Devonshire House Preparatory School
2 Arkwright Road, Hampstead, NW3 6AE

A co-educational IAPS Prep and Pre-Prep School for children from 3 to 13
with its own Oak Tree Nursery for children from 2½ to 3½

Academic / Music scholarships are available for children aged 7 or 8

For more information contact Admissions: 020 7435 1916
enquiries@devonshirehouseprepschool.co.uk
www.devonshirehouseschool.co.uk

REFERENCE COPY
please
do not take away

Hawkesdown House School

For boys
aged 3 to 8
years

Endeavour
Courage
Truth

27 Edg...

Teleph... ...o.uk

D0268723

ADD THE 2017 EDITION OF WHO'S WHO TO YOUR LIBRARY

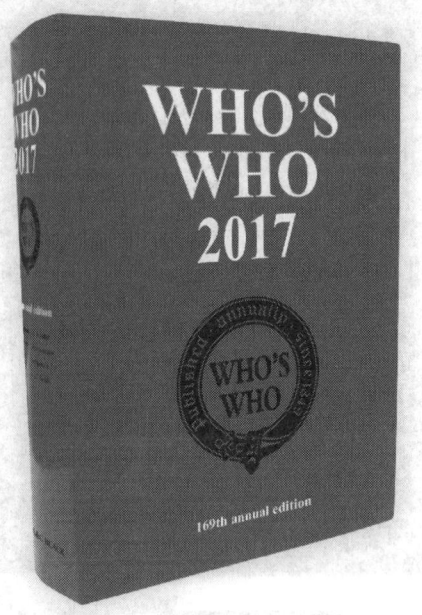

"*The unrivalled compendium of the good and the great*"

THE TELEGRAPH

9781472913609 | RRP £295.00

This essential reference book brings together over 33,000 personal entries, providing information on people of interest and influence from every area of public life.

- Around 1,000 new entries for 2017

- Entries are autobiographical

- Internationally respected and renowned

TO ORDER visit:

www.bloomsbury.com/whoswho

B L O O M S B U R Y

WHITAKER'S

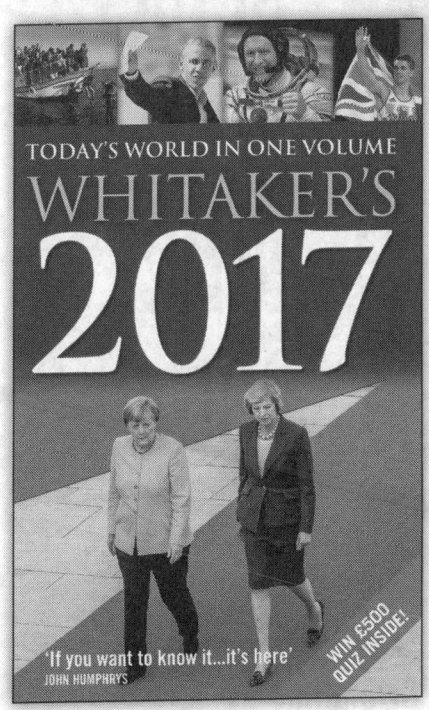

Whitaker's 2017

Published 17th November 2016

£85.00 | 9781472909336

Whitaker's 2017 is the definitive resource for anyone interested in current affairs and general knowledge.

In its 149th edition, the book has been completely revised and updated, using the most authoritative sources available. It contains a comprehensive overview of every aspect of British society, including a fully updated chapter incorporating all the changes to the UK Government since the 2016 EU Referendum, and is an excellent introduction to world politics.

The 2017 edition features a colour infographic detailing how the constituent parts of the UK voted in the referendum, plus many more new maps, charts and diagrams.

Subscribe to Whitaker's online at **www.whitakersalmanack.com** for updates throughout the year.

'Whitaker's *remains the most comprehensive compendium of information in the English language*'
– JON SNOW

'*A mighty work of reference*'
– SIR TREVOR MCDONALD, OBE

'*If you want to know it, it's here*'
– JOHN HUMPHREYS

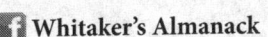 **Whitaker's Almanack** | @WhitakersAlmnck

BLOOMSBURY

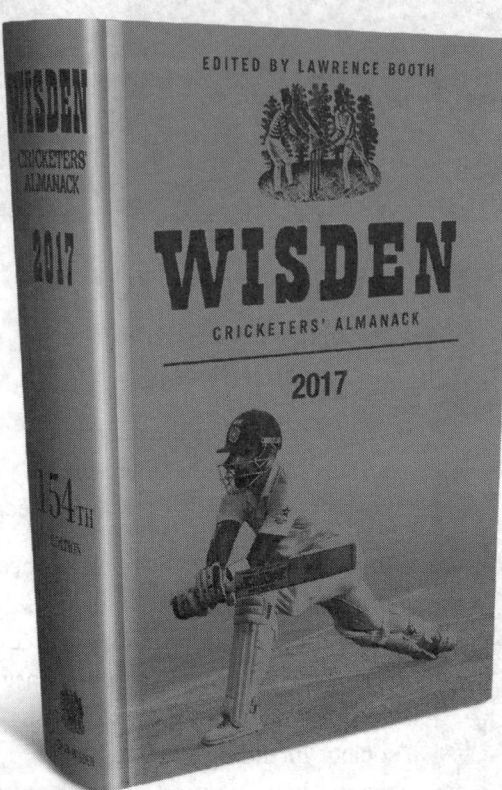

GREAT SPORTS WRITING SINCE 1864

EDITED BY LAWRENCE BOOTH

WISDEN
CRICKETERS' ALMANACK
2017

154TH EDITION

  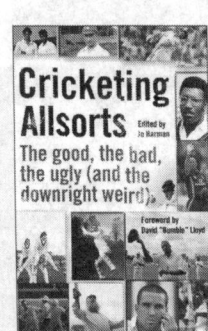 

www.wisden.com – the home of great sports writing

@wisdenalmanack | facebook.com/officialwisden

INDEPENDENT SCHOOLS YEARBOOK

2016–2017

Boys Schools, Girls Schools,
Co-educational Schools and
Preparatory Schools

Details of Schools whose Heads are in membership
of one or more of the following
Constituent Associations of the
Independent Schools Council (ISC):

Headmasters' and Headmistresses' Conference (HMC)
Girls' Schools Association (GSA)
The Society of Heads
Independent Association of Prep Schools (IAPS)
Independent Schools Association (ISA)

Edited by
JUDY MOTT

Tel: 020 7631 5600; email: isyb@acblack.com
website: www.isyb.co.uk

A&C BLACK

AN IMPRINT OF BLOOMSBURY PUBLISHING PLC

LONDON • OXFORD • NEW YORK • NEW DELHI • SYDNEY

A&C Black
An imprint of Bloomsbury Publishing Plc

50 Bedford Square　　　　　　　　1385 Broadway
London　　　　　　　　　　　　　　New York
WC1B 3DP　　　　　　　　　　　　NY10018
UK　　　　　　　　　　　　　　　　USA

www.bloomsbury.com

A&C BLACK and the A&CB logo are trademarks of
Bloomsbury Publishing Plc

© Bloomsbury Publishing Plc, 2017

All rights reserved. No part of this publication may be reproduced or
transmitted in any form or by any means, electronic or mechanical,
including photocopying, recording, or any information storage or retrieval
system, without prior permission in writing from the publishers.

The publishers make no representation, express or implied, with regard to
the accuracy of the information contained in this book and cannot accept any
legal responsibility for any errors or omissions that may have taken place.

British Library Cataloguing-in-Publication Data
A catalogue record for this book is available from the British Library.

ISBN: PB 978-1-4729-3500-7

2 4 6 8 10 9 7 5 3 1

Typeset by A&C Black Publishers
Printed an

London Borough of Richmond Upon Thames	
RTTE	
90710 000 302 216	
Askews & Holts	
371.02	£70.00
	9781472935007

Bloomsbury Publishing Plc makes every effort to ensure that the papers used
in the manufacture of our books are natural, recyclable products made from
wood grown in well-managed forests. Our manufacturing processes
conform to the environmental regulations of the country of origin.

To find out more about our authors and books visit www.bloomsbury.com.
Here you will find extracts, author interviews, details of forthcoming events
and the option to sign up for our newsletters.

INDEPENDENT SCHOOLS YEARBOOK 2016–2017

CONTENTS

PART I: HEADMASTERS' AND HEADMISTRESSES' CONFERENCE

315 schools for pupils from age 11 to 18, whose Heads are members of HMC; 54 of these are international members. They are all-boys schools (some admitting girls to the Sixth Form), co-educational schools, "Diamond" schools (girls and boys taught separately in the 11–16 age range), and some are all-girls schools. Many of the schools also have a Preparatory/Junior school or department.

PART II: GIRLS' SCHOOLS ASSOCIATION

126 schools for pupils from age 11 to 16/18, whose Heads are members of GSA. They are all-girls schools in the 11–16 age range, some admit boys to the Sixth Form and some are "Diamond" schools (girls and boys taught separately in the 11–16 age range). Some of the schools also have a Preparatory/Junior school or department.

. . ./continued

PART III: THE SOCIETY OF HEADS
87 schools for pupils from age 11 to 18 whose Heads are members
of The Society of Heads. The majority are co-educational schools,
but Membership is open to boys and girls schools. Many of the
schools also have a Preparatory/Junior school or department.

PART IV: INDEPENDENT ASSOCIATION OF PREP SCHOOLS
587 schools whose Heads are members of IAPS; 27 of these are
overseas members. Most of the schools are co-educational; some
cater for boys only or girls only. The preparatory school age range is
7 to 11/13, but many of the schools have a pre-preparatory
department for children up to age 7.

PART V: INDEPENDENT SCHOOLS ASSOCIATION
238 schools in membership of ISA. Schools in this Association are
not confined to one age range and can cater for any age range of
pupils up to 18/19 years.

ISC
INDEPENDENT SCHOOLS COUNCIL
www.isc.co.uk

"Working with its members to promote and preserve the quality, diversity and excellence of UK independent education both at home and abroad".

ISC is established to support the aims and objectives of its eight member associations; to protect and promote the sector with policy makers and opinion formers; to be a leading source of legal and regulatory guidance for the sector; to conduct and compile authoritative sector research and intelligence; and to provide online access to sector and school information to inform parental decisions.

The Constituent Associations of ISC are:

Association of Governing Bodies of Independent Schools (AGBIS)
Girls' Schools Association (GSA)
Headmasters' and Headmistresses' Conference (HMC)
Independent Association of Prep Schools (IAPS)
Independent Schools Association (ISA)
Independent Schools' Bursars Association (ISBA)
The Society of Heads

Secretariat

Chairman
Barnaby Lenon

General Secretary
Julie Robinson

Principal Legal Counsel
Sunena Stoneham

Head of Research
Donna Stevens

Head of Press and Communications
Edward Holmes

Independent Schools Council
First Floor, 27 Queen Anne's Gate, London SW1H 9BU

Tel: 020 7766 7070 • Fax: 020 7766 7071
email: office@isc.co.uk

HMC
HEADMASTERS' AND HEADMISTRESSES' CONFERENCE
www.hmc.org.uk

The HMC dates from 1869, when the celebrated Edward Thring of Uppingham asked thirty-seven of his fellow headmasters to meet at his house to consider the formation of a 'School Society and Annual Conference'. Twelve headmasters accepted the invitation. From that date there have been annual meetings. Thring's intention was to provide an opportunity for discussion at regular intervals, both on practical issues in the life of a school and on general principles in education. He believed that his guests would discharge their practical business more effectively at a residential meeting where they could also enjoy being in the company of like-minded men. Annual Meetings of the HMC still combine formal debate on current educational questions with the second element of conversational exchanges in an agreeable environment. These gatherings, which up to 1939 were usually at individual schools, then took place at a University. Nowadays they are held in major hotels and conference centres in the Autumn term. In addition to these annual conferences attended by all members, there are local meetings each term arranged by the ten branches or Divisions into which the country is divided.

Present full membership of the HMC is a total of two hundred and eighty-one, which now includes headmasters and headmistresses of boys', girls' and co-educational schools. In considering applications for election to membership, the Committee has regard to the degree of independence enjoyed by the Head and his/her school. Eligibility also depends on the academic standards obtaining in the school, as reflected by the proportion of pupils in the Sixth Form pursuing a course of study beyond GCSE and by the school's public examination results, including A Levels, the International Baccalaureate and the Cambridge Pre-U.

The Constitution provides that the full membership shall consist only of heads of independent schools in the UK and Ireland. At the same time, it is held to be a strength that the Conference includes heads of schools from the maintained sector as well as other influential figures from the world of education. There is provision therefore for the election of a small number of HMC Associates.

In addition the HMC has a number of International members, who are heads of high-quality schools from around the world. The International division meets on two occasions during the academic year and the Chair is a member of the HMC Committee. There is also a small number of Honorary Associates who have been elected to life membership on retirement.

The HMC is closely associated with the other independent sector associations that also belong to the Independent Schools Council (ISC), and with the Association of School and College Leaders (ASCL), which represents the Heads and senior staff of secondary schools and colleges in both the maintained and independent sectors.

The HMC Committee 2016–2017

Chairman	Mike Buchanan	Ashford School
Vice-Chairman	Chris King	Leicester Grammar School
Chairman-Elect	Keith Budge	Bedales School
Treasurer	Stephen Holliday	Queen Elizabeth's Hospital
Chairman – East	Nicholas Weaver	Ipswich School
Secretary – East	Stefan Griffiths	Norwich School
Chairman – Irish	David Burnett	Royal School Dungannon
Secretary – Irish	Paul Crute	Royal School Armagh
Chairman – London	Ian Davies	Brentwood School
Secretary – London	Ann Haydon	Surbiton High School
Chairman – North East	David Elstone	Hymers College
Secretary – North East	Mark Ronan	Pocklington School
Chairman – North West	Andrew Chicken	Stockport Grammar School
Secretary – North West	Philip Britton	Bolton School
Chairman – Scottish	Peter Brodie	Glasgow Academy
Secretary – Scottish	John Halliday	High School of Dundee
Chairman – South Central	Jonathan Cox	RGS Guildford
Secretary – South Central	Emma Hattersley	Godolphin School
Chairman – South East	Shaun Fenton	Reigate Grammar School
Secretary – South East	David Lamper	Kent College
Chairman – South West	Ian Wilmshurst	King's Bruton
Secretary – South West	Jonathan Standen	Plymouth College
Chairman – West	Kathy Crewe-Read	Wolverhampton Grammar School
Secretary – West	Gus Lock	Warwick School
Chairman – International	Peter Armstrong	International School Bangalore
Secretary – International	(to be appointed)	

Co-opted Members

Chairman of Academic Policy	Peter Hamilton	Haberdashers' Aske's Boys' School
Chairman of Professional Development	John Watson	Bablake School
Chairman of Universities	Chris Ramsey	King's School, Chester
Chairman of Inspection	Adam Pettitt	Highgate School
Chairman of Communications	Chris King	Leicester Grammar School
	Mary Breen	St Mary's School Ascot

General Secretary: William Richardson, BA, DPhil (Tel: 01858 469059)
Membership Secretary: Ian Power, MA (Tel: 01858 465260)

Headmasters' and Headmistresses' Conference
12 The Point, Rockingham Road, Market Harborough, Leicestershire LE16 7QU
Tel: 01858 465260 • Fax: 01858 465759 • email: gensec@hmc.org.uk

GSA
GIRLS' SCHOOLS ASSOCIATION
www.gsa.uk.com

The Girls' Schools Association (GSA) represents the heads of many of the top performing day and boarding schools in the UK independent schools sector and is the main professional association to which the heads of senior independent girls' schools belong. It is a member of the Independent Schools Council (ISC).

The GSA encourages high standards of education for girls and promotes the benefits of being taught in a largely girls-only environment. Academic performance is impressive; GSA schools are widely recognised for their exceptional record of examination achievements and 96% of students progress to university.

Nevertheless, GSA schools are just as likely to encourage excellence outside the classroom with an impressive choice of extra-curricular activities. They provide an environment in which girls can grow in confidence and ability. In a girls' school, the needs and aspirations of girls are the main focus, and the staff are specialists in the teaching of girls. Girls hold all the senior positions in the school, and are encouraged by positive role models in the schools' teaching staff and management. Expectations are high. In GSA schools, girls do not just have equal opportunities, they have every opportunity. Members of the GSA share a commitment to the values and benefits of single-sex schools for girls, and a belief that all girls, regardless of educational setting, deserve the opportunity to realise their potential, to be active and equal, confident and competent leaders, participants and contributors.

Former GSA school pupils are among the most noteworthy high achievers of the UK and indeed the world. They include world leading scientists, international charity campaigners, famous actresses, foreign correspondents, Olympic medallists and business women at the highest levels.

The GSA provides a full programme of professional development and support to members and represents their views when advising and lobbying educational policy makers.

Officers 2016

President:	Caroline Jordan	Headington School
President Elect 2017:	Charlotte Avery	St Mary's School, Cambridge
President Elect 2018:	Gwen Byrom	Loughborough High School
Treasurer:	Christine Edmundson	Palmers Green High School

Officers 2017

President:	Charlotte Avery	St Mary's School, Cambridge
Vice-President:	Caroline Jordan	Headington School
President Elect 2018:	Gwen Byrom	Loughborough High School
Treasurer:	Antonia Beary	Mayfield Girls

Committee Chairmen

Boarding:	Samantha Price	Benenden School
Education:	Sue Hincks	Bolton School Girls' Division
Membership & Accreditation:	Claire Hewitt	Manchester High School for Girls
Professional Development:	Frances Ramsey	Queen's College, London
Sports:	Jo MacKenzie	Bedford Girls' School
Universities (& GDST Representative):	Hilary French	Newcastle High School for Girls GDST

Regional Representatives

East:	Elizabeth Thomas	Abbot's Hill School
London:	Heather Hanbury	The Lady Eleanor Holles School
Midlands:	Ann Clark	King Edward VI High School for Girls
North East:	Lynne Renwick	Durham High School for Girls
North West:	Louise Robinson	Merchant Taylors' Girls' School
Scotland:	Anna Tomlinson	St Margaret's School for Girls, Aberdeen
South Central:	Jane Prescott	Portsmouth High School GDST
South East:	Paul Mitchell	Cobham Hall
South West & Wales:	Felicia Kirk	St Mary's Calne

Co-opted

ISC Vice Chairman:	Alice Phillips	St Catherine's, Bramley

Secretariat

Interim Operations Director:	Christine Edmundson
Membership Director:	Jane Carroll
Executive Assistant:	Jeven Sharma
Membership Manager:	Kate Williams
Conference & Events Manager:	Emily Hall
Digital Manager:	Imogen Vanderpump
Communications Manager:	Rachel Kerr
Finance Manager:	Jean Walklett

Girls' Schools Association
Suite 105, 108 New Walk, Leicester, LE1 7PG
Tel: 0116 254 1619 • email: office@gsa.uk.com

THE SOCIETY OF HEADS

www.thesocietyofheads.org.uk

The Society is an Association of Heads of over 100 well-established independent schools. It was founded in 1961 at a time when the need arose from the vitality and growth of the independent sector in the 1950s and the wish of a group of Heads to share ideas and experience.

The Society continues to provide a forum for the exchange of ideas and consideration of the particular needs of the smaller independent school. These are frequently different from the issues and from the approach of the larger schools. All members value their independence, breadth in education and the pursuit of excellence, particularly in relation to academic standards.

The Society's policy is to maintain high standards in member schools, to ensure their genuine independence, to foster an association of schools which contributes to the whole independent sector by its distinctive character and flexibility, to provide an opportunity for the sharing of ideas and common concerns, to promote links with the wider sphere of higher education, to strengthen relations with the maintained sector and with local communities.

Within the membership there is a wide variety of educational experience. Some schools are young, some have evolved from older foundations, some have behind them a long tradition of pioneer and specialist education, the great majority are now co-educational but we also have all-boys and all-girls schools. A good number of the member schools have a strong boarding element and others are day schools. Some have specific religious foundations and some are non-denominational. All offer a stimulating Sixth Form experience and at the same time give a sound and balanced education to pupils of widely varying abilities and interests.

The Society is one of the constituent Associations of the Independent Schools Council. Every Full Member school has been accredited through inspection by the Independent Schools Inspectorate (or Estyn in Wales and HMIE in Scotland) and is subject to regular visits to monitor standards and ensure that good practice and sound academic results are maintained. The Society is also represented on many other educational bodies.

All members are in membership of the Association of School and College Leaders (ASCL) or other union for school leaders and Full Member schools belong to AGBIS or an equivalent professional body supporting governance.

There are also categories of Additional, Overseas and Conference Membership to which Heads are elected whose schools do not fulfil all the criteria for Full Membership but whose personal contribution to the Society is judged to be invaluable. They are recorded separately at the end of the entries.

The Society has a one-day meeting for members in the autumn and summer terms and organises a two-day residential conference in the Easter term.

Officers 2016–2017

Chairman: Damian Ettinger, Cokethorpe School
Vice-Chairman: Dominic Findlay, Langley School
Chairman Designate: Gregg Davies, Shiplake College
Hon Treasurer: Stephen Fairclough, Abbotsholme School

Committee 2016–2017

Kathryn Bell, Burgess Hill Girls
Frank Butt, Langley School
Sami Cohen, d'Overbroeck's
Christine Cunniffe, LVS Ascot
Lynne Horner, Westholme School
Roland Martin, City of London Freemen's School
Adrian Meadows, The Peterborough School
Richard Palmer, St Christopher School
Sarah Raffray, St Augustine's Priory
Annette Roberts, Kirkham Grammar School

Secretariat

General Secretary: Clive Rickart

The Society of Heads
12 The Point, Rockingham Road, Market Harborough, Leicestershire LE16 7QU
Tel: 01858 433760 • Fax: 01858 461413 • email: gensec@thesocietyofheads.org.uk

Members who are also members of the Headmasters' and Headmistresses' Conference:

Anton Maree, Ackworth School
Keith J Budge, Bedales Schools
Roderick MacKinnon, Bristol Grammar School
Roland Martin, City of London Freemen's School
Joanne Thomson, Clayesmore School
Damian Ettinger, Cokethorpe School
Simon Wilson, Halliford School
Daniel Berry, Kirkham Grammar School
Nigel Williams, Leighton Park School
Mark Wallace, Lincoln Minster School

Jesse Elzinga, Reading Blue Coat School
Mark Hoskins, Reed's School
Rob Jones, Rendcomb College
Simon Smith, Rydal Penrhos School
David Buxton, St Columba's College
John Green, Seaford College
Gregg Davies, Shiplake College
Mark Mortimer, Warminster School
Chris Staley, Wisbech Grammar School

Members who are also members of the Girls' Schools Association:

Kathryn Bell, Burgess Hill Girls
Jonathan Forster, Moreton Hall
Sarah Raffray, St Augustine's Priory School

Associate Members

S Aiano (formerly Headmaster, Bearwood College)
G Allen (formerly Headmaster, The Roman Ridge School)
J C Baggaley (formerly Headmaster, Silcoates School)
S Bailey (formerly Headmaster, The Royal Wolverhampton School)
R D Balaam (formerly Headmaster, Royal Russell School)
D J Beeby (formerly Headmaster, Clayesmore School)
N Beesley (formerly Headmaster, Beechwood Sacred Heart School)
L Bergin (Headmaster, North Cestrian Grammar School)
G Best (formerly Headmaster, St John's College, Southsea)
D Boddy (formerly Headmaster, St James Senior Boys' School)
P Bodkin (formerly General Secretary, The Society of Heads)
Sue Bradley (formerly Head, Stover School)
D Bryson (formerly Headmaster, St Andrew's School)
P Cantwell (formerly Headmaster, The King's School, Tynemouth)
D Chapman (formerly Headmaster, Hampshire Collegiate School)
N Chisholm, (formerly Headmaster, Yehudi Menuhin School)
R Clark (formerly Headmaster, Battle Abbey School)
A Clemit (formerly Headmaster, Longridge Towers School)
T Cook (formerly Headmaster, Portland Place School)
P Cottam (formerly Headmaster, Halliford School)
D G Crawford (formerly Headmaster, Colston's School)
J Davies (formerly Headmaster, St Bees School)
N Dorey (formerly Headmaster, Bethany School)
J Dunston (formerly Headmaster, Leighton Park School)
M Eagers (formerly Headmaster, Box Hill School)
N England (formerly Headmaster, Ryde School)
Sarah Evans (formerly Principal, King Edward VI High School for Girls)
D J Farrant (formerly Headmaster, Abbotsholme School)
Sue Freestone (Principal, King's Ely)
M Goodwin (formerly Headmaster, Sibford School)
A Graham (formerly Headmaster, Windermere St Anne's School)
R Hadfield (formerly Headmaster, The Read School)
T Halliwell (formerly Principal, Welbeck Defence Sixth Form College)
N Hammond (formerly Headmaster, Wisbech Grammar School)
P Harvey (formerly Headmaster, St Edward's School)
Carole Hawkins (formerly Head, Royal School, Hampstead)
R Haworth (formerly Headmaster, Hull Collegiate School)
J Hewitt (formerly Headmaster, Bredon School)
G Holden (formerly Headmaster, Dover College)
Christine James (formerly Headmistress, Farringtons School)
D Jarrett (formerly Headmaster, Reed's School)
C Johnson (formerly Headmaster, The Duke of York's Royal Military School)
S Jones (formerly Headmaster, Dover College)
T Kernohan (formerly Headmaster, Fulneck School)
I Kilpatrick (Headmaster, Sidcot School)
M A B Kirk (formerly Headmaster, Royal Hospital School)
T Kirkup (formerly Headmaster, Scarborough College)

G Link (formerly Headmaster, Stanbridge Earls School)
M Long (formerly Headmaster, Tettenhall College)
C Lumb (formerly Headmaster, St Joseph's College, Ipswich)
H MacDonald (formerly Principal, Hampshire Collegiate School)
T Manning (formerly Headmaster, Longridge Towers School)
J McArthur (formerly Headmaster, Reading Blue Coat School)
A McGrath (formerly Headmaster, Leighton Park School)
Linde Melhuish (formerly Principal, Padworth College)
E Mitchell (formerly Headmaster, Abbey Gate College)
J Moreland (Headmaster, Polam Hall School)
S Morris (formerly Headmaster of The Cathedral School, Llandaff)
H Moxon (formerly Headmaster, Stanbridge Earls School)
I Mullins (Licenced Victuallers' School)
Isobel Nixon (formerly Head, Scarborough College)
T Packer (formerly Headmaster, Teesside High School)
J Payne (formerly Headmaster, Pierrepoint School)
The Hon Martin Penney (formerly Headmaster, Bearwood College)
I Power (formerly Headmaster, Lord Wandsworth College)
G Price (formerly Headmaster, Thetford Grammar School)
M Priestley (formerly Headmaster, Warminster School)
A Reid (formerly Headmaster, Hebron School)
C Reid (formerly Headmaster, St Christopher School)
Lynne Renwick (formerly Head, Our Lady's Abingdon School)
R Repper (formerly Headmaster, Wisbech Grammar School)
D Richardson (formerly General Secretary, The Society of Heads)
D Robb (formerly Headmaster, Oswestry School)
C Robinson (formerly Headmaster, Hipperholme Grammar School)
M Scullion (formerly Headmaster, Our Lady of Sion School)
Maureen Sheridan (formerly Headmistress, St Joseph's College Reading)
J Shinkwin (formerly Headmaster, Princethorpe College)
P Skelker (formerly Headmaster, Immanuel College)
P Spillane (formerly Headmaster, Silcoates School)
P Stockdale (formerly Headmaster, Oswestry School)
M Symonds (formerly Headmaster, Bedstone College)
Elizabeth Thomas (formerly Head, Stonar School)
N Thorne (formerly Headmaster, St John's College, Southsea)
A Tibble (formerly Headmaster, Ewell Castle School)
J Tolputt (formerly Headmaster, The Purcell School)
D Vanstone (formerly Headmaster, North Cestrian Grammar School)
R Walker (formerly Headmaster, Portland Place School)
N Ward (formerly Headmaster, The Royal Hospital School)
A Waters (formerly Headmaster, Kingsley School)
D Wideman (Headmaster, Silcoates School)
G Wigley (formerly Headmaster, Friends' School)
M Windsor (formerly Headmaster, Reading Blue Coat School)
S Wormleighton (formerly Headmaster, Grenville College)

IAPS
INDEPENDENT ASSOCIATION OF PREP SCHOOLS
www.iaps.uk

Together, IAPS schools represent a multi-billion pound enterprise. Our schools educate more than 175,000 children and employ more than 34,000 members of staff.

IAPS is the voice of independent prep school education, and we work with and lobby governments on an international stage to ensure the needs of our members, and the independent sector as a whole, are met.

Schools can only join IAPS if they can demonstrate the highest standards of education and care. Our member schools offer an all-round, values-led, broad education, which produces confident, adaptable, motivated children with a lifelong passion for learning.

In order to be elected to membership, a Head must be suitably qualified and schools must be accredited through a satisfactory inspection.

While the values may be the same, each of our schools is independent and distinct: we have single-sex and co-educational, boarding, day and mixed, urban and rural. Sizes vary from more than 800 pupils to less than 100.

Most of our schools are charitable trusts, some are limited companies, and others are proprietary. There are also junior schools attached to senior schools, choir schools, those with a particular religious affiliation and those that offer specialist provision.

With more than 600 members in the UK and around 50 abroad, IAPS offers excellent opportunities for fellowship and networking.

We have one of the independent sector's top training programmes, which includes a broad range of professional development courses. New members are offered an experienced Head as a mentor and members are divided into district groups by geographical location, giving them the chance to meet with fellow heads on a regular basis.

Our website with a dedicated members' area is packed with news, policy examples, advice and support. The site also actively promotes the prep school sector to parents and the media.

The Council and Officers for 2016–2017

Chairman of IAPS: John Tranmer
Vice-Chairman: Mark Hartley

Members of Council:

Jeremy Banks	Adam Edwards
Heather Beeby	Mark Gibbons
Tania Botting	Huw Marshall
Clare Bruce	Andrew Nott
Justin Chippendale	Roger Overend
Mike Crossley	David Sibson
Maureen Cussans	James Thompson
Gareth Davies	Howard Tuckett
Teresa Dunbar	

Officers:
Chief Executive: David Hanson
Director of Education: Mark Brotherton
Finance and Operations Director: Richard Flower
Membership Secretary: Petra Hancock
Association Administrator: Christine McCrudden

Independent Association of Prep Schools
11 Waterloo Place, Leamington Spa CV32 5LA
Tel: 01926 887833 • Fax: 01926 888014 • email: iaps@iaps.uk

ISA
INDEPENDENT SCHOOLS ASSOCIATION
www.isaschools.org.uk

The Independent Schools Association, established in 1879, is one of the oldest of the Headteachers' Associations of independent schools that make up the Independent Schools Council. It began life as the Association of Principals of Private Schools, which was created to encourage high standards and foster friendliness and cooperation among Heads who had previously worked in isolation. In 1895 it was incorporated as The Private Schools Association and in 1927 the word 'private' was replaced by 'independent'. ISA is a Registered Charity with a service-led approach to supporting its Members and the wider educational community. The Association's dedication to its Members, including the delivery of instant, expert advice, has resulted in growth of over 50% in the last five years and ISA is now regarded as the most representative of any organisation within the sector.

Membership is open to any independent school Head or Proprietor provided they meet the necessary criteria, which includes accreditation by any government-approved inspectorate. ISA's Executive Council is elected by Members and supports all developments of the Association through its Committee structure and the strong regional network of Coordinators and Area Committees. Each of ISA's seven Areas in turn supports Members through an extensive programme of training events and meetings.

ISA celebrates a wide ranging membership, not confined to any one type of school, but including all: nursery, pre-preparatory, junior, preparatory and senior, all-through schools, co-educational, single-sex, boarding, day, and performing arts and special schools.

Promoting best practice and fellowship for Members remains at the core of the Association, just as it did when it began 130 years ago. The 400 Members and their schools enjoy high quality national conferences and courses that foster excellence in independent education. ISA's central office also supports Members and provides advice, and represents the views of its membership at national and governmental levels. Pupils in ISA schools enjoy a wide variety of competitions, in particular the wealth of sporting, artistic and academic activities at Area and National level.

Council and Officers for 2016–2017

President: Lord Lexden OBE

Vice-Presidents:
Mr Michael Hewett
Mrs Deborah Leek-Bailey OBE
Mr Paul Moss
Mr John Wood

Honorary Officers:
Mr Stuart Nicholson (*Chair*)
Dr Sarah Welch (*Vice-Chair*)
Mr Alex Gear (*Vice-Chair*)

Elective Councillors:

Mr Amjad Ahmed	Mr Nilesh Manani
Mr Adrian Blake	Mrs Claire Osborn
Mr Andrew Hampton	Mr Phil Soutar
Mr Barry Huggett OBE	Mr Jonathan Ullmer MBE
Mrs Pam Hutley	Mr Richard Walden
Mrs Janet Lowe	Mrs Susan Webb
Mr Stephen McKernan	Mr James Wilding

Area Coordinators:

East Anglia: Mrs Clare Ogden [acting]	Midlands: Mr Matthew Adshead
London North: Mrs Lynn Maggs-Wellings	North: Mr Jeff Shaw [acting]
London South: Mrs Angela Culley	South West: Mr Paul Easterbrook
London West: Miss Vicky Smit	

Officials
Chief Executive Officer: Neil Roskilly
Deputy Chief Executive Officer: Peter Woodroffe
Professional Development Officer: Alice Jeffries
Office Manager and PA to the CEO: Karen Goddard

Independent Schools Association
ISA House, 5–7 Great Chesterford Court, Great Chesterford, Essex CB10 1PF
Tel: 01799 523619 • email: isa@isaschools.org.uk

AGBIS
ASSOCIATION OF GOVERNING BODIES OF INDEPENDENT SCHOOLS
REGISTERED CHARITY NO. 1108756

www.agbis.org.uk

The Object of the Association is to advance education in independent schools and, in furtherance of that object, but not otherwise, the Association shall have power:

(a) to discuss matters concerning the policy and administration of such schools and to encourage cooperation between their Governing Bodies;
(b) to consider the relationship of such schools to the general educational interests of the community;
(c) to consider and give guidance on matters of general or individual concern to the Governing Bodies of such schools;
(d) to promote good governance in such schools;
and
(e) to express the views of the Governing Bodies of such schools on any of the foregoing matters and to take such action as may be appropriate in their interests.

Membership

There are two categories of membership: full membership and associate membership. Schools in England and Wales applying for either category will have heads in full membership of one of the five Independent Schools Council (ISC) Heads' Associations or expecting to be so within one year. If the school is not a charitable trust, it must have either a governing body or an advisory or management committee which fulfils a similar function and is constituted in such a fashion as to provide a significant degree of oversight.

FULL MEMBERSHIP

To be accepted as full members, schools will need to demonstrate that the composition of the Governing Body and governance procedures meet the principles of good governance practice set out in the AGBIS publication 'Guidelines for Governors'. All schools must be able to demonstrate that they are financially viable and must also be able to provide a satisfactory current inspection report issued by a recognised inspectorate

ASSOCIATE MEMBERSHIP

Schools which do not meet all of the criteria above for full membership may be offered associate membership at the discretion of the AGBIS Board. The offer of associate membership can be temporary and may require a school to rectify a perceived shortcoming or weakness. Once this condition has been met, the school may apply to be considered for full membership.

Board
Chairman: Lorna Cocking (Kent College Canterbury)
Deputy Chairman: Margaret Rudland (British School of Paris, Headington,
St Margaret's School Bushey, St Swithun's, The English College Prague)
Deputy Chairman: David Taylor (Queen Anne's School Caversham,
St Lawrence College Ramsgate, Sutton Valence School)
Honorary Treasurer: Michael Goolden (Benenden School)

Yvonne Burne (Berkhamsted School)
Roger Chapman (The Mill Hill School Foundation)
Jonathan Cook (Dean Close School, Lymington Infant School, Walhampton School)
Pamela Edmonds (St Michael's Prep School)
Deborah Knight (Haberdashers' Aske's Boys' School)
David Jennings (Summer Fields School)
Katie Lancaster (Kimbolton School)
Rosanne Musgrave (St Albans High School for Girls)
Nigel Richardson (Haileybury & Magdalen College School)
Paul Voller (Box Hill School)
Ken Young (The Royal Russell School)

General Secretary: Richard Harman
Training & Membership Secretary: Andy Robinson

Association of Governing Bodies of Independent Schools
The Grange, 3 Codicote Road, Welwyn, Hertfordshire AL6 9LY
Tel: 01438 840730 • email: admin@agbis.org.uk

ISBA
INDEPENDENT SCHOOLS' BURSARS ASSOCIATION
www.theisba.org.uk

The Independent Schools' Bursars Association (ISBA) is the only national association to represent school bursars and business managers of independent schools, providing them with the professional support they need to manage their schools successfully and provide a world class education to their pupils.

The association can trace its history back seventy years to the founding of the Public Schools Bursars' Association which held its first general meeting on 26 April 1932 at the offices of Epsom College. Its name then changed to the Independent Schools' Bursars Association in 1983.

The ISBA now has more than 1000 independent school members, covering more than 1000 schools, including some 40 overseas associate members, from smaller preparatory schools to larger and well-renowned senior schools, including both boarding and day schools. Although it is the school and not the bursar who becomes a member of the association, it is usually the bursar or equivalent who is the school's nominated representative.

The association is one of the constituent members of the Independent Schools Council (ISC) and also works closely with the other seven constituent associations of the ISC. It is represented on the ISC Governing Council and a number of ISC committees and is also often called on to represent the ISC at meetings with the Department for Education, Health & Safety Executive and Teachers' Pensions providing advice on bursarial matters.

Full membership of the ISBA is open to schools who are members of one of the constituent associations in membership of the ISC. Associate membership is open to certain other schools/organisations which are recognised as educational charities.

Day-to-day the ISBA advises many different staff within a school's senior management team including the bursar, finance director, chief operations officer, business manager, deputy or assistant with areas of responsibility encompassing accounting, financial management and reporting, risk management, regulatory compliance, facilities management, HR, technology, environmental sustainability, auxiliary services and more. As part of its range of support services the association offers schools:

- guidance and legislative briefings, and model policies to download from its online reference library;
- a comprehensive professional development programme covering finance, legal, HR, inspections and other key operational issues and tailored to suit staff at all levels;
- information, advice and networking opportunities at the ISBA Annual Conference (the 2017 conference will be held at the Manchester Central Convention Complex on Wednesday 17th and Thursday 18th May 2017);
- a 'Bursar's Guide' – providing the latest information on legislation affecting schools;
- termly copies of the ISBA's magazine – The Bursar's Review – and regular e-newsletters covering the latest legal, financial and HR news and more;
- an online job vacancies page where schools can advertise any of their vacant bursary management roles for free

The Executive Committee of the ISBA consists of the Chairman of the Association, Margaret McKenna, the Bursar of Felsted School and the bursars of eleven other leading independent schools.

The Independent Schools' Bursars Association is a Registered Charity, number 1121757,
and a Company Limited by Guarantee, registered in England and Wales, number 6410037.

Chief Executive: Mr David Woodgate

Independent Schools' Bursars Association
Unit 11–12, Manor Farm, Cliddesden, Basingstoke, Hampshire RG25 2JB
Tel: 01256 330369 • email: office@theisba.org.uk

BSA
BOARDING SCHOOLS' ASSOCIATION
www.boarding.org.uk

The Boarding Schools' Association (BSA) champions boarding and promotes boarding excellence.

The BSA represents over 500 independent and state boarding schools in the UK and overseas. BSA services include professional development, government relations, communications, media, publications, conferences and events.

Aims

The BSA exists to:
- Champion boarding and promote boarding excellence
- Help member schools provide the best quality of boarding education and meet the highest standards of welfare for boarders by providing a comprehensive programme of professional development for all staff and governors of boarding schools
- Conduct appropriate research and produce regular publications on boarding issues and good practice in boarding
- Liaise with other bodies concerned with boarding – the Independent Schools Inspectorate, the Independent Schools Council, the Scottish Council for Independent Schools and Ofsted
- Engage in a regular dialogue with government on boarding issues
- Provide a platform informing parents and prospective boarders of the benefits of twenty-first century boarding and offer a conduit to individual member schools for further enquiry
- Forge links with associations of boarding schools worldwide
- Speak for boarding in today's world.

Membership

Membership is open to all schools with boarders which are members of Associations within the Independent Schools Council (ISC), to schools in membership of the Scottish Council of Independent Schools (SCIS), and also to state boarding schools. Membership may also be offered to boarding schools overseas at Associate or Affiliate level. Please contact Hayley Zimak, Membership and Marketing Manager (hayley@boarding.org.uk) for further details. Current membership comprises over 500 schools (full boarding, weekly/flexi boarding, or day schools with boarding provision; co-educational or single-sex; preparatory or secondary).

Support for Schools

THE PROFESSIONAL DEVELOPMENT PROGRAMME

In partnership with Roehampton University, the BSA has established a Professional Development Programme for all staff working in boarding schools. These BSA courses lead to university validated Certificates of Professional Practice in Boarding Education. There is a programme of Day Courses on a range of topics including Child Protection, Anti-Bullying strategies, the role of Gap Assistants, Boarding Legislation and Good Practice, Boarding Governance.

Individual courses and INSET tailored to the particular needs of a school or group of schools is also offered. BSA training is available to all staff who work in boarding schools and to the Governors of boarding schools.

BSA Training Programmes are also used by schools and boarding associations throughout the world.

RESIDENTIAL CONFERENCES

Conferences are held annually for:
Boarding House Staff
Deputy Heads & Heads of Boarding
Marketing, Communications and Admissions Staff
Heads
State Boarding Schools
Nurses & Matrons

PUBLICATIONS

These include:
- ***Running a School Boarding House – A Legal Guide for Housemasters and Housemistresses***
- ***Duty of Care***
- ***Parenting the Boarder***
- ***Being a Boarder***
- ***Mirror Mirror – Reflections on Boarding Practice 2014***
- ***Truly World Class***
- ***Boarding Briefing Papers*** – are published at regular intervals on matters concerning boarding legislation and good practice

NATIONAL BOARDING STANDARDS

The Association liaises with the Department for Education, Ofsted, and the Independent Schools Inspectorate on the inspection of boarding schools under the National Minimum Standards for Boarding schools in England and Wales, and the Care Commission in Scotland.

LIAISON WITH NATIONAL BODIES

The Association meets regularly with the Department for Education to discuss issues concerned with boarding. It also liaises with Local Government, ISI (Independent Schools Inspectorate), Ofsted (Office for Standards in Education), CEAS (Children's Education Advisory Service) and all the national educational organisations.

Organisation

At the Annual General Meeting, held at the Heads' Annual Conference, Officers of the Association are elected together with the Executive Committee The Honorary Treasurer is usually a Bursar from a member school.

Chief Executive
Robin Fletcher, email: robin@boarding.org.uk

Deputy Chief Executive and Director of Training
Alex Thomson OBE, email: alex@boarding.org.uk

The Boarding Schools' Association
4th Floor, 134–136 Buckingham Palace Road, London SW1W 9SA
Tel: 020 7798 1580 • email: bsa@boarding.org.uk

INDEPENDENT SCHOOLS EXAMINATIONS BOARD

www.iseb.co.uk

COMMON ENTRANCE

COMMON PRE-TESTS

COMMON ACADEMIC SCHOLARSHIP

Executive Chairman:
Mr J P Kirk, BSc Hons, FRSA

Chief Administrator:
Mrs K Allen, BSc Hons, PGCE

COMMON ENTRANCE

The Common Entrance Examinations are used for transfer to senior schools at the ages of 11+ and 13+. The syllabuses are devised and regularly monitored by the Independent Schools Examinations Board which comprises members of the Headmasters' and Headmistresses' Conference, the Girls' Schools Association and the Independent Association of Prep Schools.

The papers are set by examiners appointed by the Board, but the answers are marked by the senior school for which a candidate is entered. A list of schools using the examination is given below. Common Entrance is not a public examination as, for example, GCSE, and candidates may normally be entered only if they have been offered a place at a senior school, subject to their passing the examination.

Candidates normally take the examination in their own junior or preparatory schools, either in the UK or overseas.

Common Entrance at 11+ consists of papers in English, Mathematics and Science. At 13+, in addition to these core subjects, a wide range of additional papers is available in modern and classical languages, and the humanities subjects. Tiered papers are available for many subjects.

Mandarin Chinese is offered as an online examination which can be taken at any age.

Dates

The 11+ examination is held in early November or mid-January.

The 13+ examination commences either on the first Monday in November, the last Monday in January or on the first Tuesday in June.

Entries

In cases where candidates are at schools in membership of the Independent Association of Prep Schools, it is usual for heads of these schools to make arrangements for entering candidates for the appropriate examination after consultation with parents and senior school heads. In the case of candidates at schools which do not normally enter candidates, it is the responsibility of parents to arrange for candidates to be entered for the appropriate examination in accordance with the requirements of senior schools.

Conduct of the Examination

Regulations for the conduct of the examination are laid down by the Independent Schools Examinations Board.

Past Papers and Other Resources

Copies of past Common Entrance papers can be purchased from Galore Park Publishing:

website: www.galorepark.co.uk;

email: customer.services@galorepark.co.uk;

Tel: 01235 827702

ISEB-endorsed Common Entrance revision guides and practice exercises are available from a number of publishers, listed on the ISEB website.

COMMON PRE-TESTS

The Common Pre-Tests are age-standardised tests used to assess pupils' attainment and potential when they are in Year 6 or Year 7, prior to entry to their senior schools. Pupils who sit the tests will normally still be required to sit the Common Entrance examinations.

ISEB commissions the tests from GL Assessment which has long been associated with providing high-quality and reliable assessments in education. The tests are taken online, usually in the child's current school, and include multiple-choice tests in Mathematics, English, verbal and non-verbal reasoning. Senior schools will inform parents if their son or daughter needs to be entered for the tests.

No special preparation is needed for the tests and no past papers are available. Examples and practice questions are provided during the testing period so that candidates understand what they have to do.

Further details are available for schools in the Schools section of the ISEB website and for parents in the Parents section of the ISEB website.

COMMON ACADEMIC SCHOLARSHIP

ISEB sets Scholarship examination papers at 13+ which a number of independent senior schools use to assess potential scholars. Papers are set in English, Mathematics, Science, History, Geography, Religious Studies, French and Latin. Questions are based on the Common Entrance syllabuses and past papers are available from Galore Park Publications.

Candidates are entered by the senior schools for which they are registered and the papers are marked by the senior schools themselves.

Fees

The Independent Schools Examinations Board decides the fees to be charged for each candidate. Schools are notified annually in the spring term of fees payable for the following three terms. Parents seeking information about current fees should look on the ISEB website or contact the ISEB office.

Correspondence

Correspondence about academic matters relating to the Common Entrance examinations and requests for further information about the administration of the examinations should be addressed to the Chief Administrator.

Independent Schools Examinations Board
Suite 3, Endeavour House, Crow Arch Lane, Ringwood, Hampshire BH24 1HP
Tel: 01425 470555 • email: enquiries@iseb.co.uk

COBIS
COUNCIL OF BRITISH INTERNATIONAL SCHOOLS
www.cobis.org.uk
twitter: @COBISorg and @COBIS_CEO

Representing over 400 member organisations, COBIS is a responsive organisation, open to current and future opportunities. The association has developed markedly since its foundation, changing to meet the needs and aspirations of its growing global school membership base.

COBIS exists to serve, support and represent its member schools – their leaders, governors, staff and students by:

- Providing Quality Assurance in member schools
- Representing member schools with the British Government, educational bodies and the corporate sector
- Providing effective professional development for senior leaders, governors, teachers and support staff
- Facilitating, coordinating and supporting professional networking opportunities for British International schools
- Processing Disclosure Barring Service checks to promote child protection and safer recruitment and employment practices
- Engaging, challenging and inspiring students of all ages and abilities by delivering excellent interschool student competitions and events
- Providing access to information about trends and developments in UK education
- Facilitating high impact 'Member to Member' professional networking
- Promoting career opportunities within the global COBIS network
- Brokering a cost-effective consultancy service between schools and approved educational support service providers

Patron
HRH The Duke of York, KG

COBIS Executive 2016–2017

Honorary President
Sir Roger Fry CBE

Honorary Vice Presidents
The Rt Hon Lord Andrew Adonis
Sir Mervyn Brown KCMG OBE
Michael Cooper OBE
Lord Lexden OBE
The Rt Hon The Lord Macgregor OBE
Dame Judith Mayhew Jonas DBE
Jean Scott
Lord Sharman OBE

COBIS Head Office
CEO: Colin Bell

COBIS Board
Dawn Akyurek, Headteacher, King's College School La Moraleja, Spain
John Bagust, Head of Primary Schools, The Prague British School, Czech Republic
Jennifer Bray MBE, Former Principal in Hong Kong and Brussels (*Inspections and Quality Officer*) (*co-opted*)
Brian Christian, Principal, The British School in Tokyo, Japan
Dr Martin Coles, Former CEO, The British School in The Netherlands and former Vice-Dean of the National College for School Leadership (*co-opted*)
Professor Deborah Eyre, World Class Educator (*co-opted*)
Anne Howells, Principal, British International School of Stavanger, Norway
Simon O'Grady, Principal, The British International School, Cairo, Egypt (*Treasurer*)
Trevor Rowell, Governor, British School of Alicante, Spain (*Chairman*)
Eamonn Mullally, Executive Head Teacher/CEO, The Edron Academy, Mexico (*co-opted*)
Kai Vacher, Principal, British School Muscat, The Sultanate of Oman
Dr Steffen Sommer, Principal, Doha College, Qatar (*Vice Chairman*)

Council of British International Schools
55-56 Russell Square, Bloomsbury, London WC1B 4HP
Tel: +44(0)20 3826 7190 • email: pa@cobis.org.uk

INDEPENDENT SCHOOLS INSPECTORATE
AND ISI CONSULTANCY LTD
www.isi.net

School inspections undertaken by the Independent Schools Inspectorate (ISI) have two principal objectives: to nurture and encourage school improvement and to report on whether independent schools comply with the regulatory requirements of government. Its overriding aim is to help ensure that every child receives education and care of the highest quality in the schools it inspects.

ISI is the body approved by the Secretary of State to inspect schools in England in membership of Associations within the Independent Schools Council (ISC). Inspections are conducted in accordance with the Education and Skills Act 2008, the Childcare Act 2006 and the Children Act 1989. The Office for Standards in Education, Children's Services and Skills (Ofsted) monitors ISI's work on behalf of the Department for Education (DfE).

Schools are inspected regularly on a schedule agreed with the DfE. Inspection reports are published to parents and made available, with other related material, on the ISI website: www.isi.net.

What gives ISI inspections their unique quality is the element of 'peer review'. Inspections are led by professional Reporting Inspectors, mainly either former HMI or Ofsted Inspectors or former head teachers who have trained and qualified for the role. The inspection team is composed of serving headteachers or other senior staff from ISC schools, and also trained by ISI. This peer review combines professional rigour, an understanding of the reality of modern independent schools and an up-to-date grasp of current educational developments.

ISI also inspects private Further Education and English Language providers. Inspection under this voluntary scheme for colleges satisfies the inspection requirements necessary to apply for or renew a Tier 4 licence to sponsor international students under the UKVI Points Based System. ISI also inspects schools in more than 30 countries worldwide, using a framework appropriate to the schools' international setting, and is approved to inspect schools under the UK government scheme for British Schools Overseas (BSO).

Through its subsidiary company ISI Consultancy Ltd, ISI offers a range of seminars, INSET and consultancy services to schools, other organisations and governments in the UK and overseas on matters related to inspection and school improvement.

Independent Schools Inspectorate
CAP House, 9-12 Long Lane, London EC1A 9HA
Tel: 020 7600 0100 • Fax: 020 7776 8849 • email: info@isi.net

METHODIST INDEPENDENT SCHOOLS TRUST
www.methodisteducation.co.uk

Chairman: Revd Dr David Deeks
General Secretary: Mr David Humphreys
Director of Finance: Mr John Weaving

Schools for Boys and Girls

Culford School, Bury St Edmunds, Suffolk
Farringtons School, Chislehurst, Kent
Kent College, Canterbury, Kent
Kingsley School, Bideford, North Devon
Lorenden Preparatory School, Faversham, Kent
Moorlands School, Leeds, West Yorks

Queen's College, Taunton, Somerset
Shebbear College, Beaworthy, Devon
St Petroc's School, Bude, Cornwall
Truro School, Truro, Cornwall
Woodhouse Grove School, Apperley Bridge, West Yorks

Schools for Girls
Kent College Pembury, Tunbridge Wells, Kent

OTHER METHODIST INDEPENDENT SCHOOLS
Schools for Boys and Girls

Ashville College, Harrogate, North Yorks
Kingswood School, Bath, Somerset
The Leys School, Cambridge

Methodist College, Belfast
Rydal Penrhos School, Colwyn Bay, North Wales
Wesley College, Dublin

Schools for Girls
Queenswood School, Hatfield, Herts
Truro High School, Truro, Cornwall

In cases of need applications may be made to a Methodist Bursary Fund for financial help to enable Methodist children to attend these schools. This fund is available to day pupils as well as boarding pupils. Details are available from the Schools.

Information regarding other sources of assistance with fees may be obtained from The Independent Schools Council, First Floor, 27 Queen Anne's Gate, London SW1H 9BU. Tel: 020 7766 7070; email: office@isc.co.uk

Methodist Independent Schools Trust
Methodist Church House, 25 Marylebone Road, London NW1 5JR
Tel: 020 7935 3723 • email: admin@methodisteducation.co.uk

THE GIRLS' DAY SCHOOL TRUST (GDST)

www.gdst.net

Chair:	Juliet Humphries
Deputy Chairmen:	Tom Wheare, MA, DipEd, FRSA
	Helen Williams, CB, MA
Chief Executive:	Cheryl Giovannoni

The GDST (Girls' Day School Trust) is the UK's leading network of independent girls' schools, with over 3,700 staff and nearly 20,000 students between the ages of three and 18.

One of the UK's largest educational charities, with 24 schools and two academies in England and Wales, we reinvest all our income into our education. Founded in 1872, the GDST has a long history of pioneering innovation in the education of women, and is the largest single educator of girls in the UK.

At the GDST our aim is not just to provide an outstanding academic education; we pride ourselves in creating a learning environment dedicated to the development of confident, courageous, composed and committed girls, ready for any demand life may make of them.

While our schools and academies are all individual, the commitment to developing the whole person is part of our shared DNA. We have a strong network for sharing knowledge and for spreading best practice, and we also develop and promote talented teachers through this network.

We celebrate our girls' differences, reinforce their strengths, and help them overcome their challenges. Girls can be themselves, and grow at their own pace. They're not cloistered – far from it – but their individual characters can take shape in a way that isn't possible in a mixed environment. For example, girls at GDST schools and academies are over twice as likely to study A Level physics or chemistry as girls nationally, with overall nearly half the students in GDST Sixth Forms taking at least one science A Level.

Every girl is different and we make sure that, regardless, she is the best she can be, and that she tries things, reaches for things, achieves things she may have thought beyond her. And when she does this, she grows in confidence and maturity in a way that will stay with her forever.

GDST schools

Blackheath High School	Nottingham Girls' High School
Brighton & Hove High School	Oxford High School
Bromley High School	Portsmouth High School
Croydon High School	Putney High School
Howell's School, Llandaff, Cardiff	The Royal High School, Bath
Ipswich High School	Sheffield High School
Kensington Prep School	Shrewsbury High School
Newcastle High School for Girls	South Hampstead High School
Northampton High School	Streatham & Clapham High School
Northwood College for Girls	Sutton High School
Norwich High School for Girls	Sydenham High School
Notting Hill & Ealing High School	Wimbledon High School

GDST academies

The Belvedere Academy, Liverpool
Birkenhead High School Academy

Information on the schools can be found in the Yearbook or on the GDST website: www.gdst.net

The Girls' Day School Trust is a Registered Charity, number 306983.

The Girls' Day School Trust
100 Rochester Row, London SW1P 1JP
Tel: 020 7393 6666 • email: info@wes.gdst.net

CATHOLIC INDEPENDENT SCHOOLS' CONFERENCE

www.cisc.uk.net

Objects

The CISC exists to:
- promote the work of Catholic independent schools throughout the UK;
- give and coordinate support and advice to member schools;
- organise activities for member schools including an annual conference, retreats and study days;
- represent the interests of CISC schools as appropriate;
- provide a help line for those seeking a Catholic Independent School for their children.

Schools

There are 135 schools currently in membership of the CISC. Schools in membership include day and boarding schools, single-sex and co-educational, senior and junior schools and special schools.

Membership

There are two categories of Members: **Full Members** and **Associate Members**.

Full Members

Full Members may be invited by the Committee to take up membership. He/She will be the Head or Principal of a school which satisfies the following seven conditions:

(a) The school shall be recognised by the local Catholic bishop as being Catholic.
(b) The school shall have been recognised as a charitable foundation by the Charity Commissioners.
(c) The school shall be independent.
(d) The school will have been subjected to a nationally accredited inspection and found to be in good standing.
(e) The expectation is that the head of the school will be a practising Catholic. Where governors appoint a head who is not a Catholic, CISC will expect governors to provide training and support for the head to enable the head to lead a Catholic school, and will assist them in so doing.
(f) Full members only attend the AGM.

Associate Members

Associate Members may be invited by the Chairman to take up membership, but do not attend the AGM.
The following are eligible for associate membership:

(a) Heads of proprietary-owned schools, which meet the conditions of Full Membership apart from not being recognised by the Charity Commissioners as a charitable foundation.
(b) Retired full Members.
(c) Catholics, and other Christians, who are in sympathy with the aims of CISC.
(d) Heads of Foundation or Voluntary-Aided Schools, which meet the conditions of Full Membership, apart from not being recognised by the Charity Commissioners as a charitable foundation.
(e) Heads of Catholic Independent Schools outside the United Kingdom.

Officers for 2016–2017
Chair: Ms Antonia Beary, MPhil – Mayfield School
Vice Chair: Mr Michael Connolly, BSc, BA, MA, MEd – Cranmore School
Treasurer: Mr Antony Hudson, MA, PGCE, NPQH – St George's Junior School

Committee:
Mrs Sarah Conrad, BA Hons, PGCE, NPQH – St Teresa's Prep School
Mr Paulo Durán, BA, MA – St Edmund's College
Mr Michael Kennedy, BSc, MA, NPQH, CChem, MRSC – St Mary's College Crosby
Mr Gareth Lloyd, BA Hons, MSc, FMusTCL – Ratcliffe College
Mr James Murphy-O'Connor, MA – Prior Park College
Mr Stephen Oliver, BA, MLitt – Our Lady's Abingdon

General Secretary: Mr Raymond Friel, MA Hons, NPQH

Catholic Independent Schools' Conference
17 Rossiters Hill, Frome, Somerset BA11 4AL
Tel: 07949 394925 • email: raymondfriel@cisc.uk.net

CHOIR SCHOOLS' ASSOCIATION

www.choirschools.org.uk

Patron: The Duchess of Kent

Committee:

Chairman: Paul Smith, Hereford Cathedral School
Vice-Chairman: Tim Cannell, The Prebendal School, Chichester
Treasurer: Neil Chippington, St John's College School, Cambridge

Neil Blundell, Bristol Cathedral Choir School
Yvette Day, The Chorister School, Durham
Alex Donaldson, Minster School, York
Clive Marriott, Salisbury Cathedral School

Nick Robinson, King's College School, Cambridge
Clare Turnbull, Lanesborough School, Guildford
Richard White

CSA Full and Associate Members

Blackburn Cathedral
Bristol Cathedral Choir School
King's College School, Cambridge
St John's College School, Cambridge
St Edmund's Junior School, Canterbury
St John's College, Cardiff
St Cedd's School, Chelmsford
Dean Close Preparatory School, Cheltenham
The Prebendal School, Chichester
Croydon Minster
The Chorister School, Durham
St Mary's Music School, Edinburgh
King's Ely Junior, Ely
Exeter Cathedral School
The King's School, Gloucester
Lanesborough School, Guildford
Chapel Royal, Hampton Court
Hereford Cathedral School
Leicester Cathedral

Lichfield Cathedral School
Lincoln Minster School
Runnymede St Edward's School, Liverpool
St Edward's College, Liverpool
The Cathedral School, Llandaff
City of London School
The London Oratory School
St Paul's Cathedral School, London
Westminster Abbey Choir School, London
Westminster Cathedral Choir School, London
Chetham's School of Music, Manchester
St Nicholas Cathedral, Newcastle-upon-Tyne
Norwich School
Christ Church Cathedral School, Oxford
Magdalen College School, Oxford

New College School, Oxford
The King's School, Peterborough
The Portsmouth Grammar School
Reigate St Mary's Choir School
Ripon Cathedral
King's Rochester Preparatory School
Salisbury Cathedral School
Sheffield Cathedral
The Minster School, Southwell
Polwhele House School, Truro
Queen Elizabeth Grammar School, Wakefield
Wells Cathedral School
The Pilgrims' School, Winchester
St George's School, Windsor
St Peter's Church, Wolverhampton
The King's School, Worcester
The Minster School, York
Ampleforth College, York

Overseas Members:

St Patrick's Cathedral Choir School, Dublin
The Cathedral Grammar School, Christchurch, New Zealand
National Cathedral School, Washington DC, USA
St Paul's Choir School, Cambridge, MA, USA
St Thomas Choir School, New York, USA

TThe 44 choir schools in the UK are all attached to cathedrals, churches or college chapels and educate over 20,000 pupils, including some 1,300 choristers. Westminster Abbey Choir School is the only school to educate choristers and probationers only. The Association's associate membership includes cathedrals and churches without choir schools.

Choir schools offer a very special opportunity for children who enjoy singing. They receive a first-class academic and all-round education combined with excellent music training. The experience and self-discipline choristers acquire remain with them for life. There is a wide range of schools: some cater for children aged 7–13, others are junior schools with senior schools to 18; most are Church of England but the Roman Catholic, Scottish and Welsh churches are all represented.

Most CSA members are fee-paying schools and Deans and Chapters provide fee assistance while Government support comes in the shape of the Choir Schools' Scholarship Scheme. Under the umbrella of the Music and Dance Scheme, funds are available to help those who cannot afford even the reduced school fees. The Government funding, along with other monies in its Bursary Trust Fund, is administered by the CSA. Each application is means-tested and an award made once a child has secured a place at a choir school.

Each CSA member school has its own admissions procedure for choristers. However, every child will be assessed both musically and academically. A growing number of children are given informal voice tests which enable the organist or director of music to judge whether they have the potential to become choristers. Some are offered places immediately or will be urged to enter the more formal voice trial organised by the school. In some cases a family may be advised not to proceed. Alternatively, the child's voice may be more suitable for one of the other choir schools.

A number of special ingredients help make a good chorister: potential, a keen musical ear and an eagerness to sing. A clutch of music examination certificates is not vital – alertness and enthusiasm are! At the same time, school staff must be satisfied that a new recruit can cope with school work and the many other activities on offer as well as the demanding choir workload

To find out more about choir schools please visit the CSA website: **www.choirschools.org.uk**

The Association publishes a newsletter – *Singing Out*

CSA members can be contacted direct or you can write, email or telephone
for further information about choir schools to:

Jane Capon, Information Officer, Village Farm, The Street, Market Weston, Diss, Norfolk IP22 2NZ
Telephone: 01359 221333; email: info@choirschools.org.uk

Mrs Susan Rees, Administrator, 39 Grange Close, Winchester, Hampshire SO23 9RS
Tel: 01962 890530; email: admin@choirschools.org.uk

COUNCIL FOR INDEPENDENT EDUCATION
(CIFE)
www.cife.org.uk

President:
Lord Lexden OBE

Vice President:
Hugh Monro, MA

Chairman:
Sally Powell, BA, PGCE, MPhil, DPhil Oxon
Principal, Collingham

Vice-Chairman:
Tim Naylor, BA Hons, MSc, PGCE

Independent sixth-form colleges are extremely well placed to offer what is needed for students preparing for university and beyond. The best such colleges are generally members of CIFE, the Council for Independent Education, an organisation which was founded 40 years ago. There are 20 CIFE colleges, geographically spread across the country, each one offering individual features but all subject to high standards of accreditation. For example, there are some colleges that specialise in students wishing to retake in order to improve exam grades, some offering GCSE and pre-GCSE programmes as well as full A Level courses, which may be residential, homestay, day, or a mix of all three. Several colleges offer foundation programmes and are twinned with universities. In short, CIFE colleges offer a wide range of educational environments in which students can succeed.

Teaching in CIFE colleges really helps and supports students since teaching groups are small and teachers highly experienced and specialists in their subject. The 'tutorial' system derives directly from Oxbridge where it continues to be world famous. A student in a small group receives a greater degree of individual attention. Regular testing ensures that she/he maintains good progress, and the emphasis on study skills provides essential support for the AS/A2 subjects.

It is not surprising that a student gains confidence and self-belief within such an environment. Colleges engender a strong work ethic in their student communities. Many of the minor rules and regulations essential for schools are not necessary at CIFE colleges. Good manners and an enthusiastic attitude are every bit as important, but uniform, strict times for eating or homework, assemblies or games participation are not part of the picture. It can be seen from the large numbers of students going on to higher education from CIFE colleges that universities regard our students highly.

Increasing numbers of young people are deciding to move school at the age of 16, not because they are unhappy with their school, but because they see the need for a change at this stage. It may be that they wish to study a subject which their school does not offer, such as Accounting, Law, Psychology or Photography. Perhaps they are looking for a more adult environment or one where they can focus on their academic subjects to the exclusion of other things. However, it would be misleading to suggest that CIFE colleges are lacking in extracurricular activities, as every CIFE college recognises the need for enrichment of all sorts, sporting, social and creative. The difference is that activities are at the choice of the student.

As with schools, choosing a college calls for careful research. CIFE colleges undergo regular inspection either by the Independent Schools Inspectorate, Ofsted and/or the British Accreditation Council, recognised bodies which regulate the provision and standards of teaching, safety and pastoral care. While each college has its own individual character, all share the desire to provide each individual student with a superb preparation for higher education.

Members of CIFE

Ashbourne Independent Sixth Form College, London
Bales College, London
Bath Academy, Bath
Bosworth Independent College, Northampton
Brooke House College, Market Harborough
Cambridge Centre for Sixth-form Studies, Cambridge
Cambridge Tutors College, London
Carfax Tutorial Establishment, Oxford
CATS College, London
Chelsea Independent College, London

Cherwell College, Oxford
Collingham, London
DLD College, London
Duff Miller Sixth Form College, London
Lansdowne College, London
Mander Portman Woodward, Birmingham
Mander Portman Woodward, London
Oxford International College, Oxford
Oxford Tutorial College, Oxford
Regent College, London

Further information can be obtained from:

CIFE
Tel: 020 8767 8666 • email: enquiries@cife.org.uk

UNITED LEARNING

www.unitedlearning.org.uk

President
The Rt Revd & Rt Hon The Lord Carey of Clifton, ALCD, BD, MTh, PhD

Patrons
The Most Revd & Rt Hon Justin Welby, Archbishop of Canterbury
The Most Revd & Rt Hon Dr John Sentamu, Archbishop of York

United Learning – Group Board
Richard Greenhalgh (*Chair*)
Dame Yasmin Bevan, DBE, Hon DEd, BSc Econ, BA, MA
Jon Coles
Angela Crowe, JP (*Chair of Education Board – Independent Schools*)
Michael George (*Chair of Northampton Academy LGB*)
Sir Anthony Greener (*Chair of Swindon Academy LGB*)
Linda Heaver (*Chair of Lincoln Minster School LGB*)
Mike Litchfield
David Robinson (*Chair of Stockport Academy LGB*)
Nigel Robson (*Chair of Education Board – Academies*)
Sarah Squire

Executive Team:

Chief Executive: Mr Jon Coles

Director of People: Mandy Coalter
Director of Secondary Academies, South: Dame Sally Coates
Director of Estates: Graham Harvey-Browne
Chief Financial Officer: Louise Johnston

Primary Director: Darran Lee
Group Director of Technology: Dominic Norrish
Head of Strategy and Performance: Anna Bush
Director of Secondary Academies, North: Janet Woods

United Learning Independent Schools

AKS (HMC, day)
Ashford School (HMC, IAPS, boarding and day)
Bournemouth Collegiate School (The Society of Heads, IAPS, boarding and day)
Caterham School* (HMC, IAPS, boarding and day)
Dunottar School (The Society of Heads, day)
Greenacre School (GSA, day)
Guildford High School (HMC, IAPS, day)

Hampshire Collegiate School (The Society of Heads, IAPS, boarding and day)
Hull Collegiate School (The Society of Heads, ISA, day)
Lincoln Minster School (HMC, The Society of Heads, IAPS, boarding and day)
Rowan Preparatory School (IAPS, day)
St Ives School for Girls (IAPS, day)
Surbiton High School (HMC, IAPS, day)

*Associate School

Our Ethos

United Learning is a group of schools committed to providing excellent education through which all pupils are able to progress, achieve and go on to succeed in life. Our approach is underpinned by a sense of moral purpose and commitment to doing what is right for children and young people, supporting colleagues to achieve excellence and acting with integrity in all our dealings within and beyond the organisation, in the interests of young people everywhere. We summarise this ethos as 'The Best in Everyone'.

This ethos underpins our core values:

- Ambition – to achieve the best for ourselves and others;
- Confidence – to have the courage of our convictions and to take risks in the right cause;
- Creativity – to imagine possibilities and make them real;
- Respect – of ourselves and others in all that we do;
- Enthusiasm – to seek opportunity, find what is good and pursue talents and interests;
- Determination – to overcome obstacles and reach success.

As a single organisation, we seek to bring together the best of independent and state sectors, respecting both traditions and learning from each. We believe that each of our schools is and should be distinctive – each is committed to developing its own strengths and identity while sharing our core values as institutions which promote service, compassion and generosity.

Academic scholarships, exhibitions and bursaries are awarded at all schools. The tuition fees vary according to age and school; for example, tuition fees per annum in the senior schools range from £10,899 to £16,800 (day), and £25,305 to £33,750 (full boarding).

United Learning comprises: UCST (Registered in England No: 2780748. Charity No. 1016538) and ULT (Registered in England No. 4439859. An Exempt Charity). Companies limited by guarantee. VAT number 834 8515 12.

United Learning
Worldwide House, Thorpe Wood, Peterborough, PE3 6SB
Tel: 01832 864444 • Fax: 01832 864455 • email: enquiries@unitedlearning.org.uk

INSPIRING FUTURES FOUNDATION

(formerly ISCO)

Working in partnership with independent UK and
international schools to provide the full range of careers
education and development support for their students

www.inspiringfutures.org.uk

**Council of Trustees
for the Inspiring Futures Foundation**
Chairman: M E Hicks, MSc, DPhil

Hon Treasurer: R Vevers

Ms W Berliner	P Greatrix
C W Conway	K Richardson
M Elms	J Spence
Prof D Eyre	

Chief Executive: Mrs V Isaac

Contacts

Who to ask for information and help
Contact the Area or Regional Director for your area (see below) or the Information Helpline on 01491 820383

For further information on *The Inspiring Futures Foundation* or on *Inspiring Futures Careers* (now a part of the GTI Group) please contact:
Chief Executive: Virginia Isaac (email: v.isaac@inspiringfutures.org.uk, tel: 01491 820392)

Purpose and Aims

The Inspiring Futures Foundation is a not-for-profit, careers guidance organisation. It exists to help young people make decisions and develop skills which maximize their potential, enhance their employment opportunities and allow them to make a fulfilling contribution to the world in which they live. IFF oversees a School Careers Award Scheme that provides free careers support for aspiring pupils from low-income schools.

In order to do this, Inspiring Futures works with like-minded people and organisations to provide expert careers guidance, innovative learning resources and personal skills training to young people from all backgrounds, particularly those entering higher education.

Inspiring Futures Membership for independent and international schools provides a range of careers and higher education related services to complement and reinforce school programmes with impartial and professional expertise.

Services also include Futurewise, a personalised careers guidance programme for students aged 15 to 23. The web-based psychometric profile and one-to-one interview is followed by a wealth of resources and support for the student helping them with subject choices, routes to HE and alternative pathways to a career. The programme is flexible making it suitable for easy lesson planning. Futurewise courses and training events for students and a range of professional services to support independent schools' careers staff are also offered.

Inspiring Futures Careers : Area and Regional Directors

Scotland & Ireland

Area Director:	Margaret Graham (Tel: 07717 530459; email: margaret.graham@inspiringfutures.org.uk)
E Scotland:	Jane Ambrose (Tel: 07887 758166; email: jane.ambrose@inspiringfutures.org.uk)
N Scotland & Central Scotland:	Greta Weir (Tel: 07872 350696; email: greta.weir@inspiringfutures.org.uk)
W Scotland:	Margaret Graham (Tel: 07717 530459; email: margaret.graham@inspiringfutures.org.uk)

England & Wales
North, North East & Midlands

Area Director:	Sarah Frend (Tel: 07525 805007; email: sarah.frend@inspiringfutures.org.uk)
Shropshire & Midlands:	Sally Hayward (Tel: 07887 758649; email: sally.hayward@inspiringfutures.org.uk)
North West & Yorkshire:	Mike Parker-Cook (Tel: 07702 297558; email: michael.parker-cook@inspiringfutures.org.uk)
East:	Kate Coles (Tel: 07717 468074; email: kate.coles@inspiringfutures.org.uk)

London & South East

Area Director:	Emma-Marie Fry (Tel: 07702 226271; email: emma-marie.fry@inspiringfutures.org.uk)
Sussex & Kent:	Elizabeth Armstrong (Tel: 07909 972769; email: elizabeth.armstrong@inspiringfutures.org.uk)
South & West London:	Emma Paton (Tel: 07734 569968; email: emma.paton@inspiringfutures.org.uk)
North London:	Helen Barham (Tel: 07917 712603; email: hel.barham@inspiringfutures.org.uk)

South West

Area Director:	Mark Smith (Tel: 07736 821284; email: mark.smith@inspiringfutures.org.uk)
South West:	Vicki MacDonald (Tel: 07717 496523; email: vicki.macdonald@inspiringfutures.org.uk)

International

Area Director:	Mark Smith (Tel: 07736 821284; email: mark.smith@inspiringfutures.org.uk)

High quality education in an actively Christian environment for all

www.woodard.co.uk

twitter: @WoodardSchools

Members of the Board
Chairman: Mr R S Morse

The Rt Revd Dr A Russell DPhil FRAgS (*President*)
Mr S G Alder BA FCA
Ms L Ayres LLB
The Revd Canon L M Barley BA Hons MSc PGCE
Dr I Bishop CBE BEd Hons MA LLD
Mr R J Bokros
Mr T D Fremantle MBA DL

Mr M S Hedges MA FCA FRSA
Mrs M Holman MA
Mr B M Newman MA MBA CEng FIMechE FIET FIoD
  FRSA
Mrs P Pritchard BEd Hons LRAM ARCM
Mr P H W Southern FRICS

Key Officers

The Revd Canon B D Clover MA FRSA LTCL (*Senior Provost – Provost*
of Northern, Midland, Eastern and Western Regions)
The Rt Revd C J Meyrick MA Oxon, Bishop of Lynn (*Provost of Southern Region*)
Mr M Corcoran BSc ACA (*Director of Finance/Company Secretary*)
Mr C Wright MA FRSA (*Director of Education*)

Incorporated Schools (*independent*)

Abbots Bromley School
Abbots Bromley International College
Abbots Bromley Preparatory School
Ardingly College
Ardingly College Preparatory School
Bloxham School
The Cathedral School Llandaff
Denstone College
Denstone College Prep School at
  Smallwood Manor

Ellesmere College
Hurstpierpoint College
Hurstpierpoint College Preparatory
  School
King's College, Taunton
King's Hall School, Taunton
Lancing College
Lancing College Preparatory School
  at Hove

Lancing College Preparatory School
  at Worthing
The Peterborough School
Prestfelde School, Shrewsbury
Queen Mary's School, Thirsk
St James' School, Grimsby
Worksop College
Worksop College Preparatory School,
  Retford

Information on all of the schools can be found on the website www.woodard.co.uk

Woodard Schools form the largest group of Anglican schools in England and Wales. In addition to the above list of incorporated schools, a number of schools in the independent and maintained sectors choose to be associated or affiliated, respectively. Woodard also sponsors academies. The schools are not exclusive and take pupils of all faiths and of none. In total some 30,100 pupils are taught in schools throughout the group. In 2011 the members of the wider Woodard family raised sufficient funds to open the Woodard Langalanga Secondary School in Gilgil, Kenya to mark the bicentenary of the birth of the Founder, Canon Nathaniel Woodard. Doors opened to the first intake of pupils in January 2012; there are now 425 boys and girls being influenced by the Woodard ethos.

This unique partnership of schools, independent and state, boarding and day, junior and senior, co-educational and single-sex, is united by a determination to provide a first-class holistic education within a distinctive Christian ethos. The schools were founded by Nathaniel Woodard in the nineteenth century and aim to prepare children from a wide variety of backgrounds for responsibility, leadership and service in today's world.

The schools seek to provide flexible, stimulating, demanding and appropriate schemes of academic study together with a rich variety of sporting, artistic and recreational opportunities. We encourage personal success, self-confidence and self-respect whilst also stressing the importance of responsible citizenship, high moral values and a commitment to use one's gifts in the service of others.

With the geographical spread and diversity of schools included in the group it is able to offer parents a wide range of educational options for their children. Woodard incorporated schools operate bursary and scholarship schemes including all classes of concession. Fees vary from school to school and are set locally.

The Woodard Corporation is a Registered Charity (No. 1096270) and Company (No. 4659710). The objects of the charity are to promote and extend education (including spiritual, moral, social, cultural and physical education) in accordance with the doctrines and principles of the Church of England/Church in Wales by directly or indirectly carrying on schools

Woodard Schools
High Street, Abbots Bromley, Rugeley, Staffordshire WS15 3BW
Tel: 01283 840120 • Fax: 01283 840893 • email: jillshorthose@woodard.co.uk

ASSOCIATION FOR ADMISSIONS, MARKETING AND DEVELOPMENT IN INDEPENDENT SCHOOLS (AMDIS)

FOUNDED 1993

www.amdis.co.uk

Objectives:
- To promote and develop good marketing practice in admissions, marketing and development in independent education
- To help increase the effectiveness of the admissions and marketing representatives of Member Schools
- To encourage personal development within the schools' admissions and marketing profession

Achieved through:
- Seminars and workshops on a variety of admissions and marketing-led subjects held throughout the year
- Annual residential conference
- Regional networking lunches
- Training – Diploma in Schools' Marketing & Certificate in Admissions Management
- Helpline
- Website with member-only resource section
- LinkedIn Group Forum
- On-line News bulletins throughout the year
- Speakers provided for conferences, inset days and similar

Membership:
- School Membership, renewable annually by subscription
- Corporate Membership, renewable annually by subscription

The Association is directed by a Chairman, Vice Chairman and Treasurer together with a Board of Directors.

Managing Director: Tory Gillingham

AMDIS

57A Market Place, Malton, North Yorkshire YO17 7LX

Tel: 01653 699800 • email: enquiries@amdis.co.uk

ASSOCIATION OF REPRESENTATIVES OF OLD PUPILS' SOCIETIES (AROPS)

Founded in 1971

www.arops.org.uk

President:
Bill Gillen (Old Arnoldians and Belfast Old Instonians' Association)
Vice-Presidents:
Margaret Carter-Pegg (Old Crohamian), Guy Cliff (Old Silcoatian), Michael Freegard (Old Haileyburian),
Tim Neale (Radleian Society), Trish Woodhouse (GSA)

Committee
Chairman: Peter Jakobek (Old Bristolians)
Treasurer: Keith Balkham (KGS Friends)
Secretary: Hannah Baker (Queen's Gate Society)
and 12 committee members

Aim: To provide a friendly forum for the exchange of views and experiences between representatives of school alumni societies.

Membership: Open to representatives of any school alumni society. New members are always welcome. Details are available on the website – www.arops.org.uk – where you can also find information on events and member societies' news, regularly updated. Please contact us by email to: arops@arops.org.uk.

Meetings: The Conference in May is our main event and an ideal opportunity to meet up with other representatives and to share thoughts on current topics. Our very successful Conference in 2016 took place at Malvern St James Girls' School where sessions included: Trends in Secondary Education; Protecting your Alumni; Everything you wanted to know about managing data; How do you get the best out of your database provider; Careers in university mentoring; How do you engage female alumni; and The role of volunteers. The Conferences always end with a lively forum and a dinner. The 2017 Conference will be held at Prior Park College in Bath on Saturday 13th May.

Apart from the Conference and the AGM (held in London in October), AROPS now organises a series of *regional meetings* around the country which allow representatives to meet neighbouring members in a less formal environment. These have proved very popular.

Subscription: £50 per year (with discounts for smaller societies). Please email the Treasurer, Keith Balkham, on kbalkham@hotmail.com or write to him at:14 Cromwell Road, Alperton, Middlesex HAO 1JS.

MONTESSORI SCHOOLS ASSOCIATION

www.montessori.org.uk

The Montessori Schools Association (MSA) was founded to support and represent all Montessori schools across the United Kingdom. The MSA works through 9 national regions each with its own Regional Chairman, and also with the Primary Group and the Childminders' Network.

The Montessori Schools Association currently has over 3,900 members and 687 Montessori schools ranging in size from 15 to 400+ pupils covering the birth to 11 age range.

It is supported and run by the Montessori St Nicholas Charity (founded in 1954). The charity today works to support Montessori across the UK in every way it can, particularly through making awards and finance initiatives that support the development of Montessori education in the fields of training grants for individuals, equipment and advice; funding research and development into the value and effectiveness of Montessori education and facilitating the unification of the Montessori movement across the UK.

In September 2008 the Montessori St Nicholas Charity set up the Montessori Evaluation and Accreditation Board (MEAB), a national evaluation and accreditation scheme to raise standards within the Montessori Schools Association and put "best practice" at the heart of what it does. The MEAB scheme builds on Montessori's excellent track record in education. There are now 174 MEAB accredited schools.

The Montessori Schools Association
18 Balderton Street, London W1K 6TG
Tel: 020 7493 8300 • email: centre@montessori.org.uk

MEDICAL OFFICERS OF SCHOOLS ASSOCIATION

FOUNDED 1884

www.mosa.org.uk

Objects

It is the objective of the Association to offer guidance and support and to encourage the application of the highest of medical standards in the educational environment. MOSA offers its members mutual assistance in promoting school health and the holding of meetings for consideration of all subjects connected with the special work of medical officers of schools.

Membership

Medical officers of schools and medical and dental practitioners and nurses especially concerned with the health of the schoolchild are eligible for membership, and members of the teaching profession, and those related to independent school management, for associate membership. The membership currently stands at 212.

The work of the Association

The Council meets three times a year and is chaired by the current President, Dr Jonathan Holliday, MO to Eton College. MOSA council members are available for advice to members and non-members. Members have access to a secure online discussion forum where questions and topics are discussed giving access to up-to-date resources and peer support.

Clinical meetings are arranged each year together with an annual summer visit to a school. Research projects are carried out individually and collectively. The Association strongly recommends that all independent schools appoint medical officers to carry out preventative medicine duties which are undertaken in maintained schools by the School Health Service.

MOSA Consultancy Service

MOSA is pleased to announce a new consultancy service for any school which will offer a review of the medical care provided within the school environment.

This can be tailored to the school's needs but tends to be one of two types:
• A general review of the overall medical/nursing provision in the school
• A review of a specific area of concern.

Initially there will be discussion between the MOSA team leader and the school representative so that the Terms of Reference can be drawn up. MOSA will then provide the necessary team to perform the investigation with the most suitably qualified professionals, being able to draw from a pool of highly experienced school doctors and nurses. The team will then visit the appropriate areas of the school and carry out any necessary interviews.

If you are interested in this service, please contact the Executive Secretary, email: mosa.execsec@gmail.com.

Publications

The Association publishes administrative and clinical guidelines for its Medical Officers; these are found on the Association's website and updated regularly.

For further information about the Association and other related business enquiries should in the first instance be directed to:

The Hon Secretary: Dr Rebecca Pryse, MB BS, DCH, DRCOG, DFSRH
The Swan Practice, High Street, Buckingham MK18 1NU
Tel: 01280 818600; Fax: 01280 818618; email: rebecca.pryse@nhs.net

For administrative information and background please contact:
The Executive Secretary: Mrs Louise Fortune; email: mosa.execsec@gmail.com

THE ENGLISH-SPEAKING UNION

UK REGISTERED CHARITY NO. 273136

www.esu.org/sse

Secondary School Exchange Scholarships to the USA

A gap year with a difference – since 1928 the English-Speaking Union has offered young people the opportunity to spend a life-changing year or six months at a private American high school. The ESU offers the following Secondary School Exchange Scholarships:

Three-term scholarships

- The closing date for applications is in February (in your final year of A Levels or equivalent)
- Interviews are in March
- Leave for the US in September (after completion of your A Levels or equivalent)

Two-term scholarships

- The closing date for applications is in September (after completion of your A Levels or equivalent)
- Interviews are in September/October
- Leave for the US in early January

About the Scholarship

Each scholarship covers the cost of tuition, board and lodging, worth $30,000-$50,000. Scholars are fully fledged students at their host school, with access to world class facilities and a range of extra-curricular activities. Alumni of the programme include singer KT Tunstall, Sir Ian Blair, former Metropolitan Police Commissioner, Sir Richard Dearlove KCMG OBE, former head of MI6, 'City Superwoman' Nicole Horlick, the actress and comedienne Dawn French, and former HSBC chairman, Sir John Bond.

SSE is both an academic and cultural gap year programme. Scholars study a range of subjects at their host schools including some they dropped at GCSE, subjects they will study at university, and even subjects that don't feature in UK schools. The skills that can be gained from the exchange have proven to be beneficial at University: American teaching emphasises independence of thought, and discussions play a large part in the classroom. Scholars also enjoy American rites of passage such as spring break, prom, and graduation.

Scholars are responsible for additional costs including travel, insurance, and expenses. The ESU offers means-tested assistance to help towards these additional costs to successful applicants who would otherwise be unable to take up a scholarship. It also offers one full award, designed to cover all the additional costs related to the scholarship. Grants are given in the range of £200-£2,000. Many scholars use the summer holidays or the six-month gap between finishing school and leaving the US to save money for their time abroad.

Eligibility

- You must have completed your A Levels (or equivalent) and be intending to study at a UK university on your return. Your place does not need to be confirmed or deferred, and some scholars reapply during their scholarship year.
- Applications from students intending to study at a US university at undergraduate level will not be accepted.
- You must have a minimum of 3 Grade Cs at A Level or equivalent.
- You should be under 19 years and 6 months old when you take up the scholarship.
- Scholars are expected to commit to the full term of their scholarship (two-term: 6 months; three-term: 9 months).
- You must be a British Citizen and have studied/be studying A Levels (or equivalent) at a school in the UK.

About the English-Speaking Union

Founded in 1918, the ESU is an international educational charity and membership organisation that promotes mutual understanding, and fosters friendship and exchange throughout the world.

The English-Speaking Union
37 Charles Street, London W1J 5ED
Tel: 020 7529 1550 · email: education@esu.org

DURSTON HOUSE

12 Castlebar Road · London W5 2DR

A leading West London Prep School for Boys

A great spirit of community...

a real pride in achievement

Visit our *website* www.durstonhouse.org
Send for an *Information Pack* or come to see us
contact Mrs Caroline Ferns (Registrar) *telephone* 020 8991 6532
email info@durstonhouse.org

Boys Prep School 4-13 years · Registered Charity No. 294670

REDKITE
ESTABLISHED 1982

THE UK'S LEADING SUPPLIER OF SCHOOL MINIBUSES

TAKE A CLOSER LOOK

New and Used 9 -17 Seat School Minibuses
B and D1 Licence Options
Fully Type Approved and Certified by the VCA
Flexible Finance Plans to Suit all Budgets
36 Months New Minibus Warranty
12 Months Used Minibus Warranty
Comprehensive Choice of Mobility Options
Full Nationwide Service and Support

Choose with confidence, our knowledge and
support make the difference, call today

01202 827678

redkite-minibuses.com
sales@redkite-minibuses.com

Crowe Clark Whitehill

A Member of Crowe Horwath International

Listening to you

Crowe Clark Whitehill is a leading advisor to independent schools.

How we can help you:

- Technical advice in a clear and pragmatic way.
- We focus on your needs, investing time in understanding your school and being proactive in our approach.
- Always working with clear and transparent lines of communication.

Start the conversation

Tina Allison
London
Head of Education
tina.allison@crowecw.co.uk
+44 (0)20 7842 7276

Vicky Szulist
Manchester
Partner
vicky.szulist@crowecw.co.uk
+44 (0)161 214 7500

Alastair Lyon
Thames Valley
Partner
alastair.lyon@crowecw.co.uk
+44 (0)118 959 7222

Guy Biggin
Cheltenham
Partner
guy.biggin@crowecw.co.uk
+44 (0)124 223 4421

Helen Drew
Midlands
Partner
helen.drew@crowecw.co.uk
+44 (0)121 543 1900

Audit / Tax / Advisory

Smart decisions. Lasting value.

www.croweclarkwhitehill.co.uk

Crowe Clark Whitehill LLP is a member of Crowe Horwath International, a Swiss verein (Crowe Horwath). Each member firm of Crowe Horwath is a separate and independent legal entity. Crowe Clark Whitehill LLP and its affiliates are not responsible or liable for any acts or omissions of Crowe Horwath or any other member of Crowe Horwath and specifically disclaim any and all responsibility or liability for acts or omissions of Crowe Horwath or any other Crowe Horwath member. © 2017 Crowe Clark Whitehill LLP | 0003. This material is for informational purposes only and should not be construed as financial or legal advice. Crowe Clark Whitehill LLP is registered to carry on audit work in the UK by the Institute of Chartered Accountants in England and Wales and is authorised and regulated by the Financial Conduct Authority.

The Manor House & Ashbury Hotels

The Only Sport, Craft & Spa Hotels in the UK

GREAT VALUE SCHOOL ACTIVITY BREAKS IN THE HEART OF DEVON!

The Manor House and Ashbury Hotels are located on the foothills of Dartmoor National Park. We are a Sports, Craft and Leisure complex with indoor and outdoor facilities that are unrivalled anywhere in England.

INCLUDED IN YOUR BREAK:

- Full Board (3 meals a day)
- En Suite Accommodation
- Free Equipment
- Dedicated Activity Co-ordinator
- Personalised Activity Programme
- Activity Instructors to run all sessions
- Free use of all sports & leisure facilities

TENNIS COACHING

8 Indoor & 4 Outdoor Courts!

Group coaching is now available at both hotels all year round, with our LTA accredited coach. Or enjoy friendly competitions.

SPORTS PITCH

Enjoy a variety of Sports!

Our new 91mx54m sports pitch is perfect for tournaments and training. Enjoy a number of sports including: football, hockey & tag rugby.

SPORTS SIMULATORS

Enjoy Rugby, Football & Golf!

Perfect for groups, our 3 multi sports simulators will offer the opportunity to experience a wide range of sports and more!

CRAFTING FUN

Get creative with our 17 tutored crafts. All tuition is free of charge, with material costs starting from just £1!

...AND SO MUCH MORE!

OVER 70 ACTIVITIES TO CHOOSE FROM!

Tailor your programme from the 70 activities that we offer, plus enjoy our range of leisure facilities FREE OF CHARGE throughout your stay.

SELECTED JULY 2018 BREAKS... INC. 12.5% GROUP DISCOUNT STUDENTS UNDER 16 FROM £195pp FOR 4 NIGHTS FULL BOARD

0800 955 0289   sportscraftandgolfhotels.com

Authors Aloud UK

Bringing *stories* and *illustration* to life!

We are specialists in arranging author visits to schools, libraries, conferences and festivals. We can offer:

* A wide range of children's authors, illustrators, poets, storytellers and trainers
* Easy and quick booking service
* Expert advice about authors
* National and international expertise

Authors Aloud UK Ltd

T 01727 893992
E info@authorsalouduk.co.uk
www.authorsalouduk.co.uk

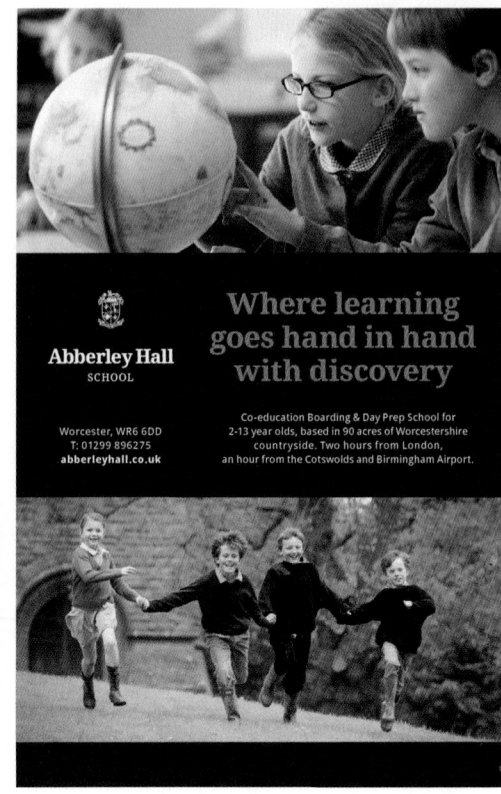

🛡 **Abberley Hall**
SCHOOL

Worcester, WR6 6DD
T: 01299 896275
abberleyhall.co.uk

Where learning goes hand in hand with discovery

Co-education Boarding & Day Prep School for
2-13 year olds, based in 90 acres of Worcestershire
countryside. Two hours from London,
an hour from the Cotswolds and Birmingham Airport.

Writers&Artists

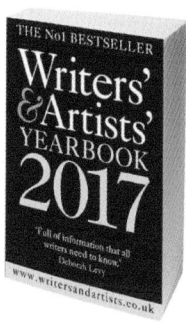

THE No1 BESTSELLER
Writers' &Artists' YEARBOOK 2017
"Full of information that all writers need to know."
Deborah Levy
www.writersandartists.co.uk

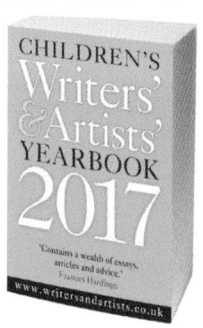

CHILDREN'S
Writers' &Artists' YEARBOOK 2017
'Contains a wealth of essays, articles and advice.'
Frances Hardinge
www.writersandartists.co.uk

❝ So much the budding writer needs
Martina Cole

❝ Full of useful stuff.
It answered my every question
J K Rowling

❝ The one and only, indispensable
guide to the world of writing
William Boyd

www.writersandartists.co.uk

We offer:

A lively online community

———

Regular writing competitions

———

Free content from authors
and industry professionals

———

Editing services and
agent consultations

———

A comprehensive directory of
publishing industry contacts

———

Creative writing workshops,
events and short courses

———

WAYB: 978-1-4729-2765-1 **£20**
CWAYB: 978-1-4729-2496-4 **£20**

Churchill Archive for Schools

From top-secret government documents to annotated copies of historic speeches, over 800,000 primary source documents are available FREE to schools and sixth form colleges worldwide until 2020 in the Churchill Archive. Visit **www.churchillarchive.com** to find out more.

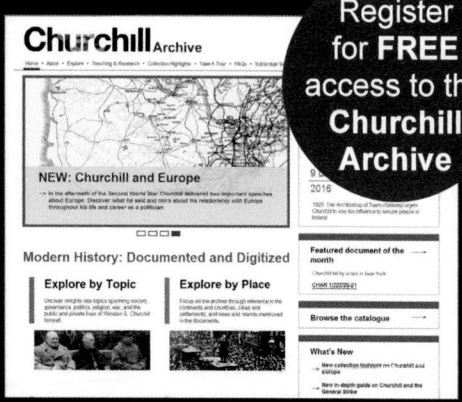

Register for FREE access to the Churchill Archive

Over 1,300 schools in more than 57 countries have already registered for access. Has yours?

It takes just a couple of minutes to get access to this unique digital resource.

❝ The Churchill Archive is very impressive. It's easy to use and navigate and the resources I have seen so far are just awesome. ❞

Sarah Hunt, Librarian,
St Theresa's School, New Zealand

Register your school today at www.jcsonlineresources.org/churchill

Use our classroom resources to help your students get the most out of the Churchill Archive

To help you introduce students to working with primary sources, we have developed a range of free classroom materials that provide a gateway into the Churchill Archive. In addition to 14 modern history topic-based investigations, you'll also find an invaluable Guide to Primary Sources which will help answer some of your students' key questions: What is an archive? Why are letters, photographs and newspaper cuttings so valuable? How do we interpret and understand historical documents?

Visit **www.churchillarchiveforschools.com**

▶ **SUPPORT THE HISTORIANS OF THE FUTURE BY DEVELOPING THEIR PRIMARY SOURCE SKILLS TODAY**

www.churchillarchiveforschools.com   BLOOMSBURY

PRIMARY

£150 RRP £230.76

BLOOMSBURY
EDUCATION

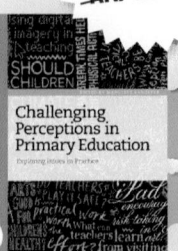

SECONDARY

£150 RRP £230.76

Exclusive Offer From Bloomsbury Education –
35% off our Book Packs for Teachers!
Visit **bloomsbury.com/ISYB** and use code **ISYB17***

All individual books are also 25% off

 @BloomsburyEd

*Use discount code at checkout to receive the discount.
Discount is valid until 31 December 2017

NEW HIGH LOW fiction for 2017

BLOOMSBURY
EDUCATION

Our high low fiction is perfectly tailored for children whose reading age is lower than their actual age.

Interest Age 8+
Reading Age 7+

PAUL MASON — SKATE MONKEY: THE CURSED VILLAGE

PAUL MASON — SKATE MONKEY: FEAR MOUNTAIN

MISSION ALERT: ISLAND X — BENJAMIN HULME-CROSS

MISSION ALERT: VIPER ATTACK — BENJAMIN HULME-CROSS

Interest Age 12+
Reading Age 9+

JO COTTERILL — ALL TOO MUCH

JO COTTERILL — STAGE FRIGHT

KAI'S STORY

LENA'S STORY

Tinted paper	✓	Dyslexia-friendly font	✓
Age-appropriate stories	✓	Perfect for those with EAL or dyslexia	✓
Approved by literacy experts at CatchUp	✓	Exciting and age-appropriate illustrations	✓

🐦 @BloomsburyEd
bloomsbury.com/education

recommended by
CatchUp
www.catchup.org

EXCEPTIONAL PUBLISHING
FOR OUTSTANDING SCHOOLS

Schools with long or distinguished histories deserve
to have their heritage set down in print.

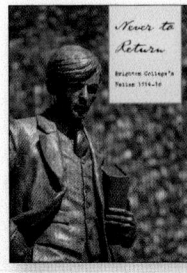

Whether to promote your story, celebrate your history or
create a beautiful product that will be treasured for years,
Bloomsbury's Bespoke Publishing services are for you.

'Bloomsbury delivered a school history meticulously copy edited,
copiously illustrated, and beautifully put together.'
Tim Hands, Magdalen College School

Contact *bespoke@bloomsbury.com* to discuss your next project.
bloomsbury.com/bloomsbury-bespoke

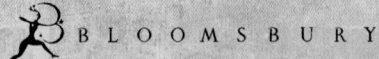

PART I
Schools whose Heads are members of the Headmasters' and Headmistresses' Conference

ALPHABETICAL LIST OF SCHOOLS
UK & Ireland

The following schools, whose Heads are members of both HMC and GSA, can be found in the GSA section:

Howell's School Llandaff
The Lady Eleanor Holles School
Putney High School
St Paul's Girls' School
South Hampstead High School
Wimbledon High School

GEOGRAPHICAL LIST OF HMC SCHOOLS
UK & Ireland

PAGE

PAGE

ENGLAND

6

Symbols used in Staff Listings

* Head of Department	§ Part Time or Visiting
† Housemaster/Housemistress	¶ Old Pupil
‡ See below list of staff for meaning	

Individual School Entries
UK & Ireland

Abingdon School

Park Road, Abingdon, Oxfordshire OX14 1DE
Tel: 01235 521563 School
           01235 849041 Registry
           01235 849022 Bursar
Fax: 01235 849079 School
email: heads.pa@abingdon.org.uk
           admissions@abingdon.org.uk
           bursars.sec@abingdon.org.uk
website: www.abingdon.org.uk
Twitter: @abingdonschool
Facebook: @abingdonschool

The foundation of the School appears to date from the twelfth century; the first clear documentary reference occurs in 1256. After the dissolution of Abingdon Abbey, the School was re-endowed in 1563 by John Roysse, of the Mercers' Company in London. It was rebuilt in 1870 on its present site, and many further buildings have been added including extensive facilities for the arts and sport and a new science centre in 2015. Abingdon Preparatory School is situated close by at Frilford (*see entry in IAPS section*).

The total establishment numbers about 1,200 boys. In the Senior School there are about 1000 boys aged 11–18, of whom approximately 135 are boarders. Boarding starts from age 13.

Boarding is organised in three houses: School House (Mr Mike Litchfield), Austin House (Mr James Golding) and Crescent House (Mr Matthew Kendry). The School values its boarding element very highly and weekly boarding features strongly as part of a policy aimed at asserting a distinctive regional identity for the School.

Pastoral Care. The Lower School has a self-contained system of pastoral care, led by the Lower School Housemaster. All boys join a senior house on entering the Middle School. Within the house system there are distinct tutoring arrangements for Middle School and Upper School boys, which are coordinated by the Middle Master and Upper Master respectively. Special emphasis is placed on the value of parental involvement and also on the provision of careers guidance at appropriate points in a boy's development. Great importance is attached to pastoral care and the School's teaching philosophy is based on a tutorial approach.

Land and Buildings. The School is surrounded by 35 acres of its own grounds, yet is within a few hundred yards of the historic centre of Abingdon, which lies 6 miles down the Thames from Oxford. A further 30 acres of playing fields are located at the Preparatory School, three miles from Abingdon. The School has additional extensive sports facilities at the Tilsley Park Sports Centre in Abingdon.

The last quarter-century has seen a considerable expansion in the School's stock of buildings. A major development in the 1990s was Mercers' Court, which celebrated the School's historical link with the Mercers' Company of London. In 2003 a £3m Arts Centre was opened providing purpose-designed facilities for music, art and drama followed in 2008 by a new Sports Centre. In autumn 2015 the School opened a new Science Centre which transformed the science facilities and enabled redevelopment of the existing science block for other subjects.

Sports facilities have been greatly enhanced by the £8m sports centre with a superb 8-lane swimming pool, fitness suites, classroom space, squash courts, climbing wall and a martial arts and fencing studio. This follows the opening in 2003 of a beautiful timber-framed boathouse situated on the River Thames a short distance from the School. In 2014 the School took over the lease for Tilsley Park Sports Centre which enhances the School's facilities still further with all-weather surfaces for rugby, hockey, football and athletics.

Courses of Study. The School is essentially academic in character and intention and levels of both expectation and achievement are high. Subjects taught include English, DT, History, French, German, Spanish, Mandarin Chinese, Latin, Greek, Ancient History, Economics, Business Studies, Geography, Mathematics, Physics, Chemistry, Biology, Art, Religious Studies, Psychology, Music and Theatre Studies. Over the last few years there has been increasing collaboration with the School of St Helen and St Katharine with joint tuition particularly in Theatre Studies and Government and Politics. The School is well equipped with computing facilities and audio-visual teaching aids.

All boys spend three years in the Middle School (13 to 16 year olds), in which many different subject combinations are possible, and there is no specialisation before the Sixth Form. In the Sixth Form many boys combine courses in arts and sciences; four subjects are normally taken in the Lower Sixth, followed by three or four in the Upper Sixth. Classroom teaching at all levels is supplemented by a programme of specialist lectures and outside visits. In general terms, the curriculum aims to combine academic discipline and excellence with the fullest encouragement of a wide range of interests and pursuits.

Games and Activities. The School enjoys some 80 acres of playing fields and has its own sports centre, swimming pool, fitness suites, climbing wall, squash and tennis courts and a boathouse on the River Thames. The major sports are rowing, rugby, cricket, hockey, football, tennis, athletics and cross-country. Special success has been achieved recently in rowing, fencing, badminton, swimming and shooting. Other sports include sailing, golf and Real Tennis.

Importance is attached to the development of a sense of social responsibility, through voluntary membership of Community Service and the Duke of Edinburgh's Award schemes. There is a contingent of the Combined Cadet Force based on voluntary recruitment.

There are numerous societies catering for all kinds of interests and enthusiasms. Music is particularly strong, with over half the boys taking instrumental or vocal lessons in school. In addition to the Chapel Choir, Choral Society and three orchestras, there are excellent opportunities for ensemble playing, including jazz.

Religion. The School is Anglican by tradition, but boys of other denominations are welcome, and normally attend by year group a short non-denominational service approximately once a week.

Health. The School has its own doctor and there is a well-equipped health centre in the school grounds. In cases of emergency boys are admitted to one of the local hospitals.

Admission. The normal ages of entry to the Senior School are 11, 13 and 16; there are occasionally vacancies at other ages. About half of each year's intake enter the School at age 11 and most of the rest at age 13. Registration by the October of the year prior to joining is recommended. Abingdon Preparatory School has its own entrance arrangements (*see entry in IAPS section*).

Details of the entrance examination procedures for all age groups are available on the School's website. Entry to the Sixth Form, at 16, generally depends on promising GCSE grades and written tests where it is appropriate, as well as on interviews and a report from the previous school.

Term of Entry. September is the usual date of entry and is preferred by the School. Boys may be accepted in any of the three terms, if vacancies occur in their age group.

Fees per term (2016–2017). The tuition fee, for dayboys, is £6,195. This includes the cost of lunches and textbooks.

For boarders, the total fee (including tuition and all extras except for instrumental music lessons and some disbursements directly incurred by individual boys) is £10,755 (weekly) and £12,875 (full).

Scholarships and Bursaries. The School offers a number of scholarships and means-tested bursaries at ages 11, 13 and 16; Scholarships and awards categories include: Academic, All-Rounder, Music, Art and Design, Sport and Drama.

Full details are published in the spring of each year and are available, on application, from the Registry or from our website www.abingdon.org.uk/scholarships or /bursaries.

The majority of awards are made at 13+ entry and are open to external and internal candidates. Some additional awards are available on entry to Sixth Form and to the Lower School. Scholarships carry an entitlement to a nominal fee remission of £300 per year plus remission of up to 100% of the tuition fee on a means-tested bursary basis. Music Scholarships also carry an entitlement to remission on instrument tuition fees.

Honours. Numerous places are won each year at Oxford and Cambridge and on other highly selective university courses.

Old Abingdonian Club. Administrator: c/o Abingdon School.

Charitable status. Abingdon School Limited is a Registered Charity, number 1071298. It exists to provide educational opportunities which are open to talented boys without regard to their families' economic standing. Its curriculum is designed to promote intellectual rigour, personal versatility and social responsibility.

Governing Body:
Mr Adrian Burn, FCA (*Chairman*)
Mr Jon Gabitass, MA (*Vice Chairman*)
Mr Andrew Saunders-Davies, MRICS, MBA (*Vice Chairman*)

The Mayor of Abingdon
Mrs Glynne Butt
Miss Penny Chapman
Dr Owen Darbishire, MA, MSc, PhD
Mrs Judy Forrest, CertEd
Mr Mark Lascelles
Dr Heather Lumsden, MA, MB BS, MRCGP, DRCOG
Mr Gareth Morris
Mrs Olga Senior, MSc
Professor Michael Stevens
Mr Matthew Tate
Mr Damian Tracey

Clerk to the Governors: Mr Tom Ayling, MA

Head: Mr Michael Windsor, BA Hons, MA, PGCE

Second Master: Mr David Dawswell, BSc
Deputy Head, Academic: Mr Graeme May, MA
Deputy Head, Pastoral: Mr Mark Hindley, LLB, UCL, MA
Director of Teaching & Learning: Mr John Davies, MA
Chaplain: Revd Dr Simon Steer, BA, MDiv, PhD
Upper Master: Mr Nick O'Doherty, BSc
Middle Master: Revd Paul Gooding, MA, DipTh, DipMin
Lower School Housemaster: Mr Adam Jenkins, BA
Director of eLearning: Mr Ben Whitworth, MA
Curriculum Director: Mr Oliver Lomax, MA
Master of Scholars: Dr Chris Burnand, MA, DPhil

Master i/c the Other Half: Mr Stuart Evans, BA

Housemasters:

Boarders:
Head of Boarding and Crescent House: Mr Matthew Kendry, MA, MEng
School House: Mr Mike Litchfield, BSc
Austin House: Mr James Golding, BSc

Dayboys:
Mr David Border, BSc
Mr David Franklin, MA
Mr Henry Morgan, MA
Mrs Emily O'Doherty, MA
Mr Robin Southwell-Sander, BA
Mr Simon James, MA

Teaching Staff:
* *Head of Department*

Art and Design:
Mrs Emily O'Doherty, MA
Ms Kate Byrne, BA
Mr James Green, BA, MA
*Ms Elizabeth Hancock, BA

Classics:
*Dr Chris Burnand, MA, DPhil
Mrs Jenny Fishpool, MA
Mr David Franklin, MA
Mr Adam Jenkins, MA
Miss Amanda Moore, BA, MA
Mr Hugh Price, BA

Computing (*ICT*):
Ben Whitworth, BA

Design and Technology:
*Mr Dan Hughes, BA
Mr Mark Johnson, MEng
Mr Steve Newton, BSc
Mr Mike Webb, BSc

Drama:
*Mr Jeremy Taylor, MA
Mr Graeme May, MA
Mr Joe McDonnell, MA
Mr Ben Phillips, BA

Economics and Business Studies:
*Mrs Nicola King, BA
Mr David Domm, BA
Mr Dean Evans, BA
Mr Simon Grills, BSc, MSc, MPhil
Mr Ben Ponniah, BSc, MSc

English:
*Mrs Jo Bridgeworth, BA
Mrs Katherine Burrows, BA, MA
Mr John Davies, MA
Mr Stuart Evans, BA
Mr Charles Griffin, BA
Mr Mark Hindley, LLB, MA
Miss Rena Papadopoulos, BA, MA
Mr Andrew Swarbrick, BA, MPhil
Miss Claire Vickers, BA
Mrs Susan Wigmore, BEd
Miss Emma Williamson, BA, MA

Geography:
*Mr Ian Fishpool, BSc, FRGS
Miss Amy Atkinson, BA
The Reverend Paul Gooding, MA, Dip Theo, Dip Min
Mr Nick O'Doherty, BSc
Mr Robin Southwell-Sander, BA

History:
*Mr David McGill, BA
Mr Peter Chamen, BSc
Mr Mark Earnshaw, BA, MA
Mr Matthew Edgar, BA
Mr James Hallinan, BA, MSt
Mr Richard Jackson, MA
Dr Carolyn May, BA PhD
Mrs Helen Wenham, MA

Mathematics:
*Mrs Samantha Coull, BA, MA
Mr Graham Cook, MMath
Mr David Dawswell, BSc, ACGI
Mr Julian Easterbrook, BA
Mrs Maris Elmore, MMath
Mr Andrew English, BA, MLitt
Mr Nathan Jones, BA
Mrs Eleanor Kaye, BSc
Mr Matthew Kendry, MA, MEng
Mr Henry Morgan, MMath
Mrs Catherine Muller, BSc
Mr Oliver Pemberton, MEng
Mr Martin Poon, MMath
Mr Alex Stuart, MA
Mr Jason Taylor, DPhil

Modern Languages:
Mrs Jane Mansfield, CAPES (*French*)
Mr Douglas Aitken, BA
Mrs Maud Cottrell, PGCE
Mr Andrew Crisp, BA
Mrs Regina Engel-Hart, MA
Mrs Chunlian Greenfield, MA
Mrs Victoria Middleton, MA
Mrs Sophie Payne, MA
Miss Sarah-Jane Poole, BSc
Mrs Victoria Pradas Muñoz, BA (*Spanish*)
Mr Nick Revill, BA
Ms Alexandra von Widdern, BA (*German*)
Ms Gao Zhang, MSc

Music:
*Mr Michael Stinton, MA, LRAM, ARCM
Mr Christopher Fletcher-Campbell, MA
Mr Jason Preece, BMus, MSt
Mrs Mariette Pringle, MMus, FTCL, LRAM, LRSM

Physical Education:
*Mr Pete Bignell, BEd
Mr Andrew Broadbent, BEd
Mr Elliot Birkbeck, BSc
Mr Matthew Gold, BA
Mr Oliver Deasy, BSc, MSc
Mr Tom Donnelly, BSc
Mr James Golding, BSc

Religious Studies:
*The Reverend George Moody, MA
Mr Henry Barnes, BA
Miss Natalie Spurling-Holt, BA
The Reverend Dr Simon Steer, BA, MDiv, PhD

Science:

Biology:
*Mr Simon Bliss, BSc
Mr Mathew Dempsey, BSc
Mrs Sarah Gibbard, BSc
Dr Robert Jeffreys, BSc, PhD
Miss Charlotte McCutcheon, BA
Mrs Su McRae, BSc
Mr Richard Taylor, BA
Mr Ben Whitworth, BA

Chemistry:
*Mr Ian Middleton, MA
Mr David Border, BSc
Mr Richard Fisher, BSc
Mr Michael Frampton, MA, DPhil
Dr Rebecca Howe, MSc, DPhil
Mr Mike Litchfield, BSc
Dr Mark Simpson, BA, MA, DPhil
Miss Kate Wylie, BSc

Physics:
*Mr John Brooks, BSc
Mrs Victoria Griffiths, BSc
Mr Simon James, MPhys
Mr Oliver Lomax, MA
Mr Daniel Mason, BSc
Miss Nelly Petrov, BSc
Mr Ben Simmons, BSc
Mr Jeremy Thomas, BSc, MSc
Dr AP Willis, BSc, PhD

Psychology:
Mrs Deborah Bennison, BSc

Librarians:
Dr Graham Gardner, BA, PhD
Mrs Wendy Hole, BSc
Mrs Lynn Mills

EFL:
Miss Katy Lee, BSocSc, MEd
Ms Vanessa Clark, BSc
Mrs Amanda Streatfield, BEd

Learning Support:
*Mrs Celia Collins, MA
Mrs Sarah Beynon, MA, MSc
Mrs Hettie Preiss-Chapman, BA

Director of Finance and Operations: Mr Justin Hodges, MSc
Director of Admissions and Marketing: Mrs Jane Jørgensen, MA

Ackworth School

Ackworth, Pontefract, West Yorkshire WF7 7LT
Tel: 01977 611401
Fax: 01977 616225
email: admissions@ackworthschool.com
website: www.ackworthschool.com
Twitter: @ackworth_school
Facebook: @AckworthSchool

This co-educational boarding and day school was founded in 1779 and occupies a large rural estate which surrounds the gracious Georgian buildings and spacious gardens and playing fields which form the School Campus. It is one of the seven Quaker Schools in England.

There are 450 girls and boys aged from 4 to 18 years, 330 of whom are day pupils. Some of the pupils are from Quaker homes, but the School has long been open to boys and girls unconnected with the Society of Friends, and these pupils are now in the majority. The pattern of school life is based on the Quaker belief that religion and life are one: that spiritual conviction directly affects the way in which people behave toward each other and determines their attitude to life in general. However, while the life of the School is based on the Quakers' interpretation of Christianity, the approach is broad-based and open-minded, for the life of the community is enriched by contributions made by those of other denominations and faiths. Although all pupils attend school assemblies and Meetings for Worship, arrangements can generally be made for pupils to worship in their own churches and boys and girls can be prepared for confirmation.

Houses. Boys and girls live separately in two houses, with resident house staff and matrons responsible for their welfare.

Curriculum. Pupils follow courses leading to GCSE, IGCSE and A Level examinations. A wide range of subjects can be taken. The main foreign languages taught are French, German and Spanish. There is a strong Music department with many ensembles and music groups; Design and Technology and Art are also very well provided for, and all of these subjects are integral parts of the core curriculum. The School also has a strong sporting tradition with many successful teams, thanks to excellent coaching and first-rate facilities. The large academic Sixth Form, which offers all of the traditional subjects as well as more recent additions such as Sport and PE and Psychology, prepares students extremely well for university entry and for life beyond School.

In our flourishing International Centre, intensive English coaching is offered to students of Fith or Sixth Form age who wish to go on to follow A Level courses and a one-year GCSE course.

Leisure Time. The many clubs and societies on offer cater for all ages and all tastes. The facilities for crafts, art and music are freely available outside the teaching day, and pupils participate in a huge range of team and individual sports. There is a very full programme of weekend activities and visits.

Buildings. A policy of expansion and upgrading has been maintained over the years and within the last decade wide-ranging improvements have been made to the School's facilities. Study accommodation for Sixth Formers is large and modern and the science laboratories have been re-equipped. The modern Music Centre and Fothergill Theatre provide spacious facilities for individual and ensemble music making, together with an excellent venue for concerts and School productions. The Design and Technology Centre houses a thriving department and numerous creative after-school clubs, and the spacious, well-appointed study, reference and careers library caters for all age groups. The superb, modern Sports Centre and fully resourced Information Technology Centre are in constant use. The most recent changes have been to boarding accommodation – the girls have specially designed, purpose-built furniture, while the boys' rooms have been re-designed to include en-suite facilities.

Scholarships and Bursaries. A number of awards are made each year to selected boys and girls entering the School who show high academic ability or exceptional talent in Music, Drama, Art or Sport.

Academic Scholarships are awarded annually. At ages 11+ and 13+ the awards are made on the basis of performance at the Entrance Tests and a subsequent interview. At Sixth Form level an offer of a Scholarship is made following a scholarship examination and interview in February.

Music Scholarships are usually awarded at age 11, 13 or 16+. The awards are made on the strength of a half-hour audition and recognise achievement and potential, preferably on two instruments. Free tuition on one or two instruments may be offered to promising musicians who do not gain a scholarship.

Art Scholarships are awarded at age 11 or 13. The awards are made on the strength of a 3-hour Art Scholarship examination and the submission and discussion of a portfolio of work, all of which must be supported by competent performance in the Entrance Tests.

Bursaries are available to Members or Attenders of the Society of Friends and others according to need.

Admission. Interested parents will be sent a prospectus upon application to the Head and visits can always be promptly arranged. There are also two Open Mornings during the year, at which parents and families are welcome to tour the School and to talk to staff and pupils. Pupils for entry at age 7 and above take the School's entrance test, while entry at age 4 is based on interview. The majority of children enter the Senior School at the age of 11, but there is also a sizeable entrance at 12, 13, 14 and 16+. Entry is always possible at other ages if places are available, and there is a direct entry into the Sixth Form for pupils who are able to take the full two-year A level course.

Coram House (Junior School). Coram House caters for day boys and girls aged 4 to 11, the majority of whom move on into the Senior School. In September 2002 a nursery opened catering for pupils aged 2 to 4 years.

Pre-prep classes are housed in new, spacious, purpose-built accommodation. From Reception onwards, emphasis is placed on a thorough understanding of the basic skills in reading, literacy, numeracy and science. In addition, a wide-ranging curriculum is provided to encourage creativity and physical ability through Art, Craft, Technology, Drama, Music and Sport.

In the Preparatory Department pupils work to a more structured timetable and are gradually introduced to specialist subject teaching. Staffing in Coram House is generous, so a thorough grounding can be given in the core subjects of English, Mathematics and Science. A broad curriculum is provided which includes French, Art and Crafts, Technology, Drama, Music and Sport – the children thus receive a rounded education and are able to develop their individual talents.

Before-school care from 8.00 am and after-school care until 5.30 pm are both available, at no extra charge.

Fees per term (2016–2017). Coram House: £2,600–£2,725 (day); Senior School: £8,335 (boarding), £4,395 (day); International Centre: £10,070–£10,810 (boarding). The day pupil fees include lunch (and other meals if required).

The Ackworth Old Scholars' Association. This is a flourishing Association with a membership of over two thousand. Annual gatherings are held at Ackworth at Easter and there are Guild Meetings held in the regions at other times in the year.

Charitable status. Ackworth School is a Registered Charity, number 529280. It was established for the purpose of providing independent education.

Governing Body:
Members appointed by The Religious Society of Friends

Clerk: David Bunney

Secretary and Bursar: Susan Allan, ACMA

Full time Teaching Staff:

Head: Mr Anton Maree, BA, HED

Deputy Head (Academic): Jeffrey D Swales, MA, PGCE

Deputy Head (Pastoral): Guy Emmett, MA, PGCE
Director of Marketing: Michael Atkins, BA, PGCE

Head of Sixth Form: Alistar Boucher, BSc, PGCE

Heads of Subject Departments:
Art: Sarah Rose-Peirson, BA
Biology: Christopher Bailey, BSc, PGCE
Business Studies: Nicola Tod, BA, PGCE
Chemistry: Nayyar Aziz, BSc, MSc, PhD
Design & Technology: Michael Windsor, BSc, PGCE
Drama: Richard Vergette, BA, PGCE, MEd
English: Alistar Boucher, BA, MA, PGCE
Food Technology: Brenda Hodge, BEd
French: Elizabeth Rayner, BA Hons, PGCE

Geography: Ros Noble, MPhysGeog, PGCE
German: Andrew Hilton, BA, PGCE
History: Thomas Plant, BA, PGCE
Mathematics: Lucinda Hamill, MA, BEd, BA
Music: Ian Lenihan, BA, PGCE
Physical Education (Boys): Patrick Roberts, BA, PGCE
Physical Education (Girls): Elizabeth Burrows, MSc,
  PGCE
Physics: Francis Hickenbottom, BSc, PGCE
Religious Studies: John Stephenson, MA, PGCE
Spanish: Caroline Wilson, BA, PGCE

Heads of Boarding Houses:
Boys: Christopher Bailey, BSc
Girls: Brenda Hodge, BEd

Coram House (Junior School):
Head: Katharine Elwis, BEd Hons

§*Librarian*: Erica Dean

Nursing Sister: Pamela Evans, SRN
Medical Officer: Gwenan Davenport, MBChB, MRCGP

AKS Lytham
United Learning

**Clifton Drive South, Lytham St Annes, Lancashire
FY8 1DT**

Tel:	01253 784100
Fax:	01253 784150
email:	headmaster@arnoldkeqms.com
	info@arnoldkeqms.com
website:	www.arnoldkeqms.com
Twitter:	@AKSSchool
Facebook:	/AKSLytham

In September 2012, Arnold (Blackpool) and KEQMS (Lytham) merged as ArnoldKEQMS (AKS), part of the United Learning group of independent schools and academies. Following a year of transition in 2012–2013, where AKS operated on each respective campus, the school co-located fully from September 2013 on the refurbished and extended Lytham campus. With an outstanding reputation of academic success, our GCSE and A Level results are currently the best on the Fylde.

With over 300 years of history and tradition, the school has a reputation for high standards and excellence in achievement, both academic and non-academic, as well as encouraging participation within an inclusive and caring community environment. Hockey has triumphed at national level, while rugby and drama also hold prestigious awards, and music has an international reputation. Sports teams tour in the UK, Europe and the Southern Hemisphere, and a large number of pupils participate in the Duke of Edinburgh's Award Scheme at bronze, silver and gold level. The school also has a popular CCF and a thriving House structure, and charity features prominently in school actions, both in support of local needs as well as international needs.

Our Location. AKS dominates an impressive position in Lytham, a delightful Victorian seaside town of charming character, overlooking the sand dunes and the Fylde coast. Preston, the Ribble Valley, the Lake District and Manchester are all within easy reach by direct motorway.

Our Opportunities. Through our membership of United Learning all teaching staff benefit from a high standard of professional training. All schools within the United Learning group communicate frequently and mutual support is always available, at all levels. The Group provides tailored CPD days for schools as well as a full range of CPD courses throughout the year for individuals to attend. The school

contributes in full to the Teachers' Superannuation Scheme and there is a fee remission scheme for children of staff who are educated at the school.

Our Co-curricular. Whilst the pursuit of high academic standards is undoubtedly important, all our pupils take advantage of the broad range of experience which our school offers, to nurture creativity and to encourage a spirit of voluntary contribution to the school and the wider community. In recent years pupils have raised tens of thousands of pounds to support charities both at home and abroad. Our main games are rugby, football, hockey, cricket and athletics, with strong fixture lists and several national and regional titles. This extensive programme provides competition and challenge for all pupils and touring sides have travelled as far afield as Argentina, Chile, the Caribbean, Canada, Australia and South Africa. As well as sport we also offer a Combined Cadet Force, Duke of Edinburgh's Award at bronze to gold levels, Young Enterprise, World Challenge, debating, dance, chess and much more. Drama and music also feature prominently and inspire countless pupils each year to take part in top quality productions, concerts and recitals.

Our Facilities. The school occupies an extensive site, overlooking the coast, with superb playing fields, including an international standard artificial all-weather sports ground. Recent investment of over 9 million pounds has resulted in: a brand new Junior School, a new Sports Hall, a new Library, a new drama studio, new Sixth Form facilities, new staff and administrative facilities, new ICT facilities, new D&T facilities, upgraded and new science laboratories, upgraded music facilities, improvements to internal accessibility, extended art facilities, and interactive whiteboards in each classroom.

Admission. Prospectus and Admissions forms can be obtained from the Admissions Secretary.

All entries to the Senior School are made through the Headmaster. Pupils are admitted to the Senior School on the basis of the School's own examinations in English, Mathematics and Non-Verbal Reasoning. The main intake to the Senior School is at 11, though entry at other times is possible depending on availability of places.

For entry at Sixth Form level, respectable GCSE grades in at least five subjects are normally expected in addition to a satisfactory report from the pupil's current Head.

Entry into the Junior School (2–11 years) is normally at the ages of 2, 4 and 7. Enquiries should be made to the Admissions Secretary.

Fees per term (2016–2017). Tuition (including books and stationery): Seniors £3,633; Juniors £2,595. Extras are minimal.

Entrance Scholarships. Several scholarships (including those for Music, Art and Sport) are available for entry at 11+. Music, Sport, Art and Drama scholarships are available in the Sixth Form. Bursaries and Assisted Places are also available. Further particulars from the Admissions Secretary (01253 784104).

Registration. Pupils may be registered at any time although this should be as early as possible if entry is requested at ages other than 2, 4, 7 or 11 years. Candidates will be called for examination in the year of entry, although those who live at a distance may have the papers sent to their schools.

Charitable status. AKS is part of United Learning which comprises: UCST (a Company Limited by Guarantee, Registered in England, number 2780748, and a Registered Charity, number 1016538) and ULT (a Company Limited by Guarantee, Registered in England, number 4439859, and an Exempt Charity).

Local Governing Body:
Chairman: Mr C R Dickson
Vice Chairman: Mrs M Towers

Mr A E P Baines, BA, BArch, RIBA
Mrs S C Carr, OBE
Mr P Cox
Ms L Grant, LLB
Mrs L Hoiles, BA
Mr A Hoskisson, Dip PFS, Cert PFS [MP&ER]
Mr A Iredale, BA, MCIM
Dr I Levitt, MA, PhD, FRSA
Mrs H Lucking, LLB
Revd D Lyon
Mr P Maguire, ACA
Mr P M Owen, ACIB
Mr L Smith
Mr D Stanhope, FCCA

Bursar and Clerk to the Governors: Mrs A Sanderson

Senior School Management:

Headmaster: Mr M H P Walton, BA, MA Ed, PGCE, NPQH

Deputy Head (Academic): Mr C W Jenkinson, MA Oxon
Deputy Head (Pastoral): Mrs J Cooper, BSc
Head of Junior School: Miss K Wright, BA
Director of External Relations: Mr P Crouch, BSc
Admissions Secretary: Mrs E Wyatt
Head of Sixth Form: Mr P Hayden, BA
Head of Middle School: Mr P Rudd, BSc
Head of Lower School: Mrs H House, BA
Director of Teaching & Staff Development: Mr A McKeown, BSc
Director of E-Learning: Mr D Culpan, BSc
External Administration & Examinations Officer: Mr P Klenk, BA

Head of Art: Miss L Heap, BA
Head of Biology: Mr S Downey, BSc
Head of Business Education: Mr C McIntyre, BA
Head of Careers: Mr K Maund, BA
Head of Classics: Mr I Morton, MA
Head of Computing: Mr D Culpan, BSc
Head of Design & Technology: Mr P Klenk, BA
Director of Drama: Miss F Horrocks, BA
Head of English: Mr J Bridges, BA
Head of Geography: Mr N O'Loughlin, MA
Head of History: Mr I Cowlishaw, BA
Head of Learning Support: Mrs E Luke, BEd
Head of Mathematics: Mr K Dawson, BSc
Head of MFL: Mrs F Burnett, BA
Director of Music: Mr D Chandler, BMus
Head of Physics: Mr J Riding, BEng
Head of PSHE: Mrs H House, BA
Head of Psychology: Mr S Collings, BA
Head of Religious Studies: Mr M Harding, BEd
Head of Science/Head of Chemistry: Dr C Jessop, BSc, PhD
Director of Sport: Mr R Jones, BEd

Aldenham School

Elstree, Herts WD6 3AJ

Tel: 01923 858122
Fax: 01923 854410
email: enquiries@aldenham.com
website: www.aldenham.com

Motto: '*In God is all our Trust.*'

The School was founded in 1597 by Richard Platt, 'Cytyzen and Brewer of London'.

Number in School. 700, of which 171 are boarders and 529 day pupils. Around one-third are girls and two-thirds boys.

Aldenham is situated in its own beautiful grounds of more than 110 acres in the Hertfordshire green belt, with excellent access to London (First Capital Connect/Jubilee Line) and within the M25, close to the M1. Aldenham's particular reputation as a close-knit, small and supportive community with a strong boarding ethos makes it the very best environment for a high-quality all-round education. The achievement of every child's academic potential remains central but the building of confidence comes too from sports, music and drama, and by living and working together within the disciplined and vigorous community that is Aldenham today.

Admission. Prospective parents are encouraged to visit the School with their sons and daughters, either individually or at one of the school's 2 open days in June and October.

At 11, entry is by tests and interview, at 13 by interview and reference and at 16 by interview and GCSE results. Every effort is made to meet parents' wishes as regards which House is chosen for their son. All girls enter Paull's House at 13.

Registration fee £75; Deposit £1,000.

Fees per term (2016–2017). Boarders £7,033–£10,462; Day Pupils £5,097–£7,138.

Scholarships and Exhibitions. Available at each point of entry, Scholarships and Exhibitions are awarded to boys and girls who have demonstrated outstanding achievement and who have the potential to make a special contribution to the School. In addition to Academic there are also opportunities for Music, Art, Sport and Design Technology scholarships and exhibitions.

Music scholarships and exhibitions are available at 11+, 13+ and 16+ under the same terms as for academic awards. Free tuition is given to Music Scholars. Any combination of choral and instrumental ability may be offered for the audition.

Art: A small number of awards at 11+, 13+ and 16+ are available each year. These are based on the candidate's portfolio and a short exercise at the school on a mutually convenient date.

Bursaries are also available to help boys and girls who will benefit from education at Aldenham but whose parents would not otherwise be able to afford the full fees.

Curriculum. From 11 to 16 the timetable closely reflects the National Curriculum. Boys and girls are prepared for GCSEs across a range of subjects including Maths, English, French, Science and a number of other Arts and language options. Care is taken that all pupils include Art, Music, Technology and IT in their programme and there is a progressive course of Theology throughout the School with GCSE taken in Year 11. The ISCO programme of tests and interviews are used as a basis for career planning and A Level choice in Year 11.

Students will take 3–4 A Levels over the two years of the Sixth Form. The majority of students go on to degree courses at universities. There are regular successes at Oxford and Cambridge.

Games and Other Activities. Great value is placed on the participation of every pupil in an extensive Games and Activities programme. Football, Hockey, Cricket and Athletics are the major sports for boys, whilst girls benefit from a breadth of in- and out-of-school activities including Hockey, Tennis, Badminton, Dance, Squash, Netball, Rounders, Trampolining, Aerobics and Sailing. In addition there is a full programme of House and School competitions in Squash, Eton Fives, Basketball, Tennis, Sailing, Table Tennis, and Cross Country. Volleyball, Horse Riding, Climbing, Judo and Golf are also available. The Sports Centre provides excellent facilities for expert and novice alike and incorporates a full-size indoor hockey pitch, dance studio, martial arts room, and keep-fit suite. Time is set apart for activities and societies; these include CCF, Adventure activities, The Duke of Edinburgh's Award scheme, Community Service, Electronics, Chess, Computing, Motor Club, Photography and Model Railway. The Debating and Philosophy societies meet regularly throughout the year

Music and Drama. Music flourishes in the School. There is a Chapel Choir, School Orchestra and wind and brass groups. A spring concert is performed annually in the School Chapel. A number of boys and girls learn to play on the fine, modern, 3-manual pipe organ in the Chapel. A music school with a recital room, practice and performance facilities and music technology classrooms was extended in September 2012.

The school theatre encourages a high calibre of Drama students. In addition to an annual School Play there are Senior and Junior House Play competitions and boys and girls have the opportunity to produce and design as well as to perform in the various productions. The School's proximity to London makes possible frequent visits to theatres and concerts. Theatre Studies is offered as a full A Level subject.

Organisation. Whilst the framework of the School is contemporary, it takes as its basis the long-established 'House' system. Each House creates an extended family and provides the formal and social focus of the School. There are four boarding and three day Houses together with a distinct yet fully integrated Junior House for 11–13 year olds. Each has a Housemaster or Housemistress and a team of tutors so every pupil has a personal tutor. In the Boarding Houses the Housemaster/mistress, his/her family, Matron and tutors live at the centre of the community ensuring the well-being of each child.

Boarding. Aldenham's unique array of day and boarding options enables it to provide the educational benefits of a boarding school to Day and Day Boarding pupils and to offer real flexibility with its arrangements for boarders, the vast majority of whom live within 20 miles of the School. Boys and girls may board from entry at 11+.

Religion. Aldenham is a Church of England foundation and seeks to maintain a strong Christian ethos to which those of other faiths are warmly welcomed.

Old Aldenhamian Society. There is a thriving Old Aldenhamian Society, details from the OA Office at the School.

Charitable status. The Aldenham Foundation is a Registered Charity, number 298140. It exists to provide high quality education and pastoral care to enable children to achieve their full potential in later life.

Governing Body:
Chairman: J T Barton [OA]
Deputy Chairman: M D Thomas

Governor Emeritus: Field Marshal The Lord Vincent, GBE, KCB, DSO [OA]

A J Bingham [OA]	Col M O'Dwyer
Mrs C Clapper	Mrs V Shah
A J S Cox [OA]	TC ff B Sligo-Young
A Day [OA]	The Ven J Smith
I A Dewar	D T Tidmarsh
A Hellman	T F Wells
Mrs D Nicholes	S Yeo
S Nokes	

[OA] *Old Aldenhamian*

Headmaster: J C Fowler, MA

Senior School Principal: A M Williams, BSc
Assistant Head (*Academic*): Dr P J Reid
Assistant Head (*Pastoral*): Mrs S H Wilson, BSc

Assistant Head (*Co-curricular & External Affairs*): R P Collins, BA, MSc

Heads of Department:
Art: Miss E J Lang, MA
Biology: Dr A D Camenzuli, MA
Business Studies: L M Flindall, BA
Chemistry: A Shead, BSc
Classics: A D B Smith, MA
Computing: M Stott, MA, BSc
Design Technology: C E C Macdonald, BA
Drama: Miss C A Martin, BA
English: C R Jenkins, MA
Geography: Mrs J Burger, BA
History: J R Kerslake, BA
Learning Support: Ms H J Southgate, BSc, MA
Mathematics: Mrs C J O Fulford, BSc
Languages: Srta M B Bustamante
Director of Music: J Rayfield, BMus
Physical Education: D L Breeze, BA
Physics: Mrs L Paine, MSc
Psychology: Mrs V Evagora, MTh, ThM
Religious Studies: Mrs A L Perry, BA
Sciences: Dr P J Reid

Head of Prep School: Mrs V Gocher, BA
Deputy Head of Prep School: Mrs C J Watts, CertEd

Houses and Housemasters:

Boarding Houses:
McGill's: M I Yeabsley, BSc
Beevor's: S Pennycook, BSc
Kennedy's: R W Pineo, BSc
Paull's: Miss E C Gratton, BA

Day Houses:
Leeman's: G L Cornock, BA
Riding's: A P Stephenson, BA
Martineau's: Mrs L Gall, BEd

Chaplain: Padre S J Chapman, BA
Librarian: A Nelson, MA, DLIS, ALA
Bursar: A W C Fraser, FCIS

Alleyn's School

Townley Road, Dulwich, London SE22 8SU

Tel:	020 8557 1500
	Headmaster: 020 8557 1493
	Bursar: 020 8557 1450
Fax:	020 8557 1462
email:	enquiries@alleyns.org.uk
website:	www.alleyns.org.uk

Motto: '*God's Gift*'

The School is part of the foundation known as 'Alleyn's College of God's Gift'. It is, with Dulwich College, the lineal descendant of "the School for twelve poor scholars" endowed by Edward Alleyn, the Elizabethan actor-manager, under a Royal Charter of 1619.

It was a Direct Grant school from 1958 until the abolition of this status in 1976. The Governors then opted for independence and at the same time opened the entry to girl pupils, making it London's first independent co-educational senior school.

Alleyn's is a co-educational day school for pupils aged 11 to 18 years, some 1000 strong, of whom approximately 300 are in the Sixth Form. The Headmaster is a member of the Headmasters' and Headmistresses' Conference.

Alleyn's Junior School, for ages 4 to 10 years, which opened in September 1992, is also on the site. (*See entry in IAPS section.*)

Entrance. A registration fee of £100 is charged for 11+ and 13+ applications, £50 for 16+ applications, and £200 for all overseas applications.

Admission to the School is by competitive examination open to both boys and girls at age 11, the normal age for transfer from primary to secondary school. Entrance is decided on the basis of the entrance/scholarship examination held in January for entry the following September. A report is requested from the Head of the applicant's school and, if they reach a satisfactory standard in the examination, boys and girls are invited for interview. The examination consists of Reasoning papers, an English paper and a Mathematics paper. Candidates should be entered for the School before the end of November (slightly earlier for 16+), for admission the following September.

There is a smaller entry by examination open to both boys and girls at age 13. The procedure is similar to that for the 11-year-old entry, with the addition of a paper in Science.

A similar procedure operates for entry at 16+, with an examination in November including subject papers and a general paper.

Opportunities for entry at other ages occasionally occur from time to time. At age 4, 7 and 9 Junior School places are awarded on the basis of an assessment held in January for entry the following September.

Fees per term (2016–2017). £6,042 (£18,126 per annum).

Scholarships, Exhibitions and Bursaries. *Academic* Scholarships, worth up to £3,000 pa, are available at 11+, 13+ and 16+ and awarded based on the results of the entrance examination and interview.

Music Scholarships, worth up to £3,000 pa plus free tuition on principal instrument, and Music Exhibitions (free tuition on principal instrument) are available at 11+ and 13+. The Hans Keller Music Scholarship, worth up to £1,500 pa, is available at 16+.

Art Scholarships, worth up to £1,000 pa, are available at 11+.

Sports Scholarships, worth up to £3,000 pa, and Sports Exhibitions (£250 pa) are available at 11+ and 13+.

Bursaries: Academic Bursary Places (up to 100% fee remission, means-tested) are available for academically able candidates at 11+, 13+ and 16+. Means-tested bursaries (up to 100% fee remission) are also available to supplement a scholarship award.

Curriculum. All pupils follow a broad and balanced curriculum in the first three years, including English, Mathematics, Spanish, Latin and/or additional foreign languages (German or French), Biology, Chemistry, Physics, Geography, History, Religious Studies, Art, Computer Studies, Music and Design Technology. In Years 10–11, pupils take nine or ten GCSE subjects which will include English, English Literature, Mathematics, Biology, Chemistry and Physics and a modern language. In addition they choose three option subjects. In Year 12, four subjects are followed. In Year 13, three or four A Levels are taken. In addition to those subjects listed above Classical Civilisation, Computing, Economics, Classical Greek, History of Art, Media Studies, Philosophy, Politics, Psychology, Physical Education and Drama and Theatre Studies are also available.

Pupils go on to universities, medical and dental schools, music and art colleges. Almost all enter higher education. Selected pupils are prepared and entered for colleges at Oxford and Cambridge, where a very good record of places is maintained each year.

Organisation. The Lower School (Years 7 and Year 8) has its own separate building and its own Head. The Middle School (Years 9–11) and Upper School (Years 12–13) each has its own Head, and pupils belong to one of eight Houses. Each Head of House is responsible, not only for organised games, but also for the welfare of each of their pupils during their time in the School. This care is supplemented by a system of form tutors for supervision of academic progress and pastoral support. Parents are invited to Open Evenings during the year, at which pupils' work and progress are discussed with the teaching staff.

Games. The School stands in its own grounds of 30 acres and offers a wide variety of sports and games including Soccer, Hockey, Cricket, Swimming, Athletics, Netball, Cross-Country Running, Rugby Fives, Water Polo, Gymnastics, Badminton, Fencing, Golf, Basketball, Tennis, Rounders, Trampolining, Aerobics, Fitness and Weight Training, Table Tennis, Squash and Horse Riding.

Religious Education. The Foundation belongs to the Church of England. Religious Education of a non-denominational nature is given throughout the School, and pupils also attend regular worship in Assembly and once each term in the Foundation Chapel or in St Barnabas Church. The School Chaplain holds voluntary Holy Communion Services during term time.

Buildings. The main school building dates from 1887. The school has a fully-equipped sports hall, with cardio-vascular room, a refurbished indoor swimming pool (with a tiered viewing gallery and Olympic timing system), a technology centre, a music school, two digital language laboratories, a new all-weather playing surface, a sports hall and pavilion, computer rooms, a library/resource centre and a RIBA Award-winning performing arts centre (the Edward Alleyn Building), containing a 350-seat theatre, a Sixth Form study centre, classrooms, lecture theatre, and a studio for the NYT. There is a refurbished science block with rooftop observatory. Some 800+ computers are networked on the School's site.

The **Fenner Library** is available to all pupils for private study. Library staff encourage reading for pleasure, with a variety of fiction and non-fiction books to borrow. Newspapers, periodicals, audio CDs and DVDs are also available.

Music, Drama and Art feature very strongly in the life of the School. There are 5 major concerts each year including an annual concert at St John's Smith Square; the School runs 3 orchestras, 3 bands, 3 choirs and has over 30 Chamber groups, chosen by ability rather than age. 5 or 6 dramatic productions are staged each year. In Art, all pupils are taught to work in different media (Painting, Drawing, Sculpture and Ceramics).

There are many clubs and societies in the school; these include, in addition to Drama groups, Debating, Dance, Photography, Chess, Politics, Science and the Christian Union.

The Combined Cadet Force has long been one of the most flourishing in the country, containing Army, Navy and RAF sections, and provides opportunities for such other activities as canoeing, rock-climbing, sailing and flying. Pupils are encouraged to join at age 14 and serve for a minimum of 2 years. Pupils who do not join the CCF are expected to join either The Duke of Edinburgh's Award scheme or the Volunteering group.

Career Guidance is given by specialised staff with the time and facilities for this important work. In Year 11 systematic aptitude testing is followed up by talks by parents themselves who give their time to talk about their own careers and who give help with offers of work experience to pupils.

An annual event, Year 12 Interview Day, is held in March. Pupils make a mock application for various and widely-ranging positions and university lecturers come in to help pupils to develop their skills.

A School Council and Learning Council, with members from each Section of the School, represents pupils' views to the Headmaster.

Relations with Parents. The Alleyn's Parents' Association is a dynamic and enthusiastic parent organisation which nurtures close links between parents and the School, and which raises considerable funds for the benefit of the School's Pupil Support Fund.

The Edward Alleyn Club. Past pupils are automatically members of the Edward Alleyn Club. This enables them to keep in touch with the school and their contemporaries, and also to take part in sporting activities if they wish. Communications should be sent to the Head of Alumni Relations, c/o Alleyn's School (alumni@alleyns.org.uk).

Charitable status. Alleyn's College of God's Gift is a Registered Charity, number 1057971. Its purpose is to provide Independent Education for boys and girls from age 4 to 18.

The Governing Body:

Chairman: Mr I Barbour, BSc Econ Hons, ACIB
Dr E F Bowen, BSc, MBBS Hons, PhD, FRCP
Dr M Campbell,
Mr Kevin Douglas, BSc, BA, Cert Ed
Mr J G Lilly, BA Hons, PGCE
Mrs L Malkin, BA Wellesley College, USA
Mr P Perry, BA Hons
Mr R Pinckard, BSc Econ, FCA
Mr I Pulley
Ms Tania Tribius, LLB Hons, AKC, Freeman of the City of London, FRSA
Revd Dr R Waller, MA Oxford, BD London, MTh Nottingham, PhD London
Mr P Yetzes, BA, JP

Headmaster: Dr G J Savage, MA Cantab, PhD, FRSA

Senior Deputy Head: Mr A W A Skinnard, MA (*Designated Lead for Safeguarding*)

Deputy Head, Personnel & Administration: Ms S P Chandler, BSc, PGDip
Deputy Head, Academic: Mrs A McAuliffe, BA

Assistant Heads:
Dr R C Atkinson, PhD, MSci, MA (*Head of Upper School; Chemistry*)
Mrs C L Heindl, BA (*Teaching & Learning, English*)
Mrs M A Joel, BA (*Head of Middle School; Modern Languages*)
Mr S W Turner, BSc, MEd (*Head of Lower School; Geography*)
Mr N J G Green, BEd (*Assistant Head Co-Curricular & Partnerships, PE*)

Bursar: Mr S R Born, BA

Registrar: Mrs L Mawer

Teaching Staff:
* *Head of Department*
† *Head of House*
§ *Part-time*

Dr M Abdalla (*Mathematics*)
Ms A K S Ackerman, MA (**Religious Studies, Philosophy, Induction Mentor*)
Mr D S Adkins, MA, MMus (*§Music*)
Mrs D E J Aird, MA (*§KS4 Curriculum Coordinator, Religious Studies*)
Mr N H Allan, BA, MA (*Art*)
Mr R J Alldrick, BA (*†Brown's House, PE, DoE Coordinator*)
Mr B D Allen, BA (*Design Technology*)
Mrs G T Anderson, MA (*English*)

Mrs C M Archard, MSc (*§Chemistry*)
Mrs V J Arter-Furlong, BA, MA (*Drama*)
Dr O J Blaiklock, BA, MA, PhD (*History*)
Miss A J Blythe, BA (*Geography 2nd in Dept*)
Mr P D Bone, BEd (*PE*)
Miss R Brett, BSc (**Biology*)
Mrs S J Brooks, BA (*§Food Technology*)
Mr A M Bruni, BSc, BEd (*Mathematics 2nd in Dept, Community Service*)
Revd A G Buckley, MA (*History, Chaplain*)
Mrs L Carey (*§Learning Support*)
Miss J R Carlsson, MA (**Geography, International Links Coordinator*)
Mrs C A Clift, BSc (*§Girls' PE & Games*)
Mr P M Cochrane, BSc (*†Roper's House, Chemistry*)
Miss C V Copeland, MA (*Director of University Admissions, Classics*)
Mrs J C Count, MA (*§Biology*)
Mrs R L Dale, BSc (*†Cribb's House, *Physics*)
Mr C W E Dearmer, MA, SSt (*Director of Music*)
Mr E S Delamare, BSc, (*Mathematics*)
Miss N A Demain, BA (*Director of Dance, Head of Outreach*)
Dr S de Silva, PhD (*Physics*)
Mrs E C Doherty, MA (*Classics*)
Miss J E Doley, LRAM (*§Music*)
Dr S Dutta, MA, DPhil (*Classics*)
Mrs H F Eagle, BSc (*§Design & Technology*)
Mr M D Eastmond, BA, MSc (*Mathematics*)
Miss R M Edwards, BA, MA (*Art*)
Miss D N Ellis, MA (*Economics, US Enrichment*)
Mr G English, BA (*KS4 Coordinator, Deputy Head of Middle School, PE*)
Mr C M Fish, BA (*Music*)
Miss C E Fleming, BSc (*2nd in Dept Biology*)
Mrs J Franco, MPhys (*Physics*)
Dr A E Galloni, BSc, PhD (**Head of Physics*)
Ms L Gardner, GRSM, LRAM, MSc (**Lower School Music*)
Mr R L Geldeard, MA (*†Spurgeon's House, Classics, *Philosophy*)
Ms J D Gibbs (*§PE*)
Ms K A Goff, BA (*§Modern Languages*)
Miss C S Goldthorpe, BA (*Head of Girls' PE & Games*)
Mrs K M Green, BSc (*§Mathematics*)
Mr M F Grogan, BA, MA (**Media Studies*)
Mrs P Hall, BA (*Spanish*)
Mr R G Halladay, BA, MA (*English, Deputy Head Middle School*)
Mr D J Harley, BSc (**History, Politics, Assistant Head of Upper School*)
Mr P J Harper, BA (*Modern Languages*)
Dr D O Hawes, BA, MA, PhD (*§History, Politics*)
Mrs M Heaton-Caffin, CertEd (*§PE*)
Miss J Hewitson, BSc (*†Tulley's House, Geography, CO CCF Army Section*)
Mrs L E Higinson, MA (*Biology*) [maternity leave]
Miss N L Hopper, BSc (*Psychology*)
Mr W J Howell, MA (*English*)
Mr N C Hughan, BA (*†Dutton's House, 2nd in Dept History, Politics*)
Mr G L H Jenkins, MA (*English*)
Miss M M V Jenney, BA (*History 2nd in Dept*)
Mr B Jones, MSc (*Director of Science, Physics*)
Mr S F Keeler, BSc, MA (*Assistant of Upper School, *Psychology, Physics*)
Dr S P Kelly, BA, MA, PhD (**German, *Universities & Careers Centre, Modern Languages*)
Mrs S Kent, MA (*Deputy Exams Officer, History, Politics*)
Ms S Kingston, MA (*Art*)

Mrs S C Latham, BA (*Assistant Head Upper School,
*Politics, History)
Mrs H E Lawrence, BA (§Deputy Head of English,
Learning Support)
Mr A J N Lea, BA (Drama)
Miss A M Legg, MA (*English, Media Studies)
Mr J W Lothian, BSc (Biology)
Mr P M MacDonagh, BSc (*Computing & ICT)
Mr E D Mann, BA (Mathematics)
Mrs S Mathieson, CertEd (*Food Technology, †Tyson's
House)
Miss M R McAteer, BEng (Maths)
Mr M McCaffrey, BA (*French)
Miss M McDonagh, BSC (Girls' PE & Games)
Mrs C A Mines, MA (§Modern Languages)
Ms E M Nicoll, BA (†Brading's House, Modern
Languages) [maternity leave]
Miss R A Norman, BSc (Chemistry 2nd in Dept)
Miss N K Oakley, BSc (Biology)
Mr R N Ody, BEd (*Head of Games and Boys' PE)
Dr A M O'Neill, PhD (Chemistry)
Miss K J Owens, BEd (Deputy Head of Lower School,
Design Technology, Head of PSHE)
Mr S R Parkin, BA (Mathematics)
Mr R D W Payne, BSc (Information Technology)
Mr J S S Piper, MA (*Drama)
Ms JA Platten, BA (Art)
Miss A M Poole, BSc (*Mathematics)
Mrs K Pryse-Lloyd, MSc (Physics)
Miss V L Rees, BA (e-Learning Coordinator, Geography)
Mr G Reid, MA (Religious Studies)
Ms S C Reynolds BA (*Art)
Mr M Riedel, BSc (Mathematics)
Mr A W Robertson, BSc, MBA (*Economics, Deputy Head
University & Careers Centre)
Mr P J Ryder, BEng (Mathematics)
Mr P N Saville, BEd (*Design Technology)
Miss A Schüller, MA (*Charities, Modern Languages)
Mr J I Shead, BEd (PE)
Mr J G Shelton, BEd, RSA Dip IT (Information
Technology)
Mrs G Silver, MA (†PSCHE, English)
Mr H G Sleath, BSc (Biology)
Mrs S C Smiddy, BSc (Deputy Head of Upper School)
Mr P A Smith, BMus, ARCM, LRAM (*Instrumental
Studies)
Mr S E Smth, BA (Classics)
Mr K Sritharan, MSc (†Acting Brading's House,
Chemistry, CCF, CO RN)
Mr V A Strain, BA (Deputy Head of Lower School,
Modern Languages)
Mr T Strange, BA (*Classics)
Mrs J M Tait, BA (§Food Technology)
Mr J D Thompson (Music)
Mrs R A Thomson, BA (§Religious Studies)
Mrs E D Thornton, BA (*Modern Foreign Languages)
Miss S C Trotter, BA, MA (English)
Miss R M Twomey, BA, MA (*Spanish)
Mrs J L van der Valk, BA (Learning Support Coordinator)
Miss M J Walker, BA (*Director of Sport & PE)
Mrs C L Wells, BSc (Deputy Director of Studies,
Mathematics)
Dr S M Whitehead PhD (§English)
Mr M Workman, MA (*Chemistry)

Ampleforth College

York, North Yorkshire YO62 4ER
Tel: 01439 766000
Fax: 01439 788330
email: admin@ampleforth.org.uk
website: www.ampleforth.org.uk/college

Motto: 'Dieu le Ward.'

Ampleforth Abbey was founded in 1607 at Dieulouard in
Lorraine by English Benedictine monks who had strong
links with the mediaeval Benedictines of Westminster
Abbey. After the French Revolution the monastic commu-
nity was resettled at Ampleforth in 1802 and the present
School was started there soon after.

The Community is dedicated, first to prayer, and then to
religious and charitable works. Ampleforth College and St
Martin's Ampleforth are the works of St Laurence Educational Trust. The other works of the Community include par-
ishes in Yorkshire, Lancashire and Cumbria, St Benet's Hall
in Oxford and pastoral involvement both at Ampleforth and
elsewhere.

Governance. The Abbot of Ampleforth is elected by the
Community for eight years at a time and presides over the
Community and its works.

The Abbot is Chairman of the Ampleforth Abbey Trustees, which is the legal institute that owns and governs its
foundation. St Laurence Education Trust is a separate limited company formed by the Abbey Trust. This also has
charitable status and is responsible for both Ampleforth College and St Martin's Ampleforth.

The governance of these works is the responsibility of the
Abbot who, with structured advice, appoints the officials,
monastic and lay, who are in charge of their administration.

Number in School. There are around 575 students, of
whom 85% are Boarders, 32% are girls and 15% are Day
Boys and Girls.

Our aims are:

• to share with parents in the spiritual, moral and intellectual formation of their children, in a Christian community
focussed on Benedictine values with which their families
may be joined in friendship and prayer for the rest of their
lives.

• to educate the young in the tradition and sacramental life
of the Church and to encourage each towards a joyful, free
and self-disciplined life of faith and virtue.

• to work for excellence in all our endeavours, academic,
sporting and cultural. We ask students to give of their best.
We ask much of the gifted and we encourage the weak.
Each is taught to appreciate the value of learning and the
pursuit of the truth.

• to help Ampleforth boys and girls grow up mature and
honourable, inspired by high ideals and capable of leadership, so that they may serve others generously, be strong
in friendship, and loving and loyal towards their families.

Organisation. St Martin's Ampleforth, an independent
preparatory school at nearby Gilling Castle, educates boys
and girls from 3 to 13 years old. (For further details, see
entry in IAPS section.)

The upper school has 7 houses for boys aged 13 to 18 and
three houses for girls aged 13 to 18. Houses are kept small
and are home to approximately 60 boarders and there are
some day students in each.

Each house has its own separate accommodation. All students eat their lunch in separate house refectories. They eat
breakfast and supper in a central cafeteria with the House
staff, chaplains and tutors.

The work and games of the whole school are centrally
organised. At least five tutors are allocated to each house to

supervise students' work and provide the appropriate guidance at each stage in their school career. The Head of Careers provides information and assistance and can arrange expert advice for pupils, parents and tutors. Some of the non-teaching life of the school is organised around the houses. House competitions help to create a strong house loyalty. We have a central school chaplaincy that acts as a social meeting place for the middle school and a sixth form social centre, the Windmill, just off the campus.

There has been over £20m invested in the school in the last 10 years.

Curriculum. The first year (year 9) provides a broad basis from which to make informed GCSE choices. In the second and third years a core of English, Mathematics, Science and Christian Theology is studied to GCSE together with a balanced selection from a wide range of subjects. In the first year of the sixth form (year 12) up to 5 subjects may be studied to AS level. One of those subjects may be AS level Christian Theology but, if not, students follow a Christian Theology short course. Normally three subjects will be taken on to A level in the second year (year 13). A comprehensive health education programme is provided in all years.

Games and Activities. There are opportunities to play a wide variety of representative sports at all levels with excellent indoor and outdoor facilities. Many activities and games take place during the week and weekends, including drama, debating, outdoor pursuits, creative arts and a wide variety of sports. These sports range from lacrosse to rugby. The school has its own outstanding 9-hole golf course and has recently completed a new all-weather hockey surface and new tennis courts. In addition, the college has its own all-weather athletics track.

Music, which is a strong academic subject, plays a major part in the extracurricular life of the school. The Schola Cantorum, our liturgical choir, sing for Mass in the Abbey and perform sacred music in Britain and abroad. They have been responsible for the production of several commercial CDs in recent years. The Schola Puellarum, our girls choir, sings with the Schola Cantorum on alternate Sundays and has its own repertoire. It has undertaken tours both at home and abroad and has also released its own CD.

Further enquiries may be made directly to the Head of Sport on 01439 766885 or the Director of Music on 01439 766730.

Admission. Applications may be made through the Admissions Office. Registration Fee: £100.

Fees per term (2016–2017). Boarders £11,130; Day Boys/Girls £7,741.

The fees are inclusive, the only normal extras being for individual tuition in Music: £30 per lesson, £28 for a second instrument; EAL £865 per term (Y12 and Y13).

Entrance Scholarships. Academic, Music and All-Rounder scholarships are awarded at 13+ and for entry to the Sixth Form.

Scholarships are awarded annually on the results of examinations held at Ampleforth. They are honorary and carry no remission of fees. However, the award of a scholarship will support a bursary application.

Academic Scholarships at 13+: ISEB Common Academic Scholarship examinations are sat in February.

Sixth Form Entry: Academic Scholarship examinations are held in November.

Music Scholarships are available for entry to the College at ages 13 and 16. All scholarships carry free music tuition.

All-Rounder Scholarships at 13+: The Basil Hume Scholarships for candidates who have a strong commitment to extracurricular activities.

Further details can be obtained from The Admissions Office, Tel: 01439 766863, email: admissions@ampleforth.org.uk.

Charitable status. St Laurence Educational Trust is a Registered Charity, number 1063808. Its aim is to advance Roman Catholic religion.

Governing Body:
The Abbot of Ampleforth is the Chairman of Governors acting with the Council and Chapter of Ampleforth Abbey. He is assisted by a lay Advisory Body.

Headmaster: Fr Wulstan Peterburs OSB, MA, PhD

Associate Headteacher: Miss D Rowe, MA, NPQH, CCRS
Director of Studies: Dr H R Pomroy, BSc, PhD
Director of Professional Development: Mr A S Thorpe, BSc, CChem, MRSC
Senior Admissions Registrar: Mrs H C McKell, BA
Head of Boarding: Mr A P Smerdon, BSc
Head of Sixth Form: Mr W F Lofthouse, MA
Assistant Head of Sixth Form: Mrs AS McNeill, BA
Head of Careers: Mrs A Toone
School Chaplain: Rev C Boulton, OSB, BA
Guestmaster: Rev H Lewis-Vivas, OSB, MA

Academic Departments:

Christian Theology:
*Mrs A S McNeill, BA
†Mr M B Fogg, BA
†Mrs G M O McGovern, MA
Mr A J J Macdonald Powney, MA
Mrs H E Pepper, BA
†Mr J D Rainer, BA
Mr R M Hudson, MA

Christian Living:
†Mrs A Le Gall, MA
Mrs M B Carter, BSc
Mrs A Rogerson, BTh

Classics:
*Mrs C J Kyrke-Smith, BA
†Mr J B Mutton, MA
Mr W F Lofthouse, MA
Miss J Sutcliffe, BA

History:
*Mr P T Connor, MA
Mr G D Thurman, BEd
Mrs M F Rainer, BA
Miss A N Rosenberg, MA
Miss G S Foster, BA

English:
*Dr C G Vowles, BA, PhD
Mr A C Carter, MA
Mr D J Davison, MA
Mrs C R Day, BA
Miss E B H Richmond, BA
*Dr E V Fogg, MA, PhD (*EAL*)
Mrs J S Adams, BA
Mrs A Mihkelson (*Learning Support*)

Modern Languages:
Mr S R Owen, MA
Mr J P Ridge, MA
Mr M Torrens-Burton, BA (*EAL*)
Rev A McCabe, OSB, MA
Mrs F Garcia-Ortega, BA
Rev J Callaghan, MA
Miss M V Serrano Fernandez

Mrs S M G Baseley, MA
Miss S Normand
Dr J M Depnering, DPhil

Geography:
*Mrs C R M Dent, BSc
Mr A P Smerdon, BSc
Mrs H E Graham, BSc
Mr B McNiff, BA

Modern Studies:
*Mr R N A Groarke, BSc
Miss J M C Simmonds, BSc
Mrs J Stannard, BA

Mathematics:
*Dr J W Large, BSc, PhD
Dr H R Pomroy, BSc, PhD
Mrs P J Melling, BSc, BA
Dr R Warren, BSc, PhD (*Head of Middle School*)
Mr D Willis, BEd, MEd
Mr C G O'Donovan, BSc
Dr J M Weston, BSc, DPhil
Mrs T M Jones, BSc
†Mr B T A Pennington, BSc
Mr E Reid, BSc

Physics:
*Mrs R L Dale, BSc
Dr L M Kessell, BSc, PhD
Mr B Townend, MPh
†Mr J Cochrane, BSc

Chemistry:
*Mr S J Howard, BSc
Mr A S Thorpe, BSc, CChem, MRSC
Mr S J Howard, BSc
Mrs E A Coop, BA

Biology:
*Mr P W Anderson, BSc
Mr A J Hurst, BSc
Mrs J Hurst, BSc
Dr O S Beveridge, BSc, PhD
Mr D J Cocks, BSc

Music:
*Mr I D Little, MA, MusB, FRCO, ARCM, LRAM
Mr W J Dore, MA, FRCO
Mr A Hardie, MA
(*Assistant Head of Music*)
Miss K Medway, BMus

Design and Technology:
*Mr B J Anglim, BEng
†Mrs V Anglim, BEng
Mr J Hart, BEng

PE and Games:
*Miss G L Atkins, BSc
Mr G D Thurman, BEd
Miss J N Horn, BA (*Assistant Head of Middle School, Head of PE*)
Mr J J Owen, BEd (*Head of Hockey*)
Mr C Booth, BSc
Miss L Hornby, BA (*Head of Netball*)

Houses and Housemasters/Housemistresses:
St Aidan's (*girls*): Mrs A Le Gall, MA
St Bede's (*girls*): Mrs V Anglim, BEng
St Margaret's (*girls*): Mrs G M O McGovern, MA
St Cuthbert's: Mr J D Rainer, BA
St Dunstan's: Mr B T A Pennington, BSc
St Edward's and St Wilfrid's: Mr A C Cooke, BA
St Hugh's: Mr M B Fogg, BA
St John's: Mr P Curran, BSc
St Oswald's: Mr J Cochrane, BSc
St Thomas': Mr J B Mutton, MA

Counsellor: Mr J G J Allisstone, BA

Medical Officer: Dr G Black, MBChB, MRCGP, DRCOG

Headmaster's Secretary: Mrs H L Richardson

Ardingly College
A Woodard School

Haywards Heath, West Sussex RH17 6SQ
Tel: 01444 893000
Fax: 01444 893001
email: head@ardingly.com
website: www.ardingly.com

Motto: '*Beati Mundo Corde*'.

Ardingly is a co-educational school in the Woodard Family founded to teach the Christian Faith.

Our aim is to enable all boys and girls to develop their love of learning, academic potential and individual talents, in a caring community which fosters sensitivity, confidence, a sense of service and enthusiasm for life.

History and development of the College. Ardingly College, the third of Nathaniel Woodard's schools, was founded in Shoreham in 1858 and moved to its present beautiful site in Mid Sussex, about halfway between Gatwick and Brighton, in 1870. The College now consists of a Pre-Prep day School and a weekly boarding and day Prep School, for boys and girls between the ages of 2 and 13, and a boarding and day Senior School for boys and girls aged between 13 and 18.

In the Prep School, which has been co-educational since 1986, there are 283 pupils, of whom 150 are boys and 133 are girls. There are 102 boys and girls in the Pre-Prep.

In the Senior School, which became fully co-educational in 1982, there are 559 pupils of whom 251 are in the Sixth

ICT:
†Mr P Curran, BSc
†Mr A C Cooke, BA

Art:
*Mr S G Bird, BA, ATC, DipAD
Mr T J W Walsh, MA
Miss A R Lister, BA

Drama and Theatre:
*Mrs E J Levahn, BA
Mrs R Clough, BA
Miss L Walsh (*Dance*)

Form. There are 327 boys and 232 girls, and 298 are boarders.

For further details about Ardingly Prep and Pre-Prep Schools, see entry in the IAPS section.

Academic. Ardingly has an extremely good academic record in both arts and science subjects achieved by boys and girls who come from a wide spectrum of ability. Both the International Baccalaureate and A Levels are offered.

Results for 2016. GCSE A*–A = 63%; GCSE A*–B = 86%; GCSE A*–C = 98%; A Level A* & IB Grade 7 = 22%; A Level A*–A & IB Grade 7–6 = 62%; A Level A*–B & IB Grade 7–5 = 86%; A Level & IB A*–C/7–4 = 97%; A Level A*–B = 77%.

Curriculum. *First year*: A broad course in which all pupils do virtually everything: second Modern Language (German or Spanish); Expressive Arts; a trans-disciplinary 'Inquiring Curriculum' and all undertake iMind research and inquiry lessons whilst completing their own chosen personal project.

GCSE (2nd and 3rd years): All take IGCSEs in English and English Literature, Maths, Sciences and the usual wide range of options.

Sixth Form Curriculum: Standard choices in a highly flexible block system at AS/A2 or in the International Baccalaureate Diploma Programme. ICT skills are developed through AS/A2 and IB courses. All Lower Sixth students follow a development course which covers life skills, careers and HE study skills. All Sixth Form students whether following the A Level route or the IB route, complete the IB Core (Extended Essay, Theory of Knowledge, and Creativity, Action and Service) which is highly valued by universities both in the UK and around the globe.

Pastoral. There are 8 Houses, four for boys and three for girls, which contain everyone from the first year to the Lower Sixth. In the Upper Sixth all boys and girls transfer to a separate, newly-built, integrated co-educational House, "Woodard", in which they are able to concentrate more fully on their studies and can be given greater responsibility for themselves and be better prepared for life at University or in the outside world. Each House has its own Housemaster or Housemistress, Assistant and House Tutors. In addition every boy and girl will have a Tutor who has responsibility for the work, progress, choices and many other aspects of the pupil's life. Tutorials are regular, weekly group tutorials and fortnightly individual tutorials. Tutors work closely with careers staff to incorporate careers guidance into their tutorials.

In Year 9 and Year 10 pupils study and discuss personal, social and health education, careers topics in small mixed groups as part of a specially designed course called Eudaimonia meaning 'human flourishing' and through Eudaimonia days in the Fifth Form.

There is an efficient Medical Centre in the centre of the school with a residential Sister in charge. The School Doctor takes three surgeries a week in the School and is always on call.

Since September 2005 School on Saturdays has been discontinued.

Expressive Arts. *Music*: Choir, Chamber Choir, Schola Cantorum, Jazz Singers, Orchestras, Concert Band, Jazz Band, Chamber Music. Instrumental lessons taken by about half the boys and girls.

Art: Painting, drawing, printing, ceramics, sculpture, fashion & textiles, photography, etching.

Design Technology: Real design problems solved in a variety of materials and forms.

Drama: Many productions in the course of the year for all ages. Large flexible theatre space and a small workshop theatre.

The expressive arts are studied throughout Year 9, are options for GCSE and A Level and offer scholarships for talented candidates, at both 13+ and for the Sixth Form.

Sport. Boys play Football, Hockey, Rugby 7s, Cricket, Tennis, Athletics; Girls play Hockey, Netball, Tennis, Rounders, Athletics. (Football and cricket are also available for girls.) Hockey and football are particularly strong at Ardingly with many country and regional competitions won and the 1XI ISFA National Boodles Cup, the most prestigious title in independent schools football for the last two years. Ardingly prides itself on developing these teams in extra coaching sessions without compromising studies.

Also (for both boys and girls) there is Cross Country, Swimming, Shooting, Golf, Volleyball, Horse Riding, Clay Pigeon Shooting, Basketball, Badminton, Karate, Croquet, Sailing, etc.

The indoor pool is open to both Prep and Senior Schools and pupils who cannot swim are taught to do so.

Activities. Combined Cadet Force (Army based), The Duke of Edinburgh's Award, Beekeeping, Modern Dance, Photography, Computers, Fencing, Astronomy, Debating, Charity Focus, Amnesty International etc.

Admission to the Senior School normally takes place at 13+ or directly into the Sixth Form at 16+. Admission is also possible at 14+ but is not advisable at the beginning of the years in which GCSE or A Levels are taken unless there are very special reasons. A Pre-IB course is offered in the Sixth Form.

At 13+ entry is by written assessments in English, Mathematics and Verbal Reasoning and satisfactory results at Common Entrance. If pupils have not been prepared for Common Entrance then they will sit our own entrance papers. We also require a report and reference from the pupil's previous school. The headmaster likes to interview prospective pupils if practicable. The selection of candidates for direct entry to the Sixth Form takes place in November of the year prior to entry. All candidates are interviewed and take an English paper and a Maths paper. A report from their Head is also required. Places will then be offered subject to the candidate gaining a minimum of 6 grade Bs or above at GCSE. Modifications of these procedures and of the timing for individuals at any stage are almost always possible.

The Prep School has entry at 7+ and 11+ or at any other time between the ages of 7 and 11. Transfer into the Senior School is by entrance assessments and Common Entrance.

Scholarships. A number of Scholarships are offered for annual competition at 13+ and 16+. They include Academic, Art, Drama, Music and Sports Awards. Ashdown Awards for all-rounders are offered for those entering at 13+. The Prep School offers Academic, Art, Music and Sports Awards at 11+. Along with other HMC schools, the maximum value of a scholarship is 40% of the basic fees pa but all may be supplemented by a means-tested bursary if need can be shown.

A limited number of bursaries are available for the children of the Clergy.

Please address all enquiries about admissions, scholarships and bursaries to the Registrar (Tel: 01444 893320; fax: 01444 893001; email: registrar@ardingly.com).

Term of Entry. Main 13+ and Sixth Form intake in September. Intake at other ages and other times on an individual basis.

Registration. The School Prospectus may be obtained from the Registrar. Registration (where a non-returnable fee of £100 is charged) can be made at any age subject to the availability of places. No separate registration is required for children transferring from the Prep to the Senior School.

Fees per term (2016–2017). Senior School: Boarding £10,160–£10,710, Day Pupils £7,460–£7,870; Occasional Boarding: £48 per night. Prep School: Weekly Boarding ranges from £240 per term for 1 night per week to £1,180 for 5 nights (in addition to Day Fees); Prep Day Pupils £4,020–£5,050; Occasional Boarding £36 per night. Pre-Prep: £2,800.

Fees are inclusive.

Further Particulars. For further information, application should be made to the Registrar.

Charitable status. Ardingly College Limited is a Registered Charity, number 1076456. It exists to provide high quality education for boys and girls aged 2½ to 18.

School Council:
Mr Jim F Sloane, BSc (*Chairman, Chair of Nominations Committee*)
Mr Peter N Bryan, BA, ACA
Mrs Claire D Cater
Mr Guy Dixon, BA Hons, Dip TP, MRTPI
Mr David F Gibbs, BA (*Chair of Education Committee*)
Mrs Liz Hewer, MA, PGCE
Mr Alan A Holmes, FCA (*Governor with responsibility for Compliance*)
Mr Douglas H T Johnson-Poensgen, BEng Hons
Dr Simon Kay, PhD
The Earl of Limerick, MA
Mrs Louise E Lindsay, FCIPD, LLM, BA Hons (*Governor with responsibility for Child Protection*)
Mr Neil Mclaughlan
Mr Graham N Turner, BSc, FCIOB (*Deputy Chairman, Chair of Finance and General Purposes Committee*)
Mr Nicholas Walker, BA Comb Hons, MSc
The Right Reverend Lindsay Urwin, OGS, MA (*Provost*)

Headmaster: **Ben Figgis**, BA, MEd

Deputy Headmaster: Philip Stapleton, BSc

Chaplain: Father David Lawrence-March, BA Hons

Head of the Prep School: Chris Calvey, BEd

Director of Operations: Paddy Jackman

Medical Officer: Dr B Lambert

Ashford School

United Learning

East Hill, Ashford, Kent TN24 8PB
Tel: 01233 625171
Fax: 01233 647185
email: registrar@ashfordschool.co.uk
website: www.ashfordschool.co.uk
Twitter: @AshfordSchool
Facebook: @AshfordSchool

Ashford School was founded in 1898 as an independent, day and boarding school and provides education for boys and girls from 3 months to 18 years. There are over 450 students in the Senior School and over 350 in the Prep School (age 3–11). There are around 150 boarders in the school cared for by resident teachers and support staff in extensive accommodation that includes en-suite rooms for many. Forty nationalities are represented and specialist English tuition is provided for those who require it. There are no lessons on Saturdays.

The school recently opened an International Centre which houses another 20 or so boarders who enjoy intensive English language tuition with iGCSEs before entering mainstream British education.

Ashford School is a member of a group of independent schools run by United Learning which provides a first-class education for more than 25,000 pupils. United Learning aims to be at the forefront of educational development, bringing the very best resources, both human and physical, to the children in its schools.

The Senior School occupies a 25-acre site in a prominent position close to the centre of Ashford and near to the International Station. A green and secure haven in a busy and growing town, Ashford is 37 minutes from London by rail and also benefits from rapid access to Paris, Lyon, Brussels, Amsterdam, Cologne and Frankfurt on the Eurostar. With easy access to the M20 motorway and local train services, the central location and easy accessibility provides an ideally located school whether you live in the UK or anywhere across the globe.

With playing fields on site, a brand new Sports Centre, two gyms, indoor swimming pool, floodlit Astroturf, tennis and netball courts, boarding houses and dining hall, the School enjoys all the specialist teaching facilities you would expect of an independent school and has embarked on a programme to refurbish and extend the facilities. The Pre-Nursery, Bridge House, is located on the Senior School site and the Prep School is located in the nearby picturesque village of Great Chart and has recently undergone major redevelopment to double its size and further improve facilities and opportunities for pupils at the school.

Almost half of the students entering the Senior School at 11+ join direct from the Prep School and the remainder from other primary and prep schools. There are then normally three classes per year through to GCSE with additional students joining other years and the Sixth Form. All Sixth Form students go on to take degree courses at leading universities in the UK and abroad.

Over the last three years an average of two thirds of A Level students have gone to Russell Group universities and one fifth to World Top Ten such as Imperial College, LSE, Durham, Warwick, Birmingham, Bristol, UCL, Nottingham, Leeds, York and Newcastle.

An inspection by the Independent Schools Inspectorate in March 2014 found the school to be 'outstanding' or 'excellent' in every category.

The Senior School curriculum is broad and provides many opportunities in the classroom and in activities. The school has interactive whiteboards in every teaching room and modern facilities throughout. Pupils follow a broad curriculum to keep their options open and in addition to the core subjects of English, maths, the sciences and a language they may study additional languages, history, geography, religious studies, information technology, art and textiles, music, drama and physical education. Throughout the Senior School, subjects are set by ability where possible and there is a strong pastoral system based around six Houses.

The school prides itself on its adventurous approach to learning.

External Examinations. Most pupils take 9/10 subjects at GCSE. Many A Level combinations are available to the Sixth Form, all of whom go on to Higher Education before entering a varied range of careers including music, design, advertising, banking, engineering, journalism, law, management, the media, medicine and veterinary science. There is a consistently high external examination success rate and pupils are prepared for Oxbridge in all subjects.

Entry requirements. School report, subject entrance tests and interview for the Sixth Form, supporting six or more A*–B grades at GCSE with at least an A grade in the subjects chosen to study at A Level. School report and written tests in English, Mathematics, Science and Non Verbal Reasoning at Years 7 and 9. Places are generally available throughout the year in all other year groups.

Scholarships. Academic scholarships are available at Year 5. Academic, art & design, sport and music scholarships are available in Years 7, 9 and 12 with theatre arts additionally in Year 12. Further details may be obtained from the Head.

Fees per term (2016–2017). Senior: £5,600 (day), £9,750 (weekly boarding), £11,250 (full boarding); Prep: £4,600; Pre-Prep: £2,975–£3,300; Nursery: £640 (one full day per week), £2,975 (full-time).

Charitable status. Ashford School is part of United Learning which comprises: UCST (a Company Limited by Guarantee, Registered in England, number 2780748, and a Registered Charity, number 1016538) and ULT (a Company Limited by Guarantee, Registered in England, number 4439859, and an Exempt Charity).

School Council:
Chairman: Mr W Peppitt, MRICS
Vice-Chairman: Mr R I Henderson, JP, DL
Mr R Coombe
Mr A J Rawlins
Mr J B Rimmer, MRICS, FAAV
Mrs E Rose, MSc
Mrs L van der Bijl
Professor P Freemont
The Ven S Taylor
Mrs E Langlands-Pearse, RCST, BCST

Head: **Mr Michael Buchanan**, BSc King's College London, HMC Chair 2016–2017

Director of Operations: Mr N Cufley, MBA Cranfield, CMgr, FCMI
Head of the Prep School: Mr R Yeates, BA Exeter
Head of the Senior School: Mr T Wilding, BA Exeter
Deputy Head & Head of Teaching and Learning (Prep School): Mrs P Willetts, BPrimEd
Deputy Head, Teaching and Learning: Mrs D Gale, BSc Rand University
Deputy Head, Pastoral: Mrs N Timms, BEng Loughborough

Ashville College

Green Lane, Harrogate, North Yorkshire HG2 9JP
Tel: 01423 566358
Fax: 01423 505142
email: ashville@ashville.co.uk
website: www.ashville.co.uk
Twitter: @AshvilleCollege
Facebook: /AshvilleCollegeHarrogate

Motto: '*Esse quam videri*'

Ashville College is an HMC independent day and boarding school for girls and boys aged 3–18 years, situated in Harrogate, one of the north of England's most attractive towns.

Ashville was founded in 1877 by the United Methodist Free Church, but has been strengthened by taking under its wing at different times two older non-conformist schools: Elmfield College, founded by the Primitive Methodists in 1864, which amalgamated with Ashville in 1932; and New College, which began in 1850 with strong Baptist connections and merged with Ashville in 1930.

Numbers. There are over 500 boys and girls in the Senior School, 285 in the Prep School (age 4–11), and approximately 30 in the Pre-School (age 3–4).

Site and Buildings. The Ashville estate consists of 64 acres of land on the south side of Harrogate.

The school boasts some of the leading teaching facilities in the North of England. 2012 saw the opening of a new all-weather surface pitch and a £2.3 million auditorium opened in 2014. These facilities complement the specialist classrooms, sports centre, which includes the longest swimming pool in the area, and extensive playing fields. The Sports centre is currently undergoing a £3 million development to include modern changing facilities, gym and fitness studios.

Curriculum. All pupils are prepared for GCSE examinations at 16 and A Levels two years later. From the age of 11 pupils spend five years on the GCSE course, which includes the study of English Language and Literature, History, Geography, Music, Art, Religious Education, French, German, Spanish, Latin, Mathematics, Physics, Chemistry, Biology, Design Technology, ICT, Food and Nutrition, Business Studies, and Physical Education. At A Level Economics, ICT, History of Art, English Language and Physical Education are also available. BTEC Sport is also available in the Sixth Form. Guidance is given by the Careers Staff in the choice of Sixth Form studies and decisions are made after consultation with parents. Over 90% of pupils who complete the A Level course go on to study at university or other institution of higher education.

Physical Education is a part of the curriculum for all pupils, and there are games afternoons for all during the week.

The main school games are Rugby, Hockey and Cricket for the boys, Netball, Hockey and Rounders for the girls. The school also has a very strong reputation for producing high quality swimmers and compete both regionally and nationally. There are also school fixtures in Cross-Country, Swimming, Athletics, Lacrosse, Tennis, Squash and Badminton. Many students represent the school at County level.

Careers. Careers guidance is regarded as a very important part of the service provided by the school. Ashville is in membership of the Independent Schools Careers Organisation, and parents are encouraged to share with the careers staff the responsibility for giving appropriate guidance from Year 9 and at Sixth Form stage. Pupils are helped in their choice of university and degree course, and arrangements are made for them to visit universities and go on careers courses.

Religious Life. All pupils attend assembly every weekday, and there is a school service for boarders on Sunday evening. Confirmation classes are held in the Spring Term each year, and boys and girls are prepared for Joint Confirmation in the Church of England and the Methodist Church. The School Chaplain is always glad to meet parents by appointment.

Leisure Activities. There are school societies which cater for a wide range of interests, and pupils are guided in the use of their free time in the early years. The school has no cadet corps, but boys and girls are enabled to take part in the Duke of Edinburgh's Award scheme. Drama has a strong following and the school play is a highlight of the year's programme.

Music is well provided for, and pupils are encouraged to take up the study of piano, organ or an orchestral instrument. The School Choir has acquired a high reputation by its contributions at the Harrogate and Wharfedale Festivals.

Admission. The school is prepared to admit pupils at any convenient time, dependent on spaces being available.

Candidates for entry at the age of 11 are required to take the Ashville Entrance Examination in the January preceding the September of entry (unless they are currently at the Ashville Prep School). The examination consists of papers in English, Mathematics and Reasoning. Candidates at Preparatory Schools seeking entry at the age of 13 are required to sit a similar examination.

Candidates for entry at other ages and into the Sixth Form are considered on the evidence of a headmaster's report and interview.

Registration forms and prospectus are obtainable from the Registrar. There is a registration fee of £100.

Fees per term (2016–2017). Tuition: Senior School £4,460–£4,600, Prep School £2,650–£3,830. Boarding (in addition to tuition fees): Full £2,590–£4,650, Lunch for Day Pupils: £270 (Year 3 to U6th), £243 (Reception to Year 2).

Scholarships and Bursaries. Discretionary Awards: Scholarships are awarded at the discretion of the Headmaster for excellence in academic performance or other disciplines, for example music. Scholarships are awarded to pupils for specific stages of their education at Ashville.

Financial Assistance: Bursaries are available at the discretion of the school and are means tested.

Forces Boarding Bursary: If a parent is serving in the armed forces and their children are boarding at Ashville, the bursary is 20% of tuition and boarding fees for junior school pupils and 10% for senior pupils.

Charitable status. Ashville College is a Registered Charity, number 529577, administered by Ashville College Trustee Ltd, company number 4552232. It aims to provide a boarding and day education for boys and girls.

Visitor: The President of the Methodist Conference

Governing Body:
Chairman: Mr P Whiteley, BSc, FCA
Deputy Chairman:

Headmaster: Mr D M Lauder, MA Aberdeen

Deputy Heads:
Mr G R Johnson, BSc Manchester
Mrs E Fisher, BSc Strathclyde

Assistant Head: Mr M Finch, BSc Surrey

Chaplain: Revd David Barker, BA Dunelm, BD, MPhil Manchester

Year Heads:
Year 7: Miss J Ellis, BA Brighton
Head of Years 8 & 9: Mrs J Wilcox
Acting Head of Years 10 & 11: Mrs F Adamson
Head of Sixth Form: Mrs V Rumsey, BA East Anglia
Assistant Heads of Sixth Form:
Mrs S O'Hara
Mr E Rintoul

Senior Housemaster: Mr G Coad, MA London

Heads of Departments:
Art: Mr S Brook, BA Canterbury
AVCE: Mrs V Rumsey, BA East Anglia
Biology: Mr P D Forster, BSc Salford
Business Studies: Mr James Austin
Chemistry: Mr D J Normanshire, BSc Bangor
Classics: Mr M Knowles
Design Technology: Mr C Pearce, BEd Leeds
Drama: Mrs J Normanshire, BA Wales
Economics: Mr J Austin
EFL: Mrs G Clift
English: Mr G Kurczij, BA, MA Leeds
Geography: Mrs V A Simpson, BSc Salford
History: Mrs H Stewart
Home Economics: Mrs J Hardy
ICT: Mr D Taylor, BSc Sheffield, MSc Manchester
Learning Support: Mrs L Mullender
Mathematics: Mr O Edwards
Modern Languages: Mr I W Kendrick, MA Leeds, BA
Director of Music: Miss A Wilby, BA Oxon, MMus RCM
PE Academic: Mr J Goldthorp, BSc Loughborough
Physics: Mr C Davies, BSc Sussex
Religious Studies: Ms C Walker
Science: Mr D J Normanshire, BSc Bangor
Director of Sport: Mr P Holmes

Prep School:
Head: Mr S Bailey, BA
Deputy Head: Mr J Thompson, BEd Dunelm

Pre-Prep (Rec–Year 2):
Head: Mrs C Berrie, BEd Hull
Deputy Head: Mrs J Hopkins, BA Liverpool

Bursar: Dr Dean White

Registrar: Mrs C Butcher

Medical Officer: Ms J Tate, MS

Bablake School

Coundon Road, Coventry CV1 4AU

Tel: 024 7627 1200
Fax: 024 7627 1290
email: info@bablake.coventry.sch.uk
website: www.bablake.com
Twitter: @bablakeschool
Facebook: @BablakeSchool

Bablake School was originally part of the College of the same name founded by Queen Isabella in 1344. After the dissolution of the monasteries, it was refounded in 1560 by the city; it is chiefly associated with the name of Thomas Wheatley, whose indentures of 1563 put its finances on a firm foundation.

Number in School. There are approx. 754 Day Pupils (including 215 in the Sixth Form) and 360 in the Junior School and Pre Prep.

Buildings. In the Home Field of 11 acres stand the main buildings which have been considerably extended to include a Sports Centre, heated indoor swimming pool and a purpose-built Modern Languages block. A purpose-built English, Music and Drama block was completed in July 2000. In 1993 Bablake Junior School was opened on the Home Field site for pupils aged 7–11 and Cheshunt Prep became Bablake Pre Prep, for pupils ages 3–7, in 2009 (*for further details, see Bablake Junior School and Pre Prep entry in IAPS section*). The school has its own nationally recognised weather station. At Hollyfast Road there are 27 acres of playing fields, a large pavilion, and two all-weather hockey pitches.

Curriculum. Pupils take and must pass the Governors' Examination for entry to the Senior School. The Senior School provides courses leading to the GCSE examinations and GCE A Levels. Subjects available include: English, Mathematics, History, Geography, French, German, Spanish, Religious Studies, Latin, Classical Civilisation, Physics, Chemistry, Biology, Music, Art, Food, Design Technology, Information Technology and Textiles. Design Technology and Food and Textiles courses are followed by both boys and girls. The separate sciences or Science and Additional Science are taught up to IGCSE. Most pupils study 10 subjects at GCSE, the majority progressing into the Sixth Form where the new A Level curriculum is followed with three subjects being examined at the end of the two years. There is a wide range of Enrichment Studies options including Art, Astronomy, Chinese, Computing, Cookery, Design, Drama, Music, Photography and many others. Some pupils take the Extended Project Qualification. All pupils follow a structured programme of PE and Games.

Games and Activities. Rugby, Hockey, Netball, Basketball, Cross-Country Running, Athletics, Rounders, Tennis, Cricket, Football, Squash and Swimming. The school has an extensive artificial turf games area, used mainly for hockey, but providing in the summer an additional 24 tennis courts. A wide range of extracurricular activities is offered, and there are approximately 50 societies and clubs. Drama and Music are strong features. All pupils are involved in the charity work of the school and there is a large Community Service programme for the Senior pupils in the Fifth and Sixth Forms.

Scholarships. The Governors award annually a number of Entrance bursaries each year for those entering at 11+. These are dependent on academic ability and on parental means. Academic, Art and Music scholarships are also available.

Academic, Sports and Music scholarships are also available in the Sixth Form.

Fees per term (2016–2017). Senior School £3,660; Junior School £2,778; Pre Prep £2,218.

Admission. Entry is via the School's own Entrance Examination held annually in January for entrance the following September. The normal age of entry is 11 but there are smaller intakes at 12, 13 and 14. Entry to the Sixth Form is based on gaining at least 5 GCSE passes at Grade B or above (with an A in the subjects chosen to study at A Level) and an interview with the Headmaster and Head of Sixth Form. Enquiries about admissions should be addressed to the Admissions Office.

Charitable status. Coventry School Foundation is a Registered Charity, number 528961. It exists to provide quality education for boys and girls.

The Governing Body is Coventry School Foundation, on which are represented Sir Thomas White's Charity, the Coventry Church Charities, Coventry General Charities, Oxford and Warwick Universities and the University of Coventry. There are also several co-opted governors.

Chairman of Governors: Mrs J McNaney

Headmaster: Mr J W Watson, MA

Deputy Heads:
Mr C R Seeley, BA, MPhil
Mr A Wright, BSc (*Academic*)
Mrs G Press, BEd (*Pastoral*)

Assistant Head: Mr J G Burns, MA

Director of Admissions & Marketing: Mrs S V Harris, BSc

Head of Sixth Form: Mrs A J Tumber, BA
Head of Fifth Year: Mrs S M Smith, BEd
Head of Fourth Year: Mrs L A French, BSc
Head of Third Year: Mr J C Hobday, BSc
Head of Second Year: Mrs K L Lenihan, BA
Head of Shells: Mrs L R T Lawrence, MA
Chaplain: Revd S Slavic, DEUG

Bursar: Mr M Shaw

Assistant staff:
* *Head of Department*

Art:
*Mr P Cleaver, MA
Miss R Brandrick, BA
Mr A J Field, BA

Biology:
*Mr A M Hall, BSc
Mrs L B Alexander, BSc
Mrs L R T Lawrence, MA
Mr C W Mohamed, BSc
Miss R F Young, BSc

Careers:
*Mr M G A Woodward, BA

Chemistry:
*Dr P J Knight, PhD
Mr I S Kalsi, MChem
Mrs A H Learmont Henry, MA

Miss S L Holyman, BSc
Mrs M R Prowse, BSc
Mr S S Sahota, BSc

Classics:
*Mr D C Menashe, BA
Mr J M Bunce, MA
Mrs K L Lenihan, BA
Mr C R Seeley, MPhil
Mr J W Watson, MA

Design Technology:
*Mr C R West, BEd
Mr P Nicholson, BEd
Mr S E Williams, BEng
Mrs J L Solomon, BA
Miss J E Kukucska, BA

Economics & Business Studies:
*Mr R G Sewell, BA

Mrs L J Alderson-
  Bolstridge, LLB
Mr J G Burns, MA
Mrs H E Sawyer, BSc

English and Drama:
Mrs K G Duke, MA
  (*English*)
Miss K E Blackie, MA
Miss K A Davies, MA
Mrs E L Hollick, BSc
Mrs A J Lister, BA
Mrs C A Martlew, BA
Mr G L Park, BA
Mrs L J Reddish, BA

Geography:
*Mr S P Enstone, BSc
Mrs A L P Bradshaw, MEd
Mrs J MacGibbon, MSc
Mrs G Press, BEd

History:
*Mrs H Skilton, MA
Mr J M Grantham, BA
Mrs K L Lenihan, BA
Mrs C A Rees, BA
Mr C R Seeley, MPhil

ICT:
*Mr M Bull, MEng
Mr L Atwal, BSc
Miss R M Blattner, BSc

Learning Support:
*Dr L S Greenway, PhD
Mrs E L Hollick, BSc
Mrs H E Sawyer, BSc

Mathematics:
*Mr K J Tyas, BEd
Dr P B M Archer, PhD
Mrs D R Booth, BSc
Mr A D Chowne, BSc
Mr J M Drury, BSc
Mrs L A French, BSc
Mrs N D Green, BSc

Junior School & Pre Prep

Headmaster: Mr N Price, BA

Deputy Head: Mr L Holder, BEd

Head of Pre Prep: Mrs T Horton, BEd

Headmaster's Personal Assistant: Mrs R Mohomed
Administrator: Mrs H Rypma, BA

Mr S Memon, BSc
Mrs H E Sawyer, BSc
Mrs S M Smith, BEd

Modern Languages:
Mrs J May, MA (*ML,
  French)
Mrs H M Billings, MA
  (*German*)
Mrs M O'Neill, MA
  (*Spanish*)
Mrs R I Bilsland, BA
Mrs M C Field, LesL
Mrs S V Harris, BSc
Mr P R Neale, MA

Music:
*Mr T Crompton, GBSM
Mr S J Cooper, GLCM
Mrs C Scott-Burt, DipTCL

Physical Education – Boys:
*Mr R L Burdett, BSc
Mr A C Phillips, MSc
Mr B G Wilson, BEd

Physical Education – Girls:
*Mrs J A Russell, BSc
Miss L J Mullan, BSc
Miss L C Watts, BA
Mrs S M Smith, BEd

Physics:
*Mr T Hyde, BSc
Mr M Duerdin, BSc
Mr J C Hobday, BSc
Miss J L Simmons, MSc

Psychology:
*Mrs A J Jones, BSc
Mrs K F Barnacle, BSc

Religious Studies:
*Dr T M P Smith, PhD
Miss K E Blackie, MA
Revd S Slavic, DEUG
Mrs A J Tumber, BA

Bancroft's School

High Road, Woodford Green, Essex IG8 0RF
Tel: 020 8505 4821
Fax: 020 8559 0032
email: office@bancrofts.org
website: www.bancrofts.org

Motto: *Unto God only be honour and glory*

By the Will of Francis Bancroft (1727) all his personal estate was bequeathed on trust to the Worshipful Company of Drapers of the City of London to build and endow almshouses for 24 old men, with a chapel and schoolroom for 100 poor boys and 2 dwelling-houses for masters. The Foundation was originally situated at Mile End, but by a

scheme established by the Charity Commissioners in 1884 the almshouses were abolished and the School transferred to Woodford Green, Essex. In 1976 the School reverted to independence, and became a fully co-educational day school, with a Preparatory School being added in 1990.

Bancroft's School is a co-educational day school of about 1,100 pupils. It stands in its own grounds with about five acres of playing fields and it has a further 16 acres of playing fields near Woodford Station. Its buildings have successfully combined the spacious style of the original architecture with the constant additions demanded by developing needs. These include a swimming pool, enhanced science facilities, music resources and art rooms. In 2006 a new building, housing kitchens, additional teaching space and a new Sixth Form Centre, was opened; a new sports centre and performing arts studio were opened in 2007. A lecture theatre seating up to 120 people, digital language lab and a new ICT suite were added in 2009. 2011 saw the addition of an enhanced Sixth Form study area, new Arts and Ceramics Workshops and additional science laboratories.

Meals are taken in a well-equipped central dining room, and there is a good variety of menu with self-service on the cafeteria principle.

Pupils are grouped in four Houses – North, East, West and School. Each of the Houses has its own Housemaster or Housemistress and a tutorial system.

The School offers a wide range of subjects at GCSE and A Level and has a strong record of academic success. Virtually all Bancroftians progress to university, with about 12 each year to Oxford or Cambridge. On average 75% of pupils will go on to study at Russell Group institutions. Bancroft's has a very strong record of pupils studying medicine and dentistry.

The major sports for girls are hockey, netball, tennis and athletics; the main curricular games for boys are rugby, hockey, cricket and athletics. Swimming, soccer, badminton and basketball are also provided. The Physical Education programme includes gymnastics, trampolining, basketball and badminton.

The School has a Contingent of the CCF (both Army and RAF sections), a Sea Scout Unit, a branch of the Duke of Edinburgh's Award scheme, and a Social Service Group, each of which caters both for girls and boys. The School has enjoyed considerable success in the Engineering Education Scheme. The wide programme of concerts and plays throughout the school year offers opportunities for pupils of all age groups.

Preparatory School. The Prep School opened in September 1990 occupying purpose-built accommodation on a separate site within the school grounds. There are 12 classrooms, a hall, a library, a performing arts studio and specialist rooms for art and science. Although self-contained, the Prep School makes extensive use of the Senior School's sports, music and drama facilities.

(*For further details, see Preparatory School entry in IAPS section.*)

Admission. 65 places are available each year for boys and girls wishing to enter the Preparatory Department at 7+; entry tests take place in the January. Transfer to the Senior School is guaranteed. At 11+ there are another 60 places available for children entering Bancroft's who sit an examination in Mathematics and English in mid-January. For candidates of other ages individual arrangements are made. Applications for 7+ and 11+ entry must be made before 1 December in the year prior to entry. There is a direct entry for boys and girls into the Sixth Form dependent upon GCSE results and performance in the School's 16+ entrance examination which is sat in the November of Year 11.

Scholarships. Each year up to 15 Scholarships, worth typically one half, one third or one quarter of the full fees, are awarded to candidates at 11+ on the basis of performance in the School's own 11+ Entrance Examination. Two will generally be awarded as Music Scholarships to children of outstanding musical talent; these are worth up to 50% of fees plus extra music tuition. Five Academic Scholarships, each worth up to 50% of the full fees, are available to external candidates entering the Sixth Form. A Music Scholarship is also awarded for entrants into the Sixth Form. A further three academic awards are available to internal candidates.

Means-tested awards (including Francis Bancroft Scholarships and Foundation Scholarships) are available at age 11, which can cover the full fees. These are awarded based on disclosure of family finances and performance in the Entrance Examination. Two means-tested Francis Bancroft Scholarships are available for entrants to the Prep School at age 7; these only cover Prep School fees. Means-tested awards may also be available for entrants into the Sixth Form.

Fees per term (2016–2017). Senior School £5,441, Prep School £4,430. Fees include lunch and books.

Old Bancroftians' Association. Hon Secretary: Mrs C Lavender, obasecretary@bancroftians.net. School contact: susan.day@bancrofts.org.

There is a strong Old Bancroftians' Association, organising a variety of social, sporting and networking event throughout the year including an annual dinner at the School and OBs Day in the summer term. The OBA also helps to organise work experience for members of the school.

Charitable status. Bancroft's School is a Registered Charity, number 1068532. It exists to provide an academic education to able children.

The Worshipful Company of Drapers

President: The Master of the Drapers' Company

Trustees and Governors:

Appointed by the Drapers' Company:
Prof P Ogden, BA, DPhil, AcSS (*Chairman*)
J Rose, BA
Prof P Kopelman, MD, FRCP, FFPH
R Williamson, BA, FRGS

Appointed by the London Borough of Redbridge:
M J Stark

Appointed by Essex CC:
R Gooding, IEng, ACIBSE

Co-opted:
Mrs B Conroy, MA (*Old Bancroftian*)
R Bhumbra, BSc, PhD, MBBS, MRCS, FRCS
Dr A V Philp, MA, MB BChir (*Deputy Chair*)
E Sautter, MA (*Old Bancroftian*)
Mrs S Siddiqui, BA, TEP
P D Southern, MA, PhD

Head: **Mr Simon Marshall**, MA, MA, MPhil

Deputy Head: M Mikdadi, MSc

Assistant Heads:
N J Maloney, MA
Mrs E F de Renzy Channer, MA
C A F Butler, BSc

Head of Sixth Form: N E Lee, BSc
Head of Section, Middle School: Mrs P R Tindall, BA
Head of Section, Lower School: J P Dickinson, MEng

Director of Studies: Mrs A M Scurfield, BSc

Head, Preparatory School: J P Layburn, MA, QTS

Assistant Staff:
* *Head of Department/Subject*
† *Housemaster/mistress*

Art:
*A D Ford, MA
Mrs S O'Sullivan, MA
Mrs N Vetta, BA
Ms I Ward, MA

Biology:
Mrs A C Carter, BSc
*Mrs F M Graham, BSc
Miss A Grimwood, BSc
Mrs S C Hampson, BSc
J H Raw, MA

Chemistry:
Dr A Ahmed, MScI
J Choy, MSci (*Head of Medics*)
*N Goalby, MEng
Dr G M Ismail, BSc (*Junior Science)
Miss H Korcz, BSc, MEd
†Miss H J Prescott-Morrin, BSc

Classics:
*Mrs M J Baker, BA
†Mrs L J Coyne, BA
A J Smethurst, MA
Miss H E Stewart, BA

Drama:
Mrs C Foinette, BA
K P Gallagher, BA
Miss H C Gartland, MA
J D Kelsall, BA, MMus
*Miss E M Middleton, BA
Dr A J Mill, MA
R E Young, BA

Economics & Business Studies:
*Mrs L R Anthony, BSc
Miss S L Brand, BA
Mrs K J Dean, BA, ACA
N J Maloney, MA (*Assistant Head Academic*)
M Mikdadi, BSSc, MSc (*Deputy Head*)

English:
†Miss C G Edwards, BA
Miss N Evans, MEd (*Junior English)
K P Gallagher, BA
*Miss H C Gartland, MA
T R C Jones, MA (*Second in Department*)
S R J Marshall, MA, MPhil
Miss E M Middleton, BA
Dr A J Mill, MA
R E Young, BA

Financial Studies:
*Mrs K J Dean, BA, ACA
MRS L R Anthony, BSc

Geography:
C A F Butler, BSc (*Assistant Head Co-Curricular*)
J S Foley, BSc
†R M Hitching, BA
N E Lee, BSc (*Head of Sixth Form*)
Mrs K Stevens, BA
*Mrs V Talbot, BA

Government and Politics:
Mrs K J Dean, BA, ACA
†R M Hitching, BA
*Dr S A Hunn, BA, MSt

History:
*L J Brennand, BA
Miss G M Carnell, BA
†R B de Renzy Channer, MA
Miss K A Hughes, MA

Dr S A Hunn, BA, MSt
†Miss A M H Wainwright, BA

Learning Support:
*†Mrs A Fryer-Green, BSc
Mrs J Collins
Mrs A Hubbard

Mathematics:
P A Caira, BSc
A M Conington, BSc
J P Dickinson, MEng (*Head of Section, Lower School*)
*M J Flaherty, MA
Dr J D Larwood, BSc
A P MacLeod, BEd
P A McGuiggan, BSc
Mrs P J F Morton, BA, MSc (*Sixth Form Mathematics*)
Mrs A M Scurfield, BSc (*Director of Studies*)
S P Taylor, BEng
Mrs S P Thompson, BSc (*Junior Mathematics*)
R Tse, MSc
Mrs E J Tynan, MEng (*KS4 Mathematics*)

Modern Languages:
Mrs A Abbott-Imboden, BA (*German*)
Mrs E F de Renzy Channer, MA (*Assistant Head Pastoral*)
Miss S Gadhvi, BA
Mrs A Gaskell, BA
Miss J Grossman, Staatsexamen (*French*)
R M A Hay, BA
Mrs M Pérez, Licenciatura en Filología Inglese
Mrs P Rasmussen, MA
†Miss J K Robbins, BA
Mrs P R Tindall, BA (*Head of Section, Middle School*)
Mr I Urreaga Gorostidi, BA (*Spanish*)
Mrs L Whalley, BA
Miss L G Williams, BA

Music:
*A E Clay, Grad RSM (*Academic Music*)
*Mrs C J Foinette, BA (*Director of Music*)
J D Kelsall, BA, MMus

Physical Education:
Mrs C Ablitt (*Swimming Coach*)
Y Aksoy, UEFA B (*Football*)
D J Argyle, BEd
Mrs S Cheshire (*Swimming Coach*)
R Faiers, BA (*Academic PE and Rugby*)
Mrs J Fryer-Green, BA (*Examinations Officer*)
C Greenidge (*Cricket*)
J K Lever, MBE, Essex CCC and England
A P MacLeod, BEd (*Boys' Hockey*)
*Miss D L Mugridge, BA (*Director of Sport*)
Ms K E Nelson, BSc (*Graduate Sports Assistant*)
J C Pollard, BEd (*PE*)
†Miss A M H Wainwright, MA (*Tennis*)

Physics:
A N Busch, MSci
J Ceeraz, BSc
N A Jaques, MA (*Science*)
*J Prole, BSc

Religious Education:
*A Berg, BA
Miss L Jones, BA
Miss H C Mead, BA
Revd I Moore, MA, BTh (*School Chaplain*, *PSHE*)

Technology:
S Burton, BA
T Peddle, BEng
*M I Salam, BA
A Whitbread, DipEd

S P Woolley, BSc

Preparatory School:

Mrs A Adams, BA
Miss S Alchin, BTEC, SES (*Graduate Sports Assistant*)
A D Baum, BA
Mrs S K Bhangal, BEd
Mrs C Biston, BA
Mrs H A Chilvers, MA, BEd
Mrs L Dalton, BA
Mrs N Doctors, BA
Miss L Ellery, MSc
C P Hall, BSc (*Graduate Sports Assistant*)
N Harrison, BSc
Miss E Hewitt, BSc
Mrs J M Hitching, BA
Miss K Johnston, BSc

Mrs S M Jones, BA
Mrs T Jones (*Learning Support Assistant*)
J P Layburn, MA (*Head*)
Mrs L Life, BA
Ms A Moor, BA
Mrs E J Norris, BSc
Mrs S O'Sullivan, BA
C Pearson, BA
Miss L C Phelps, BA
M Piper, BA (*Assistant Head*)
Mrs B Rathod, BA
Mrs S Strong, MA
N Thomas, BCom, MA (*Director of Studies*)
Mrs K Yelverton, BA

Bursar: L Green

Matron: Mrs B Sharma

Bangor Grammar School

**84 Gransha Road, Bangor, Co Down
BT19 7QU, Northern Ireland**
Tel: 028 9147 3734
Fax: 028 9127 3245
email: info@bgs.bangor.ni.sch.uk
website: www.bangorgrammarschool.com

Motto: '*Justitiae Tenax*'

Bangor Endowed School was founded in 1856 as a result of a bequest by the Rt Hon Robert Ward. The School is now known as Bangor Grammar School.

There 880 boys in the School aged 11–18.

School Buildings. The School moved into brand new premises in January 2013. The new school is a state-of-the-art establishment, located on the Gransha Road in Bangor.

Admission and Curriculum. Boys are admitted to the Senior School after the age of 11 as a result of their performance in the transfer procedure using tests provided by the Association of Quality Education. All boys follow a common curriculum for the first three years. The choice of subjects for the Fourth and Fifth Forms is kept as wide as possible to enable boys to keep their future options open right up to the GCSE examinations. The School's policy is to encourage boys to undertake a wide range of studies.

A Sixth Form of 200 plus makes possible a wide range of subjects from which boys normally take four AS Level and three or four A2 subjects.

Activities. School games include rugby football, cricket, tennis, squash, badminton, golf, hockey, swimming, athletics, basketball and cross-country running. There are numerous societies and clubs. Both drama and music flourish. There are two major play productions in the year with further smaller-scale productions in the Summer Term. Numerous opportunities are afforded for instrumental and choral performance throughout the year, both inside and outside school. Adventure training is catered for by a flourishing contingent of the Combined Cadet Force (with Army and Naval Sections) and the Duke of Edinburgh's Award scheme. Boys are encouraged to gain an experience of social work through the active Community Service Group. Frequent continental visits are arranged and an expedition under the auspices of World Challenge takes place every other year.

The School has very high standards in sport. The rugby 1st XV dominated the Ulster Schools Rugby Cup in the Eighties, with seven appearances in the final, including four victories. Other teams have been successful in the Ulster Schools Golf Championship, the major Ulster Hockey cups, the Ulster and Irish Squash and Tennis Championships and in the major Ulster Cricket cups and the Ulster Badminton Championships.

Careers. Extensive and continuous help is available to boys in connection with careers. There are five careers staff under the leadership of the Head of Careers. Careers courses, lectures, visits, interviews, work experience, work shadowing and a Challenge of Industry Conference are part of the regular careers structure for boys in Year 10 and above.

Honours. Boys from the School enter all the major universities in the British Isles. Places have been won regularly at Oxford, Cambridge and other universities.

Bangor Grammarians Association. *Hon Sec*: Norman Irwin, 10, Riverside Road, Bangor, Co Down BT20 5SA.

Governors:
The Governing Body is composed of 8 representative Governors elected by Subscribers, 6 Governors nominated by the Department of Education, 2 Parent Governors and 2 Teacher Governors.

Chairman: P Blair, MD, FRCS – Consultant Surgeon

Representative Governors:
J Adrain, BSc Econ, FCA – Chartered Accountant
K Best, MSc, RIBA – Architect
JC Harper, LIB, ACIS – Senior Bank Manager
P Hatty, BSc, MSc – Insurance
I G Henderson, OBE, MSc Econ – Chief Executive (*Chairman*)
Geoffrey Miller, QC – County Court Judge
W McCoubrey, LLB – Solicitor

Governors nominated by the Department of Education:
A Adams – Lecturer (*Retired*)
R Bailie, BA, MSW, MBA
M Burke, MBE, MSc, BA – Vice Principal, University College (*Retired*)
P Kane
D G Patterson – Civil Servant (*Retired*)
A J Preston – Career Civil Servant

Parent Governors:
P Crothers – Solicitor
W Reid – Civil Servant

Teacher Governors:
G Nicholl, MA
J Todd, BSc, PGCE

Co-opted Governors:
B McKee, MA – Barrister

Bursar and Clerk to the Governors:
Ms D Magee, BA, MSc, FCIPD

Principal: Mrs E P Huddleson, MSSc, BEd PQH NI

Vice-Principal: G Greer, BEd, MA, PQH NI
Vice-Principal: S Gilmore, BEd, PQH NI

Assistant Principals:
S Robinson, BSc
J B Wilson, BA, PQH NI

Assistant Staff:
* Head of Department

Art:
*Mrs C N Steele, BA
Mrs M-C Allsopp, BA

Business Studies:
*S Sinclair, MA

Computing:
*Ms M Garland, BA, MSc
D McShane, BSc
P Ramsey, BSc

Drama:
*Mrs J K Payne, BSc, ATD
D P Cunningham, MA

English:
*H Matheson, MA (*Acting*)
W R Stevenson, BA, ATCL
Mrs M E L Cree, BA
A M Gray, BA

Geography:
*S A Beggs, BSc
M Dickson, BSc
Mrs C Greenaway, BSc, JEB

History:
*S Wolfenden, MA
G Bond, BA
M Robinson BA

Home Economics:
*Mrs L McDermott, BA

Languages:
*G Nicholl, MA
Mrs R Shaw, BA
Mrs C Henry
Miss R Douglas, BA
Mrs K Nicholl, 1 Staatsexamen

Learning for Life and Work:
*Mrs M Faulkner, BSc, PhD

Mathematics:
*J Todd, BSc
S Robinson, BSc
A Walker, BEng, MSc
Mrs S Forbes, BSc
Mrs C McGilton, BSc
D Hinds, MEng

Music:
*P O'Reilly, BMus, LRSM
Mrs C Buchanan, BMus, LRSM

Physical Education:
*D Kennedy, BSc
D Holley, BA (*also RE*)
P Cartmill, BSc

Politics:
*J B Wilson, BA

Religious Education:
*M S Nesbitt, BD
Mrs S Crawford, BTh

Science:
N A Nowotarski, BSc MRes (*Biology*)
Mrs M Faulkner, BSc, PhD
Mrs K Bloomfield, BSc, PhD
Ms C Mills, BSc, PhD
B Smith, BSc, PhD (*Chemistry*)
B S M Christy, BSc
Dr S Cunningham, BSc
Mrs R McKee, BSc (*Physics*)
F Gilmour, BSc
S Henry, BSc

Technology:
*J T Titterington, BEng
C H M Turner, BEd (*Tech & Design*)
M Black, BEd

Headmaster's PA: Mrs S Cordner, BA

Barnard Castle School

Newgate, Barnard Castle, County Durham DL12 8UN
Tel: 01833 690222
Fax: 01833 638985
email: genoffice@barneyschool.org.uk
website: www.barnardcastleschool.org.uk

Motto: '*Parvis imbutus tentabis grandia tutus*'.

The St John's Hospital in Barnard Castle was founded in the 13th century by John Baliol, whose widow founded the Oxford College. By a Scheme of the Charity Commissioners, bequests under the will of Benjamin Flounders of Yarm were combined with the funds of the St John's Hospital and public subscriptions to build and endow the present foundation in 1883. Originally known as the North Eastern County School, the name was changed to Barnard Castle School in 1924.

Barnard Castle is a day and boarding school for boys and girls between the ages of 4 and 18.

Organisation and Numbers. There are 505 pupils aged 11–18 in the Senior School, of whom 136 are boarders. The Preparatory School comprises a Pre-Prep Department of 48 pupils between the ages of 4 and 7, and 134 pupils between the ages of 7 and 11, of whom 8 are boarders. (*See also Preparatory School entry in IAPS section.*) The Senior and Preparatory Schools are located on adjacent sites and operate separately on a day-to-day basis whilst enjoying the mutual benefits of being able to share a number of resources and facilities. Girls were first admitted in 1981 and the School has been fully co-educational since 1993.

Location. The School is situated in its own extensive grounds on the outskirts of an historic market town in an area of outstanding natural beauty. The area is well served by Durham Tees Valley and Newcastle airports and by Darlington railway station. The School also operates its own bus service for pupils from a wide area.

Curriculum. This is designed to provide a broad, balanced and flexible programme, avoiding undue specialisation at too early a stage. In the Prep School emphasis is given to literacy and numeracy skills, as well as Science, History, Geography, French (from age 8), Religious Education, Technology, Art, Music, Information Technology, Physical Education (including swimming) and Games. These subjects are developed further in the Senior School, with the addition of Latin or Classical Civilisation, Personal, Social and Health Education, and three separate sciences. German or Spanish is added at age 12, whilst Business Studies and Engineering increase the list of GCSE options at age 14. There are some twenty A, AS or Pre-U Level subjects which give a wide choice in the Sixth Form. Almost all Sixth Form leavers go on to University or College courses. A Learning Support Department provides specialist help for those who need it in both the Preparatory and Senior Schools, and tuition is offered in English as a Second Language.

Religious Education. The School is a Christian foundation and the Chapel stands at the heart of the School in more than just a geographical sense. The School Chaplain, who plays an important role in the pastoral structure of the School as well as being responsible for Religious Studies and Chapel worship, is an ordained member of the Church of England, but the School is a multi-denominational one which welcomes and supports pupils of all faiths and none. Pupils attend weekday morning assemblies in Chapel, and there is a Sunday service for boarders.

Boarding and Day Houses. There are eight single-sex Houses within the Senior School – three boarding and five day – each small enough for pupils to know each other well, but large enough to allow a mixture of interests, backgrounds and abilities, as well as opportunities for leadership. Housemasters and Housemistresses, each supported by a team of Tutors and Assistants, are responsible for the welfare and progress of each pupil in their charge.

Junior Boarders (boys and girls aged 7–11) and Senior Girl Boarders live in their own modern Houses in the School grounds, alongside their Houseparents, Boarding Tutors and Matrons. The two Senior Boys' Boarding Houses have recently undergone a major programme of restructuring and refurbishment, and offer comfortable accommodation within the main building of the School. The resident Housemasters are supported by resident boarding tutors and matrons, and by the School Sister in the School's Medical Centre. The School Doctor visits daily.

Cultural and other activities. The School has a flourishing music department in which the Chapel Choir, Orchestras, Wind and Jazz Bands and smaller ensembles perform regularly.

Drama is also prominent, with a regular programme of productions taking place throughout the year. There is a strong tradition of after-school activities; both day and boarding pupils take part in a wide range of clubs and societies, selecting from over 100 weekly activities.

Games. Rugby, Hockey, Netball, Cricket, Athletics, Squash, Cross-Country Running, Tennis and Swimming are the main sports, and other options such as soccer, badminton, basketball and golf are available. The School has extensive playing fields, a modern Sports Hall, and Fitness Centre, squash and tennis courts, and a heated indoor swimming pool. A full-size, floodlit AstroTurf-style pitch is available for all to use. Regular inter-school matches are arranged at all levels.

Outdoor Activities. There is a strong emphasis on providing instruction, opportunity and challenge in a wide range of outdoor activities. Much of this takes place under the auspices of a flourishing Cadet Force (Army and RAF sections) or The Duke of Edinburgh's Gold and Silver Award schemes.

Careers. There is a well-equipped Careers Room, and a team of careers staff work together with the Higher Education Coordinator to provide pupils at all stages of the School with expert advice and help in decision-making and application procedures.

Admission. Pupils are admitted at all stages either via the School's own Entrance Assessments. There is also direct entry into the Sixth Form subject to satisfactory performance at GCSE level. Details of the application procedure are obtainable from the Admissions Secretary (admissions@barneyschool.org.uk).

Scholarships and Assisted Places. Academic Scholarships and Exhibitions are awarded to entrants to the Senior School at Year 7, Year 9 and the Sixth Form, on the basis of the School's own entrance examinations held in February.

Music Scholarships and Exhibitions: There are two Music Exhibitions available in Year 7, a further two Scholarships in Year 9 and in the Sixth Form.

Sport Exhibitions based on potential are available at Year 7 and Scholarships are available at Year 9 and in the Sixth Form. Four Exhibitions may be awarded in Year 7, followed by up to four Scholarships in Year 9 and a further two Scholarships in the Sixth Form.

Art Scholarships and Exhibitions are available from Year 9 and in the Sixth Form.

Drama Scholarships and Exhibitions are available to candidates entering the Sixth Form.

Awards may be supplemented by means-tested Bursaries.

The School is also able to offer a small number of means-tested assisted places. Details are available from the Admission's Secretary.

Fees per term (2016–2017). Senior: £7,842 (Boarders), £8,885 (International Boarders), £4,372 (Day). Prep: £5,925 (Boarders), £6,814 (International Boarders), £3,055 (Day), Pre-Prep: £2,015. Fees are inclusive and subject to annual review.

Charitable status. Barnard Castle School is a Registered Charity, number 1125375, whose aim is the education of boys and girls.

The Governing Body:
Chairman: Mr A Fielder
Vice-Chairman: Mr P Mothersill & Mrs C J Sunley JP

Mr M Airey	Mr M McCallum
Mr S Crowe	Mrs C Newnam
Mr M H Crosby JP	D C Osborne
Mr C Dennis	Mrs K Pratt
Mrs R Dent, JP	Councillor G M Richardson
Dr J Elphick	Mr D F Starr
Mr B Hick	Dr N Thorpe
Mr P Hodges	

Clerk to the Governors: Mr M White

Headmaster: Alan D Stevens, MA (*History*)

Second Master: Tony C Jackson, BA (*History*)
Head of Sixth Form: Christopher R Butler, MSc, MA (*Physics*)
Assistant Head Pastoral: Martin T Pepper, BA (*PE, Director of Sport*)
Director of Operations: Suzanne Metcalf, BA, FCCA
Director of Studies: Michael R Truss, PhD (*Mathematics*)

Chaplain: Revd Darren Moore, MA (*History*)

Assistant Staff:
* *Head of Department*
† *Housemaster/mistress*

†Gary Bishop, BA (**Economics & Business Studies*)
Stuart Everall, BEd (**PE*)
John D N Gedye, BA (**Classics*)
Mike H Nicholson, BSc, BA (**Mathematics*)
Fiona Cover, BEd (*PE, Head of Games*)
Caroline L Shovlin, BA, ALA (*Librarian, Head of Careers*)
†Alison Armstrong, BEd (*PE*)
†David W Dalton, MA (**Geography*)
Mick Donnelly, FLCM, Cert Ed (*Music*)
†Ben C Usher, BSc (*Mathematics*)
Mandy Gorman, BA (**English, History*)
Charles H Alderson, BSc (*Geography*)
Martin P Ince, BA (**History*)
Neil Toyne, BSc (*Mathematics*)
Alan M Beaty, BSc (**Design & Technology*)
Tanya C Broadbent, BA (*PE*)
Andrea J Campbell, BA (*History & Politics*)
†Andy J Allman, MA (**Religious Studies and Psychology*)
Ian M Butterfield, PhD, BSc (**Chemistry*)
Alan R Jacobs, MA (*Modern Languages*)
Kate Baptist, BA (**Art*)
Erin E Beaty, BA (*English, History and Classics*)
Judith Brown, MSc (**ICT*)
†Luke D Monument, BSc (*PE*)
†Lesley J Burgess, BEd (*PE*)
Phil Oakley, MSc (*Technology*)
Dan G Goldberg, MA (*Mathematics*)
Alan J Maude, BSc (*Mathematics*)
Michelle Abela, BA, LLCM, ALCM (*Music*)
Nick J Connor, BA (*Bus Studies and ICT*)
Alan Owens, LLCM (*Music*)
Caroline Connor, BSc (*Biology*)
Lucy Nicholson, Mgr, Dip Trans, MCIL, DPSI (*EAL*)
Caroline J Snaith, MA, LLB (*RS, Classics, Psychology, *PSHE*)
Steven J F Tomlinson, BA (*Modern Languages*)
Sheila Butler, BA (*Religious Studies*)
Andy M Dunn, MSc, MPhil (*Physics*)
Scott Edwards, BA (*English, *Theatre Studies*)
Henry W Fairwood, BSc (*ICT*)
Elaine E McDermott, PhD, BSc (*Chemistry*)
David S Walton, PhD (**Physics*)
Sarah Rothwell, MA (*Art*)
†Carrie Burgess, MA (*Modern Languages*)
Alexander Still, BA (*Modern Languages*)
Kevin B Cosstick, JP, PhD, BSc (*Chemistry*)
Katherine Harpin, BA (*English*)
Jack White, BSc (*Maths*)
Janine Wilson, MA (*Chemistry*)
Sarah Allman, BA (*English and Learning Support*)
Simon P Dearsley, MA, MMus, BA (**Music*)
Sam S Forsyth, BSc (*Biology*)
Sebastian T Nichols, PhD (*Classics*)
Rebecca K B Gibson, MSc, BSc (**Biology*)
Helen D Kent, MPhil, BA (**Modern Languages*)
Johneena Brown (*Biology*)
Holly Creevy (*Geography*)

Diana L M Everall (*English*)
Judith Gibbons (*Learning Support*)
Edward Hodgson (*Physics*)
Olivia Hovington (*PE/Games*)

Combined Cadet Force:
Commanding Officer: Major Caroline E Hall, BSc
SSI: Martyn G Lewis, WO1

Preparatory School

Headmistress: Laura E R Turner, MA

Deputy Head: Nick I Seddon, BEd
Director of Studies: Rebecca A Robertson, BEd

Simon T Ayres, BA
Claire L Bale, BA
Lizzie J F Hairsine, BA
Fiona M Killeen, BA
Michael Killeen
Lauren Laverick
Tabitha J Michelin, BA
Claire N Priestley, BEd
Kate Roberts-Lilley
Louise E Rowlandson, BA
Sue M Seddon, BEd
Emma J Small, BA
Jennifer D Strachan
Donna J Thirling, BA, SAC Dip
Ruth Thompson, BEd
Ben E Wicling, BA
Alexandra A White, BSc Hons

Admissions Secretary: Julia Simpson, MBA

Medical Officer: Dr Robert Carter
Medical Centre:
Catherine Bainbridge, RGN

Bedales School

Church Road, Steep, Petersfield, Hampshire GU32 2DG
Tel: 01730 300100
               Registrar: 01730 711733
               Assistant Registrar: 01730 711569
Fax: 01730 300500
email: admissions@bedales.org.uk
website: www.bedales.org.uk
Twitter: @BedalesSchool
Facebook: /BedalesSchool
LinkedIn: /bedales-school

Number in School. 471 in Senior School. Equal numbers of boys and girls. 70% boarders.

Bedales stands in an estate of 120 acres in the heart of the Hampshire countryside, overlooking the South Downs. Although only one hour from London by train, this is one of the most beautiful corners of rural England. Founded in 1893, Bedales is one of the oldest co-educational boarding schools. The community is a stimulating and happy one, in which tolerance and supportive relationships thrive at all levels.

The school has strong traditions in both the Humanities and the Sciences, in Art, Design, Drama and Music. The school estate supports a thriving 'Outdoor Work' programme, including the management of livestock and a variety of traditional crafts; a stunning new Art & Design facility was opened in 2016.

The school is known for its liberal values, the individualism and creativity of its students, and a sense that the students are generally at ease with who they are. The atmosphere is relaxed (first-name terms for staff and students; no uniform), but it is underpinned by a firm structure of values, rules, guidance and support.

Admission. Entry to the School is from 3+, 7+ (see Bedales Pre-prep, Dunannie), 8+, 11+ (see Bedales Prep, Dunhurst), 13+ and 16+ (Bedales). Once in the school, pupils are assessed before proceeding to the next stage.

Entry Tests. Entry for newcomers at 10+, 11+ and 13+ takes the form of residential tests in the January preceding the September entry. Entry at 16+ is by a series of interviews spread over a single day. Contact the Registrar in the first instance.

Senior School (13 to 18). A new curriculum in Blocks 4 and 5 (Years 10 and 11) was introduced in September 2006. In order to promote more stimulating, varied and wide-ranging work in these years, and to reduce prescriptive external assessment, students will typically take a combination of externally moderated Bedales Assessed Courses (BACs) alongside IGCSE subjects. BACs are designed to give a strong basis for A Level study and are recognised by UCAS. A new curriculum was introduced for Block 3 (Year 9) in 2014 to prepare students better for the independent learning opportunities higher up in the school, starting with a week at an Outward Bound Centre in the Lake District.

All current IGCSE/BACs subjects (except Outdoor Work and Global Awareness) are also offered in the Sixth Form at A Level. Sixth Form students can opt for an assessed Extended Project in an area of interest. A new Sixth Form Enrichment Programme provides an alternative to a fourth A Level subject in the Sixth Form. A programme of personal and social education runs in Years 9 and 10, and a general course covering a wide range of topical and personal issues is taught in the Sixth Form. Students are attached to a tutor in groups of mixed ages, and meet their tutor on a regular basis.

A series of local, national and international initiatives/exchanges have been introduced as part of a new emphasis on Global Awareness. Geography and Biology departments run Sixth Form field courses, and there are special interest trips such as a History visit to Russia. IT facilities are well funded; students have access to desktop computers throughout the day, and those with their own laptops have wireless access to the school network across the campus. There are excellent recreational facilities including extensive playing fields, gymnasium, sports hall with multi-gym, indoor heated swimming pool, floodlit netball and tennis courts and a floodlit astroturf pitch. The Outdoor Work department is centred around two eighteenth-century barns reconstructed in the school grounds by students. A new Art & Design building opened in 2016. The Bedales Arts programme run public events in art, drama, dance and music, and distinguished speakers visit the school to give assemblies or as part of the 'Civics' programme. Evening assemblies ('Jaw') and other talks often have a religious or moral theme, but there is no chapel; the school is non-denominational.

There are no prefects, but students take responsibility for a wide variety of aspects of school life by running activities for younger students, taking part in committees and putting forward individual initiatives. A School Council of elected representatives provides a forum for discussion including all levels of the school. Until the final year, students sleep in small mixed-age dormitories; in the final year they move to a co-educational house with exceptional facilities. This arrangement fosters very good relationships across the age range.

Bedales Prep School, Dunhurst (8 to 13). (*See Dunhurst entry in IAPS section*).

Bedales Pre-prep School, Dunannie (3 to 8). Currently 87 pupils. Entrance at 3+ is by date of registration; after this acceptances are made following informal assessments, should vacancies arise. Dunannie has six classes including a nursery. Its aim is for children to develop a lifetime's love of learning in a stimulating environment.

The school has bright airy classrooms, an extensive library and an excellent ICT room. There are fabulous music rooms, hall and dining room which are shared with the Prep school. The children at Dunannie benefit from the indoor swimming pool, tennis courts, sports hall, pitches, farm and theatre which are all close by on the Bedales estate. The outdoor play areas include a stunning orchard with a climbing frame, Sound Garden of outdoor instruments and a hill fort.

The children have many opportunities to thrive and flourish. Dunannie offers a rich and varied curriculum that allows for rigour in basic skills, but also embraces creativity. Children are encouraged to think and be independent in their response to cross-curricular activities. First hand experiences are an integral part of learning. All children from Nursery to Year 3 go on inspiring visits that enrich their classroom experiences. There are close links between Dunannie, Dunhurst and Bedales. Children in Year 3 can automatically transfer from Dunannie to Dunhurst unless there are exceptional circumstances. There are frequent visitors to the school too. Sport is a strength with a comprehensive programme of activities including swimming, gymnastics, tennis, netball, football and orienteering. Year 3 children have sport with Dunhurst Group 1 children and have the opportunity to play inter school matches. Dunannie is a very friendly school with happy, confident children who relish being at school. Staff and parents work in partnership together and we are always pleased to welcome visitors and prospective parents to Dunannie.

Scholarships. Personal development is central to our concept of scholarship and the new approach for scholarships starting in September 2017 aims to align scholarship beneficiaries more closely with the school's aim "to develop inquisitive thinkers with a love of learning who cherish independent thought". We have introduced the new scheme for pupils with particular talents in Art, Design, Music, Drama, Sport and other academic subjects to encourage their appetite for, research, enquiry and development. Depending on their specialist subject, most scholarship holders have access to a research fund to support their individual scholarly projects. There is no reduction in school fees – research grants are non means-tested and hence have a relatively small financial value (up to £300/year for 2017/18). The award of a scholarship is reviewed annually based on student performance.

Bursaries. Ranging from part fee contributions up to full 100% bursaries (with further support for additional costs), these awards enable pupils (generally from 11+ upwards) with an appetite for learning to attend Bedales Prep School, Dunhurst and Bedales who otherwise would have been unable to pay the fees. Awards are based on an assessment of the family's financial means. Bursary awards will be reviewed in the event of a change in the family's financial circumstances – the school should be informed of any changes in personal circumstance.

Pupils can benefit from the award of either a scholarship or a bursary, or both. Although bursary financial assistance is not dependent on a scholarship award, the school aims to enable pupils with particularly strong talents to attend the school, therefore a number of bursary beneficiaries also benefit from scholarship awards. Please contact the Registrar Janie Jarman (email: jjarman@bedales.org.uk; tel: 01730 711733) if you would like to discuss suitability for a scholarship or bursary to Bedales Prep School, Dunhurst or Bedales School.

Fees per term (2016–2017). Bedales: Boarders £11,511, Day £9,046. Bedales Prep, Dunhurst: Boarders £7,908, Day £6,107–£6,319. Bedales Pre-Prep, Dunannie: £2,876–£3,639.

Charitable status. Bedales School is a Registered Charity, number 307332. Its aims and objectives are to educate children as broadly as possible in a creative and caring environment.

Governors:
Timothy Hands, BA, AKC, DPhil (*Education Committee*)
Avril Hardie, BEd, JP (*Staff Welfare*)
Owen Jonathan, LLB Hons
Michele Johnson BA (*Chair of Governor Nominations*;
    External Relations)
Dr Anna Keay, PhD (*F&GP, ER*)
Rear Admiral John Lippiett, CB, CBE
Mark Pyper, OBE, BA (*Chair of Education Committee*)
Matthew Rice, BA (*Chairman*; *F&GP Remuneration*;
    External Relations; *Bedales Association*; *Bedales
    Parents' Association*; *Governor Nominations*)
Nicholas Vetch, ARICS (*Chair of F&GP Remuneration*;
    External Relations; *Governor Nominations*)
Professor Geoffrey Ward (*Education Committee*)
Charles Watson, BA (*Chair of External Relations*; *Chair of
    Development Trust*; *F&GP*)
Timothy Wise

Clerk to the Governors and Bursar: Richard Lushington,
    BA, MCIPD

Headmaster: Keith Budge, MA University College
    Oxford, PGCE

Managing Head of the Senior School: Louise Wilson, BA
    King's College London, MA Bath

Deputy Head, Academic: Alistair McConville, MA
    Fitzwilliam College Cambridge, PGCE Gloucester

Head of Boarding: Jenni Brittain, Dip S&D Queen
    Margaret College Edinburgh, Scottish STC Moray
    House

Heads of Departments:
Art: Simon Sharp, BA
Biology: Richard Sinclair, BA St Catherine's College
    Oxford, PGCE London
Chemistry: Emily Seeber, MChem Oxon
Classics: Christopher Grocock, BA Royal Holloway
    London, PhD Bedford College London
Dance: Liz Richards, BA Chichester, MA Chichester
Design: Ben Shaw, BSc Loughborough
Drama: Phil King, BA Royal Holloway, MPhil
    Birmingham, PGCE Warwick
Economics: Shaun Ritchie, BA Essex, PGCE Greenwich
English: David Anson, BA University College London,
    MA Institute of Education, PGCE Royal Academy of
    Dramatic Art
Geography: Paul Turner, BSc Exeter, PGCE Cambridge
Global Awareness: Annabel Smith, MSc London, BA
    London, PGCE Lady Margaret Hall Oxford
Government and Politics: Jonathan Selby, BA, PGCE
    Durham
History: Matthew Yeo, MA Oxford, MA, PhD Manchester
Learning Support: Ruth Austen, BSc Swansea, PGCE
    Kingston, PGDip SEN Kingston, PG Dip SpLD
    Southampton, SpLD Assessment Practising Cert Patoss
Mathematics: Martin Hanak-Hammerl, BSc Graz, Austria
Modern Languages: Nicholas Budden, BA Unversity of
    London, MA Canterbury, PGCE Surrey
French: Marie-Pierre Hamard, MA, PGCE Goldsmiths
    College London
Spanish: Ruth Carpenter-Jones, BA Queen Mary College
    London, PGCE Bristol
Director of Music: Nicholas Gleed, MA Cambridge, PGCE
    Durham
Outdoor Work: Andrew Martin, BA Manchester
    Metropolitan, PGCE Manchester Metropolitan
Philosophy and Religious Studies: Clare Jarmy, MA St
    Catharine's College Cambridge, PGCE Cambridge
Physics: Tobias Hardy, BSc York, MA Southampton,
    PGCE Warwick

Sport: Spencer Leach, BSc West London Inst of HE, MSc,
    PGCE Exeter
Director of External Relations: Rob Reynolds, BSc, MBA,
    MCIM
Registrar: Janie Jarman
PA to the Headmaster: Pam Goff

Dunhurst (Prep School)

Head: Jane Grubb, MA Brighton, BA Newcastle, PGCE
    Leeds

Deputy Head, Pastoral and Head of Blocks: Nick
    Robinson, MSc, PGCE Portsmouth
Director of Teaching & Learning: Andy Wiggins, BA
    Kent, PGCE
Head of Boys' Boarding: Simon Kingsley-Pallant, BA
    Brighton
Head of Girls' Boarding: Alice Tang-Pullen, BA
    Newcastle, PGCE Gloucestershire

Heads of Subject Departments:
Art: Susan McFarlane, MA Edinburgh, PGCE Bath
Drama: Simon Kingsley-Pallant, BA Brighton
English: Nichola Gotel, BA Winchester, PGCE Cambridge
Geography: David Ellis, BA Portsmouth, PGCE
    Buckingham
History and PRE: Steve Jeggo, BA King Alfred's College,
    Winchester, PGCE Bath
Latin: Melissa Canter, BA Exeter, PG DipEd NSW,
    Sydney / James Beatty BA Brighton
Academic Support: Anneli Bush, MA Edge Hill, PGCE
    Homerton College
Mathematics: Darran Kettle, BEd Westminster College
    Oxford, Dip Educational Coaching Newcastle College
Modern Foreign Languages: Olivia Burnett-Armstrong,
    BA Exeter, PGCE Cambridge
Outdoor Work: Ryan Walsh, BA Northampton
Wellbeing: Nick Robinson, MSc Portsmouth, PGCE
    Portsmouth
Sport: Heather Lowe, BA & PGCE Manchester
    Metropolitan
Science: Erawin Olie, BSc Warwick, PGCE Swansea

Dunannie (Pre-Prep School)

Head: Jo Webbern, CertEd Froebel
Senior Teacher: Julia Brown, BEd Froebel

Secretary to the Heads of Dunhurst & Dunannie: Frances
    Harris

Bede's Senior School

Upper Dicker, East Sussex BN27 3QH
Tel: 01323 843252
Fax: 01323 442628
email: school.office@bedes.org
website: www.bedes.org

Founded in 1978 Bede's discovers the talents of each student through breadth of academic curriculum and co-curricular. It is academically ambitious for all and the pastoral
care, delivered through the House and Tutor systems, is
inspiring and nurturing and ensures Bede's sends its young
people into the outside world self-aware, happy and confident in what they can achieve and looking forward to the
challenges they will meet.

The Senior School owes its existence in part to the success and vitality of Bede's Preparatory School in Eastbourne, one of the first boys' Preparatory Schools to become
fully co-educational and now one of the largest co-educa-

tional Preparatory Schools in the country. The Senior School has 750 students. Of these 320 are boarders (full and weekly), 430 are day students, 340 are Sixth Formers, 60 per cent are boys and 40 per cent are girls. Bede's enjoys an enviable reputation internationally. Currently 18% of our students are from over 40 countries.

The School takes great pride in the variety of its students and the outstanding range of opportunities available to them. The breadth of choice means every student can find what they naturally excel at. Students at Bede's pick from a wide array of over 100 clubs and activities, guided by personal tutors.

Aims. Bede's aims include the provision of an outstanding education, in an inclusive co-educational environment. That education is predicated on flexibility for the student; a broad and varied curriculum; personalisation of study programmes and respect for students' choices and aptitudes. Coupled with this is the provision of an extensive and exceptional variety of co-curricular activities that allows students to find, nurture and develop their interests and talents. The programme caters for everyone, from elite performers to hobbyists, and no activity is considered more important than another.

Bede's provides pastoral care that aims to support and safeguard each student, and in so doing, develops values of respect and humanity within a framework of friendly, non-confrontational relationships between all people, adults and students alike.

Facilities. In 2007 the School opened two innovative and award-winning boarding houses and two more were opened in February 2012. The Multi-Purpose Hall, also opened in 2007, is used for School Assemblies, examinations and many sports, including basketball, badminton, cricket, football, netball and tennis. The Performing Arts Centre, in a beautiful setting next to the lake, provides studio space for both drama and dance and 2008 saw the opening of a new Music Centre. A new Multi-Purpose Games Area, water-based astro and cricket pavilion were all opened in 2015. Bede's buildings are friendly, in enviable settings and a far cry from the overbearing, institutional character of much school architecture.

Curriculum. A new first year curriculum launched in September 2015 offering a range of new, fresh courses. The programme has an emphasis on the core skills of literacy, numeracy and scientific discovery and also includes "21st Century Studies", encompassing "soft skills" such as team work and time management as well as "hard skills" including cooking and first aid. All children also study a carousel of subjects as part of a course entitled "The World", which will cover global politics, history and geography. There is also an emphasis on creative subjects with children given the opportunity to experience art in many forms.

In the Fifth Form (Year 10) most students begin two-year courses leading to the GCSE (Key Stage 4) examinations. Students usually follow nine subjects of a possible 40 at GCSE; Mathematics, Science and English are compulsory subjects. Potential optional courses include: Art and Design, Business Studies, Dance, Design & Technology, Drama, Geography, History, Home Economics, Information Technology, Latin and Greek, Media Studies, Modern Languages (French, Spanish, German), Music, Performing Arts (Dance), Physical Education, Religious Studies, Science (Triple Award), Science (Double Award), Science (Single Award). Some IGCSEs are also offered along with some short-course GCSEs. A Pre-Sixth course is offered for those who need a year of intensive English before embarking on an A Level course.

During the first three years those with particular needs, such as those with any form of Dyslexia and those who are non-native speakers of English, can follow organised pro-

grammes within the timetable taught by suitably qualified teachers.

In the Sixth Form students can follow the traditional three or four A Level courses and some Pre-U courses, which can provide a broader education. Most GCSE subjects are offered at A Level plus Economics, Media Studies, Government & Politics, Philosophy and Ethics and Theatre Studies. Bede's also offers Cambridge Pre-U in a number of subjects.

Vocational provision: BTEC National Certificate in Sport, Music Performance, Animal Management and Business Management.

Bede's also runs the Legat Professional Dance Course which is fully integrated with the academic programme.

Current class sizes average 16 up to GCSE level and 12 at A Level.

Co-Curricular Programme including Games. The extensive programme includes the many sporting and games playing opportunities open to students, The Duke of Edinburgh's Award scheme, numerous outdoor pursuits and a daily programme of activities within the fields of Art, Drama, Music, Journalism, Science, Technology, Engineering and Social Service. There are currently over 14 Club Activities running each week and an average daily choice from 40 options. Games and Sports include Aerobics, Archery, Athletics, Badminton, Basketball, Canoeing, Climbing, Cricket, Cross-Country, Fishing, Football, Golf (the School has its own practice course), Hockey, Dance, Netball, Orienteering, Photography, Riding, Rounders, Rugby, Squash, Swimming, Target Rifle Shooting, Tennis and Volleyball. Bede's has a fine sporting reputation with students past and present representing their country at cricket, football, rugby, hockey, athletics and showjumping. The Emerging Talent Programme brings together pupils across different sports who have potential to become professional sports people and provides training in areas such as nutrition, sports psychology and media handling.

Pastoral Care. There are three boys' boarding houses and two girls' houses, the numbers in each house averaging 60, with three resident staff in each. An appropriately selected tutor provides a mentor for each student during their time at the School. These tutors are responsible for ensuring that each student's academic and social well-being is carefully looked after. Tutors act in liaison with Housemasters and Housemistresses and are readily available for discussions with parents. All parents have several formal opportunities each year to meet those who teach or otherwise look after their sons or daughters. In 2015 a Day Boarding concept was launched allowing day pupils to be part of a boarding house, complete prep in house and return home on the late bus service.

Religion. The School maintains the Village Church for the local community. Confirmation classes are available, if requested. All students attend weekly meetings in the church which are appropriate to boys and girls of all religions and are of outstanding variety. Bede's does not impose any singular religious observance on its students but would rather either that their existing faith is further strengthened by their being full members of the congregation of local churches or that they grow to appreciate and value the importance of a strong spiritual life through the thoughtful and varied programme of 'School Meetings'. There is a choice of four types of observance on Sundays: the Multi-Religious School Meeting, Church of England, Roman Catholic and Free Church.

Admission. The normal age of entry to the School is between 12½ and 14 years. Admission is based on school reports and references and interview. Pupils entering the school from 2018 onwards will be invited to attend a Bede's Experience Day in Year 7. Places are open each year to those wishing to join the School as Sixth Formers and at other levels in the School.

Scholarships and Bursaries. Bede's invests in excess of ten per cent of its annual income in means-tested fee remission and academic, art, dance, drama, music and sports scholarships. Prospective students who wish to join outside of the scholarship process are able to apply for means-tested fee remission.

Further details regarding scholarships and bursaries are available from the Admissions Office, email: admissions@bedes.org.

Fees per term (2016–2017). Full Boarders £11,087, Weekly Boarders £10,431, Day Pupils £6,975, Day Boarding £6,975.

Charitable status. St Bede's School Trust Sussex is a Registered Charity, number 278950. It exists to provide quality education.

Governors:
Major-General Anthony Meier, CB, OBE (*Chairman*)
Christopher Bean, LLB Hons
John Burbidge, BA Hons, ACA
Andrew Corbett, MA Hons, PGCE
Jeremy Courtney, FRAgS, MBIAC
Peter Denison, OBE, CQSW
Christopher Doidge, MA Oxon
Louise Ellis, BA Jt Hons
Ian Hunt, BSc
Mark MacFadden, MRICS, ACIArb
Lady Rosemary Newton, MA
Catherine Nash, BEd
Peter Pyemont (*President*)
Patrick Tobin, MA Oxon, FRSA
Xavier Van Hove, BA Hons Oxon
Geraldine Watkins, JP

Senior Management:

Headmaster: Mr P Goodyer, BSc

Senior Management:
Principal Deputy Headmaster: Mr J Lewis, BA Hons, MA, PGCE
Deputy Head, Academic: Mr J Tuson, MA, GTP
Deputy Head, CPD & Staff: Mr R Frame, BA Hons, HDE
Deputy Head, Co-Curricular: Ms R Woollett, BA Hons, PGCE
School Chaplain: Revd T Buckler, BA, MA Hons, PGCE
Assistant Head of Compliance & Welfare: Mrs L M Belrhiti, BEd Hons, Dip TEFL
Senior Registrar: Mr R Mills, BA Hons, PGCE
Principal of Summer School: Mr S Wood
Director of Curriculum Management: Mr A Hayes, BSc Hons, PGCE
Director of Marketing and Admissions: Mrs R Nairne, BA Hons
Bursar: Dr Jonathan Northway, MB, FRCS

Housemasters and Housemistresses:
Bloomsbury House: Mrs M Leggett, BA Hons, MA, PGCE
Camberlot House: Mr R Jones, BA Hons
Crossways House: Mrs J Lambeth, BSc Hons, PGCE
Charleston House: Mrs M Martin, BA Hons, PGCE, MA Ed, Dip TEFL
Deis House: Mr N Driver, BCom, PGCE
Dicker House: Mr C Abraham, BSc Hons, Dip Law, PGCE
Dorms House: Mr P Juniper, BSc Hons, PGCE, CBiol, MSB
Dorter House: Mr D Leggett, BA Hons, QTS
Knights House: Mr A Waterhouse, HDE Secondary
Stud House: Mr P Jones, BSc Hons, MSc, PGCE

Heads of Departments/Subjects:

Art:
Mr J Turner, BA Hons, PGCE (*Head of Faculty*)

Mr A Hammond, BA Hons, MA, GTP (*Head of Ceramics*)
Miss E Excell, BA Hons, GTP (*Head of Photography*)
Business Studies and Economics: Mr G Parfitt, MBA
Design and Technology: Mr N Potter, BSc Hons, PGCE
Drama: Mrs K Lewis, BA Hons, PGCE
EAL: Mr J Cook, RSA, TEFLA
English: Mr M Oliver, BA Hons, PGCE
Food and Nutrition: Mrs C Ballard, BEd Hons
Geography: Mrs C Buckler, BSc Hons, MA, PGCE
Higher Education and Careers: Mr P Gibbs, BA Hons, PGCE
History and Politics: Mr R Frame, BA Hons, HDE
ICT: Mr A Hayes, BSc Hons, PGCE
Learning Enhancement: Mrs C MacGregor, BSc, QTS, PGCE
Mathematics: Mr N Abrams, BSc Hons, PGCE
Media and Film Studies: Mr R Williams, BA Hons, GTP, Dip Media Ed
Modern Languages: Mrs J Mulligan, MA Cantab, QTS
Music: Miss L Morris, BMus Hons, PGCE
Physical Education: Mrs K Merchant, BSc, PGCE
Religious Studies and Philosophy: Mr N Stannard, BA Hons, PGCE, QTS
Science:
Mr M Costley, BSc Hons, MSc, PGCE (*Head of Faculty*)
Mrs H Tilling, BSc, PGCE (*Head of Biology*)
Dr A Cumpstey, MChem Hons, MA, PhD, PGCE (*Head of Chemistry*)
Mr C Hiscox, BSc Hons, PGCE (*Head of Physics*)
Mr S Hodges, BSc Hons, PGCE (*Head of ELBS*)
Sport: Mr Andrew Hibbert, BEd (*Director of Sport*)
Legat School of Dance:
Miss L Smikle (*Principal and Artistic Director*)
Mrs A Murphy, BA Hons, PGCE (*Head of Academic Dance*)

Year Heads:
Head of First Year: Mr L Backler, BA Hons, PGCE
Head of Lower Fifth: Mr M Krause, BEd, QTS
Head of Upper Fifth: Ms J French, BSc, PGCE
Head of Sixth Form: Mr J Henham, BSc Hons, PGCE
Asst Head of Sixth Form: Mr B Jackson, BSc, PGCE

Bedford Modern School

Manton Lane, Bedford, Bedfordshire MK41 7NT

Tel:	01234 332500
Fax:	01234 332550
email:	info@bedmod.co.uk
website:	www.bedmod.co.uk
Twitter:	@BedfordModern
Facebook:	/BedfordModernSchool
LinkedIn:	/bedford-modern-school

Bedford Modern School is one of the Harpur Trust Schools in Bedford, sharing equally in the educational endowment bequeathed for the establishment of a school in Bedford by Sir William Harpur in 1566. Bedford Modern School was a Direct Grant Grammar School which became independent in 1976. It became co-educational in September 2003.

Number of Pupils. There are 258 pupils in the Junior School (aged 7–11) and 967 pupils in the Senior School (aged 11–18).

(*See also Bedford Modern Junior School entry in IAPS section.*)

Facilities. The School occupies an attractive forty-acre wooded site to the north of Bedford. The main buildings date from 1974 and there have been substantial additions since that time, most notably a new assembly hall, performance arena and classrooms to the Junior School (2002); a Sixth Form Study Centre and Refectory (The Rutherford Building – 2006) and new Library Resource Centre (2007). There are extensive facilities for Science, Technology and Information Technology. There have been recent extensions to the Music School and Performing Arts Centre. Each year group has its own common room.

A new, state-of-the-art Science Centre will be ready for occupation in September 2017. The exciting design will provide current and future generations of BMS students with an inspirational learning environment.

The playing fields are all on the School site with extensive facilities for Rugby, Football, Cricket and Athletics. There is also a large swimming pool, a fitness suite, gym and sports hall. Recent additions include two large all-weather training areas and netball courts. The School shares a large and well-stocked Boathouse with the other Harpur Trust Schools on the River Ouse.

Admissions. Pupils are admitted between the ages of 7 and 16. The School conducts its own entrance assessments which are held in January of the year prior to September entry.

Registration fee is £100.

Fees per term (2016–2017). Tuition: Junior School £3,091, Senior School and Sixth Form £4,240.

Assistance with Fees. The School offers Modern Scholarships which are available to pupils joining the School from Year 7 (11+) upwards and have been designed to provide opportunities for children with potential academically, in sport, performance arts, music and art/design and information technology. All scholarships are means-tested and are also dependent on a pupil's academic success in the entrance assessments. Further details may be obtained from the School.

Curriculum. The Junior School (ages 7–11) curriculum covers Mathematics, English, Humanities (History, Geography and RE), Science, Information and Communication Technology (ICT), Modern Foreign Languages, PE, Art, Drama, PSHE and Games. Pupils benefit both from a purpose-built practical skills centre containing art and science rooms as well as specialist computer and technology rooms, and from the Senior School, music, PE and games facilities including the swimming pool.

In the Senior School, the curriculum includes all the core subjects, as well as Technology, IT, RE, PE, Music, Art and Drama. All pupils experience French, German, and Spanish in Year 7 and Latin in Year 8 before making choices. Pupils opt for ten GCSE subjects. For the Sixth Form, pupils select four from a wide range of 29 subjects. In addition to all the traditional options, the choice of subjects also includes Computer Science, Government and Politics, Economics, Business, Religious Studies, Philosophy, DT Systems and Control, DT Product Design, Classical Civilisation, Theatre Studies, PE, Psychology, Film Studies and Music Technology. All students will sit AS exams at the end of Year 12 in all their subjects and the majority will continue three to A Level.

ICT Facilities. The School boasts a range of ICT facilities offering both staff and pupils an individual network account and email address so that they are able to access over 400 networked PCs across the School in addition to high-speed broadband Internet access, wireless classroom laptop sets, networked printing, and an extensive subject software library including a range of training courseware material.

All standard classrooms are equipped with a computer linked to ceiling mounted data projector and speakers. There are a number of interactive whiteboards and additional presentation equipment is also available for use. The School's website can be viewed at www.bedmod.co.uk.

Religious and Moral Education. The School is multi-faith and multicultural, and religious and moral education is given throughout. Personal, social and health education is a fundamental and well-established part of the timetable.

Individual Care. Every pupil has a personal tutor, who supervises and takes an interest in his or her academic progress, co-curricular activities and sporting interests. Tutors meet with their tutees on a daily basis and there is at least one longer pastoral session each week. Each Year Group has its own common room for use at break and lunchtimes and other non-taught times with a study area and recreational facilities.

We believe that common sense and courtesy lie at the heart of pastoral care. We stress self-discipline and high standards of personal conduct. The tutorial system and the academic organisation are discrete, working in parallel to complement each other. Teaching class sizes are a maximum of twenty-four and often many fewer. We aim to provide a relaxed but purposeful environment; a culture in which all feel at ease and are ambitious to achieve their best.

Drama. There are several large-scale productions each year, a Drama Festival hosted for local schools, and several smaller events. There are separate drama and dance studios and a 300-seat theatre. Speech and Drama is offered throughout the School, leading to LAMDA examinations. Ballet, tap and modern dance lessons follow the ISTD syllabus.

Music. Pupils can learn all the orchestral and band instruments as well as piano, keyboard, guitar/electric guitar and singing. The School has a large variety of choirs, orchestra, bands and ensembles. Pupils can follow courses for GCSE and A Level Music as well as A Level Music Technology. Music accommodation includes a music technology suite with ten Apple computers and state-of-the-art recording facilities.

Activities. There are many school societies and clubs catering for a variety of tastes and interests. The voluntary Combined Cadet Force is strong with Army, Navy, RAF and Marine sections. There is a structured programme of outdoor education which includes residential trips from Years 6, 7 and 8 with international expeditions available for older students. Outreach including community service and the Duke of Edinburgh's Award scheme are very popular.

Sport. Rugby, football, cricket and rowing are major sports for boys; hockey, netball and rowing for girls. Additional activities include: table tennis, water polo, badminton, hockey (boys), equestrian, snowsports, cycling, cross-country, weights and fitness, fencing, fives, sevens, swimming, dance, athletics, rounders, tennis, climbing, shooting, and gymnastics. There is regular representation at national, divisional and regional levels.

Higher Education. The great majority of sixth form leavers go on to a degree course at their chosen university. More than 30% take courses in STEM (Science, Technology, Engineering and Mathematics) subjects.

Old Bedford Modernians' Club. For further details see the OBM section of the School website or please contact externalrelations@bedmod.co.uk.

Charitable status. Bedford Modern School is part of the Harpur Trust which is a Registered Charity, number 1066861. It includes in its aims the provision of high quality education for boys and girls.

Governors and Staff:
Chairman of the School Committee: I McEwen, BPhil, MA, DPhil

Headmaster: Mr M M Hall, BA, MA, PGCE

Senior Deputy Head: Mrs S E Davis, MA, PGCE
Deputy Head Academic: Mr M R Price, MA, PGCE
Deputy Head Pastoral: Mr I C Grainger, CertEd
Head of Junior School: Mrs J C Rex, BA, PGCE

Director of Sixth Form: Mr J P White, BEd
Bursar: Mr S R Willis, MSc, BSc Hons, CDipAF
Director of External Relations: Ms J Ridge, BA

Heads of Year:
Head of Year 7: Mrs S J Sanctuary, BSc, PGCE
Head of Year 8: Mr J P Searle, BTh, PGCE
Head of Year 9: Mr J P Fitton, BSc, PGCE
Head of Year 10: Mr T E Rex, BEd Hons
Head of Year 11: Mr A D Tapper, BSc, MSt Oxon

Heads of Houses:
Senior Head of House: Mrs P Edwards, BA, MA, PGCE
Head of Bell House: Mr A G Higgens, BSc, QTS
Head of Farrar House: Mr J M Sadler, BSc, PGCE
Head of Mobbs House: Miss A L Vaughan
Head of Oatley House: Mr M Ruta
Head of Rose House: Mr A Slater, BEng, PGCE
Head of Tilden House: Mrs H Lakhani, BSc, PGCE / Miss S Sobrado Licenciatura, PGCE

Teaching Staff:

Faculty of Art, Design & Information Technology: Miss S E Milton, BA, PGCE

Art:
Mr J McGregor, BA, PG Dip, PGCE
Mrs P Edwards, BA, MA, PGCE

Design Technology:
Mr A H Jones
Mr I C Grainger, Cert Ed
Mrs L Neville
Mr A Rock, BSc Hons, PGCE
Mr J P White, BEd
Mr C Wiles, BA Hons, GTP

ICT:
Mr A Leach, BA
Miss J Hollingsworth, PGCE
Mr P J Smith, BSc Hons, CertEd

Faculty of English: Mr S D Bywater, BA, MLitt, PGCE

Dr J P Barnes, PhD, PGCE
Ms J Chumbley, BA, PGCE
Dr T Foster, BA, MA, PhD, PGCE
Mrs J L Kilbey, BA, MA, PGCE
Miss H Morey
Mr O L Roberts
Mr J J Sanders, BA, PGCE
Mrs E P Sheldon, BA, PGCE

Film Studies:
Mr J J Sanders, BA, PGCE
Dr T Foster, BA, MA, PhD, PGCE

Faculty of Humanities: Miss R Gleeson

Geography:
Mr B W Day, BSc, PGCE
Mrs D R Mistrano, BA, PGCE
Mr M R Price, MA Cantab, PGCE
Mr M Ruta
Miss A Vaughan

History:
Mrs S E Wright, MA, PGCE
Dr S Boa BA, MPhil, PhD, PGCE
Mrs D Mistrano, BA, PGCE
Mr A D Tapper, BSc, MSt Oxon
Ms C Webb, BA, PGCE

Religious Studies and Theology:
Mr J L Hooper, BA, PGCE
Mr J P Searle, BTh, PGCE
Mrs J Read, BA, QTS

Faculty of Languages and Classics: Miss R Crawley, BA, PGCE, LGSM, MEd

Classics:
Miss J Newton, MA, PGCE
Mrs S E Davis, MA, PGCE
Mr C W H Rees-Bidder, BA, MEd, PGCE
Miss E Swallow

French
Miss R Crawley, BA, PGCE, LGSM, MEd

German:
Mr R J Killen, MA, PGCE, TEFL, DipSp & DipFr

Spanish:
Mrs R Reed, BA, PGCE, TEFL
Miss S Sobrado, Licenciatura, PGCE

Languages Teachers
Mlle G Amoros, Licence Civilisation * Lit, PGCE
Miss T Le Baut Ayuso
Mr G Watkins, BA
Mrs J Williams, BA, PGCE

Faculty of Mathematics: Mr N D Shackleton, BSc, PGCE
Mr S A Brocklehurst, BA, PGCE
Miss E J Ginns
Mr I R Hay, BSc, PGCE
Mr N Hussain, BSc, PGCE
Mrs S J Jacobs, BSc, PGCE
Mr R Kay, BSc, PGCE
Mr D M King, BSc, PGCE
Mr A Leach, BA
Mr R Millar
Mr A Slater, BEng, PGCE

Faculty of Music: Mr J Mower, GRSM, ARCO, ARCM, Dip RAM

Assistant Director of Music: Mrs M Perry, BMus, PGCE, DipABRSM

Music Technology:
Mr M Gooch, BA, PGCE

Faculty of Performance Arts: Miss L Coltman, BA Hons

Drama:
Mr E I Moore
Miss L J Spence
Mrs J Goodacre, BA, PGCE, MBA

Speech and Drama:
Mrs S Leather, BA
Mr M A Burgess, Prof Dip

Dance:
Miss R Bradley, AISTD, FDI

Faculty of Politics, Philosophy and Economics (PPE): Mr D Bareham

Economics:
Mr P J Davis
Mr R Smith, BA, PGCE
Mr M Hall, BA, MA, PGCE

Business:
Mr R Smith, BA, PGCE

Government & Politics:
Mr S Baker BSc, PGCE

Philosophy:
Mrs J Morris
Mr J P Searle, BTh, PGCE

Faculty of Science: Mr N R Else, BEd, MA

Biology:
Mr R J Brand, BSc, PGCE

Mr D Donoghue
Mr D Greenfield, BSc, PGCE
Mr D A Jenkins, BSc, MSc, DipEdTech, PGCE
Mrs H Lakhani, BSc, PGCE
Miss D Randhawa [Maternity Cover]
Mrs S Sanctuary, BSc, PGCE
Mrs S Sumal, BSc MSc, PGCE

Chemistry:
Dr C M Jones, BSc, PhD, PGCE
Mrs N K Cordell, BEd Hons
Mr J P Fitton, BSc, PGCE
Mr J Sadler, BSc, PGCE
Mrs V Shehu, BSc, GTP

Physics:
Mr D C Honnor, BA Oxon, GTP
Mrs W D Hallett, BA, MA, PGCE
Mr S S Harvey, BSc, Cert. Ed
Mr J Krishna
Mr T P Mullan, BSc, PGCE
Mr T E Rex, BEd Hons

Psychology:
Miss H J Kelly, BSc, PGCE

Faculty of Sport:
Director of Sport: Mr P L Jerram, BSc
Head of Junior School Sport Development: Mr T W
   Bucktin, BSc
Head of PE: Mr T Whitehead
Head of Games: Mr D Orton, BEd, DipML
Director of Cricket: Mr P J Woodroffe, BA
Director of Rowing: Mr M Bavington
Director of Rugby/Sports Academy Manager: (*to be
   appointed*)
Coordinator of Girls Games: Miss H L Gilbert, BA, MA,
   PGCE

PE Teachers:
Mr N J Chinneck, BEd
Mr A G Higgens, BSc, QTS
Mr A D Tapper, BSc, MSt Oxon
Miss H Bodsworth
Miss H Southam

Girls' Games Coaches:
Mrs D Keep
Mrs C Orton, BEd Hons

Waterpolo and Swimming:
Mr A Bygraves

Other Areas:
Careers: Miss S Burns, DipCG
Examinations: Mr M Stellman
Librarian: Mrs M S Brown, BSc, Dip Lib, CNNA Dist,
   MCILIP
PSHE: Mrs D Mistrano, BA, PGCE
Welfare Liaison Manager: Ms M Jones
Health and Fitness Manager: Mrs L Williams, LLB, MSc
Technical Theatre Manager: Mr N Parker, BA

Director of Academic Support: Dr Sean Reid
SENCO: Miss L J Hendry

SpLD Academic Support:
Mrs D Costello, BA, MA, CertSpLD
Mrs C Setchfield, BA, PGCE, CertSpLD
Mrs M Tew, BA, PGCE

Junior School:
Head of Junior School: Mrs J Rex, BA, PGCE
Deputy Head of Junior School: Mrs P Pacyna, BA, QTS
Junior School Heads Secretary: Mrs K Smith
Head of Junior School Sports Development: Mr T Bucktin,
   BSc, PGCE

Director of Studies: Mr M Capuano, BEd, QTS

Junior School Teachers:
Mrs H Avery, BEd
Miss J Barlow, BEd
Mr C Barrow, BEd
Miss C Coyne
Mrs M Fox, BA, PGCE
Mrs F Gale, BEd
Mrs M Garton
Mrs K Hale, BA, QTS
Mrs E Hall
Mrs J Leydon, BEd
Mrs S J Nicholls, BA, Cert Ed
Mrs M Phillips, BEd
Mrs C Toumazou
Mr E Warren, BA, QTS
Mr P Wilkinson
Mrs C Kirby

Administration Assistant: Mrs C Mayfield
Learning Support Assistant: Mrs H Draycott
Learning Support Assistant: Mrs B Sehmbi
Learning Support Assistant: Miss E Lewis

Bedford School

De Parys Avenue, Bedford MK40 2TU
Tel: 01234 362216
email: admissions@bedfordschool.org.uk
website: www.bedfordschool.org.uk
Twitter: @bedfordschool
Facebook: @Bedford-School

Bedford School is a leading boarding and day school for
boys aged 13–18. The school is situated in an extensive 50-
acre estate in the heart of Bedford and is just 40 minutes
from London by train.

Established in 1552, Bedford School has an established
reputation for academic excellence and all boys are encouraged to aspire to the highest possible standards and to
exceed their expectations.

The school's success is demonstrated by a long history of
impressive exam results at GCSE, A Level, and in the International Baccalaureate Diploma. Bedford is also renowned
for its strengths in music, the arts and sport.

From the classroom to the sports field, in laboratories and
theatres, on excursions and exchanges, boys are challenged
academically, socially and culturally. They learn exciting
new skills and knowledge, and how to prepare themselves
for a successful future as well-rounded young men with confidence, compassion and critical minds.

Number in School. 690 boys aged between 13–18 years:
233 weekly and full boarders, 457 day boys.

Boarders and Day Boys. There is a balanced mix of day
boys, weekly boarders and full boarders, who combine in
lessons, games and all other school activities. There are six
Senior Boarding Houses, each containing up to 51 boys.

Academic. Academic excellence is central to life at Bedford School. Consistent high exam results at GCSE, A Level
and the International Baccalaureate set the standard for academic achievement throughout the school. The curriculum
extends learning well beyond the national requirements and
is structured to provide a balanced and varied choice of subjects which will challenge each boy's strengths.

Boys are encouraged to achieve through a balance of different teaching techniques, small class sizes and (where
appropriate) setting, well-resourced and subject-specific
classrooms, specialist teachers, prep setting, regular lecture
series and visiting speakers, lunchtime and after school aca-

demic clinics. ICT and mobile device technology is used extensively to support and enhance learning, but literacy and numeracy skills remain fundamental to all that we do.

University and Careers. A strong Careers and UCAS provision enables all boys, throughout their school years, to access tailored, professional experience and advice. In addition to an annual careers fair, regular information evenings, lectures and seminars are also held. The school is a member of the Independent Schools Careers Organisation and was awarded E2E Gold status in 2016.

Almost all leavers go on to higher education. In 2016, 77% of boys went on to Russell Group Universities including Oxford and Cambridge.

Extracurricular. The school offers a diverse programme of extracurricular activities every evening between 4.15 pm and 6.00 pm for boarders and day boys alike, many of which involve girls from Harpur Trust sister school, Bedford Girls' School. Activities include the Combined Cadet Force (CCF), Duke of Edinburgh's Award scheme, community service, fundraising groups, and more than 60 other clubs and societies from Astronomy to Young Enterprise. Concerts, plays, lectures and film performances are given in the Great Hall, the Recital Hall, the Erskine May Hall and the Quarry Theatre.

Sport. The school aims to inspire a lifelong interest in sport, promoting teamwork, well-being, fitness and fun. A team of dedicated, passionate specialist teachers and coaches are on hand to provide high-quality guidance and help each boy to develop his skills. Many boys go on to excel at sport, and the majority of major sport first teams are of county standard or beyond.

The school's major sports are rugby, hockey, rowing and cricket but the range of sports on offer extends to athletics, badminton, basketball, canoeing, cross country, fencing, fives, golf, sailing, soccer, squash, swimming, tennis, water polo and weight training/conditioning.

First-class facilities include a twin Astroturf complex with floodlights, an indoor 25m swimming pool, 28 tennis courts, four squash courts, a climbing wall and immaculate grass pitches.

Music. All boys have the opportunity to explore and perform, with a wide range of musical instruments and groups to choose from. As well as the two Senior Symphony Orchestras, a Chamber Orchestra, a Concert Band and a large Choral Society, there is a Chapel Choir trained in the English Cathedral tradition, two Junior Orchestras, a Dance Band, Jazz Band, Rock Band, a large number of chamber music groups, and a Music Club. There is a full music programme throughout each year, with at least one concert a week.

The Music department is situated in a £3 million, state-of-the-art, purpose-built development, which includes a superb recital hall, music technology suite, multi-track recording studio and the school's radio station.

Drama. All boys can get involved in Bedford School's vibrant drama scene, whether on stage or behind the scenes. Each year a range of formal and informal dramatic productions are performed by all age groups.

The drama department is housed the school's new £6m Quarry Theatre, which officially opened in June 2015 in the former St Luke's Church. The 286-seat theatre and 60-seat studio-theatre provide a superb venue for school productions and the extensive programme performed by visiting touring companies.

Art and Design. The art department works to develop each boy's individual artistic talents and encourages pupils to engage with and appreciate the world around them. Boys are encouraged to develop a lifelong appreciation of the creative arts with visits to museums and galleries, annual study tours abroad, weekly life drawing classes and a series of art lectures.

The Art School, located in a characterful mid-1750s Georgian building, has three specialist studios for painting, printmaking and sculpture. All three Art Staff are practising artists.

Admissions. The majority of boys enter the Preparatory School from seven and the Upper School at 13 or 16 years of age. The Preparatory School has its own Headmaster and specialist staff. (*See Bedford Preparatory School entry in IAPS section.*)

Parents wishing to send their sons to Bedford School should apply to the Director of Admissions. All applicants are expected to provide evidence of good character and suitability from their previous school. Year 9 applicants from Preparatory Schools wishing to enter the Upper School are assessed in Year 6 or Year 7 by an initial Pre-test and interview. In Year 8 all applicants undertake a computer-based test (designed to measure raw academic potential) at the school, along with written English and Mathematics papers.

Boys looking to join the Sixth Form are invited for an assessment day in the January before entry. Applicants sit a Verbal Reasoning paper and have an interview with a senior member of staff. In addition, the school takes up a reference with the boy's current school and considers his application along with his predicted grades at GCSE.

Additional information is also available on the website: www.bedfordschool.org.uk/admissions.

Scholarships and Bursaries. The school offers a range of Scholarships and Bursaries to boys who excel academically or show outstanding talent in art, drama, music or sport (including golf). Up to 20 Scholars receive up to a maximum of 10% of annual school fees from The Harpur Trust.

12 of these Scholars receive up to a further 25% of annual school fees if they demonstrate exceptional talent. This additional funding, from the Brian Saville Scholarship Fund, gives a total award of up to 35% of annual school fees. Any amount required beyond this is awarded on a means-tested basis through the school's Bursary scheme. Roach Scholarships are available for exceptional Sixth Form academic candidates.

Awards are available for boys joining the school at our 13+ and 16+ entry points. For more information, please visit www.bedfordschool.org.uk/scholarships

Fees per term (2016–2017). Day Boys £6,009; Full Boarders £10,163; Weekly Boarders £9,827.

Old Bedfordians Club. Tel: 01234 362262; email: obclub@bedfordschool.org.uk. For further details, visit www.bedfordschool.org.uk/the-club.

Charitable status. Bedford School is part of the Harpur Trust which is a Registered Charity, number 1066861.

School Governors:
Chairman: Professor Stephen Mayson, LLB, LLM, PhD, Barrister, FRSA
Deputy Chairman: Mr David Dixon, BA, MBA, FCA, AIB
Mr Charles Allen, BA
Dr Anne Egan, MA, BM, BCh, MRCP, FRCR
Mr Chris Johnson
Sir Clive Loader, KCB, OBE
Mr Ali Malek, QC, MA, BCL Oxon
Mr Hugh Maltby, BA
Mr Richard Miller, MA Cantab, Dip Ed Soton, Dip HA London, RAFVR[T] (*Staff Elected Governor*)
Mrs Amanda Rea, ACMA, MBA (*Parent Elected Governor*)
Mr Murray Stewart
Mrs Jennifer Sauborah Till, BSc, MSc, PhD
Mr Linbert Spencer
Revd Paula Vennells
Mr Phil Wallace, MA, FCA, FBRP
Chairman of the Harpur Trust: Mr Murray Stewart
Deputy Chairman of the Harpur Trust: Mr Anthony Nutt

Head Master: Mr J S Hodgson, BA

Vice Master: Mr D Koch, BA, DPhil
Deputy Head (Academic): Mr A G Tighe, MA
Bursar and Clerk to the Governors: Mrs J Miles, MA, MBA
Assistant Head (External Affairs): Mr R J Midgley, BA Ed
Director of Teaching & Learning: Mr W Montgomery, BSc
Director of Bedford School Association: Mr R Garrett, BA

Director of Admissions: Mrs A Steiger
Director of International Baccalaureate: Mrs E Murray, MA
Senior Boarding Housemaster: Mr C J Bury, BA
Undermaster: Mr I B Armstrong, BSc, MSc

Assistant staff:
* *Head of Department*

Academic Support (ESOL & SPLD):
*Ms J Spir, BA, RSA Preparatory Cert TEFL
Mrs K Chevallier, MA, Cert TEFL, OCNW Level 4 Cert ESOL
Mrs J Greening, BPhil, Cert TEFL
Ms J Hutt, BEd, RSA Dip SpLD, SENCo National Award
Mr T Kehoe, BA, MSt, PGCE, QTS
Mr B O'Connor, Cert Ed, Cert TEFL
Mrs M Nayar, BSc, Cert Ed
Mrs S Manning, LLB, CELTA
Mrs L Patel, BA, Cert ESOL
Mr N Pieris, MA, CELTA, MCollT
Mrs L Saunders MA, Dip TEFL

Art:
*Mr M Croker, BA
Mrs K Nicholson, BA, MA
Mrs F Whiteman, BA, MA

Biology:
*Mr M Beale, BSc, MEd (*Head of Science*)
Mrs F Bell, BSc
Mr M Mallalieu, BSc
Ms J Mainstone, BS
Mr C Palmer, BSc, MA
Ms A Swallow, BA
Mr P Whatling, BSc, BEng

Chemistry:
*Mr S Knight, BA
Dr R Jones, BEng, MSc, MRes, PhD
Mr P Lumley-Wood, BSc, CChem, MRSC
Mr M Mitchell, MA
Dr W Suthers, BSc, MSc, PhD

Classics:
*Mr A Melvill, BA
Mr N Allen, BA
Mr G McCormick

Computing:
*Mr D Wild

Design Technology:
*Mr I Armstrong, BSc, MSc
Mr L Holt, BA
Mr M Huddlestone, BA
Mr G Waite, MEng

Economics & Business Studies:
*Mr P Waterhouse, BSc
Mr C Bury, BA
Mr M Cassell, BSc
Mr R Heale, BSc
Mrs C Medley, BA
Mr H Taylor, BSc

English:
*Mr N Hopton, MA, MEd
Miss K Betterton, BA, MA
Mrs L Di Niro, BA, MPhil
Mr A Grimshaw, BA
Mrs A Smith, BA
Miss S Van Heerden, BA
Mrs R Wainwright, BA, MA

Geography:
*Mr T Rees, BSc
Mr R Campbell, BA
Mr M Gracie, BSc
Ms H Hudson, BA
Mr W Montgomery, BSc
Ms S Spyropoulos, BA

History:
*Ms E Parcell, BA
Mr N Allen, BA
Mr C Fisher, MA
Mr M Graham, BA, MA Ed
Mr M Herring, BA

Mathematics:
*Mrs J C Beale, BSc, MA
Mr S Adams, MPhys
Mr B Burgess, BA Ed
Mrs R Down, BSc
Mr R Eadie, MA
Mr F Elliott, BA, MSc
Mrs T Harbinson, BSc
Mr A Midwinter, BSc
Mrs E Murray, MA
Mrs N Tekell-Mellor, BSc
Dr D Wild, BSc, PhD
Mr J Wills, MPhysPhil

Modern Languages:
*Mrs B Bousquet, BA (*Head of French*)
Mr F Graeff, Dipl Kfm (*Head of German*)
Mr A Huxford, MA (*Head of Spanish*)
Mr A Braithwaite, BA
Mrs M Buergo, MA
Dr A Chen, MBA, PhD
Ms C Geneve, MA
Miss J Law, BA
Mr V Sánchez Jimenez, BA
Miss J Starkey, BA

Music:
*Mr J Sanders, BA
Mr B Bantock, BMus, PPRNCM
Mr G Bennett, GGSM
Mr M Green, GRSM, LRAM, ARCM, Dip RAM
Mr T Rooke, MMus, BA
Mr J Rouse, MA, FRCO
Mr R Thompson BMus, PGDip MM
Mr A Tighe, MA

Physical Education:
*Mr B Burgess, BA Ed
Mr R Midgley, BA Ed
Mr J Hinkins (*Director of Rugby*)
Mr S Mee (*Director of Hockey*)
Mr P Mulkerrins (*Director of Rowing*)
Mr G Steer (*Director of Cricket*)

Physics:
*Mr G Monaghan
Mr M Crisp, MEng
Dr A Calverley, MSci, PhD, FRAS
Mr G Green, BSc
Mr L Guise, BA

Dr E Palmer, MSci, PhD
Mr S Everitt, MEng

Religious Education:
*Mr A Finch, MA
Revd A S Atkins, MA (*Chaplain*)
Mr M Bolton, MA
Mr W Peters, BA

Theatre Studies:
Ms J Crossley, BA (*Director of Theatre*)
Mrs A Keylock, BA (*Head of Academic Drama*)
Mr J Pharoah, BA (*Theatre Manager*)

Houses and Housemasters:

Boarding Housemasters:
Burnaby: R E Heale, BSc
Pemberley: Mr H Taylor, BSc
Phillpotts: C Fisher, MA
Redburn: C J Bury, BA
Sanderson's: Miss J C Law, BA
Talbot's: M Gracie, BSc

Day Housemasters:
Ashburnham: S Everitt, MEng
Bromham: A J R Huxford, MA
Crescent: Ms A Swallow, BA
Paulo Pontine: Mrs F Whiteman, BA, MA
St Cuthbert's: L M Holt, BA
St Peter's: M Cassell, BSc

Chaplain: The Revd A S Atkins, MA

Medical Officers: Dr Goulding and Dr Murphy

Benenden School

Cranbrook, Kent TN17 4AA
Tel: 01580 240592
Fax: 01580 240280
email: registry@benenden.kent.sch.uk
          schooloffice@benenden.kent.sch.uk
website: www.benenden.kent.sch.uk
Twitter: @benendenschool

Benenden aims to give each pupil A Complete Education in which she achieves her academic potential and grows as an individual. The School wants each girl to relish all that school life has to offer so that she leaves Benenden as a confident, positive young woman truly prepared for her future.

Benenden expects each girl to be a responsible and considerate global citizen who is outward looking, courageous and compassionate. It will support her in being aspirational and in developing her interests and talents whilst learning to achieve balance in her life.

By emphasising the importance of spiritual growth, Benenden hopes that each girl will enjoy making a contribution to her happy and caring school and go on to be inspired to make a positive difference to whichever communities she finds herself in throughout her life.

Benenden aims to do this by providing:
- a safe and nurturing environment
- a challenging and responsive academic curriculum which balances the best of tradition and innovation
- excellent and inspiring teaching designed to encourage our girls to become independent, enquiring and critical thinkers
- a framework of individual support devised to help each girl experience and benefit from a full programme of study, balanced with a wide variety of cultural, creative, physical and fun activities

- a culture of encouragement and support designed to develop self-reliance, resilience, confidence and well-being
- the experience of learning to understand other people, working and living together with tolerance and compromise, whilst also offering a wide range of opportunities for leadership
- careers and higher education guidance designed to help every student achieve her own personal goals, equipped with professional and life skills for university and beyond
- a close partnership with parents so that school and home can work together to help every girl make the most of her time at Benenden.

In all that Benenden does, it aims to foster:

Belief in oneself: integrity, independence, courage, endeavour, reflection, self-respect and self-confidence

Belief in others: trust, appreciation, consultation, understanding, generosity of spirit, tolerance and respect

Commitment to learning: an enthusiasm for and love of learning

Commitment to the community: participation, service, responsibility, leadership, initiative, compassion and commitment to equality

General Information. The School is an independent girls' boarding school standing in its own parkland of 240 acres.

As a non-stop, thriving boarding school, girls at Benenden benefit from a bespoke curriculum which achieves excellent academic results and which provides huge added value in an environment where girls are stretched without being stressed.

Benenden offers the country's finest programme of Weekend activities, as well as a breathtaking array of co-curricular opportunities and numerous curriculum trips.

Benenden is a happy and safe home from home with excellent pastoral care and 24/7 medical care. Its food is much admired and would not be out of place in a top hotel.

Benenden has the perfect location: nestled in the middle of the Garden of England, the School's beautiful campus is also within easy reach of London, with the capital less than an hour by train from nearby Staplehurst Station.

The bustling modern town of Royal Tunbridge Wells is a short drive away, and girls are lucky to be less than an hour from the seaside and an hour from Bluewater shopping centre.

Girls at Benenden get the best of both worlds: life in a safe and picturesque rural location with regular trips into large towns, to the seaside and into London.

Every weekend the School organises train travel to London for girls returning home and at Exeats and other school holidays it also arranges coaches to transport girls to Sussex, London, Essex and Suffolk. It also provides transfers to Heathrow, Gatwick and City Airport at Half Term and End of Term.

Mrs Samantha Price began as Headmistress in January 2014. Previously Headmistress at Godolphin School, Mrs Price was educated at Malvern Girls' College and Edinburgh University, where she read History of Art (with modules of European History). Having graduated, she joined the Tate Britain and was responsible for marketing for Members and Patrons and became heavily involved with the Patrons of what is now the Tate Modern.

She started her teaching career in 1999 as a History of Art and History teacher at Reading Blue Coat School, where she stayed for a number of years. She then joined King's Canterbury as a Housemistress, History and History of Art teacher. Her next post was to be Deputy Head at Hereford Cathedral School and from there she became Head of Godolphin in 2010.

Samantha is married with a daughter and a son. Her husband is an Army Chaplain.

The School provides education for girls between the ages of 11 and 18 years. There are 550 students at Benenden; all are boarders and they come from a wide range of backgrounds.

Girls are taught by highly qualified staff of over 100 men and women, many of whom are leaders in their particular fields.

Each student belongs to a House in which she sleeps and spends much of her private study and leisure time: it is, in effect, her home from home. There are six Houses for 11 to 16 year olds, while Sixth Form students live in the Founders' Sixth Form Centre in one of four Sixth Form Houses.

Each House has a resident Housemistress or Housemaster, who is also a member of the teaching staff and responsible for the academic and pastoral well-being of each student in the House. Much of the day-to-day work is shared with Deputies and Day and Resident Matrons, while other non-resident members of the teaching staff are Personal Academic Tutors.

In August 2016 Benenden gained its best ever A Level results, with 32% of all grades at A*. Overall, three-quarters (74 per cent) of all results were graded at A* or A. Thirty-one girls took the Extended Project Qualification, a voluntary research project, and they all gained an A* or A.

At GCSE, a remarkable 50% of all GCSEs were graded at A* and 18 girls gained at least nine A*s. Overall, 96% of all grades were A* to B. These results were achieved alongside the full co-curricular programme of activities and academic enrichment, essential to the Complete Education on offer at Benenden.

The most popular university destinations for Benenden students are Oxford, Cambridge, London, Durham, Bristol and Exeter, with 12 girls going to Oxbridge in 2016 and one girl to Yale.

Nine girls went to university in the United States, and the School has a bespoke specialist preparation programme for the US, which is an area of expertise for the School. Seven per cent of students go to universities overseas, with British Columbia, HKU and Grenada being some of the destinations.

Three-quarters of girls gained their first-choice university, and 95% their first or second choice, with the vast majority being Russell Group or equivalent, and 50% of girls going to a university in the UK Top 10, and 14% World Top 10. Some girls go on to prestigious art or drama courses. About 25% of Sixth Formers will make a post-A Level application, with a superb careers support service for students who have left the School, including a university mentoring programme.

There are three full time members of the Higher Education and Professional Guidance team, with a robust careers programme which begins in Year 7.

The core subjects up to GCSE are English, English literature, mathematics, science and a modern language. The compulsory balanced science course ensures that all three sciences are studied (either for single sciences at GCSE or the option of Core Science plus Additional Science), and every student in Key Stage 3 studies at least two of the three modern languages offered in addition to Latin. The school boasts the prestigious Confucius Award for the excellence of its Mandarin teaching.

Cross-curricular skills and the balancing of theoretical concepts with practical applications are actively encouraged through enquiry learning models. The ability to work independently is critical to enjoyment and success, and students are given every opportunity to acquire appropriate study habits. The curriculum is innovative and imaginative, and highly bespoke for each student.

From the start of this new academic year, Benenden has introduced the Professional Skills Programme, teaching Sixth Formers practical skills that are vital for the work-place. These include teamworking, giving a business pitch, developing business plans and reading complex financial information. On the first full day of the new Professional Skills Programme, students were helped in a business challenge by Dr Margaret Mountford, one of Lord Sugar's original advisers on The Apprentice. The School has an Entrepreneur in Residence and Engineer in Residence for 2016–17.

This year the School will complete the first cycle of the Benenden Diploma – our bespoke curriculum for the Fourths and Upper Fourths (the two youngest year groups). Unique to Benenden, this is a two-year curriculum designed to capture the sense of awe and wonder that students of this age still have about discovering new knowledge and skills. The Upper Fourths will this year become the first Benenden girls to complete the Diploma, finishing with a 'prom' at School!

Year 9 (LV) also has an enquiry focus at its heart with each term being connected to the theme of Service (to the school and community, to your country, to the world) and departments regularly collaborating on investigative real-life problem-solving which allows girls to apply, connect and synthesise the work covered in the subject-based lessons.

The ACE programme (A Complete Education) uses five themes to frame the hundreds of enrichment, co-curricular, weekend and boarding opportunities: Physical Health and Wellbeing, Mind and Spirit, Life Skills, Global Citizenship and Creativity and Culture. Students are encouraged to undertake activities from all five areas and move beyond their comfort zone, and their participation is accredited in a record of achievement.

The School's facilities have been greatly enhanced in recent years. The first capital project of the Centenary Vision, the School's development programme, have just been completed – eight new staff houses and the stunning new All-Weather Sports Pitch and Pavilion. The School Hall will be redeveloped in the next few years to provide an inspiring central gathering space for the whole school community and will be equipped with the latest technology, lighting and sound management systems to create a world-class centre of music and performance. This will be followed by an enhancement of the music facilities in a new Music School adjacent to the School Hall.

The School has also recently opened a new café bar for its Sixth Form students which sells a glass of wine to over 18s on a Saturday night (with parental permission of course!)

Other facilities of particular note include the state-of-the-art Science Centre, which probably offers the best facilities for Science in any UK school; The Clarke Centre, a study centre providing modern classrooms incorporating the latest computer technology, library and IT Centre; and a beautiful eco-classroom which is completely self-sustaining, with solar power and rainwater harvesting. The School was awarded Eco-School Green Flag status in 2009. The Benenden School Theatre and Drama teaching complex is a much-used facility, staging an array of impressive School productions, which in recent years has included 'Lord of the Flies', 'Jesus Christ Superstar', a student-led production of 'Pride and Prejudice' and, most recently, 'Les Misérables School Edition'.

As well as the recent addition of the All-Weather Pitch, which is primarily used for Lacrosse and Hockey, for physical recreation there are nine Lacrosse pitches, 11 all-weather Tennis courts, a sports hall containing a further full-sized tennis court, an indoor heated swimming pool, a second sports hall (also used for Badminton, Volleyball, Netball and Fencing), a fitness centre and gym, two Squash courts and a grass running track.

The School is a Christian community, based on Anglican practice, and the ethos of the School reflects Christian principles. Members of other communions and beliefs are welcomed to the School and every effort is made to help them in the practice of their own faith, in an atmosphere of respect and tolerance for the views of others. The School is committed to every girl being a global citizen, which is achieved through the bespoke global awareness programme and a strong focus in Prayers and Form gatherings on current national and global issues.

Entrance to the School is after internal assessment at Preview Weekend, but dependent upon candidates meeting the School's standard at 11+ and 13+ Common Entrance or in entrance papers. There is also a small intake at Sixth Form level, with competitive entry by the School's own examination. All of the School's students are expected to qualify for degree courses, leaving School with at least three A Levels and at least eight subjects at GCSE. (A full careers programme is a key component of the Personal Development Programme, aimed to foster the widest range of skills.)

Benenden believes in close cooperation between School and parents and there is regular contact with them, including a weekly email newsletter. Formal reports are sent four times a year. Parents are encouraged to visit the School for concerts, plays and other events, as well as to take their daughters out for meals or weekend exeats. There is a flourishing programme of social events for parents.

Curriculum. *Lower School*: English, mathematics, biology, chemistry, physics, French, Mandarin or Spanish or Classical Greek, Latin, geography, history, religious studies, art and design including textiles, design and technology, computing, drama, music, physical education.

GCSE Core: English, English literature, mathematics, biology, chemistry, physics, one modern foreign language.

GCSE Options: French, Spanish, Classical Greek, Latin, Mandarin, geography, history, religious studies, art, design and technology, music, drama, economics, computing, Higher Project.

A Level Options: English language and literature, English literature, mathematics, further mathematics, biology, chemistry, physics, French, Spanish, Classical Greek, Latin, Mandarin, economics, business, computer science, geography, history, politics, psychology, religious studies, art and design fine art, history of art, music, theatre studies, design and technology product design, Extended Project.

(All students' programmes also include academic extension programmes – Extend, Excel, Explore – careers education, information technology, physical education, religious education, personal, social and health education, global awareness and, for the Sixth Form, Professional Skills.)

Sport. Lacrosse, netball, tennis, swimming, hockey, rounders, badminton, athletics and cross country, squash, gym, dance, fencing, rugby, judo, karate, trampolining, exercise and fitness, equestrian, scuba diving and cricket.

Opportunities in Music. Tuition is available in all orchestral and keyboard instruments as well as singing. Numerous opportunities exist for instrumental and choral performance. The School is home to a full youth symphony orchestra, in which students from other schools also play. Benenden also enjoys a strong choral tradition and hosts recitals by musicians of international calibre.

The School's Chapel Choir has recently released its first commercial CD, of Stabat Mater, which was composed for Benenden by renowned composer David Bednall. The CD has received glowing reviews, including being selected as an Editor's Choice by the respected Gramophone magazine.

The planned new Music School will offer enhanced Music facilities to further improve the standard and experience of the talented musicians at Benenden.

Opportunities in Speech and Drama. Students are able to pursue drama as an extracurricular activity throughout their School career by participating in drama workshops, House and Lower and Upper School plays. Speech and drama lessons are available and students are prepared for

both Trinity and LAMDA examinations. Many pupils are involved in MUN clubs and represent the school at MUN conferences in the UK and abroad.

Optional Extras. The Duke of Edinburgh's Award, Combined Cadet Force, Science, Technology, Engineering and Maths projects, Arabic, karate, journalism and marketing, philosophy, creative writing, satellite project, ballet, modern dance, yoga, clay pigeon shooting and many others.

Fees per term (2016–2017). £11,900 payable before the start of term. The fees include the country's finest programme of Weekend Activities at no extra charge, as well as a breathtaking array of co-curricular opportunities and numerous curriculum trips.

Scholarships. *Academic Scholarships – Lower School Entry (11–13)*: Awards of up to 10% of fees available. The examinations are held in January preceding the date of entry.

Academic Scholarships – Sixth Form Entry: Examinations are held in November preceding entry in September. Candidates take two papers in subjects which they intend to study at A Level.

Music Scholarships – Lower School Entry (11–13): Awards of up to 10% of fees available. The examinations are held in January preceding the date of entry. Candidates should have reached the standard of Grade V (or equivalent) or show great potential. Those offering piano or singing as a principal study should be fluent in an orchestral instrument. Candidates will be required to do practical tests and will be interviewed; they are also required to show that they have reached the general academic standards of any entrant either by sitting entrance papers, or by taking the academic scholarship examination.

Music Scholarships – Sixth Form Entry: Awards of up to 10% of fees available. Examinations are held in November preceding entry in September. The requirements for a Sixth Form Music Scholarship are very much the same as for Lower School candidates (see above entry), but candidates should have reached the standard of Grade VII (or equivalent). Candidates are also required to show that they have reached the general academic standard required of any entrant by taking two qualifying papers in subjects which they intend to study at A Level.

Art and Design – 13+: Awards of up to 10% of fees available. Examinations are held in January preceding entry in September. The examination for the Art Scholarship will consist of one hour on a set-piece drawing followed by an interview based on the candidate's portfolio on which particular emphasis will be placed for evidence of commitment and enthusiasm.

Design and Technology – 13+: Awards of up to 10% of fees available. Scholarships are offered to girls who show exceptional promise and commitment in this area, supported by good academic results in the normal entry papers. Applicants will be asked to produce evidence of three kinds: a record or portfolio of previous work or achievements; a response to a challenge set at Benenden; and an interview.

Sports Scholarships – 13+: Awards of up to 10% of fees available. Scholarships are offered to girls who show exceptional promise and commitment in this area, supported by good academic results in the normal entry papers. Candidates will undertake a test to measure levels of fitness, participate in a range of games to show physical ability and tactical awareness, and be given an opportunity to demonstrate their chosen specialism.

Trust Award Programme: Bursary support of up to 100% of fees (subject to means testing) to one or more local primary school pupils at 11+ or to a Sixth Form candidate at 16+.

For further information, please contact the Director of Admissions.

Admission. Prospective parents are encouraged to visit the School, either individually or with others at a Prospective Parents' Morning. Prospectuses and full details of entry and scholarship requirements may be obtained from the Registry.

Charitable status. Benenden School (Kent) Limited is a Registered Charity, number 307854. It is a charitable foundation for the education of girls.

The Council:
The Hon Mrs A Birkett MA, MBA (*Chair*)
Mr S S Smart, BSc, FCA (*Vice Chair*)
Mrs W M Carey, BA Hons
Dr F Cornish, MA, FRCGP
Mr M C C Goolden, MA (*Chair of the Finance Committee, AGBIS Representative*)
Mr M K H Leung, BA, Dip Soc (*Honorary Representative for the Hong Kong Trust*)
Mrs A McNab
Mr J McParland, BD, PGCE, MA, NPQH
Mrs A J Mogridge, BA Hons, FCIPR, FPRCA
Mr G Pugh, MA, ACMA, MBA
Mr J V Strong, MRICS (*Chair of Building Group*)
Prof L Taub
Mr W E H Trelawny-Vernon, BSc
Mr M Lander, BSc, MA (*Secretary to the Council*)
Mrs S Price, MA, PGCE
Mr M Lander, BSc, MA (*Company Secretary*)

Senior Management Team:

Headmistress: Mrs S Price, MA Edinburgh, PGCE

Deputy Head: Mr S Lambert, BA Exeter

Deputy Head Academic: Mrs L Tyler, MA Oxon, PGCE London, NPQH

Deputy Head Boarding and Pastoral Care: Miss A Steven, BA Bristol

Assistant Head Co-Curricular: Mr M J L Commander, BEng Cardiff, MEd Buckingham, QTS Sussex

Director of Finance and Operations: Mr M Lander, BSc Open, MA London

Development Director: Mrs C A Saint, BA University College Dublin, PG Dip

Berkhamsted School

133 High Street, Berkhamsted, Hertfordshire HP4 2DJ
Tel: 01442 358000 (General enquiries)
     01442 358001 (Admissions)
Fax: 01442 358040
email: enquiries@berkhamstedschool.org
       admissions@berkhamstedschool.org
website: www.berkhamstedschool.org
Twitter: @berkhamstedsch
Facebook: /berkhamstedschool
LinkedIn: /berkhamsted-school

In 1541 John Incent, Dean of St Paul's, was granted a Licence by Henry VIII to found a school in Berkhamsted, Incent's home town. Until the end of the nineteenth Century Berkhamsted School served as a grammar school for a small number of boys from the town but over the last century it has developed into a school of significance. In 1888 the foundation was extended by the establishment of Berkhamsted School for Girls. In 1996, these two schools and Berkhamsted Preparatory School formalised their partnership, offering the highest quality education to pupils from ages three to 19. More recently, Berkhamsted School merged with Heatherton House School to form the Berkhamsted Schools Group in 2011, and in May 2012, the

Group acquired Haresfoot School, which has become the Berkhamsted Pre-Preparatory School for children aged three to seven. The existing Preparatory School focuses on the education of children aged seven to eleven. *Please refer to separate entries for Berkhamsted Preparatory, Berkhamsted Pre-Preparatory and Heatherton House.*

There are 380 pupils in the flourishing co-educational Sixth Form; between the ages of eleven and sixteen 440 boys at the Boys School (Castle) and 370 girls at the Girls School (Kings) are taught in single-sex groups.

The Principal is a member of both HMC and GSA.

Aims. At Berkhamsted we believe that excellent academic results do not have to be won at the expense of the wider attributes of a good education. All pupils are supported and encouraged to reach their full potential, with appropriate teaching environments for each age group and a structure that offers the best of both co-educational and single-sex tuition. In addition to the development of the intellect, social, sporting and cultural activities play an important part within the framework of a disciplined and creative community based on Christian values. It is important that pupils come to value both the individual and the Community through school life. The School seeks to encourage spiritual and moral values and a sense of responsibility as an essential part of the pursuit of excellence.

Location. The School stands in the heart of Berkhamsted, an historic and thriving town only thirty miles from London. It enjoys excellent communications to London, the airports, to the Midlands and the communities of Buckinghamshire, Bedfordshire and Hertfordshire.

Facilities. The original site has at its heart a magnificent Tudor Hall used as a schoolroom for over 300 years. Other buildings are from late Victorian to modern periods and of architectural interest (especially the Chapel modelled on the Church of St Maria dei Miracoli in Venice). With separate Pre-Preparatory School and Preparatory School sites, and two Senior School campuses, the School is well equipped with a range of facilities. There are new Science laboratories, Library and Learning Resources Centres, Information Technology suites, Sixth Form centres located on the two Senior School campuses, Careers libraries, Dining halls, Medical centre, House rooms, Deans' Hall (an Assembly Hall) and Centenary Theatre (a modern 500-seat theatre also used for concerts and theatre productions). Recreational and sports facilities include extensive playing fields, Fives courts, Squash courts, Tennis courts, Gymnasium, Drama studio, Music school and Art studios. A Sports Hall and 25m indoor swimming pool were opened in 2004 and a state-of-the-art Design Centre in 2008. The Nash-Harris Building at Kings was completed in 2011 comprising a new dining facility, classrooms and Chapel. 2016 saw the opening of a new sports pavilion and changing rooms at the School's Chesham Road Playing Fields, as well as a high ropes course at the Haresfoot site.

Diamond Structure. The School has a "diamond" structure that combines both single-sex and co-educational teaching. Boys and Girls are taught together until the age of 11, separately from 11 to 16, before coming back together again in a joint Sixth Form.

Curriculum. The Senior School curriculum includes: English, English Literature, Mathematics, Biology, Chemistry, Physics, History, Geography, Religious Studies, French/Spanish, Latin/Classics, Mandarin (available for Years 7, 8 and 9 in September 2017), Music, Art, Physical Education and Design and Technology. Up to eleven subjects may be taken for GCSE. In the Sixth Form, courses are offered in 27 subjects and all students benefit from an Enrichment Programme with the option to complete an Extended Project Qualification or a Mini-MBA, delivered in partnership with Ashridge Executive Education at Hult International Business School. Pupils are prepared for university entrance, including Oxbridge. All pupils are taught computer skills and have access to ICT centres. Careers guidance and personal tutoring are offered throughout.

Day and Boarding. Pupils may be full boarders, weekly/flexible boarders or day pupils. The two Boarding houses, accommodating boys and girls separately, are well equipped and within a few minutes' walk of the main campus. There are up to 60 boarding places. Day pupils come from both Berkhamsted and the surrounding area of Hertfordshire, Buckinghamshire and Bedfordshire.

Pastoral Care and Discipline. The main social and pastoral unit is the House; the Head of House and House Tutors provide continuity of support and advice and monitor each individual pupil's progress.

The aim is to encourage self-discipline so that pupils work with a sense of responsibility and trust. Pupils are expected to be considerate, courteous, honest and industrious.

Pupil wellbeing is of vital importance at Berkhamsted. A Director of Wellbeing supports teaching staff across the whole school in implementing a proactive strategy that focuses primarily on keeping pupils well and looking for early signs of potential issues. There is a Medical Centre with qualified staff. The School Medical Officer has special responsibility for boarders. Qualified Counsellors are available to all pupils for confidential counselling. The School also has a full-time Chaplain.

Sport and Leisure Activities. Major sports for Girls are Lacrosse, Netball and Tennis and for Boys, Rugby, Football and Cricket. A number of other sports are also pursued including Athletics, Badminton, Cross-Country, Equestrian, Eton Fives, Golf, Hockey, Judo, Rowing, Shooting, Squash and Swimming. Team games are encouraged and pupils selected for regional and national squads.

There is a flourishing Duke of Edinburgh's Award at all levels. The CCF, community service, work experience and Young Enterprise are offered. The format of the school day allows pupils in the Senior School to choose from a wide range of clubs, societies or courses, which are attended during school hours. Regular school theatre productions, orchestral and choral concerts achieve high standards of performance.

Careers. A team of advisors, internal and external, is directed by the Head of Careers who also arranges Careers Lunches, Applying to Higher Education training sessions, Medicine and Law Careers Taster Days and an annual Higher Education, Careers and GAP Year Fair. Heads of House oversee pupils' applications for higher education, together with parents and Careers advisors. The great majority of leavers proceeds to university and higher education.

Entry. Entry to the Pre-Preparatory School is from the age of three, entry to the Preparatory School from seven, and entry to the Senior School from 11. Children are assessed for entry to the Nursery year group during a meeting with the Headteacher and attend an informal assessment day for Year 2 entry. The School's Entrance Assessments and an interview are required for entry to the Prep and Senior School. The minimum entrance requirement for the Sixth Form is 5B and 2C grades at GCSE, with A grades required to proceed to Mathematics, Science and Language A Levels, although competition amongst external candidates means that it is the norm that top grades are required.

Scholarships and Bursaries. It is the Governors' policy to award Scholarships and Exhibitions on merit to pupils whom the Governors wish to attract to Berkhamsted because of the contribution that they are able to make to School life, be that academic, musical, sporting, creative or as potential leaders.

Academic Scholarships are awarded on the basis of academic merit alone on entrance to the School.

Who can apply? Applications are welcome from pupils who qualify from their performance in the Entrance Examination and sit Scholarship Examinations in English, Mathematics and other appropriate subjects. These are usually only at 11+, 13+ and 16+.

Incent Awards are made to talented pupils from financially or socially disadvantaged backgrounds.

They are awarded to enable pupils who would not otherwise be able to attend Berkhamsted, to afford to do so.

Candidates must demonstrate academic potential or have a particular talent(s) or skill(s) so that they will make a significant contribution to some other area of School life.

The Award shall be up to 100% of the school fees, and, where appropriate, will also include financial assistance for School uniform and sports kit, travel to and from school, school trips and expeditions, extra lessons e.g. Music, Drama etc if applicable.

Whilst most applications for Incent Awards will be received from candidates who are presently in maintained sector schools, Berkhamsted does work with a number of feeder schools in the independent sector who offer awards on a similar basis and thus will entertain applications from pupils who are presently in receipt of means-tested awards of this nature.

Music, Drama, Art and Sports Scholarships are also offered.

Where there is a demonstrated need, additional means-tested funding may be available to those awarded Scholarships.

More information about Scholarships and Bursaries may be obtained from the Admissions Manager or on the School website.

Fees per term (2016–2017). Day Pupils: £5,590–£6,555. Boarding Pupils: £10,441.67 (full), £8,776.67 (weekly 4 nights).

Further information about the School's aims, its academic curriculum, facilities, activities, admissions, scholarships and awards is published in the School's prospectus and is available on the School website. Admissions enquiries should be made in the first instance to the Admissions Manager, who will be pleased to arrange for parents to visit the School.

Old Berkhamstedians. There is a vibrant and growing community of Old Berkhamstedians: www.theoldberkhamstedians.org. President: Mrs Emma Jeffrey.

Charitable status. Berkhamsted Schools Group is a Registered Charity, number 310630. It is a leading Charitable School in the field of Junior and Secondary Education.

Patron: Her Majesty The Queen

The Governors:
Mr G C Laws (*Chairman*)
Mrs S Turner (*Vice-Chairman*)

Mr J J Apthorp	Mr C Nicholls
Mr D J Atkins	Mr S Rolland
Ms A K Fahy	Mrs S Tidey
Dr M A Fenton	Mr N G Twogood
Mrs E Jeffrey [OB]	

Clerk to the Governors: Mrs M Shell

[OB] *Old Berkhamstedian*

Principal: Mr R P Backhouse, MA Cantab

Vice Principal (*Education*): Mr M Bond, BA
Vice Principal (*Business Operations*): Mr P Nicholls, MA Cantab, FCA
Headmaster Sixth Form: Mr R Petty, BSc
Head Berkhamsted Boys (*Boys 11–16*): Mr R C Thompson, BA
Head Berkhamsted Girls (*Girls 11–16*): Mrs E A Richardson, BA
Deputy Head (*Sixth Form*): Mrs M C Startin, BA
Deputy Head (*Sixth Form*): Mr D G Richardson, BSc

Deputy Head Pastoral (Boys 11–16): Mr G Anker, BA
Deputy Head Academic (Boys 11–16): Mr A Ford, BA
Deputy Head (Girls 11–16): Miss R L McColl, BA, MPhil
Director of Studies: Mr W R C Gunary, BSc

Chaplain: Reverend J E Markby, MA

Teaching staff:
* *Head of Department*
† *Head of House*

Art:
Mrs C M E Ferguson, MA (**Art & Design*)
Mrs K M Bly, BA (*Art*) [OB]
Miss J E Brodie, BA (*Art, Photography*)
Mr R B Garner, BA (*Art, Photography*)
Miss E L Gent, BA, MA, ATC (*Art*)
Miss A Kelway-Bamber, BA, MA (*Art, Ceramics, ICT*)

Classics:
*Mr I R Stewart, BA, MA
Miss R M Bradley, BA, MA (†*Hawks House*)
Mr J Cooper, BA (*also English*)
Dr A J Harker, BA, MA, PhD (†*Fry's House*)
Mrs H McCann, MA, RSA, DipTEFL, MBA (*TESL*)
Mr R K Mowbray, MA (†*Churchill House*)
Mr B Wille, BA

Design and Technology:
*Mr S R Hargreaves, BEd
Ms F M Garratt, BSc
Mrs R Knox, BSc (*Food Technology*, †*St John's House*)
Mr A M Lansdell, BSc, DipEd
Mr R Rea, BA (*Food Technology*)
Mr D S van Noordwyk, DipEd, DipMin, MCollT (†*Bees House*)

Economics and Business Studies:
*Mr P C Cowie, MA
Mr D L Foster, BA (*also History*, †*Swift's House, Fives Coach*)
Mr V Fung, BSc (*Young Enterprise*)
Mr A Ottaway, BSc (†*St George's House*)
Mr D R Pain, BA, BComm (†*Spencer House*)

English:
*Mr T A Grant, MA (*i/c Golf*)
Miss R Brims, BEd (*Head of PSHE*)
Mr J Cooper, BA (*also Classics*)
Mr A G Harrison, BA, MA, MEd
Miss A Ireland, BA (†*Holme House*)
Mr T D Lines, BA, MA, MEd
Miss R L McColl, BA, MPhil (*Deputy Head of Senior Girls*)
Mr M S Pett, BA (*i/c Fives*)
Mrs J F Phillips, BA, MA
Mrs L J Redman, BA (†*School House*)
Mrs E A Richardson, BA (*Head of Senior Girls*)
Mrs H Rossington, BA
Mrs J Simons, BA, MA (*Senior School Careers*)
Mrs M C Startin, BA (*Deputy Head of Sixth*)
Mrs K E Tomlin, BA, MA

Geography:
*Mr P Matthews, BSc, MA (*CCF Army Section*)
Mr G R Burchnall, BEd (†*Reeves House*)
Mr S J Dight, BA, DipEd
Mr L Eaton, BSc [OB]
Mrs A J Murray, BSc
Mr M J Thum, MA (*CCF RAF Section*)

History and Politics:
Mr C H Savill, BA (*History)
Mr P T Riddick, BA, MA, MSc Econ (**Politics, History, i/c Tennis*)

Miss S Afsar, BA, BSc, LLM (*also* **Psychology & Sociology*)
Mr G Anker, BA (*Deputy Head of Senior Boys – Pastoral*)
Mr M Bond, BA (*Vice-Principal – Education*)
Mrs S Bond, BA
Mr S E Bridle, BA
Mr R Falder, MA, BA
Mr D L Foster, BA (*also Economics & Business Studies*, †*Swift's, Fives Coach*)
Mr R Moseley, BA (†*Cox's House*)
Mr R Petty, BSc (*Headmaster of Sixth*)
Mr S J E Rees, BA
Mrs L Simson, BA Cantab (†*Wolstenholme House*)

Learning Support:
*Mrs A Dunmall, BSc, Dip SpLD, APC SpLD (*SENCO*)
Mrs S M Blythe, MA Cantab, OCR Dip SpLD
Mrs D Fuller, BA, MA
Mrs K Harris, BA, OCR Dip SpLD

Mathematics:
*Mr D Jeffers, BSc
Mrs J Allan, BSc
Mrs A J Casey, BSc (†*Old Stede House*)
Mr S Fraser, BA
Mr W R C Gunary, BSc (*Director of Studies*)
Dr P Khare, PhD, BSc
Mr M Middleton, BSc (†*Loxwood House*)
Miss S Parsons, MA
Mr G Reid-Davies, BSc
Mr D G Richardson, BSc (*Deputy Head of Sixth*, *Co-curricular)
Dr J Samuel, PhD, MMath
Mrs C Swarray-Dean, BSc
Mrs R H Warburton, BSc (†*Adders House*) [OB]
Mr S A Whyte, BSc, MSc

Media Studies and ICT:
Ms J D Bohitige, BA (**Media Studies, ICT*)
Ms N A V Phillips, BA (*Media Studies, i/c Community Service Pupil Development*)

Modern Languages:
*Mr N Cale, BA (*French, German*)
Mrs L M Knight, BA (*French, Spanish, Director of eLearning*)
Miss A L Y Lefrançois, MFL Licence LLCE (*French, Spanish*)
Mrs S M Shipton, DEUG Licence (*French, Spanish*, †*St David's House*)
Mr R Margerison, BA (*French*)
Mrs L C Briand, BA, DipTESOL (*German, French*)
Miss A M Ashby, BA (*Spanish)
Mr I R Cruickshanks, BA (*French, Spanish*)
Mrs C A Garcia, MA (*Spanish*)
Mr T Gayton, BA (*Spanish, French*)
Mrs E Leonard, BA (*Spanish, French*)
Ms C J Moss, BA (*Spanish*)
Mrs N Heslop, BA, MBA (*Mandarin, French*)

Performing Arts:
*Mrs S B Gunary, BA, MA (*Director of Performing Arts*)
Mr D Curtis, BA (*Academic Drama)
Miss C Anderson, BA (*Drama*)
Mrs A Gibson, BA, MA (*Drama*)
Mr O W Pengelly, BA (*Drama*)
Miss J Thackray, BA (*Drama*)
Miss D Wylie, BA (*Drama*, †*Burgh House*)
Mr R A J Crawford, MA, MMus (*Academic Music)
Mr B Noithip, BA, MMus (*Director of Co-curricular Music*)
Mrs M Brigginshaw, BA, PGDip, PGDipAdv (*Music*)
Mrs A Hatton, BA (*Music*)
Mr P J Hopkins, BA, BMus, FRCO, ARCM (*Keyboard)

Physical Education:
Mrs J Vila, BA (*Director of Girls' Sport*) [OB]
Mr D J Gibson, BSc (*Director of Boys' Sport*)
Mrs A E Bamforth, BA (†*New Stede House*)
Mr G Campbell, BA (*Cricket*)
Mr F Charnock, CertEd (*CCF*)
Mrs L J Chinneck, BSc (*Girls' PE, i/c Girls' Athletics and Cross Country*)
Miss T Cresswell, BSc
Mr B P Evers, BA (†*Incents Boarding House, i/c Hockey*)
Miss E Gray (*Lacrosse*)
Mr T Hockedy, BSc, MSc
Mrs M Levermore, BA
Mr R I Mackay, BA Ed (†*Tilman House*)
Mr B R Mahoney, BEd (*Rugby, i/c Boys' Swimming*)
Miss J Osborn, BSc (*i/c Girls' Swimming and Rounders, CCF Royal Navy Section*)
Mrs D D G Pearson, BHK, BEd (*i/c Dance and Gymnastics*)
Mr R Perrie (*Sports Coach*)
Mr R Pritchard (*Strength and Conditioning Coach*)
Mrs C Spooner (*Sports Coach*)
Mr A S Theodossi (*Fives Professional, Boys' Sports Administrator*)
Mr D Vila (*Football, i/c Squash*)
Mrs D Wates, BSc (*Netball*)

Psychology and Sociology:
*Miss S Afsar, BA, BSc, LLM (*also History*)
Miss A Ali, BSc (*Psychology*)
Mr D Officer PhD, BSc (*Sociology*)
Mrs E Taylor, BSc (*Sociology*)

Religion and Philosophy:
*Miss G Ferguson, BA, MA
Mr R W D Coupe, BA, MA (*Academic Director*)
Mr A Ford, BA (*Deputy Head of Senior Boys – Academic*)
Mr B Hopcroft, BA
Mr H R Maxted, BA
Mr G McWalter, MA
Mr M Stallard, BA (*PSHE, i/c Rowing*)
Mr A Wilkes, MA, BD

Science:
Biology:
Mr S C Robinson, BSc, FSB (*Science, *ICT*)
Mr C J Allam, BEd, BSc, MSB (*Biology*)
Mrs H A A Green, BSc
Dr P R Hatfield-Iacoponi, BA, PhD
Mr A Hopper, BSc
Dr S P S Hundal, BSc, MEd, PhD (†*Nash House*)
Ms S P Jennings, BSc
Revd J E Markby, MA (*Chaplain, Charities Coordinator*)
Mrs R E Miles, BSc (†*Greenes House*)
Chemistry:
Mrs M C Gould, BSc (*Chemistry*)
Mr D W Binnie, BSc
Mr L Hornsey, BSc
Mrs T A Kergon, BSc
Mr N Kirwan, BSc
Mr M Neill, BSc (†*Russell House*)
Physics:
Dr S A Redman, BSc, PhD (*Physics*)
Mr D Hyman, BSc, MSc
Mrs V Hyman, BSc, MSc (†*Ashby House*)
Mr P McGowan, BEng
Mr I Vovrosh, BSc

Additional Staff:
There are 23 visiting music staff offering instrumental teaching in: acoustic guitar, cello, clarinet, double bass, electric guitar, euphonium, flute, jazz piano, oboe, organ, percussion (including kit drumming), piano, recorder, saxo-phone, singing, trombone, trumpet, viola and violin. Three visiting teachers offer Speech and Drama tuition. Three additional part-time sports coaches.

Director of Human Resources: Mrs T L Evans, CIPD
Estates Director: Mr R Grant, MBIFM
Director of External Relations: Mrs C Dow, BA
Admissions Manager: Mrs L T Wesley
Sports Centre Manager: Mrs V Rees
Archivist: Mrs L Koulouris
Director of Wellbeing: Mrs J Hennigan, MSc, BSc, MBACP Accred, MBABCP
Medical Officer: Dr K Smith, MBChB, DCH, DRCOG
PA to Principal: Mrs N M Golder
PA to Vice Principals: Mrs N Murray
PA to Head of Berkhamsted Boys: Mrs T Rawlings
PA to Head of Berkhamsted Girls: Mrs S Bailey
PA to Headmaster of Berkhamsted Sixth: Mrs N Seymour

Birkdale School

Oakholme Road, Sheffield S10 3DH

Tel:	0114 266 8408
	Admissions: 0114 266 8409
Fax:	0114 267 1947
email:	headmaster@birkdaleschool.org.uk
	admissions@birkdaleschool.org.uk
	enquiries@birkdaleschool.org.uk
website:	www.birkdaleschool.org.uk
Twitter:	@BirkdaleSchool
Facebook:	/BirkdaleSchool

Motto: '*Res non verba*'

Birkdale School is an HMC day school for 850 pupils, boys from age 4 to 18 with a co-educational Sixth Form of 200 pupils. The age 4–11 Prep School is on a separate campus nearby. (*For further details see IAPS section.*) The Governing Body is in membership of the Association of Governing Bodies of Independent Schools.

Set in a pleasant residential area near the University 1.5 miles from the city centre, and 5 miles from the Peak District National Park, the school has expanded in recent years to provide for Sheffield and South Yorkshire the only independent secondary school for boys, with a co-educational Sixth Form. Birkdale Prep School for 300 boys is on a separate campus half a mile from the Senior School. School coaches bring pupils from Worksop, Chesterfield, North Derbyshire, Rotherham and Barnsley.

Birkdale is a Christian school, reflecting its foundation in the evangelical tradition. There is nothing exclusive about this: entrance is open to all, and there is no denominational emphasis. We seek to develop the full potential of each individual: body, mind and spirit. Within a framework of high academic standards, pastoral care is given a high priority, balanced by an emphasis on sport and outdoor pursuits, music and drama with a wide range of extracurricular activities available.

At 18, over 99% of pupils go on to university, with a good proportion each year gaining places at Oxford and Cambridge.

Admission. The main ages of admission are at 4, 7, 11 and 16, although it is possible to admit pupils at other ages if a place is available. Entrance examinations for candidates at 11 are held annually towards the end of January. Entrance to the co-educational Sixth Form is subject to interview and a satisfactory performance in GCSE examinations. In the first instance, enquiries should be addressed to the Registrar.

Academic Curriculum. Over 20 subjects are offered at AS and A Level. A full range of academic subjects are offered to GCSE. All pupils study English Language and Literature, Mathematics, Double Award Science, at least one Modern Foreign Language (French, German, Spanish) and at least one of the Humanities subjects (Classical Studies, Geography, History, RE). Optional subjects include Art, DT: Electronic Products, DT: Resistant Materials, PE, Latin, Drama and Music. The wider curriculum includes ICT, Religious Education, Health Education, Careers and Economic Awareness. Latin, German and Spanish are compulsory subjects in the Lower School (11–13) in addition to the usual range of National Curriculum subjects.

Games and Outdoor Pursuits. The major games are Rugby, Soccer, Cricket and Athletics, with Cross Country, Hockey, Netball, Tennis, Squash, Basketball, Volleyball, Swimming and Golf also available. The playing fields are a short bus ride away from the school. A 10-lane cricket net facility, constructed to full English Cricket Board standards was opened in 2012. The netting system is retractable and so the area can also be fully utilised for football and hockey outside of the cricket season. All members of the school play games weekly. Additional team practices take place on Saturdays or at other times, and there is a full fixture list in the major sports. The school enjoys regular use of the university swimming pool nearby. Additionally, we use two local international venues, Ponds Forge and the English Institute of Sport for basketball, netball, dance and athletics. Birkdale's Sports Hall is at the centre of the Senior School campus.

Outdoor Pursuits play an important part in the overall leadership training programme. All members of the school participate in regular training sessions leading in each age group to a major expedition. This programme culminates in the 4th Form camp held annually in Snowdonia. Virtually all members of the Third Form undertake the Bronze Award of the Duke of Edinburgh's Award scheme, and an increasing number progress to Silver and Gold awards.

Music and the Arts. Music, Art and Drama flourish both within and outside the formal curriculum. A full annual programme of dramatic and musical productions is arranged. Over 120 pupils receive weekly instrumental music lessons at school, and a wide range of orchestras and choirs provide opportunities for pupils to experience group musical activities at an appropriate level.

Extracurricular Activities. In addition to the activities above there is a broad range of clubs and societies which meet at lunchtime and outside the formal school day, providing opportunities for members of the school to explore and excel in activities such as Chess, Debating, Design and Enterprise, as well as in the usual activities such as Sport, Drama, Outdoor Pursuits, Art and Music. Awards are often won in local and national competitions.

Careers. The school is a member of the ISCO independent schools careers guidance service and there is a well equipped Careers Centre on site. A biennial Careers Convention is held in the school and regular visits are made by services liaison officers and others to give advice and help to pupils under the guidance of the school's careers staff.

Fees per term (2016–2017). Sixth Form £4,075; Senior School: £4,000 (Years 9–11), £3,925 (Years 7 and 8); Prep School £3,325; Pre-Prep Department £2,725, including lunches, textbooks and stationery (with the exception of Sixth Form textbooks).

Scholarships and Bursaries. Academic and Music Scholarships are normally available at 11 and 16, worth up to 25% of fees. Bursaries are available to increase awards up to 100% of fees in cases of proven financial need. In addition we offer Ogden Science and Arkwright Scholarships at 16+.

Charitable status. Birkdale School is a Registered Charity, number 1018973, and a Company Limited by Guarantee, registered in England, number 2792166. It exists to develop the full potential of its members within a Christian community.

Chairman of Governors: P Houghton, FCA

Bursar and Clerk to the Governors: D H Taylor, BSc

Head Master: Dr P M Owen, MA, PhD

Deputy Head: W P N Pietrek, BA

Director of Studies: P R King, BA

Heads of Departments:
Art: A Armitage, BA, Dip Ed Management
Biology: Mrs B Holder, MA, BSc
Careers: C J Cook, BSc
Classics: Mrs M A Daly, BA
Design & Technology: P S Offer, BA
Drama: A G Low, BA
Economics & Business Studies: S B Stoddard, BA
English: Mrs S J Burt, BA
Geography: H Parker, BSc
History: M S Clarke, MA
ICT: G Morton, BSc
Mathematics: M E Roach, BSc
Modern Languages: Mrs K M Higham, BA, MEd
Music: A M Jordan, BMus
Outdoor Pursuits, Chaplain: J D Allen, BSc
Physical Education: R D Heaton, BEd
Science & Physics: Dr P C Jukes, PhD, MA
Religious Education: T J Pearson, BA
Chemistry: Dr P D Myatt, BSc, DPhil
SENCO: Mrs L E Marsh, BA
Counsellor: Miss S E Brown, PG Dip Counselling

Prep School:
Head of Prep School: C J Burch, BA, PGCE
Deputy Head: J R Leighton, BEd
Director of Studies: A J Oakey, MScEd, BA
Senior Mistress: Mrs E J Arcari, BA/Mrs J Kitchen, MEd, BEd

Birkenhead School

58 Beresford Road, Oxton, Birkenhead, Merseyside CH43 2JD

Tel:	0151 652 4014
Fax:	0151 651 3091
email:	enquire@birkenheadschool.co.uk
website:	www.birkenheadschool.co.uk
Twitter:	@BirkenheadSchl
Facebook:	/Birkenhead-School

Motto: *Beati mundo corde*

Birkenhead School was opened in 1860, with the object of providing a public-school education, both Classical and Modern.

Birkenhead School is Wirral's only independent day school with boys and girls aged from 3 months through to 18 years across four outstanding schools.

Attracting students from all areas of the Wirral, Merseyside, West Cheshire and North Wales, the School enjoys a fantastic reputation for its educational successes and continues to be the best-performing school in the Wirral in terms of its public examination results.

Children thrive both academically and personally in this modern yet traditional school. Birkenhead School has a long history of providing first-class learning to its students and continues to this day to place strong emphasis on excellence in education, as well as providing a caring environment.

Our community is what binds us all; most striking is how positive and vibrant it is. Aside from our academic successes, our students succeed in the myriad opportunities available to them. Challenge and endeavour within the classroom line up alongside an exciting and varied co-curricular provision designed to enchant, excite and enable students to exceed their own potential. Everything we do is underpinned by a network of caring and supportive staff, all united in the aim of achieving the very best for our students.

School buildings are grouped around a spacious campus with a beautiful 'village green' at the centre of it. A development programme has, in recent years, extended the already extensive facilities at the School with major developments including an extension to the Prep – the Wessex Wing – and the redevelopment of the Sixth Form Centre into a central hub for Sixth Form students to study, relax and socialise.

Unique to the School is Overdale, our entry point for Year 7 and 8 students. Students in these years enjoy a smaller community of younger students, dedicated form tutors and teachers and both separate and shared facilities to help them transition smoothly from primary to secondary years.

Curriculum. All pupils follow a common curriculum in Years 7 and 8 with a choice of three languages from French, Latin or Spanish in Year 8. The wide spectrum of subjects means that pupils are then ideally placed to make GCSE option choices at the end of Year 9. As well as the compulsory subjects – Mathematics, English (including for most English Literature), and three Sciences – pupils choose four more subjects from Art, French, Design and Technology, Geography, German, Greek, Spanish, Religious Studies, History, Latin, PE and Music. Almost all combinations are possible, but attention is given to ensuring at this stage that pupils opt for appropriate subjects which will not restrict their future career choices. The School has remained committed to the teaching of Biology, Chemistry and Physics as separate subjects, but also offers Dual Award Science for some pupils. A "Beyond the Curriculum" programme has been established in Years 7 and for the Sixth Form, which includes, for example, an Etiquette course, the Environment, Drama, Philosophy and Debating. A programme of Personal Social and Health Education is provided for all pupils from Year 7 to Year 13, drawing on external agencies, as well as the School's own expertise. Compulsory Games and PE lessons not only support our highly successful sports teams but are also based on a philosophy of "games for all" with students of all abilities encouraged to enjoy physical activity by specialist games teachers.

School Chapel. The School has its own Chapel and close links with St Saviour's, the local parish church. There is an outstanding Chapel Choir which sings at daily services and at the regular Sunday Evensong. Each summer the Chapel Choir performs in cathedrals and churches both in Britain and abroad.

Parents Association. There is an active Parents' Association which provides opportunities for parents to meet informally and organises social events, as well as being involved on a day-to-day basis in the life of the School and in the funding of special projects.

Extracurricular Activities. Involvement in extracurricular activities is strongly encouraged and there is a wide range of clubs from which to choose, including scientific, cultural and recreational. There is a strong tradition of drama, with regular productions, and an annual House Drama and House Music competition. The School has an Orchestra, a Concert Band, Big Band and Brass Ensemble. The School has a fine reputation for choral music.

Games. Competitive sports are rugby, hockey, netball and lacrosse during the winter terms and cricket, athletics, tennis, rounders and golf during the summer. There are representative teams at all levels and the playing fields cover about 40 acres on three different sites. At McAllester Field there is a floodlit AstroTurf surface for hockey and tennis. A large sports complex, including a squash court, two fitness suites and a climbing wall, provides a focus for the School's comprehensive 'Sport for All' programme.

The Duke of Edinburgh's Award and Outdoor Pursuits. The School runs its own Duke of Edinburgh's Award scheme. Outdoor Pursuits form part of the curriculum and from Year 6 upwards pupils spend time away from School each year on residential outdoor pursuits activities. Climbing is available as part of the PE curriculum and as a co-curricular activity.

Admission to Seniors at 11 is by progression from the Prep or by the School's own Assessment and Taster Days. Entrance at other stages is through individual assessments and interview. Sixth Form entrants are also welcome and this selection is based on GCSE grades and interview. Prospective parents are always welcome to visit the School and the Headmaster is happy to meet parents and assist with queries over dates, methods of entry, SEN and learning support.

Fees per term (2016–2017). Seniors £3,540–£3,815; Prep £2,550–£2,880.

Scholarships and Bursaries. The Birkenhead School Foundation Trust was established in 1998 to provide Bursaries and Funded Places. Scholarships are also available. Particulars may be obtained from the Headmaster's PA, Mrs Debbie Roberts.

Charitable status. Birkenhead School is a Registered Charity, number 1093419. The charitable status means the School not only accepts fee-paying pupils but can offer places to able children from less advantaged backgrounds.

Visitor: The Rt Revd Dr Peter Forster, The Lord Bishop of Chester

President: The Rt Hon Lord Nicholls of Birkenhead, MA Cantab, LLB, Hon LLD [Liv]

Governors:
Mr A Cross, LLB Hons (*Chairman of the Governors*)
Mr I G Boumphrey
Mr A D Coates
Mrs L Dodd, BA, FSI, FRSA
Mrs J Greensmith, CBE, DL
Mr G E Jones, MA
Dr J K Moore, OBE, FRCA, MBA
Mr E N Rice, FRICS, MCIA
Mr W D C Rushworth, BA
Mr A F Watson, FCA
Mr M Cashin

Company Secretary and Clerk to the Governors: Mr M J Turner, MA Oxon, MInstLM (*Bursar*)

Headmaster: **Mr P R Vicars**, MA

Deputy Head: Mrs K Pankhurst, BA
Deputy Head (*Academic*): Mr M Hayward, BSc
Assistant Head: Mr C D McKie, MA
Assistant Head: Mr S E J Parry, BA

Art:
Mrs J Lloyd-Johnson, BA (*Head of Art*)
Mrs V J Margerison, BA

Careers:
Mrs E Reeve, BA (*Head of Careers*)

Classics:
Mrs M T Washington, BA (*Head of Classics*)
Mr W I H Allister, MA (*Examinations Officer*)
Mr G W Murdoch, MA (*Head of Overdale*)

Design Technology:
Mr S Guinness, BSc (*Head of Design Technology*)
Mr T M Higginbottom, BEng
Mr S E J Parry, BA

Economics:
Mr R A Rule, BA (*Head of Economics*; *Head of Year 10*)

English:
Mrs A J McGoldrick, BA (*Head of English*)
Mrs E K Howard, BA
Mrs K Pankhurst, BA
Mrs E Reeve, BA
Mrs H C Ballantyne, MA
Ms L Smeaton, BA (*Head of Sixth Form*)

Geography:
Mr S M Gill, MA (*Head of Geography*)
Mr G R Hill, MA

History:
Mr C D McKie, MA (*Head of History*)
Mr M Roden, BA

ICT:
Mr D R Bell, MA (*Head of ICT*)
Mr A S Davies, MA (*Network Manager*)

Mathematics:
Mr S Hope, BSc (*Head of Mathematics*)
Mr D R Edmunds, BSc
Mrs E L Hope, BSc
Mrs S E Salter, MSc
Mrs K Eassie, BSc
Mr M M Maher, BSc

Modern Languages:
Mrs M L Holgate, BA (*Head of Modern Languages*)
Mrs J H Williams, BA (*SEN Coordinator*)
Mr G W Murdoch, MA (*Head of Overdale*)
Mr M A Turner, MA
Miss D Hamblett, BA

Music:
Mr P F Robinson, BMus (*Director of Music*)
Mrs G E Coleman, BMus

PE and Games:
Mr R E Lytollis, BSc (*Head of PE and Games*)
Mr D A Hendry, BEd (*Head of Year 11*)
Mrs L Alford-Swift, BSc (*i/c Girls' PE and Games*)
Miss N M Gilbride, BA
Mr G Rickman
Miss E Nokes

Religious Education:
Mrs E A Grey, MA (*Head of Religious Education*)

Science:
Mr M Hayward, BSc (*Head of Science*)
Mr P G Armstrong, BSc (*Head of Biology*)
Mr P Lindberg, BSc (*Head of Chemistry*)
Mr P M Webster, BEng (*Head of Physics*)
Mr K M Britton, MA
Mr S W Clark, CChem
Mrs A I Harrop, BSc
Mrs B Parry-Jones, BSc

Learning Support and Special Educational Needs:
Mrs J H Williams, BA (*SEN Coordinator*)
Mrs B Cederholm, MA
Mrs P J Dale, Cert Ed, Dip Teaching SpLD
Mrs L M Oxley, MA
Mrs G M Tooley, Cert Ed, Cert Reading Recovery, RSA
   Dip TEFL, RSA Dip SpLD

Headmaster's PA: Mrs D Roberts, BA
Chaplain: Mrs S Howell-Jones, BMus
Librarian: Mrs E Reeve, BA
SSI: Captain J A Barnes, BSc
Nurse: Mrs D Rennie, BSc, RGN

Prep School:
Head of Prep: Mr H R FitzHerbert, BA
Deputy Head of Prep: Mr R A Halpin, BSc

Senior Teachers:
Mr N J Corran, BEng
Miss S J Harris, BA
Mr M G Stockdale, BA

Key Stage Two Teachers:
Mr N J Corran, BEng
Mr M G Stockdale, BA
Mrs A C Delaney, BA
Mrs S G Mills, BEd
Mrs E E Thuraisingam, BA
Dr S M Jarvis, BSc, PhD
Mrs N A Brand, BSc
Mrs B M Coyne, BA
Mr T G Brand, BSc
Mr M E Pillow, BSc
Miss A E Rushton, BEd
Mrs H J Sewell, BA
Mrs C M Pye, BA
Mrs S J Keating, BA

Mr M Ryan, BA
Mrs L Hilton, BTh

Key Stage One Teachers:
Miss S J Harris, BA
Mr T R Smith, BEd
Mrs A C Hendry, BSc
Mrs G A Mudge, BSc
Mrs J E FitzHerbert, BA

Foundation 2 Teachers:
Miss S J Parry, BEd
Mrs J Mayers, BEd

Foundation 1 Teachers:
Mrs A C Bentley-Jones, BA

Bishop's Stortford College

**Maze Green Road, Bishop's Stortford, Hertfordshire
CM23 2PJ**
Tel: 01279 838575
Fax: 01279 836570
email: admissions@bishopsstortfordcollege.org
website: www.bishopsstortfordcollege.org
Twitter: @BSCollege
Facebook: /bishopsstortfordcollege

Motto: '*Soli Deo Gloria*'.

Bishop's Stortford College is a friendly, co-educational, day and boarding community providing high academic standards, good discipline and an excellent all-round education. We aim to equip our pupils with the vital qualifications, skills, adaptability and, above all, confidence to thrive as adults in a rapidly changing world. A flourishing Prep School and Pre-Prep, sharing many facilities with the Senior School, give all the advantages of educational continuity whilst retaining their own distinctive characters.

The College welcomes boys and girls of all denominations and faiths, and, while the majority of current pupils' homes are in the Home Counties and East Anglia, a substantial number of parents work and live overseas.

There are typically 600 pupils in the Senior School (boarders and day), 460 pupils in the Prep School and 120 in the Pre-Prep.

Location. Bishop's Stortford is mid-way between London and Cambridge and can be reached quickly via Liverpool Street Station, M25 and M11. Stansted Airport is a fifteen minute drive. The College is situated on the edge of the town adjacent to open countryside. The gardens and grounds cover about 130 acres.

Facilities. Purpose-built Pre-Prep accommodation, Prep and Senior School libraries, extensive ICT facilities and campus-wide Wi-Fi, outstanding sports facilities, well-resourced centres for Design and Technology, the Sciences, Languages, Music and Drama and a superb Art Centre. The main school Library and state-of-the-art indoor Swimming Pool are notable features. All school Houses offer a welcoming, family-like environment.

At the centre of the campus stands the Memorial Hall, used daily for Assembly. Originally built in 1921, it stands in memory of Old Stortfordians who served and fell during the Wars.

Academic Organisation. The Curriculum is designed to give as broad a course of study as possible up to the specialisation at A Level and Oxbridge entry.

In addition to the three Sciences, French, Spanish, English, Maths, Geography and History, all new pupils joining the Fourth Form (Year 9) take Design and Technology, ICT, Art and Music as well as one period each of RE and PE/Swimming. Most also begin German and a significant number continue with Latin.

All Lower and Upper Fifth Forms (Years 10 and 11), take 'core' subjects; English, English Literature, Maths and the three Sciences. Four other subjects, one of which must be a modern foreign language, are chosen from History, Geography, Design and Technology, Latin, French, Spanish, German, Art and Design, Music, Drama and Religious Studies. Pupils also have one period each of RE, PE/Swimming and ICT.

At all stages, progress is carefully monitored by Housemasters, Housemistresses and Tutors, and in Staff Meetings. Throughout the Senior School, grades for Effort and Attainment are given twice termly, and full written reports are sent home twice a year for each year group.

Careers. A purpose-built Higher Education and Careers Centre is open daily with three specialist staff. The College has close ties with ISCO, local commerce and industry and the Hertfordshire Careers Service. Links with local businesses are strong and there is an extensive programme of Work Experience organised for pupils in the Upper Fifth and Lower Sixth Forms.

The Sixth Form. Pupils choose between three and four subjects in the Lower Sixth, before specialising in the Upper Sixth. Sixth Formers select from the following subjects: Art, Biology, Business, Chemistry, Classical Civilisation, Design and Technology: Product Design, Drama and Theatre Studies, Economics, English Literature, French, Geography, German, History, Maths, Further Maths, Media Studies, Music, Physical Education, Physics, Politics, Psychology, Religious Studies, Spanish.

Pupils can take an Extended Project Qualification (EPQ) which requires independent study into an area of individual interest, perhaps an extension of a particular aspect of the syllabus or something outside the curriculum. The structure of EPQ works to prepare pupils for Higher Education and employment while inspiring and motivating them.

An extensive PHSE programme operates throughout the school and there is a weekly Upper Sixth Form lecture.

Each department organises visits and invites guest speakers to meetings of Societies, which are held in lunch hours or evenings. These, together with small group teaching, seminars and excellent resources, encourages pupils to develop their self-reliance, analytical skills and their spirit of academic enquiry to equip them for Higher Education and beyond.

Progress is closely monitored, as in Senior School, with the addition of overall supervision from the Head of Sixth Form. Parents are closely involved and regular Parents' Meetings are held.

Worship. The Religious Instruction, Sunday Worship and occasional weekday services are inter-denominational. The opportunity of exploring faith and being prepared for adult membership of particular churches (including Confirmation) is offered each year through the Chaplain.

Activities. Our young people are involved in an environment of wholehearted participation. A diverse range of extracurricular activities alongside high academic standards provides the opportunity for every child to discover areas of interest.

In addition to the meetings of Clubs and Societies, Wednesday and Friday afternoons are set aside within the timetable for Activities, including The Duke of Edinburgh's Award scheme. We encourage pupils to pursue their own interests as well as introducing them to others; many carry these on into their spare time, beyond School. Projects which promote a willingness to serve others are an important aspect of the breadth of activity offered.

Music and Drama. An interest in and appreciation for all kinds of music is encouraged throughout the school. In Form One and Form Two (Years 3 and 4), all Prep School pupils are taught an instrument in class and those who show promise are encouraged to continue individually in the Senior School.

There are numerous ensembles including Orchestra, Wind Band, guitar and string quartets, brass group, a Choral Society, and Choirs. Pupils are also encouraged to make music in small groups from the earliest stages. The College has a fully equipped Recording Studio. The Music Staff includes 27 visiting teachers of singing and all the main instruments, together with the Director of Music, 2 Assistant Directors and a Musician in Residence. The House Music Competition is a major event in the school year and involves all pupils. There are regular opportunities to perform in public at Pupils' Concerts and in School Assemblies. Overseas tours also offer excellent experience.

Drama is an area of strength with significant developments in recent years to the theatre facilities, curriculum and performing opportunities in which all pupils can participate. A Level Theatre Studies is offered, as is GCSE Drama.

Sport. The College has an excellent reputation in all areas of sporting achievement. Physical Education is taught in the Fourth and Fifth Forms and facilities include a Sports Hall, an impressive indoor swimming pool, two floodlit all-weather surface hockey pitches, hard tennis courts and 100 acres of playing fields.

Health. The Medical Centre is staffed by a resident full-time Nurse, part-time Nurse and full-time Health Care Assistant. Regular surgeries are held by the School's Medical Officer.

Varied and wholesome meals, included in the fees, are provided for all pupils in the College Dining Hall; the catering team have been awarded a Gold CAP Award for five consecutive years.

Prep School. The organisation of the Prep School (for pupils up to age 13+) is largely separate from that of the Senior School, but the curricula of the two Schools are carefully integrated. Pupils are able to share resources in Sport, Design and Technology, Music and Drama.

(*For further details see entry in IAPS section.*)

Admission. The main ages of admission are 4, 7, 11, 13 and 16, but entry at intermediate stages is possible. Entry to the Senior School at 13+ is based on school reference, interview and entry test results. Sixth Form Entry Interviews and Examinations are held in the November before year of entry.

Scholarships. The following annual awards are available:

Under 11 (Year 6): Academic, Music
Under 12 (Year 7): Academic, Music, Art, Sport
Under 14 (Year 9): Academic, Music, Art, Sport
Sixth Form: Academic, Music, Art, Sport

Financial Assistance. Means-tested bursaries are awarded based on individual need. Awards range from partial assistance of 5% up to (in exceptional circumstances) 100% of the full fees.

Fees per term (2016–2017). Senior School: Full Boarders £9,151–£9,206; Overseas Boarders £9,514–£9,569; Weekly Boarders £9,061–£9,116; Day £6,065–£6,120.

Prep School: Full Boarders £6,394–£6,937; Overseas Boarders £6,680–£7,225; Weekly Boarders £6,325–£6,868; Day £4,329–£4,852.

Pre-Prep £2,804–£2,859.

Fees are inclusive except for individual music tuition.

Charitable status. The Incorporated Bishop's Stortford College Association is a Registered Charity, number 311057. Its aims and objectives are to provide high quality Independent Day and Boarding education for boys and girls from age 4 to 18.

Governing Council:

Dr P J Hargrave, BSc, PhD, FREng (*Chairman*)

Sir Stephen Lander, KCB, MA, PhD, LLD, DSc (*Vice Chairman*)

G E Baker, BSc, MRICS

Mrs L J Farrant, MSc, CPFA

Mrs M Goitiandia, BSc, MBA, FCIPD

R C V Harrison

Mrs P Mullender, MA

Mrs I M Pearman, MA, MRICS

C P Solway, BSc, MRICS

Mr R Wells, BEd, BA, Dip PE

Headmaster: Mr Jeremy Gladwin, BSc, MEd

Deputy Head (*Academic*): Mr Graham Brooks, BA

Deputy Head (*Boarding*): Mr Chris Woodhouse, BSc

Deputy Head (*Pastoral*): Ms Jane Daly, BA

Head of Sixth Form: Mrs Linda Dickinson, BA

Examinations Officer: Mr Tim Herbert, MA

Senior Teacher: Mr Keith Irvine, BA

Policy Coordinator: Mrs Beth Wheeler, BSc

Director of Studies: Mr Colin Williams, BSc

Housemasters/Housemistresses:

Sutton House: Mr Tom Atkinson, BA

Benson House: Ms Emma Chaplin, BA

School House: Mr Peter Griffin, BSc

Robert Pearce House: Mr Richard Honey, MA

Young House: Mrs Tina Hood, BSc, BEd

Hayward House: Mr Simon Lipscombe, BA

Tee House: Mrs Janet Oldfield, BSc

Collett House: Mr Alex Swart-Wilson, MA

Alliott House: Mrs Sarah Wilson, BA

Heads of Department:

Art: Mr Richard Honey, MA

Biology: Mrs Beth Wheeler, BSc

Chemistry: Mr Charlie Bannister, MA

Classics: Dr Lucy Cresswell, PhD

Design & Technology: Mr John Trant, BA

Director of Drama: Mr Richard Norman, BA

Economics & Business Studies: Mr John Birchall, MA

English as a Second Language: Mrs Fiona Williams, BA

English: Mrs Claire Bond, MA

French: Mrs Caroline Davies, BA

Geography: Dr Peter O'Connor, PhD

German: Miss Kate Gregory, BA

Higher Education and Careers: Dr Gillian Allcock, BSc, PhD

History: Mr Tom Stuart, MA

Director of IT: Mr Stephen Bacon, BSc

Mathematics: Mr Nick Alexander, MSc

Media Studies: Mr Mike Tomkys, BA

Music (*Senior School*): Mrs Helen Pervez, BA

PE (*Academic*): Mr James Rayburn, BSc

Physics: Mr Adrian Baker, BSc

Politics: Mrs Alison Self, BA

PSHE: Mr Chris Woodhouse, BSc

Psychology: Mrs Jenny Marshall, BSc

Religious Education: Mr Patrick Winter, MEd

Science: Dr Stuart McPeake, PhD

Spanish: Miss Madeline Bailey, BA

Director of College Sport: Mrs Lyndsay Shepherd, BEd

Senior School Librarian: Mrs Maggie Garrett, MCLIP

Prep School:

Head of Prep School: W J Toleman, BA

Deputy Head: Mr Graham Millard, BA

Head of Shell: Mrs Kirsty Brooks, BA

Senior Teacher (*Pastoral*): Mr Richard Clough, BA

Head of Mathematics: Mr Neil Eddom, BEd

Housemaster, Grimwade House & Senior Teacher (*Operations*): Mr Adrian Hathaway, BEd

Director of Studies: Mr Mark Self, BSocSc

Assistant Senior Teacher: Mrs Wendy Sharman,MSc

Communications Coordinator: Mr Neil Eddom, BEd

Heads of Department:

Art: Mr Aaran Donlevy, BA

English: Mr David Herd, BSc

French: Miss Emmanuelle Carme, MA

Geography: Mr Richard Clough, BA

German: Mrs Imogen Cowan, BA

History: Mr Mark Self, BSocSc

ICT: Miss Frances Sharp, BSc

Latin: Mr Sandy Barnard

Mathematics: Mr Neil Eddom, BEd

Director of Music: Mr Andrew Bruce, MA

PSHE: Mrs Laura Davies, BA

Science: Dr Jeremy Spackman, PhD

Spanish: Mrs Fiona Jones, BA

Swimming: Mrs Deborah Huggett

Prep School Librarian: Mrs Rosie Pike, BA

Pre-Prep:

Head of Pre-Prep: Miss Belinda Callow, BEd

Miss E Bruce, BA

Mrs A Cullum, BA

Mrs C Martin, MA

Miss A Strouts, BA

Miss R Ward, BA

Mrs K Cordell

Miss G Fricker

Learning Support:

Head: Mrs Elizabeth Bridle, MA

Mrs Rita Gearing, CertEd, Dip SpLD

Mrs Gerda Miller, CertEd, Dip SpLD

College Chaplain: Mr Ian Morris

Bursar: Mr Malcolm Hemingway

Senior School Admissions Officer: Mrs Marie-Louise Gough

Prep School Admissions Officer: Mrs Fiona Brett

Pre-Prep Admissions Officer: Mrs Sally McGuiness

Marketing Manager: Mrs Sarah Gowans

Bloxham School
A Woodard School

Bloxham, Banbury, Oxon OX15 4PE

Tel: 01295 724301

email: admissions@bloxhamschool.com

website: www.bloxhamschool.com

Twitter: @BloxhamSchool

Facebook: /bloxhamschool

Motto: '*Justorum Semita Lux Splendens*'

Bloxham School is an independent, co-educational boarding and day school for students aged 11 to 18. Situated in north Oxfordshire, Bloxham offers a rural setting whilst being easily accessible from London and the Home Counties.

A Bloxham education provides students with enriching educational experiences that help them to mature intellectually, physically, emotionally and spiritually. A balanced curriculum encourages the students to become leaders and creative thinkers, foster their passions, and be compassionate to others. Bloxham's outstanding teaching standards enable students to fulfil their academic potential, opening the doors of opportunity beyond the school gates and into their future careers.

An education from Bloxham School encapsulates the following five hallmarks:

- **A Passion for Learning:** fostering creativity and the capacity for dynamic, independent and critical thought. At the heart of Bloxham's teaching is the belief that all students should be inspired and encouraged to explore their learning further. Students learn to develop independent critical thought, reflect on their learning and use their intellect to problem solve.

- **A Balanced Curriculum:** academic rigour sits high on the agenda, but it is complemented by the broader curriculum to develop qualities like resilience, communication, team work and tenacity. Bloxham's broader curriculum ranges from main stream sports to minor ones, and from music, drama and art, to astronomy and kayaking.

- **A Gold Standard of Pastoral Care:** a commitment to every child's wellbeing creates the strong foundations on which Bloxham's reputation for a gold standard of pastoral care has been built. We are proud to offer full, flexi and day boarding options.

- **The Development of Character:** through promotion of responsibility, generosity, resilience and imagination. The broad and balanced curriculum, along with the experience of being part of a boarding community, creates opportunities for students to be of service to others, to lead by example, and to be part of a team. By working with others they learn to communicate, to listen, to be generous in their support and to develop empathy.

- **Christian Values:** nurturing a compassionate spirit so that students become a force for good in an ever-changing world. Bloxham aims to develop "spiritual intelligence" alongside intellectual and emotional intelligence, where students can think for themselves, question what they believe and formulate their core values, perhaps for the rest of their lives. Although the school has been built on a Christian ethos, those of faith, no faith and other faiths are welcomed and Bloxham openly encourages understanding, diversity and tolerance for all.

Admissions. Students join Bloxham at 11+, 13+ and 16+. 11+ entry is based on performance in the school's entrance exam, whilst 13+ entry is based on common entrance results (if appropriate). Students looking to join at 16+ should be predicted at least six A* to C grades, including Maths and English. Students should have at least Bs in their option subjects, with As desirable for Maths and Sciences.

Bloxham welcomes international students and supplementary English lessons are available for an additional fee if required.

Full details can be obtained from the Admissions Department.

Fees per term (2016–2017). Senior School: Full Boarders £10,815; Day £8,210 (includes all meals (except breakfast for Day students).

Lower School: Weekly Boarders £7,745, Day £5,795 (inclusive of lunch).

Scholarships and Bursaries. Students are invited to apply for Academic, Art, Drama, DT, Music, Organ and Sport Scholarships, which bring a fee remission of up to 20%.

Bursaries based on financial need are considered on an individual basis. They can be received in conjunction with a Scholarship or without.

The Development Office. The Development Office and the Old Bloxhamist Society work together to coordinate a rich programme of social and careers-orientated events for Bloxham alumni.

Charitable status. Bloxham School Limited is a Registered Charity, number 1076484. Its aim is to provide high quality academic education in a Christian environment.

Council of Governors:
Chairman: Mr Nigel Bankes

Mrs Marina Brounger	Mr Charles Mann
Mr Paul Clayson	Mr Andrew Nott
Mrs Hermione Harper	Mr Mark Pyper OBE
Mr Miles Hedges	Mrs Carol Shaw
Mr Malcolm Higgs	Mr John Spratt
Mrs Miranda Hopkins	Mrs Fiona Turner
Mrs Elisabeth Lewis-Jones	Mr Simon Wood
Mr Robert Loades	

Headmaster: Mr Paul Sanderson, MSc, MEd

Deputy Head Curriculum: Mr Matthew Buckland, MEd, BSc
Deputy Head Pastoral: Revd Michael Price, MA, MPhil
Assistant Head (Staffing and Systems): Mr David Cooper, BSc, BEd, MSc, MCollP
Assistant Head (Welfare and Boarding): Mrs Jacqui White, BEd
Head of Lower School: Mr Tom Tuthill, BA
Bursar: Mr Neil Urquhart

Heads of Departments:
Art: Mr Robert Matthew, BA, MDes, FRGS
Biology: Mr David Finch, BSc
Business Studies & Economics: Mrs Adrienne Cooper, BA, BAdmin
Design & Technology: Mrs Sian Westbury, BA
Drama (Academic): Mrs Anthea Dobry, BA
Drama (Productions): Miss Sophie Herrmann, BSc, MA
English: Mr Chris Saunders, BA
Food Technology: Ms Stella Caurie, BSc
Geography: Mr Nick Pigott, BA
Government and Politics: Mr Tom Tuthill, BA
History: Mr Robert Hudson, BA, MA
ICT: Mr Eddy Heddon, MSc, MBA, FCIPD
Latin: Mrs Christine McCaffrey, MA
Learning Support: Mrs Eleanor Russell, BA
Mathematics: Mr Julian Berry, BSc
Modern Languages: Mr Dave McLellan, BA
Music: Mr Alex Redpath, BMus RCM (*Director of Music*)
PE: Mr David Dales, BEd
Physics: Mr Andrew Millington, BSc
Psychology: Mr David Cooper, BSc, BEd, MSc, MCollP
Science: Mr Nigel Evans, BSc
Sport: Miss Becky Odlin, BSc (*Director of Sport*)
Theology: Dr Debbie Herring, BTh, PhD

Head of Careers: Dr Claire Evans, BA, MSc, PhD
Head of Scholars: Dr Julian Moyle, MA, PhD
Head of Sixth Form: Mr Robert Hastings, BA

Houses and Housemasters/mistresses:

Boys' Houses:
Crake: Mr Richard Devesa
Egerton: Mr Simon Thompson
Seymour: Mr Matt Bull
Wilson: Mr Mark Skevington

Girls' Houses:
Raymond: Mrs Jacqui White
Wilberforce: Mrs Christine McCaffrey

Lower School:
Park Close House Parents: Mr Tom Tuthill & Mrs Claire Tuthill

Headmaster's PA: Mrs Val Turner
Admissions Registrar: Mrs Fay Hand
Medical Officer: Dr Stephen Haynes, MBBS, MRCGP, DFFP
Chaplain: Dr Gerard Moate, BA, PhD, FRSA

Blundell's School

Tiverton, Devon EX16 4DN

Tel:	01884 252543
Fax:	01884 243232
email:	info@blundells.org
website:	www.blundells.org
Twitter:	@BlundellsSchool
Facebook:	/blundellsschool

The School, with its attendant connection to Balliol and Sidney Sussex Colleges, was built and endowed in 1604 at the sole charge of the estate of Mr Peter Blundell, Clothier, of Tiverton, by his executor the Lord Chief Justice, Sir John Popham. In 1882 the School was moved to its present site on the outskirts of Tiverton. It is now a thriving co-educational day and boarding school combining strong academic achievement and excellent facilities in a secure and happy environment. The deep and enduring friendships formed at Blundell's, fostered by the school's fantastic community spirit, together with the intellectual, physical and cultural interests they develop here, provide pupils with skills for life.

Admission. Entry is at 11, 13 and 16 for most pupils. This is via the Blundell's Entrance Test or the Common Entrance Examination. Most join the School in September, though a January entry is welcome.

Numbers. There are 580 pupils of whom 244 are girls; 373 board (full, weekly, flexi). There are three boys' Houses and two girls' Houses for Years 9–12 and a separate Upper Sixth House. Years 7 and 8 have a separate House with separate pastoral and academic leadership. They have no lessons on Saturdays.

Fees per term (2016–2017). Full Boarding £7,485–£10,955; Weekly Boarding £6,775–£9,360; Day £4,440–£7,035. Flexi boarding is also available. A basic tuition fee is charged for those living within ten miles of Blundell's (over the age of 13).

Scholarships and Bursaries. Open Scholarships and Exhibitions: Up to half of the chosen designation fee (ie boarding, weekly, flexi, day) are offered on the basis of our own examinations held in January (13+) and November (Sixth Form). Awards for Art, Music, Drama, Sport and All-round ability are also made. At 11+ Junior Exhibitions only are awarded for academic and musical ability (January examination) and are deducted from the basic tuition fees.

Services Package available to the sons and daughters of serving members of the Armed Forces and Diplomatic Corps.

Awards may occasionally be supplemented by means-tested bursaries at the discretion of the Head.

Full details of all scholarships and bursaries are available from the Registrars.

School Work. There are four forms at age 11 and five at age 13. During the first three years most pupils will study Art, Biology, Chemistry, Design and Technology, Divinity, Drama, English, French, Geography, History, Information Technology, Mathematics, Music (Class), Personal and Social Development, Physical Education and Physics. Latin, Greek, German and Spanish are also available.

During the GCSE years the range of subjects remains broad. Extensive advice is provided by the School to assist both GCSE and A Level choices. Parents are advised to enter their children for the Independent Schools' Careers Organisation Futurewise programme and there is a comprehensive work experience scheme on offer.

Sixth Form options enable a wide combination of subjects to be taken. Four of the following are taken to AS Level and three to A Level: Art, Biology, Business Studies, Chemistry, Classical Civilisations, Design Technology, Drama, Economics, English, Film Studies, French, Geography, German, History (Modern & Early Modern options), ICT (AS only), Latin, Mathematics and Further Mathematics, Music, Photography, Physical Education, Physics, Psychology, Religious Studies (Ethics) and Spanish.

Mark Orders, Tutorial System and Reports. Good communication is a central concept. Frequent Mark Orders and Staff Meetings are held to monitor each pupil's work. All pupils have academic tutors. Parents receive termly formal written feedback in addition to receiving Mark Order summaries every few weeks. There are regular parents' meetings and information forums.

Music and Drama. Blundell's music is excellent. Based in our own music school there are several choirs, an orchestra and varying musical ensembles. These range from a jazz band through a chamber choir to brass, woodwind and string groups. The Department has state-of-the-art recording equipment. In addition to School concerts there are visits from professional musicians. The Choir undertakes a European tour at Christmas; recent destinations have included Prague, Paris, Oslo, and Venice.

Similarly, Drama plays a key role in the School. There are three major School Plays each year, as well as House plays. The magnificent, purpose-built Ondaatje Hall offers the combined facilities of a theatre, a concert hall and an art studio. Frequent visits are made by theatre companies and Blundell's is a cultural venue for Mid-Devon.

Games and Physical Training. Boys play rugby football in the Autumn Term whilst girls play hockey. Spring Term sports include cross-country, squash, rugby, fives, hockey, soccer, fencing, basketball, netball and rugby sevens. In the Summer Term cricket, tennis, swimming, athletics and golf take place. The Sports Hall gives further scope to the range of sport, as does the all-weather floodlit pitch; there is also a Fitness Suite. Elite sportsmen and women are supported with specialised fitness programmes. A variety of other sports, such as clay pigeon shooting, fly fishing, canoeing and miniature range shooting, are available through the extensive activity programme.

Computing and Technology. All Blundellians have access to the school IT network and will develop a range of skills during their time at school to support their studies.

Recent New Facilities. There have been extensive developments at Blundell's over the past two decades which include upgrading the Science Departments, provision of advanced technological and careers arrangements as part of the resources included in the redesigned Library, a new Modern Languages block, ongoing refurbishment of all boarding houses, a Fitness Suite, a Music School, IT suites and extension to the U6 Boarding House to incorporate new study areas and a library. With the relocation of St Aubyn's School (now called Blundell's Preparatory School) onto the Blundell's site, the whole campus provides education from the age of 2½ to 18 years.

Community Service. The School is involved in a wide variety of activities, both local and national, and pupils regularly raise around £20,000 per annum for a variety of charities, as well as taking part in practical tasks locally and 'befriending' etc.

Adventure Training. Blundell's is well placed to make full use of Dartmoor and Exmoor, the coast and rivers of the area, for academic fieldwork or adventure training. For many years the School has entered teams for the Ten Tors Expedition on Dartmoor, canoes the Devizes–Westminster race and takes part in The Duke of Edinburgh's Award scheme up to Gold level.

CCF. Everyone in Year 10 serves for a year in the CCF. Thereafter it is voluntary and comprises senior pupils who provide the NCO Instructors. There are links with the 18 Cadet Training Team, Derriford, and the Rifle Volunteers.

Boarding. Blundell's is built around the ethos of boarding and all pupils (full boarding, weekly, flexi boarding and day) are accommodated in one of seven houses on the campus. A full range of weekend activities is offered including a Leadership Programme, Ten Tors, sport and a range of local trips and activities.

Religion. The School maintains a Christian tradition, while welcoming members of other faiths. All pupils are expected to attend weekday morning Chapel and boarders go to the School Service on Sundays. The Chaplain prepares boys and girls who wish to be confirmed; the Confirmation Service takes place annually in the Spring Term.

Accessibility. Blundell's is close to the M5, and is served by Tiverton Parkway Station, two hours from Paddington, London. Airports at Bristol and Exeter are close at hand.

Prospectus. Fuller details of School life are given in the prospectus, available from the Registrars. Prospective parents are invited to visit the School, when they will meet the Head and a Housemaster or Housemistress and have a full tour of the School with a current pupil. The Blundell's website (www.blundells.org) is regularly updated throughout the academic year and as well as giving details of the school and academic departments, lists the main sporting, musical and dramatic events of each term and some match results.

Preparatory School. Blundell's Preparatory School for children aged 2½ to 11 years is on its own extensive site at Blundell's. For further information apply to the Headmaster, Mr A D Southgate. (*See also entry in IAPS section*).

Charitable status. Blundell's School is a Registered Charity, number 1081249. It exists to provide education for children.

Board of Governors:
Mr C M Clapp, FCA (*Chairman*)
Mr B J Hurst-Bannister, MA (*Vice Chairman*)
Mr N Arnold, BA, App Dip Crim
Mr N P Hall, MA, FCA
Mr P M Johnson, MA, FRSA
Mr J K Macpherson, BEd
Mrs J M A Mannix, MA
Fr R Maudsley
Rt Revd N McKinnel, BA, MA
Ms L J Smith, BA, FRSA, JP
His Honour Judge William Taylor
Dr M E Wood, BA, MA, DPhil
Mrs E V Heeley, BA, Cert Ed (*Representative Governor*)
Sir Christopher Ondaatje, OC, CBE (*Honorary Governor Emeritus*)

Bursar and Clerk to the Governors: Mr D Chambers, FCA

Head: Mrs N A Huggett, MA St Hugh's College Oxford, PGCE

† *Housemaster/Housemistress*
* *Head of Department*

Second Master: B Wielenga, BCom Natal & Johannesburg, BEd (*Economics*)
Deputy Head (*Academic*): C H List, BSc Durham, PGCE (*Chemistry*)
Deputy Head (*Co-curricular*): E K S Saunders, BA Leeds, PGCE (*Physical Education*)
Senior Master: A J R Berrow, MA St Peter's College Oxford, PGCE (**Religious Studies*)

Senior Mistress: Mrs G M L Batting, BEng Exeter, PGCE (**Science, Chemistry*)
Chaplain: The Reverend T C Hunt, BD Wales Cardiff, MTh, MRICS (*Religious Studies, PSD*)

Mrs G Armstrong Williams, BA Stourbridge A&T, GDST (*Art and Design*)
G J Baily, BSc Aston, PGCE (*Biology, Chemistry, Academic Head of Sixth Form*)
Dr J T Balsdon, BSc PhD London, PGCE (*Biology*)
L P N B Barnes, BSc Gloucestershire, PGCE (*Biology*)
Mrs D E C Brigden, BEd Exeter (*Biology, PSHCE*)
G Bucknell, BSc Durham (*Geography)
Mrs A T Candler, BSc Loughborough, PGCE (*PE*)
T E Candler, BA Plymouth (**Business Studies, ICT*)
Mrs S J Clark, BA, UNISA (*Learning Support*)
J D Clayton, MSc Oxford, PGCE (*Physics)
Mrs K L Corbin, MSc C & G College, PGCE (*Learning Support)
Mrs A M Cox, MA Bristol, PGCE (*Classics*)
†Mrs R J Crease, BEd Plymouth (*PSHCE, RS*)
Mlle M Cruchon, BA Rouen (*French*)
S J Dawson, BA East Anglia, PGCE (*English*)
Miss M Delrue, LLCER Lille (*French Assistante*)
M P Dyer, MSc Dundee, PGCE (*ICT)
J P Fairclough, BSc Exeter (*PE*)
Mrs C E Francis, BA De Montfort, PGCE (*D & T, Art*)
Mrs J C Francis, BA Durham, GTC (*Politics)
T S Frappart, BA Plymouth, PGCE (*D & T*)
C L L Gabbitass, BEd St Paul's (*PE, Mathematics*)
Miss V J Gill, MEd Birmingham, PGCE (*PE)
P H Gordon, BA Rhodes, BEd (*Mathematics)
Miss E J Gore-Lloyd, BA Bristol, MA (*TESOL*)
Miss A Grant, BA Leeds College of Music, PGCE (*Music*)
T E Grant, BA University of Wales Institute, PGCE (*Art & Design*)
Mrs T R Griffiths, BA London, GTP (*Classics, English*)
Miss C R Hall, BA Bristol (*French*)
†C M Hamilton, BA Anglia, PGCE (*Geography*)
J C Hatton, BA Salford (*Spanish*)
M J Hawkins, BA Nottingham, MA, PGCE (*History)
J M Hernández-Garcia, BA Miguel H', PGCE (*Spanish*)
Miss M Ho BSc, MEd Exeter (*Mathematics*)
Mrs S Holman, BA Exeter, PGCE (*Geography*)
†Miss D J Hosking, BEd Dartford (*History, RS*)
J Hutchinson-Bazely, BMus Royal Northern College of Music (*Music & Organ*)
K D W Insull, BA UWCN, PGCE (*Art & Photography*)
Miss R S Isdell-Carpenter, BA Wales, PGCE (*English)
S P Johnson, BSc Bath, MA, PGCE (*History, Politics*)
H D Jones, BSc MSc UWE Bristol (*PE*)
P M Jones, CELTA Kent TESOL (*TESOL*)
Mrs N J Klinkenberg, BSc Swansea, PGCE (*Mathematics*)
†P G Klinkenberg, BEd Exeter (*Registrar*)
Miss E M Lacki, BA, MA, CELTA, DELTA Exeter (*TESOL*)
A Lambert, MPhys Durham (*Physics*)
Dr O J Leaman, BMus PhD Edinburgh (*Music)
N M Y Lecharpentier, BA Caen, MA, PGCE (*French)
Ms B M Lewis, MLitt, MA King's College Cambridge, DELTA, PGCE (*English*)
L J Lewis, BSc Loughborough, PGCE (*Business Studies*)
M G Lodge, BSc Exeter, PGCE (*Physics*)
†D P Marshman, BSc Loughborough, PGCE (*Mathematics, Head of School House*)
S J Mault, BSc Liverpool, PGCE (*Mathematics*)
P Mawson, MChem Edinburgh, PGCE (*Chemistry, Physics*)
A J Mead, BSc Bath, PGCE (*Chemistry)
L Menheneott, BEd St Paul's, MBA (*PE, Proctor*)
Mrs R C Milne, BA Wales, PGCE (*Speech & Drama*)

Mrs R E Milne, MA Exeter, PGCE (*Classics*)
D E Morrison, MEng Bristol (*Physics*)
T M Mycock, BSc Plymouth (*Chemistry*)
Miss S A Norman, BSc Exeter, PGCE (*Careers*)
Mrs B A Nuttall-Owen, BSc Durham, PGCE (*Geography*)
†C E D Olive, BSc Aberystwyth, PGCE (*Biology*)
Mrs J Olive, MEng London, PGCE (*Mathematics*)
Miss E C Partington, BSc Bristol, MSc, PGCE
 (*Geography*)
Dr J A Ratcliffe, BSc Nottingham, PhD, PGCE (*Biology*)
P F Rivett, MA Exhibitioner of The Queen's College,
 Oxford, PGCE (*Mathematics*)
Miss B E Rees, BSc Cardiff, PGCE (*Chemistry*)
J A Rochfort (*Drama*)
Miss E P Sage, BA Durham, PGCE (*Classics*)
Miss I G Scott, BA Reading, MA, PGCE (*German,
 French*)
J S Shrimpton, BA Bristol (*English*)
†D J Smart, BSc Birmingham, PGCE (*Biology, Chemistry*)
Mrs C St Louis, BA Bristol, BA (*Speech and Drama*)
Miss J Spencer, BA MEd Northumbria, PGCE (*Drama*)
Mrs L R M Stanton, BA Sheffield, PGCE (*French*)
Mrs A M Taylor-Ross, BA MA Nottingham, PGCE
 (*PSHCE, Geography*)
A P J Thain, BA Winchester (*English*)
Miss P E Turnbull, BA Staffordshire, PGCE (*Economics*)
Mrs E V Weaver, BSc Cardiff, PGCE (*Psychology,
 Academic Head of Yrs 7 & 8*)
Mrs L E Webster, BSc Exeter, PGCE (*Physics*)
B Wheatley, MA Loughborough, PGCE (*D & T,
 Academic Head of Yrs 9–11*)
Mrs K J Wheatley, BA Swansea, PGCE (*French*)
Mrs L J Wielenga, BEd Natal (*LS, English*)
Mrs T L Winsley, BA Exeter (*Drama*)
Mrs L Yang, MBS Sunderland (*Mandarin*)
Miss H L Youngs, BTec Somerset College (*Learning
 Support*)

Director of Development: Mrs A Oliver, MInstF
Director of Marketing and Communications: Mrs J Jeffrey,
 BA Reading

Head's PA: Mrs H L Tucker

Registrars:
†P J Klinkenberg, BEd
Mrs T L Frankpitt, BEng, MBA

Medical Officer: Dr S-J Seymour, MA, MD, BChir

Bolton School Boys' Division

Chorley New Road, Bolton BL1 4PA
Tel: 01204 840201
Fax: 01204 849477
email: seniorboys@boltonschool.org
website: www.boltonschool.org/seniorboys
Twitter: @BoltonSchool
 @Philip_Britton
Facebook: /boltonschool.org
LinkedIn: /bolton-school

Motto: '*Mutare vel timere sperno.*'

 Bolton School Boys' Division, founded ante 1516 as
Bolton Grammar School for Boys, was rebuilt and endowed
by Robert Lever in 1644. In 1913 the first Viscount Leverhulme gave a generous endowment to the Bolton Grammar
School for Boys and the High School for Girls on condition
that the two schools should be equal partners known as
Bolton School (Boys' and Girls' Divisions).

 Bolton School is a family of schools, where children can
enjoy an all-through education, joining our co-educational
Nursery for 3 and 4 year olds or Infant School before moving up to our single-sex Junior and Senior Schools with
Sixth Forms. We are strong believers that girls and boys
from 7+ perform best in a single-sex environment, but one
where there are co-educational activities – the best of both
worlds.

 Situated in imposing sandstone buildings on a thirty-two
acre site, Bolton School Boys' Division educates over 1,100
boys, all day pupils. Of these, 200 are members of the Junior
School which is housed in an adjacent separate building
close to the main site providing education for boys aged
7–11. In the Senior School of 900, 220 are in the Sixth
Form.

 Bolton School Boys' Division seeks to realise the potential of each pupil. We provide challenge, encourage initiative, promote teamwork and develop leadership capabilities.
It is our aim that students leave the School as self-confident
young people equipped with the knowledge, skills and attributes that will allow them to lead happy and fulfilled lives
and to make a difference for good in the wider community.

 We do this through offering a rich and stimulating educational experience which encompasses academic, extracurricular and social activities. We provide a supportive and
industrious learning environment for pupils selected on academic potential, irrespective of means and background.

 Curriculum. The GCSE programme comprises a core
curriculum of English Language, English Literature, Mathematics, Biology, Chemistry, Physics and Sport. In addition,
pupils select a further 4 options chosen from Art, Drama,
French, Geography, German, Greek, History, Latin, Music,
Philosophy and Ethics, RE, Russian, Science Enrichment,
Spanish and Technology. One of these choices must be a foreign language. At A Level approximately 30 different subjects are currently on offer. Boys study four subjects to AS
Level, with the majority reducing to three A2 Levels in Year
13. In addition all boys have the option of taking General
Studies to A2 Level. While many boys elect to take standard
combinations of either Arts or Science subjects in the Sixth
Form, a high degree of flexibility ensures that any desired
combination of subjects can be offered. Throughout both
years of the Sixth Form, there is an additional and extensive
programme of academic work which supports the GCE
Advanced curriculum. Some boys will take the AQA Bacc
qualification and all boys do an enrichment course and take
part in community service.

 Facilities and Organisation. The Boys' and Girls' Divisions of Bolton School are housed in separate buildings on
the same site and, though the organisation of the two Divisions provides single-sex schools, there are many opportunities for boys and girls to meet and to cooperate in the life of
the school community. This is particularly so in the new
Riley Sixth Form Centre, where boys and girls share a Common Room, cafe and learning areas equipped with the very
latest technology. Single-sex teaching remains the norm in
the Sixth Form, although in a very few subjects co-educational arrangements are in operation. The buildings of the
Boys' Division include the Great Hall, two libraries, gymnasium, sports hall, swimming pool, laboratories, art rooms,
sixth form common room and ICT learning centre, design
technology centre, performing arts centre, MFL laboratory,
classrooms and dining hall. The Junior School building has
recently been extended and refurbished and contains eight
form rooms and specialist rooms for ICT, art & design and
science & technology together with a gymnasium, library
and its own dining accommodation. Use of the sports hall,
the adjacent 25-metre swimming pool and the arts centre is
shared by all sections of the school.

 Games and PE. The extensive playing fields which
adjoin the School contain thirteen pitches. Principal games
are football, rugby and cricket. Tennis, hockey, swimming,

water polo, badminton, athletics, golf and orienteering are also all played at representative school level. All boys also undertake a gymnastics programme and play volleyball and basketball. The School is divided into four Houses for the purpose of internal competitions.

Art, Drama, Design, Music. In addition to timetabled sessions in each discipline there are many opportunities for extracurricular activities in all these pursuits. Facilities in the art department include a pottery room with kiln; within the very active musical life of the School there are choral groups, orchestras and ensembles catering for all ages and abilities. In addition arrangements can be made for individual lessons on all orchestral instruments, piano, organ and in singing. Drama is an important part of the work of the English department and boys are encouraged to develop their talents in the drama studio and arts centre. The annual major school play, musical or opera is produced in cooperation with the Girls' Division. Design and technology features strongly in the curriculum in both Junior and Senior Schools with considerable success each year in the A Level technology courses, many boys gaining industrial sponsorships as a result. In addition, a wide variety of extracurricular opportunities exists in both the design technology base and the computer rooms. All boys are encouraged to take part in the extensive lunchtime programme when over 120 clubs, societies and practices are offered to different groups.

Outdoor Pursuits. All junior school pupils and all students up to and including Year 12 in the senior school undertake an annual period of outdoor education within curriculum time. In addition, camps, trips, exchanges and expeditions go to 63 destinations over two years, 17 of them abroad. The School has its own 60-bed Outdoor Pursuits Centre, Patterdale Hall in Cumbria, used by parties of boys regularly for curriculum, weekend, holiday and fieldwork expeditions. In Year 8 boys have the opportunity to undertake sail training lessons in the Irish Sea on the School's sailing ketch. There is a large and active Scout Group with its own modern headquarters on school premises.

Religion. The School is non-denominational; all boys have periods devoted to religious education. In assemblies the basic approach is Christian although a great variety of readings and methods of presentation are adopted.

Careers and Higher Education. Careers education and guidance, and life-long learning are key elements of the curriculum. In Year 8 pupils take part in a Work Sampling Day. Careers Education is part of the Year 9 curriculum including a project marked by the Headmaster. As an aid to Sixth Form choices, the Morrisby Test with follow-up interviews and extensive feedback is undertaken in Years 10 and 11. All pupils take part in Work Experience placements at the end of Year 11 and throughout the Sixth Form.

In Year 12, all pupils attend a 3 day residential business training course at Patterdale Hall and take part in an e-business competition. Mock interviews are conducted on Interview Skills Evenings. Year 13 pupils are guided through UCAS procedures and careers advice is always available from two full-time Careers Assistants in the Careers Library. The Head of Careers oversees all these events and can be consulted by all parents and pupils.

Transport. The School provides an extensive coach service which offers secure and easy access for pupils from a wide surrounding catchment area. Over twenty routes are operated by either the School's own fleet of coaches or by contract hire arrangements.

Admission. An entrance examination is held in January annually for boys over 7 and under 8 on August 31st of the year of admission and also for those over 8 and under 9 on the same date. Fifty places are available at 7+ and a few additional places thereafter. Admission to the first year of the Senior School (140 places) is by entrance examination held annually in mid-January. Boys who are over 10 and under 12 on August 31st of the year of entry are eligible.

Entry to the Sixth Form is available to boys who have taken GCSE examinations elsewhere on the basis of interview and agreed levels of performance in these public examinations. Boys are also admitted at other ages when vacancies occur; in these cases admission is gained through satisfactory interview and test performances. There is a co-educational pre-preparatory section – Beech House Infants' School – which has recently moved to new purpose-built, state-of-the-art premises. Admission is from the age of 4 and enquiries should be made to infants@boltonschool.org. There is also a nursery providing facilities for children from 3 months to 4 years old.

Fees per term (2016–2017). Senior School and Sixth Form £3,836; Infant and Junior Schools £3,068. Fees include lunches.

Fee Assistance. Means-tested Foundation Grants are available and one in five Senior School pupils receives assistance with fees. Scholarships are also available and are offered regardless of parental income, to those pupils whose achievement in the Entrance Examination and the Interviews places them at the top of the cohort.

Prospectus and Open Day. The School holds an annual Open Morning for the benefit of prospective candidates and their parents. This is normally in mid-October. Individual tours can be arranged on working days throughout the year. Further information concerning all aspects of the School is contained in the School Prospectus, copies of which may be obtained by writing to the Headmaster at the School, or telephoning the Headmaster's Secretary. More detail can be found on the School website. Enquiries concerning admission are welcome at any time of the School year.

Charitable status. The Bolton School is a Registered Charity, number 1110703. Under the terms of the Charity it is administered as two separate Divisions providing for boys and girls under a separate Headmaster and Headmistress.

Chairman of Governors: M T Griffiths, BA, FCA

Headmaster: P J Britton, MBE, MEd

Deputy Headmaster (Pastoral): R D Wardle, BA
Assistant Head (Academic): N L Ford, BSc
Assistant Head (Activities): Dr F H Mullins, BSc, PhD

Heads of Department:
Art and Design: (to be appointed)
Biology: M A Tillotson, BSc
Business Studies: Mrs C M Edge, BSc
Chemistry: Dr M Yates, BSc, PhD
Classics: Dr J E Reeson, BA, MSt, PhD
Economics: D W Kettle, BA
English: M S Pollard, BA, MA
French: A C Robson, BA
Geography: P Newbold, BA
German: R A Catterall, MA
History: Miss S V Burgess, MA
ICT: P J Humphrey, BSc
Mathematics: D N Palmer, BSc
Music: J Bleasdale, BA
Physical Education:
P Fernside, BA (*Head of Games*)
M Johnson, BSc (*Head of PE*)
Physics: M R Ormerod, BSc
Religious Studies: Mrs C E Fox, BA
Russian: P G Davidson, BA
Spanish: Mrs J L Cotton, BA, MA
Technology: C J Walker, BA

Instrumental Music Staff:
Brass, Cello, Clarinet, Guitar, Oboe, Organ, Percussion, Piano, Saxophone, Singing, Viola, Violin

Junior School (Age 7–11):
Head: Mrs S A Faulkner, BA, MA

Deputy Head: F Morris, BA

Headmaster's Personal Assistant: Ms M M Leather
Headmaster's Secretary & Admissions Registrar: Mrs S
   Yates

Bootham School

York YO30 7BU

Tel:	01904 623261 (School)
	01904 623261 (Headmaster)
Fax:	01904 652106
email:	office@boothamschool.com
website:	www.boothamschool.com

Bootham offers Full and Weekly Boarding and Day Education to both boys and girls from 11–18, together with day education from the age of 3 at Bootham Junior School. There are now over 470 pupils in the Senior School and 130 day pupils in the Junior School (*see entry in IAPS section*).

The School was founded in 1823 by Quakers, but pupils of all denominations or none are welcomed. All pupils attend Meetings for Worship and arrangements are made for pupils to be prepared for confirmation or membership of their own churches.

Curriculum. In Years 7–9 all pupils pursue a course of study which includes English, History, Religious Studies, Geography, Classics, Latin, French, German, Spanish, Mathematics, the three separate Sciences, Music, Drama, Art and Craft, Physical Education, Design & Technology, Computer Science, Careers, Health and the Environment and Thinking Skills.

In Years 10 and 11 pupils follow a curriculum leading to 10 subjects at GCSE.

The College Classes (Sixth Form) are preparatory to university entrance. The majority of pupils remain at school until the age of 18 and each year there is a strong Oxbridge entry. A wide choice of subjects is offered. It is usual to study 3 or 4 examination subjects and to study subjects of wider interest.

Students are able to choose from a wide variety of subjects. These are: Mathematics, Further Mathematics, Physics, Chemistry, Psychology, Biology, English, French, German, Spanish, History, Classics, Latin, Geography, Economics, Business Studies, Music, Art, Design Technology, Religious Studies, Drama and Theatre Studies, and Sports Studies and Physical Education.

Site and Buildings. The School is situated close to York Minster. From the road it appears as an impressive line of Georgian houses but behind this is the spacious main school campus. There is a steady programme of development, and the buildings now include 8 well-equipped Laboratories, an impressive Arts Centre (open 2014) with Auditorium and Darkroom (photography), 2 ICT Suites, 2 DT workshops, an Astronomical Observatory, an up-to-date Physical Education Department with Sports Hall, Indoor Swimming Pool, Fitness Suite and Squash Courts, and a modern Assembly Hall, which received a national RIBA award. There are many facilities for leisure time pursuits which are an important feature of the lives of pupils at the School. The buildings are complemented by formal gardens and a beautiful Cricket Field, overlooked by the Minster. Another large Playing Field is situated nearby, in Clifton, which also houses Bootham Junior School in a new purpose-built complex.

Pastoral Care. As a Quaker School, Bootham places great emphasis on caring relationships within a friendly community. There are three boarding houses, under the special care of House staff. Each House has its own recreational facilities. Throughout the School, both boarding and day pupils are supervised and guided by form tutors. In College,

pupils have Personal Tutors who are responsible for both academic and pastoral matters, and guidance towards Higher Education.

Admission. Pupils usually enter Bootham at the age of 11. Entry is also usually possible at 12, 13 and 14. The main entrance assessment is held annually in January and this forms the basis of Scholarship and Bursary selection. Sixth form entry is welcomed and selection is on the bases of school report and GCSE performance. In special circumstances late entrants can be considered.

Leisure Time Activities. The School has long been recognised as a pioneer in the right use of leisure. The Natural History Society, founded in 1832, claims to be the oldest society of its kind with an unbroken history in this country. Other clubs and societies include Debates, Drama, Bridge, Chess, Cookery and Jazz. There are around 100 activities offered each week. Pupils follow the Duke of Edinburgh's Award scheme and are involved in Community Services.

Music. The Director of Music and his assistant are supported by 25 visiting teachers. Tuition is arranged in a wide variety of instruments and a strong tradition of music in the School is maintained. A recent leaver was named 'Young Composer of the Year' and there is a strong record of success in gaining Music College and University scholarships.

Games. Association Football, Hockey, Tennis, Fencing, Cricket, Swimming, Athletics, Netball, Basketball, Badminton, Squash, Rounders. There is no cadet force.

Fees per term (2016–2017). Boarding: £5,990–£10,170. Day: £5,295–£5,840.

Fees for instrumental music lessons are extra. Enquiries for up-to-date information are welcome.

Scholarships and Bursaries. *Academic* Scholarships (honorary and without fee reduction) are awarded on an annual basis at the end of each academic year and are based on performance throughout the year. Academic Scholarships are subject to annual reviews.

Sixth Form: We offer a means-tested scholarship/bursary to candidates from state-maintained schools who gain a minimum of 8 A/A* grades at GCSE.

Music Scholarships of up to 50% fee remission are available for candidates of good all-round musical and academic ability or potential. These are available for entry at 11+ and 13+ (Years 7 and 9) and are awarded on the basis of performance in the entrance assessment, and in tests and an audition with the Director of Music.

Means-tested Bursaries (supported by the Bootham Trust) are available:

- to assist Friend (Quaker) children, or the children of Friend (Quaker) parents, to attend the School;
- to assist children, whose families would not be able to afford an independent school education, to attend the School.

Applicants will be assessed by academic performance in the entrance assessment at 11+ and 13+ and in addition, for Music Scholars, their performance at the Music Scholarship tests and audition. Applications for bursaries need to be made in the Autumn term prior to entry to the school.

Bootham Old Scholars' Association. There is an annual Reunion in York during the second weekend in May. The Bootham Old Scholars' Association has branches in all parts of the country and Eire. The Secretary may be contacted through the School.

Charitable status. Bootham School is a Registered Charity, number 513645.

Head: **Christopher Jeffery**, BA, FRSA

Deputy Head: Suzanne Hall, BA, PhD

Academic Deputy: Ruth Crabtree, BA, MA

Head of Junior School: Helen Todd, BA Hons, MA Ed, QTS

Assistant Heads:
William Lewis, MA
Graeme Rainey, BA, MA
James Ratcliffe, BSc

Head of Boarding: Graeme Rainey, BA, MA

Bursar: Andy Woodland, BA, MA, MICE, MCIWEM

Assistant Staff:
* *Head of Department*
† *Housemaster/mistress*

Sarah Allen, BEd, BD (*Religious Studies*)
Rachel Antill, BA (*Art*)
Mathew D Aston, BEd (*Mathematics)
Joan Attwell, BA (*Drama*)
Richard M Barnes, BA, MA (*Art*)
Andrew Bell, BA Ed (*Physical Education, English*)
Simon Benson, BA, MA (*Drama)
Dina Bonner (*German Language Assistant*)
Elizabeth Brown, BSc, PhD (*Geography)
Susan Browne (*Teaching Assistant*)
Richard N Burton, BA (*Music*)
Carol L Campbell, BA (*French, Spanish,* †*Rowntree House*)
Angelica Coates (*Spanish Language Assistant*)
Kirsten S Cooper, MPhys (*Physics)
Tracey Copestake, BA (**Religious Studies*)
Ben Coxon, BA (*Physical Education*)
Steve J Elsworth, BA (*Mathematics*)
Gillian England, BA (*Classics*)
Harriet Ennis, BSc (**Psychology, Biology*)
Paul Feehan, BA (**Director of Music*)
Elizabeth Gallagher-Coates, BA (*English, Psychology*)
Robert Gardiner, BSc (*Biology)
Emma Glover, BA (*English*)
Robert E Graham, BEd (*Physical Education, Geography*)
Sally Gray, BA (*Classics*)
Craig Haggart, BA (*Design & Technology*)
Emily Harper, BA (*Art*)
Kerri Haynes-McDonnell, BA, MA, PG Cert/NASCO (*Learning Support*)
Elisabeth Hooley, BA (*Physical Education, Mathematics*)
Freya Horsley, BA, MA (*Art*)
Helen Landau, BA (*Learning Support*)
Claire Little, BMus (*Music*)
Jack MacKenzie, BA (*Music*)
Kelly McCarthy, BA, MA (*EAL*)
Elizabeth McCulloch, MA (*History)
Eamonn Molloy, BEd (**Design & Technology*)
Alison Moreland, BEd (**Physical Education, Geography*)
Catherine Morin (*French Language Assistant*)
Amanda Naylor, BSc (*Mathematics*)
Russell Newlands, MSc, BEng (*Physics,* †*Evelyn House*)
Sarah O'Keeffe, BSc (**Economics & Business Studies*)
Christina Oliver, BA, MA (**French, German*)
Anne Partridge, BSc (*Geography*)
Sue Porter, BSc (*Mathematics*)
Peter Rankin, BEng (*Information Technology, Physics*)
Lindsey Robertson, BSc (*Chemistry*)
Mark Robinson, BA, MA (*Chemistry)
Sarah Robinson, BA (*Classics)
Catherine Rowell, BSc, PhD (*Biology, Chemistry, Physics*)
Helen Sharpe, BA, MA (*English*)
Michael Shaw, BSc (*Biology*)
Mark Shuttleworth, BA (*French*)
Gill Simpson, BA, MA (*English)
David Swales, BA (**Art,* †*Fox House*)
Emma Thomas , BA, MA (*French and Spanish*)
Jay Thorpe (*Outdoor Education Instructor*)
Sue Tomlinson, BSc (*Chemistry, Biology*)
George Trifan (*Sports Assistant*)

Shazma White, BA (*Economics*)
Anne Whittle, BSc (*Mathematics*)
Catherine Wilson, BA (*History*)
Angela Woods, BEd (*Geography, Physical Education*)

Admissions Registrar: Jenny Daly

Librarian: Steven Oakden, BA

Bradfield College

Bradfield, Berkshire RG7 6AU

Tel:	General Enquiries: 0118 964 4500
	Admissions: 0118 964 4516
	Bursar: 0118 964 4530
email:	admissions@bradfieldcollege.org.uk
website:	www.bradfieldcollege.org.uk
Twitter:	@BradfieldCol
Facebook:	@BradfieldCollege
LinkedIn:	/bradfield-college-enterprises-ltd

Motto: '*Benedictus es, O Domine: Doce me Statuta Tua*'. Blessed are you, our Lord; teach me your laws (from Psalm 119).

Bradfield College was founded in 1850 by Thomas Stevens, Rector and Lord of the Manor of Bradfield.

We define our ethos by the outcome of our pupils as they leave Bradfield. We actively promote personal integrity, tolerance, understanding and independence of thought. We encourage young people to work with and learn from each other, as well as to show moral courage to stand up for what they believe in. The breadth of a Bradfield education supports our pupils in challenging themselves and develops their abilities to communicate with others. The College is a co-educational boarding school dedicated to the provision of the highest possible care for all its pupils.

Location. Bradfield College occupies the village of Bradfield, 8 miles west of Reading and 9 miles east of Newbury. It is 2 miles from Junction 12 of the M4 (the Theale access point). There are good road and rail communications with Reading, Oxford, London and Heathrow.

Organisation. The College is a fully co-educational boarding school with approximately 770 pupils, of whom about 80 are day pupils. At 13+ entry girls and boys spend their first year in Faulkner's, a purpose-built co-educational house with its own facilities and dining hall. Thereafter, the College is divided into 11 houses (7 for Boys and 4 for Girls). Day pupils are full members of the boarding houses. The Housemaster/mistress is assisted by House Tutors and a Matron. Meals are served in the central Dining Hall. About fifty girls and boys join the large and vibrant Sixth Form through 16+ entry.

Admission. 13+ candidates qualify by taking either the Common Entrance Examination, the Common Academic or Bradfield College Scholarship Examination, or the Bradfield Entrance Examination (if not taking Common Entrance); candidates are interviewed by the a Housemaster/mistress and an Admissions tutor, and school reports and references are required. All candidates are required to take the ISEB Common Pre-Test in October of Year 7. Admission to the Sixth Form is by Assessment; this comprises English and Maths tests and pastoral and academic interviews. In addition, school reports and references are required. Scholarships and Exhibitions are available.

A school prospectus and details of the entry procedure may be obtained from the Admissions Office or College website.

Fees per term (2016–2017). Boarders £11,760; Day pupils £9,408.

A fee is payable on registration. 20 months before the date of entry a Guaranteed Place fee of £1,000, which is later credited against the final account, is payable.

Entrance Scholarships. *Academic*: At 13+ scholarships are awarded on the results of a competitive examination held at the College in the Lent Term. Candidates must be under the age of 14 on 1 September. Further Honorary scholarships conferring the status and privileges of a scholar are awarded at the end of the Year 11 (post GCSE).

At 16+ Scholarships are awarded annually after competitive examinations in the Michaelmas Term.

Music Scholarships are awarded at 13+ and 16+.

Dr Gray All Rounder Scholarships are awarded at 13+ and 16+ for achievement and potential in their all-round ability, which would take into account their academic achievement as well as their aptitude in any combination of other disciplines (including Music). Individual Scholarships are also available for distinction in Art, Drama or Sport.

All awards are augmentable according to financial need. Further information and entrance forms can be obtained on application to the Admissions Office.

Academic Organisation. Pupils enter the College in September and follow a three-year course to GCSE examinations, and then a two-year course to A Level or IB.

In the first three years all the normal subjects are taught in a core curriculum, but there is also opportunity to emphasise the linguistic or the aesthetic or the practical elements through a system of options.

In the Sixth Form GCE A Level courses are offered in all subjects studied for GCSE with the addition of Economics, Film Studies, Politics, History of Art, Business and Computer Science. Sixth Formers can also choose to study the IB Diploma Programme.

A brand new state-of-the-art and environmentally-friendly Science Centre opened its doors to pupils and the local community in September 2010. It includes ten sophisticated laboratories, a living grass roof, a conservatory and a biomass boiler providing an educationally and environmentally exciting space for the teaching of science.

Academic Staff. There are 117 members of the Academic Staff who cover all the main subjects. These are almost entirely graduates recruited from British universities, although there are also native speakers of German, French and Spanish in the Modern Languages department.

Careers. The Careers Department – Bradfield Horizons – provides a wide range of careers education, information, advice and guidance to all year groups, particularly at key decision points. The College is a full member of ISCO and through them, all pupils in the Fifth Form (and new pupils in the Lower Sixth) undertake Futurewise (Morrisby) psychometric profiling, follow-up interviews and receive a detailed personal report to help them plan for the future. In the Sixth Form, pupils have opportunities to find out about various professions, industries and the Armed Services through talks, visits and courses. Specialist advice is available on University entrance in the UK and overseas, Gap Years and work-related learning.

Sports. The main Sports for girls are hockey in the Michaelmas term, netball in the Lent term and tennis and rounders in the Summer term. Girls also have the chance to play competitive lacrosse, football and cricket.

The main Sports for boys are football in the Michaelmas term, hockey in the Lent term and cricket and tennis in the Summer term.

In addition, teams represent the College at squash, fives, cross-country, fencing, athletics, golf, sailing, swimming, shooting, badminton, basketball, water polo, clay pigeon shooting, showjumping, eventing and polo. There are also opportunities to take part in dance classes, Zumba and aerobics.

There are 2 all-weather artificial grass pitches used for hockey, football and tennis, a 3-court indoor Tennis Centre, 6 other hard tennis courts, 5 netball courts, 2 fives courts, 4 squash courts and a very large and modern Sports Complex, including an indoor swimming pool. The College grounds extend to nearly 250 acres and include fine playing fields, a nine-hole golf course and fly fishing on the river Pang.

Recreation, Drama and Music. Every encouragement is given to pupils to develop their interests and talents in a wide variety of creative activities. There are modern and well-equipped studios for Art, Sculpture and Textiles, an Information Technology Centre, a purpose-built and very extensive Design and Technology Centre and a Music School with a Concert Hall and practice rooms. The Drama department stages a diverse number of productions each term and a classical Greek Play is produced every three years. In addition, there are about 30 Societies covering a wide range of other interests from Young Enterprise to Knitting.

Religion. Chapel services are those of the Church of England, and Religious Education is part of the core curriculum in Year 9. Confirmation Services are held each year for Anglicans in the College Chapel and for Catholics in the local parish.

Combined Cadet Force. The College maintains a contingent of the Combined Cadet Force which all pupils have the opportunity of joining. There is a full range of alternative activities, including Community Service and The Duke of Edinburgh's Award. All pupils take part in a programme of Adventure Training.

The Bradfield Society. The College values its links with its former pupils and parents, and a series of social and sporting occasions is held each year to enable friendships to be maintained and renewed. Address: The Bradfield Society, Bradfield College, Reading, Berkshire RG7 6AU.

Charitable status. Bradfield College is a Registered Charity, number 309089.

Visitor: The Right Revd The Lord Bishop of Oxford

Council:

M H Young (*Warden*)	Mrs C Dibble
M A Jones	Mrs J Scarrow
A H Scott	Ms S Bergqvist
D Shilton	I Davenport
P B Saunders	S Beccle
Dr S Fane, OBE	Mrs S Scrope
Professor D Paterson	Professor R Van De Noort
I M Wood-Smith	S Clarkson Webb
H P Gangsted	

Clerk of the Council: P C H Burrowes

Headmaster: Dr C C Stevens, MA, DPhil

Second Master: K J Collins, MA

Senior Deputy Head (*Admissions and Marketing*): Mrs A M C Acton, BA Hons

Deputy Head (*Academic*): N M Burch, MSci

Bursar: P C H Burrowes LLB

Houses and Housemasters:
A – Loyd: J R Preston, BSc
C – Army: A S Golding, BA
D – House on the Hill: R P Sanford, BSc
E – Stone House: P C Armstrong, BA
F – Hillside: C A Carlier, MA
G – House on the Hill: T E Goad, BA
H – The Close: J O Hanbury, BA
I – Palmer House (*Girls*): Miss G L Peel, BA [maternity cover]
J – Armstrong House (*Girls*): Mrs A L Cocksworth, MA

K – Stevens House (Girls): Mrs C van der Westhuizen, MSc
M – Stanley House (Girls): Mrs C J Kirby, BSc
L – Faulkner's (Year 9): Mr J C Saunders, BA and Mrs V T Rae

Assistant Staff:
* *Head of Department*

Creative Arts Faculty:
*M K Holmes, MA
Art:
Miss A M Cowan, BA
Miss G L Peel, BA
Ms D S Rodgers, BA
A L Whittaker, MFA
Design & Technology:
*Miss H L Knott, BA
M K Goodwin, MA

Business Studies:
*M R Rippon, BA
L A Webb, BSc

Careers and Higher Education:
*Mrs C J Taylor, BA

Classics:
*Mrs P M H Caffrey, MA
P C Armstrong, BA

Economics:
*C G Irvine, BA
L W Beith, BComm
J C Fox, BA
C W Sykes, MA

English and Film Faculty:
*Miss A L Hatch, BA (*Head of English and Film*)
English:
K J Collins, MA
A M Cocksworth, MA
Ms S R Davies, BA
Mrs E V Earnshaw, BA
A S Golding, BA
J M Longmore, LLB
Mrs H A Morris, BA
H B Peters, LLB
Miss A J Routledge, BA
J M C Saunders, BA
Ms K Terry, BA
Mrs I G Woods, BA
English Language and EAL:
*Mrs H E Bebbington, BA, MA
Mrs D Bevan, TESOL Cert
Mrs J Kingston, BA
Film Studies:
Ms J Stables, BA

Geography:
*M S Hill, BA
C B Duffell, BA
R Keeley, MA
T J Kidson, BSc
Mrs C J Kirby, BSc
J R Preston, BSc
R J Wall, BA

History:
*C M Best, BA
C J Booth, LLB
J P Shafe, BA
Miss M Winn, BSc
R J Veal, MA

History of Art:
*Mrs B H Bond, BA
T E Goad, BA

Mathematics and Computing Faculty:
*E J Clark, BA
Computing:
*A H Roush, MSc
Mathematics:
Mrs N Armstrong, BA
C B Burgess, MA, MEng
J A Carle, BSc
Mrs C de Boulay, BA
M J Green, BEng
S S Gumbs, BSc
Mrs P A Peck, BSc
Mrs C Shaikh, CertEd
C R Stoneman, MA
N J Taylor, BSc
Mrs C van der Westhuizen, MSc
S N Whalley, BSc
H Williams, MMath
J A Wilson, MEng

Modern Languages Faculty:
*M M Etherington, BA
Mrs A M C Acton, BA
Mrs B Benito Lozano, BA
C A Carlier, MA
Mrs B E D'Cruz, MA (*Head of German*)
J C Hanbury, BA (*Head of French*)
Mrs E Hayes, MA
Mrs C Jones, BA
Mrs K L Parker, BA (*Head of Spanish*)
R Somma, BA (*Head of Italian*)
Mrs F J C Wall, BA
Mrs J J Walsh, BA

Performing Arts Faculty:
Dance:
Mrs M Hunkin
Drama:
*N J Saunders, BA
Miss L R Rees, BA
Ms R M Taylor, BA
Music:
N L Cole, BA
*Mrs V S Hughes, BA
J S Mountford, BA, ARCO

PE:
*D J Clark, BA
D J Mitchell, BSc
R P P Sanford, BSc
Miss H Shergold, BSc
T M Wood

Politics:
*S H Rees, BA, PhD
A R MacEwen, MA

Religion, Philosophy and Ethics:
*Mrs M Baynton-Perret, BD Dip
J P A Ball, MA
Mrs P M Donnelly, BA
Reverend Dr P M Hansell, PhD (*Chaplain*)
S P Williams, MA, MLitt

Science Faculty:
Dr D J Brooks, BSc, PhD
Biology:
*P J J Clegg, BSc
Ms E J Appleby, BSc
Mrs C Doherty, BSc

Dr K J Ogbe, BSc, PhD
Dr L S Vat, BSc
S D Whitehead, BSc
Chemistry:
*J A F Burnside, MChem, PhD
Dr D J Brooks, BSc, PhD
N M Burch, MSci
A J Hardwicke, BSc, MA
Dr L C Hutchins, PhD
S J Lunt, BA
A J Singh, BSc
Physics:
*T C O'Toole, BSc
C P Coghlan, BEng
Miss L Allen-Mirehouse, BEng
N C Sexton, BSc
Mrs N Shackell, BEng, MA [maternity leave]

Support and Study Skills:
*Dr K A Spaulding, PhD, MSc
Mrs S S Bunyan, BA
Mrs P Donnelly, BA
Mrs K E Howells, Cert SpLD
Dr L C Hutchins, BSc, PhD
Mrs G K Mabbett, BEd, Dip SpLD
Mrs I Smith, BEd, Dip SpLD
Mrs C Wright, BA, Dip SpLD

Well-being:
*Mrs V Rae, RGN
Mrs M Hunkin
L A Webb, BSc

Bradford Grammar School

Keighley Road, Bradford, West Yorkshire BD9 4JP
Tel: 01274 542492; Headmaster: 01274 553701
Fax: 01274 548129
email: admissions@bradfordgrammar.com
website: www.bradfordgrammar.com
Twitter: @BradfordGrammar
Facebook: /bradfordgrammarschool
LinkedIn: /bradfordgrammar

Motto: '*Hoc Age*'

With a heritage dating back to 1548, Bradford Grammar School (BGS) is one of the oldest and most respected institutions in Yorkshire. Our illustrious past spans hundreds of years. In 1662 Charles II granted BGS's Charter, a document that the school proudly displays. Having occupied three locations since our establishment, the iconic building that BGS inhabits today was opened in 1949. A long history of excellence inspires BGS pupils to fulfil their potential and make their own mark upon the future of BGS.

With a 'first-class, academic and outward-looking approach' (Good Schools Guide), BGS is one of the UK's leading independent schools, providing an 'outstanding education' (ISI 2012) for more than 1,051 girls and boys aged six to 18, as well as being ranked by 'The Daily Telegraph' as one of the UK's top ten value for money independent schools. The school is fully co-educational: girls have been admitted to the Sixth Form since 1984 and in all intakes from 1999.

BGS provides every opportunity for its Junior, Senior and Sixth Form pupils to embrace academic, sporting and creative excellence within an aspirational, caring environment in which happiness is the key to an individual's success. With its impressive 'value added' provision, academic excellence is available to all.

Pupil Numbers. 1,052 day pupils (603 boys, 449 girls). Junior School (6–11): 182 pupils (85 boys, 97 girls). Senior School (11–18): 870 pupils (518 boys, 352 girls).

Location and Facilities. The school, comprising six main buildings and a separate junior school building, stands in extensive grounds situated just a mile from Bradford city centre. The School thrives upon the opportunities created by this dynamic hub of enterprise and innovation. Location Direct trains to the School's own station in Frizinghall from Bradford, Skipton, Ilkley and Leeds and many dedicated bus routes make getting to the School straightforward for pupils across Yorkshire.

There are excellent transport links between the school and areas such as Wharfedale, Airedale, Leeds City Centre, Calderdale and Huddersfield.

Facilities include a 25m competition swimming pool, sports pavilion, all-weather sports pitch, squash and tennis courts, a dedicated Sixth Form centre with full wi-fi, the Hockney Theatre, Design Technology workshops, Computer Aided Design (CAD) suites, fitness suite with rowing machines, cycling machines, treadmills and weights, a music auditorium, recording studio, debating chamber, dedicated Science building and a new state-of-the-art Library, completed in 2015. The Price Hall is the centrepiece of the main school building and provides a magnificent setting for assemblies, concerts and other major events.

Bradford Grammar Junior School occupies Clock House, a seventeenth century Manor House within the school grounds, where it enjoys its own assembly hall, Computing and Design Technology facilities and teaching accommodation. *For further details, please see separate entry in IAPS section.*

Senior School Curriculum. In Years Seven and Eight all pupils study English, Mathematics, French, German, Latin, Biology, Physics, Chemistry, Geography, History, Art, Music, Design and Technology (DT), Religious Studies (RS), Personal Development and Games.

In Year Nine pupils follow a common core of English, Mathematics, Geography, History, Physics, Chemistry, Biology, RS, Personal Development and Games, choose one core Modern Foreign Language from a choice of French, German or Spanish and choose three optional subjects from a choice of German, Russian, Latin, Greek, Art, Music, Spanish and Computer Science.

In Years Ten and Eleven pupils follow ten GCSE courses. All pupils follow a common core of English Language, English Literature, Mathematics, Biology, Chemistry, Physics, and Games, choose a core Modern Foreign Language from French, German or Spanish, and choose three optional subjects from Geography, History, German, Computer Science, Russian, Latin, Spanish, Greek, Art, Music, DT and RS.

Year 12 (Lower Sixth Form). Pupils choose four AS Level subjects from Art, Biology, Business Studies, Chemistry, Classical Civilisation, DT, Economics, Electronics, English Literature, English Language, English Language and Literature, French, Further Mathematics, Geography, Geology, German, Greek, History, Computer Science, Latin, Mathematics, Music, Music Technology, Physics, Politics, Psychology, RS, Russian, Spanish and Theatre Studies. In addition, they also take two eleven-week General Studies courses from a wide range of non-examined options, or Japanese, AS Further Mathematics or the Extended Project Qualification (EPQ).

Year 13 (Upper Sixth Form). Pupils take three or four of their AS Level courses through to A Level. It is possible to replace the fourth subject with another AS course. Pupils may follow a non-examinable General Studies course if they wish.

For further details please see the booklets A Guide to GCSE Courses and A Guide to Sixth Form Courses both of which can be downloaded from our website at www.bradfordgrammar.com.

Results. A Level: Well over half of our A Level examinations were graded A* or A in 2016, allowing the vast majority of our students entry to their university of choice. We are very proud of how successfully and smoothly run our UCAS application process is at the School, with a comprehensive programme of incredibly important Higher Education events firmly embedded within Sixth Form life. Every year a good proportion of our students go on to study at Oxford or Cambridge.

GCSE: Our results at GCSE far exceed the national average. In 2016, we achieved a record-breaking 46% pass rate at grade A*.

Co-curricular Activities. We actively encourage pupils to engage in co-curricular activities. Pupils in the Senior School currently have a choice of over 50 clubs and societies covering a wide range of sports, drama, music, academic subjects and other areas of interest – from rowing and orienteering, to war games, debating and chess. Pupils can take part in The Duke of Edinburgh's Award scheme, the Combined Cadet Force (both RAF and Army) and World Challenge expeditions.

Pastoral Care. Outstanding pastoral support contributes to the happiness of Bradford Grammar School pupils, creating a positive, friendly atmosphere for all. The school works closely with parents to ensure each child receives the best possible pastoral care during their time at BGS. The team of form tutors, Heads of Year, school nurses, counsellors and Learning Support Department work together to promote pupils' happiness and progress. They ensure that every child receives the attention they deserve. Pupils who need extra help are quickly identified by our pastoral team, who work with a team of trained mentors from Year 13 to support each child as they make their way up the school.

Beyond the classroom BGS encourages pupils to participate in physical exercise and pursue a wide range of co-curricular interests with an extensive in-house counselling programme helping pupils to avoid and overcome problems.

Admission. Boys and girls can join the school at the ages of 6, 7, 8, 9, 10 in the Junior School or 11, 12, 13 or 16 in the Senior School. Pupils are admitted into the Sixth Form on the basis of their GCSE results (at least 20 points, grade B, preferably A, in sixth form subjects), an interview and a satisfactory reference from the candidate's current school. Candidates for entry into Year 2 (6+), Year 3 (7+) and Year 4 (8+) will be invited to spend an informal day in the Junior School. Admission for all other ages is by examination in Mathematics and English in January each year.

Bursaries. Bursaries are awarded on a means-tested basis, each case being reviewed annually. The award depends on parental circumstances, the amount of capital available at the time of the examination and the academic ability of the candidate.

Fees per term (2016–2017). Junior School £3,215, Senior School £4,107, Sixth Form £4,220.

Former Pupils include Olympic heroes Alistair and Jonathan Brownlee, Team GB cyclist Abby-Mae Parkinson, actress Georgie Henley, England rugby legend Charlie Hodgson and artist David Hockney.

Old Bradfordians Association. President: Mr K Wootton, c/o Bradford Grammar School.

The Parents' Association (previously BGS Society). Chairman: Mrs C Hanafin and Mrs L Bradley, c/o Bradford Grammar School.

Charitable status. Bradford Grammar School (The Free Grammar School of King Charles II at Bradford) is a Registered Charity, number 529113. It exists to provide education for children.

Corporate Trustee: Bradford Grammar School Trustee Limited

Governors:
Chairman: Lady L Morrison, LLB

Vice-Chairman: Professor C Mellors, BA, MA, PhD
President: A H Jerome, MA

Ex officio:
The Very Revd Canon J Lepine, BA, Dean of Bradford

Co-optative:
A Chang, BSc, FCMA, GCMA, MIIA
P Cogan, BA, FCA
Mrs A C Craig, DL, DCR
Ms V Davey, LLB
D J Davies, BEng, MA
S R Davies, BA, FRSA
Professor A Francis, BSc, AGGI, FBAM, CCMI, AcSS
Mrs C Hamilton-Stewart, MBE
His Honour Judge J A Lewis
I McAleese, FCIPD
P T Smith
C M Wontner-Smith, BA, FCA
Sir David Wootton, MA

Representative:
Professor S Congdon, BSc, MA, D Health, DipN, PGCert Ed
Professor Sir Alexander F Markham, BSc, PhD, MB BS, DSc, FRCP, FRCPath
Ms S Watson, MCIPR

Governors Emeriti:
J E Barker, DL, MA
P J M Bell, JP, FCIS, CText, FTI, FRSA
R G Bowers, DL, BSc, CEng, FRSA
I Crawford, FCA
Mrs J D Fenton, MCSP, SRP
J G Ridings, FCA

Bursar and Clerk to the Governors: I Findlay, BA, ACA

Headmaster: Dr S Hinchliffe, BA, MEd, PhD, FRSA

Deputy Head: L G d'Arcy, MChem

Pastoral Director: M J Chapman, MA
Academic Director: G P Woods, MA

Department Staff:
* Head of Department/Subject

Art:
*Ms J Barraclough, BA
Mrs S E Horsfield, BA
W Norman, BA
H R Thornton, BA

Biology:
*Mrs P M A Dunn, BSc
Mrs D J Chalashika, BSc
S R Hoath, BSc
Miss Z J Smeaton, BSc
K M Smith, BSc
S Thomas, BSc

Business Studies:
*D A Pullen, BSc
Ms S L Croudson, BSc

Chemistry:
*Dr D G Proctor, BSc, MSc, PhD
Mrs S J Flaherty, MA
Mrs G M Heywood, BSc
A B R Macnab, BSc
Dr D J Mouat, BSc, PhD
Mrs N S Nicholas, BSc

Classics:
*Dr K A Meakin, PhD, BA
M J A Barr, BA

T C Bateson, MA
Mrs M J Chapman, MA (*Pastoral Director*)

Design and Technology:
*S G Taylor, BSc
D Leake, BEd, MA
J I Richards, BA

Economics:
*R D Schofield, BA
M McCartney, BSc, MA

English and Drama:
*L W Hanson, BEd, MA
Miss S J Ball, BA (*Drama*)
Miss G D'Arcy, BA, MA
Miss L A Kirk, BA
Miss A M Lancelot, BA, MA
A N Mudd, BA
S D Rees, BA
Mrs C S Swailes, MA
R Thompson, MA
Miss E K Trafford, BA, MA

Geography:
*Mrs F R Handbury, BA
D G Alcock, MA
Miss A C Hicks, BA (*Asst Head Years 8 & 9*)
Dr S Hincliffe BA, MEd, PhD, FRSA (*Headmaster*)
A G Smith, BSc
H R Wong, BA

History:
*Mrs H J Baines, BA
Miss E A Greaves, BA
J Reed-Purvis, BA, MA (*Head of Sixth Form*)
M J Roberts, BA
Mrs K E Wilde, BA (*Head of Years 8 & 9*)

Computer Science:
*Mrs C M Harvey, BA, MA
T N Birkinshaw, BSc
M Cottrell, BA

Mathematics:
*D W Fishwick, BSc, PhD
A B Baines, BSc
A Crabtree, BSc
C Finch, BSc
Dr S Harris, MMath, PhD
P Merckx, BSc (*Head of Year 7*)
R I Page, BA, MSc
V Reynolds, BSc
M A Thompson, BSc (*Head of Years 10 & 11*)
P Watson, BSc, PhD

Modern Languages:
*Mrs S L Haslam, BA (*German*)
Ms M B Cuesta-González (*Spanish*)
Mrs E J Kingsley, BA, MSc (*French*)
Miss A M Corrigan, BA
S B Davis, MA, LTCL, MCIL (*Russian*)
Miss V Martí-Fernández, BA
Ms K Murach, MA
Mrs E Tomlinson, BA (*Asst Head Years 10 & 11*)
Mrs K E Whyte, BA
Mrs S Woodhead, BA
G P Woods, MA (*Academic Director*)

Music:
*E M White, BA
R McOwen, BSc
D G Roberts, LRAM, LGSM

Physics and Electronics:
*J D Boardman, BSc

Mrs L Leach, BA
R W Morley, BSc, MA
Miss V M Powne, BSc
Dr P Shepherd, BEng, PhD
O W J Theaker, MSc
I E Walker, MA (*Head of Careers*)

PE and Games:
*Mrs C A Taylor, BA
Miss D L Bloomfield, BA
Miss H E Boughton, BSc
S Darnbrough (*Rowing Coach*)
D J Dowley, BA
A J Galley, BEd
Mrs G K Jones, BEd
S Kellett (*Cricket & Rugby Coach*)
C E Linfield, BA
J G Oakes
D R Scarbrough, BSc
B Townsend (*Swimming Coach*)
M A Wilde, BA

Politics:
*M P J Simpson, MA, DipSp
Mrs A L McOwen, BA

Psychology:
*Ms C J White, BSc

Religious Studies:
*R E Skelton, BD
Ms M E Daniel, MA, MPhil
M E Harling, BSc, MA
Mrs B R Reeves, BA

The Junior School:
Headmaster: N H Gabriel, BA, DipArch
Deputy Head: Miss K L Howes, BSc, MSc

Mrs L L Alderson, BA
Mrs J S Allen, BSc
Mr C Brook
Mrs A Buckley
Mrs E J Green, BA
Mrs L A Hepworth-Wood, BA
Ms L N Marsden, BA
C P Newsome, BA (*Head of Sport*)
Mrs C E Orviss, LLB
Mrs E D Rawlinson, BA
P Smales, BEd, BA
G P Smith, BEd
Miss H E Smith, BA
Mrs P Tatham
Mrs N J Watson, BA
Mrs A J Watts, BA
Miss D H Yates, BA

Visiting Music Teachers:
Mrs J Bryan, GMus, CT ABRSM, LRSM (*Flute & Theory of Music*)
A C Cook, GLCM (*Guitar*)
S Davis, MA, LTCL (*Recorder*)
C Francis, GMus, LTCL (*Upper Strings*)
Mrs A F Hamilton, BMus (*Saxophone*)
Ms J Harrison, GRNCM (*Singing*)
Mrs E Kenwood-Herriott, GRSM, LRAM, LTCL (*Double-reed instruments*)
Ms S Laverick, BA (*Lower Strings*)
M McGuffie, BMus (*Clarinet*)
D G Roberts, LRAM, LGSM (*Brass*)
A J Sherlock, BA, ALCM (*Piano & Keyboard*)
B G Stevens, BA (*Percussion*)
A Woodrow, MA, FRCO, FTCL (*Chamber & Senior Choir*)

Brentwood School

Middleton Hall Lane, Brentwood, Essex CM15 8EE

Tel: 01277 243243
Fax: 01277 243299
email: headmaster@brentwood.essex.sch.uk
website: www.brentwoodschool.co.uk

Motto: *'Virtue, Learning and Manners'*.

Brentwood School was founded in 1557 and received its charter as the Grammar School of Antony Browne, Serjeant at Law, on 5th July, 1558. The Founder became Chief Justice of Common Pleas shortly before the death of Queen Mary, and was knighted a few months before his death in 1567. The Foundation Stone over the door of Old Big School was laid on 10th April, 1568, by Edmund Huddleston and his wife Dorothy, who was the step-daughter of the Founder. The Elizabethan silver seal of the School Corporation is still in the possession of the Governors. In 1622 Statutes were drawn up for the School by Sir Antony Browne, kinsman of the Founder, George Monteigne, Bishop of London, and John Donne, Dean of St Paul's.

Brentwood School is a co-educational school with a total of 1,539 pupils including 411 in the Preparatory School. The Preparatory School is fully co-educational as is the Sixth Form (of 291 pupils), but boys and girls are taught separately between the ages of 11 and 16. Boarding is available for boys and girls from 11.

Buildings and Grounds. The School occupies a 75-acre site on high ground at the northern end of the town some 20 miles north-east of London. Old Big School, the original School room, is still in regular use thus maintaining a direct link with the School's founder. Over recent years a major building programme has seen extensions to the Science and Modern Languages buildings and Dining Halls; refurbishment of the Preparatory School, Boarding Houses and Sixth Form accommodation; the building of the magnificent Brentwood School Sports Centre; a Performing Arts Centre, an all-weather pitch, an Art and Design Centre and an indoor heated swimming pool. In November 2011, HRH Prince Edward The Earl of Wessex formally opened the School's new Sixth Form Centre and Wessex Auditorium. The Sixth Form Centre, which has become the intellectual powerhouse of the School, provides an exemplary educational environment for the International Baccalaureate Diploma programme. Facilities include common rooms and private study areas, 16 additional classrooms, a dedicated computer suite and multi-purpose 400-seat auditorium. The award-winning Bean Academic Centre, the intellectual heart of the School, was opened to pupils at the end of March 2016. With large classroom spaces, a lecture theatre & café, it provides a state-of-the-art environment within which pupils can develop independent learning.

Organisation. The School is one community within which, for good educational reasons, girls and boys are taught separately from age 11 to 16. They are encouraged to participate together in all co-curricular activities. The Senior School is divided into Year Groups. Each Year Group has a Head of Year and Deputy who oversee it. The vast majority of pupils join the School at 11 after successfully completing our Entrance Examination. A broad curriculum is followed through the first three years and this continues through careful choice of GCSE and IGCSE subjects to the end of the Fifth Year. Entry to the Sixth Form is conditional upon success in the GCSE examinations. In the Sixth Form students take either four of the 27 AS Level subjects or follow the International Baccalaureate Diploma programme. Most go on to University. Pass rates at Advanced Level reach 100% and many pupils gain places at Oxford and Cambridge each year.

Religion. Although Brentwood is a Christian School, pupils and staff from all faiths, or none, are welcome. There is a resident Chaplain and pupils attend Chapel weekly. Regular Communion Services are held.

Boarding. There are two Boarding Houses, both of which have been thoroughly modernised. The boys reside in Hough House which can accommodate up to 42 students; the girls reside in Mill Hill House where 27 can be accommodated. The public rooms are spacious and both Houses generously staffed. Full and weekly boarding are available. A qualified Matron runs an efficient Sanatorium.

Pastoral Care. Brentwood School has an outstanding level of pastoral care which is provided by Heads of Year, Tutors and our Pastoral Team, ably supported by the delegated senior manager, Mrs Jenkin, and by all colleagues, who together create the enabling, supportive ethos. Tutors combine pastoral care with detailed academic monitoring, thus treating the whole person. Their encouragement to their pupils to participate in a wide range of activities successfully engenders greater self-confidence and self-awareness. In addition to Mrs Jenkin, Deputy Head (Pastoral), Heads of Year and Tutors, there are two pastoral managers.

Music, Drama and Art. Music plays an important part in the life of the School, as do Drama and Art. There are four orchestras and several ensembles and jazz groups. The Big Band is internationally acclaimed. There are at least three dramatic productions each year, together with regular Art Exhibitions.

Careers. There is an excellent University Entrance and Careers Department where students receive advice and can obtain information about courses and/or careers. Aptitude Tests; Work Experience; visits to colleges, universities and places of work; visiting speakers are all part of the provision. A careers convention is held in March each year.

CCF and CSU. All pupils either join the Combined Cadet Force or, through the Community Service Unit, engage in a wide-ranging series of activities which bring them into contact with the Community. The Duke of Edinburgh's Award scheme runs alongside these activities.

School Societies. There are many flourishing societies covering a wide range of interests, catering for all ages. The Sir Antony Browne Society (SABS) at Brentwood School is a society for Sixth Form students, which provides them with an opportunity for intellectual discussion and cultural interest.

Sports Facilities. Brentwood School was one of the official training venues for the London 2012 Games. The playing fields are part of the School complex and provide ample space for soccer, cricket, hockey, rugby and tennis. There is a world-class all-weather athletics track. The Brentwood School Sports Centre includes an indoor soccer/hockey pitch, six badminton courts, indoor cricket nets, basketball courts and a fencing salle, as well as squash courts and a fitness suite. There is a heated indoor swimming pool and an all-weather pitch. Provision is made for golf, sailing and table tennis. The two Astroturfs and netball courts are floodlit for use in winter

Preparatory School. *See entry in IAPS section for details.*

Entry. Entrance Examinations for both boys and girls aged 11 are held at the School in January each year. Entries are also accepted at 13 plus, following the Common Entrance Examination, vacancies permitting. Transfers at other ages are also possible. Sixth Form entry is through GCSE success, and interview.

Scholarships and Bursaries. In addition to Academic scholarships the School offers Music, Drama, Art, Sport and Choral scholarships at 11+ and for entry to the Sixth Form. These may be supplemented by means-tested Bursaries.

The School offers a considerable number of Bursaries in addition to the awards described above. Over a fifth of pupils receive such assistance.

Fees per term (2016–2017). Day £5,800; Boarding £11,378.

Old Brentwood's Society. There is a flourishing Society for pupils to stay in touch once they have left the School. The School's Alumni Relations Officer is Rachel Cleverley, email: CleverleyR@brentwood.essex.sch.uk.

Charitable status. Brentwood School (part of Sir Antony Browne's School Trust, Brentwood) is a Registered Charity, number 1153605. It is a Charitable Trust for the purpose of educating children.

Governors:
Sir Michael Snyder, DSc, FCA, FRSA [OB] (*Chairman*)
R I McLintock, MSc, DMS, DipEd (*Vice-Chairman*)
P C Beresford, FNAEA, MARLA
Lord Black of Brentwood, MA, MCIPR, FRSA [OB]
M Bolton, MBE, BA Hons
Miss A Chapman, ACMA
D J Elms, MA, FCA, FCSI
Professor B J W Evans, BSc Hons, PhD [OB]
Mrs J M Jones, BA Hons, ARCM
Lord Flight of Worcester, MA, MBA [OB]
The Venerable D Lowman, BD, AKC
Ms R Martin, MEd, NPQH
J M May, MA, LLB
Dr C Tout, MA, PhD
J Tumbridge, CC, MCIArb, LLB Hons

Bursar and Clerk to the Governors: I F Bruton, BA Hons, MIoD

Headmaster: D I Davies, MA Oxon, FRSA

Second Master: D M Taylor, GRSM, LRAM, FASC, FRSA
Deputy Head (Staff Development & Co-Curricular): J Cohen, BSc, MEd
Deputy Head (Pastoral): Mrs N Jenkin, BA, MA
Deputy Head (Academic): J Quartermain, BA, MA, MPhil

Heads of Year:
Sixth Form: Mrs A Lawes, BSc
Sixth Form, Head of Upper Sixth: S Prest, BA
Sixth Form, Head of Lower Sixth: Dr P Tiffen, BSc, PhD
Fifth Year: I Wignall, BA
Fourth Year: Mrs J. Khush, MSc
Third Year: Mrs M E Belsham, BSc
Second Year: C Potter, BA
First Year: Miss K Crane, BA

Houses & Housemasters/mistresses:
East: J McCann, BEng
Hough: P Rees, BA & Mrs C Rees
Mill Hill: M Monro, BA & Mrs J Monro
North: S Salisbury, BA
South: C M Long, BA
Weald: S Taylor, LLB
West: Mrs L Cleaves, BA

* *Head of Department*

Art:
*D McAuliffe, BA, MA
Miss N J Bixby, MA
Miss V Cooper, BA
Miss K Gellard, BA

Biology:
*G Lewis, MSc
Mrs R Bentley, BSc
Miss J P Byrne, BSc
J Davies, BA
Mrs P Ebden, BSc, MSc
Mrs H English, BSc
K Gray, BSc
Miss V Kerslake, BSc
Mrs G Robertson, BSc [OB]
Ms S St Clair Jones, BA
Dr P Tiffen, BSc, PhD

Business Studies:
*Miss M Sorohan, BA, MA
A Giles, BA
C A Graves, BSc
Mrs K Miller, BA

Chemistry:
*D Endlar, MChem
L Brookes, BSc
S L Gonsalves, BSc
Mrs J Khush, MSc
Revd Dr A McConnaughie, BA, MA, PhD, BA
R O'Rourke, BSc
A Pask, BSc
G Pye, BSc
I Roslan, MChem
J Seaman, BSc, MSc, CChem, MRSC

Classics:
*Mr B Clark, BA
Miss K L Crane, BA [OB]
Miss Z Fleming, MA
Mrs J Gray, BA
D Hodgkinson, BA
Miss C Martin, BA [OB]
Miss F Moore-Bridger, BA
B Roberts, MA
Miss H Summerfield, BA
Miss C Tsaknaki, BA, MSt

Computing & ICT:
*J J McCann, BEng Hons
Miss I Lovelock, BA
Miss Victoria Millson, MSci
Mrs K Rajani, BSc

Design & Technology:
*A R Eckton, BSc Hons
Ms S Champion, BSc
D Murphy, BEd
M Lewis, BEd
T Walland, BA

Drama:
*M Bulmer, BA, MA
Miss M Choate, BA, MA
Mrs L Cleaves, BA
Miss F Passmore, BA
Miss R Worth, MA, BA

Economics:
*A Dean, BSc, MA
N J Carr, MA, MA EconEd, ACEM, FRSA
J Cohen, BSc, MEd
C A Graves, BSc
P Rees, BA
C Wakeling, BSc

English:
*Dr S Evans, BA, PhD
Mrs H Barker, BA
Miss S Browett, BSc
M Bulmer, BA
Ms R Coates, BA
Mrs M Callender, MA
Miss M Choate, BA, MA
R Higgins, BA, MA
R Irvine, BA
Ms P Maxwell, BA
O Murley, BA Hons
Miss F Passmore, BA
S Salisbury, BA Hons
S Taylor, LLB
C Wayne

EAL:
*C Berkley, BA

Food & Nutrition:
*Mrs C Picton, BEd
Mrs B Daly, BEd

Mrs J Franklin, BSc

Geography:
*Dr M Shepherd, PhD
Miss G Athey, BSc, MSc
Mrs R Barford, BSc, MTeach
Mrs S Davis, BSc
J Harrod, BA, MA
C M Long, BA

History:
*Ms B Fuller, BA
Mrs M E Belsham, BSc
C Berkley, BA
M Clark, BA
Mrs R Coppell, MA
Dr C Harvey, BA, PhD
J Quartermain, BA, MA, MPhil
Mrs S Sharpe, BA
M V Willis, BA

Learning Development:
*Mrs K Gorsuch, BSc
Mrs L Buck
Ms S Champion, BSc
Mrs F Quartermain, BA, MA

Mathematics:
*T Beedell, BSc, MA
T Acton, BSc
A Barnett, BSc
Dr J Benavides, PhD
P Bolton, BSc
Mrs K Bowes, BSc
L Brookes, BSc
Mrs J J Coppin, BSc, MSc
A J Drake, MA
Miss J Farrow, BSc
Prof L Hubbard BSc, PhD, BA, MSc
Miss F Hyde, BEng
Mrs A Lawes, BA
M Lewis, BSc
G J Little, MA
Ms D Porovic, MSc
Miss E Preston, BSc
Miss L Ramshaw
C Wakeling, BSc
Ms L Ward, BSc
J D Williams, BSc

Modern Languages:
*I Walton, MA (*German)
Dr E Rowlands, BA, PhD (*French)
Mr G Smith, BA, MA (*Spanish)
Mrs J Rodgers, MSc (*Mandarin)
Mrs M D Taylor, BA (*Italian)
Miss K Allen, BA
J Bowley, MA, Maîtrise, MIL, FCIEA, FRSA
Miss R Campbell, BA
Mrs L G M Dearmer-Decup, BA
Miss A Folwell, BA
Mrs N Jenkin, BA, MA
Miss C Lacotte, DEUG, BA

Mrs M Morris, BA, MA
Mrs I Penalver-Edwards, BA
R Pritchard, BA
Mrs S J Roast, BEd
Dr R M Storey, BA, PhD
Mrs A Wall, BA
Mrs M Watts-Jimenez, BA

Music:
Director of Music: Mrs H Khoo, GRSM, ARCM, Dip RCM
F Cooper, BA [OB]
W Stock, BMus

Physics:
*R Jukes, MA
M Abbott, BSc
G Davies, PhD
J Davies, BA
Prof L Hubbard, BSc, MSc, PhD, BA
L C Jenkins, MSc, FRAS
R O'Rourke, BSc
L Pollock, BSc
Ms L Ward, BSc

Physical Education & Games:
*I Wignall, BA
W Bigley, BA
Miss J Bryan, BSc (*Hockey*)
W Castleman (*Rugby*)
Miss J Farrow, BSc (*Academic*)
C Galesloot, FIE (*Fencing*)

Director of IB: J Barfield, MA
Admissions Registrar: Mrs S Hilton
Headmaster's PA: Mrs S Gilder
School Medical Officer: Dr Nasif

Miss K Herterich, ISTD (*Dance*)
G Jones MBE (*Cricket*)
Mrs W L Juniper, BEd
D Keszler
Mrs S Knightbridge, BSc
C M Long, BA (*Golf & Squash*)
Mrs C Melvin (*Swimming & Water Polo*)
M Miller, BSc (*Football*)
S Salisbury, BA (*Cricket*)
Miss J Saunders, BEd (*Netball, Rounders & Tennis*)
Miss A Simpson, BSc
J Williams

Politics:
*M V Willis, BA
Mrs R Coppell, MA
Dr C Harvey, BA, PhD

Psychology:
*Dr T Elder, BSc, PhD
Mrs L Cane, BSc, MSc
Mrs S Knightbridge, BSc
Mrs A Morris, BSc
Mrs J O'Connell, BSc

Religious Studies:
*B Clements, BA, MPhil, DipRSA
J Barfield, MA
Miss R Bishop, BA
R Jenkins, BA
M Monro, BA, AKA
C Potter, BA

Brighton College

Eastern Road, Brighton BN2 0AL

Tel: 01273 704200
          01273 704339 Head Master
          01273 704260 Bursar
          01273 704210 Prep School
          01273 704259 Pre-Prep School
Fax: 01273 704204
email: admissions@brightoncollege.net
website: www.brightoncollege.org.uk
Twitter: @BrightonCollege
Facebook: @BrightonCollegeUK

Motto: TO Δ'EY NIKATΩ (*Let the right prevail*)

The first of the Sussex public schools, Brighton College was founded in 1845. The school is located in the heart of Kemptown, Brighton, and has an historic front quadrangle with Grade II listed buildings. Over the last 10 years, there has been an ambitious building development plan focusing on the northern part of the campus, including teaching, social and boarding spaces. A new 20-classroom teaching building designed by Hopkins Architects will open in 2017. Construction will start next year on a new state-of-the-art £55 million sports and science centre designed by Dutch firm OMA.

Brighton College is a place of world-class academic excellence, not least because of an abundance of inspirational teaching. The College regularly achieves the best GCSE and A Level results in Sussex. In 2016, Brighton was placed 15th in The Sunday Times' annual survey of schools' academic performance. 39 pupils gained offers from Oxford and Cambridge in January 2016. In 2016, 92% of GCSE grades were A*/A, while 97.1% of A Level grades were A*–B (79.9% A*–A).

Brighton's reputation for innovation centres around ground-breaking developments in the curriculum, pastoral care and facilities. In 2006 Brighton was the first school in the UK to introduce compulsory Mandarin for all new pupils. Ten years later, Brighton became the first school to scrap traditional uniform rules to accommodate transgender pupils. Humanities are taught in the innovative 'Story of Our Land' course in the Third Form, which uses the framework of British history to explore geographical, philosophical and religious themes. In 2010, the College introduced a tailor-made course in entrepreneurship for all members of the Lower Sixth. All sixth formers also take a pioneering history and international politics course ('Our Island Story').

The school has been the recipient of many awards: named 'United Kingdom Independent School of the Year 2013–14' at the Independent School Awards, and Head Master Richard Cairns was named 'Public School Headmaster of the Year 2012–13' by Tatler magazine.

The principles of kindness and tolerance underpin Brighton's ethos. For ten years, pupils have worn wristbands that say 'Today's random act of kindness?', and the Head Master regularly asks pupils in assemblies how they have demonstrated kindness recently. Brighton pupils take a full and active role within the local community, with initiatives such as Respect Week, Make a Difference Day, and many others. Every year, pupils travel with teachers to Sri Lanka and to Ghana to volunteer in communities that the College has strong links with. In the 2015–16 academic year, pupils raised £53,000 for charity.

The College encourages pupils to seize opportunities and push boundaries: girls can (and do) become international cricketers, and boys become dancers who perform at Sadler's Wells. There is a wealth of extracurricular activities on offer, in particular sport, music and the performing arts.

The College became fully co-educational in 1988. There are now some 995 pupils, of whom a third are boarders. Pupils are divided into 13 houses.

In 2015, the Independent Schools Inspectorate gave Brighton College, and its Prep and Pre-Prep schools, the highest possible grade across every single inspection category, with a rare 'Exceptional' for Achievement and Learning.

Buildings. The College is situated in the Kemptown district of Brighton. The original north range and Headmaster's House were designed by Gilbert Scott in 1847. The Chapel was added in 1858 and extended in 1923 as a memorial to the Old Brightonians who gave their lives in the First World War. In 2016, the College installed a bronze memorial statue outside the Chapel to remember the men and boys of the College who died in the Great War. The south and west range of boarding houses was completed to a design by Sir Thomas Jackson (an Old Brightonian) in 1886.

An extensive programme of development is currently taking place which has seen many of the new builds win architectural awards. In 2010 the Skidelsky Building opened – home to the Lower School, a Design Technology suite and six classrooms – and the Simon Smith Building opened in 2012, providing a new social hub and café for pupils, medical centre and outdoor theatre space. Both buildings were awarded RIBA's South East regional award for outstanding architecture. In 2012 the new sports pavilion at the College's Jubilee Ground opened, and in 2013 a fifth boarding accommodation, New House, opened to meet the growing demand for boarding. New House was also awarded RIBA's South East regional award for outstanding architecture. In 2014 the new Cairns Tower (part of Sir Thomas Graham Jackson's original plans) was completed and awarded a Sussex Heritage Trust award, and in 2015 the new Music School opened, home to state-of-the-art recording facilities and a 150-seat recital hall.

Admission. Pupils are admitted to the Lower Third at the age of 11 via assessments held at the College in January; to the Fourth Form between the ages of 13 and 14 via the Common Entrance examination, the Academic Scholarship examination, or by special assessment and interview; and into the Sixth Form for A Levels between the ages of 16 and 17, subject to a minimum of 14 points at GCSE (based on three points for an A* grade, two points for an A grade and one point for a B grade) and ideally an A grade in each subject to be studied at A Level. In all cases pupils must also produce evidence of good character and conduct from their previous school. The College prospectus and registration form can be obtained from the Director of Admissions. A non-refundable registration fee of £120 is payable.

Entry for new Lower Third, Fourth Form and Sixth Form pupils is at the beginning of the Michaelmas Term.

Houses. Hampden, Leconfield, Aldrich, Durnford, Ryle, Chichester, Williams and Seldon are day houses, each with their own premises. Head's House, School House, New House, Abraham and Fenwick are boarding houses. An extensive refurbishment programme by top London designers is nearing completion across the day and boarding houses. A third of the pupils are boarders in the school and weekly boarding is increasingly popular, giving pupils the opportunity to go home on Friday afternoon and return either on Sunday evening or Monday morning.

Health. There is a Central Health Centre with a team of qualified nurses, and the Medical Officer visits regularly.

Catering. There is self-service dining room, managed by a qualified Catering Manager.

Holidays. The usual school holidays are about 3 weeks each at Christmas and Easter, and 8 weeks in the Summer. There is a half-term holiday of 1 week in all three terms.

Religion. A short morning service is held in Chapel on 2 days a week. Friday's service aims to embrace all faiths. There are services for all pupils on some Sundays to which parents and visitors are welcome. Candidates are prepared by the Chaplain for Confirmation.

Curriculum. The School is divided into 7 forms: Lower Third, Upper Third, Fourth, Lower Fifth, Upper Fifth, Lower Sixth and Upper Sixth. In the Sixth Form some 26 subjects are available at A Level. For GCSE, pupils select their subjects – usually 10 – at the end of the Fourth Form. 99% of pupils proceed to university. Preparation for the UCAS process begins in the second term of the Lower Sixth, and pupils are guided towards appropriate choices by the Head of Sixth Form in conjunction with the individual pupil's tutor.

Sport. The College enjoys a strong record of excellence at most sports. The main playing field (the Home Ground) is part of the College campus and the Jubilee Ground is a mile away at East Brighton Park. All pupils take part in the College's extensive games programme. The main sports for boys are rugby and cricket and for girls, netball, hockey and cricket. In addition, a host of other options are available including football, squash, tennis, golf, beach volleyball, aerobics, rounders, yoga, athletics and cross country.

Service. All pupils from the Lower Fifth onwards are expected to participate in a service activity on one afternoon a week. Pupils may participate in charity work or, in the Sixth Form, Community Service; alternatively they may join The Duke of Edinburgh's Award scheme or enter one of the three sections of the CCF.

Music. There is a strong musical tradition and pupils reach a very high level of performance. The Choir, Chamber Orchestra, Symphony Orchestra, Concert Band and Swing Band perform regularly both inside and outside the College. There are several Chamber groups, and the Choral Society and Orchestra usually perform major works at the annual Brighton Festival.

Drama. The College has a strong tradition of excellence in drama. There are opportunities for anyone to be involved and the College stages plays ranging from Tudor Interludes through Shakespeare, Restoration comedy and twentieth century classics. In addition to the regular calendar of a musical, Sixth Form studio production, Sixth Form play, Fourth Form play, Lower School play and House Drama festival, there are also many productions mounted entirely by pupils.

Activities. Creative activities are encouraged both in and out of school time, and the College has its own Art School and Gallery. Dance is a very popular activity with many pupils performing in regional and national productions.

Careers. Ms Olivia Upchurch heads a team of tutors who advise pupils on careers. The College is a member of the Independent Schools Careers Organisation.

Scholarships and Bursaries. The following awards are offered annually:

Academic Scholarships to pupils entering the College at age 11 and 13. Entries must be in by early January for 11+ and late February for 13+.

A number of scholarships and exhibitions will be offered each year to candidates showing outstanding ability in art, chess, choral, dance, drama, DT, music and sport. Examinations and interviews will be held at the College in January (art, choral, dance and music), February (chess and sport), April (drama and DT) for candidates intending to enter the College at 13+ in the following September. The value and number of the awards will depend on the calibre of the candidates.

All-Rounder Scholarships are available for entry at 11+ and 13+. Examinations and interviews will be held at the College in January (11+) and March (13+) for candidates intending to enter the College the following September. The value and number of the awards will depend on the calibre of the candidates.

Sixth Form entry Scholarships: All candidates sit a general paper, maths and English papers, a verbal reasoning or EAL paper, and attend two interviews. The results of these are considered for candidates who are applying for an Academic Scholarship. Scholarships are also available for sport and expressive arts (art, dance, drama, DT and music). All examinations take place mid-November.

The *Old Brightonian Bursary*, worth £1,000 per term, is available to a child or grandchild of an Old Brightonian who might otherwise be unable to afford independent education.

Further particulars can be obtained from the Director of Admissions.

Fees per term (2016–2017). Weekly Boarding: £10,430 (4th Form) to £10,750 (Upper 6th). Full Boarding: £11,710 (4th Form EU) to £13,530 (Upper 6th Non-EU). Day: £5,260 (Lower 3rd) to £7,600 (Upper 6th).

The Old Brightonians, the College's alumni network, has annual dinners and a number of flourishing sports clubs.

Preparatory School. The College has its own fully co-educational Prep School and a Pre-Preparatory School. (*For details see entry in IAPS section.*)

Charitable status. Brighton College is a Registered Charity, number 307061. It exists for the purpose of educating boys and girls.

Vice-Presidents:

The Rt Hon Sir John Chilcot	S J Cockburn
	R F Jones

Mrs J Lovegrove
D A Nelson-Smith
R J Seabrook, QC

S G R Smith
Lady H Trafford, DSc, SRN
I White

Chairman: Prof Lord Skidelsky, FBA

Governors:

N Abraham, CBE
Ms M Asmar, LLB
Mrs J Aisbitt, JP
Lady M Alexander
A Cayley, CMG QC, LLB, LLM
Ms J Deslandes, BEd, MA
P Jackson, FSA, MA Oxon
Rt Hon Lord Maude of Horsham
G R Miller, MBE, FCIB

Lord J Mogg, KCMG
A S Pettitt
R Ricci
Ms E Savage, BA Hons
C E M Snell, IAPS, Dip Ed
A J Symonds, FRICS, MCI Ard
M Templeton, MA
P Ward, BEd Hons
R J S Weir, FCA, BA Cantab

Senior Management Team:

Head Master: Mr R J Cairns, MA, FRSA

Director of Finance & Deputy Head (Bursar): Mr P Westbrook, BA, FCA
Deputy Head: Mr A R Bird, MA, MSc
Deputy Head: Mr N J Fraser, MA
Deputy Head: Mr S Marshall-Taylor, BA
Deputy Headmistress: Mrs J A Riley, MA
Deputy Headmistress: Miss L Hamblett, MA
Headmaster of Lower School: Mr G R Owton, BA
Assistant Head (Sixth Form): Mr A T Patton, MA
Assistant Head (Middle School): Mr M C Sloan, BA
Assistant Head (Co-Curriculum): Miss N J Collins, MA
Assistant Head (Director of Social Responsibility): Mr K A Grocott, MA
Director of Studies: Mr J Carr-Hill, MSc
Director of Boarding: Mrs J Hamblett-Jahn, LLB (*Housemistress, Fenwick*)
Registrar: Mrs A Withers
Director of Philanthropy: Mr S Sheridan, BA
Director of Schools, BCIS: Mr I McIntyre, MA

Heads of Department/Subject:

Director of Art: Mr R A Cuerdon, MA
Biology: Dr B N Davies, PhD
Business Studies: Mrs S A Woodmansey, DMS, MBA
Chemistry: Dr G Mancino, PhD
Classics: Mr J T Connor, BA
Director of Curriculum: Mr C Bainbridge, BA
Director of Dance: Mrs M L Porter, BA, AISTD Dip
Director of Pupil Engagement: Mr M V Lewis, BSc
Director of University Applications: Mr J Majithia, BA
Design Technology: Mr S J Harvey, MSc
EAL: Mrs J Dynes, BA
Economics: Mr C C Chong, MA
English: Miss A C Smith, MA
French: Miss C Wright, BA
Geography: Mr J R Partridge, BA
German: Mrs F M Cremona, BA
History: Mr J A M Skeaping, BA
Director of ICT: Mr R Ruz, MSc
Academic ICT: Mr B L Lambe, BSc
Director of Learning Support: Mrs S J Walker, BEng
Mandarin: Mr R Garvey, MA
Mathematics: Mr G A Brocklesby, BA
Director of Music: Mr T H Wiggall, MA
Academic PE: Mr S D Lilley, BSc
Physics: Dr A Baragwanath, PhD
Politics: Mr R I Maggs, MEd
Psychology: Mr C T Morrissey, MA
Religion & Philosophy: Mr P Sperring, MPhil
Russian: Mr B Savage, BA

Spanish: Mr R C Alvers, BA
Acting Director of Sport: Mr N Buoy, BSc
Theatre Studies: Mr J J Green, BA

House Masters and Mistresses:
Abraham: Mr P A Wilson
Aldrich: Mr C J Webster
Chichester: Ms E T M J Cody
Durnford: Mr J A Cornish
Fenwick: Mrs J Hamblett-Jahn
Hampden: Mr B M Frier
Head's: Mr R J Grice
Leconfield: Mr A J Merrett
New House: Miss K A Jones
Ryle: Mr G D Kennedy
School: Mr B A Savage
Seldon: Miss C L Davison
Williams: Ms S E Sturgeon
Lower School: Mrs K M Brown

Tutor for Admissions: Mrs A Hanna
Senior Librarian: Mrs D McCullough
Head of Careers: Ms O Upchurch, BA
Chaplain: Revd R Easton, BA, MTheol

Bristol Grammar School

University Road, Bristol BS8 1SR

Tel: 0117 973 6006
Fax: 0117 946 7485
email: headmaster@bgs.bristol.sch.uk
website: www.bristolgrammarschool.co.uk

Motto: '*Ex Spinis Uvas.*'

'The Grammar School in Bristowe' existed under a lay master in 1532 in which year, under a charter of Henry VIII, it was endowed with the estates of St Bartholomew's Hospital by the merchant and geographer Robert Thorne and others. The trust was placed in the care of the Corporation of Bristol and then the Trustees of the Bristol Municipal Charities. In September 2004 the School incorporated as a company limited by guarantee with registered charitable status and is now governed under Memorandum and Articles of Association approved by the Charity Commission in 2004.

Co-educational since 1980, Bristol Grammar School is a day school providing a wide-ranging and challenging education for c.1000 boys and girls aged between 11 and 18, while BGS Infants and Juniors, based on the same site, caters for those in the 4–11 age range.

"… *excellence in all it does within and beyond the classroom* …" ISI Inspection Report, October 2015.

Students learn in an atmosphere that motivates them to enjoy their education and as a result BGS has a deserved reputation as one of the leading academic schools in the South West. The School has a friendly and lively environment and students are encouraged to make the most of the wide-ranging opportunities available to them. Students joining at age 11 have their form rooms in the Princess Anne Building. This helps ease the transition to senior school, as well as providing an important opportunity for the year group to bond socially. This continues up the School with each year group allocated form rooms, based in separate, self-contained buildings, although teaching is spread throughout the School's specialist facilities.

Close to the city centre and adjacent to the University, Bristol Grammar School is well placed to take advantage of the city's many amenities. It is also committed to a continuing programme of investment to ensure its own facilities continue to offer the best possible opportunities to its students.

The Houses. The School is divided into six Houses, each organised by a Head of House, with the assistance of a Deputy Head of House and House Tutors. Older students become leaders within their House, whilst social, theatrical, musical, sporting and other opportunities allow those from all year-groups to work together in a friendly and cooperative atmosphere. As well as providing continuity of pastoral care and enhancing school/home links, the Houses operate as families within the school community, encouraging a real sense of belonging amongst students.

Curriculum. The school takes note of the National Curriculum but, in keeping with its academic ethos and focus on every learner being enabled to make the most of their individual ability, a far wider range of subjects and opportunities is offered. Setting is used in Maths, Science and some Modern and Classical languages to ensure optimal individual progress, but there is no streaming. In Year 7 all students follow a curriculum which includes English, Mathematics, Science, French, Spanish, History, Geography, Technology, Food & Nutrition, ICT, Latin, Religious Studies, Art, Textiles, Music, Drama, Dance and Physical Education. In Year 8 the core curriculum is continued but students are offered a further choice of languages to include German and Russian. In Year 9 students personalise their curriculum and make choices from all subjects studied thus far and other areas such as Classical Civilisation, Greek, Business Studies and Computing. From this broad base students choose their GCSE options. At the end of Year 11, most students take 11 GCSEs drawn from the core subjects of English, Mathematics, Biology, Chemistry, Physics, a Humanities subject and a Modern Language, together with a selection of other subjects, chosen from a carefully balanced range of options.

BGS currently offers the IGCSE in Mathematics, English Language, English Literature, the Sciences, Geography, History, French, German, Spanish, Business Studies and Food & Nutrition. The Sixth Form provides a flexible range of A Level options chosen from English (Language and Literature), Mathematics and Further Mathematics, the Sciences, Technology, French, German, Russian, Spanish, Latin, Greek, Classical Civilisation, History, Geography, Economics, Business Studies, Computing, ICT, Psychology, Philosophy and Theology, Theatre Studies, Sports Studies, Art (including Theatre Design), and Music. In addition, many students prepare for the Extended Project Qualification and Gold Duke of Edinburgh's Award; all students follow enrichment courses and attend a richly diverse programme of weekly lectures by visiting speakers; and many students enrichment lessons to support university preparation for Russell Group and Oxbridge and including such as Medicine, Veterinary Science and Law. A highly-experienced careers and HE advisor guides students to proceed to a wide range of faculties at universities in the UK and abroad, with the majority securing places at their first-choice universities.

There are frequent opportunities for parents to consult Form Tutors, Heads of Houses and Heads of Year and regular meetings are held for parents to meet the teaching staff. The School also has three teachers to support students with SEN (including dyslexia and EAL).

Games. The games options, which vary with different age groups, include Rugby, Hockey, Football, Cross-Country, Cricket, Athletics, Swimming, Golf, Tennis, Rounders, Netball and weight training. Facilities for Orienteering, Aerobics, Climbing, Dance, Judo, Fencing, Badminton and Squash are available. There is a Pavilion and extensive playing fields at Failand, which include an all-weather netball and Tennis area and two Astroturf hockey pitches. Below the Sixth Form, all students, unless excused for medical reasons, participate in School games; the full range of sports is available to the Sixth Form on a voluntary basis. Major sports tours are run on a three year cycle: recent destinations have been New Zealand, South America and South Africa.

Activities and Societies. Students take part in a wide-ranging programme of activities (for some years this forms part of the compulsory curriculum) and there are many clubs and societies at lunchtimes and after school. There are flourishing choirs and orchestras; tuition can be arranged in a large number of instruments. Drama productions are regularly staged by different age levels of the School and by the Houses. Ski trips are offered each year. Regular excursions are made abroad, as well as cultural exchange visits, including Japan and Russia. Students may join The Duke of Edinburgh's Award scheme in Year 10 and there is an active Community Service Unit.

Admission. Entry to the School is normally in September at age 11+ following a satisfactory performance in the entrance examination held in the previous spring and a creditable school report or reference. In addition, all applicants are invited in to meet with a member of staff to discuss their school work, interests and hobbies. An additional 10–15 places become available each year at age 13+, with a further 30–40 places at 16+. Students may be accepted into the school during any term subject to the availability of places.

Applications should be made to the Admissions Office at the School. Prospective entrants and their families are always welcome to visit the School. Please see the website for information about Open Days, Tours and Taster Days.

Bursaries. The School's Assisted Places Scheme is able to offer substantial financial assistance towards the fees of able students whose parents have limited means. The scheme is kept under regular review by the Governors who constantly seek to extend it.

Scholarships. Scholarships are available for entry at 11+ and 13+ and are awarded for academic ability; all applicants who sit the entrance examinations in January are automatically considered for these, there is no separate exam. Mathematics and Science Pople Scholarships are available at 14+ and 16+ and there is a separate exam for these. Scholarships are also available at 11+, 13+ and 16+ for Sports and Creative and Performing Arts.

The School runs a Scholars Programme designed to meet the educational needs of its most gifted students. This programme offers extended individual learning opportunities, group activities and mentoring in and out of School by the Director of Scholars. At 16+ students may apply to become Subject Scholars and work more closely with Heads of Subject.

Fees per term (2016–2017). Senior School £4,620. Juniors: Years 3–6 £3,150. Infants: Years 1 & 2 £2,930, Reception £2,590. Fees include the cost of most textbooks and stationery and lunch for Reception to Year 11 pupils.

BGS Infants and Juniors. The Junior School extended its provision to include infants, with its first Reception class in Sept 2010. The School admits children from 4–11 and is housed in its own buildings on the same site as the Senior School. (*For further details see entry in IAPS section.*)

Old Bristolians Society. Close contact is maintained with former students through the Old Bristolians Society whose honorary secretary can be contacted at the School.

Charitable status. Bristol Grammar School is a Registered Charity, number 1104425. It has existed since 1532 to provide an education for Bristol children.

Governors:
Mrs A J Arlidge, BA
Mr A Barr, LLB
Mrs B Bates, BA, MA, FRSA
Ms M Crayton, BA, MCIM
N Dawes, BSc Hons
N Fitzpatrick, BA, FIA, AllMR, FRSA
Dr J D Knox, BSc, PhD
W Lee, MA, MBA, FIA
P Meehan, BEd, FPFS
Dr J O'Gallagher, MBChB, MRCP, FRCPCH, FHEA

D Pester, BA Hons
N Pickersgill, BSc, FCA
N Reeve, FCA, CF
Dr J Selwyn, BA, MSc, PhD
D Shelton, FCIM
J Sisman, BSc, MRICS
R Vaitilingam, BA Hons Oxon, MBE (*Chairman*)
M Wilson, BSc Hons, MRICS

Senior Leadership Team:

Headmaster: R I MacKinnon, BSc

Headmaster, BGS Infants and Juniors: P R Huckle, BA, MEd
Deputy Head: P R Roberts, BSc, MSc
Deputy Head: M J Bennett, BSc
Deputy Head: Miss F A Ripley, BSc
Deputy Head: D J Stone, BSc
Bursar: G Mitchell, BA

Assistant Head: G Clark, BSc
Assistant Head: P Z Jakobek, BEd
Assistant Head: Dr A J Dimberline, BSc, PhD
Assistant Head: R M Sellers, BSc
Assistant Head: B Schober, BSc, MA
Assistant Head: Dr M G Ransome, BA, PhD
Assistant Head: J S Harford, BSc
Assistant Head: Mrs K Jones, BSc
Assistant Head: O L Chambers, BSc

* *Head of Department*

Art:
Mrs B D Barnacle, BA
Mrs S Cooper, BA
Miss D Davies, BA
P Z Jakobek, BEd
*J Lever, MA
Mrs J Troup, BA

Biology:
A Bolton, BA
Mrs R Cullen, BSc
Ms N A Diamond, BSc
   (*Head of House*)
N S Fuller, BSc, MSc, CBiol, MIBiol
*A J Goodland, BSc
J S Harford, BSc (*Director of Sixth Form*)
B Schober, MA, BSc
Ms K Surry, MA

Careers:
Miss A Humphrey, BA
Mrs D Dutton, MA

Chemistry:
T Carpenter, BSc
Mrs A Hutchings, BSc
   (*Head of SPD*)
Miss C Keevil, BSc
Dr J Macro BA, MA
A Nalty, MSc
Miss S Ricketts, MSci
Dr H Rowlands, BSc, PhD
D J Stone, BSc
*Dr J Stone, BSc, PhD

Classics:
Miss E Cox, BA
*A J Keen, BA
G C King, MA, BA
Mrs L Ray, BA
D Watkins, BA

Dance:
*Mrs K White, BA
Miss L Sampson, BA

Design & Technology:
M Hilliard, BSc (*Head of House*)
Ms L-J Knights, BA
Mrs S Muirhead, BSc
P Thomas, BA
*P M Whitehouse, BSc

Drama:
L MacKenzie, BA
Mrs C Moulds, BA
*Mrs J Walker, BA

Economics/Business Studies:
Mrs S Biggin, BA
Mrs J Carter, BA
A J Catchpole, BSc (*Head of House*)
*J Williams, BSc

English:
*D L Briggs, BA
A J Jamison, BA
Mrs C V Maddock, BA, MEd
D S Mair, BA
Ms S Robinson, BA
Miss S Thomas, MA
Mrs S Vickery, BA
Mrs J Whitehead, BAMs
E Yemenakis, BA
Mrs E Young, BA

EPQ:
*Mrs R Atkins, BSc

Food & Nutrition:
*Mrs L Bolton, Cert Ed Food & Nutrition

Geography:
Mrs R Atkins, BSc
Miss K Brimming, BSc
Dr A J Dimberline, BSc, PhD
* L Goodman, BA
A J Short, BSc (*Head of House*)
Miss A Strutt, BSc

History:
Ms S Bassett, BA
Mrs E Clare, BA
O R T Edwards, BA (*Head of House*)
N W Haines, BA, MA
*R Hambley, BA, MA
Miss A Humphrey, BA
Mrs P Lobo, BA
Dr R A Massey, BA, PhD
   (*Director of Scholars and Academic Challenge*)

Information Technology/ Computing:
*Mrs A Finney, BA
R S Jones, BSc
I Jones, BSc

Learning Support:
Mrs J Benn
Mrs A Denny, MA
*Dr M G Ransome, BA, PhD

Mathematics:
C Armstrong, BSc
J Carr, BSc
O L Chambers, BSc
B Fellows, MEng
Mrs L Hancock, BSc
G R Iwi, MSc
Mrs K H Jones, BSc
Miss H Klimach, MSc
Miss A Niamir, BSc
*Miss S M Poole, BSc
P R Roberts, BSc, MSc
A Thackray, BSc
Miss J Wall, BSc

Modern Languages:
*Miss E Corrigan, BA
   (*Head of French*)
*R J Hawkins, BA (*Head of Russian*)

PA to Headmaster: Miss C Davies

Miss C M Höelzer, MA
Mrs C Kent, BA
*Mrs A C Macro, BA
   (*Head of Spanish*)
Mrs A Pestell, BA
Dr M G Ransome, BA, PhD
Miss E J Vance, BA
*J Wall, BA (*Head of German*)
Miss M Whatmough, Hons
Ms L E Williamson, BA

Music:
Mrs A O Bassett, BMus
C Morris, BA
*D Franks, BA, MMus
*Mrs E Rees, BA, MA

Outdoor Education:
*Mrs K Murphy, BSc
PE/Games:
K R Blackburn, BSc
J Corsi, BSc
Mrs V L Dixon, BEd
P Z Jakobek, BEd
Mrs R E John, BA
*Mrs S A Johnson, BA
   (*Head of PE*)
T Lacey, BSc
Miss F A Ripley, BSc
Miss L Sampson, MSc, LABAN
B Scott, BEd (*Head of House*)
*R M Sellers, BSc
   (*Director of Sport*)
Miss R Wintle, Hons

Physics:
S Carruthers, BSc
Miss L Glenn, BEng
*S Harper, BSc
R Jervis, MEng
Dr C A Rosser, BSc, PhD

Psychology:
*Mrs L Dilley, BSc
P Ions, BSc

Religious Studies:
A Gunawardana, BA
Miss I M Milburn, BA
*R M Smith, BA
C P Wadey, MA

Bromley High School
GDST

Blackbrook Lane, Bickley, Bromley, Kent BR1 2TW
Tel: 020 8781 7000
email: bhs@bro.gdst.net
website: www.bromleyhigh.gdst.net
Twitter: @bromleyhs
Facebook: /bromleyhighschoolGDST

Bromley High School is a selective school offering an exceptional education to girls aged 4–18 years. The school is part of the GDST (Girls' Day School Trust). The GDST is the leading network of independent girls' schools in the UK. As a charity that owns and runs 24 schools and two academies, it reinvests all its income in its schools. For further information about the Trust, see p. xxiii or visit www.gdst.net.

Founded in 1883, Bromley High School was originally situated in the centre of Bromley. In 1981 it moved to Bickley to occupy modern purpose-built buildings set in 24 acres of leafy parkland. Sharing the same site, both Senior and Junior departments benefit from first-rate facilities.

Bromley High School provides a beautiful and buzzy environment where bright girls will flourish. In the classroom, each girl's intellectual potential is challenged and developed by inspirational teachers whose concern for your daughter ranges infinitely beyond her performance in examinations; teachers who have a capacity to develop a love of learning, a spirit of enquiry and an independence of mind. Girls learn to collaborate and to compete; to be creative and intellectually curious and their learning is underpinned by the school's ethos of achievement for all and by the subject passion, enthusiasm and expertise of their teachers.

Results are consistently superb. In 2016, 85% of A Level results were A*–B and Bromley High was placed 115th in the Sunday Times Parent Power Independent School League Tables. Whilst we celebrate exceptional individual academic achievement – for example, one of our A Level Chemists received the Salters' Award for achieving the second highest mark in the UK in the A Level examination – the school is most proud of its consistently impressive Value Added results at GCSE and A Level which demonstrate the care taken to bring out the best in every girl. In the 2016 ISI inspection report Learning and Achievement were graded as Exceptional.

However, outstanding success at Bromley High School is not purely academic. Bromley High girls are resilient and well-rounded young women participating with enthusiasm and commitment in Music, Drama, Sport, Duke of Edinburgh's Award and an overabundant range of activities – and where they have interest or talent or enthusiasm, it is nurtured so that they learn to excel. Sport is exceptional: with 25 acres of top-class facilities, Bromley High hosts England Netball's Regional Performance Academy. Our U16 hockey team are the reigning Kent County Champions – both indoors and out – and one of last year's Leavers has taken up a Sports Scholarship to Princeton.

Pastoral care is thoughtful and developmental, actively encouraging girls to develop key attributes: Confidence, Courage, Composure, and Commitment. Every house takes on the responsibility of supporting its own charity and the school has a highly valued tradition of volunteering and charitable activity.

Bromley High School girls are confident, cheerful, considerate and enthusiastic about the myriad of opportunities their school has to offer.

Pupil Numbers. Senior School (ages 11–18): 600 (including the Sixth Form). Junior School (ages 4–11): 312.

The Junior School. Our two-form entry Junior School provides a stimulating and happy environment in which our pupils are encouraged to strive for excellence in all they do and to derive satisfaction from their achievements both great and small. From the earliest years we offer a broad curriculum which encourages, challenges and excites the young mind. Our aim is to foster a love of learning, develop independent thinking and promote a spirit of enquiry that leads to a depth of understanding. In our approach to teaching and learning we blend the traditional with progressive insights into learning styles and the particular needs of young girls as learners in a modern world. We teach the full range of the National Curriculum, including French, Spanish, German and also Latin and accord sports and the creative arts a significant place in the timetable, whilst ensuring that the foundations of the core subjects are well established. Class

lessons are differentiated and we offer extension and support where appropriate and specialist teaching, sometimes from Senior School staff, in a number of subjects.

Bromley High believes in preparing girls for the challenges beyond school and values the importance of a holistic approach. The school provides many varied opportunities within a vibrant co-curricular programme including sporting, musical, dramatic and other creative activities. We make the most of our beautiful school grounds to provide opportunities for outdoor learning, in which our Forest School is a vital part.

Forest School is a planned programme that takes place in a woodland environment with the aim of developing opportunities for the learner to encounter the beauty, joy, awe and wonder of the natural environment. The approach is 'hands on' and seeks to promote the holistic development of the unique child, including physical, spatial, linguistic, emotional and spiritual aspects. Self-confidence and independence are increased through freedom, time and space to learn. A safe and secure environment allows the girls to extend their learning beyond their comfort zone; to challenge their existing boundaries and ideas and to tackle investigations and tasks which in the classroom may not be possible. Collaboration and cooperation between the learners, their peers and the forest school leader is at the core of the Forest School programme. Social skills develop through risk-taking and an understanding of the consequences of your own actions, whilst self-awareness, self-regulation and empathy for others are also developed. Forest School enables children to be active participants in their own education and development.

In the delivery of our curriculum we are well served by outstanding facilities which, in addition to comprehensively equipped classrooms, include a music wing, a library, ICT suite, a science room, and an art and technology room, a sensory garden and outdoor 'classrooms'. We share many other facilities with the Senior School including a swimming pool, gymnasium, sports hall, tennis courts and an all-weather pitch. Our pupils have their lunch in the main school dining room where a wide variety of hot dishes and sandwiches are served.

The Senior School. Bromley High combines a tradition of scholarship with an innovative curriculum and expansive co-curricular provision. In the classroom, an emphasis on independent learning is designed to inculcate a spirit of enquiry, an independence of mind and a love of learning. Girls participate with enthusiasm and commitment in Music, Drama, Sport and an overabundant range of activities – and where they have interest or talent or enthusiasm, it is nurtured so that they learn to excel. In 2015 the school joined the HMC and was shortlisted by Education Business Awards for the award for Outstanding Progress in an Independent School.

Consistent investment has developed new science facilities, library, sixth form centre, drama studio, and specialist teaching rooms for the creative arts enabling departments to have their own dedicated spaces for teaching and extracurricular activities. Visual and creative arts are highly valued with Photography, Drama and Dance offered to A level and students regularly progressing to study at Central St Martin's and other prestigious Arts Foundation courses.

Academic. Languages, both ancient and modern, are a particular strength with French, German and Spanish offered from Year 7. Latin and Classics are both popular A Level choices. As a girls' school, Bromley High lays great emphasis on STEM subjects – Science, Technology, Engineering and Mathematics. Teaching rooms are equipped with Smart Boards and all have Wi-Fi and digital projector facilities which allow pupils to use iPads or their own mobile computer devices. Teachers are encouraged to enrich the curriculum and teach lively, challenging lessons. Myriad trips and activities, including music tours abroad from Year

7, residential field work for Y8 geographers and Y9 Art trips to Amsterdam. The modern foreign languages department has links with France, Germany and Spain and arranges exchanges, visits and work experience placements. The school has been awarded the British Council's full International School Award.

Girls study 10 GCSE subjects including Mathematics, Biology, Chemistry, Physics, English and English Literature and a Modern Language. Three further options are chosen from French, Spanish and German, Latin and Classical Civilisation; Computer Science and Information Technology; Music, Art, Photography, Drama, Design Technology, Economics, Geography, History, Physical Education.

Sport. Sports facilities on the school's 25 acre site are superb including a large, well-equipped Sports Hall, a new fitness suite, a gymnasium, a 400-metre athletics track, two grass hockey pitches, a fine indoor heated swimming pool, and floodlit Astroturf pitches and courts. Sport is both integral to the curriculum and an important part of the extracurricular life of the school. The school is proud of its tradition of producing national level athletes and swimmers and the number of girls who play county level hockey, netball, swimming, tennis and athletics.

Sixth Form. The Sixth Form Centre provides a bright, modern setting for traditional scholarship. Students select from a broad range of A levels supplemented by Extended Project, AS Thinking Skills and electives such as Young Enterprise, Magazine Editing, Fashion, etc. Careers education, supported by the excellent GDST network of more than 65,000 alumnae. Sixth Form benefit from GDST-wide initiatives, such as leadership and Oxbridge conferences and residential course on topics such as Engineering and Environmental Sustainability.

Extracurricular Activities. A great emphasis is put on an enthusiastic involvement in music, art, sport and drama. The annual Dance production is a significant event in the school calendar and in recent years the school has staged concerts in major London venues such as the Royal Albert Hall and Southwark Cathedral.

Girls contribute to local, national and international charities and to community service. Almost all girls participate in The Duke of Edinburgh's Award scheme in Y10 with some continuing to completion of Gold Award in Sixth Form. The Eco Society promotes a keen interest in environmental issues. There are regular exchanges to France, Germany and Spain as well as Geography and Biology field trips as far as Iceland. Annual World Challenge expeditions have recently visited Madagascar and Mongolia. The Year 6 and 7 Music Tours have recently visited Paris, Brussels, Normandy and Bruges with the Senior Music Tour performing in Berlin and Prague.

Fees per term (2016–2017). Senior School £5,314, Junior School £4,285.

Fees cover tuition, stationery, textbooks and scientific and games materials as well as entry fees for GCSE and GCE Advanced Level examinations. Extra tuition in Music and Speech and Drama is available at recognised rates.

Bursaries. Bursaries are means-tested and provide, for successful applicants, assistance with fees to enable bright girls to benefit from a GDST education. For those receiving full remission of fees, the award may include uniform and trips allowances.

Scholarships. There are Academic, Art, Music and Sport scholarships for the most successful candidates in the assessments at 11+ and for entry into the Sixth Form.

Admission and Entrance Examination. Admission into the school is at 4+ (Reception) and 7+ (Year 3) by assessment and testing. Pupils from the Junior School progress automatically to the Senior School but external applicants, or those wishing to be considered for scholarship or bursary are assessed at 11+. The examination tests verbal and quantitative assessments as well as creative writing. Entry to the Sixth Form is dependent on interview and school reference, including predicted grades and is contingent on results at GCSE.

Charitable status. Bromley High School is part of The Girls' Day School Trust, which is a Registered Charity, number 306983.

Chairman of the Local Governors: Mrs P Emburey, BA, ACA

Headmistress: **Angela Drew**, BA Hons, MBA Dunelm

Head of Junior School: Mrs C Dickerson, BA Anglia

Deputy Head Pastoral: Mrs H Elkins, BA King's College London

Deputy Head Academic: Dr S Lindfield, BSc Oxon, PhD Liverpool

Assistant Head (Head of Sixth Form): P Isted, BA Bristol

Assistant Head (Co-curricular): A Morter-Laing, BSc Swansea

Director of Finance & Operations: K Ringmo, BA Southbank, MIH, FNASBM

Admissions Registrar: Mrs L Clarke

Marketing Manager: Ms D Woodfield, MCIM

Bromsgrove School

Worcester Road, Bromsgrove, Worcestershire B61 7DU

Tel: 01527 579679
email: admissions@bromsgrove-school.co.uk
website: www.bromsgrove-school.co.uk
Twitter: @bromsschool
Facebook: @bromsgroveschool

Motto: '*Deo Regi Vicino.*'

The date of the School's Foundation is unknown but it was re-organised by Edward VI in 1553 and was granted a Royal Charter 6 years later. It was refounded in 1693 by Sir Thomas Cookes, Bt, at the same time as Worcester College, Oxford (formerly Gloucester Hall). The link between School and College has been maintained ever since.

Location. This co-educational boarding and day school is situated some 13 miles north of the Cathedral City of Worcester and an equal distance south of Birmingham. Birmingham International Airport and Station are a 20-minute drive by motorway. The M5, M6, M42 and M40 motorways provide easy access to the School.

The School stands in 100 acres of grounds on the south side and within walking distance of the market town of Bromsgrove.

Facilities. The school's impressive recent building and development programme has included a major new sports complex with an eight badminton court sized sports hall, dance studios, gym, teaching rooms and hospitality suite / sports viewing room. These new facilities enhance the existing all-weather, floodlit sports facilities. The school boasts outstanding academic facilities including an award-winning Art, Design and Technology building, a new twenty-classroom Humanities building and eighteen new and refurbished Science laboratories. Work is under way on a new Performing Arts Centre consisting of a 300-seat concert hall, an entire suite of new music classrooms, recording studios and practice rooms. Connected to this by a glazed walkway is the brand new theatre with fly gallery, and flexible seating for up to 260. The new Drama department will also boast a 90-seat Performance Studio.

Boarding. Nearly half of Bromsgrove Senior School's pupil body is made up of boarders accommodated between five houses, one of which is in the town. Loyalty to House and the traditions attendant upon it are significant factors of life at Bromsgrove. The boarding environment is happy, stable, disciplined and nurturing. Pupils are very loyal their House and competitions between day and boarding houses including sport, music and debating are keenly contested.

The stability and continuity that enable boarders to thrive are provided by resident houseparents (all academic members of staff) and their families, assistant houseparents, house mothers and a team of house-based tutors. A new dining hall complete with state-of-the-art kitchens was opened in summer 2015 and all meals are taken centrally in the School, with the exception of the evening meal at Housman Hall. Boarding facilities have been enhanced by one completely new girls' boarding house and total refurbishment of the existing boys' and girls' houses to a very high standard. New wings have been being built at the off-campus Sixth Form boarding house, Housman Hall, and the existing building, formerly home of OB and poet A E Housman, has been sympathetically refurbished.

Numbers. There are 950 pupils in the Senior School, of whom 545 are boys. The Preparatory, Pre-Preparatory and Nursery School has a further 720 pupils aged 3 to 13. (*See also Preparatory & Pre-Preparatory School entry in IAPS section.*)

Curriculum. In the Preparatory School and throughout the first year in the Senior School a broadly based curriculum is followed. In addition to the usual academic subjects time is given to Art, Music, ICT, Drama, Design Technology and to a full programme of Physical Education. Languages on offer include French, German, Spanish and Latin.

As pupils move up the School other options become available and some narrowing of the curriculum is inevitable. 10 subjects is the norm at GCSE, with a broad core including the three separate sciences and a further three optional subjects chosen. The minimum qualification for automatic entry into the Sixth Form is eight B grades (or 6 grades) at GCSE. Pupils may study the IB Diploma or take the A Level route whilst BTECs are also available in Sports Performance and Excellence and Business Studies. Flexibility in timetabling aims to ensure that all pupils' subject choices are catered for whatever the combination. Many A Level subjects are available including, Art, Biology, Business, Chemistry, Classics, Design, Drama, Design, Economics, English, French, Geography, German, Latin, Mathematics and Further Mathematics, Music, Physical Education, Physics, Politics, Religious Studies, Spanish and Textiles. Under the IB umbrella, Italian, Environmental Systems, Mandarin, Global Politics and Psychology are also on offer. With two-thirds of students achieving A*/A at both GCSE and A Level and an IB average of 38 points, virtually all our pupils proceed to degree courses usually at Russell Group universities. The most popular university destinations in recent years have been University and King's Colleges in London followed by Exeter, Bath and Bristol.

Performing Arts. The performing arts are well supported at Bromsgrove School and rightly thrive. Building work is currently underway on a new Performing Arts Centre to include a state-of-the-art concert hall, full-sized theatre and large studio auditorium.

Music flourishes both within and outside the formal curriculum under the leadership of James McKelvey. House Music Competitions fill four afternoons, Pop & Jazz Festival two evenings and Music Scholars hold concerts twice a year. There is plenty of scope for involvement in the School Orchestra and String, Wind and Brass Ensembles, Chamber Groups, Jazz & Swing Bands, a 50-strong Chapel Choir and large Choral Society. The timetable is sufficiently flexible to allow special arrangements to be made for outstanding musicians. The Chapel Choir is used for broadcasts while

visits to sing Evensong at St George's Chapel Windsor Castle, York Minster and St Paul's Cathedral, as well as productions of Sweeney Todd and Cats are recent highlights. School musicians took part in the final gala concert of Bromsgrove Festival's 50th year at Worcester Cathedral, where they performed with the English Symphony Orchestra. The 120-strong Choral Society perform every year with performance venues including the splendour of Birmingham Town Hall.

Discrete Drama forms part of the curriculum for every student from Year 5 until Year 10 when the option is available for students to take the subject to GCSE level. Within the Sixth Form the school offers A Level Theatre Studies. Senior, Fourth Form and Prep school productions form the main spine of co-curricular Drama at Bromsgrove which has a reputation for high production standards. Students regularly perform as part of the National Theatre Connections scheme as well as on the Edinburgh Fringe Festival. House Drama competitions at Prep and Senior level, alongside public performances of examination pieces and a high calibre of training for aspiring theatre technicians, ensure a vibrant dramatic life within the school.

Careers. The school employs a fully qualified, full-time careers advisor and a comprehensive careers counselling programme is pursued for pupils of all ages.

Reports and Consultation. Pupils receive grades and tutor comments twice a term and there are regular reports and parents' evenings. Supervision is shared by Houseparents and House Tutors, whom parents may meet informally by appointment. There are regular parent-teacher evenings. Parents may arrange appointments to meet members of the Careers Department.

Extracurricular Activities. A wide range of sports and activities is offered, giving opportunities to participate at a competitive level in Rugby, Hockey, Netball, Athletics, Badminton, Basketball, Clay Pigeon shooting, Cricket, Cross Country, Debating, Fencing, Golf, Rounders, Soccer, Squash, Swimming, Tennis and Young Enterprise.

The Saturday timetable, in conjunction with the weekday programme, allows the activities programme more flexibility to offer both recreational and academic choices. Pupils may select from a diverse range of recreational activities including Academic extension and support, Electronics AS Level, Revision for GCSE, AS and A2, Oxbridge, Biology, Chemistry and Physics Olympiad, Aerobics, Animation Creation, Art, Astronomy, Badminton, Chess, Corps of Drums, Design Technology, Drama, EPP (Economics, Politics and Philosophy) Engineering, Golf driving range, Handicrafts, Media Club, ICT, Military skills, Music, Outdoor pursuits (including climbing, high ropes, kayaking, orienteering, raft building, sailing), Mahjong, Photography, Plaster Modelling, School Magazine, Steel Pans, Table tennis, Website design and Weight training. There are opportunities to gain qualifications in Horse riding, Modern dance, Life saving, First Aid, RADA, LAMDA, Sport/Dance Leader Awards and Martial Arts. In addition to the activities programme, Year 9 pupils participate in Bromsgrove Badge, comprising a selection of activities that help to prepare them for the Bronze Duke of Edinburgh's Award and culminating in a four-day camp at the end of the year. There is a thriving Combined Cadet Force (Army and RAF), and many pupils are involved in The Duke of Edinburgh's Award scheme. The School's Community Action programme caters for large numbers of pupils and provides a wide range of activities; examples include working in local schools and charity shops, visiting residential homes, acting as Learning Mentors and Student Listeners, helping in animal sanctuaries and supporting conservation projects.

Admission. Entrance at 13 is by Bromsgrove School Entrance Examinations. Boys and Girls may be admitted to the Preparatory School at any age from 7 to 12 inclusive. 11+ Entrance Tests take place in November and in late January for entry into other years. Places are available in the Sixth Form to boys and girls who have had their GCSE education elsewhere.

Scholarships and Bursaries. Awards are made on the results of open examinations held at the school in January. A significant number of scholarships, means-tested bursaries and Foundation bursaries for pupils of academic, artistic, sporting and all-round ability are awarded at 11+, 13+ and 16+. A number of Music scholarships and exhibitions are awarded each year at ages 11, 13 and 16, offering free tuition on up to two instruments. Means-tested bursaries may be used to supplement any scholarship. Full details are available from the Admissions Department.

Fees per term (2016–2017). Senior School (age 13+): £11,285 full boarding, £7,550 weekly boarding, £5,140 day inc lunch. Preparatory School (age 7–13): £7,400–£9,125 full boarding, £5,400–£6,530 weekly boarding, £3,585–£4,665 day inc lunch. Pre-Preparatory (age 4–7): £2,390–£2,760 day. Nursery (age 3–4): £2,680 full-time.

Charitable status. Bromsgrove School is a Registered Charity, number 1098740. It exists to provide education for boys and girls.

Patron: A Denham-Cookes

President: V S Anthony, BSc, Hon DEd, Hon FCP, FRSA

A Vice-President: J M Baron, TD, MA
A Vice-President: J A Hall, FCA
A Vice-President: N J Birch, MIMechE
A Vice-President: Prof K B Haley, BSc, PhD, FIMA, CMath, FIEE, CEng
A Vice-President: T M Horton, BA
A Vice-President: G R John, CBE

Governing Body:
P West (*Chairman*)

A Cleary	M Luckman
C Cameron	R G Noake, FCA, FCCA
R D Brookes, FRICS	B Roden
J Dillon	G Strong
R Lane, MA	Dr N Venning, BSc, PhD, MBA
J Loynton	
Dr C Lidbury	D Walters, MA, FCA
	D Waltier

Company Secretary: J Sommerville, MA

Headmaster: P Clague, BA, MBA

Bursar: Mrs L Brookes, ACMA
Assistant Head: Miss R M Scannell, BA, PGCE
Head of Senior School: J Hallows, BA, PGCE
Deputy Head (Academic): P S Ruben, BSc, MPhil, MBA
Deputy Head (Co-Curricular): P S T Mullan, BA, PGCE
Director of Staffing (Whole School): S Challoner, BSc, PGCE
School Medical Officer: Dr D Law, MA, MBChB Oxon, MRCGP, DRCOG, DFFP
Mrs C P M Maund, BSc, PGCE (*Assistant Pastoral Head*)

Staff:
* *Head of Department*
† *Houseparent*

S J Kingston, BEd (*Examinations Officer*)
Mrs C E Turner, BA, PGCE
C A Dowling MA Cantab, PGCE (*Chemistry; Academic Database Coordinator*)
Dr M R Werrett, GRSC, PhD, PGCE (*Senior Mistress*)
M A Stone, BEng, ACGI, PGCE
Mrs J A Holden, MA Oxon, PGCE
Mrs S Shinn, BSc, PGCE (*Timetabler*)
Dr A R Johns, BSc, PhD, PGCE (*Head of Sixth Form – Pupil Progress*)

Ms S J Cronin, BA, DMS, PGCE (*Business Studies*)
Mrs F K Bateman, BSc, PGCE (* *Lower Sixth Form*; **Sixth Form Enrichment Curriculum*)
J W B Brogden, BA, PGCE
Mrs S E Ascough, BSc, PGCE (*i/c Acitivities*; *Head of Fifth Form*)
Miss K E Tansley, BA, MA, PGCE (*English*)
†D G Wilkins, BA, SCITT
M A C Beet, MA Cantab, PGCE (*Modern Languages*; *i/c Oxbridge*)
Miss F E Diver, BA, PGCE (*Head of Lower Fourth Form*, *Geography*)
Miss Z L Leech, BA (*PSHE*, *UCAS*)
N C J Riley, BSc, PGCE (*Mathematics*)
Mrs E L E Buckingham, BA (*Girls' PE & Games*)
Miss S A Franks, BSc, PGCE
Miss M M Smith, BA, PGCE (*Spanish*)
Mrs T L Helmore, BA, PGCE
R O Knight, MA Oxon, ARCO (*Assistant Director of Music*)
O A Matthews, BEng, PGCE (*Design and Technology*)
Dr M Thompson, BSc, PhD, MInstP, PGCE (*IB Coordinator*)
Revd P Hedworth, BEd, BA (*Chaplain*)
Dr M K Ruben, BA, PhD, PGCE (*Gifted and Talented*)
Miss S J McWilliams, BA, PGCE
Miss S Morgans, BA, PGCE, DipND (*Art*)
G N Delahunty, BA, PGCE (*Politics*)
Ms E L Densem, BA, PGCE
†H Bell, MA, PGCE
†A McClure, BA, PGCE (*Classics*, *Senior Day Houseparent*)
Mrs S James, BSc, PGCE
†Miss L McKee, BA, PGCE
Miss J Zafar, BA, PGCE (*History*)
S Broadbent, BA, QTS
Mrs C Wedelich-Niedzwiedz, BMus, PGCE
Ms K Garratt, MA
D Tamplin, BSc, PGCE
†J D Jones, MA (*i/c Extended Project Qualification, Senior Boarding Houseparent*)
Mrs M Parkinson, BA, PGCE
†Mrs T Tweddle, BSc, CertEd FE
Mrs K Hands, BA, PGCE (*Religious Studies*)
Mrs H Barton, BA, PGCE
†D Fallows (*Director of Cricket*)
Mrs J Golightly, BA
Ms G Tyrrell, BA, PGCE
D Williams, BA, PGCE
A Carrington-Windo (*Director of Rugby*)
Miss L Davenport, BSc, PGCE
S Noble, BSc, PGCE
Miss A Baker, BSc, PGCE NQT
J Baldrey, BA, PGCE
Mrs L Newton, BEng, PGCE (*i/c DofE Silver*)
Miss E Harper, BA, PGCE
A Helmore, BA, MA, PGCE
J Holdsworth, BSC, PGCE
Miss E Johnston, BSc, PGCE (*Upper Fourth*)
Miss J Lesniak, BA, PGCE
S Matthews, BA, PGCE (*President of the Common Room*)
Mrs D Sutherland, BA, HDipMaths, QTS
Miss J Williams, BA, PGCE
J McKelvey, BA, PGCE (*Director of Music*)
B Dudley (*Director of Hockey*)
†Mrs K Hannah, BA, PGCE
†T Clinton, BSc
Mrs J Boonnak, BA, MA, PGCE (*International Education*)
L Mullan, BSc, PGCE (*Boys' PE*)
Mrs A Buckley, MA, PGCE

Miss L Hunter, BA, PGCE
†M Giles, BSc, PGCE
Miss Brain, BSc, PGCE
Mrs G Bruce, BA, PGCE
Miss R Green, BSc, PGCE (*Science*)
Ms G Hanson, BA, PGCE
S Higgins, BEd
Miss N Langford, BA, GTTP
A Laskowski, BSc, MSc, PGCE
Miss F McCanlis, BMus, PGCE
H Pothecary, BSc, PGCE
Miss R Simmons, BA
Dr R Whitehead, MA, PhD
Mrs G Wright, BSc, PGCE (*Biology*)
Mrs V Adams, BA,MA, PGCE
D Atkinson, BSc, MSc, PGCE
Miss C Berment, BA, PGCE, (*French*)
Ms K Collins, BA, PGCE
Ms M D'Angelo, BA, PGCE
Mrs A Eaton, MA, GTP
D Evans, BSc, PGCE
T Hinde, BA, MA
Ms F Jung, MA, PGCE
A Kelly, BSc, MDip Ed
Ms A Linehan, BSC, MEd, PGDipEd
Mrs N Reid, BA, PGCE
Dr D Rimmer, PhD, MA
Dr R Short, MChem, PhD, PGCE
Miss C Wadley, BA
Miss P Woolley, MChem, PGCE
Miss J Wright, BA
Mrs J Bradford, BA (*Drama*)
O Burton, BA, PGCE
P Dinnen, MA (*English*)
R Doak, BA, PGCE
M Egan, BA, PGCE (*Economics*)
D Harris, BA, PGCE
MIss L Honey, BSc
S Kettle, BSc, PGCE (*Science*, *Physics*)
Miss J Partridge, MA, PGCE
C Moore, BSc
T Norton, BA (*Performing Arts*)
R Vernon, BA, GTP
M Wakeford, BSc, PGCE

Houses and Houseparents:
Boarding:
Elmshurst (*Boys*): D Fallows
Housman Hall (*Sixth Form*): J Jones
Mary Windsor (*Girls*): Mrs T Tweddle
Oakley (*Girls*): Mrs V Adams
Wendron-Gordon (*Boys*): D Wilkins

Day:
Hazeldene (*Girls*): Mrs L McKee
Lupton (*Boys*): A L McClure
Lyttelton (*Boys*): M Giles
School (*Boys*): T Clinton
Thomas Cookes (*Girls*): Mrs K Hannah
Walters (*Boys*): H Bell

Music Staff:
J McKelvey, BA, PGCE (*Director of Music*)
R O Knight, MA Oxon, ARCO (*Assistant Director of Music*)
Mrs M Corrie (*Music, Preparatory School*)
Ms F McCanlis, BMus, PGCE
Mrs J Russell, BA, PGCE
Ms F Swadling, BA, ABSM, GBSM (*Head of Strings*)

Visiting Music Staff:
N Barry, GGSM, LTCL (*Piano*)
Miss H Bool, GBSM, ABSM, BTech Nat (*Percussion*)

Miss V Brawn (*Oboe*)
M Broadhead LTCL, DipTCL (*Cello*)
Mrs R Brown (*Singing*)
R Bull (*Guitar*)
T Bunting, BMus (*Double Bass, Bass Guitar*)
P Cambell-Kelly, GMus, RNCM, PGDip RNCM, PPRNCM (*Violin*)
Mrs S Chatt, GBSM (*Percussion*)
W Coleman, BA, LTCL (*Singing*)
S Dessanay (*Double Bass*)
J Dunlop, BA, GBSM, ABSM (*Flute*)
Mrs K Fawcett, BA, PGDip (*Viola, Violin*)
A Gittens, BTec, HND (*Electric Guitar*)
Mrs J A Hattersley, CT ABRSM, LRSM (*Brass*)
Mrs J Hiles, GBSM, ABSM (*Flute, Piano*)
Ms A Kazimierczuk GBSM, ABSM, (*Singing*)
T Martin, BA, Dip ABRSM (*Saxophone*)
Mrs C Price, BA (*Violin*)
M Roberts, BA Music (*Trumpet*)
Miss K Stevens, MMus, BMus (*Clarinet*)
A D C Thayer, MA, BMus, PG Dip (*Piano*)
Mrs K Thompson, PG Dip RNCM, PPRNCM (*Piano*)
J Topp (*French Horn*)

Preparatory & Pre-Preparatory School

Headmistress: Mrs J Deval-Reed, BEd

Deputy Head (*Pastoral*): M Marie, BA, PGCE
Deputy Head (*Academic*): Mrs J Holden, MA Oxon, PGCE
Deputy Head (*Operations*): Mrs K Ison, BEd
Director of Years 3–6: Mrs R Whiting, BA, PGCE

Miss V Barron, MA, BA, PGCE, BIAD (*Art*)
Mrs P Barton, CertEd
Mrs G BIllig, BSc, PGCE
Mrs R Boardman, BA, PGCE (*Spanish*)
Miss S Cadwallader, BA, PGCE (*Head of Year 6*)
Miss S Cartwright, BSc, PGCE (*Science*)
G Clark, BEd (*Head of Year 7*)
Mrs M Corrie, GTCL, LTCL (*Music*)
Mrs S Dakin, BA (*Forest School*)
Miss D Evans, BSc, MA, PGCE
Mr G Evans, BSc, PGCE (*Maths*)
Mrs T Faulkner-Petrova, BA, BSc, MSc, PGCE
Mrs K Finnegan, BA, PCGE (*French*)
Mrs C Goodall BA, PGCE
Mrs S Grove, BEd
J P Grumball, BSc, PGCE
Mrs P Gunn, BA, MSt, PGCE
Mrs L Hadley
Mrs R Ivison, BA, PGCE (*Year 3*)
G Jones, BA, PGCE (*Boys' PE*)
Mrs G Judson, BSc, PGCE
Mrs S Keynes, BA, OTS (*Year 5*)
C D Kippax, BA, PGCE (*MFL*)
Mrs P Kippax, BSc, PGCE
Mrs E Lalley, BA, PGCE
Mrs R Laurenson, BA, PGCE (*Year 4*)
Mrs S Le Guyader, BA, PGCE (*English*)
Mrs S M Lewis, BA, PGCE
Mrs E Mullan, BEd (*Head of Year 8*, *PSHEE*)
D Pover, BA, PGCE
Miss A Purver, BA, PGCE (*History*)
Miss A Read, BTec, BA, PGCE
Miss C Roskell, BEng, PGCE
Mrs J C Russell, BA, PGCE
Mr P Skerratt, BA, PGCE (*Latin*, *Gifted and Talented*)
Miss C Smith, BSc, PGDipEd
P Sutherland, HD Ed (*Design & Technology*)
M J Turner, BSc, PGCE (*Activities Coordinator*)
Mrs S Webley, BSc, PGCE, MEd (*Year 8*)
Mrs J Weller, BMus, PGCE (*Girls' PE*)

R Widdop, BA, DipSpPsy (*Geography*)
Mr C Woollhead, BA, PGCE (*Drama*)

Boarding House and Houseparents:
Page (*boys and girls*): Mr & Mrs T Windo-Carrington

Pre-Preparatory Staff:
*Deputy Head Pastoral, Head of Pre-Preparatory
　　Department*: B Etty-Leal, BSc, PGCE
Deputy Head Academic: Mrs K Western, BEd
Joint Head of Nursery/EYFS: Mrs S Symonds, BA

Mrs C S Abraham, BA, MA, QTS
Mrs C Cattell, BA, PGCE (*Head of Year 1*)
Mrs C Dunlop, BEd (*Head of Reception*)
Mrs L Finlay, HDip Ed (*Head of Year 2*)
Mrs J Kingston
Miss E Lewis, BA Ed
Mrs J Lockhart, BEd
Mrs M Martin, BA, GTP
Mrs N St John, BA, PGCE
Mrs J Townsend, BA, PGCE (*Joint Head of Nursery*)

Bryanston School

Blandford, Dorset DT11 0PX

Tel:　　01258 452411
Fax:　　01258 484661
email:　　head@bryanston.co.uk
website:　　www.bryanston.co.uk

Motto: '*Et nova et vetera*'.

Founded in 1928, Bryanston School aims above all to develop the all-round talents of individual pupils. A broad, flexible academic and extracurricular programme together with an extensive network of adult support encourages pupils to maximise their particular abilities as well as to adapt positively to the demands of the society of which they are part. Creativity, individuality and opportunity are the school's key notes, but a loving community is the school's most important quality. Our aim is that Bryanstonians will leave us as well-balanced 18-year-olds, ready to go out into the wider world, to lead happy and fulfilling lives and to contribute, positively and generously. We believe a school can have no more joyful, dynamic ambition.

Situation. Occupying a magnificent Norman Shaw mansion, the school is located in beautiful Dorset countryside near the market town of Blandford. There are 400 acres of grounds, which include a stretch of river used for rowing and canoeing, playing fields, woodland and parkland.

Numbers. There are approximately 380 boys and 300 girls in the school.

Admission. Boys and girls are normally admitted between 13 and 14 years of age on the results of Common Entrance or the school's own entrance exam. Sixth form entrants are admitted after interview, conditional upon securing at least 50 points at GCSE.

Scholarships. Academic, Art, DT, Music, Sport and Richard Hunter All-Rounder Scholarships are available annually for entry at 13+.

Academic and Music Scholarships and Udall Awards for Sport are available annually for entry to the sixth form.

Scholarships range in value and may be supplemented by means-tested bursaries. Music Scholarships carry free musical tuition, Alexander Technique lessons and a weekly accompaniment lesson.

Further details may be obtained from the Admissions Registrar.

Organisation. The school is organised on a house basis with five senior boys' houses, five girls' houses, and two junior boys' houses. All pupils have a personal tutor throughout their time in the school, with whom they meet on a one-to-one basis at least once a week. No tutor has more than 15 pupils. Catering and medical care are organised centrally. All sixth-form pupils in their final year have individual study bedrooms. Lower sixth formers usually share study bedrooms.

Religion. Religious instruction is widely based and is carried on throughout the school. There are two assemblies each week for the whole school. Pupils attend either assemblies or services on most Sundays during the term. Holy Communion is celebrated every Sunday and on some week days. A Chaplain is responsible for pastoral work and preparation for Confirmation.

School Work. The school aims at leading pupils, over a period of five years, from the comparative dependence on class teaching in which they join the school, to a state in which they are capable of working on their own, for a university degree or professional qualification, or in business. In addition to traditional class teaching, there is, therefore, increasing time given to private work as a pupil moves up the school. This is in the form of assignments to be completed within a week or a fortnight. Teachers are available to give individual help when required, and tutors supervise pupils' work and activities in general, on a one-to-one basis.

Every pupil is encouraged to explore a range of opportunities. All pupils follow the same broad and challenging curriculum in D (Year 9), if at all possible. This curriculum includes Latin, modern languages, three separate sciences, creative arts, technology and music as well as English and Mathematics. GCSE is taken after three years when a pupil is in B (Year 11). There is a highly flexible choice of subjects at this level and subjects are setted independently. In A (Years 12 and 13), or Sixth Form, pupils can choose between A levels and the International Baccalaureate Diploma. All lower sixth formers follow a compulsory Personal and Social Education course and the academic enrichment programme provides supplementary sessions to develop key skills and approaches to learning.

Music. A brand new state-of-the-art Music School with outstanding facilities opened 2 years ago. Bryanston has an exceptional musical tradition, and music is at the heart of school life in every aspect. Inclusion, as well as excellence, is a core value and to achieve this every pupil is their first year learns an instrument for the entire year. An extraordinary range of concerts, recitals and musical groups occur, with over 600 individual music lessons taught each week.

Drama. A well-equipped, modern theatre provides the venue for the many school productions which take place during the year and for touring professional companies. In addition to acting, pupils are involved in stage management, stage lighting and sound, and front-of-house work. There is also a large Greek Theatre in the grounds.

Sport and Leisure. A wide variety of sports is on offer at the school, including athletics, archery, badminton, canoeing, climbing, cricket, cross country, fencing, fives, hockey, lacrosse, netball, riding, rowing, rugby, sailing, squash, swimming and tennis. Extensive playing fields between the school and the River Stour provide 46 tennis courts, two astroturf pitches, nine netball courts, an athletics track and grass pitches for all major sports, an all-weather riding manège and cross-country course. A sports complex provides an indoor heated 25m Swimming Pool, gymnasium, large sports hall, squash courts and fitness centre. Sailing takes place at Poole Harbour where the school has six dinghies at its own base. In addition to sport, a number of clubs and societies, catering for a wide range of interests, meet in the evenings and at weekends.

Additional Activities. To encourage a sense of responsibility towards the community, a growing self-reliance and a practical training in the positive use of leisure, all pupils take part in all or some of the following:

- Community and Social Service
- Extracurricular activities chosen from a wide range of options
- The Duke of Edinburgh's Award
- Adventure Training

Dress. There is no school uniform but there is a dress code.

Careers. The Careers Department is well-resourced and easily accessible. Two members of staff work closely with tutors, houses and departmental heads to provide guidance at each age and stage, at a pace that is right for each pupil – one-to-one, in small groups or via PSRE classes. Pupils are empowered to develop confidence and self-awareness, to reflect on their abilities and aspirations, and are given tools to learn about career options and pathways. Psychometric profiling is offered in year 11. Higher Education and 'next steps' events are organised annually, providing the chance to meet with employers, academic subject specialists and overseas universities. Close links are maintained with Inspiring Futures, the CDI and International ACAC.

Further Education. The vast majority of pupils in the sixth form gain admission to universities or other academies of further education.

Fees per term (2016–2017). Boarders £11,882, Day Pupils £9,743.

Charitable status. Bryanston School Incorporated is a Registered Charity, number 306210. It is a charitable trust for the purpose of educating children.

Governors:
Chairman: R A Pegna, MA
S F Bowes
S O Conran
Dr K M Fleming, MA, MPhil, PhD
J A F Fortescue, BA
Mrs S Foulser, BA
J R Greenhill, MA
Mrs B Hollond, MA, FRSA
Revd J L Holt, MA
B M Irvani, MA, FCA
M A S Laurence
C G Martin, ACA, MA
Mrs V M McDonaugh, MA
Miss M E McKeown, BA, MSc
Dr H M Pharaoh, MBBS, DRCOG, MRCGP
A R Poulton, BA
Mrs L M V Soden, BA, MA
D M Trick

Bursar and Clerk to the Governors: N P McRobb, OBE, MBA, BA

Head: Ms S J Thomas, BA

Second Master: P J Hardy, JP, MA, PGCE (*Economics and Business*)
Deputy Head, Academic: Dr D A James, BA, MA, PhD, PGCE (*English*)
Director of Admissions: Mrs E M Barkham, BA, MSc, PGCE (*Biology*)

Staff:
* *Head of Department*
† *Housemaster/Housemistress*

P A L Rioch, BMus, BA
D C Bourne, MA, PGCE, FRGS (*Geography; Senior Master*)
Mrs S Stacpoole, BA (*History of Art*)
G S Elliot, BA, PGCE (*Chemistry*)
Mrs F K Pyrgos, BSc, PGCE (**Careers*)
D Fowler-Watt, MA (*Classics*)
Mrs J Ladd-Gibbon, MA (*Design*)
Mrs M F Barlow, BA (*Economics and Business*)

Mrs R A Simpson, BA (*English, Senior Tutor*)
A J Marriott, BA, PGCE (*History*)
S J Richardson, BEd, MA, FRMetS, NPQH (*Geography; Academic Registrar*)
Dr M T Kearney, MA, PhD (**Science; Physics*)
Mrs J G S Strange, BA, PGCE (*History*)
M J Owens, MA, PGCE (**Art*)
S J Turrill, BSc, PGCE (*Chemistry*)
N J Davies, BEd (*Design Technology*)
L C Johnson, BA, LTP (**French; Senior Tutor*)
Miss J F Quan, MA (*Director of Drama*)
Mrs D M Wellesley, MA (*Modern Languages*)
C T Holland, BA (**Classics*)
Dr P S Bachra, MA (*Economics and Business*)
S H Jones, BSc, PGCE (*Biology*)
Mrs A J Gilbert, BA, PGCE (*Modern Languages*)
Mrs L C Kearney, BEd (*Geography*)
†Mrs H E Dean, BA, PGCE (*Art*)
Ms L Boothman, BA, PGCE (*English*)
Mrs C L Miller, BEd (*Sports Studies*)
R J Collcott, MEng, MSc (*Mathematics and Physics*)
A J Barnes, BA, CertEd (*Director of Technology*)
†Dr H L Fearnley, BA, PhD (*Classics*)
D J Melbourne, BSc, PGCE (*Mathematics*)
†S M Vincent, BA, PGCE (*History*)
G M Scott, BA, ARCO, LTCL, PGCE (*Assistant Director of Music, Keyboard*)
Miss C L Bentinck, BA (*English*)
L C E Blanco Gomez, BA (*Spanish*)
N M Kelly, BA, PGCE (**English*)
†J J A Beales, BA, PGCE (*Economics*)
Mrs C S Scott, BMus, PGCE, FTCL, ARCM, LTCL (**Strings*)
N Welford, BSc, PGCE (**Biology*)
†Mrs K J Scott, BA, PGCE (*Drama, English*)
Ms C Cava, MPhys (**Physics*)
D M Emerson, BMus, PGCE (**Director of Music*)
T W Sellers, BA, PGCE, AKC (**History*)
A K Tarafder, BSc (*Mathematics*)
†Mrs C L Bray, BSc, PGCE (*Sport Studies*)
Mrs L M Jones, MA (*Classics*)
Mrs R Ings, BSc, PGCE (*IT, Economics*)
Revd A M J Haviland, BEd, DipCMM (**Chaplain*)
M S Deketelaere, BA, MSc, DIC (*Geography*)
Mrs A J Elliot, BSc (**Chemistry*)
Mrs C R Chourou, BA (*Fine Art*)
C J Mills, BA, PGCE, (**Design and Technology*)
†M T Bolton, BA, GTP (*Design and Technology*)
W P Ings, MA, ARCO, PGCE (*Assistant Director of Music, Academic*)
†Mrs J M I Velasco, BA, PGCE (**French*)
Dr R D Heal, BSc, PhD (*Biology*)
†M S Christie, MA, PGCE (**Economics and Business*)
†J Dickson, BA, PGCE (*Art*)
A C Hartley, MMath, PGCE (**Mathematics*)
R J Johnson, BSc, PGCE (*Chemistry*)
J M C Lyne, MA (**History of Art*)
I W McClary, MA, PGCE (**Head of Sixth Form*)
Miss J M Pike, BA, PGCE (*Modern Languages*)
L J Pollard, MA (*Religious Studies*)
A J Sanghrajka, BA, BPP (*Classics*)
R Pinzas Balesteiro, BA, PGCE (**Spanish*)
Miss C G Bloomfield, BSc (*Physics*)
Ms S D Duncker, 1/2 Staatsexamen (**German*)
P C A Dunne, BA (*History*)
R M Hallam, MPhys, PGCE (*Physics*)
Ms P L Haywood, BSc, PGCE (*Biology*)
Mrs K M Lewin, BSc, MSc, PGCE (*Mathematics*)
Miss E L Pick, BSc (*Biology*)
Miss M L Sinclair-Smith, BA (*Art*)
†S B Green, BSc, PGCE (*Mathematics*)

T W Haysom, BSc, PGCE (*Mathematics*)
Miss F Mateo-Sanz, BA (*Spanish*)
Miss I O M White, BA, MA, PGCE (*Music*)
A Fermor-Dunman, BSc, MA (*Director of Sport*)
Miss J M Grimshaw, BSc, PGCE (*Chemistry*)
J P Heritage, BSc, PGCE (*Physics*)
Ms P Quarrell, BA, PGCE (*History; Senior Tutor*)
W T Morgan, BA, PGCE (*French*)
B E Leigh, LLB, MSc (**Economics*)
Miss A R Croot, BA, PGCE (*English*)
P A Griffin, BSc, PGCE (*Mathematics*)
Mrs S Y James, BA, PGCE (*Chemistry*)
Miss K E Andrews, BA, PGCE (**Geography*)
Mrs C E Murray, BSc, PGCE (*Mathematics*)
Mr S P Nicholls, BA, PGCE (*Design and Technology*)
Miss R A Pakenham-Walsh, BA, PGCE (*Modern Languages*)
Mr A J Pattison, BSc, MSc, PGCE (*Biology*)
Mr J W Wilkes, BSc, MSc (*Chemistry*)
Mr M Wright, BEng (*Mathematics*)
Mr J G Herman, BA (*Classics*)

Admissions Registrar: Mrs L J Goodall
Head's PA: Mrs S E Simpson

Bury Grammar School Boys

Tenterden Street, Bury, Lancs BL9 0HN

Tel: 0161 696 9600
Fax: 0161 763 4655
email: boysinfo@burygrammar.com
website: www.burygrammar.com
Twitter: @bgsboys
Facebook: /BuryGrammarSchoolBoys

Motto: *Sanctas clavis fores aperit*

The School, formerly housed in the precincts of the Parish Church of St Mary the Virgin, was first endowed by Henry Bury in 1634, but there is evidence that it existed before that date. It was re-endowed in 1726 by the Revd Roger Kay and moved to its current site in 1966. The school is a selective grammar school which aims to provide a first-class academic and extracurricular education; to nurture the whole person in a safe, stimulating, challenging and friendly community in which each individual is encouraged to fulfil his potential; and to prepare each boy for an adulthood of fulfilling work, creative leisure and responsible citizenship.

Numbers of Boys. 512, aged 7 to 18.

Admission, Scholarships and Bursaries. Admission is by examination and interview. Most boys join the school at either 7 or 11, although, subject to places being available, admission is possible at other ages. A number of means-tested bursaries, based on academic performance and financial need, are awarded each year.

Fees per term (2016–2017). Senior School £3,480; Junior School £2,586.

Facilities and Development. This ancient grammar school, proud of its historic links with the town of Bury and the surrounding area, possesses a full range of modern facilities. These facilities enable the school to offer a broad and rich academic curriculum and extracurricular programme. Since 1993 the Junior School has occupied its own site opposite the Senior School. Junior School pupils are able to take advantage of the additional specialist facilities and resources in the Senior School. A new Learning Resource Centre, consisting of a Library, extensive ICT provision and private study facilities, was opened in 2002, and a new Art Centre in 2004. State-of-the-art Science laboratories were completed in 2010 and a new university-style Sixth Form

Centre for both boys and girls opened in September 2014. In September 2016 brand new sports facilities were opened to include a 3G artificial pitch and a multi-use games area so that sports can continue in inclement weather.

Pastoral Care. Each boy has a Form Tutor who has primary responsibility for his pastoral care and for oversight of his academic progress and his extracurricular programme. Form Tutors are led by Heads of Year who also oversee a boy's academic progress. There is also a strong House system for a wide range of sporting, musical and cultural inter-house competitions.

Curriculum. The Junior School offers a balanced and enriched curriculum in a friendly, disciplined and caring environment in which the boys' all-round development is of paramount importance.

In the Senior School, First Form boys study English, Mathematics, French, Biology, Chemistry, Physics, Geography, History, Religious Studies, Music, Computing, Art and CDT. All Second Form boys are taught German and either Latin or Classical Civilisation. At GCSE, all boys study English, Mathematics, Biology, Chemistry and Physics (all boys take separate sciences) and at least one Modern Foreign Language, and choose from a wide range of option subjects. Most boys offer ten subjects at GCSE.

In the Sixth Form, students study four subjects to AS Level and have the option of reducing to three subjects at A2 Level. A Level subjects are chosen from: Biology, Chemistry, Physics, Electronics, Mathematics, Further Maths, History, Politics, Economics, Business Studies, Geography, Geology, English Literature, English Language, French, German, Latin, Greek, Classical Civilisation, Psychology, Religious Studies, Theatre Studies, Music, PE, Art and Computing. All Lower Sixth Form students take AS General Studies, with the option of A2 General Studies in the Upper Sixth Form.

Art. The Art facility in the Senior School consists of two main studios and a separate sixth form studio. There is also a designated sculpture and pottery studio. In the first three years, all boys study Art and Pottery. Art is a popular choice at GCSE, AS and A2.

Music. Music is an important part of school life. As an academic subject it is offered at GCSE, AS and A2. At least three major musical events take place each year. Visiting peripatetic teachers teach over 170 pupils and also assist in running the wide range of extracurricular music, including choir, orchestra, concert band, dance orchestra and several chamber groups.

Physical Education and Games. Boys participate in Games throughout the school and in Physical Education until the end of the Fourth Form. In addition, boys in the Junior School and in the First Form of the Senior School are taught swimming in the school's own pool. Indoor facilities include a sports hall, and outdoors there are extensive playing fields, a floodlit all-weather area and tennis courts. The major sports in the autumn and spring terms are Football and Rugby. In the summer term the major sport is Cricket. Other sports which are played at inter-school level are Athletics, Basketball, Cross-Country, Golf, Hockey, Swimming and Tennis.

Outdoor Education. In the Senior School, the Outdoor Activities programme includes a residential course for all First Form boys at the National Watersports Centre at Plas Menai in Wales. Boys in the Fifth, Lower Sixth and Upper Sixth Forms can choose Outdoor Activities as part of their Games programme. This includes a variety of activities and trips, including climbing, kayaking, dry-slope skiing and cycling.

CCF. Boys may join the CCF in the Third Form, and the school contingent is a strong one. The CCF helps the boys develop qualities such as self-discipline, resourcefulness and perseverance, a sense of responsibility and skills of man-management and leadership.

Careers. The Careers Department aims to provide all boys with access to the information and advice they need to make informed and sensible decisions about their futures. In addition to a very good Careers Library, guidance is provided by individual interviews. There are regular Careers Conventions. All boys are required to complete a period of work experience during the Fourth Form.

Religion. The school has a Christian foundation but is proud of its tradition of being an open and inclusive community which welcomes boys and staff from different religious faiths as well as those who belong to no faith community.

Bury Grammar School Old Boys' Association. Secretary: Martin Entwistle, 8 Greenmount Drive, Greenmount, Bury, BL8 4HA. Tel: 01204 882502.

Charitable status. Bury Grammar Schools Charity is a Registered Charity, number 526622. The aim of the charity is to promote educational opportunities for boys and girls living in or near Bury.

Governing Body:
Chair of Governors: L A Goldberg
Vice Chair of Governors: G Winter

M Edge	A Marshall
M J Entwistle	A C Murray
The Revd Dr J C Findon	Dr J G S Rajasansir
Mrs S Gauge	J A Rigby
Mrs S Henry	A H Spencer
Mrs C Hulme-McGibbon	J S Wild

Bursar and Clerk to the Governors: Mrs J Stevens, BFocFC, ACA

Headmaster: **R N Marshall**, MSc

Second Master: D P Cassidy, BSc (*Chemistry, Designated Safeguarding Lead*)
Director of Studies, Deputy Head Academic: T J Nicholson, BA (*Mathematics*)
Assistant Head – Teaching and Learning: Mrs H M Brandon, MA (*English*)
Assistant Head – Enrichment: A E Dennis, BSc (*Mathematics, Head of Outdoor Activities*)
Head of Sixth Form: N Parkinson, BA (*Economics & Business Studies*)

Assistant Staff:
M Ahmad, BSc (*Physics*)
B Alldred, MSc (*Mathematics*)
Miss E L Bailey, BSc (*Biology*)
M J Beesley, BSc (*Biology*)
D S Benger, MA (*Music*)
D A Bishop, BSc (*Head of Geology*)
M R Boyd, BA (*Head of French*)
Mrs R L Bradley, BA (*Classics*)
Mrs H Campion, BA (*Head of Economics & Business Studies*)
Mrs S G Cawtherley, BA (*Religious Studies, Head of Fourth Year*)
A P Christian, BA (*History & Politics, Head of Learning Support*)
M J Cooke, BEd (*CDT & Electronics, Assistant Head of Sixth Form*)
P F Curry, BSc (*Head of Physics*)
Miss J H Downing, BMus (*Director of Music*)
J Eastham, BA (*History, Head of Third Year*)
W Elf, BSc, MA (*Mathematics*)
G D Feely, MA (*Head of Classics, Oxbridge Coordinator*)
D A Ferguson, BA (*Computing*)
Mrs G L Fern, BSc (*Chemistry*)
Miss V L Frisby, BA (*French*)
Miss K J Gittins, BA (*Art, PSHEE Coordinator*)
Miss K A Gore, BA (*Head of Art*)
D Hailwood, BEd (*Head of CDT & Electronics*)

G Hall, BSc (*PE & Sport*)
Mrs J M Hill, BSc (*Head of Science, Head of Chemistry*)
M J Hone, MA (*Head of History & Politics*)
Mrs S J Howard, BA (*French & German, Head of First Year, E-Safety Officer*)
P Meakin, BSc (*Head of Computing*)
D T Newbury, BSc (*Geography, Head of Fifth Year*)
P O'Sullivan, BA (*Head of Mathematics*)
L A Purdy, BSc (*PE & Sport*)
Mrs J G Smith, BA (*English*)
Miss E A Stansfield, BA (*English, Head of Second Form*)
Mrs K E Stedman, BA (*Head of Religious Studies*)
Miss V Tandon, BSc (*Mathematics*)
Mrs T J Taylor, MA (*Head of Geography*)
A D Watts, BSc (*Head of Biology*)
Miss N M Whittaker, BA (*Head of English*)
S Williams, BSc (*Director of Sport*)
B Wong, PhD (*Chemistry*)

Junior School:
Head of Junior School: M J Turner BSc
Assistant Head of Junior School: Mrs C A Howard, BSc
P F Burrell, BSc
Mrs F M L Hartwell, BSc
Mrs K A Marshall, BA
Miss L A Moffitt, BA
Mrs C M Murphy, BA
N G Robson, BA
S H Sheikh, BA

Headmaster's PA: Mrs J M McCoy

Campbell College

Belmont Road, Belfast, Co Antrim BT4 2ND, Northern Ireland

Tel:	+44 (0)28 9076 3076
Fax:	+44 (0)28 9076 1894
email:	hmoffice@campbellcollege.co.uk
website:	www.campbellcollege.co.uk
Facebook:	/Campbell-College

Motto: '*Ne Obliviscaris*.'

Campbell College, which was opened in 1894, was founded and endowed in accordance with the will of Henry James Campbell, Esq (Linen Merchant) of Craigavad, Co Down. It has a reputation as one of the leading educational environments in the country. Our commitment is to welcome, challenge and inspire each and every pupil to be the very best they can be, to push themselves and to stand tall as contributors to a global society.

Ethos. Our commitment is to welcome, challenge and inspire each and every pupil to be the very best they can be, to push themselves and to stand tall as contributors to a global society.

Confidence, commitment and achievement are at the heart of everything we do. From the classroom to the extra-curricular activities, we are dedicated to ensuring that boys make the most of their talents within Campbell and beyond.

We nurture the individual and prepare them for the world. Academic achievements are important and we expect our pupils to strive for high grades; it is also our duty to harness the potential in every pupil whether it is academic, creative, physical or otherwise.

We want boys to leave the school with an assured set of values; we want them to believe they can truly make a difference in society. We want our boys to leave the school with things that are going to matter to them for the rest of their lives.

Pastoral Care. We believe that pupils learn best when they are happy, safe and secure and the purpose of our pastoral care is to provide such an environment. The strong, caring ethos of the College is demonstrated by its commitment to the welfare of the pupils and staff.

In Senior School all boys are allocated a Personal Tutor as the first point of contact for parents and our comprehensive Child Protection Policy is issued to all parents before their child commences school. Above and beyond this level of care we have a dedicated medical centre on campus led by the College Matron and a School Doctor who visits our boarders three times a week.

Boarding. We have a successful boarding department which brings an international dimension and unique character to the College; this will enable our pupils to thrive in the increasingly global world in which we all must live and work. We have approximately 133 boarders.

The Curriculum. This is focused upon giving our boys the maximum opportunity to produce the best possible examination results from a varied choice of subjects which meet the needs of the 21st century.

Class sizes are capped at 26 throughout Key Stage 3 to allow boys to grow in confidence and security in their learning as they make the transition from Primary School to Senior School. The teacher to pupil ratio is a generous 1:14, and the curriculum followed at Year 8 comprises English, Maths, Science, Geography, History, Religious Education, French, Art, Drama, Music, Technology, ICT, PE and Learning for Life and Work.

The Campus. Campbell College stands in a secure and impressive 100-acre wooded estate where the academic, boarding, artistic and sporting pursuits are all catered for on site. The College has its own indoor swimming pool, Astro-Turf pitches, squash courts, shooting range, running track and numerous rugby and cricket pitches. It has a variety of sports and assembly halls, drama studio, computer suites and technology areas.

Other Activities. Campbell College is able to provide boys with a host of activities which naturally complement the culture of learning promoted within the school. Whilst the College is widely acknowledged for its sporting excellence, especially in rugby, hockey and cricket, there are many other opportunities available. Alongside a diverse range of sports there are opportunities to participate in The Combined Cadet Force, Duke of Edinburgh's Award scheme, Drama and Music productions and the Charity Action Group.

A competitive House system allows all boys to compete, with camaraderie and collegiality, in numerous inter-House competitions so all have an opportunity to represent their House as well as their school.

Holidays. There are three annual holidays: two weeks at Christmas and Easter, and eight in the summer. In the Christmas and Easter terms there is a half-term break of one week, during which parents of boarders are required to make provision for their sons to be away from school.

Admissions. Campbell College welcomes students at a variety of entry levels. Day boys can begin in Kindergarten and stay through to Sixth Form; boarders may start at Year 8. The school structure is designed to offer our students easy transitions as they grow and mature; they begin in Junior School, then move aged 11 to Middle School, before progressing to Senior School to prepare for their public examinations (GCSE, AS and A2 Level).

There are approximately 895 students in the Senior School of whom 133 are boarders, and 300 students in the Junior School.

Fees per annum (2016–2017). Tuition (Years 8–14): £2,515 (EU citizens), £7,845 (Non EU citizens). Boarding (Years 8–14): £12,955 (EU citizens), £18,280 (non-EU citizens). Junior School: £3,905–£4,190.

As a Voluntary B Grammar School, Campbell College charges an annual fee to all pupils for development and maintenance. The Board of Governors seeks to support applications to the College by offering scholarships and bursaries, the details of which may be found in the Prospectus.

Prospectus. Further information is included in our prospectus which can be obtained from the College Office or you may download a copy from the College website.

Old Campbellian Society. There is a link from the College website.

Charitable status. Campbell College is registered with the Inland Revenue as a charity, number XN45154/1. It exists to provide education for boys.

Governors:
Mrs F Chamberlain, MA (*Chair*)
Mr I Jordan, FCA, MA Cantab (*Vice-~Chari*)
Mr J Andrews, BSc Hons, FCA
Mr G C Browne, BEng Hons, CEng, FIStructE, MICE, MaPS, MConsE
M G B Campbell, BA Hons (*Parent Governor*)
Mr A F W Devlin, LLB Barrister-at-Law
Mr M E J Graham, BSc, MSc, FCIOB
Mr G F Hamilton, BA, FIFP
Mr J R Hassard, MA, BEd, DASE, AdvCertEd, PQH
Sir Mark Horner, QC
Mr H J McKinney, BSc, CertEd (*Staff Governor*)
Mr M A D Moreland, LLB, FCA
Mr J I Taggart, ARICS
Mr W B W Turtle, LLB
Mrs C M Van der Feltz, BA Hons, MCIPD
Mr T R Wilcox, BSc, DipM (*Parent Governor*)
Mr A W J Wilson, BA Hons, MSc, ACMA

Headmaster: **Mr R M Robinson**, MBE, BSc, PGCE, MEd, PQH NI

Vice-Principals:
Mr W E Keown, MA, PGCE
Mr C G Oswald, BSc, PGCE, AdvCertEd, MEd

Senior Teachers:
Mr H J McKinney, BSc, CertEd
Mr H H Robinson, BSc, PGCE
Mrs K E Sheppard, MSc, BSc, PGCE (*Learning Support*)
Mrs S L Coetzee, BMus, PCGE, PGCE Careers
Mr C McIvor, MA, PGCE

Assistant Teachers:
Mr S D Quigg, BSc
Mr A Doherty, BMus Hons, PGCE
Mr C G A Farr, BA, DASE, AdvCertEd, MEd, CertPD
Mr D M McKee, BA, PGCE, DipModLit
Ms B M Coughlin, BEd, PGCertComp
Mrs G E Wilson, BMus, MTD
Mr D Styles, BA, PGCE, Dip IndStudies
Mrs K P Crooks, BA, ATD
Mr B F Robinson, BA, PGCE, MSc
Mr A W Templeton, BSc, PGCE
Mr N R Ashfield, BSc, PGCE
Mr S P Collier, BA, PGCE
Mrs R McNaught, MA, PGCE
Mr G Fry, BA, PGCE
Mr D Walker, BEd
Mrs K-A Roberts, BA, PGCE
Mr B Meban, BSc, PGCE
Mr J McCurdy, BD, MA, PGCE
M P Cousins, BSc, PGCE
Mrs L Haughian, BA, PGCE
Miss D H Shields, MA, MSc, PGCE
Mr M G Chalkley, BA, PGCE, MEd, PQH
Mr N McGarry, BA, PGCE
Mrs M Debbadi, BA, PGCE, MSc

Dr J A Breen, BSc, PGCE, PhD
Mr R D Hall, BSc, PGCE
Mrs E McIlvenny, BA, PGCE
Mrs K Magreehan, BA, PGCE
Ms L Anderson, BA, QTS
Mrs J Bailie, BA, PGCE
Mrs C A M Irwin, BSc, PGCE
Mr P D A Campbell, BEd
Mr T R Thompson, BSc, PGCE
Mr A McCrea, BEng, PGCE
Mrs W Pearson, BEd
Mr J H Rea, BSc, PGCE
Mrs K Murphy, BSc, PGCE
Mrs V Spottiswoode, BA, PGCE
Mr F N Mukula, BSc, AssDipTh, PGCE
Miss J-A Taylor, BA, PGCE
Miss G Lamont, BEd, MSSc
Mr G P Young, BEd
Mrs C M Crozier, BSc, PGCE, MSc
Mr J P Cupitt, BSc, PGCE
Mrs W Shannon, BA, PGCE
Ms K M Marshall, MA, QTS
Mrs K McGarvey, MSci, PGCE
Mr J McNerlin, BSc, PGCE
Mr J Smyth, BSc, PGCE
Mrs E Kennedy, BA, PGDip ESL
Mrs J L Hempstead, MA, PGCE
Ms S Kirsch, BA, PGCE
Dr A Dunne, MA, PhD, PGCE
Mrs E McInerney, BSC, MEd
Mr M Brown, MA, PGCE

Visiting Music Teachers:
Mrs M Fenn (*Woodwind*)
Mrs J Leslie (*Brass and Piano*)
Mrs K Lowry (*Lower Strings*)
Mrs H Neale (*Upper strings and Piano*)
Mr M Wilson (*Brass*)
Mrs L Lynch (*Percussion*)
Mr R Nellis (*Guitar*)

Bursar: K J Wilson, FCA
Headmaster's Secretary: Mrs L Crawford
Medical Officers:
Dr G Millar, BMSc, MBChB, MRCGP
Dr D Best, MRCGP, MRCSed, MBBch
Matron: Mrs E M Hoey, SRN

Junior School:
Head: Miss A Brown, BA, PGCE, MEd, PQH

Mrs E M Gwynne, BEd	Miss K Courtney, MA,
A P Jemphrey, BEd, DASE	PGCE
Mrs P McGarry, BEd	Ms C Martin, BA, PGCE
Mrs F Mottram, BA, ATD	Mrs C Glenn, MA, MEd,
Mr J S Anderson, BEd	PGCE
Mrs H M Jennings, BEd	Mrs S Smith, BSc, PGCE
Hons, Dip PD	Miss S Busby, BSc, PGCE
Mrs L M Leyland, BEd	Miss L Reid, LLB, PGCE
Mr S Montgomery, BEd	Mr A Russell, BA, PGCE

Kindergarten:
Mrs L Wilson, BA, PGCE
Mrs H Reid

Caterham School

Harestone Valley Road, Caterham, Surrey CR3 6YA
Tel: 01883 343028
Fax: 01883 347795

email: enquiries@caterhamschool.co.uk
             admissions@caterhamschool.co.uk
website: www.caterhamschool.co.uk

Motto: *Veritas Sine Timore*.

Caterham School is one of the leading co-educational schools in the country. We are committed to providing an environment in which all pupils are challenged to be the best they can be and one in which pastoral care and well-being underpin academic, co-curricular and sporting excellence. The majority of our pupils are day pupils but we are also a thriving boarding community, which enriches the educational opportunity and experience for all. We believe in providing an education for life for all Caterhamians and we seek to ensure that the learning experience at our school blends the best of tradition with the exciting opportunities provided by new technology. Learning how to learn is a key facet of a Caterham education and is in our view an essential skill for life in the twenty-first century. We believe that a truly excellent school is about more than academic achievement alone: it is also about developing a passion for learning, a capacity for independent and critical thinking, self-awareness and resilience, self-confidence without arrogance and genuine interests that extend beyond the confines of the classroom.

Number in School. In the Senior School there are around 900 pupils, of whom 164 are boarders. In the Preparatory School there are 300 pupils.

Aims. At Caterham School we focus on developing the whole person, aiming to ensure that each pupil leaves here ready for the challenges of life at university and beyond and understanding their responsibilities towards others. We want our pupils to leave Caterham well equipped to engage positively with a rapidly changing world as accomplished problem-solvers and innovators, confident in their ability to lead and with a clear appreciation of and respect for the views and potential of others. In so doing we remain true to our founding Christian principles and values.

Situation. Caterham School is in a rural location in north Surrey just 22 miles from the centre of London. The 200-acre campus is in the beautiful, wooded Harestone Valley, less than a mile from the centre of Caterham, and only five minutes' drive from Junction 6 of the M25. The journey by taxi to London Gatwick airport is 20 minutes and about 50 minutes to London Heathrow.

Caterham Railway Station is a 15-minute walk – a morning shuttle bus to school is available. The frequent trains to London (Victoria or London Bridge) make connections to the capital easy and convenient.

There are separate boarding houses for boys (Townsend and Viney) and girls (Beech Hanger). Common rooms, dormitories (for younger pupils) and study-bedrooms are comfortably furnished, many with en-suite facilities.

In recent years there has been a substantial building and development programme. The boarding accommodation has been extended and refurbished. The sports centre (with indoor pool, fully-equipped fitness suite and sports hall, language laboratory and IT facilities have all benefited from extensive investment. A new all-weather pitch was opened in early 2016 and an expanded performing arts centre will open in September 2016.

The Preparatory School. *Please see entry in IAPS section.* Continuity of education is provided as boys and girls move from the Preparatory School to the Senior School at the age of eleven.

Admission. Intake is by selection on academic merit and on assessment of a pupil's likely positive contribution through good behaviour to the aims, ethos and co-curricular life of the School. All candidates must sit our examinations.

For day pupils the main intake ages are 11+ years, 13+ years and for the Sixth Form. All day pupil candidates are required to attend an interview and a report from the pupil's current school will be required prior to an offer of a place being made in addition to sitting the School's entrance examinations.

Places in the Sixth Form are offered subject to a minimum of six GCSE passes (or equivalent) at Grade A. Additionally, pupils will be expected to meet the specific subject entry requirements for their AS and A Level choices. This is a pass at grade A or B (or equivalent) depending on the subject.

All international applicants for boarding places must pass our examinations which are usually taken at the offices of the British Council or one of our overseas agents. For all international applicants we require a school report at registration.

For further details please contact the Registrar, Mrs A Jones, Tel: 01883 335058, email: admissions@caterham school.co.uk.

Details concerning the admission of pupils to the Pre-Preparatory and Preparatory School are published separately (*see entry in IAPS section*).

Term of Entry. Pupils are normally accepted for entry in September each year, but vacancies may occur at other times.

Scholarships. Scholarships are assessed with a view to encouraging pupils. The breadth and depth of the awards can vary each year depending on the quantity and quality of applicants.

Academic Scholarships: These are awarded at 11+, 13+ and 16+ and can represent up to 50% of the fees

At 11+ and 13+: All external candidates who have registered, and those pupils progressing from Caterham Preparatory School, are automatically considered for an Academic Scholarship. The scholarships are awarded solely on the basis of our entrance examinations, interviews and Head Teacher reports.

At 16+: Candidates applying for Academic Scholarships are required to sit a general paper and two other papers in subjects of their choice that they will be studying at A Level. Examinations and interviews take place in the November preceding entry the following academic year. These scholarships are available to all external candidates, and to internal candidates not already holding an award. Candidates must still satisfy the entry requirement for Sixth Form. In addition to Academic Scholarships, awards may be made for specific subjects, eg languages.

All Rounder Scholarships: These are awarded at 11+ and 13+ and can represent up to 25% of the fees. These scholarships are awarded to candidates who are academically sound and achieve scholarship standard in two of the following subjects: Art, Drama, Music or Sport. They should be a genuine 'all-rounder' with real evidence of potential leadership.

Art & Design Scholarships: These are awarded at 11+, 13+ and 16+ and can represent up to 25% of the fees. Candidates wishing to be considered for a scholarship will initially be asked to submit a portfolio of their work for assessment by the Head of Department. The portfolio should reflect the breadth and depth of personal interest and may include paintings, prints, drawings and photographs of three-dimensional work. Portfolios will be returned. Successful candidates will be invited to attend a scholarship interview and to undertake a practical examination. Sketchbooks and a selection of the work from the portfolio should be made available at the interview. All Art & Design Scholars are expected to be fully committed to the school's Art & Design programme.

Music Scholarships & Awards: Music Scholarships are awarded at 11+, 13+ and 16+ and can represent up to 25% of the fees. In addition, up to four exhibitions may be offered, each to the value of free instrumental music tuition on one or more instruments in school. These awards are made on the basis of musical potential as well as actual achievement. As a guide we would expect students to have achieved grade 4 or above aged 11+; grade 5 or above at 13+ and grade 7/8 at 16+ on their principal instrument. Auditions take place early in the Spring Term during which candidates are required to perform one substantial piece (or two shorter pieces) on their principal instrument, and one piece on a second instrument (if studied). There are also sight-reading, aural tests and an informal viva voce with members of the Music department.

All Music award holders are expected to be ambassadors for the music department taking part in the annual music award holders concert and playing active roles in the co-curricular music programme.

Performing Arts Scholarships: These are awarded at 11+ and 13+ and can represent up to 25% of the fees. They are awarded on the basis of performance in the entrance examination and interview, together with performance in the following disciplines: dance, drama or music. Candidates will be expected to excel in two of these disciplines, with potential to develop the third.

Sports Scholarships: These are awarded at 11+, 13+ and 16+ and can represent up to 25% of the fees. Candidates are expected to show exceptional promise in at least one sport and have an established record of achievement in one of Caterham School's major sports at their current school, and at club/county level. Candidates will be required to take part in drills and game situations to show evidence of their positional and tactical awareness as well as skill, agility and fitness level. Records of achievement and school recommendations will be taken into consideration. All Sports Scholars are expected to be fully committed to the School's annual sports programme.

Boarding/International Scholarships: We are prepared to consider awarding a scholarship of up to 25% of the fees to a pupil who is judged to have the potential to make a significant contribution to the boarding community. If applicable at 16+, arrangements can be made for Academic Scholarship assessments to take place overseas. Please contact the Registrar for details.

Science Scholarships: These are awarded at 16+ and can represent up to 25% of the fees. Candidates are expected to show exceptional promise in at least two subjects (chosen from Biology, Physics, Chemistry or Maths) and have an established record of achievement in the subjects at their current school. The Head of Science will interview candidates. All Science Scholars are expected to be fully committed to the School's curricular and co-curricular science activities.

Drama Scholarships: These are awarded at 16+ and can represent up to 25% of the fees. Candidates will be required to perform and discuss two contrasting monologues, one of which must be from the classical repertoire. They will be required to attend an interview to which they should bring a portfolio of their experiences and achievements.

Bursaries. We wish to ensure that Caterham School is accessible to talented students, irrespective of parental income. Therefore, any prospective pupil from a low-income family is eligible to apply for a Caterham Bursary to obtain means-tested financial support in respect of day fees. Bursaries do not preclude pupils from holding a scholarship award.

Bursaries can be offered to new pupils and those who are already in the school and whose families have suffered sudden and unexpected financial hardship. All Bursaries are reassessed annually.

A fully-funded day place for a Sixth Form student is provided by a Wilberforce Bursary. Bursaries are also available for the sons and daughters of URC Clergy, Regular Forces and FCO personnel.

Fees per term (2016–2017). Full Boarding £10,395–£10,954; Weekly Boarding £10,312–£10,871; Day £5,566–£5,826. Lunch for Day Pupils: £220.

Curriculum. Preparatory School: A wide range of subjects is provided following National Curriculum guidelines. (*For further details see entry in IAPS section.*)

Senior School: For GCSE the core curriculum is English Language and Literature, Mathematics, Physics, Chemistry, Biology and a Modern Language as well as PE and Games and RPSE. To this core is added three further subjects from Latin, Greek, Modern Languages (French, German, Spanish, Italian), Art, 3D Design, Music, Drama, GCSE PE, Economics and Business Studies, History, Geography and Religious Studies. All of the subjects offered at GCSE are available at A Level, as well as Further Mathematics, Economics, Business Studies, Photography, Psychology, Politics and Textiles. The curriculum is supplemented by an innovative, non-examined 'Forum' programme that includes expert led lectures and seminars designed to prepare students for the opportunities and responsibilities of adult life. Sixth Form students can also participate in the Caterham Award which recognises public speaking, community service and leadership development.

Music, Drama and Creative Arts. Music is an important feature of the life of the School. Individual lessons are given on the piano, in string, brass and wind instruments, and the organ. The Choral Society performs at least one major choral work each year. Each term there are several School concerts and a programme of recitals is arranged. Drama is also well-supported and popular. Each year there are three major productions which involve a large number of pupils both on and off stage. The expertise within the Art Department is broad, including painting, printmaking, textiles, fashion, ceramics, photography, digital media and sculpture and pupils are encouraged to pursue their interests in creative work, as diverse as ceramics, textiles, digital manipulation, drypoint etching and mixed media.

Societies and Hobbies. All pupils are encouraged to pursue a hobby or constructive outside interest, and there are a large number of active School Societies, including: Art, CCF, Chess, Amnesty International, Astronomy, Dance, Debating, Duke of Edinburgh's Award, Film, Greek, ICT Club, Kit Car Club (Caterham 7), Moncrieff-Jones (Sixth Form Science), Music, Circus, Textiles, Young Enterprise. The School has an active charity committee and significant funds are raised annually to support partner schools in Tanzania and Ukraine.

Games. Most of the playing fields adjoin the School including an all-weather synthetic grass pitch for Lacrosse, Hockey and Tennis. Overall there are many sporting activities, but in each term at least one major game is played. For boys it is Rugby in the Autumn Term, Hockey in the Spring Term and Cricket in the Summer. Girls play Lacrosse, Netball, Rounders and Tennis. Pupils can also participate in Athletics, Fencing, Equestrian, Swimming, Badminton, Basketball, Cross Country, Squash, Soccer, Taekwondo and, in the Summer Term, Sailing, Windsurfing and Canoeing.

Health. There is a well-equipped Health Centre with a SRN Sister. The School Doctor attends regularly.

Careers. The Careers staff are available to give advice. The School has membership of the Independent Schools Careers Organisation and parents are encouraged to enter their sons or daughters for the ISCO Aptitude Test in the Sixth Form year. The School arranges Careers and Higher Education Forums and the Headmaster and Careers staff are available to discuss careers with parents.

Old Caterhamians' and Parents' Associations. The School has flourishing Old Caterhamians' and Parents' Associations. Information about these may be obtained from the School.

Charitable status. Caterham School is a Registered Charity, number 1109508. Its aim is to develop the academic and personal potential of each pupil in a Christian context.

Board of Trustees:
Chairman: Mr J E K Smith, CBE
Vice Chairman & Honorary Treasurer: Mr I R M Edwards [OC]
Mr D P Charlesworth [OC]
Dr S R Critchley
Mrs A M Crowe
Mrs T Eldridge-Hinmers
The Reverend N J Furley-Smith
Mr J Joiner [OC]
Mr M H P Smith
Mrs S M Whittle
Mrs P H Wilkes
Mr A P Wilson

Clerk to the Trustees: Mr J C L King, MBE

[OC] *Old Caterhamian*

The School Staff:

Headmaster: Mr Ceri Jones, MA Cantab

Principal Deputy Head: Mr Daniel Gabriele, MA Oxon
Deputy Head (Academic): Mr Tom Murphy, MA Oxon
Deputy Head (Boarding): Mrs Catherine Drummond, BA Hons
Deputy Head (External Relations): Mr Matthew Godfrey, MA
Director of Learning and Teaching: Mr Kim Wells, MA Cantab

Senior Teacher (Social Responsibility and Engagement): Anthony Fahey, BA
Senior Teacher (Pastoral): David King, BA Oxon
Senior Teacher (Operations): Andrew Taylor, BSc
Senior Teacher (Academic): Rob Saleem, MA Oxon
Senior Teacher (Director of Innovation): Adam Webster, BA Oxon

Ms Ana Ambles, ASCENTIS (*Spanish*)
Mr Magnus Anderson, MA Cantab, MEng (*Physics, Head of Fifth Year*)
Mr Adam Assen, BMus (*Director of Music*)
Dr Rachel Avery, PhD (*Psychology*)
Mr Jonathan Batty, BSc (*Master in charge of Cricket and Assistant Director of Sport*)
Mrs Charlotte Bell, MA (*Head of Art and History of Art*)
Mr Christopher Bovet-White, BSc (*Biology*)
Mrs Clare Brown (*Head of Careers, PSHEE*)
Mr Rob Clarke, BSc (*Director of Sport*)
Mrs Catherine Clifton, BA (*Head of German*)
Mr Philip Comerford, MSc (*Physics*)
Mr Toby Cooper, MA, AKC (*Head of Politics, History*)
Miss Angela Cox, BA (*English*)
Mr Nick Crombie, BA (*English, Second in Department*)
Miss Nancy Dawrant, MA Oxon (*Mathematics, House Coordinator*)
Mrs Victoria de Silva, BA (*Economics and Business Studies*)
Mr Michael Dimakos, PhD (*Mathematics*)
Mrs Jackie Driscoll, BA (*Drama*)
Mrs Cecile Ellis, MA (*French Language Assistant*)
Mrs Louise Fahey, BA (*Head of Drama & Theatre Studies*)
Mr Peter Friend, BSc (*Hockey Academy Manager*)
Mr Carlos Garcia, BA (*Modern Languages Coordinator, Spanish*)
Miss Elisabeth Gibbs, MA (*Head of EAL*)
Miss Rebecca Goddard, BSc (*Biology, Head of Harestone*)
Mr Tim Graham, BA Cantab (*Teacher of Classics, Graduate Assistant Boys Games*)

Dr Emily Gray, PhD (*English*)
Mr Tristan Hall, BMus (*Music*)
[Dr Kate Hanford, PhD (*Chemistry*)]
Miss Rachel Hart, BA (*PE, Head of Fourth Year*)
Mr Harry Hawkridge, BSc (*Chemistry, Head of Underwood*) [Maternity cover]
Mr Adam Hicks, MEng (*Physics, Assistant Head of Fourth Year*)
[Mrs Holly Howden, BA (*English*)]
Mrs Harriet Howgego, MChem (*Chemistry*)
Mrs Becky Hunter, BA Oxon (*Classics, Religious Studies*)
Mr Colin James, BSc, MBA (*Economics and Business Studies, Director of Sixth Form – Lower Sixth*)
Mrs Katy James, BA (*Head of History, Politics and Resident Tutor Beech Hanger*)
Miss Lucy Jones, MChem (*Chemistry*) [maternity cover]
Mr Warren Jones, BA (*Modern Foreign Languages*)
Mr David Keyworth, MSc (*Head of Chemistry*)
[Mrs Katie Koi, BA (*Head of Lacrosse, PE*)]
Mr Darron Kokott, BA (*Head of Psychology, Head of Third Year*)
Mr Stephen Lander, MA Oxon, MSc (*Mathematics*)
Dr Anthony Langdon, PhD (*Head of Mathematics*)
Mrs Julia Laverick, BEd (*French, German*)
Miss Jaclyn Leach, BSc (*Head of Examination PE*)
Mrs Natalie Lomas, BA (*Head of Second Year, PE*)
Mr Ronan MacManus, MMus (*Head of Strings*)
Mr John Mansell, BA Oxon (*Head of Physics*)
Mr Steven Marlow, MBioChem Oxon (*Biology*)
Mrs Nicole McVitty, DEUG, Licence d'Anglais (*Head of French, Spanish, Deputy Director of Sixth Form – Lower Sixth*)
Revd Dr Rick Mearkle, BA, MDiv, DMin (*Chaplain, Head of Religious Studies, PSHEE*)
Mrs Vanessa Mesher, MA (*Geography*)
Mr Nick Mills, BA (*Head of Viney, History*)
Mr Alexander Moore, BSc (*Economics and Business Studies, Dance, Assistant Head of Second Year*)
Mr Robert Mugridge, BA (*Geography, Head of Aldercombe*)
Miss Alice O'Donnell, MA (*Head of English*)
Mr James Ogilvie, BSc (*Mathematics, Internal Examinations Officer*)
Ms Helen O'Hare, MA (*Head of Textile*)
Mr Mathew Owen, MA Oxon (*Classics, CCF*)
Mr Neil Parker, MSc Econ (*Head of Spanish, Italian, Head of Newington*)
Mrs Penny Parker, BA MEd (*Mathematics, Assistant Head of Fifth Year*)
Miss Collette Pateman, BA (*Head of 3D Design*)
Mr Andrew Patterson, MA (*Sports and Events Coordinator*)
Mrs Rachel Pearce, MA (*Mathematics, Assistant head of Third Year*)
Dr Rachel Pilkington, PhD (*Chemistry*)
Mrs Clare Quinton (*Head of Beech Hanger*)
Mr Dan Quinton, MA Oxon, FSB (*Head of Science, Head of Biology*)
Mr Daniel Richards, BA (*Head of Rugby, History, Politics*)
Mrs Helena Richards, BMus (*Assistant Director of Music, Composer in Residence, Dance*)
Miss Jemma Riches, BMus (*Music, Head of Wind*)
Mrs Zoe Roberts, BA (*Spanish, Assistant Head of First Year*)
[Dr Jamie Robinson, PhD (*Biology, Duke of Edinburgh's Award Bronze*)]
Miss Francesca Ryan (*Graduate Assistant Girls Games*)
Mr Robbert Schenk (*School Sports Coach, Head of Hockey*)
Mrs Fiona Scott, BSc (*Assistant Head of Mathematics*)
Mr Nicholas Sharman, BA (*3D Design*)

Mrs Aimee Seal, BSc (*Biology, Head of First Year*)
Mrs Louise Sheridan, BA (*Textile*)
Miss Jennifer Simpson (*Lacrosse Coach, Assistant Head of Ridgefield*)
Dr Christopher Sinclair, MSc, PhD (*Physics*)
Miss Rebecca Smith, BA (*Philosophy and Theology, Head of Ridgefield*)
Mr Ross Smith, BSc (*Swimming Academy Manager*)
Mrs Isabelle Solley, BA (*Drama Assistant, Assistant Head of Lewisham*)
Dr Robert Soltysiak, MChem (*Chemistry*)
Mr Richard Stamper, MA (*Teacher of EAL*)
Ms Catherine Stedman, MA Cantab (*English*)
Mr Neil Stokes, BSc, MA (*Head of Computing and Digital Creativity*)
Mrs Gaelle Sullivan, MA (*SENDCo, Assistant Director of Learning and Teaching*)
Ms Anne-Marie Sutcliffe, MA Cantab (*History*)
Mr Alistair Taylor, BSc (*Games & PE, Sports Coach and Head of Strength and Conditioning, Deputy Head of Viney House*)
Mrs Lorraine Temple, LRAM, ACRM, Prof Cert, DipRAM (*Head of Brass*)
Mr Stuart Terrell, MPhil (*Head of Geography, Deputy Director of Sixth Form – Upper Sixth*)
Mr Daryl Todd, MA Oxon (*Mathematics, Head of Lewisham*)
Mr Andion van Niekerk, BA (*Head of Townsend, English, Geography*)
Mr Kristian Waite, MA Oxon (*Head of Classics*)
Ms Amelia Wallace, MA (*Head of Photography, Art*)
Mrs Cathriona Wallace, BA, ACIB (*Economics and Business Studies*)
Miss Hannah Walters, BSc (*Physics*)
Mr Conrad Ware, BSc (*Mathematics*)
Mr John Weiner, LLB, ACA (*Director of Sixth Form – Upper Sixth*)
Mrs Isis Whitwell, BSc (*Biology*)
Mr Jan Whyatt, MA, BA (*Philosophy and Theology*)
Ms Hannah Wildsmith, BA (*English*)
Mr Ben Wilkinson, BA (*3D Design, Head of Outdoor Learning, Duke of Edinburgh's Award Gold and Silver and Coordinator*)
Mrs Alexandra Yankova, BA (*English, Drama*)

Registrar: Mrs Alison Jones

Preparatory School:
Head: Mr Howard Tuckett, MA
Deputy Head: Miss Emma Neville, BA Hons, MEd Cantab

Charterhouse

Godalming, Surrey GU7 2DX

Tel:	Admissions: +44 (0)1483 291501
	Headmaster: +44 (0)1483 291601
	Bursary and Enquiries: +44 (0)1483 291500
Fax:	Admissions: +44 (0)1483 291507
	Headmaster: +44 (0)1483 291647
email:	reception@charterhouse.org.uk
	admissions@charterhouse.org.uk
website:	www.charterhouse.org.uk
Twitter:	@CharterhouseSch

Motto: '*Deo Dante Dedi*'

Charterhouse was founded in 1611 by Thomas Sutton who made provision for 40 scholars, or 'Gownboys', to be housed in fine Tudor buildings on the site of the fourteenth century Carthusian monastery near Smithfield in London.

In 1872 the School moved to its present magnificent 250 acre site near Godalming, Surrey.

Today the School has around 800 pupils, all of whom, except for about 30 day boarders, are boarders. Charterhouse accepts boys at 13+ and girls at 16+.

Academic. The highly qualified teaching staff combines academic excellence with sympathetic and imaginative teaching to foster a love of knowledge and study. The emphasis is on developing independent thinking and enquiring minds, not simply on fulfilling the requirements of public examinations. The curriculum follows the normal path to (I)GCSEs in Year 11, followed by a choice of Cambridge Pre-U courses or the IB Diploma Programme in the Sixth Form. We aim to stretch and challenge all our pupils, in many cases well beyond the demands of the syllabus. Academic results are excellent, and the university destinations of our leavers reflect both their abilities and the quality of the education we provide.

Extracurricular activities have a high profile, and pupils are encouraged to develop a variety of interests. Music, art, technology and drama are popular and successful, with work of the highest quality from the most talented, and wide participation from others of all abilities. A remarkable variety of games are played, with school teams at all levels, and a large number of house matches for those who wish to participate. The Queen's Sports Centre, three Astro-Turf pitches and new tennis courts complement many acres of playing fields.

Pastoral Care. Charterhouse provides both a stimulating and a supportive environment, and we ensure that our pupils' time is engaging, inspiring and happy. We hold an induction programme for new pupils, social and cultural outings for sixth formers, and numerous clubs and societies for all ages.

Daily life for all pupils at Charterhouse revolves around the twelve houses. Each Housemaster takes responsibility for the welfare and progress of the pupils in his or her house and is the principal point of contact with their parents. Housemasters and their families live in the houses, as do the Matrons.

Each girl is a member of one of the houses, which will act as her base during the school day. Girl boarders spend the night in their own very comfortable Halls of Residence or in the separate girls' wing of the Sixth Form House.

A Tutor oversees the academic and social development of each pupil. The Tutor's role is to nurture and encourage, and to ensure that pupils make the most of their time at school. Tutors can also help to sort out any problems, and take an active interest in their tutees, attending concerts, plays and sporting events in which they participate.

Admissions.

13+ entry. Most boys arrive at Charterhouse from prep schools at the age of thirteen. Parents wishing to enter their sons for the School should contact the Director of Admissions at least 3 years before they are due to come to the School.

Some boys are admitted from other schools in Britain and overseas after taking our own tests, usually in the January of the year of entry.

Sixth Form. Parents wishing to enter their sons or daughters to enter Charterhouse in the Sixth Form should contact the Director of Admissions at the beginning of the summer term in the year before the September entry.

Visits. Prospective parents and their children are warmly invited to visit Charterhouse where they normally meet the Headmaster or the Director of Admissions and other staff and members of the School.

Full details on the Admissions processes are available on the School website: www.charterhouse.org.uk.

Fees per term (2016–2017). Boarders £12,258, Day Boarders £10,129. The Governing Body reserves the right to alter the School fee at its discretion. At least one term's notice is required before the removal of a pupil from the School.

Scholarships, Exhibitions and Bursaries.

13+ entry:

Ten Foundation Scholarships and up to five Exhibitions are offered. The examination is held in May.

A Benn Scholarship is offered for proficiency in Classics.

Up to five Music Scholarships and two Exhibitions are offered. The examinations are held at the School at the end of January. Music tuition on two instruments is free for Music Scholars and on one or two instruments for Exhibitioners.

Two Art Scholarships are offered as a result of an examination held at the School at the end of January.

One Design and Innovation Scholarship is offered after an assessment in February.

Five Peter Attenborough Awards are made annually to candidates who demonstrate all-round distinction.

Up to two Bob Noble Awards are made annually to exceptional sportsmen.

Sixth Form entry:

Up to six Sir Robert Birley Academic Scholarships and seven Academic Exhibitions are offered annually on the basis of performance in the entrance examination and interview.

Two Art Scholarships are offered; the examinations for these awards will normally be held in November.

Five Music Scholarships are offered annually, normally awarded in December. Music tuition on two instruments is free for Music Scholars. In addition, there is the John Pilling Organ Scholarship.

The Fletcher Scholarship is offered to a pupil from a local state school to attend Fletcherites, the Sixth Form House.

Charterhouse in Southwark offers a biennial Scholarship to a boy or girl from Southwark to attend the Sixth Form at Charterhouse.

Bursaries. All Awards (except Exhibitions) may be increased to the value of the full School fee in cases of proven financial need.

Two Entrance Bursaries are offered to boys in Year 6 after a selection day in May.

Charitable status. Charterhouse School is a Registered Charity, number 312054. Its aims and objectives are the provision of education through the medium of a secondary boarding school for boys, and girls in the Sixth Form.

Governing Body:
Chairman: N J Kempner, BSc
J N B Bovill, BA
Ms S Chao, BSc
Professor M J Collins, MA, DPhil
Cllr Mrs C M Curran, BSc
Professor V C Emery, PhD, FSB
The Very Revd Dianna Gwilliams, MA
D F Jennings, MA, Dip Arch, RIBA
P M R Norris, MA
A Reid, MA, MBA
W S M Robinson, BA
Dr R Townsend, MA, DPhil
Professor K R Willison, BSc, PhD

Clerk to the Governing Body: Ms S L Gowland, BSc, MA Ed, ACIS

Headmaster: A J Turner, BA, LLM

Second Master: J H Kazi, MA

Deputy Headmaster (Academic): S P M Allen, MA, MEd

Deputy Headmaster (Pastoral): D P Corran, MA

Assistant Head (Pastoral): Miss A J A Hawkins, BA

Assistant Head (*Wellbeing*): J S Wilson, BA

Assistant Staff:
T J Aberneithie, BA (*Head of Design & Technology*)
Miss P Aguado, BA (*Head of Modern Languages*)
A Aidonis, MA, PhD (*Master of the Scholars*)
Mrs S C Allen, MA
Mrs A Alonso, BA
P A Bagley, MA (*Head of Biology*)
G Balasubramanian, MSc, PhD
Miss L F Batty, BSc
W R Baugniet, LLB, LLD, LLM
N E Beasant, BA (*Director of Sport*)
M J Begbie, MA (*Master of Creative Arts*)
M P Bicknell
J A H Bingham, MA
M L J Blatchly, MA, FRCO
Miss A Boggian, BA
S F C Brennan, BA
Miss A C Brooking, MA
K D Brown, BSc (*Deputy Director of Sport*)
R Brown, MPhys, PhD (*Master of the Specialists*)
The Revd C A Case, BA MTh (*The Senior Chaplain*)
N L Coopper, BSc, MA
M J Crosby
D A Cruse, BA, MA, PhD (*Head of Science*)
M J Dobson, BA
M K Elston, BSc (*Head of Mathematics*)
O P Elton, BA
Miss E A Fletcher, BA
Major R N D Follett, BA
D R Fox, BA
Miss E J Fox, BA (*Master of the Under School*)
J D Freeman, BA (*Director of Drama*)
J P Freeman, MA
P Funcasta, MA, MSc
N S Georgiakakis, MSc
G H M Gergaud, L-ès-L (*Head of French*)
M R Gillespie, BA (*Head of History*)
N Hadfield, MA
E Hadley, BA (*Head of Theology, Philosophy & Ethics*)
C R G Hall, MA
I J M Hamilton
R W T Haynes, MA
J S Hazeldine, BA (*Head of Careers and Tutoring*)
S T Hearn, MSc, MInstP
D G Howells
I A Hoffmann de Visme, MSc
D G Howells
Miss D Huang, BA
A R Hunt, MA
S D James, MA (*Master of the Fifths*)
A G Johnson, MSc (*Master of Examinations*)
A Johnston, MA, PhD (*Head of Academic Monitoring*)
G M Kemp, MSc, MMath, PhD
D Lancefield, CPhys, MInstP, MIEE, MIEEE, PhD (*Head of Physics*)
P J Langman, PhD
T Marlow, MSci, PhD
C W Marsh, MA
S P Marshall, MMath, DPhil
D P Martucci, BSc
R N C Massey, MPhys (*Master of the Removes*)
D J McCombes, MA (*Master of the Specialists*)
Mrs C L McDonald, MA (*Head of History*)
Ms E McGowan, BSc
Mrs E M McIntyre, MA
R C D Millard, MA, MPhil (*Head of Academic Music*)
P Monkman, MA (*Director of Art*)
J D L Moore, BSc, MSc
R W Morgan

M W Nash, BA
J Nelmes, MA (*Head of Classics*)
G W Nelson, BSc, MSc, DPhil
Mrs E P Nelson, MSc
B Nicholls, MA, AMusTCL, FRSA (*Director of Social Responsibility*)
S J Northwood, BA, PhD
Mrs M H Orson, BA
Miss J Oxley, BA (*Head of Business & Management*)
R J Paler, MA (*Head of Government & Politics*)
J N Parsons, BA, LRAM, ARCM
N S Pelling, MA
Miss H E Pinkney, BA
S R Plater, BSc
Miss C L R Pounder, BSc
E F Poynter, BA
J L Price, BA (*Head of German*)
P Price, MA (*Head of Geography*)
Mrs S J Pritchard, BA, MA, MCLIP
Miss H K Punnett, BSc
P J Rand, BA, PhD
Miss E J Rees, BSc
E J Reid, MMath
A N Reston, BA, MSt
T E Reynolds, MA, MSc
I S Richards, MA
J M Richardson, BA (*Safeguarding Officer*)
B A Shah, BA, MMath
Miss N C Sheddon, BSc
M N Shepherd, MA, FRCO, ARCM (*Director of Music*)
J M Silvester, BSc
R W Smeeton, ARCM, LRPS, MLC
G Smith, MChem, PhD
R H Snell, BSc, MChem, DPhil (*Head of Chemistry*)
C A M Sparrow, MA (*Master of the Yearlings*)
P S Stimpson, MEng
Mrs M H Swift, BDs
W T Taylor, MSci, MA
Miss R C Thomas, BA
W R Tink, BA
Miss J Tod, MSc
J C Troy, BSc, MBA (*Head of Economics*)
J F Tully, BEng, FICS, FRGS
Mrs L J Wakeling, MA (*Head of Higher Education*)
N P Wakeling, MA (*Head of English*)
The Revd A J M Watkinson, BA, MA (*Chaplain*)
A Wiscombe, BA
S K Woolley, MA
D G Wright, LTCL
E H Zillekens, BA, DPhil (*Master i/c of Archives*)

Archivist: Mrs C R I Smith, BA, MAA

Medical Officer: Dr A Borthwick, MA, MB, Bchir

Senior Chaplain: The Revd C A Case, BA, MTh

Counsellors:
Ms J Symes, BA, MBACP, UKCP, SRN, CQSW
Mrs V Gordon-Graham, MA Psych & Counselling, PG Dip CBT

Director of Finance & Strategy: D S Armitage, MBE, MSc
Director of Admissions: Mrs I Hutchinson, BA
Estate Bursar: Mrs E Humphreys, RIBA
Finance Bursar: Mrs V Western, BA, FCA

Director of Cricket: M P Bicknell
Director of Football: D Howells
Director of Hockey: D R Fox
Head of Racquets: M J Crosby

Houses and Housemasters:
Saunderites: Mrs S C Allen

Verites: E J Reid
Gownboys: A N Reston
Girdlestoneites: Dr P J Langman
Lockites: A R Hunt
Weekites: E F Poynter
Hodgsonites: I S Richards
Daviesites: J F Tully
Bodeites: Dr A Aidonis
Pageites: N S Pelling
Robinites: S T Hearn
Fletcherites: Miss A C Brooking

Cheltenham College

Bath Road, Cheltenham, Gloucestershire GL53 7LD

Tel: College: 01242 265600
         Admissions: 01242 265662
         Bursar: 01242 265686
Fax: College: 01242 265630
         Headmaster: 01242 265685
         Bursar: 01242 265687
email: info@cheltenhamcollege.org
website: www.cheltenhamcollege.org
Twitter: @cheltcollege
Facebook: @CheltCollege

Motto: *Labor Omnia Vincit*

Situated in 72 acres of beautiful grounds in the heart of the Cotswolds, Cheltenham College is one of the country's leading co-educational independent schools for boarding and day pupils aged 13–18. Combining a strong academic record with a considerable reputation for sport, drama, music and outward-bound activities, College offers an outstanding all-round education. Founded in 1841, it was the first of the great Victorian schools.

Location. Stunning buildings and first-class playing fields provide a magnificent setting near the centre of Regency Cheltenham. Situated in the heart of the beautiful Cotswolds with excellent road and rail connections with London and the major airports, Cheltenham College offers all the advantages of life in a thriving town community, whilst maintaining a separate campus life.

Numbers. Boys: 310 boarders; 65 day boys. Girls: 220 boarders; 60 day girls.

Admission. Entry to College is into Third Form at 13+ or Lower Sixth at 16+. Pupils may also be admitted into the Fourth Form at 14+. Entry at 13+ can be secured in three ways: Common Entrance, College Entrance papers or College Academic Scholarship papers. Entry at 16+ can be secured by scholarship and entry tests in November or March, good GCSE predictions and a testimonial from previous school. Full details, prospectuses and application forms can be obtained from the Admissions Office who will always be glad to welcome parents who wish to see College. There is a registration fee of £150 and a final acceptance fee of £1,000 (for pupils aged 13–16) or £1,350 (for Sixth Form entrants) which is deducted from the final term's account.

Scholarships and Bursaries. Scholarships and Exhibitions are available for entry at both 13+ and 16+ (as well as 11+ into Cheltenham Prep). They are offered in Academic, Art, Design Technology, Drama, Music (including 16+ Organ and Choral awards) and Sport. Discounts for Armed Forces Families and bursaries are also available.

Fees per term (2016–2017). Boarders £11,550, Day pupils £8,660. Sixth Form: Boarders £11,865, Day pupils £8,975.

Chapel. There is a ten-minute service in the Chapel most weekday mornings and a main service each Sunday. There is a Confirmation service every year.

Houses. The 10 Houses, eight boarding and two day, are at the heart of College life and all located around the College campus. Girls are in four houses and boys are in six houses. Accommodation and pastoral care is outstanding for both boys and girls.

Planned Developments. There has already been significant refurbishment of the College Library, Big Classical Theatre and, most recently, the Science Centre in the last few years. Looking forward, a rolling programme of boarding house refurbishment will continue whilst at the same time completing many exciting new development projects including the creation of a new rowing base and new business and economics learning centre.

Curriculum. On entry at 13+, pupils follow a broad course for one year, before embarking upon GCSE in the Fourth Form. The core of the curriculum comprises: IGCSE English Language and English Literature, IGCSE Mathematics, and all three Sciences (either as Dual Award or Triple Award). All then choose at least one Modern Language (French, German, Spanish); and four options from Art, Classical Civilisation, Design Technology (Resistant Materials, Textiles), Drama, Geography, Greek, History, Latin, Music, PE and Theology, Philosophy and Ethics. In the Sixth Form, twenty five A Level subjects are offered and all students complete an EPQ. Boys and girls and given extensive preparation for entrance to Oxford, Cambridge and other top Russell Group universities. Over 98% of leavers go on to university.

Cultural Activities. The Arts are central to the life of College, with at least six plays being staged each year in the school's various theatres. Boys and girls are encouraged to attend concerts, plays, films and lectures not only in Cheltenham but in nearby Oxford, Stratford, Bristol and London. College is also significantly involved in Cheltenham's Jazz, Science, Literature and Music Festivals. Art is housed in Thirlestaine House, a beautifully elegant early nineteenth century mansion, with a Gallery that houses an exhibition of current Art and that also serves as an excellent chamber music concert hall, housing the superb Steinway concert grand piano. The beautiful Chapel houses a magnificent 3-manual Harrison & Harrison organ. Music plays a vital part in College life, with pupils able to learn just about every orchestral instrument imaginable, even bagpipes. The Chapel Choir, Chamber Choir and Barbershop groups enable singers to reach very high standards and many achieve university Choral Scholarships. The numerous instrumental groups and ensembles, from the Orchestra, Chamber Orchestra and Wind Band to the Jazz Bands and String Quartets, regularly perform in Cheltenham Town Hall, the town's Pump Rooms, as well as in the College Chapel and other venues. Both the top Jazz Band 'JIG' and the Chamber Choir have recorded CDs in the last few years.

Sports. Cheltenham College is one of the strongest schools nationally in a wide cross section of sports and benefits from top-level sports professionals and coaches. The main boys' games are rugby, hockey, tennis, cricket and rowing. The main girls' games are hockey, netball, tennis and rowing. In addition to the two astroturf pitches, the Sports Hall and swimming pool, there are excellent facilities for other sports available, which include rackets, squash, equestrian, golf, athletics, cross country, badminton, polo, and shooting.

Activities. On entry to College, a structured programme of outdoor pursuits, team building exercises and leadership initiatives are provided for one year. Following this, CCF is compulsory for one year at age 14, optional thereafter. The Duke of Edinburgh's Award scheme operates at Bronze and Gold level and a wide range of expeditions is available, including an annual trip to Nepal. College offers a full range of activities in the period after GCSEs. Up to 30 clubs operate weekly, including shooting, dance, pottery, film-making and drama.

Service. There is a strong Community Service scheme which serves the town, and an Industrial Link scheme enables all College Sixth Formers to experience the world of work. The College's Humanitarian Aid Project raises funds for building and refurbishment work in a number of orphanages and schools and the members of the group regularly visit Romania and Kenya to provide practical assistance. Wherever possible, all College facilities are made available to the town, especially the festivals, and other schools.

University entry and Careers. There is a full-time teacher in charge of Higher Education and Careers, and a Higher Education and Careers Advisor. In addition, every Sixth Former has a tutor who is charged with ensuring that he or she is fully aware of the opportunities and challenges available.

Cheltonian Association. Tel: 01242 265694.

Cheltenham College Preparatory School. *For details see entry in IAPS section.*

Charitable status. Cheltenham College is a Registered Charity, number 311720. As a charity it is established for the purpose of providing an efficient course of education for boys and girls.

Visitor: The Rt Revd The Lord Bishop of Gloucester

The Council:
President: Mr WJ Straker-Nesbit
Deputy President: Dr R Acheson

Mr R Badham-Thornahill	Mrs R Lewis
Mrs J Blackburn	Mr H Monro
Mr P Brettell	Mr T Smith
Mr C Cooper	Dr G Valori
Miss K Cox	Dr P Wingfield
Mrs K Hickey	Mr M Wynne

Headmaster: **Dr Alex Peterken**, BA Durham, MA London, EdD Surrey

Senior Deputy Head (*Pastoral*): Mr Crispin Dawson, BA Bristol
Deputy Head (*Academic*): Mr Simon Brian, MA Edinburgh
Deputy Head (*Learning and Wellbeing*): Dr Mary Plint, BEd Johannesburg, MEd, PhD Gloucestershire
Assistant Head (*Co-curricular*): Mr Stephen McQuitty, BSc Nottingham
Assistant Head (*Pastoral*): Mrs Anna Cutts, BEd Middlesex
Assistant Head (*IT*): Ms Suzanna Harris,
Bursar: Mr John Champion, FCIB
Director of Admissions & Marketing: Mrs Amanda Naylor
Senior Housemistress: Mrs Anna Cutts, BEd Middlesex

Special Responsibilities:
Head of Upper College: Mr Daniel Evans, BA Manchester
Head of Lower College: Mr Graham Cutts, BA Sheffield City
Head of Third Form: Mr Simon Conner, BSc Durham
Chaplain: Revd Dr Adam Dunning, BA Oxford, PhD Birmingham
Head of Prep School Liaison and Parental Relations: Mr Simon Conner, BSc Durham
Scholarships Coordinator: Mrs Alexandra Eldred, BA Durham
Director of Extracurricular: Mr Dominic Faulkner, BSc Imperial College London
Head of Higher Education & Careers: Mr Daniel Evans, BA Manchester
Librarian: Mr Beren-Dain Delbrooke-Jones, MA Bristol
Head of PSHCE: Mr Tom Carpenter, BSc Bristol
Examinations Officer: Mr Dominic Meason, BA Gloucestershire
Director of Internationalism and Culture: Mr Nick Nelson, BA East Anglia

Development Director: Mrs Christiane Dickens, BA Nottingham
Assistant Development Director: Mr Sebastian Bullock, BA Exeter

Heads of Departments:
Art: Ms Jo Millar, BA Bath Spa
Art History: Mr Nick Nelson, BA East Anglia
Classics: Mr Tom Lambert, BA, MPhil King's College Cambridge
Design & Technology: Mr David Lait, BSc Brunel
Economics: Dr Graham Mallard, MA Cambridge
Business Studies: Mr Jonathan Mace, BA Durham, MSc Leicester
English: Mr Tim Brewis, BA Exeter
English as an Additional Language: Miss Helen Davies, BA Lancaster
Drama: Miss Sian McBride, MA Warwick
Geography: Miss Emily Hartley, MA St Andrews
History: Miss Jo Doidge-Harrison, MA Cantab
Learning Support: Dr Mary Plint, BEd Johannesburg, MEd, PhD Gloucestershire
Mathematics: Dr Brendan Enright, BSc, PhD Hull
Modern Languages: Mrs Ester Leach, BA UWE
Music: Mr David McKee, MA Exeter
Psychology: Dr Tricia Norman, BSc Durham, PhD Reading
Theology, Philosophy & Ethics: Revd Dr Adam Dunning, BA Oxford, PhD Birmingham
Science: Mrs Isabella Mech, BSc Johannesburg, MA Johannesburg
Biology: Mrs Ruth Kramer, BSc King's College London
Chemistry: Mr Daniel Townley, MChem
Physics: Mr Stuart Cooper, BEng Nottingham
Sports Science: Mrs Rebecca Faulkner, BSc Exeter

CCF:
Mr Ben Rees, BSc Manchester (*Contingent Commander*)
WO2 QMSI Jason Gwynne (*SSI*)

Housemasters and Housemistresses:
Ashmead (*Girls*): Mrs Anna Cutts, BEd Middlesex
Boyne House (*Boys*): Mr Richard Penny, BSc Swansea
Chandos (*Girls*): Mrs Annette Poulain, BSc Brunel
Christowe (*Boys*): Mr Jonathan Mace, BA Durham, MSc Leicester
Hazelwell (*Boys*): Mr James Coull, BA Thames Valley
Leconfield (*Boys*): Mr Chris Reid, BA Portsmouth, MA Ed Anglia Ruskin
Newick House (*Boys*): Mr James Hayden, BA Bristol
Queen's (*Day Girls*): Mrs Wandrille Bates, MA Nanterre Paris & Mr Will Bates, BA Exeter
Southwood (*Day Boys*): Mr Matt Coley, BSc Leeds
Westal (*Girls*): Mrs Jenny O'Bryan, MSc Nottingham

Preparatory School:
Headmaster: Mr Jonathan Whybrow, BEd Exeter
Deputy Head – Academic: Mrs Vicky Jenkins, BA
Deputy Head – Pastoral: Mr Noll Jenkins, BA
Deputy Head – Operations: Mr Bob Wells, BSc
Director of Studies: Mr Phil Williams, BEd, BA
Director of Learning: Mrs Gill Barrett, MA, Adv Dip SEN, Cert SpLD
Head of Pupil Wellbeing: Mr Fergus McCracken, BSc
Boarding Houseparent: Mr Bob Wells, BSc
Head of Kingfishers: Mrs Rachael Buttress, BSc
Head of Lower School: Mrs Amanda Grieves, LLB
Head of Middle School: Miss Lindsay Gooch, BA
Head of Upper School: Mrs Sarah Reid, BA
Head of Co-Curricular: Mr Kit Perona-Wright, BA

Cheltenham Ladies' College

Bayshill Road, Cheltenham, Glos GL50 3EP

Tel: 01242 520691
email: enquiries@cheltladiescollege.org
website: www.cheltladiescollege.org
Twitter: @cheltladiescoll
Facebook: /CheltLadiesColl

A College education gives girls the best possible opportunities to achieve their potential in both the academic and personal spheres.

Academic excellence forms the basis of College life, but just as important is the formation of character. We are committed to making our girls ready for their lives well beyond College. We recognise also that an education in the 21st century needs to inspire, prepare and equip young women to sustain a lifetime of independently sought learning, and to give them the flexibility and resourcefulness to flourish in our rapidly changing world.

With this in mind, we give serious thought to our ethics and the source of our emotional and spiritual nourishment, holding the wellbeing of the girls to be equally as important as their academic outcomes. Attention to ensuring the security and sustainability of the former will enable the achievement of the latter. Pupils are encouraged to be self-determining and genuinely caring towards others, building the foundations of character and self-sufficiency for both success and fulfilment in the years beyond school.

Girls are encouraged to embrace a broad range of co-curricular activities to suit their passions and interests, from the sporting to the intellectual and cultural. Added to this, a global outlook encourages girls to play a part in the wider world, creating young women who value the communities to which they belong. The curriculum promotes the values of mutual respect, integrity and courage, while nurturing intellectual curiosity, creativity, confidence and an enduring love of learning.

Girls are at the heart of all College does; we are ambitious for their futures, collectively and individually.

Numbers. Approximately 170 day and 680 boarding.

Fees per term (2016–2017). Day £7,680, Boarding £11,440. New Entrants to Sixth Form: Day £8,740, Boarding £12,890. Some extras are charged, e.g. music, riding.

Admission. Entry at 11+, 12+, 13+ and 16+ via College's own examinations. An interview is also required for some entry points.

Academic. Our curriculum aims to instil in each girl a curiosity about the world in which she lives and equip her with tools to question, reason and communicate articulately. Our Lower College curriculum provides exceptional breadth, building foundations for the GSCE years. The girls study separate sciences, computing, humanities and a language acquisition course, as well as music, drama, art and design, and engineering, enterprise and technology. As a large school, College is able to offer extraordinary advantages in resources and choices. Girls have a free choice of options for GCSE but are encouraged to maintain a broad curriculum whilst tailored to their individual strengths and interests. In Sixth Form, girls have the option of taking A Levels or the International Baccalaureate Diploma programme. Our A Level exam results are consistently outstanding and College was named top girls boarding school in the UK for IB results in 2015 and 2016.

Pastoral Care and Wellbeing. As a large school, College is able to offer extraordinary advantages in resources and choices, but we are also divided into small groups too, through the three academic Divisions (LC, UC & SFC), the Tutor groups and the House system. These create interlocking layers of pastoral care, which work alongside our whole-school Wellbeing Programme, to enable every girl, the reserved as well as the extrovert, to find opportunities to lead a confident, fulfilled and enjoyable life at College. This network is backed up by an experienced and well-resourced Medical Centre based in College, an informed and skilled Catering department and the support of the College Chaplain. Pastoral care isn't something that happens when things go wrong; it's a constant support network for every girl throughout her time in College.

Buildings and Grounds. College is set in a 23-acre dispersed estate in the centre of Cheltenham. The single teaching site is built in a Gothic revival style, complete with the stunning Princess Hall and complemented by more recent additions such as an Art and Technology block, housing College's new Engineering, Enterprise and Technology Department, and the Parabola Arts Centre, with a 325-seat theatre. The day and boarding houses and a large sports complex are located in nearby residential areas within a short walking distance of the main site.

Houses. There are six Junior Boarding Houses and three Day Houses. All girls move into one of six houses at Sixth Form, which is an excellent stepping stone to university life. Each of the Houses is run by a Housemistress, Deputy Housemistress and a team of staff, as well as a dedicated Chef. All Houses have dining rooms, common rooms, prep rooms, computer rooms, space for music practice and laundry facilities. Day girls are fully integrated into all College activities, regularly joining boarders on weekend trips and expeditions.

Music, Drama and Dance. More than 1,000 individual music lessons take place each week, with many choirs and orchestras running throughout the academic year. There are also at least five productions put on each year, with Sixth Form girls often taking a piece to the Edinburgh Fringe Festival. Dance and gymnastics are also available and very popular.

Sport and Co-curricular. It is important that College can support each girl in striking a successful balance between academic and co-curricular activity. To this end, our provision in this area is exciting and well-resourced, and presents every girl with an opportunity to find her niche. At College, we are deeply committed to promoting the health, fitness and wellbeing of all pupils and to developing talent and a lifelong enthusiasm for sport and exercise, regardless of ability or expertise. The main sports are hockey, lacrosse, netball, swimming, athletics and tennis, but College aims to provide what girls enjoy and more than 30 different sports are offered, including rowing, cricket, football, squash and golf. As part of a multimillion pound redevelopment, College's new Health and Fitness Centre will open in 2018. Alongside the existing 25m swimming pool, tennis and netball facilities, and AstroTurf pitches, new facilities will include a second sports hall, multi-purpose studios, and a gym and fitness suite. More than 170 co-curricular opportunities are on offer, including art and design, computer programming, dance, debating, drama, fencing, journalism, yoga, martial arts, Model UN, music, natural science, philosophy, street dance, young engineers, Young Enterprise, environmental clubs and international clubs.

Scholarships and Bursaries. A number of Academic, Art, Day Girl, Drama, Music and Sport Scholarships and other awards are made annually for girls of all ages.

Applications for bursaries are welcome from girls whose parents require financial assistance in order to help their daughter join College.

Beyond College. Our dedicated Professional Guidance Centre provides specialist careers and higher education advice to girls throughout their time at College. Sixth Form tutors also provide significant support in this area. The majority of our girls gain places at Russell Group universities, including Oxbridge, or at top US universities to study a diverse range of subjects.

Former Pupils (Guild). There are over 8,000 Guild members throughout the world, and many are actively involved in helping current girls prepare for the future, including supporting networking dinners, interview preparation, hosting careers events, and arranging speakers from universities and the professions.

Charitable status. Cheltenham Ladies' College is a Registered Charity, number 311722. It exists to provide a high standard of education for girls.

Chairman of the Council: Ms Libby Bassett, MA, ACA

Principal: **Ms Eve Jardine-Young**, MA

Vice-Principal: Mr Richard Dodds, BSc
Vice-Principal (Academic): Miss Jackie Adams, BSc

Chief Operating Officer: Mr Nigel Richards, BSc
Director of Admissions: Dr Hilary Laver, BSc
Finance Director: Mr Jeffrey Speke, BSc, MPhil, ACA
Development Director: Ms Samantha Bagchi, BSc
Director of Marketing and Communications: Mrs Dragana Hartley, BSc
Curriculum Director: Mr James Pothecary, MSci
Head of Pastoral Care: Miss Caroline Ralph, BEd
Head of Sixth Form College: Mr Jonathan Marchant, BA, MA
Head of Upper College: Dr David Gamblin, MChem, MRSC
Head of Lower College: Mrs Charlotte Oosthuizen, BEd Hons

Chetham's School of Music

Long Millgate, Manchester M3 1SB
Tel: 0161 834 9644
Fax: 0161 839 3609
email: chets@chethams.com
website: www.chethams.com

Chetham's is a co-educational school for boarding and day students aged eight to eighteen. The School teaches a broad curriculum set within a framework of music. At the centre of every child's course is a 'musical core' of experiences rooted in a determination to educate the whole person. Originally founded in 1653, through the Will of Humphrey Chetham, as a Bluecoat orphanage, the School was re-constituted in 1969 as a specialist music school.

The School numbers 301 students, of whom 160 are girls. There are 210 boarders. Admission is solely by musical audition, and any orchestral instrument, plus keyboard, guitar, voice or composition, may be studied. Each student studies two instrumental studies, or voice and one instrument, as well as following academic courses which lead to GCSE and A Levels and to university entrance and music college. The School stands on the site of Manchester's original 12th century Manor House adjacent to the Cathedral, and is housed partly in the fine 15th century College Buildings, and partly in the New School (2012) which houses all the instrumental, musical and academic teaching, an Outreach Centre and two performance spaces.

Music. Instrumental tuition is guided and monitored by the advisers in each specialism, who visit regularly to survey students' work, conduct internal examinations and give masterclasses. Internationally renowned musicians hold residences at the School for string, wind, brass, percussion and keyboard players. The Director of Music has responsibility for the full-time Music Staff and also for about 100 visiting tutors. All students receive three sessions of individual instrumental tuition each week. Practice is rigorously set and supervised. Academic Music is normally studied at A Level.

Boarding. There are two boarding houses for girls and boys aged 13 to 18 and one for Juniors aged 8 to 13. Each House is run by House Parents in residence, with resident assistants. All full-time teachers act as Tutors and are involved with pastoral care. In addition, when necessary, students have open access to the School Counsellors.

Recreation. Serious attention is paid to recreation, PE and games and the students' physical well-being. On-site facilities include an indoor swimming pool, gym, multi-gym and a squash court.

Applications, Visits. Entry is by audition only. Preliminary assessment auditions are held throughout the year, with final auditions in the Christmas and Spring terms.

The Prospectus and application forms are sent on request and are available on the School's website. Parents and prospective students are welcome to visit the School by arrangement with the Head's PA.

Fees, Grants. All entrants from the United Kingdom are eligible for grants under the Department for Education's Music and Dance Scheme. Parental contributions are calculated according to means and parents on low incomes qualify automatically for full fee remission. The Bursar will be glad to advise about the scales.

Choristers. The School is a member of the Choir Schools' Association and Choristerships at Manchester Cathedral for day boys and girls are available under a separate scheme. Choristers' Fee: £9,480 pa (subject to Cathedral Bursaries).

Charitable status. Chetham's School of Music is a Registered Charity, number 526702. It exists to educate exceptionally gifted young musicians.

Governors:
Dame A V Burslem, DBE (*Chairman*)

Dr B Brennan	M Edge
Canon Philip Barratt	K Jaquiss
Ms C Baxendale	Ms Newman
Ms A Corcoran	J Wainwright
Councillor J Davies	S Webb

Staff:

Head: **Mr Alun Jones**, LTCL, LWCMD

Director of Music: S Threlfall, GRNCM Hons, FRSA
Bursar: Mrs S C Newman, BSc Hons, FCA
Deputy Head, Pastoral: Ms C Rhind, BA
Deputy Head, Curriculum: C Newman, MA, MSc

Music:

PA to the Director of Music: Mrs J Scott
Music Department Coordinator: I Mayer
Concert Administrator: Ms H Bull
Music Department Timetabler: Miss N Prestt
Auditions and Administration Secretary: Mrs A Herbert
Music Department Secretary: Ms S Self

Key:
Chamber Music Tutor
[Hallé] *Member of Hallé Orchestra*
[BBC] *Member of BBC Philharmonic*
* *Tutor at Royal Northern College of Music*
[O.North] *Member of Opera North Company*
[RLPO] *Member of Royal Liverpool Philharmonic Orchestra*
X *Manchester Camerata*
[CBSO] *Member of City of Birmingham Symphony Orchestra*

Brass:
Head of Department: David Chatterton
Euphonium Tutors: Bill Millar #, David Thornton #*

Horn Tutors: Elizabeth Davis #*, Julian Plummer [Hallé], Helen Varley

Percussion Tutors: Sophie Hastings (*Latin percussion and Kit*), David Hext [Hallé], Paul Patrick [BBC]#*

Trombone Tutors: Robert Burtenshaw #[O.North], Philip Goodwin [BBC]#, Les Storey #

Trumpet Staff: David Chatterton #

Tutors: John Dickinson *#, Murray Greig *#[O.North], Tracey Redfern #X, Gareth Small [Hallé]#

Tuba Tutors: Brian Kingsley *#[O.North]

Keyboard:

Head of Department: Dr Murray McLachlan *

Staff: Simon Bottomley #

Tutors: Graham Caskie, Hazel Fanning, Benjamin Frith #, Duncan Glenday, John Gough, Alison Havard, Marta Karbownicka, Helen Krizos *, Jonathan Middleton, Dina Parakhina *, Masa Tayama, Marie-Louise Taylor, Lulu Yang, Jeremy Young #

Harpsichord Tutor: Charlotte Turner

Jazz Piano Tutor: Les Chisnall

Organ Tutors: Christopher Stokes, Joshua Hales

Chamber Tutors: Benjamin Frith, Jeremy Young

Strings:

Head of Department: Nicholas Jones

Assistant: Owen Cox

Senior Chamber Music Tutor: Graham Oppenheimer

Violin Staff: Owen Cox

Tutors: Jiafeng Chen, Connie del Vecchio [RLPO], Kristoffer Dolatko, Ruth Hahn, Benedict Holland *, Linda Janowska, Jan Repko *, Yumi Sasaki, Katie Stillman, Deirdre Ward, Qian Wu #

Viola Tutors: Sebastian Mueller, Graham Oppenheimer #,

Cello Staff: Nicholas Jones # *, Stephen Threlfall #

Tutors: Elinor Gow, Barbara Grunthal X, Li Lu, Anna Menzies, David Smith #, Gillian Thoday

Double Bass Tutor: Yi Xin Salvage [Hallé], Steve Berry (*jazz*)

Harp Tutor: Eleanor Hudson, Marie Leenhardt [Hallé]

Guitar Tutors: Jim Faulkner (*jazz*), Wendy Jackson #

Woodwind:

Head of Department: Belinda Gough

Recorder/Baroque Ensembles Tutor: Chris Orton

Baroque Flute and Historical Performance: Martyn Shaw

Oboe Tutors: Rachael Clegg X, Matthew Jones, Stephane Rancourt [Hallé]

Flute Tutors: Katherine Baker [Hallé], Rachel Forgreive *, Fiona Fulton, Belinda Gough #, Linda Verrier #*

Clarinet Tutors: Jim Muirhead [Hallé]#, Marianne Rawles, Tom Verity

Saxophone Tutors: Iain Dixon (*Jazz/improvisation*), Jim Muirhead [Hallé], Carl Raven * (*Jazz/improvisation*), Andrew Wilson #

Bassoon Tutors: Ben Hudson [Hallé], Graham Salvage *

Contra-Bassoon Tutor: Simon Davies

Vocal Department:

Tutors: Helen Francis #, Margaret McDonald, Stuart Overington, Diana Palmerston #

Staff Accompanists:

Heads of Department: Brenda Blewett, Nicholas Oliver

Staff: Elena Namilova, Martyn Parkes, Hilary Suckling

Composition:

Head of Department: Dr Jeremy Pike, MA, MPhil, PhD, LRAM, Hon ARAM

Staff: Dr Gavin Wayte

Music Technology:

Adrian Horn, BMus

Dr Jeremy Pike, MA, MPhil, PhD, LRAM, Hon ARAM

Practice Team Leaders:

Diane Hammond

Lulu Yang

Big Band:

Directors: Richard Iles, Jim Muirhead [Hallé]

Improvisation:

Steve Berry *, Les Chisnall (*Keyboard*), Iain Dixon

Alexander Technique:

Patrick Grundy-White, Anne Whitehead

Academic Music:

S King, BA, MA, MPhil, PhD

Ms R Aldred, BMus

Miss C Campbell Smith, MA

J LeGrove, BA

D Mason, BA

Dr S Murphy, PhD, BA

Mrs S Oliver, BA

Art:

Miss A Boothroyd, BA

Mrs J Jones, BA

Compensatory Education/Special Needs:

Mrs B L Owen, BEd, RSA Dip SpLD

Miss L Fogg, MA

Miss C Lynch, BA

Learning Support Assistants

Drama & Theatre Studies:

Mrs J Sherlock, MA

English:

Mrs J Harrison, MA

Miss L Jones, BA

J Runswick-Cole, MEd

Mrs J Sherlock, MA

Humanities & PSHE:

A Kyle, BA

M Clarke, BSc

Mrs S Cox, BA

C Newman, MA

Information Technology:

Mrs F Holker, BSc

Miss C Whittaker, BA

Junior Department:

D Harris, BA

Languages:

C Law, PhD, MA

P Chillingworth, BA

Mrs R Jordan, BA

Mrs S Hales, BA

Mathematics:

Mrs A Marsden, BSc

C Bramall, BA

Mrs F Holker, BSc

Mrs S Wegg

Recreation:

Ms I Staszko, BEd, MA

Miss C Whittaker, BA

Sciences:

A Henderson, BA

J Blundell, BSc

Mrs L Gartside, BSc

P Przybyla, BSc

Ms E Storey, BSc

Librarian: Mrs G Wood, BMus

Careers:
Dr S Murphy, PhD, MMus, BA (*Music Colleges*)
C Newman, MA (*Universities*)

Houses:
Mr & Mrs J Runswick-Cole (*Boys' House*)
Mrs I Merrett (*Girls' House*)
Mr G Taylor (*Victoria House*)

School Doctor: Dr J Tankel
Nurse: Mrs K Scott, RGN
Head's PA: Mrs L Haslam

Chigwell School

Chigwell, Essex IG7 6QF

Tel:	020 8501 5700
Fax:	020 8500 6232
email:	hm@chigwell-school.org
website:	www.chigwell-school.org

Motto: '*Aut viam inveniam aut faciam*', '*Find a Way or Make a Way*'.

The School was founded in 1629 by Samuel Harsnett, Archbishop of York, "to supply a liberal and practical education, and to afford instruction in the Christian religion, according to the doctrine and principles of the Church of England". William Penn, founder of Pennsylvania, is the most famous Old Chigwellian.

Today the School welcomes boys and girls from all backgrounds and is a lively, happy community in which pupils are encouraged to develop all their talents to the full.

The School became co-educational in September 1997 and currently there are over 920 pupils aged 4 to 18 pupils, including 27 international boarders.

Location. Chigwell School stands in a superb green belt location in 100 acres of playing fields and woodlands, midway between Epping and Hainault Forests and enjoys excellent communications. It is easily accessible from London (by Central Line Undergound network). Both the M25 and M11 motorways are close by, while Heathrow, Gatwick, City of London, Stansted and Luton Airports are all reachable from the School within the hour.

Buildings. The original building is still in use and houses the Senior School Swallow Library. There has been a considerable amount of building in the past years and all the older buildings have been modernised while retaining their character. New facilities include a Junior School classroom block, a new Junior School library, a state-of-the-art Drama Centre, new catering facilities, upgraded boys' boarding houses, a superb floodlit all-weather pitch, refurbished science block and a purpose-built Pre-Prep School. The latest addition is the stunning Risham Sarao Sixth Form Centre which opened in September 2016.

Organisation. The School is divided into the Senior and Junior Schools but is administered as a single unit with a common teaching staff.

The Head of the Junior School is responsible for all pupils between the ages of 7 and 13, although teaching from Year 7 upwards is coordinated by the Senior School. The Junior School is on the same site as the Senior School and all facilities and grounds are used by Junior pupils. Assembly, Games and Lunch are all arranged separately from the Senior School. (For further details, see Junior School entry in IAPS section.)

The Head of Pre-Prep is responsible for children aged 4 to 7 and they are largely self-contained in the new Pre-Prep School.

In the Senior School, all the day pupils and boarders are divided into four Day Houses. Each House has a large House room and a Housemaster's or Housemistress's study.

Curriculum. Pupils follow a broad based course leading to GCSE. Maths, English, Science and one modern language form the common core of subjects. Science is taken either as three separate subjects (Physics, Biology, Chemistry) or as Coordinated Science. In addition, a wide range of options is taken at GCSE including Art and Design, Graphic Design, Design Technology, French, German, Spanish, Latin, Greek, Geography, History, Religious Studies, Drama and Music.

Sixth Form. Students take 4 AS Level subjects in the first year and 3 or 4 A2 Level subjects in the second year. Subjects taken include, Latin, Greek, Classical Civilisation, French, German, Spanish, English, Economics, History, Geography, Maths, Further Maths, Physics, Chemistry, Biology, Music, Art, Design and Technology, Psychology, Religious Studies and Theatre Studies.

Games and Activities. Cricket, Football, Netball, Hockey (Boys and Girls), Athletics, Cross-Country Running, Swimming, Tennis, Golf, Basketball and Badminton. There are numerous School Societies and a Scout Troop. Many pupils join The Duke of Edinburgh's Award scheme. There is a swimming pool, two Sports Halls and extensive playing fields on site.

Art & Design, Ceramics, and D & T. Art is taught throughout the School and there is excellent provision for Ceramics and D & T which form part of the curriculum for all pupils between the ages of 10 and 14.

Music. There are three Orchestras, two Wind Bands, one Swing Band and six Choirs. Many other ensembles flourish and perform at major concerts during the year, some of which take place in the local community. Pupils may learn any instrument (including the Organ).

Boarding. Boy Boarders are accommodated in Church House, run by Mr and Mrs Rabbitte, and Harsnett's House, run by Mr and Mrs Saunders. Sandon Lodge, set in the middle of the beautiful School Grounds, accommodates Sixth Form Girl Boarders under the care of Dr and Mr Lord. Hainault House, under the supervision of Mr and Mrs Goddard, lies adjacent to the Junior School and offers accommodation for girls.

Fees per term (2016–2017). Full boarding £9,310; Day pupils £3,590–£5,500. Fees vary depending on age. Fees are inclusive of all tuition, meals (lunch and afternoon tea), textbooks, societies and most clubs.

Admission. Pupils usually join Chigwell School at 4+, 7+, 11+, 13+ or 16+.

Scholarships and Bursaries. Academic scholarships are awarded each year, primarily at 11+ and 16+. They are awarded in recognition of academic merit, irrespective of financial means. A competitive examination for Academic scholarships is held each year during the Lent Term for pupils aged 11+ and during the Michaelmas Term for pupils aged 16+.

Music scholarships are offered each year at 11+ and sometimes at 13+ and 16+ and these make a substantial contribution to school fees. In return, scholars are expected to play a full role in the performing life of the department. Currently, two scholars attend the Junior Guildhall School of Music on Saturdays.

Art and Drama scholarships are available at 16+.

Chigwell has always tried to ensure that children who would benefit from an education at the School are not excluded for financial reasons. A number of means-tested Bursaries are offered.

Further details can be obtained from the Admissions Registrar (email: admissions@chigwell-school.org).

The Old Chigwellians' Association. c/o Development Office, Chigwell School, Essex.

Charitable status. Chigwell School is an Incorporated Charity, registration number 1115098. It exists to provide a rounded education of the highest quality for its pupils.

Governing Body:
Chair: Mrs S L Aliker, BA, MBA, ACMA
Vice Chairman: D Morriss Esq, BSc, CEng, FIET, FBCS, CITP
Mrs E Brett, ACA
J Cullis Esq, MBE, BA, MSc
Sir Richard Dales, KCVO, CMG, MA
Dr G Dixon, MA, BMus, PhD, MBA, ARAM, FRCO, FRSA
N Garnish Esq, BSc, MBA, CMgr, FCMI, MCSI
Mrs J Gwinn, BSc
M Higgins Esq
R Howard Esq, MA
A N Howat Esq
The Revd B W King, BA, MA
Mrs I Peck, BA
Dr A Pruss, BSc, PhD, MBBS, LRCP, MRCS, AFOM
R H Youdale Esq, MA

Clerk to the Governors: G Norman Esq, BSc Econ, CPFA, ACIS

Bursar: J Rea, MA, FCA, CTA

Headmaster: M E Punt, MA, MSc, PGCE

Deputy Head: D J Gower, BSc, PGCE

Deputy Head, Staff and Systems: Mrs A Savage, FTLC, GTCL, PGCE

Head of the Junior School: A Stubbs, BA, PGCE

Deputy Head of the Junior School: Mrs J Botham, BSc

Head of the Pre Prep School: E Gibbs, BA, PGCE, NPQH

Assistant Staff:
* *Head of Department*
† *Housemaster/mistress*

Mrs A M Aitken, MA
E Aitken, MA (*Art and Design*)
Mrs M Baldwin, BSc (*Girls' Games*)
Ms S Bell, BA, PGCE (†*Caswalls*)
Mrs L E Bengtson, BSc, PDAP, PGCE (†*Lambourne*, *Psychology*)
Mrs K S Bint, BSc, PGCE
Miss J E Bonner, BA, PGCE
Miss G Brien, MA, BSc, PGCE
A J Bruce, BA, PGCE
Miss C A Cassell, BSc, MSc, PGCE
Mrs M F Chan, BA, PGCE
S M Chaudhary, MA, PGCE (*Mathematics*)
Mrs L Chery, MA
Dr P G Clayton, PhD, DIC, ARCS
S Coppell, MA, PGCE (†*Penns*, *Modern Languages*)
Ms E Creber, BSc, PGCE
A J Crockatt, BA, BMus, PGCE
W P Eardley, BSc (*Biology*)
H J G Ebden, BA, PGCE (*Music*)
K Ennis, BA, PGCE, BSc
K Farrant, BEd (*Boys Games*, *PE*)
Mrs E M P Feeney, L-ès-L, PGCE (*French*)
Dr E M Ferreira, PhD, MSc, PGCE
P R Fletcher, MA, Dip TEFL, PGCE
Miss J R Foster, BA, PGCE
E. Gamwells, BA, PGCE
A Goddard BSc, PGCE (*Boarding*)
I C Goddard, BA (*History*)
Dr G M Groszewski, BA, PGDip, MPhil, PhD
J W Harley, BA, PGCE (*Economics*)

D J L Harston, MA, DCEG, PGCE
D W Hartland, MA, PGCE, FRGS
Mrs Y A Hizer, BA, PGCE
G S Inch, BA, PGCE (*Senior Master*)
Mrs S Inch, BEd
Miss J L Ireland, MA, PGCE
Mrs V C James, BEd
Mrs N A Jermyn, MEd, BA, PGCE (*Design & Technology*)
Ms J Kershberg, BA, PGCE
Mrs S L Lawrence, BSc, GTP (†*Swallow's*)
Miss F M Leach, BMus
Miss D Le Bas, BA, PGCE
A Long, MSc (*Head of Sixth Form*)
R A F Lonsdale, MA, DipEd
C J Lord, MA (*Classics*)
H J Lukesch, 1st & 2nd STEX (*German*)
J L Maingot, BA, PGCE (*Drama*)
R D Maynes, BSc
J P Morris, BSc, PGCE, FRGS
Miss K V Morris, BA, PGCE
D J Morse, BA QTS, MCSE, MOS, MBCS
Ms C M Nairac, BA
Miss A M J Ochana, MSc, BEng, PGCE
Ms J Osborne, MEd, PGDip, PSE, AMBDA (*Learning Support*)
D I Patel, BSc, PGCE
The Revd S N Paul, BA, PGCE (*Chaplain*)
S B Pepper, MA, PGCE (*Government & Politics*)
Miss RA Pettingill, BSc, PGCE (*Chemistry*)
Mrs P Pewsey, BSEd, Dip EFL, PGCE
Mrs R J Philip, BEd
B W Porter, BSc, PGCE (*Physics*)
D P Rabbitte, BA, LLB, PGCE (*Geography*)
Mrs E R Rawlings, BA
Mrs E R Rea, MA, PGCE (*English*)
Ms P S Rex, BA, PGCE (*Religious Studies*)
R C Richardson, BA, MA, PGCE
Mrs M A Saunders, BA, PGCE
N M Saunders, BSc, PGCE (*Director of Studies*)
G J Sexton, BSc
R S Spicer, BA, MSc, PGCE
Mrs E C Stoker, BA, PGCE
Mrs J Summers, BEd
Miss H M Tate, BA, PGCE
Miss L C Tellwright, BA, PGCE
Mrs L M Thurtle, BA, PGCE
Mrs C E Tilbrook, BEd, Dip SEA
Mrs H E Tomsett, BSc, QTS
W Tomsett, BSc
J J Twinn, BA, PGCE
Mrs T Tyson, BA, PGCE
Miss A D van Bergen, BEd
Miss S E Wales, MA
Mrs S E Welsford, BEd, Dip IT
B Wille, BSc, PGCE
S C Wilson, MEd, BSc (*Science*)
Dr G Winfield, PhD, PGDipEd

Christ College
Brecon

Brecon, Powys LD3 8AF
Tel: 01874 615440 (Head)
          01874 615440 (Bursar)
Fax: 01874 625174

email: enquiries@christcollegebrecon.com
website: www.christcollegebrecon.com

Motto: '*Possunt quia posse videntur.*'

Founded by Henry VIII, 1541. Reconstituted by Act of Parliament, 1853.

Christ College, Brecon lies in a setting of outstanding natural beauty at the foot of the Brecon Beacons on the edge of the small market town of Brecon, two minutes' walk away on the opposite side of the river. The River Usk flows alongside the playing fields providing good canoeing and fishing while the nearby Llangorse Lake is available for sailing and windsurfing.

The school was founded by King Henry VIII in 1541 when he dissolved the Dominican Friary of St Nicholas. The 13th Century Chapel and Dining Hall are at the centre of school life and the school's mix of important, historic buildings and modern architecture represents the continuity of education at the school. In the last ten years additional boarding capacity has been added to a girls house, all of the houses have been refurbished, an Astroturf built as well as Fitness Suite, the Art School re-located and expanded while a Sixth Form Centre renovated as well as extensive landscaping of the school campus. In recent years, new additions to the built environment include a £1.5m Science Centre and a new Centre for the Creative Arts – Y Neuadd Goffa: The Memorial Hall. In September 2014, St Nicholas House, a junior day and boarding house for pupils aged 7–11 years, was opened.

Estyn, Her Majesty's Inspectorate for Education & Training in Wales, inspected the school in 2011 and rated the school's current performance as 'Excellent' with 'Excellent prospects for improvement'.

Organisation. Christ College was a boys' only school until 1987 when girls were admitted to the Sixth Form. In 1995 the school became fully co-educational. There are 400 pupils in the school of whom 210 are boys and 190 girls. Approximately 60% of pupils board and there are three senior boys' houses, School House, Orchard House and St David's House, three senior girls' houses, Donaldson's House, de Winton House and Banau and a lower school house, Alway House, for 11–13 year old boys and girls. Alway House also offers weekly boarding for our younger boarders in St Nicholas House. St Nicholas House is a junior day and boarding section for boys and girls aged 7–11 years.

Chapel. Chapel services are conducted in accordance with the liturgy of the Anglican church, but entrance to Christ College is open to boys and girls of all faiths. The ownership of Chapel by the boys and girls, demonstrated through their participation in services and their singing, is a feature of the school. Pupils are prepared for Confirmation by the School's Chaplain who lives on site.

Curriculum. Up to the Form 5 (Year 11) pupils follow a balanced curriculum leading to GCSE at which most pupils take 10 subjects. Options are chosen at the end of Form 3 (Year 9). Current subjects taught include Art, Creative Art, Computer Science, English Language, English Literature, Mathematics, French, Spanish, Physics, Chemistry, Biology, History, Geography, Religious Studies, Art, Music, Physical Education, Photography, Drama, Information Technology and Welsh.

In the Sixth Form a similar range of subjects is taken at AS and A2 Level plus opportunities to take Economics, Further Maths, Business Studies. All pupils have timetabled tutorial periods and in the Sixth Form periods are set aside for Careers advice. The Extended Project Qualification (EPQ) is also available for Sixth Form pupils.

Class sizes rarely exceed 20 up to GCSE and average fewer than 10 at A Level.

Games. The main school games are Rugby Football, Cricket, Hockey, Soccer, Netball, Cross-Country and Athletics. Tennis, Badminton, Squash, Volleyball, Basketball, Golf, Fishing, Swimming, Shooting, Mountain Biking, Canoeing, Fencing, Indoor Cricket, Climbing, Triathlon and Aerobics are also available. The playing fields are extensive and lie adjacent to the school. Christ College has entered into a corporate partnership with Cradoc Golf Club, two miles outside of Brecon, to encourage pupils of all ages and experience in the fundamentals of the game of golf. The opportunity to play at Cradoc Golf Club and receive professional instruction is also extended to all parents of pupils attending Christ College. A recent initiative with The Pony Club also means that equestrians now have access to a British Eventing standard course at the nearby Glanusk Estate.

Thursday Afternoons. On Thursday afternoons the CCF Contingent meets. There is a choice between Army and Royal Air Force sections and the CCF has its own Headquarters, Armoury and covered 30m Range in the school grounds. Pupils take their proficiency certificate after two years and may then choose to continue as Instructors, undergo training for the Duke of Edinburgh's Award scheme or leave the CCF and may become involved in community service.

Music. The Chapel Choir is large and enjoys an excellent reputation with radio and television broadcasts as well as overseas tours to its credit. As befits a school in Wales singing on all school occasions is committed, energetic and frequently with natural harmony. The school has a Chamber Choir, plus multiple wind, brass and string ensembles and its pupils play a prominent role in the South Powys Youth Orchestra and works in partnership with the Welsh Sinfonia to provide opportunities for pupils to play alongside professional musicians. There are many other opportunities to play in ensemble groups throughout the school. Individual instrumental and singing lessons are delivered by visiting musicians.

Activities. In addition to sporting pastimes a wide range of activities are available to pupils including Sixth Form Film Society, Advanced Chemistry, Art, Badminton, Basketball, Brass Group, Canoeing, Chamber Choir, Chess, Choir, Climbing, Community Service, Disability Sport, Drama, Fencing, Fitness, Golf, Indoor Cricket, IT Projects, Mandarin Chinese, Modern Dance/Jazz, Modern Language Film Society, Music Practice, Music Theory, Percussion Group, Project Science, Railway Modelling, Shooting, Stage Management, String Group, String Quartet, Technology, Wado Kai Karate, Wind Sinfonia, and Young Enterprise. The Duke of Edinburgh's Award scheme has been popular for many years and the majority of pupils gain at least a Bronze award, and a significant number go on to achieve the Gold award.

Overseas Travel is frequent and extensive. In recent years tours, expeditions and exchanges have taken place to Beijing, Canada, Japan, Nepal, New York, South Africa, Shanghai, Tibet and Barbados as well as a number of European destinations.

Careers. Two members of staff also serve in the Careers department which also enlists the help of the Independent Schools Careers Organisation as well as the local Careers organisations. Former pupils return annually for Careers evenings and in this the Old Breconian Association is very helpful.

Entrance. Pupils are admitted at the age of 7+, 11+, 13+ and 16+ following the school's own entrance papers in English and Mathematics plus an IQ test, school report and interview. These tests are usually held in Jan/Feb, but individual arrangements can be made. The majority of 11 year old entrants come from local State Primary Schools, those at 13 from Preparatory schools when, instead of the Common Entrance examination, pupils face the same entrance procedures as at 11. Boys and girls also enter the Sixth Form on the basis of GCSE grade estimates, an IQ test and an interview. Although these are standard entry points, pupils will be considered for entry in Years 4, 5, 6, 8 and Year 10.

Term of Entry. Pupils are accepted in the Michaelmas, Lent and Summer terms.

Scholarships. Scholarships are available for entry at age 11, 13 and 16.

Academic: Up to 10 Academic scholarships and exhibitions, tenable at 11+, 13+ and 16+ and ranging in value from 10 to 20% of the fees, are offered annually.

Music: Up to 8 Music scholarships in total are available each year, for award at 11+, 13+ or 16+ ranging in value from 10 to 50% of the fees, together with free tuition on one instrument.

Drama: One exhibition awarded annually at 13+ and Sixth Form.

Art: One Art exhibition may be awarded each year at 13+, up to the value of 20% of the fees.

Science scholarships are available at 13+ and 16+, also ranging from 10 to 50% of the fees.

Sports scholarships are available annually at 11+, 13+ and 16+ to candidates showing outstanding talent ranging in value from 10% to 20% of the fees.

All-Rounder: W G Fryer All-Rounder Scholarships are available at 13+ and 16+ each year.

In addition, three scholarships are awarded each year to those entering the Sixth Form each worth £1,500 a year: a Lord Brecon, a Roydon Griffiths and a G John Herdman Scholarship.

The value of any award may be augmented in case of need.

Bursaries are available at all ages and are subject to a means test.

There is a 25% fee remission for sons and daughters of the Clergy, and 10% bursaries are available each year for the children of serving members of the Armed Forces.

Fees per term (2016–2017). Years 3–6: Day £2,876–£3,777, Boarding £5,433–£5,606; Years 7 and 8: Day £4,872, Boarding £6,701; Years 9–11: Day £5,547, Boarding £8,563; Years 12–13: Day £5,821, Boarding £8,994.

Charitable status. Christ College, Brecon is a Registered Charity, number 525744. Its aims and objectives are to provide a fully rounded education for boys and girls between the ages of 7 and 18.

Visitor: Her Majesty The Queen

Governing Body:
Sir E P Silk (*Chairman*)
The Rt Revd The Lord Bishop of Swansea and Brecon
The Venerable The Archdeacon of Brecon
Prof M C R Davies, BSc Eng, AKC, MPhil, PhD Cantab, CEng, FICE, FGS, FIPENZ, FRSE
C I Dytor, MC, KHS, MA Cantab, MA Oxon
M Gittins
Mrs S A E Gwyer Roberts, BA, MEd, NPQH, FRSA
R J Harbottle, BA
D James
Mrs J James
Mrs H Johnson
The Hon Dame E S J Legge-Bourke, LVO, Lord Lieutenant of Powys
A L P Lewis
Mrs A Mathias
Ms H Molyneux, LLB
H Warman
A Whittall

Head: **Mrs Emma Taylor**, MA Oxon

Deputy Head (*Academic*): J D Bush, MA Cantab

Deputy Head (*Pastoral*): S Hill

Assistant Staff:
* *Head of Department*
† *Housemaster/mistress*

†Mrs R E Allen, BA (*History*)
†Mrs E Blatt, BSc (*Biology*)
N C Blackburn, BSc (*Mathematics*)
P Chandler, BA (*EAL, Careers*)
J T Cooper, BA, ARCO (*Director of Choral Music*)
†A Copp, BSc (*Economics*)
M Cornish, MA (**RS*)
Ms A M Doran, BA (*French and Spanish*)
Miss A Derrien (*Languages Assistant*)
P K Edgley, ARPS (*Photography*)
Dr G Evans, MA, PhD (*English*)
R Evans, BSc (*Geography*)
Mrs U Feldner, BA (*Art*)
†Mrs C N Forde-Halpin, BA (*Mathematics*)
†Mrs A Golding, MA (*Computer Science*)
B Goodrich, MSc (**Geography*)
R Goodrich, MA (*Religious Studies*)
Mrs J Gould, MA (**Drama*)
†G Halpin, BSc (*Business Studies*)
Mr R Heysmond, MA (*Information & Communication Technology*)
Mrs D Houghton, BA (**Art*)
Mrs J Hope, MA (**English*)
Miss S Hunter, BA (**PE*)
Miss S E Jones, BSc (**Biology*)
Mrs F Kilpatrick, BA, RSA Dip SpLD, AMBDA (**Learning Support*)
J Ling, BA (**Director of Music*)
Mrs L McLean, BA (**Modern Languages*)
I McMillan, MEng Hons (*Mathematics*)
Dr G Meredith, BSc, PhD (**Chemistry*)
I J Owen, BSc (**Mathematics*)
Mrs E Owen (*Welsh*)
Dr D Phelps, MA, PhD (**History*)
A Reeves, BSc (**Physics*)
C Rees, BA (*Modern Languages*)
Mrs R Sandhu, BA (**PSE*)
†M P Sims, BSc (*Biology*)
C Thomas, BSc (*Physics*)
T J Trumper, BEd (*Director of Sport*)
Mrs H Williams, BA (*Modern Languages*)
Mrs A Zhu (*Mandarin*)

Junior Section
Mrs J Lewis, BA Ed (*Head of Juniors*)
Miss J Brunsden-Brown, BSc (*KS2*)
G Kerr, BA Ed (*KS2*)
Miss G Kent, BA Hons (*KS2*)
Miss A Hallinan, BSc (*KS2*)
Mrs J Gardner (*Classroom Assistant*)

Visiting Music Staff:
T Cronin
A S Davies, GWCMD
G Hamlin
J C Herbert
R Johnston
J Pickford
Miss E Priday, LRAM, ARAM
Mrs D Taylor
Miss K Thomas
Mrs C E Walker, MA Oxon, ARCM

Bursar: M Allen
Admissions Registrar: Mrs M L Stephens
SSI: WO2 M Bevan
OBA Liaison: H L P Richards
Marketing and Communications Manager: Mrs R Johnston

Christ's Hospital

Horsham, West Sussex RH13 0LJ

Tel:	01403 211293
Fax:	01403 255283
email:	hmsec@christs-hospital.org.uk
website:	www.christs-hospital.org.uk

Christ's Hospital was founded in the City of London by King Edward VI in 1552. In 1902 the boys moved to Horsham, where they were joined by the girls from their Hertford school in 1985.

Christ's Hospital is now a fully co-educational 11–18 boarding and day school for up to 880 pupils set in over 1000 acres of magnificent Sussex countryside.

Christ's Hospital is in many ways unique, offering an independent education of the highest calibre to children with academic potential, from all walks of life in a caring, boarding and day environment.

Pupils' fees are assessed according to family income, so that it is a child's ability and potential to benefit from a Christ's Hospital education that determines their selection. This results in a social and cultural diversity that enriches our school community and offers our pupils unique opportunities as we prepare them to take their place in the modern world.

We believe in the benefits of a rounded and balanced education for our pupils. In practice, this means that as well as a challenging academic programme, pupils are also involved in music, art, drama, public speaking, community action and sport.

The School has an impressive history of high academic achievement with an average of 10 pupils each year taking up places at Oxford or Cambridge, and 98% of leavers going on to top Universities in this country and abroad.

Facilities. The Christ's Hospital campus is nothing short of majestic. From the moment you arrive you'll see that it is a very special place. Sweeping sports fields, beautiful buildings and our spectacular Quad are immediately visible.

We also have 16 boarding houses, two Upper Sixth Form residences, our own purpose-built theatre, modern sports centre, music school and art school. The School has recently implemented a major programme of refurbishment, which has included a complete modernisation of the boarding houses.

The majority of pupils and teachers live on site, creating a community where children are happy and secure, with a wide range of activities on their doorstep. The seven-day week boarding school environment provides the time and space for pupils to develop their interests and talents, and to live and work successfully with others from a diverse range of backgrounds.

Christ's Hospital welcomes day pupils who are within a commutable distance from the School. Day pupils enjoy all the advantages of a top boarding school with access to an exceptional co-curricular programme.

Admission. Normally entry to Christ's Hospital is at Year 7, Year 9 or Sixth Form. Occasionally, we can admit children at Year 8 or 10. The Admissions Office will be able to advise you if places are available.

We encourage you to visit CH on one of our termly Open Mornings to enable you to see the school in action.

Our selection process is designed to determine whether a child will flourish in a busy boarding school environment with a strong academic ethos, enjoying the wide range of opportunities on offer, and feel at home at Christ's Hospital.

Parents are advised to start the Admissions process as early as possible and ideally at least eighteen months before their child would be due to enter the school.

Places at the school are academically selective and are offered on the basis of Christ's Hospital's own assessments.

Year 7 Entry. As a guide, children entering at age 11 into Year 7 need to show evidence of academic potential, working towards the higher end of the ability range in both the Mathematics and English National Curriculum syllabuses (ie predicted level 5 in the Key Stage 2 SATs tests).

Year 9 Entry. Entrants will be expected to be working at SATs level 6/7 across the board or to be predicted to achieve an average of 60% at Common Entrance.

Candidates for entry at age 13 into Year 9 who are coming from independent prep schools or choir schools may choose to apply to be tested at age 11 and have their places deferred. Offers will be made on the basis of Christ's Hospital's own assessments but will be subject to satisfactory completion of Common Entrance.

Alternatively candidates from independent prep schools or choir schools may choose to apply during Year 8 for a Year 9 place following the same assessment process and subject to places remaining available.

Sixth Form Entry. Offers of places at age 16 into Year 12 (Sixth Form) are conditional upon an applicant achieving 6 As or A*s in their GCSE exams.

Additional Entry Information. In all cases reports will be requested from a candidate's current school and it is recommended that parents contact their child's current school early in the admissions process to ask about their child's predicted SATs/Common Entrance/GCSE results.

Fees per term (2016–2017). Boarding £10,500; Day £5,430 (Years 7–8), £6,830 (Years 9–13).

Charitable status. Christ's Hospital School is a Registered Charity, number 1120090, supported by the Christ's Hospital Foundation, Registered Charity number 306975.

Head Master: **John Franklin**, BA, MEd

Deputy Heads:
J E Perriss, BA (*Geography*)
Mrs M A Fleming, BA (*Classics*) [Acting]

Chaplain:
Revd S Golding, BA, MA (*Theology & Philosophy*)

Assistant Staff:
* Head of Department

Miss R A Ahmed (*English*)
S J Albutt, BSc (*Sport Science & PE*)
R Allcorn, MSc (*Biology*)
P A Andersen, BA (*History*)
Miss J Azancot, BA (*Design & Technology*)
R E Barlow, BA (*Geography, Sport*)
Dr R Brading, BA, MA, PhD (*English*)
P W Bromfield, BSc (*Mathematics*)
Miss L Brown, MA (*French and English*)
P J Bryant, BA (**Economics*)
Miss H C Burt, BTh (*Theology & Philosophy*)
Mrs E A Callaghan (*Theology & Philosophy*)
T J Callaghan, BMus, LRAM (*Music*)
J B Callas, BSc (**Biology*)
Miss A Cassidy, MA (**French*)
Miss R Catterall, BA (*Art*)
G N Chandler, BA (*German, French*)
Mrs C Cherry, MA (*English*)
A M C Cleary, BA (**Music*)
Miss J A C Copley, BA (**History*)
S A Cowley, BA (**Art*)
Mrs C C C Cowley, BA (*EFL*)
I E Davies, MSc (*Chemistry, Sport*)
P Deller, BA (**Art*)
D N Don, MA (*English*)
Mrs N D Dotor Cespedes, BSc (*Biology*)
Mr J D Duffield, BSc (*Mathematics*)

P L Dutton, MA, ARCO (*Music*)
Mrs V C Dutton, BEng, MSc (*Physics*)
D J Farnfield, BA (*Geography*)
Mrs M A Fleming, BA (*Classics*)
N M Fleming, BA, DipArch, LRPS (**Archaeology*)
Mrs A K Franklin, BA, MA (*English*)
Z Gan, BA (**Mandarin*)
Miss S Gamba, BMus (*Music*)
Mr J-M Gonzalez (*Spanish*)
Miss S M Gorman, BSc (*Physics*)
Mrs J I Green, BSc (*Chemistry*)
D Griffiths, BSc (*Mathematics*)
J A Grindrod, BA (**Sports Science & PE*)
P H Hall-Palmer, BA (**Design & Technology*)
Dr K H Hannavy, BSc, DPhil (*Chemistry*)
Mr E L Hansen, BA (*Biology, Chemistry*)
E W G Hatton, BA (**Classics*)
Mr E J Hawkins, BSc (*Mathematics*)
Mrs C M Hennock, MA (*Mathematics*)
A E Henocq, BSc (*Chemistry*)
Miss A E Henry (*Physical Education*)
Mrs C Y Hitchcock, BA (*Economics*)
H P Holdsworth, BA, CcrtEd (*English*)
Miss E F Holmes, BA (*Mathematics*)
A Y Hughes, BMus LRSM, MMus (*Music*)
M R Jennings, BA, PhD (*History*)
Mrs G N Jerrit, MA (*Biology*)
J S Johnson, MA (**Drama & Theatre Studies*)
E Jones, MA (*Music*)
J P Keet, MA (*History*)
Mrs C E Kelley, BA (*Drama*)
D M L Kirby, BA (*English, Theology & Philosophy*)
Mrs R J Krebs, BA (*Geography*)
Miss F MacKenzie, MA (**Librarian*)
Mrs I M Mainwaring, BA (*Mandarin*)
R B Malpass, PhD (*English, Classics*)
Miss R L Manby, BA (*Geography*)
Mrs J A Marks, BA (*ESL, Teaching & Learning Skills Support*)
E A Marquez, BSc (**Spanish*)
S Mason, BSc (**Physics*)
K McArtney, BA (**Computer Studies*)
Mrs D McCulloch, MSc (*Mathematics*)
F McKenna, BTech (*Computer Studies, Design & Technology*)
G C McPheat, BSc *(Learning Support*)
K J Mead, BA (*Art*)
M I Medley, MSc, PhD (**Chemistry*)
D H Messenger, BA (**Director of Sport*)
Mrs I J Morgan, MA (*Classics*)
D Mulae, BSc (*Biology, General Science*)
Miss Z M Munday, BA (*Drama & Theatre Studies*)
Miss H N Nwandu, BSc (*Sports Science & Physical Education*)
S J O'Boyle, BSc, ARCS (*Mathematics*)
P I O'Regan, BSc (*Physics*)
Mrs C E P Page, BSc (*PE & Sport*)
H Parker, BSc (*Mathematics*)
Miss D L Petford, BSc (**Geography*)
A R B Phillips, BA (*Languages*)
Miss A P Phillips, BA (*Art*)
Mr A J Presland, BSc (*Mathematics*)
Miss E M Purvis, BA (*English*)
Mrs L V Ransley, BA (**Modern Languages*)
Miss S R Redfern-Jones, MA (*Theology & Philosophy*)
Mrs E A Robinson, BA (**Food & Nutrition*)
Mrs L B Russell, MA (*Biology*)
A Saha, MA, BA (*English*)
J P Salisbury, BSc (*Chemistry*)
Miss I Savidfoluschi, BA (*German*)
T D Scrivener, MSc (*Economics*)

Mr R D Sharkey, BA (**Economics*)
Mr W F Snowball, BA (*History*)
Mrs D J Stamp, BEd (*Mathematics*)
I N Stannard, BA (**Theology & Philosophy*)
Mr M S Stephens, BSc (*Mathematics*)
J G Tamvakis, BEd (*Biology*)
A G Taylor, BA (*Theology & Philosophy*)
Dr S R Thomson, BA, DPhil (*Classics*)
Miss L E A Thornton, MA (*History*)
S M Titchener, BA, MMus (*Music*)
Miss B Torres Casado (*Spanish*)
S W Walsh, MA (**English*)
Ms R L Watson, BSc (*Design & Technology*)
Dr P J Webb, BA, PhD (*Physics*)
Miss G M Webster, BA, PG Dip (*Music*)
G P Whitely, BA (*Art*)
T W Whittingham, BA, LTCL (*Music, Bandmaster*)
A R Wines, MA, PhD (*History*)
S C Young, MSc (*Chemistry*)
Mrs M E Young, BSc (*Geography*)

Clerk: G Andrews
Bursar: K J Willder, MBE
Assistant Head Admissions : Dr A R Wines
Head Master's PA: Mrs C Clark

Churcher's College

Petersfield, Hampshire GU31 4AS

Tel: 01730 263033
Fax: 01730 231437
email: enquiries@churcherscollege.com
website: www.churcherscollege.com

Motto: 'Credita Cælo' – Entrusted to Heaven

The College was founded in 1722 by a local philanthropist, Richard Churcher, who provided an endowment for boys to be taught English, Mathematics and Navigation in preparation for apprenticeships with the East India Company. The school relocated to more spacious grounds and accommodation in 1881.

The College roll is 1105 pupils. The Sixth Form totals 231 and the Junior Department (ages 4 to 11 years) totals 231. The school is fully co-educational.

Admission. The normal ages of admission to the Senior School are 11+ and 16+, and 4+ and 7+ in the Junior School after Churcher's assessment in the Spring Term. However, if vacancies exist, pupils are considered for admission at other ages.

A prospectus and application form, with details of fees, are available from the Headmaster.

The Sixth Form. Students are prepared for GCE A and AS Levels.

A wide combination of choices is offered from English, History, Geography, Economics, French, German, Spanish, Latin, Art & Design, Music, Drama, Philosophy & Ethics, Business Studies, Mathematics, Further Mathematics, Physics, Chemistry, Biology, Classical Civilisation, Design & Technology, Sport and Physical Education and Computing. All students take a course to prepare them for AS Level General Studies.

There is a fully-equipped Sixth Form Centre, for both study and recreation, a floor of the Library dedicated to Sixth Form private study, an excellent Careers Library and full-time Careers Officer and specialist Sixth Form teaching rooms and ICT facilities.

Years 1–5. From the 11+ entry all pupils follow a common academic programme comprising Mathematics, English, French, Physics, Chemistry, Biology, Latin, Classical Civilisation, Geography, Religion and Philosophy, Music, Art, Design & Technology, ICT, Drama and PE. In Year 2 an additional Modern European language (German or Spanish) is added to the programme. All pupils follow a broad curriculum and are not asked to specialise until they reach GCSE. All pupils follow GCSE courses in Mathematics, English, Language and Literature, Biology, Chemistry, Physics, a Modern Language, a Humanity and at least 2 additional optional subjects.

Pupils are tested and examined regularly with formal assessment procedures each half term and each end of term.

Facilities. Churcher's academic facilities include impressive purpose-built teaching accommodation, ICT suites, drama studios, art and design studios, design technology workshops, music centre and science block. Sports facilities include a swimming pool, sports halls and on-site tennis courts, netball courts, rugby pitches, all-weather hockey pitches and cricket squares. Churcher's has the facilities and resources to support an extensive range of extracurricular activities. The Sixth Form enjoys extensive recreational and teaching facilities. The Junior School is situated on its own spacious 10 acre site in Liphook, close to Petersfield.

Games and other Activities. The major sports played are Rugby, Hockey, Netball, Cricket and Rounders. There are also facilities for Badminton, Basketball, Volleyball, Tennis, Athletics, Aerobics and Cross-country, to name but a few. The School has a strong CCF unit with Army, Air Force and Naval Sections, and a flourishing Duke of Edinburgh's Award programme. Other activities include Mountain Biking, Canoeing, Gliding, Climbing, Adventurous Training, Young Enterprise Companies, Dance, Karate, Fencing, Football, Sailing, Horse Riding, Bridge, Chess, Debating, Drama and Photography.

Music, drama and dance are very strong in the school with School and House plays produced regularly and a wide range of out-of-school activities. The school also has a significant range of orchestras, wind bands and choirs and many more ensembles.

Careers. The College has a full-time Careers Adviser on the staff and regular visits are made by other professional Career Advisers. Talks are given to pupils in the Third Form and above, and individual interviews are arranged.

A **Parents' Association** was formed in 1967 and meetings are held each term.

Fees per term (2016–2017). Senior School £4,740; Junior School £3,020–£3,225. Fees include charges for examination fees and textbooks, but exclude lunches and individual music lessons.

Charitable status. Churcher's College, Petersfield, Hampshire is a Registered Charity, number 307320. Its aims and objectives are to provide a school for boys and girls between the ages of 4 and 18 in the Parish of Petersfield.

Governing Body:
M J Gallagher, DipArch Hons, RIBA, MIOD, FIMgt (*Chairman*)
Mrs J Bloomer, LLB (*Vice-Chairman*)
S Barrett
S Beecham
Mrs D Cornish, BA, MLitt
A Cox, BA Hons, FCA (*Nominated Governor for Parents' Association, Senior School*)
S Flint, BSc, MBA
R Hastings, LLB Hons
Mrs C Herraman-Stowers
W A Jones, MA
R May, MIOD
Mrs D Moses, FCA (*Nominated Governor for Parents' Association, Junior School*)
A Robinson, BSc, PGCE, MCGI
Ms A J Spirit, BA Hons, AMCM
Mrs L Warner, FCA, CTA

Headmaster: **S H L Williams**, BSc, MA

Deputy Heads:
Mrs S M J Dixon, BSc (*Staff and Co-curricular*)
C D P Jones, MA (*Pastoral*)
I G Knowles, BSc (*Academic*)

Head of Sixth Form: W Baker, BA, MSc, FRSA
Senior Teacher (Pastoral): Mrs J E Jamouneau, BEd, MSc
Senior Teacher (Public Relations): Mrs J B Millard, BSc, MSc, ARCS
Academic Registrar: I M Crossman, BA

Creative Arts Faculty:
Head of Faculty/Art: A Saralis, BA
Mrs G Heath, BA
Mrs G Roff, BA
D Heath, BA [maternity cover]

English Faculty:
Head of Faculty: Dr D P Cave, BA, PhD (*i/c The Academy*)
Miss P Harper, BA, PG Dip Broadcast Journalism (*Publications Editor*)
Mrs S Herrington, BA (*Head of Drake House*)
Ms J Jarrett, BA
Mrs A Jones, BA
Mrs C Lilley, BA
S Reeves, MA
Mrs L Wade, BA
Mrs B Williams, BEd

Humanities Faculty:
Head of Faculty/Classics: J Hegan, BA
Head of Economics/Business Studies/Politics: M Hill, BA (*Deputy Head of Sixth Form, i/c Young Enterprise*)
Head of Geography: D J Nighy, BSc, FRGS (*PSHE Coordinator*)
Head of History: Mrs C Hill, MA
Head of Religion & Philosophy: T Ostersen, BA
W Baker, BA, MSc, FRSA (*Head of Sixth Form*)
P Cheshire, MA, BA
Mrs S M J Dixon, BSc (*Deputy Head Staff and Co-curricular*)
G Glasspool, BSc, MA
J Harris, BSc
M Hoebee, MA
C D P Jones, MA (*Deputy Head Pastoral*)
Miss L Jenkinson, BA
Mrs H Jolliffe, MA (*Assistant Head of Sixth Form*)
J Lofthouse, BA, MMus, PGDip
J McLearie, MA
M Murray, MA (*Assistant Head of House*)
Mrs N Plewes, BSc (*Deputy Head of Sixth Form*)
Miss L Roberts, MA
B Seal, BA (*Head of Collingwood House*)
P Shipley, BA (*EPQ Coordinator*)
G M Strachan, BA (*Assistant Head of Sixth Form*)
R West, BSc, PGDip

Mathematics Faculty:
Head of Faculty: Mrs T L Greenaway, BSc
Miss L A Holmes, BSc, ACA
Dr N Jackson, DPhil, MSc
J Seaton, BA (*Head of Grenville House*)
Mrs L J Selby, BSc
Mrs R Tindal, BSc (*Assistant Head of House*)
Mrs A Thomas, BSc [maternity cover]
Mrs J Trench, BSc
G Wilson, BSc

Modern Languages Faculty:
Head of Faculty/French: Mrs K A Shaw, BA
Head of German: Mrs P Sykes, BSc
Head of Spanish: Mrs A-M Giffin, BA
Miss I Constantin, BA

I M Crossman, BA (*Academic Registrar*)
Ms A Louis, BA
Mrs M Robertson, BSc
Mrs N Sparks, BA (*OSCA Admin*)
H Sutherland, BA

Performing Arts Faculty:
Head of Faculty: Mrs H J Purchase, BA (*Director of Music*)
Head of Drama: Ms S Stokes, BA
Mrs L Cox, BA
P Cree, BA (*Assistant Director of Music Academic*)
S Fort, BA
M Greenwood, BA (*Assistant Director of Music Performance*)
J James, BA
R Peck, BA
Miss E Stretch, BA

Science Faculty:
Head of Faculty: Ms M J Westwood, BSc (*Head of Biology*)
Head of Chemistry: D J Dunster, MA
Head of Physics: M C Kelly, BSc
Mrs S L Cockerill, BSc (*Director of Studies*)
G Glasspool, BSc, MA
R M Hoe, BSc (*Head of Nelson House*)
Mrs J E Jamouneau, BEd, MSc (*Senior Teacher Pastoral*)
I Knowles, BSc (*Deputy Head Academic*)
J Lucraft, MBA, MEng, CEng
Mrs J B Millard, BSc, MSc, ARCS (*Senior Teacher Marketing & Public Relations*)
Dr V Raeside, BSc, PhD
Mrs N Rivett, BSc (*Assistant Head of Sixth Form*)
Mrs E Smith, BSc (*Coordinator of Springboard*)
Miss L Hattersley, BSc, MSc
R West, BEng
Dr R Whittle, MEng
J G Yugin-Power, BSc (*Head of Rodney House*)

Sports Faculty:
Director of Sport: D R Cox, BA, MSc (*Head of Boys' PE, i/c Rugby*)
P Beard, BA
R Cardwell, BA
Miss E Chambers, BSc
J Daniel (*First Challenge*)
Miss S Gardner, BSc, MSc
Miss L K Howe, BSc (*Fifth Year Pastoral Coordinator*)
Mrs T Jenkins (*i/c tennis*)
K Magurie, BA (*Assistant Head of House*)
R Maier (*i/c Cricket*)

Technology Faculty:
Head of Faculty: M Parrish, BSc, Dip Arch
Head of Design & Technology: S Atkinson, BA
Head of Computing: Mrs K McCathie, BSc
Miss C Evans, BA
S Reid, BSc
A Sangster, BSc

Adventure Faculty:
Head of Faculty: P Pearson, ML, SPA (*Head of Adventurous Activities, OSCA, DofE Manager, Climbing Wall Manager, QM for Adventure Stores, Ten Tors, i/c Expeditions*)
M J B Adams, BEd (*i/c CCF Navy Section, Devizes to Westminster Canoe Marathon*)
R Cardwell, BA
J Daniel (*First Challenge*)
D Dugan (*CCF School Staff Instructor*)
Miss L K Howe, BSc, ML (*OSCA, Elite Skiing*)
Mrs N Sparks, BA (*OSCA*)

Dr K Verney, BSc, BDS (*Careers and HE Advisor, Assistant Head of Sixth Form, CCF Contingent Commander*)
J G Yugin-Power, BSc, HDipEd (*Skiing*)

Curriculum Support:
Mrs L Blackman, BEd, Dip SpLD, Dip Counselling Children and Adolescents (*Head of Curriculum Support, School Counsellor*)

Junior School

Head of Junior School: I Adams, BSc, MBA

Deputy Head: Mrs P Yugin-Power, BSc, MA Ed, QTS
Head of Infant Department: Miss K M Humphreys, BEd
Senior Teacher Middle School: Mrs S J Moore, ARCM, GRSM
Senior Teacher Upper School: N Rushin, BSc, MSc
Senior Teacher Staffing: Mrs S Roberts, BEd

Miss H Parry, BA (*Class R Teacher*)
C Taylor, BSc (*Class 1 Teacher*)
Miss K M Humphreys, BEd (*Class 2 Teacher*)
Mrs J Gillard (*Class 3G Teacher*)
Miss K Shipton, BA (*Class 3S Teacher*)
Mrs A Knowles BSc (*Maternity cover*) (*Class 4K Teacher*)
Ms K Pendry, BA [maternity leave]
Mrs S J Moore, ARCM, GRCM (*Class 4M Teacher*)
Miss R Morris, BA, MSc (*Class 5M Teacher*)
Mrs K Tkaczynska, BEd (*Class 5T Teacher*)
Mrs S Roberts, BEd (*Class 6R Teacher*)
N Rushin, BSc, MSc (*Class 6N Teacher*)
Mrs R Cameron, CertEd, DipSpLD (*Learning Support*)
H Newport, BMus (*Head of Music*)
M Forbes, BSc (*Head of Sport and Outdoor Learning*)
Mrs A C Chilton, BEd (*PE*)
Mrs P Clemens, BEd (*Maths, PE*)
J Daniel (*Assistant Sports Teacher*)
Mrs R Drummond, BSocSc (*ICT*)
Mrs L M Eddy, BA (*English, PE*)
Mrs G Roff (*Art*)
Mrs S Penfold, BA (*MFL*)
W Pook, BSc (*ICT*)

Librarians:
Mrs L M Robbins, BSc, MIEH (*Junior School*)
Ms S Grant, BA, MSc
Mrs V Johnson, BSc

Bursar: D T Robbins, BSc Econ, FCCA

City of London Freemen's School

Ashtead Park, Surrey KT21 1ET

Tel: 01372 277933
Fax: 01372 276165
email: admissions@freemens.org
website: www.freemens.org
Twitter: @HelloFreemens
Facebook: @HelloFreemens

Motto: '*Domine dirige nos*'

The City of London Freemen's School is an independent co-educational day and boarding school which provides continuity of education for children aged 7 to 18. The School was founded in Brixton in 1854 by the Corporation of the City of London to provide 'a religious and virtuous education' for the orphaned children of Freemen of the City of London; Christian principles remain at the heart of its ethos, although the School is non-denominational. It is one of 3 schools governed and maintained by the City of London Corporation.

In 1926 the School moved to Ashtead Park, its present site and now educates approximately 915 girls and boys. Most of these pupils are day pupils, but the School remains firmly committed to the provision of boarding for a number of its pupils.

Alongside excellent academic results, our innovative enrichment programme is at the heart of our commitment to developing the whole person. We have the facilities, staff and grounds to ensure our students are happy, secure and fulfilled. We place particular emphasis on the individual and their needs and in providing the opportunities to identify and develop their skills to flourish throughout their time at Freemen's, and beyond.

There are 913 pupils in the School, approximately equal numbers of boys and girls, including up to 30 female and 30 male boarders. There are 515 pupils over the age of 13, including a Sixth Form of approximately 225.

The School stands in 57 acres of playing fields and parkland between Epsom and Leatherhead with easy access to Heathrow and Gatwick – both of which are only 22 miles away – via the M25. Buildings include a central Georgian Mansion, an Assembly Hall, a floodlit all-weather pitch and a Sports Hall complex completed in 1995. A multimillion pound building programme in the 1990s saw the addition of a Sixth Form Centre, an Art and Design Centre and a Science and Technology Centre. New teaching facilities for all subject Departments including Library and IT facilities were completed with the opening of the Haywood Centre in September 2000. A Studio Theatre was opened in October 2001, providing an auditorium for all productions, recitals, concerts and lecture facilities. The all-weather pitch has been replaced, bringing both up to modern national representative standards. A state-of-the-art music school, including a Steinway-D concert grand piano, and a co-educational boarding house for 60 pupils were completed and opened in 2014. Work has begun on the re-building of the swimming pool, which will be followed by the refurbishment of Main House.

Junior School. Since September 1988 the Junior School, ages 7–13, has been accommodated in a new complex in Ashtead Park. This provides 20 classrooms for up to 400 pupils. The Junior School is fully integrated within the framework and policies of the whole school and other facilities include specialist rooms for Art and Design, Science, Music and an integrated Technology Centre as well as an Assembly Hall and extended Library.

See Junior School entry in IAPS section.

Organisation and Entry. The School is divided into two sections but is administered as a single unit. The Junior Department has its own specially trained staff and its own self-contained building, but otherwise all staff teach throughout the School.

Junior entry is by the School's own examination at 7+ or 11+ (normally in January).

Senior School entry is by passing the Common Entrance examination, normally at the age of 13+, or by the School's own 13+ examination. Screening tests for Senior School entry have been introduced for Year 6 and Year 7 pupils; these take place in January. Freemen's Junior School pupils may expect to transfer satisfactorily to the Senior School at 13+ without sitting a special examination.

Sixth Form entry is by obtaining good GCSE grades with a minimum of 55 points from 10 subjects (or equivalent average for fewer subjects) with at least 8 passes at GCSE (grade C or better) including English and Mathematics. In addition, most subjects have specific entry requirements. At least four grade B passes must be obtained at GCSE in appropriate subjects. (A*=8, A=7, B=6, C=5)

Foundation entry is open to orphan children of Freemen at any age from 7+ to 16+, subject to satisfactory academic potential.

(Except for Foundationers, it is not necessary for applicants to be children of Freemen of the City.)

Curriculum. The first four years (7+ to 10+ in Years 3 to 6) are largely taught by class teachers up to Key Stage 2 following the broad outlines of the National Curriculum. Up to the age of about 14 all pupils have substantially the same curriculum which comprises English, French/German/Spanish, Mathematics, Physics, Chemistry, Biology, History, Geography, Religious Education, Latin, Design Technology, Computing, Food Technology, Art and Music. Thereafter, apart from a common core of English, French or German or Spanish, Mathematics and the 3 separate Sciences, selection is made for the course to GCSE from 15 other subjects including Spanish, German, French, Computing, Drama, Geography, History, Latin, Sociology and Design Technology so that the average pupil will offer 10 subjects. The principles of the National Curriculum are followed at all levels. Physical Education and Personal, Social and Health Education are included in the curriculum at all levels and all age groups have an Enrichment afternoon.

Sixth Form courses include the following: English Literature, Mathematics, Further Mathematics, Physics, Chemistry, Biology, History, Geography, Government & Politics, Classical Civilisation, French, German, Spanish, Art & Design, Business Studies, Drama, Music, Physical Education, Design Technology, Economics, Psychology and Philosophy and Theology. Pre-U courses are also offered in Art & Design. From September 2016, the Sixth Form will also study the Free Minds Programme: a course to run alongside A Levels that allows students to study a range of subjects to provide an even broader base to students' knowledge.

All pupils follow an Enrichment Curriculum which consists of an Extended Project, Physical Education, Leadership Skills and Community Service. Computing is well equipped and established, with specialist rooms in both the Junior and Senior Schools.

The School has an excellent academic record. Recent GCSE results have been excellent, with more than 80% of examinations awarded A* or A grades. A Level results have been equally impressive with over 90% of examinations awarded A or B grades, and nearly all leavers go on to degree courses at universities or other higher education institutes.

Each pupil is allocated to a House comprising a cross-section of boys and girls, both day and boarding, throughout the School. House teams compete in all forms of sport as well as music, drama and debating.

Games. *For Boys*: Principally Rugby, Cricket, Football, Athletics, Fencing, squash, Swimming, and Tennis.

For Girls: Principally Hockey, Netball, Tennis, Athletics, Rounders, Fencing, Squash, Swimming and Horse Riding.

There is a very wide choice of extracurricular activities throughout the School. The Duke of Edinburgh's Award scheme is a very popular option in the Senior School.

Fees per term (2016–2017). Senior School: £5,732 (day), £9,289 (boarding); Junior School: £4,229–£4,588 (day). Instrumental Music lessons: £217.

Scholarships and Bursaries. Scholarship awards are intended to attract and reward pupils of high academic ability and talent. Parents of scholars will be offered up to a maximum 5% discount of the fees. Bursary funds are available for those families requiring support to meet school fees and can be as much as 100% of the school fees. City of London Scholarships, open to both internal and external applicants, are awarded as follows:

At 11+ Scholarships of not more than 5% of the tuition fee, tenable for seven years. These Scholarships are awarded on the basis of performance in the School's Entrance Examination, school reports and an interview.

At 13+ Scholarships of not more than 5% of the tuition fee, tenable for five years. These Scholarships are awarded on the basis of performance in the 13+ Scholarship examinations, school reports and an interview.

At 16+ (Sixth Form entry) Scholarships are awarded of not more than 5% of the tuition fee tenable for two years. These Scholarships are awarded on the basis of performance in the Sixth Form Scholarship papers, school reports and an interview.

Music Scholarships are awarded as follows:

At 11+ awards of not more than 5% of the tuition fee. Applicants must have reached Grade 3 in one instrument and be able to offer a second study. Auditions and interviews are held with the Director of Music.

At 13+ awards of not more than 5% of the tuition fee. Applicants must have reached Grade 5 in one instrument and be able to offer a second study. Auditions and interviews are held with the Director of Music.

At 16+ (Sixth Form) awards of not more than 5% of the tuition fee. Applicants must have reached Grade 7 in one instrument and be able to offer a second study. Auditions and interviews are held with the Director of Music.

In all cases, music scholarships include free tuition in one instrument provided by teachers at the School.

A significant number of Bursaries, from our Bursary funds and Livery Companies, are also available.

Board of Governors:
Chairman: Mr Roger Chadwick
Deputy Chairman: Mr Stuart Fraser CBE
Mr John Bennett, Deputy
Mr Nicholas Goddard (*co-opted*)
Mr Timothy Hailes (*Alderman*)
Mr Brian Harris
Mr Michael Hudson
Mrs Clare James (*ex officio*)
Mrs Vivienne Littlechild
Mr Andrew McMillan (*co-opted*)
Mr Hugh Morris
Mr Graham Packham
Mr Matthew Richardson (*Alderman*)
Ms Elizabeth Rogula
Mr Ian Seaton (*ex officio*)
Sir Michael Snyder (*ex officio*)
Cllr Chris Townsend (*co-opted*)
Mr Philip Woodhouse
Mrs Gillian Yarrow (*co-opted*)

Clerk to the Governors: Jacqui Daniels

Headmaster: Mr Roland Martin

Deputy Head: Mrs Evelyn Guest
Academic Deputy Head: Mr Andrew McCleave
Head of Sixth Form: Mr Gareth Hughes
Head of Upper School: Mr Richard Dolan
Head of Junior School: Mr Matthew Robinson
Bursar: Mrs Susan Williams
Director of Marketing & Admissions: Mr Jason Harrison-Miles
Head of Boarding: Mrs Jemima Edney
Deputy Houseparent: Mr Alan Auld
Assistant Head (Junior School): Mrs Louise Jowitt
Assistant Head (Sixth Form): Mr Adrian Parkin
Head of Year 9: Miss Georgia Hill
Head of Year 10: Ms Sarah Chamberlain-Webber
Head of Year 11: Mr Alex Buhagiar

Subject Departments:
* Head of Department

English:
*Mrs Sarah Parkin
Mrs Sarah Stewart
Mr Christopher Bloomer
Ms Sarah Chamberlain-Webber
Mrs Evelyn Guest
Miss Charlotte Hughes
Mrs Emma Leigh (*p/t*)
Ms Fiona Moncur (*KS2 Coordinator*)
Mr Patrick New
Miss Ashleigh Callow (*EAL Teacher*)

Mathematics:
*Mr Ewan Bramhall
Mrs Marie Cast (*2nd in Department*)
Mrs Zara Field
Mrs Stella Hippolyte (*p/t*)
Mr Marc Holmes
Mrs Cecilia Inns (*p/t*)
Mrs Louise Jowitt (*KS2 Coordinator*)
Mr Tom Marsden
Mrs Elizabeth Newhouse
Mr Adrian Parkin
Mrs Elizabeth Rowlands (*p/t*)
Mr Robin Retzlaff

Modern Languages:
*Mrs Sarah Hankin

French and German:
*Mrs Sarah Hankin
Mrs Linda Headon
Mrs Catherine Leighton (*p/t*)
Mrs Julia Rosin (*p/t*)
Miss Lorna Vickers
Miss Rebecca Willis

Spanish:
*Mrs Christina Salisbury
Miss Rebecca Willis
Mrs Maria Willis-Jones

Classics:
*Mr Alan Chadwick
Mrs Ida Ashworth (*p/t*)
Mr William Ash (*p/t*)

Science:
*Mr James Hallam
Mrs Michelle Restall (*KS2 Coordinator*)

Biology:
*Mrs Judith Vatcher
Mrs Raylene Fox
Mr John Graham
Mrs Susan Meek

Chemistry:
*Dr Sarah Pinniger
Mrs Torna Burton (*p/t*)
Mrs Marina Corosio
Mrs Joanna Dickson
Dr Julia Lister

Physics:
*Mr James Hallam
Mr Richard Calladine
Mrs Helen Irwin
Mr Mark Newcome
Mr Brandon O'Donnell
Mrs Penni Thornton

Technology:
*Mr Steve Sarsfield

Design Technology:
Mr Rami Al-juboori

Mrs Joy Heafford (*KS2 Coordinator*)
Mr Max Hicks

Electronics:
Mr Steve Sarsfield

Food Technology:
*Mrs Margaret Smith
Mrs Tina Judge (*p/t*)

Art & Design:
*Mrs Bridget Downing
Mrs Rebecca Houseman
Ms Ginny Humphreys (*p/t*)
Mrs Vanessa Symonds (*KS2 Coordinator*)

Economics and Business:
*Mrs Justine Marvin
Mr Richard Dolan
Mr John Scullion (*p/t*)

Computing & Information Technology:
*Mr Ian Bartram
Mr Oliver James
Mrs Janet Wilby (*KS2 Coordinator*)

Drama:
*Miss Joanne Warburton
Ms Sarah Chamberlain-Webber

Enrichment:
*Mrs Elizabeth Newhouse
Mr Alex Buhagiar (*Enrichment Coordinator Yrs 7, 8, 9*)
Miss Harriet Pennington (*EPQ Coordinator*)
Mr Simon Davies (*KS2 Coordinator*)

Geography:
*Mr Richard Bustin
Miss Georgia Hill
Mrs Harriet Pennington
Mrs Emma Smith (*KS2 Coordinator*) (*p/t*)
Mrs Philippa Whiteley (*p/t*)

History & Politics:
*Mrs Katherine Edwards
Mr James Brooke
Mr Robbie Davies (*KS2 Coordinator*)
Mrs Elizabeth Joss
Mrs Nicky Sanderson

Music & Music Technology:
Mr Paul Dodds (*Director of Music*)
Mrs Natalka Eaglestone (*Assistant Director of Music*)
Mrs Ida Ashworth (*p/t*)
Mrs Sarah Gillespie (*KS2 Coordinator*)

RE:
*Mr Tim Wright
Miss Nicola Bax
Mr Andrew Illingworth
Mrs Louise Jowitt
Mrs Catherine Williams (*KS2 Coordinator*)

Psychology:
*Miss Joanna Vinall

PE and Games:
Mr Jamie Shore-Nye (*Director of Sport*)
Mrs Alison Bennett (*p/t*)
Miss Rachel Blackburn
Mr Alexander Buhagiar (*Head of Cricket*)
Mr Peter McKee
Mr Jon Moore (*Head of Rugby*)
Miss Frankie Paul (*Head of Hockey*)
Miss Sophie Robertson
Mrs Louise Shaill (*Head of Tennis and Athletics*)
Mrs Philippa Whiteley (*p/t*)

Physical Education A Level (*Sport Studies*):
*Mr Jon Moore
Mr Alex Buhagiar
Mrs Louise Shaill

Mr Neil Stewart (*Cricket Coach*)
Mr James Earl (*Hockey Coach*)
Mrs Alison Bennett (*Netball Coach*)
Mr John Thistlethwaite (*Tennis Coach*)
Mr Mike Cudmore (*Rugby Coach*)
Mr Marc Crump (*Rugby Coach*)
Mr Jeremy Colton (*Squash Coach*)

PSHE:
Mr Adrian Parkin (*Sixth Form Coordinator*)
Mrs Evelyn Guest (*Upper School Coordinator*)
Mrs Sue Meek (*Upper School Coordinator*)
Mrs Louise Jowitt (*Junior School Coordinator*)

Careers:
Miss Rebecca Willis (*Head of Sixth Form Careers*)
Miss Lorna Vickers (*Assistant Careers Advisor*)

Learning Support:
Mr Andrew Illingworth (*Learning Support Manager*)
Ms Fiona Moncur (*Learning Support Coordinator, Junior School*)

Junior School:

Year 3 (*Form 1*):
Mr Simon Davies (*Head of Year*)
Mrs Emma Smith (*p/t*)
Mrs Catherine Williams

Year 4 (*L2*):
Mrs Vanessa Symonds (*Head of Year*)
Mrs Jenny Cooper
Mrs Michelle Restall (*p/t*)
Mrs Vanessa Ielpi (*p/t*)

Year 5 (*U2*):
Mrs Sarah Gillespie (*Head of Year*)
Mr Richard Metcalfe
Mr Martin Valkenburg

Year 6 (*L3*):
Mrs Janet Wilby (*Head of Year*)
Mrs Nicola Sanderson
Miss Rosemary Kempster

Year 7 (*U3*):
Ms Fiona Moncur (*Head of Year*)
Mr Brandon O'Donnell
Dr Julia Lister
Mrs Philippa Whiteley (*p/t*) / Mr Jamie Shore-Nye
Mr Max Hicks

Year 8 (*L4*):
Mr Marc Holmes (*Head of Year*)
Miss Nicola Bax
Mrs Stella Hippolyte
Miss Francesca Paul
Miss Sophie Robertson
Mrs Louise Shaill

Heads of Houses:

Gresham:
Miss Nicola Bax
Mrs Catherine Williams (*Junior School*)

Hale:
Mrs Helen Irwin
Miss Rosemary Kempster (*Junior School*)

Whittington:
Mr James Brooke
Dr Julia Lister (*Junior School*)

Staff Induction:
Mrs Natalka Eaglestone (*New Staff Induction Coordinator*)
Miss Joanna Vinall (*NQT Coordinator*)

Duke of Edinburgh's Award Scheme:
Mr John Graham (*Senior D of E Coordinator*)
Miss Rosie Kempster (*D of E Coordinator*)

Boarding House:
Mrs Jemima Edney (*Head of Boarding*)
Mr Alan Auld (*Deputy Houseparent*)
Mrs Lin Retzlaff (*Day Matron*)
Mr Alex Buhagiar (*Boarding House Tutor*)
Miss Georgia Hill (*Boarding House Tutor*)
Mr Patrick New (*Boarding House Tutor*)

Combined Cadet Force:
Miss Rosemary Kempster (*CCF Staff in charge of CCF*)
Mr Colin Davies (*CCF School Staff Instructor*)

Medical Centre:
Mrs Anna Corbett (*School Nurse Manager*) (*p/t*)
Mrs Lizzie Dyer (*p/t*)
Mrs Bernadette O'Connor (*p/t*)

Non-Teaching Staff:
Bursar: Mrs Susan Williams
Headmaster's PA: Mrs Kelly Montague
Assistant Bursar: Mrs Anna Atkins
HR Officer: Miss Helen Lambert
Finance Manager: Mr Cedric Ngassam
Finance Officer – Fees: Mrs Debbie Widmer
Finance Officer – Creditors: Mrs Michelle Ilbert (*p/t*)
Finance Administrator: Mrs Jane Arnett (*p/t*)
Finance Administrator: Mrs Gillian Daniel (*p/t*)
Lettings Administrator: Mrs Suzanne Wilding (*p/t*)
Director of Marketing & Admissions: Mr Jason Harrison-Miles
Admissions Officer: Mrs Jodi-Lynne Shalgosky
Admissions Assistant: Mrs Nicola Navamani
Outreach Officer: Mrs Kerri Martin
Development Officer: Mrs Jo Patel
Senior Management Secretariat Team Leader: Mrs Amanda Moss
Deputy Head's Secretary: Mrs Rebecca Whiteway
Senior School Secretary: Mrs Lucy Ryckaert
Senior School Receptionist: Mrs Tracey Clarke
Secretary to Head of Junior School: Mrs Gillian Anklesaria
Junior School Administrator: Miss Natalie Holdway
Music Administrator: Mrs Samantha Grover (*p/t*)
Sports Administrator: Mrs Antonietta Caprano-Wint
Examinations Officer: Mrs Nicketa Williams
Senior Reprographics Officer: Mr Nigel Fairhurst (*p/t*)
Reprographics Officer: Mr Steve Butcher
Senior Librarian: Mrs Sue Dawes
Assistant Librarian: Mrs Nicola Mason (*p/t*)
Assistant Librarian: Ms Charlotte Bellsham-Revell
Senior Science Technician: Mrs Julie Mayhew (*p/t*)
Technician – Chemistry: Dr Janet Johnson (*p/t*)
Technician – Science, Junior School: Mrs Jane Dallyn (*p/t*)
Technician – Electronics: Mr David Mayhew (*p/t*)
Technician – General Science: Mr David Dunn
Technician – Art & Design: Ms Emma Hughes-Phillips
Technician – Art & Design: Mr Geoff Coates (*p/t*)
Technician – Design Technology: Mr Rami Al-juboori (*p/t*)
Technician – Food Technology: Mrs Sarah Baxter (*p/t*)
Technician – Physics: Mrs Mary Marrett
Facilities Technician – Theatre Facilities: Mr Chris Ruby
ICT Manager: Mr Adam Cohen
Data Manager: Mr Anthony Richmond
ICT Technician: Mr Stephen Miller
Head of Grounds & Gardens: Mr Gary Marshall
Senior Groundsperson: Mr Clive Fisher

Groundsperson: Mr Stuart Dare
Gardener: Mr Lawrence Aggett
Maintenance Assistant: Mr Michael Bartlett
Maintenance Assistant: Mr Sean Hayes
Maintenance Assistant: Mr Andrew Mills
Chaplain: Revd Jonathan Prior

Visiting Music Teachers:
Ms Nicola Berg (*Singing*)
Mrs Alice Bishop (*Singing*)
Mrs Victoria Brockless (*Violin, Viola*)
Miss Ruth Chappell (*Flute*)
Mrs Hilary Dilnot (*Piano*)
Mr David Eaglestone (*Trombone, Tuba, French Horn*)
Ms Jennifer Janse (*Cello, Double Bass*)
Miss Jan Lewis (*Piano*)
Miss Sally MacTaggart (*Clarinet, Saxophone*)
Mr James O'Carroll (*Percussion, Drums*)
Ms Elenlucia Pappalardo (*Piano*)
Mr Tim Peake (*Piano*)
Miss Leah Perona-Wright (*Singing*)
Mr Nigel Peronal-Wright (*Flute, Singing*)
Mr Paul Smith (*Saxophone, Clarinet, Oboe, Piano*)
Mr Simon Sturgeon-Clegg (*Trumpet, Trombone, Euphonium*)
Mrs Hilary Taylor (*Piano*)
Miss Gillian Wallace (*Violin*)
Mr John Wallace (*Guitar*)

City of London School

Queen Victoria Street, London EC4V 3AL
Tel: 020 3680 6300
Fax: 020 3680 6328
email: admissions@cityoflondonschool.org.uk
          head@cityoflondonschool.org.uk
website: www.cityoflondonschool.org.uk
Twitter: @CityLondonBoys

The City of London School occupies a unique Thameside location in the heart of the capital and has 925 day boys between the ages of 10 and 18 from all parts of the capital. It traces its origin to bequests left for the education of poor boys in 1442 by John Carpenter, Town Clerk of the City. The Corporation of London was authorised by Act of Parliament in 1834 to use this and other endowments to establish and maintain a School for boys. This opened in 1837 in Milk Street, Cheapside, and moved to the Victoria Embankment in 1883. In 1986 the School moved again, to excellent purpose-built premises provided by the Corporation on a fine riverside site in the City, to which a new Technology building was added in 1990. The School lies on the riverside next to the Millennium Bridge with St Paul's Cathedral to the north and the Globe Theatre and Tate Modern across the Thames to the south. The School's Board of Governors is a committee of the Court of Common Council, the Corporation of London's governing body and four independent co-opted members.

Admissions. Pupils are admitted aged 10, 11 and 13 (as on 1st September of year of entry), on the results of the School's own entrance examinations held each year in January. Note that boys applying for entry at age 13 are examined when they are in Year 6. Those admitted at 16 into the Sixth Form are selected by test and interview in the previous November. Applicants must register for examinations using our online system.

Fees per term (2016–2017). £5,211.

Entrance Scholarships. Academic, Music and Sports Scholarships, with a value of up to quarter of the school fees are awarded annually. These Scholarships are available at any of the normal entry points. At 16+ an Academic Scholarship may be awarded on the strength of a candidate's GCSE results.

Candidates for entry to the School may also apply for Choristerships at the Temple Church or the Chapel Royal, St James's (the choristers of both choirs are pupils at the School). Choristers receive Choral Bursaries whose value is two-thirds of the school fee. Potential choristers may also take auditions and academic tests in Year 4; successful applicants will be offered a conditional place in the School for the year after their 10th birthday.

Sponsored Awards. The School offers a number of bursaries, up to full fees, to assist those parents of academically very bright boys, who otherwise could not contemplate private education. These awards are only available at 11+ and 16+.

Curriculum. All boys follow the same broad curriculum up to and including the Third Form. In the Third Form boys spend some eight afternoons throughout the year on educational visits to institutions and places of interest in and around the City. Latin, French and Mandarin are started by all in the First Form and two choices from Greek, Classical Civilisation, Drama, German and Spanish may be added as options in the Third Form. Fourth and Fifth Form boys take a core of English, Mathematics, three Sciences (the core subjects are all IGCSEs), and at least one Modern Foreign Language (which can include Russian), and choose three other subjects from a wide range of subjects available for study to GCSE/IGCSE. In the Sixth Form boys study either four A Levels, or three and any one of an EPQ (Extended Project Qualification), AS Photography, an IT&C Qualification or a Financial Services Qualification. Virtually all boys leaving the Sixth Form proceed to their first or second choice of Russell Group University or Medical School.

Games. The School's 20 acres of playing fields, at Grove Park in south-east London, offer excellent facilities for football, cricket, athletics, and tennis. Sporting facilities on the School site include an astroturf pitch, sports hall, a gymnasium with conditioning room, three squash courts, a fencing salle, and a 25-metre swimming pool.

School Societies. There is a large number of School Societies, catering for a very wide range of interests, and a Freshers' Fair is held early each year to allow societies to promote themselves. Every opportunity is taken to benefit from the School's central position by participation in the cultural and educational life of London, and of the City in particular. The School has a strong musical tradition; tuition is available in a large range of instruments, and membership of the School choirs and orchestras is encouraged. Choristers of the Temple Church and of the Chapel Royal are educated at the School as bursaried scholars provided that they satisfy the entrance requirements. There is much interest in Drama, and the School has a fully-equipped Theatre and a Drama Studio. There is a large CCF Contingent which boys may join from the age of 13, with Army, Navy and RAF Sections. There is also a successful Community Service programme. Many boys also take part in the Duke of Edinburgh's Award scheme.

Alumni Association. There is a flourishing Old Boys' Society known as the John Carpenter Club, website: www.jcc.org.uk. The Alumni Relations Officer can be contacted at the School.

Chairman of Governors: Mr Ian Seaton

Head: Mrs S K Fletcher, MA

Senior Deputy Head: R M Brookes, MChem, DPhil
Assistant Head Academic: Miss N H Murphy, BA
Assistant Head Pastoral: Mrs C B Stephenson, MA
Assistant Head Professional Development: A J V McBroom, BA

Assistant Head Teacher and Learning: J T Silvester, BA, MA
Assistant Head Strategic Development: E Whitcomb, BSc

Bursar: C B Griffiths, LLB
Head of Admissions: P S Marshall, MA

Head of Sixth Form: I Emerson, BSSc, MA
Deputy Head of Sixth Form: Miss Z L Connolly, MA
Deputy Head of Sixth Form: J P Santry, BEng
Deputy Head of Sixth Form: M N Everard-Pennell, MChem, PhD
Head of Fifth Form: S S Fernandes, BSc, MA
Deputy Head of Fifth Form: Mrs K L Pattison, BSc, PhD
Head of Fourth Form: J Norman, MA
Deputy Head of Fourth Form: G W Dawson, BSc
Head of Third Form: M P Kerr, BA
Deputy Head of Third Form: S A Swann, BA MSc
Head of Second Form: Mr M C Chataway, BA
Deputy Head of Second Form: Miss K A Saunt, BA
Head of First Form and Old Grammar: C E Apaloo, BSc
Deputy Head of First Form: N C Hudson, BA
Deputy Head of Old Grammar: Miss C A Hudson, BSc

* *Head of Department*

Classics:
*W Ellis-Rees, MA
Miss C L Rose, BA
Miss Z L Connolly, MA
J E Pile, BA
S A Swann, BA, MPhil
J E McArdle, MA
Mrs C B Stephenson, MA

Design & Visual Arts:
*I P Dugdale, Dip
Miss A E Gill, BA
Miss B Easton, BA
Miss N Cleary, BA
S R Lewington

Drama:
*Miss S H Dobson, BA
Miss M L Franklin, BA

Economics:
*D P Rey, BSc, MA
M Wacey, BSc
C R Webb, BSc

English:
*R A Riggs, BA, MA
J Norman, MA
Miss H M Sénéchal, MA
B Bellak, BA
N C Hudson, BA
Miss E J Green, BA
Miss L O Longhurst, BA
MIss H C Cowen, BA

Geography:
*O J Davies, BSc, MSc
P S Marshall, MA
Miss V J Robin, MA
Miss A E Low, BA

History and Politics:
*A J Bracken, BA
Miss N H Murphy, BA
A J V McBroom, BA
Mrs V W Arnold, BA
Miss K A Saunt, BA
S J Brown, BA, MA
M C Chataway, BA, MA
J T Crowther, MA

Mrs K Molteni, BA
J N Millard, BA

Information Technology:
*Mrs S L Ralph, BA
Mrs A M MacDonagh, BSc, BSc

Mathematics:
*D R Eade, BA
D J Chamberlain, BSc, MSc
Miss C A Hudson, BSc
S S Fernandes, BSc, MA
Mrs C S Musgrove, MA
Miss J C L Mesure, BA
Miss E L McCallan, MA
S J Dugdale, BSc, PhD
Ms N Bigden, BSc, MSc
Mr B P Broadhurst, MSc
T G Betchley, BSc, MA
Miss S E Golleck, PhD, MPhil

Modern Languages:
*R Edmundson, MA
P A Allwright, MA
G J Dowler, JP, MA
Miss V Vincent, MA
Mrs A L Robinson, BA
C B Fillingham, BA, MA
P R Eteson, BA (*French)
Ms M J Ciechanowicz, MA
I Emerson, BSSc, MA
B Pollard, MA (*German)
Miss F G Easton, BA
T H White, BA, MA

Music:
*P Harrison, GLCM, MA
Miss J E Jones, BA
J Harrison, BA

Physical Education:
*N F Cornwell, BEd
M P Kerr, BSc, MSc
B J Silcock, BPE
J P Santry, BEng
C E Apaloo, BSc

Religious Education:
*J M Fenton, MA
J T Silvester, BA, MA
Mrs K E Weare, MA, MA
Mrs A Giannorou, BSc,
  BA, MPhil
Miss S K Wallace, MA

Science:
Mrs P C McCarthy, BSc
  (*Chemistry*, * *Science*)
A A Wood, MSci
  (*Physics*)
A Zivanic, BA, MA
  (*Biology*)
N O Mackinnon, BSc, PhD

R Mackrell, BSc
G W Dawson, BSc
E Whitcomb, BSc
K P Rogers, MChem
P J Naylor, BSc
Mrs K L Pattison, BSc,
  PhD
G H Browne, BA, BSc
M N Everard-Pennell,
  MChem, PhD
R J Dharamshi, BA
A Jackson, BSc, MA,
  MPhil
T L Robinson, BSc
Miss H Stanley, BSc

There are Visiting Music Teachers for Bassoon, Cello, Double Bass, French Horn, Flute, Guitar, Jazz, Oboe, Organ, Percussion, Piano, Saxophone, Singing, Trombone, Trumpet, Tuba, Viola, Violin.

Learning Support:
*Ms A C DiStefano Power, BAH, BEd
Mrs A J Fountaine, MSci, MA
Mrs J de Stacpoole, Hornsby Dip SpLD
M C Biltcliffe, BA
Mrs K J Ireland, BA

Library:
*D A Rose, BA, Dip Lib, ALA
Ms J Grantham, MA
Miss R Stocks, BA
M Evans

Registrar: Mrs V J Haley
Human Resources Manager: Mrs V Wheatley
Development Director: Mrs J Lancaster

City of London School for Girls

St Giles' Terrace, Barbican, London EC2Y 8BB

Tel: 020 7847 5500
Fax: 020 7638 3212
email: info@clsg.org.uk
website: www.clsg.org.uk
Twitter: @clsggirls
Facebook: /clsggirls
LinkedIn: /city-of-london-school-for-girls

Motto: *Domine Dirige Nos*

City of London School for Girls is an academically selective, non-denominational, independent day school for girls aged 7–18. There is an infectious vibrancy and energy at "City". Its distinctive location in the Barbican Centre provides immediate access to the wealth of London's educational and cultural opportunities, while the teaching staff and girls imbue the place with a sense of happiness, purpose, enthusiasm and fulfilment.

The School Course includes English Language and Literature, History, Geography, Religion, Philosophy and Ethics, Latin, Greek, French, German, Spanish, Mathematics, Biology, Chemistry, Physics, Economics and Politics, Art, Music, Physical Education, Classical Civilisation, Design and Technology, Theatre Studies, and Chinese.

Pupils are prepared for GCSE, AS and A2 Level Examinations offered by Edexcel, OCR and AQA. They are also prepared for entrance to Oxford, Cambridge and other Universities. The Sixth Form courses are designed to meet the needs of girls wishing to proceed to other forms of specialised training.

Facilities are provided for outdoor and indoor games and the school has its own indoor swimming pool and an all-weather sports pitch. Extracurricular activities before school, in the lunch hour or at the end of afternoon school include Debating, Football, Drama, Science, Technology, Fencing, Netball, Gymnastics, Swimming, Tennis, Climbing and classes in Chinese, as well as many more. Guest speakers are frequently invited to the school, especially in the Sixth Form. There are also Junior and Senior Choirs, a Madrigal group, a Barbershop group, Junior and Senior Orchestras, a Wind Ensemble, a Chamber Orchestra and a Swing Band. Lunch hour music recitals, with visiting professional players, are encouraged. Many girls take the Duke of Edinburgh's Award scheme at bronze, silver and gold level.

Admission. Main entry points to the school are at 7 and 11 and 16 years of age. For girls over 11 years old, vacancies are only occasional. The entrance examinations for age 11 admission in September will usually be held in the previous January. For age 7 the entrance exam is held in the Autumn Term. Admission to the Sixth Form is also by written examination and interview during the Autumn Term.

Applications for 11+ and 16+ should reach the Admissions Officer by the start of the previous October. Specific deadlines can be found on the website.

Scholarships and Bursaries. The School has a variety of art, music and drama scholarships and means-tested bursaries for entry at 11+ and 16+.

Further details may be obtained from the Admissions Officer.

Fees per term (2016–2017). Preparatory Department: £5,352 (including lunch); Main School: £5,352 (excluding lunch).

Senior School lunches are paid for with a cashless system based on credited payment cards. Pupils in the Preparatory Department are expected to take school lunch for which there is no extra charge. After-school supervision is also available at £182 per term.

Extra Subjects: Pianoforte, Violin, Cello, Flute, Clarinet, Organ, Guitar and a wide variety of other instruments, including Singing: £258 per term (fees are all payable in advance).

School Governors:
Chairman: Mrs Clare James, MA, CC
Deputy Chairman: Mr Nicholas Michael Bensted-Smith, JP

Headmistress: Mrs E Harrop, BA Salamanca, MA Munich, MPhil Cantab, MA London

Deputy Head (Pastoral): Mrs K N Brice, MA Cantab
Deputy Head (Staff): Mrs C Tao, BSc Surrey, MSc LSE
Deputy Head (Academic): Mr N Codd, BA Hons Oxon

Head of Sixth Form: Miss R Lockyear, BA Hons Cantab

Assistant Head of Sixth Form: Mrs C Williamson, BA Cantab

Head of Senior School: Mrs S Gilham, BA Oxon

Assistant Heads of Senior School:
Miss N Ispahani, BSc York
Mr A Wright, BSc Bournemouth

Head of Lower School: Ms J Singleton, BEng Hons Southampton

Assistant Head of Lower School: Miss R Robertson, MA St Andrews

Head of Preparatory School: Miss J Rogers, MPhil, BA London

Deputy Head of Preparatory Department: Mrs L Hall, BA Hons Bristol, MA Herts

Heads of Department:

Art:
Miss J Curtis, BA Hons London, St Martin's School of Art, ATC London

Classical Languages:
Mr D Themistocleous, BA Oxon

Drama:
Mr S Morley, Dip Acting CCSD

Economics:
Mr A Kanwar, BA Oxon

Politics:
Miss R Lockyear, BA Hons Cantab

English:
Mr B Ward, BA The New University of Ulster

Geography:
Miss E A Moore, BA Liverpool, FRGS

History:
Mr J Murray, MA Oxon

Mathematics:
Mr T Bateup, BSc Warwick

Modern Languages:
French: Mr G Tyrrell, BA Oxford Brookes, MA
German: Mrs A Marett, BA Oxon
Spanish: Miss M Leturia, BA Granada, MA London
Italian: Miss E Perkins, BA Leeds
Chinese: Ms E Garner, BA Hons York, MA SOAS, MSc Manchester

Music:
Dr S Berryman, BMus Wales, MMus London, PhD Wales, FRSA

Physical Education:
Ms C Castell, BA Loughborough

Religion, Philosophy and Ethics:
Mrs K Bullard, MA Cantab

Sciences:
Biology: Miss N Brown, BSc Hons Edinburgh, MRes Edinburgh
Chemistry: Mr A Stylianou, BSc Hons London
Physics: Mr M Wilkinson, BSc Hons Nottingham

Technology:
Miss S McCarthy, BSc Brunel

ICT:
Mr D Libby, BSc West of England

Careers and PSHCEE:
Miss E Perkins, BA Leeds

Library:
Mrs R Trevor, BA Hons, MCLIP

Bursar: Mr A Bubbear, MBA Open
Facilities Manager: Mr J Valentine
Finance Manager: Mr R Woodvine, MA RCA
Registrar: Mrs R Kearney, MA Dunelm
Senior Administrative Officer: Mrs V Pyke

Health & Support Network:
School Doctor: Dr D Soldi, MB, ChB, DCH
School Counsellors:
Ms D Marcus, BA Counselling Tavistock Institute, Dip Psychodynamic Counselling Westminster Pastoral Foundation
Ms C Nancarrow
Learning Support Coordinators:
Mrs C Cole, BA East Anglia, RSA Dip London
Miss E Herbert, BA London, PGCE Secondary

Clayesmore School

Iwerne Minster, Blandford Forum, Dorset DT11 8LL
Tel: 01747 812122
email: margaret@clayesmore.com
website: www.clayesmore.com
Twitter: @clayesmore

Developing the unique gifts of every girl and boy

Infused with an atmosphere of warmth and friendliness, Clayesmore is a flourishing co-educational school with Senior and Preparatory sharing the same stunning 62-acre site. The Senior School was founded in 1896 and in 1975 was joined by the Prep at Iwerne Minster. Despite Clayesmore being one big happy family, the two schools each have their own Headmaster, staff and separate teaching areas.

Clayesmore has been deemed 'excellent' across the board following its most recent Independent Schools Inspectorate inspection that included pupils' achievements, quality of teaching and quality of boarding. The report strongly praised the school's remarkable achievements and its rise to becoming one of the South West's premier independent boarding and day schools.

Buildings and Grounds. The excellent facilities have been radically improved in recent years providing even greater opportunities for pupils. The attractive main building functions as the school's HQ with the upper floors used as a girls' boarding house. The ground floor features a charming library complete with computer facilities for private study and research, as well as delightful reception rooms for a variety of uses.

Recent development has included a £2.8m state-of-the-art Business School, a greatly expanded Design & Technology facility, and a girls' boarding house to accommodate growing pupil numbers. This stylish Business School houses teaching facilities for Business Studies, Economics, Psychology and a Careers Centre. Future development plans include the building of a new theatre, sports pavilion, English & Drama faculty and boys' boarding house.

The Sports Centre has a 25m indoor pool, squash courts, fitness suite, four badminton courts and indoor cricket nets. Outside, as well as the many pitches and netball courts, there is a floodlit, all-weather hockey pitch that provides 12 tennis courts for summer use.

There is a dedicated Music School and self-contained Art School, as well as a Chapel, built in 1956, as a memorial to the Old Clayesmorians who gave their lives in two World Wars. The parkland grounds are quite outstanding, with extensive playing fields, a lake, and wonderful views towards Hambledon Hill.

Houses and Pastoral Care. The Senior School has five houses (three for boys and two for girls) each with resident, married house staff, and resident tutor, who provide nurturing pastoral care. Boarding pupils and day pupils live and learn together – there are no day houses and all pupils have a tutor to oversee academic progress and support them through school. Clayesmore has a real family feel and its comparatively small size enables the Headmaster and the staff to really get to know the pupils.

Academic work. Year 9 serves as a useful foundation year prior to GCSE courses starting in Years 10 and 11. Sixth Form students study four AS Levels in the Lower Sixth, taking three of these on to A2 in the Upper Sixth. The school has also introduced new A Level subjects and a number of BTEC options to broaden choice. The Sixth Form really helps to prepare students for life after Clayesmore, with supportive tutors, work experience opportunities and expert careers advice.

Clayesmore pays close attention to the needs of individual pupils, both in academic as well as other spheres, and the school has earned a strong reputation for successfully helping pupils with dyslexia.

Scholarships. A wide range of bursaries and scholarships really open doors, including those for HM Forces families.

The wider life at Clayesmore. Sport is well supported at Clayesmore with rugby, hockey, cricket, athletics, netball, swimming and cross-country complemented by popular subsidiary sports such as badminton, squash, sailing and orienteering.

Year 10 and 11 pupils can experience the challenges and excitement of the Combined Cadet Force with many enthusiasts continuing as NCOs into the Sixth Form. Clayesmore also offers the chance to achieve the well-respected Duke of Edinburgh's Award, as well as a marvellous mix of other activities.

Music and drama play a vibrant role in the life of the school and provide pupils with numerous opportunities to perform. Encouragement is given to pupils of all ages to learn instruments and sing in choirs. There are all sorts of ensembles and new ones are formed to match different pupil interests. The purpose-built theatre is a practical, intimate space, used with great imagination, not only for various termly productions, but also for GCSE Drama and the BTEC in Performing or Production Arts.

Entry arrangements. Entrance to Clayesmore Senior School is at 13 with those from preparatory schools taking the Common Entrance examination. For entrants from maintained schools, there are tests in English, Mathematics, Science and French. Girls and boys may join Clayesmore earlier if they attend Clayesmore Preparatory School and it is quite normal for new pupils to arrive at age 11 and undertake Years 7 and 8 at the Prep School. Each year, between 10 and 20 young people join as Sixth Formers, and the total number in the Sixth Form is roughly 170.

Clayesmore Preparatory School. Clayesmore is an 'all-through' school with both Prep and Senior sharing the same idyllic setting and it offers a seamless transition at 13 that is perfect for parents, particularly of boarders, who are keen to keep siblings together. Entrance to the Preparatory School may take place into any year group assuming a place is available, and is dependent upon an interview with the Headmaster and a report from the pupil's present school.

Fees per term (2016–2017). Senior School: £11,370 (boarding), £8,340 (day). Preparatory School: £5,620–£7,990 (boarding), £2,450–£5,970 (day).

Charitable status. Clayesmore School Limited is a Registered Charity, number 306214.

Council of Governors:
Mr J Andrews, LLB (*Chairman of F&GP*)
Mr D Haywood, MA, FRGS (*Vice Chairman – Education*)
Mr A Beaton [OC]
Mr P Dallyn, FRICS, FAAV
Mrs F Deeming, BA, PGCE
Mrs D Geary, CertEd
Mr D M Green, MA, FRSA
Mr T Ingram, MA, MBA, FCIB
Mrs R Stiven
Major General J Stokoe, CB, CBE
Mr S Symonds, BA Ed
Dr R Willis, MA, BM, BCh

Governors Emeritus:
Mr R C Kingwill, BSc, MS
Mrs J H Lidsey

Head: Mrs Joanne Thomson, BA

Deputy Head: Mr J R Carpenter, BA, FRSA

Second Deputy: Mrs E M Bailey, BA, PGCE

Director of Teaching & Learning: Mr A R West, BA, MA, PGCE

Head of Sixth Form & Senior Master: Mrs S J Newland, BSc, PGCE

Head of Learning Support: Mrs A Cowley, BSc, PGCE, MEd SEN, Dip SpLD, AMBDA

Director of Co-curriculum: Mr J A Reach, BEng, PCGE

Bursar: Mr M J M Dyer

House Staff:
Mrs H N Christmas, BA
Mr M McKeown, BA, PGCE
Mrs R V Readman, BA, PGCE
Mr M I Newland, BSc, MA, PGCE
Mr D I Rimmer, MA

Assistant Staff:
Mr T M Andrews, BA, PGCE
Ms B Barrie, BA, MA
Mr R G Berry, BSc, PGCE
Mrs M Bleeze, BA
Mrs I Browse, BA, MA
Miss S A Buckland, BSc, PGCE
Mr C L Burton, BSc, PGCE
Mrs A L Cheverton, BSc
Mrs L Chmielewski, BA, PGCE
Mrs H N Christmas, BA
Mr P W Coates, BEd, CertEd
Mr D O Conway, BSc, PGCE
Mrs H Cook, BA, PGCE
Miss E C Cummings, BA, MA, PGCE
Mr C B A Didier, MFLE, PGCE
Mrs E L Dorey, BA, PGCE
Miss L Downton, BA
Mrs A E Easterbrooke, MA
Mrs C B W Ellis, BA, PGCE
Mrs J M Essex, BSc, PGCE
Mrs H B Forster, MA, PGCE
Mr M S Fraser, BA, PGCE
Mrs K D Gallagher, BA, PGCE
Dr J Gammon, MChem, PhD, PGCE
Mr H J Gibbons, BSc, PGCE, CPhys, CSci, MInstP
Mr W H Gibbs, BSc, PGCE
Mr G Glasspool, BSc, MEd
Mrs C Godfree, BA, PGCE
Ms J Gregory, BA, MA, PGCE
Dr J Harrison, BA, MA, PhD, PGCE
Mrs M Herry, BA, PGCE
Mrs R M Hunter, CertEd, BA, RSA SpLD
Miss C E Jacks, BA, PGCE
Dr A P G Jancis, BSc, PhD, CBiol, MIBiol, PGCE
Mr M I Jones, BA
Mr R Kerr, MA
Mrs K R Mareau-Jones, BA, PGCE
Miss S E May, MA
Mr M McKeown, BA, PGCE
Mr C R Middle, BA
Mr R S Miller, BSc, PGCE
Mrs W Mills, BEd
Mrs T J Moussalli, BA, PGCE
Mrs J A Murphy
Mr P Musson, BA
Mr M I Newland, BSc, MA, PGCE
Mrs S J Newland, BSc, PGCE
Miss K E O'Rourke, BA, MA, PGCE
Mrs N E Patterson, DipCOT
Miss G Penny, BA, PGCE
Mrs H A Perrett, BA, PGCE
Mrs N L Potter, BSc, PGCE
Mr A K Powell-Young, BSc, PGCE, MRSC

Mr P J Randall, BA, PGCE
Miss R V Readman, BA, PGCE
Miss S J Rhead, BSc, PGCE
Mr K A Richards, BA, PGCE
Mr D I Rimmer, MA
Mr E R Robeson, MA, PGCE
Mr K A Samoluk, BA, PGCE
Mrs M J Simpson, BCom, PGCE
Mrs C L Smith, BSc, PGCE
Mr H C Smith, BA, PGCE
Mrs K Smith, BSc, PGCE
Mr S A Smith, BSc, PGCE, MInstPhys
Mr H P Stevenson, BA, PGCE
Dr F M Thomason, BSc, PhD, OCN Cert SpLD, PGCE
Mr F Thomson, BEd, MA
Miss L Thomas, BA
Mrs M Walker, PGCE
Mr T E Wansey, BA
Mrs J Willoughby, BSc, PGCE
Mrs T F Woolford, BSc, PGCE

Administrative Staff:
Headmaster's Secretary & Registrar: Mrs M B McCafferty
Assistant Registrar: Mrs H de Bie
Head of Marketing: Mrs L Smith, BA
Clayesmore Society Officer: Mrs L Steele
School Secretary: Mrs R Rutherford
Assistant School Secretary: Mrs E Maxwell
Transport Manager: Mrs H Horley
Pupil Registration/Absence: Mrs S J Lockwood
Exams Officer: Mr A Jancis, BSc
Assistant Exams Officer: Mr J Goodman, BA

House Matrons:
Mrs A West (*Wolverton*)
Mrs W Everest (*Gate*)
Mrs A Goates (*King's*)
Mrs S Hughes (*Devine*)
Mrs C McKeown (*Wolverton/The Bower*)
Mrs K Willetts (*Manor*)

Medical Officers:
Dr N Berry, BM, BS, BMedSc, DRCOG, MRCGP
Dr S Nixon, BA, MB, BChir

Nurses:
Sister in Charge: Mrs D J Amphlett, RGN
Sister: Mrs G Hakimzadeh, RGN
Sister: Mrs J Morris, RGN, RSCN, HV
Sister: Mrs M Sandiford, RGN
Sister: Mrs R Sheridan, RGN
Medical Centre Assistant: Mrs L Cox, BSc

Director of Sport & Enterprise: Mr C Humpage, BH, PGCE
Assistant Directors of Sport & Enterprise: Mr R S Miller, BSc, PGCE; Miss T S Cook, BA
CCF School Staff Instructor: Mr I Rockett
Buildings & Estates Manager: Mr J Handley
Building & Estates Secretary: Mrs V McKinley
Catering Manager: Mr A Croft
Head Groundsman: Mr I Lucas
Librarian: Mrs J A Murphy, Mrs A Elms

Clayesmore Prep School

Headmaster: Mr W G Dunlop, BA

Deputy Head: Mr S Reeves, BA, QTS
Deputy Head (Academic): Mrs E L Reach, BA, Cert SpLD
Head of LSU: Mrs A Cowley, BSc, PGCE, MEd SEN, PG Dip SpLD, AMBDA
Head of Pre-Prep & Nursery: Mrs J E Jackson, CertEd
Head of Boarding: Mr D J Browse, BA, QTS

Assistant Staff:
Mrs H Bignold, BLib, MA, MCLIP
Mr D Blackburn, BSc, PGCE
Dr S Bragg, BA, PhD
Mrs I J Browse, BA, MA
Mrs S Bunnell, BA, Cert Ed, RSA Dip TEFL, BTEC, HND, MIfL
Mrs C Caiger, BA, PGCE, PG Dip Dys
Mrs F Carless, BA, MA, PGCE, MEd
Mrs S M Chinnock, BA, PGCE
Mrs A Coombes, BHEd, PCES SpLD
Mrs J Coplan, BMus, MA, PGCE
Mr D A Harrison, BSc, PGCE
Mrs S L Hart, BA, PGCE
Mrs M Herry, BA, PGCE
Mr T Manley, BSc
Miss S May, MA
Mrs P A Middle, BA, PGCE
Mr R S Miller, BSc, PGCE
Miss E Oakley, BMedSci
Mrs M M Oakley, CertEd, RSA SpLD
Mrs S Panton, BSc, MA, PGCE
Mrs E F Pogson, BEd, Cert RSA SpLD
Mrs P Price, CertEd
Mrs E L Reach, BEd, SpLD
Mrs C Ritchie, BA, MA
Mrs I Rose, BA, PGCE
Miss N Rowse, BEd, Cert RSA SpLD
Mr J Smith, BMus, PGCE
Miss D Spokes, BSc, PGCE
Mrs E Stewart, BA, PGCE
Mrs C Townsend, MA, PGCE
Mr R Wilson, BA, QTS
Mrs E Vaughan-Johncey, BEd

Nursery Staff:
Miss R Howell, Diploma in Childcare
Mrs S Maitland, BSc, PGCE
Mrs H Martin, City & Guilds NVQ3

Administrative & Pastoral:
Head's Wife: Mrs C Dunlop, BA, PGCE
School Secretary: Mrs H Breakwell
Registrar: Mrs S Lambert
Assistant School Secretary: Mrs G Hewlett

Sister in charge: Mrs S Hillyard, RN
Deputy Sister: Mrs R Flute, RGN
Matron: Mrs H Galley

Librarian: Mrs H Bignold, BLib, MA, MCLIP

Clifton College

Guthrie Road, Clifton, Bristol BS8 3EZ

Tel:	+44 (0)117 74058417
	+44 (0)117 4058396 (Preparatory School)
Fax:	+44 (0)117 315 7101
email:	admissions@cliftoncollege.com
	prepadmissions@cliftoncollege.com
website:	www.cliftoncollege.com
Twitter:	@Clifton_College
Facebook:	/CliftonCollegeUK
LinkedIn:	/Clifton-College

Motto: '*Spiritus intus alit*'

Clifton College was founded in 1862, and incorporated by Royal Charter in 1877. It is situated in the city of Bristol, on the edge of Clifton Down and not far from open country. The School is well placed to take advantage of the many cultural and educational activities of the city, and to gain much else of value from its civic and industrial life. There are friendly links with the Universities and with other schools of various types.

Admission. Boy and girl boarders and day pupils are normally admitted in September between the ages of 13 and 14, and most are required to pass the Common Entrance examination, which can be taken at their Preparatory Schools. Credentials of good character and conduct are required. Registration Forms can be obtained from the Director of Upper School Admissions, Guthrie Road, Clifton, Bristol, BS8 3EZ.

Houses. It is usual for a pupil to be entered for a particular House, but where parents have no preference or where no vacancy exists in the House chosen, the Head Master will make the necessary arrangements.

Day Pupils and Day-Boarders. Day boys are divided into Houses: North Town, South Town and East Town. Day girls enter West Town or Hallward's. The town Houses have the same status as Boarding Houses and day pupils are encouraged to take a full part in the various activities of the School. A number of day-boarder places are available for boys and girls.

Catering is managed by our own experienced caterers and boarders take all meals in the School Dining Hall. Day pupils and day-boarders are required to have their midday meal at School, and arrangements are made for their tea and supper at the School when necessary.

Fees per term (2016–2017). Years 9–13: Boarders £11,340–£11,685; Day Boarders (4 nights) £10,315–£10,610; Day Pupils £7,670–£7,800. Sixth Form Joiners (from other schools): Boarders £12,260; Day Boarders (4 nights) £11,080; Day Pupils £8,110.

Scholarships, Bursaries and Awards. All awards on merit are limited to 25% of the fees, but they may be augmented by means-tested bursaries. The following awards are offered each year:

13+ entry: Academic, Music, Art scholarships and Sport awards. Boys and girls who are already in the School may compete for all 13+ scholarships and awards.

Sixth Form entry: Up to 10 Academic scholarships per year are available for entrants from other schools to the Sixth Form. A limited number of Sport awards, Music scholarships and an Organ scholarship are also available.

All Music awards include free tuition in two instruments (one of which may be singing).

Bursaries: these are means-tested awards and may be awarded in addition to scholarships (or in their own right). In exceptional circumstances, bursaries may be awarded up to 100% of the fees.

Academic structure. Boys and girls enter the School in the Third Form, following a general course for their first year. Most GCSEs are taken at the end of the Fifth Form.

Thereafter boys and girls enter Block I (Sixth Form) and take an advanced course consisting of 4 subjects at AS Level, then 3 at A Level. A great many combinations of subjects are possible.

Service. All pupils are given a course in outdoor pursuits and other skills in the Third Form. In the Fourth Form they are given more advanced training, which may include involvement in The Duke of Edinburgh's Award scheme, and at the end of the year they decide whether to join the Army, Navy or Air Force sections of the CCF or to take part in Community Service. There is regular use of a property owned by the school in the Brecon Beacons for all these activities.

Societies. Voluntary membership of Scientific, Historical, Literary, Dramatic, Geographical, Debating and many other Societies is encouraged.

Music and Art. The musical activities of the School are wide and varied, and are designed for musicians of all standards. They include the Chapel Choir, Choral Society and Chamber Choir, a full orchestra, 2 string orchestras, 2 wind bands, a jazz band, as well as numerous chamber music activities. Visiting concert artists regularly run masterclasses, and there are wide opportunities for performance. Teaching is available on virtually all instruments and in all styles. Instrumental and vocal competitions are held at House level and individually annually. The well-equipped and recently refurbished Music School includes practice facilities, computers, recording studio, an extensive sheet music library and a large record/compact disc library.

Drawing, Painting, Sculpture, Pottery, Textiles and various Crafts are taught under the supervision of the Director of Art in the Art School. There is an annual House Art Competition and various exhibitions throughout the year.

Theatre. Drama and Dance play an important part in the life of the School with an increasing number of pupils achieving success in LAMDA, PCERT LAM and RAD examinations. The Redgrave Theatre is used for School plays, the house Drama Festival, and for other plays that may be put on (eg by individual houses, the staff or the Modern Language Society). Each House produces a play each year. It is also used for teaching purposes, and in addition for concerts, lectures and meetings.

Information and Communication Technology. The ICT Centre at the heart of the School houses the most advanced internet facility of any school in the South West.

Physical Education. Physical Education is part of the regular School curriculum and games are played at least twice per week by all age groups.

In the Michaelmas Term, boys play Rugby and girls play Hockey. There is a multi-sport option for seniors who are not in team squads. In the Lent Term, Hockey and Soccer are the main options for the boys whilst the girls mostly play Netball. Rowing, Running, Squash, Swimming, Shooting, Tetrathlon and Fives are among the alternative options for senior boys and girls. In the Summer Term, Cricket is the main sport for the boys and Tennis for the girls, with Tennis, Athletics, Rowing, Swimming and Shooting as alternatives for seniors. The Clifton College playing fields in Abbots Leigh include three floodlit all-weather Hockey and Football pitches, six floodlit Tennis courts, a 3G artificial pitch for Soccer and Rugby, a water-based Hockey pitch with training D, and a Real Tennis court. An indoor facility for Tennis and Netball is one of the best in the region.

Careers. Careers advice is the shared responsibility of the Head Master, Housemasters, Housemistresses, Heads of Departments and the Head of Sixth Form. The School is a subscribing member of the Independent Schools Careers Organisation and of the Careers Research and Advisory Centre at Cambridge. The proximity of the city of Bristol enables the Careers Department and other members of the staff to keep in close touch with Universities, business firms and professional bodies about all matters affecting boys' and girls' careers.

Clifton College Preparatory School. *Headmaster*: J Milne, BA, MBA

The Preparatory School has separate buildings (including its own Science laboratories, Arts Centre, ICT Centres and Music School) and is kept distinct from the Upper School. The two Schools nevertheless work closely together and share some facilities, including the Chapel, Theatre, sports complex, all-weather playing surfaces and swimming pool. Most boys and girls proceed from the Preparatory School to the Upper School. Pupils are also prepared for schools other than Clifton. There is a Pre-Prep School for day pupils aged between 2 and 8. Boys and girls are accepted at all ages and scholarships are available at age 11.

For further details see entries for Clifton College Preparatory School in IAPS section.

The Cliftonian Society. *Administrator*: L Nash, The Garden Room, 3 Worcester Road, Clifton, Bristol BS8 3JL (Tel: 0117 3157 665).

Charitable status. Clifton College is a Registered Charity, number 311735. It is a charitable trust providing boarding and day education for boys and girls aged 2–18.

Council:
President: Dr J Cottrell, PhD, MA, FCA
Chairman: Mr R M Morgan, MA
Vice-Chairman: Mrs A Streatfeild-James, MA
Treasurer: Mr S Smith, BSc, DPhil, FCA

Dr C K Beale, MBA, FIMechE, FRAeS
Mr R Cartwright, CTA
Ms T Fisk, MA, FCA
Mr L Gray, MA, PGCE, ARCO, FRSCM
Mr H Harper, MA
Mrs L Harradine, BA
Mrs C Lear, BA
Mr D Maggs, MA
Mr P McCarthy, BSc, MBA, CEng, FI ET
Brig R J Morris, BA
Sir H Sants, MA
Mr N Tolchard, BSc
Mr C Trembath, BSc

Secretary and Bursar: Mrs L K J Hanson, BSc, FCA

Head Master: Dr T M Greene, MA, DPhil

Deputy Head (Pastoral): Miss A Tebay, BSc
Deputy Head (Academic): Mr G E Simmons, BSc
Chaplain: Mr P Hansell MA, MPhil, PhD
Director of Admissions: Mr J S Tait, BA, MA
Head of Sixth Form: Mr J H Greenbury, MA

Heads of Department:
Art: Mr A J Wilkie, BA
Biology: Mrs J Wood, BSc
Boys' Games: Mr J C Bobby, BA
Chemistry: Mr J Older, BA, PhD
Classics: Mr T Patrick, MA, DPhil
Design & Technology: Miss N O Hall, MA
Director of Drama: Mrs K J Pickles, BA
Economics & Business Studies: Mr N Luker, BA
English: Miss S A Clarke, MA
French: Miss C Bloor, BA
Geography: Mr M Williams, BA
German: Mr O G Lewis, MA
Girls' Games: Mrs L A Catchpole, BA
History: Mrs A Sim, BA, MA
Information Technology: Mr D Dean, MA, PhD
Mandarin: Ms E L Cordwell, BA
Mathematics: Mr G E Simmons, BSc
Modern Languages: Mr L Siddons, MA
Director of Music: Mr D Robson, BA
Physical Education: Mr A Wagstaff, MA
Physics and Science: Mr A Hasthorpe, MSc
Politics: Mr P G Lidington, BA
PSHE and Psychology: Ms S Griffin, BSc
Religious Studies and Philosophy: Mrs J M Greenbury, BA
Spanish: Miss M Harris, BA
Director of Sport: Mr P Askew, BEd

Houses and Housemasters/mistresses:

Boys Boarding:
Moberly's: Mr G J Catchpole, MEng
Watson's: Mr N Doran, BA
School House: Mr J H Hughes, MA
Wiseman's: Mr W J Huntington, MA

Girls Boarding:
Worcester: Mrs A J Ballance, BSc
Oakeley's: Mrs K A Jeffery, BSc
Hallward's: Mrs K J Pickles, BA

Boys Day:
North Town: Mr D Janke, BA
South Town: Mr J T J Hills, BA
East Town: Mr N Mills, BA

Girls Day:
West Town: Mrs M Beever, BA

Clongowes Wood College

Clane, Co Kildare, Ireland
Tel: 00 353 45 868202
Fax: 00 353 45 861042
email: reception@clongowes.net
website: www.clongowes.net

Motto: '*Aeterna non Caduca*'

Clongowes Wood College was founded in 1814 in a rebuilt Pale castle – Castle Brown in North Kildare, about 25 miles from Dublin. A boarding school for boys from 12–18, the school has developed steadily ever since and now has 500 pupils on the rolls, all of whom are boarders.

The College is situated on 150 acres of land, mostly comprising sports fields and a 9-hole golf course. It is surrounded by about 300 acres of farmland. Clongowes is listed as an historic building.

Admission. Application for admission should be made to the Headmaster. There is a registration fee of €50. An assessment day is held in early October prior to the year of entry and entry is determined by a variety of factors including family association, geographical spread including Northern Ireland and abroad, date of registration, and an understanding of the values that animate the College. Normal entry is at the age of 12; entry in later years is possible in exceptional circumstances if a place becomes available.

Curriculum. A wide choice of subjects is available throughout the school and pupils are prepared for the Irish Junior Certificate and the Irish Leaving Certificate. This latter is the qualifying examination for entry to Irish Universities and other third-level institutions. It is acceptable for entry to almost all Universities in the United Kingdom, provided the requisite grades are obtained. All pupils take a Transition Year programme following the Junior Certificate. This programme is recommended by the Department of Education in Ireland. Work experience modules, social outreach programmes, exchanges with other countries and opportunities to explore different areas of study are all included in this programme.

Religious Teaching. Clongowes is a Jesuit school in the Roman Catholic tradition and there are regular formal and informal liturgies. Boys are given a good grounding in Catholic theology and are encouraged to participate in retreats, prayer groups and pilgrimages (Taize, Lourdes). Social Outreach is part of the curriculum in Transition Year and is encouraged throughout the school. A small number of boys of other faiths are pupils in the school.

Sport. All boys play rugby in their first year in school. They then have the choice to continue in that game or to play other games. Rugby pitches, a golf course, tennis courts, soccer pitches, squash courts, a cross-country track, an athletics and cricket oval, a gymnasium and a swimming pool provide plenty of opportunity for a variety of activities. Athletics, Gaelic football and cricket are popular activities in the third term. Clongowes has a strong rugby tradition and has won the Leinster Championship twice in the last decade.

Other activities. Following the Jesuit tradition, the school has a fine reputation for debating and has won competitions in three different languages (English, Irish, French) in the last decade. A large school orchestra and school choir gives a formal concert at Christmas and another before the summer holidays. Drama productions take place at every level within the school. A large-scale summer project for charity has been undertaken each year. A residential holiday project for children with disabilities takes place in the school each summer and is animated by teachers and pupils. The College has recently created link programmes with schools in Hungary and Romania.

Pastoral Care. The school is organised horizontally into Lines. Two 'prefects', or housemasters look after each year within a Line, composed of two years, with a Line Prefect in charge of the Line itself. In addition, an Academic Year Head oversees the academic work of each of the 70 pupils within each year. A Spiritual Father or Chaplain is attached to each line. There is a strong and positive relationship with parents and a good community spirit throughout the school. The school seeks to foster competence, conscience and compassionate commitment in each of the boys in its care.

Fees per annum (2016–2017). €18,650. Parents are also asked to support the continuing development of the College through various fundraising activities.

Clongowes Union. This association of past pupils of the school can be contacted through: The Secretary, The Clongowes Union, Clongowes Wood College, Clane, Co Kildare; email: development@clongowes.net.

Trustee of the School: Fr Tom Layden, SJ, Provincial of the Society of Jesus in Ireland

Chairman of the Board of Management: Mr Peter Gray

Headmaster: **Mr Chris Lumb**, BSc, HDip, MEd

Assistant Headmaster: Mr Martin Wallace, BA, HTE

Deputy Assistant Headmaster: Mr Frank Kelly, BComm, HDip

Cokethorpe School

Witney, Oxfordshire OX29 7PU

Tel: 01993 703921
email: hmsec@cokethorpe.org
        admissions@cokethorpe.org
website: www.cokethorpe.org.uk
Twitter: @cokethorpe

Motto: Inopiam Ingenio Pensant

Cokethorpe School, founded in 1957, is a vibrant and dynamic day school for around 660 girls and boys aged 4 to 18. It is set in 150 acres of parkland, two miles from Witney and ten from Oxford. There are 133 children in the Junior School and 528 pupils in the Senior School (including 147 Sixth Formers).

Curriculum. A curriculum is offered that gives pupils the chance to pursue individual passions, with both traditional and modern subjects, those that are highly academic and others that are more practical. The National Curriculum is broadly followed up to GCSE. All pupils study core subjects of English, Maths and Science at GCSE and have a wide choice of subject options. There is also a full programme of personal, social and health education.

Sixth Formers typically choose four subjects to study at A Level and complete the EPQ. The small size of teaching groups is particularly conducive to individual attention and encouragement. The usual courses are supplemented by Economics, Government and Politics, Philosophy and Classical Civilisation.

The Junior School offers a fully balanced curriculum with the focus on developing high standards and providing intellectual challenges. Whilst the National Curriculum is followed, the freedom to offer breadth is embraced. (*See Cokethorpe Junior School entry in IAPS section.*)

Parents are kept closely informed of their child's progress and achievement, both academically and socially.

Facilities. Teaching takes place in a range of modern buildings set around the elegant Queen Anne Mansion House. The most recent addition is the Dining Hall and dedicated Sixth Form Centre that sit alongside the contemporary glass and stone library. A 200-seat auditorium is the centre for Performing Arts and a perfect setting for visiting speakers. As well as extensive sport pitches, astroturf pitches, tennis and netball courts, a nine-hole golf course, climbing tower and clay pigeon shoot, Cokethorpe also has a full-size Sports Hall with a fitness suite. The Sports facilities are rounded off with the Boat House situated close to the School on the River Thames.

Pastoral. The House system, personal tutoring (including day-to-day care, pastoral welfare and academic progress), year-group specific social and health programmes and a joint Anglican and Roman Catholic foundation creates an excellent support structure. Small classes and dedicated teachers help pupils champion their strengths and challenge their weaknesses.

Sport. The School has a strong and successful sporting tradition. Principal sports include rugby, hockey, netball, football, cricket and tennis. A wide variety of subsidiary sports are also available including kayaking, clay pigeon shooting, badminton, athletics, cross-country, golf, judo, squash, swimming and sailing, designed to suit all tastes and abilities. All pupils do PE as part of the curriculum. There are regular county, national and international successes. The most talented pupils will be considered for the School Sports Academy.

Other Activities. The extracurricular programme (known as 'AOB') plays a prominent part in a pupil's timetable and includes over 150 activities such as Dance, Engineering, Dissection Club, Fencing, Web Design, Chess, Debating, Climbing and The Duke of Edinburgh's Award scheme. There is also a strong tradition of fundraising. Other activities include language exchanges, ski trips, sports tours abroad and cultural trips to Africa and Greece.

Music, Drama and Creative Arts. The Arts are extremely important at Cokethorpe. All pupils are encouraged to learn a musical instrument and join the choir or one of the range of orchestras and ensembles. Peripatetic teachers cover a very wide range of instruments, and there are regular concerts and recitals during the year. Drama flourishes with two to three whole-School productions and the Inter-House competition annually, numerous GCSE and A Level performances, a programme of lunchtime recitals from all years and frequent trips to the theatre. Art, Textiles and Design Technology (Resistant Materials and Graphic Design) are all offered at GCSE and A Level. There is also a vibrant and varied range of art, design and craft activities as part of the extended curriculum.

Higher Education and Careers. The majority of Sixth Form leavers go on to Higher Education, enrolling in a wide variety of foundation courses, degrees or apprenticeships. A careers programme is followed throughout the Senior School, including work experience, careers conventions and psychometric profiling. Help and advice is given by experienced Careers teachers and the latest literature is available in the Careers Library.

Admission. Pupils usually enter the Junior School at age 4 or 7 (the latter based on an assessment day in January) and the Senior School either at age 11, 13 or 16. There are occasionally vacancies at other ages. Candidates at age 11 are required to sit assessments in Maths and English, at age 13 either assessments or Common Entrance and at age 16 GCSEs or equivalent. Places are offered on the basis of these results, plus interviews and school reports. There is a registration fee of £75. Registration forms and details of entrance examination procedures are available from the Registrar.

Scholarships. Scholarships are assessed separately and awarded annually. Academic, Art, Design and Technology, Music, Sport and Drama scholarships and awards are available.

Bursaries. Financial assistance is available, through the award of means-tested bursaries, to those families entering the School from ages 11 through to 18 (and occasionally into the Junior School). The value of the bursary can be up to 100% of fees.

Fees per term (2016–2017). Junior School: £4,050 Reception–Year 2, £4,150 Years 3–6; Senior School £5,950. Fees include lunch. Extras are kept to a minimum.

The Cokethorpe Society. c/o Events and Alumni Administrator: Nicole Bartlett-Dunn, Cokethorpe School (society@cokethorpe.org).

Charitable Status. Cokethorpe Educational Trust Limited is a Registered Charity, number 309650. It aims to provide a first-class education for each individual pupil.

Governing Body:
Chairman: Sir John Allison, KCB, CBE, FRAeS
Vice-Chairman: Mr S K Dexter, FCA
Mr A Bark, ACIB
Mrs C Bartlett, MA
Mr M Booty
Mrs R Gunn, MA Cantab
Mr W E Hart, CFQ, MA, ICAEW
Mr R F Jonckheer, LLB Hons
Dr W W Lau, PhD, MSc, BSc
Mrs G McAndrew, CQSW, BA
Mr P G Riman, BA, LL Dip
Mr P Tolley, BSc, FRICS
Governor Emeritus: Mr M St John Parker, MA

Headmaster: D J Ettinger, BA, FRSA, MA, PGCE

Deputy Headmaster: J C Stevens, BEng
Bursar: Mrs S A Landon, BA, ACMA
Head of Junior School: Mrs C A Cook, BEd
Director of Studies: A E Uglow, BA, PGCE
Director of Co-Curricular: G J Sheer, BA, PGCE
Registrar: Mrs S M L Copeland, BA, PGCE, AdvDipPsych
Head of Sixth Form: S D White, BA, PGCE
Third Master: C Maskery, MSc, BA, PGCE, FBAPT
Senior Administrator and Sacristan: E J Fenton, BD, AKC, PGCE
Deputy Head of Sixth Form: Mrs C S L Mason, BSc, PGCE
Deputy Head of Sixth Form: J A W Capel, MA, PGCE
School Nurse: Mrs J E Homewood

Housemasters and Housemistresses:
Feilden: S G Carter, MA, PGCE
Gascoigne: Mrs E Semenzato, DLit, PGCE
Harcourt: W G Lawson, BA, PGCE
Queen Anne: Mrs S A Orton, BA, PGCE
Swift: Mrs M H D Cooper, BA, PGCE
Vanbrugh: T J Walwyn, BA
Lower House: Mrs J L Pratley, BA, MCertSpLD

Heads of Departments:
Art: Ms E F Williams, BA, PGCE
Business Studies and Economics: R D Hughes, BA
Classics: P A R Goulding, BA
Design Technology: Mrs H V Brown, BA, PGCE
Drama: Mrs C L Hooper, Dip Act, DCL
English: Miss D C H Jackson, BEd, Dip EFL, FRSA
Geography: J A W Capel, MA, PGCE
History: Dr R W L Power, DPhil, MA, BA
Learning Support: Mrs C M McCormick, BA, PGCE, AMBDA, Dip SpLD

Mathematics: Mrs C S Scaysbrook, BSc, PGCE
Modern Foreign Languages: Miss M Bertholle, BA, PGCE
Music: J E Hughes, BA, BMus
Philosophy, Religion and Ethics: Miss A J Cottingham, BA, PGCE
Physical Education: Miss A M Woodcock, BSc
Psychology: Miss K J Rogers, BSc, PGCE
Science: Dr C Flaherty, PhD, MSc, PGCE, MRSC

66 full-time academic teaching staff, plus 20 part-time.
17 visiting teachers for Piano, String, Wind and Brass instruments, Percussion and Singing.
22 part-time sports coaches.

Colfe's School

Horn Park Lane, London SE12 8AW

Tel: 020 8852 2283
Fax: 020 8297 1216
email: head@colfes.com
website: www.colfes.com

Mottos: '*Soli Deo honor et gloria*' (Leathersellers) ~ '*Ad Astra per Aspera*' (Colfe)

Colfe's is one of the oldest schools in London. The parish priest of Lewisham taught the local children from the time of Richard Walker's Charity, founded in 1494, until the dissolution of the monasteries by Henry VIII. Revd John Glyn re-established the school in 1568 and it was granted a Charter by Queen Elizabeth in 1574. Abraham Colfe, Vicar of Lewisham, became a Governor in 1613 and the School was re-founded bearing his name in 1652. Colfe declared that the aim of the School was to provide an education for "pupils of good wit and capacity and apt to learn", reflecting the School's emphasis on sound learning and academic achievement since the earliest times. Colfe's original vision was to educate the children of "the hundred of Blackheath" and although today our pupils travel to the School from all parts of London, a strong sense of local community remains, with most of the pupils coming from the four boroughs which surround the school. One of Abraham Colfe's wisest moves was to invite the Leathersellers' Company, one of the oldest of the city Livery Companies, to be the Trustee of his will. Links between the School and the company are strong.

Admissions. There are 625 pupils in the Senior School, including 170 in the Sixth Form. The Junior School caters for a further 440 pupils. All sectors of the school are fully co-educational. The main points of entry to the Junior School are 3+ and 4+ (EYFS, KS1) and 7+ (KS2). The majority of the Junior School pupils transfer to the Senior School at 11. Approximately 65 pupils from a range of local state primary and Prep schools enter the Senior School directly at 11 and there are a limited number of places available to pupils wishing to join in the Sixth Form at Year 12.

Buildings. All the teaching accommodation is modern and purpose built. Specialist on-site facilities include the Sports and Leisure Centre, comprising sports hall, swimming pool, and fitness suite. The Leathersellers' Sports Ground, located less than a mile from the main school campus, provides extensive playing fields and related facilities. The school also holds the freehold of the Old Colfeians' ground at Horn Park. Recent developments include the Performing Arts centre and the Pre-prep and Nursery expansion. The opening of the Stewart Building in 2015, comprising a purpose-built Sixth Form suite and eight hitech classrooms, marked the end of a £10 million phase of site improvement.

Curriculum. The curriculum follows the spirit of the National Curriculum in both Junior and Senior Schools.

Pupils are entered for the separate Sciences at GCSE and follow the IGCSE Maths course. A wide range of subjects is available at A Level, 26 in total, including Drama, Government and Politics, Media Studies, Psychology and Philosophy.

Physical Education and Games. Physical Education and Games are compulsory for all pupils up to and including Year 11. Full use is made of the wide range of facilities available on-site, including a fully-equipped Sports Centre, swimming pool and all-weather surface.

The main sports for boys are rugby, football and cricket. Girls play hockey, netball, tennis and athletics. Other sports available include badminton, basketball, cross-country running, squash and swimming. Girls' cricket introduced in 2013. Girls' teams national champions in netball and county champions in cricket (2013).

Music and Drama. Music and Drama thrive alongside each other in the purpose-built Performing Arts Centre. The music department is home to a wide range of performance groups ranging from beginners to advanced ensembles in both classical and contemporary genres. There are regular performance opportunities given throughout the year, some held in the purpose-built recital hall and others in external venues. A team of 20 visiting instrumental teachers provide further opportunities for pupils to enjoy making music. Drama is a popular subject at both GCSE and A Level, with large numbers of pupils also involved outside the classroom. We recently staged a full-scale production of *One Flew Over The Cuckoo's Nest* at the Greenwich Theatre, London.

Careers. The Careers and Higher Education Department is staffed on a full-time basis. Regular events include University Information Evenings and Careers Fairs.

Fees per term (2016–2017). Senior School £5,370 (excluding lunch); Junior School (KS2) £4,395 (excluding lunch); KS1 £4,155 (including lunch); EYFS £3,978 (including lunch).

Scholarships and Bursaries. Academic Scholarships are awarded mainly on the basis of outstanding performance in the Entrance Examinations. The exams are designed to identify and reward academic potential, as well as achievement.

Means-tested bursaries are also available at 11+. Bursaries may, in exceptional circumstances, cover the total cost of tuition fees. Application forms are available from the Director of Admissions.

A limited number of Music, Drama and Sports awards are also available at 11+. In the case of Music scholars, free instrumental tuition may accompany the award. Details of Music and Sports awards can be obtained from the Director of Admissions.

A number of scholarships, bursaries and other awards are also available to candidates entering the school at 16+. Details can again be obtained from the Director of Admissions.

Junior School. The purpose-built Junior School was opened by HRH Prince Michael of Kent in 1988. Specialist rooms of the Senior School are also used. While the curricular emphasis is on high standards in basic Mathematics and English, a wide range of other subjects is taught, including Science and French. There is also a range of activities similar to those enjoyed by the Senior School and all pupils are expected to participate. All pupils proceed to the Senior School if they achieve the qualifying standard. It is expected that virtually all pupils from the Junior School will proceed to the Senior school at 11.

(*For further details see entry in IAPS section.*)

The co-educational EYFS/KS1 department for pupils aged 3 to 7 is housed in modern accommodation (substantially expanded in 2013) adjacent to the KS2 department (7–11).

The Colfeian Society. Enquiries to the Alumni Relations Officer, Colfe's School, London SE12 8AW. Tel: 020 8463 8119.

Charitable status. Colfe's School is a Registered Charity, number 1109650. It exists to provide education for boys and girls.

Visitor: HRH Prince Michael of Kent

The current Governors provide between them a broad range of relevant experience and qualifications. A majority are Members or appointees of the Leathersellers' Company to which Abraham Colfe entrusted the School in his will when he died in 1657.

The activities of the Leathersellers are many and varied but the School and its fortunes continue to feature prominently on the Company's agenda. The Master of the Company is, *ex officio*, a member of the Board of Governors.

Board of Governors:
Mr Ian Russell, MBE (*Master of the Leathersellers' Company*)
Mr Matthew Pellereau, BSc, FRICS (*Chairman*)
Mr Andrew B Strong, BSc
Mr Sean Williams, MA Oxon, MPA Harvard
Miss Serena Cheng, MA, LLB
Mr Mark Williams
Prof Angela Brueggemann, DPhil
Dr Robert Abayasekara, BSc, PhD
Mr John Guyatt, MA Oxon
Mrs Belinda Canham, BA
Mr David Sheppard, BA

Headmaster: **Mr R Russell**, MA Cantab

Deputy Head: Mrs D Graham, GRSM, LRAM
Bursar and Clerk to the Governors: Mrs J Lerbech, MA Cantab, MSci, CA
Director of Studies: Mr A Pearson, BSc Hons
Assistant Head, Pastoral: Mrs J German, BA Hons
Director of Sixth Form: Mr S Drury, BA Hons, MA
Senior Master: Mr J King, BSc Hons, MA
Head, Junior School: Miss C Macleod, MSc

Heads of Departments:
Art: Mrs J Burton, BA Hons
Classics: Miss C Le Hur, MA Cantab, MPhil
Design & Technology: Mrs C Cox, BA Hons
Drama: Miss L Atkinson, BA Oxon, MA
Economics & Business Studies: Mr R Otley, BA Hons
English: Miss M Schramm, BA, MA
Geography: Mrs H Nissinen, BSc Hons, MA
Government & Politics: Mr S Drury, BA Hons, MA
History: Mr J Patterson, BA Hons
Learning Support: Miss A Coode, BA Hons, DTLLS Literacy
Maths: Mr A Guy, MEng Hons
Media Studies, General Studies: Mr C Foxall, BA Hons
Modern Foreign Languages: Mrs E Biggs, BSc Hons, MA
French: Miss E Harris, BMus with French
German: Mr M Koutsakis, MA
Spanish: Mr A Seddon, BA Hons, MIL
Music: Mrs E Bond, BMus Hons, MA
Outdoor Education: Major C Cherry, BSc Hons
Physical Education: Mrs N Rayes, BEd Hons, EMBA
Religion & Philosophy: Miss E Henderson, BA Hons
Science: Mr J Worley, BSc Hons, DIS
Biology: Dr G Zimmermann, BSc, PhD
Chemistry: Mr D Fisher, MA
Physics: Mr J Fishwick, BSc Hons
Psychology: Dr J Lea, PhD, BSc Hons

Director of Admissions: Mrs S Walker, BA Hons

Colston's

Bell Hill, Stapleton, Bristol BS16 1BJ

Tel: 0117 965 5207
Fax: 0117 958 5652
email: admissions@colstons.org
website: www.colstons.org
Twitter: @colstonsschool
Facebook: @Colstons-School

Motto: '*Go, and do thou likewise.*'

Colston's is a thriving co-educational day school for pupils aged 3 to 18 located on a spacious 30-acre site in Stapleton village in north Bristol. Our traditional pastoral structures and house system promote a sense of community and belonging amongst pupils.

A Colston's education extends far beyond the classroom with opportunities for sport, music, service and co-curricular activities all playing their part in creating the unique experience on offer at the school.

Organisation. There are approximately 720 pupils at Colston's. The Lower School, which caters for the 3–11 age range, includes a nursery and is adjacent to the main site which accommodates the Upper School, which pupils attend from 11–18.

For details of the Lower School, see entry in IAPS section.

Admission. Pupils are admitted at 11+ and 13+ through the school's own examinations. Pupils also join the school for the Sixth Form. Academic scholarships are available as well as scholarships for pupils excelling in art, drama, music and sport. Bursaries are also available which are means tested.

Work. Colston's offers a wide ranging and engaging curriculum which avoids premature specialisation and is in line with the provisions of the National Curriculum. Art, Business Studies, Computing, Drama, Design Technology, French, Geography, History, Music, Physical Education, Religious Studies, Spanish are optional subjects. There is a wide choice of A Level subjects and some BTECs available in the Sixth Form.

Chapel. Colston's is a Church of England Foundation, and use is made of neighbouring Stapleton Parish Church for morning assemblies and other services. Pupils of other denominations are also warmly welcomed.

Sport and Games. Colston's has a shining sporting legacy, perhaps unsurprisingly given the impressive on-site facilities that are unique in Bristol. Sport plays a huge part in the life of pupils and while excellence is pursued for those with talent, everyone is encouraged, regardless of ability, to get involved. Opportunities to represent the school are abundant and an impressive number of teams are fielded each week. The main sports for boys are rugby, hockey and cricket and hockey, netball and rounders for girls.

Music and Drama. The drama department is one of the most successful in the country. It is based in the Harry Crook Theatre which offers an exceptionally well-equipped 200-seat auditorium. Music is vibrant and inclusive, with one-third of pupils taking individual instrumental lessons. Performances are given regularly in the dedicated concert hall.

Careers. Colston's is proud of its careers provision which is available to all pupils. The school is a member of the Independent Schools Careers Organisation. Through a highly successful programme of careers guidance, pupils are helped to make the right decisions to ensure success. The careers library and interactive resources help pupils think about career options and the Head of Careers and Employability meets with each pupil regularly throughout their time at Colston's.

Service and Community. Pupils are given many opportunities to contribute to the wider community. Colston's Combined Cadet Force, one of the most successful in the South West, allows cadets to regularly take part in expeditions and activities. Pupils also undertake The Duke of Edinburgh's Award which seeks to develop lifelong skills. Pupils relish the opportunity to get involved in a diverse range of volunteering projects across the city.

Fees per term (2016–2017). £4,395 (Lunch £200).

Modernisation. An extensive building programme has been carried out to provide new teaching classrooms, a 210-seat concert hall and purpose-built CCF headquarters. Additionally the library, laboratories and Sixth Form facilities have been completely refurbished to create a 21st century learning environment.

Situation. Colston's is located in Stapleton village which is within the city of Bristol, and enjoys the advantage of having all its playing fields and facilities on site. The 30-acre campus provides a wonderful environment for pupils to explore, learn and excel.

The school is large enough to sustain a wide range of activities at a high level and yet small enough for each boy or girl to contribute actively and be known as an individual. Every effort is made to provide for and develop pupils' abilities in academic, cultural and other co-curricular activities. The school aims to encourage a strong sense of community and service, and to fully develop and extend the talents of every boy and girl.

Charitable status. Colston's School is a Registered Charity, number 1079552. Its aims and objectives are the provision of education.

Governors:
Mr T Kenny (*Chair*)

Mrs B Allpress	Mr C Lucas
Mr A Baker	Mr D Mace
Mr N Bhadresa	Mr J McGeehan
Mrs A Burrell	Mr T Ross
Mrs C Duckworth	Dr A Seddon
Mr I Gunn	Mr N Wilson
Mr M Hughes	Mrs J Worthington

Headmaster: Mr J McCullough, MA Oxon

Deputy Headmaster: Dr P Hill, BSc, PhD

Ms C Allen, BA (*English*)
Miss T Anderson, BSc (*PE/Games*)
Mr C Banning, BSc (*Head of Roundway House, PE*)
Mrs K Bates, BA Ed (*Art*)
Mr E Beavington, MA (*Assistant Head Co-Curricular, History*)
Mr B Berry, BA (*Head of Psychology*)
Miss A Boys, BA (*English*)
Ms L Brown, BSc (*Head of Learning Support*)
Mr R Butterfield, BSc (*Mathematics*)
Mrs S Campbell, BA (*Humanities*)
Mr M Castle, BA (*Music*)
Miss L Coates, (*Director of Faculty – Humanities, Head of RS and Philosophy*)
Mrs K Connolly, BSc (*Biology*)
Mr S Cope (*Business*)
Dr K Dawson, BA, PhD (*Assistant Head Curriculum, Examinations Officer, Geography*)
Miss O De Zarate, BA (*Spanish*)
Mr N Drew, BA (*Head of History*)
Mr L Evans, BSc (*PE/Games*)
Mr M Eyles, BSc (*Head of Geography*)
Miss C Flay, BA (*Head of Aldington House, RS, Geography*)
Mr R Gash, BSc (*Head of Computing*)
Mr J Gwilliam, BA (*MFL*)

Mr J Harper, MA (*Head of Physics*)
Mrs A Hart, BSc (*Biology*)
Mrs E Hayett, BEd (*Mathematics*)
Dr P Hill, BSc, PhD (*Chemistry*)
Mrs R Johnson, BA (*Director of Faculty – Maths/ Computing, Head of Mathematics*)
Mr P Jones, BSc (*Mathematics*)
Mr D Kaye, BA (*Head of Dolphin House, History*)
Mr J Layland, BA (*Head of Business Studies*)
Mr L Masters, BSc (*Head of King's House, RS and PSHE*)
Miss S Matthews, MA (*Oxon*) (*Geography*)
Miss S Mills, BA (*Design and Technology*)
Miss E McCoy, BSc (*Careers and Employability*)
Mr J McCullough, MA Oxon (*Mathematics*)
Dr N Morse, BSc, PhD (*Director of Faculty – Science, Head of Biology*)
Mrs C Parry (*Design Technology*)
Mrs J Poppy, BA (*English*)
Ms K Porter, BA (*Drama*)
Mrs R Power (*Learning Support*)
Mr S Proudman, BA (*Director of Faculty – Languages, Head of English*)
Mr T Richardson, BA (*Head of Music, Contingent Commander CCF*)
Miss A Roberts, BEng (*Mathematics*)
Mr C Russell, BSc (*Mathematics*)
Mr R Simes, BSc (*Computing and Data Manager*)
Mr R Smith, BA (*Director of Faculty – Expressive Arts, Head of Drama*)
Mrs K Snell, BA (*Director of Faculty – Creative Arts, Head of Design and Technology*)
Mr P Temple, BSc (*Head of Chemistry*)
Mr P Thornley, BEd (*Director of Physical Education*)
Dr J Tovey, BA, PhD (*Assistant Head (Academic), English*)
Mr R Troy, BSc (*Biology*)
Miss S Victor, BEd (*MFL*)
Mr N Vittle, BA (*Head of Government and Politics, History, Management of D of E*)
Mr D Wall, BEd (*Head of PE/Games*)
Mrs S Ward, BA (*Head of Girls PE/Games*)
Mr B Warlow, BSc (*Physics*)
Miss A Willis, BA (*Assistant Head (Pastoral), Drama*)
Mrs V Wilson, BA (*English*)
Mr N Yaxley, BEd (*Head of Art, Community and Service Coordinator*)

Director of Finance: Mrs N Prosser, BSc, ACA
Head of Marketing and Admissions: Ms B Gorman
Headmaster's PA: Miss M Bailey
Lower School Head's Secretary: Mrs C Pullin
School Administrator: Mrs D Thomas
Facilities Manager: Ms J Prince
Matron: Mrs D Head
Commander CCF: Major T Richardson
SSI CCF: Sgt R Cain

Cranleigh School

Horseshoe Lane, Cranleigh, Surrey GU6 8QQ

Tel:	01483 273666
Fax:	01483 267398
email:	admissions@cranleigh.org
website:	www.cranleigh.org
Twitter:	@cranleighschool
Facebook:	/Cranleigh

Motto: '*Ex cultu robur*'

Cranleigh is a leading co-educational weekly boarding and day school set in a stunning rural location in more than 280 acres on the edge of the Surrey Hills. Cranleigh's beautiful campus is exceptionally well equipped, with outstanding classrooms, studio, performance and sports facilities, including three theatres, twelve rehearsal and performance spaces, competition pitches, stables, sports centres, golf course, outdoor education centre and swimming pool.

There are strong links between the School and nearby Cranleigh Preparatory School and pupils also join from a wide variety of other prep schools across London and the home counties, creating a lively, House-based community of young people who are drawn together by their inherent love of life and getting involved in everything Cranleigh has to offer.

Cranleigh School's principal aim is to provide an environment in which pupils can flourish, enabling them to capitalise on the diverse range of opportunities offered by the School and to achieve to the best of their ability within a framework of shared values and standards. The School's 280-acre site, situated eight miles from Guildford on the Surrey-West Sussex border, lies on the outskirts of Cranleigh Village and within 45 minutes of London. The School is fully co-educational, with some 200 girls and 400 boys between the ages of 13 and 18, including a Sixth Form of about 280. It is a predominantly boarding community, attracting boarders from both the local area and further afield; it also, however, welcomes day pupils, who are fully integrated into the Cranleigh community, playing their part in the activities of their respective Houses and benefiting from the advantages thereby offered.

Each House (separate for boys and girls) has a resident Housemaster or Housemistress, a resident Deputy, a Warden, two Matrons and a team of tutors for both the Lower School and Sixth Form. There is also a strong and active partnership between parents and the School.

Cranleighans are encouraged to relish challenge, to feel they are known as individuals, and to become talented and wise adults with an inherent ability to adapt to a fast-changing world. Aligned with this, the School boasts an impressive record in academic achievement. Almost all pupils achieve three A2 Levels (with a record number of A*s in 2015), and in recent years more than 99% have gone on to university, with 80% to their first-choice university (including Oxbridge and Russell Group universities).

Academic Patterns. Our aim is to act within the spirit of the National Curriculum, but to offer more, taking full advantage of our independence and the extra time available to a boarding school. We therefore retain a very broad curriculum in the Fourth Form, and have an options system in the Lower and Upper Fifth Forms which enables a pupil to take between nine and eleven GCSE subjects before moving on to A Levels in the Sixth Form. We offer the opportunity to do Double or Triple Award Science, as well as giving good linguists the chance to take two foreign languages (with Latin if they wish). In the Sixth Form, pupils can select from a wide choice of subjects.

Work on languages, with an emphasis on commercial and colloquial fluency, is encouraged for non-specialist linguists, and much use is made of the Language Laboratory. Exchanges take place with pupils in schools in France, Spain and Germany. We have comprehensive facilities for Science, with an emphasis on experimental work. All members of the Lower Sixth Form study a course in Critical Thinking, or attend a series of lectures on a variety of topics, to help broaden their education.

Information Technology is incorporated into the teaching of all other subjects, with each academic department having its own IT policy, coordinated by the Director of IT. Most teaching rooms have networked PCs, and every House and academic department has PCs available for use, all linked to the School's network and the Internet.

Creative and Performing Arts. Cranleigh has maintained an enviable reputation for Music over many years, and the Merriman Music School offers pupils some of the finest facilities available. We send Choral Scholars to Oxford, Cambridge and major Music Departments and Colleges elsewhere; boys and girls of all ages successfully take part in national competitions and well over a third of the School learns a musical instrument. Keyboard players have access to a new Mander two-manual tracker organ, purposefully designed for versatility and teaching, and to two Steinway concert grand pianos. Cranleigh's exciting Cranleigh Music initiative is now well established, bringing together the Music Departments of Cranleigh School and Cranleigh Preparatory School under a single performing, management and administrative structure. Whilst facilities remain on separate sites (both sides of Horseshoe Lane), the ethos is that of a single Music Faculty encompassing the full 7–18 age range, whose cohesive structure will help to nurture and progress talent from a very young age, so ensuring that all pupils are able to perform in an environment commensurate with their individual ability.

Cranleigh also boasts a strong Drama tradition. Regular large-scale productions take place in the Devonport Hall, to which is linked a studio theatre, the Vivian Cox Theatre, while a flourishing Technical Theatre department encourages the development of 'backstage' skills. The School's proximity to London allows for regular attendance at professional theatre, music and opera productions.

Art & Design are brought together under one Faculty, housing a talented mix of practising artists, teachers and designers. The spectacular Rhodes Art & Design School is spread over several buildings, with a mix of dedicated airy studios and manufacturing and prototyping areas. A comprehensive range of disciplines across drawing, painting, sculpture, printmaking, ceramics, graphics, product and industrial design, prototyping and CAD/CAM are delivered. The studios are open every day and appropriate use is made of the Faculty library, ICT and digital video and photo facilities. External visits are encouraged (both nationally and internationally). All students exhibit throughout the year.

Sport. Cranleigh provides an extremely diverse range of sporting activities for all pupils.

The School possesses an impressive array of sports facilities, including four full-size Astroturf pitches (one of which is floodlit), a 9-hole golf course, an Equestrian Centre with floodlit sand-school, 4 squash courts, 6 fives courts, 24 tennis courts, 8 netball courts and an indoor swimming pool. The large Sports Hall complex (the Trevor Abbott Sports Centre) provides a popular venue for netball, tennis, badminton and basketball, and also includes a separate dance studio and a fully equipped fitness suite. There is also a separate Indoor Cricket Bubble for year-round development. High standards are set for the numerous competitive teams, with an extensive programme of fixtures at all levels and for all ages. 'Sport for All' is a key philosophy at the School, supported by an experienced and talented team of coaches, many of whom have competed themselves at county, national and Olympic level. The School has witnessed some outstanding team and individual successes in recent years, including National representation in hockey, rugby, riding and cricket; taking National titles in horse riding (show jumping and dressage), kayaking, cricket, rugby 7s, swimming and hockey and also seeing several recent Old Cranleighans continue to compete in the international arena and as Olympic hopefuls.

In the Michaelmas term the majority sports are hockey for girls and rugby for boys; in the Lent term the majority sports are netball for girls and hockey for boys. During the winter terms, pupils can also compete in lacrosse, crosscountry, golf, water polo, soccer, fives, rugby-sevens, basketball, riding and squash, plus badminton and canoeing for the Sixth Form. All pupils in the Fourth and Lower Fifth Forms take part in the majority sport, while an element of choice is gradually introduced for the older pupils. All pupils in the School take part in sport, even in the Sixth Form.

In the Summer term, the main team sport for boys is cricket, whilst some boys compete in tennis, swimming, athletics and golf. For girls the main sport is tennis, with competitive swimming, athletics, rounders and cricket popular additional offerings.

Service Activities. There are opportunities for pupils to take part in a range of 'service' activities. Boys and girls may join the CCF or get involved with community service, ecology or first-aid training. Cranleighans help local elderly people in community settings and also have links with local schools for children with learning difficulties and with a home for adults with similar problems. Many Houses and the Fundraising Group raise money for various charities. Wider initiatives also include the School's 'Beyond Cranleigh' initiative – a key partnership between Cranleigh School and Beyond Ourselves, a London-based charity that works to improve the lives of disadvantaged young people in both London and in Zambia. This partnership has led to Cranleigh's sponsorship of a primary school in Kawama, to which Sixth Form pupils regularly make visits to help with building and teaching initiatives. This year Cranleigh has also pledged to support social enterprise projects in Kawama to provide jobs and skills training for locals posteducation. Such initiatives are designed to focus pupils' thoughts on life beyond the School.

Outdoor Education. Cranleigh operates a large Duke of Edinburgh's Award scheme group, with many pupils completing the Gold Award before leaving school. By way of introduction, all Fifth Form pupils undergo an Outdoor Education programme in order to improve their self-awareness and confidence. There are many other opportunities for Outdoor Education through the CCF, there is a well-attended climbing club (which has its own bouldering wall), and the School enters the annual International Devizes-to-Westminster Canoe Race (which the School won in 2015).

Religion. The striking, neo-Gothic Chapel was built as a central point of the School, and Cranleigh maintains its concern to present the Christian way of life. It welcomes pupils of all faiths and none.

Developments. The latest in a line of major building projects, the Emms Centre houses the Modern Languages, Science and Mathematics Departments, while the new Faculty of Art & Design offers fabulous work spaces for these disciplines (see Creative and Performing Arts section). A timber-pole Workshop, designed using sustainable principles, has won numerous Awards. A premier 1st XV rugby pitch, newly resurfaced hockey astroturf and additional cricket pitches have recently been added to the School's impressive sporting facilities. A proposed programme of development will see a new girls boarding house and a new teaching block open in 2017.

Planning for our Pupils' Future. Cranleigh takes the future of its pupils very seriously. It maintains good contacts with the professions, industry and commerce, through links developed as part of the careers advice structure. All pupils are regularly assessed during their time at the School, and this process includes a period of Work Experience at the end of the Upper Fifth year. Closely linked with the Old Cranleighan Society and the School, the Cranleigh Network oversees skills training, CV advice, post-graduate work experience and mentoring.

Admission and Registration. Entry at 13+ is normally via Common Entrance or as an Academic Award holder, although separate provision is made for candidates not being prepared specifically for Common Entrance.

The Senior School admissions process is changing for applicants from 2018 onwards. For 2018 applicants Holistic Interview and Assessment Days will take place during October and November 2016. For 2019 these will take place in January 2017. Our intention is not to pre-test but we will be including a short written English assessment in our Holistic Review as well as a Maths Challenge. However, the Prep School Headmaster's reference and the one-to-one interview will continue to play the largest part in our decision to make an offer of a place. Prospective parents are welcome to meet the Headmaster and have a tour of the School at any time.

Registration forms are available to download or from the Admissions Office. Telephone 01483 276377 or email admissions@cranleigh.org

For Sixth Form Entry: A limited number of places is available to boys and girls who are likely to achieve good results in their GCSE examinations. For further details telephone the Admissions Office on 01483 276377 or email admissions@cranleigh.org

Awards. The Master of Scholars has a specific responsibility for all Scholars. They are members of their Houses and attend normal lessons, but also have an additional programme throughout their time at the School that covers a wide variety of academic, cultural, social and commercial areas beyond the syllabus and which encourages independent thinking and research.

At age 13, Cranleigh School offers a variety of awards and scholarships. Music Exhibitioners receive free instrumental (including singing) lessons. In certain circumstances, additional consideration may be given to sons or daughters of public servants, members of the armed forces and the clergy of the Church of England.

Fees per term (2016–2017). Boarders £11,790, Day Pupils £9,630.

It is the policy of the School to keep extras down to an absolute minimum, and limited to such charges as individual music tuition. Textbooks are supplied until the Sixth Form, at which point pupils are encouraged to buy their own so that they may take them on to university. A scheme is available for the payment of fees in advance.

Preparatory School. The School has its own Preparatory School and boys and girls are normally admitted at seven or eight, but also at other ages. For further information, apply to the Headmaster of the Preparatory School (*see entry in IAPS section*).

Charitable status. Cranleigh School is a Registered Charity, number 1070856. It exists to provide education for children aged 13–18 and the Preparatory School for those aged 7–13.

Governing Body:
Chairman: J A V Townsend, MA
Deputy Chairman: A J Lajtha, MA, FCIB

R A de Blaby, BSc, MRICS
Dr R M Chesser, MA, MB BChir, MRCP
Mrs M M S Fisher, MA
Mrs N A Huggett, MA
J A M Knight, BA Hons
Mrs A J Lye, BA
Mrs L A Muirhead, BA
The Revd Canon N P Nicholson, DL
R A Robinson, MBA, FCA
The Revd Dr T J Seller, BSc, PhD
Mrs E Stanton, BSc, ACA
N D L Sweet, Dip LA, MA, MLI
O A R Weiss, MA
Prof T D Wilkinson, BEng, PhD, MIET
Mrs M J Williamson
S J Watkinson, BSc, ACA
R L Johnson, BSc, MRAES
M Foster, MA Oxon

Bursar and Clerk to the Governors: Mr P T Roberts, MBE, DChA

Headmaster: Mr Martin Reader, MA Oxon, MPhil, MBA

Deputy Head: Mr S D Bird, BA, MEd, QTS
Deputy Head (*Pastoral*): Dr A Saxel, BSc, PhD
Deputy Head (*Academic*): Mr D R Boggitt, BEng, PGCE
Assistant Head (*co-curricular*): Mr C H D Boddington, BA, PGCSE, MEd
Assistant Head (*Director of IT*): Mr D J Futcher, BSc, MBCS, QTS
Assistant Head (*Learning, Teaching and Innovation*): Dr J L Taylor, BA, BPhil, PhD, PGCSE
Head of Admissions: Mr S J Batchelor
Head of External Relations: Mrs J R Cooksley, BA Hons, MA

Members of Common Room:
† *Housemaster/mistress*

Mr I M Allison, MA, PGCE
Mrs M C Allison, BEd
Ma S C Ashton
Miss M Baffou, LLCE
Mr A K Barker, BSc, PGCE
Mr J Bartlett, BSc, CIMA
Mr S J Batchelor
Mrs S E Baumann, BA, PGCE
Mr E J P Bradnock
Mrs P Bigg, PGCE
Mr S D Bird, BA, MEd, QTS
Mr C H D Boddington, BA, PGCE
Mr B W Browne, BSc, PGCE
Mrs G L Bukowska, BSc, MSc
Mrs O Burt, BA, MA
Mr E J Carson, BSc
Mr S T Cooke, BA (†*Cubitt*)
Mr J N M Deacon, BA, PGCSE
Mrs E G M Dellière, BA
Mr N Drake, BA
Mr D M Eaglestone, BSc, PGDip
Mrs E L Ellin, BA, PGCE
Mrs H B Fearn, BA, PGCE
Mr T R Fearn, BSc, PGCE
Mr A P Forsdike, MA, PGCE (†*North*)
Mr D J Futcher, BSc, MBCS, QTS
Mrs C Gangemi, BSc, PGCE
Miss R S Gibson, BTh
Ms C S Gray SpLD
Miss S L Greenwood, BA (*Ed*)
Miss Z E S Griffiths, BA
Mr A J Guppy, BA
Dr D A W Hogg, BA, MSt, DPhil
Miss E M Holland, BA, PGCE
Mr A R Houston, BSc
Miss S J Houghton, BSc
Mr M R Jenkins, BA
Mr R C E K Kefford, BSc, PGCE
Dr S L Kemp, BSc, PhD, PGCE
Mr R G Lane, MEng
Miss S J Leach, BA, PGCE
Mr T G Leeke, BSc
Mr P Leggitt, MA
Mrs B L Lewis, MA, MSc
Revd T M P Lewis, MA, MTh
Mr A A G Logan, BA, PGCE (†*Loveday*)
Mr R W Mansel Lewis, BA, PGCE
Mrs C J Lock, BSc, PGCE (†*South*)
Mrs S E McLaughlin, BEd
Miss H Mallory, BSc
Mrs L Mercer, BA, PGCE
Miss H K Merry, BSc
Mr N G A Miller
Mr A Moore, BA
Mr J B Nairne, BFA, PGCE
Mr G J N Neill, BA, MA, PGCE

Miss C E Nicholls, MA, PGCE
Mrs C L Oldfield
Mrs K K Opie, BSc, MSc, PGCE
Mr R J Organ
Miss D E Parkes, BA, PGCE
Miss S R Parry, BA, PGCE
Mr M C Pashley, BMus
Mrs J A Pimm, BEd
Ms N Plowman, BA, QTS
Mr G V Pritchard, BSc, PGCE
Mr T D S Pym, BCom, GDipEd
Mrs O D Ravilious, BA, PGCE
Mrs A E Reader, BA, PGCE
Mr D C Reed, BA, MSc
Mr A D Robinson, BS, PGCE
Mr I P Rossiter, BSc
Mr A S J Rothwell
Mr G C Royall, BSc
Dr A P Saxel, BSc, PhD
Mr R J Saxel, BA, DipRam, LRAM
Mr J H Schofield-Newton, BA, MA
Mr P N Scriven, BA, MA, LRAM, MM (*Organist in Residence*)
Miss H E O Shairp, BA, PGCE
Mr W Sherrington-Scales, BA, PGCE
Mrs A M Simpson, BA, PGCE
Miss E R Sinclair, BA, PGCE
Miss R J Singleton, BEng
Mr C P G Stearn, BA, MPhil
Mrs A C Smuts, BSc, PGCE
Mrs S D Thomson, BSc
Mr J J Taylor, BA
Dr A L J Thomas, BMus, MPhil, PhD
Dr B R Tyrrell, MChem, DPhil
Mr D N Vaiani, MA
Miss E L Wallis
Dr M Ward, BA, PhD, LGSM, MMus, Dip RCM, ARCM
Mr K W Weaver, BA Music, PGDip
Mr M J Weighton, BA, PGCE
Miss S L Webb, BA
Mr S D Welch
Miss J D Wiles, BSc, PGCE
Mrs R A Williams, BMus, PGDip, PGCE
Mr J M Witcombe, BSc, PGCE (†*East*)
Mrs A Worsley, BSc, PGCE (†*West*)
Mr M A Worsley, LLB
Mrs U C Yardley, BA, PGCE
Ms W L Yates, Cert Ed
Dr S A H Young, BSc, MSc, PhD, PGCE

Medical Officer: Dr G Tyrrell, MB BS, DObst RCOG

Preparatory School
(*see entry in IAPS section*)

Headmaster: Mr M T Wilson, BSc Keele

Deputy Head (*Pastoral*): Mrs S D Gravill, BA, PGCE

Members of Common Room:
Mrs S E Awwad, MEd, BA, QTS
Mr E T Batchelor, BSc
Mrs C A Beddison, BMus, PGCE
Mr D Britt, BA, PGCE
Mrs J Brown, HND
Miss Z Burrell, BSc
Mr R B P Carne, MA, PGCE
Mrs P Charlesworth, BA
Mr J Dale-Adcock, BA, PGCE
Miss V Diacono, BA, OCR, CLANSA
Mr B M Dixon, BA, CertEd
Mrs C Elliott, BA, PGCE, OCR Dip SpLD

Mr N French, BSc
Mr D Futcher, BSc, PGCE
Mrs S D Gravill, BA, PGCE
Mr N Green, MA, PGCE
Mr M J Halstead, BSc, PGCE
M S F Howard, BA, CertEd
Mrs K Laidler, ISTD
Mrs S Johnston, BSc, PGCE
Mrs A Jolly, BSc, PGCE
Mr D S Manning, EDE
Mrs J J Marriott, BA, PGCE
Miss L R Martin, BA, PGCE
Mrs N M C McCormack, BA, OCR, Dip SpLD, PGCE [NMcC]
Mrs S E McLaughlin, BEd
Mrs P R Meadows, BEd
B Monks, BA
Miss J Moore, BSc
Mrs A Morgan, BA
Mrs H L H Pakenham-Walsh, BA
R Perry
Mr M Poeti, BSc
C Preece, Dip RLP, BSc
Mrs E Reed, BSc, PGCE
Miss C Sanders, BSc, PGCE
Mrs K Schutte, BA, MA Ed
Mr G Simpson, BSc, PGCE
Mrs L J Smith, BA
Mr T M Stroud, BSc
Mr M Till, BSc
Mrs E Unwin, MA, BA, PGCE
Mr P G Waller, BEd
Mrs J Witcombe, BSc, IPGCE
Mrs C J Wilson, BEd, RSA Dip SpLD, Cert TESOL
Mrs L Yule, BA

Registrar: Mrs F M J Bundock
School Secretary: Mrs J M Cooke

Culford School

Bury St Edmunds, Suffolk IP28 6TX
Tel: 01284 728615
Fax: 01284 728631
email: admissions@culford.co.uk
website: www.culford.co.uk
Twitter: @CulfordSchool
Facebook: /culfordschoolocs

Motto: '*Viriliter Agite Estote Fortes*'

Culford School was founded in 1881 in Bury St Edmunds and moved to its present site on the Culford estate in 1935. The School is one of twelve owned by the Methodist Independent Schools Trust and is administered by a Board of Governors, to whom local control is devolved.

About Culford School. Culford is a co-educational boarding and day school for 670 pupils aged between 2¾ and 18 across three schools: the Pre Prep & Nursery, Prep and Senior Schools, all of which are situated within 480 acres of beautiful Suffolk parkland.

Where is Culford School? Culford is conveniently located four miles north of Bury St Edmunds and is within easy reach of Cambridge and Norwich (to which the school runs a daily bus shuttle service), Ipswich and Stansted Airport, and Heathrow and Gatwick airports are within two hours of Culford.

Teaching & Learning. We believe education should be challenging, enriching and fun and are committed to helping our pupils achieve excellence in all areas of school life.

Hard work in the classroom is complemented by full sporting and extracurricular programmes.

Curriculum. We aim to give a broad and balanced education that enables every pupil to fulfil their academic potential. Core subjects at GCSE are English Language and Literature, Mathematics, the three sciences and a foreign language. Pupils can choose additional subjects from a wide range of options and receive guidance from the Deputy Head, their teachers and personal tutor who, along with the Housemaster or Housemistress, has responsibility for their academic and social progress. To support this Culford pupils also experience Personal, Social, Health and Citizenship Education (PSHCE) courses.

Culford Sixth Formers usually study three or four subjects at A Level. The majority of students go on to university, including Oxbridge and the prestigious Russell Group universities. Sixth Formers may also study for an Extended Project Qualification (EPQ) which enables students to study beyond the confines of A Level specifications; it can be an essay, a film, a composition or even something created in Design and Technology.

Facilities. Culford is centred on the magnificent Culford Hall, an 18th century mansion formerly the seat of Marquis Cornwallis and Earl Cadogan. The Hall houses Culford's Music School and purpose-built Studio Theatre. In September 2015 the School's facilities were further enhanced with a brand new £2.2m landmark library at the academic heart of the school.

Teaching Facilities. Teachers are specialists in their fields and are united by a passion to help the children in their care achieve their goals, whatever they may be. Classrooms are modern and well equipped, and in the case of specialist subjects, such as languages and sciences, have the latest technologies installed. The School also has excellent Art, Design and Technology facilities in the Pringle Centre which boasts its own exhibition gallery.

Sports Facilities. Culford's fantastic £2m Sports and Tennis Centre is a state-of-the-art facility which comprises a four-court, championship-standard Indoor Tennis Centre, a 25m indoor pool, gym, strength and conditioning suite, squash court and a large sports hall with a climbing wall and indoor cricket nets. Outside there are further tennis courts, two of which are seasonally covered, two artificial turf pitches (one in partnership with Bury Hockey Club) and numerous rugby and hockey pitches.

Pupils can also pursue athletics, horse riding, canoeing, sailing, scuba diving and even fishing in our own lake. Culford launched a new Golf Academy programme in 2015 to sit alongside its already well-established high-profile Tennis and Swimming programmes.

Boarding. Culford accepts boarders aged 7 to 18 and for a whole host of reasons, including an 'Excellent' ISI rating, boarding is extremely popular with over half of Senior pupils boarding. Boarders enjoy an amazing range of weekend activities and have full access to Culford's impressive Sports and Tennis Centre.

Culford's boarding Houses offer children a comfortable, secure and fun place to live during term time. Boarders in their first year share study-bedrooms and move into single rooms in the Upper Sixth. Culford offers flexible arrangements for other boarders where possible: part and occasional boarding is available providing space is free. We do not have an enforced exeat at the weekends; children may stay at school throughout the term, going home at the weekend or to stay with friends only when they or their parents wish them to.

All pupils have access to our fully-equipped Medical Centre, supervised by a resident nurse, and this includes provision for residential care when necessary.

Culford Pre-Prep & Nursery School. Our purpose-designed Nursery accepts children from 2¾ and the Early Years Foundation perfectly prepares them for School life.

Culford's Nursery is located within the Pre-Prep and has its own well-equipped play area and secure garden.

Culford Pre-Prep occupies a combination of new and entirely refurbished buildings and provides teaching for 80 children from Reception through to age seven in a delightful setting within the grounds.

Both Pre-Prep and Nursery schools take part in Forest School activities, a way of learning outdoors that helps children to develop personal, social and technical skills in a woodland setting.

Music & Drama. Music plays an important part in the life of the School. There are numerous choirs, orchestras and bands and regular concerts are held to give pupils the chance to perform in public. Individual music tuition is offered in voice, piano, organ and all orchestral instruments. Drama is also very popular and there are regular House plays and concerts as well as major productions: these include musicals and plays for different sections of the School.

Activities. There is a huge array of clubs and societies on offer – from academic and creative to sporting and community. Pupils are encouraged to take part in Community Service Activities and many participate in the Duke of Edinburgh's Award Scheme or choose to join the Combined Cadet Force (CCF).

Staff regularly take pupils out on visits and expeditions too, and every summer a group of Sixth Formers and teachers spend 3 weeks in Malawi helping with various development projects; a trip that is universally viewed as a life-changing experience. Other recent trips have included tours to New York, skiing in France and scuba diving in Tobago as well as sports tours worldwide.

Entry. The majority of pupils join in September at ages 2¾–7 (Pre-Prep), 7+, 8+ and 11+ (Preparatory School); and at 13+ and 16+ (Senior School). Entrance examinations are held in January and February of the year of entry or pupils may enter having passed Common Entrance in June. Entry to the Sixth Form is on the basis of GCSE performance or its equivalent for overseas candidates.

Entry to Culford Pre-Preparatory School is by informal assessment just prior to enrolment.

Applications are welcome from individuals throughout the year, subject to places being available.

Visiting Culford School. If you would like to visit Culford, the Headmaster will be delighted to welcome you. Please contact the Admissions Office to arrange an appointment and a tour on 01284 385308 or to request a copy of the School prospectus. We also hold regular Open Mornings each term, please visit www.culford.co.uk to find out more. Please follow this link to view the School Videos: www.culford.co.uk/video.

Scholarships and Exhibitions. Culford holds its Scholarship examinations between November (Sixth Form) and January/February for entry in the following September. Scholarships and Exhibitions are awarded according to merit in the following categories:

11+: Academic, Music, Swimming, Tennis, Cricket and Golf

13+: Headmaster's Foundation Scholarship, Academic, Art, Design & Technology, Drama, Music, Hockey, Rugby, Swimming, Tennis and Sport

16+: Headmaster's Foundation Scholarship, Professor Watson Scholarship, Academic, Art, Drama, Music, Design & Technology, Hockey, Rugby, Swimming, Tennis, Golf and Sport

11+, 13+ and 16+: Jubilee Scholarships for all-rounders who board are worth up to 25% of boarding fees.

16+: The William Miller Scholarship for a pupil studying sciences is worth up to 25% of tuition fees. The Arkwright Scholarship for a pupil studying Design & Technology allows an amount over two years to be shared between the pupil and the School.

Swimming and Tennis Scholarships and Exhibitions may be available at any age from 10+.

The Headmaster's Foundation Scholarship is worth up to 50% of tuition fees; the Professor Watson Scholarship (restricted to pupils coming from state schools) is worth 25% of day or boarding fees; all other scholarships are worth up to 25% of tuition fees, and Exhibitions are worth up to 10%.

Bursaries are available to those in genuine financial need.

A generous Forces Allowance is available to parents who are serving members of the Armed Forces and are in receipt of the MOD CEA.

For further details please apply to The Registrar, Tel: 01284 385308, Fax: 01284 385513 or email: admissions@culford.co.uk.

Fees per term (2016–2017). Day £6,150 Boarding £9,495–£9,995.

Charitable status. Culford School is a Registered Charity, number 310486. It exists to provide education for boys and girls.

Visitor: The President of the Methodist Conference

Patron: The Rt Hon Viscount Chelsea

Governors:
Chairman: Air Vice Marshall S Abbott, CBE, MPhil, BA
Mrs P Abbott, BEd, ECP
Prof S Challacombe, BDE, PhD, FRC Path, FDSRC Ed, FMedSci, DSc [hc], FKC
A Atkinson, LLB, MBA, MA, JP
A P Crane, BSc, CEng, FIET
M Donougher
N Gillis, MA
J M Hammond, MA
M King
T C Matthews, BSc, FRICS
P Moore, BA, MBA, MIC
S Pott, FRICS, FRAgS, FinstCPD, FRAU
The Revd J M Pursehouse
Mrs V Sanderson

Headmaster: J F Johnson-Munday, MA, MBA

Deputy Heads:
Dr J Guntrip, BSc, PhD

Assistant Head: D V Watkin, BEd

Chaplain: The Revd Simon Crompton-Battersby, BTh

Members of the Common Room:
* *Head of Department*
† *Housemaster/mistress*

Art:
*Mrs B A Hunt, BA
L Hoggar, BA
Miss K Noorlander

Business Studies and Economics:
*D Nichols, BSc
†S Arbuthnot, MSc

Classics:
*Mrs S Deering, MA

Design Technology:
*I C Devlin, BEd
Miss J Cooke, BA

Drama:
*Miss M Jackson, MA
Miss S Borley, MA

EAL:
*Mrs H F Baker, BSc

Mrs A Burge BA
Mrs C Byrne MA
Mrs B Recknell BA MA

English:
*Miss E Williams, BA
Mrs C Byrne, MA
Mrs A Glassbrook, BA
J Holiday-Scott, BA
Mrs R Radlett, BA
N Murray, BA

Geography:
*M H Barber, MA
†Miss H Mayhew, BSc
Mrs A Burge, BA
Miss L Bryant

History:
*M Rackowe, BA
G E Draper, BA

†Miss J Kaye, MSc

Information & Communication Technology:
*J W Tyler, MA, BSc

Mathematics:
*N J Tully, BSc
Dr Brian O'Riordan, PhD
Mrs S J Flack
†G Reynolds, BEng
J Veitch, BA, BSc

Modern Languages:
*A R Deane, BA
Miss K McCarthy, MA
Ms K Waghorn, BA
Miss P Kirby-Smith, BA

Music:
*P R Burge, MusB, ALCM
D Bolton, Dip Mus
J D Recknell, MA, FRCO
Mrs J Welsh, BMus, LRSM

Physical Education:
*Mrs K Kemp, BEd
Mrs C Almond, FISTC
Mr L Dodd (*Director of Golf*)
Miss L Kammerijer
M Bolton, BSc
Mrs E Long, BSc
Mr A Northcote (*Director of Cricket*)
†Miss C Olley
Mrs C Reynolds, BEd

Finance Director: Mrs E Boardley, BA, FCCA
Medical Officer: Dr N Harpur, MB BS, MRCGP, DRCOG
Headmaster's PA: Mrs A Buttery
Registrar: Mrs K Tompkinson

D Hall (*Director of Tennis*)
J D Yates
Miss H Grant, BA

Religious Studies:
*Revd Dr A G Palmer, MTh, PhD
Revd S C Crompton-Battersby, BTh
Miss S Haughey, MA, MPhil

Science:

Chemistry:
*D Rees, BSc
Mrs S L Antonietti, BSc

Physics:
*†J Fox, BSc
J Christopher, BSc
Dr D Edwards, BSc, PhD

Biology:
*A P Fisk, MSc, BSc
Dr J Guntrip, BSc, PhD

Psychology:
*Dr A Butler, PhD, BSc

Learning Development:
*†Mrs B Murray, TTHD, Dip SpLD
Mrs J Cope, BA, Cert SpLD
Mr N Murray, BA, PGCE

Library:
Mrs L Martin, MA, MCLIP

Preparatory School
(*see entry in IAPS section*)

Headmaster: M Schofield, BEd

Deputy Head (Pastoral): Miss J Hatton, BEd
Deputy Head (Academic): Mrs C Bentley, BEd

Miss S Ahrens, MA
Mrs K Allum, BEd
Mr N Anns, BEd
Mrs D Barker, Maîtrise, FLE
Mrs T Black
Mrs C Blake
*M Bolton, BSc
Mrs A Bunting, BA
Mr B Burrows, BEd
J Calvert, BA
Mrs K Clarke, BEd
Mrs S Combes
Mrs K Dearman
Mrs S Deering, MA
Mrs R Drake, BA
S Clay, BMus
Mrs S Guntrip, BSc

Mrs N Gumbleton, MA
Mrs A Haffermann, MA
Miss P Kirby Smith
Mrs E Herd, BA
†J Herd, BSc
Mrs A MacKenzie
Mrs B Murray, TTHD, Dip SpLD
Miss S O'Neill, BA
Mr W Pook, BSc
Mrs R Ratcliffe, BEd
Mrs B Recknell, MA
Mrs C Rosten, BSc
Mrs E Veitch, BEd
Mr D Venables, BSc
Mrs K Waghorn
Mrs C Wakefield
*Mrs H Whiter, BA

Pre-Preparatory School:

Headmistress: Mrs S Preston, BA

Nursery Manager: Miss K Trow, BA

Mrs M Anderson

Mrs N Brown, NNEB

Mrs S E Combes, BA
Mrs E Grey, DPP
Miss K Harrison, BEd
Mrs H Hansgate, BSc
Mrs R Lesley, BA
Mrs A McKenzie, TFL Dip French

Mrs A Morrell, BEd
Mrs D Rampling
Mrs R Ratcliffe, BEd
Miss N Rodwell, BTEC
Miss C Rossiter, BEd
Mrs J Suckling
Miss S Widger, BSc

Dauntsey's School

West Lavington, Devizes, Wiltshire SN10 4HE

Tel: 01380 814500
Fax: 01380 814501
email: info@dauntseys.org
website: www.dauntseys.org
Twitter: @DauntseysSchool
LinkedIn: /dauntsey's-school

Dauntsey's was founded back in 1542, here in Wiltshire, under the will of Alderman William Dauntesey, Master of the Worshipful Company of Mercers. Today it has grown into a thriving, friendly, co-educational boarding and day school of some 800 11–18 year olds with continued close links to the Mercers' Company. They are actively involved in the School and several members of the Company sit as Governors. Warmth, laughter and lasting friendships built on trust and mutual respect are the hallmarks of daily life at Dauntsey's. Perhaps this is due in some part to the spirit of our Mercer founder.

Number. 827 Pupils aged between 11–18 years: 420 boys, 407 girls, approximately 40% board.

Situation. The School is set in an estate of over 100 acres in the Vale of Pewsey in Wiltshire. The Manor House, a mansion with its own woodland and playing fields, is the co-educational Junior boarding house for pupils in the First to Third Forms.

The Community. Our house system is the cornerstone of our community, giving pupils a secure source of support and guidance on every aspect of life, as well as the chance to get together and have fun. Every pupil joins either a boarding or day house, which are co-educational in the Lower School (ages 11 to 13) and single sex in the Upper School (ages 14 to 18). Each house is run by a housemaster or housemistress and a team of tutors who take a close and active interest in pupils' academic and social development, as well as encouraging them to make the most of the activities on offer. Above all, they really do make sure that the house is a home from home.

Curriculum. Throughout the School, the curriculum is broad and balanced, offering the opportunity to study an extensive range of subjects. The academic curriculum is well balanced, very wide ranging and offers a good amount of choice. The timetable offers a great deal of flexibility, with well-structured weekly lessons and extensive options that cater for the different interests and aptitudes of all our pupils. Dauntsey's especially promotes independent learning, enabling pupils to fulfil their potential and develop the key skills they will need in later life. Gifted and talented pupils have access to work and experiences at the higher cognitive levels, to stimulate interest and develop advanced thinking skills, while pupils with mild learning difficulties get expert help and support from a dedicated team of specialist teachers.

Games. The major sports are Rugby, Football, Hockey, Cricket and Netball. Other games options include Tennis, Squash, Athletics, Swimming, Soccer, Water Polo, Fencing, Badminton and Basketball. In the Sixth Form further options include Triathlon training, Canoeing, Basketball, Rifle-shooting, Yoga, Cross-Country, Ballet, Dance, Conditioning and Riding. Sixth Formers can also choose to do volunteer work within the community. Special attention is given to Physical Education.

Extra-Curricular Activities. Our adventure education and extra-curricular programmes set us apart, encouraging pupils to try new experiences. From drama, dance, music, sport and a huge range of clubs and societies, to our lecture series, adventure programmes and volunteering initiatives – there are opportunities to suit everyone. We aim to push our pupils out of their comfort zone, inside and outside the classroom, and we bring that spirit of adventure to everything we do.

Fees per term (2016–2017). Boarders £9,900; Day Pupils £5,980; International Pupils £11,430. There are no compulsory extras.

Admission. Boys and girls are admitted at 11 on the results of a competitive examination; at 13 on the results of Scholarship and Common Entrance examinations; to the Sixth Form dependent upon academic record and reports, with a minimum of six GCSE passes, three at grade A and three at grade B.

Scholarships and Bursaries. Academic Scholarships are awarded on merit following examinations held in January (First Form), February (Third Form), and November (Sixth Form) for entry the following September.

There is a wide range of Scholarships and Awards available for entry to the First, Third and Sixth Form:

First Form (Year 7): Academic, Music, Sport.

Third Form (Year 9): Academic, Science, Sport, Performing Arts (Music, Drama, Dance), Head Masters Award (Art, Design Technology), Jolie Brise All-Rounder (boarding only).

Sixth Form (Year 12): Academic, Sport, Performing Arts (Music, Drama, Dance), Boarding.

Bursaries: The school funds three new, 100% bursary places each year to pupils whose parents would otherwise be unable to fund any portion of the school fees. In addition, there is a fund to provide short-term bursarial support for current pupils whose parents or guardians who meet financial difficulties.

For further details please contact the Registrar.

Charitable status. Dauntsey's School is a Registered Charity, number 1115638. It is dedicated to the education of boys and girls.

Governors:
Mr R G Handover, CBE (*Chairman*)
Mr R M Bernard, CBE
Mr N B Elliott, QC
Mr N J S Fisk, BA, ACA
Mrs P L P Floyer-Acland, BSc
Mrs S E S Gamble, BA
Mr D Goodhew, BA
Professor L M Harwood, MA, BSc, MSc, PhD, CSci, CChem, FRSC
The Venerable A P Jeans, BTh MA
Air Chief Marshal Sir Richard Johns, GCB, KCVO
Mr M J H Liversidge, BA, FSA, FRSA
Mr P J Lough, MA
Mr C H de N Lucas, FRICS, FAAV
Mr A S Macpherson, BA, ACA
Mrs V P Nield, BSc, MBA
Dr R E L Quarrel, BA, MA, DPhil
Brigadier P P Rawlins, MBE
Mr F W Scarborough
Mr N W Smith
Mrs L F Walsh Waring, BA (*Vice Chairman*)

Head Master: Mark Lascelles, BA

Deputy Head: Mrs J F E Upton, BSc

Second Master: Mr M C B McFarland, BA

Deputy Head (Academic): Mr J M Tyler, BA

Head of Lower School: Miss E S Conidaris, BSc

Heads of Department:
Art: Mrs V A Rose, BA Bath Spa
Careers: Mr J F O'Hanlon, BSc Wales
Classics: Mrs A Webb, MA Cambridge
Design Technology: Mr A Pickford, BA Wales
Drama and Dance: Mr R M Jackson, BA Warwick
Economics and Business Studies: Mr A Poole, BA West of
England
English: Mr A Brown, BA Warwick
EFL: Mrs A Whitchurch, BA Swansea, TESOL
Geography: Mr A J Palmer, BSc London, FCIEA
History: Mr B H Sandell, BA Exeter
Information Technology: Mr G R Parry, BSc London
Language Development: Mr C W W Wilson, BA Exeter,
Dip SpLD
Mathematics: Mr P A Mobbs, BSc Bath, MSc LSE
French: Ms P J Harrison, BA Birmingham
German: Mrs V A H Wilks, BA Exeter
Spanish: Mrs A L Jackson, BA Nottingham and Mrs A L
Evans, BA Portsmouth
Music: Mr G G Harris, BMus Manchester
Physical Education: Mr J Devney, BSc Cardiff and Met
Complementary Curriculum & PSE: Mrs D C Hills, BA
Bristol
Religious Studies: Mr J Holland, BA Stirling
Science: Mr A J Crossley, BSc Newcastle
Biology: Mr V R Muir, BSc Canterbury NZ, BSc Open,
MIBiol
Chemistry: Mr A J Crossley, BSc Newcastle
Physics: Dr R V Lewis, BSc, PhD Wales, FRAS
Sailing: Mr T R Marris, DTP, YME
A Level PE: Mr J Devney, BSc Cardiff and Met

Houses and Housemasters/Housemistresses:

Upper School:
Evans: Mr & Mrs N Yates
Farmer: Mr W P J Whyte
Fitzmaurice: Mr J A Spencer
Hemens: Mrs V A H Wilks
Jeanne: Mrs A L Jackson
King-Reynolds: Mrs E Crozier
Lambert: Mrs K S Clark
Mercers: Mr A J Sheffield

Lower School:
Manor: Mr A M P Hurst
Forbes: Mrs E C Gardiner
Rendell: Mr M Olsen
Scott: Mrs G S Ward

Chaplain: Revd D R Johnson, MA, BSc
Bursar: Air Cdr S Lilley, RAF Retd
Registrar: Mrs J H Sagers, BA
Head Master's Secretary: Mrs D Caiger

Dean Close School

**Shelburne Road, Cheltenham, Gloucestershire
GL51 6HE**

Tel: 01242 258000
Fax: 01242 258004
email: registrar@deanclose.org.uk
website: www.deanclose.org.uk
Twitter: @DeanCloseSchool
Facebook: /DeanCloseSchool

Motto: *'Verbum Dei Lucerna.'*

Sitting on a beautifully landscaped 50-acre site in the Regency town of Cheltenham, Dean Close School is an attractive mixture of old, traditional buildings and modern, hi-tech structures. The School was opened in 1886 in memory of Francis Close, Rector of Cheltenham 1826–55 and later Dean of Carlisle, and has been co-educational since 1967. Dean Close is a Christian school which believes that education is as much about building character and relationships as it is about gaining knowledge. An independent Preparatory School was established in 1949.

Admission and Withdrawal. Admission to the Senior School at 13 is through Common Entrance or direct entrance tests in English, Maths and Verbal Reasoning. Sixth Form: examination and interview, 6 Bs minimum at GCSE. We advise pupils to have at least an A in the subjects they wish to study at A Level. Prospectus and application forms are available from the Registrar who is also happy to arrange a visit at a time to suit. There is a non-returnable registration fee of £100 and a returnable deposit of £750 payable one year before entry. One term's notice is required before a pupil is withdrawn from the School.

Fees per term (2016–2017). Boarders £11,260, Day Boarders £8,592, Day Pupils £7,772.

Term of Entry. We prefer to accept pupils in September but will make exceptions at any time of year, even in the middle of a term, if a good reason exists.

Scholarships and Bursaries. The School offers scholarships, exhibitions and bursaries at age 13 and for entry into the Sixth Form. The six areas of talent which are recognised are academic, music, sport, drama, art and design technology. The size of award is set according to performance. Dean Close Prep School also offers scholarships at ages 7 and 11.

Academic: The 13+ ISEB Common Scholarship Examination, for which specimen papers are available from the ISEB, is held annually at the school in February. Candidates for academic scholarships from state schools should contact the Admissions Tutor. The Sixth Form Scholarship examination takes place in November.

Music (including Choral and Organ) and Drama Scholarships are based on audition, interviews and exam (Drama). Individual specialist tuition is free to all scholars and exhibitioners.

Carducci Strings Scholarship: linked to the Carducci Quartet.

Art and Design Technology Scholarships may be awarded, based on portfolio, drawing / technical test and interview.

Sports Scholarships are awarded to reflect all-round sporting ability and commitment. Assessment by conditioning tests, skills tests in two or more sports and interviews.

Means-tested bursaries for sons and daughters of clergy and missionaries. Automatic discounts, known as Thierry Awards, are offered to parents serving in HM Armed Forces on a scale according to rank. Foundation Bursaries for families in the locality unable otherwise to benefit from a Dean Close education.

Number and Organisation. There are 481 in the Senior School (13–18). The Sixth Form comprises approximately 40% of the School. There are nine Houses: three for boarding boys (one Sixth Form only), two for day boys, three for boarding girls (one Sixth Form only) and two for day girls. Housemasters take immediate responsibility for pupils' work, careers, applications for universities and further education. A tutorial system ensures that all pupils have a member of the teaching staff who takes a particular interest in them, both academically and pastorally. There is a Careers department. The Prep School (2–13) has approximately 427 pupils of whom 170 are girls.

Work. In the lower part of the School pupils are set rather than streamed. Included in the Lower School timetable is a

Creative Studies course introducing pupils to a wide range of artistic and creative subjects, embracing DT, Art, Drama, Music and Physical Education. The language centre, high-tech seminar room, music school, art school, sports hall, modern laboratories, computer, electronics and creative workshops combine excellent teaching and leisure facilities which are available both in timetabled and extra-curricular time. Much of the accommodation has been built in the last twenty years and is modern and purpose-built. A professional 550-seat theatre houses an ambitious programme of productions. There is also an open-air theatre. As well as several orchestras, wind band, many ensembles and the Chapel Choir, the School has a Choral Society which performs a major work at least once a year. The Strings Department is headed up by the internationally renowned Carducci Quartet. Tuition in any number of musical instruments is available as an extra. Free tuition is provided for music award holders and high-grade musicians. The theatre also affords first-class concert facilities.

Religious Education. The teaching and Chapel services are in accordance with the Church of England and the School's strong Evangelical tradition is maintained. The Chaplain prepares members of the School for confirmation each year. Most services are in the School Chapel. There is a thriving Christian Union and each House hosts voluntary weekly bible studies groups.

Games. The School has a 25m indoor swimming pool and a £3m sports hall, both used all the year round. There are two astroturf pitches and a large number of tennis courts. Hockey, rugby, cricket, basketball, netball, rounders, badminton, athletics, tennis, squash and cross-country are the main sports.

Health. The School has three qualified Sisters with Assistants and visiting Doctors. There is a surgery and a medical centre.

Outside Activities. There is a huge range of clubs, activities and societies, from climbing to creative writing, salsa dancing to Warhammer, theatre tech to horse riding. A very active Combined Cadet Force with RN, RAF and Army sections trains every Wednesday afternoon and some pursue Bronze and Gold Duke of Edinburgh's Award. There is an active outward bound club and a large Community Action group gets involved with projects on a local, national and international level, particularly with a link school in Uganda.

President of Council of Members: The Lord Ribeiro, CBE

Board of Trustees:
Mrs K Carden, MPhil, BA (*Chairman*)
J M Carter
M J Cartwright, BA, FCA (*Treasurer*)
The Revd R M Coombs, BSc, MA
Mrs H Daltry, BA
C S S Drew, MA
I Duffin, FCA, BCom
R S Harman, MA
Mrs S L Hirst, BEd
The Revd D J S Munro, MA, MBA
Mrs K Riding, LLB
M P Smith, MA

The Trustees are elected by the Members of Council and oversee the overall governance of the School. They carry a substantial burden of financial and legal responsibility on an entirely voluntary basis and the School is greatly indebted to them.

***Interim Warden*: R Jones**, LVO, BEd

Headmaster: B J Salisbury, MEd, PGCE

Senior Master (Communications): D R Evans, MA
Deputy Head Pastoral: Mrs J A Davis, MA, PGCE

Deputy Head Academic: M D Tottman, MA, MBA, QTS
Bursar: A P Bowcher, MBA, FCIB, DipFS

Director of Studies, Sixth Form: M Wilkes, BA
Director of Studies, Years 10 & 11: B P Price, BSc, PGCE
Director of Studies, Year 9: A J George, MA, PGCE
Assistant Director of Studies: Miss R J Donaldson, BSc, PGCE
Chaplain: Revd J Ash, BA
Admissions Tutor: Mrs M-A McClaran, MA

Housemasters & Housemistresses:
Brook Court: J Slade, MA (*2004*)
Dale: B P Price, BSc, PGCE (*2016*)
Fawley: Mrs J Abbott, BA, PGCE (*2011*)
Field: P S Montgomery, MA, PGCE (*2005*)
Gate: M D Tottman, MA, MBA, QTS & R E Tottman, MA, PGCE, SpLD (*2008*)
Hatherley: Mrs K E Milne, BA (*2011*)
Mead: Mrs C M Feltham, MA, PGCE (*2016*)
Shelburne: Mrs J D Kent, GDLM (*2001*)
Tower: B S Poxon (*2015*)

Heads of Department:
Art & Design: Mrs C J Evans, BA, PGCE
Biology: Mr M Wilkes, BA
Chemistry: A R Needs, BSc, PGCE, MRSC
Classics: J M Allen, MA, PGCE
Design Technology: D D Evans, BSc
Drama: L S Allington, BA
Economics & Business: J Hardaker, BA, PGCE
EAL: Miss R J Vest
e-Learning & Computer Science: D F Fitzgerald
English: Mrs K Ledlie, MA, PGCE
Equestrianism: Mrs F Cradock, BA
Geography: A Cradock, BSc, PGCE
History & Politics: Mr J Sheldon, MA, BA, PGCE
Learning Support: Mrs R E Tottman, MA
Mathematics: P J J Garner, MA, PGCE
Modern Languages: C J Hooper, BA, PGCE
Music: Mrs H L Porter, BA, LRAM, PGCE (*Director of Music*)
Choral Music: S A H Bell, MMus, BMus, FRCO
Physical Education: G N Baber-Williams, BA, PGCE (*Director of Sport*)
Academic PE: Miss R J Donaldson, BSc, PGCE
Physics: P Harvey, BA, PGCE
PSHE: Miss D-M Richards, BSc, PGCE
Psychology: Miss T L Williams, BSc, PGCE, GTP
Religious Studies: Mr D Mochan, MA, BA
Speech & Drama: Miss R M O Vines, BA, FVCM, LALAM, ALAM
Careers & UCAS: D M Fullerton, MA
Examinations Officer: Dr P J P Anstis
Librarian & Study Skills: Z Suckle, MA, PGCE

Medical Officers (both Schools):
Dr J Wilson & Partners, MBBS, DRCOG, Dip Pall Med, FRCGP
Overton Park Surgery

SSI, CCF: WO1 B G Lloyd

Preparatory School:
(*see entry in IAPS section*)
Headmaster: P Moss, BA
Deputy Head: J Harris, BA, PGCE
Deputy Head Academic: M Walters, BA QTS
Senior Master: E Harris, BEd
Senior Mistress: Mrs E Bailey, BSc, PGCE

Pre-Preparatory School:
(*see entry in IAPS section*)
Headmistress: Dr C A Shelley, PhD
Deputy Head: J E Cowling, BA, PGCE

Early Years Foundation Stage Coordinator: Mrs R Cowling

Deputy Bursar (Finance): L Connel
Deputy Bursar (Estates): A T W Maynard, MMs, FCIM
Registrar (Senior): K Serjeant, BA
Director of Marketing: Mrs T C Colbert-Smith, BA, MCIM
Admissions (Prep): Mrs R Chaplin, BSc
Headmaster's PA (Senior): Mrs J Priest
Headmaster's PA (Prep): Mrs E Materacki

Denstone College
A Woodard School

Uttoxeter, Staffs ST14 5HN
Tel: 01889 590484
Fax: 01889 591295
email: admissions@denstonecollege.net
website: www.denstonecollege.org
Twitter: @DenstoneCollege
Facebook: /DenstoneCollege

Motto: *'Lignum Crucis Arbor Scientiae.'*

Achievement, Confidence and Happiness are central to the College philosophy, through which girls and boys are always encouraged to aim high and so reach their full potential. Founded in 1868, the College is rich in tradition and history, but combines this with a forward thinking approach to education.

Denstone College offers a rounded education, where proper emphasis is placed on academic achievement and high standards are the top priority. A wide range of other opportunities, however, ensures that every individual finds and develops his or her own special talents. Denstonians emerge with a degree of self-esteem and confidence, possible only as a result of so much opportunity and challenge. They have the qualifications, skills and personality to make their mark in today's competitive world.

Location. Denstone College is situated on the Staffordshire/Derbyshire border, 6 miles north of Uttoxeter in 100 acres of grounds. The site is located in magnificent countryside, but is well served by road, rail and air.

Organisation. The College is divided into the following units: Junior School (ages 11–14, Years 7, 8 and 9), Middle School (ages 14–16, Years 10 and 11), and Senior School (ages 17–18, Sixth Form which typically numbers around 200 pupils).

All girls and boys are in one of the six houses, each numbering about 100 members, with a total roll of 600. Weekly boarding is a popular option. Just over a quarter of our pupils board, and one third are girls, who have separate boarding accommodation. The College does not believe in vertical boarding.

Denstone College Preparatory School at Smallwood Manor, also a Woodard School, is 9 miles away. Age range 3–11.

Buildings. The main building contains classrooms, day and boarding areas, studies, Dining Hall, Chapel, Theatre and resident staff accommodation. A great deal of school life is thus centred in this main block, which also includes IT facilities, library, and a language laboratory.

The Sports Hall, laboratories, other classrooms, indoor heated swimming pool, Art Centre, Design and Technology Centre, and other buildings, such as the Medical Centre and School Shop, are elsewhere in the grounds.

Recent and Future Developments. Over £7 million has been spent on improving our buildings and on building new facilities in recent years.

The most recent development is the College Library, which was refurbished and extended and opened in September 2013. A purpose-built 9-classroom block, Tookeys, which houses English and RS classrooms, was completed in June 2012. Other developments include a second Astroturf and £750,000 invested in the kitchens and dining area, and the updating of boarding facilities, including the development of a Sixth Form girls' boarding house. Another classroom block with Maths and Modern Language classrooms is currently under construction and should be completed by the Summer of 2017.

A £2 million Music School and classroom block was completed in May 2010. As well as practice rooms and two music classrooms with interlinking recording studio, there are also two History classrooms, a Psychology classroom and three IT classrooms in the building.

Future plans include building more top-quality teaching facilities, extending and developing girls' boarding spaces, enhancing teaching space for Art and DT including gallery areas, and creating still further sports provision by increasing the number of astroturf pitches.

Curriculum. In the Junior School (ages 11 to 14, Years 7, 8 and 9) all follow roughly the same spread of subjects: English, Drama, French, Spanish, Mathematics, Physics, Chemistry, Biology, History, Geography, Art, Music, DT, Religious Studies, Information Technology, and PE.

Girls and boys enter the Middle School at the beginning of Year 10. Subjects are studied in option blocks. Mathematics, English Language and Literature, a Modern Language, RS and Science are core subjects, and three others are chosen from those listed above, along with Business and Economics GCSE.

Girls and boys then specialise in AS and A2 Levels, chosen in an option system appropriate to the current discussions regarding Sixth Form Curriculum nationally. Four AS Levels will normally be taken in the Lower Sixth. Subjects offered are Mathematics, Further Maths, Physics, Chemistry, Biology, English Language, English Literature, French, Spanish, History, Geography, Economics, Psychology, Politics, Art, Theatre Studies, PE, and DT. There will also be a minority who will study, in varying numbers from year to year, Music and Religious Studies. An extremely flexible timetable is possible and we aim to offer as many combinations of subjects as possible.

The vast majority of pupils take A Levels, with the aim of going on to University. Each year, some girls and boys are prepared for Oxford or Cambridge entrance. A majority of the Upper Sixth are typically accepted into one of the Russell Group Universities and almost all to their first-choice or second-choice university.

The School is well-equipped with computer rooms, laboratories, and a 200-seat Theatre. Each department remains up-to-date with subject development and members of staff regularly attend courses and conferences.

Class sizes are relatively small. Up to Year 11, 20 is an average class size, and in the Sixth Form sets vary from 6 to 14.

In addition to having a Head of School and Head of House each pupil has a Tutor with whom he or she meets regularly to discuss work and progress, and both half termly and end of term grades and reports are issued.

Pupils in both Junior and Middle School have a number of staff supervised Homework sessions incorporated into the school day. Boarding members of Fifth Form, Lower Sixth and Upper Sixth have shared or single studies.

Out of Class Activities. The aim is to provide as wide a variety of opportunities for pupils of differing aptitudes and inclinations as possible.

Games: The College has 2 full-size all-weather hockey pitches, one of which is floodlit and provides 9 tennis courts in the Summer Term. A nine-hole handicap-standard golf course has been laid out to the west of the College. There is an indoor heated swimming pool, and the main Sports Hall accommodates indoor sports as well as a fitness room. The Drill Hall provides further games space and a CV gymnasium, with cycle machines and rowing machines.

The main sports in the Michaelmas Term are rugby for the boys and hockey for the girls, with opportunities for other games. In the Lent Term these change to hockey and football for the boys and netball for the girls, along with swimming, cross country, aerobics, and others. In the summer there is a degree of choice between cricket, athletics, swimming, golf, and tennis and rounders for girls.

In the course of the year there is opportunity for boys and girls to take part in a wide variety of sports, in which they can represent both their House and the School.

CCF and Pioneers: There is also a Combined Cadet Force with Army and Royal Air Force sections and The Duke of Edinburgh's Award scheme.

The Arts: There are set times each week when priority is given to non-sporting clubs and activities, giving pupils opportunities in a wide range of experiences. Music plays a central role in College life. There is a School Orchestra, Swing Band, and Jazz Ensemble. There is a Girls chamber choir, and the Chapel choir sings at the main service each Friday. In addition, there are also other specialist ensembles and small instrumental groups. Music is included in the curriculum of Years 7–9 and in addition tuition in most instruments from both resident and visiting staff is available. A number of musical events takes place annually, including the Junior School Music concert, and the Summer Serenade, the showcase concert, held in May.

Traditionally there is a major play or musical at the end of the Michaelmas term. The College has a proud record of 104 Shakespearean productions. The 2015 School Play was *Les Misérables*. Each year there is also a Junior School Play (7 Golden Dragons in 2016), the Junior Drama Festival and performances from GCSE Drama and A Level Theatre Studies students.

The DT Department is fully equipped with Art and Pottery centres. These facilities are housed in the Centenary Building and allow pupils to fulfil abilities in design, woodwork, metalwork, painting, drawing, ceramics, and printing.

Entrance. Pupils wishing to join Year 7 (age 11+) or Year 9 (age 13+) sit examinations at the College in January and February. Pupils wishing to join Year 9 (age 13+) from Independent Preparatory Schools offering Common Entrance, sit the Common Entrance examination in June. There is also entry in the Sixth Form, an increasingly popular option for girls and boys after their GCSEs.

Occasionally pupils enter at other ages and times. They need to show that they have attained the necessary academic standard either by public examination results or by sitting papers set by the College.

The Registration Fee is £50 and the deposit is £400.

Scholarships, Exhibitions and Bursaries. Scholarships and Exhibitions are available in the following categories – Academic, Art, Design and Technology, Drama, Music (instrumental and choral), Sport and All-Rounder – and are at the discretion of the Headmaster. They are awarded at the ages of 11, 13 and for Sixth Form entry. Scholarships carry a remission of up to 20% of the fees which may be supplemented by means-tested Bursaries. Recently launched awards, which are usually made annually, are the Alastair Hignell Scholarship and the Governors' Award.

In all Scholarships, in addition to academic excellence, all-round ability and out-of-school activities and interests are taken into account.

A number of bursaries may be awarded to those in genuine financial need. Special consideration is given to the children of Clergy, Old Denstonians and members of the Armed Forces.

Fees per term (2016–2017). Boarding: £5,922 (Year 7), £7,848 (Years 8 & 9), £8,603 (Years 10–13) including items of board and education other than music lessons and extra tuition. Day: £4,088 (Years 7–9), £4,941 (Years 10–13).

The Old Denstonian Club. *Secretary*: Mr M S Smith, Denstone College, Uttoxeter, Staffs. Regional Clubs based in London, Manchester and at the College.

Charitable status. Denstone College is a Registered Charity, number 1102588. It exists to provide Christian education for children.

Visitor: The Bishop of Lichfield

School Council:
K P Threlfall (*Custos*)
The Revd Canon B D Clover MA, LTCL (*Senior Provost*)
A D Coley
His Honour Judge R T N Orme, LLB (*Vice Custos*)
J S F Cash, BSc, MRICS
Mrs B C Hyde, BA Hons, Dip MS, MBA
C J Lewis
Mrs J Dickson, BSc, OT
Mrs B McNally-Young
Mrs E Bell
Mrs E Evans
M F Coffin MA, FCA
B W Hinton, MBA, FCIPD, MCIM
G R Bowe, BA, PGCE
D T Brown, ACA

Headmaster: **D M Derbyshire**, BA, MSc

Second Masters:
M R M Norris, BA
J Hartley, BA (*Registrar*)

Chaplain: The Revd R C M Jarvis, MA, MPhil, Cert Th

Masters and Mistresses:

Miss J R Morris, GMus	J I Young, BA (*Selwyn House*)
T P S O'Brien, DA	
R C Menneer, BSc, CNAA (*Head of Senior School*)	Mrs A M Jones, BA
	G A Jones, BA
M P Raisbeck, BA, CNAA	Miss S Jones, BA
Mrs S A Leak, BEd	Miss L Finat-Duclos, MSc
Miss J H Plewes, BA	N Horan, BA
A J Wray, BA	R Lightfoot, MSc
J M Tomlinson, BSc (*Heywood House*)	Mrs L A Gater, BA, MA
	R C Neal, BSc, MEd
Mrs V A Derbyshire, BA	C M Ashurst, BA (*Head of Middle School*)
Mrs P A Provan	
A C Bonell, BEd (*Head of Junior School*)	Mrs C L Ashurst, BA
	Mrs S J Burrows, BA
Mrs K Hood, BSc (*Senior Mistress*)	Mrs G Butler, BSc
	Mrs R E Maddocks, BA
P D Brice, BA (†*Meynell*)	J A Taylor, BA
C J Sassi, MA (†*Philips*)	T A H Williams, BSc
B J R Duerden, BSc	Mrs R C Abson, BA
Mrs K Rylance, BSc	Dr D P Baker, BA, MA, MPhil, PhD
S R Francis, BSc (*Shrewsbury House*)	Miss O J Barraclough, BA
T J Bell, BA (*Director of Studies*)	R H W Hinton, BA
	Mrs V Sykes, MSc, BSc
Miss A K Smart, BA	P Nye, BSc
Mrs M Silvey, BA	Miss J R Pitt, BA, MA
Mrs J A Teather (*Head of Moss Moor*)	M E H Rankin, BA
	Mrs L E Stanley, BSc
Mrs C A Tuxford, BA	Mrs J Westacott, MSc
I A K Sherwani	F S J Hardy, MA
Mrs C L Burrows, BA	Mrs G M Butler
Mrs C G Bailey, MA	Dr R Norris, MA, MPhil, DPhil
A D Pearson, BSc	
N J Parrans-Smith, MA,	Dip TCL

T Quinlan, BSc   Miss A K Smart, BA
Mrs D Williams-Jenks, BA   S Guy

Visiting Music Staff:
Mrs A O'Brien, DRSAMD, PGDip RSAMD, ARCM
  (*Piano, Singing, Recorder*)
A Gatford (*Guitar*)
Mrs A Hardy, GBSM, ABSM (*Flute*)
R Shaw, BA, GRSM, PGDip, ARCM, ABSM (*Saxophone,
  Clarinet*)
S J Ryde, ARCM, ARCO (*Piano*)
Ms C M Thomson, LRAM, GRSM, PGCE, CDRS (*Piano,
  Flute, Singing*)
W Raffle, BA, LVCM, AVCM (*Guitar*)
Ms L Kaniewski, BA (*Cello, Guitar*)
Mrs R Theobald, LRAM, ALCM (*Voice, Piano, Oboe*)
Mrs R Melland, GRSM, PG Dip (*Brass*)

Chapel Organist: G Walker, MA, ARCO, FRSA
Finance Bursar and Clerk to the School Council: D M
  Martin, ACIB
HR Manager: Mrs V L Astley
Headmaster's Secretary: Mrs T F Wedgwood, BA
Admissions Secretary: Mrs A Taylor

*Denstone College Preparatory School at Smallwood
  Manor*:
Headmaster: J Gear, BEd
(*For further details about the Preparatory School, see
  entry in IAPS section.*)

Dollar Academy

Dollar, Clackmannanshire FK14 7DU
Tel: 01259 742511
Fax: 01259 742867
email: rector@dollaracademy.org.uk
website: www.dollaracademy.org.uk
Facebook: /dollaracademy

Motto: '*Juventutis veho fortunas*'

The Academy, founded in 1818 and the oldest co-educational boarding and day school in Britain, is situated in forty acres of its own grounds on the southern slopes of the Ochil Hills, 30 miles from Edinburgh, 38 from Glasgow, 40 from St Andrews and 10 miles east of Stirling. The Academy is renowned for its academic reputation, for its inclusive international outlook, and for its range of co-curricular activities. In recent years, all the boarding houses have been extensively refurbished, and the quality of the facilities throughout the school campus is of the highest order; a Sixth Form Centre was opened in 2010 and a new Modern Languages centre opened in 2015. The A-listed Playfair Building of 1821 is surrounded by a number of impressive modern buildings named after distinguished Scots.

Organisation. The Academy is divided into the Senior School (ages 12–18, 850 pupils); the Junior School (ages 10–12, 162 pupils) and the Prep School (ages 5–9, 204 pupils). It is fully co-educational throughout, and has been from 1818.

Academic. Pupils follow a course of study based upon the Scottish Curriculum for Excellence, leading to qualifications that are highly regarded and which are valid for entry to all world universities. In the Senior School, pupils are prepared for examinations at National 5 level (generally in 7 or 8 subjects) and Higher Grades (usually in 5 subjects); and then afterwards for a range of Advanced Highers, further Highers or wider interest modules. Three Modern Languages are offered from age 10, with Mandarin optional at age 12, and co-curricular Japanese and Russian. The separate sciences are available from 13. The timetable is created around the needs of the pupils rather than requiring them to slot into pre-arranged subject blocks.

Beyond Dollar. Senior staff offer advice on Careers and Higher Education to current and former pupils. In addition, all pupils are offered the services of a professional careers adviser, and both Planitplus and Centigrade programmes are used. Dollar has a flourishing Work Experience programme for seniors locally, and in France, Germany and Spain. Volunteering, community service and charitable activities are widely supported throughout the school.

International links. Contact with other countries has increased notably in recent years. For example, the Art department visits Paris, Berlin, London and Madrid; the geographers visit USA, Iceland and the Swiss Alps; the biologists visit Costa Rica; the Modern Languages department runs exchange programmes and trips to France, Germany, Spain and China, while sporting links are firmly established elsewhere in Europe, in Japan, Ireland, Australia and South Africa. The Pipe Band has toured in Sri Lanka, the Far East and mainland Europe. The boarding community includes boys and girls from throughout the world.

Games and Activities. The extensive playing fields and new all-weather playing surface are immediately adjacent to the school, as are the Games Halls, the Sports Centre with fully-equipped Fitness Suite, 25-metre indoor heated swimming pool and the rifle range.

Teams represent the school in rugby, hockey, cricket, tennis, athletics, swimming, skiing, shooting, curling, football, golf, badminton, basketball and ultimate frisbee.

The Duke of Edinburgh's Award scheme is widely supported at all three award levels. The Combined Cadet Force has equal numbers of boys and girls in a Royal Signals troop, an Infantry section, a REME section, an RAF section, an RN section and two Pipe Bands.

Dollar follows the principle of allowing pupils to opt into co-curricular activities as well as games, and an extraordinarily wide variety of clubs is on offer, from surfing and croquet to climbing and childcare.

The Arts. Music is taught as part of the curriculum, and tuition is offered as an extra in most orchestral instruments, besides bagpipes, guitar, drums and clarsach. There are six choirs, four orchestras, two Jazz bands and one Celtic Rock Orchestra. Junior and Senior Musical productions are performed annually. Drama productions and clubs are found throughout the age range; a range of performance spaces is used including the purpose-built Studio Theatre. Many Art Clubs take place outwith the timetabled lessons and exhibitions are held throughout the year. Dance – whether it be Scottish Country or Latin American – is taught at all levels. Debating and Public Speaking are popular and competitive activities both within Dollar and in national competitions, where success is regularly achieved.

Boarding. Boarding pupils are accepted from the age of nine. There is one Boys' and two Girls' Houses. Weekly or flexible boarding arrangements can be made to suit pupils' and parents' needs.

Fees per term (2016–2017). Tuition: £3,018 (Prep), £3,468 (Junior), £4,035 (Senior). Boarding fees (including tuition): £8,769 (Junior; full), £8,259 (Junior; weekly) £9,336 (Senior; full), £8,826 (Senior; weekly).

Admission. This is by interview and/or test with the Head of the Prep and Junior School for ages 5–14; and by interview and current school report for ages 14–18. The biggest single intakes are at age 5, and at 10 and 11 to the Junior School; there are intakes in other years as vacancies occur.

Charitable status. The Governors of Dollar Academy Trust is a Registered Charity; it exists to provide education for boys and girls.

Governors:
Chairman: Professor J McEwen, MBChB, FFPH, FFOM, FRCP, FMedSci, FDSRCS

Vice-Chairmen:
Mrs J M Smith, BA
Professor R E Morris, MA, DPhil

Members:
Mr M W Balfour, BCom, CA
Mr V J Buchanan
Mrs D A Burt, MCSP
Cllr A D Campbell, CA
Dr G B Curry, BA Mod, PhD, DIC
Mr R W Fraser, LLB, DipLP, Advocate
Sheriff W E Gibson, BA, LLB, sheriff
Mr I C Glasgow, BSc, Dip Surv, Dip IA, ASIP
Mr R P S Harris, BCom, Dip Com, CA
Mrs E C C Heath, MA
Professor M A Hogg, LLB, LLM, PhD, NP, FRSA
Mr C J Milne, BSc
Mr D C Walker, BArch, Dip Arch, ARB, BSc
Mrs D D Weir
Mr E D White, BCom, FIoD

Bursar and Clerk to Governors: J StJ Wilkes, MA
Assistant Bursar: Mrs S Dunsire
Bursar's PA: Mrs M Campbell, BA

Rector: D J Knapman, BA, BSc, MPhil

Rector's PA: Ms E C Gallagher

Deputy Rector: G P Daniel, MA, MA

Assistant Rectors:
Dr J T Brooks, BSc, PhD
Mrs K B Miller, BSc, PGCE
Mr S Burbury, MMus, BA Hons, NPQH
Mrs A M Morrison, BA (*also Head of Prep & Junior School*)

Head of Communications: Mrs E Gunn, MA, Dip IDM

Former Pupil Registrar and Development Officer: Mrs K J Molnar, BSc

Prep & Junior School:
Deputy Head, Prep & Junior School: Mrs M Barbour, BEd
Assistant Head, Junior School: Miss S Horne, BEd

Senior School:
Heads of Departments:
Art & Design: Mrs C Kelly, BA
Biology: Mr C K Ainge, BSc
Business Education:
Mr M C Moore, BSc, Dip IDM
Chemistry: Mr D J Lumsden, BSc
Classics: Mrs H S Lumsden, MA
Computing: Ms R McGuinness, MSc
Drama: Mr P G Russell, BA
Engineering, Design & Technology: Dr D A Keys, BA, PhD
English: Mrs C Murray, MA, MPhil
Geography: Mr A M McConnell, BSc
History & Modern Studies: Miss M D Sharp, MA
Home Economics: Mrs C Maciver, Dip HomeEc
Mathematics: Mrs V Mason, BSc
Modern Languages: Mr D Delaney, MA
English as an Additional Language (EAL): Mrs S Brooks, MA
Music: Mrs K Fitzpatrick, MSc, BMus (*Director of Music*)
Physical Education: Mr S R Newton, BSc
Director of Hockey: Ms L Allan, BEd
Director of Rugby: Mr D W Caskie, BEd
Physics: Dr S Fulton, BSc, PhD
Support for Learning: Mrs L S McDougall, MA

Boarding Houseparents:
Argyll: Mr & Mrs M Hose
Heyworth: Mr & Mrs E Duncan
McNabb & Tait: Mr & Mrs N J McFadyean

Downe House

Cold Ash, Thatcham, Berks RG18 9JJ
Tel: 01635 200286
Fax: 01635 202026
email: correspondence@downehouse.net
website: www.downehouse.net
Twitter: @DowneHouse1
Facebook: @downehouse

Founded 1907.
Numbers on roll. 569 Boarding girls, 19 Day girls.
Age Range. 11–18.

Downe House is situated in 110 acres of wooded grounds, five miles from Newbury and within easy reach of Heathrow Airport. The school's proximity to London allows the girls to take part in a rich variety of cultural activities outside the school.

Buildings. There are two newly-built Lower School Houses for girls aged 11+ and 12+ and five recently refurbished mixed-age Houses for those between 13 and 16. When girls enter the Sixth Form they move into one of two Sixth Form Houses, where they have twin-shared or single study-bedrooms and facilities appropriate to their needs. All the Housemistresses are members of the teaching staff and are responsible for the coordination of the academic, pastoral, social and moral development of the girls in their care.

The school buildings include up-to-date Science Laboratories, an Art School, Design and Technology suite, a Music School, an indoor Swimming Pool and Squash Courts and a Library. The games facilities are excellent; a Sports Centre and all-weather pitch. The school also has a Performing Arts Centre and a Concert Room which are used for lectures, concerts and plays, and a recording studio.

Religion. Downe House is a Church of England school with its own chapel, which girls attend for prayers and for a service of either Matins or Evensong on Sunday. Holy Communion is celebrated once a week and girls are prepared for confirmation if they wish. Other denominations are welcome. Girls can go to mass on Sundays and are prepared for Roman Catholic Confirmation.

Curriculum and Activities. The curriculum includes the study of English, History, Geography, Religious Studies, French, German, Spanish, Italian, Mandarin Chinese, Latin, Greek, Mathematics, Physics, Chemistry, Biology, Design and Technology, Information & Communication Technology, Music, Art, Drama and Theatre Studies, Food and Nutrition and Textiles. In addition, Classical Civilisation, Business Studies, Sports Science, Politics, Economics, Photography and History of Art are offered at A Level or Pre-U, as well as Global Perspectives and writing a 5000-word Independent Research Report. Leiths Food & Wine Certificate is also offered to girls in the Sixth Form. Girls are prepared for GCSE, IGCSE, AS, A Level and Pre-U examinations, with the vast majority of girls going on to University or some other form of Higher Education.

ICT skills are developed across the years with all girls following a general ICT course. All girls have their own Downe House email address.

All girls in the Lower Fourth, aged 12, spend a term at the School's House in France in the Dordogne, to study French and increase their awareness of themselves as global citizens.

Careers Specialists give help to the girls in selecting their careers and a Careers Resource Centre is available to all ages.

There are many extracurricular activities, including a variety of musical instruments, Drama, Sub Aqua, Pottery, Photography, Art, Craft, Singing, Speech & Drama Training, Cookery, Dance (Tap, Modern, Ballet, Hip Hop, Street). There is a regular programme of varied weekend activities, including The Duke of Edinburgh's Award scheme, which develops leadership qualities, plus Young Enterprise which offers an insight into business practice in the UK.

Fees per term (2016–2017). £11,720 for boarders and £8,480 for Day Girls.

Admissions. Girls may enter the school at 11+, 12+ or 13+ after assessment, interview and Common Entrance. A few girls annually are given places in the Sixth Form after interview and entrance test.

Application for entry should be made well in advance. Prospective parents are asked to make an appointment to see the Headmistress, at which time they are offered a comprehensive tour of the school.

Scholarships. Scholarships are awarded to recognise girls with strong academic, musical, artistic, sporting or dramatic potential from a variety of backgrounds and who will benefit from the overall education offered by Downe House.

The School offers a number of Academic Scholarships at 11+, 12+, 13+ and for entry into the Sixth Form. Scholarships are also awarded in Music, Art and Sport (11+ and 13+) and Drama (13+ and 16+) and there are Headmistress's Awards for outstanding all-round performers.

All Academic, Art, Sport and Drama Scholars receive recognition in the form of £600 per annum remission in fees. Exhibitioners receive a remission of £450 per annum.

Music Scholars will receive free tuition in two instruments, which may include the voice, up to a maximum of 30 lessons per year. Exhibitioners will receive free tuition in one instrument, up to a maximum of 30 lessons per year.

Candidates who are successful in gaining an award, but require greater remission in fees in order to be able to take up their place may apply for an Academic, Art, Music, Sport or Drama means-tested Bursary, as appropriate.

Academic Awards. The Olive Willis 13+ Scholarships, 12+ and 11+ Downe House Scholarships are awarded on the results of examinations and interviews with the Headmistress, Head of Upper School and Head of Lower School, held each year in January. In addition to these major awards, Exhibitions may be awarded in each age group. Further Minor Awards for excellence in specific fields may be made if candidates of sufficient merit present themselves. Candidates sit papers in English, Mathematics, Science, French (12+ and 13+ only), a General Paper, plus Latin (optional).

Sixth Form Scholarships are year round and candidates sit papers in two subjects of their choice, together with a General Paper. Candidates will also be required to undertake an interview with the Headmistress and Head of Sixth Form.

Age of entry will normally be in line with general entry, ie 11+, 12+, 13+ and Sixth Form (16+). Candidates must be under 12, under 13 or under 14 on the 1st September following the examination. Girls sitting for entry to the Sixth Form must be in the final year of their GCSE studies or equivalent.

Music Awards will be made on the results of auditions and aural tests held at Downe House in February each year

Art Awards will be made on the results of a girl's portfolio and a practical test held at Downe House in June each year.

Drama Awards will be made on the results of a one-hour written paper and a one-hour practical examination held at Downe House in May/June each year.

Sports Awards are made in March each year. It is expected that potential candidates will be at the top level of their year group in a minimum of two major sports. Candidates will be invited to undertake a programme that will test general principles of fitness and skill acquisition. All candidates will also be assessed in swimming.

A number of *Headmistress's Awards* may be awarded, at the discretion of the Headmistress, to reward outstanding all-round performers.

For Music, Art, Sport and Drama awards junior candidates must be under 14 on the following 1st of September of the year of entry. Potential award holders are required to reach a satisfactory standard in the Common Entrance examinations for their age group before taking up their Award. Senior candidates (i.e. those entering the Sixth Form) must achieve Grade B or above in seven IGCSE subjects before taking up their Award and at least an A/A* grade in the subjects they wish to pursue in the Sixth Form.

Bursaries. The School is able to award a small number of full means-tested Bursaries for girls to join the School at 11+, 12+ or 13+. Girls should be able to meet the entry requirements and benefit from a busy boarding environment.

Alumnae Bursaries are available for the daughters of alumnae if their parents are in need of financial assistance.

Charitable status. Downe House School is a Registered Charity, number 1015059. Its aim is the provision of a sound and broadly based education for girls, which will fit them for University Entrance and subsequently for a successful career in whatever field they choose.

Governors:
Chairman: Mr M J Kirk, MA
Mr S Creedy-Smith, BA, ACA
Lady Cunningham, BSc, FRCP
Mrs V Exelby, MA
Mr N Gold, FCA
Mrs J M Grant Peterkin, BA
Ms F Hazlitt
Mrs F Holmes
Mr Nicholas Hornby, BSc
Dr Christopher O'Kane, MA, MB BChir, MSc, DPhil
Mr Christopher Radford, BSc, (*Chairman of Estates Sub-Committee*)

Headmistress: Mrs E McKendrick, BA Liverpool, PGCE, FRSA

Deputy Head: Mrs A Bizior, BSc, PGCE, BEd University of South Africa
Academic Deputy: Mr M Hill, BA Hull, MA Reading, MEd Open, PGCE
Boarding Deputy: Mrs G Ford, BA Bristol, PGCE
Head of Sixth Form: Ms M Stimson, MA Edinburgh, PGCE
Head of Upper School: Mrs Anna Dourountakis, BA Hons, HDE PG
Head of Lower School: Mrs J Gilpin-Jones, LWCMD
Assistant Headmistress (Foundation): Mrs M Scott, BEd Brisbane
Finance Bursar: Mr C Cockburn, FCCA
Director of Information Systems: Mr S Finch
Director of HR: Mrs K Tuttle, MCIPD
Director of Estates, Property and Services: Mr A Heath

Director of Admissions: Mrs L Ogilvie-Jones, BSc, PGCE, PGDip CEG, QCG
Director of Operations: Mrs Y J Charlesworth, BSc Reading, PGCE (*also Head of Science*)
Director of Studies (Assessment and Reporting): Mrs P Toogood, BA Hons, MSt Oxon, PGCE
Director of Studies (Data Management): Mrs K Henson, BA, MA, PGCS, MEd

Heads of Department:
Art: Mrs S J Scott, BA Central England, PGCE

Biology: Miss C M Pugsley, BSc Warwick, PGCE
Business & Economics: Mrs Orla Cahill, BA
Higher Education and Global Initiatives: Mrs M Ahktar, BA, MA, PGCE, PG Cert
Chemistry: Mr A Reynolds, BSc Loughborough, PGCE
Classics: Mrs L Dakin, MA Cantab
Co-Curricular: Mr Matt Ilott, BSc, PGCE, W-ENT, ML, SPA
Design & Technology: Miss S Singh, HDE Natal, South Africa, QTS
Drama: Mr Sam Brassington, BA, MA, PGCE
English: Mrs Johanne Harrington, BA, PGCE
Geography: Miss Kathryn Rawlinson, BSc Hons, MSc, PGCE
History: Mr W Lane, MA, PGCE
ICT: Mr Gareth Bouwer
Learning Skills: Mrs T Evans, BA, PG Dip SpLD, RSA TEFL, AMBDA
Library: Ms L Scott-Picton, BA, MLib, PGCE, MCLIP
Mathematics: Mr R S Barnes, BSc East Anglia, PGCE
Modern Languages: Mrs J Basnett, BA Westminster, MA, PGCE
Music: Dr C Exon, BMus, PhD Birmingham, PGCE
Physical Education: Mrs L J M Rayne, BEd Hons
Physics: Mr M Rivers, MA, PGCE
PSHE: Mrs N Riddle, B PhysEd, Dip T
Religious Studies: Mr P Evans, BD London, MA London, PGCE
Science: Mrs Y J Charlesworth, BSc Reading, PGCE
Speech & Drama: Mrs R Watson, BA Hons, AVCM

Housemistresses/Housemaster:
Hermitage House: Mrs A Nash, BTchg, Lng Canterbury, NZ
Hill House: Miss Annabel Brown, BA Hons, PGCE
Darwin: Mrs F V Capps, CertEd Bedford College
Veyrines (France): Mrs D Scotland
Aisholt: Mrs J Boswell, MA, PGCE
Ancren Gate North: Miss K Anger, BMus Hons, GSMD
Ancren Gate South: Mrs S McClymont, LLB, PG Dip LPC
Holcombe: Mrs Mears-Smith, BA, PGCE FE, TEFL
Tedworth: Mrs S Barnard, MA
Willis House East: Mrs T Reeve, MA, PG Dip
Willis House West: Mrs V Ryan, BA Bangor, PGCE
York House North: Miss Ellen Clark, BA, QTS
York House South: Mrs C Walton-Walters, BSc Open, Cert Ed

Chaplain: Revd Andrew Taylor
Nurse Manager: Mrs G Murray, BSc RGN, BSc RM

Downside School

Stratton-on-the-Fosse, Radstock, Bath, Somerset BA3 4RJ

Tel: 01761 235100
Fax: 01761 235105
email: admin@downside.co.uk
website: www.downside.co.uk

Downside School is one of England's oldest and most distinguished Catholic schools. It is an independent, full-boarding school for boys and girls aged 11–18. Founded in 1606 in Douai (in France), the School sits in a 500-acre estate at the foot of the Mendip Hills in Somerset, twelve miles south of the City of Bath. Voted as one of the 'Top 10 Most Beautiful Schools in the UK' by the Daily Telegraph.

Downside is a strong academic school with outstanding examination results. Everyone is encouraged to aspire beyond their expectations and the School has a thriving aca-

demic life with excellent admission rates to all the top UK universities. Importantly, Downside was also voted "Best for well-being" by The Week Independent Schools Guide in 2015. The happy atmosphere which pervades is remarked on by all visitors.

Academic. Strong intellectual traditions focusing on academic subjects, with a range of additional options to encourage independent learning and an enquiring mind. 12% of leavers to Oxbridge, as well as places to read Medicine and Veterinary Science last year. In 2016, 46% of A Level results were at A*/A, with 28% of pupils gaining at least 3 A*/A grades.

Boarding. 82% of Downside pupils are 7-day-a-week boarders and approximately 28% are international from all over Europe and worldwide. Weekends for boarders are busy with Saturday morning lessons, sports fixtures in the afternoon and a full programme of activities; film nights, theatre trips, cookery and quiz competitions to name but a few. Pupils are all invited to celebrate Mass in the Abbey Church on a Sunday morning.

Downside has six boarding houses: Powell, Isabella, Caverel, Barlow, Roberts and Smythe, with boarders and day pupils integrated together in all the houses. Junior boys join Powell House at 11, 12 & 13, before moving up to one of three senior boys' houses: Barlow, Roberts or Smythe, whilst girls join Caverel or Isabella House.

Each House has its own spirit, character and traditions. Pupils have friends across the Houses but avidly compete in inter-house games, drama, music and other activities.

Downside School is proud to provide 24/7 professional nursing care, with access to three GP surgeries on site each week.

Sport. Pupils compete in a range of high quality fixtures throughout the year in Rugby, Hockey, Netball, Cricket, Tennis, Cross-Country, Athletics and Football. Additional disciplines are offered as activities, ranging from Judo to Squash, and Zumba to Polo.

Downside School believes that physical activity plays an important role in every pupil's life. Sport for All is a central part of the school's philosophy as is the desire for every pupil to enjoy sport and achieve their own personal best. With all our facilities on campus pupils can also swim, use the gym and play tennis in their own time and for budding athletes a cross country run need never leave the estate.

Arts. You'll discover that Art, Drama, Music, and Design & Technology are very popular amongst Downside pupils, both at GCSE and A Level, and as additional activities. The department is open on Sunday afternoons for recreation or to catch up on work and our association with Hauser Wirth Somerset means that top quality art installations are on our doorstep.

Concerts are held in the magnificent Abbey Church throughout the year, with plays performed in our new Performing Arts Centre. We have an Artist-in-Residence who continually inspires the children, and the very latest equipment in our Design workshops: from 3D printers to an iMac suite.

Founded over a century ago, Downside's Schola Cantorum is the oldest Roman Catholic school choir in the UK. Formed of boys and girls, it gives concerts of large-scale sacred works throughout the year and has topped the charts with its CDs, The Abbey and Gregorian Moods. There are three Chamber Choirs at Downside, plus opportunities in orchestral, band and chamber music, with frequent concerts and recitals as well as a new recording studio for budding professionals.

Development. In the last few years, Downside has developed a brand-new Learning Support Centre, a new Performing Arts Centre, a refurbished Sports Hall and Swimming Pool complex, and a new Art and Design faculty. The Monastic Library, subject to a Lottery Grant to make its treasures available to a wider public, is now a wonderful new resource for serious historians and scholars studying at the School.

Alumni.

Tom Bethell (Journalist)
Rocco Forte (Hotelier)
Brion Gysin (Artist)
Jared Harris (Actor)
Christopher Jamison (Monk)
Emmanuel de Merode (Conservationist)
David Mlinaric (Designer)
William Nicholson (Writer)
Anthony Palliser (Artist)
John Pope-Hennessy (Art Historian)
Auberon Waugh (Journalist)
Adam Zamoyski (Historian)

Fees per term (2016–2017). Boarding £7,854–£10,536; Day £4,980–£5,904.

Scholarships are available for gifted and talented pupils in a range of areas. Please contact our Admissions Department for the latest assessment deadlines.

Charitable status. Downside School is a Registered Charity, number 1158507. Its purpose is to advance the cause of Catholic Education.

Prior of Downside Abbey, Chairman of Downside Abbey Trust and Chairman of Governors: Dom Leo Maidlow Davis

Head Master: **Dr J S Whitehead**, MA Oxon, MPhil, PhD, FRSA

Deputy Head Master: A R Hobbs, MA

Senior Leadership:
Director of Studies: D M Gibbons, BA
Director of Pastoral Care: A N Falzon, MA
Chief Executive (*Downside Trust*): S Treloar
Director of External Communications: Mrs J Vines

House Mistress of Caverel: Mrs B Bouchard, MA
House Mistress of Isabella: Mrs C Murphy, BSc
House Master of Barlow: S J Potter, BA
House Master of Roberts: S Ottewell, BA
House Master of Smythe: J Storey, BA
House Master of Powell: J Dolman, BSc

School Chaplains: Dom James Hood, Dom Boniface Hill

Director of Music: J McNamara, MA
Director of Sport: R Jones, BA

Heads of Faculty:
Art & Design: N J Barrett, BEd
English: Mrs L Pickering, BA
Humanities: O G Simper, BA
Languages: R C Rawlins, MA
Mathematics: Miss S Moody, BSc
Science: N M Cox, BSc
Theology & RS: H F Walters, MA

Learning Support: Mrs M Morrison

Head of Nursing Care: Mrs Tania Bartholomew

Registrar: Mrs A Hatvany
email: registrar@downside.co.uk

Dulwich College

Dulwich Common, London SE21 7LD
Tel: 020 8693 3601
Fax: 020 8693 6319

email: info@dulwich.org.uk
website: www.dulwich.org.uk
Twitter: @DulwichCollege
Facebook: /DulwichCollege

Motto: '*Detur gloria soli Deo*', ('Let Glory be given to God alone')

Dulwich College was founded in 1619 by Edward Alleyn, the Elizabethan actor, and is approaching its 400th anniversary.

The College is an academically selective, independent day and boarding school for boys aged 7–18; full and weekly boarding is available for boys aged 11–18. Situated in over 70 acres of grounds and playing fields, the campus is just 10 minutes by train from London Victoria. A Dulwich education ensures each pupil fulfils their academic potential whilst taking advantage of the wide range of sporting, cultural and adventurous activities on offer.

Boys move on to universities, medical and dental schools, music and art colleges. Almost all enter higher education, but an increasing number of boys are following vocational paths. Pupils are prepared for entry to the most competitive universities such as Oxford, Cambridge and Imperial, where a very good record of places is maintained each year.

The College's principal aims for all its boys are:

- to offer an appropriate academic challenge which enables each pupil to realise his potential;
- to create an environment which promotes an independent work ethic and encourages all boys to acquire a love of learning;
- to provide a wide range of sporting, cultural and adventurous activities for pupils to enjoy and through which they can learn to work co-operatively and to take a lead;
- to nurture a supportive community that encourages a sense of social responsibility and spiritual and personal development;
- to ensure that pupils from a broad variety of backgrounds can feel equally secure and valued;
- to offer boys and staff opportunities to benefit from and contribute to the College's international and UK educational partnerships.

Organisation. The College, comprising some 1,500 boys, has four specific schools: Junior School, Lower School, Middle School and Upper School. Each of these has its own Head who is responsible to the Master for that part of the College. Within each School there are Heads of Year and Form Tutors who have daily contact with boys in their care. These teams are responsible for overseeing the pastoral and academic welfare of the boys and they ensure that close links are fostered between parents and the College.

DUCKS. Dulwich College's Kindergarten and Infants' School is the only co-educational element of the College providing a secure foundation for future learning and development for children from 6 months to Year 2. Most children from DUCKS enter leading independent schools in south London, and many boys will pass the entrance examination for the College.

Day House system. A thriving Day House system offers boys the opportunity to take part in a wide range of competitive activities including art, chess, poetry, general knowledge, debating, drama and music. They can also compete in a number of sports throughout the academic year, including rugby, soccer, hockey, cricket and athletics.

Curriculum. In Years 7 and 8 all boys follow a broad and balanced curriculum, including all standard core subjects and French or Spanish, Chinese, Latin, Wellbeing, PE, Computing, Drama, DT, Art and Music. In Year 8, boys make a choice between Latin, Chinese or German; this reduces the number of languages studied to two, allowing boys the time to engage rigorously in their chosen languages and make significant progress. In Year 9 boys continue with the core subjects, Wellbeing and PE together with French or Spanish, and they choose a second language from German, Chinese, French, Spanish, Latin or Italian. This second language may be a continuation of languages they have previously studied, or they may start them from scratch. In Years 10 and 11 boys take between nine and 10 GCSE subjects, comprising English, English Literature, Mathematics, Biology, Chemistry, Physics and French or Spanish plus three optional subjects; they all continue with Wellbeing and PE. In the Upper School (Years 12 and 13), there is a free choice of three A Level subjects (four if they are studying Further Mathematics) and from 2017 every pupil will opt for an A Level 'Plus' option which is an in-house qualification that aims to provide enrichment, cross-curricular links and programmes that reflect the likely courses boys choose at university. Boys will also choose a 'Link' course in conjunction with James Allen's Girls' School that will provide breadth to their educational profile, including a regular lecture series and community service options. The concept of Free Learning (supra-curricular and other learning beyond the curriculum) is now fully embedded in the life of the College across all year groups.

Facilities. Over the years the College has developed its complex of buildings to meet the needs of boys' education in the twenty-first century, and this development continues.

The latest addition is The Laboratory, a new state-of-the-art building that brings together the twin cultures of Science and Art. There are 21 laboratories, three preparation rooms and the James Caird Hall, which houses the rescue boat of one of the College's most famous Old Alleynians, Sir Ernest Shackleton. There are five adaptable 'Informatics' suites with free-thinking spaces for creative learning and cross-curricular collaboration and a seminar room with full video-conferencing facilities. In addition there is a versatile 240-seat auditorium which will be available to the whole Dulwich community for events and exhibitions and an outdoor piazza for recreation and performance.

Extensive IT facilities are available to all pupils. The IT network gives pupils and staff access to a wide range of centrally stored learning resources through the College's own virtual learning environment, 'MyDulwich'. Three separate libraries, all staffed by professional librarians, cater to the specific needs of different age groups. Exhibitions, drawn from the College archive, are regularly mounted in the Wodehouse Library.

The College has two separate dining areas which provide a wide choice of food, including a vegetarian option, on a cafeteria basis for both pupils and staff. The College also has its own shop, the Commissariat, where uniform, equipment and stationery can be purchased. The Richard Penny Medical Centre provides professional nursing care on a round-the-clock basis for boarders and day boys. The College Counsellor, based in the Medical Centre, provides confidential consultation for pupils and parents.

Sport is integral to life at Dulwich College both within the curriculum and as part of the wider co-curricular programme. There are over 70 acres of playing fields. The PE Centre includes a substantial sports hall and a modern indoor 25-metre swimming pool. The College owns a boathouse on the Thames, accommodating the thriving Boat Club, and an Outdoor Centre in the Brecon Beacons which is used for a variety of activities and residential courses. The sports programme provides a continuity and breadth of experience across the age range, with 24 different sports on offer, giving all boys the opportunity to reach their sporting potential.

Music and Drama. A professionally equipped, purpose-built Music School provides all pupils with the opportunity to study a musical instrument. More than 500 pupils receive individual tuition every week from 35 experienced specialist musicians, led by the Heads of Strings, Wind, Brass, Keyboard and Singing. The College Chapel Choir, an ancient foundation, leads regular services in the Foundation Chapel and also at other venues throughout the country. The Edward Alleyn Theatre is a fully rigged auditorium with a capacity of 250; over 50 events are staged annually and the facility includes rehearsal and teaching spaces, as well as dressing rooms.

Clubs and Societies. A wide variety of clubs and societies, many run by the boys themselves, take place during the lunch break and after school. These range from Lego for the younger boys to the Political Society which is responsible for inviting prominent public figures to speak. The College is particularly renowned for its Debating success that in 2016 culminated in a Year 12 boy captaining Team England to victory in the World Schools Debating Championships. The College encourages boys to take part in expeditions as well as many community-based activities which can include membership of the Combined Cadet Force, Scouts, the Duke of Edinburgh's Award scheme and Community Service. Academic, cultural and sporting excursions take place at various points throughout the school year.

Careers. Specialist careers staff, professional external advisors, dedicated IT facilities and an accredited library provide an up-to-date service assisting boys in planning higher education and careers. Boys and their parents attend the annual Courses and Careers Convention to consult with representatives from key employers, professional institutes and around 25 universities. Upper School boys receive guidance on how degree course choices might influence their future careers.

Boarding. There are three boarding houses in Dulwich College, all situated within or close to the campus. Each house has a Housemaster who is resident with his family. Boys in Years 7–13 live in Old Blew and The Orchard and boys in the Upper School live in Blew House and Ivyholme, where each boy has his own room with en-suite facilities. At present, there are around 140 boarders. Boarding at Dulwich is truly international with boys coming from all over the world and this adds to an atmosphere of cultural tolerance and intellectual curiosity.

ISI Inspection November 2014. ISI Inspectors awarded Dulwich College, Dulwich College Junior School and DUCKS 'Excellent' in every category, 'Exceptional' for 'the quality of pupils' achievements and learning' for the senior school – the only category for which this grading can be given – and 'Outstanding' for the EYFS (Kindergarten, Nursery and Reception).

Entry. Boys are admitted to the College as day boys, boarders or weekly boarders. Places are available at age 7, 11, 13 and 16. Casual vacancies occur from time to time at ages 8, 9, 10 and 12. At age 7 places are awarded on the basis of interview, report and practical assessment during the Lent Term. At age 11 places are awarded on the results of the Combined Entrance and Scholarship Examination held in the Lent Term. Candidates take papers in English and Mathematics and also a Verbal/Non-Verbal Reasoning test. At age 13 boys may take the College's own Entrance Examinations held in the Lent Term. Entrance is by examination and interview. At 16+ places are offered on the results from subject specific tests, interview and GCSE grades. Application should generally be in the year before desired date of entry. For further information please see the Admissions section on the College website. A non-refundable registration fee of £100 is charged for all applications and £200 for overseas applications.

Fees per term (2016–2017). Day £6,305 (includes lunch for Junior and Lower School pupils); Full Boarding £13,160; Weekly Boarding £12,339.

Scholarships and Bursaries. A significant number of academic scholarships are awarded each year up to one-third of the tuition fee. There are also scholarships for Music, Art and Sports. Scholarships can be enhanced by Bursaries in cases of financial need. A substantial number of Bursaries are awarded annually to new boys entering Year 3, Year 7 or Year 9 where parents are unable to pay the full tuition fee. Bursaries are means-tested and reviewed annually. All applicants will be considered on the basis of their performance in the entrance examination and interview.

Old Alleynians. Founded in 1873, The Alleyn Club is a flourishing former pupils' association with over 10,000 Old Alleynian (OA) members. The club's name acknowledges the founder, Edward Alleyn, actor, theatre manager and contemporary of William Shakespeare.

Charitable status. Dulwich College is a Registered Charity, number 1150064.

The Governing Body:
Chairman: The Rt Hon P J R Riddell, CBE, MA, FRHistS
Vice Chairman: Ms J Hill, MA [née Black]
Sir Brian Bender, KCB
Dr I Bishop, CBE, BEd, MA, LLD
Ms V Flind, BA
Mr R J Foster, BEd
Mr B Ghosh, BA, MA
Mr P L Hogarth, CA, MSI
Dr A H Köttering, BSc, MSc, DPhil
Mr J D Lovering, BA, MBA [OA]
Mr P M Thompson, RD, MB BS, FRCS [OA]
Mr G N C Ward, CBE, MA, FCA

Honorary International Advisor to the Governors:
His Excellency Khun Anand Panyarachun, Hon KBE, MA [OA]

Special Advisor to the Governors: Sir John H Riblat, FRICS, Hon FRIBA [OA]

[OA] *Old Alleynian*

Clerk to the Governors: Ms K Jones, LLB

Master of the College: Dr J A F Spence, BA Hons, PhD

Deputy Masters:
Mrs F M Angel, BA (*Pastoral*)
Mr D A P King, MA (*Academic*)
Dr C S B Pyke, MA, MMus, PhD (*External Relations*)
Mr I L H Scarisbrick, BSc (*Co-curricular*)

Chief Operating Officer: Mr S J Yiend, MA
Director of Finance: Mr N Prout, BA, ACA
Director of Communications: Ms J M Scott, MA, MBA
Director of Development: Mrs L A Hindley, BA

Head of Upper School: Mr R P Berlie, MA
Head of Middle School: Dr N D Black, BA, PhD
Head of Lower School: Mr S Tanna, BA
Head of Junior School: Dr T G A Griffiths, PGCE, MA, MSc, DPhil
Head of DUCKS (*Kindergarten and Infants' School*): Mrs N A Black, BA

Registrar: Mrs S Betts
Archivist: Mrs C M Lucy, BA, MCLIP
Head of Academic Administration: Dr J Kinch, BA, BPhil, DPhil
Director of Expeditions and Activities: Miss S G Wood, BSc
Examinations Officer: Mr M Grantham-Hill, BSc
Staff Tutor: Mr A J Threadgould, BSc

Heads of Departments:
Art: Mrs S Mulholland, BA (*Director of Art*)
Classics: Dr J-M Hulls, MPhil, PhD
Design & Technology: Mr M Ross, BA
Drama:
Mr P V Jolly, BA, DipRSA (*Director of Drama*)
Mrs K Norton-Smith, BA (*Head of Academic Drama*)
EAL: Miss S E Horsfield, BA

Economics: Mr N Fyfe, BA
English: Mr R F Sutton, BA
Geography: Miss J K Woolley, BA
Higher Education & Careers:
Dr R E McIlwaine, MChem, PGCE, PhD (*Director of University Admissions*)
Mrs E H Soare (*Head of Careers*)
History and Politics: Mr D Flower, BA
ICT:
Mr J D Cartwright, MA (*Head of Computing*)
Dr A C Storey, BA, MSc, PhD (*Director of ICT*)
Learning Support:
Mrs A J Owen, CertEd SpLD (*Joint Head*)
Mrs A T Burrows, BA, PGCE
Libraries:
Mr P J Fletcher, BA, DipLib, MCLIP (*Head of Libraries*)
Mr R Weaver, BA, MA, FSA Scot (*Keeper of the Fellows' Library*)
Lower School Science: Mr Graham Wilson, MPhys
Mathematics: Mr C J Ottewill, BA, MPhil
Modern Languages:
Mr R S Baylis, MA, MA (*Head of Modern Languages*)
Mr N Mair, BA (*Director of Languages*)
Chinese: Mr A M Stark, BA, DMS, MA
French: Mr J G Brown, BA
German: Mr W Dugdale, BA
Italian: Mrs J Briggs, BA
Spanish: Mr A Iltchev, BA
Music:
Mr R G Mayo, MA, MusB, FRCO (*Director of Music*)
Dr J Carnelley, BMus, MMus, ARCO (*Head of Academic Music*)
Physical Education:
Mr P C Greenaway, BSc (*Director of Sport*)
Mr M Burdekin, BA (*Head of Academic PE*)
Religion and Theology: Mr J H Fox, BA
Scholars and General and Liberal Studies: Dr N T Croally, MA, PhD [OA]
Science:
Biology: Dr P J Cue, BSc, PhD
Chemistry: Miss L V A Rand, MChem
Physics: Dr S P Parsons, BA, MSci, PhD, PGCE

DUCKS (*Dulwich College Kindergarten and Infants' School*):
Mrs N A Black, BA (*Head of DUCKS*)
Miss S Donaldson, NNEB, MA (*Head of Kindergarten*)

Medical Centre Charge Nurse: Mrs C Baxter-Wilks, RN, BSc, MSc
College Counsellor: Ms J De Heger, BEd, Dip Art Therapy
Medical Officer: Dr R A Leonard, MBE, MA, MB, BChir, MRCGP, DRCOG
PA to the Master: Mrs M Wood
PA Governance & Finance: Ms S White

The High School of Dundee

Euclid Crescent, Dundee, Tayside DD1 1HU
Tel: 01382 202921
Fax: 01382 229822
email: enquiries@highschoolofdundee.org.uk
website: www.highschoolofdundee.org.uk
Twitter: @HSofDundee
Facebook: /highschoolofdundee

Motto: '*Prestante Domino*'.

The present School traces its origins directly back to a 13th century foundation by the Abbot and Monks of Lindores. It received a Royal Charter in 1859. Various Acts of Parliament in the 19th Century were finally consolidated in an Order in Council constituting the High School of Dundee Scheme 1965, which was revised in 1987.

Admission. The School comprises three sections:

The Nursery – 41 pupils (age 3–5; pre-school and ante pre-school).

The Junior School – 337 pupils (Primary 1 to Primary 7).

The Senior School – 667 pupils (S1 to S6).

The normal stages of entry are Nursery, Primary 1 and S1. Entry to Primary 1 (age 4½ to 5½ years) is by interview held in January and to S1 (age 11 to 12 years) by an Entrance Examination held in January. Where vacancies exist entrance is usually available at all other stages subject to satisfactory performance in an entrance assessment.

Bursaries. A number of means-tested bursaries are provided for entry to P6/7 and from S1 in the Senior School, to help those who otherwise could not afford the fees.

Fees per term (2016–2017). Primary: £2,833 (P1 to P3), £2,969 (P4 to P5), £3,372 (P6 to P7); Secondary £4,021. Nursery varies according to the number of sessions selected.

Buildings. The five main school buildings are in the centre of the city and form an architectural feature of the area. Two excellent, extensive playing fields – Dalnacraig and Mayfield – are situated some 1½ miles to the east of the school. As well as grass pitches, the facilities include an international standard synthetic water-based hockey surface and a sand-dressed synthetic hockey pitch which is up to national standard. The school's Mayfield Sports Centre, comprising a state-of-the-art games hall, dance studio, gymnasium and fitness suite, is adjacent to the playing fields. The Nursery is also located at Mayfield. In 2013 the School acquired the former Head Post Office Building, located just yards from the city centre campus, and has recently launched one of the most ambitious capital campaigns ever embarked upon by a UK independent school in order to realise its vision of transforming the landmark building into a flagship multimillion pound centre of excellence for performing and visual arts.

Curriculum. The Junior School follows a wide-ranging primary curriculum. Subject specialists are employed in PE, ICT, Music, Science, Modern Languages, Art, Drama and Health and Food Technology.

In the Senior School, after two years of a general curriculum, some specialisation takes place with pupils currently being prepared for the Scottish Qualifications Authority examinations at National 5, Higher and Advanced Higher which lead directly to university entrance. Results in public examinations are amongst the best in Scotland, with pupils regularly achieving the top marks nationally in individual subjects, and 90–95% of leavers enrolling at universities in the UK or abroad.

Co-Curricular Activities. Almost 100 co-curricular activities are offered. Sports teams compete at the highest levels and each year a number of pupils represent their country in a wide range of sports. Music plays an important part in the life of the school, with a large number of orchestras, bands, choirs and musical ensembles to choose from. Special tuition is provided in a wide variety of instruments.

There is a flourishing contingent of the Combined Cadet Force including a pipe band. Drama, Public Speaking and Debating, Chess and The Duke of Edinburgh's Award Scheme are examples of the wide variety of activities available.

Charitable status. The Corporation of the High School of Dundee is a Registered Charity, number SC011522. The school is a charity to provide quality education for boys and girls.

The Board of Directors comprises:

Chairman, 2 ex officiis Directors, viz, The Lord Dean of Guild and The Parish Minister of Dundee. The Guildry of Dundee, the Nine Trades of Dundee, the Old Boys' Club and the Old Girls' Club and the Parents' Association each elect one Director. Six Directors are elected by Friends of the High School and up to 6 co-opted by the Board.

School Staff:

Rector: Dr J D Halliday, BA Hons, PhD

Deputy Rectors:
Mrs L A M Hudson, MA
Mrs V A Vannet, MA, Dip Ed, FRGS, FRSGS

Assistant Rector – Junior Years and Nursery: Mrs J Rose, BEd

Bursar: C M Sharp, FCCA

Deputy Heads – Senior School:
Mr D A Brett, BSc
Mr D G Smith, BSc
Mrs S J Watson, MA

Deputy Heads – Junior Years:
Mr R Petrie, BA
Mrs C E Proudfoot, MA, DELL

Director of Development: Mr O A Jackson-Hutt, MA

Director of ICT: Mrs W Wilson, BSc

Junior Years:

Mrs L J Mooney, Dip CE, IE	Miss L Carrie, MA, MPhil
Mrs L Docherty, Dip CE	Mrs K Goldie, BEd
Mrs M A Mordente, BEd	Mrs M R Leburn, MA
Miss M Cardno, MA, CEEd	Miss J Wallace, BEd
Mrs L Smith, BEd	Mrs D Sager, MA
Mrs A Davie, MEd	Mrs F A Trotter, BSc
Mrs C Powrie, BSc	Mrs L Duff, MA
Mrs F S Wilson, BEd	Miss H Brian, BEd
Mrs L Coupar, MA	Mrs G Johnson, BEd
Mrs C Reid, BEd	Mr N Joss, MA
Mrs S Fish, BEd	Miss R E Stewart, BEd
Miss K A Reith, MEd, DELL	Mrs C E Proudfoot, MA, DELL
	Mr R Petrie, BA

Nursery:
Manager: Mrs S C Tosh, MA

Mrs L C Yule, BA	Miss C Cosgrove
Mrs D M Irving, BA	Miss N V Whyte
Miss A A Balfour	Mrs K Roberts

Senior School:
* Head of Department

English:	*History and Modern Studies*:
*Ms J V Cortazzi, BA, MA, MEd	*Mr G Fyall, BA, Dip Ed
Mrs D M MacDonald, MA	Miss K McKie, MA
Mrs D E Keogh, MA	Miss L Hegan, MA
Mrs M Ovenstone-Jones, MA	Mrs L A Hudson, MA
Miss E Whatley-Marshall, MA	Mr C Melia, MA
Mr D P Campbell, MA	Mr R W Welsh, MA

Drama and Media Studies:
*Mrs L M Drummond, Dip Drama
Miss L E Ashton, BA

Geography:
*Miss J L Stewart, BSc
Mr C R McAdam, MA
Mrs S B Williams, MA
Mrs V A Vannet, MA, Dip Ed, FRGS, FRSGS
Mrs R Lloyd, MA, MSc
Mrs S J Watson, MA

Philosophy and Religion:
*Mr D J Goodey, BA, MA
A W Cummins, BD, Dip Min

Business Education:
*Mrs C A Laird-Portch, BA
Mr N S Higgins, BSc

Classics:
*Mr E Faulkes, BA
Mrs C Meeuwsen-Findlater, MA

Modern Languages:
*Mr N A MacKinnon, MA
Mrs I M McGrath, MA
Mrs J Brown, BA
Ms A Aguero, BA, BEd
Mr F M McAvinue, MA, MSc
Dr J D Halliday, BA, PhD
Mr J P Nolan, MA
Mrs D M Wedderburn, MA
Mrs Y Murdoch, MSc
Mrs H A Yellowley, BA

Mathematics:
*Mr G A Mordente, BSc
Mr A G Blackburn, BSc
Mr R C Middleton, BSc
Miss D MacDonald, BSc
Mrs L A Craig, BSc
Dr F Spiezia, MSc, PhD
Mrs E V Collins-Mcintyre, MMathPhys

Chemistry:
*Mrs R J Broom, BSc
Mr D A Brett, BSc
Mr A S Downie, BSc
Dr P Taylor, PhD, BSc, MRSC, CChem
Dr E R T Robinson, MChem, PhD

Biology:
*Dr E Duncanson, BSc, PhD
Dr M W Fotheringham, MA, PhD
Mr G M S Rodger, BSc
Mr R H Bunting, BSc

Physics:
*Mr J Darby, BSc
Dr D G Brown, BSc, PhD
Dr P Taylor, PhD, BSc, MRSC, CChem
Dr G MacKay, BSc, MSc, PhD

Technology:
*Mr F Walker, BSc
Mr D F Preston, MEd, BEd

Computing:
*Mr S McBride, BSc
Mr D G Smith, BSc
Mr A N Wilson, BA

Art and Design:
*Mr A Kerr, BA
Mrs M Angus, BA
Mrs A Ross, BDes

Miss J Cura, MDes

Music:
*Dr L S Steuart Fothringham, MA, PhD, FRCO
Mr D G Love, Dip MusEd, DRSAMD
Ms G Simpson, Dip Mus, ALCM
Mr S Armstrong, DRSAMD
Mrs S Sneddon, LTCL, ALCM
Miss A Evans, BA, LTCL
Ms S Morgan, BMus
Mrs J Petrie, BA, CPGS
Mrs E M J Stevenson, MA
Mrs S Colgan, BEd, LRAM
Mr D W S Wilton, BA

Learning Skills:
*Mrs P A Maxwell, BEd, DPSE, Cert SpLD
Mrs J M Downie, MA, Cert SpLD
Mrs J Chalmers, DPE SIQ
Mrs L Duff, MA
Mrs P M Spowart, BEd
Mrs C McDonald, BEd

Physical Education:
*Mr E D Jack, BEd
Mrs P M Spowart, BEd
Mr G R E Merry, BSc
Mr W Nicol
Mrs S McKenzie, BEd
Miss J McMullen, BSc
Mr I Strachan
Mr C K Allan, BSc
Mrs L S L Baxter, BEd
Ms L Clement, BEd (*Head of Hockey*)
Mr P J Godman (*Head of Rugby*)
Mr C D O'Donnell, BSc

Home Economics:
*Mrs L J Ross, MA
Mrs O Anderson, BSc

Library:
*Miss I McFarlane, MA, MSc
Mrs J S Hutton, MA
Miss E A Charlett

Guidance:
Mrs S J Watson, MA (*Deputy Head with responsibility for Guidance*)

Principal Teachers:
Mr R W Welsh, MA
Mrs P M Spowart, BEd
Mrs J Brown, BA
Mr C R McAdam, MA

Assistant Principal Teachers:
Mr C K Allan, BSc
Mrs L S L Baxter, BEd
Mr A S Downie, BSc
Mrs S B Williams, MA

Head of Careers:
Mr G M S Rodger, BSc

Outdoor Activities Coordinator:
Mr G M Ross, BA

Head of Academic Administration:
Mrs I M McGrath, MA

Durham School

Quarryheads Lane, Durham City, County Durham DH1 4SZ

Tel: 0191 386 4783
Fax: 0191 383 1025
email: enquiries@durhamschool.co.uk
website: www.durhamschool.co.uk
Twitter: @dunelmia
Facebook: /DurhamSchool1414

Motto: Floreat Dunelmia – Let Durham Flourish

Durham School is one of the oldest schools in England. It probably has a continuous history from Saxon times and has always been closely associated with the Diocese of Durham. As the Bishop's School it was re-organised and endowed by Cardinal Langley in 1414 and was re-founded in 1541 by Henry VIII as a Lay Foundation under the control of the Dean and Chapter of Durham. In 1995 it left the Cathedral Foundation to become a separate body. The school is now fully co-educational 3–18, incorporating Bow, Durham School (3–11). 2014 marked 600 years of providing outstanding education.

Location. The School is magnificently situated above the steep banks of the River Wear, overlooked by the west towers of Durham Cathedral on the opposite bank, and has occupied its present site since 1844. The School is physically compact – all the buildings are within 5 minutes' walk of each other; the playing fields and the river are adjacent. The School still has connections with Durham Cathedral and all pupils attend Chapel on a regular basis and the cathedral once a term.

Aims. While pursuing the highest academic standards, the School has an intellectual range which includes both prospective Oxford or Cambridge entrants and pupils who will succeed at A Level with the careful teaching and support the School provides. The School's main objective is to bring out the best in every pupil. Everyone is expected to contribute fully to the life of the School and thus to develop all their talents to the full. The School provides the care, the teaching and the facilities to do this in happy and attractive surroundings.

Size. Numbers are relatively small, around 410, with an excellent staffing ratio. The Preparatory School (age 3–11) currently caters for a further 150 day girls and boys.

The House System. The House system is one of the great strengths of the School, enabling pastoral care of the highest order. There are 5 Houses at the Senior School: three for boys (School House, Poole House and Caffinites House) and two for girls (Pimlico House and MacLeod House). Junior House staff look after the interests of Years 7 and 8 and in the boys' Houses Assistant/Deputy Housemasters are in charge of Years 9, 10 and 11. The School offers full, weekly or occasional boarding and has some 120 boarders (girls and boys). Day pupils enjoy all the benefits of a "boarding style" education during the day (including breakfast and supper, included in the fee), the same leisure facilities as the boarders and space for private study.

Admission. At the Prep School, admission is possible at any age and entry is based on an interview with the Headmistress and (if appropriate) an assessment test. Entry at age 11 is by way of the Durham School 11+ Entrance Examination. Pupils joining at age 13 sit the School's 13+ Entrance Examination. It is also possible to join in the Sixth Form. Such admission is by interview, testimonial and GCSE results. Entrance and Scholarship examinations and interviews generally take place in late January/early February, although Sixth Form scholarships take place in December (see scholarships below). A prospectus with full details can be obtained on application to the Admissions Office.

Academic. Academic courses are followed to GCSE, AS and A2 Levels. A broad programme is pursued during the years up to GCSE and there is a wide choice and flexible programme for the Sixth Form. There is a fully developed Careers Advisory Service as well as a dedicated EPQ coordinator and Elite-Course coordinator.

Extra-Curricular Activities. A very wide and growing variety of musical, dramatic, sporting and other activities is available. Sports on offer include rugby, hockey, rowing, cricket, netball, rounders, squash, swimming, athletics, cross-country, tennis and water polo. The School has an all-weather sports pitch. Various types of Adventure Training are pursued through the Combined Cadet Force (CCF) and pupils can take part in world expeditions and the Duke of Edinburgh's Award scheme. The Durham School Boat Club is proudly the 3rd oldest Boat Club in the world and the School is also the 5th oldest Rugby Club in the world.

Scholarships and Bursaries. A range of prestigious Academic, Drama, Music, Art, Design and Technology and Sports Scholarships is available at 11+, 13+ and 16+ entry. The King's Scholarship award can be awarded to top performing candidates at 11+ and 13+ entry and the Burkitt Scholarship is awarded at 16+. The Peter Lee Scholarship for applicants of Chinese origin is available for academic entry to the Sixth Form.

Financial support in the form of means-tested Bursaries is available at all ages where appropriate and bursaries can be held alongside academic and non-academic awards. Langley Foundation Bursaries are available. These are means-tested awards which can be up to 100% of the school fee.

Music Scholarships are available at 11+, 13+ and 16+ entry. At least one scholarship is available at each age group in each of the following categories: strings, brass, woodwind, piano. A Sixth Form organ scholarship is available annually. All holders of Music Awards receive some free music tuition.

Drama, Sports, Art and DT Scholarships are also available at 11+, 13+ and 16+ entry.

Fee concessions are available for brothers and sisters and children of clergy and the Armed Forces (in addition to the CEA Boarding allowance).

Fees per term (2016–2017). Day Pupils: Nursery £1,750; Reception & Years 1–2 £2,857; Years 3–6 £3,607; Years 7–8 £4,662; Years 9–13 £5,493. Weekly Boarders: £6,931 (Years 7–8), £8,289 (Years 9–13). Full Boarders: £7,981 (Years 7–8), £9,289 (Years 9–13). Overseas Full Boarders: £8,662 (Years 7–8), £9,990 (Years 9–13). The overseas fee includes a Saturday Language Activity Programme and EAL teaching as required. Extras are kept to a minimum.

Bow, Durham School is Durham School's Preparatory School and caters for around 150 girls and boys from age 3–11. It is situated in its own beautiful grounds half a mile away from the Senior School and makes full use of the Senior School facilities. It has been situated on its present site, half a mile from the Senior School and overlooking the Cathedral, since 1888. Bow has its own extensive facilities including a fully-equipped science laboratory, IT suite, sports hall and library. Pupils also benefit from all the excellent facilities at the senior site, such as the swimming pool, all-weather sports pitch, the chapel and the theatre.

Bow has a fine record of academic achievement over the years and results in externally-marked examinations, such as the Key Stage I and 2 tests, are regularly impressive. The overwhelming majority of pupils move into the Senior School at the age of 11 at which point a range of prestigious awards are available. A high pupil-teacher ratio is maintained and small classes are considered vital as staff seek to ensure that each child fulfils his or her academic potential.

Bow has an outstanding tradition in competitive sport, many former pupils having represented their country. A wide range of sports is on offer to all pupils. Music and drama form an integral part of life at Bow, with an active choir, ceilidh band and fiddle group performing regularly. There are three drama productions each year. Pupils are encouraged to take part in these productions whether it is on the stage or behind the scenes. Bow offers a wide range of extra-curricular activities which are seen as a vital ingredient in the daily diet of every Bow pupil. In addition further activities and hobbies are available as voluntary after-school clubs.

Charitable status. Durham School is a Registered Charity, number 1023407. It exists to provide a high quality education for boys and girls.

Governing Body:
Mr A MacConachie, OBE, DL, FRSA (*Chairman*)
Mrs M Coates
Miss G Kerr
Mr A Martell
Prof S Hackett
Mrs S Langridge
Canon D Kennedy
Mr R Ribchester
Mr N Turner
Mrs J Cowie
Mr G Hodgson
Miss J Kirkley
Mr R Salkeld (*President of the Old Dunelmian Society*)

Clerk to the Governors: Mrs S Spence

Headmaster: Mr K J McLaughlin, MA, PGCE

Deputy Head: Mr J M Webb, MA, PGCE
Deputy Head (Pastoral): Dr J M Burns, BA, PhD
Bursar: Mrs D J Leigh, BA, FCA
Senior Master, Head of Boarding: Dr M P Alderson, BA, MA, PhD
Head of Bow, Durham School: Mrs S Harrod, BA, QTS
Director of Sixth Form Studies: Mr P C Gerrard, BEd
Director of Operations: Mr N Millen, OBE
Director of Co-Curriculum & Pimlico Housemistress: Mrs K L Rochester, BA
Director of Admissions and Marketing: Mrs J Dinning, LLB
Director of Development: Mr A Beales, MSci, MInstF Dip
Headmaster's PA: Mrs S Spence

Heads of Department – Senior School:
Art and DT: Mr M C T Baldwin, BA, PGCE
Biology: Mr M F Burke, BSc, PGCE
Boys' Games: Mr M Bedworth, BA
Chemistry: Mrs T Moore, BSc, MChem
Classics: Mr C Hope, BA, MA, MPhil
Co-Curriculum: Mrs K L Rochester, BA
Drama: Miss A Parkin, BA
Economics and Business Studies: Mr O J Hughes, BA
EAL: Mrs C Pinan, BA
English: Mrs F Swan, BA, MA, PGCE
Geography: Dr C Scott-Warburton, BSc, PhD
Girls' Games: Mrs K E Dougall, BA, QTS
History: Mr D Tyreman, BA, MA, PGCE
ICT: Mr A McMillan, BSc
Learning Support: Mrs J Wood, BA
Mathematics: Mr T Middleton, BSc
Modern Languages: Mrs K Wilkinson, BA

Music: Mr R A Muttitt, BMus, MA, ARCO
PE and Games: Mr P C Gerrard, BEd
Physics: Mr A Smith, BSc
Politics: Mr S McNair, BA, MSc
Psychology: Mr B Brownlee, BA
Religious Studies, PSHE and General Studies: Revd S
  McMurtary, MA
Director of Sport: Mr M Bedworth, BA

Eastbourne College

Old Wish Road, Eastbourne, East Sussex BN21 4JX

Tel: Headmaster: 01323 452320
          Bursar: 01323 452300
email: reception@eastbourne-college.co.uk
website: www.eastbourne-college.co.uk
Twitter: @EBCollegeLife
Facebook: /EastbourneCollege
LinkedIn: /eastbourne-college

Founded 1867; Incorporated 1911.

Situation. The College is situated 400 metres from the sea in the prime residential part of the town of Eastbourne, adjacent to the national Tennis Centre at Devonshire Park, the Congress Theatre, and at the heart of the cultural quarter of the town. There is easy access to a wide range of cultural opportunities. The train to Gatwick Airport and London Victoria is under ten minutes walking distance; it is 1½ hours travel to London. The College links closely with the local community in a variety of ways including assisting people through its extensive S@S (Service at School) programme. There are a number of successful partnership schemes with local schools in the maintained sector. We also have a partnership with Glyndebourne and host rehearsals, auditions, masterclasses and performances.

Organisation and Pastoral Care. The College is a medium-sized boarding and day community where the ethos is of full boarding education. The College is co-educational with a ratio of girls to boys of 41:59. In 2016–2017 there are 639 pupils, of whom nearly a half are full boarders. There are five boarding houses, three of which are for boys (Gonville, Pennell and Wargrave) and two are for girls (Nugent and School). There are six day houses, three of which are for boys (Craig, Powell and Reeves) and three are for girls (Arnold, Blackwater and Watt). Day and boarding houses have similar facilities and are run on similar lines with resident house staff and full tutorial teams. All day pupils can take supper at school and do prep in houses. School buses leave at two different times in the evening and pupils choose which time best suits their programme for the day. There is great commitment from staff and pupils in all areas and there is strong system of pastoral care.

Curriculum. Pupils study the full range of subjects in their first year which includes the opportunity to study both Latin and Classical Greek along with a second or even third modern language. For GCSE, pupils study biology, chemistry, English, a modern foreign language, mathematics and physics, as well as four other subjects from a choice of 16. In September 2016, the College introduced a bespoke Sixth Form curriculum. In addition to its academic core of studying three A Level subjects, a programme of individually-tailored, on-timetable development and support is offered. Pupils will be able to select a programme to meet their needs and aspirations. Opportunities include dedicated scholarship activity, Extended Project Qualification and leadership courses. ICT is central to the teaching and learning experience and the College is networked with its own Intranet.

Sport. A wide variety of sports is offered: major sports are rugby, hockey and cricket for boys; and hockey, netball and tennis for girls. Athletics, basketball, equestrian (show jumping), fencing, fives, football, golf, rowing, sailing, squash and swimming all have fixtures as well. All games pitches are within a short walking distance including two Astroturf hockey pitches, seven rugby pitches, four highly maintained cricket squares, four netball courts and 28 tennis courts in the summer including professional quality grass courts at Devonshire LTC. Current building development will see a new sports hall and six-lane swimming pool plus squash courts, gym and dance studio, due for completion in 2018. Most major sports enjoy international tours at regular intervals (for example, cricket to Dubai and Nepal 2016, girls hockey to Hong Kong, Singapore and Malaysia in 2015, and rugby to South Africa in 2014). Sport is offered to all pupils; almost the whole College is involved in fixtures. There are also current and former pupils achieving county, regional and national recognition. In September 2015 the College was a team base for South Africa during the Rugby World Cup.

Religion. The College is a Church of England registered school with an Anglican Chapel and Chaplain. All pupils experience Christian worship at least once a week. There is a long choral tradition and the Chapel Choir continues to contribute to the worshipping life of the community. Religious studies is compulsory in Year 9, with many pupils opting for the subject at GCSE and A Level.

Developments. All boarding and day houses continue to be refurbished on a rolling programme. The Birley Centre, a whole-school performing arts facility that includes a new music school, was opened in September 2011 and is much in demand from within the school and from outside groups including Ballet Rambert and Culture Shift. College pupils and those from other schools reap the benefits of collaborations with such organisations. A new day-girl house (Arnold) opened September 2014. The College is currently working towards a game-changing development to be completed in celebration of the 150th anniversary of its founding which falls in 2017. Well over an acre of land is being transformed with buildings over three and four floors comprising a new dining hall, café and function suites, 31 state-of-the-art classrooms, a new pavilion and conference facilities, new squash courts, and a six-lane swimming pool and sports hall.

Activities. A wide variety of activities are undertaken as part of the junior school programme and numerous and diverse clubs and societies flourish throughout the school. All pupils are encouraged to do something well and standards in art, drama, dance and music are all high. The Birley Centre (opened in September 2011) provides state-of-the-art facilities for the performing arts. The school has three other theatres: Big School Theatre, the Le Brocq Studio and the Dell Theatre for outdoor productions. The CCF, Duke of Edinburgh's Award Scheme and S@S (Service at School) all offer opportunity for leadership, initiative testing and service to the community. There are regular College expeditions abroad while a wide range of other outdoor activities thrive on the Sussex "Sunshine Coast".

Admission. Boys and girls are generally admitted between the ages of 13 and 14 years in Year 9 or for the Sixth Form in Year 12 after GCSE examinations. A prospectus and application form may be obtained from the Admissions Officer. The website contains more information and parents and prospective pupils who wish to visit the school are welcomed. Early registration for a place is recommended, preferably a year in advance; a registration fee (£75) is charged and places are confirmed with a guaranteed place deposit (£750 for UK; £12,000 for overseas) within a year of entry. All pupils start in September, although exceptional cases are occasionally considered at other times.

Scholarships and Bursaries. At 13+, academic, art, drama, music and sports scholarships are offered. In line with most top independent schools, the great majority of awards given at the College are between 5% and 20% of the day or boarding fees but more may be offered in exceptional circumstances (up to a maximum of 50%). Applicants must be under 14 on 1 September in the year they are due to enter the College. At 16+, academic scholarships (including the Scoresby-Jackson Science Award and the Bernard Drake Award), art, drama, design and technology, music, and sports scholarships are offered to pupils who join the school in Year 12 after GCSEs. A 10% boarding discount is available to HM Forces and Diplomatic Service families.

Bursaries are awarded in appropriate circumstances. All are means tested according to the Charity Commission criteria.

Entry forms for scholarships can be obtained from The Registrar.

Fees per term (2016–2017). Boarding: £10,875 (Years 9–11), £11,000 (Sixth Form); Day: £7,130 (Years 9–11), £7,250 (Sixth Form). An additional supplement for overseas pupils of £155 per term applies. Fees include meals and most extras.

Preparatory School. The charitable bodies governing Eastbourne College and the independent prep school, St Andrew's, amalgamated in February 2010 to become one charity. Collaboration between the two schools had always been extremely close but, until then, there had been no formal financial or governance links between them. This was a change of governance and not of the school. The schools continue to operate independently and St Andrew's prepares boys and girls for a variety of schools including the College.

The **Eastbournian Society** brings together all those with a College connection: parents of current and former pupils, current and former staff, Old Eastbournians, friends, neighbours and local businesses. In particular, strong links are maintained with former pupils who offer careers assistance to current pupils (there is a convention every year to support the careers and higher education programme). The Society provides a series of social events and career and business networking opportunities. It comprises also the College's fundraising activity, providing funds for bursaries and new developments.

The **Devonshire Society** (legacy club) meets annually.

Charitable status. Eastbourne College Incorporated is a Registered Charity, number 307071. It exists for the purpose of educating children.

Board of Governors:
President: His Grace The Duke of Devonshire, KCVO, CBE, DL

Vice-Presidents:
The Bishop of London
The Earl of Burlington
¶General The Lord Richards of Herstmonceux, GCB, CBE, DSO, DL
¶Mr D Winn, OBE, MInstM

Members:
¶ *Former Pupil*

¶Mr M T Barford, MA Cantab, FCA
¶Mr P A J Broadley, MA Oxon, MSc, FCA (*Vice-Chairman*)
Mrs A C Coxen, LLB
Dr C R Darley, MD, FRCP
¶Mr R V Davidson-Houston, BA
Mr C M Davies, FRICS, ACIArb
Mrs N L Eckert, BA
¶Mrs V J Henley, BA
¶Mrs C P Locher
Mr G Marsh, MA Oxon
¶Dr R A McNeilly, MBBS, DCH, MRCGP, DOccMed, MBA
¶Mr D L Meek, LLB, FCA
¶General Sir Kevin O'Donoghue, KCB, CBE (*Chairman*)

Mrs M J Richards
Mr T S Richardson, FRICS
Mr A M Robinson, BA, ACA
¶Mr J H Ryley, BA, AMP
¶Dr A M Spencer, BA, PhD
Mrs H J Toole, MBA
¶Mr J P Watmough, LLB

In attendance:
Mr G Ferguson, BSc
Mr G E B Jones, BA, MEd
Mr T N M Lawson, MA Oxon
Mr C W Symes, BSc, MEd, MCGI

Bursar and Clerk to the Board of Governors: Mrs C Meade, MA Cantab

Senior Management Team:

Headmaster: Mr T N M Lawson, MA Oxon

Deputy Head: Mr C W Symes, BSc, MEd, MCGI
Bursar to the Eastbourne College Charity: Mrs C Meade, MA
Assistant Head (Curriculum): Mr J M Gilbert, BSc, MBA, MRSC
Assistant Head (Co-curricular): Mr A T Lamb, BA, DipEd, DL
Assistant Head (Teaching and Learning): Mr D J Ruskin, BA
Assistant Head (Pastoral): Mrs G E Taylor-Hall, BA
Registrar: Mr L Chu, BA
Marketing and Communications Director to the Eastbourne College Charity: Mrs J S B Lowden, BA
Eastbournian Society Director: Mr D A Stewart

* *Head of Department*
† *Housemaster/mistress*
§ *Part-time*
¶ *Former Pupil*

Art:
*Mrs J L A Harriott, BA
Miss K M Hobden, MA
¶§Ms J Lathbury, DipFA
Mrs S A Martin, BA
Miss I Pocock, BA
(*Photography*)

Classics:
*Mr P J Canning, MA, MTeach
Mr T L Cowper, BA
¶Miss J H Howell, BA
†Mr H B Jourdain, BA
Miss K L Morton, BA
¶†Mr I P Sands, MA

Dance:
Dr J R M Gabelman, MA, PhD
§Miss K A H Reid, ISTD, LicDip

Design and Technology:
*Mr M J Clover, BA, PGCertArch
Mr N J Clark, BA
Mr S J Norris, BEd
Mr W L Trinder, BEd, EITB

Drama:
*Mr T W Marriott, BA
Mrs A F Marriott, BA, MA Ed
Mrs L A Salway, BA, MA

Economics / Business:
*Mr G R Newlyn-Bowmer, BA
¶Mr J M Bathard-Smith, MA
Mr T J Holgate, BA
Mr M J McVeigh, BSc
Mr M J Pringle, BA

English:
*Mr C A Davies, BA
§Mrs L J Ablewhite, BA
§¶Mrs J E Bathard-Smith, BA, MA
Dr D P Gabelman, BA, MA, PhD (*Deputy HoD Lang*)
§Mrs L J Jourdain, BA
Mr P H Lowden, MA
†Mrs L J C Mackenzia, BA
Mr O K Marlow, MA
Miss P M H Squire, BA (*Deputy HoD Lit*)
Mr S P Young, BA

English as an Additional Language:
§*Miss K Briedenhann, BSecEd Sci, CELTA
§Mrs G L Williams, BA, RSA Dip TEFL

Geography:
*Mr W M Longden, BA
†Mr R K Hart, BA

†Mr R W Hill, HND
Mr A T Lamb, BA, DipEd, DL
Mr S Mason, BSc
§Mrs L Price, BSc
Mr C W Symes, BSc, MEd, MCGI
Mr A O Wingfield Digby, BA, MA

Government and Politics:
*Mr R H Bunce, MA

History:
*Mr S A Gent, MA
Mr R H Bunce MA
Revd C K Macdonald, BA
†Mr J C Miller, MA
Mr T J Spiers, BA

Information and Communication Technology:
*Mr I R Shakespeare, BSc
Mrs M A Ambler, BSc

Learning Support:
*Mr A J Spraggon, BA
Mrs E D Harter, BSc, MPhil
§Dr E B Miller, MBBS
§Mrs H J Williams, BA, CELTA

Life and Learning Skills:
*Mr E V Protin, MA

Mathematics:
*Mr J R Wooldridge, MA
¶Mr S E Beal, BA (*Deputy HoD*)
Mr O L Dennis, MA, LRAM, ARAM
§Ms C E Hewson, BSc, MSc
¶§Mr L G Karunanayake, MA
Miss J K Lusty, BSc
Mrs K F MacGregor, MA, MSc, MBA
Mrs E M Sheridan, BSc
†Mrs J C Wood, MA

Modern Languages:
*Mr E V Protin, MA
Mrs M C Tripp, BA, CMIL, DipTrans IoL (*Deputy HoD*)
§Miss M-M Bourda, BA
†Miss V E Burford, MA
Mr L Chu, BA
Mrs A-L Davies, MA
†Mrs M J De La Torre, BA
§Ms A G Del Angel, BA, MA

Visiting Music Staff:
Mrs A Boothroyd, MA, ARCM (*Vocal Studies*)
Miss S Carter, GMus (*Flute*)
Miss M M Davis, BA, Dip RCM (**Strings*)
Miss R K Dines, ARAM, MMus, BMus, LRAM, ARCM (*Piano*)
Mr P Edwards, MMus, GRSM (**Woodwind*)
Mr M D Fields, AGSM, LRAM (*Guitar*)
Mr D Fuller, BMus, LGSMD (*Horn*)

§Mrs R Entwisle, MA
§Mrs H R Rünger-Field, BA
Mr D J Ruskin, BA
§Mr J Thornley, BA
Mrs G A Webb, BA
Mrs E M Wingfield Digby, BA

Music:
*Mr D K Jordan, MA
Mr A C Eadon, BA, LRAM, ARCO, FASC, FGMS
Mr T J G Gilbert, BA
Mr B M Holmes, BA, PGDipRCM

Physical Education:
§*Mrs J M Simmonds, BA
Mr M T Harrison, BSc
¶§Mrs J M Kirtley, BA
Mrs G E Taylor-Hall, BA
Mr O M Torri, BA, MBA
Mrs C Whiddett-Adams, BA

Religious Studies and Philosophy:
*Mr A P Wood, BA, MA, MSc
Miss C M Ball, BA, MA
Revd D J Peat, BA, MA (*Chaplain*)

Textiles:
*Ms Z B Cosgrove, BA, MA, LTI
†Ms A Young, MA

Biology:
*Mr D J Beer, BSc
Mrs R N Cooke, BSc
Mr C C Corfield, BSc
¶Mr P J Fellows, MBioMedSc

Chemistry:
*¶Mr D C Miller, BSc, MRSC, CChem
Mr J M Gilbert, BSc, MRSC, CChem
Revd D P Ibbotson, BSc
Miss H L Simmons, BA
Mr A D Swift, BSc

Physics:
*Mrs E J Livingstone Greer, BSc
Dr A Ball, BSc, PhD
Mr J M Hall, BSc, CPhys, MInstP
§Mr D J Hodkinson, BSc (*also *Science*)
Mr A T Roberts, MSc

Mrs N Fuller, BMus, LGSMD (*Piano*)
Mr K Goddard (*Guitar, Bass Guitar*)
Mr P T Greatorex (*Drums*)
Mr C D Greenwood, BA (*Jazz Piano*)
Mr S A Hollamby, ARCM, Dip RCM (*French Horn, Trumpet, Trombone*)
Mr J L Kotz, BA (*Oboe, Vocal Studies*)
Mrs J H Lakin, GRSM, ARCM, LRAM (*Piano*)
Mr R C Lakin, GRSM, Dip RCM piano, Dip RCM (*Violin, *Keyboard*)
¶Mr A R Mackenzie-Wicks, BA (*Vocal Studies*)
Mrs E J Mansergh, FTCL, LTCL, ARCO (*Piano*)
Miss C S Mumford, Dip ABRSM (*Cello*)
Mr M Simmonds, BMus (*Percussion*)
Ms L P Wigmore, GRSM, ARCM (*Violin*)
Mr T A Williams (*Guitar*)

The Edinburgh Academy

42 Henderson Row, Edinburgh EH3 5BL

Tel:	0131 556 4603
	0131 624 4987 (Admissions)
Fax:	0131 624 4990
email:	enquiries@edinburghacademy.org.uk
	admissions@edinburghacademy.org.uk
website:	www.edinburghacademy.org.uk
Twitter:	@edinburghacad

The Edinburgh Academy is a co-educational day school for pupils aged 2 to 18 with a proud history and outward vision. Founded in 1824 with the aspiration to create a school where excellence could always be achieved, the School motto translates as 'Always Excel'. The Edinburgh Academy is built on strong traditions but is always seeking to innovate.

The Edinburgh Academy consists of a Nursery of 98 children, a Junior School of 390 children and a Senior School of 557. The School's size allows it to cater for the individual needs and ambitions of each child whilst high staff ratios means that at each stage it can tailor the teaching and pastoral care to the needs of each pupil, giving them the best possible chance to develop their unique talents. Through a rounded education Academy pupils enhance their social, emotional and spiritual capacities; equipping them for citizenship in a challenging and changing world. The attributes of an Academy Learner are that they are curious, creative, independent, collaborative and resilient.

Campus. A strength of the Academy is the split campus. This allows for purpose-built facilities and high-quality teaching at each age and stage through which all children can flourish.

Situated in Edinburgh's New Town since 1824, the Senior School is a stunning architectural blend of traditional and modern buildings. The most recent additions have been the splendid Science Centre (inspired by an alumnus of the school, mathematical physicist James Clerk Maxwell) and the Salvesan Performing Arts Centre.

The Junior School, Nursery and Playing Fields are on Arboretum Road: next to the world-renowned Royal Botanic Gardens. The recently opened McTavish Wing at the Junior School has created a new library, learning resource centre and four additional classrooms whilst the purpose-built Nursery provides a bright, functional and fun environment ensuring the best of opportunities for learning through play and experience both inside and out.

Academic. The Academy supports each child on their preferred education path and gets to know each individual extremely well in helping them to reach their personal goals and achieve to the best of their ability. The pre-14 curriculum offers flexibility; giving a very good grounding in basic skills whilst allowing pupils to progress through developing the critical higher order skills inherent in the best parts of 'A Curriculum for Excellence'. Older Senior School pupils present for exams in a wide range of subjects at National 5, Higher and Advanced Higher.

In keeping with the stated vision of producing children who are 'Grounded in Scotland, Ready for the World', the school takes pride in the fact that there are Academicals (alumni) around the globe who look back on their Academy education as their first crucial step on the ladder to success.

Class Sizes. Class sizes are kept relatively small to allow teachers to identify and nurture each child's strengths. In the Junior School the aim is to keep class sizes of around 22 children. In the Senior School, no teaching group is larger than 24 pupils, and most are substantially smaller.

Courses of Study. A very wide general curriculum is taught at the Edinburgh Academy between the ages of 2 and 14. Away from the valuable lessons taught by their class teacher, Nursery pupils receive specialist teaching in Science, PE, Modern European Languages and Music. In Junior School this is further complimented by Art and Mandarin (from Primary 5) whilst in Senior School specialist Latin, Drama and Design Technology are introduced. Maths is set from Primary 3 and all subjects are taught by Secondary School specialist teachers from Primary 7 (Geits).

Eight subjects are taken for National 5 (GCSE equivalent): English, Maths, a foreign language and a science must be taken and it is recommended that pupils complete the balance by adding either History or Geography, and one of Art, Music, Drama, PE or a technical subject.

In the final years of the Senior School the emphasis increasingly moves towards preparing young people for higher education and beyond. The penultimate year sees the breadth inherent in Scottish Highers followed by the greater depth of Advanced Highers. In Art and Music a two-year A Level course is offered in the belief that this is better suited to the needs of pupils looking to progress in those specialisms.

Physical Education. All Academy pupils are encouraged to stay active and healthy. Over 25 acres of sports pitches, including four all-weather surfaces, squash, tennis and fives courts and a sports centre, are coupled with top-class coaching to help them enjoy their chosen sports. Pupils can choose from a full range of winter and summer sports and teams represent the School in rugby, hockey, football, cricket, tennis, squash, badminton, fives, athletics, skiing, shooting, golf, shooting, sailing, swimming, cross country running, basketball, netball and dance.

In March of 2015 the Academy opened a brand new state-of-the-art Climbing and Bouldering Facility that is without doubt the best school arena of this type in the country.

Outdoor Education. The Edinburgh Academy has invested significantly in its recently established 'Spirit of Adventure Fund'. As well as the Climbing Wall this has allowed for the recruitment of both a Head of Outdoor Education and an Early Years Outdoor Learning specialist. This example of 'EA Innovation' means that all Academy children from the youngest in the Nursery to those completing their Gold Duke of Edinburgh's Award benefit from the resilience and character most easily developed in the outdoors.

Music, Drama, Art. The Creative Arts are an important part of Edinburgh Academy life and pupils are encouraged to take part from Junior School and beyond. Most pupils learn a musical instrument and are members of the various choirs, orchestras, bands and ensembles. All Junior School pupils take part in an annual drama production whilst the Senior School produces extremely high-quality performances at regular intervals throughout the year.

In Art, a large number of pupils take the A Level and the success rate for being accepted into Art College is very high. A number of students join the Academy each year with their primary objective being to study Fine Art. This is complemented in Design and Technology where there is a fully furnished Jewellery Studio. At the end of each year there is a major exhibition in these subjects where pupils' work is displayed and sold.

Extra-Curricular. The Academy recognises that significant learning takes place outside the formal classroom and believes in a balance between academic and co-curricular activities; offering a wide range of opportunities to participate and represent the Academy in sport, music and a variety of expressive and creative arts.

There is an extremely broad range of co-curricular activities available including Debating, Photography, Computing, Model United Nations, Modern Languages, Jazz, Politics, Scripture Union, Film Club, Bridge, Chess, Eco Group, Sailing, Cross Country, Climbing, Football and many, many more.

Combined Cadet Force and The Duke of Edinburgh's Award. All pupils over the age of 14 must participate in either the CCF (Army, RAF or Pipe Band sections) or The Duke of Edinburgh's Award scheme for a period of three terms after which further participation is voluntary. The CCF sections offer training in field craft, weapons handling, orienteering, drill and first aid and affords young people the opportunity to develop their leadership potential.

Fees per term (2016–2017). Nursery £2,106–£2,748. Junior School P1–P6 £2,636–£3,279. Senior School: £3,555 (Geits), £4,416 (2nds–7ths).

When 3 or more siblings are in attendance at the School (excluding Nursery) at the same time, a reduction of one-third of the tuition fees is made for each sibling after the first two.

The Academy is currently in partnership with Edinburgh City Council regarding Nursery Provision. For further details about the financial package available please contact Accounts on 0131 624 4916.

Scholarships and Bursaries. Means-tested Bursaries of up to 100% of fees are offered to pupils who are most able to benefit from an Edinburgh Academy education; irrespective of financial means. These are generally available to Senior School pupils.

A number of Scholarships (age 11+) are offered to candidates of very high ability either academically or in Art, Music or Sport. Examinations and assessments are held in January.

Admissions. The majority of new pupils join at the beginning of the Autumn Term in late August though some also join during the session. Other than for Nursery, all candidates for admission to the Edinburgh Academy must be assessed by the School and assessment days are held in November (Junior School P2–6) and January (P1 and Senior School). The Academy is always delighted to welcome families outwith this time. Initial enquiries should be made to the Admissions Registrar: Tel: 0131 624 4987; email: admissions@edinburghacademy.org.uk.

Edinburgh Academical Club. There is a strong former pupil community and the Club works hard to remain in contact with former pupils all over the world. They host events each year, both from a social and career perspective, and have established a career mentoring and internship service to help former pupils. Contact: Ms Eve Macdonald, Tel: 0131 624 4958, email: accies@edinburghacademy.org.uk.

Charitable Status. The Edinburgh Academy is a Registered Charity, number SC016999. It exists for the advancement of education and the contribution to the educational life of Scotland in its widest sense.

Court of Directors:

Chairman: M W Gregson, MBA, BSc

Extraordinary Directors:
Lord Cameron of Lochbroom, PC, FRSE
Professor J P Percy, CBE, LLD, CA
J H W Fairweather, MA
S A Mackintosh, MA, LLB, WS

Elected Directors:
B E Beveridge, LLB, Dip LP, NP (*Chair EA Foundation*)
Dr A E Gebbie, MB ChB, FRCOG, FFSRH, DCH
Dr B A Hacking, MA Hons, D Clin Psychol
G T Hartop
Dr A Huntingdon, BA, PhD, FSI
M McNeill, LLB, LLM, Dip LP
P H Miller, BLE, MRICS
C C R Robertson, MA
Sheriff Principal CAL Scott, QC
J F Smith, MA Hons, BSc Hons
V Khurana LLB, Dip LP, MB ChB, DRCOG, JCCC, MRCGP, DCCH
V Skene, MCIPD
P Dollman, BSc Hons
R A Fletcher
D J Knapman, BA, BSc, MPhil

Co-opted Members:
The Rector
The Headteacher of Junior School
The Senior Deputy Rector of the Senior School

Bursar and Clerk to the Court:
G G Cartwright, MA CA

Rector: Mr M G Longmore, MA, FRSA

Junior School Staff:
Head of the Junior School: Mr G A Calder, MA Hons, PGCE, Dip Ed Leadership
Deputy Head of the Junior School: Mrs L Htet Khin, LLB Hons
Deputy Head (Admissions and Early Years): Mrs L Paterson, DCE, INSC

Heads of Departments:
Support for Learning: Mrs P A Macnair, BA, MEd
Middle Years: Mrs B G G Robertson, BEd, DPSE
Upper Years: Mrs C A Petrie, BEd
Music: Mrs L A Russell, BEd Hons

Senior School Staff:
Senior Deputy Rector: Mrs D K Birrell, BSc Hons
Deputy Rector (Director of Studies): Dr R Wightman, BSc, PhD
Deputy Rector (Pastoral and Personnel): Mr M Bryce, BSc
Deputy Rector (Learning and Teaching): Mrs C E Hancox, MA, PGCE,

Head of Sixth Form: Mrs F B Slavin, MA

Heads of Departments:
Art: Mr D L Prosser, BA
Biology: Mr A W MacPherson, BSc, MSc, PhD
Business Studies/Economics: Mr W J Turkington, BA
Careers: Mrs Y D Harley
Chemistry: (*to be appointed*)
Classics: Mr A K Tart, MA
Computing: Mr D G Stewart, BSc
Design & Technology: Miss S M Hennessy, BA, MA
Drama: Miss G D M Henderson, BA
English: Mr J R Meadows, BA
Geography: Dr D J Carr, BSc, PhD
History, Politics and Modern Studies: Mr J Lisher, BA Hons

Mathematics: Mr C A Brookman, BSc, PhD, GRSC, MInstP
Modern Languages: Mr Youssouf Kassime, PGCE Masters
Music: Dr P N Coad, MA, PhD, FRCO (*Director*)
Physical Education: Mr M J de G Allingham, MSc
Curricular PE: Mr M E Appleson, BA
Physics: Mr N Armstrong, MA, CPhys, MInstP
Religious Education: Mr H Jarrold, M Theol
Support for Learning: Mr C Gerrard, BSc Hons

Admissions Registrar: Mrs J Murray Brown
PA to the Rector: Mrs F Bell
PA to the Headteacher: Mrs T Maguire

Elizabeth College

The Grange, St Peter Port, Guernsey, Channel Islands GY1 2PY

Tel:	01481 726544
Fax:	01481 714839
email:	office@elizabethcollege.gg
website:	www.elizabethcollege.gg
Twitter:	@Eliz_Coll

Motto: Semper Eadem

Elizabeth College was founded in 1563 by Queen Elizabeth I in order to provide education for boys seeking ordination in the Church of England. It is one of the original members of HMC and has Direct Grant status. It provides a broad education while maintaining the Christian aspirations of its Foundress. There are approximately 770 pupils in the College, of whom about 270 are in the Junior School. Girls are accepted into the Junior School. The Sixth Form is mixed through a partnership with nearby Ladies' College.

Buildings and Grounds. The Upper School (for pupils over 11 years) is situated in imposing buildings dating from 1829 which stand on a hill overlooking the town and harbour of St Peter Port. The classrooms and laboratories, all of which are equipped with appropriate modern teaching aids, the Hall, Sports Hall and Swimming Pool are accommodated on this site. Improvements in recent years have included a new Refectory, Performing Arts Suite, six new Mathematics classrooms and an additional classroom at the Junior School. There are two large games fields, one of which includes an artificial pitch for hockey. Elizabeth College Junior School comprises Beechwood, a prep school, and Acorn House, a pre-prep and nursery school. The Junior School has its own site some ten minutes' walk from Elizabeth College. It takes boys and girls from 7 to 11 years old. Acorn House accepts boys and girls from 4 to 7 years old and also has a pre-school facility for younger children.

Academic Curriculum. At Key Stage 3, boys follow a broad curriculum which is common to all, covering arts, sciences, creative and practical subjects. Information Technology is timetabled in all three years to develop the skills needed for the demands of GCSE and A Level courses. Opportunity is also afforded to boys to sample both Latin and a second Modern Foreign Language in addition to French. PSHE, RS, PE, Games and Drama are timetabled throughout. In Years 10 and 11 the aim is to produce a high level of achievement and choice at GCSE by offering flexibility wherever possible. Three separate sciences or Core and Additional Science are studied. At least one modern language should be taken, although more are available as options. English Literature is studied within the English teaching groups, but is not compulsory for all. Other GCSE options combine the traditional with the contemporary: Art, Business Studies, Ancient History, Computing, Drama, Graphics or Resistant Materials, History, Latin, Music and PE are currently offered. Alongside the GCSE courses

PSHE and PE continue to be taught. The Sixth Form is run in partnership with The Ladies' College, with interchange of pupils between schools and shared teaching of many groups. The Sixth Form offers a very broad array of subjects across the two schools enabling a wide variety of choices, with subjects ranging from the traditional to the new, including Computing. Tutorial periods enable vocational, careers and pastoral guidance to be available.

Music. There is a lively extra-curricular music programme which includes the College Orchestra, Wind Ensemble and Brass Jazz Band, with numerous small ensembles running alongside these larger groups. There is a variety of choral groups, with the College choir making regular visits to France to sing in Cathedrals and at concerts. Individual instruction is available in instrumental and vocal studies, catering for a wide range of interests including piano, organ and traditional orchestral studies as well as contemporary and jazz styles. The Junior School has its own choirs, orchestra, recorder group and steel pan band. Each summer holiday the College hosts a week-long orchestral course when tuition is provided by eminent professionals to over two hundred and fifty boys and girls drawn from the islands, the UK and other parts of Europe.

Games. The sports fields cover some 20 acres. The Junior School has its own small playing field, and also has access to the facilities of the Upper School. The major College games are Association Football, Hockey and Cricket. Athletics, Badminton, Basketball, Cross-country Running, Fencing, Golf, Rugby Football, Sailing, Shooting, Squash and Swimming also flourish. Physical Education forms a regular part of the curriculum for all boys up to the end of Year 11. Some seniors specialise in Outdoor Pursuits as their Games option under the guidance of a fully qualified expert. Despite the size of the Island, plentiful opposition for sports fixtures is available. The College competes against other Island schools, has a traditional rivalry with Victoria College in Jersey, makes regular tours to the UK mainland and hosts return visits from UK schools.

Combined Cadet Force. This is voluntary and optional from Year 10, and is Tri-Service. Cadets travel regularly to the UK and beyond for proficiency training, camps, courses, qualifications and competitions, as well as adventurous training. Competition shooting forms a major part of the CCF and there is a long and distinguished record at Bisley. The CCF has an important role in providing Guards of Honour for Island ceremonial occasions.

Duke of Edinburgh's Award. Boys are encouraged to participate in this scheme. Both Bronze and Gold Awards are offered as extra-curricular activities. Bronze expedition work takes place locally in the Channel Islands whilst the expedition work necessary for the Gold Award takes place on the UK mainland during the Easter and Summer holidays.

Community Service. This is an alternative option to CCF for pupils in Year 10 and above. Pupils actively contribute to a wide range of service activities including sports leadership in primary schools, subject leadership in junior lessons, the environmental Ruskin group and support of local charities.

Scouts. There is an active Elizabeth College Scout Group, whose headquarters are situated on the College Field. At the Junior School there is a Cub Scout Group.

Clubs and Societies. The College stresses the importance of extra-curricular activity. Among over thirty currently active clubs are those which foster Bell Ringing, Chess, Climbing, Debating, Design Technology, Fencing, Life Saving, Model Railways, Sailing, Shooting, Squash and War Gaming.

Pastoral Care. In the Upper School each year has a Head of Year assisted by four Tutors. Acorn and Beechwood have Form Tutors. All these staff provide pastoral care and academic guidance for their own sections of the College. They are supported by a Chaplain who conducts services in all three schools as well as preparing boys for Confirmation.

Parental Involvement. Parents are strongly encouraged to take an active part in their child's education. There are regular assessments and reports, parents' evenings, pastoral information evenings and parent workshops. Heads of Year keep in regular contact with parents through newsletters and email. A Parent Teaching Learning Group acts as a consultative body enabling exchange of information and ideas. The Heads of Year and pupils' tutors are always available to meet with parents to discuss any concerns.

Admission. The principal ages for admission into the school are 4, 7, 11, 13 and 16, but there are usually vacancies for entry at other ages. Entry is by means of tests and/or interview which are adapted to the age of the applicant. There is a £110 non-refundable registration fee. Applications for entry should be addressed to the Principal.

Scholarships to the College. The Gibson Fleming Trust provides Awards on a means-tested basis for current pupils to support them in their involvement with extra-curricular activities.

Choral and Instrumental Scholarships. The Gibson Fleming Trust provides Choral and Instrumental Scholarships to current pupils. Details of the scholarships may be obtained from the Principal or Director of Music.

Scholarships to the Universities. The College Exhibitions, Scholarships and Prizes include the Queen's Exhibition, the Lord de Sausmarez Exhibition, the Mainguy Scholarship, the Mansell Exhibition and the Mignot Fund.

Travel. There are several flights each day from Southampton (half an hour), Gatwick (about three quarters of an hour) and Stansted (about one hour). There are also regular flights to the West Country and to Midlands and northern airports. There are frequent sailings to and from Portsmouth and Poole, which offer vehicle transportation.

Old Boys. The Honorary Secretary of the Old Elizabethan Association is James Ovenden who may be contacted via www.oea.org.gg.

Fees per term (2016–2017). Acorn House (Pre-Prep): £3,125; Beechwood (Prep): £3,480; Upper School (11–18): £3,585.

Visitor: The Assistant Bishop of Winchester

Directors:
The Very Revd T Barker, Dean of Guernsey (*Chairman*)
J D Perkins
D G Le Marquand
D E Preston
M R Buchanan
Mrs A-M Collivet
K Roberts
M R Thompson
S Falla

Principal: **G J Hartley**, MA Cantab, MSc

Vice-Principal (Academic): R J W James, BA
Vice-Principal (Pastoral): J M Shaw, BA, MA
Assistant Principal (Sixth Form): C R W Cottam, MA, CT ABRSM
Assistant Principal (Pupil Progress and Inspection Compliance): Mrs P E Cross, BA, ARCM

Members of Teaching Staff:

E C Adams, BA	A P Carey, BA, MA
T I Addenbrooke, BEng, MSc, PhD	Mrs E J Chamberlain, BSc, MEd
B E H Aplin, BSc	J J Conner, BSc
Mrs N C Brown, BA	D J Costen, BA
Mrs C S Buchanan, BA	G S Cousens, BA
M A M Buchanan, BA	Mrs G Dallin, BSc
Mrs M Campbell, BA, MA	P G Davis, BSc

R M Davis, BA
T R de Putron, BSc
Miss A C M Demongeot, BA, MA
Mrs J-A Dittmar, BSc
T P Edge, BA, MA
T P Eisenhuth, BPhysEd
M Garnett, BA
A J Good, BSc
Mrs M E Gordon, MA
M N Heaume, BSc
S J Huxtable, MA
D R L Inderwick, BA, MA
Mrs C Keeley, BA
Ms B C Knox, BA, MA
Miss P S Le Poidevin, BA
R G Le Sauvage, BSc
Mrs S Lee, Mgr
Ms E A Loveridge, BA

D R Loweth, MA, MEd
Mrs H M Mauger, BA
R A Morris, BA
S G D Morris, BSc
A R Mulholland, BSc, MA
Mrs K A Norman, BA
Mrs J B Odlin, BSc
S Over, BTech
Ms J M Pendleton, BA
Mrs P J Read, MSci, MA
J R D Rowson, BA
Miss M Schofield, BA
Miss R L Seymour, BSc
Mrs K M Shaw, BA
T C Slann, Dip NEBSS
M A G Stephens, BA
A G Stewart, BSc
Mrs A J Tautscher, BSc
Mrs W I York, BA, MA

Chaplain: The Revd P A Graysmith
Director of Music: Miss E D Willcocks, BMus, MA
Games and Physical Education: D Wray, BEd

Head of the Junior School: J E Walton, BA

Prep:
Deputy Head Pastoral: Mrs E Bott, BEd
Deputy Head Academic: Miss E J Brooker, BSc

Mrs M Brady, BA
Mrs S Crittell, BA
Mrs D Dowding, BA
Mrs D M McLaughlin, BSc
Mrs E Parkes, BEd
Mrs A M Pollard, BEd
Mrs K Reed, BA

Mrs J Ricketts, BA
P Sargent, BA
Mrs B Santi
Mrs N Stevens, BEd
R Sutton, BA
Mrs M Walton, BA
Mrs C Wray, BSc

Pre-Prep:
Deputy Head: Mrs J Atkinson, BEd

Mrs C Bowden, BA
Miss R Curtis, BA
Mrs L Du Port, BEd
Miss C Gillman, BA

Mrs J Hamilton, BA
Mrs E Jones, BA Ed
Mrs L Le Lievre, BA Ed
Miss C Price, BEd

Bursar and Clerk to the Directors: M F Spiller, MSc, BSSc, FCILT

Ellesmere College
A Woodard School

Ellesmere, Shropshire SY12 9AB

Tel: 01691 622321
Fax: 01691 623286
email: hmsecretary@ellesmere.com
website: www.ellesmere.com
Twitter: @ellesmerecoll
Facebook: @Ellesmere-College

Motto: '*Pro Patria Dimicans.*'

Ellesmere College is a fully co-educational school set in the beautiful English countryside. Founded in 1884, the school offers students between the ages of 7 to 18 the chance to achieve success in both their studies and a wide range of activities, including music, art, sport and drama, in a happy, friendly atmosphere. We prepare students for their GCSEs, A Levels and the International Baccalaureate as well as giving them the opportunity to enjoy a full and varied sports and social programme. Standing in its own stunning grounds covering more than 50 hectares, the school is conveniently located near the small, historic town of Ellesmere, and is

less than 100 kilometres from both of England's second major cities, Manchester and Birmingham.

The College Building. The main school building contains three boys' Boarding and Day Houses, as well as a mixed 10–12 junior Boarding and Day House, bachelor and married accommodation for Housemasters and Housemistresses and/or Assistant Housemasters and Housemistresses, the Chapel and the Dining Hall. St Luke's Boarding House completes the main quadrangle. A 13–16 girls' Boarding and Day house has its own wing in the main building and was opened in response to demand in 1996. The girls' Sixth Form Boarding and Day House which accommodates girls in a combination of shared and single study bedrooms and dayrooms was completed in 1986. A Gymnasium, Big School (Assembly Hall) which houses the Schulze Organ, and three subject Departments are also located in the main building. September 2004 saw the opening of the College's new Sports Hall, which adds to facilities that include two other gymnasia and squash courts.

Additional wings contain the Library and Sixth Form Centre. Other subjects are taught in their own Departmental blocks close to the main building, and include Science Laboratories, a Modern Languages Department with a Language Laboratory, an Art School, a Design & Technology Centre, and a Business Studies Department with its own computer suite. A purpose-built Lower School for Years 3–8 was opened in 1999.

The House System. The Lower School (ages 7–13) has a competitive system based on 3 Houses. The Senior School has a competitive system based on 4 Houses all of which are co-educational and combine boarding and day pupils. Separate from the competitive Houses is the residential House system for living arrangements. There are 2 Girls' Houses, catering for age 13–16 and Sixth Form respectively; there are 4 Boys' Houses: two for age 13–16 and two Sixth Form Houses; there is also a Mixed House catering for boarders of ages 10–12.

Curriculum. In the first year in the Senior School a full range of fourteen subjects is studied, including Art, Design and Technology, Computing and Technical Drawing. This curriculum is designed to give all pupils a comprehensive introduction before reducing to a basic eight subjects for GCSE. At GCSE all pupils take English, Mathematics, and either Dual Award Science or the three Sciences studied separately. Other subjects depend on individual aptitude and choice.

In the Sixth Form over 20 different academic subjects are available for study to A Level or IB Diploma to prepare for University Entrance or entry to the Services and the Professions.

Music. The College has a very strong musical tradition. It possesses two of the finest organs in the country, including the internationally renowned St Mary Tyne Dock Schulze Organ. The Chapel Choir has a wide repertoire of Church Music. There is a Big Band, a Choral Society, a Jazz Group and other ensembles, all of which give regular concerts. There are House Music Competitions every year.

An annual programme of Celebrity Concerts brings distinguished musicians to the College.

The Music School is part of the College Arts Centre which provides first-class facilities, including 8 Practice Rooms, a Recording Studio, Teaching Rooms and a Studio Theatre designed for small concerts and seating 220 people.

The department has 2 full-time and 16 part-time teachers.

Arts Centre. This purpose-built complex was opened in 1976 for Drama, Dance, Film, Music and Art Exhibitions. A programme is organised in which international artists in all these fields visit the Centre, which shares its facilities with the local community.

Careers. At all levels pupils are encouraged to seek advice from the College careers masters and mistresses as well as representatives from the Independent Schools

Careers Organisation. The ISCO aptitude tests are available for all pupils in their GCSE level year. A Careers Convention is held each year for pupils in Year 11.

Games and Physical Education. Ellesmere has a long tradition of sporting excellence particularly in rugby and tennis. The sporting excellence is supported by the Rugby Academy programme (3 leavers turned professional in 2008), the Tennis Academy, and the joint College and Community Ellesmere College Titans Swimming Team. The Cricket Academy was launched in 2009 and the Shooting Academy in 2010.

All members of the School are required to participate in a regular programme of games, though particular inclinations and aptitudes are taken fully into consideration. Facilities include a sports hall, a floodlit multi-sports area, a fitness centre, squash courts, a heated indoor swimming pool, indoor and outdoor shooting range, a gymnasium, 6 floodlit all-weather tennis courts, a golf course, rugby pitches, all-weather hockey pitches, cricket squares, and an athletics track. Ellesmere has a long tradition of sporting excellence, particularly in rugby and tennis.

Ellesmere is superbly placed for outdoor pursuits. Easily accessible lakes, rivers and hills provide opportunities to develop talents and interests.

Sailing takes place on Whitemere. The School owns six boats and pupils are allowed to bring their own craft. Canoeing takes place on the Ellesmere canal and on local rivers such as the Dee and the Severn.

All pupils are expected to join one of the following: Outdoor Training Unit; CCF; Social Service. These activities occur on one full afternoon a week, but, in order to extend their activities, twice a year 3 days are set aside when all members of the School participate in 48-hour expeditions. In the Lent Term a single day is devoted to expeditions.

Admission. Boys and girls are admitted at all points of entry into the school. Entrance examinations are held in February for Lower School entry. Scholarships for Prep School candidates are held in May, while others take the Common Entrance Examination in June.

Scholarships and Bursaries. A wide range of Awards recognising a range of talents is available:

Academic: Available at 8+, 9+, 11+, 13+ and 16+ entry worth up to a maximum of 50% fee remission.

All-Rounder: Available at 11+, 13+ and 16+ entry worth up to a maximum of 25% fee remission.

Art: Available at 13+ and 16+ entry worth up to a maximum of 25% fee remission.

Drama: Available at 13+ and 16+ entry worth up to a maximum of 25% fee remission.

Music: Available at 8+, 9+, 11+, 13+ and 16+ entry. Scholarships are worth up to a maximum of 50% fee reduction and free tuition in two instruments. Exhibitions are worth up to a maximum of 25% fee reduction and free tuition in one instrument.

The *Schulze Organ Award* is reserved for Sixth Form candidates and is valued at 50% of fees.

Sports: Available at 13+ and 16+ entry and may be worth up to a maximum of 50% fee remission. (Awards below Sixth Form level are unlikely to exceed 25% fee reduction.)

In cases of need, all awards may be supplemented by means-tested bursaries.

There are reduced fees for children of the Clergy. Foundation and Regional awards are available for children of parents of limited means.

Fees per term (2016–2017). Upper School: Boarders £10,296, Weekly Boarders £7,524, Day £5,826. Lower School: Boarders £8,250, Weekly Boarders £7,317, Day £3,555–£4,086. Fees are inclusive of general School charges.

Music lessons are given at a charge of £267 for ten lessons and individual tuition for dyslexic pupils also incurs an extra cost. A scheme of insurance is in force under which the School Fees may be insured for a small termly premium for any number of years and which enables a pupil to remain at Ellesmere to complete his/her education free of all board and tuition fees, if a parent dies before the pupil's School career is ended. There is also a School Fees Remission Scheme for insurance of fees in cases of absence through illness and of surgical and medical expenses. Arrangement can be made for a single advance payment of fees.

'Old Boys and Girls'. Former pupils of the school normally become members of the Old Ellesmerian Club, which in turn enables them to take part in a number of societies and activities. For further information contact: Nick Pettingale, Director of Development, Ellesmere College, Ellesmere, Shropshire, SY12 9AB.

Charitable status. Ellesmere College is a Registered Charity, number 1103049. It exists to provide education for children.

Founder: The Revd Nathaniel Woodard, DCL, then Dean of Manchester

Visitor: The Rt Revd The Lord Bishop of Lichfield

College Council:

D C Brewitt	C E Lillis
Mrs F M Christie	J A Mathias, FCA
The Reverend Canon B C	A L Morris
Clover	Mrs C S Newbold, BA
Mrs S Connor	Mrs R E Paterson
J S Hopkins	The Reverend M J Rylands
R A K Hoppins	M D T Sampson

Headmaster: B J Wignall, BA, MA, MCMI, FRSA

Deputy Head (Pastoral): Dr R Chatterjee, BSc, MSc, PhD, Cert SpLD

Deputy Head (Academic): Mrs S V Pritt-Roberts, BEd, MEd, NPQH

Head of Sixth Form: P A Wood, MA (*General Studies*)

Head of Middle School: Dr T Gareh BSc, MSc, PhD, CSci, CChem, MRSC

Head of Lower School: Mrs S Owen, BEd

Director of Activities: Mrs D Joynson-Brooke, BEd

Chaplain: The Revd Phillip Gration

Director of Finance: N Haworth, ACMA, BA

Director of Operations: M McCarthy, BSc, DMS

Teachers:
* *Head of Department*
† *Housemaster/mistress*

Ms C Allen, BA (*EAL*)
R Bach BA (*Economics*)
†J J Baggaley, BA
Mrs S J Bogue, BSc
C Baurance, DEUG, LLCE
A Chaloner, BSc
M P Clewlow, BSc
Mrs J Chatterjee, BSc
Dr J K Collins, BSc, PhD (*Biology*)
T Coupe, BMus (*Music*)
J H Cowley, BSc, NPQH (*Mathematics*)
D W Crawford, MA, MSc, MPhil
Miss A C Darrant, BSc (*Physics*)
Mrs H L Davenport, BSc (*Physical Education*)
T Davidson, MA (*English*)
C R Davies, BA
Mrs J M Davies, BA
J Dilks, BA
†Mrs A Done, HD
Mrs J Evans
†Mrs Z Fisher
P J Hayes, MA

Dr R Hansford, BSc
Miss G Heald, BA
Mrs J M Hibbott, BA
Mrs V M Howle, BEd, Cert SpLD, Dip RSA
Mrs M E Hutchings, MA, MA (*Media Studies*)
W J Hutchings, BEd
G Hutchinson, MA
J Haycock, BA
T Hurst, BEng
Mrs D Joynson-Brooke, BEd
Miss E A Killen, BEd
Ms D Lensing, BA
G Macdonald, BSc
R J Macintosh, BSc
Miss J M Manion, BA, NPQH (*Support for Learning*)
†D J Morgan, BSc
Mrs S E Morgan, BEd
Miss K Marshall, BSc
S B Mullock, BA (*Business Studies and Careers*)
A Murphy, BSc
Mrs J R Nicolson, MA
H B Orr, BD (*Religious Studies and Sociology*)
†G Owen, BEd
Mrs L A Paton, BA (*History & Classics*)
Mrs R Paul, BA
Mrs E Phillips, BSc
Mrs S Phillips, MA (*Art and Design Technology*)
R J Purnell, BSc
S Prescott, BA
D M Roberts, BSc, MEd
†I Roberts, BA
S Shakibi, BA (*Computer Science*)
Ms R Schubert, BA (*Director of Drama*)
P E Swainson, BSc (*Chemistry*)
Ms M J Tarrega, MA
Miss M Thomas, MA
Dr I G Tompkins, MA, BD, DPhil (*IB Coordinator*)
J Underhill, MA
Mrs R Waddams, BSc (*Geography*)
S Welti, LTA Club Coach
Mrs C Westwood, BA (*MFL*)
I L Williams, BEd

Registrar: Ms K Randall

School Medical Officer: Dr E A M Greville, MBChB
Sanatorium Sisters:
Mrs M Moore, RGN
Mrs M Haynes, SEN

Eltham College

Grove Park Road, London SE9 4QF

Tel:	020 8857 1455
email:	mail@eltham-college.org.uk
website:	www.elthamcollege.london
Twitter:	@ElthamCollegeUK
Facebook:	@ElthamCollegeOfficial
LinkedIn:	/Old-Elthamians

Eltham College is a thriving independent day school for boys aged 7 to 18, with a co-educational Sixth Form. It is a highly successful and exciting school which aims to provide a broad and balanced education to both boys and girls that will prepare them for the modern world. The College is regularly found amongst the leading academic schools in the country and boasts many county and national players in a range of sports. The co-curricular programme is wide and diverse.

The school has a distinctive character, born out of its Christian heritage, and continues to focus on the care of the individual. Strong pastoral care and a relaxed and unpretentious atmosphere make the school a happy and vibrant place.

There is an ambitious programme of development and expansion as well as a strong emphasis on staff development. Many staff choose to stay; but equally others are prepared and trained for future promotion in leading HMC schools.

History. The College was founded in 1842 as the School for the Sons of Missionaries and it began life as a small boarding school catering for these children whose parents were serving overseas, famously including the Olympic athlete Eric Liddell. The College moved to its present extensive site in Mottingham in 1912, with just under 70 acres of playing fields surrounding an elegant 18th century mansion. The College has developed into a day school primarily for boys and has been admitting girls into the Sixth Form since 1980. Eltham College now numbers 910 students in total, with 240 boys in the associated on-site Junior School and 240 students in the co-educational Sixth Form.

Location. The College is fortunate to occupy a spacious and pleasant site with extensive playing fields in the London Borough of Bromley, adjacent to the boroughs of Royal Greenwich and Lewisham. The College has easy access to the Kent countryside and the M25, which is just 15 minutes away. There are frequent fast trains to London Bridge, Charing Cross and Victoria (15–20 minutes). The majority of students live locally but the catchment area is expanding and students are drawn from Kent, Dulwich, Croydon and Docklands.

Facilities. The College, set in almost 70 acres of land, enjoys superb facilities which have been improved considerably in recent years, including the Gerald Moore Gallery, new Science laboratories, a floodlit all-weather AstroTurf pitch and our extended Dining Hall. The building of a substantial new Sixth Form centre is due to commence this year, along with new Languages and Mathematics centres.

The existing Eric Liddell Sports Centre will be augmented with a further £5 million sports stand, complete with a second weights and fitness suite and physiotherapy facilities that will enable the College and Elthamians to compete in the premier divisions for Rugby and Hockey. The students benefit from an extensive modern and bright library, providing huge amounts of resource which extends online to the virtual library and resource links.

Curriculum. The College has maintained its grammar school ethos and puts academic achievement as its first priority. The curriculum is broad and balanced, incorporating both traditional and modern elements: for example, all students in Year 7 study both Latin and Mandarin. All students study at least one Modern Language to GCSE, and separate Sciences are available to all. Most students take ten GCSEs and three or four A Levels, chosen from a wide range of subjects. Recent examination results placed us amongst the top day schools in the country: at GCSE 97.5% of grades were A* to B and the vast majority of Sixth Formers start with straight A*/A profiles. A Level results are consistently around 85% A* to B. Almost all students get in to their first choice university with over 80% at Russell Group universities and more than 20% of the cohort studying either medicine or courses at Oxford and Cambridge.

Co-Curricular. We are equally proud of our co-curricular activities which provide an impressively wide range of opportunities while ensuring that academic potential is fulfilled. We have an enviable reputation in Sport, Music and Drama: the College has a number of international and Olympic standard sports coaches; the quality and range of Music compares favourably with specialist Music schools; and audiences are frequently treated to spectacular school productions in our purpose-built theatre.

The majority of students participate in the vast amount of clubs and societies available, including (to name but a few), The Duke of Edinburgh's Award, Debating Society, Chess, Japanese Club, Eco-Eltham, Rocket Club and Water Polo. We encourage students to help those less fortunate than them by participating in charity fundraising events and the Lower Sixth Formers take part in our Community Service scheme.

Trips and expeditions are a major feature of life at Eltham College. These range from the traditional UK visits to more ambitious overseas trips, which in recent years have included Norway, Nepal, Tanzania, Italy and China. Language trips and exchanges are encouraged. Sport, Drama and Music tours are frequent occurrences, and have included the USA, Australia and South Africa.

Admission. Students are mainly admitted at the ages of 11, 13 and 16 via our own entrance examination. The College is academically highly selective, with over three applicants for every place. Approximately half our students come from primary schools and half from the preparatory sector, and the College has an unusually wide social mix, thanks, in part, to our generous Bursary scheme, which provides financial assistance for those unable to afford the full fees. In the most deserving cases, remission of up to 100% of fees is available.

Scholarships. It is our aim to provide as much assistance with the fees as we can to attract the brightest and most talented students to the College. Scholarships and Bursaries (financial assistance) are available to all students applying to the Senior School and Sixth Form.

Scholarships of not more than 50% of fees are awarded on Academic performance at 11+, 13+ and 16+. Awards are also made for Music (11+, 13+ and 16+), Sport and Art (11+ and 16+), and Drama (16+ only). The Leverhulme Trust Scholarship is also available for Sixth Form entry.

Bursaries. As befits a school founded for the sons of missionaries and a former Direct Grant School, many students receive financial support to attend. Bursaries are available up to 100% of fees subject to ISBA confidential means test. Community Scholarships (for 11+ boys from the immediate neighbourhood) are assessed on financial need.

Term of Entry. The College normally accepts students only for the beginning of the academic year in September but, if gaps in particular year groups occur, it is willing to interview and test at any point in the year with a view to immediate or subsequent entry.

Junior School. The Grange, a large house on the College estate was converted and extended and now accommodates about 240 day boys in classes of approximately 22. The form rooms are complemented with an Assembly Hall, Science Room, Music Room, and Art, Design and Technology Room. With an emphasis on English and Mathematics, the curriculum, which includes Mandarin as the main Modern Foreign Language along with French in Year 6, provides an excellent foundation.

Excellence is also pursued outside the classroom whether on the sports field, stage or concert hall. In recent years we have had rugby teams with 100% wins, trebles singing at world famous venues and actors earning hosts of awards at local festivals. The Junior School is managed by its own Master who is responsible to the Headmaster.

Admission is at the age of 7, though there may also be an opportunity for boys to enter at 8+, 9+ and 10+ if there are places available. There is no entrance test for boys from Eltham College Junior School wishing to enter into the Senior School. Recommendation for is made on the basis of a boy's performance during their time in the Junior School and on their potential to flourish in the Senior School. Almost all boys therefore progress seamlessly through to Eltham College Senior School. This transition provides an opportunity for 11 years of uninterrupted education in healthy surroundings.

Junior School applications should be made to the Registrar.

Fees per term (2016–2017). Senior School £5,415, Junior School £4,780. Lunch: £262.

Charitable status. Eltham College is a Registered Charity, number 1058438. It exists to provide education for boys and girls.

Governors:

The Governing Body comprises the Chairman and Vice Chair, ten Trust Governors and eight Nominated Governors representing the Baptist Missionary Society, the Council for World Mission, the United Reformed Church, the London Boroughs of Bexley and Bromley, the Parents (two representatives elected by the parental body) and the Staff Common Room (one representative elected by the Teaching Staff).

Chairman of the Board: Mr S Wells, RIBA

Headmaster: Mr G Sanderson, MA Oxon, FRSA

Bursar: Mrs S Roxby
Deputy Head: Mr J Cooper, BSc, MA
Director of Studies: Mr E Wright, MA

Senior School Teaching Staff:

Art:
Ms E Brass, BA, MA
Mrs M Franklin, MA (*Head of Well-being*)
Mrs A C E Richards, BA (*part-time*)

Biology:
Mrs C M Hobbs, BSc
Mrs H C Clough, BSc (*part-time*)
Mr P J Ormanczyk, BSc
Mrs J C Perry, BSc

Business:
Mrs S Potter, BA (*part-time*)

Chemistry:
Dr F Morris, BSc, PhD (*NQT Induction Coordinator*)
Mr J Copley, MSci
Dr J N Hill, BSc
Mrs J C Perry, BSc

Classics:
Miss A Bolland, MA (*Head of Oxbridge*)
Mr B R d'Arcy, MA, GDL, BPTC (*Head of Upper Sixth*)

Computing, ICT and Computer Science:
Mr J P Pringle, BSc (*Curriculum Coordinator*)

Design and Technology:
Mr M E L Gennari, BSc (*Head of Universities and Enrichment*)
Mr D J Boydell, MSc (*Head of EPQ*)
Mr P J Wren, BSc, TEng

Drama:
Mrs K Robinson, BA, MA
Miss A Strong, BA, PGCE
Mr T C Mitchell, BA

Economics:
Mr S G Milne, MA (*Head of Lower Sixth*)
Mr D Connolly, BA
Mrs K Evans, BSc [maternity leave]
Mrs S Potter, BA (*part-time*)

English:
Mr T C Mitchell, BA
Mr N J Amy, MA
Miss H Conway, BA
Miss V K Edgar, BA (*Deputy Head of Lower School*)
Mr J Owen, MA (*Head of Academic Scholarship*)

Geography:
Mr D K Cotterill, BSc
Mr P Angel, MA, BSc, NPQSL
Mr A D Beattie, MA (*part-time*)
Mr J P Chesterton, BSc (*Deputy Head of Middle School*)
Mr J Cooper, BSc, MA (*Deputy Head and Designated Safeguarding Lead*)
Miss K Richard, BSc
Mr J Willatt, BSc (*Assistant Head – Co-curricular*)

Geology:
Mr P Angel, MA, BSc, NPQSL
Miss K Richard, BSc

History:
Mr D R Grinstead, BA (*Head of Chalmers*)
Mr M E R Chesterton, BA (*Head of Moffat*)
Mr J Clark, BA
Mr S Marlow, MA
Mr M P Wearn, BA

Mathematics:
Mrs N Bilsby, BSc, MA (*Senior Tutor – Girls*)
Mr J L Baldwin, BSc (*Master in charge of Cricket, Head of Livingstone and Assistant Head of Maths – Lower School*)
Mrs R E Bevington, BSc
Mr V Broncz, BSc
Mr J P Crowley, BEng
Ms R Gordon, BSc (*Assistant Head – Teaching and Learning*)
Mr L Watts, BSc (*Assistant Head – Head of Middle School*)
Mrs S Wood, BSc (*part-time*)

Modern Languages:
Mr D Boudon, L-ès-L
Mr P G Cheshire, MA (*part-time*)
Mr J Houghton, MA (*Chaplain and Head of Spanish*)
Mr P A Howls, BA (*Head of German*)
Miss M Mateos, BA
Mrs A McCullough, BA
Mr F Meier, MA (*Assistant Head – Head of Lower School*)
Miss L Scarantino, BA (*Head of French*)
Mrs A Senior, L-ès-L (*part-time*)
Ms M Su, BA, MA (*Head of Mandarin Chinese*)

Music:
Mr P Showell, BMus (*Director of Music*)
Mr K A Hughes, BA (*Head of Academic Music*)
Mr N R Miller, BA (*Musician-in-Residence*)
Miss G Reece-Trapp, BA, FRCO

Physics:
Mr A Hindocha, BSc
Mr J P Crowley, BEng
Mr J P Hesketh, BSc, MA
Mr S Whittaker, MSc (*Head of Science*)
Mr E B Wright, MA (*Director of Studies*)

Politics:
Mr S Marlow, MA
Mr J Clark, BA

Psychology:
Ms M M Pokorny, BSc
Mr G E Marshall, MA, MSc

Religious Studies:
Ms E G Haste, BA
Mr P G Cheshire, MA (*part-time*)
Mr G E Marshall, MA, MSc
Revd P Swaffield, BA, MA (*Chaplain*)

Sport:
Mr J L Baldwin, BSc (*Master in charge of Cricket, Head of Livingstone and Assistant Head of Maths – Lower School*)
Mr A Brown, BSc
Mr T Brown, BSc (*Head of Sport Scholarship*)
Mr S D Howard, BSc (*Director of Rugby*)
Mr B King, BSc
Mr D Lespierre, BSc
Mr T Sullivan
Mr A Thomas, BEd (*Activities and Transition Coordinator*)
Mr E T Thorogood, BSc (*Acting Coordinator of Sport*)
Mr M Wilkins (*part-time*)

Learning Support:
Mrs D Rabot, BA

Library:
Mrs C M Roche, MiL
Mrs J Angel

Development Director: Mr S McGrahan, MSc
Registrar: Mrs C St Clair-Charles

Junior School:

Master: Mr E R Cavendish, MA

Director of Studies: Mrs L Evelyn-Rahr, BA Ed, MA (*Assessment Coordinator*)

Junior School Teaching Staff:
Mrs L Wrafter, Cert Ed (*General Subjects*)
Mrs A Hallett (*General Subjects*)
Mr J P Easy, BA (*General Subjects*)
Miss H L Reed, BSc (*Form Tutor Year 3*)
Mrs N Devon, BA (*Head of English, Form Tutor Year 5*)
Mrs V Meier, MA (*Head of Years 3 and 4, Form Tutor Year 3*)
Mrs L E Kanellis, MA (*Subject Leader History, Form Tutor Year 3*)
Miss N L Tutchings, BEd (*Subject Leader PSHE, Form Tutor Year 4*)
Mr S Oliver, BSc (*Head of Mathematics, Form Tutor Year 5*)
Miss M S Johnson, BA (*Subject Leader Design and Technology, Form Tutor Year 4*)
Mrs N J Chamberlain, BEd (*Learning Support Coordinator, Form Tutor Year 5, PTA Rep*)
Mr W Schaper, BEd (*Subject Leader Geography, Form Tutor Year 6*)
Mr N Dale, BA (*Head of Science, Form Tutor Year 5*)
Mr M O'Dwyer, BEd (*Subject Leader PE and Games, Head of Years 5 and 6, Form Tutor Year 6*)
Mrs A Carey, BA (*Deputy Head of English, Form Tutor Year 6*)
Mr M Alexander, BA (*Head of Junior School Music*)
Mr D Boudon, L-és-L (*French Teacher – Senior and Junior School*)
Mrs A McCullough, BA, TCAFL (*Head of Junior School Mandarin*)
Mrs J M Smith, BSc (*General Subjects*) (*part-time*)
Ms M Su, BA, MA (*Mandarin Teacher – Senior and Junior School*)
Mrs K Newham, BEd SpLD (*Learning Support Tutor*) (*part-time*)
Mrs H Mansell (*Teaching Assistant*)
Mrs J Cable (*After School Care*)

Emanuel School

Battersea Rise, London SW11 1HS

Tel:	020 8870 4171
Fax:	020 8877 1424
email:	enquiries@emanuel.org.uk
website:	www.emanuel.org.uk

Motto: *Pour bien désirer*

The School was founded in Westminster by Lady Anne Dacre in 1594, and moved to its present site on the north side of Wandsworth Common in 1883 as one of the three schools of the United Westminster Schools Foundation.

Emanuel is a fully co-educational day school. We have approximately 895 pupils including about 200 in the Sixth Form.

Admission. Each September about 40 pupils are admitted at age ten, 95 pupils at age eleven and 10 to 15 at age thirteen. There are also about 10 external candidates admitted into the Sixth Form each year.

Entry at age ten, eleven and thirteen is by competitive examination, held at the school each year in January. Applications for 10+ entry are capped at 180, 11+ entry is capped at 600 and 13+ entry at 150 in order to interview every child. Early registration is a must. Entry to the Sixth Form is by interview and tests held in the November before entry. Unconditional or conditional offers may be made.

Prospective parents are warmly encouraged to visit the school and there are many opportunities to do so. Please see our website or telephone for details.

Fees per term (2016–2017). £5,858 covering tuition, some stationery, books and lunch. Extras charged are for individual instrumental tuition and some external visits and trips.

Site and Buildings. Emanuel was founded in 1594. In 1883 it moved from Westminster to the present site in Wandsworth. The original building is the core of the school, with most of its classrooms and a fine library and chapel. The first addition made was the new building of 1896, which now houses our concert hall and music rooms and the science laboratories. These have been completely refurbished in the last few years to a very high standard.

Over the last century many further additions have been made, including a large sixth form centre. The school's playing fields adjoin the school buildings together with a full-sized indoor swimming pool. Our facilities include fives courts and a sports hall. The new library and theatre are superb resources for the whole school. A new arts and humanities centre is under construction. The school has a boathouse on the Thames by Barnes Bridge and further pitches on the A3 near Raynes Park.

Scholarships, Exhibitions and Bursaries. There are three types of scholarship at Emanuel: Foundation Scholarships (50% reduction in fees), Dacre Scholarships (25%) and Normal scholarships (10%).

All types of scholarship can be topped up using school bursaries to a maximum of 100% of the school fee, depending on financial need. It is also possible for a pupil to apply for and be awarded a scholarship in more than one category. Categories can be added together.

Academic scholarships are awarded at 10+, 11+ and 13+ on the basis of outstanding performance in the school entrance examinations held in January. At 16+ Academic scholarships are awarded to internal candidates on the basis of internal tests and to external candidates on the basis of their performance in the interviews and assessment tests.

Candidates applying for Music, Art, Drama and Sports scholarships must meet the general criteria for admission to Emanuel (eg reach the required standard in the academic entrance examinations) before a scholarship can be awarded. Thereafter each department has specific criteria for their scholarship requirements.

Exhibitions are awards of up to £1,000 on the basis of a pupil's high attainment in the entrance exams and scholarship assessments.

Bursaries are intended to help parents of pupils who can demonstrate financial need. Most bursaries are used to top up scholarships.

Full details of Scholarships, Exhibitions and Bursaries can be found on the school website or by contacting the Admissions Secretary.

Organisation. There are two forms for pupils who join at age ten (Year 6). Pupils joining at age eleven (Year 7) are streamed by ability in six forms. Primary responsibility for their care rests with the form teacher and the head of year, under the overall supervision of the Head of the Lower School, who deals with Years 6, 7 and 8. As all pupils move from Year 9 into Year 10 there is a re-grouping along the lines of the subjects chosen for GCSE examinations. In the Sixth Form a tutor system operates.

Pupils are placed in houses when they join the school and they stay in these houses throughout their school career. Although originally intended as a means of fostering competition in games, these houses have developed over many years a strong community spirit.

For fuller details please ask for the school prospectus or go to the website (www.emanuel.org.uk).

Times. The normal school day runs from 8.30 am to 3.45 pm, but many activities extend into the late afternoon after school. Many school activities, especially games, also take place on Saturday mornings.

Curriculum. Pupils are prepared for the GCSE. There is a wide range of options with most pupils taking nine subjects.

Thereafter, in the Sixth Form, there is a further range of options from which pupils choose three or four A Level subjects leading to examination at the end of the Upper Sixth. The vast majority of Sixth Form leavers go on to university, art college or other forms of higher education.

Religious Education. There are two Chaplains who work in the school, whose general religious tenor is that of the Church of England. A daily service is held in the school chapel. Pupils in Years 6, 7, 8 and 9 receive one or two periods per week of religious education, which continues into Years 10, 11 and Sixth Forms as a GCSE or A Level option.

The Arts. Emanuel has a long-standing tradition of excellence in these areas and all pupils are encouraged to participate in one or more of these activities. The school has a chapel choir and a chamber choir, an orchestra and ensemble groups and a major musical production is presented each year.

There is a specialist suite of art rooms with facilities for all kinds of creative activity. A great deal of high quality work is displayed around the school and several pupils a year go on to foundation courses at art college.

Drama is taught throughout the school and there is a major school production every year, usually in the autumn term, with many smaller-scale events during the year. The Theatre has been rebuilt and opened in September 2013.

We have an annual arts festival in July with an art exhibition, summer serenade, performances by pupils and visitors and a series of talks by visiting speakers.

Games and Activities. At present cricket, rowing, rugby and athletics are the main school games for the boys. For the girls the main activities are netball, hockey, rowing, tennis, athletics, and swimming. Many other activities become available as a pupil moves up the school. Each pupil will have one games afternoon each week and other opportunities for physical education and swimming. The school has its own playing fields, sports hall, swimming pool, fives courts and boathouse on the Thames.

The Duke of Edinburgh's Award scheme is offered at all levels to pupils from Year 9 upwards. Community service is arranged for senior pupils and can involve hospital visiting or voluntary work in local primary schools, charity shops or our local hospice. More formal work experience is offered as part of an extensive careers and further education advice programme from Year 9 upwards. There is a very strong Young Enterprise programme in the Lower Sixth.

Careers. Careers and further education advice is readily available from an experienced team. There is an annual careers convention for the senior school when many representatives from the professions and commerce visit the school to talk about career options. All pupils become members of the Independent Schools Careers Organisation (included in the fees).

Old Emanuel Association. *Membership Secretary*: Mr R Udall, 43 Howard Road, Coulsdon, Surrey CR5 2EB.

Charitable status. Emanuel School (administered by the United Westminster Schools' Foundation) is a Registered Charity, number 309267. Its aims and objectives are for "the bringing up of children in virtue and good and laudable arts".

Governing Body:

Chairman: F R Abbott, BA
Vice Chairman: C F Scott
B F W Baughan,
Mrs S Chambers
Lady Emily Dacre
M Jaigirder, MA
Dr F Lannon, MA, DPhil LMH Oxford
Ms M A D'Mello, BSc, MSc
R Naylor
Mrs M M Parsons, MA
The Very Revd V A Stock, OAM, Hon D Surrey, AKC, FRSA
Mrs J Sutcliffe, MA
J G M Wates, CBE

Clerk and Receiver: R W Blackwell, MA

Headmaster: M D Hanley-Browne, MA Oxon

Second Master: J A Hardy, MA
Director of Studies: Mrs J L Peters, MA Oxon
Registrar: P M McMahon, MA Cantab
Assistant Head, Academic: Dr R M Evans, DPhil Oxon
Assistant Head, Curriculum: Dr S J Wakefield, PhD King's College London
Assistant Head, Co-Curricular: J P Layng, BSc Nottingham, MCIEA, MSB
Assistant Head, Pastoral: Mrs S M Williams-Ryan, L-ès-Lettres Geneva, MA
Head of the Lower School: S J Gregory, MA Oxon, ARCO
Head of Middle School: S P Andrews, BA Swansea
Head of Sixth Form: Ms K Bainbridge, MA King's College London
Senior Chaplain: Revd P M Hunt, BA Dunelm, MA, MTh
Chaplain: Revd R F Walker, BSc, BD Glasgow, ThM

Teaching staff:
* Head of Department

S Andrews, BA
R Arnott, BA
Ms K Bainbridge, MA
A Ball, BA
J Barber, BA (*MFL, *French)
Miss H Blaikie, BSc
P Blum, BA, PhD
Mrs M Brennand, MA (*Mathematics)

Ms R Brown, MA Oxon (*Chemistry)
Ms O Bueno-Lopez, MA (*Geography)
Ms H Burnett, BA
Ms U Casais, BA
Ms R Chetwood, MA
Miss L Cleveland, BTh Oxon, MTh
Ms V Cojbasic, BSc
D Conington, BSc
Ms R Cottone, MA
Miss H Coulson, BA
C Csaky, BSc, MA Ed
Dr M Dancy, BSc, PhD
W Davis, BA
Mrs B Dawson, BA (*Creative Arts and Design, *Drama)
Ms V Dittmer, BSc
J Dunley, BA
Miss L Elliot, MA Cantab
Dr R Evans, DPhil Oxon
N Fazaluddin, BSc
Miss L Fitzgibbon, BSc
W Ford, MA (*Classics)
Miss C Forrest, BA
S Gregory, MA Oxon, ARCO
T Gwynne, BSc
J Hale, BA
D Hand, BA
W Hanson, BA
J Hardy, MA
Mrs J Haxby, MA Cantab
Miss J Henderson, BA
Z Higgins, BA
Miss L Holden, BA
N House, MA
Revd P Hunt, MA, MTh
H Jackson, BA (*German)
Miss J Johnson, MA Oxon (*English)
S M Jones (*History)
Miss A Jordon, BSc
A Keddie, MA Oxon, ACIB
P King, BSc
C Labinjo, BSc
W Lai, MA, MEng Cantab
J Layng, BSc, MCIEA, MSB
A Leadbetter, BSc
Ms C Lepetre, Licence d'Anglais
Ms S Leslie, MA
Mrs R Lewis, MA
Ms S MacMillan, BA (*Art)
Miss C Maison, MA Oxon (*Religious Studies)
Miss H Malik, BSc
P McMahon, MA Cantab
Miss K Moore, BA
Mrs J Morrison-Bartlett, BSc (*Science, *Physics)
Miss R Mott, BA
N Mullen, MA Cantab
N Nilsson, BA
Ms D Patel (*Biology)
Mrs J Peters, MA Oxon
Miss S Potts, BMus
R Price, BSc (*DT)
C Reed, BA
T Rhodes, BMus (*Music)
E Rice, BA Cantab
J Rice, BSc
Mrs S Riley, MBA
M Roberts, BSc
B Rogers
Mrs S Shaw, Dip SpLD
M Shetzer, MA
Miss L Stoby, BA
M Swift, BA

Mrs N Tawil, BA
R Tong, LLB (*Humanities *Business Studies & Economics*)
Dr S Wakefield, PhD
The Revd R Walker, BSc, BD (*Chaplain*)
Ms V Walton, BA Oxon
Miss H Watson, BA Oxon
Mrs L Whipp, BEd
Mrs E Wilbraham, MA
Mrs S Williams-Ryan, MA
Mrs L Wilson, BSc (*Psychology*)
Miss H Windsor, BA
Miss C Yeoman, BSc
Ms A Zaratiegui, MA (*Spanish*)

Visiting Music Teachers:
F Baird, Dip TCL, ARCM
Ms J Bauser, BMus RCM, Dip RAM
Ms C Boushell, MMus, PG Dip, ArtDipOp, RCM
Mrs Y Burova, BMus GSMD
F Crowther, BMus
Ms L Easton, BA
R B Harker, MA Cantab, MA RAM, LRSM
Ms J Hayter, BMus RAM, LRAM, PG Dip RCM
Ms K Lauder, BMus RNCM, PPRNCM
J McCredie, MMus, CertEd
Ms A Mowat, BMus RAM, LRAM
M O'Leary, ARAM
J Oldfield, MA Cantab, PG Dip RCM, ArtDipOp RCM
G Philips, BMus GSMD
P Sharda (*Guitar*)
Dr F Tarli, MMus, PhD
D Watts, BMus RNCM
T Williams, MA

Librarian: T Jones, BA
Assistant Librarian: G J Dibden
Director of Finance and Administration: J E Sharp, MA Cantab, ACA
Development Officer: Miss E Symmonds, BA
Headmaster's Secretary: Ms J Kiaer
Admissions Secretary: Ms D Shuttleworth

Epsom College

College Road, Epsom, Surrey KT17 4JQ
Tel: 01372 821004 (Headmaster)
            01372 821234 (Director of Admissions)
            01372 821133 (Bursar)
email: admissions@epsomcollege.org.uk
website: www.epsomcollege.org.uk
Twitter: @EpsomCollegeUK
Facebook: /Epsom-College

Motto: '*Deo non Fortuna*'.

Founded in 1855, Epsom College is situated in 84 acres of parkland estate close to Epsom Downs and is only 15 miles from central London. Epsom has become one of the most successful co-ed boarding and day schools for able all-round girls and boys aged 11–18. Almost all leavers go on to degree courses, especially at the research led universities, with historic strengths in Medicine, but now in all subjects. Art, music, drama and sport are very strong, with national representatives at Rugby, Netball, Hockey, Cricket, Golf and Target Rifle Shooting. Boarding is central to the College with 380 boarders, many living within 25 miles; the House system ensures a strong sense of community and support. Academic results are high: 85% of A2 results at A*–B, with 61% at A*–A, 86% of all University places were secured at Russell and 1994 Group Universities in 2016.

Numbers and Houses. The College has been fully co-educational from September 1996. There are 800 pupils in the School, 380 full and weekly boarders and 420 day pupils, divided among 7 boarding houses and 5 day houses. There are 325 in the Sixth Form. The College has 19% of pupils from overseas and a spread of 38 nationalities. The boy/girl ratio is 2:1 in the junior year groups and 1:1 in the Sixth Form.

There are 5 separate houses for girls: two boarding houses, Crawfurd and Wilson; two day houses, Raven and Rosebery; and a Sixth Form house, White, for both boarding and day girls.

The boys' boarding houses are: Fayrer, Forest, Granville and Holman. All boarding Sixth and Fifth Formers and Upper Fourth Formers have study-bedrooms in the modernised Houses. In the Michaelmas Term there are two weekend exeats roughly halfway through each half of term, in addition to a two week half-term holiday. In each of the other two terms there is one exeat in the first half followed by a one week half-term holiday. Weekly boarders can go home every weekend.

The day boy Houses are: Carr, Propert and Robinson. Day boys and girls are full members of the School community and have lunch and tea in College. All members of the School, boarders and day, eat centrally in the Dining Room which makes for efficiency and strengthens the sense of community.

Pupils who are ill are looked after in the School Medical Centre which has 8 beds with a qualified sister always on duty. One of the two (one male, one female) School Doctors visits daily except Sundays.

Academic Work. In the Lower School the design of the curriculum follows a number of key principles: Skills for the future, learning to learn, wellbeing and 21st century education.

Middle Fourth (Year 9) pupils take English, Mathematics, Physics, Chemistry, Biology, Religious Studies, Drama, Geography, History, Art, Music, Information Technology and Design Technology. Normally two languages are studied, chosen from French, German, Spanish and Mandarin. The College will select two sets of pupils to study Latin from those who perform well on Latin papers at Scholarship and CE. The normal programme is to enter the Middle Fourth at the age of thirteen and take the main block of GCSEs at the end of the Fifth Form (Year 11). Almost everyone then enters the Sixth Form of approximately 325 pupils. Students will choose 3 principal subjects to study at A Level or Pre-U. These will then be enhanced by choices from the core curriculum where they can choose from: Internationalism, Research & Analysis or Core Skills. They will also benefit from a varied lecture programme and Epsom's award winning service programme. A wide range of A Level subjects are offered. Options in Business Management, Politics and Government, Photography and Economics are introduced to complement the broad range of subjects already available at GCSE. The courses are linear meaning all examinations are taken at the end of Upper Sixth.

There are excellent facilities for work in one's own study, in the main Library or one of the specialist Departmental Libraries. The school is fully networked and has the latest Wi-Fi router system, including all Houses, and has over 600 computers alongside a further 600 personal computer points, as well as digital projectors and electronic whiteboards used across the curriculum. There are five fully-equipped Information Technology rooms and Design Technology is housed in award-winning buildings, with state-of-the-art, industrial-standard CAD and CAM facilities.

Higher Education. Almost all students go on to university, with the occasional student choosing to follow another path, such as Art Foundation. In recent years, Medicine, Law, Engineering, Economics and Business degrees have proved particularly popular degree options, but Epsom students have been successful in gaining places on a broad variety of competitive courses. Approximately 70% of all pupils go to Russell Group or 1994 Group universities each year.

Careers. Careers education is offered from the first term at Epsom and is particularly well developed in the Sixth Form. Epsom has an experienced team of careers tutors with specialists in Medicine, Oxbridge Entrance, Engineering and American University Entrance. There is a well-stocked Careers Room attached to the Library, and much care is taken to assess a pupil's potential and aptitude and to provide proper guidance on careers. All pupils belong to the ISCO Scheme and all Fifth Form pupils take careers aptitude tests through Futurewise. There is a well-established work experience programme and a Careers Convention is organised each year for the Fifth Form and Lower Sixth. The College also hosts a GAP Year Fair.

The **Religious Teaching** and the Chapel Services follow the doctrines of the Church of England, but there are always pupils of other denominations and faiths. Multi-faith services take place regularly. There is a Senior Chaplain who works together with a visiting Rabbi and a Hindu priest to ensure a multi-faith approach. Muslim pupils attend prayers at the College.

Games and other Activities. Games contribute much to the general physical development of girls and boys at Epsom and the College has a strong tradition of high standards in many sports. The very large number of teams means that almost all pupils are able to represent the School each year. A wide range of sports is available: Rugby, Hockey, Netball, Cricket, Tennis, Athletics and Swimming, Squash (6 courts), Target Rifle Shooting (with an indoor range), Soccer, Cross-Country, Fencing, Golf, Badminton, Rounders, Basketball, Judo and Sailing. The Indoor Sports Centre, housing two sports halls, a fencing salle and climbing wall, was opened in 1989 by the Patron of Epsom College, Her Majesty the Queen. In January 2007 a new extensive fitness suite was completed. The Target Rifle Team has a long history of excellence at Target Rifle Shooting, both small-bore and full-bore, and over the last 20 years has consistently been the premier rifle shooting school in the UK. The College Rifle team has won the National Championships – the Ashburton Shield – 14 times in the past 26 years and 15 times overall. The College holds the record for the highest number of Ashburton wins by a single school.

The CCF has Naval, Army and RAF Sections and pupils over the age of 14 are expected to join for 2 years when much time is spent on camping and expeditions. Older boys and girls may join instead The Duke of Edinburgh's Award scheme, while others are involved with the service programme in Epsom where they contribute to the community and take a leadership role in service projects.

The College ensures that all pupils take advantage of an extensive range of activities from Dance to Design Textiles.

Music, Art and Drama. There are three full-time Music teachers and a large staff of visiting music teachers. Over one-third of the pupils learn musical instruments and virtually any instrument can be taught, and many take singing lessons. There are four Choirs, a School Orchestra and seven major instrumental ensembles, including Big Band, Clarinet, Saxophone and Classical Guitar. Visits are arranged each term to concerts in London and elsewhere. The Music School has a Concert Hall and 18 practice rooms. Recent productions have included *The Coronation of Poppea, Sweeney Todd, Les Misérables, Jesus Christ Superstar and Cabaret.*

Art, which includes pottery, printing and sculpture as well as painting and drawing, is housed in a spacious building with 8 studios, a Library, an Exhibition Room and an Exhibition Hall. There are two full-time Art teachers and one part-time, and Art is studied up to GCSE and A Level.

There are several major Drama productions each year, from classical theatre to the modern musical, produced by a range of staff and pupils. These give boys and girls an opportunity to develop their talents and interests in Drama. In 2004 staff and pupils wrote their own show which was performed at the Royal Albert Hall, with over 1,000 performers, to mark the 150th Anniversary of the College.

Admission. Almost all pupils enter Epsom College in September. There are now 3 entry levels 11+, 13+ and 16+.

For those entering at 11+ candidates will be assessed for entry in January of Year 6. They will sit papers in English, Mathematics and verbal reasoning, and these tests will be supported by a short interview and a report from their current school.

For those entering at 13+ after reaching a satisfactory standard in the Common Entrance or Scholarship Examination or the Epsom College January Entry Test examination set specially for those who are not prepared for Common Entrance. All boys and girls will be expected to sit a Pre-Test Examination in their Year 6 of corresponding entry at 13+. If the required standard is achieved, a pupil will be offered a place for entry at 13+, conditional upon maintaining the same standards at the present school and they will also sit a test in the year of entry for setting purposes. Some enter the school later than this and there is always a direct entry into the Sixth Form, both for girls and boys.

A boy or girl may be registered at any age by sending in the registration form and fee. All enquiries should be sent to the Director of Admissions from whom a prospectus may be obtained.

Fees per term (2016–2017). Boarders £11,539; Weekly Boarders £10,482; Day Pupils £7,824, Third Form £5,700.

The fees are inclusive and cover the normal cost of a pupil's education. The main extras are for examination fees, private tuition and a pupil's personal expenses. Fees for day pupils include lunch and tea.

There is a College Store for the provision of uniform, clothing and other requirements.

Entrance Scholarships. Scholarships are available at 11+ (Academic, Drama, Music, Sport), 13+ and 16+ entry in the following areas: Academic, All-Rounder, Art, Design Technology, Drama, Music and Sport.

Music candidates compete for all Open Scholarships. Music can be offered at a lower level as part of a candidature for an All-Rounder Award.

Drama/Dance awards are based upon a performance audition, interview and authorised record of achievement.

Art candidates compete for Open Scholarships. They should submit a varied portfolio of about 15 pieces of work and they will then be invited to Epsom to discuss their work at interview and, at 13+, to do a timed drawing test.

Design Technology awards are based upon a portfolio presentation composing several contrasting items and, at 13+, a timed design test.

Sport awards are based upon a combination of skills tests and authorised records of achievement.

All-Rounder awards require applicants to offer an academic element plus two or more elements to be selected from Art, Design Technology, Drama/Dance, Music and Sport. The latter are assessed through tests and interviews.

Scholarships and bursaries are also available for children of the medical profession.

Bursaries. Over the past six years, Epsom has reduced the value of non means-tested Scholarships and Awards, which can be worth up to 10% per annum. This has enabled us to double the bursary fund which is allocated to families with demonstrable financial need. In turn this has helped us, with Educational Trust support, to 'Widen our access' to disadvantaged families which is one of the College's declared aims in line with both Government and HMC guidance. Potential scholarship applicants are encouraged to seek extra financial support, if appropriate, by way of a means-tested Bursary. Application forms are available on request from the Bursar or Admissions Registrar.

Old Epsomians. The Old Epsomian Club promotes sporting activities, social gatherings and networking events among its former pupils, with eight international chapters and an online database. On leaving the College, all pupils automatically become lifelong members of the OE Club and they are invited back regularly for reunions, the OE Dinner and Founder's Day. They also receive several publications each year, including the OE magazine. Bursaries are available for the sons and daughters of OEs who wish to attend the College.

Charitable status. Epsom College is a Registered Charity, number 312046. It exists for the advancement of education.

Patron: Her Most Gracious Majesty The Queen
President: Lord McColl, CBE, MS, FRCS, FACS

Visitor: The Right Reverend The Lord Bishop of Guildford

Chairman: Dr A J Vallance-Owen, MBE, MBA, FRCS Edin
Vice Chairman: Dr A J Wells, MB BS, DRCOG, MRCGP
Treasurer: Ms S J Williams, MEng FCA
Dr J Bolton, MA, MB BChir, FRCPsych
Mrs F Boulton, BSc, MA
Dr H H Bowen-Perkins, LMSSA, MRCS Eng, LRCP Lond, MB BS
Mr K Budge, MA Oxon
Mrs B Dolbear, LLB
The Very Revd D Gwilliams, BA, MA
Mr J A Hay
Dr S Lipscomb, MA Oxon, MSt Oxon, DPhil Oxon
Mr D Mahoney, MA Cantab
Mr D Maunder, MA Oxon
Mr A J Pianca, FCA
Mr G B Pincus, MBE, MIPA
Mrs S Piper, BA, MA
Mrs K Thomas, BM Soton, FRCS Orth
Mr C Watson, ACA

Bursar and Clerk to the Governing Body: Mrs S E Teasdale, BSc Lond, FCA

Headmaster: Mr J A Piggot, BA Cardiff, MA Liverpool

Second Master: Mr P J Williams, BSc Dunelm
Deputy Head Academic: Mr R Alton, MA Cantab
Director of Academic Operations: Mrs T Muller, MA Oxon
Assistant Head, Total Curriculum: Mr A J Bustard, BA Swansea
Assistant Head, Teaching Staff: Dr M A L Tod, MA, PhD Glasgow, FSA Scot
Assistant Head, Sixth Form: Mr N Russell, MA Liverpool
Head of Lower School: Mrs A Martineau, BA Bristol

Heads of Year:
Head of Sixth Form: Mr N Russell, MA Liverpool
Head of Lower Sixth: Mr M C Conway, MA Cantab
Head of Fifth Form: Ms T St Clair-Ford, BA Cantab, MA Chichester
Head of Upper Fourth: Mrs C C Winmill, MA Bordeaux
Head of Transition: Mrs F C Drinkall, BSc Loughborough
Head of Third Form: Mr R C G Young, BSc Bath

Director of Transformation & IT: Mr M Blahut, BSc Matej Bel, Slovakia
Head of Higher Education & Careers Guidance: Mrs R J B Harrop, BA Bristol
Director of Lower School Co-Curriulum: Mrs F C Drinkall, BSc Loughborough
Director of Learning and Innovation: Mr J Short, BA UCL
Head of Core Curriculum Sixth Form: Mrs K Hancock, BSc LSE

Director of Welfare: Mrs H E Keevil, BA Exeter
Activities Coordinator: Mr M Ruxton, BSc Birmingham

Housemasters /Housemistresses:

Carr (boys' day):
Mr L Matthews, BSc Exeter
Matron: Ruth Boyce

Crawfurd (girls' boarding):
Mrs H H Hynd, BA Nottingham, MA Dunelm, FRSA
Matron: Jill Ballinger

Fayrer (boys' boarding):
Mr S J Head, BSc UWE
Matron: Corinne Roy

Forest (boys' boarding):
Mr J F Stephens, BSc Liverpool
Matron: Yvette Tolson

Granville (boys' boarding):
Mr A Day, BSc UWE, MEd Cantab
Matron: Karen Clarke

Holman (boys' boarding):
Mr T A Stone BSc Plymouth
Matron: Silvana Ispani

Propert (boys' day):
Mr A J Wilson, BSc MSc Warwick
Matron: Eileen Cornwell

Raven (girls' day):
Dr R L Stone, BSc Bristol, PhD Birmingham
Matron: Gina Frost

Robinson (boys' day):
Mr P J Gillespie, BA Exeter
Matron: Tracey Pointing

Rosebery (girls' day):
Mrs R J B Harrop, BA Bristol
Matron: Patricia Martins

White (girls' VI form boarding & day):
Miss F Smith, BSc Bristol
Matron: Diane Liquorish

Wilson (girls' boarding):
Mrs K R Tod, BA Lond
Matron: Tania Moore

Chaplain:
Revd Fr P Thompson, BA Oxon (*Senior Chaplain*)

Department for Academic Support:
Mrs R Doyle, BEd Glasgow, BA, BPhil Birmingham, RSA Dip TEFL, Advanced Dip Sp Ed
Mrs M-A Barnett, BA Manchester, TEFL Advanced Dip (*EAL*)
Mrs I Chistyakova, BA Vernadsky
Mr Gareth Davies, BEng Warwick
Mrs Joanna Desmier, BA Kent
Ms N Strivens, BA Edinburgh

Art:
Mrs K H P Lenham, BA Soton
Mr N Arvanitis, MA University of the Arts, London
Miss J Moore, MA Cantab

Biology:
Mr W Keat, MA Lond
Mr M D Hobbs, BSc Lond, CBiol, MSB
Dr V Patel, BSc Leeds, PhD Lond
Dr R L Stone, BSc Bristol, PhD (*Birmingham*)
Mr N J Smith, BSc Portsmouth
Dr R Storey, BSc Dunelm, PhD

Chemistry:
Mr J Styles, BSc UCL
Miss S Heyes, BSc Newcastle
Mr L Matthews, BSc Exeter
Mrs T M Muller, MA Oxon
Mr N S A Payne, BSc Salford
Mrs S E Williams, MA Cantab

Classics:
Miss J Saul, BA Oxon
Mrs K Cole, BA Durham

Design Technology:
Miss A M R Wickham, BEd Exeter MEd Open
Mr M Day, BEd Trent Polytechnic
Mr P G Lewsey, BSc Coventry

Economics & Business Studies:
Mr G R Watson, BA Cantab
Mr J Bailey, BSc Nottingham
Mr P J Gillespie, BA Exeter
Mr S J Head, BSc UWE
Mr F Pearce, BSc Cardiff
Mr R C G Young, BSc Bath

English:
Mr W M A Burn, BA London
Miss N Bubbear, BA Newcastle
Dr B Elliot Lockhart, BA Southwestern, MPhil Cantab,
    MPhil Columbia, PhD Columbia
Mrs C E Jeens, MA Soton
Mr N Russell, MA Liverpool
Ms T St Clair-Ford, BA Cantab, MA Chichester
Miss S H Wilson, BA Nottingham
Mr R M Wycherley, BA Leeds

Geography:
Mr S Powell, BSc Dunelm, MEd Cantab
Miss A Furlong, BA Sussex
Mrs A Venables, BSc Bristol
Mr R I Whiteley, MA Cantab

History, Government & Politics:
Ms F Ring, BA MA Cantab
Mr A J Bustard, BA Swansea
Mr M C Conway, MA Cantab
Mr L Fisher, BA Cantab, MA Lond
Mr R E T Moore, BA Manchester
Mr J Short, BA UCL
Mr P Swainson, BA Exeter
Dr M A L Tod, MA, PhD Glasgow, FSA Scot

ICT & Computing:
Miss S Biletchi, BSc Bucharest
Mr A Day, BSc West of England, MEd Cantab
Mr R A Johnstone, BTheol Brunel
Mr A Stride, BA Cantab

Mathematics:
Mrs C Gamble, BA Cantab
Ms F G Buzzacott, BSc Exeter
Mrs K Hancock, BSc LSE
Mr S Hibbitt, BA York
Mr D T Reeve, BSc, MRes Lancaster
Miss F Smith, BSc Bristol
Mr J F Stephens, BSc Liverpool
Mr T A Stone, BSc, Plymouth
Mr J D Wallace, MEng Oxon
Mr P J Williams, BSc Dunelm
Mr A J Wilson, BSc, MSc Warwick

Modern Languages:
Mr M Fries, BA Open University
Mrs X Cheng, BA Henan, MSc Conservatoire National des
    Arts et Métiers
Mrs N Cholet, BA Open University (*French Assistante*)

Miss C L Creevey, BA Nottingham
Mr L Gimenez, BA Madrid (*Spanish Assistante*)
Mrs C Guyon, Teacher's Cert (*French Assistante*)
Miss U Herwig, MA Bonn (*German Assistant*)
Mr M P Hynd, MA Glasgow
Mrs H E Keevil, BA Exeter
Mrs Z Liu, BEd Shenyang (*Mandarin*)
Mr N Mayer, BA Ruhr, Bochum
Miss J Pizarro, BA MA Salamanca (*Spanish Assistante*)
Miss G Ramos Zorrilla, BA Granada, MA Valladolid
Mrs C C Winmill, MA Bordeaux

Music:
Mr G A Lodge, MA, BMus Cardiff, LTCL, ACIEA
Mr C I Holiday, BEd Leeds, ACP
Mr P Johnson-Hyde, BMus Birmingham Conservatoire

Visiting Instrumental Tutors:
Mr M E Allsop, BA, RSAMD (*electric/acoustic guitar and
    music technology*)
Mr P S Becher, BA, ACM (*electric/acoustic guitar*)
Mr T Carey, MA, BMus, ARCM, LTCL (*organ and piano*)
Mr A Dennant (*violin*)
Mrs L Egan, BMus, Cert Ed, LRAM, LTCL (*oboe and
    bassoon*)
Mr P G Evans (*bass guitar*)
Miss G Ford (*piano*)
Miss L Geldard, Dip RCM Performers, ARCM, PGRCM
    (*flute*)
Mr C Goldsack, MA, PGCE (*singing*)
Miss A Goldy, PGCPerf TCL, Dip-TCL, PGCE UCL
    (*singing*)
Mr N Hassall, BMus, PGDip RCM (*saxophone and
    clarinet*)
Mr A Hooley (*clarinet and saxophone*)
Mrs K Humphries, GRSM (*piano*)
Mrs N Johnson-Hyde, BMus Hons, MMus, MPerf (*singing*)
Mr P Johnson-Hyde, BMus Hons (*piano*)
Mr D C Marrion (*clarinet, saxophone and flute*)
Miss B Meek, DipMusEd RSAM, DRSAM Performers,
    Cert Ed (*singing*)
Mr C Moore (*trumpet*)
Miss D Morley, BMus (*singing*)
Miss S D'Oliveira Teixeira, BMus, MSTAT (*Alexander
    Technique*)
Mr J O'Carroll (*drum kit*)
Mr M W Osborn (*drum kit and percussion*)
Miss S Pedley, BSc, BA, BTEC National Diploma (*Music*)
    (*beatbox*)
Mr N Perona-Wright, LRAM, LTCL, LLCM TD (*flute and
    recorder*)
Mr G R D Rowland, ARCO, ARCM (*piano and
    harpsichord*)
Mr R H W Slade, MA Cantab Cert Ed (*singing*)
Mr D Smith, AGSM (*electric and acoustic guitar*)
Dr J Spooner, MA Cantab, MA, PhD Lon, ARCM, LRAM,
    Dip RAM (*cello*)
Mrs B Stevens, ARCM (*violin*)
Mrs C Stewart, BMus, PGCE (*piano*)
Mr G Straw, BA (*trumpet and french horn*)
Mrs H Taylor, BA, LGSM (*piano*)
Mr J S D Taylor, LRAM (*Teachers*) Professional Cert
    (*classical guitar*)
Miss N Veal, BA Hons, PGCE (*harp and piano*)
Miss D Xenakis, BMus Hons (*violin*)
Mr S Walker, BA Hons (*saxophone, clarinet and jazz
    piano*)
Mr A Waterson, BSc, EBOR (*electric and acoustic guitar*)
Mr D Whitson, LRAM, ARCM, ARAM (*trombone*)

Physical Education:
Mr M E Johnson, BSc Loughborough (*Director of Sport &
    Head of Hockey*)

Mr M Ruxton, BSc Birmingham (*Head of Physical Education & Activities Coordinator*)
Miss J L Bennett (*Sports Coach*)
Mrs B Bostock (*Head of Netball Development*)
Mr P A Burke, BSc Loughborough (*Director of Rugby*)
Mrs S L Church-Jones, BA Exeter (*Head of Girls' Games & Head of Tennis*)
Mr G Davies, BEng Warwick (*Acting Head of Shooting*)
Mr M Day, BEd Trent Polytechnic (*Head of Football*)
Mrs F C Drinkall, BSc Loughborough (*Director of Lower School Co-Curriculum & Head of Transition*)
Mr J M Drinkall, BSc Durham (*Head of Basketball*)
Mr S Hibbitt, BA York (*Head of Volleyball*)
Mrs C E Jeens MA Soton (*Shooting Coach*)
Mr P G Lewsey, BSc Coventry (*Head of Cross Country*)
Mr B G MacDowel, MTheol (*St Andrews Head of Golf*)
Mr R E Moor, BA Manchester (*Director of Cricket*)
Mr N Smith, BSc Portsmouth (*Head of Fencing*)
Dr R L Storey, BSc Dunelm, PhD King's College London (*Head of Swimming*)
Mr N Taylor (*Head of Cricket*)
Mr A Thompson, MSc Durham (*Sports Development Coach*)
Mr M A L Tod, MA, PhD Glasgow, FSA Scot (*Head of Squash*)
Miss L Watson (*Shooting Coach*)

Visiting Coaching Professionals:
Mr D Bangerter (*Table Tennis & Badminton*)
Mr R Barcellona (*Strength & Conditioning*)
Mrs H Blakeburn (*Netball*)
Mr R Chappell, MA Lond, MEd Kentucky, MSc Leicester (*Athletics & Basketball*)
Mr J Culver, Licensed CCA LTA (*Tennis*)
Mr R Dennis, ITF 5th Degree (*Taekwon-do*)
Mr N Frankland (*Squash*)
Mr J Franklin (*Tennis*)
Mr C Hanson-Khan (*Badminton*)
Mr M Homes (*Rugby, Football & Cricket*)
Mrs K Jordan (*Netball*)
Mr C Keevil, BSc Bath (*Hockey*)
Mr A Mason (*Swimming*)
Mrs L McQuade (*Hockey*)
Mr N Payne (*Fencing*)
Mr D N Rice, BSc Loughborough (*Athletics*)
Mrs T Thompson, BSc Loughborough (*Netball*)
Mr S Whatling (*Rugby*)
Mrs S White (*Hockey*)
Mrs P Winsor (*Hockey, Cricket*)
Mr A Wolstenholme, BEd Exeter (*Rugby*)

Physics:
Mr C C Telfer, BSc, MA UWE
Mr R J Alton, MA Cantab
Mr R D B Burgess, BSc Soton, ACMA
Mr J M Drinkall, BSc Dunelm
Mr M W D Perrins, MEng Oxon
Mr V Singh, MSc IIT Roorkee, India

Religious Studies:
Mr G Greenbury, BA Cantab, MA Warwick, EdM Harvard
Mrs H H Hynd, BA Nottingham, MA Dunelm, FRSA
Mr B G MacDowel, MTheol St Andrews
Mrs A Martineau, BA Bristol
Revd Fr P Thompson, BA Oxon

Theatre Studies:
Miss K Chandley, BA Birmingham
Mr P Henson, MA De Montfort

Headmaster's Office:
Headmaster's PA: Mrs C Beesley
Assistant to Headmaster's PA: Mrs M McDonald
Deputy Heads' Secretary: Mrs E Bauchop, Mrs S Lawrence

Admissions and Marketing Office:
Director of Admissions: Mrs C Kent
Acting Director of Marketing: Mrs C Sender, BA Hons Bournemouth
Admissions Manager: Mr M Day, BEd Trent Polytechnic
Marketing & Events: Ms J Busby
Admissions Assistant: Mrs D Upot

Bursars Office:
Bursar's PA: Ms K Plimmer

Epsom College Education Trust and OE Club:
Director of Education Trust: Ms Karen Doyle, BA Warwick
Education Trust Coordinator: Mr C Collins
OE Club Secretary: Mrs S Croucher
Education Trust Administrator: Mrs C Mowbray

Examinations Office:
Database Administrator: Mrs N Elliott

The Royal Medical Foundation:
Administrator: Mr C Titman
RMF Caseworker: Mrs H Jones

Other Staff:
Archivist: Ms Rebecca Jallot
CCF Instructor: WO1 RLS Bonner, IG Combined Cadet Force
Medical Officer:
Dr M Sevenoaks, BSc, MBBS, MRCGP, DRCOG, DFFP
Dr K A Bryce, BSc, MBBS, MRCP, MRCGP
Music Administrator: Mrs J Bustard, BSc Swansea
School Counsellor: Ms Alice Allen, BSc UCL, PGDip UEL
Senior Sister: Mrs L Hendry, RN DPNS
Service Coordinator: Mrs R Watkins
Sports Centre Manager: Mr C Field
Co-curricular Coordinator: Mrs L Romano

Eton College

Windsor, Berkshire SL4 6DW

Tel: 01753 370611 (Admissions)
         01753 370100 (Head Master)
         01753 370541 (Bursar)
email: admissions@etoncollege.org.uk
website: www.etoncollege.com

Eton College is a full boarding school for boys with 1,300 pupils, situated next to the historic town of Windsor, Berkshire. It was founded in 1440 by King Henry VI with the purpose of educating 70 poor, but talented boys. The school's ethos is to take talented pupils with character and give them the skills to progress through life as happy, successful and socially responsible adults. Academic results are important but so too are the skills gained from co-curricular activities including music, drama, art, sports and the many different societies. At Eton the emphasis is on finding, nurturing and giving value to each pupil's unique talents.

One fifth of the boys at the school currently receive means-tested bursary support and there are also a number of scholarships available. See our website www.etoncollege.com for further details.

Recent Developments. Eton College's Head Master, Simon Henderson, joined in September 2015. Simon was previously at the helm of Bradfield College and has built a reputation as a progressive and innovative head. He knows Eton well having taught history here for eight years; four as head of department. Simon is a graduate of Brasenose College, Oxford and is married with a young family.

Centre for research and learning. The world of teaching and the way young people learn is set to be transformed through the advent of new technologies (including apps) and a better understanding of neuroscience. The Tony Little Centre for Research and Innovation in Learning was opened in May 2015, with the aim of putting Eton into the forefront of global teaching and learning development.

The centre works alongside schools and universities around the world to exchange ideas and share best practice, carry out research and analyse new developments – with the aim of continually improving our outstanding teaching and learning experience for our pupils, as well as society more widely.

Academic achievement. Academic excellence is central to Eton life, with the vast majority of our pupils going on to attend leading universities; an increasing number are also attending leading universities in the United States. Our pupils go on to study a range of subjects as under-graduates including the sciences (inc. medicine), humanities/English, modern languages and economics/business. Eton has its own dedicated Learning Support centre for boys with special educational needs or specific learning challenges, such as dyslexia or dyspraxia.

Sport (known as Games) plays a central role in school life, both within and outside the curriculum. There are nearly 30 different activities on offer, ranging from the more familiar football, rugby, cricket and rowing to Eton's own unique sports – the Wall and Field Games.

We have a range of highly skilled professional coaches and masters leading our extensive games programme. Bringing home the silverware is very important and we have provision for elite athletes, but at Eton we consider the central ethos of sport – encouraging teamwork as well as leadership, dedication, respect, physical fitness and well-being, to be the real goal for our pupils.

The Arts. Over 1,300 music lessons are taught each week at The Music Schools by a staff of seven full-time masters and 70 specialist visiting teachers. Our facilities include a modern concert hall, orchestral rehearsal hall, recording studio, rock studio, numerous teaching and practice rooms, and a music library. There are three chapel choirs, a concert choir, a choral society, three orchestras, two concert bands, two big bands and a large number of smaller ensembles. Senior boys regularly put on their own concerts – a tradition initiated by Hubert Parry during his time as a boy at Eton. A number of music scholarships are available.

Eton's Director of Drama is actor and director Scott Handy, who is a former member of the RSC, with numerous film and television credits to his name. More than 20 theatrical productions are staged at the school each year, affording boys the opportunity to take part both onstage and behind the scenes; these opportunities have seen a number of former pupils forging very successful careers in the industry. The facilities include the 400-seater Farrer Theatre, a flexible auditorium with a scenic workshop, wardrobe, make-up studio and dressing rooms. The smaller Caccia Studio seats 100.

More than 20 theatrical productions are staged at the school each year, affording boys the opportunity to take part both onstage and behind the scenes. The facilities include the 400-seater Farrer Theatre, a flexible auditorium with a scenic workshop, wardrobe, make-up studio and dressing rooms. The smaller Caccia Studio seats 100.

Our stunning Drawing Schools have opportunities for printmaking, computer graphics and digital photography, painting and drawing. There are also two purpose-built 3D studios with facilities for sculpture (in wood, metal, plaster) and ceramics. Regular exhibitions are staged and there is also an ambitious Artist in Residence programme. Art and design features in the curriculum but pupils are also encouraged to use The Drawing Schools in their free time.

Additional activities. Eton societies are extremely popular and there are a large number available (around 50 at any one time), covering a broad range of topics – from the Mountaineering Society to the Political Society, the Culinary Society to the Medical Society and the recently formed Tech Club and Investment Society.

Pupils are also encouraged to develop a sense of social responsibility and they give back in a number of ways, including volunteering with school children or the elderly and taking part in charity fundraising events, such as the annual Eton Community Fair.

Pastoral Care. The welfare of boys at Eton College is taken extremely seriously and a robust system is in place, specifically designed to enable staff to spot problems as early as possible. The house structure, tutor groups, a professional psychologist, our own health centre and the chaplaincy teams (the chaplaincy team has representatives of all faiths) all play a role within this system. Our pastoral care procedures are reviewed regularly by the Head and Lower Masters.

Admissions. The majority of pupils are admitted to the school aged 13. For entry up to and including 2019 registration is required by the age of 10 years and 6 months. For entry in 2020 and beyond registration is required by 30th June in UK School Year 5 (the academic year in which a boy reaches the age of 10); please note these are strict deadlines. There are scholarships for entry aged 13 – the academic King's Scholarship and the Music Scholarship – as well as means-tested bursaries. There are also a small number of Sixth Form Scholarships and Sixth Form admissions available.

The Admissions process for entry up to and including 2019 consists of a report from the pupil's current school, an interview and a specially designed computer test. For entry in 2020 and beyond the process will also include the ISEB Common Pre-tests and an assessed group activity. A visit to the school either before registration or before assessment is recommended. Please contact the Admissions Team via www.etoncollege.com for further details.

Fees per term (2016–2017). £12,354.

Charitable status. Eton College is a Registered Charity, number 1139086.

Visitor: The Right Revd the Lord Bishop of Lincoln

Provost: The Lord Waldegrave of North Hill, PC, MA

Vice-Provost: Dr Andrew Gailey, CVO, MA, PhD

Fellows:
Professor Michael Proctor, MA, MMath, ScD, FRS, FRAS, FIMA (*Provost of King's College Cambridge, Senior Fellow*)
Professor Christopher Dobson, MA, DPhil, ScD, FRS
Sir Michael Burton, MA
The Duchess of Wellington, OBE, BA
Mr David Reid Scott, MA
Professor Kim Nasmyth, PhD, FRS
Dr Caroline Moore, MA, PhD
Mr Hamish Forsyth, MA
Mr John Varley, MA
Mr Mark Esiri, LLB, MBA

Honorary Fellows:
Mr John Butterwick, TD
Sir Simon Robertson
Sir Eric Anderson, KT, MA, MLitt, DLitt, FRSE
Lady Smith, OBE, BA

Head Master: **Mr Simon Henderson**, MA

Lower Master: Dr Robert Stephenson, BSc, PhD

Director of Curriculum: Mr Gerard Evans, MA

Senior Tutor: Mr Ian Harris, MA

Director of Outreach & Partnership: Mr Tom Arbuthnott, MA, MPhil

Conduct: The Revd Canon Keith Wilkinson, BA, FRSA

Senior Chaplain & Conduct Elect: The Revd Stephen Gray, MA

Precentor: Mr Tim JOHNSON, MA

Steward of the Courts: The Rt Hon the Lord Carrington, KG, GCMG, CH, MC, PC

Bursar: Miss Janet Walker, MA, FCA

Clerk & Legal Advisor to Provost & Fellows: Ms Serena Hedley-Dent, MA

Buildings & Facilities Director: Mr Ian Mellor, BA, FRICS

HR Director: Miss Kate Bradley, MA

Finance Director: Mrs Catherine Taylor, BA, ACA

Director of Development: Mrs Rachael Henshilwood, BA

Heads of Departments:
Art: I Burke, MA
Classics: C J Smart, MA
Computing & Digital Education: J W F Stanforth, MA
Design & Technology: K R N Ross, BSc
Divinity: Revd N G Heap, BA, DPhil
Economics & Politics: M Tanweer, MA
English: B B Cooper, MA, MPhil, PhD
Geography: D E Anderson, BA, DPhil
History: D Yuravlivker, BA, MSc, PhD
Mathematic: R J Gazet, MA
Modern Languages: R A Fletcher, BA, MPhil
Music: T J Johnson, MA
Options: A J Maynard, MA
Physical Education: P I Macleod, BEd, BA
The Sciences: K Frearson, MA

Head of Teaching & Learning: J M Noakes, MA
Head of Career Education: G D Fussey, BSc

Exeter School

Victoria Park Road, Exeter, Devon EX2 4NS
Tel: 01392 273679 (Headmaster/Registrar)
           01392 258712 (Bursar/Office)
Fax: 01392 498144
email: admissions@exeterschool.org.uk
website: www.exeterschool.org.uk
Twitter: @ExeterSchoolUK

Motto: ΧΡΥΣΟΣ ΑΡΕΤΗΣ ΟΥΚ ΑΝΤΑΞΙΟΣ

Founded in 1633, Exeter School occupies a 25-acre site, located within a mile of the city centre, having moved from its original location in the High Street in 1880. Some of its well-designed buildings date from that time but many new buildings have been added over the past twenty years and the school now enjoys first-rate facilities on a very attractive open site.

The school is fully co-educational and offers education to boys and girls from 7 to 18. It has its own Junior School of around 200 pupils, nearly all of whom transfer to the Senior School at the age of 11. The Senior School has around 720 pupils, including a Sixth Form of 220. (*For further information about Exeter Junior School, see entry in IAPS section.*)

Exeter School is a well-run school with high all-round standards and very good academic results. It prides itself on strong cultural, sporting and extra curricular achievement. Its music is outstanding and there is a strong tradition of performance drawn from all age groups in the School. It offers a very wide range of sports and maintains consistently high standards especially in hockey, rugby and cricket. It is well placed for outdoor pursuits (e.g. Duke of Edinburgh's

Award scheme and Ten Tors on Dartmoor) and has its own very large voluntary CCF unit. The School is closely involved with the life of the City of Exeter and its university and it has a substantial commitment to support the local community.

Buildings, Grounds and General Facilities. The Senior School block includes a large multi-purpose assembly hall, a library, a private study area, dining hall and Sixth Form Centre as well as many well-appointed classrooms. A major refurbishment of the former boarding accommodation to include a new Library and Study Centre was completed for September 2006. There are separate buildings on the site housing the Chapel, the Music School, the Science Centre, Art Studios, Drama Studio, Design and Technology Centre and Exonian Centre. The Science Centre provides 14 laboratories and there are four fully-equipped computer rooms. All departments have access to their own computers and the School has a wide, controlled access to the internet. In 2005 the school opened a new dance studio and a fitness suite to add to the existing sports facilities of a large modern well-equipped Sports Hall with its own squash courts and access to on-site floodlit all-weather sports arena, top-grade all-weather tennis/netball courts and a heated swimming pool. The playing fields, which are immediately adjacent to the School buildings are well kept and provide, in season, rugby, cricket, hockey, football, rounders and athletics areas. The Junior School, which was extended in 2012 to provide four new modern classrooms, has access to all the Senior School facilities but is self-contained on the estate.

Admission. The majority of pupils enter the Junior School at 7 or 9 and the Senior School at 11 or 13. Admission is also possible at other ages where space allows and a significant number of pupils join at the age of 16 for Sixth Form Studies.

Entrance to the Junior School is by assessment in January. This includes a report from the child's previous school, classroom sessions in the company of other prospective pupils, and literacy, numeracy and general intelligence tasks.

Entrance examinations for the Senior School are held in January.

Assessment for entry to the Sixth Form at 16 is by interview and a report from the applicant's previous school. Dedicated interview days are held monthly from December to March each year and the entry requirement is a minimum of 3 A and 3 B grades at GCSE, including English and Mathematics, with normally an A grade in the subjects chosen for study.

Registration Fee £100.

Fees per term (2016–2017). Junior School: £3,700 (includes lunch which is compulsory). Senior School: £4,105.

Sibling discount of 10% for the second child and 20% for the third or subsequent child attending concurrently.

Scholarships and Financial Awards. Academic Scholarships and Exhibitions, in the form of an individual prize, are offered annually to pupils who excel in the school's entrance tests at 7+, 11+ and 13+. Music Scholarships and Exhibitions are offered at 13+ and 16+ following an audition and interview.

The School annually makes available a number of means-tested Governors' Awards. These are for external candidates joining the School, who meet the academic entry requirements and whose parents could not afford to send them to Exeter School without financial assistance. As a general guide, gross parental income will need to be below £60,000 per annum to allow consideration for a Governors' award. In addition, there are also a number of special awards made possible by donations from local benefactors for able pupils whose parents require financial assistance.

Curriculum. In the first 3 years in the Senior School all pupils take English, History, Geography, a carousel of

French, German, Spanish and Latin, Mathematics, IT, Physics, Chemistry, Biology, Art, Design Technology, Drama, Music and Religious and Physical Education. After this there is a wide choice of subjects at GCSE level, including English, one compulsory Modern Foreign Language, Mathematics, dual or triple award Science, Religious Studies and 3 of the following: Latin, French, German, Spanish, Classical Civilisation, History, Geography, Music, Drama, Art, Design and Technology, and Information Technology.

Pupils enter the Sixth Form choosing over 20 different subjects for A Level study and are prepared for university scholarships, university entrance and admission to other forms of further education or vocational training. Over 95% go on annually to Degree Courses.

Houses. There are nine Pupil Houses. Each is under the personal care of a Head of House and his/her deputy, with whom parents are invited to keep in touch on any matter affecting their child's general development and progress throughout the school.

Religion. All pupils attend Religious Education classes, which include Sixth Form discussion groups. Pupils may be prepared for Confirmation.

Games. Rugby, Hockey, Cricket, Swimming, Athletics, Dance, Cross Country, Tennis, Badminton, Squash, Shooting, Basketball, Netball, Fencing, Cycling and Golf. Further activities are available for the Sixth Form, including Football and Multi-Gym sessions.

Community and other Service. All pupils learn to serve the community. Many choose to take part in Social Service, helping old people and the handicapped young. There is a voluntary CCF Contingent with thriving RN, Army and RAF Sections. The CCF offers a large variety of Outdoor Activities, including Adventure Training Camps, Ten Tors Expedition Training as well as specialist courses. Pupils are encouraged to participate in the Duke of Edinburgh's Award Scheme.

Music. Pupils are taught Singing and Musical appreciation and are encouraged to learn to play Musical Instruments. More than one third of all pupils have individual lessons on at least one instrument. There are 4 Orchestras, a Choral Society which annually performs a major work in Exeter Cathedral and 4 Choirs, 3 jazz bands, and numerous smaller groups from string quartets to rock bands. There are over 30 visiting instrumental teachers. Over 20 public concerts are given each year. Recent Summer Music trips have included Lake Garda and Barcelona.

Drama. Drama is developed both within and outside the curriculum. The School Hall with its large and well-equipped stage provides for the dual purpose of studio workshop and the regular production of plays, operas and musicals. The recently refurbished Drama Studio is used for smaller productions.

Art and Design. Art lessons are given to junior and senior forms. Apart from the formal disciplines of GCSE and A Level, which can be taken by those who choose, all pupils have opportunity for artistic expression in painting, print-making, photography, pottery, construction in many materials and carving wood and stone. All younger pupils learn to develop craft skills in wood, metal and plastic and to use them creatively in design work. Some then follow GCSE or A Level courses in Design and Technology. There is an annual art exhibition in July.

Expeditions. Throughout the school a large number of residential field trips and expeditions take place each year including a Third Form new pupils' Dartmoor weekend, various departmental excursions, several foreign exchanges and Duke of Edinburgh's Award expeditions. Pupils are also encouraged to compete for external expeditions and, following years of representation on its expeditions, the school has been awarded Star status by the British Exploring Society (BES). In recent summers, the school has run its own adventure trips to Namibia, Peru, Vietnam and the Himalayas and canoeing trips to Peru and Slovenia. There is a programme of major and minor sports tours.

Societies and Clubs. Pupils are encouraged to pursue their interests by joining one of the School Societies. Groups of enthusiasts can form new Societies or Clubs, but the following are at present available: Art, Badminton, Basketball, Canoeing, Chess, Choral Society, Computing, Dance, Drama, Electronics, Model Railway, Music, Politics, Sailing, Shooting and Squash.

Social. Close contact is maintained with the City and the University. Association between members of the School and the wider society outside is fostered wherever opportunity offers.

The staff believe strongly in the value of association with parents, who are invited to meetings annually throughout their sons' or daughters' time at the School. A termly lecture by a visiting speaker is provided for parents. The Exeter School Parents' Association exists to promote closer relations between the School and its parents.

Careers. Careers education begins at the age of 13 and continues on a progressive programme until students leave the school. Careers evenings are held annually when pupils and their parents have the opportunity to consult representatives of the professions, industry and commerce. A work experience programme is organised for Year 11 pupils each summer, and a scheme of mock interviews with career professionals for pupils in the Sixth Form. A major Careers Convention is held at the school each Autumn for pupils from Years 9 to 13.

Honours. Pupils regularly gain admission to Oxford and Cambridge. The School encourages application to the leading universities, including the Russell and 1994 Groups.

Leading musicians have gained places at the Royal College of Music and the Royal Academy of Music.

Charitable status. Exeter School is a Registered Charity, number 1093080, and a Company Limited by Guarantee, registered in England, number 04470478. Registered Office: Victoria Park Road, Exeter, Devon EX2 4NS.

Patrons:
The Lord Lieutenant of the County of Devon
The Right Reverend the Lord Bishop of Exeter
The Right Worshipful the Lord Mayor of Exeter

Governors:
Appointed by the Devon County Council:
Mrs R Brook

Appointed by the Exeter City Council:
G J Prowse

Appointed by the Governors of St John's Hospital:
¶A C W King (*Chairman*)
Miss R Edbrooke, BEd

Representatives of the Universities of Exeter and Oxford:
Exeter: Professor S C Smart, BA, PhD
Oxford: Dr M C Grossel, MA, PhD

Co-opted Governors:
J D Gaisford, BSc, ACA (*Vice-Chairman*)
¶T E Hawkins (*Vice-Chairman*)
Mrs B Meeke, LLB (*Vice-Chairman*)
¶A P Burbanks, BA
K Cheney, BA
Mrs H Clark
¶Ms G A Hodgetts, BA, MSc
Professor A F Watkinson, MSc, FRCS
¶Brigadier S P Hodder, BSc

Headmaster: **R Griffin**, MA

Deputy Headmaster: M J Hughes, MA
Assistant Head: Miss L J Hilton, MSc
Assistant Head: G S Bone, BSc, CSci

Assistant Head: Mrs N A Fairweather, BA
Director of Alumni Relations: J W Davidson, MA, MSc

Assistant Staff:
* Head of Department
† Housemaster/mistress
§ Part-time or Visiting
¶ Former pupil

Art & Design:
*Mrs A J Dyer, BA
Miss J H White, BA

Biology:
*Mrs J H Metcalf, MA
†P J C Boddington, BSc
Mrs J M Clark, BSc
Mrs A C Johnson, BSc
Mrs K A Coe, BSc

Chemistry:
*R F J Tear, BSc
Miss L J Hilton, MSc (*Assistant Head*)
M K Chitnavis, BSc, CSci, FRSC (*Universities Adviser*)
Dr S P Smale, BSc, PhD
Dr A M Rowland, PhD
§Mrs F J Tamblyn, BSc

Classical Subjects:
*Mrs S Shrubb, MA
N P L Keyes, MA
Mrs E K J Dunlop, MA, MPhil

Computing & Information Systems:
*Mrs R Cull, BSc, MIITT, CMath, MIMA
N F Howard, BA
§D E Sims, BSc

Design Technology:
*J Parry, BA
I R Lowles, BA

Drama:
*J S Brough, BSc
§Ms P E Marriott, BA

Electronics:
*Dr A W Houghton, MA, MSc, PhD
M E Schramm, BSc

English:
*A S Dobson, MA
†Mrs J H Daybell, MA
†Mrs E K J Dunlop, MA, MPhil
†Mrs E A Whittall, BA, MEd
Miss K L Ridler-Murray, MA
R O Evans, BA
E J Seaton-Jones, BA

Geography:
*Mrs H M Sail, BA
J W Davidson, MA, MSc (*Director of Alumni Relations*)
Mrs M J Webb, MA
Mrs N A Fairweather, BA (*Assistant Head*)
Mrs A Roff, BSc
P M Hyde, BSc

History:
*G N Trelawny, BEd, MA
Mrs A-J Culley, BA, BSc
Ms J R Hodgetts, BA

Languages:
*M F Latimer, MSt
M C Wilcock, BEd
Mrs A M Francis, MA
§Mrs S C Wilson, BA
R A Charters, BA

Mrs D D S Masters, BA
Mrs R Alborough, BA
J J Marshall, BEd

Mathematics:
*Miss E V Marshall, BSc
†G R Willson, BSc
†Dr P M Smallwood, BSc, PhD
A J Reynolds, BSc
M J Hughes, MA (*Deputy Head*)
Dr G J D Chapman, BSc, MSc, PhD (*CCF Contingent Commander*)
Mrs A J James, BSc
F E Malone-Lee, BA
Miss M McCluskey, MSc

Music:
*P Tamblyn, MA, MMus (*Director of Music*)
T P Brimelow, MA
Mrs T M Guthrie, BA
§A Gillett, ARCM
§D Bowen, BEd
§P Painter, DipMusEd, Cert Ed
§B Moore, BA

Physical Education and Games:
*A C F Mason, BA (*Director of Sport*)
Mrs A J Marsh, BEd (*Head of Sixth Form*)
E P M Jones, BSc
Miss R A Carter, BSc
§F L Smith (*CCF SSI*)
§G Skinner, BEd
Miss H J Rhodes, BSc
T N Ross, BSc

Physics:
*Dr J L Wilson, MPhys, DPhil (*Director of Science*)
G S Bone, BSc, CSci (*Assistant Head*)
Dr A W Houghton, MA, MSc, PhD
M E Schramm, BSc
M K Chitnavis, BSc, CSci, FRSC (*Universities Adviser*)
Dr G B N Robb, PhD
D I Trim, BSc

Religious Studies:
*†M H R Porter, BA
†Mrs J M K Murrin, BA
Mrs A J Marsh, BEd
Revd T P Carson, MTh, MA (*Chaplain*)
Mrs C Gooddy, MSc

Social Studies:
*S K Mackintosh, BA (*Economics*)
*Miss M F Dunn, BA (*Politics*)
†R J Baker, BA
P Bell, MA

Learning Support:
§Mrs A Reeves, BSc
§Mrs S E Oliver, BEd

Junior School

Headmistress: Mrs S Marks, BSc, PGCE

Assistant Head: J S Wood, BA

Assistant Staff:
R Bland, BEd
¶G E L Ashman, BA
Mrs P A Goldsworthy, BA, LTCL
R J Pidwell, BA
Mrs R M Parkin, CertEd
Ms J A Barnes, MSc
Mrs C H Handley, BEd
Mrs L L Hardy, MA
Mrs K J Daws, BA

Mrs R E Pettet, BA
Mrs K L Jones, BSc

Bursar and Clerk to the Governors: Cdre R C Hawkins
RN, BA
Deputy Bursar and Company Secretary: Mrs G M Robins,
BA, ACCA
Registrar: Mrs S M Chamberlain, BA
Headmaster's PA: Mrs K Leach
Bursar's PA: Mrs J W Furniss
Head of Information Systems: W R T Lines, MSc, CEng
Librarian: Mrs E G Taylor, BSc, DipLib
School Nurse: Mrs M R Sanders, RGN

Felsted School

Felsted, Essex CM6 3LL
Tel: 01371 822606 (Headmaster)
           01371 822605 (Admissions Registrar)
Fax: 01371 822697 (School)
           01371 822607 (Headmaster)
email: info@felsted.org
website: www.felsted.org
Twitter: @felstedschool
Facebook: /felstedschool
LinkedIn: /Felsted Network

Founded in 1564 by Lord Richard Riche, Felsted celebrated its 450th anniversary in 2014, and was honoured by a
visit from Her Majesty The Queen. Educating boys and girls
aged 4 to 18, Felsted is is ideally situated in a picturesque
North Essex village, close to both London and Cambridge,
and within easy reach of Stansted and other international airports. Felsted is a Church of England foundation but welcomes pupils from all Christian denominations and those
from other religious traditions. The Senior School, for 13 to
18 year olds, has around 530 pupils; the majority are boarders and weekend arrangements are flexible. The Preparatory
School boasts 510 pupils, with a buoyant boarding house,
home to full, weekly and flexible boarders.

The School is a Global Member of the Round Square
Organisation offering international exchanges and collaboration, and offers both A Levels and the International Baccalaureate in the Sixth Form. Felsted's prospectus can be
found online at www.felsted.org along with much other
information and news, details of forthcoming events and
location maps. Each Boarding House has its own web page
and several videos, including one called 'Boarding at Felsted', can be downloaded. Felsted had an Ofsted boarding
and welfare inspection in 2011 and was rated 'outstanding'
in every aspect, with no recommendations for improvement.
Felsted also received an 'excellent' in all aspects rating by
the Independent Schools Inspectorate in 2013, and passed
with flying colours in a full compliance inspection across
both the Preparatory and Senior School in 2016. Details are
available from their website.

The Houses. There are ten Houses at Felsted, a day
house for boys, a day house for girls, three boarding houses
for boys, three boarding houses for girls, an Upper Sixth
House for boys and an Upper Sixth House for girls. Each
House is under the direction of a resident Housemaster or
Housemistress.

Each House Parent is supported by a pastoral team comprising a resident Assistant House Parent, a matron responsible for overseeing the domestic arrangements, and several
House tutors.

The Curriculum. All pupils study English Language,
English Literature, Mathematics and Sciences (Science/
Additional Science) to GCSE and choose a further five sub-
jects from the following: History, Geography, Religious

Studies, French, German, Spanish, Latin, Classical Civilisation, Art and Design, Music, Drama, Triple Science (instead
of Science/Additional Science), Design & Technology
(Resistant Materials or Graphic Products), Physical Education and Computing.

One of the options must be a Modern Foreign Language
and one must be a Humanities subject.

In the Sixth Form pupils have a choice between A Levels
and the International Baccalaureate.

Those studying A Levels choose four subjects to study to
AS Level and then continue with either three or four subjects to A Level. The following subjects are offered: Art and
Design, Business Studies, Classical Civilisation, Computing, Design Technology, Drama and Theatre Studies, Economics, English Literature, Geography, Government and
Politics, History, History of Art, Latin, Mathematics, Mathematics (Further), Modern Foreign Languages (French, German, Spanish), Music, Music Technology, Physical
Education, Psychology, Religious Studies, Sciences (Biology, Chemistry, Physics). Students also complete the EPQ.

IB pupils study six subjects, one from each of the following categories: Language and Literature (English, German,
Italian, Self-Study Language, Spanish and French), Language Acquisition (French, German, English, Spanish,
Latin. Mandarin, Spanish and Italian 'ab initio'), Individuals
and Societies (Economics, Geography, History, Philosophy,
Psychology), Sciences (Biology, Chemistry, Design Technology, Physics, Sports Exercise and Health Science), Mathematics (Maths, Maths Studies), The Arts (Visual Arts,
Music). They also follow a course on the Theory of Knowledge, write an extended essay and are fully involved in the
Creativity, Action and Service Programme.

Scholarships and Bursaries. Academic, Music, Drama,
Art, Design & Technology and Sports Scholarships are
awarded annually for entry at 13+ and to the Sixth Form, up
to the value of 20% of the fees.

The examinations for the 13+ Scholarships take place in
February and May and for the Sixth Form Scholarships in
November.

Mary Skill Awards, which recognise all-round ability or a
specific ability in one area, are also available.

Means-tested Bursaries may be available to increase an
award.

Up to two Open Bursaries (100%) each year are available
to those who might otherwise not be able to consider Felsted, due to financial circumstances.

Talented students in Design are also entered at 16+ for
Arkwright Foundation Scholarships.

Scholarships are also awarded at 11+ at Felsted Preparatory School and these may be carried through to the Senior
School.

Fee reductions are available for children of those serving
in the Armed Services.

Full details are available at www.felsted.org and from the
Admissions Registrar.

Registration and entry. Boys' and girls' names can be
registered at any time. Registration fee £100.

Before admission to Felsted all pupils at other prepara-
tory schools must pass the Common Entrance or Common
Academic Scholarship Examination. Entry from other
schools is by Head Teacher's Report and Felsted Entrance
Test, or, for Sixth Form entry, 6 B Grades at GCSE, Head
Teacher's report, Felsted Entrance Test and interview.

Fees per term (2016–2017). Senior School: Full Boarding (7 nights) £10,995, Weekly Boarding (5 nights) £10,345,
Contemporary Boarding (3 nights) £9,195, Day £7,375. Preparatory School: Day £2,905–£5,550, Weekly Boarding
£7,195, Full Boarding £7,540.

Felsted Preparatory School, whose Head is in membership of IAPS (The Independent Association of Prep
Schools), shares the same governing body with Felsted

School. It has its own campus, with 510 pupils aged 4 to 13. There is a dedicated teaching centre for 11–13 year-olds and a state-of-the-art Pre-Preparatory Department, which opened in 2011. (*For further information, see entry in IAPS section.*)

Old Felstedian Society organises both social and sporting activities, plus networking opportunities across a variety of industries. The Old Felstedian Liaison Master, Mr N S Hinde, would be pleased to answer queries about the Alumni and further information can be found at www.archives.felsted.essex.sch.uk.

Charitable status. Felsted School is a Registered Charity, number 310870. The charity is based upon the Foundation established by Richard Lord Riche in 1564 with the objective of teaching and instructing children across a broad curriculum as ordained from time to time by its Trustees.

Governing Body:
J H Davies OBE (*Chairman*)

P G Lee	B Grindlay
P J Hutley	N Stuchfield
Mrs B Davy	Mrs A Carrington
Dr J Nicholson	R Brown
O Stocken	G Boult
J Tibbitts	J Abel Smith
Mrs J Crouch	B Lewis
W Sunnucks	

Bursar & Clerk to the Governors: Mrs Margaret McKenna, MA, MBA, FCMA

Headmaster: Mr Christopher J Townsend, MA

Deputy Headmaster: Mr George Masters, PGCE

Deputy Head (Welfare): Mrs Karen A Megahey, BSc (*Designated Safeguarding Officer, *PSHE*)

Assistant Head (Academic): Mrs Sarah R Capewell, MA (*Classics*)

Staff:
* *Head of Department*
p/t *Part-time*
† *Housemaster/mistress*
AHM *Assistant Housemaster/mistress*

Mrs Catherine J Allen, BA (*Geography*)
Mr G Charles Allen, BA, MA (**Classics*)
Mr Chris Allen (*Mathematics*)
Mr Joseph Andrews, MA (*Mathematics*)
Mr Christopher J Atkinson, MSc (*Mathematics*)
Mrs Meredith Atkinson-Wood, MA (**History of Art*)
Mr Francis M Barrett, BBS (*Economics and Business Studies, †Windsor's, Senior HM*)
Mrs Lucy T Barrett, BSc (**Chemistry*)
Mrs Sarah Barrett, BSc (*PE, †Garnetts*)
Mr Gordon Bates (*Geography*)
Ms Suzanne Beale, BA (*SFL*)
Mr Peter G Bennett, AGSM (*Director of Music*)
Mrs Mandy J Bonnett, MSc (*Biology*)
Ms Maria E Burns, BA (**English*)
Mr Barny J Bury, BA Ed (**PE, AHM Windsor's*)
Mrs Melissa Cacace, BA (*Psychology, *Theory of Knowledge*)
Mr Michael J Campbell, MSci (**Mathematics, AHM Gepps*)
Mr Alan G Chamberlain, MA (*Modern Foreign Languages*)
Mrs Holly Charlton-Ricks, BA (*Design & Technology, AHM Manor*)
Miss Kelly Cleaver (*Exams Officer*)
Ms Roslyn Cox (*Tennis*)
Mrs Caroline Croydon, MSc Hons (*ICT, Timetabler and Curriculum Coordinator*)

Ms Zoe Defoe, BA (*HLTA, EAL*)
Miss Patrizia Dellea, MA (*Italian and French*)
Miss Constance Donaldson, BSc (*Mathematics*)
Mrs Mel Donaldson, BA (*Director of Performing Arts*)
Maj William H Eke, MBE (*CCF Adjutant*)
Mr Daniel P Emmerson (*Director of Holiday Courses, Round Square Coordinator*)
Ms Anna Fazekas, MA (**German, Modern Languages*)
Mr Richard L Feldman, MSc (*Mathematics, Director of Data Administration*)
Mr Edward Fenning, MA (*Mathematics, AHM Elwyn's*)
Mrs Helen A Fenning, MA (*SfL*)
Mr Jason E R Gallian (*Geography, Director of Cricket, AHM Montgomery's*)
Mr Thomas Galvin, BSc (**Geography*)
Mrs Rebecca Grant, BA (*Modern Foreign Languages, Round Square Coordinator*)
Mrs Dianne K Guerrero, BA (**EAL, International Coordinator*)
Mr Thomas J Hietzker, FSB (**Biology, Deputy Designated Safeguarding Officer*)
Mr Jeff Hipkin, BA, QTS, MEd (*SfL*)
Mr A Martin Homer, MA (*English, Drama, Director International Education and IB*)
Mrs Nichola Howarth, BA, DipLib, MCLIP (*Librarian*)
Mrs Catriona M James, BA (*English*)
Mr Joseph Johnson, BA (*English, AHM Deacon's*)
Ms Nicola J Johnson, CDip (*SfL*)
Mr Charles S Knightley, BA (*PE, Director of Sport, †Deacon's*)
Mr Andrew Le Chevalier (*Rugby, †Montgomery's*)
The Revd Nigel Little, BA (*Chaplain, RE, Charities*)
Mr Nick J Lockhart ECB3, EH2 (*Head of Grounds and Cricket Professional*)
Mrs Lauren Macey, BA (*Drama*)
Ms Janine K Mallett, BA (**French*)
Mr Lewis Mann, BA (*Drama*)
Mrs Andrea Manzi-Davies (*English*)
Mrs Joy E McArdle, BA, MBA (**Business Studies and Economics, Director of Business and Enterprise Education*)
Dr Sufia McGuire, BSc, MSc, PhD (*Chemistry, †Thorne*)
Mr Luke McIlvenna, MEd (*Business Studies and Economics, †Gepps*)
Miss Elizabeth M McLaren, BA (*Classics*)
Miss Charlene Menet (*MFL*)
Dr Peter H Milner, BSc, PhD, CChem, MRSC (*SfL*)
Mrs Aarti Mohindru, LLB (*Economics*)
Mrs Katherine Moir-Smith, BA (*Geography*)
Mrs Heather Mollison, BSc (*Chemistry, *Science*)
Ms Nicola F S O'Brien, MA (*Spanish, †Follyfield*)
Mrs Tina Oakley-Agar, BSc (*ICT*)
Mrs Abbey Overall (*Dance*)
Mr Clifford H Palmer, MA (*CCF Contingent Commander, Physics*)
Mr Rakesh Pathak, BA (**History*)
Mr Ben R Peart, BSc (*Biology, †Elwyn's*)
Miss Rocio Perez Cabrera (*MFL Language Asst*)
Mrs Carolyn M Phillips, MCLIP (*SFL, †Manor, Magic Bus Coordinator*)
Mr Nicholas J Phillips, BA (*PE, *Boys Hockey*)
Mr Mick A Pitts, BEng (**Design Technology*)
Miss Rebecca Purdy, BA (*English, MUN Coordinator & Felsted Diploma and Co-Curricular Coordinator*)
Mr Mark Redding (*ICT*)
Mr David A Rees, BA (*Classics, Business Studies*)
Mrs Beth S Roberts Jones, BSc (**RE*)
Ms Elizabeth K Rose, BA (*Geography*)
Miss Carla E Rudd, BSc (*Sport/PE*)
Mrs Anna L Salmon, BA (**Support for Learning, †Stocks's*)

Mr Felix Sanchez del Rio, Licenciatura (*Modern Languages*, *Spanish*)
Ms Louise Scofield, BA (*History and Politics*)
Ms Loren Sherer, BSc, MA (*Director of Girls Sports, AHM Follyfield*)
Miss Katie Shirtcliffe, BA (*Art*)
Miss Alex L F Simpson, BSc (*Biology, Director of Lower Sixth and Work Education*)
Mr David J Smith, BA (*Art*)
Mr David T Smith, BSc (*Physics*)
Mrs Vicki L Smith, BSc (*Psychology*)
Mr Nicholas J Spring, MA (*English, Director of Professional Guidance, President of Common Room*)
Mrs Lorne Stefanini, BSc, MA (*Religious Studies*)
Mrs Shirley Stone (*Exams Officer*)
Sra Marta M Valls, BA (*Spanish, French*)
Miss Rachel Ward, BA (*History*)
Miss Rebecca Warner, MSc (*SFL, AHM Stocks'*)
Mr William Warns, BA, FNCM (*Academic Music, Choirmaster & Organist*)
Mr Christian L Watkinson, BSc (*Chemistry*)
Mrs Dee L Whittock (*DofE Manager*)
Miss Laura Wigglesworth, BA (*Religious Studies*)
Mr Nigel Wilson (*Tutor*)
Ms Sonia D Wilson, BA (*Business Studies and Economics, AHM Garnetts*)
Mrs K L Woodhouse, BSc (*Physics*)

Houses and Housemasters/mistresses:

Boys' Houses:
Deacon's: Charlie Knightley
Elwyn's: Ben Peart
Gepp's: Luke McIlvenna
Montgomery's: Andrew Le Chevalier
Windsor's: Francis Barrett

Girls' Houses:
Follyfield: Nicola O'Brien
Garnetts: Sarah Barrett
Manor: Carolyn Phillips
Stocks': Anna Salmon
Thorne: Sophie McGuire

Head of the Preparatory School: Mr Simon James, BA
Director of Marketing: Mrs Sophy Aitken
Admissions Registrar: Mrs Ruth Wyganowski
School Chaplain: Reverend Nigel Little
Medical Officer: Mrs Sally Staines

Fettes College

Carrington Road, Edinburgh EH4 1QX

Tel: +44 (0)131 311 6744
Fax: +44 (0)131 311 6714
email: admissions@fettes.com
website: www.fettes.com
Twitter: @Fettes_College

Motto: '*Industria*'.

Founded in 1870 by Sir William Fettes and designed by David Bryce, Fettes College is uniquely situated in extensive grounds and woodland close to the heart of Edinburgh, and enjoys a reputation as one of the pre-eminent co-educational boarding schools in the UK. Fettes College has 757 pupils aged 7–18 (205 in the Prep School and 552 in The College), boarders and day pupils at a ratio of 80:20 in the Senior School and 30:70 in the Prep School. Fettes students are drawn from all over the British Isles and from abroad and this diverse and healthy mix of backgrounds provides a richness that contributes to the stimulating, warm and energetic community that is Fettes College.

Fettes College has over 5,000 Old Fettesians who remain in touch with us for one very compelling reason: being educated at Fettes was one of the most important and beneficial aspects of their lives.

Fettes is where their confidence was built, horizons broadened, talents nurtured and lifelong friendships made, where they achieved exam success, broke sporting records, were inspired by teachers and learnt the skills which would equip them for later life.

Fettes is where they were enthused, praised and encouraged to work hard and achieve the very best they could, while being surrounded by like-minded peers and caring staff.

To this day, a Fettes education is an incredible start to life.

Situation and Buildings. Fettes stands in 80 acres of parkland close to the centre of Edinburgh. Being just 20 minutes' walk to the city centre, means that Fettes students can take full advantage of the wealth of cultural resources on offer in Scotland's Capital city such as galleries, museums and theatres. Students also have every opportunity to enjoy the majestic Scottish outdoors with a full programme of trips and experiences from hillwalking to canoeing, camping to white water rafting. Regular national and international school trips further broaden the experience Fettes students are offered.

Transportation links by road, rail and air are excellent.

Organisation. Each member of the School is the responsibility of a Housemaster or Housemistress. In the Senior School there are four Houses for boys, four for girls, and a co-ed Upper Sixth Form house. The Upper Sixth Form boarding house provides individual and twin study-bedrooms with en-suite facilities for all boarders. There is a strong tutorial system for the encouragement and guidance of each pupil.

Aims. Our mission at Fettes is to develop broadly educated, confident and thoughtful individuals. The hopes and aspirations of each and every one of our students are of central importance to us, and the happy, purposeful environment of the College encourages the boys and girls to flourish and develop fully the skills and interests that they possess.

Curriculum. For GCSE all students take English, Mathematics, Physics, Chemistry and Biology. Students then choose four subjects from the following list: Art & Design, Computer Science, Classical Civilisation, Classical Greek, Drama, Economics, French, Geography, German, History, Latin, Mandarin, Music, PE and Spanish. Students must choose at least one modern foreign language.

Fettes offers a very broad range of subjects in the Sixth Form with students choosing either A Levels or International Baccalaureate, therefore allowing a choice of curriculum to best suit the needs of the individual student. Over 98% of pupils gain university entry with up to 15 students securing places at Oxford and Cambridge each year.

Careers. The School is a member of the Independent Schools Careers Organisation, and a team of Staff are responsible for providing specialist advice on careers and Higher Education and for developing links with industry and commerce. Fettes Community & Fettes Career Partnership was launched in 2014 providing business networking links between Old Fettesians, current parents, past parents, Fettes students and recent Fettes graduates.

Chapel. The College Chapel, situated in the heart of the School, is central to life at Fettes with the daily Chapel service forming the core of the moral and spiritual guidance offered at Fettes. Fettes has a strong Christian tradition but members of other faiths and those with no faith are warmly welcomed, and this is reflected in the tolerant and questioning character of the School.

Games. All students are involved in sports at least 3 afternoons per week. All major sports are offered at Fettes in fact there are very few sports you cannot pursue. Rugby, cricket, hockey, lacrosse, netball, athletics, tennis, squash, fives, swimming, badminton, fencing, basketball, volleyball are an example of what is on offer. Fettes College is very proud of the individual and team success at school and national levels across a range of sports including rugby, fencing, sailing and cross-country. Fettes College also has excellent sporting facilities including a purpose-built sports centre, all-weather pitches, indoor swimming pool, climbing wall, courts for fives and squash, shooting range and a separate specialist gym for Sixth Form pupils.

Other activities. There are 50+ societies, clubs and extra-curricular activities, and each pupil is encouraged to develop cultural interests. On Saturday evenings, in addition to lectures, plays and concerts, there are regular dances and discos, and committees of pupils, with the assistance of members of Staff, are responsible for planning and organising social events for different age groups.

Music. The College possesses a strong musical tradition, and many pupils receive instrumental tuition. In addition to the orchestras there are ensembles, a swing band, Chapel Choir and Concert Choir. A major concert is held at the end of every term. Standards are very high and the Chapel Choir has achieved notable success, being recorded by the BBC and performing by invitation at Westminster Abbey and St Paul's Cathedral.

Drama. Drama is lively and of a high standard. Each year the School Play and House plays offer great opportunities for large numbers of boys and girls to act and to participate in Lighting and Stage Management.

Art. The Art School is flourishing, and the standards of pupil attainment are very high. Regular House art competitions and gallery display of current work occur.

Combined Cadet Force, Duke of Edinburgh's Award, Outside Service. Pupils are members of the CCF for two years and may choose to extend their service while they are in the Sixth Form. Training is offered in Shooting, Vehicle Engineering, Canoeing, Rock-Climbing, Skiing, Sub-Aqua and Sailing.

In the Sixth Form many pupils pursue the Gold Standard of the Duke of Edinburgh's Award Scheme, and some 70 members of the School join the Outside Service Unit which provides help for others in difficult circumstances and raises funds for Charities.

Outdoor Activities. The School aims to make full use of its proximity to the sea, the Dry Ski Slope, and the rivers and mountains of Scotland. Outdoor activities are encouraged for the enjoyment that they give and the valuable personal qualities which they help to develop. A number of members of Staff are experts in mountaineering, skiing and watersports, and all pupils have opportunities for receiving instruction in camping, canoeing, sailing, hillwalking and snow and rock climbing. There are regular expeditions abroad.

Preparatory School. The Preparatory School for 205 boys and girls aged 7 to 13 is situated in the School grounds. Boarders stay in the modern purpose-built Houses. Pupils in the Prep School share the facilities of the senior school and participate in the full range of activities enjoyed by the College as a whole. (*For further details see entry in IAPS section.*)

Admission. Personal interviews assess the promise of each individual and determine those who will gain most from a Fettes education. Entrance exams are also required for entry. Pupils may join the Preparatory School at any stage (7–13) with students normally joining the Senior School at 13+, 14+ and 16+. Further details are available from the Registrar.

Scholarships and Bursaries. All applicants can apply for a means-tested bursary which can cover up to 100% of the fees. There is a finite amount of funding available each year and therefore not all applicants will be successful. Bursaries are awarded independently of any Scholarship or Award. The process for applying for a bursary is completely separate to the admissions process and must be done through the Bursar's Office.

There is a wide range of Scholarships and Awards available at 13+ and/or 16+ including Academic, All-Rounder, Sport, Music, Art and Piping. There is great kudos associated with being a scholar or award holder of The College. Scholarships also attract reductions of up to 10% of the fees while Awards can also attract reductions of up to 5% of the fees unrelated to parents' financial circumstances.

Children of members of HM Forces qualify for a reduction in fees and Special Bursaries (Todd) are available for descendants of Old Fettesians.

Past papers are available and further enquiries should be made to the Registrar.

Fees per term (2016–2017). Senior School: Boarders £10,780, Day Pupils £8,515. The fees cover all extras except books and stationery, music lessons and subscriptions to voluntary clubs and activities.

Registration Fee £100.

Old Fettesian Association. *Liaison*: Old Fettesian Association Office, Fettes College (Telephone +44 (0)131 311 6741).

Charitable status. The Fettes Trust is a Registered Charity, number SC017489. Fettes aims to provide a quality education at Junior and Senior level.

Chairman of Governors: The Hon Lord Tyre, CBE, QC

Senior Management Team:

Headmaster: M C B Spens, MA Selwyn College Cambridge

Deputy Head: Mrs H F Harrison, MA Cambridge
Assistant Headmaster & Director of Studies: A Shackleton, MA Cambridge
Headmaster of the Preparatory School: A A Edwards, BA London
Director of Teaching & Learning: A J Armstrong, MA St Andrews
Assistant Director of Studies: L J Whyte, BSc PhD Norwich
Head of Pastoral Care: Mrs C M Harrison, BA Cambridge
Head of PSE: Mrs S A Bruce, BSc St Andrews
Director of Sport: S M Bates, BSc London
Director of Digital Strategy: Mrs YEA Mitchell, BSc Durham
Bursar: P J F Worlledge, BSc Bristol
Director of Marketing and PR: Mrs G G Gray, MA Edinburgh
Director of Development: Ms N Pickavance, LLB Aberdeen

Chaplain: Revd Dr A Clark, BA York, PhD St Andrews

Heads of Departments/Subjects:
Art: Miss B J Conway, BA Edinburgh College of Art
Biology: Dr S A Lewis, BSc London, PhD Glasgow (*Head of Science*)
Business Studies and Economics: P F Heuston, BSc Cape Town (*i/c Outdoor Pursuits*)
Chemistry: Dr C R Mathieson, MChem, PhD St Andrews
Classics: Miss C L Nicholls, BA Oxford
Computer Science: A R Cheadle, MA Reading
Drama: E M J Boulter-Comer, BA Edinburgh
English: A J Speedy, BA Durham
Geography: Miss H E Cockburn, BSc Queen's Belfast
Government and Politics: D B McDowell, MA Oxford
History: Miss T J McDonald, BA Salford
History of Art: R E Hughes, MA Edinburgh, MPhil London

Mathematics: Miss J M Maguire, MSc Belfast
Modern Languages: Ms J M Berganza, BA Grenoble
Music: D A Goodenough, GGSM, FTCL, ARCO, ALCM
    (*Director of Music*)
Bagpipe Music: C R Drummond, BA RSAMD
Physical Education:
S M Bates, BSc London, MBA Durham (*Director of Sport*)
Miss F Ermgassen, BSc Bath (*Head of Girls' Games*)
J D Pillinger, BSc Surrey (*Head of PE*)
Physics: N C R Ward, BSc Manchester
Support For Learning: Miss P Bailey, MA Lancaster

Forest School

London E17 3PY

Tel: 020 8520 1744
Fax: 020 8520 3656
email: info@forest.org.uk
website: www.forest.org.uk
Twitter: @ForestSchoolE17
Facebook: /ForestSchoolE17

Motto: '*In Pectore Robur*'.

Established in 1834, Forest School is London's only diamond structure school located at the edge of capital's largest open space, Epping Forest.

There are currently more than 1,377 pupils in the School (1,105 boys and girls in the Senior School, 272 boys and girls in the Pre-Preparatory and Preparatory School). All pupils share the main school campus and facilities such as the Chapel, Dining Hall, Sports Hall, playing fields, Deaton Theatre and the Martin Centre for Innovation. Sixth Form pupils enjoy use of a dedicated Sixth Form Centre including collaborative IT work spaces, group study areas and a careers room. The School site and playing fields cover nearly 27 acres.

Diamond Structure. Boys and girls are taught in co-educational classes when they join Forest School in the Pre-Prep, then in single-sex classes within the Prep School from Y3. At 11, pupils join the Senior School and single-sex teaching continues until the Sixth Form, where classes are once again co-educational. Co-curricular activities are largely co-educational although boys and girls follow different sports programmes.

While the existence of the diamond structure at Forest is a result of evolution rather than initial design, the Forest School of today regards the mix of single-sex and co-educational teaching as an educational model of which to be proud, and thought and effort goes into making it a structure that we might indeed have designed from scratch.

Curriculum. The Forest curriculum parallels the National Curriculum, although the School exercises its independence to enable teachers to exploit the high academic ability of the pupils. In Y7–Y9 a range of core subjects is taught, including Modern and Classical Languages and the three Sciences. Options in Y9 include Computing, Ancient Greek and Food & Nutrition, as well as more mainstream subjects. At GCSE, all pupils follow a core curriculum of English Language & Literature, a Modern Foreign Language, Maths and Science (separate or Double Award, according to preference) as well as a choice from around 15 optional subjects. A distinctive feature of the curriculum is that all pupils also submit work for the Higher Project Qualification (HPQ) – a research-based dissertation on a subject of the pupil's own choosing, following a taught course of critical thinking and project skills, assessed at GCSE level.

In the Sixth Form, pupils take the Forest Diploma. A Levels provide the core academic element and Sixth Formers can choose from 26 different A Level subjects, with most choosing three main subjects, examined at the end of the two-year course, and taught in small teaching groups of typically around ten to fifteen pupils. All Diploma pupils begin a course in Project Skills in Year 12 and will continue to produce an EPQ, which may take the form of a dissertation-style essay, or perhaps a 'creative artefact', like a film, composition or even a computer program.

The School places considerable emphasis on teaching the effective use of Information and Communications Technology. Every pupil in the Senior School is required to have with them a keyboard-enabled device in school, and all pupils are trained in the use of mobile devices. All teachers incorporate digital materials and applications within their teaching, to a greater or lesser extent. Computing, with an emphasis on programming, is available from Y9 as an academic subject.

The curriculum is augmented by a wide range of popular academic co-curricular activities which supplement timetabled subjects. Lessons in Brazilian Portuguese, Italian, Mandarin Chinese and Russian are offered, as well as opportunities to develop skills in Music Technology, through Science and Maths competitions, societies and online courses.

Co-Curriculum. The School has a large Music Department with more than 50 visiting staff teaching a wide range of instruments and voice, regular concerts in school venues and outside, House Music and Classical competitions. Drama offers two major productions a year and House Drama competitions as well as regular showings for curricular drama. Art presents regular exhibitions and cross-curricular projects with English and other departments. Other activities include Forest's Combined Cadet Force, which is linked to the Royal Green Jackets, and the Duke of Edinburgh's Award which offers Bronze, Silver and Gold levels delivered by Forest staff. Other activities include raising money for charity, taking part in public speaking competitions, community work – such as visiting the elderly and riding for the disabled – student-led societies and publications, video techniques, theatre lighting, additional languages, musical theatre, dance, speech & drama and journalism. The Forest Portfolio monitors pupil involvement and encourages a rounded approach to co-curricular involvement.

Games. The main games are association football, hockey, cricket, netball, athletics, basketball and swimming. The sporting facilities are extensive and include an all-weather astroturf facility, tennis and netball courts, indoor and outdoor cricket nets, gym, sports hall, two swimming pools and acres of sporting field.

Fees per term (2016–2017). Reception to Year 2: £3,869, Year 3: £4,146, Year 4 to 6: £4,487, Year 7 to 13: £5,660.

Careers. Almost all pupils go on to universities to take degree courses, including 10 each year to Oxford and Cambridge.

Admission – Preparatory School. In principle, pupils are assessed on the basis of:

4+ entry:

A series of activities such as alphabet and number work, sequencing, picture recognition, responding to a story and drawing

7+ entry:

- Initial computer-based assessments in reasoning, mathematics and reading
- Upon selection for the second stage: a written test in English, collaborative activities and reading test
- A written confidential report from the present school is also requested

Admissions – Senior School. In principle, pupils are assessed on the basis of:

11+ entry and 13+ entry:

- Performance in English and Mathematics examinations

- An interview with a senior member of staff
- A written confidential report from the present school

16+ entry:
- The entrance examination consists of a compulsory critical thinking paper and two GCSE-standard papers
- An interview with a senior member of staff
- Entry into the Forest Sixth Form requires at least grade 4/C in English and Maths; and at least two 7/A grades and four 5/B grades; and the required grade at I/GCSE in the qualifying subject/s required for their chosen courses.

Full GCSE grade requirements can be found on the School website: www.forest.org.uk. A written confidential report from the present school will also be requested.

Scholarships and Bursaries are available at 11+, 13+ and 16+ entry. The maximum non-means-tested fee remission awarded in respect of any one pupil is 50% of full fees, whether in one area of excellence or in a combination of one or more areas of excellence.

Bursaries are means-tested and are awarded in addition to Scholarships, up to and including the total remission of fees; in other words, a free place. Bursaries are only given in conjunction with a Scholarship.

11+ entry:
Up to the equivalent of 14 places may be given annually to pupils at 11+ following Scholarship assessment in January of the year of entry. This figure includes both Scholarships and Bursaries.
- Academic Scholarships
- Music Scholarships
- Sport Scholarships

13+ entry:
Up to the equivalent of 2 places may be given annually to internal and external applicants at 13+ following Scholarship assessment.
- Academic Scholarships
- Music Scholarships
- Sport Scholarships
- Excellence Scholarships

Excellence Scholarships are awarded in recognition of exceptional attainment or potential in a minimum of two areas: Academic, Art, Dance, Drama, Music or Sport.

16+ entry:
Scholarships are awarded for outstanding Academic ability and exceptional attainment in Art, Drama, Music and Sport.

Up to the equivalent of six places may be given annually to both internal and new entrants to the Sixth Form.

Fee reductions are available for children of the Clergy.

For full details visit www.forest.org.uk.

Old Foresters Club. *President*: Martin Oliver, c/o Forest School.

Charitable status. Forest School, Essex is a Registered Charity, number 312677. The objective of the School is Education.

Governing Council:
Chairman of Governors: D Wilson, LLB
The Venerable Elwin Cockett, Archdeacon of West Ham
Mrs J Davies
W Fuller
G S Green, MA
Mrs G Jenkinson, AGSM, Dip Ed
His Honour Judge W Kennedy
Mrs P Oates, BEd
M Robinson
Dr E M Sidwell, CBE, PhD, FRSA, FRGS

***Acting Warden*: Mr M Cliff Hodges**, MA University College Cardiff

Bursar and Clerk to the Governors: Mrs D E Coombs, BSc Cape Town, Hons B&A MBA Stellenbosch

Head of Preparatory School: Mr A M Noakes, MA Ed Open

Deputy Head Academic: Mr J W J Mitchell, MA St Andrews, NPQH

Deputy Head Co-Curricular: Mr J E R Sanderson, BMusPerf Hons Elder Conservatorium, BMus Adelaide

Deputy Head Pastoral: Mr J H Kayne, BSc Nottingham Trent

Head of Sixth Form: Ms K Spencer Ellis, MA Christ Church Oxford (*Head of English*)

Head of Middle School: Mrs J K Venditti, BEng University College Swansea

Head of Lower School: Ms L E Lechmere, BA Sheffield

Chaplain: Reverend P K Trathen, MA York

Assistant Staff:
[P] *Prep School*
HM *Housemaster or Housemistress*

B D Adams, BSc Exeter (*Director of Sport*)
K C Adams, BA Exeter (*Head of Spanish*)
Y Ahmed, MA London (*Acting Head of Government and Politics*)
A Amirthananthar, BSc Queen Mary & Westfield London (*Chemistry*)
F Anwar, BA Huddersfield (*Learning Support*)
L P Arnold, BA Exeter [P] (*Art Subject Leader*)
T J Arnold, BSc Exeter [P] (*Head of Prep School Sport*)
P T S Aspery, BA Lady Margaret Hall Oxford (*Head of Physics*)
L M Baber, BSc Baylor, MSc Harvard (*Biology, HM*)
L D Barker, BA Brighton (*Head of Design and Technology*)
T A Barlow, MA Birmingham (*English*)
C A Barras, BSc Loughborough (*Head of Girls' Games*)
G R Barton, BA University College London (*Mathematics*)
G M Bassett-Jones, BSc Manchester (*Biology*)
R Begom, MSc London School of Hygiene and Tropical Medicine (*Biology*)
A N Bergès, Lic-ès-Lettres Paris (*Modern Languages*)
H R Betteridge, BA Durham (*RS and Philosophy*)
L S Bishop, BSc London (*Food and Nutrition, Examinations Officer*)
L Bouzguenda, BSc Salford (*Biology*)
C D Brant, MA Queens' College Cambridge (*Head of History*)
R L Broom, BSc Aston (*Economics, Acting Head of Economics and Business*)
M Broughton, BA Leeds Metropolitan (*PE and Games, Master i/c of Football*)
C P A Browne, BEd Surrey, MA Institute of Education, London [P] (*Deputy Head of Preparatory School*)
M D Bullock, BSc Nottingham (*Mathematics, Timetabler*)
T J Burnside, MA Manchester (*English, Forest Diploma Coordinator*)
S L Campbell, BA Worcester [P] (*Coordinator Extra-Curricular Activities & RE Subject Leader*)
R N Chipman, MSc Auckland (*Physics*)
K L Clark, BEd Homerton College Cambridge [P] (*Head of Prep School Girls' Pastoral Care*)
M Clifford, BSc Queen's Belfast (*Biology*)
A J Clifton, BA Sussex (*Learning Support*)
H W Clough, BA Somerville College Oxford (*History*)
N Coghlan, BA Roehampton Institute (*Head of Inclusion*)
H Cole, BA Wales Lampeter (*Geography*)
J Connell, BA Warwick (*English, HM*)

P R Cooper, BSc Leeds Beckett (*Graduate Assistant Teacher – Sport*)

H Corbett, MA Northampton (*Art and Textiles*)

P Cordón, BA Vigo, Spain (*Spanish*)

O Critchfield, MSc Queens' College Cambridge (*Maths*)

M Dean, MBA Stellenbosch, South Africa (*Economics and Business Studies, Assistant Head of Sixth Form – Careers*)

O Dhani, BSc City University London (*Mathematics*)

S Dhanjal, BSc University College London (*Art and Design*)

O Dicker, BSc University College London (*Physics*)

M Dowd, BMus King's College London (*Assistant Director of Music*)

P Drennan, Digby Stuart College, Dip DT Middlesex (*Design and Technology*)

JC Duncalf, MA Wales (*Head of Art and Textiles*)

H Dyke, BA Nottingham (*French and Spanish, HM, Community Service Coordinator*)

H Edwards, MA Edinburgh (*Classics*)

M A Ellis, MA Cambridge (*Religious Studies and Philosophy, Project Qualification Coordinator*)

P M Faulkner, BSc Leeds, MSc Edinburgh [P] (*Master i/c of Pre-Preparatory School*)

S F Firek, BSc Leicester, PhD Portsmouth Polytechnic (*Head of Biology*)

A E Foinette, MA Nottingham (*Classics*)

S J Foulds, BA Royal Holloway London (*Modern Languages, HM*)

S Gadd, BA Birmingham [P] (*Head of Prep School Boys' Pastoral Care*)

A Gillham, BA Queens' College Cambridge (*English*)

E F Golden, BA Williams College USA (*History, HM*)

H Golding-Fuller, MSc Middlesex (*Graduate Assistant Teacher – Sport*)

A G Gould, MA Balliol College Oxford (*Head of Classics*)

J L Gordon, BA Anglia Ruskin [P] Geography Subject Leader)

F J Grace, BSc Sussex (*Chemistry*)

M Gray, BA Lancaster, MA, Middlesex (*Design and Technology*)

T F Grayson, BSc Kent at Canterbury (*Chemistry*)

R Greasley, BEd Liverpool John Moores (*Design and Technology*)

E Greatorex, BA University College Swansea (*Geography*)

K Hall, BA Nottingham (*RS and Philosophy, Assistant Head of PSHE*)

A Hargitt, MA Christ Church Oxford, MA Durham (*Classics*)

S M Harris, BA Southampton, MA East London (*School Counsellor*)

A Hartley-Mottram, BA Brighton [P]

J E Hayes, BSc London Metropolitan (*Food and Nutrition, HM*)

C A Heath, BA Queen Mary & Westfield London (*Head of French, HM*)

A K Henriksen, BA Sussex [P]

I R Honeysett, MA Selwyn College Cambridge (*Head of Science*)

K J Hopkin, BA Durham [P]

D Hordok, BA Liverpool (*Modern Languages*)

F Hoxha, BSc Royal Veterinary College, London (*Biology*)

S Jacques, BA Greenwich [P]

M S Jalowiecki, BA Queen Mary London (*Computing*)

R K Jeffries, BA University College London (*Classics*)

J J Kay, BA Leeds (*English, HM*)

R H Kay, MA Warwick (*History, HM, Head of PSHE*)

A Kelly, BSc Surrey (*Physics*)

J R Kendall, BA East London [P]

V Kieu, MSc Cranfield Institute of Technology (*Computing*)

A Landi, MA City University [P]

M Y M Lau, BA Hong Kong [P] (*MFL Subject Leader*)

I M Leitão, MSc Glamorgan (*Physics*)

A Lindsey, BSc Sheffield City Polytechnic (*Head of Computing*)

O E Ling, BA Queen Mary & Westfield London (*Government and Politics, HM*)

R Lokier, BA Downing College Cambridge (*Head of MFL*)

B J D P Lumley, MA Leeds Metropolitan (*Head of Boys' Games*)

R Mackie, MA, MEd Fitzwilliam College Cambridge (*RS and History, Assistant Project Coordinator*)

A Manlangit, BEd McGill [P] (*Head of Pre-Preparatory School Teaching and Learning*)

N Marie, BMus Edinburgh (*Music*)

K Mather, BSc Warwick (*Mathematics*)

S McCabe, BA Oxford Brookes (*Graduate Assistant Teacher Sport*)

I A McGregor, MA Fitzwilliam College Cambridge, MA, Keele (*Director of Music*)

A J McIlwaine MA Sidney Sussex College Cambridge (*Director of Drama*)

S Merali-Smith, MA Manchester (*Classics*)

V J Middleweek, BA Middlesex (*Design and Technology*)

H P R Miller, BA University College London (*Head of German, HM*)

J Miller, BA Exeter (*Modern Languages, HM*)

R L Miller, BA Queen's College Oxford (*Music*)

L C Moore, BA Anglia Ruskin (*Art and Textiles*)

L A R Morrell, BA Brighton (*Girls' PE and Games*)

E W Morris, BSc Cheltenham & Gloucester College of HE (*Head of Geography, Assistant Examinations Officer*)

G Morris, BA King's College London (*Religious Studies*)

S P Morris, BSc York (*Head of Chemistry*)

G Moss, BA Worcester [P]

S Mozakka, BSc University College London (*Mathematics*)

Z A Munir, BA Westminster (*Economics and Business Studies*)

Z H Nazir, BSc DPhil Sussex (*Mathematics*)

E Newman, MA Sheffield (*History and Religious Studies*)

C L Nightingale, BA Corpus Christi College Cambridge (*Head of English*)

R Nolan, BA Anglia Ruskin (*Art and Textiles*)

C M Nortier, BSc Free State, SA (*Mathematics, Director of Studies*)

B O'Brien-Blake, BA St Anne's College Oxford (*Economics and Government & Politics, Assistant Head of Sixth Form – Higher Education*)

J F O'Riordan, BA College of Marketing and Design, Dublin (*Design and Technology*)

C R E Pepys, BA Durham (*Head of Religious Studies and Philosophy*)

F M Pereira, MA Middlesex (*Computing, Assistant Head of e-Learning*)

J Perham, BSc West of England (*Graduate Assistant Teacher – Sport*)

B M J Phillips, BSc Cardiff Metropolitan (*PE*)

M M Pickwick, BSc City of London Polytechnic [P] (*SEND*)

D R Potter, BA Birmingham, PG Dip Acting Webber Douglas Academy (*Drama*)

J S Pryke, BA St John's College Cambridge [P] (*ICT Subject Leader*)

C M Ranger, PhD Essex (*English*)

B A Richardson, BSc Witwatersrand, South Africa (*Mathematics*)

K J Ridley, MChem St Andrews (*Chemistry*)

C Risk, BSc, BPhD Otago, Dunedin, NZ (*Girls' PE and Games*)

L Roberts, MA Gastronomic Sciences, Italy (*Design and Technology/Food and Nutrition*)

R D Seager, MSc London (*Physics*)
J B Scott, BA Reading [P] (*Maths Subject Leader*)
K A Scott, BA Ulster [P] (*English Subject Leader*)
E J Sharpe, BE Western Sydney (*Head of Food and Nutrition*)
B J Shuler, BEng, Durham (*Physics*)
J T Sloan, BA Royal Holloway London (*History, HM*)
M J Smith, BSc University College Swansea, MBA Open University, FRGS (*Geography*)
M H A Stern, PhD Kent at Canterbury (*English*)
D J Supperstone, MA Gonville and Caius College Cambridge (*Modern Languages*)
C E Taylor, BA Bristol [P] (*PSHE Subject Leader*)
M J Taylor, MA Jesus College Oxford, MSc Manchester (*Head of Mathematics*)
L W Thompson, BSc East Anglia (*Mathematics*)
D L Tubb, BEd IM Marsh College of PE, Liverpool (*Girls' PE and Games*)
K Vidos, BSc Nottingham (*Biology, Junior Science Coordinator*)
K White, MA Canterbury Christ Church [P] (*Preparatory School Music Coordinator*)
J A C Whitmee, BA Sheffield (*Geography, HM*)
S E Williams, MChem Bradford (*Chemistry*)
T E Wilson, MSc Imperial College London (*Physics and Mathematics, Assistant Timetabler*)
J H Wyn-Thomas, MA Trinity College Cambridge (*English*)

J Clifton (*Teacher's Assistant, Reception*)
L Crisp (*Classroom Assistant*)
B Eiras Reboiras (*Spanish Language Assistant*)
H Fellowes (*Y3 Teacher's Assistant*)
D Groves (*Y1 Teacher's Assistant*)
G Henze (*German Language Assistant*)
K Kelsey (*Y2 Teacher's Assistant*)
F Matson (*Teacher's Assistant, Reception*)
N Messalti (*French Language Assistant*)
J Randall (*Y4 Teacher's Assistant*)
S Sahins (*Y2 Teacher's Assistant*)
D Young (*Y1 Teacher's Assistant*)

Bursar's Department:
Chief Accountant: Mr N Asghar, BA Hons East London
Assistant Accountant: Mrs T Prior
Accounts Clerk: Mrs E Kearney
Assistant Accounts Clerk: Ms S Morl
Estates Helpdesk Administrator: Miss A Vickers
Estate Manager: Mr J Stalley
Head of Maintenance: Mr C Blanchard
Carpenter/Joiner: Mr R Coles
Head Groundsman: Mr P J Gleaves
Assistant Groundsman: Mr D Mackenzie
Facilities Supervisor/Porter: Mr S Zieba
School Porter: Mr S Grant
Reception: Mrs J Bell
Heath, Safety & Compliance Director: Mr W Bishop, IOSH, CIMSPA

Network Support:
Director of Information & Technology: Mr D Lundie, MBA Stellenbosch Business School
Network Manager: Mr G Triggs, MCSA, MCSE, MCDBA, ACE, IT Dip
Assistant Network Manager: Mr S Aparicio
Database Manager: Mr I Gulma
Network Support: Mr M Allen, Mr T Uzice
Junior Support Engineer/Trainee: Mr K Dearing
Data Analyst: Ms Z Fookeer, BSc Westminster
Head of e-Learning: Ms L Golding-Hann, BSc UWE Bristol, PG Dip Hertfordshire

Secretarial:
PA to the Warden: Miss S Woolston
PA to the Deputy Warden: Miss A Buck
School Registrar: Mrs S Martin
Assistant Registrar: Mrs D Carbonaro, BA Nottingham
School Office Manager: Mrs K Wolstenholme
School Office Assistant: Mrs E Ruiz Rull
School Office Assistant: Mrs A Patuto
PA to the Deputy Head Pastoral: Miss D Tardioli
PA to the Deputy Head Academic: Mrs T Hogg
Sixth Form Secretary: Mrs D O'Brien
Sixth Form Administrator: Mrs E Campbell
PA to the Head of Preparatory School: Mrs Y Farquharson
Preparatory School Secretary: Mrs T Petherbridge
Admin Assistant: Mrs I Green
Head of Resources: Mrs D Bryant

Co-Curriculum:
Co-Curriculum Manager: Mrs D Cleveland-Hurley
Music School Manager: Mrs S Roach
DofE Manager: Mr J Moore-Hurley
Technical Theatre Manager: Mr C Tindall
Sports Administrator: Ms N Okey
Activities Administrator: Mrs A Lincoln

Marketing and Communications:
Press and Communications Officer: Mr J-L Squibb, BSc Royal Holloway London
Marketing Secretary: Mrs L Wiggins

Sports Centre:
Centre Manager: Miss Lydia Cooper, BSc Bangor

Medical:
Matrons:
Mrs G Delaforce, RGN
Mrs S Dempsey, RGN

Framlingham College

Framlingham, Woodbridge, Suffolk IP13 9EY

Tel: 01728 723789
Fax: 01728 724546
email: admissions@framcollege.co.uk
website: www.framcollege.co.uk
Twitter: @FramCollege
Facebook: @framcollege
LinkedIn: /framlingham-college

Motto: '*Studio Sapientia Crescit.*'

Location. The school is situated close to the wonderful Suffolk Coast, in the historic market town of Framlingham, overlooking the Mere and Castle, and is served by good road and rail links to London, Cambridge, Colchester, Norwich and all the main London airports.

History. The School was founded in 1864 by public subscription as the Suffolk County Memorial to Prince Albert and was incorporated by Royal Charter.

Organisation. Mr Taylor became Headmaster in September 2009; he was formerly Lower Master (Deputy Head) at King's School in Canterbury. He now leads a school that has recently received an excellent ISI Inspection Report, which described the College as highly successful in meeting its stated aims and mission of providing a first-class, holistic education, in a safe and inspiring environment, accessible to a broad range of boys and girls. The Senior School numbers some 415 pupils of whom 236 are boarders. All students are accommodated in seven fully-integrated boarding and day houses: three for girls and four for boys.

Preparatory School. Framlingham College Prep School, located less than 5 miles away at Brandeston Hall, is a leading preparatory school for boys and girls aged 2–13. All students are prepared for the ISEB Common Entrance Examination. (*See entry in IAPS section.*)

Facilities. An imaginative buildings programme has produced an exciting range of facilities which include the Headmaster Porter Theatre, a state-of-the-art drama and music facility. Science, Technology and Art enjoy purpose-built accommodation, and the Leisure Centre houses an indoor swimming pool and fitness suite, thereby enhancing the superb range of sports facilities. The flourishing Sixth Form is 200 strong and students enjoy their own Centre, which overlooks an attractive central concourse used extensively for informal gatherings. There are further plans to improve the warm and friendly boarding houses. A new state-of-the-art Cricket Pavilion will be finished in the Summer of 2017.

Curriculum. The College has a fine record in stretching the most able, while the 'value added' rating for those pupils who are not automatically destined to achieve A grades at GCSE and A Level stands among the very best in the country. Department for Education figures covering recent years confirmed this when placing the College among the top 5% in the country at improving pupils' grades between GCSE and A Level, and this is reflected in the ISI Inspection report which describes much of the teaching as *outstanding*.

Extra-Curricular Activities. Our academic success rates are mirrored by outstanding sporting achievements, commitment to the popular and extremely successful Duke of Edinburgh's Award scheme and the outward-bound work of the voluntary Combined Cadet Force. From the cut and thrust of the debating society there are visiting speakers and musical performances, charity competitions, formal house suppers and many cultural, educational and recreational visits. Whether it is cookery or the choral society, equestrianism or aero-modelling, a round of golf on campus or trekking in Nepal, there is something for everyone.

Games. Framlingham College enjoys an enviable reputation for sport and fields a large number of teams. The major sports are rugby, hockey, cricket, athletics and tennis for boys, and hockey, netball, tennis and athletics for girls. There is a wide range of other sporting opportunities, including squash, football, badminton, basketball, rounders, swimming, archery, shooting, volleyball and table tennis. The immaculately tended grounds include four rugby pitches, two floodlit artificial pitches, a golf course and one of the finest cricket squares in the East of England. The facilities also include a sports hall, indoor swimming pool, fitness centre, gym, squash courts, netball courts and tennis courts. Students benefit from Golf fixtures and practice at Aldeburgh Golf Club.

Music and Drama. Framlingham has a very strong choral tradition, and there is a wide range of orchestras and instrumental ensembles. In the past seven years, three pupils have reached the finals of BBC Radio 2 Chorister of the Year. The College's dramatic productions enjoy a very high reputation. The main productions each year generally include one musical, a major drama and a junior play.

Religion. The College has a strong Christian foundation, but students of all backgrounds are welcomed.

Admission. Common Entrance and interview form the normal means of entry to the College at 13+, but special provision is made for students for whom this is not appropriate. Entrance at 16+ is normally on the basis of GCSE results and interview or testing, but special arrangements are made for overseas students who are not following the British Curriculum. Visits from interested parties are welcomed; please contact us to make an appointment.

Scholarships and Bursaries. A wide range of scholarships are awarded every year at the following points of entry:

11+ (Prep School): Academic, Music, and Sports.

13+: Academic, Art, Design & Technology, Drama, Music, and Albert Memorial (All-Rounder including Sport).

The Porter Science Scholarship is awarded at 13+ for excellence in Science.

Sixth Form: Stapleton (Academic) Scholarships are available to students who are attaining academic excellence and have the potential to achieve at least 3 Grade As at A Level. Art, Design & Technology, Drama, Music, and Albert Memorial (All-Rounder including Sport) Scholarships are also available.

Successful candidates can be offered further assistance through bursaries in cases of proven financial need.

Special bursaries are available for the children of serving members of HM Forces.

Fees per term (2016–2017). Boarding £9,660.50, Day £6,211.50 (including lunch).

Charitable status. Albert Memorial College (Framlingham College) is a Registered Charity, number 1114383.

Chairman of Governors: A W M Fane, MA, FCA

Headmaster: **Mr P B Taylor**, BA Hons

Senior Deputy Head: Miss S M Wessels, BSc Hons, MEd
Deputy Head Academic: D G Ashton, BA Hons, Dip Ed
Deputy Head Co-Curricular: M D Robinson, MA, BEd Hons (*Head of History*)
Deputy Head Pastoral: T J Caston, BA Hons, MSc

Heads of Department:
Art: Mrs S Tansley, BA Hons, PGCE
Business Studies & Economics: A W Bennett, BA Hons, PGCE, Dip C inst M
Careers: Miss C Cranmer, BA Hons, PGCE, Dip Speech & Drama
Universities: R W Skitch, BSc, ACCEG, ACIB, PGCE
Computer Science: J Harrod, BA Hons, PGCE
Design & Technology: W Judd, BSc Hons, PGCE
Drama: Ms D Englert, BA Hons, PGCE, Dip Speech & Drama
ESL: Mrs K Cavalcanti, BEd Hons, RSA Dip EFL
English: L Goldsmith, BA Hons, MBA, PGCE
Geography: D Lyon, MSc, BA, PGCE
Languages: Mrs D Hardman, MA, PGCE
Learning Support: Mrs L Wrigglesworth, BA Hons
Mathematics: A Bailey, BSc Hons
Director of Music: Mrs L Bloore, Dip TCL, LTCL, PGCE
Psychology: Mrs J S Hobson, BA Hons, PGCE
Religious Studies & Philosophy: Dr P Giles, BD Hons, PGCE, MEd, PhD
Science: Dr D R Higgins, MA, PhD, PGCE
Director of Sport: N Gandy, BA Hons, PG Dip

Finance Director: N J Chaplin, BA Hons, FCCA
Operations Director: A L Payn, Chartered FCIPD
Development Director: M K Myers-Allen, BSc Hons, PGCE
Admissions Registrar: Miss E Rutterford, BA Hons
Headmaster's Personal Assistant: Mrs H Alcoe

Francis Holland School

Regent's Park

Ivor Place, London NW1 6XR

Tel: 020 7723 0176
Fax: 020 7706 1522
email: admin@fhs-nw1.org.uk
website: www.fhs-nw1.org.uk
Twitter: @FHSRegentsPark
Facebook: /FHSRegentsPark

Founded 1878.

There are 485 day girls and entry by examination and interview is normally at 11+, with a number joining at 16+ for the Sixth Form. The school was founded in 1878 and is affiliated to the Church of England, but girls of all Christian denominations and other faiths are accepted.

Curriculum. Girls are prepared for GCSE, A Levels, and for admission to Universities, and Colleges of Art, Education and Music. Sport takes place in Regent's Park and full use is made of the museums, theatres and galleries in central London. Extra lessons are available including fencing, music, pottery, Speech and Drama, Alexander Technique, kickboxing, Mandarin Chinese and cookery. For the first five years, to GCSE, girls follow a broad curriculum and normally take 10 GCSE subjects. Careers advice is given from the third year, and all pupils receive individual guidance through to the Sixth Form. In the Sixth Form a wide choice of A Level subjects is combined with a general course of study, including the opportunity to take the Extended Project. All girls are expected to stay until the end of the A Level course.

Scholarships and Bursaries. We will consider awarding a bursary to girls who demonstrate the ability to succeed at Francis Holland, but whose parents might not have sufficient financial resources.

A bursary is a means-tested award and is determined by the family's financial circumstances, taking into account income, realisable assets and other relevant circumstances. The level of assistance provided will depend on individual circumstances, which will be reviewed annually. The number of bursaries awarded each year is at the discretion of the Governors and may vary.

Remission of a third of the fees is available to places offered to daughters of the clergy.

Fees per term (2016–2017). £6,130.

Situation. The school is situated just outside Regent's Park and is three minutes from Baker Street and Marylebone stations. Victoria and Hampstead buses pass the school.

Charitable status. The Francis Holland (Church of England) Schools Trust Limited is a Registered Charity, number 312745. It exists to provide high quality education for girls.

Patron: The Right Revd and Right Hon The Lord Bishop of London

Council of Governors:

Chairman: Mrs M Winckler, MA
Vice Chairman: Mrs A Edelshain, BA, MBA, MCIPD
Mr P Ashton, BSc, ACA
Mr A Beevor, BA, MBE
Ms C Black, MCSI
Rev Dr M Bowie, BA, DPhil
Ms J Briggs, BA, MA, PGCE, Adv Dip CIPFA
Mr D Dowley, MA, QC
Mrs S Graham-Campbell
Dr M Harrison, BA
Mr J Hawkins, BA
Mrs S Honey, BSc, MRICS
Mr R Owen, BA, FRICS
Professor J Parry, MA, PhD
Mr S Pitchford, MA
Lady R Robathan, BSc
Miss S Ross, BSc, FInstP (*Safeguarding*)
Dr H Spoudeas, MBBS, DRCOG, FRCPCH, FRCP, MD
Mr G Stead
Professor J Yeomans, MA, DPhil, FRS

Bursar Mr G Wilmot, BA, ACA
Clerk to the Governors Mrs G Shaw, BSc

***Headmaster*: Mr C B Fillingham**, MA King's College London

Senior Deputy Head: Mrs K Whiteman, MA Oxon
Academic Deputy Head: Miss J Zugg, BSc Cape Town South Africa
Pastoral Deputy Head: Miss C Mahieu, BEd Sydney Australia
Director of Extra-Curricular Activities: Miss C MacDonnell, MA London
Head of Sixth Form: Mrs A Francisco, BA Sydney Australia
Joint Head of Sixth Form, Director of Higher Education, Oxbridge and University Applications: Ms A Slocombe, MA Cantab
Senior Teacher: Mr D Ward, MA Physics OU
Assistant Academic Deputy Head: Ms S Hack, BA Portsmouth
Director of Communications: Mrs V McKinley, BA London
Director of Information Systems: Mr T Oladuti, BA Winchester MBCS

Teaching Staff:
* *Head of Department*

Art:
*Miss J Orr, BA NkU, MA Sussex
Miss H Gardner, BA Hons Nottingham
Mrs R North, PG Dip RA
Miss L Evans, BA Wimbledon College of Art

Classics:
*Mrs C Wood, BA Oxon
Mrs J Cohen, MA Oxon
Mrs A Hillier, MA Cantab
Miss V Greenhalgh, BA Cantab
Miss H Williams, MA Durham

Economics:
*Miss A M Conway, MA St Andrews

English:
*Miss E Williams, BA Leeds
Mrs N Foy, MA London
Mrs K F Oakley, BA London
Dr F De Bono, PhD London
Mr A Smith, BA York
Mrs A Phillips, MA Oxon

Geography:
*Ms S Hack, BA Portsmouth
Mrs P Freeley, BA Durham
Miss E O'Neill, BSc St Andrews

History and Politics:
*Miss F Barton, BA Cantab
Mr H Clayton, BA Liverpool
Mrs K Whiteman, MA Oxon
Mr P Glavin, BA Liverpool
Mr D Bryson, MA Warwick

History of Art:
*Mrs A Montgomery, BA Newcastle
Miss C MacDonnell, MA London
Mrs A Francisco, BA Sydney Australia

Information Technology:
*Miss V Rusu, BEd Alberta
Mrs M Anastasi, BSc Open University

Learning Enhancement:
*Mrs F J Forde, CertEd Dartford College
Mrs M Wynne, BA Dunedin New Zealand
Mr T Carew Hunt, MA Oxon

Librarian:
Mrs E Aves, BA Gloucestershire

Mathematics:
*Mrs C Thornhill, MSc Oxon
Miss N Murugan, BSc Heriot-Watt, MA King's College London
Miss R Le Roux, MSc Essex
Miss J Zugg, BSc Cape Town South Africa
Miss H Blazewicz, BSc Bristol

Modern Languages:
*Mr N Gridelli, BA Bologna Italy
Mrs B Edwards, BA Hull
Miss A Spera, BA Pisa
Herr R Diesel, Technische Universitat Berlin
Miss M Gustave, MA Montpellier
Mrs R Pithouse, BA Lyon France
Ms A Slocombe, MA Cantab
Mrs F Boschi, AVCE
Miss N Lamas, MA King's College London
Ms A Diaz-Cespo, MA Cadiz
Ms R Iksilara, MA IoE London
Mrs A McBurney, MA Cantab

Music:
*Mr R Patterson, MA Cantab, FRCO
Mr J Ingham, BA Southampton
Mr A Smith, BA York

Visiting:
Mr K Abbs, FTCL (*Clarinet/Saxophone*)
Ms K Bennett, MMus (*Flute*)
Ms F Firth, LTCL (*Voice*)
Ms K Gilham, BA, MMus (*Piano*)
Miss C Graham, MMus (*Cello*)
Mr E Hackett, LRAM (*Percussion & Kit*)
Mrs C Hall, LRAM (*Voice*)
Miss J Harris, BMus (*Trumpet*)
Mr O Lallemont, MA Cantab, FRCO (*School Organist*)
Ms C Marroni, MusB, MPerf (*Bassoon*)
Ms J McLeod, ARCM (*Theory*)
Mr D Parsons, ARCM (*Guitar*)
Miss C Parker, BMus (*Violin*)
Mr S Queen, MA Cantab (*Singing*)
Ms J Schloss, BMus Qld (*Piano*)

Also visiting teachers for:
aerobics, kick boxing, self-defence, pottery, cookery, fencing, yoga and Alexander Technique, according to demand.

Physical Education:
*Miss J Tucker, BEd Queensland Australia
Mrs F Forde, CertEd Dartford College
Mrs K Lombard, BEd Canterbury New Zealand [maternity leave]
Miss C Mahieu, BEd Sydney Australia
Miss M Merrigan, BSc Loughborough
Miss K Evans, BA Deakin Australia
Miss E Slattery, BA Sydney Australia

Psychology:
*Miss A Langley, BSc UWE

Religious Education:
*Miss J Farthing, BA Bristol
Mrs S Bexon, BA King's College London

Speech and Drama:
Ms K Mount, BA Rose Bruford College

Science:
*Mr D Ward, MA Open University
Mr J Peters, BSc Swinburne
Miss K Hotchkiss, MChem Oxon
Mrs R Grant, BSc Sheffield
Mrs M Lockwood, BA Oxon [maternity leave]
Mr J Bossé, BSc BEd Moncton

Miss B Shah, MSc Queen Mary's
Miss T Ahmed, MSc Strathclyde
Miss C Till, BSc St Andrews

Non Teaching Staff:
Admissions Registrar: Mrs S Bailey
Deputy Registrar and School Secretary: Mrs D Hesketh
PA to the Headmaster: Miss O Birkby, BA Bristol
School Secretary: Ms Lynn Bosch
Art Technician: Miss H Holden, BA Leeds
Display & Art Technician: Miss N Stowell, BA London
Assistant Librarian & Admin Assistant: Ms L Barlow, MA Loughborough
Director of Information Services: Mr T Oladuti, MBCS, BA Winchester
Systems Manager: Mr S Andrews
ICT Technician: Mr M Jaskiewicz
Database Manager: Mrs M Anastasi, BSc Open
Examination Officer: Mrs A McBurney, MA Cantab
Assistant Examination Administration: Mrs S Gurini
Development Manager: Mrs L Richmond
Marketing Executive: Mrs L Taylor-Mitchinson, BA London
Marketing Assistant: Miss L Payn, BA Exeter
Alumni Relations Officer: Mr A Brown, MA Durham
Resources: Mrs E Sheriffs
Science Technicians
Mrs G Unwin, BSc Greenwich
Mrs N Kazemi, BSc North London
Ms S Kazemi, BA Roehampton
Caretakers:
Mr C Alarcon Mejia
Mr J Saguiguit
Mr K Bright
Catering Manager: Mr S King
School Counsellor: Ms C Vincenti, MA School of Psychotherapy and Counselling

Frensham Heights

Rowledge, Farnham, Surrey GU10 4EA

Tel:	01252 792561
Fax:	01252 794335
email:	admin@frensham-heights.org.uk
website:	www.frensham.org

Founded in 1925, Frensham Heights is a highly distinctive school in a world of educational conformity. We have developed from the progressive school movement and are acknowledged as one of the most successful liberal day and boarding schools in the country. We believe every child is an individual and we will feed their imaginations, expect them to ask questions – and indeed pursue their own answers, and therefore help them grow into confident, generous and happy young adults. At the heart of this is personal development and responsibility alongside excellent academic achievements.

Pupil numbers. 500 boys and girls aged 3 to 18 years. Average class size: 18.

Entry. Children entering from Nursery to Year 6 have an assessment day, with older children called during a two-week period in February. Children entering the school at the age of 11+ and 13+ sit the Frensham Heights Entrance Examination, held in January. Entrance to the Sixth Form is by examination and interview with a minimum of six GCSE passes at Grade C or above (A/B grades in A Level subjects). The school recommends that parents first visit on an Open Day, after which individual appointments tailored to their specific requirements can be made through the Admissions Registrar.

Curriculum. Most students take nine GCSE subjects of which the compulsory elements are English Language and Literature, mathematics and triple or double award science. The top set take triple award science. Students then choose from geography, history, business studies, a second modern language, art, 3D design, dance, design technology, drama, music, music technology or PE. Photography is taught to GCSE as an extracurricular activity and as part of the curriculum at A Level. There are 24 subjects to choose from at A Level. The AQA Extended Project Qualification is also offered for suitable candidates. PSME is taught throughout the school.

Academic Results. Examination results are very good. There is a strong Sixth Form, the vast majority of whom go on to further education, including Oxford, Cambridge and Russell Group. Public examination results 2016: A Level – 11% A*, 25% A*/A, 73% A*–C grades; GCSE – 16% A*, 40% A*/A, 89% A*–C.

Sport. The school's excellent sporting facilities include an astroturf, playing fields, swimming pool, tennis courts and an indoor sports centre. Sports include basketball, football, netball, hockey, rounders and cricket. Annual ski and surfing trips take place in the holidays.

Outdoor Education. Outdoor education is part of the curriculum for all pupils in Year 7 and above. Training takes place in the school's extensive adventure centre and leads to weekend and holiday expeditions in camping, climbing, caving, canoeing, scuba-diving and trekking, including World Challenge and Duke of Edinburgh's Award.

Extracurricular Activities. All pupils are expected to take part in extracurricular activities. An extensive and varied selection of activities includes sports of all sorts, art, music, dance, drama, hobbies and clubs.

Facilities. 100 acres of parkland in beautiful countryside, a Performing Arts Centre (the Aldridge Theatre), drama studios, music school with recital room and recording facilities, state-of-the-art photography suite, science laboratories (to be extensively refurbished and extended over the summer of 2016), art & design centre, Mac and PC computer suites, junior and senior libraries, sixth form centre and boarding house, completely refurbished Middle School boarding houses (separate houses for younger and older students).

Music. Music is held in high esteem at the school and regarded as an essential part of a student's education. It is studied by all students until the end of Year 9. The school has an impressive record for its choral and instrumental music. There are senior and junior choirs, two orchestras and a large number of instrumental groups. Concerts are put on regularly.

Boarding. Boarders are housed in small and friendly boarding houses. Each has a resident housemaster or housemistress and house tutor. There is a varied programme of weekend activities for the boarders. Weekly boarders may leave on Friday afternoon, returning on Sunday evening or Monday morning. The School organises a coach to London at weekends. All three boarding houses (Hamilton House – age 11 to 14; Main House – GCSE years; Roberts' House – Sixth Form) are co-educational, with boys and girls occupying separate wings.

Religion. Frensham Heights is non-denominational and there are no religious services during the school day.

Dress. There is no uniform but students follow a dress code based on respect for others.

Welfare and Discipline. The school's discipline is firmly based on good relationships between staff and students and reflects the values of the school, including respect, tolerance, self-discipline, cooperation and creativity. Every student has a personal tutor. Senior pupils act as mentors to younger members of the school. The boarding house staff are supported by a school nurse and a part-time counsellor.

Learning Difficulties. The school is sympathetic to those with dyslexia and other specific learning difficulties and offers limited support.

Overseas Students. The school admits a small number of boarders from overseas each year (6% in 2016) and provides tuition in English as a Second Language as part of their curriculum.

Frensham Heights Junior School. Nursery to Year 3 students aged 3–8 are in their own recently enlarged buildings and gardens within the main school grounds. Years 4–6 are situated in purpose-built classrooms within the main body of the school. The Junior School provides firm foundations in English and Mathematics, supported by a well-balanced curriculum that includes Science, French, Information Technology, Music, Drama and Dance at a level appropriate to the year group. Students have access to all the main school's facilities.

Fees per term (2016–2017). Nursery (EYFE Scheme): £18.20 (morning session, including lunch), £32.13 (afternoon session, including lunch); Reception £2,175; Years 1–2 £2,665; Year 3 £3,190; Year 4 £3,260; Years 5–6 £4,030; Years 7–8: £5,790 (day), £8,200 (boarding); Years 9–13: £6,070 (day), £9,240 (boarding); New Sixth Form Entrants: £6,450 (day), £9,595 (boarding).

Scholarships and Bursaries. Scholarships will be awarded for Academic distinction or exceptional promise in Music, Art, Dance, Drama and Sport at 11+, 13+ and for Sixth Form entry. These do not have monetary value but they recognise and celebrate excellence. Scholars access dedicated Enrichment activities. Bursaries are awarded on the basis of a means-tested assessment.

Charitable status. Frensham Heights Educational Trust is a Registered Charity, number 312052. It exists to provide high quality education for boys and girls.

Patrons:
¶Professor T Sherwood, MB, MA, FRCP, FRCR (*Emeritus Professor of Radiology, Cambridge, Fellow of Girton College*)
¶Mrs J Read, BA, FCIPD (*Semi-retired HR Consultant*)
Chairman: Mr M Chadwick, ACA, ATII (*former Head of Group Taxation, Friends Provident plc*)
Vice Chairman: Mrs M Coltman, BA LLB (*Group General Counsel and Company Secretary at Prudential plc*)
Treasurer: Mr R Lowther, CIMA, MSc (*Finance Consultant*)
Company Secretary and Clerk to the Governors: Mr P Lane, MBA, BSc, FCIPD, FCMI

Governors:
Mr W Bird BA, MA, MBA, MBCS, FRAeS, MBE (*Consultant specialising in defence and commercial management programmes*)
Mr A Brown DArch, MA, RIBA (*Retired Chartered Architect and Founder of IID Architects*)
¶Mr D Eley (*CEO of The Dan Eley Foundation*)
Mr J Hynam Cert Ed, ACP, BEd, MPhil (*Former Bursar of Winchester College*)
Mr A Lawman, AFA, FIAB, FCMA (*Finance Director*)
Mr M Lupton, MRCOG, MBBS, MA, Cert MEd, Dip MEd, MEd (*Consultant Physician*)
¶Mr W Marriott, BA (*Partner with Meadows Fraser LLP*)
Mrs K Poulsom (*Managing Director of an Agricultural Contracting and Plant Hire Company*)
Mrs J Sullivan, RICS (*Chartered Surveyor*)
Mr P Ward BEd (*Headmaster of Thomas's Preparatory School, Clapham*)

Head: **Andrew Fisher**, BA, MEd, FRSA

Deputy Head: Becks Scullion, BSc, PGCE
Deputy Head (Academic): Rachel Burnett, BA, MSc, PGCE

Heads of Schools:
Sixth Form: Peter Unitt, BSc, PGCE
Middle School: Andy Spink, BSc, QTS
Junior School: Nic Hoskins, BA, QTS

Departments:
* *Head of Department*
TiC *Teacher in Charge*

English:
Lisa Graham, BA, PGCE
Deirdre Gannon, BA, Dip Ed
Jennifer Hodge, MA, PGCE
Rachel Burnett, BA, MSc, PGCE
Alison Bundy, BEd

Mathematics:
*Steve Powell, BSc, PGCE
Russell Crew, BEng, PGCE
Andrew Ellison, BSc, QTS
David Stevenson, BA, PGCE
Paul Hughes, BEng, PGCE
Daniel Pullen

Sciences:
*Tom Bacon, BSc, PGCE
Peter Unitt, BSc, PGCE
Nick Arnell, BSc, PGCE (*TiC Biology*)
Charlotte Douglass, BA, PGCE (*TiC Chemistry*)
Susan Millerchip, BSc, PGCE (*TiC Physics*)
Andrew Ellison, BSc, QTS
Jeff Loomis, PhD, QTS
Andrew Melbourne, BSc, PGCE
Janette Wiggs (*Senior Science Technician*)
Kerry Howard (*Science Technician*)

Modern Foreign Languages:
*Tim Seys, BA, PGCE (*Spanish/French*)
Angela Schock-Hurst, MA (*TiC German*)
Richard Arthur, BA, PGCE
Kate Godeseth, BA, PGCE
Emma Wyld, BA, Dip TESOL TiC EAL
Valerie Taylor-Meysonnet, BA, PGCE

History:
*Matthew Burns, BA, PGCE
Charles Bennett, BA, PGCE
Sophia Colley, MA, PGCE
Amanda McCallum, BSc, PGCE

Geography:
*Nicola O'Donnell BA, MEd, PGCE
Karen McBride, BSc, PGCE
Will Paskell, BSc, PGCE
Amanda McCallum BSc, PGCE

Economics & Business Studies & Sociology:
*Hugh Robertson, BSc, PGCE, MBA
Barry Carr, MA, PGCE
Becks Scullion, BSc, PGCE
Hannah Manton, BSc, PGCE

Psychology:
Hannah Manton, BSc, PGCE

IT:
*James Clarke

PE & Games:
*Joanne Dalziel, BSc, PGCE
Andy Spink, BSc, QTS
Sian Owens, BSc, QTS
Lucy Fox, BSc, PGCE
David Lloyd Coach

Outdoor Education:
Linn Kathenes, BSc, PGCE

Art & Design:
*Brendan Horstead, BA, PGCE
Alexander Allan, BA, PGCE (*TiC Design Technology*)
Sarah Farr (*TiC Photography*)
Michele Rickett, BA, PGCE
Ashley Howard, MA
Steffi Cottle-Bailey, BA
Robert Russell (*Art Technician*)
Robert McGuigan (*DT Technician*)

Dance:
*Robert Keane
Lynn Goodburne, BPhil, Dip LCDD, QTS

Drama:
*Amanda Liddle, BA
Clare Esterhuysen, MA, PGCE
Sara Winthrop

Music:
*James Casselton
Laura Eaton, BMus

Learning Support:
Beverley Wrigglesworth (*Senior SENCO*)
Chris Vardy, BEd (*Junior SENCO*)

PSME:
Kate Godeseth, BA, PGCE

RE:
Karen McBride, BSc, PGCE

Librarian:
Noel Rasmussen

Junior School:
Nic Hoskins, BA, QTS (*Head of Junior School*)
Nick Oram-Tooley, BA (*Class Teacher Year 6*)
Paul Allams, BSc, PGCE (*Class Teacher Year 6*)
Rosemary Giraudet, BEd (*Class Teacher Year 5*)
Clive Esterhuysen, BA (*Class Teacher Year 5*)
Sally Heighington, BEd (*Class Teacher Year 4*)
Rosemary McMillan, CertEd (*Class Teacher Year 3*)
Rachel Greenfield, BA, PGCE (*Class Teacher Year 2*)
Olivia Aylott, BEd (*Class Teacher Year 1*)
Esme Lee, BEd (*Class Teacher Year 1*)
Lucinda Edwards, BA, PGCE (*Class Teacher Reception*)
Clare Kerr BA, PGCE (*Class Teacher Reception*)
Jo Maiklem (*Maternity Cover*) (*Class Teacher Reception*)
Caroline Rand (*Nursery Teacher*)
Lydia Hardcastle, LLB, PGCE (*Forest Class Teacher*)
Robin Park (*Teaching Assistant*)
Lisa Neave (*Teaching Assistant*)
Debbie Hunt (*Teaching Assistant*)
Penny Gibbs (*Teaching Assistant*)
Sanya Birch (*Teaching Assistant, Extended Day Supervisor*)
Liz Waite (*Nursery Assistant*)
Maria Colebrook (*Nursery Assistant*)
Samantha Moulton (*Junior School Administrator*)

Boarding House Staff:
Becks Scullion (*Deputy Head, Director of Boarding*)

Hamilton House (*Years 7 to 9*):
Clive Esterhuysen (*Housemaster*)
Lucy Fox (*Deputy Housemistress*)
Debbie Hunt (*House Parent*)
Sian Owens (*Visiting Tutor*)
Nick Oram-Tooley (*Visiting Tutor*)

Main House (*Years 10 and 11*):
William Paskell (*Housemaster*)
David Lloyd (*Boys' Deputy Housemaster*)
Lin Kathenes (*Visiting Tutor*)

Sarah Dedman (*House Parent – West Wing*)
Colette Hill (*House Parent – East Wing*)
Romuald Guerville (*Resident Staff*)

Roberts House (*Sixth Form*):
Richard Arthur (*Housemaster*)
Jenny Hodge (*Resident Tutor*)
Matthew Burns (*Resident Tutor*)
Brendan Horstead (*Visiting Tutor*)
Dan Pullen (*Visiting Tutor*)

Medical Centre:
Carys Willman (*Senior School Nurse*)
Charlotte Lee (*School Nurse*)
Debbie Huddlestone (*School Nurse*)
Vanessa Edworthy (*School Counsellor*)
Dr Paul Adams (*Medical Officer*) (*visiting*)
Dr Liz Colyer (*Medical Officer*) (*visiting*)

Support Staff:
Headmaster's Office:
Lindsey Boyce (*Headmaster's PA*)
Helen Evans, BA (*School Secretary*)
Lulu Spurling (*Receptionist*)
Vicki Maule (*Receptionist*)
Sally Vivian (*Receptionist*)

Marketing & Admissions:
Emily Wood, BA (*Director of Marketing & Admissions*)
Peter German, BA (*Marketing & Admissions Manager*)
Sarah Windsor, BA (*Admissions Registrar*)
Sarah Conway, BA (*Marketing & Admissions*)

Bursary:
Paul Lane MBA, BSc, FCIPD, FCMI (*Bursar & Clerk to Governors*)
Susie Birdsall, BA (*Bursar's Secretary*)
Karen Anderson, FCCA (*Finance Manager*)
Rachel Goddard, MATT (*Senior Financial Administrator*)
Julie Cox (*Accounts Assistant*)
Barbara Smale (*Accounts Assistant*)
Louise Moore BEng (*IT Manager*)
Sean Connor, BA (*Theatre Manager*)
Ruth Wilde (*Resources*)
Karen Heath (*Resources & IT Support*)
Kerry Guy (*Enterprises Manager*)
Christine Barrett (*Housekeeper*)
Gordon Duncan (*Estate Bursar*)
Liz Bownass-Clark (*School Administrator/Assistant Exams*)
Michael Hoy (*Head of Maintenance*)
Kevin Barrett (*Plumber*)
Russell Finbow (*Carpenter*)
Doug Paine (*Maintenance Assistant*)
John Clark (*Maintenance Assistant*)

George Heriot's School

Lauriston Place, Edinburgh EH3 9EQ

Tel: 0131 229 7263
Fax: 0131 229 6363
email: enquiries@george-heriots.com
website: www.george-heriots.com

Motto: '*I distribute chearfullie*'

Heriot's Hospital was founded in 1628 to care for the fatherless children of Edinburgh. Today it is a fully co-educational day school, deeply rooted in the Scottish tradition.

The School is attractively situated in its own grounds close to the city centre and within easy walking distance of bus and rail terminals. A number of bus routes also service the School. Edinburgh Castle forms a magnificent backdrop, and Edinburgh's flourishing financial centre, the University of Edinburgh, the College of Art, the National Library and the Royal Scottish Museum are located close by.

The original building, described as a "bijou of Scottish Renaissance Architecture", has been carefully preserved and, as a historic monument, is open at certain times to the public during school holidays. The Chapel, Council Room and Quadrangle are particularly notable.

Over the years a succession of new buildings has provided the full complement of educational facilities. A state-of-the-art Sports Centre was opened in 2012. The School has excellent sports fields and facilities at Goldenacre and sole use of an outdoor centre in the Scottish Highlands.

Our aim is to introduce all our pupils to the broadest possible spectrum of academic, cultural and sporting interests and experiences, which will enable them to develop into articulate, self-reliant, hard-working and kind adults who play their full part in an ever-changing society. The School had a highly successful QUIPE inspection by HMISS in September 2016.

Heriot's has long enjoyed a reputation for academic excellence, with outstanding examination results and we value scholarship and effort. In the same spirit, every pupil is encouraged to participate in an extensive array of extra-curricular activities. We encourage participation and success in an unusually wide range of sports; the main sports are cricket, cross-country running, hockey, rowing, football, rugby and tennis but we also strongly encourage more minority sports.

We have an outstanding record in music, both choral and instrumental and in Drama. Both Junior and Senior schools boast a huge range of clubs, with particular strength in our Combined Cadet Force, our Debating Society, our Pipe Band, our Quiz Teams and in the Duke of Edinburgh's Award. The School proudly holds Level 2 of UNICEF's Rights-Respecting Schools Award. There is a heavy emphasis throughout the School on charitable fund-raising and community service including our award-winning S6 Voluntary Service programme.

The Nursery (32 children). The Nursery accommodates children in their pre-school year. It is part of the Early Years Department. Admission to the Nursery is open to all.

The Junior School (614 pupils). The Junior School curriculum follows the central aims of Curriculum for Excellence, but with a focus on academic rigour and solid subject content, particularly with regard to literacy, numeracy and science. Art, Drama, Modern Languages, Music, Computing and all areas of Physical Education are taught by specialists, and Junior School staff liaise closely with their secondary colleagues to provide curricular continuity throughout a pupil's time here.

The Senior School (1027 pupils). For the first two years, a broad curriculum is followed. An unrivalled choice of subjects is available from S3 to S6 in preparation for Scottish Qualifications Authority examinations at every level. Most pupils stay on for our carefully designed Sixth Year and proceed to university or other forms of tertiary education.

Heriot's enjoys a reputation as a caring community. The greatest importance is given to pastoral care and a sophisticated careers advisory programme is in place. The Support for Learning Department provides invaluable help to many Junior School and Senior School pupils.

Admission: Admission (other than for Nursery) is by assessment or examination. Application for occasional places is welcome at any time, but for the main stages should normally be submitted by the end of November.

Fees per annum (2016–2017). Junior School: £7,737 (Nursery, P1 & P2), £9,393 (P3 to P7); Senior School: £11,604.

A limited number of Bursaries is available in Senior School and there are Scholarships for entry at S1. Fatherless and motherless children may qualify for free education and other benefits through the Foundation and James Hardie Bursaries. Full information is available from the Finance and Business Office on request.

Charitable status. George Heriot's Trust is a Registered Charity, number SC011463. It exists to provide education for children.

Governors of George Heriot's Trust:
Chairman: Mr M J Gilbert
Vice-Chairman: Mr A D Paton
Finance Convener: Mr J D M Hill
Education Convener: Dr P Sangster
Buildings Convener: Dr N M Irons
Mr H Bruce-Gardyne
Mrs K Cherry
Revd Dr R Frazer
Mr I Herok
Mr G Robertson
Councillor C Rose
Prof M W J Strachan
Mr J Thomson

Principal: Mr C D Wyllie

PA to the Principal: Miss C Macleod

School Management Team:
Mrs J A Alexander (*Bursar*)
Mr R C Dickson (*Head of Senior School*)
Miss S P Donnelly (*HR Manager*)
Mrs J J Easton (*Director of External Relations*)
Mrs L M Franklin (*Head of Junior School*)
Mr A MacLachlan (*Estates Manager*)
Mrs K S O'Hagan (*Deputy Head of Junior School*)
Mr A Semmler (*Director of IT*)

Deputes, Senior School:
Mrs C W Binnie
Miss K A Macnab
Mr K J Ogilvie
Mr N J Seaton
Mr R H Simpson

Deputes, Junior School:
Mr C W McCloghry
Mrs K L Stevens
Mrs K L Reid

Chaplain: Mrs A G Maclean

Art:
*Mrs A J E Thomson
Mrs R E Billett
Mrs J R Coombs
Mrs C M Fraser
Ms N L Garriock
Mrs S L Jamieson
Mrs C J McGirr
Mr A Rahimian

Biology:
*Miss A McKenzie
Mrs L J Anderson
Ms D Barnaby
Miss M E Gralewicz
Mrs A Macleod
Mr A A N Ramage
Mrs G Stevenson

Business Education:
*Mrs J Arnott
Miss K C Coltart
Mrs A Donaldson

Mrs G Line
Mr G MacGregor
Miss K A Macnab
Mr J Payne

Chemistry:
*Mrs F Donaldson
Mrs J Blaikie
Miss E L Maclean
Mr F I McGonigal
Mr J Wilson

Citizenship:
*Mrs G K Hay

Classics:
*Mr D Carnegie
Mr D R Underwood

Computing:
*Mr J T Scott
Mr A Semmler
Ms J McColgan
Mr M P Hill

Drama:
*Mrs J H Arya
Miss K Henderson
Mrs E R Mackie
Miss K H Morgan

English:
*Mr K Simpson
Mr R C Dickson
Mr R Gray
Mrs G K Hay
Mr P J Lowe
Mrs M C Massie
Miss K H Morgan
Mr J R Muir
Dr A Neilson
Mr D J Stenabaugh
Mr C D Wyllie

Geography:
*Mrs A Hughes
Mr D Armstrong
Mrs S E A Harris
Miss R Hay
Mr K J Ogilvie

History and Modern Studies:
*Mr M A McCabe
Miss M Buchanan
Mr T J Clancey
Ms A Connor
Mr C D Francis
Miss T Peters
Miss L P Robertson
Mr N J Seaton

Food, Health & Consumer Studies:
Miss L Ballantyne

Support for Learning:
*Mrs H A Staines
Mrs H R Fennell
Ms S G Gallacher
Mrs C Guy
Mrs S C Harrod
Mrs J Jackson
Miss N Knopfel
Mr I J Smith
Mr D Thain

Mathematics:
*Mr R G Kearsey
Mrs G Bateman
Mr G A Dickson
Mrs J H Dickson
Mrs P E Hart

Junior School Teachers (including Nursery):

Miss M Anderson
Mrs V E J Clark
Mrs E S Clarke
Mr G Cockburn
Miss G L Downey
Miss M S M Esplin
Mrs L Gilmour
Mrs G Happs
Mrs B I S Hunt
Mr C Johnstone
Ms A Josiffe
Ms A J McNeill
Miss L E Meikle
Mrs C F Milne

Miss K Henry
Mrs K Lydon
Miss F Moir
Mr C Walker

Modern Languages:
*Mr M G Grant
Mrs C W Binnie
Miss C Boscher
Ms E Bottaro
Miss A Chen
Mrs H Davies
Mrs M D Hansen
Ms H Loughlin
Ms E R Mackie
Ms J Murphy
Dr S T S Tonini
Miss F Yang
Ms G H Zhang

Music:
*Mr G C W Brownlee
Mrs J Buttars
Mrs S C Lovell
Mr G D Maclagan
Mrs R S J Weir

PE/Games:
*Mr M J J Mallinson
Miss A L Brodie
Miss L Brown
Mr A D Easson
Mr E Harrison
Mr G Hills
Mrs N Kesterton
Mrs K F Rutherford
Mr R Stevenson

Physics:
*Mr R M Bush
Dr F M Baumgartl
Mrs R D Mayo
Ms W C Morgan
Mr I Oliphant
Dr K Ward

Philosophy and Religion:
*Mr J C Rodger-Phillips
Mrs L Beilby
Mrs A G Maclean
Mr C Mackay

Design & Technology:
*Mrs E L Watson-Massey
Miss K Eaglesfield
Mrs A Johnson
Miss H L O'Boyle
Mr I Purves
Miss A D Williamson

Mrs C H Noble
Miss H Oliver
Miss S Renton
Mr N J Ross
Mr E P Santer
Mrs M Scott
Mrs R S Sweetman
Mrs E S R B K Szczypka
Mr B Tyler
Mr R J Waters
Mr A Weir-Addie
Mr I J A S Woolley
Miss L J Wormald

Junior School Principal Teachers:
Miss S Gordon
Mrs R McKinnon
Miss L M Waddell

Learning Enhancement:

Miss J Attenborough	Mrs M Hogg
Ms H A Bassam	Mrs H Murphy
Miss K A Duncan	Mrs L J Smith
Mrs C Humphreys	Mrs S E Wilken

Giggleswick School

Giggleswick, Settle, North Yorkshire BD24 0DE
Tel: 01729 893000 Headmaster's Office
              01729 893012 Bursar's Office
Fax: 01729 893150
email: admissions@giggleswick.org.uk
website: www.giggleswick.org.uk
Twitter: @giggschool
Facebook: /GiggleswickSchool

Giggleswick School is based on the edge of the Yorkshire Dales National Park, offering affordable independent education and academic excellence for girls and boys aged 3 to 18. In 2015 our senior school was awarded 'excellent' in an impressive six aspects of provision by the Independent Schools Inspectorate (ISI).

The School sits amongst 200 acres of stunning Yorkshire countryside, where you'll find 500 years of heritage, exceptional modern facilities and a happy, welcoming community. Approximately 400 boys and girls attend Giggleswick, either as full-time or flexi boarders or day pupils. It is a traditional British boarding school with 60% of pupils boarding, 17% of which are from military families and 19% from the International community. The approach to education combines excellent academic achievement, ambition and strong self-belief, creating well – rounded individuals with a lifelong desire to learn.

In 2016, the school announced record-breaking A Level results with 68% of pupils achieving A*–B grades, 10% of candidates achieving at least one A* and 32% A*/A grades. Average UCAS points have also risen to 331, opening up plenty of fantastic opportunities at leading universities. The School's A*to B results have increased by 18.3% over the last two years and many of the Upper Sixth have also achieved exceptional results in their EPQs (Extended Project Qualifications) with 75% at A*/A grades. 81% of pupils were accepted into their first or second choice of Russell Group or 1994 university.

Over half of GCSE pupils achieve A* grades and more than a quarter of them have been awarded six or more A*/A grades, with 66% achieving A* to B grades. Even more impressive this year are the value added scores of the pupils with many achieving over two grades higher than their target GCSE scores.

Life is about more than great grades at Giggleswick though. The extended day and boarding ethos gives all pupils the chance to participate in any of over 60 co-curricular activities that encourage pupils to explore new horizons, challenge themselves and often achieve beyond their expectations. 50% of pupils take part in music lessons at Grade 6 or above with 120 pupils in drama productions. Average class sizes are 14 in Key Stage 3 and 4 and seven in Sixth Form.

All boarders live in one of seven boarding Houses, where they are looked after by a team of House Staff. A Housemaster or Housemistress, appointed by the Headmaster, supervises each house and is responsible for the academic and personal progress and general welfare of all the pupils in the House within a caring, disciplined framework.

There are excellent sports coaches at all levels, superb facilities and regular programmed training sessions. Each year a number of pupils gain representative honours in a range of sports and a place on the Elite Sports Programme. This includes specialist coaching, mentoring, professional sports visits and strength and conditioning training.

Facilities include a floodlit AstroTurf, fully equipped fitness centre, two indoor sports halls and an indoor swimming pool. The Outdoor Pursuits Department is staffed with seven Mountain Leaders and five Rock Climbing Instructors, with 34 crags within 10km of the school and the school's own mountain bike trail and shooting range.

Giggleswick's Art Department provides a lively and stimulating environment where pupils can explore and develop their creative skills. The department includes a resident ceramic artist, Matthew Wilcock, who works and teaches in the Department and recently won the BBC's Great British Pottery Throw Down. There is a well-equipped ceramics studio, a vacuum silkscreen printing bed, plus facilities to make photo silkscreens, and a large etching press.

Drama takes place in the state-of-the-art Richard Whiteley Theatre, a 250-seat professional venue. There are opportunities to develop skills in stage management, sound and lighting as well as acting in productions such as Les Miserables.

In the music department there is a Head of Instrumental Music as well as a Head of Department and four full-time musicians. They are assisted by a team of 13 visiting teachers, and ensembles include the School Orchestra, Concert Band, Chapel Choir, Concert Choir, a Brass Ensemble and a String Quartet as well as a number of rock bands. Numerous performance opportunities are offered including trips abroad.

We are not a selective school. The school has an equal opportunities policy and is happy to consider applications from any child so long as other entrance criteria are met. Various scholarships and bursaries are also available. Please visit http://www.giggleswick.org.uk/applying-to-giggleswick for more information

The school is an hour's drive from Leeds, Manchester and The Lakes. It can be reached from the M6 or M1 motorways or by rail via Settle or Giggleswick stations. Overseas students fly to Leeds/Bradford or Manchester Airports.

Fees per term (2016–2017). The fees are fully inclusive. Senior School: Boarders: £7,400 (Years 7 & 8), £10,100 (Years 9–11), £10,600 (Sixth Form); Flexi Boarders: £6,700 (Years 7 & 8), £8,100 (Years 9–11), £8,600 (Sixth Form); Day Pupils: £4,900 (Years 7 & 8), £6,100 (Years 9–11), £6,600 (Sixth Form). Junior School: Boarders £6,678 (full), £5,152 (3-night flexi); Day Pupils £2,506–£4,010.

Charitable status. Giggleswick School is a Registered Charity, number 1109826.

The Governing Body:
Chair: Mrs H J Hancock, MA, LVO
Vice-Chair: A R Mullins, BSc, MBA, ACA

Bursar & Clerk to the Governors: M Z Hodge, BA, CPFA

Headmaster: M M Turnbull, BA, MA

Deputy Heads:
N A Gemmell, BA West London Inst of HE
Ms S L Williamson, BA Liverpool

Assistant Head (Academic): Miss A L Wood, MA New College Oxford

PA to the Headmaster: Mrs C A Jowett
Director of External Relations: Mrs J Paul

The Glasgow Academy

Colebrooke Street, Glasgow G12 8HE

Tel: 0141 334 8558
Fax: 0141 337 3473
email: enquiries@theglasgowacademy.org.uk
website: www.theglasgowacademy.org.uk

Motto: '*Serva Fidem.*'

Founded in May 1845, The Glasgow Academy is the oldest continuously independent school in the west of Scotland. It has been co-educational since 1991, when it joined forces with Westbourne School for Girls. Mergers with Atholl Preparatory School in Milngavie (1999) and Dairsie House School in Newlands (2005) have given parents a choice of three locations for their children in the Nursery to Prep 4 age group, contributing to the school's enduring success as a school covering the whole of west central Scotland. Children from TGA Milngavie and TGA Dairsie transfer to the main Academy site at Kelvinbridge at Prep 5. The school's affairs are managed by the Glasgow Academicals' War Memorial Trust, formed to commemorate the 327 former pupils killed in the war of 1914–18.

Organisation. The Preparatory School contains some 635 pupils (325 boys, 310 girls) between the ages of 3 and 11 and educates pupils from the earliest stages for the work of the Senior School. The Senior School contains 690 pupils (365 boys, 325 girls). They are prepared for the National Qualifications at National 5 level at the end of S4, Higher at the end of S5 and Advanced Higher or Higher at the end of S6. The Sixth Form provides courses in most subjects leading to presentation at Advanced Higher. Pupils are prepared for entrance to Oxford and Cambridge. The Academy has a history of successes at Oxford, Cambridge and the Scottish Universities. It aims to offer a unique combination of academic, musical, dramatic, sporting, co-curricular, social and outdoor education opportunities, backed up by high levels of pastoral care. There are numerous opportunities for children to develop leadership skills and take on responsibilities.

Buildings. The magnificent main building (1878) contains the Senior School library as its centrepiece and classrooms. Recent purpose-built facilities include a Music School (1994), Art and Design School (1998), Preparatory School (2008) and award-winning Science centre, auditorium and hospitality/social area (2015). Two drama studios, a dance studio, rowing studio, medical centre and fitness area were also created in 2015. There are extensive sports facilities, including new astros, rugby/cricket pitches and a water-based hockey pitch. The school's Wi-Fi network covers the entire campus and supports pupils' own laptops, smart phones and tablets. The Academy VLE is used to engage pupils and parents in the learning experience.

Music and Drama. Music tuition is offered in a wide range of instruments by 21 tutors. There are Senior, Junior and Theatre Choirs, a Concert Band, Pipe Band, Brass Group, Percussion Ensemble, Orchestra and various Prep School groups. Concerts and large-scale drama productions take place regularly and are supplemented by plays mounted by smaller groups. There are music tours to places such as New York, Rome and Barcelona.

Societies and Activities. These range from Basketball, Chess, Debating and Public Speaking to Engineering, Fairtrade and Research clubs. Very large numbers of pupils undertake each section of the Duke of Edinburgh's Award and there is a thriving Young Enterprise group. Residential education is an integral part of the curriculum at various stages of both the Prep and Senior schools. These experiences augment the PSE programme by promoting team building and personal and social development through outdoor challenges.

Games. Teams represent the school in Hockey, Rugby, Cricket, Swimming, Golf, Tennis, Athletics, Rowing, Football, Shooting and Squash. Options include Badminton, Cross-Country running and Dance.

Combined Cadet Force. The Academy has a strong voluntary contingent with RN, Army and RAF Sections.

Childcare outside school hours. The Academy provides care before and after school for its younger pupils. There is also provision for children between the ages of 3 and 12 through the holidays.

Entrance. Pupils may be registered at any age. The main entry points are (a) in the Preparatory School: age 3, 4 and 10; (b) in the Senior School: age 11 or 12 or for Sixth Form. Bursaries are available for P7–S6.

Fees per term (2016–2017). Preparatory School: P1 £2,648/£2,882, P2 £2,727/£2,967, P3–P4 £3,015/£3,238, P5 £3,238, P6–P7 £3,793. Senior School: S1–S2 £3,621, S3–S5 £3,929, S6 £3,929 (Autumn & Spring Terms), £3,205 (Summer Term).

Charitable status. The Glasgow Academy is a Registered Charity, number SC015638. It exists to provide education for girls and boys.

Chairman of Governors: Graham Scott, FCIBS

Nominated and Elected Governors:
Mrs C F Abercrombie, BAcc, CA
A Barr
J Beattie
S Binns, DipED, BEd, PGDip School Leadership and Management (*SQH*)
Mrs K Dinardo, CEng, MICE, MIStructE, MCIHT, FIES
Jeremy Glen, LLB, Dip LP, NP
D Mackison
Professor Andrew Marshall, BA, MPhil
S J McCaffer, BCom, CA
Mrs N Mahal, MA, DCG
Dr K Percival, MB ChB, MRCGP
W Sinclair, MA, MFB, MIDE, MIOD, MSExpE, MICM, MAPS
A Waddell, MA, CA, ASIP

Secretary: T W Gemmill, LLB, NP

Rector: **P J Brodie**, MA Oxon, MA Management of Education, Canterbury Christ Church University College

Deputy Rector: M K Pearce, BA, Dunelm

Deputy Heads:
Dr J Andrews, BSc Glasgow, PhD London
A L Evans, BSc Strathclyde
A N MacRae, BSc Strathclyde

Heads of Department:
English: Mrs A F Watters, MA St Andrews
Mathematics: Mrs L S Moon, BSc Southampton, CMath, FIMA, CertGuid
Modern Languages: Mrs E B Holland, MA Glasgow
Biology: J M Shields, BSc Glasgow
Chemistry: Dr R J Sowden, MChem St Andrews, DPhil Oxon
Physics: S M Brunton, BSc Glasgow
Art/Craft & Design: J M McNaught, BA Glasgow
Classics: S A A McKellar, MA Glasgow
Computing Science: Mrs J E McDonald, MA Glasgow
Drama: G E Waltham, MA Glasgow
Economics & Business Studies: Mrs S McKenzie, MA Glasgow, PGDip BusAdmin Strathclyde
Food Technology: Ms C Dolan, BSc Manchester Metropolitan University
Geography: Mrs V Magowan, MA Glasgow
History & Modern Studies: S M Wood, MA St Andrews
Music: T E Mills, BMus Bangor

Physical Education/Sport:
S W McAslan, BEd Jordanhill (*Head of PE*)
Miss R I Simpson, BEd Heriot-Watt (*Director of Sport*)
PSE: Mrs M T Muirhead, BA East Anglia, Dip Guid &
    Pastoral Care Glasgow
Outdoor Education: Miss R Goolden, Mountain Instructor
    Certificate, Outdoor Education Diploma & National
    Governing wards, Newbury College
Learning Support: Mrs A A Harvie, BA Strathclyde,
    PGDip Ind Admin Glasgow Caledonian
Careers: A J McCaskey, MA Glasgow

Preparatory School:
Head: A M Brooke, BEd Southampton
Deputy Head: Mrs H A Kirkhope, BEd Strathclyde
Depute:

TGA Milngavie:
Head: Miss J McMorran, DCE, PGDip, DipTEFL

TGA Dairsie:
Head: Miss H J Logie, BEd Oxon

After-school Care:
After-school Care Manager: Mrs C Bremridge, BA
    Childhood Practice Glasgow

Chaplains:
Revd D J M Carmichael, MA, BD
Revd A Frater, BA, BD
Revd G Kirkwood, BSc, BD, PGCE
Revd S Matthews BD, MA

Combined Cadet Force:
OC CCF: Squadron Leader A L Evans
SSI: WO2 C J Duff

Administration/Finance:
General Manager: Dr W R Kerr, LLB Glasgow
    Caledonian, PhD Strathclyde, MBA Glasgow, MSc
    Glasgow Caledonian, FCIS, FCIM, FHCIMA

Rector's PA: Ms A K Cain, MSci University College
    London
Administration Manager: Miss I Kovacs, BA Strathclyde
School Secretary: Mrs A M Farr
Database Coordinator/Administration Secretary: Mrs D
    Hegedus, BA Budapest, MA Pecs

Development:
Director of Admissions and External Relations: M R
    McNaught, MA Glasgow
Director of Development: M G Taylor, MA Aberdeen

The High School of Glasgow

637 Crow Road, Glasgow G13 1PL
Tel: 0141 954 9628
email: rector@hsog.co.uk
website: www.highschoolofglasgow.co.uk
Twitter: @HSofG

Motto: '*Sursum semper*'.

The new, independent, co-educational High School of Glasgow came into being at Anniesland in 1976 following a merger involving the Former Pupil Club of the High School, a selective state grammar school, and Drewsteignton School in Bearsden.

Buildings. The Senior School occupies modern purpose-built buildings at Anniesland on the western outskirts of the city immediately adjacent to twenty-three acres of playing fields. The Junior School is in the extended and modernised former Drewsteignton School buildings in Bearsden about three miles away. New facilities opened during the last few years include a purpose-built Science extension, a water-based artificial pitch and 3G multi-sports area, a Junior School extension, a Drama Studio, a Refectory, a Fitness Centre, a Grandstand and an Information and Communications Technology building.

Organisation. The School is a day school with about 1,022 boys and girls. The Junior School, which includes a pre-school Kindergarten, has some 348 pupils (ages 3½–10). Primary 7 pupils are included in the Senior School which has about 674 pupils (ages 11–18). A general curriculum is followed until the Third Year of the Senior School when, with the Scottish Qualifications Authority examinations in view, a measure of choice is introduced. In Fifth Year Higher examinations are taken and in Sixth Year courses for Advanced Highers are offered. Whilst the majority of pupils are aiming for the Scottish universities, places are regularly gained at Oxford, Cambridge and other English universities.

Throughout the School, time is allocated to Art, Music, Personal, Social and Health Education, Physical Education and Religion and Philosophy. All pupils will also take courses in Computing Studies, Drama and Health and Food Technology at various stages in their school careers.

Games. The main sports are hockey, rugby, athletics, cricket, tennis and swimming. Pupils participate in a wide variety of other sports, including badminton, basketball, netball, volleyball, golf, cross-country running and skiing.

Activities. Pupils are encouraged to participate in extra-curricular activities. Clubs and societies include debating, Scripture Union groups, computer, table tennis, chess, art, bridge, chemistry, electronics, drama and film clubs. Pupils take part in the Duke of Edinburgh's Award Scheme and the Young Enterprise Scheme, and parties regularly go on tour. There are choirs, orchestras, jazz and concert bands and a pipe band and tuition in Instrumental Music is arranged as requested. Each year there are several concerts and dramatic productions. The Chamber Choir was BBC Songs of Praise Senior School Choir of the Year 2013.

Admission. Entrance tests and interviews are held in January. The principal points of entry are at Kindergarten (age 3½–4), Junior 1 (age 5), Transitus (age 11) and First Year (age 12) but pupils are taken in at other stages as vacancies occur.

Fees per term (2016–2017). Junior School: £1,375–£3,412; Senior School: £3,457–£3,973.

Bursaries. The School operates a Bursary Fund to give assistance with fees in the Senior School in cases of need.

Former Pupils' Club. The Glasgow High School Club Limited is the former pupils' association of the old and new High Schools. Former pupils all over the world maintain an interest in the life and work of the School. *Secretary*: Murdoch C Beaton, LLB.

Charitable status. The High School of Glasgow Limited is a Registered Charity, number SC014768. It is a recognised educational charity.

Governing Body:
Honorary President: Lord Macfarlane of Bearsden, KT
Chairman: B C Adair, TD, LLB
Mrs P Galloway, FCA
A Horn, MA, LLB
E W Hugh, CA
Mrs L Keith, MA, Cert Ed, ITQ
S J MacAulay
C M Mackie, BSc, FFA
S C Miller, LLB Hons, Dip L
Professor V A Muscatelli, MA, PhD, FRSE, FRSA
K M Revie, LLB Hons
Dr C M Stephen, MBChB, DGM
Mrs M A Stewart, LLB Hons, Dip LP, DFM

R M Williamson, MA, LLB, FRSA, FRSAMD
R G Wishart, FCMA

Rector: J O'Neill, MA

Senior Deputy Rector: K J A Robertson, BSc

Deputy Rectors:
Mrs S Gibson, BEd
I S Leighton, BSc
G Robertson, MA, CA

Staff:
* *Head of Department*

English:
*P A Toner, MA
†G Baynham, BA
Mrs R A Baynham, MA
†P D C Ford, MA
Mrs S de Groot, MA
†T Lyons, MA
Mrs J Muir, MA
Mrs S L Patterson, MA
Mrs M Noonan, BA
    (*Drama*)

Mathematics:
*S Welsh, BEng
†Mrs C V M Anderson,
    BSc
†J G MacCorquodale, BSc
D K Hamilton, BSc, PhD
T Lockyer, LLB
D MacGregor, BSc
Mrs H S Mills, MEng
P Moon, BSc
Mrs N Morrison, BSc

Computer Studies:
*N R Clarke, BSc
D Muir, BSc
I R Purdie, BSc

Science:
A E Baillie, BSc (**Physics*)
N M E Dougall, BSc, MSc,
    (**Biology*)
Mrs K S M O'Neil, BSc
    (**Chemistry*)
Dr M McKie, BSc, PhD
Mrs A E McNeil, BSc,
    MSc
Dr L A A Nicholl, BSc,
    PhD
Mrs M Peek, MSc
Dr N J Penman, BSc, PhD
K J A Robertson, BSc
I J Smith, BSc
Dr D R Went, MSci, PhD

Modern Languages:
*N F Campbell, MA, LLB
†Mrs K J Bhatia, BA
Miss M Cranie, BA
Mrs K Evans, MA
†Mrs J M Horne, MA
Miss K Peron, BA
Mrs A M T Drapeau-
    Magee, L-ès-L, M-ès-L
Mrs V MacCorquodale,
    MA
Mr A Fernandez Lucas
Mrs A Hilt, MA

Classics:
*A H Milligan, MA
T W Ingham, MA
Mrs B Roarty, MA

*Economics and Business
    Studies*:
*T J Jensen, MEd, BComm
Mrs E A Milne, BA,
    MCIBS

*Geography and Modern
    Studies*:
*Miss N L Cowan, MA
K F FitzGerald, BSc
I S Leighton, BSc
Miss J A McAteer, BA
Mrs L McFarlane, BSc
Miss K Macpherson, MA
G J Robertson, MA, CA

History:
*C MacKay, BA
R J Broadbent, BA, MEd
    (**Careers*)
Miss N Sutherland, MA
Mrs G A Lindsay, MA

Art:
*Mrs C J Bell, BA
Ms N Henderson, BDes
Mrs J Stewart, BA

*Health and Food
    Technology*:
*Miss K Moore, BA
Mrs J Sellar, BA, TQFE

Learning Support:
*Mrs R E Hamilton, BA
Mrs N Morrison, BSc

Music:
*Mrs S C Stuart, MMus
    Oxon, MSt Oxon,
    PGAdvDip RCM
L D Birch, BA, LRAM,
    DRSAMD
M Duncan, DRSAMD
Ms W MacDougall, MMus,
    BA, LLCM TD
N G McFarlane, BA
R McKeown, DRSAMD
Mrs C Mitchell, MMus,
    BMus, PGDM, PGDE
Mrs J Tierney, BMus
F Walker, BA, ARCO

Religion & Philosophy:
*C F Price, MTheol
Mrs G A Lindsay, MA

Physical Education:
*D N Barrett, BEd
Mrs A Cox, BEd (**Girls'
    PE*)
Mr R Baillie, BEd
K F FitzGerald, BSc
S Leggat, BEd
Mrs H Cannon, BEd
Mrs S Dougan, BEd
Mrs M J Gillan, DPE

F J Gillies, BSc
S Ingles
J McConnell, UKCC Level
    2 (*Rugby*)
Mrs D McCluskey, BSc
A W Meikle, MA
Mrs S Mitchell, BEd
Mrs R Owen, BEd
Mrs M Stevenson, DPE

Junior School Staff:
Head Teacher: Miss H Fuller, BEd
Mrs G Morrans, BEd (*Deputy Head*)
Mr R Baillie, BEd
Mrs C Brown, NNEB
Miss C E Carnall, BMus, MA
Mrs L Cowan, BEd
Mrs A Dougherty, BA
Mrs A M T Drapeau-Magee, L-ès-L, M-ès-L (*French*)
Mrs H M Eustace, BEd
Mrs S A Foster, MA
Mrs E Gibson, BEd
Mrs M J Gillan, DPE, Dip Sfl, ATQ
I Hallahan, BA, PG Dip (*Educational Support*)
Mrs A Kiyani, BEd (*Principal Teacher of Kindergarten*)
Mrs L A Lambie, BEd
Mrs S McCarron, BA Dip Lib (*Librarian*)
Mrs E McCormick, DCE
Miss M MacLean, BA (*Principal Teacher*)
Mrs I W McNeill, DA (*Art*)
Mrs C Mitchell
Mrs M Moreland, DCE, AEE
Mrs J O'Neill, NNEB
Miss I Rashid
Mrs G Reid, MA (*Principal Teacher*)
Mrs C Ritchie, DCE
Miss I Skinner, MSc (*Principal Teacher*)
Miss A Taylor
G J Walker, BSc
Mrs M C Watt, DCE

Bursar: Mrs J M Simpson, BAcc, CA

Rector's PA: Ms J Mackay

Glenalmond College

Glenalmond, Perth, Perthshire PH1 3RY
Tel: 01738 842000
            Admissions Office: 01738 842144
Fax: 01738 842063
email: registrar@glenalmondcollege.co.uk
website: www.glenalmondcollege.co.uk
Twitter: @GlenalmondColl
Facebook: /GlenalmondCollege

Motto: '*Floreat Glenalmond*'

Glenalmond College, was founded by Mr W E Gladstone
and others in 1841 and opened as a School in 1847.

The College is built on the south bank of the River
Almond, from the north bank of which rise the Grampian
mountains. It is about 50 miles north of Edinburgh and 8
miles from both Perth and Crieff.

The College Buildings, grouped round a cloistered quadrangle, comprise the Chapel, Hall, Library, houserooms and
studies, study bedrooms, classrooms and laboratories. A
separate block houses additional laboratories and a Theatre.
A few metres away are the Art School and the Design and

Technology Centre. Next to these are the Music practice rooms and a Concert Hall.

The Sports Complex consists of squash courts, a gymnasium, an indoor sports hall and a heated indoor swimming pool and fitness suite.

The College also has a state-of-the-art Science Block and IT Resources Centre.

Houses. There are 5 houses for boys, and 3 for girls. Each house has accommodation for the resident Housemaster or Housemistress and their family. Senior boys and girls have study-bedrooms of their own.

Religion. The College has an Episcopalian foundation and has a splendid Chapel. However pupils from a wide range of ethnic, religious and cultural backgrounds are welcomed; the needs of other religious groups and recognised faiths will be observed and supported.

Admission. In line with the College's foundation and tradition, entry to Glenalmond is academically selective. Boys and girls may be registered for admission at any time after birth and enter the College between the ages of 13 and 14 via the Common Entrance Examination or Entrance Scholarship papers. Pupils leaving Primary Schools may qualify by tests and examinations for junior entry at age 12. Girls and boys may also qualify for entry into the Lower Sixth, or at other points during their school career. Boarding and Day pupils are accepted throughout the school.

For those applying from overseas, or whose first language is not English, we expect, as a minimum, an Intermediate standard of written and spoken English (IELTS Grade 4 or equivalent).

Curriculum. In the Second and Third Form (Years 8 and 9, S1 and S2) all pupils take a wide range of subjects including English, Mathematics, History, Geography, French, Spanish or German, Latin or Ancient Civilisation, Biology, Chemistry, Physics, Technology, Music, PSHCE, Drama, Art and ICT. In the Fourth and Fifth Forms pupils may choose three options from a wide range of subjects (including Latin and Greek), along with the core subjects of Mathematics, English Language and Literature, French and the three Sciences. Each pupil is guided by an academic tutor who meets regularly with their tutor group.

The Sixth Form curriculum is designed to allow pupils as wide a choice as possible with 24 A Level subjects being offered ranging from Business and Music Technology to Physics and Philosophy. There are weekly lectures from outside speakers on social, economic and cultural subjects which foster academic excellence across the age ranges. The more able pupils are encouraged to join the William Bright Society which promotes cross year group discussion on relevant academic and moral issues.

Careers. Over 98% of pupils continue to university; a few go direct to professional careers, industry, the Services, etc. Around half of pupils go to Russell Group universities, with a good number gaining places at Oxbridge each year. Great emphasis is placed on careers guidance: careers talks, visits and advice along with a well-stocked careers room assist pupils in their choice. All pupils are encouraged to take psychometric careers aptitude tests at age 16.

The computer network extends to all parts of the campus. ICT is available in libraries and all classrooms, and all pupils have access to email and the internet within their Houses.

Art, Drama and Music. Music plays a central part in the life of the school: there is an Orchestra as well as smaller String, Woodwind and Brass Groups. A large Choir and Choral Society perform at the College, in Perth and in Edinburgh. A new Harrison and Harrison pipe organ supports Glenalmond's central Chapel tradition. The Concert Society arranges recitals and concerts at the College; frequent visits are made to concerts in Perth and elsewhere. There are currently two Pipe Bands.

The Drama and Art departments flourish, in conjunction with the well-established Design and Technology Centre. Both Art and Music as well as Design/Technology form part of the normal curriculum and can be taken at GCSE and A Level.

Sport and Recreation. Rugby (boys) and Hockey (girls) are played in the Michaelmas Term and there is a wide variety of activities to choose from in the Lent Term, including Lacrosse and Netball for girls and Hockey, Football and Cross-Country for boys, with Cricket, Athletics, Basketball, Shooting, Sailing, Tennis and Golf in Summer. Shooting on the Miniature Ranges takes place during the two winter terms. There is a large indoor heated Swimming Pool and pupils are trained in personal survival and Lifesaving. Instruction in Sub-aqua and Canoeing is given. There are also Squash Courts, Tennis Courts, a nine-hole (James Braid) Golf Course, and two full-size all-weather pitches for hockey, netball and tennis.

During the Summer, pupils have the opportunity to explore the hills and the neighbouring countryside. There is also a Sailing and Windsurfing Club which uses a neighbouring loch. Weekend camping expeditions are arranged to encourage self-reliance and initiative.

Glenshee is just over an hour away and there are opportunities for skiing in the Lent Term.

Combined Cadet Force. There is a contingent of the Combined Cadet Force which has strong links with the Armed Forces and the Royal Regiment of Scotland (Black Watch Battalion) in particular. The ceremonial dress, as worn by the Pipe Band for example, is the Highland dress with the Murray of Atholl tartan.

Army and Air sections, with a Pre-Service section for Junior Pupils, are organised on the basis of the Duke of Edinburgh's Award. Shooting and Adventure Training figure prominently; pupils may also be engaged on Conservation, Community Service Work or Mountain Awareness Group.

Fees per term (2016–2017). £10,743 Boarders; £7,318 Day Pupils (for whom free transport is arranged); £8,049 Junior Boarders; £5,490 Junior Day.

These fees include extras common to all pupils, such as membership of the CCF, Games, Subscriptions, journeys to matches, the use of the Golf Course, etc.

Sibling discounts are available. Children of serving members of the Armed Forces and members of the Clergy receive an automatic 10% fee discount.

Term of Entry. Entry is normally in September. Entry in January or April can be considered where special circumstances exist.

Scholarships and Bursaries. Academic Scholarships and Exhibitions are awarded. Junior Scholarship candidates must be under 14 on 1 September of the year of entry. A short statement showing the scope of the examination will be forwarded on application, and copies of last year's papers may be obtained. Scholarship candidates will be examined at Glenalmond. The Entrance Scholarships Examinations are usually held in March for younger pupils and in November for entrants to the Sixth Form.

Music Scholarships may be available to entrants at 12+, 13+ or Sixth Form. Candidates will usually offer two instruments at least to Grade V. Promising string players and singers will be considered with great interest. Award holders receive free musical tuition.

An Organ Scholarship, Piping Awards and Art & Design Scholarships are also available. There are also Outstanding Talent Awards for Sport.

All-Rounder Awards are available to 13+ entrants only; candidates must demonstrate strength in at least two of the following areas: Drama, Sport, Music, Art.

All Awards can be increased in cases of need. A number of means-tested bursaries are available each year for up to

100% of fees. Applications should reach the Director of Finance no later than 1 February in the year of entry.

The Old Glenalmond Club. *Hon Secretary*: D Sibbald, 21 Ravelston Park, Edinburgh EH4 3DX.

Charitable status. Glenalmond College is a Registered Charity, number SC006123. It exists for the all-round education of Boys and Girls in the tranquillity of a rural setting.

Council:
*President of Council: The Primus of the Episcopal Church in Scotland, The Most Reverend David Chillingworth, Bishop of St Andrews, Dunkeld & Dunblane
*Chairman of Council: The Rt Hon Lord Menzies PC [OG]
*Chairman of Committee of Council: N S K Booker, BA Hons [OG]
The Earl of Home, CVO, CBE
**D G Sibbald Esq, BArch Hons, RIBA, FRIAS (*OG Club Secretary*)
Mrs C S C Lorenz, AA Dipl
**J M Squire Esq, MBA, MSc
J V Light Esq, MA
**M A J Miller Esq, BSc, MRICS
**J G Thom Esq, LLB, Dip LP, NP, TEP [OG]
D M S Johnston Esq
Prof A McCleery, MA, PhD
J Smelt Esq, MA, FCSI
**K R Cochrane Esq, BAcc Hons, CA, DSC
T J O Carmichael Esq
Mrs L White, LLB
The Rt Revd Dr G D Duncan, Bishop of Glasgow and Galloway
R N B Morgan Esq [OG] (*OG Club Chairman*)
H Ouston Esq, MA, PGCE, Dip Ed [OG]

* *Committee of Council*
[OG] *Old Glenalmond*

Warden: Ms Elaine Logan, MA, PGCE

Sub-Warden: C G Henderson, BSc, PhD St Andrews
Deputy Head – Academic: Dr S N Kinge, BSc, PhD
Deputy Head – Teaching and Learning: Dr M Gibson, BSc, PhD, PGCE
Deputy Head – Pastoral: Mrs S Sinclair, BSc Edinburgh, PGCE
Registrar: M T Jeffers, BSc, PGCE
Chaplain: The Revd G W Dove, MA, MPhil, BD
Chief Operating Officer: S Johnstone, ACMA
Chief External Relations Officer: Dr C Fleming, BSc, PhD
Head of Marketing: Ms L M Nowell, BA, DipM, Dip DigM, MCIM
Head of Careers: A Norton, BA, BEd
Lead Nurse: Miss J Moffat, RGN

Teaching Staff:
* *Head of Department*
† *Housemaster/mistress*

English:
**J Hathaway, BA, MA, PGCE
Miss V M Dryden, BA, PGDE
Mrs W Youlten, MA, PGCE
Miss L Kirk, RSAMD Glasgow, PGCE
Mrs L Swaile, MA, PGDE

Mathematics:
**G G O'Neill, BSc, PGCE
M T Jeffers, BSc, PGCE
S P Erdal, BSc, PGCE
Mrs S Sinclair, BSc, PGCE (†*Lothian*)
M A Orviss, MA Cantab, PGCE
Mrs S Smith, BSc, PGCE
Miss R Mullan, BSc, PGCE

Classics:
**G W J Pounder, MA Oxon, PGCE
Mrs I Reynolds, MA
Miss R Masson, MA, MLitt

Modern Foreign Languages:
**Mrs J Davey, MA, PGCE
J A Gardner, BA, PGCE
Mrs S Baldwin, MA Cantab, PGCE
Mrs I Reynolds, MA
T J O Carmichael, BA, PGDE

Geography:
**S Smith, MA, PGDE
C S Swaile, MA, PGCE
M Gibson, BSc, PhD, PGCE, FRGS (†*Reid's*)
R L Myers, BEd, BA

History:
**L W R Rattray, MA, MLitt, PGDE (†*Matheson's*)
C D B Youlten, BA, PGCE
Miss J H Kaye, MSc Aberystwyth (†*Lothian*)
D Tolan, MA, PGDE

Biology:
**A C Hughes, BSc, PGCE
C G Henderson, BSc, PhD, PGCE
Dr S Colby, BSc, PhD, PGCE
Mrs L Tosh, BSc, PGCE

Chemistry:
**Dr T S Wilkinson, BSc, PhD, PGCE
Dr S N Kinge, BSc, PhD
Mrs T T Hughes, BSc, PGCE
Mrs L Tosh, BSc, PGCE

Physics:
**R Benson, BSc, PGCE
Dr S N Kinge, BSc, PhD
D M Smith, BSc, MEng, PGCE

Economics and Business:
**J C Robinson, BA, PGCE
P J Golden, BSocSc, MA, PGCE (†*Goodacre's*)

Computer Science:
**Ms J MacDougall, BSc, MLitt, Dip Ed

Drama:
**C D B Youlten, BA, PGCE (*Head of Academic Theatre Studies*)
**Miss L Kirk, RSAMD, PGCE (*Head of Drama and Performance*)

Music:
**T J W Ridley, GRSM, PhD, LRAM, FRSA
B J Elrick, LLB
Ms J Neufeld, BA, BEd

Art and Design:
**B Wang, BA, MA
Mrs C V Norton, BA
Mrs N J Beaumont, BA, PGCE (†*Cairnies*)

History of Art:
**Mrs C J R Butler, MA (†*Home*)

Divinity and Religious Studies:
**Revd G W Dove, MA, MPhil, BD

Library and Archives:
Mrs E Mundill, MA, DipLib, MCILIP, Cert TM, TESOL

Design Technology:
**A A Purdie, BSc, BEd
Mrs N J Beaumont, BA, PGCE (†*Cairnies*)
Miss G Granger, BTecEd

Physical Education:
*A P N Rowley, BSc, PGCE
Miss C Bircher, BEd
Miss G Douglas, BPE
D Stott, CMI, MMI
D Best
G Smith
C Williamson

Learning Support:
*Mrs N Henderson, BSc, PGCE
Mrs E Critchley, Montessori Diploma
Miss G Douglas, BPE
Mrs W Youlten, MA, PGCE
Mrs S Spiers, BA, PGCE

English as an Additional Language:
J A Gardner, BA Hons, PGCE, Cert TESOL
Mrs M Gardner, BA, PGDE, Cert TM, TESOL, CELTA
Mrs E Mundill, MA, Dip Lib MCILIP, Cert TM, TESOL

Godolphin

Milford Hill, Salisbury SP1 2RA

Tel:	01722 430500
	Preparatory School: 01722 430652
Fax:	01722 430501
email:	admissions@godolphin.wilts.sch.uk
website:	www.godolphin.org
Twitter:	@GodolphinSchool

Motto: *Franc Ha Leal Eto Ge* (Frank and Loyal art though)

Founded by Elizabeth Godolphin in 1707; date of the will of the Foundress, 24 June 1726; a new scheme made by the Charity Commissioners and approved by HM, 1886, and re-issued by the Charity Commissioners in February 1986. Godolphin is an independent boarding and day school for girls aged 11–18, with its own purpose-built preparatory day school for girls from the age of 3. Of the 435 girls in the senior school, 100 are in the Sixth Form.

Godolphin stands in 16 acres of landscaped grounds on the edge of the historic cathedral city of Salisbury, overlooking open countryside.

A strong academic life combines with thriving art, drama, music and sport. A five-studio art centre provides excellent art and design facilities, while the Blackledge Theatre provides a professional environment for drama and music performance. Other notable developments include the Baxter Pool and Fitness Centre, a new boarding house and a dedicated Sixth Form Centre, the latter providing a focus for careers and higher education advice, and the Sixth Form social programme, as well as study-bedrooms, work space and recreational areas. Sciences are taught within the well-equipped laboratories and have a strong tradition of Oxbridge success. The whole site is served by a wireless network.

Religious Instruction. Godolphin has strong affiliations with the Church of England, but religious instruction covers all the major world faiths.

Curriculum. High academic standards (81% A* to B grades at A Level and 96% A* to C grades at GCSE and IGCSE in 2016) are combined with a wide range of clubs, societies and weekend activities; also an outstanding programme of trips and expeditions. Activities include: cookery, photography, Duke of Edinburgh's Award, Combined Cadet Force, community service, debating, creative writing, academic societies and wide ranging opportunities in art, drama, music and sport. 24 subjects are available at A Level, and virtually all students continue to higher education, most to universities, including Oxbridge; some to art colleges, drama schools and music conservatoires. There is considerable emphasis on Careers guidance, including an excellent work shadowing scheme.

Physical Education. Strong sporting record with pupils regularly selected for county and regional teams; also at national level. 22 sporting options include lacrosse, hockey, netball, tennis, athletics, swimming, gymnastics, dance, rounders and cross-country. Each girl is encouraged to find at least one sport she really enjoys during her time at Godolphin.

Entrance Examination. Godolphin's own assessment and interview at 11+ and Common Entrance Examination at 13+. Examination and interview at all other levels, including Sixth Form.

Scholarships and Bursaries. 11+ and 13+ for outstanding merit or promise in academic work, music, sport or art. Candidates for music awards should have attained at least Grade 4 at 11+ (Grade 6 at 13+) on one instrument. They are also expected to reach an acceptable academic standard.

Sixth Form Academic, Art, Drama, Music and Sports scholarships are also available.

Six Foundation Bursaries are available to boarding candidates from single parent, divorced or separated families who have been brought up as members of the Church of England.

The Old Godolphin Bursary, a means-tested bursary, is awarded from time to time by the Old Godolphin Association to the daughter of an Old Godolphin.

Fees per term (2016–2017). Senior School: Full Boarding £8,416–£9,880, 5-day Boarding £8,171–£9,592, 3-day Boarding £7,876–£9,248, Day £5,854–£6,505.

Prep School: Full Boarding £7,637, 5-day Boarding £6,522, 3-day Boarding £5,667, Day £2,179–£4,210.

Fees include tuition, textbooks, stationery, sanatorium, laundry, and most weekday and weekend clubs and activities.

Extra Subjects. Individual tuition in music, speech and drama, tennis, fencing, judo, EFL and learning support.

Old Godolphin Association. *Secretary*: Miss H Duder, Keith Cottage, Cold Ash, Thatcham, Berkshire RG18 9PT, or via Development Office, Tel: 01722 430570.

Charitable status. The Godolphin School is a Registered Charity, number 309488. Its object is to provide and conduct in or near Salisbury a boarding and day school for girls.

Governing Body:
M J Nicholson (*Chairman*)

Mrs R Hawley	A F R Boys
Revd I Woodward	R Franks
G W Green	Mrs N Huggett
S Hill	Mrs A Burchmore
J S Lipa	Mrs C Mannion-Watson
Dr R Griffiths	Dr Elizabeth Shaw
J Kelly	K Thompson
J Booker	

Bursar and Clerk to the Governors: K Flynn, BSc, FCMA

Headmistress: Mrs Emma Hattersley, BA Dunelm

Deputy Head: R Dain, MA Oxon
Academic Deputy: G Budd, BA Hons Durham
Pastoral Deputy: Mrs N Green, MA Sussex
Director of External Relations: Mrs M Rowney
Deputy Head Communication and Innovation: N Everett, BSc South Bank

Registrar: Mrs C Heritage, BA Manchester

Staff:
* *Head of Department/Subject*

Art and Design:
*N Eggleton, BA London, ATC
Mrs S Duggan, BA Winchester

Miss E Findley, BA Leeds Metropolitan
Mrs J Josey, C&G TCert Basingstoke
C Wright, BA Napier

Business Studies and Economics:
*D Miller, BA Nottingham
Mrs N Owers, BA Nottingham

Classics:
*A Mackay, MA Cantab
Mrs P Campbell, MA Edinburgh
Mrs S Radice, BA Reading

Drama:
*D Hallen, BA Middlesex, PGCE
Miss N Strode, BA Cardiff
Miss R Harris, BA Goldsmiths

Speech and Drama: Mrs M Ferris, LGSM, LTCL

English:
*Mrs C George, BA Hons London
Mr Ryan-East, BA Plymouth
Mrs M Edouard, BA London
Mrs T Nicholls, MA Keele, BEd Cambridge
Miss A Richards, BA Sheffield
Mrs C Smallwood, BA Lancaster
R Dain, MA Oxon

Geography:
*Miss S Collishaw, BSc Swansea
Mrs J Morris, MA Bath
Mr G Budd, BA Dunelm

History:
*Dr A Dougall, LLB London, MA, PhD Southampton
Mrs S Eggleton, MA Aberdeen
Miss J Miller, BA Belfast, MEd Open
Dr S Wood MA, DPhil Oxford

History of Art:
*Mrs S Radice, BA Reading

Information and Communication Technology:
Mrs W Laptain, BEd Manchester
*Mrs S Davis, MSc Bath

Learning Support (*SEN*):
*Mrs C Firth, BA, BSc Open, MSc, SpLD Southampton
Mrs J Dunne, BEd Oxon, CELTA
Mrs A Eccles, BA Exeter
R Tarlton, MA Leicester

Mathematics:
*Mrs K Healey, BSc Bristol
Mrs J Robson, BSc Bristol
Mrs R C Stratton, BSc Exeter
Mrs N Owers, BA Nottingham, PGCE
Mrs A Bacon, BSc Southampton PGCE
D Roberts, BSc Warwick

Modern Languages:
*Ms N Daubeney, BA Exeter
Mrs C England, BA Hons Warwick
Ms M Cibis, BA Sheffield
Dr L Rojas-Hindmarsh, DPhil Leeds
Miss M Reyes Avila Cabrera, Lda Alicante
Mrs N Monediere, BA Reading
Mrs E Bally (*Assistentin*)
Sr J-M Verdu Cortes (*Assistentin*)

Music:
*R Highcock, BMus London
Mrs O Sparkhall, BA Dunelm
C Guild, BMus RCM

Physical Education:
*Mrs S Pokai, BA Brighton

Mrs L Banks, BA Wagner College, New York
Mrs L Edwards, BSc Loughborough
Mrs S Harvey, BEd Exeter
Mrs A Venn, BA Manchester, PGSC Physical Education
Miss R Bond, MA St Andrews
Mrs J Melhuish (*LTA Tennis Coach*)
Ms J Caplen (*LTA Tennis Coach*)
Mrs S Drummond (*Netball Coach*)
Mr J Routledge (*Fencing Coach*)
Mrs K Addison (*Swimming & Equestrian*)

Psychology:
Miss A Bowler, BA Manchester, BA Wimbledon

Religious Studies:
F Spencer, BA Essex, BTh Southampton
*P Sharkey, BA London

Science:
Dr C Thrower, PhD, MSc, BSc Manchester (**Chemistry*)
Dr B Medany, BSc London, PhD Nottingham (**Biology*)
C Hillman, MS, PhD Southampton (**Physics*)
Mrs M Foster, BA London
P Hill, BSc London
Miss A Masson, BA Cambridge
J McNulty, MSc Leicester
R Pocklington, BEd Southampton

Technology (*Design & Food*):
*Mrs S McNulty, BEd Hons Sheffield Hallam
Mrs C Complin, BSc Bath College of HE
Mrs P Parry-Jones, BSc Bath College of HE

Chaplain: Dr S Wood, MA, DPhil Oxford
Librarian: Ms D Jones, BA Oxford
Head of Sixth Form and Higher Education Adviser: Dr A Dougall, LLB London, MA, PhD Southampton
Upper School Tutor: D Hallen, BA Middlesex
Middle School Tutor: Mrs S Eggleton, MA Aberdeen
Lower School Tutor: Mrs W Laptain, BEd Manchester
Careers Adviser: Mrs B Ferguson, BA Newcastle upon Tyne

Sixth Form Centre:
School House:
Ms S Jones, BA Wales (*Housemistress*)
Mrs S Hallen, (*Assistant Housemistress*)
Jerred House:
Miss E Findley, BA Leeds Metropolitan (*Housemistress*)
Ms M Cibis (*Assistant Housemistress*)

Houses:
Cooper:
Mrs M Edouard, BA London (*Housemistress*)
Mrs V Wilson (*Day Matron*)
Miss R Harris, BA London (*Resident Tutor*)
Walters:
Mrs W Laptain, BEd Manchester (*Resident Tutor*)
Mrs M Reyes Avila Cabrera, Lda Alicante (*Housemistress*)
Miss H Longley (*Matron*)
Sayers:
Mrs S Ramsdale, BEd Liverpool (*Housemistress*)
Miss J Tatem, BEd Southampton (*Assistant Housemistress*)

The Godolphin and Latymer School

Iffley Road, Hammersmith, London W6 0PG
Tel: 020 8741 1936; 020 8563 7649 (Bursar)
Fax: 020 8735 9520

email: office@godolphinandlatymer.com
website: www.godolphinandlatymer.com

Motto: *Francha Leale Toge*

Foundation. Godolphin and Latymer, originally a boys' school, became a girls' day school in 1905. It was aided by the London County Council from 1920 onwards and by the Inner London Education Authority when it received Voluntary Aided status after the 1944 Education Act. Rather than become part of a split-site Comprehensive school it reverted to Independent status in 1977.

Godolphin and Latymer is an independent day school for 820 girls, aged 11 to 18. The school stands in a four-acre site in Hammersmith, near Hammersmith Broadway and excellent public transport. The original Victorian building has been extended to include a pottery room, computer studies room, language laboratory, science and technology laboratories, art studios, a dark room and an ecology garden. The girls benefit from a recently renewed all-weather surface for hockey and tennis, as well as netball courts and a Sixth Form Centre. Since September 2006, the school has leased St John's Church and its Vicarage, both adjacent to the existing site. The Vicarage, renamed the Margaret Gray Building, provides additional classrooms. The new Rudland Music School opened in the Autumn Term 2008 and the renovated church, The Bishop Centre, for the performing arts was completed in early Spring 2009. These state-of-the-art developments provide a range of teaching and performance spaces, recording studios and a music technology suite. The Bishop Centre provides an auditorium to seat over 800. In September 2015 a new Sports Complex, the Hampton Centre, was opened.

The Godolphin and Latymer School aims to provide a stimulating, enjoyable environment and to foster intellectual curiosity and independence. We strive for a love of learning and academic excellence, emphasising the development of the individual, within a happy, supportive community.

While girls are expected to show a strong commitment to their studies they are encouraged to participate in a range of extracurricular activities. We aim to develop the girls' self-respect and self-confidence, together with consideration and care for others so that they feel a sense of responsibility and are able to take on leadership roles within the school and the wider community.

Pastoral Care. The school has a close relationship with parents, and every member of the staff takes an interest in the girls' academic and social welfare. Each girl has a form teacher and a deputy form teacher and there is a Head of Lower School, Head of Middle School and a Head of Sixth Form, each with at least one deputy.

Curriculum. We offer a broad, balanced curriculum including appropriate education concerning personal, health, ethical and social issues. During the first three years Philosophy and Religion, English, French, Spanish or German, Mandarin, Latin, History, Geography, Mathematics, Physics, Chemistry, Biology, Food Technology, Design Technology, Art, Music, and Physical Education are studied. In Year 10 Italian, Greek, Classical Civilisation and PE and Drama become available. Girls take ten or eleven subjects to GCSE. Drama is studied in Years 7, 8, 9 and 10.

In the Sixth Form there is a choice of curriculum between the Advanced Level and the International Baccalaureate Diploma. All subjects offered to GCSE can be continued into the Sixth Form with the addition of Ancient History, Drama and Theatre Studies, Economics, Government and Politics and History of Art. Sixth Formers also undertake the Extended Project Qualification (AL) or Extended Essay and Theory of Knowledge (IB) and attend lectures given by outside speakers.

The Sixth Form. The Sixth Form facilities include a Common Room, Work Room and Terrace. The 220 girls in the Sixth Form play a leading role in the school, taking responsibility for many extracurricular activities, producing form plays and organising clubs. They undertake voluntary work and lead our Raising and Giving programme.

Higher Education and Careers Advice. A strong careers team offers advice to girls and parents. Our specialist room is well stocked with up-to-date literature and course information, and lectures and work shadowing are arranged. Almost all girls proceed to Higher Education degree courses (including an average of 15 a year to Oxford and Cambridge).

The Creative Arts. Music and Drama flourish throughout the school. The Rudland Music School has outstanding facilities for music: 20 soundproofed rooms for individual or group work, a recording studio, ICT suite and two classrooms which open out into a very large rehearsal space for choirs and orchestras. There are four choirs, two orchestras and several small ensembles, and a joint orchestra and choral society with Latymer Upper School. Individual music lessons are offered in many different instruments. Each year there is a pantomime, Year 10 and Sixth Form plays as well as the school productions. The refurbished church, known as The Bishop Centre, offers a superb performing arts space for music, drama and dance.

Physical Education is a vital part of a girl's development as an individual and as a team member. Younger girls play netball, hockey, tennis and rounders and have gymnastic and dance lessons. In the senior years there is a wider range of activities offered, including rowing and squash off site. A state-of-the-art Sport and Fitness Centre opened in September 2015 providing a Sports Hall, climbing wall, dance studio and fitness suite. Tennis/netball courts and an astroturf hockey pitch are also on site.

Extracurricular Activities. The many opportunities for extracurricular activities include the British Association of Young Scientists, Computing, Chess, the Young Enterprise scheme, Debating, Creative Writing, Classics Club and the Duke of Edinburgh's Award scheme, as well as a wide range of sporting activities such as karate, fencing, rowing and canoeing.

Activities outside the School. We organise language exchanges to Germany and France and a musical exchange to Hamburg and Sixth Form work experience in Versailles and Berlin. There is also an exchange with a school in New York. Each year, Year 9 girls ski in the USA and there are study visits to Spain, Italy and France and History of Art visits to Paris, Bruges, Venice and Florence.

We take advantage of our London location by arranging visits to conferences, theatres, exhibitions and galleries. Field courses are an integral part of study in Biology and Geography.

Admission. Girls are normally admitted into Year 7 (First Year Entrance) or into our Sixth Form. Examinations for First Year entrance are held in January and for the Sixth Form in November. There are occasional vacancies in other years. Entry is on a competitive basis.

Fees per term (from January 2017). £6,716. Fees may be raised after a term's notice. Private tuition in music and speech and drama are extra. Most girls have school lunch, but it is an option from Year 8.

Scholarships. Music scholarships are available on entry to Year 7 and in the Sixth Form and include free tuition in one instrument.

An Art scholarship is available in the Sixth Form.

All scholarships are worth up to 30% of fees and may be topped up by means-tested bursaries in cases of need. For all awards, candidates must satisfy the academic requirements of the school.

Bursaries. A number of school bursaries are available annually.

Uniform. Uniform is worn by girls up to and including Year 11.

Charitable status. The Godolphin and Latymer School is a Registered Charity, number 312699. It exists to provide education to girls aged 11 to 18.

Governors:
Chairman: Mr Clifford Hampton, BA, FCA
Mr Sean Carney, BEcon, LLB
Miss Julia Collins, BA, ACCA
Miss Sarah Davies, MA
Mr Simon Davies, BA Oxon
Mr Jonathan Eley, MA
Mr Jon Gabitass, MA
Mr Timothy Howe, QC
Professor Dame Julia Higgins, DBE, FRS, FREng
Mrs Gillian Kettanah Priestley, PhD, MA, BSc
Mrs Sue Kinross, BA
Mr Kevin Knibbs, MA Oxon
Mrs Susie Lane
Dr Leonard Magrill, PhD, BSc, MCom
Mrs Alison Paines, MA, BA
Mrs Penelope Stout-Hammar, BA
Mrs Elizabeth Watson, BA

Clerk to the Governors: Mrs Diana Lynch, BSc Kingston, FCCA

Staff:

Head Mistress: Mrs Ruth Mercer, BA London, PGCE Oxford

Senior Deputy Head (Pastoral): Mrs Anna Paul, BA
Deputy Head (Curriculum and Academic): Dr Sara Harnett, DPhil, BA Oxon

Senior Teachers:
Dr Claire Badger, PhD, MSc Cantab
Mr John Carroll, BSc Durham
Miss Caroline Drennan, MA Oxon, MA UEA
Miss Julia Hodgkins, MA Brunel, BEd CNAA
Ms Amanda Triccas, MA, BA London

Teaching Staff:
Mrs Zoe Allan, BA Nottingham
Mr Adam Abdulla, MA Oxon
Ms Sarah Adams, BEd Melbourne
Miss Sue Adey, BEd Brighton
Mrs Lisa Afifi, MA, BA Kent
Mrs Genevieve Andrade, MA UEL, BSc Imperial College
Mrs Anna Armstrong, BA York
Mrs Eszter Backhausz, BA Cantab
Miss Emily Bannister, BMus Birmingham
Miss Karen Barac, BSc, BEd British Columbia
Miss Ella Barden, BSc Durham
Mr Julian Bell, BA Cantab, MA Sussex
Dr Pamela Bickley, PhD London, BA London
Miss Katy Blatt
Ms Diana Blease, MA Oxon, BA Open
Mrs Ebiere Bolu, BSc Loughborough
Miss Neala Brennan, BSc Bath
Mrs Sancha Briffa, MA Kingston, BA Central St Martins
Dr Aimee Bunting, PhD Soton, MA Soton, BA Soton
Miss Clare Butterworth, MA London, BA Oxon
Miss Karen Casterton, BSc Keele
Miss Zara Cheng, MPhil, BA Cantab
Miss Alison Clark, BA Oxon
Mrs Matilda Cockbain, MA Oxon
Mrs Angela Connell, BSc Bath
Miss Lucy Cooper, MA Wimbledon School of Art, BA Staffordshire
Mrs Celine Corcoran, MA Soton

Ms Patricia Cordeiro Deiros, MSc Cranfield, MSc Catalunya
Mr Matthew Corry, MSc Oxon
Mr Peter Cosgrove, BA Bristol College of Art & Design
Miss Maria Jose Coto Diaz, MA Santiago de Compostela
Miss Virginie Dall' Acqua, MA, BA Toulouse
Mr Adrian Davies, BA Cardiff Institute
Mr Quintin Davies, MA Keele
Mrs Marianne Davis, MA BA Surrey
Miss Tara Dean, BSc Edinburgh
Mrs Amertha Devadoss, BSc London
Mr Nikhil Dholakia, MBA, MEng London
Miss Audrey Dubois, Maître FLE, LLCE Boulogne-sur-mer
Mrs Louise Duffett, MA London, BA Oxon
Miss Natalie Earl, BA Manchester
Miss Ellen Elfick, BEd Exeter
Mrs Sara Farago, BA Winchester School of Art
Mrs Ursula Fenton, Diploma PH Freiburg
Miss Elizabeth Fox, MA Oxon, MSc LSE
Miss Kate Frayling, BSc Bristol
Mr Andrew Furnival, BA Oxon
Mrs Jennifer Garcia, BMus Surrey
Mr Miles Golland, BA London
Miss Ruth Gordon, BA Durham
Miss Hannah Graham, BSc Durham
Mrs Deborah Halifax, LPC, Grand Dip Law BPP, Dip Lancaster, BA Canterbury
Mrs Veronique Halls, BA Sorbonne
Miss Nicola Hanger, BA Oxon
Miss Sophie Harley-Mckeown, MA Cantab
Dr Eilis Harron-Ponsonby, PhD, BA, MSci Cantab
Ms Rachel Hart, BA Oxon
Miss Faye Hasteley, BA Falmouth
Miss Kate Healy, BA Leicester
Miss Charlotte Hegarty, BA Durham
Mrs Rachel Hollis, PhD Birmingham, BSc Portsmouth
Miss Isabell Jacobson, BA Bristol
Dr Ian Jones, PhD CNAA, MSc Cardiff, BSc Liverpool
Miss Lorna Jones, BA Durham
Miss Vicklyn Joseph, BA Surrey
Miss Manuella Kanter, BA Oxon
Miss Veronique Kehr, MA, BA Nancy
Mr Mark Laflin, MA Oxon, ARCO, ATCL
Miss Eva Lerche-Lerchenborg, MA RCA, BA Edinburgh
Mrs Christine Lee, MA London, BEd Exeter
Miss Jennifer Lloyd, MChem Cardiff
Miss Emma Lorys, BA Exeter
Mr David Mahoney, BSc London
Mrs Daniela Malone, MA London, MEng Oxon
Ms Monica Martins, BA Leeds
Mrs Harsha Mason, MA London, BA Durham
Miss Helena Matthews, BA Cantab
Miss Lisa McAdam, MA Cantab
Miss Nicola McDonald, BA Bristol
Mr Justin McGrath, MSc Cranfield, BSc Wales
Miss Emma McLaren, MChem Oxon
Mrs Fiona Meyers, BA Kent
Miss Athina Mitropoulos, MPhil, BA Oxon
Miss Sophie Nicholas, BA Loughborough
Mrs Helen Nohlmans, BSc Durham
Miss Louise Ockenden, MA RCA, BA Central St Martins
Miss Eleanor Odell, BSc Bristol
Mrs Grace Oliver, MA Cantab
Miss Caroline Osborne, MA, BSc London
Mrs Caroline Osborne, MA Sussex
Mrs Victoria O'Shea, BA London, BA Manchester
Miss Luigia Padalino, BA Bologna
Mrs Christine Preston, BSc Bath
Mrs Sylvia Rendall, BA Manchester
Mrs Catriona Roberts, MA Oxon

Dr Madeline Row, MSc Brunel, BSc Brunel
Miss Lucy Shackleton, BA Cantab
Mr Avinash Shah, MEd Sheffield, BA City
Miss Kirsty Smith, MA Middlesex, BA Oxon
Dr Ben Snook, PhD Cantab, MPhil Cantab, BA Cantab
Mrs Helena Spooner, BA Oxon
Dr Jenny Stevens, PhD London, MA London
Miss Emily Strang, BA Oxon
Mrs Susan Sutherland, BA Aberystwyth
Miss Katherine Tallett-Williams, MA Cantab
Mrs Rini Tan, BEd Ji Nan University
Miss Jennifer Taylor, BA Durham
Mr Carl Thomas, LPC Westminster, LLB North London,
    BSc London
Mrs Thania Troya, BA Santa Cruz de Tenerife
Miss Sarah Valentine, BSc Wellington
Mrs Sarah Vantini, BA Bristol
Miss Stephanie von Haniel, MA Edinburgh
Miss Lucy Wallace, BA Reading
Dr Rik Werker, PhD Cantab, BSc Bangor
Mrs Susan Whittaker, BA Durham
Miss Camilla Williams, BA Kent
Mr Jonathan Wong, BSc Imperial
Mr Alastair Wood, MA Edinburgh
Dr Richard Woodberry, PhD, MA Bristol, BA Oxon
Mrs Jennifer Wright, BA Bristol, BEd Bath College
Miss Wendy Zhang, MSc Birmingham, BSc Manchester

Visiting teachers in Music and Speech Training:
Mrs Letitia Allen, PG Dip RCM, PG Dip Trinity, BMus
    Edinburgh
Miss Emily Bannister, BMus Birmingham
Mrs Christina Birchall-Sampson, BA Cantab
Miss Ruth Buxton, BMus RCM, LGSM Guildhall
Miss Davina Clarke, BMus Manchester
Mrs Jane Clark-Maxwell, BMus London, LTCL
Mr David Cuthbert, PG Dip, BMus RAM
Miss Eva Doroszkowska, BMus Manchester, RNCM
Mrs Kasia Feltrin, MA Cracow, PG Dip Guildhall
Miss Avril Freemantle, MA RAM, BMus RNCM
Miss Victoria Galer, BA York
Miss Rebecca Lea, MMus RNCM
Mr Martyn Lewington, Dip RCM
Miss Ching-Ching Lim, MMus RCM, LRSM, FRCL,
    LTCL
Mrs Eloise Marson Chowdhury, BMus RCM
Ms Paola Martinez, BMus RCM
Mrs Laura Moore, PG Dip CSSD, BA Birmingham
Miss Catherine Morphett, BMus Sydney
Ms Vivien Munday, BMus Sydney
Mr David Neville, BA RCM
Miss Camilla Pay, BMus RAM, LRAM
Ms Catherine Riley MMus Auckland NZ, LRSM
Mrs Joanna Roughton-Arnold, BA Wellington NZ, PG Cert
    Trinity, MMus London, DSCM NSW
Mrs Kate Ryder, MMus London, DSCM NSW
    Conservatorium
Mr Christopher Stell, LRAM, Dip RAM
Miss Emma Tingey, LWCMD, ACC WCMD, TCM
Miss Lindsay Tricker, BEd CSSD
Mrs Penny Whinnett, GMus RNCM
Mr Ryan Williams, MMus Guildhall, BMus Exeter
Mrs Sophie Willis, PG Dip, BMus RCM
Miss Emilia Zakrzewska, BMus RAM, RSAMD, Dip
    RAM, LRAM

Bursar: Mrs Diana Lynch, BSc Kingston, FCCA
Registrar: Mrs Felicity Lundberg
Head Mistress's PA: Mrs Vivienne Cox, BA
School Doctor: Dr Samia Hassan, MBBS Imperial,
    MRCGP, DSFRH, PGCE
School Nurses:

Mrs Victoria Dickins, RN, BSc Clinical Practice, Dip
    SpLD Hornsby
Mrs Tessa Vardigans, RN, SpCPHN-SN

Gordonstoun School

Elgin, Morayshire IV30 5RF
Tel: +44 (0)1343 837837
Fax: +44 (0)1343 837808
email: principalspa@gordonstoun.org.uk
            admissions@gordonstoun.org.uk
website: www.gordonstoun.org.uk
Twitter: @gordonstoun
Facebook: @GordonstounSchool

Introduction. As well as preparing students for exams, Gordonstoun prepares them for life.

The school's uniquely broad curriculum encourages every individual to fulfil their potential academically and as human beings. The school motto is 'Plus est en vous' – There is more in you. At Gordonstoun, this sense of possibility is presented to its students, every single day.

'It wasn't until we saw the curriculum and the schedule of what they would be doing each day that we truly understood the difference between Gordonstoun and other schools.' Current parent.

Gordonstoun's location on a 200-acre woodland estate in the North of Scotland provides the background for its world-beating outdoor education. Expeditions to the Scottish Highlands or sail training on the School's 80ft boat are an integral part of school life.

Active engagement in service to the local community also comprises a core part of Gordonstoun's 'working week', further expanding the students' sense of personal and social responsibility and building self-esteem.

Gordonstoun follows the English GCSE and A Level curriculum. Every student's progress is carefully overseen by their tutor and they go on Universities, Colleges and Art Schools all over the world.

Gordonstoun students inhabit a community which is both balanced and internationally dynamic, living and learning alongside fellow students from across the social, cultural and geographical board. The school's seven day programme ensures that students are happily integrated and engaged.

The uniquely all-round education on offer at Gordonstoun provides its students with the chance to develop intellectually, emotionally, physically and spiritually because Gordonstoun understands that the broader the experience, the broader the mind.

The School. Gordonstoun is a co-educational boarding and day school for children aged 6–18. Our main entry points are at age 6 for the Junior School, age 13 for the Lower School (Years 9–11) and age 16 for the Sixth Form (Years 12 and 13), though students can be admitted into any year group as space allows. There are approximately 100 pupils in the Junior school and a further 425 in the Senior School. Gordonstoun prides itself on the international make-up of the student body with approximately one third from overseas, one third from Scotland and one third from the rest of the UK. Gordonstoun is a founding member of The Round Square Organisation and in Year 10 approximately 20 students each year participate in a term's exchange with other Round Square schools in countries such as New Zealand, Australia, Canada, South Africa, Germany, Denmark and the USA. A corresponding number of students from the recipient schools arrive at Gordonstoun each Spring Term.

Boarding. Gordonstoun is one of the few remaining full-boarding schools in the UK and nearly 90% of students in the Senior School are full boarders. This ensures that a full programme of activities is offered throughout weekends and Leave-out weekends. Day pupils join in with weekend activities. There are 8 boarding houses in the Senior School, all but one of which are all-through Houses for boys or girls aged 13–18. One House is for Sixth Form boys only.

Pastoral Care. Gordonstoun's commitment to the well-being, care and protection of every child and young person in our Junior and Senior Schools is paramount. In every aspect of the pastoral care and curriculum experience we endorse the national focus on 'getting it right for every child' and our commitment to ensuring our compliance with the Children and Young People's Act (Scotland) 2014 supports this focus. We place particular importance on ensuring that all students at Gordonstoun have their wellbeing carefully and sensitively managed. Any student joining the school is well cared for, and monitored throughout his or her education. Our systems are built around our pastoral aims, which closely reflect the Gordonstoun ethos and our aim of developing the whole person. This is achieved by an exceptional pastoral team, who devote boundless time, energy and expertise to developing, encouraging and advising students.

Curriculum. Year 9 students carry out a broad and balanced curriculum in both the core and non-core GCSE subjects. Maths, Core Languages (French/Spanish) and Physical Education are set independently of each other and students are streamed according to ability. For the remainder of the curriculum time students are assigned to one of four form sets. The form set will also be the class in which students are grouped together to carry out humanities and creative arts. A second language, chosen from French, Latin, German and Spanish is available as an option across the year.

Gordonstoun follows the English National Curriculum of GCSE and A Level examinations. There are a wide range of subjects available at both levels.

At GCSE students take the core subjects of English (Language and Literature), Maths, Combined Science or Triple Science and a Language (French, Spanish or German) with a choice of two or three optional subjects. Non-examinable subjects in the Core include International & Spiritual Citizenship – a course encompassing and enhancing Religious Studies and Personal & Social Education – and Physical Education.

In Year 12 most students choose three A Level subjects and an optional EPQ. Most non-English speaking students take their native language at A Level. The School offers a range of A Levels allowing students to choose the course that suits them. The School is continually looking to develop new opportunities for students so new courses may become available. In addition to academic subjects, students attend a weekly lecture and International and Spiritual Citizenship lessons where they explore what they believe and their role as an international citizen.

Gordonstoun has a wide support network for those students requiring Learning Support and there is the opportunity to receive one to one or small group teaching. We also offer lessons to prepare international students for IELTS (the International English Language Testing System) for entry into a British University and to acquire the skills they need to study in English in the Sixth Form and beyond.

Academic Results.

Three Year Average Exam Results:
GCSE results (average 2014–16)
Percentage of A*–C grade 78%
Percentage of A*–B grades 51%
Percentage of A*/A grades 28%
A Level results (average 2014–16):
Percentage of A*–C grades 70%
Percentage of A*–B grades 46%
Percentage of A*/A grades 23%
Value Added. The school's success in fulfilling academic potential is reflected, too, in 'value added' measure-

ments. These show students' progress between the start of their courses, when they sit a series of baseline tests which generate predicted grades, and their eventual results in examinations.

An overwhelming number of Gordonstoun students' examination results either match or exceed their baseline scores. Over the last three years these have averaged out at 80% at A Level.

Destination of Leavers. Nearly all students go on to universities and colleges of Higher Education either straight from school or some, after a year of broader experience. In the last three years these have included Oxford, Cambridge, St Andrews, Imperial College, Exeter, Durham, University College London, Edinburgh, as well as the Royal Academy of Music, London and the Royal Conservatoire, Scotland. There are an increasing number of students making successful applications to universities abroad, including MIT (Massachusetts Institute of Technology, USA), Georgetown (USA), Hong Kong University and universities in Canada, Austria, Germany, Spain and Holland.

Our students study a very diverse range of subjects at university from history, geography and psychology to mathematics, physics and engineering. From architecture, textile design, classical archaeology, veterinary medicine, psychology and sports science to music composition and drama.

Sport and Activities. The Gordonstoun Activities programme is carefully designed to enhance and enrich the experience and opportunities of the student body. Students are encouraged to maximise these opportunities by experiencing a wide range of activities whilst also pursuing their passions and strengths. There are many different activities available at Gordonstoun using both the School's facilities and facilities further afield. These activities range from the physical to the cerebral, from team to individual.

The School has competitive teams in rugby, football, hockey, basketball, cricket, tennis, athletics and squash for the boys; hockey, netball, tennis, athletics and squash for the girls; and mixed teams in golf and tennis. These teams participate in national competitions and players are regularly chosen to represent district and regional teams. There are also opportunities to compete in swimming galas, cross-country running, skiing, sailing and adventure races. There is a wide range of recreational sports available including: riding, target shooting, badminton, golf, aerobics, yoga, mountain biking, cycling, climbing, kayaking, orienteering and table tennis.

Cultural activities are designed to give the students opportunities to taste other areas of intellectual stimulation. They include: conversational French and Spanish; cooking, newspaper editing, Jazz dance, electronics, web design, arts, crafts, debating, film and digital art, drama, dance, chess and music practice.

The Performing Arts. Gordonstoun prides itself on the strength of its Performing Arts. Dance, Drama and Music are available to all students and there are regular collaborations between the three departments to produce major theatrical productions. A weekly Dance activity is available to all students and there is also an annual Dance Show, regular Shakespeare productions and an annual Theatre Festival. The School also routinely takes shows to the Edinburgh Fringe Festival. Music students are encouraged to become accustomed to performing in front of audiences large and small via a weekly series of relaxed lunchtime concerts as well as full-scale, formal musical events. Nearly half of the student body receives individual musical tuition in a wide range of instruments.

Outdoor Education and Sail Training. Gordonstoun's outdoor education and learning programmes of expeditions and adventure activities aim to provide experiences that encourage greater personal understanding within individual students. The programmes and sessions look to instil effective learning habits that develop confidence, resilience, tenacity and creativity into the core of all students. The School's fantastic location means that Gordonstoun can provide students with a structured and inspiring programme of mountain, river and sea-based wilderness expeditions. Gordonstoun uses a variety of beautiful and remote settings for Year Group, House, DofE and PE expeditions and journeys which allow students to learn more about and develop a respect for the natural environment while encouraging independence, resourcefulness and effective collaboration.

Sail training is an essential component of Gordonstoun's broader curriculum. It helps to develop teamwork and leadership skills, which complement personal challenge. All students undergo seamanship training in cutters at nearby Hopeman Harbour and on the Moray Firth where they learn basic skills in preparation for a voyage off the Scottish coast in the School's own 80-foot sail training vessel, Ocean Spirit of Moray. Year 8 pupils at the Junior School participate in a two day voyage, Year 10 students are on board for six days and Sixth Formers undertake a week-long Sail Training voyage. These experiences are unique in British mainstream education, combining the challenge of the sea with the development of interpersonal skills, teamwork and leadership. In the Sixth Form there are other opportunities to sail on Ocean Spirit during holiday periods, including participation in a Tall Ships Race or voyaging to the Svalbard Archipelago.

Services. Service at Gordonstoun is concerned with fostering and developing a sense of responsibility and a feeling of care towards all fellow beings. It builds on the experience of responsibility within the School community, transferring this to society at large. It involves each student demonstrating a willingness to give up his or her time and effort to benefit another individual or group without expecting return or reward and is an excellent way of fostering links with the local community and of increasing self-esteem. There are nine Services each of which has a particular set of skills it requires or develops to put something back into the community. Many include training which leads to nationally recognised qualifications that will be useful beyond School life. The Services provide an opportunity to develop and use existing skills or a chance to learn new skills. Every student from Year 11 onwards is expected to take part in one of the services on offer at Gordonstoun.

Admissions. Entry to the Junior school is by interview and a report from the pupil's previous school. Scholarships are awarded by written examination, a day assessment and interview.

Entry at Year 9 and Year 12 is by interview and a report from the previous school. Scholarships in Year 9 are awarded through our own examination or ISEB examinations, interview and report from the previous school. Scholarships at Year 12 are awarded by our own examination, group assessments, interviews and a report from the previous school.

We are looking for candidates with a diverse range of backgrounds and aptitudes who will thrive on, and contribute to, everything that a Gordonstoun education offers regardless of ability to pay. Scholars are awarded a 10% fee reduction with further fee reduction based on means testing. Approximately one third of our students receive support of up to 100%.

The admissions department is always happy to talk to potential parents about Gordonstoun and how to join.

Fees per term (2016–2017). Day fees range from £4,491 (Junior School) to £8,869 (Sixth Form direct entry). Boarding fees range from £7,304 (Junior School) to £11,974 (Sixth Form direct entry). Weekly boarding is available in the Junior School only.

Scholarships and Bursaries are available for entry to the Junior School, Lower School and Sixth Form. The range of Scholarships include: Academic, All-Round, Music and Art; additionally, Sport, Drama, IT and Design in the Sixth

Form. The award is generally for 10% of the annual fee. Additional awards (fee reductions) may be available, based on means testing. Further information on this is available from Gordonstoun's Finance Department.

Charitable status. Gordonstoun Schools Limited is a Registered Charity, number SC037867.

Chair of Governors: Dr Eve Poole

Principal: **Simon Reid**

Head of Senior School: Titus Edge

Head of Junior School: Robert McVean

Deputy Head (Pastoral Care): Richard Devey

Deputy Head (Staffing and Planning): Roberta Keys

Head of Sixth Form: Suzy Morton

Year 11 Leader: Gillian McCrum

Year 10 Leader: Alix Dickinson

Year 9 Leader: Richard Cavaye

Director of Admissions: Sabine Richards

Finance Director: Hugh Brown

Campaign Director: Andrew Davies

Director of Gordonstoun International Summer School: Claire McGillivray

The Grange School

Bradburns Lane, Hartford, Northwich, Cheshire CW8 1LU

Tel: 01606 539039
Fax: 01606 784581
email: office@grange.org.uk
website: www.grange.org.uk
Twitter: @GrangeHartford
Facebook: /thegrangeschool

Motto: *E Glande Robur*

The Grange was founded in 1933 as a Preparatory School, the Senior School opening in 1978. The School is co-educational, with 1,177 pupils from 4–18 years, and is situated in the village of Hartford, half an hour away from Chester and Manchester and eight miles from the M6 motorway.

The Kindergarten and Junior School (432 pupils). 1996 saw the opening of a brand new, purpose-built Kindergarten and Preparatory School for children aged 4–11. In 2010 an additional extension was added incorporating a sports hall, Music Department, Science, Design Technology and Art rooms. These developments have brought together all the children of this age group on to one attractively landscaped eleven acre site which is within walking distance of the Senior School. The main teaching takes place in 21 large, self-contained classrooms on two floors, with the younger children located on the ground floor separated from the older children. The school has its own extensive playing fields and generous play areas while three large halls provide facilities for dining, teaching, sports and school productions. Rooms are provided for specialist teaching in Science, Art, Design Technology and a Music Department with no fewer than 6 individual music practice rooms. As well as a broad curriculum, junior pupils study ICT and a modern language; they have regular swimming lessons and compete in sport with other schools. Close attention is given to each child's progress with two parents' evenings each year. Children learn to use computers from Kindergarten, there is a junior orchestra, and opportunities for private music and drama lessons. Extra-curricular activities are held both at lunchtimes and after school. Before and after school care is available from 7.30 am and until 5.45 pm during term time.

The Senior School (744 pupils). The pupils benefit from excellent extra-curricular and study facilities. The Grange has never been a school to stand still, as a very young school in a lively and competitive market, we spent many of our early years in 'catching up', in terms of our facilities, with the more established schools around us; the physical development of both sites was a top priority at that time.

In more recent years, while the process has slowed and the quality of our provision inside our classrooms has been our major focus, we have still built several new buildings development of The Grange Theatre; The Junior School sports hall, music and science extension and the pavilion on the seven acres of playing fields – which have greatly enhanced the life of our community, and demonstrate the quality we now aspire to as an established and successful institution.

The new Sixth Form facility, completed in September 2014, offers a two storey, pavilion-style building, with a terrace and garden to the rear. Whilst still closely connected to the rest of the school, the Sixth Form Centre provides our senior students with unique and largely self-contained social facilities, careers room and seminar suites. The ground floor is largely given over to a substantial Common Room with room for over 200 and a café only open to Sixth Formers and staff.

Curriculum. Years 1, 2 and 3 follow a broad curriculum with all Third Year pupils studying two modern languages. In the Third Year pupils continue to study English, Mathematics, Biology, Chemistry, Physics, History, Geography, Classical Civilisation or Latin, Religious Studies, Information Technology, PE/Games, two Modern Languages, and select three of five practical subjects. At the end of the Third Year pupils opt for nine subjects which must include Mathematics, English, at least one science and at least one modern language. Personal and Social Education is taught in Years 1 to 5.

From the Third Year advice and assistance is available to all pupils on a wide range of career possibilities. The careers team arrange a biannual careers convention supplemented with regular visits and talks when advice is given by consultants from a variety of professions. There is a fully equipped careers room.

Pastoral Care. The School provides a disciplined, caring and secure environment in which pupils may work and play without being subjected to harm or distress, in which they may develop their personalities to the full and enjoy their time at school. The Form Teacher is the key figure in each pupil's academic and pastoral welfare and is the first point of contact with parents. The Form Teacher is supported by Heads of Year and regular meetings are held to ensure that the pastoral needs of all our pupils are met. The system is enhanced by a Peer Support scheme which allows trained senior students to listen to younger pupils' concerns.

House Activities. Each pupil is allocated to one of four Houses on entry to the school; siblings are allocated to the same House. A House Convener arranges meetings with Heads of House to discuss policy, procedure and House activities. These activities range from sporting competitions to an art and a literary competition. Each year the pupils produce their own play for the drama competition and their own repertoire for the music competition. The organisation of such activities is carried out by the pupils themselves with staff providing support and guidance. All pupils are actively encouraged to participate in the full range of activities in order to raise their self-esteem and to allow each to shine; they gain much from the experience. Junior, Intermediate and Senior House Assemblies are held on a weekly basis.

Sixth Form and Higher Education. Students take four or five subjects plus General Studies to AS Level in the Lower Sixth. They continue with three or four of those subjects plus General Studies to A2 Level in the Upper Sixth. The subjects are chosen from an extensive range with 27 presently available. All Sixth Formers participate in Games lessons, where a wide choice of activities is provided. Supplementary courses provided include Information Technology, Application of Number and Communication and ab initio language courses.

Careers guidance is given considerable emphasis in the Grange Sixth. Each student is attached to a member of the careers team and linguists are given the opportunity to undertake their work experience abroad. Almost all the students progress to higher education, with around 15% going on each year to Oxford and Cambridge.

Sixth Formers are expected to play a leading role in school life. They also participate in the extensive programme of House activities as well as in the Duke of Edinburgh's Award scheme, outward bound courses, Young Enterprise, and the Engineering Council Award scheme.

All students are required to participate in the execution of duties around school and there is a Sixth Form Council, run by the Head Girl and Head Boy, to coordinate the various aspects of Sixth Form life. Students have the use of their own common rooms.

Reporting to Parents. The School recognises that our pupils are best served when parents and the School work together and to this end we consider it important to report to parents fully and regularly. We encourage full discussion of the pupils' progress and well being. Each pupil receives at least two full reports per year. Each half term brings a progress report with academic grades and a profile of the pupil's extra-curricular involvement and pastoral welfare. There are two parents' evenings each year for all Junior School pupils and Years 1, 4 and Lower Sixth in the Senior School, and one for all other year groups. If parents have any concerns, they are encouraged to discuss these with the relevant staff at the earliest opportunity and the School will always contact parents and invite them to discuss issues should we feel it necessary.

Games. The School has 22 acres of sports fields across both schools, an all-weather sports area including a 60m athletics track and a low ropes course. The principal games are hockey, netball, rugby, rowing, football, cricket, cross country, athletics and tennis. There are four all-weather tennis courts as well as three badminton courts.

Art, Design, Drama, Music. In addition to timetabled lessons for these subjects there are numerous opportunities to participate in extra-curricular activities.

In the music department no less than 15 peripatetic teachers provide 420 private lessons a week. There are two orchestras, jazz, string, wind and saxophone ensembles, senior choir and choral society. Cantores Roborienses, the School's senior singing group, and the Chamber Orchestra perform at the many informal concerts held during the year and at numerous public events.

Considerable emphasis is placed on Drama in the school with two part-time and two full-time members of staff and pupils participate in a number of drama festivals with a high degree of first and second placings. Over 80 private Speech and Drama lessons take place each week, with all these pupils entering Trinity-Guildhall examinations, from Junior Preliminary to Grade 8. Regular school productions take place each year with frequent theatre trips.

Religion. The School is Christian based but pupils of all faiths and none are accepted as long as they are prepared to take a full part in the life of the School. Full School Assemblies take place twice a week.

Transport. Hartford is served by two main line stations, Manchester to Chester and Crewe to Liverpool. The majority of children travel to and from school by car or by one of the private buses which cover a 30-mile radius.

Admission. Kindergarten by informal assessment at the end of January; Senior School by entrance assessment on the first Saturday in February; Sixth Form by interview and good GCSE results.

Pupils are also admitted at other ages as vacancies occur. Admission is gained by interview and test performance. Enquiries for admission are welcome at any time of the year and a copy of the school prospectus may be obtained by contacting the Admissions Secretary.

Open Morning. The School holds two Open Mornings in the Autumn term when prospective parents and pupils are welcome to see the facilities available and to talk to the pupils and staff. Appointments to view the school can be made at other times by contacting the Admissions Department.

Fees per term (from January 2017). £2,700 (Kindergarten & Form 1); Junior School £2,925 (Forms 2–6); Senior School £3,610.

Scholarships. Several scholarships are offered for entry to the Senior School for exceptional academic ability and music. A number of Sixth Form Scholarships are awarded for outstanding academic potential after an examination held at the end of spring term preceding Sixth Form entry.

Bursaries worth up to full fees and assessed according to means are available to new entrants to the Senior School.

Charitable status. The Grange School is a Registered Charity, number 525918. It exists to provide high quality education for boys and girls.

Governing Body:
Chairman: Mrs K Williams,

Mrs A Arthur	Mrs C Stanton
Mr S Batey	Mr N Brougham
Mrs S Hudson	Mrs C Bregal
Mrs K Jones	Mr L Fairclough
Mr N Parkinson	Mr J Simpson
Mr J Stamer	Mr D Akka
Mr C Oglesby	

Head: **Mrs D Leonard**, BEd, MEd

Deputy Head (*Staff & Pupils*): Mr A Testard, BA
Deputy Head (*Communications & Enrichment*): Mrs P Duke, BA
Deputy Head (*Academic*): Mr A Crook, MA, MPhil
Head of Sixth Form Studies: Mr A Reeve, BA York, MCIEA
Director of Finance and Operations, Mrs D Torjussen, BA Eng, ACA
PA to the Head: Mrs J Ward, BA
Bursar: Mrs L Foxley, ACA
Estates Manager: Mr I Grant, MRICS
Marketing Manager: Mrs P Watson-Peck BSc

Assistant staff:
* *Head of Department*

Mr P J Ackerley, BA (*English*)
Mrs L Aherne, BA, MA (**Politics*)
Mrs P Allison, BA (*History*)
Miss I Arbones, BA, (*Spanish*)
Miss A Barsoum, BSc (*Geography*)
Mrs N Beardsall, BA (*Art and Technology*)
Ms N Benzerfa, MA (*Spanish*)
Mrs J Bloor, BA (*Director of Performing Arts*, **Speech & Drama*)
Mr A Boardman, MA (*History*)
Miss A Brace, BA (*Art*)
Miss J Breton, BEd (*Food and Nutrition*)
Mrs B A Broderick, BSc (*Chemistry, Geography*, **Outdoor Pursuits*)

Mrs S Brunt, BA (*Economics*)
Mr P Challinor, BA, MSt (**Classics*)
Mrs H Chaplain, BA, MA (*English*)
Mrs G Clough, MA (*English*)
Mr N Cusick, BSc (*PE & Games*)
Miss L Davenport, MA (*Religious Studies*)
Miss A Dostalova, BSc (*Biology*)
Mrs H Eaton, MA (*Geography*)
Mrs M Ellis, BSc (*Mathematics*)
Mrs V Farrell, BA, MA (*Graphic Design*)
Miss J Fowler, BSc (*PE & Games*)
Mr T H Giles, BA (*PE & Games*)
Mr P Grattage, BSc (*Director of Sport*)
Mrs H Hackett, BA, MSc (*German & French*)
Mrs J Hardy-Kinsella, BA (*Drama & English*)
Mr R A Hibbert, BA (**Modern Languages*)
Mrs C Hill, BSc (**Mathematics*)
Mrs H Horsley, BSc (*Physics*)
Mr R A Hough, BA (*Religious Studies*, **Philosophy*)
Mr C Howe, BSc, MRSC (**Chemistry*)
Mr S Howells, BA (**French*)
Mrs S Hoyle, BA (*Religious Studies, Philosophy*)
Miss A Jackson, BSc (*Biology*)
Ms P H Janson, MA (*Mathematics*)
Mrs S Johnson, BA (*Art*)
Mr D W Jones, MA (*History & Politics*)
Mr G Jump (**Rowing*)
Mr M Langridge (*Rowing*)
Miss F Livesey, BSc (*Mathematics*)
Mr H Kelly, MA (*English*)
Mr S Kenyon, BSc (*Geography*)
Mr D Kereszteny-Lewis, BA (*Director of Art & Design*, **Art*)
Mrs V Kereszteny-Lewis, BA (**German*)
Mr M Lambert, BSc (*Mathematics*)
Mrs M Kaipainen, MA (*English*)
Mr R Latham, BA (**Religious Studies, Public Benefit Co-ordinator*)
Miss H R Lawson, BA (*Assistant Director of Physical Education*)
Mrs G Lewis, BSc (*Mathematics*)
Mr A Lumley, BSc (*Mathematics*)
Mr B Madden, BA (*Music*)
Mr A Masters, BA (**ICT, Director of E-Learning*)
Mrs J Masters, BA (*Biology and Maths*)
Mr P McAleny, BA (**Graphic Design*)
Miss P McKeown, BA (*English*)
Mr A J Millinchip, MA, FRCO CHM (*Director of Music*)
Mr A Milne, BSc, MSc (**Science*, **Biology*)
Miss E Moore, BA (*French*)
Mr W Morrison, BA (**Economics & Business Studies*)
Mrs J S Oakes, BSc (*Biology*)
Mrs C J Osborne, BSc (*Mathematics*)
Mrs K Osorio, BA (**Spanish*)
Mr J M Pearson, BA (**Geography*)
Mr S Petts, BA (**Physics*)
Miss B Picken, BA (*Art*)
Mrs M Plant, MA (*French & German, Head of Pupil Support*)
Mr A Reeve, BA (*Economics*)
Mr R K Robson, BA (**History*)
Mr G Sgroi, BA (*Classics*)
Mr L Snelson, BSc (*ICT*)
Mrs A Stewart (*Food & Nutrition*)
Miss J Stockton (**English*)
Mrs L Sunners, BA (*Drama*)
Mr W Sutton, MInstP (*Physics*)
Mr J Taylor, BSc (*Biology*)
Mrs J Thayer, BSc (*Mathematics*)
Mrs S Thornes, BSc (*Physics*)
Mrs K Tomlin, BA (*Drama*)

Dr S Wharton, PhD, MChem (*Chemistry*)
Miss M Wright, MSc (*Physics*)

Junior School

Head of Junior School: Mr G Rands, BSc
Deputy Head: Miss A Evans, BEd (*Head of Pastoral Care*)
Deputy Head: Mr J Land, BEd (*head of Academic Development*)
PA to the Headmaster/Admissions Secretary: Mrs M Shaw

Mrs J Batchelor, BEd	Mrs V Houghton, MA, BEd
Ms K Blakeley, BA	Mrs C Jones, BSc
Mrs C Carson, CertEd	Mr H Jones, BEd
Mrs L Collier, BA	Mrs S Jones, BEd
Mrs A Copping, BA	Mr J P Land, BEd
Miss A Dalzell, BA	Miss J Lloyd, MA
Mrs R Davies, BA	Mrs S Lucchesi, BA
Mrs M Dewhurst, BEd	Mrs H Oliver, BA
Mr T Eddy, BA	Mrs Z A Pidcock, BA
Mr G H Evans, BEd	Miss V Ravenscroft, BA
Miss D Fuller, BMus	Mrs G Ruddick, BSc
Mrs H Greaves, BA	Miss C Sales, BA
Mrs K Hales, BA	Mrs A Sneath
Mrs V Heath, BEd	

Peripatetic Staff:

Mrs A Barnett, BMus, LRAM, PG Dip RAM (*Clarinet, Saxophone*)
Mrs N Boardman, GRNCM (*Violin*)
Mrs M Bushnell-Wye, ARCM, LGSM, GRSM Hons (*Clarinet, Saxophone*)
Mrs B Elsby, BMus Hons, MMus Perf RNCM (*Cello*)
Mr C Gandee, ARCM, LLCM [TD], FFLCM (*Brass*)
Mrs S Hoffman, BMus Hons, PG Dip RNCM (*Flute*)
Mr G Hogan, BA, LRAM, LGSM, LLCM (*Keyboard, Piano*)
Ms R Holt, GMus RNCM, PPRNCM (*Flute*)
Mrs C Hughes, GNSM, ARCM (*Piano*)
Mr M Jackson, Grad Dip Jazz & Cont Music (*Guitar*)
Mr B Madden, BA (*Cello, Piano*)
Mr A Millinchip, MA, FRCO [CHM], ATCL, (*Director of Music*)
Miss P MacMillan, BMus, PG Dip RNCM, ALCM [TD] (*Percussion and Drum Kit*)
Mrs A Powell, BMus, PG Dip RNCM, PPRNCM (*Oboe*)
Miss L Turner, CT ABRSM (*Guitar*)
Mr S Watkiss, CT ABRSM (*Guitar*)
Miss S Wilkes, GMus RNCM (*Singing*)

Gresham's School

Cromer Road, Holt, Norfolk NR25 6EA

Tel: 01263 714500
          01263 714614 (Admissions)
email: admissions@greshams.com
website: www.greshams.com
Twitter: @Greshams_School
Facebook: @greshamsschool

Motto: Al Worship Be To God Only

The School was founded in 1555 by Sir John Gresham Kt and the endowments were placed by him under the management of the Fishmongers' Company.

There are 480 pupils in the Senior School, 275 boys and 205 girls, of whom 213 are in the Sixth Form and 262 are boarders.

The School is situated about 4 miles from the breathtaking north Norfolk coast, in one of the most beautiful parts of England. Gresham's enjoys a spacious setting of 200 acres including 50 acres of woodland. Numbered amongst its alumni are W H Auden, Benjamin Britten, Stephen Spender, Lord Reith, Ben Nicholson and Olivia Colman on the Arts side, Christopher Cockerell, inventor of the hovercraft, Ian Proctor, yacht designer, Sir Martin Wood, co-founder of Oxford Instruments, Sir James Dyson, inventor and engineer, Sir Alan Lloyd Hodgkin, biophysicist and Nobel Prize winner in Physiology or Medicine, and, more recently, Tom and Ben Youngs, international rugby players. It offers excellence in a wide range of fields, from which pupils gain an outstanding, all-round education.

Gresham's is a Church of England foundation but all religious denominations are welcomed. The School has its own Chaplain and counsellor. Both are available to advise and help pupils throughout their time at Gresham's. In addition, a 24-hour Health Centre provides a multi-disciplinary professional health service.

In the Senior School, there are four boys' boarding houses and three girls' houses. Students joining in Year 9 share a small dormitory, while older pupils share study-bedrooms, and most Sixth Formers have their own room.

Curriculum. In their first year (Year 9), students study the complete curriculum, including exposure to the full set of sciences, humanities, creative subjects, IT and up to three languages. There is a comprehensive language tuition programme and pupils can select up to three language choices from French, Spanish, German, Latin, Mandarin and Japanese. The curriculum is designed to allow students to experience the full range of subjects prior to making their choices for their two year GCSE programme. For their GCSEs all students follow a compulsory curriculum of English, Maths, a language and either dual award or all three sciences, together with an option system allowing for up to a further four subject choices (including further languages) to be made. In Years 10 and 11, students study up to ten IGCSE and GCSE subjects which enable them to keep open a wide diversity of career opportunities. It is possible to take Maths early and for top-set mathematicians to additionally sit AO Maths in Year 11. The flexibility built into our option system allows for virtually all subject combinations to be accommodated.

Since September 2007, we have offered a one-year Pre IB course to a small number of students each year. This course is specifically designed to integrate overseas students into life at Gresham's and most students will gain approximately 8 full GCSEs as a result. The course offers the ideal preparation for the IB Diploma Programme and students follow an individually tailored curriculum centred on English Language, Maths, (usually) two sciences and two or three other option subjects.

Entry into the Sixth Form is dependent on students achieving a minimum of six GCSE passes at A* to B grade, to include passes in Maths and English. Students can either opt for A Levels or the IB Diploma. All students receive advice, information and guidance on academic choices and full support for university entrance.

For those students following the A Level course, three subjects are normally taken, though four or more are possible for very able students. All A Levels at Gresham's are now linear. Students are also encouraged to complete an Extended Essay on a subject and topic of their choice. A supplementary course is offered providing enhancement skills in advanced thinking techniques, numeracy, literacy and ICT skills.

For those students entering our IB Diploma, six subjects have to be taken, at least three at higher level and three at standard level. In addition, a Theory of Knowledge (TOK) course is taken, a Creativity, Action and Service (CAS) course followed and an Extended Essay (effectively a research project on a subject of the student's choosing) has to be written. This rigorous programme helps pupils become lifelong and independent learners and the IB qualification is recognised by universities throughout the world.

Pupils entering the Sixth Form receive continual, consistent and experienced support and guidance on the UCAS process to help them make realistic and informed decisions about their futures. Lower Sixth pupils are included in the Career and Course Bites sessions where they hear from visiting career professionals and university lecturers. They also participate in a number of careers events throughout the year.

A varied programme of enrichment is offered across the school. In Year 9, students select an area of specialism – academic, drama, art, music or sport. In Year 10, all pupils experience an academic enrichment carousel, whilst there is a stimulating Friday night lecture programme for Sixth Formers. Lower Sixth pupils also experience a successful well-being programme. There are many societies to take part in which are dedicated to English, the humanities, foreign languages, the sciences and philosophy. Wider scholarship is also nurtured through activities like debating, Model United Nations, and Electives.

Sport, Music and Drama. The School has abundant playing fields, AstroTurf pitches, tennis courts, as well as a swimming pool, gym, sports hall and its own indoor shooting range. The main sports are athletics, cricket, hockey, netball, rugby and tennis. Shooting, sailing, swimming, squash, badminton, football, cross-country, running and trampolining are also very popular, and a number of pupils have gone on to achieve international success in rugby, shooting, sailing and hockey.

There is a flourishing CCF contingent and Duke of Edinburgh's Award section and approximately 25 gold awards are achieved each year. The School has a talented choir which performs regularly in East Anglia and travels overseas on its annual choir tour. Several of its members have recently sung in the National Youth Choirs of Great Britain. The school has its own theatre as well as an outdoor amphitheatre in the woods. Art and Drama are also exceptionally strong with Drama and Theatre Studies offered at GCSE, A Level and IB.

Entrance. Those entering at Year 9 from Preparatory Schools take Entrance Examinations in January. Gresham's Prep pupils take Year 8 exit examinations. Tests in Maths, English and a General Paper are given to those entering from independent schools and from the maintained sector. Candidates applying from overseas sit assessments in Maths and English.

Scholarships and Bursaries. The School is extremely grateful to benefactors, in particular the Fishmongers' Company, for financing many of the awards below.

Senior School: There are Academic scholarships available for entry into Year 9 and Sixth Form, as well as scholarships for those who are exceptional in Music, Art, Drama and Sport.

Year 9: Academic scholarships are worth up to 50% of the fees. Music, Art, Drama or Sport scholarships are worth up to 20% of the school fee. A means-tested bursary may also be awarded.

Sixth Form: Academic, Music, Art, Drama and Sport scholarships are worth up to 20% of the fee.

Prep School: Scholarships are available for entry into Year 7 and enquiries should be directed to the Headmaster at the Prep School (prep@greshams.com).

Fees per term (2016–2017). Senior School: £10,990 (boarding), £7,900 (day). Prep School: £8,050 (boarding), £5,720 (day). Nursery and Pre-Prep School: £3,075–£3,385 (day).

These are inclusive fees; no extra charge is made for laundry, games, medical attention, etc, although some areas, such as individual music tuition, trips, English as a Second Language and learning support, attract extra charges.

Day pupils' meal charges are included in the fees.

Honours. In 2016, 93.5% of pupils achieved A*–C grades at GCSE. At A level pupils achieved a pass rate of 96% with 63.6% achieving A*–B grades. In the IB Diploma, the average point score was 35 points. With 8 pupils gaining 38 points or more, placing them among the top 10% of global IB Diploma achievers. We consistently send around 95% of our Upper Sixth leavers on to higher education, most of these going to their first-choice courses.

Gresham's Prep School is a flourishing boarding and day co-educational Prep school of 257 pupils within half a mile of the Senior School. Its Headmaster is a member of IAPS. (*For further details see our entry in the IAPS section.*) There is also a Pre-Prep School of approximately 80 pupils.

The Old Greshamian Club. The Club is active on behalf of present and former members of the School and it can be contacted through its Alumni Manager, Mrs J Thomas-Howard, at Gresham's School.

Charitable status. Gresham's School is a Registered Charity, number 1105500. The School is a charitable trust for the purpose of educating children.

Governors:
Mr N Bankes (*Prime Warden of Fishmongers' Company*)
Mr A Martin Smith, BA Hons (*Chairman of Governors*)
Mr C Boag, CB CBE (*Clerk to Fishmongers' Company*)
Mr J fforde
Mr S Gorton
Mrs V Graham
Mr D Jones MA Cantab
The Rt Reverend Jonathan Meyrick, The Bishop of Lynn
Mr P Peal
Mrs S Smart, MA Oxon, PGCE
Mr G Able, MA Cantab, PGCE (*Chairman of the HR & Staff Conditions Committee*)
Mr M Goff (*Chairman of GSEL*)
Mr E Gould, MA Oxon (*Chairman of Education Committee*)
Mr P Marriage, MA Oxon
Mr P Mitchell, MEng Cantab (*Deputy Chairman of Governors, Chairman of Finance & General Purposes Committee*)
Mr J Morgan, LLB (*Chairman of the Estates Committee*)
Mr S Oldfield (*Chairman of the Audit, Risk and Compliance Committee*)
Dr S Ruben, FRCPCH, FRCP

Headmaster: Mr D Robb, MA, MEd

Deputy Head – Academic: Mr T Hipperson, BA, MA, QTS, PGCE (*English*)
Deputy Head – Pastoral: Mr W Chuter, BA (*English*)
Business & Finance Director: Mr J Stronach, ACA
Director of Admissions & Marketing: Ms S V Wilson, BA, MCIM
Director of Development: Mrs K Bromham, BCom, LLB, FCIM

Staff:
* *Head of Department*
† *Housemaster/mistress*

Mr S Adams, BEd (*Sports Development Director*)
Mr D Atkinson, BA, PGCE (*Geography,* †*Farfield*)
Mr D Bailey, ONC/HND (*Design & Technology*)
Mrs L Barden, BA, PGCE (**MFL, French*)
Mr A Bealey, BA, PGCE (*Activities Coordinator*)
Mrs S Botley, BSc, PGCE (**Mathematics*)
Mr J Bowley, MA Cantab, ARCM PG (*Director of Music*)
Mr S Brown, BA, PGCE (**Geography*)
Mr A Coventry, BA, PGCE (*Business Studies*)
Mr C Cox, BA, PGCE (**History*)
Mr S Curtis, BSc, PGCE (*Mathematics*)

Mr P Detnon, BSc, PGCE (*Economics*)

Mrs S L Ellis-Retter, BA, PGCE (*ESL, Overseas Pupil Coordinator*)

Mrs V English, BEd (*Careers Coordinator, Learning Support*)

Dr E Fern, BA, MA, PhD, PGCE (*History, †Edinburgh*)

Mr A Fletcher (*English*)

Mrs J Flower, Dip Boarding Education (*Director of Pastoral Care, Designated Safeguarding Lead, Games*)

Mrs L Futter, BA, MA, QTS (*Assistant Director of Drama*)

Mr S B Gates, BA, MA, PGCE (*Philosophy*)

Mrs S Gates, BA Hons, PGCE, OCR Dip SpLD, Cert TESOL (*Head of Learning Support, SENCo*)

Miss F Gathercole, BA (*Assistant Head Co-curricular, Biology, Environmental Systems and Societies*)

Mr M Gillingwater, MSc, BSc, PGCE (*Head of Sixth Form, Biology*)

Mr A Gray, BA, PGCE (*Art*)

Mrs H Green, MA Cantab, PGCE Oxon (*Biology*)

Mr B Green, BSc, PGCE Oxon (*Biology*)

Dr C Hammond, MPhil, PhD (*French, Spanish*)

Mr T Howland, BA, PGCE (*Mathematics*)

Mr N Humphrey, BA, PGCE (*Design Technology*)

Mrs C Jefford, BA (*French, Spanish*)

Mr T S Keen, Cert Ed, QTS, Dyslexia Guild (*Learning Support*)

Mr M Kemp, BSc, PGCE (*Chemistry*)

Mr S A Kinder, BA, PGCE (*Head of Teaching and Learning, History*)

Miss S E King, BSc, PGCE (*Geography*)

Mr P Laidler, BSc, PGCE (*Biology, †Tallis*)

Mr J Lewis, BA (*Physical Education*)

Mr S Lowe, BA, QTS (*Mathematics*)

Mr C Mack, BA Hons, FCCA (*Economics*)

Mr M Masters, BA Hons, PGCE (*ESL*)

Mr M Matthams, BSc, MA, PGCE (*Science*)

Mrs E McNamara, LLB, QTS, PGCE (*Mathematics*)

Mrs K Mousley, BA, PGCE (*French, Spanish, †Oakeley*)

Mr J G N Myers, DipHE, GSMD (*Music Technology*)

Mrs M Myers, BEd, RSA Cert TEFL, Cert SpLD (*Head of Wellbeing & SRE, Learning Support*)

Mrs S Nakajima, AGSM, BA Oxon (*Assistant Director of Music*)

Mrs L Nicols, BA, PGCE (*Art*)

Mr C Nichols, BSc, PGCE (*Religious Studies*)

Mr J Norris, BA, MA, MSc, PGCE (*Chemistry*)

Mrs N Norris, BA Hons, PGCE, PG Dip (*English*)

Miss B O'Brien, BA, PGCE (*Drama*)

Mr T O'Donnell, BS, QTS (*History*)

Mr M Peacock (*Classics*)

Miss S Pink, BA, PGCE (*Art*)

Mr C Reed, BEng, PGCE (*Physics*)

Mr F J V Retter, BA, PGCE (*German, †Woodlands*)

Revd B R Roberts, BD, DipTheol (*School Chaplain, Religious Studies*)

Mrs H Robinson, BA, MA (*History of Art*)

Mrs K Robinson, BA, PGCE (*ESL*)

Mr D Saker, BSc, MSc, PGCE (*Physics*)

Mr M Seldon, BA, MA (*Director of Studies, English*)

Mrs V Seldon, BA, PGCE (*†Queens', *Spanish*)

Mrs C Stevens, BA Hons, STC, QTS, PGCE (*English*)

Mr A Stromberg, BEng, MSc, AFRIN, PGCE (*Head of Lower Years, Mathematics, †Howson's*)

Mr A Stoppani, BSc Hons, MSC, PGCE (*ICT*)

Miss K Thompson (*English*)

Mr J R P Thomson, BEng, PGCE (*Mathematics*)

Mr L Tao, BA, PGCE (*Head of Academic Music, Organist*)

Miss E Thornbury, BA, PGCE (*PE*)

Dr K C Tsai, MA, PhD, DipEd (*Mandarin*)

Mrs C van Hasselt, BA, PGCE (*English*)

Mrs K Walton (*DofE Coordinator, Games*)

Mrs A Watt, BA, PGCE (*French*)

Mr J Wheeler, BSc Hons, PGCE (*Chemistry*)

Mr R West, MMath, PGCE (*Japanese*)

Miss E Whittle, BA, QTS, PGCE (*Psychology*)

Miss M Zechiel, Staatsexamen Degree, QTS (*German*)

Prep School:

Headmaster: Mr J H W Quick, BA Hons, PGCE

Deputy Head: Mr R T N Brearley, CertEd (*Geography*)

Deputy Head Academic: Mrs C Braithwaite, BA Ed Hons, QTS (*Mathematics, Science, Physics, Sport*)

Assistant Head: Mrs S Vare, BA (*Classics, Modern Languages*)

Special Projects and Outreach Coordinator: Mrs K Quick, BA, PGCE (*Head of Charity Fundraising, Staff representative for the Parents' Association*)

Prep School Staff:

Mr T Appleton, BA (*Music*)

Mrs J M Andrews, BA, QTS (*Learning Support*)

Mrs E Ashcroft, BA, PGCE (*Modern Languages, French Coordinator*)

Mr G Baird, MA, BA, PGCE (*History, Geography*)

Dr L Betts, MB BS, MS (*Science, Chemistry Coordinator*)

Mrs S Bracey (*Games*)

Mrs J Brearley, BA, Dip ELS (*Librarian, English, Learning Support*)

Mrs H Buckingham (*Sport*)

Mrs R Casey, BA Hons QTS, PGCE (*Music*)

Mr N P Cornell, BSc, PGCE (*Science, Biology Coordinator*)

Mrs C Cozens-Hardy, MTD (*Art, Design & Technology*)

Mrs E Curtis, BSc (*Sport*)

Mrs N J Doran, MEd, LIB, QTS, PGCE

Mrs K Edwards, MA, BA (*Head of Dance and Junior Performing Arts*)

Mrs S Fairbairn-Day, BA, PGCE (*Junior Science Coordinator, Science, Religious Studies, PSHE Coordinator*)

Mrs J Fenn, MEd, DipHD (*English, *Learning Support, Designated Safeguarding Lead*)

Mrs K Fields, BEd (*Geography, History, Religious Studies, †Crossways, Learning Support, Designated Safeguarding Lead*)

Mr S Fields, BSc, QTS (*Mathematics, Sport, †Crossways*)

Mrs K Gill, BA, PGCE (*Head of Juniors, Mathematics, English, Science, Sport*)

Miss V Harvey, BA (*English, *Drama*)

Mrs K Heal, BA, PGCE (*Teacher Junior Years*)

Mr K Hobday, Violin teacher

Mr A Horsley, BA, PGCE (*Mathematics, Sport*)

Mrs A Horsley, BSc, QTS, PGCE (*Head of Girls' PE and Girls' Games, Mathematics*)

Ms J Howard, BA (*Modern Languages, Learning Support*)

Mrs G Kretchetov, MA, RSA CTEFLA (*EAL, Learning Support*)

Mr P M Laycock, BA, BSc, PGCE (*Design Technology, Sport*)

Mrs S Li-Rocchi, MA, BA, PGCE (*Art*)

Miss M J Lister (*Games*)

Mrs P Matthams, BSc (*Games*)

Mr P Moore, BSc, PGCE, PGDAA (*Physics*)

Mrs A Nash, BA, PGCE (*Religious Studies, Modern Languages, Sport, Gifted and Talented Coordinator*)

Mrs S O'Leary, BA (*History, English*)

Mrs A O'Sullivan, MA Hons, PGCE Oxon (*English*)

Mrs A Pitkethly, BA, PGCE, PG Dip (*Learning Support*)

Miss L B Roberts, BA, ARCM, AGSM, DipNCOS (*Director of Music*)

Mrs C Sankey, BA, PDSEN (*Learning Support*)

Mrs C Smith, BA, PGCE (*English, Mathematics*)

Mr M Smith, BA (*Mathematics, Sport*)

Mr N Thomas, BA, PGCE (*English, Modern Languages, Sport, †Kenwyn*)
Mrs F Thomas (*†Kenwyn*)
Mrs K Walton (*Sport*)
Mrs H E Witton, BA (**ICT, Learning Support, Sport*)
Mrs L Worrall (*Sport*)
Mr S C Worrall, BA, PGCE (*Geography, *Boys' PE*)

Pre-Prep School:
Headmistress: Mrs S Hollingsworth, PGCE, QTS, BSc, DSL
EYFS Coordinator: Miss J Sandford, BSc, PGCE (*Learning Enrichment*)

Pre-Prep Staff:
Mrs N Adams, BEd Hons
Miss L Connon, MSCi, QTS, PGCE
Miss B Court, BEd Hons
Mr T Hadley, BSc Hons, QTS, PGCE
Mrs K Kinder, BSc, PGCE
Mrs E Langton, BEd
Mrs E Richardson, NVQ4 (*Nursery Leader*)
Mrs R Casey, BA Hons QTS, PGCE (*Music*)

Health Centre Staff:
Dr Roebuck (*School Doctor*), Mrs T Roebuck, Mrs R Richardson, Miss D Needs, Mrs J Smith, Mrs K A Barnes, Mrs E Mingins, Mrs J M Bix, Mrs A Main
School Counsellor: Mrs R Lubbuck
SSI: C C Scoles, MBE

Guildford High School

United Learning

London Road, Guildford, Surrey GU1 1SJ
Tel: 01483 561440
Fax: 01483 306516
email: guildford-admissions@guildfordhigh.co.uk
website: www.guildfordhigh.surrey.sch.uk
Twitter: @GuildfordHigh

Motto: *As one that serveth*

Established in January 1888.
Number of Girls. 700 Day Girls aged 11–18 years.
Guildford High School is a successful school in which high expectations are set for all pupils, with learning as its key focus. It is a community in which everyone is known, valued and feels secure. Pupils are supported and encouraged to reach their potential.

The school has outstanding pastoral care: it is key to its happy and successful environment. It has a system of Form Tutors, Heads of Year and, of course, a Deputy Head responsible for pastoral matters. When the girls arrive in Year 7, they are assigned a 'buddy' from Year 8 who will steer them through the first term and beyond.

Guildford High School has an extensive extra-curricular and curriculum-enrichment programme, encompassing sport, drama, music, debating and much more besides.

As a result, the girls achieve outstanding success at all levels from SATs to GCSE and A Level. In 2016, the A Level pass rate was 100%, with 84% of girls achieving A* or A grades and 34% of all grades were A* grade. At GCSE, 96% of the results were A or A* with 77% being A*. Most importantly, the vast majority of leavers go on to their first-choice university with an average of 20% gaining offers from Oxford or Cambridge each year.

Sixth Form. There is a strong Sixth Form and most girls take four AS Level subjects from the wide range offered and continue with three of these subjects to A Level. They also follow a non-examined General Studies course. All girls proceed to University or to other areas of Higher Education. The Sixth Form has its own accommodation, which has been extended and refurbished as part of a major development plan.

Music. There is a lively musical tradition and girls are encouraged to play musical instruments and to join one of the orchestras, choirs, chamber groups or the wind bands. GHS has recently opened the doors to its stunning 2016 Hall for the first time; housing a recording studio and teaching studios, this new music Recital Hall has been designed for a variety of events – not just concerts but also lectures from visiting speakers.

Drama. Drama is taught as part of the curriculum. GCSE Drama is available as well as A Level Drama and Theatre Studies. There are major productions every term which are actively participated in by girls of all ages taking on acting, directing, producing and backstage roles.

The Duke of Edinburgh's Award Scheme. Around 90% of girls take part in this fun and challenging scheme, which is run jointly by parents and teachers and which offers opportunities for developing character through service, skills and expeditions.

Physical Education. Lacrosse, netball, tennis, rounders, athletics, gymnastics, dance and swimming take place within games lessons. A wide range of sports including cross-country running, rowing, taekwondo, yoga, badminton, indoor climbing, football, hockey, golf, fencing and trampolining are also available as extra-curricular activities. The girls compete locally, nationally and internationally with excellent results and a 'sport for all' policy provides many opportunities to take part for fun and recreation. Sixth Formers can select from a wide choice of activities for their timetabled games lesson.

Situation and Facilities. The school is pleasantly situated near the centre of Guildford on a bus route and close to London Road Station; frequent trains to the main station provide links over a wide area. Facilities include libraries, eleven well-equipped laboratories, whiteboards in every classroom, an Information Technology Centre, a Design Technology Centre, Art and Design Studios, a Food Technology Room, Music Rooms, Music Technology Studio, a Careers Room and Dining Hall. The school also opened a £5 million Sports Hall and indoor swimming pool in 2006, and a new Music Recital Hall in 2016.

The Junior School at Guildford High School combines a warm, caring atmosphere with a stimulating environment, and offers careful preparation for entry to the Senior School. (*See Junior School entry in IAPS section.*)

Normal ages of entry. 11 years and Sixth Form level (the Junior School takes girls at age 4 and 7).

Admissions. The school sets its own entrance examination. Academic standards are high.

Fees per term (2016–2017). £5,344. Fees exclude lunches. Textbooks and stationery are provided.

Extra Subjects. Instruments (orchestral) £201.

Scholarships and Bursaries. Academic Scholarships are offered at 11+ and 16+. Academic Exhibitions (lesser award) are also available at 11+ and 16+. Music Scholarships are also offered at 11+ and 16+. United Learning Assisted Places are available at 11+. These places are awarded on the basis of financial need. Bursaries are available throughout the School for daughters of Clergy.

Charitable status. Guildford High School is part of United Learning which comprises: UCST (a Company Limited by Guarantee, Registered in England, number 2780748, and a Registered Charity, number 1016538) and ULT (a Company Limited by Guarantee, Registered in England, number 4439859, and an Exempt Charity).

Governing Body: The Council of United Learning

Patron: The Most Revd and Rt Hon Justin Welby, Archbishop of Canterbury

Local Governing Body:
Chairman: Mr Dan Perrett
Dr David Ashton
Canon Robert Cotton
Mrs Anna Lise Gordon
Prof Ortwin Hess
Miss Zip Jila
Mr John Rigg
Miss Karen Braganza

Staff:

Headmistress: Mrs Fiona J Boulton, BSc Hons Cardiff, MA London (*Biology*)

Deputy Heads:
Academic: Mrs Victoria M Bingham, BA Keble College Oxford (*Classics*)
Pastoral: Mrs Karen J Laurie, BA Hons Leeds (*History*)
Co-curricular: Mr William H Saunders, BA Hons Bristol, MA St Mary's Twickenham (*History*)

* *Head of Department*

Art and Design:
Dr Ursula C A Weekes, PhD London
*Mrs Susan C Kew, BA Hons Kingston
Mr Roderick C R Laughton, BA Hons Liverpool John Moores

Classics:
Mrs Victoria M Bingham, BA Keble College Oxford (*Deputy Head Academic*)
Mrs Alison G George, BA Hons St John's College Oxford
*Mr Andrew S James, MA Worcester College Oxford
Miss Sophie M Oakes, BA Hons Cambridge
Ms Clare L Weightman, BA Capetown, MA Capetown

Computer Science:
Mr Javier González Abia, BA Hons Valladolid, Spain (*Word Press Coordinator*)

Critical Thinking:
Mrs Samantha J Buxton, BA Hons Cardiff (*Assistant Head of Years 10 & 11*) [maternity]
Mr William H Hack, BA Hons MSci Cambridge (*Assistant Examinations Officer*)
Mrs Katie M C Perrin, BA Hons, MPhil Trinity Hall Cambridge
*Miss Katrina M Sloan, BA Hons Reading (*Deputy Head of Sixth Form*)

Design & Technology:
*Mrs Wendy A Bengoechea, BEd Hons Bath (*Head of Year 7, Head of Faculty*)
Mrs Helen P Gowers, BSc Hons Surrey
Mr Christopher T McGhee, BA Hons Loughborough
Mrs Janine E Sankey, BA Bristol [part-time maternity cover]
*Mrs Jenni L Wilkinson, BA Hons Sheffield Hallam (*Head of Resistant Materials*) [maternity]

Economics:
*Mrs Carol L Jones, BA Hons Sheffield (*Young Enterprise*)
Mr Ian J W Pethick, BA Hons Oxford

English & Theatre Studies:
Mrs Lucy E Cowie, BA Hons King's
Miss Molly R F Edwards
Ms Ashley L Fenton, BA Hons Aberystwyth (*Head of Drama*)
Mrs Judith A Gibson, BA Hons Liverpool (*Assistant Head of Year 7*)

Mrs Sarah L Glyn-Davies, BA Hons East Anglia (*Head of Year 9*)
Miss Amy E Gray, BA Hons Leeds (*2nd in English*)
Mrs Joanne L Holt, BA Hons York, MA London (*Senior Teacher Curriculum*)
*Miss Jemima M Kettle, BA Hons Keble College Oxford
Mrs Nicola J Lewis, BA Hons York
Miss Katharine Whiteman, BA Hons Lancaster

Geography:
Mrs E Ruth Cook, BA Hons Oxford
*Mrs Sharon R Howitt, BA Hons Belfast (*Eco-Schools, People and Planet*)
Mr Daniel G Martin, BA Cambridge (*Head of Ruby House*)
Mr Philip K E Truman, BSc Hons Leeds

History:
Mrs Tamsyn L Houlden-Stanley (*Assistant Head of Years 8 & 9*)
Mrs Karen J Laurie, BA Hons Leeds (*Deputy Head Pastoral*)
*Mrs Ann L Minear, BA Hons Exeter (*New Staff Mentor*)
Mrs Katie M C Perrin, BA Hons, MPhil Trinity Hall Cambridge
Mr William H Saunders, BA Hons Bristol, MA St Mary's Twickenham (*Deputy Head Co-curricular, Oxbridge Coordinator*)
Miss Katrina M Sloan, BA Hons Reading (*Head of Critical Thinking, Deputy Head of Sixth Form*)

Mathematics:
Mrs Laura A Celiker, BSc Surrey
Mr Tom D Collier, BSc Hons Surrey
*Mrs Kate M Denny, BSc Hons London
Mr William G Forse, BSc Hons Southampton (*Head of Amethyst House*)
Miss Sarah E Holliday, MA MEng Gonville & Caius Cambridge (*Director of Studies*)
Mr Martin W Holtham, BA St John's Cambridge (*Senior Teacher Digital Learning, Examinations Officer*)
Mrs Catherine L Joyce, BA Hons St Hilda's College Oxford (*People and Planet*)
Mrs Elisabeth A Mulgrew, MA St Hilda's Oxford (*2nd in Maths*)
Mrs Katie E Perryman, BSc Hons York
Mr Ian J W Pethick, BA Hons Oxford
Mrs Gillian T Rackham, BSc Hons Sheffield
Mr Michael J Walden, MSci Bristol
Mrs Anna Worthington, BSc Hons London

Modern Languages:
Miss Kathy A Buckley, BA Hons Exeter (*Head of Sixth Form*)
*Mrs Valerie A Callaghan, BA Hons Portsmouth (*Head of French*)
Mr Javier González Abia, BA Hons, Valladolid, Spain (*Word Press Coordinator*)
Ms Alice Hello, Licence Langues et Cultures Etrangeres et Regionales
*Ms Carol Igoe, BSc Hons Georgetown, Washington DC (*Head of German*)
Mr Andrew S James, MA Worcester College Oxford (*Head of Classics*)
Miss Donna E Jenkins, BA Hons Bath
Mrs Audrey J Lewis, MA Université François-Rabelais France
Mr Thomas G M'Clelland, BA Hons King's College London
*Mrs Zoë N Rowe, BA Hons Exeter, MA Bristol (*Acting Head of Spanish*)
*Mrs Róisín P Watters, BA Hons Ulster (*Senior Teacher Staff Development, Head of Modern Languages*)

*Mrs Charlotte H Wilkinson, MA Queens' College Cambridge (*Head of Spanish*) [maternity]

Music:
Mrs Emilie A Forrest-Biggs, MA Downing College Cambridge (*Head of Year 10*)
Mr Andrew C Hadfield, BA Hons St Catharine's College Cambridge (*Examinations Assistant*)
*Mr Grayson T Jones, BMus Hons Birmingham
Mr Nicholas A H Tudor, BA York

Physical Education:
Mrs Sally P Appleton
Mrs Rachel E Byrne, BEd Hons De Montfort (*Assistant Director of Sport*)
Miss Catriona H Coutts-Wood, BA Durham (*Head of Opal House*)
Miss Sarah A Gill, BA Bath
Mr Glyn S Groom, BA Hons Manchester (*Head of Outdoor Education, Unit Leader D of E*)
Mrs Keely M Harper, BSc Hons Loughborough (*Head of Year 8*)
Miss Katelyn E Hoffman, BA North Carolina
Mrs Helen Le Page, BA Hons East Anglia
Mrs Tara J Oxley, BSc Hons Birmingham
*Mrs Louise Stone, BEd Hons Bedford College (*Director of Sport*)
Mrs Amanda J Whybro, BA Hons Chichester (*Assistant Head of Years 10 & 11*)

Politics:
*Mr David Cleaver, MSc Econ Swansea, MA Econ Manchester
Mr Ian J W Pethick, BA Hons Oxford

Psychology:
*Mrs Carol A Benson, BA Hons Manchester
Dr Jane E Boyd, BSc Newcastle, PhD London, King's College (*Director of Careers & Higher Education*)
Miss Daisy M Evans, BSc Hons Southampton

Religious Studies:
Mrs Samantha J Buxton, BA Hons Cardiff [maternity]
Miss Rosanna L Cocksworth, BA Hons Durham (*Scholarship and Sixth Form Entrance Exam Coordinator, Head of Emerald House*)
*Mrs Julie A Shopland, BA Hons Lampeter

Science:
Mrs Ruth L Batchelar, MA St Hilda's College Oxford
Mrs Fiona J Boulton, BSc Hons Cardiff, MA London (*Headmistress*)
Dr Jane E Boyd, BSc Hons Newcastle, PhD London (*Director of Careers & Higher Education*)
Miss Amy V H Dixon, BSc Southampton
Mrs Amy L Dutton, MA Hons Durham
Mrs Penny L J Gilbert, BSc Hons Durham
Mrs Catherine B Gilmore, BSc Hons Bath (*Head of Year 11*)
Dr Kerry J Goodworth, PhD, PGCE, MSc
*Mr William H Hack, BA Hons MSci Cambridge (*Head of Chemistry, Assistant Examinations Officer*)
Dr Nicholas Harries, PhD Oxford
Mr Tom A Helliwell, BSc Hons Southampton (*Head of Topaz*)
Miss Sarah E Holliday, MA MEng Gonville & Caius Cambridge (*Director of Studies*)
Mrs Rachael J Ling, MChem MSc Oxford (*2nd in Chemistry*)
Dr Lucinda M Lockett, BA Hons Hertford College Oxford, MSc London, DPhil York
*Mrs Tiffenny Nelson, BA Hons Cambridge, MA Cambridge (*Head of Biology*)

*Mr Brad J Russell, BEng London (*Senior Teacher Pupil Progress, Head of Science*)
Mrs Gail A Scott, BSc Hons Surrey
*Miss Kimberley F Walrond, BSc King's (*Head of Physics, Head of Sapphire House*)
Mrs Hazel J Webb, BSc Strathclyde

Specialist Teacher and Assessor: Mrs Joanna I Bayley

Administration:

PA to the Headmistress: Mrs Helen J Thompson

Facilities Manager: Mr Iain G Hazell, MBIFM

Human Resources Manager:
Mrs Susan M Mooney, BSc Hons Leicester, PG Dip Personnel Mgt Kingston, MCIPD

Language Assistants:
Miss Estefania Alarcon Andreu (*Spanish*)
Mrs Susann G Beasley (*German*)
Mrs Dominique F J Hopgood, MA Stendhal (*French*)

Library:
*Mrs Yvonne A Skene (*Librarian*)
Mrs Alison Hewson, BA Hons, MCLIP (*Assistant Librarian*)

Marketing and Admissions:
Mrs Jane R Bak (*Assistant Registrar*)
Mrs Louise E Miles, BA Hons Warwick, MA Swansea (*Director of Marketing*)
Mrs Helen E Moffat (*Director of Admissions*)
Mrs Sara J Saunders, BA Hons Bristol (*Admissions Assistant*)

Music Administrator:
Mrs Diana R G Baumann, MA MusB St Catharine's College Cambridge

Teaching Schools Coordinator and Senior Administrator:
Miss Marta Z Bednarek, Warsaw University

Junior School:

Head of Junior School:
Mr Michael D Gibb, BA Hons London

Deputy Head of Junior School:
Mr Toby W Day, BA Hons Southampton
Miss Sheina C Wright, BA Hons UWE

Teaching Staff:
Miss Dawn L Aytoun, BSc Hons Portsmouth
Mrs Clare J Burch, BA Hons Exeter
Mrs Lisa C Cartwright, BA Hons Newcastle upon Tyne
Miss Camilla Flint, BA Hons Cardiff
Miss Jemima Grimke-Drayton, BA Hons Nottingham
Mrs Harriet A Guest, BA Hons Southampton
Mrs Diane Hall BEd Joint Hons Exeter
Miss Henrietta R Henry, BSc Hons Loughborough
Miss Kathryn L Holland, BSc Hons Brunel
Mrs Rachel F Kemp, BSc Hons Exeter
Mrs Jane E Kinch, BEd Birmingham
Mrs Clare Kirkham, BA Hons Leeds
Miss Amy C Langfield, BA Hons Bournemouth
Miss Ashley K Lovegrove, BSc Hons Open Universtiy
Mrs Maria Mager, BA Hons Durham
Miss Sarah Martyn-Fisher, BSc Buckingham
Miss Lucy Matthews, BA Hons Brighton
Mrs Karen L Nanson, BEd Bedford College
Mrs Jodie Newberry, BA Hons Cardiff
Mrs Beth Pinkerton-Smith, BA Hons Exeter
Mrs Heather M Stamp, BEd Hons East Anglia
Mrs Laura Sunckell, BSc Leeds
Mrs Rachel J Wardell, BMus Hons London

PA to Head of Junior School: Mrs Helen K Burling-Smith, BSc Hons South Bank, MRICS, ALCM

Visiting Music Teachers:

Bassoon:
Miss Rosemary Cow, MMus, BMus Hons

Cello:
Mr Richard Bridgmont, FTCL, ARCM, LTCL
Miss Jennifer Kimber, BMus

Clarinet:
Miss Claire Henry, ARCM, LRAM

Double Bass:
Miss Nicola Bailey, ARCM, LRAM

Flute:
Mrs Deirdre Ball, LTCL
Miss Ruth E Chappell, AGSM
Mrs Fiona J Howe, ARCM

French Horn and Trumpet:
Miss Francesca Moore-Bridger, MA Cantab, Dip RAM, LRAM

Guitar:
Mr Peter L Howe, ARCM

Harp and Piano:
Mrs Jane Carr, BMus

Oboe:
Miss Joanna Lees, ARCM

Percussion:
Mr James Morley, BA Hons

Piano:
Mrs Irene Bridgmont, BMus, LTCL, ARCM
Miss Helen Dives, LTCL
Mrs Naoko Law, BMus
Miss Gillian Young, LRAM, ARCM, DipMT Nordoff-Robbins, Grad Dip Mus

Saxophone:
Mr Simon D West, GTCL, LTCL

Singing:
Miss Katherine Walker, BMus Hons, LRAM
Miss Jennifer Ward, AGSM

Trombone, Trumpet and Tuba:
Mr Rupert Whitehead, BMus, MA

Violin and Viola:
Miss Lucy Hill, LTCL, FTCL
Mrs Catherine A Woehrel, Grad Lucerne (*Head of Strings*)

The Haberdashers' Aske's Boys' School

Butterfly Lane, Elstree, Hertfordshire WD6 3AF
Tel: 020 8266 1700
Fax: 020 8266 1800
email: office@habsboys.org.uk
website: www.habsboys.org.uk
Twitter: @habsboys
Facebook: /habsboys

Motto: *Serve and Obey.*

The School was founded in 1690, endowed by an estate left in trust to the Haberdashers' Company by Robert Aske, Citizen of London and Liveryman of the Haberdashers'

Company. In 1898 it was transferred from Hoxton to Hampstead and in 1961 to Aldenham Park, Elstree, Hertfordshire.

The aim of the School is the fullest possible development of the varied talents of every boy within it, and to this end a broad curriculum is provided, together with extensive facilities for the development of each boy's cultural, physical, personal and intellectual gifts. The School sets out to achieve high academic standards and sets equally high standards in cultural and other fields. In matters of behaviour a large degree of self-discipline is expected, and of mutual tolerance between members of the School community.

Organisation. The School, which is a day school, has 70 boys in the Pre-Prep (ages 5–7) and over 200 boys in the Preparatory School (ages 7–11), 300 in the Junior School (ages 11–13), 500 in the Senior School (ages 13–16) and over 300 in the Sixth Form (over 16). There are 6 Houses. The School regards pastoral care as important; all the Housemasters and Deputy Housemasters and Heads of Section have a large responsibility in this field but so also do House Tutors, the Senior Master and the Chaplain, as well as other members of the staff.

Forms. In the Pre-Prep school there are two forms in Years 1 and 2 with approximately 18 boys in each form. In the Preparatory School there are three forms in Years 3, 4, 5 and 6 each with about 18 boys. In the Senior School there are 6 forms in Years 7 and 8 with approximately 25 boys in each form. There are 12 forms in Year 9 each with about 14 boys. Years 10 and 11 are divided amongst 18 forms each with 17–18 boys. The usual size of teaching groups in the Sixth Form is about 10–15.

Facilities. The School and its sister Girls' School, Haberdashers' Aske's School for Girls, enjoy the use of a campus of over 140 acres with extensive woodlands. The playing fields surround the buildings, which in the Boys' School include the following: Assembly Hall, Dining Hall, Sixth Form Common Room, Music Auditorium, special accommodation for Classics, English (including a Drama Room), History, Geography, Mathematics, Information Technology, Modern Languages including 2 Languages Laboratories, Music School, Science and Geography Centre with 19 laboratories and 8 classrooms, a Design Centre for Art, Craft and Technology, Sports Centre, Gymnasium, Indoor Swimming Pool, two Artificial Grass Pitches and School Shop.

The Preparatory School is situated on the same campus in a new building of its own. (*For further details, see Preparatory School entry in IAPS section.*) The Pre-Prep is situated on its own nearby campus.

The Curriculum up to the age of 13 is common for all, with no streaming or setting except in Mathematics in Year 8. From the age of 11 in addition to the usual subjects it includes three separate Sciences and two foreign languages which are taught as a carousel to ensure all boys have sampled all languages before making informed choices. From the age of 13, subjects are taught in sets of mixed abilities. GCSE courses start in Year 10, when boys take ten subjects. In the Sixth Form students study four subjects to AS in the Lower Sixth, narrowing to three A2 subjects in the Upper Sixth. The School takes seriously its commitment to Enrichment and Enhancement; this non-examined part of the curriculum occupies 10% of the week in both Upper and Lower Sixth. Boys are entered for the GCE examination at A Level at the age of 18 and are prepared for entry to degree courses at Universities. The wide scope of the School's curriculum gives ample opportunity for all its boys whether preparing for University (overwhelmingly their primary interest), for a profession, for the services, or for commerce or industry. The University Applications and Careers Departments have their own modern facilities, and careers advice is readily available to parents and to boys.

Religious Education. The School is by tradition a Church of England school, but there are no religious barriers to entry and no quotas. It is part of the ethos of the School that all its members respect the deeply-held beliefs and faith of other members. The School Chaplain is available to, and holds responsibility for, all boys in the School of whatever faith. He prepares for Confirmation those who wish it, and there are weekly celebrations of Holy Communion and an annual Carol Service in St Albans Abbey. The morning assembly and class teaching, however, are non-denominational in character. Faith assemblies are held on Thursday mornings, and comprise separate meetings for Christians, Jews, Muslims, Hindus, Jains and Sikhs.

Physical Education. A wide variety of sports is available, including Athletics, Badminton, Basketball, Cricket, Cross-country running, Fencing, Golf, Gymnastics, Hockey, Rugby Football, Sailing, Soccer, Squash, Shooting, Swimming, Tennis, Table Tennis and Water Polo. All boys are expected to take part in physical education unless exempt on medical grounds.

Out of School Activities. The extensive range includes a period of 2 hours on Friday afternoon when boys can choose one of a large variety of activities of a service nature. This includes Community Service, both on the School campus and among those who need help in the surrounding district. It also includes the Combined Cadet Force, which has Royal Navy, Army and Royal Air Force sections, and Adventure Training.

Music and Drama. Both have a prominent place in the School. The Music School has a Recital Hall and some 12 other rooms; 20 visiting instrumental teachers between them teach 500 instrumental pupils each week covering all the normal orchestral instruments together with Piano and Organ. There is a Choir of 250, and several orchestras. For Drama the facilities include a generously equipped stage and a separate Drama Room with its own lighting and stage equipment.

School Societies. School Societies and expeditionary activities in term time and holidays include Amnesty, Archery, Art, Badminton, Bridge, Canoeing, Chess, Choral, Classical, Crosstalk, Debating, Duke of Edinburgh's Award, Dramatics, English, Football, History, Jazz, Jewish Society, Life-saving, Life Drawing, Modern Languages, Mountaineering, Philosophical, Photography, Politics, Puzzles and Games, Rifle, Sailing, Science, Squash, Stamp Club, Windsurfing.

Transport. There is a joint schools coach service providing an extensive network of routes and some 110 pick-up points, to enable boys and girls to attend the School from a wide area, and to remain for after-School activities.

Admission. Boys are admitted only at the beginning of the school year in September. They may be admitted at the age of 5 and may remain in the School until the end of the academic year in which the age of 19 is attained, subject to satisfactory progress at each stage of the course and to compliance with the School Rules currently in force. Each year approximately 18 boys are admitted at age 5, a further 18 boys at age 7, approximately 100 at age 11, approximately 25 at age 13 and a very small number at age 16. There are competitive examinations including written and oral tests of intelligence, literacy and numeracy at the ages of 7 and 11, held in January for admission in the following September. Applicants aged 13 also take examinations at the beginning of January and are interviewed later in the month for entry in September. An Open Day for prospective parents is held each year early in October. Registration Fee: £100.

Scholarships and Bursaries. A number of Academic Scholarships are awarded annually to pupils entering the Main School. A smaller number of Music Scholarships are also awarded each year to candidates showing special promise in music.

A significant number of means-tested Governors' Bursaries are awarded at age 11+, valued from a few hundred pounds to full fees (and in some cases coach fares), depending upon financial need. Open equally to boys progressing

from the Prep School and to those applying from other Schools.

Full details of all these awards are included in the prospectus available from the School Registrar who is glad to answer enquiries. Alternatively you can request a prospectus via the school's website: www.habsboys.org.uk.

Fees per term (2016–2017). Main School £6,152 exc lunch; Preparatory School (Years 3–6) £6,152 exc lunch; Pre-Preparatory (Years 1 & 2) £4,638 inc lunch.

Piano, Organ and Orchestral instruments (individual tuition) £210 per instrument; Orchestral classes £138; Aural classes £67; Instrument hire £30. Speech & Drama group lessons £25.

Honours. In 2016, 33 boys secured a place at Oxford or Cambridge, 90% of the year group accepted a university place.

Charitable status. The Haberdashers' Aske's Charity is a Registered Charity, number 313996. It exists to promote education.

The Governors:
Richard Glover (*Master of The Haberdashers' Company*)
Sir Robert Fulton, KBE (*Chairman of the Aske Board*)

Boys' School Committee:
D A Hochberg (*Chairman of the Boys' School Committee*)

S Ajitsaria	S Behr
R Gokhale	M Scribbens
Dr L Goldman	J Gatehouse
T Jackson-Stops	J Gregory
A Kirk	

Girls' School Committee:
T Johnstone-Burt, CB, OBE (*Chairman of the Girls' School Committee*)

S Cartmell, OBE	Dr J Maxton
Mrs E Howarth	R Ohrenstein
R C Hughes-Penney	T Dolan
L Leigh	H Rosethorn
A Manz	

Clerk to the Governors: C M Bremner

Headmaster: P B Hamilton, MA

Bursar: S B Wilson, MSc
Second Master: M L S Judd, BA
Deputy Head Academic: J Maguire, MSc
Deputy Head Pastoral: Mrs M J C Jones, BEd
Deputy Head Staff: Mrs C B Lyons, MA

Director of ICT: I R Phillips, MA
Director of Admissions: Mrs K R Pollock, MA
Head of the Sixth Form: R Amlot, MA
Head of the Middle School: G J Hall, BA Hons, BSc Hons, MBA
Head of the Junior School: Mrs D J Bardou, BA
Head of the Preparatory School: M L S Judd, BA

Teaching Staff – Main School:
* Head of Department

Art:	*Computing & ICT*:
*Mrs J E Gleeson, CertEd	*I R Phillips, MA
Miss L M Bird, BA	Ms D F Blyth, BSc
Miss K Norris, BA	V Connolly, MEd, MPhil
Miss K Shaw, BA	D Franks, MSc
S N Todhunter, BA	
	Design & Technology:
Classics:	* S Vincent, MA
Dr C J Joyce, PhD	G Cox, C&G (*Design
M Pfeffer, BA Hons	Technician*)
*Ms E M Simons, BA	P I Dathan, BEd
	T B W Hardman, BEd
	N P Holmes, BEd

P I Roncarati, BA, MSc

Drama:
* I Wheeler, BA
Miss S Leadbetter, BA
Mrs D H Morris-Wolffe, BA
H Silver, BA (*Drama Technician*)
J Talboys
R Weinman, BA Hons

Economics:
*M Catley, BA
P H Bartlett, MA
G J Hall, BA Hons, BSc Hons, MBA
Mrs K Shah, MPhil
C Raatz, MSc, FRSA
D Tomkins, MSc

English:
*I D Wheeler, BA
R Amlot, MA
C R Bass, BA
T Eyre-Maunsell, MA
W D Hall, BA
D Jewison, BA, MPhil
T Lunn, MA
Mrs C B Lyons, MA
E Nairne
A Pearson, MA
S Pinkus
J Plotkin, BA Hons, MA, MA
Mrs K R Pollock, MA

Geography:
*J S Bown, BA
M Baird, MA
Mrs M A Carrick, BA
R Cooper, BA
Mrs N Fielden, BSc
M L S Judd, BA
J Maguire, BSc
A McGrath, MA Hons
D C Taberner, MSc

History:
*Dr A Courtney, MA, MPhil, PhD
Mrs D J Bardou, BA
S P H Clark, BA

Music:
*R Osmond, NA, ARCO
P Bainbridge, ARCM, DipRCM (*Trumpet*)
D Bentley GGSM (*French Horn*)
H Brink
S Byron, BMus (*Trombone and Tuba*)
R Carter, FRCO CHM, FTCL, ARCM, LRAM (*Pianoforte and Organ*)
R Fisher, BMus
Miss U Galuszka, MMus (*Guitar*)
L Gee, BA, GBSM, ABSM (*Violin*)
O Gledhill, PhD MA ARCM (*Cello*)
R Gozzard, MA
Mrs R Heathcote, BMus, LGSMD (*Oboe*)
M Herd, BMus
H Legge, LRAM (*Bassoon*)
Miss C Maguire, LRAM (*Double Bass*)
Miss I Mair, GRSM, MMus, LRAM, ARCM (*Pianoforte*)
D O'Hare, BA

T M Handley, MA
E Leung
N P Saddington, BA
A P A Simm, BA
Dr I St John, DPhil
I Tsakiropoulou, BA, MSt, DPhil

Mathematics:
*A M Ward, BSc
J A Barnes, BSc
Mrs A C C Baron, BSc
P A Barry, PhD, ARCS, DIC
Mrs M Brock, BSc
B Brown, MA
S D Charlwood, BSc, CMath, MIMA
J Hails, BSc
B Haria, BSc Hons
S Haring, BA
N Harte, BSc Hons
Dr I B Jacques, DPhil
T I Jones, BSc
N Jovanovic, BSc
G P Kissane, BSc
A Lee, BSc
R Mehta, MSc
R D Oldfield, BSc
Mrs A Thakar, BSc

Modern Languages:
*R J Thompson, BA
Ms K Adams, MA
A Drake, BA
N Geering, MA
E Gomez, BA
P B Hamilton, MA
Ms S E Hanlon, BA Hons, MA
Miss A McKenzie, BA Hons
Mrs D Miller-Smith, BA
A Perdikis, MA Merit
E Poisson
Mrs J Robson, BA
O Garcia Rochera, BA, BSc
A Schwochow
Mrs J B Swallow, BA
J C Swallow, MA
Miss L von Truchsess, BA

R Nathwani
J Ormston, MA, LRAM (*Percussion*)
Miss M Parrington, ARCM (*Violin*)
Miss L Rive (*Violin*)
A J Simm, BA
T Taylor, MMus
D Woods, BMus
Miss P Worn, LRAM, ABSM, ALCM (*Viola*)

Physical Education:
*R J McIntosh, BA
Miss K Brandon, BSc
J Carville
D Cooper, BA
M Griffin, MSc
D H Kerry, BSc
C Mack
A F M Metcalfe, BSc
L Spain, BSc Hons
P D Stiff, BSc
M Woodlock

Games:
S D Charlwood (*i/c Cricket*)
D Cooper (*i/c Hockey*)
T B W Hardman (*i/c Sailing*)
J Hails (*i/c Tennis*)
S Lowe (*i/c Athletics*)
A F M Metcalfe, BSc (*i/c Rugby*)
R D Oldfield (*i/c Orienteering*)
P D Stiff, BSc (*i/c Swimming & Water Polo*)
A M Ward (*i/c Association Football & Golf*)
C K Whalley (*i/c Badminton*)

Politics:
*S P H Clark, BA

Science:
*G R Hobbs, PhD
A C Bagguley, BSc, CBiol, MIBiol
R Cachuela, BSc
A Chapman, MSci, PhD, MRSC
G Chapman, PhD
B Chaudhry, PhD
A Citron, PhD
Mrs H Dawda, HND
Mrs L I Dixon, BSc

Preparatory School:
*M L S Judd, BA (*Executive Head*)
*J J Evans, MA (*Deputy Head Academic*)
*Mrs C M Griggs, CertEd, Dip S&D (*Deputy Head Pastoral*)
*Mrs H Pullen, BEd (*Senior Teacher*)
Mrs S Adat, BA
R Bloch, MA
N Bowley
M Brown, BSc
Mrs K Bruce-Green, BEd
R Fisher
K Fradd
Mrs E F Hall, BA
L Harrington, BA Hons

D S Endlar, MChem
T Fyfe, MEng
C Gannarelli, PhD
H Gauntlett, BSc
C Glanville, BSc, BA (*i/c Biology*)
E Hanson, BSc Hons
C L Harrison, PhD
Mrs M J C Jones, MEd
R O Kerr, BSc (*i/c Physics*)
R J Kingdon, MSc, CPhys, MInstP
S Krishmadasan, PhD, MRSC, MinstP
Miss F Letts, BSc
Mrs J Letts, BSc
A Lynch, BSc
K Morris, BSc
Mrs S Patel, BSc
E Pauletto, BSc
A D S Perera, PhD
Miss A Pindoria, BSc
R Randall, PhD
Miss D Scammell, MGeoSci
J Teague, MEng
Mrs D Vekaria, BSc
J B Ward, BSc
C K Whalley, BSc

Theology and Philosophy:
*R J Cawley, MA
Revd M Brandon, MA, MTh
L Charman, MA
R C Garvey, MA
J S Green, PhD
A Lawrence, BA
E Lennon, MA, MA
P Milton, BA
B Rylands, MA

Combined Cadet Force:
Lt Col N Woodall (*Contingent Commander*)
WO2 J Sandercock (*School Staff Instructor*)

Ms D Jones (*School Secretary/Reception*)
Dr C A Lessons, PhD
S S Lipscomb, BA
S Lowe, BEd
Mrs J I Magnus, BA
Mrs D A McKever, NNEB
Mrs W Morelli
Mrs M Newfield, BEd Hons
Mrs H Pritchard
Mrs H Pullen
A Thomas (*Prep School Administrator*)
G Thomas, BA Hons
Mrs J Valente, PGCE

Pre-Preparatory School:
*Mrs V G Peck, BSc (*Deputy Head, Pre-prep & Yr2 Form Teacher*)
Mrs J Barber
Mrs H Elliott
Mrs A Fielden, CertEd
Mrs T Grossman, BEd
Mrs M Gunn
Mrs R Hodis
Mrs S McLeigh, MA
Mrs N Patel, BA
Mrs H Pieri
Mrs P Porter
Ms T Redmon (*Catering Manager*)
Ms S Thompson
M Williams (*Caretaker*)
Miss N Young, BA Hons

Chaplain: The Revd M Brandon, MA, MTh

Library:
*Mrs S Stanbury, MA, MCLIP
Ms C Wright BA, ACLIP
Mrs A Sellen
Mrs A Leith
M Clifford (*Archivist*)

Support Staff:
PA to Headmaster: Mrs C Russell
PA to Bursar: Miss T Phipps
PA to 2nd Master: Miss J Woodham
PA to Deputy Head (Academic): Miss L El-Beih
PA to Deputy Head (Pastoral): Mrs S Muller
Preparatory School Secretary/Receptionist: Mrs D Jones
Admissions & Database Officer: Miss C Allison
Catering Manager: K Nolan
Director of Foundation: R de H Llewellyn, MA
Estates Manager: R A Hamzat
Marketing & Communications Officer: J Suchak, BA
Finance Manager: M O'Donnell
Grounds Manager: J Lewis
HR Manager: Mrs R Titley
ICT Support Director: I R Phillips, MA
Payroll: Mrs L Meighan
School Counsellor: Ms L Nolte
School Nurses: Mrs G McGrath, RGN; Ms M McGrath, RGN
School Office Manager: Mrs S Vithlani
School Shop Manager: Mrs F Hogberg
Transport Manager: Ms R Caterer
Assistant ICT Director: G Byrne

Haberdashers' Monmouth School for Girls

Hereford Road, Monmouth NP25 5XT
Tel: 01600 711100
Fax: 01600 711233
email: admissions@hmsg.co.uk
website: www.hmsg.co.uk
Twitter: @HMSGHead
Facebook: /Habsmonmouth

Motto: *Serve and Obey*

Haberdashers' Monmouth School for Girls is one of the five schools of the William Jones Foundation, arising from a bequest in 1614, and administered by the Worshipful Company of Haberdashers. The School stands high on the outskirts of the town of Monmouth, in the beautiful countryside of the Wye Valley.

There are 480 girls in the senior school including a Sixth Form of 142. Pupils aged from 7 to 11 years have their own preparatory school, Inglefield House, of 144 girls on site. A thriving Boarding Community with accommodation on the school site, includes a Junior House and modern Senior House with study-bedrooms and Augusta House, the Sixth Form Boarding House with 47 en-suite bedrooms.

Classrooms and laboratories are extensive, with special Sixth Form provision. Specialist workshops are provided for DT and Drama. Full use is made of the ample sports facilities: spacious playing fields, all-weather pitch, tennis courts, newly upgraded sports hall with climbing wall, indoor swimming pool and gymnasium. All are adjacent to the School. A recent classroom extension, including 4 new ICT suites, an updated Sixth Form block and Library and a new Sixth Form Boarding House in 2012 provides a vibrant and modern learning environment.

The School has a Chaplain and is a Christian foundation. Girls are encouraged to attend the places of worship of their own denomination.

A large and fully qualified staff of graduates teaches a modern curriculum, which aims to achieve high academic results within a broader education, acknowledging our cultural inheritance and technological and social needs.

Classics is taught throughout the School. At examination level, Latin GCSE, Latin AS/A Level, and Classical Civilisation AS/A Level are offered. Classical Greek is offered by request as an extra-curricular activity. The school excels in a variety of STEM programmes, gaining many accolades in 'The Big Bang' and ESSW competitions.

Almost all pupils progress to Higher Education. With excellent careers advice, girls are aware of the scope of degree subjects. A number annually enter Oxford, Cambridge and Russell Group universities.

Every encouragement is given to creative and practical work, especially Music and Drama. Girls frequently attend concerts, plays and exhibitions, and an active interest is taken in industry and management. Local businesses lend support to the School's Young Enterprise schemes.

Girls participate in the Duke of Edinburgh's Award scheme, CCF, overseas expeditions and community projects and many also belong to local voluntary organisations.

Main sporting activities include lacrosse, netball, softball, rowing, fencing, hockey, dance and equestrian. Many girls play at County, National and International level. A newly established Tennis Academy makes the most of the impressive site.

Fees per term (2016–2017). Day £4,643, Boarding £9,003–£9,545. Inglefield House: Day £3,484, Boarding £6,333.

Entry is usually at 7, 11, 13 or post GCSE, although occasionally other vacancies occur. Informal assessments for entry at 7+ to Inglefield House are held in the Lent Term. Entry to the Senior School is by examination, interview and report from the current school. The interviews and entrance examinations are held for 11+ in January, 13+ in February/ March (or Common Entrance in June), and for 16+ in November.

Further information and a Prospectus is available from the Admissions Registrar, Tel: 01600 711104, email: admissions@hmsg.co.uk.

Scholarships and Bursaries. A number of academic scholarships are awarded at 11+, 13+ and 16+ to the best candidates on the basis of the school's entrance examination, interview and report from the current school. Music scholarships, also available at 11+, 13+ and 16+, are awarded on the basis of audition and interview held in the Lent Term for 11+ and 13+ and the Michaelmas Term for 16+.

Sport and Dance Scholarships are available at 11+, 13+ and 16+ entry and are awarded on the basis of assessment and interview, held in the Lent Term for 11+ and 13+, and Michaelmas Term for 16+. Creative Arts (Art and Drama) scholarships are awarded following an assessment day held at HMSG in the Lent Term for 13+ and the Michaelmas Term for 16+.

Means-tested Bursaries and Assisted Places of up to 100% of fees are also available at all entry points.

Further information may be obtained from the Admissions Registrar (as above).

Old Girls' Association. *Mrs C Anning*, c/o Haberdashers' Monmouth School for Girls, Monmouth. The OGA Annual General Meeting is held at the school on the second Saturday in November.

Charitable status. William Jones's Schools Foundation is a Registered Charity, number 525616. The object of the Foundation shall be the provision and conduct in or near Monmouth of a day and boarding school for boys and a day and boarding school for girls.

Trustees: The Worshipful Company of Haberdashers

Governing Body:
Chairman: Mr A W Twiston-Davies

The Master of the Worshipful Company of Haberdashers (*ex officio*)

Mr P M Alderman	Dr J Kelly
Mr M H C Anderson	Mr M Kerrigan
Dr P E G Baird	Mr N F H Manns
Mrs J Booth	Mrs M Nordal
Mrs S Clayton	Mrs T Pike
Mr M E Davidson	Mrs R F Rose
Mrs C J Davis	Dr D S Watkins
Mr C R S Hardie	Councillor Mrs S White
Mrs M K Henderson	

Clerk to the Governors: Mrs F Creasey, BCom, ACMA

Bursar: Mrs T Norgrove

Headmistress: Dr C A Pascoe, BSc Hons Bristol, MSc Leicester, PGCE Roehampton

Deputy Head: Mr T Arrand, MA Oxon, PGCE Cantab
Deputy Head (*Academic*): Mrs O E Davis, BSc Joint Hons Salford, MA Ed, PGCE York
Assistant Head (*Academic*): Mr D R Evans, BA Hons Coventry, MA Wales, PGCE Wales
Assistant Head (*Sixth Form*): Mrs J A Poyner, BSc Hons Exeter, PGCE Wales, MBA Ed Keele
Assistant Head (*Co-curricular*): Mrs N Clayton, BA Hons Central England, PGCE UWCN

Chaplain: Reverend D P Ibbotson, BSc Manchester, FDA Winchester

* *Head of Department*

Art:
*Mrs V E Reynolds, BA Hons Oxford Brookes, MA Brighton, PGCE Wales
Mr C Beer, BA Hons, PGCE UWIC
Miss L Porritt, BA Hons Wales, PGCE Wales

Business Studies:
*Mr D R Evans, BA Hons Coventry, MA Wales, PGCE Wales
Ms M C Attrill, BTEC Dip Bus Studies, CertEd UWCN

Careers:
*Mrs A Johnson, BA Hons, Dip Careers Guidance

Classics:
*Mrs L Beech, BA Hons Birmingham, PGCE Cambridge
Dr C H Geisz, Licence BA France, MA Paris IV, DPhil Oxon

Drama & Theatre Studies:
*Miss E Leyshon, BA Hons Oxford, PGDip, PGCE Aberystwyth
Mr C Beer, BA Hons, PGCE UWIC

Economics:
*Mr D R Evans, BA Hons Coventry, MA Wales, PGCE Wales
Ms M C Attrill, BTEC Dip, CertEd UWCN

English:
*Mrs Z Harvey, BA Hons Wales, PGCE London
Mr J A Edwards, BA Hons, MA Warwick, PGCE Wales
Mrs J Hastings, BA Hons Westfield College London, MSc LSE, PhD LSE, BA Hons Open Univ
Ms J Knight, BA Hons Cardiff, MA Cardiff, PGCE UWE
Ms S White, BA Hons UEA, PGCE Bristol

Geography:
*Mr N Meek, BA Hons Middlesex, MA Leicester, PGCE Wales, MEd Birmingham
Mr L Jones, BSc Hons Reading, PGCE Swansea, MA Worcester
Mrs J E Harper, BSc Hons, PGCE Aberystwyth

History:
*Mr M Seaton, BA Hons, PGCE Swansea
Mrs R Griffiths, BA Hons Wales, MA Wales, PGCE Wales
Mr P Grant, BA Hons Durham, BA Hons OU, PGCE Swansea

ICT:
Mrs E Martin, BA Hons Wolverhampton, MSc Dip Swansea, PGCE London
Mrs L C Arnold, BA Hons Oxford

Mathematics:
*Mr A Skailes, BSc Southampton, PGCE St Martin's London
Mrs B M Keyton, BSc Hons Wales, PGCE Wales
Dr S Lawlor, BSc Hons Dublin, PhD Leeds, PGCE UWIC
Mrs J E Morris, BSc Hons, PGCE Wales
Mrs J A Poyner, BSc Hons Exeter, PGCE Wales, MBA Education Keele
Mrs V R Price, BSc Ed UWCN

Modern Languages:
*Mrs H K Smail, MA Reading, PGCE Birmingham (*French, *German)
Mrs K Wellings, BA Hons Hull, PGCE London (*French*, *Spanish)
Mrs O E Davis, BSc Jt Hons Salford, MA, PGCE York (*Spanish*)

Mrs H English, BA Hons Michel de Montaigne Bordeaux III, PGCE Wales

Mrs C A Griffiths, BA Hons London, PGCE Reading (*German, French*)

Mrs A Hutchings, BA Hons Bath, PGCE UWIC (*French, German*)

Mrs R Rees, BA Hons Manchester, PGCE Bristol (*French, German*)

Miss C Villemagne (*French Foreign Language Assistant*)

Mr S Klein (*German Foreign Language Assistant*)

Music:
*Mr M Conway, BMus Hons, MA, PGCE Wales, LTCL, ARCM (*Director of Music*)

Mrs A Clouter, BA Hons Bristol, MA Cardiff, PGCE UWIC

Mrs R Friend, LRAM, LRAM TD

Personal and Social Education (Confidence 4 Life):
Miss J Johnson, BSc Hons OU, PGCE Carmarthen

Physical Education and Sport:
*Miss L Scott, BA Hons QTS PE Chichester (*Acting Director of Sport, PE & Dance*)

Mrs C F Crawford, BA Hons UWIC, PGCE UWIC (*Head of Inglefield House Sport, PE & Dance*)

Ms R V Parry, BA Hons, PGCE Bedford (*Dance*)

Mrs K A Callaghan, BA Hons Surrey (*Rowing*)

Mrs R Harris, BSc Hons UWIC, PGCE Exeter

Mrs C E Jones, BSc Hons Wolverhampton, MSc Wales, PGCE

Ms Z Pritchard, TCert RAD, Teaching Associate ISTD, Dip Dance Ed

Mrs S J Rossiter, BSc Hons South Bank, PGCE Wales

Mr K Williams, Rowing Coach and Boatman

Psychology:
*Mrs K Smith, BSc Hons Bath Spa, Dip Teaching

Ethics & Philosophy:
*Dr H Whatley, PhD King's College London, PGCE London, MA Humboldt University, Germany, BA Hons Edinburgh

Mr T Arrand, MA Oxon, PGCE Cantab

Miss J Johnson, BSc OU, PGCE Carmarthen

Science:
Mrs D E Clarke, BSc Hons Newcastle, PGCE Durham (*Chemistry*)

Miss L J Woodburn, BSc Hons, PGCE Glasgow (*Biology*)

Mrs D L Davies, BSc Hons, PGCE Wales (*Physics*)

Mrs L C Arnold, BA Hons Oxford (*Physics*)

Mrs C Avila-Jones, BSc Hons Wales, PGCE UWIC (*Physics*)

Mrs C Levick, BA Hons Oxford, PGCE Bristol (*Biology*)

Mrs V Lyons, BSc Hons Cardiff, PGCE (*Biology*)

Mrs S P Marks, BSc Hons OU, PGCE Wales (*Chemistry*)

Mrs C Natt, BSc Hons Swansea, PGCE Worcester, MA Ed OU (*Biology*)

Dr I Wallace, BSc Hons Newcastle, PhD Cantab, PGCE OU (*Chemistry*)

Speech & Drama:
*Mrs M Hill, BA Belfast, Cert Ed, LGSM

Mrs A Baker, BPhil Warwick, Cert Ed

Mr D Murray, MA Hons Aberdeen, PGACA RWCMD

Technology:
*Mr S McCluskey, BSc Hons Wales, PGCE Wales

Mrs N Clayton, BA Hons Central England, PGCE UWCN

Mrs J Vickers, CertEd Wales

Learning Support:
Mrs J Jefferies, BEd Liverpool, PGCE Gloucestershire

Mrs C Bown, CNAA Jt Hons, PGCE Exeter

Duke of Edinburgh's Award Coordinator:
*Miss L Scott, BA Hons QTS Chichester

Inglefield House (Preparatory Department):
Headmistress: Mrs H J Phillips, BA, BEd Exeter

Deputy Head: Mr T Evans, BA Hons Aberystwyth, PGCE Cardiff

Mrs P M Champion, Dip Prim Ed Moray House

Mrs M Corker, TCert Durham

Mrs M E Dummett, BSc OU

Mrs A Griffiths, BA Hons Bristol

Mrs J A Jones, BA Hons Surrey, PGCE Kingston

Mrs S Latheron, BSc Hons Brighton, BSc OU, PGCE Bristol

Mrs L Partridge, BA Hons Wales

Miss C Pledger, BA Plymouth, PGCE UWIC

Mrs S Ridyard, BEd Hons CNAA, MA Ed Brighton

Mrs A Roskilly-Green, BA Hons Kent, PGCE Brighton

Dr T Murcott, BSc Hons York, PhD Bristol

Learning Support for Inglefield House:
Mrs A Copley, BHEd Kingston Polytechnic

Halliford School

Russell Road, Shepperton, Middlesex TW17 9HX

Tel:	01932 223593
Fax:	01932 229781
email:	registrar@halliford.net
website:	www.hallifordschool.co.uk

Halliford School was founded in 1921, moved to its present site in 1929. The Headmaster is a member of both HMC and the Society of Heads.

Facilities. Halliford School is situated on the Halliford bend of the River Thames. The old house, a graceful eighteenth century building, which stands in six acres of grounds, is the administrative centre of the school. Some 500 yards from the school gate there are six additional acres of sports fields. Over the years there has been a steady development programme, including a new 320-seat theatre, a refurbished kitchen and dining room, new classrooms and a new Science laboratory. In September 2005 a new Sports Hall with new changing facilities, Library and additional classrooms was opened. In September 2012 the Philip Cottam building was opened. This incorporates the Sixth Form, Art Studios, Music Centre and the Vibe Café.

Admission. There are approximately 400 pupils on roll with a three-form entry at Year 7 (approx. 60 pupils). There is a further entry at Year 9 and admission is possible into other Year Groups dependent on the availability of places. Entrance is by examination (English, Mathematics and Reasoning) and interview. Siblings are given priority as long as they can benefit from a sound academic education. This policy creates a strong feeling of a family community and helps reinforce the close partnership that exists with parents. Girls and Boys are admitted the Sixth Form on the basis of their GCSE predictions, a report from their current school and an interview.

Curriculum. In Years 7 to 9 pupils study the following subjects: English, Mathematics, two languages (French, German or Spanish), Latin/Classical Civilisation, Biology, Chemistry, Physics, History, Geography, Art, Drama, Music, Design and Technology, Computing, Religious Studies and Physical Education. In Years 10 and 11 (GCSE) there is a compulsory core of English Language and Literature, Mathematics (some also take Further Mathematics), a Modern Foreign Language (French, German or Spanish), and the three separate Sciences. Pupils choose a further three subjects: a second Modern Foreign Language, Latin,

Classical Civilisation, History, Geography, Religious Studies, Art, Drama, Music, PE, Business Studies, Design Technology (either Resistant Materials or Graphic Products) or Computing Science.

In the Sixth Form some 25 subjects are available at A/AS Level and all teaching is co-educational. Many pupils also complete an extended project.

Games. Rugby, Football, Cricket are the main games played at Halliford. Athletics, Basketball, Badminton, Volleyball and Golf are available, plus a number of other activities. There is also a Climbing Club which makes use of the climbing wall in the new Sports Hall.

Pastoral Organisation. There are four Houses and pupils are tutored in House groups. Parents receive either a grade card or full report every half term. Tutors are always willing to see parents and the Headmaster can usually be seen at very short notice.

Out of School Activities. These include very successful Drama, Music and Art Departments.

There is a long list of clubs including Chess, Design, Computing, Film, Creative Writing, Modern Languages, Science and Art. In addition there are Senior and Junior Debating and Academic Societies and Interhouse Public Speaking and Unison Singing Competitions. The Duke of Edinburgh's Award is available as an additional activity.

School Council. Each Tutor group elects a representative to the School Council. This is not a cosmetic exercise and in recent times the School Council has effected real changes. Halliford believes that pupils do have good ideas which can be utilised for the well-being of the School as a whole.

Prospective Parents. The main school Open Day is held in October on a Saturday. Further Open Days are held in November, March and May during the school week. Also in October the school holds a Sixth Form Open Evening. Prospective parents are welcome at other times by appointment.

Fees per term (2016–2017). £4,900.

Scholarships and Bursaries. The School offers scholarships to the value of 10% of the annual school fees for entry at 11+. The scholarships awarded are: Academic, Art, Drama, Music and Sport. All those taking the 11+ entrance examination will be considered for the academic scholarships and applications for the remaining scholarships are taken during the registration process.

Sixth Form Scholarships are also available in the same areas as above to those in Year 11 or to external candidates.

The school is also keen to help those who could not otherwise afford the fees and means-tested Bursaries are available on application.

Old Hallifordians. *Chairman:* Darren Allen.

Charitable status. Halliford School is a Registered Charity, number 312090. It exists to provide high-quality education.

Governors:

Mr K Woodward
Mr C S Squire
Mrs N F Cook
Mr M A Crosby
Mr R Davison
Mrs K Gulliver
Mr W J Hargan
Mr B T Harris

Mrs T Harrison
Mrs P A Horner
Mr A Lenoel
Mr R J Parsons
Professor J P Phillips
Mr P Roberts
Dr M Sachania

Headmaster: Mr Simon G Wilson

Bursar: Mrs E Sanders
Deputy Head: Mr M Duffield
Director of Studies: Mr A Nelson
Senior Tutor: Mr J Carrington
Head of Sixth Form: Mr S Slocock

Academic Staff:
* *Head of Department*

Art:
*Mr N Moseley
Mrs S Regan

Business Studies:
*Mr P Gale
Mr S Slocock
Mr M Daniel

Classics:
*Mr M Shales
Mrs V Wagner-Hall
Mr A Cunningham

Design Technology:
*Mr C Heeney
Mr J Carrington

Drama:
*Mr B Bruno

Economics:
*Mr P Gale
Mr S Slocock
Mr M Daniel

English:
*Mrs D Mitchelmore
Miss J Butler-Smith
Mr N De Cata
Miss H Searle
Mr M Duffield
Ms E Lagast

Geography:
*Mr J Willcox
Mrs K Gilbert

Government & Politics:
*Mr L McMillan
Mrs F Bootle-Wilbraham

History:
*Mr L McMillan
Mrs F Bootle-Wilbraham
Mrs V Wagner-Hall

Computing:
*Mrs D Duffy
Mr A Nelson

Mathematics:
*Mr P Diamond
Mr P N Booth
Mr L Cupido
Mr T Ackroyd
Dr M Yacoot

Mr J Carrington
Mr P Hodgkinson
Mrs M Turner-Smith
Mr S Wilson

Media Studies:
*Mr N De Cata

Modern Languages:
*Mr M Gruner
Mrs A Wain
Mrs E Whitticase
Mr I Arriandiaga
Miss C Wilcockson
Mr P Sweeting
Mrs M Moon

Music:
*Mrs R Greaves
Mr A Williams
Mrs H Head

PE:
*Mr I P Bardget
Mr P Hodgkinson
Mr J Greggor

Religious Studies:
*Mr A Cunningham
Mrs V Wagner-Hall

Science:
*Mrs D Samarasinghe

Biology:
*Mr D Howard
Dr S Brooks
Mrs D Samarasinghe
Mr T Ackroyd
Mrs M Turner-Smith

Chemistry:
*Mrs D Samarasinghe
Mrs M Turner-Smith
Mr T Ackroyd
Miss H Foster
Dr G Matthews

Physics:
*Mr V Harden-Chaters
Mrs D Samarasinghe
Mr T Ackroyd
Mrs M Turner-Smith

Learning Support:
Mrs M Rogers

Visiting Staff:
Mrs H Head (*Piano*)
Mr W Brown (*Percussion*)
Mr J Fryer (*Woodwind*)
Mr P Savides (*Guitar*)
Mr S Tanner (*Piano*)

Administrative Staff:
Registrar: Mrs F Clatworthy
Headmaster's Secretary: Mrs C Worrell
Assistant Bursar: Mrs T Trevorrow
Accounts Assistant: Mrs S O'Hara
Facilities Assistant: Mrs L Gabb (*part-time*)
School Fee Clerk: Mrs J Egginton
School Administrator: Mrs M Hammond
Alumni Secretary: Mrs K Smallbone
School Receptionist (am): Mrs A Grainger

School Receptionist (pm): Mrs L Gabb
Librarian: Mr T King
Matron: Mrs C Brooks (*Mon-Wed*)
Mrs K Davis (*Thurs-Fri*)

Technical Staff:
Science:
Mrs S Luterbacker
Mrs H Spellman
Mr A Parnell
Art: Miss E Waters
ICT: T Hext-Stephens, Mr J Chamberlain
Design: Mr R Wiedemann
Theatre: Mr P Abbott
Learning Support Assistant: Ms N Kritzinger

Caretaker: Mr R Knight
Catering Manager: Mr A Murphy
Cafe Bar Supervisor: Mr S King

Visiting Chaplain: The Revd Christopher Swift, MA,
Rector of Shepperton

Hampton School

Hanworth Road, Hampton, Middlesex TW12 3HD
Tel: 020 8979 5526
Fax: 020 8783 4035
email: headmaster@hamptonschool.org.uk
             admissions@hamptonschool.org.uk
website: hamptonschool.org.uk

Motto: *Praestat opes sapientia.*

Founded in the academic year of 1556/57 by Robert Hammond, a Hampton merchant, and re-established in 1612. From 1910 the School was administered by the local authority, latterly as a voluntary aided school, but in 1975 reverted to independent status.

Hampton is a day school of around 1,250 boys aged from 11 to 18, including a Sixth Form of about 340. The School achieves all-round excellence, encouraging academic ambition, personal responsibility and independent thinking in an energetic, happy and well-disciplined community. It aims to provide a challenging and stimulating education for boys of high academic promise from the widest possible variety of social backgrounds.

In the most recent ISI inspection (March 2016) Hampton was awarded the highest judgement possible in each individual category. The quality of pupils' achievements in academic and co-curricular areas is exceptional and the contribution of arrangements for pastoral care excellent. The School achieves excellence in the spiritual, moral, social and cultural development of pupils and meets its aim to provide a friendly and supportive environment. The teaching at the School is described as excellent and teachers display expert subject knowledge which is used to inspire and guide pupils. Many lessons have a real sense of scholarly collaboration between teachers and pupils, based on mutual respect and a shared love of learning. It was also noted that the curriculum is enriched by an extensive, varied range of co-curricular activities and strong links with the community. The inspection report confirmed the School's success in meeting its aim of producing mature, confident yet unpretentious young people who aim for personal success while supporting those around them.

Hampton is academically selective and virtually all boys go on to elite universities, the Russell Group and Oxbridge with increasing numbers to American Ivy League Universities. Examination results in 2016 at A Level (91% A*, A and B grades) and GCSE (91% A*/A grades) were extremely strong: 30% A* grades at A Level and 67% at GCSE. 23 boys achieved their Oxbridge offers. The Sixth Form has a strong emphasis on deep academic enquiry, breadth of study, critical thinking and independent learning.

An annual exchange programme offers boys the chance to visit Spain, Germany, France, Italy and Russia as well as Asia, Africa and the Far East. Boys visit many other countries through academic and sporting initiatives and there is an extraordinary range of trips available.

The extensive co-curricular programme forms an essential part of the balanced education which Hampton provides. Music and drama are central to the character of the School and concerts, musicals and plays involve all age groups throughout the year. Over half the boys learn musical instruments and there are frequent music and choir tours abroad. A notable number of Organ and Choral Scholarships to Oxbridge colleges have been won over recent years.

Drama is included in the curriculum, in addition to regular School and Year group productions. There are major joint musical and drama productions regularly with neighbouring LEH. Recent highlights include *West Side Story, Mack & Mabel, Jekyll & Hyde, Chicago, Les Misérables,* Shakespeare's *The Tempest,* Joseph Kesselring's *Arsenic and Old Lace,* Jez Butterworth's *Jerusalem* and *Oliver Twist,* a joint production with Waldegrave School for Girls.

Hampton has an outstanding reputation for sport and standards are very high indeed; many boys play at county and national level in a wide range of sports. Particular strengths are cricket, football, rowing, rugby, tennis and chess. Boys benefit from superb facilities and specialist coaching. Hampton has produced many schoolboy internationals in a wide range of sports and also Olympic rowers; the School shares a nearby boathouse on the River Thames with LEH.

Integrity and social conscience are encouraged implicitly through the daily interaction of boys and teachers, as well as explicitly through School assemblies, PSHE lessons, extensive Charity, Environment and Community Service programmes, and long-standing links with the Hampton Safe Haven in Malawi. The School became the first 'climate neutral' school in the country by offsetting all of its carbon emissions. The School was one of the two founding schools of the 'Mindfulness in Schools Project' promoting pupil well-being and emotional resilience.

Hampton School and LEH are served by 22 coach routes across south-west London, Surrey and Berkshire.

Buildings and Grounds. The School has been situated on its present site since 1939. Its premises and facilities for both academic work and co-curricular activity have been greatly improved and extended since 1975 when the School, formerly Hampton Grammar, reverted to independence.

Set within grounds of some 27 acres all facilities (with the exception of the Boat House) are on site including four rugby pitches, seven football pitches, six cricket squares and six hard tennis courts. Buildings include an Assembly Hall, Dining Hall, large multi-purpose Sports Hall, fully-equipped Library and specialist facilities for Art, Science, Technology, ICT and Languages.

The Millennium Boat House, located on the nearby River Thames and shared with LEH, was opened in 2000 by Sir Steve and Lady Redgrave and provides the focal point for the popular and highly successful Boat Club.

The magnificent Hammond Theatre provides exceptional facilities for the performing arts, doubling as a theatre and concert hall.

A rigorous development programme ensures that all boys continue to benefit from excellent facilities. A three-storey Atrium extension opened in September 2011, comprising 11 classrooms, a new Biology lab and a large display area and a state-of-the-art, all-weather 3G sports ground, opened in 2013, for football, rugby and recreational use. The 3G area is a unique facility for a school and has dual accreditation from FIFA and the Rugby Football Union. A new Sixth Form Centre will open in 2018.

Community. Hampton School has developed extensive partnerships both locally and internationally. The School enjoys particularly strong links with two neighbouring schools, Hampton Academy and LEH. These two schools participate in various activities with Hampton pupils, especially Drama and Music, Combined Cadet Force and the very popular visiting speakers '*Talk*!' programme. A 'United Nations Youth & Student Association' (UNYSA) branch involves pupils meeting to discuss issues of national and international significance. Strong links are maintained with the numerous local state primary schools which provide around 65% of the First Year intake. Year 5 and Year 6 pupils from a number of local state primary schools attend teaching sessions in a range of subjects on Saturday mornings. The School also works in partnership with other local independent and state secondary schools offering GCSE revision courses and a range of academic and co-curricular activities.

In addition, Hampton School has a busy Community Service programme and also hosts many events for schools in Richmond Borough. All members of the Lower Sixth undertake a placement in a local primary school as part of their Curriculum Enrichment Programme, working with young children on literacy, numeracy, computing and sport. Many boys in the Fourth Year and above volunteer their assistance in primary schools, residential homes for the elderly, or the local Barnardo's project. Various joint activities are run with LEH, including an annual Christmas Party for the elderly, and a trip to the Science Museum for children with special needs. Several senior boys participate in holiday schemes for young people from more deprived parts of East London each summer.

Curriculum. Boys in the Lower School follow a wide curriculum, including Technology, Coding and Computing, Physics, Chemistry, Biology, a Modern Language (French, German or Spanish) and Latin. Mandarin has recently been added to the curriculum; Greek, Ancient History and Russian are optional subjects begun in the Third Year. In the Fourth and Fifth Years all boys continue to study, in addition to PE, Games and Religious Studies, the following: English Language, English Literature, a Modern Language, Mathematics and the three sciences for either GCSE or IGCSE. They choose three subjects from the following: Art, Ancient History, Drama, French, Geography, German, Greek, History, Latin, Mandarin, Music, Religious Studies, Russian, Spanish and Technology. Most of these GCSEs/IGCSEs are taken at the end of the Fifth Year. The most able mathematicians take GCSE/IGCSE at the end of the Fourth Year and then move on to A Level study in the Fifth Year.

The Sixth Form offers a free choice of A and AS Level subjects, in addition to a wide range of courses leading to A Level General Studies, and the option to enter for Critical Thinking. The Cambridge Pre-U is offered in addition to the standard AS/A2 in Art, Physics, Chemistry, History, German, Mandarin and Philosophy. Additional teaching and preparation is provided for boys seeking entrance to Oxford or Cambridge, to which around twenty-five to thirty boys are admitted each year. About fifty boys a year also opt for the Hampton Extended Project, a substantial piece of independent research of around 5,000 words.

Games. Sport and Physical Education are part of every boy's School week. A very large number of boys also take part in voluntary sport on Saturdays; fixtures, at a range of ability levels, are arranged for each age group. Whenever possible boys are able to choose which sport to follow, with a wider range of options available to Sixth Form boys. In winter, the major games are Rugby, Association Football and Rowing; in summer, Cricket, Athletics and Rowing. Other sports include Tennis, Real Tennis, Fencing, Squash, Skiing, Windsurfing, Wakeboarding, Sailing, Climbing, Cycling and Swimming.

Careers. Each boy receives advice from the careers staff at those points when subject choices should be made. The School is a member of ISCO, who provide Morrisby testing as part of the Fifth Year advice programme. A Careers Convention is held annually, there are advice evenings for parents on A Level choice and on university decision-making, and comprehensive work experience is arranged.

Pastoral Care. This is one of the strongest features of the School. A boy's Form Tutor is responsible in the first instance for his academic and pastoral welfare and progress. The work of Form Tutors is supported and coordinated by Assistant Heads of Year and Heads of Year under the direction of one of the Deputy Heads. The School works in partnership with parents who are always welcome to discuss their son's work with any of these tutors; Parents' Evenings provide an opportunity to meet subject teachers. Year group Pastoral Forums provide parents with an opportunity to meet staff responsible for pupil welfare and to discuss a variety of pastoral issues. The School was one of the first in the country to develop a course in Mindfulness, which is delivered to all pupils in the Fourth Year. There is also an active Parents' Association.

Societies. The School's large CCF contingent, run jointly with LEH, and more recently an intake from Hampton Academy, comprises Army and RAF sections and has a programme which includes adventurous training, orienteering and gliding. The very active Adventure Society provides opportunities for kayaking, climbing, orienteering, camping and expeditions both in the UK and abroad. A very large number of boys regularly undertake The Duke of Edinburgh's Award – Gold, Silver and Bronze.

The Music Department fosters solo and ensemble performance as well as composition, and offers pupils an opportunity to perform in the School's orchestras, bands and choirs including National Choir of the Year Finalists and Voice Festival finalists, Voices of Lions. Singing is very popular and there are eight different choral groups. The Joint Choral Society, with the neighbouring LEH, gives a performance of a major choral work annually. The number of drama productions is increasing. There is at least one dramatic production each term, and also an annual musical. In all these activities, as in the Community Service work, the School enjoys close cooperation with LEH. Hampton is also an *All-Steinway* school.

A programme of visiting speakers, '*Talk*!', holds lunchtime and evening meetings and offers boys the opportunity to hear and question distinguished politicians, writers, academics and scientists.

There is also an extensive range of co-curricular societies, among which Chess, Debating, the Technology Club and the Creative Writing Society are particularly strong.

Admission. Boys are usually admitted to the School into the First Year (Year 7), Third Year (Year 9) and the Sixth Form. Approximately 120 boys join the First Year at 11+ each September and a further 60–70 join the Third Year at 13+. A small number join the Sixth Form each year.

Entry at 11+ is via the School's own entrance examination, which is held in the January of Year 6. Entry at 13+ is through the Common Entrance examination following a Pre-test which candidates sit in the January of Year 6. A further Pre-test is held in Year 7 for those who sat the Year 6 Pre-test without gaining an offer, as well as to those who have not sat before.

Boys may also be admitted to fill occasional vacancies at other ages at the discretion of The Headmaster. Further details may be obtained from the Head of Admissions (Tel: 020 8979 9273).

Fees per term (2016–2017). £6,125 inclusive of books and stationery.

Scholarships and Bursaries. Scholarships (remitting up to 25%) are awarded for academic, musical, artistic and all-round merit at 11+ and 13+. Choral Scholarships, awarded in conjunction with the Chapel Royal, Hampton Court Palace, are also available at 11+ entry.

The School also has a Bursary Fund from which awards are made according to parental financial circumstances. A number of free places are also awarded each year.

Further details on all Awards may be obtained from the Admissions Manager.

Old Hamptonians' Association. Leavers are entitled to life membership of this association which provides regular communication with members and has active sporting and dramatic sections. The OHA Office is located at School and can be contacted by email: oha@hamptonschool.org.uk.

Charitable status. Hampton School is a Registered Charity, number 1120005.

Governors:
Chairman: N J Spooner, BA
Vice-Chairman: J S Perry, BA
S A Bull, BSc, ACA
R C Davison, MA, LRPS
Mrs M Ellis, Cert Ed
R C Kelly
His Honour Judge S E Kramer, MA, QC
L R Llewellyn, BSc, MMus, MBA, FCMA, FRSA
J A Livingston, MA, Dipl Arch RIBA
A H Munday, LLB, QC
A J Roberts, CBE, BA, FRSA, FColl
S C Naidu
Air Vice Marshal [Retd] G Skinner, CBE, MSc, CEng, FIMechE, FILT, FRAeS
R M Walker, MA
R J K Washington, MA Oxon, MBA
The Revd D N Winterburn, BSc, MA, Vicar of Hampton
Ms A Yandle, MA Oxon

Clerk to the Governors: M A King, BSc

Senior Management Team:

Headmaster: Kevin Knibbs, MA Oxon

Deputy Heads:
Pippa Z S Message, BSc
Philip D Hills, MA Cantab, PhD
J Owen Morris, MA Cantab

Bursar: Mike A King, BSc
Director of Studies: Alasdair N R McBay, BSc, MSc
Assistant Head: Mark A J Nicholson, BA

Senior Tutors:
David R Clarke, BHum
Ski Paraskos, MA Oxon
S Andrew Wilkinson, MA Oxon
Richard D Worrallo, MA Oxon

Departmental Staff:
* *Head of Department*

Art:
*Karen A Williams, BA
Joel Baker, BA
Adrian J Bannister, MA
§Stephanie Kirby, BA
Jerry Blighton (*Technician*)

Biology:
*Phil H Langton, BSc, Dip Env Sci
Guy K Baker, MBiochem (*Head of Fifth Year*)
Christopher J Barnett, MA Oxon
Richard J Davieson, BSc
Polly A Holmes, BSc (*Head of Upper Sixth*)
Katya L Martin, MA Oxon

Pippa Z S Message, BSc (*Deputy Head, Designated Safeguarding Officer*)
Katie Mimnagh, BMedSci
§Laura A Holmes, BSc
§Emily Libbey, BSc
Janice Green (*Senior Technician*)
Christina Baptiste (*Technician*)
Jenita Jeyarajan (*Technician*)

Chemistry:
*David Schofield, MA
Phil A Coleman, BSc
Jo S Cooper, BSc
Neil J I Double, BSc (*Asst Head of Upper Sixth*)
Aidan Doyle, BSc
Polly A Holmes, BSc (*Head of Upper Sixth*)
J Francesca Knibbs, BSc
Sarah R Langdon, MChem, PhD (*Asst Head of Fifth Year, Charities Coordinator*)
Jonathan Neville, MChem (*Asst Head of Fourth Year*)
Maria G Stuart, DPhil
Lorna Jones (*Senior Technician*)
Vijaya Mallula (*Technician*)
Mary-Ann Palmer (*Technicians' Assistant*)
(*To be appointed*) (*Technicians' Assistant*)

Classics:
*J Wesley Barber, MA Oxon
Gemma J Busby, BA
Philip D Hills, MA Cantab, PhD (*Deputy Head*)
Samuel Hitchings, BA, MA
Tim J Leary, MLitt, PhD (*Keeper of the Archives*)
§Helen M Carmichael, BA, MA
§Alice H Jacobs, MA Cantab

Design Technology:
*Oliver Rokison, MEng
Michael Richards, BSc
Joseph O Sarpong, BSc
Diane C Woodward, BSc
W [Bill] Jones (*Senior Technician*)
A [Tony] Barun (*Technician*)

Drama:
*Joanne Davis, BA (*Head of Drama*)
Max J Duda, BA
Ravi K Kothakota, BA (*Head of Fourth Year*)

Economics and Business Studies:
*§Ski Paraskos, MA Oxon (*Senior Tutor*)
Ferdinand Doepel, BSc
Tom F Rigby, BA (*Asst Head of Third Year, Charities Coordinator*)
John D Slater, BA

English:
*Catherine E Goddard, BA
Michael M Baker, MA
Tessa Bartholomew, BA
Martha B Bedford, BA
Daniel C Phillips, BA
Sian E Smith, MA
Louise A Teunissen, BA
Paul D Thomas, BA, MSc
Steve Timbs, BA (*Master i/c Sporting Conduct*)
§Helen V Booker, BA
§Alexandra C McLusky, BA
§Martyn Payne, BA, MA
§Peter Smith, BA, MA

Geography:
*Barney S Bett, BA, MA
Charlotte Brown, BA
Thomas E Hill, BA (*Asst Head of First Year*)
Rachael Kugele, MSc

James Odling, BSc
Dominic Saul, BSc
Harriet Slator, BA

History:
*A Jon Cook, MA Oxon
Esther Arnott, BA
David R Clarke, BHum (*Senior Tutor*)
Kevin Knibbs, MA Oxon (*The Headmaster*)
Andy J Lawrence, BA
J Owen Morris, MA Cantab (*Deputy Head, Designated Safeguarding Lead*)
Jim Parrish, BA (*Head of Lower Sixth*)
Jennifer L Peattie, BA (*Head of First Year*)
Victoria M Smith, BA Head of Tennis, Asst Head of Upper Sixth
Richard D Worrallo, MA Oxon (*Senior Tutor Careers & UCAS, Talk!*)
§Martin P Cross, BA
§Holly E Partridge
§Alan Thomas, BA

Information and Communications Technology:
*Ian Trevena, MCSA (*Head of IT Services*)
Harjit Singh (*Asst Systems Manager*)

Learning Support:
*Caroline Conway (*Head of Learning Support*)
Susanne Harradine, CertEd, BDA Dip SpLDs, PG Dip Ed (*Specialist Teacher*)
Nicola Day BEd (*SpLD Teacher*)
Sam Day (*Learning Support Assistant*)
Kim Riches (*SEN Administrator*)

Library:
Karl Hemsley, MA
Liz Colvine, PhD (*Asst Librarian*)

Mathematics:
*Joanna R Condon, MMath Oxon
Christopher G Aubrey, MA Oxon (*Head of Key Stage 4 Maths*)
Ami Banerjee, BSc, MBA (*Head of Cricket*)
Sean Boret
Hannah Clarke, BSc
Mark P Curtis, MSc Oxon, DPhil (*2i/c Maths*)
Daniel Griller, BA Cantab
Bethany Hart, BSc (*Asst Head of Lower Sixth*)
James Hope, BSc
Aidan W Kershaw, BSc Cantab
Floriane D Latulipe, BSc
Jeremy J Lee, MA Cantab
Alasdair N R McBay, BSc, MSc (*Director of Studies*)
Tim N Passmore, MEng
Jan Perz, PhD, MSc, BSc
Christopher M Schurch, BSc
Verity Short, MA
Nick Stebbings, BEng
Michael Thornton, BA, MSci
Rohit R Trivedi, MA (*Key Stage 4 Maths Coordinator*)
Marta Watson-Evans, BSc
§Adrienne Burke, BA
§Mei-Wah Field, BSc (*Head of SIMS*)
§Caroline Reyner, MSc

Modern Languages:
*Duncan E Peel, MA
Haig Agulian, BA
Thomas R Aucutt, BA (*Spanish*)
Christopher J Blachford, BA
Marc Boardman, BA (*Asst Head of Fourth Year*)
Shirley A Buckley, BA
Francesca G Byrne, MA (*Asst Head of Second Year*)
Frederic C Chaveneau, BA (*French*)

Katya N Dubova, BA (*Russian*)
Silvia Garrido-Soriano, BA (*Academic Extension and Think!, Coordinator for KS3*)
Charles Malston, BA
Jill C Owen, BA (*Head of Second Year*)
Augusta Samuel, BA
Philipp Studt, BA, MA (*Asst Head of Third Year*)
Paddy G Turner, BA
Katherine Willett, BA
Sophie C Yoxon, MA
Hong Zhang, MA (*Mandarin*)
§Margaret Chandler, MA
§Ms Maria Doncel-Cervantes, BA
§Ms Y Isaeva (*Russian Conversation*)
§Sophie E May, BA Oxon
§Ludmilla Wilson, BA (*Russian Conversation*)
§Hong Zhou, BA, MBA
Joanne Iredale, BA, DipIM (*Languages Resources*)
Clemence Daudu (*French Assistant*)
Judith Kalinowski (*German Assistant*)
Natalia Lara Hinojosa (*Spanish Assistant*)
Patricia Lobato Vázquez (*Spanish Assistant*)
Antoine Stevenin (*French Assistant*)

Music:
*Iain C Donald, BA
Daniel E Roland, MusB (*Assistant Head of First Year*)
Matthew Ward, BA, PhD Cantab
Charlotte Carnes (*Performing Arts Administrator*)
§Miss J M Ainscough, LTCL, GTCL, FTCL, MMus FRCO (*Organ*)
§Mr J Akers, BMus (*Classical Guitar*)
§Mr T Barry, GGSM (*Percussion*)
§Mr K Christiane, DPLM (*Saxophone*)
§Mr C Clague, ARCM, BA (*Trumpet*)
§Miss J Clare, GRNCM (*Violin and Viola*)
§Mr P Dennis, RAM, LRAM (*Singing*)
§Miss J Estall, GTCL, FTCL, COS Dip Dist (*Clarinet, Head of Woodwind*)
§Mr A Gibson (*Director of Jazz Band*)
§Mr S Hvartchilkov, BMus, LRAM (*Classical Guitar*)
§Mrs J Jaggard, AGSM, NCOS Dip (*Oboe*)
§Mr J A Jones, GMus, ARCM (*Pianoforte, Head of Keyboard Studies*)
§Miss J Koster, GRNCM, PPRNCM (*Flute*)
§Mr T Law, BMus RCM, MMus GSMD (*Saxophone*)
§Mr M Lewandowski (*Double Bass*)
§Mr D Nair, BMus (*Jazz Piano*)
§Laura Oldfield, BA
§Mr A Pym, RGT (*Modern Guitar*)
§Mr M Schofield, GMus (*Violin & Viola*)
§Mr M Steward (*Modern Guitar*)
§Mr L Taylor, ARCM, FTCL (*Trombone*)
§Angharad Thomas (*Bassoon*)
§Miss Tshui Fei Lim, ARCM, LRAM (*Pianoforte*)
§Miss E van Ments, GMus RNCM, PG Dip PPRNCM (*Violin and Viola, Head of Strings*)
§Mr D Ward, AGSM (*Trumpet*)
§Miss S Whale, LRAM (*Cello*)
§Mr S Willmott (*Percussion*)

Personal, Health & Social Education:
*Jack H Talman, BA
§Rebecca J Nicholson, MPhys Oxon

Physical Education and Games:
P [Billy] D Bolton, BSc (*Athletics*)
Andrew Beattie, BSc
David R Clarke, BHum (*Senior Tutor*)
Colin Greenaway (*Director of Rowing*)
Carlos T Mills, BSc (*Head of Sport*)

Matthew K Sims, BSc (*Sports Rehabilitation & Asst Head of Second Year*)
Sean Thomson (*Director of Rugby*)
Steve Timbs, BA (*Master i/c Sporting Conduct*)
Paddy Walsh, BA (*Outdoor Pursuits Specialist*)

Physics:
*Mark G Yates, PhD
Peter D Armstrong, BSc
Christopher P Arnold, BA, DPhil Oxon (*Asst Head of Fifth Year*)
Gordon H Clark, BSc (*Head of Computing Science*)
Dan J Fendley, BEng (*Induction Tutor, Designated Safeguarding Officer*)
Stephen Gray, BSc
Kathryn E Millar, BEng (*Head of Third Year*)
Christine Reilly, MSc
Leonard O Rouse, BSc
Amy White, BA, MA
Nicholas D Woods, BA, MEng Cantab (*Head of Third Year*)
§Joanne L Boon, MA Oxon
§Rebecca J Nicholson, MPhys Oxon (*Asst Head of PHSE*)
David A Hughes, HNC (*Senior Technician*)
Rebecca Galan (*Technician*)

Politics:
*Jenny A Field, MA
Holly E Partridge, BA
Tom F Rigby, BA (*Assistant Head of Third Year, Charities Coordinator*)
Victoria M Smith, BA (*Head of Tennis, Asst Head of Upper Sixth*)
Richard D Worrallo, MA Oxon (*Senior Tutor Careers & UCAS, Talk!*)
§Martin P Cross, BA

Psychology:
*Stephen J Wakefield, BSc
Alice Goodman, BSc (*Asst Head of Careers, Asst Head of Lower Sixth*)

Religious Studies & Philosophy:
*Neal K Carrier, BA, MPhil, PhD (*Asst Head of UCAS*)
Tom Jenkins, BA
Mark A J Nicholson, BA (*Assistant Head*)
Peter D Rowntree BEd
Jack H Talman, BA (*Head of PHSE*)
S Andrew Wilkinson, MA Oxon (*Senior Tutor*)
§Judy A Perkins, BA, MA, MPhil

Combined Cadet Force:
Jeremy Schomberg (*Commanding Officer CCF Contingent*)

Administrative Staff:
Examinations Officer: Michelle Barnes
Headmaster's PA: Valerie Conroy
Admissions & Marketing Manager: Dorothy Jones, BA, Dip Mar
Deputy Admissions Manager: Caroline Elia
Admissions Assistant: Kathy Hadrill
School Nurse: Elizabeth Searle

Harrow School

Harrow on the Hill, Middlesex HA1 3HP
Tel: +44 (0)20 8872 8000 (Enquiries)
           +44 (0)20 8872 8003 (Head Master)

           +44 (0)20 8872 8007 (Admissions)
           +44 (0)20 8872 8320 (Bursar)
Fax: +44 (0)20 8423 3112 (School)
email: harrow@harrowschool.org.uk
website: www.harrowschool.org.uk

Mottos: *Stet Fortuna Domus; Donorum dei dispensatio fidelis*

Harrow School is a full-boarding school for boys aged 13 to 18. It was founded in 1572, under a royal charter from Queen Elizabeth I, by a local landowning farmer, John Lyon, whose original intention was to provide 30 boys of the parish with a classical education. Today, the School's purpose is to prepare boys with diverse backgrounds and abilities for a life of learning, leadership, service and personal fulfilment; distinguished Old Harrovians include seven British prime ministers and the first prime minister of India, Pandit Nehru, as well as poets and writers as diverse as Byron, Sheridan and Richard Curtis. This statement of purpose is borne out through our various areas of activity: teaching that helps boys achieve their best academically, pastoral care that matures them both emotionally and spiritually, and an extra-curricular programme that develops their characters and interests. The School's 300 acres have a collegiate feel, its historical architecture complemented by modern buildings that meet its pupils' developing needs. Approximately 820 boys 18 attend Harrow, from across the UK and further afield.

Academic. In 2015, the School's A Level results were in line with the robust performance of recent years, in light of the major examination reforms that have led to a national deflation of A*/A grades for two consecutive seasons. Our A*/A rate this year was better than last year, at 67.5%. Maths is our most popular A Level subject and here a third of our candidates earned an A*. In seven subjects, the A*/A rate was 100% and more than 80 of our leavers – nearly half of the year group – earned three or more A*s or As, securing them places at the top universities. At GCSE, our A* rate over the past three years has been at the highest ever, with this year topping last year at 58% A*. 50 boys in this year group achieved 10 A*s, which qualifies boys who are not already academic scholars to become honorary academic scholars in the Sixth Form. Seven subjects achieved 100% A*/A. Visit http://www.harrowschool.org.uk/The-Curriculum for details of our curriculum.

The Super-Curriculum. Beyond the examination syllabus, our Super-Curriculum focuses on the aspects of scholarship that are not formally assessed: habitual reading, independent research, reflection and debate. Central to this is the electives system, in which boys select a challenging off-syllabus course that is taught in small groups. These courses promote lateral thinking, problem-solving and the articulation of profound thought, while also allowing boys to lead their own learning. On virtually every night of the week, there are seminars and society meetings, and we are able to attract eminent speakers from all walks of life to enrich and broaden the boys' experience of academic and cultural life.

Boarding. Our leafy 300-acre estate contains 12 Boarding Houses. The buildings are quite individual, with their own gardens and facilities, helping to set each house apart. The Houses inspire fierce loyalty from the boys and old boys, who take pride in their own part of Harrow. House Masters and their families live in the houses, and are assisted by an Assistant House Master, Matron, Year Group Tutors and Health Education Tutors. In addition, the chaplaincy, full-time psychologist and pastoral support committee provide further layers of nurturing and support. Approximately 70 boys live in in each House. There are no dormitories: a boy shares his room with a boy of the same age for the first year or so, and thereafter has a room to himself. Every boy has a computer in his room and each house has common rooms and shared kitchens. All teachers live in the School. Typically, for the first two weekends of a term, all pupils are in the School. If they are able to, parents come and visit. On the third weekend – an exeat – all pupils go home or to friends; the weekend starts at 12 noon on Friday and ends at 9.00 pm on Sunday. The next two weekends are followed by a nine-day half term.

Sport. With afternoon games available in 32 sports, five times a week, sporting fixtures against other schools and the chance to compete regularly in House matches, boys are kept healthy and active. Under the expert guidance of some of the country's leading coaches, boys develop their skills, character and confidence. Through games such as rugby, soccer, cricket and Harrow football, they learn how to be team players. Equal emphasis is placed on the many individual sports offered here that cultivate resilience, self-discipline and enjoyment. Surrounded by acres of sports fields, AstroTurf pitches, a golf course, swimming pool, sports centre, tennis, rackets and fives courts, Harrow has a breadth of sporting opportunities. Our elite sportsmen have an impressive record of achieving excellent standards and some go on to enjoy successful, professional sporting careers. Unique occasions like the annual cricket match versus Eton at Lord's provide memorable highlights in the School year.

The Arts. The arts are an extremely important part of Harrow's packed calendar of activities. Whether it's learning a musical instrument, playing in orchestras and ensembles, singing in choirs or in houses, performing in plays or discovering beauty in fine art, sculpture and ceramics, the opportunity for creative expression at Harrow not only sets our boys on a lifetime of personal enrichment and enjoyment, but also teaches them to be more self-disciplined, attentive and better at planning and organising their busy lives. Boys who participate in the vast spectrum of Harrow's creative and performing arts also find that this involvement has a broader, more beneficial effect on their overall academic performance. By encouraging boys to perform in the highest-quality School and house concerts, plays and competitions, we see them finding their own voice and the confidence to express their individual creativity, regardless of innate talent.

After Harrow. Virtually all of our boys take up places at selective universities. Boys who are heading towards Oxbridge, Ivy League and other competitive institutions are given specific guidance and preparation from their House Masters and our dedicated Universities Team. In 2015, our most popular destinations were Oxford (14), Edinburgh (14), Durham (12), Newcastle (12), Bristol (11) and UCL (11). All boys holding Oxbridge places made their offers and 16 boys are off to top universities in America, including Stanford, Duke, Chicago, UVA and seven different Ivy League universities. Harrow is one of only four schools in the country to get two of its leavers into Harvard this year. The Harrow Association, Harrow's Old Boys' Society, has a thriving membership of over 10,000. Tel: 020 8872 8200, email: ha@harrowschool.org.uk.

Admission. Boys are typically admitted for entry at 13 and a smaller number at 16. Visit http://www.harrow-school.org.uk/Admissions-Home for more information.

Fees per term (2016–2017). £12,450, including board, tuition, textbooks, a stationery allowance and laundry. For any subject requiring additional tuition, there is an extra charge.

Scholarships and bursaries. A large number of scholarships are awarded every year. Scholarships have a value of 5% of the fee and are held throughout a boy's time at Harrow, subject to satisfactory performance. Boys may apply for more than one of the different types of scholarship, which include Academic, Music, Art, Sport and Outstanding Talent. Scholarships can often be supplemented by a means-tested bursary of up to 100% for parents who might not otherwise be able to afford the fees.

Charitable status. The School is constituted as a Royal Charter Corporation known as The Keepers and Governors of the Possessions Revenues and Goods of the Free Grammar School of John Lyon, which is a Registered Charity, number 310033. The aims and objectives of the Charity are to provide education for the pupils at the two schools in the Foundation, Harrow School and The John Lyon School.

Visitors:
The Archbishop of Canterbury
The Bishop of London

Governors:
J P Batting, MA, FFA (*Chairman*)
R C W Odey, BA, FRHS (*Deputy Chairman*)
Professor D J Womersley, MA, PhD, FBA
C H St J Hoare, BA
K W B Gilbert, BA, FCA
E J H Gould, MA
M K Fosh, BA, MSI
Professor G Furniss, BA, PhD, FBA
Professor Sir D Wallace, CBE, FRS, FREng
The Hon R Orr-Ewing
Mrs S Whiddington, AB
Admiral Sir G M Zambellas, KCB, DSC, BSc, FRAeS
Professor P Binski, MA, PHD, FBA
C G T Stonehill, MA
Dr I Dove-Edwin, BSc, MDCM, MRCP
G W J Goodfellow, QC, MA, LLM
J M P D Stroyan, MA
Mrs M S Brounger, LLB
A C Goswell, BSc, MRICS
The Hon Andrew Butler, MA
D G P Eyton, FREng, FIOM^3, FIOD
J C Faber, MA
A D Hart, ACA, FRSA
R T G Winter, BA, FCA

Clerk to the Governors: The Hon Andrew Millett, MA, Pemberton Greenish, 45 Cadogan Gardens, London SW3 2AQ

Head Master: J B Hawkins, MA

Deputy Head Master: A K Metcalfe, MA, FRGS, CGeog

Senior Master and Director of Boarding: P J Bieneman, MA

Senior Tutor: A R McGregor, MA

Director of Studies: A J Chirnside, MA

Registrar: E R Sie, BSc, PhD, CChem

Academic and Universities Director: N Page, BA, MCIL

Bursar: N A Shryane, MBE, BA, MPhil

Head of Departments:
Astronomy: Dr C M Crowe, MSci, MASt, PhD, FRAS
Director of Art: L W Hedges, BA, MA
Biology: N S Keylock, MSc
Chemistry: Dr A F Worrall, MA, MSc, PhD
Classics: Dr J L Roberts, BA, MA, PhD
Computing: N J Marchant, BEng
Critical Thinking: C D Barry, BSc
Design and Technology: T M Knight, BA
Drama and Theatre Studies: Dr J K Bratten, BA, PhD
EAL: H E Rhodes, BA
Economics and Business Studies: C T Pollitt, BA
English: Dr J K Bratten, BA, PhD
French: O Syrus, BA
Geography: S M Sampson, BSc, FRGS
German: Dr A J Hills, BA, MA
Government and Politics: Dr M E P Gray, BA, MA, PhD
History: A D Todd, BA, MPhil

History of Art: L W Hedges, BA, MA
ICT: Dr C D O'Mahony, BA, DPhil
Italian: H A Haldane
Mathematics: I Hammond, BSc
Modern Languages: W Turner, BA
Director of Music: D N Woodcock, MA, FRCO, [Dip CHM], FRSA
Oriental Languages: R M Tremlett, BA, MA
Painting: S N Page, BEd
Photography: D R J Bell, BA
Physical Education: J J Coulson, BA, MA
Physics and Digital Learning: C D Barry, BSc
Russian: K A Fletcher
Spanish: A D T Turner
Director of Sport: J J Coulson, BA
Theology and Philosophy: R J Harvey, BA

Houses & House Masters:
Bradbys: Dr D Earl
Druries: Mr M J M Ridgway
Elmfield: Mr M J Tremlett
Lyon's: Mr N J Marchant
Moretons: Mr P J Evans
Newlands: Mr E W Higgins
Rendalls: Mr S N Taylor
The Grove: Mr C S Tolman
The Head Master's: Dr S A Harrison
The Knoll: Dr S J Abbott
The Park: Mr B J D Shaw
West Acre: Mr M G J Walker

Hereford Cathedral School

Old Deanery, The Cathedral Close, Hereford HR1 2NG

Tel:	01432 363522
Fax:	01432 363525
email:	schoolsec@herefordcs.com
website:	www.herefordcs.com
Twitter:	@Herefordcs1
Facebook:	/HerefordCathedralSchool

Founded ante 1384. No record of the School's foundation survives, although its close association with the Cathedral is indicated by Bishop Gilbert's response to the long-standing right of the Chancellor to appoint the Headmaster in a letter of 1384, and it is probable that some educational institution was always associated with the Cathedral, which was founded in 676.

It is a fully co-educational 11–18 day school of 505 pupils.

Admission. Pupils are normally admitted at the ages of 11, 13 or 16. Admission at ages 11 to 14 is by sitting the Senior School Entrance Examination at the School. Suitably qualified boys and girls may be admitted at Sixth Form level. The School operates a Deferred Entry Scheme at 11 for 13+ entries.

Facilities. The School is situated in the lee of the Cathedral. It occupies many historic buildings and some later ones, all adapted for School use, as well as purpose-built facilities. On the main campus are, in addition to some of the main departments, eight science departments, five which are new, a large music school, an Art, Design and Technology and Computer Centre (that gained Hereford's first RIBA award for architecture), the Gilbert Library and a refurbished Dining Hall. The Zimmerman Building provides 20,000 square feet of robust working space for Classics, Modern Languages, examination/functions hall, Geography and Drama departments and the Sixth Form Centre. A new on-site Sports Hall was opened in April 2009, which has first-class facilities for badminton, five-a-side football, net-ball, basketball and four sets of cricket nets. Rugby and outdoor cricket is held at the School's Wyeside sports ground, alongside the HCS rowing club.

Curriculum. Pupils are divided on entry at 11 into four forms (a maximum of 24 pupils per form) for academic and pastoral purposes. Below the Sixth Form, pupils take a broad range of subjects. Option choices are made at the end of the third year (Year 9).

In the Sixth Form pupils are prepared for A (AS/A2) Levels, for which there is a wide choice of subjects: Latin, Greek, English Literature/Language (Combined), English Literature, French, Philosophy and Ethics, Classical Civilisation, Spanish, Economics, History, Geography, Mathematics, Further Mathematics, Biology, Physics, Chemistry, Design and Technology, Fine Art, Textiles, Business Studies, Music, Drama and Theatre Studies and Physical Education. Almost all students go on to Higher Education degree courses and the vast majority to the university course of their choice.

Religious instruction throughout is in accordance with the doctrines of the Church of England. The School is privileged to have the daily use of Hereford Cathedral for Chapel.

Sports/Activities include Rugby, Cricket, Football, Badminton, Tennis, Hockey, Netball, Athletics, and Rowing. There is a CCF Group and a wide range of societies active within the School. The School is an Operating Authority for the Duke of Edinburgh's Award scheme. Drama flourishes, with several productions each year. The School has a national reputation in debating.

Music. The School is also particularly strong in Music: over half the pupils receive tuition in the full range of orchestral instruments, piano, organ and classical guitar. There is a Senior Symphony Orchestra, Senior Wind Quintet, Junior and Senior String Quartet, a Jazz Ensemble, Senior Chamber Choir, a Chapel Choir and a Junior Choir and many chamber music groups. There is at least one Concert each year and operas are produced from time to time. The musical tradition is strengthened by the presence of the Cathedral Choristers (and former Cathedral choristers) in the School.

Fees per term (2016–2017). £4,447.

Extras. CCF £15 per term from Year 10; DoE from £210 Bronze level; Instrumental Tuition £17.25 per lesson, plus public examination fees; PTA £20 per family annually.

Scholarships. Up to eight Dean's Scholarships are awarded as a result of the Senior School Entrance and 11+ Scholarship Examination. Up to three Dean's Scholarships are also awarded at 13+. Up to eight Dean's Scholarships are competed for entry to the Sixth Form. Art and Drama Scholarships are available at 13+ and 16+ entry. Sports and All-Rounder Scholarships are available at 11+, 13+ and 16+ entry. All Scholars are admitted to the Foundation by the Dean of Hereford each Autumn term.

Up to four Music Exhibitions are awarded each year as a result of auditions held in the first half of the Spring Term. 11+, 13+ and Sixth Form Music Scholarships are also available. Details are available from the Director of Music.

Cathedral choristers are members of the School from entry. They are accepted from the age of eight as probationers following voice and educational tests held in May each year, and are educated initially at the Junior School. The Governors and the Chapter award choral scholarships jointly annually. Two-thirds reductions in tuition fees are available for Cathedral Choristers.

Assisted Places (Bursaries). A number of means-tested bursaries are awarded competitively to able children from families of limited means.

Old Herefordian Club. *Alumni Coordinator*: Mrs Helen Pearson.

The Junior School. This is situated close by the main school. (*For details, please see Junior School IAPS entry*).

Charitable status. Hereford Cathedral School is a Registered Charity, number 518889. Its aims and objectives are to promote the advancement of education by acquiring, establishing, providing, conducting and carrying on residential and non-residential schools in which boys and girls of all sections of the community may receive a sound general education (including religious instruction in accordance with the doctrines of the Church of England).

Governing Body:
President: The Very Revd M Tavinor, Dean of Hereford, MA, MMus
Chairman: R Haydn Jones, BSc, MRICS
C D Hitchiner, LLB, ACIS
Rear Admiral P Wilcocks, CB, DSC, DL
Prof E Ellis, MA, PhD
Mrs V Oliver-Davies, JP
A Teale, BSc, PGCE
Major L C Glover, BA
Mrs K Usher, DL
W Hanks, BDS Lond
S Borthwick
T Keyes, MA
The Right Revd A Magowan, BSc, Dip HE, MTh Oxon

Clerk to the Governors: R Pizii, MA, BSc

Headmaster: P A Smith, BSc

Deputy Head: B G Blyth, BA

Deputy Head (*Academic*): J P Stanley, MA, MBA

Assistant Head: M J Blackburn, BA

Head of Sixth Form: J R Terry, BSc

Heads of Department:
Art: C A Wilkes, BA
Biology: Mrs E Segalini-Bower, MSc
Chemistry: Mrs A J Burdett, MSc
Classics: Miss A M Wright, MA
Drama: Ms L D A Zammit, BEd
Economics: M R Jackson, BA
English: B E Abbott, BA
Geography: Mrs R M Floyd, BSc
History: P A Wright, BA
Junior ICT:
Learning Support: Miss L R Stevens, BA, Cert SpLD
Mathematics: M Taylor, BSc, ARCM
Modern Languages: Mrs N J Teale, BA
Music: D R Evans, MA, GBSM
PE and Games: M J Blackburn, BA
Physics: Dr S J B Rhodes, BEng, PhD
Religious Studies: Dr N Williams, BLitt, BA, PhD
Technology: C J Howells, BA

Careers Adviser: Mrs M McCumisky, BA
OC CCF: Gp Capt J Andrews RAFVR[T]
Director of Finance and Resources: R Pizii, MA, BSc
Headmaster's PA: Mrs S Gurgul
Marketing Manager: Mrs S Corness
Development Director: Mrs C M Morgan-Jones
Admissions Officer: Mrs S D A Fortey
Tel: 01432 363506, email: admissions@herefordcs.com
Examinations Officer: Dr D Summers
School Office Administrator: Mrs L G Harding

The Junior School
Headmaster: C Wright, BSc, MSc, PGCE
Deputy Headmaster: J M Debenham, BEd
Head of Pre-Prep: Mrs E Lord, Bed
Head of Nursery: Mrs J Windows, BA

Heads of Department:
English: J Bond, BA
Maths: Miss N Jeynes, BEd
Science: Dr I Barber, BSc
French: Miss C Lambert, BA
Humanities: T Brown, BA
Drama: Miss A Sutton, BA
ICT: T Hutchinson, BSc, CertEd
Art: Mrs K Gummerson, BA
Music: Miss R Toolan, BMus, PG Dip Perf Hons
PSHE: Mrs S Price, LLB, PGCE
Learning Development: Mrs T Denny, BSc
Boys Games: S Turpin, BA
Girls Games: Miss K A Davies, BEd
Gifted & Talented:

Secretary: Mrs S Stick
Admissions Secretary: Mrs A Phillips
Tel: 01432 363511, email: enquiry@herefordcs.com
Nurses:
Mrs S Warner, RGN
Mrs F Jennings

Highgate School

North Road, London N6 4AY
Tel: 020 8340 1524 (Office)
        020 8347 3564 (Admissions)
email: office@highgateschool.org.uk
        admissions@highgateschool.org.uk
website: www.highgateschool.org.uk

Motto: *Altiora in votis.*

Highgate School was founded in 1565 by Sir Roger Cholmeley, Knight, Chief Justice of England, and confirmed by Letters Patent of Queen Elizabeth in the same year. The School has three principal aims: to be a place for learning and scholarship; to be an exemplar for the healthy life; and to be a reflective community.

There are 1,180 boys and girls in the Senior School. The Junior School has some 365 boys and girls, aged 7 to 11, and prepares them for entry to the Senior School. The Pre-Preparatory School has 150 boys and girls aged 3 to 7. The School is fully co-educational and admits girls and boys at each entry point.

Situation and Grounds. The academic centre of the Senior School is in the heart of old Highgate, which has retained much of its village atmosphere. In addition to the Victorian buildings, such as the Chapel and Central Hall classrooms, the pupils have the benefit of modern facilities such as Dyne House, with its 200-seat auditorium and dedicated recital space, an Art, Design & Technology Centre opened in 2005 and the Charter Building, housing the English and Geography Departments, a science laboratory and ICT suite which opened in 2012; the Sir Martin Gilbert Library opened in Big School in 2013, and an extension to the Garner Building, providing two new science laboratories and three new modern languages classrooms, opened for use in September 2014.

Highgate underground station, on the Northern line, is a short walk away and there is also easy access to the School by bus. It is four miles to central London (City or West End).

A few hundred yards along Hampstead Lane in Bishopswood Road lie more than twenty acres of playing-fields together with the Mallinson Sports Centre, indoor swimming pool and other extensive sporting facilities, the dining hall, the newly re-built Junior School which opened in September 2016, and the Pre-Preparatory School. Hampstead

Heath and Kenwood, the largest expanse of open country in London, are adjacent.

Pastoral Care. In the Senior School, pastoral care for Years 7 and 8 is organised by form, with a Head of Year in overall charge. From Year 9, each pupil is a member of a House. There are twelve Houses based on particular areas of North London. A Head of House, helped by five tutors, is responsible for monitoring the day-to-day progress and welfare of the fifty or so pupils in his or her care and for liaising with their parents.

Academic Curriculum. Pupils enter the Senior School at 11+ (Year 7); there is a further, limited, entry at 13+. There are eight forms in Years 7 and 8 and the curriculum is broad. At present, in addition to the usual range of subjects in Years 7 to 9, Art, Music and Design Technology Engineering are taken by all; the vast majority of pupils take Latin, and two sets study both Latin and Greek in Year 9 as a single timetable option; all pupils take a second modern language option in Year 9. Mandarin has been offered at GCSE since 2011 and is offered as a Pre-U in the Sixth Form. By the time they start their GCSEs, pupils have developed an appropriate pattern of work, both in the classroom and out of school. Homework is an integral part of each pupil's programme of study.

The two-year GCSE courses begin in Year 10. The core subjects, studied by all, are: English, English Literature, Mathematics, Biology, Chemistry and Physics as single award separate sciences. A further four subjects (including a modern language) are then chosen from: Ancient History, Art, Classical Civilisation, Design Technology Engineering, Drama, Geography, French, German, Greek, History, Latin, Mandarin, Music, Religious Studies, Spanish and Russian. In addition to their GCSE subjects, all pupils take courses in Religion and Philosophy and Sport and Exercise. All GCSEs are taken at the end of Year 11. The IGCSE qualification is taken in English Language, English Literature, the Sciences, History, French, German and Spanish.

The teaching staff are experienced and well-qualified subject specialists and the teacher/pupil ratio is about 1:9. Class sizes are generally in the low twenties in Years 7 to 9 and just under twenty in Years 10 and 11, although for some subjects they will be much smaller; in the Sixth Form classes of 6–14 are usual.

Educational resources include a new learning platform, HERO, which enables pupils to access learning materials and extension work and to submit assignments and receive feedback on them. This complements an extensive intranet on a large information technology network and parent and pupil portals for remote access. The use of all these is guided by trained professionals and they complement the facilities available in the academic departments, which have specialist teaching rooms, equipment and, where appropriate, technicians, computers and libraries. Fieldwork and visits to galleries, museums, exhibitions and lectures are an integral part of the academic programme.

When they enter Year 12, girls and boys choose four subjects from the wide range of A Level and Pre U courses on offer. Prospective Sixth Formers are assisted in selecting the best programme of study according to their known ability and future plans. A booklet listing the options available and containing details of the courses is published each year and given to Year 11 and their parents before those choices are made. Both new and old-style A Levels are taught in a linear fashion and pupils will not take any public examinations at the end of Year 12.

All Year 12 pupils follow a Critical Method programme which introduces them to the criticism and formation of logical argument. This is followed by a Critical Independence course for one term in Year 13, which pursues the aims of the Year 12 course at a higher level. The Extended Project has been introduced as an additional option in Year 12.

Emphasis is placed on learning to work independently and to develop more advanced study skills. At this stage a pupil will for the first time have a number of private reading periods. Two Sixth Form Common Rooms act as a social and recreational base for senior pupils.

Each Sixth Former has a tutor who, in conjunction with the Housemaster, exercises supervision over general academic progress and who advises on and monitors higher education applications in conjunction with the Director of Higher Education.

Religion. Highgate has a Christian tradition but pupils from all faiths and denominations or none are welcome. Pupils attend Chapel once a week, by houses, and there are weekly voluntary celebrations of Holy Communion; Choral Evensong is sung on some Sundays, at which parents are welcome. There are weekly meetings of the Jewish Circle and an assembly for those of other faiths.

Music, Drama and Art. Highgate music has a long and distinguished tradition and many former pupils are now leading composers, conductors or performers. A wide range of musical activities is designed both to encourage the beginner and to stimulate and further the skills of the talented musician. State-of-the-art performance spaces for orchestral and chamber music, complete with computerised recording facilities, are available in Dyne House.

There are five main instrumental ensembles: a symphony orchestra, a chamber orchestra, a symphonic wind band, and string orchestra and a concert band. Two choirs provide music for Choral Evensong on Sundays, with a further three choirs covering a wide range of sacred and secular repertoire. There are four main concerts each year, one taking place in a major central London venue. Numerous chamber groups rehearse weekly and regular concerts are arranged, together with masterclasses, workshops and an annual house music competition.

Individual music lessons are available with specialist visiting teachers in all the main instruments and in singing. Certain orchestral instruments can be hired by beginners who may be offered a free term's trial of lessons.

Every encouragement is given to participate in drama, as actors, in stage management, or by assisting with sound and lighting. Major productions in recent years have included *South Pacific, West Side Story, Romeo and Juliet, Midsummer Night's Dream, Sweeney Todd, Les Misérables, The Trojan Women, The Bacchae, Medea, Bugsy Malone, Oklahoma, Much Ado about Nothing* and *The Tempest*. Small-scale plays are staged in most terms, some by younger pupils, and there is a biennial play performed in French. A separate drama studio provides additional rehearsal and performance space. Regular visits to the professional theatre are also arranged. In 2015, Highgate held its second Festival, celebrating excellence in the performing arts and sport, which culminated in a show at Camden's Roundhouse.

The excellent Art department has facilities for painting, print-making, life drawing, sculpture, pottery, photography, and film-making. Whether taking part in formal classes or working in their free time boys and girls are encouraged to explore their own ways of expressing ideas visually. Their work is regularly exhibited, both in the department and elsewhere in the school.

Sport and Exercise. Highgate is exceptionally fortunate in its sports facilities. The extensive playing fields are complemented by the Mallinson Sports Centre and by courts for squash, tennis and Eton fives, and a new all-weather pitch which opened for use in 2009.

The Sport and Exercise (Games and PE) curriculum aims to maximise participation, promote enjoyment and ensure progression. Sport (one afternoon per week) and exercise (a double period in Years 7–10) are integrated to ensure pupils develop skills and strength relevant to the sport which, from Year 8 onwards, they choose from a wide range, including the team games of football, rugby, cricket (boys) and netball, hockey and rounders (girls), and the following options: athletics, aquatics, cross-country, climbing, fives, fencing, golf, gym and dance, kayaking, martial arts, rowing, sailing, softball, squash and tennis. Specialist sports coaches lead the teaching which is complemented by early-morning, lunch-time and after-school training. There is a High Performance Programme for outstanding sports pupils. Tours take place annually, either to short- or to long-haul destinations.

Activities. We aim to provide as many opportunities as possible in which pupils will develop qualities of self-reliance, endurance and leadership, in which they can serve the community and in which they can develop their own interests and enthusiasms. There are a large number of societies and clubs, usually meeting in the lunch-hour or after school. The School is an operating authority for the Duke of Edinburgh's Award scheme and each year many gain the bronze award and often go on to gain the silver and gold awards. There is also a Community Service scheme and an Urban Survival award scheme.

Admission. Normal entry to the Junior School is at the age of 7. All candidates take an entrance examination in January and a proportion are recalled for interview shortly thereafter, for entry the following September. Application should be made in writing to the Principal of the Junior School, 3 Bishopswood Road, London N6 4PL.

Boys who enter the Senior School at 11+ are mainly from primary schools while girls come from prep and primary schools. The remainder enter from Highgate Junior School. Places for the very limited entry at 13+ will be offered on the basis of pre-tests in the September of Year 7, conditional on passing Common Entrance. 13+ pupils not in preparatory schools should contact the Admissions Office for advice. Girls and boys from other schools are also admitted to the Sixth Form at Highgate following a thinking skills test and interviews. Only occasionally are there vacancies at other levels of the School. All enquiries concerning admission to the Senior School should be addressed to the Director of Admissions, admissions@highgateschool.org.uk.

Fees per term (2016–2017). Senior School: £6,530; Junior School: £5,990; Pre-Preparatory School: £5,655 (Reception–Year 2), £2,825 (Nursery).

Fees are inclusive of lunch (exc Nursery) and the use of books.

Scholarships and Bursaries.

Bursaries: The Admissions Officer (Widening Access) (admissions@highgateschool.org.uk) can provide information about the process for bursary applications and on the number of bursaries held by pupils in the school at any one time. Preference will be given to bursary candidates who currently attend state schools. There would need to be particular and unusual circumstances for us to award a bursary to a child attending an independent school.

Scholarships: Academic scholarships are honorary and do not bring with them any remission of the school fee. We do not award academic scholarships on the strength of the entrance tests alone. We believe that we gain a much more accurate picture of a child's academic ability after we have had an opportunity to see the quality of their work within the School. Therefore we award academic scholarships towards the end of Years 7, 8, 9 and 10, and then again in the Sixth Form. In Year 7, usually six of these are awarded to external 11+ entrants and six to those coming from the Junior School. Two further scholarships are awarded at the end of Years 8, 9 and 10 on the basis of examination results, the pupil's class work and homework, and teachers' assessment of the pupil's effort and performance. There are also a small number of lesser awards, Academic Exhibitions, awarded at the end of each year.

Music awards: We make music awards (scholarships and exhibitions) for pupils joining the school at 11+, by means of audition at the point of entry. Awards are also made to pupils already in the school at these points, too, where they have met the standard for a scholarship or exhibition. Music scholarships bring up to a maximum of 10% remission of the school fee and free tuition on two instruments, provided tuition is given by instrumental teachers employed at Highgate. More detailed guidance may be obtained from the Admissions Office (admissions@highgateschool.org.uk) or the Music Department (natasha.creed@highgateschool.org.uk).

Old Cholmeleian Society. Former pupils are known as Cholmeleians. Enquiries should be addressed to the Foundation Office at the School, oc@highgateschool.org.uk.

Charitable status. Sir Roger Cholmeley's School at Highgate is a Registered Charity, number 312765, committed to meeting its responsibilities to the society that lies beyond the school gates. The importance that Sir Roger Cholmeley's School at Highgate attaches to its social responsibilities has become more focused, but is not new; the objects stated in the charity's constitution are:

- the advancement of education by the provision of a school in or near Highgate, the provision of incidental or ancillary educational activities, and the undertaking of associated activities for the benefit of the public;
- in so far as the Governors think fit (and so long as they in their discretion consider that the first object is being properly provided for) the relief of the poor.

The principal ways in which the charity meets these objects are:

- the provision of bursaries and scholarships;
- training teachers;
- running educational summer schools;
- supporting applications to selective universities;
- partnerships with local primary and secondary schools, including the sponsorship of the London Academy of Excellence, Tottenham;
- sharing our facilities with community groups;
- an extensive programme of community service;
- events in support of other charities.

More detailed information can be found on the School's website.

Visitor: Her Majesty The Queen

Governors:
J F Mills, CBE, MA, BLitt (*Treasurer and Chairman*)
R M Rothenberg, MBE, BA, FCA, CTA, MAE (*Deputy Chairman*)
Mrs G Aitken, BA
M Clarke, MA, FCA
J Claughton, MA
Mrs J Coleman, MA, LLDip
M Danson, MA
B Davidson, MD, FRCS
Miss R Langdale, QC, LLB, MPhil
Dr K Little, MB BS, BSc
P E Marshall, BSc, MRICS
K Panja, BA
A Patel, BA
J D Randall, BSc
P Rothwell, MArch

Bursar and Secretary to the Foundation: J C Pheasant, BSc, LLDip, Barrister

Head: A S Pettitt, MA

Deputy Heads:
T J Lindsay, MA (*Principal Deputy Head, Senior School*)
S M James, BA, MA (*Principal of the Junior School, Deputy Head and Director of Admissions*)
D M Fotheringham, MA (*Deputy Head, Academic*)
Miss L M Shelley, BA (*Pupils' Personal Development and Employability*)

Assistant Heads:
S N Brunskill, MA (*Head of Sixth Form*)
S Evans, BA (*Head of Lower School*)

B S Weston, BSc, PhD, FSB, CBiol (*Assistant Head, Teaching and Learning*)
[Mrs H Evans BA (*Head of Middle School*)]
S A Pullan, LLB, MA (*Assistant Head, Staff*)
P Johnston, BSc, PhD (*Assistant Head, Projects and Logistics; Director of Learning Support*)
G A Waller, MA (*Acting Assistant Head, Middle School*)

Teachers:
* *Head of Department*
† *Head of House*

Art:
C M Finnegan, BA
*Ms C M Goldsworthy, BA
[Ms S Keay, BA, MA]
Mrs A M Murphy, BA
Mrs M J Nimmo, BA
Mrs J L Sacks, BA, MA
Ms M E J Vasey, BA, MA

Classics:
N A Bowling, BA, MSt
†Mrs A J Brunner, BA
T L Corcoran, BA
D M Fotheringham, MA
†Ms H J P Isaksen, BA
J S Morrow, BA
Ms M V Neckar, MA, MA
*H E Shepherd, MA
†Miss V L Smith, BA, MA
G A Waller, MA

Computing:
*M A O'Connor, BA

Design Technology Engineering:
S M A Henderson, BSc
A B H Sursok, BA
*A F Thomson, BSc
W H Y Tang, MEng, MA

Drama and Theatre Studies:
Miss A M Beyer, BA MA
*Ms J E Fehr, BA
Mrs K A Hale, BA
T J A Hyam, BA

Economics:
Miss E L Cowell, BA, MPhil
*M J Feven, BSc, MA
T R D Goddin, BA
†Miss K P Norris, BA

English:
S G Appleton, MA
G J H Catherwood, BA
E Gault, MA, MLitt
*Mrs R J Hyam, BA
Dr C S Maclean, BA, MSt, MA, PhD
†Miss J E McLoughlin, BA
A J Miles, BA
M E Morgan, MA, MSt
[Miss O R Orlans, BA]
A J Plaistowe, MA
[R J Powell, BA]
†M W M Seymour, BA
Miss L M Shelley, MA
N J S Taylor-Collins, BA, MA, PhD

Miss S K Wijesuriya, BA, MA

Geography:
*M J Beloe, BSc
W J C Blackshaw, MA
D G Brandt, BA
[Mrs H J Broadbent, BA]
†P J Harrison, MA
†Miss R E Joss, BA
Miss G S Y Kwong, BA, MPhil

History:
B J Dabby, MA, MPhil, PhD
A T Davies, BA, MA, PhD
T J Lindsay, MA
P P McClory, BA, MA
*Mr J P R Newton, BA, MSc
J B Pearson, BA
S A Pullan, LLB, MA
Mrs E H Roberts, MA, MA
Miss E A Worthen, BA
J F Young, MA, MSc

History of Art:
*Ms J E W Jammers, MA, PhD
Miss S K Wijesuriya, BA, MA

Learning Support:
Mrs S M Bambrough, BA
G S Dhillon, BSc
*P Johnston, BSc, PhD
Ms J Hamilton, BA

Mathematics:
A D Bottomley, MMath, MRes
Miss J R Brewin, MMath
KRC Brown, MMath
Miss P F D Brownlee, BSc, MSt
A G Dales, MA
T J Dessain, MMath, PhD
[Mrs H Evans, BA]
†J S Galdal-Gibbs, BA, BA
G W Grasso, MSci
Miss S L Hutchinson, MMath
M P Kwasigroch, BA, MSci, PhD
Mrs N S Levin, MA, MBA
Mrs M C Murphy, MA
Mrs J L Newton, BSc, MSc
Mrs H A Nicholls, BA
D J Noyce, MMath
N V Salvi, MA, MBA
M Scala, MSc, PhD

A F Strangeway, MMath, PhD
M P Streuli, MA, MBA
*D J Vaccaro, MA
J Wright, MMath
[Mrs L A Wright, MMath]

Modern Languages:
Mrs N Y Arnold, BA
Miss N Arosemena Manso, BA
Ms M R Bolster, BA, MA
S N Brunskill, BA
J A Brydon, BA, MSt, DPhil (**French*)
G D C Creagh, BA (**German*)
J E Flowers, BA
Mrs C C Hayes, L-ès-L (**French*)
S P Keeble, BA
Ms C E Lary, BA, MLitt
P A Munoz, BA (**Spanish*)
Mrs C B Pettitt, L-ès-L
Ms E M Roessler, BA
Mrs R J Russell, MA (**Russian*)
[F J Santaniello, L-ès-L]
Mrs Q W Wallis, BA (**Mandarin*)
Miss Y Wang, BA, MA
J A J Watts, BA (**Modern Languages*)

Music:
V J Barr, LRAM
A Cannière, BM, MM
R J Costin, BA, ARCM
G Hanson, BMus, LRAM, FRSM
Miss C D Harrison, BA
S J King, BMus
M A Noble, BMus, LRSM, ARCO
*J P Murphy, GRNCM
Miss E C Price, BMus, MA
Miss L S Stott, BA, MPhil, MMus

Politics:
R R X Miller, MA
S A Pullan, LLB, MA
*Mrs K B Shapiro, MA

Sport and Exercise:
Mrs S J Addicott-Clarke, BSc
Miss L Cripps, BSc
S Evans, BA

*C L M Henderson, BEd (*Co-Director of Sport and Exercise*)
J Humphrey (*Head of Football*)
Ms H L Millns, BSc
*Ms S Pride, BSc (*Co-Director of Sport and Exercise*)
Mrs L Sursok, BA
†A G Tapp, BEd

Religious Education and Philosophy:
C M Ajmone-Marsan, BMus, BA
S J H Bovey, BA
R N Davis, BA
*R Leigh, MA, MPhil, PhD
Ms D Saywack, MA, MA
[Miss E A Shipp, MA]
Miss P C Voute, BA, MA
Revd RSS Weir BA, Dip TH, MTh

Science:
W J Atkins, BA
†J T M Barr, MEng
Ms A M Blackmore, BSc
Dr C F Carter, MSc, PhD
A C Cheung, BA, MSci, PhD (**Physics*)
S R Crawford, BA, PhD (**Biology, *Science*)
Ms C L Cunningham, MPhys
I R Davies, MChem, PhD (**Chemistry*)
P Doyle, BSc
A C Dyson, MA
Mrs C A Gruer, BSc
Miss G V Gulliford, BSc
P Johnston, BSc, PhD
[Dr D Kuipers, BSc, MRes, PhD]
Ms W Y Li, MSci
†P A Liebman, BA
A C McBride, BA
Miss N Muhara, BSc, MSc
Miss E M Richardson, BSc
Miss C E Steers, MChem
Dr V E C Stubbs, BSc, PhD
A Z Szydlo, MSc, PhD
C J Tooze, MChem
[Dr V Vaccaro, BA, PhD]
Mrs J C Y Welch, BSc, MSc, PhD
B S Weston, BSc, PhD
W Whyatt, MPhys, PhD

Highgate Junior School
3 Bishopwood Road, London N6 4PL
Tel: 020 8340 9193; Fax: 020 8342 8225
email: jsoffice@highgateschool.org.uk

Principal of the Junior School: S M James, BA, MA
(*For further details, see entry in IAPS section.*)

Highgate Pre-Preparatory School
7 Bishopswood Road, London N6 4PH
Tel: 020 8340 9196; Fax: 020 8340 3442
email: pre-prep@highgateschool.org.uk

Principal: Mrs D Hecht, DCE

Hurstpierpoint College
A Woodard School

College Lane, Hurstpierpoint, West Sussex BN6 9JS

Tel: 01273 833636
Fax: 01273 835257
email: registrar@hppc.co.uk
website: www.hppc.co.uk
Twitter: @Hurst_College
Facebook: /HurstCollege

Motto: *Beati mundo corde*

Founded 1849 by Nathaniel Woodard, Canon of Manchester.

Hurstpierpoint College is a co-educational day and boarding school for boys and girls aged between 4 and 18 years. Pre-Prep, Prep and Senior Schools are linked by common values and a common academic and administrative framework, to provide a complete education. There are currently 406 boys and 332 girls. 51% of the pupils are boarders. The Preparatory School has a further 292 boys and girls and the Pre-Prep currently has 54 pupils.

The school is truly co-educational throughout and offers boarding for boys and girls in the Senior School. Boarding is a particularly popular option at the school with many day pupils and flexi-boarders later opting to become weekly boarders. In their Upper Sixth year at Hurst, pupils join St John's House, a co-educational day and boarding house where, appropriately supervised, they enjoy greater freedom and are encouraged to further develop their independent learning skills in preparation for university.

Buildings and Facilities. At the heart of the school's large country campus lie the core school buildings and Chapel arranged around three attractive quadrangles built of traditional Sussex knapped flint. Key facilities nearby include two floodlit Astroturfs, art school, sports hall, music school, dance and drama studios, 250-seat theatre, indoor swimming pool and Medical Centre. Other facilities include a new Library and fully-equipped IT Centre. The extensive grounds are laid mainly to playing fields and include one of the largest and most attractive school cricket pitches in the country.

Chapel. As a Woodard School, Hurstpierpoint is a Christian foundation and underpinned by Christian values, although pupils of other faiths or of no faith are warmly welcomed. Pupils attend up to three assemblies during the week. The main Eucharist, which parents and friends are most welcome to attend, takes place early on Friday evenings, although there are also occasional Sunday services in addition to voluntary celebrations of the Holy Communion. Pupils who wish to do so are prepared in small classes for the annual Confirmation taken by one of the Bishops of the diocese.

Curriculum. The five-day academic week is structured to allow boys and girls to study a variety of subject options that can be adapted to suit their natural ability. The entry year (Shell) gives pupils the chance to experience most of our GCSE subjects before they choose their options. It involves the study of English, History, Geography, French, Spanish, Latin, Ancient Greek, Mathematics, Physics, Chemistry, Biology, Religious Studies, Art, Design & Technology, Music, Drama, Physical Education and IT. In the second (Remove) and in the third (Fifth) years students study between 8 and 10 GCSE subjects. In addition to the core subjects there are five option blocks offering a choice of 17 subjects, including Ancient Greek, Applied Business and Dance.

Students entering the Lower Sixth study A Levels, with the majority studying four AS Levels in the Lower Sixth.

The choice is wide, with 28 AS subjects to choose from. Art, Business Studies, Classical Civilisation, Computing Science, Dance, Economics, Government and Politics, Further Maths, Music Technology, Photography, Philosophy of Religion, Psychology and Religious Ethics are introduced in addition to the GCSE options. There is also a General Studies programme. The Upper Sixth can take a varied programme with the most able studying four or five full A Levels, whilst others build a valuable qualifications portfolio by studying a varying number of AS subjects along with at least two full A Levels.

All pupils' work is overseen by academic tutors and we take particular care to ensure that university applications are properly targeted to suit the students' aspirations and talents.

Games. The School operates a "Sport for All" policy that seeks to place pupils in games most suited to their tastes and abilities. During the first two years they are expected to take part in at least some of the major sports but thereafter a greater element of choice occurs. The major sports are Rugby, Hockey, Cricket and Athletics for boys; Hockey, Netball, Athletics and Tennis for girls. Recent tours for major sports include Rugby (Italy), Netball (Barbados), Dubai (Cricket), South Africa (Hockey). In addition there are teams in Basketball, Cross Country, Football, Golf, Polo, Rounders, Shooting, Squash, Swimming, Triathlon, boys' Tennis, girls' Cricket and girls' Rugby. The Sports Hall and indoor Swimming Pool provide opportunities for many other pursuits such as Aerobics, Badminton, Equestrian, Fencing, Gymnastics, Power Walking, Weight Training and Water Polo, while the Outdoor Pursuits enable pupils to enjoy challenges such as Rock Climbing, Mountain Biking, Sailing, Kayaking and Canoeing.

Service Afternoons. On Wednesdays all pupils other than the Shell (Year 9) are expected to take part in The Duke of Edinburgh's Award activities alongside the Combined Cadet Force (Army, RN or RAF sections), Community Service or Environmental Conservation.

Music. There has always been a strong musical tradition at Hurstpierpoint with an orchestra and other more specialised ensembles. A large proportion of the pupils, currently 160, take individual instrumental lessons and give frequent recitals. The Chapel Choir plays a major part in regular worship and there are several other choral groups.

Drama. The Shakespeare Society is the oldest such school society in the country and organises an annual production and an annual musical. Drama covers a wide range and varies from major musicals to more modest House plays and pupil-directed productions. The 250-seat Bury Theatre also gives the more technically minded ample opportunity to develop stage management, lighting and sound skills.

Other Activities. The Thursday afternoon activity programme is for Shell and Remove pupils (Years 9 & 10) and includes Art, Climbing, Dance, Self-Defence, Car Maintenance, Girls' Football, Hurst Farm, Robotics, Japanese, LAMDA, Ningitsu, Shooting, Horse Riding, Polo, Karate, Golf Range, Squash, Clay Pigeon Shooting, Dinghy Sailing and Surfing alongside a variety of music clubs and literary clubs. Other activities also take place during the school week.

Hurst Johnian Club. In addition to providing facilities and events for Old Pupils, the Club also assists with careers and supports the current pupils in various ways, eg Gap Year travel fund and tour sponsorship contributions. Contact the Hon Secretary, c/o Hurstpierpoint College.

Fees per term (2016–2017). Senior School: Full Boarding: £10,425–£10,990; Weekly Boarding £9,320–£9,400; Flexi Boarding £8,745–£8,825; Day £7,395–£7,475.

Scholarships and Bursaries. Awards available at 13+: Academic, 'Hurst' All-Rounder, Art, Drama, Music and 'Downs' Sports. Please note that candidates entering for awards other than Academic are not eligible to apply for All-Rounder awards. Such candidates will be considered for

All-Rounder awards as part of their other applications. Awards available at 16+: Academic, Art, Drama, Music and 'Downs' Sports.

Academic Award examinations are held annually in May for 13+ candidates. Assessments for All-Rounder, Art, Drama and Sports Awards are held in February.

Music Award assessments are held in January of the year of entry for entrants to the Prep School and in February of the year of entry for entrants to the Senior School. Awards are offered with free musical tuition in two instruments. Informal auditions are encouraged and may be held at any time by arrangement with the Director of Music. The Awards are given subject to satisfactory Scholarship or Common Entrance results or the College's own entry tests.

Art Scholarships: A folio of work is presented and there is an objective test as well as an interview.

Assessment for Sixth Form awards takes place in November of the year prior to entry.

Means-tested bursaries may be available to supplement awards.

Admission. For 13+ entry, pupils must be registered on the School's list and will sit the Common ISEB Pre Test in Year 7. Offers are made subject to passing Common Entrance or Scholarship examinations. Entry from Hurst Prep school is by the College's own examinations. Entrants from maintained schools and from overseas undergo separate tests and interviews.

Places in the Sixth Form are available to students who achieve an A/A* grade at GCSE in the subjects (or, if a new subject, then in a subject closely related to it) that they intend to study for A Level. Students should also have a minimum of a C grade at GCSE in Mathematics and English.

Please contact the Senior School Admissions Office for further information.

Preparatory School. See entry in IAPS section.

Charitable status. Hurstpierpoint College is a Registered Charity, number 1076498. It aims to provide a Christian education to boys and girls between the ages of four and eighteen in the three schools on the campus.

School Council:
Chairman: Mr A Jarvis, BEd, MA, FRSA

Members:
Professor J P Bacon, MA, MSc, PhD
Dr S Brydie, MBBS, MD, MRCGP
Mr R P Dean
Mrs L J Corbett
Mr P M Dillon-Robinson, BAFCA, MBA
¶R J Ebdon, BSc, MAPM, MCIOB, FRSA
Mrs F M Hampton
The Revd J B A Joyce, BA, DipEd
Mrs K M Mack
Mr K S Powell FCA
¶Mr J P Ruddlesdin, FCA
¶Mr G A Rushton
Mrs S M Shaw
¶Mr G J Taysom, BSc, FRSA

Headmaster: Mr T J Manly, BA Oriel College Oxon, MSc LSE

Deputy Head Pastoral: Mrs C E Jacques, BSc Southampton
Deputy Head Co-Curricular: Mr T F Q Leeper, BSc Edinburgh, CBiol, MIBiol
Deputy Head Academic: Mr L P Dannatt, MEng Imperial College London
Head of Senior School: Mr D W Mott, MA Queens' College Cantab
Head of Prep School: Mr I D Pattison, BSc Southampton

Director of Academic Administration: Mrs K J Austin, BSc Edinburgh, CChem FRSC CSci
Director of Operational Technology: Mr D M Higgins, BA, Cert Ed Loughborough
Director of Professional Development and Performance: Mrs M Zeidler, BEd Homerton College Cantab, MEd OU
Director of Pastoral Care and Boarding, i/c Head of Careers: Mrs J Leeper, BA University College London
Prep School Deputy Head: Mr N J Oakden, BA Wales, NPQH, MEd Buckingham
Bursar: Mr S A Holliday, BSc, ACIB, MAPM

Directors:
Mr Liam J Agate, BA Sidney Sussex College, Cantab (*Director of Academic Development*)
Mr Robert J Ashley, BA Manchester, MA Melbourne (*Director of Learner Development*)
Mrs Keramy J Austin, BSc Edinburgh, CChem, FRSC, CSci (*Director of Academic Administration*)
Mr Nicholas D D Beeby, BA Roehampton London, LGSMD (*Director of Drama*)
Mrs Kate V Doehren, BEd Sussex, RSA DipSpLD (*Director of Learning Support*)
Mr Dan M Higgins, BA, Cert Ed Loughborough (*Director of Operational Technology*)
Mr Rob M Kift, BEd Madeley College of PE (*Director of Sport*)
Mrs Jan Leeper, BA University College London (*Director of Pastoral Care and Boarding, i/c Head of Careers*)
Mr Neil Matthews, BA St John's College Durham (*Director of Music*)
Mrs Sarah Miles, BEd Nottingham Trent (*Director of PSHCEE*)
Mr Fred Simkins, GCGI, CVQO Surrey (*Director of Outdoor Education*)
Mrs Debbie K Stoneley, BEd London (*Director of Safeguarding*)
Mrs Michelle Zeidler, BEd Homerton College Cantab, MEd OU (*Director of Professional Development and Performance*)

Housemasters/Housemistresses:
Mr Nicholas D D Beeby, BA Roehampton London, LGSMD (*Housemaster – St John's*)
Mr Nick Creed, BSc UWIC (*Housemaster – Crescent*)
Miss Nicola C Dominy, BA Surrey (*Housemistress – Shield*)
Mr Chris J Eustace, MA Queens' College Cantab (*Housemaster – Eagle*)
Miss Tania C Fielden, BA Brighton (*Housemistress – Pelican*)
Mrs Helena E Higgins, BA, Cert Ed Loughborough (*Housemistress – Phoenix*)
Mr Adam J Hopcroft, MEng Bath (*Housemaster – Red Cross*)
Mrs Sarah Hyman, BA Lancaster (*Housemistress – Fleur*)
Mr Mike J Lamb, BSc Nottingham (*Housemaster – Chevron*)
Mrs Kathren Lea, BSc Brighton (*Housemistress – Martlet*)
Mrs Rebecca J Scott, BA Brighton (*Housemistress – St John's*)
Mr Rob Shearman, BSc Brighton, MSc Aberdeen (*Housemaster – Star*)
Mr Andrew J Smith, BA Warwick, MA Royal Holloway London (*Housemaster – Woodard*)

Heads of Years:
Shell: Mr D E Parry, MA Edinburgh
Remove: Miss A L Taylor, BSc Leeds
Fifth Form: Mr O J J Gospel, BEng Liverpool
Sixth Form: Mr B T Schofield, BA Pembroke College Oxon

Teaching Staff – Heads of Department:

Art: Mrs J N West, BA Nottingham Trent
Business Studies: Mr S C Bale, BSc Warwick
Classics: Miss K S E Barker, MA Exeter College Oxon
Dance: Miss N C Dominy, BA Surrey
Design Technology: Mr K D K MacDonald, BA Brunel
Drama:
Mr N D D Beeby, BA Roehampton London, LGSMD
  (*Director of Drama*)
Mr A J Smith, BA Warwick, MA Royal Holloway London
  (*Head of Academic Drama*)
Economics: Mrs J S Jedamzik, BA, MA Sussex
English: Mrs S N M Watson-Saunders, BA Surrey, MA
  OU
ESL: Mrs K L B Goddard, MA The Queen's College Oxon
Geography: Mr R J Ashley, BA Manchester, MA
  Melbourne
Government & Politics: Mr W G D Bradley, BA Essex
History: Miss J C Clarke, BA Edinburgh
IT/Computing:
Mr R J S Cooke, BSc Hatfield College Durham (*Head of
  IT*)
Mr S J Crook, BSc East Anglia (*Head of Computing*)
Learning Support: Mrs K V Doehren, BEd Sussex, RSA
  Dip SpLD (*Director of Learning Support*)
Modern Foreign Languages:
French: Mr D J Wickenden, BA, MSc, Birkbeck
Spanish: Ms E M Paull, MA Gonville & Caius College
  Cantab, MSc Bristol
German: Mrs J B Smith, MA King's College Cantab
Mathematics: Mrs L J Mackinder, BSc Nottingham
Music:
Mr N Matthews, BA St John's College Durham (*Director
  of Music*)
Mr D Jameson, GTCL Trinity College of Music, MA York,
  LRSM, LTCL (*Head of Academic Music & Music
  Technology*)
PE & Sports Science: Mr S J May, BSc Chichester
Psychology: Mr S P Poole, BEd Exeter, CBiol, MIBiol,
  MBA Ed Man Leicester
Philosophy and Theology: Mr J W Cherry, BA, MPhil
  Magdalene College Cantab
Science:
Mr A G Daville, MA Lady Margaret Hall Oxon (*Head of
  Faculty*)
Physics: Mr A G Daville, MA Lady Margaret Hall Oxon
Biology: Mrs N Coxon, BSc Durham
Chemistry: Mrs S Crickmore, MA Newnham College
  Cantab
Enrichment: Mr L J Agate, BA Sidney Sussex College
  Cantab
Library: Ms D B Collins, MA UCL
Sport: Mr R M Kift, BEd Madeley College of PE (*Director
  of Sport*)

Head of Admissions: Mrs D S Allison

Hutchesons' Grammar School

21 Beaton Road, Glasgow G41 4NW

Tel: 0141 423 2933
Fax: 0141 424 0251
email: rector@hutchesons.org
website: www.hutchesons.org
Twitter: @hutchesons
Facebook: /HutchesonsGrammar

Motto: *Veritas*.

Founded in the 17th Century and endowed by the brothers George and Thomas Hutcheson (Deed of Mortification 1641). The School is governed by Hutchesons' Educational Trust.

Hutchesons' Grammar School is a recognised Glasgow institution, which has been synonymous with excellence in education for over 350 years.

The modern School, spread over two well-provisioned campuses in the city's Southside, is a dynamic place of tremendous vitality and diversity which merges tradition and positive values with cutting-edge educational innovation. There is a sustained and historical commitment to understanding the needs of bright children, from all backgrounds, and to help them push the limits of what they can achieve.

At Hutchesons', from P1 to S6, the curriculum is broader and more flexible, the list of subject specialisms is wider, and the pace is faster than in most other schools – but that's what suits Hutchesonians! The School attracts great teachers, because it's something of a privilege to be part of such a vibrant, well-resourced learning community, where new opportunities just keep arising.

Hutchesons' results (which are freely available online) are consistently among the best in the country. 66% of Higher entries at Hutchesons' were awarded A grade in the last session. You shouldn't be surprised to learn that Hutchesons' pupils excel at music, drama and sport as well. Intelligent children enjoy new challenges and they have opportunities here to find things that excite and motivate them, amongst others who'll share their enthusiasms.

First-class facilities offer more opportunities for individual development. The Primary is now home to a new purpose-built infant playground and stunning outdoor classroom. At the Secondary the curtain rose on a purpose-built, state-of-the-art, Drama Studio in 2012 which houses an adaptable theatre, specialised practice studios and a cutting-edge lighting and technical gallery. The Alix Jamieson Stadium, another world-class facility, provides an arena for sporting achievement with a contemporary floodlit Hockey pitch and international-standard Athletics track.

At Hutchesons' research is regarded as a lifelong and life-enhancing activity that develops an individual's intellectual, personal, academic and professional success. Unique to the School is the Hutchesons' Centre for Research, a community for scholars producing innovative research projects and promoting collaboration between Hutchesons' and the academic community.

At every level the key values of honesty, resilience, independence, creativity, curiosity and compassion are instilled in pupils, preparing them for university and future success. Generations of former pupils retain a strong sense of community with their old School, affectionately known as 'Hutchie', and share the belief that making the most of your intelligence alongside others like you is, ultimately, life changing.

Admissions. Pupils are normally admitted on interview at age 4/5 and by examination at age 9/10 to the Primary School or at age 11/12 to the Secondary School, but applications for vacancies at other stages are welcomed. New pupils normally start at the beginning of the academic year, but intermediate entries are possible from time to time where circumstances dictate. Please call our Admissions Registrar, Aileen Burns, for a chat on 0141 433 4402 or email admissions@hutchesons.org to arrange a personal tour and meet current pupils and staff.

Fees per term (2016–2017). Primary £3,032.67–£3,481.67. Secondary 1–2 £3,858. Secondary 3–6 £3,768. All fees from Primary 1 to Secondary 2 include books.

Financial Assistance. The School offers financially means-tested bursaries by competitive entry for entry to S1.

Religion. The School is non-denominational, but many pupils opt to attend regular Christian, Muslim and Jewish assemblies. The School also hosts interfaith events and Religious Studies are taught in S1 and S2.

Curriculum. We aim to provide a happy, purposeful environment for the academic, social and emotional development of all pupils at Hutchesons'. The foundation for excellence starts at Primary 1 with a tailored and comprehensive curriculum.

Even the youngest pupils benefit from specialist teaching in Art, Music and Physical Education. A range of Modern Languages is introduced from Primary 4. These, combined with Latin in Primary 6 and 7, provide an excellent grounding for the study of English and Modern Languages in the transition to Secondary School. In addition the Primary has an ICT specialist and a full-time librarian, rare assets in junior education.

At every stage the formal curriculum is enriched by a varied programme of educational visits, guest speakers and workshop activities. A natural passion for discovery and love of learning is carefully nurtured creating a strong platform for academic success at the Secondary school.

S1 Compulsory Subjects: Art, Biology, Chemistry, Drama, English, Geography, History, Computing, Latin, Mathematics, Modern Language, Music, Physics, Religious Education, *Personal and Social Education, *PE/Games. (*Non-examined subjects)

At the beginning of S1, pupils will choose a Modern Language from French, German or Spanish on which to focus in S1 and S2. In general, pupils are prepared for universities and higher education, including Oxbridge. They are given vocational and pastoral guidance throughout the Secondary School.

S2 Compulsory Subjects: Art, Biology, Chemistry, Drama, English, Geography, History, Computing, Latin, Mathematics, Modern Language, Modern Studies, Music, Physics, Product Design and Marketing, Personal and Social Education, *PE/Games, RMPS. (*Non-examined subjects)

S3/S4 Compulsory Subjects: English, Mathematics and a Modern or Classical Language. A broad and balanced choice of other subjects from Science, Social Science and the Humanities is appropriate at this stage. In addition, all pupils take Personal and Social Education and PE/Games. Option/Subject Choice forms change from year to year. Twilight Courses in Art, Computing Studies, Engineering Science, Classical Studies, Greek, Latin, Graphic Communication and Music are also offered.

S5 Compulsory Subjects: English, Games, PSE. Apart from PSE and Games, at least five subjects and up to six Highers may be taken in S5. Subject choice forms again change from year to year.

S6: Pupils are expected to follow a challenging and rewarding individual programme of study. The year can include Advanced Higher and Higher courses as well as other levels of study and there is a full S6 Prospectus available.

Ethos & Values. The Hutchie ethos encourages compassion, respect, honesty, tolerance and responsibility. Hard work, creativity and independence are celebrated and pupils aim high in both in co-curricular and academic endeavours.

As individuals, Hutchesons' pupils are encouraged to develop qualities based on our core values:

- Honesty
- Resilience
- Independence
- Curiosity
- Creativity
- Compassion

Your children will be encouraged to mature into thoughtful, articulate and well-read young adults with clear self-direction and the motivation to realise their ambitions beyond school and university.

Pupil Council, Drama and Sport calendars offer the chance to support and participate. The School hosts many environment and charity initiatives and is currently fundraising for The Prince and Princess of Wales Hospice.

Pupils run their own Amnesty Group and support Scottish Refugee Week. There is also an established set of campaigning 'J8 groups' who tackle inequality and world issues.

Sport. Pupils can enjoy a wide range of competitive activities including cricket, football, netball, athletics, rowing, tennis, golf and cross-country. Curling, volleyball, badminton, aerobics and rock climbing are other alternatives. Our teams compete with the nation's best and many Hutchesonians enjoy sport to a very high level. Pupils are regularly selected to represent both District and National teams. There is also the opportunity for international travel with recent sport tours to Barcelona and South Africa.

The excellent facilities at the Secondary School include the Sports Hall and a fantastic athletics arena. There are also excellent playing fields at Auldhouse and we use the adjacent Clydesdale Cricket Club and Titwood Tennis Club.

Trips & Tours. There are a great number of tours and academic excursions per year. Recent destinations include Morocco, Belgium, Spain, Italy, the Swiss mountains, the European Parliament and Everest Base Camp. There is a rewarding partnership with a school In India and growing links to Australia, Tanzania and the USA. There are cultural trips to China and Russia and to our partner schools in Nuremberg, Germany, and Radomsko, Poland. Pupils take part in Model UN Conferences and outward bound expeditions offer the chance to kayak, canoe and sail for Silver and Gold Duke of Edinburgh's Award.

Activities, Clubs & Societies. The rich mix of drama, musical productions, sport and many extra-curricular activities enriches the more formal areas of the curriculum, providing all pupils with the confidence and skills to move on to the next stage of their educational careers. There are many co-curricular activities available to pupils throughout their time at Hutchesons', including Art, Archaeology, Chess, Chemistry, Climbing, Creative Writing, Bridge, Debating, Model United Nations, J8, Photography, Film and Scripture Union. Sports include Hockey, Rugby, Table Tennis, Volleyball, Basketball, Netball, Kickboxing and Running, while Drama and Music offer various clubs, choirs, Ceilidh Band, Orchestra, Wind Band and Guitar Ensemble. A major highlight is the end-of-session Senior Show, a joint Music and Drama production involving up to 100 pupils on stage, in the orchestra and backstage. More than 500 pupils receive specialist instrumental and vocal tuition. There is also a very strong tradition of fundraising for charity, community service, Young Enterprise and The Duke of Edinburgh's Award. School pupils publish the School Annual, "The Hutchesonian", every June.

Charitable status. Hutchesons' Educational Trust is a Registered Charity, number SC002922.

Governors:
Not more than 17 in number.

Representatives of the following Bodies:
Glasgow Presbytery of the Church of Scotland (2), Senatus Academicus of Glasgow University (1), Merchants' House of Glasgow (1), Trades House of Glasgow (1), Patrons of Hutchesons' Hospital (2), Glasgow Educational Trust (1), Senate of the University of Strathclyde (1), FP Club (1), School Association (1) and not more than 9 persons co-opted by the Governors.

Chairman: Prof Brian Williams, CBE, MD, Hon DSc, FRCP, FRCS

Rector: Mr Colin Gambles, BSc

Senior Depute Rector: Mr M Martin, BSc Hons

Bursar: Mr I T Keter, BA, CA

Depute Rectors (Secondary School):
Mr C Bagnall, MA, MA
Mr D G Campbell, MA Hons, MEd Hons, MSc
Mrs G Fergusson, MA, MEd
Mr J McDougall, MA Hons

Depute Rectors (Primary School):
Miss F Macphail, BA Edinburgh, MBA
Miss H Gibson, BEd
Mrs A Wilson, BSc Hons, PGCE

Heads of Departments:
Art: Mrs S Breckenridge, BA Hons
Biology: Mr A Kerr, BSc Hons
Chemistry: Mr P H B Uprichard, BSc Hons
Classics: Mrs E Carey, MA Hons, BA
Drama: Mrs V Alderson, DipSD
Economics & Business Studies: Mrs C Keddie, BA Hons
English: Mr M J Symington, MA Hons
Geography: Mrs Elaine Prentice, BSc Hons
History: Mrs M Windows, BA Hons
ICT: Ms R Housley, BSc Hons, DipCompEd
Law: Miss R Hems, MA, MEd
Mathematics: Mr A Eadie, BSc Hons
Modern Languages: Mrs E M Bertram, MA Hons
Modern Studies: Mr G F Broadhurst, BA Hons
Music – Curriculum: Mr E W M Trotter, BMus Hons
Music – Performance: Mr K D Walton, BMus Hons
Philosophy: Dr P Tonner, MA Hons, MA, PhD
Physical Education:
Director of Sport: Mr S Lang, BEd Hons
Head of Boys' PE: Mr R Dewar, BEd Hons
Head of Girls' PE: Mrs K Robertson, BSc Hons
Head of Girls' Hockey: Mrs Gillian Green, BEd Hons
Physics: Dr S Lonie, BSc Hons, MSc, PhD
Psychology: Mr J Firth, MA Hons
Religious Studies: Mr S J Branford, MA Hons
Technology: Mr C McCormick, BTechEd Hons

Rector's Secretary & Admissions: Mrs S Burrowes and Mrs A Burns
Development Manager: Mrs C Biggart
Communications & Marketing Manager: Mrs C Biggart

Hymers College

Hymers Avenue, Hull, East Yorkshire HU3 1LW
Tel: 01482 343555
Fax: 01482 472854
email: enquiries@hymers.org
website: www.hymerscollege.co.uk
Twitter: @Hymers_College
Facebook: /HymersCollege

Hymers College in Hull was opened as a school for boys in 1893, when the Reverend John Hymers, Fellow of St John's College, Cambridge, and Rector of Brandesburton, left money in his Will, for a school to be built 'for the training of intelligence in whatever social rank of life it may be found among the vast and varied population of the town and port of Hull'. Although the school has remained true to its Founder's intentions, the catchment area now stretches across East Yorkshire and North Lincolnshire and the school became fully co-educational in 1989.

Number of Pupils. 972.

The Junior School has 198 pupils aged 8–11. There is a full range of academic, sporting, music and extra-curricular activities.

The Senior School has 537 pupils in Years 7–11 and the Sixth Form has 237 pupils.

Admission is by competitive examination at ages 8, 9 and 11, together with an interview with the Headteacher. Most pupils proceed at age eleven into the Senior School by an examination taken also by pupils from other schools. Almost all pupils qualify for the Sixth Form through GCSE results. Pupils from other schools are admitted to the Sixth Form on the basis of good GCSE results and interview with the Headmaster.

Pupils are prepared for the GCSE in a broad curriculum including music, business-related subjects, computer studies, technology and the arts.

There is a full range of courses leading to AS and Advanced Level examinations, and special preparation is given for Oxford and Cambridge entrance.

Facilities. The buildings consist of 35 classrooms, 11 specialist laboratories, a 30-booth language laboratory, extensive ICT facilities, audio-visual room, art rooms, theatre, Art/Design Technology Centre, a gymnasium and very large sports hall. A new Music Block opened in September 2014 providing a full range of music facilities including a Recital Hall, Rehearsal and Music Technology Rooms and a Recording Studio. A new Learning Resource Centre is under construction for completion in December. The Junior School building contains 9 classrooms and specialist rooms for music, DT, art, ICT and science, along with a library, hall and changing rooms. The grounds, which extend for over 40 acres, include an all-weather hockey pitch, 12 tennis courts and a swimming pool/sports centre.

Extracurricular Activities. All pupils are strongly encouraged to participate in the very wide range of extracurricular activities. The main school games are rugby, cricket, hockey, netball, tennis and athletics. There are also school teams in swimming and fencing. The school regularly competes at national level in these sports and provides members of county and national teams. Many pupils take part in The Duke of Edinburgh's Award scheme and the school has an impressive track record in Young Enterprise. Other clubs include ACF, chess, debating, photography, community service and journalism. Drama is particularly strong, with several productions a year. Music is a major school activity; there are three full orchestras, a large choir, and several chamber groups in each part of the school. Individual tuition is available in most instruments.

Fees per term (2016–2017). (including textbooks) Senior School £3,534; Junior School £2,943–£3,108. Hymers Bursaries are awarded at ages 8, 9, 11 and 16.

The Old Hymerians Association, c/o Alumni Relations Manager, Hymers College, Hull HU3 1LW.

Charitable status. Hymers College is a Registered Charity, number 529820-R. Its aims and objectives are education.

Governors:
Chairman: M de-V Roberts, FCA
Vice Chairman: District Judge P J E Wildsmith, LLB
J R Wheldon, LLB, MRICS, ACI ArB
Mrs B E Elliott, MSc, BN, RGN, RSCN, RHV, NNDNCert
Mrs G A Greendale
J G Robinson, BA
D J Stone, BA
M C S Hall, BSc
P A B Beecroft, MA, MBA
Mrs T A Carruthers, RGN
D A Gibbons, BSc, MRICS
C M Read, MRICS
J M V Redman, BSc, FIDM, MIOD
W H Gore, BSc, MSc, PhD, ACA
Prof P G Burgess, MA, PhD, FRHistS
Dr A Pathak, MBBS, MAMS
Mrs J Lloyd, MSc, FCIPD
Mr J G Leafe
Mrs N Shipley, FCA

Mrs G V Vickerman, BSc, MSc, MRICS

Headmaster: D C Elstone, MA Ed Mgt

Deputy Head (Management): A N Holman, MA Cantab
Deputy Head (Pastoral): Mrs H Jackson

Head of Junior School: P C Doyle, BSc

Teachers:
* Head of Department

Mrs M Armstrong
Miss N Batch (*Geography*)
Dr R Bennett, BSc Hons
R Bird
R Burrell
Mrs J M Brown, BA (*Art*)
A D Cadle, BSc
Mrs C Cook, BA
P Cook, BA (*ICT*)
A Copeland
Mrs C Copeland, BSc
M Couzin
Dr J Denton, MA (*History & Politics*)
P C Doyle, BSc
Mrs J I Duffield, BA
Mrs R Elstone, MA (*English*)
Miss R England
Mrs A Exley, BA
N Exley, BA
Mrs T Ferguson
Mrs J Fillingham
S R Fincham, MSc
A Garmston
C Gaynor-Smith, BA (*Sixth Form*, *RE*)
Mrs Z L Gillett, BSc
Mrs H Griffith
L Griffiths-Bartlett
G R Hambleton, BA
D Harrison, MA
Mrs H L Harrison, BA
D Hickman, BSc
Mrs S Hickman, BA
M Hodston
A Holman
Mrs S Holman
Mrs M Humblet
A Irving, BA
Mrs H Jackson, BSc
Dr S Jardine
Dr J M Jarvis, BSc
A Z Javed, MSc
Ms W Johnston (*Sport*)
Mrs B Lewis
J Lucas
P Lusvardi
Dr J Martin
Mrs C McDonough-Bradley, BSc
Ms N McLeod (*Drama*)
S McLoughlin
D McPherson, BA (*Latin*)
M McTeare, BA
P Meadway, BSc
D Mills, BEd (*Design Technology*)
W Murray (*Head of Hockey*)
J Mutter (*Business Studies & Economics*)
Mrs K R Oatridge, MChem
G Oglesby
R O'Hara, BSc
A Pailing
Miss T Parker
Miss M Pearson

A Penny, GRNCM, ARNCM
Dr M J Pickles, MEng, ACGI, PhD
Mrs A J Powell
G Prescott, MA (*Chemistry*)
Dr R Pybus, BSc Hons, MRSC
R Quick, ALCM, ARCM
A Raspin, BSc
Mrs T Redhead
Mrs M Riley
Mrs F Rix, BA Hons
Mrs L L Roberts, MSc
P J Roberts, MA (*Biology*)
I R Sanderson, MA Cantab
A Sanz-Caro (*Modern Languages/Spanish*)
C Setterington
R Shaw
J Shepherd
R Simpson
Mrs S E Sinkler, BPharm
B D Skirving (*Head of Rugby*)
Dr A H Smith
A Stirk
R J Summers, BSc
E Tame, MMath (*Mathematics*)
J Tapley
N A Taylor, BA
D Thompson, BSc
D Thompson
G Tipping
Mrs L Turner (*Music*)
Mrs L A Walmsley, BA
S J Walmsley, BA (*PE*)
A Whittaker, BA
Ms J Willan, MA Hons
Mrs C Wogan, BA
Mrs K Wylde
B J Young (*Physics*)
Mrs R Young

Immanuel College

Elstree Road, Bushey, Hertfordshire WD23 4EB

Tel: 020 8950 0604
Fax: 020 8950 8687
email: enquiries@immanuel.herts.sch.uk
website: www.immanuelcollege.co.uk

Motto: *Torah im Derech Eretz* (Jewish learning leading to secular success)

Immanuel College is a selective, co-educational day school founded in 1990 by the late Chief Rabbi, Lord Jakobovits to fulfil his vision of a school affirming orthodox Jewish values and practice in the context of rigorous secular studies. The College aims at giving its pupils a first-class education that encourages them to connect Jewish and secular wisdom, to think independently and to exercise responsibility. Its ethos is characterised by attentiveness to individual pupils' progress, high academic achievement and the integration of Jewish and secular learning. There are both Jewish and non-Jewish teachers at the school, the common element being enthusiasm for their work and concern for their pupils. In 2016 Immanuel College was ranked 34 in the Daily Telegraph Independent Schools' league table.

Age Range. 4–10 and 11–18. The Preparatory School opened in September 2011 and now includes Reception to Year 6 classes.

School Roll. There are 632 pupils on roll, of whom 286 are girls and 346 are boys. There are 128 pupils in the Sixth Form.

Buildings and Grounds. The College is situated in a tranquil 11-acre site dominated by Caldecote Towers, a Grade II listed 19th-century mansion. Facilities include the Joyce King Theatre, two suites of science laboratories, a fitness suite, a large all-weather surface for tennis and netball, cricket and football pitches, and grounds for field events and athletics. Professor Lord Winston opened a new multi-functional 8-classroom building in September 2010, and a further building for an enhanced Jewish Learning facility (Atar-Zwillenberg Beit K'nesset), additional classrooms and state-of-the-art laboratories was opened in November 2014 by Chief Rabbi Ephram Mervis.

Admission (Senior School). Most boys and girls enter in September, though pupils are accepted in all three terms. Admission into the Senior School is on the basis of performance in the College's entrance examination and interview. The principal entry is at 11+, but the school considers pupils for admission at any point. A number of boys and girls join the College in the Sixth Form; offers of places are gained by interview and are conditional upon GCSE results and suitability for A Level courses.

Admission (Preparatory School). Admission into Reception and Year 1 is on the basis of informal assessment consisting of a play session and a focus activity. For Year 2 there is a short Mathematics activity and a reading/writing task.

Fees per term (2016–2017). Senior School: £5,500; Lunch £295. Preparatory School: £3,130; Lunch £200.

Scholarships and Bursaries. Immanuel Jakobovits, Academic, Jewish Studies and Science Scholarships are awarded on a competitive basis to outstanding 11+ entrants. Exhibitions to the value of £2,000 per annum are awarded to pupils who show exceptional promise in Art and Music. Means-tested bursaries are awarded to a number of boys and girls from less affluent families who are academically and personally suited to the education the College provides.

Curriculum. The articles of the College's faith are that Jewish and secular learning shed light on one another, that the appreciation of each is deepened by study of the other, and that the life of the mind and spirit should not be compartmentalised but holistic. As such, the school offers a wide range of secular subjects, including English, Mathematics, Further Mathematics, Computing, Electronics and the Sciences, as well as Art and Design, Photography, Drama, Geography, History, French, Spanish, Music, Personal, Social and Health Education and Physical Education. At A Level, additional subjects include Economics, Government & Politics, Media Studies and Psychology. Throughout a pupil's time at Immanuel, Jewish Studies forms part of the core curriculum. Jewish ethics, philosophy, history and religion and Israel Education are studied by way of close textual learning and through guest speakers and seminars, developing *Chochma* (wisdom) and well-founded Jewish identities. All members of the College have informal and formal opportunities to deepen their understanding of Jewish faith and practice with team members from the school's Jewish Study Centre, the Beit.

Pastoral Care. The College prides itself on attentiveness to the needs of individual pupils. The Pastoral Team includes Form Tutors and Heads of Section, who in Years 7 to 11 work under the direction of the Deputy Head for Pastoral Education and Pupil Progress. The Director of Sixth Form is in charge of a team of Form Tutors. Parental consultation evenings take place regularly. The School Council, which meets fortnightly with the Deputy Head for Pastoral Education and Pupil Progress, gives pupils the opportunity to express their views and make suggestions about further improving school life.

Religious Life. The College commemorates and celebrates landmarks in the Jewish and Israel calendar such as Purim, Chanukah, Succot and Yom Ha'atzmaut. Each January, on Holocaust Memorial Day, Lower Sixth Form students share the knowledge and insights that they have gained on their trip to Poland with pupils in the first five years of the Senior School. The College also commemorates Yom Hazikaron. Pupils attend morning and afternoon prayers on a daily basis.

The **Inclusion and Learning Support Department** supports teachers to help pupils become independent and successful learners. In addition to the programme followed by all pupils, the Department provides a range of tailored programmes to pupils whose learning needs are more specific. Pupils with a variety of learning profiles are thereby helped to develop confidence and to exceed their predictions and reach their potential.

Art, Music and Drama. The College enjoys a tradition of excellence in the visual arts (the annual Gottlieb Art Show being the highlight of the artistic year) and drama (recent school productions have included *Macbeth, An Inspector Calls, The Happiest Days of Your Life, Pygmalion, The Trojan Women, Twelfth Night and Oliver*). There is a yearly Music Festival and the calendar includes a number of concerts and recitals involving soloists, ensembles and orchestra.

Games. The PE and Games staff involve pupils in activities that range from aerobics, golf, and trampolining to athletics, cricket, football, hockey, table tennis, netball, badminton and tennis. Over twenty sports clubs meet weekly. Physical Education may be studied for GCSE and A Level. Sports facilities include an all-weather surface and a fitness suite. The College has won trophies in many sporting competitions.

Enrichment activities. The many co-curricular activities on offer include opportunities for pupils to participate in leadership programmes, volunteering schemes, The Duke of Edinburgh's Award, public speaking, debating competitions and Young Enterprise. There are also clubs in areas such as philosophy, chess, art, science and modern European languages.

Educational Journeys. In Year 7 pupils visit Amsterdam; in Year 8 they visit Paris; in Year 9 they spend three and half weeks in Israel; in Year 10 they visit Strasbourg and Madrid; and in the Lower Sixth they spend eight days in Poland. These experiences encourage pupils to understand themselves, bond with one another and comprehend the forces that have shaped contemporary Jewry. Photography students benefit from trips to foreign locations of great natural beauty.

Careers. The guidance provided by the College supports pupils in their research about choices beyond Immanuel. Through assemblies, the lower years are encouraged to start thinking about their own strengths and weaknesses and likes and dislikes which lead to discussions about future pathways. Even at this stage, any experience in the labour market is encouraged and supported. By the time GCSE subject choices need to be made, pupils are aware of the wider world around them and are closely monitored throughout the process. During Year 10 and Year 11, pupils make use of the weekly CEIAG Clinic, where they often collect information about relevant courses, one-day events and other opportunities to engage directly with people from specific areas of work. Year 11 pupils may also undertake testing for the Morrisby Profile and this, along with a personal interview after mock examinations, helps pupils and their parents to feel confident about making the right A Level choices. Pupils continue to enrol in career-specific courses and events throughout the Sixth Form, and all are welcomed to our Careers Fair.

Charitable status. Immanuel College is a Registered Charity, number 803179. It exists to combine academic excellence and Jewish tradition in a contemporary society.

Board of Governors:
Mr Edward Misrahi, BA Econ Hons (*Co-Chairman*)
Professor Anthony Warrens, DM Oxon, PhD, FRCP, FRCPath, FEBS, FHEA (*Co-Chairman*)
Mr Richard Werth, BSc Hons, ACA (*Vice Chairman*)
Mrs Valerie Eppel, BA Econ Hons, ACA (*Treasurer*)
Mrs Erica Marks, BA Comb Hons, MBA (*Compliance*)
Mrs Annette Koslover, LLB (*Designated Child Protection Governor*)
Mrs Lynda Dullop, BA Hons (*Director of Admissions, Parental Liaison, Fundraising & PR*)
Mrs Michelle Sint, MA (*Jewish Life & Learning*)
Mrs Ruth Hoyland, BSc Hons (*Immanuel College Preparatory School*)
Mr Tim Isaacs, BSc Econ Hons, ACA
Mr Henry Clinton-Davis, BA Hons Cantab, Dip Law
Rabbi Eliezer Zobin, MA

Rabbinic Advisor: Dayan Ivan Binstock, BSc

Clerk to the Governors: Mr Martin Blain, MA Cantab, NPQH (*Interim Chief Operating Officer*)

Head Master: Mr Charles Dormer, MA Cantab

Deputy Head – Pastoral Care and Pupil Progress: Mrs Beth Kerr, BSc

Deputy Head – Jewish Life and Learning: Rabbi David Riffkin, BA, MA

Senior Leadership Team:
Mr Paul Abrahams, BA (*Assistant Head – Operations & Examinations*)
Mr Martin Blain, MA Cantab, NPQH (*Interim Chief Operating Officer*)
Mr Richard Felsenstein, BA (*Assistant Head – Community & Communication*)
Mrs Jo Fleet, BA (*Assistant Head – Personalisation, Transition {13–17} and Guidance*)
Mrs Alexis Gaffin, BEd Hons Cantab (*Head of Immanuel College Preparatory School*)
Mr Lee Rich, BA (*Assistant Head – Teaching Quality and Pupil Learning*)
Mrs Sharron Shackell, BA (*Assistant Head – Director of Sixth Form Studies*)
Rabbi Eliezer Zobin, MA (*Rosh Beit HaMedrash*)

Heads of Department:

Art (*Fine Art*): Mrs Alison Ardeman, BA

Art (*Photography*): Ms Neha Vadera, BA

Business and Economics:
Mr Ben Freedman, BSc
Mr Mark Gavin, BA, MA

Electronics: Ms Kirsti Cullen, BSc

English: Mr Gordon Spitz, BA, MA

Geography: Mrs Anna Blain, BA, MA

Higher Education: Ms Natalie Lancer, MA Oxon, MA Director of Special Projects and Higher Education

History, Government and Politics: Mr Geordie Raine, MA, BA, BEd

Computing: Mr Mario Brzezinski, BSc (*Senior Teacher*)

Jewish Education: Mr Danny Baigel, BA

Head of Beit HaMedrash: Rabbi Eliezer Zobin, MA

Learning Support Department: Mrs Janine Lewinton, BA Hons

Library and Independent Learning: Mr Alex Coope, MA

Mathematics: Ms Kalpana Patel, BA, MBA

Media Studies: Mr Jonathan Meier, MA Oxon

Modern Foreign Languages: Mrs Nicola Fahidi, BA

Performing Arts:
Mrs Sara Green, BA (*Head of Drama*)
Mr Stephen Levey, LLB (*Head of Music*)

Physical Education: Mr Philip Monaghan, BA

Psychology: Mrs Helen Stephenson-Yankuba, BSc

Science: Mr Felix Posner, BSc (*Assistant Director of Studies – Timetable and Curriculum*)

Heads of School:
Mr Richard Felsenstein, BA (*Assistant Head – Community & Communication, Joint Head of Year 7*)
Miss Susan Ribeiro, BA (*Deputy Head of Art, Joint Head of Year 7*)
Mrs Deborah Unsdorfer, BSc (*Head of Lower School Jewish Studies*)
Ms Naomi Amdurer, BA (*Head of Middle School, Head of Charity & Social Action*)
Mrs Anne Pattinson, BA (*Assistant Head of English, Head of Upper School*)

Safeguarding and Child Protection:
Mrs Beth Kerr, BSc (*Deputy Head – Pastoral Care & Pupil Progress, Designated Senior Person in Charge of Child Protection*)
Mrs Alexis Gaffin, BEd Hons Cantab (*Head of Immanuel College Preparatory School, Designated Senior Person in Charge of Child Protection for Preparatory School including EYFS*)
Mr Charles Dormer, MA Cantab (*Head Master, Deputy Designated Senior Person in Charge of Child Protection*)
Mrs Jo Fleet, BA (*Assistant Head (Personalisation, Transition {13–17} and Guidance), Deputy Designated Senior Person in Charge of Child Protection for Senior School*)
Ms Jacyn Fudge, BSc (*Deputy Head of Immanuel College Preparatory School and Head of EYFS, Deputy Designated Senior Person in Charge of Child Protection for Preparatory School*)
Mrs Janine Lewinton, BA Hons (*Head of Inclusion and Learning Support, Deputy Designated Senior Person in Charge of Child Protection*)

Admissions:
Mrs Lynda Dullop, BA Hons (*Director of Admissions, Parental Liaison/Fundraising & PR*)
Mrs Elaine Essex (*Senior School Secretary – Head Master's Office*)

Ipswich School

Henley Road, Ipswich, Suffolk IP1 3SG

Tel: 01473 408300
Fax: 01473 400058
email: enquiries@ipswich.school
website: www.ipswich.school
Twitter: @ipswichschool

Motto: *Semper Eadem.*

The School was founded in the fourteenth century by the Ipswich Merchant Guild of Corpus Christi. Its first Charter was granted by Henry VIII and this was confirmed by Queen Elizabeth I.

At Ipswich School we pride ourselves on a passion for learning, and the care and attention we give to our pupils. Through these we help our pupils to unlock their potential and develop their talents.

Ipswich School occupies an attractive site adjacent to Christchurch Park. The cricket field lies within the perimeter of the school buildings and a further two sports sites, Notcutts playing fields and Ipswich School Sports Centre (Rushmere) – with its three astroturf hockey pitches and six netball courts – are owned by the school locally.

There are 783 pupils in the Senior School (11–18), including 47 boarders. Of these 235 boys and girls are in the Sixth Form. There are 285 pupils in the Preparatory school (2–11).

The Boarding House stands in its own grounds a short distance from the school. There is a choice of full, weekly and occasional boarding for pupils in the Senior School.

All academic subjects have been housed in new or refurbished rooms in the last few years and visitors comment on the quality of the buildings, which are grouped around one of the School's playing fields.

The Preparatory School is housed in purpose-built accommodation on an adjacent campus; it benefits from all the amenities of the Senior School including the Sports Hall, Swimming Pool, Performing Arts Centre and Playing Fields. (*For further details, see entry in IAPS section.*)

Admission. Entry to the Preparatory School after Nursery is by means of an assessment. Pupils must show language and number skill levels that are above their chronological age and acceptable behaviour. The main entry to the Senior School at 11 is by examination in English, Mathematics and a Reasoning test, taken in late January/ early February. At 13, more pupils enter the Senior School, taking the Common Entrance Examination in June or the School's own Entrance and Scholarship Examination in March. Admission to the Sixth Form for girls and boys from other schools is by attainment of the required grades at GCSE, a report from the previous Head and an interview in November. Application forms may be obtained from the Director of Admissions. A registration fee of £50 is payable (£25 for brothers or sisters).

Religious Education. There is religious education throughout the age range and weekly chapel services for different sections of the school; there are also occasional Chapel Services on Sundays and after School at which pupils and their parents are most welcome.

Careers. Computer analyses of interests and aptitudes complement carefully planned advice about GCSE, A Level choices, higher education and professional training. There is also a wide variety of talks, seminars and work experience options throughout the year.

Curriculum. In the Preparatory School pupils study English, Mathematics, Languages, Computing, History, Geography, Religion, Science, Music, PE, Games, Art and Design Technology, PSHE and Outdoor Education.

Senior School pupils follow a common curriculum in the first two years with a choice between French and Spanish, plus Classical Civilisation in Year 7 and Latin in Year 8. German or Russian are introduced in Year 9. Mathematics and English are taken at IGCSE, one or more Modern Foreign Languages and separate Sciences are taken by all pupils to GCSE level. Apart from these compulsory subjects, pupils are examined in three other subjects chosen from French, Latin, History, Geography, German, Russian, Spanish, Drama, Design and Technology, Classical Civilisation, Art and Design, Philosophy, Religion and Ethics, and Music.

In the Sixth Form AS and A Level subjects are chosen from the following:

Mathematics, Further Mathematics, Physics, Chemistry, Biology, Latin, Classical Civilisation, Economics, Business Studies, Art, Design Technology, Music, History, Geography, English, French, German, Russian, Spanish, Psychology, PE, Philosophy, Religion and Ethics, and Theatres Studies.

In addition to their A Level studies, all Sixth Formers participate in an Enrichment Programme designed to complement and broaden the conventional curriculum. Students are also able to gain qualifications in a range of subjects such as Critical Thinking, ICT, Mandarin, Politics, Photography, Law and Spanish, and the Extended Project Qualification (EPQ).

Clubs, Trips and Activities. All are encouraged to participate in a variety of co-curricular activities which take place in lunchtimes, after school, at weekends and during the holidays. One afternoon a week is devoted to a host of community service activities, such as music and drama in the community, volunteering at local Primary schools and Special schools, journalism for internal publications, CCF (Army and RAF contingents) and a variety of sports and other pursuits. Sixth Formers may participate in the School's Leadership Programme at this time.

Drama in the school is particularly strong; continuous activity in this sphere maintains a succession of productions throughout the year, in all age groups. Productions in 2015–2016 included: *Much Ado About Nothing, What Are They Like?, Be My Baby, The Exam and Alice in Wonderland.*

Ipswich School Britten Faculty of Music has an impressive reputation as a place where musicians thrive, finding unstinting support from expert staff. Opportunities abound for enjoyable music-making, including Symphony, Intermediate and Chamber Orchestras; Chapel Choir; Wolsey Consort; Show Choir; Lower School Choir; Choral Society; Intermediate String Ensemble and various Chamber Music Groups; Big Band, Stage Band, Sax Ensemble, Jazz and Rock Bands. Tours have taken the Chapel Choir to residencies in Durham, Salisbury, Winchester and Wells Cathedrals, and visits to New York, Poland, Switzerland and Italy. The Chapel Choir has also sung Evensong in St Paul's Cathedral on several occasions. In 2016 the Chapel Choir sang live on the BBC Radio 4 Daily Service. Our annual concerts at Snape Maltings have featured Mozart's *Requiem*, Rutter's *Feel The Spirit*, MacCunn's *The Land of the Mountain and the Flood*, Saint-Saëns' *Carnival of the Animals* and Ben Parry's *You will go out in joy*, commissioned by Ipswich School for the 450th anniversary of the reaffirmation of its Royal Charter by Elizabeth I. We have a popular annual music competition which culminates in a "Young Musician of the Year" final. The Preparatory School runs its own Summer Strings course. Our annual Festival of Music brings world-renowned musicians into the school environment. Highlights in 2016 include Joe Stilgoe, Swingles and the Royal College of Music Strings. Our newly-built state-of-the-art Music School was officially opened on 18 March 2016 by Julian Lloyd Webber.

Duke of Edinburgh's Award. The School runs a successful Duke of Edinburgh's Award scheme. In 2016 we have over 90% of our Year 10 pupils enter the Bronze Award. In 2017, there will be Silver expeditions to the Wye Valley and Gold expeditions to Southern Snowdonia. Some of our Gold candidates in 2016 participated in a community project in the mountains of Ecuador, working with a village that had their own small school destroyed by a mudslide.

Games. Our key aim is to support the development of individuals at every level, whatever their sport of choice. In line with the school's core values, our sports ethos centres around passion, potential and performance. We aim to develop an environment where athletes set realistic but challenging goals, are encouraged to be curious, creative and take risks, and are given opportunities to express themselves without fear of failure. Success is judged and celebrated not just on the outcome, but on the process and the spirit of sport. It is our goal that every pupil who participates in sport at School feels important, supported and has a sense of belonging to not just their team, but Ipswich Sport as a whole. The termly sports for boys are Rugby, Hockey and Cricket and for girls, Hockey, Netball and Cricket/Tennis in the summer. These take place on our excellent Notcutts playing fields and our recently opened Sports Centre at Rushmere, which boasts 3 hybrid hockey pitches and 6 netball/tennis courts. In addition to termly sports pupils have the opportunity to be involved in a range of other sports including indoor hockey (U18 Girls National Champions and U16 Boys National Runners-Up, 2015), athletics, rounders, golf (Senior National Finalist 2015 & 2016), tennis, Eton fives, football, squash, sailing, badminton, paddleboarding and swimming. Ipswich School has links with a number of external clubs and academies and we are proud of our range of sports touring opportunities on offer to our pupils.

Fees per term (2016–2017). Day: Senior School £4,801; Lower School £4,379; Preparatory School: £3,805 (Years 4–6), £4,002 (Year 3 inc lunch); Pre-Preparatory School (Reception, Years 1 & 2) £3,652 (inc lunch); Nursery (inc lunch): £31.95 (am/pm session), £60.43 (whole day).

Boarding (inclusive of tuition fees): Full Boarding: £8,881 (Years 9–13), £7,745 (Years 7 and 8); Weekly Boarding: £8,046 (Years 9–13), £7,154 (Years 7 and 8).

Scholarships. These are available for external candidates at 11, 13 and 16. Academic Scholarships, known as Queen's Scholarships commemorating the Royal Charter granted to the School by Queen Elizabeth I in 1566, of up to half fees are awarded on the basis of examinations and interviews at 11 and 13. Music and Art Scholarships at 11 and 13 are awarded on the basis of excellence in these areas as demonstrated by audition or portfolio. Music auditions for promising instrumentalists entering Years 7 and 9 are held in January/February. A Sports Scholarship at 11 is awarded to a pupil who will make a significant contribution to the quality of sport at the school and an All-rounder Scholarship is available at 13.

Sixth Form Scholarships are awarded for academic excellence, for exceptional musical talent and for an all-rounder who will do well academically and contribute outstandingly in other areas of school life such as sport or drama. Academic Scholarships are awarded on the basis of school reports, predicted GCSE grades, interview and scholarship essay. Sixth Form Music Scholarship auditions are held in November. A Sports Scholarship is also available at 16. We also offer Arkwright Scholarships, which focus on Design Technology.

Awards may be supplemented by bursaries in cases of proven need.

Bursaries. These are available on a means-tested basis, up to full fee remission, for entry at 11, 13 and 16.

The Old Ipswichian Club. Annual dinners are held in London and Ipswich. Many less formal socials are held in a variety of venues each year. Sports gatherings are held for cricket, fives, golf and rugby, with an annual sports festival for football, hockey, netball and tennis

Charitable status. Ipswich School is a Registered Charity, number 310493. It exists for the purpose of educating children.

Visitor: Her Majesty The Queen

Governing Body:
H E Staunton, BA, FCA (*Chairman*)
N C Farthing, LLB, (*Vice Chairman*)
T Baxter
C D Brown, MA
J A Caudle, LLB
The Revd Dr G M W Cook, MSc, PhD, FIBiol, FRSC
Mrs Jane Crame, BSc, ACA, PGCE

Mrs Elizabeth Garner, MEd, BA, PGCE
Dr Orla Goble, MBBS, DRCOG, DFFP, JCPTGP
Dr R E Gravell, PhD, BMEdSci, BSc, MRCSLT, MUKCP
E B Hyams, BSc Eng, ACGI, CDIPAF, MIET
C Oxborough, BSC, FCA
J W Poulter, MA
A C Seagers, BA
N H H Smith, MA, FCA
M Taylor, BA, ACA
The Rt Revd M Seeley, MA, STM, Bishop of St Edmundsbury & Ipswich (*ex officio*)
Dr R A Watts, MA Oxon, DM Oxon, FRCP
Dr T Wilkinson, MA, PhD
R P E Wilson, MA, ARCM

Headmaster: **N J Weaver**, BA, MA

Senior Deputy Head (Pastoral): Mrs A Cura, BSc
Deputy Head (Academic): Mrs A Allen, BSc
Head of Sixth Form: Mrs Z Austin, MA
Head of Middle School: A R Bradshaw, BA
Head of Lower School: B Cliff, MA
Chaplain: The Revd Holly Crompton-Battersby, BA, BTh

Heads of Houses:
J W Orbell, BSc
S J Blunden, BA
D J Beasant, BA
Ms C J Chapman, BSc
Ms A Caston, BSc
Dr N Kerr-Boyle, PhD, MA

Heads of Department:
Art and Design: R Parkin, BA
Biology: Mrs H Blee, BSc
Sixth Form Careers: A M Calver, BSc
Chemistry & Science: D J P Halford-Thompson, BSc
Classical Civilisation: Miss K Hutton, BA, MEd
Design Technology: J M Smith, BA
Drama: Mrs L Ward, BEd
Economics & Business Studies: E Wilson, BEd
English: Ms J S Clarke, BA
Geography: R G Welbourne, BA, FRGS
History: Mrs O Tollemache, BA
Latin and Greek: Dr K Michalopoulou, BA, PhD
Life Skills: S J Duncombe, BA
Mathematics: M J Core, BSc
Modern Languages: J A Thompson, MA
Music: S W Parry, BMus
Physical Education: S Field, MSc, BSc (*Director of Sport*)
Curriculum PE: Miss S Holden, BA
Physics: S A Arthur, BEng
Psychology: Ms L Cross, BA
Religious Studies: Ms T Walker, BA

Head of Preparatory School: Mrs A H Childs, BA QTS, PGC PSE, DipEd, MA

Bursar: P Wranek
Director of Admissions: Mrs Y M Morton
Headmaster's PA: Mrs R G Connor

James Allen's Girls' School (JAGS)

East Dulwich Grove, London SE22 8TE

Tel: 020 8693 1181
Fax: 020 8693 7842

email: enquiries@jags.org.uk
website: www.jags.org.uk

The school was founded in 1741 as part of the Foundation of Alleyn's College of God's Gift and is the oldest independent girls' school in London.

JAGS is set in 22 acres of grounds in North Dulwich, with extensive playing fields and long-established Botany gardens. The school buildings include a well-equipped modern library, 13 science laboratories, a purpose-built suite of language laboratories, 6 art rooms, 4 computer rooms, design technology workshops, new indoor swimming pool, floodlit artificial turf pitch, dance studio, sports hall with squash court, fitness studios and a climbing wall, a professionally-managed theatre and a music school. The Sixth Form Centre has its own tutorial rooms, common rooms and lecture theatre. A new two-storey dining hall and teaching block opened in 2008.

There is a five-form entry at 11 and JAGS senior school has approximately 800 pupils with 200 in the Sixth Form. About a third of girls come up from our junior department, James Allen's Preparatory School (qv) with about two-thirds entering from other preparatory and state primary schools.

Girls follow a broad curriculum with a wide choice of GCSE/IGCSE options, structured to ensure a balanced programme. Advanced Level courses are available in all the usual subjects as well as Classical Civilisation, Greek, Latin, Russian, Spanish, Italian, Japanese, Economics, Philosophy, Physical Education, Politics, Music and Theatre Studies. Art is a particular strength throughout the school. The Pre-U English course is followed.

The extracurricular programme is a key part of the JAGS education. The excellent Prissian Theatre enables first-class, full-scale drama productions, while the active music department plays a central role, offering some 30 ensembles including 6 choirs, 4 orchestras, brass ensembles, wind ensembles plus jazz and big bands. A great variety of other interests is encouraged, from The Duke of Edinburgh's Award, debating, photography, and the Literary Society, to Politics and Amnesty International. Study visits to Russia, France, Germany, Italy, and Spain are regularly organised. The choirs, orchestras and sports teams also visit overseas. Community Action plays an important part in school life, and there are extensive partnership activities with other local schools and community groups.

Sports: Hockey, netball, football, aerobics, basketball, gymnastics, dance, tennis, rounders, swimming, athletics and self-defence are taught in the curriculum, with opportunities for yoga, fencing, rugby, badminton, sailing, ice skating and golf.

Individual lessons in Instrumental Music and Speech and Drama are available (fees on application).

Fees per term (2016–2017). £5,505.

Admission. Girls are mainly admitted at 11+ and also into the Sixth Form. Casual vacancies at other ages. Registration fee: £100.

Entrance Examination. Every candidate for admission will be required to pass a pre-selection assessment and an entrance examination. For details and method of admission, please visit www.jags.org.uk.

Scholarships and Bursaries. Up to twenty Academic Scholarships are awarded every year to girls of 11 years of age on entry to the School. There are also Scholarships on entry into the Sixth Form. Scholarships are awarded for academic ability, but are also available for Music, Sport and Art up to a potential value of £4,000 per annum. Music Scholarships are on the same basis as academic scholarships but also include instrument tuition. Candidates must satisfy the academic requirements of the school and pass an audition. All Scholarships are augmented by a means-tested element where there is need.

Following the demise of the Government Assisted Places Scheme, the School has introduced James Allen Bursaries to continue to enable talented girls from families of limited means to enter JAGS. Fee support up to 100% is available.

Charitable status. James Allen's Girls' School is a Registered Charity, number 1124853 and exists for the purpose of educating girls.

Governors:
Mrs Frances Read, MA Cantab, FCA, MSI (*Chair*)
Mrs Alison Fleming, BA Hons, MA Ed, PGCE
Mrs Geraldine McAndrew, BA Hons Sussex, CQSW Herts
Dr Jane Marshall, MB BCh, BAO Hons, DCH, MRCP, MRCPsych & FRCPsych
Mr David Miller, MA, FCSI
Ms Helen Nixseaman, MA, FCA
Mrs Jane Onslow, MA
Dame Erica Pienaar, BA Hons, MBS, FRSA
Mr Simon Smith, BA Hons, Dip Arch, ARB, RIBA
The Hon Dr Rema Kaur Wasan, MA Cantab, MBBS Lon, MRCP, FRCR UK
Mr Nick Wood, MA

Director of Operations & Clerk to the Governors: Mrs Justine Addison

Headmistress: Mrs Sally-Anne Huang, MA Oxford, MSc

Senior Deputy Head: Mrs Deborah Bicknell, BSc Hons Durham, MEd Belfast (*Biology*)

Deputy Head, Academic: Laurence Wesson, BSc Hons London (*Biology*)

Deputy Head, Pastoral: Samantha Payne, BA Hons Central St Martins (*Art*)

Assistant Head, Head of Extra & Co-Curricular Activities: Miss Fiona Murray, BEd Hons London (*PE*)

Assistant Head, Head of Schools Partnership: Mr Robert Wallace, MA Birmingham, MBA Nottingham (*DT*)

Assistant Head, Head of Sixth Form: Mr Matthew Weeks, MA Hons Oxford (*Geography*)

Assistant Head, Head of Years 10 and 11: Miss Lucy Mitchell, BA Hons Oxford, MA London (*Geography*)

Assistant Head, Head of Years 7–9: Mrs Ann Massey, MA Oxon (*History*)

Deputy Heads of Sixth Form:
Miss Rachel Barnes, BA Hons Belfast (*Religious Studies*)
Mrs Katharine Firth, BA Hons CNAA

Head of Year 11: Mrs Anna Jones, BA Hons Nottingham (*English*)
Head of Year 10: Miss Gina Thomson, BA Hons Brighton (*PE*)
Head of Year 9: Mrs Jessica Drucker, BA Hons Hull (*Drama*)
Head of Year 8: Miss Nicola Roden, BSc Hons Bristol (*Biology*)
Head of Year 7: Mrs Luisa Alonso, BA Hons Durham (*Spanish*)

Art:
Mr Michael Grant, MA Royal College of Art (*Head of Art*)
Ms Rose Aidin, BA Hons East Anglia, MA London (*History of Art*)
Mr Andrew Carter, BA Hons, Central St Martins
Mrs Katharine Firth, BA Hons CNAA
Miss Chantal Gilou, BA Hons Norwich
Ms Irene Riddell, BA Hons Glasgow
Mrs Rachel Marshall, MA Oxford
Mr John Luttick (*Art Technician*)

Classics & Philosophy:
Mrs Rachel Hyde, BA Hons, Oxford (*Head of Classics*)
Mrs Saltanat Hanif, BA Hons Cambridge
Mrs Sonia McGarr, BA Hons KCL
Dr Howard Peacock, BA Hons Oxford, MPhil London,
    PhD UCL
Mrs Frances Shaw, MA Oxford

Drama:
Mrs Joanna Billington, BA Hons Middlesex (*Director of
    Drama*)
Miss Holly McKinlay, BA Hons Bristol
Miss Jessica Payne, BA Hons Hull
Miss Louise Roberts, BA Hons Leeds
Miss Linda Bloomfield, BA Hons London (*Drama
    Assistant*)
Mr Will Feasey, BA Hons (*Theatre Technician*)

English:
Dr Matthew Edwards, BA Hons, PhD Bristol (*Head of
    English*)
Ms Katherine Bishop, BA Hons Cambridge
Ms Melanie Duignan, MA Manchester
Mrs Rachel Edwards, BA Hons Cambridge
Mrs Catherine Ferrar, MA Cambridge
Mrs Alison Holmes-Milner, BA Hons York
Mrs Anna Jones, BA Hons Nottingham
Miss Jane Quarmby, BA Hons Bristol
Miss Rachel Wilkinson, BA Hons Ulster

Humanities:
Mrs Monica Buckley, MA Oxford, History (*Head of
    History & Politics*)
Mr Thomas Hamilton-Jones, BA Hons Oxford (*Head of
    Economics*)
Mrs Deborah Lewis, BA Hons Sheffield (*Head of Religious
    Studies*)
Mrs Alice Mollison, MA Hons Edinburgh (*Head of
    Geography*)
Ms Verity Aylward, BA Hons Leicester (*History &
    Politics*)
Mrs Corrine Barton, BA Hons Sheffield (*History &
    Politics*)
Mr David Burns, BA Hons London (*Economics*)
Mr Jonathan Chesterman, BA Hons King's College London
    (*History*)
Dr Mark Fowle, MA & BA Hons Sheffield, PhD Warwick
    (*History & Politics*)
Mrs Elizabeth Gerhardt, BA Hons London (*History &
    Politics*)
Mr Stuart Labran, BA Hons Leeds, MPhil Cambridge
    (*Religious Studies*)
Mrs Imogen Mules, BSc Hons Leeds (*Geography*)
Ms Hermione Taylor, BSc Cambridge (*Economics*)
Miss Rachel Wilson, BA Hons King's College London
    (*Geography*)

Languages:
Ms Cristina Sanchez-Satoca, BA Hons Barcelona, MA
    London (*Head of Spanish, Head of Modern Foreign
    Languages*)
Mr Arvind Arora, Staatsexamen Germany (*Head of
    German*)
Mrs Claire Gene, Licence LCA, Paris (*Head of French*)
Mrs Giulia Marchini, Dottoressa Bari (*Head of Italian*)
Mrs Sally George, MA London, BA Hons London (*Head of
    Russian*)
Mrs Luisa Alonso, BA Hons Durham (*Spanish*)
Mrs Laurence Arora, BA, MA & DEUG UCO (*French*)
Mr Timothy Billington, BA Hons London (*German, ICT*)
Ms Georgina Legg, BA Hons Sussex (*French*)
Ms Lorna Macleod, BA Hons Bristol, MBA Warwick
    (*French*)

Ms Lola Merino, BSc Hons London (*Spanish*)
Mr Hiroshi Okura, BA Waseda (*Japanese*)
Mme Charline Reddihough, Licence Maîtrise Strasbourg
    (*French*)
Mr Jerome Roussel, Licence France (*French*)
Mrs Marta Totten, BA Hons Bergamo (*Italian*)
Mrs Ksenia Wesson, BEd Hons Krasnoyarsk (*Russian*)

Mathematics:
Ms Sara Glover, BSc Hons London (*Head of Mathematics*)
Ms Antonia Buccheri, BSc Hons Manchester
Miss Jessica Higgitt, BSc Cardiff
Mrs Jessica Millar, BSc Hons Nottingham
Mrs Lucy Rose, BSc Hull, BA Hons, MA London
Mrs Gillian Oxbrow, BSc Hons Exeter
Mr John Pattison, BSc Hons Newcastle, MA Lancaster
Mrs Natalie Plant, BSc Hons Bristol
Mrs Tracey Walton, BSc Hons Cambridge

Music:
Mr Peter Gritton, BA Hons Cambridge (*Director of Music*)
Miss Elinor Corp, BA Hons Bristol, MA
Mrs Caroline Davis, ARCM (*Head of Strings*)
Ms Kay Dickson, GRSM, Dip RCM London
Mr Jonathan Lee, BA Hons & MA Chichester, PhD Exeter
Mr Andrew Tait, MA Middlesex, MMus London
Mrs Samantha Clare-Hunt (*Music Department
    Coordinator*)

PE:
Mrs Elizabeth Head, BA Brighton (*Head of PE*)
Mr Jonathan Baxter, BMus Hons Middlesex (*Hockey
    Coach*)
Miss Wendy Johnson, BEd Hons London
Mrs Leanne King, BSc St Mary's University College,
    Ireland (*PE*)
Miss Angela White, BSc Hons Brighton

Science:
Mr John Watson-Reynolds, BSc Edinburgh, BA Hons
    Open University (*Head of Science*)
Miss Angela Newton, MSc LSE (*Head of Chemistry*)
Mr Andrew Hicklenton, BSc Hons Southampton (*Head of
    Physics*)
Mr Christopher Adams, BSc Hons KCL (*Physics*)
Miss Eleanor Baker, BA Hons Oxford (*Chemistry*)
Miss Hedy Canessa, BSc Southampton (*Physics*)
Miss Natalie Davidson, MChem Durham (*Chemistry*)
Mrs Wendy Barratt, BSc Hons Kent (*Biology*)
Mr Paul Davies, BSc Hons Newcastle (*Physics*)
Ms Karen Giles, BSc Hons York (*Biology*)
Mr Dominic Gillespie, BSc Manchester (*Physics*)
Mrs Clare Grant, BSc Hons Sussex (*Chemistry*)
Miss Yihuan Huang, MSc Imperial (*Chemistry*)
Mrs Nicola Hunt, BSc Hons UCL (*Biology*)
Miss Elizabeth Parker, BSc Hons London (*Biology*)
Dr Anna Parrish, BSc Loughborough, PhD Exeter
    (*Chemistry*)
Mrs Christine Bobrowicz, HNC Applied Biology (*Biology
    Technician*)
Miss Pamela Kettle, BTEC Science (*Science Technician*)
Mr Kevyn Knight, BSc Hons Thames Poly (*Chemistry
    Technician*)
Mr Mark Standing, BSc Hons Thames (*Physics
    Technician*)
Ms Elisabeth Temuena, BSc Hons Imperial (*Science
    Technician*)
Mrs Sylvia Thompson, HND Microbiology (*Biology
    Technician*)

Technology:
Miss Louise Cook, BA Hons Wolverhampton (*Head of
    Technology*)
Ms Lara Brookes, BEng Hons London

Mr Andrew House (*Design & Technology Technician*)
Ms Paula McCormick, BA Hons London

SENCO:
Years 7–9: Mrs Joyce Hepher, BEd Hons, Dip SpLD,
CCET, ACC
Years 10 & 11: Mrs Catherine Winter, BSc Hons Bristol

IT Support:
Mr Guy Downer
Mr Daniel Szenasi-Holland, BA Hons Leeds
Mr Paul Low
Mr Joe Williams

Librarians:
Mrs Elen Curran, BA Hons Reading, Dip Lib, MCLIP
Mrs Susan Stacey, BA Hons Manchester
Mrs Nel Yiend, BA Hons Exeter, ACLIP

Administration & Secretarial:
Mrs Elizabeth Allan, BSc Hons London (*Assistant to the
Head of Sixth Form*)
Mrs Christine Allen, SLT (*Administrator*)
Miss Helen Barefoot, BA Hons Birmingham (*PA to
Headmistress*)
Mrs Elizabeth Handslip, BA Leeds (*Assistant Registrar*)
Mrs Sejal Joshi, Dip Hons Gujarat, India (*Data
Administrator*)
Mrs Henrietta Kiezun, BA Hons Keele (*Registrar*)
Miss Lindsey McDonald (*Pupil Attendance Administrator*)
Mrs Victoria Rees, BA Hons Reading (*Staff Resources
Assistant*)

School Nurses:
Mrs Karen Cattanach, RGN
Mrs Helen Mandefield-Chang, RGN
Ms Jacqueline Martin, RGN

Bursary:
Mr Kevin Barry, ACA (*Finance Coordinator*)
Mr Nazir Badshah, BA Hons London (*Senior Accountant*)
Miss Henrietta Smith, BA Hons Warwick (*PA to the
Director of Operations*)
Mrs Samantha Dock (*Assistant Accountant*)
Mrs Sarah Hand (*Purchase Ledger Clerk*)
Miss Laura Rance (*Purchase Ledger Clerk*)

Human Resources:
Mrs Salome Osibogun, BA Hons, MA, HRM Middlesex,
Assoc CIPD (*HR Coordinator*)
Miss Manuela Forina, HRM Italy, CIPD (*HR
Administrator*)

Communications, Marketing and PR:
Mrs Alison Venn, BEd Hons Cambridge (*Director of
Communications*)
Mrs Jo Denham, BA Hons (*Marketing Manager*)
Ms Yang Ming Ooi, BA Hons Oxford (*Database and
Research Coordinator*)
Miss Kate Cheshire (*Marketing Coordinator*)

Reception:
Ms Lucy Geoghegan
Mrs Rebecca Goddard

Facilities & Estates Manager: Mr Simon Willoughby

Maintenance Department:
Mr Jim Double (*Maintenance Manager*)
Mr Bert Kingsford (*Maintenance Assistant*)

Schoolkeeping Department:
Mr Robert Thompson (*Head Schoolkeeper*)
Mr James Norris (*Deputy Head Schoolkeeper*)
Mr Luis Cagica
Mr Michael Norris
Mrs Christine Rousseaux

Mr Jim Stevens
Mr Keith Van Ackeren

Grounds Department:
Mr Peter Hammer (*Head Groundsman*)
Mr Jamie Adams
Mrs Jennifer Morriss

Botany Gardens Manager: Mr David Benson, BSc Hons
Reading

Catering Manager: Mr Martin Benson

The John Lyon School

Middle Road, Harrow, Middlesex HA2 0HN

Tel: 020 8515 9400
Fax: 020 8515 9455
email: enquiries@johnlyon.org
website: www.johnlyon.org
Twitter: @TheJohnLyonSch

Motto: *Stet Fortuna Domus*

The John Lyon School was established as a Day School
in 1876 under the Statutes made by the Governors of Harrow School, in pursuance of the Public Schools Act, 1868.

There are 600 boys in the School.

Admission. Admission is at 11+ for Year 7, 13+ for Year
9 and 16+ entry into the Sixth Form.

The closing date for 11+, 13+ and 16+ Application Forms
is the 31st October in the year prior to entry. Entrance examinations for 11+ and 13+ entry are held in early January of
the year of entry. For more information see www.john-
lyon.org.

11+ selection is based upon a two-part examination lasting approximately 1½ hours and a separate interview prior
to the examination. The first part is an online test, designed
to identify potential rather than 'taught' skills. The online
test consists of English, Maths and Verbal Reasoning. The
second part of the examination is a short test of creative
writing completed by hand. The approximate intake is 60
boys at 11+.

13+ selection is based upon performance in our entrance
examinations in Maths, English, French and Science and,
most importantly, a personal interview with the Head. The
School takes special note of potential and achievement in
Music, the creative and performing Arts as well as the
capacity of any candidate to contribute fully to the extra-curricular life of the School. The School looks for potential and
achievement in at least one major academic subject.
Approximate intake is 40 boys at 13+.

Entrance Examinations for 16+ entry are held in March
of the year of entry. For more information see the website. A
completed application form and confirmation of predicted
GCSE grades are required. We also write to the candidate's
current school requesting a reference. 16+ candidates are
invited into school to take an entrance exam based around
the four subjects they would like to take for A Level. Conditional and Unconditional Offers are made pending entrance
examination results and GCSE results.

The closing date for 11+, 13+ and 16+ applications is
31st October 2016.

Registration Fee: £100.

Fees per Term (2016–2017). Years 7 to 11: £5,544
(including lunch); Sixth Form: £5,756. Key textbooks are
covered within the fees.

Scholarships. Scholarships usually provide for
£800–£2,000 of the tuition fees each year.

All boys who take the 11+ and 13+ entrance examination
are assessed for an academic scholarship.

Art, Drama, Music and Sport scholarships are also available. A separate scholarship application form is available on the School Website.

Art, Drama, Music and Sport scholarship assessments are held in November of the year prior to entry.

Potential candidates are called for selection interviews and tests as appropriate.

Bursaries. A small number of means-tested bursaries of up to 100% of School Fees are available from the John Lyon's Charity for boys living in specific postcodes. More information is available on the School Website.

Closing date for Scholarship and Bursary applications is 31st October in the year preceding the year of entry.

School Buildings. The School buildings are on the West side of Harrow-on-the-Hill and include a range of facilities. Additions and investment are regularly undertaken. The main School building houses the Science Laboratories, Drama studios, Art studios, Gallery and the Boyd Campbell Hall. The Music School has a 120-seater Recital Hall, two Steinway Concert Grand Pianos, a recording studio and eight individual practice studios. The Sports Complex comprises a 25-metre indoor swimming pool, fitness studio and sports hall. Recent developments include a new catering extension in January 2012. The Thomas Blackwell Sixth Form Centre was opened in September 2012 in the restored Old Building, the original 1876 School house.

Games. A floodlit Multi-Use Games area opened in 2016 allowing for all-weather hockey and tennis at the 25-acre School playing fields, just a 5-minute minibus journey on the south side of the Hill. There are 4 cricket squares, 7 football pitches, a challenge course, pavilion and archery range. In addition, the School can access the sporting facilities of Harrow School including cricket nets, an athletics track, a nine-hole golf course, tennis, squash and badminton courts.

The main games are Association Football and Hockey in the Winter Terms, Cricket, Athletics, Tennis and Swimming in the Summer Term, supported by Badminton, Basketball, Archery, Waterpolo, Squash and other games. PE and Swimming are in the curriculum.

Curriculum. The School Curriculum at present includes English, Mathematics, Physics, Biology, Chemistry, French, Spanish, Latin, Ancient Greek, History, Religious Studies, Geography, Drama, Art, Computer Science, Business Studies, Classical Civilisation, Economics, Psychology, Government & Politics, ICT, Music and Music Technology. PE and PSCHE are also part of the curriculum but are not examined.

Out of School Activities. Boys are strongly encouraged to play an active part in a wide range of activities. The School is well known for the breadth and range of its musical offering, the range of musical clubs and activities is unusual for a School of its size. All boys are encouraged to play an instrument or sing. There is a String Ensemble, Brass Ensemble, R&B Group, Flute Choir, Jazz Band, Woodwind Ensemble as well as Rock Jam Sessions and a parent choir.

Drama, as well as being taught in the curriculum, is developed through House and School Plays with many opportunities to work with national Drama groups and neighbouring Schools. There are over 70 School Clubs and Societies.

One in every four boys at the School takes an active part in the Duke of Edinburgh's Award scheme, under the care of a full-time Head of Outdoor Education. The School's CCF operates in conjunction with Harrow School.

Community Service has been developed through various projects which are undertaken in the Harrow Area. Each year the School devotes considerable time to fundraising for a charity chosen by the boys.

Careers. Advice on Careers is given by the Head of Careers. Specialist advice concerning entrance to Higher Education is given and there is a team of 7 specialists in the Sixth Form Centre to offer guidance and support with UCAS, University choices and careers. Morrisby testing is undertaken.

Entry to Universities. The Sixth Form on average consists of 140 boys who will usually apply for Degree courses at leading Universities and of these typically 75% or more will achieve or exceed their first choice. Usually half of all boys take up places at Russell Group Universities.

The Lyonian Association. All boys on leaving the School from the Sixth Form become life members of the Association. The Association has its own ground and pavilion at Sudbury Fields.

Charitable status. The Keepers and Governors of the Free Grammar School of John Lyon is a Registered Charity, number 310033. The purpose of the charity is the education of boys living within reach of Harrow between the ages of 11–18.

Governors:
Mr Giles Goodfellow, QC, MA, LLM (*Chairman of Governors*)
Mr K W B Gilbert, BA, FCA (*Deputy Chairman*)
Mr J H Dunston, MA, ACIL, FRSA [OL]
Mrs S Symonds
Professor J S Chadha, BSc Econ, MSc Econ [OL]
Mr R Fox, LLB [OL]
Mr G Stavrinidis, BSc Eng, MBA, DipM [OL]
Dr S Jollyman, MB ChB, DCH, DRCOG, DFFP, MRCGP
Mr J Mark PD Stroyan MA LLB
Mr I Kendrick, MA, BEd
Mr D Tidmarsh, BSc
Mr J H Graham, BSc, MRICS [OL]
Mr Liam Halligan, MPhil Econ, BSc Hons [OL]
Mr Neil Enright, MA Oxon, MBA, NPQH, FRSA [OL]
Mrs Michelle Beresford-Smart

[OL] *Old Lyonian*

Clerk to the Governors: The Hon Andrew C Millett, MA

Head: **Miss K E Haynes**, BA Warwick, MEd Birmingham, NPQH

Deputy Heads:
Mr J O M Pepperman, MA Cantab
Mr A J Sims, MA, MEng Cantab

Bursar: Mr M E Gibson, BA, MSc Trinity Dublin

SMT:
Mrs L C Cottrell, BA, MA Manchester (*Director of Marketing & Admissions*)
Mr S L Lythgoe, BA Huddersfield ACA (*Director of Finance & Business Systems*)
Mr I R Parker, BSc Loughborough (*Co-Curricular*)
Mrs L S Plummer, BA Middlesex (*Links & Community*)
Mr S Rana, MSc Birmingham (*Director of Studies*)
Mr A Tamattiris, BA, MSc, CIPD (*HR Manager*)
Mr A S Westlake, BA Southampton, BA Bristol, MA King's College London (*Staff*)

Academic Staff:
* *Head of Department*

Art:
*Ms L Hope, Dip VA Alberta College of Arts
Mr E R Collard-Walker, BA Central St Martins, MA Royal College of Art

Biology:
*Mr L A Ulakanathan, BSc, MSc, MA King's College London
Mr C D James, BSc South Africa
Ms N M Lagos, BSc Brunel
Mr S Rana, MSc Birmingham

Business Studies:
*Mr D P Boylan, BEd Queen's Belfast

Chemistry:
*Mr C J McDonald, BSc Nottingham
Mr O Damree, BSc Mauritius
Miss A James, BSc Durham
Mr D F Weedon, MA Oxon

Chinese:
Ms J C Lin, BA, BBA Chinese Cultural University, MA
　Westminster

Classics:
*Mr P J Cowie, BA, MA Sydney
Mr J E Ahsan, BA UCL
Mr J E Blenkinsop, BA King's College London

Computer Science:
*Mr A R Hadwen-Bennett, BSc UEL, MSc Westminster

Drama:
*Mr S G Jones, BA Birmingham
Mr L H Felgate, BA Goldsmiths London

Economics:
*Dr M E White, BA, MA, PhD Manchester
Mr W P T Fernando, BA Nottingham, MLitt St Andrews

English:
*Mr J W Peel, BA King's College London
Miss J M Boyle, BA Loughborough
Miss B R Davies, BA Leicester
Mr G R Iveson, MA Cantab
Mrs M L Trafford, MA Glasgow, BTh Brunel

French:
*Mr F Troublé, BA, MA Paris-Sorbonne, BComm St Denis
Ms N E Dunston, BA Leeds
Mr A K Ferguson, BA Reading [OL]

Geography:
*Mr J D Bruce, BSc, Dip EIA Aberystwyth
Miss K M Littlefield, BSc UCL
Mr I R Parker, BSc Loughborough

History:
*Mr C K Longhurst, BA Hull
Mr A D Hartrup, BA Southampton
Mr J O M Pepperman, MA Cantab
Mr T W Yardley, BA, MA Cardiff

Learning Support:
*Ms S C Blanchard, BA Bordeaux, MA Paris VII Diderot,
　Dip RSA SpLD
Mrs F Attar, BA Manchester, Dip RSA SpLD
Mrs N Walker, BSc Manchester

Mathematics:
*Mr T J Lewis, MA, MEng Cantab
Mr S J K Andon, MSc UCL
Mr J Chen, BSc Imperial College
Mrs L J James, BSc Exeter
Mr J McNaughton, BSc Swansea
Dr K Sudhakar, BSc, PhD London
Mr M W Vickery, BEng Exeter

Music:
*Mr H R Jones, MA Cantab, FRCO, ACA
Mr A J Furniss, MA Oxon, FRCO

Music Technology:
*Mr R E Marshall, BND Stanmore Music College

Physical Education:
*Mr K J Paradise, BSc Surrey, MSc Brunel
Mr A L Jones, BSc Brunel
Mr A S Ling, BSc Brunel

Physics:
*Mr T J Mahon, BSc UCL, BA Surrey, MA London
　Institute of Education
Dr T A Choudhury-Fieret, BSc, PhD Aston
Dr S J Mills, BSc Sheffield, PhD Sheffield Hallam
Mr A J Sims, MA, MEng Cantab
Dr F R Weinberg, BSc, MSc, PhD Imperial College

Politics:
*Dr C J Clews, BA, MA, PhD London
Mr J A Armstrong, BA York, MA Durham (*Head of Sixth
Form*)

Psychology:
*Mrs E McMillan, BSc Birkbeck London, MSc London

Religious Studies:
*Miss F L Baldwin, BA Bristol, MA Heythrop College
　London
Miss S B Patel, BA Birmingham
Mrs L S Plummer, BA Middlesex
Mr A S Westlake, BA Southampton, BA Bristol, MA
　King's College London

Spanish:
*Mr P D Berry, BA Bristol
Ms E D Murtagh, BA Cantab

Kelvinside Academy

33 Kirklee Road, Glasgow G12 0SW

Tel:　　　0141 357 3376
Fax:　　　0141 357 5401
email:　　rector@kelvinsideacademy.org.uk
website:　www.kelvinsideacademy.org.uk
Twitter:　@KAGlasgow
Facebook: /KelvinsideAcademy

Motto: ΑΙΕΝ ΑΡΙΣΤΕΥΕΙΝ

The Academy was founded in 1878. Since May 1921, it has been controlled by the Kelvinside Academy War Memorial Trust, which was formed in memory of the Academicals who gave their lives in the War of 1914–18. The affairs of the Trust are managed by a Board of Governors, mainly composed of Academicals and parents.

Kelvinside Academy is a co-educational day school for some 580 pupils, aged 3 to 18.

The main building is in neo-classical style and Grade A listed but has been extensively modernised within. Further buildings and extensions provide excellent facilities for all subjects and interests, and are symptomatic of the school's progressive approach. Recent additions include state-of-the-art IT and multimedia suites, custom-built nursery and new sports pavilion.

Curriculum. Junior School pupils (from J1) benefit from specialist input in Art, Music, PE and Modern Languages. The Senior Prep (P7) year is a transitional year with a core curriculum taught by the class teacher but science, languages, art, music and PE are delivered by secondary specialists. Computing is a core compulsory subject up to S4.

Senior 3 and 4 pupils follow eight National 4 or 5 courses, followed by Higher and Advanced Higher courses in Senior 5 and 6.

Combined Cadet Force. The hugely popular CCF is compulsory for one year in Senior 3. Pupils embark upon the Duke of Edinburgh's Award scheme at this stage.

Games. Rugby and hockey are the principal team games in the winter terms with athletics, tennis and cricket in the summer. A range of additional sports and games, from football to basketball and dance, is offered.

Activities. A rich programme of extra-curricular and House activities contributes significantly to the broad educational experience enjoyed by all pupils.

The Expressive Arts. Music, drama, dance and the visual arts have a central role in both the curriculum and the co-curriculum.

Fees per term (2016–2017). Nursery £1,260–£2,850, Junior School £2,500–£3,590, Senior School £3,745–£3,960.

Admission. For Nursery and P1, children undergo an informal assessment. For P2 to Senior 3, children sit an entrance test and informal interview. For Senior 4 to Senior 6, entry is by interview, school report and exam results.

Bursaries. Financial support with fees (ranging from 10%–100%) is available to P7 and Senior School pupils.

Charitable status. The Kelvinside Academy War Memorial Trust is a Registered Charity, number SC003962. The purpose of the Trust is to run a combined primary and secondary day school in memory of those former pupils of the school who gave their lives in the war of 1914–18.

Board of Governors:
Mr D Wilson, BAcc, CA (*Chairman*)
Mr C Neill, BA (*ex officio*)
Mr K Cairnduff
Professor W Cushley, BSc, PhD, FSB
Mrs E M Davis, BA Hons, PGCE
Mr C J Mackenzie, LLB, Dip LP, NP
Mr S MacKenzie, MRICS
Mrs A McDowall, LLB Hons, Dip LP
Mr H Ouston, MA
Mr A Palmer, BAcc, CA
Mrs J Rowand, FIRP

Rector: **Mr I H Munro**

Deputy Rector: Mr D J Wyatt
Academic Deputy: Miss L A Thrippleton
Head of E-Learning and Professional Development: Mrs J Maclean
Head of Support for Learning: Miss L Jackson
Head of Guidance: (*to be appointed*)

Head of Senior 6: Miss K Leckie
Head of Senior 5: Mr B Parham
Head of Senior 4: (*to be appointed*)
Head of Senior 3: Miss L Bruce
Head of Senior 2: Miss S Crichton
Head of Senior 1: Mrs F Kennedy

House Staff:
Buchanan: Mrs F Cafolla
Colquhoun: Mrs L FitzGerald
MacGregor: Mrs F Kennedy
Stewart: Miss L Preston [Mr B FitzGerald]

Leadership Coordinator: Miss K Leckie
Enterprise Coordinator: Mrs J Shields

Faculty of Language (*English, Modern Languages*):
Mr J Gilius (*Head of Faculty*)
Mrs A Mullan (*Deputy Head of Faculty*)
Mrs J Hepburn
Miss S Jeen
Mrs H Jephson
Mr S Klimowicz
Mr D O'Neil
Miss M Orr
Miss L Preston

Faculty of Maths, Science and Technology (*Maths, Physics, Chemistry, Biology, Computing*):
Mr J I O Cuthbertson (*Head of Faculty*)
Mrs D Macgregor (*Deputy Head of Faculty*)
Mr A G Mulholland (*Deputy Head of Faculty*)

Miss L Bruce
Mr S H Connor
Mrs L C FitzGerald
Mr B FitzGerald
Mr G Guile
Miss K Leckie
Mr I Nicholson
Mr B Parham
Miss L Thrippleton

Faculty of Social and Business Studies (*History, Geography, Modern Studies, Business Subjects, Religious Education*):
Mrs J Clark (*Head of Faculty*)
Mr J Calder (*Deputy Head of Faculty*)
Mr J Brown
Mrs J Hannah
Miss D Laverick
Mrs N Mathews
Mrs B Meikle
Mr N Reid
Mrs J Shields
Mr C Simpson

Faculty of Expressive Arts (*Art & Design, Music, Drama*):
Mrs J Cunningham (*Head of Faculty, Director of Music*)
Mrs J Hardy (*Deputy Head of Faculty*)
Miss S Crichton
Mrs A Gallie
Mrs A H M Schneeberger
Mrs F Whittle

Faculty of PE, Games & Extra-Curricular (*Games, PE, Outdoor Education, Extra-Curricular*):
Mr D J Wilson (*Head of Faculty, Director of Games*)
Mrs F Cafolla
Mr C J Lawson
Mr M McAlister
Mr R W J Moir

Teachers of Senior Prep:
Mrs F Kennedy
Mrs J Rynn

Support for Learning (*SfL*):
Miss L Jackson (*Head of Department*)
Mrs N Anderson

Timetabler: Mrs F Whittle
SQA Coordinator: Mrs C Campbell

Librarians:
Ms S Tipping
Ms S McLay

Duke of Edinburgh's Award Coordinator: Mr N Reid

Head of Junior School: Mr A L Dickenson

Junior School Class Teachers:
Junior 1A: Mrs A Stevenson, Mrs G Robertson
Junior 2A: Mr N Armet
Junior 2B: Mrs L McColl, Mrs L Hill
Junior 3A: Mrs E Laird-Jones, Mrs L Hill
Junior 4A: Miss C Brown
Junior 4B: Mrs S Rodger, Mrs G Robertson
Junior 5A: Mrs E Henderson
Junior 5B: Mrs G Flanigan
Junior 6A: Mrs S Paterson, Mrs J Rynn
Junior 6B: Mrs A McAllister

Teachers with a specific remit:
Senior Teacher, Upper Primary: Mrs S Paterson
Senior Teacher, Early Years: Mrs A Stevenson

Nursery Staff:
Head of Nursery: Mrs T Nugent

Deputy Head of Nursery: Miss P Argue
Early Years Practitioner and Holiday Session Coordinator:
   Mrs J Hartley
Early Years Practitioner: Mrs J Pettigrew
Early Years Practitioner: Mrs G Stewart
Early Years Practitioner: Mrs L Ramsay
Early Years Practitioner: Miss S Singleton
Apprentice EYP: Miss Demi Mardon
Apprentice EYP: Miss Ashleigh Harvey
Supportworker: Mrs M Brown

Non-Teaching/Support Staff:
Bursar: Mr D Pocock
Finance Officer/Deputy Bursar: Mrs E Cummings
Bursar's PA: Mrs L Andonovic
Finance Assistant: Mrs J Arthurs
Finance Administrator: Miss P Sabau
Director of Admissions and Communications: Mrs K L
   Bottomley
Development Manager: Mrs E Solman
Marketing Officers: Mrs L Young
PA to the Rector: Miss A-M Cormack
School Receptionist/Secretary: Mrs C Craig, Mrs P Lindsay
Junior School Secretary: Mrs I Lindsay
School Nurse: Mrs L MacDonald, Mrs E Semple
ICT Systems Manager: Mr J Paterson
IT Technician: Mr E Longmore
Laboratory Technician: Mrs P McArthur
Classroom Assistant: Catherine Campbell
Classroom Assistant/After School Club Supervisor: June
   Ghomashchian
Classroom Assistant/After School Club Supervisor: Ann
   Marie Gunn
Classroom Assistant: Janice Park
After School Club Supervisor: Emma Cowan
CCF Head of Army Section: Mr J Ferguson
CCF School Staff Instructor: Mr M McAlister
Facilities Manager: Mr C Shaw
Head Janitor: Mr D Anderson
Assistant Janitor: Mr S Lau
Head Groundsman: Mr D Boyd
Assistant Groundsman: Mr B Fenton
Road Crossing Patrol Staff: Mr A Craig

Kent College

Canterbury, Kent CT2 9DT
Tel: 01227 763231
Fax: 01227 787450
email: admissions@kentcollege.co.uk
website: www.kentcollege.com
Twitter: @kentcollegehm
Facebook: /kentcollege
LinkedIn: /kent-college-canterbury

Motto: *Lux tua via mea*

This outstanding boarding and day school is situated on the rural edge of the beautiful City of Canterbury. Students come to the school from the age of three through to eighteen. The majority of students live within an hour of the school. However, the school also has a strong and fully integrated boarding community of children from the age of seven; these children come from all over the world and add an exciting international aspect to the school. Academic, sporting and musical achievements are nationally acclaimed. Parents choose the school for its warm, friendly and welcoming nature where their children are encouraged to achieve all that they can, in a happy and supportive environment.

Facilities. The Junior and Senior schools occupy two independent sites. All of the six boarding houses are situated on site. Both of the schools are surrounded by extensive playing fields which are used throughout the school day. Modern classrooms and provision of laptops to senior school students, distinguishes Kent College as a market leader in education. Excellent sport, music and drama facilities are augmented by the highest level of teaching and coaching. The school also runs its own farm and equine unit.

Curriculum. The curriculum is aligned to the National Curriculum but a greater range of subjects is provided. It is not the aim to specialise in any one group of subjects but to provide a balanced curriculum which will give full opportunity for students to get a good grounding of general knowledge and later to develop particular talents to a high standard. We pride ourselves on being able to provide a personalised learning experience, where we can organise the curriculum to suit the child.

The International Baccalaureate is offered alongside A Levels in the Sixth Form with outstanding results in both.

Dyslexia Unit. The Dyslexia Support Centre is a haven of help for those amongst the school intake that need extra support. Students are taught all the mechanisms that they need to access the whole curriculum. Support remains a constant throughout the child's time here.

International Study Centre. Small group lessons and specific language assistance provide a useful platform for those students who arrive without an adequate level of English. These students are then integrated into the mainstream classes at a pace that suits them.

Pastoral Care. The school operates closely with each student and the student's parents to ensure that there is an open line of communication. Each student is individually supported by a strong team: house parents; year heads; tutors; teachers and peer mentors all of whom take a significant interest in looking after the needs of each individual.

Religion. As a Methodist school a strong Christian ethos purveys all that the school does. Students of all faiths and no faith are welcomed in the school.

Games and Activities. The school possesses 28 acres of playing fields and a floodlit all-weather hockey pitch. The major games for boys are Rugby, Hockey, Tennis, Cricket and Athletics and for girls Netball, Hockey, Tennis, Cricket, and Athletics. Hockey is a particular strength with teams regularly attaining National championship status. Representative honours are common occurrence in all sports. The boarding community enjoys full use of the facilities in the evening with regular activities in Basketball, Football and Fitness Training. Senior pupils take part in various forms of community service in the City and the school also has its own Duke of Edinburgh's Award group. There is a full range of optional school activities, including Art, Debating, Chess, Conservation, CDT and Photography. The School has its own farm and developing equine unit which provides countless opportunities for outdoor adventure and agricultural experiences.

Music and Drama. Music and drama play an important part in the life of the school.

There are four choirs, two orchestras, a jazz band, rock groups and a variety of other specialist ensembles and singing groups. Many concerts are given each year, including the annual Carol Service in Canterbury Cathedral. The last whole-school production was *Oklahoma*, which was a great success!

Admission. The usual ages of admission to the Senior School are 11, 13 and 16. Entrance Examinations usually take place in the Spring Term for admission the following September.

Fees per term (2016–2017). Day Pupils: £5,327–£5,897; Boarders: £10,916–£11,160 (full). International Study Centre: £1,325 extra.

Entrance Scholarships. The school awards academic, music, sport, drama and art scholarships to pupils for entry into Years 7, 9 and 12. Scholarships normally carry a value equivalent to a percentage remission of the tuition fees which would not exceed a maximum of 50% and would be at the discretion of the Head Master. Full particulars may be obtained from the Registrar.

Academic scholarships for Years 7 and 9 are awarded as a result of performance in our Entrance Test, usually held in the Spring Term, for entry the following September. Sixth Form academic scholarships are awarded on the basis of existing performance, a detailed report from the Head of Year or current school, and confirmation of high levels of performance in the final GCSEs. The school also offers specific scholarships for the International Baccalaureate.

Music/Drama GTX scholarships of up to half the tuition fee are offered in conjunction with the Entrance Test to candidates for entry into Years 7, 9 and 12. Free tuition on two instruments is offered to Music Scholars.

Sports GTX scholarships of up to half the tuition fee are awarded to pupils for entry into Years 7, 9 and 12. For Years 7 and 9 these will be awarded in the Spring Term in conjunction with the Entrance Test and on the basis of assessment at Kent College. For Year 12, Sports scholarships will be based on current performance and other assessment methods during the year. Scholars receive 1:1 coaching, physiotherapy support and enjoy a programme of nationally recognised motivational speakers.

Bursaries will be awarded in accordance with, and after consideration of, the financial circumstances of parents. Parents will be invited to complete a financial assessment form and the scale of bursary awarded will be based on the information provided and the financial criteria which the school applies to all bursary awards. All bursaries are reviewed annually.

In addition, the school operates an awards system for the children of HM Forces, NATO and War Graves Commission personnel, whereby the parents pay a set figure, normally 10% of the inclusive fee, plus the amount of Boarding School Allowance which they receive. The balance is treated as a Bursary Award.

Honours. Most school leavers go on to Russell Group and other top universities both in the UK and abroad. Each year a number of pupils secure offers of places at Oxford and Cambridge.

Charitable status. Kent College, Canterbury is a Registered Charity, number 307844. The School was founded to provide education within a supportive Christian environment and is a member of the Methodist Independent Schools Trust.

Governors:
Chairman: Lorna Cocking, BA
Secretary to the Governors and Bursar: Mrs A C Hencher, AInstAM

Executive Head Master: Dr D J Lamper, EdD Hull, BMus, MA London, AKC

Senior School Head Master: J G Waltho, MA Oxon

Director of Studies: G Letley, BA Kent

Chaplain: Revd Dr P Glass, BA Leeds, MA Cantab, PhD Leeds

Registrar: Mrs J Simpson
Executive Head Master's PA: Miss M Lucas
Senior School Head Master's PA : Mrs K Simpson

Junior School Head Master: A J Carter, BEd
Junior School Head Master's PA: Mrs C Goldsmith
(*See entry in IAPS section*)

Kent College Pembury

Old Church Road, Pembury, Tunbridge Wells, Kent TN2 4AX

Tel: 01892 820218
Fax: 01892 820239
email: admissions@kentcollege.kent.sch.uk
website: www.kent-college.co.uk
Twitter: @KentCollegePemb
Facebook: @KentCollegePemb
LinkedIn: /kent-college-pembury

Kent College Pembury is a leading day and boarding school for girls aged 3 to 18. A happy thriving school with high academic standards and an ethos of providing a bespoke education and outstanding opportunities for enrichment and success. The school provides for the educational and cultural needs of day students and boarders from all over the world. Set in beautiful countryside, just 35 miles from London, students benefit from innovative teaching and excellent resources in a superbly equipped environment, within a caring Christian community. All girls participate in the imaginative and extensive programme of extracurricular activities which include various music, drama and sports clubs and other exciting activities such as film-making, scuba-diving, canoeing and clay pigeon shooting amongst others. Performing Arts and Science are major strengths of the school and the school was delighted to open a state-of-the-art multi-purpose second Sports Hall in September 2015. The school is accredited by HMC, GSA and IAPS.

Ethos and Aims. The Prep School (ages 3–11) and the Senior School (ages 11–18) are part of a group of Methodist Schools, which have an ethos of being caring, Christian environments, and welcoming pupils from all faiths or none. Kent College is a happy school with high academic standards and pupils achieve excellent results in public examinations. With 200 girls in the Prep School and 470 in the Senior School there is a real community feel and teaching staff know each girl as an individual. Building self-esteem is at the heart of our ethos. All girls get a chance to shine, try something different, feel good about themselves and develop new and existing talents. Exciting opportunities to develop confidence are an integral part of school life: overseas music, drama and sports tours, an Australian exchange, 80 extracurricular activities, Kent College Gym, Theatre and Swimming Academies to name a few. Our aim is to equip students with the confidence, skills and positive attitude to succeed in their examinations, at university, in their chosen career and in life ahead.

Location and Facilities. The Prep School and the Senior School share the site which is set in 75 acres of beautiful green countryside in Pembury, three miles from Royal Tunbridge Wells. It is just forty minutes to London by train and within easy reach of Gatwick, Heathrow and Luton airports, channel ports and the Channel Tunnel. The Senior School campus comprises an elegant Victorian manor house, used for offices and boarding, and purpose-built facilities include language laboratories, a music school, Sixth Form Centre, science laboratories, dance studio and on-site outdoor adventure confidence course. The Susanna Wesley Arts and Library Centre opened in March 2013 and provides an open-plan Library space, ICT areas and a coffee shop on the ground floor with art studios and offices above. The two schools benefit from an excellent range of shared facilities including two large sports halls, state-of-the-art theatre, an indoor heated swimming pool and dining hall; excellent ICT facilities include Apple Mac suite, wireless laptops and smart boards in the majority of the teaching rooms. The boarding house Hawkwell and Hargreaves is home to all boarders in Year 9 and below while James and Osborn is home to all boarders in Year 10 and above. The Prep School is based in its own modern, purpose-built building with spacious playgrounds. The Preparatory School has its own range of after school clubs and also offers supervised prep, late after prep care facility including supper and an early morning breakfast club.

(*See also Prep School entry in IAPS section.*)

Curriculum. In the first years of the Senior School all girls follow a wide curriculum which includes academic as well as creative and practical subjects. They learn keyboard skills and develop confidence in the use of computers and technology. At GCSE level, all girls take English language, English literature, mathematics, science, and select other GCSE option subjects. At 16+, girls take the two-year Advanced Level course in four subjects and all follow a structured Curriculum Enrichment programme. In addition to A Levels, students can take the prestigious Leith School's Basic Certificate in Food and Wine. All students are given extensive careers and higher education advice and academically able students are prepared for admission to Oxford and Cambridge, as well as other high achieving courses and Russell Group universities. The majority of students proceed directly to their first-choice universities and colleges of higher education.

Sport. Sporting activities include hockey, netball, rounders, football, basketball, athletics, cross country, fencing, horse riding, swimming, tennis, trampolining, dance and gymnastics. The school has a strong reputation for high achievement in gymnastics, athletics, swimming and netball. There are regular wins at Inter-school matches, county and national competitions. The superb facilities include a brand new all-weather pitch, indoor heated swimming pool, two state-of-the-art sports halls, dance studio and spacious grounds with a variety of courts and pitches. The school also runs its own Gymnastics and Swimming Academy.

Extracurricular Activities, Music and Drama. The school prides itself on offering an extensive programme of extracurricular activities at lunchtimes, after school and at weekends which are open to day girls and boarders. Senior School pupils are expected to take part in at least two activities from an extensive list. There are frequent visits to London theatres and overseas trips and exchange visits in the holidays. The school has a strong reputation for high standards in music and drama. There are opportunities for girls of all ages to take part in drama productions and there is a Saturday Theatre Academy from ages 4–18.

Christian Community. Kent College was founded by the Wesleyan Methodist Schools' Association in 1886. The school continues to benefit from having its own resident Chaplain. There are Christian assemblies on certain weekdays and a school service each Sunday.

Entrance. Main intakes to the Prep School are to the Nursery (aged 3) and Reception (aged 4) classes. The school will take girls into other year groups subject to places being available. Entrance is based on a place being available; however entrance into Years 3–6 pupils is based on the school's own entrance tests.

The main entries to the Senior School are at 11+, 13+ and 16+. Entrance is by the school's own Entrance Examinations, interview and a report from the previous school. At 13+ entry we also accept the Common Entrance as a means of entry. Girls wishing to study A Levels are required to gain at least six GCSE passes at grade C or above. Boarders are welcomed from age 10.

Scholarships and Bursaries. Academic, Drama, Music and Sport Scholarships are awarded to outstanding entrants at 11+. Academic, Drama, Music, Art and Sport Scholarships are awarded to outstanding entrants at 13+ and 16+. A maximum of two practical scholarships may be applied for and these may be worth up to 10% of the tuition fees.

Bursaries: Fee assistance may be offered to those applying to the senior school. This fee assistance is for those girls who would benefit from all the school offers but whose parents cannot meet full fees. Such fee assistance is means tested on application.

Fees per term (2016–2017). Senior: Day £6,400, Full Boarders £10,200, Weekly Boarders £8,000. Prep: Day: £2,943–£4,390, Full and Weekly Boarders £8,000. Sixth Form Entrant: £6,900. 20% discount for Forces personnel. Discounts for sisters.

Charitable status. Kent College Pembury is a Registered Charity, number 307920. It exists for the education of children.

Board of Governors:
Chairman: Mr E Waterhouse
Vice-Chair: Mrs J Stevens

Mrs J Day	Mrs G Morgan
Mr M Haftke	Mr I Pattenden
Revd J Hellyer	Mr D Robins
Mr J Ingram	Mrs G Boutillier-Scott
Mrs G Langstaff	Mrs E Thomas
Mr I Leroni	Mrs C Veall
Mr G MacKichan	

Headmistress: **Ms Julie Lodrick**, BA Hons University College, Chichester, West Sussex, NPQH National College for School Leadership, Cert Professional Practice in Boarding Mgt BSA and Roehampton, MA Ed Mgt Open University, PGCE Kingston

Bursar: Mrs A Jenkins, BA Hons Aberystwyth, ACA

Deputy Head: Mr A Kirk-Burgess, BSc Bath, PGCE, MSc Oxford

Senior School Staff:

** *Head of Subject Group*
* *Head of Department*
§ *Part-time*

§Mr N Ashton, BA Hons Worcester College, PGCE London (*Drama*)

§Miss A M C Church, BA Oxford, PGCE Birmingham (*English*)

Miss S Clark, BEd Hons De Montfort (**Director of Sport*)

Mrs C Davidson, BA Hons QTS Kent, AEP Dib Brighton (*PSHE, *Head of Pastoral & Outdoor Education, Senior School Deputy DCPO, *Head of Eco & Sustainable Issues*)

§Mrs N Denton, BSc Hons Loughborough QTS (* *PE*)

Mr A Dixon, BA Hons Kingston, PGCE Canterbury (*Art & Photography*)

§Mrs J Dooley, BA Hons Kent, MA Nottingham, PGCE Chi Chester (*Film Studies, English*)

Mrs L Hallam, BA Hons Southampton (*Assistant Head Lower School*, Spanish*)

§Mrs M Hambleton, BA Hons Reading, PGCE London (*Geography*)

Ms D Hopper, BSc Hons Canterbury Christ Church, QTS (**Head of Sciences, *Biology*)

§Mrs A Hutchinson, BA, MA, PGCE Oxon (*Classics, Latin, Greek*)

Mrs J Jenkins, BEd Hons Exeter (*Mathematics*)

Mrs T Karalius, BA Hons Aberystwyth, PGCE Canterbury Christ Church (*Economics and Business Studies*)

Mr M Kent-Davies, BMus Hons Sheffield, PGCE Manchester Polytechnic (*Director of Music, Boarders Band & Services*)

Mrs S Kruschandl, BA Hons Lancaster, PGCE Nottingham (*English & Housemistress Hawkwell & Hargreaves*)

Mr D Lee, BSc London Guildhall, QTS (**Humanities and Social Sciences, *Psychology, Gifted and Talented Coordinator*)

Mrs H Levett, BA Hons, PGCE Leeds, MA York, MEd OU (*SENCO*)

Ms C Lusher, BA Hons Middlesex (*Food Technology*)

Mrs B Mitchell, BA Hons Durham, MA London, PGCE London (*Religious Studies, Assistant Chaplain*)

Miss C Mortlock (*ICT and Business Studies, Assistant Exams Officer*)

Mr J Mossman, BA Hons, MA, PGCE King's College London (**Linguistics, Classics, Assistant Head Sixth Form*)

Mrs A Nieto, BA Madrid, PGCE London (*MFL, *Spanish*)

§Miss C Noyek, BA Hons Surrey, PGCE (*Dance*)

Mrs C Smith, BA Hons Somerset, PGCE Cardiff (*Textiles*)

Mrs G Cable, BA Hons Lancaster, QTS (**Performing and Creative Arts, Second in Dept Drama, Theatre Manager, Housemistress James & Osborn*)

Mrs J Tobin, BA Hons, PGCE Canterbury Christ Church (*Assistant Head Middle School, Religious Studies*)

Mrs A Wharton, BA Hons, PGCE Leeds (*Politics & History, Director of Career Pathways, Assistant Head of Years 12–13*)

Mr M Wilson PGCE Birmingham, MA London, BA Hons Nottingham (*History of Art*)

§Ms W Yang, BSc Guangxi Normal University China, MSc Reading (*Chinese Tutor*)

Mrs W Young Min, BA Hons London, PGCE Nottingham (*MFL, *French*)

Plus 16 Visiting Instrumental Staff.

Chaplain: §Revd J Todd

Head of Careers:
Mrs A Wharton, BA Hons, PGCE Leeds (*Politics & History, Director of Career Pathways, Assistant Head of Years 12–13*)

§Mrs G E Shukla, BEd Bradford College, PGCE Reading

Library & ICT:
Mrs S Waller, BA Hons Anglia Ruskin, MCLIP (**Learning & Life Skills, Librarian*)

Duke of Edinburgh's Award:
Mrs C Davidson, BA Hons QTS Kent, AEP Dib Brighton

House Staff:
Mrs S Kruschandl, BA Hons Lancaster, PGCE Nottingham (*English & Housemistress Hawkwell & Hargreaves*)

Mrs G Cable, BA Hons Lancaster, QTS (**Performing and Creative Arts, Second in Dept Drama, Theatre Manager, Housemistress James & Osborn*)

Admissions & Marketing Office:
Director of External Relations: Ms S Evans
Director of Marketing: Miss E Donovan, ACIM, BA Hons Surrey Institute
Head of External Relations: Miss K Minihane, BSc Hons Oxford Brookes, ILM Level 2
Director of Admissions: Mrs D Sainsbury
Admissions Officer: Mrs N Sneddon, BEd Hons Cheltenham

Bursar's Office:
Bursar: Mrs A Jenkins, BA Hons Aberystwyth, ACA
Estates Bursar: Mr D Middlehurst, MBIFM

Kent College Preparatory School:

Prep School Head: Mr N Pears, BEd Hons Cantab

Mrs P Dabin, CertEd London, BSc Hons OU (*Early Years Coordinator, Reception Class*)

Mrs V Harte, BA Hons Warwick, PGCE London (*Assistant Head KS1, Year 1, ICT Coordinator*)

Mrs S Hall, BSc Hons Wales, PGCE Canterbury (*Assistant Head KS2, Year 5*)

Mrs H Levett, BA Hons, PGCE Leeds, MA York, MEd OU (*SENCO*)

Miss G Lucy, BSc Hons Southampton, PGCE (*Prep School PE, Year 6*)

Mrs T Youdale, CertEd Brighton, BA Hons Manchester (*Assistant Head Pastoral, PSHE Coordinator, Year 5*)

School Administrator: Mrs A Cyster

Kimbolton School

Kimbolton, Huntingdon, Cambs PE28 0EA

Tel:	01480 860505
Fax:	01480 860386
email:	headmaster@kimbolton.cambs.sch.uk
website:	www.kimbolton.cambs.sch.uk
Twitter:	@KimboltonSchool
Facebook:	@KimboltonSchool

Motto: *Spes Durat Avorum.*

The School was founded in 1600 and was awarded Direct Grant status as a boys' day and boarding school in 1945. Girls were first admitted in 1976. The Preparatory School (ages 4–11) and the Senior School are fully co-educational with day boys and girls (4–18) and boarding boys and girls (11–18). As a result of the withdrawal of the Direct Grant the School assumed fully independent status in 1978. There are around 300 pupils in the Prep School and 660 pupils in the Senior School. There is almost a 50:50 ratio of girls to boys.

Mission Statement. Kimbolton School creates a caring, challenging environment in which all pupils are encouraged to fulfil their potential and are given opportunities to flourish in a wide variety of curricular and extra-curricular interests.

It provides a close family environment where young people are educated to be tolerant, socially responsible and independent of mind, equipping them for our changing world. It is a community that challenges pupils to discover their talents, develop socially and excel.

Facilities. The Senior School facilities are situated in and around the main school building, Kimbolton Castle, once the home of Queen Katharine of Aragon and for three centuries the home of the Dukes of Manchester. Now, with its Vanbrugh front and Pellegrini murals, it is a building of considerable beauty and architectural importance. The former Staterooms are study areas for senior pupils and the Castle Chapel is used each day for prayers.

The Queen Katharine Building is a state-of-the-art teaching and learning centre, complete with a 120-seat multimedia lecture theatre. Its new two-storey Science and Maths wing, opened in September 2015, provides outstanding facilities including 12 new laboratories and a digital learning suite. The Lewis Hall caters for the performing arts and daily assemblies and provides modern theatre and concert facilities. The Design Technology Centre is up-to-date and well-equipped, as is the Music School.

A large sports complex, incorporating squash courts, gymnasium, sports hall, multi-gym and changing rooms stands in the Castle's parkland. Closer to the Castle itself, lie a modern Art Centre, Library and an indoor swimming pool. The School has two fine all-weather hockey pitches, one of which is floodlit.

Our separate girls' and boys' boarding houses stand adjacent to the grounds in the picturesque Kimbolton High Street. The boarding community is an important part of the School.

The Prep School is located to the west of Kimbolton village, at the opposite end of our 120 acres of parkland and playing fields. It has, on site, a dining hall, library, digital suite, assembly hall, music teaching and practice rooms, science laboratory, art and design technology room, and sports hall, as well as large, light and airy classrooms.

We are very much one school: the curricula of the Prep and Senior Schools are aligned, our warm caring ethos starts at Reception Year and continues through to the Upper Sixth; and some of our staff teach at both the Prep and Senior Schools.

Admission and Organisation. The Prep School admits children at 4+, 7+ and 9+ (as day pupils) with the expectation that they will complete their education in the Senior School. Entry at other ages is sometimes possible. Tests for entry at the Prep School are held in February. Entry into the Senior School at the age of 11 is open to boarders and day pupils; the Senior School Entrance examinations are also held in February. There are significant entries at 13+ usually by the Common Entrance Examination in June. Those not preparing for Common Entrance may sit the School's own 13+ examination in February. Entry into the Sixth Form is based on interview and GCSE/iGCSE results.

Arrangements can be made for overseas candidates to take the entrance examination at their own schools.

Pupils are accepted in September at the start of the academic year, but a few places may be available for entry in other terms.

The relationship between the Prep and Senior Schools is a close one and contributes to the strong 'family' atmosphere of the whole School. In the Senior School, there are four senior houses and one junior house. It is an important element of our pastoral care that boarding pupils and day pupils are together – there are no day houses. Housemasters/ Housemistresses, assisted by Tutors, look after the general well-being and progress of their charges.

Work and Curriculum. For the first two years in the Senior School there are four or five parallel forms; in each of the third, fourth and fifth years there are five smaller forms with sets for some subjects. Boys and girls entering at 13 join one of the five Third Forms. An option scheme is introduced in the Fourth Form. In the Sixth Form specialisation occurs, and pupils will usually study three subjects from the following list: English Language and Literature; English Literature: History; Geography; French; Spanish; Maths; Further Maths; Physics; Chemistry; Biology; Music; Art (Fine Art); Art (Critical and Contextual); Design Technology and Engineering; Drama and Theatre Studies; Physical Education; Economics; Business; and Politics. All Sixth Formers follow a 'Preparing for Citizenship' series of lectures, seminars and debates and may opt to take A Level General Studies. Almost all leavers gain places at the universities of their choice, with many heading to Oxbridge colleges and Russell Group universities.

Religious Teaching. Our school is non-denominational with a Christian ethos and attracts children of all religions and none. Pupils attend Chapel once a week and have RS lessons each week in the First to Third Form. Other services are held in the School Chapel during each term for pupils and parents to attend. Sunday Services are held in the Chapel and occasionally the School worships in the Parish Church.

Sport and Activities. The School owns over 120 acres of land, more than 20 of which are laid out as playing fields. The major sports for boys are association football, hockey and cricket. For girls the main sports are hockey, netball and tennis. Other sports include athletics, gymnastics, dance, climbing, archery, swimming, golf, fitness training, rifle shooting, clay pigeon shooting, squash, badminton, rowing, basketball and rounders. Swimming is popular with before and after school sessions and numerous galas. Extensive use is also made by the sailing club of nearby Grafham Water, both for recreational sailing and inter-school matches. Canoeing is popular and each year a team competes in the highly demanding 125-mile Devizes–Westminster chal-

lenge. The equestrian club competes in around twenty fixtures during the course of the year. The aim is to find a sport that each pupil loves and will continue to enjoy long after leaving Kimbolton.

Music and Drama play an important part in the life of the School and almost half of the pupils take lessons in a great variety of instruments. There is a Choral Society, two orchestras, several bands and many ensemble groups. The School stages plays, musicals or concerts each term.

The School contingent of the CCF is a voluntary, keen and efficient body, divided into Navy, Army and RAF Sections with a national reputation for excellence; Community Service is an alternative. There is a successful Duke of Edinburgh's Award scheme with a growing number of participants.

There are many other activities and societies that meet on a regular basis, such as debating, public speaking, Latin, Young Enterprise, forensic science, photography, chess, robotics, bookworms, beekeeping, gardening, modelling, pottery and philosophy.

All pupils are able to participate in the large number of trips in the UK and abroad.

Careers. Advice can be sought at any time by pupils or their parents from the Careers Staff, three of whom specialise in university entrance. There is a well-stocked Careers Room, and the School is a member of the Independent Schools Careers Organisation. Fifth Formers take the Morrisby careers tests administered by ISCO. An annual Careers Fair is held for Fourth to Sixth Formers.

Dress. The School colours are purple, black and white. Boys wear blazers and grey flannels (shorts until the final year in the Prep School). The girls' uniform includes a standard skirt, blouse and blazer. Sixth Formers wear a black suit.

Scholarships and Bursaries. A number of scholarships are awarded at 11+ and 13+ to candidates who perform with distinction in the Entrance Examination or in Common Entrance.

Further Scholarships, known as William Ingram Awards, may be awarded at 13+ to external candidates with strengths in music, art, games or leadership.

Sixth Form Scholarships and Exhibitions are awarded to those who achieve outstanding results in GCSE.

There is a bursary scheme for deserving candidates aged 11 or over; bursaries may be awarded on their own or in addition to scholarships.

Fees per term (2016–2017). £3,185 (Lower Prep), £4,035 (Upper Prep), £4,950 (Senior Day), £8,235 (Senior Full Boarding), £7,740 (Senior Weekly Boarding). A 2% discount is applied if fees paid by termly direct debit.

The fees are inclusive of lunches and there is no charge for laundry, books, stationery and examination entries.

There is a reduction of 2½% in tuition fees when siblings attend at the same time.

Music Tuition Fee: £233–£273 per term for individual lessons. (Half a term's notice must be given in writing before a pupil discontinues music lessons.)

Old Kimboltonians Association. All correspondence to: Mrs H M Hopperton, Alumni Officer, OKA, Kimbolton School, Kimbolton, Huntingdon, Cambridgeshire PE28 0EA; email: alumni@kimbolton.cambs.sch.uk.

Charitable status. Kimbolton School Foundation is a Registered Charity, number 1098586.

Governing Body:
Mr C A Paull, MPhil, FCA (*Chairman*)
Mr J W Bridge, OBE, DL (*Vice Chairman*)
Mr P F R D Aylott, MA, MNI
Prof F Broughton Pipkin, MA, DPhil, FRCOG
Mrs S M Brereton
Miss E M C Coles [Colonel]

Mrs J L Doyle
Mrs S E Duberly, DL
Mr P J Farrar
Cllr J A Gray
Cllr Mrs S Hawkes, BSc, DIC, MBA
Dr T P Hynes, BA, MA, PhD
Mrs K E S Lancaster, MC Cantab, LPC/CPE
Mr M C Neale, LLB, PG Dip
Mr S J F Page, BA Hons, Cert Ed
Mr G K Peace
Mrs J L Rice
Mr G Yeandle

Headmaster: **Mr J Belbin**, BA, FRSA

PA to the Headmaster: Mrs J Nelson-Lucas

Senior School:

Senior Deputy Head: Mr M J Eddon, BSc
Deputy Head (Academic): Mr C J A Bates, BA, MA
Assistant Head (Extension & Enrichment): Mr J C
  Newsam, MA, MEd
Assistant Head (Pastoral): Mrs C A Stokes, BEd
Assistant Head (Staff): Mrs L A Hadden, BA
Director of Activities: Mr R E Knell, BA
Head of Sixth Form: Mr A J Bamford, MA

School Chaplain: Revd L N Bland, BEd
Head of Careers: Mrs A J Bates, BA

Heads of Departments:
Art: Mrs L D Bamford, BA, MA
Design, Technology & Engineering: Mr K Spencer, BEd,
  MSc, MInstMI
Digital Learning: Mr M Reed, MEng
Drama: Mrs J C Webber, BA
Economics & Business Studies: Mr J R Saunders, BA
English: Mr S K Pollard, MA
Food & Nutrition and Textiles: Mrs C E Bennett, BSc
French: Mr R E Knell, BA
Geography: Mr S Wilson, BA
History: Mr A J Bamford, MA
Maths: Mr A S Jessup, BSc, MA
Music: Mr D Gibbs, MA, FRCO
Physical Education: Mr M S Gilbert, BEd
Politics: Mr F W B Leadbetter, MA, BD, AKC, FRSA,
  FRHistS
Religious Studies: Mrs L Stone, BEd
Spanish: Mr J C Gomez, BA
Director of Science: Mr A Gray, BSc
Biology: Mr A J Treharne, MBE, BSc, PhD, CBiol, FLS,
  FRSB
Chemistry: Mr E C Drysdale, BSc
Physics: Mr C A M Holmes, BSc, BA
Academic Support: Ms R Stewart, BEd
Outdoor Pursuits: Mr J Sweet, BA

Preparatory School:

Head of Preparatory School: Mr J P Foley, BA
Senior Deputy Head: Mr O C Stokes, BEd, MEd
Lower Prep Coordinator: Mrs L K Collins, BA

Bursar & Clerk to the Governors: Mr E F P Valletta,
  MBIFM
Registrar: Mrs J Simpson

King Edward VI School
Southampton

Wilton Road, Southampton, Hampshire SO15 5UQ
Tel: 023 8070 4561
Fax: 023 8070 5937
email: registrar@kes.hants.sch.uk
website: www.kes.hants.sch.uk

King Edward VI School was founded in 1553, under Letters Patent of King Edward VI, by the will of the Revd William Capon, Master of Jesus College, Cambridge, and Rector of St Mary's, Southampton. The original Royal Charter, bearing the date 4th June 1553, is preserved in the School. The first Head Master was appointed in 1554.

There are about 963 pupils in the School, of whom over 230 are in the Sixth Form.

Admission. An entrance examination is held in January for boys and girls seeking to enter the First Year at age 11 or the Third Year at age 13 that September. Applications from able under-age candidates will also be considered. Smaller numbers of entrants are accepted into the other school years if there is space, provided the applicants are of suitable academic ability. Students may also apply to join the Sixth Form. In order to qualify for entrance to the Sixth Form a student will normally be required to have grade B or above in six subjects at GCSE, including English Language and Mathematics, and A grades in the subjects to be studied at A Level.

Registration for entry may be made at any time on a form obtainable via the school website or from the Registrar, who can supply current information about fees, bursaries and scholarships.

Class sizes average 22; the average size of Sixth Form sets is 8.

Curriculum. All pupils follow a common course in the first two years: this includes French or German or Spanish with Latin, Mathematics, Science and an Extended Studies programme. In years 3, 4 and 5 all pupils study eight 'core' subjects to IGCSE: Biology, Chemistry, English Language, English Literature, a Modern Foreign Language, Mathematics, Religious Studies and Physics. In addition there is a range of 'option' subjects: Art, Computing, Design and Technology, Economics, Geography, German, Greek, History, Italian, Music, PE, Philosophy, Sports Science, Theatre Studies and Spanish. The syllabus leading to the IGCSE Examinations, in which most pupils take eleven subjects, is designed to avoid any premature specialisation. In the Sixth Form, students may either take 3 Advanced Level subjects along with one AS course or four full Advanced Level subjects. In addition, all have an afternoon of games in both years and follow a Foundations Studies programme in both the Lower and Upper Sixth Year.

On entering the First Year pupils join a form of about 22, with a Form Tutor responsible for their general welfare and progress. The other years are organised on a system of pastoral groups of about 16. Each group has its own Year Head. In addition there is a Head of Lower School who has general responsibility for the first three years; a Head of Upper School and a Director of the Sixth Form have similar responsibilities in their respective areas.

Our aim is to provide a congenial atmosphere and a disciplined environment in which able pupils can develop as individuals.

School Activities. 10% of a student's timetable is devoted to physical education as sport and games are regarded as forming an integral part of life at King Edward's. The major sports played in the three terms are rugby, hockey, cricket and tennis for boys; and netball, hockey, tennis and rounders for girls; other sporting activities include athletics, basketball, badminton, fencing, squash, swimming and a number of other games. The School has a large sports hall and a fully equipped fitness studio and an all-weather pitch for Hockey and similar games which provides twelve Tennis Courts in Summer. There are a further 33 acres of off-site sports fields which include a second astro pitch and floodlit netball and tennis courts.

A considerable range of clubs and societies meets during lunchtime, after school, at weekends and in school holidays, catering for pupils of all ages and many differing tastes. All are encouraged to join some of these societies, in order to gain the greatest advantage from their time at the School.

In addition to a large number of sporting teams representing the School, there are such activities as charitable and community work, dance, drama, debating, chess, Duke of Edinburgh's Award scheme, International Expeditions, sailing, collectors' clubs and music. The School has flourishing choirs, as well as orchestras and a large number of smaller instrumental groups. Art and Design and Technology occupy up-to-date premises. The studios and workshops are usually open during lunchtimes and after school. Over the past 6 years the whole school has been expanded and refurbished with modern classrooms and specialist rooms.

Fees per term (2016–2017). £4,995. Fees can be reduced in appropriate cases by the award of Bursaries and Scholarships. Scholarships are available on entry at age 11, 13 and 16. Further Scholarships may be awarded during a pupil's career in the School. Some Scholarships are awarded for proficiency in the Creative Arts. Foundation Bursaries are available at age 11, 13 and into the Sixth Form.

Charitable status. King Edward VI School Southampton is a Registered Charity, number 1088030. The object of the Charity is to advance education and training in or near Southampton or elsewhere, including the carrying on of school or schools or other educational establishments and ancillary or incidental educational or other associated activities for the benefit of the community.

Patron: The Lord Lieutenant for the County of Hampshire

Governors:
Mr B E Gay (*Chair*)
Mr P W Brazier, BSC, FCIOB (*Vice-Chair*)
Incumbent Team Rector City Centre Parish Southampton, Revd Dr J E Davies, MA, DPhil
Dr Y Binge, MBChB
Dr R B Buchanan, FRCP, FRCR, MBBS
Mr M Chaloner, MA
Mrs M L Chant
Dr N J England, MA, DPhil, DL
Mrs S J Mancey
Miss J C May
Mr M H Mayes, MSc, MA, MBA
Mr J W J Mist, FCA
Mr A J Morgan, MA Oxon, FCA, ATII
Councillor R Perry, BA
Mrs C Pierce, DCH, DRCOG, MRCGP
Mr B W Richards
Dr A L Thomas, MA, PhD
Mrs J L Wadsworth
Mr K St J Wiseman, MA

Bursar and Clerk to the Governors: Mr Ray Maher, BA Econ, ACA

Head: Mr Julian Thould, MA (*History*)

Senior Deputy Head: Mr Adrian Dellar, BSc (*Chemistry*)
Deputy Head (*Academic*): Dr Bruce Waymark, BA, MA Ed (*Geography*)

Assistant Head (*Pastoral*): Mr William Collinson, BA (*English*)
Assistant Head (*Registrar*): Mrs Emma Sheppard, BSc (*Chemistry*)
Assistant Head (*Staff Development*): Mr Stephen Hall, BSc (*Biology*)
Assistant Head (*Co-Curriculum*): Miss Hilary Smith, BSc (*Biology*)
Assistant Head (*Co-Curriculum*): Mrs Paula Burrows, MSc (*Physics*)
Assistant Head (*Digital Strategy and ICT*): Mr Bob Allen, BSc (*Computing*)

Director of Sixth Form: Mr Nick Culver, MA (*Economics*)
Head of Upper School: Dr Emma Thomas, BSc, PhD
Head of Lower School: Mrs Clare Kelly, BA (*PE*)
Director of Student Guidance: Mrs Lem Millar, BSc
Senior Master: Mr Kevin Fitzpatrick (*PE*)

Teaching Staff:
* *Head of Department*

Art:
*Mr Graham Piggott, BA
Miss Alex McGinn BA
Mrs Nicola Moxon, BA
Mr Ed Lewis, BA

Biology:
*Mr Simon Aellen, BSc
Mrs Josephine Barnes-Wardlaw, BSc (*Junior Science Coordinator*)
Mrs Laura Burnett, BSc
Miss Lucinda Downing, BSc
Mr Stephen Hall, BSc
Mrs Lem Millar, BSc
Mr Mark Miller, MA, DPhil
Mrs Rachel Moody, BA
Miss Liz Porter, BSc
Miss Hilary Smith, BSc
Miss Katrina Yerbury, BSc

Chemistry:
*Mr Richard Cross, BSc
Mrs Jan Collinson, MChem
Mrs Claire Costello-Kelly, BSc
Miss Lucinda Downing, BSc
Mr Adrian Dellar, BSc
Dr Stuart Gamblin, BSc, PhD
Mrs Emma Sheppard, BSc
Dr Viv Green, MSc, PhD

Classics:
*Mrs Jacqui Meredith, BA
Mr Chris Giles, BA
Mr Julian Halls, BA

Computing:
*Mr Peter Mapstone, BSc
Mr Bob Allen, BSc
Mr Gerard Eyssens, BEd
Miss Rachel Jones, BA, MA, MPhil

Design & Technology:
*Mr Simon Barker, MA
Mr David Blow, BSc
Mrs Nicola Moxon, BA
Mrs Helen Sheridan, BA
Miss Amelia Stone, BSc

Economics/Business Studies:
*Mr Paul Sheppard, BSc
Mr Nick Culver, MA
Mrs Sue Quinn, BA
Mr Matthew Laverty, BA

English:
*Dr Alistair Schofield, MA
Mrs Hannah Arnold, BA
Miss Rebekah Champion, BA
Mr William Collinson, BA
Miss Emer Cullen
Mrs Sam Evans, BA
Ms Ruth Greenwood, MA
Mrs Joanna Gunton, BA
Mrs Julia Hardwick, BA
Ms Andrea Gadsbey, BSocSc

Geography:
*Miss Laura-Jane Grant, BA
Mr David Brown, BA
Mr Andy Gilbert, BA
Mr Geoff Havers, BSc
Dr Bruce Waymark, BA, MA Ed
Mr Garry Hunt, BSc
Mrs Alice Penfold, BA

History:
*Mr Nick Diver, MA (*Head of Humanities*)
Miss Jacky Barron, BA
Mr Kevin Coundley, MA
Dr David Filtness, MA
Mrs Rosemary Potter, BA
Mr Julian Thould, MA
Mrs Shona Burt, BA

Mathematics:
*Mrs Kathryn Platten, BSc
Mrs catherine Asiki, BA
Mr Peter Collins, BSc
Mr Gerard Eyssens, BEd (*2nd in Maths*)
Mrs Clare Kelly, BA
Mr Ian Hardwick, BA
Miss Emma Ridley, BSc (*2nd in Maths*)
Mr Paul Robinson, BEng
Mr Ian Rosenburg, BEd
Mr John Singleton, BSc
Mrs Jennifer Thimbleby, BSc
Mr Gareth Westwater, BSc
Mr Richard Wood, BEd

Modern Languages:
Mrs Susan Allen, MA (*Head of Foreign Languages*)
Mrs Jenny Jones, BA (*French*)
Mr Martin Kukla, MA (*German*)
Mrs Elisa Ladislao, BA (*Spanish*)
Mr Stuart Ayers, BA
Miss Emily Ball, BA
Miss Rebecca Enfield, BA
Mr Daniel Fernandez, BA
Mrs Hong Deng, MA
Mr Gavin Lawson, MA
Mrs Sophie Rugge-Price, MA

Music:
Mrs Heather Freemantle, MA, LLCM, ALCM (*Director of Creative Arts*)
Miss Irene Anderson, MA
Mr James Belassie, MA
Mr Chris Evans
Mr Harun Kotch

PE:
Mr Daniel Kent, BA (*Director of Sport*)
Mrs Jessica Ferrand, BA (*Deputy Director of Sport*)
Mr Matt Mixer, BSocSc (*Sports Science*)
Mr Calum Crichton, BA
Mrs Lisa Henderson, BEd
Mrs Clare Kelly, BA
Mrs Janis Kent, BA

Mrs Hannah Penn, BA
Mr Lloyd Powell, BSc (*Performance & Fitness Coordinator*)
Mr Richard Wood, BEd (*Physical Education Coordinator*)

Psychology:
*Mrs Rachel Moody, BA
Mr Mark Miller, MA, MPhil
Miss Hilary Smith

Physics:
*Mr Rob Simm, BSc
Mrs Paula Burrows, MSc
Dr Helen Dean, BSc, PhD
Mr John Foyle, BSc
Mr Lawrence Herklots, BSc (*Head of Science*)
Mrs Maryam Mahdavi, BSc
Mr Jamie Shadbolt, BA

RE:
*Mrs Helen Searles, MA
Mr Tim Tofts, MA, Dip Phil
Mrs Rachael Kairis, BA
Revd Julian Poppleton, BA, Dip RS

Theatre Studies:
*Mrs Hannah Arnold, BA
Mrs Hayleigh Hawker, BA
Mrs Caroline Piggott, BA

Curriculum Support:
*Mr Stefan Smart, BA, MPhil
Mrs Susie Smart, BA
Mrs Jane Thould, BA

King Edward's School
Bath

North Road, Bath BA2 6HU

Tel: Senior School: 01225 464313
         Junior School: 01225 463218
         Pre-Prep School: 01225 421681
Fax: Senior School: 01225 481363
         Junior School: 01225 442178
         Pre-Prep School: 01225 428006
email: reception@kesbath.com
website: www.kesbath.com
Twitter: @KESBath
Facebook: /kesbath

As the city's former grammar school, founded in 1552, KES has a very healthy tradition of nurturing academic excellence and ambition, reflected these days in the School's outstanding results which consistently place us in the top five independent schools in the South West. The ethos of the School is one that encourages all pupils to play as hard as they work and to make the most of all the wonderful opportunities here, both in and out of the classroom, that enable them to grow and thrive within a supportive and caring framework. We set the bar high, but we also give our pupils all the tools that they need to reach those ambitious standards. We aim to foster talent in all its forms and to open doors to enquiry and discovery. Independent-mindedness and creative spirit are strong suits, but so too is the sense of community that seeks to respect and value all its members.

As a family of three schools, the Pre-Prep, Junior and Senior sections of King Edward's offer an inspiring and supportive environment for children age 3 to 18. Some join us just for the Sixth Form, many stay for their entire school career. All pupils are encouraged to be the best they can be and all are nurtured along the pathway to leading happy, ful-filled and successful lives at school and beyond.

ISI Inspection report. In 2015 the School was inspected by the ISI and was judged as 'excellent' across all eight aspects of school life under review including pastoral care and co-curricular provision. The report noted that "The success of the school lies in the strength of the ethos which permeates it from the EYFS to the sixth form. All three sections of the school encourage the pupils to strive for excellence and to achieve to the best of their ability in a stimulating environment so that they acquire a love of learning which goes beyond the formal curriculum."

Organisation. King Edward's is a co-educational day school. The School consists of a Senior School of 768 pupils, a Junior School of 182 pupils and Pre-Prep & Nursery of 98 pupils.

Facilities. The Senior School is situated on a 19-acre campus with stunning views across Bath. A further 17-acre site at nearby Bathampton is home to the School's playing fields and sports pavilion. Senior School buildings include the Wroughton Theatre, extensive laboratories for Biology, Chemistry, Physics and ICT and a Modern Foreign Languages suite. The newly refurbished Holbeche Centre includes a Sixth Form Centre with adjoining café, an extended Careers and Higher Education Centre, a Drama studio, Art Gallery and Design Technology studios. There is also a modern Sports Hall, together with an artificial playing surface. The newest addition to the site is the stunning Wessex Building: a three-storey, glass-fronted structure with a dining room and servery on the first floor, a multi-purpose second floor for assemblies, presentations, concerts and social gatherings, and a state-of-the-art Library on the ground floor.

Admission. King Edward's Pre-Prep and Nursery is non-selective upon joining. Children can join the Nursery after they turn three. Thereafter, children progress to Reception and then on to Years 1 and 2. Space allowing, children are also welcomed throughout the academic year.

Junior School: Children joining from our own Pre-Prep do so via internal assessment. They do not sit an entrance examination. Pupils from other primary schools and preparatory schools are offered places based on assessment and interview. The main entry is in Year 3 but other vacancies may occur.

Senior School: All potential Year 7 pupils are interviewed and assessed via an entrance examination testing Verbal Reasoning, Mathematics and English. Older pupils may enter the Senior School, if and where places are available, by sitting an entrance examination appropriate to their age.

Pupils may also seek direct entry into the Sixth Form. Such pupils are expected to acquire a sound set of GCSE passes before transfer for advanced study. Applicants are interviewed and a reference is sought from their present schools.

Application forms and further information concerning entry are obtainable from the Registrar or available online. Open Days are held in the Autumn and Spring terms.

Fees per term (2016–2017). Pre-Prep £3,175, Junior School £3,520, Senior School £4,455–£4,525.

Scholarships. Scholarships are awarded in Year 7, either for academic excellence or for an outstanding special talent in art, drama, music and sport.

Bursaries. Income-related entrance Bursaries may be awarded to children entering Years 7 and 12, whose parents are unable to pay the full fee. A general Bursary fund is also available to assist parents during times of unforeseen family circumstances, when they may find themselves unable to fund full school fees. Further details are obtainable from the Bursar's office.

Senior School Curriculum. We start in Years 7 and 8 with a broad range of subjects, to which we add choice and greater range in Year 9. By the time pupils are choosing their GCSE options, they will have a clearer idea of their strengths and enthusiasms and be able to select the best range of subjects to go alongside the core subjects of English, Maths, all three sciences and a modern foreign language.

For A Level, further specialisation and greater focus on personal interest and academic strengths come into play as pupils look to their education and potential careers after life in the Sixth Form. We offer careers guidance and testing to support these fundamental choices and then UCAS and Higher Education guidance as they look to make the move to their chosen degree subject from the A Levels they will complete in Year 13.

No two pupils are the same and so we work to provide as much choice and flexibility as we can in our options schemes for Years 9, 10 and 12. All combinations are possible in principle and a broad mix of subjects is as supported as more traditional routes of sciences, languages or humanities.

Throughout, there is an underlying appreciation that pupils succeed best when taught interesting and engaging lessons by enthusiastic, specialist staff. We want our pupils to leave here with valuable study skills, having found their intellectual and academic passion and having fulfilled their potential in that area.

Music and Drama. There is a healthy musical tradition in the School, with over 20 instrumental and choral groups affording opportunities to explore differing musical styles. Partnerships with Bath Abbey and Bath Philharmonia Orchestra help to further extend the experience of our musicians and choirs.

King Edward's is known for producing exceptional theatrical work and is regarded as a centre of excellence for its creative and challenging performance work, the professional standards of its productions, and its consistently outstanding academic results. In addition to two big productions each year, the Senior School also offers inter-form competitions, Duologue performances, drama clubs, tech club and an end-of-year 'Spectacular'. The School has also recently introduced LAMDA exams and taken a show to the Edinburgh Fringe.

Sport. Sport plays a significant role in the life of King Edward's School. The School enjoys a strong sporting tradition, where all pupils are encouraged to take an active role in the curricular and co-curricular opportunities available to them. Each pupil is encouraged to develop their potential, creating the opportunity to allow later involvement at recreational level or within a competitive environment. We aim to nurture teamwork, leadership, commitment and a passion for sport through the opportunities available to all pupils at KES. The major games are rugby, hockey, cricket and netball. Minor sports include athletics, cross-country, tennis, soccer, rounders, badminton, golf, basketball, dance, gymnastics, table tennis and trampolining.

School Societies and Activities. The School aims to challenge and stimulate all pupils by offering a wide range of activities and experiences beyond the classroom. The 2015 ISI Report found our extra-curricular provision to be "outstanding", and we truly believe that there is something for everyone from among the 100 clubs and societies running each year.

Outward bound opportunities include joining the School's CCF, founded in 1896, or taking part in the Duke of Edinburgh's Award scheme. The School also enters the Ten Tors Competition each year. Lunchtime clubs include Lego Robotics, KES Amnesty Club, the Socrates Debating Club and IFS Student Investor Club.

Pastoral Care The Deputy Head (Pastoral) coordinates the pastoral team. Every child has a Form Teacher who is at their foremost contact during daily life at school. Tutors work in teams managed by Heads of Year or Senior Tutors who are in turn assisted by Heads of Sector (Lower, Middle School and Sixth Form). The pastoral staff are ably supported by a School Nurse and Counsellor. The School prides itself on its family atmosphere and the excellent relationships between pupils of all ages and staff.

Honours. In 2016 pupils performed exceptionally in their A Levels: 27.6% at A*, 63.4% at A* or A and 88.3% at A*–B. At GCSE: 44.3% at A* and 71.8% at A* or A.

King Edward's Junior School and Pre-Prep and Nursery. For further details please see separate entries for the Junior School and Pre-Prep and Nursery under IAPS.

The Association of Old Edwardians of Bath. c/o The Development Office.

Charitable status. King Edward's School Bath is a Registered Charity, number 1115875. It is a charitable trust for the purpose of educating children.

Chairman of Governors: Mrs W Thomson, MEd, BEd Hons, LLCM TD

Headmaster: Mr M J Boden, MA (*French & German*)

Second Master: Mr M J Horrocks-Taylor, BSc, MEd (*Geography*)

Bursar and Clerk to the Governors: Mr J Webster, BSc, ACA

Deputy Head Academic: Mr T Burroughs, BA (*History & Politics*)

Deputy Head Pastoral: Ms C Losse, MA (*German & French*)

Assistant Heads:
Head of Middle School, Compliance: Mr A Bougeard, BSc (*Chemistry*)
Staff Development: Mrs P Bougeard, MA (*Spanish & French*)
Head of Lower School, Events: Mr D Chapman, BA (*Mathematics*)
Curriculum: Mr D Middlebrough, BA (*Mathematics*)
Head of Sixth Form: Mr P Simonds, BSc (*Geography*)
Co-curricular: Mr J Tidball, BSc (*Geography*)

Teaching Staff:
* *Head of Department*
[1] *Head of Year/Sixth Form Senior Tutor*
[..] *On leave*

Miss F Bains, BA (*Religious Studies & Philosophy*)
Mr M Barber, BA (*Economics & Business Studies*)
Mr N Barnes, MA (*Chemistry*, *Careers*)
Mrs S Bird, BA (**Drama/Theatre Studies*)
Mrs J Blair, BMus (*Learning Support*)
Mrs H Blamire, BDes (*Art*)
Mr D Bloomer, BSc, MBA (*Mathematics*)
Mr M Boden, MMus (*Music*)
Mrs E Brown, BA (**English*)
Mr G Brown (*Physical Education & Games*)
Mrs C Bruton, BA (*English*)
Mr M Bull, MA (**Classics*)
[Mrs J Burchell, MA (*Classics*)]
Mr M Buswell, ME (**Religious Studies & Philosophy*)[1]
Mr G Butterworth, BA (**Economics & Business Studies*)[1]
Mrs B Charlton (**Spanish*)
Mr M Cooney, BA (*Classics*)
Mr P Craven, MA (*History & Politics*)
Ms R Davies, BA, MSc (**History & Politics*)[1]
Mrs T Dawson, BSc (*Mathematics*)[1]
Mrs L Dias, BSc (*Economics & Business Studies*)
Mr T Dore, BSc (*Biology*)
Mrs O Doughty, BA (*English*)
Mr R Drury, BA, LRAM (**Music*)
Dr A Fewell, BSc, PhD (*Biology*)

Mr T Fisher, MA (*English*)
Ms O Fitzgerald, BA (*Classics*)
Mr J Garner-Richardson, BSc (*Chemistry & Biology*)
Mr C Graham, BSc (*Mathematics*)
Mrs H Graham, MA (*History & Politics*)[1]
Mrs E Grainger, BA (*French & Spanish*)
Mrs L Gwilliam, BSc (**Physical Education & Games*)
Mr D Hacker (**Physical Education & Games*)
Mr M Harrison, BSc, MSc, CPhys, MInstP (*Physics*)
Miss C Hartley, BA (*English*)
Mr R Haynes, MA (**Physics*)
Miss L Hews, BA (*Classics*)
[Dr M Heywood, BSc, PhD (*Chemistry & Biology*)]
Mr J Holdaway, BEng (**Design & Technology*)*
Mr M Howarth (*Physical Education & Games*)
Mrs F Hughes, MA (*Art & Photography*)
Miss L Hughes, BA (*Spanish & French*)
Miss S Hurst, BA (*Design & Technology*)
Mrs C Jones, BA (*German & French*)
Miss Z Kayacan, BA (*English*)[1]
Mrs A Kean, BSc (*Biology*)
Mr J Kean, MA (*English*)
Mr L King, BA, MSc, (*Physical Education & Games*)
Dr J Knight, BSc, PhD (**Geography*)
Mr T Laney, BSc (**Biology*)
Mr B Lang, BSc (*Physics*)
Mrs R Lang, BSc (*Mathematics*)
Mr D Lehmann, BSc (*Mathematics*)
Mr C Lilley, BSc (*Physical Education & Games*)
Mr S Lilley, BSc (*Physical Education & Games*)
Mr P Livesey, BEd (*Physical Education & Games*)
Mrs P Mason, BSc (*Biology & Chemistry*)
Mr J Mawer, BSc (*Geography*)
Miss S McCrorie, MA (*Mathematics*)
Mrs K Moreno, BA (*Physical Education & Games*)
Mr T Medhurst, BEd (**Information Technology*)
Miss L Miners, MSc (*Chemistry*)
Mrs A Munn, BA (**Learning Support*)[1]
Mrs C Nightingale, BSc (*Chemistry*)
Mr M Oehler, BSc (**Chemistry*)
Mr R Pagnamenta, MEng (**Mathematics*)
Mr M Pell, BA (**Art & Photography*)
Miss L Perris, BMus (*Music*)
Mr N Purcell, MA (*Design & Technology*)
Miss S Richardson, MSc, MA (*Physics*)
Mr W Satterthwaite, MA (**German, French*)
Mrs J Scott Palmer, BSc (**Psychology*)
Mrs K Simonds, BSc (*Learning Support & Geography*)
Ms S Stanford-Tuck, BScEd (*Biology*)
Mrs V Stevens-Craig, BA (*Drama/Theatre Studies*)
Mrs D Tamblyn, BEd (*Drama/Theatre Studies*)
Mr R Thomas, MA (*History & Politics*, **HE/UCAS*)
Miss K Trump, BA (*Physical Education & Games*)
Mrs A Tse, BSc (*Biology*)
Mr A Vass, MA (*French*)*
Ms S Vernon, BA (*English*)
Dr L Wainer, MSc, PhD (*Mathematics*)
Mr T West, BA (*ICT*)
Miss A White, BA (*English*)
Mrs J Wilcox, BSc (*Mathematics*)
Mr D Willison, BA (*Art*)
Dr M Wood, MA, PhD (*Religious Studies*)
Mr D Woods, BA (*Physical Education & Games*)
Miss E Young, BEd (*Physical Education & Games*)

Examinations Officer: Mrs S Moles
School Chaplain: Revd Caroline O'Neill
School Librarian: Miss L Bowman, BA, MLS (*Head of PSHE*)
SSI KES CCF: CSgt P H Jones

Finance Manager & School Accountant: Mrs N Rowlands, AAT
Headmaster's PA: Ms L Wolfe, BA
School Secretary (Academic): Mrs K Tedstone
School Secretary (Pastoral): Mrs V Gibbens, BA
School Receptionist: Mrs A Budgett
Registrar: Miss A Rashid
Admissions Administrator: Miss H Lane
Development Director: Ms K Teague, BA, MInstF Dip
Development Officer: Mrs C Davies, BA
Communications Officer: Mrs K Gentle, MA
Marketing Communications Officer: Mr G Goold, BA
Music Administrator: Miss K Folan, MMus
PE Administrator: Mrs R Worsdall, BA
School Nurse: Mrs C Morris, RGN

Junior School:
Head of Junior School: Mr G Taylor, BA Ed, NPQH
Deputy Head: Mr M Innes, BA, PGCE
Deputy Head (Pastoral): Mrs R Hardware, BEd
Mrs R Barrett, MA, PGCE
Mr S Carr, BEd
Miss L Chapman, MA, PGCE
Mr J Corp, BSc, PGCE
Mr D Cousins, BA
Mrs F Dore, BSc, PGCE
Mrs E Heaney, BEd
Mrs C Hutchings, BMus, PGCE
Mrs A Jabarin, BA, PGCE
Mrs C Lewis, CertEd
Mrs G Oliver, CertEd, ASM
Mrs E Pike, BA, PGCE
Mr J Roberts-Wray, BA, PGCE
Miss S Paul, BSc, PGCE
Miss A Young, BSc, PGCE

Junior School Administrator: Miss S Hunt

Pre-Prep School Staff:
Head of Pre-Prep & Nursery: Ms J Gilbert, BEd, NPQH
Deputy Head: Mrs D Bright, BA, QTS
Mr S Boydell, BA, PGCE, MEd, MRHistS, PGCert
Mrs H Blakey, BSc, PGCE
Mrs J Carter, BA
Ms L Williams, BSc, PGCE

Pre-Prep Administrator: Mrs A Fairlie

King Edward's School
Birmingham

Edgbaston Park Road, Birmingham B15 2UA
Tel: 0121 472 1672
Fax: 0121 415 4327
email: admissions@kes.org.uk
website: www.kes.org.uk
Twitter: @KESBham
Facebook: /KESBham

Motto: '*Domine, Salvum fac Regem*'.

King Edward's School, Birmingham, was founded in 1552 and occupied a position in the centre of the city until 1936 when it moved to its present 50-acre site in Edgbaston, surrounded by a golf course, lake and nature reserve and adjacent to the University. It is an independent day school with 850 boys aged 11 to 18. Approximately 50 boys in each year receive financial assistance with fees from scholarships and the Assisted Places Scheme. The school belongs to the Foundation of the Schools of King Edward VI in Birmingham (two independent, five grammar schools and one acad-

emy), and its sister-school, King Edward VI High School for Girls, is on the same campus. Academically one of the leading schools in the country, King Edward's is also renowned for the scale of its provision and its excellence in sport, music, drama, outdoor pursuits and trips and expeditions.

Admission. Most boys enter the school at 11+, although a small number join at 13+. In addition, applications at 16+ to enter the Sixth Form are encouraged. At both 11+ and 13+ candidates take papers in Mathematics, English and Verbal Reasoning at a level appropriate to the National Curriculum. A large number of pupils are also interviewed as part of the admissions process. At 16+ entry is decided by interview, report from current Headteacher and predicted GCSE grades.

The names of candidates must be registered at the School before the closing date as stated in the prospectus. Evidence of date of birth and a recent photograph must be produced when the name of a candidate is registered for the examination.

Term of Entry: Autumn term only.

Scholarships and Assisted Places. Approximately 15–20 Academic scholarships varying in value from 15% to 50% of the fees are awarded each year. Most of these scholarships are awarded at 11+, but awards are also made to outstanding candidates at 16+ and, very occasionally, at 13+. Music scholarships are also available.

Scholarships may be increased to full fees in cases of financial need.

The Assisted Places Scheme offers means-tested support to up to 35 boys a year. The scheme targets primarily 11+ entrants but 16+ entrants are also eligible to apply.

Fees per term (2016–2017). £4,125.

Academic Success. In 2016 the school's fifth International Baccalaureate results were world-class with an average points score of 39.2. 54% of the boys gained 40 points or over, the equivalent of 4 A*s at A Level. Almost all leavers go on to university, some after a gap year, with over 91% of them gaining a place at their first-choice university. 25 pupils gained places at Oxford and Cambridge. Additionally, 26 boys will study Medicine.

At GCSE 61% of results were at A* and 87% A* or A grades. Furthermore 26 pupils gained 10 A* grades, 49 gained 9 A*s, and 72 boys achieved only A*s and As.

Curriculum. *Lower School*: The following subjects are studied by all boys to the end of the third year: English, Mathematics, French, Geography, History, Physics, Chemistry, Biology, (General Science in first year), Latin, Art, Design, Drama, Music, PE and Religious Studies. All boys study one of German, Spanish or Classical Greek in the third year and may take their choice to GCSE or IGCSE and beyond. In addition, boys are required to undertake familiarisation courses in Information Technology. In the Fourth and Fifth year all boys study Mathematics, English, English Literature, a Modern Foreign Language and either Physics, Chemistry, Biology plus three other optional subjects, or two Sciences plus four other optional subjects, which are taken to GCSE or IGCSE. At present, the school offers IGCSE in Mathematics, Biology, Chemistry, Physics, English, English Literature, History, Modern Languages and Music.

Sixth Form: Since September 2010, A Levels have been replaced entirely with the International Baccalaureate Diploma. The school believes that this diploma provides a more challenging and broad Sixth Form education with greater opportunity for independent learning and is a better preparation for university study and life thereafter.

The school's curriculum goes beyond preparation for examinations. For example, PE and games are compulsory for all and Friday afternoon is set aside for the entire school to pursue non-academic activities: Combined Cadet Force,

Leadership, service in the community, outdoor pursuits, Art, Information Technology etc.

Music and Drama. The school has a very rich musical and dramatic life. Many of the musical groups and theatrical productions take place jointly with King Edward VI High School for Girls. There are ten different musical groups and choirs. The school has recently opened a Performing Arts Centre with a main hall seating up to 500 and excellent facilities for music and drama.

Games. Rugby, Cricket, Hockey, and Athletics are the major team games in the school. However, many other games prosper including archery, badminton, basketball, chess, cross-country, cycling, fencing, Fives, golf, kayaking, squash, swimming, table tennis, tennis, water polo. The School has extensive playing fields for all these activities plus its own swimming pool, all-weather athletics track, sports hall, gymnasia and squash courts. In 2015 the school opened its new hockey pavilion and astro pitch.

Societies and Clubs. The school has a very wide range of clubs and societies including Christian Union, Islamic Society, Literary Society, Classical and Junior Classical Societies, Historical and Junior Historical Societies, Living History Society, Economics Society, Musical Society, Senior and Junior Dramatic Societies, Shakespeare Society, Art Society, Geographical Society, Debating and Junior Debating Societies, Scientific Society, Biological Society, Mathematical Society, Meteorological Society, Modern Language Society, Chess Club, Photographic Section, School Chronicle, Film Society, Hard Rock Society.

CCF, Outdoor Pursuits and Expeditions. The Royal Naval, RAF and Army Sections of the Combined Cadet Force are very popular amongst pupils. In addition, the KES Award and the Duke of Edinburgh's Award Scheme have grown substantially in recent years, so that the majority of pupils in the third year gain the KES Award and about 20 each year gain the Gold Duke of Edinburgh's Award. All of this forms part of a strong tradition of trips and expeditions, ranging from cycling and caving and walking and skiing trips, to language trips to Europe to major expeditions to Honduras, Venezuela, Peru, Egypt, Morocco. There have also been very successful rugby tours to Australia, South Africa and China.

Forms and Houses. In the first five years there are five forms in each year, with an average of 24 pupils. In the Sixth Form, forms are on average 12 in number, and often comprise pupils together from the Lower and Upper Sixth. There is also a house system, comprising eight houses, which continues to provide an important element of pastoral support and competition in sport, music, debating and general knowledge.

Charitable status. The Schools of King Edward VI in Birmingham is a Registered Charity, number 529051. The purpose of the Foundation is to educate children and young persons living in or around the City of Birmingham.

Governing Body:
Mr Tim Clarke (*Chairman*)

Dr B Adab	Mr I Metcalfe
Mr G Andronov	Ms L Pearson
Mrs G Ball, OBE	Dr J Sherwood
Mr J Beeston	Mr S M Southall
Mr P Burns	Ms S Stobbs
Mr P Christopher	Mr G Thomas
Mr G Marsh	Mrs A Tonks

Chief Master: Dr Mark Fenton

Deputy Head (*Administration and Pupil Discipline*): Mr K D Phillips, BA
Deputy Head (*Pupil Welfare/Health & Safety*): Mr R D Heathcote, BSc
Deputy Head (*Academic*): Mr J C Fern, MA

Assistant Teachers:

Dr T F P Hosty, BA, PhD	Mrs E J Wareing, BA
Mr L W Evans, BA	Dr D C Wong, BEng, PhD
Mr J C S Burns, MA	Ms L C Seamark
Mr L M Roll, BA	Mrs K S Charlesworth-Jones, BA
Mr T Mason, BSc	
Mr E J Milton, BA	Mr M P Barratt, BA, MA
Mr B M Spencer, BA	Ms H A Ferguson, BSc, MSc
Mrs G A Ostrowicz, BA	
Mr C D Boardman, BSc	Mrs G J Babb, BA, MA
Mr S J Tinley, BSc	Mr T J Wareing, BA
Mrs C M L Duncombe, BA	Dr C Arico, MSc, PhD
Mr J Porter, BSc	Miss F C Lee, BA
Mr T A McMullan, BSc	Dr M Romon Alonso, MSc, PhD
Dr G Galloway, PhD	
The Revd D H Raynor, MA, MLitt	Mr J J W Fair, BSc
	Dr T S Miles, MSc, PhD
Mr M J Monks, GRSM, Dip RCM	Mr P R Ollis, BSc, MA
	Mr J M Pavey, BSc
Mr R W James, BA	Dr L A L Rackham, MA, MSc, PhD
Mr S L Stacey, MA	
Mr T F Cross, BSc	D L N Tuohey, BSc
Mr D J Ash, MA	Ms D K Poole, BA
Ms R Leaver, MEng	Mr T Burdett, BSc
Mr J P Smith, BA	Dr H M Cocksworth, MA, PhD
Mr R E Turner, BA, MPhil	
Ms D E McMillan, BSc	Mr A M Dutch, BMus
Mr P A Balkham, BA	Dr J Fennell, BSc, PhD
Mr D M Witcombe, MSc	Mrs C L Gillow, BA
Mr I J Connor, BSc	Dr S P Kulkarni, BSc, MPhil, PhD
Mr R D Davies, BSc	
Ms S-L Jones, BSc	Dr M D Leigh, MA, PhD
Dr J L Amann, BA, PhD	Mr B A Orlin, BA
Ms E K Sigston, BA	Mr N A Shepherd, BSc
Mr P W L Golightly, BA	Ms S Alam, BA
Mr M J Bartlett, BA	Mrs S L Behan, BSc
Mrs P J R Esnault, MA	Mr G P J Browning, BA
Senora A Estevez, BA, MA	Mr A Bussey, BA
Mr C A P Johnson, BA	Mr J M Butler, BA
Dr M R Follows, BSc, PhD	Mr A D Langlands, BSc
Mrs F M Atay, BA	Miss R V Morris
Mr D H Corns, MA, MPhil	Mr A W J Petrie, BA
Mr H M Coverdale, BScEcon	Miss R A Smedley, BSc
	Mr C R Turford, BA, MA
	Dr A D Webb, MChem

Part-time Teachers:

Mr D C Dewar, BSc	Mr J C Howard, BEd
Mr J P Davies, MA	Mr R J Deeley, MA
Mrs G S Hudson, BEd	Mr E J Aston, BSc
Mrs C R Bubb, BA	Ms B Dehame-Hare, MA
Mrs H J Cochrane, BA	Ms A Havel, BA
Mrs S Thorpe, BSc, MEd	Ms P K Higgins, BA
Mrs C Smith, BA, MA	Ms N B Lockhart-Mann, BA
Mr R W Symonds, BSc	

Librarian: Ms K A Fletcher-Burns, BA, MSc Econ

School Medical Officer: Dr M Forrest, MBChB, DRCOG, MRCGP

King Edward's Witley

Petworth Road, Godalming, Surrey GU8 5SG
Tel:	01428 686700
Fax:	01428 682850
email:	admissions@kesw.org
website:	www.kesw.org
Twitter:	@KESWNews

Facebook: /King-Edwards-School-Witley
LinkedIn: /king-edward's-school-witley

King Edward's Witley was founded in 1553 by King Edward VI as Bridewell Royal Hospital. Originally housed at the Bridewell Palace, which was given under Royal Charter to the City of London, the School moved to Witley in 1867, simultaneously changing its name; it became co-educational again in 1952. The School is an independent boarding and day school for girls and boys aged 11–18. The School has 415 pupils; approximately a third are day pupils. There are a substantial number of bursaries, currently over 100, available to help boys and girls whose home circumstances make a boarding style of education a particular need.

The School is situated in a 100-acre campus in an Area of Outstanding Natural Beauty in the Surrey countryside, approximately ten miles south of Guildford, with Heathrow and Gatwick international airports both within a 45-minute drive.

King Edward's Witley is steeped in history, but combines its traditional strengths with a modern outlook. The School prides itself on its ability to provide a school community that reflects the real world admitting pupils from a broad range of academic, social, economic and cultural backgrounds – 65% are English native speakers and over 43 countries are represented. All children are nurtured to encourage independent thinking and a spirit of respect and understanding for others, resulting in a mature and well-rounded outlook on life and a commitment to upholding the strongest moral values.

King Edward's Witley is proud to be one of the first English boarding schools in the area to offer the IB Diploma Programme and in 2014 celebrated 10 years of the IB. In 2016 pupils achieved a 100% success rate and King Edward's has evolved to become one of the top 20 boarding IB schools in the country, as acknowledged by an award from Best Schools UK.

From 2015, King Edward's has also offered the new A Level course as an alternative to the IB, ensuring pupils have a choice of routes to secure a place at university. In 2016 44% pupils gained A*–A and 96% gained A*–C at GCSE. The School also runs a one-year Pre-Sixth Form course for overseas pupils, representing an opportunity to improve English language skills and trial both IB and A Level subjects on offer, allowing for more Sixth Form choices.

Renowned for its ability to nurture pupils so they excel in their academic studies, King Edward's Witley also provides a highly motivating and inspiring environment for children to equally thrive in other sporting / creative activities. The School has an excellent reputation for its welcoming community and the provision of high-quality pastoral care.

The 1st and 2nd Forms constitute the Lower School and are accommodated in Queen Mary House with shared communal facilities for boys and girls. From the 3rd Form upwards boys and girls live in seven modern, purpose-built paired houses where the accommodation and study areas are completely separate but everyone can come together in the shared communal facilities on the ground floor.

Facilities at the School are second to none and include a brand new state-of-the-art Business and Finance Centre, indoor swimming pool, all-weather hockey and tennis playing fields and a newly refurbished central dining hall, which delivers an outstanding standard of catering. The School pioneered paired boarding houses with communal areas, where everyone can come together in their spare time to enjoy games, TV, music and conversation in the common rooms, kitchen, music and television rooms. For the Sixth Form, a lively common room and new study area and careers library provide an environment for independent learning and recreation.

Admission. Children are normally admitted at 11+, 13+ and 16+ but if there is room they may be admitted at other times, and occasionally a child who should clearly be working alongside older children is admitted at 10+. Admission is by pre-testing or by the School's own entrance examination and interview taken normally in the January prior to entry.

Fees per term (2016–2017). Boarders: Lower School £9,155, Forms 3–5 £9,495, (Pre) Sixth Form £9,865, including all boarding and tuition fees, books and games equipment, and the provision of school uniform and games clothing.

Day Pupils: Lower School £4,995, Forms 3–5 £6,245, (Pre) Sixth Form £6,650, including meals and uniform. Individual music tuition in piano, organ, singing and all orchestral instruments is available.

Bursaries. Bursaries are available for both boarding and day pupils. The School has an endowment providing support for children whose circumstances make boarding a particular need. Awards are reviewed annually with regard to parental circumstances and to school fees. They may be given in conjunction with Local Education Authority grants or help from a charitable trust. The School has a dedicated Bursaries officer who works with applicants to source the financial support needed to enable worthy candidates to join the School.

Scholarships. Academic, Art, Drama, DT, Music and Sports Scholarships are offered at 11+, 13+ or 16+ for entry to the Sixth Form. These awards will be up to a maximum of 30% of full fees but may be augmented in case of financial need. A discount of 10% of full fees is available to children from service families. There is a special IB Sixth Form Day scholarship available, awarding 100% of fees.

Charitable status. King Edward's Witley is a Registered Charity, number 311997. The Foundation exists to provide boarding education for families whose circumstances make boarding a particular need, though the excellent facilities and the high standards of academic achievement and pastoral care make it attractive also to any family looking for a modern and distinctive education.

Treasurer and Chairman of Governors: Mrs J Voisin, BA

Headmaster: J Attwater, MA

Senior Deputy Head: S J Pugh, MA

Academic Staff:
* Head of Department
† Housemaster/mistress

D Abraham, BA (*Director of Football*)
Mrs J A Abraham, BSc (*Mathematics, †Elizabeth*)
Mrs S Antill (*Information and Communication Technology*)
Miss K Apfelstedt, BSc (*Learning Support*)
Mrs V Attwater, BMus (*Music*)
Dr P Attwell (*Science*)
R Arch (*Head of IB and Sixth Form, Economics & Business Studies, Theory of Knowledge*)
A Baynes, MA (*Modern Languages*)
Mr M Bennett (*History*)
Mrs S Butler, BA (*Learning Support*)
T Campbell (*Geography*)
B Cochrane, BEng (*Science*)
Miss S Condy (*Religious Studies & Philosophy*)
J G Culbert, BSc (*Physics*)
Mr R Davies (*Mathematics*)
Miss Dibb-Fuller (*Learning Support*)
Miss R Di-Salvia, BSc, BA, MA (*Modern Languages*)
Miss H Duncan, BA Ed (*Science, †Queens'*)
N Emsley, BSc, Dip Com, PGCE (*Science, Physics, †Grafton*)
M-A Eysle (*Director of Sport*)

Dr E K Foshaugen, BA, MPhil (*Theory of Knowledge and Critical Thinking*)
D G Galbraith, BSc (*Science, *Chemistry*)
Mr S Gardner (†*Mathematics*)
Mrs H Hanley, BSc (*Geography, ICT*)
Mrs E Harman, BSc (*Economics & Business Studies*)
Mrs J Harris (*Library, Extended Essay Coordinator*)
Ms L Harris Jones (*Religious Studies and Philosophy*)
M Harrison, BA (*Modern Languages, †Ridley*)
P W Head, BSc (*Mathematics*)
Mrs A E Hill, BSc (*Science, Biology, Theory of Knowledge*)
Mrs S J Hinde-Brown, BA (*Modern Languages, Theory of Knowledge*)
Mrs J A Hinton, BSc (*Modern Languages*)
J Hole, BA, MA (*Deputy Head Academic, English and Drama, Physical Education*)
A N K Johnson, BSc, MSc (*Design & Technology Resistant Materials, Mathematics*)
J C Langan, BA (*English & Drama*)
D Laurence, BA (*Economics & Business Studies*)
Dr A Lennard, PhD, BSc (*ICT*)
G Lynch-Frahill, BSc, BEd (*History, Physical Education, Religious Education*)
Mrs J M Lyttle, BA (*English*)
A Macmillan, BA (*Design & Technology, †Wakefield*)
S McDonald, MA (*Classics*)
Mrs A Meyer, BSc, BEd (*Mathematics*)
Dr H Mir, PhD (*Mathematics*)
Mrs L Moore (*Art and Photography*)
Mrs P V Nash, BEd (*Science*)
Mrs M Pevreall, BSc, MSc (*Biology*)
Mrs C Pitt (*Art & Photography*)
D K Poulter, BSc, FRGS (*Deputy Head Co-curriculum, Geography*)
Mrs H Pullen (*Sports Coach*)
S J Pugh, MA (*Senior Deputy Head, Classics*)
N Rendall, BA (*English, Assistant Head of Sixth Form*)
Mrs C Shadforth, BA, MA (*Learning Support, Modern Languages*)
Mrs C Shouksmith (*Art*)
Mrs N Skau, BAc (*Careers, Modern Languages, Library*)
A Sibacher (*Mathematics*)
D Slater, BA (*English*)
S Sliwka, BMus, FRCO (*Director of Music*)
Miss A Small, BSc (*Design & Technology Food & Textiles*)
Rev Dr D Standen, BA, AKC, CTM (*Classics, School Chaplain*)
Mrs K Standish (*Chemistry*)
M Tate (*Artist in Residence*)
Mrs H Thorpe (*Geography*)
S L Todd, BSc (*Examinations Officer, Physical Education, Science, Mathematics*)
Mrs J Todd (*Examinations Officer*)
J Tudor, BSc, MSc (*Physical Education*)
Mrs L M Vitagliano, MA (*History*)
Miss B Ward (*Learning Support*)
Mrs B Waters, BEd (*Modern Languages*)
Mrs K A Wilson, DipM, ACIM (*Economics and Business Studies, English*)
Mrs E van Rooyen, BA,BSc (*Learning Support*)

Houses and Housemasters/Housemistresses:

Queen Mary House (*Junior Boys and Girls*): S Gardner and Mrs K Gardner
Senior Paired Houses:
Wakefield (*Boys*): A Macmillan and *Elizabeth* (*Girls*): Mrs J A Abraham
Edward (*Boys*): D Tobias and *Tudor* (*Girls*): Mrs N Skau

Ridley (*Boys*): M Harrison and *Queens'* (*Girls*): Miss H Duncan
Grafton (*Boys*): N Emsley

Director of Finance and Administration: A Lewis
Director of Admissions & Communications: J Benson
Head of Marketing: Miss N Dimmock
Development Manager: Mrs E Harrison
Headmaster's Secretary: Ms C Todd

King Henry VIII School
(Part of the Coventry School Foundation)

Warwick Road, Coventry CV3 6AQ

Tel: 024 7627 1111
email: info@khviii.net
website: www.khviii.com
Twitter: @KHVIIISchool

Founded in 1545 by John Hales, Clerk of the Hanaper to the King, under Letters Patent of King Henry VIII, King Henry VIII School has a deserved reputation as one of the finest independent, co-educational day schools in the UK.

"Success, responsibility and enjoyment – these are our prime aims", states Jason Slack, Headmaster.

The school is represented on the Headmasters' Conference and on the Association of Governing Bodies of Independent Schools. The governing body is the Coventry School Foundation, on which are represented Sir Thomas White's Charity, the Coventry Church Charities, Coventry General Charities and Birmingham, Coventry, Oxford and Warwick Universities. There are also several co-opted Governors.

There are 400 boys and 321 girls in the Senior School, and 258 boys and 230 girls in the Prep School.

Facilities. The school moved to its present extensive site in a pleasant part of Coventry in 1885. The Governors have continually improved, extended and restored the buildings which are well equipped to cope with the demands of an up-to-date, relevant and challenging curriculum. The school has extensive playing fields, some of which are located on the main site. Other playing fields are five minutes away by minibus.

The Governors have committed themselves to a major building programme at the school. A new Prep School, Art facility, Sixth Form Centre and Sports Hall have recently been completed. Both Senior and Prep Schools have a first-rate computer network available to all pupils. A six-lane, 25m swimming pool (and fitness suite) opened in 2009. An Archive was opened in 2014 containing a timeline from 1545 to 2014 and original Tudor artefacts.

Curriculum. The curriculum is broad and balanced, integrating National Curriculum principles and practices where appropriate. The Senior School curriculum provides courses leading to the GCSE examinations and GCE AS and A Levels. Subjects available currently are Art, Biology, Business Studies, Chemistry, Classical Civilisation, Computing, Design and Food Technology, Drama and Theatre Studies, Economics, English, French, Geography, German, Greek, History, Information and Communication Technology, Latin, Law, Mathematics, Music, Photography, Psychology, Physics, Religious Studies and Spanish. Physical Education and Sport are also considered to be a vital part of the curriculum and are available as an AS and A2 Level option. All students follow a structured PSHE course.

Courses in Key Skills/Complementary Studies and Critical Thinking are offered in the Sixth Form. The Extended Project Qualification was introduced for Year 13 in 2012. Examination results at all levels are excellent.

Games. Rugby, Hockey, Netball, Basketball, Cross-Country Running, Athletics, Rounders, Tennis, Cricket, Swimming, Golf, Orienteering and Fencing. Prep School games include Tag Rugby, Swimming, Soccer, Rounders, Athletics, Cricket and Cross-Country Running. In 1986 the largest artificial turf games area in the country was created, and refurbished in 2014, used mainly for hockey, but providing an additional 24 tennis courts in the summer. This facility is shared with Bablake School.

Extra-Curricular Activities. The School is noted for the excellence of its sport, music, drama, debating, public speaking and outdoor pursuits. All pupils are encouraged to make a contribution to the extra-curricular life of the school. The School has close connections with many universities including Oxford and Cambridge.

Admission. Admission is via the School's own Entrance Examination, held annually in January for entrance the following September. The normal age of entry is 11, but there are additional intakes at other ages and also at Sixth Form level. All enquiries about admission to the school should be addressed to the Headmaster.

Scholarships. The Governors award annually a number (not fixed) of entrance bursaries and scholarships. Full details regarding financial assistance are available from the Headmaster at the school.

Old Coventrians Association. Email: alumni@ khviii.net; website: www.khviii.com.

Fees per term (2016–2017). Senior School £3,660; Prep School £2,778–£2,960.

Prep School. The Prep School is based on two nearby sites and enjoys excellent facilities which include an Early Years Centre, a Library, ICT rooms with networked PCs, an Art and Design rooms, a Science room, Astroturf and Sports Hall and a Music room. Children are accepted by competitive examination from 7+ to 10+. The emphasis is on a broad education based upon the National Curriculum and children are prepared for the Entrance Examination for entry to the Senior School.

(*For further information about the Prep School, see entry in IAPS section.*)

Charitable status. Coventry School Foundation is a Registered Charity, number 528961. Its aim is to advance the education of boys and girls by the provision of a school or schools in or near the City of Coventry.

Chairman of Governors: Mrs Julia McNaney

Senior School

Headmaster: Mr Jason Slack, BSc, MA Ed

Deputy Heads:
Mr Warren Honey, BSc, MEd
Mr David Morton, BA
Miss Ann Weitzel, MA, NPQH

Teaching Staff:

Mr Naz Amlani, BSc
Mr Tom Andrews, BSc
Mr Conn Anson-O'Connell, BA
Miss Marysia Bancroft, MA
Dr Steven Barge, BA
Miss Emma Barwell
Mrs Michelle Bayne-Jardine, MA, MPhil, LLB
Mr Matthew Blake, MPhys
Mrs Sally Bradley, BA
Mr Ben S Bramley, BSc
Miss Sally Burton, BA

Dr Helen Buttrick, MA, MSCi
Mr James Cannock, BEng
Mr James Carlyle, BA
Mrs Anna Clegg, BA
Miss Rosalyn Coull, BMus, MMus, PhD
Dr Michele Cuthbert, BSc, MEd, HDipEd, WITS
Mrs Clare Dempsey, BSc
Mr Niall Doherty, BA, LTCL
Mrs Carrie Dowding, BSc
Mrs Tracy Ferguson, BSc
Mr Jon Fitt, BSc

Miss Angelique Giordano, BA
Miss Margot Griffiths, BSc
Mr Richard Harrington, MA
Dr Debbie Hayton, BSc
Mrs Anna Heathcote, BA
Miss Hannah Hemskerk, BA
Mr John Henderson, BA
Mrs Julie Holland, BA
Dr Tim Honeywill, MMath
Mrs Linda Horton, MA
Mrs Loraine Hughes, BSc
Mrs Karen Hunt, BEd
Mrs Kathryn Hunt, BSc
Mr Peter Huxford, MA
Mrs Anna Jewell, BA
Mr Nicholas Jones, MA
Mrs Victoria Kaczur, BA
Mr Alistair Kennedy, BA, BA Mus
Mr Duncan Lovell, LLB, MA
Mr Peter Manning, MA
Mrs Rachel Mason, BSc
Mrs Jaynita Mattu, BSc
Mr Craig McKee, BTEC NDip, BSc
Dr Mary McKenzie, MA
Mr Nick Meynell, BA
Miss Sarah Mould, BA
Mrs Jenny Morris, BSc, MA
Mrs Cindy Neale, MA
Dr Donna Norman, BSc
Mr Francis O'Reilly, BA
Mrs Kerry Owens, BEd

Mrs Michelle Oxtoby, BSc, BSc
Mrs Kulwinder Pabla, MSc
Mrs Denise Pandya, BMus
Mr Andrew Parker, BEd
Mr Guy Parker, BSc
Dr Noel Phillips, BSc
Mrs Dolores Pittaway, BA, PG Dip
Mrs Amanda Pontin, CertEd
Mrs Jessica Proudlock, BA
Mrs Debra Quinn, BA
Mr Alastair Rendle, BEng
Dr Lynn Reynolds, BSc
Ms Sally Ridley, BA, MBA
Mr Paul Robbins, MEng
Mrs Lynne Roote, BSc
Miss Tajinder Sanghera, MA
Mr Shaun Schofield, BSc
Miss Charlotte Southall, BSc
Mrs Julie Spraggett, BMus
Mrs Christine Spriggs, BSc
Miss Grace Spring, BA
Mrs Amy Stickels, MA
Mr Stuart Sweetman, MA
Mr Neil Tingle, BA
Mrs AJ Tracey, BSc
Mrs Anne Wade, BSc, MA, CBiol, ML
Mrs Kate Whitehead, BSc
Mrs Lisa Whiteman, Nat Dip Perf Arts, Higher Nat Dip Dance
Mr Chris Wilde, BA
Mr Steve Wilkes, BEd

Administrative Staff:
Bursar: Mr Michael Shaw
School Administrator: Mrs Julie Low, HND
Headmaster's PA/Admissions Secretary: Mrs Amanda Skinner
Examinations Officer: Mrs Belinda Leslie, MBA
Careers Advisor: Mrs Sally Pike, BA, Dip Careers Guidance
Chaplain: Revd Alison Hogger-Gadsby, BA, Dip HE, Clerk in Holy Orders
School Nurse: Mrs Wendy Bolland, RGN
School Network Manager: Mr Tim Lees
Office Manager: Mrs Jacky Matthews
Sports Centre Manager: Mr Dominic Bell
Librarian: Ms Helen Cooper, LLB, PGCE
Alumni Relations Officer: Mrs Amanda Garman, BSc

King Henry VIII Preparatory School

Head: Mrs Gill Bowser
Deputy Head (Swallows): Miss Caroline Soan, GMus, PGCE
Deputy Head (Hales): Mrs Helen Higginson, BSc, MA
Director of Studies: Mr Steven Dhaliwal, BEd, MSc

Teaching Staff:

Mrs Rachel Avlonti, BEd
Ms Emma Barwell, BA
Miss Nicola Bawcutt, BMus, PGCE
Mr Greg Beaufoy, BSc
Mrs Sarah Brand, BEd
Mrs Claire Brindley, BSc

Miss Lynn Brown, BSc
Mrs Jane Coles, CertEd, BPhil, MSc
Mrs Emma Curran, BEd
Mr Steve Dhaliwal, BEd, MSc
Mrs Lucy Duckers, BA, PGCE

Mrs Jane Duffield, BSc, PGCE

Mrs Charlotte Ferguson, BA

Mr Steve Hall, BA

Mrs Julia Halstead, BA

Mrs Helen Harvey, BA

Mr Brian Hewetson, BA

Mrs Catherine Jeffcoat, BA

Mr Lau Langkilde

Mrs Jane Lovell, BEd

Miss Emily Manship, BSc, PGCE

Mr Philip McGrane, BSc

Mrs Lesley McKenzie, BEd

Mrs Helen Mellor, BEd

Mrs Ruth Morris, BA

Mr Neil Mosedale, BSc

Mrs Elizabeth Ochieng, BEd

Mrs Kelly Osman, BA, PGCE

Mrs Manisha Patel, MA, PGCE

Mr Ken Pearson, BEd

Mrs Beverley Piercy, BTEC Dip

Mrs Amanda Pontin, CertEd

Miss Jenna Sainsbury, BA

Mr Phil Savage, BA

Miss Tamsin Slack, BSc

Mrs Jill Sutherland, BA, QTS

Mrs Sian Westmancoat, BA Ed

Mrs Helen Williamson, BSc

Miss Nicola Wood, BA

Mrs Karen Wormald, BEd

Miss Kate Wozencroft, HND, BEd Hons

Mrs Sophia Wright, BA

Administrative Staff:

Bursar: Mr Michael Shaw

School Administrator: Mr Alan Shaw

Headmaster's PA/Admissions Secretary: Mrs Lesley Batson

School Nurse: Mrs Wendy Bolland, RGN

School Network Manager: Mr Tim Lees

Librarian: Mrs Kate Batchelor

King William's College

Castletown, Isle of Man IM9 1TP

Tel: 01624 820400
Fax: 01624 820401
email: admissions@kwc.im
website: www.kwc.im

Motto: '*Assiduitate, non desidia.*'

King William's College owes its foundation to Dr Isaac Barrow, Bishop of Sodor and Man from 1663 to 1671, who established an Educational Trust in 1668. The funds of the Trust were augmented by public subscription and the College was opened in 1833 and named after King William IV, 'The Sailor King'.

In 1991, the College merged with the Isle of Man's other independent school, The Buchan School, Castletown, which had been founded by Lady Laura Buchan in 1875 to provide education for young ladies. The Buchan School has been reformed as the junior section of the College for boys and girls up to age 11. (*For further details of The Buchan School, see entry in IAPS section*).

The Isle of Man, being internally self-governing, has a very favourable tax structure and the independence of College would not be affected by changes in UK legislation.

The College is set in superb countryside on the edge of Castletown Bay and adjacent to Ronaldsway Airport. The Isle of Man is approximately 33 miles long and 13 miles wide and is an area of diverse and beautiful scenery. The Isle of Man is an unusually safe environment with a very low crime rate.

There are approximately 370 pupils at College and a further 200 pupils at the Preparatory School. There is also a Nursery School for 2 to 4 year olds on the Buchan site. Both King William's College and The Buchan School are fully co-educational.

Entry. New pupils are accepted at any time, but most begin at the start of the September Term. Boys and girls are admitted to the Preparatory School up to the age of 11 at which point transfer to King William's College is automatic. Entry to College, including Sixth Form level, is by Head's report and, where possible, by interview.

Further details and a prospectus may be obtained from the Admissions Office to which applications for entry should be made.

Organisation. The school is divided into three sections: Fourth Form (Years 7 & 8), Fifth Form (Years 9, 10 & 11) and Sixth Form (Years 12 & 13). Each section is led by a Head of Year, assisted by a team of tutors who monitor the academic progress and deal with all day-to-day matters relating to the pupils in their charge. In addition, all pupils are placed in one of three co-educational Houses for internal competitive purposes, which provides an important element of continuity throughout a pupil's career at the School.

Boarders. There are two houses: one for boys and the other for girls. The living and sleeping accommodation is arranged principally in study-bedrooms for senior pupils with junior pupils sharing dormitories in small groups. Each House has its own Houseparent who is responsible for the pastoral welfare of the pupils. He or she is assisted by two or three tutors, of whom at least two are resident.

Chapel. The College is a Church of England foundation but pupils of all denominations attend Chapel; the spirit of the services is distinctly ecumenical.

Curriculum. Pupils at both Schools follow the National Curriculum in its essentials.

The curriculum is designed to provide a broad, balanced and challenging form of study for all pupils. At 11–13 pupils take English, Mathematics, French and Spanish or Latin, Science, History, Geography, Design Technology, ICT, Art, Music, Drama, Religious Studies, Physical Education, PSHE. Pupils then go on to study typically 9 subjects at GCSE/IGCSE level from a wide number of options.

In the Sixth Form King William's College offers the **International Baccalaureate**. Students choose 6 subjects, normally 3 at higher level and 3 at standard level, which must include their first language, a second language, a science, a social science and Mathematics. In addition, students write an extended essay (a research piece of 4,000 words), follow a course in the Theory of Knowledge (practical philosophy) and spend the equivalent of one half day a week on some form of creative aesthetic activity or active community service (e.g. Duke of Edinburgh's Award fulfils this requirement).

Music and Drama. There are excellent facilities for drama with House plays and at least one major school production each year, together with regular coaching in Speech and Drama. There are Junior and Senior Bands and Choirs, and a very flourishing Chapel Choir. The House Music competition is one of the many focal points of House activity.

Games. The College has a strong tradition and a fine reputation in the major games of rugby, hockey and cricket. There are regular fixtures with Isle of Man schools and schools in other parts of the British Isles. Netball, athletics, soccer, cross-country and swimming all flourish and there are both House and College competitions. Senior pupils may opt to play golf on the magnificent adjoining Castletown Golf Links or to sail as their major summer sport. There are approximately thirty acres of first class playing fields, an indoor heated swimming pool which is in use throughout the year, a miniature rifle range, a gymnasium for basketball and badminton with an indoor cricket net, hard and grass tennis courts, two squash courts and a sand dressed all-weather pitch.

Other Activities. There is a wide range of societies and activities to complement academic life. The Duke of Edinburgh's Award Scheme flourishes and expeditions are undertaken regularly both on the Island and further afield.

There is a thriving Combined Cadet Force and Social Services group. There are strong links with the Armed Services who help regularly with Cadet training. There are regular skiing trips, choir tours and educational trips to the UK and abroad.

Travel. King William's College is easily accessible from the UK and from abroad. Some boarders come by sea from Heysham or Liverpool using the regular service to Douglas but the majority of boarding pupils and parents come by air from the British Isles and much further afield. There are direct flights to London, Belfast, Dublin, Liverpool, Manchester, Bristol and other UK cities. Boarding House staff are fully experienced in arranging international flights and younger pupils are met at the airport.

Health. The health of all pupils is in the care of the School Doctor. There is a sanatorium supervised by a qualified nursing sister and high standards of medical care are available at Noble's Hospital in Douglas.

Fees per term (2016–2017). Day: £4,931 (Years 7 & 8), £6,159 (Years 9–11), £7,012 (Years 12 & 13). Boarding Fee: £3,133 in addition to Day Fee.

A reduction of one-third of the fee for boarders and one half of the fee for day pupils is allowed to children of clergy holding a benefice or Bishop's licence and residing in the Isle of Man. There is a similar arrangement for children of Methodist Ministers.

A reduction of 15% is allowed for serving members of the Armed Forces of the Crown. Once a pupil is accepted, the reduction continues even though the parent may leave the Services.

A reduction of 10% is made for the second, third and fourth child.

Scholarships and Bursaries. Year 7 Academic Scholarships are offered up to the value of 20% of the current tuition fee and examinations take place in late January. There are papers in English and Mathematics and an interview.

Sixth Form Academic Scholarships are offered up to the value of 20% of the current tuition fee and examinations are normally held in November of the year prior to entry. There are papers in Mathematics, English, one other subject chosen by the candidate and an interview.

Music Scholarships, Drama and Sports Awards to the value of 20% of the tuition fee are available to candidates entering either the Lower Fourth or the Lower Sixth Form who demonstrate exceptional talent or potential. Examinations and auditions take place by arrangement.

There is also a Bursary fund to support students if the financial circumstances of parents make this necessary.

Further details of all scholarships may be obtained from the Admissions Office and on the website.

Charitable status. King William's College is a Manx Registered Charity, number 615 and is operated as a Company limited by guarantee.

Visitor: The Most Revd and Right Hon Dr J Sentamu, Lord Archbishop of York

Trustees:
Chairman: His Excellency Sir Richard Gozney, KCMG, CVO, Lieutenant Governor of the Isle of Man
S G Alder, BA, FCA
Professor R J Berry, RD, MA, DPhil, MD, FRCP
The Ven Andrew Brown, MA, Archdeacon of Man
T W B Cullen, MA
Professor Ronald Barr, Chief Executive Officer, Department of Education and Children
M J Hoy, MBE, MA
The Rt Revd Robert Paterson, MA, The Lord Bishop of Sodor and Man

Secretary to the Trustees and Bursar: J V Oatts, BA, MSc, Dip Surv

Governors:
Chairman: N H Wood, ACA, TEP
S Billinghurst, BA Hons, ACA
P B Clucas, BA, BSc
A C Collister
M Grace, BSc Hons, MRICS
Mr P Harwood, BSc, FIA
Dr W Henle, LLM NYU
Mrs E J Higgins, BSc, ACA
Dr L Hulme, LRCP, MRCS
Miss S J Leahy, LLB, Dip LP
R Raatgever, ACA, CA SA

[Principal: **M A C Humphreys**, MA]
Acting Principal: J H Buchanan, BA

Acting Vice Principal: Miss C L Broadbent, MA
Head of Senior School: Mr S L Corrie, BMus

* *Head of Department*
† *Housemaster/mistress*

Mr J M Allegro, BA
Mrs M Bailey-Barnes, BA
Mrs E J Ballantyne, BSc
Mrs A G Beesley, BA
Miss C R Beswick, MSci
Mrs K E Brew, BEng
Mrs A Z A Clarke, MA (**English*)
Mr S N Cope, BA (**Geography*)
Mr M C Crabtree, BSc (**Boys PE & Games*)
Mrs D J Currie, BA (**Religious Studies*, *History*)
Mr C Davidson, MA
Miss M de Andres Marquiegui
Miss E F Drane, BA
Mrs B Dunn, BEd (*Director of Sport*)
Mrs S M Ellson, MA
Mrs R J Foxon, BSc
Mrs J M Finch, MA
Miss C Ganzo Perez, BA
Miss B C Harkin, BA (*Acting Head of Sixth Form*)
Miss S Hathaway, BA
Miss F Heckel, MA (**French*, **Modern Languages*)
Mr N A Howell-Evans, BA (*Head of Science*)
Mrs P Howell Evans, BA
Mr E J Jeffers, BA (*Head of Boarding*, †*Colbourne House*)
Mrs S A Jeffers, BA
Mr S B Jelly (*Head of Fourth Form*)
Mr S P Kelly, BA (**Art*)
Miss A Kerr, MA
Mrs B Kneen, BSc (*Head of Fifth Form*)
Miss C V Ledger, BA (**Drama*)
Mr D M C Matthews, BSc (**Mathematics*)
Mrs Z A McAndry
Mr D McConnell, BSc
Mr G E Moore, BMus (*Director of Music*)
Mrs A L Morgans, BA Ed, BSc (*Head of Sixth Form*)
Dr P H Morgans, BSc, PhD (**Science*, **Chemistry*)
Mrs J Munro, BA
Mrs G R Murphy, MCLIP (*Librarian*)
Mr R C Parry, BSc
Mrs S Parry, BA (†*School House*)
Mr R Riekert, BComm (**Economics*)
Mrs A M Schreiber, MA
Mr C Smith, BSc
Mr M C D Taylor, BA
Miss K K Teare, BSc
Mr A D Ulyett, BSc (**Biology*, *IB Coordinator*)
Mr P Verschueren, MSc
Ms M Westall, BSc
Miss E C Winstanley, BA
Mr J J Wood, MSc

Part-time Staff:
Miss J Busuttil, BA
Mr D Cowley, BSc
Miss P Cloux Valle, BA
Miss R Lloyd, BMus
Miss R R Pate
Ms S Roper, BA
Mrs S A Ross, BEd
Reverend E J Scott, BA (*Chaplain*)
Mrs E Smith
Mrs O Stone, BA
Miss C C Temps, MA

Principal's PA: Mrs J Bateson
Admissions Registrars: Mrs S Gibson & Mrs M Taggart
School Medical Officer: Castletown Medical Centre

King's College School

Wimbledon Common, London SW19 4TT
Tel: 020 8255 5300
Fax: 020 8255 5309 (Porters' Lodge)
email: admissions@kcs.org.uk
website: www.kcs.org.uk
Twitter: @KCSWimbledon
Facebook: @kingscollegeschool

Motto: *Sancte et Sapienter.*

King's College School was founded as the junior department of King's College in 1829. According to the resolutions adopted at the preliminary meeting of founders in 1828, "the system is to comprise religious and moral instruction, classical learning, history, modern languages, mathematics, natural philosophy, etc., and to be so conducted as to provide in the most effectual manner for the two great objects of education the communication of general knowledge, and specific preparation for particular professions". In 1897 it was removed from the Strand to its present site on Wimbledon Common.

Organisation. King's College School is a day school. Boys only are admitted below the sixth form. The sixth form is co-educational. The school consists of a senior school of 912 pupils aged 11 to 18 and a junior school of 449 pupils aged 7 to 13 who are prepared for entry to the senior school. On entry to the senior school, pupils are placed in a house. Every pupil has a tutor who is responsible for their progress and welfare throughout their school career.

Admission. Entrance at 13+ to year 9 is via a pre-test which boys sit in year 6 followed by the CE or scholarship in year 8. Since September 2016, the senior school has admitted boys in year 7 after entrance tests in year 6. Candidates from King's College Junior School sit either the transfer examination or the scholarship examination. Places for girls and boys are available each year for entry to the sixth form. Preliminary enquiries about entry should be made to the admissions registrar. A non-refundable registration fee of £150 is charged.

Junior School. Entrance examinations, graded according to the ages of the pupils, are held in the January of the year of entry. Enquiries should be made to the junior school secretary. (*For further details of the junior school refer to entry in IAPS section.*)

Scholarships and Bursaries. A system of scholarships helps to set high academic standards and create opportunities for pupils from a variety of backgrounds to benefit from what the school offers at both 11+ and 13+.

11+ scholarships for entrance into the senior school, will be available in 2017. Further information will be available closer to the entrance exam.

13+ Academic scholarships: Up to 20 academic scholarships may be awarded. The number will vary according to the quality of the candidates. Candidates must be under 14 years of age on 1st September of the year in which they sit the examination. This is held at King's College School in early May. The maximum award for major scholarships will be £1,500. Smaller awards will be fixed sums of £1,000, or £500. If a pupil is awarded two or more scholarships, the maximum fee remission will be £2,000 pa. All additional financial benefits will be means tested, so that any award would be supplemented by fee remission of up to 100% inclusive of the scholarship.

13+ Art scholarships: One or more art scholarship and/or exhibition worth up to £1,500 of the school tuition fee per annum may be awarded annually to a boy of high artistic ability or potential. Selection will be by folio inspection and by invitation to a half-day of practical work in an informal and friendly atmosphere in the King's studios.

13+ Drama scholarships: One or more drama scholarships or exhibitions worth up to £1,500 of the school tuition fee per annum may be awarded annually. The school's intention is to offer awards to drama enthusiasts of outstanding ability and potential as performers, technicians or practitioners.

13+ Music scholarships: Three or more music scholarships or exhibitions worth up to £1,500 of the school tuition fee, in addition to free instrumental tuition on two instruments, may be awarded annually. The school's intention is to offer awards to instrumentalists of outstanding ability and potential. As a guideline, a boy of at least Grade 6 standard would be considered a promising candidate.

13+ Sport scholarships: One or more scholarships or exhibitions worth up to £1,500 of the school tuition fee per annum may be awarded annually to boys of exceptional ability or potential, determination and enthusiasm. Sports scholars should have exceptional talent in one or more sports, normally at least two. Candidates for all scholarships must be under 14 years of age on 1 September in the year of entry.

It is a condition of the award that the scholar achieves the King's pass mark in the common entrance examination, the King's scholarship examination or the transfer examination.

Sixth Form Academic scholarships: Rossetti and Fawcett scholarships which recognise academic performance in the entry examinations are available for boys and girls entering the Sixth Form.

Sixth Form Music scholarships: One or more music scholarships and exhibitions worth up to £1,500 may be awarded annually following auditions in November. The school also awards an organ scholarship. Recipients of these awards additionally receive free tuition on two instruments.

Sixth Form Drama scholarships: One or more drama scholarships or exhibitions worth up to £1,500 of the school tuition fee per annum may be awarded annually. The school's intention is to offer awards to drama enthusiasts of outstanding ability and potential as performers, technicians or practitioners. Selection takes place in the summer term of Year 11 through auditions and a workshop day.

Sixth Form Sport scholarships: We will consider awarding sports scholarships to sixth form entrants based on the pupil's track record and/or their impact in their first term at King's.

Bursaries: The school is making increasing provision for bursaries both from its own resources and as a result of the generosity of its many benefactors. Bursaries may be awarded at any of the points of entry to the junior and senior schools. Bursaries are means tested and may offer up to 100% fee remission, inclusive of any scholarships. Parents should make their initial application in advance of any entrance examination.

Fees per term (2016–2017). Tuition: senior school £6,800, junior school £5,530–£6,125.

The Curriculum – Junior School. The curriculum of the junior school is designed to lead naturally into that of the senior school in content and style. All boys within a year group follow the same timetable.

Transition, First and Second Forms (years 3, 4 & 5): English; Mathematics; Science; History; Geography; Religious Studies; Music; Drama; Art; Technology (year 3); ICT; Personal, Social, Health and Economic Education (PSHEE); Think Tank (in years 3 and 4); French (from year 5); three double sessions of PE and Games.

Third and Remove Forms (Years 6, 7 & 8): English; Mathematics; Science; French; Latin; Geography; Religious Studies; Music; Drama; Art; Design & Engineering; ICT; Personal, Social, Health and Economic Education (PSHEE); PE and two afternoons of Games.

Homework in the Junior School: Homework is graduated according to age, starting with enough to form a regular discipline.

The Curriculum – Senior School. The lower and middle school curriculums offer a wide range of options which enable the maximum choice of subjects in the sixth form. A very wide range of subjects is available at GCSE and IGCSE (International GCSE), with the majority of subjects now being taken at IGCSE. In the sixth form, pupils choose to study either A Levels or the International Baccalaureate diploma (IB).

Religious Education. King's is an Anglican foundation but welcomes pupils from all churches and faiths. The practice of other faiths is encouraged. The school has a Chaplaincy through which pupils are prepared for confirmation and there is a Chapel for voluntary worship and communion.

Music. There is a purpose-built music school and a new music school, with a 200-seater concert hall, is currently under construction (due to be completed in 2018). Four orchestras, three choirs and two wind bands, as well as various smaller groups and jazz groups, perform a number of major choral and orchestral works each year. There are regular performances at major London venues including Westminster Abbey, Cadogan Hall, St Paul's Cathedral and St John's Smith Square. Also, the choir and orchestra undertake international tours. Some 30% of the pupils have individual music lessons at the school.

Games. After an introduction to a range of games in the fourth form, pupils have a free choice of termly sports. The major sports are rugby, hockey, soccer and cricket and the games programme also includes athletics, badminton, basketball, cross-country running, fencing, fives, hockey, karate, rowing, sailing, shooting, squash, swimming, tennis and water polo. The school has its own indoor heated swimming pool. The sports hall has a floor area providing four badminton courts, as well as volley and basketball, indoor tennis and cricket nets, together with a fitness training room and four squash courts. There are two all-weather surfaces for hockey and tennis at the Kingsway ground. The school's boathouse is on the Tideway at Putney Bridge.

School societies and activities. Every pupil is encouraged to take part in extracurricular activities. Societies meet in the two extended lunch breaks and after school. Friday school finishes early to allow pupils to participate in a range of activities such as the CCF and community service. The school runs an impressive outreach programme supporting a number of neighbouring state schools. There are active drama and debating societies, together with a wide range of other societies.

Honours. Places offered at Oxford and Cambridge for 2014: 54, 2015: 52, 2016: 57.

Charitable status. King's College School is a Registered Charity, number 310024. It exists to provide education for children.

Governing Body:
Mrs P L Hughes, CBE

Mrs F R Cahill, BA Hons
Mr R J Cairns, MA
Mr O L Carlstrand, BSc, CEng, MICE
Mr A J M Chamberlain, MA, FIA
Dr P A Fraser, PhD
Mrs S Hobbs, BA, PGCE
Mr D G Ingram, MA
Mr G W James, MA
Sir Robert Jay, QC
Prof D A Lievesley, CStat, AcSS, CBE
Mr R S Luddington, MA, MPhil
Mrs P Reed-Boswell, CertEd
Mr M D J Sharp, BA
Mr D R J Silver, MA
Mr G C Slimmon, MA, MBA
Mr P J L Strafford, MA, MBA
Mrs D A Walls

Bursar & Secretary to the Governing Body: Mrs A M Clarke, MA Oxon

Senior School

Head Master: **Mr A D Halls**, MA, FRSA

Principal Deputy: Miss M Hunnaball, BSc, MA
Deputy Head (Pastoral): Mr R Milne, BA
Deputy Head (Academic): Mr W Brierly, BSc
Senior Master (Learning Resources): Mr B J Driver, MA

Assistant Heads:
Mr M D Allen, MA (*Head of IB Diploma*)
Mr K Gross, MA (*Director of Overseas Schools*)
Dr S A Hendry (*Head of Lower School*)
Dr E Laurie (*Head of Sixth Form*)
Mr R J Mitchell, MA (*Public Occasions*)
Mr J H Renwick, MA (*Head of Middle School*)
Mr M P Stables, MA (*Director of Studies*)

Chaplain: The Revd Dr J W Crossley, BA, MA, PhD

Biology:
Dr R C Clark (*Head of Science*)
Mr N E Edwards, MSc (*Head of Examinations*)
Mr N J Gardner, BSc
Mr J E Grabowski, BSc
Miss R A Harris, MSc
Dr S A Hendry
Mr P M Lavender, BSc
Dr A C Stewart

Chemistry:
Dr A M Hayes
Dr I I F Boogaerts
Mr I M Davies, MA
Mr M P Gibson, BSc
Dr P M Lloyd (*Deputy Head of IB*)
Dr R A McCarthy
Miss H L McKissack, MBE, BSc, MA (*Senior Teacher*)
Mr R J Mitchell, MA
Dr R A L Winchester

Physics:
Mr D Miller, BSc
Mr T S Banyard, BA (*Head of Teaching & Learning*)
Mr G Cawley, BSc
Miss M Hunnaball, BSc, MA
Miss N J Kersley, BSc
Miss A Langerman, BSc
Mr D J Lavender, MA, ALCM
Ms M A G Spottiswoode, BSc

Classics:
Mr B M Baulf, MA (*Head of Classics*)
Mr G E Bennett, BA
Miss V R Casemore, BA (*Head of Safeguarding*)

Dr E C Park
Mr A E Sharpe MA [maternity cover]
Miss C L Tedd, MA [maternity leave]
Mr S L C Young, BA

Economics & Social Sciences:
Mr G J A Simpson, BSc (*Acting Head of Economics*)
Mr W P Brierly, BSc
Mrs S M Danaher, BBS [maternity leave]
Mr H J Phillips, BSc
Mrs S Williams BCom
Mr W W Wilmot, BSc

English:
Dr J P D Cannon (*Head of English*)
Miss P C Alisse, MSt [maternity leave]
Mr M D Allen, MA
Mrs K L Bird, MA, MPhil
Miss J L Blunden, MA
Mr B L Bransfield, MA
Miss E C Collin, BA (*Head of Sixth Form Girls*)
Miss C F Crothers, BA
Miss A V Eilert, MA
Mr L P Maxted, MSt [maternity cover]
Mr R Milne, BA, MSc
Mr J L B Trapmore, MA (*Head of Curricular Drama*)
Mr H R Trimble, BA

Drama:
Ms D J Barron, MA (*Director of Drama*)
Mr J L B Trapmore, MA (*Head of Curricular Drama*)

Geography:
Miss M J Clarke, BA (*Head of Geography and A Level*)
Mr M V Christou, BA
Mr J A Galloway, BA (*King's Ambassador*)
Dr E R Laurie
Miss J M Lawton, BSc (*Head of Maclear House*)
Mr J M Stanley, BSc (*Head of Glenesk House*)

History:
Mr M A Stephenson, MA (*Head of History*)
Miss E J Campbell, MA
Miss R M Davis, BA (*Director of Staff Development*)
Mr N J S Knowland, MA
Mr J G Lawrence, MA, MLitt
Mr J G Ryan, BA
Mrs S E Wiseman, MA
Mrs J I Woodward, MA

Mathematics:
Mr S J Nye, BSc (*Head of Mathematics*)
Mr S A Williams, BSc (*Deputy Head of Mathematics*)
Mr C G Bell, DPhil
Mr H Bond, BSc
Mr S J Bradley, BEng
Mr B J Driver, MA, ARCO
Mr D S Fickling, MMath
Mr J A Harris, MEng (*Deputy Head of Sixth Form*)
Mrs E C Nicholl, BSc
Miss L Y Owens, BA
Mrs A J Panaite, BSc
Dr T R Squires (*Head of Alverstone House*)
Mr M P Stables, MA
Miss K E Sullivan, BSc
Mr A M R Trosser, MSci

Modern Languages:
Mrs H M Mulcahy, BA (*Head of Modern Languages*)
Mr B P Andrews, BA (*Deputy Head of Middle School*)
Mrs A J Ansbro, MA [maternity leave]
Miss B P Cerda Drago, BA
Mr H Chapman, MA (*Director of Partnerships and Outreach*)

Mr C C D Fowler, BA (*Head of Kingsley House*)
Mr K Gross, MA
Mr J T Hyam, MA
Mr S C Kent, MA
Miss M M E Kidwell, MA
Mrs H M Lindsey-Noble, BA
Miss R C Peel, BA (*Head of Major House*)
Mrs J E Purslow, MA
Mr J M A Ross, BA (*Head of Layton House*)
Mr J R C Saxton, BA
Miss J Turquin, BA
Ms R Cagigas (*Spanish Assistant*)
Mr E Boulzennec (*French Assistant*)
Ms S G Doettling (*German Assistant*)
Mr C Gonzalez Ruiz (*Spanish Assistant*)
Miss B Habimana-Ishimwe (*French Assistant*)
Mr A Scasciafratti (*Italian Assistant*)
Mrs X Yang (*Chinese Assistant*)
Dr E G Keys (*Russian Assistant*)

Psychology:
Dr G M Bamford (*Head of Psychology*)
Mrs E S Britton, MSc

Theology & Philosophy:
Mr T J Davies, BA (*Head of Theology & Philosophy*)
Mrs R R Catterall, MA, MPhil
Revd Dr J W Crossley (*Chaplain*)
Mr J H Renwick, MA
Miss E R Tozzi, BA

CCF:
Mr D Goodall, MBE (*School Staff Instructor, Combined Cadet Force*)

Memorial Library:
Mrs B Ferramosca, MSc (*Head Librarian*)
Mrs H I Mavin, BSc Econ (*Assistant Librarian*)

Junior School
Tel: 020 8255 5335; Fax: 020 8255 5339;
email: jsadmissions@kcs.org.uk; HMJSsec@kcs.org.uk

Headmaster: Dr G A Silverlock, BEd Hons, MLitt, PhD

Deputy Heads:
Mrs H J Morren, MA (*Pastoral*)
Mr D Jones, BA (*Academic*)

Assistant Head: Mr J E Hipkiss, BSc Hons (*Head of Communications & Head of Science*)

Head of Rushmere: Mrs C S Madge, BEd

Junior School Staff:
Mr R D Anderson, BComm (*Head of Windsor House*)
Miss V J Attié, BA (*Head of Tudor House*)
Mr N G Attwood, BA (*Head of English*)
Mr A Baker, BEd (*Professional Tutor*)
Miss C M Bitaud, BA (*Head of Lower & Upper Remove*)
Mrs J C Blight, BEd
Mrs C Bourne, BEd (*Head of Norman House*)
Mr P K Brady, BA (*Head of Stuart House*)
Mr D Cheers, BEd
Mr S F Connolly, BSc
Mr M D Cuming
Mrs S J de Montfort, MA
Miss E J Emmott, BA
Miss L S Gillard, MA, ATC (*Head of Art & Design*)
Mrs O M Hamilton, MA (*Head of Religious Studies*)
Mr M J Hortin, MA (*Head of Classics*)
Mrs S V D Howes, BA (*Head of Drama*)
Mrs A Huckerby, BA
Miss F C Hutchison, BA
Mrs J C Lewis, BA Ed

Mr E H Lougher, BA (*Head of Modern Languages & Academic Administrator*)
Mrs S J Martineau Walker, BA
Mr J K McAuslan
Ms C P McGregor
Mr R McCluskey, MA (*Head of PE & Games*)
Mr M J McLaughlin, MMus
Mrs R K Moore, BSc (*Head of Mathematics*)
Mr I D Morris, BA
Mr P Nash, BEd (*Head of Years Second and Third Forms*)
Mr M L Nixon, BMus (*Head of Keyboard*)
Mrs S K Phillips, BEd Hons
Mrs R F A Rose, BSc
Miss E E Savitt, MEd
Mr M N Sayer, MA
Mr P J Scott, MRes
Mr J A Streatfeild, BA (*Head of Geography*)
Mrs A C Tingle, BA, Dip SpLD
Mr P P Thomas, MA (*Head of ICT*)
Mr E T Watkins, BA (*Head of History*)
Mr R Weber (*Head of Music*)
Mrs J R McSweeney (*Teaching Assistant*)
Mr S S Baron (*Teaching Assistant*)

Joint Junior and Senior Departments

Art:
Mr R A Carswell, MA (*Head of Art*)
Miss E-J Emmott, BA
Miss L S Gillard, MA, ATC (*Head of Junior School Art & Design*)
Mrs S J Martineau Walker, BA
Mr N A Pollen, MA

Design & Engineering:
Miss L E L Spicer, BA (*Head of Design & Engineering*)
Miss D Langenberg, BA (*Coordinator of International Links*)
Mr J D Broderick, BA
Mr R W Entwisle (*Engineer in Residence*)

ICT & Computing:
Miss C A Ramgoolam, BEd, MA (*Senior School ICT Coordinator, Staff Cover, EVC & Head of Examinations*)

Learning Enrichment:
Mrs E Goodchild, BSc, Dip SpLD
Mrs L Charlesworth, MA
Mrs A C Tingle, BA

Music:
Mr D G Phillips, MA, FRCO (*Director of Music*)
Mr P A Hatch, MusB (*Assistant Director of Music and Head of PSHE*)
Mr C A Jackson, MA (*Organist and Teacher of Academic Music*)
Mr M L Nixon, BMus (*Head of Keyboard*)
Mr L Silvera, BMus (*Head of Strings*)
Mr R Weber (*Junior School Head of Music*)
Mr T A Vorias (*Gap year student*)

Physical Education:
Mr M F Baggs, BA (*Director of Sport*)
Mr R McCluskey (*Head of Junior School Games & PE*)
Mr G P Butcher (*Sports Coach*)
Mr M P Culverhouse, BA
Mr P Duggan (*Director of Rowing*)
Mrs N L Edwards, BA (*Head of Girls' Games*)
Mr J S Gibson, BA (*Deputy Director of Sport*)
Mr L B D Kane, BSc (*Director of Co-Curricular Education*)
Mr L O'Sullivan (*Swimming & Water Polo Coach*)
Mr N C Roberts (*Director of Rugby*)
Mr B D Tibble, BSc (*Head of Hockey*)
Mr P Scott, MRes

Mr H D Lovelock (*Gap year student*)
Mr C J Moore (*Gap year student*)
Mr J J Barrington (*Graduate Assistant – Sports*)
Mr M R Latham (*Graduate Assistant – Sports*)
Mr M W Lawton (*Graduate Assistant – Sports*)
Miss M Suter (*Graduate Assistant – Sports*)

Support Staff:
Bursar & Secretary to the Governors: Mrs A M Clarke, MA Oxon
PA to the Head Master: Mrs S Carrett
Admissions Registrar: Ms S J W Dowling, BA Hons
PA to Junior School Headmaster: Mrs S Richards

King's College
A Woodard School

South Road, Taunton, Somerset TA1 3LA

Tel:	Headmaster: 01823 328210
	Reception: 01823 328200
Fax:	01823 328202
email:	admissions@kings-taunton.co.uk
website:	www.kings-taunton.co.uk

Motto: *Fortis et Fidelis*

A Woodard school, Canon Nathaniel Woodard renamed the school King's College in memory of King Alfred, when he bought it in 1879, but its historical links go back to the medieval grammar school which was founded by Bishop Fox of Winchester in 1522.

King's College, Taunton is an independent co-educational boarding and day school for 460 boys and girls aged 13–18 years.

Situated on the outskirts of Taunton, the county town of Somerset, on a splendid 100-acre site, King's College offers high academic standards, a friendly and caring day and boarding community, and has an enviable reputation for music, drama and sport. Kindness, consideration for others, honesty and self-discipline are the values which King's hopes will provide its pupils with the inner resources not just for school, but for life.

King's College, Taunton, delivers success at all ages whilst offering a friendly, happy and safe living and working environment. The school provides an extraordinary breadth of opportunities to pupils and has very high academic standards. As well as the school's academic success, pupils also enjoy the highest levels of achievement in sports, art, drama and music. The school won the 2007 BBC Songs of Praise Senior School Choir of the Year title, as well as the Rosslyn Park 7s Rugby Cup – a taste of the breadth of opportunity available to pupils.

King's College has produced a large number of Oxbridge entrants over the years and is well regarded by the top universities in the UK. Pupils can join the Third Form (Year 9) at 13, going on to take GCSE exams, or in the Sixth Form (Year 12) at 16 or 17 to study for A Levels. The school is blessed with highly-qualified and committed members of staff who see their role as ensuring the happiness and successful development of each individual member of the school community. The word community is very prominent at King's: Boarders and day pupils benefit from a strong Christian ethos: an environment where self-respect and kindness to others are highly-regarded qualities.

Admission. All entries are made through the Headmaster. Pupils normally enter at 13 years in the Michaelmas term and are admitted via Common Entrance or the Scholarship Examination.

The registration fee is £75.

Fees per term (2016–2017). Boarders £10,370 Day Pupils £6,995. The fees are inclusive of all extra charges of general application.

Scholarships. Scholarships are available to boys and girls going into the Third Form (13+) and Sixth Form. Major Academic scholarships are awarded, as well as scholarships for Music, Drama, Art, DT and Sport.

Auditions for Music and Drama Scholarships and Awards are held in February (13+), and in November for Sixth Form.

Applicants for Art and Design & Technology Scholarships are invited to visit the school during the Lent term with a portfolio of work.

13+ Sports Scholarships are available for competition each February and Sixth Form Sports Scholarships are available in November.

Old Aluredian's Association. *Secretary*: P J Scanlan, MA, c/o King's College.

Charitable status. Woodard Schools Taunton Ltd is a Registered Charity, number 1103346. King's College exists to provide high quality education for boys and girls aged 13–18.

Senior Provost: The Revd Canon Brendan D Clover, MA, FRSA, LTCL

School Council:
R D V Knight, OBE, MA, DipEd (*Custos*)
Dr R A K Mott, BA, PhD (*Vice-Custos*)
The Revd Canon Mrs L M Barley, BA, MSc, PGCE
S J Carder, MA, MBA
Mrs C A Cavaghan-Pack, BEd, JP
C F B Clark, MA, MRICS, FAAV
T A Close, FCA
The Reverend B D Clover, MA, FRSA, LTCL
The Rt Revd J D G Kirkham, MA
Mrs C Cooper
G P Davis, FCA
Sir Harry Farrington Bt, MRICS
C H Hirst, MA
J E R Houghton, MA
R D A Lloyd, BSc, MRICS
Mrs L Nash
M F Trimble, BSc, ACA, FCSI
Mrs L C Scott

Headmaster: R R Biggs, BSc Cape Town, MA Oxon

Chaplain: The Revd M A Smith, BA, DipTh St Paul's

Deputy Head (Academic): J J B Lawford, BA
Deputy Head (Pastoral): Mrs K L McSwiggan, BA

Assistant Head (Administration) & Director of Music: C J Albery, BMus
Director of Extra-Curricular Activities: D J Cole, BSc
Director of Finance: M C MacEacharn, BSc, FCA
Director of Operations: A J Prosser, BSc
Director of Marketing: Mrs J M Hake, ACIM
Director of Development: Mrs L M Lavender, MBE
Admissions Registrar: Mrs K J Rippin

Assistant Teachers:
* *Head of Department*
† *Housemaster/mistress*

Ms H Agg-Manning, BA
J Arliss, BA (*Philosophy of Religion and Ethics*)
Mrs S Brownlee, MBA, BA, DipHM
Mrs L S Cashmore, BA (*Classics*, *Induction*, †*Meynell*)
Mrs K E Cole, BA (*Learning Support*, †*Carpenter*)
Mrs P Corke, BA
Mr B D Craggs, BSc
Mrs L L M Cruttenden, BA (*Modern Foreign Languages*)
Miss K M Davies, BA (*Careers*)

Mrs M V Duckham
A G Edwards, BA (*Geography*)
Mrs EM Edwards, BA,(†*Taylor*)
S Florey, BSc (†*King Alfred*)
Miss E Forward, BA
Ms B M Goldsmith, BSc
Mr M P Graven, BSc
Mrs L H Graven, BA
Mrs L Gregory (*Economics and Business Studies*)
Mrs J A Gresswell, BSc (*Physics*, * Science*)
N S Gresswell (*Director of Sport*)
J H Griffiths (*Boarding*)
J W Grindle, BSc (*Design and Technology*)
Ms Hayashi, BSc
Mrs C Hayes (* Hockey*)
C J Heayns (*Football*)
S Henderson BSc
Mrs A R Hildreth, BSc
R M Hooper, MA
P D Lewis, BSc (†*Tuckwell*)
R R Llewellyn-Eaton, MA
N D Lorimer, BCom
W H Mackenzie, BA
Miss C S Mann, BSc
C R Mason, MMath
Miss M R Menheneott, BSc
Miss K E Orr, BSc
Mrs I S Pardoe, BSc
Mrs K J Paul, BA (*Assistant Director of Music*)
Mrs A M Powell, MA
O Ridley, BA (*Sixth Form*)
J K Round, MA (*Mathematics*)
P J Scanlan, MA (*History*, *Teaching Strategies*)
Mrs C Schmidt, BA
Miss A L Schultz, MA
Mrs S A Similien, BSc
T D H Smith, MA
Dr D J Snell, BSc, PhD (†*Woodard*)
Miss E Stevens, BA
A J Wood, BA (*Drama*, †*Bishop Fox*)
Mrs L D Wrobel, BA
G Wrobel, BSc

CCF:
Lt Col D J Cole (*Officer Commanding*)
S Sgt R Mason (*SSI*)
Lt Cdr M A Smith, BA
Capt S J Shaw (*Army*)
Capt S King (*RM*)
Dr B M Greedy (*Chindits*)

Medical Officers:
Dr Yvonne L Duthie, MB BS, DCH, MRCGP
Dr A F C Fulford, MB ChB, DRCOG, MRCGP
Dr J Martin, MB BS, MRCPCH, DRCOG, MRCGP

ICT Manager: M M Lang, BSc

The King's Hospital

Palmerstown, Dublin 20 D20 V256, Ireland
Tel: 00 353 1 643 6500 Reception
            00 353 1 643 6564 Admissions
Fax: 00 353 1 623 0349

email: reception@thekingshospital.ie
website: www.kingshospital.ie
Twitter: @Kings_Hospital
LinkedIn: /the-kings-hospital

Voluntary Church of Ireland (Anglican), co-educational, secondary school for boarders and day pupils aged 12–18 with 720 pupils, of whom 275 are boarders and 445 are day pupils. We maintain an equal balance of boys and girls.

The King's Hospital, one of the oldest boarding schools in Ireland, was founded in 1669 as The Hospital and Free School of King Charles II. In 1971 the School moved from the centre of Dublin to its present, modern setting in spacious, scenic grounds of over 85 acres on the banks of the River Liffey in Palmerstown, yet remains only 15 minutes from Dublin International Airport. The King's Hospital attracts pupils from all over Ireland with approximately 10% from overseas.

The fundamental values of a Christian conscience, a sense of duty and loyalty and a love of learning are actively promoted.

The school offers five-day teaching programme with quality 5 and 7 day boarding options at extremely competitive rates. Our Saturday Programme of activities is designed to support the school curriculum and offer the pupil the opportunity to expand his/her knowledge base. Workshops in Web Designing and Coding, Extra English classes, Indoor Sports are a sample of the options available on Saturday mornings. The students also have organised social evenings, cultural trips and can join one of our many extra-curricular clubs at the weekend.

The King's Hospital believes that every child should achieve his or her true potential intellectually and socially, through personal endeavour and the encouragement and support of our staff, parents and governors. Through our academic, pastoral and extra-curricular programmes, we strive to develop core values of:

- a love of learning which makes all study a discovery and a joy, and which leads to standards of academic excellence appropriate to each child's ability;
- a Christian conscience and awareness which enables our pupils to develop a personal faith in God, to lead fulfilling lives which will enrich the communities in which they live, to uphold truth and show respect for others as well as for themselves, and to accept responsibility for their own actions;
- a sense of duty and loyalty which encourages participation in, and commitment to, every aspect of school life.

Academic. The school has an excellent academic record (97% progression to Higher Education in 2016), numbers that are not captured accurately in school league tables as they only count students who entered Irish Universities. In 2016 12% of our students took places in Universities in the UK, Europe and the US.

Most pupils pursue a 6 year course on entering the school at the age of 12. The first three years lead to the Junior Certificate Examination, followed by a Transition Year, and the final two years are devoted to the Irish Leaving Certificate Examination (equivalent to 4 A Levels) providing access to universities in the UK and throughout the World. Streaming is not a policy at The King's Hospital and the consistently high level of academic achievement is a reflection of the manner in which the School has always adapted to the ever-evolving education process and the ever-changing needs of its pupils by providing a comprehensive and progressive range of subjects, extensive specialist facilities and a highly qualified teaching staff.

The specialist facilities range from laboratories, workshops and computers to technical equipment and instruments, with Computer/PowerPoint facilities in all classrooms. A highly trained and well-equipped Special Needs department is available for both gifted children and those with learning difficulties. Media technology in the Harden Library provides access to national and international databases for project work as well as a computerised resource centre for information and guidance on careers.

Extra-Curricular. In addition to academic pursuits, The King's Hospital is renowned for its choice of recreational activities and offers a wide variety of sporting, music, drama and academic clubs and societies with unrivalled facilities. Pupils are encouraged to participate and all have the opportunity to represent the School at various levels in the activities of their choice.

An ultra-modern Sports Hall incorporating a fully-equipped fitness centre, a 25-metre indoor heated swimming pool and a floodlit astroturf pitch are among the outstanding facilities providing ample opportunity for Rugby, Hockey, Athletics, Swimming, Canoeing, Rowing, Cricket, Soccer, Basketball, Badminton and Tennis.

The promotion of cultural activities is catered for through Arts and Crafts, Choirs, Orchestras and Drama and Musical productions. A dedicated Performing Arts Centre is a recently built facility with the School's Assembly Hall/Theatre.

A diverse array of recreational activities is covered with clubs and societies, a Student Council, social work and European Studies, theatre and concert trips and trips abroad, both sporting and cultural.

Pastoral. Cooperation and mutual respect between pupils and staff, as well as a specified code of behaviour, are central to the daily life of the School. There are ten houses whose Housemaster or Housemistress has specific responsibility for the general welfare and development of pupils under his or her care. Peer mentoring in the form of Prefects and Mentors also provides a very supportive environment for the pupils. The diverse aspects of health education are included in the School's programme and 24 hour nursing care and a counsellor are available. Worship, according to the rites of the Church of Ireland and led by the resident Chaplain, is an integral part of daily life and pupils gain an understanding of and respect for all religious persuasions.

The Future. A vision for the future of the School is embodied in an ever-evolving School Plan and the Board of Governors is committed to implementing the development strategies within that plan. The School maintains its position as one of Ireland's leading educational institutions through this ambitious development programme, the most recent addition being the completion of a new Form 6 Centre, complete with ensuite accommodation for boarders. The King's Hospital is a school firmly rooted in tradition while continuing to be at the cutting edge of modern education.

Fees per annum (2016–2017). Pupils with an Irish Passport: 5-Day Boarding €15,580, 7-day Boarding €14,275, Day €6,895. Pupils with a EU Passport: 7-Day Boarding €18,696. Pupils with Non-EU Passport €19,475.

Chairman of Governors: Mr Ken Peare

Headmaster: **John Rafter**, BA MOD, BSc, HDipEd

Deputy Head: Louise Marshall, BEd Hons

Assistant Heads:
Siobhán Daly, BA, HDipEd (*Academic Affairs*)
John Aiken, BA, HDipEd (*Pastoral Care*)

Chaplain: The Revd Canon Peter Campion, MPhil, MA, PGCE

Subject Coordinators:
Detta Brennan, Dip Fine Arts, Dip ADT (*Art*)
Orla Cummins, BA, HDipEd (*Mathematics*)
Dean Maguire, BComm, HDipEd (*Mathematics*)
The Revd Canon Peter Campion, MPhil, MA, PGCE (*Religious Education*)
Jean Atkinson, BBS, HDipEd (*Business*)

Annabel Browne, BA, HDipEd (*Geography and CSPE*)
Glenda Ua Bruadair, BA, PGCE (*English*)
Janet Nelson, MSc, BA, HDipEd, DSEN (*Special Education Needs*)
John Huggard, BA, HDipEd (*History*)
Emma Ryan, BSc QTS (*Physical Education*)
Caroline Brady, BEd (*Home Economics*)
Dymphna Morris, BA, DipComp (*Information Technology*)
Michelle Murray, MEd Mgt, BA Special, HDipEd (*Irish*)
Patrick O'Shea, BTechEd (*Design and Communication Graphics*)
Aileen Polke, BA, HDipEd (*Modern Languages*)
Miriam Wright, BMus, HDipEd (*Music*)
Susan Tanner, BSc, HDipEd, HDCG (*Career Guidance and SPHE*)
Ciaran Whelan, BSc, HDipEd (*Science*)
Cormac Ua Bruadair, BA, HDipEd (*Transition Year*)

Housemasters/Mistresses:
Dean Maguire, BComm, HDipEd (*Desmond House*)
Rachelle Van Zyl, BComm Hons, HDipEd (*Grace House*)
David Plu-mmer, BSc, PGCE (*Ivory House*)
Denise Farrelly, BA Hons, HDipEd (*Ivory House*)
Caroline Brady, BEd Hons (*Mercer House*)
Elizabeth Peoples (*Stuart House*)
Alison Gill, BA Hons, PGCE (*Swift House*)
Cormac UaBruadair, BA Hons, HDipEd (*Morgan House*)
Niall Mahon, BSc, HDipEd (*Ormonde House*)
Raymond Mcllreavy, MEd, BA, HDipEd (*Bluecoat House*)
Amy Fitzgerald, BA Hons, HDipEd (*Bluecoat House*)

Head of Finance and Operations: Tony Kearney

Marketing & Admissions Manager: Síle Jio

Headmaster's PA: Lorraine Walker

The King's School
Canterbury

25 The Precincts, Canterbury, Kent CT1 2ES
Tel: 01227 595501
Bursar: 01227 595544
Admissions: 01227 595579
Fax: 01227 766255
email: headmaster@kings-school.co.uk
website: www.kings-school.co.uk

St Augustine's foundation of a monastic school in Canterbury in 597 AD marks the origin of The King's School: hence, its claim to be the oldest school in the country. It was re-founded by King Henry VIII in 1541. More recently, a Junior School has been established on the former estate of Lord Milner outside the city. The close relationship with the Cathedral Foundation has been there throughout.

King's Scholars. Many schools cherish the notion that they are the oldest school in the country, but there is little doubt that there has been a school on the present World Heritage site of King's School, Canterbury since the Augustinian mission to E ngland in 597 AD. The name of the school and its intimate relationship with the Cathedral community of the mother church of the Anglican Communion date from the Henrician settlement, as do the King's Scholars who, along with the Headmaster and the Senior Deputy Head, form part of the original Foundation of Christchurch, Canterbury. So much for the history, the King's Scholars continue to occupy buildings and be taught in classrooms that predate the Reformation. Besides their function in the Cathedral, the King's Scholars are at the heart of the vibrant and open-ended academic life of the school. Each year, some of the King's Scholars are on full means-tested bursaries, keeping alive the original vision of the school. The modern King's Scholar discovers a school which is fully co-educational, diverse in its catchment and intentions, as well as in tune with the wider life of the city of Canterbury and national/international context beyond its immediate compass.

Scholarships and Bursaries. Up to twenty King's Scholars and Exhibitioners are elected each year following competitive examinations and interviews in February. A further group of King's Scholars are added at the Sixth Form entrance stage (competitive examination and interviews in the November preceding entry). These academic awards have a meritocratic value of 10%, but the crucial thing is that they can be augmented by means-tested bursaries up to 100%. The extremely strong tradition of music at King's, both instrumental and choral, means that Music Scholarships (about 20 are awarded annually) are generously provided for. The school is particularly welcoming for those who have come on to King's from the choir schools of Cathedrals and Colleges. There are further Music Scholarships made for Sixth Form entry.

There are further Scholarships and Exhibitions at 13+ for exceptional ability in Art and Sport – the Gower Sports Scholarships named after the former England cricket captain – and the school also grants awards for DT and Drama.

Academic Life. The King's curriculum is distinct for its combination of striving for the very highest standards in the most appropriate Public Examinations (IGCSEs at the end of Year 10 for a few subjects, but mainly at the end of Year 11; A Levels and Pre-U courses in the Sixth Form) on the one hand, and the pursuit of learning and the development of the intellect for its own sake (self-standing courses, tutorials and lectures in the evenings and extended project qualifications, as well as independent research). The school puts particular emphasis on studying Mandarin, German and Russian, as well as 'new' subjects like Photography and Computer Science. A wide degree of choice of subject in the Sixth Form (Geology and Philosophy, for example) is often an engine for academic success.

Some 20–25 offers of admission to Oxford and Cambridge are received each year.

All round vision. Christopher Marlowe, William Harvey and Thomas Linacre number amongst King's pupils and the pursuit of the Renaissance ideal still resonates in the contemporary school. The strongest encouragement is given to Music, Drama, Sport, CCF and the Visual Arts. This stems from belief in the value of these activities in themselves, but also since recreation and success in these fields leads to growth in self-confidence and better academic performance. Alongside these activities are opportunities to get involved in Partnership projects and pursue the Duke of Edinburgh's Award.

Numbers and Organisation. There are currently 861 pupils on the school roll, 448 boys and 413 girls, of whom 79% are boarders. There are 6 boys' boarding houses, 7 girls' boarding houses and 3 (mixed) day houses. Junior King's School, the prep school of King's, occupies a site on the River Stour, in Sturry, 3 miles from Canterbury. There are currently 356 pupils at Junior King's, 198 boys and 158 girls of whom 80 are boarders. To the east of the main school buildings in the Cathedral Precincts is St Augustine's, home to 5 boarding houses, the original Medieval Hall and magnificent school library. There are 2 major sites for sport, Birley's and Blore's, each with extensive sports facilities.

Admission. Application should be made to the Assistant Registrar. It is advisable to register pupils at an early age. Admission is normally through the Common Entrance Examination, the King's School entrance examination (for non-CE candidates) or, if academically appropriate, through the King's Scholarship Examination. The age of entry is about 13.

Fees per term (2016–2017). Senior School: £11,765 for boarders and £8,900 for day pupils. Junior School: £8,080 for boarders and £5,295–£5,890 for day pupils.

OKS (Old King's Scholars). *Coordinator*: Dr K Mason, OKS Association Office, Tel: 01227 595669; email: oks@kings-school.co.uk.

The King's Society exists for all parents, past and present. A termly programme of social and cultural events is open to all members and is published on the school website.

Charitable status. The King's School of the Cathedral Church of Canterbury is a Registered Charity, number 307942. It exists to provide education for boys and girls.

Visitor: The Lord Archbishop of Canterbury

Governors:
Chairman: The Very Revd Dr R A Willis, DL, DCL, DD, Dean of Canterbury Cathedral
Vice-Chairman: N S L Lyons, MA
Dr C R Prior, DPhil
Mrs E McKendrick, BA
The Revd Canon D C Edwards, SRN, RSCN, BTh
Sir Roger De Haan
The Revd Canon C P Irvine, BTh, MA, PGCE
J D Tennant, MRICS
R C A Bagley, LLB
Mrs C Evelegh, Dip CE, Dip SpLD
Miss F J Judd, QC
M W S Bax, FRICS
T M Steel, MA, DL
The Revd Canon N Papadopulos, MA
Dr M L Sutherland, BSc, MSc, PhD
Mrs C Swire

Clerk to the Governors: M R Taylor, FRSA

Governors Emeriti:
The Very Revd J A Simpson, OBE, MA, DD
The Lady Kingsdown, OBE, DCL
The Very Revd D L Edwards, DD

Headmaster: **P J M Roberts**, MA

Headmaster's PA: Mrs A S Kelly, BA
Headmaster's Office PA: Miss C J M Finch
PA/Receptionist: Miss J M Henderson, BA

Senior Deputy Head: Mrs E A Worthington, MA

Deputy Head Academic: L G Bartlett, BA, MRSC
Deputy Head Pastoral: Miss T Lee, BA

PA to Senior Deputy Head/Deputy Head Pastoral: Miss A L Tamblyn, BA
Academic Assistant: Mrs G V Hone, BSc Econ
Examinations Officer: Mrs L A Renault

Head of Sixth Form: Mrs C D Cornell, BA, MA
Heads of Middle School: M W Browning, BA and Miss C E Anderson, MA
Head of Lower School: R P Cook, BSc
Head of Oxbridge: Dr R A B Johnson, MSc, PhD
Head of Extended Projects: Miss A K Fraser, MA, MPhil

Bursar: M R Taylor, FRSA
Estates Bursar: L Dudas, BSc, Dip Surv, Associate RICS
Deputy Finance Bursar: Mrs M Brown, FCCA, MBA
Human Resources Manager: J Hadlow, BA, Associate CIPD

Foundation Director: Mrs K E Chernyshov, BA

Head of Strategy and Planning: I S MacEwen, MA

Marketing Coordinator: K L Orwin, BA

Registrar: G E Sinclair, AGSM, FRSA
Assistant Registrar: Mrs B Skilton

Senior Tutor: M J Miles, MA
University and Careers Adviser: Ms P D Williams, MA, DipCG

Senior Chaplain: The Revd Canon C F Arvidsson, DipTheol
Assistant Chaplain: The Revd M Robbins, BA, BTh

Librarian: Miss P K Rose, FDA, MA, PGCHE, ACLIP

Medical Officers:
Dr W Lloyd Hughes, MB BS
Dr T Crook, MB BS, MRCGP, DRCOG

* *Head of Department*
† *Housemaster/mistress*

Art:
Mrs G C Burrows, BA
*P K Cordeaux, BA
Mrs I A Dutton, BA
M McArdle, BA
Mrs J Taylor-Goodman, BA, MA
I S Wallace, BA
D K Willis, BA

Classics:
M W Browning, BA
Dr G M Longley, MA, DPhil
*Miss J Taylor, BA
Miss H L Warwicker, BA

Design & Technology:
M J Franks, BEd
*M J Rolison, BEd
G J Swindley, BSc

Drama:
*Mrs R J Beattie, BA, FRSA
Miss F R Mountjoy, BA

Economics:
*S N Chester, BA
Mrs L A Horn, BSc
†R W Ninham, MA
A Rodriguez, MSc
M D Bell, BCOM, CIMA

English:
Dr H Barton, MA, PhD
Mrs L Carlyle, BA, DPhil
†Mrs J M Cook, BA
Mrs C D Cornell, BA, MA
E J Flower, BA
*Dr A T H Latter, MA, PhD
A J W Lyons, BA, MA, FRSA
Mrs K J Newsholme, BA
Dr C E Pidoux, MA, PhD, ALCM
†Mrs C J Shearer, BA
†Mrs A L Young, MA

Geography:
†S E Anderson, BA
†A J Holland, BSc
*R P Sanderson, BA
Mrs S J Sensecall, BSc
M C E Turner, BSc

History:
Miss C E Anderson, BA, MA

Mrs D J Ardley, BA
W M R Flint, MA
S J Graham, MA
G W H Harrison, MA
*D J C Perkins, BA, MA, Dip Law, PhD
L J W Philipps, MA
Mrs E A Worthington, MA

History of Art:
*D J Felton, BA, MA
Miss D M Francis, BA, Dip Ecol, Cert Vis

ICT and Computing:
Mrs L M Cousins, BA
*†A J Holland, BSc
B D M Katz, BA, MSc
Dr S Kerridge, BA, BSc, PhD
M C E Turner, BSc
*C P Wooldridge, BSc

Mathematics:
M O Cox, MA, MEng, Dip ITEC
M P H Dath, L-ès-ScM, M-ès-ScM
Mrs J J de Villiers, MA
J P E Dickson, BSc, MSc, RN
Dr R A B Johnson, MSc, PhD
Miss E R Laughlin, MSci
†Mrs J Gorman, BSc
B D M Katz, BA, MSc
Dr S Kerridge, BA, BSc, PhD
A McFall, BSc
*S P Ocock, BA
Dr K J Palmer, BSc, PhD
R C Stuart, BSc
R N Warnick, MA

Learning Support:
Mrs D J Ardley, BA
*Mrs P J Brown, BA, MA
Miss C J Grannell, MA
*Ms G R Moorcroft, BEd, MA
Mrs M L Orders, BA
Mrs R A Simmons
Mrs C R Titterton, BA

Modern Languages:
†Mrs Z T Allen, MA
Miss L N Bernardo Otamendi, Lda, MPhil, MA

Mrs A Browne, LSc
Miss H C Davies, MA
Mrs M B Garcés-Ramón, Lda
Mrs N Geoffroy, L-ès-ScEd
*Mrs R E Heskins, BA
Mrs C L Kelly, MA, BEd
*Mrs L Liu, BA, MPhil
Miss J M Maréchal, BA, MSc
M J Miles, MA
C P Newbury, BA
Miss A M Pedraza Rascado, BA, MA
*B R Pennells, BA
J P Priegue-Patino, MA
Mrs L Waitt, MA Ed
Mrs L J Warnick, MA
Miss F Zanardi, MA

Music:
K Abbott, Dip RCM
*W Bersey, BMus
S J R Matthews, MA
A Pollock, MA
G R Swinford, BA
N G Todd, MA

Politics:
Mrs D J Ardley, BA
I S MacEwen, MA
*O T Moelwyn-Hughes, BA, LLB, MSt

Physical Education:
Miss K V Batty, BSc
*M E Lister, BSc, MSc
L W Portsmouth, BSc
R A L Singfield, BEd (*Sport*)

Religious Studies and Philosophy:
The Revd Canon C F Arvidsson, Dip Theol
G R Cocksworth, BA, MA
*Mrs C A Cox, BA, MPhil

Houses and Housemasters/mistresses:

School House: M J Thornby
The Grange: M C Orders
Walpole: Mrs A L Young
Meister Omers: R W Ninham
Marlowe (*day*): S E Anderson
Luxmoore: Ms L Cousins
Galpin's: J M Hutchings
Linacre: J W Outram
Tradescant: A S D Stennet
Broughton: Mrs C J Shearer
Mitchinson's (*day*): Mrs E S Ladd
Jervis: Mrs J Gorman
Harvey: Mrs J M Cook
Bailey (*Sixth Form*): Mrs Z T Allen
Carlyon (*day*): A J Holland
Kingsdown: Mrs C A Hayes

The Junior King's School
Milner Court, Sturry, Nr Canterbury, CT2 0AY.
Tel: 01227 714000
Headmaster: P M Wells, BEd
(*For further details see King's Junior School entry in IAPS section.*)

Miss A K Fraser, MA, MPhil
Mrs C A Hayes, BA
Miss T Lee, BA
†J W Outram, BA
The Revd M Robbins, BA, BTh

Science:

Biology:
Miss K Budden, BSc
Dr H E Cunnold, BSc, PhD
†J M Hutchings, BA
Mrs E H Lockwood, MA, BSc
Miss S A Rajska, BSc
M J W Smiley, MA
†M J Thornby, BSc
*S J Winrow-Campbell, BSc, MIBiol, CBiol

Chemistry:
D M Arnott, BSc, PhD
R P Cook, BSc
Miss A R Donkin, MChem
*S T Hayes, MSci, PhD, MRSC
L W Hynes, BSc PhD
D A Scott, BSc, MSc, MA Ed, MRSC (*Science*)
†A S D Stennett, BSc
Dr T J Waite, BSc, HND, PhD

Physics:
*Miss L M Comber BSc (*Science*)
Mrs S K Dieu, BAppSc
F Elias Schliserman, Ldo, PhD
Miss L M Kendrick, BSc
†Mrs E S Ladd, BEng
†M C Orders, BSc
D M Tanton, MA, MSc, DipD'I, PhD

Geology:
*M R Mawby, BSc

The King's School
Chester

Chester CH4 7QL
Tel: 01244 689500
Fax: 01244 689501
email: info@kingschester.co.uk
website: www.kingschester.co.uk

Motto: '*Rex Dedit, Benedicat Deus.*'

The School was founded AD 1541 by King Henry VIII, in conjunction with the Cathedral Church of Chester. It was reorganised under the Endowed Schools Act in 1873, and by subsequent schemes of the Ministry of Education. The School is now Independent. The aim of the School is to prepare pupils for admission to Universities and the professions, and at the same time provide a liberal education.

Organisation. The School, which at present numbers 1073, consists of (i) an Infant School for pupils aged 4 to 7 years, (ii) a Junior School for pupils aged 7 to 11 years, and (iii) the Senior School. The Infant and Junior Schools are housed in separate buildings, but are run in collaboration with the Senior School.

Admission. Please refer to our admissions policy which outlines the criteria and selection process for entry: www.kingschester.co.uk/school-policies. Selection is by academic merit alone.

Academic. The subjects offered for study in the Sixth Form are – on the Arts side: Art, Business Studies, Classical Studies, Drama, Economics, English, English Language, French, Geography, German, History, Latin, Music, Philosophy, Politics, Religious Studies, Spanish; and on the Science side: Biology, Chemistry, Computing, Further Mathematics, Mathematics, Physics, Sports Science and Design Technology. It is possible to take most combinations of subjects in the Sixth Form.

Spiritual life. The School is part of the Cathedral Foundation and regularly holds its own services in the Cathedral. Spiritual assemblies are held regularly in school.

Music. Music is part of the general curriculum for all pupils up to the age of 14. After this music may be taken at GCSE and A Level. Private tuition in orchestral instruments, piano and organ is available. There are many musical ensembles and choral groups including the Schola Cantorum which leads the worship in Cathedral services.

Cadet Corps. There is a CCF contingent which gives pupils opportunities to develop leadership skills and to undertake adventurous training.

Outdoor Education. Opportunities are provided both within and outside the curriculum for outdoor education, and all pupils in each of the first three years of the senior school spend some days away at centres specialising in outdoor activities. In addition many pupils participate in the Duke of Edinburgh's Award Scheme at all levels.

Games. Football, Hockey, Netball, Rugby, Cricket, Rowing, Swimming, Badminton, Basketball, Athletics, Netball, Tennis, Squash, Golf, Rounders.

Buildings. Formerly situated adjacent to the Cathedral, the school moved into new buildings in 1960 situated in rural surroundings nearly 2 miles from the centre of Chester. Since then there has been an impressive programme of additional building development. These include the Wickson Library, a new Music School, the Vanbrugh Theatre and extensions to the Sixth Form Centre. In September 2014 the Junior School was extended to provide a new Junior School Library and Learning Centre, and in September 2015 a purpose-built Infant School was opened by the Duke of Westminster. The school celebrated its 475th anniversary in September 2016.

Alumni associations. Please see the website (www.kingschester.co.uk/kings-alumni) for details of OAKS (the Organisation for the Alumni of the King's School) and CAOKS (Chester Association of Old King's Scholars).

Fees per term (2016–2017). Tuition: Senior School £4,296, Junior School £3,294, Infants £2,830. Lunches: £258.

The School offers a small number of bursaries annually.

Scholarships. Academic scholarships of up to £500 are awarded to pupils during their early years in the Senior School. Scholars carry the title 'King's Scholar' throughout their time at the school.

Tenable in the Sixth Form: A number of scholarships are awarded to students on entry to the Sixth Form and during their Sixth form years. These include: (1) Alfred McAlpine Scholarship of £1,000; (2) Keith Oates Scholarship of £1,000; (3) Investec Scholarship of £1,000; (4) King's School Parents' Association Scholarship: £500.

Tenable at Universities: (1) Old King's Scholars Exhibition: £750; (2) Robert Platt Exhibition: £500; (3) John Churton Exhibition: £500; (4) Haswell Exhibition: £500; (5) Finchett Maddock Exhibition: £500; (6) King's School Parents' Association: two exhibitions of £600.

Charitable status. The King's School, Chester is a Registered Charity, number 525934. The aim of the charity is to provide a sound education to all boys and girls who can benefit from it regardless of their economic and social background.

Governors:
Mrs J L Clague, BA, ACA (*Chairman*)
The Rt Revd the Lord Bishop of Chester
The Very Revd the Dean of Chester
R Arnold, BSc, ACA
Prof R Ashford, PhD, FCIM, FHEA, BEd
Prof J H P Bayley, MA, PhD, FRS
Prof J Billowes, MA, DPhil, FInstP
Mrs J Carr, BA, FCA
J C Davies, MSc, CEng, FICE, MCIOB, MIWM
S Docking, BA
Revd Canon P Howell-Jones, MA
P M H Jessop, BA
Mrs E M Johnson, JP
Mrs K Kerr, MBA, BA
D Monk, MBChB, FRCS
I O'Doherty, BE, MSc, MBA
Dr D Pawson, BSc, PhD
Mrs R J Phillipson, BA, FCIPD
G P Ramsbottom, BSc, MSc, MRICS
R A Storrar
W J Timpson, OBE
N H Wood, BSc, MRICS, IRRV

Clerk to the Governors: S P Cross, MSc, LLB

Headmaster: **C D Ramsey**, MA, late scholar of Corpus Christi, Cambridge

Deputy Head: Dr J M Byrne, BA, PhD
Deputy Head (Academic): J E Millard, BA
Deputy Head (Pastoral): M J Harle, BSc
Head of Sixth Form: J P Carter, MA
Head of Academic Administration: S Neal, BA
Head of Co-curricular: R G Wheeler, BA
Director of Learning Support: Mrs S Glass, BA

Assistant staff:
* *Head of Department*

Art and Design:
*S Downey, BA

Ms L Black, BA
Mrs A L Hollingworth, BA

Biology:
*Dr H C Faulkner, BSc, DPhil
J A Dunn, MSc
R D J Elmore, BSc, MIBiol, CBS
R H Jones, BSc, PhD
L A Parkes, BSc, MSc

Chemistry:
*A Cook, BSc, PhD
Dr C A Gleave, BSc, PhD
M J Harle, BSc
Mrs J E Jepson, BSc
Dr J R Macnab, BSc, PhD
Mrs K L Russon, BSc

Classics:
*P R Wilcock MA
Mrs S H Gareh, BA, MA
M J P Punnett, MA

Design Technology:
*R J Curtis, BSc
N J Dudderidge, BA, MSc
Miss E Hodgson, BA

Drama:
*Mrs C L Howdon, BA

Economics:
*S D Walton, BA, MSc
Miss E M Rowley, BSocSc
G F Smith BA
Mrs C A Rule BA

English:
*R J Aldridge, BA, MBA
M A Boyd, BA
Mrs A C Leake, BA, MEd
Dr A M McMahon, MA, DPhil
Mrs A E Richards, BA
R G Wheeler, BA

Geography:
*M J Prestshaw, BSc
Mrs R H Aldridge, BA
J A D Blackham, BA
J F Day, MSc

History & Politics:
*P G Neal, BA
J P Carter, MA
Mrs G K Chadwick, BA
R J M Hensman, BA, MA, PhD
S Neal, BA

Information Technology:
*R J Higgins, BSc, MSc
Mrs E E Simpson, BA, MBA

Head of Junior School & Infant School: Mrs M A Ainsworth, LLB

Deputy Head (Junior School): A Griffiths, BA
Director of Studies (Junior School): T W Griffin, BA

Deputy Head (Infant School): Mrs J C Callaghan, BEd

Assistant Staff (Junior School & Infant School):

Miss J M Anderson, BA, CertEd
Mrs J Benson, BA
H J Duncalf, BEd

Mathematics:
*A J Dewberry, MA
Mrs H E Sugarman, MMath
S D Bibby, BSc
C J Canty, BSc
Mrs S Cooper, BSc
Mrs A Ignata, BSc
Mrs C E Lanceley, BSc
Mrs C Plass, BSc
Mrs C N Ranson, BSc
Miss D Roberts, BSc

Modern Languages:
*Miss L E McCutcheon
Miss R E Lindesay, BA
Mrs M Rowley-Williams, BA, MEd
Mrs K L Shapland, MA
Mrs K J Thurlow-Wood, BA
Mme F Vergnaud, MA

Music:
*T M Harvey, BA, ARCO (*Director of Music*)
Ms K Z Andrews, BMus, MA (*Head of Academic Music*)
Mrs V L S Latifa, BMus
J E Millard, BA

Personal & Social Education:
*M S Lee, MA

Physical Education:
*R Lunn, BEd (*Director of Sport*)
Mrs K Jones, BA (*Assistant Director of Sport*)
R I D Hornby, BA
B Horne, BSc (*Director of Football*)
Ms J Huck, BA
C Morris, BEd
Mrs C Sumner, BA

Physics:
*S Bosworth, MA, DPhil, FRAS
Ms H M Davies, BSc, MSc
N A Grisedale, MPhys
N Heritage, MSc, PhD, MInstP, CPhys
B Horne, BSc

Religious Studies:
*J R Rees, BA
M S Lee, MA
Ms J E Rutberg, MA

Mrs H George, MA
Miss J M L Hartley, BA
K A Hollingworth, BEd
Miss K Johnson, BA

Miss S Ley, BA
J B Melville, BEd
Mrs N C M Moffatt, BA
Mrs M D O'Leary, BA
D M O'Neil, BSc
Mrs S Parker BEd
Mrs D L Rudd, BA

Miss K A Savage, BA
J N Spellman, BEd
Mrs N J Stevens, BMus
Mrs A Stevenson, BEd
Mrs N M Tomlinson, BA
Mrs S Tomlinson, BEd
Mrs K Williams, BEd

Peripatetic Staff:
W Armstrong, BA, PGRNCM (*Oboe*)
Miss C Barker, BA (*Cello*)
Ms S Boryslawska, BA
S J Hall, BSc (*Bass Guitar*)
Mrs V L Ierston, LTCL (*Piano & Flute*)
Miss R Jones, GMus, RNCM, LRAM, ARCM, FLCM
   (*Piano*)
G Macey, ATCL (*Woodwind*)
Ms S Marrs, FTCL (*Voice*)
N Middleton, BA (*Drums*)
D Ortiz, BMus (*Head of Brass*)
A Parker, MA (*Saxophone*)
M Reynolds BA (*Piano*)
Mrs J Riekert, ATCL (*Flute*)
S A Rushforth (*Head of Strings*)
Mrs S E Tyson, MA (*Woodwind, Voice*)
Mrs J Williams, BA (*Bassoon*)
T Wyss, ARCM, LRAM, LTCL (*Brass*)

Extra-Curricular Staff:
Director of Rowing: J A D Blackham, BA
Contingent Commander, CCF: Maj M S Lee, MA
Duke of Edinburgh's Award Coordinator: D A Brown
Educational Visits Coordinator: R I D Hornby, BA

Bursar: Mrs J H Beer, ACMA, CGMA, CIPS
Director of Human Resources: Mrs E R Davidson, BA,
   CIPD & Mrs A H Millard, BSc, MCIPD
Director of External Affairs: Ms V M Titmuss, BA
Director of Development: A Hopkinson, BA
Director of ICT: J K Warne, BSc, MCSA
Admissions Manager: Mrs E R Sears, BA
Head Librarian & Archivist: Mrs R Harding, MA
Examinations Officer: R D J Elmore, BSc
School Nurse: Mrs L Jones, RN
Care Scheme Supervisor: Mrs L Hornby

Headmaster's PA: Mrs A M E Wilson, BA

King's Ely

Ely, Cambridgeshire CB7 4DB
Tel: 01353 660701 (Principal's PA)
          01353 660707 (Head of Pupil Recruitment)
Fax: 01353 667485
          01353 660712 (Business Manager)
email: admissions@kingsely.org
website: www.kingsely.org
Twitter: @kings_ely

Energy, Courage, Integrity
An independent, co-educational school, with day and
boarding facilities, offering a seamless education for students from 1 to 18. With over 1000 years of experience educating young people, King's Ely is a school that is
innovative, challenging and inspiring. Boasting as its school
chapel one of the world's finest cathedrals, with easy access
to London, King's Ely offers a very special and very tranquil
environment, with one of the best stretches of training river
in the UK.

King's Ely is a school where education really is an adventure. Students of all ages are encouraged to take risks in their

learning, pushing themselves beyond the boundaries of their
expectations, discovering more about the world around
them, and, in so doing, more about themselves. What makes
us special is our determination to instil in the young people
in our care a real enthusiasm for learning and a belief that
drives us all, that all students can achieve if the teaching is
approached in a way that suits the learning style of each student. This is not easy necessarily; it is challenging, often
uncomfortable, but King's Ely students know that they are
well supported, that their teachers believe in them, and so
they are willing to step out of their 'comfort zone' and take
the very risks that will bring about high-level learning.

Our long and illustrious past provides a dynamic springboard to the future; our confidence is born of tradition, our
aspirations reach for the stars.

Organisation. The school is fully co-educational from
the ages of 1 to 18. The total roll is 985 and more than a
quarter of pupils over the age of eight are boarders.

The school is divided into four parts: King's Ely Acre-
mont, the Nursery and Pre-Prep for children aged 1 to 7
(Year 2). standing in its own grounds at Acremont House;
King's Ely Junior for children aged 7–13 (Years 3–8);
King's Ely Senior for students aged 13–18 (Years 9–13) and
King's Ely International Years 7–8 and 10–11.

Buildings. The Old Palace on Palace Green, home for
centuries to the Bishops of Ely, serves as the entrance to the
school, housing the Sixth Form Centre, the Head's Offices
and Admissions as well as the Development Office. The
school still uses many of Ely's medieval monastic buildings
– as boarding houses, as classrooms and as the dining hall.
The 14th century Porta, the great gateway to the monastery,
has been converted into a magnificent Senior School library.
Other recent buildings show the continuing and substantial
investment in modern facilities: the renovated Georgian
villa that now houses the Nursery and Pre-Prep section of
King's Acremont; a brand new Art School and Performance
Studies block, housing the new Dance Studio and 'Black
Box' Drama Studio; a Technology Centre; a senior Music
School and Recital Hall and a self-contained, two-storey
accommodation including seven classrooms and a science
laboratory for Years 7 and 8.

King's Ely Acremont. At King's Ely Acremont, children
thrive in a happy, safe environment where they feel secure
and valued and quickly develop a sense of belonging. Children from 1 to 7 are encouraged to question, explore and
have the confidence and security to take risks in their learning. A rich, creative curriculum sets the children on the road
to becoming lifelong thinkers and learners. Courage and
courtesy are valued, encouraged and celebrated publicly.

Children may start in King's Ely Nursery in the term in
which they turn one. The Nursery is sessional and it is recommended children attend three sessions a week from the
outset. However, flexibility to suit the needs of each individual child is important. As children progress through the
Nursery, the number of sessions should increase to a minimum of five sessions per week. The children are very well
prepared for a smooth transition into Reception through regular visits ensuring that they are very familiar with both staff
and setting in the next stage of their journey through King's
Ely. Please contact Admissions to discuss suitable sessions
for your child.

Children start Reception in the September following their
4th birthday. Reception, Year 1 and Year 2 are all taught in
Acremont House. Small class sizes, with a Teacher and
Teaching Assistant in each, allow children to flourish, preparing them well for the transition to King's Ely Junior.

King's Ely Acremont offers working parents the option
of an 8 am Breakfast Club, After School Care until 6 pm and
Holiday Club.

King's Ely Junior. In King's Ely Junior, celebrates the
many ways that students learn and is keen to embrace different learning styles. Students are encouraged to develop their

autonomy as they mature and there is an expectation of an ever-increasing use of information literacy, technology and study skills during the students' time at King's Ely Junior. Individual responses, such as films being made for homework, or a computer generated response to a task are equally as welcome as a formal written piece of work. Students can be characterised by their flexibility of approach and it is seen as an important life skill for the next generation.

Ensuring that every student is challenged to fulfil their potential and encouraged along the way, requires that the progress of each student is measured and supported well at all times. Form Tutors shoulder this role on a day to day basis. However, each student has a Head of Year who monitors their work and considers how well they are progressing against our predictions. Weekly meetings ensure that speedy intervention is offered to support or extend students appropriately.

From Year 5 onwards, students are set for Maths and English. At this point the students are split between four sets of about 14. These groups are reviewed frequently by the subject teachers and the Head of Year and any adjustments to the sets are made by the Director of Studies, following discussion with parents. As students progress through the school more subjects are set, such as languages and Science. In Years 7 and 8 subjects are linked according to the English, Maths and Science or Language sets. Students are taught in four or five groups, depending on subject.

Every term is punctuated by a host of academic challenges that serve to inspire the pupils and encourage them to push the parameters of their learning. The overtly enriching activities this year have all been provided as additional activities beyond the timetabled lessons:

- King's Ely awarded Gold medals in the Biology Olympiad
- King's Ely Junior takes part in their first ever Big Outdoor Day
- A week of Masterchef Finals concluded in a cook-along session for Jamie Oliver's Food Revolution Day
- Visit from Rt Hon John Bercow MP – The Speaker of the House of Commons
- Breakfast Week goes International – Students take part in Shake Up Your Wake Up's Breakfast Week
- King's Ely International students visit Free the Children's We Day at Wembley as part of the We Act programme
- King's Ely Crews bring home 10 trophies from the Bedford Star Regatta
- Year 9 students win the Modern Foreign Languages round of the Real Business Challenge
- King's Ely Sixth Form launches The Big Thinking Club

Examination results are high and the school prides itself on being at the forefront of developments in the educational world.

During the school day all children are divided among four co-educational Houses for pastoral and competitive purposes; each of these houses is staffed by male and female members of the teaching staff. King's Ely Junior has one co-educational boarding house and one for the boy choristers of Ely Cathedral who are all pupils of King's Junior School. There is a wide range of extra-curricular opportunities both at lunch times and after school.

King's Ely Senior. The amount of academic choice that pupils can exercise grows as they move through the Senior School: options in the Sixth Form are very flexible, and the sets are often small. Up to GCSE (Year 11) there is a compulsory core of English, Mathematics, Religious Studies and Sciences. In addition every pupil chooses up to four option subjects from: Art, Business Studies, Classical Civilisation, Design & Technology (Resistant Material Technology, Food and Nutrition), Drama, English as a Foreign Language, French, Geography, German, History, Latin, Music, Physical Education, Spanish. Inter house competitions in disci-

plines such singing, Ely Scheme, debating are keenly participated in.

King's Ely International. At King's Ely International, students are welcomed from all over the world to engage with the unique community that is King's Ely. The aim is to ensure a smooth and successful transition into the vibrant environment of a UK boarding school, steeped in history but offering an innovative educational experience.

King's Ely International offers effective support academically for international students between the ages of 14 and 16 who may be studying for the first time in the UK. The one-year intensive GCSE course suits students who wish to complete their GCSEs in a year. The Pre-GCSE programme is for students between the ages of 14 and 15 who need support in their English. It is also a "stand-alone" course and may be seen as a sabbatical year, especially for European students who wish to return to their home countries after a year abroad improving their English.

Extra-Curricular Activities. Music, art, drama, outdoor pursuits, sports, practical hobbies and interests – all are catered for in a large range of lunchtime and after-hours activities.

The Ely Scheme. All pupils in Year 9 are introduced to the school's distinctive outdoor pursuits programme, the Ely Scheme, which provides a training in practical and personal skills and in teamwork, initiative and leadership. For some pupils it leads on to the Duke of Edinburgh's Award Scheme or to specialised activities such as climbing.

Art, Drama and Music. Music is strong, as one would expect in a school that is so closely linked to the Cathedral. There is a full programme of performances for school and public audiences, and regular tours overseas. Nearly half of all pupils have personal tuition in a musical instrument; many learn two or even three. An outstanding new Art School, opened in March 2010, inspiring fine art, sculpture, ceramics, photography and textiles. All parts of the school present plays every year in addition to productions by year or ad hoc groups.

Games. The main sports are rowing, rugby, soccer, netball, hockey and cricket. Athletics, badminton, basketball, tennis, sailing, squash, swimming, golf and horse riding are also available. All pupils are encouraged to take part in team games, and there is a full programme of fixtures against other schools.

Religious Worship. The Junior and Senior Schools worship regularly in Ely Cathedral. Other services weekly are also in accordance with the principles of the Church of England. The Bishop conducts a confirmation service for pupils in the Lent term. However, all denominations (or none) are warmly welcome.

Exeats. Boarders are granted weekend exeats on the written request of a parent or guardian. Weekly and flexi boarding are increasingly popular.

Admission. Registration forms can be obtained from the Admissions Department and £100 (£150 international) fee is payable at first registration.

Admission to King's Ely Acremont is by interview

Admission to King's Ely Junior by interview and INCAs and Lucid screening for dyslexia; King's Ely Junior entrance assessments are held in January prior to the following Michaelmas Term. Small groups of children are invited to attend assessments throughout January.

Admission to King's Ely Senior at 13+ entrance is by the school's entrance examination consisting of English, Maths, Science and Lucid are held on a Monday in a late January.

Admission to Year 12 at 16+ is by interview with the Principal and predicted GCSE grades. The entry qualification for the Sixth Form is not less than six C grades with B grades in subjects selected for A Level. Twenty-seven AS/A2 Level subjects are offered in Years 12 and 13. Taster Days are held throughout November and December.

Pupils may enter the school at any time, depending on availability of space and assessment.

Scholarships and Exhibitions. Entrance Scholarships and Exhibitions up to a cumulative total of 10% of tuition fees are awarded for achievement and potential in academic work, music and sport, and 5% in art, design technology, drama.

A competitive examination is held in January each year and successful candidates enter Year 9 the following Michaelmas term. These Scholarships will be continued until the end of Year 11, subject to satisfactory progress, after which an application for a Sixth Form Scholarship may be made.

King's Ely Senior:

Academic Scholarships are for the three years from Year 9 leading to the GCSE examinations and are made on the basis of a competitive examination set by the school in January. Successful candidates are also interviewed.

Music Scholarships are available for choral and/or instrumental excellence, including organ-playing, and may include free weekly tuition on two musical instruments. Candidates for entry into Year 9 are invited to the school for auditions in January.

All boy Choristers of Ely Cathedral are full boarders of King's Ely Junior and receive a choristership worth 50% of fees while they remain in the choir and a bursary worth 33% of fees on transfer to King's Ely Senior. Members of the Cathedral Girls' Choir are all boarders in King's Ely Senior and receive a bursary worth 33% of boarding fees. Additional means-tested funding may be available. Chorister auditions are held in February for boys who will be aged 8 and for girls who will be 13 by the following September.

Sports Awards, for entry into Year 9 are open to boys and girls with potential for major county, regional or national representation or with all-round sporting excellence. Reports will be sought from the candidates' coach(es) and practical tests, if required, will be held at the school in January.

Art, Drama and Design Technology Exhibitions are available for entry into Year 9 and assessments are held in January.

Sixth Form:

Academic Scholarships are for the two years of the A Level course and are made following an examination in November and an interview with the Vice Principal (Academic) and Head of Sixth Form (Academic). Candidates should be on course for at least six A* or A passes at GCSE.

Music Scholarships are available for choral and/or instrumental excellence, including organ-playing, and may include free weekly tuition on two musical instruments. Candidates for entry into Year 12 are invited to the school for auditions in November.

Sports Awards, for entry into Year 12 are open to boys and girls with potential for major county, regional or national representation or with all-round sporting excellence. Reports will be sought from the candidates' coach(es) and practical tests, if required, will be held at the school in November.

Art, Drama and Design Technology Exhibitions are available for entry into Year 12 and assessments are held in November.

Full particulars of all awards are available on the King's Ely website.

Bursaries. Awards may be supplemented by a means-tested Bursary if there is genuine financial need. Bursary support may be available to new pupils over the age of 7 whose parents are unable to pay the full tuition fee.

Fees per term (2016–2017). King's Ely Acremont Nursery and Pre-Prep: Nursery places are booked by the session (morning or afternoon) and the day of the week; Daily rates range from £40–£68. The fee for Pre-Prep Reception to Year 2 is £3,110 (no boarding). Pre- and after-school care and holiday club are available at extra charge.

King's Ely Junior: Years 3 and 4: £4,393 (day); £7,004 (boarding); Years 5 to 8: £4,794 (day); £7,394 (boarding).

King's Ely Senior: Years 9 to 13: £6,623 (day); £9,588 (boarding).

Flexi boarding: It may be possible to offer overnight accommodation for day pupils on an occasional basis at a cost of £50.00 per night. The cost of extended flexi boarding will be quoted in advance upon application to the Bursar.

Concessions: A 10% discount in fees is available from age 4 for children of clergy serving the Christian faith and boarders who are children of Services personnel in receipt of CEA. Sibling discounts may be available.

Old Eleans. Former pupils receive news of the school and of their contemporaries and are invited annually to events.

Charitable status. The King's School, Ely is a Registered Charity, number 802427. Its aims and objectives are to offer excellence in education to day and boarding pupils.

Visitor: The Rt Revd S Conway, Bishop of Ely

Governors:
Chairman: Mr J Hayes
Vice-Chairman: ¶Mr R Phillips, QC
Chairman of Finance and GP Committee: Mr D Day
Chairman of Education Committee: The Revd Canon D Pritchard, BA, FRCO, LTCL
¶Air Vice-Marshal C Bairsto, CBE, CMgr, FRAeS, FCMI, RAF
The Revd Canon M Bonney, Dean of Ely
Mr GF Chase, FRICS C.Arb FRSA FInstCPD
Mrs A East
Mrs A Kenna, MEd, LRAM
Mrs F Martin-Redman
Mr ME Myers, MA
Mrs I Newport-Mangell
Rt Hon Sir J Paice, MP
Prof M Proctor, FRS
¶Dr K Skoyles, LLB, LLM, PhD
Mr P Cantwell

¶ *Old Elean*

Principal: **Mrs S E Freestone**, MEd, GRSM, LRAM, ARCM, FRSA

Vice Principal (Academic) Senior: Mrs J R Thomas, MA, PGCE
Vice Principal (Pastoral) Senior: Miss S E Knibb, BA, PGCE

Head of King's Ely Junior: Mr R J Whymark, BA Ed
Deputy Head, King's Ely Junior: Mr A Marshall, BSc, PGCE
Assistant Head, King's Ely Junior: Mrs L H F Roberts, BSc, PGCE
Director of Studies, King's Ely Junior: Mr J A Lowery, BA, PGCE

Head of King's Ely Acremont: Mr J Willcocks, BA, PGCE
Deputy Head, King's Ely Acremont: Mrs S Stevens, BSc, PGCE M, CIM Dip Marketing
Head of Nursery and EYFS, King's Ely Acremont: Mrs A G Ballanger, BEd, MA

Academic Manager, King's Ely International: Mr M Norbury, BA

Head of Pupil Recruitment: Mrs J Formston, BA, PGCE
Head of Admissions: Mrs D Burton
Chief Operating Officer: Mr M Hart
Business Manager: Mr S Drew

Medical Officer: Dr A S Douglas, BMedSci, BMBS,
    DRCOG, FP Cert; Dr J Kitson, MBCLB, DRCOG,
    DFFP, MRCGP
PA to the Principal: Mrs P Martin

King's Ely Senior Heads of Department:
Director of Art: Mrs A J Rhodes, BA, MA
Biology: Miss I Smyth, BSc, MA, PGCE
Business Studies: Mr A Wilson, BA, MA, PGCE
Chemistry: Mr M Newman, BSc, PGCE
Classics: Mr J Burden, MA Oxon
Design & Technology: Mrs C Poole, BEng, MA, PGCE
Director of Drama and Theatre: Mr N Huntington, BA,
    PGCE
Economics: Mr N Williams, MEd, BA, PGCE
English: Miss R Watkins, MEd, BEd (*Acting*)
Film & Media Studies: Mr S Merrell, BA, TCert
French: Mr A Reall, BA, PGCE
Geography: Mr A Birkhamshaw, BA, PGCE
German: Miss K Walter, BSc, MEd, PGCE
History: Mr C Currie, MA, PGCE
Government & Politics: Mr A J Thomas, BA, MEd, PGCE
ICT & Computing: Mr M G Hawes, BA, PGCE
Mathematics: Dr C P Skeels, BSc, DPhil, PGCE
MFL & Spanish: Mrs E Salgado, BA, PGCE
Director of Music: Mr J Kingston, BMus, PGCE
Director of Outdoor Education: Miss S Cheng, BSc, PGCE
Personal Development: Mr T Humphry, BA, MA
Physical Education: Mr K R Daniel, BA, PGCE
Head of Science & Physics: Mr E W M Kittoe, BSc, PGCE
Psychology: Mr S Quinn, BSc, MSc
Religious Studies: Ms G Smith, MA, MTh, PGCE
Director of Sport: Mr B Edmondson, BHSPE Australia
KS3 English: Miss R Watkins, MEd, BEd
KS3 Mathematics: Ms A Bezzina, BSc, MSc
KS3 MFL: Mrs M Delaveau-Fillmore, BA, CPLP2, PGCE

King's Ely Junior Heads of Department:
Director of Learning Development: Miss C Kyndt, BA,
    MSc, PGCE
English: Miss R Watkins, MEd, BEd
Geography: Miss C Kyndt, BA, MSc, PGCE
Girls' Games: Miss A E Kippax, BSc, HND, Dip SpLD
History: Mr E J Davis, BA, MA, PGCE
Information Technology: Mr D Everest
Mathematics: Ms A Bezzina, BSc, MSc
MFL: Mrs M Delaveau-Fillmore, BA, CPLP2, PGCE
Director of Music: Mr N Porter-Thaw, LTCL, Dip TCL,
    QTS
Physical Education: Mr D A Boothroyd, BEd
PSHE: Mrs K Prior, DipSpLD, CertEd
Religious Studies: Mrs Linda Hill, BA, DipMus, DipTheo,
    MSc, PGCE
Science: Mrs L H F Roberts, BSc, PGCE

King's Ely Acremont Staff:
Mrs A Black, BA, PGCE
Mrs C M Burgess, BA, PGCE
Miss N Cochrane, BA, PGCE M
Miss T Miller, BSc, PGCE
Mrs H Monk, BMus, PGCE
Miss I Robinson, BA, PGCE
Mrs J Lyall

In addition, 29 visiting music teachers and 18 external
    sports coaches.

The King's School
Macclesfield

Cumberland Street, Macclesfield, Cheshire SK10 1DA
Tel: 01625 260000
Fax: 01625 260022
email: mail@kingsmac.co.uk
website: www.kingsmac.co.uk

The King's School is the top performing independent
school in Cheshire East for both GCSE and A Level results
and is in The Telegraph Top 150 Independent Schools for
exam results in 2014, 2015 and 2016.

Founded in 1502 and situated in rolling Cheshire countryside, King's offers an academic education through a
unique combination of mixed and single-sex education
(known as a diamond structure school). It places an emphasis on excellent teaching and academic standards combined
with an extensive range of extra-curricular activities and
exceptional pastoral care.

Number in School. Infants 3–7: 51 boys, 47 girls.
Juniors 7–11: 121 boys, 100 girls. Boys (11–16) 400; Girls
(11–16) 265. Sixth Form: 130 boys, 111 girls. Total: 1,225.

Organisation and Curriculum. The King's School is
organised into four Divisions: on one site, an Infant & Junior
Division (co-educational 3–11) and a Senior Girls' Division
(11–16); on the other, a Senior Boys' Division (11–16) and a
Sixth Form (co-educational 16–18). Each Division is run by
a Principal, who is responsible for day-to-day organisation,
and the pupils in the 11–16 divisions of the school are taught
separately but undertake a number of joint extra-curricular
activities (e.g. music, drama, trips, etc.)

The King's School has one Board of Governors, one
Head and two Deputy Heads who manage the school and
plan regularly with the Divisional Principals to carry out the
aims and objectives of the school. Girls and boys from 3–18
enjoy the same opportunities.

King's aims include 'to challenge our pupils to aspire,
work hard and achieve' and 'to develop lively and enquiring
minds'. The curriculum is broad and rich throughout all year
groups offering pupils of all ages choice and a range of
experiences.

The School's most recent ISI Inspection Report (2015)
graded King's as 'excellent' – the highest ranking – in all
eight aspects. As well as teaching and pupils' achievements
being excellent, so too is Pastoral care, which is a high priority within the school. The divisional structure is key to
enabling each unit to be small and operate as a community.
Coupled with the aim of 'fostering a friendly, polite and caring community', King's is definitely a happy place to be a
pupil.

Students are assigned to a personal tutor responsible for a
group of 10 or so pupils throughout their Sixth Form course.
Any justifiable combination of available A Level subjects
may be pursued, complemented by an IGCSE Global Perspectives (in Year 12), EPQ and Recreational Activity. Students choose from a wide range of options designed to
extend their breadth of cultural interest and intellectual
inquiry, whilst Recreational Activities are designed to
encourage the positive use of leisure time and offers initial
experience in sports and activities new to the individual.
Pupils are also prepared for University Entrance Examinations where appropriate.

Arts and Craft. Well-equipped art rooms and Design &
Technology (DT) workshops are also available for use by
the members of the Art Club, STEM Club, Textile Club and
Craft societies outside the timetable.

Music. Over 400 pupils receive tuition in the full range of
orchestral instruments, the Piano, Organ, Classical Guitar

and Singing. An introductory tuition scheme enables all new entrants to assess their talent. There are three orchestras, a Concert-band, two Jazz bands, three Choirs and many ensembles, all of which provide regular performing experience. The Foundation Choir was the first BBC Songs of Praise Choir of the Year in 2003. Pupils regularly enter music profession in addition to those pursuing academic training.

Drama. Theatre Studies is an important creative option at GCSE and AS Level and covers all aspects of the theatre. Great importance is attached to the regular school plays and musicals, which involve large numbers of pupils and enjoy a distinguished reputation. Pupils regularly take examinations and study for LAMDA qualifications in performance and public speaking.

Games. All pupils take part in games and athletic activity appropriate to the season. Junior School sports include Football, Cricket, Netball, Hockey, Tennis, Rounders, Rugby, Swimming, Athletics and a wide range of individual games. In the Senior School, boys' sports include Rugby, Hockey, Cross-Country, Squash, Badminton, Cricket, Tennis, Athletics and Basketball; the girls' sports include Hockey, Netball, Tennis, Football, Cross Country, Volleyball, Cricket, Gym and Athletics. In addition there is a varied programme of sports in the Sixth Form, including Rugby and such activities as Caving, Fell Running and Rock Climbing which are actively pursued by boys and girls. In the last 4 years, the school has opened new netball courts, Junior cricket wickets, two adventure playgrounds, two new astro pitches for hockey, as well as new tennis courts, netball courts and cricket nets.

Outdoor Pursuits. This is a thriving part of the school. There is a regular programme of activity weekends including canoeing, gorge scrambling, surfing, coasteering, etc. In addition, numerous expeditions are arranged in the many favourable areas near the school and also abroad. Sailing and Orienteering are popular and The Duke of Edinburgh's Award scheme attracts around 100 pupils each year. King's is one of the largest DofE authorising centres in the UK.

Clubs and Societies. There is a wide range of other clubs catering for most interests and hobbies, ranging from Astronomy, Debating, Dance, Chess and Squash to Sailing, STEM Club, Equestrian Society and Taekwondo.

Fees per term (2016–2017). Senior School £4,075, Junior School £3,300, Infants Department £3,200.

Scholarships and Bursaries. Bursaries are available for entry at 11 and 16 years of age. In addition a number of Academic Scholarships are awarded based on performance in the Entrance Examination. Senior School Music Scholarships are available for instrument or singing. Academic, Music and Organ scholarships are also available in the Sixth Form. Funds are available to assist pupils attending courses and field trips and to help in cases of urgent need.

Admissions. Admission for the Infants is non-selective. Admission for the Juniors and Seniors is normally for September each year through competitive examination of age-appropriate Entrance papers. Girls and boys are admitted to the Sixth Form subject to academic attainment, interview and course requirement: a minimum of four A grades (7) and two B grades (6) is standard. Further details of Admission arrangements are available on the website and upon request. Immediate admission, e.g. for new arrivals in the area, is possible.

Former Pupils' Association. Chairman: David Barratt; email: formerpupils@kingsmac.co.uk. An annual magazine and termly newsletter are provided to former pupils.

Visit the Website. The award-winning website is found at www.kingsmac.co.uk.

Charitable status. The King's School, Macclesfield is a Registered Charity, number 1137204. It exists for the education of boys and girls between the ages of 3 and 18.

Chairman of the Governors: J Kennerley
Vice-Chair of Governors: J Sugden, MA, FIMechE, CEng

Senior Management Team:

Headmaster: Dr S Hyde, MA, DPhil

Deputy Headmaster (*Development*): T Seth, MA Cantab
Deputy Headmaster (*Academic*): R Griffiths, MA Cantab
Director of External Relations: Mrs C Johnson, BSc, DipM
Director of Finance: Mr J M Spencer Pickup
Senior Teacher: Mrs R Roberts, BA, PGCE

Principal of Boys: Mr I J Robertson, BSc
Principal of Girls: Mrs H L Broadley
Principal of Infants & Juniors: Mrs C J Hulme-McKibbin, BEd
Principal of Sixth Form: Dr J H Cocker, MA, PhD

Vice-Principal of Boys: P M Edgerton, MA
Vice-Principal of Girls: Mrs J Seth, BA, MA, PGCE
Vice-Principal of Juniors: Mrs A Lea, BMus
Vice-Principal of Infants: Mrs E L Warburton, BEd

Heads of Departments:
Art & Design: Mrs D Inman, BA
Biology: Miss E Hall, BSc, MSc, PGCE
Chemistry: Miss L C Watkins, BSc
Classics: M T Houghton, BA
Design & Technology: J Nichols, BEd
Drama: D A Forbes, BA
Economics & Business Studies: J S MacGregor, MA
English: Mr R Kellett, BA, PGCE
Geography: A S Puddephatt, BA
Geology: Dr J A Fitzgerald, BSc, MSc, PhD
German: Mrs J Houghton, BA
History: Mr G Barker, MA, PGCE
Computing: Mr C O'Donnell, BSc
Learning Support: Mrs N S Davis, BA, Dip Psych, PG Cert
Modern Languages: I E Dalgleish, BA
Director of Music: I Crawford, BMus
Physical Education (*Director of Sport*): C S Thompson, BA, PGCE
Physics: Dr S J Hartnett, BSc, DPhil, PGCE
Psychology: Mrs C Bell, BSc, PGCE, MA Ed
Religion & Philosophy: R N Jackson, BA
Science: J Street, BSc, PGCE
Spanish: Mrs S Jones

King's Rochester

Satis House, Boley Hill, Rochester, Kent ME1 1TE

Tel:	01634 888555
Fax:	01634 888505
email:	admissions@kings-rochester.co.uk
website:	www.kings-rochester.co.uk
Twitter:	@Kings_Rochester

The School traces its history to 604 AD, when St Justus, the first Bishop of Rochester, formed a school in connection with his Cathedral; it was reconstituted and endowed by Henry VIII as the King's School in 1541. The School has been fully co-educational since 1993.

The School is situated close to the Cathedral and Castle in the centre of the city and in a secluded conservation area; it enjoys the open spaces of the Precincts, the Vines and the Paddock, which is one of the School's playing fields. The other playing field, the Alps, is 10 minutes from the School. The School recently acquired a local Sports Centre which it is currently refurbishing at a cost of half a million pounds. This new facility will expand the School's current sporting facilities with 9 additional external tennis/netball courts, a large gymnasium, a fitness gym, physio suite and changing rooms in addition to the indoor swimming pool and playing fields already on the 1400 year-old school's town centre site.

The Main School dates from the mid-nineteenth century but the School also has a number of fine listed buildings from the eighteenth century, and considerable extensions of more recent date. Recent additions include a £3 million Conference Centre and dining facility, a girls' boarding house, and a Pre-Prep building with Sports Hall and a modern, self-contained nursery was added in 2010. There is an indoor swimming pool and a well-equipped language laboratory.

The School numbers about 650 pupils, including a small but significant community of 70 boarders from the local area, London and overseas. The School is fully co-educational and divided into a Pre-Preparatory School of approximately 140 pupils (4–8 years), plus 33 in the nursery, a Preparatory School of approximately 200 pupils (8–13 years) and a Senior School of approximately 300 pupils (13–18 years); this provides 3 units of an intimate size, which are regarded as a single community working closely together. While catering for the whole of a pupil's career from 3 to 18, there is a large entry of pupils at 11, 13 and 16 who bring experience from other backgrounds, and enjoy the advantages of coming into a stable community with a strong family atmosphere.

The boarders, some of whom are weekly, play an important part in the life of the School. Although a small community, they are a large enough part of the School to make a very significant contribution of their own, and enjoy a more intimate atmosphere than is possible in a larger boarding environment.

King's is the Cathedral School. The Dean and Chapter are ex officio Governors, the Principal and King's Scholars are members of the Cathedral Foundation, and the Cathedral Choristers are members of the Preparatory School. The School uses the Cathedral for worship.

Work. In the Pre-Preparatory School, the pupils follow a four year curriculum of Maths, Science, English, Divinity, Geography, History, Information Technology, Art and Craft, Design & Technology, Music, and Physical Education. Daily spoken German lessons taught by native German teachers form part of the curriculum from the age of 4 with German fun and games sessions twice weekly in the nursery.

In the Preparatory School, the syllabus covers Art, Religious Studies, English, General Science, History, Geography, Mathematics, Information Communication Technology, Latin, French, Music, Drama, Physical Education and Design & Technology.

In the Senior School, all pupils continue with the same range for the first year. In the Fifth Forms, a core of subjects is continued and pupils add a balanced choice of options in preparation for the GCSE and IGCSE examinations at the end of the two-year course.

In the Sixth Form, a wide range of AS and A Level subjects are available. Pupils study 4, or occasionally more, AS and then 3 A Level subjects. Some pupils also take the Extended Project Qualification as additional study alongside their A Levels.

All Sixth Formers, who wish to, go on to university or other further education, and are encouraged to think carefully about their ultimate careers. Careers talks are given by outside speakers during the GCSE year, and the advice of specialist careers advisers and the careers teachers is available at all stages.

Activities. The School aims to develop pupils through a wide range of activities, both within the School programme and outside it.

There is a large CCF contingent, with Army, Navy and Air Force sections. Strong Service connections locally give particularly wide scope for CCF activities.

Pupils also undertake a variety of activities in Community Service and participate in the Duke of Edinburgh's Award scheme.

Out of School there is a range of over 20 school societies in all three parts of the School, and in the holidays there is a strong tradition of annual cultural and outdoor expeditions in this country and abroad for Preparatory and Senior School pupils.

Art, Drama and Music. The School sets great store by the Arts, and uses the comparative proximity to London to take pupils to art exhibitions, concerts and the theatre. The School stages major drama productions each year, recently *Les Misérables, Dido, Sweeney Todd, Joseph and the Amazing Technicolor Dreamcoat* and *The Merchant of Venice* have been the main presentations. There is a strong musical tradition enhanced by visiting music staff, and pupils are encouraged to learn instruments. In addition to concerts in the School and the Cathedral, the Orchestra gives a number of outside performances each year, some by invitation. The choral tradition is strengthened by the presence of the Cathedral choristers in the School who regularly undertake overseas tours. In 2011, the senior choir reached the semi-final of the BBC Songs of Praise Choir of the Year Competition. In 2014, Drama at GCSE level and Theatre Studies at A Level were added to the curriculum.

Games. The boys' games are Rugby, Hockey, Football (Preparatory School) and Cricket and for girls' Hockey, Netball and Tennis. Other team sport options are Rowing (from our River Medway boathouse), Athletics, Cross Country, Fencing, Tennis and Swimming, and there are opportunities in addition for Squash, Badminton and Sailing. Physical Education is a regular part of the School curriculum and all pupils are required to take part in games. 80% represent the School competitively.

Religious Education and Worship. Although there is no denominational requirement for entry to the School, religious instruction is in accordance with the principles of the Church of England. All three parts of the School begin the day with an assembly or chapel service, some of which are held in the Cathedral.

Admission. Pupils can enter the School at any age from 3 to 18, although the main entry points are: 4+, 7/8+, 11+, 13+ and 16+. Entrance to the Senior School is either by Common Entrance at 13 or by the School's own examination for pupils who have not been prepared for Common Entrance.

Sixth Form entry is on the basis of interview and School report, together with satisfactory GCSE results (a minimum of 5 A*–C passes, and grade requirements for A Level courses).

Choristers. Choristerships to Rochester Cathedral (8+/ 9+) from Cathedral and School are awarded to boys following voice trials and a satisfactory performance in the Preparatory School Entrance Examination. Under normal circumstances, the choristership will continue until a boy transfers to the Senior School or until he leaves the choir.

Scholarships and Bursaries. *Senior School*: Up to five Major King's Scholarships (30%) and five Minor King's Scholarships (15%) may be awarded annually. At least five scholarships are for pupils from maintained sector schools. King's Scholars become members of the Cathedral Foundation.

Preparatory School: Five King's Exhibitions valued at 30% of fees are available at 11+. Two are for pupils from maintained Primary Schools.

Music: Up to five Music Scholarships may be awarded annually with a value of up to 30% of fees.

A range of Chesterfield Organ Scholarships have recently been introduced for 11+, 13+ and 16+ entry and details of these generous Scholarships are available from the Registrar on 01634 888590, admissions@kings-rochester.co.uk.

Free tuition on all instruments studied in School is given to holders of major and minor awards.

The Scholarships, available from 11+, will be awarded after an examination, usually in February, consisting of aural, sight reading and practical tests, and a viva voce. In addition, candidates at 13+ will be expected to be of Grade 5–6 standard and capable of passing Common Entrance, or a genuine A Level candidate if 15+. 11+ candidates should be at about Grade 4 level.

The Peter Rogers Scholarship of £3,000 per annum is awarded from time to time to assist an exceptionally talented musician, and a Dame Susan Morden Choral Scholarship of £2,500 is occasionally available to a Cathedral Chorister.

Boy Choristerships to Rochester Cathedral (8+/9+) from Cathedral and School.

Governors' Exhibitions are means-tested academic awards and may be of value up to 100% of fees.

To celebrate the acquisition of the new King's Rochester Sports Centre, the Principal introduced a range of Sports Scholarships for entry at 11+, 13+ and 16+.

Additional means-tested bursaries may be available.

Fee Remissions. Children of Church of England ministers are given an annually means-tested reduction in tuition fees.

Children of Service Personnel are given a 20% reduction in tuition fees.

Where parents have three or more children at the school a reduction after the second child is given, amounting to 10% of the third child's tuition fees, 20% for the fourth child and 40% for the fifth and subsequent children.

Fees per term (2016–2017). Senior School: Boarders £9,860, Day Pupils £6,070. Preparatory School: Boarders £6,860, Day Pupils £4,140–£4,700 (inc lunch). Pre-Preparatory School (Day only): £3,190–£3,460 (inc lunch).

Charitable status. King's School, Rochester is a Registered Charity, number 1084266; it is a charitable trust for the purpose of educating children.

Patron: The Lord Bishop of Rochester, The Rt Revd James Langstaff

Governing Body:
Chairman: Mr R W Hoile, MS, FRCS
Vice-Chairman: The Revd Canon Dr P Hesketh, PhD, BD, AKC
Assistant Vice-Chairman: Mr P J Webb, MS, FRCS
Mr B Bell, BSc Hons, CIMDIP, FCIM
Mr M A Blanning, BSc Econ
The Venerable S Burton-Jones, MA, BTh
Mr M J Chesterfield
Mr J K Daffarn, FRICS
Mr S J Douglass
Mr J Franklin, BA Med Admin
Mrs J Glew, BA, CIMDIP, MA
Mr P L Rothwell, LLB Hons
Mrs R A Rouse, MSc
Mr C R Shepherd, BSc, CEng, FICE, FRSA
Miss J A Shicluna, MA Oxon
The Revd Canon N Thompson, BEd, MA

Executive Board:

Principal of King's Rochester & Headmaster of the Senior School: Mr J Walker, MA Oxon, MA London
Headmaster of the Preparatory School: Mr R P Overend, BA, FTCL, ARCM, FRSA
Headmistress of the Pre-Preparatory School: Mrs C E Openshaw, MA Ed
Bursar and Clerk to the Governors: Mr G R Longton, BSc, FCMA

Senior School:

Principal of King's Rochester & Headmaster of the Senior School: Mr J Walker, MA Oxon, MA London
PA to the Principal: Miss B J Senior
Deputy Head (Academic): Miss N Steel, BSc
Deputy Head (Pastoral): Mr C H Page, BA
Deputy Head (Operations): Miss H L Catlett, BA
Chaplain: The Revd S J Padfield, MA

Heads of Department:
Art: Mr A J Robson, BA
Biology: Mr B Liddle, BSc
Chemistry: Mr N J McMillan, BSc Hons
Classics: Mr S C Janssens, MA
Design & Technology: Mr S J Johnson, BEd
English: Mr W E Smith, BA
French: Mrs A Warne, Maîtrise
Geography: Miss L Costelloe, BA
German & Russian: Mr B W Richter, BA
History: Mr C M Hoile, BA Hons
ICT: Mr S Lea, BA Hons
Mathematics: Mr P G Stevens, BSc
Music: Mr D B McIlwraith, BA Hons, ARCO, PGCE
Physics: Mrs E L Parren, BSc
Physical Education: Mrs A J Richter, BSc
Religious Studies: Mrs L A Rogers, BA
Sport: Mr M Hebden, BA

Head of Admissions and Marketing: Mrs R Hall
Librarian: Mrs X Guo, MA
CCF Contingent Commander: Major S Short

Preparatory School:
Headmaster: Mr R P Overend, BA, FTCL, ARCM, FRSA
Deputy Headmaster: Mr P N Medhurst, BA, MA

Pre-Preparatory School:
Headmistress: Mrs C E Openshaw, MA Ed
Deputy Headmistress: Mrs K Crozer, BEd
Honorary Pre-Preparatory School Lay Chaplain: Dr S Hesketh, MB BS, MRCGP, AKC, PRCOG, DCH, DFSRH

Music Department:
Director of Music: Mr D B McIlwraith, BA Hons, ARCO, PGCE
Preparatory School Director of Music & Head of Strings: Mrs J M Hines, BA
Head of Woodwind: Mr G Vinall, BA, LRAM
Cathedral Director of Music: Mr S Farrell, BMus Hons, ARCO, ARCM, PGCE

Medical Officer: Dr M Ojedokun, MB BS, MRCGP

The King's School
Worcester

5 College Green, Worcester WR1 2LL

Tel:	01905 721700 (School Office)
	01905 721721 (Bursar)
	01905 721742 (registrar)
Fax:	01905 721710
email:	info@ksw.org.uk
website:	www.ksw.org.uk
Twitter:	@KingsWorcester

A Cathedral School appears to have existed at Worcester virtually continuously since the 7th century. In its present form, however, The King's School dates from its re-foundation by King Henry VIII in 1541, after the suppression of the Cathedral Priory and its school. In 1884 the School was reorganised as an Independent School and in 1944 the Cathedral Choir School was amalgamated with The King's School.

Today, the King's School Worcester is a foundation comprising two junior schools and a senior school – all three are co-educational day schools.

The School still occupies its original site south of the Cathedral. The buildings are grouped around College Green and the School Gardens. They range in date from the 14th century College Hall and Edgar Tower through the 17th and 18th century buildings surrounding College Green, to a range of modern, purpose-built accommodation, much of which has been constructed in the last twenty years. Recent additions in a continuing development programme include a library located in the heart of the school, the John Moore Theatre, a new boat house opened in 2012, a covered Swimming Pool and upgraded House accommodation. A new Sports and Performing Arts centre, the Keyes Building, is now open. There are centres for English and Mathematics and a Music School. A Languages Computer Centre with the latest software for the teaching of French, German and Spanish has been established.

There are two Junior Schools. King's St Alban's stands in its own grounds on the edge of the main school site, offering education from age 4–11 with a purpose-built pre-prep department for girls and boys aged 4–7. King's Hawford is in a spacious rural setting just to the north of the city and offers education from age 2–11.

Numbers and Admission. The school is fully co-educational. King's St Alban's has 214 pupils. King's Hawford has 310 pupils. The Senior School has 912 pupils, including 270 in the Sixth Form.

Entrance to the school is by the Junior Entrance Test at 7, 8 or 9, or by the School's Examination at 11, 12 and 13. Boys and girls also join the School at Sixth Form level; this entry is by test, interview and GCSE results.

Term of Entry. Pupils are normally admitted annually in September.

Religion. The School has an historic connection with the Cathedral. Religious education, given in accordance with the Christian faith, is non-denominational. Pupils of all denominations and faiths are welcomed.

Curriculum. Pupils are prepared for the GCSE, and A, AS and Advanced Extension papers, and for Higher Education, the Services, the professions, industry and commerce. The curriculum is designed to give all pupils a general education and to postpone specialisation for as long as possible. Further details will be found in the Prospectus.

Games. The major sports are Rugby, Netball, Hockey, Football, Rowing and Cricket. Other sports include Tennis, Athletics, Cross Country, Badminton, Rounders, Fencing, Squash, Golf, Swimming, Sailing and Canoeing. PE and games are compulsory for all; a wide choice is offered to Sixth Formers. The school has been awarded the Sportsmark Gold award.

Other Activities. The school has a Choral Society and two other Choirs, 3 Orchestras and a Wind Band; there are at least 20 concerts each year. There are more than a dozen dramatic productions each year, including two or three major School plays, one of which is usually a Musical. The School takes part in the Duke of Edinburgh's Award scheme; there is a CCF and a Welfare and Community Service group. Young Enterprise companies in the Sixth Form are well subscribed and highly successful. A large number of societies and groups cater for a wide variety of other out-of-school activities and interests. The School has an Outdoor Activities Centre in the Black Mountains which is widely used both during the term and in the holidays. The Himalayan Club takes about 25 pupils on expeditions each year.

Scholarships and Bursaries. Both Music and Academic Scholarships are available at 11+, 13+ and 16+ in the Senior School, value up to one third of tuition fees. Academic scholarships at 11+ and 13 + are awarded on the basis of the Entrance Test and an interview; at 16+ on the basis of an aptitude test and interview, along with a report from the candidate's school.

Means-tested bursaries up to 100% of fees are available to academically-able candidates and can be combined with a scholarship. Full details are available from the Registrar.

Fees per term (2016–2017). Senior School £4,360; Junior Schools £2,184–£4,120.

Chorister Scholarships. Entry to the Choir is by means of Voice and Academic Tests which are held at various times throughout the year. A high vocal and musical standard is naturally required and boys must also have sufficient intellectual ability to hold their own in the Choir and the School. Boys should be 7–9 years old at the time of entry.

The **Prospectus** and information about Entrance Tests, Awards and Chorister Scholarships can be obtained from the Registrar.

Charitable status. The King's School Worcester is a Registered Charity, number 1098236. It exists to provide high quality education for boys and girls.

Visitor: The Lord Bishop of Worcester

The Governing Body:
Mr H B Carslake, BA, LLB (*Chairman*)
The Very Revd P G Atkinson, MA, FRSA (*Vice-Chairman*)
Mr M Atkins, MRICS
Professor M Clarke, CBE, MA, DL
Mr D Dale, MA, FCA
Mr J W R Goulding, MA Oxon
Mr D L Green, LLB
Mrs J H Jarvis, BA, MCIPD
Mr R S McClatchey, BA
Revd Canon Dr A Pettersen, BA, PhD
Mrs C Pike, OBE
Mrs P Preston, MA Oxon, DipM
Mr A E Reekes, MA, MRes, FRSA
Dr H Swift, MA, MSt, DPhil Oxon
Mrs I Taylor, MA Cantab, FCA
Professor J Vickerman, BSc, PhD, DSc
Mr P Walker, MBE, BSc, MPhil, CEng, MIMMM

Clerk to the Governors and Bursar: Miss H L Jackson

Headmaster: Mr M G Armstrong, MA

Senior Deputy Head: Mr J Ricketts, BSc
Second Deputy Head: Miss C Mellor, BA
Director of Studies: Mr R C Baum, MA
Academic Deputy Head: Mr D S King, BSc

* *Head of Department*
§ *Part-time*

Art:
*Miss G Terry, MA
Mr C Haywood, BA
Miss J Hewitt, BA
§Mrs C Horacek, BA
Mrs G Hardy, BA
Miss J Wallace-Mason, BA [maternity cover]

Biology:
*Dr M Parkin, MA, PhD
Mr S M Bain, BSc, MSc
§Dr C L Brown, BSc, PhD
Mrs N Essenhigh, BSc
Mr M J Newby, BEd
Mr J H Chalmers, BASc
Mrs R Worth, BSc

Careers:
*Mrs H Riddell, BA
Mrs E Friend, BA

Chemistry:
*Mr R P Geary, BSc, CChem, MRSC
Mrs C E Battrum, MA
Dr R J James, BSc, PhD
Mr T B Jeavons, BSc
Dr M C Poole, BSc, PhD
Mr J R Ricketts, BSc
Mrs R Roberts, MSc

Classics:
*Mrs S C Bradley, BA
§Miss R M Lewis, MA
Mr P J Garland, BA
Mrs E Shepherd, MA

§Miss G Bradley, BA

Critical Thinking:
*Revd Dr M R Dorsett,
BA, MTh, PhD,
CertTheol (*Chaplain*)

Design and Technology:
*Mr C W S Wilson, BA
Mr A G Deichen, BA
Miss R A Ellender, BA
Mr E Lummas, BA

Drama & Theatre Studies:
*Ms J Price-Hutchinson,
BA
Mrs S Parry, MA
Mr S Le Marchand, BA

*Economics & Business
Studies*:
*Mrs E Friend, BA
Mr R Mason, BA
Mr G L Williams, BA
§ Ms C Westley, BA

English:
*Mr A J M Maund, MPhil,
MA
Mr S Le Marchand, BA
Mr R J Davis, BA
Ms L L Guy, BA
Mrs A J Fellows, BA
Mrs S H Le Marchand, BA
§Mrs L Walmsley, BA
§Mr M Warren, MA

Geography:
*Mr S C Cuthbertson, BA
Mr W J Joyce, BSc
Mr A W Longley, BA
Mrs C M Neville, BSc
Mrs E Woodward, BA
Mr D King, BSc
Mr J C Barnard, BA
[maternity cover]

History:
*Miss E Cameron, BA
Mr T Sharp, BA
Mr A J Ford, BA
Mrs N J Sears, BA
§Mrs S E Stuart, MA

Information Technology:
*Mr D N Branchett, BSc

Key Skills:
Mrs C M Neville, BSc

Learning Skills:
*Mrs J L Lucas, BA,
DipSpLD, NDT [NPP]
Mrs C J Knipe, BA,
DipSpLD, APC SpLD
§Miss R M Lewis, MA

Library:
*Ms A Jeffery, MA,
DipLIS
Mrs A Haywood, BA
Mrs M Capell

Mathematics:
*Mr O Heydon, BSc
Ms K Conroy, BA
§Mrs K Beever, MA, CEng

Mrs E L Darby, MA
Mr J N Gardiner, BSc
Mr J Hand, BA
Mr A A Kerley, BEng
Mrs M M Longley, BEd
Mrs D Salkeld, BSc
Mr E J Lewis, BSc
Miss A-M Simpson, BSc
Mr A R Swarbrick, BSc
§Mrs D J Clarke, BSc

Modern Languages:
*Mr R A Ball, MA
  (*German*)
Mrs C Yates, BSc
  (*French*)
Mrs R Shearburn, BA
  (*Spanish*)
Miss C Mellor, BA
Mr N J Pilborough, BA
Mr E D Houghton, BA
Mrs R M Rutter, BA
Mr J Sarriegui, BA
Ms L Ruiz Pelaez, BA
§Mrs A Azzopardi
  (*German Assistant*)
§Mrs I Houer-Milton
  (*Spanish Assistant*)
§Miss A-C Rolland
  (*French Assistant*)

Music:
*Mr S Taranczuk, MMus,
FRCO (*Director of
Music*)
Mr G M Gunter, GTCL,
LTCL
and visiting teachers

PE & Games:
*Mr J J Mason, BSc
  (*Director of Sport*)
Mr A A D Gillgrass, BA
  (*Boys' Games*)
Mrs S C Parkinson-Mills,
BSc (*Girls' Games*)
Mr J Chalmers, BApplSc
  (*Rowing*)
Mr C Atkinson, BSc
Mr S M Bain, BSc, MSc
Miss E K McKenzie, BSc
Mrs M M Longley, BEd
Mrs F L Short, BA
Miss L C Symonds, BSc
§Mrs K M Armitage
§Mrs J D Clark, BEd

Physics:
*Dr D J Haddock, MA,
DPhil Oxon
Mr R C Baum, MA
Mrs L E Haddock, BSc
Mr I C Robinson, BSc
Mrs S K Stone, BEng
Mr A Knights, MPhys

Politics:
*Miss E Cameron, BA
Mr A A D Gillgrass, BA
Mr A J Ford, BA

PSHE:
*Dr R Head, BA, MPhil,
PhD

Religion and Philosophy:
*Dr R Head, BA, MPhil,
PhD

Cover Supervisor: Mrs A Sansome, BA, ACA

Headmaster's PA: Mrs C Swainston
Registrar: Mrs V Peckston, BA
Medical Officer: Dr A Woof, MBChB
Sister: Mrs C F Furber, RGN, DipN

The King's Junior Schools

King's St Alban's
Tel: 01905 354906; email: ksa@ksw.org.uk

Head: Mr R A Chapman, BSc
Deputy Head: Mrs R Duke, BA
Director of Studies: Mr D Braithwaite, BEd

Mr T Dudley
Mrs K Etherington, BMus
Mrs K Beauchamp, BA
Mrs K Chatterton, BSc
Mrs K Hadfield
Mrs V Gunter, GTCL,
  LTCL
Mrs H Haggarty, BMus
Mrs A Hind, BSc
Mrs K Kear-Wood, BSc
Mrs L Kilbey, MA, LRSM
Mrs J Knipe, BA, DipSpLD

Mrs N Ricketts, BSc
Mrs E Lewis, BEd
Mrs J Pitts, BEd
Mrs L Thorp, BA
Miss E Chadwick, BA
Mrs E Majhu, BEd
Mrs P White
Mrs R Woodger
§Mrs F Atkinson, BSc
§Mrs N Cain, BA
§Mrs L Hand
§Mrs J Clark

Registrar: Mrs L Robins
Secretary: Miss S Hurley
Matrons: Mrs K Jenkins, Mrs A Withnall
Teaching Assistants: Mrs A Cinao, Mrs C Holden-Milner,
  Mrs E Monkhouse, Mrs J Stenson

King's Hawford
Tel: 01905 451292; Fax: 01905 756502;
email: hawford@ksw.org.uk

Head: Mr J M Turner, BEd, DipEd, ACP
Deputy Head: Mrs L Baxter, BSc
Assistant Head: Mrs P M Bradley, BEd (*Head of Pre-Prep*)
Assistant Head: Mrs A Marshall-Walker, BA
Director of Studies: Mr J Turvey, BA

Prep Department:
§Mrs J Atkins, BA
Mrs J Chambers
Mrs K Chapman, BA
Mr R Cook, BSc
Mrs H Fowler, BA, OCR
  Cert
Mr S Hodgkins, BSc
Mrs S Hughes, BA
§Mrs L Hyde, BA
Mrs C Knight, BEd
§Mrs T McCullough
Mr I Percival, BA
Mrs C Rawnsley, BA
Mrs J Redman, BEd
Mrs L Stephens, BA
§Ms K Turk, BA, MA

Pre-Prep:
Head: Mrs P M Bradley,
BEd
Miss A Kingston, BA
Mrs J Rand, MSc

Early Years:
Head: Mrs J Willis, BEd
Mrs G Riley, BSc

Mrs A Leatherdale, BSc
Mrs A Jeavons, BA

Classroom Assistants:
Mr K J Bethell
Mrs H Chapman
Mrs S Doorbar
Mrs K Goodman
Mrs C Green
Mrs M Griffiths-Garbett
Mrs E MacDonald
Mrs S Hodson
Mrs S Routledge
Mrs S Surey
Mrs J Ireland
Mrs A Hershman
Mrs E Jennings
Mrs R Pearman

Sports Assistants:
Miss G Holtham
Mr D Austin
Mr W Hollis

Kindergarten:
Mrs D Field
Mrs K Farrow

Revd Dr M R Dorsett, BA,
MTh, PhD, CertTheol
(*Chaplain*)
Miss A-M Simpson, BSc

Mrs S A Gwilliam Miss J Obrey
Mrs J Hooper Mrs S Powell
Mrs M Jones Mrs J Simons
Mrs C Kennedy Mrs S Watts

Registrar: Mrs D Wenyon
Head's PA/Office Secretary: Miss L Crowe
Office Secretaries: Miss G Woolley
Matron: Mrs F Geary, RGN

Kingston Grammar School

London Road, Kingston-upon-Thames, Surrey KT2 6PY
Tel: 020 8546 5875
email: enquiries@kgs.org.uk
website: www.kgs.org.uk

Motto: *Bene agere ac laetari.*

A school is believed to have existed in the Lovekyn Chantry Chapel since the fourteenth century. However, in 1561, Queen Elizabeth I, in response to a humble petition from the Burghers of Kingston, signed Letters Patent establishing the "Free Grammar School of Queen Elizabeth to endure for ever". In 1944 the School accepted Direct Grant Status and became fully independent in 1976. Two years later the School became co-educational, initially with girls in the Sixth Form, but in the following year joining in the First Year, to progress through the School. There are still close links with the Royal Borough of Kingston upon Thames, but no residential qualification for entry to the School. There are around 820 pupils and the proportion of boys to girls is approximately 54%–46%.

Buildings. Starting with the medieval Lovekyn Chapel, the site of Kingston Grammar School has been developed over 450 years. The refurbishment of the Fairfield Building has provided modern, energy-efficient classrooms and science laboratories. The Queen Elizabeth II building, opened by Her Majesty in 2005, has a Performing Arts Centre, a Music Technology Suite, Sixth Form Centre and classrooms. Pupils have access to an extensive networked computer system which they can access from home. The school is easily accessible by road and rail links to Kingston. The 22-acre sports ground includes an indoor training area, sports pavilions, 4 cricket squares, 6 netball courts, 8 tennis courts, 6 cricket nets, 2 hockey pitches plus practice area, 4 football pitches and the recently refurbished KGS Boat House.

Entry to the School. Admission to the School is by examination and interview at 11+ and 13+ and GCSE grades, examination and interview at 16+. Candidates sit the School's own examination papers; for 13+ in November prior to entry year and for 11+ in January of the year of entry. We also hold a 10+ deferred entry exam for candidates in Year 5 at primary school to enter in Year 7.

Term of Entry. Pupils enter in September. Occasional vacancies considered.

Fees per term (2016–2017). £6,015; this covers all charges except examination fees and lunch.

Scholarships and Bursaries. The Governors award scholarships (on merit) and means-tested bursaries to pupils entering the School at 11+ and 16+.

At age 11 there are Academic Scholarships attracting a fee remission which are awarded on the results of a scholarship examination and interviews, which is by invitation only following the Entrance Examination.

Academic Scholarships are also awarded to entrants to the Sixth Form, following written entrance examinations, interviews and successful GCSE results.

Music Scholarships, plus free tuition on one instrument, are available. Auditions are in January for candidates who are applying for entry at either 11+ or 16+.

Art Scholarships may be awarded at 11+ and 16+ following practical test, interview and submission of a folder of work.

Sport Awards for candidates demonstrating outstanding sporting potential are available at 11+ and 16+, based on practical assessment.

Drama Scholarships are also available at 16+, based on auditions.

Curriculum. The academic curriculum through to GCSE emphasises a proper balance between varied disciplines and a range of intellectual experience, with all taking Maths, English, the three sciences and at least one modern foreign language as part of 10 IGCSE/GCSE subjects. Maths IGCSE may be taken early by the most able candidates. There is a Learning Support Department and mentoring for pupils with specific needs. A full Careers Programme is offered with support for university entry as well. Pupils are encouraged to view academic pursuit as a desirable end in itself, using a profiling process to develop their commitment to study. In the Sixth Form, students choose 4 A Level subjects in the Lower Sixth and normally continue with 3 into the Upper Sixth. In addition, students in the Lower Sixth undertake an academic enrichment programme, designed to develop the skills necessary to learn independently and to broaden their horizons. They are able to choose from courses such as the Extended Project Qualification (EPQ), MOOCS, OU courses or Critical Thinking. They also engage in community service. All Sixth Form students attend fortnightly lectures on wider social issues and international themes. Almost 100% of the Sixth Form elect to proceed to higher education, including Oxford and Cambridge, with a high proportion gaining entry to Russell Group institutions.

Care. A pupil's Form Tutor is responsible for welfare and progress. Heads of Year, supported by Senior Tutors, coordinate the work of form tutors. There is a full-time qualified nurse and a School Counsellor visits two days a week to support any pupils who have concerns in and out of school. Parents' meetings are held regularly and pupils receive two written reports per year, in addition to twice termly grade cards. Pastoral evenings are also held, where parents can discuss with each other and staff the difficulties and anxieties faced by young adults.

Games. The School's sports grounds are beautifully situated at Thames Ditton, by the River Thames opposite Hampton Court Palace. Kingston Grammar School prides itself on the large number of pupils who represent Great Britain in hockey and rowing.

Hockey (in both winter terms) and Rowing (all the year round) are main games with teams at all levels regularly competing in National Championships. The School also has representative sides in Football, Athletics, Cricket, Tennis, Golf, Cross-Country and Netball, with an emphasis on sport for all and participation as well as on training for performance athletes.

Societies. The School is proud of its extensive co-curricular provision and its programme of House-based activities. A large number of School societies provides for the interests of pupils of all ages. They range from Chess and Debating, to Natural History and Young Enterprise. The Duke of Edinburgh's Award scheme is popular and overseas travel is a regular feature of many activities. The Music Department has a vigorous programme of concerts and tours, and a flourishing Drama Department provides a wealth of opportunity for pupils in all aspects of dramatic production.

Community Service. A large number of pupils are involved in over ten external organisations as a result of the Community Service Programme at KGS, including MENCAP, the Joel Community Project, Kingston Food Drive, local primary schools, Kingston Hospital, St Stephen's homeless shelter and Elmbridge Community Link. While older pupils are directly involved in the projects, younger pupils also support groups through activities that take place within school. Volunteering helps pupils to develop awareness and understanding of elements within society that frequently go unnoticed by young people. Although KGS already offers a wide range of activities to choose from, staff are also willing to help pupils find other projects. In addition, the School has a partnership with a school in Ghana; gap year students undertake periods of work experience at the school, whilst younger pupils are involved in fundraising activities and co-curricular links.

Combined Cadet Force. The CCF is divided into Army and RAF sections with a variety of activities ranging from night exercises and flying to outward bound and adventure training. Camps are held in school holidays and pupils attend courses in a range of subjects. This is an entirely voluntary activity which pupils may take up in the Third Year.

Careers. The Careers Staff assist pupils in their choice of options at all levels, and give advice on possible future careers. They are in close touch with employers in professions, commerce and industry, and all Fifth Year pupils undertake a period of work experience after their GCSE examinations. An annual Careers Convention is held at the School. Particular attention is given to advice on entry to the universities to which the majority of Sixth Form students go. The School is in membership of the Independent School Careers Organisation and pupils are able to take advantage of several computer assessment programmes.

Parents' and Staff Association. The Association exists to further the interests of the School in the broadest possible way and does much to strengthen the links between staff, parents and students. The Sherriff Club (rowing), The Hockey Society, Music Society, and Drama & Dance Society also support school activities.

KGS Friends (our Alumni Society) does much to foster a spirit of unity and cooperation. All pupils and their parents automatically join the Friends on leaving the School.

Honours. An average of 10 places are gained each year at Oxbridge.

Charitable status. Kingston Grammar School is a Registered Charity, number 1078461, and a Company Limited by Guarantee, registered in England, number 3883748. It exists to enable children to adapt their talents to meet the needs of an ever-changing world, whilst holding fast to the principles of self-reliance, a sense of responsibility and a determination to seize opportunity.

Governing Body:
D Rice, LLB (*Chair*)
E A Kershaw, MA, MPhil (*Vice Chair*)
Mrs L Adam, BSc
M Annesley, BA, ACA
R W Brown, MA, ACMA
Mrs C Chevallier
D P D Combe, BA
A D Evans, BSc, ACA
N Khandan-Nia, BSc
Ms F C Le Grys, MA
A N McLean, BA, LLM, JP
R O'Dowd
Mrs K Sonnemann, Dipl-lng Architect TU Berlin RIBA

Head Master: S R Lehec, BA

Deputy Head Pastoral: Mrs V S Humphrey (*Geography*)
Deputy Head Academic: W Cooper, MPhil (*Religion & Philosophy*)
Assistant Head: Mrs D M Sherwood, BSc (*Geography*)
Assistant Head: Mr A J Beard, BA (*History*)
Assistant Head: Mrs A Lett, BSc (*Chemistry*)

Staff:
* *Head of Department*

Miss L S Andrews, BSc (*Mathematics*)
Mrs A Angell, BA (**History, Joint Head of Academic Monitoring*)
Mrs J Barkey, BA (*Art*)
M Behnoudnia, BSc (*Second in Physics, Assistant Head of Academic Scholars*)
T G Benson, MSci (*Physics, Head of Third Year*)
C Bequignon, MA (*French & German*)
Miss S J Boulton, MA (**Director of Drama*)
Miss K A Brackley, BA (*English*)
T A Braine, MA (*Design Technology*)
Mrs J Butcher, BA (*History & Politics*)
D G Buttanshaw, BEd (*PE, Mathematics, *Hockey*)
B Campbell, BA (*HMCTT English*)
Miss E Carlstedt-Duke, BSc (*HMCTT PE*)
Miss S E Christie, BA (*Art*)
Mrs H L Cleaves, MA (*Librarian*)
Ms S Clifford, BSc (*Mathematics*)
K Connor, MEng (*Second in Mathematics*)
Mrs H B Cook, BSc (*Mathematics*)
Mrs S J Corcoran, BEd (*Learning Support)
Dr A Crampin, BSc, PhD (*Physics, Head of Fourth Year*)
S R Crohill, BA (*Assistant Director of Drama*)
M Daly (*Director of Sports Scholars & Outreach*)
J M Davies, MA (*History*)
I Deepchand, BSc (**Physics, Assistant Head of Year Sixth Form*)
Dr A Deters, MA, PhD (*English*)
J A Dyson, BA (*Art)
Mrs A L Edwards, MA (**Psychology, Joint Head of Academic Monitoring*)
D Farr, BA (**Design Technology*)
A R Fitzgerald, MA (*Director of Careers & Universities*)
N S Forsyth, BSc (*Biology, Head of Pastoral Training & Outreach*)
O P Garner, BA (*French & Italian, Deputy Head of Sixth Form*)
Mrs P S Garside, BA, MA (*English)
M S Grant, BA, MA (*History, Director of Educational Visits & Student Leadership Development*)
Ms Y Greaves, BSc (*ICT*)
Miss C M Hall, BSc (*Science)
J Halls, BA (*Design Technology*)
Miss A Henderson, BA (*History*)
Mrs R L Hetherington, BA (*Design Technology, Head of Second Year*)
Mrs N L Hempstead, L-ès-L (*French, Spanish*)
Miss A L Hicks, BSc (*Biology*)
Mrs H Hunt, BA (**PSHE, Religion & Philosophy*)
Miss E M Hyde, MA (*Assistant Director of Music*)
Mrs M-J Jeanes, BSc (*Chemistry*)
Miss L M Jenkins, MSc (*Geography, Senior Tutor First Year*)
Mrs C A Jones, BSc (*Mathematics, Assistant Head of Year Fourth & Fifth*)
Dr K Kennedy, MSt (*HMCTT History*)
Miss L Knight, BA (*English, Deputy Head of Community Service*)
H R Lawrence, BSc (*Religion & Philosophy*)
Mrs N Maclean, BSc (*Director of Sport*)
Miss R M McBrien, MSc (*Mathematics*)
J B McClenaghan, BSc (*Mathematics*)
Miss B A McDonald, BA, MA (*Classics, Director of Sixth Form*)
S R Morris, BSc (*Mathematics, Deputy Director of Careers & Universities*)
Miss H M Naismith, MSc (**PE, *Girls' Hockey*)
Miss E Noble, MSc (*HMCTT Geography*)

J P Orr, MA (*Mathematics*)

Miss R Pastore, MA (*Spanish, Assistant Head of Third Year*)

Mrs K D Pinnock, BA (*French & Italian, Head of Community Service*)

Mrs A Plumridge, BSc (*Biology, Head of Fifth Year*)

P R C Powell, BA (*Economics*)

Mrs E Pytel, BA (**Classics*)

Mrs N A Reilly, MSci (*Mathematics*)

Miss N Reynolds, BA (*Spanish*)

Mrs L Rhys, BSc (*Mathematics, *Young Enterprise*) [maternity leave]

P J Ricketts, MA (**Economics, University Admissions Tests Tutor*)

Mrs M Robinson, BSc (*Psychology*)

M J C Rodgers, BSc, MSc (**Biology, management of Golf Programme*)

Mrs T M Russell, Mag Phil (**Modern Foreign Languages*)

Miss C Searl, MSc (*Geography*)

M D Scott, BA (*Religion & Philosophy*)

Miss R J Sharp, BA (*French & Spanish, Second in Modern Foreign Languages*)

P J Simmons, BSc (**Rowing*)

J W Skeates, MA (**Mathematics*)

C R Smalman-Smith, BA (*Mathematics, *Junior Rowing*)

J S Smith, BA, MPhil (*English*)

Dr L J C Snook, MPhil, PhD (*Classics*)

D A R Sorley, BA (**Politics, History, Professional Tutor*)

Mrs J Stapleton (**Netball*)

Mrs P W E Stones, MA (*Deputy Second in English, Head of Academic Scholars*)

S Symington, MSc (*HMCTT Economics*)

J J Tierney, BMus (*Music*)

K Turner, BA (*German*)

Ms E K Varley, BA (*Second in English, Assistant Head of Year Sixth Form*)

M P Von Freyhold, PG Dip RCM, Diplom Musiklehrer Karlsruhe (**Director of Music*)

H Waddington, MPhil, FOLSIG (**Geography*)

Mrs R Wakely, BA (*Art*)

C G Wenham, BA (*Second in Chemistry*)

Mrs A R Whitby-Smith, MSc (*HMCTT Mathematics*)

Ms A Williams, BSc (*Chemistry, Head of First Year*)

Mrs C Williams, BA (**Religion & Philosophy*)

M P Williamson, BEd (*PE, Director of Coaching, Boys' Hockey Head Coach*)

Dr L H Winning, MChem, DPhil (**Chemistry*)

S J Woodward, BSc (*Assistant Director of Sport*)

Bursar and Clerk to the Governors: Mrs P J Smith, BA, ACIS

Facilities Manager: J Farmer

Development Director (Acting): C Conneely, BA

Head Master's PA: Mrs C Pink

Registrar (Acting): Miss K Riches

Marketing Manager: Mrs N Man, BA

Kingswood School

Lansdown, Bath BA1 5RG

Tel:	01225 734200
Fax:	01225 734305
email:	admissions@kingswood.bath.sch.uk
website:	www.kingswood.bath.sch.uk

Motto: *In via Recta Celeriter*

Kingswood is one of the top independent, co-educational schools in the UK and is currently placed 62 in the UK league tables. It was founded by John Wesley in 1748 and moved to its stunning 214-acre site overlooking the World Heritage City of Bath in 1851. Kingswood combines academic excellence with a concern for the development of each individual's talents. Boarders and day pupils are fully integrated within a happy and caring community environment. There are currently 768 pupils (410 boys and 358 girls) at the Senior School and 321 pupils at the Prep School.

Site and Buildings. Kingswood is located in 214 acres of superb parkland overlooking the world heritage City of Bath and within easy reach of the M4 and M5 motorways, as well as rail and air links. In addition to the beautiful main Victorian buildings, there is a state-of-the-art Theatre; a spacious Sixth Form Centre with facilities for private study and a modern common room; a stunning contemporary café, a series of specialist centres for ICT, DT, Drama Studio, Art Studio and a Music School with its own recording studio. The library and resources centre is engaging and is fully equipped with a Wi-Fi facility. All academic departments also have well-resourced areas including a new modern Language Laboratory. There are seven houses for boarding and day pupils, a stunning Chapel and excellent sporting facilities, including a Sports Hall, indoor swimming pool, two floodlit astroturfs, and extensive playing fields. The school also boasts a sports pavilion with first-class sports changing facilities and excellent hospitality areas.

The School also has its own Prep School in a Georgian mansion and award-winning modern buildings in a separate section of the parkland.

Curriculum. Kingswood encourages its students to develop lively, enquiring and well-informed minds and the high standard of attainment reached by its pupils has been highly praised. From 11 to 13 pupils follow a broad and balanced curriculum. Each pupil has a tutor to supervise progress and to offer advice and encouragement. At 14 the pupils choose at least eight and up to twelve GCSE subjects to develop their particular talents whilst maintaining a broad range of skills. They are also encouraged to develop independent learning plans which they work on with their tutors. Most sixth formers specialise in three subjects plus an EPQ and all participate in a General Studies programme. Sixteen subjects are offered at GCSE level as well as over twenty at A Level, including Politics, Business Studies, Sports Studies, Theatre Studies, Psychology and Critical Thinking.

Organisation. *Preparatory*: Pupils are drawn from a wide variety of schools, but Kingswood also has its own prep school for boarders and day pupils. Kingswood Prep School (KPS) caters for c320 boys and girls between the ages of 3 and 11, and offers a variety of activities alongside the academic curriculum. A boarding house for boys and girls aged 7–11 opened in September 1998. This "family-based" unit of 20 boarders is cared for by house-parents who also teach at the school. Children from the prep school are expected to move on to Kingswood, but parents are advised if children are felt to be academically unsuitable for entry to the Senior School at the end of Year 6. (*See Kingswood Preparatory School entry in IAPS section.*)

Westwood: A junior house operates for boys and girls aged 11–13. This is designed to settle new pupils into the school at 11+ or 12+ and provide the special environment that the younger pupils require before going into the senior houses. In effect, it means the pupils enjoy the atmosphere associated with a prep school whilst also enjoying all the facilities of a senior school. Sixth formers are especially selected to act as elder "brothers/sisters" and prefects to the younger pupils. The house is run by four resident house staff, together with house assistants.

Senior Houses: From the age of 13+ pupils are assigned to one of six houses, three for boys and three for girls, each under a resident Housemaster or Housemistress and assisted by other teaching staff. The houses ensure a good and friendly 'home from home' environment and there are also shared social areas in the centre of school. It would be normal to have c240 students in the Sixth Form, which has its own special building.

Houses. The seven houses are all very distinctive and five are set within their own grounds. Emphasis is placed on creating a family atmosphere in each house and the pastoral care provided has been judged at ISI inspection as 'exceptional'. Tutors monitor each pupil's progress and welfare. The school has a number of houses and flats for single and married staff. Many of the staff at the senior school live on the campus which cultivates exceptionally good relationships between teachers and students. Two state-of-the-art senior boarding houses were opened in both 2014 and 2016 and work is already under way to develop the other houses.

Sports and Games. The sporting and leisure activities programmes have around 90 activities with particular emphasis on sport, drama, music, art and outdoor pursuits. Sporting activities include athletics, badminton, basketball, cricket, cross-country, fencing, golf, hockey, netball, rugby, swimming and tennis. Other activities range from the Duke of Edinburgh's Award scheme to Computing, from Orienteering to Photography, and Bird Watching to Dance Express. Regular group activities in the instrumental field include orchestra, an award-winning jazz band, string group and wind band. There are also junior and senior choirs and a large-scale choral society and an extensive performance programme. Over 50% of the school are involved in extra music lessons. At least four dramatic productions take place each year.

Health. The well-equipped School Medical Centre is under the supervision of a fully qualified resident Sister and the School Medical Officer.

Religious Activities. Kingswood welcomes pupils from all denominations. In addition to regular morning worship, there is a wide variety of guest speakers and the Christian Fellowship organises its own events. There are regular fundraising activities for charities and a Community Service programme. Every year a joint Methodist-Anglican Confirmation service is held and there are special services in Bath Abbey for the whole school Carol Service and for Commemoration Day.

Careers. From the earliest stage possible, students are encouraged to participate in all decisions affecting their future. Kingswood subscribes to the Independent Schools Careers Organisation and has links with local career guidance organisations. A programme of work experience is followed by all members of the Lower Sixth and is aimed at providing experience of the entire process of job application, interview and work itself. The School has established close links with local employers to make all this possible. A series of lectures and discussions with visiting employers is also organised and endorsed by the Head of Sixth Form.

Leavers. It is normal for all of our Sixth Form pupils to go on to university courses, around 98% to the place of their first choice.

Fees per term (2016–2017). £4,794 (day), £8,626–£10,704 (full boarding), £7,536–£9,336 (weekly boarding).

EAL teaching is provided for students who do not speak English as their first language – this is invoiced separately as required.

Entry Requirements. Entry is based on Kingswood's entrance examination; a report from the candidate's previous school and, where possible, a personal interview. Candidates at 13+ may also enter by Common Entrance or Scholarship papers. Entry to the Sixth Form is by a minimum of six or more GCSE passes – four at Grade B plus two at Grade C, plus school report and interview. There are some subject specific criteria, details of which are found on the school website. (Most applicants achieve considerably more than the minimum entry grades.) There are normally around 25 places available due to the extended facilities available at Sixth Form level.

Scholarships and Bursaries. Academic and Special Talent scholarships (up to a maximum of 25% of the basic fees) are available annually to day and boarding pupils entering Years 7, 9 and Lower Sixth. Special Talent scholarships are awarded for excellence in a particular field: Art, Drama, Music, Sport, Design Technology. John Wesley All-Rounder Awards are also available for boarders only.

Means-tested bursaries, worth up to 100% of fees, are available in Years 7, 9 and Lower Sixth, awarded annually at the discretion of the Headmaster and the Governors.

Very special provisions are made for the children of Methodist Ministers (up to 100% bursary assistance) and consideration may also be given to assist the sons and daughters of clergymen of other denominations, with a reduction in fees according to circumstances.

HM Forces families receive a reduction in boarding fees of up to 20% for each child and Kingswood is one of the top boarding schools for Forces children.

Further details of scholarships and bursaries can be obtained from the school website: www.kingswood. bath.sch.uk.

Charitable status. Kingswood School is a Registered Charity, number 309148. Founded by John Wesley, it maintains its Methodist tradition in providing preparatory and secondary education.

Chairman of the Governing Body: Tim Westbrook

Clerk to the Governors & Bursar: Mr P A Sadler

Headmaster: Mr S A Morris, MA

Deputy Head Academic: Mrs S C Dawson, BEd
Deputy Head Pastoral: Mr G D Opie, BEd
Chaplain: Revd D A Hull, BTh, MLitt

Senior School Teaching Staff:
† *Senior Housestaff*
§ *Part-time staff*

Mr E T Allchorne, BSc (*Biology*)
Miss N J Beale, MA (*French, German*)
§Mrs M L Brennan, BEd (*Mathematics*)
Miss S Brookes, BA (*Head of French*)
Mr B N Brown, BSc Ed (*Head of Design Technology*)
Mr J O Brown, BSc (*Head of Boys' Games*)
†Mrs M L Brown, BSc (*Physics, Timetabler, Senior Housemistress Summerhill*)
Mr S T Brown, BDes, MA (*Head of Art*)
§Mr C W Burkinshaw (*Computer Science*)
Mr R E Burton, BSc (*Head of Physics*)
§Mrs A E Campbell, BA (*English*)
Mr S J Campbell, BA (*Head of English*)
Miss O A Chapman (*English*)
Mr J J Chua, MMath (*Mathematics, Head of Activities*)
§Mrs J Cook, Cert Ed (*Head of Study Support*)
Mrs N L Curtis, BA (*Head of Academic PE*)
Mrs S Dakin, MA (*Head of Classics*)
Mr D M Darwin, BA (*History and Politics*)
Mr J W Davies, BA (*History and Politics, Director of Co-Curricular, Member of SMT*)
Miss K M Donovan, BSc (*Geography*)
Mr R J Duke, MA (*Head of Languages and Head of German*)
Miss K J Duncan (*Sports Assistant*)
Mr G D Edgell, BA (*Head of Computer Science [Academic]*)
Mrs C E Edwards, MBA, BSc (*Head of Psychology, Assistant Head of Sixth Form*)
Miss S V Elliott, BA (*Art*)
Mr S J Forrester, MA (*Head of EAL*)
Mrs S C Fountain, MA (*Humanities*)
§Mrs E K Francis, LRAM (*Music*)
Mrs J T Hallett, Cert Ed (*Study Support*)

†Mr D T Harding, BA (*Drama & Theatre Studies, Senior Housemaster Hall*)
Mr M Haynes, MA (*Director of Music*)
§Mrs S F Herlinger, BA (*History and Politics*)
Mr J P Hills, BA (*Head of Economics*)
†Mr P J Hollywell, BA (*PE, Geography, Senior Housemaster Westwood*)
Mrs A Holsgrove, MBA (*Study Support*)
§Miss M G Huckle, BA (*Music*)
§Miss H J Hughes (*French, Spanish*)
Mrs D J Jenner, BA (*Head of Geography*)
Mr M P Jones, BCom (*Economics*)
Miss S A Jones, MA (*English*)
Mrs A M Knights, BSc Ed (*Mathematics*)
Mr J Knights, BA (*Music*)
Mr J-M Legg, BA (*French, Spanish*)
Mr P P G MacDonald, MA (*Head of History and Politics*)
†§Mrs J L Mainwaring, MA (*English, Housemistress Westwood*)
§Mrs S J Marshall, BA (*Head of PSHCE, Religious Studies*)
Mr L J Matheson, MEng (*Head of Science*)
§Mrs A K Matthews, BSc (*Geography*)
†Mr J Matthews, BA (*PE, Senior Housemaster Middle*)
Miss A E Moore, BA (*English*)
Mrs C D Morris, BA (*French and German*)
§Mrs R H Murchison (*Mathematics*)
Mr W T Musgrove, MSc (*Physics*)
Mr G J Musto, MPhil (*Mathematics, Director of CPD, Member of SMT*)
Mrs K L Nash, LLB (*Head of Drama & Theatre Studies*)
Mr G S Newbould, MA (*History and Politics*)
Miss M Newman (*PE*)
Miss A Nicholson, BA (*Art & Design Technology*)
Mrs J R Opie, MA (*Head of Biology*)
§Mrs E Pasco, MA (*French, Spanish, Head of Careers*)
Mrs M K Patterson MSc (*Biology*)
†Miss U J Paver, BA (*PE, Biology, Senior Housemistress School*)
Mr E C Peerless, BSc (*Physics*)
Mr S D Pentreath (*Chemistry*)
§Mrs A V Phillips (*Classics*)
Ms J Reeman, BEd (*Mathematics*)
Mr T P Reeman, BA (*Director of Sport and Head of PE*)
Miss N Robinson, BA (*French, Spanish*)
§Miss B G Rolfe, BSc (*Biology*)
†§Mrs C M Sergeant, BA (*Computer Science, Senior Housemistress Fonthill*)
Mrs V M Sim, BA (*Head of Girls' Games*)
Mr M D Smith, BEng (*Mathematics*)
Mr M W Smith, MA (*Head of Mathematics*)
§Mrs L Smyth, MSc (*Biology*)
Mr S D Smyth, BSc (*Geography*)
§Mrs J Solomon-Gardner, BA (*Computer Science*)
Miss N J Sparks, MChem (*Chemistry*)
Miss K A Sutherland, MSc (*Librarian*)
Mr M S Thatcher, BA (*Head of Religious Studies and Critical Thinking*)
Mr S R Thomas, BSc (*Design Technology*)
Mr D Walker, BA (*Head of Spanish*)
§Mrs E L Ward, BA (*Drama*)
Mr D C Webb, BSc (*Athletic Development Coordinator*)
†Mr J R White, BSc (*Mathematics, Senior Housemaster Upper*)
Mrs J-A Wilcock, BSc (*Chemistry*)
Miss H C Wilson, BA (*Religious Studies*)
Dr J M Wood, PhD (*Head of Chemistry*)
Mr C B Woodgate, MA (*History and Politics, Head of Sixth Form, Member of SMT*)
Miss C E Wormald, BA (*English*)

Miss A T Wright, MEd (*Psychology, Head of Boarding, Member of SMT*)

Director of Marketing & International Relations: Mrs H Lightwood
Registrar: Mrs D W Patterson
Director of Development: Miss S Mansfield

Kirkham Grammar School

Ribby Road, Kirkham, Preston, Lancashire PR4 2BH

Tel:	01772 684264
Fax:	01772 672747
email:	info@kirkhamgrammar.co.uk
website:	www.kirkhamgrammar.co.uk

Kirkham Grammar School, founded in 1549, is a co-educational independent School of 830 pupils aged between 3 and 18. The Senior School of 620 pupils, 65 of whom are boarders, incorporates a Sixth Form of 200, and the Junior School, for day pupils, has 210 on roll.

Kirkham Grammar School prides itself on developing well-balanced and confident young people, the vast majority of whom go on to University. As well as excellent academic results and a good Oxbridge entry record, the School introduces pupils to as wide a range as possible of cultural, sporting and creative activities and encourages them to participate in those which appeal to them. Great emphasis is placed on preparing pupils for life beyond university.

The School has a strong Christian ethos, with an emphasis on care for the individual, traditional family values, good manners and sound discipline.

It is a friendly close-knit community where staff and pupils work closely together, fostering leadership and self-discipline, and encouraging cheerful, friendly and supportive relationships within the framework of 'one family'.

Facilities. Occupying 30 acres of its own grounds, Kirkham Grammar School boasts some excellent facilities, which include a large multi-purpose hall, a superb floodlit all-weather pitch, a Sixth Form Centre, an outstanding Technology Centre and Languages Centre, and a magnificent Dining Complex. The School has built a new Science Centre alongside a new extended classroom block incorporating interactive facilities and also a new Performing Arts Centre. The school has developed a new Music Centre and new Sports Hall.

Boarding. The School is a member of the Boarding Schools' Association. The refurbished Boarding House is pleasant and comfortable and is run by a House Parent (Academic), whose residence is attached to the boarding wing of the School. The House also has a team of full-time support staff and tutors.

Academic Programme. The courses lead to GCSE and A Level. In the first three years, the basic subjects studied are English, French, Mathematics, German, Spanish, Geography, History, Physics, Chemistry, Biology, Music, Art & Design, Drama, ICT, Design and Technology, and Religious Studies. The first stage of specialisation takes place on entering the Fourth Form where the core subjects of English, Mathematics, Physics, Chemistry and Biology are taught in sets, and there is a further choice of subjects from four option blocks, which include: Art & Design, Design and Technology (Product Design; Electronic Products), Drama, Economics & Business Studies, French, Geography, German, History, ICT, Latin, Music, Physical Education, Religious Studies, Religion, Philosophy & Ethics, and Spanish.

In the Sixth Form, A and AS Level subjects are chosen from the following: English Language and Literature, Maths, Further Maths, Biology, Chemistry, Physics, French, German, Latin, Spanish, Art & Design, Music, Design Technology, Geography, History, Psychology, Philosophy, Government & Politics, Theatre Studies, Religious Studies, Economics, Business Studies, Physical Education & Electronics.

In addition many Sixth Formers voluntarily continue in the CCF and the Duke of Edinburgh's Award, Young Enterprise or Community Service. Extra tuition is provided for Oxbridge candidates. Students are also offered the opportunity to undertake an Extended Project Qualification (EPQ) alongside their A Levels.

A comprehensive careers service is available. The School is an active member of ISCO and is also served by Careerlink.

Sport. The School has a strong sporting tradition and ranks among the very best schools in the country for rugby and girls hockey. The other main sports played are cricket, athletics, tennis, netball, cross-country, badminton, squash, swimming, rounders, volleyball and basketball.

Music. There is a very active musical life at the School, with regular Concerts both at lunchtime and in the evening, providing a platform for the Orchestra, various ensembles and Soloists.

Extra-Curricular Activities. An impressive range of extra-curricular activities is offered by a School renowned for its sporting prowess, but with strength across the board in music, art, and drama. There is a strong and popular Combined Cadet Force contingent, with Army and RAF sections, and a flourishing House System. A large number of societies cater for a wide range of interests including archery, broadcasting society, drama, debating, the very popular Duke of Edinburgh's Award scheme, chess, public speaking, badminton, climbing, magic circle, music and many others.

Admission to Senior School. Four form entry. Pupils are usually admitted at 11 years after passing the entrance examination held in January each year. Admissions to the School in other year groups, especially the Sixth Form, are possible. Day/Boarding applications should be made to the Headmaster who will be glad to provide further details.

Fees per term (2016–2017). Day (excluding lunches): Senior School £3,599; Junior School £2,699; Pre-School: £233 (full week), £47.80 (full day).

These fees cover tuition, use of class, text and library books, school stationery, scientific equipment, games apparatus.

Senior School Boarding: £3,232 in addition to the Day fee. The boarding fee is discounted by 5% for children resident Monday to Friday (weekly boarders) and for children whose parents are current members of HM Forces.

Scholarships and Bursaries. The School offers an impressive number of Scholarships and Bursaries at 11+ and 16+. Further details are available from the Registrar.

Junior School (3–11 years). An integral part of the School under the same Board of Governors, the Junior School comprises a Pre-School, an Infant Department and a Junior Department, housed in splendid, purpose-built accommodation. The curriculum is organised in close consultation with the Senior School to ensure that education in its broadest sense is continuous and progressive from the age of 3 to 18.

The curriculum is broadly based and balanced. The core subjects – English, Maths, Science and ICT – are given priority as set in the National Curriculum. History, Geography, RE, Music, ICT, Design and Technology, Art, PSHE, PE and Games are studied as pure subjects and also as they relate to one another in a cross-curricular manner. In the Early Years we offer a fun, stimulating and caring environment, which follows the Early Years Foundation Stage Framework.

Application should be made direct to the Headmistress's PA from whom a separate prospectus may be obtained.

Old Kirkhamians Association. For further details contact the Secretary, Mr A R Long, via the School.

Charitable status. Kirkham Grammar School is a Registered Charity, number 1123869. The object of the Charity shall be the provision in or near Kirkham of a day and boarding school for boys and girls.

Chairman of Governors: Mrs R F Cartwright

Headmaster: Mr D H Berry

Senior Deputy Head: Mrs D C Parkinson, BSc, NPQH
Deputy Head (Operations): Mr M J Hancock, BEd, MA, MBA
Deputy Head (Pastoral)/Head of Sixth Form: Mr M P Melling, BA, MA Ed

Heads of Year:
Sixth Form: Mr M P Melling, BA, MA Ed
Assistant Heads of Sixth Form:
Mr M Gaddes, MA Cantab
Mrs J Stanbury, BA
Fifth Year: Mrs N Walter, BA
Fourth Year: Mrs A Walker, BA
Third Year: Mr D Gardner, BEng
Second Year: Mr S Duncan, BA
First Year: Mrs G R Latham, BA

Heads of Departments:
Art: Mr S P Gardiner, BA
Boys' Sport: Mr J P Roddam, BA
Business Studies & Economics: Mrs L E Hargreaves, BA
Chemistry/Biology: Dr A B Rollins, BSc, PhD
Design & Technology: Mr D Gardner, BEng
Drama: Ms J E Barrie, BA
English: Mrs K C O'Flaherty, BA
Geography: Mr S R Whittle, MA Cantab
Girls' Sport: Mrs L D Osborne, BA
History: Mrs H L Atkinson, BA
Latin: Mrs S P Long, BA
Learning Support: Mrs B P Batty, BSc
Librarian: Mrs G R Latham, BA
Mathematics: Mr D R Carter, BSc
Modern Foreign Languages: Miss L E Vicquelin, BA
Director of Music: Miss J Z Crook, BMus
Physics: Mr M Gaddes, MA Cantab
Politics: Mr M P Melling, BA, MA Ed
Psychology: Mrs J Stanbury, BA
Religion, Philosophy & Ethics: Mrs L Bowles, BA

Houses & House Parents:
House Parent (Academic): Mr A E Trenhaile, BA, MEd
Kirkham House: Mr G S Partington, BA
Fylde House: Mr S R Whittle, MA Cantab
School House: Mr J R Lyon, HND
Preston House: Mrs J M Glover, BEd

Bursar: Mrs C E Brown

Headmaster's PA/Registrar: Mrs C M Seed

Junior, Infant and Pre School:
Headmistress: Mrs A S Roberts, BEd
Deputy Headmistress: Mrs H Shuttleworth, GMus, RNCM
Assistant Head: Mr S Lewis, BA
Pre-School Manager: Mrs A Blanco-Bayo, QTLS

Junior School Headmistress's PA: Miss J Stewart
School Secretary: Mrs A Taylor

Lancing College

A Woodard School

Lancing, West Sussex BN15 0RW

Tel: 01273 452213
Fax: 01273 464720
email: admissions@lancing.org.uk
website: www.lancingcollege.co.uk
Twitter: @lancingcollege
Facebook: /lancingcollege

Motto: *Beati mundo corde.*

Founded in 1848 by the Revd Nathaniel Woodard, Lancing College is one of the first schools of the Woodard Foundation.

There are 580 pupils in the school, accommodated in nine houses.

Location. The school stands on a spur of the Downs, overlooking the sea to the south and the Weald to the north, in grounds of 550 acres, which include the College Farm.

By train, Lancing is 10 minutes from Brighton, 30 minutes from Gatwick Airport and 75 minutes from central London.

Buildings and Facilities. The main school buildings, faced with Sussex flint, are grouped around two quadrangles on the lines of an Oxford or Cambridge College.

The Chapel, open to visitors every day, has the largest rose window built since the Middle Ages.

The College has extensive laboratories, a purpose-built Music School, a Theatre with a full-time technical manager and a modern Design and Technology Centre with computerised design and engineering facilities. Alongside this, a strikingly modern Art School provides vast studio space and a photography suite. More recently a café has been created in the centre of the school for use by pupils and staff. There are over 350 private studies for boys and girls, many of which are study-bedrooms. There is a sports hall, indoor swimming pool and a miniature shooting range. Sporting facilities also include Squash, Tennis and Fives courts and an all-weather surface and full-sized AstroTurf hockey pitch. The College will be opening an Equestrian Centre in January 2017, which will provide livery as well as additional centre horses for co-curricular activities.

Admission. Boys and girls are normally admitted at the beginning of the Autumn Term in their fourteenth year. Admission is made on the result of either the Entrance Scholarship, the Common Entrance Examination or by private testing. A registration fee of £100 is paid when a child's name is entered in the admission register. Entries should be made via the Registrar, who will assign a House, following as far as possible the wishes of the parents. After a pupil has joined the school, parents usually correspond with the Housemaster or Housemistress directly.

Sixth Form Entry. Applications for entry should be made to the Registrar one year prior to the year of entry. Testing takes place in November or by private arrangement.

Curriculum. Designed as far as possible to suit every pupil's potential with a wide range of subjects on offer including over 20 at A Level. Pupils work closely with academic staff and personal tutors to help them consider future options, entry to universities and to a wide range of professions. The College prides itself on the individual support available for pupils.

In a pupil's first three years the curriculum provides a broad, balanced education without premature specialisation. The total of subjects taken at GCSE is limited to about nine or ten, the object being to promote excellence in whatever is studied and to lay firm foundations for the Sixth Form years.

The following subjects are studied in the Senior School: English Language and Literature, Religious Studies, Mathematics, Physics, Chemistry, Biology, French, Spanish or German, Geography, History, Physical Education, Music, Art, Design and Technology, Latin or Classical Civilisation and Drama.

In the Sixth Form there is a choice of over 20 subjects which can be studied to A Level. A BTEC qualification is also available in Sport, and a Pre-U in Photography. Pupils are also encouraged to carry out an EPQ (Extended Project Qualification) to enhance their studies.

A close connection has been established with schools in Germany and Spain, with which individual and group exchanges are arranged.

Tutorial System. In addition to the Housemaster or Housemistress there are pastoral Tutors attached to each House who act as Academic Tutors to individual pupils. The Tutors' main functions are to supervise academic progress and to encourage general reading and worthwhile spare time activities. A pupil usually keeps the same Tutor until he or she moves into the Sixth Form, where this function is taken over by an Academic Tutor chosen from one of the specialist teachers.

Music and Art form an important part of the education of all pupils. There are orchestras, bands, ensembles and choirs. Organ and Choral awards to Oxford and Cambridge and Colleges of Music are frequently won. There is a full programme of extra-curricular **Drama**. The **Art School** and **Design & Technology Centre** provide for a wide range of technical and creative work.

Other Activities. Boys and girls in their first year are given the opportunity to sample the many activities on offer at the College. A well-organised extra-curricular programme is followed by pupils of all age groups and participation is strongly encouraged under the supervision of the Director of Extra-Curricular Activities.

Up to twelve plays are produced each year and pupils are able to write and perform their own plays and to learn stagecraft.

In the Advent Term the main sports are Association Football for boys and Hockey for girls; in the Lent Term Football and Hockey for boys and Netball for girls. Squash, Fives, Badminton, Basketball, Volleyball, Cross Country and Shooting (the College has an indoor range) take place during both terms for boys and girls. Some Rugby is played in the Lent Term. Cricket, Tennis, Sailing, Athletics and Rounders take place in the Summer Term, and there is Swimming all year round in the College's indoor heated pool.

The College has a CCF contingent (with Army and RAF sections) and takes part in the Duke of Edinburgh's Award scheme. There is also a flourishing Outreach group, which works in the local community. Pupils help to run a small farm (including sheep, goats, pigs, alpacas and chickens) and participate in conservation projects under the supervision of the Farm Manager.

Links have been established with local industries and pupils are involved in business experience through the Young Enterprise scheme.

Careers and Higher Education. A number of the teaching staff share responsibility for careers advice and there is a well-equipped careers section in the Gwynne Library. Over 56 per cent of pupils go on to Russell Group universities; popular universities include Bristol, UCL, LSE, Imperial, Exeter and Durham; five to Oxbridge in 2016; several to other international universities. All members of the Fifth Form attend the annual Careers Symposium and most enrol in the ISCO Futurewise scheme. Lancing also offers the Sixth Form a new "Leaving Lancing" programme with activities to help pupils develop practical, team working and leadership skills.

Scholarships and Exhibitions. Candidates for the following awards must be under 14 years of age on 1st September in the year of the examination. The age of the candidate is taken into account in making awards. A candidate may enter for more than one type of award, and account may be taken of musical or artistic proficiency in a candidate for a non-musical award; but no one may hold more than one type of award, except in an honorary capacity.

A number of Open Scholarships ranging in value from £1,000 per year to half of the annual school fee.

A number of Music Scholarships ranging in value up to a maximum 10 per cent of the annual school fee. Scholarships may be offered to pupils from schools where the time for Music is less than in some others, and where a candidate may have less musical experience but greater potential.

One Professor W K Stanton Music Scholarship for a Chorister from Salisbury Cathedral School, or failing that any Cathedral School. A Stanton Exhibition may also be awarded.

A number of scholarships in Art, Drama and Sport, ranging in value up to a maximum 10 per cent of the annual school fee.

The Peter Robinson Cricket Scholarship is awarded to an outstanding young cricketer at 13+ entry.

A number of Ken Shearwood Awards, ranging in value up to a maximum 10 per cent of the annual school fee, are made to pupils of all-round ability and potential who have made outstanding contributions to their present schools.

Entry Forms for Academic, Art, Music, Drama, Sport and All-Rounder (Ken Shearwood) awards are obtainable from the Admissions Officer.

Sixth Form Awards: Scholarships are available for new entrants to the Sixth Form with special proficiency in Academic subjects, Music or Art. There is also one Organ Scholarship. The candidate's general ability to contribute to the life of a boarding school community will also be taken into account. A small number of Scholarships is also available internally on the strength of GCSE results.

The value of all Entrance Scholarships may be augmented by bursaries, according to parental circumstances.

Fees per term (2016–2017). Boarding £11,305; Day £7,950.

Further details about fees, including the scheme for payment in advance of a single composition fee to cover a pupil's education during his/her time in the School, are available from the Bursar.

Charitable status. Lancing College is a Registered Charity, number 1076483. It exists to provide education for boys and girls.

Governing Body:
The Provost and the Directors of Lancing College Ltd

Visitor: The Archbishop of Canterbury

Governors:
Chairman: Dr Harry Brünjes, BSc, MBBS, DRCOG, FEWI
Vice-Chairman: Mr Martin Slumbers, BSc, ACA [OL]
Mr David Austin, BSc
Mrs Philippa Berry, GTCL, LTCL
Baroness Cumberlege, CBE, DL
Mr Roger M Dancey, BA Hons, MA, DUniv Hon [OL]
Mrs Anne-Marie Edgell, LLB
Mr Anthony Evans, MA, MPhil, FICL, FKC
Mrs Charlotte Houston, BSc, ACMA, CGMA [OL]
Mr Henry Lawson, MA Cantab, MBA Harvard [OL]
Mr Simon Moll, BEd Hons [OL]
Major General David Rutherford-Jones, CB [OL]
Mr Richard Stapleton, FRICS (*Chairman of Estates Committee*)
Mrs Pauline Bulman, FCA (*Clerk to the Governing Body*)
Mr Simon J O Gurney (*Co-opted Chairman of Finance Committee*)

Head Master: D T Oliver, BA, MPhil

Bursar: M B Milling, CA
Senior Deputy Head: Mrs H R Dugdale, MA
Deputy Head: J R J Herbert, BA, PhD
Assistant Head (Pastoral): D S Connolly, BA, FRSA
Assistant Head (Academic): S J Ward, MMath, MASt, MPhil
Registrar: A J Betts, BA, PhD
Director of Co-Curricular Activities: C P Foster, MA [OL]
Director of IT: A C Brown
Chaplain: The Revd R K Harrison, BA, MA
Foundation Director: Ms Catherine Reeve, BA [OL]

Common Room:
Miss L M Agg, BA (*Graduate Assistant, Girls' Games*)
Miss K O J Allan, BSc (*Mathematics*)
Mr T S Auty, BA (*Photography, Art*)
Dr A J Betts, BA, PhD, MIL (*Registrar, French*)
Mr G D Bird, BSc, MSc (*Psychology*)
Mrs K J Blundell, BA, BA (*Head of Art*)
Mrs M Brookes, Referendarstudium 2 (*German*)
Mr N A Brookes, BSc, MSc (*Mathematics*)
Mr J J Bullen, BSc (*Head of Mathematics*)
Mrs E Campbell, MA, BTh (*Mathematics*)
Miss J K Champ, BSc (*Mathematics*)
Mr A M Chappell, BSc (*Biology, Chemistry*)
Mr A R Coakes, BA, MSc (*Design and Technology*)
Mr D S Connolly, BA, AdDip, FRSA (*Assistant Head Pastoral, Head of Politics*)
Mr D N Cox, MA, FRCO, FTCL, LRAM, ARCM (*Director of Music [Chapel]*)
Mrs M J Creer, BA (*English*)
Mr C P E Crowe, BEd (*Director of Sport*)
Mr D G Cutler, MPhys (*Physics*)
Mr D G Davies, BA, ALCM (*Head of Spanish, French*)
Mr O DE Sales, BA (*Spanish, French*)
Mr S A Drozdov, BEd (*Head of MFL, Head of German*)
Mr G A Drummond, BSc (*Head of PSHE, Economics, Politics*)
Mrs H R Dugdale, MA (*Senior Deputy Head, English*)
Mr J R J East, BSc (*Mathematics*)
Ms K V Edwards, BA (*Head of Girls' Games*)
Mrs P S Faulkner, BSc (*Head of Biology*)
Mr C P Foster, MA (*Head of Geography, Director of Co-Curricular Activities*)
Miss L J Freeland, BA, MPhil (*English*)
Mrs L Fryer, BA (*Head of French, Spanish*)
Miss L J Gaukroger, BA (*Classics*)
Mr J A Grime, BSc (*Geography*)
Mr D J Harman, BA, MA (*Head of English*)
The Revd R K Harrison, MA, BA (*Religious Studies, History*)
Mr D J Harvey, BSc (*Biology*)
Mrs H L Harvey, BA (*Mathematics*)
Dr J R J Herbert, BA, PhD (*Deputy Head, English*)
Mrs A M Johnson, BSc (*Business, Economics*)
Dr E P Keane, BA, PhD Cambridge, MA New York (*English, Politics*)
Dr D A Kerney, MA, PhD, FRSA (*Head of History*)
Mrs C M Krause, BA, MEd (*English, History, Religious Studies*)
Miss R Lawrence, BA (*Art, Classics*)
Mrs S E Lawrence, BA (*Design and Technology*)
Mrs Q Liang, MA (*Chinese*)
Mrs K Lindfield, HND (*Art*)
Mrs R Loftin, BA (*Library Supervisor*)
Mrs C H Mann BA (*Spanish, French*)
Mr D N Mann, BSSc (*Head of PE, Biology*)
Mrs S E Marchant, BA, MCLIP (*Librarian*)
Mr R J Maru, NCA Advanced Coach & ECB Level III (*Director of Cricket*)
Ms A McKane, MA (*English*)

Mr T J Meierdirk, BFA (*Head of Design and Technology*)
Mr R P Mew, MA, BA LitHum (*Head of Classics*)
Mr C M Mole, BSc (*PE, PSHE*)
Mrs C R Mole, BA (*Head of Economics and Business*)
Dr I Morgan-Williams, GMus RNCM, DPhil (*Director of Music [School]*)
Mrs M P Muggeridge, BA (*Learning Support*)
Mr J Naughalty, BSc (*Director of Hockey*)
Dr S R Norris, BSc, PhD (*Chemistry*)
Mrs C E Palmer, MA (*History*)
Dr M S W Palmer, BA, PhD, MIL (*German, Italian*)
Mr N L Payne, BA (*English*)
Mr K Perrault, Masters Nanterre Paris-Ouest la Défense (*French*)
Mrs M S Porter, MSc (*Physics*)
Mr A W Pratt, BA, MA (*Economics*)
Dr G A Preston, BSc, PhD (*Head of Science, Physics*)
Mr P C Richardson, MA, MA (*Head of Religious Studies, Drama, History*)
Mrs H M Robinson, BSc (*Chemistry*)
Mrs J M Scullion, BEd (*Learning Support Coordinator*)
Mr J L Sherrell, MA (*Economics*)
Mr M J H Smith, BA (*Head of Drama, Religious Studies, Classical Civilisation*)
Ms II A Stevenson, BLib, MCLIP (*Assistant Librarian*)
Mr P W Tarbet, BSc (*Mathematics*)
Mr G C Thomas, BEng, MInstP (*Physics*)
Mrs A W Tritton, BSc, MA, FRGS (*Geography*)
Dr M E Walsh, DPhil, BSc (*Head of Chemistry*)
Mr S J Ward, MMath, MASt, MPhil (*Assistant Head Academic, Mathematics*)
Mrs R M Webber, MBA, BSc (*Biology*)
Mr A P Williamson, MA (*Chemistry*)

Houses & Housemasters/mistresses:

Boys:
Head's: Mr A M Chappell
Second's: Mr D J Harvey
School: Mr C M Mole
Gibbs': Mr M J H Smith
Teme: Mr J A Grime

Girls:
Field's: Mrs M J Creer
Sankey's: Mrs E Campbell
Manor: Mrs C M Krause
Handford (*Sixth Form*): Ms A McKane

Head Master's Secretary: Mrs H L Betts, BSc
Acting Admissions Officer: Mrs S L Linfield

Medical Officers:
Dr H Bentley, MBBS, MRCGP, DA, DRCOG
Dr I Cox, MBChB, BSc, DRCOG, MRCGP
Dr V Figuera, DM, MRCGP
Dr C Huckstep, MBBS, DRCOG, DCH
Dr E Lerner, BSc, MBBS, MRCGP

Latymer Upper School

King Street, Hammersmith, London W6 9LR
Tel: 020 8629 2024
Fax: 020 8748 5212
email: head@latymer-upper.org
website: www.latymer-upper.org
Twitter: @LatymerUpper

The Latymer Foundation owes its origin to the will of Edward Latymer, dated 1624. It is a Day School of 1,179 pupils, of which 350 are in the Sixth Form. The School is fully co-educational with 51% boys and 49% girls. There are also 160 pupils in the co-educational Latymer Prep School which shares the same grounds. (*Please see entry in IAPS section.*)

Admission. This is by competitive examination and interview at 11. The 11+ examinations are held every year in January followed by interviews for selected candidates in late January/early February. Entry to the Sixth Form is based on interview in November of the year before entry and conditional offers at GCSE.

Details of Open Days and Entry are obtainable from the Registrar.

Preparatory School. Pupils sit the 11+ Entrance Exam for the Upper School from Latymer Prep School. (*For further details see entry in IAPS section.*)

Fees per term (2016–2017). £6,170.

Bursaries. A number of means-tested bursaries are awarded every year assessed on academic merit and family circumstances. These range from 25% of fees to full fees and are available at 11+ and 16+. Currently 16% of pupils are in receipt of fee assistance.

Scholarships. *11+ Entry*: Music Scholarships of varying amounts are offered, together with music awards of free tuition on two instruments. Scholarships will only be offered to candidates who are successful in the school's competitive entrance examination.

16+ Entry: Scholarships for Music, Drama, Art and Sport. Candidates who have satisfied the academic requirements will be invited to an interview and assessment in January.

Further details are available from the Director of Admissions (020 3004 0478; csh@latymer-upper.org).

Curriculum. A full range of academic subjects is offered at GCSE and A Level. Languages include French, German, Spanish, Mandarin and Italian (European Work Experience and exchanges are run every year), Latin and Greek. Science is taught as separate subjects by subject specialists from Year 7. Form sizes in the Lower School of around 22 and smaller teaching group sizes ensure the personal attention of staff. Our own World Perspectives Course, now UCAS accredited, comprising elements of Geography, History, RS, Politics, Philosophy, and Economics is enjoyed by Years 10 and 11.

Pastoral Care. The School has a strong tradition of excellent pastoral care led by the Deputy Head Pastoral. There are three Divisions (Lower School, Middle School, Sixth Form) and each Division is led by an Assistant Head. A Head of Year is responsible for the pupils in each year. Teams of Form Tutors deliver a coherent PSHE programme which promotes involvement in the community, charity work, and the personal, social and academic development of the Form.

Sixth Form. The large co-educational Sixth Form offers around thirty-five A Level choices; students opt to take four subjects at A Level including the very popular Extended Project. Students have the opportunity to undertake work experience in Paris or Berlin and receive extensive Careers and Higher Education guidance. All students expect to go on to University or Art College; more than 20 went to Oxbridge last year and 16 to Universities in North America. The Sixth Form has its own Common Room as well as a University and Careers Centre.

Music and Drama. These activities play a large part in the life of the School. The Latymer Arts Centre houses music practice rooms and a 300-seat Theatre in addition to increased facilities for Art. The Latymer Performing Arts Centre houses a 100-seat recital hall, music classrooms and more practice rooms and a dance/drama studio. There are several orchestras and bands and a number of major concerts each term, both here and in Central London venues. There are five major drama productions each year, and opportunities for all pupils to perform in events.

Science and Library. A state-of-the-art building, housing Science Laboratories, a Library, Sixth Form Study Common Room and Study Centre, opened in September 2010. All year groups have the use of these facilities.

Sport. The new Sports Centre – opened by Sir Steve Redgrave – features outstanding facilities including a 6-lane, 25m pool with an adjustable floor, a large sports hall, fitness suite, and three studios all providing a full programme of indoor sporting activities and fitness training throughout the year.

The School has a Boat House on site with direct river access and on-site netball courts. The Wood Lane complex (a short coach drive away) features all-weather, floodlit playing surfaces including 4 rugby/football pitches, 3 cricket squares, a floodlit Astroturf for hockey, netball, football and tennis and a modern pavilion and changing rooms. Out of school hours the facilities are used for training by the England Rugby Team and visiting international teams.

The emphasis is on involvement, participation and choice. School teams enjoy great success in the major sports of rugby, football, netball, hockey, rowing, cricket and athletics; other sports such as karate, judo, dance, swimming, pilates and power walking for individual interests. The School maintains excellent fixture lists for all major sports.

Extra-Curricular Activities. There is a wide range of clubs and societies at lunch time and after school. In addition, every pupil has the opportunity to have residential experience and to take part in outdoor pursuits as part of the annual Activities Week. Fundraising by a very active Parents' Gild ensures that nobody is excluded from an activity for financial reasons. The Duke of Edinburgh's Award scheme flourishes with a number of students achieving the Gold Award each year.

Charitable status. The Latymer Foundation is a Registered Charity, number 312714. It exists to provide education for children.

Chairman of Governors: James Graham, MA, FRSA

Co-opted Governors:
Stephen Hodges, MA
Nicholas Jordan, MA
Tracey Scoffield, BA
Professor Jim Smith, MA, PhD, FRS, FRSA, FMedSci
Professor Julius Weinberg, BA, BMBCh, DM, MSc, FRCP
James Priory, MA
Ros Sweeting, LLB
Joanna Mackle, BA
Hugh Sloane, BSc, MPhil
Alex Plavsic, MA Oxon, FCA
Gubby Ayida, MA, FRCOG, DM
Charlie Wijeratna, BA
Annamarie Phelps, MA, CBE

Ex officio Governor: The Reverend Simon Downham, LLB, DipMin, MA

Clerk to the Governors: Lucinda Evans

Head: David Goodhew, MA, FRSA Corpus Christi College Oxford

Deputy Heads:
Andrew Matthews, MA Sidney Sussex College Cambridge (*Academic*)
David Boyd, BA, MA (*Pastoral*)
Angela Tomlinson, BSc Cardiff, MA Open University (*Staff Welfare & Development*)
Richard Niblett, BA Liverpool (*Co-curriculum*)

Finance Director: John Tyrwhitt, MA, FCA

Director of Development: Amanda Scott, MA

Assistant Heads:
Amy Sellars, BSc Cardiff (*Lower School*)
David Boyd, BA, MA UCL Institute of Education (*Middle School*) (*[Acting]*)
Rachel Collier, MA Corpus Christi College Oxford, MA Birkbeck London (*Sixth Form*)
Charlie Ben-Nathan, BA Exeter, MBA Middlesex (*Director of Studies*)

Prep School Principal: Stuart Dorrian, BA, Dip Drama, PGCE

Director of Development: Catriona Sutherland-Hawes, MA

Heads of Year:
M G Holmes, BA Bristol (*Head of Upper Sixth*)
Mrs S M T Adams, BA Birmingham, MA Surrey (*Head of Lower Sixth*)
Miss R Monahan, BSc Birmingham (*Head of Year 11*)
Ms D Kendall, BA Leeds (*Head of Year 10*)
P Goldsmith, BA Leeds, MBA Cass Business School, FRSA (*Head of Year 9*)
Mrs K Temple, BA Durham (*Head of Year 8*)
G Cooper, BSc Port Elizabeth (*Head of Year 7*)

Heads of Departments:
Academic Mentoring: Jacqueline Heywood, BSc LSE, SENCO
Art & Design: David Mumby, BA Wolverhampton, PGCE Goldsmiths
Biology: Miranda Patterson, BSc Bristol
Chemistry: Arthur Dabrowski MSc Bristol
Classics: Marcel Lewis, BA Durham
Computing/IT: Edward Charlwood, BSc Aston
Director of Drama: Justin Joseph, BA London
Economics: Mark Wallace, BSc Birmingham
English: Will Goldsmith, MA Edinburgh
Geography: Michael Ashby, BA Middlesex, MSc King's College, FRGS, CGeog
History: Jonathan White, MA Selwyn College Cambridge
History of Art: Ruth Bell, BA Bristol, PG Dip Art Gallery/Museum Studies Manchester
Mathematics: Patrick MacMahon, MA Emmanuel College Cambridge, MSc Open University
Modern Languages: Cameron Palmer, BA, MA UCL Institute of Education
Director of Music: Tony Henwood, MA Exeter College Oxford, ARCO, FRSA
Physics: Dr J [Zen] Rogers, BSc MSc Bristol, PhD Cranfield
Politics: John Gilbert, MA Wadham College Oxford
Religious Studies & Philosophy: Keith Noakes, MA Corpus Christi College Cambridge, MA Manchester
Director of Sport: Tallan Gill, BA Manchester Metropolitan

The Grammar School at Leeds

Alwoodley Gates, Harrogate Road, Leeds LS17 8GS

Tel:	0113 229 1552
Fax:	0113 228 5111
email:	enquiries@gsal.org.uk
website:	www.gsal.org.uk
Twitter:	@TheGSAL
Facebook:	/grammarschoolatleeds

The Grammar School at Leeds is one of the UK's leading independent, co-educational schools. It enjoys the heritage of both Leeds Grammar School and Leeds Girls' High School with a lineage traceable back to 1552 with a long history of academic excellence. It benefits from a magnificent site on the outskirts of the north of Leeds.

We are committed to caring for our pupils as well as educating them. Our aim is to help them develop their individual abilities and talents within an ethic of teamwork, friendship and mutual respect.

We teach with pleasure and our pupils learn with enjoyment. That essentially sums up our mission. How well we accomplish it depends on much more than just excellent exam results. Our satisfaction lies in guiding children and young adults to become, quite simply, the best of their generation.

Structure. Pupils are taught using the structure that has come to be known as the 'diamond model'. Classes are fully co-educational from age three to eleven and again in the Sixth Form. Between the ages of eleven and sixteen, boys and girls are taught separately, but enjoy mixed extra-curricular and pastoral activities. Pupils therefore have both the social benefits of co-education and the academic benefits of single-sex teaching in the adolescent years.

Junior School pupils progress to Senior School, in most cases automatically. Junior School begins with Year 3, Senior School Year 7 and Sixth Form Year 11.

Religion. The School has a Chaplain and its own Chaplaincy centre which serves as a focus for worship and pastoral care. Although an Anglican foundation, the School welcomes boys and girls of all faiths and separate meetings are held for Jewish, Muslim, Hindu and Sikh pupils.

Facilities. The Grammar School at Leeds occupies a modern, purpose-built site whose facilities are unrivalled anywhere in the country. They include:

- Specialist suites of teaching rooms for all subjects with the necessary support systems for each faculty.
- Centres for each section of the School, with generous common rooms, locker and cloakroom areas.
- A large assembly hall.
- A newly extended Junior School, having its own identity, specialist resources and operating an independent timetable.
- A library incorporating multimedia facilities.
- IT centre with three interlocking suites.
- A dedicated art, design and technology unit with computer aided design suite.
- Seventeen specialist science laboratories.
- A fully resourced music school.
- Theatre with fully-equipped lighting gantry.
- A new Food Technology Suite.
- Extensive playing fields with changing facilities and hospitality areas.
- A large indoor sports complex with 2 sports halls, climbing wall, squash courts, conditioning room, a 25m swimming pool of competition standard.
- Extensive grounds with pitches, tennis courts, athletics track.
- Large play and recreation areas for each section of the School.
- Refectory for breakfast, lunch and snacks.
- Provision for a wide variety of indoor and outdoor extra-curricular pursuits.
- Conservation areas.
- A versatile Chaplaincy Centre.
- A new Sixth Form Centre with its own cafeteria, study area and IT and leisure facilities.

Curriculum. Rose Court Nursery and Pre-Prep establishes the foundation for a long and rewarding education – pursuing a broad and balanced curriculum, which builds upon the natural aptitudes, learning skills and interests of each child, whilst enabling each to develop at his/her own pace. We use our own schemes of work, broadly based upon the early years of the National Curriculum, but refined by our own expertise and experience.

In the Junior School pupils concentrate upon the core subjects of English, Mathematics and Science. History, Geography, French/German, Religious Studies, Music, Art and Technology are also taught.

Pupils follow a broad curriculum, including two foreign languages in Years 7–9.

At the end of Year 11 pupils are presented for the GCSE examination.

In the Sixth Form students choose to study up to 5 AS and 3 A2 Level subjects and are encouraged to choose a broad range of subjects.

Games. Rugby, Football, Cricket, Athletics, Swimming, Tennis, Basketball, Badminton, Cross-Country, Volleyball, Hockey, Netball, Rounders, Squash, and Golf. There is a running track, swimming pool and a sports centre, including squash courts.

Other Activities. The School's many clubs and societies offer pupils the opportunity to participate in a wide range of out-of-school activities from Mountaineering and Skiing to Choral Singing, Dancing and Drama. There are regular tours and visits abroad and there are long-established exchanges with French and German schools.

The School has an extensive Arts Programme which covers music, film, drama, debating and creative art and includes visiting groups with national reputation as well as the students' own contributions.

The School provides a contingent of the CCF (Army & RAF sections), and has a Scout Troop, with Cub Pack and Venture Scout Unit. The School participates in the Duke of Edinburgh's Award scheme and Community Service is compulsory in the Sixth Form.

Admission. The entrance procedure takes place in the Spring term for entry the following September and is based upon an examination, an interview and school report. Very young boys and girls are assessed through a series of observed activities. The usual points of entry are 3+ for Nursery, 4+ for Reception, 7+ for Junior School and 11+ for Senior School, although applications can be made at any time for any age. Entry to the Sixth Form is based upon interview and report and the attainment of good GCSE grades.

Details of the entrance procedure together with copies of sample papers are available from the Headmaster's Secretary.

Fees per term (2016–2017). Senior School £4,302; Junior School £3,210; Rose Court Nursery & Pre-Prep: £2,943 (full-time), £1,767 (part-time).

Bursaries. A number of means-tested bursaries (some full fee) are currently awarded each year to pupils entering the school at 11+ and 16+ (Sixth Form).

GSAL Alumni. This includes the Old Leodiensian Association – Leeds Grammar School and the Old Girls Club – Leeds Girls' High School. See Alumni section of school website, email: alumni@gsal.org.uk.

Charitable status. The Grammar School at Leeds is a Registered Charity, number 1048304. It exists for the advancement of education and training for boys and girls.

Governors:

Mr D P A Gravells, JP, MSc (*Chairman*)
Dr H Luscombe, MB BS, DA, DRCOG, MRCGP (*Joint Deputy Chairman*)
Mr P N Sparling, MBE, LLB (*Joint Deputy Chairman*)
Mrs E E Bailey, BChD, LDS, RCS, DOrthRCS
Sir Stephen Brown, KCVO
Mr J Cross, BA Oxon, ACA
Mr I Jones, MA, ACA, MBA
Mrs D Kenny, BEd
Mr A M Martin, MA, FCA
Mr K Morton, MRICS
Mr C R Obank, LLB

Mrs S A Solyom, BA, ACA
Professor D Sugden, PhD
Mr A J Walsh, ACIB
Mr J Woodward, MA
Mr E M Ziff, HonDBA

Teaching Staff:

Principal & Chief Executive: Sue Woodroofe

Head of Junior School: Robert Lilley
Head of Rose Court (Pre-Prep): Jo Hall
Senior Deputy Head (Pastoral Care): Helen Stansfield
Vice Principal & Head of Senior School (Co-Curricular):
  Neal Parker
Deputy Head (Academic): Debbie Danks
Director of External Relations: Helen Clapham
Director of Finance: David Naylor

Director of Sixth Form: Paul Rushworth
Head of Student Development: Christine Jagger
Head of Upper Sixth: Pat Brotherton
Head of Lower Sixth: Petra Turner
Head of Year 11: Sean Corcoran
Head of Year 10: James Veitch
Head of Year 9: Carol Heatley
Head of Year 8: Rachel Haywood
Head of Year 7: Stephen Gibbin

Heads of Department:

Art, Design & Technology: Stuart Kelly
Biology: Lynne Gilbert
Chemistry: Ruth Boddy
Classics: Martin Gibson
Economics/Business Studies: Christopher Law
English: Jenny Bolton
Food Technology: Yvonne Wilson
French: Nick Hele
Geography: Simon Knowles
German: Emma Whittaker
History: Keith Milne
ICT: Tim Street
Mathematics: Orla Fitzsimons
Music: Andrew Wheeler
Physics: Tom Rogerson
Politics: Andrew Stodolny
Psychology: Alison Wilson
Religious Studies: Fiona Fishburn
Spanish: Rowan Reed-Purvis
Sport: Paul Morris

Admissions: Angela Boult
Principal's Secretary: Elaine Green

Leicester Grammar School

London Road, Great Glen, Leicester LE8 9FL
Tel: 0116 259 1900
Fax: 0116 259 1901
email: admissions@leicestergrammar.org.uk
website: www.leicestergrammar.org.uk
Twitter: @LGS_Senior
Facebook: @Leicester-Grammar-School

Leicester Grammar School was founded in 1981 as an independent, selective, co-educational day school to offer able children in the city and county a first-class academic education. Its founders sought to create a school which would maintain the standards and traditions of the city's former grammar schools lost through reorganisation and develop them to meet the demands of a rapidly changing environment. The School moved to a new state-of-the-art

building on the south-east side of Leicester in September 2008.

There are 860 day pupils in the Senior School (393 girls, 467 boys), of whom 239 are in the Sixth Form. A further 385 pupils, aged 3–11, attend the Junior School.

Admission. An entrance examination is held in the Lent Term for boys and girls seeking to enter the Preparatory (10+) and Year 7 (11+) forms in the following September. Papers are taken in verbal reasoning, English and Mathematics. In addition admission into Years 9 and 10 takes place at ages 13 and 14 and there is provision for direct entry into the Sixth Form, offers of a place being conditional upon the GCSE grades gained. The normal entry requirement to the Sixth Form is a minimum of two A and four B grade passes at GCSE. Visitors are always welcome to make an appointment to see the school and meet the Headmaster. All applications are handled by the Head of Marketing & Admissions, from whom all Registration forms are obtainable. Candidates at all levels may be called for an interview.

Scholarships and Bursaries. Academic, music, art and sports and all-rounder scholarships are offered to outstanding candidates on examination and assessment.

Academic scholarships (maximum 25%) are available at all ages from 11+ upwards and are given on the results of the Entrance Examination (or, at Sixth Form entrance, GCSE results).

Up to four music scholarships are offered at any age. The scholarships are given on audition in recognition of achievement and potential in musical ability and are confirmed by a pass in the Entrance Examination.

A small number of art scholarships are awarded on examination and portfolio.

Sports scholarships are available linked to ability in the school's major sports.

The School has some funds available for Bursaries. It has always been the policy of governors to try to ensure that children capable of benefiting from education at the School should not be prevented by financial considerations from entry. All awards can be supplemented by bursaries when appropriate.

Curriculum. Class sizes are about 20 to 24 in the first three years; the average size of a GCSE group is 19, of a Sixth Form group 12.

All pupils in the first three years (and those entering the preparatory form) follow a balanced curriculum covering the National Curriculum core and foundation subjects, Religious Studies and Latin (Classical Studies in the preparatory form). Classes are split into smaller groups for the creative and technological subjects, so that all pupils can gain practical experience, whether in the School's ICT suite or on its extensive range of musical instruments. From Year 8 the three science subjects, Biology, Chemistry and Physics, are taught separately. There is no streaming and setting occurs only for Mathematics and French from Year 8. In Year 9 an element of choice is introduced and pupils must opt from a choice of third languages and from a list of five creative subjects.

In Years 10 and 11 pupils prepare for GCSE examinations in ten subjects, as well as doing PE/Games. All study a 'core' of five subjects: English Language and Literature, Mathematics, French and Chemistry. The range of 'options' includes Art, Biology, Chemistry, Classical Civilisation, Design and Technology, Drama, French, Geography, German, Greek, Religious Studies, History, Latin, Music, Physics, Spanish and PE.

Students in the Sixth Form normally study 4 A Levels from a choice of 19 subjects, including Further Mathematics, Economics, Physical Education, Politics, Computer Studies and Theatre Studies. There is no rigid division between arts and science sides. To ensure that breadth of education does not suffer, the majority of the Sixth Form complete an Extended Project. The school has an excellent record of success at public examinations and university admissions, including Oxbridge. The Careers Department is very active in giving help and advice to students.

School activities. A broad range and variety of activities complements the academic curriculum. Participation rates are high.

Music, drama and sport form an integral part of life at LGS. Every pupil in the First Year learns a musical instrument and a high proportion continue afterwards with private weekly lessons. The School Orchestra gives two major concerts a year, whilst a training orchestra, a jazz band, a dance band, recorder groups and various chamber ensembles explore other avenues. The School Choir is the resident choir for the Crown Court Services and tours regularly. Links with the Leicestershire School of Music orchestras and several pupils play in national orchestras. Senior and junior drama clubs function throughout the year, a major play or musical and a junior play are staged regularly and house drama extends the opportunity to act to most pupils.

Games are seen as an important means not only of promoting health and fitness but also of inspiring self-confidence. Major winter games are hockey, netball and rugby and in summer athletics, cricket and tennis. Opportunities occur for individuals to follow their interest in badminton, basketball, squash, golf, table tennis, gymnastics, dance, sailing and cross-country running whilst swimming is an integral part of the PE programme. The School's own facilities are extensive and meet all modern standards for sport. Teams represent the School in the main games at all age groups and several students achieve recognition at county or even national level. The school is proud of the fact that it is one of only eight other schools to have been awarded the Sportsmark Gold with Distinction, for the quality of the delivery of sport within the school.

Societies and clubs complement these activities, ranging from chess to The Duke of Edinburgh's Award scheme, history and Lit Soc to model aeroplanes, debating to art, design and technology, for which the workshop and art rooms are usually open during lunchtimes and after school.

Religion. The school espouses the principles of the Church of England, teaching the Christian faith, its values and standards of personal conduct, but also prides itself on welcoming children of all faiths, who play a full part in the life of the community. Very strong links exist with Leicester Cathedral and there is a flourishing Guild of Servers and University of Leicester clergy participate in school life and prepare confirmation candidates.

Pastoral Care. Responsibility for a wide-ranging system of pastoral care and for the creation of the caring, friendly and disciplined environment, resides in eight Heads of Year, assisted by form teachers, personal tutors and a very active house system.

Junior School. Entry to the Junior School is by interview and, where appropriate, assessment at 3+, 4+, 7+ and into other school years, when places are available. Pupils are prepared for entry to the Senior School. A balanced curriculum is followed covering National Curriculum Key Stages 1 and 2 and beyond; French (from 5 years), classical studies and ICT are also taught. A wide range of activities complements the academic curriculum, with a strong stress on music and a rapidly growing games programme. The School is a Christian foundation and lays great emphasis upon the pastoral care of young children. (*See also Junior School entry in IAPS section.*)

Fees per term (2016–2017). Senior School £4,114; Junior School (Years 3–6) £3,496; Kinders to Year 2 £3,312.

Old Leicestrians Association. All correspondence to the OL Secretary, c/o the School.

Charitable status. Leicester Grammar School Trust is a Registered Charity, number 510809. Its aims and objectives are to promote and provide for the advancement of education and in connection therewith to conduct, carry on, acquire and develop in the United Kingdom or elsewhere a School or Schools to be run according to the principles of the Church of England for the education of students and children of either sex or both sexes.

Governors:
Dr S M Dauncey, MRCGP (*Chairman*)
Mrs E Bailey, MA Cantab
Mrs J Burns, BA (*Vice Chairman, Academic*)
S Gasztowicz, QC
D Green, BSc, CEng, MICE, MCIWEM
Dr S E Hadley, BMedSci, BM, BS, FP Cert, DRCOG, DCM, MRCGP, PGCME
M J Holley, MA (*Vice Chairman, Financial*)
N J Imlach, CA FCSI CF
K J Julian, MA
Dr D H Khoosal, MB, BCh, LLM RCS, FRCPsych
Dr L C Mongan
Mrs A O'Donovan
Prof J Saker, BSc, MSc

Business Director: Mrs A Shakespeare, MA Fitzwilliam, Cantab, ACA, FCA

Headmaster: C P M King, MA Dunelm

Deputy Head (Academic): J W Rich, BA Cardiff (*History*)
Deputy Head (Pastoral): Mrs A Ewington, MA Nottingham, CBiol, MIBiol (*Biology*)

Assistant staff:
Miss R E Adams, BA Italia Conti Academy (*Drama*)
Dr S W Ainge, BSc, PhD Newcastle, CChem, FRSC (*Head of Chemistry*)
Miss E S Allcoat, BSc Bristol (*Physics*)
T P Allen, BA Kent (*History, Politics, Head of Sixth Form*)
D J Armitage, BA St Hugh's College Oxford, MA, PhD Nottingham (*Biology*)
J M Barker, BMus, MMus Royal College of Music (*Assistant Director of Music, Duke of Edinburgh's Award*)
Mrs A C Barre, BA Birmingham (*French*)
Mrs J A P Barrow, BEd Liverpool (*Textiles, Design & Technology*)
Dr D D Boyce, MPhys Lancaster, PhD Leicester, CPhys, MinstP (*Physics*)
W D Burns, BSc Edinburgh Napier (*Design & Technology*)
Mrs A J Button, BA Loughborough (*Physical Education*)
Mrs C Calland, BA De Montfort (*Physical Education*)
Mrs J R Carr, BA Roehampton (*Head of Religious Studies*)
Miss Z Carter, BSc Leicester (*Mathematics, Duke of Edinburgh's Award*)
Mrs C E Charles, BA Selwyn College Cambridge (*Learning Support*)
Miss M J Clapham, BA Hons, MBA Ed, PGC SpLD Leicester, PGC SENCO Northampton, SpLD APC and TPC Patoss (*Head of Learning Support*)
Mrs P Clare, BSc Leicester, MSc Imperial College (*Biology, PSD Coordinator*)
F W Clayton, BA Wolverhampton (*Religious Studies*)
P Cox, BSc UCW Bangor (*Biology, Duke of Edinburgh Award*)
Miss L Crampton, MEng Hull (*Design and Technology, ICT, Staff Development Officer*)
Dr D M Crawford, MA, DPhil Jesus College Oxford, MEd Bristol, MA Ed OU, MSc OU (*Head of Mathematics*)
Mrs A J Davies, MA De Montfort (*Art*)
G D Davies, MA De Montfort (*Head of PE and Games*)
Mrs K R Douglas, BA Liverpool (*French, Italian & EAL*)
A N Duffield, BSc UCW Cardiff, CBiol, MSB (*Head of Biology*)
H A Ellis, BSc Loughborough (*Physical Education*)

K Esmail, BA Portsmouth (*Economics*)

Dr S L Ewers, BSc, PhD Bristol (*Biology*)

Mrs S M Faire, BSc Surrey (*Mathematics, Maths Learning Support*)

Dr C H Fearon, BSc Liverpool, PhD Birmingham (*Biology, AQA Baccalaureate EPQ Centre Coordinator for Enrichment Programme*)

Mrs H T Feasey, BA Stellenbosch, South Africa (*Geography*)

T E Fishpool, BA Newcastle (*Geography*)

Miss N J Fletcher, BA Dunelm, MEd Homerton College Cambridge (*French and Italian, Head of Year 7*)

Dr K L Fulton, BSc Dunelm, PhD Nottingham (*Biology*)

C I J Gilham, BA London (*Classics*)

Miss E Graff-Baker, MA Queen's College Oxford (*Music*)

Mrs A L Griffin, BA Essex, MA Loughborough (*Head of Drama*)

J M Griffin, MA Fitzwilliam College Cambridge (*Deputy Head of English, Theatre Studies*)

P M Handford, MA Queen's College Oxford (*Chemistry*)

Mrs W E Harvey, BA Loughborough College of Art & Design (*Head of Design & Technology*)

Ms S Haywood, BEd Worcester College, BA OU (*Art*)

Mrs M Higginson, BEd, MA Toronto (*English, Editor of Leicestrian*)

Mrs A J Hillier, BA Nottingham (*Religious Studies*)

Mrs V Hird, BA Leicester (*History*)

Miss L Howd, BSc East Anglia (*Mathematics*)

C W Howe, BEd CNAA Crewe & Alsager College (*Director of Sport*)

Miss N Hughes, BA London (*English, Staff Induction & Teacher Training*)

J T Hunt, BA Reading (*English, AQA Baccalaureate & Extended Project Team Leader, Head of Sixth Form*)

Mrs J Hutchinson, BEd Durham, MA Ed OU (*Physical Education, i/c Academic PE, Mathematics*)

G Inchley, BSc Hull, MSc Bristol (*Deputy Head of Mathematics*)

R A Jacobs, BSc Leeds, BA Open University (*Mathematics*)

C S James, MA Girton College Cambridge (*Mathematics, Director of Studies*)

Mrs C L Jess, MA Gonville & Caius College Cambridge (*French & Spanish, AQA Baccalaureate Taught Skills Programme Coordinator, Head of Year 11*)

Dr A J Kendall, MA Wadham College Oxford, DPhil Linacre College Oxford (*Chemistry*)

Mrs R E Kendall, BA Dunelm, MA Goldsmiths (*English*)

R W S Kidd, BA, MA Ulster (*Head of English*)

A T King, MChem Loughborough (*Chemistry*)

Miss J L Knight, BA De Montfort (*Art & Design*)

Mrs N L Laybourne, BSc Hons, MSc Loughborough (*Physical Education*)

T A Lemon, BA Bedfordshire (*Physical Education, Head of House – Masters*)

R L Longson, BA UCW Aberystwyth, Dip CG LGMB Swanley, MICG (*Head of Careers*)

D M Lupton, BA Exeter (*Deputy Head of Modern Languages*)

D W Maddock, BA Bristol Polytechnic, MA Leeds Polytechnic (*Head of Art, AQA Baccalaureate VLE Coordinator*)

Sra I Manktelow, BSc Instituto Politécnico Nacional, Mexico (*Spanish*)

Sra P Matalobos, BA, MA Santiago dé Compestela (*Spanish Assistant*)

Mrs H C May, BA UCW Aberystwyth (*Head of Geography*)

D McCann, BEd Leicester (*Physical Education*)

R J McLean, BA Lady Margaret Hall Oxford (*Head of Classics*)

P Moore-Friis, BA De Montfort, PG Dip Oxford, CIM Dip (*Head of Economics, Young Enterprise Coordinator*)

Miss J Mould, BEd Bedford College of HE (*Head of Preparatory Department*)

N Murray, BSc Imperial, MA London, MSc Sheffield Hallam (*Mathematics*)

Mrs E J Nelson, BA Northumbria (*German*)

Mrs E Nisbet, BEd Trent Polytechnic (*Food Technology*)

Mrs F Paton, DEUG and Licence Bordeaux (*French*)

Miss A M Patterson, BSc Sunderland Polytechnic (*Chemistry, Head of House – Duke's, Community Service Coordinator*)

J J Peake, BSc Coventry University (*Geography*)

Miss L Percy, BA Derby (*Graduate Sports Fellow*)

A J Picknell, BA Manchester, MA London (*Head of History*)

D Pilbeam, MChem Nottingham (*Chemistry, Examinations Officer*)

Mrs K G Pollard, BSc Loughborough (*Mathematics*)

L Potter (*Physical Education, Head of Year 8*)

R J K Preece, MA Warwick (*History and English*)

S J R Radford, BSc Sheffield (*Mathematics*)

P T G Reeves, BSc Manchester (*Head of Physics, Head of Science*)

Mrs S J Sains, MA Lady Margaret Hall Oxford (*Mathematics*)

Mrs M Sian, BA Middlesex (*Head of Information & Communications Technology and Computing*)

Miss L M Sicard, BA Sorbonne (*French Assistant*)

Dr A E MSchofield, MA, PhD Manchester (*Classics*)

Mrs S Stout, BSc Aston (*Head of Modern Languages*)

T A Thacker, BEd CNAA Crewe & Alsager College (*Physical Education, Head of Year 9*)

Mrs J Tompkins, BA Leicester (*Religious Studies, Head of Year 10*)

Dr A Vassilliou-Abson, BA Athens, MPhil, PhD Birmingham (*Classics, Charities Coordinator*)

J R Walker, BA Warwick (*Classics*)

Dr M Wheeler, BSc, PhD Bristol, CPhys, MInstP (*Physics*)

Dr D M T Whittle, BMus, PhD Nottingham BMus, PhD (*Director of Music*)

D R Willis, BSc CNAA: Portsmouth Polytechnic (*Science, Senior Head of House, Head of House – Vice Chancellors*)

Ms Y Yau, BA De Montfort (*Extracurricular Mandarin Chinese*)

Dr S Yeomans, MA, PhD Loughborough (*Head of Politics, School Council Link Teacher*)

Headmistress, Junior School: Mrs C M Rigby, BA

Leighton Park School

Shinfield Road, Reading, Berkshire RG2 7ED

Tel: 0118 987 9600
Fax: 0118 987 9625
email: admissions@leightonpark.com
website: www.leightonpark.com
Twitter: @LPSchool
Facebook: /leightonparkschool
LinkedIn: /leighton-park-school

Leighton Park is a forward-thinking, co-educational day and boarding school for students aged 11–18. Founded in 1890 on Quaker values and set in 60 acres of beautiful parkland in Reading, Berkshire, Leighton Park provides a unique and inspirational learning environment, where students live, learn and grow as individuals.

Students at Leighton Park experience and benefit from the provision of a holistic educational experience. The curriculum is academically rigorous, yet strives to achieve greater coherence by making connections between academic subjects and the strong pastoral and extra-curricular programmes.

Students develop their intellectual curiosity while becoming independent, lifelong learners with the skills to respond positively to the challenges of a rapidly changing world. This curriculum framework affords greater opportunities for creativity, individuality and independent learning.

Our commitment to academic excellence is balanced by our commitment to the development of every individual, deriving from our Quaker heritage. You will find outstanding teaching and excellent academic results at Leighton Park, as well as a real feeling of mutual respect, tolerance and tranquility. The last ISI inspection (2014) stated, 'Pupils' personal development is excellent and they fulfil the school's aim to educate young people to have integrity and honesty, and be a force for good.'

In 2016, 41.2% of candidates received A*/A grades at A Level, 6% higher than the national average and the average points score was 327 points per student. The 2016 cohort of International Baccalaureate students averaged 35 points against a world average of 29.9 points. At GCSE 45.2% of candidates achieved A*–A grades with particularly notable success in the STEM subjects.

Curriculum. Our creative curriculum provides a distinct educational experience, where academic depth and rigour are balanced by breadth and coherence. Mandarin Chinese has been introduced in Year 7 which can be followed through to GCSE and A Level. Year 10 students are expected to follow a full GCSE course of nine or ten subjects, comprising both compulsory and optional subjects. In the Sixth Form, a wide range of academic subjects in A Level and International Baccalaureate courses is complemented by a broad extension programme, including Critical Thinking, Film Studies, European Computer Driving Licence and Dance.

Facilities. Excellent facilities and resources include a new Food Technology facility, a newly refurbished ICT Centre, a digital recording studio, a drama studio, a heated indoor swimming pool, a wonderful library and dedicated Individual Learning Centre. Oakview, the dining centre, offers a first-rate choice of meals (breakfast, lunch and tea).

Ethos and Pastoral Care. Within Leighton Park's distinctive Quaker ethos, students of many faiths and backgrounds flourish in an atmosphere of tolerance, harmony and understanding. They know they will be challenged in their work to achieve the highest standards of excellence.

Boarding and Day Boarding. We offer a highly flexible approach to boarding with full, weekly and day boarding options to suit family and student needs. The five houses provide a comfortable base in which all students, whether boarding or day, genuinely feel at home. Boarders and day students both have individual study facilities in the houses. Day students are welcome for breakfast and to stay for tea, prep and extra-curricular activities, included in the fees. All day boarders are given the opportunity to stay overnight at no extra charge for two nights each term.

Sport. Sport plays an important role in life at Leighton Park with many individual performers and teams reaching county and regional level. First rate coaching and superb facilities – which include a heated indoor swimming pool, floodlit AstroTurf pitch, 22 tennis courts and a cricket square ensure that talented and enthusiastic students can develop their sporting abilities to the full.

Music. Music has for a long time been one of Leighton Park's particular strengths with around half our pupils learning instruments and performing a wide range of styles. Our facilities for practice and performance include nineteen new Yamaha pianos, a suite of ten practice rooms, a digital recording studio, a suite of Apple Macs, a recital room and concert hall. A state-of-the-art Music and Media Centre including a 'Live Lounge' style recording studio will be finished and ready for use in autumn 2017. Opportunities to perform include regular concerts and tours abroad, most recently to Croatia and Bosnia in 2016.

Hobbies and other activities. Pupils can participate in an enormous variety of activities during the week and at weekends and both before school and after school. The Duke of Edinburgh's Award scheme is well established and flourishing, with students completing Bronze and Silver Award programmes. In keeping with our Quaker perspective many Leighton Park students are involved in community service and fundraising initiatives that benefit the local community as well as larger charities such as Refugee Relief. Sixth Form students participate in a biennial trip to Uganda, Malawi or Tanzania lending practical support to the school's fundraising efforts in Africa.

Careers. Students have access to the well-resourced Careers Library, including software to help them research and evaluate their options. Thorough preparation and support for entry to university is given.

Entry. Entry to the school is by exam and interview, with an additional English test where appropriate. Pupils are normally admitted at one of three points: Year 7 (age 11); Year 9 (age 13), and the Sixth Form. Entry to the Sixth Form requires 5 GCSE passes or equivalent at Grade B or above.

Fees per term (2016–2017). Full Boarding £8,623–£10,808; Weekly Boarding £7,583–£9,302; Day £5,563–£6,940.

Scholarships and Bursaries. Several Academic, Music, Drama, Art & Design and Sports Awards are made each year for entry in Year 7, Year 9 and the Sixth Form and are also available to existing pupils. Candidates may apply for any combination of scholarships, but can only receive the financial benefits of one (in the region of 10% of Day Boarder fees). Bursaries may be available, in cases of financial hardship, to existing and prospective pupils. Bursaries are always means-tested and subject to annual review. Additional awards may be made by the David Lean Foundation.

Old Leightonians. Website: www.leightonpark.com/old-leightonians.

Charitable status. The Leighton Park Trust is a Registered Charity, number 309144. It exists to provide education for young people.

Governors:
David Isherwood (*Chairman*)

Liz Banks	Chris Houston
Simon Best	Bruce Johnson
Sally Jayne Bonner	Zella King
Simon Clemison	Martin Lloyd
John Crosfield	Nathan Pearce
Jan Digby	Liza Phipps
Elaine Green	John Walmsley
Simon Hollands	

Head: **Nigel Williams**, BA Bristol, MA London, PGCE

Deputy Head: Edward Falshaw, MA

Bursar: Keith Eldridge, BA, FCA

Teaching Staff:
* *Head of Department*
§ *Part-time*
† *Housemaster*

Spartakos Anagnostaras, MS, QTS (§*Modern Foreign Languages*)
Jeremy Belas, BSc, QTS (**Director of Sport*)
Ruth Bell, MA, QTS (**Modern Foreign Langauges*)
Julian Berrow, BA (*Modern Foreign Languages*)
Simon Booth, MEng, PGCE, QTLS (*Head of Physics)
Naomi Bonthrone, BA, QTS (*English*)
David Bradford, MA (*ICT, CEM Data Manager*)

Tom Cartmill, BA (*English as a Second Language*)
Bridget Clarke, BSc (*Mathematics*)
John Clarke, BSc (*Physics*)
Maddie Cottam, MA (*Music*)
Harriet Custance, MA, BA (**English as a Second Language*)
Matthew Dawes, BA, QTS (**Economics*)
Katherine Donegan, BSc (*Biology*)
Deborah Duggan, BA (§**Spanish, German*)
Beverley Eldridge, MBA, BA, QTS (§*Economics*)
Eddie Falshaw, MA (*History, Games, Educational Visits Coordinator, Deputy Head*)
Kate Findlay, BA (§**History*)
Chris Fisher, BEd (*Sports*)
Pablo Gorostidi Perez, MBA (*Spanish*)
Karen Gracie-Langrick, MA, BA (*History, Deputy Head Academic Studies*)
Claire Gray, BA (*Individual Learning Centre*)
Tim Green, BSc (*Games, †Field House*)
Claire Gulliver, BSc PGCE (*Psychology*)
David Hammond, MSc, BSc, QTS (§*Biology*)
Anwar Haque, MBA, BSc, PGCE (**Computing and ICT*)
Emilia Hicks, BSc (*Biology and Science*)
Deborah Ince, BA, PGCE (*Art and Textiles*)
Elaine King, BA (**Careers, Art, Games*)
Adél Kiss, BSc, BEd (**Mathematics*)
Lan Kuang, MA, BA (**Mandarin Chinese*)
Eithne Laird, BSc, MSc, PGCE (**Geography, †Fryer House*)
Isabelle Lauzeral, MA, BA (*Modern Languages*)
Zoe Macpherson, BSc (*Graduate Trainee, Girls*)
Alexander Leighton, MA, BA, PGCE, (*English*)
Maureen Lenehan, MA (§*English*)
Cookie Liu, PhD, PGCE, (*Mathematics*)
Robin Longworth, MA, BSc (*Geography, †Reckitt House*)
Zoe Macpherson (*Graduate Teacher, Girls Games*)
Jakki Marr, BEd, (**Girls Games, †Field House*)
Rachael Martin, BEd (*Individual Learning Centre, †Reckitt House*)
Mair Mayers, BSc (§*Mathematics*)
Rachel Mayne, BSc (§*Physics*)
Chris Mitchell, BA (§*Assistant Director of Music and Media Arts Development*)
Jane Mulvihill, BSc (*Mathematics*)
Ann Munday, BSc (*Mathematics*)
Myles Nash (**DT, †School House, Head of Boarding*)
Lynne Parry, BA (*Individual Learning Centre*)
Joanna Terry, BSc (**Chemistry*)
Jonathan Porter-Hughes, BA, PGCE (*English, †School House*)
Thomas Rawlings, BA, PGCE, (**English*)
Patricia Robson, MA, BEd (*ILC*)
Jeanne Rourke, BA, PGCE (*English as a Second Language*)
Ian Rowe, BSc (*Head of Individual Learning Centre, SENCO*)
Elizabeth Samuels, BSc QTS (*Mathematics*)
Premnath Samyrao, MSc, MEd (*Mathematics*)
Rosemary Scales, BA, MA (**Director of Music*)
Peter Scoggins, BA, PGCE, QTS (**Head of Drama*)
Howard Shaw, BA (*History, Government and Politics*)
Mark Simmons, BEd (*PE, Games, Senior Master, Head of Middle School*)
Gemma Sims, MSc, BSc (*Acting Head of Biology*)
Graham Smith, BA (*Games, Geography, †Grove House*)
Mark Smith, BEng, BSc (*Design Technology*)
Ken Sullivan, MA, BSc, PGCE (*Head of Teaching and Learning, Biology*)
Adrian Stewart, BPrimEd South Africa (*Geography, Games, Head of Fryer and Lower School*)
Rod Tait, QTS (*Physics*)

Shazia Taj, BA, MA, PGCE (**Beliefs and Values*)
Helen Taylor, BA, PGCE (*Science, *Sixth Form, IB Coordinator*)
Nicholas Tickell, BA, PGCE (*Modern Foreign Languages*)
Michael Ward, BEd, MA (**Information Technology, Director of IT*)
Sherilyn Wass, BSc, PhD (§*Chemistry*)
Mitch Whitehead, BA, MA (*Beliefs and Values, *Learning Technologies*)
Nicola Williams, BEd (*PE, Dance, *PSHE, *Pastoral Welfare and Safeguarding*)
Nigel Williams, BA, MA, PGCE, (*Head, History*)
Mark Wood, BA, PGCE (**Art*)
Jennifer Yabsley, DPhil, BSc (**Biology*)
Damon Young, BA (*Drama, Theatre Studies, †Grove House*)

Registrar: Rachael Bolding
Head's PA: Virginia Cashin
Librarian: Chris Routh

The Leys

Trumpington Road, Cambridge CB2 7AD

Tel: 01223 508900
email: office@theleys.net
website: www.theleys.net
Twitter: @LeysCambridge
Facebook: @TheLeysSchoolCambridge

Motto: '*In Fide Fiducia.*'

The Leys is situated half a mile from the centre of the university city of Cambridge, close to the River Cam and Grantchester Meadows. The School was founded in 1875 on the initiative of a group of leading Methodists to provide a liberal Christian education, establishing a tradition which has continued unbroken to this day. The School was incorporated as a Charitable Trust in 1878. All the buildings are grouped around the Main Field and lie within the estate originally acquired for the purpose; there is a second extensive playing field nearby.

The Leys is a friendly, caring and happy community, large enough to offer many opportunities, but not so large as to lose sight of the individual. The School is fully co-educational; of a total of over 560 pupils, 200 are in the Sixth Form. Girls and boys are accommodated in separate houses. 70% of the pupils are accommodated in the boarding houses, but all, including the 160 day pupils, are able to enjoy all the opportunities offered by boarding school life.

Buildings and Facilities. There is a continuing development programme involving all areas of the School. A state-of-the-art Music School was opened in 2005. There is an excellent Humanities Building with first-class facilities for Geography, History, Classics and Divinity together with a Museum and Archives Centre, and an award-winning Design Centre, which contains workshops (metal, plastic and wood), a 3D printing and laser cutting area, Art School, Ceramics Studio, Computer Centre, together with facilities for Design, Photography, Cookery and an Exhibition Centre. A Sports Hall and all-weather pitch were built in 1995. In 2008 the Sports Hall was extended to include a superb fitness suite and cricket pavilion, and a second Astroturf pitch was added. A new climbing wall was constructed in summer 2007. A major capital development has been added, which provides a new theatre, Assembly Hall, Drama and Dance Studios, Drama Department, School Café and three new Science Laboratories. This project, known as Great Hall, was completed in summer 2013. There are 40 acres of playing fields, an indoor heated swimming pool open all the year, a recently re-furbished boat house on the Cam shared with

King's, Selwyn and Churchill Colleges, and synthetic as well as grass tennis courts. A radical re-designing and refurbishment of all boarding houses began in summer 2006, with the aim of providing the most comfortable and homely of boarding facilities. To date six of the seven Senior Boarding Houses have been refurbished. The School Library underwent a major refurbishment in 2008.

Admission. Admission for girls and boys is mainly at 11+, 13+ and 16+. Entrance tests for 11+ and 13+ entry are held in the January prior to entry. Places in the Sixth Form are available for both girls and boys who have successfully completed their GCSE or equivalent courses elsewhere. Application for admission should be made to the Admissions Office in the first instance.

Scholarships. Scholarships are available for entry at 11+, 13+ and to the Sixth Form, valued at a maximum of 5% fee remission, which can be supplemented by means-tested bursaries up to a total concession of 100%.

Academic Scholarships are available for entry at 11+, 13+ and for entry to the Sixth Form at 16+. Scholarships are also available for entry at 13+ in Music, Art, Design Technology, Sport, Drama and all-rounders, and for entry to the Sixth Form at 16+ in Music, Art, Sport and Drama.

The School also participates in the Arkwright Scholarship Scheme, which is an external examination offering Scholarships for those wishing to take Design and Technology in the Sixth Form and who are aiming to read Engineering, Technology or other Design-related subjects in Higher Education.

The Scholarship Examinations at 11+ and 13+ take place in the Spring Term and the Sixth Form Scholarship Examination takes place in the November of the year prior to entry.

Bursary awards are made on a means-tested basis, and applications for bursaries must be made before entrance tests are taken.

Special awards for children of Methodist Ministers and members of HM Forces are available. Special consideration is given to the sons and daughters of Old Leysians.

Further particulars may be obtained from the Registrar.

Curriculum. The academic curriculum broadly conforms to the National Curriculum but is not restricted by it. Each pupil has an Academic tutor who, in conjunction with the Director of Studies and the Housemaster or Housemistress, works to tailor the pupil's programme to suit the needs of the individual wherever possible. Pupils follow a broad programme in the first three years (Years 7, 8 and 9). At the end of Year 9 they choose three from a wide range of options to add to the basic core of IGCSE English Language and Literature, separate Sciences and a Modern Foreign Language, and GCSE Mathematics and Religious Studies. The GCSE examinations are normally taken at the end of Year 11, but Religious Studies is taken by all pupils in Year 10.

In the Sixth Form, a similar option scheme operates with pupils choosing from a total of 25 subjects to take normally 3 A Levels in the Sixth Form. Double Maths (Maths and Further Maths) is regarded as one subject leading to two A Levels.

There is considerable flexibility of combinations possible at both levels, and choices are made after consultation between parents, tutors, careers staff and subject teachers. The most able pupils are given an enrichment programme under the guidance of the Director of Academic Development, including extension projects, visits to Gifted and Talented seminars, and seminars with Cambridge undergraduate or postgraduate students. In addition, departments organise extension groups and societies and the school has a thriving Debating Society and a Model United Nations group. The school runs its own Independent Research Project to help senior pupils develop independent study skills.

About 95% of the A Level candidates proceed to degree courses. A Reading Party for potential Oxford and Cambridge candidates is held during the Summer Term.

Personal and Social Education forms an integral part of the curriculum at all levels. In the Sixth Form this is supplemented by a year-long programme that draws on the cultural resources of Cambridge University and the city as a whole.

The Chapel. The School Chapel is at the heart of the community in every sense. From the time of its Methodist foundation The Leys has been firmly based on non-sectarian Christian principles. It welcomes boys and girls of all denominations and religions, encouraging them to see the relevance of a personal faith of their own. Religious Education forms part of the curriculum. Preparation is also given for Church membership, and a combined confirmation service is held.

Physical Education. The physical education/games programme aims at introducing a wide variety of physical activities. Sports available are Rugby, Hockey, Cricket, Tennis, Athletics, Netball, Badminton, Basketball, Gymnastics, Golf, Rowing, Sailing, Dance, Shooting, Climbing, Squash, Swimming, Volleyball, Water Polo. Outdoor activities such as Camping, Orienteering, Canoeing, and Climbing are also encouraged through CCF and The Duke of Edinburgh's Award. PE is offered at GCSE and A Level. The School has close links with many Cambridge University Sports Clubs, with the Sixth Form competing in University Leagues.

Careers. In the Lower School, careers guidance forms part of the PSHE programme and is carried out by tutors and members of the Careers Department. Year 9 are supported in their option choices by tutors and Careers staff and are introduced to the Careers Library. Year 11 take the Preview Careers Selection Programme. It matches pupils' interests and abilities to appropriate career fields and is followed up by two individual interviews with career specialists. Year 11 pupils are also encouraged to participate in the Work Experience scheme. Support continues into the Sixth Form with all Lower Sixth being interviewed by Careers staff. An annual Careers Forum is organised in the Lent term, enabling pupils to investigate various career paths before embarking on their UCAS applications. Work experience is organised throughout the Sixth Form.

Societies. All are encouraged to participate in out-of-school activities of their choice. These range from Literary, Philosophical, Scientific, Mathematical, Languages, Debating, Music and Drama societies to any of the activities available in the Design Centre, which are available after School and at weekends. The life of the School is enriched by its proximity to Cambridge; distinguished visiting speakers are available, and pupils are encouraged to go to plays, concerts and lectures in the town. The programme of visiting speakers is largely run by the pupils themselves, overseen by a member of staff. A programme entitled the Cambridge Experience ensures that all Sixth Form pupils avail themselves of the cultural opportunities afforded by the school's location.

Combined Cadet Force. Except in special circumstances, pupils in Year 10 join the CCF (Army or Navy section) and also follow The Duke of Edinburgh's Award scheme. CCF camps take place annually. There is a miniature range, and a Rifle Club exists for small-bore shooting. The School is an authorised centre for the organisation of activities within The Duke of Edinburgh's Award scheme and pupils work towards the Bronze, Silver or Gold awards in the four sections: community service, expeditions, physical recreation and skills or hobbies.

Fees per term (2016–2017). Years 7 and 8: £7,535 Boarders; £4,995 Day Pupils. Years 9 to Sixth Form: £10,345 Boarders; £7,780 Home Boarders; £6,920 Day Pupils.

St Faith's Preparatory School is part of the same Foundation. It was founded in 1884 and acquired by the Governors of The Leys in 1938. There are 547 boys and girls, aged 4–13 years. The buildings, which include the Keynes Building opened in 2006 and a new Sports Hall opened in May 2011, stand in 10 acres of grounds. Full particulars may be obtained from the Headmaster of St Faith's, Mr N Helliwell, MA. (*For further details, see entry in IAPS section.*)

The Old Leysian Society. *Secretary*: J C Harding, MA, The Leys School, Cambridge CB2 7AD. Handbook and Directory, twenty-second edition, 2010.

Charitable status. The Leys and St Faith's Schools Foundation is a Registered Charity, number 1144035. It aims to enable boys and girls to develop fully their individual potential within a School community firmly based on Christian principles.

Governors:
Chairman: Sir Tony Brenton, KCMG
Mrs H Arthur, Cert Ed
¶R Ashby-Johnson, MA
M D Beazor, BA, FRSAHH
¶HH Judge Revd M A Bishop, MA
Mrs A M Brunner, BA
Miss J H E Burton, BA
¶M A Elliott, BSc
Mrs P M Graves, MA, Dip S W
¶B Haryott, BSc, FREng, CEng, FICE, FIStructE, FRSA, CRBCCC
R B Hewitson, LLB
Mrs E Hooley
¶C M Kidman, ACIOB
P R Lacey, MA, PGCE, FRSA
A S MacGregor BSc CertEd
Mrs M E Mackay, RGN
¶T C Moore
R Norfolk
Mrs J Plows, BA
Revd J M Pursehouse
R C Sadler, FRICS
¶A V Silverton, BSc, FCSI
¶D Unwin, MA, ACA
Dr R D H Walker, MA
R B Webster, FCA
R J Willmott, MCIOB

¶ *Old Leysian*

Headmaster: **M J Priestley**, MA Oxon

Deputy Head: Mrs C E Mayo, MA Cantab

R Adamson, BSc, PhD
B A Barton, BA
A R C Batterham, BA
Miss C E Battison, BA
D R Bell, MA
A Bennett-Jones, BSc
Ms E Bonnaud, BA, MA
N R Born, MA
M A Brown, BSc
Miss S J Byrne, MA, PGCE
D Cassidy, BPhEd
Ms H S Clark BA
Ms L J Clark, BA
Miss L Corble, BA
Mrs K J Cox, BSc
P J Crosfield, BA
Mrs E R Culshaw, MA
T Dann, BSc
P M Davies, BSc
G J Deudney, BSc, BEd
D A Divito, BSc, MSc, PGCE
N J Dix-Pincott, BA, MA
R J Driscoll, BA, BEd
T P Dunn, BA, MSc, MEd Cantab, CPsychol, FRSA
Mrs C M Earl, BSc
W J Earl, BSc
Miss K E Eaves, MA
Miss H Edmondson, BA
M A Egan, BSc
A S Erby, BSc
J W Fawcett, BA, MA
D K Fernandes, BSc
R Fielden, MA, DPhil, PGCE
R Francis, MA, MEd
Revd C I A Fraser, BA, MA Ed, MCMI, PG Dip, FRSA
M C Gale, BEd
Miss G H Jefferies, BA
¶E M W George, BEd
Mrs J George, FIMLS
S G Hancock, BA, MA

A P Harmsworth, MA, FRAS
Ms J L Hebden, BA, MA
L D J Higgins, BA
R A D Hill, BA
Mrs A Hodges, BSc, RSA Cert SpLD
Ms C C Howe, BA
Mrs C L Howe, BSc, PhD
G K Howe, BSc, MSc, MA, MEd
R I Kaufman, BA
M J Kenworthy, BMus
Miss C A Knights, BA
Mrs A Lainchbury, BA, MCLIP
S N Leader, BA
Mrs C E Leigh, BA, MEd
Mrs G L Lester, MA, BA, DipSpLD
M P J Lindsay, MSc
A C R Long, BA
Mrs C E Mayo, MA Cantab

R S McAlinden, BA
Ms S J McEwan, BA
Revd C J Meharry, BEd, BTh
S A Newlove, BSc, PhD
D J Nye, BSc
Ms E F Prosser, BSc
T L Reed, MA, MSc
Mrs L A Reyes, MA
N P Robinson, BSc, MBA, CEng
R T Roe MA PGCE
Mrs J A Samuel, BSc
Mrs J Schofield, BSc
Mrs J Stobbart, BA
B R Stuttard, BA
W P Unsworth, BSc, PhD
P R Wallace, BSc, MPhil, DPhil
A J Welby, BA
P White, BEd
Mrs C E Wiedermann, MA
Mrs H Williams, BA

¶ *Old Leysian*

Housemasters and Housemistresses:
Barker House: Mr G J Deudney
Barrett House: Mr M C Gale
Bisseker House: Miss E F Prosser
Dale House: Miss C E Battison
East House: Rev C J Meharry
Fen House: Mrs K J Cox
Granta House: Mrs H Williams
Moulton House: Miss A Macpherson
North A House: Mr B A Barton
School House: Mr T L Reed
West House: Mr A C R Long

Director of Studies: P J Crosfield
Director of Pastoral Care: Mrs C E Wiedermann
Senior Tutor: A S Erby
Director of Wider Curriculum: M A Brown
Chaplain: Revd C J Meharry
Director of Sport: W J Earl
Examinations Officer: Miss Anna Hunt
Head of Careers: N P Robinson
Head of Outdoor Education: R S McAlinden
Higher Education Coordinator: M A Egan
Bursar: P D McKeown, BA
Finance Bursar: Mrs M Cooksey, FCCA
Bursar's PA: Ms Helen Hammond [maternity cover]
Headmaster's PA: Ms R C Silcock, BA
Registrar: Mrs J A Cooper, BA
Head of Marketing: Mrs A M Cox, CIM
Medical Officers:
Dr A J Stewart, MA, MB BCh, DRCOG, DCH, MRCGP, AFOM
Dr C Lea-Cox, BSc, MB BS, MRCGP, DCH, DFFP
Nursing Staff:
Sister M A Williams, SRN, SCM
Sister L Gate, RGN
Sister J Rhodes, RGN

Lincoln Minster School
Part of United Learning

The Prior Building, Upper Lindum Street, Lincoln, Lincolnshire LN2 5RW

Tel: 01522 551300
Fax: 01522 551310
email: admissions@lincolnminsterschool.co.uk
website: www.lincolnminsterschool.co.uk
Twitter: @MinsterSchool
Facebook: /LincolnMinsterSchool
LinkedIn: /Lincoln-Minster-School

Lincoln Minster School is an independent co-educational HMC day and boarding school for pupils aged 2½–18 years. We aim to provide an inspirational all-round education which combines academic achievement with a wealth of co-curricular opportunities.

Structure and Organisation. Lincoln Minster School educates pupils from nursery to A Level over several sites in the heart of historic Lincoln close to the Cathedral and Castle.

A new £10 million Music Centre and Sports Hall, redeveloped and extended Preparatory School and refurbished boarding accommodation have augmented the School's facilities dramatically and are bolstering the School's growing reputation for excellence. With a new strategy to open its doors worldwide, the School is seeking to build on a growing national reputation to become a school of international renown, especially in the field of Music.

Inspired teaching, individual focus and small classes create an excellent learning environment. There is excellent pastoral care and award-winning careers provision designed to equip youngsters for life beyond the classroom. The Nursery and Early Years department attained 'outstanding' status in their current Ofsted inspection report, underlining the quality of provision across all areas.

Lincoln Minster School is a member of United Learning, which owns and manages independent schools and academies across England. There is no doubt that membership of a group of this size gives Lincoln Minster School strength and breadth of contact.

Curriculum. A full range of subjects is offered and the school is proud of its excellent track record of examination success.

The curriculum is supported by a wealth of trips, visits and activities, too numerous to list, plus a comprehensive sports programme to cater for all tastes.

Pupils of all ages are encouraged to develop intellectual curiosity, resilience and self-confidence.

Music. As the Choir School for Lincoln Cathedral, Lincoln Minster School provides for the all-round education of boy and girl choristers. About 70% of pupils receive individual instrument lessons. Music is a focal point of school life and opportunities for public performances abound.

Boarding. Weekly and termly boarding is offered. The large family of boarders is very much at the heart of the School. There are 3 boarding houses, all in close proximity to the School and within the beautiful conservation area of uphill Lincoln.

Admissions. Lincoln Minster School welcomes pupils of a wide range of ability and all faiths. Admission is by interview and report, and subject to availability of a place.

Chorister Auditions, open to boys and girls 7–10 years, are held in November and March. These are worth up to 50% of boarding and tuition fees. Other dates by arrangement. For further details apply to The Registrar.

Scholarships. Art, Sport, Drama and Academic Scholarships are available. Music Scholarships are available for entry into Y7, 9 and 12.

Fees per term (2016–2017). Day (including lunch): Nursery & Early Years £2,799 (all day), Pre-Prep £3,002, Prep £3,785, Seniors £4,325. Termly Boarding: £7,521 (Up to Y6), £8,730 (Y7–13), £10,350 (Overseas Boarders); Weekly/Flexi Boarding: £6,830 (Up to Y6), £7,904 (Y7–13).

Charitable status. Lincoln Minster School is part of United Learning which comprises: UCST (a Company Limited by Guarantee, Registered in England, number 2780748, and a Registered Charity, number 1016538) and ULT (a Company Limited by Guarantee, Registered in England, number 4439859, and an Exempt Charity).

Chair of Local Governing Body: Mrs Linda Heaver

Members:
Mrs Helen Clarke
Revd Canon Gavin Kirk, MA, Precentor of Lincoln Cathedral
Professor Ieuan Owen
Dr Barry Devonald
Mrs Sally Mundy
Mr Terry O'Halloran
Dr Anne Craven
Dr Karin Crawford
Mrs Cordelia McCartney
Mr Robin Wright
Mrs Angela Crowe (*UCST Board*)

Senior Leadership Team:

Headmaster: Mr Mark Wallace, MBA

Deputy Head: Mrs C McKenzie, MA, BSc Hons, PGCE
Assistant Head Learning & Teaching: Mr R Eastham, MEd, BSc Hons, PGCE
Assistant Head Pupil Support & Progress: Mrs J Muir, BA Hons, PGCE
Director of Studies: Mr S Grocott, BSc Hons, PGCE
Head of Sixth Form: Mr P Norman, MSc, BSc Hons, PGCE
Head of Preparatory School: Mrs F Thomas, BEd Hons, NPQH
Head of Pre-Preparatory School: Mrs Victoria Whitworth, BSc Hons, QTS
Deputy Head of Preparatory School: Mr Mark Burton, BEd Hons

Heads of Department:
Mrs E Barclay, BEd Hons, PGCE, Dip RSA SpLD (*Learning Support*)
Mr N Boot, BA Hons, DipLaw, QTS (*History*)
Mrs R Hewitt, MEd, BA Hons, PGCE (*English*)
Mr J Cochrane, BSc, PGCE (*Mathematics*)
Mr C Freckelton, BSc Hons, GTP (*Food Science*)
Mr A Ganfornina, BA Hons, PGCE (*Modern Foreign Languages*)
Mrs A Gilbert, BSc Hons (*PE & Games*)
Mrs R Gladwin, BA Hons, PGCE (*Religious Studies*)
Mrs J Glenn-Batchelor, BA Hons, GTP (*Geography*)
Mr S King, BEng Hons, PGCE (*ICT*)
Mrs H Mason, BSc Hons, PGCE (*Science*)
Mrs N Hutchinson, MEd, BMus Hons, PGCE (*Music*)
Mrs C Servonat-Blanc, BA Hons, PGCE (*Art, Graphics & Photography*)
Miss A Tweedale, BA Hons, PGCE (*Business Studies*)
Mrs J Wafer, BA Hons, PGCE (*Drama*)

Executive Assistant to the Headmaster: Miss C Swallow
Registrar: Mrs A Stuffins
Examinations Officer: Mr J Hart, MSc, BSc Hons, PGCE

Lingfield Notre Dame

St Piers Lane, Lingfield, Surrey RH7 6PH

Tel: 01342 832407
email: office@lingfieldnd.co.uk
website: www.lingfieldnd.co.uk
Twitter: @lingfieldnd

Age Range. 2½–18.
Number in School. 922.
Fees per term (2016–2017). £3,610–£4,684. Nursery according to sessions attended.

Situation. The School is located just outside the village of Lingfield on the Surrey, Sussex, Kent border. Lingfield station has a line to London Victoria via Hurst Green, Oxted and Woldingham and is 5 minutes' drive or ten minutes' walk. The School also operates an extensive bus service.

Entry. Senior School: at 11+ and 13+ by Entrance Examination and report from previous school. At 16+ by 6+ GCSEs results and school report.

Scholarships. Available to existing pupils from Year 4. To existing and external pupils at 11+ (Academic, Art, Music and Sport) and at 13+ (all those available at 11+ as well as Drama). Means-tested Bursaries may also be available to Scholars. Scholarships are also available for the Sixth Form.

Academic. In Years 7–9, the pupils study the core subjects and a range of other options within the Lower School Curriculum. Pupils typically take 10 GCSEs which consist of English Language and Literature, Triple Science (although some may take Dual Science) at least one Language and 3 other subjects of their choice which include Computing, Media and Economics. IGCSEs are taken in the majority of subjects. The top Maths set takes Additional Maths as well as IGCSE Mathematics. 23 subjects are offered at A Level and many students also sit the Extended Project Qualification.

The School offers an extensive Scholars' Programme for its Academic Scholars and Award Holders. Seminars are held and special excursions planned as part of the Scholars' enrichment programme. Headmaster's Lectures are held every term. The School is dedicated to a progressive and innovative approach to learning and has invested heavily in digital learning (including a new Mac Suite and i-Pads plus an interactive lecture theatre), whilst valuing traditional methodology.

Pastoral. Pastorally, the School was considered 'outstanding' in its last inspection. Since then, improvements such as smaller tutor groups, more parent focus groups, regular school council and House meetings have further enhanced the feel of a forward-thinking, family-focused school. Communications between the Lingfield village community, staff, students and parents are both open and honest. The School also employs a part-time councillor to support and advise pupils where necessary.

Sport. The School has a sporting ethos of 'Opportunity, Participation and Excellence' and the students have access to a wide range of sporting activities which take place at lunchtime and after school. Students represent the School across a full range of sports at all levels and age groups, as well as participating in regional and national competitions. Hockey, netball and football form the core of major team sport representation in the autumn and spring terms whilst cricket, athletics, tennis and rounders provide the main options for the summer term.

The Rugby Club runs for both the autumn and spring terms and provides an option for those who want to play rugby to represent the School. Golf, equestrian, swimming, cross country, badminton, basketball and table tennis are some of the other competitive team sports available. We also offer performance dance.

Pupils who hold Sport Scholarships benefit from the Elite Sports Mentoring Programme which helps aspiring young athletes fulfil their potential.

Extracurricular. The School has an extensive extracurricular programme with over 120 clubs on offer, taking place both at lunchtime and after school. The clubs vary from arts and crafts to sporting and practical activities and have been designed to assist pupils develop their hobbies, strengths and skills. There are numerous trips for the students to go on. These include departmental trips, languages exchanges and sports tours.

The Duke of Edinburgh's Award programme is particularly popular. More than 90% of pupils take the Bronze Award in Year 10 and about 40% of them proceed to the Silver and Gold Awards.

In the Sixth Form a wide programme of activities is arranged such as Zumba, Ballroom Dancing, Self Defence, Car Maintenance, Orienteering, Cooking, Youth Parliament, Debating, Public Speaking, Critical Thinking and Safe Driving Talks. In addition to this, an extensive range of outside speakers visits the School to hold seminars and lectures, offering pupils the chance to broaden their horizons.

Music. A substantial number of students subscribe to instrumental lessons and participate in the numerous ensembles available to them. The School maintains two orchestras, three choirs, a jazz band, ukulele group and various chamber ensembles, including String, Flute, Percussion, Woodwind and Brass Ensembles, which are run by a team of specialist instrumental tutors. As well as the main school concerts and productions, regular informal recitals are given.

Drama. The Drama Department offers a full range of theatrical experience to its actors and audiences alike. The Department explores challenging texts from the classics and from modern writers which push both the academic and performance boundaries of the students. All pupils are taught Drama in the Lower School and it is a popular and successful option at both GCSE and A Level. They are all accommodated in the School's newly extended and refurbished teaching suite which includes two fully equipped studio spaces, technical, costume and make-up workrooms as well as a specialist Speech and Drama room.

Religion. Lingfield transferred to a lay management in 1987. It maintains its Christian ethos and welcomes students and staff of all faiths, and of none. Its philosophy is based on a strong belief in the development of the whole person. The School has a tradition of providing a caring, friendly and disciplined environment.

Buildings. The School has experienced substantial redevelopment in the last 15 years. Recent improvements include a new Sports Hall, Drama Centre, Science Rooms and Art and Photography facilities. A state-of-the-art Sixth Form Centre was opened in September 2014, offering a university-style lecture theatre, modern, interactive classrooms, atrium coffee shop and student-designed common room. A new Music Centre is due to open in April 2017. There are 40 acres of grounds which include 4 football pitches, a floodlit astro and cricket nets.

Charitable status. Lingfield Notre Dame is a Registered Charity, number 295598. It exists to provide education.

Chair of Governors : Mrs S Rutherford

Headmaster: Mr R W Bool, BA Hons, MBA

Deputy Heads:
Mrs J Richards, MA
Mr D Snowden, MA

Assistant Heads:
Mr I Copeland, BSc Hons
Mrs A Folkard, BSc Hons

Mr J Wale, BA Hons
Mr S Casey, BA Hons

Heads of Departments:
Academic PE: Mrs K Davis, BA Hons
Art: Miss K Muir, MA, BA Hons
Boys' Games: Mr N Harrison, BA Hons, QTS
Chemistry: Dr D Thompson, BSc Hons MSc PhD
Drama: Mrs E Jolly, MA ,LGSM
Economics: Mr R Dewey, BA Hons
English: Mrs A Saunders, BA Hons
Food & Nutrition: Mrs S Jenn, BSc Hons
French: Miss C Murie, MA, BA Hons
Geography: Mr C Roberts, BSc Hons
German: Mrs B Edwards, BA Hons
Girls' Games: Miss L Biddulph, BSc Hons
History: Mrs S Milivojevic, BA Hons
Learning Support: Mrs S Sevier, BA Hons
Mathematics: Mr M Maranzano, BSc Hons
Media: Mrs S House, BA Hons
MFL, Spanish: Mr J Martinez, MA
Physics: Mr C Fast, BEd, BSc
Psychology: Miss R Hase, BSc Hons
Religion and Philosophy: Mr A Gaunt, BA
Science, Biology: Mr J Grant, BSc Hons

Junior School:
Headmaster: Mr R W Bool, BA, MBA
Head of Junior School: Mrs J Shackel, BA Hons
  (*SENDCO*)
Deputy Head of Junior School: Mrs E Margrett, BA Hons,
  MA, CCRS
Senior Teacher: Mrs H Roll, MA Ed, AMBDA

Peripatetic Staff for Bassoon, Brass, Cello, Clarinet,
  Classical Guitar, Drums, Flute, French Horn, Guitar,
  Harp, LAMDA, Oboe, Percussion, Piano, Saxophone,
  Trombone, Viola, Violin, Voice.

Finance Manager: Mrs A Brassett
Registrar: Mrs M O'Neill
Marketing Manager: Ms M Morgan
Headmaster's PA and Clerk to Governors: Mrs T Unwin
Deputy Heads' PA: Mrs P Kohlbeck
Junior School Head's PA: Mrs S Wood

Lomond School

**10 Stafford Street, Helensburgh, Argyll and Bute
G84 9JX**

Tel: 01436 672476
Fax: 01436 678320
email: admissions@lomondschool.com
website: www.lomondschool.com
Twitter: @LomondSchool

A superb quality of life. Lomond School is a co-educational independent school, for children aged 3 to 18 years, positioned in the elegant suburbs of the coastal town of Helensburgh located only 10 minutes from Loch Lomond and the Trossachs National Park. We make the most of our unique location by providing and encouraging participation in a wide range of opportunities for outdoor learning, sports and activities. Students can enjoy a superb quality of life in a beautiful and safe environment.

Personalised Education. At Lomond School we believe passionately that education should be about supporting our young people to develop and grow, both academically and personally, as rounded individuals with strong values who are ultimately prepared to embark confidently and successfully on their life beyond Lomond School.

We uphold this commitment with six **Guiding Principles** which are delivered throughout our curriculum and co-curriculum. These include: Internationalism; Environmentalism; Adventure; Leadership; Lifelong Learning and Service. To find out more visit our website at www.lomondschool.com.

Inclusive Ethos. Our focus is on preparing our students for their future by ensuring that they learn the skills necessary to be successful in the 21st century whilst developing the traditional values and qualities that they require to be responsible and active global citizens.

We provide small class sizes, an extensive programme of extra-curricular activities, attention to the individual and a strong record of academic achievement which opens the door to allow new experiences, skills and talents to be explored. All aspects of development are accorded importance, be they academic, musical, dramatic, sporting or in wider outdoor activities.

We were one of the first schools in the UK to integrate an ICT strategy which provides all our P6 to S6 students with their own personal iPad.

The Lomond Family. Our experienced pastoral care team ensures the welfare and onward progression of all of our students. Our young people are well known by staff and teachers and we see ourselves as a large family where any issues or problems are identified and dealt with promptly and effectively.

Extra-curricular and Outdoor Learning. Our location means that there is a particular emphasis on outdoor pursuits. The Duke of Edinburgh's Award is, without doubt, a significant feature and we have enjoyed great success carrying out expeditions both locally and abroad. Many of our trips and excursions revolve around our passion for the outdoors and have included trekking in Morocco, canoeing in Norway and skiing in Austria.

We also build many cultural and educational trips into the school year with visits to Paris, Berlin, Brussels and Iceland, as well as Hockey and Rugby tours to South Africa or more locally. We support and encourage our young people to make the most of the opportunities available, recognising both the immediate and long-term benefit of the personal development these experiences and activities can offer.

Living at Lomond. Our boarding facility adds a distinctive dimension to the school; the mix of cultures and backgrounds enriches our curriculum and co-curriculum, supporting all of our pupils to develop their global awareness and understanding.

Our infrastructure boasts a mix of modern, purpose-built structure and characterful listed buildings, which make for an inspirational setting for our young people. We continually invest in our facilities and take a cutting-edge approach to every new project we initiate.

Entry and Scholarships. Means-tested bursaries are available for entry between T2 and S6 with fee assistance ranging from 10% to 100% depending on circumstances. In addition, means-tested bursaries are available for services personnel with children who board at Lomond.

Admission is by assessment in Mathematics and English for 11 to 18 year-olds. For younger pupils, placement in classes is the main requirement, whilst for senior pupils reports and examination results are given due weighting.

Fees per term (2016–2017). Tuition: £2,414 (Nursery net of Local Council Funding), £2,660 (Junior 1–2), £3,110 (Junior 3–5), £3,390 (Transitus 1), £3,600 (Transitus 2), £3,700 (Senior School).

Boarding (inc Tuition Fees): £8,410.

A levy of £50 per pupil per term is payable along with tuition fees.

Charitable status. Lomond School Ltd is a Registered Charity, number SC007957. It exists to provide education for boys and girls.

Board of Governors:
Chair: Mr A J D Hope, LLB
Vice-Chair: Mr C Burnet, LLB, CA
Mr D Bowman, FNAEA
Professor R Brown, BSc Hons, PhD
Mrs D Cook
Mr D Girdwood
Mr J Kemp, BA Hons
Captain C M Mearns, Royal Navy
Mrs L Pender, BA, PGCE
Dr T Reitano, MB ChB

Staff:

Principal: Mrs J Urquhart, BSc Hons, PGCE, MEd

Academic Depute: Mrs C Chisholm, MA Hons, PGCE
Pastoral Depute: Mr A B H Minnis, MA Hons, PGCE, Cert PP
Head of Junior School: Mrs A Lawn, BSc Hons, PGCE
Bursar: Ms A Sheehan, BA, MSc, CSBM
Marketing: Mrs J Scullion
Admissions: Mrs J Dixon ACIM

* Head of Department

Subject Teachers – Secondary:

Art & Design:
*Mrs B Croft, BA Hons, Cert Ed
Mrs L Jack, BA Hons, PGCE
Mrs D Aitken, BA Hons, Cert Ed

Business Studies & Economics:
*Mrs C McElhill, BA Hons, MSc, PGCE

Drama:
Miss S Gibbs MA PGDE

EFL:
Mrs A Riches, BA, PGCE
Mrs J Robertson, BEd

English:
*Mr D Torbet, BA Hons, PGDE
Dr M Cotter-MacDonald, MA Hons, PhD, PGDE
Mrs M McKillop, MA Hons, MPhil, PGCE
Mrs C Chisholm, MA Hons, PGCE

Geography:
*Mrs N McKenzie, MA Hons, PGCE

Graphic Communication:
Mr J Stewart, BSc, PGDE

Health & Food Technology:
Mrs N Harwood, BSc Hons, PGCE, MEd

History and Modern Studies:
*Mrs S Guy, MA Hons, PGCE
Mr J Forrest BA Hons PGDE
Mr A B H Minnis, MA Hons, PGCE, Cert PP

ICT:
*Mr S J Kilday, DipTechEd, DipComp

Learning Support:
*Mr H Hunter, BA Hons, PGDE
Mrs C Greaves, BSc Hons, PGCE
Mrs S Bell, BEd, PGDE

Mathematics:
*Mr G Macleod, BSc Hons, MEd, CMath, CSci, FIMA, PGCE, Adv Dip Hist Oxon
Mrs E Cameron, BSc Hons, PGCE

Modern Languages:
*Mr A Greig, MA Hons, PGCE, PGDip
Mrs E Bruce, MA Hons, PGDE
Miss E Clarke, BA Hons, PGDE

Mrs J Robertson, BEd
Ms I Skowronski, LLCE English, PGDE

Music:
*Mr D Fleming, BMus Hons, PGCE
Miss M-C Brown, BA Hons, PGDE

Physical Education:
*Mrs M G Taylor, BEd
Mr C Dunlop, BEd Hons
Mr S Louden, BA, MEd, PGCE
Miss Julia Hodgson

RME:
Mr S J Kilday, DipTechEd, DipComp
Mrs L Jack, BA Hons, PGCE

Science:
Biology:
*Mr J Laycock, BSc Hons, PGCE
Chemistry:
*Mr D L Dodson, BSc Hons, Cert Ed
Miss M Ward, BSc Hons, PGCE
Physics:
*Dr A MacBeath, BEng Hons, PhD, PGDE
Mr C Butler, BSc Hons, Cert Ed
General Science:
Mrs A Lawn, BSc Hons, PGCE

Careers Advisor:
Mr Terry Chambers, BSc MSc PGDE

School Nurse:
Mrs Lesley Serpell, RGN, MPH

Head of Junior School:
Mrs A Lawn, BSc Hons, PGCE

Class Teachers – Junior School and Transitus:

Class Teachers – Transitus:
Mrs C Greig, BA Jt Hons, PGCE, Dip Ed Tech
Mrs V McLatchie, DCE
Dr M Cotter-MacDonald, MA Hons, PhD, PGDE

Class Teachers – Clarendon
Mrs L Canero, BA, PGDE
Mrs V Cassels, MA Hons, MA, BSc, PGCE, Dip Env Dev, Cert Con Sci, Cert French
Mrs J Fullarton, BA Hons, PGCE
Mr J Grafton, BEd Hons
Mrs J Macleod, BEd Hons, MEd, Dip RSA, Dip APS, Dip Ed Lead, SQH
Mrs K Muggoch, MA Hons, PGDE
Mrs S Bell, BEd PGDE

Nursery/Pre-School Group:
Head of Nursery: Mrs L Canero, BA, PGDE
Miss L Lovell, HNC
Mrs J McArthur, SNNEB
Mrs G Thomas, HNC
Miss J Wardle
Miss L Burnside
Mrs K Ross

Lord Wandsworth College

Long Sutton, Hook, Hampshire RG29 1TB

Tel:	01256 862201 (Main Office)
	01256 860348 (Headmaster)
	01256 860200 (Admissions)
Fax:	01256 860363

email: info@lordwandsworth.org
website: www.lordwandsworth.org

Motto: '*Vincit Perseverantia.*'

Lord Wandsworth College is a co-educational secondary school for 580 pupils between the ages of 11 and 18. Approximately 55% of the pupils are boarders, either full, weekly or flexi.

Location and accessibility. The school occupies a magnificent rural setting on the North Hampshire/Surrey border just five miles from Junction 5 of the M3 and only an hour from London by road or rail.

History. Lord Wandsworth died in 1912 and left a large sum of money for the foundation of a school. The College that bears his name now occupies a 1,200 acre site. The Lord Wandsworth Foundation awards a number of places annually to children who have lost the support of one or both parents through death, divorce or separation with priority to those who have lost a parent through death.

Mission statement. LWC is a socially inclusive non-denominational boarding and day Foundation school for boys and girls. We focus on the needs of each individual, while developing in each child a concern for others and a love for and loyalty towards the school community. We ensure that each pupil shapes their values and aspirations within a stimulating and supportive environment, and strive constantly to improve the quality of teaching and learning. We aim to equip pupils with character attributes, passion, resourcefulness, independence, skills, knowledge and qualifications so they can become the best possible version of themselves and make a great contribution to a changing world.

The outstanding features of the school are
- that almost all academic staff live on campus allowing them to provide a high level of pastoral care;
- that Character Education is imbedded into the curriculum and co-curriculum. By promoting Character Education, we believe we will give all pupils the best chance of realising their full potentials.
- that all pupils, whether full, weekly, flexi boarding or day, belong to one of the eight houses and are fully integrated into the social life of the school;
- that the school is purpose-built with an outstanding range of facilities for both academic and extra-curricular activities;
- that the school is an unusually unpretentious, happy and caring community.

Curriculum. The aim of the curriculum is to provide a full and flexible range of subjects to fit the needs of each individual. The school's policy is to follow closely the National Curriculum.

Subjects taught to GCSE are: English (Language and Literature), French, Geography, Mathematics, History, Latin, Classical Civilisation, Drama, Physics, Chemistry, Biology, Spanish, German, Art, Music, Design & Technology, Computer Science and Religious Studies.

Most pupils continue into the Sixth Form where the subjects taught at A level are: English, History, Geography, Economics, Business Studies, Classical Civilisation, Music, Latin, French, Spanish, German, Physics, Chemistry, Biology, Mathematics, Further Mathematics, Art, Design, Theatre Studies, PE, Philosophy and Ethics and Psychology. We also offer the EPQ.

ICT. There has been, and continues to be, significant investment into IT provision. There is a wireless networked system across the whole school.

Games. The school lays great store by its games involvement and has a local and national reputation for many of its pursuits. The main boys' games are rugby, hockey and cricket and for girls hockey, netball and cricket. In addition swimming, athletics, tennis, squash, badminton, basketball, golf, cross-country running and canoeing are all on offer.

Drama. Drama has a high profile and several shows are staged each year. There is a musical production every other year as well as showcases, reviews and workshops. Pupils are encouraged to participate in all fields of drama either acting, writing, set design, lighting, stage management, prop-making or sound.

Music. There is a large variety of instrumental ensembles, including a swing band, chamber and rock groups. Pupils sing in two choirs. Tuition is available in singing, all orchestral instruments, piano, organ, percussion and guitar. Musicians regularly perform formally and informally both within school and at local venues.

Other activities. There is an extensive extra-curricular programme. Some of the activities on offer are: Cookery, Soccer, Chess, Community Service, Pottery, Drama clubs, Mountain Biking, Dance, Photography, LWC Tv, Riding, Life-saving, Debating and Climbing.

The Duke of Edinburgh's Award scheme is thriving and the College has its own licence to run the scheme. There is an active CCF programme for Year 10 pupils and above which has an Army and Air Force Section.

Organisation. There is a two or three form entry at age 11. For the first two years all pupils are in the co-educational Junior House. At 13 there is another entry, mainly from children who have taken Common Entrance. All houses are in the charge of Houseparents assisted by a team of tutors and matrons.

Scholarships and Awards on offer are:

First Form (Year 7): Academic, Performing Arts (Music, Drama and Dance) and Sport.

Third Form (Year 9): Academic, Performing Arts (Music, Drama and Dance), Art, Sport, All-Rounder and Character.

Sixth Form (Year 12): Academic, Performing Arts (Music, Drama and Dance), Art, Sport, All-Rounder and Character.

Foundation Awards are available for children who have lost the support of one or both parents through death, divorce or separation.

Further details for all scholarships and awards may be obtained from the Admissions Office.

Fees per term (2016–2017). Senior Full Boarding £10,290; Senior Weekly Boarding £9,820; Senior Flexi Boarding £8,530; Senior Day £7,250; Junior Full Boarding £9,025; Junior Weekly Boarding £8,750; Junior Flexi Boarding £7,650; Junior Day £6,430.

Charitable status. Lord Wandsworth College is a Registered Charity, number 1143359. It exists to provide education for boys and girls.

Chairman of Governors: R J Hannington

The Governing Body consists of 12 governors.

Headmaster: Adam Williams, MA

Senior Deputy Head: Gareth Pearson, BEng
Deputy Head, Teaching and Learning: Stephen Badger, MA Cantab
Deputy Head, ISI Compliance, Inspection & Academic Systems: Jackie Davies, MA
Bursar: Richard Gammage, MSc, MA

Teaching Staff and Assistants:
† *Houseparent*

Vic Allan, BA (*Head of Performing Arts*)
Marie-France Allen (*French Assistant*)
Sharon Allmark, BA (*Careers & Higher Education*)
Andrea Maresa Amo (*Spanish Assistant*)
Alice Asbury, BSc (*Biology*)
Sarah Badger, MA (*Head of French and MFL*)
David Beven (*Sports Assistant, Head of Cricket*)

Sue Brown, MA (*Librarian*)
Portia Cantwell, BMus (*Musician in Residence*)
†Eduard Coetzer, BA (*ICT*)
Diane Crichton, BSc (*Chemistry*)
Alte Gerstenkorn (*German Assistant*)
Lauren Griffin, BMus, MA (*Head of Music*)
Sally Dawson-Couper, MA (*Head of Mathematics,
     Assistant Deputy Head, Academic Systems*)
Natalie Eley, BSc (*Chemistry*)
Margaret Ellwood, MA (*Senco*)
Ann-Marie Engelbrecht, BA (*Geography*)
Elaine Faulkner, BA (*Psychology*)
Alison Fisher, BA (*EAL*)
Peter Gilliam, MSc (*Mathematics*)
Danielle Green, BA (*Assistant Director of Music*)
Alex Hamilton, MA (*Head of Latin and Classics*)
Ben Hazell (*Sports Assistant*)
Clive Hicks, MA (*Latin and Classics*)
†James Hine, BA (*History*)
Andrew Howard, MA (*English*)
Holly Hunter, BA (*Artist in Residence*)
†Chris Irvine, BSc (*Physics*)
†Richard Kimber, BEng (*Mathematics*)
Beverley Lane, BSc (*Mathematics*)
Andrew Lay, BSc (*Head of Economics*)
Jennifer Leopold, BA (*English*)
Claire Liggins, BA (*Head of Design & Technology,
     Assistant Deputy Head, Pastoral*)
Jonathan Lilley, BA (*Head of History*)
Jeni Loud, BSc (*Physics & Chemistry, Assistant Deputy
     Head, Teaching & Learning*)
Samantha Ludlow, BSc (*Geography*)
Audley Lumsden, BSc (*Physics*)
Pete Maidment, BA (*Chaplain*)
David Machin, MA (*English*)
Jessica McKinnon, BA (*German, Deputy Head of Co-
     Curriculum*)
Lucie McNabb, BA (*Head of German, Head of 5th Form*)
Donna McPhee, BA (*Design & Technology*)
Chris Millington, BA (*ICT & Computer Science*)
†Jane Mitchell, BA (*German*)
Graham Mobbs, BA (*Head of Art*)
Vincent Murtagh, BSc, PhD (*Head of Chemistry*)
Ahmed Musleh, BSc (*Biology*)
Gill Neighbour (*Head of 1st Form & PE*)
Jan Norgaard, BSc (*Head of Geography*)
†Jonathan Pitt, BSc (*Geography*)
†Kay Price, BA (*History*)
Chris Radmann, BA (*Head of English, Head of 6th Form &
     Enrichment*)
Lesley Radmann, BA (*English*)
James Rayner, BA (*Sports Assistant, Head of Rugby*)
Jacob Read, BA (*Sports Assistant*)
Noel Reeson, BA (*French & Spanish*)
Rosana Rial Garcia (*Spanish*)
Tim Richardson, BA (*Head of PE & Co-Curriculum*)
Stephanie Richardson, BA (*Spanish, Head of 3rd Form*)
Webster Richardson, BSc (*Design & Technology*)
Liz Scott, BA (*Classics*)
†Tom Shedden, BA (*History*)
Soma Singh, BA (*Head of Sport*)
Susan Stevens, BA (*Art*)
Peter Summers, MA (*Head of Science & Physics*)
Richard Thorne, BA, MSc (*Biology*)
Jane Turner, BA (*Senco*)
Jonathan Turney, MA (*Biology, Head of 4th Form*)
Edward Walker, BSc (*Business Studies*)
Ian Watson, MEng (*Mathematics*)
Christian White, MA (*Head of Philosophy & Ethics*)
David Widdowson, BSc (*Mathematics*)
Colin Wiskin (*Ceramics*)

Sylvie Yvon Case, BA (*French*)

Librarian: Sue Brown

Director of Admissions & Marketing: Mary Hicks

Headmaster's Secretary: Nicolette Grossmith

Medical Officers:
Dr R Assadourian, MB BS, BSc Hons, MRCGP, DRCOG,
     DFFP
Dr C Shand, MB BS, LMSSA, MRCGP, DRCOG, DFFP

Loretto School

Linkfield Road, Musselburgh, East Lothian EH21 7RE
Tel: School: 0131 653 4444
              Headmaster: 0131 653 4441
              Admissions: 0131 653 4455
Fax: School: 0131 653 4445
              Admissions: 0131 653 4401
email: admissions@loretto.com
website: www.loretto.com

Loretto has flourished as a school since its establishment
in 1827, 6 miles from Edinburgh, on the banks of the River
Esk and surrounded by the beautiful countryside of East
Lothian. It is a non-denominational, co-educational boarding and day school and provides for full and flexi boarders,
as well as for day pupils, with a distinctive emphasis on the
full development of the individual through academic, intellectual, sporting, musical, dramatic and artistic pursuits in a
fine, secure environment. Loretto is a small school, big on
heart and big on ambition. Its distinctive ethos fosters in its
pupils a quiet confidence in themselves and a spirit of readiness to succeed in the changing world beyond school.
Loretto is a small community where staff and pupils know
each other personally. Classes are deliberately small so that
proper individual attention is possible; recent examination
results have been outstanding. Boys and girls take part in a
very wide range of activities. Its pupils, from 0 to 18 years,
are known and valued for themselves and are expected to
respect and support each other. The School makes fullest use
of its proximity to Edinburgh, enabling pupils to take advantage of the music, drama, museums and art galleries, as well
as giving opportunities for sport and leisure in this capital
city. To the east lie the golf courses which provide the fair-
way for The Golf Academy at Loretto.

The Senior School consists of 400 boys and girls with
almost 75% of pupils boarding.

Academic. An excellent staff/pupil ratio (1:8) ensures an
environment that stimulates, supports and nurtures the
potential in everyone. The academic programme aims to
challenge pupils and to recognise and reward effort and
attainment. A full range of curricular subjects – humanities;
drama, music and art; languages and sciences; ICT and business; physical education – is offered. The depth, breadth and
quality of a Loretto education encourages each pupil to
achieve his or her personal best and to enjoy doing so.
Pupils are prepared for success in GCSE, AS and A Level
and for a choice of good university careers thereafter. The
School is also running the AQA Extension Project Scheme
which contributes to UCAS points. In 2016 30.7% of all A
Levels sat were at grade A*/A. 87.5% of GCSEs were at
A*-C grades. Virtually all pupils go on to higher education
and 95% of pupils enter their chosen university. Loretto is
ranked in the top 7% of schools nationally for value-added
at A Level.

The facilities keep abreast of changing national academic
demands, with modern, well-equipped specialist areas in
languages, art and design, music, drama and the sciences.
The Communication and Resource Centre provides a tradi-

tional library as well as a Sixth Form Centre and computer network which can be accessed from academic departments and Houses. All pupils become familiar both with modern technology and with books, to facilitate independent learning, essential for success in Higher Education and beyond. The Support for Learning department assists the academically gifted as well as those who have a learning difficulty or those who simply want to improve essential study skills. 2015 saw the opening of a state-of-the-art Indoor Golf Centre.

Pastoral Care. There are seven houses where full and flexi boarders and day pupils can relax "at home", socialise and develop their studies under the experienced supervision of dedicated resident pastoral teams. The House structure is: 6 boarding houses (4 for Sixth Form and 2 for Second, Third, Fourth and Fifth Form), and 1 day house (boy and girl). There is excellent pastoral care, nurturing an atmosphere of mutual care and support in which children mature at their own pace and older pupils are encouraged to take responsibility, not just for themselves, but for their young housemates.

Younger pupils sleep in small dormitories, while sixth formers have double or individual study-bedrooms.

The day pupils at Loretto have access to the same broad and full education provided for boarders, and are able to take full advantage of the facilities of a boarding school, while returning home to sleep.

All academic staff are involved in the boarding houses and so staff are always on hand to guide and encourage. The aim is always to ensure that the well-being and development of every pupil is closely and sympathetically monitored. An excellent programme of personal, social and health education is an integral part of the curriculum.

Health. A medical centre staffed with nurses who are qualified and registered with the NMC. The Doctors surgery is located off site. All health/medical appointments for boarding pupils are made through the Loretto School Medical Centre Staff. There is a school counsellor who visits the school twice a week.

Music, Drama and Art. Loretto is well known for the excellent quality of its Expressive Arts. Pupils are encouraged to enjoy the creative arts and to develop their individual talents. A purpose-built Music School enables a very high proportion to learn individual instruments or to take voice lessons and there is a range of concerts, recitals and performances both in School and in venues in Edinburgh and East Lothian. Loretto is Europe's first All-Steinway School. The choir and orchestra practise weekly. All pupils enjoy whole School choral singing in chapel, while performance music extends from rock, through jazz to classical music. The Loretto Pipe Band competes successfully in national competitions and has a busy schedule of appearances. A theatre is the base for much drama work, with performances – both musical and dramatic – each term involving pupils of all ages. LAMDA exams are also available. The theatre and dance studio facilities have been refurbished to provide performance areas and technical facilities to the highest specifications. There is also a campus radio station to complement the modern well-equipped studio theatre and recording studio. The Art department offers drawing, painting, mixed media, ceramics, sculpture and linoprinting. The School's art gallery allows pupil work to be displayed as well as housing outside exhibitions that encourage pupil experimentation with different techniques and styles.

Games and Activities. Pupils are encouraged to enjoy exercise and to develop their skills. The Golf Academy at Loretto is widely recognised as one of the best independent golfing schools in Europe, with on-site facilities, including a new state-of-the-art indoor centre and professional coaching. Cricket is also a major strength with the employment of former Scotland player, John Blain, as Head of Cricket and ex-England international, Rob Hardwick as Head of Rugby.

Provision is also made for rugby, hockey, lacrosse, athletics, cricket, tennis, fives, badminton, swimming, shooting, and basketball, to name but a few. A well-equipped fitness centre and an astroturf pitch are also on site. Riding, sailing, skiing and snowboarding are available using excellent local facilities. Team games are important: boys play rugby, hockey and cricket; girls, hockey, lacrosse and netball. There is an extensive range of fixtures for both boys and girls at all levels. Participation in the Duke of Edinburgh's Award scheme is strong and Community Service, the Combined Cadet Force and outward bound programme offer additional experience of a range of skills and challenges. A full programme of activities, from karate to hip hop dance, operates each day and all weekend.

Sixth Form. Preparing its pupils for the world beyond school is something that Loretto takes very seriously. Loretto's Sixth Form is structured to encourage boys and girls to take responsibility for their work and organise their time. Loretto offers a wide range of academic subjects in the Sixth Form and fosters a purposeful work ethic. Academic tutors and pastoral mentors are on hand at every step to provide encouragement and guidance. A comprehensive enrichment programme has been developed which enables students to enjoy concerts, theatre trips, social evenings and outings to Edinburgh.

There is a thriving lecture society which organises visiting speakers from University and industry to enthuse and advise the Sixth Form. Additionally, the school runs a series of seminars and workshops on the humanities, literature, politics, creative writing, science and more. Pupils also volunteer to research and deliver lectures to their peers. A dedicated, experienced team of teachers are on hand to guide every pupil through their university applications, gap year choices, career paths and work-experience ventures

Beyond academic matters, Loretto furnishes each pupil with a range of leadership and teamworking opportunities. Positions of responsibility and trust are earned. Prefects are selected on the basis of a rigorous application and interview process which mirrors that of the business world. Loretto runs a range of specific leadership and teamworking exercises for Sixth Formers in the form of CCF and adventure activities. These are complemented by sessions on interview techniques, organisational skills and "CV loading". After all, in such a competitive job market, Lorettonians need to be well prepared and well informed.

Religion. Services are held in the School Chapel every week. The services are non-denominational and boys and girls are prepared for confirmation in both the Church of England and the Church of Scotland; they are confirmed at a combined service held in the Chapel. Whole School singing is a long-standing tradition at Loretto and continues to be memorable.

Developments. A Loretto Foundation has been established to provide for the mid to long-term future of the School with a particular emphasis on raising money to support scholarships and bursaries. In recent years, a major programme of development has taken place to provide an indoor golf centre, six science laboratories, four new classrooms, a further Art room and ICT room, a lecture theatre, and a recording studio and radio station, all equipped to a very high standard. There is also an ongoing programme of refurbishment in the houses.

Uniform. The uniform is practical and comfortable. Formal dress on Sundays is the kilt for boys and girls. Ordinary School dress is charcoal trousers for boys, navy skirts for girls, with white shirts and the distinctive red jacket.

Entrance. Boys and girls are required to pass either the Common Entrance Examination or the Open Assessment Examination in English, Mathematics and Verbal Reasoning before being admitted, as well as an interview. Entrance to the Lower Sixth is based on interview and a conditional offer subject to satisfactory performance at GCSE/Standard Grade or international equivalent.

Junior School. 'The Nippers' enjoy many of the facilities of the Senior School, such as the playing fields, Theatre, Sports Hall, Music School and Chapel. The boys and girls are under closer adult supervision than in the Senior School but in other respects the system is similar. There are over 200 boys and girls aged between 0 and 12. The majority are day pupils, but occasional and flexi boarding are available. (*For further details, see entry in IAPS Section.*)

Fees per term (2016–2017). Boarding: £6,950–£10,650; Flexi Boarding (3 nights p/w): £5,900–£8,850; Overnighting £50 per night. These fees include all the expenses of board, lodging, most textbooks (though in the sixth form textbooks may have to be purchased), stationery, games material, medical attendance and medicine, CCF, transport to matches and internal school entertainments.

Day Fees (including meals): £2,850–£7,250.

Optional Expenses. These will be kept to a minimum, but include individual voice and instrumental music lessons; extra-curricular visits and expeditions.

Scholarships and Bursaries. *Senior School*: Academic, Art, Golf, Music and Sports are available for 12+ entry.

Academic, Golf, Music, Sport, Art and Drama are available from 13+ to Sixth Form entry.

Means-tested bursaries up to 105% are also available.

Bursaries are available to support scholarship and non-scholarship award candidates who pass Loretto's entrance criteria and who the School feels would benefit from a Loretto education. Bursaries can be used to supplement a scholarship award if the financial amount of a scholarship is insufficient to allow a pupil to attend Loretto. Bursaries are means-tested and are available for prospective pupils as well as existing pupils who experience unforeseen financial difficulty. Bursary funds are limited.

Please contact the Admissions Department on 0131 653 4455 for further details.

Leaving Scholarships. A number of awards are given to assist with university education to those who have 'deserved well of Loretto' in recognition of their loyalty and service to the School.

Old Lorettonian Society. *Hon Secretary*: Charles T D Craig, Loretto School, Musselburgh.

Charitable status. Loretto School is a Registered Charity, number SC013978. It exists in order to educate young people in mind, body and spirit.

Governors:
Brigadier S J M Graham (*Chairman*)

Mrs R Caughey	Mrs T Laing
K Dobson	Mrs S Lang
Mrs K Eyre	Major General P C
Mrs C Fleming (*Clerk to*	Marriott, CBE
the Board)	J Miller
W Frain-Bell	T McCreath
B GIbson	S Pengelley
Dr S Gillies	Rt Revd B Smith
J Grant	

Headmaster: **Dr Graham Hawley**, BSc, PhD

Vicegerent: N C Bidgood, BSc, MSc, PGCE, FRGS

Head of Junior School: P Meadows, MA

Staff:
* *Head of Department*
† *Housemaster/mistress*

Dr David J Adamson, MA Hons, PhD (*History, Government and Politics, Head of Sixth Form/Senior Tutor, University Guidance*)
Ms Aisling Agnew, MMus (*Music – Flute*)

Mrs Emily Alexander, BSc Hons, PGDE Secondary Geography, PGDE and MSc Outdoor Education (*Acting Head of Geography,*)
Mr Neil Allan, BLE Hons MRICS PGCE (*Head of Hockey, Housemaster – Pinkie*)
Mr Christopher Ash, PGDE, BA Hons (*Head of Business Education, House Assistant – Hope*)
Mr Edward Barker, MSc, MEd, PGCE, MA Hons (*History/ Politics, House Assistant – Seton*)
Mr Chris Baxter (*Music – Piano*)
Mr Nigel C Bidgood, BSc, MSc, PGCE, FRGS (*Vicegerent, Biology*)
Mr John Blain, Master Cricket Coach (*Head of Cricket*)
Mrs Madeline Bonner, PGCE, MA Fine and Applied Arts, BA Hons Textile and Fashion Design DIS (*Director of Pastoral Care/Child Protection Coordinator*)
Mrs Seonaid Boyd, PGCE, BSc Hons (*Part-time Teacher of Science, Psychology*)
Mrs Ann Buchanan, MA Fine Art (*Head of Art and History of Art*)
Mr James Burnet, MA, PGCE (*Head of Modern Languages*)
Ms Alina Bzhezhinska (*Music – Harp*)
Mrs Charlotte Cadzow, BA Ceramics (*Art, Ceramics*)
Mrs Margarita Campbell, BA English Literature (*Modern Languages (Spanish)*)
Mrs Nina Capaldi (*Art Technician*)
Mr W Edward Coleman, MMus, ARCO (*Director of Music*)
Ms Abigail Cooper, BA Hons, PGCE (*English, Drama, House Assistant – Holm*)
Mrs Catharine Davidson, BA Hons, MA DIS, GTCS (*Part-time Teacher of Art*)
Mrs Helen Day, MA Hons English Language and Literature, PGCE (*Head of English, University Guidance, House Assistant – Balcarres*)
Mrs Rachael Delaney, MA, PGCE (*Temporary Teacher of English, House Assistant – Holm*)
Mr Sergei Desmond, BSc, BMus (*Music – Piano, Music Tech*)
Mr Robert Dick (*Music – Violin*)
Mr W Dennis Dickinson, BEd (*Geography, Housemaster Schoolhouse*)
Mrs June Dunford, BA History, MA Librarianship (*Head Librarian, Editor of the Lorettonian Magazine*)
Mr Paul S Dunn, BSc, PGCE, GTCS Registered, ECDL (*Mathematics*)
Mrs Silvia Feria, Spanish, English Philology, BA in English with Spanish Literature and Post Grad Diploma in Secondary Teaching (*Modern Languages, House Assistant – Holm*)
Dr Ian Fox, BSc Hons, PhD (*Head of Physics*)
Mrs Rebecca Fox, BA Hons, PGCE (*Music, ICT, House Assistant – Balcarres*)
Ms Shelagh Fuller, BA Hons, CPGS, MMus (*Music – Cello*)
Mrs Monique Galloway, MA Hons French, Dip Trans (*Modern Languages, Housemistress – Holm, Head of Second and Third Form*)
Ms Fiona Grant-Macdonald (*Physics Technician*)
Mr Nick Guise, DipEd, PGCSE, GTCS Cert Dyslexia (*Support for Learning*)
Mr Geoff Harbison, BSc Hons, MSc Dist, MRICS (*Business Studies and Economics, Housemaster – Hope*)
Mr Rob Hardwick (*Head of Rugby*)
Miss Justine Henning (*French Assistant*)
Miss Jo Hepton, BSc Hons, PGCE (*Mathematics, House Assistant – Seton*)
Mrs Carol Hewitt (*Lab Technician*)
Mrs Alison Horsey, BA, MA, PGCE (*Classics*)

Mr David Howie, MIC, BCU, BASI 3N, APIOL, ILM L5Mgt (*Head of Outdoor Pursuits*)

Dr Jonathan Idle, BSc, PhD, PGCE, PQH NI (*Director of Teaching and Learning, Chemistry*)

Mr Ross Johnston, BSc, PGDE (*Physics, House Assistant – Seton*)

Mr Alan Jordan (*Music – Tenor Drum*)

Dr Julian Karolyi, BA French and Spanish, PhD French, PGCE, TESOL (*Modern Languages, Higher Education, Careers and University Guidance, EPQ Coordinator*)

Rev Andy Keulemans, BSc, BTh, PGCE (*Mathematics, Housemaster – Seton*)

Miss Zoe Law, BSc Hons, PGDE (*Mathematics, House Assistant – Hope*)

Mrs Carol Lekkas, BSc Hons Physiology, Dip TEFL/TESL (*Head of English as a Second Language, Biology, Overseas Pupil Coordinator*)

Mr Simon J M Lowe, MA Oxon, Cert Adv Studies Guildhall School of Music & Drama, PGCE MMU (*Artistic Director, Modern Languages, Music, House Assistant – Eleanora Almond*)

Mr Stuart Lucas, BA Hons, MLitt, PGCE English, PG Dip SpLD Dyslexia, PGC Autism, CPT3A (*Head of Support for Learning Specialist Assessor*)

Miss Fiona Lund (*Music – Brass*)

Miss Jennifer Macdonald, BSc Hons, PGCE (*Support for Learning, House Assistant – Holm*)

Mr Michael Macdonald, BA (*PE*)

Mr Graham Mackay, PGA Professional UKCC Level 3, (*PGA Professional*)

Mr Jamie MacKenzie, BA Hons History, CELTA, PGCE (*English as a Second Language, History, Assistant Housemaster – Pinkie*)

Dr Marjory MacLeod, PGDE, PhD, MSci (*Mathematics, House Assistant – Balcarres*)

Miss Lorna McDonald (*Music*)

Mr Daniel McLean Steel, BA Hons BA Hons Goldsmiths' College London (*English, Theatre Studies, Head of Drama, House Assistant – Eleanora Almond*)

Mrs Kate McMillan, BSc Earth Science, PGDE (*Head of Geography, House Assistant – Balcarres*) [Maternity Leave]

Ms Jenny Mcque, BA, ALCM, LLCM (*Music – Clarinet/Saxophone*)

Ms Carole Melrose (*Music – Double Bass*)

Miss May Millburn-Fryer, BA Hons Sport (*Head of Girls Games, House Assistant – Holm*)

Mrs Fiona S Monk, PGCE, TESOL, BA Hons (*Economics and Business Studies, Assistant Housemistress – Seton*)

Ms Isabella Morton, MBA (*Part time Teacher of Mandarin*)

Ms Alexandra Opie, PGCE, BA Hons (*English, House Assistant – Holm*)

Mr David R Pierce, BSc Hons Maths Stats, PGCE Maths (*Head of Mathematics, Alis Coordinator*)

Mrs Johanna Prior, MA Oxon, PGDE, GTCS (*Head of Fourth and Fifth Form, English, UCAS, Debating, House Assistant – Hope*)

Mr Martin Presavage, BMus Performance Hons, PG Dip Mus Performance Dist, PG Dip Mus (*Music – Guitar*)

Mrs Nicola Presavage, BA Mus (*Music – Percussion*)

Dr Richard Phillips, BSc Astrophhysics, PGCE, BSc Geology, DPhil (*Physics/Science teacher, House Assistant – Pinkie*)

Mr Colin Pryde, Institute of Piping (*Pipe Major and Instructor*)

Mrs Kim Reid, BSc Biomedical Sciences (*Senior Science Technician, Assistant Housemistress – Hope*)

Miss Ana Rodriguez (*Spanish Assistant*)

Mrs J Katie Rudge, BSc Biochemistry, PGCE (*Chemistry, SAT Supervisor, Assistant House Mistress – Balcarres*)

Mrs Elspeth Scott, MA Fine Art (*Art*)

Mr Ryan Scott, Advanced PGA Professional, PG Dip, UKCC Level 3, QCF, (*Golf Professional*)

Mr Scott Smith, PG Dip, PGA Assistant Professional (*Golf Assistant Professional*)

Ms Clare Stubbs, Dip SMS, MMus, PGCE (*Music – Singing*)

Mr Peter R B Sutton, AKC, BD, MTh, PG Cert Counselling (*Chaplain. Head of Religious Studies*)

Ms Samantha Tassiker, BA Hons, PGCE, MEd (*English, House Assistant – Holm*) [Maternity Leave]

Dr David Tidswell, PGCE, PhD, BA (*Head of History and Politics,*)

Dr Michael G Topping, BSc Hons, PhD Zoology, PGCE Biology and General Science (*Biology, Director of Academic Progress*)

Mr Richard I Valentine, BSc Hons, Adv PGA Professional, UKCC Level 4, PG Dip (*Director of Golf*)

Mr Scott Walsh (*Music – Snare Drum*)

Mrs Susannah Ward, BSc, PGCE (*Head of Science, Chemistry*)

Mr Roger P Whait, BSc, CDipAF, PGCE (*Maths, Coordinator of Activities,Examinations Officer*)

Ms Lucy Willmott, BSc Hons Zoology, PGCE Science Biology (*Head of Biology, House Assistant – Hope, Duke of Edinburgh's Award Coordinator/Manager*)

Mrs Ginny Wilson, BMus Performance, PG Dip, MMus (*Music – Singing*)

Ms Jenny Woodhead (*Geography, House Assistant – Balcarres*) [Maternity Cover]

Mr Paul (*Ged*) Woolley (*Contingent Commander of the CCF, House Assistant Hope and Seton*)

Ms Jacqueline Young, BA, Cert TESOL (*English as a Second Language*)

Houses and Housemasters/Housemistresses:

Boys Boarding:
Hope House: G Harbison
Seton House: A Keulemans
Pinkie House: N Allen

Girls Boarding:
Balcarres House: Mrs S Meadows
Holm House: Mrs M Galloway
Eleanora Almond House: Mrs Y McLean-Steel

Day (Boys and Girls):
Schoolhouse: W D Dickinson

Bursar: S Howard
Director of Communications: J Hewat
Director of Admissions: Mrs F Gordon
Director of Development: R Baird

Junior School
Head: P Meadows, MA Hons, PGCE

Staff:
Mrs E Burgess, BEd Hons (*Head of Early Years / Year 2*)
Mrs N Coleman, BMus Hons (*Early Years Music and Drama*)
Mrs A Gauld, DCE, ACE (*Year 2*)
Mrs S Gold, BEd Hons (*Year 5*)
K Hutchison, DipTMus (*Director of Music – Junior School*)
J Jackman, BA Hons, PGDE (*Year 6*)
Mrs F Kelly, BA Hons, PGCE (*Support for Learning*)
Mrs S Keulemans BEd Hons (*Year 4*)
Mrs F Ferguson, BSc Hons, PGDE (*Year 5*)
Mrs E Károlyi, MA Hons, PGCE (*Director of Studies – Junior School*)
Miss S A Kettlewell, BA (*Art and Drama*)
P McDouall, MA Hons, PGDE (*Year 7*)
Mrs K MacKinnon, MA Hons, PGDE (*Year 6*)
D J Pearce, BSc Hons (*Year 7*)

Mrs S Scott, BEd Hons (*Year 2*)
Miss K Seabra, BEd Hons (*Year 1*)
Mrs J Selley (*Classroom Assistant*)
Mrs C Robertson, DipEd (*Nursery Teacher*)
Mrs E Shaw, BA Hons, PGCE (*Year 3*)
Mrs K Wells, BA, PGDE (*French Nursery–Year 6*)

Loughborough Grammar School

Burton Walks, Loughborough, Leicestershire LE11 2DU

Tel:	01509 233233
Fax:	01509 218436
email:	admissions@lesgrammar.org
website:	www.lesgrammar.org

Motto: *Vires acquirit eundo.*

Loughborough Grammar School was founded in 1495 by Thomas Burton, Merchant of the Staple of Calais, though it is probable that the Trustees of the Town Charity were managing a free school well before that date. The School is itself part of a larger 'family' known as the Loughborough Endowed Schools. Situated in the spacious and attractive grounds surrounding the Grammar School are Loughborough High School for Girls (*see GSA entry*) and Fairfield School, our co-educational Preparatory School (*see IAPS entry*). Links between all three are very strong.

There are just under 1,000 boys in the School, including 60 boarders.

The School moved to its present site of some 27 acres in 1852 and is situated away from the centre of the town in attractive grounds containing the beautiful avenues of trees known as Burton Walks. At its centre is a handsome Victorian College quadrangle. There has been an impressive development programme in recent years – a new Music School was opened in September 2006; a new state-of-the-art Chemistry building in September 2009; a refurbished and extended Biology building in September 2011; a new Physics building in September 2012 and a new Mathematics building and boarding provision in 2013, completing the Science Park.

Admission. Entry to the School is by the school's own examination at all levels and also by Common Entrance at 13+. Sixth Form entry is dependent on GCSE results and interview with the Headmaster and other senior staff.

Boarding Arrangements. Boys are admitted to Denton House at the age of 10 or over; Sixth Form boys are in School House. Termly and Weekly boarding is available.

Fees per term (2016–2017). Day £3,925 (includes books and stationery); Full Boarding £8,643 (includes laundry, board, medical attendance).

The School offers a 25% boarding fee remission to sons of HM Forces and sons of Clergy.

Scholarships and Bursaries. A number of Scholarships are offered at 10+, 11+ and 13+/Common Entrance, based on performance in the Entrance Examination. Sixth Form scholarships are based on GCSE results. Choral and instrumental scholarships are also awarded at 10+, 11+, 13+/Common Entrance and Sixth Form. There are also a number of bursaries, dependent on parental income.

Foundation Bursaries. Free or discounted places based on financial need are offered for boys entering the school at 11+ (Year 7) and 13+ (Year 9). Such places are means-tested and an application for one requires the completion of a form declaring income, an interview with the Headmaster and, in some cases, a home visit.

Religious Teaching. The School is non-denominational though there is a strong Christian tradition. The Chaplain teaches Religion and Philosophy but is available for boys at any convenient time. On Wednesdays, Boarders attend the School Chapel and, on request, are prepared for Confirmation by the Chaplain.

Curriculum. The aim of the School is to give a broad and balanced general education to GCSE with greater specialisation afterwards. In Year 6, boys follow a curriculum similar to that of their last year of junior school; subjects included are English, Mathematics, Art, Sciences, Drama, Design and Technology, Geography, IT, History, Music, PE, RE. In Year 7, all boys study English, Mathematics, Biology, Chemistry, Physics, French, History, Geography, Latin, and Music. Additionally, all boys have lessons in RE, PE, PSHE and Games. In Year 8, Design and Technology and Classical Civilisation are introduced and, in addition to French, boys choose a second language from either German or Spanish, and the boys are taught separate sciences. In Year 9 pupils continue with both MFLs, and make some choices from their existing subjects as well as Ancient Greek and Drama.

In Years 10 and 11, for GCSE, boys study English Language and Literature, Mathematics, a modern Foreign Language, and at least two sciences. They also choose three subjects from an extensive options list. Some more able boys study a tenth subject.

The Sixth Form contains 300 boys. In Year 12, boys study 4 subjects to AS Level and in Year 13 they will take 3 or 4 of them to A2 Level. A wide range of subjects and combinations is available, along with General Studies, EPQ, Games and other activities. There are some joint teaching lessons with the Girls' High School.

Games. The School has an excellent First XI field and a junior field of over 13 acres within its precinct and within two miles are well-equipped playing fields extending to nearly 70 acres.

The School runs teams in Rugby, Soccer, Hockey, Cricket, Athletics, Tennis, Cross Country, Swimming, Badminton, Fencing and Squash. In addition there is a Sailing and Canoe Club. The School prides itself in an array of Mind Sports, with teams in Bridge, Chess, Go and Chinese Chess.

Combined Cadet Force. There is an efficient and keen CCF of about 250 boys from Year 10 onwards, run on an optional basis, with 17 Officers, an SSI and a RQMS. Boys have the choice of joining the RAF, Army or Royal Navy Sections. The CCF complex is purpose-built with excellent facilities and many varied and Adventurous Training courses are available to members.

Scouts. There is a flourishing Scout Troop of 35 boys and 1 Scouter.

Duke of Edinburgh's Award Scheme. Over 250 boys are actively involved in the scheme and each year a large number earn Gold, Silver and Bronze awards.

Music (of which most is joint with the Girls' High School) takes place in our award-winning music school, which has "All-Steinway School" status, and instrumental ensembles involve all the schools in the Foundation. For boys at LGS, there are 4 Choirs, 3 Orchestras, 3 Wind Bands, 3 Jazz Bands and over twenty smaller instrumental ensembles, which rehearse weekly. Our top ensembles perform on the national stage regularly, and there are annual music tours and residencies for instrumental and vocal groups alike: recent tours have taken in Barcelona (2014), Truro (2015) and Prague (2016). Our sacred choirs sing services regularly at cathedrals around the UK, having performed in Southwell Minster, as well as Coventry, Birmingham, Leicester, Gloucester and Worcester Cathedrals in the past couple of years. We put on a large-scale concert each spring at De Montfort Hall, involving all Year 7 pupils and other choirs performing a choral masterpiece (Carmina Burana, Mozart's Requiem, Rutter's Magnificat) with our symphony orchestra.

Drama. The School has a fine Studio/Theatre and all boys in Years 6, 7 and 8 participate in a dramatic production.

After that, there are productions for other age groups in conjunction with the Girls' High School each term.

Careers. Careers advisors are available to inform boys on options for their futures, with special regard to University or Professional careers. The School is a member of the Independent Schools Careers Organisation.

Academic Successes. An average of 10 boys per year gain admission to Oxford and Cambridge, and over 98% each year begin degree courses at Universities.

The Loughburians Alumni Association. All former pupils of the school have automatic free membership to the Loughborough Endowed Schools alumni association. All enquiries to info@loughburians.com.

Charitable status. Loughborough Endowed Schools is a Registered Charity, number 1081765, and a Company Limited by Guarantee, registered in England, number 4038033. Registered Office: 3 Burton Walks, Loughborough, Leicestershire LE11 2DU.

Governing Body:
Chairman: Mr G P Fothergill, BA
Deputy Chairman: Mr H M Pearson, DL, DUniv Hon, BA Econ

Vice-Chairs:
Mrs M Gershlick
Professor J Feather, MA, PhD, FRSA
Dr P Cannon, MA Cantab, BM BCh Oxon, FRCS, MRCGP
Professor A Dodson, BSc Hons, PhD, DSc

Co-optative Governors:
Mr P Alexander
Professor R Allison, BA, PhD
Mrs E K Critchley, MA Oxon
The Lady Gretton, JP, Lord-Lieutenant of Leicestershire, LLD Hon, DUni Hon, Hon DLitt
Mr R Harrison, MA Cantab, Dip Arch RIBA
Mr P M Jackson, FIMI
Mrs K Jenkins
Mr A D Jones, BA, FCA
Professor J Ketley, BSc Hons, PhD Bham, CBiol, MSB
Mrs R J E Limb, MA Cantab
M Mulla, BSc, MSc, MIM
Mrs P O'Neill, MA Cantab
Mrs G Richards, BA Hons, MEd, Hon EdD
Admiral Sir Trevor Soar, KCB, OBE, DEng Hon, FCMI
Mr J Stone

Nominated Governor:
Sister C Leydon

Ex-Officio Governors:
Dr A de Bono, MA, MB, FRCGP, FFOM (*Bursary Committee member*)
Dr P J B Hubner, MB, FRCP, DCH, FACC, FESC (*Bursary Committee member*)

Foundation Secretary & Treasurer: J Doherty

Headmaster: Mr D J Byrne, MA, MEd Trinity College Cambridge

Deputy Headmasters:
Dr T G Willmott, BSc, PhD London, MBA Leicester
Dr C G Walker, MA Glasgow, DPhil Balliol College Oxford

Assistant Headmaster (*Pastoral*): Mr A J Dossett, BSc Loughborough
Assistant Headmaster (*Staff*): Mr B McCabe, MA Balliol College Oxford

Director of Studies: Dr R C Healey, BEng London, PhD Pembroke College Cambridge
Head of Sixth Form: Mr R B Parish, BSc, MSc Bristol

Chaplain: The Revd D R Owen, BA Natal, HDE Natal, BA Hons Natal, MTh Rhodes
Director of Admissions/Marketing: Mr C J Feakes, BSc Leicester, MSc Leicester
Director of Boarding: Mrs D P Briers

Academic Departments:
* *Head of Department*

Art and Design:
*Miss E E Johnson, BA Loughborough
Miss S L Mackie, BA Nottingham Trent
Miss E Notman, BA Cumbria

Biology:
*Mrs M C Herring, BSc St Andrews
Mr R B Parish, BSc, MSc Bristol
Miss E S R Clingain, MSc Nottingham
Mr J S Parton, MA Girton College Cambridge (*Head of Year 7*)
Dr A D Waters, BSc Cambridge, PhD Bristol
Dr T G Willmott, BSc, PhD London, MBA Leicester
Mr L N Mantell, BA Oxford
Dr A J Bingham, BSc, PhD Southampton
Dr P S Rhodes BSc, PhD Nottingham

Chemistry:
*Mr B J Arrowsmith, BSc Leeds
Dr R J Ball, BSc, PhD Queen's Belfast (*Head of Yates*)
Dr N M A Ebden, BSc Nottingham, PhD Nottingham
Mr C B Faust, BSc Manchester, MEd Nottingham, CChem, FRSC (*Head of Sixth Form Enrichment*)
Mr P M Marlow, BSc Durham, PGCE Homerton College Cambridge
Mr T D Morse, BSc Sheffield, MSc Dundee
Dr P S Rhodes BSc, PhD Nottingham (*Head of Pulteney*)

Classics:
*Mr N D Pollock, BA, Queens' College Cambridge
Dr N Lipatov-Chicherin, BA, PhD University of St Petersburg
Mr P L Harper, MA Corpus Christi College Oxford
Mr R N Fielden, MA Trinity College Cambridge

Computing and Information Technology:
*Mr R Statham, BSc Open
Mrs D Kaur, BA Wolverhampton (*Head of Information Technology*)
Mr D M Starkings, BSc Nottingham, BA Open
Mrs C M Winship, BSc Reading

Design and Technology:
*Mr P P A Jackson, BSc Nottingham Trent
Mr R Michalak, BA Bristol
Mr T A Moseley, BA Loughborough

Drama:
*Mrs S Bruton, BA Liverpool John Moores
Miss R L Hooper, BA De Montfort University

Economics and Business Studies:
*Mr R J Lightfoot, BA Birmingham, MA Warwick
Ms S A Bell, BA York
Mrs H E James, BA Durham, Dip ABRSM
Mr G I Sutcliffe, BA Rhodes South Africa

English:
*Mr R M Hunter, MA St Andrews
Mr B McCabe, MA Balliol College Oxford
Dr K Buckley, BA Birmingham, MA Cardiff, PhD Cardiff
Mrs S Daya, BA South Africa
Miss RM Hannah, BA Lancaster, MLitt Glasgow
Mr A J N Morris, BA Reading (*Assistant Head of Sixth Form*)
Mrs A J Quigley, BA New College Oxford
Miss A Whitehead, BA Warwick

Miss S Rouse, MA Durham
Mr M Sollars, BA Loughborough

Geography:
*Mr M D Butcher, BSc Lancaster, MSc Lancaster
Mr D L Evans, BSc Reading
Mr N A Hewitt, BSc Leicester, MSc DIC, Imperial, FGS
Mr I O G Potter, BSc Southampton
Mrs D Outwin-Flinders, BEd Bristol
Miss S E Durden, BA Leicester

History and Politics:
*Mr C W Blackman, BA Bristol
Mr M I Dawkins, BA De Montfort, MA De Montfort
   (*Head of Politics*)
Miss S H Jenkins, BA UCL (*Head of Year 9*)
Mr D J Murphy, BA Oxford
Dr C G Walker, MA Glasgow, DPhil Balliol College
   Oxford
Mr P J Dowsett, BA Nottingham (*Head of EPQ*)
Dr T J McKay, BA Leicester
Miss S E Durden, BA Leicester

Mathematics:
*Dr C J Luke, BSc Sidney Sussex College Cambridge, PhD
   Manchester
Miss N Bahl, BSc Loughborough (*Head of Year 8*)
Dr D C Barrett, BSc Nottingham, PhD Loughborough
Mr R Bhattacharyya, BA Trinity College Cambridge
Mrs R L Cooch, BSc East Anglia
Mr A J Dossett, BSc Loughborough
Mr D A Happer, BSc Loughborough
Mr C J Feakes, BSc Leicester, MSc Leicester
Mrs R French, BEd Leeds (*Head of Year 10*)
Mr P Gacs, MSc Budapest (*Head of Abney*)
Mr S D Hatfield, BEng Sheffield (*Head of Year 11*)
Dr R C Healey, BEng London, PhD Pembroke College
   Cambridge
Mr J D Jackson, BSc Nottingham (*Head of Davys*)
Mr D M Starkings, BSc Nottingham, BA Open
Mr T J Pearson, BSc Birmingham

Modern Languages:
*Mr M M Jackson, BA Leeds (*Head of Spanish*)
Mr R F Kerr, MA Queen's College Oxford (*Head of
   German*)
Miss Z Mir, LLB Leicester, LPC Guildford (*Head of
   French*)
Mrs H J Coles, BA London
Mrs L E Gosling, BA Churchill College Cambridge
Mrs N V Lorente, BA Zaragoza, BA Barcelona
Ms V M Perino, BA Nottingham
Mr D Reavie, BA Hull
Mr R Ward, BSc Salford
Mr B Korosi, BA Durham

Music:
*Mr R J West, MSc, BA, LGSMD, LRSM, PGCert
   MusTech, PGCE (*Director of LES Music School*)
Mrs N M Adkinson BA Durham (*Deputy Director of LES
   Music*)
Dr P J Underwood, MA Downing College Cambridge,
   MMus London, PhD Birmingham, FRCO CHM, FTCL,
   LRAM, ARCM, ADCM, FCIEA (*Head of Senior
   Curriculum Music*)
Mrs A McGee, GTCL, LTCL, CSAT (*Head of Junior
   School Music*)
Miss C Revell, BMus (*KS3 Coordinator*)
Mr N Ellum, BA (*Class Music Teacher*)
Mr A Geary, GLCM (*Head of Percussion*)
Mr D Morris, LRAM (*Head of Vocal Studies*)
Miss M Reinhard, ARCT, LPRCM (*Head of Keyboard*)

Instrumental Teachers:
Dr A P Bean, BMus, LRAM, AMusD (*Piano*)
Mr J W Bean, LRAM, LGSM {MT}, Cert Ed (*Cello*)
Mr P Bennett, LTCL, FTCL (*Brass*)
Mr J Boyd, Dip Mus (*Guitar*)
Mrs K Burns, BA Birmingham, LLCM, ALCM, CSAT
   (*Head of Strings*)
Mr D Cowen, MA, FRCO, LRSM (*Piano, Organ*)
Mrs S Douglas, ARCM, ABSM (*Clarinet & Saxophone*)
   CertEd
Mrs K Geary, GLCM (*Violin, Viola*)
Mrs A Gillies-Loach, GMus Huddersfield, LTCL, LRSM
   (*Flute*)
Mr C L Groom, RMAM (*Brass*)
Miss J Kirkwood, BMus, AdvPGDip Music {professional
   performance} (*Flute*)
Mrs C A Lee, LRAM, Prof Cert RAM (*Violin and Viola,
   Piano*)
Mr W Mee, LRAM (*Brass*)
Mrs J Neal, JP, BA (*Voice*)
Mr M Newnham, BA (*Percussion*)
Mrs A Parker, BA, ABRSM (*Piano, Flute*)
Miss F Richardson, LRAM (*Guitar*)
Mr A Thomas, MMus, BMus (*Guitar*)
Mr C White, ACRM, Dip RCM (*Violin, Viola*)
Miss S Vermeulen, BMus (*Harp*)
Mrs K Goss, BLIB, LTCL, FTCL (*Bassoon*)
Miss S Griffiths, BA, PG Dip WCMD (*Oboe*)
Miss C Slominska, BMus (*Percussion*)
Mrs V Watson, BA, PGDip (*Clarinet, Saxophone*)
Ms J Saunders, LRAM (*Voice*)

Physical Education:
*Mr M S E Broadley, BA Leeds
Mr M I Gidley (*i/c Cricket*)
Mr D J Miles, BSc Loughborough (*Senior Housemaster, i/c
   Cross Country*)
Mr E O Lewis, BSc UWIC (*i/c Rugby*)
Mr J Clarke (*i/c Hockey*)

Physics:
*Mr G J Kerr, BSc Birmingham
Miss K Cartwright, BEng Birmingham
Dr R M Green, BSc Nottingham, PhD Nottingham
Mr N B Khan, BSc Bangladesh, MSc London
Mr A Lloyd, BSc Leicester
Mr R C Wright, BEd Nottingham Trent

PSHE:
*Dr C Livingstone, BA, MA, PhD Durham

Religion and Philosophy:
*The Revd D R Owen, BA Natal, HDE Natal, BA Hons
   Natal, MTh Rhodes (*Chaplain*)
Mr D E Berner, BA Durham (*i/c Football*)
Dr C Livingstone, BA, MA, PhD Durham
Mrs M Hiebert, BA Chester College

Year 6: Mrs M L Marlow, BSc Nottingham Trent

Head of Learning Support: Mrs H L Baker, BEd Bedford,
   PG Dip Dyslexia and Literacy
Head of Careers: Mr R J Lightfoot, BA Birmingham, MA
   Warwick
PA to the Headmaster: Mrs K Rajput
Librarian: Mrs V Bunn, ALA
Examinations' Officer: Miss S A Hawkins, BSc
   Birmingham
Catering Manageress: Mrs J Johnstone, Mrs H M North
Medical Officer: Dr P M Cannon, MA, BMBCh, FRCS,
   MRCGP, Dip Occ Med
School Nurses: Mrs J Bryan, RGN; Mrs N Krarup, RGN
OC CCF: Lt Col J W Doherty, HAC

CCF SSI: Mr M J Hall
Head of Duke of Edinburgh's Award: Mr P T Moffett, BA
Derby

Magdalen College School
Oxford

Oxford OX4 1DZ

Tel: 01865 242191
Fax: 01865 240379
email: admissions@mcsoxford.org
website: www.mcsoxford.org

Motto: *Sicut Lilium.*

Magdalen College School consists of 595 boys aged 7–16 with a co-educational Sixth Form of 305. Academic standards are amongst the highest in the country and there is a strong emphasis on study beyond the syllabus, most of all in the Waynflete Studies programme, which allows Sixth Formers to develop a personal project which is finally supervised by university academics. Almost all pupils go on to higher education with about a third each year progressing to Oxford or Cambridge. The school seeks to develop the individuality and interests of each pupil. There is a strong emphasis on extra-curricular activity, with particularly proud traditions in sport, music and drama. The school was Sunday Times Independent School of the year in 2004–5 and again in 2008–9.

History. William of Waynflete, born in 1398, rose from unexceptional social origins to become Bishop of Winchester and Lord Chancellor. Having been Headmaster of Winchester, school of the church, and Provost of Eton, school of the court, he determined to use his wealth to repay his debt to the transformative power of education. He determined to found something altogether new, a school of that exciting and rapidly expanding proposition – the university. This school would link primary, secondary and tertiary education in a novel way, and be named after his patron saint, Mary Magdalen.

Magdalen College School opened in 1480, and rapidly acquired an international reputation as a pioneer of new renaissance methods of learning. Early Masters included Thomas Wolsey, early pupils Richard Hooker, John Foxe, Thomas More and William Tyndale. The school, which from an early stage provided choristers for the College choir, was accommodated entirely in College until the late 19th century, when expanding numbers led to the acquisition and erection of buildings on the other side of the Cherwell, opposite the University Botanical Gardens and adjacent to St Hilda's College. Today's school still occupies this picturesque and privileged site.

Buildings. The school buildings include a Chapel which also serves as a theatre, a library, classrooms, science laboratories, Music School and art department. New science laboratories were opened in 1991 and totally refurbished in 2001. The expanded Junior School was opened in 1993. New classrooms, lecture theatre, Careers Centre and a Sixth Form Centre were opened in September 1998. In June 2001, a £2m sports complex was opened. In 2002, additional science laboratories were provided and in 2005, the school opened its new Sir Basil Blackwell library. In Autumn 2008 a new building was opened which houses a modern refectory, the Art and Design department, Senior Common Room and reception. In 2010 a redesigned and enlarged Sixth Form Common Room was opened, to accommodate and welcome the first intake of Sixth Form girls, and the computer suites were refurbished in 2011. In 2012 the Sports Hall was extended to incorporate a studio and additional classrooms, and a climbing wall has also been added. A new

building programme has been agreed by the Governors and work started in August 2016.

Pastoral. From 7–11, boys are in form groups. Their Tutor is responsible for day-to-day care, pastoral welfare and academic progress. Boys from age 11 and Sixth Form girls are allocated to one of the six Houses. Houses are divided into eight Houserooms. A Housemaster or Tutor in charge of each section is responsible for the pastoral and academic welfare of pupils in his or her Houseroom. The Heads of Departments, SENCO, Chaplain and Matron also play their part in the pastoral organisation.

Organisation and Curriculum. All boys study a core of subjects to GCSE level, consisting of English, Maths, Science and at least one modern foreign language. In addition, there is a wide variety of options taken by pupils in their GCSE years including Latin and Greek, Geography, German, Spanish, History, Computing and Art. There is no streaming and very little setting.

Pupils study four subjects in the Lower Sixth and sit rigorous internal exams in the Trinity Term. Pupils have the opportunity to focus on just three subjects in the Upper Sixth, but a significant proportion sit four or even five A Levels. MCS has a busy curriculum in the Sixth Form, as well as their A Levels, all pupils complete an independent research project (Waynflete Studies), follow a course in Thinking Skills, have Games sessions and take part in our Community Service Programme. The provision is further enriched by regular seminars and lectures delivered by members of the MCS community and visiting speakers.

Careers. There is a well-equipped Careers Room, and there is a team of Careers Staff. Careers Aptitude Tests are offered to all boys in the Fifth Form, and there is a regular programme of careers workshops.

Games and Societies. In addition to Physical Education which is taught in the curriculum, games play a major part in the School. Major sports are rugby in the Michaelmas Term, hockey and rowing in Hilary, and cricket, rowing and tennis in the Trinity Term. Other sports include basketball, football, fencing, cross-country, sailing and athletics. There are Army and Air Force sections of the CCF and a Community Service Organisation. Many pupils participate in the Duke of Edinburgh's Award scheme. Girls from Oxford High School participate in the CCF.

The main playing field, surrounded by the River Cherwell, adjoins the grounds of School House and covers 11 acres. In addition, the school enjoys the daily use of the adjacent Christ Church playing fields, and also uses regularly a number of other university sporting and cultural facilities. An additional field of 13 acres with its own pavilion and changing rooms has been developed at Sandford-on-Thames, three miles from the school. The school also has use of the Magdalen College sports fields one mile from the School.

Music is extremely important in the school and there is a large Choral Society, a Madrigal Group, Senior and Junior Orchestras, a Jazz Band and other ensembles. Many pupils are involved in drama and there are several productions in the year. There are many other societies and clubs covering cultural and recreational activities. The main school concert is held annually in the Sheldonian Theatre. The school is the founder and main sponsor of the Oxford Festival of Arts which features events throughout the City and pupils throughout the county take part.

Admission. The main entry points are at 7, 8, 9, 11, 13 and 16. Around 25 boys are taken at 7, a further 15 or so at 8 and 9, and about 70 at the age of 11. Up to 25 boys are taken at 13. Around 60 boys and girls join the school directly into the Sixth Form.

Admission at ages 7, 8, 9 and 11 is by a School Entrance Examination held in January or February each year.

Admission at age 13 is by pre-test at 11 followed by the Common Entrance Examination for most candidates at preparatory schools and by a School Entrance Examination held in March each year for candidates at maintained schools.

Offers of Sixth Form places are made after interview, and are conditional on good GCSE grades.

Candidates can be registered at any age. Full particulars can be obtained from the Registrar.

Term of Entry. Pupils enter the school in September. Exceptionally, for example if parents move into the Oxford area, other arrangements can be made.

Fees per term (2016–2017). Day pupils: £5,705 (Years 5–13); £5,495 (Years 3 and 4). They are payable in advance and are inclusive of textbooks and stationery. The Registration Fee (non-returnable) is currently £75.

Scholarships, Exhibitions and Bursaries. Scholarships, Exhibitions and Governors' Presentation Awards are awarded at all points of entry.

Bursaries are available subject to testing of parental means. Ogden Trust Sixth Form Scholarships are available to candidates of sufficient merit from state schools.

At age 13, up to 16 Scholarships of up to £300 are awarded each year based on the results of a two-day scholarship examination in February. Candidates should be under 14 on the subsequent 1 September. Closing date for entries: 13 January.

Music, Art, Drama and Sports Scholarships are awarded each year on the results of assessments held in January (Music), February (Art and Drama) and November (Sports). Music award holders also receive free tuition in one instrument.

Further information can be obtained from the Registrar.

Choristerships. There are 16 Choristerships. Entry is by Voice Trial and candidates should normally be between the ages of 7 and 9. For a Chorister two-thirds of the tuition fee is remitted. All enquiries about Choristerships should be addressed to the *Informator Choristarum, Magdalen College, Oxford OX1 4AU.* Choristers normally continue at the school after their voices have broken. In deserving cases, further financial help may be available.

Honours. Almost all pupils go on to higher education when they leave – to Oxford and Cambridge and other universities.

Old Waynfletes. Representative Old Waynfletes of the 20th century include Olympic athlete and soldier, Noel Chavasse, VC and bar; bookseller Sir Basil Blackwell; Nobel Prize winner Sir Tim Hunt; composer Ivor Novello; educationalist Tom Wheare; theatre directors John Caird and Sam Mendes, and sports commentators Nigel Starmer Smith and Jim Rosenthal.

Contact: Waynflete Office, Magdalen College School, email: waynfleteoffice@mcsoxford.org.

Charitable status. Magdalen College School Oxford Limited is a Registered Charity, number 295785. Its aims and objectives are to promote and provide for the education of children.

Governors:
T P W Edwards (*Chairman*)

Dr C Benson	Dr S Mackenzie
Ms P Cameron Watt	Ms J Philips
Professor C Coussios	N P Record
Mr A James	Dr N P V Richardson
Mrs S Kerr Dineen	The Revd Canon K H
Prof Dr D Kroening	Wilkinson
Mrs J Brooks Longworth	Mr P Withers
	C G Young

Master: **Miss Helen Pike**, MA Oxon, MA Michigan, MA London

Usher: T G Beaumont, MA (*History*)

Deputy Head (Academic): B D White, BA (*Mathematics*)
Deputy Head (Education Learning): Dr A K Cotton, BA, MA, MSt, DPhil (*Classics*)

Teaching Staff:
* *Head of Department/Subject*

Miss F J Amswych, BA (**Learning Support*)
S J Andrews, MSc, MPhil (*Mathematics*)
Ms S-J Arthurs, BSc (*Physics*)
G C Atkin, BSc (*Rowing Professional*)
Miss J C Attia, MA (*French*)
A J Awcock, BsC MA (*Rugby Professional*)
A Baker-Munton, MA (*French and German*)
D S Barr, BA, MA (*English*)
Miss E J Beardmore, MA, MSc (*Physics*)
D Bebbington, BSc, DPhil (**Cricket, Chemistry*)
Dr C L Bell, BSc, MPhil, DPhil (*Chemistry*)
A T Berry, BA (*Tutor to Choristers*)
T D Booth, MA (**Geography*)
C J Boyle, BA (*PE, Games*)
N D Brittain, BA (**French, German*)
M R Burchett, BSc, MSc (**Junior School Sport*)
Dr J C Carter, MA, MA, MSt, DPhil (**Theology*)
Miss E H Churcher, MA, LRSM (*Music*)
B W Cole, MA (**Classics*)
A C Cooper, MSc, BA (*Senior Teacher, Mathematics*)
T P Cooper, BSc (*Head of Middle School, Mathematics*)
J D Cullen, MA (**Director of Music*)
A Duncan (*Cricket*)
E Dupee, BSc (*PE Coordinator*)
Mrs L D Earnshaw, MA (**Mathematics*)
T J Elton, MMath (*Mathematics*)
A England, MA (*Deputy Head of Lower Sixth Academic, Deputy Head of Mathematics*)
Dr S Floate, BSc (*Chemistry*)
B Ford BSc (*PE and Games*)
Mrs L Frith Powell, BA (*Art*)
Mrs M-J Gago, BA (**Spanish*)
Mrs J L Gladstone, MA (**Biology*)
C E Hack, MSc (**Physics*)
Mrs D Hackett, BEng (*Junior School*)
Dr R Hamer, BA, DPhil (*Biology*)
R Hemingway, BA (*Head of Lower School, *History*)
Miss J E Henman, BA (*Geography*)
A G Hepworth, BSc (**Economics*)
Mrs H C Hinze, BA (*English*)
N J Hinze, BA (**Chemistry*)
Dr C Howell, BA, MA, DPhil (*History, Learning Support*)
T P Hunter, BA (*Artist in Residence*)
Mrs C Kelly-Eldridge, BMus, MA (*Junior School*)
Mrs A C S Kenyon, MA (*NQT Mentor, Classics*)
A I Kostyanovsky, BA, PhD (*Deputy Head of Sixth Form Waynflete Studies, Theology*)
Revd Dr Tess Kuin-Lawton, BA, MPhil, DPhil (*Chaplain, Theology*)
Mrs R E Lambert, BSc (*Deputy Head of Sixth Form Pastoral, Biology*)
Mrs C A C Lewis, BA, MEng (*Mathematics*)
C-W Liu, BA (*French*)
O Marjot, BA, MA (*French*)
P J McDonald, MA (*Director of Higher Education, Classics*)
Dr E C McKenzie-Edwards, BSc, MBBS (*Medical Admissions Advisor*)
A J McLarin, BA, MA (*History, Politics*)
J Methven, DPhil (*Deputy Head of English*)
St J E J Mitchard, BA, MA (*Special Educational Needs*)
Miss N M Moloney, BA (**Junior School Music*)
E Monaghan, BA (*Deputy Head of Upper Sixth Pastoral, Deputy Head of English*)
Mrs L A Moylan, BA (*Spanish*)

C E Newbury, BA (*Junior School Director of Studies*)
J C Otley, BA (**Art*)
S Pahl, BSc (**Head of Tennis*)
J K Panton, MSc, MPhil, DPhil (**Politics, Philosophy*)
T J Parker, MA (*Chemistry*)
Mrs H C Parry, BSc (*Chemistry*)
L A Pearce, MA (*Mathematics*)
C Pearson, BSc, DPhil (**Head of Sixth Form, Biology*)
M Penton, BA (*Surmaster, Deputy Head of Lower School 3rd Form, PE*)
Dr J C Petersen, BSc, PhD (*Physics*)
Miss L W Pinching, BA (*English*)
J F Place, BA (*Chess*)
R E Presley, MA (*Economics*)
Mrs F J Pritchard, BA (*Deputy Head of Lower Sixth Admissions, Art*)
R Pygott, MA (*Deputy Head of Middle School L4th, Geography*)
T D Quayle, BA (*English*)
C J Reid, BSC, MLitt, MSc (*Physics*)
M H Rigby, MPhys, DPhil (*Physics*)
Miss F Roddis, BA (*Biology*)
Miss K J Rooney, BSc (*Biology*)
A Rush, BA (*Deputy Head of Lower School Extra-curricular, *Design and Technology*)
Mrs H Rutter, BA (*Art*)
A J Scriven (*Cricket*)
G L Seely, BA (**Rugby*)
Miss S Shortland, BA (*Assistant Director of Music*)
P A Shrimpton, MA, MEd, PhD (*Mathematics, *Careers*)
T E Skipwith, BSc (*Head of Junior School*)
P D Smith, MA, LTCL (*Music*)
Mrs J A Soave, BA (*Junior School Learning Support*)
S A Spowart, BA (*Master of Boats*)
Mrs H R Stammers, BA (*Theology, PSHCE*)
Mrs E Stapleton, BHum (*Deputy Head of Junior School*)
L A Stone, BEd, MSc (**Hockey*)
Mrs J A Taylor, BSc (**Rowing, Geography*)
J P Terry, BA, MSt (**Junior School English*)
A D Thomas, BA (**Drama, History*)
J Unwin, BA (**Philosophy, *Sailing*)
D Tuck, BSc (*Tennis Professional*)
J P Unwin, BA (**Philosophy*)
T J M Vallance, BA (*Classics*)
Mrs J M Wade, BA (*Junior School*)
P S Walter, MPhil (**Computing, Mathematics*)
A Watts, BSc (**Director of Sport*)
T R Williams, BA (**Coaching Education*)
Mrs C E Winstone, BA (*Junior School*)
M P Wood, BA (*Deputy Head of Upper Sixth Academic, History*)

Assistant Music Staff:

Miss M Ackrill (*Flute*)
Ms K Bailey (*Saxophone*)
Dr E M Baird (*Violin*)
C Becke (*Piano*)
Ms A Bendy (*Guitar*)
V Bijeloviv (*Piano*)
Ms E H Churcher (*Piano*)
A Cole (*Trombone and Tuba*)
R Cutting (*Trumpet*)
P B Davidson (*Drumkit*)
B G Davies (*Singing*)
T Dawes (*Double Bass, Bass Guitar, Drums*)
Miss J A Ellis (*Violin*)
K Fairbairn (*Percussion, Drums*)
Dr J Faultless (*Horn*)

B J Hall (*Piano*)
Ms E Harre (*Double Bass*)
G Hoddinott, BMus (*Brass*)
Mrs L Howarth, BA, MPerf, MMus (*Singing*)
M R Jones (*Piano*)
P D Judge (*Trombone, Tuba*)
P Manhood (*Guitar*)
Miss E Mantle (*Singing*)
D C McNaughton (*Trumpet*)
Ms V Murby (*Viola*)
Miss M Nasidlak, MA (*Piano*)
J Newell (*Organ*)
T Payne (*Clarinet*)
M Pickett (*Piano*)

W Purefoy (*Singing*)
B P Skipp (*Oboe*)
B Twyford (*Drumkit*)
O Weston, BA (*Saxophone*)

Dr J P Whitworth (*Guitar*)
S J Wilson (*Cello*)
Mrs D J Wyatt (*Violin*)

Clerk to the Governors and Bursar: T M Knowles, BA

PA to the Master: Mrs A Sweeney, BA

Registrar: Mrs B Mallett, MA

Malvern College

College Road, Malvern, Worcestershire WR14 3DF
Tel: 01684 581 500
Fax: 01684 581 617
email: enquiries@malverncollege.org.uk
website: www.malverncollege.org.uk
Twitter: @malverncollege
Facebook: /MalvernCollege

Motto: *Sapiens qui prospicit.* Wise is the one who looks ahead.

Malvern College was founded in 1865 and incorporated by Royal Charter in 1929. The College is co-educational for children aged 13 to 18. There are five girls' Houses and six boys' Houses, each of which accommodates boarding and day pupils. Malvern is a proper boarding school with the majority of its pupils in residence at weekends. It is associated with The Downs Malvern, a co-educational preparatory school for pupils aged 3 to 13 (*for further details, see IAPS entry*).

Malvern College is particularly fortunate in its location. Situated on the lower slopes of the Malvern Hills and close to the centre of Great Malvern, the main College campus commands striking eastward views across the Severn Valley towards the Cotswolds.

The school is justly proud of its high academic standards and the high level of pastoral care it provides. The College was rated 'Outstanding' by Ofsted in its 2010–11 report. In the Sixth Form about half study for the International Baccalaureate and half for A Levels, which gives pupils a real choice of subjects in each course of study. Facilities are excellent: a state-of-the-art science centre has recently been opened in the College's 150th year.

Curriculum. In the Foundation Year (Year 9), pupils study a wide range of subjects. In addition to English, Mathematics, all three Sciences, French, History, Religious Studies, Geography, Art, Drama, Design Technology and Music, nearly all pupils are introduced to a second modern foreign language and most study Latin. All pupils study Debating and web design as well as Physical Education. The object of this year (as in co-curricular activities) is to show pupils as much as possible of what the College has to offer. On entering the Remove (Year 10), pupils choose their GCSE or IGCSE subjects to be taken at the end of the Hundred (Year 11). The compulsory subjects are English, Mathematics, Biology, Chemistry, Physics and one Modern Foreign Language. Pupils also choose optional subjects from Art and Design, Design Technology, Drama, Geography, French, German, History, Latin, Music, Physical Education, Religious Studies and Spanish. Greek is available for those who began it in the Foundation Year (Year 9). A Separate Sciences option enables pupils to extend the core Double Award Science to the three separate science IGCSEs. Pupils choose either four or five options, according to their academic ability. Pupils decide on their choices in consultation with their Tutors, Housemasters/Housemistresses, Heads of Year and parents.

In the Sixth Form, there is a choice between A Levels and the International Baccalaureate. In the IB, combinations of the following subjects are offered: Visual Art, Biology, Chemistry, Business Management, Economics, English, Environmental Systems and Societies, French, German, Geography, Greek, History, Italian, Latin, Mathematics, Further Mathematics, Music, Physics, Spanish, Technology, Philosophy and Sports, Health and Exercise Science. All pupils take the valuable Theory of Knowledge (ToK) Course. A Levels are available in all of the subjects listed above for the IB (except Environmental Systems and Societies and Italian) and also in Classical Civilisation, Photography, Politics, Physical Education and Psychology. Most pupils take three subjects to A Level. Pupils studying A Levels also choose, in addition, one option from the Enrichment Programme, which includes the Extended Project, beginner Italian and beginner Spanish.

Sport. Pupils are offered a range of sports throughout their time at Malvern College. Each term there is a focus on priority sports; for girls these are Hockey in the Autumn term, Netball in the Lent term and Tennis and Athletics in the summer. In addition to these, regular fixtures are offered for girls in Football, Cricket, Badminton, Golf, Fives and Cross Country. The boys' priority sports are Rugby in the Autumn term, Football in the Lent term, and Cricket in the summer. In addition to these, regular fixtures are offered for boys in Hockey, Tennis, Badminton, Golf, Cross Country, Athletics, Squash, Rackets, Basketball and Fives.

The co-curricular activity programme provides an extensive range of physical activity for pupils to engage in to develop their health, fitness, confidence, leadership and social skills.

Exceptionally talented pupils are invited to join the Elite Performance Programme, which comprises specialist strength and conditioning sessions and offers support with lifestyle management and progression through their sport performance pathway. We foster strong links with clubs such as Worcestershire County Cricket Club, Worcester Warriors Rugby Club, Stourport Hockey Club and Malvern Netball Club.

A state-of-the-art Sports Complex includes a 25m swimming pool, a double sports hall (eight badminton courts), a shooting range, squash courts, fitness studio, climbing wall and fitness suite. The Sports Complex has a Cricket Centre which is the official training venue for Worcestershire County Cricket Club. The College has recently refurbished its two Rackets courts, which now offer tournament standard Rackets facilities. In addition there are 10 hard court Tennis/Netball courts and Fives courts. In our extensive playing fields there is a Grandstand overlooking the athletics track, six football/rugby pitches, a water-based all-weather pitch and an all-weather AstroTurf which host regular local club fixtures including the Worcestershire Hockey Junior Development Centres. The Malvern Hills and Peachfield Common offer marvellously challenging terrain for the College's cross-country runners and mountain bikers.

Co-Curricular Activities. Pupils have the opportunity to take part in a range of additional activities such as sailing, trampolining, jewellery-making, volleyball, fencing, photography, golf, polo, cookery, speech & drama, mountainbiking, canoe-polo, kayaking, judo, silversmithing, archery, and Zumba.

The College has a strong tradition of expedition training and outdoor pursuits, including rock-climbing, kayaking, paragliding and mountaineering (summer and winter, UK and abroad). Opportunities exist for the use of the College's cottage in the Brecon Beacons. Annually expeditions go to Scotland and have also recently been to Iceland, the Alps, Malta, Namibia, Costa Rica, Ghana and Swaziland in the school holidays. Many of these activities are an integral part of the voluntary CCF (which has RM, Army and RAF sections) and The Duke of Edinburgh's Award scheme. There is also a flourishing Community Service Volunteering Organisation.

Music is strong at Malvern. Approximately 40% of pupils learn a musical instrument and there are eight musical ensembles including orchestras, concert band, jazz band and choirs. The well-equipped Music School (22 practice rooms, three large rehearsal rooms) includes a soundproofed practice pod for percussion and an IT suite. Attached to the Music School is St Edmund's Hall, a 150-seat recital hall with a fine Steinway piano. Pupils of all standards are encouraged both instrumentally and vocally, and regularly give performances (internal, locally and further afield). Inter-House competitions are held throughout the year. The Music department works collaboratively with the Drama department and the most recent productions were *Grease, Dido and Aeneas* and *Oh What a Lovely War*. The Elite Music Programme offers further opportunities for pupils to meet performers and composers in both the classical and contemporary realm, and to attend concerts and workshops.

Drama is a thriving creative force within the community of the school. Pupils are encouraged to play a full part in all aspects of theatre, whether as actor, theatre maker or technician. This might be through academic study at GCSE or A Level, participation in the many co-curricular productions staged each year, or the annual House Drama Competition. Recent productions staged in the College's Theatre include *The Great Gatsby, Henry V, The Sound of Music, Noughts and Crosses, The Odyssey, A Midsummer Night's Dream, South Pacific, Jane Eyre, Blue Stockings, Private Peaceful* and *Les Misérables School Edition*. Speech and Drama tuition is a popular option for many, with pupils receiving preparation for LAMDA examinations or local public speaking festivals. Regular attendance at the Malvern Theatres in town is complemented by visits to Stratford, London and Bristol.

Art. The purpose-built Art School has a focus on Fine Art and Photography. There are facilities for Painting, Drawing, Intaglio and Relief Printmaking, Photography and Digital Imaging. Pupils of all abilities develop a rich visual vocabulary in these media from the Foundation Year, enabling work to become increasingly fluent and sophisticated as they progress through the school. Pupils visit galleries and exhibitions in the UK as part of their course and the department organises regular overseas visits. The department is open during the evening and at weekends to enable pupils to develop their work. A rich co-curricular programme is offered in areas such as Life Drawing, Photography and Digital Imaging. The Elite Art Programme offers further opportunities for pupils to meet artists and designers, attend talks and workshops to extend and nurture their work. The standard of work produced is exceptionally high with a focus on technique, especially drawing, together with an informed understanding of others' art practice.

Design and Technology. There is a well-equipped Design & Technology Centre ensures that pupils have the opportunity to develop their knowledge and skills through project work in this exciting subject. Facilities include Textiles Technology, Resistant Materials, Computer Aided Design and Manufacture including 3D Printing, Product Design, Architectural Design and Engineering.

Careers. In their GCSE year pupils take the Inspiring Futures 'Futurewise New Generation' on-line Morrisby careers guidance tests which assess ability, personality, aptitude and interests. An in-depth interview with an experienced IF careers advisor helps pupils to make sensible and informed choices about their future. A Careers and Futures evening which takes place in March every year gives pupils the opportunity to learn from current parents and alumni about a variety of careers and pre- and post-university activities. All pupils in the Lower Sixth are encouraged to spend at least one week in the holidays on work experience. Pupils are given advice on choice of course at University (both UK and international) and help with their application (including interview and SAT preparation) by teachers in the Careers and Higher Education Department, and by their Sixth Form Tutor and Housemaster/Housemistress. Malvern College is a member of Inspiring Futures (the new name for ISCO: the Independent Schools Careers Organisation).

Pastoral Care. The Housemaster or Housemistress are House parents and pupils also have the direct support of House Tutors and an Academic Tutor who share the responsibility for pupils' overall personal development and well-being. Members of the Sixth Form choose their own Tutor in collaboration with the Head of Sixth Form and Head of Lower School. There is also a full-time Chaplain (who is a member of the pastoral team in addition to the Senior Deputy Head, Deputy Head: Pastoral and Safeguarding Lead) and two Independent Listeners available by phone or email. In addition, pupils have access to school counsellors. Chapel Prefects, Heads of House and Peer Mentors also provide support.

Health Care. There is a modern and well-equipped Medical Centre staffed 24 hours a day by Registered Nurses.

Coaches. During the school year there are three half-term holidays and about five leave-out weekends. On these occasions, school coaches are run to Guildford, London Paddington and Birmingham airport, according to demand. A coach service to Heathrow airport runs at the start of half term and the end of term.

Admission. Most pupils start school at Malvern between their thirteenth and fourteenth birthdays and may qualify for admission to the school by a satisfactory performance in the Common Entrance Examination or the annual Scholarship Examination. Pupils who wish to enter from schools which do not prepare pupils for Common Entrance are required to sit internal entrance tests in Maths, English and Science.

Pupils are also admitted to the Sixth Form at 16 on the basis of GCSEs/IGCSEs, interviews and entrance tests.

Application for admission should be made to the Registrar.

Scholarships. Malvern College offers a generous number of Scholarships and Exhibitions at 13+ each year, varying in value according to merit and financial circumstances up to 50% of the current fees. Scholarships and Exhibitions are offered for Academic potential, Art, Drama, Music, Sport and Design and Technology, as well as the Malvernian Society All-Rounder Award. Entries must be received three weeks before the examination. Entries must be received three weeks before the examination. Entry forms are available from the Preparatory School or the Registrar at Malvern College. For academic scholarships, Malvern College offers the Common Academic Scholarship Examination. Details and entry dates are available from the ISEB, the Preparatory School or Malvern College. Three Academic Scholarships are also awarded for the Sixth Form: an all-rounder academic award; a science award and an all-rounder award for a pupil from the state sector. The Richard Nieper Art Award is awarded to one talented artist entering the Sixth Form every other year.

Further particulars may be obtained from the Registrar, Tel: 01684 581515, or email: registrar@malverncollege.org.uk.

Fees per term (2016–2017). Senior School: Boarding: £11,950–£12,638; Day £7,921.

The Malvernian Society. On leaving, Malvernians retain contact with the College by joining the Malvernian Society. They also become members of the OM Club which organises various teams and a number of social functions. Secretary of the Malvernian Society: Syd Hill (Tel: 01684 581517).

College Council:
Ten members of the Council may be nominated, one each by the Lords-Lieutenant of the Counties of Gloucestershire, Herefordshire and Worcestershire, by the Vice-Chancellors of the Universities of Oxford, Cambridge and Birmingham, by the Service Boards of the Navy, Army and Air Force, and by the Headmaster and Teaching Staff. Ten members are elected by the Governors, and between six and ten are appointed by the Council.

President and Visitor: The Lord Bishop of Worcester

Chairman: Mr R Black [OM]
Vice Chairman: Mr G E Jones
Treasurer: Mr C Leonard, JP
Dr N Bampos
Mrs F P Bridge
Mr P G Brough
Mr W J Burke III [OM]
Mr P J Cartwright [OM]
Professor K J Davey, OBE
Miss S R Duff [EOG]
Mrs J Edwards-Clark, MVO [EOG]
Mr N C S Engert [OM]
Ms C Fairchild
Mr J Foxall [OM]
Mr F R R Francis
Professor L J Gullifer
Mr J M J Havard [OM]
Mr S M Hill
Professor P Jackson
Dr A Kennedy
Revd K U Madden
Mr P Nicholls [OM]
Mrs S Raby-Smith
Mr D G Robertson
Dr D C Sandbrook [OM]
Dr C W O Stoecker [OM]
Mr T D Straker, QC [OM]
Mr A Trotman
Mr R T H Wilson [OM]
Dr H M Wright

[OM] *Old Malvernian*
[EOG] *Ellerslie Old Girl*

Clerk to the Council & Bursar: Mr G R H Ralphs

Headmaster: Mr A R Clark, MA Cantab

Senior Deputy Head: Dr R A Lister, BA, MTS, PhD
Deputy Head: *Pastoral*: Mrs S G Angus, MA
Deputy Head: *Logistics*: Mr P Godsland, MA
Deputy Head: *Academic*: Mr J A Gauci, BA

Heads of Department:
Art: Mr S Callister, BA, MA
Drama: Mr K R C Packham, BA
Economics, Politics and Business Studies: Mr S C Holroyd, BA
English: Mr B M Wells, BA, MA, PhD
Geography: Mr R Needham, BSc
History: Mr J C Herod, MA
Psychology, Life Skills and e-Safety Coordinator: Mrs S Godsland, BA
Mathematics: Mr C Thomas, BEng
Modern Languages: Mr P Godsland, MA
Music: Mr J M Brown, BMus
Religious Studies: Mr D O'Keeffe, BA
Science: Dr N V Watson, BA, PhD
Sports (boys): Mr N R Tisdale
Mr M E A Hardinges, BSc
Mr M W Cleal, BA
Sports (girls): Miss C A West, BSc

Boarding Houses:
Mr M E A Hardinges, BSc (*School House*)
Mr A J Wharton, BTh (*No.1*)
Mr J J W E Major, BA (*No.2*)
Mrs F C Packham, BSc (*No.3*)

Mrs A I Sharp, BA (*No.4*)
Mr T P Newman, BSc (*No.5*)
Mrs V E Young, BA (*No.6*)
Mr D J Eglin, BSc (*No.7*)
Mrs R Grundy, BMus (*No.8*)
Mr P Wickes, BSc (*No.9*)
Mrs E Brown, BA (*Ellerslie*)

Chaplain: The Revd A P Law, DipTh
Registrar: Mr G Vosper-Brown

The Manchester Grammar School

Old Hall Lane, Manchester M13 0XT

Tel: 0161 224 7201
Fax: 0161 257 2446
email: general@mgs.org
website: www.mgs.org
Twitter: @MGSMagic
LinkedIn: /the-manchester-grammar-school

Motto: 'Sapere Aude' ('dare to be wise')

The Manchester Grammar School was founded in 1515 to promote 'godliness and good learning' and it has endeavoured throughout its history to remain true to these principles, while adapting to changing times. It is now an independent boys' day school with around 1,500 pupils. Almost all leavers go on to university, and there is a strong tradition of boys progressing to Oxford and Cambridge (27 boys were offered places for entry in 2016) and other leading Russell Group universities. 26 boys proceeded to medical school in 2015. A number of pupils each year obtain offers from prestigious US universities. Over 150 qualified teaching staff provide all pupils with a broad, traditional and flexible curriculum; for example, boys may study up to five languages at GCSE, from a choice of Latin, Greek, French, German, Italian, Mandarin, Russian and Spanish. Arabic and Czech are available as part of the options programme in the Sixth Form. The School offers a vast and diverse range of co-curricular opportunities.

The tradition of offering places to clever pupils regardless of their background is maintained by MGS bursaries. Over 250 pupils in the school are fee-assisted. Our pupils come both from primary and preparatory schools and represent a wide variety of cultural, ethnic and religious backgrounds.

Registration and Entry. Entry to the Junior School is considered at age 7, 8, 9 and 10, subject to availability at any stage during the academic year. Junior School pupils progress automatically to the Senior School. Entry for most other boys joining the School is at age 11, although entry at other ages is considered, subject to availability and applicants for Sixth Form entry are particularly welcomed. At all levels the normal assessment for entry involves prospective pupils spending a day in School, being taught and assessed in small groups. Alongside these assessment days, there is an entrance exam for entry at age 11. Sixth Form entrants have to meet GCSE grade requirements. Further details are available from the Admissions Office.

Fees per term (2016–2017). Tuition: £3,990.

Bursaries. The School offers means-tested bursaries of up to 100%. There are currently over 220 boys in receipt of financial support from the School and the majority receive full-fee support (the average fee support is currently 91%). The School does not offer academic scholarships.

Junior School. The Junior School opened in September 2008 in award-winning accommodation. It admits boys from age 7 and currently has 243 pupils. There is a strong focus in its curriculum on creativity, academic enrichment and skills-based learning. Specialist teachers from the Senior School contribute to the academic enrichment in Years 5 and 6.

Senior School Organisation and Curriculum. During the first two years the boys will study English, Mathematics, a modern foreign language (French, German, Russian, Spanish and Mandarin Chinese are offered), Classics (including Latin) History, Geography, General Science, Religious Studies, PSHE, Computing, Music, Art & Design, Drama, PE, Swimming and Games. Greek, Italian and Electronics are introduced as options in Year 9; there is also the opportunity for pupils who have not already done so to take up languages offered in Year 7. In Year 10 pupils may opt to study for an AS Extended Project Qualification; Classical Civilisation is also offered. Pupils make IGCSE/GCSE choices towards the end of Year 9 and typically take ten subjects, including Mathematics, English, English Literature, a language and at least one science subject.

In the Sixth Form A Level, Pre-U and International A Level courses are offered, with each department selecting the course which offers the best preparation for university; in addition, all students participate in the School's own non-examined enrichment programme, which includes a philosophical and critical thinking course (Perspectives).

Pastoral Care. Each form in the school is looked after by a Tutor, who is responsible, with the appropriate senior members of staff, for the academic and general progress of each pupil. In the Senior School Tutors work with no more than 13 boys. Regular written reports are supplemented by Parents' Evenings. The School Medical Room is staffed by a part-time doctor and two full-time Nursing staff. The older pupils selected as prefects are encouraged to help younger pupils in running societies and other co-curricular activities.

Creative Arts. All pupils experience Music, Art & Design and Drama within the curriculum; in addition, each of these areas offers activities to large numbers of pupils during the lunch-hour and after school. There are choirs, orchestras and instrumental tuition; plays, drama workshops and musicals; clubs for art, pottery, and computer design. There are regular exhibitions and public performances both in school and in public venues. The School has a well-equipped theatre and drama studios, providing many opportunities for pupils both to perform and provide technical support for productions.

Sport. All boys take part in timetabled games and the school produces successful teams in most sports. A new sports hall opened in 2015; there are extensive playing fields, a gymnasium, indoor swimming pool, squash courts, tennis courts and fitness suite. The choice of sport increases with age, to include rowing, climbing and golf in addition to mainstream sports.

Outdoor Pursuits. The school has a long tradition of camping and trekking and there are numerous weekend and holiday excursions. The School is the largest centre for D of E in the North West. Mountain activity days are offered most weekends, free of charge. Four annual camps cater for the full age range and offer a wide choice of activities. In recent years expeditions have visited the Alps, the Pyrenees, Morocco and Scandinavia. The school has two centres in Cumbria and one in Derbyshire.

Foreign Visits. Many trips abroad are organised each year, providing enjoyable holidays of broad educational value. Destinations include France, Germany, Spain, Russia, Italy, Greece, Mexico, Argentina, Peru, Mexico, Egypt, Tunisia, South Africa, India and China.

Societies and Activities. There are over 200 clubs, societies and activities catering for a variety of interests, including Chess and Bridge Clubs, and a school newspaper produced by pupils. The School is active in charitable fundraising and has a very extensive community action programme, including projects in Manchester and Salford, as well as in Uganda.

Prizes and Scholarships. In addition to bursaries, funds are provided for grants to help deserving pupils with the expense of a range of co-curricular activities. Prizes are awarded in all subjects in the curriculum.

Old Mancunians' Association and MGS Parents' Society. The Old Boys' Association has many regional sections. There is an annual Old Boys' Dinner in Manchester. The Development Office Secretary is Mrs Jane Graham who can be reached at the School.

The MGS Parents' Society has a membership of parents and friends and exists to support school activities and promote a programme of social events.

Charitable status. The Manchester Grammar School is a Registered Charity which provides Public Benefit. The aim of the School is to prepare able boys from the Manchester area, regardless of their financial background, to proceed to university and make a positive contribution to society in their adult life.

Co-optative Governors:

B Dixon, CBE
Professor T A Hinchliffe
J Kingsley
J Luca

C Bolton
J P Wainwright
J Young
E M Watkins, CBE
    (*Chairman*)

Dr T Westlake, The University of Manchester
Professor D A Cardwell, The University of Cambridge
Dr J R W Prag, The University of Oxford

Ex officio Governors:
The Dean of Manchester
The Lord Mayor of Manchester

Bursar and Clerk to the Governors: Mrs G M Batchelor, BSc

High Master: M A Boulton, BEng, PhD

Deputy High Master: P A M Thompson, BA, DPhil, MA Ed
Academic Deputy Head: N D Smith BA
Pastoral Deputy Head: A N Smith, BA
Surmaster & Head of Co-Curriculum: J W Mangnall, MA
Head of Junior School: Mrs L A Hamilton, BEd
Head of Lower School: Mrs S C James, BA
Head of Middle School: S G Crawshaw, BSc, PhD
Head of Sixth Form: C P Thom, MA
Director of Development: S P Jones, BA
Assistant Head: S Foster, BA, MA
Proctor: S J Burch, BSc, PhD, MIBiol
Director of Admissions: M Strother, MA, MPhil
Director of Studies: D Jeys, BSc, MA

Academic Staff:
* *Head of Department/Subject*
¹ *Language Assistant*
² *Teaching Assistant*

Art & Design:
R E Berry
Mrs J Dobbs, BA, MA Ed
A Lyth
*Mrs L J Murphy, BA, MA
Miss S Taylor, BA
K Yearsley, BA

Mrs N A Loughlin, BSc
Mrs C Morgan, BSc
M J Smedley, BSc, PhD
Miss A Wicking, BA

Biology:
*J Blair, BSc
Dr S J Burch, BSc, PhD, MSB
Dr S G Crawshaw, BSc, PhD
P W Freeman, BSc, MSc
Dr E Loh, BSc, MSc, PhD

Chemistry:
T Ahmed, BSc
I Airth, BSc
*C Buckley, BSc
M Facchini, BSc, MSc
Dr S Graham, MSci, PhD
Mrs H M Hughes, BSc
Mrs T C James, BSc
D Moss, MA
Miss F C Roberts, MChem
G M Tinker, MEng

Classics:
*Miss H L Eckhardt, MA
B S Edwards, MA
Miss C A Owens, BA, MA
Dr P A M Thompson, BA, MA Ed, DPhil
J O Ross, BA
N G Williams, BA
Dr R G Williams, BA, DPhil

Computing:
*S J Duffy, BSc, MSB, CBiol

Drama:
S Abbs, BA
Mrs K Hellier, BA
*M J Nichols, BA
Mrs J Sherratt, BA
K Tetley, BA
B J Turner, BA
J M Williams, BA

Economics:
Miss H L Dangerfield, BA
G J McSherry, BSc
D Wilson, BA

Electronics:
*M S R Hesketh, BSc, MSc

English:
Mrs R E Adams, BA
R J L Geldard, BA, MA, MA
J C Gibb, MA
Mrs V E Horsfield, BA, MEd
Mrs S C James, BA
Miss A Lloyd-Hughes, BA
C McCarthy, BA, MA
Miss L E Nelson, BA, MA
O N Nzelu, BA
H Sargent, BA, MA
B Townsend, BA
J N Tucker, BA, MA
*N Warrack, MA, MA
Miss J Welsh, BA, MA

General Science:
*D L Virr, BSc

Geography:
F C G Baker, BA
M D Corbett, BSc
Mrs A Curry, BSc
Miss P J Higgins, BSc
S P Jones, BA, MBA
J W Mangnall, MA
M A Nowell, BSc
S P G Spratling, BA
*P J Wheeler, BSc

History:
*Mrs E Carter, MA
S R Garvey, BA
A R T Hern, BA, MPhil, MPhil
D O Lacey, BA, MEd
Ms M A S Lowe, BA, MPhil
Dr S Orth, BA, MA, PhD
W B Pye, BA

A M Smith, MA
M G P Strother, MA, MPhil
D M Taylor, BA

Junior School:
Miss K V Atty, BA
Mrs D R Barnett, BEd
Miss C Beattie, BA
A J Bentley, LLB
A G Bird, BSc
Mrs L E Brunsden, BA
²Mrs C Burke, BSc, MSc
Mrs S M Callaghan, BA
²Dr T Campbell-Green, BA, MA, PhD
²J S Claverly
G Clayton, BSc
T Glennie, BA
²Miss R L Glynn, MA
*Mrs L A Hamilton, BEd
B A Hanson, BA
S Howarth, LLB
Mrs N Humphreys, BA
²Miss A Y Leigh, BEd
Mrs H Mortimer, BSc, MEd
Mrs T C Neild, BA
²Mrs S Reed, BA
²Miss N Reynolds BSoc-Si
²Mrs J Robinson, BA
Mrs V Shingler, BA
Miss E J Thorpe, BSc
²Mrs V J Tierney
²W J van Zyl, BSc
Mrs J M Ward, BA
Mrs Z L Ward, LLB

Learning Support:
²Miss A Batchelor, BSc
*Mrs H Butchart, BA, LTCL
²Miss S Cocker
²Miss R Daws, BSc
²Miss S T Kukoyi
¹C M Lyndon, BSc
Mrs L Merlo, BA, MA
²Miss R Williams, BA

Mathematics:
Mrs J Allinson, BA, MA
N T Burin, BSc, AFIMA
Dr J J Burke, BSc, PhD
Dr A P Burrows, BSc, PhD
Mrs A E Carolan, BSc
A R Davies, BSc, MSc
Dr A C Hunter, BSc, MSc, PhD
D Jeys, BSc, MA
I Z Khan, BSc
S J Leigh, BEng
O W J Llewelyn-Smith, BSc
G J Morris, BSc
D V Naughton, MM, PhD
*T J Pattison, BSc, MIMA, CMath
S E Phillips, BMus
Dr H G Read, BSc, PhD
Miss R L Sharkey, BA, MA
Mrs N M Williams, BSc, FRGS

Modern Languages:
E C F Cittanova, L-ès-L,
  M-ès-L, DEA
[1]Miss H Closa, MA
Mrs E R Dalton, L-ès-L
A P Dobson, BA, MA
  (*German*)
[1]Miss S Fragagnano
Miss E A Garnett, BA
[1]Mrs I Kovtunenko, BA
*Mrs A V Hemsworth, BA
  (*Italian*)
Miss A Jacinto, BA
C M Jarrett, BA, MA
Mrs O Kelly-Saltaleggio,
  BA
Mrs R Lan, BA, MA
S Lu, BA
Mrs D Minguito-Pantoja,
  BA
R J Neal, BA, MA, MEd
B Parolin, BA, MA, PhD
[1]L Patzl
Mrs S J Paulson, BA
L M Rigby, BA
[1]Miss M Robert
Mrs G Rrugeja
N J Sharples, BA, MA
  (*Spanish*)
R W Simpson, BA
  (*French*)
Mrs L Speed, Mosc Dipl
C P Thom, MA
Miss K J Tinslay, BA

Music:
G Blackwell
Mrs F A Bradley, BMus
Mrs H Butchart, BA, LTCL
*R M Carey, MA (*Director
  of Music*)
D E Francis, MusB,
  GRNCM, ARNCM,
  LRAM, LTCL, ATCL

C L Carey, ABSM
Miss E M Shercliff, BA
  (*Junior School Music*)
L E Stoker
R A Waldock

Physical Education:
T A Grainger, BSc
R F Jennings, BA
J L Leggett, BA
M J Roe, BSc
J H Shoard, MA
S Swindells
M Watkinson
G Wilson
*M A Walmsley, BSc
S R Walsh

Physics:
Dr M A Boulton BEng,
  PhD
Ms S M Hewett, BSc
Dr P Holt, BSc, DPhil
*S J F Hunt, MA
Dr D W F Inglis, BSc, PhD
Dr D P Smith, MEng, PhD
Miss L Thewles, BSc

Politics:
S Foster, BA, MA
*R N Kelly, BA, MA,
  MPhil
Miss E C Kilheeney, BA,
  MA
D O Lacey, BA, MEd

Religion & Philosophy:
Mrs L J Anderson, BA
Mrs E L Bellieu, BA
*D Brown, BD, STM,
  MLitt
M P A Coffey, MA
D Farr, MA
A Greggs, BA
A N Smith, BA
Mrs J A Whittell, BA

Medical Officer: Dr J L Burn, FRCP, FRCPCH
PA to the High Master: Lorraine Coen
Admissions Office Manager: Kath Heathcote

Marlborough College

Marlborough, Wiltshire SN8 1PA

Tel: Main Switchboard: 01672 892200
           The Master's Office: 01672 892400
           The Bursary: 01672 892390
           Admissions: 01672 892300
Fax: Main No: 01672 892207
           The Master's Office: 01672 892407
email: master@marlboroughcollege.org
           admissions@marlboroughcollege.org
website: www.marlboroughcollege.org
Twitter: @marlboroughcol

Founded 1843. Incorporated by Royal Charter.

The College is fully co-educational and there are 936 boys and girls in the 16 Houses of whom 910 board. The normal age of entry is either 13 or 16.

Registration. For entry to the College at 13+ registrations are accepted no earlier than four years before entry. Registrations for entry at 16+ are accepted at any time. The College assesses all applicants 20 months ahead of entry and offers places accordingly. After this date a small number of able candidates may still win a place in the College by being accepted onto the Master's List. All applicants to the College must meet our entry criteria and take either the Academic Scholarship or the Common Entrance examination. Please see our website for details of this policy: www.marlboroughcollege.org. The 13+ Scholarship examination is in March of the year of entry and the Sixth Form Scholarship examination is in the November before entry.

Scholarships. All Awards enable those with a financial need to receive bursarial assistance with the fees. The degree of support given will be subject to a means test. Candidates for entry in the Shell (Year 9) must be under 14 on 1st September. The closing date for entries is late January of Year 8. There are up to 16 academic scholarships at 13+ and a further 22 Awards in Music, Art, Design and Sport. There are also William Morris All Rounder Awards based upon strengths in academic work, Sport, Art, Drama or Music. Up to 20 awards are made at Sixth Form entry. From time to time there are a number of other special categories of scholarship based upon parental occupation and particular abilities. The College offers a limited number of Foundation (Clergy) places and Armed Services closed scholarships.

A Scholarship Prospectus and copies of past papers may be obtained from the Admissions Office. Applications and enquiries about entries and scholarships should be addressed to The Senior Admissions Tutor, tel: 01672 892300; email: admissions@marlboroughcollege.org.

Academic. The College's curriculum follows and extends the National Curriculum to allow for a proper combination of breadth and specialisation. It is designed to stimulate, challenge and support all pupils and to ensure that they maximise their potential. There is a clear focus placed upon success in public examinations, where standards are very high, but the College prioritises pupil success at university and in their subsequent careers.

Almost all pupils go on to study at university either in the United Kingdom (currently 85% annually to Russell Group universities) or, increasingly, overseas with destinations ranging from Europe to North America and beyond.

In the Lower School a wide-ranging curriculum is followed. Central to this is "Form", an innovative and unique humanities course which embraces English, History and Religious Studies. It gives pupils a sense of the history and evolution of human culture, and our place within it. It aims to develop the skills and habits of mind that will lead to success at the College and beyond – wide reading, critical analysis, synthesis and evaluation of ideas, the confidence to have a go and voice their opinions. Choices are made at the end of the Shell (Year 9) leading to 10 or more GCSEs and IGCSEs. In the Sixth Form, pupils choose from 30 subjects, following the A Level or Pre–U systems. In subjects where the new linear A Levels are already available, the College does not offer the AS.

The curriculum is supported by an enormous range of academic extension and enrichment activities through societies, lectures, theatre trips, museum and gallery visits, debates, poetry readings, conference and concerts, creating a full co-curriculum which recognises that qualifications alone do not produce an educated person.

Universities & Careers. Nearly all pupils who come to Marlborough go on into the Sixth Form and virtually all proceed to degree courses. The well-resourced Guidance Department is located at the heart of the College and assists Housemasters and Housemistresses in advising boys and girls and their parents about Sixth Form subject selection, higher education options, gap year projects, work experience and careers.

Co-Curricular. Sports facilities are outstanding. There are two brand new floodlit astro-turf pitches, acres of sports pitches, a tartan athletics track, 24 tennis courts and nine netball courts. The main sports for boys are rugby, hockey, cricket, football, athletics and tennis, and for girls, hockey, netball, tennis, lacrosse and athletics. Alternative sports include aerobics, badminton, basketball, beagling, clay pigeon shooting, fencing, golf, rackets, riding, rugby sevens, fives (Rugby & Eton), shooting, squash, swimming, water polo and yoga. There are regular fixtures in many of these sports.

An Outdoor Activities Department offers the Gold Duke of Edinburgh's Award, canoeing, climbing, kayaking, mountain biking and sub-aqua. The annual Devizes to Westminster kayak race has become a feature of the Lent Term for up to 10 Upper School crews. There are numerous OA activities each Sunday in term-time in House groups and more adventurous trips further afield in the school holidays. Recent destinations include the Brecon Beacons, Snowdonia, The Swiss Alps, Peru, Iceland and Tanzania.

The College's Combined Cadet Force is thriving. It is compulsory in Year 10 and optional thereafter. It provides excellent leadership training and there is a strong record of College pupils winning Sixth Form Army Scholarships. All year groups take part in Field Days or CCF Camps both in the UK and abroad; recently the Upper School cadets have visited the US Navy Seals in California.

The College also offers a comprehensive Outreach Programme in the local community. The mantra "with privilege comes responsibility" is the underlying philosophy. Many of the pupils are involved with local primary schools, a special school and care homes for the elderly. The College has a partnership with Swindon Academy which involves College staff and pupils providing academic support. Swindon Academy pupils also attend some themed residential weekends at the College. There are also partnerships with Pewsey Vale School and St John's Academy.

The College has a large array of thriving academic and intellectual societies which complement and support the academic programme, attracting impressive speakers each term.

There is a programme of Day Trip and Study Trips in the holidays which support and enrich the academic curriculum. There is also a strong tradition of Sports Tours. In summer 2016 the boys' rugby tour to Japan was a great success. A girls' hockey tour to the Netherlands is planned for October, and in February 2017 the cricket XI are touring Barbados.

The College has recently been voted "Great for extra-curricular activities" by "The Week".

Music. Music at Marlborough plays an essential part in the cultural life of the College.

Based in the state-of-the-art, purpose-built Henry Hony Centre, the Department is home to some 40 Music scholars and with over 55% of pupils taking instrumental lessons. The major groups are Chapel and Chamber Choir, Symphony Orchestra, Chamber Orchestra and Senior Wind Orchestra. Unique to Marlborough is the College's professional orchestra in partnership, London's Southbank Sinfonia.

Drama. Drama at Marlborough is all about collaboration, creative debate, experimentation and excellence. With an average of 16 productions a year diversity of style is at the heart of what we offer; from contemporary productions of classical tragedy to musicals and farcical comedy. Independent productions give the opportunity for pupils to write, direct and produce, working alongside visiting practitioners and influenced by the wide range of touring productions that visit our three well-equipped theatres. Drama is offered as an option in the Shell (Year 9) and is popular thereafter.

Art and Design. The Art Department is a vibrant, inspirational and engaging creative environment, where every pupil's individuality, visual literacy and potential to fully realise their artistic ambitions is highly valued. All pupils study Art in their first year and many go on to take the sub-

ject at GCSE or A Level. Pupils may specialise in Fine Art or Photography at A Level.

The purpose-built Art School houses painting, drawing, relief and intaglio printmaking studios, a photography darkroom, lecture room and an IT suite within the main building. In addition, there is a well-resourced art library. Two annex buildings accommodate ceramic workshops, a drawing studio, the Mount House Gallery and an Apple Mac digital editing and animation suite.

There is also a purpose-built Design and Technology Centre.

Fees per term (2016–2017). £11,760 Boarding; £9,995 Day Pupils.

The Marlburian Club. www.marlburianclub.org

Charitable status. Marlborough College is a Registered Charity, number 309486 incorporated by Royal Charter to provide education.

Visitor: The Most Revd The Lord Archbishop of Canterbury

Council:
President: The Rt Revd The Lord Bishop of Salisbury
The Rt Hon The Lord Malloch-Brown, KCMG, PC (*Chairman*)
P J Manser, CBE, DL
The Revd Rachel Weir
Ms S Hamilton-Fairley
J K Baker (*Chairman Finance Committee*)
C H Pymont, QC
Dr Tracy Long, CBE
S M W Bishop
The Venerable Dr Jane Steen
W Mills
Sir John Hood
Lieutenant General Sir J G Lorimer, KCB, DSO, MBE
P Freeman

International Council:
Y A M Tunku Ali Redhauddin ibni Tuanku Muhriz
T D P Kirkwood

Master: **J Leigh**, MA Corpus Christi College Cambridge, FRSA

Second Master: W D L Nicholas, BEng, MSc
Deputy Master & Director of Corporate Resources: P N Bryan, BA, ACA
Deputy Head (Academic): J M Barot, MA, MSc
Deputy Head (Boarding): Lady Cayley, MA
Deputy Head (Co-Curriculum): Mrs D J Harris, MA
Senior Admissions Tutor: Dr N G Hamilton, BA, PhD

Assistant Staff:
* *Head of Department*
† *Housemasters/Housemistresses*

P R Adams, BEd (**Design and Technology*)
Miss A L Adderley, BA
B R Allen, MA
Miss N L Allen, BSc
M W Alleyne
N M Allott, BSc
D I Andrew, MA, MSci (**Economics & Business Studies*)
A J Arkwright, BA
D R Armitage, MA
M Baldrey, BMus, FTCL
C E Barclay, BSc, FRAS, FRSA (*Director of the Observatory*, *Director of EPQ*)
T A Birkill, BSc
M B Blossom, MA
A J Brown, MA (*Modern Languages)
Ms V R Brown, MA
Mrs R L T Bruce, BA

M P L Bush, BA
J P Carroll, BEd (†*B House*)
D T Clark, MTheol (*Religious Studies*)
Mrs M E Clarke, MA
S C Clayton, BA
M Conlen, BSc (†*Cotton House*)
D R Cowley, BEd
Mrs H A M Cox, BSc (†*Elmhurst*)
Miss J Darby, BA, GMus
A H de Trafford, MA (*Spanish*)
Miss V G M Delalleau, BA
S M D Dempster, BA (†*C3*)
Mrs I D Dennis, BA
S J Dennis, MBE, MSc
Revd J G W Dickie, MA, BLitt
Dr G A Doyle, BSc, MSc, PhD, DIC, CChem, MRSC
 (*Science*)
P T Dukes, FGSM, ARAM (*Artistic Director*)
Mr J J Duplock, MA
A S Eales, BMus
S J Ellis, BSc (†*Barton Hill*)
[P A Finn, BA]
[Mrs S A Finn, BA]
Mrs A J Finn, MSc (*Mathematics*)
Dr S D Flatres, MSci, PhD
P G M Ford, MA
Mrs L F W Ford, MA (*English*)
C A Fraser, MA
[Mrs J L Fruci, BA]
B W Giles, MA
A Gist, MA (*IB Coordinator & Form Coordinator*)
N O P Gordon, MA
M A Gow, BA (*Politics*)
[Mrs C E Green, MA Ed]
Miss O F Grimley, BSc
C L Harrison, BSc (†*Summerfield*)
P A J Hodgkinson, BA (*Choirmaster*)
Mrs J Hodgson, BA (†*Morris House*)
J A Hodgson, BSc
Mrs R F Horton, MA
Mrs K M Hudson, MSc (*Director of Sport*)
Miss J C Isitt, BA
H E B Jones, BA
P N Keighley, BEng
Mrs A L Keighley, BA (†*Ivy House*)
D Kenworthy, BA, MFA (*Drama*)
T A Kiggell, MA
Mrs K J Kiggell, MA (†*Dancy House*)
G D M Lane, BSc
Mrs J E Lane, BSc
J T W Lane, BA
Miss A C Langdale, MSc
T C M Lauze, BA, MBA (*Director of Teaching &
 Learning*)
Ms Q Li, MA (*Mandarin Chinese*)
Mrs D L Lilley, MA (†*Mill Mead*)
J F Lloyd, BA, MPhil (*Classics*)
J J Lyon Taylor, BSc (†*Littlefield*)
G I Macmillan, BA, (†*Turner House*)
D J Madden, BEng
T G R Marvin, MA (†*Preshute*)
Ms R L McAuley, BA (*Psychology*)
Mrs J McClean, BA (*Acting *Learning Support & Study
 Skills*)
Mrs J McFarland, BSc
Dr F S McKeown, BA, PhD (*History of Art*)
M McNally, BSc
G J McSkimming, BSc
Miss H L Meehan, BSc
B H Miller, BSc
W J Molyneux, BA

Mrs Y Momota
N J L Moore, MA
Ms L M Morey, MA
P N Morley-Fletcher, BA (*French*)
E S D Mortimer, BA
C A F Moule, MA (*History*)
N Nelson-Piercy, BA (*Russian*)
J N Newman, BSc
E G Nobes, MA (*Careers*)
P J O'Sullivan, BA
Mrs C E Page, MA
J H Parnham, MA (*Art*)
Mrs A E Paterson, MA (*Biology*)
Mrs C N Pembroke, BA
G R Playfair, MA (†*C2*)
Dr M J Ponsford, BA, PhD
A C Pountney, BA (*Rugby*)
S G Quinn, BSc
Miss T C Rainer, MA (*Acting *German*)
M S Ramage
K J D Richards, MA (*Geography*)
Dr L J Richards, BSc, PhD
Dr D G Roberts, MSc, PhD
Mrs E J Ross, MA
Dr E Ryder, BSc, PhD
[Mrs M C Sandall, BA]
R A Sandall, BCom, BA
Mrs R Scott, MA
Miss H M Scott, BSc, ICAS
H M H Scott, DRSAMD
M J Sharrad, BSc (*PE*)
G B Shearn, BSc (*ICT*)
Mrs S Shearn, BEd (†*New Court*)
C S Smith, BEng, MSc
Mrs E C Smith, BA
K G A Smith, BA
C O Stewart, MA
V J Stokes, BA
Dr J P Swift, BSc, PhD (†*C1*)
H L R Tilney, BA (*Academic Scholarship & Leadership
 Programme*)
Mrs M Tollit, MA
R Tong (*OA Coordinator*)
Miss C Toomer, GGSM
Mrs C A Walsh, BSc (*Chemistry*)
C J Wheatland, MPhys (*Physics*)
Ms J M White, MA
I A Wilkins, MFA
R D Willmett, BA
[Mrs B S Wingfield Digby, BA]
Mrs A T Woodford, BA (*Italian*, *Oxbridge Coordinator*)
Mr J Wright, BSc

Senior Chaplain: The Revd Dr D Campbell, MTh, DMin
Medical Officers:
Dr R W Hook, MB BS, MRCGP, DRCOG
Dr J Campbell, MBBS, DRCOG, DFFP, MRCGP
Librarian: J E Burton, BA
Master's Assistant: Mrs S Nicholas

Merchant Taylors' Boys' School
Crosby

186 Liverpool Road, Crosby, Liverpool L23 0QP
Tel: 0151 928 3308 (General Enquiries)
          0151 949 9323 (Headmaster)
          0151 949 9326 (Bursar)
          0151 949 9333 (Admissions Office)

Fax:　　0151 949 9300
email:　　infomtbs@merchanttaylors.com
website:　　www.merchanttaylors.com
Twitter:　　@MerchantsCrosby
Facebook:　/merchanttaylorscrosby

Motto: *Concordia parvae res crescunt – Small things grow in harmony*

The Boys' School was founded in 1620 by John Harrison, Citizen and Merchant Taylor of London. In 1878 the School was transferred to its present site where it is now housed beneath the iconic red brick clock tower.

The Senior Boys' School is attended by over 550 boys aged eleven to eighteen, 158 of whom are in the Sixth Form. There is also a Junior Boys' School with 145 boys aged between seven and eleven.

The school has a reputation for academic excellence and the majority of our leavers go on to study at Russell Group universities including Oxford and Cambridge. The emphasis throughout is very much on developing learners who are able to work independently and who have a genuine curiosity in their studies.

Curriculum. In the first three years of the Lower School boys study a wide variety of national curriculum subjects including separate sciences as well as the opportunity to pick up extra modern and ancient languages. They gradually specialise in the Middle School where there is the flexibility to study between 8 and 11 GCSEs including an accelerated IGCSE mathematics course. There is an additional timetabled Friday afternoon in Years 7–9 for enrichment activities. The Gifted and Talented extension programme offers practical lessons in beekeeping, skateboard design, shooting, fencing, ceramics, scuba diving and many others.

In the Sixth Form the following subjects are available at A Level: Mathematics, Further Mathematics, Physics, Chemistry, Biology, Latin, Greek, Classical Civilisation, English Language, English Literature, History, Geography, Economics, French, German, Spanish, Design and Technology, Art & Design, Music, Theatre Studies and Physical Education. In addition, students in the Sixth Form will have an opportunity to follow a course in General Studies.

Games. Facilities include a £5 million sports centre with climbing wall, fitness suite, sports hall and dance studio. There is a heated indoor swimming pool on site, extensive playing fields, cricket nets, a share of Northern Club's facilities and three tennis courts.

Games played are Rugby, Hockey, Cricket, Athletics, Rowing, Football, Swimming, Tennis and Cross-Country. All boys are encouraged to try at least one of the many games options available during their time at school.

School Societies. A wide range of activities and interests is covered by School Societies.

Music and Drama. About 200 boys receive weekly instrumental tuition and there is a subsidised scheme for beginners on orchestral instruments. There is a School Choral Society, Junior School Choir, Concert Band, Swing Band, a Chamber Orchestra along with various woodwind and brass ensembles. Boys regularly perform both in and out of School at a variety of events and are given many opportunities to perform publicly.

There are two full-time teachers, plus a team of visiting specialist instrument teachers. There are links in Music with our sister school, Merchant Taylors' Girls' School. There are also close links with the Girls' School in Drama, which now forms an integral part of the Senior School curriculum as well as being a major extracurricular activity.

Combined Cadet Force. The School has a voluntary contingent of the Combined Cadet Force with Royal Navy, Army and Royal Air Force Sections. Activities include mountaineering, camping, sailing, flying and shooting, and there is the opportunity to attend a variety of camps and courses, both in Great Britain and overseas. There are around 250 members of the CCF, many of whom are girls from our sister school.

Admission. Boys are admitted to the Junior School at age 7 and to the Senior School at 11, 13 or at Sixth Form. Some Assisted Places are available at age 11.

Fees per term (2016–2017). Tuition: Senior School £3,650, Junior School £2,728.

Old Boys. There is an active Old Boys' Association (The Old Crosbeians) whose Secretary may be contacted via the School and from whom a handbook/register may be obtained (please email Miss Kate Thomas in our Development Office if you wish to get in contact: k.thomas@merchanttaylors.com). The OBA is a lively and sociable association which organises events up and down the country throughout the year.

Charitable status. The Merchant Taylors' Schools Crosby is a Registered Charity, number 1125485, and a Company Limited by Guarantee, registered in England, number 6654276. Registered Office: Liverpool Road, Crosby, Liverpool L23 0QP.

Governors:
Chairman: Mrs B Bell, LLB Hons, FCILT, FRSA
Mr P G Magill, MSc, FCIPD
Miss A M Dobie, BA Hons
Mr S A Wilkinson, BA Hons, FCA
Mr D S Evans, MA Oxon
Ms L C Martin Wright
Dr J Fox, MBCh Birm, DRCOG, MRCGP
Mr J Sutcliffe, BEng Hons, CEng, MICE, MRICS, MCIOB
Mr C Williams, FCA FIMC

Clerk to the Governors: Mrs J Baccino
Accounts: D Norton

Headmaster: David Cook, BA, MA

Deputy Headmasters:
R A Simpson, MA, MCIEA, BA Hons, PGCE
D Williams, BSc Hons, PGCE

Head of Sixth Form: G Bonfante, BSc Hons, MA, PGCE
Head of Middle School: S G Fletcher, MSc, BSc Hons, PGCE
Head of Lower School: N A Hunt, BA Hons
Assistant Headmaster Operations: J B Green, MA, BA Hons
Head of Pastoral Care: J E Turner, BA Hons, MA, PGCE
Director of Music: D Holroyd, MA, GMus Hons RNCM, PPRNCM, ARCO
Emeritus Chaplain: Revd D A Smith, BA

Teachers:
* Head of Department

Art:
*Miss B Baker, BA Hons
Miss S Murphy

Biology:
*Miss J M Whitehead, BSc, PGCE
G Bonfante, BSc Hons, MA, PGCE
Mrs R J Wright, BSc, PGCE
R Yates, BSc, PGCE
D Williams

Careers:
Mrs V Mee, BA Hons

Chemistry:
*Dr I M Buschmann, Dip Chem, MSc, PhD

Mrs A C Byrne, BSc, PGCE
Dr C M Clay, MChem, PhD, PGCE
Dr S J Hardy, BSc, PhD

Classics:
P Fentem, MA Hons, PGCE
Miss H Hoath, BA Hons, PGCE
*Mrs S Rohrer, BA Hons

Cookery:
Mrs M Taylor

Design Technology:
Miss A Evans, BA Hons, PGCE
I McKie

*I Taylor, BEd, MA Ed

Economics:
M Cooper
*S J Kay, BSc Hons

English and Drama:
Mrs M Casaus, MA, PGCE
Ms J Finnegan, BA Hons
Dr J S Gill, BA Hons, MPhil, PhD
Mrs N Rice, BA Hons, MA
*R A Simpson, MA, MCIEA, BA Hons, PGCE
M A Stanley, MA, BA Hons, PG Dip, PGCE
Miss L Quinn

Geography:
*Miss R Clint, BA Hons
J Green, MA, BA Hons
N A Hunt, BA Hons
J E Turner, BA, MA, DipC, PGCE

History:
*J C Heap, BA Hons
S P Sutcliffe, BA Hons, MA
Mrs C Croxton
Miss E Cuthbert, MA, BA Hons

ICT:
*T Higham, BSc Hons

Learning Support:
*Mrs A Edwards, BA Hons
Mrs A O'Brien, LLB
Mrs J Ascroft
Mrs C Swift

Library:
Mrs E Rea, BA Hons, MCLIP

Mathematics:
Mrs M Cunliffe, BSc Hons, PGCE
Mrs C Hobbs, BA Hons, PGCE

Duke of Edinburgh's Award Manager:
M Slemen, BEd, Dip PE

Junior School:
Head: Mrs J E Thomas, BEd Hons, MEd, NPQH
Deputy Head, Pastoral: D K J Youngson, BA Hons
Deputy Head, Academic: Mrs Y Bonfante, BEd Hons
PA to the Headmistress: Mrs A Hodson

N Benbow, BA Hons
Mrs Y Bonfante, BEd
Miss C Fraser, BA Hons, PGCE
Mrs P Graham, Dip Tch Asst
Miss R Hargreaves BA Hons
D I Lyon, MA, PGCE
Mrs M Mellor, BA Hons, MMS Dip, PGCE

Admissions: Mrs P Saffer
PA to the Headmaster: Mrs S Maitland and Mrs C Austin

Mrs C Hunt, BSc Hons, PGCE
Mrs J R Marshall, BA Hons, PGCE
W K Miles, BSc, PGCE
J O'Brien, BSc, PGCE
*Mrs E C Peacock, BA Hons, PGCE

Modern Foreign Languages:
Mrs S A Dunning, BA Hons
F J Rubia Castro, BA Hons
S G Fletcher, MSc, BSc Hons, PGCE
*P E Howard, MA, BSc Hons, PGCE
Miss A Nielsen, BEd
A Scott, MA, BA Hons
Mrs G Eden

Music:
*D Holroyd, MA, GMus Hons RNCM, PPRNCM, ARCO
R Richardson, BA Hons

Physical Education:
J Carew, MSc, Level 2 Coaching Rowing
S Cooke, BSc Hons
D W King, BA Hons
*I D McKie, CertEd
G T Stiff, BA Hons
M Whalley, ASA CC L3, ASA Swimming L2, NRTSTC

Physics:
*P J Cooper, BSc Hons, MA, PGCE
M Toney, BSc Hons, PGCE
Miss M Liang, MA, BSc Hons, PGCE
J Furlong, BSc Hons
Dr M Liang

Religious Studies:
*R M Fawcett, BEd, DipTh
I Mckie

Mrs H O'Sullivan, BSc Hons
J O'Shaughnessy, BA Hons
Mrs L Rogers, BEd Hons
Mrs P Rule
P A Wardle, BEd
M Whalley, ASA CC L3, ASA Swimming L2, NRTSTC
Mrs H White, BA Hons
Mrs A Wynne, BEd

Merchant Taylors' School

Sandy Lodge, Northwood, Middlesex HA6 2HT

Tel: Head Master's PA: 01923 821850
Reception: 01923 820644
Admissions Officer: 01923 845514
Bursar: 01923 825669
Fax: 01923 845522
email: info@mtsn.org.uk
website: www.mtsn.org.uk
Twitter: @MerchantTaylors
Facebook: /MerchantTaylors
LinkedIn: /merchanttaylorsschoolnorthwood

Motto: *Concordia parvae res crescunt*

The school has enjoyed a distinguished history since its foundation by the Merchant Taylors' Company in 1561. It was one of the nine original "Clarendon" public schools and its pupils have achieved distinction throughout its history. The school enjoys close links with the Company, which, to this day, constitutes its Governing Body. In 1933 the school moved from central London to its present superb, rural setting of 280 acres at Sandy Lodge, Northwood. We are within easy reach of parents in Buckinghamshire, Hertfordshire, Middlesex and North-West London by car, train or school coach service, as well as a mere half hour by tube from Baker Street.

Four distinct boys' day schools share the campus. The nursery school, pre-prep and prep cater for 330 boys from 3 to 13 years of age (the prep school shares some of its facilities with the senior school, but is a separate school in its own right), while the senior school has approximately 890 pupils from 11–18, with over 300 in the sixth form.

All pupils have an individual tutor who looks after them during their school career in small House tutor groups. They are encouraged to cultivate interests at which they can excel, to have confidence in their abilities and to gain self-knowledge as well as knowledge. The academic achievements of the school are first-rate and are achieved in a humane, civilised and unpressured atmosphere. We place a great emphasis on encouraging boys to organise many activities themselves and to take responsibility for others.

Admission. Entry to the senior school at 11+, 13+ and 16+ is by the School's own Entrance Examinations, together with an interview; for entry to the Prep school, see Merchant Taylors' Prep entry in the IAPS section.

Term of entry. September unless there are very special circumstances.

Scholarships and Bursaries. There are no separate Scholarship papers in the Entrance Examinations. We make awards to boys who perform exceptionally well in these examinations and at a separate interview; we take into account information received from the boy's current school.

11+ entry: Up to 5 major Academic Scholarships are awarded, each to the value of at least 10% of the School fee. Up to 5 minor Academic Scholarships each to the value of £200 per annum. Up to 2 All-Rounder scholarships, each to the value of at least 10% of the School fee. Scholarships for Sport, Art, Design Technology & Drama (a maximum of 2 per subject) each to the value of a £200 department programme and associated materials.

13+ entry: Up to 5 major Academic Scholarships each to the value of at least 10% of the School fee. Up to 12 minor Academic Scholarships each to the value of £200 per annum. Up to 2 All-Rounder scholarships each to the value of at least 10% of the School fee. Up to 8 scholarships for Sport, Art, Design Technology & Drama (a maximum of 2 per subject) each to the value of a £200 department programme and associated materials.

16+ entry: Scholarships in Art, Design Technology, Sport and Drama – a maximum of one per subject, each to the value of a £200 department programme and associated materials. One bursary up to the value of the full School fee is available.

Music Scholarships: Four Music Scholarships (one of up to 25% of the School fee; one of up to 15% and two of up to 10%) awarded across 11+, 13+ and 16+. A Scholarship includes free instrumental and/or singing tuition on two instruments (or instrument and voice). Additional awards of free tuition may be made if there are boys of sufficient merit. All Scholarships can be supplemented by means-tested bursaries should there be a proven need.

Bursaries: The School welcomes applications from parents whose sons would benefit from attending Merchant Taylors' School, and who will contribute strongly to the life of the community, but who require financial assistance. Means-tested bursarial support is available up to the value of 100% of the School fee; further details can be obtained from the Admissions Office.

Other Awards: There is a generous variety of awards open to Sixth Formers for travel, Outward Bound and Sail Training, as well as leaving scholarships to assist at University.

Scholarships at Oxford and Cambridge Universities. At the end of their first undergraduate year, Old Boys are eligible for election to a maximum of three Sir Thomas White Scholarships at St John's College Oxford, a Matthew Hale Scholarship at The Queen's College Oxford and a Parkin & Stuart Scholarship for Science or Mathematics at Pembroke College Cambridge.

Curriculum and Organisation. The curriculum in years 7, 8 and 9 (Thirds, Upper Thirds and Fourths) is a broad one: Art and Design, Biology, Chemistry, Computing, Design Technology, Drama, English, French, Geography, History, Latin, Mathematics, Music, Physical Education, Physics, PSHCE, and Religious Studies. Greek, German, or Spanish are started when 13+ boys enter the school. All boys take nine or ten GCSEs, chosen from the subjects above. Boys are entered for IGCSEs and GCSEs. A student entering the Lower Sixth embarks upon a two-year course in which all boys initially study four subjects to A Level, with most certifying three and some four. An extensive choice of supercurricular options is available, including the EPQ, Thinking and Study skills and Careers Preparation.

Music. All orchestral and band instruments, piano, organ, percussion and guitar are taught to boys throughout the school. Choirs, orchestras, bands and chamber groups give frequent concerts throughout the year.

Games and Physical Education. Magnificent playing fields include over 55 acres dedicated to Rugby, Cricket, Soccer and Hockey. There are Fives, Squash and Tennis Courts; an athletics track and two floodlit, all-weather pitches. The Sports Hall accommodates four badminton courts, a multi-gym, a climbing wall, a fencing salle and indoor cricket nets. The school's lakes provide a marvellous facility for our Sailing Club, canoeing and windsurfing. Physical Education is compulsory for all pupils, and all pupils learn to swim. There is an indoor swimming pool and Water Polo is offered. Coaching in Fencing, Basketball, Judo and Karate is excellent. MTS is one of only two schools in the country to host first-class cricket fixtures and is the home of Middlesex Youth Cricket.

Service Sections. The school has a Contingent of the Combined Cadet Force with RN, Army, and RAF Sections. The CCF includes girls from St Helen's School, Northwood. There is a Rifle Range for the use of the Contingent (and we send a team to Bisley every year). The Duke of Edinburgh's Award Scheme allows boys to achieve Bronze, Silver and Gold Awards, and the Community Service programme provides an opportunity for a wide range of activities in the local area. All boys in Years 10 and 11 take part in the CCF,

The Duke of Edinburgh's Award Scheme or Community Service teams.

The school places great emphasis on charitable endeavour and the boys run a great many societies to support good causes. A special feature of the school's charity work is Phab, a week-long residential holiday for handicapped children held every Easter and organised by Sixth Form boys together with the girls of St Helen's School. The school also has a charitable partnership with two schools in India.

School Societies. A large number of societies cover a wide field of interests and activities.

Careers. There is an outstanding Careers Advisory Service, which organises annual Careers and Higher Education Conventions at the school and a range of work experience.

House and Tutorial Systems. The school is divided into eight Houses. Each House is under the care of a Head of House and a team of tutors, who are responsible for the pastoral care of boys in that House.

Fees per term (2016–2017). £7,808 (Autumn Term), £5,856 (both Spring Term & Summer Term); these cover not only tuition, games, and lunch but also a lifetime alumnus subscription (OMT). There is a non-refundable registration fee of £100; separate admission fee deposits are charged later.

Merchant Taylors' Prep, the Preparatory school to Merchant Taylors', adjoins the senior school.

(*For further details see Merchant Taylors' Prep entry in IAPS section.*)

Charitable status. Merchant Taylors' School Charitable Trust is a Registered Charity, number 1063740. It exists to provide a first-class all-round education for boys, irrespective of their background.

The Governors of the School:
Chairman: C P Hare

G Barrett	D Haria
S W Bass	Mrs S Morgan
R J Brooman	A J Moss
Dr J M Cox	Mrs J Redman
A Eastwood	D J Shah
D G M Eggar	Dr J H S Sichel
Ms L Gadd	R-J Temmink
R C G Gillott	Sir M Tomlinson

***Head Master*: S J Everson**, MA

Bursar: I D Williams, MBA, CMgr, FCMI, MAPM, MCIL
Second Master: M C Husbands, MA
Senior Deputy Head (Academic): B J C Horan, MA
Senior Master: C R Evans-Evans, BA, MEd, NPQH
Registrar: J G Taylor, MA
Deputy Head, Information Services: Dr A R H Clarke, MA, DPhil
Development Director: N J Latham, LLB Law
Head of Upper School: R C Harvey, MA
Head of Middle School: T W Jenkin, MA
Head of Lower School: T C H Greenaway, BSc
Chaplain: The Reverend D M Bond, BA, BTh

Assistant Staff:

Art & Design:
Ms I Lumsden, BA (*Head of Art and Design*)
Miss H C Blowes, BA
S N Leech, BA
J B Rogerson, BA

Biology:
Mrs S N Stuteley, BSc (*Head of Biology*)
F J Canales-Navarrett, BSc, BEd
C W Gray, BSc
T C H Greenaway, BSc (*Head of Lower School and SCR President*)

Mrs L Pruden-Lawson, MA (*Head of Clive House*)
Dr B J Stallwood, PhD (*Head of Ccommunity Service and Charities*)
Dr T R Stubbs, BSc, PhD, CBiol, MIBiol (*Second Master*)

Careers:
Mrs H Armstrong, BA, PG Dip (*Head of Careers*)
Mrs C M Andrews, BA, Dip TransIoLET (*Work Experience Coordinator*)
I A Jacob, BA (*Computing and Entrepreneur in Residence*)

Chemistry:
T J Hingston, MA (*Head of Chemistry*)
R I M Alexander, BSc (*Head of Hockey & Deputy Leader of Co-Curricular Activities*)
J E L Coote, MChem
Dr S Khan, MSc, PhD
Dr M Lomas, PhD (*Assistant Examination Officer*)
M P Powell, MA (*Assistant to Head of Upper School*)
Mrs F A Rashid, BSc (*Head of Science*)

Classics:
P D Harrison, MA (*Head of Classics*) (*SCR Representative on the Governing Body*)
Miss M L Bergquist BA (*Temporary*)
Mrs C D Fielding, BA (*Staff Tutor*)
M C Husbands, MA (*Second Master*)
X J Pollock, MA, MPhil (*Temporary*)

Computing:
G N Macleod, BA (*Head of Academic Computing*)
E E W Williams, MEng
I A Jacob, BA (*Entrepreneur in Residence*)

Design & Technology:
G M Stephenson, BSc (*Head of Design and Technology*)
J B Coleman, CertEd, MA
H J Hutchings, BA
N J Kyriacou, BEd (*Assistant to Head of Middle School*)

Drama and Theatre Studies:
D D Garnett, BA (*Director of Drama*)

Economics & Politics:
D C Halliday BA (*Head of Economics*)
Dr M I Beacham, PhD York (*Head of Andrewes House*)
Mrs H V Butland, MA (*Director of Teaching and Learning*)
E P James, BA, MSc (*Subject Leader for Politics*)
Miss A C Thornton, MPhil (*Second in Oxbridge*)

English:
M G Hilton-Dennis, BA (*Head of English*)
P M Capel, BA (*External Links Coordinator*)
Mrs J M Cox, BA
D A Gibbons, MA
T W Jenkin, MA (*Head of Middle School*)
J D Manley, MA (*Head of Mulcaster House*)
I J Mitchell, BA, BSc (*Head of Psychology*)
A J Richardson, MA
Mrs K Shockley, BA (*Second in English*)
Ms L V Smith, MA (*Head of Hilles House*)
J H Tyler, MA (*Head of Spenser House*)

Geography:
J D Innes, BA (*Acting Head of Geography*)
Miss N M Innes, BA (*Temporary*)
Mrs C B Jones, BA
[Mrs E J Lemoine, BA]
Miss H J Maxfield, BA
M J Prestshaw, BSc (*Head of PSHCE*)
Mrs S A Riddleston, BA
R Simmonds, BSc (*Head of PSHCE*)

History:
R J Try, MA, MSt (*Head of History*)

M Flower, BA (*Head of White House*)
M W S Hale, BA, MPhil (*Head of Walter House*)
B J C Horan, MA (*Senior Deputy Head, Academic*)
Miss F E Pace, BA (*Second in Enrichment*)
J G Taylor, MA (*Registrar*)
A A Watts, BA (*Deputy Director of Communications*)

Information Technology Systems:
Dr A R H Clarke, MA, DPhil (*Deputy Head, Information Services*)
P Gregory, HND (*Technical Services Manager*)
J P Beck (*Senior Network Engineer*)
J R Cho-Yee (*Network Engineer*)
P A J G Gregory (*Network Engineer*)
A Karr BSc (*ICT/AV Technician*)
I Rudling (*Webmaster*)

Learning Support:
Ms E J Sadler, BA Hons, MEd (*Head of Learning Support*)
Mrs G M Kantor, BA Hons, OCR Dip SpLD
M J S Paynter, BA (*Graduate Assistant*)

Library:
Mrs A J South, BSc, Dip Lib (*Senior Librarian*)
Mrs P J Jones, BA, PG Dip (*Library Assistant*)
Mrs R J L Millard, BA, MA (*Assistant Librarian*)

Mathematics:
A S Miller, BSc (*Head of Mathematics*)
Dr F R Andrews, BSc, PhD, DIC, ARCS
W J Beaumont, MA (*Head of Duke of Edinburgh's Award*)
P Davidson-Reiber, MMathPhil
M A Fothergill, BSc
Mrs D C Gedalla, MA
S F Hardman, BSc
Mrs G M Hazan, BA (*Temporary*)
M F Illing, MA
Mrs N Manek, BA (*Examinations Officer*)
Mrs T A Omert, BEng
Miss S M Peers, BSc (*Second in Mathematics, Tracking Manager and Second in DofE*)
S L Rowlands, BSc, MSc Cardiff (*Head Manor House*)
[Mrs N K Turton, BA]

Modern Foreign Languages:
R P Bailey, BA (*Head of Modern Foreign Languages*)
Mrs M C R Castro, BA (*Spanish*)
Miss R G Haye, Licence LCE (*French and Spanish*)
Ms V M Kotsuba BA, MA (*French*)
Miss H E McCullough, BA (*German and French*)
M W Pacey, BEd, Grad Cert Arts (*Subject Leader for German*)
J M S Rippier, BA (*French and Director of Communications*)
T P Rocher, L-ès-L (*French*)
Mrs C E Udell, MA (*German and French*)
F R Vignal, DipHE (*Subject Leader in French and Second in Modern Foreign Languages*)

Music:
S J Couldridge, DipTCL (*Director of Music*)
Dr R L Couchman, BA, MPhil, PhD (*Head of Academic Music*)
Mrs J H Stubbs, MusB, ARCO, ALCM (*Assistant Director of Music*)

Physical Education:
L D Foot, BSc (*Director of Sport*)
R I M Alexander, BSc (*Head of Hockey, Deputy Leader Co-curricular Activities and Joint Head of Academic PE*)
C R Evans-Evans, BA, MEd, NPQH (*Senior Master*)
I McGowan, BSc, MSc (*Graduate Assistant*)
A J Mills, BSc (*Head of Rugby and Joint Head of Academic PE*)

M J Penny, BSc (*Graduate Assistant*)

T Webley, BSc (*Head of Cricket, Assistant Head of Lower School and Joint Head of Academic PE*)

Physics:

[Mrs A Mayadeen, MPhys (*Head of Physics*)]

D W Hivey, BA (*Acting Head of Physics*)

Dr A R H Clarke, MA, DPhil (*Deputy Head, Information Services*)

S J Day, BSc

Dr J E Honeysett, PhD

C P Hull, BSc

D J Spikings, BA, MEng (*Director of Studies*)

Psychology:

I J Mitchell, BA, BSc (*Head of Psychology*)

Religious Education & Philosophy:

I L Smith, MA (*Head of Religious Education and Philosophy*)

The Rev D M Bond, BA, BTh (*School Chaplain and Head of Phab*)

M Flower, BA (*Head of White House*)

School Counsellor:

Ms P Llewellyn, BSc Hons, PG Dip

Visiting Teachers:

J Atkins, DipRAM (*Trumpet*)

G Boyd, DipMus (*Double Bass*)

S Byron, BMus Hons RCM (*Trombone*)

Miss S Clark, MA, LRSM, ARCM, Dip RCM, CTABRSM (*Piano*)

Mrs N S Coleman, CertEd (*Flute*)

Miss K Cormican, GTCL, PDOT (*Violin*)

G Cracknell, LRAM (*Violin*)

A Francis, LRAM (*Clarinet*)

J Francis (*Saxophone & Clarinet*)

A Gathercole, GGSM (*Trumpet*)

R Halford (*Guitar*)

Ms N Hawkins, (*Guitar*)

D Hester, LTCL, DipTCL (*Bassoon and Music Technology*)

C Hooker, LRAM, ARAM (*Oboe*)

J Lawrence, BA (*Percussion*)

D Lewis, LRAM (*Brass*)

Mrs N Manington, BMus LGSM (*Piano and Jazz Piano*)

N Martin (*Percussion*)

Ms P O'Sullivan, BA (*Recorder*)

D Rowland, MMus Perf (*Harp*)

D Saunderson, GGSM (*Singing*)

Mrs M Stone, MMus (*Piano*)

Mrs N Tait, LRAM Hons (*Cello*)

Sports:

A Bruce (*Strength and Conditioning*)

N Buckman (*Tennis*)

J Burley (*Rugby, Performance Analyst*)

P Cladd (*Tennis*)

R Crane (*Rugby*)

S Dokic (*Athletics*)

D Emms (*Tennis*)

L Fazekas (*Fencing*)

A French (*Watersports*)

G Furber (*Cricket*)

L Gick (*Physiotherapist*)

J Honeyben (*Rugby – WASPS*)

A Ibbetson (*Fives*)

J Jones (*Judo*)

M Khalifa (*Squash*)

N Lambert (*Rugby*)

P Loudon (*Hockey*)

A Morris (*Sports Psychologist*)

I Taplin (*Rugby – WASPS*)

D Thorpe (*Squash*)

L Wooldridge (*Cricket*)

Head Master's PA: Mrs C Herbert

Admissions Officer: G McCann

Bursar's Secretary: Mrs A Johnson

Merchant Taylors' Prep:

Head of School: Dr Karen McNerney, BSc Hons, PGCE, MSc, EdD

Assistant Head of School: Mr Michael Hibbert, BEd QTS

Deputy Head: Mr Andrew Crook, BA Hons, PGCE

Merchiston Castle School

Colinton, Edinburgh EH13 0PU

Tel: 0131 312 2200
       Headmaster: 0131 312 2203
       Admissions: 0131 312 2201

Fax: 0131 441 6060

email: headmaster@merchiston.co.uk

website: www.merchiston.co.uk

Twitter: @MerchiNews

Facebook: /MerchistonEdinburgh

LinkedIn: /merchiston-castle-school

Motto: *Ready Ay Ready*.

The School was established in 1833 and moved in 1930 from the centre of the city out to its present spacious and attractive site, bordered by the Water of Leith and close to the Pentland Hills.

There are 460 boys in the School, of whom 300 are boarders.

Admission. The normal ages of entry are 7–14 and 16, though from time to time there may be vacancies at other ages. Entry at 7–12 is by entrance assessment, interview and current school report; entry at 13 by the Common Entrance or Merchiston entrance examinations and current school report. Entry at 14 is by Merchiston entrance examinations. Entry to the Sixth Form at 16 depends on a successful showing in GCSE or National 4 and National 5 examinations as well as on interview and a school report. There are approximately 160 pupils in the Sixth Form. Entry is possible in all three terms where vacancies permit.

A prospectus and further details may be obtained from the Registrar. Prospective parents are encouraged to visit the School. Information may be also found on our website: www.merchiston.co.uk.

Video Gallery. Please follow this link to view videos of Merchiston life: Merchiston Video Gallery.

Courses of study. In the Juniors the curriculum comprises English, English Literature, Mathematics, Biology, Chemistry, Physics, History, French, Latin, German, Spanish, Mandarin, Geography, Religious Studies, Art and Design, Music, PE, Electronics, Design and Technology, and Information Technology.

In the Middle School a 2-year course leading to GCSEs is followed, consisting of a core curriculum: English, English Literature, Mathematics, a foreign language (French, German, Spanish, Mandarin), IGCSE Biology, Chemistry and Physics, and a wide range of optional subjects, including History, a second foreign language, Electronics, Information Technology, Geography, Latin, Religious Studies (Philosophy and Ethics), Art and Design, Design and Technology, and Music. Many boys take 10 subjects.

In the Lower Sixth, most boys study 4 subjects at AS Level. In the Upper Sixth, boys study generally 3 subjects to A2. A Level options include English Literature, Mathematics, Further Mathematics, Biology, Chemistry, Physics, French, German, Spanish, History, Geography, Economics, Government and Politics, Classical Civilisation, Religious Studies, PE, Information Technology, Latin, Design and Technology, Electronics (AS only) and Art. Other languages at A Level (including Classical Greek, Italian and Russian) are available on request and at additional charge. In addition to his main subjects, each boy follows a General Studies course offering Moral and Social Studies and Careers Guidance. Classes are small throughout the School, and all subjects are set by ability. The School prepares boys for entry to Oxford and Cambridge.

The School makes provision for specialist ESOL teaching for International students, including an opportunity to study GCSE English in the Upper Sixth year.

In 2015, the A Level A*–B pass rate was 76% with 65% of pupils gaining entry to their first choice and 88% gaining entry to their first or second choice of University.

Support for Learning Provision. Able boys with learning difficulties, including dyslexia, enjoy successful careers at Merchiston. Our aim is to enhance self-esteem through genuine praise. We encourage each pupil to find success in his area of strength, whether inside or outside the classroom. The objective is that all pupils have access to a wide and varied curriculum, and that, as a result, each discovers his own personal strengths and talents, and enjoys the resulting success. All are expected to follow mainstream GCSE courses.

Houses. Each of the boarding houses caters for a particular age group and the atmosphere and activities are tailored accordingly. The purpose-built Sixth Form boarding house opened in 2009 offering 126 en-suite bedrooms, with modern kitchens, a multi-gym and open plan social spaces with stunning views of Edinburgh and Fife. The Housemaster and his House Tutors pay special attention to the care of the individual and to the development of both his studies and interests.

Day boys. The life of day boys is fully integrated with that of the boarders.

Games. The principal games are rugby, played in the Autumn and Lent Terms, and in the Summer Term cricket and athletics. In 2011 Merchiston launched The Golf Academy at Merchiston, which is based both at the School's 100-acre campus and also at nearby Kings Acre Golf Course, where coaching, practice and tutorial work take place. Launched in 2007, The Tennis Academy provides specialised coaching and a full training and sports science programme. There is a large indoor heated swimming pool and a sports hall, and there are good facilities for other sports including tennis, football, squash, fives, shooting, sailing, skiing, basketball, golf, badminton and hockey.

Music. Music plays an important part in the life of the School. Tuition is available in all keyboard and orchestral instruments; currently about fifty per cent of the School are learning a musical instrument, and two choirs flourish. There is also a School orchestra, a close harmony group, a jazz band and two pipe bands. The choir and instrumentalists frequently go on tour, eg to the USA, the Far East, and Europe.

Drama. There is at least one major drama production a term, jointly staged with our sister school, as well as frequent House plays or drama workshop productions in a well-equipped, purpose-built theatre.

Art, Craft, Design and Technology, and Ceramics. The Art and Design Centre offers scope both within the curriculum and in the pupils' free time for painting, pottery, metalwork, woodwork and design work. Courses in Computing and Electronics are also available both within the curriculum or in free time.

Societies. There is a wide variety of clubs, including chess, debating and electronics. Visits to theatres, concerts and exhibitions are a frequent part of a boy's life at Merchiston. The Enlightened Curriculum uses Edinburgh as a prime resource for cultural experiences for all age groups.

CCF. All boys join the CCF for a period of three terms, after which point participation is voluntary. This includes outward bound activities such as climbing, hillwalking, canoeing and camping. All senior boys at Merchiston also undertake a Bronze Duke of Edinburgh's Award expedition, with participation at Silver and Gold level on a purely voluntary basis.

The School is also very active in community service work.

Girls. The School does not take girls but has a special relationship as brother/sister school with St George's School for Girls, Edinburgh and Kilgraston School in Perthshire. This includes joint expeditions, concerts, tours, seminars, debating, drama, social events and study courses. Merchiston operates a joint fees scheme with St George's School for Girls; Kilgraston School and Queen Margaret's School, York.

Careers advice. An expert careers adviser supplements the advice of the Academic Management Team, Housemasters and Academic Tutors. In the LVI year, pupils attend timetabled lessons in Careers as part of the General Studies Programme of the Sixth Form, where they are also encouraged to take a Work Experience placement and to visit local universities in the month of June. When pupils start in the Shell, they undertake Cambridge Occupational Analysts (COA) Preview and Profile assessments. These assess each individual's interests and abilities in several key cognitive areas. In the Fifth Form each individual has a discussion with the Head of Careers, during which interests are explored and feedback from the COA assessments is given. The discussion is focused on career areas of interest – as identified by the individual and the COA feedback – and identifying areas to be investigated, as well as touching on potential A Level programmes. There is an annual HE & Careers Fair to which other local schools are invited.

Links with parents. There are regular parent/staff meetings and parents are fully briefed and consulted with regard to all academic and career decisions. There is also a parents' forum, which holds regular meetings.

Health. There is a medical centre in the charge of the School Nursing Sisters and the School Doctor visits regularly.

Fees per term (2016–2017). Junior School: Boarders £6,550, Day boys £4,700; Forms 2 and 3: Boarders £7,615, Day boys £5,610. Senior School (Forms 4 and above): Boarders £10,220, Day boys £7,570.

Sibling, Forces and Teaching Profession (means–tested) fee reductions are available.

Scholarships and Bursaries. Scholarships are offered for competition from 10+ up to 16, with an emphasis on 13+ entry from Prep Schools.

Junior (10+-12+): Academic, Music (including a Piping Exhibition), All-Rounder.

Senior & Sixth Form (13+, 14+, 16+): Academic, Music (including a Piping Exhibition), Sports, All-Rounder, Art & Design, Design & Technology.

Scholarships no longer carry an automatic fee concession.

Means-tested financial assistance: where parental income is not sufficient to allow the pupil to attend Merchiston, parents may apply for means-tested financial assistance, which may be up to 100% of the day or boarding fees.

International Scholarships include European, Kenyan and Hong Kong. Merchiston also supports the HMC Projects in Eastern and Central Europe Scholarship scheme.

Forces: 10% fee remission is available to the sons of serving members of HM Forces.

Trust Applications: The School can apply to charities on behalf of prospective candidates who can demonstrate financial need.

Old boys. The Secretary of The Merchistonian Club, c/o the School. Former pupils include: The Rt Hon Lord John MacGregor, MP; Sir Peter Burt, former Chief Executive, Bank of Scotland; The Rt Hon Lord Kenneth Osborne PC, longest-serving judge of the current Scottish bench; Air Marshal Sir John Baird, Surgeon General of the British

Armed Forces between 1997 and 2000, International Rugby Union players: N G R Mair, W S Glen, I H P Laughland, A C W Boyle, A H W Boyle, Q Dunlop, G R T Baird, J Jeffrey, P Walton, C Joiner, B R S Eriksson, D W Hodge, N J Mayer, I A Fullarton, P J Godman, F J M Brown, Sam Hidalgo-Clyne.

Charitable status. Merchiston Castle School is a Registered Charity, number SC016580. It aims to give each boy in his way the capacity and confidence to live in an uncertain world and to make that life as rich as possible; more specifically, to encourage him to work hard and to take pride in achievement, to think independently, to face up to challenges, to accept responsibility, to show concern for others and the environment, and to develop wider skills and interests.

Governors:
Chairman: G T G Baird, HND, FRAgS

Members of the Board:
H P G Maule, MA
Prof L Waterhouse, BA, MSW
Mrs S Kuenssberg, CBE, BA, DipAdEd, FRSA
R M Ridley, MA
S P Abram
J L Broadfoot, BA, MEd
B M McCorkell, BA, MA Cantab
I McAteer, LLB
R W Nutton, MB BS, MD, FRCS
D R Whiteford, OBE, BSc, FRSA, ARAgs
R S Elliot
P W Yellowlees
D C M Moore BSC, MPhil, PhD

In Attendance: Mrs P Marshall, MA

Secretary to the Governors and Bursar: A G Clayton, BA University of North Wales, MBA Warwick

President of the Merchistonian Club: W A McDonald, BA

School Leadership Team:

Headmaster: **A R Hunter**, BA Manchester

Senior Deputy Head: P K Hall, MA Oxford
Deputy Head Academic: S Campbell, BSc Glasgow
Deputy Head Co-Curricular: R A Charman, BA Canterbury
Deputy Head Pupil Support: A W Johnston, MA Edinburgh
Head of Merchiston Juniors: Ms N G Waldron, BA Kent

Academic Leadership Team:
Deputy Head Academic: S Campbell, BSc Glasgow
Assistant Head Academic: D D J Cartwright, BSc PhD Edinburgh
Assistant Head Academic: W J J Clayton, MA Edinburgh

Pupil Support Leadership Team and Delegated Named Persons:
Deputy Head Pupil Support: A W Johnston, MA Edinburgh
Assistant Head Pupil Support: B G Campbell, BSc Paisley
Assistant Head Pupil Support: Mrs I Stewart, BEd Glasgow
Senior Deputy Head: P K Hall, MA Oxford

Assistant Head – Professional Standards:
R P Nicholls, BSc Durham

Housemasters:
Laidlaw South: M R Hillier, MA Cambridge
Laidlaw North: D P Rowlands, MA Cambridge
Evans: R L McCorkell, BSc Edinburgh
Rogerson: P K Rossiter, MA Oxford
Chalmers East: F P J Main, BEd Edinburgh
Chalmers West: R S R Pyper, BSc Leeds
Pringle: Ms N G Waldron, BA Kent

Academic Departments:
* *Head of Department*

Art & Design and Design & Technology:
*J M V Cordingley, MA London
Miss F M Blakeman, Dip Des Napier
J D Loftus, BSc Robert Gordon
F P J Main, BEd Edinburgh
C F Thomson, BSc Heriot Watt

Biology:
*MS King, BSc Bristol
D M George, BSc Edinburgh
N M Lieberman, BSc Northumbria
Mrs H J Williams, MSc Glasgow

Chemistry:
*K G Pettigrew, BSc PhD Edinburgh
S R Belding, MA Edinburgh, MChem DPhil Oxford
D D J Cartwright, BSc PhD Edinburgh
Ms C Gilfillan, MSc Strathclyde

Classics:
*Mrs R J Fawthrop, BA Oxford
M R Hillier, MA Cambridge
Mrs C R Smith, BA Cambridge
Ms C M B Batey, MA Cambridge

Economics:
*W J J Clayton, MA Edinburgh
J D Ferguson, MA Edinburgh

Electronics:
*R P Nicholls, BSc Durham
J D Loftus, BSc Robert Gordon

English:
*Mrs S J Binnie, MA Edinburgh
Ms G Cunningham, BA Stirling
S H Kristjansson, BA Iceland (*Director of Drama*)
Ms L K Wellingsclare, BA Oxford, MLitt St Andrews
P S Williams, BA Leicester

English as an Additional Language:
*Mrs S J Hardman, BA Sheffield
Miss J M Bowman, MA Aberdeen
S J Horrocks, MA Cambridge

Geography:
*Dr T A S Bower, BA London, MSc Toronto, DPhil Oxford
S I Buchanan, BSc St Andrews
B J Hall, BSc Strathclyde
M Harkins, BA Stirling
M K Raikes, MA Manchester

History and Politics:
*S R Thompson, MA Edinburgh
F E Newham, MA Oxford
Mrs L McDiarmid, BA Warwick
J Troxler, BA Stirling

ICT:
*Mrs M B Watson, BSc Glasgow
J B Bisset, MA MSc Aberdeen (*Director of ICT Services*)
D H Thomson, MA Glasgow
D M Turner, MA Oxford (*Data and Website Manager*)

Mathematics:
*Ms F Vian, PhD Parma
S Campbell, BSc Glasgow
R A Charman, BA Canterbury
W J J Clayton, MA Edinburgh
M Harkins, BA Stirling
R C Lucas, MEng Aston, MA Sheffield
R L McCorkell, BSc Edinburgh
M R Monteith, MSci Belfast

Mrs M A S Muetzelfeldt, BSc London
Miss N M Steen, MSci PhD Belfast
J C O Vaughan, BSc Edinburgh
Ms J R Vaughan, BA Newcastle
Mrs M B Watson, BSc Glasgow

Modern Foreign Languages:
*Mrs M H Gray, MA Lyon
Ms J M Bowman, MA Aberdeen
F Calvo-Martin, BA Salamanca
F Geisler, LAS11/1 Bochum
S J Horrocks, MA Cambridge
Mrs J C Robertson, MA Bournemouth, BA BSc Taiyuan
D P Rowlands, MA Cambridge

Music:
*S M Dennis, BMus Edinburgh
D M Turner, MA Oxford

Physical Education:
*C R Harrison, BSc Napier
D W Blair, BSc Stirling
R C Deans, BSc Abertay (*Director of Rugby*)
R D McCann, BSc Ulster (*Director of Sport*)
R S R Pyper, BSc Leeds
M K Raikes, MA Manchester (*Director of Junior Sport*)

Physics:
*A M Roache, BSc St Andrews
Miss M L Aiken, BSc Edinburgh
Mrs A E Manners, MSc London
R P Nicholls, BSc Durham
Mrs S M Twyford, MSc Strathclyde, PhD Glasgow

Support for Learning:
*Mrs I Stewart, BEd Glasgow
Ms J R Vaughan, BA Newcastle
Mrs C Weaving, BSc Leeds

Religious Studies:
*Revd N G D Blair, MA Edinburgh

Pringle Centre:
Ms N G Waldron, BA Kent (*Head of Merchiston Juniors*)
Ms J R Vaughan, BA Newcastle (*Deputy Head Academic – Juniors*)
Miss R E Foster, MA Aberdeen (*Leader of Pringle Centre*)
M R Boyd, BEd Stranmillis
M Harkins, BA Stirling
M K Raikes, MA Manchester

Accounts and Human Resources:
*A G Clayton, BA North Wales, MBA Warwick (*Bursar*)
Ms A Lees, BSc Oxford (*Financial Controller*)
Mrs C McIntosh, HNC Stevenson (*Assistant Bursar*)
Mrs K M Morrison (*Purchase Ledger*)
Ms C L Hall (*HR Administrator*)

Administration:
Mrs S Nicholson (*Executive PA to Headmaster*)
Mrs L W Campbell (*Senior Deputy Head's Secretary*)
Mrs L Campion, BSc St Andrews, BM Napier (*Assistant Secretary*)
Mrs E Firoozi (*Academic Secretary*)
Mrs G B Gibson (*Receptionist*)
Mrs H McIntosh (*Admin Assistant*)
Miss B R Lawson, MA Stirling, MSc Napier (*Admin Assistant*)

Admissions:
Mrs K Wilson (*Admissions Manager*)
Miss H Aitken, BA Napier (*Admissions Assistant*)

Chapel Team:
Revd N G D Blair, MA Edinburgh (*Leader of the Chaplaincy Team*)

P K Rossiter
S M Dennis

Departmental Technical Assistants:
R Shepley, MChem Edinburgh (*Lab Technician*)
Miss N A Farrugia, BSc London Metropolitan (*Lab Technician*)
Mrs K Ryan, BSc Abertay (*Lab Technician*)
A C MacNeill (*IT Network Manager*)
C A Brown, BSc Heriot Watt (*Network Admin*)
N P Burt (*Design & Technology*)

Development:
D Rider, MinstF (*Cert*) (*Director*)
Miss G Imrie, BA Napier (*Assistant*)
Miss L M Pert (*Assistant*)

Domestic and Catering Management Team:
Mrs A J Hanna (*General Manager*)
C Afrin (*Head Chef*)
Ms K Macdonald (*Domestic Manager*)
Mrs J Hogg (*Duty Manager*)
Ms A Slodownik (*Domestic Supervisor*)

Examinations:
T J Lawson, BA Sheffield, PhD Edinburgh, FSAScot (*Examinations Officer*)
F E Newham, MA Oxford (*Assistant Examinations Officer*)

External Relations:
Mrs T I Gray, BA Napier (*Manager*)
Miss M C White, BA Stirling (*Assistant*)

Library:
Mrs J M Williams, BA Leicester (*Librarian*)

Medical Staff:
Dr K Robertson (*Medical Officer*)
Dr D A Reid (*Medical Officer*)
Ms J Bennington-Lloyd, RGN (*Senior Medical Sister*)
Mrs J N Fisher, RGN (*School Nurse*)
Mrs N Fallowfield, RGN (*School Nurse*)
Mrs D Marshall, Scottish Ambulance First Responder (*Health Assistant*)
Mrs L Benn, BSc Robert Gordon, MCSP (*Physiotherapist*)

Specialist Sports Coaches:
S Gilmour, MSc Edinburgh (*Cricket*)
A Evans (*Cricket*)
D Brewer (*Tennis Academy Leader*)
N Lundy, MA Sunderland (*Tennis Academy*)
G Soutar (*Tennis Academy*)
A Murdoch (*Golf Academy Leader*)
K Mungall (*Golf*)
S Capaldi (*Basketball*)
J Hay (*Squash*)
Mrs S Legget, CertEd Durham (*Swimming*)
A Young (*Swimming*)
I M Noble, BSc Napier (*Strength & Conditioning*)

Support Staff:
Major A D Ewing, BSc Napier (*School Staff Instructor*)
G Campbell, MA Aberdeen (*Master i/c Pipe Bands*)
Mrs M Lucas, BA Edinburgh College of Art (*Masterchef*)
Mrs F Blair, BSc Edinburgh, BA Queen Margaret's (*School Counsellor*)
Mrs J A Ghazal (*Support Assistant – Juniors*)
Mrs C L Nugent, BSc Northumbria, MEd Edinburgh (*Pringle Housemother*)
Mrs P Wearmouth, CertEd Dunfermline (*Pringle Assistant*)
Mrs A McGregor, BA Edinburgh (*Chalmers East and Rogerson Housemother*)
Mrs R Pyper, BMus University College Dublin (*Chalmers West Housemother*)
Mrs M Cordingley, BA Roehampton (*School Shop Manager*)

Mrs F Horrocks, BA South Africa (*School Exchange Shop*)
Mrs L Millard (*Bookshop*)
D Holliday, BA Durham (*Graduate Assistant Teacher*)
B T Lothian (*Transport Manager Health & Safety Coordinator*)

Visiting Instrumental Music Teachers:
Miss J Beeston (*Upper Strings*)
Ms M C Bell (*Oboe/Bassoon*)
B Davidson (*Piano*)
B Donaldson (*Bagpipes*)
Ms S Sahyouni (*Singing*)
A McGrattan (*Brass*)
C Macgregor (*Kit*)
A Rankin (*Percussion*)
A Mitchell (*Guitar*)
Ms K M Nicholls (*Piano*)
J Walker (*Drums*)
Mrs L Bell (*Woodwind*)
Mrs R Pyper (*Voice/Theory*)
G McDiarmid (*Guitar*)
Ms J Pearce (*Flute*)
Ms S Lee (*Cello*)
Mrs R Banyuls-Bertomeu (*Saxophone*)
P A Chamberlain (*Accordion*)

Visiting Language Teachers:
Mrs J L McKinlay (*ESOL Consultant*)
Mrs R Nazipova-Petherick (*Russian*)
Mrs N Davidson (*Japanese*)
Mrs K Kelly (*Japanese*)
Ms C Van Wengen (*Dutch*)
Dr M Breatnach (*French*)
Miss A Rodriguez-Macias (*Spanish*)
Miss C Gaudiano (*Italian*)
Miss N Walsh (*Language Assistant*)
Miss T Birkner (*Language Assistant*)

Works Staff:
D M Stenhouse (*Master of Works*)
Mrs K Stables (*Secretary*)
M Yan Hip (*Head Groundsman*)
J W Hutchison (*Groundsman*)
D A Stewart (*Groundsman*)
J House (*Groundsman*)
S Chalmers (*Groundsman*)
A Campbell (*Joiner*)
B McLeish (*Joiner*)
A Brooks (*Painter*)
S Thomson (*Painter*)
B Begley (*Electrician*)

Mill Hill School

The Ridgeway, Mill Hill, London NW7 1QS
Tel: 020 8959 1221 (Admissions)
Fax: 020 8906 2614
email: registrations@millhill.org.uk
website: www.millhill.org.uk

Mill Hill was founded by Samuel Favell (1760–1830) and Revd John Pye Smith (1774–1851) as a grammar school for the sons of Protestant dissenters and opened in 1807. The School's motto, *et virtulem et musas* ('both virtue and learning') continues to characterise the aims of the School. Indeed in September 1997 the School became fully co-educational.

Location. The School is part of Mill Hill village and is situated in a conservation area, on the borders of Hertfordshire and Middlesex, approximately 12 miles from the centre of London. Set in 120 acres of parkland originally formed by the famous botanist Peter Collinson, the grounds provide a spacious setting for the academic buildings, boarding and day houses and offer extensive facilities for sports and activities.

Buildings. Mill Hill combines a rich traditional heritage with modern educational facilities. The present School was designed by Sir William Tite, architect of the Royal Exchange and opened in 1826. Since the late 19th century numerous buildings have been added, including the Chapel, Library, Assembly Hall, Music School and Science Block. Other additions include the Art and Design Technology Centre, a modern Sports Hall, a new Sixth Form Centre and Innovation Hub, the Piper library and learning resources centre, a multimedia language centre, two networked IT suites, a music technology centre including a hard disk recording studio, a theatre, a studio theatre, an indoor swimming pool and three Eton Fives Courts.

As well as these facilities, a brand new academic teaching block, The Favell Building, was opened in 2007. This houses 25 new classrooms with libraries, seminar rooms, and departmental offices for the Geography, History, Business Education, Classics, Religious Education and the Modern Foreign Languages departments.

Houses. There are 678 pupils in the School (463 boys, 215 girls) of whom around 100 are boarders. Weekly and full boarding is available for entry at Year 9, Year 10 and Sixth Form and we currently have 40 weekly boarders. There are five boarding Houses and seven day Houses all of which have been recently refurbished. Day pupils take a full part in the activities of the School. Full boarders have a full range of activities and workshops on Saturday mornings. These sessions are optional to day and weekly boarding pupils.

Admission. Application may be made as early as parents wish. The majority of boys and girls enter at the age of 13 and candidates are selected on the basis of interviews, examinations and a Head's confidential reference.

Pre-testing is offered in Year 6 for unconditional places at Year 9 (13+ entry). For Year 6 track candidates, the test is a computer-based assessment of aptitude in Reading Comprehension, Verbal, Non-Verbal and Numerical Reasoning. Results are age-standardised, enabling us accurately to compare candidates born at different times of the year.

For the Year 8 track, the tests remain as traditional entrance examinations in English, Mathematics, Science and French, with Latin as an optional paper. Year 8 examinations assess against the Common Entrance syllabus in each subject, and act as our Academic Award examinations.

Scholarship candidates are identified through the entrance tests (Year 8 Track) and candidates are called back for interviews on the basis of their scores. Single subject awards may be made. Awards are also made for Art, Music, Drama, Sports and Design Technology.

There are two other methods of entry:

(a) A limited number of places are available at 14+. Candidates are selected on the basis of interview, performance in the 14+ Entrance Examinations (English, Maths, Science and French) and a Head's confidential reference.

(b) Sixth Form Entry: Admission to the Sixth Form is based on an entry requirement of five GCSE passes, at least two at Grade A plus three at Grade B, together with at least C grades in Mathematics and English, or equivalent qualifications for overseas pupils. More detailed entry requirements for specific AS courses are given in the School's Sixth Form Curriculum Guide. Candidates unable to offer the number of subjects required (e.g. some overseas candidates) will be considered on their individual academic merit.

Selection is by interview at the School (there are no examinations) and by reference from the candidate's present school. Offers made are conditional on meeting the entry requirements detailed above. International candidates may be asked to complete entry tests in the subjects they wish to study in the Sixth Form and are interviewed either in person or by Skype. All pupils with English as a second language will be asked to sit an EAL paper. Scholarships are awarded on the basis of examinations and interviews in January.

Pastoral Care. Pastoral care is organised by House and individual House identities are a significant feature of Mill Hill. All of the Houses (including day Houses) have their own designated space including recreational facilities and areas for relaxation and/or study. In the School's most recent full ISI Inspection in 2012, the overall quality of pastoral care was rated as *Outstanding* and genuine pride is taken in maintaining and developing this aspect as a real strength of the School as a whole. Boarding was also rated as *Excellent* in all five categories.

The report also portrayed *teachers and tutors as knowing their pupils very well* and described *pupils' behaviour as showing a high degree of maturity.* The provision of boarding too was rated as *Excellent* and the School received particular praise for providing *a lively supportive and caring environment that allows boarders to grow in confidence, independence and sensitivity to the needs of others, in line with its aims.*

One of the principal features of the Mill Hill approach to pastoral care is the continuity of support and involvement offered by Housemasters/Housemistresses throughout a pupil's career at Mill Hill, aided by Tutors and House Parents who work within a House dealing with day-to-day matters for specific year groups.

Another particularly notable element of Mill Hill's pastoral care is the wide range of dynamic pupil councils which meet regularly covering areas as diverse as anti-bullying and mentoring, boarding, charity, environmental issues, food, Fourth Form (new Year 9 pupils), inter-faith and Sixth Form-specific issues. In addition there is a Full School Council which offers an opportunity for the pupils' voices to be heard on key whole-School issues.

Curriculum. The School's academic curriculum is broad, flexible and forward-looking and is designed to encourage among pupils intellectual curiosity, sound learning and a spirit of enquiry in the pursuit of academic excellence. It seeks to enable pupils to acquire core knowledge and skills in English, Mathematics, Science and a Modern Language and, in addition, to develop their own particular academic interests. It also incorporates a full programme of Personal, Social and Health Education, appropriate guidance and information for pupils on subject choices, higher education and careers. Detailed information on the curriculum for each Key Stage is set out in a series of three curriculum guides, which are available on the School website and from the Admissions Office.

Organisation of the Curriculum. Pupils normally enter the School at 13+ (Year 9). There are normally 7 core subject sets in each of Years 9, 10 and 11. The Year 9 curriculum aims to consolidate what has been learned in the previous two years, to enable pupils to experience a comprehensive range of subjects and to maintain pace and progression as they prepare for their GCSE courses.

When choosing their GCSE option subjects, pupils are encouraged to select a combination of subjects which maintain a sensible breadth of study. This will vary between pupils and is balanced against each pupil's relative strengths in his/her subjects. Greater emphasis is nevertheless given to each pupil choosing option subjects which they enjoy and in which they are likely to do well, than mere breadth for its own sake. In Years 10 and 11 English Language, English Literature, Mathematics, three separate Sciences or Dual Award Science and a Modern Language (French, German or Spanish) are core examination courses, in addition to PE and Games. Pupils also choose three GCSE option subjects from

Art, Classical Civilisation, Computer Science, Design Technology, Drama, Geography, German, History, Information and Communication Technology, Latin, Music, Physical Education, Religious Studies and Spanish. Further Pure Mathematics IGCSE is offered to the ablest mathematicians, and there are opportunities to take Ancient Greek outside the regular timetable.

The **Sixth Form Curriculum** offers a wide and flexible choice of A Level courses. It aims to encourage and develop personal skills of study, research and thought and to encourage pupils to consider and discuss issues relevant to them as they move towards adulthood and participation in the full range in rights and responsibilities as citizens. The School keeps its range of Sixth Form subjects under continuous review, and has recently added Psychology to its offer.

In the **Lower Sixth** pupils have traditionally taken four academic courses. In addition they follow a course in Personal, Social, Health and Religious Education. The most able mathematicians take Mathematics and Further Mathematics together as one of their courses. For a small number of pupils, a programme of three, rather than, four courses is appropriate. Guidance is given to pupils and their parents about making subject choices; this includes an external academic/careers guidance test report and interview and discussions with tutors, Housemasters/mistresses and senior members of staff.

In the **Upper Sixth** most pupils take three subjects plus a weekly timetabled session of Personal, Social, Health and Religious Education.

Provision for Pupils with Special Educational Needs and/or Disabilities (SEND) and Learning Difficulties and/or Disabilities (LDD). The School provides those pupils who have a statement of educational need or a learning difficulty or disability support to meet their requirements and a suitably adapted curriculum, where this is appropriate. The Learning Support Department plays a key role in this work, seeking to identify, through screening and ongoing monitoring, the particular needs of individual pupils and putting in place strategies (and, where necessary, additional assistance) designed to help them fulfil their potential. Pupils who have a Special Educational Need and/or Disability may have their curriculum modified to take account of their particular needs, as appropriate. Where a pupil has a statement of Special Educational Needs, the requirements of the statement are closely followed in order to ensure that the School provides an effective and accessible educational experience. The progress of all pupils on the School's Learning Support Register is regularly reviewed and support is amended as appropriate.

Academic and Careers Guidance. Through the tutor system, presentations and information evenings, pupils are helped to make the best possible choices of GCSE and Sixth Form courses and to make well-informed and appropriate higher education choices. In the Sixth Form the School arranges visits to universities as well as presentations, workshops and information evenings. The School has a full-time Head of University and Post-School guidance and an active Careers Department which provides information and advice on possible future careers paths. Careers Education is included within the School's Personal, Social, Health and Religious Education programme and careers interviews are arranged for pupils in Year 11 and in the Lower Sixth, and also on request for other pupils. Careers guidance was rated as *Excellent* in the 2012 ISI inspection.

Support for pupils with English as an Additional Language. For pupils whose first language is not English, class or individual tuition in EAL is provided as appropriate, to enable them to maximise their academic opportunities and to enjoy all of the social and cultural aspects of life at the School. Some EAL pupils follow a modified curriculum in order to accommodate their needs, where this is appropriate. EAL pupils are prepared for IGCSE English as a Second Language, ideally in Year 10, and IELTS in Year 11 or the Lower Sixth, depending on the point at which they enter the School. Extra, individual, EAL tuition in addition to class lessons can be arranged if required.

Academic Enrichment. The School prides itself on offering a broad variety of opportunities for pupils to pursue their curiosity and extend their knowledge and skills outside the formal curriculum. There is a plethora of subject societies operating in both the Lower School (Years 9–11) and the Sixth Form. Academic departments enter pupils of all ages for external competitions such as essay prizes in Humanities and Classics, Olympiads in Science subjects and national debating competitions for Modern Languages. A number of current and past pupils have held Arkwright Engineering Scholarships. Sixth Formers can opt for the Extended Project Qualification. The School uses its proximity to Central London to take pupils to lectures, plays, concerts, exhibitions and seminar days. There is a wide variety of academically based trips on offer, such as: Modern Languages exchanges and study visits to many destinations in Europe; Art trips to New York and the Venice Biennale; Design Technology trip to the Centre for Alternative Technology in mid-Wales; Geography field trip to Iceland.

Art, Drama and Music. The Creative Arts have a long and successful tradition at Mill Hill and are a key part of the academic curriculum. In addition to achieving excellent results in public examinations, relevant academic departments have a high success rate in preparing students for further study in the Arts. For example, six of the School's eight A Level Art candidates in 2016 have gone on to Art-related degrees.

Alongside academic successes, there is a substantial and varied programme of co-curricular activities in these subjects. The Art Department offers facilities and expertise for pupils to develop their interest and skills in painting and drawing, alternative media, film, illustration, multimedia, photography (including digital photography), printmaking, sculpture, textiles, theatre design and video.

In addition to the very extensive range and number of drama performances relating to examination courses there is a biennial inter-House Drama festival, which alternates with the biennial inter-House Music Festival; both attract a high level of pupil participation. There is a regular programme of School plays, ranging from Shakespeare to musicals. The School's musical ensembles include an orchestra, wind band, string ensemble, jazz band, four choirs and numerous ad hoc pupil bands and chamber ensembles. Individual tuition in most instruments and in singing is available from high quality specialist teachers. There is an extensive programme of concerts, competitions and recitals throughout the year, some of which include recitals by professional performers.

Tours have included drama performances at the Edinburgh Festival and choir tours to New York and Paris, plus a Chapel Choir residency at Canterbury Cathedral.

Sport. Mill Hill School is renowned for its sporting excellence. Every pupil, regardless of physical ability, is encouraged to participate in both competitive and non-competitive sport. The major sports for the boys are Rugby, Hockey (although we are currently reviewing the offer of Football) and Cricket and for the girls are Hockey, Netball, Rounders and Tennis. Other opportunities include Athletics, Basketball, Cross Country, Eton Fives, Golf, Horse Riding, Soccer, and Swimming. For our most able pupils we run a fantastic sports scholarship scheme which aims to increase the breadth of sporting experience of our youngest pupils and is increasingly sport focused at the top end of the School. There are a range of awards and bursaries (including full bursaries) available for talented sporting pupils designed to supplement our home grown talent. The level of professional coaching skills is exceptional. In addition to the excellent full-time staff members, we benefit from having a team of external coaches; including Strength, Conditioning and Kicking coaches from Saracens RFC and Middlesex CC to professional coaches in Netball and Tennis. The School has a 25-metre indoor swimming pool, three Eton Fives Courts, a shooting range, an all-weather pitch and a Sports Hall including a refurbished Fitness Suite and a Free Weights Room. Mill Hill is the home to the London Golf Academy which benefits from our own Golf professional, an on-site short course facility, indoor golf coaching facilities as well as having a link and access to the amazing facilities at The Shire Golf Club. Finally, the pupils are given the opportunity of participating in overseas sports tours for all of the major and many of the minor sports at the School.

Co-curricular Activities. Year 9 pupils are introduced to the range of minor sports (as above) and aspects of adventure training. All pupils are also offered a range of other activities such as debating, drama, chess, jewellery-making and computing. In Year 10 the focus is 'teamwork and leadership'. Pupils choose from a number of options including the CCF (Army, Navy and RAF), a Sports Leaders programme and Business Enterprise. In addition, many Societies exist to cater for a variety of out-of-school interests.

Fees per term (2016–2017). Boarding £10,442, Weekly Boarding £8,834, Day (including lunch) £6,547. Fees include the games fee and the cost of most textbooks and stationery.

Scholarships and Bursaries. Scholarships, which attract a maximum of 10% fee remission, are available to pupils showing exceptional talent in a variety of areas both in the classroom and on the sports field. Academic, Music, Drama, Art, Design and Technology, and Sports Awards are available at 13+ and Academic Scholarships are available to candidates entering the Sixth Form. In addition to major Awards, there are a number of minor Awards or Exhibitions also on offer. The Head, Deputy Head (External Relations) the Registrar and the Assistant Registrar are happy to advise parents and feeder schools about any of these Awards.

Bursaries are available for those entrants able to demonstrate a financial need. Parents will be asked to complete a detailed statement of their financial circumstances. Applicants for Bursaries will be selected in the normal way. There is provision for the award of full-fee Bursaries for entrants at all levels. It is possible for bursary funds to be used to top up Scholarship Awards. As with scholarship queries, the Head, Deputy Head (External Relations) or the Assistant Registrar are happy to offer advice.

There are also a number of special scholarships and bursaries available, further information of which is available on the School's website www.millhill.org.uk.

The Mount, Mill Hill International is a new co-educational boarding and day school for international pupils which opened in September 2015 on a newly refurbished site adjacent to the main School campus. Mill Hill International is an important part of the Mill Hill School Foundation, a family of four co-educational schools for boys and girls aged 3 to 18. It offers a traditional British educational experience and an academic curriculum up to GCSE/IGCSE and specialist EAL teaching. Pupils for whom English is not their first language receive English language tuition while at the same time studying an appropriate range of other subjects in order to equip them for further study whether at Mill Hill School or elsewhere. Suitable also for British pupils returning to the UK after a period abroad, Mill Hill International offers an intensive one year GCSE/IGCSE course for pupils entering Year 11. For further information visit the website – millhillinternational.org.uk.

Charitable status. The Mill Hill School Foundation is a Registered Charity, number 1064758. It exists for the education of boys and girls.

Court of Governors:

Chairman: Dr R G Chapman, BSc, MB BS, FRCGP
Deputy Chairman: A L Brooke Esq, BA Cantab, MBA
Professor E W F W Alton, MA, MB BS, MD, FRCP,
    FHEA, FERS, FMedSci
Dr A P Craig, MBBS, DRCOG
D J Dickinson Esq, DipQS, MRICS
R A Eliott Lockhart Esq, MA Cantab, MPhil
Mrs S Freestone, MEd, GRSM, LRAM, ARCM, FRSA
D Harris Esq, BSc, FCA
E Lipton Esq, MBA, BSc Hons, ACGI, DIC, FRSA,
    FRICS
Mrs S J Miller, BA Hons
G Nosworthy Esq
Mrs M Patel, MBA, BCS, BFSS
R L Tray Esq, BA Hons, MA Cantab, MBA
A W Welch Esq, BA, MA Oxon
Mrs P H Wilkes, BEd, FRSA

Director of Operations and Finance [Interim]: A Flanagan,
    CIPFA, Ad Dip
Clerk to the Court: Dr R L Axworthy, JP, BA Hons, PhD

Head: Mrs F M R King, MA Oxon, MA London, PGCE,
    MBA

† *Housemaster/Housemistress*

Principal Deputy Head: Mrs J Sanchez, BSc (*also PHSRE*)
Deputy Head (Academic): A T W Frazer, MA (*also
    Modern Languages*)
Deputy Head (External Relations): A J Binns, BA (*also
    English*)
Foundation Director of Boarding: Miss L J Farrant, BA
    (*also English*)
Assistant Head (Pastoral): K M Seecharan, BA (*also
    History and Politics*)
Assistant Head (Academic): S Baldock, MA, FRSB (*also
    Biology*)
Director of Academic Administration: J M Lewis, MA
    (*also English*)
Director of Sixth Form: J A Barron, BSc, MA (*also
    Coordinator of Sixth Form Chemistry*)
Director of Sport: T J Vercoe, BSc, MA (*also Physical
    Education*)

Chaplain: Revd Dr R J Warden, BA, MTh, DMin (*also
    Head of RE*)

Assistant Teachers:

Art & Design:
A D Ross, MA (*Head of Art and Design*)
N G Cheeseman, BA
Miss V C Dempster, MA

Business Education:
M S Smith, BA (*Acting Head of Business Education*)
P H Edwards, BA
Mrs V G Miner, MSc
Mrs P Stoughton-Harris, BA

Classics:
A R Homer, BA (*Head of Classics*)
†S T Plummer, BA

Design Technology:
Ms B D Banks, BEd (*Head of Design Technology*)
C M McKay, BA

English & Drama:
R W Searby, BA (*Head of English*)
D S Proudlock, BA (*Head of Drama*)
Ms K E Ferson, MA (*Head of EAL*)
†D T Bingham, BA
Mrs S R Hope, BA

Mrs S Isaacs, BEd
Mrs E Kaplan, BA
Miss S Martinez, BA, MEd
Mrs A L Murphy, BA
Mrs S Stagg, LLB
Mrs N Stimler, BA
Mrs P Wright, Dip ACT
Mrs J S L Young, BA

Geography:
†Ms S J Bull, BSc (*Head of Geography*)
N R Hodgson, MA
D R Woodrow, BA (*Coordinator of Activities*)

Higher Education:
Miss L H Sharples, BA (*Head of University and Post
    School Guidance*)

History & Politics:
M Dickinson, MA (*Head of History*)
D W Hine, MA (*Head of Government & Politics*)
Mrs C E Adams, BA
Mrs R E Bradley, MA (*Extended Project Qualification
    Coordinator*)
Mr A Granath, BA
K G Pearson, BA

Information Technology and Computer Science:
L A C Minett, BSc (*Head of ICT & Computer Science*)
Ms P A Newsome, BSc

Mathematics:
K P Bulman, BSc (*Head of Mathematics*)
Miss W Ashraf, MEng, MBA
M J Carruthers, BEng (*Assistant Examinations Officer*)
P J Kwok, BEng
G W Roberts, BA
Mrs L R Sandu, BSc
A H Slade, BA
Miss E Stewart, BA
T Trhlik, BSc (*Second in Department, Time-Tabler*)

Modern Languages:
M S V Bardou, BA, (*Head of Modern Languages, French
    & Spanish*)
Mrs B K Hazeldine, MA (*Head of German*)
Miss V S David, Maîtrise d'Anglais
Miss A C Ellerington, BA
†P R Lawson, MA
Mr A B Mansilla, BA
Miss M Soriano Florez, MA

Music:
H E Brink, BA (*Director of Academic Music*)
K Kyle, BMus Hons, LRAM, PG Dip RAM (*Director of
    Musical Performance*)
A Chakravarty, MA, ARCM
†Dr R Peat, BMus, MA, PhD

Visiting Instrumental Teachers:
J Bradford, BA, BMus, LGSM, LLCM, ALCM, PGCE,
    AdvDip, Cert Berklee (*guitars*)
A Cucchiara, GRNCM (*violin*)
Mrs C Emanuel, Dip Perf RCM, Dip RAC (*violin*)
J Fleeman, GCLCM, Adv Cert GSMD (*percussion*)
Dr O Gledhill, MA Mtpp, PGCA, ARCM, PhD
    (*violoncello*)
Miss R Havel, BMus, MPerf (*voice*)
Miss C Hopper, BMus, LRAM, DipRam (*voice*)
P Jaekel, GRSM, LRAM, ARCO (*pianoforte*)
Mrs H Kearns, BA, LTCL (*pianoforte*)
Mrs H Kyle, BMus, LRAM (*voice*)
A Martin, AGSM (*percussion*)
A R McAfee, BA, PGCE, TCM (*flute/piccolo*)
Mrs M L Payne, BMus TCM, LTCL (*saxophone/clarinet*)

Dr A Poole, BSc, MA, PhD (*double bass, guitar*)
Mrs A Starr, BMus RCM, MMus TCM (*pianoforte*)
Miss J Tate, BA Mus, Grad RNCM, Dip MTP (*voice*)

Physical Education:
D L Townson, MSc (*Head of PE*)
D M Halford, PGA (*Director of Golf*)
†S Hendy, BSc
†Miss R L Jakeman, MEd (*Head of Girls' Games & Head of PHSRE*)
Mr B H Kerr, BSc (*Director of Rugby and Gifted & Talented Coordinator of Sport*)
†A T Morton, BSc, MEd

Religious Education:
Revd Dr R J Warden, BA, MTh, DMin (*Head of RE and Chaplain*)
Miss N F Anders, MA
Miss L E Miller, BA, MEd

Sciences:
L J Stubbles, MSc (*Head of Science and Head of Physics*)
Dr K R Damberg, BSc, MD (*Head of Biology*)
G N Saint, BSc (*Head of Chemistry*)
†Miss A Bignell, BSc, MA
Miss L E Fox, BSc
M E Jennings, BSc, MRSB
Miss H V P Kimber, BSc (*Teacher in charge of Psychology*)
J M Murphy, BSc (*Lower School Gifted & Talented Coordinator*)
Dr S Radojevic, BSc, PhD
R Savva, BSc
G C Stead, BSc
†G M Turner, BSc
M J Uddin, BSc
J G W Watson, BSc
C M G Watterson, BEng, MSci

Learning Support:
Miss L N Silverman, BA, Dip SpLD (*Head of Learning Support*)
Mrs A Fryatt, BEd, MA, Dip Counsel APC
Mrs J R Herbert, BA

Head of Careers: Miss N F Anders, MA (*also Religious Education*)

Officer Commanding CCF: Major A Norrington

Medical Officer: Dr J Peter

Nurse:
Miss A Whatford, RGN (*Nurse Manager*)
Miss R Kelly (*Resident Health Care Assistant*)
Mrs Jane Simpson, RGN

Belmont, Mill Hill Preparatory School
The Ridgeway, Mill Hill, London NW7 4ED
Tel: 020 8906 7270; Fax: 020 8906 3519
email: office@belmontschool.com
website: www.belmontschool.com

Head: L Roberts, MA, PGCE

Senior Deputy Head (*Pastoral*): P Symes, BSc, PGCE
Deputy Head (*Academic*): Mrs R Alford, M.Ed
Deputy Head (*Operations*): J Fleet, BSc, PGSE
Head of Lower School: Ms R Sutherns, MA, SESI
Assistant Head (*Marketing, Communications and Admissions*): J Pym, MEd, PGCE
Assistant Head (*Teaching & Learning*): Miss J Harrison, BSc, PGCE

Heads of Department:
Mr J McNulty, BA, PGCE (*Art*)
Mr J Clement, BA, PGCE (*Classics*)

Mr A Warden, BA, QTS (*Design Technology*)
Miss L Olsson BA, GDE (*English*) [Maternity]
Miss S Bufton BA, PGCE (*Acting Head of English*)
Mrs C McRill, BA, PGCE (*French*)
Mr A Hayward, BSc, PGCE (*Geography*)
Mrs C Smith, BA, PGCE (*History*)
Mrs A Gritz, BSc, QTS (*ICT*)
Mrs G Perrin, BA, PGCE (*Music*)
Mrs C Pugh, MA, PGCE (*Mathematics*)
Mr N Bird, BA, GTP (*Boys' Games*)
Miss J Southam, BSc, PGCE (*Girls' Games*)
Mrs H Lawson, BA, PGCE (*RE*)
Mrs J Fisher, BSc, PGCE (*Science*)
Miss K Hockley, BA, PGCE (*PE*)
Miss A Desai, BSc, PGCE (*PSHEE*)
Mrs L Russo, BA, PGCE (*Learning Support, Drama*)
Miss P Southall, MA, BSc (*EAL Coordinator*)

Subject Teachers:
Miss R Ali BA, PGCE (*English*)
Mrs M Allen BA, PGCE (*French*)
Miss K Anderson BA, PGCE (*PE/Girls' Games*)
Ms Y Aslam, BA, (*Mathematics*)
Mr R Baker BEd (*Science/Boys' Games*)
Mr J Billows, BSc, PGCE (*PE/Games*)
Mr A Haigh, BSc, PGCE (*Science, Boys' Games*)
Miss E Hayman BSc, PGCE (*PE/Girls' Games*)
Mr J Ince, BA, PGCE (*English/Classical Studies/Boys' Games*)
Mr O McGuiness BA, PGCE (*Mathematics/Boys' Games*)
Mrs A Passer BA, PGCE (*RE, Classical Studies*)
Mrs K Paul, BEd (*Humanities*)
Miss V Risianova, BA (*DT, Girls' Games*)
Mrs S Roberts, BA, PGCE (*Mathematics*)
Mrs E Semp, BA, PGCE (*English*) [Maternity]
T Spink, BSc, PGCE (*Mathematics, Boys' Games*)
Miss V Thwaites BA, GDE (*English*)
Mr C. Unwin M.Ed (*English/Boys' Games*)
A Warren, GTCL (*Music, RE*)

Lower School Tutors:
Miss H Barnes, BEd
Miss S Black, BA, PGCE
Mrs T Bridge, BA, PGCE
Miss A Desai, BSc, PGCE
Mrs J de Souza Dark, BEd
Mrs N Harris, BSc, PGCE, Dip IT
Mr H King BA, PGCE
Mr J Norbury, MA, PGCE
Mrs E Pendred, BA, PGCE
Mrs N Sawdaye, BA, PGCE
Miss M Sevani, MA
Mrs M Slade, BEd
Mr A Wright, BEd

Mrs A Caldwell BSc (*Learning Support*)
Mrs M Corcoran, BEd, PGCPSE (*Learning Support*)
Mrs H Hardy, BA, PGCE (*Learning Support*)
Mrs T Ftaiha (*Learning Support*)
Mrs S Lewin, RSA Dip SpLD (*Learning Support*)
Mrs K Pople, BA, PGCE (*Learning Support*)
Mrs S Sulkin (*Learning Support*)
Mrs S Wiltshire (*Learning Support*)

Support Staff:
Head's PA: Mrs G Ellen
Registrar & Marketing Assistant: Mrs I Manfredi
School Secretary: Mrs N McDavid
Librarian: Mrs C Hunt, MA
School Nurse: (*to be appointed*)
School Counsellor: Mr S Kohon, BA
Network Administrator: Dr J White, PhD, BSc
Science & DT: *Technician*: Mrs P Daly

Rugby Coach: Mr J Matthams
Netball Coach: Mrs J Nicol
Hockey Coach: Mrs L Briscoe
Fives Coach: Mr A Rennie
Gap Students: Miss K Heath, Mr E Schiller, Mr L Snaddon
& Miss K Wade

Peripatetic Music Staff:
Mr J Bailey, MMus (*Piano*)
Mr M Blake, LRAM (*Brass*)
Mr J Bradford, BMus, PGCE (*Guitar*)
Mrs K Bywater, ARAM, Dip RAM, LRAM (*Woodwind*)
Mr A Cucchiara, GRNCM (*Violin*)
Mr L Daniel, BMus (*Clarinet and Saxophone*)
Ms C Emanuel, Dip RCM, ARCM (*Violin*)
Mr M Flourendzou (*Drums*)
Dr O Gledhill, PhD, MA Mtpp, PGCA, ARCM (*Cello*)
Miss R Havel, BMus (*Voice*)
Mrs K Hopper, BMus (*Voice*)
Mrs H Kyle, BMus (*Voice*)
Miss S Llewellyn, BMus GSMD (*Piano*)
Mr A McAfee, BA (*Flute*)
Mr J Preiss, MMus (*Guitar*)
Ms A Starr, MA, BMus (*Piano*)
Miss J Tate, BA Mus, Grad RNCM (*Voice*)

Grimsdell, Mill Hill Pre-Preparatory School
Winterstoke House, Wills Grove, Mill Hill,
London NW7 1QR
Tel: 020 8959 6884; Fax: 020 8959 4626
email: office@grimsdell.org.uk
website: www.grimsdell.org.uk

Head: Mrs K Simon, BA Hons, PGCE

Deputy Head: K Dobson, BA Hons (*also Safeguarding,
Health & Safety and Assessment Coordinator*)
Director of Studies: Mrs T Weeks, BA Hons, PGCE (*Year
2 Coordinator*)

Teachers:
Mrs J Baddick, BSc Hons, PGCE (*Part-time Learning
Support Teacher, Enrichment Coordinator*)
Mrs J Barnett, BA Hons, PGCE (*Part-time Learning
Support Teacher, PSHE Coordinator*)
Mrs S Broom, HNC Early Childhood Studies (*Nursery
Teacher, Art & Display Coordinator*)
Mrs L Dobson, BA Hons QTS (*Class Teacher, History
Coordinator*)
Mrs F Ellis, Diplôme d'Études (*Part-time French Teacher*)
Mrs M Gold, DCE Primary Education, Dip Support for
Learning (*SENCO Head of Learning Support, Part-time*)
Mrs J Golden, BMus Hons, PGCE (*Part-time ICT Teacher*)
Mrs C Harvey, MA, PGCE (*Part-time ICT Teacher*)
Mrs E Jenner, BA Hons, PGCE (*Class Teacher, EYFS
Coordinator*)
Miss Y Matsushita, BA Hons QTS (*Class Teacher,
Literacy Coordinator*)
Mrs A Moir, BSc Hons QTS (*Class Teacher, Computing
Coordinator*)
Mrs S Dean, BEd Primary (*Class Teacher*)
Mrs T Patel, BA Hons (*Class Teacher, Geography
Coordinator*)
Mrs N Satariano, BA Hons (*Class Teacher*)
Mrs F Smith, BSc Hons, PGCE (*Class Teacher, Maths
Coordinator*)
Miss L Corrigan, BSc, MA QTS (*Class Teacher*)
Ms V Suarez Rivas, BA Hons (*PE Specialist*)
Ms Caroline Freeman, BA Hons (*School Counsellor*)
Mrs C Cox, MA (*Music Specialist*)

School Administrator: Mrs S Webb
Registrar & Assistant Administrator: Ms K Andrews

Millfield

Street, Somerset BA16 0YD
Tel: 01458 442291
email: office@millfieldschool.com
website: millfieldschool.com
Twitter: @millfieldsenior
Facebook: /MillfieldSchool

The school was founded in 1935 by R J O Meyer with the philanthropic aim of using its resources to generate places for boys who were gifted but not wealthy. The school became co-educational in 1939. In 1945 Edgarley Hall was acquired and the junior pupils were transferred there. This is now Millfield Prep School. The school expanded through the 50s and 60s offering a more orthodox curriculum, although it was never a 'normal' public school. C R M Atkinson became Headmaster in 1971, and carried out a major building programme that established modern purpose-built facilities throughout the academic and recreational areas of the school, including a prize-winning Library and Resource Centre and a large Fine Arts Centre, completed in 1992, a year after his death. Further improvements to the campus include a purpose-built Mathematics Centre, and 500-seat Theatre and Dining Hall. Nine new boarding houses have been opened since 2003. A Design & Technology building with high-tech equipment was completed in 2005 and a Music School complex housing the 350-seat Johnson Concert Hall was completed in September 2006. New Science laboratories and a Science lecture theatre were completed in September 2009. The main part of the school is surrounded by over 100 acres, which includes an equestrian centre, stabling for 64 horses, a 50m Olympic swimming pool, a golf course and an indoor Tennis Centre.

The school is fully co-educational with 765 boys and 486 girls; there are 938 boarders.

Housing. There are 16 single-sex, Year 10 to Upper Sixth, boarding houses. Most Sixth Formers have their own rooms whilst younger pupils share either in pairs or fours. Since the launch of Nine at Millfield dedicated Year 9 houses have been introduced for boarding and day. All Year 9 houses lie in the heart of the campus and have a higher staff to pupil ratio to oversee every aspect of each pupil's well-being and academic progress. There are four day houses for Year 10 to Upper Sixth; they have their own base on site and may stay in the evenings to do supervised prep.

The Curriculum. The academic programme is consistent with the broad principles laid down in the National Curriculum pre-16. Thus those moving to Millfield from a wide range of independent preparatory and maintained secondary schools should find both common academic ground and unrivalled choice for GCSE, Vocational Courses, BTEC and AS/A2 Level. A five-year course in Personal and Social Education is also included within the curriculum.

All pupils entering Year 9 (at age 13), regardless of ability, study English, Mathematics, three Sciences, at least one language, Art, Design and Technology, ICT, Food and Nutrition, Geography, History, Religious Studies, Physical Education and Music. The pupil : teacher ratio is 6.5:1. Pupils have a structured co-curricular programme.

In Years 10 and 11 pupils follow courses leading to GCSEs in the core subjects of English, Mathematics, Science and a Modern Language. In addition, there is a wide choice of options: Art & Design, Business Studies, Mandarin Chinese, Computing, Drama, Economics, Food & Nutrition, French, Geography, German, Greek, History, ICT, Italian, Latin, Music, Music Technology (BTEC), Physical Education, Product Design, Religious Studies and Spanish. The Learning Support Centre provides individual support for all pupils in need of this.

At Sixth Form level, a wide range of subjects is on offer leading to AS and A2 qualifications. These include Accounting, Art, Biology, Business Studies, Chemistry, Chinese Mandarin, Drama, Economics, English Literature, French, Further Mathematics, Food, Nutrition and Health, Geography, German, Government & Politics, History, ICT, Italian, Latin, Mathematics, Media Studies, Music, Philosophy, Physical Education, Product Design, Psychology, Religious Studies, Spanish, and World Development. Also on offer are the vocational courses of BTEC Business Studies (equivalent to a two A Level course), BTEC National Diploma in Art & Design (equivalent to a three A Level course), BTEC Sport Performance and Excellence (equivalent to 2 A Level courses), BTEC Music Technology, the Leith Cookery Course and the British Horse Society Preliminary Instructor Certificate (BHSPI). Most pupils choose four AS Level subjects in the Lower Sixth and then take three of these to the full A Level in the Upper Sixth. Wider enrichment opportunities are available to all Sixth Formers. The curriculum offers breadth, depth and flexibility in course choice. Pupils are also prepared for STEP papers and Scholastic Aptitude tests for American Universities. English as an additional language (EAL) and Learning Support is available at all levels.

Every pupil is guided through his or her school career by a Group Tutor. Each Tutor cares for between 10 and 14 pupils within a House, taking a close personal interest in each and maintaining regular contact with parents on academic matters.

Sport and Activities. Millfield runs an unparalleled range of sports and activities to engage all pupils. Pupils in Years 9, 10 and 11 generally choose from one of the core games of the term, including athletics, basketball, cricket, dance, football, hockey, netball, riding, rugby and tennis depending on term and gender. In Sixth Form, the range extends to include all of the above plus archery, badminton, canoeing, chess, clay shooting, climbing, karate, sailing, skiing, squash, trampolining, triathlon, and various fitness activities such as aerobics, pilates and yoga. Throughout the School, pupils may also specialise in one of our high performing programmes including athletics, cricket, fencing, golf, modern pentathlon, squash, swimming and tennis.

In addition, pupils in Years 9, 10 and Lower Sixth take part in the school's Activities Programme where they can further broaden their experiences through a choice of more than 100 activities, ranging from athletics to street dance, building a Caterham car or guitar, film clubs, photography, scuba diving and The Duke of Edinburgh's Award.

Fees per term (2016–2017). Boarding £11,925, Day £8,010.

Scholarships and Bursaries. Scholarships of up to 15% are awarded for exceptional talent in Academic, All-rounder, Art, Drama, Dance, Design & Innovation, Music, Sport and Chess. A limited number of Headmaster's Scholarships of up to 50% are also available. Where parental resources are limited, these may be augmented by means-tested bursaries of up to 100%.

Charitable status. Millfield is a Registered Charity, number 310283. Its aim is to provide independent boarding and day education for boys and girls, and to maintain an extensive system of bursary aid to gifted pupils or those in financial need.

Governors:
Chair of Governors: Sir J G Reith, KCB, CBE

S Burns	C Hirst
W J Bushell	A Jackson
R J R Clark	J Lever
Mrs C Cripps	J Maudslay
R Exley	A A Patel
Mrs C Flood	R Rudd

Mrs A Sexton	R P Thornton
M A L Simon	D S Williamson
T M Taylor	

Clerk to the Governors: Mrs R Summerhayes

***Headmaster*: Craig Considine**, MEd, BAppSc, DipEd, MACE

Bursar: M Suddaby, MA Hons, PGCE, ACA
Deputy Head (Academic): F J Clough, BSc Hons, PhD, QTS
Deputy Head (Pastoral): C P Seal, BA Joint Hons, PGCE
Assistant Head (Teaching and Learning): Dr C Fiddes, BA Oxon, PhD
Assistant Head (Housing): A Collins, BA, Dip, QTS
Assistant Head (Co-Curriculum): E Jones, BSc
Assistant Head (Sixth Form): Ms C Bowring, BA Hons
Director of Sport: D Faulkner, Olympic Gold Medallist
Registrar: J Postle, BA Hons, PGCE, FRSA
Head of Marketing: Ms T Denbigh, BA Hons
Director of IT: G Henderson, BA Hons, MA

Heads of Department:
Art, Design & Technology: P Maxfield, BA Hons, PGCE
Biology: S J Whittle, BSc
Chemistry: J Hope, MA
Computing and ICT: M Shields, BSc Hons, PGCE
English as an Additional Language (EAL): H Winkley, MA
Economics and Accounting: A Shaw, MA Oxon, PGCE
English, Drama and Media: J C Baddock, BA Hons
Equine Studies: D Anholt BHSI HT
Geography: Miss A Starling, BA Hons, PGCE
History: Dr D Burton, MA, DPhil
Home Economics: Mrs J Moore, BSc Hons, PGCE
Languages: Ms C Coutand-Moore, L-ès-L, PGCE
Learning Support Centre: Mrs P Barnes, MA Ed SEN, BSc Hons, PGCE, PG CertEd, CPT3A
Library: D Trevis, BA, MEd
Mathematics: T Bowley, MSc, BSc
Music: M Cook, BA Hons Music, PGCE Secondary Music
Physical Education: S Maddock, BA Hons, MEd
Physics: J Hudson, MA Hons Cantab, PGCE
Religious Studies: Ms E Earl, BA, MA Oxon
Sciences: Mrs R Landrigan, BA Hons, MA Oxon, PGCE

Houses and Houseparents:

Boarding Houses:
Abbey House: Mr and Mrs K Shelver
Acacia House: Mr and Mrs B J McEwen
Butleigh: Mr and Mrs B C Boyd
Etonhurst: Mr and Mrs T P Akhurst
Holmcroft: Mr and Mrs R Owlett
Joan's Kitchen: Mr and Mrs M A Speyers
Keen's Elm: Mr and Mrs T Sawrey-Cookson
Kernick: Ms C Coutand-Moore
Kingweston: Mr and Mrs T J Greenhill
Martins: Ms Garcia
Millfield: Mr Kemp
Orchards: Mr S Robertson
Portway: Mr & Mrs Trainor
St Anne's: Mr & Mrs C D Gange
Shapwick: Mr and Mrs J A Mallett
Southfield: Mr R Baxter and Ms T Allen
The Grange: Mr T B Kingsford
Walton: Mr & Mrs A J Whatling
Warner: Mr and Mrs C J Middleton

Day Houses, Boys:
Great: Mr J A Bishop
Mill: Mr B McEwen

Day Houses, Girls:
Overleigh: Mrs A E S Brade

The Lakes: Miss E A Dando

Day House (*Year 9 Girls & Boys*):
Ivythorn: Mrs K Butt

Heads of Sport:
Athletics: A Richardson, BA Hons, IAAF Level 5 Elite coach
Tutor i/c Badminton: J Anderton
Tutor i/c Basketball: C Seeley
Tutor i/c Chess: M Turner, MA, Grand Master
Master i/c Cricket: R Ellison, ECB Level 3
Cross Country: J Allen
Tutor i/c Dance: K Leader
Director of Fencing: T Parris, BAF Advanced Coach
Football: T Akhurst, UEFA A
Director of Golf: K Nicholls, PGA/LET member
Director of Hockey: R Keates, HA Coach Level 2
Martial Arts: T Cheung, purple belt in Washinkai Karate and Kickboxing, blue belt in Shotokan karate
Modern Pentathlon: T Parris, BAF Advanced Coach
Netball: C Mitchell, UKCC Level 3
Outdoor Activities: P Bond, MLA
Polo: D O Anholt, BHSl, HT
Director of Riding: D O Anholt, BHSI, HT
Rowing: E Green
Director of Rugby: J A Mallett, RFU Level 4
Skiing: R W Smith, BASI Coach Level 1
Squash: I Thomas, High Performance Coach
Director of Swimming: J Finck, Australia Gold Licence Coach
Director of Tennis: Ms K Warne-Holland
Trampolining: Mrs C Mitchell, Level 4
Triathlon: P Guthrie, BTF Level 3 Cert Coaching

Monkton School

Monkton Combe, Bath BA2 7HG

Tel: 01225 721102
Fax: 01225 721181
email: admissions@monkton.org.uk
website: www.monktoncombeschool.com
Twitter: @monkton
Facebook: @monktoncombeschool

Monkton School, just a mile from the World Heritage City of Bath, is an independent, co-educational boarding and day school for pupils aged 2–18. We pride ourselves on our lively Christian ethos, excellent exam results and our strong pastoral care. At Monkton, we are setting standards for life; giving young people the qualities of character they need to become trusted employees, inspiring leaders, valued friends and loving parents.

Situation. The Senior School faces south across the Valley, or Combe, from which the place takes its name, while the Pre-Prep and Prep School are at the top of the hill above with magnificent views over Avon and Wiltshire.

Organisation. The Pre-Prep and Prep (ages 2–13) and Senior School (ages 13–18) each have their own Heads and the Principal of the Senior School has overall responsibility for the two schools; they share the same Board of Governors and there are close links between them.

(*For further details see Monkton Preparatory entry in IAPS section.*)

Numbers. *Preparatory School*: There are 309 pupils of whom 31 board and 75 are in the Pre-Prep.

Senior School: There are 391 pupils (245 boys, 132 girls), of whom 253 are boarders. The Sixth Form has 163 pupils.

Admission. *Prep School*. For those entering the Prep at age 7 years through to 13 years, admission is by tests in English and Mathematics, a Reasoning Test, a reference from the candidate's current school and an interview.

Senior School. (a) For pupils entering the Senior School from a Prep school, the usual means is via the Common Entrance Pre-Test at age 11 years, taken in the Lent Term of Year 7. Arrangements for sitting the examination are usually made by the Head of the candidate's prep school. A school reference and report will also be sought. Results of the Pre-Test will be conveyed to the candidate's parents by Monkton Senior School. Offers will be conditional upon the candidate completing the Common Entrance courses at his/her school from whom a reference would be sought.

(b) For those entering the Senior School at age 14 admission is by tests in English and Mathematics and a Reasoning test, a reference from the candidate's current school and an interview.

(c) For entry into Year 12, candidates will usually sit a Reasoning Test and attend an interview, where possible. A school reference will be sought and any place then offered is subject to pupils obtaining a minimum of at least five GCSE grades A*-C, together with an average score of at least 6.0 in all of the GCSE subjects taken. At GCSE, an A* grade scores 8, an A – 7, a B – 6, a C – 5, a D – 4 and so on. A pupil whose score is just below 6.0, but who is admitted into the Year 12, will, in the first instance, be offered a one-year course to AS Level. Progression to A2 will depend upon a satisfactory performance throughout the year and in the AS examinations in June. Please note that to study certain AS subjects, a minimum grade at GCSE in that subject may be a prerequisite. Pupils are normally expected to attain at least 2 D grades at AS Level for entry into Year 13, and at least D grades in subjects they wish to pursue to A2.

Sport facilities. The School has extensive playing fields, an AstroTurf all-weather playing area for Hockey and Tennis, Boathouses on the River Avon, 3 Netball Courts, 18 Tennis Courts, a covered Rifle Range, a Rowing Tank, 2 Squash Courts, a Sports Centre and a 25m indoor Swimming Centre and Fitness Centre.

Chapel. There is a full-time resident Anglican Head of Chaplaincy. A short service or assembly is held three times each week. There is a Confirmation Service each year. The pupils run a Christian Union, which is popular, and attended by 70–100 pupils each week.

Houses. The four boys' Houses, two girls' Houses and Sixth Form House are all under the care of Houseparents, who together with their tutorial teams of colleagues are responsible for the boys' and girls' general welfare.

Day Pupils are fully integrated into the boarding houses and the total life of the School and are encouraged but not obliged to stay until the end of evening prep. Senior pupils are given opportunities for responsibility as School or House Prefects during their Sixth Form careers.

Tutor System. Each pupil has a Tutor, normally a member of staff of his or her own choice, who keeps in touch with parents and provides guidance and advice over every aspect of School life and over making choices for the future.

Curriculum. Our aim is to provide a broadly based curriculum in the years leading to GCSE. Those who show particular ability in French or Mathematics may proceed to work more advanced than GCSE before the end of Year 11. Personal, Social and Health Education is included up to Year 11. In Year 10, pupils have two supervised study periods to develop the skills they will especially need when in the Sixth Form, but which ultimately underpin genuine success at GCSE as well.

In Year 9 all pupils study English, Mathematics and the Sciences with a foundation course normally comprising two Foreign Language, Art, Design Technology, Drama, Geography, History, Information Technology, Music, PE and Religious Studies. In addition, pupils develop study and research skills with a library period. In Years 10 and 11 all pupils take IGCSE English, Mathematics, and either Dual

Award or Separate Sciences (Biology, Chemistry and Physics), and almost all choose at least one Modern Foreign Language (French, Spanish and Mandarin). Pupils choose three other subjects from Art, Business Studies, Design Technology, Drama, Geography, History, Latin, Music, Photography, Physical Education, and Religious Studies. English and Maths support is available as an option instead of a Modern Foreign Language for those with particular needs in these areas. Pupils with English as a Second Language receive lessons according to their level of English.

Most pupils stay on for two years in the Sixth Form. The subjects offered are broad and include 27 subject areas. All pupils are given the opportunity to take the Extended Project Qualification. Most pupils entering Year 12 study four subjects for one year to AS and continue with three to full A Level. A notable feature of the Sixth Form programme is the wide variety of lectures and presentations delivered by visiting speakers prominent in their field.

Careers Advice and Staff/Parent Meetings. An experienced Careers Teacher works closely with Tutors in advising pupils. There is also a member of staff responsible for advice on higher education. Parents, Old Monktonians and local people are invited to help pupils in their thinking about careers. The School belongs to the Independent Schools Careers Organisation which arranges Aptitude and Interest tests. Annual staff/parent meetings are held at the School to discuss pupils' progress. Parents are of course always welcome at other times.

University Entrance. The great majority of leavers go on to degree courses at Universities and Colleges of Higher Education. Over 90% of leavers go to their first-choice university and many of our pupils go to the top universities in the country including Oxford, Cambridge, UCL, Edinburgh, Durham, Exeter and Warwick.

Games. Those with particular abilities are encouraged to aim for excellence, but we also believe that regular games and exercise are important for all, helping to build a healthy lifestyle for the future and fostering leadership, teamwork and cooperation.

The major sports for boys are: in the Michaelmas Term, Rugby; in the Lent Term, Hockey or Rowing; in the Summer Term, Cricket, Rowing or Tennis.

The major sports for girls are: in the Michaelmas Term, Hockey; in the Lent Term, Netball or Rowing; in the Summer Term, Tennis or Rowing.

Other sports include: Athletics, Badminton, Basketball, Cross-Country, Football, Golf, Judo, Squash and Shooting.

CCF and Community Service. There are sections for all three Services, besides various specialist activities such as Venture Section (through which the Duke of Edinburgh's Award scheme is offered) and car maintenance. There is also an active Community Service group.

Leisure Activities. Monkton encourages as many worthwhile leisure pursuits as possible. Between 35 and 40 different activities are offered. All the facilities of the School, including the Art and DT Departments, Music Rooms and ICT Centre are available to pupils during their free time. The Choir, Orchestra, Jazz band and other less formal music groups play an important part in the School's life and tuition is available in all orchestral instruments. There is a major School drama production in the Michaelmas Term. The School is conveniently close to Bath and Bristol for taking parties to concerts and theatres. Some 30 clubs and societies figure on the School List, ranging from the Bridge Club to the Literary Society and the Christian Union. Bible Study groups meet weekly.

Health. The School Medical Officer visits regularly and all boarders are required to register with him. The Medical Centre on site is under the care of a fully qualified Sister and Assistant.

Catering. Catering is provided by an external company, offering nutritious home cooked meals everyday. All pupils take their meals in the Dining Hall, with a range of choices available in cafeteria service.

Dress. All required items can be purchased in the School Shop.

Scholarships and Bursaries. Scholarships are awarded on entry to the School for candidates at Year 9 and Year 12. The Principal reserves the right to award up to two Year 10 Scholarships at his discretion; no application for this award is required. Scholarships recognise the contribution to School life which is made by exceptional performers by raising the aspirations of other pupils, by stimulating greater achievement in their peers and by enabling higher levels of performance in collaborative activities such as music, drama and sport. All scholarships awarded are conditional on this continued contribution to the area of School life which is recognized in the award. In addition, all scholarships are awarded for the duration of the pupil's time at the School. Moreover, candidates for all awards are expected to achieve satisfactory standards in Common Entrance, GCSE exams or other entry tests.

Monkton Senior School seeks to give bursaries to pupils who would otherwise not be able to come to the School. Such bursaries are available for 5–100% of fees, and special consideration is given to the children of clergy and missionaries, in accordance with the School's charitable objectives. Where a bursary and a scholarship are awarded to the same pupil, the scholarship is subsumed into the bursary (assuming this is the larger of the two); the bursary will never be reduced below the level of the original scholarship. Where a bursary has already been awarded, the scholarship will not increase the bursary unless it is greater than the bursary.

Where two scholarships are won by the same pupil, the second scholarship will have a percentage value against the remainder of the fee, rather than the total (gross fee). If the first was 20% and the second 10%, the second scholarship would be worth 10% of the remaining 80% of fees (i.e. 8% of full fees). Internal scholarships are offered for pupils moving from Year 11 to 12, who intend to board in the Sixth Form.

Details of all awards can be obtained from the Registrar.

Fees per term (2016–2017). Senior: £10,355–£10,630 (boarders); £6,345–£6,665 (day pupils). Preparatory: £7,300–£7,870 (boarders); £3,750–£5,460 (day pupils). Pre-Prep: £2,983–£3,194.

Old Monktonian Club. No additional charge is made for pupils to become full Old Monktonians. Details from the Development Office at the School.

Charitable status. Monkton School is a Registered Charity, number 1057185, and a Company Limited by Guarantee, registered in England, number 3228456. Its aims and objectives are to provide education for girls and boys combined with sound religious training on Protestant and Evangelical principles in accordance with the doctrines of The Church of England.

Governors:

Chair of Governors: Prof H Langton, RGN, RSCN, ACNT, RNT, BA Hons, MSc

Mr C J Alexander, BA Hons Oxon

Revd S Barnes, BA QTS Hons, MA, Cert BA

Mrs R Coates, BA Hons

Mr J R Myers, BEng Hons

Mrs J J Perry, BPharm Hons, MRPharmS, Dip Clin Pharm

Mr R J Pringle, BSc Hons

Mrs M K Townsend, BSc Hons

Mr M R A Womersley, MA Cantab

Mr S B M Young, BA, FCA, ACA

Executive Leadership Team:

Principal: Mr C J Wheeler, BA Durham, PGCE Bristol

Prep School Headmaster: Mr M Davis, BEd Hons

Head of Pre-Prep: Mrs C Winchcombe, BEd Hons, MA Ed

Bursar: Mr T Davies, BA, ACA, DChA

Director of External Relations: Mr T Reid

Monmouth School

**Almshouse Street, Monmouth, Monmouthshire
NP25 3XP**

Tel: 01600 713143
Fax: 01600 772701
email: enquiries@monmouthschool.org
website: www.habs-monmouth.org
Twitter: @habsmonmouth
Facebook: /Habsmonmouth

Motto: *Serve and Obey*.

The School was founded in 1614, by William Jones, a merchant of the City of London and a Liveryman of the Worshipful Company of Haberdashers, who was born near Monmouth and bequeathed a large sum of money to found a school and almshouses in the town. The School has derived immense advantage from this unusual association with the City of London.

The School is controlled by a Board of Governors appointed variously by the Haberdashers' Company, the Universities of Oxford, Cambridge and Wales, and local representative bodies.

There are approximately 530 boys in the Senior School, of whom 150 are boarders. The Grange, the School's Preparatory Department, caters for 130 day boys aged 7 to 11, with boarding available at age 9. (*For further details see entry in IAPS section.*)

Situation and Buildings. The School was founded in 1614 by William Jones and is one of the schools of the Worshipful Company of Haberdashers. A generous endowment enables the School to provide superb facilities and an excellent academic education whilst keeping fees at a reasonable level. There are many scholarships and bursaries and the Haberdashers' Assisted Places Scheme, which replaced the Government scheme in 1998, ensures that an education at Monmouth School can be available to boys who will benefit from it, irrespective of their parents' income.

The School is enriched by close cooperation with Haberdashers' Monmouth School for Girls in many areas of school life, especially at Sixth Form level.

The School is set in the delightful landscape of the Wye Valley and much use is made of the surrounding countryside for expeditions and other outward-bound activities. There is a strong tradition of music and drama as well as excellence in sport. A new sports complex was opened in Autumn 1999, a studio theatre in January 2001 and additional outdoor facilities, including an all-weather pitch, in Autumn 2001. The Blake Theatre (500 seats) was completed in Summer 2004. Other recent developments have included greatly expanded ICT facilities and refurbished boarding houses and classroom blocks. The Sixth Form has a dedicated Sixth Form Centre. A superb new Sports Pavilion opened in 2008 and the Prep School, The Grange, moved to an innovatively designed and exciting new building in February 2009. An ambitious development, *The Heart* Project, saw its completion in October 2013. The William Jones Building provides excellent facilities in classrooms for three departments as well as a completely new reception and administration area. This move has allowed the School to release space to expand and further enhance the boarding accommodation.

Boarding. The boarding community forms the core of the School. Junior boarders (9–12 year olds) are accommodated in Chapel House for their first few years and benefit from the care of a dedicated house team who also provide an ambitious and popular programme of extra-curricular activities, tailored to the interests of the age group.

There are three senior boarding houses for boys between 13 and 18. The School has a flexible boarding policy which provides a considerable degree of freedom for families to make boarding arrangements which fit in with their lives, but which encourages boys to take full advantage of the many sporting, cultural and extra-curricular activities for which the School is renowned.

September 2011 saw the opening of Buchanan House, a sixth form boarding house with single study-bedrooms and en-suite facilities.

Admission. The main admission points are 7, 10, 11, 13 and 16, but other stages will be considered if places are available. Candidates aged 7 and 11 sit the School's own entrance tests. At 13, candidates take the Common Entrance Examination, the School's own Foundation Scholarship Examination or its 13+ examination. Entrants to the Sixth Form are accepted either after sitting the Sixth Form Scholarship Examination or on the basis of GCSE results (or equivalent).

Candidates from overseas are welcome. Those whose first language is not English take a preliminary test of proficiency in English before proceeding to the appropriate entrance test.

The School accepts pupils with Dyslexia or similar specific learning difficulties. They are taught in mainstream lessons and additional study support is available.

Curriculum. The curriculum is designed to provide both flexibility and breadth and to be in step with the National Curriculum without being constrained by it. Those in Forms I and II (Years 7 and 8) study a wide range of subjects including Latin, French and combined Science. In Form III (Year 9) the three Sciences are taught separately and pupils have the option of starting Greek.

Pupils normally take nine or ten GCSE subjects, four of which are of their own choosing. There is a cross-curricular ICT scheme to enable pupils to make full use of the School's extensive facilities.

We offer a Foundation 1 Year GCSE course in up to 6 GCSEs including English, Mathematics and the three Sciences.

In the Sixth Form a range of approximately 30 AS subjects is offered along with an enrichment programme. This programme and many of the AS subjects are offered in cooperation with Haberdashers' Monmouth School for Girls.

A particular feature of the curriculum is the extensive range of Modern Languages. French is taught at all levels and Spanish and German are available from Form III. Welsh is available as an after-school conversational class and Russian is available at AS/A Level.

The Chapel. The School is an Anglican foundation and the Chapel plays an important part in its life. All pupils attend Chapel at least once each week and there is a weekly service for boarders. A varied programme of preachers is organised, including clergy and lay people of many denominations. The Bishop of Monmouth officiates at the annual Confirmation Service.

Games. The main sports are rugby, rowing, cricket and soccer. Many other sports are also available at a highly competitive level including athletics, cross-country running, golf, softball, squash and swimming. Several members of staff have international sporting honours and pupils regularly gain places to represent Wales in a variety of sports.

Activities. There is an extensive programme of activities throughout the School. Pupils in Form IV and above may join the CCF (Army and RAF sections) which enjoy excellent links with locally based regular and territorial forces.

Community Service is a popular option and many boys participate in the Duke of Edinburgh's Award scheme. There is a very strong musical tradition with many pupils taking part in choirs, orchestras and bands which achieve high levels of success in competitions, and play to appreciative audiences locally and on the regular overseas tours which take place. Drama is also strong and good opportunities are provided for participation at all levels. A wide range of School clubs and Societies further enriches the life of the School.

Fees per term (2016–2017). Day £4,969, Boarding £9,003–£9,545; The Grange: Day £3,484, Boarding £6,333.

Scholarships and Bursaries. A generous number of Entrance Scholarships are awarded to day boys or boarders on the basis of performance in the Year 7 Entry Assessments (11+) held in February, on the Foundation Scholarship Examination (13+) held in February/March, and the Sixth Form Scholarship Examination (16+) held in February. In cases of need, Scholarships may be augmented by a Bursary.

Music Scholarships and Exhibitions may be awarded at 11, 13 and 16 up to the value of half of the fees and carrying free instrumental tuition. Sixth Form organ or instrumental scholarships also available.

Sports Awards are available to suitable candidates at 11, 13 and Sixth Form entry.

Old Monmothian and Mountjoy Awards are available for candidates who show all-round ability and potential.

The E F Bulmer Award is available to suitable Sixth Form candidates living in Herefordshire; awards range in value from 50% to 100% of the fees. A new Sixth Form Boarding Scholarship is available, which is means-tested and can cover up to 75% of the fees.

Bursaries and the Haberdashers' Assisted Places Scheme can also provide up to 100% remission of fees, in certain circumstances.

Service Bursaries are available for the sons of serving members of HM Armed Forces, thus guaranteeing no more than the minimum 10% of fees is payable by parents.

Old Monmothians. Past members of the School are eligible to join the Old Monmothian Club which enjoys a close relationship with the School. The Membership Secretary is Roger Atkins, c/o Old Monmothians, Monmouth School, Almshouse Street, Monmouth NP25 3XP.

Charitable status. William Jones's Schools Foundation is a Registered Charity, number 525616. Its aims and objectives are to provide an all-round education for boys and girls at reasonable fees; also to carry out the Founder's intention that local boys qualifying for entry should not be prevented from attending the School by lack of funds.

Governors:
Acting Chairman of Governors: A W Twiston-Davies
The Master of the Worshipful Company of Haberdashers (*ex officio*)
[1]P M Alderman (*Safeguarding Governor*)
M H C Anderson
Dr P E G Baird
[1]Mrs J Booth
Mrs S Clayton
[1]M E Davidson
Mrs C J Davis
[1]C R S Hardie
Mrs M K Henderson
[1]Dr J Kelly
M Kerrigan
N G H Manns (*Chairman, Haberdashers' Monmouth School for Girls Committee*)
[1]Mrs M Nordal
[1]Mrs T Pike (*Grange Governor*)
Mrs R F Rose
[1]A W Twiston-Davies (*Chairman, Monmouth School Committee*)

Professor D S Watkins
Councillor S White

[1] *Member of the Monmouth School Committee*

Headmaster: Dr A J Daniel, BSc, MEd, PhD, PGCE

Second Master: S H Dorman, MA, MPhil
Director of Studies: A J Winter, BSc, PhD
Head of Sixth Form: J Boiling, BA

Assistant Staff:
* *Head of Department*
† *Housemaster/Housemistress*

Mrs E A Aldridge, BSc
Mrs E R Arrand, BA (†*Severn House*)
Mrs S G Atherton, BA
Miss E K Barson, BSc, MSc (*Biology)
J W Bateman, LLB
J Boiling, BA
K D Chaplin, BSc
Dr M D Clarke, BSc, PhD (*Chemistry)
Mrs E R Cole, BSc
Dr J P Danks, BSc, DPhil (†*Dean House*)
A J Dawson, BSc, MSc
J Despontin, BSc, MSc
S H Dorman, MA, MPhil
G Dunn, BSc, MSc
Dr E Evans, BSc, PhD
Dr H B Evans, MSc, PhD (*Mathematics)
Miss S L Fowler, BSc
J F Geraghty, BA
L M P Godfrey, BSc
N J R Goodson, BSc
Miss L M J Goupil, BA
P M Griffin, BA (*Drama)
J D Griffiths, BSc
Mrs J R Gunn, BA
B H Hague, BA
Dr J M Harrison, BA, PhD (*History)
A Hawley, BA (†*Town House*)
Mrs S M Holmes, BA
D G Hope, BA (†*Weirhead House*)
Mrs L A Hope (*ICT)
R Howe, BA (†*Monmouth House*)
P D Jefferies, BSc
Mrs R E M Jenkins, BA, MA
Mrs J A Johnston, MA
A J Jones, BA (†*Chapel House*)
Dr D G Jones, MPhys, PhD (*Physics)
D K Jones, BSc (*Head of Boarding*)
I J Lawrence, BSc, MSc (†*Buchanan House*)
D F Lawson, BA (*Director of Music and Organist*)
Mrs L E Lewis, BA
M Lewis, BA (†*School House*)
Mrs L R Livingston, BA
K J Madsen, BA (*Economics, †*Glendower House*)
Mrs R J Marsh, BSc
Mrs T L Matthews, BA
Ms S M Mone, BA
Miss H T Morton, BA
D G Murray, MA
Mrs L C Parr, BEng, BSc
Mrs L Parsons, BA (*Modern Languages)
A K Peace (†*New House*)
Mrs G S Peace, BA, MA
M Peake, BA (*Art)
D J Pearson, BSc
Mrs S E Phillips, BEd, MA, Dip SpLD
R D Picken, BA (*English)
A E Shakeshaft, BA
G F Stentiford, MSc (*Geography)

M J Tamplin, BSc (†*Hereford House*)
O P Thicknesse, BA
P Vaughan-Smith, BA
D M Vickers, BEd (*Director of Physical Education,* †*Tudor House*)
A J White, BA (**Design Technology*)
R C Whiteman, BA (**Classics*)
Mrs R Widdicks, BA (**Study Support*)
O T R Williams, BSc, MA
P R Williams, BA
Miss S E L Williams, BA, MA (†*Wye House*)
Dr A J Winter, BSc, PhD
Mrs R L Wynne Lord, MA (**Religious Education*)

Chaplain: Revd. C R Swartz, BA, MA

The Grange (Preparatory Department)

Head: N D Shaw, BA
Deputy Head: Mrs KE Kirman, BSc

A J Ahmad, BSc

Mrs L Davies, BA	Mrs A M Taylor, LRSC
D G Hayden, MA	Dr S R Wall, BSc
S C Huson, BA, BA, MA	J D Walton, BMus
P N Morris, BEd	Mrs E R Waters, BA
D G Murray, MA	Mrs H C Simpson, BEd
K J Shepherd, BA	

Foundation Bursar: Mrs T Norgrove, MBA

Medical Officer: Dr J Knowles

Morrison's Academy

Ferntower Road, Crieff, Perthshire PH7 3AN
Tel: 01764 653885
Fax: 01764 655411
email: principal@morrisonsacademy.org
website: www.morrisonsacademy.org
Twitter: @macmorrisons
Facebook: @morrisonsacademy

Motto: *Ad summa tendendum – Striving for the highest*

Morrison's Academy Boys' School was opened in 1860 with a Girls' Department in 1861, an arrangement which continued until 1889 when a separate school for Girls was opened within the ten acres of the original site. In 1979 these two schools were brought together to become the one Morrison's Academy. The original foundation was possible through the generosity of Thomas Mo(r)rison, a native of Muthill who became a builder in Edinburgh and who in 1813 executed a Trust Deed directing that the fee of the reversion of his estate should be used to found and erect 'an institution calculated to promote the interests of mankind, having particular regard to the Education of Youth and the diffusion of useful knowledge ... a new institution which may bear my name and preserve the remembrance of my good intentions for the welfare and happiness of my fellow men'.

The School. Morrison's Academy is an integral part of the community in Crieff and comprises a 10-acre main campus supplemented by 45 acres of sports fields, main hall, after-school/holiday club and Nursery. The school provides education for 442 boys and girls from 3 to 18 years. The Nursery was recently inspected by HMIE and the Care Commission and received an outstanding report, where all areas received 'excellent' or 'very good' indicators.

The Primary School, housed in a separate building on the main campus, educates 149 pupils in small classes. Transfer between primary and secondary is helped by our Transitional Year (P7), which provides teaching in the primary school by a class teacher supplemented by lessons in the secondary school taught by subject specialists.

The Secondary School has 293 pupils studying towards Scottish Qualifications and entry to universities in Scotland, the rest of the UK and abroad. Academic expectations and achievements are high and small groups encourage individual learning and development. Over ninety-seven percent of our S6 go on to university.

Staff and pupils mix easily and the scale of the school allows for every individual to be known and valued by all.

Situation. Morrison's Academy is situated in the beautiful market town of Crieff on the edge of the Scottish Highlands in Perthshire. Strathearn is a beautiful area of mountains, rivers, lochs and rich agricultural land. Pupils attend from the local area and travel from Perth, Pitlochry, Dunkeld, Auchterarder, Stirling and Dunblane.

Curriculum. Pupils in Primary and lower Secondary follow broadly the Scottish 5–14 programme of study, leading in upper Secondary to Intermediate and then to Higher and Advanced Higher National Qualifications. Emphasis is placed upon academic achievement, while the pupils are also always encouraged to develop broad skills and interests outside the classroom. Co-curricular activities are extensive and Morrison's Academy makes good use of its glorious location.

Houses. All pupils are placed in one of the four houses named after local families: Campbells, Drummonds, Grahams and Murrays. There is healthy, competitive rivalry between the houses and senior pupils are encouraged to take charge of teams for sporting, music, debating and other events.

Games and Activities. Morrison's Academy encourages pupils to participate in a wide range of co-curricular activities and sports. All pupils use the playing fields and facilities on the main campus or walk to the 45 acres of playing fields and pavilions at Dallerie. Main sports are rugby, hockey, cricket, tennis and athletics. From upper primary fixtures against other schools take place, generally on Saturday mornings. Other sporting activities include soccer, basketball, netball, swimming, golf, weight training, sailing, short tennis, skiing, climbing, karate and more. To complement the sporting activities, pupils are active in The Duke of Edinburgh's Award Scheme, the Combined Cadet Force, drama, music, debating, chess, Pipe and Drum Band, environment group, Young Enterprise, charity fundraising, Christian groups, highland dancing and more. Pupils are challenged to make the most of their time and all within the wonderful environment of Perthshire.

Fees per term (2016–2017). Day: Primary £2,779–£3,962, Secondary £4,210.

The fees include tuition, textbooks, stationery, external examination fees, sports and curriculum-related travel.

Admission Procedure. Admission to the school is by entrance test and school report and/or exam results and entrance interview. The school's main entrance testing/interview days are at the beginning of February and beginning of May, for entry to the academic year commencing the following August.

For a prospectus pack and any queries please contact the Admissions Registrar.

Scholarships and Bursaries. There are Academic Scholarships for S1. There are also a number of Sixth Form Scholarships which are awarded after examination and interview in May. The awards, which carry a nominal financial value, recognise both achievement and potential. Means-tested Bursaries are also available.

The *Thomas Morrison Scholarship* provides means-tested assistance with tuition fees and is available to both existing pupils and new applicants, the main awards being made at entry to Form 1 in the Secondary School.

A limited number of awards are granted at other stages of the Secondary School but these are determined by the availability of funds at the time. Many of these awards are intended to assist existing pupils where there has been a significant change in financial circumstances, such as loss of income, which threatens the pupil's continued attendance at Morrison's Academy. Further details are available from The Rector.

Charitable status. Morrison's Academy is a Registered Charity, number SC000458. The school is a recognised charity providing education.

Board of Governors:
Chairman: Mr L C Johnston
Mr P J Brodie
Mr E J Cameron
Mr H Campbell
Mr A E Christmas
Mr P J H Cook
Mrs K M Elwis
Mr G Ferguson
Mr A P Godfrey
Mr M A Johnson
Councillor M Lyle
Mrs J F Morrow
Mr D Cloy
Mr J W Stewart

Clerk to Governors: Mrs C M Adams

Staff:

Rector: **Mr G Warren**

Depute Rector: Mr D Johnston
Assistant Rector: Mr P J Lovegrove
Assistant Rector: Miss A McCluskey
Bursar: Mr A U Beaton
Head of Primary: Miss M Bulloch
Depute Head of Primary: Mrs L S Anderson
Director of Development and Alumni Relations: Ms C Dingwall
Head of Nursery: Mrs B Thomson

Teaching Staff:

Art & Design:
Ms P M O'Neill
Miss G D McLaren

Business Studies:
Mrs M Stirling

CDT:
Mr R G McDermott

Computing & IT:
Mrs P Boal

English:
Mr P G O'Kane
Mrs T Lafferty
Mrs L McNaughton

Drama:
Miss K V Haddow

Geography:
Mr A Wylie
Mr R S Anderson

History/Modern Studies:
Mr M J Clayton
Mr P J Lovegrove
Mr D Johnston
Miss C M Cully

Home Economics:
Mrs H McDermott

Mathematics:
Mr I K O Barnett
Mr A M Jack
Mrs M T O'Kane
Mrs J McConville

Modern Languages:
Mr E Coffey
Miss A McCluskey
Mrs C Bergeron
Miss K Henderson
Mrs J White

Music:
Miss S Herbert (*Director of Music*)
Mrs S Smart

Physical Education:
Mr S G Weston (*Director of Sport*)
Mr L Howell
Mrs J C Lee
Miss E McCormick
Mrs D J McMillan

Science:
Mr J B Beedie

Mr R S Armstrong
Mr F Black
Mrs A S Harper
Mr M McKeever
Mrs S Steven, BSc

Primary:
Mrs L S Anderson
Ms M Anderson
Mr I Barr
Mrs A Beavington
Mr G Chater
Mrs G M Lauchlan
Mrs J A Longmuir

Mrs C Marchbank

Nursery:
Mrs B Thomson (*Head of Nursery*)
Mrs C Senior
Mrs G Thomson
Mrs M Thomson

Learning Support:
Mrs G Wilkie
Mrs S M Keating

Early Years Assistant:
Mrs M Thomson

Mount Kelly

Parkwood Road, Tavistock, Devon PL19 0HZ
Tel: 01822 813193
Fax: 01822 813168
email: admissions@mountkelly.com
website: www.mountkelly.com
Twitter: @Mount_Kelly
Facebook: /MountKellyFoundation
LinkedIn: /mount-kelly

Mount Kelly is a fully co-educational, Independent day and boarding school for children between the ages of 3 and 18. Mount Kelly was established in June 2014 following the merger of two neighbouring Schools, Kelly College (founded in 1877) and Mount House School (founded in 1881).

Mount Kelly combines academic excellence with an outstanding range of opportunities beyond the classroom and exceptional pastoral care. The School offers day, weekly and full boarding places, currently for over 575 pupils (299 at the Prep and 276 at the College). Boarding is available from the age of 7.

We have high expectations and this encourages our pupils to believe in themselves, to be inquisitive, to be resilient and to show ambition both in and out of the classroom. Our pupils feel happy and valued, which in turn gives them the confidence, social awareness and enthusiasm for lifelong learning needed to succeed in a fast changing world. Respect for tradition and an openness to innovation are valued and we encourage our pupils to work with and learn from each other, whilst also showing moral courage to stand up for what they believe in.

Children at Mount Kelly are nurtured, guided and inspired to develop their own skills and interests. Each pupil joins one of the School's Houses, which serves as a boarder's 'home from home' and a day pupil's working base. Boarders and day pupils are integrated throughout the School with small class sizes offering exceptional levels of individual focus. Each pupil is cared for by a Housemaster or Housemistress and assigned a dedicated tutor who oversees their academic, pastoral and co-curricular progress. This comprehensive tutoring system produces happy pupils who are confident, well-rounded and ambitious.

Site and Buildings. Mount Kelly is set in over 100 acres of green fields and woodland on the edge of Dartmoor National Park and on the outskirts of the historic town of Tavistock, Devon. The buildings comprise the School Chapel, Assembly Hall, Performing Arts Centre, Dining Hall, Library and ICT Centre, Art Studios, Technology workshops, Science Laboratories, Swimming Pools (50m, 25m indoor and 25m outdoor), Sports Hall, Gym, Climbing Wall, Fives and Squash Courts, floodlit All-Weather Pitches, Golf course, an Armoury and Rifle Range. There is also an on-site residential Adventure Centre, including a high-ropes course and trapeze jump. The School also has its own Trout and Salmon fishing.

Term of Entry. Pupils may be accepted at any stage in the school year from the nursery though to the Lower Sixth Form.

Scholarships. Each year, Mount Kelly makes available a number of scholarships and awards to pupils hoping to join us in Year 7, Year 9 or the Sixth Form. Scholarships and awards are competitive on entry, and provide exceptional opportunities for able pupils. Awards may be given in the following disciplines: Academic, Art, DT, Music, Sport and Swimming.

Curriculum. The GCSE curriculum is flexible and aims to stretch each pupil appropriately. The core subjects are Mathematics, English, Science, a Language and ICT (ECDL qualification). The range of option subjects include Art & Design, Business Studies, Product Design, Geography, History, Latin, Modern Foreign Languages, Music, Physical Education and Religious Studies.

Pupils entering the Sixth Form need to possess 6 GCSE passes. Mount Kelly pupils study for 3 A Levels. A Level option subjects include Mathematics, Further Mathematics, English Literature, Biology, Physics, Chemistry, Fine Art, Photography, Business & Economics, Geography, History, ICT, Music, Physical Education, Product Design, Psychology, Religious Studies, Modern Foreign Languages and EPQ. All pupils in the Lower Sixth year receive tuition in Public Speaking.

Co-Curricular Activities. Mount Kelly has a strong commitment to co-curricular activities and the majority of College pupils are involved with the Combined Cadet Force, Duke of Edinburgh Awards, the Devizes to Westminster International Canoe Race or the Ten Tors Challenge.

Academic staff, in collaboration with the on-site Adventure Centre, run the innovative Learning Outside the Classroom Programme. Children in the Pre-Prep attend a weekly Forest School activity and the Shackleton outdoor programme is run for 9 to 13 year olds.

All pupils are encouraged to explore new interests and to make the most of their spare time. Societies and Activities include LAMDA, Debating, Current Affairs, Drama, Choir, Orchestra, Ensembles, Chess, Computer Programming, Photography, Robotics, Chess, Fine Arts, Surfing and Textiles.

Sport. Mount Kelly has a strong sporting tradition, particularly known for its elite international swimming programme, and has produced more Olympians and Internationals than any other school of its size. Sports undertaken are Rugby, Hockey, Cricket, Tennis, Athletics, Swimming, Netball, Rounders, Climbing, Cross Country, Golf, Horse Riding and Fives, Squash, Basketball, Sailing, Surfing, Tennis, Football and Yoga.

Fees per term (2016–2017). Day Pupils £2,300 to £5,570 and Full boarding: £5,750 to £9,700.

Charitable status. The Mount Kelly Foundation is a Registered Charity, number 306716.

Chairman of the Governors: Rear Admiral Chris Snow, CBE, DL

Head Master and Principal of the Foundation: Mr Mark Semmence, BA, MA Warwick, MBA, PGCE

Principal Deputy Head: Mr Adam Reid, MSc, PGCE
Deputy Head (Academic): Mr James Dixon, MA, PGCE
Deputy Head (Pastoral): Mr Drew Bott, BA, PGCE
Head of Prep: Mr Dominic Floyd, BA, PGCE, QTS
Bursar and Clerk to the Governors: Mr Steven Webber, MA, FCMA, FCIS
Commercial Director: Mr Richard Smith

Mount St Mary's College

College Road, Spinkhill, Nr Sheffield, Derbyshire S21 3YL

Tel: 01246 433388
Fax: 01246 435511
email: headmaster@msmcollege.com
website: www.msmcollege.com
Twitter: @MountSpinkhill

Motto: *Sine Macula.*

Mount St Mary's College, a co-educational boarding and day school, and its preparatory school and nursery, Barlborough Hall, educate children from age 3 to 18 in the Jesuit tradition. Mount St Mary's is a member of BSA and CISC, the Governing Body is a member of AGBIS and the Headmaster is a member of HMC.

Mount St Mary's College was founded in 1842 by the Society of Jesus in order to provide an education for the country's growing Catholic population. The manor of Spinkhill in North East Derbyshire was the first home of the College, forming the nucleus of the present school. The Elizabethan manor of Barlborough Hall, 1¼ miles away, is the home of the Preparatory School to the College (*see also Barlborough Hall entry in IAPS section*).

Educating children since 1842, we have over a century of teaching and pastoral expertise as well as long-standing traditions that embed charm and character in school life. Boys and girls excel during their time with us, growing in knowledge, confidence, humility and aspiration.

We follow a traditionally robust GCSE and A Level curriculum and the quality and quantity of our music and sporting departments is immense. In addition, we offer a varied range of popular co-curricular opportunities Combined Cadet Force, fencing and Latin, to name but a few. Our teaching nursery ensures children are school-ready when they join Reception.

Numbers. College 290 (11–18); Preparatory School (3–11 years) 190. Boarders, Weekly Boarders and Day Pupils (girls and boys) are accepted at the College.

Aims. Mount St Mary's College is a Jesuit Catholic school inspired by the ideals of St Ignatius of Loyola. The College seeks to develop the whole person and encourages an appreciation of the needs of others both in the College community and the world at large. Mount St Mary's prepares its pupils for an active life commitment through the development of 'a faith that promotes justice'. The College seeks to produce young men and women for others. Pupils of other and no religious denominations are most welcome.

Special Features. Mount St Mary's College is well known for its family atmosphere. Pupils benefit from the close interest and encouragement which they receive throughout their time at the College and parental involvement is particularly encouraged. The strong emphasis on extra-curricular activities illustrates the Jesuit commitment to developing each pupil's individual talents in all areas – academic, spiritual, cultural and physical.

Situation. Located in beautiful private grounds in villages in north east Derbyshire, between Chesterfield, Worksop and Sheffield, the schools are easily accessible from Junction 30 of the M1. A fleet of school minibuses operate throughout the region.

Organisation. Each pupil is guided by a tutor and Heads of Line, who is responsible for overseeing academic progress, pastoral care, recreation and discipline. Heads of Line work closely with the Academic Subject Leaders, Prefect of Studies and the School Pastoral Leader.

Boarding. Full and flexi boarding options are available for pupils in Year 7 upwards. Boarders live in the boys' or girls' houses, under the care of a Resident Boarding Pastoral Leader and Senior Boarding Tutor, assisted by resident House Tutors. The majority of rooms are en-suite, with either 2–3 sharing or in single rooms. Boarders, both domestic and international, enjoy a full evening and weekend programme incorporating studies, the arts, sport and social time.

Curriculum. Pupils at Mount St Mary's are prepared for GCSEs, AS and A Levels, and University entrance. The curriculum for the first three years (ages 11–13) broadly follows National Curriculum at KS3 with opportunity to pursue a second foreign language and a range of creative arts subjects. The standard GCSE package is nine GCSEs, although more or less is negotiable according to ability; this includes a core of English, Mathematics, a foreign language and between one and three separate Sciences. Several subjects follow the IGCSE curriculum. Other subjects are chosen from a range of options. In the Sixth Form pupils follow AS Levels (usually four) in the Lower Sixth. The most able pupils can continue with four A Levels in the Upper Sixth, although many pupils will choose to focus on three subjects. The College also runs an "A Level Plus" programme to stretch the more able students. In keeping with the school's Ignatian ethos, all pupils follow a Religious Studies course at every stage in addition to a full programme of Games and Physical Education at every level. Specialist tuition is available in a variety of musical instruments and in speech and drama training. Assessment and monitoring of work is built into the tutorial system and there is a regular timetable of reports, pupil progress interviews and communication with parents. Academic excellence and breadth of knowledge are characteristics of Jesuit education and the curriculum is constantly reviewed to ensure that the widest opportunities are available to each pupil.

Religion. Mount St Mary's College is a distinctively Jesuit school, that welcomes children of all denominations to share its ethos. Ignatian principles inform the College's work in fostering a realistic knowledge, love and acceptance of self and of the world in which we live and this underpins our main objective: the formation of young men and young women for others. There are school masses, year masses and other liturgical celebrations regularly throughout the school year, as well as retreats and pilgrimages. The College enjoys close links with the Hallam Diocese and participates in the diocesan pilgrimage to Lourdes. Religious Education is a part of the curriculum to GCSE and either as an examination or non-examination option in the Sixth Form. The Arrupe programme provides opportunities for Sixth Formers to give service to the local community. The College maintains a strong link with Jesuit missions in different parts of the world, finding ways to further the work of the Society in this area. Pupils have the opportunity to be involved in gap year projects supported by the Jesuits. Pupils and their parents are expected to recognise and endorse the religious commitment of the College.

Sports. The College has extensive playing fields for rugby, hockey, cricket and football. Rugby, for which the College has a strong regional and national reputation, is the major boys' sport. Cricket facilities are excellent with all-weather practice wickets and indoor practice nets. The main girls' sport in the winter term is hockey, for which there is a floodlit all-weather hockey pitch. There is a full-time Level 4 Athletics Coach. Other sports include swimming, tennis, basketball, volleyball, badminton, shooting, netball and fencing.

Art, Drama and Music. There are many opportunities to be involved in the Arts within the school, both within the curriculum and as part of the extra-curricular activities. Within the Art and Design department pupils can study fine art, textiles, resistant materials within the workshop, and photography. On Saturday mornings activities are run involving sculpture, textiles, art and photography.

Music is particularly strong, and popular at all levels. Pupils are encouraged to take up a musical instrument, and can participate in a wide number of musical activities, ranging from three choirs and a barber shop group to symphony orchestra, concert band, jazz band and many ensembles. Drama is also strong in the College, and several Senior and Junior productions are put on every year. The music and drama departments collaborate to produce a whole-school musical.

Combined Cadet Force and other Extra-Curricular Activities. All pupils in Year 10 participate in the Combined Cadet Force, in the Army or RAF section. They can continue to be a member, if they choose, in Year 11 and the Sixth Form. The CCF gives opportunities for external leadership courses and adventure training and fulfilling Duke of Edinburgh's Award options. There are extensive opportunities for extra-curricular activities at lunchtime, after school and on Saturday mornings. Pupils can pursue interests in drama, music, sports, the Duke of Edinburgh's Award and many other clubs and societies.

Facilities. Facilities include a Sixth Form Centre, a Drama Studio, ICT suite of three fully-equipped rooms, Music School with practice rooms, Recital Hall and Music Studio, College Theatre, Library with ICT facilities, various pupil common rooms, Fitness Centre, heated indoor swimming pool, Sports Hall, Rifle Range, Outdoor Pursuits Centre, all-weather tennis courts and 30 acres of games fields. A grade A accredited athletics track was opened in 2007.

Admissions. Entry to the College at age 11 is via the College's entrance examination, taken early in the Spring term at the College. At 13+, pupils either sit the College entrance examination or Common Entrance exam through their prep schools. At other ages, pupils are accepted on the basis of school reports, with College entry tests as appropriate and in the Sixth Form, pupils are accepted on the basis of GCSE results, or their equivalent.

Private tours of the school take place all year round. The Headmaster, Dr Nicholas Cuddihy, extends a warm welcome to families to visit Mount St Mary's College or its Preparatory School. Call the Admissions team on 01246 433388 or email: admissions@msmcollege.com.

Fees per term (2016–2017). Full Boarders: £9,332 (Years 9–13), £7,109 (Years 7 and 8). Weekly Boarders: £7,528 (Years 9–13), £5,848 (Years 7 and 8). Day Pupils: £4,307 (Years 9–13), £3,749 (Years 7 and 8). Barlborough Hall: £3,315 (Upper School), £2,487 (Pre-Prep).

Scholarships. Academic scholarships are awarded at 11+, 13+ and Sixth Form on the basis of the College's Scholarship Examination papers. GCSE results also form an aspect of Scholarship awards at Sixth Form. Music and sports scholarships are also available and the College will be happy to provide further information on these. In keeping with the College's ethos, bursaries are awarded in cases of demonstrable need. The Old Mountaineers offer post-graduate scholarships to former pupils of the College and applications are considered annually for these. All scholarships take place early in the Spring Term at the College.

Charitable status. Mount St Mary's is a Registered Charity, number 1117998. The College was founded in 1842 to provide an education for children.

Governing Body:

Chairman: Fr A Porter SJ

Vice Chairman: Mr R Gilbert

Fr M Beattie SJ	Dr L Merrick
Mr J Ridley	Mr C Emmott
Rev John Twist SJ	Mr G Smith
Mrs M Bolton	Mr J Dickson
Mr J McNally, MBA	Prof M Staub
Mr M O'Hara	

Executive Team:

Headmaster: **N Cuddihy**, EdD Dublin, BRelSc, MSc

Head Teacher, Barlborough Hall School: N Boys, BA Australia

Bursar: H Ewins, Accountancy Hons Degree Liverpool

Deputy Headmaster: A Hutchings

Director of Marketing, Development, Admissions & Communications: Mrs V McAllister

Assistant Head – Prefect of Studies: C McAllister, BA Leeds

Assistant Head – Head of Higher Line, Sixth Form: J Murphy, BA York, FRSA

Jesuit Community:

Fr Simon Ellis, Director of Chaplaincy

Fr Michael Beattie SJ, STL Rome, MA London (*Resident Jesuit Priest*)

Fr Peter Knott SJ (*Resident Jesuit Priest, Barlborough Hall Chaplain*)

New Hall School

The Avenue, Boreham, Chelmsford, Essex CM3 3HS

Tel:	01245 467588
Fax:	01245 464348
email:	registrar@newhallschool.co.uk
website:	www.newhallschool.co.uk
Twitter:	@NewHallSchool
Facebook:	/newhallschool

Pupil numbers. Senior School (11–18): 833 (Day 617, Boarding 216). Preparatory School (3–11): 334.

Location. New Hall School benefits from a magnificent campus and stunning heritage setting, with a grade I listed main building part of a former Tudor palace occupied by King Henry VIII.

We aim to educate the whole person: academically, creatively and socially, in a community which also nurtures the spiritual dimensions of human life. All benefit from the outstanding facilities on offer within our stunning 85-acre campus.

New Hall is set in an idyllic and convenient location, just 30 minutes by train from London and within easy reach of all major airports. We offer a distinctive education of real quality that is designed to give students the best start in life.

Diamond Model. At New Hall, students are educated in co-educational classes up to age 11 and again at Sixth Form, however, from 11 to 16 they are taught in single-sex lessons.

The main benefits of the 'diamond model' and five years of single-sex teaching derive from the ability to tailor pastoral and academic provision more sensitively and expertly to the needs of young people going through the physical, emotional and social upheaval of adolescence. Young teenagers are liberated from the negative peer pressure of having to perform in mixed classes.

Gender stereotyping of subjects is also removed. Girls and boys follow an identical curriculum and do not learn to perceive subjects as being more suited to either girls or boys.

Curriculum. The New Hall curriculum is distinctive in its breadth and academic rigour. An imaginatively taught and well-balanced curriculum is appropriately tailored to the needs of the individual. The experienced and dedicated staff endeavour to bring out the best in everyone.

New Hall has its own Most Able and Talented programme, which is proven to add exceptional value at GCSE and A Level. We believe that giftedness can be created and that students' academic skills can be developed at ever higher levels if they are given intellectual challenges.

New Hall encourages able students to apply for Oxford or Cambridge universities. The school has a good track record of students winning Oxbridge places in a wide range of subjects, including sciences, arts, humanities and languages.

We are proud that our examination results are consistently among the best of any independent school in the area.

Co-Curriculum. Our co-curricular programme is designed to add breadth to the New Hall education, which enables us to develop the well-rounded young men and women of whom we can be proud.

Our educational philosophy is reflected in the extensive array of challenging co-curricular activities. Educational visits to countries such as India and China, alongside our societies and clubs, create a stimulating environment for your son or daughter to develop his or her passions, learning and talents.

Through activities such as debating, Model United Nations and political philosophy, students can become independent thinkers with a broad and rich experience of social and academic life.

Our Ethos. Our Catholic foundation and ethos is central to all that we do, supported by the work of our lively Chaplaincy Team. At New Hall, a special value is placed on love and forgiveness, which encourage relationships based on trust, kindness, self-respect and care for those in need.

All students participate in our award-winning New Hall Voluntary Service (NHVS), where they gain confidence, leadership and team-working skills and a desire to serve others. They will develop a sense of charity and community that will remain with them beyond their years at New Hall.

Boarding. We have a thriving full boarding community and options for weekly or flexible boarding. The six boarding houses offer their members a strong sense of identity and opportunities to forge new friendships. There are dedicated boarding houses for younger boarders (age 7–11), for students in the senior division (age 11–15) and for Sixth Form (age 16–18).

Although each of our boarding houses has its own individuality, a common theme throughout is the exceptional pastoral care and dedication of the residential team. This is a significant strength of our school.

Music and Performing Arts. Our dedicated Performing Arts Centre and theatres allow students opportunities for group or individual performances, which develop talent and encourage confidence.

Music has a long and fine tradition at New Hall. There is a host of performing groups, including chamber choir, chapel choir, senior orchestra, strings academy and jazz band. Students can participate in the London Academy of Music and Dramatic Arts (LAMDA) programmes, which develop presentation and public speaking skills. Drama performances range from Shakespeare to modern plays and musicals. Dance is a particular strength, with the annual dance show attracting a cast of more than 200 girls and boys.

Students take part in regional and national festivals and competitions and groups regularly perform in major venues across Europe.

Sport. New Hall students are able to develop their team spirit and physical development through our rich programme of sporting opportunities.

Under the guidance of expert coaches, including former international sportsmen and women, New Hall balances first-class training for those with particular sporting talents, with an inclusive 'sport for all' approach.

Our elite sportsmen and women compete at county, regional and national levels, at which they have enjoyed individual team success.

Our facilities set us apart and the rich variety of sports on offer include rugby, hockey, netball, cricket, swimming, athletics, golf, skiing and tennis.

Fees per term (2016–2017). Senior School: Day £5,830–£6,243; Weekly Boarding £7,697–£8,932; Full Boarding £8,514–£9,585.

Preparatory School: Day: £1,817.40–£4,572; Boarding (from age 7): £6,114 (weekly), £6,754 (full).

There is a Prompt Payment Discount of £100 per term in Years 1–13 (not included in the Fees shown).

Entry requirements. Entrance examination, school report, and interview.

Scholarships and Bursaries. Scholarship candidates follow the normal entrance procedure and, dependent on the type of scholarship, a further assessment. All candidates for Year 7 entry are entered for the Academic Scholarship, which is awarded to the highest achieving student from the entrance examination results. Other scholarships at Year 7 entry 2013 are available in Drama, Music and Sport. There are also scholarships available for Catholic students. Similar scholarships are available for Year 9 entry. For Sixth Form entry, there are scholarship awards available based on GCSE examination results as well as an Open (all rounder) scholarship, Boarding scholarship and Special Talent Award.

Means-tested Bursaries (up to 100% remission of fees) are available to new and current students.

Further information on Admissions, Scholarships and Bursaries is available from the Registrar and on the school website.

Charitable status. New Hall School Trust is a Registered Charity, number 1110286. Its aim is the education of children within a Christian environment.

Chair of Governors: Mrs Clare Kershaw, LLB Hons, MCMI

Senior Leadership Team:

Principal: Mrs K Jeffrey, MA Oxon, PGCE Surrey, BA Div PUM, MA EdMg OU, NPQH

Deputy Principal: Mrs C Goddard, MA Oxon, PhD, AMBDA

Vice Principal: Mr J Sidwell, BSc Loughborough, PGCE London

Head of Sixth Form: Mr J Alderson, BA Manchester, PGCE Cantab

Director of Boarding: Mrs E Searle, BA ARU

Head of Finance: Mrs D Came, IPFA, IoD

Preparatory School Headteacher: Mrs C Goodwin, BA Hons QTS, MEd, NPQH

Heads of Academic Departments:

Art:
Mr G Hughes, BA Coventry, MFA Reading

Classics:
Miss H Morrison, MA Oxon, PGCE Cantab

Critical Thinking:
Mr D Yates, BA, PGCE Lancaster

Dance:
Mrs S Molina, AISTD

Design Technology & Food:
Mrs L Curtis, BA Oxford Brookes

Drama:
Mr D Rutter, BA Middlesex, PGCE Middlesex, LCM Dip

Economics & Business Studies:
Miss R Walters, BSc Surrey, GTP

English:
Dr S Foster, BA PhD Loughborough, PGCE Anglia Ruskin

English as an Additional Language (EAL):
Mrs C Edmunds, BA Soton, PGCE Soton

Geography:
Mrs J Lewis, MA Cantab, PGCE Cantab

Gifted & Talented Coordinator:
Mr D Yates, BA, PGCE Lancaster

History:
Dr L Shaw, MA Cantab, PhD, GTP

Information & Communication Technology:
Mr G Kiff, BA London

Learning Development:
Mrs J Fawdry, BSc Hull, PGCE London, PG Dip SpLD, AMBDA

Library:
Ms J Tait, BSc Otago, CertLibSt Wellington, Dip Tchg Dunedin

Mathematics:
Mr I Tanner, BSc UEA, PGCE UEA

Modern Languages:
Mrs S Reid, BA Bristol, PGCE Homerton, MFLE

Music:
Mr A Fardell, BA Kent, LRAM (*Director of Music*)

Physical Education:
Mr G Kirkham, BSc Lough (*Director of Girls' Sport*)
Mr O Cobbe, BA QTS St Mary's (*Director of Boys' Sport*)

Politics:
Miss R Walters, BSc Surrey, GTP

Theology:
Mr P Bray, BA, MA Dunelm, GTP

Science:
Mrs L Willson, BSc Roehampton, GTP (*Head of Biology*)

Examinations Officer:
Mrs G Newton

Careers:
Mrs S Haddrell

Housemasters/Housemistresses:
Earle House: Mr C Coupland
Magdalen House: Mrs R Mackay, MSc Loughborough, BSc Reading
Petre House: Mr J Marriott, BA Leeds, PGCE Lancaster
Hawley House: Miss J Palmer, MA Northumbria, PGCE Northumbria, BA Cumbria
Dennett House: Mrs J Murray-Turner
Campion House: Mr J Aiken

Registrar: Ms H Rogers

Newcastle-under-Lyme School

Mount Pleasant, Newcastle-under-Lyme, Staffordshire ST5 1DB

Tel:	01782 631197
Fax:	01782 632582
email:	info@nuls.org.uk
website:	www.nuls.org.uk
Twitter:	@NuLSchoolUK
Facebook:	/NewcastleunderLymeSchool

Newcastle-under-Lyme School, which attracts pupils from a large area of North Staffordshire, South Cheshire and North Shropshire, is a co-educational day school for 800 pupils aged 3–18. The present School was formed in 1981 through the amalgamation of Newcastle High School and the Orme Girls' School, two schools which were endowed as a single foundation in 1872 under an educational charity scheme for children in Newcastle-under-Lyme which has its roots in the 1600s. The two schools enjoyed a reputation for scholarship and for service to the community throughout North Staffordshire, a reputation which has continued with the formation of Newcastle-under-Lyme School. The School is also well known for its high standards in sport, music and drama, which play a major part in the co-curricular life of the School. The Junior School is adjacent to the Senior School and has some 300 pupils aged 3–11.

Buildings and Grounds. Set in 30 acres of grounds, the School is pleasantly situated on high ground in a quiet conservation area close to the centre of Newcastle-under-Lyme. The original buildings still form part of the School and extensions have been added from time to time. A fine dining hall was opened in one of the wings of the original building, part of the continuing programme of development and refurbishment which was begun when the School reverted to full independence in 1981. The Millennium Sixth Form Centre opened in March 2000 affording spacious new accommodation for senior students. The new Stinton building was opened in September 2014. The library, lecture theatre, new and refurbished laboratories and the enhanced indoor social space and cafe have transformed the whole building. The School has a Language laboratory, workshops, a Music School, an Art and Design Centre, a gymnasium, and a Sports Centre which includes a sports hall, a fitness suite and an indoor swimming pool. Computers are accessible in subject areas and in four modern laboratories, where machines are linked on a network basis. There are also tennis and netball courts and extensive playing fields, providing pitches for cricket, rugby and hockey, adjacent to the School. An all-weather pitch with floodlighting was opened in March 2002.

Organisation. The School is organised in two sections: the Junior School – nursery (2004), pre-preparatory (2004) and preparatory (1982) – which has up to 300 pupils in the age range 3 to 11 and the Senior School of some 500 pupils, including the Sixth Form numbering more than 150 students.

Form Tutors and Heads of Year have particular responsibility for the pastoral welfare of the pupils in their charge.

In Year 7 and Year 8 boys and girls have their own inter-form and inter-house competitions, with separate Lower School assemblies. This structure gives to the Lower School forms a separate identity within the Senior School. The Senior House structure, which extends from Year 9 upwards, consists of four co-educational houses.

Curriculum. A broad curriculum in the first five years has English (Language and Literature), Mathematics, Biology, Chemistry, and Physics as core subjects. All pupils also take a Modern Foreign Language, selected from French, Mandarin, German and Spanish, Latin, Greek, History, Geography, Religious Education, Music, Art, Food and Nutrition, Design and Technology, ICT, PE, Swimming and Games. Pupils have the option of taking Biology, Chemistry and Physics as a dual-award GCSE or as three separate GCSEs in Year 10 and Year 11.

Pupils take nine GCSEs and the great majority will proceed to take between three and five A Level subjects in the Lower Sixth Form. There may also be the possibility of taking the Extended Project Qualification.

Optional choices in the Sixth Form include A Level Business Studies, Psychology, Economics, British Government and Politics and Physical Education in addition to AS Levels in the subjects available at GCSE. Pupils are also prepared for Oxford and Cambridge Entrance.

Co-Curricular Activities. The main school games are Rugby, Cricket, Hockey, Athletics, Tennis and Cross-Country for the boys and Hockey, Athletics, Netball, Tennis and Rounders for the girls. Swimming, Water Polo, Life Saving and Synchronised Swimming, Water Polo and Life Saving also feature strongly and there are usually opportunities for Shooting, Squash, Aerobics, Basketball, Badminton, Golf and other physical activities in the Sixth Form.

There are also strong traditions in both Music and Drama and standards are very high. More than 200 pupils receive instrumental tuition and there are a number of concerts in each year with major performances being given in local churches and in the Victoria Hall in Hanley. There are several major drama productions each year including one each at Upper School and Lower School levels.

The flourishing Combined Cadet Force has naval, army and air-force sections and there is also a large Scout troop, which enrols both boys and girls. Pupils also participate in the Duke of Edinburgh's Award scheme.

Clubs and Societies meet during the lunch hour and after school.

Careers. The School places much emphasis on the importance of careers guidance, both in the GCSE years and in the preparation for higher education. The School is an all-in member of the ISCO Careers Guidance Scheme, through which all pupils in Year 11 receive a careers report based on tests of ability, personality and aptitude. Pupils receive full advice on applications to Universities and other Institutes of Higher Education.

Honours. Between 1987 and 2016 288 of our students gained places at Oxford and Cambridge, while in 2016 some 95% of all Upper Sixth leavers gained entry to degree courses in Higher Education.

Admissions. Entry to the Nursery is on a first-come first-served basis. Entry to the Junior School and Years 7, 8, 9 and 10 of the Senior School is by examination/assessment only. Pupils moving into the area may be considered for entry at any time.

Entry at Sixth Form level is by interview and GCSE qualifications.

Registration forms, and copies of the Prospectus, are available on request.

Scholarships and Bursaries. The following Scholarships and Bursaries are available:

Governors' Scholarships: Scholarships of up to £2,000 per annum for up to five years following entry to be awarded on the results of the 11+ and 13+ Entrance Examinations.

Sports Scholarships: A number of Sports Scholarships may be awarded to candidates on their entry to the Senior School demonstrating particular sporting prowess in major School sports. These will be of value up to £1,000 per annum for one year following entry.

The Robert S Woodward Scholarships: One or Two Scholarships, of value up to £1,000 per annum, to be awarded annually to students entering, or in, the Sixth Form, for outstanding performance in the field of Mathematical Sciences.

The JCB Sixth Form Scholarship: One Scholarship, of value up to £1,000 per annum, to be awarded annually to pupils entering, or in, the Sixth Form, for outstanding performance in the field of Physics.

Music Scholarships: A number of Music Scholarships may be awarded to candidates entering the Sixth Form at 16+ and on entry at 11+, to cover the cost of music tuition throughout the student's school career.

Bursaries: A number of Bursaries are available for pupils applying for entry to the Senior School. Bursaries offer assistance with School Fees, depending upon parental income.

Further details may be obtained from the Registrar.

Fees per term (2016–2017). Senior School £3,838; Junior School: Preparatory £3,136; Pre-Preparatory £2,794; Nursery £39.50 per day (£25.50 per morning, £23.00 per afternoon session).

Charitable status. Newcastle-under-Lyme School is a Registered Charity, number 1124463. The object of the Charity shall be the provision and conduct in or near Newcastle-under-Lyme of a day or a day and boarding school or schools for boys and girls.

Governing Body:

Chair of Governors: Professor G I Russell, MB, ChB, MD, FRCP
M Caulkin, Cert CIB
D H Cook, MA
Mrs S Edmends
Mrs R E Evans, LLB
Mrs E Gillow, BA
Professor P W Jones, BSc, MSc, PhD, CStat
Mrs K A Miller, BSc, ACA
G Neyt
J S Rushton, BSc, FCA, CISA
D P Wallbank, BA
M R Warren, BA, MArch
D Webster, BA, DUniv

Bursar: J P Longdon, MCGI

Headmaster: **D M Williamson**, BA, MA, FRGS

Deputy Heads:
Mrs J A Simms, BA, MSc (*Pastoral*)
M S Snell, BSc, MA (*Academic*)

Head of Sixth Form: Mrs B A Godridge, BA

English:
*Mrs A A Keay, MA
Mrs J Betts-Nicholson, BA
Mrs B Joughin, BA
R Lench, BA
Mrs L Marrable-Griffiths, BA

History:
*D Dunlop, BA, PhD
D A Cawdron, BA
Mrs S J Stockdale, BSc

Mathematics:
*Miss J M Griffiths, BSc
Mrs C M Barber, BSc
D T Buckley, BSc
Mrs J C Cliff, BSc
Mrs J A Cryer, BSc
Mrs O Exley, BSc, PhD
E J Griffiths, BA

ICT:
*S Luck, BSc

Chemistry:
*P Thomson, BSc, PhD
M S Lunt, BSc
G J Moore, BSc, PhD

Physics:
*N P Migallo, BSc
A Fishburne, MEng
Mrs K Rigby, BSc

Biology:
*N J Simms, BSc
N C Carter, BSc
Miss J Galvin, BSc
D R Pepper, BSc, PhD
   (*Deputy Head of Sixth Form*)
Mrs A Sparrow

Geography:
*T P Jowitt, BSc
Miss N J MacKintosh, BSc
D P Sherratt

Modern Languages:
*Mrs M T Holmes, BA
Mrs M Barnes
Mrs S Graham, MA
Mrs M Isherwood, BA
D G Murtagh, BA
Mrs K H Tan, BA
Mrs D A Woodcock, BA

Religious Studies:
*A Poole, BA
J S Preston, BA

Latin:
*Ms T A Thomas, BA
Mrs E Scullion, BA

Economics:
*Miss L Barton, BA
A R Sparks, BEd

Art and Design:
*Mrs S Parkinson, BA
Miss L Herian, BA
Mrs B W Jones, CertEd
Mrs F Jones

Design and Technology:
*J S Meredith, BEd
P Finney, BA

Home Economics:
*Mrs J Machin
Mrs N G Swindells, BEd

Physical Education:
*G M Chesterman, BSocSc
Miss R E Bradley
G M Breen, BSc
P J Butler, FISTC, AIST LS
Mrs D Glenn, BEd
S A Robson, BEd

Music:
*T Sagar, MA
Mrs C Hughes, BA, MusEd
Mrs J Perkin

Mrs M Potter, GGSM, ARCM, PGCE

Careers:
Mrs B Joughin, BA

Learning Support Coordinator: A R Sparks, BEd

Librarian: Miss W F Butler, BA, MA, DipLib, MCLIP

Newcastle-under-Lyme Junior School:

Head: N J Vernon, BSc, MA

Deputy Head: M J Erian, BA, MA
Head of Pre-Prep: Mrs A M Burgess, BA
Nursery Manager: Mrs A Smith, NNEB, NEBS

Mrs C Deakes, BA
Miss R L Edwards, BA
Mrs N J Erian
Mrs A Farnsworth
Mrs J Grisdale, BEd
Mrs M Johnson, BA
Miss P D Knighton, BEd
G Lewis, BEd
Mrs L Moss, BA
Mrs E L Oram, BEd
Mrs S Quinn, BEd
Miss J E Stanton, BEd

Norwich School

70 The Close, Norwich, Norfolk NR1 4DD
Tel: 01603 728430
email: admissions@norwich-school.org.uk
website: www.norwich-school.org.uk

Motto: '*Praemia virtutis honores*'

Norwich School is a co-educational, independent day school for pupils aged seven to eighteen. Currently there 1080 pupils attending the school. Set in the Cathedral Close, Norwich School is a traditional, yet lively place where boys and girls enjoy a rounded and stimulating education. The school is characterised by strong, warm relationships and a profound appreciation of scholarship.

The school achieves exceptional results but we believe that an education for life is about more than statistics. Here we enjoy local character, beautiful surroundings and a remarkable history. Staff and pupils together create a supportive atmosphere and boys and girls benefit from specialised facilities and a broad curriculum.

Ethos. Learning and scholarship are at the heart of the broad education that Norwich School provides. Christian values – notably love and compassion for one another – underpin our activities and relationships.

Aims. Norwich School is committed to producing scholarly, reflective young people who are capable of handling difficult concepts and expressing profound thought; providing a rich, varied and broad education that develops the diverse talents of the boys and girls; equipping pupils for leadership and service.

Pastoral. The Senior School is organised by Houses. Pupils are allocated to a House upon joining the school, and stay with that House as they move up through the year-groups. Many of a pupil's first and firmest friendships will be forged within the House.

Each of the eight Houses is managed by a Housemaster, a senior member of staff who comes to know the pupils and their parents very well during their years of association with the House, and who brings compassion and continuity to a pupil's life. If a problem arises, the tutor will involve the Housemaster in its resolution; they are familiar figures in the school who offer a blend of experience and encouragement.

Sixth Form. Life in the sixth form is a busy and rewarding experience, combining rigorous academic scholarship and commitment to a range of extra-curricular activities, as well as leadership and service roles. Our aim is to ensure that all pupils reach their potential and are able to apply for the university courses and career paths of their choice.

Extra-curricular activity. There are many areas of life beyond the classroom which serve to fulfil the aim of a broad and varied education. Encompassed within the programme are challenges, opportunities for service, group cooperation, team participation and leadership. All are seen as central to the educational experience of each school member.

It is hoped that every pupil will find something from the programme which will influence and stay with them far beyond their school days.

Bursaries. Norwich School sets aside generous funds to enable pupils to attend the school who would otherwise not be able to do so without financial help.

All bursaries are means-tested and can result in a reduction in fees of up to 100%; there is a sliding scale based on family income and finances and resources of the school.

Scholarships. Scholarships are assessed by: examination, interview and audition and reward pupils with outstanding ability and flair that will make a significant contribution to the School in their area of particular skill. Pupils may apply for more than one scholarship but may only be awarded a maximum of two scholarships at any one time. Academic, Music and Sport Scholarships are offered at 11+, 13+ and 16+ entry. Design, Art and Drama are offered at 16+ entry.

Admission. The main points of entry are at ages 7, 11, 13 and 16.

Fees per term (2016–2017). Senior School £5,020; Lower School £4,575.

Old Norvicensians. All enquiries should be made to Mrs R Lightfoot, Norwich School, 71a The Close, Norwich NR1 4DD.

Charitable status. Norwich School is a Registered Charity, number 311280. It exists solely to provide education.

Governors:
P J E Smith, MA, FIA (*Chairman*)
T J Gould, MA (*Vice-Chairman*)

Dr S C Bamber	J A E Hustler
Mrs A Fry, MA	Ms M Jarrold, MA Cantab
A R Grant, MA, FRSA	I Reid, BSc, MRICS
E J H Gould, MA	D W Talbot, ACA
Mrs A J C Green, BSc	J W Walker, BEd Cantab
C W Hoffman, ACIB	Miss T Yates, BA

Representative Governors:
Professor C Andrew, MA, University of Cambridge
A R Burdon-Cooper, MA, LLB, Worshipful Company of Dyers
J R Chambers, FCA, Worshipful Company of Dyers
The Revd Canon J M Haselock, BA, BPhil, MA, Dean & Chapter
The Very Revd Dr J B Hedges, Dean & Chapter
J Holme
Professor R J Last
A Little
Dr Kay Yeoman, PhD, University of East Anglia

Senior Management Team:

Head Master: S D A Griffiths, MA Oxon

Principal Deputy Head: Miss L E Péchard, BA, MA
Acting Deputy Head: Mrs N J Hill, BSc
Deputy Head (Director of Studies): Dr D N Farr, BA, PhD, FRHS
Deputy Head (Co-Curriculum): N M Plater, MA Oxon
Assistant Head (Fifth Form, Admissions and Marketing): M D Barber, BA
Director of Development and Engagement: P D Goddard, BEd
Assistant Head (Head of Sixth Form): C Hooper, BA

Assistant Head (Teaching & Learning); *Head of General Studies*: P A Todd, MA Cantab
Bursar: Mrs M W T Cherry, BEng

Heads of Department and Pastoral Leads, Senior School:
R P Allain, BMus, FTCL (*Director of Music*)
Miss R Anderson, MA (*Head of Religious Studies*)
D P Bateman, BSc (*Head of Politics*; *Housemaster, Valpy*)
J Bendall PhD (*Head of Chemistry*)
Miss A E Boyt, BA (*Head of Classical Civilisation*)
C Child, BA, MA (*School Chaplain*)
J Cowan, BSc (*Director of Sport*)
W H J Croston, BA (*Head of Careers and Higher Education, Head of Common Room*)
A P Curtis, BA (*Housemaster, Seagrim*)
A L Fisher, BA (*Housemaster, Parker*)
J C Fisher, BSc (*Senior Master*)
J C Gent, BSc (*Head of Biology*)
A E Grant, MA (*Head of History*)
I M Grisewood, BA (*Housemaster, School House*)
Mrs K Grote, MA (*Head of Classics*)
G A Hanlon, BSc (*Housemaster, Coke*)
T J Hill, BSc (*Head of ICT*)
M D Hopgood, BA (*Head of Geography*)
Mrs V L Hood, BA, MA (*Deputy Head – Sixth Form, Head of German*)
S Kirby, BSc, PhD (*Head of Mathematics*)
J Large, BSc (*Housemaster, Nelson*)
M Mulligan, BA, MPhil (*Head of Philosophy*)
A Murray, MA (*Head of English*)
Miss T M Mounter, BA (*Housemaster, Brooke*)
Mrs C Norton, BSc (*Head of Sports Science, Head of Girls' Games*)
Mrs L E D Parkhouse, MA (*Head of French*)
Mrs G Parsons, MA (*SENDCo*)
I R Passam, BA (*Head of Design*)
Mrs N Robinson, BA (*Head of Spanish*)
A M Rowlandson, BA (*Acting Head of Fourth Form*)
R Sims (*Housemaster, Repton*)
Dr M Venables, MA, PhD (*Head of Physics*)
Mrs S Ward, MA (*Head of Greek*)
Mrs K Watkinson, BA (*Acting Head of French*)
T J Watts, LLB (*Head of Community Service*)
D Whatley, BSc (*Head of Chemistry*)
T P White, BA (*Head of Economics*)

Lower School:
J K Ingham, BA (*Master of the Lower School*)
C M W Parsons, BSc (*Deputy Head – Academic*)
A Wilson, BSc (*Principal Deputy Head*)

Support Staff:
Head Master's PA: Mrs J Grapes, BA
Bursar's PA: Ms R Peters
Principal Deputy Head's PA: Mrs K Smith
Registrar: Mrs V A Gaskin, BSc
Chief Examinations Officer: Mrs M Brown, MA
School Nurse: Georgina Valpied, DipHE
Archivists: H Bedford-Payne, J Fisher

Nottingham High School

Waverley Mount, Nottingham NG7 4ED
Tel: 0115 978 6056
Fax: 0115 979 2202
email: info@nottinghamhigh.co.uk
          enquiries@nottinghamhigh.co.uk
website: www.nottinghamhigh.co.uk

Motto: '*Lauda Finem*'

This School was founded in 1513 by Dame Agnes Mellers, widow of Richard Mellers, sometime Mayor of Nottingham. The first Charter was given by Henry VIII, and supplementary Charters were given by Philip and Mary, and by Queen Elizabeth. The School, which remains independent, is now administered under the terms of a scheme issued by the Charity Commissioners.

Organisation. There are 987 day pupils, of whom 250 are in the Infant and Junior School and 215 in the Sixth Form. Nearly all Junior School pupils go on to complete their education in the Senior School. (*For further details about the Infant and Junior School, see entry in IAPS section.*) From 2015 the school became co-educational in the Sixth Form and Infant school, followed by the other year groups from 2016.

Curriculum. The Senior School curriculum leads to examinations at GCSE in the normal range of subjects. The Sixth Form are prepared for AS and A Levels. The range of subjects is wide: Latin, Classical Civilisation, Drama, Modern Languages, English, History, Economics, Politics, Design Technology, Geography, Mathematics, Physics, Chemistry, Biology, Music, Art, Philosophy, Psychology, RS, Classical Greek, Music Technology.

Admission. Entrance Examinations and assessments are held in January each year. Applicants for the Infant School should be between the ages of 4 and 7 years, for the Junior School between the ages of 7 and 11 years, and for the Senior School/Sixth Form between 11 and 16 years on 1 September of the year of entry. Entry is also possible higher up the School, subject to places being available and a successful interview (entry to Sixth Form is also dependent upon a minimum of 5 As at GCSE).

Fees per term (2016–2017). Tuition: Senior School £4,608, Junior School £3,670, Lovell House Infant School £3,155.

Entrance Scholarships and Bursaries. The Entrance Examination for the Senior School is held in January each year for the award of Entrance Scholarships. Part-Scholarships of a fixed sum may be awarded. They are not linked to parental finances and will normally continue throughout a pupil's school career. Application does not have to be made for part-scholarships as these are awarded at the discretion of the Headmaster, subject to entrance examination performance and interview.

Following the ending of the Government Assisted Places Scheme, Nottingham High School has introduced its own means-tested Bursaries to be awarded to pupils entering the Senior School at age eleven. All Bursaries will be awarded at the Headmaster's discretion and will normally continue until a pupil leaves the School.

Games. The Playing Fields, covering 20 acres, are situated about a mile and a half from the School with excellent pavilion facilities. There are also indoor cricket nets at the school. The School games, in which all pupils are expected to take part unless medically exempted, are Rugby, Hockey, (together with Association Football in the Junior School) in the winter, and Cricket or Tennis and Athletics in the summer. Other alternatives provided for seniors include Cross Country, Squash, Association Football (Sixth Form), Badminton, Golf, Shooting and Basketball. Swimming (the School has its own 25m pool) forms part of the Physical Education programme. Girls play Hockey, Netball and Rounders in the winter and summer terms respectively.

Combined Cadet Force. The School maintains a contingent of the CCF based on voluntary recruitment and consisting of Navy, Army and Air Force sections. There is a small bore range, and the School enters teams for various national competitions.

Societies. Individual interests and hobbies are catered for by a wide range of Societies which meet in the lunch break or at the end of afternoon school. These include Drama, Modern Languages, Mathematics, Chemistry, Biology, English, Politics, Arts, Music and Debating Societies, the Chess Club, the Bridge Club, Christian Union, and the Scout Troop. Over 120 pupils a year participate in the Duke of Edinburgh's Award Scheme. The Community Action Group, the Explorer Scouts and other Societies meet jointly with the neighbouring Nottingham Girls' High School.

Music. Apart from elementary instruction in Music in the lower forms, and more advanced studies for GCSE and A Level, tuition is offered by 3 full-time and 18 part-time teachers in the full range of orchestral instruments. There are 2 School orchestras of 50 and 30 players, 2 Choirs, a concert band (wind) of 50, a Training Band and Big Band and choral and orchestral concerts are given each year. Four instrumental bursaries, covering fee tuition on one instrument, are available to pupils entering Year 7.

Honours. 13 Places at Oxford and Cambridge in 2014.

Charitable status. Nottingham High School is a Registered Charity, number 1104251. It exists to provide education for pupils between the ages of 4 and 18 years.

Governing Body:
The Lord Lieutenant of Nottinghamshire
The Lord Mayor of Nottingham
Two Representatives of the City Council
One Representative of the Nottinghamshire County Council
Four Representatives of the Universities
Eleven Co-optative Members

Chairman of the Governors: Mr David Wild

Headmaster: Mr Kevin Fear, BA

Deputy Head (*Pastoral*): Mr Paul Spedding, BSc
Deputy Head (*Academic*): Dr Nick Dennis
Assistant Head (*Co-Curricular*): Mr Kieron Heath, BSc
Assistant Head (*Academic*): Ms Sally Peacock, BSc
Assistant Head (*Pastoral*): Miss Lisa Gritti, MSci
Assistant Head (*Head of Sixth Form*): Mrs Wilma Robinson, MA
Head of Infant & Junior School: Mrs Clare Bruce, MA
Director of Finance and Estates: Mr Rob Dunmore, BA, ACA

Academic Staff:
* *Head of Department*

Art:
*Mrs Gemma Hainsworth, BA
Miss Melanie Kirbyshire, BA
Mrs Gillian Riley Gill, BA, BArch
Mrs Sue Radford, BA

Biology:
*Mrs Joanne Day, BSc
Mrs Judith Poole, BSc
Mr Aaron Duckett, MA
Miss Natalie Willsher, BSc
Mr Sam Robinson, BSc MRes
Mr Malcolm Saperia, BSc

Chemistry:
*Mr Iain Adshead, MSc
Mrs Hollie Matthews, BSc
Dr Katharine Linton, PhD
Mrs Kate Costante, MA
Mr Kieron Heath, BSc
Mrs Helen Wood, MSci

Classics:
*Mr Robert Grant, BA
Mr Ben Harrison, BA
Mrs Jane Packer, BA

Design Technology:
*Mr Paul Gray, BSc
Mr David Thomas, BEd
Mr Ian Thorpe, BEd

Drama:
*Miss Charlotte Webster, BA
Mrs Lisa Rogers, BA

Economics & Politics:
*Mr Peter Cramp, BA
Mrs Wilma Robinson, MA
Mrs Lynne Woolliscroft, BSocSci
Mrs Vicky Wicks, BA

English:
*Mr Scott Hiebert, BA
Dr Benjamin Burton, MA
Miss Michaela Green, BA
Mr Matthew Neale, BA
Dr Rachael Pearson, BA, MA, PhD
Mrs Rhian Wheeler, BA

Geography:
*Mr Neil Brown, BSc
Mrs Amy Lemon, BA
Mr Colin Sedgewick, MA
Mr Richard Kelsey, BSc

History:
*Miss Katherine Rich, MA
Mr Simon Williams, BA, MA
Mr Michael Stratford, BA
Miss Cara Thompson, MA, MSc

ICT:
*Mrs Kerry Turner, BA, HDip (*Computer, ICT and E-Learning*)

Learning Support Coordinator:
*Mr Mark Glarvey, MSc

Mathematics:
*Mr Darren Brumby, BSc
Mrs Caroline Howat, BSc
Mrs Rachel Adams, BA
Mr John Allen, MA, MSc
Mr Simon Barr-Smith, BSc
Mr Richard Batchelor, BSc
Mrs Rachael Northedge, BA
Mr Artie Smith, MA
Mr Paul Spedding, BSc
Mr Peter Hurrell, MSc

Modern Foreign Languages:
Mr David Allerton, BA (*Spanish*)
*Mr Grahame Whitehead, MA
Miss Sophy McCabe, MA (*French*)
Mrs Victoria Pidgeon, BA
Mr Adam Brown, BA
Mrs Alison Griffin, BA
Mr Tony Holding, BA
Mr Franz Rosas
Mr Andrew Winter, BA

Music:
*Mr Stefan Reid, MA, MMus (*Director of Music*)
Mr David Williams, BA (*Assistant Director of Music*)
Miss Natasha Giddens, BMus
Mrs Melissa Woodhead

Physical Education:
Mr Martin Smith, BEd (*PE & Games*)
Miss Georgie McAndrew (*Girls PE & Games*)
Mr Mark Baker, BSc (*Director of Cricket*)
Mr Paul Allison, MSc
Mr Chris Farman, BSc
Mr Ian Cowley (*Hockey*)
Mr Simon Payne
Mr Paul Smith
Mr Stuart Whitehead, BEd (*Director of Rugby*)

Physics:
*Mr Alex Robson, MEng
Mr Ben Hayton, BSc
Mr Chris Martin, BEng
Mr Rory Mellows, BEng
Miss Lisa Gritti, MSci

Psychology:
*Mrs Rachel Kersey, MSc, PhD

Religious Studies:
*Mrs Toni Ford, BA
Mrs Elaine Nicolson, BA, MA

Heads of Year Groups:
Head of Year 7: Mr Christopher Farman
Head of Year 8: Mr Anthony Holding
Head of Year 9: Mr Simon Barr-Smith
Head of Year 10/11: Mrs Judith Poole
Head of Year 10/11: Miss Michaela Green
Head of Year 12/13: Mr Ben Harrison
Head of Year 12/13: Mr Stuart Whitehead

Support Staff:
Headmaster's EA: Miss Rebecca Winch
Deputy Heads' PA: Miss Grace Cooper
Receptionist: Mrs Kathryn Ready
Receptionist: Mrs Keri Wardle
Director of Finance & Estates: Mr Rob Dunmore
PA to Director of Finance & Estates: Mrs Christine Winter
Operations Manager: Mr Paul Dunwell
Estates Manager: Mr Chris Scott
Bookings Co-ordinator: Miss Katy Spray
Finance Manager: Mr Barry Nicholls
Finance Officer: Mrs Kelly Hinds
Finance Officer: Mrs Serena Beckford
Head of Marketing and Admissions: Miss Amy Chambers
Admissions Co-ordinator: Mrs Lynda Goodwin
Development Director: Mr Andy Shields
Development Assistant: Mrs Deborah Penney
Alumni Relations and Events Officer: Miss Kamala Newton
Librarian and School Archive: Mrs Yvette Gunther
Library Assistant: Mrs Sally Blythe
School Nurse: Ms Sarah Jacob
School Councillor: Mr James Hawes
School Shop Manager: Mrs Irene Epworth
Catering Manager: Mr Moz Lynch

Infant and Junior School:

Head: Mrs Clare Bruce, MA
Deputy Head (*Academic*): Miss Lucy Thorpe, MA, MSc
Deputy Head (*Pastoral*): Mr Eddie Jones, BA

Academic Staff:
Miss Jennifer Abell, BA
Mrs Susan Allan
Mrs Emma Baker (*KS1 Coordinator*)
Mrs Alison Barker
Mrs Deborah Bonney
Mrs Jane Cash, BA
Mr Martin Crossland, BA (*Head of Humanities*)
Mrs Claire Farman, BA
Miss Julie Higgins, BA
Mrs Lynn Kawalec, BEd (*Head of Music*)
Ms Lesley McCluskey (*Head of EYFS*)
Mr Richard Miller, BA
Mrs Lynne Sedgewick, BEd (*Head of Mathematics*)
Mrs Gunmeet Sethi, BA, MA (*Head of Science*)
Mr Richard Shaw. BA
Mr Anthony Simpson, BEd (*Curriculum Coordinator*)
Mrs Rachel Slater, BA (*Head of English*)
Miss Victoria Walster, BA (*Head of MFL*)
Mrs Helen Whittamore, BA
Mrs Andrea Williams, BEd

Teaching Assistants:
Mrs Julie Bignall
Miss Tara Bradbury
Miss Amanda Clarke
Mrs Julie Falkner
Miss Elaine Gleadell
Mrs Claire Jones
Mrs Judith Robinson

Learning Support: Mrs Karen George, CertEd

Support Staff:
Head's PA: Mrs Michelle Cartwright
Infant School Secretary: Mrs Barbara Marson
Library Assistant: Mrs Christine Martin
Early Morning Supervisor: Mrs Christine Martin
After School Club Manager: Miss Elaine Gleadell
After School Club Deputy Manager: Mrs Tara Bradbury
After School Club Supervisor: Ms Sarah Hackett
After School Supervisor: Miss Wendy Staples
Lunchtime Supervisor: Miss Katrine Ritchie
Lunchtime Supervisor: Mrs Tara Bashire

Oakham School

Chapel Close, Oakham, Rutland LE15 6DT
Tel: 01572 758500
            Admissions: 01572 758758
Fax: 01572 758818
email: admissions@oakham.rutland.sch.uk
website: www.oakham.rutland.sch.uk
Twitter: @OakhamSch

Motto: '*Quasi Cursores Vitai Lampada Tradunt*'

Oakham School is a fully co-educational boarding and day school for 10–18 year olds. Located in the historic market town of Oakham, on the edge of Rutland Water, the School's rural location is balanced by being only 30 minutes by road from Peterborough, and from there under an hour by train to London. The School embraces a holistic approach where academic excellence flourishes alongside a strong tradition in the Arts, Music and Sport. Beyond the classroom, we offer many opportunities for pupils to develop into well-rounded individuals through an extensive activities and Community Action programme. Oakham is a caring community where we nurture yet challenge our pupils and teach them how to be independent, thoughtful and responsible young adults, who are ready to take on the challenges of life beyond School.

Founded in 1584 by Archdeacon Robert Johnson, Oakham was the first independent secondary school to go co-educational in 1971. Today there are 1,058 pupils (551 boys, 507 girls) aged 10–18 and a 50:50 ratio of boarders to day pupils. The overall staff : pupil ratio is 1:7. Oakham is one of only a few schools in the UK that offers the choice between the International Baccalaureate Diploma and A Levels in the Sixth Form; our students achieve consistently outstanding results whichever pathway they choose.

Facilities. Oakham's facilities include one of the best school libraries in the country, state-of-the-art Science and Design Technology facilities, an art gallery, a new Social Sciences Faculty, a theatre and a music school. Sports facilities are extensive with 40 acres of superbly maintained fields, all-weather pitches for hockey and tennis, a sports complex with an indoor swimming pool, squash courts, fives courts and fitness centre, and access to nearby Rutland Water for sailing and Luffenham Heath for golf.

Organisation and Curriculum. Oakham has 16 houses: four in the Lower School (age 10–12), ten in the Middle/Upper School (age 13–17), and two houses for final year girls and boys where they can concentrate more closely on their studies and enjoy increased freedom in preparation for university. The Housemaster or Housemistress is responsible for pastoral support. Each pupil has a tutor, who is responsible for pupils' personal and academic development, and for keeping a balance between academic, creative and social activities.

The curriculum is tailored so that an education at Oakham develops the potential of all our pupils, opening up academic and commercial opportunities around the world. The Lower School offers a unique and exciting programme combining the full range of traditional subjects with the development of essential learning habits. In the Middle School, pupils can choose their GCSEs and IGCSEs from a comprehensive range of subjects. In the Upper School Oakham is unusual in offering a choice between A Levels or the highly-regarded IB Diploma Programme.

GCSE/IGCSE: All pupils take English Language, English Literature, Dual-Award Science (which comprises Biology, Chemistry and Physics), and Mathematics, together with a choice from History, Geography, Religion and Philosophy, French, Spanish, German, Drama or Music and a variety of Creative Arts subjects (Fine Art – Painting and Mixed Media, Textile Design or Sculpture, or Design Technology focusing on Electronics Products, Resistant Materials or Graphics Products). Other academic options include: Citizenship, Classical Civilisation, Computer Science, Creative iMedia, Greek, Latin and Physical Education. We expose pupils to a rich cultural environment, providing an exciting programme of projects and visits to enhance learning beyond the classroom and the exam syllabus.

16+: Upper School pupils may opt either for A Levels and equivalent stand-alone qualifications or the International Baccalaureate Diploma. A Level subjects on offer include Art: Critical and Contextual Studies, Art (Cambridge Pre-U course), Biology, Business, Chemistry, Classical Civilisation, Design Technology, Theatre Studies, Economics, English Language, English Literature, French, Geography, German, Greek, History, Italian, Latin, Mandarin, Mathematics, Further Mathematics, Music (Cambridge Pre-U course), Philosophy, Sport Science (A Level and BTEC), Physics, Politics, Spanish. The International Baccalaureate programme offers a similar range, but students study six subjects: three subjects are studied at Higher Level and three at Standard Level. Additionally, all students take the three Core Elements of the Diploma: Theory of Knowledge, the Extended Essay and a programme of Creativity, Action and Service.

Music. Around half of all pupils play in musical ensembles, choirs, bands, orchestras, and musical theatre productions. Nearly 80 concerts each year present a wide variety of performing opportunities both in and out of School, as well as international tours. Pupils are regularly selected for national youth ensembles and the School Chamber Choir were finalists in the BBC 'Songs of Praise' School Choir of the Year Competition in 2016.

Drama plays an important part in the life of the School with five major productions each year. A majority of pupils at all levels takes part in at least one dramatic production a year.

Art, Design and Technology. The Richard Bull Centre and the state-of-the-art Jerwood School of Design together offer an extensive array of creative and Design Technology opportunities, including painting, pottery, sculpture, textiles, print-making, photography, computer aided design and electronics, working in wood, metal and plastics. Pupils regularly compete for and win nationally-recognised awards and scholarships, such as the Arkwright Scholarship.

Sport and Activities. Our major sports are rugby, hockey, cricket, athletics, netball and tennis. Some 30 other sports options are also offered. A typical year will see over 100 pupils progress to the national finals in 10 different sports. Oakham is proud to be a well-recognised training ground for national squads.

We offer a comprehensive activities programme (over 135 on offer) and each week pupils follow an activity (or hobby) and, from the Middle School upwards, a Service Option. They can try something new or pursue an existing passion. Our Service Options develop skills and values for life. Pupils choose from an extensive volunteering programme, the Combined Cadet Force or the Duke of Edinburgh's Award.

Entry. Normal entry points are 10+, 11+, 13+ and 16+. Pupils are accepted mainly in September at the start of the academic year. Full admissions information is available from the Registrar.

Scholarships and Bursaries. The following scholarships are available: Academic and Music (11+, 13+ and 16+), All-rounder (13+), Art, Design and Technology, Drama and Sport (13+ and 16+). The basic value of a scholarship is up to 10% (academic up to 20%) and top-up means-tested support may be available. For further information including bursaries please request an information booklet from the Registrar, Tel: 01572 758758.

Fees per term (2016–2017). Lower School (age 10–12): £8,580 (full boarding), £6,750–£8,150 (transitional boarding: 2 to 5 nights), £5,715 (day).

Middle and Upper Schools (age 13+): £10,525 (full boarding), £10,000 (flexi-boarding: up to 5 nights), £6,450 (day).

Honours 2016. With a 99.5% A Level pass rate, 43% of students gained A*/A grades and 74% of all grades were A*–B. Oakham's cohort of 60 IB students achieved a 100% pass rate and an average points score of 37.2 out of a possible 45 (well above the international average of 30). 27% gained 40 or more points and 52% scored 38 or more points (equivalent to 5 As at A Level. In another excellent GCSE year 62% of pupils achieved A*/A grades with 42 pupils gaining straight A*/As. 97% achieved A*–C grades. Nearly all leavers go to university or college; 12 pupils received Oxbridge offers; 8 gained places at medical and veterinary schools.

Charitable status. Oakham School is a Registered Charity, number 1131425, and a Company Limited by Guarantee, registered in England and Wales, number 06924216. Registered Office: Chapel Close, Market Place, Oakham, Rutland LE15 6DT. It exists for the purpose of education.

Trustees:
Chairman: P O Lawson, DL, BSc, CITP, MBCS, DipMus
Deputy Chairman: T F Hart, DL, MA

Ex officio:
The Rt Revd D Allister, MA, Bishop of Peterborough
Dr L Howard, OBE, Hon LLD, JP, Lord-Lieutenant of Rutland
The Very Revd C Taylor, MA, Hon FGCM, Dean of Peterborough

Co-optative:
J Czarnota, MBA
P S Douty
R Foulkes, MA
Mrs J Gibson, MA, BEd
Professor N T Gorman, DL, BVSc, PhD, DVSc, DVMS, DVM, DACVIM, Dip-ECVIM, FRCVS, FRSA
Mrs J Grundy
H Haefeli, BCom, CTA SA
N D G Jones, BSc
A R M Little, MA
Mrs J Lucas, MA
Mrs J Osborne, BA, LLM
G J Schanschieff, MBE, BA
M G Wilson, BA, Dipl Arch RIBA
S Woolfe, LLB

Headmaster: N M Lashbrook, BA

Director of Operations and Strategic Planning: S Piggott, MA, MBA
Deputy Head: Mrs L M North, BA
Deputy Head (Pastoral and Co-curricular): Mrs S J Gomm, BSc
Deputy Head (Academic): D A Harrow, MA

Senior Members of Staff:
Head of Upper School: Mrs S Lorenz-Weir, MA
Head of Middle School: J H Robinson, BA
Master of the Lower School 'Jerwoods': V J Harvey, BSc
Director Teaching and Learning: J M Andrews, BA
Senior Housemistress: Mrs C Latham, BEd
Registrar: N S Paddock, BSocSc
Marketing Director: Mrs S Rowntree
Foundation Director: Ms A E Bentley

Heads of Department:
Activities: A V Petit, MA, MBA
Careers: Mrs P C Gibbs, BSc, MBA
Computer Science: M D Crofts, BSc
Creative Arts: S L Poppy, BA
English: M M Fairweather, MA
Geography: H A Collison, BSc, MPhil
History: J N J Roberts, MA
Languages: Dr S T Glynn, MA
Learning Support: Mrs C D Hill, MA, DipSpLD
Mathematics: Mrs W Singhal, BSc
Music: P Davis, MA, ARCO
Religion and Philosophy: Mrs M J Fairley, BA
Social Sciences: P Nutter, BA
Science: Dr J A Chilton
Sport: I Simpson, BSc

Chaplain: The Revd T F Tregunno, MTh

Housemasters/mistresses:

Lower School:
Ancaster: Mrs A Petit, LLB
Lincoln: Mrs H M Foster, BA, DipLA
Peterborough: S B Foster, GRSM
Sargants: A S Denman, BA

Middle School:
Barrow: N P Favill, BA
Buchanans: Mrs C L Latham, BEd
Chapmans: D W Bonanno, BA
Clipsham: T Dixon-Dale, BA
Gunthorpe: Mrs K M Hegarty, MA
Hambleton: Mrs S M Healey, BSc
Haywoods: D M Taylor, BA
Rushebrookes: Mrs T Drummond, GRSM, LRAM
Stevens: Mrs A M Lear, BA, MCLIP
Wharflands: J J Cure, BA

Upper School:
Round House: Mrs E L Durston, BSc
School House: C J Foster, BSc

Oldham Hulme Grammar School

Chamber Road, Oldham, Lancs OL8 4BX

Tel: 0161 624 4497
email: admin@ohgs.co.uk
website: www.ohgs.co.uk
Twitter: @OhgsPrincipal
Facebook: @OldhamHulmeGrammarSchool

Motto: *Fide sed cui Vide.*

The school, founded in 1611, was reconstituted in the 19th century under the Endowed Schools Act. The main buildings of Oldham Hulme Grammar School were opened in 1895 on a commanding south-west facing site overlooking the city of Manchester.

The Oldham Hulme family of schools is renowned for delivering outstanding levels of education at each stage of a child's development. With unbeatable standards and outstanding achievements, the schools cater for boys and girls aged three to 18 and offer a caring, orderly and academically stimulating environment.

At the age of 3 school life begins in the Nursery which has recently moved into new modern premises. Confidence is then built throughout the infant, junior and secondary years and great care is taken in the sixth form to create extremely capable, well-balanced young adults.

The schools' primary aim is to provide a caring, friendly and lively school environment that fosters a desire to learn and at all times, pupils are encouraged to think and work independently. With a reputation for academic excellence and outstanding extra-curricular activities, pupils benefit from the right environment which enables them to achieve their full potential in life so that they go on to become successful, happy and confident young men and women.

The Hulme family of schools value academic achievement and standards are high. Consequently there is an excellent record of examination success at GCSE and A Level. Pupils are taught within small classes by a team of dedicated, well-qualified staff.

The schools also offer an excellent pastoral care system which guides and supports pupils, promoting their personal development within the wider school community.

The comprehensive careers education programme on offer widens each pupil's understanding of the opportunities available in the changing world of work, while equipping them with the skills to manage their future career.

A stimulating range of extracurricular activities provides opportunities for fun, challenge, initiative, leadership and service, while activities within the wider community encourage active involvement and promote a genuine concern for the needs of others.

Fees per term (2016–2017). Nursery, Infants and Juniors £2,620; Senior School and Sixth Form £3,582; International Students £13,000 per annum payable in advance.

A number of bursaries are awarded annually to pupils entering at the ages of 11 and 16. These awards are based on parental income and academic ability and will remain in place for the time in school subject to satisfactory progress by the pupil.

Charitable status. The Oldham Hulme Grammar School is a Registered Charity, number 526636. It exists to provide a balanced academic education for pupils aged 3 to 18.

Patron: The Lord Clitheroe of Downham

Governors:
Chairman: Mr V A K Srivastava, LLB Hons (*Chairman of the Finance and General Purposes Committee*)
Vice Chairman: Mrs A Richards, BSc (*Child Protection Governor*)
Hon Treasurer: Mr D M Meredith, CCB

Elected Governors:
Mr S A Corns, MA, FRSA (*Chairman of the Education Committee*)
Mr R S Illingworth, BSc
Mr R Lobley, MRICS (*Chairman of the Health & Safety Committee*)
Mr A Milnes, BA Hons, FCA (*Chairman of the Audit Committee*)
Mr K Sanders
Mrs V Stocker, LLB

Representative Governors, Metropolitan Borough of Oldham:
Mr Z Chauhan
Mr J Sutcliffe

Bursar and Clerk to the Governors: I Martin, BSc, FCA, FCMA

Principal: C J D Mairs, MA Edinburgh

Deputy Principal – Pastoral: J C Budding, BEd Sheffield Hallam
Deputy Principal – Academic: N G H James, MA York
Deputy Principal – External Relations: D J Dalziel, BSc London, PG Dip Leeds

S P Adamson, MA Manchester (*English, Duke of Edinburgh's Award, Careers, Head of Booth/Platt House*)
W L M Atkins, BSc Keele (*Head of Biology, CCF*)
Dr P M Beagon, MA, DPhil Oxford (*Head of Classics*)
D Berry, BSc Huddersfield (*Head of Psychology*)
Mrs N Bibi, BSc Manchester (*Mathematics*)
Miss J C Brown, BA Liverpool (*Physical Education, Head of Year 10*)
Miss L E Bowden, BSc Manchester (*Biology, Head of Year 7*)
N P Buckley, BA Sheffield (*Business Studies and Economics, Head of Year 8*)
N J Chesterton, BA Leeds (*Physical Education and Games, Head of Assheton House*)
G W Conroy, CertEd Leeds (*Physical Education and Games*)
T M J Cotton, BEd MMU (*Design Technology*)
Ms L J Cowan, MA Dundee (*History, Duke of Edinburgh's Award, Head of Year 9*)
Mrs N L Cross, BSc Manchester (*Mathematics, Duke of Edinburgh's Award*)
Mrs C Davies, BA Kent (*Head of Drama, Careers*)
M N Dowthwaite, BA Manchester (*Head of History and Politics, School Functions Officer*)
Miss C W Duffy, BA, MPhil Aberystwyth (*History*)
Mrs C A Eliot, BA Heriot-Watt (*Head of Textiles, PSHE Coordinator*)
O M Gandolfi, BSc Bangor (*Biology, Head of Year 11*)
Mrs H Garside, BA North Wales (*Modern Languages*)
Ms R M Glover, MA Sussex (*Head of English*)
M J A Grant, MA Newcastle (*Modern Languages*)
Miss J V Graystock, BA Liverpool (*Head of Art*)
J J W Gumpert, MA Cambridge (*Head of Religious Studies*)
Mrs E Harris, BA Liverpool (*Physical Education*)
J R Hesten, BA Manchester (*Physics*)
Mrs A H Howarth, BEd, Manchester Metropolitan, PG Dip, Dip SEN, PG Cert SpLD AMBDA, SpLD APC Patoss (*Head of Learning Support*)
Mrs D Howarth, BSc Manchester Metropolitan (*Head of Home Economics*)
A H B Hurst, BA Manchester Metropolitan (*Head of Physical Education*)
M C Jones, MPhys Manchester (*Head of Physics*)
Mrs T A Kershaw, BA Salford (*Head of Modern Languages*)
Miss J P Knighton, BEd Leeds Metropolitan (*Head of Physical Education*)
M F Kostecky, BSc Manchester (*ICT*)
Mrs J A Lamb, BSc Liverpool (*Head of Mathematics*)
P Langdon, BEd Manchester Metropolitan (*Head of Information Technology*)
Miss L Lavin, BSc Manchester Metropolitan (*Biology*)
Mrs J Leach, BA Hull (*English*)
T A Leng, BA Leeds (*History, Teacher i/c Politics, i/c Newsletter*)

Mrs A Longley, MA Manchester (*Economics, Business Studies, Head of Year 6th Form*)

Mrs D Maders, BSc Leeds, MRSC (*Head of Chemistry*)

A H Marshall, BSc Hull (*Geography, Director of Pastoral Care*)

Miss G McCarrick, BSc Manchester Metropolitan (*Geography*)

Mrs J McCarthy, MA, PG Dip Liverpool (*Art, Design Technology*)

Dr C R Millington, BSc Durham, DPhil Oxford, MEd Cambridge (*Chemistry*)

Ms E Mills, BA Manchester (*English*)

S McRoyall, BA Sunderland (*Art*)

Mrs H M North, BSc Liverpool (*Chemistry*)

Miss V B Pastor, MA Madrid (*Spanish*)

A Peacockc, BA Glamorgan (*Head of Geography*)

Miss H R Plews, BA Liverpool, MPhil Cantab (*Classics, Head of Lees House, Peer Mentoring Coordinator, Academic Tutor 6th Form*)

S G Rawlings, BEng Aston (*Mathematics, Physics, Head of Year 6th Form*)

D R A Rees, BSc Bradford (*Head of Business Studies and Economics*)

M Richmond, BSc Leeds (*Mathematics, Master i/c Football*)

D G Robertson, BMus Aberdeen, ALCM (*Director of Music*)

Mrs A G Robinson, BSc Romania, MSc Manchester (*Physics*)

Mrs R S Shapey, BMus Birmingham, LRSM (*Music*)

Miss S E Shepherd, BA London (*i/c French*)

A D Smith, BSc Salford (*Mathematics, Head of Hulme House*)

C J Travis, BEd Crewe and Alsager (*Head of Design Technology*)

Mrs J Travis, DipM (*Head of Careers, Food Technology*)

Miss R L Turner, BSc Loughborough (*Mathematics, Duke of Edinburgh's Award*)

Mrs D Y Wheldrick, BA Preston Polytechnic (*Information Technology*)

Mrs J C Wood, BA Leeds (*Religious Studies, Director of Pastoral Care*)

Nursery, Infants and Juniors:

Head of Nursery and Infants: Miss C Barnett, BA Edge Hill

Head of Juniors: Mrs R Knott, BA Surrey

Deputy Head of Nursery and Infants: Mrs A A Summers, BA Manchester Metropolitan

Deputy Head of Juniors, Upper KS2: A Booth, BA Central England

Deputy Head of Juniors, Lower KS2: M G Cowley, BSc Stirling

Miss L Lavin, BSc Manchester Metropolitan (*Science Coordinator*)

M P Bumford, BSc Chester

Mrs R L Christo, BEd, Birmingham (*Literacy Coordinator*)

P S Coulson, BSc Edge Hill College (*ICT Coordinator*)

S Davies, BA Edge Hill University (*PSHE Coordinator*)

Mrs S Dockerty BA Huddersfield

Miss K V Evans BA Sheffield

Miss G A Fulford-Brown, BA Manchester Metropolitan

A J Halliwell, BEd Manchester, CertEd Manchester

Mrs B Humphreys, NNEB, HNC

Miss S E Oates, LTCL, LGSM, CertEd Reading

Miss M Wall, BA Manchester/Lancaster

Mrs E White, BA Durham

Mrs H A Whitwam, BA Bradford College (*PSHE Coordinator*)

Visiting Music Teachers:

Miss C Babington, BMus, PG DIp, MMus RNCM, MusM VU Manc (*Cello*)

D Browne, GRNCM (*Cello*)

Miss A Cooper, GGSM (*Oboe & Bassoon*)

Mrs V Eastham, MA, FTCL, LRSM (*Piano*)

Ms S Gibbon, GRNCM (*Violin*)

K Heggie, GRNCM (*Guitar*)

Mrs M Hulme, BSc, LTCL (*Violin*)

Mrs J Kent, CT, ABRSM (*Brass*)

Miss G Murray, BMus RAM, PG Dip TCL (*Singing*)

O Patrick, BMus RCM (*Percussion*)

Miss J Puckey, BMus (*Clarinet & Saxophone*)

Mrs S Walker, GRSM, PPRCM (*Flute*)

The Oratory School

Woodcote, Reading, South Oxfordshire RG8 0PJ

Tel:	01491 683500
Fax:	01491 680020
email:	enquiries@oratory.co.uk
website:	www.oratory.co.uk

Motto: '*Cor ad cor loquitur*'

The Oratory School was founded in 1859, by Blessed John Henry Newman, at the request of a group of eminent Catholic laymen. The Chaplain apart, the School is administered and staffed entirely by laymen.

Number in School. There are 330 boys: 165 boarding and 165 day boys.

The School is situated in an area of outstanding natural beauty in grounds of approx. 400 acres, in South Oxfordshire. There are four Senior Houses (13–18) and one Junior House called St Philip House (11–13). Each House is run by a married Housemaster and staffed by a House team, which includes a Housemother. There is at least one other adult in each Boarding House and over three-quarters of the staff live on site or in the local village.

The School has completed a ten-year development programme. Two new boarding Houses have been constructed along with new Art & Design, DT, English, History, Maths, and Theology Departments. A new Performing Arts facility, the Hilaire Belloc Theatre, opened in 2013 and a major Sports Centre redevelopment costing £5 million opened in May 2015.

Organisation. Four Senior Houses and St Philip House offer living facilities for 380 boys, both day and boarding. Particular care is taken to provide an environment which facilitates the assimilation of new boys.

Health. The School Medical Centre is under the supervision of a fully qualified resident Sister and the School Medical Officer visits once a week.

Admission. Boys enter at age 13 through the Scholarship or Common Entrance Examinations, or at 11 by informal interview and exam. Boys also enter in the Sixth Form.

Religious Education. Catholic spirituality pervades the school in an unobtrusive way. It is at the heart of the school and to be an Oratorian is something special. Respect for the individual within the larger framework of this society is the hallmark of this Oratorian ethos. There is a Resident Chaplain who looks after the needs of both boys and staff. All boys study religions.

Studies. Boys are prepared for A Levels and GCSE. A wide range of subjects is offered in the Sixth Form. There is no rigid division into Arts and Science subjects; almost any combination of subjects can be taken. Pre-U is offered in some subjects.

Games. In addition to the main games – Rugby Football, Soccer, Cricket, Shooting and Rowing – boys take part in

Athletics, Cross-Country Running, Swimming, Tennis, Badminton, Basketball, Squash, Golf, and Real Tennis. There is a nine-hole golf course on the 400-acre site and a four-lane indoor shooting range. National awards have been won for sport.

CCF. There is a flourishing contingent of the CCF which, in addition to the Army section, includes the following subsections: RN, RAF, REME, Signals, and Adventure Training. The Duke of Edinburgh's Award scheme is popular with the gold expedition going to Morocco. The school ranks in the top five shooting schools in the country with some team members shooting for Great Britain.

Extracurricular activities. There are frequent theatre outings, visits to museums and art galleries, careers visits, as well as talks and lectures given in the School by visiting speakers. There is a wide range of clubs and societies.

Optional Extras. Instrumental Music, coaching in Real Tennis, Lawn Tennis, Squash and Golf.

Careers Guidance. The Head of Sixth Form provides guidance for boys in their choice of future occupation. There is also a Careers Master who organises speakers and a Careers Fair.

The School is a member of ISCO.

Fees per term (2016–2017). Boarders: £10,865 (Junior House £7,180); Day Boys: £7,900 (Junior House £5,350).

The fees include board, tuition, consolidated extras, and games. An optional insurance scheme is in operation which covers remission of fees in the event of a boy's absence through illness. A full term's notice of withdrawal is required; failing such notice a term's fees are payable. There may be a reduction for younger brothers and sons of old boys.

Scholarships. A number of Academic Scholarships and Exhibitions, and Awards in Music, Art and Sport, are offered. Awards are of varying values. Music awards include free music tuition in two disciplines. All-rounder awards are made on the recommendation and reports from Prep School Heads.

The Preparatory School is at 'Great Oaks', a property situated in grounds of 45 acres on the same ridge of the Chilterns, about 2 miles from the Main School, between Cray's Pond and Pangbourne. This is co-educational. (*For further details, see entry in IAPS section.*)

The Oratory School Society. *Chairman:* David Connolly.

Charitable status. The Oratory Schools Association is a Registered Charity, number 309112. It is a charitable trust dedicated to continuing the aims of its Founder, Blessed John Henry Newman.

President: The Rt Hon Lord Judge

Vice-Presidents:
His Eminence Cardinal William W Baum
J J Eyston, MA, FRICS, KSG
Archbishop Vincent Nichols, MA, STL, PhL, MEd

Chairman: Dr C B T Hill Williams, DL, MA, FRGS, FRSA
Vice-Chairman: C J Sehmer, FCA

The Governors:
M J Berkeley, JP, BSc, BA, IMC, MCSI
B F H Bettesworth, FRICS, ACIArb
The Very Revd R Byrne, BD, AKC, Cong Orat
Mrs M Cochrane
Mrs M Edwards
Professor P W Evans, MA, PhD
F J Fitzherbert-Brockholes, MA
C J French, FRAgS
Mr M H R Hasslacher
H H K A D Hornby, BA
N R Purnell, MA, QC
The Revd J N Saward, MA, MLitt

M W Stilwell
Mr N J Tanner, MSc

Clerk to the Governors & Bursar: M W Halsall, MBA, FCMI

Head Master: J J Smith, BA, PGCE

Second Master: T J Hennessy, BSc
Lower Master: M H Green, MBE, MEd, FRSA, MRAeS
Chaplain: Revd K E MacNab, BA, MA (*Religious Education*)

Academic Staff:
* *Head of Department*
† *Housemaster*
§ *Part-time*

Mrs E K Aldington, Dip AD (§*Art*)
J Aldridge, BSc (*Mathematics*)
J Berkley, BA, MA (*French, Italian,* *Languages)
S Bosher, BSc, DipDes (*Design and Technology, CCF,* †*Faber*)
S A Bowles, BSc, PhD (*Chemistry*)
J A Brooke, BA, MA (*English)
P W Brown, BSc (*Physics*)
S P S Burrows, BA (**Director of Music*)
I A N Campbell, BSc (*Physics)
P J Chaundy, BA (*Director of Art & Design*)
T N Danks, BSc, PhD (*Chemistry)
A P Dulston, BA (*Religious Education*)
P J Easton, BSc (*Biology*)
Revd D J Elliot, MA (*Theology)
M G Farnan, BSc (§*Curriculum Support, CCF, Shooting*)
M R Fec, BA (**History,* †*Norris*)
D Forster, MA, MSc (*Director of Studies, Mathematics, Philosophy*)
M H Green, MEd, MBE, FRSA, MRAES (**Design and Technology, Lower Master*)
Mrs S Green, BA (*Curriculum Support*)
Mrs L Haddock, BVSc, MRCVS (*Mathematics*)
T J Hennessy, BSc (*Mathematics, Second Master*)
M D Hennessy, BA (*History*)
V B A Holden, BSc, PGCE (*Science, Mathematics,* †*St John*)
N C Jones, BA, ARCO (**Academic Music, Examinations Officer*)
I P Jordan, BEd (*Physical Education, Mathematics,* †*FitzAlan*)
Mrs S D Kenyon, BSc Hons, PGCE, QTS (*Biology)
Mrs K S Lambert, BA (*Curriculum Support*)
R A O'Sullivan, BA (*English*)
Mrs S O'Sullivan, BA (*English*)
P E Poynter, BA (*Geography)
A N Stroker, BA, MA, PhD (*English, Drama*)
C J Sudding, BEng Hons (*Mathematics)
M P Syddall, MA (*Classics, Head of Sixth Form*)
S C B Tomlinson, BSc (**Director of Games*)
Mrs A D T Tuite-Dalton (§*French*)
C Watson, BA (*Junior Humanities,* †*St Philip House*)
Miss S E Wethey, BA (*English*)

Music Staff:
C Caiger (*Guitar*)
T D Carleston (*Singing*)
J Donnelly (*Drums, Percussion*)
Mrs S Ellison, BA, LRAM (*Oboe and Piano*)
Mrs S L Dytor, ARCM (*Violin*)
G Howarth, BSc, MA (*Brass*)
C C King, FRICS (*Drums & Percussion*)
M Knowles, AGSM (*Brass*)
Miss E V Krivenko, MMus Dip (*Piano*)
Miss R Watson, BA (*Cello*)
Mrs K E Laughton, BA (*Saxophone, Flute*)

Miss E L Mallett, BA (*Singing*)
Ben Giddens BA, ARCO (*Organ*)
G Williams, FTCL, FLCM, LRAM, ARCM (*Bassoon*)

School Health Centre:
Dr A Goode (*Medical Officer*)
Mrs C Thompson, RGN, BA (*Practice Manager*)
Mrs S Atkins, RGN
Mrs N L Barker, RGN
Mrs I Courtney-Hatcher, RGN
Mrs C M Fleming, RGN
§Mrs M Gates, RGN
Mrs C McSoley, RGN
Mrs J H Routledge, RGN, BSc

Non-Teaching Staff:
Miss C Bleimschein (*Bursar's Secretary*)
M W Halsall, MBA FCMI (*Bursar*)
T R Brittan, MCSA, CEH (*Network Manager*)
Mrs N Brouard (§*Reception*)
Mrs L Coupland (*Marketing & Public Relations*)
Mrs M Lee (*School Secretary*)
Mrs C Macnab (*Librarian*)
Mrs J Martin (*Registrar*)
K Mackowski (*Payroll Manager*)
R Squizzoni (*Estates Manager*)
Mrs G Munoz (§*Reception*)
Mrs D Nash, MA (§*Archivist & Society Officer*)
A Rajan (*Finance Manager*)
M Sixsmith, BSc, MPhil (§*Computer Services*)
Mrs J Stoner, Assoc CIPD (*Human Resources Manager*)
Mrs N Moran (*Head Master's PA*)
Mrs K Warren (§*Secretary*)

Sports Centre Staff:
D Housego (*Cricket Professional*)
M Seigneur (*Professional Real Tennis*)
P B Duncan (*Sports Centre Manager*)
H Ritchie (*Gap Student*)
C Anderson (*Graduate Sports Assistant*)

Oundle School

Oundle, Peterborough, Northamptonshire PE8 4GH

Tel:	01832 277122 (Reception)
	01832 277142 (Head's Office)
	01832 277125 (Admissions Office)
	01832 277116 (Undermaster's Office)
Fax:	01832 273564
email:	admissions@oundleschool.org.uk
website:	www.oundleschool.org.uk

Motto: '*God Grant Grace*'

Oundle School originated from the bequest of Sir William Laxton, a native of Oundle, to the Grocers' Company in 1556. The School was established with the object of providing a liberal education in accordance with the principles of the Church of England. The aims of the School are: to promote excellence and allow pupils to reach their full academic and intellectual potential; to develop independence and team players who will contribute to the community; to develop strong values, encourage involvement and an understanding of adult life, and prepare pupils for life beyond Oundle; to provide a full-boarding programme such that its excellence is recognised worldwide.

Oundle became fully co-educational in September 1990. Its buildings, dating from the 17th to the 21st centuries, are dispersed throughout the attractive market town of Oundle, giving the School a distinctive and unique charm. Oundle is the third largest independent boarding and day school in

England, with national boarders coming from over 120 feeder schools all over the UK. 19% of pupils come from over 34 overseas countries. Laxton Junior School, a co-ed day School in Oundle for pupils aged 4–11, also comes under the Corporation of Oundle School.

Number of pupils (2016–2017). 859 boarders and 249 day pupils.

Admission. Main entry is at 11+, 13+ and 16+ with a small number of places available at other stages, including boarding places at 12+. Most pupils sit the June Common Entrance Examination or the Oundle Scholarship Examination at thirteen before joining in September. Those joining the School at eleven sit a written examination in January before entry in September, with papers in English, Mathematics, Science and Ability tests.

Facilities. Academic departments are situated in the Cloisters, the Needham building, the Adamson Centre, the Gascoigne building, Old Dryden and SciTec, Oundle's impressive and spectacular home of the STEM subjects, with its extensive 'green' credentials. The teaching areas are very well equipped; the Information Technology Centre includes two fully-equipped computer rooms and there are 'cluster networks' around the School. Thin Client terminals are located for each boarder in the Houses. Electronic whiteboards and computer-driven projectors feature in most teaching rooms. The Adamson Centre for Modern Languages opened in September 2013 and is equipped with two state-of-the-art language laboratories, six language assistant pods, fourteen teaching rooms and an International Suite.

Art, Music, Drama and Design and Technology are all very strong and well provided for. The Art Studios are large, airy and well equipped and the department includes the Yarrow Gallery. Facilities in Music include the Frobenius Organ and an electronic Music Studio. The Drama Department is centered on the Rudolph Stahl Theatre, a cleverly converted chapel in the middle of the town, where numerous productions of both the School and visiting companies take place. The long tradition of the Oundle Workshops continues, incorporating courses and large-scale projects in Engineering. In September 2016, the aforementioned SciTec building opened, bringing together the STEM subjects of Science, Technology, Engineering and Mathematics and embracing developments in new fields such as nanotechnology and mechatronics.

The Chapel was built as a memorial shortly after the Great War and its East windows, designed by John Piper, were installed in 1956. Thirty-two stained glass windows by Mark Angus, added in 2005, compliment Piper's original vision. Religious instruction accords with the Church of England, but other faiths are welcomed.

The School is part way through a major development that has to date resulted in the opening of JM Mills Cricket Pavilion, two additional astroturf pitches and forty new cricket nets. The next phase of the development will bring and impressive sports centre which will house a 50m pool, an 8-court sports hall, a fitness suite, dance studios and externally a new athletics facility.

Oundle has fifteen houses: eight boys' boarding houses, five girls' houses, a junior boarding house and a day house. A continuous cycle of renovation and refurbishment is in operation. Each house has its own distinct community, with in-house dining a hallmark of the School's character.

Academic Curriculum. Third Formers (Year 9) take a general course consisting of English, Mathematics, French, Latin, Physics, Chemistry, Biology, History, Geography, Religious Studies, Art, Design and Technology, PE, Music, Drama, Computing, and German or Spanish or Chinese or Greek. A unique 'Trivium' course introduces pupils to ideas, culture and pursuit of knowledge outside a prescribed syllabus. The First and Second Form curriculum is similar.

The traditional importance of Science and Technology is still maintained, with all pupils being taught the three Sciences to IGCSE level (both Triple Award and Dual Award on offer) and all Third Formers spending time in both the Art and the Design and Technology Departments. Computing and Microelectronics are available at all levels.

Pupils take English, Mathematics and the three Sciences as the core of their GCSE/IGCSE curriculum and choose a further five subjects from Arabic, Art, Chinese, Classical Greek, Computing, Design Technology, Drama, Electronics, French, Geography, German, History, Italian, Latin, Music, Physical Education, Religious Studies, Russian, and Spanish. Almost every pupil studies at least one modern foreign language (seven are timetabled), many study two or more.

In the Sixth Form, pupils choose four subjects from Art, Biology, Chemistry, Chinese, Classical Civilisation, Computing, Design and Technology, Economics, Electronics, Literature in English, French, Geography, German, Government and Politics, Greek, History, History of Art, Italian, Latin, Mathematics, Further Mathematics, Music, Philosophy and Theology, Physical Education, Physics, Psychology, Spanish, Sports Science and Theatre Studies. Of these, Chemistry, Chinese, Literature in English, German, History, History of Art, Italian, Physics and Spanish are assessed by the linear Cambridge Pre-U qualification; other subjects are assessed as A Levels.

Studies in the Sixth Form are enhanced by an extension block, in which is available the School's bespoke *Quadrivium* course – which is a selection of different courses divided into four topics looking at a central theme, and other options, such as one-year *ab initio* courses in Italian and Russian, Music Technology, preparation for Music Diplomas, and Projects. The last of these leads to AQA Extended Project Qualification.

Honours. 99% of Upper Sixth Former pupils go on to higher education at good universities; in 2016 thirty pupils secured places at Oxford and Cambridge.

Sport. The main School sports are Rugby, Hockey, Cricket, Rowing, Netball and Tennis, but others available include Aerobics, Athletics, Badminton, Clay Shooting, Cross Country, Cycling, Fencing, Fives, Golf, Horse Riding, Sailing, Shooting, Soccer, Squash, Swimming and Volleyball.

Activities. A full range of activities take place which are an integral part of the wider school curriculum. Events in Drama and Music feature prominently in the School calendar, and Art Exhibitions are held regularly in the Yarrow Gallery. A large number of Societies meet on a regular basis. Links have been established with schools in France, Germany, Spain, Hungary, the Czech Republic, Russia, China, America and Australia, with annual Exchanges taking place. Pupils are able to participate in the very large number of expeditions and trips in the UK and abroad. There is a flourishing CCF comprising Army, Navy, RAF, Fire and Adventure Training sections and a thriving Duke of Edinburgh's Award scheme is in operation. Community Action plays an important part in school life and contributes significantly to the wider community. Much time and energy are devoted to fundraising activities in support of national charities, international aid programmes and holidays run at Oundle for MENCAP and inner-city children.

Entrance Scholarships. An extensive series of entrance scholarships is offered each year.

Scholarships at 13+:

Fifteen Academic scholarships at 10% of fees. A qualifying examination takes place in January, with final papers in May.

Twelve General (All-Rounder) scholarships at 10% of fees. Assessment in March.

Ten Music scholarships at up to 30% of fees, including One Junior Organ Scholarship. Audition and interview in January.

One Drama scholarship at 10% of fees. Audition and interview in March.

Two Art scholarships at 10% of fees. Assessment and interview in May.

Two Design and Engineering scholarships at 10% of fees. Examination and interview in May.

Five Sports scholarships at 10% of fees. Assessment and interview in November.

Scholarships at 11+:

Four Junior Academic scholarships for entry to The Berrystead or Laxton at 10% of fees. Examination in January.

Two Junior Music scholarships at up to 20% of fees. Audition and interview in January.

Scholarships at 16+:

Two Academic scholarships at 10% of fees. Examination in November.

One Music scholarship at 10% of fees. Audition and interview in November.

One Art scholarship at 10% of fees. Examination and interview in November.

One Design and Engineering scholarship at 10% of fees. Examination and interview in November.

Three Sport awards at 10% of fees. Examination and interview in November.

Further details of all awards may be obtained from the Registrar (Tel: 01832 277125, email: admissions@oundleschool.org.uk) or the Undermaster's Assistant (Tel: 01832 277116, email: hev@oundleschool.org.uk).

Bursaries. Financial help towards the payment of fees in cases of proven need is available in some instances. This assistance is available in the form of bursaries which vary in size according to circumstance; some may be as high as 100%. Bursaries are not dependent on scholastic merit but are awarded to pupils who are likely to gain most from an Oundle education and who will contribute fully to the life of the School. The pupils in question must satisfy the School's academic entry requirements and continue to work to capacity as they progress through the School. Parents who feel that they may need the support of a bursary are encouraged to discuss the matter with the School well in advance of the child's due date of entry. Decisions regarding bursary assistance are made approximately two years ahead of entry. Judgements are dependent on a supporting reference from a candidate's previous school, an informal interview and on scrutiny of the family's financial circumstances.

Fees per term (2016–2017). Boarders: Berrystead Year 1 £8,725; Berrystead Year 2 £10,125; Years 3–7 £11,480. Day Pupils: Year 1 £5,595; Year 2 £6,490, Years 3–7 £7,355.

Details of extras are given in the School prospectus. The registration fee is £125.

Laxton Junior School caters for 4 to 11 year old boys and girls and has 250 pupils on roll. (*For further details, see entry in IAPS section.*)

Charitable status. Oundle School is a Registered Charity, number 309921.

Governing Body:

[1]J G Tregoning (*Chairman*)

D C L Miller (*Vice-Chairman*) [OO]

C Bartram [OO]

[1]J H Cartwright [OO]

The Countess Howe, DL

D A Hutchinson [OO]

Mrs J C Kibbey

Mrs R Lawes

[1]R H Ringrose [OO]

Dr P J Rogerson

M C B Spens

Lady Stringer

[1]T W Stubbs

[1]P J Woodhouse

Ex officio:
[1]O Wise (*Second Warden*)
[1]A R Gavin (*Third Warden*)
[1]J N Whitmore
J H O'Hare, OBE, MBA, BSc (*Bursar and Secretary*)

[1] *Member of the Court of The Grocers' Company*
[OO] *Old Oundelian*

Head: Mrs S J Kerr-Dineen, MA

Deputy Head and Director of Pastoral Care: Mrs D L
  Watt, MA
Senior Master: P S C King, BSc, MSc
Undermaster: A B Burrows, MAEd, BSc
Deputy Head Academic: I C Smith, MSc
Bursar: J H O'Hare, OBE, MBA, BSc
Senior Chaplain: Revd B J Cunningham, MA
Director of Professional Development: Mrs J T Coles, BA
Director of IT: Mrs L Waide
Registrar: G Phillips, BA
Director of Marketing and External Relations: Miss R J
  Vicary, BA
Director of Development: M J Dear, BTh, GDL, FInstPa
Deputy Bursar (Finance): Ms J Jones, BSc, FCA, DChA
Deputy Bursar (Estates): R M C Tremellen, BSc, AIMBM

Houses and Housemasters/Housemistresses:
Bramston: A J Sherwin
Crosby: H Roberts
Dryden: Ms K A Francis
Fisher: N J T Wood
Grafton: W W Gough
Kirkeby: Mrs A E Meisner
Laundimer: J R Hammond-Chambers
Laxton: Mrs V Gascoine
New House: Mrs M L Smith
Sanderson: Mrs S L Ratchford
School House: A E Langsdale
Sidney: Dr C J Quiddington
St Anthony: P J Kemp
Wyatt: Dr N M Mola
The Berrystead: Mme S Fonteneau

Medical Officers:
Dr M J Richardson, BSc, MBChB, MRCGP, DRCOG
Dr K Newell, MBChB, MRCGP, DRCOG

* *Head of Department*

Art:
*J D Oddie, BA
Ms C L B Dent
Mrs G C King, BA, MA
Ms K A Hannant, MA

Biology:
P S C King, BSc, MSc (*Senior Master*)
A E Langsdale, BSc, MSc
*Dr P J Rowe, DPhil
W W Gough, BSc
O E A Peck, BSc (*Head of Science*)
S K Burman-Roy, MA
Miss E A C Byatt, BA
Miss K M Morris, MSc

Chemistry:
R J McKim, PhD, CChem, MRS, FRAS
R F Hammond, BSc (*Proctor*)
M J Bessent, MChem, PhD, AMRSC (*Sanderson Fellow*)
C J Quiddington, MChem, PhD
Miss T A Dorman, MChem
*J Peverley, MA
C Davison, MSc
Ms M E Sandford, BSc
I C Smith, MSc

Classics:
Mrs M P R James, MA
Mrs D L Watt, MA (*Deputy Head and Director of Pastoral
  Care*)
N J Aubury, MA
*T J Morrison, BA
Ms C L Westran, BA (*The Academic Assistant*)
P A Liston, MA
Miss R L Hodgson, BA
Miss C L Harrington, MA

Computing:
*R J Cunniffe, BSc (*Head of Academic Computing*)
D S Barnes (*Head of Digital Strategy*)

Design and Technology:
D A Vincent, CAPET, MEd
R H Lowndes, BSc, MEng
Mrs R L Lowndes, BSc
*J M Baker, BA

Drama:
A D Martens, BA
Ms K A Francis, BA
*M Burlington, BA
Miss N M Jones, MA (*Director of the Stahl Theatre*)

Economics:
A P Ireson, MA (*Examinations Officer*)
J Röhrborn, MA
Mrs F L Quiddington, BEcon, MT
Mrs J A Barnes, MSc, MA
*O R C Butterworth, BSc

Educational Support:
Mrs C M Redding, BA, MA
*Mrs A M J Taylor, MA
Mrs C M Nolan, BA
Mrs V K E Brown, BEd
Mrs A Larter, BA
Mrs Z Thomas, BA

English:
Ms M K Smedley, BA
N J T Wood, MA
Mrs J T Coles, BA (*Director of Professional Development*)
A D Martens, BA
B Raudnitz, MA (*Child Protection Officer*)
A J Sherwin, MA
Mrs H M Wells, BA
Mrs H K Hopper, BA
*R J Smith, BA
Mrs A J Gould, MA

Geography:
Mrs M S Turner, BA
J R Hammond-Chambers, BA
Mrs J L L Banerjee, BSc, MEd
A C Mansergh, MA
*Mrs M T Chapman, MEd
P G Pitcher, BSc
Mrs M L Smith, MA

Government and Politics:
*M J G King, LLB
Mrs J A Barnes, MSc, MA

History:
P J Pedley, BA
I D Clark, BA
*M P H von Habsburg-Lothringen, MA, PLD
A J Brighton, BA
P J Kemp, BA
Mrs T E Harris, BA
J M Allard, BA
J P Crawley, MA

Library:
Mrs L Guirlando, BA, MSc, MCLIP
Mrs K Stidston, BA
Mrs E Shawyer, MA
Mrs R Cook, BA

Mathematics:
A P Ireson, MA, DipFM (*Examinations Officer*)
D A Turner, BSc
R Atkins, BSc
N D Turnbull, BA
D B Meisner, BA, MSc, PhD
D P Raftery, BSc
*S G Dale, MEng, MA
M A Blessett, MA
M M Sanderson, BSc
S D Coates, BSc
Miss E C Matthews, BSc
R G Montgomery, MSc
Miss A M Strachan, BSc
R G Macdonald, PhD
Miss X Yu, BSc

Modern Languages:
Dr N M Mola, BA
B Béjoint, L-ès-L
J Röhrborn, MA
Mlle G M Skinner, L-ès-FLE, L-ès-LCE
Mlle S Fonteneau, L-ès-L
T D Watson, MA (*Head of Italian*)
*Mrs S J Davidson (*Head of Modern Languages*)
Mrs L M Brighton, MEd (*Head of Girls' Games*)
S Jessop, BA (*Head of French*)
H Yan, BA (*Head of Chinese*)
R F Charters, MA
Miss C H Hignett, BA
Miss K Paone, LDML
Miss B K Gannon, MA
W D Gunson, MPhil
Miss S Naga, DUEL (*Arabic Coordinator*)
Miss M Viruete Navarro, MA (*Head of Spanish*)
Miss E J Wagstaffe, MEd (*Head of German*)
Ms S Russo-Lai

Music:
Director of Music: Q P Thomas, BA
Organist: J C Arkell, MA, FRCO, FTCL, FLCM, FRSA
Head of Woodwind: D P Milsted, BA, LTCL
Head of Brass: Mrs A S Hudson, GRNCM, PPRNCM
Head of Keyboard: A Hone, BMus, ARCM, ARCO
Head of Strings: A P Gibbon, GRNCM
Academic Music: Mrs S L Ratchford, BA
Music Fellow: J E R Thomas
and 38 peripatetic teachers

Physical Education and Games:
D J Grewcock, BA (*Director of Sport*)
R A J Finch, MSc
C J Olver, WLIHE
M Walker, BA
Miss R S Goatly, BA
G Terrett, BA
Mrs L M Brighton, MEd (*Head of Girls' Games*)

Physics:
*M N Wells, MA
A B Burrows, MA Ed, BSc (*Undermaster*)
Mrs L E Kirk, BSc
Mrs T E Raftery, BSc
H Roberts, BSc
D J Talbot, MPhys
B A Letts, BSc
Miss C A Rees, MSc

Mrs S J Waring, BEng

Psychology:
S R Heath, BA, MSc
*R Banerjee, BSc

Religious Studies:
Mrs V Gascoine, BEd (*Head of Laxton*)
Mrs A E Meisner, BA
*B T Deane, BA
Revd B J Cunningham, MA
Mrs C A Deane, BA
Miss H A Dawes, BA

Teaching Fellows:
L V S Bezerra
Miss T M Brown

Pangbourne College

Pangbourne, Reading, Berkshire RG8 8LA

Tel: 0118 984 2101
email: registrar@pangbourne.com
website: www.pangbourne.com
Twitter: @PangColl

Motto: '*Fortiter ac Fideliter*'

Pangbourne College was founded in 1917 by Sir Thomas Devitt of the Devitt & Moore Company to train boys for a career at sea. It is now a modern, friendly boarding and day school for approximately 420 girls and boys aged 11 to 18. The College offers sound academic results, first-class sports coaching and an excellent pastoral structure prioritising the happiness and well-being of the individual. It will celebrate its centenary in September 2017.

Location and Facilities. Set in 230 acre grounds designated an Area of Outstanding Natural Beauty, a mile from Pangbourne village and neighbouring the town of Reading, the College combines a rural environment with easy access to London and Heathrow. The extensive school facilities include the Falkland Islands Memorial Chapel opened in March 2000, two new girls' boarding houses, a new drama studio, ICT suite and Music School. The modern, excellently equipped sports hall, floodlit Astroturf hockey pitch, spacious playing fields and boathouse on the River Thames provide sporting facilities of a professional standard. Boarding and day pupils are integrated across the seven fully-refurbished or new boarding houses. Senior pupils share study-bedrooms and most have single rooms in the Sixth Form. Meals are taken in a central dining hall although boarding houses contain kitchens too. Most academic staff live on the campus in College houses and there is an extremely strong community spirit.

Junior House. The Junior House, Dunbar, offers excellent, purpose-built accommodation and common room areas for 11 and 12 year old pupils in the heart of the College. Fully integrated into the academic, cultural and social life, Dunbar pupils enjoy full use of all the senior school's facilities and its specialist teaching. Pupils transfer automatically to the senior school without further examination.

Academic Study. Pupils aged 11–16 follow a broad curriculum which reflects, but is not determined by, the National Curriculum. This covers all of the core and foundation subjects of the National Curriculum: English, Mathematics, Science, French, German, History, Geography, Design Technology, Religious Study, Personal, Social, Health and Citizenship Education (PSHCE), Art, Music, Drama, Physical Education and Computing. Pupils in Forms 1–3 are assessed by the College's own assessment and reporting system. A Learning Support Unit, staffed by specialist qualified teachers, is available to help.

In the Sixth Form students follow the A Level programme with 25 subject options on offer. Sixth Form class sizes are typically between 8 and 12 and each student works with a Tutor, a Housemaster/Housemistress and the Head of Sixth Form who help them successfully navigate their way through their academic study.

Although the College's primary focus is the pursuit of academic excellence, it does nonetheless cater for a wide spectrum of abilities. Pupils are given considerable opportunities to discover and develop additional skills and talents through the extensive music, art, sport, drama and leadership programmes.

Careers. The Head of Sixth Form and the Careers Adviser work closely with the individual's Tutor to ensure that wise, informed choices are made. Whilst many students go on to Russell Group universities and a few to Oxford and Cambridge, the College champions as equals and provides guidance for the minority of students who do choose to take the vocational route.

Games. For a small school Pangbourne has an outstanding reputation for sport and thrives at National level in several games. The College has had many successes at Henley Royal Regatta making it one of the top rowing schools in the country and competes at a high level in rugby, consistently making good progress in the Berkshire Cup and national NatWest competitions. The hockey club regularly produce County players and have recently finished fourth in the National Hockey Championships. Pangbourne Equestrian provides professional and dedicated riding training and claimed victory at the National Schools' Equestrian Association Championships in October 2015. Other sports and activities offered include cricket, netball, tennis, football, athletics, golf, sailing and basketball. Pupils have regular access to the College's gym which is supervised by a member of the sporting faculty and the resident Strength and Conditioning coach.

Adventure Training. Led by the Head of Adventure Training and Duke of Edinburgh's Award Coordinator, the College provides an extensive range of activities designed to foster teamwork, leadership and communication skills. There is a full programme of adventure training built into the curriculum from Form 1, with weekend and holiday expeditions. As well as the opportunity to take part in a major expedition abroad every two years, pupils have regular, supervised access to the College's on-site high and low ropes course.

The Combined Cadet Force (CCF) programme at Pangbourne allows students to split into Army, Royal Navy and Royal Marine Sections, with each providing tailored exercises and expeditions. Despite being mandatory only in Forms 3 and 4, many of Pangbourne's pupils currently take part in the CCF.

All Form 3 pupils are entered for the Bronze Duke of Edinburgh's Award with the majority moving on to the Silver and Gold programmes.

Music and Drama. Pangbourne has a long tradition of excellence in Music and Drama. The newly constructed Nancye Harding Recital Centre has provided the College with its own recital hall, music technology facilities and extensive rehearsal space, adding further performance space to the existing Chapel and school hall. The Centre – which was opened in 2012 – houses the College's Steinway pianos, which gives Pangbourne its prestigious All-Steinway School status. There is also the opportunity to perform with the College choirs, Choral Society, orchestra, swing band and Marching Band, and the many professional musicians working around the College, including the Organist in Residence, Head of Brass and Cello Tutor, allowing students to pursue individual musical excellence.

Enrichment. The Enrichment programme is a dedicated time in the afternoon put aside for students and teachers to explore their interests and passions. Under the broad Enrichment banner rests a multitude of activities, clubs and societies, from academic support and extra language tuition to the code breaking, clay pigeon shooting and sailing clubs.

Admission. Children normally enter the Junior House, Dunbar, at 11+ through an interview and the College entrance examination. They are joined by more boys and girls at age 13+ through the Common Entrance or Scholarship Examinations. Sixth Form entry is based on interview, a satisfactory report from the previous school and good GCSE examination results. A prospectus and registration form may be obtained from the Registrar, Mrs Margaret Smith, who is always pleased to arrange visits to the College.

Scholarships and Bursaries. Scholarships and Awards of up to 20% of fees may be offered at 11+, 13+ and 16+ for excellence in the academic, music, drama, art, technology and sporting spheres. Means-tested Bursaries are also available.

Scholarship and Exhibition assessments are set and held at the College in January and February of the year of entry. All candidates applying for an award – academic or practical – must be registered and fulfil the standard entry requirements of the College.

Academic: Scholarships or Exhibitions may be offered at 11+, 13+ and 16+, and are the most important scholastic awards made by the College. They are based on academic merit in a range of subjects and the potential to produce an outstanding performance at GCSE and A Level.

Art: Scholarships of up to 20% of fees may be offered at 13+ and 16+. Candidates must present a portfolio of work completed over the previous two years and attend an interview.

Drama: Scholarships may be offered at 13+ and 16+. Candidates are invited to attend an audition consisting of two prepared monologues, an improvised piece and sight reading.

Music: Several Music Scholarships or Exhibitions of up to the value of 20% of College fees are available at 11+, 13+ and 16+. For consideration, candidates should be approximately Grade 3 at 11+ entry, Grade 5 at 13+ entry and Grade 7 at 16+ entry on their main instrument. A second instrument or experience as a chorister is an advantage. Awards normally carry free tuition on two instruments.

Sports: Scholarships or Exhibitions may be offered at 11+, 13+ and 16+ to candidates who have the sporting potential to be a significant member of the College's first teams, in one or more of our major sports, and the ability to compete at County or higher representative level.

Technology: Scholarships may be offered at 13+. Candidates are expected to design and make an item out of scrap materials and be prepared to discuss their work at interview.

Please contact the Registrar (registrar@pangbourne.com) for more information.

Fees per term (2016–2017). At age 11 and 12: Boarders £7,736; Part Boarders £6,895; Day Pupils £5,493. At 13 and above: Boarders £10,949; Part Boarders £9,741; Day Pupils £7,741.

Charitable status. Pangbourne College Limited is a Registered Charity, number 309096. The objective is to provide an excellent all-round education for boys and girls between the ages of 11 and 18.

Governing Body:
Chairman: Rear Admiral R C Lane-Nott, CB
Vice-Chairman: Revd A T Bond

Headmaster: Mr T J C Garnier

Senior Deputy Head and Deputy Head Academic: Mr W Williams

Deputy Head Co-Curricular: Mr R Bancroft

Deputy Head Pastoral: Mrs C Bond

Bursar: Mr R Obbard

The Perse Upper School

Hills Road, Cambridge CB2 8QF

Tel: 01223 403800
Fax: 01223 403810
email: office@perse.co.uk
website: www.perse.co.uk

The Perse School is Cambridge's oldest surviving secondary school, founded in 1615 by Dr Stephen Perse, a Fellow of Gonville and Caius College. The school still maintains close links with both Gonville and Caius and with Cambridge University.

The Perse Upper School is a co-educational independent day school for pupils aged 11–18.

Ethos. A Perse education is an adventure, full of curiosity, discovery and challenge. Students come from a wide range of social and economic backgrounds thanks to the School's significant bursary programme and a commitment to keeping fee rises low. The School's values are: intellectual curiosity and scholarship, endeavour, breadth and balance, and valuing one another. The School encourages all pupils and staff "*To love learning and strive for the greater good*."

History. The School remains true to its historic roots, with close links to the University of Cambridge and a £1 million per annum means-tested bursary programme that supports more than 120 pupils. In 2015/16, The Perse School celebrated its 400th anniversary.

Admission. There are approximately 1145 students in the Upper, including 340 in the Sixth Form. The main entry points are Year 7, Year 9 and the Lower Sixth. For Years 7 and 9 candidates are examined in maths, English and verbal reasoning, and undertake a short humanities video/questions exercise. Sixth Form applicants sit entrance tests and offers are conditional on GCSE results.

Facilities. The Perse has invested more than £40 million in new facilities over the last decade. The Upper occupies an attractive 27 acre green field site with extensive playing fields and recreational areas. Yet at just over two miles from the centre of Cambridge, and adjacent to the University's biomedical campus, it benefits from easy access to world-class facilities. Pupils enjoy high specification science labs and classrooms; a purpose built sports centre; on-site sports fields and all weather surfaces; a music centre including a rehearsal hall; art studios and a gallery; a lecture theatre; and an outdoor pursuits centre, climbing wall and shooting range. There is a 20,000 volume library and high-speed wired and wireless networks to ensure ready access to online learning resources. There are also plans to create a performing arts centre ready for the 2017 academic year.

Academic excellence. Perse pupils learn in a purposeful and supportive environment where they are taught to think independently and to make sense of a diverse and complex world. The School achieves some of the best A Level and Pre-U results of any co-educational school in the country, regularly appearing in the top 10 schools nationally. In 2016 more than three quarters of A Level entries were graded at A or A*. 94% of students' GCSE and IGCSE results are A* or A, and the School was the top ranking co-ed institution in The Times and The Telegraph GCSE league tables. Pupils regularly excel in science and maths olympiads, economics and business challenges, drama and poetry contests and essay and fiction writing competitions.

Rounded education. There is a buzz about daily life at The Perse. There are more than 100 clubs and societies on offer. The School was awarded the Pro Corda Special Award for Schools for outstanding contribution to chamber music making; there are more than 70 coached or directed ensembles and a typical year will see around 50–60 separate performance opportunities. There are at least eight productions each year and the Perse Players drama group performs at the Edinburgh Fringe. The main sports are cricket, hockey, netball, rugby, tennis, athletics and rounders. There is an extensive fixtures list; the School fields more than 160 teams in 30 different sports and regularly enjoys regional and national success. More than 400 pupils are involved in the Perse Exploration Society, learning outdoor skills as well as life skills such as team working and resilience. Other popular outdoor pursuits include adventure racing, shooting, the Combined Cadet Force and the Duke of Edinburgh's Award programme.

Supportive community. The Upper is a happy school where pupils feel safe, secure and supported. The School works hard to strike the right balance of work and play, comfort and challenge, instruction and discovery, rules and common sense, and guidance and independence. Each student has a pastoral tutor who monitors their progress and there are peer listeners, form prefects and a system of heads of year, heads of section, senior tutors and school counsellors. The Perse has a very active programme of charitable fundraising and outreach, and pupils have the chance to become involved in the wider community. Perse pupils work with children from local primary schools, teach the older generation digital skills, and volunteer in developing countries.

Global perspective. The Perse has strong international links including foreign language and cultural exchanges, a partnership with Christel House (a charity that educates some of the world's poorest children) and membership of the SAGE global alliance of leading schools. Pupils regularly travel overseas and increasingly collaborate remotely through the latest technology.

Fees per term (2016–2017). £5,344.

Bursaries and scholarships. Means-tested bursaries are available, ranging from 5% to 100% of annual tuition fees. At Year 7 and Year 9 the School offers a small number of academic and music scholarships to pupils of exceptional merit. Sixth formers are able to apply for a maximum of two scholarships. All sixth form applicants who sit our entrance tests are automatically considered for an academic scholarship and general scholarship.

The Perse Prep is a co-educational preparatory school for pupils aged between 7 and 11. Tel: 01223 403920; email: prephm@perse.co.uk. (*See The Perse Prep School entry in IAPS section.*)

The Perse Pelican Nursery and Pre-Prep is for children aged 3 to 7. Tel: 01223 403940; email: pelicanschoolsec@perse.co.uk. (*See The Perse Pelican Nursery and Pre-Prep entry in IAPS section.*)

Alumni. Tel: 01223 403 836; email: development@perse.co.uk.

Charitable status. The Perse School is a charitable company limited by guarantee (company number 5977683, registered charity number 1120654) registered in England and Wales whose registered office is situated at The Perse School, Hills Road, Cambridge CB2 8QF.

Governing Body:

Sir David Wright, GCMG, LVO, MA, Hon LLD (*Chairman*)

Representing Gonville & Caius College:
Dr A M Bunyan, BA, PhD
Dr E M Harper, BA, MA Cantab, PhD

Representing Trinity College:
Dr M T J Webber, MA, DPhil, FRHistS, FSA

Co-opted:
J C Aston, OBE, MA, ACA
H Bettinson, MA, PhD
S Dorrian, BA, PGCE
Dr C J Edmonds, BSc, PhD

I G Galbraith, MA
R G Gardiner, MA, FCA
S W Graves, BSc, MBA
Dr R C St H Mason, BSc, MBBS, MRCP, MBA
M P H Pooles, QC, LLB
D M Shave, MA, MBACP
B P Smith, MA, CPFA, FCIHT
C J Stenner, LLB (*Vice Chairman*)
Dr V J Warren, MA, MD, FFPH

Bursar & Clerk to the Governors: G A Ellison, MA

Head: E C Elliott

Deputy Head (Staff): D R Cross

Deputy Head (Pupils): E W Wiseman

Deputy Head (Curriculum): P D Baker

Assistant Head (Welfare and Admissions): G F Hague

Assistant Head (Extra-curricular): S A Richardson

Plymouth College

Ford Park, Plymouth, Devon PL4 6RN

Tel:	01752 505100 (School Office)
	01752 505104 (Headmaster)
	01752 505107 (Finance Director)
	01752 505115 (Registrar)
Fax:	01752 203246
email:	mail@plymouthcollege.com
	slambie@plymouthcollege.com
	lfisher@plymouthcollege.com
website:	www.plymouthcollege.com
Twitter:	@plymouthcolleg1
Facebook:	@PlymouthCollege

Plymouth College, based in the maritime city of Plymouth with the moorland, countryside and coastal landscapes of Devon and Cornwall close to hand, has been at the forefront of education in South West England since its foundation in 1877. It amalgamated in 1896 with Mannamead School for boys in Plymouth, founded in 1854. The School became fully co-educational in 1995 and in 2004 merged with St Dunstan's Abbey for girls.

Numbers. Currently there are 500 pupils in the school (160 in the Sixth Form) and of these 215 are girls.

Buildings. The Senior School stands on high ground in Plymouth. The buildings include Science Laboratories, Art and Craft rooms including extensive facilities for photography and print-making, the Dining Hall, an Assembly Hall in which concerts and plays are performed. A well-equipped Design and Technology Block was opened in 1979. The grounds in Ford Park include a rifle range and an indoor, heated swimming pool. Playing fields at Ford Park are supplemented by two other fields close by. The Sports Hall was opened in 1986 and a new library was opened in 1996. An astro surface was built in 1999 and upgraded in 2012 and the school has use of a full-size astro for Hockey. In 2004 a new hospitality suite and Music School opened. In 2011 two new boarding houses were established. There is a dedicated Sixth Form Centre with its own Bistro and 2016 saw the opening of the Michael Ball Drama Studio, opened by its namesake who is an old boy of the school. There is also an outdoor education centre located on Dartmoor.

The Preparatory School at The Millfields is approximately half a mile from the Senior School and has its own playing field and sports hall.

Organisation. Below the Sixth Form, pupils are set in some areas so that pupils may proceed at a pace best suited to their abilities. Pupils are organised in 4 Houses. Each

pupil is under the supervision of a Tutor and Head of Year who report to the Assistant Head. In Years 7–10 Form Prefects are appointed. Every pupil is expected to play a full part in games and other school activities outside the classroom. Pupils in Years 10 and above also take part in our enrichment programme which includes The Duke of Edinburgh's Award, CCF (all 3 sections), Sports Leaders Award and a wide range of other activities. All pupils take part in our active PSHEE programme, with careers advice starting in Year 7.

English (Language and Literature), a Modern Language, Mathematics, Physics, Chemistry and Biology are taken by all to GCSE. Normally three more are chosen by the pupils.

Sixth Form. The Sixth Form is based on tutor groups with about twelve in each group. Pupils usually study three subjects at A Level, with four being studied in exceptional circumstances. In addition, our Sports Baccalaureate is an alternative to A Levels which includes A BTEC in Sport and Outdoor Education as well as qualifications in other sporting and outdoor activity areas. Tutors keeps a pastoral and academic watch on the pupils' performance, feeding information to the Head and Assistant Heads of Sixth Form.

Sixth Formers are well prepared for universities and careers both in the UK and overseas, including scholarship advice for the US, with detailed university advice starting in Year 9.

Games. Rugby, Football, Cricket, Hockey, Netball and Swimming are the major sports. There is also Athletics, Badminton, Basketball, Cross-Country Running, Sailing, Shooting, Squash and Tennis. Games are compulsory but more senior pupils have a wide range of options available to them.

School Activities. Pupils take part in a very good range of activities. There is a contingent of the CCF with Navy, Army and Air Force Sections. There is also The Duke of Edinburgh's Award scheme and Adventure Training as well as Ten Tors. Pupils in Year 10 participate in a JSLA scheme with local primary schools. A number of overseas expeditions are also organised each year. School Societies cover a range of activities from Archery to Young Enterprise.

Music & Performing Arts. There is an excellent school choir that sings at all major school events, concerts, and church services throughout the school year. The school orchestra, like the choir, provides music at school events and concerts. Both the choir and the orchestra receive invitations to support large-scale events in and around Plymouth. In addition to these groups the school has various small ensembles that are run by the visiting specialist instrumental teachers. The school has a thriving house drama and music competition that attracts whole school support. As well as the formal/organized music making there are innumerable student-led bands that help to ensure that the music department is a vibrant environment. Tuition is provided on all orchestral instruments, including percussion. Voice, piano, organ and all types of guitar lessons are also available. Speech and drama lessons (LAMDA) are offered to all students. The music and drama departments work together on large-scale productions. The drama department offers drama clubs to all year groups. The lower school clubs focus on all aspects of stage technique and improvisation while the upper school groups tie their work in with current productions. A sound and lighting club runs which trains students in all aspects of the technical side of theatre. Both departments work with a number of visiting performers/practitioners throughout the year; these are usually focused on specific year groups or examination groups.

There are annual music and drama scholarships and instrumental exhibitions.

Boarders. With pupils from all over the world, the boarding houses are run by an enthusiastic, experienced and friendly team who are responsible for all aspects of boarding pupils' welfare. There is also a good mix of activities for boarders at the weekends including ten-pin bowling, ice skating, cinema trips, surfing, moorland walking and horse riding.

In the Senior School there are 5 Boarding Houses situated on the senior school campus: one for boys, one for girls (approx. 50 in each) and three smaller Sixth Form houses. They are located close to the school field and are equipped with small dormitories, common rooms, sickroom and games rooms. Meals are taken in the Dining Hall, supplied by a modern, well-equipped kitchen.

Admission. Admission to the Senior School is normally based on the College Entrance Examination for boys and girls over 10½ and under 12 on 31 August of the year of entry, but it is also possible to enter at 13 via the Common Entrance Examination or a Year 9 Scholarship/Entrance test. Occasional vacancies are available at other ages. Application forms may be obtained from the Registrar.

Admission to the Preparatory School is from the age of 3+. Application should be made direct to the Secretary to the Headmaster of the Preparatory School.

Scholarships and Bursaries. For pupils entering at 11 there are 2 Major Scholarships (50% of fees pa) and 3 Ordinary Scholarships (one-third of the fees pa). Two of these awards are restricted to pupils coming from Plymouth College Preparatory School. There are also smaller awards for Art, Music, Performing Arts, Drama and Sport and on occasion All-Round awards are given. Awards are made on the basis of the Entrance Examination.

At 13+ there is one Major and one Ordinary Scholarship and these are awarded on a Scholarship Examination.

For those entering the Sixth Form two further awards are made based on interview and GCSE results.

There are eight Scholarships and Awards for Art, Music, Drama and Sport. Four of these are awarded at 13 and four to Sixth Form entrants. The value of these awards is up to one-third of the fees.

Bursaries of up to half fees are available.

Further information from the Registrar.

Fees per term (2016–2017). Preparatory School: Infant Department: Kindergarten £2,430, Reception £2,540, Years 1 & 2 £2,985. Junior Department: Years 3–4 £3,200, Years 5–6 £3,345.

Senior School: Day: Years 7–8 £4,340, Years 9–11 £4,935, Sixth Form £5,140. Boarding: Years 7–8 £8,665, Years 9–11 £9,535, Sixth Form £9,930. Weekly and occasional boarding are also available.

These fees include stationery and games. Music lessons and lunches are extra.

Armed Forces and sibling discounts are available.

Charitable status. Plymouth College is a Registered Charity, number 1105544. Its aim is to provide private education for boys and girls.

Governing Body:
Chairman: C J Robinson, MA
Vice Chairman: D R Woodgate, BSc, MBA
Dr P Atkinson
T J Burke
Professor A Edwards
S Elford
Mrs R Hattersley, BA
Professor D A Huntley, BA, MA, PhD
P H Lowson, FCA
Mrs C Magill, BSc Econ
Mrs J McKinnell
Mrs A Mills, ACIS, MCIPD
I Penrose
Professor P Shears, BA, LLB, LLM
C P Thomson, BSc, FCA
Dr S Thorpe

Clerk to the Governors: Mrs S Wills MEng, ACA (*Senior & Preparatory School*)

Headmaster: **Mr Jonathan Standen**, BA Nottingham, NPQH

Deputy Head: Mrs J Hayward, MA Downing College Cambridge

Assistant Head: Mr C S Irish, BSc Birmingham

Teaching Staff:
Miss P J Anderson, MA Emmanuel College Cambridge (*Head of Classics*)
Mrs J E Ashenbury, BEd Reading
Miss N K Baker, BA Exeter, MA Exeter (*Head of History*)
Miss M Becker, Diplom-Ingenieur University of Applied Sciences, Berlin (*Head of German*)
Mr M Bennett, BA Exeter
Miss A C Blunden, BA Exeter
Mr K C Boots, BA Wales, MEd Exeter, AMBDA
Mrs P M Brockbank, Cert Ed (*Head of EAL*)
Dr J L Burns, BSc Oxford Brookes, DPhil Oxford
Mr M Byrne, BSc Loughborough (*Director of Cricket*)
Mr A R Carr, MA St Andrews (*Head of Sixth Form & MFL Faculty*)
Mr R Chapman, BEd College of St Mark & St John
Mrs A-L Chubb, BA Wolverhampton
Mrs L E S Clark, BA Open
Mrs R L Connor, BA Nottingham
Miss S Currie, BA Stirling (*Head of English*)
Mr R L Edwards, BA University of Wales (*Director of Rugby*)
Mrs N E Glasgow, BA Aberystwyth
Mr J P Gregory, BA Birmingham (*Head of Economics & Business Studies*)
Dr A Green, BA Exeter
Mrs A E Green, BSc Nottingham
Mr D Green, BA Dartington College of Arts (*Head of Music & Performing Arts*)
P J Grey, BSc Open, AMInstP (*Head of Academic Progress & Monitoring*)
Mr C J Hambly, BSc Manchester (*Head of Chemistry*)
Mr D R Hawken, PG Dip, BMus Hons, PGCE, Dip ABRSM, Royal Welsh College of Music and Drama (*Head of Year 10*)
Dr A Hawker, BSc Plymouth, PhD
Ms J Herod, BA Nottingham, MSc East London (*Head of SEN, Educational Psychologist*)
Mrs C Herroro-Shaw, BA Middlesex
Miss N S L Husband, BA Queen Margaret
Mr D A Jones, BSc Birmingham (*Head of Mathematics*)
Dr S Jordan, PhD Dundee (*Head of Biology*)
Mrs N Lilley, BA Nottingham Trent
Mr G J Llewellyn-Rees, BEng Brunel, MEng Heriot-Watt, MBA Imperial College
Mr A N Longden, BSc Plymouth
Mr D J Martin, BA Warwick (*Head of Religious Studies*)
Mrs P M Martin, BA Southampton
Dr A Miller, BSc PhD Bristol, CChem, MRSC, CPhys, MInstP (*Head of Computer Science*)
Mr P M Mutlow, BA Durham (*Director of Sport*)
Mr C G Nicol, Duncan of Jordanstone College of Art, Diploma (*Head of Art*)
Dr A Norris, BSc Liverpool, PhD
Miss L M Odendaal, BA Stellenbosch
Mrs H J Owen, BA College of St Mark & St John
Mrs N Paice, BA College of St Mark & St John (*Head of Geography*)
Mr R G Palmer, BA College of St Mark & St John (*Head of Year 7*)
Mrs M Paton, Maîtrise d'Anglais Université de Bretagne Occidentale

Mr R J Prichard, MA London
Mr D P Prideaux, BSc Bristol
Mr P J Randall, BA Oxford Brookes (*Head of French &*
Spanish)
Miss L M Russo, MSci Imperial College
Mrs A Savage, BSc Exeter (*Head of Psychology*)
Miss C P Sherratt, BSc Plymouth
Mrs T K Shields, MSc Leeds
Mrs L E Smith, BSc Exeter
Mrs S Sullivan, BA Glasgow School of Art
Mr A G Summons, BSc MSc Exeter (*Head of Year 9*)
Dr C Taylor, BSc Bath, PhD Bath
Mr M P Tippetts, BA Exeter (*Head of Boarding*)
Mrs Z P Thurston, BSc Exeter
Miss E D Tremaine, BEd De Montfort (*Head of PE*)
Miss F Venon, Licence d'Anglais Université de St Etienne,
Maître
Mr M P Wesley, BSc Nottingham Trent (*Head of Design
Technology*)
Mrs V J Willden, BA Plymouth
Miss E Williams, BA Greenwich
Mrs E Wright, BA University College London
Mr R P Wilson, BEng University College London

Preparatory School:
Plymouth College Preparatory School
St Dunstan's Abbey
The Millfields
Plymouth PL1 3JL

Headmaster: Mr C D M Gatherer, BA

Pocklington School

**West Green, Pocklington, York, East Yorkshire
YO42 2NJ**

Tel: 01759 321200
Fax: 01759 306366
email: enquiry@pocklingtonschool.com
website: www.pocklingtonschool.com
Twitter: @PockSchool
Facebook: /PocklingtonSchool
LinkedIn: /pocklington-school

Inspired for Life
Pocklington is a thriving independent school, 12 miles east of York, providing outstanding day and boarding education from 4–18 years. Pocklington School delivers an excellent all-round education and a vibrant co-curricular life within a supportive and caring community, all founded on a 500 year tradition.

Set in a safe and picturesque rural setting, the school focuses on the needs of the individual, inspiring each pupil to achieve their full potential.

Highly-skilled staff encourage an enthusiasm for learning and independent thought, helping pupils develop into motivated adults who are valued members of society.

Number of Pupils (2016–17). There are 546 pupils (297 boys, 249 girls) at Pocklington School (ages 11–18) and 224 pupils (119 boys and 105 girls) at Pocklington Prep School (ages 4–11). These numbers include 92 boarders aged 8–18.

Pocklington Prep School is on the same site as the Senior School. (*For further details, see entry in IAPS section.*)

Curriculum. Pocklington's curriculum has been developed to motivate and stretch pupils. Following foundations at Pocklington Prep School and in the Lower School at Pocklington, there are wide-ranging options in Year 9 and GCSE. Sixth Form AS and A2 subjects offer a diverse selection of subjects and combinations. There is excellent careers and university advice. Music, drama and art thrive, as do

sport, outdoor education, community service, the CCF and other extra-curricular activities. The main sports are athletics, badminton, basketball, cricket, cross-country, football, hockey, netball, rounders, rugby, squash, swimming and tennis.

Location, Campus and Development. The school is set in extensive grounds on the edge of Pocklington, a market town 12 miles east of York. Emphasis is given to the importance of personal achievement in an attractive, high-quality learning environment with very good facilities.

Admission in Years 7–9 is subject to vacancy and to a satisfactory entry exam result and school report. Interviews may also be held. Year 9 applicants sit either a Senior School entry exam or Common Entrance. There is no entry test for Sixth Form applicants who are expected to have a minimum of 4 B grades and 2 C grades at GCSE. Subject to these entry criteria, the school seeks to admit candidates who will benefit from what it has to offer and whom it will be able to support. Children with mild learning difficulties can be supported, as can those who will in due course seek entry to the most demanding university courses.

Scholarships and Bursaries. Three academic scholarships up to the value of 10% of the annual day fee and three exhibitions up to the value of 5% of the annual day fee are offered to entrants in each First Year and Third Year. Two further academic scholarships up to 10% of the annual day fee and two exhibitions up to the value of 5% of the annual day fee are offered to Sixth Form entrants. Means-tested Sixth Form bursaries providing up to 100% of annual day fees are also available. Pocklington School awards a maximum of four music scholarships annually, valued at 5% of the annual day fee.

Awards are available to internal and external candidates. Tenure of all awards is for the duration of the pupil's time at Pocklington School subject to satisfactory performance and behaviour.

Fees per term (2016–2017). Day £4,538, Boarding £8,844, 5-Day Boarding £8,135, Extended Day Pupil (1–5 nights per week) £183–£860.

Charitable status. The Pocklington School Foundation is a Registered Charity, number 529834.

Governors:
Chairman: Mr T A Stephenson, MA, FCA
Vice-Chairman: Mr C M Oughtred, MA, DL
Mrs J Atkinson
Mrs E Bryers
Mr J L Burley, BSc, MRICS
Mr D G Buttery, BA, DL
Mrs E Duncan, BA, MA
Mr J A Farmer, FCA
Mrs D Flint, MBA
Mrs J Good BA (*representing the Lord Lieutenant*)
The Reverend G Hollingsworth (*Ex-officio, Vicar of
Pocklington*)
Rt Hon Sir Greg Knight, MP (*Ex-officio, MP for Yorkshire
East*)
Mr K B Morrow, BA
Professor R C Nolan, MA (*nominated, representing St
John's College Cambridge*)
Dr D A Nott, BA, MA, PhD, Dip Soc Admin
Mrs S M Oughtred, BSc
Councillor G Perry, CEng, MIMechE, FIHEEM
(*nominated, representing Pocklington Town Council*)
Mrs L Rickatson, LLB Hons
Mr S M Shastri, BTech Mining Engineering, MSc, FRSA,
FRGS (*nominated, representing the University of Hull*)
The Reverend L Slow, BSc, MSc (*nominated, representing
the Archbishop of York*)
Dr A J Warren, MBE, MA, DPhil, FRHS (*nominated,
representing the University of York*)

Life Patrons:
Mrs J S Davies, DL
Rt Hon D M Davis, MP
Mr B Fenwick-Smith, MA
Mr R E Haynes, MA
Mrs N Jennings
Mr J L Mackinlay, DL, FCA, FCMA
Mr D V Southwell
Major General H G Woods, CB, MVO, MBE, MC, DLiH, MA, FRSA, FBIM

Clerk to the Governors & Bursar: Mr P S Bennett, BSc, FLS

Headmaster: **Mr M E Ronan**, MA Cantab

Deputy Head, Professional Development Director: Miss C L Bracken, MSc

Heads of Departments:

English: I Hashim, BA
Drama: A W J Heaven, MA, BHum
Mathematics: J F Cullen, BSc
Modern Languages (French, German, Spanish): D A Galloway, MA
Science:
Biology: M J Butcher, BSc
Chemistry: Mr M R Evans, BSc
Physics: Mr G Binks, BSc
Psychology: Dr S McNamee, BSc, PhD (*External Relations Director*)
Classics (Latin/Ancient Greek): Mr M J Adams, BA, MPhil
Creative & Technological:
Art: Mr D A Cimmermann, BA
Design: Mr S D Ellis, BA
Cookery: Mrs A-M Salmon, BSc
ICT & Computing: Mrs H T Alexander, BA
Music: M Kettlewell, BA, ATCL (*Director of Music, Co-Curriculum Director*)
Peripatetic Music Teachers for: Flute, Woodwind, Classical Guitar, Piano, Percussion, Brass, Violin and Viola, Electric and Bass Guitar, Cello, Clarinet, Saxophone, Voice.
Humanities:
Economics, Business Studies and Politics: Mr G J Shephard, MA
History: Mr G J Hughes, MA (*Head of Middle School*)
Geography: Mrs R H Brennan, MA
Religious Studies: Mr M J Davies, BA
Games, Sport and PE:
Mr D Byas (*Director of Sport*)
Mr A E Towner, BA (*Head of Physical Education*)
Careers and University Advice: Mrs G J Jones, DipCG
English as an Additional Language: Mrs A J Chenery, BA, CELTA (*EAL Coordinator*)
Learning Support: Miss H M Young, MA Cantab, PGCert SpLD Dyslexia, AMBDA
School Librarian and Archivist: Mrs A J Edwards, BA, PGDipILS
Chaplain: Revd Dr J Goodair, BA, PhD

Boarding Houses & Housemasters/mistresses:
Fenwick-Smith (*Senior Boys*): Mr P M H L Dare, BA, MA, RSA Dip TEFL
Dolman (*Junior Boys*): Mrs W J Wright, MA
Faircote (*Senior Girls*): Miss C Thackray, BA
Orchard (*Junior Girls*): Mrs L Scrowston

Day House Staff:
Dolman:
Mr M J Adams, MPhil, BA (*Sixth Form*)
Mr S D Ward, BSc (*Middle School*)
Mr I J Andrews, BA (*Lower School*)
Gruggen:

Mrs H T Alexander, BA (*Sixth Form*)
Mrs A K Hallam, BA (*Middle School*)
Mrs L J Walker, BSc (*Lower School*)
Hutton:
Mr A W F Hall, BA (*Sixth Form*)
Mr T M Loten, BA (*Middle School*)
Mr S A Houltham (*Lower School*)
Wilberforce:
Mr R P Bond, BEd (*Sixth Form*)
Mr P Oatridge, BSc (*Middle School*)
Mrs M S Wilson, BA, MSc (*Lower School*)

Pocklington Prep School:

Head: Mr I D Wright, BSc
Assistant Head (Pre-Prep): Mrs S A Cobb, BSc
Assistant Head (Co-curriculum): Mr J R Parker, BA
Assistant Head (Curriculum): Mrs C L Sweeting, BA Hons

The Portsmouth Grammar School

High Street, Portsmouth, Hants PO1 2LN

Tel: 023 9236 0036
Fax: 023 9236 4256
email: admissions@pgs.org.uk
website: www.pgs.org.uk
Twitter: @PGS_1732
Facebook: /ThePortsmouthGrammarSchool

Motto: *Praemia Virtutis Honores*

The Portsmouth Grammar School is a happy and vibrant independent school located in the historic heart of Portsmouth and only a few minutes' walk from the Solent.

The support our pupils experience at PGS and the challenges they encounter have a shared purpose: that each individual should be happy and successful, in that order. In the spirit of our founder, Dr William Smith, we seek to provide excellence in all areas of school life and encourage our girls and boys to think not only about where they will be at 18 but where they aspire to be at 25. Portsmouth is, after all, a city concerned with destinations.

The Portsmouth Grammar School is a fully co-educational school which assumed full independent status in 1976. There are 1,143 pupils in the Senior School and 357 pupils in the Junior School. There are no boarders.

The Nursery School offers outstanding care and education for boys and girls from 2½ to 4 years old in a safe and stimulating environment. Currently there are 56 children in the Nursery.

The Junior School for boys and girls aged 4–11, is a thriving, dynamic and popular school, committed to giving pupils the best possible start to their educational lives. Juniors benefit greatly from an increase in specialist teaching and from learning in subject-specific rooms. This allows the school to immerse pupils in a stimulating and connected curriculum that combines the learning of skills and knowledge with an understanding and ability of how best to apply them. The main ages of entry are 4 and 7 however there are places available for intermediate entry. (*For further details see entry in IAPS section.*)

Since September 2015, pupils in the Junior School no longer sit the 11+ entrance assessments for entry in to the Senior School. The Headmaster of the Junior School will recommend entry to the Senior School following its programme of continuous assessment.

Senior School. Admission is by the School's Entrance Assessment at 11+ and at 13+. Entrants at 13 are usually pre-tested at 11 to accommodate high demand for places. Pupils are admitted at other ages, should vacancies occur, subject to assessments and satisfactory reports from previous schools. Admission to the Sixth Form, which numbers 352, is subject to satisfactory standard at GCSE and interview.

Curriculum. Pupils are educated for life as well as for academic achievements through initiatives such as The Portsmouth Curriculum in Year 7 and the wide-ranging General Studies Programme in the Sixth Form. After GCSE, pupils enter the Sixth Form, which seeks to prepare pupils for the challenges of university education and subsequent competitive employment. Pupils have the choice of either studying for the International Baccalaureate Diploma or A Levels. A Level subjects include: Art, Biology, Business Studies, Chemistry, Classical Civilisation, Design and Technology, Drama, Economics, Electronics, English Literature, French, Geography, German, Government and Politics, Greek, History, Italian, Latin, Mathematics, Further Mathematics, Music, Physical Education, Psychology, Religious Studies and Spanish. The General Studies Programme is mainly taught by outside professionals and is aimed at widening personal and academic horizons as well as offering some further academic opportunities. The Sixth Form prepares candidates for entry to Higher Education, and the Universities and Careers Department provides excellent support with UCAS applications and close relations with various forms of employment.

Religion. The Portsmouth Grammar is the Cathedral school. However, Religious Instruction, given in accordance with the principles of the Christian faith, remains, in accordance with a long tradition of latitudinarianism, non-denominational. The School has a Chaplain.

Pastoral Care. Pastoral Care is of paramount importance. On entry to the school pupils are allocated to one of four Houses. Heads of House and their House Tutors are responsible for the pastoral and academic welfare of all pupils, supported by Heads of Year, and provide a focal point for communication between teaching staff and parents. Particular emphasis is placed on the triangular relationship between pupil, parents and teaching staff, including a programme of telephone calls from tutors to new parents in which all senior staff and the Headmaster have a monitoring role.

Games. Rugby football, netball and hockey are the main games in Winter and Spring, cricket, tennis, athletics and rounders in the Summer. Cross-country running, squash, judo, badminton, gymnastics, basketball, aerobics, swimming and sailing are also available. The School has enjoyed national success in recent years in sports such as football, hockey, netball, athletics, cricket and rounders.

The Co-Curriculum. There are significant opportunities for co-curricular involvement at the school. Music, Sport, Drama, CCF and Outdoor Pursuits including Ten Tors and participation in the Duke of Edinburgh's Award scheme, play a huge role in the development of pupils and provide them with a diverse and popular range of activities. Service to the local community and charity work is also an important feature of the school's ethos. Many clubs and societies cater for a considerable range of co-curricular interests from the Model United Nations to Wildlife Club. Numerous expeditions, holiday activities and trips are actively encouraged and include many foreign tours for sports teams and music ensembles. The School has a flourishing exchange scheme with French, German and Spanish schools. Sports teams have recently gone on tour to Singapore, Malaysia and South Africa. Recent expeditions have seen pupils travel to Madagascar, Uganda, Cambodia, Argentina and Cuba.

Fees per term (2016–2017). Senior School: £4,939. Junior School: £3,170–£3,515. (Fees quoted include direct debit discount.)

Scholarships and Bursaries. An extensive programme of scholarships and means-tested bursaries is offered in the Senior School from 11–18 years and we are extremely grateful to all those, whose generosity makes it possible for a growing number of pupils to join PGS each year regardless of their financial situation.

Scholarships are non means-tested and awarded to recognise exceptional academic or co-curricular ability. Where appropriate, these awards may be augmented by a bursary.

Bursaries are entirely means-tested and reflect the outstanding academic potential of an individual pupil regardless of ability to afford the school's fees.

All candidates are automatically considered for academic scholarships at 11+, 13+ and 16+.

Additionally, scholarships can also be awarded for excellence in Art, Drama, Music and Sport at 13+ and 16+. Existing PGS pupils may also apply for consideration for these awards once they become eligible during their time at the school.

Full details of all scholarships and bursaries are available on the School's website.

Buildings. The School is located within the historic quarter of Portsmouth. The Grade II listed buildings of the Junior and Senior School sit comfortably next to modern developments such as the Bristow-Clavell Science Centre which opened in 2010, and the Sixth Form Centre which opened in September 2014. The School sports facilities are located at the Hilsea Playing Fields and include an all-weather pitch and Sports Pavilion.

Honours. In 2016 sixteen pupils took up places at Oxbridge, with 63% going to Russell Group Plus universities and a further 25% going to other universities. The vast majority of Sixth Formers gained a place at their first-choice University. Sportsmen include England Cricket Captain Wally Hammond, Athletics International Roger Black, and Paralympian Ross Morrison. Military distinction in abundance, including 3 VCs (one the first VC submariner), several Admirals, Generals and Air Marshals. Medicine is also a continuing theme – from pioneer ophthalmologist James Ware to Viagra researcher Ian Osterloh. Arts are well and diversely represented: dramatist Simon Gray, poet Christopher Logue, novelist James Clavell, film director James Bobin, Sky News entertainment reporter Joe Michalczuk, cathedral organist Christopher Walsh, and pop singer Paul Jones. Civil Servants, Judges and barristers galore, plus entrepreneur industrialist Alan Bristow.

Old Portmuthian Club. This maintains links with former pupils not least by holding reunions in Portsmouth, London and Oxford, and is enhanced by its relationship with the School's Development Office.

Charitable status. The Portsmouth Grammar School is a Registered Charity, number 1063732. It exists to provide education for boys and girls.

Governing Body:
Chairman: Mr B S Larkman, MBE, BSc, ACIB
Vice Chairman: Mrs M Scott, BSc
Mrs K Bishop, BA
Mrs F Boulton, BSc, MA
The Dean of Portsmouth,
The Very Revd D Brindley, BD, MTh, MPhil, AKC
Mr W J B Cha, BA
Mr M R Coffin, BA Econ, FCA
Mrs R Duff
Dr M Grossel, BSc, PhD, MA
Mr N D Latham, CBE, MSc, CEng, FIMarEST, FIMechE
His Honour Judge Lodder QC, LLB
Mr B Martin, MA
Mr P G Parkinson, BA, Dip Arch
Professor C B R Pelling, MA, DPhil
Mr M J Pipes, MA, MBA, FInstP
Commodore Jeremy Rigby RN, MA
Mrs A Stanford
Mr H W G Tuckett, MA
The Right Worshipful the Lord Mayor of Portsmouth

Senior Team:

Headmaster: Mr J E Priory, MA

Second Master: Mr B P H Charles, BA, FRSA
Deputy Head (Academic): Mr B C T Goad, BSc
Deputy Head (Co-curriculum and External Relations): Mr C J Hamlet, MA
Assistant Head (Sixth Form): Mr L F Rees, BA
Assistant Head (Teaching and Learning): Dr G T Purves, MPhys, PhD
Assistant Head (Head of Middle School): Mrs J Jackson, BSc
Bursar: Mr D J Kent

Senior School:
‡ *Senior Teacher*
§ *Part-time*

Mr J M Addyman, BSc (*Mathematics*)
Mr D P Ager, BSc, MSc (*Mathematics, Timetabler*)
Mr L A Ansell, BSc, MA (*Design and Technology*)
Mrs L C Ashdown, MA (*Mathematics, Second in Department*)
Mr J D Baker, BSc (§*Mathematics*)
Mr J P Baker, TD, BSc, MA Ed, FRGS, FGS (*Geography and Geology*)
Mrs E E Bell, BA (*English, Second in Department*)
Mrs M C Bodman-Flack, BA (*Head of Design and Technology*)
Ms A E Bolton, BA, MA (*Classics*)
Mr G Brown, FLCM, LLCM (*Head of Brass*)
Ms S H Brunner, MA (§*English*)
Miss L V Burden, BA, MA (*Head of English*)
‡Mr J E Burkinshaw, BA (*English, Head of Careers and Universities*)
Mrs S A Burkinshaw, BA (§*English*)
Miss L J Burton, MA (*Geography & Geology*)
‡Miss F E A Bush, BA (*History, Head of Whitcombe House*)
Mrs A S Casillas-Cross, BA, MA (*History, CAS Coordinator, Deputy Head of Smith House*)
Mrs K E Clark, BSc, MSc (*Biology/Chemistry*)
Mrs A M L Clarke, MA (§*Classics*)
Mrs R H Clay, BA (*History, Deputy Head of Sixth Form and General Studies Coordinator*)
Mrs B Clifford, BA London, BA Wales (*Classics*)
Miss R L Close, BSc (*Head of Economics and Business Studies*)
Miss C L Coward, BA (*Head of German*)
Miss E J Cox, MSc, CPhys, MInstP (*Physics*)
Mrs A Cross, BTh, MA (*Philosophy and Religious Studies, Deputy Head of Careers and Universities*)
Ms D J Curteis, MA Ed, FDE SNE SpLD, AMBDA (*Head of Learning Support*)
Mr S J Curwood, BEd (*Head of Cricket, Deputy Head of Latter House*)
Mrs A J Day, BEd (§*Head of Athletics*)
Mr S J Dean, BEd (*Mathematics*)
Mr S G Disley, BSc (*Physics*)
‡Mr C J Dossett, BSc, MSc (*Director of Sport*)
‡Mr D T Doyle, BA (*Modern Languages, Head of Latter House*)
Mrs M G Dray, BA, HDipEd (*Learning Support*)
Mr J Dunne, MA (*English*)
Mrs L C Erricker, BA (*History and Politics*)
Mr T M Fairman, BA (*Mathematics*)
Mrs M Fake, BSc (*Head of Physics*)
Miss S J Farmer, BA (*Head of Physical Education*)
Mrs S L Filho, BA, MA (*Drama*)
Mr P R Fisher, BA (§*Economics and Business Studies*)
Mr D J Frampton, BA (*History*)
Ms R H Fry, BEd (*Learning Support*)

Dr P W Galliver, MA, MPhil, EdD (§*History*)
Mr P M Gamble, BA (*Head of French*)
Mr J R C Gillies, BSc (*Mathematics, Head of Grant House*)
Mr S J Gladstone, BA (*Director of Music*)
Mrs C A Gozalbez-Guerola, BA (§*Modern Languages*)
Mrs K I Greenslade, BSc (*PE and Games, Head of Eastwood House*)
Mr O G A Hancock, BA, MMus, FRCO (§*School Organist*)
Miss P A Hardisty, BSc, MA (*Biology*)
‡Mr S J Harris, MA (*Chemistry, Surmaster, CCF Contingent Commander, DofE Manager*)
Ms B C Hart, MA (*English, Deputy Head of Whitcombe House*)
Mr S D Hawkswell, BA (*PE and Games, Head of Barton House*)
Miss S Heath, BMus (*Head of Academic Music*)
Mr J K Herbert, BSc (*Physics*)
Miss J Horn, BA (*PE and Games*) [Maternity Cover]
Dr M R Howson, BSc, PhD, CChem, MRSC (*Head of Chemistry, Head of Science*)
Revd S C Hunt, BA (*Philosophy and Religious Studies, School Chaplain*)
Miss K Kingsley GRSM, LRAM (§*Music*)
Mrs T A Knott BSc, MSc (§*Geography & Geology*)
Mrs E M Kirby, MA (§*English*)
Mrs P I Langtry, BA (§*Modern Languages*)
Mr S D Lavery, BSc, MSc (*PE and Games, Cricket Professional*)
Mr A D Leach, BSc (*PE and Games, Head of Hawkey House*)
Mr D D Lee, BSc (*Mathematics, Computing*)
‡Mr S Lemieux, MA (*Head of History and Politics*)
‡Miss H V Linnett, BSc (*PE and Games, Deputy Head of Sixth Form*)
‡Mr B P Lister, BA (*Head of Classics*)
Mrs F E Lyon, MChem, (*Physics, Coordinator of Physical Science, Bronze DofE Coordinator*)
Mr D J E Lyons, BA, MSc (*Head of Rugby*)
Miss G Meadows, BEd (*Drama*)
Mr A S Milford, BA (*History and Politics, Second in Department*)
Mrs J L K Morgan, BA (*Philosophy and Religious Studies, Head of Pastoral Curriculum*)
Mr J H Murphy, BA (*Coordinator of Modern Languages, Coordinator of Pupil Council*)
Mrs R L Nash, BSc (*Mathematics, Deputy Head of Yrs 9–11, Silver DofE Coordinator*)
Mr T J D Neal, MA, MPhil (*Music*)
Ms F J Nicholson, BSc, MPH (§*Geography*)
Dr P A O'Neil, BSc, PhD (*Chemistry*)
Mr S Page, BA (§*Modern Languages*)
Mrs S E Palmer, BA, Dip SpLD (§*Learning Support*)
Mr R A Peebles, BA (*Head of Art*)
Mrs H E Prentice, BA (§*Head of Girls' Tennis*)
Mrs S R Pye, BSc, MSc (*Psychology, Coordinator of Aspirant Medics*)
Miss J J Read, BSc (*Mathematics, Head of Examinations*)
Mrs K C Rees, BSc (§*Design and Technology*)
Mr M P Richardson, BA, MA (*English*)
‡Dr R J I Richmond, MA, PhD (*Head of Philosophy and Religious Studies*)
Miss S J C Robert, MA (*Modern Languages*)
Ms S L Roberts, BA (§*Design and Technology*) [Maternity Cover]
Mr J F Robinson, LLB (*Drama*)
Mr D P Rogers, BSc (*Biology*)
Mrs A V Russell, BSc (*Chemistry*)
Mr G J Ryan, BSc (*Biology, Deputy Head of Yrs 9–11*)
Miss K Sanders, BA (*Economics and Business Studies*)
Mrs H E Sands, BSc (§*Geography and Geology*)

Mr A J Seddon, BSc (*PE and Games, Head of Eastwood House*) [Maternity Cover]

Mrs C D E Smith, BSc (*Chemistry*)

Ms L A M Smith, BA (*Philosophy and Religious Studies, Head of Summers House*)

Dr M J Smith, MChem, DPhil (*Chemistry, Second in Department*)

Mrs S Smith, BSc, MA (§*Mathematics, Assistant Timetabler*)

Mrs K Sparkes, BSc (*Biology, Deputy Head of Middle School*)

Mr H C Stayte, BA (*Head of Digital Learning*)

Dr P G Stephenson, BSc, PhD (*Head of Biology*)

Miss S L Stewart, BSc (*Head of Geography and Geology*)

†Mr O G Stone, BA (*Head of Modern Languages*)

‡Mr S C Taylor, MA (*Classics, Director of IB*)

Miss K G Thomas, MA (*Mathematics*)

Dr N Thomas, BSc, PhD (*Biology*)

Mr G T de Trafford, BA, MA (*Physics, Head of Smith House*)

Mrs J L Tweddle, BSc (*Head of Netball*)

Mrs J M H Tyldesley, BSc (§*Biology*)

Mr V Valera-Ramiro, BA (*Spanish and French*)

Mr M van Willigen, MA (*Head of Hockey*)

‡Mr N G Waters, BA (*Modern Languages, Head of Yrs 9–11*)

Mrs W Whitaker, CertEd (*Design and Technology*)

Mrs D J Willcocks, BA, AKC (§*Modern Languages*)

Mr S P H Willcocks, BA (*Art*)

Mrs L A Williams, BA (*Art*)

Mr C M Williamson, MA, MSci (*Chemistry, Deputy Head of Grant House*)

Mr I C Wilson, MA (§*Mathematics*)

Mr J Winship, BEd (*Design and Technology*)

Mrs K E Winship, BA (*Head of Mathematics*)

Ms A J Wood, BA (*Head of Psychology*)

Mrs M J Worley, BA, MSc (§*Economics and Business Studies*)

Modern Languages Assistants:
§Mme E Doize
§M. A Guillaume
§Frau S Kolb
Mrs M Chapero, BA

Junior School:

Headmaster, Mr P S Hopkinson, BA, PGCE

Deputy Head, Mr J Ashcroft, BSc, PGCE

Assistant Heads:
Mrs P Giles, BA, PGCE (*Assistant Head Co-curriculum, Head of Years 5 & 6*)
Mr C Williams, BA, QTS (*Assistant Head Academic*)

Head of Nursery: Mrs K Moore, BA, QTS

Mrs J M Albuery, BEd (*PRS Leader*)

Mrs A Ayres, BA, PGCE (*Computing Leader, Infants*)

Mr G Brown, FLCM, LLCM TD, ALCM (*brass*)

Mrs L Budd, BEd (*Food & Nutrition Leader, Juniors*)

Mrs J Budgen, BSc, PGCE (*Geography Leader, Juniors; Acting Digital Learning Leader*)

Mrs S Carlin, BA, PGCE (*Reception Leader; PSHE Leader, Infants*)

Miss E Carter, BA QTS (*History & Geography Leader, Infants*)

Mr A Chappell, BA QTS (*Head of Boys' Games*)

Mrs P Crysell, MMus, PG Dip

Mrs L Dean, BA, PGCE (*English Leader, Juniors; Year 6 Leader*)

Mr C Ellis, BSc, QTS (*Resources Leader*)

Mrs A Evans, BPE, MEd (*Director of Sport & Physical Education*)

Mr G Evans, BA, PGCE (*Director of Drama*)

Mrs R Evans, BA, QTS, (*Senior Teacher, Head of Lower Juniors; House Leader*)

Mrs V Francis, BA, QTS (*Year 1 Leader*)

Mr O Griffin, BSc, PGCE (*PSHE Leader, Juniors*)

Mrs J E Ingamells, ARCM (*Head of Strings*)

Miss D H Jennings, BA, MA, ALCM, LTCL, Mus Ed, Dip Class St Open, PGCE (*History Leader, Juniors; Junior School Archivist, UJS Librarian*)

Mr M Le-Clercq (*PE & Games*)

Miss J McFadzean, BA, QTS (*PE & Games*)

Mrs K Martin, BA, GTP (*Digital Learning Leader*)

Mrs J L Millward, BEd (*Senior Teacher, Head of Infants; English Leader, Infants*)

Mrs F Nash, BEd (*Assistant Director of Music*)

Mrs J Neilson, BA, MA, PGCE (*Year 3 Leader, Able, Gifted & Talented Leader*)

Mrs K Park, BA, PGCE

Mrs J Pereira, BA, BSc, MA, PGCE

Mrs E Peskett, GGSM, PG Dip RNCM (*Violin*)

Mrs A Porter, BEd, Cert SpLD (*Learning Support*)

Mrs S Powlesland, BA, PGCE (*French Leader, Juniors*)

Mrs M Price, BEd

Mrs A Reader, BA, QTS (*Year 5 Leader, Maths Leader & SMSCD Leader, Juniors*)

Mr J R Sadler, BSc (*Games*)

Mrs C S Sayers, BEd (*PE & Games*)

Mrs E G Sharrock, BMus Perf, LRAM (*Cello, String Scheme*)

Mrs V Shoebridge, BA, PGCE (*Science Leader, Infants*)

Mrs M Smith, BSc, Cert Ed (*Science Leader, Juniors*)

Mrs T Squire, BA, PGCE, SpLD (*Learning Support Coordinator*)

Mrs G Stainton, BSc, PGCE

Mrs L Summerskill, BEd (*Mathematics*)

Mrs B E Tilling, BSc, PGCE (*Art & Design Technology Leader, Juniors; Display Leader, Juniors*)

Mrs N R Townsend, BA, QTS Dance and Education (*Dance Leader, Juniors; Charities Leader; Year 4 Leader*)

Mrs S P Tyacke, BEd (*Art Leader, Infants; Display Leader, Infants*)

Miss P Watkins, BA, QTS (*Year 2 Leader; Maths Leader, Infants*)

Mr I Webber, BA Ed (*Director of Music*)

Mrs S Webb, BA, PGCE (*Design Technology & Food & Nutrition Leader, Infants*)

Mrs L Younger, BSc, PGCE (*Design Technology & Science*)

Assistants in The Junior School

Mrs A Atkinson	Mrs S Jennings
Miss K Bradley	Mrs M Millerchip
Mrs S Buckett	Mrs K Moffitt
Mrs C-A Elsley	Mrs J Northey
Miss H Green	Mrs C O'Leary
Mrs K Hinks	Mrs D Pascoe
Mrs B Holloway	Mrs C Shahran
Mrs M Hopkinson	Mrs L Staley
Mrs N Hutton	Mrs C White
Mrs C Iliffe	

Princethorpe College

Princethorpe, Rugby, Warwickshire CV23 9PX

Tel:	01926 634200
Fax:	01926 633365

email: post@princethorpe.co.uk
website: www.princethorpe.co.uk
Twitter: @PrincethorpeCol
Facebook: /princethorpecollege

The school, which has a Catholic foundation, was founded as a boys' school in 1957 in Leamington Spa by the congregation of the Missionaries of the Sacred Heart (MSC), moving to its present site, a former Benedictine monastery, in 1966. The College became co-educational in 1996, and in September 2001 formed a partnership with Crackley Hall School in Kenilworth in order to provide continuous education from 2 to 18 years. A further merger took place in September 2016 with The Crescent School, Rugby. All schools are members of an independent trust – The Princethorpe Foundation.

Number in School. The school has about 880 day pupils from 11 to 18 years with 210 in the Sixth Form. An extensive network of private coaches transports pupils from a wide area.

Aims. The College provides a caring, Christian environment for children where their needs can be met and their talents, confidence and self-esteem developed. There is a healthy balance between freedom and structure and an emphasis on self-discipline through responsibility and trust, which develops confidence and independence.

The College draws on a rich tradition of Catholic teaching and the spirituality of the Missionaries of the Sacred Heart, whose ethos is central to its character and disciplinary system. In welcoming families of a variety of faiths, the school community is a living example of ecumenism. The College motto, *Christus Regnet* – let Christ reign – is a reminder of Christ's love, service, forgiveness and generosity of spirit.

Academic. A broad-based, stimulating curriculum satisfies a wide range of ability and fosters a love of learning. A favourable pupil-teacher ratio, permitting personal attention, contributes to impressive value-added achievements. High fliers are stretched and provided with intellectually challenging assignments through our da Vinci Programme, ensuring that they achieve at the highest possible levels. The curriculum is well supported by a magnificent library and ICT. Qualified specialists give tuition to dyslexic pupils.

Pupils in Years 7 to 9 have a broad-based curriculum which avoids early specialisation and usually go on to take nine or ten GCSEs.

Supervised homework and free extended day are offered until 6.00 pm.

The Sixth Form. Students in the Sixth Form are prepared for AS Level and A2 Level examinations after which the vast majority proceed to university. The Head of Sixth Form and the team of tutors monitor the academic progress of Sixth Formers through regular discussions with the students and their teachers. Visits to university Open Days, together with professional careers advice enables students to make the best choices about their next stage of education.

There is a strong emphasis on the acquisition of key skills and the education of the whole person. Sixth Formers are offered residential outward bound courses, training programmes and retreats which provide an opportunity for reflection and exploration, to develop a mature and balanced perspective. Guest lecturers, debates and theatre outings all enhance Sixth Form life.

All Sixth Formers enjoy privileges and have the responsibilities of leadership and example; certain members are elected to perform prefectorial duties. Prefects attend a leadership course and learn valuable management skills. They organise activities for younger pupils and chair the School Council, which offers a forum for lively discussion and gives the students an influential voice in the running of the College. The House Captains have a pivotal role in the organisation of inter-house events.

Princethorpe Diploma. Open to all Sixth Form students the innovative Princethorpe Diploma brings together six components (work experience, community and ethos, service to others, extra-curricular, academic studies and attendance and punctuality) that we believe are critical in today's world, helping our students leave us as mature, confident, resilient, well-rounded young adults, with a strong set of moral values to guide them through adult life

Careers. The Careers Advice Programme commences in Year 9 and regular tutorials are held concentrating on option subject choices and developing careers awareness. Interview technique is developed and students are assisted with work experience placements which are undertaken at the end of Year 10 and Lower Sixth. The College also holds a biennial Careers Fair for pupils in Year 10 to Sixth Form and their parents.

Art & Design. A feature which immediately strikes all visitors to the College is the outstanding display of canvases. Superb examination results and successes in national competitions are commonplace. The study of drawing, painting, graphics and ceramics are central and they are enhanced by using the work of great artists as stimulus material.

Technology includes Food, Graphics, Resistant Materials, Information and Communications Technology, Textiles and Electronics. Pupils can work with a variety of materials, realising their technical designs in the well-resourced workshops, which includes CAD/CAM facilities.

Music and Drama. Music is studied by all pupils in their first three years and as an option at GCSE and A Level. The College choir gives regular performances and tours extensively overseas. Many pupils learn instruments and are encouraged to join the orchestra. Peripatetic staff offer tuition in most instruments. There is a state-of-the-art studio with digital recording facilities for Music Technology and there is an acclaimed Binns organ in the magnificent Chapel built by Peter Paul Pugin.

The College has a well-equipped theatre and regular productions are staged including pantomimes and revues. Productions involve a large number of pupils and staff and provide an excellent way for pupils of different years to get to know each other. There are thriving Dance and Drama Clubs. Theatre Studies is offered in the Sixth Form.

Physical Education. All pupils participate in games and Physical Education classes. Physical Education can also be studied as an examination subject at GCSE and A Level along with the new BTEC Physical Education option introduced in 2015. The major sports are rugby, netball, hockey, cricket, rounders, tennis and athletics; they are run in tandem with badminton, soccer, squash, basketball and trampolining.

The Sports Centre has a sports hall, fitness gym and a climbing wall; a floodlit all-weather surface was laid in 2003. Extensive outdoor facilities include an internationally recognised cross-country course, tennis courts and over sixty acres of games pitches.

Extra-Curricular Activities. There is always a wide range of clubs, societies and activities such as art, board games, chemistry clinic, choir, computing, cookery, debating, drama, history, jazz band, mathematics workshop, meditation, music workshop, orchestra, photography, Spanish, technology and textiles. The Duke of Edinburgh's Award scheme, World Challenge, Camps International and Outward Bound courses are also offered. The Arts Society provides a cultural programme of lectures, poetry evenings, music recitals and play readings.

Admissions. Admission is by examination, usually towards the end of January, generally at 11 and 13 and at other ages as space allows. Students from other schools join the Sixth Form after their GCSE courses.

Scholarships. There is a variety of Scholarships available for particularly able or talented candidates ranging from Academic, Art and Music to All-Rounder. Additionally, for the Sixth Form there are Academic, Organ and Sports Scholarships available. Scholarships to a maximum reduction of 50% of tuition fees are on offer.

Academic Scholarships: Candidates applying for entry in Years 7, 8, 9 and 10 will be considered automatically for an academic scholarship when taking the Entrance Examination. Pupils to be considered for major Academic Scholarships of between 25% to 50% will be invited for interview by the Headmaster following the Entrance Examination.

All Rounder Scholarships: Sometimes there are students who are both academically able and gifted in a variety of areas and the most outstanding of these can be awarded an All Rounder Scholarship. Supportive evidence is required, such as references from team coaches or activity leaders.

Art Scholarships: Candidates must submit a portfolio and attend an Art Scholarship day, usually in early January. Further details and an Art Scholarship application form are available from the Registrar.

Music Scholarships – Instrumental and Choral: Candidates must attend an audition. The timing of auditions is usually staggered over a week in early January. Further details and a Music Scholarship application form are available from the Registrar.

Sixth Form Academic Scholarships: Sixth Form Academic Scholarships are open to all external candidates who are expected achieve A and A* grades at GCSE. The candidates will sit a Verbal Reasoning examination and will have an interview with the Headmaster. They will also be expected to submit a personal portfolio of achievements to support the application.

Sixth Form Sport Scholarships: Senior Sport Scholarships may be awarded to internal or external candidates entering the Sixth Form. Full details are available from the Registrar.

Sixth Form Organ Scholarship: A Sixth Form Organ Scholarship of up to 50% of tuition fees is available to candidates who have a high level of ability and are committed and enthusiastic performers. Full details are available from the Registrar.

Fees per term (2016–2017). £3,903 excluding transport and meals. Instrumental tuition, external examinations and some targeted support for those with learning needs are charged as extras.

Charitable status. The Princethorpe Foundation is a Registered Charity, number 1087124. It exists solely for the education of children.

Governing Body:
Chair of Trustees Mrs Mary O'Farrell, BEd, QTS, CTC
Trustees Sister Mary Jude Bogie, SP, BEd
Quintin Cornforth, BSc
Mrs Elizabeth Griffin, BSc, PGCE, CTC
David Jackson, MInst AM, HNC Business Studies
Mrs Sarah Kershaw
Mrs Cecilia Lane
Mrs Pat Lines, Cert Ed
Mrs Catherine MacDonald, BA, PGCE, PQH NI, MEd
Ms Teresa McNamara, BPhil, Cert Ed
Jean-Pierre Parsons, BA, MA, MSc
Eur Ing Peter Rush, BSc, CEng, FIMechE, MBA
Colin Russell, IEng, ACIBSE, MBA
Commodore Bernard Warner

Staff:

Headmaster: Ed Hester, MA Oxon, PGCE (*Mathematics*)

Deputy Head – Pastoral: Mrs Beth Sharpe, BSc, PGCE (*Design and Technology*)
Deputy Head – Staffing and Assessment: Dr Digby Carrington-Howell, BSc, MA Ed, EdD, PGCE, NPQH (*Biology*)

Assistant Head – Co-curricular: Greg Hunter, BEng, Grad Dip Ed (*Physics*)
Assistant Head – Development: Alex Darkes, BEd
Assistant Head – Director of Studies: Mrs Sarah McKeever, BEng, PG Cert, QTS (*Mathematics*)
Assistant Head – Marketing, Admissions and Communications and Old Princethorpians Secretary: Mrs Melanie Butler, BA
Head of Sixth Form: Dr Michael Reddish, LLB, LLM, PhD, PGCHE (*Law*)
Foundation Bursar, Company Secretary and Clerk to the Trustees: Eddie Tolcher, BA, ACIB, MCMI, TechIOSH

Art:
Paul Hubball, BA, PGCE (*Head of Art; also Head of Photography*)
Mrs Rebecca Blunsom-Washbrook, BA, GTP (*also Photography*)
Ms Catherine Gregg, BA, PGCE (*also Design and Technology*)
Mrs Susan Harris, BA, PGCE (*Head of Transition and Induction*)

Careers:
Mrs Margaret Robinson, BEd (*Head of Careers; also Joint Head of Sixth Form; also CoRE Programme*)
Mrs Kerry Low, BA, Dip CG (*Careers Adviser*)
Dr Michael Reddish, LLB, LLM, PhD, PGCHE (*Joint Head of Sixth Form; also Oxbridge Coordinator*)
Mike Taylor, BA, PGCE (*Head of Geography; Work Experience; also Games*)

Classics:
Mrs Rachel Taylor, BA, QTS (*Joint Head of Classics*)
Dr Melinda Palmer, MA, DPhil Oxon, QTS (*Joint Head of Classics*)

CoRE Programme:
Mrs Anne Allen, BSc, PGCE (*Assistant Head of Sixth Form; also Geography*) [Maternity Leave]
Adam Depledge, BSc (*Head of Information and Communications Technology and Computing*)
Mrs Louise Harrison, BSc, PGCE (*Acting Assistant head of Sixth Form; Head of Academic PE*)
Roderick Isaacs, MA Cantab, MA, CertEd (*Assistant Head of Sixth Form; also Religious Studies*)
Kieran McCullough, BA, PGCE (*Director of Ethos; also Religious Studies and Games*)
Matthew Newsome, BA (*also Economics and Business*)
Mrs Helen Pascoe-Williams, BA, PGCE (*Coordinator of Provision for the Most Able; also English*)
Dr Simon Peaple, BA, PhD, CGTC (*Head of History and Politics*)
Dr Michael Reddish, LLB, LLM, PhD, PGCHE (*Joint Head of Sixth Form; also Oxbridge Coordinator*)
Mrs Margaret Robinson, BEd (*Head of Careers; also Joint Head of Sixth Form*)

Design and Technology:
Paul Scopes, BEd, AST (*Head of Design and Technology*)
Ms Angie Ash, BA, PGCE
Ms Catherine Gregg, BA, PGCE (*Also Art*)
Matt Parsons, BA, PGCE (*House Activities Leader for Fisher; TA Coordinator; also Games*)
Mrs Sarah Sellars, BA, QTS
Mrs Beth Sharpe, BEd, PGCE (*Deputy Head – Pastoral*)

Drama and Theatre Studies:
Ms Aileen Cefaliello, BA, PGCE (*Joint Head of Drama and Theatre Studies; also English*)
Ms Michelle Baker, BA Oxon, PGCE (*also English*)
Mrs Jessica Newborough, BA, PGCE (*also English*)
Mrs Helen Pascoe-Williams, BA, PGCE (*Coordinator of Provision for the Most Able; also English*)

Miss Vicky Roberts, BA, PGCE (*Joint Head of Drama and Theatre Studies*)

Visiting (Drama) LAMDA Staff:
Mrs Katherine Buckingham, LAMDA
Mrs Chris Carpenter, LAMDA
Mrs Mary McDonald, LAMDA

Economics and Business:
Mrs Elizabeth Gane, BA, PGCE (*Head of Economics and Business*)
Matthew Newsome, BA (*also CoRE Programme*)
Kenny Owen, BSc (*Head of Austin House; also Games*)

English:
Chris Kerrigan, BA, MA, PGCE (*Head of English*)
Ms Michelle Baker, BA Oxon, PGCE (*Joint Second in Department; also Drama*)
Mrs Lisa Challinor, BA, PGCE (*Head of Benet House*)
Ms Emma Litterick, BA, PGCE, TESOL (*Staff Development Coordinator; also Foundation Cross Phase Coordinator*)
Miss Rachael Mack, BA (*also Hockey Coach*)
Mrs Fiona Moon, BA, PG Cert Dyslexia and Literacy (*also Special Educational Needs*)
Mrs Jessica Newborough, BA, PGCE (*Joint Second in Department; also Drama*)
Mrs Helen Pascoe-Williams, BA, PGCE (*Coordinator of Provision for the Most Able; also CoRE Programme*)
Jonathan Washington, MA

Geography:
Mike Taylor, BA, PGCE (*Head of Geography; also Careers – Work Experience and Games*)
Mrs Anne Allen, BSc, PGCE (*Assistant Head of Sixth Form; also CoRE Programme*) [Maternity Leave]
Mrs Helen Baker, BA [Maternity Cover]
Stewart Dear, BSc, QTS (*also Games*)
Mrs Sarah Evans, BSc, PGCE
Mrs Chris McCullough, BA, QTS (*Head of Fisher House; also Academic PE and Special Educational Needs*)

History and Politics:
Dr Simon Peaple, BA, PhD, CGTC (*Head of History and Politics; also CoRE Programme*)
Peter Bucknall, BA, MA (*KS4 History Teaching and Learning Coordinator; also Head of Rugby*)
Mrs Felicity Coulson, GMus, PGCE (*Peripatetic and Exam Coordinator for Music; History*)
Miss Katharine Darwood, BSc (*House Activities Leader for More; History and Politics; also Games*)
Ms Stephanie Hawkins, BA, MA, PGCE (*KS3 History Teaching and Learning Coordinator*)
Mrs Tracey Hester, BA Oxon, PGCE (*History*)

Information and Communications Technology (ICT) and Computing:
Adam Depledge, BSc (*Head of Information and Communications Technology and Computing*)
Benjamin Packwood, BSc, PGCE

Law:
Dr Michael Reddish, LLB, LLM, PhD, PGCHE (*Joint Head of Sixth Form; also Oxbridge Coordinator*)

Mathematics:
Mrs Karen Bannister, BSc, PGCE (*Head of Mathematics*)
Mrs Clare Callaghan, BSc, PGCE (*also Special Educational Needs*)
Mrs Tanya Cowan, BSc, PGCE
Ed Hester, MA Oxon, PGCE (*Headmaster*)
Mrs Christina Howe, BSc
Ms Helen Lewis, BA
Mrs Sharon McBride, BSc, PGCE (*Second in Department*)

Mrs Sarah McKeever, BEng, PG Cert, QTS (*Assistant Head – Director of Studies*)
Ms Davinya Munford, BSc, PGCE [Maternity Cover]
William Uglow, BSc, MA, DipABRSM (*KS3 Mathematics Coordinator*)
Mrs Fenola Whittle, BEd

Modern Languages:
Mrs Stella Keenan, MA, PGCE (*Head of Modern Languages; Spanish Subject Leader and French*)
Ms Katherine Boothroyd, BA, MA, PGCE (*House Activities Leader for Benet; Spanish and French*)
Mrs Lourdes Camargo-Mantas (*Spanish Assistant*)
Mrs Finola Coy, BA, City and Guilds Teacher Cert (*German*)
Mrs Suzanne Ellis, BA, PGCE, Cert TESOL (*French Subject Leader; also Second in Department; German*)
Miss Bérénice Galano, Licence LLCE Anglais (*French*)
Ms Kristina Grosser, BA, MA (*German Subject Leader*)
Miss Abi Raffan, BA (*French and Spanish*)
Miss Charlotte Verleure (*French Assistant*)

Music:
Gil Cowlishaw, BMus (*Director of Music*)
Peter Marshall, BA, Cert Ed [Maternity Cover]
Mrs Alison Wakeley, BMus, MMus, PGCE [Maternity Leave]
Visiting Music Staff:
Mrs Felicity Coulson, GMus PGCE (*Peripatetic and Exam Coordinator for Music; also History; Flute, Oboe, Clarinet and Saxophone*)
Tom Durham, BMus (*Guitar*)
Miss Jodie Fisher, ATCL Brass (*also PE and Games*)
Andrew Hughes, ABSM (*Violin and Viola*)
Mrs Joanna Kunda-Jedynak, MA (*Vocal Studies*)
Adrian Moore, BA, ARCO (*Organ and Piano*)
Ms Clare Preston, BMus Flute
Matthew Prior, BMus (*Classical and Electric Guitar*)
Mrs Abigail Rhodes, MA Oxon, LLCM, FLCM, ADPA (*Vocal Studies*)
Miss Tori Rushton Cello and Bass
Mrs Susan Shepherd, MA, ARCM, ARCO, LRAM, CertEd (*Piano, Harpsichord and Keyboard*)
Alan Wickett (*Drum Kit and Percussion*)
Mrs Bev Wickham (*Steel Pans*)

Photography:
Paul Hubball, BA, PGCE (*Head of Photography; also Head of Art*)
Mrs Rebecca Blunsom-Washbrook, BA, GTP (*also Art*)

Physical Education and Games:
Neil McCollin, BA, QTS (*Foundation Director of Sport; also Coordinator of Elite Sports Programme*)
Will Bower, BSc, PG Dip with QTS (*Head of Outdoor Education*)
Mrs Deborah Brookes, BA, QTS (*Head of Girls' Games*)
Miss Holly Brookes (*Trampoline Coach*)
Peter Bucknall, BA, MA (*Head of Rugby; also KS4 History Teaching and Learning Coordinator*)
Ms Hannah Carminati, BSc
Ms Suzanne Cox, MSc (*Trampoline coach*)
Miss Katharine Darwood, BSc (*also History and Politics*)
Stewart Dear, BSc, QTS (*also Geography*)
Adam Depledge, BSc (*Head of Information and Communications Technology and Computing*)
Colin Dexter, MAAT (*Hockey Coach*)
Philip Duckworth, BA, MA, PGCE (*also Physics*)
Marc Edwards, BSc (*Head of Hockey; House Activities Leader for Austin*)
Miss Jodie Fisher, ATCL (*Sports Coach; also Peripatetic Music – Brass*)
Stuart Friswell (*Rugby Coach*)

Mrs Elizabeth Gane, BA, PGCE (*Head of Economics and Business*)

Mrs Louise Harrison, BSc, PGCE (*Acting Assistant Head of Sixth Form; Head of Academic PE*)

Ms Stephanie Hawkins, BA, MA, PGCE (*KS3 History Teaching and Learning Coordinator*)

Roderick Isaacs, MA Cantab, MA, CertEd (*Assistant Head of Sixth Form; also CoRE Programme*)

Ms Rachael Mack, BA (*Hockey Coach*)

Ms Danette Matthews (*Netball Coach*)

Mrs Chris McCullough, BA, QTS (*Head of Fisher; also Geography and Special Educational Needs*)

Kieran McCullough, BA, PGCE (*Director of Ethos; also CoRE Programme and Religious Studies*)

Kenny Owen, BSc (*Head of Austin House; also Economics and Business*)

Benjamin Packwood, BSc, PGCE (*also ICT and Computing*)

Matt Parsons, BA (*House Activities Leader for Fisher; also Design and Technology*)

Adrian Pilgrim (*Table Tennis Coach*)

Simon Robertson, BSc, PGCE (*Head of More House; also Biology*)

Rob Sothern, BSc, PGCE (*also Physics*)

Mike Taylor, BA, PGCE (*Head of Geography; also Careers – Work Experience*)

Mike Turns, BSc, PGCE

Cyprian Vella, BA, MA, PGCE (*Primary School Liaison Teacher; also Religious Studies*)

Paul Whitehead (*Hockey Coach*)

Psychology and Sociology:
Adam Rickart, BSc, PGCE (*Head of Psychology and Sociology; also CoRE Programme*)

Ms Jo Powell, BA PGCE

Mrs Fionnuala Schofield, BSc

Mrs Clare White, BSc, PGCE

Religious Studies:
Ian Lane, BA, PGCE (*Head of Religious Studies*)

Roderick Isaacs, MA Cantab, MA, CertEd (*Assistant Head of Sixth Form; also CoRE Programme*)

Kieran McCullough, BA, PGCE; (*Director of Ethos; also Games*)

Mrs Eleanor Russell, BA, PGDipEd

Cyprian Vella, BA, MA, PGCE (*Primary School Liaison Teacher; also Games*)

Special Educational Needs Department:
Ms Lorna Prestage, BSc, PGCE (*Special Educational Needs Coordinator*)

Ms Kat Brittain (*Learning Support Assistant*)

Mrs Clare Callaghan, BSc, PGCE (*SEN Mathematics Support; also Mathematics*)

Mrs Caroline Hardware (*Learning Support Assistant*)

Mrs Holly Hinks, BSc (*Learning Support Teacher*)

Mrs Anna Jelec, Med (*Learning Support Teacher*)

Mrs Amanda Kelly (*Learning Support Assistant*)

Mrs Chris McCullough, BA, QTS (*Head of Fisher; also Academic PE and Geography*)

Mrs Fiona Moon, BA, PG Cert Dyslexia and Literacy (*also English*)

Mrs Lee O'Gorman (*SEN Teaching Assistant*)

Mrs Judi Smith, PGCE SEN, Dip SpLD Dyslexia

The Sciences:
Mrs Gill Smith, BSc, PGCE (*Head of Science; Head of Chemistry*)

Dr Digby Carrington-Howell, BSc, MA Ed, EdD, PGCE, NPQH (*Deputy Head – Staffing and Assessment; Biology*)

Ben Collie, BSc (*Chemistry and Biology*)

Phil Duckworth, BA, MA, PGCE (*Physics; also Games*)

Greg Hunter, BE, Grad Dip Ed (*Assistant Head – Co-curricular; Physics*)

Dr Stuart Rimmington, MChem, PhD, PGCE (*Chemistry*)

Miss Faye Roberts, BSc, MSc, PGCE (*Head of Biology; House Activities Coordinator*)

Simon Robertson, BSc, PGCE (*Head of More House; Biology; also Games*)

Mrs Sophie Rose, BSc, PGCE (*Head of Physics*)

Mrs Joanne Smith, MChem, PGCE (*Chemistry*)

Rob Southern, BSc, PGCE (*Physics*)

Mrs Catherine Warne, BSc, PGCE (*Biology*)

Dan White, BSc, PGCE (*Chemistry*)

Non Teaching Staff:
Amraize Ajaib (*IT Intern*)

Mrs Keren Andrews, BA (*Recruitment Coordinator*)

Dr Nick Baker, BA, MA, PhD, PGDipHerInt, DipEurHum, FRSA, MAHI (*Archivist*)

Will Bayley, MEng, PhD (*Senior Science Technician*) [Paternity Leave]

Mrs Mary Benham, BA, CertEd (*Chaplaincy Coordinator*)

Mrs Katie Boon, BSc (*Administrator/Receptionist*)

Miss Hattie Brember, BA, MA (*Marketing and Communication Coordinator*)

Miss Liz Brown, MAAT (*Management Accountant*)

Miss Nicola Browne (*Shop Manager*)

Mrs Cynthia Carpenter (*Estates*)

Mrs Jennifer Cook, BA (*Administrator/Receptionist; job share*)

Ms Alison Cox, BEd (*Laboratory Technician*)

Mrs Loretta Curtis (*Development Assistant*)

Mrs Helen Cutter (*Assistant Matron*)

Mrs Shellagh Dodds (*Examinations Officer*)

Mrs Kathryn Else, BA (*Pastoral Secretary; job share*)

Mrs Claire Fletcher, BA (*Finance Manager*)

Dean George, BSc (*IT Engineer*)

Ben Gregory (*IT Engineer*)

Mrs Paula Greig, SRN (*Senior Matron*)

Andy Hadley (*Estates*)

Mrs Rachel Hadley-Leonard, BEd (*Foundation Development Director*)

Mrs Ruth Hedderwick, BA (*Pastoral Secretary; job share*)

James Hester (*Estates*)

Mrs Charlotte Hetherington, BEng (*Design and Technology Technician; also teaches Textiles*)

Mrs Carmel Hopkins (*Headmaster's Personal Assistant and Office Manager*)

Tim Humpries-Tattam (*Teaching Assistant*)

Tom Knowles (*Estates*)

Ms Ruth Laband, MA, CPCAB (*Counsellor*)

Miss Barbara Lewandowski (*Finance Assistant*)

John Lewis (*Electrician*)

Gerry Lovely (*Estates*)

Mrs Kerry Low, BA, DipCG (*Careers Adviser*)

Mrs Gina Malin (*Finance Assistant*)

Mrs Valerie McFadden (*Reprographics and Sports Administration Assistant*)

Miss Mia Mead (*Teaching Assistant*)

Mrs Denise Morgan (*PA to Foundation Bursar*)

Miss Helen Morgan, BA (*Assistant Registrar*)

Mrs Angela Morris, Cert Ed (*Laboratory Technician*)

Miss Sophie Nicholls (*Teaching Assistant*)

Mrs Karen O'Connor (*Library Assistant*)

Aidan Oakley (*IT Intern*)

Mrs Elena Pope (*Purchase Ledger Clerk*)

Mrs Gill Price, BSc (*Special Projects Officer and Parent Portal*)

John Price (*Teaching Assistant*)

Tom Probert (*Grounds*)

Clive Randle (*Grounds*)

Steven Rawson (*Estates*)

Nathan Reynolds (*Grounds*)
Edd Robertson (*Foundation Grounds Manager*)
Mrs Vanessa Rooney (*Registrar*)
Mrs Julie Satchwell (*Student Support Officer*)
Mrs Celia Scott, BA, ALA (*Associate Librarian*)
Tom Secher (*Estates*)
Michael Small (*Foundation Estates Manager*)
Robert Thomas (*Teaching Assistant*)
Graham Thomson (*Estates*)
Dr Michael Tideswell, BSc, PhD, QTS (*Curriculum Coordinator*)
Mrs Heather Tocher, MBACP Dip (*Counsellor*)
Mrs Becky Underhill, BTech, ATT (*Sixth Form Administrator*)
Robert Van Spelde (*ICT Manager*)
John Vasquez (*Estates Supervisor*)
Mrs Judy Vick (*Estates*)
Charlie Warner (*Estates*)
Peter Wilkes, BA (*Assistant Estates Manager*)
Fr Alan Whelan, MSC, BA (*Chaplaincy*)
Paul Whitehead (*Estates*)
Miss Lauren Whitfield (*Marketing, Admissions and Communications Intern*)
Ms Claire Wong (*Laboratory Technician*)

Prior Park College

Ralph Allen Drive, Bath BA2 5AH

Tel: 01225 835353
email: info@priorparkschools.com
website: www.priorparkschools.com
Twitter: @priorpark
Facebook: /prior.park.37

Motto: '*Deo Duce, Deo Luce*'

Prior Park College is a fully co-educational Catholic Boarding and Day School. Founded in 1830 by Bishop Baines, it was under the control of the Bishops of Clifton until 1924, when it passed to the Congregation of Christian Brothers. Since 1981, Prior Park has been under lay management and has more than doubled in size. Prior Park is a friendly, thriving community of around 600 pupils, with a strong boarding community, excellent academic standards and a strong devotion to educating the whole person.

The College is housed in magnificent Palladian architecture, built by John Wood for Ralph Allen, with glorious views of the World Heritage City of Bath. The 57-acre site combines an elegant setting for boarding and day education with access to Bath and its numerous cultural attractions. Proximity to the M4 and M5 motorways places the College within easy reach of London, the Midlands, the South-West and Wales. Good rail links and proximity to Bristol, Heathrow and Gatwick international airports allow easy transfer for our international students.

Structure of the School. Prior Park is a friendly, thriving community of approximately 600 pupils. The annual three-form entry of day pupils aged 11–13 makes up our co-educational Baines Junior House. A further forty enter the school at 13, when we admit both boarders and day pupils. Each boy and girl between 13 and 18 is a member of a boarding or day single-sex Senior House. Year groups also meet regularly for assemblies. Weekly and full boarding is available.

Objects of the College. The College provides an outstanding education, within the framework of a caring, Catholic community which warmly welcomes members of other denominations. Our A Level and GCSE results are consistently excellent, with our EPQ (Extended Project Qualification) results among the best in the country. Our resident Chaplain serves the needs of the whole community and great importance is attached to the commitment of all staff to the ethos of the school. Pastoral care is perceived by the current parent body to be outstanding and great efforts are made to ensure that all pupils are nurtured and supported.

Buildings and Grounds. Ranked by the Oxford Royale Academy as the UK's most beautiful boarding school. The Houses, Administration and College Chapel are to be found in the fine 18th century architecture grouped around Ralph Allen's celebrated Palladian Mansion. A major programme of modernisation has enhanced the accommodation for residential staff and their families, and added to the attractive environment for the residential community. A major refurbishment programme of boys' and girls' boarding accommodation has provided comfortable study-bedrooms, quiet areas and recreational rooms. A rolling programme of refurbishment continues, including the opening of a new Art & Design Faculty in September 2014 and a new Sports Centre in February 2015.

Curriculum. The academic curriculum conforms to and goes beyond the requirements of the National Curriculum. Core subjects to GCSE are Mathematics, English, the Sciences, a Modern Language and Religious Studies. The curriculum in Year 7–9 is broad. Great care is taken to ensure that careful guidance is given to pupils in Year 9 and Year 11 when GCSE and AS/A2 choices are being made. The Academic Deputy, his assistant and the House staff work with pupils and their parents to tailor a programme which reflects the strength and interests of the individual. The majority of pupils will study ten in eleven GCSE subjects, four AS/A2 subjects in the Lower Sixth, and drop to three A2 in the Upper Sixth.

We currently offer twenty-three AS/A2 courses and there is considerable flexibility of combinations at both GCSE and A Level. The Extended Project Qualification (EPQ) is also offered in the Sixth Form. We are delighted to have added Psychology to the A Level curriculum due to popular demand.

Music. The College has a highly-deserved reputation for musical excellence. Two chapel choirs provide high quality music for the weekly sung Mass in the glorious surroundings of the Chapel of Our Lady of the Snows. The John Wood Chapel, within Prior Park Mansion, offers a further concert and rehearsal venue for the many musicians in the school.

The Music Department, also in the Mansion, houses a recording studio and teaching and practice rooms. Around half the pupils learn a musical instrument and there are several thriving orchestras, chamber groups and bands, as well as a large and ambitious Choral Society, annual competitions and festivals. Many Prior Park musicians have gone on to Oxbridge and a graduate from the class of 2014 was awarded the Trinity Choral Scholarship to Cambridge. Other graduates go to major conservatoires and play in NYO, NCO, etc.

Performing Arts. The students stage around twenty drama productions a year, Dance, Inter-House Music Competitions, Band Nights and charity events all feature prominently in the life of the school. The Julian Slade Theatre is a wonderful setting for this extensive and diverse performing arts programme. It has been extended to provide a Dance Studio and further teaching and technical support areas. There is also a full-time theatre technician.

Physical Education and Games. Physical Education is included in the curriculum. Games are an important part of school life. Main school games are Rugby, Hockey, Cricket and Tennis for boys; with Hockey, Netball and Tennis for girls. Provision is made for Swimming, Badminton, Cross-Country, Football, Volleyball, Basketball, Table Tennis, Fencing, Athletics and Rounders.

Activities Programme. The voluntary Combined Cadet Force includes Navy and Army Sections. Adventure training takes place both in the UK and overseas. Cadets are encouraged to participate in the Service and Contingent Camps and Courses.

The Duke of Edinburgh's Award scheme operates at Bronze and Gold Award level. Participants work on the four sections: volunteering, skills, physical, and expeditions; plus a residential project section at Gold Award level.

Boarders and day pupils alike participate in a wide range of activities after school. Public speaking and debating thrive. All full-time boarders in Years 9 to 12 take part in Saturday Active.

Careers. Our careers guidance programme combines the traditional strength of the House system with the benefits of a specialised central careers department. Every pupil receives individual guidance through the five years from Form 4 (Year 9) to Upper Sixth, with particular support at the three critical stages of choice for GCSE, A Level, and university entrance. At the same time, professional careers advice is available from the Head of Careers, who provides objective information and guidance via a programme of interviews, supported by psychometric testing and on line guidance tools.

Admission. Main points of admission are at 11+, 13+ and 16+ but pupils may transfer into the College at 12 and 14 if places are available. Early registrations are encouraged. Prospective families are encouraged to visit the College on Open Days or on an individual visit.

Entrance and scholarship examinations for 11+ and 13+ take place in January and February prior to entry in September. 16+ scholarship examinations and interviews take place in November. Please contact the Registrar, admissions@thepriorfoundation.com, for the relevant entrance/scholarship admission booklet.

Scholarships and Bursaries. Academic Scholarships are available at 11+, 13+ and 16+. Art, All-Rounder, Drama, Music and Sporting Excellence awards are available at 11+, 13+ and 16+. All awards carry with them a fee remission.

Bursaries are available, including HM Forces Bursaries of up to 20% of fees. The Bursar is pleased to discuss individual cases. Sibling discounts apply.

Fees per term (2016–2017). Boarding £9,815, International Boarding £10,170, Weekly Boarding £8,095; Day 13+ £5,305; Day 11+ £4,805.

Prior Park Preparatory School. The Preparatory School is situated at Cricklade, Wiltshire, 35 miles from Prior Park and within easy reach of Swindon train station, Cirencester and the M4. It has ample boarding and recreational facilities for 180 boys and girls aged 7–13+. In addition, the adjacent nursery and pre-prep offer a wonderful educational environment for day children up to the age of six. Extra-curricular activity is an important element and the school has excellent standards in Music, Drama and Sport.

Headmaster: Mr Mark Pearce, BA Hons, QTS

For further details, see entry in IAPS section.

The Paragon School, Bath – Junior School of Prior Park College. The Paragon School is part of Prior Park Educational Trust. Housed in an impressive Georgian mansion, the co-educational school for 3–11 years is set in beautiful wooded grounds, only a few minutes drive from Prior Park College. A broad and balanced curriculum is delivered within a happy, caring environment.

Headmaster: Mr Andrew Harvey, BA Hons

For further details, see entry in IAPS section.

Prior Park School, Gibraltar. Opened in September 2016, Prior Park School is the first Independent co-educational senior school in Gibraltar for children 12–18 years.

Headmaster: Mr Peter Watts, BSc, CPhys

For further details please visit the website www.prior-parkschools.com

Charitable status. Prior Park Educational Trust is a Registered Charity, number 281242.

Patrons:
His Eminence Cardinal C Murphy-O'Connor, STL, PhL
The Rt Revd D R Lang, BA, Bishop of Clifton
Miss J Bisgood, CBE
Mr C J B Davy, CB
Mr D R Hayes
Sister J Livesey, CJ, MA
Mr F J F Lyons, KSG
Sir Cameron Mackintosh
The Rt Hon the Lord Patten of Barnes, CH, PC
The Revd Monsignor Canon R J Twomey, VF
Commodore C B York, FCMI, Royal Navy

Governors:
Mr A M H King (*Chair of Governors*)
Mr A Bury, MBA, BSc Hons
Mr S Eliot, MA Cantab
Mrs N Freeman, BA Hons, MA, PGCE
Mr J Garcia, BA Hons, PGDL, BVC
Dr J Haworth, MBS, MSc
Mr J Jarvis, LLB Hons, BVC, Barrister at Law
Mrs A Lloyd, MA Ed, Cert Ed, LGSM
Fr W M McLoughlin, PhL, BD, MTh, OSM
Mr P S J O'Donoghue, MA, FCA
Mrs N Pearson, BA Hons, PGCE
Rear Admiral N J Raby, OBE, MSc
Mrs M Rae, MSc PH, Dip Ed, FFPH, FRIPH
Ms A Shepherd, MBE, BA Hons
Mr J Shinkwin, MA Oxon, PGCE
Mrs J Singleton, BA Hons, Dip TEFL
Mr P Vaughan Fowler, BA Hons
Mr J Webster, BA, BArch, MCD, RIBA, MRTPI

Headmaster: Mr James Murphy-O'Connor, MA Oxon

Business Director: Mr A McNiff, LLB FCA
Senior Deputy Head: Miss C Cummins, MA Oxon
Senior Master and Deputy Head Academic: Mr T J Simons, BSc, BA Hons
Director of Communications: Mrs J Kearney, BA, DipSp
Deputy Head Pupil Progress: Mrs S Forshaw, BSc Hons
Deputy Head Operations: Mrs L Blake, BA Hons
Deputy Head Pastoral: Mr S Cane-Hardy, BA

Heads of Departments:
Art: Ms S Seville, BA Hons, BA Fine Art
Biology: Dr R Trott, BSc, PhD Newcastle & Bristol
Chemistry: Mr K Chard, BSc Leeds
Classics: Mrs S Hearn, BA Oxon
Drama & Theatre Studies: Mr D Langley, BA Manchester
Design & Technology: Mr R Faulkner, BSc Nottingham
Economics and Business Studies: Mrs L Stotesbury, BA, MA
English: Dr K McGowran, BA, MA, PhD Hull
English as an Additional Language (*EAL*): Mr P Stroud, BA UCL, MSc Surrey
Geography: Mr S Burt, BSc Reading
History: Mr C Bartlett, BA
ICT: Mrs E Knechtli, MSc Bristol
Learning Development Programme (*LDP*): Mrs K Mason, BA Hons, MA
Library: Ms L Smith, BA, MA Lancaster
Mathematics: Mrs J Jones, BSc Belfast
Modern Languages: Mr J George, BA
Music: Mr R Robertson, MA Cantab, ARCO
Physical Education & Sports Science: Mr R Gwilliam, BA Hons Cardiff
Physics: Dr M French, MSci, PhD Bristol
Psychology: Mrs R Bird, MA, Dip Psych
Theology and Philosophy: Mr T Maxwell, BA London

Visiting Music Staff for Acoustic/Electric Guitar, Bass Guitar, Bassoon, Cello, Clarinet, Drums, Flute, Oboe, Piano, Saxophone, Trumpet, Violin, Viola, Voice.

Foundation Executive Personal Assistant: Ms D Miller
College Executive & Headmaster's PA: Miss K Finlayson
Registrar: Mrs V Quinn
Chaplain: Revd Father Anthony McNeill
Director of Development: Ms M Ball

Queen Anne's School

6 Henley Road, Caversham, Berkshire RG4 6DX

Tel:	0118 918 7300
Fax:	0118 918 7310
email:	office@qas.org.uk
website:	www.qas.org.uk
Twitter:	@QASCaversham
Facebook:	/Queen-Annes-School-Caversham

Queen Anne's is an independent boarding and day school for girls with over 445 pupils aged 11 to 18 years. High aspirations combined with a positive approach to learning creates an environment where girls can grow into motivated, decisive and self-assured individuals. We are renowned for academic success alongside a rich programme of extra-curricular opportunities and excellence in the arts, drama, music and sport.

We are a Church of England School and part of The Grey Coat Hospital Foundation, Westminster, London. Located in Caversham, Berkshire, the school is situated to the north of Reading near Henley-on-Thames and is just over 40 minutes from London. School transport is available throughout the local area; a coach service runs every Friday and Monday to London.

Here at Queen Anne's, understanding what is happening in the brain can help us to be more efficient learners and more effective people and as a result, live happy and fulfilled lives. Our BrainCanDo: Life and Learning Programme has helped us to understand that learning about the brain and mindset is critical to improving our learning and to making things happen.

In September 2016 we officially opened 'The Space', our new state-of-the-art Sixth Form Centre. The new centre is home to a common room/café (Café 6), a digital library featuring innovative learning pods, a new dining hall and a walled garden for relaxation. The upper floor contains themed breakout rooms, designed by the students themselves, and digitally enhanced seminar and teaching rooms to facilitate collaborative learning for our Sixth Form students.

The best way to find out about Queen Anne's is to talk to those at the heart of our community – our pupils! Our website www.qas.org.uk contains images, videos and narratives drawn from their experiences. We look forward to welcoming you to Queen Anne's!

Pastoral organisation. Queen Anne's has an excellent reputation for pastoral care. Girls can attend Queen Anne's daily or on a full, weekly, flexi or occasional boarding basis according to individual family needs. Each girl, whether day or boarding, belongs to a House and the House system is integral to our academic and pastoral care.

The staff believe that students perform best when they are happy and secure, and Queen Anne's has effective pastoral systems in place to ensure this. The support network includes Housemistresses and the House Pastoral Team, Academic Staff and Tutors, and Heads of Year.

Curriculum. All girls follow a broad and varied curriculum up to GCSE. Separate subject sciences are taught, as well as Dual Award; mathematics and music follow IGCSE;

Spanish, German or Mandarin may be taken from Year 9; Latin is studied from Year 7. Music, art and drama form part of the girls' timetable until the end of Year 9. Information technology is taught throughout the school. A wide range of A Level subjects is offered. A programme of personal, social and health education is followed by all girls.

Careers. All girls go on to Higher Education, many to top universities in the UK and overseas.

Extra-curricular activities. Queen Anne's is reputed for many of its achievements. It offers a full extra-curricular programme and excellent opportunities for sport, including tennis, lacrosse, 'rock' climbing and rowing on the nearby Thames. Music, drama and art are very strong. The Duke of Edinburgh's Award, WOHAA, public speaking and debating (National and International finalists), photography, dance, riding, socials and many more activities are available. A full programme of optional activities is available on Saturday mornings for pupils and parents.

Admission. Girls are admitted at 11+, 13+ and at Sixth Form by Queen Anne's Entrance Examination or by Common Entrance. Sixth Form places are offered on the basis of GCSE results. For further information please contact the Registrar.

Scholarships are offered for entry at 11+, 13+ and 16+ and are awarded for excellence in one or more fields of the life of the school. Awards may be made in respect of Academic Excellence, All-Round Contribution, Art, Drama, Music or Sport.

Fees per term (2016–2017). Full Boarding £10,870; Flexi Boarding £9,800–£10,330; Day pupils £7,375.

Charitable status. Queen Anne's School is part of The Grey Coat Hospital Foundation, which is a Registered Charity, number 312700.

Governing Body: The Grey Coat Hospital Foundation

Chairman: Vice-Admiral P Dunt, CB, DL
Vice-Chairman: Mr J M Noakes, MA
Mrs C Gray, BA
Ms A Kiem, MA, BMath, DipEd
Lady Laws, BLitt, MA
Ms K Parsons
Mr R F Penfold, MBE
Mr M Sharrock
Mr J Slater, ACA
Mr D Taylor, MA, FRSA
Ms S A Thewlis
Mrs L Troake, BA
Miss A Wiscarson, BSc

Clerk: Mr R W Blackwell, MA

Headmistress: Mrs Julia Harrington, BA Exeter, PGCE, NPQH, Dip Counselling

Deputy Head (Pastoral): Ms Maggie Chodak, BA Birmingham, PGCE
Deputy Head (Academic): Mr Mark Richards, BMus Wales, MMus King's College London, Research Fellowship Cardiff, FRSA
Head of Lower School: Mrs Linda McGrenary, BEd Strathclyde
Head of Middle School: Mr Daniel Boyes, BA MA Oxford, PGCE Cambridge, Dip Theology and Political Studies Oxford
Director of Sixth Form: Dr Dawn Bellamy, BA Leicester, MA, PhD Bristol
Director of Teaching and Learning: Mrs Gill Little, BSc St Andrews, PGCE Cantab

Heads of Departments:
Art and Design: Ms Sarah Beales, MA Norwich, PGCE London

Classics, Philosophy and Theology: Mr Daniel Boyes, BA MA Oxford, PGCE Cambridge, Dip Theology and Political Studies Oxford

Drama: Mr Rhodri Punter, BA Wales

Economics and Business Studies: Mr Ian Chapman, BSc Bristol

English: Mrs Eileen Green, BA MA PGCE Reading

EAL: Ms Lesley McNeil, MEd Exeter, TESOL

Geography: Mr Will Warwick, BSc Birmingham

History (Acting Head): Dr Juliet Ingram, PhD MA BA Warwick, PGCE (*Reading*)

Information Technology: Mr Thomas Lange, Dipl-Ing FH, BEng Germany

Mathematics: Ms Jenny Clubbe, BA London, PGCE Buckingham

Modern Languages: Mr Antoine Rogeon, Licence of English France, Masters France, QTS Reading

Principal Director of Music: Mr John Padley, BMus London, LTC, ACPID, FRSA

Psychology: Dr Amy Fancourt, BSc Durham, MSc London, PhD Goldsmiths London

Science: Mrs Sarah Eagle, BSc PGCE Southampton

Director of Sport: Mrs Nicola Burley, BA North Staffs, PGCE Exeter

Director of Marketing and Admissions: Mrs Sarah Holgate, BSc Surrey, Dip Marketing, MCIM

Queen Elizabeth's Hospital (QEH)

Berkeley Place, Clifton, Bristol BS8 1JX

Tel:	0117 930 3040
email:	headmaster@qehbristol.co.uk
	office@qehbristol.co.uk
website:	www.qehbristol.co.uk

Motto: '*Dum tempus habemus operemur bonum.*'

Patron: Her Majesty The Queen

By his Will dated 10 April 1586, John Carr, a Bristol merchant, founded Queen Elizabeth's Hospital, a bluecoat school in Bristol on the lines of Christ's Hospital which was already flourishing in London. The Charter was granted to the School by Queen Elizabeth I in 1590. Originally composed entirely of boarders, the School continued so until 1920 when foundation day boys were admitted. Direct Grant status was accorded in 1945. The School is now independent and day only and, as of September 2017, has a co-educational Sixth Form.

Admission. There are 588 boys in the Senior School, ranging in age from 11 to 18. Entrance examinations for both Year 7 and Year 9 applicants are held in January each year; Sixth Form and other Years by arrangement. From September 2017, girls are able to join the QEH Sixth Form.

Term of Entry. Usually September.

Entrance Scholarships. A significant number of scholarships are offered at Year 7, Year 9 and Sixth Form. These are awarded purely on academic merit for outstanding achievement in the entrance procedures and may also carry with them generous assistance for applicants whose parents' means are limited.

Music and Sports scholarships are available at Year 7 and Year 9.

Assisted Places. There are many School assisted places available. The School has a substantial foundation income and is able to give generous support to parents whose means are limited.

Buildings. The School was originally close by the City Centre but moved to new premises on Brandon Hill in 1847. A major building and improvement programme has included the building of the QEH Theatre (1990), refurbishment of the Art School (2000), new Mathematics rooms and heavy investment in ICT (2004). An 80-strong Junior School opened in 2007 (increasing to over 100 in 2012) along with a new Sixth Form Centre. In 2008 a multimillion pound development programme, in conjunction with Bristol City Football Club, saw new football pitches on 23 acres at the Sports Ground at Failand. A new £3 million Science and Art Building was opened in October 2016 and there are future development plans which include improvements to Music and Art facilities and other areas of the school. An expansion of the Sixth Form Centre is also under way, due to open in September 2017.

Curriculum. Students are prepared for the GCSE (IGCSE in Mathematics and English) and GCE A Level, and for university entrance. The usual school subjects are offered at GCSE level, and the AS/A2 Level subjects are: English Literature, English Language, Drama, Economics, Latin, Greek, History, Geography, French, German, Spanish, Art, Music, Mathematics, Further Mathematics, Music Technology, Physics, Chemistry, Biology, PE and Sport, Business Studies, ICT, Ethics and Philosophy, Politics and Psychology.

Music & Drama. There is a School Orchestra, Choir, Jazz Band, Brass Group, and Wind Band. Music is included in the timetable for all the junior forms. GCSE and A Level music is part of the School curriculum, and tuition is arranged for a wide range of instruments. The Choir and Instrumentalists perform regularly and also undertake joint ventures with other schools in Bristol. Drama flourishes and the school has its own high-tech purpose-built theatre which seats 220.

Art. The Department is well equipped and offers ceramics, screen printing, photography and computer imaging.

Religious Studies. The School is a Christian one which welcomes students of all faiths, or none. Religious Studies is part of the curriculum and students attend two services a year in Bristol Cathedral.

Games. Rugby, Football, Athletics, Cricket, Swimming, Tennis, Badminton, Sailing, Squash, Fencing, Judo, Climbing and Mountain Biking. A large number of students also participate in The Duke of Edinburgh's Award and Ten Tors.

Dress. Boys wear either grey trousers and a blazer or a plain dark suit. Sixth Form girls wear smart business dress. Traditional bluecoat uniform is worn by some for special occasions.

General. All parents are encouraged to join the Friends of Queen Elizabeth's Hospital, a society whose aim is to promote a close relationship between parents and staff and to further the welfare of the School. There is a flourishing Old Elizabethans' Society, which holds regular meetings and circulates a newsletter. A panel of former pupils, formed from all professions, and working with the Head of Careers, is available to give advice on careers to students.

The School has long been known in Bristol as 'The City School' and its links with the Lord Mayor and Corporation are strong. Students read the lessons and sing in the Lord Mayor's Chapel, and groups are in attendance for such occasions as Mayor-making and Council Prayers.

The central position of the School, close to the University, the Art Gallery and Museum, the Central Library, the Bristol Old Vic and the Colston Hall, affords ready access to a wide range of cultural facilities which students are encouraged to use.

Junior School. 100 Boys aged 7–11. (*For further details see QEH Junior School entry in IAPS section.*)

Fees per term (2016–2017). Senior School £4,553, Junior School £2,975. Fees include text and exercise books, and essential educational trips but do not include public examination fees or lunches (which are £3.55 per day).

Charitable status. Queen Elizabeth's Hospital is a Registered Charity, number 1104871, and a Company Limited by Guarantee, number 5164477. Queen Elizabeth's Hospital has existed since 1590 to provide a first class education.

Governing Body:
D A Smart, BSc, FCA (*Chairman*)
S Speirs, MA (*Vice-Chairman*)

Ms S Blanks, MSc
J Buchanan, LLB Hons, CTA
E Corrigan, BA, FCS, MAE
Mrs S Cosgrove, BSc
T Davis, BSc, MRICS
J Eyles, BEd, RSA

P N Gibson, MA, FCA
R J Hill, LLB Hons, TEP
P A Keen, SCIB
P J Kilmartin, BSc
C Russell-Smith, BSc, FRICS
Mrs J Scarrow, BA

Bursar: R N Cook, FCA

Headmaster: S W Holliday, MA

Deputy Head (Pastoral): J Sharrock, BA
Deputy Head (Academic): J Martin, MA
Assistant Head (Staff Development): C Brotherton, BA
Assistant Head (Operations): W R Ellis, BSc
Assistant Head (Sixth Form): Mr R Porter, MA
Head of Marketing and Communications: E A Down, BSSoc, LLB

S Albon, BSc
Mrs S K Allen, BSc
P M Amor, BA
T Appleby, BA
A A Berry, BSc
A Burns, BA
A E Calder, BA
A C Clements, BSc
Mrs E Conquest, BA
C B Conquest, BEd
P A Davies, BSc
Mrs M M Dimes, BSc
R Dixon, BSc
T J Dunn, BSc
M Dutton, BEd, MA, EdD
Miss N Dyer, BA
Miss L Fenner, BA
C Gamble, BSc
C Gardner, BA
E M Gent, BA
R J Harris, BA
S A Harris, BSc
T Harrison, BA
D T Hawkes, BSc
Mrs P Hockenhull, BA
S Hofkes, BMus, PG Dip
Miss N Holcombe, BA
G A R Huband, BSc
A R Hughes, BA
P M Jones, BA

Dr J Jönsson, MSc, PhD
P E Joslin, BEd
J Kelly, BSc
Mrs S J King, MA
P J Kirby, BA
H L Kyle, BSc, PhD
Ms S Maltin, BA
Miss L Mantle, BA, MA
R Martineau, MEng
J R Matthews, BEd
Mrs M McGowan, BA
C Miller, BSc
S Mitchell, BSc
P C Moore, BEd
Mrs S Moritz, BSc
S J Munnion, BA
A Pegg, BA
H Pike, BA
W G Plowden, BA
N Pursall, BA
C Ryan, BSc
Mrs L Shaw, BA
Mrs H Shields, BA
Mrs R Steven, BA
A W H Swithinbank, BA
Mrs R Thwaites, BA, MA
Z Verry, BA
Mrs F Waite-Taylor, BA
R J Waldron, BA

Junior School:
Headteacher: M J Morris, BA

Visiting Teachers:
J Bacon, MMus
P Barrett, BA, PG Dip
Mrs D Dickerson, Dip LCM, Dip ABRSM, Dip ESA
K Figes, LGSM, PG Dip
Mrs A Howell, BMus, FRCO, LGSM, BA
Miss C Lindley, BA
C McCann, Dip Mus MoD
B Mullan, BMus
G Robinson, BMus

T Shevlin, BMus, PG Dip
N Shipman, BMus, LGSMD
A Stewart, BMus
Miss L Tanner, BMus, MMus, PG Dip
J Whitfield, BMus

Chaplain: The Revd S B Taylor, BA
Headmaster's Secretary: Mrs E Davies
Admissions Registrar: Mrs C Matthews
Librarian: Mrs A Robbins

Queen's College
Taunton

Trull Road, Taunton, Somerset TA1 4QS
Tel: 01823 340830 Admissions
email: admissions@queenscollege.org.uk
website: www.queenscollege.org.uk
Twitter: @QueensTaunton
Facebook: @queenstaunton

Motto: '*Non scholae sed vitae discimus*' (*We learn not for school but for life*)

Introduction. Queen's College is one of the South West's leading independent day and boarding co-educational schools.

Queen's has a well-deserved reputation for the quality of its teaching and all pupils are cared for in small tutor groups. Pastoral care is outstanding. The staff work tirelessly to encourage students to develop their personal skills and abilities. Class sizes are small and the atmosphere is friendly and supportive – students are happy and motivated here.

The boarding community is strong with excellent houseparents, full activities programme and lots of support. Communication and relationships with parents are valued and all are included in the wider Queen's family.

Queen's is very strong in sport, in particular hockey, rugby, athletics and swimming. It also has an outstanding reputation for the visual and performing arts and the School currently has some outstanding musicians in the National Youth Orchestra.

Queen's operates a strong co-curricular programme including a wide variety of performing arts, sports, arts and outdoor pursuits and considerable emphasis is placed on participation in The Duke of Edinburgh's Award scheme. All students take Bronze, many go on to Silver and to date, over 300 Sixth Form students have achieved their Gold Awards. Queen's hosts its own Model United Nations conference and is a centre of excellence in the South West.

Number of Pupils. The Queen's College Nursery, Pre-Prep, Junior and Senior Schools are based on the same site with some facilities shared: continuity of education is assured. The Senior School (11 to 18 years) has 540 pupils of whom 200 are boarders. The Junior School and Pre-Prep (4 to 11 years) has 175 pupils, with a junior boarding house. The full College complement is an excellent size of 715 meaning that there are enough pupils for good friendship groups, team sports and school plays but it is still personal enough so that the Head Teacher knows every pupil. A happy, friendly, family school which doesn't stand on ceremony.

Situation and Buildings. Queen's College was founded in 1843 within Taunton's Castle walls but was relocated to the south western outskirts of Taunton three years later when the present main school buildings were constructed. It is in an excellent situation with fine views of the Quantock and Blackdown Hills, within easy reach of Exmoor and Dartmoor, just a short distance from Taunton town centre, easily accessible by road or rail, junction 25 of M5 is 2 miles away and serviced by Heathrow, Bristol International and Exeter Airports.

The 1846 original Grade II* listed building contained a School House, the School Hall and a Dining Room. Later a Junior School was added, an indoor heated Swimming Pool and a Music Department. Over the past 20 years there has been an extensive building programme which has included: nine classrooms for the Junior school, applied science, technology centre, new changing rooms, day girl and day boy accommodation, enlargement and modernisation of girl and boy boarding houses, school hall for the Junior school, new music school, concert/assembly hall for the Senior school, and a sixth form centre. Latest additions are a new Art & Drama building; Leisure and Performing Arts Centres; a new Science Block and major expansion of Pre-Prep facilities. Recently, a state-of-the-art Sixth Form Centre has provided an excellent interim between school and university, equipped with multimedia, social spaces, collaborative and quiet study areas. Other additions have included a new Medical Centre, new Languages Centre and new boarding wing with top-quality boarding accommodation. Definitely a school on the up which is modern in its outlook and does not rest on its laurels.

Organisation. There are two day boy houses and two day girl houses and each has a House Parent and set of Tutors for each year group. The boarding set-up is superb with some really committed House Parents who offer a combination of stability and fun. There are two boys' boarding houses and one large girls' boarding house and House Parents are supplemented by a resident Assistant House Master/Mistress. Tutors are attached to each house and are responsible for academic progress. They guide each student through GCSE and A Level choices, in conjunction with the Head Teacher, Deputy Head and Head of Sixth Form. In the Sixth Form students are able to choose their tutor, who will advise them on university selection and choices of career and the academic, careers and social programmes are excellent. All who want to go on to university, with 75% going on to Russell Group universities.

Curriculum. Pupils in the first three years of Senior School follow the national curriculum providing them with a sound base in the arts, sciences, humanities and technology based subjects as well as games and PSHME. They are streamed and taught as a form for most subjects and are set for mathematics, English and French. At GCSE there is a common core of English language and literature, mathematics, three sciences and a modern foreign language. Pupils then choose three option subjects.

In the Lower Sixth pupils usually choose three A Level subjects and the Extended Project Qualification. Throughout the Sixth Form some periods of curriculum time are devoted to a General Studies course which includes RE, PSHME and key skills and significant emphasis is placed on gaining good leadership, organisation and communication skills.

Co-Curriculum. In addition to games, music and drama, pupils are encouraged to participate in a range of activities including Model United Nations – a real strength at Queen's, debating, public speaking, general knowledge quizzes, ICT, chess, photography, robotic design, electronics and cookery. There are also a number of academic societies. Outdoor pursuits such as canoeing, mountain bike riding and rock climbing are popular and participation in The Duke of Edinburgh's Award scheme is a particular feature with a stunning 300 Queen's College pupils having now achieved their Gold Award.

Music. The music staff provides teaching for keyboard, strings, brass, woodwind, percussion and singing amongst others. The purpose-built Music Department comprises classroom, six large teaching rooms, five practice rooms, electronic studio for keyboard studies, audio studio for computer-based composition (GCSE and A Level).

The Music Department also uses the beautiful Old Music Room and Performing Arts Centre in the main building for rehearsals and small concerts as well as the stunning Queen's Hall with its 570-seat multi-purpose auditorium, two-manual pipe organ and Steinway Concert Grand Piano.

Musical organisations include a variety of choirs including Chapel Choir, girls musical choir, boys barbershop and younger youth choirs; First Orchestra, Chamber Orchestra and Middle School Orchestra; Wind Band, Swing Band, Sound School, Open Mic Nights and bands.

There is also a wide variety of small ensembles and chamber groups for strings, brass, woodwind with or without piano. A number of concerts are staged each year. Opportunities are available to help prepare for the National Youth Orchestra, Somerset Orchestra and Guildhall.

Drama. The provision for performing arts at Queen's is outstanding. The programme is extremely active throughout the College with the Senior School Drama department providing courses from Year 7 to Year 13. The department aims to involve all those wishing to develop their co-curricular and academic interests and sends many students on to drama school. A number of students have attended the National Musical Youth Theatre over recent years. Over seven different types of dance are studied ranging from ballet and tap to hip hop and jazz with a large-scale production and professional dancers coming in to give workshops. The school also runs an annual professional arts festival with performers and artists from all over the UK, also open to the general public.

In the Senior School, productions take place once a term. There are both Senior and Pre-Prep productions at the end of the Autumn Term, a major Dance Show at the end of the Spring Term, and Middle School and Junior plays at the end of the Summer term. Major productions and concerts take place in the Queen's Hall, drama and comedy in the Drama Studio and the Performing Arts Centre and Old Music Room stages smaller scale concerts and readings.

PE/Games. The playing fields are both extensive and adaptable and sport is strong at the school – in particular hockey, swimming, cross country, athletics and riding. However all abilities are welcomed.

In the Autumn Term the grass area provides seven rugby pitches which are also used for sevens in the Spring term.

In the Summer there are five cricket squares, a 400-metre athletics track and numerous rounders pitches.

The three AstroTurf pitches are used frequently – daily for hockey in the Autumn and Spring Terms – and are of such quality that Queen's has often been called upon to host County hockey tournaments. The hockey academy has produced a number of international players. The pitches are converted to tennis courts in the Summer, giving a total of 30 courts.

The hard court surface in the middle of the field is used for netball in the Spring term and for tennis in the Autumn and Summer terms.

The Sports Hall is used for gymnastics, basketball, badminton, volleyball, indoor hockey, football and indoor tennis. There is also a fully-equipped fitness centre adjoining the Sports Hall. Within the complex is an indoor heated pool that is used at various times for swimming from Pre-Prep through to Sixth Form lessons. Team swimming, canoeing, canoe polo and sub aqua are regular activities throughout the year.

Admission. Education at Queen's starts on entry to the Highgrove Nursery. The majority of pupils join the Pre-Preparatory school from the age of 4 years. Junior School pupils start at age 7. Entrance to the Senior School is by examination and those who are successful in gaining places to the Junior School transfer to the Senior School at the age of 11. There are places for boys and girls from primary schools at the age of 11 based on entry tests in Maths, English and verbal reasoning. There are places for boys and girls at the age of 13 from Preparatory schools also with entrance examinations and a number enter the Sixth Form direct on GCSE Level results.

Scholarships. 11+ scholarships are awarded in January, 13+ in February and Sixth Form in November.

Academic Scholarships: Up to 50% of fees for students of proven academic ability.

Music Scholarships: Worth up to 50% of fees for the most gifted musicians.

Performing Arts Scholarships: Worth up to 50% of fees for the students of best ability.

Art Scholarships: Worth up to 50% of fees for the most talented scholars. Scholarships are for talented students with an existing standard and potential for considerable development. Candidates to be aged 11+ or 13+ at projected time of entry to the college. Sixth Form scholarships included. Art scholarships are based on portfolio and interview.

Sport Scholarships: Worth up to 50% of fees for the students of best ability.

Fees per term (2016–2017). Pre-Prep £2,000–£2,060 (day pupils only); Junior Day Pupils £2,460–£4,070; Junior Boarders £4,430–£6,703; Junior Overseas Boarders £5,510–£7,800; Senior Day Pupils £4,900–£5,800; Senior Boarders £7,910–£9,770; Senior Overseas Boarders £8,990–£10,860. The fees are inclusive of most books and stationery, but exclude external examination charges.

Charitable status. Queen's College, Taunton is a Registered Charity, number 310208. The College is a leading Charitable Trust in the field of Junior and Secondary education.

Visitor: The President of the Methodist Conference

Governors:
Chairman: Mr Mark Edwards
Vice Chairman: Mr Michael F Powell, BSc, FRICS, FAAV
Mrs Rachel Davies
Mrs Kate Gardner, LLB
Sir Nicholas Harvey
Mr Paul M Hughes, BSc, ACIB
Mr J David Jones, LLB
Brig Thomas H Lang, QVRM, RD, FRICS, DL
Mr Pradeep Madhavan, Dip NB Surg, FRCS, Ed Tr & Orth
Revd Stephen Mares
Mrs Deborah Perreau
Mr David Savill, LLB, FCA
Mr Brian Tanner, CBE, DL, BA
Revd Graham Thompson
Mr David Turner, LLB, FCCI
Mrs Janet Walden

College Leadership Group:

Head Teacher: Dr L Earps

Junior School Headmistress: Mrs T Khodabandehloo
Finance Director: Mr G Taylor
Deputy Head: Mr A Free
Director Outreach and Partnerships: Mrs J Evans
Director Marketing, Development and Admissions: Mrs K Howard

Senior Curriculum Group:
Head Teacher: Dr L Earps
Deputy Head: Mr A Free
Head of Curriculum, Monitoring and Reporting: Mrs P Pawley
Head of Thinking & Learning: Mr T Jolliff
Head of Curriculum Planning: Mr N O'Donnell
Head of Learning Development: Mrs A Free
Head of EAL: Mrs V Orme-Dawson
Head of English: Mrs J Brierley

Senior Pastoral Group:
Head Teacher: Dr L Earps
Deputy Head & DSL: Mr A Free
Head of Boarding: Mr J Shepherd
Head of Sixth Form: Mrs S Wilde
Head of Learning Development: Mrs A Free
Head of EAL: Mrs V Orme-Dawson
Head of PSHME: Miss C Harrison
Head of Outdoor Pursuits: Mr M Neenan
Senior Nurse: Mrs S Parratt

Senior School Teaching Staff:
Melissa Allan (*Head of History*) [Maternity Leave]
Donna Ashman (*History*)
Claire Barker (*Psychology & Anthropology*)
Jon Bird (*Mandarin & EAL*)
Geoff Bisson (*History*)
Kay Bloxham (*Learning Development*)
Roger Bowden (*Maths*)
Jenny Brierley (*Head of English*)
Yvonne Brooks (*English & RS*)
Alison Brothwood (*Learning Development*)
Sarah Brown (*Business Studies*) [Maternity Leave]
Laura Burgoyne (*Art*)
Rebecca Cade (*Art*) [Maternity Leave]
Dave Cooke (*Biology*)
Ruth Copeland (*English, RS & Anthropology*)
Simon Copeland (*Director of Sport*)
Paul DeJaeger (*Geography*)
Henrietta Drummond (*Maths*)
Joanna Elliott (*Performing Arts/Dance*)
Jane Evans (*Performing Arts*)
Steve Evans (*Performing Arts*)
Andrew Exley (*Maths*)
Amanda Free (*Head of Learning Development*)
Andrew Free (*PE*)
Andrew Garton (*Computing*)
Paul Gibson (*Maths*)
Helen Goodall (*EAL*)
Donna Greenow (*Spanish*)
Darren Haggerston (*Physics*)
Ian Haley (*Director of Hockey*, *PE*)
Angus Hamilton (*Head of RS*)
Claire Harrison (*Biology*)
Julie Harrison (*PE*)
Oona Hazell (*Business Studies*)
David Hedges (*Music*)
Ian Henden (*Chemistry & Computing*)
Lisa Henden (*Head of Biology*)
Jenni Hill (*Maths*)
Ed Jenkins (*Director of Music*)
Tim Jolliff (*Head of Chemistry*)
Rachel Knowlman (*Performing Arts*)
Caroline Lewis (*PE*)
Yvonne Mackey (*Head of Food Technology*)
Grace Mainstone (*EAL*)
Sarah Male (*French*)
Philip Mann (*PE*)
John Marston (*English*)
Mary Mason (*Chemistry*)
Karen McIntyre (*EAL*)
Chris Monks (*Maths*)
Mark Neenan (*Head of Geography*)
Kate Newsome (*Maths*)
Richard Newsome (*History*)
Nick O'Donnell (*Head of Physics*)
Eoin O'Donnachadha (*Business Studies*)
Valerie Orme-Dawson (*Head of EAL*)
Adrian Palmer (*Chemistry*)
Pamela Pawley (*Head of Maths*)
Sheila Platt (*Maths*)

Laura Schofield (*Head of Spanish*)
Jonathan Shepherd (*Biology*)
Alicia Shortman (*Performing Arts*)
Roger Simon (*PE*)
Sandra Spall (*Art*)
David Steele (*Learning Development*)
Elizabeth Storrs-Fox (*Biology & Food Technology*)
Arul Suppiah (*Director of Cricket, Business Studies*)
Pete Vicary (*Head of Business Studies, Economics & Politics*)
Michael Wager (*Head of Foreign Languages*)
Kirsten Webber (*German*)
Sue Wedge-Thomas (*Biology*)
Claire Western (*Head of Art*)
Sarah Whitehouse (*Physics*)
Sharon Wilde (*English*)
Gareth Wilson (*Design Technology*)

PA to the Headmaster: Mrs Pam Chapman
Admissions Registrar: Mrs Sarah Frost
Academic Administrator: Miss Judith Poole
Sixth Form Administrator: Mrs Rebecca Mockridge

Junior School Teaching Staff:

Headmistress of Junior, Pre-Prep and Nursery: Mrs Tracey J Khodabandehloo

Deputy Head: Mr Dick Wilde

Linda Alcock	Rebecca Milby
Charlotte Baker	Shirley Neale
Doug Baker	Barbara Newsham
Sam Chislett	Hannah Newsham
Andy Clark	Andrew Owen
Philip Dudman	Sarah Scutt
Jo Elsmore	Abbey Thresher
Jill Fear	Candice Thompson-Gardiner
Pat Fox	Teri Underwood
Gill Harrison	Anne Wade
Helen Hitchin	Anthea Watkins
Clare Hood	Dick Wilde
Samantha Horner	Sharon Wilde
Bel Hoskins	Jan Williams
Sue Marston	Nicola Williams

Queenswood School

Shepherd's Way, Brookmans Park, Hatfield, Hertfordshire AL9 6NS

Tel: 01707 602500
Fax: 01707 602597
email: admissions@queenswood.org
website: www.queenswood.org
Twitter: @QueenswoodSch
Facebook: @Queenswood-School-Hertfordshire-UK

Motto: 'In Hortis Reginæ' – 'In the Queen's Gardens'.

The School was founded in 1894 in Clapham Park, London. It moved to its current site in Hertfordshire in 1925.

Queenswood is a progressive boarding and day school for around 440 girls, aged between 11 and 18, where boarders make up half of the School. An all-round education focuses on equipping the girls with all the life skills required of women in the 21st century. Within a caring and supportive framework, the girls enjoy a dynamic academic curriculum, supported by a diverse and exciting co-curricular programme.

It is a warm and friendly community where everybody knows each other. Girls thrive within a nurturing House structure tailored to meet their needs as they progress from the Lower School, through the Middle School, and on into the Sixth Form. Day girls are fully integrated within the Houses, are able to enjoy all the facilities and opportunities available to the boarders, but choose to go home at night after a packed school day. There is a flexible approach to boarding to meet the varying needs of individual families; girls may choose to be full boarders or just to remain in School for four or five nights a week.

Queenswood is proud to be an international community with an outward-looking approach; overseas girls make up around 20% of the pupils. We welcome girls of all faiths and none, recognise and support an individual's adherence to her own faith, but expect all girls to embrace the School's broad spiritual ethos.

The girls are ambitious high achievers, winning places at the top universities both at home and abroad prior to embarking upon a range of exciting careers. The School is, however, resolutely neither an academic hothouse nor overly selective. Individual talent also flourishes in sport and the creative and performing arts. As important as individual achievement is the development of a sense of responsibility for each other and the world in which they live. Queenswood girls are thoughtful young people with a secure set of values and self-confidence.

The beautiful Queenswood estate provides the perfect educational environment. Being just 25 minutes from central London, it also has the advantage of easy access to the cultural richness of the capital. At the same time, its proximity to major international airports provides ease of travel for both our overseas girls and for those participating in the School's foreign exchange and visit programmes.

Curriculum. With over twenty-five subjects in the curriculum and more than ninety co-curricular activities available, girls have every opportunity to discover their strengths and to become exceptional learners and leaders. We offer a holistic educational experience which supports and encourages intellectual, physical, moral and spiritual development.

Spiritual Life. Queenswood encourages intellectual curiosity of which the spiritual dimension is an important part. Girls are therefore welcome to discuss their thoughts, feelings and faith in an open and supportive context. Since true education is holistic it includes spiritual and moral development. All pupils of the school, whatever their religion, are encouraged to explore and develop their own faith in an atmosphere of tolerance.

Boarding. We strongly believe that fun and friendship should be the foundation of our boarding community. So, we invite you to enter a world where your daughter will be able to embrace diversity, firmly establish her independence while still fostering a sense of care and concern for the community, sample more to achieve more and certainly make friends for life.

Lower School. Our ultimate aim in the Lower School is to help girls to become independent students with enthusiasm for learning and the ambition to develop their skills and qualities to their fullest extent. Beyond the classroom, there is a wealth of opportunities for younger girls to enrich their education. These include a wide range of over 90 co-curricular clubs and activities and a diverse programme of House outings and excursions.

Entry. Entrance to Queenswood is by examination (CEE or Queenswood's papers), interview and a report from the pupil's current Headteacher.

Scholarships. Academic, art, dance, drama, golf, music, sports and tennis scholarships (honorary) are available at 11+, 13+, and Sixth Form entry. Bursaries are means-tested and reviewed annually.

Fees per term (2016–2017). Boarders: Sixth Form £11,250; Years 9–11 £10,900; Years 7–8 £10,150. Day: Sixth Form £8,275; Years 9–11 £8,125; Years 7–8 £6,975.

Old Queenswoodians' Association (OQA) with 4,000+ members and an active young membership that support current Queenswoodians after their time at School has come to an end.

Charitable status. Queenswood School Limited is a Registered Charity, number 311060, which exists to provide high-quality education for girls.

Governors:
Chairman: Mr E M Sautter, MA
Vice-Chairman: Mr H J De Sausmarez, BA Hons, FCIS
Mr R Baines, BSc Hons, CIMA, CEng, MICE
Reverend David M Chapman
Mr T C Garnham, BSc Hons
Dr O McGuinness, BSc Hons, MBBS, FRCP
Mr S Morris, MA
Mrs V R Neale (*Old Queenswoodian Representative*)
Mr A D Poppleton, BEng, AKC, FIET, FBSC
Mrs J Sotiriou
Reverend T Swindell, BA Hons, BSc Hons, FCA
Mrs P M Wrinch

Principal: Mrs J Cameron, BSc Hons Surrey, PGCE

Bursar and Clerk to the Governors: Mr I Williams, BEng Hons RMCS Shrivenham, CEng
Deputy Head Academic: Mr I Sheldon, MChem Oxon, PGCE, MRSC
Deputy Head Pastoral: Mrs A Wakefield, BMus Hons Sheffield
Deputy Head Staff: Mrs S Sanders, BA Hons London, PGCE
Head of Sixth Form: Mr P Merrell, BA Hons UCL, MPhil Birmingham, PGCE
Head of Middle School: Ms C De la Pena, MA London, PGCE
Head of Lower School: Mrs H Mackay, BA Hons Yale, MA London, PGCE

Head of Boarding: Ms S Hurndall-Waldron

Art and Design: Mr A Wright, BA Hons Sunderland, PGCE
Classics: Mrs C Tarrega, BA Hons, MIL, QTS
Dance: Mrs R McGregor, BA Hons Roehampton
Design & Technology: Miss L Tillotson, BA Hons Lancashire, PGCE
Drama: Mrs A Kelley, BA Hons Wales, MA Portsmouth
Economics & Business Studies: Mr S Lovell, BA Hons Southampton, PGCE
EAL: Ms D Eastwood, BA Hons Leeds, TESOL
English: Miss L Morton, BA Hons Oxon, PGCE
Geography: Mrs E Barnard, BA Hons Manchester, PGCE
History: Mr S Daughton, BA Hons Sunderland, PGCE
History of Art: Dr W Bird, BA Hons Leicester, PGCE, PhD Reading
ICT: Mr J Earle, BSc Hons, MA Beds, PGCE
Languages: Mrs L Law, BA Hons Middlesex, PGCE
Leaning Support: Mrs G Helks, BEd, MA, OCR Dip SpLD, Adv Dip SEN
Mathematics: Mrs H Wolohan, BSc Hons Dunelm, PGCE
Music: Mr J Dobson, Prof Cert Hons RAM, LRAM
Physical Education: Mrs J Wakeley, BEd Hons London
Practical Cookery: Mrs J Lee
PSHCEE: Mrs A Wakefield, BMus Hons Sheffield, QTS
Religious Studies: Mrs K Sunderland, BRelSc Dublin, MA Ed Derby, QTS

Science: Mrs N Grant-Stevenson, BSc Hons Nottingham, MEd Belfast, PGCE

Head of Marketing, Admissions & Foundation: Mr Guy Ranford, BA Hons Derby

Radley College

Abingdon, Oxfordshire OX14 2HR

Tel:	01235 543127 (Warden)
	01235 543122 (Bursar)
	01235 543174 (Admissions)
	01235 543000 (General Enquiries)
Fax:	01235 543106
email:	warden@radley.org.uk
website:	www.radley.org.uk

Motto: '*Sicut Serpentes, sicut Columbae*'

St Peter's College, Radley, was founded by the Reverend William Sewell, Fellow of Exeter College, Oxford, to provide an independent school education on the principles of the Church of England. It was opened on 9 June 1847 and incorporated by Royal Charter in 1890. It stands in a park of some 700 acres.

General Arrangements. There are 690 boys in the school, all of whom board. On admission, boys enter one of the 10 houses known as Socials. All are close together within the grounds. All meals are served in Hall on a cafeteria system. There is a daily Chapel Service for all boys.

Admission. The 13+ admissions process for 2019 onwards will be held when boys are in Year 6. Boys will be assessed using the ISEB Common Pre-Test, a current school report and an interview with the Warden or Senior Master at Radley. Those who have registered early on the Radley List (generally before a boy is 3 years old) will go through this process in the Michaelmas Term of Year 6 with offers being made on 1st March of Year 6. Those who have not registered, or who are on the waiting list, go through the same assessments from 1st November to end of March in Year 6, with offers being made by May of Year 6. This process is called Open Entry. Offers will be unconditional, but boys are required to sit 13+ Common Entrance (or Maths and English exams for those abroad) and Radley reserves the right to refuse entry in exceptional circumstances. Any 2017 or 2018 candidates can apply to Radley through the scholarship process.

A few places are sometimes available for Sixth Form entry: details are available on our website.

Scholarships and Bursaries. Up to twelve Academic Scholarships and Exhibitions are awarded each year. In addition All-Rounder, Music, Sport, Drama and Art Awards are offered. All awards may be supplemented by a means-tested bursary. Details of all awards are available from our website or the Registrar, admissions@radley.org.uk. Further means-tested bursaries are available for boys who would otherwise be unable to come to Radley.

Music: On average five Instrumental Scholarships and several Exhibitions are offered annually with free tuition.

Drama: Around two awards will be offered annually.

Art: Around two Art Scholarships and an Art Exhibition will be offered annually.

Work. In the Shells, Removes and Fifth Form a broad curriculum is followed. There is some choice at GCSE with boys generally taking nine or ten subjects.

In the Sixth Form a boy can specialise in a combination of Classics, French, Spanish, German, Theatre Studies, English, History, Religious Studies, Geography, Geology, Biology, Chemistry, Physics, Mathematics, Economics, Politics, Economics and Business, Music, Art or Design, leading to AS/A2 examinations.

Careers. Advice and assistance is available to all boys on a wide range of career possibilities through the Director of Careers. The School is a member of ISCO (The Independent Schools Careers Organisation) and close connections are maintained with the professions, with firms, with the services and with Old Radleians. Visits and talks by experts in these fields are a special feature.

Games. In the Michaelmas Term rugby football is the major school game. In the other two terms the 'wet-bobs' row; the 'dry-bobs' play hockey (the major game) and soccer in the Lent Term, cricket (the major game), athletics and tennis in the Summer. There are also numerous minor sports which involve boys in competition with other schools. The playing fields are close to the main buildings.

The College has its own boathouse, and the use of a stretch of the River Thames between Sandford and Abingdon. The VIIIs compete in regattas and Head of the River races.

There are three all-weather hockey pitches, an athletics track, five squash courts, a Real Tennis court, a rackets court, two covered Fives courts, 20 hard tennis courts and a 9-hole golf course. There is a large, well-equipped gymnasium and an indoor, heated swimming pool attached to a multi-purpose sports hall and a state-of-the-art rowing tank.

CCF and Duke of Edinburgh's Award. All boys, in their fourth term, join the Radley College Contingent, Combined Cadet Force (Army, Navy and Air sections). They work for the Proficiency examination, which takes three terms. When they have passed Proficiency and done a week's Corps Camp in the holidays they either stay on in a special section for further training or join one of the many Community Action Projects on offer. There is a thriving Duke of Edinburgh's Award scheme.

Fees per term (2016–2017). £11,830 (inclusive of medical attendance). Insurance is available a system of insurance against loss of fees caused by illness, accident, or infection. Particulars can be obtained from the Bursar.

Charitable status. St Peter's College, Radley is a Registered Charity, number 309243. It exists for the purpose of the education of youth in general knowledge and literature and particularly and especially in the doctrines and principles of the Church of England.

Visitor: The Rt Revd The Lord Bishop of Oxford

Council:
Chairman: M E Hodgson, MA, FRICS
Vice-Chairman: N J Henderson, MA, FRCS

T O Seymour, MA	R H Warner, MA, ACA
M J W Rushton, MA	A C Mayfield, MBA
D C S Smellie, MA	Sir John Holmes
A P G Holmes, MA	R N L Huntingford
Mrs D J Pluck, FCA	P E F Watson, FRGS
G A Kaye, BSc	Mrs E J Martineau, FRGS
Mrs E McKendrick, BA	H J R Willis, MA
W S H Laidlaw, MA	Rt Revd S Conway
T M Durie, BA, ACA, FSI	S J B Shaw
J C Bridcut, MA	

Warden: **J S Moule**, MA

Sub Warden: B J Holden, MA, BTech
Academic Director: S R Rathbone, MA, MA

Senior Masters:
H D Hammond, BSc
R D Shaw, MA
N Murphy MA

Under Masters:
D C K Edwards, MA
R M C Greed, BSc

Teaching Staff:

G Wiseman, BA	P J Miron, BSc, DPhil
J C Nye, MA	M P Hills, MMath
P W Gamble, MA	E J Tolputt, MEng
I P Ellis, BA, DipRASchls	E O Holt, BA
S Barlass, BA	†C A San Jose, BA (*F Social*)
†A J McChesney, BSc	
C M Bedford, BA, PhD	D J Cresswell, BA
I S Yorston, MA	M J Pringle, BA
W O C Matthews, BA	J W Schofield, BA, MSc
†T R G Ryder, BA, MFA (*A Social*)	D L Cox, MMath
	Mrs K C Ison, BA
R A King, BSc, MRSC, CChem	Ms P E Henderson, BA
	J M Ambrose, BA, DPhil
†J M Sparks, BSc	Ms L E Nott, BA
S A Hall, BA, MPhil, PhD	K J Reid, MSc
M R Jewell, BA	M G Noone, MA
R Johnson, BSc	R D Woodling, MChem
J R W Beasley, MA	T A Barfield, MSt
I K Campbell, BA	S J Perkins, BSc
Mrs M C Hart, BA	J M Sumner, BA
B R Knox, BEd	M E Walker, BA, MA, PhD
P M Fernandez, MA	Mrs R E Murphy, BA
D W S Roques, MA	Ms M M Carter
K A Mosedale, MA, MSc	M C F Brown, BA
Mrs K J Knox, BA	Miss L P Gregory, BA
†H Crump, LLB, BA (*D Social*)	R E P Hughes, BSc
	T C H Norton, MA
S H Dalrymple, BA	Dr A R Rhodes, BA, MA, DPhil
K Halliday, BSc, PhD	
R M Lowe, BA	Mrs L R I Smart, BA
†G H S May, MA (*H Social*)	Mrs C E Piller
	N M Martin, BA
†G R King, BA (*G Social*)	M G D Glendon-Doyle, BA
D J Pullen, BSc	J P J Dodd, BA
R K McMahon, MA, MPhil, DPhil	K W S Willis-Stovold, BSc
	Miss M Hurley, BA
C J Ellott, BA, LLB	Mrs G M Maybank, BA
J E Gearing, BA	Mrs C E Piller
D S Borthwick, DPhil, MChem	P Asbury, BA
	S R Molyneux, BA
Mrs G C Porter, MA, MSc	A F C Nash, BA
†O H Langton, MA (*J Social*)	A C N Norman, MSc
	D Scott, BA
Mrs T Scammell Jackson, BA, MPhil	Mrs R Tufnell, BA
Ms E E N Danis, BA	R J Adams, BA
†S R Giddens, BSc, MSc, PhD (*C Social*)	E J Pearson
	C McKegney
†T C Lawson, BA (*E Social*)	L Clogher
	Miss L Taft
†C J Lee, BA (*K Social*)	I Ashpole
†C E Scott-Malden, BA, MA (*B Social*)	J Gaunt
	Mrs E Ellis
A D Cunningham, MA, PhD	J Sheldrake
	S Townsend

Chaplain: The Revd D Wilson, BSc, BA, MLitt, PhD
Assistant Chaplain: The Revd T J E Fernyhough, BA
Librarian: Ms A K Muhlberg

Music:
Precentor: S D J Clarke, MA, ARCO
A J A Williams, MMus, DipRAM, GRSM, LRAM
Miss S-L Naylor, MA
T M Morris, MA, DPhil, FRCO

There are 36 peripatetic music staff.

Bursar and Secretary: A Ashton, MA, ACIB
Medical Officer: Dr J N B Moore, BSc, MB BS, DRCOG, MRCGP
Development Director: C J Dudgeon
Registrar: Mrs V M G Hammond

Ratcliffe College

Fosse Way, Ratcliffe on the Wreake, Leicester, Leicestershire LE7 4SG

Tel: 01509 817000 School Office
            01509 817072/817031 Registrar
Fax: 01509 817004
email: registrar@ratcliffe.leics.sch.uk
website: www.ratcliffe-college.co.uk
Twitter: @RatcliffeCol
            @RColPrepSchool
            @RatcliffeSport

Motto: '*Legis Plenitudo Charitas*'

Ratcliffe College is a co-educational Catholic day and boarding school. The School was founded in 1844 and opened in 1847; the original buildings, designed by the famous architect of the Houses of Parliament, Augustus Pugin, were erected with funds provided by Lady Mary Arundel of Wardour, who also bequeathed money for subsequent extensions.

Age Range. 3–18.

Number of Pupils. 823: 374 girls, 449 boys. Sixth Form 160; Boarders 93.

Aims. The vision of the College is to educate young people in the spirit of the Gospel and the traditions of the Catholic Church, seeking to nurture the God-given talents and potential of each individual, so that each one may become a confident, responsible and useful member of society. Whilst Ratcliffe is a Catholic school, it welcomes children of other denominations and faiths, whose parents feel they can share in and benefit from the School's ideals and environment.

Location. Ratcliffe College is set in over 200 acres of rolling parkland on the A46, seven miles north of Leicester. It is easily accessible by road and benefits from being free of congestion at peak times. The M1/M6 motorways, main line railway stations and airports of Birmingham and East Midlands are all within easy travelling distance. For day pupils, school buses operate daily from Leicester, Loughborough and Nottingham.

Site and Buildings. The main Senior School buildings surround a quadrangle and contain the Administration offices, Church, Refectory, Library, Medical Centre, Computer Rooms and Common Rooms, together with a number of subject departmental areas. In addition, there is a Music Department with Concert Hall; a fully-appointed Theatre; and a Science Centre with additional classrooms for Food Technology. Sporting facilities include extensive playing fields, athletics track and floodlit all-weather hockey pitches; the state-of-the-art Sports Centre comprises sports changing rooms, swimming pool and sports hall with a modern fitness suite. A complex of recently refurbished buildings nearby provides departmental bases for Geography, Modern Languages and Mathematics. Modernised Boys' and Girls' boarding accommodation is situated on the upper floor of the main building, in separate wings, with individual study bedrooms for older students.

The Rosmini Sixth Form Centre, named after Blessed Antonio Rosmini, the founder of the Rosminian Order, has an upper floor wholly dedicated to independent academic study with full IT accessibility, and ground floor areas providing for social and extracurricular usage, the Centre provides a flagship modern setting for Sixth Formers.

In September 2014, the College invested £4.5 million opening a brand new purpose-built Preparatory School building on the school site. The new Preparatory School has twelve classrooms located over two floors, as well as a dedicated technology and languages centre, science and food technology laboratory, library, central assembly hall and music room for the young pupils. It has been developed to be sympathetic to the original school building.

The Nursery is located nearby in purpose-built accommodation also on the campus.

Organisation. The College is divided into 2 sections: Senior School (11–18 year olds) and Preparatory School (3–11 year olds, including the Nursery for 3–5 year olds). The sections are closely integrated, allowing continuity of education from 3 to 18. Boarding girls and boys are accommodated in separate wings within the main Senior School building, under the supervision of the resident Senior Housemistress and Housemaster, together with their Assistants. There is a strong emphasis on pastoral care for all pupils. The teacher:pupil ratio in the Senior School is 1:10 (the ratio in the Sixth Form is much lower).

Curriculum. In the Nursery, the emphasis is on early Literacy, Numeracy and the development of personal and social skills, all of which contribute to a child's knowledge, understanding and skills in other areas of learning. Programmes of study are based on the Early Years Foundation Stage Curriculum, but extend well beyond these guidelines to develop a child's interests, talents, outlook and general knowledge and understanding of the world.

The Preparatory School offers small class sizes, well-resourced classrooms, a clear focus on the National Curriculum, an extended school day and a varied extracurricular activities programme. The curriculum is broad and balanced including extensive provision for Drama, Music, Modern Foreign Languages, Physical Education and Latin, taught by specialist teachers. Each classroom has the most up-to-date teaching and learning resources, with specialist classrooms for Art, Music, Science, Food Technology, ICT and Performing Arts. As the children move into Year 6, approximately half their timetable is taught by Senior specialists. This enables the highest academic standards at the end of Key Stage 2, which means that all pupils move very happily into Year 7.

In the Senior School a broad and balanced curriculum is followed, which aims to identify and provide for individual needs. Most students take at least nine GCSEs. Core subjects consist of English Language, Mathematics, Religious Studies, a Modern Foreign Language and Science (Core and Additional or Triple Award). This is augmented by up to three further option subjects.

In the Sixth Form, most students start 4 A Levels in Year 12 and continue with 3 in Year 13. During the autumn term of Year 12, the large majority of students will then decide which three of these subjects they wish to continue to A Level, perhaps with an Extended Project Qualification (EPQ) to be completed in Year 12. In addition, students can opt to study the EPQ and the European Computer Driving Licence (ECDL) Level 3 along with two A Level subjects. To ensure a balanced programme, Games lessons and the Enrichment Programme are also part of the curriculum.

Games. The playing fields, which surround the College buildings, cover over 200 acres. All pupils participate in Games, including Cricket, Hockey, Rugby, Football, Tennis and Athletics for boys, and Hockey, Netball, Rounders, Tennis and Athletics for girls.

Extracurricular Activities. Pupils' talents and interests are developed through an extensive programme of activities on weekdays and at weekends. As well as many sporting opportunities, 25% of pupils learn a musical instrument; there are many musical groups, including brass ensemble, orchestra and choirs; all Year 4 pupils have free year-round orchestral instrumental tuition. Many pupils are involved in school productions and film-making, and other media activities are popular. The Combined Cadet Force and The Duke of Edinburgh's Award scheme both flourish. Pupils are encouraged to be caring and to have consideration for others through Chaplaincy groups and Voluntary Service activities.

Admissions.

Nursery: Entry is by school report (if applicable) and informal assessment.

Preparatory School: Years 1–3: children spend a half day in School and, during this time, take assessments in English and Mathematics. Years 4–6: children spend a half day in School and, during this time, take assessments in English, Mathematics and Non-Verbal Reasoning. Entry is normally at age 7+ and 9+ (when an additional class of 18 pupils is admitted), but a small number of places may be available for entry to other years if there are vacancies.

Senior School: Entry is normally at age 11+, and age 13+ (when an additional form of entry is admitted), but a small number of places may be available for entry to other years if there are vacancies. Papers are set in English, Mathematics and Non-Verbal Reasoning.

Sixth Form: Entry is based on successful performance in GCSE (or equivalent examinations) and interview. Applicants should obtain at least six GCSE passes at grade B or better, including English and Mathematics. For any subject to be studied in the Sixth Form, applicants should have at least GCSE grade B in that subject (or, for subjects not taken at GCSE, at least grade B in related GCSE subjects). Further to this, GCSE grade A or A* is normally required in order to study the following subjects in the Sixth Form: Mathematics, Sciences, Languages and English Literature.

Non-Native Speakers of English from Overseas: It is strongly recommended that overseas applicants should provide an IELTS or ESOL examination certificate to confirm their ability in English language. In addition, students may be tested in subjects such as Mathematics and Science. Overseas applicants are also interviewed, via Skype.

Scholarships and Bursaries. Ratcliffe College offers a wide range of scholarships to recognise academic, sporting, musical, dramatic and artistic talent amongst applicants for the Senior School.

Each scholarship is worth up to 20% off the fees. Points at which scholarships are offered are Years 7, 10 and 12.

A limited number of Bursaries are available, generally on entry to Years 7 and 12. Sixth Form Talent Bursaries are also available in Sport, Music, Drama, Art and Design.

For further details, please contact the Registrar.

Fees per term (2016–2017). UK Students: Full Boarding (Years 6–13) £8,236; Weekly Boarding (Years 9–13) £7,342; Weekly Boarding (Years 6–8) £6,560. Boarding fees include the full cost of the programme of boarding weekend trips throughout the year.

Overseas Students: Full Boarding £9,576. Boarding fees include the full cost of the programme of boarding weekend trips throughout the year. Boarding fees include the cost of additional teaching of English as a Foreign Language with a minimum of 10 one-hour sessions per term.

Day: £2,950–£3,313 (Nursery aged 3–5); £3,328–£3,832 (Years 1–5); £4,339–£5,219 (Years 6–13).

Fees are subject to such termly increase as may prove necessary. Additional charges are made for: private Music lessons at £230 per term for 10 half-hour sessions (for individual tuition for each instrument); Where additional teaching of Learning Skills is required and agreed with parents, this will be charged at £42 per lesson. There is a non-refundable registration fee of £99 (£125 overseas) and a deposit (refundable on leaving school) of £500 for UK students and £1,000 for students from overseas.

Charitable status. Ratcliffe College is a Registered Charity, number 1115975, for the education of children.

Governing Body:
Consists of two members of the Board of Directors of the Company Limited by Guarantee which owns the College (Ratcliffe College Ltd), together with up to 10 additional governors, appointed by the Directors, who hold office for a period.

Governors:
Mr Louis Massarella (*Chairman of Governors, Current Parent and Past Pupil*)
Cllr Margaret Smidowicz (*Vice-Chair of Governors*)
Mr Richard Gamble (*Foundation Governor, Past Pupil*)
Mrs Mary Goldstraw
Mr Enzo Lallo (*Current Parent*)
Ms Bridget Lavin (*Past Pupil*)
Mrs Louise Marsden (*Current Parent and Past Pupil*)
Mr Abe Mee (*Current Parent and Past Pupil*)
Mr Patrick Mulvihill (*Current Parent*)
Fr Philip Sainter (*Foundation Governor, Past Pupil*)
His Hon Judge Stokes, QC (*Current Parent*)
Mr Martin Traynor, OBE

Headmaster: Mr G P Lloyd, BA Hons, MSc, FMusTCL

Senior Deputy Head (*Pastoral*): Mr J Reddin, BSc, MSc
Deputy Head Academic: Mr K Ryce, BA, MSc
Assistant Head: Mr G J Sharpe, BA, MBA
Assistant Head Academic: Ms J Davis, BA, MSc
Director of Finance: Mr D Robson, BCom Accounting, ACA
Development Director: Mr A Yell, BSc
Head of Preparatory School: Fr C Cann, MA St Andrews, MA Oxon, Cert Theol
Head of Nursery: Mrs S Rankine, BEd
Father President: Fr T Mullen IC

Teaching Staff:
* Denotes Head of Department
Mrs T Allen, BSc (*Biology*)
Mrs L Arnold, BSc, MPhil (*Information and Communication Technology*)
Mr W Ballard, BSc, MA (*Chemistry**)
Mr M Balmbra, BSc (*Physical Education, Geography, OC CCF*)
Mrs A Batten, BSc (*Learning Support Assistant*)
Miss S Beddoes, BA (*Languages*)
Mr M Benjamin, BA (*English*)
Mrs C Bennett, BA (*Media Studies*, English*)
Mr D Berry, BA (*Art and Design**)
Mrs K Burton, BA (*Food Technology**)
Mr J Cantrill, BA (*History**)
Mrs J Cartwright, BA (*Deputy Head Preparatory School*)
Miss M Casas-Ojeda, BA, MA (*Spanish*)
Mrs C Caven-Henrys, AISTD, Dip LCCD (*Drama*, Dance*)
Mr A Chorley, MSc (*Science**)
Mrs S Clarke, BA (*Mathematics*)
Mrs J Cluley, BEd (*Special Educational Needs Co-ordinator**)
Mrs C Cole, MA (*Mathematics*)
Mrs A Crebbin, DEUG (*French and Spanish*)
Mrs S Cushing, BA (*Languages**)
Mrs D Darlington, BSc (*Science*)
Mr M Darlington, BSc (*Curriculum Director, Physics*)
Miss L Davids, BSc (*Learning Support*)
Miss R Doig, BA (*Media Studies*)
Mrs A Dungey, BSc (*Science, Food Technology*)
Mr A Dziemianko, BSc (*Geography*)
Mr P Enoux, BA (*Preparatory School*)
Mrs L Evans, BSc (*maternity leave*) (*Mathematics*)
Mr W Faulconbridge, BSc (*Head of Prep School Sport*)
Mr A Ferrari, BSc (*Preparatory School*)
Miss D Gatt, BSc (*Biology*)
Mrs N Gilchrist, BEd (*Preparatory School*)
Mr P Gilchrist, BSc (*Senior Housemaster*)
Mrs D Grant, BEd (*Preparatory School*)
Miss R Green, BSc (*Preparatory School*)
Mrs J Harlock, BA (*Learning Support*)
Mr G Higham, BSc (*Mathematics**)

Mr J Imrie, BA (*English*)
Miss C Jeyes, NNEB (*Early Years Practitioner, Nursery School*)
Mr M Jones, BSc (*Information and Communication Technology**)
Dr S Jones, PhD (*Mathematics*)
Mr M Kaye, BA (*Physical Education, History*)
Mr A Kellighan, BA, MA (*Religious Studies*)
Mr D Kent, BA (*Preparatory School*)
Mr M Lambert, BSc (*Geography**)
Dr C Layfield-Hartle, PhD (*Specialist Learning Support Assistant*)
Mrs J Leite, BA (*Learning Support (Preparatory School), Senior Housemistress (Girls' Boarding)*)
Miss C Llewelyn, BA (*Preparatory School*)
Mrs F Lodder, BA, MA (*History*)
Mrs M Markham, BA (*Music (Preparatory School)*)
Mr E McCall, BMus, MMus (*Music**)
Mr P McCrindell, BA (*Head of Year 11, German*)
Mr P Michel, BA (*Lay Chaplain*)
Miss J Monk, BA (*Drama*)
Mrs S Neuberg, BA (*Nursery School*)
Mr M Newman, BA (*Head of Year 13, History*)
Mr A Nott, BSc (*Biology, Physics*)
Mr T Oakley, HND, TEFL (*Learning Support Assistant*)
Mrs Y O'Connor, BA, Med (*Religious Studies*)
Mrs S Owen, BA (*Early Years Practitioner*)
Miss C Papadopoulou, MSc (*Geography, Teacher of PE, Boarding Assistant*)
Mr C Price, BMus (*Music*)
Mrs S Rankine, BEd (*Head of Nursery School*)
Mrs J Reddin, BA (*French*)
Mrs M Reeves, BA, MSc (*EAL, English*)
Mr P Rogers, BA (*Design Technology*)
Ms E Sellars, BSc (*Mathematics*)
Mr A Seth, BSc (*Design and Technology**)
Mr M Sleath, BSc (*Mathematics*)
Mrs H Smith, BSc (*Mathematics*)
Mrs P Smith, BA (*Religious Studies*)
Mr P Spencer, ACIB (*Business/Economics**)
Miss T Spencer, BA (*PSHCE*, Business Studies, Careers Co-ordinator*)
Miss A Stafford, BSc (*Acting Head of Sport*)
Miss B Stanley, BSc (*Preparatory School*)
Dr L Stannard, BA, MA, PhD (*Acting Head of English*)
Dr S Standen, BSc, PhD (*Head of Year 9, Science*)
Mrs A Taylor, BEd (*Academic PE**)
Mr N Taylor, BEd (*Head of Year 12, Physical Education, History*)
Miss E Thompson, BA (*English*)
Mr S Thorpe, BSc (*Head of Year 7, Biology*)
Mr P Trotter, CChem MRSc (*Science*)
Mr D Turner, BEd (*Preparatory School, Assistant Boys' Housemaster*)
Mrs E Walker, BA (*Preparatory School*) [maternity leave]
Mr N Walsh, LLB (*Religious Studies**)
Mr T Walsh, BA, MPhil (*Classics**)
Mrs E Waters, BEd (*Learning Support*)
Miss F Watson, BA (*Preparatory School*)
Mrs L Whieldon, BA (*English*)
Mrs M Williams, BA (*Librarian*)
Mr E Woodcock, BA, MSc (*Head of Year 8, Physical Education*)
Mrs E Worthington, BA (*English**) [maternity leave]
Miss A Wright, BA (*Art and Design*)

Sports Coaches:
Miss L Cluer
Mr L Deacon
Mr D Jelley
Mr D Willcock

Mr S Yassin
A Stanley
G Mullen

Peripatetic Music Staff:
Mr D Beavan
Mr P Bennett
Mr J Boyd
Mr C Earp
Mrs S Forrester
Ms S Hall
Mr G Henderson
Mr S Johnson
Mrs C Lee
Mr M Nicholls
Miss R Reedman
Mrs C Spencer

LAMDA Teachers:
Mrs M Johnson
Mrs G Courtney [maternity leave]
Miss S Green

Teaching Assistants:
Miss R Argo (*Music*)
Miss H Bray (*Sport*)
Mr N Cairns (*Sport*)
Miss R Lowe (*Sport*)
Mr L Robinson (*Sport*)
Mr B Teil (*Languages*)
Mr P Varga (*Languages*)

Boarding Assistants (*Girls' Boarding*):
Mrs D Grant
Mrs H Grant
Miss C Papadopoulou
Mrs T Nightingale

Teaching Assistants (*Preparatory School*):
Mrs R Deacon
Mrs L Finn, NVQ III
Mrs D Hately
Mrs A Leake, NVQ II
Mrs E Sleath, NVQ II
Mrs S Wereszczyinski
Mr D Wilcock
Mrs J Yapa, BA

Ratcliffe Development:
Mr A Yell (*Development Director*)
Mrs L Liston (*Foundation Manager*)

Reading Blue Coat School

Holme Park, Sonning, Berks RG4 6SU
Tel: 0118 944 1005
Fax: 0118 944 2690
email: reception@rbcs.org.uk
website: www.rbcs.org.uk
Twitter: @ReadingBlues
Facebook: /ReadingBlueCoatl

The School was founded in 1646 by Richard Aldworth, a merchant of London and Reading, and a Governor of Christ's Hospital. There are 750 pupils (aged 11–18) including a co-educational Sixth Form.

Aims. The School aims to provide a stimulating and friendly atmosphere in which each pupil can realise his or her full intellectual, physical and creative potential. Pupils are encouraged to be self-reliant and adaptable and we hope that they will learn the basis of good citizenship founded on honesty, fairness and understanding of the needs of others.

Our School is a Church of England Foundation, and emphasis is placed on Christian values and standards.

Buildings. The School is set in an attractive 46-acre site by the banks of the Thames in the village of Sonning. School House, originally built in the eighteenth century and extensively remodelled in the Victorian era, stands at the heart of the School. The School's facilities have undergone a continuous programme of improvement over the last decade, including a new IT Centre, a new Design Technology Centre, improvements to the school's entrance and dropoff/pickup area, a new geology and psychology block, a 23-classroom teaching facility, a cricket pavilion, improvements to the swimming pool and a boathouse on the banks of the Thames. The School has recently expanded its facilities for the Sixth Form and has plans for further development.

Curriculum. In Years 7 to 9, pupils study a broad range of subjects, including Classics, two modern foreign languages and Religious Studies. In Years 10 and 11, pupils follow IGCSE courses in Mathematics and Science and also opt to complete four further courses in a wide range of additional subjects, such as History, Geography (IGCSE), Geology and Physical Education, with a modern foreign language being compulsory. A wide range of subjects is offered at A Level, including subjects such as Psychology, Economics, Business, Government and Politics, and Drama and Theatre Studies, with nearly every pupil going on to university, including Oxford and Cambridge.

Sixth Form. The co-educational Sixth Form Centre accommodates more than 250 students. Girls are fully integrated into all activities. In addition to A Level courses, all Sixth Formers follow a compulsory enrichment programme.

Games and Activities. A wide range of sports and activities is offered within the curriculum and regular school fixtures for all year groups are arranged. Full advantage is taken of the River Thames and rowing is a popular sport for both boys and girls. The main boys' games are Rugby in the Autumn Term, Football in the Spring Term, and Cricket and Athletics in the Summer Term. Girls play Netball, Rounders and Hockey. Other sporting activities include Squash, Basketball, Tennis, Golf, Table Tennis, Climbing, Swimming, Lacrosse, Kayaking, Archery, Cross Country, Badminton, Kickboxing, Mountain Biking, Yoga and Sailing.

The Cadet Force includes Army, RAF and RN Sections. Camping and adventure training activities take place during holidays and at weekends. There is a wide range in the Activities Programme, which includes The Duke of Edinburgh's Award, overseas expeditions, community service and sports leadership.

Music and Drama enjoy a high profile in the life of the School. Well over a third of the pupils receive individual instrumental lessons and pupils are encouraged to join in activities such as the Choir, Chamber Choir, Piano Trio, String Group, Concert Band, Saxophone Group, Guitar Ensemble, Orchestra, Wind Band, Brass Group, Jazz and Swing Bands. Concerts, plays and musicals are presented regularly.

Admissions. The two main points of entry in September are at 11+ and 16+. 11+ entry is by entrance examination taken the previous January. Entry at other levels is by examination and interview and is subject to vacancies. Entry to the Sixth Form for girls and boys is by assessment, interview and GCSE results.

The Foundation makes provision for awards of scholarships and bursaries, including academic, music and art awards, based on merit and need. Foundation Scholarships up to 100% of fees are available according to financial need.

Fees per term (2016–2017). £5,220.

Charitable status. Reading Blue Coat School is a Registered Charity, number 1087839. Its aim is the provision of secondary education for pupils aged 11 to 18.

Chairman of Governors: P Bertram

Headmaster: J R Elzinga, BA, MSt

Second Master: P J Thomas, BA Hons, GTP (*Geology*)
Deputy Head, Staff: Dr K J Magill, MPhil, BA, PGCE, PhD (*Religious Studies*)
Deputy Head, Academic: P C K Rowe, MEd, MA, PGCE (*Classics/Latin, Government & Politics*)
Deputy Head, Pastoral: P D Wise, BSc Hons, PGCE (*Geography*)
Bursar: S A Jackson, BSc, MBA

* *Head of Department*

Mrs K M Anderson, BA, PGCE (*English*)
M J Baker, BA Hons, PGCE (**Geography*)
Mrs C E Bamforth, MA, PGCE (*Biology*)
S D Bateman, BA (*Business, Economics*)
Mrs K E Bayliss, BA (**Business, *Economics*)
Mrs L J Bennett, BEd Hons (*Religious Studies*)
Mrs S E Berry, BA, PGCE, Dip SpLD, AMBDA (**Learning Support, French*)
T Blackburn, BA Hons, MPhil (*Religious Studies*)
J Bowler, BA Hons, PGCE, LTCL, ARCM (**Director of Music, Performance Studies/Drama and Theatre*)
J P Brown, BSc, PGCE (*Chemistry*)
M Brownsell, BSc, MBA (*Physics*)
Mrs N E Bruce-Lockhart, BA Hons, PGCE (*English*)
M R Budge, MEng, UMIST (*Mathematics*)
B J Clark, BA Hons, MSt, PGCE (**Religious Studies*)
Mrs M A Clews, BA, PGCE, PG Cert (**Psychology, Classics*)
Mrs D Coccia-Clark, BA Hons, MA (**Performance Studies/Drama and Theatre*)
A W Colville, BSc Hons, BSc (**Biology*)
S J Cook, CertEd, BA (**Physical Education*)
Mrs R L Crossland, MESci, PGCE (**Geology*)
Mrs C Dance, BA Ed Hons (*Mathematics, *Girls' Games*)
PJ Davies, BSc (*Sport & Physical Education*)
Mrs A M Dewar, BA Hons, PGCE (*French, German, Spanish*)
Dr S M Dimmick, BSc, DipEd, MSc, PhD (*Biology*)
R G Edmondson, BSc, BSc (*Geography*)
R N Ennis, BA, PGCE (*Art*)
Miss N Evans, BA Hons, PGCE (**Classics*)
Mrs G R Finucane, BSc, MSc (*Geology*)
Mrs J L Forward, BSc (*Mathematics, Physics*)
W E Gilbertson, MEng (*Physics*)
Mrs S A Head, MA (**Modern Foreign Languages, German, French*)
Miss G Higgins, BA Hons, PGCE (*Information Technology, Religious Studies*)
Miss C A Holliday, BA, PGCE (*German, French*)
M J Jerstice, BSc, PGCE (**Integrated Science, Chemistry*)
L B Johnson, BA Hons, PG Law Diploma (**Government and Politics*)
Mrs G M Kelly, BA Hons, PGCE (*Religious Studies, French*)
Mrs R Kennedy-George, MA, MPhil, PGCE (*English*)
J Leigh, BA, MA (*History*)
Mrs P J Leonard, BA, PGCE (*Mathematics*)
A J Maddocks, BA (**French, German*)
Mrs T A McConalogue, BEd (*Mathematics*)
S R McFaul, MEng, PGCE (*Mathematics, Physics*)
H J McGough, BSc Hons (**Design Technology*)
Mrs I A McGough, BA, PGCE (*Design Technology*)
A G McMahon, BMus, LTCL (*Music Technology*)
R E Mellows, BEng (*Physics*)
W E Mitchell, BA, PGCE (*Geography*)
W Nash-Wortham, BA Hons, PGCE (*Business, Economics, *Careers*)
G E Morton, BA Hons, PGCE (*English*)

D H Oldfield, BA Hons (*Music*)
Mrs H J Oliver, BA Hons, PGCE (*French*)
M J Pink, BA Hons, MSc (*Psychology, Information Technology*)
Miss G Plowman, BA Hons (*History*)
Mrs H E Rancombe, BSc Hons, PGCE (*Psychology, Biology*)
S R Roberts, BSc, PGCE (*Mathematics*)
Mrs C Rule, BA Hons, OCR SpLD Diploma (*Learning Support*)
D L Salmon, MA, Computing Dip, PGCE (**Physics*)
Dr F B Santos, BSc, MSc, PhD (*Chemistry*)
D H R Selvester, BA, PGCE (*Design Technology*)
T E Seward, MSc (*Sport and Physical Education*)
R I Shuttleworth, BSc Hons, PGCE (**Mathematics*)
J R Slack, BSc, PGCE (*Mathematics*)
Mrs J P Smith, BSc, PGCE (*Physics*)
R P Starr, BA Hons, PGCE (*Spanish, French*)
H R Stephens, BSc Hons, PGCE (*Geography, Geology*)
M J Stewart, BA Hons, MA, PGCE (**English*)
Mrs A D Tapley, BSc (*Biology*)
R H Taylor, BA Hons (*History*)
Miss B A Truman, BA Hons, MA, PGCE (*English, French*)
Mrs J M Turton, BSc, PGCE (**Chemistry*)
Miss T van der Werff, MA, PGCE (**History*)
W Voice, BA Hons, PGCE (*Information Technology, *Sport*)
T C Walford, BSc, PGCE (*Information Technology*)
R J Wallis, BA, PGCE (**Art*)
N J Warde, BSc, PGCE (*Biology*)
Mrs N Watmough-Starkie, BMus Hons, PGCE (*Music*)
S Yates, BSc Hons, PGCE (**Information Technology*)
R W Yue, MSc, BSc, PGCE (*Mathematics*)
Mrs J F Zambon, BA Hons, PGCE (**Spanish*)

Headmaster's Secretary: Mrs L A Bell
Director of Marketing and Admissions: Mrs J Jarrett
School Nurse: Mrs G F Montgomery, RGN
Sports Centre Manager: C Bate
Archivist: P J van Went, MA, CertEd

Reed's School

Cobham, Surrey KT11 2ES

Tel: 01932 869001
email: admissions@reeds.surrey.sch.uk
website: www.reeds.surrey.sch.uk

Reed's is a boarding and day school for boys with girls in the Sixth Form, founded by Andrew Reed in 1813 and incorporated by Act of Parliament in 1845 under the presidency of the Archbishop of Canterbury, the Duke of Wellington and the Marquis of Salisbury. When the School was founded, its facilities were reserved for boys whose fathers had died. In 1958 the School expanded and all boys became eligible for entrance. Sixth Form girls became eligible for entrance in the 1980s. Foundation awards are still granted each year to boys and Sixth Form girls who have lost the support of one or both parents.

The School is situated near Esher in 40 acres of heath and woodland. It can be reached in 30 minutes by train from Waterloo and is within half an hour's drive of both Heathrow and Gatwick Airports.

To the original buildings have been added in the last 15 years Chemistry laboratories; four Computer suites; two artificial turf hockey pitches; a new library; a new teaching block for the Physics and Mathematics departments; a Music School; an Indoor Tennis Centre; new Biology,

Geography and History departments; extensions to the Day Pupil Centre and an extension to the Sixth Form House which incorporates a lecture theatre; a new Language laboratory and new Language and English classrooms; a new Design and Technology building (FutureTech).

There are 704 pupils, just under 20% of whom are boarders, divided among 5 senior houses, Blathwayt, Bristowe, Capel, Mullens and School House, and one junior house, the Close, for those under 13. There is also a separate Sixth Form House. Admission at the age of 13 is normally by the Common Entrance examination, with a pre-test in Year 6; admission at the age of 11 by means of the School's own examination. There is admission into the Sixth Form for boys and girls by means of an entrance test sat in the November of Year 11.

Pupils are prepared for GCSE and GCE, AS and A Levels, and virtually 100% of Upper Sixth leavers go on to good universities. The games are Rugby, Cricket, Hockey, Athletics, Swimming, Squash, Netball and Basketball with sports Academies for Tennis, Skiing and Golf. The School has its own Combined Cadet Force with RAF and Army sections. The Duke of Edinburgh's Award can also be undertaken at Bronze, Silver and Gold levels. Special scholarships may be awarded for tennis, skiing and golf.

Pupils are all involved in a wide-ranging Activities Curriculum. There is also a broad range of Inter-House competitions. There is a School Choral Society, a Chapel Choir, an Orchestra, a Jazz Orchestra and various ensembles.

Religious instruction, which promotes religious tolerance, is in accordance with the principles of the Church of England. An annual Confirmation Service is held in the School Chapel for which pupils are prepared by the Chaplain. Pupils of all denominations are accepted into the School and are expected to attend chapel.

The National Curriculum is broadly followed in Years 7 to 9 and early specialisation is avoided. There is a Careers Team which advises pupils and arranges suitable visits and interviews and gives advice on University degree courses. The main responsibility for each pupil is undertaken by his or her Housemaster, supported by a Tutor. The health of the pupils is in the care of the School Doctor, and a State Registered Nurse is in charge of the Medical Centre.

Fees per term (2016–2017). Day Pupils (including meals): £6,205 (Years 7 & 8), £7,755 (Years 9–13). Boarders: £8,270 (Years 7 & 8), £9,995 (Years 9–13). All boarders may exercise a weekly boarding option. There are no compulsory extras.

Scholarships and Bursaries. Academic Scholarships are offered each year at age 11, 13 and 16.

Scholarships may be awarded for Music, Drama, Art and Sport at age 11, 13 or 16. Design & Technology scholarships are available at age 13 or 16. Headmaster's Awards may be given to candidates who offer a high performance in more than one area.

A large number of Foundation awards are made each year to boys and girls who have lost one or both parents, or whose parents are divorced or separated or whose home life is for some special reason either unhappy or unsatisfactory. The awards, which are means tested, vary according to circumstances.

All applications should be made to the Registrar.

Charitable status. The London Orphan Asylum (Reed's School) is a Registered Charity, number 312008. Its aims and objectives are to provide an education for pupils who have lost the support of one or both parents.

Patron: Her Majesty The Queen

Presidents:
Viscount Bridgeman
P B Mitford-Slade, OBE

G M Nissen, CBE
I Plenderleith, CBE

Governors:
I Wheeler, CBE, BCom, FCA (*Chairman*)

U D Barnett
D R Blomfield, BSc
Mrs M Donald
J Fulton, BA
Dr A M McLean, MB,
  BChir, FRCP, FRCR
Mrs L F Napier, FSI
Ms B O'Brien-Twohig,
  MA
Mrs D M Peacock, BSc
S T Poole, MSc
H M Priestley, MA Oxon

Miss K Richardson, MA
M Robinson, BA Arch,
  Grad Dip RIBA
Prof P Sellin, BSc, PhD,
  MInSEP, CPhys, IEEE
B Shepherd, BA
J Simpson, BEd, MSc,
  MPhil
R Stewart, FCIB
N D Taunt, FCA
P H H Verstage, BCom
  Hons

Bursar & Secretary to the Governors: Mrs L Hurford, BSc,
  ACMA

Headmaster: M W Hoskins, BA, MA

Senior Deputy Headmaster: G D Spawforth, MA
Deputy Head (*Academic*): D J Atkins, BA
Deputy Head (*Pastoral*): †A R Balls, BEd
Senior Master: I A Clapp, BEd
Development Director: Mrs K Bartram, BA
Assistant Head (*Teaching & Learning*): Ms C F St Gallay,
  BA
Assistant Head (*Sixth Form*): †L G Michael, BA (*Media Studies*)
Assistant Head (*Middle School*): L Pytel, BA
Assistant Head (*Academic Tracking*): J S Ross, MA
  (*Geography*)
Assistant Head (*Curriculum*): D Thompson, BSc (
  Physics, *Science*)
Chaplain: The Revd A Winter, BSc, BD
Head of Communications: Mrs J G Hart, BA (*Psychology*)

Assistant Staff:
* *Head of Department*
† *Housemaster*

†J E Allison, BSc
J M Anderson, BA
Ms L Ashby, BA (*Spanish*)
Mrs L Balls, BA (*Girls' Sport*)
J O Bishop, BA
†A J Blackman, MA
S M Bramwell, BA
Ms J A Brewster, BSc (*Chemistry*)
Mrs S E Butler, MA (*Academic Music*)
I B Carnegie, MA (*Director of Music*)
J E Clatworthy, MA
C E Cole, BA (*Printing*)
Mrs C C Cook, BA
Miss FL Cramoisan, MA
A J Davey, BA
P P Davies, MA
Miss A Di Mond, BSc
Miss Z C Davison, BA
J K Ditchburn, BA
J B Douthwaite, BA
M R Dunn, HND
B J Edwards, BA (*Head of Sport*) (*Physical Education*)
J M Finnerty, BSocSci
Ms M Fitzgerald, BA (*Librarian*)
Mrs M Francis, BA (*CPHSE*)
S A Gibbins, BA
Mrs K D Goden, BSc
T D Ha, BSc
†B J Haining, BSc

Mrs R F Harris, MA
T A Harrison, MSc (*Mathematics*)
†G S Hart, HEd (*Head of Digital Learning*)
Ms S M Hashmi-Lewis, BSc
C J Hawley, BA (*Head of Activities*)
Miss S L Hughes, BSc
Miss A M Jiménez, BA
Miss A N Johnson, MA (*Art*)
W A Jolly, BSc
Mrs D L Kane, BSc (*Head of Girls*)
Mrs J A Lawrence, BA
Ms E McGhee, BA (*Learning Support*)
K T Medlycott
P L Millington, BSc (*Design Technology*)
Mrs T A Millington, BEd
Miss K Morland, MA (*Head of Scholars*) (*Classics*)
†J W Norman, BA
Miss A O'Donovan, BSc
C J Osgood, MA
A R Pascoots
Mrs L Paterson, BSc (*Biology*)
Miss J L Pauley, BA
Mrs E Peyton, BSc
S J Pyburn, BSc, PhD
Miss M K Rai, BSc
Miss Z H Rice, BA
T J Rimmer, BSc
P W Rocket, BSc
Mrs H T Salford, BA (*French*)
C Sandison-Smith, MA (*German*)
T P Silk, BA (*Drama*)
G Stuckey, BSc
Mrs R L Sullivan, BA
E M Swift, BA (*Religious Studies*)
A R Talbot, BEd
T H Tam, BSc, PhD
A M Thompson, BSc, PhD
C S Thomson, BA
Mrs A Trehearn, BA (*English*)
M C Vernon, BSc
Mrs V Wakefield, BSc
A J Waller, BA (*History*)
J M Wallis, MEng
T A Webb, BA
S D Whiteley, BA (*Economics & Business Studies*)
R D Willey, GLCM
J Wright, BSc

Visiting Music Teachers:

J Dalgleish (*Piano*)
G Duggan (*Cello*)
J Dunning (*Electric Guitar*)
K Garrett (*Jazz Piano*)
D Hawkins (*Guitar*)
H Morgan (*Clarinet*)
E Spevok (*Drums*)
P Von Wielligh (*Flute*)

G Sutton (*Violin, Viola*)
A Marshallsay (*Percussion*)
S Rommer (*Double Bass*)
S James (*Classical Guitar*)
S Smith (*Oboe*)
M Hickman (*Voice*)
D Larkin (*Saxophone,
  Violin*)
D Deam (*Voice*)

Headmaster's Secretary: Mrs V Cox
Registrar: R M Gilliat, MA
Assistant Registrar: Mrs R Morris
Medical Officer: R Draper, MBChB, DCH, DRCOG, DA,
  MRCGP

Reigate Grammar School

Reigate Road, Reigate, Surrey RH2 0QS

Tel:	01737 222231
Fax:	01737 224201
email:	info@reigategrammar.org
	admissions@reigategrammar.org
website:	www.reigategrammar.org
Twitter:	@ReigateGrammar
Facebook:	@ReigateGrammarSchool

Reigate Grammar School is a co-educational day school for pupils aged 11 to 18.

The school was founded in 1675 as a free school for boys. It became an independent Grammar School during the nineteenth century, but after the 1944 Education Act it came under the control of Surrey County Council. On the abolition of the direct grant in 1976, Reigate Grammar School reverted to independent status. At the same time girls were admitted for the first time, initially in the Sixth Form only, but throughout the school from 1993. The school now numbers 950 pupils, of whom 250 are in the Sixth Form. In September 2003, the school merged with Reigate St Mary's Preparatory and Choir School (*see entry in IAPS section*), which provides education to 330 boys and girls aged from rising 3 to 11.

The school is situated in the historic market town of Reigate, just outside the M25 yet with easy transport links into London, Surrey and Sussex. Pupils come from a wide geographical area and from across the social spectrum, thanks to the school's own bursary programme, and to the generous support of the Peter Harrison Foundation which provides substantial financial support each year. Around 50% of pupils come from primary schools, the remainder coming from the preparatory sector.

The Governors have invested considerable sums in new buildings in recent years; a new science and humanities building opened in 2011, a new indoor swimming pool opened in January 2009; and new science laboratories and classrooms were completed in 2011. A new centre of learning incorporating a new library and Sixth Form Centre is due for completion in summer 2017. In addition to the main school site, the sports ground at Hartswood, two miles from the school, provides some 32 acres of playing fields and two floodlit all-weather pitches.

Organisation. The school is divided into three sections: Lower School (First and Second Forms – Years 7 and 8), Upper School (Third, Fourth and Fifth Forms – Years 9–11), and Sixth Form (Years 11 and 12). The welfare of pupils is overseen by the Heads of Section and Heads of Year. Recently the school has reintroduced a House system with the four houses taking the names of previous Headmasters of the school.

Curriculum. The range of subjects on offer is traditional in the early years, but allowing for a broadening of options in the Sixth Form. Prior to GCSE (the courses for which start in the Third Form) all pupils study a core curriculum of Mathematics, English, Science, one or two Modern Languages (French, German or Spanish), Latin, History, Geography, Religious Studies, ICT, Art, Design Technology, Food Technology, Music, Drama, PE and Games. Most pupils take ten GCSEs or IGCSEs, chosen from the above, with the added options of Sports Studies and Greek. Both Dual Award Science and the separate sciences are offered.

Most pupils stay on into the Sixth Form and take subjects to A2 level. Subjects available include all of the above, with the added options of Business Studies, Economics, Politics and Philosophy and Ethics. Further details are available on the website.

Extracurricular activities. Reigate Grammar School has a strong tradition of excellence in a wide variety of extracurricular activities, including an enviable reputation in sport, music and drama; large numbers of pupils participate in the Combined Cadet Force and in The Duke of Edinburgh's Award. The school has raised up to £45,000 for charities during the last year. The main sports are rugby, hockey and cricket for boys, and hockey, netball and rounders for girls, but other sports on offer include athletics, badminton, basketball, gymnastics, football, squash, swimming and tennis. There is a plethora of musical groups which rehearse regularly, including two orchestras, a Swing Band and three choirs. There are frequent concerts both inside and outside the school, including tours overseas. The Drama department presents at least one major production each term, sometimes in collaboration with the music department.

Admissions. Pupils are normally admitted to the School at 11+, 13+ or 16+, although vacancies occasionally occur at other ages. There is a registration fee of £100. All candidates are required to sit an entrance examination and attend an interview (normally in January or November) details of which are available from the Admissions Secretary. All enquiries concerning admission to the school should, in the first instance, be addressed to the Admissions Secretary.

Fees per term (2016–2017). £5,820. Sibling discounts are available.

Scholarships and Bursaries. The school offers a wide range of scholarships and bursaries, aimed at enabling parents who might not otherwise be able to consider an independent school to send their child to Reigate Grammar School. Discretionary Headmaster's Awards in addition to Academic, Music and Sports Scholarships are awarded at 11+, 13+ and 16+. Applicants should contact the Admissions Secretary for further details.

Bursaries may also be available, dependent on parental income and assets. Candidates living in the Borough of Reigate and Banstead may be eligible for a Harrison Scholarship, which is also means-tested and made available through the generosity of the Peter Harrison Foundation. Further details are available from the Bursar.

Junior School. Reigate St Mary's Preparatory and Choir School (*see entry in IAPS section*) is the junior and nursery school of Reigate Grammar School. It numbers approximately 330 pupils aged 3 to 11 and is one of the few choir schools in the country not attached to a cathedral or college.

Charitable status. Reigate Grammar School is a Registered Charity, number 1081898. Its aim is to provide high-quality education for boys and girls.

Governing Body:
Chairman: Mr A Walker
Vice-Chairmen: Sir Colin Chandler, Mrs J Langham

Mr D Adams	Mr E Elsey
Mr M Benton	Mrs E Fieldhouse
Mr C Cobain	Mrs J Forbat
Mr D Cole	Mr L Herbert
Mr B Day	Dr K Knapp
Mr J Dean	Mr R Newstead
Mr W Dunnet	Professor S Sayce

Headmaster: **S A Fenton**, MA Oxford, MEd Oxford

Senior Deputy Head: Mrs M A Collins, BEng Bristol (*Physics*)
Deputy Head: Miss S J Arthur, BA Durham (*History*)
Deputy Head: B P Stones, BSc, PhD Edinburgh (*Mathematics*)
Assistant Head: S J Rushby, BMus Surrey (*Director of Music*)
Assistant Head: A J Boothroyd, BSc Bradford (*Physics*)

Head of Sixth Form: H T Jones, BA Durham, MSt Oxford
(*History*)
Deputy Head of Sixth Form: R T James, BSc Bristol
(*Geography*)
Deputy Head of Sixth Form: Miss C Green, BA East Anglia
(*History/Politics*)
Deputy Head of Sixth Form: Dr T J Carter, MPhys Oxford,
PhD London (*Chemistry/Physics*)
Head of Upper School: N M Buchanan, BSc Edinburgh
(*Chemistry*)
Head of Fifth Form: N J Lobb, BA Bretton Hall (*Music*)
Head of Fourth Form: Ms H Robinson, BA Manchester,
MTeach IoE UCL (*English*)
Head of Third Form: Miss T Williams, BA Holloway
(*Spanish, MFL*)
Head of Lower School: Mrs C Lawson, BA Liverpool
(*Classics*)
Head of Second Form: M H Hetherington, BA Nottingham
(*Mathematics*)
Head of First Form: Mrs K Scaglione, BA Keele (*English*)

Chaplain: P J R Chesterton, BA OU, CertEd St Luke's
Bursar & Clerk to the Governors: S P Douty, FCMA
Development Director: S Davey, BSc, MA, MInstF Cert

Heads of House:
Bird: Mrs A McConnell, BSc Durham (*Biology*)
Cranston: B S Ellis, BA Southampton, MA Reading
(*History*)
Hodgson: W J Byfield, BSc Bath (*Biology*)
Williamson: Mrs C L Cline, BSc St Mary's College
(*Geography, Girls' PE & Games*)

* *Head of Department*

Teaching Staff:
Miss R J Aczel, BA Cambridge MLitt Aberdeen (*Classics*)
R I Alvarez, BDesignTech UWA Australia (*Design
Technology*)
G A Armstrong, BSc Sussex (*Biology*)
D G Bader, BSc Bath (*Mathematics*)
Mrs E L Bader, BEd Worcester College (**Food and
Nutrition*)
Miss S Branston, BA Wales (**Drama*)
Mrs E J Burns, BA Canterbury (**Art & Design*)
M J Buzzacott, BA Durham (*Classics, *Careers*)
T J Carden, MA Bristol (**Music*)
Miss S Carraro, BA Ca Foscari (*Spanish, French, MFL*)
Mme F Chartrain, MA Nantes (**French, *Modern
Languages*)
Mrs B Channon, Adv Dip SpLD Worcester (*Learning
Support*)
S T Chevalier, MA Oxford (**English*)
Miss E R Childs, BA Warwick (*Theology & Philosophy*)
Ms S Clarke, MA Sussex (*English, *Learning Support*)
M G Cline, BA Southampton (**Geography*)
Mme B F Collett, MA Aix-en-Provence (*French, Spanish*)
S A Collins, BA Durham (**Outdoor Training, Geography*)
D Cooper, BA Exeter (**PE, Sport Studies*)
Miss G B Cooper, BSc Exeter (*Physics, *PSHEE,
Electives)
Mrs K G Cooper, BA Leeds, MA Durham (**Theology &
Philosophy*)
Mrs A L Crook, BSc Edinburgh, MSc Bristol
(**Mathematics*)
R S Crook, BSc Southampton (**Chemistry*)
Miss H T Cuthbert, BSc York, MSc East Anglia (*Biology*)
T S Dare, MA Cambridge, MSc Sussex (*Biology*)
Mrs A J Davies, BEd Brighton Polytechnic (*Girls' PE &
Games*)
A R Davies, BSc Bristol (*Mathematics*)
Mrs G C Dexter, BA Queen's Belfast, Cert SpLD
(*Geography, Learning Support*)

H W Edwards, BA Aberystwyth (*Drama*)
W H Edwards, BA Staffordshire Polytechnic (*Art &
Design*)
Mrs R S Ellen, BA Brighton (*Art & Design, CCF
Contingent Commander*)
Mrs V R Ellwood, BA Durham (*English*)
J R Evans, BSc Warwick (*Mathematics*)
Mrs A R Fenton, BA De Montfort (*Food Technology*)
Mrs S M Garcia, BSc Queen's Ontario, BEd Kingston
(*Physics*)
Mrs S J T Genillard, ATC Goldsmiths (*Art & Design*)
Mrs T J Glynne-Jones, GRRNCM RNCM (**Choral Music*)
Miss V Godbold, BA Hull (*Geography, Careers*)
Mrs F Grant, BEd Bulmershe College (*Mathematics*)
Mrs F A Gunning, MA Oxford (**History, *Politics*)
M D Hallpike, CertEd Crewe & Alsager (*Design &
Technology*)
Miss K S Hancock, BSc Bath, MEd OU (*Mathematics*)
Miss M G Hare, BA Guildford School of Acting (*Drama*)
R I Hare, BMus Royal Academy of Music (*Music*)
J T Haskey, BA Kent (*History, Politics*)
Miss R A Haycox, BSc Leeds, MSc Leeds (*Mathematics*)
E R Hogarth, BA Lancaster, MA Exeter (*Theology &
Philosophy*)
Mrs R E Hogarth, BA Kent, MA Kingston (*Learning
Support*)
Mrs K Holbrook-Wilson, BA Rand Afrikaans South Africa
(*English*)
Miss C L Hollis, BA Oxford, MPhil Cambridge (*History*)
Mrs C M Hosegood, BSc Bristol (**Biology*)
H G Ingham, BA MA Oxford (*Classics*)
D A Jackson, BA Middlesex (*Drama*)
Mrs C J Jones, BA Durham (*English, Academic PE*)
Dr S L Lawson, BSc PhD Plymouth (*Biology*)
J M C Leck, BA East Anglia (**Cricket*)
Mrs S L Leck, MA Cambridge (*English*)
A L Lewis, BA Aberystwyth (*ICT, Business Studies*)
Miss P Lewty, BA Brighton (**Computing*)
P R Mann, BSc Loughborough (**Director of Sport*)
Miss R L Mansfield, BA Southampton Institute, MA
Camberwell (*Art & Design*)
Mrs E J Mitchell, BEd Exeter (**Academic PE*)
L W Morgan, BA MA Cardiff (*History, Communications &
E-Learning*)
Miss J A Morris, BSc Greenwich (*Chemistry*)
Mrs S Nasim, LLB Sussex MA Sussex (*Economics*)
N R Newman, BA Newcastle (**Business Studies,
Economics)
C S Nicholson, BSc Loughborough (*Head of Boys Hockey*)
Miss M Parque, BA Montpelier/Cardiff, MA Avignon
(*Spanish, French, MFL*)
Mrs C J Peats, BA Nottingham (*History, Economics*)
Mrs R Pegg, BA Queen Mary London, MA Nottingham
(*English*)
Miss M L Pope, BA MSc Cambridge, MA Sussex (*Biology,
Scholarships)
Mrs D Pricopie, BA, BSc Romania (*Physics*)
Dr M S Purcell, MEng Loughborough, PhD Nottingham,
MA Canterbury Christ Church (*Chemistry*)
Mrs V Ramsden, MSc Nottingham, BSocSc Birmingham
(*Geography*)
A G Reid, BSc MinstP London (*Physics, Extended Project
Coordinator*)
A K Reid, BEd St Luke's College Exeter (*Boys' Games*)
M R Russell, BEd Bulmershe (*Mathematics*)
P A Saunders, BEng Southampton (**Physics, *Electronics*)
J M Sergeant, BSc King's College London (*Chemistry,
Examinations)
R P Shaughnessy, BA Leeds (**English*)
G J Sillience, BSc LSE (*Mathematics*)
C A Smith, BSc Warwick (*Mathematics*)

C W Smith, MPhys Bath, MEd Exeter (*Physics*)
Miss M A Sowa, BA Kent (**German, French*)
Dr M J Stenning, BA MA East Anglia, DPhil Sussex (*English*)
Mrs L J Stephens, BEd Cambridge (*Mathematics, Examinations*)
Mrs S Sullivan, BEd Exeter (*Girls' PE & Games*)
Mrs C S Tate, BA Oxford (*Classics, Mathematics*)
Mrs D S L Trewinnard, BA Chichester (*Girls' PE & Games*)
Miss N Vasanthakumar, BSc KCL (*Mathematics*)
Miss A-M Vaughan, BA Durham (**Spanish, French*)
A Welch, BA Cambridge (*Chemistry*)
Mrs R J Wickham, BA Ed Exeter (*Girls' PE & Games*)
C T Wileman, BA Greenwich (*English*)
P J Williams, BSc Plymouth (**Design & Technology*)
Miss T R Williams, BA Royal Holloway (*Spanish*)
Mrs J Wright, BA Wales (*Spanish, French*)

PA to the Headmaster: Mrs B G Eustace

Rendcomb College

Rendcomb, Cirencester, Gloucestershire GL7 7HA

Tel: 01285 832306
Fax: 01285 831331
email: admissions@rendcombcollege.org.uk
website: www.rendcombcollege.org.uk
Twitter: @RendcombCollege
Facebook: @Rendcombcollege
LinkedIn: /rendcomb-college

Rendcomb College is a co-educational, independent day and boarding school for children aged 3 to 18 in the heart of the Cotswolds, UK. The College was founded in 1920 by Noel Wills and is set within a stunning 230-acre parkland estate which is equidistant from Cheltenham and Cirencester.

Our Mission. Our mission is to develop thoughtful, adventurous and academically ambitious young people who are lifelong learners. We aim to prepare them with the character and skills to succeed in the ever-changing world after school. Our pupils have the freedom to experience, explore and enquire about the world around them. We aim to encourage independence and tolerance in a safe, caring community and magnificent natural environment.

To achieve this we will:

* Promote a growth mindset, where abilities can be developed through dedication and hard work;
* Provide a co-curriculum that will challenge and support character development, leadership and teamwork;
* Encourage individualism, creativity and contribution to a nurturing and collaborative community;
* Engender physical, spiritual and mental wellbeing through a strong pastoral system;
* Prepare pupils for a life beyond school;
* Develop an appreciation for and responsible attitude towards their environment and surroundings.

Admission. Pupils join the Junior School from Nursery or Reception or join the Senior School at age 11, 13 or 16. The entrance examination at 11 is taken at Rendcomb and comprises three papers: English, Mathematics and Verbal Reasoning. At 13, pupils are admitted by Common Entrance or Rendcomb Examination and at 16 by interview, school reports and GCSE results.

Curriculum. Rendcomb College's curriculum extends well beyond the confines of the classroom and the core teaching day. Our small size in both the Junior and Senior schools enables all students to participate in a number of sports, in addition to a wide range of activities which begin after the end of formal lessons each day. Our philosophy is to consider these to be co-curricular, aimed at combining with the academic elements to genuinely develop the whole person and ensure that we provide a fully-rounded education.

Academic Success.
A Level Results 2016:
88% Pass Rate A*–C
68% Pass Rate A*–B
49% Pass Rate A*–A
GCSE Results 2016:
88% Pass Rate A*–C
69% Pass Rate A*–B
47% Pass Rate A*–A

University Entrance. In 2016, leavers went on to a number of prestigious Higher Education institutions including Oxford University, Imperial College London, King's College London, Loughborough, Keele, Exeter and Leeds. One student received a double scholarship to study at Keiser University in Florida securing both an academic and lacrosse award. The Head Girl was accepted into the Royal Military School of Music where she continues with her clarinet studies.

Houses. Both Day pupils and Boarders share the same Houses, enabling strong friendships and comradery to flourish among all pupils throughout the College.

Pupils can board when they join the Senior School in Year 7 though to Sixth Form. From Year 10 upwards, all Boarders have their own modern, comfortable study bedrooms which can be personalised, whilst the younger pupils share dormitories with two or three other students.

Our boarding is very flexible, especially at weekends; from Saturday teatime onwards, Boarders choose to stay at school to work, relax or join in family life at home. There are beds for Day pupils too if they wish to try boarding, or if they need to stay over.

Pupils are allocated to the House relevant to their age and gender until they join Sixth Form when they may join the dedicated co-educational Sixth Form house.

Boarders' weekends are full, busy and purposeful through the provision of an extensive programme of activities run by our Boarding Activities Coordinator.

The five Houses at Rendcomb College are located on the school's campus and within easy reach of classrooms and sports facilities. Each with their own character and style, the Houses offer an ideal setting for all pupils to thrive and develop under the guidance of the Houseparents and their pastoral and domestic teams.

Bursaries. A number of contributory bursaries are awarded in keeping with the original charitable aims of the College's Founder. The amount of the bursary award is not influenced by the level of the child's academic ability but by the extent of need and each case is assessed on its own merits with awards being made accordingly.

Scholarships. A number of Scholarships (Academic, Art, Music, Drama and Sport) are awarded each year at 11+, 13+ and 16+ with additional Scholarships awarded at 7+. Scholarships are based on the assessment of a pupil's potential and the value that we believe they will add to the life of our school. We also award the Noel Wills Scholarship and the Rendcomb Scholarship at 11+.

All awards are reassessed annually and are subject to satisfactory academic progress and behaviour. The number of individual Scholarships awarded each year depends solely on the calibre of the candidates. There is no limit to the number of Scholarships the school awards; Rendcomb looks for a level of excellence in order to award a Scholarship.

Fees per term (2016–2017). Senior School: Boarding £6,950–£10,180, Day £5,000–£7,330. Junior School: Day £2,225–£3,730.

Charitable status. Rendcomb College is a Registered Charity, number 1115884.

Chairman of Governors: Sir Francis Richards, KCMG, CVO, DL

Headmaster of College: **Mr Robert Jones**, BA, MEd

Head of Juniors: Mrs Victoria Beevers, BEd

Bursar: Mrs E Sharman, BSc

Registrar: Miss E Townsend, BA

Repton School

Repton, Derbyshire DE65 6FH

Tel: 01283 559222 (Registrar)
          01283 559200 (School)
email: registrar@repton.org.uk
website: www.repton.org.uk
Twitter: @ReptonSchool

Situated in the heart of England, Repton School has been home to a spiritual community for over 800 years and the inspiring buildings of the 12th century Priory remain at the centre of our life together today.

Over its 450 years Repton has established a strong tradition of distinguished alumni in public life, sport and the arts including Roald Dahl, Archbishop Michael Ramsey, C B Fry, Graeme Garden and Jeremy Clarkson.

The 21st century Repton is a fully co-educational school with a strong boarding ethos and is home to 650 pupils. Individuality flourishes within the context of a real community and every Reptonian is encouraged to discover those areas in which he or she can excel, and to prepare for the world of possibilities that lie beyond the Arch.

Admission. Pupils are admitted at 13+ (Year 9) and 16+ (Year 12) but exceptions may be made in other years. Application for admission should be made to the Headmaster. There is a registration fee of £100. Candidates will normally have passed Common Entrance at their preparatory schools, but there is also an entrance examination for candidates not being prepared for CE.

Fees per term (2016–2017). Boarders £11,342; Day pupils £8,414. Some additional expenses (for books, stationery, pocket money, etc) will be incurred.

There is a Bursary Fund from which grants in the form of remissions from full fees may in certain circumstances be made. No remission of fees can be made on account of absence.

Scholarships and Bursaries. A number of scholarships and exhibitions are offered annually, generally at 13+ and 16+, though in exceptional circumstances candidates may be considered for awards at other entry points. The value of any award may be increased where need is shown.

Entrance Scholarships at 13+: The examination for non-academic awards is held at Repton in January for entry the following September, and the examination for academic awards is held at Repton in May for entry the following September. Candidates must be under 14 on 1 September in the year of the examination.

16+ Scholarships: The examination for both academic and non-academic awards takes place in November for entry the following September. A number of awards are available for pupils joining Repton from both the maintained and independent sectors.

Music Scholarships and Exhibitions are awarded, usually at 13+ and 16+. Examinations take place in November (16+) and January (13+). An open day for potential music scholars is held in October.

Drama Scholarships are also offered, usually at 13+ with auditions and interviews taking place in January.

Art Scholarships and Exhibitions are offered, usually at 13+ and 16+. Examinations take place in November (16+) and January (13+). Candidates will be assessed by examination, interview and an assessment of their portfolio.

Design and Technology (DT) Scholarships and Exhibitions are offered, usually at 13+. Examinations take place in January. Candidates will be asked to complete a practical session and interview and to provide a folder of work for assessment.

Sports Scholarships are offered, usually at 13+ and 16+, to pupils of exceptional talent. Assessments are held by arrangement with the Director of Sport, during the Lent Term.

C B Fry All Rounder Award: awards worth up to 20% of the Repton boarding fee may be offered at 13+ to candidates exhibiting outstanding all-round leadership potential. Assessments take place in March or April when candidates are in Year 7.

Bursaries may be available to those who would not otherwise be able to attend an independent school. These may, in appropriate circumstances, be used to supplement Academic or non-academic awards. Means-tested bursaries are also available to Forces families.

Curriculum. The curriculum in Year 9 is broad to enable pupils to make an informed choice of GCSE subjects at the beginning of Year 10.

In Years 10 and 11, pupils study a combination of core and optional subjects. All pupils study English, Mathematics, Biology, Chemistry and Physics (leading either to two GCSEs in Science and Additional Science or three GCSEs in separate sciences for the more able students). The vast majority of pupils also take English Literature and French as core GCSEs. Pupils choose three subjects as optional GCSE subjects from: Art, Business Studies, Classical Civilisation, Classical Greek with Latin ("Gratin"), Design and Technology, Drama, Geography, German, History, Latin, Music, Physical Education, Religious Studies, Spanish and Three Dimensional Studies. Art and Music may also be taken "off the timetable" to provide pupils with the choice of a fourth optional subject. In Year 10, all pupils also receive one lesson in ICT and one lesson in PSHCE per week.

Most pupils study four subjects in the Lower Sixth at AS Level, though Further Mathematics can be taken as a fifth option. In the Upper Sixth many pupils choose to take three of these subjects to the full A Level; some opt to continue with all four or indeed five. The following are available as full A Levels over two years or as AS Levels over one year: Art, Biology, Business Studies, Chemistry, Classical Civilisation, Classical Greek, Design and Technology, Drama and Theatre Studies, Economics, English, French, Geography, German, Government and Politics, History, Latin, Mathematics, Further Mathematics, Music, Physical Education, Physics, Religious Studies, Spanish and Textiles. In the Lower Sixth, most pupils take "Civics", a course designed by the School to consolidate and extend their AS Level studies. In the Upper Sixth, there is a timetabled lecture programme where pupils have the opportunity to hear distinguished speakers talk on a wide variety of subjects.

Potential Oxbridge candidates are identified by the end of their second term in the Sixth Form and prepared for interview.

Chapel services are those of the Church of England and boarders are expected to attend a service every Sunday unless specially excused. A Confirmation is held each year.

Other activities. Every opportunity and encouragement is given to pupils to develop their creative interests in Art, Music, Drama and Design Technology. Facilities include dedicated Art, Drama and Music Schools, newly renovated Theatre, Studio Theatre and Textiles Studio. There are numerous School societies, covering a wide variety of interests.

Games and sports. Football, hockey (three astroturf pitches – 2 water-based, 1 sand), cricket, netball, rugby, fives, squash, tennis (2 indoor courts and 14 hard courts), cross-country, athletics, sailing, climbing, canoeing, swimming, fencing, golf and horse riding. Superb facilities are provided for physical education including a sports hall, fitness suite, gymnasium and indoor swimming pool.

Combined Cadet Force. The School maintains a contingent of the Combined Cadet Force and every pupil is a member in Year 10. Subsequently pupils may remain in the CCF to take part in The Duke of Edinburgh's Award scheme or specialise as instructors. Sixth Formers have the additional choice of Community Service.

Houses. All pupils belong to a House, which is their home in the School, where they eat all meals, and is at the heart of their life at Repton. The Housemaster or Housemistress, who has overall responsibility for an individual pupil's work and development, lives in the House with his/her own family and is supported by a resident Matron and team of Tutors.

Repton Preparatory School and Pre-Preparatory School at Foremarke Hall are approximately 1½ miles from the main school and house 63 boarders, 273 day boys and girls and 110 pre-prep day boys and girls. Pupils are taken from age 3 and prepared for entrance to Repton and other schools. Academic Scholarship examinations take place in January.

Further information may be obtained from The Headmaster, Foremarke Hall, Milton, Derbyshire DE65 6EJ. (*See Foremarke Hall's entry in IAPS section.*)

Charitable status. Repton School is a Registered Charity, number 1093166. It exists to provide high quality education for boys and girls.

Chairman of Governors: Sir Henry Every Bt

Headmaster: **W M A Land**, MA Trinity College Cambridge

Second Master: Mrs S A B Tennant, MA late Scholar of Somerville College Oxford
Deputy Head (*Academic*): T C Owen, MA late Exhibitioner of St Edmund Hall Oxford
Deputy Head (*Pastoral*), *Senior Master*: J G Golding, BA King's College London
Chaplain: The Revd N C Robert, BA King's College London

Heads of Department:
Classics: R G Embery, BA Durham
Modern Languages: Mrs C R Watson, MA Pembroke College Oxford
English: Miss K J Campbell, MA St Andrews
Drama: Mrs F J Bardsley, BA Durham
History : Dr N F Pitts, BA, PhD Leeds
Government & Politics: A R Couldray, BA Lady Margaret Hall Oxford
Geography: R G De Rosa, BSc Durham
Economics: D A Exley, BSc York
Business: Mrs M K Court, BA Durham
Mathematics: P V Goodhead, MA late Scholar of Pembroke College Oxford
Ethical & Religious Studies: Mrs A V E Sanders, BA Leeds
Physics: M W T Hunt, BSc UCL
Biology: Dr S M Ingleston-Orme, BSc, PhD Nottingham
Chemistry: V R Jones, BSc Hull
Director of Music: O M Walker, BA Keble College Oxford
Director of Art: I J Whitfield, MA Royal College of Art
Design and Technology: I Setterington, BEd Loughborough
Physical Education: S J Clague, BSc Crewe and Alsager College of HE

Boys' Boarding Houses:
School House: T H Naylor
The Priory: N F Pitts
The Orchard: M M Carrington
Latham House: S O Merlin
The Cross: S Earwicker
New House: J D Wilton

Girls' Boarding Houses:
The Abbey: Mrs L E Wilbraham
The Garden: Ms S J Lees
Field House: P J Griffiths & Mrs J Griffiths
The Mitre: Mrs A F Parish

Bursar: C P Bilson, MA, MBA Jesus College Cambridge
Registrar: Miss J Shone
Headmaster's Secretary: Miss J J Taylor

Robert Gordon's College

Schoolhill, Aberdeen AB10 1FE

Tel:	01224 646346
Fax:	01224 630301
email:	enquiries@rgc.aberdeen.sch.uk
website:	www.rgc.aberdeen.sch.uk
Twitter:	@robertgordons
Facebook:	/robertgordonscollege
LinkedIn:	/robertgordonscollege

Motto: 'Omni nunc arte magistra'

An HMC independent co-educational day school from Nursery to Sixth Year.

Robert Gordon's College is an independent school in the heart of Aberdeen. Our pupils' success is built on a strong sense of who they are, what they can achieve, and what it feels like to be part of a happy and purposeful school community. Our school motto translates as 'Be the Best You Can Be'. Every individual child deserves this ambition; Robert Gordon's College is a school which will prepare your child for a life where ambition, success and confidence are rooted in security, happiness and a sense of who they are.

Robert Gordon's College is now home to the largest school teaching centre for science education in Britain – The Wood Foundation Centre for Science and Technology alongside The Craig Centre for Performing Arts, a new performance and digital recording venue. We will continue this momentum as we look towards the creation of a new sports facility to complement our on-site swimming pool at Schoolhill and our renowned sports grounds at Countesswells. Our ambitious plans demonstrate our commitment to our pupils and their future locally, nationally and internationally.

History. Robert Gordon was a merchant from Aberdeen who spent much of his life based in Poland. On retiring to Aberdeen, he left his fortune to found a 'Hospital' for boys' accommodation and education. The school opened in 1750. In 1881, the 'Hospital' was reconstituted as a day school under the name of 'Robert Gordon's College'. It continued to attract support from benefactors. In 1909 its charitable constitution changed to allow the development of adult education, a move which developed in the course of time into the Robert Gordon University. The next major change in the nature of the school was in 1989 when girls were admitted. Robert Gordon's College is now a co-educational day school in the Scottish tradition, which remains true to the charitable and educational principles on which it was founded by Robert Gordon over 250 years ago.

Number of Pupils. Nursery (age 3½–5): 35 children; Junior School (Primary Classes 1–7): 537 pupils; Senior School (Secondary Forms 1–6): 1074 pupils.

Admission. The main entry points are Primary 1, Primary 6 and Secondary 1. Entry to Primary 1 (age 4½–5½ years) is by interview held in January/February, and to Primary 6 (age 9½–10½ years) by Entrance Test held in January/February.

Entry to Secondary 1 is by an Entrance Examination held in January.

Entry at other stages depends upon vacancies arising, and the offer of a place is subject to satisfactory performance in an Entrance Test and interview.

Fees per annum (2016–2017).
Nursery (whole day): £8,990 (exc lunch), £9,400 (inc lunch)
Nursery (half day): £4,495 (exc lunch), £4,905 (inc lunch)
Primary 1: £7,905 (exc lunch), £8,365 (inc lunch)
Primary 2: £7,905 (exc lunch), £8,385 (inc lunch)
Primary 3: £10,740 (exc lunch), £11,220 (inc lunch)
Primary 4–7: £10,740 (exc lunch) £11,350 (inc lunch)
Secondary: £12,305 (exc lunch)

Bursaries. Robert Gordon's College offers means-tested Bursaries to between 10 and 18 pupils every year for entry into Secondary 1 from any school. Burnett Scholarships offer up to half-fee discounts to pupils of outstanding talent in academic subjects, in music, or in sport. Burnett Scholarships are available to pupils currently in Fourth or Fifth Year at other schools.

Buildings. The centre block was erected in 1732, but there have been many modern additions. The College is fully equipped with Assembly Hall, Library, Laboratories, Art Rooms, Computing areas and Workshops. There are two Gymnasia and a Swimming Pool on site at the School. Countesswells Sports Field was opened in 1992 on a 40-acre site 3 miles from the school incorporating first-class accommodation and facilities, including a water-based hockey pitch and an astroturf all-weather sports surface. A five-storey teaching block, incorporating a Dining Hall, was opened in 1994, and a new Library and Information Centre in 2000. A new Junior School building opened in Spring 2009, with newly located and renovated Senior classrooms following in Summer 2009. A new Science and Technology Centre, and Performing Arts Centre opened in 2015.

Curriculum. In the Junior School the usual subjects of the primary curriculum are covered, with specialist teachers in Art, Drama, French, Music, Physical Education, ICT and Science. In the Senior School S1–S2 builds on the primary curriculum and as a foundation to the S3–S4 curriculum based on CfE principles. S3–S4 study eight National 5 subjects; S5–S6 Higher Grade and Advanced Higher. S6 pupils have Higher courses particular to them and specifically designed Enhancement courses.

The tradition of academic success continues at Robert Gordon's College with the vast majority of pupils annually going on to University.

Games. Rugby, Hockey, Cricket, Netball, Tennis, Athletics, Cross-Country Running. A wide range of other sports is offered, including Badminton, Basketball, Volleyball, Golf, Squash, Skiing, Swimming, Orienteering, Hillwalking and Kayaking.

Extra-Curricular Activities. There is a strong Combined Cadet Force (Army, RAF and Pipe Band). The Choirs, Concert Band and Orchestras play a prominent part in the life of the School, as do Literary and Debating Societies who meet weekly, and dramatic societies, which present a variety of performances. Many other clubs and societies flourish, making over 100 in all. A very large proportion of pupils undertake The Duke of Edinburgh's Award.

Charitable status. Robert Gordon's College is a Registered Charity, number SC000123. It exists to provide education for boys and girls.

Board of Governors:

Nominated Governors:
Chairman of Governors: Professor James Hutchison (*University of Aberdeen*)
Mrs Elizabeth Clark (*University of Aberdeen*)
Councillor Bill Cormie (*Aberdeen City Council*)
Councillor Jean Morrison MBE (*Aberdeen City Council*)
Councillor Ian Yuill (*Aberdeen City Council*)
Councillor Alan Donnelly (*Aberdeen City Council*)
Revd B Stephen C Taylor (*Presbytery of Aberdeen*)
Revd Marian Cowie (*Presbytery of Aberdeen*)
Mr Robin Whyte (*Gordonian Association*)
Mr Graeme Nicol (*Gordonian Association*)
Dr George S Stevenson (*Seven Incorporated Trades of Aberdeen*)
Mr Alfred Cordiner (*Aberdeen Endowments Trust*)
Mr Victor Beamish (*Aberdeen Endowments Trust*)
Mr David Rennie (*Aberdeen and Grampian Chamber of Commerce*)

Co-opted Governors:
Mr Paul de Leeuw (*Vice Chairman*)
Dr Tracey J H Menzies
Mr William Rattray
Mr Kevin Reynard
Mr Christopher Shepherd
Mr Alistair Hector

***Head of College*: Simon Mills**, MA, BA

Head of Senior School: Andrea Angus, BSc

Deputy Head (S1): Stefan Horsman, MA, BA
Deputy Head (S2–S3): Robin Fish, MA
Deputy Head (S4–S5): Claire Cowie, MLiH
Deputy Head (S6): Michael S Elder, MA

Guidance Staff:
Blackfriars (B1, B2): Gail E Clark, BSc; Sarah Coates, MSc
Collyhill (C1, C2): Kevin Cowie, BSc; Anne Watson, BA
Sillerton (S1, S2): Colin Filer, BEd; Tracy Reid, BA, FCCA
Straloch (T1, T2): Arthur Jamieson, BSc; Louisa McEwan, MA
Head of Careers: Dawn Pirie, BSc, MRes, RSci
Head of University Guidance: Daniel Montgomery, MA

Principal Teachers (Learning):
Carolyn Armstrong, BEd
Donna Ellis, BSc (*Tracking & Monitoring*)
Craig Harper, BEd BSc (*Boys' PE*)
Wendy Smith, BEd (*Girls' PE*)
Roy Wakeford, BSc (*Numeracy*)
Gemma West, BSc (*Health & Well-being*)
Margaret Wood, BA (*Transition*) [Maternity Leave]

Heads of Department:
Art: Louise Charlton, BA
Biology: Owain Bristow, MA
Chemistry: Jane Kennedy, BSc, PhD
Classics: Caig Galbraith, PhD
Computing Studies: Mark Hay, BSc
Drama: Andrew Milarvie, BA, DipDA
Economics and Business Studies: Jackie Farquhar, BA
English: Marion Waters, MSc
Geography: Jennifer Gray, MA, PhD
History and Modern Studies: Noel Shearer, MA
Mathematics: Simon Fogiel, MA, PGDip
Modern Languages: Nadine Clark, MA
Music: Kevin Haggart, BMus, MMus
Physical Education:
Stacey Stewart, BEd (*Head of PE*)
Richard Anderson, BA (*Head of Sport*)

Physics: Stuart Farmer, BSc, MBA, CSciTeach, FInstP
Religious Education: Kenneth Primrose, MA, MTh
Support For Learning: Allie Smith, BA
Technology: David McLaren, DipTechEd

Junior School:
Head of Junior School: Mollie Mennie, MBA

Deputy Heads:
Sally-Ann Johnson, BEd, MEd
Varie Macleod, BEd

Principal Teachers Learning and Teaching:
Susan Jamieson, MEd, MA (*Health and Well-being*)
Claire Rae, BSc
Tracy Geddes, MA
Susie Robertson, MA

Whole College Support Staff:
Director of Finance: Andrew W Lowden, MA, CA
Director of Development, Marketing and Admissions:
  Laura Presslie, BA
Director of IT Services: David Stone, BSc, MSc

Full staff list is available to view at
www.rgc.aberdeen.sch.uk/stafflist.

Roedean School

Roedean Way, Brighton BN2 5RQ

Tel: 01273 667500; Admissions: 01273 667626
Fax: 01273 676722
email: info@roedean.co.uk
website: www.roedean.co.uk
Twitter: @RoedeanSchool
Facebook: @RoedeanSchool

Introduction. Roedean is a day, flexi, weekly and full boarding school for 500 girls aged 11–18. The school has grown from 360 girls in the last two years, and, due to increased demand from UK parents, it now has a three-form entry to Year 7. In 2016, the school has received an outstanding ISI Inspection report, awarded 'excellent' in every category, and the girls also achieved the school's best-ever A Level and GCSE grades.

The three Lawrence sisters founded Roedean in Brighton in 1885 and the school was Incorporated by Royal Charter in 1938. Their original aims were to give due emphasis to physical and outdoor education, to encourage independence and self-reliance, 'to give as much liberty as can be granted with safety' and to supply a sound intellectual training.

Today the school community is made up of 40 different nationalities and remains committed to the founders' emphasis on independent learning and the development of self-confidence in readiness for professional life. The school buildings are set on a spacious, yet safe, 45-acre site surrounded by a further 70 acres of farmland. The campus commands enchanting views of the English Channel.

Philosophy. The Roedean philosophy is strongly focused on a holistic education, with success in all areas of school life complementing each other. Pupils are encouraged to challenge themselves and everything around them, and to be self-reliant, to explore their talents, to strive for excellence, to develop their intellectual curiosity, to lead as well as to be part of a team, and to appreciate cultural diversity. A girl educated at Roedean will have respect for herself and others, be qualified to enjoy a fulfilling career and feel confident she has the skills to balance her personal and professional life – she will grow up at her own pace within a warm, supportive, and enabling community.

The boarding approach is ideally suited to the school's holistic philosophy as it provides a rich and balanced programme of learning and activities in a structured yet informal environment. Day girls benefit from this ethos as they are well integrated into the House system. The single-sex environment has particular advantages for girls: it prevents stereotyping, raises expectations, and develops self-confidence by offering ample opportunities for leadership and responsibility.

Curriculum. Girls are given a structured grounding in basic skills and offered a very broad programme of knowledge and experience. Subject specialists work together in a coordinated approach to achieve maximum reinforcement and continuity across 30 subjects. The benefits of traditional subjects, including Latin, are balanced by Psychology, Design and Technology, and Critical Thinking. Girls in KS3 take part in an academic enrichment programme called HHH (Heads, Hands, and Hearts), which includes Russian, cookery, and Sign Language, among others. Class-sizes are consistently small, ranging between 14 and 20 girls in the Lower School, with smaller groups in the Sixth Form.

Each girl's GCSE programme is individually tailored to provide a broad, balanced education and to ensure that requirements for higher education are met.

The strong Sixth Form offers an extensive range and combination of A Levels, covering over 20 subjects. Over time, the school has developed a strong link with the University of Sussex, enabling the most able Sixth Form mathematicians to study undergraduate geometry alongside their A Level courses.

Results in public examinations were excellent in 2016, with 62.2% of A2 grades at the highest level of A* and A. At GCSE, 46.2% of examinations were awarded A* grades, and 74.3% were A*–A grades.

Co-curricular Activities and Physical Education. The range of music, art and design, speech, debating, drama and dance opportunities within the curriculum are further supported by optional private tuition and club activities. The school is particularly strong in the performing arts: music (choirs and orchestras), drama and dance.

The school has an excellent record in The Duke of Edinburgh's Award and Young Enterprise Business Scheme which offer girls opportunities to develop a spirit of discovery and independence and encourage links with the wider community.

Netball, hockey, tennis, swimming, athletics, cricket and rounders are the principal sports, with sailing, lacrosse, football, badminton, basketball, volleyball, squash, trampoline, gymnastics, fencing, golf, scuba diving and karate also available. Inter-school fixtures are part of all the major sport programmes and girls are encouraged to enter local, county and national tournaments.

Boarding. The House system provides the supportive and caring environment necessary for each girl, boarder or day, to flourish as an individual and a member of the community.

The four main Houses (for girls 11 to 17) and the separate Sixth Form House, Keswick, each have a dedicated team of staff in close contact with parents. Facilities range from bedrooms shared by 2 or 3 younger girls to university-style study-bedrooms for Sixth Formers. The girls in the four main houses are composed of a mixture of boarding and day students from each of the six year-groups.

Continuity of individual guidance and care is ensured by the school's tutorial system. Tutors monitor each girl's academic progress and involvement in extracurricular activities and liaise with House staff on a regular basis to maintain a balanced, realistic timetable which meets each individual's needs and abilities.

Health. The School Health Centre is run by a Registered General Nurse who is assisted by a team of similarly qualified nurses. A doctor visits the School and holds clinics regularly each week. She is "on call" in case of an emergency.

There is also a Counsellor who runs sessions in school each week.

Religion. The School welcomes students of all faiths, or none. Arrangements are made for Anglicans to be prepared for Confirmation, for Roman Catholics to attend Sunday Mass locally, and for Jewish girls to receive instruction.

Facilities. All subjects are taught in specialist rooms, and students have Wi-Fi access throughout the school to support their studies. There is a main library and resources' centre to support individual study. There are two art studios adjacent to a Design & Technology Centre, a multimedia Language Centre, a Performing Arts complex (including a theatre which seats 320 people, dance studios, music suite) and a Science wing with nine laboratories for Biology, Chemistry and Physics. A multi-purpose sports hall with gym, heated indoor pool, 13 newly-refurbished hard tennis and netball courts, squash courts, ample playing fields and the use of two astroturf pitches close by support the PE/Sports programme. An all-weather pitch will be added on site over the coming year.

School Year and Leave Out. There are three terms, beginning in September, January and April. The summer holidays last eight weeks and Christmas/Easter up to four weeks each. Girls go home for half term and there are two weekend exeats each term. All boarders are free to go home at weekends and weekly boarders are escorted back to London on the train. The school provides a full boarding programme, but there is considerable flexibility to accommodate the individual needs of families.

Admission. Entry at 11+, 12+, 13+ and 16+ is through Roedean Entrance Examination papers in English, Maths, and Non-Verbal Reasoning, which can be taken at any time up to two terms before entry. A good number of suitably qualified girls are admitted each year to the Sixth Form.

Scholarships and Bursaries. Academic, Art, Dance, Drama, Music, and Sport scholarships (worth up to 10% of fees) and exhibitions (worth up to 5% of fees) are available for girls entering Year 7, Year 9, and the Sixth Form.

Junior Scholarship examinations are held in January; Sixth Form Scholarship examinations are held in November.

Means-tested Bursaries are available. Details of scholarships and bursaries may be obtained from the Registrar.

Fees per term (2016–2017). Full Boarders £9,960– £12,060; Weekly Boarders (5 days) £9,225– £10,290; Flexi Boarders (3 days) £7,390–£8,935; Day Girls £5,165– £6,720. For girls entering the Sixth Form from other schools, there is an additional supplement of £1,300 per term (boarding). Parents who wish to pay a single composition fee should apply to the Director, Finance and Administration.

Extra fees are charged for individual tuition in musical instruments, speech training, ballet and some athletic activities.

For further details please contact the Registrar.

Charitable status. Roedean School is a Registered Charity, number 307063. It exists to provide quality education for girls.

President:
Lady Patten of Barnes, BA [OR]

Vice-Presidents:
Mrs S M Fowler-Watt, RGN [OR]
Dr J M Peacey, MB BS, MRCGP [OR]

Chairman of Council:
Ms A Whitaker MA Oxon ACA

Vice-Chairman of Council:
Mrs M S Chaundler, OBE, BA [OR]

Council:
Ms J Barnard-Langston, BA, MA, Dip Couns, JP
Ms F Cook, BSc [OR]

Dr A Edwards, MA Oxon FRCP
Dr H Fajemirokun, MA Oxon, PhD
Ms S Glynn, BSc, LLB [OR]
R S H Illingworth Esq, BA
Ms A-M Martin, MBE, BSc, MSc
Mrs C Nightingale, BA, MBA [OR]
Ms C Oram, MA Cantab, ACIB, Dip Trans
Mrs T Outhwaite, BA, PG Dip [OR]
Ms D Patman, FRICS
R Sanders Esq, OBE
Dr G Savage, MA Cantab, PhD, FRSA
Mrs V Smiley, BA [OR]
Mrs S Walton, MA Cantab [OR]

[OR] *Old Roedeanian*

Clerk: Mr R Poffley, BA, FCCA

ORA President: Ms Virginia Stephen

Staff:

Headmaster: Mr O Blond, BA Essex

Senior Deputy Head: Miss T Keller, BSc Manchester, PGCE, NPQH
Deputy Head, Academic: Dr J Hobbs, BA Leeds, PhD King's, PGCE
Deputy Head, Pastoral: Mrs S Ellis, BA Brighton, PGCE
Director of Finance and Administration: Mr R Poffley, BA Sussex, FCCA

Head of Key Stage 3 and Boarding: Mrs S Bakhtiari, BA QTS Brighton, MA Brighton
Head of Key Stage 4: Mrs D Robins
Head of Sixth Form: Miss C Carragher, BSc Southampton, PGCE
Director of Sixth Form: Dr G Hannan
Director of Communications: Dr R Barrand, BA Durham, PhD Leeds, PGCE
Senior Boarding Mistress: Mrs J Chandler
Senior Boarding Mistress: Mrs O Waller
Assistant Head, Academic: Ms A Kazem, MA Cantab, PGCE
Assistant Head, Co-Curricular: Ms H Boobis, MA Cantab, BA Cantab, MEd Open, PGCE

Heads of Department:
Art: Mr G Earl
Classics: Mrs P Wynne
Dance: Miss S Abaza
Design Technology: Miss E Griffiths-Moore, BA Edinburgh, PGCE Brighton
Drama: Mrs C Rigby, BA, MA Rose Bruford College of Speech & Drama
Economics, Government & Politics: Mr K Camburn (*Acting*)
English: Mr D Woodhouse, BA Anglia, MA Sussex, PGCE Brighton (*Acting Faculty Lead*)
Geography: Mrs R Herridge
History: Mr R Chamberlain
ICT & Business Studies: Ms S Bakhtiari, BA, MA Brighton
Learning Support: Miss S Maguire. BA Essex, MA Open, PGCE Chichester, RSA Dip TEFL
Mathematics: Mr D Orys
Modern Languages: Mr J Sampieri
Music: Miss V Fewkes, BA Bath, PGCE
Personal & Social Education (PSHE): Ms L Harknett, BA Warwick, PGCE Oxford
Philosophy & Religious Studies: Miss K Balnaves, BA Birmingham, MA UCL, PGCE Liverpool Hope
Physical Education: Miss K Andrew, BA De Montfort, PGCE Cheltenham
Psychology: Ms F Alexander, BA Durham, PGCE Brighton
Science & Chemistry: Mr A Wood

Biology: Miss P Harrison

Physics: Mr J Higginson

Registrar: Mrs D Banham

Rossall School

Fleetwood, Lancashire FY7 8JW

Tel:	01253 774201
Fax:	01253 772052
email:	admissions@rossall.org.uk
website:	www.rossall.org.uk
Twitter:	@RossallSchool
Facebook:	/RossallSchoolUK
LinkedIn:	/RossallSchool

Motto: '*Mens agitat molem*'

Rossall has been described by the Good Schools Guide as 'a warm, inclusive and remarkably happy place to be'.

Set on an historic 160-acre campus on the picturesque Lancashire coastline, Rossall is one of the country's leading independent co-educational boarding and day schools, where boys and girls aged 2–18 are nurtured in a safe, secure and supportive environment.

With a history dating back to 1844, Rossall combines a traditional British education with a modern approach which focuses on developing the whole child.

With nearly fifty different nationalities living and learning together at Rossall, we truly are a global village. The combination of UK day students and students from right across the world creates an exciting international dimension and an appreciation of diverse cultures, religions and politics.

Academic Curriculum. We deliver a broad and balanced curriculum with the principles of the International Baccalaureate learner profile at its heart. At Nursery level, we follow the Early Years Foundation Stage (EYFS) learning goals. From the age of 3 to 11, we offer the IB Primary Years Programme (PYP).

At age 16, students sit GCSE and iGCSE examinations, then have the option to choose either the IB or A Level route in the Sixth Form. The IB principles run through our teaching and learning in every phase of the school and underpin a dynamic and enjoyable yet rigorous learning experience.

All subjects are equally valued at Rossall, giving students the freedom to experience a broad and balanced portfolio of learning up to the age of 16 so they can make informed choices about their Sixth Form studies.

Facilities. Rossall's generous facilities support our aims for teaching and learning excellence. From our dedicated Science building and state-of-the-art Design Technology workshops to our bright, spacious art studios complete with a computer-rich Graphics suite, the school provides every student with the space and resources to pursue their academic studies and outside interests.

For those with musical ambitions, the Beecham Music School, with its own practice organ, orchestra rehearsal room and Sibelius suite, offers students the opportunity to develop their skills, whilst our theatres, performance and exhibition spaces provide budding singers, actors and artists with the chance to explore their talents.

With the recent renovation of the Sixth Form study room (based on designs created by the students themselves) and the opening of a new kitchen classroom to support the development of Food Studies skills, Rossall is a school which is constantly evolving to meet the needs of its students as well as the curriculum.

Beyond the classroom, our spacious 160-acre campus has extensive sports and recreation facilities, including a 25-metre indoor heated swimming pool, squash courts, tennis courts, fives courts, a modern all-weather sports pitch, a multi-use games area, two indoor sports halls, extensive sports pitches and a fitness room. That's not to mention our own beach, which is put to good use for our own exclusive sport of Ross Hockey.

Rossall is also proud to be one of the few schools in the country with an on-site Astronomy Centre.

The House System. For younger pupils (aged 7–13), Anchor House, our dedicated Junior Boarding House, has a home-from-home family atmosphere.

Anchor House is full of fun and laughter; from baking in the kitchen, to celebrating a birthday or taking part in one of our many house trips, there's always something to do and someone to do it with. As well as a varied activities programme, all of the house staff are committed to developing and supporting all students with their academic needs, ensuring that all of our children succeed and reach their maximum potential.

There are seven Houses for Senior boarders: three for girls (Rose, Wren and Dolphin) and four for boys (Maltese Cross, Mitre Fleur de Lys, Spread Eagle and Pelican).

All Houses have triple, double and single bedrooms, a common room, a large games room, a kitchen for snacks and weekend baking and a library with computer workstations and internet access.

While each House has its own unique history and personality, all foster an environment in which boarders are encouraged to achieve their true potential and develop valuable skills and qualities such as communication, teamwork, leadership, empathy and cultural understanding.

Religious Instruction. Rossall was founded as 'the Northern Church of England School' and Chapel remains central to the well-being of the community. Pupils of all faiths are encouraged to share in this community, and the School has its own Chaplaincy with resident Chaplain.

Games. 45 acres of playing field and a gymnasium, floodlit Astroturf, MUGA and indoor 25-metre swimming pool, along with squash, tennis, and fives courts allow all pupils to pursue a sporting interest. The boys mainly play rugby, hockey, cricket, football and basketball, with the girls playing hockey, netball, rounders and tennis. All pupils are taught to play the unique game of RossHockey on the sandy beach owned by the School. The brand new Golf Academy boasts state-of-the-art technology, and with close links to major golf clubs, including Royal Birkdale and Royal Lytham and St Annes, students have the opportunity play at some of the most prestigious golf clubs in the world. There are full programmes of competitive fixtures against other schools and clubs. House matches occur in all major games, including football, cross country in the Lent Term. Archery, athletics, shooting, horse riding and many other activities are offered.

The CCF. Rossall's CCF contingent is the oldest in the country. Currently most of Years 8–10 are in either the Army, Navy or Air Force sections. The school has a shooting range, keeps boats on the Wyre and there is opportunity to fly at RAF Woodvale.

Activities and Clubs. We are pleased to offer our biggest selection of extracurricular activities ever at Rossall.

Through our Activities Programme, our students have the opportunity to learn new skills, socialise with other students and, most importantly, have fun.

We encourage our students to try new activities, to help them broaden their horizons, so that they can meet the challenges of the wider world.

The extensive range of clubs we offer at Rossall include: Debating Club, Scuba Diving, The Duke of Edinburgh's Award, Robotics and Electronics, Creative Writing, Volleyball, Choir, International Cookery, Hockey, Photoshop and

Creative Graphics, Knitting, Rugby, Ceramics, Basketball, Orchestra, and Climbing.

Admission. Any term in the year for boys and girls aged 7+ and 13+, September preferably at 16+ or 17+. All applications for entrance should be made to the Admissions Team. On registration, a fee of £50 will be charged to day applicants and £175 to boarding applicants.

Fees per term (2016–2017). Day £2,550–£4,150; Full Boarding £6,540–£11,850; Weekly Boarding £4,400–£7,150.

Scholarships and Bursaries. Scholarships are offered for academic, music, art, drama, sport and all-round achievement. Scholarships are awarded solely on merit and range in value. In exceptional circumstances the special Trapnell Scholarship for excellence in Maths and Science may award up to 100% fee remission.

A number of clerical bursaries are awarded on a means test to sons of Clergy who can sustain a proportion of the Fees themselves but who need extra help. Bursaries are also available to families from the British Armed Forces.

All enquiries about Scholarships and Bursaries and other awards should be addressed to the Admissions Team.

Rossall Junior School. Rossall has its own Junior School for children aged 7–11 situated within the same grounds. There is also a Nursery and Infants School for day boys and girls aged 2–7.

Access. Motorway: 15 minutes from M55 (spur off M6). Railway: Blackpool North (6 miles). Air: Manchester International Airport (55 miles by road).

Alumni. A network of Old Rossallians is managed by Sharon Potts, Alumni Relations Manager at the school.

The Rossallian Club. This club for former pupils keeps a record of more than 5,000 members and coordinates the activities of eight Branches. A Newsletter is published twice each year.

Charitable Status. The Corporation of Rossall School is a Registered Charity, number 526685.

Life Governors:
The Earl of Derby, President of Corporation
Mrs H N Trapnell
Mr A N Stephenson, MA

Governors:
Chairman: Mr Chris Holt, BSc, MBA, ACMA
Vice Chair: Mr S J Fisher, MA
Mr M J Reece, MA
The Revd G Ashton, BA
Mr J Parr
Mrs C Preston, BSc, ARICS
Mr M Craven, MA
The Revd Canon J Hall, MA
Dr H O Fajemirokun
Mr M R Mosley, MA
Mr S J Fisher, MA
Mr N K Ward, BSc
Dr D M Elliott, BSc, MBChB
Mrs L Croston, BSc, PGCE, ALCM
Mrs M Smith, MSc, FFA, MInstF Dip, JP
Mrs K Thomas, MIFST, BSc, RSci
Mr C Littler, FCA

Secretary to the Corporation and Council: Mr B E Clark, MBE

Head: Ms Elaine Purves, BA Hons, PGCE

Deputy Head: Mr Robert Robinson, BA Hons, PGCE, MA
Bursar: Mrs Emma Sanderson, PGCE, MA Hons, MBA
Deputy Head (Academic): Mrs Gillian Pryor, BSc Hons, PGCE
Head of Dragon, Juniors, Infants & Nursery: Mrs Katie Lee, MA, CPP, Cert Ed

Head of EAL: Mrs Cheryl Wolstencroft, MEd TESOL, BA Hons
Head of Sixth Form: Mr Mark Bradley, BSc Hons, PGCE
Senior Master: Mr Mark Pryor, BSc Hons, PGCE

Heads of Departments:

Art: Mrs Sarah Holder-Williams, MA, RSA Dip PA
Business Studies: Mr Graham Wallace, MA, BEd, HND
Economics: Mrs Elizabeth Almond, BA, MA, PGCE
English: Mrs Sheila J Cross, BA, PGCE
Mathematics: Mr Philip Butterworth, BSc Hons
Modern Foreign Languages: Mrs Isabelle Wallace, BA Hons, MA, PGCE
EAL: Mrs Cheryl Wolstencroft, MEd TESOL, BA Hons
Director of Music: Miss Margaret Young, BA Hons, LTCL, LRSM
Science and Chemistry: Mr Ky Hutchinson
Physics: Ms Jane Mercer, BSc, PGCE
Biology: Mrs Alison Forster, BSc Hons, PGCE
Geography: Mr Anthony Fairhurst, BA Hons, PGCE
History: Mr Michael Holder-Williams
ICT: Mrs Susan Byrne, BSc, PGCE
Physical Education (Academic): Mrs Emma Williams, BSc, PGCE
Director of Sport: Mr Oliver Rogers, BA, PGCE
Design & Technology: Mr Lee Hodgetts, BA Hons
Religious Studies, Philosophy and Ethics: Mrs Francesca Saponiere, BA, PGCE
Psychology: Miss Nik Allen, BSc Hons, MSc, MBPsS, Unicert TEFL, LTCL, Dip TESOL
Learning Support: Mrs Siobhan Edge, BA Ed Hons

Houses/Houseparents:
Anchor House: Mr Lee & Mrs Helen Gair
Dolphin House: Miss Jocelyn Merris
Maltese Cross House: Mr Graham & Mrs Isabelle Wallace
Mitre Fleur de Lys House: Mr Stuart Corrie
Pelican House: Mr Anthony Fairhurst
Rose House: Mr Tim & Mrs Adele Fletcher
Spread Eagle House: Mr Ian McCleary
Wren House: Mrs Emma Williams

Instrumental Music Teachers for:
Brass, Flute, Guitar, Composition, Piano, Organ, Clarinet, Saxophone, Violin, Voice, Percussion

Director of Admissions, Marketing and Communications: Mrs Lucy Barnwell
International Registrar: Ms Gillian Leggett
UK Registrar: Mrs Julie Barkhuizen
Careers: Mr Jonathon Holland
IB Coordinator: Dr Doris Dohmen, DPhil, PGCE
Examinations Officer: Mr Ron Asher, BSc, PGCE
Librarian: Mrs Beth Simmons, BA Hons
Marketing Manager: Mrs Nancy Fielden
Medical Officer: Dr P G Carpenter, MBChB, MRCGP, DRCOG, FPA

Rougemont School

Llantarnam Hall, Malpas Road, Newport, South Wales NP20 6QB

Tel: 01633 820800
Fax: 01633 855598
email: registrar@rsch.co.uk
website: www.rougemontschool.co.uk
Twitter: @rougemontschool
Facebook: /Rougemont-School

Rougemont was founded in a house of that name immediately after the First World War as a co-educational day school taking children through to grammar school entrance at 11. It moved to Nant Coch House just after the Second World War and grew to about 200 pupils.

In 1974 the school was re-founded as a Charitable Trust. Since then it has bought extensive new buildings and has approximately 550 pupils on roll in the Preparatory School (Infant Department – Nursery to Year 2 and Junior Department – Years 3–6) and Senior School (Years 7–13).

The Preparatory Junior Department and Senior School moved to a new site at Llantarnam Hall, a large Victorian mansion set in 50 acres of grounds, between 1992 and 1995, with the Infant Department joining them in April 2004. The grounds have been landscaped to provide playing fields and an extensive building programme has taken place on the site. During 1998 a Liberal Arts area including Sports Hall, Music suite and Drama Studio was completed. In 1999 a new classroom block and library was completed and in 2000 additional classrooms together with Art studio were built. New Science and Technology buildings were completed in 2009.

Admission to the Preparatory and Senior Schools is by interview and assessments. Entry to the Sixth Form is dependent on GCSE results.

The following paragraphs refer to the Senior School although peripatetic specialists work in both and there is some interchange of teachers.

Curriculum. Pupils follow a wide syllabus to age 14. For the two years to GCSE pupils normally study nine subjects of which English Language and Literature, Mathematics, a language, science and a humanities subject are normally compulsory. 18 subjects are available.

Sixth Form. 19 AS/A2 Levels are available. Sixth Form pupils have their own common room and study area. Sixth Form pupils can also take part in a range of extracurricular activities and games.

Religion. Rougemont School has no direct affiliation to a Christian Church or denomination. However, the religious instruction, corporate worship and moral value system of the School is based on that of the broad tradition of the mainstream Christian Churches.

Careers. The School belongs to the Independent Schools Careers Organisation. The Senior teachers advise on all aspects of further education and careers.

Music. In addition to specialist teachers of music a large number of peripatetic teachers cover the range of orchestral instruments. There are choirs and instrumental ensembles for all ages.

Drama. In addition to the Infant Department's Spring Festival and the Senior School Eisteddfod, two major plays and two musical events take place each year.

Elocution and Dance. Visiting staff hold weekly classes for LADA courses, ballet and modern dance.

Sport. The School has developed a high standard of performance in most major sports. There is a wide fixtures programme for both boys and girls, as well as the opportunity to participate in numerous coaching courses.

Clubs. A wide variety of extracurricular activities and clubs are available at lunch time and after school, as is supervised prep.

The Duke of Edinburgh's Award. This is a very successful activity within the school and over 60 pupils have gained the Gold Award in the last twenty years.

Fees per term (2016–2017). Preparatory School: Infant Department £2,333–£2,856, Junior Department £3,256; Senior School: £3,768–£4,232.

Scholarships. An annual scholarship examination is held for entry to Year 7. A limited number of means-tested bursaries are offered from Year 7 upwards, with a separate scheme for Sixth Form entry.

Further information. A prospectus and other details are available from the Registrar (Tel: 01633 820800, email: registrar@rsch.co.uk).

Charitable status. Rougemont School is a Registered Charity, number 532341. It exists to provide education for boys and girls.

President: Mr I S Burge

Governors:
Chair: Mrs S Desai, BPharm, MRPharmS
Vice-Chair: Mrs A C Thomas, JP, SRN, SCM
Mr I G Short
Mrs J Clark, BA, PGCE
Mr R Pugsley, MSc, FCCA
Dr J N Tribbick, FCMI, JP
Miss J Sollis, BA, AKC
Mr M Tebbutt
Prof D Fone, MB BS, MD, FFPH, FRGS, MRCGP, DCH, DRCOG
Mr I Hoppe
Mr H Clark
Mr R Green, BSc, BArch, ARB, RIBA
Mr M Cordner
Mr P Harris

Headmaster: **Mr R Carnevale**, MA Ed, BSc, PGCE

* Head of Department
§ Part-time

Head of Preparatory School: Mrs L Pritchard, BA, PGCE
Deputy Head of Senior School: Mrs S Archer, BSc, PGCE (*Biology*)
Director of Staffing: Mrs S Roberts, BSc, PGCE (**Mathematics*)
Assistant Head (Curriculum): Mrs P Rogers, MA Ed, BSc, PGCE (*Director of Studies, Geography, ICT Coordinator*)
Director of Co-Curriculum: Mr A Rees, BA, PGCE (*Physical Education, Head of Years 10 and 11, DofE*)
Academic Registrar: Mr M James, MA Ed, BEd, BA, BSc, CBiol, MIBiol, Cert Maths Open (*Biology*)
Business Manager: Mr A Knight, ACA
Operations Manager: Mr M Baldwin

Senior School:
Miss S Ashton, BA, PGCE (**Spanish*)
Mrs L Bateman, BA, PGCE (**Art*)
Mr K Bell, BA, PGCE (*Director of Sport*)
Mrs K Benson-Dugdale, BMus, MA, QTS, PGEM (*Higher Education Advisor, *Music*)
Mr M Bowman, BSc, PGCE (*Mathematics*)
Ms A Clason-Thomas, BA, MA, PGCE (*Learning Resources Manager, French, English*)
Mr D Cobb, BSc, PGCE, Cert Maths Open (**Biology*)
Mrs L DeCruz, BA, PGCE (**Religious Studies*)
Miss C Dugdale, BA, PGCE (*§PE, Religious Studies*)
Mrs S Elson, LLB (*§Latin*)
Mrs E Ferrand, BEd (*Mathematics*)
Miss S Fletcher, BA, PGCE (*Art, DT*)
Mrs H Garratt, BSc, PGCE (*§Physical Education, DofE*)
Mrs R Garrod, BA, PGCE (*§History, Editor of School Magazine*)
Mr A Griffiths, BA, PGCE (*Spanish*)
Mrs J Goodwin, BSc (**Physics, Head of Pupil Performance Y8–Y11*)
Mr J Hardwick, BSc, PGCE (*Biology, Science, Careers*)
Mrs K Hughes, BSc, PGCE (**Geography*)
Miss R Hayes, BA, PGCE (*Design & Technology, DofE*)
Miss J Jones, BA, PGCE (**English*)
Mrs A Jenkins, BSc (*Chemistry, Physics*)
Mr M Jenkins, MA Cantab, PGCE (**History*)
Mrs C Langford, BSc, PGCE (*Chemistry*)

Mrs J Livings, BEd, PG Dip Dys and Literacy, AMBDA,
SpLD Assessor
Mr P McMahon, MSc, BSc, QTS (*Computing and IT,
Mathematics*)
Miss A Mintowt-Czyz, BA, PGCE (*English*)
Mrs D Moore, BA, PGCE (*Drama*)
Mrs D Morgan, BA, PGCE (*French*)
Mrs S Munro, DEUG, Licence, PGCE (*French, Year 7
Pupil Progress Coordinator*)
Miss C Owen, BA, PGCE (*Business Studies, IT, House
Tutor*)
Miss K Page, BSc, PGCE (*Physical Education, House
Tutor*)
Mr E Price, BSc, PGCE (*Mathematics*)
Mr A Richards, BSc, PGCE (*Mathematics, Head of Year
12*)
Mrs A Robst-Cross, BA, PGCE (*English, Media Studies*)
Mr M Savery, BA, PGCE (*Economics, Spanish*)
Mrs C Sims, BA, PGCE, AMBDA, CCET (*Learning
Development Centre, Latin, Spanish*)
Mr H Singer, MA Ed, BA, PGCE (*Head of Key Stage 3,
Design & Technology)
Mrs L Singer, BSc, PGCE (§*Physical Education*)
Miss A Sutton, MA(*Ed*), PGCE, BA, PG Dip SpLD
(*Learning Development Centre*)
Mrs L Thickins, BA, PGCE (*English, Media Studies*)
Mrs T van der Linde, MA Ed, BSc, PGCE (*Chemistry,
Head of Year 13*)

Preparatory School, Junior Department:
Mr A Bevan, BA, PGCE (*Junior Department Class
Teacher*)
Mrs R Carroll, BA, PGCE (*Junior Department Class
Teacher, Able and Talented Coordinator*)
Mr C Dobbins, BMus, DipMus, LRSM, PGCE (*Music,
Games*)
Mrs S Elson, LLB (*History, Religious Studies*)
Mrs K Galloway, KS2 (*Teaching and Learning Assistant*)
Miss L Hallas, BA, PGCE (*Deputy Head, English, History*)
Mrs R Payne, NNEB (*Teaching and Learning Assistant*)
Mr A Pritchard, BSc, PGCE (*Mathematics*)
Mrs C Poore, BEd (*Science, Geography, Curriculum
Director (Juniors)*)
Mr S Rowlands, BA, QTS (*Junior Department Class
Teacher, House Tutor*)
Mrs L Singer, MA Ed, BSc, PGCE (*Junior Department
Class Teacher, PE*)
Miss A Sutton, MA Ed, PGCE, BA, PG Dip SpLD
(*English*)
Mrs K Williams, BEd (*Junior Department Class Teacher*)

Preparatory School, Infant Department:
Mrs H Ashill, NNEB (*Teaching and Learning Assistant*)
Mrs A Burridge, BSc, PGCE (*Infant Department Class
Teacher*)
Mr C Dobbins, BMus, DipMus, LRSM, PGCE (*Music*)
Mrs S Hotchkiss, BA, QTS (*Deputy Head, Class Teacher*)
Miss C Leaves, BA, QTS (*Infant Department Class
Teacher*)
Mrs L McLoughlin, NVQ3 (*Teaching and Learning
Assistant*)
Mrs T Mountford, BEd (*Infant Department Class Teacher*)
Mrs N Noor, BA, PGCE (*Class Teacher, Curriculum
Director, Infants*)
Miss Z Rees, NNEB (*Teaching and Learning Assistant*)
Mrs C Townsend, NVQ (*Infant Department Class Teacher*)

Preparatory School, Rougemont Nursery:
Mrs J Forouzan, NNEB (*Nursery Teacher*)
Mrs A Exley (*Teaching and Learning Assistant*)
Mrs E Mian, NNEB (*Teaching and Learning Assistant*)

Registrar: Mrs N Bates

Royal Grammar School
Guildford

High Street, Guildford, Surrey GU1 3BB
Tel: Headmaster: 01483 880608
             School Office: 01483 880600
Fax: 01483 306127
email: office@rgsg.co.uk
website: www.rgsg.co.uk
Twitter: @RGSGuildford
Facebook: /RGSGuildford

Located in the centre of the historic town of Guildford,
the RGS is an independent day school for around 900 boys
aged 11 to 18, some 270 of whom are in the Sixth Form. As
a flagship for boys' education, the School has a national reputation for academic excellence but also prides itself on its
traditional values of decency and respect, supported by outstanding pastoral care. RGS boys have the opportunity to
experience the widest range of enriching activities providing
them with a broad and balanced education. Academic excellence is at the very heart of the School's philosophy. The
RGS aims to encourage the growth of intellectual curiosity
and creativity and to inculcate a life-long love of learning in
the boys. The RGS is consistently one of the top five boys'
schools in the country at both A Level and GCSE, and is
extremely proud of its Oxbridge record; in the last decade
341 offers have been made including 42 offers in the recent
round of admissions.

Buildings and Facilities. The Tudor buildings in Guildford's High Street have been at the very heart of the RGS for
over five centuries. The School was founded by Robert
Beckingham in 1509 and established by King Edward VI's
Charter of 1552, which decreed that there should be "… one
Grammar School in Guildford … for the Education, Institution and Instruction of Boys and Youths in Grammar at all
future times for ever to endure". Among the first in the
country to be purpose-built, the original buildings contain a
remarkable Chained Library, which is now the Headmaster's Study. The School enjoys facilities appropriate to education in the 21st century, including a state-of-the-art Music
School, Art School, purpose-built Sixth Form Centre, Sports
Hall and the recently-opened John Brown Building which
houses the innovative Design and Technology centre. The
Sports Ground at Bradstone Brook provides twenty acres of
pitches, tennis courts and a recently refurbished pavilion.
The School also benefits from the use of nationally
renowned sports facilities in the immediate proximity,
including Surrey Sports Park.

Curriculum. The school day is from 8.45 am to 4.00 pm;
there are no lessons on Saturdays. Many extracurricular
activities and clubs take place after school, however. In the
first three years (Years 7, 8 and 9 nationally), all boys follow
a common curriculum embodying the programmes of study
for Key Stage 3 of the National Curriculum. The subjects
studied are English, French or Spanish, Geography, History,
Latin, Maths, Information Technology, RE, PE, Art, Music,
Design and Technology, and Science. In the second year, the
boys study the separate sciences and in the third year (Year
9) all boys choose between Spanish, German and Greek as
an additional language.

GCSEs and IGCSEs are offered with boys taking ten subjects out of the 17 available. At GCSE there is a range of
ancient and modern languages including Ancient Greek and
Latin, as well as French, Spanish and German. There is the
opportunity to study Arabic, Mandarin, Japanese and Russian off timetable.

All Sixth Form boys take four subjects at AS Level and
then three or four at A Level; over twenty AS and A Level
subjects are offered. A broad curriculum also includes the

Independent Learning Assignment, the Extended Project Qualification and a General Studies programme organised in conjunction with Guildford High School.

Religion. The ethos of the RGS is firmly based on traditional Christian principles and the School has strong links with Holy Trinity Church in the centre of the town and Guildford Cathedral; however, as a non-denominational school, boys from all faiths are welcomed. A diverse, stimulating assembly programme provides the opportunity for collective worship and broadens the boys' horizons while establishing a tolerant set of values. Religious Education lessons, which are an integral part of the School's curriculum, further contribute to developing each individual's moral compass.

Pastoral Care. Respect, tolerance and understanding of others characterise daily life at the RGS and the very strong rapport between boys and teachers makes for a vibrant environment. The boys establish lasting relationships within the year group; in addition, the house system, mentoring, and role of all senior boys as prefects ensure friendships are forged throughout the School. The outstanding pastoral care on offer from dedicated form tutors, heads of year and personal tutors, all overseen by the Deputy Head (Pupils), enables the boys to thrive in a mutually supportive environment where every boy can flourish as an individual.

Extracurricular Activities. The exceptional range of extracurricular activities offered is one of the greatest strengths of the School; there are currently over seventy societies at the RGS. These range from air rifle, chess, christian union, contraptions society, drama, Model United Nations, music, philosophy, squash to Young Enterprise. Boys have the opportunity to take Bronze, Silver and Gold Duke of Edinburgh's Award through the Combined Cadet Force, Scouts or Outdoor Pursuits. Over 30% of pupils learn a musical instrument and they can join a variety of instrumental groups including Big Band, School Orchestra, Choir and a strong Choral Society. There are many opportunities for boys throughout the School to get involved in drama productions, both for the School and their house.

Games. The School's principal games are rugby, hockey and cricket, although as boys move up the School their sporting options widen considerably. Sports available include athletics, badminton, basketball, cross-country running, fencing, football, golf, sailing, shooting, swimming and tennis. Professional coaching and outstanding facilities develop the skill levels of boys of all abilities; the School takes pride in providing competitive sport and opportunities for all while nurturing the very best of sporting talent. The School currently has a significant number of boys who are competing for county, national and international honours.

Admission. Boys may be considered for entry to the RGS at any age between 11 and 18. The usual ages of entry, however, are at 11, 13 and 16 into the Sixth Form. Applicants at 11 take the School's entrance examination in the January before the year of entry; those for 13+ entry take the Common Entrance examination or Scholarship papers after 11+ assessment. New boys are admitted in September of each year. The Headmaster is pleased to meet parents, arrange for them to see the School, and discuss the possibility of their son's entry to the School. Appointments may be made through the Registrar, who can supply a hard copy of the School's prospectus; it is also available on the RGS website.

Fees per term (2016–2017). £5,645 (plus £263 for lunches, which are compulsory for First and Second Forms) inclusive of all tuition, stationery and loan of necessary books.

Scholarships. Scholarships of up to 20% fee remission are awarded in recognition of outstanding academic merit. For boys entering the First Form at 11 there is a competitive examination in English and Mathematics, held in January. For boys entering the Third Form at 13 there is a two-day examination covering all Common Entrance subjects, held in March. The top scholar of a year group is designated the King's Scholar.

Music scholarships of up to 20% fee remission are available at 11 and 13. It is hoped that a King's Scholarship can be awarded each year to a boy of outstanding musical potential.

One Art Scholarship and one Sports Scholarship of 10% fee remission at 13+ is available annually.

Full details of Scholarships and Bursaries are available from the Registrar.

Charitable status. The King Edward VI Royal Grammar School, Guildford is Registered Charity, number 312028.

Governing Body:
Chairman: Mrs S K Creedy, MA
Vice-Chairman: His Honour Judge C Critchlow, LLB, DL
Mr C D Barnett, MA
Mrs C F Cobley, MCIPD
The Revd Canon RL Cotton, MA, DipTh
Mr D J Counsell, FCA [OG]
Mr B J Creese, BA, MA
The Earl of Onslow, High Steward of Guildford
Mr J D Fairley, BA
Mr S G S Gimson, MSc
Cllr Mrs J Jordan, BA
Dr L S K Linton, MA, MB ChB, MRCP
The Mayor of Guildford
Dr H J Pearson, OBE, MA, PhD, CMath, FIMA
Mr P G Peel, FCA
Professor S Price, MSc, PhD, FBTS, ERT, FHEA
Mr C T Shorter, CEng, MIStructE, FConsE, FFB
Mr J A Smith, CEng, FCIBSE
Mrs H Styche-Patel, BSc, MBA
Mr N E J Vineall, QC, MA Cantab and Pittsburgh [OG]
Mrs R Weir, MA

[OG] *Old Guildfordian*

Chief Operating Officer: Mr R A Ukiah, MA
Bursar and Clerk to the Governors: Mrs C M Perceval, BA

Headmaster: Dr J M Cox, BSc, PhD (*Biology*)

Deputy Head (Staff): Mr G T Williams, MA (*History*)
Deputy Head (Pupils): Mr A U Woodman, BSc, MA (*Biology*)
Director of Studies, Careers and Higher Education: Mr P J Dunscombe, BSc (*Mathematics*)
Senior Master: Mr J W Pressley, MA (*Classics*)

Assistant Head (Learning): Miss N S Goul-Wheeker, MA (*Classics*)
Assistant Head (Partnerships): Mr T W Shimell, MChem (*Chemistry*)
Assistant Head (Teaching): Mr H R Wiggins, MA (*History**)
Assistant Head (Operations) : Mr N E Wild, BA (*Religion and Philosophy*)
Assistant Head (Co-curricular): Mr S J H Yetman, BSc

* *Head of Department*

Art:	Mr A J Skitt, BSc
*Mr A M J Curtis, MA	Mrs J S Thorpe, BSc
Miss K E Price, BA, MA RCA	Mrs K Walker, BSc
Mr A N Rozier, BA	*Chemistry*:
Mrs R F Shepherd, BA	*Mr W-S Lau, MChem, MRSC
Biology:	Mr S W Armstrong, MA
*Dr E J Hudson, MA, MSc, PhD	Dr E T Batchelar, MChem, DPhil
Mr A H Dubois, BSc	Dr J L Bodmer, BSc, PhD, MBA
Mr J J Richards, BSc [OG]	

Dr J S Braithwaite, BSc,
PhD
Dr L A Whall, BA, PhD

Classics:
*Mr E K D Bush, MA
Mrs S E Besly-Quick, BA
Mrs S Cooper, BA
Mr P G Nathan, BA, LIB
Mr H A L Prentice, BA
[OG]
Mr D J Woolcott, BA

Design & Technology:
*Mr J B Kelly, BA, MA,
MA RCA
Mr D M Hoyle, BEng
Mr K J Knight, BSc, MSc

Drama:
*Ms N C McClean, BA,
MA

Economics:
*Mr D S J Wright, BA
Miss S K H Blair, BSc,
MSc
Mrs P A Brooks, MBA
Mr N W Gough, BSc, MSc
Dr J M Wisson, BSc,
MPhil, DPhil

English:
*Mr A F E Quenault, BA,
MA, MA
Mr D Amis, BA
Dr A H S Barras, BA, MA,
PhD
Ms C J Clarkson, BA
Mrs H M Curtis, BA
Mr P M Leamon, BA
Miss E J Newton, BA, MA
Miss L Simpson, BA
The Revd J P Whittaker,
MA

Geography:
*Mrs R G Waters, MA
Miss G M Clements, BA
Mr W D Cowx, BSc, MSc
Mr T A J Rothwell, MA
[OG]
Mr R E J Seymour, BEd,
FRGS
Mrs P A Thomas, BSc,
MSc, FRGS, MSB, Dip
Counselling
Mr J C Witts, BSc

History:
Mr J A R Bass, BA, MA
Mr A C Dodd, BA, MA
[OG]
Dr V L Henshaw, BA, PhD
Mr T J J Owens, BA
(*Politics*)
Mr J R Saxton, MA
Mr A J Shakeri, BA

Mathematics:
*Mr S G Black, MMath
Mr J A Casale, BSc, MBA
Mr C George, BSc
Mr A R Gyford, MSci

Admissions Registrar: Mrs K L Sweet, BA, MCIPD

Mrs F A Hobbs, BSc
Mr M R Jenkins, BSc
Mr M J Jennings, BA
Mr A W J Jessett, MMath
Mr A B Kirkland, BSc
Dr A A Page, BA, MSci,
PhD
Mrs S J Perrett, BA
Mr N C Pinhey, BSc
Mr A J W Thorn, MA
Mrs F M Wimblett, BSc

Modern Languages:
*Ms A V E Tournier, Lic
Mr S J Baker, BA
Dr M M Creagh, BA, MSc,
PhD
Mr P J Hosier, BA, MEd
Mr R J A Lemaire, BA
Mr A R Lowe, BA
Mr J Marchiafava, Lic
Miss M-L McCarter, Lic,
MA
Mrs R J Rathmell, BA
Mrs C E Smith, BA
Miss G E Spencer, BA
Mrs N Wilson, BA

Music:
*Mr P H White, MA
(*Director of Music*)
Mr D H Chambers, BMus,
PCASS
Miss J Newman, AGSM,
CRD
Mr S J Orchard, BMus,
MMus
Dr E R Thackrey, BMus,
MMus, PhD

Physical Education:
*Mr I Wilkes, BEd
(*Director of Sport*)
Mr G D G Cover, BSc
Mr B Dudley, BSc
Mr C R Mullon, BSc
Mr T P Rogers, BSc
(*Rugby*)
Mr C J L Sandbach, BA
(*Cricket*)

Physics:
*Mr J P Hood, MA, MSci
Mr C S Bradford, MPhys
Mr M A Burbidge, BSc,
BA
Mr L M Holland, BSc
Mrs N L Odhams, MA,
MEng
Dr D Patel, BSc, PhD
Dr S G Thornhill, MA,
DPhil
Mrs D Whitehead, BTech

Religion and Philosophy:
*Mr R B Meadowcroft,
BA, MA
Mr M P Burgin, BA [OG]
Mrs L Griffiths, BA
Mrs H K Suenson-Taylor,
BA
Mr K Tayar, BA [OG]

Royal Grammar School
Newcastle upon Tyne

Eskdale Terrace, Newcastle-upon-Tyne NE2 4DX

Tel: 0191 281 5711
Fax: 0191 212 0392
email: admissions@rgs.newcastle.sch.uk
website: www.rgs.newcastle.sch.uk

The Royal Grammar School was founded and endowed in 1545 by Thomas Horsley, and by virtue of a Charter granted in 1600 by Queen Elizabeth it became 'the Free Grammar School of Queen Elizabeth in Newcastle upon Tyne'. For over 450 years and on six different sites the School has been of major educational importance in Newcastle and in the North East as a whole. It has valued its close links with the city and region, and its Governing Body consists largely of representatives of important companies, Local Authorities and Universities.

The School benefits from its central position, being within easy walking distance of the Civic and City Centres and of Newcastle's two Universities, and linked with the whole region by easily accessible rail, bus and metro services.

The School is a Day School and moved towards full co-education in 2006 with places being allocated to boys and girls at all entry points (7+, 9+, 11+, 16+). There are about 1320 students, including 1065 in the Senior School (age 11–18) and 255 in the Junior School (age 7–11).

Curriculum. The aim of the curriculum up to Year 11 is to offer a general education, culminating in GCSE in a wide range of subjects. All students study English (Language and Literature), a Modern Language (French, German or Spanish), Mathematics, Biology, Physics and Chemistry to this level and three further examination subjects are taken at GCSE level from Ancient History, Art, Economics, Geography, German, Greek, History, Latin, Music, Spanish, Design & Technology and Drama. Additionally there is a programme of Art, Drama, Music and Technology for all in Years 7 to 9.

From September 2017 Sixth Formers will normally choose three A Level subjects. In addition, students will be required to select either a fourth A Level or a combination of two complementary courses from EPQ, two-year AS subject or non-examined subject. The range of A Level subjects is currently: Ancient History, Art, Biology, Chemistry, Design Technology, Economics, English, Film Studies, French, Geography, German, Greek, History, Latin, Mathematics, Further Mathematics, Music, Philosophy, Physics, Physical Education, Politics, Psychology, Spanish and Theatre Studies. There is also a compulsory series of lectures and talks/workshops designed to provide cultural and personal broadening and development.

Almost all Sixth Formers go on to University, and success in gaining entry at Oxford and Cambridge, and medical schools, has been an outstanding feature of the school's record.

Physical Education. All students are required to take part in a Physical Education programme which, up to Year 10, includes Rugby, Football, Cross-Country, Cricket, Athletics, Gymnastics, Hockey, Netball, Tennis, Rounders, Swimming. At the upper end of the School a wider range of activities is offered: in addition to the above students may opt for Badminton, Basketball, Climbing, Fencing, Fitness training, Karate, Orienteering, Squash, Tennis, Table Tennis, Volleyball and Dance. A wide range of activities is available to all through voluntary membership of various Sports Clubs.

Activities. Art, Drama and Music are strong features in the life of the School, all of them overflowing from scheduled lessons into spare-time activity. There is a large number of wide-ranging music groups and ensembles from choirs and orchestras to bands, jazz ensembles and rock groups. There are several productions in the theatre each term. Numerous societies meet in the lunch-break or after school, some linked with school work but many developing from private enthusiasms. There is a thriving Duke of Edinburgh's Award scheme. There is an entirely voluntary Combined Cadet Force Contingent. Annual overseas visits include ski-parties, sporting tours, Classics trips, visits to art galleries and to the battlefields of World War I.

Supervision and Pastoral Care. Each student is within the care of (a) Form Supervisor and (b) Tutor. The latter will normally be associated with the student throughout their school career, and the aim is to forge a personal link with students and their families.

The Careers programme begins in Year 9; in Year 11 and the Sixth Form every possible care is taken to advise each student individually about Careers and Higher Education.

The School's Medical Officers are available regularly for consultation; there are also male and female School Counsellors.

Buildings. Some of the School's buildings date from 1907 and are described by Pevsner as "friendly neo-Early-Georgian". Recent years have seen many developments and improvements, including the opening in February 1996 of a new Sports Centre, a new Science and Technology Centre which opened in 1997, and new Maths and ICT departments in 1998. A new Junior School extension opened in 2005 and a Performing Arts Centre opened in 2006. A new 6-lane, 25m swimming pool was completed in August 2015 as part of an additional sports complex which includes a second sports hall, a dance and fitness suite and new indoor and outdoor changing facilities.

Junior School. Years 3 and 4 of the Junior School are separately housed in Lambton Road opposite the Senior School playing fields. Years 5 and 6 are housed in a new extension on the main school site. Junior School students use the Sports Centre, Swimming Pool, games fields and dining hall. English and Mathematics are taught by Form Teachers, while History, Geography, French, Science, Religious Education, Music, Art and Physical Activities are taken by specialists.

Entrance. Entry is by examination. Application forms are available from the Admissions Secretary.

Junior School at 7+ and 9+. Prospective students attend Assessment Days held in November (9+) and January (7+) when they take part in a number of activities and sit a number of short tests. A reference is sought from previous/current school.

Senior School at 11+. The Senior School examination is held each January for prospective students who will be 11 on 1 September of the year in which entry is desired. Applications by 15 December (later application at School's discretion). A reference is sought from previous/current school.

Sixth Form at 16+. Applicants are considered for direct entry to the Sixth Form if their GCSE results are likely to form an adequate basis. All external candidates are interviewed and a reference is sought from the previous/current school.

Each year a small number of places may be available at entry points other than the main ones listed. Please contact the Admissions Secretary for details.

Term of Entry. Autumn, although a small number of places may become available throughout the year.

Fees per term (2016–2017). Senior School £4,056, Junior School £3,417.

Bursaries. Some bursaries, awarded on the basis of parental income, are offered. They include those awarded by the Ogden Trust, which may cover all fees and expenses depending on parental income. Details are available from the Bursar.

Charitable status. The Newcastle upon Tyne Royal Grammar School is a Registered Charity, number 1114424.

Governing Body:

Co-opted Governors:
Chairman: Mr P A Walker, BA
Vice-Chairman: Professor A C Hurlbert, BA, MA, PhD, MD
Mr A J Applegarth, BA
Mr P A Campbell, MA, DBA, FRSA
Ms N C D'Cruz, LLB
Dr I O Evbuomwan, MBBS, MD, FRCOG
Mr R H Fell, FRICS
Mr N A H Fenwick, MA
District Judge P A Kramer, LLB
Mrs C S E Murphy, BSc
Mr I R Simpson, ACIB
Mrs J Drummond, BA, MA
Ms T Hartley, MRICS, BSc, MSc, MBA

Nominated Governors:
Professor S Ali, BSc, MSc, PhD
Professor S Hambleton BA, BM, BCh, MRCPCH, DPhil
Professor E W N Glover, MA, PhD, CPhys, FInstP, ILTM
Dr J G Holland, MA, MS, DPhil
Councillor T Robson

Clerk to the Governors and Bursar: Dr M J Pitkethly, CEng, FIMMM, BSc, PhD

Headmaster: Dr B St J Trafford, MA, MEd, PhD, FRSA

Deputy Head: Mr A A Bird, BMus, MEd, LRAM

Assistant Staff:
* *Head of Department*
§ *Part-time*

Art:
*Mr G P Mason, BA
Mr P Edwards, BA
Mrs C Egan-Fowler, BEd
Mrs K Nowicki, BA
§Miss H C Bray, BA, MA

Biology:
*Mr P J Heath, BSc
Dr M H Bell, BSc, PhD
Mrs J A Malpas, BSc
Dr C J Murgatroyd, BSc, DPhil
Mr L Shepherd, BA
§Mrs S F Hutchinson, BSc
§Mr C J H Wancke, BSc

Chemistry:
Dr A J Pulham, BA, DPhil (*Science)
*Mr R W Wiggins, BSc
Mr G A Corner, BA
Dr J L Greenhalgh, BSc, PhD
Mr T Kelso, BSc (*Head of Year 13)
Dr E A Smith, BSc, PhD
Mrs N Wright, BSc
§Dr R Campbell, BSc, PhD
§Mrs S L Coates, MSc
§Mrs M C Slack, BSc

Classics:
*Mrs V C Mee, BA, MA

Mr T C Clark, BA (*Head of Year 7)
Mrs P R Coningham, BA, MA
Dr L E Hope, PhD, MA, BA
Miss S V Tucker, BA
Miss P L Whitworth, BA

Economics/Politics:
*Mr J D Neil, MPhil
Mrs L E Davison, MA, BA
Mr R C M Loxley, BSc, MEd (*Director of Studies)
Mr S O'Dwyer, BA
Mr P Shelley, BA, MSc
Mr M J Smalley, BA
§Mr D Leightley, BA

English:
*Dr S J Barker, BA, PhD
Miss S G Davison, BA
Mr L J Gilbert, BA
Dr C Goulding, BA, MLitt, PhD
Mrs K J Keown, BA
Mr A R D King, BA, MA
Dr S C Masters, BA, MA, PhD (*Film Studies)
§Mrs L A Stadward, BA, MA

Geography:
*Mr D A Wilson, BSc
Mr M G Downie, BA
 (*Head of Careers*)
Mrs R J L Laws, MA
 (*Assistant Head of
 Careers*)
Miss S J Longville, BA
 (*Head of Year 11*)
Miss Z C Morrow, BSc,
 MA

History:
*Mr S E Tilbrook, BA
Mr O L Edwards, BA
Mr D C Greenhalgh, BA,
 MA (*Head of Year 8*)
Dr E S Matthews, MA,
 PhD
Mr W Simmons, BA
§Mrs A J Palmer, MA

Mathematics:
*Mr J A Smith, BSc
Dr J Argyle, BSc, MSc,
 PhD
Ms L Atkinson, BA, MA
Mr H M W Bingham, BA
Mr A Delvin, BSc, MSc
Mr G D Dunn, BSc
Dr P M Heptinstall, BSc,
 PhD
Mr D A Jardine, BSc
Mr T E Keenan, BSc, MSc
 (*Head of Sixth Form*)
Mr M J Poole, BSc
Mr H Rashid, BSc, MSc
Mr A Snedden, BSc
Mr S D Watkins, BSc
Miss R M Watterson, BSc

Modern Languages:
*Miss K E Sykes, BA
Mr M S Bailie, BA, MA
 (*Head of Year 10*)
Miss S Demoulin, DEUG
 (*French*)
Miss B Membrado-Dolz
 (*Spanish*)
Miss J Budd, BA (*Head of
 Year 12*)
Mrs C L Diaz-Crossley, BA
Miss E L Hayes, BA
Mr M Metcalf, BA, MPhil
 (*Head of Year 9*)
Mrs C Towns,
 Staatsexamen
Mrs D Williams, BA
 (*German*)

Junior School:
Mr R J Craig, BEd (*Headmaster*)
Mr J N Miller, BA (*Deputy Head*)
Dr A J Spencer, BSc, PhD (*Deputy Head*)

Miss K L Barnes, BA
Ms C Bolam, BA
Miss H Close, BSc
Mrs C M Cree, BSc
Miss C E Gardiner, BA
Mr T G Lloyd, BA
Miss S J McCulloch, BA
Miss M A Noble, BA

§Mrs C A M O'Hanlon,
 BA

Music & Performing Arts:
*Z Fazlic, BA (*Director*)
Miss S L Bolt, BA
Mrs K Clappison, MA
 (*Head of Junior School
 Music*)
Mr F Mullaly, BA
Mr T Walters, BA
§Mrs R A Shaw-Kew, BA

Pastoral:
Mrs S J Baillie, BA
 (*Pastoral Director*)
Ms A E Lee, MSc, BA
 (*Director of Student
 Progress*)

Philosophy and Religion:
Dr M B A Read, MA,
 MPhil, PhD

Physical Education:
*Mrs A J Ponton, BSc
Mr M R Davidson, BSc
 (*Deputy Director*)
Miss H J Atkinson, BA
Mr A G Brown, BSc
Miss O Chapman, BA
Mr F Dickinson, BEd
Miss J Harrison, BSc
Miss K M Smith, BSc
Mr A E Watt, BA
Mr J A Wood, BA
§Mr R V MacKay, BSc

Physics:
*Mr E T Rispin, BSc
Mr J L Camm, BSc
Dr R M Houchin, MSci,
 PhD
Miss B Milburn, BSc
Mr P Wilson, BSc, MSc
§Mrs P M Gill, BEng

PSHE:
Mrs K E J Hammill, BA

Psychology:
*Dr C M Bone, PhD, BSc
 (*Complementary
 Studies*)
Miss K A Jacques, BSc

Design & Technology:
*Mr P M Warne, MEng
Mrs C A Pipes, BA
Miss R Harvey, MFA, BA

Mr J A Pollock, CertEd
Miss R S Scott, BA
Mrs L M Stairmand, BA
Mrs R S Towers, MEd
Mrs K Wall, BA
Ms A J Whitney, BA
Miss L R B Wood, BA,
 MA
§Mr G Scrafton, BA

School Medical Officer: Dr K Hermuzi, MBBS, MRCGP
Admissions Officer: Mrs A Perry

RGS Worcester

Upper Tything, Worcester WR1 1HP

Tel:	01905 613391
Fax:	01905 726892
email:	office@rgsw.org.uk
website:	www.rgsw.org.uk
Twitter:	@RGSWorcester
Facebook:	/rgsw.org.uk

School Aims. The aim of the family of RGS Worcester schools is to provide an excellent all round education for children aged 2–18 years, supporting them in their passage to adulthood by developing character, intellect, physical and emotional well-being and cultural understanding within a supportive community.

The School and its staff aim to cultivate an ethos in which each pupil is cared for individually, valued equally and achieves their potential.

RGS Worcester sets out to achieve these aims by:

- Encouraging the growth of intellectual curiosity, creativity and a positive attitude to learning, including the preparation of each child for life through a broad, coherent and balanced curriculum, the use of digital technology to enhance teaching and learning, and educational and enrichment opportunities

- Developing in every child quiet self-confidence, aspiration, responsibility, resilience, spiritual values and a personal moral code, leading to the highest standards of behaviour, consideration for others, tolerance and understanding of other cultures, awareness of British values, and pride in, and loyalty to, the School community

- Offering a wide range of co-curricular activities through which children can develop their social, sporting and cultural interests, explore and enhance their leadership skills and learn the importance of working together

- Providing well-qualified and able staff who are highly committed to delivering excellent teaching, enabling pupils to enjoy learning and achieve to their full potential

- Promoting opportunities for higher education and career options, and creating an awareness of the world beyond the School and a sense of service to the local and wider community

- Pursuing positive relationships with parents through open communication and opportunities to attend school events

It is hoped that, by our schools fulfilling these aims, our pupils will leave RGS Worcester as flexible, independent thinkers, who have quiet self-confidence, treat others with respect and kindness, and go on to make a very positive contribution to the community and to society as a whole.

History. The Royal Grammar School Worcester was founded ante 1291, received its Elizabethan Charter in 1561 and was granted its 'Royal' title by Queen Victoria in 1869. The Alice Ottley School was founded in 1883 as Worcester High School for Girls. The two schools merged to form RGS Worcester & The Alice Ottley School in September 2007 and was renamed RGS Worcester in September 2009.

Location and Buildings. The Senior School is situated a few minutes' walk from the centre of the City and is convenient for rail and bus stations. The Headmaster's office is housed in the Grade II* listed Britannia House, and there are several other historic buildings on the site, including the RGS Main Block, dating from 1868. Educational facilities are outstanding: there are two Sports Halls, specialist Art, IT, Technology and Textiles rooms, a Theatre, Library, Science Block, Music Technology room, and a Lecture Theatre, as well as several assembly halls. The playing fields and boathouse are close by and the School has good use of the local swimming pool. A full-size, floodlit all-weather pitch was opened in 2007 and a state-of-the-art fitness centre in 2008. A new Dance Studio plus changing facilities, two new Science Laboratories and a Digital Language Laboratory were also completed in 2008.

There are two co-educational Preparatory Schools. RGS The Grange (*see IAPS entry*) is set in 48 acres of grounds to the north of the city and has a 16-classroom, £4.5 million extension to complement the original Victorian building that houses the Pre-Prep. RGS Springfield (*see IAPS entry*) is housed in a beautiful Georgian building in the centre of the nearby Britannia Square, close to the city centre. It is secluded and secure, and benefits from its close proximity to the Senior School.

Organisation. The Senior School population is c768 (349 girls and 419 boys). The Senior School is divided into three sections – Lower (Years Seven and Eight), Middle (Years Nine and Ten) and Sixth Form – with an Assistant Head responsible for each. The basic unit is the form, and the form tutor, under the Head of Year, is responsible for all day to day matters relating to the pupils in their charge. In addition all pupils are placed in Houses which exist mainly for internal competitive purposes, but which do provide an important element of continuity throughout a pupil's career at the School. Both Preparatory Schools admit pupils from the age of two, and most proceed to the Senior School at the age of eleven, into Year Seven. RGS The Grange and RGS Springfield are both well known for the high standard of their pastoral care and for stretching the brightest children. Learning Support is particularly well organised.

Curriculum. Pupils follow a common curriculum for the first three years in the Senior School which includes the usual academic subjects, plus IT, Design Technology, Music, Drama and PE. The GCSE option arrangements (Years Ten and Eleven) allow a wide choice, subject to final selection, giving a balanced curriculum which does not prejudice subsequent career decisions. Normally nine to ten subjects are studied: IGCSE English, Mathematics, a Modern Foreign Language and Sciences being setted and compulsory, plus three from French, German, Latin, Spanish, Geography, History, RE, Drama, Art, Music, Textiles, Design Technology. Most members of the Sixth Form study four subjects to AS Level and at least three to A2 Level. In addition to those subjects studied at GCSE Level, PE, Classical Civilisation, Business Studies, Economics and Politics may be taken up. The Digital Learning Programme was launched in September 2014, which saw iPads become an integral part of the teaching and learning experience.

Careers. The School is a member of ISCO; the award-winning careers service is readily available and the Head of Careers is responsible for ensuring that all pupils receive basic careers education, and subsequently, access to all the necessary information and experience on which a sound decision may be made regarding future career and Further or Higher Education.

Physical Activities. The School aims to satisfy a wide range of sporting interests and abilities. For boys, Rugby Football, Association Football, Cricket and Athletics are the main activities. Girls take Netball and Hockey in the winter and spring, and Athletics, Tennis and Rounders during the summer Term. Cross-Country Running and Rowing have a full programme of fixtures. A wide range of other activities share priority in the Sports Halls throughout the year, and high-quality cricket coaching is given throughout the winter months.

Outdoor Pursuits. Combined Cadet Force and The Duke of Edinburgh's Award scheme: all pupils may choose to join one or the other at the end of Year Nine. The strong CCF comprises Royal Navy, Army and Air Force sections. Good opportunities exist for attachments to regular units in UK and abroad, for flying training, for leadership training and for Adventure Training. Those who choose The Duke of Edinburgh's Award scheme may work for the Bronze, Silver and Gold Awards, and undertake adventure training and community service.

Other Activities. There is a wide range of clubs and societies. All Lower School pupils receive drama lessons as part of the curriculum and school productions take place each term. School music is also strong: in particular, there is a fine organ, a Big Band, several brass ensembles, two choirs, several smaller vocal ensembles and a very popular Jazz Band. The School fosters a range of international links including regular exchanges with schools in France, Germany, Spain, China and the USA. The School has strong links with schools in the developing world via the World Challenge Organisation, and the school community raises large sums for a range of local, national and international charities every year.

September Admission. This is by examination held in January, mainly at 11+ but also at 12+ and 13+. Pupils are also admitted into the Sixth Form on the basis of a test, interview and GCSE results. Exceptionally, pupils may also be examined and admitted at any time of the year. Admission to the Preparatory Schools is by assessment from age 6+ and by classroom visit before this age.

Fees per term (2016–2017). £3,984.

Scholarships and Bursaries. Scholarships are offered for academic achievement as well as for music, art, design, textiles, drama and sport of up to 50% remission of fees. Bursaries of up to 100% are also available according to parental means and academic potential. Further details can be obtained from the Registrars at the schools.

Charitable status. RGS Worcester is a Registered Charity, number 1120644. The aim of the charity is the education of boys and girls.

Board of Governors:
Chairman: Mrs R F Ham

Mrs L Cook	Quentin Poole
Mr N Fairlie	Mrs J Preedy
Sir R G Fry	B W Radford
H Kimberley	Dr E Robinson
Ms K Meredith	A Greenaway
J G Peters	P Lee

Bursar & Clerk to the Governors: I T Roberts, OBE, MA

Headmaster: J D C Pitt, MA

Deputy Head : Mrs C S Smee, BSc, MA

Assistant Heads:
Dr L J Andrew BSc, PhD (*Pastoral*)
T Rounds, BA (*Co-curricular*)
R J Houchin, BA (*Academic*)

Preparatory School: RGS The Grange

Headmaster: G W Hughes, BEd Hons

Deputy Head (*Academic*): Mrs S Atkinson, BEd
Deputy Head (*Pastoral*): Mrs W Wreghitt, BA
Assistant Head (*Co-Curricular*): D Bousfield, BA

Preparatory School: RGS Springfield

Headmistress: Mrs L Brown, BA

Deputy Head: Mr Ian Griffin, BEd

The Royal Hospital School

Holbrook, Ipswich, Suffolk IP9 2RX

Tel: 01473 326200
Fax: 01473 326213
email: admissions@royalhospitalschool.org
           reception@royalhospitalschool.org
website: www.royalhospitalschool.org
Twitter: @RHSSuffolk
Facebook: @RoyalHospitalSchool

The Royal Hospital School was founded in 1712 in Greenwich, London, to 'improve navigation' through education and, as it prepared boys for a life at sea, many went on to become explorers and pioneers of their time. The School is immensely proud of these historic links and discovery, exploration and challenge continue to shape its ethos. The traditional values of loyalty, commitment, courage, respect, service and integrity have underpinned the School's core aims and philosophy from the very beginning. 300 years later, they are still as relevant to the education it provides as they were then. Today the School is set in 200 acres of Suffolk countryside overlooking the Stour Estuary and it is a co-educational HMC boarding and day school for 750 pupils providing a full and broad education, fit for the modern world. It aims to inspire its pupils to have the courage and commitment to be ambitious for their futures, whichever path they choose, challenging pupils of all academic abilities, steering them to look beyond the moment, and beyond the confines of the classroom, and to approach life with an open and receptive mind.

House System. 65% of pupils board and there is a strong diamond-shaped House System. An ongoing programme of refurbishment and development provides superb facilities and accommodation for both boarders and day pupils.

Pupils joining the School at 11+ are accommodated in the Junior House purpose-built to accommodate 11 and 12 year olds in 4/6-bedded rooms, with facilities, routines and pastoral care that assist the transition between junior and senior school. Weekly boarding and the opportunity to stay overnight on an ad hoc basis are available.

At Year 9 (13+) pupils join a Senior House. Two are co-educational Day Houses and one is a boys' Day House with flexi boarding facilities enabling the boys to board up to 3 nights per week. There are 3 boys' and 3 girls' Senior Boarding Houses which are each home to approximately 60 full and weekly boarders. Boarders in Years 8 and 9 share rooms with up to four other pupils and older pupils have double or single studies with en-suite facilities.

In the Upper Sixth both boarding and day boys and girls join Nelson House, where they learn to live more independently in preparation for university.

Curriculum and Academic Development. The School's curriculum shadows the National Curriculum Key Stages 3 and 4. On joining the School, pupils are placed in sets on the basis of assessed ability from entrance testing or at 13+ the results of Common Entrance examinations. The School subscribes to the Durham University Value Added Measuring Scheme at all levels, allowing tutors to map pupil progress. In core subjects setting takes place from the outset and at GCSE level setting occurs in all core curriculum subjects. There are 66 x 55min periods over a two weekly timetable.

Lower School (Years 7–8): The subjects studied are English, mathematics, science (biology, physics and chemistry), modern foreign languages (French, Spanish and German), Latin, geography, history, design technology, art, drama, IT (Information Technology), music, religious studies, RHS Compass (digital literacy, Personal, Social and Health Education, thinking and study skills) and PE. There are four forms in Years 7 and 8 and the average class size is

18 pupils. Homework is set daily and completed within supervised sessions during the working day by both boarders and day pupils. All junior pupils must take part in at least three co-curricular activities after lessons.

Middle School (Years 9–11): The subjects studied in Year 9 are the same as in the Lower School and a further intake of pupils from prep schools means that there is an additional class. GCSE courses start in Year 10 and most pupils will study 10 subjects including English language and literature, mathematics, a modern foreign language, physics, chemistry, biology (either as three separate sciences or as the dual award) as the core subjects and four options from science (if taking separate sciences), history, geography, PE (Physical Education and Sports Science), French, German, Spanish, media studies, religious studies, art, music, theatre studies, design technology and business studies.

Sixth Form (Years 12 and 13): Pupils choose three from 27 A Level subjects. Subject choice depends upon average point scores at GCSE and grades gained in specific subjects. As well as three A Level subjects, pupils must choose one from a range of academic Elective subjects which can range from an Extended Project Qualification to a BTEC Level 2 First Award in Information and Creative Technology. RHS+ provides sessions on careers, managing finances, cooking on a budget, digital effectiveness and safety and coping with stress and mindfulness. RHSXtra runs a series of talks and seminars on topics aimed at broadening horizons and inspiring curiosity. Around 90% of pupils go to the University or Higher Education institution of their choice and approximately 50% to Russell Group and other top-class universities. An increasing number of pupils are gaining places on Higher Degree Apprenticeship schemes with leading corporations.

Pupil progress is formally monitored by means of at least two assessments or reports per term which grade the academic performance of the pupil against their target or challenge grades. Every pupil has a personal tutor and bi-weekly tutorial meetings are an opportunity to deal with any problems and check on progress.

All pupils have access to iPads, a suite of mobile learning apps and Wi-Fi throughout the site. Additional networked computers are available in Boarding or Day Houses as well as in computer suites around the school. Mobile learning is embraced by the teaching staff with the aim of enhancing teaching and learning.

Through high quality, enthusiastic teaching, excellent resources and dedicated tutorial support, every pupil is encouraged to aim high and achieve his or her personal best. The most able pupils' potential is realised through the mentoring of scholars, the Stretch and Challenge scheme and Oxbridge preparation.

Sport and Leisure. Facilities include ninety-six acres of playing fields, a golf course, shooting range, sports hall, fitness suite, gym, climbing wall, large heated indoor swimming pool, squash courts, tennis and netball courts and an all-weather sports surface.

The School has a strong sailing tradition and all pupils joining in Year 7 receive sailing instruction to RYA Level 2. Through the School's RYA-accredited Sailing Academy, pupils have access to a fleet of 40 racing dinghies on adjacent Alton Water Reservoir, as well as traditional Cornish Shrimpers on the River Stour and Orwell. The School is widely known as one of the top in the country for both fleet and team sailing and offers an elite training programme for those wishing to follow Olympic pathway.

The recently launched Graham Napier Cricket Academy aims to provide a centre of cricketing excellence developing aspiring young cricketers to reach their full potential and promoting participation by girls and boys at all levels and ages.

The other main sports are rugby, hockey, netball, kayaking, athletics, cross country, climbing, basketball, football, tennis, riding and swimming. The swimming pool also offers opportunities for kayak-polo, life-saving training and sub-aqua.

Music and Drama. The School has a particularly strong musical tradition and the state-of-the-art Music School provides a recital hall, specialist rooms, recording studio, technical suite and "rock room". Almost half the pupils in the School are involved in music on a regular basis. The Chapel is of cathedral proportions and has one of the finest organs in Europe, much used by pupils as well as professional performers. Peripatetic teachers offer tuition in a wide range of instruments and the choir and chamber choir perform both nationally and internationally. As well as drama in the curriculum and LAMDA classes, productions are often combined with the music department for whole-school performances and there is a full programme of plays, competitions and festivals each year.

CCF and Community Service. All pupils participate in the Combined Cadet Force in Years 9 and 10 and are able to choose between Army, Navy, RAF and Royal Marine sections. The emphasis is on adventure training and personal development. More than 300 pupils take part in The Duke of Edinburgh's Award scheme and 100 of these to Gold Award. The Community Action Team promotes the School's social responsibility and is actively involved in a wide range of charitable activities in the local community.

Religion. The core values of the School are based on the Christian faith but pupils from a variety of religions and cultural backgrounds attend the School and all beliefs are respected. The magnificent Chapel, that holds over 1,000 people, is the spiritual hub of school life and the whole community gathers there most mornings for worship.

Admission. Entry to the School is normally at 11, 13 and 16 years. Pupils are asked to sit an entrance examination, comprising papers in English, mathematics and verbal reasoning, in the January prior to the September of the year of entry unless following Common Entrance for entry in Year 9. Entry into the Sixth Form is subject to a minimum average GCSE point score and specific grades in chosen A Level subjects. Entry is also subject to an interview and satisfactory reference from the pupil's current school.

Fees per term (2016–2017). Full Boarding: £7,795 (Years 7 and 8), £9,995 (Years 9–13). Weekly Boarding: £7,495 (Years 7 and 8), £9,260 (Years 9–13). Day: £4,845 (Years 7 and 8), £5,300 (Years 9–13). Day Boarders: £6,845 (Years 9–13). Discounts are available for services families eligible for the MOD Continuity of Education Allowance (CEA) and siblings where three or more children are in the School at any time.

Scholarships, Exhibitions and Awards are awarded annually for academic excellence, musical talent, drama, art, sport and sailing. All scholarship candidates are required to sit the School entrance examination (unless taking Common Entrance or GCSE examinations), have an interview and undergo an assessment in their relevant field. Full details from the Admissions Office, Tel: 01473 326136 or email: admissions@royalhospitalschool.org.

Bursaries. Pupils in receipt of a scholarship or award are eligible to apply for additional assistance by way of a means-tested bursary, should the financial circumstances of the family necessitate it. The School's parent charity, Greenwich Hospital, can award generous means-tested bursaries to the children of seafarers, particularly serving or retired Naval or Royal Marines personnel.

Charitable status. The Royal Hospital School is owned by Greenwich Hospital which is a Crown Charity.

Director, Greenwich Hospital: Mr H Player

Governors:
Chair of Governors: Mr H C T Strutt

Mr J Agar
Brig K Beaton, OBE, QHP
Mrs V Bidwell
Mr J Gamp
Mr T P J Hill, QC
Mr A Kerr

Mr J Lynas
Dr P Marshall
Mr P Smith
Capt A Tate, RN Retd
Mrs E Todd

Senior Management Team:

Headmaster: **Mr Simon Lockyer**, BSc, MEd

Director of Finance and Operations (Bursar): Mr P Church, BA
Second Master: Mr S J Dixon, MA
Deputy Head (Pastoral): Mrs S E M Godfrey, BA
Deputy Head (Academic): Mrs C A Stevens, BSc
Assistant Head (Co-Curricular): Mr C A Rennison, BSc
Assistant Head (Pastoral): Mr L M Corbould, BSc
Director of Curriculum, Teaching & Learning: Mr M R Christmas, MA
Director of Communications: Mrs S Braybrooke, BA
Head of Sixth Form & Careers: Mr C Graham, BSc

Chaplain: Revd J W P McConnell, BEd, MA, BD, DASE

Head of Middle School: Mr A Wynn, BSc
Higher Education Coordinator: Mr C D Barker, MA
Academic Challenge Coordinator: Dr J L Evans, BSc
Head of Digital Learning: Mr H Mackenzie, BA
Examinations Officer: Mr A J Loveland, ACGI, MA

Heads of Department:
Art: Mr G D Ravenhall, BA, ATD
Biology: Mr B A Raybould, BSc
Business Studies: Mr L Thompson, BEd, BA
Chemistry: Ms M Egan-Smith, BSc (*Head of Science*)
Classics: Mr M Routledge, BA
Director of Cricket: Mr G Napier
Design Technology: Mr O Millington, BA
Drama: Mr D Kerr, BA
Economics: Mr C Terry, BA
English: Ms J L Stone, BA
English as an Additional Language: Mr D P Coleman, BA
Film & Media Studies: Mr M Vickers, BA
French: Mrs J Routledge, BA
Geography: Miss H Izod, BSc
German: Mrs N J Mann, MA
History and Politics: Mr R S Watson-Davis, BA
Information & Communication Technology: Mr P C Du Toit, BComm, HDE
Learning Support: Mrs E Burge, MA
Librarian: Miss R Gitsham, BA
Mathematics: Mr G Mears, BA
Director of Music: Mr W Saunders, BMus
Bandmaster: Mr R Harvey, BMus
Head of Academic Music: Mr E C Allen, BA
Director of Sport: Mr D P Hardman, BA
Head of Academic PE: Mrs S J Williams, MA, BEd
Physics: Dr M R Gibbs, BSc
Psychology: Mrs M R Price, BA
Religious Studies: Mr M R Christmas, MA
Director of Sailing: Mr A C Nutton
Spanish: Mr R G Encinas, BA

Health Centre Sister: Mrs A Thompson, RGN
Head of Ceremonial: Lt Cdr Retd N Griffiths
CCF Contingent Commander: Lt Col M H Godfrey
CCF School Staff Instructor: WO1 [RSM] K Weaver
Duke of Edinburgh's Award: Sgt P Ryan

Registrar: Mrs K Evers, BA

The Royal Masonic School for Girls

Rickmansworth Park, Rickmansworth, Herts WD3 4HF

Tel: 01923 773168
Fax: 01923 896729
email: enquiries@royalmasonic.herts.sch.uk
website: www.royalmasonic.herts.sch.uk
Twitter: @RMSforGirls
Facebook: @RMSforGirls

There are 931 pupils in school, of whom 235 are in Cadogan House (Pre-Prep and Prep Department) and 60 are in Ruspini House, our co-ed Pre-School. There are 167 girls in the Sixth Form. 100 of the current school population are boarders and day girls and boarders are fully integrated through the Houses.

Premises and Facilities. Founded in 1788, the School came to Rickmansworth in 1934. It stands in over 150 acres of parkland on an attractive site overlooking the valley of the River Chess. The buildings are spacious and well-appointed. They include excellent ICT facilities, a well-equipped Science building, a Planetarium, a Chapel and Resource Centre of exceptional beauty. A new Sixth Form Centre, Hind House, opened in 2012.

The Sports Hall is equipped to the highest international standards. There is a heated indoor swimming pool, 12 tennis courts, four squash courts and superb playing fields. In 2015 the School opened its brand new All-Weather Pitch, funded by the Campaign for Excellence. The School has been awarded Sportsmark status.

Location. Central London is 15 miles to the south and Amersham is just north of the town. The M25 is one mile from the school and links it to London (Heathrow) – 30 minutes, London (Gatwick) – 50 minutes, and Luton Airport – 30 minutes. London Underground services (Metropolitan Line) and British Rail from Marylebone enable Central London to be reached by train in 30 minutes.

General Curriculum and Aims. The first three years of Senior School provide a broad general education which fulfils the requirements of the National Curriculum and reaches beyond it. As well as the traditional academic subjects of English, Mathematics, Science, History, Geography and Religious Studies, girls study Design Technology, Information Technology, Home Economics, Art & Textiles, Performing Arts, Physical Education and Life Skills. Language Studies begin with French or Spanish and Latin. In Year 8 German and Mandarin are also offered.

GCSE options are chosen from among all the subjects taught in Years 7 to 9 and new possibilities, such as Child Development, Performing Arts, Drama and Business are introduced at this stage. Most pupils take nine or ten GCSE subjects and girls are guided in their choices by subject teachers, in full consultation with parents. Triple Science is available.

The Sixth Form. The School offers a wide range of A Level subjects in flexible combinations. Politics, Economics, Performance Studies, Classical Civilisation, Photography, Sociology and Psychology are all new additions to the curriculum at this stage. There are also practical and vocational courses leading to qualifications in Business and Health and Social Care. Virtually all Sixth Formers go on to higher education.

Religion. Girls of all faiths and none are welcome. School assemblies are traditional and inclusive in nature and Chapel Services for boarders are held according to the rites of the Church of England.

Health. The School Doctor attends the Health Centre regularly. There are two Nursing Sisters and a Medical Assistant.

Admission. Applications should be made to the Admissions Manager (admissions@royalmasonic.herts.sch.uk). The School sets its own entrance examinations at all levels. New boarding and day pupils are accepted into the Sixth Form where there are wide-ranging opportunities for girls of all abilities.

Scholarships and Bursaries. Scholarships are offered by the School to encourage and reward excellence. Scholarships are awarded in recognition of outstanding achievement, or promise in a particular sphere, and involve financial support, not exceeding 25% of the annual fee.

A number of scholarships are available at 11+, 13+ and 16+, and some means-tested bursaries. The former are for open competition; the latter are restricted to certain categories of pupils in need. A scholarship and bursary could run concurrently in the case of a scholar who needed financial assistance.

At 11+: Awards are given in recognition of excellence with regard to academic achievement in the entrance examination, Sport, All-Rounder potential and Music.

At 16+: Awards are given for academic excellence, Music, Art, Sport and Performing Arts.

Bursaries enable suitable girls whose parents could not otherwise afford the fees to benefit from an education at The Royal Masonic School for Girls. Bursaries are awards made to girls who reach the School's required standards but who require financial assistance to take up a place. These awards are subject to means testing, under a standard formula widely used within the independent sector, at the time the offer is made and biennially thereafter. The number of awards made in any one year will vary according to the quality and circumstances of candidates and the availability of funds.

Fees per term (2016–2017). Senior School: Full Boarders £9,380; Weekly Boarders £8,645; Day Pupils £5,305.

Cadogan House: Full Boarders: £6,450 (Years 3–6); Weekly Boarders: £6,115 (Years 3–6); Day Pupils: £3,485 (Reception, Years 1 and 2), £4,040 (Years 3–6). Ruspini House Pre-School (boys and girls aged 2–4): please visit our website for range of fees.

Charitable status. The Royal Masonic School Limited is a Registered Charity, number 276784. Its aims are the advancement of education.

Board of Governors:
Mr J Gould (*Chairman & Trustee*)
Mr K S Carmichael, CBE (*Honorary Life President*)

Prof J Brewer	Mr J Knopp
Mrs P Dyke	Mr N Springer
Mr D Ellis, OBE	Mr K Surry
Mr K Emmerson	Mr M Woodcock (*Trustee*)
Mr J Flecker	Mr D Yeaman
Ms A Gray	

Head: Mr K Carson, MPhil Cantab, PGCE

Bursar: Mrs D Robinson, BSc Hons Bristol, ACA

Assistant Heads:
Mr D Cox, BEng Brunel, PGCE, NPQH
Mrs K Young, BSc Notts, PGCE

Head of Sixth Form: Mrs C Freeman, BSc Dunelm, PGCE

Senior Teachers:
Mrs R L C Bloomfield-Proud, MA London, BA Leeds, PGCE
Mrs C Bomford, MA Greenwich, BA Manchester, PGCE
Ms V Gunn, MA York, BA Hons Cape Town, HDE Cape Town, PGCE

Chaplain: Reverend John Quill

Housemistresses:
Connaught: Miss K Batty (*Head of Boarding*)

Harris House: Mrs D Dwyer
Zetland House: Mrs R Dobson

Heads of Year:
Miss H S Stanley, BEd Liverpool (*Year 7*)
Miss K Cook, BSc Reading, PGCE (*Year 8*)
Mrs S Bayless, BSc Bath, PGCE/Mrs S Baron MA UCL, BA Nottingham, PGCE (*Year 9*)
Mrs D E Heaffey, BA Middlesex, PGCE (*Year 10*)
Miss J Simmonite, BA Loughborough, PGCE (*Year 11*)
Mrs C Freeman, BSc Dunelm, PGCE (*Sixth Form*)

Heads of Departments:
Art: Mrs L Kingston, BA De Montfort, PGCE
Business Studies and Economics: Mrs V Bannister, BCom Dublin, MBA
Computing: Mr D Buddie, BSc Dundee
Design Technology: Miss M Dines, BA Bucks
English: Mrs C Gardner, MA Open, LLB Leicester, PGCE
Food and Nutrition: Mrs H Clivaz, BSc Oxford, PGCE
Geography: Mrs S McMonagle, BSc London, PGCE
History: Mr F Grogan, BA York
Latin & Classical Civilisation: Mr N M Young, MA Oxon, MCIBS
Learning Support: Mrs A Ralph, BSc Lancaster
Mathematics: Mrs S Cubbon, MSc London, PGCE
Modern Languages: Mr J Piqueiras, BA Spain, PGCE Spain
Music: Mrs J Whitbread, MA Trinity, LRAM, CertRAM
Performing Arts: Mr D Hyde, BMus Birmingham, ALCM
Physical Education: Mrs E Spendiff, BSc Staffordshire
Psychology: Mrs S Reeve, MSc London
Religious Studies: Mrs S Elder, BA Durham, PGCE
Science: Mrs N Timoney, MSc Warwick, PGCE [maternity leave], Mrs Z Sears, MSc Hungary, PGCE
Textiles: Mrs R Bloomfield-Proud, MA London, BA Leeds

Cadogan House:
Head: Mr I Connors, BA Hons, NPQH
Deputy Head: Mrs A Brown, BA Reading

Ruspini House:
Acting Head: Mrs L Sumner

Visiting Music Teachers for bassoon, brass, cello, clarinet, drum kit, flute, guitar, oboe, organ, percussion, piano, saxophone, singing, steel pans, viola, violin.

Peripatetic Staff for Dance, Learning Support, Speech and Drama, EAL.

Estates Bursar: Miss J Horsnell
School Doctors: Dr C Orsi, Dr C Quinn
Personal Assistant to the Headmistress: Mrs J Beal
Admissions Manager: Mrs G Braiden

Royal Russell School

Coombe Lane, Croydon, Surrey CR9 5BX

Tel: 020 8657 4433
Fax: 020 8657 0207
email: headmaster@royalrussell.co.uk
website: www.royalrussell.co.uk
Twitter: @Royal_Russell

Motto: *Non Sibi Sed Omnibus*

Royal Russell School is an exceptional co-educational boarding and day school, for children aged 3 to 18 years, founded in 1853. Set in 110 acres of woodland, it enjoys excellent access to London, the South, and the airports at Gatwick and Heathrow.

Number in School. There are 1023 pupils in the school: 692 pupils in the Senior School, of whom 180 are in the Sixth Form, and 331 in the Junior School. In the Senior School there are 123 boarders and 569 day pupils; of these 417 are boys and 275 are girls. In the Junior School there are 186 boys and 145 girls, all day pupils.

Admission. Most pupils enter the school in the Autumn term at the age of 3+, 11 or 13. Space permitting pupils may be considered and admitted at other ages, and there is a direct entry into the Sixth Form for eligible students.

Religion. The school's religious affiliation is to the Church of England but pupils of all persuasions are welcome. Our approach to daily life is founded on Christian principles and we maintain an atmosphere of mutual respect and understanding.

The resident Chaplain is responsible for the conduct of all services and the teaching of Religious Education throughout the school. Weekly Chapel assemblies allow a brief act of worship and an opportunity to share ideas and concerns. The Sunday service is compulsory for those boarding at school, and the voluntary Eucharist is specifically for those with a Christian commitment. Enquiries regarding Confirmation to the Church of England are encouraged.

Curriculum. The keynote of curriculum organisation is flexibility and there is close alignment with the requirements of the National Curriculum. All pupils follow a curriculum designed to provide a sound foundation across a broad range of subjects. Equipped with this experience, pupils are helped in selecting their GCSE examination subjects from a wide range. Great care is taken to achieve balance in each pupil's timetable and to ensure that an appropriate number of subjects is studied.

A high proportion of pupils continue to the Sixth Form where, typically, four subjects are studied in Year 12 with three continuing into Year 13. At present A Level courses are available in Mathematics, Further Mathematics, Computing, History, Geography, Geology, Physics, Chemistry, Biology, English, Business Studies, Economics, Politics, French, Spanish, German, Drama and Theatre Arts, Media Studies, Art and Design, Photography, Design and Technology, Music, Food Science and Physical Education.

It is our expectation that all pupils will leave the Sixth Form to go on to higher education and we regularly secure places at Oxford and Cambridge for our strongest students.

Facilities. The School lies in 110 acres of stunning private grounds providing excellent academic and sporting facilities for all age groups.

There are 3 Boarding/Day Houses and six Day Houses, a well-resourced School Library and Sixth Form Study Centre. Recent refurbishment has provided new, spacious areas for Art, Design Technology, Food Science and Photography along with a new Media Studies Suite. A new Sport Pitch development has further enhanced our impressive sports facilities, providing a floodlit all-weather pitch, multi-use games area, new natural turf areas for cricket, athletics and football and re-surfaced and extended netball courts. These are in addition to our Sports Hall and indoor swimming pool.

A detached Science building contains seven modern and very well-equipped laboratories.

An outstanding purpose-built Music and Performing Arts building was opened in December 2010 along with new dining rooms, kitchen, servery and Sixth Form Café facility.

Careers. The Head of Careers coordinates Careers advice, giving individual counselling and helping with all University applications. The School is a member of the Career Development Institute whose services are available to all pupils. Towards the end of the Summer Term work experience placements are organised for those who have completed GCSE examinations, and members of the Lower Sixth participate in organised visits to Universities and Colleges.

Organisation. The Senior School is divided into nine Houses, 2 boarding and 3 day for boys, 1 boarding and 3 day for girls. Each House has its own premises, Housemaster or Housemistress and assistant House Tutors. It is expected that all pupils should be able and encouraged to participate as fully as possible in the co-curricular life of the school, becoming involved in evening and weekend activities irrespective of their status as a Boarder or Day pupil. Supervised homework sessions and drop-in subject clinics are provided for day pupils participating in evening activities and they attend supper with the boarders. Tutors play a vital pastoral and academic role, monitoring overall progress and development.

Games. Popular sports are hockey, cricket, football, netball, tennis, swimming and athletics. Badminton, basketball, table tennis, trampolining and volleyball are also played.

Music, Drama and Art. Music in the Senior School is in the hands of the Director of Music whilst the Assistant Director of Music concentrates on the Junior School. They are assisted by a large number of visiting teachers. There is a Senior School Orchestra and wind, brass, jazz, swing and string ensembles. Choral Society, Chapel Choir, Barbershop and Junior School Choir and Orchestra meet and perform regularly.

Drama is taught as part of the Creative Studies programme in the lower school and is available at GCSE and A Level where pupils make use of our Drama Studio, Auditorium and Technical Room.

In Art and Design, instruction is offered in a wide range of Artistic techniques using a variety of materials – paint, ink, screen printing, ceramics and pottery.

Clubs and Activities. Senior School pupils choose from a programme of over 60 regular activities, with a participation rate of over 98%. Many activities are open to pupils in both Senior and Junior Schools, and the annual House Activities Cup is keenly contested by pupils in all year groups. The school's involvement in the Model United Nations programme is unique in this country, with our annual IMUN conference each October attracting over 500 student delegates from all over the world. There is a flourishing voluntary Combined Cadet Force unit and Duke of Edinburgh's Award Scheme, the Theatre Society takes advantage of the school's proximity to London's West End, and the annual ski trip is always over-subscribed.

Junior School. The aim in the Junior School is to instil a lifelong love of learning with a strong academic focus and extensive range of clubs and activities. A Breakfast Club and After-School Care is available. The majority of children progress to the Senior School. The Junior and Early Years Section provides a happy, secure and purposeful environment. (*For full details please see our entry in the IAPS section.*)

Scholarships. A number of scholarships are available each year to pupils aged 11+ to 13+ who show particular academic, musical, drama or sport promise and talent. Sixth Form scholarships are also awarded annually.

For further details or an appointment to visit the school apply to the Headmaster.

Fees per term (2016–2017). Senior School: Boarders £11,325 (Years 9–13), £8,385 (Years 7 & 8); Day £5,730 (inclusive of lunch and supper). Junior School: Years 5–6 £4,410 (inclusive of lunch, after-school clubs and supper), Years 3–4 £4,235 (inclusive of lunch, after-school clubs and supper), Reception–Year 2 £3,460 (inclusive of lunch), Nursery £1,940–£3,460.

Charitable status. Russell School Trust is a Registered Charity, number 271907. It exists solely for the education of boys and girls.

Patron: Her Majesty The Queen
Board of Governors and Trustees:

Chairman: Mr K Young

Mrs A D Greenwood
Dr D J Begley
Mr S Kolesar
Mr A Merriman
Dr A Fernandes
Mrs J Burton
Mr J Penny

Mrs A Martin
The Hon Sir Philip Moor
Mrs L Jessup
Mrs J Stevens
Mr J D Lacey
Mr A Lorie

Senior School:

Headmaster: Mr Christopher Hutchinson, BMet, FRSA

Director of International Relations: Mr Graham Moseley, BEd Hons, MA
Deputy Head (*Performance and Operations*): Mr David Selby, BA Hons
Deputy Head (*Pastoral and Designated Safeguarding Lead*): Mrs Natalie Hart, Licence D'Histoire, PDC
Deputy Head (*Academic*): Mr Daniel Botting, MSc, MA
Head of Sixth Form: Mrs Sandra Culbert, BEd Hons, MA, MA Ed Man, Dip M, ACCEG (**Careers*)

Teaching Staff:
Miss Sophia Ahmad, BA Hons
Ms Cathi Allison, BEd Hons, MA, NPQH, NCSL, CIEA
Mrs Nicky Archer (*Administrator – Music*)
Ms Deborah Baldwin, BA Hons, QTC (*Art*)
Miss Rachael Bainbridge, MA (*Mathematics*)
Mr John Baron, BSc Hons (*Admin and Activities Manager*)
Mrs Joanne Barton, BSc Hons
Mr Johnnie Blows (*Media Instructor/Technician*)
Mr Jose Bueno, BSc Hons (*Modern Languages*)
Mr Michael Callow, MA Cantab (*Mathematics*)
Miss Sandrine Calvet, BA, MA FLE (*French*) (*Modern Languages*)
Mrs Sarah Clarke, BEng (*Physics*)
Mrs Mary Colyer (*Librarian*)
Miss Alba Conde del Rio, BA Hons, MA (*Modern Languages*)
Mrs Alex Cook, BA Hons (*Science Technician*)
Mr Peter Cook, BSc Hons (*Mathematics*)
Mrs Victoria Corcoran, Cert Ed, MA (*Food Technology*)
Ms Elayine Cripps, Cert Ed (*Head of Drama*)
Miss Sarah Culliford, BSc Hons (*PE*)
Mrs Melanie Davies, BA Hons (*Drama*)
Mr John Davies, BSc Hons (*Head of Boys' PE*)
Mrs Saira Dean, BSc Hons (*Mathematics*)
Mr Colin Dear, BA Hons (*Head of Media Studies*)
Mrs Regine Demuynck-Mandinga, BTec, HND, BTS, BA Hons (*Modern Languages*)
Mr Dominic Dureau, BA Hons, MA (*English*)
Mr Jonathan Edwards (*Drama Technician*)
Mrs Kate El-Asmar, BA Hons (*English and Literacy Support*)
Mr Paul Endersby, BSc Hons (*Head of Science*)
Mrs Lynn Faulkner, BA Hons (*Business Studies & IT*)
Mr Steve Greaves, BSc Hons (*Mathematics*)
Mr David Grindrod, BSc, MSc (*Geography*)
Miss Lydia Green, BA Hons (*English*)
Mrs Helen Hadjam, BCom Hons (*Head of Economics*)
Mrs Jennifer Harris (*Library Assistant*)
Ms Sophia Hewett, BA Hons (*Head of Art and Design*)
Mr Ed Hutchinson, BA Hons (*Head of History*)
Mrs Marion Januszewski (*Senior Science Technician*)
Mr David Jewiss, BEd Hons (*PE*)
Mr Andrew Kay, BA Hons (*Head of Design and Technology*)
Mr Simon Keable-Elliott, BA Hons (*Politics & Business Studies*)
Revd Henry Kirk, BA, BD Hons, MA, Dip Hist Art (*Head of Religious Studies*)

Miss Maria Latessa, DLing, RSA Cert, TEFLA (*Head of EFL*)

Mr Colin Leggatt, RAF VR T (*Contingent Commander CCF*)

Mrs Susan Lower, BA Hons, MSC (*Head of Support for Learning*)

Mr Jordi Major, BA Hons (*Head of Food Technology*)

Mr Neil Marshall, BEd Hons (*Head of Biology*)

Mrs Anne Mawer, MA, BA Hons (*Head of Modern Languages*)

Mr Alan McKenna, BSc Hons (*Head of Chemistry*)

Mrs Stephanie Milton-Thompson, BSc Hons (*Science*)

Mr Philip Millward, MA Hons, FRCO (*Head of Music*)

Miss Geeta Missan, BSc Hons, BA Hons (*Head of Spanish*)

Mr Martin Muchall, MA, BA Hons (*Religious Studies*)

Mrs Karen Muldoon (*Drama Support Assistant*)

Miss Claire O'Sullivan, BSc, MSc (*Science*)

Miss Karen Palenski, BA Hons, MA (*Modern Languages*)

Mr Martin Parham, BSc, PhD (*Head of Geography*)

Mr Gunvantrai Parmar, Cert Ed/Dip Ed CDT & IT (*Design and Technology*)

Miss Lisa Parish, BA Hons (*Music*)

Ms Tamsin Pearson, BA Hons (*Art & Design*)

Mrs Angharad Pelling, BA (*Art & Design*)

Mrs Donna Pepperdine, BA Hons (*English*)

Miss Ruth Pringle, BA Hons (*English*)

Mr Nigel Rocca, BA Hons (*Head of Business Studies*)

Miss Celia Roe, BSc Hons, RSA Dip, TEFL (*EFL & Spanish*)

Mr Michael Salvage, BA (*History & Humanities*)

Mrs Michelle Saunders (*Food Technology/Art & Design Technician*)

Miss Olesia Sava, BA, MA (*English, EFL & Modern Languages*)

Miss Malica Scott, BA Hons

Mrs Lindsay Smith, BSc Hons, MA (*Mathematics*)

Mr Michael Stanley, BA Hons, MBA (*Head of Mathematics*)

Mr Alexander Stathopoulos, BSc Hons (*Head of Computing*)

Mr Alexander Sternfeld, MA, TESOL, Delta, BSc Hons (*Head of EAL*)

Miss Helen Stevens, MA (*Head of English*)

Mrs Susan Strutt, BSc Hons (*Biology*)

Mr Martin Tanner, BSc Hons, MA (*Head of Geology*)

Mr Adam Tansley, BSc Hons (*Mathematics*)

Mr Greg Thurstans, BSc Hons (*Director of Sport*)

Mrs Maria Wade, BA Hons (*Modern Languages*)

Miss Catherine Walton, BSc Hons (*Computer Science*)

Miss Lauren Welham, BSc Hons

Miss Scarlett Williams, BSc Hons

Miss Tiffany Wood, BA Hons

Miss Michele Worsfold, MSc, MA Hons (*History*)

School Counsellor:
Ms J Bovingdon, BA Surrey, Dip HE, MBACP Accred, UKRCP Registered

Houses and House staff:

Boarding:
Cambridge: Mr A McKenna
Oxford: Mr S Greaves
Queen's: Miss M Davenport

Day:
Buchanan: Mrs D Pepperdine
Keable: Mr E Hutchinson
Madden: Mr A Stathopoulos
Reade: Miss K Palenski
St Andrews: Mr A Tansley
Hollenden: Mrs S Strutt

Junior School:
Headmaster: Mr James Thompson, BA QTS
Head of Lower Juniors: Mrs Amanda Burton Smith, BA QTS, MA Ed
Head of Upper Juniors: Mrs Sarah Pain, BSc, PGCE, MA Ed Mgt

Mrs Emma Austin, BA Hons
Mrs Jan Bennett, BA Hons, PGCE
Mrs Abigail Cummings, BA Hons, PGCE
Mr James Davis, BSc
Mr Varun Footring, BA Hons, PGCE
Miss Siobhan Fox, GTCL, LTCL (*Head of Music*)
Miss Bethan Frisby, BA Hons
Mrs Judy Houlden, BA
Mr John Janowski, BSc Hons
Mrs Caroline King, BSc Hons, PGCE
Mr Mark Lloyd BSc, PGCE (*Boys' PE*)
Mrs Laura Lloyd, BA (*Girls' PE*)
Mr Chris Lottering, BEd (*Science*)
Mrs Sue Lower, BA, PGCE, MSc (*Head of Learning Support*)
Miss Holly Luke, BA Hons, PGCE
Mrs Judy Moseley, CertEd
Mrs Alys Netherway, BSc, PGCE
Mrs Laura Pasquel, BA Hons, QTS
Mrs Jozie Quinn, BEd Hons
Miss Aimee Rance, BA Hons, PGCE (*Head of Modern Foreign Languages*)
Mrs Fizza Rizvi, MA, PGCE
Miss Natasha Rogers, BA Hons
Miss Stephanie Scanlon, BA Hons, PGCE
Mrs Sujata Sharma, BSc, QTS
Mrs Louise Taylor, BSc
Miss Melanie Thompson, BSc Hons, PGCE
Mr Steve Urie, BA, PGCE, QTS
Mrs Ceri Warner, BA Hons, PGCE
Miss Danielle Willmott, BA Hons, PGCE
Mrs Sue Wilson, BEd, MA

Teaching Assistants:
Mrs Teresa Bridgewater, CACHE Level 3 Dip Pre-School Practice
Mrs Lynne Bruce, NNEB, CCE
Mrs Adele Cane, Level 3 Dip
Mrs Susan Haig, NVQ Teaching & Learning L3
Mrs Yayoi Ikeda, Level 3 Dip, Adv Level Apprenticeship
Mrs Nicola Jordan, OCR Level 3 NVQ
Mrs Sharmaine Nemar, NVQ Early Years L2, Level 3 Dip, Adv Level Apprenticeship
Mrs Karen Parsons, NNEB
Mrs Kelly Payne, CACHE Level 2 NVQ
Mrs Janette Vallance, Level 3 Dip
Miss Emilie Webber, Early Years Foundation Degree
Mrs Anne Willis, CACHE Level 3 Dip Pre-School Practice

Operations Director & Clerk to the Governors: Mr D Neely
Admissions Registrar: Mrs Melanie Stone
Marketing Manager: Mrs Ciara Campbell

The Royal School Dungannon

2 Ranfurly Road, Dungannon BT71 6EG, Northern Ireland

Tel:	028 8772 2710
Fax:	028 8775 2845 Headmaster
	028 8775 2506 Bursar

email: info@rsd.dungannon.ni.sch.uk
website: www.royaldungannon.com
Twitter: @RoyalDungannon

Motto: *Perseverando* (*Excellence through Perseverance*)

In 1608 James I made an order in Privy Council establishing six Royal Schools in Ulster of which Dungannon became, in 1614, the first to admit pupils. In 1983 plans were first drawn up to incorporate the neighbouring girls' grammar school and to use both campuses' excellent facilities for co-educational purposes. This development came to fruition in 1986. A £9 million building and refurbishment programme began in 2000 and was completed in 2003, providing very high-tech specialist accommodation in science, technology and IT. In 2007 an international standard Astroturf hockey pitch was completed with flood lighting and four new all-weather tennis courts were opened. Annual investment by Governors in the school's infrastructure has continued allowing RSD staff and pupils to enjoy excellent facilities.

For nearly four centuries the Royal School has aimed at providing an education which enables its pupils to achieve the highest possible standards of academic excellence and at developing each pupil into a mature, well-balanced and responsible adult, well-equipped for the demands of a highly complex and technological world.

There are four Houses which foster the competitive instincts and idiosyncrasies of young people. Pastorally, each year is supervised by a Head of Year who guides his/her pupils throughout the child's career in a caring school environment.

The Boarding Department provides accommodation for 52 Boarders with the Girls and Boys housed in separate wings of the modernised Old School building dating from 1789. The recently refurbished facilities include a new kitchen/dining area, recreation area with flat screen TV and games console, new furniture in all dormitories and fully regulated wireless internet throughout. There are a number of staff who assist in the Boarding Department, including a Head of Boarding, a team of seven resident teaching staff, a team of 5 day and evening matrons, and a large number of support staff. These staff all work together to ensure that high standards of care and support are maintained. The School is also serviced by a team of local doctors and dentists who support the Boarders. A major hospital is less than 30 minutes from the campus.

The extensive buildings are a mixture of ancient and modern, with recently opened technology and science accommodation. Eight well-equipped Science Laboratories, Audio/Visual Room, two Libraries, Sixth Form Centre and Study Rooms, Technology, two Music and Art Studios and two Information Technology Suites are supplemented by a Boarding Department housed in well-appointed accommodation which has been completely renovated in the recent times. Boarders are able to make use of a wide range of facilities such as Sports Hall, Computer Laboratory, Multigym, Badminton Courts, Television Lounges, satellite TV, high-speed broadband (including Skype) and nearby facilities such as the local swimming pool and extensive parkland walks. Situated in its own spacious grounds in a quiet residential area of this rural town, the School is linked directly by motorway to Belfast (40 minutes), two airports, cross-Channel ferries and railway stations.

The establishment of good study skills and practices is considered to be of crucial importance. The size of the School ensures that no child is overlooked in any way.

At A Level new subjects are offered such as Economics and, in collaboration with partner schools, Media Studies, Politics, Psychology and Business Studies.

Pupils are prepared for GCSE and A Levels under all the major UK Examination Boards and there is a tradition of Oxbridge successes as well as a high rate of entry to the University of Ulster, Queen's University Belfast and other leading British Universities. In most years around 95% of the Upper Sixth Form proceed to Higher Education. The School's overseas students typically choose to enrol both at UK universities and universities in their home country.

Many co-curricular pursuits are encouraged during lunchtime or after school, such as Choir, Orchestra, Duke of Edinburgh's Award scheme, Chess, Charities, Debating, Public Speaking and many more.

Alongside the School's academic achievements in both Arts and Sciences may be placed its record in the sporting world: in Rugby, Hockey, Cricket, Badminton, Shooting, Table Tennis and Tennis.

Fees per annum (2016–2017). Day: £150. 7-Day Boarding: £16,950 (non-EU passport holders), £9,600 (EU passport holders). 5-Day Boarding: £15,150 (non-EU passport holders), £7,800 (EU passport holders).

Charitable status. The Royal School Dungannon is a Registered Charity, number XN46588 A. It was established by Royal Charter in 1608 for the purpose of education.

Board of Governors:
Chairman: Ven A J Forster, BA, BTh
Vice Chairman: H McLean, LLB, MBA

Members:
Mrs J Anderson, BA Hons, MCIPD
Mrs J Archer
F Bain, BSc, MCOptom
Mrs K Bain, BEd
D N Browne, MIB, MIMgt
Dr C Cassidy, MB BCh, FRCPsych
J C M Eddie
R Eitel
Mrs R Emerson
Mrs Y Halliday, BEd Hons
Mrs E Harkness, BL
Mrs L McDonald
K McLean, MRICS
Lord Maginnis of Drumglass, PC
Dr D Maguire, BDS
J C McCarter, BA, DipArch, RIBA
Dr H G McNeill, BA, MB, FFARCSW
Mr P G Moore, MA, PGE, GC, TEFL, DELE Int
Mrs P L Matthews, BD, PGCE
Dr P G Steen, PhD, BSc, CPhys, MInstP
Mrs E V Stitt, BA, PGCE, DELE Sup
Revd A S Thompson, MA, BD
Dr G Walsh, BEd, PhD, ALCH, FHEA
Mrs L Watt, BA, Dip IT Adv
Mrs J Williamson, BA, MSc, PGCE, CPsychol AEP, HPCP
J G Willis LLb
Mrs G Leonard
R Patton, BA

Secretary to the Governors: The Headmaster

Headmaster: Dr D A Burnett, BA, PhD, NPQH

Teaching Staff:
* *Head of Department*
[1] *Head of Year*
[2] *Head of House*

Deputy Head: R J Clingan, BSc, MEd, PGCE

Senior Teacher: *G R Black, BSc, PGCE
Senior Teacher: *[1]Miss A E Chestnutt, BSc, MEd, PGCE
Senior Teacher: [1]Mrs C L Kerr, BA, MEd, PGCE

Head of Boarding: Mrs C J Mawhinney, BEd

Mrs A Best, BA, PGCE
A D Boyd, BMus Hons, PGCE, ALCM

*N J Canning, BEng, PGCE
*R E Chambers, BSc, PGCE
*Mrs W Y Chambers, BSc, MEd, PGCE, Dip IT
*[1]Mrs M E Clingan, BA, ATD
Miss S A Colgan, BSc, PGCE
*S J Cuddy, BMus, PGCE
Mrs G S Glenn, BSc, PGCE
[1]J R Graham, BA, MSc, PGCE
*Mrs R L Hampton, BSc, PGCE
*J W Hunniford, BA, MA, PGCE
*Mrs S J Jackson, BA, MEd, PGCE
Miss A Williamson, MSc, PGCE
*[1]P S Kerr, BA, MSc, PGCE
[1]G S R Lucas, BSc, PGCE
[2]Mrs P L Matthews, BEd, PGCE
*[2]G W McClintock, BSc, PGCE
Miss D McCombe, BSc, PGCE
Mrs C E McMcCormick, BA, PGCE
Mrs S J McCullough, BA, PGCE
M McDowell, BA, MA, PGCE
*K McGuinness, BSc, PGCE
*[1]Mrs P McMullan, BEd, PGCTEd
*Miss H Montgomery, BSc, PGCE
*P G Moore, MA, PGCE, GC, TEFL
*Ms A M Prescott, BEd, MEd
*[2]A S Ritchie, BSc, PGCE
*[2]Mrs D Robb, BSc, PGCE
Miss L Robinson, BSc, PGCE
Mrs J Stewart, BSc Hons, PGCE, DIS
Mrs E V Stitt, BA, PGCE
*Mrs A R Straghan, BSc Econ, PGCE
A T Turner, BSc, PGCE
[1]G T Watterson, MSc, PGCE
J W Willis, BEd
I A Wilson, BSc, PGCE

Chaplain: Ven A J Forster, BA, BTh

Administrative Staff:
Bursar: Mr D Wheeler, BSc Econ, FCA
Headmaster's Secretary: Mrs A Cullen

Matrons:
Mrs M Willis, SRN (*Day*)
Mrs M McNeill (*Evening*)
Miss R Nelson (*Evening*)

Rugby School

Rugby, Warwickshire CV22 5EH
Tel: 01788 556216 (Head Master)
           01788 556260 (Bursar)
           01788 556274 (Admissions Registrar)
Fax: 01788 556277 (Admissions Registrar)
email: head@rugbyschool.net (Head Master)
           bursar@rugbyschool.net (Bursar)
           admissions@rugbyschool.net (Admissions
           Registrar)
website: www.rugbyschool.co.uk

'*The School is storming ahead on all fronts*' (Tatler Schools Guide 2016).

'*Rugby puts an enormous amount of time and effort into its pastoral care*' (Good Schools Guide 2015/16).

Ethos. Rugby School pupils flourish in a supportive and spiritually aware community which challenges learners, develops resilience and encourages intellectual risk-taking. We foster academic excellence, nurture individual talents and ignite that spark enabling our students to develop a life-long love of learning, while achieving outstanding results.

Our greatest Head Master, Dr Thomas Arnold, knew that education is all about transforming lives and ever since, we have sought to hold onto the conviction that education is much more than the sum of academic results: it is about forming character because at Rugby, the whole person is the whole point.

Founded in 1567, Rugby is one of the UK's oldest schools and was an influential force in the development of independent education. This remarkable and innovative institution has every right to be seen as the leading co-educational boarding school in the country.

Number of pupils (2016–2017). 807 (45% girls and 55% boys).

Location. Enjoying a central location just 48 minutes by train from London and close to the M6, M1 and Birmingham Airport, Rugby School offers the best of all worlds – a leafy green 150-acre campus of the edge of the countryside but still part of the town.

Facilities. A rich, cultural heritage runs through the core of the School with many buildings of architectural distinction from the impressive Chapel to the splendid Temple Speech Room. Step away from the town and pupils enter another world of ancient cloisters and elegant quads punctuated by swathes of green.

The facilities are, however, state-of-the-art including a purpose-built Modern Languages building, an impressive Science Centre, a Design Centre featuring The Lewis Gallery with its dedicated art and exhibition space, a Media Centre with professional TV Studio and most recently, a huge new sixth form centre for A Level only subjects, complete with a debating chamber modelled on the House of Commons.

The Music Schools have recently been extended and refurbished to include 40 teaching/practice rooms, technology classrooms, recording studio and a small concert hall. Pupils regularly get to play with the School's professional orchestra.

Sports facilities are equally impressive including a modern Sports Centre, with its 25m pool, fitness suite and courts, three new astroturf hockey pitches, soccer and rugby fields and hard courts for tennis and netball. Our polo fields mark the boundary of this wide-reaching campus. Sport at Rugby includes Athletics, Badminton, Basketball, Cricket, Cross-country, Fencing, Fives, Football, Golf, Gymnastics, Hockey, Netball, Polo, Rackets, Rugby, Sailing, Squash, Swimming and Tennis. Pupils also have access to professional sports coaching and conditioning.

Boarding Houses. The House structure at Rugby is central to our strong sense of community. Ideas flourish best where they were originated and it was Dr Arnold who initiated the boarding house system to ensure exceptional pastoral care and provide the ideal social environment in which young people could thrive.

Much copied but never bettered, Rugby's 200 years of 'House' experience has resulted in a genuine and uncompromised care plan which supports every single student.

There are now 16 Houses at Rugby, each with their own unique character, in different locations and of varying sizes, but all offering a true home away from home, a real family to which every pupil belongs and is rightly proud of.

The ethos at Rugby that the whole person is the whole point is undeniably apparent within this perfected and seamless House structure. The role of Housemaster or mistress as head of the 'family' is to create and maintain a happy and balanced home with the able support of their deputy and the Matron, who importantly are all resident. Totally committed to the well-being of their young people, this nucleus of staff provides 24-hour care that is second to none.

Academic. *GCSE*: All the usual subjects are offered as well as Computing, German, Spanish, Latin, Greek, Design, Art and Music, PE, Theatre Studies and Religious Studies.

A Level/Pre-U: A Level is offered in all the GCSE subjects as well as in Business Studies, Economics, Graphics, History of Art, Textiles and Politics. The option of following Pre-U courses is available in Chemistry, Art and Design, Modern Foreign Languages, Mathematics and Physics. All pupils have the opportunity to pursue an Extended Project and all go on to Higher Education with around 10 per cent receiving Oxbridge offers.

A diverse programme of academic enrichment is an integral part of a Rugby education with all pupils attending at least three clubs and societies each week. Academic societies, many of which are pupil driven, invite a wide range of eminent figures to the School – speakers have included Rowan Williams, Ambassador Frank Wisner, Anthony Horowitz and Dame Tanni Grey-Thompson.

Spiritual Life. A well-balanced individual needs a sense of spiritual awareness along with academic achievement and physical ability. The experience of holiness, an understanding of right and wrong, and respect for the worth of each human being; these things are the invisible glue holding our community together. These values are learned in every part of our lives, but the School Chapel and the activities connected with it are a particular focus for our spiritual development.

The Chaplains get to know the boys and girls by sharing meals, visiting the Houses and involving themselves with all the School's activities. They also share the teaching of the younger pupils, giving them regular contact with the entire Lower School.

Co-curricular. Life here at Rugby is enhanced by a co-curricular programme that challenges, inspires and helps to create that 'whole person'. We recognise every pupil is an individual and we say make the most of every opportunity while you are here.

Youngsters are encouraged to take part in a School play or in the smaller House plays, join the CCF, belong to one of the many inspirational clubs – live, learn, grow and find out who you are within this incredibly inspiring community. Activities include canoeing, camping, CCF, choirs, climbing, Duke of Edinburgh's Award, First Aid, orienteering, pottery, sculpture, target and clay-pigeon shooting, Social Service, television production and School journalism.

There are some incredible trips organised annually – 2016 included a girls' hockey and netball tour to New Zealand and Singapore, a boys' rugby tour to Japan and a Philosophy expedition to Northern India when pupils met the Dalai Lama.

Admission. At 11+ local boys and girls may be assessed for entry into Year 9 as day pupils. At 13+: offers of boarding places on the basis of previous school's report and interviews during Year 7, subject to CE at average 55% at least, or the School's own Maths and English tests, or scholarship entry.

At 16+: offers of places for boarders and day pupils on the basis of previous school's report, interview and written entrance tests during Year 11, subject to at least three A (or 7) grades and three B (or 6) grades or above (including English and Mathematics, and in the subjects chosen for A Level if applicable) at GCSE.

Scholarships. Our scholarship provision is designed to attract boys and girls of outstanding talent and skill in a variety of fields. We value scholarship of all sorts. Through the excellence of our academic provision and of our facilities we aim to foster high achievement at all levels and to challenge expectations. The interplay of teaching and learning, and the experiences to be gained from being part of a rich and diverse community, encourage all pupils to develop their talents and to emerge as confident, well-rounded individuals.

13+ (Year 9) Academic Scholarships: Examinations are held in February of Year 8.

16+ (Year 12) Academic Scholarships: Scholarship interviews are held in mid-November of Year 11. Candidates must first take the Sixth Form Entrance Examination and those showing scholarship potential will be called for Scholarship interviews.

Music Scholarships: Awarded each year at 11+, 13+ and 16+. At 11+ and 13+ with assessment auditions held at Rugby School in late January of the year of entry. At 16+ the audition is held in November as part of the 16+ entrance procedure.

Art Scholarships: Awarded each year at 13+ and at 16+. At 13+ the assessment takes place in March of Year 8. At 16+, it is in November as part of the 16+ entrance procedure.

Design and Technology Scholarships: Awarded each year at 13+ and at 16+. At 13+ the assessment takes place in March of Year 8. At 16+ it is in November as part of the 16+ entrance procedure.

Sports Scholarships: At 13+ and 16+ for candidates with outstanding ability or potential in the major team games for boys (rugby, hockey, cricket and tennis) or girls (hockey, netball and tennis). At 13+ the assessment takes place in October of Year 8. At 16+ it is in October of Year 11.

Drama Scholarships: A number of Drama Scholarships are awarded each year at 13+ and 16+ to candidates with outstanding acting ability or potential. At 16+ there are also scholarships for technical ability in drama. At 13+ the assessment takes place in October of Year 8. At 16+ it is in October of Year 11.

Computing Scholarships: Awarded each year at 13+ and 16+. At 13+ the assessment takes place in May of Year 8. At 16+ it is in November as part of the 16+ entrance procedure.

Foundation Awards: Several Foundation Awards are made annually to day boy and day girl candidates at 11+, 13+ and 16+. These candidates must live within a radius of 10 miles from the Rugby Clock Tower – excluding the city of Coventry.

Awards and Augmentation: The value of a Scholarship Award or a Foundation Award (including more than one award) is a maximum fee concession of 10%. Support can be augmented up to 100% of the day fees subject to means assessment.

The Arnold Foundation aims to raise funds through charitable donations to support the education of talented boys and girls whose families would not be able to fund boarding school fees. Funds are available for several awards for entry to the sixth form and at 13+. Pupils offered a place through this scheme may be awarded up to 100% of the full boarding fee plus extras. The final selection is through interviews. Candidates are expected to pass the School's normal entrance requirements. Initial enquiries should be made via the Admissions Office

For further information and details of all Scholarships, Foundation Awards and the Arnold Foundation please contact the Admissions Registrar, Tel: 01788 556274, email: admissions@rugbyschool.co.uk.

Fees per term (2016–2017). The consolidated termly fee for boys and girls: £11,357 (boarding), £7,126 (day). Junior Department: £4,197 (Marshall House). Optional charge for instrumental or singing tuition: £315.

Further Information. Log on to www.rugbyschool.co.uk. Enquiries and applications should be made in the first instance to the Registrar.

Charitable status. The Governing Body of Rugby School is a Registered Charity, number 528752. It exists to provide education for young people.

Governing Body:
Mrs L J Holmes, BA Hons (*Chairman*)
R C A Hingley, MA (*Deputy Chairman*)
Prof C H E Imray, PhD, FRCS, FRCP

The Rt Revd the Lord Bishop of Birmingham, D A
  Urquhart
Dr E Wood, OBE, DL, MSc, EdD, Hon LLD
P Bennett-Jones, CBE, MA.
D J Bennett, MA
Prof C J Howe, ScD
S Lebus, MA
C J Edwards, MA
B J O'Brien, LLB
S R T Penniston (*until 24.11.16*)
HM Lord-Lieutenant of Warwickshire, T B Cox
P Smulders, BA, MBA
Ms C J Marten, MA
Ms G Woodward, BA
Mrs J Eastwood, BA
Mrs H Jackson, BSc
G V Lloyd-Jones (*from 24.11.16*)

Bursar and Clerk to the Governing Body: G Lydiatt, BSc,
  FCCA

Medical Officer: Dr S Brown, MA, MB, ChB, LLB, LLM,
  DCH, DRCOG, DFSRH, FRCGP

Head Master: P R A Green, MA, PGCE

Deputy Head: Dr N G Hampton, MA, PhD, PGCE

Deputy Heads:
Mrs S A Rosser, BEd (*Pastoral*)
G Parker-Jones, MA, PGCE (*Academic*)

Assistant Head (*Upper School*): Dr J D Muston, MA,
  MPhil, DPhil
Assistant Head (*Middle School*): E S Davies, BA, MSc,
  PGCE
Assistant Head (*Co-Curricular*): N A Gutteridge, BEd

Admissions Registrar: H G Steele-Bodger, MA

Assistant Teaching Staff:

Chaplaincy:
The Revd R M Horner, BSc (*Chaplain*)
Miss L Greatwood, BSc, DipMin, PGCE
D R Shaw, MA, PGCE

Classics:
Mrs A D Henderson, BA, MA, MPhil (*Acting Head of
  Department*)
T J Day, BA, PGCE
Miss S R Harris, BA, MSt
A E L Thomson, BA

Design:
P A Byrne, BA (*Director of Design Faculty, Head of D&T*)
Mrs A Bradbury, Dip AD (*Art/Graphics*)
Mrs A K Farrelly, BSc
Miss A K Janulewicz, BA, PGCE
Mrs S E Phillips, BA, QTS (*Art/Ceramics*)
J Ryan, BA, BTech, PGCE, MFA
B J Welch, BEng, PGCE
Dr G M Williams, MA, BA, PhD

Drama and Theatre Studies:
A K Chessell, BA, MSc, PGCE (*Artistic Director*)
Dr T D Coker, BA, MMus, MPhil, PhD (*Head of Drama*)
Dr S L Hancox, BA, MA, PhD

Economics and Business Studies:
C J Fisher, BA (*Head of Department*)
A J Darby, BA
P J Rosser, BA
H G Steele-Bodger, MA, PGCE
J D Walker, BSc, PGCE

English:
J A Sutcliffe, PhD (*Head of Department*)

Mrs E C Ademokun, MA, QTS
Mrs E M Beesley, MA
J B Cunningham-Batt, BA
Miss I C Marks, MA, BA, PGCE
A J Naylor, BA, PGCE
A N Smith, MA, PGCE

Geography:
R Ghosh (*Head of Department*)
Miss A Abrahams, BA
J C Evans, BA, PGCE
Dr L E Milner, MA, MSc, PhD
Miss E Price, BA, MPhil
Mrs S A Rosser, BEd

History:
Dr T D Guard, MA, MSt, DPhil, PGCE (*Head of
  Department*)
Dr E A Beesley, BA, PhD
E S Davies, BA, MSc, PGCE
Miss K Hollings, BA
Dr J D Muston, MA, MPhil, DPhil
Mrs A Naylor, BA, PGCE
G Parker-Jones, MA, PGCE
Ms M H Pink, MA, GDL, LPC, PGCE

Information Technology:
T E Rennoldson, BSc, PGCE (*Head of Department*)
Mrs L A Bell, BEng

Learning Development:
Mrs L J E Stevenson, LLB, Dip SpLD (*Head of Learning
  Development*)
Mrs A L Cunningham-Batt, MA, OCR Cert SpLD
Mrs F J Fleming, MA, Cert TESOL
Mrs B Green, MA, MEd, PGCE

Mathematics:
M R Baker, BA, PGCE (*Head of Department*)
Dr M A Hennings, BA, DPhil (*Second in Department*)
R J Baker, BSc, PGCE
P K Bell, MA, Msc, PGCE
Miss R J Force, BSc
J E Ingram, MMath
B L Lane, MA, MSc
Mrs S C McGuirk, BSc, PGCE
L P Rao, MA
B Rigg, MA, ACA
D R Shaw, MA, PGCE
A J Siggers, BSc
I S Tipler, BSc

Modern Languages:
D Gillett, BA, PGCE (*Head of Department*)
Mrs C A O'Mahoney, BA (*Head of Spanish*)
Mrs S Trelinska, BA, MEd, PGCE (*Head of French*)
Mrs W J Corvi, BEd, PGCE
R M Horner, BSc
N D Jarvis, MA, BA, PGCE
Mrs R P Kayada, BA, PGCE
Dr A C Leamon, MA, BA, PhD
A M Maguire, MA, BA, PGCE
Dr B Parolin, BA, MA, PhD
Dr J C Smith, MA, DPhil, PGCE

Music:
R J Tanner, MA, FRCO, ARAM, HonFGCM (*Director of
  Music*)
D Blackadder, DipRCM, ARCM (*Head of Brass*)
Mrs A Brogaard, DipRDAM (*Head of Strings*)
R F Colley, MA, BSc, LRAM, ARCM, DipRAM, PGCE
  (*Head of Piano*)
A R Davey, LTCL (*Head of Woodwind*)
J T Oxley, MA, ARCM

J A Williams, MA, BA, DipABRSM, PGCE (*Head of Academic Music*)

Philosophy and Theology:
D J McLean, BA (*Head of Department*)
Mrs A L Parker-Jones, MA, PGCE

Physical Education:
F J Hemming-Allen, BEd, MEd (*Head of PE*)
Mrs D L Skene, BSc, PGCE (*Head of Girls' Games*)
Mrs L M Hampton, MSc, BEd

Politics and International Relations:
P Teeton, BA (*Head of Department*)
Miss E Price, BA, MPhil
E E Trelinski, MA

Science:
Dr M A Thompson, BSc, PhD, PGCE (*Head of Science*)
Dr G C E Joyce, BSc, PhD, PGCE (*Head of Biology*)
T M White, BSc, PGCE (*Head of Chemistry*)
Dr A G Davies, BSc, PhD, PGCE (*Head of Physics*)
P A Berry, BSc, PGCE
Mrs E Brien, MChem
P Calleja, MChem
R Dhanda, BSc
O Gardner, MSci, MA, PGCE
Miss L J Greatwood, BSc, DipMin, PGCE
Mrs L M Hampton, BEd, MSc
Dr N G Hampton, MA, PhD, PGCE
Dr M C Jones, MA, MSc, PhD
Miss R J Lambert, BSc, PGCE
R B McGuirk, BSc, MSc, PGCE
M A Monteith, BSc, PGCE
Dr N J Morse, BSc, PhD, CChem, FRSC
R Parker, BSc, PGCE
Mrs E L Sale, BSc, PGCE

Careers and Higher Education:
Mrs D J Horner, BA (*Head of Department*)
Ms L Waweru, BPhilEd, PQCG
Mrs J A Higgins
Mrs A L Parker-Jones MA, PGCE

PSHE Education:
Miss L J Greatwood, BSc, Dip Min, PGCE (*Head of Department*)

Sport:
S J Brown, BSc (*Director of Sport*)
Miss L Blair (*Netball Development Officer*)
M J Powell (*Cricket Professional*)
M Pugh, BSc, ASCC (*Strength and Conditioning Coach*)
P J Rosser, BA (*Rackets Professional*)
Mrs D L Skene, BSc, PGCE (*Head of Girls' Games*)
J M Stedman, BA (*Director of Hockey*)
J Taylor, BSc (*Tennis Development Officer*)
M Taylor (*Hockey Development Officer*)

Houses and Housemasters/mistresses:

Boarding Houses (*boys*):
Cotton: Mr Ed Trelinski
Kilbracken: Mr James Walker
Michell: Mr Tim Day
School Field: Mr Mindy Dhanda
School House: Mr Peter Bell
Sheriff: Mr Maurice Monteith
Whitelaw: Mr Chris Evans

Day Boy House:
Town: Mr Tony Darby

Boarding Houses (*girls*):
Bradley: Mrs Liz Sale
Dean: Mrs Amy Farrelly
Griffin: Mrs Anne Naylor

Rupert Brooke: Miss Katie Hollings
Stanley (*Sixth Form only*): Mrs Lara Hampton
Tudor: Mrs Debbie Horner

Day Girl House:
Southfield: Mrs Lizzie Beesley

Junior Day House (*boys and girls*):
Marshall: Mr Barrie Cunningham-Batt

Director of Development: Mrs K Wilson, BA

Rydal Penrhos School

Pwllycrochan Avenue, Colwyn Bay, North Wales LL29 7BT

Tel:	01492 530155
Fax:	01492 531872
email:	info@rydalpenrhos.com
website:	www.rydalpenrhos.com
Twitter:	@RydalPenrhos
Facebook:	@rydalpenrhosschool

Penrhos College was founded by Thomas Payne in 1880 as a Methodist girls' school; its neighbour, Rydal School, was founded five years later by Thomas Osborn, also as a Methodist boarding school. In 1999, after just over a century of co-existence, the Schools merged under the name of Rydal Penrhos; now Rydal Penrhos School. A second merger took place in 2003 when Rydal Penrhos Preparatory School merged with another local prep school, Lyndon School. The school is fully co-educational from 2½ to 18, with a total roll of 539 pupils.

Situation and Buildings. Rydal Penrhos School is 45 minutes' drive from Chester and 95 minutes' drive from Manchester and Liverpool airports, giving easy access to Europe and beyond. There are also excellent rail links to London and the Midlands. The school is located in Colwyn Bay and is close to the Snowdonia National Park. It is therefore ideally placed to combine a broad academic curriculum with a rich variety of outdoor activities that make the most of the sea and the mountains. The Preparatory School (Rydal Penrhos Preparatory School), which takes pupils from 2½ years, overlooks Colwyn Bay and is adjacent to Rydal Penrhos School.

Teaching facilities include nine science laboratories, dedicated study areas for senior pupils, specialist art, music and design technology centres, a lecture theatre and a drama studio. There are also information technology suites, a well-stocked library and a recently built Sixth Form centre. A sports hall, swimming pool, fitness suite, dance studio and Astroturf pitch complement the outdoor sporting facilities.

Many of the boarding houses started their existence as large Victorian or Edwardian residences in the fashionable seaside resort of Colwyn Bay. As a result, each has a very distinctive character, and a strong sense of being a 'home-from-home'. There are four boys' houses and one girls' house. Each boarding house is supervised by resident housemaster or housemistress, with the assistance of a team of tutors and matrons.

Numbers and Organisation. There are currently 313 pupils in the senior school (182 boys and 131 girls) of which 124 are boarders. There are 161 pupils in Rydal Penrhos Preparatory School, comprising 89 boys and 72 girls.

The Prep School is divided into Early Years (age 2½–4), Pre-Prep (Reception to Year 2) and Prep (Year 3 to Year 6) departments, with separate and distinct curricula and routines. The senior school is arranged into the Lower School (Years 7–8), Middle School (Years 9–10 and pre-Sixth) and Sixth Form (IB and A Levels), each with its own Head of School. Pupils in the Prep and senior schools are also allocated to competitive Houses for academic, sporting and cultural events. The well-being and academic life of the school is driven by a tutorial structure that creates a strong framework bringing pupils, teaching staff and parents together in an effective partnership.

Religious aims. Rydal Penrhos School is a Christian school in the Methodist tradition, but welcomes pupils from all faiths or none. Prayers are held daily in St John's Church, ownership of which has now been transferred to the school. Special services are held to mark key festivals and occasions in the Church year, and there is an annual confirmation service for members of the School community.

Curriculum. The National Curriculum is shadowed and supplemented to afford the best opportunities and choices for the pupils.

In Years 7 to 9 (KS3), pupils study English, Mathematics, the three sciences, Religious Studies, French, German, Geography, History, Drama, Art & Design, Home Economics, Design & Technology, Music, ICT, Physical Education, and PSHE. Pupils have a choice of language options into Years 8 and 9.

In Year 10, the core GCSE subjects are English and English Literature, Mathematics, Science (either separate sciences or Dual Award), a modern foreign language and Religious Studies. Pupils will choose two further subjects to complete their GCSE options, and all pupils participate fully in both Physical Education and the PSHE programme. GCSEs in other languages (notably Welsh and Latin) are also available by request. EFL and Learning Support are provided to support pupils at the appropriate level and allow them to take full advantage of the academic programme.

The School welcomes new entrants into the Sixth Form, which offers both the International Baccalaureate Diploma programme and A Levels in a full range of subjects. Pupils are expected to have Grade C or above in at least 5 subjects at GCSE before entering the Sixth Form. With a wide range of options available, pupils are able to choose courses that reflect their own particular strengths and interests.

Sports and Activities. All pupils undertake a balanced programme of extra-curricular activities, with the aim of acquiring a range of physical and social skills, and developing talent. The importance of competitive sport is recognised, and the School has a strong fixture list in rugby (it is a partner and host of the WRU North Wales Rugby Academy), cricket, netball, hockey (its teams are regular National champions at various age levels), athletics and tennis. The sailing, skiing and swimming teams also enjoy considerable success and School teams compete and win at regional and national level in the full range of sports available at Rydal Penrhos.

The school's coastal location within a few miles of the Snowdonia National Park offers unrivalled opportunities for a full programme of adventurous activities including mountaineering, climbing, hillwalking and kayaking. The Duke of Edinburgh's Award is very well supported by pupils. The school runs its own sailing training centre and hosts the annual Rydal Penrhos School Regatta; sailing is an integral part of the core activities programme.

The Arts. The school has a fine tradition in both music and drama, and pupils are actively encouraged to develop an enthusiasm for the performing arts. The Music department presents two full school concerts at Christmas, Spring and in early Summer, with many other performance opportunities on offer. Pupils also perform regularly in chapel and at other whole-school occasions. The Drama department has enjoyed real academic success for many years, and this is reflected in the high standard of performance in school plays, musicals and other performances throughout the year.

Careers. The school prides itself on the quality of its advice on careers and higher education, and the library has a well-equipped careers centre to support this function. All pupils in Year 11 are expected to arrange work experience in collaboration with the Careers department, and the School holds an annual careers convention and industrial conference. In the Spring term of Year 11, pupils are given an individual interview to discuss their Sixth Form programme to ensure that they are fully informed about their options. In preparation for university mock interviews are arranged with local businesses and the professional community. Sixth Form pupils are expected to move on to university, and the vast majority do so.

Admission. Pupils can be admitted at the beginning of any term after their 11th birthday; the largest entry is in September. Entry is normally via the school's entrance examination, held in February, or equivalent tests.

Scholarships and Bursaries. Academic, Art, Drama, Music and Sport Scholarships worth up to 50% of school fees are available for Year 7, Year 9 and Sixth Form entry. An award may be increased through a means-tested bursary up to 70% of the school fees.

There are 2 fully-funded (means-tested) day places for Year 7 entry reserved for candidates residing in North Wales.

Children of Methodist and Anglican ministers are admitted at substantially reduced fees. Bursaries for children of serving members of the Armed Forces are also available. Forces families may also be eligible for the North Wales Day Allowance.

For full details of all awards, please apply to Mrs Jenny Marsden, Admissions, email: JMarsden@rydal penrhos.com.

Fees per term (2016–2017). Boarding £8,700–£10,715, UK Weekly Boarding £6,630–£7,420, Day £4,470–£5,380.

Rydal Penrhos Preparatory School. Co-educational Day School for children aged 2½–11.

Charitable status. Rydal Penrhos Limited is a Registered Charity, number 1063489, and a Company Limited by Guarantee. The object of the charity is the advancement of education in accordance with Christian principles.

The Governors:
Chairman: Mr J I Morris

Mrs A M Watson	Dr N Bickerton
Revd P Barnett	Mr I M Williams
Mr P D Slater	Mr J Barnes
Mr R W Dransfield	Dr D Fazey
Dr Revd S Wigley	Mr J Waszek
Mr J P Burgess	Mrs N Rutherford
Mr J M A Wilford	Mr P Rigby
Mr J Payne	Revd J P Atkinson
Mrs D A Draper	

Honorary Governors:
Mr A J Hollis
Mrs E P Jones

Headmaster: **Mr S R Smith**, BA

Director of Finance: Miss K Baines
Deputy Head: Mr T Cashell, BEd
Director of Studies: Mrs S A Harding, BA
Head of Sixth Form: Mr P J Lavery, BA
Head of Middle School: Mr J B Murphy, BA (†*Netherton*)
Head of Lower School: Mrs G S Murphy, BA
Chaplain: The Revd N Sissons, MA

Assistant staff:
* *Head of Department*
† *Housemaster/Housemistress*

Mr D Baker, BSc (†*Asst Housemaster*)
Mr P Baxter, BEd
Mrs A Beaumont, BA (†*Asst Housemistress*)
Mrs S Boxleitner, MA
Mr A M Boyd, MA (*Director of Sport*)

Mrs C Boyd, BA
Dr M F Brown, BSc, PhD (†*Walshaw*)
Dr S Brown, BA, MSc, PhD (†*Matron*)
Mrs M Burgess, MA
Mrs A Cashell, BEd (**Learning Support*)
Mrs S Chatburn, BA (†*Asst Housemistress*)
Mrs L Crimes, MA (**English & Drama*; †*Asst Housemistress*)
Mr R A Davies, BA
Ms F Earle, BA (†*Edwards*)
Mr M J Farnell, BA (**Economics, Business Studies & ICT*)
Miss H Freeman, BA
Mrs N J Head, BA (**Girls' Games*)
Miss S James (†*Asst Housemistress*)
Miss F H Jones, BA
Mrs R Jones, MA
Mrs C Lavery, BSc
Mr P Lavery, BA (**MFL*, †*Asst Housemaster*)
Mr M T Leach, BSc
Mrs S Leach (†*Matron*)
Dr J T Lewis, BSc
Mrs S Livingstone, BA
Miss F Lloyd, BA
Ms A Margerison, BSc (**Biology*)
Mr P J Mather, BEd (**Boys' Games and Activities*; †*Hathaway*)
Mrs K Mather (†*Matron*)
Mrs D Maughan, BA
Dr D Molinari, MA, PhD
Mrs S Morris, BA
Mrs W Murphy (†*Matron*)
Mr E Parri, BA
Mrs M Pearce, BA, MSc
Mr M W Pender, BSc (**Chemistry, UCAS & Careers*)
Mr A Price, MA (**History*)
Mrs A Price, BA
Mr I L Richardson, BSc, MSc (†*Beecholme*)
Mrs A M Richardson, BA (**Religious Education and PSHE*; †*Beecholme*)
Mr P Richmond, BSc (**Mathematics, †Asst Housemaster*)
Ms D Riley (†*Matron*)
Dr G R Roberts, BSc, PhD
Mr D M Robson, BSc, BEng (**Science*)
Mr P W Russell, BA
Mr P A Sanders, BA
Mr J M Sherrington, BA (**Art*)
Miss J K Simpkins, BA (**EFL*)
Mr P Sutton, BEng (**Design & Technology*)
Ms C A Vallée Licence, LLCE
Mrs L Williams, BSc (**Home Economics*)
Mr P Williams, Mus Dip (**Music*)
Mrs R E Williams, BA

Admissions Officer: Mrs J Marsden

Preparatory School:

Headmaster: Mr Roger McDuff, BEd Hons, MA

Deputy Head: Mrs Alison Hind
Head of Pre-Prep: Mrs Gaynor Davies
Head of Early Years: Mrs L Roberts

Mrs Clare Chamberlain
Mrs Catherine Culver
Mr Richard Davies
Mrs Frances Devilleforte
Mr Andrew Edgley (*Swimming*)
Mrs Anna George
Mrs Lavinia Lewis (*Learning Support*)
Mrs Emma McDuff
Mr James McLeod
Mrs Nicola Merrick

Mrs Suzanne Morris
Mrs Judith Pyves
Miss Dawn Roberts (*Early Years*)
Miss Hannah Rushton (*Gym*)
Mrs Helen Rushton (*Gym*)
Mr Maciej Ruszkowski (*Swimming*)
Mrs Nicola Shilton (*Early Years*)
Revd Nicholas Sissons
Miss Nikki Taylor (*Early Years*)
Miss Charline Vallée
Mrs Caroline Williams
Mr Peter Williams (*Head of Music*)
Mrs Julie Woodthorpe
Ms Nerys Wynne-Jones

Teaching Assistants:

Mrs Rebecca Curle
Mrs Deborah Edwards
Mrs Beth Hughes
Mrs Hayley Hughes

Mrs Elizabeth Hutin
Mrs Holly Roberts
Miss Clare Tebbits
Mrs Catherine Williams

Preparatory School Admissions: Mrs Susan Williams

Ryde School with Upper Chine

Queen's Road, Ryde, Isle of Wight PO33 3BE
Tel: 01983 562229
Fax: 01983 564714
email: school.office@rydeschool.net
website: www.rydeschool.org.uk
Twitter: @rydeschool
Facebook: @rydeschool2013

Motto: '*Ut Prosim*'

Ryde School with Upper Chine is a day and boarding school which provides education for boys and girls aged two and a half to eighteen. It is situated on the Isle of Wight. Ryde School was founded in 1921 to provide a Christian education for boys. In 1992 the School opened Fiveways, which caters for pupils in the Nursery, Reception and Years 1 and 2. Upper Chine was founded as a Girls' School in Shanklin on the Isle of Wight in 1914. The two schools merged in 1994 to form Ryde School with Upper Chine and in 1996 the School took over Bembridge School. As a result of these acquisitions and mergers the School is now fully co-educational. Boarding provision is situated on a coastal site of 117 acres in nearby Bembridge and in a newly-opened boarding house for 10 Sixth Formers in Ryde itself.

Situation and Buildings. The School stands in its own grounds of 17 acres in Ryde with stunning views over the Solent and is easily accessible from all parts of the Island and the near mainland. It is within walking distance of the terminals which link Ryde to Portsmouth by hovercraft (10 minutes) or catamaran (15 minutes) and a number of pupils travel daily from the mainland. In recent years there have been many additions to the School buildings. The School now enjoys up-to-date and extensive facilities. New Art and CDT departments opened in 2011, alongside a new dining hall in the award-winning Bembridge Building and new Chemistry labs opened in 2015.

Organisation and Curriculum. The School aims to provide a secure and nurturing environment from which pupils gain the ambition, courage and values to face the world. It enjoys an enviable reputation on the Island for high standards both inside and outside the classroom.

In the Junior School strong emphasis is laid on core skills and on proficiency in reading, writing and number work. Pupils are prepared in this way for entry into the Senior School and, following a recommendation from the Head of the Junior School, they are offered places in the Senior School at the age of 11. All pupils in the Junior School get the opportunity to sail and engage in outdoor learning.

The programme of work in the Senior School is designed to provide a broad but challenging education up to the end of Year 11 with all pupils working towards the EBac. The subjects taught to IGCSE/GCSE level are English, English Literature, Mathematics, Physics, Chemistry, Biology, French, Spanish, Latin, Geography, History, Religious Education, Business Studies, Art, Music, Physical Education, Drama and Design Technology. All pupils also follow a programme of Personal Development (PD) and Games.

In the Sixth Form pupils may choose from three courses: the IB Diploma, 'A Level Plus' (3 A Levels plus various enrichment and extension options) and the IBCP (An IB certificate that combines academic courses alongside professional qualifications in one of Finance, Engineering, Art & Design or Sports Science). In addition, pupils are encouraged to take the Extended Project Qualification, designed to add breadth to their academic studies. Courses lead to entrance to universities, the Services, industry and the professions. The Careers Department provides advice and guidance to all pupils who go to a variety of universities and careers, over half to Russell Group universities in the last three years.

Tutorial System. Each pupil has a tutor who is responsible for his or her academic and personal progress and general pastoral welfare. The tutorial system encourages close contact with parents, which is further reinforced by parents' meetings which are held at regular intervals and a parent portal. The School aims to maintain sound discipline and good manners within a traditionally friendly atmosphere and encourages pupils to live up to the School motto "Ut Prosim".

Games. The main games in the Senior School are hockey, sailing and athletics, with rugby football and cricket for the boys, and netball and rounders for the girls. In the Junior School, Association football is also played. Other games include basketball, squash, golf, swimming and tennis. Regular matches are arranged at all levels against teams both on the Island and the mainland. There are growing opportunities for sailing and the School keeps some sailing dinghies at Seaview Yacht Club.

Music and Drama. The Music School incorporates practice and teaching facilities and a well-equipped recording studio. The School has a flourishing choral tradition, with opportunities for participation in a variety of choirs and instrumental groups. Concerts and musical plays are performed in both Senior and Junior Schools, and concert tours abroad have taken place in recent years. Full-length plays are produced each year by both Senior and Junior Schools, and special attention is given in the English lessons of the younger forms to speaking, lecturing and acting. Musical Theatre is a particular strength. The School has its own theatre and studio theatre, a School Poet and an artist-in-residence.

Activities. There are many societies which cater for a wide range of individual interests. The School has a contingent of the Combined Cadet Force with Royal Navy and Royal Air Force sections. Sailing, canoeing, gliding, and other forms of venture training are strongly encouraged. There is a flourishing Duke of Edinburgh's Award scheme; last year around a quarter of the Upper Sixth achieved their Gold Award. Holiday visits and expeditions are regularly arranged, and there are opportunities for exchange visits with schools on the continent.

Boarding. Boarding for both boys and girls is available for pupils on the Bembridge campus which offers approximately one hundred acres of playing fields and woodland in a beautiful setting overlooking Whitecliff Bay and Culver Cliff, some six miles from Ryde. Transport is provided to and from Ryde for the school day. A new boarding house for up to ten Upper Sixth Formers has recently opened in Ryde.

Fees per term (from January 2017). Tuition: Foundation Stage: £2,150–£2,380 (full day), £1,090 (half day); Pre-Prep £2,580–£3,295; Junior School £3,990; Senior School £4,125.

Boarding (excluding tuition): Senior School: £4,960 (full), £3,985 (weekly).

Rates for payment by Direct Debit.

Scholarships and Bursaries. Scholarships may be awarded on merit to external or internal candidates for entry at 9+, 11+, 13+ and 16+. All scholarships may be supplemented by bursaries, which are means-tested.

Charitable status. Ryde School is a Registered Charity, number 307409. The aims and objectives of the Charity are the education of boys and girls.

Governors:
Chairman: Dr C J Martin, BSc, DPhil, MBA, FIChemE, CEng
Vice-Chairman: Mr C Lees, MB BS, BSc, MD
Hereditary Governor: Mr A McIsaac, MA, DPhil
Chair of Finance & General Purposes Committee: Mr N Wakefield, MA
Chair of Education Committee: Ms C R Clark, MA, BA
Mrs J Bland, Cert Ed
Ms C Doerries, QC
Mr S Drew, MA
Mr J H [Danny] Fisher, MBE, DL
Mrs D Haig-Thomas, BA
Mrs A Harvey
Dr M Legg, BSc, MB BS (*Safeguarding responsibility*)
Mrs E Millett, BA
Mrs J Minchin
Mr P Weeks

Clerk to the Governors: Mr P C Taylor, JP, FCA, FRSA

Headmaster: Mr M A Waldron, MA Cantab, MEd

Deputy Head (*Academic*): Mr P R Moore, MA
Deputy Head: Mr B Sandford-Smith, MEd
Head of Junior School: Mrs L M Dennis, BEd
Head of Fiveways: Mrs S A Davies, BEd
Bursar: Mr J A F Marren, BSc
Chaplain: The Revd Canon G Morris
Head of Boarding: Miss A Sutton
Director of Boarding: Mrs L Nestor-Powell, BA
Second Master: Mr K J Dubbins, BEd
IB Coordinator: Miss K Gallop
Head of Sixth Form: Mr M J Windsor, BSc
Head of Pastoral Care: Miss C B Vince, BA

Senior Teachers:
Mr S R Baxter, BA (*Careers, Skills and Lifelong Learning*)
Mr D P C Blewitt, MSc (*Director of Studies*)
Mrs S E Evans, BA (*Alumni and Events*)

§ *Part-time*

Senior School:
Mr M Alderton, MPhys (*Head of Year 8, Physics*)
Mrs J Barclay, BA (*Librarian, English*)
Mrs S L Bayley (*Head of Learning Support, Economics*)
Mr S Baxter (*Head of Careers, Skills & Lifelong Learning, Art, IBC, TOK*)
Ms K E Bishop, BSc, BA Hons (*Head of Psychology, Science*)
Mr D P C Blewitt, MSc (*Director of Studies, Mathematics*)
§Miss S Blewitt (*English, Languages*)
§Mr G Bowen, BEd (*IB Self-Taught Language*)
§Miss S Broyé, BA, MA (*Languages*)
§Mrs J Bryant (*Languages, SEN, ESL*)
Mr T Bull, BA (*Head of Drama, i/c Global Rock*)

Mrs M E Burgess, BSc (*Head of Social Sciences, Head of Geography*)

Mr MG Chalmers, BSc (*Head of Chemistry*)

Miss J Coates (*Graduate Teacher, English, Drama*)

Mr J C Comben, BA (*Head of Year 9, Bronze Duke of Edinburgh's Award, History, Politics*)

Miss O E Crean, MA (*Head of Art*)

Miss J Drabble, BA (*Head of Seaford, Geography*)

Miss A Drinkwater, BEd, MA (*Head of Games, Head of Netball, PE*)

Mr K J Dubbins, BEd (*Second Master, Contingent Commander CCF, Biology*)

§Miss J A Dyer, BA (*Head of Spanish, Languages*)

Mr H Edwards (*Graduate Sports Teacher*)

Mrs S Evans (*Senior Teacher Alumni & Events, Drama*)

§Mrs K Gavin, BA (*Languages*)

Mr M J Glasbey, BSc (*Head of DT, Head of Year 10*)

Mr A M Graham, BA, HNTD (*Mathematics*)

Mr A Grubb, BMus (*Director of Music*)

Mrs T A Hall, BA (*Director of Languages*)

Mr O Herbert (*Graduate Sports Teacher*)

Mr R Hoare, BA (*Head of Personal Development, DT*)

Miss E Holloway (*Graduate Sports Teacher, Geography*)

Mr P A Johnson, BSc, BA (*Mathematics, Squash*)

Mr A Johnston, BA (*Head of ICT*)

Ms E C Jones, BA (*English*)

Miss A Lengersdorf, BA (*Languages*)

Miss C Manser (*Economics & Business Studies, Head of Sailing*)

Ms H McComb, BA, TEFL Dip (*Head of Religious Education, IB Spanish*)

Mr S M Mead, BEd (*Chemistry*)

Mr J H Mitchell, BHum (*Head of Hanover, Head of Athletics, Head of Ac PE*)

Mr P R Moore, MA (*Deputy Head Academic, Maths, Science*)

Ms A J Newman, BA Hons (*IB TOK Coordinator, Head of Year 11, Chinese, History*)

§Mrs M L Newte, MEng (*Physics*)

Mrs L E O'Sullivan, BSc Ed (*Head of Trinity, Mathematics*)

Miss C Parkes, MA, BA (*History, Latin, Languages*)

§Mr B W Penn, BSc, CBiol (*Science*)

Miss B Percy, BA (*Graduate Sports Teacher, Head of Rounders*)

Dr M Postelnyak, MA, DPhil (*Head of Mathematics*)

§Mrs J Ratcliff, BA (*Art, IB, Visual Arts*)

Mrs K J Snow, BA (*History*)

Dr G R Speller, BSc, MPhil, PhD Cantab (*Head of Science*)

Mr B Sanford-Smith, MA (*Deputy Head, Psychology*)

Miss G S Stenning, BA (*Head of English*)

Mr P J Stott, BA (*Head of History & Politics*)

Mr P G Swann, BSc (*Head of Physics*)

Mr C G S Trevallion, BSc (*Head of Biology, Silver Duke of Edinburgh's Award*)

Mrs R F Tweddle, GTCL, LTCL (*Choir Director, Music*)

Miss C Vince, BA (*Head of Pastoral Care, English*)

Mrs L L Waldron, BA Hons, MA Ed (*Mathematics*)

Mr M A Waldron, MA Cantab, MEd (*Headmaster, German*)

§Mrs J J Whillier, BSc QTS (*Mathematics, Science*)

Mr M Whillier, BSc (*Head of Year 7, Physics, Chemistry*)

Mr J Willetts, BSc Econ (*Head of Business, Economics and Finance, Head of Rugby*)

Miss N Wilson (*English*)

Mr M J Windsor, BSc (*Head of Sixth Form, Gold Duke of Edinburgh's Award, Geography*)

Junior School:

Head: Mrs L Dennis, BEd

Director of Studies: Mrs G Elsom, BEd

Senior Teacher: Mr E Marsden, BSc

Mrs M Bawdon	Mr C Sammons, BSc
Mrs S Burgess, BA	Mrs A Selby
Mr A Gallerwood, BA	Ms R Shaw
Mrs G Gallerwood, BA	Mrs D Shepherd, Cert Ed
Mrs D Grubb	Mrs T Simons
Mrs J Jeffery	Mrs R Tweddle, GTCL,
Mr J Mathrick, BSc	LTCL
Mr J McGouran, BA	Mrs H Vann, BA

'FIVEWAYS' Nursery and Pre-Prep:

Head: Mrs S A Davies, BEd

Miss K Clarke, NNEB	Miss N Noott, BA Hons
Mrs F Curtis, MA, EYPS	Mrs P Ong, DPP
Miss S Glover, NNEB	Mrs G Packer
Mrs S Griffiths, BTech, NN	Mrs T Simons, BEd
Mrs S Lea, NTD	Miss A Townson, NVQ3
Miss V Lovell, BEd Hons	

St Albans High School for Girls

3 Townsend Avenue, St Albans, Hertfordshire AL1 3SJ

Tel: 01727 853800
Fax: 01727 792516
email: admissions@stahs.org.uk
website: www.stahs.org.uk
Twitter: @STAHS
Facebook: /stalbanshighschoolforgirls

Motto: *The fear of the Lord is the beginning of wisdom*

St Albans High School for Girls is a selective, independent day school for girls aged 4–18 years. It is uniquely placed in being able to offer all the advantages of a continuous education in two very different settings; the Preparatory School is based in the picturesque village of Wheathampstead whilst the Senior School enjoys a more urban setting in the heart of the historic City of St Albans.

Mission. Fostering scholarship and integrity, the High School provides inspirational opportunities and strong support to develop a lifelong love of learning and respect for others.

Aims.

- Scholarship: to offer an education for girls, which promotes intellectual confidence, curiosity and the joy of learning.
- Adventure: to build an outward looking community through local, national and international curricular and co-curricular programmes.
- Integrity: to sustain a community in which every girl feels supported, confident and ready to shape society in a school which builds a strong ethic of service and responsible citizenship.

Academically curious, girls here have high expectations of themselves; results are exceptional and learning fun, with the majority of girls going on to their first-choice university. We took a decisive stance by choosing to adopt linear A Levels across all of our A Level and AS Level subjects from September 2015, creating time for students to enjoy learning. As they approach the Sixth Form, students are expertly guided in choosing their programme of study.

Excellent facilities for all subjects include the Jubilee Centre – a Performing Arts Centre and Art & Technology block; a Music School and a newly refurbished and expanded Science block. Girls are encouraged to embrace broad horizons through participation in an extensive programme of co-curricular activities and a wealth of wide educational opportunities. Sport and music feature strongly, as do an impressive selection of clubs and societies.

Outstanding pastoral care, based on a thriving house system, ensures that girls flourish with firm support around them. They are encouraged to feel valued for their contributions to the life of our outward-looking community. Inter-house sporting, drama and public speaking competitions are held throughout the year.

We are experts in girls' education and believe that they learn best in an all-girls environment. Our aim is that they leave the school as strong, resourceful young women, equipped with the skills of independent learning and enriched by the friendships they have made here.

Enjoying the benefits of membership of the GSA and the HMC, which support the country's leading independent schools, the school is embarking on an exciting new phase under the leadership of Mrs Jenny Brown who took up post in September 2014.

Fees per term (2016–2017). Reception (age 4) £4,405 (inc Lunch), Years 1 and 2 (age 5–6) £4,650 (inc Lunch); Years 3–6 (age 7–11) £4,650 (exc Lunch); Senior School (age 11–16) £5,600 (exc Lunch); Sixth Form (age 16–18) £5,600 (exc Lunch).

Private music lessons, special tennis coaching, school lunch (from Year 3) and daily school coaches are all optional extras.

Scholarships. Academic and Music Scholarships are awarded annually at entry to Year 7 and Sixth Form. In addition to these, scholarships are also available for both internal and external candidates on entry to Sixth Form in Art/DT, Drama & Theatre Studies, and Sport. Fees Assistance up to 100% may be awarded in cases of hardship.

Admission. Pupils are normally admitted in September at 4+, 6+ and 7+ to the Preparatory School and at 11+ and 16+ to the Senior School. However, applications for places occasionally available in other year groups are welcome. Girls are expected to have at least 5 GCSE subjects at A grade or above, and an A or A* in the subject to be taken at A Level. However, entry is subject to interview, and there may be flexibility in the number of A grades required.

Open Events. Prep School in Action: Friday 4 November 2016; Prep School Open Morning: Saturday 1 October 2016; Senior School Open Morning: Saturday 8 October 2016. Senior School in Action: Wednesday 9 November 2016 and Thursday 17 November. Sixth Form Open Evening: Wednesday 21 September 2016; Sixth Form in Action: Wednesday 5 October.

Charitable status. St Albans High School for Girls is a Registered Charity, number 311065. It exists to provide an education for girls "in accordance with the principles of the Church of England".

Visitor: The Right Reverend The Lord Bishop of St Albans

Council:
Mr R Allnutt, LLB
Mr D Alterman, MA Oxon
Mr P Brewster
Mrs C Callegari, BA Hons, CertEd
Mr N Enright, MA Oxon, MBA, FRSA, NPQH
Mr G Follows, BEng, DChA, FCA
Ms E de Galleani, BA Hons
Mrs H Greatrex, BA, MSc Hons ACA
Mrs W Hazley-Payne, BA Hons, ACMA, CGMA
Miss D Henderson, MA Cantab, MA (*Chairman*)
The Very Revd Dr Jeffrey John, MA Oxon, DPhil Oxon
Mr B Kettle, FRICS, MCIArb, MAE
Miss R Musgrave, MA, MA
Mr D Roe, BSc Hons, MRICS
Mrs J Ross, BA Hons, NPQH
Mrs J Stroud, MA Cantab, PGCE

Mr J Thomson, CA
Mr R Ward

Headmistress: **Mrs J Brown**, MA Oxon

Senior Leadership Team:
Mr F Campbell, BSc Glasgow, FCMA (*Bursar*)
Mrs J Taylor, MA Cantab (*Senior Deputy Head*)
Ms J Healy, MA Oxon, MPhil Trinity (*Deputy Head Strategy & Communications*)
Mrs K Gorman, BA Birmingham, MEd Cambridge (*Deputy Head Curriculum*)
Mr N Hamshaw, MMath Oxon (*Deputy Head Academic*)
Mr B Kerr-Shaw, BA Cantab (*Assistant Head Co-Curriculum*)
Mrs J Rowe, BEd Durham (*Head of the Preparatory School*)
Dr S Legg, DPhil Oxon (*Head of Chemistry*)

Senior Management Team:
Mrs J Douglas, BA Durham (*Senior Housemistress*)
Mrs R Frost, MA Ed, BA Open, BEd Dundee (*Senior Teacher*)
Mrs G Lusby, FCIPD (*HR Manager*)
Mrs R Mason (*Registrar*)
§Mrs R McDermott, MSc Bristol (*Director of Higher Education and Careers*)
Mr I Thomson, BA London (*Head of Sixth Form*)
Mrs K Guille, MA Bath, BA Birmingham (*Head of Modern Languages*)

§ Part-time

Senior School Teaching Staff:

Art:
Mr S McGuinness, BA Manchester Polytechnic (*Head of Art*)
Mrs S Brown, MA Manchester (*Assistant Head of Sixth Form*)
Miss R Marsh, BA Southampton

Classical Civilisation:
Miss A Dugdale, MA London, MA Oxford (*Head of Classics*)
Miss A Fox, BA Oxon, Mst Oxon
Mr P Northcroft, BA UCL

Drama:
Mrs Anna Bullen, BA Wales Aberystwyth (*Acting Head of Drama*)
Mr S Brownett, BA Winchester

Design & Technology:
Mrs G Davies, MSc Wales (*Head of Design & Technology/ Young Enterprise Coordinator*)
Ms J Cooper, BEd Cambridge
Mr D Fitzgibbons, BSc De Montford
§Mrs A Wigg, BSc Sheffield
Mrs W Emes, MSc Reading
§Mrs E Wadey, BA Winchester

Economics:
Mr J Stanford, BA York (*Head of Economics*)
§Mrs R McDermott, MSc Bristol (*Director of Higher Education and Careers*)

English:
Miss E Coutts, BA Cantab (*Head of English*)
Mrs J Douglas, BA Durham (*Senior Housemistress*)
Mrs K Gorman, BA Birmingham, MEd Cambridge (*Deputy Head Curriculum*)
Ms J Healy, BA Oxon, MPhil Trinity (*Deputy Head Strategy & Communications*)
Mrs J Powell, BA Durham
Mrs P Ray, BA Leeds
Ms P Willmott, BA London

Geography:
Mr S Ramsbottom, BSc Reading (*Head of Geography/ Director of eLearning*)
Miss E King, BSc Durham
§Mrs A MacDonald, BA Cambridge
Mrs K Thomson, BSc London

History and Government & Politics:
Mr S Mew, MA Essex (*Head of Government & Politics*)
Mrs S Darbar, MA Cantab (*Head of History*)
Mr R Hillebrand, MA Oxon (*More Able/Oxbridge Coordinator*)
§Mrs S Jenkins, BA York, MA York
Mrs E Schaffer, BA Nottingham
§Mrs L Ryan, MA Cantab
Mrs J Taylor, MA Cantab (*Senior Deputy Head*)

ICCT:
Mrs C Wright, BA Anglia Ruskin (*Head of ICCT/Director of eLearning*)
Mr A Byfield, BSc Hertfordshire (*Computing Subject Leader*)
Mrs G Sapsford, BA Anglia Ruskin

Mathematics:
Miss K Sumner, BSc Warwick (*Head of Mathematics*)
Mr R Bailey, BSc Bath
Mrs R Frost, MA Ed, BA Open, BEd Dundee (*Senior Teacher*)
Mrs J Grimmette, MA Cambridge
Mr N Hamshaw, MMath Oxon (*Deputy Head Academic*)
§Mrs V Jacques, MA Oxford
§Mrs D Lewis, MA Oxon, MPhil Cantab
§Mrs J Major, MA Cambridge
Mrs V Parton, MA Hertfordshire, BSc York (*Head of Careers*)
Mrs G Sapsford, BA Anglia Ruskin

Modern Foreign Languages:
Mrs K Guille, MA Bath, BA Birmingham (*Head of Modern Languages*)
Miss A Burgess, MA Cantab
§Mrs S Cooper, BA Exeter
§Mrs E Crowther, BA UCL
Miss M C Foster, BA Manchester, MEd Hertfordshire (*EPQ Centre Coordinator*)
Miss S Jost, MA Université de Lausanne
§Mrs E Kelly (*Cover Supervisor*)
§Mrs H Monighan, BA Durham (*eSafety Officer*)
Mrs S Pearse, BA Durham
Mr I Thomson, BA London (*Head of Sixth Form*)
Mrs K Trenor, BA Sheffield

Mlle M Gauthier (*French Assistant*)
Sra V Gonzales-Lorente (*Spanish Assistant*)
Frau L Petersen (*German Assistant*)

Music:
Mrs C Turkington, BMus Ed Cape Town (*Head of Academic Music*)
Mrs L Amador, BMus Royal Academy of Music
Dr N Springthorpe, PhD, BMus Surrey, FLCM, PG Cert RCM
§Miss S Dumbrill, BMus, PGDip RNCM
§Mr E Kay, BA Durham, LTCL Trinity College of Music
§Ms J Rowley Jones, MusB Manchester
Mr S Stanley, BMus Royal College of Music (*Head of Keyboard/Piano*)

Physical Education:
Miss K Eddison, MA Birmingham (*Director of Sport*)
Miss A Hedley, BEd Edinburgh
§Mrs M Galea, BEd Exeter
§Mrs E Gray-Brown, BA Brighton

Miss R Griffiths, BSc West of England, MSc Loughborough
Mrs E Greenall, BSc Birmingham
Mrs R Hepworth, BA Leeds
§Mrs D Whiting, BSc De Montfort
Miss B Dingley Physical Education Assistant
Mr S McDermott Lacrosse Coach

Religious Studies:
Mrs H Harper, BA/MA Leeds (*Head of Religious Studies/ Debating & Public Speaking*)
Mr B Kerr-Shaw, BA Cantab (*Assistant Head Co-Curriculum*)
Miss J Broman, BA Birmingham
§Mrs M Patel, BA Aberystwyth

Science:
Mr D Thomson, BSc Edinburgh (*Head of Science*)
Dr S Legg, DPhil Oxon (*Head of Chemistry*)
Ms J Scott, MA Oxford (*Head of Biology*)
Miss N Collins, BSc Brunel
Miss S Day, MChem Oxon
Mrs C Gissane, BSc Edinburgh
Miss L Hicks, BSc Durham
§Mrs A Jallport, MA Institute of Education, BSc Hertfordshire
Mrs J Jennings, BSc Auckland
Mrs E Marsden, BSc UCL, MSc Sussex
§Mrs H McSherry, BSc Plymouth (*Head of PSHEE*)
Dr T Seaby, PhD, MRes, Msci, Imperial College
Mrs R Shah, BSc Warwick
Mrs S Stewart, BSc Leicester
Mr A Tickner, MSci Durham, MA East Anglia (*Head of Physics*)
§Mrs M Walker, BSc Manchester
Mr C White, BSc London (*Examinations Officer*)

Learning Support:
Mrs T Corbett, SENCO Hertfordshire, BA Humberside (*Head of Learning Support SEND*)

Mrs E Kelly, BA Exeter (*Cover Supervisor*)

Library:
Mrs J Foster, BA North London Polytechnic, CILIP (*Senior School Librarian*)
Mrs C Brailsford, MA Loughborough, BA Leicester (*Sixth Form Librarian*)

Pastoral:
Revd D FitzGerald Clark, BA Rhode Island, M of Divinity GTS, NYC (*Chaplain*)
Mrs J Douglas, BA Durham (*Senior Housemistress*)
Mr I Thomson, BA London (*Head of Sixth Form*)
Mrs S Brown, MA Manchester (*Assistant Head of Sixth Form*)
Mrs K Trenor, BA Sheffield (*Julian Housemistress*)
Miss J Broman, BA Birmingham (*Assistant Julian Housemistress*)
Mrs S Stewart, BSc Leicester (*Mandeville Housemistress*)
Mrs C Gissane, BSc Edinburgh (*Assistant Mandeville Housemistress*)
Mrs E Schaffer, BA Nottingham (*Paris Housemistress*)
Miss N Collins, BSc Brunel (*Verulam Housemistress*)
Miss A Fox, BA Oxon, Mst Oxon (*Assistant Verulam Housemistress*)
Miss S Jost, MA Université de Lausanne (*Assistant Paris Housemistress*)
§Mrs H McSherry, BSc Plymouth (*Head of PSHEE*)
§Mrs H Monighan, BA Durham (*eSafety Officer*)

Senior School Support Staff:
Mrs R Simpson (*PA to Headmistress*)
§Mrs L Lord (*Association*)
Mr F Campbell (*Bursar*)

Mr P Crossey (*Hospitality & Catering Manager*)
Mrs G Lusby (*HR Manager*)
Mr B Tavakoli (*Head of IT Services*)
Mrs R Mason (*Registrar*)
Mrs T Parker (*Estates Manager*)

School Medical Officer: Dr L Wasson, MBCHb Cape Town

Visiting Speech & Drama Teachers:
Mrs A Berzigotti Williams, DPSI Institute of Linguistics (*Italian*)
Mrs L Ashton, BA, PCertLAM (*Speech and Drama*)
Mrs E Elliott, Cert Ed, Birmingham, LGSM, P Cert LAM (*Speech and Drama*)
Mrs A Downey (*Speech and Drama*)

Visiting Music Teachers:
Mrs A Bosatta, BA Reading (*Oboe*)
Mrs K Bradley, LRAM (*Violin/Viola*)
Mrs P Burgess, BSc Middlesex, DipABRSM, ALCM (*Piano*)
Mr D Coleman, PGDip RCM, BMus Birmingham (*Brass*)
Miss S Dumbrill, BMus, PGDip RNCM (*Flute*)
Miss R Edmonds, GRSM, PGDip UCLA (*Bassoon/Flute*)
Ms L Hayter, BMus PGDip RCM (*Oboe*)
Mrs C Heller-Jones, BMus, PGCE, PGCert GSM (*Singing*)
Mr J Holling, DipTCL, LTCL (*Percussion*)
Miss P Jeppesen, PGDip GSM (*Violin*)
Mr S Jones, GTCL, LTCL, MTC (*Singing*)
Mr K Milton, MSc, AMusA AMB, Dip T&P, Kunstl Dip Lübeck (*Violin/Viola*)
Miss F Nisbett (*Cello, Piano, Double Bass*)
Mr M Onissi, LTCL (*Saxophone/Flute*)
Mr B Palmer, BMus, Phil Birmingham (*Conductor in Residence*)
Ms G Pevy, LTCL, FTCL (*Recorder/Piano*)
Mrs H Shabetai, BMus (*Piano*)
Mr S Stanley, BMus Royal College of Music (*Head of Keyboard/Piano*)
Mr W Smith, Trinity BMus, PGDip (*Brass*)
Mrs H Templeton BA York (*Singing*)
Miss A Tysall, BMus (*Piano*)
Mrs B Valdar, AGSM (*Clarinet*)
Mrs H Wild, BMus, LRAM (*Harp*)

Visiting PE Teachers:
Mr L Allen (*Golf*)
Ms B Amos (*Tennis*)
Mr H Boty (*Skiing*)
Mrs W Burdett (*Gymnastics*)
Ms L Cairns (*Swimming*)
Ms E Carder (*Netball*)
Mrs E Coles (*Karate*)
Mr K Coles (*Karate*)
Mrs E Davies (*Games*)
Mr T Dyball (*Tennis*)
Mr B Figg (*Tennis*)
Miss M Godfrey-Evans (*Tennis*)
Mr J Grant-Bailey (*Tennis*)
Ms J Hoare (*Swimming*)
Mr D Lawlor (*Tennis*)
Mr S Mardle (*Football*)
Miss N Marshall (*Ballet*)
Mrs M Moody (*Fitness Instructor*)
Mrs P Moxham (*Trampolining/Gymnastics*)
Mrs C Peers (*Yoga*)
Mr J Simpson (*Tennis*)
Ms S Stephens (*Swimming*)
Mrs D Szokolovics (*Fencing*)

Preparatory School Teaching Staff:

Mrs J Rowe, BEd Durham (*Head of the Preparatory School*)

Mrs L Perry, BSc Liverpool (*Deputy Head Pastoral, Preparatory School; Science Coordinator*)
Mr M Vandewalle, BSc Middlesex (*Deputy Head, Preparatory School*)
Mrs E Courtney-Magee, BEd Reading (*Head of Pre-Prep, Preparatory School*)
Miss H Ennett, BEd Limerick (*Curriculum Development Lead*)

Miss H Watts, MA RAM, BMus GSMD (*Director of Music*)

§Miss C Allin, Licence LLCE (*French Coordinator*)
§Mrs J Byron, BA Wales, MSc City University London, (*SENCO/Learning Support*)
Dip Literacy Difficulty Oxford Brookes
Mrs C Caruso, BA Manchester (*Art Coordinator*)
Miss L Fidgeon, BSc Royal Holloway
§Mrs A Fletcher, BSc Bath (*PE Specialist*)
Miss E Grant, BEd Hertfordshire
Miss L Hill, LLB Hertfordshire (*Geography Coordinator*)
Mrs D Horton, BA Bedfordshire (*PE Specialist*)
§Mrs L Hughes, BA Canterbury (*History Coordinator*)
§Mrs W Job, BEd Brighton (*PE Specialist*)
§Mrs J Julians, MSc Loughborough (*PE Specialist*)
Mrs H Lee, BSc Exmouth
Miss M McClean, BEd Hertfordshire (*Maths Coordinator*)
Mrs S Millac, BSc London (*ICT Coordinator/eLearning Coordinator*)
Mrs C Miller, BA East Anglia (*History Coordinator*)
Mrs S Munday (*Librarian*)
Miss A Northen, BA Roehampton (*PSHEE Coordinator*)
Mrs C Petronella-Thakarer, BA Royal Holloway
Mrs A Rogers, MA Sheffield, BSc Sheffield (*English Coordinator*)
Mrs P Ross, BA Bedfordshire
Miss T Skuse, BSc Manchester (*RE Coordinator*)
Mrs L Still, BA Exeter (*PE Coordinator*)
Mrs L Storey, BA Birmingham (*DT Coordinator*)

Preparatory School Support Staff:
Mrs C Gibbs (*Secretary/PA to Head of the Preparatory School*)
Mrs R Dean (*Chef/Manager*)
§Mrs J Scrimgeour, RGN (*Nurse*)

Teaching Assistants:
Miss R Barnett
Mr T Cooke
Miss E Daley
Mrs A Di-Lieto, BA Hull, NVQ3+
Mrs J Englebright
Mrs S Holmwood, BA Manchester
Mrs E Osborne, BA Open
Mrs S Smith, Teaching Assistant Diploma Level 3
Mrs C Strang

St Albans School

Abbey Gateway, St Albans, Herts AL3 4HB

Tel: 01727 855521
Fax: 01727 843447
email: hm@st-albans-school.org.uk
website: www.st-albans.herts.sch.uk
Twitter: @SASHerts
Facebook: /stalbansschoolherts

The origins of the School date back, according to tradition, to the monastic foundation of 948, and there is firm evidence of an established and flourishing school soon after the Conquest. Following the Dissolution, the last abbot,

Richard Boreman, sought a private Act of Parliament to establish a Free School. Charters, granted to the Town Corporation by Edward VI and Elizabeth I, together with endowments by Sir Nicholas Bacon from the sale of wine licences, secured the School's continuance.

St Albans is a day school of about 850 pupils which, after being for many years part of the Direct Grant System, reverted to full independence. Girls were admitted into the Sixth Form in September 1991. Its atmosphere and ethos derive from its long tradition and its geographical position near the city centre of St Albans in close proximity to the Abbey and overlooking the site of the Roman City of Verulamium. Whilst maintaining a high standard of academic achievement, it offers wide opportunities for development in other fields, and a strong emphasis is laid upon the responsible use of individual talents in the service of the community.

Buildings. For more than 3 centuries the School was in the Lady Chapel of the Abbey. It moved in 1871 into the Monastery Gatehouse, a building of considerable historic and architectural interest, where teaching still continues. There were extensive additions made to the campus during the twentieth century which in recent years has been extended significantly by the purchase of a very large building on an adjacent site and its conversion to a superb Art school, Sixth Form Centre and a suite of classrooms and the building of a Sports Centre.

The School has close historical and musical ties with the Cathedral and Abbey Church of St Alban. By permission of the Dean, morning prayers take place twice weekly in the nave, where the School Choir sings regularly and an annual oratorio is performed in collaboration with St Albans High School for Girls.

Admission. The majority of boys enter at the age of 11 or 13 but there are also entries at 16, when girls are also admitted; candidates are accepted occasionally at other ages. For the main entry at 11 an examination in basic subjects is held at the School each year, normally in January, and parents of interested candidates should contact the School for a prospectus and application form. Most candidates at 13 enter through the Common Entrance examination, and conditional offers of places are normally made about one year before entry, following a preliminary assessment. Ideally parents should apply to the School at least 2 years in advance for entry at 13.

Pupils are admitted only at the start of the Autumn Term unless there are exceptional circumstances.

Enquiries about entry should be addressed to the Registrar.

Fees per term (2016–2017). £5,746.

Bursaries and Scholarships. Some assistance with tuition fees may be available in cases of proven need from the School's own endowments. Such Bursaries are conditional upon an annual means test and will be awarded according to a balance of merit and need.

Numerous scholarships are awarded on academic merit at each age of entry. Scholarships in Art, Music and Sport are offered to existing pupils or new entrants at 13+ who show exceptional talent. Choral Scholarships are offered only at 11+.

Curriculum. The curriculum for the first three years is largely a common one and covers a wide range. All boys study three sciences and two languages, and devote some part of their timetable to Art, Drama, Music, ICT and CDT. Mathematics IGCSE is taken in the January of the Fifth Form (Y11), and in the Fourth and Fifth Forms a system of compulsory subjects and options leads in most cases to the taking of at least a further nine GCSEs or IGCSEs. In the Sixth Form most pupils study four subjects at AS Level in the Lower Sixth Form and three or four A2s in the Upper Sixth. The choice is wide, and the flexibility of the timetable makes it possible for almost any combination of available subjects to be offered. In addition, all pupils take General Studies either as an AS or a full A Level and are prepared for an AS in Critical Thinking. Many also undertake an Extended Project Qualification. Virtually all Sixth Form leavers go on to universities or other forms of higher education, a good proportion to Oxford or Cambridge and the vast majority to Russell Group universities.

Out-of-school activities cover a wide range and there are clubs and societies to cater for most interests. Several of these are run in conjunction with other schools. Musical activities are many and varied and include regular concerts and recitals by the School Choir, Choral Society and ensembles and by professional artists. Plays are produced 3 or 4 times a year either in the New Hall, the Drama Centre Studio, the English Centre Studio Theatre or in the Open-air Theatre, and there is ample opportunity for creative work in the Art school and the Design Technology Centre. There is a strong contingent of the CCF with sections representing the Army and RAF. Many pupils join the Duke of Edinburgh's Award scheme and do various forms of social service and conservation work in and around the city of St Albans. The School owns a Field Centre in Wales which is used for research and recreation in holidays, as part of the Lower School curriculum and as a base for field studies and reading parties.

Games. The School competes at a high level in Rugby Football, Hockey, Cross-country, Cricket, Tennis, Athletics, Netball and Lacrosse, in addition to a range of other sports including Association Football, Squash, Shooting, Sailing, Swimming, Orienteering, Basketball, Golf and Table Tennis. The new Sports Centre with swimming pool, sports hall, fitness centre, dance studio and climbing wall was opened in 2012. The School also owns a working 400-acre farm within 3 miles of the school where the Woollam Playing Fields, extending to 75 acres, were opened in 2002 by HRH The Duke of Gloucester. The grounds include an Astroturf all-weather pitch and a superb state-of-the-art pavilion. There are good links with Saracens RUFC, whose training is based at the Woollam Grounds.

The playing fields are within easy reach of the School, and the spacious and pleasant lawns on the School site, stretching down to the River Ver, give access to the open-air theatre, tennis courts and shooting range.

Old Albanian Club and the St Albans School Foundation. Information may be obtained from the Development Director: Mrs Kate Gray at the School address or at: development@st-albans.herts.sch.uk.

Charitable status. St Albans School is Registered Charity, number 1092932, and a Company Limited by Guarantee, number 4400125. The aims and objectives are to provide an excellent education whereby pupils can achieve the highest standard of academic success, according to ability, and develop their character and personality so as to become caring and self-disciplined adults.

Visitor: The Rt Revd The Lord Bishop of St Albans

Governors:
Chairman: Mr S P Eames
Vice Chair: Miss L M Ainsworth, MA Oxon
Mr P G Brown
Mr A L Dalwood, BSc, BA Cantab, ASIP, CFA UK
Mr D Foster, FCA
Sir R Gardner
Ms A Hurst
Mrs C Leach, BSc, FCA, DChA
Mr R R Lucas, BEng
Prof J P Luzio, FMedSci
Mr S Majumdar, BA
Mr C McIntyre, BA
Dr M Pegg, MB BS, BSc, FRCA, LLM
Mr M E Punt, MA, MSc
Mr A Woodgate, BA, MRICS

Advisory Council:
The Mayor of St Albans
The Dean of St Albans
The President of the Old Albanian Club
Mr D S Mercer, BSc, FCSI
Prof R J C Munton, BA, PhD, ACSS
Mr N C Moore, LLB, MA, CNAA
Mr C Oglethorpe
Mr P M Rattle, BA
Mr L Sinclair, BSc, MRICS
Mrs J Tasker, FCCA
Mr B C Walker, BA, PGCE, CELTA
His Honour Judge Wilding

Bursar and Clerk to the Governors: Mr R Hepper, MA, FCA

Director of Operations and Finance: Mr D Todd, MA, FCA, DChA

Staff:

Headmaster: Mr J W J Gillespie, MA Cantab, FRSA

Second Master: Ms M Jones, BSc

Deputy Head Academic: Mr M E Davies, MA

Senior Master: Mr P W Taylor, BEd

Head of Sixth Form:
Mr G J Walker, MA, FRSA
Dr R G Hacksley, BA

Head of Middle School: Miss R J Baxter, BA

Assistant Head – Co-Curricular and Head of Third Form:
Mr G S Burger, HDip Ed SA

Head of Lower School: Mr D Swanson, Dip RADA

Assistant Head – Teaching and Learning: Mr M J Smyth, BSc

Director of Marketing, Admissions and Communications:
Ms A J Crombie, BA

* *Head of Department or Faculty*

Art:
*Mrs S J Forbes-Whitehead, BA
Ms K K Lillian, MA

Classics:
*Mr D M Rowland, MA (*Deputy Head of Middle School*)
Miss L J Benson, BA, MEd
Mr M E Davies, MA
Mrs V L Ginsburg, BA

Computing:
*Ms R A D'Cruz, MSc

Design & Technology:
*Mr G J Calvert, BEd (*Head of Creative, Technical and Performing Arts*)
Mr A J Brien, HNC, BEd, MSc (*Deputy Head of Sixth Form*)
Mr D J Phillips, BA
Mr C A Roberts, BEng
Mr P W Taylor, BEd (*Deputy Designated Safeguarding Lead*)

Drama:
*Miss M L Bruton, BA
Miss R O Olaleye, BA
Mr D Swanson, Dip RADA (*Designated Safeguarding Lead*)

Economics:
*Mr G D Nichols, BA
Mrs L A Bonner, MA
Mr A Rowley, BA

Mr A C R Thompson, BA
Mr B D Tobias, BSc

English:
*Mr J D Hughes, BA
Miss R J Baxter, BA
Dr M C Brereton, MA (*Deputy Head of Sixth Form*)
Mr N J Cassidy, BA (*Head of Publications*)
Miss E C Crowe, MSt
Dr R G Hacksley, BA
Mr A K Jolly, BA (*Academic Librarian*)
Miss S K Routledge, MA

Geography:
*Mr C C Johnston, BA, FRGS
Ms L H M Andrews, BSc (*Deputy Head of Lower School, Deputy Designated Safeguarding Lead*)
Mr C P A Gould, BSc (*Director of e-learning*)
Mr J P Hickman, BSc

History:
*Miss E L Milton, MA
Mr A C Alcoe, MA
Mr T D Asch, BA (*Head of Government & Politics*)
Mr D J Forbes-Whitehead, BA (*Head of Hampson*)
Mr T J Martin, BA
Miss G Mendes da Costa, MA (*Head of Hawking*)
Mr G J Walker, MA, FRSA

Maths:
*Miss J Higgins, BSc, ARCM
Mr C D Bradnam, BEng
Mr G S Burger, HDip Ed SA
Mr P R Byrom, MSc
Mr I Charlesworth, MA
Mr C J Ellegard, BSc, DipEng Auckland
Mrs T J Gott, BSc, ARCS
Mrs H J Robertson, BEng (*Deputy Head of Third Form*)
Mr L V Robinson, BSc
Mrs C J Rogers, BSc
Miss E C Russell, BA
Dr J H Saunders, MA Cantab, PG Dip GSMD (*Data and Curriculum Manager*)
Dr D M Young, MSc

Modern Languages:
*Mr J R Russ, BA (*Head of French*)
Mrs D S Percival, MA, MIL (*Head of Spanish*)
Mr K J Squibb, BA (*Head of German*)
Mrs A A Butcher, Lda en Filosofia
Ms S Charalambous, MA
Mrs C Coudert, BA
Dr J P Dray, MA (*Head of Oxbridge Applications*)
Mrs G Renz, MA, MPhil
Mrs G E Tomsett-Rowe, BA
Mrs D P L McGorrian, BA (*French Assistant*)
Mrs P Gamble (*German Assistant*)

Music:
*Mr M R Stout, BMus (*Director of Music*)
Mr T H Young, MA, PG Dip (*Head of Academic Music*)
Mr P F G Craig, BMus (*Percussion*)

Visiting Staff:
Mr P A Bainbridge, Dip RCM ARCM (*Brass*)
Mr D Bentley, GGSM (*Brass*)
Mrs R Boswell (*Strings*)
Ms R Edmonds, GRSM, ARCM
Mr T Gill, BA Cantab, FRAM (*Cello*)
Ms L Hayter, BMus, PG Dip (*Oboe*)
Ms C Ireland, BMus (*Recorder*)
Mr S Jones, GTCL, LTCL, MTC (*Singing*)
Ms J Koos, MA Cantab, Dip RAM (*Cello*)
Miss A Le Hair, BMus, DipRCM Teachers, ISM Fellow (*Piano*)

Mr A Lucas, BMus, GRSM, FRCO, LRAM, ARCM, Hon FGCM (*Organ*)
Ms V Parker, LTCL, FTCL, DipTCL, ARCM (*Clarinet*)
Mr R Patterson, BMus (*Percussion*)
Mr O Roberts (*Electric Guitar*)
Miss J E Simmons, BMus (*Saxophone*)
Mrs Z Smith, BMus, GRNCM, PPRCNM (*Flute*)
Ms J Trentham, GLCM, LLCM, TD (*Strings*)
Mr N Woodhouse, FLCM, LTCL, LLCM, ALCM (*Guitar*)
Mr M Woodward, BMus (*Piano*)
Ms C Wright, LLCM, GLCM, LRAM Cert Adv Studies RAM (*Double Bass*)
Miss V Yannoula, BMus Hons, PG Dip, MMus (*Piano, Chamber Music*)

PE:
*Mr M J Langston, BSc (*Director of Sport, Head of Academic PE*)
Miss V L Sandell, BSc (*Head of Girls' Games*)
Mr K Bracken, LLB
Mr R D Daurge, BSc (*Head of Marsh*)
Mr M C Ilott
Mr T R Smith, BSc
Mr J F Walmsley, BSc
Mr J R White, BSc

Religious Studies/Philosophy:
*Mrs C A Malacrida, MA
Mr T O Eames-Jones, BA (*Head of PSHE*)
The Revd Dr C D Pines, MB BS, MA (*Deputy Head of Sixth Form*)
Mr J Qasim, BA

Science:
*Dr M J Guy, MSc (*Head of Physics*)
Dr K A Agyei-Owusu, MSc (*Head of Chemistry*)
Mr R J Lockhart, MA Cantab, MRSB (*Head of Biology*)
Mrs J C Crouch, BSc (*Deputy Head of Sixth Form*)
Dr J E Eastmond, MA
Dr L F Gray, BSc
Dr S A Hughes, BSc
Mrs J M Jex, BSc
Ms M Jones, BSc (*Deputy Designated Safeguarding Lead*)
Mrs V C McClafferty, BA
Mrs P M Mills, MA
Mr D S Russell, MChem
Dr I M Shillcock, BSc (*Head of Renfrew*)
Mr G L Smithson, BSc
Mr M J Smyth, BSc
Mr G Spencer, BSc
Dr R E Tanner, BSc (*Director of Cross-Curricular Learning*)
Mrs H Zaver, BSc

Chaplain: The Revd Dr C D Pines, MB BS, MA

Public Examinations: Mr C J Ellegard, BSc, DipEng Auckland

Dean of Sixth Form: Mr T J Martin, BA

Learning Support:
*Mrs R E Taylor, MSc
Mr A J Bateman, BA

Development Office:
Mrs K Gray, BSc (*Development Director*)
Mr C J Harbour, BA (*Development and Alumni Relations Manager*)
Mrs H Nelson, BA (*Development and Archive Assistant*)

IT Services Manager: Mr N S Cragg, BSc, MBCS

Technical Support Manager: Mr R E Hagon, BA

Librarians:
*Dr H McCabe, BA, MLIS

Mrs S Feyisetan, BSc
Mrs J Vance, BA

Graduate Assistants:
Mr J A Cox, BSc
Mr C K Dobson, BSc

Medical Officers:
Dr M Bevis, BSc, MRCGP, DCH, DRCOG
Dr T Jollyman, MB ChB, MRCGP, DCH, DRCOG

School Nurses:
Mrs V Blackman, RGN
Mrs S M Green, RGN, RSCN
Mrs C Russell, RGN, DN

Combined Cadet Force:
OC CCF: Major K J Everitt, D of E Coordinator
SSI CCF: WO1 Mr W J Wilson

St Aloysius' College

45 Hill Street, Glasgow G3 6RJ
Tel: 0141 332 3190
Fax: 0141 353 0426
email: mail@staloysius.org
website: www.staloysius.org
Twitter: @StAlsGlasgow
Facebook: /StAlsGlasgow

Motto: *ad majora natus sum* (I was born for greater things).

Founded in 1859, St Aloysius' College is a Catholic school for boys and girls aged 3 to 18. The school is fully co-educational at all stages (Kindergarten to S6) with a total roll of 992, drawn from a wide catchment area.

As a Jesuit school, it shares in a tradition of educational excellence which is almost 500 years old and it is part of a worldwide network of schools and universities whose mission is the "*Improvement in living and learning for the greater glory of God and the common good*" (*St Ignatius Loyola*).

The College creates an environment which is underpinned by mutual respect, friendship and care for others. It prides itself on upholding a clear set of religious, moral and spiritual values.

Great stress is placed upon educating the whole person, with pupils encouraged to develop confidence, leadership and teamwork through sport, outdoor activity, music, drama, and many other activities.

Entrance. Pupils from P7–S2 will sit an entrance exam. In the Junior School, children are assessed according to the current curriculum. Informal meetings with parents at all stages are also part of the application process.

Buildings. St Aloysius' College is located in the historic Garnethill area of central Glasgow with additional facilities in Millerston.

The College's main Garnethill campus is made up of a number of school buildings and is well-served by public transport.

The College campus is varied, providing examples of both award-winning modern architecture and construction, as well as historic listed buildings. The original Jesuit residence, now part of the school, is a listed building, as is The Mount where Art and Music are taught, and the magnificent St Aloysius' Church which the College uses regularly.

Two further additions to the St Aloysius' College campus, The Junior School and The Clavius Building used for Maths, Science and Computing, have attracted widespread critical acclaim. Not only have the buildings been the subject of great praise, but they have won many architectural awards, including the Best New Building in Scotland 2004.

The Kindergarten building is the most recent addition to the College buildings. This purpose-built facility is located beside the Junior School and is the ideal place for younger pupils to learn and play.

In addition to the aforementioned buildings, the College acquired the Convent of Mercy on Hill Street in 2009. The sports pavilion and playing fields are located at Millerston, and provide an excellent range of outdoor facilities. A new sports hall is currently being built at the Garnethill campus.

Curriculum. The Junior School and lower years of the Senior School follow internally devised courses which are suitable for academically able children. All Junior School pupils study specialist subjects such as science, art, music, IT and languages from Kindergarten and P1. National 5 is taken at the end of S4 and pupils take five Highers in S5. A wide range of Advanced Highers and other courses are available in S6.

Co-Curricular Activities. The main sports are Rugby, Hockey, Athletics and Cross Country. Pupils are extensively involved in community service and charity work. The College has now established a choral music programme which continues to go from strength to strength. In 2013 the Junior Schola performed on stage with world-famous tenor Andrea Bocelli.

Fees per annum (2016–2017). £6,522–£11,214.

Bursaries are available on consideration of parents' income.

Charitable status. St Aloysius' College is a Registered Charity, number SCO42545.

Board of Governors:
Chairman: Mr John Hylands
Rev Dermot Preston, SJ (*Jesuit Provincial*)
Rev James Crampsey, SJ
Brother James Spence, SJ
Sir Harry Burns
Mr Greg Hannah
Mr Nigel Kelly
Dr John Halliday
Mr Matthew Reilly
Mr Mike Smith
Mr Joseph Hughes
Ms Jane Stuart-Smith
Sir Jim McDonald

Safeguarding Commission: Dr Amy Kerr

Bursar and Clerk to the Board: Mrs Kathleen Sweeney, FCCA

Head Master: Mr Matthew Bartlett, MA, PGCE, NPQH

Head of Senior School: Mr Frank Reilly, BSc

Senior School Depute Head: Mrs Isabelle Erskine, BSc

Director of Christian Formation: Mrs Lynn McWilliams, BA, MA, HDipEd

Head of Admissions and Communications: Miss Laura McLachlan, LLB Hons, MLitt

Head of Junior School: Dr Aileen Brady, BSc Hons

Head of Early Years: Mrs Marie Forbes, DipEd

PA to the Head Master: Mrs Monica Harper

St Bede's College

Alexandra Park, Manchester M16 8HX
Tel: 0161 226 3323 (Senior School)
            0161 226 7156 (Preparatory School)

Fax: 0161 226 3813 (Senior School)
            0161 227 0487 (Preparatory School)
email: headmaster@stbedescollege.co.uk
            enquiries@stbedescollege.co.uk
            prepschool@stbedescollege.co.uk
            admissions@stbedescollege.co.uk
website: www.sbcm.co.uk
Twitter: @StBedesCollege
Facebook: @St-Bedes-College-Manchester

Motto: '*Nunquam otio torpebat*'

St Bede's was founded in 1876 by Bishop Herbert Vaughan, who later, as Cardinal Archbishop of Westminster, went on to found Westminster Cathedral. From small beginnings the College has grown and changed whilst remaining faithful to Bishop Vaughan's ideals.

St Bede's College welcomes Catholic and non-Catholic pupils. Every pupil should experience educational excellence and exhibit values through the unique contribution each member makes to the rich diversity of the College community.

We therefore seek the highest standards of performance so that pupils are stretched to, but never beyond, their personal limit. The provision of this education within a Catholic environment remains one of the chief characteristics of the College. High expectations of personal behaviour and discipline are rooted in our faith.

The Governors introduced co-education in 1984, so that they could offer girls from Greater Manchester and beyond the benefits of a Catholic Grammar School education.

Admission. Most pupils enter St Bede's at 11+ by taking the College Entrance Examination. There are occasional vacancies in other age groups, and there is an additional intake of students from outside the College into the Sixth Form each year.

The College Entrance Examination takes place in January and is open to Catholic and non-Catholic boys and girls who will not have reached the age of 12 by 31st August in the year of the examination. Details of the examination may be obtained from our Admissions Officer, Helen Taylor, email: admissions@stbedescollege.co.uk. There is also direct entry to the Sixth Form for boys and girls who expect to obtain good GCSE results. Interviews are held from the beginning of the Easter Term.

Curriculum. Curriculum provision is constantly monitored to ensure the best possible educational provision for all students.

A common Lower School curriculum offers all expected subjects together with Latin, Computer Science, Technology, ample PE/Games and pastoral time. In the Middle School four subjects are chosen from French, German, Spanish, Latin, Classical Civilisation, Economics, Business Studies, Computer Science, Design & Technology, Art and Music for a one year course to further enhance GCSE options.

At GCSE/IGCSE, 9 or 10 subjects are taken from a wide choice of 23 and these are available in almost any combination. Our latest additions at GCSE level are Classical Civilisation and PE.

Students must usually achieve 7 GCSE passes (grades A*–C) to be admitted to the Sixth Form where the most common model is to take four subjects to AS Level in the Lower Sixth and then three A2 subjects in the Upper Sixth. The 25 subjects available can be combined in any way and no group exceeds 12 students for A Level. All Sixth Form students in addition have pastoral time, General Religion lessons and Supplementary Studies (which amongst many other things offers opportunities to take the ECDL and EPQ).

Co-Curriculum. Our co-curricular programme allows students of St Bede's an exciting opportunity to experience a range of cultures, arts, activities and sports, outside of their formal academic lessons, that cater to their individuality and allow them to exercise their potential to become multi-talented. Our programme is designed so that it fits in with our continued endeavour to develop a well-rounded student who has had the opportunity to experience a broad range of activities that; inspire, motivate and heighten interests.

All activities have, at their core, value that links in with the College ethos found within the mission statement; being inspiring excellence and instilling values. Our goal is to develop wider skills for lifelong learning as well as helping to prepare students for the major ideas, innovations and challenges that they face in a rapidly changing society.

The autumn programme sees over 60 clubs, sports and societies taking place, with hundreds of students participating daily. These activities occur whenever there is time outside the classroom: lunch times, weekday afternoons and evenings, at weekends and during the holidays. The clubs are diverse in nature and include: charity, chess, cooking, debating, drama, photograph and science clubs along with forums for aspiring business, medical and law students and the introduction of new languages such as Portuguese and Italian which are proving quite popular. In the sporting arena traditional sports such as rugby, football, hockey and netball have been joined by badminton, basketball, volleyball, indoor cricket, rock climbing and table tennis with fencing, skiing and scuba diving to be offered in the near future.

Fees per term (2016–2017). Senior School £3,595, Preparatory School £2,475.

Preparatory School. St Bede's College Preparatory School, a co-educational day school for pupils aged 3–11, was founded in 1985. The school has the same Governing Body as the College and the Prep School is situated within the main College campus and has full use of College facilities.

Charitable status. St Bede's College Limited is a Registered Charity, number 700808. Its aims and objectives are the advancement and provision of education on behalf of St Bede's College.

Governors:
Chair: Mr T Walsh, LLB Hons, PG Dip Law
Joint Vice-Chair: Mrs R Kennedy, MA
Joint Vice-Chair: Mr D Coffey, Cert Ed London
Revd P Daly, PhB, STL
Mr J Ainscough, BSc Hons
Mrs J Johnson, MBE
Mrs Z Kwiatkowska, BA Hons
Mr P Lanigan, BA, FCA, ATII
Mr G MacMillan, LLB Hons, PG Dip Law
Mr J Moynihan, BA, Cert Ed
Mr T Richards, BSc Hons

Clerk to Governors: Mr M Lynch, ACMA

Headmaster: Dr R Robson, BA Hons, CCRS, MA, EdD

Senior Deputy Head: Mrs S Pike, BSc
Deputy Head: Mr D Grierson, MA
Director of Studies: Dr A Dando, BSc, PhD
Bursar: Mr M Lynch, ACMA
Head of Sixth Form: Mrs M A Gallagher, BSc
Senior Master: Mr B V Peden, MA

Heads of Faculty:
Mr S Bargery, BSc (*Mathematics and Enterprise*)
Ms F Cochran, MA (*World Languages*)
Mrs J Hudson, BA (*Humanities*)
Mr P McDaid, BSc (*Science*)
Miss A Smith, BMus (*Performing Arts*)
Mr A Wright, BA (*Sport*)

Sixth Form Pastoral Team:
Mrs M A Gallagher, BSc (*Head of Sixth Form & Transition*)
Mr M Gallagher, BBus, BEd (*Assistant Head of Sixth Form, Pastoral*)
Mrs R Lockett, BA (*Assistant Head of Sixth Form, UCAS & Careers*)

Assistant Staff:
* Subject Leader

Art:
*Mrs S Dittman, BA
Mrs J Hudson, BA (*Head of Faculty*)
Mr H Peers, BA

Business/Economics:
*Mrs J Hatton, BA
Mrs M Corbett, BA
Mr M Gallagher, BBus, BEd (*Director of Co-Curricular*)
Mr D Grierson, MA (*Deputy Head*)

Classics:
Mr G Yates, MA (*Assistant Head of Campion House*)

Performing Arts and Drama:
Miss A Smith, BMus (*Head of Faculty*)
*Mrs N Alderson, MA

English:
*Mrs C Boylan, BA (*Assistant Head of Upper Fifth*)
Mrs N Alderson, BA (*Head of Siena House*)
Mrs K Barber, BA
Miss F Cochran, MA (*Head of Faculty*)
Dr A McMonagle, PhD
Mr B Peden, MA (*Senior Master*)
Mrs S Sullivan, BA
Mrs A Vyce, MA (*Head of Lower Seniors*)

Geography:
*Mr D Parkes, BA
Mrs C Smith, BA
Mrs M Vidouris, BA (*Leader in Learning Difficulties & Disabilities*)

Geology:
*Mr M Parker, BSc

History:
*Mr A Power, BA
Mr J Bowden, BA
Mr T Fisher, Cert Ed

Computer Science:
Mr P McDaid, BSc (*Head of Faculty*)
Mrs C Earles, MSc, BITM

Mathematics:
*Mr C Wright, BSc (*Internal Assessments*)
Mr S Bargery, BSc (*Assistant Head of Upper Seniors*)
Mrs C Brewer, BA
Dr A Dando, BSc, PhD (*Director of Studies*)
Mrs T Davie, BSc, MSc (*Head of Campion House*)
Mr D McCotter, BSc
Mr J Parkinson-Jones, MMath (*Assistant Head of Siena House*)
Mr K Wardell, BSc

Modern Languages:
*Mrs M Reid, MA
Mrs M B Girolami, BA (*Head of Upper Seniors*)
Mrs I Morillo, Licenciatura en Filología
Mrs N Perry, BEd
Mrs A Welch, BA (*Assistant Head of Bosco House*)

Music:
*Mr A Davies, BMus (*Head of Bosco House*)

PE:
*Mr A Wright, BEd (*Director of Sport*)
Mrs N McCormick, BEd
Mrs N Lavorini, BEd
Mr L Mitchell, BA
Miss C Whitney, BA

Politics:
*Mrs R Lockett, BA (*UCAS*)

Religion:
*Mr L Hughes, BA
Mrs M Andrews, Cert Ed
Mrs M A Gallagher, BSc
Mrs E Meakin, BA

Science:
Physics:
*Mrs C Aspinall, BSc
Mr A Coyle, BSc
Mr P McDaid, BSc (*Head of Faculty*)
Chemistry:
*Mr S Hepburn, BSc
Mrs S Ball, BSc
Mrs S Pike, BSc (*Senior Deputy Head*)
Mrs R Prince, BSc (*Assistant Head of Lower Seniors*)
Biology:
*Miss C Hennity, BSc
Mrs S Powell, BSc, PhD

Technology:
*Mr A Hennigan, BEd
Mrs M Collins, BEd
Mr S Fallon, BEd (*Director of Marketing*)

EAL:
Mrs S Alexopoulou, BEd, TEFL

Preparatory School:
Head of Prep: Mrs C Hunt, BEd

Examinations Officer: Mrs M Tierney
Medical Officer: Dr M Cunningham, BA, BM, BCh,
   MRCGP, DCM, DRCOG
College Nurse: Mrs K Taylor, RSCN
Headmaster's PA: Mrs B McGoff

St Benedict's School

54 Eaton Rise, Ealing, London W5 2ES

Tel: 020 8862 2000 (School Office)
          020 8862 2010 (Headmaster's Office)
          020 8862 2254 (Admissions)
          020 8862 2183 (Finance Director)
Fax: 020 8862 2199
email: headmaster@stbenedicts.org.uk
          enquiries@stbenedicts.org.uk (Admissions)
          marketing@stbenedicts.org.uk (Marketing)
website: www.stbenedicts.org.uk
Twitter: @stbenedicts
Facebook: /StBenedictsSchool
LinkedIn: /st-benedicts-school

Motto: *A minimis incipe*

St Benedict's is London's leading independent Catholic co-educational school. Our Mission of 'Teaching a way of living' is at the core of the holistic Catholic education that is provided to boys and girls throughout the School from Nursery through Junior School and Senior School to Sixth Form. We nurture their growth and prepare them for future challenges in an increasingly secular world.

St Benedict's is committed to supporting all children to develop their full potential and has a proud academic record. Inspections by ISI (November 2012) and Westminster Diocese (September 2013) have endorsed our success in fulfilling the School's aims and have recognised the many strengths of the School. In August 2015, The Telegraph included St Benedict's among its list of 'ten best value private schools in the UK'. The school welcomes children of other Christian denominations and other faiths.

In the Senior School pupils are encouraged to think and express themselves creatively, to work independently, to take pride in all their achievements and to enjoy the rewards that scholarship brings. High standards are expected, but our pupils are not just educated – they are given the tools with which to attain knowledge and wisdom. In the Sixth Form students are encouraged to take on leadership roles and all contribute to a variety of projects, which raise funds for communities across the world.

There has been huge recent investment in buildings and facilities, including a full size all-weather facility at the playing fields. The latest project, a £6 million Sixth Form Centre and Art, Design and Technology building, was officially opened in January 2016.

St Benedict's is renowned for its sporting tradition and has a national reputation for rugby. Whilst promoting the highest sporting aspirations, the school is committed to sport for all. A wide range of co-curricular activities is offered including music, drama and opportunities for Christian service. In the Senior School there are over eighty different clubs and societies. There is something for everyone and all are expected to take an active role.

St Benedict's School is unique. We are an extended family in which pupils can thrive and we are proud of our cohesive community. Come and visit and see what we have to offer. You can be sure of a warm Benedictine welcome.

Admission to the School is in September at the age of 11, by interview and special examination. Admission to the Sixth Form is subject to good GCSE results. Application for admission should be made to the Headmaster. Registration Fee: £75.

Religion. A specifically Christian and Catholic atmosphere with a Benedictine ethos is the hallmark of the School. There are regular periods for liturgy, both formal in the Abbey Church and informal in small groups. However the School welcomes pupils of other denominations and faiths.

Curriculum. In the Senior School, for the first year all pupils follow a common curriculum including ADT, French and Music. In the second year additional languages are offered: German or Spanish. Religious Studies is undertaken by all in every year. Pupils normally take between 9 and 11 GCSE subjects. A wide choice of subjects is available at A Level. The Sixth Form is large, over 200, and almost all proceed to University or further education. In 2016, 99% of students received 4 or 5 offers from universities, the majority from their first-choice university. Students are also prepared for Oxford and Cambridge entrance, where there is an impressive record.

Sport. St Benedict's is renowned for its sporting tradition. Whilst promoting the highest sporting aspirations, the school is committed to sport for all. Physical Education and Games are part of the curriculum throughout the School. Rugby, hockey and cricket are the principal games for boys and netball, hockey, rounders and athletics for girls. Fencing is available for both boys and girls. Other sports are also promoted, including tennis, swimming, volleyball and table tennis. The School has 15 acres of playing fields nearby at Perivale, with a state-of-the-art Pavilion and changing rooms. St Benedict's has a national reputation for rugby.

Arts. The arts at St Benedict's are thriving and performances in music, drama and dance are of an extremely high standard. There is a wide range of musical ensembles and choirs on offer, to suit every musical taste and ability. Drama productions are staged termly, and recent performances include Bernstein's *West Side Story* and Moliere's *Le Malade Imaginaire*. Rehearsals are currently under way for Schaffer's *Amadeus* and Shakespeare's *A Midsummer Night's Dream*.

Facilities. In the past ten years there has been huge investment in computer technology, new classrooms, the award-winning £6.2 million Cloisters complex, and a full-size all-weather facility at the playing fields. Most recently, in September 2012, a new servery adjacent to the dining hall and a conference room were opened and the library was enlarged and refurbished. A new £6m Art, Design, Technology and Sixth Form building is scheduled to open in January 2016.

Activities. There are nearly 90 lunchtime or after-school clubs and societies including Combined Cadet Force, the Duke of Edinburgh's Award scheme, music, drama and opportunities for Christian service. There are two major Drama productions each year. Provision for Music is extensive and almost any instrument can be learnt. Activities include five choirs, two orchestras and twenty-six ensembles across the whole school. Public concerts are held several times each term. Art is outstanding, with a large number of pupils passing from the Sixth Form to Art Colleges each year. Considerable use is made of opportunities available in London for visits to concerts, theatres, museums and art galleries.

Careers. Careers advice and guidance on university choice and application is available throughout the upper years and particularly in the Sixth Form. This is delivered through seminars, a dedicated and well-resourced Careers Room and individual tutorials.

Fees per term (2016–2017). Tuition fees: Senior School £5,100, Junior School £4,490, Pre-Prep £4,040.

Contact with parents is frequent and regular.

Charitable status. St Benedict's School Ealing is a Registered Charity, number 1148512, and a Charitable Company Limited by Guarantee, number 8093330. Its aim is to promote the Christian and Catholic education of young people.

Governing Body: The Governing Board of St Benedict's School

Headmaster: Mr Andrew Johnson, BA

Deputy Heads:
Mr L Ramsden, BA, MSt
Ms F Allen, MSc

Finance Director: Mrs C Bedwin, BSc

Headmaster's PA: Mrs R Wynne

Registrar: Mrs L Pepper

Old Priorian Association: Mrs T George, Development Director

St Columba's College

Whitechurch, Dublin 16, Ireland

Tel: 00 353 1 490 6791 (Warden's Office)
         00 353 1 493 2860 (Bursar's Office)
Fax: 00 353 1 493 6655
email: admin@stcolumbas.ie
website: www.stcolumbas.ie

Motto: '*Prudentes Sicut Serpentes et Simplices Sicut Columbae*'

St Columba's College was founded in 1843 by the Revd William Sewell, the Lord Primate, the Earl of Dunraven and others. The College was incorporated by Royal Charter in 1913.

The College is a co-educational boarding school of about 300, with a number of day pupils. Boarding is seven day a week and there is school on Saturdays, which is unusual in Ireland. It is situated on the slopes of the Dublin Mountains about 7 miles south of the city overlooking Dublin Bay in an estate of 138 acres, which includes a 9-hole golf course and a deer park.

Having occupied its present site for over 170 years, the College combines the best of architecture old and new. Recent additions include a new Library and Reading Room, a Sports Hall, a Computer Centre, a Careers Library and an Arts Centre. Two completely new boarding houses, four classrooms, a new Music School, a second astroturf hockey pitch and an additional dining hall were also added in recent years. In 2016 the science labs were refitted and represent an outstanding state-of-the-art facility.

The College prides itself on its enviable academic standards, aided by very small class sizes. Pastoral care is exceptional and all pupils do six afternoons of sport a week. It is a very busy, happy and supportive environment.

Admission. Application for admission should be made to the Warden. There is a registration fee of €100. There are two junior Houses for entrants between the ages of 11 and 13 years. An assessment day is held for 11/12 year old entrants in October prior to the year of entry. Entry is determined by a number of factors, including family association, geographical spread (including Northern Ireland, the UK and overseas), date of registration and an understanding of the values which underpin the College. Entrants from Preparatory Schools take the Common Entrance Examination. Admission may also be made at 16–17 years.

Curriculum. In the Upper School, a wide choice of subjects and a large number of courses are available for the Irish Leaving Certificate. This examination keeps many options open for third-level colleges. It is the qualifying examination for entry to Irish universities and is acceptable to the faculties of all British universities. The Irish Junior Certificate is taken in the third form. A compulsory Transition Year programme follows the Junior Certificate.

Religious Teaching. Chapel services are held daily for the whole school. Religious instruction is based upon the liturgy and doctrine of the Church of Ireland. Boys and girls of other denominations and faiths are included and welcome.

Other Activities. Music, Art, Pottery and Technical Graphics (which are part of the curriculum in the Lower School) and Drama, Debating, Photography, Computers and various other clubs and societies function at all levels.

Games and Pursuits. Rugby, Hockey, Cricket, Athletics, Cross-country Running, Tennis, Badminton, Basketball, Golf, Swimming, Hillwalking, Horse Riding, Polocrosse, Sailing, Archery and Aerobics. The proximity to the Dublin Hills creates wonderful opportunity for outward bound activities.

Fees per term (2016–2017). Day Pupils €2,667, Day Boarding €3,467, Full Boarding €6,207–€8,940.

The above fees are expressed in Euros. Fees may be paid in the Sterling equivalent.

Entrance Scholarships. Junior and senior awards are made at age 12 (entry to Form I), 15 (entry to Form IV) and 16 (entry to Form V). Entrance exhibitions are often awarded to candidates for entry to Form II through the Common Entrance Examination. Generous discounts are available for the sons and daughters of the Clergy of the Church of Ireland. Old Columban and sibling discounts are also available. Details on request.

Leaving Scholarship. Norman Scholarships, for three years or more at all university colleges in Britain, Ireland

and elsewhere are open to the sons and daughters of Clergy of the Church of Ireland.

St Columba's Former Pupils' Society. Old Columban Society. *Hon Secretary*: G Symes, St Columba's College.

Charitable status. St Columba's College is a Registered Charity, number 4024. Its aims and objectives are the provision of Secondary Education facilities.

Visitor: The Most Revd Dr Richard Clarke, Archbishop of Armagh and Primate of All Ireland

Fellows:
C D S Shiell, BSc, MSc, FCIS, PGDip EDM
P F Myerscough (*Chairman of the Board of Management*)
G D Crampton, MA, BBS
I Roberts, BA, BAI, CEng, FIEI, FIStructE, FICE
J Bailey, MA
G Caldwell, BBS (*Chairman*)
Ms T Banotti, MA
M Gleeson, MA, MSc
The Most Revd M Jackson, MA, PhD, Archbishop of Dublin
J R P Wardell, MA, ACA
Mrs R Johnson
M H T de la Poer Beresford, MLitt
A W McPhail, MA
D J Reade
C Carroll, BA
Ms J Bulbulia, BA, HDip Psych, Barrister at Law

Warden: **M Boobbyer**, BA, PGCE

Sub-Warden: J M Girdham, BA, HDipEd

Bursar: Mrs S Gibbs, MA, MSc, HDipEd

Assistant Staff:
* *Head of Department*
† *Housemaster/mistress*

F H Morris, BA, HDipEd (*Senior Master, French*)
P J Jackson, BSc, HDipEd, MIBI (*Biology and Chemistry*)
J R Brett, MA, MSt, HDipEd (**Latin, Senior Tutor, Librarian*)
P R Watts, DipArt, HDipADE (**Art*)
Mrs A Morris, BA, HDipEd (*Director of Girls' Boarding*)
B A Redmond, BTech, HDipSGC, DipID (**Technical Graphics and *Construction Studies*)
G R Bannister, MA, PhD, HDipEd (**Irish, Liaison with day pupils and parents*)
L Canning, BA, HDipEd (*Director of Sport, English, †Stackallan*)
Miss A E Maybury, BA, HDipEd (*Irish, *SPHE, Deputy Liaison for Child Protection*)
Ms A Kilfeather, BA, HDipEd (*French, Spanish*)
P G McCarthy, MA, HDipEd (**Business Studies, *Classical Studies, Transition Year Coordinator*)
Ms S McEneaney, BA, PGCE (*Learning Support, Asst †Beresford*)
Mrs F G Heffernan, PGCert SLD, CertEd, ACLD, ILSA, AMBDA (**Learning Support*)
Dr M Singleton, MSc, PhD, HDipEd DipEdMan (*Registrar, Director of Studies, *Physics, Asst †Hollypark*)
Mrs G Malone-Brady, MA Mus, LRAM, ARCM, LRSM (*Director of Music*)
Mrs D Sherwood (*Learning Support, †Iona*)
D Higgins, MA, HDipEd (*Director of Pupil Behaviour, Designated Liaison Child Protection, Mathematics*)
Miss D Cullen, BEd Art and Design (*Art, †Beresford*)
P Cron, MA, NDipCMA,GDEd (**Sports Coordinator, †Gwynn, RE, Business, Economics*)
R Swift, BA, HDipEd (**CSPE, Classical Studies,†Glen*)
Ms K Hennessey, BSc (*Biology, Physics and Astronomy*)

Ms R Howell, BA, HDipEd (**Economics, Business Studies, House Tutor Iona*)
N Coldrick, BSc (*Mathematics, House Tutor Tibradden*)
S G Crombie, BSc (*Director of ICT, House Tutor Glen*)
H Jones, BScEd, PGDipGC (*Guidance and Careers, *Agricultural Science, Science, House Tutor Gwynn*)
Mrs S-J Johnson, BEd, BTEC ND (**Sports Coordinator, PE, Geography*)
M Patterson, MSc, MEd, PGCE (*†Tibradden, *Mathematics, Applied Mathematics, Director Extra-Curricular Activities*)
B Finn, MA, HDipEd (**History, House Tutor Glen*)
[E Jameson, MA, HDipEd (*English*)]
M O'Shaughnessy, MA (**Modern Languages, Asst †Stackallan*)
Ms J Robinson, BA, HDipEd (*Mathematics, †Hollypark*)
W E Gibbs (*Asst †Tibradden*)
T Clarke, BA, PGDipEd (*French, Music, Irish, Asst †Gwynn*)
Ms K Smith, BA, PGDipEd (*English*)
Mrs H Kavanagh (*Learning Support*)
T de Brit, BSc, PhD, HDipEd (**Geology, IT Administrator*)
Ms J Pyz, MA (*Asst †Iona*)
G Dean (*House Tutor Stackallan*)
S Duffy, BSc, MTeach, PGCE (**Geography, Asst †Glen*)
P Stevenson, BA, PGDE (*Geography, House Tutor Tibradden*)
The Revd D Owen, BSc, BTh, Chaplain (**Religious Education*)
A Mitchell, MSc, (*Science, House Tutor Stackallan*)
Ms A Thompson, BSc (*House Tutor Beresford*)
T McConville, BA (*Librarian*)
M O'Toole (*Learning Support*)
Mrs S Owen (*House Tutor Hollypark*)
A Donnelly, MA, PGCE (*English*)
E Duggan, MA, PGCE (*History, English*)
L Harrahill, BScEd (*Biology, Chemistry, Science*)

A Grundy, MA Mus, HonVCM, FTCL, LRSM, ALCM (*Guitar*)
Ms S Taylor, MBA, BA, LTCL (*Piano & Theory*)
Ms K Snowe, BA, ALCM (*Piano*)
Ms A Murnaghan, BA Mus, LRAM (*Cello, Piano, Theory*)
Ms T Lawlor, ALCM, (*Guitar*)
D Hatch, BMus (*Clarinet, Saxophone*)
F Moran (*Percussion*)
Ms E Shannon, MA Mus (*Singing*)
Ms A Brady, BMus (*Singing, Piano*)
Ms M Buicke, BA Mus (*Singing*)
Ms M O'Reilly (*Flute*)
Ms B Robinson (*Violin*)
R Sheldrick (*Trumpet*)

Warden's Secretary: Ms E Bainton
Admissions: Mrs Amanda Morris
Accountant: Mr N Grannell, FCA
Assistant Account: Ms C McLerie
Medical Officer: Dr A Khourie
Infirmary Sister: Ms A Getty, RCN, RGN
School Nurses:
Mrs R Cron, RGN, RM
Mrs J Newell, RGN
Ms M Merriman, RCN, RGN

St Columba's College

King Harry Lane, St Albans, Hertfordshire AL3 4AW

Tel: 01727 855185
Fax: 01727 892024
email: admissions@stcolumbascollege.org
website: www.stcolumbascollege.org

Motto: *'Cor ad Cor Loquitur'*

St Columba's College was founded in 1939, and has been a school in the tradition of the Brothers of the Sacred Heart (New England Province) since 1955. It is a Catholic, selective boys' school, with a little over half of its pupils coming from other denominations and faiths. The predominantly lay staff works together with pupils and parents to provide a Christian education based on traditional values, balancing a friendly community with sound discipline and academic rigour.

St Columba's College stands in its own grounds overlooking the picturesque vale of St Albans and the Roman settlement of Verulamium. In the last few years extensive improvements have been made to Science, English and Drama, Sixth Form and Preparatory facilities, and a major building development at the heart of the College was completed in September 2013.

Entry. St Columba's College admits boys from 4–18. Currently there are 255 boys in the Preparatory School, aged 4–11, and 625 boys in the Senior School, aged 11–18. The main entry for the Senior School is at 11, by Entrance Test and interview, with a smaller group being offered deferred entry at 13+.

Scholarships. Academic Scholarships are awarded at 11, 13 and for the Sixth Form. Additionally, the College offers two Music Scholarships each year and means-tested Coindre Bursaries.

The Curriculum. This is kept as broad as possible up to GCSE, pupils usually taking 9/11 subjects from the traditional range of Arts and Science options. There are 21 A Level (A2) subjects for pupils to choose from, all of which are also available as a fourth option up to AS. Sixth Form education is complemented by an enrichment course which prepares students for extra qualifications including the Extended Project, ICT and Personal Finance. Almost all of the Sixth Form go on to universities, including Oxford and Cambridge.

Careers. A full-time Head of Careers and Higher Education works from a fully-equipped Careers Centre to ensure that all students receive high-quality guidance in order to make informed decisions about subject choices and university courses with subsequent career options in mind.

Pastoral Care. St Columba's is a Catholic foundation welcoming students from all traditions. The spiritual and moral well-being of our pupils is a matter of primary importance for all of our staff, the majority being tutors. The six Housemasters and their teams are supported by a Ministry Team. Relations between the College and parents are open – a strength of the Foundation – and they are in regular contact with each other in monitoring the progress of the boys. The College seeks to nurture the academic and personal talents of each individual.

Sport. All boys participate, and the College has a strong sporting reputation. A rich variety of sports is available, including Rugby, Basketball, Football, Tennis, Cricket, Athletics, Swimming and Cross Country. For Sixth Form boys, not selected for the major sports, an even wider range of activities is available. Facilities include a large gymnasium and sports field on site. The Sports Department makes extensive use of soccer and rugby pitches, an athletics track, swimming pool and a golf course which are all immediately adjacent to the College site.

Extended and Extra-Curricular Activities. The College offers a mix of activities both at lunch-time and after school. These include sports clubs, such as archery and lacrosse, drama, art, chess, computing, Young Enterprise and many others, as well as a variety of academic and social clubs. There is a number of music ensembles, including a choir, orchestra and jazz band and four choirs of handbell ringers.

CCF. The Combined Cadet Force includes an Army and an RAF section. A full-time SSI (School Staff Instructor) is employed and the sections now include girls from The Princess Helena College, Hitchin and Loreto College, St Albans. The Duke of Edinburgh's Award scheme comes under the same management.

Preparatory School. The Preparatory School is on the same site as the Senior School and shares many of its facilities. The College has a strong family atmosphere, providing a secure and purposeful environment in which expectations are high. It admits boys only, by assessment, into the Lower Prep and Upper Prep phases. In their final year, most Preparatory School pupils are offered unconditional places at St Columba's College Senior School, following recommendations by Prep School staff.

(*See also St Columba's College Preparatory School entry in IAPS section.*)

Fees per term (2016–2017). Senior School £4,801, Prep 4–6 £4,186, Prep 3 £3,795, Reception–Prep 2 £3,360.

Charitable status. St Columba's College is a Registered Charity, number 1088480. It exists to provide a well-rounded Catholic education for pupils from 4–18 years of age.

Governors:
Chairman: Mrs J Harrison, BEd
Vice Chair:

Trustee and Dean of the College: Brother Daniel St Jacques SC, BA, PGF HG Dip Counselling, MBACP

Bursar and Clerk to the Governors: Mr Neville De Lord, BSc

Headmaster: Mr David Buxton, BA, MTh, MA

Deputy Head: Mrs K Marson, MA
Academic Deputy Head: Mr I Devereux, BEd
Head of Sixth Form: Mr R McCann, BA
Assistant Head: Mrs C Powlesland, BA
Assistant Deputy Head: Mr S Leadbetter, MA
Head of Preparatory School: Mrs R Loveman, BSc
Prep Pastoral Deputy: Mr K Boland, BA
Prep Academic Deputy: Mr M Ioannou, BEd

Heads of House:
Charles: Mr S Murphy, BSc
Guertin: Miss C Treacy, BA
Joseph: Mr J Tatham, BA
Martin: Mr A Lowles, BA
McClancy: Mr M Livesey, BSc
Stanislaus: Mrs R Paterson, BA

Heads of Department/Subject Leaders:
Art: Mr W Gurney, MA
Biology: Mrs M Mester, BSc
Careers: Mr P Kelly, BA
Chemistry: Ms R Tuckwell, BSc
Classics: Mr S Graves, BA Cantab
Design Technology: Mr B Barnett, BA
Economics & Business Studies: Mrs A D'Arcy, BA and Miss K Fitch, BSc
English & Drama: Mr E Waters, BA
Geography: Miss A Ellis-Jones, BSc

History: Mr K Roberts, MA
Information & Communications Technology: Mr S
    Leadbetter, MA
Learning Support: Mrs N Taylor Imrie, BSc, OCR Dip
    SpLD
Library/Media: Mrs S Mathieson, Dip Lib
Mathematics: Mrs K Parsons, BSc
Modern Foreign Languages: Mr R Childs, BA
French: Ms S Jasieczek, BA
Spanish: Mr R Childs, BA
Music: Mr K Brown, MusB
Director of Sport: Mr E Lowe, BSc
Politics: Mr R McKenzie, BA
Religious Education: Ms L Cronin, MA Cantab
Science & Physics: Dr R Clarke, DPhils (*Physics SL*)
Sociology: Mr N Hogan, BA

Administration:
Registrar: Brother Denis Bessette, SC, BA
Headmaster's PA: Mrs R Coakley
Head of Prep's PA: Mrs C Tominey

St Columba's School

Duchal Road, Kilmacolm, Inverclyde PA13 4AU

Tel: 01505 872238
Fax: 01505 873995
email: secretary@st-columbas.org

Junior School:
Knockbuckle Road, Kilmacolm, Inverclyde PA13 4EQ

Tel: 01505 872768
email: juniorsecretary@st-columbas.org

website: www.st-columbas.org

Motto: *Orare Laborare Literisque Studere*

Founded in 1897, St Columba's School is a non-denomi-national, co-educational day school for pupils aged 3–18. The School currently has just over 700 pupils with around 340 at Senior School. It is situated in the small rural community of Kilmacolm, surrounded by delightful countryside and located only 7 miles from Glasgow Airport.

With a roll of just over 700 across both the Junior and Senior Schools, teachers know each child by name. Considerable effort is made to create an environment which encourages each pupil to realise their potential, and nurtures polite, articulate and informed young people. The School consistently achieves excellent academic results, regularly placing it as one of the highest-achieving schools nationally. St Columba's was awarded Gold Investor in People status in 2013.

Facilities. The School buildings and sports facilities are located within a quarter of a mile radius of each other. The new Girdwood Building was completed in October 2016 and houses the new library, 13 additional classrooms, Transitus and Guidance.

Sports facilities include: gym area for gymnastics and dance, large purpose-built sports hall including fitness suite, all-weather floodlit hockey/tennis ground, access to three rugby pitches and a large playing field used for athletics and cross-country running.

The School has a dedicated transport service and an after-school care facility.

Curriculum. St Columba's School follows the Scottish Curriculum at all stages. Junior School pupils are taught French, music and PE by specialist staff. Transitus (P7) is a transitional year with core curriculum taught by the class teacher and science, languages, art, music and PE delivered by specialist secondary teachers. Pupils in SIV are presented

for National 5 examinations followed by Higher Grade and Advanced Higher Grade examinations in SV and SVI.

Games. Rugby, hockey, tennis, athletics, badminton, gymnastics, swimming, volleyball, basketball, soccer, dance (girls), orienteering. Optional: netball, squash, cricket, golf, skiing/snowboarding, curling, street dance, weight-training.

Extra-Curricular. The importance of extracurricular activities is emphasised at both Junior and Senior School level. The School offers over 20 clubs including The Duke of Edinburgh's Award, debating, sport, chess, drama and music (choirs, orchestras, ensembles, pipe band, jazz band). Individual tuition in a wide range of instruments and in Diction is available. Public performances and school shows are arranged on a regular basis.

From SIII upwards, The Duke of Edinburgh's Award Scheme attracts very large numbers with its emphasis on skills, service, sport and the expedition section at bronze, silver and gold level.

There is a very strong tradition of fundraising for charity and community service within the School.

St Columba's has strong links with schools in Australia and Canada and has annual exchanges between students for periods of time.

Organisation. The school is organised into four Houses for both pastoral and competitive purposes. Each house has a Head of House as well as pupil Captain and Vice-Captain. Career guidance is supported by ISCO.

Admission. Entry to St Columba's is by a combination of entry test, interview and, where applicable, a report from the applicant's previous school. An open week is held in November and entrance tests are held in January. The main entry points are Junior 1 and Transitus however pupils are taken in at other stages as places become available.

Fees per annum (2016–2017). Early Years £2,885, J1 & J2 £8,220, J3 £9,000, J4 £9,560, J5 & J6 £10,035, Trans & SI £11,185, SII £11,565, SIII–SV £11,185, SVI £11,245.

A number of bursary places, ranging from 10–100% of fees, are available for new applicants entering Transitus (P7), SV to study Highers and SVI to study Advanced Highers.

Charitable status. St Columba's School is a Registered Charity, number SC012598. It exists to provide education for pupils.

Governing Body:

Honorary President: Mr Guy Clark, Lord Lieutenant of
    Renfrewshire

Honorary Vice-Presidents:
John C Ritchie
Dr Helen M Laird, OBE, MA, PhD, DL
Ron M Kennedy, TD, FCCII, FLIA

Board of Directors:
Calum Paterson, BA, MBA, FRSE, CA (*Chairman*)
Dr Aileen Findlay, BSc, MBChB Ed, MRCGP (*Deputy
    Chairman*)
Hugh M Currie, BSc, CEng, MICE
Jo Halliday, BSocSc
Katharine Hardie, LLB Hons, DLP
Glen Watson, BA, CA
Kenneth Wilson, MA, CA
Paul Yacoubian, BAcc, CA

Rector: **Mr D G Girdwood**, DL, BSc St Andrews, MEd
    Stirling, SQH

Head of Junior School: Mrs A Duncan, MA St Andrews,
    Dip EdMan, SQH

Senior Depute Rector: Mrs V Reilly, MA Edinburgh

Depute Rector: Mr M J McLaughlin, MA Greenwich, BA
    Thames

Depute Rector: Ms A Berry, BA MRes Kent, MEd Buckingham

Depute Head of Junior School: Mrs J Andrews, BA King Alfred's, MA Ed Open

Senior Master: Mr C S Clark, BEd Glasgow

Registrar: Mr B A Manson, DipPE Jordanhill

Rector's PA: Mrs Moira McWhirter

Heads of House:
Strathgryffe: Mrs A Moran, MA Glasgow [Mrs N Smith, MA Glasgow]
Kilallan: Dr L Hay, BSc Aberdeen, PhD Strathclyde
Craigmarloch: Mrs J Scott, BA Edinburgh, DipSL
Duchal: Mr A Tait, BA Stirling, BEd Edinburgh

Senior School Teaching Staff:
* *Head of Faculty*
‡ *Chartered Teacher*

Ancient & Modern Languages:
*Ms L Rodger, MA Edinburgh
Mrs V Reilly, MA Edinburgh
Mrs N Smith, MA Glasgow
Mrs J Hepburn, MA Glasgow
Mme V Bretaudeau-Eteiba
Mrs P Kennedy, MA Glasgow
Mrs K A Ingham, MA St Andrews
Mr S Branford, MA Glasgow
Mr G Paterson, MA Glasgow
Mrs D Staber, MA Munich

Design:
*Mrs H Mathie, BA Reading
Mrs M R Robinson, BA Glasgow School of Art
Mr A Morrison, BEd Strathclyde
Mr T Boag, Dip TechEd Jordanhill

English:
*Mr G McNicol, BA Hertfordshire
Ms A Berry, BA MRes Kent, MEd Buckingham
Mrs K Brash, MPhil Queensland
Mrs V Kennedy, BA Stirling
Mrs A Moran, MA Glasgow
‡Mr G Smith, MA Glasgow, MEd West of Scotland
Mr M J McLaughlin, MA Greenwich, BA Thames

Humanities:
*‡Mr R Arbuckle, MA Dundee
Ms F Fowler, BSc Glasgow
Mrs J Scott, BA Edinburgh, Dip SL
Dr C Gilmour, BA, PhD Stirling
Mrs A Gillen, MA Glasgow
Miss R Henderson, MA Glasgow
Mrs R Kerr, MA Glasgow
Ms Z Shaw, BA Glasgow Caledonian

Mathematics & ICT:
*Mrs F I Bruce, BSc Glasgow
Mrs E Brunton, MA Glasgow
Mr C S Clark, BEd Glasgow
Mrs F Houston, BSc Strathclyde
Mr A Walkey, BSc, MSc Glasgow
Mrs N Gardner, BA, MPA Indiana
Mrs B Mackenzie, MA Glasgow

Music:
*Ms Y Carey, Dip MusEd Glasgow
Mrs K Fleming, BA RSAMD
Miss C Patterson, BEd RSAMD

Outdoor Education:
*Mrs C Marr, MBE, Dip PE I M Marsh College PE

Physical Education:
*Mr E Milligan, BEd Edinburgh
Mrs L Carlton, BEd Edinburgh
Mr B A Manson, Dip PE Jordanhill
Mrs J Bellew, BEd Dunfermline
Miss E Martin, BA Strathclyde
Mrs L Urie, BEd Dunfermline
Mr A Tait, BA Stirling, BEd Edinburgh
Miss F Ramsay, BSc Stirling

Science:
Biology & Psychology:
*Mrs E Wilson, BSc Paisley
Mrs P Nicoll, BEd St Andrews Coll
Dr L Hay, BSc Aberdeen, PhD Strathclyde
Ms Barnard
Chemistry:
*Mrs T Munro, BSc Paisley, PG Dip Comp Jordanhill, SQH
Ms L Robertson, BSc Strathclyde, PG Dip IT Paisley
Physics:
*Mr I Weir, BSc Paisley, MBA Strathclyde
Miss J Boyle, MSci Glasgow

Junior School Teaching Staff:
*Mr A MacKay, BEd Strathclyde
Mrs G Annetts, BA RSAMD
Miss C Bertram, BEd Glasgow
Mr F Campbell, BA Strathclyde
Miss A Kelly, BEd Strathclyde
Mrs G Hall, MA Cantab
Miss Hannah, BA Strathclyde, PGDE Glasgow
Mrs G Henderson, BA Paisley
Miss Hopkins, BA Northumbria, PGCE Bangor
Mrs K Leighton, MA Glasgow
Miss S MacLean, MA Glasgow
Mrs H Manceau, MA Glasgow
Mrs G Maxwell, BEd Dundee
Mrs K Fleming, BA RSAMD
Mrs R Porter, BEd Strathclyde, CertLSGlasgow
Mrs L Reid, BSc Caledonian, DipASN Edinburgh
Mrs J Wolfe, DipEd Jordanhill

Early Years Manager/Principal Teacher: Mrs E Corbett, BEd Jordanhill

St Dunstan's College

Stanstead Road, London SE6 4TY
Tel: 020 8516 7200
Fax: 020 8516 7300
email: info@sdmail.org.uk
            admissions@sdmail.org.uk
website: www.stdunstans.org.uk
Twitter: @StDunstansColl
Facebook: /StDunstansColl

Motto: '*Albam Exorna*'

The College was founded in the 15th Century in the Parish of St Dunstan-in-the-East, part of the Tower Ward of the City of London. In 1888 the school was re-founded in Catford, South East London. It became co-educational in 1994.

Buildings. The College is located in mainly Victorian buildings on a 15-acre site three minutes' walk from Catford and Catford Bridge railway stations. Facilities include an imposing Great Hall, a well-equipped Learning Resource Centre, a drama studio, three state-of-the-art ICT suites and refurbished chemistry laboratories. To complement extensive playing fields on site, St Dunstan's has a sports hall, fully-equipped fitness rooms, floodlit netball/tennis courts, rugby fives courts and an indoor swimming pool, recently modernised to a very high standard. In addition to the on-site acreage, the College has bought the Private Banks Sports Ground which is in Catford on Canadian Avenue. This 20-acre property doubles the land available to St Dunstan's College and further enhances the sporting and other facilities available to all of its pupils.

Organisation and Curriculum. The College educates boys and girls from the ages of 3 to 18. The Junior School comprises a nursery class for 20 children (3+), a Pre-Prep Department for 120 children aged 4–7 and a Prep Department of 160 children aged 7–11.

In the Junior School great emphasis is placed on letting children learn in a friendly, caring and stimulating environment. Pupils study a broad curriculum and participate in a wide variety of extra-curricular activities. The Head of the Junior School is a member of IAPS (*see entry in IAPS section*).

The Senior School, with a total of 570 pupils, comprises Key Stage 3 (Years 7–9), Key Stage 4 (Years 10 and 11) and Key Stage 5 (Years 12 and 13). A considerable choice of subjects is on offer – English, Drama, French, German, Spanish, Italian, Latin, History, Geography, Religious Studies, Economics, Business Studies, Mathematics, Physics, Chemistry, Biology, Environmental Systems & Societies, Design & Technology, ICT, Physical Education, Music, Art & Design, and Personal, Social and Health Education (PSHE).

In the Sixth Form students can choose whether to study for the International Baccalaureate (IB) Diploma, or for AS/A2 Levels. The College received accreditation from the IBO in 2004. Virtually all students proceed to Higher Education.

The College is a vibrant, academic community with a friendly atmosphere. It values cultural diversity and has a reputation for high academic standards and excellent pastoral care.

Pupils have the opportunity to join a wide range of extracurricular activities to develop their special interests and personal strengths, for example:

- A thriving Combined Cadet Force
- The Duke of Edinburgh's Award scheme – among London schools, the College has very strong numbers of pupils involved at all Award levels
- Community service – every year the College supports a range of British and overseas charities and local organisations
- The Armstrong Society (Science)
- Modern Languages Society
- The Stanford Tuck (History) Society
- Debating Society
- Christian Forum
- Literary Society
- Puzzle Club
- Drama Club
- Chess Club
- Electronic Workshop
- Visual Arts Society

Music. Pupils from all parts of the school participate in a variety of choirs, orchestras and instrumental ensembles. There is an annual Choral & Orchestral Concert for the whole College at St John's Smith Square.

Sport. The chief sports are cricket, hockey, netball, rounders, rugby, soccer and swimming. Students also have opportunities to take part in cross-country running, fives, tennis, basketball, badminton, sailing, golf and fitness training.

Entrance. The main entrance points are at the age of 3, 4, 7, 11 or 16. Admission to the College is competitive in all years with the exception of the Nursery, and depends on academic ability and the demonstration of potential. At 11+ an Entrance Examination is held annually in January.

Entrance Scholarships. Scholarships are offered for academic merit and also for excellence in Music, Sport, Art and Design and Drama. Means-tested bursaries are available.

Fees per term (2016–2017). The consolidated fees (including lunch) are: Nursery £3,137; Junior School £3,998–£5,038; Senior School £5,326.

Old Dunstonian Association. The ODA has 4,000 members. All pupils subscribe to the ODA while at school and automatically become life members when they leave.

St Dunstan's College Family Society. This parent-run fundraising body works to support the educational, social and extra-curricular activities of the school for the benefit of all pupils. All parents are automatically members of the Family Society.

Charitable status. St Dunstan's Educational Foundation is a Registered Charity, number 312747.

Governors:
Chairman: ¶Alderman & Sheriff Sir Paul Judge, MA, MBA, LLD Hon
Deputy Chairman: P L Coling, Esq, FRICS
Mrs S Ahmed, BSc
Mrs V Alexander
Ms J Clements, OBE
I Davenport, Esq
P Durgan, Esq
¶P W France, Esq
Professor P Leonard, BSc
Mrs L Kiernan, MA, DipEd
K L Marshall, Esq, RD, FICS, ACII
Revd B Olivier
Mrs C Price, MA, FRSA
Miss D Robertshaw, BSc
S Rahman, Esq

¶ *Old Dunstonian*

Clerk to the Governors and Bursar: Colonel N Wallace

Senior School Academic Staff:

Headmaster: Mr Nicholas Hewlett, BSc

Deputy Head (Academic): A Johnson, BA
Deputy Head Pastoral: Mrs A Waite, BSc
Deputy Head (Communication & Development): T Kirk, MA
Assistant Head – Head of Sixth Form: N Fieldhouse, BA
Assistant Head – Head of Middle School: Mrs G L Davies, BSc
Assistant Head – Head of Lower School: Mrs J McLellan, BA

* *Head of Department*

J Apweiler, BSc	Mrs G L Davies, BSc
G Armstrong, BSc	R W Davies, BA
Mrs J Atkinson, GRSM, NCOS	P Dawson, BA
	B Doherty, BA
R Austin, BSc	Miss F Du Sauzay, BA
Mrs H S Baptiste, BSc	*J P H Elmes, MA
Mrs C Bird, BA	Miss F Fairley, BA
Miss R Biggs, BSc	Ms A Gomez-Ramos, BA
S Bowering, BA	*D Gower, BSc
M Bradley, BA	*Miss F Hardy, BA
Mrs O Brigue, MA	B Harrild, BA
Miss E Burrowes BA	Mrs L Hartwell, BSc
*Ms R E Butryn, MA	Mrs S Hearn, BSc
*Mrs J Byrne, MA	R A Hill, BSc
*Ms M M Callaghan, BA	*J Holmes, BA
*Miss G Charleton, BA	Miss G Joyce, BA
Mrs S Cheeseman	Miss A Karmock-Golds, BA
C Cox, BSc	

Miss S Kervella, MA

O Knell, BSc

*Miss F Low

L Merrony, BA

*Mrs K Molteni, BA

*Mrs S Otley, BA

Miss S Penny, BA

*G S Phillips, BSc, MSc

*D Preece, PhD

*D Read, BSc

T Scambler, BA

D Sharples, BA

Mrs A Sobota, BSc

G Stewart, BA

X Tan, BSc

Miss I Taylor

*Miss D M Warren, BEng

*Miss R Watkins, BSc

D J Webb, BA

Mrs J V Williams, BEd

M Wood, BA

M Woodward, BA

PA to the Headmaster: Mrs P Phillips

Marketing & Admissions Officer: Miss S Stammers

Marketing Officer: Miss K Atti

College Chaplain: Revd C Boswell

Junior School Secretary/Registrar: Mrs R Scard

St Edmund's College

Old Hall Green, Ware, Hertfordshire SG11 1DS

Tel: 01920 824247

email: admissions@stedmundscollege.org

website: www.stedmundscollege.org

Twitter: @stedmundsware

Motto: '*Avita Pro Fide*'

St Edmund's College, England's oldest Catholic school, is a leading Independent day and boarding, co-educational Catholic School for boys and girls aged 3–18. From the Nursery to the Sixth Form St Edmund's College offers an education that challenges and stimulates, developing the whole person in the intellectual, physical, emotional and spiritual areas of life; the richness of our extra-curricular provision and our high academic standards are testament to the College's success and popularity.

Located on a beautiful site in rural East Hertfordshire, only 40 minutes to London by train, St Edmund's has outstanding transport links to the surrounding area and makes full use of the excellent facilities on its 450-acre site including floodlit astroturf pitches and and indoor swimming pool.

Scholarships are available at 7+, 11+, 13+, 16+ and we welcome applications for entry to all years if places are available. St Edmund's welcomes students from all faiths who support our ethos.

Admission. Pupils are mainly admitted at the ages of 11, 13 and 16, although entry is always considered at other ages if there are spaces available.

Scholarships. The College offers the following scholarships:

St Edmund's College 11+ Scholarships:

Douay Academic Scholarships are decided by the mark in the 11+ Entrance Exam, the school report, the confidential school report and the interview with the Headmaster.

Old Hall Academic Scholarships are restricted to Catholic students who are in a catholic school (and have been for the last two years). As above, this award is decided by the mark in the 11+ entrance exam, the school report, the confidential school report and the interview with the Headmaster or Registrar.

All Rounder Scholarships are decided by interview, school report, confidential report and mark in the Entrance Exam. For this award, the child will be competent academically and also be able to make a substantial contribution to other areas of life at St Edmund's. This will be as agreed with the Headmaster but contributions might be to one or more aspects, such as drama, music, technology, the Catholic life of the College, specialised sports or outdoor pursuits.

Art Scholarships are decided by examination of a portfolio and a test. Scholars are required to make a significant contribution to the artistic life of the College.

Music Scholarships are decided by audition and include the provision of free tuition in two instruments. Scholars will normally be required to play two instruments with at least one to a high standard (voice can be counted as one instrument).

Music Exhibitions may also be awarded which give free tuition in either one or two instruments. Those in receipt of Music Scholarships and Exhibitions are required to make a significant and sustained contribution to the musical life of the College.

Sport Scholarships are decided by open competition and references from sport clubs or teachers where the child is already involved in sport at a very high level for example County level. Scholars will be expected to play a full and sustained role in the sporting life of the College.

The closing date for Year 7 scholarship applications is in November for entry the following September.

St Edmund's College 13+ Scholarships:

Students will sit an examination in English and Mathematics with an assessment in the relevant field if the application is for Music, Art or Sport.

Academic Scholarships are decided by the mark in the 13+ Entrance Exam, the school report, the confidential school report and the interview with the Headmaster.

Music Scholarships are decided by audition and include the provision of free tuition in two instruments. Scholars will normally be required to play two instruments with at least one to a high standard (voice can be counted as one instrument).

Art Scholarships are decided by examination of a portfolio and a test. Scholars are required to make a significant contribution to the artistic life of the College.

Sport Scholarships are decided by open competition and references from sport clubs or teachers where the child is already involved in sport at a very high level for example County level. Scholars will be expected to play a full and sustained role in the sporting life of the College.

The closing date for Year 9 scholarship applications is in December for entry the following September.

Sixth Form Scholarships:

At 16+, the Cardinal Allen Academic Scholarships are decided by open competition using the results of specially set scholarship examinations, interview and previous school reports. Candidates for these scholarships would be expected to achieve all A/A* grades in their GCSEs. Music, Sport and Art scholarships may also be offered through competitive test.

The closing date for Year 12 scholarship applications is in October for entry the following September.

Bursaries. We also offer a limited number of means-tested Bursaries at 11+, of up to 100% of fees. The closing date is in November.

Further details are available from the Admissions Office on 01920 824247.

Fees per term (2016–2017). College: Day Pupils: £5,110–£5,520; Weekly Boarders: £7,275–£8,320; Full Boarders: £8,165–£9,370.

There are reductions for siblings and for sons and daughters of serving members of the Armed Forces.

Curriculum. All pupils follow the National Curriculum. At the end of Year 11, pupils take GCSE examinations in all courses that they have followed, usually more than is required by the National Curriculum.

In Rhetoric (Sixth Form) students study A Levels and the majority leave St Edmund's to progress to Russell Group universities including some to Oxford and Cambridge.

The International Baccalaureate is also taught at St Edmund's College alongside A Levels. The programme is an alternative to the traditional A Level programme, suited to all-rounders and recognising the St Edmund's aim of not solely focusing on academic excellence, but on developing well-balanced, spiritually grounded people, well prepared to face the challenges of modern life.

Religious Instruction. St Edmund's is a College for all those who appreciate the values of a Catholic Education. All students receive instruction in Christian doctrine and practice from lay teachers. Importance is attached to the liturgical life of the College and the practical expression of faith. All faiths and denominations are welcomed.

Sport. Great importance is attached to sport and physical education throughout the College. All pupils are required to participate in a variety of sports. The major sports for boys are rugby, football, cricket and athletics, while for girls they are hockey, netball, rounders and athletics. The other sports available are cross-country, tennis, swimming, basketball and badminton. A floodlit astroturf pitch, large sports hall, indoor swimming pool, tennis courts, fitness room, new outdoor astroturf cricket nets together with 450 acres of grounds provide excellent facilities.

Extracurricular Activities. At St Edmund's we believe our responsibility reaches far beyond the academic success of our students. We have a commitment to the whole person, which is reflected in the broad range of activities on offer to everyone and we wish to encourage the notion that success can be achieved in many ways, not just in the classroom.

Each day between 3.30–4.30 pm, time is set aside for students to pursue an interest or activity. Wednesday afternoons are also dedicated to our activities programme.

The CCF (RAF and Army sections), Community Service and The Duke of Edinburgh's Award play a prominent part in developing a self-reliant and confident individual.

Careers. There is a Careers teacher and Careers Library. Careers advice is available to pupils from the age of 13. There are regular careers lectures and visits to industry and Universities.

Prep School. St Edmund's also includes a Prep situated on the same estate. It consists of a Nursery, Infants and Junior School for pupils from age 3 to 11, which feeds into the Senior School at 11. The pupils are able to make use of many of the amenities of the Senior School such as the Refectory, Chapel, Swimming Pool and Sports Hall. There is no boarding at the Prep School.

(*For further details, see entry in IAPS section.*)

Charitable status. St Edmund's College is a Registered Charity, number 311073. It aims to provide a Catholic Education for students of all faiths between the ages of 3 and 18.

President & Patron: His Eminence Cardinal Vincent Nichols, Archbishop of Westminster

Governors:
Chairman: Mr Patrick J Mitton, MSc
Deputy Chairman and Chair of PR and Marketing Sub-Committee: Dr Frances MacIntosh, MA, MRCP, MFPM
Members:
Mr Neville Ransley, MA, MEd (*Chair of Academic Sub-Committee*)
Mr John Bryant, BA
Fr Alban McCoy, OFM Conv, BA, MLitt
Mrs Madeline Roberts, FCA
Mrs Jane Ranzetta, BA Hons, PGCE
Mr Stephen Grounds, BSc, DPhil

Senior Leadership Team:

Headmaster, DSM Child Protection: Mr P Durán, BA, MA London

Deputy Head, DSL Child Protection: Mr M Barber, BA Oxon, MSc Manchester, MA Oxon

Bursar: Mr B Tomlinson, BA Hons London, ACMA

Head of Prep School: Mr S Cartwright, BSc Surrey

Assistant Head, Director of Studies: Mrs K MacDonald, BA Hons, PGCE, PQH NI Belfast

Assistant Head Pastoral, Deputy DSL Child Protection, Registrar: Mr A D Petty, BA Wales, MSc Herts, PGCE Cantab, FRSA

Priest in Residence: Revd Father P H Lyness, MA Rhodes

Senior Teacher in Charge of Religious Life, Charities Coordinator: Mrs P Peirce, BD AKC London

Head of Boarding, Director of Activities, Educational Visits Coordinator & DofE Coordinator: Miss E Cobb, BSc Liverpool

Human Resources Directors:
Mrs H Duffy, LLB Hull, PGDL
Mrs L Nice, BA Hons Herts

Director of the International Department: Miss C M Hugo, Cert Ed Newcastle, Dip RSA

Deputy Head of St Edmund's Prep, DSL Child Protection, Head of Academics: Dr F J F McLauchlan, MA, PhD Cantab (*Director of Music and Performing Arts*)

Head of Music Department (*Performance*): Mrs K L Salter-Kay, GTCL, LTCL, ALCM

St Edmund's College Teaching Staff:

* *Head of Department*

Art, Design and Technology:
*Miss A M Healy, BA Luton
Mrs S Applegate, BA Herts, MA, PGCE (*Lead Art Teacher*)
Mrs D Stringer, BA Hons Surrey, PGCE
Mr R Ireson, BEd Winchester
Mrs J Daly, BSc Strathclyde, MFC (*Careers Adviser*)

Business Studies and Economics
*Ms L Smith, BA Hons Lancaster, PGCE IOE
Mr D R Davies, BSc Plymouth, Cert Prof Practice Boarding Education (*Head of Douglass House*)
Mr W Fulford-Brown, BA Hons Leeds Beckett, PGCE Nottingham
Miss L Sargent, MA Edge Hill, BSc Brunel

Drama:
Mr J Bonnett, BA Hons Hull

English:
*Mrs P Ager, BA Hons Middlesex, PGCE Anglia
Mrs K Evans, BA Hons Cantab, PGCE Cantab
Mr J Hayes, MA Oxon
Miss N Larkin, BA Hons Sheffield
Mrs M McCann, BA London, MA Birkbeck
Miss J McCarthy, BA Hons Lancaster, PGCE Westminster
Mrs P O'Neill, BA Roehampton
Mr A Simmonds, BA, MA Keele, PGCE King's

Geography:
*Ms Elizabeth Tucker, BA Hons Leeds, PGCE London
Mrs C McNiece, BA Hons Belfast, PGCE Dunelm [Maternity Leave]
Mrs N Pitman, BA Hons Wales, PGCE Bath
Mrs T York, BSc Hons Wales, MA Canterbury, PGCE IOE

History:
*Mr J R Stypinski, BA York
Mr D Brett, MA Hons St Andrews, PGCE Leeds
Mrs C McNiece, BA Hons Belfast, PGCE Dunelm
Mr A D Petty, BA Wales, MSc Herts, PGCE Cantab, FRSA (*Assistant Head Pastoral, Deputy DSL Child Protection, Registrar*)

Miss C Regan, MA Glasgow, PGCE Glasgow (*IB Coordinator, CAS Coordinator*)

IB Coordinator:
Miss C Regan, MA Glasgow, PGCE Glasgow (*IB Coordinator CAS Coordinator*)

Information Technology:
Director of ICT, Computing and E-learning: Mr K R Fry, BSc Brunel, MSc Herts, PGCE Exeter
Mr B Kovacevic, BSc Middlesex, BSc Croatia
Mr R Sharma, PGCE Newman PgDip Birmingham, BSc Leicester

International Department:
Director: Miss C M Hugo, Cert Ed Newcastle, Dip RSA
Mrs E Hawkes, MA Cantab
Mr L Hawkes, MEd Open, BA Hons Open, PGCFSE Open

Languages:
Mr M Belt, MA de Reims, BA Kent
Miss F Di Carlo, MA Palermo, BA Palermo, TFA equivalent to PGCE Palermo
Miss A Dunning, BA Bath (*Head of Talbot House and Head of German*)
Mr P Durán, BA, MA London
Mrs E Franco, MA Leon (*Head of Spanish*)
Mrs K MacDonald, BA Hons, PGCE, PQH NI Belfast (*Assistant Head Director of Studies*)
Ms L Nye, BA Sussex, PGCE Reading (*Acting Head of French*)
Miss S Rinaldi (*Head of Italian*)
Miss M C Simon, Licence Bordeaux (*Second in Department Head of Elements*)
Mr N Yuille, BA Hons Manchester, MA, PhD, PGCE York
Language Assistants:
Spanish Assistant: Mirian Leticia Ramos Gines

Mathematics:
*Mrs R A K West, BEd Exeter
Dr L Banahan, BSc, PhD, PGD Dublin
Mr M Barber, BA Oxon, MSc Manchester, MA Oxon (*Deputy Head/DSL Child Protection*)
Mrs G A Burrows, BA Essex
Miss L Dunhill, BSc Hons, PGCE Nottingham (*Head of Poynter House*)
Mrs H Fraser, BSc, PGCE East Anglia (*Assistant to Director of Studies – Tracking in Bounds*)
Mr N Harding, BA Hons Middlesex, PGCE Bath
Mr J Hounsell, BSc BCA Wellington, NZ (*Head of Challoner House*)
Mr S Mohana, BEd, MSc Bangalore
Mr G Perkins, MA Cantab, PGCE Greenwich
Mr G West, BSc East Anglia (*Head of Pole House*)

Media Studies:
*Mr L Woodward, BA Hons Bournemouth

Music:
Head of Music Academic: Mrs C Noble, BA Hons Exeter, PGCE Canterbury (*Co-Director Rhetoric*)
Head of Music Performance: Mrs K L Salter-Kay, GTCL, LTCL, ALCM
Mr C Benham, BA Colchester

Physical Education:
Mr K D Jones, BA Greenwich (*Head of PE*)
Miss A Hebdon, BA Hons Brunel (*Head of Girls' Games*)
Miss E Cobb, BSc Liverpool (*Director of Activities, Educational Visits Coordinator, Head of Boarding & DofE Coordinator*)
Mr A Cunnah, BA Brighton (*Head of Boys' Games*)
Mr O Plummer, BSc Hons Bristol
Miss E Wilkins
Sports Coach: Neil Kimsey

Graduate Assistant: Clara Barreda-Gomez
Graduate GAP Assistants: Francisco Nodrid Domenech, Rachael Murley, Benito Villegas Perez

Psychology:
*Mr C Hack, BA Hons Dunelm
Mrs M Inglessis, BA Dunelm, MA Kent, PGCE London (*Teacher in charge of Staff Development*)
Miss J-A Murphy, BA Hons Liverpool (*PSHE Coordinator and NQT/GTP Mentor*)

Religious Studies:
*Mrs A Moloney, BA Hons Surrey, PGCE Roehampton
Mr D D'Cruz, BA India, BA Middlesex, PGCE Surrey
Mrs M Inglessis, BA Dunelm, MA Kent, PGCE London (*Teacher in charge of Staff Development*)
Mrs P Peirce BD AKC London (*Senior Teacher in Charge of Religious Life & Charities Coordinator*)
Mr B Powell, BA Australian Catholic Bachelor of Teaching New England, Australia (*PHSE Coordinator Co-Director Rhetoric*)
Miss J-A Murphy, BA Hons Liverpool (*PSHE Coordinator and NQT/GTP Mentor*)
Mr A J D Robinson, BEd Exeter (*Head of Boys' Boarding – Allen Hall*)

Religious Volunteer:
Brother Ignacio Golmayo Pardo de Santayana

Science:
*Miss M Towns, BSc West of England (*Head of Science*)
Dr N Cairns, MSc Dunelm (*Director of Key Stage 3*) [Maternity Cover]
Mr R Chapman, PGCE Aberystwyth, BSc UWE Bristol
Mr M Connor, PGCE Herts, BSc Nottingham (*Director of Key Stage 4*)
Mr D Essien BSC London [Maternity Cover]
Dr J Eves, BSc Berkeley, USA, MSc, PhD Dublin (*Gifted and Talented Coordinator*)
Dr J Heslin, BSc Canterbury, PhD Imperial College, Grad IPM Middlesex, PGCE Herts
Mrs V Jauncey, PGCE Cantab, BSc Durham
Mrs D Mallabone, BSc, PGCE Southampton (*Director of Key Stage 3*) [Maternity Leave]
Ms J Marrinan, MA Open, BSc Hons London (*TOK & EE Coordinator*)
Mr D Webster BEng, PGCE Science (*Director of Key Stage 5*)

Cardinal Hume Centre, Learning Support:
*Mrs S Nicholson, BA Hons Manchester, PGCE Lancaster
Mrs L Barley (*SEN Assistant*)
Mrs M Sargent NVQ3 (*SEN Assistant*)
Mrs N Wells SEN Assistant

Careers:
Mrs J Daly, BSc Strathclyde MFC
Mrs C Noble, BA Hons Exeter, PGCE Canterbury (*Co-Director Rhetoric*)
Mr B Powell, BA Australian Catholic Bachelor of Teaching New England, Australia (*PHSE Coordinator, Co-Director of Rhetoric*)

Librarian:
Mrs J Tyne, BA Newcastle-Upon-Tyne MCLIP

St Edmund's Prep School:

Head of St Edmund's Prep: Mr S Cartwright, BSc Hons Surrey

Deputy Head of St Edmund's Prep, DSL Child Protection: Dr F J F McLauchlan, MA, PhD Cantab
Assistant Head of St Edmund's Prep: Mr G Duddy, BEd Wales (*Year 5, RE, Activities*)
Head of EYFS, Deputy DSL Child Protection: Mrs V Penfold, BA London Metropolitan

St Edmund's Prep School Teaching Staff:

Nursery & Reception:
Mrs K Purves, BA Birmingham EYFS Herts (*Nursery Teacher, Library*)
Mrs V Penfold, BA London Metropolitan (*Reception Teacher, Head of EYFS*)

Years 1–6:
Mrs G Boulter Diplôme Universitaire de Technologie France (*French & Humanities*)
Mrs A Chick, BA Hons Bristol, PGCE Bristol (*Prep Learning Support Manager*)
Ms E Christen, BA Hons London Cert Ed London (*Year 4, Maths*)
Mrs N Crick, BA Twickenham (*Year 6, Assessment*)
Mrs A Cutler, BA Leeds (*Year 4, English*)
Mr G Duddy, BEd Wales (*Year 3, RE, Activities*)
Mr G Goodfellow, BA Northampton (*Year 5/6 Maths, PE/ Games, Director of Sport Prep*)
Ms S Harvey, BEd Hons Herts (*Year 2, PSHE*)
Mrs A Gardiner, BEd Herts (*Year 3, Science*)
Mrs Z Kirton, BSc Hons Derby, MSc London QTS Herts (*Year 1, Head of Pre-Prep*)
Mrs C Mitton, BEd Cantab (*Year 5*)
Mrs M Murphy, BEd Hons Surrey (*Form 6*)
Mrs E Roper, BA Surrey (*Art*)
Mrs A Sayer, PGCE Greenwich, BA Hons Bournemouth (*Year 5, English*)
Miss K Simpson, BA Bradford (*Year 5, ICT*)

Nursery and Teaching Assistants:
Mrs S Brown
Miss C Dee (*Art, Tea-time Club Worker*)
Mrs A Drabwell (*Swiss Level 2, NVQ Level 3 and ASA Level 1 Swim Coach*)
Mrs S Goodfellow, NNEB
Mrs J Heraud, BA Hons Herts
Miss L Ingrao, NVQ Level 3 (*Nursery Nurse & Tea-time Leader*)
Miss S Jones
Miss S Piacquadio
Mrs L Simson (*Breakfast Club Leader, TA, Midday Supervisor*)
Mrs S Smith

Technician: Mr C Hull

Swimming Coach: Mrs L Short, Royal Life Saving Society UK, National Rescue Award for Swimming Teachers and Coaches

Administration & Secretarial Support:
Prep School Secretary: Mrs T Leader
Prep School Admin Assistants: Mrs T Dickinson, Mrs C Land

St Edmund's School Canterbury

Canterbury, Kent CT2 8HU

Tel:	01227 475601 (Admissions)
	01227 475600 (General Enquiries)
Fax:	01227 471083
email:	admissions@stedmunds.org.uk
website:	www.stedmunds.org.uk
Twitter:	@stedscanterbury
Facebook:	/StEdsCanterbury

Motto: '*Fungar Vice Cotis*'

St Edmund's is an independent, co-educational day and boarding school for pupils aged between 3 and 18 years, comprising the Pre-Prep, Junior and Senior Schools. Its aim is to provide varied opportunities for academic, sporting, artistic, musical and dramatic achievement. The school has excellent teaching facilities and numerous options for extra-curricular activities.

First established in 1749 as the Clergy Orphan School in Yorkshire, the School later moved to London and settled in its present location in 1855. The School's commitment to its origins endures, as does its Christian ethos. However, the School welcomes pupils from all backgrounds and places a particularly strong emphasis on pastoral care.

St Edmund's is situated on a beautiful site at the top of St Thomas Hill, adjacent to the University of Kent and over-looking the historic city of Canterbury. It is within easy reach of the towns of East Kent, and is just over an hour from London. The proximity to London's airports, the Channel ports and Eurostar stations at Ashford and Ebbsfleet gives international pupils convenient access to the School.

The school is owned by St Edmund's School Canterbury, a charitable company limited by guarantee, registered in England and Wales.

St Edmund's is a distinctive and historic boarding and day co-educational school where a family atmosphere is fostered, individuals are valued, the spiritual element is explored, and pupils enjoy a rich academic and cultural experience. We are committed to producing happy and successful pupils who can access a high quality education, while enjoying a wealth of stimulating and exciting extra-curricular activity. Set within a beautiful and extensive green field site affording spectacular views of the city and Cathedral of Canterbury, St Edmund's not only enjoys a stunning location, but also offers a happy, vibrant and creative environment within a supportive community.

The school offers a nurturing, yet challenging, environment where an emphasis is placed upon academic rigour and extracurricular involvement. Its extracurricular provision is broad, but also encourages excellence in each individual area. Its tradition of housing and educating the Choristers of Canterbury Cathedral brings much to the richness and diversity of our community.

Academic standards are set high. Its dedicated and talented teaching and support staff work alongside pupils to encourage them to develop into caring, resourceful and confident young men and women who are well equipped to tackle the demands of the modern world.

Organisation. The Pre-Prep, Junior and Senior Schools are on the same site and are closely integrated, using the same Chapel, music and art facilities, theatre, dining hall, science laboratories, sports facilities, and so on. However, for practical day-to-day purposes the Junior School is under the control of the Head of the Junior School and the Pre-Prep under the Head of Pre-Prep. St Edmund's derives much of its strength and its capacity to work efficiently and economically from its close-knit structure.

The Senior School is divided into four Houses: Baker, Wagner, Warneford and Watson, the respective Housemasters each being assisted by a team of Deputies and Tutors.

The Chapel. All pupils attend at least two of the morning services a week. Confirmation is conducted annually by the Archbishop of Canterbury (as Patron of the School) or by the Bishop of Dover acting on his behalf; the candidates are prepared by the School Chaplain. The School Carol Service is held in Canterbury Cathedral, by kind permission of the Dean and Chapter.

Buildings and Facilities. Over the past twenty years there have been extensive additions to and modernisation of the school's buildings and facilities: a new Junior School building; a purpose-built music school; a new Sixth Form Centre; the main hall with tiered auditorium and exhibition area; the sports hall; the technology department; additional classrooms and major extensions to science, art, IT and the Pre-Prep School; as well as the conversion of all Senior

School boarding accommodation to study-bedrooms and refurbishment of Junior boarding premises. Recent additions include: new recreational facilities for Senior School boarders; Gorsefield, Sunfield and Clare boarding houses; a refurbished library; an AstroTurf pitch; a new medical centre; upgrading of classrooms, boarding and House facilities.

Academic Organisation. At St Edmund's, the academic expectations are high. The breadth and balance of the academic programme exceeds the requirements of the National Curriculum and pupils begin to be grouped by ability while they are in Junior School. This approach encourages children to apply their talents and aptitudes with diligence and perseverance. Comprehensive reports are sent regularly throughout the school year. A system of interim reports, as well as regular parents' meetings, ensures close communication with parents.

Pre-Prep School: The Pre-Prep School has its own classroom buildings and playground, creating a warm, secure and friendly learning environment in which pupils can develop to the full. The happy and purposeful atmosphere helps pupils develop their confidence.

The School has a wide range of excellent activities and teaches a broad-based curriculum that emphasises academic development as well as art, music, drama and sport. The teachers have many years' experience of working with Early Years' children and the small classes allow staff to focus on the needs of every pupil.

Junior School: The aim of the Junior School is to produce independent learners who are confident and motivated. In Forms 3 to 5, the National Curriculum is broadly followed and, while placing particular emphasis on English, Maths and Science, there is also focus on subjects such as Art, French, Geography, History, Information Technology, Latin and Music. Subject specialists teach Forms 6 to 8, helping to prepare pupils for Senior School. Music (from Form 3), Technology and Art (from Form 6) and Science and Drama (from Form 7) is taught in specialist facilities.

The House system gives older pupils the opportunity to experience the skills of organisation, cooperation and leadership, by helping and encouraging younger members of their Houses and assisting with the organisation of House teams and events. Taking on more responsibility and developing greater initiative is valuable in smoothing their passage to Senior School.

Choristers: The 25 choristers of Canterbury Cathedral are all members of the Junior School. They board in the Choir House (in the Cathedral Precincts) in the care of Houseparents appointed by the school. All their choral training is undertaken in the Cathedral by the Master of Choristers and Cathedral Organist; the remainder of their education takes place at St Edmund's.

Senior School: In the first year of the Senior School (Year 9) pupils follow a core curriculum in English, Mathematics, French, Physics, Chemistry, Biology, History, Geography, Art, Music, Information Technology, Religious Education, PSHE, Physical Education, and Technology. Drama, Spanish and Latin are options.

GCSE core subjects are: English, English Literature, French, Mathematics and the three (separate) Sciences. Options include Latin, Spanish, Arabic, Greek, History, Geography, Art (Ceramics), Art and Design, Technology: Food Technology, Product Design, Computer Science, Music, Drama, Dance, Physical Education and Religious Studies.

The following subjects are offered for A Level examinations: Art, Biology, Business Studies, Ceramics, Chemistry, Classical Civilisation, Design and Technology, Economics, English Literature, Film Studies, French, Geography, Government and Politics, History, Mathematics and Further Mathematics, Music, Music Technology, Photography, Physics, Psychology and Theatre Studies. In addition to their A Level choices, Lower Sixth pupils have the option to undertake an EPQ (Extended Project Qualification) and the Leiths Academy Diploma.

Careers and Higher Education. The School is affiliated to the Independent Schools Careers Organisation and the Careers Research and Advisory Centre. Pupils have the opportunity to undergo careers aptitude testing in the GCSE year, and all pupils are assisted in finding a placement for a week or more of work experience in the GCSE year. The careers and higher education staff give all possible help in the finding of suitable careers and in selecting appropriate universities and colleges of further education. Most A Level candidates go on to degree courses after leaving school; others join Art or Music conservatoires.

Music. Music is woven into the fabric of school life at St Edmund's, reinforced by the presence of the Canterbury Cathedral Choristers. In the purpose-built Music School, specialist teachers give lessons to pupils from Pre-Prep through to the Sixth Form. Pupils of all ages participate in numerous musical ensembles which cater for a range of vocal and instrumental abilities. As a result, there is an exceptional practical examination record, with more than 80% of entrants achieving Distinction or Merit. Over twenty-five concerts and performances take place each year, from the Pre-Prep's 'Little Voices' festival and small lunchtime recitals in the Recital Hall to large gala concerts in Canterbury Cathedral. The school acts as a focus for musical excellence for children throughout East Kent and enjoys a creative partnership with the Tippett Quartet.

Performing Arts. Dramatic performance is included in the curriculum from the earliest years. Every term, the Pre-Prep School holds thematic drama workshops. Pupils in Junior and Senior Schools participate in school plays and other performances with vitality and enthusiasm, as an outlet for expressing their talents in acting, dancing, singing, music, choreography and technical production. The consistently outstanding GCSE and A Level results are testament to the emphasis placed on drama within the curriculum and school life in general.

Art. The emphasis St Edmund's places on creative subjects means that art is embedded in the curriculum across the three Schools. Pupils studying Art and Design enjoy excellent facilities and teaching. Drawing, painting, print-making, photography (traditional and digital), sculpture and ceramics are offered to pupils in the Junior and Senior Schools.

Sport. Association football, hockey, cricket, athletics, tennis, squash and (for girls) netball and rounders are the principal sports but there are opportunities for many other forms of exercise, including cross-country running, indoor rowing, golf, badminton, basketball, volleyball, swimming and gym-based fitness training. There is an astroturf pitch and large playing fields that adjoin the school buildings. There is an open-air heated swimming pool. The sports hall is well-equipped. There are eight tennis courts (both hard and grass), a compact golf course and a rifle range.

Activities. For those in the first four years of Senior School one afternoon a week is given over specifically to a broad range of activities. A number involve helping the local community, while other pupils learn new skills, eg archaeology, broadcasting, Eco-Schools, Japanese language and culture, kite making, literary and debating societies, photography, Rotary Interact and yoga.

In the second year all Senior School pupils join the Combined Cadet Force, a highly successful unit commanded by a member of the teaching staff and administered by an ex-soldier. There is an annual camp in the summer and an adventurous training camp at Easter, attendance at which is voluntary. Cadets may remain in the CCF for the duration of their school career if they wish, and are encouraged to do so if contemplating a career in the armed forces.

Pupils may also participate in The Duke of Edinburgh's Award scheme and the British Association of Young Scientists. There are regular field trips, choir and music tours, sports tours and many other one-off trips.

In Junior School, too, there is a diverse range of extracurricular activities, many of which draw on the school's excellent facilities for sport, music and drama. There is a Year 8 outdoor activities week in Spain, an annual sports tour and skiing trip.

Health. The School Medical Centre is staffed by state registered nurses and provides medical care at all times. The health of the pupils is supervised by a senior local general practitioner under the NHS. A counselling service is available.

Admission. *Pre-Prep School*: Entry at any age from 3–7. Once registered, children are invited to visit the School for informal assessment.

Junior School: Entry at any age from 7–12. Candidates will sit entrance tests and all prospective pupils will be interviewed or attend an assessment day.

Choristers: St Edmund's is the school of the Canterbury Cathedral choristers. For details of the voice trials please contact the Junior School Secretary.

Senior School: Entry at 13 from preparatory schools is through the Common Entrance Examination. Candidates from other schools will be tested appropriately or sit the School's own entrance tests. There is also a large entry of pupils into the Sixth Form, usually on the basis of interview and GCSE grade estimates from their present school.

Fees per term (2016–2017). Senior School: Boarders £10,572; Weekly Boarders £9,855; Day pupils £6,557. Junior School: Boarders £7,389, Weekly Boarders £6,734, Choristers £7,083, Day pupils £4,909–£4,996. Pre-Prep: £3,009–£3,478, Nursery £2,450.

Music fees: £253 per term. Extras have been kept to the minimum.

Entrance Scholarships. Competitive scholarships of up to 25% of tuition fees are offered in academic achievement, music, drama and sport at 11+, 13+ and 16+. In addition, art scholarships are available at 13+ and 16+. At the discretion of the Head an All-Rounder scholarship may be made to a candidate whose combination of talents merits an award. Such a candidate will have sat the academic scholarship paper and been assessed for a scholarship in at least one other discipline.

Bursaries and Fee Concessions. Originally founded to provide a free education for the fatherless sons of the clergy of the Church of England and the Church of Wales, St Edmund's now accepts applications from boys and girls for Foundationer status. Bursaries to provide a temporary (no more than 12 months) cushion are granted on a means-tested basis to existing pupils. Fee concessions, also means-tested, can be provided to the children of the clergy, members of the armed forces and to the third and subsequent children of the same family in the school at the same time.

The St Edmund's Society (for former pupils). President: Mr D Knight.

Charitable status. St Edmund's School Canterbury is a Registered Charity, number 1056382. It exists to educate the children in its care.

Patron: The Lord Archbishop of Canterbury

Governors:
Chairman: Mr M C W Terry, FCA
Dr M Carnegie, MB BS
Dr P Eichorn, MD
Mr C Harbridge, FRICS, FCIA, ISVA
The Revd Canon C Irvine, MA, BTh
Mrs M L Lacamp, CertEd London, DipRSA
Mrs N Leatherbarrow, BSc, MBA
Dr L Naylor, BSc, PhD
Air Marshal C M Nickols, CB, CBE, MA, FRAeS
Mr M Punt, MA, MSc

Mr Q L Roper, BA, NPQH
Mr S M Sutton, BA, FCA
Councillor P A Todd

Head: **Mrs L J Moelwyn-Hughes**, MA Cantab, MEd

Head of the Junior School: Mr M J Jelley, BA Hons UEA, PGCE

Head of the Pre-Prep School: Mrs J E P Exley, BEd Hons CCCU

Chaplain: The Revd M S Bennett, MusB Hons Canterbury NZ, BA Hons CCCU

Bursar: Mr N C Scott-Kilvert, FCCA

Deputy Head: Mr E G O'Connor, BA Cantab, MPhil Oxon, MEd Cantab

Assistant Head: Mr L A Millard, BSc Loughborough, PGCE

Assistant Director of Studies: Mrs J J Mitchard, BSc Hons London

Heads of Departments:
[1] *Department serving both Senior & Junior Schools*

Additional Educational Needs:
Mrs A E Bensberg, BSc LSE, MA UCL, CELTA Cantab, Dip SpLD Northampton, APC

[1]*Art*:
Mrs A A Slater-Williams, BA Hons Glasgow School of Art, PGCE (*Director of Art*)

Business Studies and Economics:
Mr R N Comfort, BSc Hons Wales

[1]*Design and Technology*:
Ms M Florence, BTec, BA Hons

Drama and Theatre Studies:
Mr M Sell, NCDT Acc Diploma ALRA, PGCE (*Director of Drama*)

English:
Mr M J Whitman, BA Nottingham Trent, PGCE

EAL:
Mrs H E Copland, TESOL Trinity College

Film Studies:
Dr M G Caiazza, BA MSMC, MA Kent, PGCE, PhD Kent

[1]*Geography*:
Miss D T Burren, BSc Hons Middlesex, PGCE

History/Politics:
Mr D J Morrissey, BA Hons, MSc Keele, PGCE

Computer Science:
Mrs J J Mitchard, BSc Hons London

Latin:
Mrs A I Heavens, MA Hons St Andrews, PGCE

[1]*Mathematics*:
Dr E R Jones, BSc Wales, MSc Liverpool, PhD Wales

Modern Languages:
Mrs D F Micheloud, BA Hons Kent, MA Fribourg, Dip MG (*Head of French*)

[1]*Music*:
Mr S J Payne, BA Hons MA, ARCM, LTCL, ARCO, PGCE (*Director of Music*)

Personal, Social and Health Education:
Mr J M Clapp, BSc, MA Reading

Physical Education:
Mr A R Jones, BSc Sheffield

Psychology:
Dr C F Sotillo, MA, PhD Edinburgh

Religious Studies:
Mrs V A Gunn, BA OU, BA Kent, MA Kent

[1]*Science*:
*Dr L J Ashby, BSc, PhD London

Biology:
Dr G Jones, MBChB Hons Birmingham, PGCE Warwick

Chemistry:
Dr L J Ashby, BSc, PhD London

Physics:
Dr J C Horn, BSc Hons, PhD Leeds

Junior School:
Deputy Head: Mr R A Austen, BEd Hons Bulmershe
Director of Studies: Mr M Christodoulou-Jones, BSc Hons
    Bristol, PGCE CCCU
Head of Pastoral Care: Mr A J McKean, BA/BSc, PGCE
    CCCU
Senior Master: Mr T Hooley, MA Cantab
Head of Lower School: Mrs A J Swatman, BA Ed Hons
    Kent

Support Staff:
Senior School Librarian: Ms S A Scally
Medical Officer: Dr G Manson
Head's PA: Ms E Ottaway, BA Hons Essex
Junior School Secretary: Mrs Y King
Head of Admissions: Ms A Selmon

(*Please refer to the school website for full staff list*)

St Edward's, Oxford

Woodstock Road, Oxford OX2 7NN
Tel: Warden: 01865 319323
            Bursar: 01865 319321
            Registrar: 01865 319200
Fax: 01865 319242
email: registrar@stedwardsoxford.org
website: www.stedwardsoxford.org
Twitter: @TeddiesOxford

Motto: '*Pietas Parentum*'

St Edward's was founded in 1863 by the Revd Thomas Chamberlain to educate the sons of middle class clergy in the Anglican tradition. The somewhat cramped original premises in the centre of Oxford soon proved inadequate for the growing school, so the decision was taken in 1873 to move to what were then the farmlands of Summertown. Today, the School – fully co-educational since 1997 – sits on a vast 100-acre estate complete with riverside boat house, pitches, courts, sports centre, elegant Quad, golf course and canalside towpath – yet is only a 2-minute walk from the busy urban village of Summertown and less than a mile from the centre of Oxford, a city world famous for education and culture. The school has around 680 pupils, 85% of whom board, and 40% of whom are girls. Pupils live in one of 12 houses (five for girls, seven for boys) and, in addition to having the run of extensive playing fields, benefit from access to the Nuffield Health Fitness & Wellbeing Gym (owned by the school but managed by Nuffield), the North Wall Arts Centre (celebrating its 10th anniversary in 2016), and all the amenities of a lively international city. A brand new £7m Music School opens in January 2017.

Ethos. The St Edward's ethos is underpinned by a firm emphasis on the far-reaching benefits of participation and engagement. We ask each of our pupils to engage in their academic work with real belief – in themselves and in their ability to achieve – and we encourage all pupils to take advantage of the many opportunities on offer to them at Teddies. An important touchstone for the St Edward's educational ethos is the conviction that those pupils who derive joy and satisfaction from a wide range of activities outside the classroom are those who go on to perform exceptionally well in their academic work.

Pastoral Care. The comprehensive pastoral care system at St Edward's has long been regarded as one of the school's great strengths – a point highlighted by successive ISI reports. The system is underpinned by a highly-effective network of relationships offering distinct but interwoven levels of care. Each pupil sits at the centre of his or her network, surrounded by a range of people who can offer guidance and support. The Housemaster or Housemistress is a vital member of this web of care and in this role they are supported by an Assistant HM and a Matron. Also key are Tutors who monitor the academic and pastoral life of six to 10 pupils, meeting with them regularly to offer advice as necessary. Within the school community, Sixth Formers are trained to offer a peer listening service and a great many other leadership and support roles; the Head Boy and Girl meet regularly with senior staff to raise any areas of concern.

Academic Work. Academically, it would be hard to overstate the importance to St Edward's of being in Oxford, within easy reach of the stimulating academic life of the university. Academic endeavour lies at the heart of the school; pupils are expected to work consistently hard, to take responsibility for their own learning and to engage actively in the myriad opportunities open to them for broadening their intellectual horizons. The school offers GCSE (IGCSE in most subjects), A Level with the Extended Project and the IB Diploma. Alongside these qualifications, the school offers its own bespoke courses: the Shell Curriculum in the first year teaches the skills necessary for successful study, the Warden's Project in the Fourth Form introduces the idea of an independent research project and the Taught Skills Course in the Lower Sixth teaches such vital topics as critical thinking, presentation and precis-writing. The Learning Development Department supports pupils who are mildly dyslexic or dyscalculic.

In 2016, 47% of pupils achieved the highest grades in their Sixth Form exams (A*/A at A Level, Levels 6/7 in the IB). 70% of A Level results were awarded within the A* to B grades with 63% of GCSE results graded at A* or A. In the IB Diploma, our average point score was 35.8. On average, some 80% of sixth form leavers take up places at Russell Group or equally prestigious universities, including Oxford and Cambridge, and increasingly, pupils look to study overseas. In recent years, pupils have gone on to study at US and Canadian universities, including Columbia, New York; Dartmouth, New Hampshire; Georgetown, Washington; Berkeley, California; and McGill, Montreal. Pupils have also been successful in their applications to universities in Hong Kong and Japan, and to universities in a number of European cities including Dublin, Amsterdam, Leiden and Madrid.

Higher Education and Careers. The new Careers Department is firmly rooted in the real world of work. Our Head of Careers, a former Head Hunter with first-hand knowledge of a wide range of industries, runs a structured programme. Every Fifth Former benefits from a termly, compulsory careers session to help them identify and secure the most relevant work experience placements. Some 12 or so informal careers receptions are organised each year covering everything from financial services, law, engineering and fashion to marketing services, manufacturing and design.

Higher Education advice is highly personalised and quite exceptional. The new Shell Curriculum is designed to feed directly into pupils' career planning by explicitly teaching the skills required for today's workplace: research, self-regulation, innovative thinking, presentation, collaboration and teamwork. Pupils are given every assistance in choosing the right course of further study and in preparing a strong application, including visits by representatives of UK and US universities, mock interviews and personal statement workshops. Tailored advice is given to Oxbridge and Ivy League candidates, to those aiming for highly competitive courses, such as medicine or veterinary science, and to those looking to study overseas.

Music, Drama and the Arts. The cutting-edge programming of the award-winning North Wall Arts Centre enriches the cultural life of both the school and the wider community, placing St Edward's at the forefront of developments in arts education. As a result, the arts are highly valued and enormously successful at St Edward's. The Drama Department is flourishing: main school productions, including musicals, are complemented by devised pieces, House plays, Shell plays and a Speech and Drama programme. The Art Department is strong and vibrant, benefiting from recently enhanced facilities and the stream of visiting exhibitions to The North Wall. The Dance programme is extensive, with over 30 classes every week – covering styles from ballet to hip hop – generating a range of material for the dance shows. The Music Department, moving into an elegant new building in 2017, delivers about 450 lessons every week, taught by a team of 40 visiting specialists. The main school groups include the Orchestra, Chamber Orchestra, Chapel Choir, Chamber Choir, St Edward's Singers, Concert Band, Big Band, Jazz Band and various Chamber Music groups. There are around 60 concerts a year, in school and further afield, with regular foreign tours.

Sport, Games and Activities. A wide variety of sports, games and activities is on offer. We compete at the highest level in several sports and can boast of county and national representatives. We encourage all our pupils to participate and to enjoy playing at all levels. We have fielded as many as 27 teams on one day – over 400 children representing the school. These sports, games and activities include rugby, football, hockey, cricket, rowing, athletics, netball, squash, tennis, swimming, cross-country running, sailing, golf, football, canoeing, ceramics, theatre crew, filmmaking, debating, investment, textiles, cycle maintenance, volunteering, charitable challenges, community service – and much more. We operate a Combined Cadet Force with Navy, Army and RAF sections, and offer all levels of The Duke of Edinburgh's Award.

Admission to the School. Registration forms may be downloaded from the website or obtained from the Registrar. There is a registration fee of £75. Places in the School, conditional upon performance in the entrance exam, are offered 18 months before entry at 13+. Boys and girls are expected to take the Common Entrance Examination or Scholarship in their last Summer term at their Preparatory School. Separate assessment arrangements can be made for applicants from schools not preparing candidates for the Common Entrance Examination. Lower Sixth scholarship and entrance examinations are held in November prior to entry; offers of places in the sixth form are subject to good performance at GCSE (at least six B grades and above) and a satisfactory report from the previous school.

Scholarships. Academic, Music, Art, Dance, Drama and Sports Scholarships are available at both 13+ and 16+ entry. All-Rounder and Design Technology Scholarships are available at 13+ only.

Academic, Music, Sports and All-Rounder Scholarships, both for entrants at 13+ (into Year 9) and 16+ (into Year 12), can be increased on means testing up to a total of 100% fee reduction. There is no means-tested increase available for Dance, Drama or Art Scholarships.

Academic: Up to fifteen scholarships and exhibitions are available each year. 16+ academic scholarships take place in the November prior to entry in the September, 13+ academic scholarships take place in the March prior to entry.

Music scholarships: Most candidates perform on two instruments, and many offer singing as one of these options. Composition can also be considered. We look for potential rather than attainment to date, although the minimum standard required is about grade 5 for 13+ and grade 8 for 16+.

Dance and Drama scholarships: Candidates for both these awards will be expected to demonstrate considerable natural ability and should be able to confirm that they have begun to reach high standards on the stage.

Music, Dance and Drama 13+ scholarships take place in the January/February prior to entry, 16+ in the November prior to entry.

Art scholarships: Candidates must submit a portfolio of work prior to the assessment. On the day of the award they will be asked to complete an observational drawing task. 13+ scholarships take place in the January/February prior to entry, 16+ in the November prior to entry.

Sport scholarships for both 13+ and 16+ entry take place in the November prior to entry. Candidates will show considerable natural ability in at least one sport. We are particularly looking for players of rugby, cricket, hockey, netball, tennis and rowers.

All-Rounder awards are available at 13+ only. Candidates must be academically sound, expecting to obtain over 65% at Common Entrance, show strong leadership qualities and be able to demonstrate considerable talent in two of the following areas: art, design technology, music, dance, sport or drama. The All-Rounder Award takes place in the February prior to entry.

Bursaries. The School may offer bursaries for children of clergy at the Warden's discretion.

Fees per term (2016–2017). Boarding £11,890; Day £9,515.

Charitable status. St Edward's, Oxford is a Registered Charity, number 309681. The aims and objectives of the school are to provide an outstanding education to pupils between the ages of 13–18 in order to prepare them for happy, fulfilled and productive adult lives.

Visitor:
The Rt Revd The Lord Bishop of Oxford

Governing Body:
Mike Stanfield [OSE] (*Chairman*)
Caroline Baggs, BSc
Georgina Dennis, BA, MA [OSE]
Professor Louise Fawcett-Posada, MA, DPhil
George Fenton [OSE]
Alexandra Holloway, BM, MRCGP
David Jackson, LLB
Chris Jones, MA, FRSA [OSE]
Kenneth MacRitchie, MA, BD, LLB
Jo Peach, MA, DPhil
The Very Reverend Professor Martyn Percy, BA, MEd, Phd
Sir Bob Reid, MA
Michael Roulston, MBE, MEd
E Wilfrid Stephenson, MA
Oliver Watson, BA [OSE]

Warden: Stephen Jones, BA, MSc, MLitt, FRSA

Bursar: Stephen Withers Green, MA, ACA

Sub-Warden: Thomas James, BSc, MSc

Deputy Head Pastoral: James Cope, BA, MA
Deputy Head Academic: Matthew Albrighton, BA, MA

Assistant Head Academic: Nicola Hunter, BA

Assistant Head Academic: Margaret Lloyd, BSc

Registrar: (*to be appointed*)

Assistant Head Co-Curricular: Nick Coram-Wright, MA
Assistant Head Co-Curricular: Judy Young, BSc

Teaching Staff:

Art:
*Adam Hahn, BA
Jane Bowen, BA
Tova Dalgleish, BFA
Philip Jolley, BA, BEd
Peter Lloyd-Jones, Dip FA
Nicholas Permain, BA
Lorraine Turley, BA
Instructor: Richard Siddons
Technician: Sharon Keen

Classics:
*Mark Taylor, BA
Edmund Hunt, BA, MA
George Macpherson, BA, MA
Flora Nelson, BA, MSt.
Simon Palferman, BA, MPhil
Matthew Parker, MA, MSc

Design & Technology:
*Oliver Barstow, MEng
Laura Allen, BSc
Susan Holland, BSc
Ben Pyper, Dip AD
Technicians:
Stuart Giles
Susannah Chant
Lucian Taylor

Drama:
*Katrina Eden, BA, MA
David Aldred, BA
Lauren Mackrell, BA

Economics:
*Yvette Ramadharsingh, BSc
Jeremy Mather, BA, MSc
David Finamore, BSc

English:
*Jason Clapham, MA, MSc
Lucinda Gallagher, MA, PhD
Rose Glendon-Doyle, MA
Catherine Greves, BA
Nicola Hunter, BA
Jonathan Muir, MLitt, MA
Finola Picknett, MA
Millie Pumfrey, BA, MA
Simon Roche, BA
Ashley Somogyi, BA

Geography:
*Gavin Turner, BSc, MSc
Matt Albrighton, BA, MA
James Cope, BA, MA
Andrew Dalgleish, BSc, MSc (*Director of Sport*)
Richard Howitt, BSc
Garrett Nagle, MA, DPhil
Sue Webb, MA, MA

History:
*Jonathan Lambe
Elizabeth Boast, BA
Anna Fielding, BA
Peter Rudge, BA, BA
Huw Thomas, LLB, MEd
Fiona Wickens, BA, MA

History of Art:
*Nicola Hunter, BA
Charlotte Schofield, MA

Learning Development:
*Debra Clayphan, BA, MSc
Edmund Edwards, BEd
Joanna Sephton, BA

Mathematics:
*Dominic Barker, MMath
Annie Blair, MEng
Henry Chitsenga, BSc
Andrew Grounds, BA, MSc
Catherine James, BSc
Stephen Jones, BA, MSc, MLitt, FRSA
Margaret Lloyd, BSc
Tom Phillips, BSc
Anneli Ruele, BA
John Simpson, BEng
John Wiggins, MA

Modern Languages:
*Marie-Laure Delvallée, Licence d'Anglais (*French)
Katherine Cole, BA (*German)
Jamie Davies, BA (*Spanish)
Stuart Bartholomew, MA
Solana Cabello Malfetano, BA
Nick Coram-Wright, MA
Robert Cottrell, BA
Paula Diaz Rogado, BA
Anna Heeren, BA, MA
Trevor Hunt, BA, MA
Denise Kohlhepp, MA
Barney Norman, BA, MA, PhD
Catherine Phillips, BA, MA
Nicoletta Simborowski, MA
Technician:
Lucy Bentley
Language Assistants:
Albane d'Arodes de Peyriague (*French*)
Isabell Haas (*German*)
Belen Sanchez Alonso (*Spanish*)

Music:
*Alex Tester, MA (*Director of Music*)

Neville Creed, MA (*Director of Cultural Activities*)
Gabriele Damiani, BMus, GSMD, ARCO
Richard Powell, GRSM, IRAM, ARCM
Mark Sellen, BA, MMus, ARCM

PHSE:
Beth Steer, BA (*Head of Pupil Wellbeing*)
Eve Singfield

Psychology:
Rachel Bellamy, BA, MA
Alastair Summers, BSc
Rona Summers, BSc, MSc

Politics:
Jonathan Thomson, BA
Robert Fletcher, BA, MA, MLitt
Huw Thomas, LLB, MEd

Sciences:

Biology:
*Richard Storey, BSc
Lucy Baddeley, MA
Louise Bowen, BSc, PhD
Andrew Davis, BSc, PhD, FRGS
Lewis Faulkner, MA, MA
Tom James, BSc, MSc
Alastair Summers, BSc
Kendall Williams, BSc, PhD
Technicians:
Beata Kolodziej
Gail Benson

Chemistry:
Matthew Fletcher, MA, PhD, MRSC

Graduate Assistants:
Hannah Fullelove, BA (*Drama Department*)
Joe Guppy, BSc (*PE Department*)
Sam Lapage, BA (*English Department*)
Elizabeth Preece, BMus, MMus (*Music Department*)
Emily Wilson, BA (*French Department*)

Houses and Housemasters/Housemistresses:
Cowell's: Jeremy Mather
Sing's: Matthew Parker
Field House: Mark Hanslip
Macnamara's: Kate Newson
Apsley: Oliver Richards
Tilly's: Lewis Faulkner
Segar's: Simon Roche
Kendall: Philip Waghorn
Oakthorpe: Elizabeth Boast
Corfe: Eve Singfield
Avenue: Rachel Bellamy
Jubilee: Phaedra Gowen

Chaplain: Revd E Charles Kerr, MA, MTh
Examinations Officer: John Simpson, BEng
Head of Careers: James Vaughan-Fowler

Medical Officers:
Dr Matthew Cheetham
Dr Lorna Monteith
Dr Hannah Peters

Phaedra Gowen, BSc
Monica Islam, BSc
Sophie Pollard, BSc, MRSC
Oliver Richards, MA
Technician: Judy Roberts/ Liz May

Environmental Science:
*Andrew Davis, BSc, PhD, FRGS
Garrett Nagle, MA, DPhil

Physics:
*Katherine Richard, MPhys, DPhil
David Bickerton, BA, MA, MSc
Tom Holdsworth, BEng
Natalie McDaid, MChem
Heather Murphy, BSc
David Roche, BEng
Philip Waghorn, BSc, MSc
Judy Young, BSc
Technician: Graham Quelch

Sports Science:
*Becky Drury, BSc
Rachel Bellamy, BA, MA
Nicholas Bond, BA
Mark Hanslip, BEd

Theology, Philosophy & Ethics:
*Philip Mallaband, BA, MA, PhD
Michael Bunch, MEd
Charlie Kerr, MA, MTh (*Chaplain*)
Bethany Steer, BA
Kate Newson, BA, MSt
Jonathan Thomson, BA

St George's College, Weybridge

Weybridge Road, Weybridge, Surrey KT15 2QS

Tel: 01932 839300
Fax: 01932 839301
email: contact@stgeorgesweybridge.com
website: www.stgeorgesweybridge.com
Twitter: @sgweybridge
Facebook: /stgeorgescollegeuk

Motto: *Amore et Labore*

Founded by the Josephite Community in 1869 in Croydon, the College moved in 1884 to its present attractive grounds of 100 acres on Woburn Hill, Weybridge. Within its particular family orientated ethos, the College seeks to encourage a wide, balanced Christian education in the Catholic tradition encouraging excellence and achievement across a broad spectrum of academic, sporting and extra-curricular activities. Almost all pupils move on to higher education, the vast majority gaining places at Russell Group universities, including Oxford and Cambridge.

The College is co-educational throughout the school and there are approximately 940 girls and boys.

Admissions. Entry is normally at age 11 (First Year), 13 (Third Year) or 16 (Sixth Form). Students are accepted in September each year. Entry is also possible during an academic year if a place is available.

Admissions details may be obtained from the Admissions Department.

Entrance Scholarships. Academic Scholarships are awarded at 11, 13 and for the Sixth Form. Additionally, at age 11 Music and Sports scholarships are offered and at 13 and 16 Music, Drama, Sport and Art Scholarships are offered.

Details of the number of scholarships at each year group, process for application and guidance on expected standards are to be found on our website under the Admissions section. Scholarships are awarded equally to boys and girls and a certain number are allocated to Junior School candidates each year.

Bursaries. The College provides short-term financial assistance for existing families who find themselves in difficult financial circumstances. Further information is available from the Bursar.

Assisted Places Scheme. St George's offers financial assistance of up to 100% relief on fees via its means-tested Assisted Places Scheme. The scheme allows families, who would not normally be able to consider the independent sector, to seek a St George's education for their academically able son or daughter. Places are awarded from the age of seven at the Junior School and eleven at the College. As with all applications, children will need to reach the academic entry standards required at both schools.

Facilities. Our new state-of-the-art Sixth Form building provides group and silent study rooms, social space, five History and five Geography classrooms, staff offices and meeting areas. Refurbishment over the past three years has provided modern facilities for Music, Languages, English, Mathematics, Theatre and Technology. There is an extensive Arts Centre, an impressive Library and a large indoor Sports Hall with an adjacent fitness training room. The College has 19 tennis courts, including three international standard grass courts, clay courts and an impressive four-court Indoor Tennis Centre. In addition, there are floodlit netball courts, an all-weather athletics track and two astroturf hockey pitches. The College Boat Club is situated nearby on the Thames.

The Curriculum. This is kept as broad as possible up to GCSE, with a balance between Arts and Science subjects. Students usually take a maximum of 10 GCSEs, A Level candidates may choose from over 20 subjects. The vast majority of the Sixth Form go on to Russell Group universities including Oxford and Cambridge.

Careers. Guidance is given throughout a student's career but particularly in making GCSE, A Level and university choices. The Careers Coordinator has a modern well stocked Careers Room and makes effective use of testing, portfolios, work experience, trial interviews, Challenge of Industry days and computer software.

Art. The Art Department attracts large numbers of students at GCSE and A Level who achieve consistently high results in public examinations. A large proportion of A Level candidates successfully apply to Art Colleges, often each receiving several offers in this highly competitive field.

Music. Music plays a vital part in school life. There is a wide range of music-making encompassing early music, madrigal groups, jazz, rock, African Drumming as well as more traditional ensembles, orchestras and wind bands. The choir and orchestra give regular performances (including radio broadcasts), and tour Europe annually. Tuition is available on all orchestral instruments from a team of 36 visiting specialists who teach over 400 students each week. Students play in youth orchestras and have gained scholarships to the major conservatoires.

Responsibility and Service. Many girls and boys are engaged in the care for the elderly at home or in old people's homes, as well as the mentally and physically handicapped. Each Easter and Summer, groups of Sixth Formers accompany handicapped people on visits to Lourdes. Students find these activities a rewarding exercise in Christian service. The Prefect system and the mentor system offer positions of responsibility to the oldest students. The Duke of Edinburgh's Award scheme is encouraged and there is a flourishing College Council.

Pastoral Care. The spiritual, moral and academic well-being of the students is the concern of every member of staff at the College. Nearly all staff act as Group Tutors with particular responsibility for the daily care of their students and for forging links with parents. Each Year Group is led by a Head of Year, and the Chaplain has a general pastoral role. All groups have a day of retreat away each year. The College also has four Houses to which the students are affiliated and all students have one period per week as part of their PSE programme.

Extra-Curricular Activities. There is a very wide range of clubs and societies taking place both at lunchtime and after school. In addition to music and sport, a broad range of interests is catered for such as the Science Club, Cookery, Young Enterprise, Philosophy and Model Clubs.

Sport. All students participate and there is a variety of sports: rugby, hockey, netball, cricket, tennis, rowing, and rounders, plus a wide range of other activities such as golf, athletics, badminton, basketball and cross country. Each student has the opportunity to develop his or her own talents in small coaching groups. The College has its own boat house on the Thames, nineteen tennis courts (including four indoor), two floodlit artificial pitches with viewing stand, floodlit netball courts, six artificial cricket nets, one main pavilion and two smaller cricket pavilions, eight rugby pitches. The College has access to the Junior School heated outdoor swimming pool. Attendance at national hockey finals is an annual event and the College hosts a very popular Under 18 Hockey Sixes every year. International honours have recently been gained in hockey, cricket, rowing and tennis.

Junior School. St George's Junior School is located nearby in Thames Street, Weybridge, and is co-educational, catering for boys and girls from 3 to 11.

(*For further details, please see Junior School entry in IAPS section.*)

Fees per term (2016–2017). First and Second Years £5,190; Third Year to Upper Sixth Form £5,915. Lunches (compulsory for First and Second Years) £290.

Charitable status. St George's College Weybridge is a Registered Charity, number 1017853, and a Company Limited by Guarantee. The aims and objectives of the Charity are the Christian education of young people.

Governing Body:
Chairman: Mr M Davie

Mr D Anderson	Ms I McCormick
Mr D Bicarregui	Ms A Muggeridge
Mrs D Ewart	Rev W M Muir, CJ
Mr M Falmer	Mrs K Patterson
Mr C Jansen	Mr C Prescott
Mr K Jones	Mr J F Rourke
Mr J Lewin	

Clerk to the Governors and Bursar: Mr G Cole

Headmistress: Mrs R F Owens, MA Oxon, PGCE, NPQH

Deputy Head Academic: Ms F M May, MA, BA, PGCE (*English*)
Deputy Head Pastoral: Ms R Ross, BSc, GTP (*PE*)
Deputy Head Staff: Mr D Wright, MA, BA, PGCE (*History and Politics*)

Assistant Head Reporting: Mr J E Davies, BA, PGCE (*Geography*)
Assistant Head College Entry: Miss S L Hall, BSc, PGCE (*Geography*)
Assistant Head Timetabling: Mr P J Robinson, BEng, PGCE (*Mathematics*)
Assistant Head Sixth Form: Mrs M D Smith, BA Hons, PGCE (*History*)

College Chaplain: Fr Martin Ashcroft CJ, MA, MA, STB, BPhil, BA, CertEd
Assistant Chaplain: Miss K E Snowden, MA, DMP, CBTS, ARAD Hons
Assistant Chaplain: Miss A M Colantuoni, BE, MA

Miss S Arif, BSc Hons, MEd, PGCE (*Head of Mathematics*)
Mr M J Barham, BA Hons, PGCE (*Head of History*)
Mr A Barton, BA Hons, PGCE (*Head of 4th Year, Music*)
Mrs L Y Batten, BA Hons French & German, PGCE (*Languages*)
Dr J A Baur, BSc, MSc, MPhil, PhD (*Chemistry*)
Mrs M Bigwood, BSc, HDE (*Mathematics*)
Mr N M Bissessar, BA Hons (*Drama*)
Mr G A Bowman, BSc (*Mathematics*)
Mr G D Boyes, BSc, GTP (*Head of Geography*)
Mr D J Bradford, BHum, PGCE (*Mathematics*)
Mrs E M Brambell, BA Hons, PGCE (*Religious Studies*)
Mr M Bryant, BSc Hons, PGCE (*Biology*)
Mr L R Buckingham, BSc, PGCE (*Head of Southcote House, Geography*)
Ms C A Butler, BA, PGCE (*Art*)
Mrs S Carpenter, BA Hons, PGCE (*Languages, i/c Latin*)
Miss T V Castledine, MA, MMus, FRCO (*Director of Music*)
Mr O J Clayson (*PE/Games; Head of Cricket*)
Miss V M Clayton, BA, PGCE (*Government and Politics*)
Mr M J Cullen, BSc, PGCE (*Economics & Business Studies*)
Mr J M Cunningham, BA, PGCE (*Religious Studies, i/c D of E*)
Mr D P Danaher, MTL, BA, PGCE (*Head of Economics & Business Studies*)
Mr T Deive, BA, PGCE (*Head of Languages*)
Mrs E L Doyle, BSc, PGCE (*Biology*)
Mrs V G Emad, BA Hons, PGCE (*Art*)

Mr I C Facey, BSc Hons, QTS (*Technology*)
Mr J V Fialho, BA, PGCE (*English*)
Miss A Fincher-Jones, BA Hons (*Head of 2nd Year, Girls' Games/PE*)
Mr I Findlay-Palmer, BSc, PGCE (*Head of Physics*)
Mrs N D Flash, BSc, PGCE (*Science*)
Mr N J Galanis (*Languages, i/c French*)
Miss N Gavin, BA Hons, PGCE (*History & Politics*)
Mrs L E Gibson, BSc, PGCE (*Head of Girls' Games, Acting Director of Sport*)
Ms S E Goodfellow, MA Oxon, BA Hons, PGCE (*Head of Chemistry*)
Mr A D Gradon, BSc, QTS (*Mathematics*)
Mr A J Graham, BSc Hons, PGCE (*Chemistry/Science*)
Dr F Grant, PhD, BSc, MA, PGCE (*Mathematics*)
Mr P J Graves, BSc, PGCE (*Languages, Head of Activities*)
Mr D A Green, BSc Hons, GTP (*Biology, Head of U6th*)
Mr R P Grimmer, BSc, PGCE (*Physics*)
Mrs G Hale, Deug LL France (*Languages*)
Mrs T A Hall, BSc, MSc, PGCE (*PE/Games, Head of 3rd Year, A Level PE*)
Mrs L C Hanlan BA, PGCE (*Languages*)
Miss T Haynes, BSc (*PE & Games*)
Miss N I Houston, BA Hons, PGCE (*Religious Studies, Head of 5th Year*)
Mr A Hudson, BA, PGCE (*Mathematics*)
Mr M S Hughes, MA, BA (*Head of Boys' Hockey*)
Miss C Hulf, BA Hons, MA, GTP Cert Ed (*Rowing Coach*)
Mrs A S Huysamen, BA Hons Design, PGCE Art & Design (*Art*)
Mr B Johnston, RFU Level 3 Coaching Rugby Union (*Head of Rugby*)
Miss S A Kent, MA, PGCE (*History*)
Mrs S M Knights, BSc, PGCE (*Geography, Head of Careers*)
Mr M P Lakin, MA, BA, PGCE (*English*)
Miss M T Lane, BA Hons History, PGCE (*Head of Religious Studies*)
Mr R J Lawrence, BA, PGCE (*English*)
Miss E M Marshall, BA Hons Modern History, PGCE (*History*)
Mr J G Martin, BA, PGCE (*Economics & Business Studies*)
Mr T A McIlwaine, BA Hons, PGCE (*Head of Art*)
Ms T E Medhurst, BA Hons, PGCE, Dip Dyslexia (*Academic Support*)
Miss S L Morris, BSc Hons, PGCE (*Head of Computing*)
Miss S J Napier, BA, PGCE (*Geography*)
Mr M Parnham, BEd Hons, CertEd (*Head of Technology*)
Mr B J Peake, BSc, PGCE (*Physics*)
Miss S G Peters, BA Hons, QTS (*History & Politics*)
Miss H M Pothecary, BA Hons, PGCE (*Mathematics*)
Miss R A Potter, BSc Hons, PGCE (*Biology*)
Mrs S Rowlatt, BA Hons, MA, PGCE, DipLE (*Head of English*)
Mr M A Schofield, MA (*Director of Drama*)
Mrs J M Sciortino Nowlan, BA Hons, PGCE, MPhil (*Religious Studies*)
Mrs I A Seymour, BSc, MSc, GTP (*Mathematics*)
Mr D I Shingles, BSc Hons, PGCE (*Head of Girls' Hockey*)
Mr M T Stather, BSc Hons, PGCE (*Head of Biology*)
Mrs M Strachan, BSc Hons Computer Science, PGCE (*Mathematics*)
Mr C Tapscott, BA Hons, PGCE (*History*)
Mrs C A Taylor, PhD, MSc, BSc, PGCE (*Science*)
Mr M F Tierney, MChem, PGCE (*Head of L6th, Chemistry*)
Mr M P Tiley, MA (*History*)
Mrs S H Turner, MA, BA, PGCE (*Religious Studies, Extension Programme Coordinator*)
Mr O J Vella, MMath, MSc, PGCE (*Mathematics*)

Mr N Waight, BA Hons, PGCE (*English, PSHE Coordinator*)
Mr G P Walters, BSc (*Biology, i/c Rowing, Head of Petre House*)
Miss J A Ward, MA, BA (*English*)
Mr J T Ward (*Head Tennis Coach*)
Miss K B Wardil, BA Hons, PGCE (*Music*)
Mr A P Waring, BSc, PGCE (*Biology, Head of Stirling House*)
Mrs J B Weaver, BA Hons, PGCE (*Food Technology*)
Miss C J Wilde, BSc Hons, PGCE (*Chemistry, Head of Kilmorey House*)
Mrs K Wilkinson, BSc, PGCE (*Physics*)
Mrs E L Williams, BA Hons, PGCE, GTP Art (*Art*)
Mrs L L Willis, BA Hons, PGCE (*Drama, Head of 1st Year*)
Miss L M Willis, BA, PGCE (*Languages*)
Mr N Wingrove, BA Hons, PGCE (*Languages*)
Ms S J Wragg, DPhil, MPhil, BA (*English*)
Mr O Yanez Vila, BA Hons, PGCE (*Religious Studies*)
Miss C N Yeoman, BA (*PE/Games*)

Librarian: Mrs I Monem
Head of Marketing and Admissions: Mr R Morris
Headmistress's PA: Miss P Bell
Admissions Manager: Mrs D Palmer-Smith
Matron: Mrs C Jones

St Lawrence College

Ramsgate, Kent CT11 7AE
Tel: 01843 572900 (Principal)
         01843 572912 (Junior School)
         01843 808080 (Bursar and General Office)
         01843 572931 (Registrar)
Fax: 01843 572901 (Principal)
         01843 572913 (Junior School)
         01843 572915 (Bursar and General Office)
         01843 572901 (Registrar)
email: principal@slcuk.com (Principal)
         jsoffice@slcuk.com (Junior School)
         bursar@slcuk.com (Bursar and General Office)
         admissions@slcuk.com (Registrar)
website: www.slcuk.com

Co-educational, Day: age 3–18 years, Boarding: age 7–18 years.

Number of Pupils. Senior School: 407: 220 boys (109 boarders, 111 day), 187 girls (82 boarders, 105 day).

Junior School: 12 boarders, 195 day pupils (of whom 24 attend the Nursery).

Educating children from the age of 3 to 18 years, this safe and caring school is set in over 45 acres of spacious, stunning grounds which house beautiful old architecture combined with new modern builds and facilities. Founded in 1879, it is home to just over 600 day and boarding pupils from local, UK and international families and welcomes boarders from 7 years of age.

A medium-sized school – small enough to ensure that individual pupils receive the attention and care they require, but large enough to provide outstanding facilities – and with something of a reputation for punching well above its weight in school competitions!

Academic. St Lawrence has a long record of providing an excellent academic education within a supportive community, but is also modern in its outlook and very well suited to preparing pupils for a rapidly changing world. Class sizes are small and pastoral support is strong. Academic standards are high and impressive results are achieved across all years in the school. An extensive choice of GCSEs and A Levels are offered, with an excellent success rate of pupils going on to their first-choice university.

Boarding. Boarding pupils enjoy a 'home from home' experience, both in terms of comfort and atmosphere. In recent years, a massive programme of investment has created some truly remarkable facilities for boarders, including the opening of a new girls' boarding house and a modern purpose-built home for junior boarders. All senior boarders are housed in single or double rooms with en-suite facilities and younger boarders are placed in rooms of between two and five pupils with modern streamlined en-suite bathrooms.

Facilities & Extracurricular. Sporting facilities are exceptional and expert coaching is provided at all levels in a variety of disciplines including rugby, netball, hockey, cricket and swimming. The magnificent Sports Centre houses a fitness suite, squash courts, climbing wall, dance studio and a large sports hall for badminton, basketball, etc. Music and drama flourish, enhanced by a 500-seat Theatre. Alongside the traditional chapel and library sits the school's modern coffee shop and boarders are able to use all of the facilities in the evenings and at weekends. All pupils benefit from an extensive activities programme which includes the CCF (Combined Cadet Force) and the Duke of Edinburgh's Award scheme, as well as chess, archery, golf, fencing, horse riding, table tennis, musical theatre, and many more activities.

Location. The school is set in a safe, self-contained campus situated within easy walking distance of the historic seaside town of Ramsgate. It has excellent transport links to the continent, being near both Dover and the Channel Tunnel. London is only 75 minutes away by high-speed rail link to St Pancras International. Both Gatwick and Heathrow are under 2 hours away.

Exam Results. Outstanding results are achieved by the most academic students who progress to top universities. The school is also regarded as a centre of excellence for 'value added'; students who need additional support perform well beyond expectation.

2016 GCSE results: 5+ A*-C grades including English and Maths: 91%; A*/A grades: 33%

2016 A Level results: A*/B grades: 53%; A*/A grades: 27%

Admissions. At 11+ admissions are based on an Interview with the Principal. A copy of a recent school report will also be required. Testing will be carried out where appropriate.

At 13+ the offer of a place will be dependent on the Common Entrance Examination, GCSE predictions and/or an assessment of a recent school report.

At 16+ the offer of a place will be dependent on a minimum of 5 GCSEs passes.

EU and Overseas Students will be admitted on the basis of current performance, references and a short language test as interviews are not always possible. Our special EFL centre will assess and integrate overseas pupils into the curriculum by offering a range of English teaching options, including an intensive English course.

Fees per term (2016–2017). Boarders £10,995, Day £4,667–£5,985. Fees are due and payable before the commencement of the relevant school term. St Lawrence College offers generous sibling allowances.

Individual Private Tuition: £53 per hour. Individual Instrumental Music: £39 per hour.

Bursaries. Parents in HM Forces pay the MOD CEA (Continuity of Education Allowance) plus 10% of our main boarding and tuition fees. Bursaries are awarded annually to pupils in need of financial assistance and who are likely to make a positive contribution to the life of the school. Bursaries may be awarded to new or existing pupils of the College and pupils who have been awarded a scholarship which requires supplementing. Parents may apply to the Governors' Bursary Committee for assistance and will be required to complete a confidential grant application form. Bursaries are means tested.

Scholarships. Scholarships can be offered in Years 7–11 for outstanding all-round ability, academic, sporting or music disciplines, worth up to 25% of fees. Sixth Form scholarships are also available.

Charitable status. The Corporation of St Lawrence College is a Registered Charity, number 307921. It exists to provide education for children.

The Council:

President: C Laing

Vice-Presidents:
The Baroness Cox, BSc, MSc, FRCN
¶Sir Martin Laing, CBE, MA, FRICS
G H Mungeam, MA, DPhil
S Webley, MA
The Revd Canon Nigel M Walker
A T Emby, FCA
¶B J W Isaac
M G Macdonald, MA, LLM

Chairman: D W Taylor, MA Oxon, PGCE, FRSA

Members:
¶M Iliff, MSc
G E Page
J B Guyatt, MA
A G Burgess, TCNFF, ACP
J H Tapp, BSc
¶N G Marchant
¶T L Townsend, LLB
A Truphet
M J Bolton, MBE, BA
¶J Laslett, BA Hons, FCMA
Rev G Warren, RN Hon, DMin Oxon
J Challender, BEd, MA

¶ *Old Lawrentian*

Clerk to the Governors and Bursar: J A Connelly, MA, MBA, BEng, CEng, MIET

Principal: A Spencer, MA Oxon, ACA

Deputy Head (Pastoral): D Jackson, BA Durham
Deputy Head (Academic): W M Scott, BSc St Andrews
Deputy Head (Registrar): S Heard, BA Exeter
Director of Studies: I D Dawbarn, BA York, MSc Oxon
 (*Head of Careers, Mathematics*)
Chaplain: Revd P R Russell, BA, Dip Theo Min, PG Dip OM, CCCU (*Religious Studies*)
Assistant Head, 6th Form: E Matthews BA West of England (*Head of Drama*)

Heads of Department:
A E Bailey, BEd London, MA Sussex (*Head of PSHE, Games, English*)
C Brown, BA Exeter (*Head of Economics and Business Studies*)
G Burson-Thomas, BSc Nottingham (*Head of Biology*)
M F Ebden, MSc Bristol (*Head of Science, Chemistry*)
S Fraczek, BA Cambridge, MA Durham (*Head of English*)
J Gale, BA Oxon, MA Oxon (*Head of Modern Languages*)
S J Glynn-Brooks, BSc CCCU (*Head of Academic PE*)
J Good, BA Manchester Metropolitan (*Head of Design Technology*)
A J Izzard, BA Chichester (*Director of Sport*)
S F King, BA RSA/Cambridge (*Head of EAL*)
E Kouthouri, BSc N&C Univ, Athens (*Head of Physics*)
D P Lewis, BA KIAD (*Head of Art*)
T Moulton, BA Leeds (*Head of History, Universities*)

E L Pegden, BSc Greenwich (*Head of Chemistry*)
¶J M Rawbone, BA Leeds, PG Dip Aspergers Sheffield Hallam (*Head of AEN*)
J E Van-Ebo, BA CCCU, MA CCCU (*Head of Religious Studies*)
N Watts, BA Hons Brighton, QTS (*Head of Geography*)
¶R B Wilkening, BA London, MA Kent (*Head of ICT*)
Mrs W J Wilkening, BSc York (*Head of Mathematics*)
J R Woodhall, BMus, MMus Surrey (*Director of Music*)

Houses and Housemasters/mistresses:
Lodge: S Palacios, BMus CCCU (*Music*)
Tower: G Davies, BSc Hons Cheltenham, PGCE (*Geography*)
Newlands: N Watts, BA Hons Brighton, QTS (*Head of Geography*)
Bellerby: A Izzard (*Pastoral*)
Laing: F E Jackson, BA Leeds (*French*)
Kirby House: C E Sharp, MEng Sheffield (*Mathematics, Physics*)
Kirby House Boarding: D D Spencer, BSc Hons Southampton, PGCE (*Mathematics, Games*)

Junior School
Head: Mrs E Rowe, BA Hons, PGCE

St Leonards School

St Andrews, Fife KY16 9QJ

Tel: 01334 472126
Fax: 01334 476152
email: contact@stleonards-fife.org
website: www.stleonards-fife.org
Twitter: @StLeonards_Head
Facebook: @stleonardsschool

Motto: *Ad Vitam*

Situated in the heart of idyllic St Andrews, St Leonards offers day and boarding education for 5–18 year old boys and girls, combining academic achievement and opportunity with an inspirational atmosphere.

There are approximately 530 pupils in the School with an equal number of boys and girls and around 130 boarders.

Ethos. Founded in 1877, St Leonards aims to prepare young people for the challenges of life ahead and to provide them with the skills and abilities that will enable them to step into the world with confidence and integrity. We offer a broad, rigorous education and exceptional opportunities, while instilling confidence, responsibility and independence.

Location and Campus. St Leonards combines a beautiful, historic campus with the inspirational buzz that comes from being in the heart of the university town of St Andrews.

The School is situated in a picturesque and secure, self-contained campus within the medieval walls of the former St Andrews Abbey. Our campus has served as a place of learning since the 16th century and contains several buildings of historical significance, including our library, a building once used by Mary Queen of Scots as lodgings.

On their doorstep our pupils have golden sandy beaches, historic landmarks, world-famous golf courses and the friendly town of St Andrews itself, in which our pupils are made to feel very much part of the community.

St Andrews is only 45 minutes from the cultural highlights and international airport of Edinburgh and just 20 minutes from Dundee (a one-hour flight from London).

Curriculum. The Sixth Form at St Leonards prepares pupils for the International Baccalaureate Diploma and the

School is the only in Scotland to have an all IB Diploma Sixth Form.

The Senior School (Years 8–11) prepares boys and girls for GCSEs – typically around ten.

The Junior School (Years 1–7) follows the St Leonards Junior curriculum based on the principles of the Primary Years Programme from the International Baccalaureate, delivering a seamless and coherent transition into the Senior School.

University Link. The School has close links with the University of St Andrews and each year appoints an Associate Researcher, a postgraduate student who provides a link for the pupils to the research community at the University. St Leonards students also have access to the University Library and regularly attend special lectures.

Sport, Drama, Art and Music. Opportunities in sport, music, drama and art abound. Our pupils regularly enjoy success on the sports field, earning team success and individual recognition in sports including rugby, lacrosse, hockey, tennis and football. They are also encouraged to make the most of living just a few hundred yards from the most famous golf links in the world. The School has close links with SALJGA (St Andrews Links Junior Golf Association) and has its very own world-class three-tier school Golf Programme.

All pupils have the opportunity to learn a wide variety of musical instruments, leading to ABRSM recognition.

Drama students have the chance to take part in a number of professional quality productions which are staged both within School and in the wider local community. Our Art students show off their inspiring work every year in an exhibition that is open to the public.

Co-Curricular. There is a wide range of activities in which pupils can take part, including Duke of Edinburgh's Award expeditions, falconry classes, rock climbing, skiing and debating. Foreign trips are also regularly organised with recent destinations including New York, Rome, the Italian Alps and Dresden. Community awareness is important at St Leonards and in the past few years our pupils have raised over £30,000 for charity.

Boarding. The School excels in its boarding provision, our boarding houses offering friendly and welcoming 'home from homes'. According to a Care Commission inspection report, St Leonards offers its boarding pupils, "an outstanding, Scottish, boarding experience", with the quality of care and support and the quality of the environment rated as "excellent". Both weekly and full boarding options are available and boarding is now offered from as early as Year 7.

Fees per term (2016–2017). Junior School: £3,208 (Years 1–5), £3,595 (Years 6–7). Year 7 Boarding: £9,896; Senior School and Sixth Form: Day £4,379; Boarding £10,680.

Admission. Applications can be considered for any year group, at any time during the School year. Bursary support may be given, based on need. Full details are available from the Registrar.

Charitable status. St Leonards School is a Registered Charity, number SC010904.

Members of Council:
Chairman: Mr James Murray, MA, LLB, DL
Mr Ian Adam, CA
Lord Balniel, BA
Mrs Victoria Collison-Owen, MA
Mr Neil Donaldson, MSc
Col Martin Passmore, MA, GCGI, FRSA
Mr David Pattullo, MA
Mrs Heidi Purvis, BA, PGCE
Mrs Rosaleen Rentoul, BSc Hons, Dip Ed, PGCE
Mr Sandy Richardson, MA, MBA, FRRSA

Mr Graeme Simmers, CBE, CA
Mrs Clare Wade

Academic Staff:

Headmaster: Michael Carslaw, BSc Hons Newcastle, MBA Nottingham, PhD London

Deputy Headmaster & Deputy Head Pastoral: Geoffrey Jackson-Hutt, BSc Hons, PhD Southampton
Deputy Head Academic: Dawn Pemberton-Hislop, BA Hons Sheffield, MBA Keele
Head of Sixth Form: Aileen Rees, MA Hons Cambridge
Diploma Curriculum Coordinator: Ben Seymour, BSc Hons UEA Norwich
Head of Year 10 & Pre IB: Andrew Durward, BEd Hons Edinburgh
Head of Years 8 & 9: Dan Barlow, MA Hons St Andrews

Art & Design:
Donna Rae, MA Glasgow, BFA Chicago
Margaret Behrens, BA Hons Edinburgh, Dip PG Edinburgh
Lisa Donald, BEd Manchester
Linda Jackson, BA Hons DJCA Dundee
William Clark, MA Winchester, BA Hons Dundee

Classics:
Andrew Laing, MA Hons St Andrews
Roseanna Bochenek, MA Hons St Andrews
Maria Franzoni, BA Bolonga, MSc Edinburgh
Douglas Underwood, BA UCLA, MA Missouri

Economics:
John Lambert, MA Hons Dundee
Paula Prudencio-Aponte, BSc Boliviana, MSc Manchester, MSc St Andrews

English:
Rupert Crisswell, BA York, MEd Cambridge
Katherine Gilbertson, MA Hons St Andrews
Denise Johnston, BA Hons Cardiff
Mick Kitson, BA Hons Newcastle
Vanessa Samuel, BA Hons Cantab

Geography:
Ben Seymour, BSc Hons UEA Norwich
Catherine Goldsmith, BSc Durham, MSc London
Shaun Oakey, BSc Hons Plymouth, MSc London
Amy Henderson, MA Hons Dundee

History & Politics:
Jam Fulton, BA Hons Sitrling, MA Hons Durham
Lorna Greenwood, MA Hons Edinburgh
Susannah Adrain, MA Hons Dundee

ICT:
Christian Hoehn, Dip Ing Dresden

Learning Support:
Rona Wishart, MA Hons Edinburgh
Lisa Ann Donald, BEd Manchester
Gillian Greenwood, MA Hons Cambridge
Ann Stephens, BEd Dundee

Library:
Angela Tawse, MA St Andrews, PG Dip St Andrews, MA UCL, MCLIP

Mathematics:
Graeme Baxter, BSc Hons Aberdeen
Jonathan Edwards, BEd Hons Wales
Paul McDonald, BSc OU, MSc Napier
Louise Toye, BSc Hons St Andrews
Kristina Struck, State Exam MA Berlin

Modern Languages:
Annabelle Bossard, BA Tours
Rie Adya BA MA Rissho, MPhil PhD Delhi

Susana Aranzana-Gonzalez, BA, MA, CAP Valladolid
Dan Barlow, MA Hons St Andrews
Anne Bavaj, First State Examination MA Bonn, Second
State Examination Aachen (*maternity leave*)
Anna Beck, BA Columbia, MBA Cornell
Barbara Beedham, BSc Hons Salford
Sofia Dogan
Nora Gannon, Masters History of Law Aix-Marseilles
Ana Kotarcic, BA Bern, BA Bern, MSt Oxon
Irene Kretschmann, BA Bonn
Kathryn McGregor, BA Hons Southampton
Darya Owren Mario Prisco, MA Hons Napoli
Helene Sicard-Cowan, PhD MA California, MA Nantes
Christina Steele, MA Hons St Andrews
Anouk Vermeulen, BA MPhil Radboud, Nijmegen
Tadeusz Wojtych Haiyan Wang, BA MA Sichuan,
Chengdu, MSc Dundee

Music:
Fiona Love, BMus Hons Glasgow
Marjorie Cleghorn, LGSM Napier (*Music School
Secretary*)
Aisling Agnew, BMus Hons,MMus
Robin Bell, BMus Glasgow
Douglas Clark, Dip Mus Ed RSAMD
Martin Dibbs, MA, MLitt, PhD St Andrews, DMS ARMC
Marie Downes, BA Hons Sussex
Winston Emmerson, BSc Hons Rhodes, MSc, PhD UPE
Andrew Foden, BMus Hons RSAMD
Stuart Foggo
Janice Gibson, ALCM London College of Music, Dip
ABRSM
Kyle Howie, HNC Music Dundee College RSAMD
Kenneth Irons, SADJ
Dorothy McCabe, GRSM, ARCM, ATCL, Cert Ed London
Louise Major, BMus, BSc Hons Victoria, PhD Otago
Matthew McAllister, BMus Hons RSAMD
Simon Milton, BSc Reading, MMus Sheffield
Melanie O'Brien, Dip TCL TCM London, ALCM, LLCM
Napier
Rachel Pettican, BA Applied Music Hons Strathclyde
Megan Read, MA Glasgow, PG Dip Mus RSAMD
Lynne Ruark, DRSAM, LRAM, Glasgow, CertEd
Edinburgh
Toni Russell, BA Hons Applied Music Strathclyde
Paul Shiells, BEd Hons Aberdeen

Physical Education:
Clare Muir, BEd Edinburgh
Mark Baxter, BEd Hons Edinburgh
Louise Carroll BEd Hons Edinburgh
Rosie Dawson, BA Hons Bangor
Andrew Durward, BEd Hons Edinburgh
Neil Ronaldson Dip PE Jordanhill
Fintan Bonner BA Ireland
Andrew Turnbull, BSc Napier

Psychology:
Lin McLean, PhD St Andrews, BSc Hons OU, BA
Edinburgh, MEd Sheffield

Religious Studies:
Gillian Greenwood, MA Hons Cambridge
Catherine Gratwick MA Hons St Andrews

Science:
Aileen Rees, MA Hons Cambridge
Catherine Dunn, BSc Hons, PhD St Andrews
Carla Grilli, BSc Hons St Andrews
Charlotte Kirby, BSc Hons St Andrews
Diane Lindsay, BSc Hons Aberdeen
Anna Radons-Harris, BSc Hons Lancaster
Rebecca Cornwell, BSc Durham, MRes St Andrews, CPhys

Alison Hill, MSc Glasgow, BSc Hons Aberdeen PhD
Belfast
Leanne Hunter Cert HE Open
Elaine Nolan, BSc Hons Liverpool

Theatre:
Nichola Ledger, BEd Hons London
Elizabeth Dunsmuir, DipPE
Laura Stewart, Cert HE Open

St Leonards Junior School:

Headmaster: William Goldsmith, BA Hons Durham, QTS
Reading

Senior Staff:
Julianne Pennycook, BEd Hons Jordanhill (*Deputy*)
Dianne Cormack, BSc Hons St Andrews
Katie Jones, BEd Hons Sussex (*Acting*)

Nicola Arkwright, BEd Hons Coventry
Marina Barclay, PDA (*Classroom Assistant*)
Claire Boissiere, MA Hons Dundee
Mickael Bosphore-Ward, BA Limoges
John Davie, Cert Ed Liverpool, MPhil Dundee (*maternity
cover*)
Valerie Donald, MA Hons St Andrews
Anna Fisher, MA Hons Dundee
Charlotte Jackson-Hutt, MA Hons St Andrews
Billie Paterson Herd, NC Childcare & Education
Kenny McDonald, BEd Dundee
Kathleen McKimmon, BCom Edinburgh
Karen Napier, BSc Abertay
Adele Neave, BSc Hons Glasgow
Nicola Nejman, MA Hons St Andrews
Teresa Sherratt, MA Hons Edinburgh
Caroline Soutar
Laura Stewart, MA Hons Kent

Bursar: Gerald Brown, BSc Dist Heriot-Watt, Dip H-WU,
FCMI
Registrar: Caroline Routledge, BSc, PhD

St Mary's Calne

Curzon Street, Calne, Wiltshire SN11 0DF
Tel: 01249 857200
Fax: 01249 857207
email: admissions@stmaryscalne.org
website: www.stmaryscalne.org
Twitter: @StMarysCalne
Facebook: /stmaryscalne
LinkedIn: www.cgacalne.org/linkedin

St Mary's Calne is a boarding and day school of around
350 girls aged 11–18. Around 80% of the girls board and it
is a rich boarding life with all girls taking part in the full curriculum and extra-curricular activities on offer. Situated two
hours west of London, escorted travel is provided to and
from London and airports at all holidays and exeats.

St Mary's is committed to providing a broad and fulfilling education that will challenge and inspire its pupils, as
well as helping them to achieve fantastic public examination
results. All girls go on to higher education; the overwhelming majority are awarded places at their first-choice university and approximately 15% go on to Oxbridge every year.
A new, purpose-built Sixth Form Centre, a tailor-made lecture programme, a Women in Corporate Culture Conference, debating competitions, careers advice, leadership roles
and much more prepare the girls for university and beyond.

Pastoral Care. The school, which has a strong Sixth
Form (115+ girls) is renowned for its outstanding pastoral

care. Every girl is known and cared for as an individual and has a Tutor to support and guide her through every aspect of school life, from organisational skills and subject choices through to university application. St Mary's organises boarding specifically on the criteria of age. Within the seven residential Houses girls live with their own age group. This offers the maximum opportunity to establish firm friendships and fellowship across the year group which will last throughout school and beyond. Girls are therefore cared for by Housemistresses who are particularly aware of the needs of their charges' own individual age group.

Extra-Curricular Activities. Outside the classroom, there is a wide range of extra-curricular activities, clubs and societies. Sport at St Mary's is very successful and there have been many individual and team successes. Large numbers of girls play lacrosse at County level, with many going on to play for the South West and National Teams. Girls compete in Athletics at County, Area and National level and we have a number of International Equestrians. The St Mary's Calne Tennis Academy (SMCTA) offers a structured programme of tennis at all levels, from beginners up to our elite players. As well as the mainstream sports, girls also compete in fencing and ski racing and participate in many other clubs, such as rowing and archery.

All girls work for the Bronze Duke of Edinburgh's Award with large numbers going on to higher levels. 80% of girls play musical instruments and take part in a wide variety of ensembles, including the award-winning Chamber Choir. Drama productions transfer to the London stage and the Edinburgh Festival Fringe and the department boasts a unique relationship with RADA. We have a dynamic Art Department and in November 2015 we hosted a spectacular exhibition in London, with exhibits from former and current girls; we were honoured to have Sir Antony Gormley awarding the prize for the best piece of work by a senior girl at this prestigious event.

St Mary's offers a holistic education and the girls benefit from trips which enrich this experience. Recent expeditions have included a Cultural trip to China, a Lacrosse tour in the USA, a Science expedition to Montserrat, a Classics trip to Sicily, a Language trip to Rouen and a Geography trip to Iceland. The girls are also involved in an ongoing project working with a charity to help to build a school in Zambia.

St Mary's girls play an important part in the local community; a number of our Sixth Form take part in a mentoring programme with a nearby specialist school for children with learning difficulties. Over the summer holiday, a number of girls also volunteered and worked in a camp for disabled girls; they shared this rewarding experience with the school through a presentation in assembly, encouraging other girls to volunteer.

Fees per term (2016–2017). Boarding £12,150, Day £9,050.

Scholarships and Bursaries. Scholarships available at main entry points include Academic and All-Rounder, which are means-tested and could be worth up to 40% of the fees; Music and Choral, which receive free musical tuition, and Art, Drama and Sport which are worth £1,000 per annum. Exhibitions may also be available to pupils showing outstanding ability in a single subject. Foundation Scholarships are means-tested and could be worth up to 100% of the fees.

All awards are retained to the end of Sixth Form and are reviewed at regular intervals. Candidates who are successful in gaining an award, but require greater remission in fees in order to be able to take up their place may apply for a means-tested Bursary. HM Forces discounts are available.

Charitable status. St Mary's School (Calne) is a Registered Charity, number 309482 and exists for the education of children.

Chairman of Governors: Mr S Knight, FRICS

Headmistress: **Dr Felicia Kirk**, BA University of Maryland, MA Brown University, PhD Brown University

Deputy Head: Mrs D Harrison, MA Cantab

Senior Mistress: Mrs A Davies-Potter, BSc Hertfordshire, MEd Bristol, PGCE

Senior Master: Mr J Rothwell, MA Oxon

Director of Development: Mrs C Depla, MA St Andrews

School Chaplain: The Reverend J Beach, BSc Essex, BA Bristol, MTh Cardiff

Bursar: Mr R Gordon, MA Aberdeen, MBA Edinburgh

St Mary's College

Everest Road, Crosby, Merseyside L23 5TW
Tel: 0151 924 3926
Fax: 0151 932 0363
email: office@stmarys.lpool.sch.uk
website: www.stmarys.ac
Twitter: @stmarys_college
Facebook: /stmaryscollegecrosby

Motto: '*Fidem Vita Fateri*'

St Mary's College is an Independent Catholic School for boys and girls of all faiths aged 0–18. We are a thriving community which places a high value on outstanding academic achievement and all-round personal development. Our school is built on strong values which emphasise the importance of caring for others and striving for excellence in all we do. Boys and girls can start at our Bright Sparks & Early Years department (0–4 years) soon after birth and progress to our Preparatory School (4–11 years) before moving on to the College (11–18 years), where typically they achieve up to 100% pass rates at both GCSE and A Level. Our rich programme of extracurricular activities equips our pupils with the skills and values which will guide and support them throughout their lives. Scholarships and bursaries are available.

Numbers. There are 418 pupils in the Senior School and 264 in the Preparatory School. There are no boarders.

Preparatory School. Open to boys and girls up to the age of 11. There is an Early Years Unit (0–4) comprising baby unit and kindergarten. Pupils are admitted to the Preparatory School after an interview at 4, 5 and 6 years of age and by informal assessment during a day visit.

The Prep School has a strong family atmosphere, providing a secure and lively environment in which expectations are high. The school takes what is best from the National Curriculum and follows an enhanced programme with greater emphasis on the 3 Rs and fostering self-discipline.

Sciences play an important part in the curriculum. Sport and Music are particularly strong. Tutoring in a wide range of musical instruments is provided. French and Spanish are taught in small groups from Reception.

The Head of the Preparatory School, Mr J Webster, will be pleased to meet you and show you round.

Senior School. Fully co-educational, the Senior School admits pupils at 11 both from the Prep and from primary schools over a wide area. An Entrance Examination is held in January each year. Generally speaking, pupils must be between the ages of 10½ and 12 on 1 September of the year in which they wish to enter the School. Sixth Form entry and entry into other year groups is also possible if places are available. A Registration Fee of £40 is payable with the form of application for admission.

The **Curriculum in the Senior School** includes English Language and Literature, French, German, Spanish, History, Geography, Classical Studies, Latin, Physics, Chemistry, Biology, Mathematics, Information Technology, Art, Music, Drama, Design and Technology and Physical Education. A broad curriculum of 14 subjects is followed for the first 3 years. In the Fourth and Fifth Years, pupils normally take 10 subjects at GCSE, including either single Sciences or Core plus Additional Science, and all pupils study for GCSE Religious Studies and an ICT qualification. In the Sixth Form there are Advanced courses in all the subjects mentioned above. Business Studies, Psychology, and Further Maths may also be taken at A Level. The Sixth Form options system is flexible allowing combinations of 3 or 4 A Levels.

St Mary's is a pioneer school on Merseyside in the inclusion of **orchestral music** as a normal feature of the School curriculum. All pupils are given the opportunity to play an orchestral instrument. The School Band and Orchestra give an annual Concert in the Liverpool Philharmonic Hall, win regional contests and undertake tours abroad.

Religious Education. Religious Education is a core subject through to GCSE. Religious Education in the Sixth Form is integrated through Outreach Work in the community.

Careers. The College works in partnership with the Independent Schools Careers Organisation. Arrangements are made each year for interviews for Fifth Formers to which parents are invited. Sixth Formers are interviewed several times to help them choose appropriate courses at University or in Higher Education. Advice is given to Third Year pupils in choosing options.

Games. Games periods provide opportunities for Rugby, Cricket, Football, Hockey, Netball, Squash, Golf, Cross-Country, Tennis and Basketball. The main games for girls are Netball and Hockey. There is an adjacent modern Sports Centre.

Activities. Some 40 extracurricular activities and societies are available, including The Duke of Edinburgh's Award scheme.

Combined Cadet Force. There is a very active Combined Cadet Force which contains Army and Air Force sections. Membership of the Combined Cadet Force is voluntary.

Fees per term (2016–2017). Senior School £3,541; Preparatory School £2,402.

Open Academic Scholarships. There are up to six Open Scholarships based on performance in the College Entrance Examination, worth up to half fees. The awards are based on academic merit alone and are currently irrespective of income. There is also a small number of Art, Music and Sports Scholarships.

There are also School Assisted Places, known as Edmund Rice Scholarships, at 11+. These are income-related and are open to pupils whose parents' joint income would have brought them within the Government scheme.

Sixth Form Scholarships. Edmund Rice Scholarships (worth approximately 10% of fees) are available on merit, and are awarded on the basis of a Scholarship Examination in January.

Charitable status. St Mary's College Crosby Trust Limited is a Registered Charity, number 1110311. The aims and objectives of the Charity are to advance religious and other charitable works.

Governors:
Mrs S Ward, FCMA, BSc (*Chair of Governors*)
Mr M McKenna, LLB Hons (*Deputy Chair*)
Mr C Cleugh
Mrs M Burrows
Mr R Burrows
Mr N Campbell

Mrs A Daniels, MA, PGCE
Mr A Duncan, BA Hons, MBA
Mr D Magill, BA Hons
Mrs L Martindale, MA, BEd Hons
Mrs P Old, LLB
Mrs H Thompson, ACA, BSc
Mr C Wright, BSc Hons, MRSC, MIoD

Principal: **Mr M Kennedy**, BSc, MA, NPQH, CChem, MRSC

Vice Principal: Mrs J Thomas, BSc

Senior Leadership Team:
Mrs C Killen, BEd (*Head of Sixth Form*)
Mr N Rothnie, MA (*Extended Learning Coordinator, *History*)
Miss A Fletcher, (*Business Director*)
Mr J Quint, BA Hons, PG Cert (*Director of Marketing, Admissions & Development*)

Teachers:
* *Head of Department*

Miss N Addy, BSc (**Biology*)
Mr J Armstrong, BA
Mrs S Bartolo, BEd
Miss L Brace, BSc
Mr A Byers, BA (**Music*)
Mrs L Clark, BSc (**Chemistry*)
Mr P Duffy, MPhil (**Religious Studies*)
Mrs K Fallon, BA
Mrs E Ford, BA
Dr A Giafis, PhD (**Mathematics*)
Mr T Hammersley, MSc (**Psychology*)
Mrs C Hearty, BEd
M Ireland, BEng, MSc (**Design & Technology*)
Mrs N Moore (**Classics & Latin*)
Mrs A Nichols, BA
Miss H Orrett, BA
Mr M Prescott, BA, MA
Mr D Rasores-Parry, BA (**Art*)
Mr P Ravenscroft, BA (**English*)
Mr I Rhead, BSc
Mrs J Sargison, BA (**Geography*)
Miss J Simpson, BA (**Business Studies*)
Mrs A Smith, BA
Mr A Stagogiannis, BA (**Modern Foreign Languages*)
Miss N Sykes, BSc, BA (**Physics*)
Dr J Thorne, PhD
Mrs S Townsley, BSc (**Girls' PE*)
Mr N Vagianos, BSc, MBA (**Information Technology*)
Mr D Williams, BA (**Boys' PE*)

Preparatory Department:
Headmaster: Mr J Webster, BA

Teachers:

Miss J Battisti, BSc
Mrs J Booth, BEd
Mr D Cooke, BA
Mrs K Gallagher, BA
Miss V Johnson, BA
Miss S Moran, BA
Miss P Walton, BA

Mr A Chow

Claremont House:
Head of Early Years: Mrs A Haigh, BEd
Mrs A Fielding, NNEB
Miss R Malone, NNEB

St Mary's School Ascot

St Mary's Road, Ascot, Berks SL5 9JF
Tel: 01344 296600 (Main Switchboard)
            01344 296614 (Admissions)
email: admissions@st-marys-ascot.co.uk
website: www.st-marys-ascot.co.uk

St Mary's School Ascot is a Roman Catholic boarding school founded by the Religious of the Institute of the Blessed Virgin Mary. St Mary's today is a self-governing, self-financing school.

Founded in 1885, the school is set in 55 acres within easy reach of London and Heathrow and close to the M4, M3 and M25 motorways.

Numbers on roll. Boarders 374, Day pupils 19.

Age range. 11–18.

Method of Entry. 11+ and 13+ School's own examination and interview. There is a small entry at Sixth Form.

Scholarships and Bursaries. At 11+ and 13+ there are three Academic Scholarships available worth 5% of the fees.

At 16+ there is one Academic Scholarship available worth 5% of the fees and the Sixth Form Science Scholarship worth up to 5% of the fees.

One Music Scholarship worth up to 5% of the fees and free tuition on two instruments is awarded annually to a pupil entering the School at 11+ or 13+. Candidates must have qualified to at least Grade V on the first study instrument at the time of application.

One Art Scholarship worth 5% of the fees is awarded annually to a pupil entering the School at 11+, 13+ or 16+.

One All-Rounder Scholarship is is awarded annually to a pupil entering the School at 11+ and another at 13+.

One Sports Scholarship worth up to 5% of the fees is awarded annually to a pupil entering the School at 13+.

Means-tested Bursaries are available.

Fees per term (2016–2017). Boarders £11,790, Day pupils £8,390.

Curriculum. All pupils follow a broad curriculum to GCSE including Religious Education, English, History, Geography, Maths, Biology, Physics, Chemistry, French, German, Italian, Spanish, Latin, Music, Drama, Art and Design, Information Technology and Physical Education. Tuition is also available in Piano, most String and Wind Instruments, Ballet, Tap Dancing, Speech and Drama, Ceramics and Craft activities, Tennis, Photography.

All pupils are prepared for GCSE at 16+ and typically take 10 subjects.

Sixth Formers have a choice of 25 A Level subjects and normally study 4 subjects. Interview, CV and course choice preparation is offered to all Upper Sixth including Oxbridge candidates. They are encouraged to undertake some of the many extra activities on offer and develop skills outside their A Level curriculum. Sixth Formers also have their own tutor who liaises closely with the Careers Specialist. Careers advice forms an integral part of the curriculum. This is supported by work experience, work shadowing placements and talks from external speakers, including Ascot Old Girls. The majority of Sixth Formers go on to university, and preparation is offered to Oxbridge candidates.

The School is a member of ISCO (Independent Schools Careers Organisation).

Religious Education is an integral part of the curriculum and the chapel holds a central position in the life of the school.

Sport. A varied programme is offered depending on age group. It includes Netball, Hockey, Gym, Swimming, Rounders, Tennis, Squash, Badminton and Athletics.

Purpose-built sports complex with sports hall, dance studio, squash courts and fitness suite. A floodlit 400m athletics track and hockey pitch provides a year-round, all-weather sports facility.

Drama. Performing Arts Centre which includes a flexible auditorium with lighting catwalks and control room with teaching facilities, fully-equipped drama studio and make-up and dressing rooms.

Art, Drama, Music, Science, Modern Languages and English. Specialist buildings are provided for all of these subjects and all pupils are encouraged to develop their musical, artistic, scientific and linguistic skills.

Libraries. The senior and junior libraries form the academic heart of the school. The senior library was built to meet the specific needs of Year 11 and Sixth Form girls and includes seminar rooms, which are used for teaching and careers advice.

Other Activities. Senior pupils are encouraged to participate in Community Service Projects, and those interested may enter the Duke of Edinburgh's Award Scheme. There is a wide range of club activities for all ages, and, as a termly boarding school, generous provision is made for evening and weekend activities.

Charitable status. St Mary's School Ascot is a Registered Charity, number 290286. Its aim is to provide an excellent education in a Christian atmosphere.

Board of Governors:
Chairman: The Hon Mr M Hunt
Mrs A Ayton
Mrs C Colacicchi
Miss J Ebner
Dr A Gailey
Mr P Gaynor
Mr E Horswell
Professor R Parish
The Revd Dr D Power, BA, BDSTL
Sr M Robinson
Mr V Thompson
Ms C Vaughan

Council:
Chairman: Mr G van Cutsem, FRICS
Mr M Armour
Mr N Davidson
The Lord Hemphill
Baroness S Hogg, MA
Sr C Kenworthy-Browne CJ, BA
Mrs P Mathias
Mr M Milbourn
The Hon Mrs O Polizzi
Mr B Stevens

Senior Management Team:

Headmistress: Mrs Mary Breen, BSc Exeter, MSc Manchester

Senior Deputy Headmistress: Mrs V Barker, BSc Reading, PGCE
Pastoral Deputy Headmistress: Mrs C Ellott, BA Oxon, MA London, PGCE
Academic Deputy Head: Mrs J McPherson, BA Western Australia, DipEd Edith Cowan, MA Sydney
Director of Sixth Form: Dr G Williams, BA MA Cambridge, EdD Cardiff
Bursar: Mr G Brand, BA Leeds

Support Staff:
Mrs R Brand (*Chapel Housekeeper/Resources Assistant*)
Mrs Jacquelene Carrington (*Catering Manager*)
Mr T Clark (*Estate Manager*)
Mrs P Dewes, BA Leeds (*Development Director and Assistant to the Headmistress*)

Mrs Denise Fossey (*Housekeeper and Lettings Manager*)
Mrs F Green (*School Secretary*)
Mrs C Holland (*Assistant Registrar*)
Mrs R Johnson (*Estate Manager's Administrator*)
Mrs C Leneghan (*Administrative Assistant to the Development and Alumnae Director*)
Mr R Liles (*Reprographics/Resources*)
Mrs N MacRobbie, LLB Southampton (*Recruitment Administrator*)
Mrs E Mari Sanmillan (*Account's Assistant*)
Mrs E May (*Accountant*)
Ms C Morgan-Tolworthy (*Accountant's Assistant*)
Mrs J Osborne (*PA to the Bursar*)
Mrs C Sitta, Lic Phil I Zürich (*Administrative Assistant to the Senior Deputy Head*)
Mrs V West (*Administrative Assistant to the Academic Deputy Head*)
Mrs H Williams (*Administrative Assistant to the Director of Sixth Form*)
Mrs S Young (*Registrar*)

Reception Staff
Mrs S Hickmott (*Receptionist*)
Mrs S Austin (*Saturday Receptionist*)
Mrs A Hoolan (*Weekend Evening Receptionist*)
Mrs L Peacock (*Sunday Receptionist*)
Mrs C Roberts (*Evening Receptionist*)
Mr S Jackson (*Night Porter*)
Mr G Watts (*Night Porter*)

Heads of House:
Mary Ward: Mrs K Jenkinson, BSc Nottingham, MA London, PGCE
Babthorpe: Mrs H West, BA Surrey, PGCE
Bedingfeld: Mr T Parsons, MA York and Mrs K Parsons, BA York, MA Warwick
Poyntz: Ms R Toner, BA Cantab, MA London, PGCE
Rookwood: Mrs H Jansen, BEd Central School of Speech & Drama
Wigmore: Mrs V Hutchinson, BA Cork, Dip CompSc, DipEd HDGC and Mr N Hutchinson, GBSM, ARCO, ARCM, LTCL

Sixth Form
Dr G Williams (*Director of Sixth Form*)
Miss M Fisher (*US Universities Advisor*)
Mr D Hillman (*Oxbridge Coordinator*)
Miss E Hyde (*Academic Coordinator for LVI*)
Mrs C Norvill (*Deputy Director of Sixth Form*)
Mr J Powell (*Academic Coordinator for UVI*)
Mrs H Williams (*Administrative Assistant to the Director of Sixth Form*)

Pastoral and Residential Staff:
Mrs C Marchant, BA CCAT, PGCE (*Senior Boarding Mistress*)
The Revd Dr D Power (*School Chaplain*)
Mrs M McGeown, RGN SCM (*School Nurse*)
Mrs P Perera, RGN RM (*School Nurse*)
Mrs L Steele-Perkins, RGN RM (*p/t School Nurse*)
Dr G Tasker, MBRBS, DRCOG, MRCGP, DHC (*School Doctor*)
Miss J Bennett
Mrs S Blackman
Mrs Beverley Green
Miss K Horwood, BA Plymouth, FRGS
Mrs B Lister
Mrs S Malyon, CertEd, MA Ed
Miss V Shipley
Miss S Strongman
Miss V Swire
Miss S Tate

Graduate Assistants:
Miss A-R Fenner
Miss R Howard
Miss K Murray
Miss L Spencer

Cover Staff:
Miss K Clements, BSc Brunel (*Cover/Department Administrator*)
Mrs A Heath (*Cover/Lunch Supervisor*)
Mrs S McLachlan (*Cover/Lunch Supervisor*)

Academic Departments:

Art and Design:
Miss C Atwill, BA Loughborough, PGCE (*Head of Department*)
Miss L Clarke
Miss L Green, BA De Montfort, Reigate College of Art & Design, PGCE (*Art and Design*)
Mrs A Harle, BA Cardiff, PGCE
Mrs X Harrison, BA Wales, PGCE (*Ceramics*)
Mrs E Klein
Mrs G Neville, BA Coventry, MA Edinburgh (*Photography*)

Classics:
Mrs L Povey, BA Nottingham, MPhil London (*Head of Department*)
Miss M Fisher, BA Wales, BA OU, ACCEG, PGCE
Mrs A Golding, BA Bristol, PGCE
Miss E Hyde, BA Oxford
Ms I Inskip, BA Oxford, PGCE

Drama:
Ms J Brayton, BA Lancaster (*Director of Drama*)
Miss B Carr, BA Southampton
Mrs H Jansen, BEd Central School of Speech & Drama
Mr I Warboys (*Rose Theatre Manager*)
Mr M Barker (*Assistant Drama Technician*)
Mr C Dexter, Dip ALRA (*Assistant Drama Technician*)

Economics & Politics:
Mr J Powell, BA Leeds, MSc London, PGCE
Mr D Hillman, BA Oxon, MSc London
Mr P Smith, BA Wales, MA Warwick, PGCE
Dr G Williams, BA MA Cambridge, EdD Cardiff

English:
Mrs H Trapani, BA Leicester, MA Hong Kong, PGCE (*Head of Department*)
Mr C Ellott, LLB UCL, BA OU, PGCE
Miss F McDermott, BA Cantab, PGCE
Mrs J McPherson BA Western Australia, DipEd Edith Cowan, MA Sydney
Mr T Parsons, MA York (*History of Art*)
Dr D Richards, BA MA PhD King's College London, PGCE
Miss D Staunton, BA York, MA York, PGCE
Mrs M Vandenberg, BA London, PGCE
Mrs L Waltho, BA, MLitt Newcastle

Food Technology:
Ms J Sherrard-Smith, BSc Westminster, PGCE
Mrs S Malyon, Cert Ed, MA Ed

Geography:
Mrs S Tailby, BA Birmingham, MSc Oxford Brookes, PGCE
Miss L Pitt, BSc Bath Spa, PGCE
Mrs H Tarasewicz, BA Cantab, MA Cantab

History:
Mr P Smith, BA Swansea, MA Warwick, PGCE
Miss R Evans, BA Durham, PGCE
Mr D Hillman, BA Oxon, MSc London, PGCE

Mr J Powell, BA Leeds, MSc London, PGCE
Miss H Rider, BA Bath, PGCE

History of Art:
Miss H Oakden, BA Manchester, MA Courtauld (*Head of Department*)
Mr T Parsons, MA York

ICT & Computing:
Ms B Hudson-Reed, BA Natal Univ, HDE, FDE (*Head of Department*)
Mrs V Hutchinson, BA Cork, DipComSc, DipEd, HDGC
Miss V Parsons, BSc Portsmouth
Mr R Wakeford
Mr A West, BA UWE Bristol (*Network Services Manager*)
Mr A Luther (*Network Services Supervisor*)
Miss N Arnold (*Network Services Technician*)
Mr T Nicholson (*Network Service Engineer*)
Mr M Shrestha, BSc Surrey (*Junior Systems Developer*)

Mathematics:
Mrs B Breedon, BEd Queen's Belfast, MSc Ulster (*Head of Department*)
Mrs V Barker, BSc Reading, PGCE
Mrs W Dutton, BSc Southampton, PGCE
Miss C Hicks, BSc Royal Holloway, PGCE
Mrs K Jenkinson, BSc Nottingham, MA London, PGCE
Mrs J Love, BA Sussex, PGCE
Miss S McCarthy-Brown, BSc Cardiff, QTS
Mrs G Miles, BSc London, PGCE
Mrs S Mwanje, BSc Makerere, MSc Hertfordshire, PGCE
Dr R Torcal Serrano, PhD Surrey, PGCE

Modern Languages:
Mme E Cook, DEUG Licence Toulouse, AdvDip English Studies, PGCE (*Head of Department, French*)
Mrs R Cabrera, Lic en traducción Granada and GTP, Cilt and Leeds Univ (*Spanish*)
Miss E Caretti, MA Milan, PGCE (*Italian*)
Mrs S Chasemore (*German Assistant*)
Ms T Correa-Sanchez, BA Salamanca (*Spanish*)
Miss S Doyotte, DEUG Nancy, PGCE (*French*)
Mlle V Feuillet, DEUG Licence Maître Sorbonne, PGCE (*French*)
Mrs L Harrison, BA Oxford, MA Oxon, PGCE (*French*)
Mlle M Hervi, Licence Maître Rennes, PGCE (*French*)
Mrs M Kuo (*Mandarin*)
Mrs C Marchant, BA CCAT, PGCE (*French & Italian*)
Mrs C Morrier, BA Bretagne (*French*)
Mrs S Webb, BA Cantab, PGCE (*German*)

Music:
Mrs A Rees, BA Surrey, MMus Royal Holloway, PGCE (*Director of Music*)
Mr N Burrage, BA Salford
Mrs L Flockhart (*Secretary*)
Miss J Green (*Music Assistant*)
Mr N Hutchinson, ARCO, ARCM, GBSM, LTCL
Mr J Rees, ARCM

Physical Education & Sport:
Miss G Eamer, BSc Coventry, PGCE (*Head of Department*)
Mr A Bennett, BSc St Mary's (*Head of Tennis*)
Mr B Challenger
Mrs J Freeme, BEd Johannesburg, PGCE
Miss L Gow (*Sports Assistant*)
Miss A Haylett, Dip Sports Psychology Newcastle College
Mr R Huysamen, BSc Stellenbosch, PGCE
Miss M Joseph (*Sports Assistant*)
Mrs L Lock, BSc Worcester, PGCE
Mrs J Obertell (*Department Administrator*)
Miss A Stollery, BSc Birmingham
Miss S Windle, BSc, PGCE De Montfort

Mrs A Wright, BA OU, CertEd Chelsea College

Religious Studies:
Mr J Ware, BA Oxford, MA Oxford, PGCE (*Head of Department*)
Mr P Golden, BA Stirling, MA London, PGCE
Mrs M-T Slater, BA London, PGCE, DPSE
Ms R Toner, BA Cantab, MA London, PGCE
Mrs M Vandenberg, BA London, PGCE
Mrs H West, BA Surrey, PGCE

Science:
Mr S Barker, BSc Bangor, PGCE (*Head of Department*)
Mr M Breen, BSc Exeter, MSc Manchester (*Science*)
Mrs L Carlsson, BSc London (*Biology*)
Mr R Dibsdall, BSc Exeter, MSc Exeter, PGCE (*Biology*)
Mrs A Finlay, BSc Anglia Ruskin, PGCE (*Biology*)
Mr N Jones, BSc Wales, MSc Wales, PGCE (*Biology*)
Dr D Lampus, MSci Cagliari, PhD Nottingham, PGCE (*Chemistry*)
Mr D Marsh, MChem Surrey, PGCE (*Chemistry*)
Mr D May, BA Manchester, PGCE (*Physics*)
Mr D Riding, MPhys Sheffield, PGCE (*Physics*)
Mrs S Senior, BSc Durham, PGCE (*Physics*)
Mrs J Ford, ONC and HNC Med Lab Sciences (*Senior Technician*)
Mrs S Howard, BSc UMIST, MSc UMIST (*Technician*)
Mrs K Sidhu, BSc Wolverhampton (*Technician*)

Special Needs:
Mrs J McPherson BA Western Australia, DipEd Edith Cowan, MA Sydney (*Most Able Coordinator*)
Mrs A Bingham, BA Durham, PGCE (*Learning Support Teacher*)
Mrs V Manders-Wood, BA Bretton Hall (*Learning Support Teacher*)
Mrs M Vandenberg, BA London, PGCE (*SENCO*)
Dr G Williams, BA MA Cambridge, EdD Cardiff (*Academies Coordinator*)

Careers:
Mrs C Norvill, BA Lib, CCEG

Duke of Edinburgh's Award Scheme:
Mrs A Wright, BA OU, CertEd Chelsea College (*Coordinator*)
Mr P Edmunds, CertEd, MA Oxford Brookes
Mr N Jones, BSc Wales, MSc Wales, PGCE
Mrs Fran Kenden, CertEd ML
Miss L Pitt, BSc Bath Spa, PGCE
Mrs M Vandenberg, BA London, PGCE (*Administrator*)

Exam Office:
Ms A Siddiqui (*Examinations Officer*)
Mlle V Feuillet, DEUG Licence Maître Sorbonne, PGCE
Mr N Hoad (*Invigilator*)
Mrs A Nash (*Invigilator*)
Mrs E Greengrass (*Invigilator*)

Library:
Mrs C Norvill, BA Lib, CCEG

Skills for Life:
Mrs S Malyon, CertEd Gloucs, MA OU

Independent Listener
Mrs Marion Jemmett, HE Dip Counselling

St Paul's School

Lonsdale Road, Barnes, London SW13 9JT
Tel: 020 8748 9162
Fax: 020 8746 5353

email: reception@stpaulsschool.org.uk
website: www.stpaulsschool.org.uk
Twitter: @StPaulsSchool
Facebook: /StPaulsSchool1509
LinkedIn: /st-paul's-school-189071

Motto: '*Fide et literis*'

St Paul's School is one of the UK's leading independent schools, offering an outstanding all-round education for some of the brightest boys in the country.

Founded by John Colet, Dean of St Paul's Cathedral, in 1509 to educate boys "from all nations and countries indifferently," regardless of race, creed or social background, St Paul's School remains committed to his vision today.

Erasmus, the greatest scholar of the northern Renaissance, advised Colet in the original planning of St Paul's School and wrote textbooks for the School's use. Today, a sense of scholarship, a commitment to all-round excellence and a culture of venturing beyond the syllabus continues to pervade life at St Paul's, which is known for its inspirational and responsive teaching, and outstanding academic results. Recent statistics show 80% of Paulines enter the top 12 UK Universities in the QS World rankings, with 13% going to North American universities (Ivy League or equivalent).

Admission. Application for Admission to St Paul's is to be made via an online application form on the School's website. 13+ candidates can register when they are in Year 5. In the autumn term, three years before entry, they must take the ISEB Common Online Pre-Test. The results of this, together with a detailed report from their current school will be used to select candidates for interview. Boys offered conditional places on the Main List must achieve 70% at Common Entrance Examination in June prior to entry in September. For 16+ applications should be made one year in advance. Further details can be found on the School's website.

There is a registration fee of £175.

A Deposit of one third of the termly day fee is required when a parent accepts the offer of a place for his son after interview. The Deposit will be returnable only if the boy fails to reach the necessary standard in the entrance examination or when the final account has been cleared after the boy leaves St Paul's.

Fees per term (2016–2017). The Basic Fee for St Paul's is £7,827 and £6,257 for St Paul's Juniors. This covers Tuition, Games, Loan Books, Stationery, Libraries, Medical Inspection, a careers aptitude test in the GCSE year, certain School publications and Lunch, which all boys are required to attend. Charges are made for the purchase of some books (which become the personal property of boys) and Public Examination Fees.

There are facilities for up to 35 boarders (ages 13 to 18) and boarding is flexible allowing boys to go home at weekends as they wish. The Boarding Fee is £11,723 per term.

Bursaries. St Paul's takes pride in giving the best possible education to talented boys, irrespective of their family's financial circumstances. Each year there are funds available for free and subsidised places for those with household incomes below £120,000. Bursaries are means-tested each year and may change as a family's financial situation improves or deteriorates. More information can be obtained from the School's website.

Scholarships. *Foundation Scholarships*: A few Foundation Scholarships may be awarded to 11 year old boys in St Paul's Juniors on the basis of examinations. The Scholarship Examination for St Paul's is held in May. Candidates must be under 14 on 1 September. There are 153 Scholars at any given time and about 30 vacancies arise each year. All new Academic Scholarships are honorary, and carry an award of £60 per annum.

Music: A number of Music Scholarships and Exhibitions may be awarded at St Paul's each year. Auditions take place at the end of January/beginning of February. Candidates must be under 14 on 1 September following the audition and all boys must be registered for entry to St Paul's to apply for music awards. Candidates are normally expected to have attained at least Grade 6 standard on their principal study, but this is just a guide.

The Sharp Music Exhibition Award and the Dennis Brain Memorial Exhibition are awarded from time to time to a boy entering St Paul's for his A Level years.

Several South Square Choral Scholarships are awarded to senior boys each year who show full commitment to school choral activities.

Full particulars are available from the Director of Music.

Art: One or more South Square Art Scholarships are available each year to boys who have taken GCSE to assist them in following a career in practical art. These scholarships can be awarded for the candidate's A Level course at St Paul's.

Arkwright Scholarships: The School is a member of the Arkwright Scholarship Scheme which offers financial assistance to sixth-formers who intend to pursue a career in Engineering, Technology, or other Design-related subjects.

Leaving Scholarships or Awards. A number of Prize Grants and Exhibitions (including the Lord Campden's exhibitions, founded in 1625 by Baptist Hicks, Viscount Campden) are given by the Governors every year to boys proceeding to Oxford or Cambridge or to any other place of further education.

Curriculum. All boys follow a broadly based course up to GCSE. Thereafter in Y12 & Y13, A Level and Pre-U subjects are so arranged that boys can combine a wide range of Arts and Science subjects if they so wish. In Y12, boys take four subjects and may also undertake an Extended Project, followed by three or four subjects in Y13. Subjects are all taken in a linear way and there are no public exams in Y12.

Games. Games offered include: Athletics, Cricket, Fencing, Fives, Golf, Judo, Rackets, Rowing, Rugby, Sailing, Soccer, Squash, Swimming and Tennis (hard and grass).

The School has its own Swimming Pool, Fencing Salle, Tennis, Squash, Fives and Rackets Courts, and its own Boat House. The Games Centre also comprises a Sports Hall and Gymnasium. The Sports Hall is equipped for Tennis, Badminton, Basketball and indoor Cricket nets. There are Cricket and Rackets Professionals.

Music. All boys are taught music in the classroom in the first year. In subsequent years, GCSE is taught as a two-year course, and A level taught in the final two years. Additional tuition is available in piano, organ, all the standard orchestral instruments, jazz, music theory and aural. There are a wide range of ensemble activities – chamber music, jazz and big band, two full orchestras, two training orchestras and several choral/vocal groups. The music school contains a professional standard concert venue, the Wathen Hall, several rehearsal rooms, two large teaching rooms and a music technology suite. There are regular concerts and recitals, as well as music competitions, musicals and external engagements, workshops and festivals.

School Societies. There is a wide choice of more than 30 Societies, including Musical, Artistic and Dramatic activities, Debating, Historical and Scientific Societies, Politics and Economics, Bridge, Chess, Natural History, Photography, European Society, a Christian Union and Social Service.

St Paul's Juniors adjoins the School. (*For details see entry in IAPS section.*)

Charitable status. St Paul's School is a Registered Charity, number 1119619. The object of the charity is to promote the education of boys in Greater London.

Governors:
Chairman: J M Robertson, BSc

Deputy Chairman: A Summers, BSc, MSc

Appointed by the Mercers' Company:
S Barker, LLB
N J Doyle, BEd
N A H Fenwick, MA
Lord Grabiner QC
Lady Hall, MA
P Higgins, MA
Professor R Luckin, BA, DPhil
Ms A Macleod, BSc, MA
The Earl St Aldwyn, MA
B V R Thomas, MA
C J Vermont, MA

Clerk to the Governors: T C Owens, LLB, MSc, ACIS

St Paul's Staff:

High Master: Prof Mark Bailey, BA Dunelm, PhD Cantab

Surmaster: Richard Girvan, MA, MEng Cantab

Director of Studies: Paul Woodruff, MA, MSc Oxon

Director of Teaching & Learning: Simon Hollands, MA Dunelm

Director of Admissions: Andy Mayfield, BSc Manchester, MSc, DPhil Oxon

Senior Tutor: George Boss, BA Oxon (*Lower Eighth Form*)

Director of Outreach and Academic Partnerships: Ken Zetie, MA, DPhil Oxon

Head of Wellbeing & Mental Health: Samuel Madden, BA Exeter, MA LSE

Undermasters:
Caroline Gill, MA Cantab (*Fourth Form*)
Paul Motion, BSc Massey (*Fifth Form*)
Michael Howat, BA Cantab (*Sixth Form*)
Thomas Killick, MA, PhD Cantab (*Lower Eighth Form*)
Alex Wilson, BA Exeter (*Upper Eighth Form*)

Art:
Nigel Hunter, BA Bristol Polytechnic, MEd Oxon (*Director of Art*)
Tom Flint, BA Leeds Met, MA London
Penny Holmes, BA, UED Natal
Michael Page, BA UCL, MA Royal College of Art
Erasmia Stravoravdi, MA Oxon, PG Dip RA
Ian Tiley, MA Newcastle, ATC London
Jonathan Williams, MA RCA

Biology:
Jonathan Bennett, BA, DPhil Oxon, MSc Edinburgh (*Head of Biology*)
Ben Burrows, BSc, MSc Canterbury, NZ
Sarah Field, BSc Edinburgh, DPhil Oxon
William Kricka, BSc UEA, PhD TCD
Alexander Langley, MA, PhD Cantab
Martyn Powell, BSc Surrey, PhD Reading (*Assistant PSCHE*)
Sam Roberts, MA Oxon
Camille Shammas, BSc Sheffield, PhD Bristol

Chemistry:
Matthew Smith, MChem Oxon (*Head of Chemistry*)
Simon J Clarke, MChem Oxon, MRSC
Martin Fitzpatrick, BSc, PhD (*UCD*)
James Gilks, PhD Nottingham
Tom Lowes, MChem Oxon
Barnaby Martin, BA Cantab
Janet Mitchell, BSc Bristol, MSc Open
Thomas Orr, MChem Newcastle
Suzanne Squire, MSc London

Classics:
Simon May, MA Cantab (*Head of Classics*)
Alex Wilson, BA Exeter (*Upper Eighth Form*)
Douglas Cairns, MA Glasgow
James Harrison, MA Oxon
Hannah Mervis, BA Oxon (*PSCHE Coordinator*)
Matthew McCullagh, MA, MPhil, PhD Cantab
Robert Taylor, MA, MLitt St Andrews
Katharine Waterfield, BA, MPhil Oxon

Computing:
Richard Barker, BA Oxon (*Head of Computing & Examinations Officer*)
Roisin Flanagan, BSc PGCE Brighton
Vincent Ting, BSc London, MSC Kingston

Drama:
Edward Williams, MA Cantab (*Director of Drama*)
Christian Anthony, BA, MA London (*also English*)
Alex Kerr, MA Edinburgh (*also History*)

Economics:
Samuel Schmitt, BSc Bristol (*Head of Economics*)
Felix Allen, BA Oxon
Stuart Block, MA Cantab
Thomas Passmore, BA Dunelm
Joanna Pick, BA Bristol
Andrew Sykes, MA Oxon, MSc London

Engineering:
Allan Gardam, BSc London, MSc Open, PhD Lancaster (*Director of Engineering*)
Edward Bailey, BSc Harper Adams, MSc Oxford Brookes
Brian Clark, BA Liverpool John Moores
Katie Douglass, BA Open
David Emery (*Electronics Technician*)
Tomi Herceg, BSc Princeton, PhD London
Stephen Patterson, MSc, PhD London

English:
Tristram Hager, MA Cantab (*Head of English*)
Andrew Broughton, MA Cantab
Andrew Copeman, MA Newcastle, MSc Oxford Brookes
Matthew Gardner, MA Oxon, MA Manchester
John Hudson, MA Cantab, PhD Kingston
Nicholas Kemp, BA Oxon, MPhil Cantab
Judith McLaren, MA Cantab, MA Westminster
Bernard O'Keeffe, MA Oxon

Geography:
Alexander Isaac, MSc Bristol, MA London (*Head of Geography*)
Rebecca Burridge, BSc Edinburgh
Rhiannon Cogbill, BA Cantab, MPhil Cantab
Linda Johnson, BA, MSc Rhodes
Nicholas Troen, MA Oxon, MSc LSE

History:
Graham Seel, MA St Andrews (*Head of History*)
Philip Joy, BA York, GDL Nottingham
Suzanne Mackenzie, BSc Brunel, MA London
Neville Sanderson, BA, MA London (*Head of Universities and Careers*)
Nick Watkins, BA Oxon (*Boarding Housemaster*)

Mathematics:
Andrew Ashworth Jones, BSc PNL (*Head of Mathematics*)
Sebastian Allon, BSc Bristol
Richard Baxter, BSc, PhD Queen's Belfast
Robert Breslin, BA Sheffield
Luis Cereceda, MPhys Warwick, MSc Oxon, PhD London
Paul Charlton, BEng Nottingham (*Head of Junior Mathematics*)
Chris Harrison, MSc, PhD London
Adrian Hemery, MMaths Cantab, MSc, PhD Lough

Thomas Lyster, BA Dunelm, MSc London
Alex Milne, MSc (*Imperial*)
Tim Morland, MA Oxon
Paul Motion, BSc Massey
James Ramsden, BSc Dunelm
Amrita Shravat, BSc London, DPhil Oxon
Owen Toller, MA Cantab

Modern Languages:
Eliza James, BA Manchester (*Head of Modern Foreign Languages*)
Peter Davies, MA London (*Head of Spanish*)
David Hempstead, BA, MPhil Bath (*Head of French*)
Douglas Perrin, MA Cantab (*Head of German, President of the Boat Club*)
Alexander Tofts, BA Dunelm (*Head of Italian*)
Paul Collinson, MA Oxon
Amy Grogan, BA Bristol
Rebecca Kemal-ur-Rahim, BA UCL
Larissa Lapaire, BA UCL, MA London
Guy Larlham, BA Newcastle
Ruth Williams, BA Cardiff

Music:
Mark Wilderspin, MA Oxon, MMus RCM (*Director of Music*)
Thomas Evans, BA, MPhil Cantab, PhD KCL (*Assistant Director of Music*)
Craig Greene, BA Oxon, MPerf RCM

Physics:
Simon Holmes, MPhys, DPhil Oxon (*Head of Physics*)
Michael Jacoby, BSc Bristol, MA Cantab
James Perkins, MPhys, PhD Warwick
Joshua Turnball, BSc UCL
Thomas Weller, MSc, PhD London
Ryan Buckingham, MPhys Oxon, DPhil Oxon
Chongyu Qin, BA, MSc Cantab
Mark Robinson, BA Cantab, MA Cantab, MEng Cantab

Politics:
Rohan Edwards, MA Oxon, MSc Birkbeck (*Head of Politics*)

Theology & Philosophy:
Rufus Duits, MPhil Cantab, PhD UCL
Jim Blackstone, PhD Cantab
Natasha McKeever, BA, MA, DPhil Sheffield

Sport:
Glenn Harrison, BSc Brunel (*Director of Sport & Head of Physical Education*)
James Blurton, BSc St Mary's (*Head of Rugby*)
Nigel Briers, BEd London (*PE, Head of Cricket*)
Alastair Fraser (*Head of Football*)
Andy Mcguire (*Head of Athletics*)
Roxana Roman (*Head of Elite Swimming*)

Learning Support:
Helena Howard, MA Oxon (*Learning Support Coordinator*)

Universities and Careers:
Neville Sanderson, BA, MA London (*Head of Universities and Careers*)
Carol Graham, BSFS, MAAS, MA Georgetown (*Head of US Universities*)

Chaplain: Revd Dr Jim Blackstone
Finance Director: Haley Richardson, BCompt UNISA
Chief Operating Officer: Ed Flute, MBA, PGCE
Communications & Marketing Director: Zeena Hicks, MCIM, PGCE
Medical Officer: Dr Owen Evans, BSc, MBBS, MRCP
Counsellor: Dr Robert Bor, CPsychol, AFBPsS, UKCP
Librarian and Archivist: Mrs Alex Aslett, BA, ALA

St Paul's Juniors
(*For further details see entry in IAPS section.*)

St Paul's Juniors Academic Staff:

Head of St Paul's Juniors: Maxine Shaw, BSc London, PGCE Hull, PG Dip Brunel

Deputy Head: John Barlow, BSc PGCE Liverpool (*Head of Third Years, Mathematics*)

Director of Studies: Jayne Gordon, BA Wales, PGCE Oxon (*History*)

Head of Second Years: Tim Young, BA Kent, PGCE Cantab (*Lay Chaplain, Theology & Philosophy and PSCHE*)

Head of First Years: Pippa Kershaw, BA Oxon QTS (*Upper First Year*)

[2] teaches at St Paul's and St Paul's Juniors

Art:
Neil Groom, BFA DipT Christchurch, NZ (*Director of Art*)
[2]Tom Flint, BA Leeds Met, MA London
Jakob Rowlinson, BA Oxon
[2]Erasmia Stravoravdi, MA Oxon, PG Dip RA

Computing:
[2]Roisin Flanagan, BSc PGCE Brighton (*Director of Computing*)

Classics:
Alexander Games, MA Cantab (*Head of Classics; also History*)
Emily Evans, BA Manchester (*also Theology & Philosophy*)
Georgina Tomaszewska, BA Oxon (*also English*)

Drama:
[2]Jonathan Boustead, BA Cumbria, MA York (*Director of Drama*)
[2]Alex Kerr, MA Edinburgh (*also History*)

Engineering:
Sally Hamma, BSc Huddersfield, PGCE Goldsmiths (*Head of Engineering*)
[2]Edward Bailey, BSc Harper Adams, MSc Oxford Brookes
[2]Brian Clark, BA Liverpool
[2]Katie Douglass, BA Open
Ruth Hannah, BA Leeds, PGCE Nottingham Trent

English:
Jemima Waller, MA Cantab, PGCE Inst Ed, Dip Ed Birkbeck, Dip Law City (*Head of English*)
[2]Andrew Copeman, MA Newcastle, MSc Oxford Brookes
Tiffany Masters, MA St Andrews
Josephine Wielebinska, BA PGCE Manchester

Upper First Year:
Andrea Bartlett, BEd London (*also Geography and Theology & Philosophy*)
Amanda Bodley, BSc Bristol, PG Dip Law College of Law, PGCE Roehampton (*also Geography*)
Emma Howe, BA Leeds, PGCE Surrey
Tom Taylor, BSc PGCE Dunelm (*Head of PSCHE*)
Laura Moss, BA York

French:
Valerie Nolk, LèsL Sorbonne Institut Britannique de Paris (*Head of French, Archivist; also PSCHE*)
Anna Baker, BA Reading, PGCE Oxon
Quentin Brunson, BA Reims (*French Assistant*)
Patrice Reutenauer, LèsL Strasbourg, PGCE Brunel

Geography:
Nick Howe, BEd Westminster College Oxford (*Head of Geography, Head of Rugby, Educational Visits Coordinator*)

[2]Rhiannon Cogbill, BA Cantab, MPhil Cantab
Gwyn Page, BA Southampton, PGCE Buckingham (*Head of Tennis*)
[2]Nicholas Troen, MA Oxon, MSc LSE

History:
Simon Motz, MA Oxon, PGCE London (*Head of History, Timetabler*)
[2]Caroline Gill, MA Cantab

Learning Support:
Iona Mitchell, MA Open, BSc Edinburgh, PGCE, AMBDA (*Head of Learning Support*)

Lower First Year:
Anna Cuthbertson, BA London, MSc Bath, PGCE Worcester (*Head of Lower First Year; also Computing*)
Sarah Sammons, BSc MA London, PGCE Kingston
Camilla Waterworth, BA Newcastle, PGCE Roehampton

Mathematics:
George Tsaknakis, BSc Ed Exeter (*Head of Mathematics*)
Samuel Bailey, BA Oxford Brookes
Michael Burke, BSc Western Sydney, GDE New England
Benedict Rowan, BA Oxon, PGCE UCL

Music:
Philip Berg, MVO, FRCO, ARCM (*Director of Music, Organist at St Paul's School*)
Gordon Waterson, BMus London (*Assistant Director of Music*)

Science:
Michael McRill, BTech Brunel, PhD N Wales, PGCE Keele, MRSB, CBiol, NPQH (*Head of Science*)
David Alsop, BSc Newcastle, PGCE Sunderland
Alexander James, BSc Open, QTS Hertfordshire
Jennifer Kinrade, BSc Glasgow, PGCE Oxon (*Assistant Director of Studies*)

Theology and Philosophy:
Sophie Walton, BA Oxon, GDL Oxford Brookes, LPC BPP Law Sch, QTS UCL (*Head of Theology & Philosophy*)

Sport:
Daniel Stewart, BA UWE QTS (*Director of Sport, Head of Cricket*)
Matthew Young, BA Reading, PG Dip Law QTS (*Head of Football*)
Simon Cattermole, BA Exon
[2]James Blurton, BSc St Mary's, PGCE Brunel
Kiyo Jason

St Peter's School, York

Clifton, York YO30 6AB
Tel: 01904 527300
Fax: 01904 527302
email: enquiries@stpetersyork.org.uk
website: www.stpetersyork.org.uk
Twitter: @stpetersyork
Facebook: /stpetersschoolyork

Motto: Super antiquas vias

Founded in 627AD, St Peter's is one of the world's oldest schools. It provides outstanding boarding and day education for boys and girls from 13 to 18. Pupils at St Peter's School achieve some of the best grades in the North of England at GCSE and A Level. Its Prep School, St Olave's, admits boarding and day boys and girls from 8 to 13 and Clifton School and Nursery admits day girls and boys from 3 to 8.

St Peter's is a co-educational boarding and day school with 571 boys and girls aged 13–18. There are 138 boarders housed in four boarding houses, and all day pupils are assigned to a day house, all of which are on the campus. St Peter's offers full boarding.

Buildings & Facilities. The School occupies an impressive 47-acre site just a few minutes' walk from the historic centre of York. Playing fields stretch down to the River Ouse and the School boat house, and the sports facilities are further supplemented by three sports halls, a fitness suite, an astro pitch and a 25m 6-lane swimming pool.

Recent developments have seen the introduction of Harkness tables in some rooms, the refurbishment of the Memorial Hall and a new entrance for the Senior School. There are three performance spaces of varying capacities, a music school, an outstanding art school with its own exhibition gallery and a superb library.

Entrance. Pupils are admitted through the School's entrance examinations held at the end of January for 13+ and in mid-November for 16+. The School is oversubscribed and application before the entrance exam is strongly recommended.

Scholarships and Bursaries. Honorary scholarships are awarded to those performing extremely well in the entrance examination.

Various music awards covering a proportion of the fees and free tuition on up to three musical instruments are available for entrants at 13+ or Sixth Form. Interviews and auditions for these awards are held in January or February.

Help with Fees is available at 13+ and 16+. Full particulars on Help with Fees and scholarships are available from the Admissions Officer, Mrs Gillian Daniells, Tel: 01904 527305 or email: g.daniells@stpetersyork.org.uk.

Curriculum. St Peter's offers a very broad middle school curriculum including Music, PE, Art, Design & Technology, Community Action and courses in personal and social education, among many others.

Nearly all pupils proceed into the Sixth Form, and A Level courses are available in all subjects studied for IGCSE/GCSE, and in Economics, Politics, Business Studies, Further Mathematics and PE.

Academic and pastoral care. A comprehensive house and tutorial system with interim assessments and reports during the term ensure the close scrutiny by all the teaching staff of pupils' academic and general development.

Religious education and worship. Religious Studies are part of the curriculum, and Chapel is seen as an opportunity for pupils to be made aware of the School's Christian heritage.

Careers and university entrance. The School is an 'all-in' member of the Independent Schools Careers Organisation. Careers staff are available for consultation, maintaining an extensive library relating to careers and higher education and organising a full programme of events for the Sixth Form. In 2015 the School's Careers Department was accredited by Career Mark, 'The mark of Quality for Careers Education and Guidance'.

Games and Physical Education. Physical education is a significant part of the curriculum. There is an extensive games programme and excellent sports facilities. Rugby, netball, hockey, cricket and rowing are major sports, and many other options including swimming, athletics, cross country, basketball, squash, badminton, tennis, fencing, golf, mountain biking, trampoline, fitness and weight training are available.

Combined Cadet Force. A flourishing and voluntary CCF contingent, with army and air sections, allows the pursuit of many activities including a full programme of camps, expeditions and courses.

The Duke of Edinburgh's Award is also on offer with expedition training for all levels as part of the activities programme and 150 pupils are currently participating.

Music. Musical ability is encouraged throughout the School. There is an orchestra, bands, choirs, choral society, Barbershop and Barbieshop groups and numerous smaller activities. Concerts and tours abroad are a regular feature of the school year. Tuition in all instruments is provided, and music is offered at GCSE and A Level.

Art. Drawing, painting, print-making, ceramics and sculpture may all be taken up both in and out of school hours in an outstanding department.

Drama. The School has three performance spaces: the Memorial Hall, the Shepherd Hall and the smaller, more flexible Drama Centre. There are various productions through the year giving opportunities for acting and back-stage skills.

Clubs and societies. Many societies flourish including chess, debating, Radio 627 and numerous others. The Community Action programme has over 100 regular participants.

Travel and expeditions. Recent opportunities for trips and tours have included skiing trips, Classics trips to Greece, trekking in Morocco, a Rugby tour to Canada and the USA, among many others.

The Friends of St Peter's. Parents are encouraged to join the Friends, a society whose aim is to promote a close relationship between parents and staff.

Fees per term (2016–2017). Full Boarding £9,380, Non-EU Full Boarding £9,615, Day £5,645. Tuition fees include the costs of stationery and textbooks. There are no compulsory extras except for examination fees. Lunches are included in day fees.

Further information. Prospectuses are available on request: tel: 01904 527305, email: enquiries@stpetersyork.org.uk, or via the website: www.stpetersyork.org.uk.

(*See also entries for St Olave's School and Clifton School and Nursery in IAPS section.*)

Charitable status. St Peter's School, York, is a Registered Charity, number 1141329.

Visitor: The Rt Honorable the Lord Archbishop of York

Board of Governors:
Chairman: Mr W Woolley
Vice Chair: Mr J E Burdass
Vice Chair: Rev Canon Dr C Collingwood

Members of the Board

Mrs C Bailey	Miss S L Palmer
Dr D M Haywood	Mr A Taylor
Mr P B Hilling	Mr S Town
Ms P Kaur	Mr P Widdicombe
Dr A Lees	Mrs C Bailey
Professor M D Matravers	

Clerk to the Board: Ms Sara Esler

Head Master: Mr L Winkley, MA Oxon, MEd OU

Deputy Head: Mrs J R Wright, BA, PGCE

Academic Deputy: Mr D H Gillies, BA, MSc

Heads of Departments:
Art: Mrs C Chisholm, BA Hons
Biology: Mrs S E Mckie, BSc, PGCE
Careers: Mrs J Loftus, BSc
Chemistry: Mr G Smith, BSc
Classics: Mr E Noy-Scott, BA, PGCE
Design and Technology: Mr P Cooper, BSc, QTS
Drama: Miss H K Lindley, BA, PGCE
Economics/Business Studies: Mr B D White, BA, PGCE
English: Mrs J D Lawrence, MA
Geography: Miss E C Ullstein, BSc
Government & Politics: Mr B Fuller, BA, PGCE
History: Mr R J Trevett, MA
Mathematics: Mr D J Spencer, BSc

Modern Languages: Mr M J Duffy, BA
Director of Music: Mr P Miles-Kingston, MA, LRAM, QTS
Director of Sport: Mr S J Williams, BEd
Physics: Mr M Edwards, MA Ed, BSc, MInstP
Religious Studies: Mr C D Bembridge, BTh, PGCE
Science: Mr D K Morris, BSc

All other St Peter's academic staff are listed on the school website.

Administrative Staff:
Bursar: Mr R M Schofield, FCA
Director of External Relations: Miss H E M Hamilton, MA, ACIM
Head Master's PA: Mrs S V Emson
Admissions Officer: Mrs G Daniells

The Prep School – St Olave's
Master: Mr A I Falconer, BA, MBA
Master's Secretary: Mrs C Murgatroyd

Deputy Head: Mr M C Ferguson, HDE
Senior Master: Mr C W R Lawrence, BEd, MIBiol
Director of Teaching & Learning: Mrs C Lees, BEd
Chaplain: Mr J Dodsworth, BA, MA

All other St Olave's academic staff are listed on the school website.

Clifton School and Nursery
Head: Mr P C Hardy, BA, PGCE
Head's Secretary: Mrs C Fattorini

Deputy Head: Mrs A Clarke

All other Clifton School and Nursery academic staff are listed on the school website.

Seaford College

Lavington Park, Petworth, West Sussex GU28 0NB

Tel:	01798 867392
Fax:	01798 867606
email:	info@seaford.org
website:	www.seaford.org

Motto: *Ad Alta – To The Heights*

The College was founded in 1884 at Seaford in East Sussex and moved to Lavington Park at the foot of the South Downs in 1946 in West Sussex. The picturesque grounds cover some 400 acres and include extensive sports facilities. The campus includes a Prep School for pupils aged 6–13 (*see IAPS entry*), a superb Art and Design department, a Sixth Form Centre, purpose-built boarding houses, a state-of-the-art Mathematics and Science block, and a Music School, which has its own performance arena, rehearsal rooms and recording suite.

Seaford is controlled by an independent non-profit making Charitable Trust approved by the Department for Education and the Charity Commissioners, and is administered by the College Board of Governors.

Pupils. Seaford College offers day and boarding facilities, with options of full, weekly and flexi boarding. There are over 700 pupils at the College with almost 200 in the Sixth form. There are two boys houses, a girls house, a junior house and two Sixth Form boarding houses.

Aims. Seaford College's aim is to bring out the best of each individual, by helping every pupil to reach their full potential and to achieve personal bests both inside and outside the classroom. The aim is to enable pupils to leave the College feeling confident in their own abilities and able to contribute in the external world.

Academic. The Prep School (incorporating Years 2–8) offers a wide-ranging curriculum, which includes the core subjects of English, Mathematics, Science, Spanish, French and Information Technology, as well as Geography, History, Art, Music, DT, Sport, Forest School and PSHCE.

Years 10 and 11 lead up to the GCSE examinations. Students study the core subjects of English Literature, English Language, Mathematics and Science and then choose four other syllabuses to follow from a comprehensive list of subjects, which include: Art, Business Studies, Computing, Drama, Design and Technology, Geography, French, History, Music, Physical Education, Religious Studies and Spanish.

The A Level subject list is comprehensive. In the Lower Sixth, pupils choose up to four subjects to study but may choose to drop one subject after the first term, then continue with three subjects through to A Level. Over and above this in their first year students may undertake The Duke of Edinburgh's Silver Award. In the Upper Sixth students concentrate on their three A Level subjects or BTEC courses in Business, Sport, Countryside Management or Hospitality.

Music is an important part of life at Seaford and the Music School offers the latest in recording and performing facilities. The College boasts an internationally-renowned College Chapel Choir, who have sung on tour with Gary Barlow and have performed many concerts for charity. The College also has an orchestra and offers lessons for all instruments. Music can be studied at GCSE and A Level.

Sports. With superb facilities available in the grounds and staff that have coached and played at international level, the College has a reputation for sporting excellence. Facilities include: eight rugby pitches, eight tennis courts, three cricket pitches, a water-based all-weather hockey pitch, enclosed swimming pool, a large indoor sports hall that allows tennis and hockey to be played all year round, and a 9-hole golf course and driving range.

Art. The College has an excellent Art department, which allows students to exercise their talents to the fullest extent in every aspect of art and design, whether it is ceramics, textiles, fine art, animation, or any other medium they wish to use. Many pupils from Seaford go on to study at design school and work for design and fashion houses or advertising companies. Students display their work throughout the year in the department's large gallery.

Combined Cadet Force. The College has strong ties with the Military and has a very well supported Combined Cadet Force, with each wing of the armed forces well represented. Weekend exercises and training are a regular feature in the College calendar and include adventure training, canoeing, climbing, sailing and camping.

Admission. Entry at age 7 consists of a trial day and assessment. Entry at age 10, 11 and 13 is determined on cognitive ability testing, references and a trial day at the school. 13+ pupils will still be expected to take the Common Entrance Examination. Sixth Form entry is dependent upon GCSE results, Trial Day and interview. Pupils are required to have at least 45 points at GCSE (=9 C grades) and these should include English and Mathematics. Pupils may enter the school without one of these subjects on condition they retake. Overseas students are required to take an oral and written examination to determine level of comprehension in English.

Scholarships and Bursaries. Academic, Music, Art, Design Technology and Sports scholarships may be awarded to boys and girls entering the prep and senior school at 11+, 13+ and 16+. These scholarships are worth a fixed value of £500 per annum. Scholarship examinations take place in February of the year of entry.

Bursaries are available on a means-tested basis. A potential scholarship recipient in need of further financial assistance may apply for a means-tested bursary.

Sibling and Forces discounts are also available. Please contact the Admissions Secretary for more details.

Fees per term (2016–2017). Years 9–13: £10,395 (Full Boarding), £9,060 (Weekly Boarding), £6,720 (Day). Years 7 & 8: £7,155 (Weekly Boarding), £6,410 (Day). £6,700 (Year 6 Weekly Boarding), £3,220–£4,910 (Years 2–6 Day).

Extras. Drama, Clay Pigeon Shooting, Fencing, Duke of Edinburgh's Award, Golf, Kayaking, Museum & Theatre trips, Creative Writing, Debating Club, Rock Climbing, etc.

Charitable status. Seaford College is a Registered Charity, number 277439. It exists to provide education for children.

Governing Body:
R Venables Kyrke (*Chairman*)
Mrs S Sayer, CBE (*Vice Chair*)

A G Mason, MBE	N Karonias
R Norton	J R Hall
J Cooper	H A Phillips
Mrs E Lawrence	A Hayes

Headmaster: J P Green, BA Hons, PGCE

Academic Deputy Head: Mrs B Jinks, BA Jt Hons, MA, NPQH
Deputy Head (*Middle School*): J A Passam, BA, FRSA
Deputy Head (*Sixth Form*): W Yates, BSc Ed
Prep School Head: A Brown, BE
Deputy Head Prep School: J Harte, BSc

Teaching Staff:
* *Head of Department*

Art & Design:
*A G Grantham-Smith, BA, PG Dip ArtEd
Mrs K Grantham-Smith, BA (*Photography*)
Mrs H Hatton, BA (*Ceramics*)
A Kirkton, BA Hons

Business Studies:
M Pitteway, BComm Hons

Classics:
T Farmer, BA

Design Technology:
*D Shaw, BEd
Miss A Prince-Iles, BA Hons, PGCE
P Harker, MDes Hons

Drama:
*Dr J Askew, BA Hons

EAL:
Ms Y Clarke, CELTA, BA Hons

Economics:
E Bowden, BSc Hons
E Reynolds, BA

English:
*Ms H Johnson, BA Hons
J Doy, BA Oxford, PGCE
Mrs S Roberts, BA Hons, PGCE
Mrs P White, BA, PG DipSpLD
Mrs A Doy, BA, PGCE
D Pilgrim, BA, PGCE (*Media Studies*)
G Vernon, BA, MA

Food Technology:
Mrs A Wilkins Shaw, BSc Hons, PGCE

Geography:
*N Q Angier, BSc, MA
J Hart, BA, PGCE
J Follows, BA Hons, PGCE
Miss E LeBarthe, BSc Hons

History:
*J Gisby, BA Hons, PGCE
Miss M Beard, BA Hons
R Stather, BA
Mrs L Stitt, BA Hons

Information Technology:
*D Crook, BA
P Bain, BA
M Townsend, CE, BA, MA

Learning Support:
*Mrs P A Angier, BA, Dip CG, Dip SpLD
N Foster, BA, Hornsby Dip SpLD
Mrs M Gilbert, BA Hons, PGCE, OCR SpLD
Ms A Jensen, Dip SpLD
Mrs L Ferris, OCR SpLD
Mrs H Russell, BA, OCR Cert SpLD
Mrs E Jones, CE
Ms S George
Mrs B Vernon

Mathematics:
*S Kettlewell, BA
Mrs B Jinks, MA, BA, NPQH
Dr N Pothecary, PhD, BA
J Percival, BA, PGCE
Mrs J Percival, BSc, PGCE
D Lockyer, BSc, PGCE
Mrs E Bloem, BA

Modern Languages:
*Ms A Loten, BA Hons, PGCE
Ms H Martin, PGCE (*French*)
C Thorpe, PGCE, BEd, MA
Mrs J Lingford, BA Hons, PGCE
Miss M Molinero Quiralte
Miss J Stroudley, BA, PGCE

Music:
*J Weaver
Mrs J Hawkins, PGCE, BMus
Mrs S Reynolds, BA Hons (*Choirmaster*)
Tim Sheinman, BA, MA

Physical Education:
*A Cook, BA, PGCE
J Thompson, BA Hons, PGCE
Miss E Teague, BA Hons QTS
T W Gregory, BEd
Mrs D Strange (*Coach*)
J Halsey (*Golf Professional*)
D Barnes, BA, PGCE
Mrs G Hegarty, BA Ed, PGCE
Miss L Bryant, BA Hons
D Joseph, QTS PE
C Adams (*Head of Cricket*)
J Bird (*Head of Tennis*)
C Greenway (*Head of Hockey*)

Psychology:
Mrs A Yates, BS, PGCE

Religious Studies:
Revd M Barter, BA

Science:
*D Priest, BSc, DMS, NPQH
Mrs G Pasteiner, BSc (*Biology*)
S D'Agar, BS Hons, PGCE (*Biology*)
E Barkham, MA Hons
P Nazir, BSc, PGCE (*Physics*)
Ms K Bloomer, BSc Hons, PGCE
G Barham, BSc Hons, PGCE
Dr N Street, PhD, MBA, PGCE
A Plewes, BSc Hons, PGCE

KS2 Teachers:
Mrs A Hobbs, BA
Mrs S Lewis, BEd Hons
Mrs H Stevens, BA Hons
Mrs F Jones, CertEd
Mrs S Page, GRSM, LRAM, PGCE (*KS2 Music, PSE*)
Mrs M Mitchinson, BA, PGCE

Exams:
Mrs L Goddard

CCF:
A Plewes, BSc Hons, PGCE
M Gough

Chaplain: Revd M Barter
Finance Manager: A Golding
Facilities Manager: G Burt
IT Systems Manager: G Bell
Marketing Manager: S Twigger
Headmaster's Secretary: Mrs A Thornley
Admissions Secretary: Mrs J Mackay-Smith

Sevenoaks School

High Street, Sevenoaks, Kent TN13 1HU

Tel: 01732 455133
Fax: 01732 456143
email: regist@sevenoaksschool.org
admin@sevenoaksschool.org
website: www.sevenoaksschool.org
Twitter: @SevenoaksSchool
Facebook: /SevenoaksSchoolUK
LinkedIn: /Old-Sennockians-Sevenoaks

Motto: *Servire Deo Regnari Est*

Founded in 1432, Sevenoaks School is a co-educational day and boarding school for pupils aged 11–18. Alongside academic excellence, it offers strong pastoral care, co-curricular breadth, innovative thinking, and an inclusive global dimension inspired by the International Baccalaureate.

Sevenoaks is one of the top schools in the UK, providing an outstanding modern education. In 2015, Sevenoaks was the highest performing fully co-educational school in the Sunday Times Parent Power's list of the top 50 fee-paying schools for the IB, and the top UK fully co-educational IB school in the Education Advisers Ltd rankings. In 2013 the Independent Schools Inspectorate (ISI) awarded Sevenoaks School the rare accolade of 'Exceptional' for its students' achievement.

There are seven boarding houses: a co-educational junior house (11–13), two boys' houses (13–18), two girls' houses (13–18) and two single-sex Sixth Form houses (16–18). All welcome students from the UK and around the world. Accommodation ranges from a charming Queen Anne house to modern, purpose-built facilities. There are lessons and sport for all pupils on Saturdays and a full programme of activities for boarders on Sundays.

Sevenoaks has a reputation for exploring new ideas. The school has taught the International Baccalaureate since 1978 and was the first HMC school to offer the IB Diploma Programme exclusively. More recently, Sevenoaks was among the first schools in the UK to devise its own externally accredited qualification, the Sevenoaks School Certificate (SSC), which is taken at the end of Year 11 and is fully recognised by UCAS. A wide range of subjects is offered at GCSE, IGCSE and SSC, with setting in core subjects. In the Sixth Form all pupils study the International Baccalaureate Diploma Programme – a rigorous two-year diploma designed to provide a broad and balanced education. It is a well respected qualification for leading universities world-wide. Academic results in the school are excellent, with an average IB Diploma score of 39.8 points (world average around 30 points) and some 30 students achieving a score of 45 or 44 points. In 2016, 82 per cent took up a place at one of the leading UK universities, while 17 per cent accepted places at top US, Canadian, European and other international universities.

There is a strong emphasis on the co-curriculum, from sport to music, drama and art. Pupils are regularly selected for regional and national orchestras and choirs, the NYT, and compete at county, national and international level in a number of sports. A variety of clubs and societies provide opportunities for all pupils to find and develop their interests. Sevenoaks was one of the first UK schools to incorporate voluntary service as a compulsory element of the co-curriculum, pioneering a local Voluntary Service Unit in the 1960s and continuing with a strong service programme today. There is also a CCF and involvement in The Duke of Edinburgh's Award scheme.

The facilities are first class: recent developments include a sports centre providing outstanding facilities, and an award-winning world-class performing arts centre. Work has begun on a state-of-the-art science and technology centre which will unite the four core fields of science, and an innovative new Sixth Form centre, both due to open in 2018.

Admission. The main points of entry to the school are at 11, 13 and 16 years. A small number are admitted at other levels. At 11+, pupils are admitted on the basis of a competitive examination held in January, an interview and school report. At 13+, candidates take part in an assessment process in the May of their Year 7. A reference from their current school is also required. Candidates studying at a UK Preparatory School will then take either the school's academic scholarship examinations in the May of Year 8 or the Common Entrance examinations in the June of Year 8. At 16+ students are admitted into the Sixth Form based on their performance in interview and academic entrance tests, and on the strength of their current school reports. There are boarding and day places for boys and girls at all ages. All applications for entry should be addressed to the Director of Admissions (regist@sevenoaksschool.org).

Fees per term (2016–2017). Boarders £11,493; Day Pupils £7,197 (including lunch). Fees for pupils entering directly into the Sixth Form are £12,468 (boarding) and £8,172 (day).

Scholarships and Bursaries. Up to 50 awards are available at 11+, 13+ and 16+ for outstanding academic ability or promise, as well as outstanding ability in music, sport, art and drama (at 13+ and 16+ only).

Scholarships are awarded to the value of £1,000 or 10% of the day fee.

Applicants are invited to apply for 11+ scholarships on the basis of performance in entrance tests and interviews, and for music scholarships when confirming their application. For 13+ awards, candidates may be invited to take part in the Academic Scholarship exams, or those who attend a UK prep school may be put forward by their school. Internal candidates may apply for co-curricular scholarships.

Sixth Form academic scholarships are offered on the basis of performance in entrance tests and interviews. Applications for Sixth Form Art, Music, Drama and Sport scholarships should be made by expressing an interest during the application procedure.

Means-tested bursaries are available for pupils who could not otherwise afford the fees. Priority is given to local candidates. Scholarships may be augmented by bursaries in cases of financial need.

Charitable status. Sevenoaks School is a Registered Charity, number 1101358. Its aims and objectives are the education of school children.

Governing Body:
Chairman: R N H Gould, BA
Vice-Chairman: Mrs S Dunnett, BA

Governors:
Ms A Beckett, MBA, MA
A Boulton, MA
Mrs S Carr, BA
Lord Colgrain, MA
I Doherty, MA
Mrs E Ecclestone, LLb, Dip LP
Dr C Goh, MA, MB, BChir, MRCP
Prof S Iversen
A R M Little, MA
J London, LLM
N May, MA, MSc
D M Phillips, BA, ACA
P Shirke, MBA
Dr A Timms
Prof I Wilson

Bursar and Clerk to the Governors: Air Vice-Marshal A J Burton, OBE, BSc Econ, FCIS, Chartered FCIPD

Academic Staff:

Head: Mrs C L Ricks, MA, DPhil

Senior Deputy Head: Miss T M Homewood, BSc, MA
Deputy Head (Pastoral): Miss H P Tebay, MA
Deputy Head (Academic): T R Jones, BA, MA
Deputy Head (Co-curriculum): G E Stanford, MA, MBA
Director of Administration: Miss A A Franks, MA
Director of Admissions: Mrs A M Stuart, BSc, MEd
Director of Development: M D Joyce, BA
Director of Higher Education and Careers: Mrs W J Heydorn, MA
Director of Information Systems: Mrs S J Williamson, BA, MSc
Director of Innovation: G A Lawrie, BSc
Director of Curriculum: M P Beverley, BA, MA
Director of International Baccalaureate: N T Haworth, BA
Head of Sixth Form Admissions: Mrs K E Lewis, BSc
Head of Boarding: Mrs N J Haworth, MA
Head of Sixth Form: M T Edwards, BA, MPhil, PhD

Assistant Teachers:
* *Head of Department*
† *Housemaster/mistress*

Miss N L Atkinson, BSc (*Technology*)
†Mrs E M Bassett, BA (*Chemistry*)
P R Bassett, MA (*Mathematics*)
C P Bates, BSc (*Biology*)
J H Beck, BA, MA (*Philosophy*)
Miss F J Bolton, BSc, MSc (*Mathematics*)
Miss H M Bonsall, BSc (*Biology*)
Mrs L D Boulianne, BA, MSci, PhD (*Physics*)
Mrs R L Brown, BA (*Technology)
M Burnett, MChem (*Chemistry*)
I C Campbell, BSc (*Psychology)
Mrs R Campbell, BA (*English*)
M R Capelo, BSc (*Modern Languages, *Spanish*)
S Carr, MA (*Classics*)
J Cheetham, BA (*English*)
Miss C-Y Chiang, BSc (*Mandarin*)
Mrs C H Collier, BA (*Classics*)
Miss M T Connolly, BSc (*Physics*)
T G Cook, BA (*English*)
†S A J Coquelin, MA (*French*)
Miss O Corbett, BA (*History*)
J D Cullen, BSc, MSc (*Physical Education*)
T J Danby, BSc (*Geography*)
A G Day, MA (*Economics*)
Miss E B Delpech, BA (*Art*)

J H Dickinson, MPhys (*Physics*)
Ms L A Dolan, BA (*English*)
Miss L E Dollman, BA (*English*)
J Drury, MA (**Russian*)
Mrs C Duran-Oreiro, DegEd (*Spanish*)
Miss A M Durnford, BA (*English*)
†Mrs C E Dyer, BA (*French, German, LS*)
C H J Dyer, BA (**Music*)
†Mrs T G Edwards, MChem (*Chemistry*)
J C Emmitt, BA (**Physical Education*)
P L Eversfield, MA (**Economics*)
Mrs S C Eversfield, BA (*English*)
Miss N M Fayaud, MA (*French*)
T J K Findley, MSc, PhD (*Chemistry*)
Mrs V J FitzGerald, BA (**History*)
I A Fletcher, BSc (*Chemistry, *Service*)
P Freeman-Jones, BA (*Mathematics*)
Mrs C E Glanville, BA, MA (*Higher Education, English*)
R C Glass, MSci (*Mathematics*)
Mrs N A Glover, BSc (*Mathematics*)
Mrs S E Golding, BA (*Mathematics*)
J W Grant, BA (*Drama, Literature & Performance*)
D C Hall, MA, MPhil (*History*)
S A Hall, BSc (*Psychology*)
C M Harbinson, BA, MA (*English*)
Mrs P O Hargreaves, BA (**PSHE, Drama*)
Miss A Harmer, BA, MA (*Classics*)
Miss E R Harris, BSc (*Geography*)
J Harris, BA (*Geography*)
P Harrison, MA (*English*)
P Harvey, BA, MA (*Drama, English*)
M K Heighway, BA (*Music*)
G E Henry, BA, MA (**Drama*)
Mrs C J Henshaw, BA (**English*)
Miss A Hill, BSc (*Mathematics*)
S Holden, BEd (*Physical Education*)
G Howden, BSc, MA (**Mathematics*)
P J Hulston, BSc (*Economics*)
H J Jarvis, BA (*Physical Education*)
R M Jones, BSc (*Technology*)
Mrs E A Joseph, BA (*Physical Education*)
Mrs J L Kiggell, MA, ARCM, AMus, TCL (*Music*)
L C Kiggell, MBA (*Economics*)
E Kirby, BSc (*Biology*)
N Kunaratnam, BA, MA (**Theory of Knowledge, French*)
P C Lilley, BA, MA (*Geography*)
R D Lyle, BA, MA (*English*)
T MacBain, BA (*History*)
Mrs A Mack, BA, MA (*History*)
C R Martin, MA, PhD (**Science, *Chemistry*)
S B Mavroleon, BSc (*Physics*)
P G de May, BA (*Classics*)
Mrs A J Maynard, BA (**Head of Learning Support, French*)
Mrs R V McCullagh (**French, Russian*)
Miss R L McQuillin, MA (*History*)
Miss C Y Mehta, BSc (*Chemistry*)
Mrs K A Mylod, BSc (*Biology*)
Mrs C de Nanteuil, MChem (*Chemistry*)
Miss A E Nairn, BHPE (*Physical Education*)
Mrs C E Nicholson, BA (*Physical Education*)
G Oberti Oddi, BA, MA (**Spanish*)
C W Openshaw, BA (**Art*)
Mrs D Orme, BSc, MSc, PhD (*Mathematics*)
M Otero Knott, MA, MLitt, PhD (*Philosophy*)
†S M Owen, MA, PhD (*Chemistry*)
S Palmer, BA, BSc (*Music*)
M Parsons, BA, PhD (*Chemistry*)
R D Patterson, BSc, PhD (*Mathematics*)
Miss C M Pearson, BSc (*Physical Education*)
Mrs K L Pitcher, BSc (**Biology*)

C D Potts, BA, MPerf (*Music*)
Miss O C Power, BA (**Systems of Belief, Theory of Knowledge*)
R Rands-Webb, MA (*Spanish, French*)
Mrs J E Redding, BA (**Entrepreneurship*)
Mrs H E Roff, BSc, DPhil (*Physics*)
Miss A K Russell, MA (*French*)
Miss E S Schaefer, BA, MA (*French*)
Miss M C Schirn, BA, MEd (**German, French*)
Ms L U Seetharaman, BA, MA (*English*)
Miss S A Shah, BA (*Art*)
S J Sharp, BSc, PhD (**Physics*)
A C Smith, BComm (*Economics*)
E Spindler, BA, DPhil (*History*)
Miss O Springer, MA (*German*)
Ms N Y Strabić, MMath, PhD (*Mathematics*)
C P Taylor, MA (**Classics*)
A W Thomas, BSc (*Technology*)
P R Thompson, BA, MA (**Geography*)
Mrs A J Turner, BSc, MRes (*Biology*)
Miss A W White, BA (*Mathematics*)
Mrs G P Williams, BSc, PhD (*Mathematics*)
†G J Willis, BA (*Geography*)
A G Wilson, MA (*English*)
J L Witton, BSc (*Biology*)
Miss Y Yin, BS, MSc (**Mandarin*)

Part-time Staff:
Ms A Ashwell, MusB, MMus (*Instrumental and Vocal Studies*)
O C Barratt, BA (*Art*)
Mrs L Carda, BA, MA, PhD (*Spanish*)
A J Cornah, LLB, MSc (**Sailing*)
Mrs E M Cummins, BA (*Girls' Games*)
Miss A E Downton, BA (*Spanish*)
Mrs S K Harvey, MA (*Higher Education*)
Mrs J Hendry, Dip RSAM, ARCM (*Music*)
Mrs A M Hulston, BA (*English as an Additional Language*)
Mrs E Kelly (*Russian*)
Miss G P Low, BA (*Artist in Residence*)
Mrs S J MacLeay, MA (*Geography*)
Mrs H de May, BA (*Classics*)
D Merewether (*Photography*)
A C Mitchell, BA (*Film, Video*)
Miss S Rahman, BA (*English*)
Mrs A E Rochdi, BA (*French, Spanish*)
Mrs H Smith, BA (*Learning Support*)
Mrs A Symons, MSc (*Italian*)
C J Tavaré, MA (*Biology, Physical Education*)
T T Wey, MA (**Keyboard*)
Mrs A Williams-Walker, BSc (*Mathematics*)

Head of Library: Ms C Woodhouse
Head's PA: Mrs M Thomas

Sherborne Girls

Bradford Road, Sherborne, Dorset DT9 3QN

Tel: Admissions: 01935 818224
        School: 01935 812245
        Bursar: 01935 818206
Fax: 01935 389445
email: registrar@sherborne.com
website: www.sherborne.com
Twitter: @sherbornegirls
Facebook: /sherbornegirls
LinkedIn: /Sherborne-Girls

Sherborne Girls, founded in 1899, provides an outstanding education for 11 to 18 year olds in the beautiful county of Dorset and is proud of its co-curricular programme and exceptional pastoral care. Girls are admitted at 11+, 12+, 13+ and into the Sixth Form. There are 473 girls: 430 Boarders, 43 Day girls. The International Baccalaureate Diploma is offered in addition to A Levels, which provides education tailored to each girl's needs. A close relationship with Sherborne School allows co-ed opportunities including some joint lessons in the Sixth Form, music, drama, activities, clubs and societies and social occasions. The schools have the same term dates.

Terms. Three terms of approximately 12 weeks each. Christmas holidays 4 weeks; Easter holidays 4 weeks; Summer holidays 8 weeks. Term dates are in common with those of Sherborne School.

Admission. Common Entrance Examination to Independent Schools. Scholarship Examinations and interviews. The School's own entrance examinations where Common Entrance is not possible. Girls should be registered in advance and reports will be requested from their current school. Pre-assessment for 13+ entry takes place 18 months before entry. For entry into the Sixth Form girls are required to gain 5 good passes in relevant subjects.

Registration fee £100. A deposit of £1,000 is required before entry (a term's fees for overseas pupils) and credited to the last term's bill.

Scholarships and Bursaries. Academic Scholarships are offered at 11+, 13+ and 16+ annually as a result of examination and interview. There are also scholarships offered for outstanding promise in Music, Art, Drama and Sport. All examinations are held in January and February apart from Sixth Form in November. Scholarship awards are made on merit with a maximum merit award of 15% of the fees. Scholarships may be combined with means-tested Bursaries which can raise considerably the effective amount of an award. Bursarial support (up to 100%) may be available in cases of demonstrable need.

Music Awards (Junior and 16+): Scholarships of up to 10% of the current fees with free music tuition for up to three lessons per week. Music Exhibitions offer free music tuition for up to three lessons per week.

Art Scholarships (Junior and 16+): Awards of up to 10% of the current fees. Candidates will be required to bring a portfolio with them and would be asked to do some work in the Art Department whilst they are here.

Sport Scholarships (Junior and 16+): Awards of up to 10% of the current fees. Candidates will offer one or more sports, preferably reaching county standard or higher.

Drama Awards (13+): Scholarships of up to 10% of the current fees with free drama tuition for one lesson per week. Drama Exhibitions offer free drama tuition for one lesson per week.

All-Rounder Award (Junior): Awards of up to 15% of the current fees. All-Rounder Awards take into account ability in two areas of activity outside of the classroom (art, drama, music and sport) as well as academic potential.

Fees per term (2016–2017). 13+: Boarders £11,100, Day Boarders* £8,100, Day Girls £6,580 11+: Boarders £8,950, Day Boarders* £8,100, Day Girls £6,580. *Day Boarders are girls who wish to stay overnight on the odd occasion and for whom a bed space will be made available on request.

Houses. There are five Houses for 13–17 year olds and one Upper Sixth House. 11 and 12 year old girls spend their first years together in Aldhelmsted West House.

Religion. The School has a Church of England foundation, but it values the presence and contribution of members of all the Christian traditions and of other faiths. Regular services are held in the Abbey, some jointly with Sherborne School.

Examinations. Girls are prepared for I/GCSE, A Levels and the International Baccalaureate Diploma. There is a wide choice of subjects to be studied. Some subjects at A Level are studied jointly with Sherborne School.

Games. Hockey and Lacrosse/Netball are played in the Michaelmas and Lent terms and Tennis, Rounders and Athletics during the Trinity term. There is a performance swimming programme for regional and national swimmers. Oxley Sports Centre in partnership with Sherborne Girls contains a 25m pool and state-of-the-art fitness suite. There are Squash Courts, floodlit Astroturf, Sports Hall, Dance Studio and Climbing Wall. Riding, Badminton, Cross-Country Running, Golf, Aerobics, Judo, Sailing, Trampolining are some of the alternative games.

Sherborne Old Girls. All enquiries should be made to Mrs Fiona James at the School, Tel: 01935 818329.

Prospective parents and their daughters are invited to the School for Tour Mornings (approximately monthly during term time), or private visits by appointment. Please visit the school's website or telephone Admissions on 01935 818224 for further details.

Charitable status. Sherborne School for Girls is a Registered Charity, number 307427. It exists to provide education for girls in a boarding environment.

Council:

Chairman: Mr S H Wingfield Digby

Vice Chairs: Mr R Strang, Lady Plaxy Arthur

Mrs K Brock	Mrs A Harris
Mrs I Burke	Mr R A L Leach
Dr S Connors	Mr P Pilkington
Mr I Davenport	Mrs A L M Simon
Lt Gen Sir Robert Fry	The Hon Mrs C Townshend
Mr W J A Gordon	Mr P Ward
The Rt Revd Karen Gorham	Mrs M Wingfield Digby
	Mr N Wordie
Mrs L Hall	

Clerk to the Council: Mr S D Miller

Senior and Pastoral Staff:

Headmistress: **Mrs Jenny Dwyer**, BEd Hons Cantab

Bursar: Mr S D Miller, MA Cranfield, BA

Deputy Head External Affairs: Mrs Fiona Clapp, MBA, BSc Hon London PGCE

Deputy Head Teaching and Learning: Mrs Louise Orton, BSc Swansea, PGCE

Deputy Head Pastoral and Planning: Mr Ben Gudgeon, MA, BA, AMusTCL, FRSA

Head of Sixth Form: Mrs Florence Corran, MPhil Oxford

Director of Boarding: Miss Bex Brown

Director of Development and Marketing: Mrs Katherine Massey, BA Hons Oxford Brookes

Chaplain: Revd Rebecca Ayers-Harris, BA Nottingham, Dip Theology, PGCE

Housemistresses of Boarding Houses:

Aldhelmsted East: Mrs D Miller, BEd Manchester

Aldhelmsted West: Mrs H Vanstone, BSA, Dip

Dun Holme: Mr R Garnsworthy, BE Australia and Mrs H Garnsworthy

Wingfield Digby: Mr O McManus, BA Hons Nottingham, PGCE and Mrs K McManus, BA Hons Bournemouth, PCE

Reader Harris: Mr J Hammond, BEd Hons Gloucester & Mrs S Hammond, BEd Wellington NZ

Kenelm: Mrs F Barnes, BSc Lancaster, PGCE

Mulliner: Miss C Howell Evans, BSc Hons Dunelm, PGCE

Staff:
* Head of Department

Art, Design and Food Technology:
*Mrs C Mason, BA Reading, MA, PCE
Mrs A D Heron Watkins, BA Southampton
Miss T Farris, Leiths, BSc Texas
Mr I McCarthy, BEng Leeds, PGCE
Ms P Ellis, MA London, BA Courtauld Institute, London
Mr J Casely, BA Hons, MPhil Birmingham
Miss F Bugg, BA Hons, PGCE
Mra A Diggle Perry, BA Hons Middx, PGCE
Mr N Wright, BA, MA, PGCE
Mrs D Miller, BEd Hons
Miss E Hobson, BA Hons
Miss E Smith, BA Hons, PGCE

Classics:
Mrs R M Allen, BA Birmingham
Miss S Haslam, MA Cantab, PGCE

Drama and Theatre Studies:
*Miss E Nurse, BA Manchester, PGCE
Ms J Moore, MA Warwick, BA Leicester, PGCE, Dip Ed Brighton

English:
*Mr P R Cantrell, Cert Ed, BA Nottingham
Ms K Chapman, BEd Southampton
Mr J Hammond, BEd Hons Gloucester
Mrs J Ward, BA OU, Dip SpLD, TESL Toronto, AMI Toronto, PGCE
Mr S P Wood, BA Oxon, PGCE
Mrs F Corran, MA Oxon, MPhil Oxon
Miss L Suttle, BA Birmingham
Mr O McManus, BA Hons Nottingham, PGCE

Geography, Economics and Business Studies:
*Mrs E Morray-Jones, BSc Surrey
Mrs C Morgan, BSc Wales, PGCE
Revd Rebecca Ayers-Harris, BA Nottingham, Dip Theology, PGCE
Mr D Banks, BSc Cardiff, PGCE
Mrs K Creswell, MA Edinburgh
Miss S Hardman, BSc Hons Bangor, PGCE
Mrs K McManus, BA Hons Bournemouth

History:
*Mrs S Elliot, BA Hons Reading
Mrs S Francis, MA Oxon
Ms S Haslam, MA Cantab, PGCE
Mrs K Scorer, MA Oxon, PGCE

ICT:
Mrs S Hammond, BEd Wellington
Dr G Collins, MMath Durham, PhD Birmingham

Mathematics:
*Mrs D Kirby, BA Leicester, PGCE
Mrs L Orton, BSc Hons Swansea, PGCE
Miss J Davidson, BSc UMIST, PGCE
Mrs J Edmondson, BSc, MA
Dr A Moore, BEng, PhD Bristol, MA Nottingham
Mr S Payne, BSc Kent, PGCE

Modern Languages:
*Mr M Felstead, MA Cantab
Mme M-D Bonelli-Bean, Licence LLCE Paris
Mrs G Carvia-Ruiz, PGCE
Mrs P J Fieldhouse, MA London, BA Rhodes, PGCE
Mrs G Henderson, BA Exeter, PGCE
Mrs L Plant
Mr D Woods, BA Hons Loughborough
Senora Lopez, BA Castellon
Miss M Calle Drapela

Music:
*Mr J M Jenkins, BA Dunelm, ARCO
Mr S Clarkson, BMus Edinburgh, FRCO, ARCM
Mr B Gudgeon, MA, BA, AMusTCL
Miss A Manero, BMus, PGDip, MMus
Mrs J Nelson, MEd, Dip RAM, LRAM, RAM
Miss C Win Morgan, BMus Manchester, Dip RAM, LRAM
30 visiting teachers

Musical tuition in:
Flute, Clarinet, Saxophone, Percussion, Singing, Alexander Technique, Oboe, Bass/Electric/Classical Guitar, Baroque Recorder, Brass, Violin/Viola, Cello, Piano and Harp.

Physical Education:
*Mr M Spivey, BAS Australia
Mr D Woods, BA Hons
Mrs N Matthias, BEd
Mr J Brooker, BA London, PGCE
Mr R Garnsworthy, BE Australia
Miss S Hardman, BSc Bangor
Mrs H Vanstone, BSA Dip
Mr M Rawle
Miss C Pitt
Mrs E Spivey, BA Exeter
Mr E Dower
Miss S Walls, BEd

Religious Studies:
*Mr S D Loxton, PhD Seattle, BEd Sussex, MPhil Hull
Revd Rebecca Ayers-Harris, BA Nottingham, Dip Theology, PGCE
Mrs S Hammond, BEd Wellington, NZ
Mrs H Bajorat, BA Manchester, PGCE
Mrs M Tillyer, BA, PGCE

EAL and Learning Support:
Ms S Aristotlous, MEd, TEFL
Ms R Standish, CELTA
Mrs J Trew

Sciences:
*Mr D Thompson, BSc Hons Exeter, PGCE
Mr A Angelosanto, BSc, PGCE
Mrs K Smith, BSc Manchester, PGCE
Miss P Abbott, BSc, Southampton
Mr M Crabtree, BSc, LRPS, PGCE
Mrs F Clapp, MBA, BSc London, PGCE
Miss R Brown, BSc London, PGCE
Mrs A Cochrane, BSc Nottingham
Dr J Hopper, BSc Birmingham, PhD London, PGCE
Mrs J Massey, BA, MA
Miss C Howell Evans, BSc Hons, PGCE

Sanatorium Sister: Mrs A Watson, RGN
Registrar: Mrs J Hinks
Librarian and Learning Resource Manager: Miss J Noble, BA Hons
Head of Higher Education and Careers: Mrs P Utting, BA Hons Portsmouth
Headmistress's PA: Mrs J Dart, BSc
Outdoor Activities Instructor: Mr T Fremlin, BA York, MA

Sherborne School

Abbey Road, Sherborne, Dorset DT9 3AP
Tel: 01935 812249
          01935 810403 (Admissions)
Fax: 01935 810426
email: admissions@sherborne.org
website: www.sherborne.org

Royal Arms of Edward VI: *Dieu et mon droit.*

The origins of Sherborne School date back to the eighth century, when a tradition of education at Sherborne was begun by St Aldhelm. The School was linked with the Benedictine Abbey, the earliest known Master was Thomas Copeland in 1437. Edward VI refounded the School in 1550. The present School stands on land which once belonged to the Monastery. The Library, Chapel, and Headmaster's offices which adjoin the Abbey Church, are modifications of the original buildings of the Abbey.

Situation. The School lies in the attractive Abbey town of Sherborne. By train, Salisbury is forty minutes away, London and Heathrow two hours.

Organisation. There are about 520 boarders and 40 day boys, accommodated in eight houses, all of which are within easy walking distance of the main school.

Admission. Entry is either at 13+ (Year 9) or 16+ (Sixth Form) with a small number of places available at 14+ (Year 10) Assessment days take place for 13+ entry when pupils are in year 7. Pupils may then sit scholarship examinations or Common Entrance in year 8. Other entrance tests take place throughout the year of enrolment.

Parents who would like to enter their sons for the School or have any queries, should contact the Director of Admissions.

Visits. Visits can be arranged at any time of the year by contacting the Admissions Office, Tel: 01935 810403.

Scholarships and Exhibitions. Sherborne offers a wide range of scholarships and exhibitions at 13+ entry: Academic (February); Music (January); Art, Design & Technology, Drama, Sport (February), All Rounder (February). Sixth Form Academic and Sports Exhibitions are also offered annually.

Open Scholarships: For 13+ entry, a number of Scholarships of up to 20% of fees (the top scholarship being the Alexander Ross Wallace Scholarship) and up to eight Exhibitions of up to 10% of fees may be awarded. In awarding one of these Exhibitions regard will be paid to special proficiency in a particular subject.

In addition Awards are available to those who are able to demonstrate outstanding ability in one of the following areas: Art, Design & Technology, Music, Drama and Sport.

A number of Music Awards are available at 13+. In addition one Marion Packer Scholarship of £600 pa for an outstanding performance on the piano may be offered. Those given Awards receive free instrumental tuition.

A number of all-rounder awards are available for pupils showing talent and passion across a range of disciplines.

Closed Awards: Raban Exhibition of 10% of fees for the sons of serving or ex-service officers; a Nutting Exhibition of 10% of fees for sons of RN Officers.

The maximum value of any award is 20% of the fees but this may be supplemented by bursarial assistance in cases of financial need.

Further details of all awards are available from the Director of Admissions.

Sixth Form Entry. Places are available for boys who wish to join the Sixth Form to study A Levels for two years. Scholarship and entrance examinations take place by arrangement with the Director of Admissions. There are up to two scholarships offered annually. Also available, for good A Level candidates, is the Arkwright Scholarship for Technology. Offers of Sixth Form places are dependent on satisfactory performance in GCSE examinations.

Curriculum. All pupils follow a broadly based curriculum for their first three years to GCSE. In the Sixth Form boys study at least three A Levels drawn from a wide choice of available courses. There is also a diverse and stretching enrichment programme as a part of the compulsory curriculum. Opportunities for research projects are available to broaden the scope of pupils' studies. Some of the courses for A Level are run jointly with Sherborne Girls.

Careers and Universities. The Careers Department has an enviable reputation. Boys experience work shadowing programmes in the fifth and lower sixth forms – these are followed by careers conventions, university visits, parents' forums and lessons in interview techniques. There is an encyclopaedic, fully computerised Careers Room with regularly updated contacts with those at university and at work. The department has visited all universities and places of higher education. Virtually all leavers go on to university.

Pastoral Care. The boys in each house are in the care of a Housemaster and his wife, a resident tutor and a resident matron. In addition a team of tutors assists the Housemaster in the running of the House and boys have many avenues of support and advice available to them. The School Chaplain also plays a major role and will talk with a boy whenever required. A School Counsellor is available.

Tutor. Each boy has a personal Tutor who not only monitors his academic progress but provides a useful contact point for parents.

Religion. The weekly pattern of Christian services in the school Chapel or Sherborne Abbey underpin the spiritual rhythm of the school. There is a wide variety of voluntary Christian groups and services including a Friday night candlelit Eucharist which is well attended. Boys can be prepared for Confirmation into the Church of England and the Roman Catholic Church. Theology is taught throughout the school and boys can opt for a GCSE Religious Studies course and a Philosophy and Ethics A Level course.

Community Service. Boys take part in a busy programme aimed at encouraging a sense of responsibility towards the local community. Entertainment, fundraising, clubs and assistance are organised for the young and elderly in and around Sherborne.

Art. The Art School is a dynamic and highly successful department achieving outstanding academic results at all levels. The core disciplines are based around the study of Fine Art, which enables students to approach a broad curriculum encompassing an eclectic mix of approaches such as painting, photography, 3D, digital media, printing and performance.

Design and Technology. In recent years the Design and Technology Department has been through a programme of complete refurbishment. The subject is taught from year nine right through to A Level and pupils can go on to higher education courses in Product and Aeronautical Design, Architecture and Engineering. The department has developed links with local industries where pupils can see CAD/CAM production, commercial furniture design and precision casting in process. It runs afternoon activities and is open on both Saturdays and Sundays.

Music. There is a strong music tradition in the School – over 400 music lessons take place every week. There are two full orchestras, various chamber music groups, many different types of jazz band, a brass group, a swing band, Chapel choir and a choral society, not to mention rock bands. Many of these groups tour both home and abroad. Numerous concerts, recitals and musical productions are held throughout the year. Lunch time concerts take place every Friday. Regular subscription concerts are given by visiting professional musicians.

Drama. Drama productions of all kinds are a major feature of school life, from large scale musicals to classical drama, substantial modern works and fringe performances, many staged with Sherborne Girls. The sophisticated technical resources of the Powell Theatre attract programmes from professional touring companies. The newly instated, state-of-the-art drama studios underpin the school's ambition for this important part of the pupils' learning.

Information Technology. The school has a fast wireless network that is available throughout the school, including in boarding houses. Safe filtering systems and time restrictions are in place to protect pupils. Pupils are encouraged to connect their own devices to the network, but there are also a large number of fixed terminal computers, including six major computer suites around the school. The school is embracing new technologies and runs a sophisticated Virtual Learning Environment to support pupils' learning away from the classroom.

Sports. There are over fifty acres of sports fields, where, at any one time, seventeen various games or matches can take place. Other facilities include two AstroTurf pitches, twenty tennis courts, Rugby fives courts and a shooting range. Within the School's sports centre there is a sports hall, a twenty-five metre swimming pool, a fitness suite and squash courts. A wide variety of sports and activities are offered including athletics, badminton, basketball, canoeing, cricket, cross-country, fencing, fives, golf, hockey, polo, riding, rugby, sailing, shooting, soccer, sub-aqua, swimming and tennis.

Societies and Activities. In addition to a full sporting, music and drama programme, numerous academic societies meet regularly throughout the term. Other activities and clubs take place on Wednesday afternoons and whenever time allows. They include: bridge, chess, computing, debating, photography, dining, life drawing, cooking for university, film making, community service, speech and drama and United Nations.

The school has a strong tradition of outdoor education and, in addition to The Duke of Edinburgh's Award scheme, there are walking, climbing, kayaking and sailing trips. These are local or further afield in Scotland, the Lake District, Wales, Exmoor, Dartmoor and occasionally abroad. Boys also take part in the annual Ten Tors Challenge.

Membership of the Combined Cadet Force is voluntary and the Army, Royal Navy and Royal Marine sections attract about 150 boys each year. A large number of trips and camps are arranged during the term time and the holidays.

Old Shirburnian Society. Mr John Harden, Secretary, tel: 01935 810557, email: OSS@sherborne.org.

Girls' Schools. There is close liaison with the neighbouring girls' schools, which allows us to offer many of the real benefits of co-education with all the advantages of a single-sex secondary education. As well as the Joint Sixth Form academic courses with Sherborne Girls, drama, music and social activities are arranged throughout the year.

Fees per term (2016–2017). Boarders: £11,675; Day Boys: £9,450.

Charitable status. Sherborne School is a Registered Charity, number 1081228, and a Company Limited by Guarantee, registered in England and Wales, number 4002575. Its aim and objectives are to supply a liberal education in accordance with the principles of the Church of England.

Governors of the School:

Chairman: R S Fidgen Esq, FRICS
Vice-Chairman: Major General P A J Cordingley, DSO, DSc

Ex officio:
The Representative of Her Majesty's Lord Lieutenant for the County of Dorset, A Campbell Esq
The Vicar of Sherborne, The Revd Canon E J Woods, DL, MA

Co-opted:

Dr S E Ball, BM, MRCPsych
Mrs I Burke, MB BS, MRCGP
A Charlton Esq, CMG, CVO
Mrs V Cotter, LLB Hons, LLM
M L French Esq, FCA
Professor R Hodder-Williams, MA, FRSA
G A Hudson Esq
R A L Leach Esq, MA
G Marsh Esq, MA, Cert Ed
R-J Temmink Esq, MA, BL, FCIArb
The Revd Canon K Willkinson, BA, FRSA
Mrs G Staley, BSc, MSc, CMIOSH
Mrs A Lane, BA, FCA

Staff Nominated: M Whittell Esq

Bursar and Clerk to the Governors: Mrs L Robins, BSc, MRCIS

Headmaster: D A Luckett, BA, DPhil, FRSA, FHA

Usher (*Senior Deputy*): R A Barlow, BSc, FRSA, CMath, FIMA
Deputy Head (*Academic*): T W Filtness, BA, MA, PhD
Deputy Head (*Pastoral*): M I Jamieson, BA

Housemasters:
Abbey House: M J McGinty, AKC, BA, MSc (Tel: 01935 812087)
Abbeylands: S J Clayton, CertEd & Mrs VA Clayton, BA, MCLIP (Tel: 01935 812082)
The Digby: M J Brooke, MA (Tel: 01935 810170)
The Green: A M Hatch, BA (Tel: 01935 810440)
Harper House: J J B Wadham, BSc, PhD (Tel: 01935 812128)
Lyon House: B P Sunderland, BEng (Tel: 01935 812079)
School House: K Jackson, BA (Tel: 01935 813248)
Wallace House: G T W Robinson, BA (Tel: 01935 813334)

Director of Admissions: Mrs Vanessa Hicks
Head of Admissions: Mrs J Gilbert
Admissions Manager: Mrs D Lewis

Staff:
* Head of Department/Subject

Art:
*J E Wright, BA, MA
Mrs E S Drake, BA
M Bone, BA

Ms B Darnley, BA
J Donnelly

Biology:
*J-P A Manning, BSc, PhD, MEd
D J Ridgway, Bsc
T W Filtness, BA, MA, PhD
G R Harwood, BSc
Miss E L Southall, BSc, MSc
J J B Wadham, BSc, PhD

Chemistry:
*W E Buckley, BSc
Miss S L Cummings, BSc, MSc, BA
C G B Hamon, PhD, CCSci, CChem, MRSC
N C Scorer, MChem
D A Watson, BSc

Classics:
*S A Heath, BA
Miss G A Free, MA
P Rogerson, MA (*Head of Careers*)
S L Tremewan, BA, PhD

Design and Technology:
*P R Chillingworth, BA
J Salisbury, BEd

Drama:
*I C C Reade, BA
Mrs V A Clayton, BA, MCLIP

Economics and Business Studies:
*R T B Harris, BA, MBA
A R Duncan, BA
M C Ewart-Smith, MBA, CEng
C M O'Donnell, BA
Mrs S Salmon, BA, MA

English:
*Mrs R E C de Pelet, MA
M J Brooke, MA
Miss H L Cant, BA
M P O'Connor, BA, Cert SpLD
T W Payne, BA
G T W Robinson, BA
J L Winter, MA

Geography:
*T R J Mason, BSc
A M Hatch, BA
Miss K L Millar, BA
M Ollis, BA
J P A Wilson, BSc

Government and Politics:
*R C Le Poidevin, MA, MA, MSc
M J McGinty, AKC, BA, MSc

History
*G D R Reynolds, MA
J P Crouch, BA
P S Francis, MA
M I Jamieson, BA

B L Wild, MA, PhD

Learning Support:
*Mrs S G Collis, BA
Mrs E J H Ashton, BBA
Mrs C M Dillow, BA
Mrs L J McMillan, BSc
M P O'Connor, BA,
    CertSpLD
Mrs S M L Reade, BSc

Mathematics:
*S C Lim, MSc
R A Barlow, BSc, FRSA,
    FinstM
Miss A E R Civardi, BSc
T A J Dawson, BSc, Dip
    Stats, MA
N A Henderson, BSc, MBA
Mrs L J McMillan, BSc
S K Mertens, BA, MA,
    MSc, PhD
A C Morgan, BSc, MSc,
    FRSA
P C D Spencer, BSC
Miss C M Standen, MA,
    ACA
B P Sunderland, BEng
Mrs C L Tatham, BSc

Modern Languages:
*Mrs J R Thurman, BA
Miss A Bailon Artal, MA
    Hons
S K Byrne, BA
D B Cameron, MA
W E Chadwick, BA,
    DipLaw
R Dillow, BA, MA
Mrs C E Greenrod, BA,
    Cert TEFL
A D Nurton, BA
A R Oates, BA, MLitt
    (*French*)

Medical Officers:
C P Cleaver, MB, ChB, MRCGP
K Dixon, MB BS, MRCGP, DFFP
I A Latham, MB BS, MRCP, DFFP

Nurse Manager: Mrs M Hutchings, RGN
Sports and Uniform Shop: Mrs M Reade

T J Scott, BA
Mrs J M Slade, BA

Music:
*J E C Henderson, MA
B J Davey, GRSM, LRAM
Miss S J Drury, GRSM,
    ARCM
M Lehnert, BA, MMus

Physical Education:
*R P McGuire, BA, MPhil,
    PhD
S J Clayton, Cert Ed PE,
    Dip Sp Psy
D A R Guy, BA (*Director
    of Sport*)
D N Muckalt, BSc (*Deputy
    Director of Sport*)
M Pardoe
C Roberts
C Smith, BA

Physics:
*M C Thurman, BSc
J J Kimber, BSc
J S Mitchell, BSc
D J Murray, BSC
J G Willetts, BA, CPhys,
    MInstP, MBCS

PSHE:
*R C Le Poidevin, MA,
    MA, MSc

Theology:
*J A Crawford, MA
Revd L R F Collins, BD,
    AKC, MTh (*Chaplain*)
K G Jackson, BA
Revd N J Mercer, BD,
    LLM, MTh
H F Tatham, BA, MA
P M Ward, BA

Shiplake College

Henley-on-Thames, Oxon RG9 4BW

Tel: 0118 940 2455
email: info@shiplake.org.uk
website: www.shiplake.org.uk
Twitter: @ShiplakeCollege
Facebook: @shiplakecollege

Motto: '*Exemplum docet*' (Example teaches)

Shiplake College is an independent boarding and day school for boys aged 11 to 18 and girls aged 16 to 18. Situated in 45 acres of beautiful Oxfordshire countryside near Henley-on-Thames, we offer an outstanding education based on small class sizes, excellent facilities and dedicated teaching staff. Shiplake has a wholly inclusive environment spanning all areas of College life.

Ethos. Whilst Shiplake College has evolved and moved forward since its founding in 1959, many principles remain the same. We ensure that every pupil is challenged and supported according to their need and ability, providing an education that is tailored to the individual. We firmly believe that in addition to a solid academic grounding, sporting, social and cultural achievements are vital to a pupil's long-term development. Shiplake offers a wide range of challenging enrichment activities to ensure an all-round education.

Academic. We aim to admit a well-balanced intake of pupils with a variety of skills and talents. Pupils are selected on his or her potential to make the most of the opportunities that Shiplake can offer and the value we can add to their education. We are proud of our superb value-added results. At Shiplake, teaching and learning concentrates on delivering excellent teaching through small classes and individual attention with a supportive but stimulating environment. Our teaching is delivered through a mixture of conventional teaching and inspirational multi-sensory methods to provide for a range of learning styles.

Pastoral Care. Shiplake College is renowned for delivering outstanding pastoral care – a reputation that has been built and maintained over a sustained period of time, largely due to the belief in a holistic approach to education. Houses are a huge part of the Shiplake community, creating a sense of togetherness and spirit. Boys joining at 11+ enter the Lower School which houses Year 7 and 8. From Year 9 all pupils become a member of one of the five houses: Burr, Skipwith, Welsh, Everett or Orchard. Both day and boarding girls join Gilson House, the purpose-built girls' house, but are attached to one of the boys' houses for social purposes, duties and inter-house competitions. The Upper Sixth boys enjoy the separate facilities of College House which helps establish independence before the move to university or a career.

Each house is run by a Housemaster who is supported by a strong team of staff including the House Matron, House Tutor, Visiting Tutors, the Medical Staff and the Chaplain. The houses provide excellent support for the pupils in addition to ensuring a comfortable, homely environment for pupils to study or relax. There is a strong house spirit in evidence with competitions organised for arts, games and academic progress.

Knowing our pupils well enables us to ensure that they get the best from their education at Shiplake. We know that every pupil is different and we aim to tailor the support and guidance they receive to suit their individual needs.

As a Christian School there is an extensive programme of worship, very often provided in the neighbouring Parish Church. The Chaplain, whose role is purely pastoral, is always available to any member of the College community. Shiplake also welcomes pupils of other faiths.

Boarding. Boarding is an integral part of life at Shiplake. Full, weekly, flexi boarding and overnight stays (all available from Year 7) allow pupils to fully benefit from all the academic and co-curricular opportunities that we offer. 150 weekly and full boarders enjoy a busy weekend and evening programme, which covers a mixture of cultural, social and sporting trips and activities. International pupils, including a balance of British and non-British students resident abroad, represent approximately 5% of the current school population.

Location. The College is situated in 45 acres of beautiful Oxfordshire countryside, just two miles upstream of the world famous Henley Royal Regatta town of Henley-on-Thames.

Although pupils love the acres of sports pitches and the country trails, parents appreciate the fact that Shiplake is conveniently placed for access to the M4 and M40 and the railway stations at Henley and Reading. This idyllic countryside location is just an hour from London and within easy reach of Heathrow and Gatwick airports.

Facilities. Shiplake House, built in 1889 as a family home, is at the heart of the school. Pupils and staff take their main meals in the wood-panelled Great Hall. The College is fortunate to have the use of the twelfth-century Parish Church for assemblies and worship.

In addition to the main school buildings, Shiplake boasts a range of facilities including the innovative 'Thinking Space', Lecture Theatre, Recording Studio, Tithe Barn Theatre, Sports Hall, Fitness Suite and award-winning Sports Fields. The boathouses are a short walk from the main buildings, allowing direct access to the Thames. The College has state-of-the-art ICT and computing facilities, including site-wide Wi-Fi, available to all pupils.

Academic Structure. Boys entering the College in Year 7 follow the specially designed curriculum for Years 7 and 8 before moving on to the Upper School. In the Upper School they will enjoy the broad and balanced Year 9 curriculum which provides a strong foundation for GCSE. Following the A Level forms, Sixth Form pupils now select three subjects from a choice of twenty-two.

Learning Development. Shiplake has a dedicated Learning Development Department to provide tailored additional help for both those who are academically gifted and those who find certain subject areas difficult to access. The purpose-built Department is situated in the revolutionary John Turner Building, and provides a first-class environment for pupils to receive additional support, to improve pupils' confidence and self-esteem and equip them with the necessary skills. We are a school with small class sizes and our teachers are committed to providing individual attention for all abilities. Pupils are able to approach their subject teachers for additional support whenever necessary.

Sport. Sport is an integral part of life at Shiplake College. Our extensive site on the banks of the River Thames makes Shiplake an ideal location for pupils who love sport. The College has an excellent sporting reputation and most pupils take part in a sporting activity every day. The College enjoys direct access to the river and boathouses, hockey, cricket and rugby pitches, tennis courts, squash courts and an outdoor swimming pool. The sports hall offers a variety of indoor sports, a weight-training gym and a fitness room.

Almost all boys play rugby in the autumn term. In the spring term boys play hockey, football or row, and in the summer term there is the choice of cricket, tennis or rowing. The girls enjoy hockey, netball and rounders as part of a mixed programme of sports and activities using the sporting facilities available. Basketball, badminton, squash, judo, cross-country running and athletics provide additional activities to develop skills and fitness.

For a small school, Shiplake has a remarkable number of crews and teams taking part in events and competitions with national success. There have been a number of overseas tours involving the rugby, cricket, hockey and rowing clubs.

Music, Art and Drama. The College has a thriving mixture of Arts activities and performances and all pupils are encouraged to enjoy the Arts. The annual House Music Competition ensures that every pupil in the school is involved in preparing for a performance and every term there is at least one concert for pupils to demonstrate the progress they have made. The Drama Department provides a range of opportunities for the theatrically inclined, to explore and experiment with the subject beyond the constraints of the curriculum.

Activities. Two afternoons are dedicated to a Co-Curricular programme where pupils choose from a wide range of activities including art, ballroom dancing, cookery, debating, Japanese, log-chopping and canoeing. The College has a thriving Combined Cadet Force with Air Force, Army and Navy sections. Pupils take part in community service activities and the school has links to a Kenyan School for which fundraising activities are regularly undertaken. The College also runs a Duke of Edinburgh's Award scheme with a number of pupils each year collecting Gold Awards. In addition there are drama productions, debates and music recitals.

Careers. There is an experienced Careers Adviser and particular attention is paid to the choice of university and career from Year 11 onwards. The School is a member of ISCO.

Admission. The Registrar is the first point of contact for all admissions enquiries. Boys are admitted at 11+ into Year 7 and at 13+ into Year 9. There is an intake into the Sixth Form for boys and girls. Places are offered following an assessment day. Please contact the Registrar for further details. Occasional places arise in other years.

Scholarships. Means-tested scholarships and bursaries are offered for academic excellence and to outstanding sportsmen, artists, actors or musicians at Year 7, Year 9 and in the Sixth Form.

Fees per term (2016–2017). Full Boarders £10,300; Weekly Boarders: Years 9–13 (6 nights) £9,990, Years 7 & 8 (4 nights) £7,700; Flexi-Boarding (2 nights) Years 9–13: £7,950, Years 7 & 8 £6,550; Day: Years 7 & 8 £5,550, Years 9–13 £6,950.

Alumni. The Old Viking Society has an annual programme of events including sports fixtures and a formal dinner. The Society produces an annual magazine for Old Vikings, as well as frequent newsletters.

Charitable status. Shiplake College is a Registered Charity, number 309651. It exists to provide education for children.

Governing Body:
Chairman: The Rt Hon T J C Eggar
Vice-Chairman: M G E Mackenzie-Charrington
A Ashton
R Dempster
Mrs M Carey-Elms
C Eve
J S Gordon
J R B Hobbs
I Howell
R C Lester
The Hon Sir William McAlpine
Lady Phillimore
Mrs S J Ryan
D W Tanner
J Welsh

Headmaster: A G S Davies

Senior Staff:
Bursar and Clerk to the Governors: J N Walne
Deputy Headmaster (*Academic*): Dr G Hughes
Deputy Headmaster (*Pastoral*): N J Brown
Assistant Head (*Sixth Form*): R Curtis
Assistant Head (*Academic Studies*): P Jones
Assistant Head (*Co-Curricular*): A Hunt
Director of Sport: D Traynor
Director of Learning Development: Mrs A Higgins

Housemasters:
Miss S G Andrew (*Gilson*)
T M Armstrong (*Everett*)
R Curtis (*College*)
A D Dix (*Senior Housemaster and Burr*)
A P R Duncan (*Skipwith*)
J Howorth (*Welsh*)
Mrs A Higgins (*Lower School*)
A Mallins (*Orchard*)

Chaplain: The Revd S Cousins

Shrewsbury School

The Schools, Shrewsbury, Shropshire SY3 7BA

Tel:	01743 280500 (Switchboard)
	01743 280525 (Headmaster)
	01743 280820 (Bursar)
	01743 280552 (Director of Admissions)
Fax:	01743 243107 (Reception)
	01743 280559 (Director of Admissions)
email:	admissions@shrewsbury.org.uk
website:	www.shrewsbury.org.uk

Motto: '*Intus si recte, ne labora*'

Shrewsbury School was founded by King Edward VI in 1552 and augmented by Queen Elizabeth in 1571. In 1882 it moved from the centre of the town to its present site overlooking the town and the River Severn.

Number in School. There are 789 pupils in the School (633 boarding and 156 day).

Admission. Most admissions are in September. Girls and boys are admitted at 13 or (direct to the Sixth Form) at 16. Registration forms and other information can be obtained from the Admissions Office. The registration fee, which is non-returnable, is £100.

Entry at 13: Pupils usually take the Common Entrance Examination or the Scholarship Examination in the term preceding that in which they wish to come. The School has its own entrance test for pupils who have not followed the Common Entrance syllabus.

Sixth Form Entry: Direct entry into the Sixth Form depends on examination at Shrewsbury, an interview, and a favourable report from the applicant's present school.

Scholarships. Shrewsbury School has had a tradition, since its founding Charter in 1552, of making generous scholarship awards. Scholarships fall into various categories – Academic, Music, Art, Drama, Design & Technology, Sport and All-Rounder. Awards are made either to pupils under the age of 14 joining the school in the Third Form, or to those entering the school at Sixth Form level.

Buildings. The school operates a rolling programme of refurbishment for all boarding houses. Similarly, large-scale refurbishment of the teaching accommodation is currently under way. All classrooms are professionally equipped to a very high standard. A Music School, including an auditorium and a large ensemble room, was opened in February 2001, a cricket academy and a new house (now accommodating day and boarding girls) opened in 2006, a new swimming pool opened in 2007, a new sixth form centre was completed in 2008, and two further houses for girls opened in September 2011 and September 2014 respectively. A new, 19-classroom academic block opened in October 2015.

The Moser Library houses the School Library, the Moser collection of watercolours, and the Ancient Library, which contains medieval manuscripts and early printed books.

Courses of Study. All pupils follow a general course as far as GCSE (or IGCSE) examinations. In the Sixth Form, pupils study either three or four subjects leading to A Level (or Pre-U) qualifications. Many also complete an Extended Project or follow the Pre-U Global Perspectives course.

Games. Rowing, Cricket, Association Football, Swimming, Lacrosse, Hockey, Netball, Cross-Country, Eton Fives and Rugby. The School has its own indoor Swimming Pool, Gymnasium, Multi-gym, Miniature Rifle Range, all-weather playing surface, Tennis Courts, Squash Courts and Fives Courts. The River Severn flows just below the Main School Building and the Boat House is within the School grounds.

Activities. Pupils are offered a considerable range of outdoor activities via the Combined Cadet Force, leadership courses and the Duke of Edinburgh's Award Scheme. The programme of activities and opportunities continues to broaden as a pupil moves up the School.

Art and Design. Art and Design are taught to all pupils in their first year. For those not doing GCSE or A Level courses they subsequently become activities followed mainly, but not exclusively, out of school hours. The Art and CDT centres are available seven days a week. The CDT department offers the chance of advanced design work and of creative work in a variety of materials.

Societies. These range from Literary, Political, Debating, Drama and Language societies to those catering for practical skills. Hillwalkers and Mountaineers make use of the unspoilt country on the doorstep and of the Welsh hills.

Music. Teaching is available in any orchestral instrument, as well as the Piano and Organ. The charge for this is £22.94 per 40 minute lesson for all instruments. Regular Choral, Orchestral and Chamber Concerts both at the school and elsewhere (e.g. St John's, Smith Square; Birmingham Town Hall) are given by the pupils. In addition concerts are given during the winter months by distinguished visiting artists.

Drama. Drama is a major feature of school life, with two school plays and a range of house plays every year, together with regular accolades at the Edinburgh Fringe.

Field Study Centre. Shrewsbury owns a farmhouse in Snowdonia, which is used at weekends throughout the year as a base for expeditions.

Careers. There is a full-time Careers Fellow and a Higher Education Adviser. Pupils receive a programme of Careers guidance throughout the school.

Community Service. In association with other schools in the town, pupils play an active part in caring for the old and needy in the Shrewsbury area.

Shrewsbury House. Founded in Liverpool as a Club for boys in 1903, it was re-built as a Community Centre in association with the Local Authority and the Diocese in 1974. There is residential accommodation in the Centre and groups of pupils from the School have the opportunity to go there on study courses.

Shrewsbury International School. The school has close links with Shrewsbury International School in Bangkok. Teaching and pupil exchanges take place between the two schools, and Governors of Shrewsbury School serve on the board of management of the International School.

Fees per term (2016–2017). Boarders: £11,250, including tuition, board and ordinary School expenses. There are no other obligatory extras, apart from stationery. Day Pupils: £7,875.

Application for reduced fees may be made to the Governors through the Headmaster.

Old Pupils' Society. Most pupils leaving the school join the Salopian Club, The Schools, Shrewsbury SY3 7BA; email: oldsalopian@shrewsbury.org.uk.

Charitable status. Shrewsbury School is a Registered Charity, number 528413. It exists to provide secondary education.

Governing Body:

Chairman: M H Collins
Vice-Chair: Mrs Lyndsey O'Loughlin, LLB
S R Baker, BSc, FCA, CF
T H Biggins, MA
R Burbidge, OBE, BA, DL
J R Clark, MA
Prof C Dobson, FRS
Mrs D Flint, DL
Dr Fiona Hay, MA, BM, BCh, DRCOG, MRCGP, DFFP
T H P Haynes, MA
Mrs C Howarth, LLB
W R O Hunter, QC

Prof E W Jones, OBE, BSc Hons, PhD, FRAgS
R J Kendall, BSc
D Kerr, BSc, MRICS
Prof A J McCarthy, BSc, PhD
Cllr C M Motley, BA
Prof M R E Proctor, FRS, FIMA
P StJ Worth, FCA

Headmaster: **M Turner**, MA

Bursar and Clerk to the Governors: M J Ware, MA, ACA
Second Master: M J Tonks, BA
Senior Master and Director of Admissions: M J Cropper, MA
Deputy Head (Academic): M H Walters, MA
Deputy Head (Pastoral): Ms A R Peak, BA
Deputy Head (Co-Curricular): P J Middleton, BA
Director of Teaching & Learning: S H Cowper, MA
Director of Shrewsbury School Foundation: J G E Rolfe

Assistant Masters/Mistresses:
* *Head of Faculty*
† *Housemaster/Housemistress*

Mrs R W Adams, BEc, BEd
Revd A C V Aldous, BA (*Chaplain*)
J C Armstrong, BA (**Mathematics*)
J Balcombe, BSc
Mrs K H Balcombe, BEd, OCR Cert SpLD (**Learning Support*)
A S Barnard, BA (†*Port Hill – day boys*)
M W D Barrett, BSc (†*Rigg's Hall*)
R Barrett, MSc, PhD
G StJ F Bell, BA
H R D Besterman, MA (†*School House*)
M C Bird, BA
Mrs N J Bradburne, BA (*Head of Girls' Games*)
A D Briggs, BSc, PhD (**Science*)
Miss H R Brown, MA (**Director of Drama*)
Miss N M Buckley, BA
Miss J M M Burge, BSc
J R Burke, BSc
R A J Case, BSc, PhD (†*Radbrook – day boys*)
M D H Clark, MA
C E Cook, MA
S K P Cooley, MEng
T A C Corbett, BSc (**Chemistry*)
A Dalton, BA (**Philosophy & Theology*)
N P David, BSc
Mrs L J Drew, BA
M S Elliot, MA, PhD
H A S M Exham, BSc
R T Fitton, MEng
P G Fitzgerald, MA (**Classics*)
Mrs S Fletcher, BSc
T R Foulger, BSc, PhD
S A A Fox, BA
J R Fraser-Andrews, MA, MMus
J Gabbitas, MA
P D Graham, BSc
M H Hansen, BSc
M J Harding, BA
I P Haworth, MA
Miss E C Higgins, BA
R T Hudson, MA (†*Churchill's Hall*)
W A Hughes, BA (†*Ridgemount*)
A T Hundermark, BSc (**Director of Rowing*)
M D B Johnson, BSc, BA (†*Oldham's Hall*)
D M Joyce, Dip RCM, ARCM
P A Kaye, BEng (**Educational ICT*)
C W Kealy, BComm (**Business Studies*)
Mrs E J Kelly, BA
M A Kirk, BSc (**Physics*)

Mrs V L Kirk, BSc
P H Lapage, BA
Mrs S G Latcham, BA
D A Law, BA, MA, PhD
Mrs K Leslie, BA (**English*)
K M Lloyd, BA (**DT*)
J V Lucas, LLB
H G Mackridge, MA (**History*)
A E Mason, BA, MMus
Mrs J A Matthews, BSc
P A Merricks-Murgatroyd, BA (**Economics*)
Miss S I Milanova, BA
J F Moore, BA, LRAM (**Music*)
T S Morgan, BSc, PhD (**Biology*)
R H Morris, BEd
A J Murfin, BSc (**Director of Sport*)
D A G Nicholas, BA (†*Severn Hill*)
Mrs D B Nightingale, BMus, LTCL, ACCEG (*Higher Education Adviser*)
C L O'Rooke, MA
C W Oakley, MMath, DPhil
J L Pattenden, MA, DPhil
P Pattenden, MA, DPhil, CPhys, MInstP (†*Moser's Hall*)
H R W Peach, BA (**German*)
T P Percival, MA
D Portier, BA, MA
A P Pridgeon
Mrs N M Pritchard, BA (†*Mary Sidney Hall*)
F O L Reid, MA
W R Reynolds, BSc
D M Roberts, BSc, MEd
Miss C E Rule, BSc
O J Russell, MPhil (**Geography*)
C M Samworth, BSc, PhD
Mrs E L Sandhu, BA
Miss A Schmaller, BA
M Schofield, BSc
Mrs S L M Shantry, BSc
Mrs R Shawe-Taylor, BA, MA (**Art*)
J A Sheppe, MPhil
W M Simper, BSc
Miss E J Stokes, BA
Mrs L R Temple, BA
Miss L E Walker, BSc
T D J Warburg, MA
Miss R B Weatherstone, BA
N J Welch, BSc
Mrs K M Weston, MSc (†*Emma Darwin Hall*)
T C Whitehead, BA (**French*)
S P Wilderspin (*Master i/c Football*)
Mrs C H L Wilson, BA (†*The Grove*)
R M Wilson, MEng Hons
Miss R Witcombe, BSc
Miss G Y Y Woo, MSc
D M Wray, MA
M P J Wright, BA (†*Ingram's Hall*)
Mrs P A Wright, BA, BEd (**Spanish*)

Careers Fellow: Mrs C M Dry, BA Nottingham

Visiting French Fellow: Miss C Piquard, MA Université de Montesquieu, Bordeaux IV

Visiting Hispanic Fellow: Miss M L Fernandez, BA Univ Nac de Rosario, Argentina

School Doctors:
The General Practitioner Team, Mytton Oak Surgery, Racecourse Lane, Shrewsbury

Dental Adviser: R J Gatenby, BDS, DGDP, RCS

Headmaster's Personal Assistant: Mrs E J Gibbs

Silcoates School

Wrenthorpe, Wakefield, West Yorkshire WF2 0PD

Tel: 01924 291614
email: head@silcoates.org.uk
website: www.silcoates.org.uk

Motto: '*Clarior ex ignibus*'

Founded in 1820 and retaining its links to the United Reformed Church, Silcoates School is set in 50 acres of grounds in Wrenthorpe, near Wakefield. It offers an all-through, fully co-educational experience for children from age 3 to 18. The Pre-School is for 3 year olds, the Junior School for 4 to 11 year olds and the Senior School for 11 to 18 year olds, which includes its own distinctive Sixth Form. It seeks to provide an all-round education with an academic edge.

Admission. There are 610 pupils at Silcoates. Boys and girls are admitted to the Pre-School at 3, the Junior School from the age of 4 and the Senior School from the age of 11. Places are available for girls and boys wishing to study for A Level in the Sixth Form.

Entrance Assessments for the Senior School take place in January for admission the following September. Pre-School and Junior School admissions take place throughout the year.

Curriculum. Recent inspection reports have been highly complimentary about the school's academic performance. Nearly all pupils sit a minimum of 9 GCSEs and 3 A Levels, and the vast majority go on to degree courses. There is great flexibility of subject choice at GCSE and A Level. Small class sizes and excellent facilities create a positive atmosphere for learning. Value added scores are good.

Games and Activities. Sport, music, art and drama all flourish at Silcoates. The school has an excellent record of individual and collective achievement in all of its extra-curricular activities. The outstanding sports facilities include an indoor pool, an astroturf, netball and tennis courts, and extensive sports pitches. There is a well-equipped Music School. Our very successful Duke of Edinburgh's Award programme makes extensive use of various venues in the north of England.

Pastoral Care and Careers Guidance. With a generous pupil : personal tutor ratio, the quality of pastoral care is first class. We provide a full programme of careers advice and guidance for university entrance.

Fees per term (2016–2017). Senior School: £4,420; Junior School: £2,360–£3,490.

Scholarships and Bursaries. Academic and All-Rounder Scholarships are offered at 11+ and above; Sixth Form entrants are eligible for these awards. Means-tested Bursaries are available.

Charitable status. Silcoates School is a Registered Charity, number 1158796.

Board of Governors:

Chairman: Mrs Mary Chippendale, BSc
Vice-Chairman: Mr John Lane, LLB, AKC, TEP

Mrs Rachel Copley
Mrs Dianne Elson, CertEd, Dip PE
Dr Moira Gallagher, MBE
Ms Alison Malecki-Ketchell, MSc
Revd Steven Knapton, MA
Mrs Sue Lee, BPharm, MRPharmS
Mr Adrian Lingard
Mr David Payling, MA, ACA
Mrs Debbie Procter, BA

Mr Mark Willings, BDS, MFGDP UK, Dip Imp Dent RCS Eng, FFGDP UK

Staff:

Headmaster: **Darryl Wideman**, MA (*History*)

Deputy Head: Dan Coll, BEd (*Psychology*)

Director of Studies: Rebecca Dews, BEng (*Mathematics*)

Director of Teaching & Learning: Sue O'Leary-Hall, BA, MA (*English*)

Head of Sixth Form: Anand Mistry BA (*Design & Technology*)

Head of Upper School: Carol Marsh, BEd (*Religious Studies*)

Head of Middle School: Richard Fenn, BEd (*Geography*)

Head of Junior School: Adrian Boyer, BEd (*Junior Subjects*)

Director of Admissions: Helen Lindenmayer, EYP

Chaplain: Revd Janet Lees, PhD, MPhil, MTh, MRCSLT

Assistant Staff:

* *Head of Department or Year*
† *Head of House*

Malcolm Affleck, BA (**Religious Studies*)
Tom Andrews, BA (*Junior Subjects*)
James Bentley, BA (**Business Studies & Economics*, *Careers)
Naomi Chambers, BA (*Junior Subjects*)
Sandra Coll, BA (*Modern Languages*, *Latin)
Julia Conlon, BA (*English*)
Sandra Cooke, BA (*Early Years*)
John Cooling, BSc, MMedSci, PhD (*Biology*)
David Coulson, BSc (*Biology*, *PSHCE)
Angela Eckersley, MA, BSc (*ICT)
Rebecca Elliott, BA (*Junior Subjects*)
Helen Emmett, BSc (*Geography*)
Jenny Everingham, BA, MA (*History)
Ross Falloon, BSc (*Geography**)
Wendy Forge, BA (*Junior Subjects*)
Chris Green, BA, MA (*Religious Studies*)
Paul Grooby, BSc, PhD (*Chemistry*)
Samantha Harder, BSc (*Physics*)
Joel Hinchliffe, BA (*Learning Support)
Nicki Hoare, BA (*Music)
Laura Hoyland, BA (*Design & Technology*, †*Yonge's House*)
Cale Hugill, BSc (*Mathematics*)
Brian Hutson, BEng, MEng, MA (*Physics)
Mark Jeanes, BSc (*Mathematics*, †*Evans' House*)
Emma Jones, BA (*Early Years*)
Amy Knowles, BA (*Physical Education*, †*Spencer's House*)
Sarah Lloyd (*Pre-School Coordinator*)
Joanne McManus, BA (*Modern Languages*, *PSHCE*)
Claire Moore, BA (*Art*)
Dawn Naylor, BSc (*Design & Technology*)
Isabel Nicholls, BA (*English*)
Liz Nuttall, BA (*Physical Education*, **Duke of Edinburgh's Award Scheme*)
Liz Olumegbon, BSc (*Junior Subjects*)
Beatriz Pelaez, BA (*Modern Languages*)
Alex Paling, BSc (*ICT*)
Hilary Peach, BA (**Physical Education*, †*Moore's House*)
Rachel Platt, BA, LTCL (*Music*)
Andy Potter, BEd (*Physical Education*, *Games)
Cathryn Powell, BA (*Junior Subjects*)
Lauren Reynolds, BSc (*Mathematics*)

Glenn Roberts, BEd (*Physical Education*)
Chris Rowe, BA (**Design & Technology*)
Barbara Shaw, BA (**Modern Languages*)
Kathryn Shuttleworth, BA (*Junior Subjects*)
Tom Sprott, BSc (**Psychology*)
Helen Stalker, BA (*Modern Languages*)
Lorrie Sugden, BSc, MSc (*Learning Support*)
Diane Townsend, BSc (*Mathematics*)
Tom Verinder, BA (**Politics, History*)
Simon Wardle, BA, MSt (**English*)
Pat Watkin, BSc (**Biology*)
Nigel Wears, GCLCM (*Music*)
Laura Whitworth, BA (**Art*)
Graham Wickstead, BSc (**Mathematics*)
Fiona Wideman, MA (*History*)
Victoria Wilkinson, BA (*Junior Subjects*)
Peter Wright, MSci, PhD (**Chemistry*)

Jan Alkadi, RGN (*School Nurse*)
Sandra Beeching-Smith (*Classroom Coordinator*)
Lisa Boyer (*Classroom Coordinator*)
Sophie Brooke (*Classroom Coordinator*)
Michael Cole (*Chemistry Technician*)
Michael Collinson (*ICT Systems Manager*)
Heather Cooper (*Classroom Coordinator*)
Nicola Ferry (*Classroom Coordinator*)
Simon Gibson (*Design Technician*)
Beryl Hancock (*Head of Catering*)
Matthew Johnson (*Bursar*)
Louise Leach (*Marketing Officer*)
Karen Lingard (*Librarian*)
Hannah Masser (*Classroom Coordinator*)
John Nelmes (*Biology Technician*)
Phil Noble (*Head Porter*)
Amanda Obridge (*School Secretary*)
Jane O'Brien (*Accounts Assistant*)
Lindsay Parker (*Payroll Officer & Finance Assistant*)
George Pearson (*Physics Technician*)
Fiona Reed (*Operations Manager*)
Dan Stevens (*Classroom Coordinator*)
Sharron Taylor (*Accounts Office Supervisor*)
Kath Thackray (*Projects Manager*)
Rebecca Thompson (*Data Manager & Examinations Officer*)
Michelle Wardman (*Classroom Coordinator*)
Teresa Watkin (*Sixth Form Supervisor*)
Lauren Watson (*Classroom Coordinator*)
Paul Webb (*ICT Technician*)
Gillian Wood (*Cleaning Supervisor*)
Carol Woodhead (*Headmaster's PA*)

Solihull School

Warwick Road, Solihull, West Midlands B91 3DJ

Tel: 0121 705 0958 (Headmaster)
            0121 705 4273 (Admissions)
            0121 705 0883 (Bursar)
Fax: 0121 711 4439
email: admin@solsch.org.uk
website: www.solsch.org.uk
Twitter: @solsch1560
Facebook: /SolihullSchool

Motto: '*Perseverantia*'

Solihull School was founded in 1560 with the income from the chantry chapels of the parish of Solihull. The School is particularly proud of the richness and diversity of the education that it provides. The school has always been closely involved with the community, making its sporting and theatrical facilities available for local schools.

Organisation. The school now provides education for approximately 1,030 day pupils aged between 7 and 18. The Junior School, which occupies its own separate building on the site and has its own Headmaster, has more than 210 pupils aged from 7 to 11. In the Senior School there are approximately 560 pupils from Year 7 to Year 11 and around 250 pupils in the Sixth Form. In 1973 girls were accepted into the Sixth Form. From September 2005 the school became fully co-educational.

Site and Facilities. The school moved to its present site in 1882 and the original school building, School House, survives. The site now comprises over 50 acres of buildings and playing fields, which enable all teaching, games and activities to take place on the one site. In the last decade there has been a very substantial building programme. This programme originally involved the extension of the Science Department and Design and Technology Centre, the laying of an Astroturf pitch and three squash courts, and the substantial redevelopment of School House. In 2002 a new hall/theatre, the Bushell Hall, was built, which can accommodate a theatre audience of 600 and an assembly for 1000. At the same time, the old hall was transformed into a library and IT rooms. In 2003, a new pavilion, the Alan Lee Pavilion, was completed. In September 2005 a new teaching area, the George Hill Building, was unveiled to provide 16 new classrooms and an extensive social space. The Junior School, which has grown considerably in recent years, has been extended and entirely refurbished. A new music school was unveiled in September 2009 – The David Turnbull Music School. In September 2015 a new four-floor, state-of-the-art Sixth Form Centre, the Cooper Building, opened. It was designed to transform the Sixth Form teaching and learning and incorporating the latest multimedia technology. Throughout the school there are excellent IT facilities for staff and pupils.

Curriculum. In the Junior School particular emphasis is placed on establishing high standards in core subjects and key skills that permeate the children's learning across the curriculum. The Junior School has specialist teaching rooms for Art, Design and Technology, ICT, Music and Science and benefits from the additional facilities it shares with the Senior School on the same 55-acre campus.

At the beginning of the Senior School, all pupils take at least one year of Latin and Spanish. In the second year French and German are optional subjects. English Language and Literature, Mathematics, a Modern Foreign Language, Physics, Chemistry and Biology remain compulsory subjects to GCSE. Three other subjects are chosen from a wide range of options.

The size of the Sixth Form enables the school to offer a very wide range of subjects and combinations. These subjects are Art and Design – Fine Art, Biology, Business, Chemistry, Classical Civilisation, Design & Technology, Drama & Theatre Studies, Economics, English Literature, French, Geography, German, History, Latin, Mathematics (and Further Mathematics), Music, Photography, Physical Education, Physics, Politics, Psychology, Religious Studies (Philosophy and Ethics) and Spanish. There is also a substantial programme of Enrichment for all pupils in the Sixth Form, ranging from Mandarin Chinese to Cookery.

Academic Success. In 2016 we recorded another great year of A Level results with 85 per cent of all grade achieved at A* to B grades and over a third of pupils gaining three A* or A grades or more. We were named the Top Independent School for A and AS Levels in the West Midlands 2015 by the Birmingham Post. At GCSE, a record breaking 79% per cent of pupils were awarded A* to A grades in 2016 and 70 pupils achieved an incredible 8 or more A* to A grades.

Games. Games are an integral part of the school curriculum and all pupils in the school are involved. PE is compulsory until Year 11 and all pupils in the school have a games afternoon. The school has a very strong tradition in the major team games for both boys and girls, but also offers a very wide range of other options. The principal team games are rugby, cricket, hockey (for both boys and girls) and netball. The Junior School pupils play football in addition to these sports. The school also has teams in tennis, athletics, swimming, clay-pigeon shooting, cross-country, badminton, basketball and fencing to name but a few. In recent years the school has organised very extensive tours for pupils of differing ages: in 2015 our 1st XI cricket team toured Barbados, and this summer our senior rugby players are touring South Africa while our girls hockey and netball teams are visiting Singapore and Malaysia. Individual and team national success is a regular feature of Solihull sporting life.

Music and Drama. The school has a very strong tradition in music and drama, which has been enhanced since the building of the Bushell Hall and the David Turnbull Music School. Over a third of all pupils learn a musical instrument and there are over 25 different musical groups in the Senior School. This ranges from orchestras, bands and choirs to piano, string and wind ensembles. Several of these groups are very successful in competition at local festivals. There are many opportunities for pupils to perform at concerts, both formal and informal, throughout the year. A busy programme of masterclasses is given by visiting professional musicians. There is also an excellent Chapel Choir that performs during the school week and at the chapel services each Sunday. Each term the choir sings Evensong in a cathedral (including an annual visit to St Paul's in London) and performs on BBC Radio 4's Daily Service. In 2015 the school joined the Steinway Initiative, purchasing three new Steinway grand pianos.

The drama and music departments come together each year for the staging of an ambitious musical, which always involves a large number of pupils. There are two major dramatic performances each year: a school musical (*Phantom of the Opera* 2013, *Spamalot* 2014, *Les Misérables 2015, Carousel 2016*) and a school play (*Macbeth* 2013, *Blood Wedding 2014, His Dark Materials (Part 1) 2015*). In addition, there are several smaller productions in the course of the year.

Outdoor Pursuits. Outdoor pursuits play a major part in the school's life. In the Third Form pupils take part in an outdoor activities programme called Terriers. In the Shell Form every pupil spends a week at the school's mountain cottage in Snowdonia. From the Shell Form pupils are able to participate in the CCF, which has an Army and an RAF section, and from the end of the Fourth Form, they can pursue the Duke of Edinburgh's Award scheme. There are approximately 80 pupils in the CCF and 160 are involved at different stages of the Duke of Edinburgh's Award scheme, with 20 Gold Awards achieved in 2015. The school has a popular Mountain Club and organises biennial major expeditions: Chile in 2009, Alaska in 2011, Cambodia in 2013, and Ladakh India in 2015.

Admissions. Pupils are accepted into the Junior School through examination at 7+, 8+, 9+ and 10+, although the majority of pupils enter at 7+. Pupils joining the Junior School in Years 3, 4 or 5 (in most cases) have their places in the Senior School confirmed at the end of Year 5. The major point of entry is at 11+ (Year 7). Places are awarded on the basis of written exams in English and Mathematics and, in some cases, an interview. Some pupils are also accepted to enter the school at 12+, 13+ and 14+. A substantial number of pupils enter the school at Sixth Form level. Offers for admission to the Sixth Form are made on the basis of an interview, predicted GCSE grades and a personal profile. Such offers are conditional on receiving a pupil's school report which should indicate high levels of effort and attainment, excellent conduct and a positive attitude to school life plus achieving a minimum of 2 A grades and 4 B grades at GCSE, normally including B grades in Mathematics and English. A or A* grades at GCSE are strongly recommended for those subjects to be studied at A Level particularly in Mathematics, Biology, Chemistry, Physics and Modern Foreign Languages.

The dates for entrance examinations and the Sixth Form scholarship examinations are available on the school website.

Fees per term (2016–2017). Tuition: Senior School £4,000, Junior School £3,250–£3,384. Lunch charges per day: £3.20 Junior School, £3.60 Main School. There are few obligatory extras.

Scholarships and Assisted Places. The school offers approximately 25 academic scholarship awards at 11+ and 13+ and around 30 at Sixth Form. The number of awards and their value is at the discretion of the Headmaster. There are also Sport, Art and Music, Choral and Organ Scholarships which are awarded at 11+, 13+ and Sixth Form. These are awarded based on a musical, art or sporting assessment. Sixth Form Academic scholarships are available in all A Level subjects on the basis of examination and interview.

In addition to scholarships, means-tested Assisted Places are available to offer opportunities to able pupils with financial needs. Applicants for such assistance are considered at Senior School and Sixth Form entry.

Children of the clergy are offered a 50% fee remission.

Old Silhillians Association. *Secretary*: Mr P Davies, Memorial Clubhouse, Warwick Road, Knowle, Solihull. The aim of the Old Silhillians is to support and maintain links with the school. They also have their own clubhouse and extensive sports facilities.

Charitable status. Solihull School is a Registered Charity, number 1120597. It exists to provide high-quality education for pupils between 7 and 18 years old.

Chairman of the Governors: Mr Mark Hopton, FCA

Bursar and Clerk to the Governors: Mr Richard Bate, MA Cantab, ACMA

Headmaster: Mr David Lloyd, BSc

Senior Deputy Headmaster: Mr Sean Morgan, BA
Deputy Headmaster (Academic): Mr David Morgan, BA, MA Cantab

Assistant Headteacher (Pastoral Care): Mrs Lisa Fair, BA, MA
Assistant Headteacher (Co-Curricular): Mrs Hannah Fair, BA, MA
Assistant Headteacher (Academic): Ms Daniele Harford, BA Oxon
Assistant Headteacher (ICT): Mr Dave Reardon, BSc

Head of Sixth Form: Mr Thomas Emmet, BSc
Head of the Middle School: Mrs Ruth Lancaster, BSc
Head of the Lower School: Mr Owen Bate, BSc
Head of the Junior School: Mr Mark Penney, BA

Assistant Staff:
* *Head of Department*

Ms Aisha Abid, BSc
Mr Gareth Affleck, BA (*History*)
Miss Rachel Airdrie, BA
Mr Oliver Anderton, BSc
Mrs Nicola Atkins, BEd
Dr Richard Atkinson, BA, DPhil Oxon
Mr Matthew Babb, BSc
Mrs Katie Baden, BSc
Mr Owen Bate, BSc
Mr Mark Bishop, MSc (*Mathematics*)
Mrs Claire Black, BA

Mr David Brough, BSc
Mrs Julie Brown, BA, MA
Mrs Lindsay Browning, BA
Miss Tracy Bryan, BA
Mrs Denise Buckle, BSc
Ms Libby Campbell, BA
Miss Yolanda Cánovas, BA
Miss Suzannah Compton, BSc
Miss Joanne Collier, BSc
Mr Neal Corbett, BA (*Design Technology*)
Mr Martin Covill, BSc
Mrs Petra Cramb, BA (*German*)
Miss Sara Crowther, BEd
Mr Geddes Cureton, BSc
Mrs Nicola Dickerson, BA
Ms Helen Dolby, AGSM, ATCL
Mr Andrew Dowsett, BA
Mrs Samantha Durkan, BSc
Mr Thomas Emmet, BSc (*Psychology*)
Miss Natasha Evans, BA, MA
Mrs Hannah Fair, BA, MA
Mrs Lisa Fair, BA, MA
Mr David Farrington, BSc (*Physics*)
Mr Patrick Ford, MA
Dr Sian Foster, MA, MPhil, DPhil, MBA
Mr Martyn Garner, BSc
Mr Michael Gledhill, BA, LLB
Mrs Corinne Goodman, BSc (*Chemistry*)
Miss Christa Greswold, GLCM, AMus LCM, ALCM
Mrs Kate Griffiths, BSc
Mrs Helen Hallworth, BSc
Mr James Hammond, MA (*Drama*)
Miss Jennifer Hanlon, BSc
Ms Daniele Harford, BA
Mr Stuart Hart, BA, MPhil (*English*)
Mr Stephen Hifle, QTS
Mr Phil Higley, BA, CertEd
Mrs Janet Humphreys, BEd Cantab
Mrs Eleanor Hurst, BA, Cert SpLD (*Learning Support*)
Revd Canon Andrew Hutchinson, BA, MEd
Mr Peter Irving, BA, ARCM, FRCO (*ICT*)
Mr Paul Jackson, BSc
Mrs Joanna Johnson, BA, MPhil (*Classics*)
Mr Andrew Jones, BSc (*Science*)
Mr Michael Jones, MA, BA
Miss Lijana Kaziow, BSc
Mr Tim Kermode, MA (*Director of Music*)
Mrs Ruth Lancaster, BSc
Mr Nick Leonard, BEd
Miss Lydia Lynch, BSc
Mr Darren Maddy
Mrs Jane Mander, BA
Mrs Hanlie Martens, MA
Mr Philip May, BSc
Mr Chris Mayer
Mrs Wendy Meigh, BEd
Mrs Hayley Middleton, BEng, BCom
Mrs Marion Mitchell, BA
Mr Stephen Mitchell, BSc
Mrs Clare Mollison, BA
Mr Paul Morgan, BA (*MFL*)
Mrs Rachel Morgan, BEd
Miss Saranne Moule, BSc
Mrs Ulrike Mynette, MA
Mrs Dawn Parker, BSc (*Biology*)
Dr Mary Partridge, BA Oxon, MA, PhD
Mrs Donna Penney, BSc
Mr Simon Phillips, BA
Dr Andrew Powell, PhD, MBA
Mrs Betty Richardson, BSc, MSc
Miss Stephanie Roberts, BA, MA

Mrs Alex Roll, BA (*Geography*)
Mrs Pilar Roman-Blythe, MA
Mrs Beatrice Rossay-Gilson (*French*)
Dr Amy Routledge, PhD
Miss Laura Rutherford, MA Cantab, MEd (*Religious Studies*)
Dr Szymon Sawicki, BA Cantab, MSc, PhD
Mrs Jane Sixsmith, MA & Honorary Doctorate
Mrs Helen Smith
Mr Michael Smith, BSc
Miss Rebecca Smith, BSc
Mrs Laura Spratley, BA
Dr Peter Spratley, BA, MA
Mr Dan Super, BA
Miss Amy Thacker, BA
Mrs Sharron Thomas, BSc
Mr Steve Thompson, BSc (*Director of Sport*)
Mrs Donna Trim, BA (*Art*)
Miss Francesca Wernham, BA
Mrs Ruth Whaley, MA
Miss Danielle Wilcox, BA (*Girls Games*)
Mr Alex Woodrow, MA, FRCO, FTCL
Mr Mark Worrall, MA
Mr Liam Worth, MA

Careers: Mrs Julia Skan, BA

Director of Development and Alumni Relations: Mrs Susie Jordan, BA
Head of Marketing: Mr Sean Morgan, BA

OC CCF: Major Nick Leonard
SSI: WO2 Philip Dean, MBE

Medical Officer: Dr Sunil Kotecha, MBChB, FRCGP, MSc
Senior Nurse: Mrs Sarah Serle, RGN
School Nurse: Mrs Helen King, RGN

Headmaster's PA: Miss Lisa Else
Admissions Registar: Mrs Nicolette Mullan
Bursar's PA: Ms Suzanne Baldwin
Librarian: Mrs Alison Vaughan, BA

Stamford School

Southfields House, St Paul's Street, Stamford, Lincolnshire PE9 2BQ

Tel: 01780 750300
Fax: 01780 750336
email: headss@ses.lincs.sch.uk
website: www.ses.lincs.sch.uk
Twitter: @SpedeNews
Facebook: @stamfordendowedschools

Motto: *Christe me spede*

Founded by William Radcliffe, of Stamford, 1532.

Introduction. Stamford School is one of three schools within the overall Stamford Endowed Schools Educational Charity, along with Stamford High School (girls) and Stamford Junior School, the co-educational junior school.

Buildings and Grounds. Stamford School dates its foundation to 1532. The grounds include the site of the Hall occupied by secessionists from Brasenose Hall, Oxford, in the early 14th century. The oldest surviving building is the School Chapel, which was formerly part of St Paul's Church, but which from 1548 until restoration in 1929 was used as a schoolroom. Extensive additions to the School continued to be made throughout the nineteenth and twentieth centuries. In 1956 the Old Stamfordians gave the School a swimming pool as a war memorial. The science school was built in 1957 and extended in 1973 when a new dining hall and kitchens also came into use. These were subsequently completely redesigned and upgraded in 2003. A music school was built in 1977 and extended in 1984. A further extensive development programme was begun in 1980 and included the building of one new senior boarding house (Browne), opened in 1981, and extensive and comparable provision in the other (Byard). Development works in 2009 saw the creation of a new Research and Learning Centre in the School House building, providing a library, study space and additional IT facilities. The Sixth Form Common Room is now located in a newly-renovated section of Brazenose House, containing quiet study areas, IT and recreation facilities. A glass atrium linking School House and the Hall has been erected, providing a new focal point for the School in a unique architectural style. The Science rooms were also upgraded. A new Sports Centre, which includes a fitness suite, gymnasium and 25m swimming pool, has recently been completed and forms a central part of the curricular and extracurricular sports provision. The old gymnasium will now be renovated to become a state-of-the-art Performing Arts Centre.

School Structure and Curriculum. The school consists of around 680 boys divided into Lower School (11–14), Middle School (14–16) and Sixth Form. The Heads of each section, with their assistants and Form Tutors monitor the academic progress of each boy and manage the pastoral arrangements.

The National Curriculum is broadly followed but much more is added to the curriculum to make it stimulating and rewarding. Information Technology, Art & Design and Design Technology form an integral part of the curriculum and from Year 8 boys may begin German, Spanish or Russian. All boys are prepared for a complete range of GCSE examinations; the great majority of them continue into the Sixth Form and then on to higher education.

In the Sixth Form of about 190 boys (and 190 girls) the timetable is so arranged that a wide range of combinations of subjects is possible. In partnership with Stamford High School all Sixth Form students can choose from the full range of 27 subjects available across the two schools.

Activities. Art, Music, Drama, Games and Physical Education form part of the normal curriculum. There is a choral society, an orchestra, a band and a jazz band, and a chapel choir. The musical activities of the school are combined with those of the High School under the overall responsibility of the Director of Music for the Endowed Schools. The school maintains RN, Army and RAF sections of the CCF and there is a rifle club. A large number of boys are engaged at all levels of The Duke of Edinburgh's Award scheme.

The school plays rugby, football, hockey, cricket, tennis, golf. The athletics and swimming sports and matches are held in the summer term. In winter there is also badminton, cross-country running and basketball. There are squash courts and a full-sized, floodlit Astroturf hockey pitch.

There are many school clubs and societies and a thriving weekend activity programme.

Close links are maintained with the local community. The school welcomes performances in the hall by the music societies of the town and uses the excellent local theatre in Stamford Arts Centre for some of its plays.

Careers. The school is a member of ISCO and has a team of careers staff. There is an extensive new careers library, computer room and interview rooms.

House Structure. Boarding: Byard House (11–16) Mr & Mrs Colley; Browne House (16–18) Mr L H Ware.

Weekly and three-night boarding are available, as well as full boarding.

Competition in games, music and other activities are organised within a house system. Housemasters with their assistants monitor boys' commitments to the wider curriculum and act as counsellors when boys need to turn to someone outside the formal pastoral and disciplinary system.

Admission. Registration Fee £75; Acceptance Fee £250.

The main point of entry is at age 11, but boys are considered at any age. A number join at age 13 or directly into the sixth form. Application forms for admission may be obtained from the school office. The school's entrance examinations take place in late January, but arrangements may be made to test applicants at other times. Entry into the sixth form is considered at any time. Boys who enter through the Stamford Junior School progress automatically on to Stamford School at age 11 without having to take further entrance tests.

Fees per term (2016–2017). Day £4,755; Full Boarding £8,809; Weekly Boarding £7,680; 3-Night Boarding £6,674.

These fees include stationery, textbooks and games. School lunches for day boys are at additional charge.

Scholarships and Bursaries. The Schools offer a range of scholarships for pupils entering into years 7, 9 and 12 (Sixth Form). Scholarships are less common for pupils entering into other years but may at times be available. There are scholarships for Academic, Music, Art, Sports and All-Rounder performance. Means-tested bursaries can be applied for by families of pupils who would otherwise not be able to benefit from a Stamford education. Please see our website for full details.

Charitable status. As part of the Stamford Endowed Schools, Stamford School is a Registered Charity, number 527618.

Chairman of the Governing Body: Dr Michael Dronfield

***Principal of the Stamford Endowed Schools*: William Phelan**

Vice-Principal, Head: Nicholas Gallop

Deputy Head: William Chadwick
Director of Studies: Harvey Hewlett
Head of Sixth Form: Geoffrey Brown
SES Chaplain: The Revd Mark Goodman

Teaching Staff:
Justin Backhouse (*Maths*)
Lorna Blissett (*Deputy Head of English*)
Michael Blissett (*Head of Classics*)
Edmund Board (*Maths*)
Christopher Brace (*Head of Physics*)
Pierre Braud (*Head of French*)
Richard Brewster (*Head of Geography*)
Emma Calvert (*Biology*)
Martin Caseley (*English*)
Kenneth Chapman (*Senior Master Staff*)
Annette Chauvaux (*Head of German*)
Helen Chew (*EAL Teacher*)
Charlotte Clifton (*Religious Studies*)
Alexandra Colley (*History*)
David Colley (*PE*)
Anne Corrigan (*Speech and Drama*)
Jack Cropper (*Head of Hockey*)
Anneke Davies (*Head of Drama*)
Amber Dewey (*Drama*)
Rupert Dexter (*History*)
Dion Di Cataldo (*PE*)
Charles Esson (*PE*)
Julia Fox (*Deputy Head of 6th Form*)
David Gloucester (*History*)
Amy Halliday (*Business Studies*)
Faye Harrison (*Head of Religious Studies*)
Dean Headley (*Cricket*)
Richard Henry (*English*)
Eleanor Herdale (*Head of Economics*)
Carrie Hill (*Drama*)
Ashley Hilton (*Biology*)
Jonathan Hodgson (*Senior Master Co curricular*)

Michael Holdsworth (*DT*)
Annabelle Holland (*Head of Art*)
Peter Jones (*Head of Chemistry*)
Timothy Jones (*Chemistry*)
Samuel Jordan (*Physics*)
Louise Kemp (*Head of English*)
Austin Kersey (*Head of PE*)
Jamie Laird (*Physics*)
David Laventure (*Director of Sports*)
Karen Leetch (*English*)
Sarah Macaulay (*Head of Business Studies*)
Suzanne MacCarthy (*Business Studies*)
Susan Manning (*Head of Maths*)
Constanza Marquez-Godoy (*Spanish*)
Felicity McClarty (*French*)
Lisa McKenna (*Art*)
Kendal Mills (*Senior Master Pastoral*)
Malcolm Milner (*DT*)
James Mitchell (*Geography*)
Hannah Moody (*Geography*)
Brendan Morris (*Geography*)
Kieran Nally (*Maths*)
Alister Pike (*History*)
Catherine Pike (*Head of Spanish*)
Roxana Popa (*MFL*)
Nicholas Porteus (*Head of Science*)
Andrew Ramsey (*Geography*)
James Rushton (*Drama*)
Bryan Russell (*Maths*)
Bonita Smart (*Chemistry*)
Edward Smith (*Director of Outdoor Education*)
Daniel Stamp (*Head of History*)
Amanda Steven (*Maths*)
Rachel Tomlinson (*Art*)
David Tuck (*Head of Politics*)
Leigh Ware (*Biology*)
Victoria Washbrooke (*Biology*)
Mark Webb (*Maths*)
Gary Whitehouse (*Head of Learning Support*)
Paola Wigmore (*Speech and Drama*)
David Williams (*PE*)
Katherine Woodward (*Chemistry*)
Caroline Wray (*Head of MFL*)

SES Music Department:
Giles Turner (*Director of Music*)
Duncan McIlrae (*Assistant Director of Music*)
Stephen Chandley (*Head of Brass*)
Daniel Leetch (*Head of Strings*)

Visiting Music Staff:
Steven Andrews (*Drum Kit, Percussion*)
Jonathan Aughton (*Flute*)
Margaret Bennett (*Singing*)
Karen Bentley (*Cello, Double Bass*)
Tatiana Boison (*Pianoforte*)
Susan Bond (*Singing*)
David Brown (*Clarinet*)
Alexander Crutchley (*Lower Brass*)
Julie Dustan (*Flute*)
Frances Gill (*Saxophone*)
Nicholas Gray (*Electric Guitar*)
Nan Ingrams
Sarah Latham (*Violin, Viola*)
Alexander MacDonald (*Classic Pianoforte*)
Margaret Maclennan (*Pianoforte*)
Anne McCrae (*Bassoon, Pianoforte*)
Elizabeth Murphy (*Violin, Pianoforte*)
Janet Roberts (*Cello*)
Kieran O'Riordan (*Percussion*)
Elizabeth Taylor, BA (*Violin, Viola*)
Nicholas Taylor

Eleanor Turner (*Harp*)
Lynn Williamson, LTCC (*Pianoforte*)

Medical Officer: C S Mann, MBChB, BSc

The Stephen Perse Foundation

Union Road, Cambridge CB2 1HF
Tel: 01223 454700
email: office@stephenperse.com
website: www.stephenperse.com
Twitter: @SPFSchools
Facebook: @stephenpersefoundation

Founded 1881.

The Stephen Perse Foundation comprises Stephen Perse Pre-Prep, Dame Bradbury's School (see entry in IAPS section), the Stephen Perse Foundation Junior and Senior Schools, and the Stephen Perse 6th Form College.

We are now welcoming boys throughout our family of schools, from kindergarten through to university entrance. Boys started at our Junior School in Cambridge in September 2014 and they will start at the Senior School in Year 7 from 2017. From Year 5 through to Year 11, there will be parallel, single-sex classes for boys and girls (a structure known as the diamond formation). Our 6th Form is fully co-educational.

In September 2013, Dame Bradbury's in Saffron Walden joined our family, making the benefits of a Stephen Perse Foundation education available outside Cambridge for the first time. This non-selective school for boys and girls aged three to 11 shares our ethos of learning for life rather than exams, helping children to become confident, happy and eager to tackle every challenge.

The Stephen Perse Foundation is different. We achieve exceptional exam results without sticking blindly to the syllabus or cramming facts and figures – but what pupils learn in class is only half the story. What happens on the sports field, in our art and music department, on the stage or in our clubs and societies is just as important.

We applaud success but nurture a diverse, inclusive community in each of our schools and our 6th Form College. We're small enough to know each other but large enough to provide challenges and stimulate debate. As you would expect, we have great facilities and offer one-to-one attention but the key is brilliant teaching in an unusually warm, relaxed atmosphere and the way we encourage our pupils and students to think – independently, analytically, logically, creatively and imaginatively.

Admissions. We hold our own entrance tests and interviews; these are held annually for applicants at 7+, 8+, 9+, 10+, 11+ and 13+. We also offer regular entry at 6th Form, based on an interview and GCSE results. Entry is available outside of these testing dates if places allow; please contact the relevant school if you would like more information.

Cambridge is our campus. Located in the heart of Cambridge, we consider this historic University City to be our campus; it offers our students access to a wide range of museums, sporting facilities and a host of additional places that can help our students expand their learning and encourage critical thinking – supplementing the outstanding facilities available at each of the schools within the Foundation.

Across the Foundation we offer a superb range of facilities, including a dedicated sports facility complete with all-weather pitch and tennis courts, high-spec science laboratories, a dedicated music block with 18 individual teaching rooms and performance area, a superb visual arts centre complete with mac suite, print room, textiles room and ceramics room, and multiple learning resource centres. In

2016 we refurbished our STEM building and started to build our new development with 10 classrooms, an indoor sports hall and a rooftop games area; this will be ready in 2017.

Education. For us our students are more than a set of subjects. They are individuals with their own hopes and ambitions. Our staff within the six school communities pride themselves on truly understanding what makes each student tick, offering an educational experience which is not just about what learning is today, but what it needs to be for tomorrow.

What does this mean for our students' learning? They need to be critical thinkers. This is in many respects an old-fashioned discipline. However, in a digital age of unknowns, the capacity for independent thought has never been so important. Students also need to be creative, able to collaborate and to communicate. Education needs to prepare youngsters for a life beyond examinations where the metric of success will not just be a simple grade on a certificate.

We help students to fulfil their potential by learning how to bring ideas together creatively, to solve problems and find their own perspective. We help them discover the way they learn most effectively and teach them in the way they find most inspiring and stimulating. The best education is one where children learn effortlessly because they are immersed in their learning. Inspirational teaching and a focus on the needs of individuals go hand-in-hand here.

Whether we're introducing the small boys and girls in our Pre-Preps to the world beyond their families, helping the students in our Junior and Senior Schools to grow in confidence and courage as they grow up or encouraging the young adults in our 6th Form College to broaden their intellectual, personal and social horizons, we celebrate individuality and curiosity.

We know that, in order to succeed, you have to lose your fear of failure, because nobody gets everything right first time. Have a go – you'll discover something useful about yourself anyway. It's an exciting journey, wherever you start. You don't have to be a genius to come here and you don't have to come from a privileged family. Our pupils and students are as mixed as any group of young people – but they all have bright, enquiring minds, whether they're artistic or academic, sporty or in need of educational support.

All schools tell you they're wonderful but the only way to know it's right for you is to see for yourself. At the Stephen Perse Foundation you'll find pupils and students who bubble with enthusiasm, teachers who love what they do and a place where young people blossom and have amazingly good fun. They'll be delighted to show you what being here is really like.

Diamond. Focusing too much on testing fails to take account of the importance of inspiring children to believe in themselves and to believe they can dream. To make this possible we create small communities of learners. That's where the best pastoral support, teaching and guidance happens. Our commitment to this is absolute. We have introduced a diamond system because we believe for certain subjects, and at certain ages, boys and girls learn better in single-sex classes. Pupils from 9 to 16 will have single-sex classes for core subjects like English, Maths and Sciences. It's a 21st century version of single sex education – the single-sex education that's right for the future.

Results. Our results, and our students, speak for themselves. In 2016, 88% of GCSE grades were A* or A, with 62% of our students securing 8 or more A* grades. At A Level, 75% of grades achieved were A* or A and 100% of all results were graded A*–C. At IB, the average score for students gaining their diploma was 40.2 points (out of total of 45). This is equivalent to almost A*A*A*A* at A Level plus an additional A in AS Level. A score of around 40 points places students within the top 5% globally.

Our students go to a wide variety of destinations – in 2016 examples included: Law at Cambridge, Physics at Oxford, Engineering at Imperial and Music at Durham, as well as Social Sciences at the world-renowned Sciences Po university in France and a place on the prestigious Deloitte BrightStart scheme. Around 25% gain places at Oxbridge universities, while many others opt for one of the other leading Russell Group institutions or universities abroad.

Fees per term (2016–2017). Pre-Prep £3,750; Junior School £4,710; Senior School £5,480; 6th Form College £5,325. Extras: Individual music lessons in most instruments, speech and drama.

Scholarships, Exhibitions and Bursaries. Academic Scholarships and Music awards are available in the Senior School. 6th Form Scholarships are awarded on academic merit based on written papers and interviews. 6th Form Music and Art Scholarships are also offered. Bursaries are available for pupils throughout the Foundation. Information about these may be obtained from the Bursary.

Pastoral Care. We place a great emphasis on pastoral care and the well-being of all our students. Established pastoral structures support the students and foster personal development, responsibility and informed choices. Subject teachers and year staff care for the academic progress and individual welfare of each student.

Charitable status. The Stephen Perse Foundation is a Registered Charity, number 1120608, and a Company Limited by Guarantee, number 6113565.

Governors:
Dr G Sutherland (*Chairman*)

Dr H Allen	Dr G Johnson
Dr C Barlow	Mr R Lee
Mrs S Barlow	Mrs K Ollerenshaw
Dr J Burch	Prof S Peacock
Dr V Christou	Mrs A Powell
Mr A Crouch	Dr A Thomas
Dr M Ellefson	Mr Sven Töpel
Mr J Dix	Mr D Walker
Prof R Foale	Prof G Ward
Mr S Galbraith	

Principal: **Miss P M Kelleher**, MA Oxon, MA Sussex

Bursar: Mrs J Neild, BSc Southampton

Head of Senior School: Mr D Walker, BSc Hons Bristol

Head of 6th Form: Mr S D Armitage, BA Hons Oxon, MPhil Cantab

Head of Pre-Prep: Mrs S Holyoake, BA Hons Cantab

Head of Junior School: Miss K Milne, BEd Hons Cantab

Director of Guidance: Mr S D Armitage, BA Hons Oxon, MPhil Cantab

Director of Innovation & Learning: Mr D Edwards, BSc Hons Loughborough

Director of Teaching & Learning: Mrs C Petryszak, BSc York

Head of Dame Bradbury's: Mrs T Handford, MA

Stewart's Melville College

Queensferry Road, Edinburgh EH4 3EZ

Tel:	0131 311 1000
Fax:	0131 311 1099
email:	admissions@esms.org.uk
website:	www.esms.org.uk

Twitter: @esmsedinburgh
Facebook: /esmsedinburgh
LinkedIn: /erskine-stewart's-melville-schools

'Daniel Stewart's Hospital' was founded (1855) by Daniel Stewart and has been administered since its inception by the Company of Merchants of the City of Edinburgh. Melville College, formerly The Edinburgh Institution, was founded in 1832 by the Reverend Robert Cunningham. The two schools combined in 1972 to form Daniel Stewart's and Melville College (now Stewart's Melville College). Since 1989 management of the School has been delegated by the Merchant Company Education Board to the Erskine Stewart's Melville Governing Council.

The School enjoys a commanding position on Queensferry Road, a mile from the City Centre. The original College building is occupied by the Senior School while the Junior School is in a modern building. There are a number of excellent facilities including a Sixth Form Centre, Games Hall, Swimming Pool and The Tom Fleming Centre for Performing Arts.

Since 1978 the school has been twinned with The Mary Erskine School (*see entry in GSA section*). This includes a fully co-educational Junior School for children between the ages of 3 and 11, single-sex but very closely twinned secondary schools between the ages of 12 and 17 and a fully co-educational pre-university Sixth Form which provides the ideal bridge between school and university. Boys and Girls from Stewart's Melville College and The Mary Erskine School come together in the Combined Cadet Force, in orchestras, choirs, drama and musicals and in numerous outdoor education projects.

The Senior School (744 boys). S1 and S2 follow a broad curriculum, whereby boys are equipped to pursue all routes to National 5. In S3 boys commence eight courses, including English, mathematics, at least one modern language, at least one science, and a social or creative subject. In S5 boys are expected to take 5 subjects at Higher level. A majority will continue their studies for a Sixth Year, usually three Advanced Highers to provide a firm foundation for degree courses in Scotland and England. Most boys proceed to such courses.

The School has a sophisticated system of guidance. Boys in the first year are with a Form Tutor, under the overall direction of an Assistant Head Teacher. The next four years are spent in Houses of approximately 90 boys, each with its own Head of House and House Tutors. The Sixth Form is a co-educational year, as the girls from The Mary Erskine School join with the boys of Stewart's Melville College in a completely 'twinned' Sixth Form. There is a well-established Careers department. The Support for Learning Department helps boys with specific learning difficulties.

Games. Rugby and Cricket are played on the school playing fields at Inverleith, while Hockey and Tennis are played at Ravelston. There are also opportunities for Athletics, Curling, Golf, Swimming, Squash, Sailing and Shooting as well as the many sports played in the Games Hall. Boys from the school are frequently selected for national teams in many sports.

Music is much-valued and flourishes within the school. Approximately 500 instrumental lessons are given each week by an enthusiastic staff of 25 visiting teachers. Most orchestral activity is combined with The Mary Erskine School, including junior and senior orchestras, two concert bands, a jazz band and numerous chamber groups. Choral singing is also very strong, from large junior choirs to more specialised groups for madrigals and close harmony. A full programme of public performances includes two major musicals every year and large choral and orchestral concerts in which our musicians combine with an active parents' choir.

Activities. The School encourages boys to take part in The Combined Cadet Force which comprises Army and RAF sections or in The Duke of Edinburgh's Award scheme. Each week the School offers approximately 70 clubs and societies to suit the appetites of all boys. In sport the school has particular strengths in rugby, swimming, sailing, basketball, hockey, athletics and skiing with representation at district or national level.

Boarding. Dean Park House, adjoining the school grounds, serves as the Boarding House for up to 25 boys. They share dining and recreational facilities with The Mary Erskine boarders next door in Erskine House.

Fees per term (2016–2017). Day: Nursery to Primary 7 £2,546–£2,853; Secondary £3,639. Full Boarding: Primary 6 and 7 £6,515; Secondary £7,301. Weekly Boarding: Primary 6 and 7 £6,333; Secondary £7,119.

Scholarships and Bursaries. Means-tested Bursaries worth up to 100% of the tuition fee may be available to parents of children entering any year group in the Senior Schools and at P7 in the Junior School. Academic scholarships worth £300 annually are offered to boys applying to enter S1, following a competitive selection process. These are known as Merchant Company Scholarships. The top scholarship holder at Stewart's Melville College receives the Cunningham Scholarship, worth £1,250 annually. Scholarships are paid to the pupil and are held in trust by the school until completion of their Sixth Form year. Music Scholarships of £300 per annum are offered from S3.

ESMS Junior School. In The Junior School (1,254 pupils), girls and boys are educated together from age 3 to 11. Children in Nursery to Primary 3 are based on The Mary Erskine School site at Ravelston, while boys and girls in Primary 4–7 are taught on the Stewart's Melville College site. Normal entry points are Nursery (age 3 or 4), Primary 1, Primary 4, Primary 6 and Primary 7. The school is remarkable for the breadth of its educational programme and the quality of its sporting and cultural activities, in particular the professional standards attained in Music and Drama.

Daniel Stewart's & Melville College Former Pupils' Club. *Sec:* Bobby Clark, Tel: 0131 551 2331.

Charitable status. The Merchant Company Education Board is a Registered Charity, number SC009747. It is a leading charitable School in the field of Junior and Secondary education.

Governing Council:
Chairman: Mr M Sims

Clerk to the Governors: Mr D Wright, LLB

Principal: Mr J N D Gray, BA

Bursar: Mr J B Molloy, MA Hons

Deputy Headmaster: Mr N G Clark, MA
Director of Studies: Mrs K Siljehag, MA
Head of Upper School: Mr M S Kemp, MA, PGCE
Director of Sixth Form: Dr I Scott, MA, PhD, FRSA
Assistant Head Teacher, Regent: Mrs M Elswood, BA, Dip TESL
Assistant Head Teacher, Guidance: Mr G F W Park, BD
Director of Administration: Mr G J Brown, BEd
Director of ICT: Dr K Hussain

* *Head of Department*
† *Head of House*

Art:	Mr R D Miller, BSc, CBiol,
*Mr M Crichton, BA	MIBiol
Mr C A Nasmyth, BA	Mr S W Primrose, BSc
Biology:	Chemistry:
*Mr D Lloyd, BSc, MEd	*Mr P Johnson, BSc
Mrs L A Lim, BSc	Mr C P Kerr, BSc
	Mr G Mitchell, BSc

Classics:
*Mr M Williams, MA Hons, PGCE
Mr I Crosbie, MA
Mr M T Garden, BA

Computer Studies:
*Mr A Thomson, BA
Mr S Love BA, MA, CEng, MBCS

Design & Technology:
*Mrs L Burt, BSc, FRSA
Mr S Longair, BEd Des Tech
Mr A Scott, BEng (†*Kintyre*)

Drama:
*Mrs D Sobolewska, BA
Ms E Shackleton, BA Hons, PGDE

Economics:
*Ms S Burns, MA
Mr S McMahon, BBS, ACCA, PGDE

English:
*Dr D Higgins, BA, MA, PhD
Mr J C Allan, BA (†*Appin*)
Mrs G Bakewell, MA
Mrs M Bryce, MA
Mr N G Clark, MA
Mrs S Frost, BA, MPhil
Mr S Hart, MA
Mr I A Major, BA
Mr I McNally, BA, MA
Mr S Hart, MA Hons, PGCE
Mr A Millar, MA Hons, PGDE

Geography:
*Mr K Turnbull, MA
Mr D Foulds, BSc, LLB
Mr N Williamson, BSc, ACA, PGCE
Mr M Kemp

History:
*Mr M Longmuir, BA, CAM
Mrs J D Bennett, MA (†*Ettrick*)
Mr T J M Spowart, MA, PGDE
Mr D C Clarke, MA Hons, PGDE

Mathematics:
*Mr A J T Dunsmore, BEng, MSc
Mr R I Canter, BSc, HDE
Dr G Henderson, BA, BSc
Mr G Johnston, MPhys
Mr S Love, BA, MA, CEng, MBCS
Mr J J Robertson, BSc (†*Galloway*)
Mr G Smith, BSc
Mr C Kerr, MA Hons, MSc

Media Studies:
*Mr D A Orem, MA, MPhil, Cert Media Ed, DipEd

Modern Languages:
*Mr M Z Hamid, MA
*Mrs C R Siljehag, MA
Mrs V Chittleburgh, BA, MA
Mr N A C Connet, MA
Mr M Constable, BA
Mrs V Longbottom
Mr J F Marsh, BA
Mrs I Richardson, MA
Ms N Alexander, MA Hons, PGDE

Music:
*Mr S Chenery, BA Hons, MA, PGDE
Miss R Millar, BEd Mus RSAMD, ATCL
Mr R Burns (*Pipe Major*)
Mr J Matthews, BMus, GRNCM
Mr J Skuse, BA Hons, PGCE
Mr J Smith, BA Hons
Mr S Walsh, (*Drumming*)
Mrs J Wilson, BA, PGCE
Ms D Smith, LRAM, Prof Cert RAM Hons

Physical Education:
*Mr B G Lockie, BEd
Mr J Moran, BA, BEd
Mr A Brogden, BSc Hons, GTP
Mr M R Burgess, BA Ed
Mr S T Edwards, BEd Hons
Ms P Johnston, BEd Hons
Mr H Lingard, BSpLS
Mr D Roxburgh, BEd Hons
Mr C S Spence, BEd
Mr G Wood, BSc, PGDE
Mr G Brown, BEd

Physics:
*Miss J Macdonald, BSc
Mr J Balfour, BSc
Dr C Broughton, BSc, PhD
Mr S D Jackson, MSc, BSc, BEd

Product Design:
*Mrs L Burt, BSc, FRSA
Mr S Longair, BEd Des Tech
Mr A Scott, BEng (†*Kintyre*)

Religious, Moral and Philosophical Studies:
*Mr L H F Woolley, MA Hons, PGDE
Mr G Innes, BD (†*Lochaber*)
Mr D S Chalmers, BA, PGDE
Mr G Park, BD Hons, PGCE, PG Dip

Ms L Crichton, MA Hons, PGDE

Support for Learning:
*Mrs C G C Maxwell, BA

Junior School:
Head Master: Mr M Kane, MA
Senior Deputy Head (*Primary 4–7*): Mrs G Lyon, DCE, DipRSA
Deputy Head (*Early Education*): Miss S Mackay, ALCM, LLCM, BMus Hons, PGCE
Assistant Head (*Primary 4–7*): Mr D McLeish, DCE
Assistant Head (*Primary 4–7*): Mrs J Hewitt
Assistant Head (*Early Education*): Ms C Macpherson, BEd

Miss R Meredith, BSc, PGDip
Mrs M Nimmo, BEd

Stockport Grammar School

Buxton Road, Stockport, Cheshire SK2 7AF

Tel: 0161 456 9000 Senior School
            0161 419 2405 Junior School
Fax: 0161 419 2407
email: sgs@stockportgrammar.co.uk
website: www.stockportgrammar.co.uk
Twitter: @stockportgs
Facebook: /stockportgrammar
LinkedIn: /Stockport-Grammar-School-Alumni

Motto: *Vincit qui patitur*

Founded in 1487, Stockport Grammar School is one of England's oldest schools. The founder, Sir Edmond Shaa, was a goldsmith, 200th Lord Mayor of London and Court Jeweller to three Kings of England. The School's rich history and traditions are celebrated in the annual Founder's Day Service in Stockport.

A co-educational day school, Stockport Grammar School is non-denominational and welcomes pupils from all faiths and cultures. Almost all leavers go on into Higher Education, including many to Oxbridge. Although academic performance is formidable, it is not the be-all and end-all of life at Stockport Grammar School.

Stockport Grammar School aims to provide the best all round education to enable pupils to fulfil their potential in a friendly and supportive atmosphere. The backbone of the school is academic excellence, with a clear framework of discipline within which every activity is pursued to the highest level. Entry is at 3, 4, 7, 11 and 16, but vacancies may occur at other stages. There are over 1,400 pupils aged 3–18 years, with 350+ in the Junior School and over 250 in the Sixth Form.

The Senior School. Admission at age 11 is by competitive entrance examination. This is held in January, for admission in the following September. There are several open events: see website for details. Occasional vacancies are considered on an individual basis and a few places are available in the Sixth Form each year. Visitors are always welcome to make an appointment to see the school.

Curriculum. The emphasis is on how to learn. The GCSE philosophies are introduced in the first three years as part of a broad general education. The sciences are taught as separate subjects and all pupils study Latin, French and German.

On entering the fourth year, at the age of 14, pupils retain a core of subjects but also make choices, so that individual aptitudes can be fully developed. GCSE examinations are taken in the fifth year; the percentage pass rate is historically 96% or above. In 2016, 62% of GCSE entries gained an A* or A with 83% of entries at grade B or better. On entering the Sixth Form, pupils begin with four subjects. The pass rate at A Level was 100% in 2016, with 81% of all entries gaining A* to B and 52% of entries at A* or A.

Art. A high standard is set and achieved. There are facilities for all aspects of two-dimensional work and textiles, plus a fully equipped ceramics area and a sculpture court. There are regular exhibitions in School and pupils' work is displayed annually at The Lowry.

Music. The curriculum provides a well-structured musical education for all pupils for the first three years. GCSE and Advanced Level are offered for those who aspire to a musical career as well as for proficient amateurs. Three main areas of musical ensemble – choirs, orchestras and wind bands – are at the centre of activities with opportunities open from First Year to Sixth Form. Emphasis is on determination, commitment and a sense of team work. All ensembles are encouraged to reach the highest standards.

Drama. A particularly strong tradition has been fostered over many years and regular productions involve all year groups. There are drama clubs, trips to local theatre groups and workshops in school.

Physical Education. The Physical Education curriculum is diverse, with activities including aerobics, ball skills, badminton, basketball, dance, gymnastics, health-related fitness, squash, swimming and volleyball. The main winter games for boys are rugby and football, and for the girls hockey and netball. In the summer, boys concentrate on cricket and athletics, whilst the girls focus their attention on tennis, athletics and rounders. Extra-curricular clubs provide further sporting opportunities including archery, climbing and fencing. Up to 400 pupils represent the school at Saturday fixtures and the teams have an excellent reputation, gaining success in regional and national competitions. Almost fifty pupils have represented their country, region or county in the last year.

Information Technology. Dedicated Computer Suites accommodate full classes. All pupils have their own password and email address, and are able to use the Internet for research. The rooms are available to everyone as a computer resource at lunchtimes and after school. Information Technology skills are taught as part of the curriculum and academic departments incorporate the use of computers and interactive whiteboards into their everyday lessons. The subject is also available as a GCSE option.

Houses. Every pupil is a member of one of the four Houses, each led by two Heads of House staff assisted by a team of senior pupils. The Houses organise and compete in a wide range of sporting and non-sporting activities.

Clubs and Societies. The School has many active clubs and societies covering a wide variety of extra-curricular interests, for example, debating, where Fifth and Sixth Formers have the opportunity to participate in up to four Model United Nations Assemblies around the world each year.

Development. In the summer of 2012 the School completed a major project providing new classroom accommodation on the Woodsmoor site for History, Classics, English, Economics, Business Studies and Psychology.

Visits. Well-established language exchange visits are made every year to France, Germany and Spain in addition to hillwalking, camping, mountaineering, skiing, sailing and cultural trips.

Assembly. Formal morning assemblies are held for all pupils; there are separate Jewish, Hindu and Muslim assemblies. House assemblies, which sometimes include Junior School pupils, are on Wednesdays; the Sixth Form have an additional weekly assembly.

Pastoral Care. Form Tutors get to know each pupil in the form individually, and are supported by Year Heads, by the Head of Lower School (years 1 to 3), the Head of Middle School (years 4 and 5), the Head of Sixth Form and the Deputy Head (Pastoral).

Discipline. This is positive and enabling. Much importance is attached to appearance and to uniform, which is worn throughout the school.

Fees per term (2016–2017). Senior School £3,678; Junior School £2,835.

Bursary Scheme. The School's own Bursary Scheme aims to provide financial assistance on a means-tested basis to families who have chosen a Stockport Grammar School education for their children. Details available from the Bursar.

Stockport Grammar Junior School. (*See also entry in IAPS section.*) With its own Headmaster and Staff it has separate buildings and a playing field on the same site. The Junior School has boys and girls between the ages of 3 and 11 years.

Boys and girls join the Nursery when they are three. In its own building and with a designated play area, the Nursery is very well resourced. The children are looked after by qualified and experienced staff.

Entrance is by observed play at the age of 4 years into two Reception forms, and by assessment in February for an additional form at the age of 7. All pupils are prepared for the Entrance Examination to the Senior School at the age of 11.

The Junior School buildings provide special facilities for Art, Technology, Music and Computing. The winter games are soccer, rugby, hockey and netball, with cricket and rounders in the summer. There are swimming lessons every week; other activities include the gym club, life saving, athletics and chess. There are clubs running each lunchtime and after school for both infants and juniors. Matches are played every Saturday against other schools in the major sports. Many pupils have instrumental music lessons and there is an orchestra, band, recorder group and a choir. The musical, held in May each year, is a very popular event in which all pupils participate. Visits are made annually to the Lake District in May. Short annual residential visits, are introduced from age 7.

Charitable status. Stockport Grammar School is a Registered Charity, number 1120199. It exists to advance education by the provision and conduct, in or near Stockport, of a school for boys and girls.

Patron: The Prime Warden of the Worshipful Company of Goldsmiths

Governing Body:
C Dunn, MA (*Chairman*)
P A Cuddy, BA (*Vice-Chairman*)
F A Booth, FCA
P J Britton, MBE, MA
A P Carr, MA
Miss S E Carroll, BA
Professor J Dainton, MA, DPhil
P L Giblin, MA, MEd (*Teaching Staff*)
Mrs S Lansbury, LLB
K Lansdale, MRICS
P H Locke, BVSc, MRCVS
P Milner, BA
Dr E M Morris, MBChB, DCH
J A Shackleton, BA
A C Simpson, BSc, ACA
R P Yates, FIMI

Clerk to the Governors and Bursar: C J Watson, MA

**Headmaster*: A H Chicken*, BA, MEd, FRSA

Senior Deputy Headmaster: D W Howson, MA
Deputy Headmistress – Academic: Mrs D L Harris, BSc
Deputy Headmistress – Pastoral: Mrs J White, BA
Deputy Headmaster – Staffing & Co-Curricular: E B S Bowles, MEng, MSc

Head of Lower School: Mrs H R Lawson, MA
Head of Middle School: Mrs J L Smith, BA
Head of Sixth Form: D J Stone, BA, MEd

Assistant Masters and Mistresses:
* Head of Department

Art:
*R A Davies, BA, MA
Miss R J Upton, BA

Biology:
Miss K L Chandler, BSc
*P J Grant, BSc
Mrs E Niven, BSc
Mrs A R Reid, BSc
Miss C R Sutton, BA, MSc
Mrs J White, BA
Mrs M Whitton, BSc
Mrs L J Withers, BA

Chemistry:
Miss J Berry, BSc
Mrs K L Britton, BSc
*Mrs A L Glarvey, MChem, PhD
R D Heyes, BSc
Miss R F Hindley, MChem
W Krywonos, BSc, MSc, PhD
Mrs L Pitts, BSc, PhD

Classics:
Miss L E McAllister, BA
*A C Thorley, BA
P A Urwin, BA
Mrs E Zanda, BA, PhD

Drama:
Mrs A K Moffatt, BA

Economics:
*Miss L Curl, BA, MA
R Young, BEd

English:
T Byrne
Mrs R V Cross, BA
*Mrs G A Cope, BA
D W Howson, MA
Mrs R G Johnson, BA, MA
Mrs H R Lawson, MA
Miss E MacDonald, BA, MA
Mrs S L Moore, BA
Mr M Sallabank, BA
Mrs E E Suttle, BA, MEd

French:
Mrs S L Belshaw, BA
*Miss S M Gibson, BA
D Lorentz, BA, MA, DEA
Miss C L Stevenson, BA
J D Wilson, BA

Geography:
A Cooke, BSc
Mrs H J Crowley, BSc
Mrs G N Miles, BA
Miss J Perkins, BSc
*D J Preston, MA, MSc
Mrs J L Smith, BA

German:
Mrs T Kampelmann, MA, PhD

Mrs L M Morgan, BA

History:
Mrs H R Ashton, BA
Mrs K J Chesterton, BA, MA
A H Chicken, BA, MEd, FRSA
Ms C F Griffiths, BA, MA
S A Moore, BA
*S J D Smith, BA, PhD
D J Stone, BA

Information Technology:
N S Clarke, BA
*M J Flaherty, BSc

Life Studies:
*A G Ehegartner, BA
Miss H Morgan, BA

Mathematics:
P J Arthur, BSc
A B Cheslett, BSc, MSc
Mrs M Evans, BA
*G D Frankland, BSc
M Hamilton, MSc, PhD
Mrs D L Harris, BSc
Miss M E Higgins, BSc
Mrs L Lammas, BA
Mrs A S Larkin, BSc
Mrs C L Marshall, BSc, MSc
R J Silk, BSc
Mrs R C Taylor, BSc

Music:
*M G Dow, MA, ALCM
P J Kennedy, BMus, MA
Mrs J Matthews, BA
Mrs E N Short, MA, LLCM

Philosophy/RS:
D Breffit, BA
Rev L E Leaver, MA, BTh
*J Swann, BA, MA

Physics:
Miss A Curtis, MEng
Mrs Z Dawson, MSc
*Mrs H M Fenton, BSc
Mrs C M Hird, BSc
I Killey, BSc, BEng
Miss R H Moore, MSc
C Shaw, BSc

Physical Education:
R Bowden, BA
E H Corbett, BA
Mrs L E Goddard, BSc
A S Hanson, BEd
Mrs J Maskery, BEd
Mrs K Wilkinson, BA
Miss S Withington, BEd
*C J Wright, BA

Psychology:
*Miss H K Barton, BSc
N I Browne, MA

Spanish:
Miss K A M Psaila, BA
Mrs K Christmann, MA

Technology:
Mrs R E Groves, BA
Miss S Hodkinson, BSc
Mrs H Tadman, BEng

Mrs Z A Vernon, BEd
G M Whitby, BSc
*N Young, MA

Learning Support:
Mrs S Boardman, BA
Mrs D H Meers, BA, MEd
Mrs D M Flint, CEd

School Chaplain: Revd L E Leaver, MA, BTh
Director of Music: M G Dow, BA, MA
Director of External Relations: Mrs R M Horsford, BA
Headmaster's Secretary: Mrs J E Baker
Admissions Secretary: Mrs M Connor
Librarian: Ms J Pazos Galindo, BA, MA
School Nurse: Mrs P Ward, RGN, DipHE

Junior School

Headmaster: T Wheeler, BA, MA

Assistant Masters and Mistresses:

Mrs C Bailey, BA
Miss H Baker, BEd
Mrs S Barrowman, BA, MSc
Mrs H Carroll, BEd
Mrs L Carr, BA
Mrs R Cole, BA
Miss S Coleman
Mrs K Franklin, ASA
Mrs C Hampson, BA
Mrs L Hudson, BA
Mrs N Hurst, BEd
Mrs V Hutchinson, BA
Miss C Jeans, BA
Mrs N Jones, BA
Miss S Knowles, BSc
D Makinson, HNC Eng

Mrs J Mercer, BA
S Milnes, BA
Mrs C M Nichols, BEd
Mrs J Noble, BA, PGDip, AMBDA
Miss J Pepper, BA, ASA
Miss E Ripley, BA
Mrs K Roberts, BEd, MA
Mrs C Smith, BA
Mrs A Sullivan, BEd
Mrs J Swales, BA, ALCM
A Taylor, BSc
Mrs L Turner, BEd
Mrs K Wells, BA
Mrs S Westaway, BSc
Mrs C Woodrow, BA

Nursery Manager: Miss C Peake, BTEC, HND Ed
Headmaster's Secretary: Mrs B Cheyne

Stonyhurst College

Stonyhurst, Clitheroe, Lancashire BB7 9PZ
Tel: 01254 826345; 01254 827073 (Admissions)
Fax: 01254 827135 (Admissions)
email: admissions@stonyhurst.ac.uk
website: www.stonyhurst.ac.uk
Twitter: @Stonyhurst
Facebook: /stonyhurstcollege

Motto: 'Quant je puis'

Stonyhurst is an outstanding 3–18 co-educational boarding and day school in the Jesuit tradition. Academic standards are excellent, with an extraordinary range of co-curricular opportunities and focused individual pastoral care in a stunning location.

Stonyhurst College is a co-educational Catholic boarding and day school. We are a Jesuit school, which means that we attach particular importance to emotional and spiritual development as well as academic excellence. Founded in 1593, it stands in its own estate of 2,500 acres in the beautiful Ribble Valley on the slope of Longridge Fell, ten miles from the M6 motorway, and just over 1 hour by car from Manchester International Airport. We are 2 hours away from London by train.

The College houses a remarkable collection of items relating to the history of the Church in England. These are used as a learning resource. The College has a full-time curator.

Aims. The School curriculum is intended to reflect the ideals of the founder of the Jesuits, St Ignatius Loyola: the importance of trying to find God in all things; the development to the full of each individual's talents whatever his or her gifts; the need for thoroughness and breadth in learning, helping pupils to think for themselves and to communicate well; above all an awareness of the needs of others. We aspire for our pupils to be men and women of competence, conscience and compassion.

Religion. The College is Roman Catholic and strives to educate its pupils in the principles and practice of their Faith. Pupils of other denominations are welcomed and encouraged to be active in the school's worship and spiritual life.

Organisation. There are 470 pupils in the College, with 260 in the adjacent preparatory school, Stonyhurst St Mary's Hall, which admits boys and girls from 3 to 13 (*see Stonyhurst St Mary's Hall entry in IAPS section*). About a fifth of the Prep school pupils and about two-thirds of the College students are boarders. The school is fully co-educational from 13 to 18. The pastoral care is based on 5 year groups called 'Playrooms' or horizontal houses, each of which is in the care of married Playroom staff assisted by others including a Jesuit priest acting as Chaplain and a Lay Chaplain. The younger girls are in the care of a resident Housemistress, and occupy their own designated area of the College. A resident Housemistress takes particular responsibility for the boarding and day girls in the Sixth Form. The Health Centre is self contained but within the main building; medical care is available on a 24 hour basis.

Academic organisation. A broad curriculum is offered up to GCSE in an attempt to avoid undue specialisation at an early age. Over 50% of pupils achieve A and A* grades. There are 26 AS/A2 Level subjects available and we offer the IB Diploma alongside A Levels, achieving results well above the world average. Over 70% of pupils achieve A* to B grades, with 41% achieving A and A*. All Sixth Formers must follow a course in General Theology. Academic progress at all ages is monitored on a regular basis by Tutors and progress reports are sent to parents throughout the term. There are five central ICT resource centres with Video Conferencing facilities. Sixth Formers have their own ICT resource centre and networked computers in their rooms with email and controlled internet facilities. Recent developments have created the highest quality teaching areas across the whole curriculum, with a particularly impressive Science Department and provision for the Performing Arts. There is also a splendid Library/Learning and Resource Centre. Staff from the Special Needs Department are available to give help and support where required and EAL classes are held on either an individual or group basis without extra charge.

Music, Art, Design and Technology. These subjects form an integral part of the curriculum. The opportunities for both formal and informal music are extensive: there are several orchestras, a Concert Band, small string ensembles, several Choirs and other groups. Design and Technology is taught to all first-year pupils along with Art, prior to the choice of GCSE subjects; the facilities for both these subjects are outstanding thanks to recent developments. Drama is strong and there are opportunities for taking part in a wide range of dramatic productions throughout the year either in our own Theatre or in the nearby Centenaries Theatre at Stonyhurst St Mary's Hall.

Games. The main games are Rugby Football, Cricket, Hockey, Netball and Athletics, but it is our aim to offer the widest possible range of sporting and recreational opportunity to all pupils. In addition to playing on our own golf course, pupils can take part in Soccer, Tennis, Badminton, Squash, Fencing, Basketball, Netball, Shooting, Sub Aqua and Cross Country. Our indoor six-lane swimming pool offers first-class opportunities for both competitive and recreational swimming, and the Sports Hall provides the usual range of indoor activities. An aqueous-based all-weather pitch is available for Hockey and other sports.

Cadet Corps and Other Extra-Curricular Activities. In Year 10 all pupils are members of the Cadet Corps, which introduces pupils to a number of activities such as canoeing, orienteering, climbing, trekking and shooting, in addition to an extensive programme of Army-based training. After the second year, membership of the Cadet Corps is by selection; it is invariably over-subscribed. An active Outdoor Pursuits Department offers opportunities for climbing, sailing, fell-walking and caving; the Duke of Edinburgh's Award Scheme is very popular with boys and girls at all ages.

Voluntary Service. Active work in the Community is a hallmark of Stonyhurst's commitment to others. Weekly programmes of community work are arranged and thousands of pounds a year are raised for charitable causes, in particular the College's own annual holiday for children with disabilities.

Higher Education and Careers. Most of our leavers go on to higher education either in the UK or abroad, with several every year to Oxbridge. We also send a number of students to medical schools each year. An average of 50% of our leavers have entered The Russell Group of Universities in the last few years. Our Careers department, based in a well-stocked Careers library with extensive research facilities, enables pupils to be fully informed about university choices and Tutors are actively involved at all stages in the decision making. Careers conferences are regularly organised.

Fees per term (2016–2017). Boarding £11,143, Weekly Boarding £9,287, Day £6,205.

Scholarships and Bursaries. A large number of scholarships are awarded each year at 11+, 13+ and the Sixth Form. A number of bursaries up to half fees are awarded annually to pupils whose parents are in need of financial assistance and who are likely to benefit from a Stonyhurst education and make a positive contribution to the life of the school.

Open Major and Minor Scholarships are awarded annually at 13+ on the basis of academic achievement or potential after competitive examinations in May. These vary in value up to a maximum of half fees. Sixth Form Academic scholarships are available. Music, Art and All-Rounder scholarships are awarded each year at 13+ and 16+. Our SFX scholarship award offers up to 70% off fees for ten boarding pupils who, in the opinion of the selection panel, are most likely to benefit from and contribute to life at Stonyhurst.

Open Major and Minor Music scholarships are also awarded annually in February on a generous scale related to parents' income and pupils' talent.

Applicants for Art scholarships are invited to submit portfolios of their work, personal as well as set pieces, which demonstrate a lively interest in and enthusiasm for the subject(s). There should also be evidence of proven ability through a variety of media and approaches. Portfolios should be sent or brought by the applicant early in May.

Admission. Enquiries about admission should be addressed to the Registrar, Tel: 01254 827073 or 827093. Candidates entering at 13+ are normally required to pass the Common Entrance Examination, but alternative entrance tests are available for candidates from maintained schools or from abroad. Applications for Sixth Form boarding and day places for girls and boys are particularly encouraged.

Charitable status. Stonyhurst College is a Registered Charity, number 230165. The Charity for RC Purposes exists to provide a quality boarding and day education for boys and girls.

Governors:
Chairman: Mr J Cowdall
Deputy Chairman: Mr M I Davis

Mr M J Belderbos	Dr Nuala Mellows
Mr R Brumby	Fr P Nicholson SJ
Mr A Chitnis	Fr M Power SJ
Mr D FInn	Mr M Riley
Dr M Guzkowska	Mr J Stoer

Headmaster: Mr John Browne, MA

Second Master: Mr Matthew Mostyn, BA, MA Ed
Deputy Head (Pastoral): Mr Patrick MacBeth, BA
Deputy Head (Learning): Mr Vincent Sharples, BA
Director of Studies: Mrs Lorraine Wright, BA
Deputy Head (Higher Line): Mr Neil Hodgson, BSc

College Chaplains:
Fr J Twist SJ
Miss S Young, BA, MA (*Lay Chaplain*)
Mr P Warrilow, BD (*Lay Chaplain, Religious Studies*)

Assistant Staff:
Mrs H Addy, BA (*Hispanic Studies*)
Mr E Allanson, MA (*Head of Theology and Humanities Faculty*)
Mr P R Ansell, BA (*Modern Languages*)
Ms E Ashe, BA (*Business Studies, Head of Enterprise*)
Mr K Athimoolam (*Graduate Assistant*)
Miss E Austin, BA (*Maths*)
Miss L Banks (*Gap Assistant/Tennis Coach*)
Lt Col A Barber (*Contingent Commander CCF*)
Mr J Bickerstaff, BSc (*Physics*)
Ms M Brecken, BA (*Art*)
Mr B Burgess, BA (*Head of The Creative and Performing Arts Faculty*)
Mr A J Callinicos, BA, MA (*Classics*)
Mr D Caro, BA, MA (*Spanish*)
Ms K Cavaleri, BA (*Religious Studies*)
Ms A Carvajal (*Language Assistant*)
Mr S J Charles, BA, MSc (*Asst Head Co-curricular*)
Dr A Chadwick, BSc, PhD (*Science*)
Ms D Clayton, BA (*English*)
Ms J Cockle, BA (*Art*)
Ms L Copley, BSc (*Mathematics*)
Mrs E Corns, MAG Phil (*German*)
Mrs R Crossley, BA (*Head of Geography*)
Mrs J Eachus (*Non-Teaching Assistant, Registration*)
Mr M Evans, BSc (*Head of PE*)
Miss L Fielding, BA Hons
Mrs L J C Fisher, MA (*Head of Sciences Faculty*)
Mrs H Flatley, BSc, MSc (*Biology*)
Mrs C Frankland, BA (*Geography*)
Mr P Garlington, BEd (*History*)
Ms L Gentle, BA Hons (*Graduate Assistant*)
Ms J Greenwood, MA (*Theology & Religious Studies, CAS Coordinator*)
Dr D Hallam, BDS, BSc, DMS (*Biology/Chemistry*)
Ms S Haworth, BA (*Head of Biology*)
Mrs L Heaven, BSc (*Mathematics*)
Mr M Heaven, BSc (*Design & Technology*)
Mrs J Hines, BA (*Art*)
Mr P E Hodkinson, BSc, MSc (*Mathematics*)
Mr T Holden, MA (*Politics*)
Mr J Hopkins BA (*English*)
Mr J Hopkins (*Graduate Assistant*)
Ms R Jackson, BSc (*Mathematics*)
Mrs H Johnson, BA Hons (*Classics*)
Mrs E Kay, BEd (*Head of Girls' Games*)
Mrs D J Kirkby, BSc (*IB Coordinator*)
Miss S Klasan, MA (*German*)
Ms Z Livingstone, BA (*Spanish*)
Mr D Lloyd, MEng (*Mathematics*)

Mr L Loveridge, BSc (*Graduate Assistant*)
Mrs Y Luker, BEd (*Girls' Games, Senior Tutor LLGH*)
Ms J Lynch, BSc, MPhil (*Chemistry*)
Mrs C M Markarian, BSc, MS (*Mathematics*)
Mrs K Marshall, BA (*Head of Art*)
Mr M Marshall, BA (*Director of Music*)
Mr J McGarvey, BA (*ICT*)
Miss K Mitchell, BA (*English as a Second Language*)
Dr K Morgan, BA, MA, PhD, FRCO, FISM, Hon FNMSM, LRAM, LTCL (*College Organist, Head of Keyboard and Master in charge of Music Scholars*)
Mr D Morley, BA (*Head of Languages Faculty*)
Mrs S Morley, MA (*English*)
Mrs L Morris, BSocSc (*Learning Mentor*)
Mr B P J O'Connor, BSc (*Physics*)
Miss S Oliver, BSc (*Girls' Games*)
Miss J M Parkinson, BA, MA, MPhil (*Head of Classics*)
Miss J S Pontoizeau (*Language Assistant*)
Mrs R Procter, BSc, MSc (*Mathematics*)
Miss J Pye (*Graduate Assistant*)
Dr L Quigley, BA, DPhil (*History*)
Mr D N Rawkins, BSc (*Head of Mathematics Faculty*)
Mr D C Ridout, BA
Dr C Robinson, BEd, PhD (*English*)
Mrs J Robinson, BEd (*Art*)
Ms L Rushworth, BSc (*ICT*)
Mr P Schimmenti, PhD (*Italian*)
Mr J M B Sharples, MA Oxon (*Modern Languages*)
Ms J Shelley, MChem (*Head of Chemistry*)
Mr S Shields, BSc (*Biology*)
Ms A Southward, BA, RAD, AISTD, CDE, ISTD (*Dance*)
Miss A Stevens (*Graduate Assistant*)
Mrs M Strain, BA (*SEN/EAL*)
Mr T J Strain, BEd (*Economics/Business*)
Mr G Thomas (*Games*)
Mrs L W Timmins, BA (*Head of Economics*)
Mr M J Turner, MA (*Head of History*)
Mr P A Warrilow, BD (*Religious Studies*)
Mr J Weld-Blundell (*Graduate Teaching Assistant*)
Mrs E Whalley, BSc (*Geography*)
Ms E Winstanley, BA (*Head of Literacy and English Faculty*)
Miss A Woodhouse, BA Hons (*Drama*)
Ms L Woodcock, Phd, MChem (*Chemistry*)
Mrs K Wright, BA (*Head of Social Sciences Faculty*)

Visiting Music Staff:
Mr G Banks, BA (*Brass*)
Mr P Greenhalgh, BMus, LRSM, LTCL, LLCM, LGSMD[P] (*Piano*)
Mr A Hession (*Saxophone*)
Mr M Jones (*Oboe*)
Mr D Lewis, MPhys, BGDip, RNCM (*Percussion*)
Mr G Lister (*Drum Kit*)
Mrs C Lorriman (*Flute*)
Mrs J Moon, BA, ALCM, (*Singing*)
Mrs M Rigby, GRSM, ARMCM (*Violin*)
Ms M Turner (*Cello*)
Miss S E White (*Violin*)

Development Director: Mrs R Hindle
Director of Admissions and Marketing: Mrs R Hughes, BA, PGThp, HE3
Registrar: Mrs L Carr
Admissions Secretary: Mrs T Erskine
Admissions Assistant: Mrs S Holgate
Careers Coordinator: Mrs C Anderton
Domestic Bursar: Miss F V Ahearne
Headmaster's PA: Mrs R Taylor

College Doctors:
Dr Ibbotson MBChB, MRCGP, DRCOG, DSM SA
Dr S Owen, MBChB, BA Hons, MRCGP, DRCOG, DFFP

Senior Nursing Officer: Mrs L Hindle, RNC
Nurses:
Mrs A Bell, RGN, RSCN, DipFN, DN
Ms A Salter, RGN
Mrs G Kellet, RGN
Ms I Haigh, RGN

Stonyhurst St Mary's Hall
Stonyhurst Preparatory School
Boys and Girls aged 3–13
(*see entry in IAPS section*)

Headmaster: Mr Ian Murphy, BA

Stowe School

Stowe, Buckingham, Bucks MK18 5EH

Tel:	01280 818000
Fax:	01280 818181
email:	enquiries@stowe.co.uk
website:	www.stowe.co.uk
Twitter:	@stowemail
Facebook:	/stoweschool

Motto: '*Persto et Praesto*'

Stowe provides an all-round education of the highest standard, supporting Stoics in their passage to adulthood by developing individual talents, intellectual curiosity and a lasting sense of moral, social and spiritual responsibility. Confidence and tolerance of others flourish in a close community. The School provides a caring environment which promotes academic excellence, sporting prowess and artistic and musical creativity. Through teaching of the highest calibre, Stoics are encouraged to think for themselves, challenge conventional orthodoxies and pursue their own enthusiasms. Stoics acquire skills that enable them to live happily, work successfully and thrive in their future lives.

Stowe is a country boarding school with boys and girls from 13 to 18. The School roll is 785, comprising 670 boarders and 115 day pupils. Pupils are also accepted each year for 2-year A Level courses.

Houses. There are eight Boys' and four Girls' Houses, six of which are within the main building or attached to it and six at a short distance from it. In 2014 a new Sixth Form House, West, opened for boys and girls.

The Curriculum allows pupils to enjoy a wide variety of subjects before they settle down to work for their (nine or ten) GCSEs taken in the Fifth Form. A flexible Options system operates at this stage. Most boys and girls will go on to take 4 A Levels. Throughout the School, boys and girls have a Tutor to look after their academic welfare and advise them on higher education. In the Lower School all pupils take the Vanguard Programme which is designed as a vehicle to help pupils develop an understanding of how learning happens and how challenge (and also failure) is essential to achieving progress. There is also a course in Visual Education for boys and girls in their first year at Stowe. It promotes an understanding of Stowe's architecture and landscape gardens in particular and the built environment in general.

Art, Design and Information Technology. All pupils are introduced to these subjects in their first year at Stowe. Art and Design are popular both for those pursuing hobbies and for those studying for formal examinations. Traditional skills are covered alongside more modern techniques such as computer-aided design and desktop publishing.

Music and Drama flourish as important and integral parts of the School's activities both within and outside the formal curriculum. There is plenty of scope to get involved in the School Orchestras, Jazz Band, Clarinet Quartet, Choirs, School plays, House plays and House entertainments. The timetable is sufficiently flexible to allow special arrangements to be made for outstanding musicians to study outside school. Drama Clubs and Theatre Studies groups have a fully-equipped theatre at their disposal. The refurbishment of the Theatre and classrooms, alongside a brand new Music School, allows these creative arts to flourish.

Careers Guidance. Pupils are provided with a variety of opportunities which allows them to make sound career decisions. Seminars, Gap Year advice and an interview training programme are all offered. The Careers Centre is extremely well-resourced, with a suite of computers and appropriate software, DVD facilities and a wealth of literature. Every encouragement is given to pupils to make regular visits to the Centre at Stowe and parents are always welcome to attend Careers events and to spend time using the available resources.

Religion. The School's foundation is to provide education in accordance with the principles of the Church of England and this is reflected in its chapel services on Sundays. Pupils of other faiths and other Christian Churches are welcomed and in some cases separate arrangements are made for them on Sundays. Every pupil attends the chapel services on weekdays.

Games. The key sports for boys are rugby, hockey and cricket, and for girls, hockey, lacrosse and tennis. The other main sports range from badminton, basketball, cross country, football, Eton Fives, fencing, golf, netball, squash, swimming and water polo in the winter to athletics, golf, polo, rowing, sailing and swimming in the summer; there are inter-school fixtures in most of these sports.

The School enters national competitions in many sports and encourages pupils to challenge for representative honours. The School has a heated 6-lane 25m indoor swimming pool with electronic timing system, a sports hall, squash courts, Eton Fives courts, a weight training/fitness room and two floodlit Astroturf pitches which also provide 24 tennis courts in the summer. There are also hard tennis courts available all the year round, plus outdoor netball and basketball facilities, an 8-lane sandwich surface athletics track, an indoor shooting range, a clay-pigeon shooting tower, a nine-hole golf course where the National Prep Schools (IAPS) annual tournament is played, and extensive playing fields for rugby, hockey, football, cricket and lacrosse. Sculling, canoeing, sailing and fishing take place on a lake within the Landscape Gardens as well as at Northampton Rowing Club and Glebe Lake, Calvert. The School opened its Equestrian Centre in 2012 and enters local and regional competitions.

Other Activities. Pupils complement their games programme with a broad variety of extra-curricular activities, including clubs and societies. There is a full weekend programme of events and activities. Stowe's grounds lend themselves to outdoor pursuits such as fishing and clay pigeon shooting, and the School has its own pack of beagles. On Mondays a special activities programme is based on Service at Stowe and at the heart of this is the Combined Cadet Force with all three service arms, the Duke of Edinburgh's Award scheme, Community Service (in the neighbourhood) and Leadership skills.

Fees per term (2016–2017). Boarders £11,490, Day Pupils £8,260 payable before the commencement of the School term to which they relate. A deposit is payable when Parents accept the offer of a place. This deposit is repaid by means of a credit to the final payment of fees or other sums due to the school on leaving.

Scholarships and Bursaries. A range of Scholarships and Exhibitions, up to the value of 25% of the School fees, is awarded annually. Scholarships may be supplemented by means-tested bursaries, with a limited number of fully-funded places, where there is proven financial need.

Academic Scholarships up to the value of 25% of the School fees are available for pupils at age 13+ entering Stowe's Third Form, and are awarded to gifted children already following the ISEB Common Academic Scholarship syllabus at their Preparatory School.

Stephan Scholarships are awarded to academically bright pupils from independent or state schools which do not follow the ISEB Common Academic Scholarship syllabus.

Academic Scholarships are also available to pupils wishing to join the School in the Lower Sixth Form after GCSE at 16+. Competitive Entry Examinations are held in the November of the candidate's GCSE year consisting of a Verbal Reasoning paper, two subject papers related to their AS Level choices, and an interview. Successful Scholarship candidates would normally be expected to gain A* and A grades in all their subjects at GCSE.

Music Scholarships: Candidates at age 13 should be at least Grade Five standard on at least one instrument and preferably nearer Grade Six. An Exhibitioner may be around Grade Four standard. Candidates at age 16 should be the equivalent standard of Grade Six or above on one instrument and be of a good standard on a second instrument or voice. A candidate gaining a Minor Scholarship of up to 10% or an Exhibition may be around Grade Five standard.

Some *Art and Design & Technology Scholarships* are available for pupils entering Stowe at age 13 or 16, and are offered to candidates who submit evidence of outstanding ability and a strong interest in these areas.

Sixth Form Arkwright Scholarships: Stowe is affiliated to the Arkwright Scholarships Trust which provides a number of scholarships available to students, both internal and external, who will be studying Maths and Design and Technology in the Sixth Form and intend to read Engineering, Technology or another Design-related subject at university.

Sports Scholarships may be awarded to exceptional candidates at 13+ and 16+ showing outstanding potential in at least one of Stowe's key sports: hockey, lacrosse, netball or tennis for girls and rugby, hockey or cricket for boys.

Roxburgh (All-Rounder) Scholarships at 13+ and 16+ are intended to enable any boy or girl of outstanding all-round ability and leadership potential to benefit from Stowe's unrivalled environment to develop fully his or her talents. In addition to strong academic potential, which will be demonstrated in Stowe's Entry Examinations, candidates would be expected to demonstrate a high level of ability in at least one of the following: sport, music, art and drama.

Full details may be obtained from The Registrar.

Admissions. Boys and girls can be registered at any age. Full details can be obtained from the Admissions Department, who will supply entry forms. The School is always prepared to consider applications from pupils to enter the School at 14 if they have been educated overseas or in the maintained sector. The date of birth should be stated and it should be noted that boys and girls are normally admitted between their 13th and 14th birthdays.

The Old Stoic Society. Director: Anna Semler. Old Stoic Society Office: Tel 01280 818252, email oldstoic@stowe.co.uk.

Charitable status. Stowe School Limited is a Registered Charity, number 310639. The primary objects of the charity, as set out in its Memorandum and Articles of Association, are to acquire Stowe House, which was achieved in 1923, and to provide education in accordance with the principles of the Church of England.

Visitor: The Rt Revd The Lord Bishop of Oxford

Governing Body:
Simon C Creedy Smith, BA, ACA (*Chairman*) [OS]
The Revd Peter Ackroyd
John R C Arkwright, FRICS [OS]
Jonathan M A Bewes, BA, FCA [OS]
Ms Julie C Brunskill, BSc, MRICS
Admiral Sir James Burnell-Nugent, KCB, CBE, MA
    Cantab [OS]
David Carr, MA Cantab [OS]
David W Cheyne, MA Cantab (*Vice Chairman*) [OS]
Ms Juliet Colman, BA, Dip Arch, RIBA, SCA
Professor Guy Gibson, BA, DPhil, FMedSci, FRCPsych
Mrs Joanne Hastie-Smith
David Hudson, MA Cantab
Mrs Andrea Johnson, BSc, PGCE
Robert A Lankester, MA Cantab
Mrs Catriona Lloyd, MA Cantab
The Lord Magan of Castletown
Mrs Elizabeth Phillips, OBE, BA, MA, AKC
Lady Stringer, BSc, MB BS, LRCP, MRCS
Christopher J Tate, BA, MIMC [OS]
Jonathon Hall, FIDM (*Chairman of the Old Stoic Society*)
    [OS]
Michael B M Porter, BA, MSc (*Secretary to the*
    Governors)

[OS] *Old Stoic*

Administrator to the Governors: D J Critchley, MA

Headmaster: A K Wallersteiner, MA, PhD

Deputy Headmaster: C C Robinson, MA, MPhil
Assistant Head – Director of Studies: Mrs J Potter, MPhil, BA
Assistant Head – Senior Housemaster: P A Last, BA
Assistant Head – Senior Master: M D G Wellington, BSc
Registrar: D Fletcher, BEd

Assistant Staff:
* *Head of Department*

Art:
*Mrs A Jorgensen, BA, MA
Ms A Cammish, BSc
C J Grimble, BA
Mrs S U Harmon, BA, MA
B L Johnson, MA

Biology:
*Mrs L M Carter, BSc
R R Akam, BSc, MEd
Miss A S Davies, BSc, MSc
Mrs J M Gracie, BSc
M A Righton, MA

Business Studies & Economics:
*R B Corthine, MA
D Beniston, BA
P John, BSc
G West, MBA, LLM, DBA

Chemistry:
R G Johnson, BSc, MA
Mrs K M McMahon, BSc
J M Tearle, BA
*Dr A Waine, MA, MSc, PhD
C J Warde, BSc, MSc

Classics:
*M J Bevington, MA, MEd
J A Smith, BA

Computing:
*A C Gabriel, BA
N J Mellor, BA, MSc

Design & Technology:
C T McGhee, BA
C Peratopoullos, BEd
*M D G Wellington, BSc

Drama & Theatre Studies:
N D Bayley, Dip Acting & Theatre
Mrs L I Miller, BA, MA
*Ms R E Clark, BA
C D Walters, BEd

EAL:
*Mrs J Y Johnson, BA, MA
Mrs P J S Kitchen, BSc

English:
Mrs E J Ackroyd, BA
P S Miller, MA, PhD
J W H Peppiatt, MA
*Ms S A H Puranik, BA, MPhil
D A Roberts, MA
Ms E Sheard, BA, Cert SpLD

Games Coaching:
*I Michael, BEd
K Bennett (*Track and Field, Cross Country*)
S A Cowie, FIST (*Swimming*)
Mrs J M Duckett, BEd (*Lacrosse*)
A Hughes (*Rugby*)
J A Knott (*Cricket, Hockey*)
J S Skinner (*Tennis*)

Geography:
*Mrs S A Murnane, MA
Mrs S L Akam, BA
Mrs L C Campbell, BA
L Copley, BA
Mrs A J Dawson, BA
P J Deakin, BSc
P A Last, BA, Adv DipEd

History:
*P Griffin, BA
S G Aston, BSc, MA
H J Hoare, BA
J R H Sayers, BA
C T Standley, BA
H J L Swayne, BA

History of Art:
*Ms E M A Chubb, BA,
    Ad Dip
C C Robinson, MA, MPhil

Library:
Mrs L Foden

Mathematics:
Ms V A Green, BSc,
    CertEd
Mrs F C James, BEng
R D Knight, BSc
A McDaid, BEd
*M B Møller, BA

Modern Languages:
*Mrs T L Jones, BA
Mrs H Browne, BA
S G Dobson, MA
G D Jones, BA
G R Moffat, BA
Mrs M L D Peña, BA
Mrs A P A Savage, BA
Miss C Stirzaker, BA
Mrs A R G Tearle, MA

Music:
A Aitken, BA, LRSM,
    LTCL, ARCO
B C Andrew, BMus
N C Gibbon, BSc
M R H Nottage
G L Silver, BA, MPhil
C Windass, ABSM, GBSM

Philosophy and Religion:
*C S Bray, BA, BPhil
The Revd C M B Huxtable,
    BA *(Chaplain)*
A A Macpherson, BA, MA
M P Rickner, BA

Physics:
*R J Carpenter, BSc
B Hart, BEng
S H Malling, MSc, CPhys,
    MInstP
T C O'Toole, BSc
P A Thompson, BSc

PSHE:
*Miss K J McLintock, BA,
    MA

Politics:
*C Barker, BA
J P Floyd, MA

Skills Development:
*Mrs S Carter, BA, MA,
    MEd
Mrs F E Atherton, BA,
    AMBDA
Mrs E A Birks, MA
Mrs E N Hughes, BA
Ms L C Powell
Mrs S Rawlins, HLTA, Dip
    ADHD
Mrs S D Rookley, BA
    HLTA

Sports Science:
*P R Arnold, BSc
Mrs J M Duckett, BEd
I Michael, BEd
R C Sutton, BA
Mrs S E Sutton, BA

Houses and Housemasters/mistresses:

Boys' Houses:
Bruce House: R C Sutton
Temple House: A A Macpherson
Grenville House: A D D Murphy
Chandos House: P J Deakin
Cobham House: J W H Peppiatt
Chatham House: L Copley
Grafton House: G R Moffat
Walpole House: G D Jones

Girls' Houses:
Nugent House: Mrs J M Duckett
Lyttelton House: Ms V Green
Queen's House: Mrs F C James
Stanhope House: Mrs S U Harmon

Sixth Form House:
West House: Mr R Johnson & Mrs J Johnson

Medical Officer: Dr R D Pryse, MB BS, DCH, DRCOG,
    DFSRH

Director of Finance: Mrs J L Hill, MA, FCA
Director of Marketing & Admissions: Mrs V M Roddy,
    BSc, MSc
Director of Operations: N Morris, BA, MSc, FRSA,
    FCILT, MIL

Strathallan School

Forgandenny, Perth, Perthshire PH2 9EG

Tel: 01738 812546
Fax: 01738 812549
email: secretary@strathallan.co.uk
website: www.strathallan.co.uk
Twitter: @StrathallanSch
Facebook: /strathallanschool

Motto: '*Labor Omnia Vincit*'

Strathallan School was founded by Harry Riley in 1913 and moved to its present site in Forgandenny, Perthshire in 1920. The School is fully co-educational and numbers 540 pupils, of whom 216 are day pupils and 324 are boarders.

Situation. Strathallan School is located 6 miles south of Perth in the village of Forgandenny. It occupies a glorious rural location, situated in 150 acres of richly wooded estate on the northern slopes of the Ochils and overlooks the Earn valley. At the same time, Strathallan is within easy reach of the international airports – Edinburgh (35 minutes) and Glasgow (1 hour) – and Perth (10 minutes).

At the centre of the School is the main building which dates from the 18th century and was formerly a country house and home of the Ruthven family. The School continues to invest in outstanding facilities. These include modern laboratories, a Theatre, Computer Centre, Library, Design Technology Centre, Sports Hall, Fitness and Weight Training Room, 2 Floodlit Synthetic Hockey pitches, Indoor Multi-Sports Facility, Dance and Drama Studio, Medical Centre, Art School and newly refurbished Boarding Houses. All boarding houses have been built within the last thirty years with modern facilities and a single study-bedroom for every boarder in the last four years.

Aims. At the heart of the School's philosophy is the commitment to provide opportunities for all to excel, to help pupils to make the most of their abilities within the framework of a caring environment.

Organisation. The School is primarily a boarding school yet also takes day pupils who are integrated into the boarding houses. There are four Senior Boys' houses (Ruthven, Nicol, Freeland and Simpson). There are three Girls' houses (Woodlands, Thornbank and Glenbrae). All boarding houses have their own resident Housemaster or Housemistress, assisted by House Tutors and a Matron. Boys have single study-bedrooms from the Fourth Form and Girls have single study-bedrooms from the Third Form.

The Junior House, Riley, is designed to cater for boys and girls wishing to enter the School at 9+. Riley is run by a resident Housemistress, assisted by tutors, two of whom are resident, and a resident Matron. After Riley, pupils move directly to one of the Senior houses. Riley is situated within its own campus, yet also enjoys the facilities of the main School. It has its own Common Room, Library, dormitories and music practice rooms.

The whole School dines centrally and there is a wide choice of hot and cold meals as well as vegetarian options. All boarding houses have "brew rooms" for the preparation of light snacks.

Religion. Strathallan has a Chapel and a resident Chaplain who is responsible for religious studies throughout the School.

Curriculum. Two of the keys to academic success are an ethos of continuous improvement and support from teachers who are high quality practitioners and passionate about their subject – we pride ourselves on providing just such a learning environment. In addition, all pupils receive support from a tutor linked to the pupil's House; there is also a full time

Careers Advisor to help with opportunities available beyond school.

Junior. Boys and Girls entering Riley House follow a course designed for the transition between the school which they have previously attended and joining the senior part of the School at the age of 13. The following wide range of subjects is taught: Art, Computing, Design Technology, Drama, English, French, Geography, History, Latin, Maths, Music, PE, Personal and Social Development, Religious Education and Science. Courses are generally based on English Key Stages Two and Three.

The aim is to give pupils experience in specialist areas while at the same time ensuring that they have an appropriate basis in the core subjects to move on to further study. Pupils in the Junior House benefit from the facilities available in the whole School and are taught specialist subjects by specialist teachers. Classes are organised to take into account both ability and previous experience to ensure that each pupil moves at his/her appropriate level.

Third Form. Pupils in the Third Form participate in the following wide range of subjects: Art, Biology, Chemistry, Computing, Design & Technology, English, French, Geography, German and Spanish, History, Latin, Mathematics, PE, Physics and Religious Education. They are given a grounding in the skills necessary to pursue the subjects in the future should they wish, and an experience which is worthwhile in itself. All subjects are taught by specialists.

Fourth Form and the start of GCSE study. The two year GCSE course begins in the Fourth Form. All pupils study English, Mathematics, at least one Modern Language and the three Sciences. In addition each pupil studies History or Geography (and can study both), plus two other subjects from an extensive choice. The aim is to ensure that pupils keep their options open, pursue a well-rounded curriculum, and establish a good basis for Sixth Form study.

Pupils are supported in their study not only by the individual teachers and the Heads of Department but also by a tutor who is linked to the House. A system of Merits and Distinctions rewards both individual pieces of outstanding work and continuous hard work and achievement. It is a central aim of the academic programme that pupils' efforts and achievements are recognised.

Sixth Form. Nearly all pupils stay on into the Sixth Form where the normal entry requirement is five passes at grade C or above at GCSE level. It is a special feature of Strathallan's Sixth Form that there is the flexibility to choose either A Levels or Scottish Highers. The choice is determined by the needs of the individual pupil. There is a wide range of subjects: Art, Biology, Business Management, Business Studies, Chemistry, Classical Civilisation, Computing, Design & Technology, Economics, English, French, Geography, German, History, Latin, Mathematics, Music, RMPS, Physical Education, Physics and Spanish.

The formal academic curriculum is supplemented by an enhancement programme of talks, visits and exchanges. We have well-established links with continental schools, and visits to theatres, galleries, courses and conferences in the UK and abroad often take place. Extracurricular activities and societies complement the formal academic courses and extend pupils' interest in learning and discussion, through activity beyond the classroom.

Each pupil is allocated a tutor who is a member of the academic staff and one of the duty staff of the boarding house. The tutor monitors pupils' academic and social progress and is responsible for discussing their regular reports with them. Teacher : Pupil ratio 1:7.

Games. The main School games are rugby, cricket, hockey, netball, athletics and tennis, and standards are high. Other sports include skiing, squash, rounders, football, fencing, judo, badminton, table tennis, basketball, swimming, golf, horse riding and cross-country running in all of which

national and regional success have been achieved in recent years.

Strathallan has 2 squash courts, 15 hard tennis courts, 3 netball courts, 2 floodlit synthetic pitches, a heated indoor swimming pool, sports hall, gymnasium and a fitness and weight training room. The sports hall comprises a basketball court, three badminton courts, a rock climbing wall as well as facilities for six-a-side hockey and indoor cricket coaching. Sailing, canoeing and skiing are recognised pastimes, and pupils participate in School ski days in the Spring term. Strathallan also has its own nine-hole golf course as well as Tennis and Shooting Academies.

Activities. All pupils are encouraged to take part in a range of activities for which time is set aside each day. There are over 50 weekly activities to choose from including dance, drama, pottery, chess, photography, first aid, life-guarding, judo, horse riding, shooting (both clay pigeon and small bore) and fishing. There are also many societies and a programme of external speakers who visit the School. Pupils also work towards awards under The Duke of Edinburgh's Award scheme. They are also encouraged to take part in Community Service.

Music. The Music department has its own concert room, keyboard room and classrooms, together with a number of individual practice rooms. Music may be taken at GCSE, Higher and AS/A2 Level. There are choirs, traditional music ensembles, jazz band, wind band, an orchestra, folk bands and rock bands. A house music competition takes place annually and there are regular concerts throughout the term. Individual tuition is available for virtually all instruments. Recitals and visits to concerts in Edinburgh, Perth and the environs are arranged. The School has a Pipe Band and a full-time Piping Instructor. There is also a specialist Choral Scholarship programme.

Art. Art is recognised as an important part of the School's activities and there are opportunities to study the subject at GCSE and AS/A2 Level. Pupils benefit from regular art trips abroad and have the opportunity to exhibit their work both locally and further afield. A purpose-built Art School features facilities for ceramics, sculpture and print-making. National awards reflect pupils' achievements in this area.

Drama. Drama thrives throughout the School and the department makes full use of the theatre. There are junior and senior performances each year and pupils are encouraged to become involved in all aspects of production. The School also provides tuition in public and verse speaking and pupils regularly win trophies at the local festivals. There is also an annual Musical and pupils enter musical theatre exams.

Combined Cadet Force. There is a large voluntary contingent of the Combined Cadet Force with Navy, Army and Marines Sections.

Careers. Careers guidance begins in the Third Form. The Careers Adviser maintains close links with universities and colleges and regularly visits industrial firms. We have exchange programmes with schools in Australia, New Zealand and South Africa. There is a dedicated Careers Library, well-stocked with prospectuses, reference books and in-house magazines. Strathallan is a member of the Independent Schools Careers Organisation, a representative of which visits regularly and of the Scottish Council for Development and Industry.

All pupils have the opportunities to gain work experience in the Fifth Form, after their GCSEs. There is also a GAP year programme which provides placements for pupils to work overseas prior to going to university. Strathallan is developing particular links with Charities in Kenya.

Pastoral Care. There is a strong emphasis on pastoral care. The School has drawn up its own welfare guidelines in consultation with parents, governors and Perth and Kinross Social Work Department.

Medical Centre. Strathallan has its own purpose-built Medical Centre with consulting and treatment rooms. There are nursing staff at the Centre and the School's Medical Officers visit four times a week. Physiotherapy, chiropody, and relaxation also take place in the Centre during term time.

Entrance. Junior Entrance – Boys and girls are admitted to the Junior School (Riley House) at either age 9, 10, 11 or 12. An Entrance Day (including those sitting scholarship examinations in January) is held in early Spring each year for those who are available. Entry is based on a satisfactory school report and assessments in Maths and English.

Entry to the Senior School – Candidates for entry into the Senior School at 13 may enter via the Open Scholarship examination in February, Common Entrance or a satisfactory school report.

Sixth Form – Boys and girls may also enter at Sixth Form level, either via the Sixth Form scholarship examination in November or on the basis of a satisfactory school report and GCSE/Standard Grade results.

Scholarships. Awards are made on the basis of competitive examination/assessment. Bursary help is available to supplement awards for outstanding candidates on a financial need basis.

Awards are available in the following categories to candidates entering the school at three levels:

Junior School: Academic and Music/Choral/Performing Arts/Piping/Drumming, Drama and Sport. Candidates should be under 13 on 1 September in the year of entry. Scholarship Examination: January.

Third Form: Academic, Music/Choral/Piping/Drumming, Art, Design Technology, Drama and Sports. Candidates should be under 14 on 1 September in the year of entry. Scholarship Examination: February.

Sixth Form: Academic, Music/Choral/Piping/Drumming, Art, Design Technology/Arkwright, Drama and Sports. Candidates should be under 17 on 1 September in the year of entry. Scholarship Examination: November.

Further information is available on the School's website, www.strathallan.co.uk, or from The Admissions Office, Tel: 01738 815003, email: admissions@strathallan.co.uk.

Bursaries. Bursaries are awarded dependent on financial circumstances and are available to pupils who have qualified for entry through exam or school report or both. It is not necessary for successful candidates for bursaries to have achieved scholarship standard but it may be possible to add a bursary award to a scholarship to enable a pupil to come to Strathallan.

Fees per term (2016–2017). Junior School (Riley House): £7,397 (boarding), £4,616 (day). Senior School: £10,372 (boarding), £7,038 (day).

Prospectus. Up-to-date information is included in the prospectus which can be obtained by contacting the Admissions Office or via the School's website.

Charitable status. Strathallan School is a Registered Charity, number SC008903, dedicated to Education.

Board of Governors:

Chairman: Mr R K Linton, LLB, NP
Deputy Chairman: Professor J S Cachia, BSc, MBChB, MD, FRCGP, DRCOG, FRCPE
Mr J G Barrack
Professor J A Cleland, BSc, MSc, PhD, DClinPsychol, FHEA, AFBPsS
Mr K C Dinsmore, BA, LLB, Dip LP
Mrs K J Dunn, LLB
Mr D Gillanders
Mr M Griffiths, LLB Hons, CA
Mr R G A Hall, BArch, Dip Arch, RIAS, RIBA
Mr S J Hay, BA, MBA, MSc
Professor T Hoey, MA, PhD, Hon FRSGS

Mr N Houston, MA, Dip MusEd, PG Dip EdTech CNAA, PG Dip Couns, MScR Mus, FHEA
Mr J Leiper, CA, BA
Mrs E Lister, BSc, Dip Ed
Mrs C Miller, MA Hons
Mrs P A Milne, BA, MBA, MCIPD
Miss R Sandison, MCIM
Mr A M D Wilkinson, MBA, MA, FSI
Mrs G M Wilson, MA, PGCE

Headmaster: **Mr B K Thompson**, MA Oxon

Assistant Staff:
Mrs T Ailinger, Staatsexamen, Cert TESOL
Mr Y Banda, BSc, PGCE
Mr D J Barnes, BSc, PGCE, PGCG, FRGS (*Deputy Head Pastoral*)
Mr G J Batterham, BSc, PGCE (*Simpson House*)
Mr M Bergin, BSc, PGCE
Mr D E Billing, MA, PGCE (*Nicol House*)
Mrs D Billing, MA, PGCE
Dr K E M Blackie, PhD, PGDE, BSc
Miss C Brownbridge, BA, PG Dip, PGDE
Mr F Burnett, BSc, PGDE
Miss E de Celis Lucas, BA, CAP
Dr A N Collins, BSc, BA, PhD
Dr B Cooper, BSc, PhD, PGCE
Mrs M-L Crane, BA, PGCE
Mrs L E Davies, BA, PGCE
Mr S Dick, BEd
Dr S B Downhill, BA, MSc, PhD, PGCE, FRGS
Mr S Drover, BSc, PGCE
Mrs E C Duncan, MA, PGCE
Mr A L M Dunn, MA, PGCE
Dr S R Ferguson, MA, PhD, MSc, PGCE
Mrs S E Fleming, BEd
Mr N P Gallier, MBE, MA, MSc, PGCE
Mr G N Gardiner, BSc, PGCE
Mr D R Giles, BA QTS, Cert PP
Mr S Glass, BSc
Mrs S E Halley, BSc, PGDE
Mr S Hamill, BA (*Deputy Head Academic*)
Mr N A Hamilton, BMus
Mr B A Heaney, BSc, Dip Ed (*Freeland House*)
Mr A D Henderson, UKCC
Mr M Henderson-Sowerby, BSc, PGCE
Mr D M Higginbottom, MA, PGCE
Mrs J Higginbottom, MA, PGCE
Mrs R Hodson, MA, PGCE, MSc
Mrs C G Howett, BA, Dip Ed
Miss H Jassim, BSc, PGDE
Mr E Kalman, BSc, MPhil
Mr P J S Keir, BEd, Cert SpLD
Mr L Kent, BSc, PGCE (*Thornbank House*)
Mr E G Kennedy, BA, PGCE
Mrs E C Lalani, BEd, Dip Man (*Riley House*)
Miss C Laurie, BSc, PGCE
Mr E Lee, MA, PGCE
Mrs F MacBain, MA
Mr I McGowan, BCom Dip Teaching (*Ruthven House*)
Miss S Mackay, BA, MSc, PGCE
Mr K McKinney, BSc, BEd
Ms G McLean, BA, PGCE
Dr I Mitchell, BSc, PhD
Mr S Mitchell, BSc, PGCE
Miss J L Morrison, BTechEd
Mr C Muirhead, BA
Mr R Newham, BSc, PGDE
Mr T Ogilvie, LTA CC
Mr G S R Robertson, BA, DMS
Mr S W Robertson, MA, BSc, PGCE
Mrs M C Robertson-Barnett, MA, PGCE

Dr J D Salisbury, MA, PhD, PGCE
Mrs L Salisbury, BA, Dip Ed, PGCE, ALCM
Mrs C A Sim Sayce, BMus, PGCE
Miss A Sime, BEd (*Director of Sport*)
Mr J Storer, BEd, MA
Mr A C W Streatfeild-James, MA, PGCE (*Director of Studies*)
Mrs K L Streatfeild-James, BA, PGCE, Dip SpLD
Mrs R C W Stuart, MA, PGDE
Mrs J A Summersgill, BSc, PGCE
Mrs A J Tod, MA, PGCE
Mr M R A J B Tod, BSc, PG Dip
Mr P M Vallot, BSc
Mr R C A Walmsley, MA (*Director of Music*)
A Watt, BComm, BComm, HDE
Mrs L Waugh, BA, PGDE
Ms K Wilson, BSc, PGCE (*Glenbrae House*)
Dr I Woodman, MA, MLitt, PhD, PGCE
Revd J Wylie, BSc, BD, MTh
Mr D Yeaman, MChem, PGDE
T Zhou, MSc, PhD

Bursar and Clerk to the Governors: Mr A C Glasgow, MBE, BEng, MSc, CEng

Director of Marketing & Development: Ms F Duncan
Marketing Manager: Mrs L Leslie
External Relations: Mrs A Wilson

Medical Officers:
Dr A M Lewis, MBChB, MRCGP
Dr L D Burnett, MBChB, BSc, DRCOG, MRCGP

Sutton Valence School

Sutton Valence, Maidstone, Kent ME17 3HL

Tel: 01622 845200
Fax: 01622 844103
email: enquiries@svs.org.uk
website: www.svs.org.uk
Twitter: @SVSchoolKent
Facebook: /SuttonValenceSchoolKent

Motto: *My Trust is in God alone*

Founded in 1576 by William Lambe, Sutton Valence School has over 425 years of proud history. Today the School is co-educational and includes a preparatory school on a neighbouring site. Both schools are situated on the slopes of a high ridge with unequalled views over the Weald of Kent in the historic, beautiful and safe village of Sutton Valence.

Our greatest strength is our community. The relationships we enjoy between staff, pupils and parents allow us to craft an educational journey that is individually-suited to every pupil. During a family's association with the School we hope they will feel involved, listened to and informed.

Through the high expectations and standards we set, all our young people are encouraged and helped to go further than they had thought possible in their academic, co-curricular, community and leadership journeys. We want them to become confident, civilised, tolerant and open-minded individuals who possess a love of learning and a strong sense of self-discipline along with a set of values reflecting our principles as a Christian Foundation.

Ethos. A community where each cares for all and individuality is cherished.

Sutton Valence is an educational community whose philosophy embraces a breadth of challenges. Through a diverse curriculum and a wide range of activities we cultivate an appreciation of academic excellence, responsibility,

leadership, kindness and friendship amongst our pupils. All members of the School develop a sense of spiritual, moral and ethical awareness and, in so doing, come to appreciate their own place in the world.

At Sutton Valence every person is valued as an individual with their own distinct sense of worth and potential. Each member of the community has abilities, talents and skills unique to them. Our School strives to provide the seedbed to allow these gifts and talents to grow, develop and ultimately flourish.

Our community is founded on the principles of trust, tolerance and openness. As such, we expect all at Sutton Valence to treat each other with respect, humanity and care. Individuals therefore are obliged to recognise that the differences between us make us collectively stronger. It is essential that we understand, appreciate and celebrate the diversity of backgrounds, world views and attitudes expressed by those in our community.

At the foundation of our community is the expectation that every student will achieve their potential. Our commitment is to strive for excellence as pupils and teachers. To achieve this it is essential that every member of the School strives to give of their very best in all that they do.

Results. Sutton Valence School has an inclusive intake, however, our academic strength lies in enabling our students to achieve beyond their benchmarked potential, whatever their ability. On average, our students will gain results at A Level that outperform their predicted grade on entry to the School by 0.5 of a grade per subject. As measured by Durham University's Centre for Evaluation and Monitoring, which has a thirty-year history of computing these statistics, this year Sutton Valence is in the top 10% of schools for adding academic value (amongst those participating). That means that children at Sutton Valence do significantly better in their exams than they would do in 90% of other schools, nationally.

It is the combination of outstanding teaching and consistent effort by our students that brings these enviable results. For example, this year our top set students (many of whom did not pass the 11+) achieved 98% A* to B grades at A Level. Overall, our A Level results in recent years are similar to, or better than, those of the highly selective Kent grammar schools.

Curriculum. The academic curriculum is innovative and aims to achieve a balance between the needs of the individual and demands of society, industry, the universities and the professions. Classes are small and the ratio of graduate teaching staff is 1:9.

Our First and Second Forms (Years 7 and 8) follow our innovative, challenging and stimulating Junior Curriculum, which has academic excellence at its heart and continues to promote our pupils' love of learning by emphasising the Sutton Valence Learning Habits of Being, Thinking, Doing and Relating. We also ensure that the fundamental study skills required for success are mastered so that our pupils can move on fully prepared to excel at GCSE and beyond. These pupils also pursue our excellent Junior Leadership programme which promotes those essential skills required in addition to academic study for them to become truly successful and make the most of all that is on offer; leading others, team membership, organisation, time-management and perseverance, as examples. In addition they each produce a Junior Portfolio which records their achievements over the two years and 'graduate' in readiness to join the Senior School with the award of the Sutton Valence School Junior Curriculum.

Many pupils join us in the Third Form from other schools. In this Form we concentrate even more on developing a high level of competence in the essential numeracy, literacy and ICT skills, across all subjects, in targeted-ability groups, with the most able often undertaking extension programmes, in preparation for GCSEs in Core (English, Mathematics, Sciences, Humanities and Languages) and Option (Music, DT, Art, Drama, HE and PE) subjects, which are then studied in the Fourth and Fifth Forms. Every pupil is set 'Target Agreed Grades' (TAGs) in discussion with their teachers and their attainment and effort level in relation to their TAGs is reviewed half-termly. These grades are benchmarked against the performance of pupils of similar ability in other independent schools. Our aim is that Sutton Valence pupils will aspire to and achieve highly ambitious outcomes relative to their ability profile and thus amply fulfil their true potential. They are also heavily involved in our extensive co-curricular programme.

In Fourth and Fifth Form (Years 10 and 11) pupils usually study nine or ten subjects to GCSE level. These are divided between the core – English and English Literature, Mathematics, a Modern Language (French, Spanish, German), Science, Religious Studies, PSHE and ICT – and option groups. Each group contains a number of subjects, offering a choice which allows every pupil to achieve a balanced education whilst, at the same time, providing the opportunity to concentrate on his or her strengths. Subjects on offer are History, Geography, Drama, Business Studies, a second Language, DT, Home Economics, Art, Music, iMedia and PE.

Sixth Form Pupils, either progressing from our Fifth Form or joining us from elsewhere, pursue an A Level course in three or four carefully-chosen subjects, along with individual research in a specialist topic in preparation for submission of an extended project qualification (EPQ) or the BTEC Level 3 in Uniformed Public Service, which counts for university entry. As in the younger years, all pupils work towards ambitious TAGs based on Durham University's independent school benchmarking system. In recent years, our pupils have significantly outperformed these national expectations, achieving strong positive value added results which show that there is something special happening here relative to similar institutions. They can also expect to receive plenty of individual support and expert, bespoke, advice on appropriate Higher Education applications, interview practice, CV writing and careers in general. In addition there are numerous opportunities to be fully involved in wider School life and take on positions of leadership. The vast majority will continue their academic journey at university level, although employment-based training routes are becoming an increasingly popular option for some.

Potential Oxbridge candidates are identified in the Lower Sixth year and suitable tuition is arranged.

Choice of Subjects: Separate booklets on GCSE and A Level options are available.

Setting, Promotion, Reporting. In First to Fifth Form Mathematics and French are setted. In First to Third Form a top group is selected.

The minimum qualification for entry into the Sixth Form is normally considered to be five B grade passes at GCSE Level, or the equivalent for overseas students.

Academic progress is monitored by tutors and at regular intervals throughout the term every pupil is graded for achievement and effort in every subject for their classwork and for effort in their prep. Parents are invited to a 'monitoring morning' at every half term to discuss their child's progress and to set targets for improvement next half term, if required. At the end of term full subject reports are written on all pupils. Promotion between sets is always possible.

ICT (iMedia). In addition to well-equipped computer suites the School has developed a sophisticated campus-wide network with its own intranet and online systems of communication with parents.

The school network serves the whole site providing open access for pupils in the computer rooms and throughout the

school via a Microsoft Windows-based system working on industry-standard software. The library stocks many CD ROMs and there is a CAD system in Design and Technology. Access to the network is available to pupils in their own rooms in boarding houses.

Higher Education and Careers. Sutton Valence has a modern and well-equipped Sixth Form Centre which incorporates a careers library and the latest technologies to help in degree and career selection.

Every pupil sits a series of aptitude and ability tests during the two years prior to GCSE. This is followed by a thorough interview with trained members of staff in conjunction with the Kent Careers Service, when suggestions are made for Sixth Form academic courses and possible degrees or careers are explored.

In the Sixth Form further interviews are conducted, the Higher Education Coordinator gives advice on university and college applications and a range of career lectures and visits are laid on, including trips to Oxford and Cambridge universities.

Music. Music plays a very important part in the life of the school, and we have a deservedly fine reputation for the quality and range of our music-making. The music school contains a concert hall, five teaching rooms, ten practice rooms and an ensemble room.

Approximately 40% of the pupils learn a musical instrument or have singing lessons; there are four choirs, an orchestra, wind band, string group, jazz band, and a very full programme of concerts. Music tours to Europe are arranged, and the Music Society organises a programme of distinguished visiting performers every year.

Drama. As with Music, Drama is central to the life of the school and the creative expression of our students. Every year there will be a number of productions, in addition to theatre workshops and reviews. Drama scholars and others also receive one-to-one drama coaching lessons in preparation for LAMDA exams. The Baughan Theatre provides an adaptable venue seating up to 250 for drama, music and lectures, along with rehearsal rooms, technical gantry and scene dock.

Sport and Physical Education. Sutton Valence has a deserved reputation as a strong sporting school, competing in seventeen sports. On average, forty pupils will have representative honours at County, Regional and National levels in the main sports as well as in other disciplines. On a typical Saturday afternoon, half the school will be engaged in matches.

The Talented Athlete Group (TAG), which includes sports scholars, helps those students, both inside and outside of Sutton Valence, who are performing at a very high level (county and beyond). Once identified, the student will have regular meetings with their coach, either as a group or individually, where aims and objectives will be set and a variety of subjects will be covered. Individual strength and conditioning programmes and sessions are offered for all senior teams and are monitored by professionally qualified staff.

Our 100-acre site has one of the best cricket squares in Kent, two floodlit Astroturf pitches for hockey, a six-lane indoor swimming pool, tennis, netball and squash courts, a sports hall encompassing a full-size indoor hockey pitch, sprung-floor cricket nets and fitness suite, six golf practice holes and a floodlit all-weather running track. In all, there is a tremendous range of choice for both boys and girls, all of whom will have timetabled sport on at least two days every week and could be involved in a sporting activity every day, if they wished. Additional sports, such as football, judo, dance, horse riding, badminton, basketball, fives and fencing are offered through our activities programme.

Pastoral System. The School is arranged vertically in houses, with the Juniors (Years 7 and 8) in a separate house. Each House has a Housemaster or Housemistress and is divided into Tutor Groups containing pupils from each year and from day and boarding. Pupils meet with their Tutor every day and this allows their progress to be monitored, as well as giving pupils an opportunity to seek guidance. In addition to monitoring academic progress, tutors help pupils develop their potential through the Personal, Social and Health Education (PSHE) programme.

The School is a Christian foundation, however, our values are very much based on openness, tolerance and inclusivity. As such, we welcome students from all faith backgrounds, as well as those families who have no faith commitment.

Community Service, CCF and Duke of Edinburgh's Award. The CCF provides an organisation within Sutton Valence School which enables boys and girls to develop self-discipline, responsibility, self-reliance, resourcefulness, endurance, perseverance, a sense of service to the community and leadership. It complements the academic and other co-curricular aims of the School in preparing our pupils for adult life. All the three service elements of Army, Navy and RAF are offered. Pupils may join in the Third Form (Year 9) and CCF is also one of the option choices in the Fourth Form (Year 10). Cadets are encouraged to join the Duke of Edinburgh's Award scheme where there is the opportunity for planning and undertaking expeditions. Sutton Valence School CCF is affiliated to the Princess of Wales's Royal Regiment.

The Duke of Edinburgh's Award scheme is, similarly, well supported with, on average, 18 Gold Awards being achieved each year. Others participate in Community Service activities whereby pupils visit local primary schools, old people's homes, hospitals, undertake charity work and help out with local conservation projects.

Clubs and Activities. Time is specifically set aside each week for clubs and activities. Every pupil spends time pursuing his or her own special interests, and with up to forty clubs or activities from which to choose, the range and scope is very wide. In addition, various school societies and some other activities take place out of school hours, for example the Kingdon Society for Academic Scholars.

Scholarships and Bursaries. Academic, Art, Design Technology, Music, Sport and Drama Scholarships are awarded at 11+, 13+ and Sixth Form entry. Candidates may apply for a maximum of two non-academic scholarships.

The Westminster Scholarship supports well-motivated and able pupils who enter Sutton Valence School at Sixth Form level and who are expected to achieve 5 A* grade passes at GCSE.

Bursaries are awarded according to financial need at the discretion of the Scholarship and Bursaries Committee, and are reviewed annually. Forces bursaries are available.

Further details may be obtained from the Admissions Officer.

Fees per term (2016–2017). Senior Boarding (in addition to Tuition): £3,750 (Full), £3,015 (5 nights pw), £2,460 (4 nights pw), £1,950 (3 nights pw). Junior Boarding (in addition to Tuition): £2,985 (Full), £2,605 (5 nights pw), £2,205 (4 nights pw), £1,745 (3 nights pw). Tuition: Junior £5,150–£5,855, Senior £6,725. Lunch for Day pupils and occasional boarders: £270.

Instrumental Music: £250 per term (10 lessons).

Extras: Books, stationery and clothing are charged for as supplied. A small charge is also made for entry at each stage to The Duke of Edinburgh's Award scheme. Any other extras are those expenses personal to the individual. We have a series of bus routes available to families from areas across Kent costing up to £300 per term. Further details of routes can be obtained on request.

Charitable status. United Westminster Schools Foundation is a Registered Charity, number 309267. Its aims are to promote education through its two independent schools and one state comprehensive school.

Visitor: The Lord Archbishop of Canterbury

Foundation: United Westminster Schools

Director/Clerk: R W Blackwell, MA

Governing Body:
Lady Vallance, JP, MA, MSc, PhD, FRSA, FCGI
Major Gen D L Burden, CB, CBE
Mrs J Davies, BSc
A J Hutchinson, MA Cantab
T D Page
The Revd Canon D Stanton
Mrs G Swaine, BSc Hons, MEd (*Vice-Chair*)
D W Taylor, MA, FRSA
E L Watts, OBE, BA, FRSA
Mrs A Westbrook, LLB Hons, PG DiP

Headmaster: **B C W Grindlay**, MA Cantab, MusB, FRCO CHM

Senior Deputy Head: J J Farrell, MA Cantab (*History*)
Academic Deputy Head: Mrs R C Ball, BA (*Media Studies*)
Assistant Head: D R Sansom, BSc (*Geography*)
Bursar: S R Fowle

Academic Staff:
† *Boarding Housemaster or Housemistress*
‡ *Day Housemaster or Housemistress*

‡G N Alderman, BEd Avery Hill College (*Games, Mathematics*)
‡A R Bee, BSc Manchester (*Head of Geography*)
Miss H Blackhall, BA Exeter (*MFL*)
Dr M Brown, BSc Kent (*Physics, Chemistry, Astronomy, Junior Science Coordinator*)
‡Miss L J Burden, BA Anglia, BSc OU, Dip Hyp (*Head of Psychology, Community Service, Head of PSHE*)
‡R H Carr, BA St John's College Durham (*History, Games, Head of the Juniors and Prep School Liaison*)
W G A Clapp, BA Exeter (*Geography*)
D E Clarke, BSc Bristol, CBiol, MSB (*Biology and Photography*)
Miss E J Clement-Walker, MSc, BA Loughborough (*DT and Art*)
‡T P Cope, MEng Loughborough (*Maths, CO RAF*)
†C M Davenport, BA Keele (*Head of English*)
Miss E R Davies, BA Coventry (*HE and Drama*)
G A Davies, BA Wales Lampeter (*Chaplain, Religious Studies*)
Mrs S H de Castro Franco, BA Manchester (*Head of MFL*)
L Ellmers, BA Oxford (*MFL*)
B E Fewson, BA Hull (*Director of Drama*)
D Frost, BSc Wolverhampton (*Head of Learning Support*)
Mrs F M Gosden, BA Rhodes University (*English*)
Miss L Gray, BA Bangor (*Religious Studies, Junior Leadership Coordinator*)
Dr E J Grindlay, MA Cantab (*English, Head of Academic Scholars*)
Miss M A Halleron, BSc Leeds (*Head of Physics*)
Miss P L Hallett, BA Brighton (*Head of Academic PE, Head of Tennis and Rounders*)
A P Hammersley, BSc York (*Biology*)
G Harris, BA King's College London (*Assistant Head of Mathematics*)
Mrs E Head, MA Dundee (*SEN*)
†S J Head, MSci Bristol (*Chemistry and Head of Boarding*)
Mrs H E Heurtevent, BA Caen, DEUG I and II Université Catholique, Angers (*MFL*)
Dr S P Hiscocks, BSc, CChem, FRSC, CSciTeach Essex, MA King's College London (*Head of Chemistry*)

D W Holmes, LRAM, Prof Cert Royal Academy of Music (*Head of Strings*)

P J Horley, PG Dip RNCM, BA, ARCO, ATCL, ALCM College of Ripon and York St John (*Director of Music*)

M D Howell, BSc University College Worcester (*Director of Sport, Head of Rugby*)

Ms S Morávek-Hurst, MA Dundee (*Mathematics*)

J Ings, BA Southampton (*Geography*)

†M B James, MEd Macquarie University Sydney, Grad Dip Ec New England University, Australia (*Head of Business Studies and Economics*)

M A Jones, BSc East Anglia (*Geography*)

D J J Keep, MA Greenwich, BEd Avery Hill College (*Head of DT*)

Mrs C J Kitchen, BEng Bradford, MSc Birmingham, BSc OU (*Mathematics, Timetabler and Academic Data Coordinator, Assistant DofE Coordinator*)

Mrs W M Loy, MSci Durham, MSc Birmingham (*Physics*)

Miss J A Manning, BA Kent, PG Dip Dyslexia & Literacy York (*Head of ESL*)

†Mrs A Mathews, BA Canterbury Christ Church (*PE, Games, Dance*)

D R Mathews, BSc Brunel (*Head of Boys' and Girls' Hockey, Golf, Geography*)

Miss K J McConnachie, BSc Birmingham (*PE, Games, Head of Netball, ICT, Assistant D of E Coordinator*)

G J Millbery, BA Wales Lampeter (*Director of ICT, Contingent Commander CCF, Assistant D of E Coordinator*)

Mrs L A Mitchell-Nanson, BSc Kent (*Head of Mathematics*)

B P O'Donovan, BA Southampton (*MFL*)

Miss E J Oliver, BSc Bangor University (*Biology and ICT*)

A J F Penfold, BA Surrey (*Head of Religious Studies*)

R W J Plowden MA Wales, BA Newcastle (*History*)

Mrs F H Porter, BA Leeds, MA Ed Christ Church Canterbury (*English, Head of Sixth Form*)

Miss S Pritchard, BA Greenwich (*Business Studies and Economics*)

Miss Z Radford, BSc Swansea (*Head of Biology*)

Mrs A P Simpson, BSc London, PGCert (*Dyslexia*), PGCert (*Educational Testing*) (*SEN*)

Mrs S Rose, BEd Bishop Otter College (*Assistant Head of the Juniors, English, Games, Child Protection Coordinator*)

J D Soman, BA Oxford (*Assistant Director of Music*)

Mrs A J Sunde, BA Sheffield (*Head of History*)

Mrs N R Sutton, BA Canterbury, Christchurch, NZ (*Art*)

M J Thompson, BA Wolverhampton (*Head of Art*)

Mr V Wells (*Head of Cricket, Games*)

Mrs C Westlake, BA Sussex (*Assistant Head of English*)

C J Westlake, BSc Glamorgan (*Mathematics*)

Ms L J Williams, BA Open University (*English and Drama*)

Mrs H M Wood, MSc, BSc Hull (*Chemistry, CO Navy*)

Mr J Zane, MA City University, BA Exeter (*Head of Media Studies*)

Assistant Bursar: Mrs D van Leeuwen

Headmaster's PA: Mrs S O'Connell

Admissions Officer: Mrs K Webster

Development Manager: Mrs H Knott, BSc

Preparatory School

Acting Head: Miss C L Corkran, MEd, BEd Hons Cantab

Head of Pre-Prep: Miss P McCarmick, MA, BSc QTS, AMBDA

Director of Studies: Mrs R Harrison, BEd Hons

Head's Secretary and Admissions: Mrs A Leckie

Tonbridge School

Tonbridge, Kent TN9 1JP

Tel:	01732 365555
Fax:	01732 363424
email:	hmsec@tonbridge-school.org
website:	www.tonbridge-school.co.uk

Motto: '*Deus dat incrementum*'

Tonbridge School was founded in 1553 by Sir Andrew Judde, under Letters Patent of King Edward VI.

Tonbridge is an all-boys, 13–18, boarding and day school. 780 boys from a variety of backgrounds are offered an education remarkable both for its breadth of opportunity and the exceptional standards routinely achieved in all areas of school life.

The school aims to provide a caring and enlightened environment in which the talents of each individual flourish. We encourage boys to be creative, tolerant and to strive for academic, sporting and cultural excellence. Respect for tradition and an openness to innovation are equally valued. A well-established house system at the heart of the school fosters a strong sense of belonging. We want boys to enjoy their time here, but also to be made aware of their social and moral responsibilities. Ideally, Tonbridgians should enter into the adult world with the knowledge and self-belief to fulfil their own potential and, in many cases, to become leaders in their chosen field. Equally, we hope to foster a life-long empathy for the needs and views of others.

Tonbridge boys are extremely successful at obtaining places at leading universities. 37 leavers in the summer of 2015 have so far gone to Oxford or Cambridge, with more applying post A level. Other popular destinations include Durham, Bristol and Imperial.

Visitors to Tonbridge are always welcome and full information about the school is available on our website: www.tonbridge-school.co.uk.

Location. Tonbridge School is just off the M25, on the edge of the Kent / Surrey / Sussex borders and attracts families from all over southern England and beyond. It lies in about 150 acres of land on the edge of the town of Tonbridge, and thus provides a good balance between town and country living.

Admissions. The majority of boys join the school at the age of 13, having gained admission through the Common Entrance Examination or the school's own Scholarship Examination (held in early May). About 140 boys are admitted at the age of 13 each year. An additional 20 places are available for entry to the Sixth Form at the age of 16. We also have up to 6 places for boys aged 14 (Year 10).

Registration for a boy at 13+ entry should be made as early as possible, and preferably not later than three years before the date of intended entry. Boys will then be asked to come to Tonbridge to sit a short computer-based cognitive test. The results of this test, in conjunction with the current school Head's report, will determine whether the offer of a place may be made, conditional upon either Common Entrance or Scholarship entry at 13 years old. Applications for 14+ and Sixth Form entry are best made by September a year before entry, but may be considered later. Admission at 14+ (and at 13+ from schools who do not prepare boys for common entrance) is gained via our own Maths and English exams. Boys sitting for entry at 16+ will take papers in the 4 subjects they wish to study for A Level.

Parents wishing to send their sons to Tonbridge should apply to the Director of Admissions for a copy of the Prospectus, which gives full details of the registration procedure. Information is also available on the website: www.tonbridge-school.co.uk.

Scholarships and Bursaries. About 45 scholarships are offered each year: up to 21 Academic Scholarships (awarded by examination in early May); 10 or more Music Scholarships (examination in early February); up to 10 Art, Drama or Technology Scholarships (examination in early February); up to 4 Cowdrey Scholarships, for sporting ability and sportsmanship (assessment in early February); Choral Boarding Awards, for Choristers of Cathedral or other Choir Schools. 3 or 4 Sixth Form Academic or Music Scholarships are also awarded.

The value of a Scholarship may be increased by any amount up to the full school fee, if assessment of the parents' means indicates a need.

For boys over 10 and under 11 on 1st September, two Junior Foundation Scholarships are awarded, tenable at a Preparatory school. Candidates must be attending a State Primary School. Junior academic and music awards may also be made to 10 or 11 year old sons of parents requiring financial help in fee-paying Prep Schools. They are awarded as 'advance' Scholarships by competitive examination in November two-three years before entry to Tonbridge.

Foundation Awards provide means-tested support (up to 100% of the full school fee) for a Tonbridge education to boys who can clearly and substantially benefit from what the school has to offer. Awards may be made at three ages: in Year 6 (for entry to Tonbridge in Year 9), in Year 8 (for entry to Tonbridge in Year 9) and in Year 11 (for entry to Tonbridge in Year 12). Boys from the State sector who earn an Award in Year 6 will receive means-tested support through preparatory school (for Years 7 and 8); this should put them in a position to sit the Tonbridge School Scholarship Examination in Year 8 (although the place at Tonbridge is guaranteed from Year 6).

Forces bursaries are available for children of serving members of the armed forces.

Entry forms and full particulars of all Scholarships and Foundation Awards may be obtained from the Admissions Secretary; Tel: 01732 304297; email: admissions@tonbridge-school.org.

Fees per term (2016–2017). Boarders £12,513; Day Boys £9,386.

Charitable status. Tonbridge School is a Registered Charity, number 1097977. It exists solely to provide education for boys.

Governors:
J L Cohen, QC (*Chairman*)

T M Attenborough	G M Rochussen
D P Devitt	Professor C J Rudge, CBE
M Dobbs	Dr M S Spurr, DPhil
R J Elliott	Professor S Stallebrass
Mrs S Huang	Dr G E Taggart
A Mayer	Mrs K Wheadon
Mrs J Naismith	The Earl of Woolton

Clerk to the Governors: Major General A Kennett, CBE

Headmaster: T H P Haynes, BA

Second Master: Dr P H Williams, PhD
Director of Studies: J C Pearson, MA
Director of Teaching and Learning: M J Weatheritt, MA
Director of Admissions and Marketing: A J Leale, BA
Bursar: A C Moore, MA, MBA, INSEAD
Upper Master: J R Bleakley, BA
Development Director: A R Whittall, MA

Assistant Staff:
* Head of Department/Subject

Art:
*F J Andrews, MA, BA
T W Duncan, BA
Mrs E R Glass, MA
Mrs B L Waugh, BA

Artist-in-Residence: Mrs J de Pear, MA
Art Librarian: Mrs M P Dennington
Art Technician: Mrs J M Brent

Classics:
*J A Burbidge, BA, MSt, DPhil
J A Nicholls, MA
P W G Parker, MA
A P Schweitzer, MA
R J M Stephen, BA

Design Technology and Engineering:
*R L Day, BSc
W D F Biddle, BSc
A O Cooke, MEng, DPhil
J M Woodrow, BA
Engineering Advisor: D L Faithfull, BTech, MSc, CEng
Technology Technicians: R Davies; O Longson
Teaching Assistant: C Martin

Digital Creativity:
*P J Huxley, BSc
Technology Tutors: D P Love MIET, C D Walker
Media Tutor: Mrs E R Sim, BA, MPhil

Divinity:
*J C F Dobson, MA
R Burnett, MA
S J Dungate, BA
The Revd D A Peters, MA
H J M Swales, BA

Drama:
*G D Bruce, MA
R J Hartley, BA
L Thornbury, DipDrama

Modern Languages:
*L S McDonald, MA
Mrs E Saurel, BA, MA (*French*)
S Kerr (*German*)
R Lokier, BA (*Spanish*)
X J Wu, MA (*Mandarin Chinese*)
Mrs C Clugston, MA (*EAL*)
Mrs C Cordero, Lda en Fil
R D Hoare, MA (*International Coordinator*)
Miss D M McDermot, MA
J A Nicholls, MA
P W G Parker, MA
A B F Pruvost, BA
Mrs R Thomson, BA, DipHE, TESOL
Mrs A Troletti-Harlow, MA
C E Wright, BA
Mrs X Yu, BA

English:
*N J Waywell, BA
J P Arscott, MA
J R Bleakley, BA
P S D Carpenter, MA
A J Edwards, MA
R H Evans, MA
Mrs D M Hulse, MA, DipModDrama
Mrs S Pinto del Rio, BA
W van Asperen, BA

Geography:
*C M Battarbee, BA
C M Henshall, BA
G P Gales, BEd
Miss J H Green, BA
Mrs J M Watson-Reynolds, BA

History:
*C D Thompson, BA, MPhil, PhD
D Cooper, MA
Mrs F C Dix Perkin, MA
J C Harber, MA
R W G Oliver, MA
Miss M L Robinson, MA

Mathematics:
*I R H Jackson, MA, PhD
S Burns, BSc
T G Fewster, BSc
R J Freeman, MA
K A Froggatt, MA
Miss J A D Gent, BA
J D King, MA, PhD
M J Lawson, BA
N J Lord, MA
V Myslov, BA
A A Reid, MChem, PhD
S J Seldon, MA, MEng
Dr J D Shafer, PhD, MA, BSc
A J Sixsmith, BA

Music:
*M A Forkgen, MA, ARCO (*Director of Music*)
J R P Thomas, MA, FRCO (*Head of Academic Music & Choirmaster*)
A E L Pearson, BMus, ARCM, LRAM (*Strings*)
D L Williams, GRSM, ARCM, LRAM (*Piano*)
S J Hargreaves, MA, MEd
Mr C Bentley

Physical Education:
Director of Sport and Head of PE: C D Morgan, BSc

Science:
*W J Burnett, BSc, PhD
P G Deakin, MEng, BA
A O Cooke, MEng, DPhil
R L Fleming, MA, MInstP
A G McGilchrist, MA
J K Moore, BA
D S Pinker, PhD, MSci
C T E Powell, BSc, MRes
M J Weatheritt, BSc, MA
Dr C R Lawrence, MA, PhD
J A Fisher, BSc
M J Clugston, MA, DPhil
D P Dickinson, MChem
G C Fisher, BSc, MA
A V Nagar, BSc, ARCS
J C Pearson, MA
Dr D P Robinson, MEarthSci, DPhil
H M Grant, MA
M R Ackroyd, BSc, PhD
W J Burnett, BSc, PhD
P M Ridd, MA
A T Sampson, BSc
C J C Swainson, MA
Dr P H Williams, PhD

Social Science:
J Blake, BA, MSc (*Economics and Business*)
Miss K E Moxon, MA (*Politics*)
I J Black, MA, BA
A J Leale, BA
P J North, MA, BA
N R V Rendall, BA
J D W Richards, MA, PhD
P T Sadler, BA
A J Sixsmith, BA

Director of ICT Services:
C J Scott, BA

University Entrance and Careers:
Mrs A Rogers, BA

Learning Strategies:
Mrs H F McLintock, BA
Mrs N M Gerard, BA

Houses & Housemasters:

Boarding:
School House: R Burnett
Judde House: G P Gales
Park House: A T Sampson
Hill Side: P J North
Parkside: C D Thompson
Ferox Hall: J A Fisher
Manor House: C J C Swainson

Day:
Welldon House: R H Evans
Smythe House: C M Henshall
Whitworth House: W D F Biddle
Cowdrey House: J C Harber
Oakeshott House: G M Barnes

Administration:
Librarian: Mrs B Matthews, MCLIP
Headmaster's PA: Mrs L R O'Neill
Admissions Secretaries:
Miss R G Hearnden (*Senior Admissions Officer*)
Mrs V C Larmour (*Admissions Officer Lower Sixth Entry*)
Mrs R Griffiths (*Admissions Officer Pre-testing*)
Examinations Officer: Miss B J Shepherd

PA to the Second Master: Miss E J Day
Music Dept Administrator: Mrs J Marsh

Trinity School
Croydon

Shirley Park, Croydon CR9 7AT

Tel: 020 8656 9541
Fax: 020 8655 0522
email: admissions@trinity.croydon.sch.uk
website: www.trinity-school.org

Motto: '*Vincit qui Patitur*'

The School was founded by Archbishop John Whitgift in 1596. The full title of the school is Trinity School of John Whitgift.

One of the three governed by the Whitgift Foundation, the School is an Independent Day School for boys aged 10–18 with a co-educational Sixth Form since September 2011. The School aims to give a wide education to students of academic promise, irrespective of their parents' income.

Buildings and Grounds. Trinity School has been in its present position since 1965, when it moved out from the middle of Croydon (its old site is now the Whitgift Centre) to a completely new complex of buildings and playing fields on the site of the Shirley Park Hotel. The grounds are some 27 acres in extent, and a feeling of openness is increased by the surrounding Shirley Park Golf Club and the extensive views to the south up to the Addington Hills. There are additional playing fields in Sandilands, ten minutes' walk from the School.

The resources of the Whitgift Foundation enable the School to provide outstanding facilities. All departments have excellent and fully equipped teaching areas.

Admission. The main ages of admission are at 10, 11 and 13. Entry is by competitive examination and interview. A reference from the feeder school will also be required. The School attracts applications from over 150 schools, with approximately 60% entering from state primaries. Entries of boys and girls into the Sixth Form are also welcomed.

Fees per term (2016–2017). £5,302 covering tuition, books, stationery and games.

Bursaries. Whitgift Foundation Bursaries (means-tested) are available providing exceptionally generous help with fees.

Scholarships. Academic, Art, Design Technology, Drama, Music and Sport Scholarships are available annually to boys applying for entry at 10+, 11+ or 13+. Boys must be the relevant age on 1 September of the year of entry. Awards are based on the results of the Entrance Examination, interview and current school reference. They are awarded without regard to parental income and are worth a percentage (maximum 50%) of the school fees throughout a pupil's career.

Academic, Art, Music and Sport Scholarships are also available for entry to the Sixth Form, based on GCSE results.

Scholarships may be supplemented up to the value of full fees if there is financial need.

Music Scholarships of up to 50% fee remission include free tuition in two instruments. Applicants are required to play two pieces on principal instrument and show academic potential in the Entrance Examination. Awards are available for all instruments and singing ability can be taken into consideration. Further details from the Director of Music.

Organisation and Counselling. The School is divided into the Lower School (National Curriculum Years 6–9) and the Upper School (Years 10–13). The Pastoral Leader in charge of each section works with the team of Form Tutors to encourage the academic and personal development of each boy. There is frequent formal and informal contact with parents.

A counselling service is provided to pupils as part of the pastoral provision and a fully qualified School Counsellor is on hand to help students with their individual needs. Pupils can refer themselves to the Counsellor or they may be referred by staff.

There is a structured and thorough Careers service, which advises boys at all levels of the School and arranges work experience and work shadowing.

While the academic curriculum is taught from Monday to Friday, there is a very active programme of sports fixtures and other activities at the weekend, and all boys are expected to put their commitment to the School before other activities.

Curriculum and Staffing. The School is generously staffed with well qualified specialists. The organisation of the teaching programme is traditionally departmental based. The syllabus is designed to reflect the general spirit of the National Curriculum while allowing a suitable degree of specialisation in the Upper School.

The normal pattern is for pupils to take 9 or 10 GCSE subjects, and to proceed to the Sixth Form to study an appropriate mixture of AS and A2 level subjects, complemented by a wide-ranging General Studies programme, before proceeding to university.

Games and Activities. The main school games are Rugby, Football, Hockey, Cricket and Athletics, with the addition of Netball for girls in the Sixth Form. Many other sports become options as a boy progresses up the School. Games are timetabled, each pupil having one games afternoon a week.

At the appropriate stage, most boys take part in one or more of the following activities: Community Service, CCF, Duke of Edinburgh's Award scheme, Outdoor Activities. There are many organised expeditions during the holidays.

Music. Music at Trinity has an international reputation, and every year Trinity Boys Choir is involved in a varied programme of demanding professional work. The Choir has performed at the BBC Proms for the past seven years and sings at the Royal Opera House, the English National Opera, Glyndebourne or Garsington 3–4 times each year. Recently the choristers have travelled to Vienna, Brussels, Venice, Dusseldorf and Wachock Abbey, Poland. They also appear regularly on radio and television. Trinity Choristers, who specialise in religious music, hold an annual residential Easter Course at a British cathedral. Choral Scholarships are awarded annually and enable boys to receive additional professional voice training without charge.

Many boys learn at least one musical instrument, and a large visiting music staff teach all orchestral instruments, piano, organ and classical guitar. There are numerous orchestras, bands and other instrumental groups for which boys are selected according to their ability. Musicians recently travelled to Canada and instrumentalists are regular finalists in the Pro Corda National Chamber Music competition.

Drama. There are two excellently equipped stages in the school and a lively and developing programme of formal and informal productions directed by pupils, staff and members of the Old Boys Theatre Company. Drama forms part of the formal curriculum in Years 6–9 and can be studied for GCSE and A Level.

Art and Design Technology. As well as the formal curriculum, which has led to 70% of the School taking a GCSE in art or design technology, pupils are encouraged to make use of the excellent facilities to develop their own interests.

Charitable status. The Whitgift Foundation is a Registered Charity, number 312612. The Foundation now comprises the Whitgift Almshouse Charity for the care of the elderly and the Education Charity which administers three schools.

Visitor: His Grace The Archbishop of Canterbury

Governing Body:
Chairman: C J Houlding
His Honour William Barnett, QC, MA Oxon
The Revd Canon C J L Boswell, The Vicar of Croydon
Mrs R A Jones, MA
Cllr T Letts, OBE
G H Wright, TD, DL, FCIOB
Cllr D Mead, FCCA, FCMA, FCIS, MBE
D C Hudson, MA
Mrs P Davies, BSc, MEd
Cllr M Mead, JP
The Rt Revd Jonathan Clark, The Bishop of Croydon
M A Proudfoot, MA, MLitt
D C Q Sutton, JP, FRICS
Cllr A Fleming
D C Q Sutton JP, FRICS
Viscountess Stansgate, MA, OBE

Chief Executive: M C Corney

Headmaster: A J S Kennedy, MA

Deputy Headmaster: E A Du Toit, MA London
    (*Economics, Mathematics*)
Deputy Head and Head of Upper School: Miss S L Ward,
    BSc Birmingham (*Psychology**)
Director of Extra-Curricular: J G Timm, BA Cambridge
    (*History, Politics*)
Director of Studies: N H Denman, MA Oxford
    (*Mathematics*)
Director of Teaching & Learning: A J Corstorphine, MPhil
    Cambridge (*Classics*)
Head of Lower School: G Du Toit, BEd Pretoria (*Religious
    Studies*)
Designated Safeguarding Lead: Mrs M R Sanders, BEd
    London (*Drama*)
Bursar: Mrs J Stanley, BA, CCAT, ACA
Director of Admissions: Mr J G Timm, BA Cambridge
    (*History, Politics*)

Assistant Staff:
* *Head of Department*
§ *part-time*

P G Abbott, BSc Cardiff (*Economics and Business, Head
    of Upper Sixth*)
M I Aldridge, BEd London (*Design Technology, Head of
    Lower Sixth*)
S R Allison, BA Durham (*Spanish**)
Mrs J L Anderson, BSc Bath (*Biology*)
M Asbury, BSc Bath (*Mathematics, Internal Exams**)
Dr M S Asquith, BA, MA, PhD London (*English§*)
Ms D S Balasubramaniam, BDS Chennai (*Biology*)
Ms N M Beaumont, MA Oxford (*Mathematics*)
L D Benedict, BA Bristol (*English*)
O J Benjamin, BA Durham (*German, Spanish*)
Ms H A Benzinski, BSc London (*Mathematics, DofE
    Coordinator*)
G C Beresford-Miller, BA Rhodes (*Physical Education,
    Clubs and Societies Coordinator*)
J Bird, BSc Kent (*Biology*)
P J Blanchard, BSc Exeter, MA Warwick (*Chemistry*)
Mrs N Blamire-Marin, BA Granada (*Lectora, Spanish*)
Miss V J Boorman, BA King's London (*Classics*)
M E Brennan, BA Oxford (*History, Politics, Head of Fifth
    Year*)
L A Brito-Babapulle, BA, MA, MSt Oxford, FRCO
    (*Music**)

M Bromberg, MSc Imperial (*Chemistry, Biology*)

T M Brooks, BA Leeds (*Geography*)

C R Burke, Port Elizabeth (*Physical Education*)

Mrs S I Cater, BA King's London, MPhil Queensland (*English, Drama, Assistant Head of Year – Sixth Form*)

Ms C D Cesar, BA Oxford (*Religious Studies, Drama*)

T W Chesters, BSc Strathclyde (*Design Technology, Assistant Director of Studies, Head of Information Management*)

S W Christian, BA Liverpool (*French, Spanish*)

Mrs M A Chitty, CertEd, Dip SpLD (*Learning Support*§)

D B Clifford, BA Oxford, MSc LSE, MBA Toronto (*Mathematics*)

M J Cole, BA MSc Cambridge (*Physics*)

A Cornick, BA Nottingham Trent (*Physical Education*)

D W G Currigan, BA, MA Chelsea, Kingston (*Design Technology**)

T Deakin, BSc Brunel (*Head of Hockey, Physical Education*)

T J Desbos, LCE Lille (*French*)

A B Doyle, MA Glasgow, MA Open (*English**)

T D Drake, BSc St Mary's Twickenham (*Junior Science*)

Dr T E Durno, MA, MPhil, PhD Cambridge (*English, EPQ Coordinator, Gifted and Talented Coordinator*)

R Earl, BSc UCL (*Economics and Business**)

J S Eminsang, BA Manchester (*Mathematics, Head of Junior Maths*)

T Escacena, BA Seville (*Spanish*)

N S Evans, BA Nottingham (*History, Politics*)

R E Evans, Dip Perf Royal College of Music (*Head of Piano*)

R G Evans, BSc Aston (*Electronics**, *Design Technology*§)

L M Flanagan, BA Cambridge (*Physics**)

Mrs A A Fulker, BA Oxford Brookes (*Art*)

A M Godfrey, BA Bretton Hall (*Drama, Drama Productions**§)

R M Greenberg, MA Oxford (*Biology*)

R E Hodder, BA SOAS London (*History*)

S M Hodge, BA Exeter (*Religious Studies*)

O J Hutchings, BA, MA York (*History, Politics*)

J A Inglis, BEng Open (*Design Technology*)

M V Johnson, BSc London (*Biology*)

Ms R Kanji, BSc, MEd Auckland (*Chemistry*)

I Kench, BSc Loughborough, MSc Oxford (*Geography, Physical Education, Head of Fourth Year*)

S D King, BA Manchester Metropolitan (*Physical Education*)

Mrs G C Kitchen, BA Durham (*Music*)

S D Kpodar, BA Lyon (*French*)

R E Lee, MA Oxford (*Religious Studies**)

A Liffchak, BA Hertfordshire (*Head of Rugby, Physical Education*)

Ms P-S Lin, BA National Taiwan University (*Chinese**)

A E Magee, MA St Andrews (*English*)

Dr M Mariani, BSc Kent, PhD UCL (*Physics*)

P Mazur, BA Wales, MA London (*Drama**, *English*)

Mrs S J McDonald, MA St Andrews (*Head of Learning Support*§)

S A McIntosh, MA Oxford (*German**)

R D Moralee, BSc Johannesburg (*Biology**)

D P Moran, BSc, MSc Dublin (*Chemistry*)

Mrs H C Murray, MEng Cambridge (*Mathematics*)

S Orungbamade, BEd Nigeria (*Economics and Business*)

Miss C A Parkinson, BSc Sussex, MSc UCL (*Psychology, Science*)

B J Patel, MA Cambridge (*Mathematics, Physics*)

B Patel, MSc UCL (*Mathematics*)

J A Paterson, BA Cambridge (*Classics*)

C P Persinaru, Dip RAM, LRAM (*Music, Head of Strings*)

Mrs R J Petty, MA Oxford (*English, Drama, Deputy Designated Safeguarding Lead*)

Mrs X L Phasey, MA Schiller International (*Chinese*§)

A Prestney, BA Durham (*Geography*)

J E Pietersen, BA Cambridge (*History, Politics, Head of Second Year*)

D K Price, BA Wimbledon College of Art (*Design Technology, Head of First Year*)

Mrs S J Rapoport, BEd Twickenham (*Academic Mentor*)

Mrs L Regan, BMus, LRAM (*Music*§)

Miss M-T Rembert, BA Cambridge (*History, Politics**)

M D Richbell, BSc Liverpool (*Director of Sport**)

R J Risebro, BSc Manchester Met (*Head of Cricket, Physical Education*)

A J Rogers, BA Plymouth (*Art and Photography, Head of Film*)

K A Roy, BSc Queen Mary London, MSc PhD Imperial (*Physics*)

Dr K R Rogers, BSc Cardiff, PhD London (*Chemistry*)

C P Ruck, BSc Southampton (*Geography*)

Dr J N Rush, BA, PhD, MPhil Cambridge (*English*)

M P Ryan, BA Oxford (*English*)

R M Salmanpour, BSc London (*Chemistry*)

Mrs V C Salin, MA Rouen, Northumbria (*French**)

L Signorelli, BSc Bath (*Economics*)

M D Smith, BEng Bath (*Mathematics*)

A E Smith, BA, MA York, MSc London (*Religious Studies*§)

J J Snelling, BSc Swansea, MA London, CGeog (*Geography, Head of Staff Development*)

G Spreng, MA Glasgow (*History**)

Mrs B J Steven, BA Cape Town (*English*)

Ms T Stevens-Lewis, BA, MA Goldsmiths (*Art, i/c Photography*)

Miss E E Stewart, MSc Leeds, MPhys Oxford (*Physics*)

J E Stone, BA Cambridge (*Classics**)

Ms C S Story, BA Durham (*English*)

Ms E M Suarez, BA Juan Carlos 1, Rey de Espana (*Lectora, Spanish*)

Miss A Sukiennik, BA, MA Paris X (*Lectrice, French*)

D J Swinson, MA, FRCO, ARCM, LRAM, Cambridge (*Director of Music**)

Mrs S Z Taylor, BSc Exeter (*Mathematics*)

W S Tucker, BSc Exeter (*Science**, *Physics*)

Mrs T A Upton, BSc Warwick (*Mathematics*)

S T Van Dal, BA Cambridge, MA UCL (*Classics*)

R van Graan, BA Canterbury Christ Church (*E-Learning**, *Computing*)

R J Venables, MEng Durham (*Mathematics*)

Miss R M Walker, BMus Birmingham Conservatoire (*Music, Drama*)

Mrs R E Wallace, MA Oxford (*Geography**)

Miss H C Whiteford, BSc Durham (*Religious Studies, Head of Third Year*)

Mrs C-J Wilkinson, BSc Glasgow (*Biology*)

R J Wickes, BSc Warwick (*Mathematics**)

C J Wilkinson, BSc Glasgow (*Biology*)

Miss J Wiskow, MA Wuppertal, Berlin (*German, Girls' Games**)

Ms H E Yovichich, BA Durham (*Geography*)

Admissions Registrar: Mrs P S Meyer

Sixth Form Admissions: Ms S Redican

Headmaster's Secretary: Mrs K Carr

Truro School

Trennick Lane, Truro, Cornwall TR1 1TH

Tel: 01872 272763
email: enquiries@truroschool.com
website: www.truroschool.com

Motto: *Esse quam videri*

Truro School was founded in 1880 by Cornish Methodists. In 1904 it came under the control of the Methodist Independent Schools Trust (MIST) and is now administered by a Board of Governors appointed by the Methodist Conference. Although pupils come from all parts of the country and abroad, the roots of the school are firmly in Cornwall and it is the only HMC school in the county.

The religious instruction and worship are undenominational though the school is conscious of its Methodist origins.

There are 790 pupils (456 boys, 334 girls; 720 day, 70 boarders) in the Senior School (age 11+ and above). There are another 240 pupils in the Preparatory School, where boys and girls may start in the pre-prep section at the age of 3.

The school is fully co-educational throughout and there is a strong Sixth Form of some 200+ pupils.

Boarding. At the Senior School girl boarders live in Malvern (Sixth Form) and Pentreve; boy boarders (5th–U6th) live in Trennick House; boy boarders (1st–4th) live in Poltisco House. All are supervised by resident teaching staff and families. Pupils eat in the central dining room with a cafeteria system. There is a School Medical Centre on site.

Campus and Buildings. The *Prep School* campus is built around a country house acquired by the school in the 30s. It has an indoor heated swimming pool, a large assembly hall and extensive areas for science, modern languages, computing, art and crafts, as well as a modern sports hall. A new Dining Hall was opened in 2013. The Pre-Prep is housed in a purpose-built unit, with a new extension opened in September 2009.

The *Senior School* occupies an outstanding site overlooking the Cathedral city and the Fal Estuary; it is only five minutes from the centre of the city but the playing fields reach into the open countryside. The school is excellently equipped. There is a first-class Library, extended and refurbished in 2010, extensive science laboratories, excellent Technology and Art facilities, a computer centre, music school, Sixth Form centre, a Sixth Form cafeteria and a range of classroom blocks. The fine block containing the Burrell Theatre, six classrooms and a drama centre has been extended to provide a Modern Languages Centre in The Wilkes Building. An attractive and newly-refurbished chapel provides a focus for the life of the school. A new Dining Hall and social area opened in November 2009. The Sir Ben Ainslie Sports Centre, completed for September 2013, provides an eight-court multi-use sports hall, two county standard glass-backed squash courts with viewing gallery, large fitness suite with a range of aerobic, strength and conditioning equipment, a multi-purpose dance and exercise studio with a sprung wooden floor, adding to the existing excellent facilities of 25m swimming pool, cricket nets, tennis courts, 40 acres of pitches and cricket pavilion. Following a link with Truro Fencing Club in September 2014 the school has its own designated Fencing Salle.

Organisation and Curriculum. Our academic programme up to GCSE provides a balance between the three Sciences, Humanities, Creative Arts and Modern Languages. In the 1st to 3rd Year, pupils study English, Mathematics, Biology, Chemistry and Physics, French and German, Geography, History, Religious Studies, Art, Design & Technology, Drama, ICT and Music. Spanish is optional from 3rd Year. All pupils have PE as well as Games each week. Every pupil in the 1st Year is taught touch typing, and ICT lessons culminate in a City & Guilds certified qualification by the end of the 3rd Year.

At GCSE the norm is to study nine subjects at full GCSE, with all pupils also studying a short course in Religious Studies (equivalent to a half GCSE). Compulsory subjects are English Language, English Literature, Mathematics, Double Award or Triple Award Science; the options include French, German, Spanish, Geography, History, Art and Design, Design and Technology, Music, Drama, Computer Science, PE and Geology.

Sixth Formers usually study for four AS Levels in the Lower Sixth and these include the same subjects as at GCSE, but with the introduction of Further Mathematics, Religious Studies (with Philosophy and Ethics), Economics, Business Studies, Psychology and the Extended Project Qualification. Our Extension Studies programme includes modules on Photography, Philosophy and Film Studies. As part of this we provide advice on careers and university applications, with a specialised programme for potential Medics, Dentists and Vets. The Community Sports Leadership Award is a popular option for the Upper Sixth. Three subjects will be most commonly continued into the Upper Sixth at A Level and the vast majority of Sixth Formers go on to further education when they leave.

Out-of-School Activities. Extra-curricular life is rich and varied. There is a choir, school orchestra, a jazz group, a brass band and many other ensembles. Facilities such as the ceramics room, the art room and the technical block are available to pupils in their spare time. A huge variety of activities includes fencing, squash, sailing, golf, basketball, debating, surfing, and many others. Many boys and girls take part in the Ten Tors Expedition, an exceptional number are engaged in the Duke of Edinburgh's Award scheme, as well as local Community Service. The School has an outdoor activities centre on Bodmin Moor and pupils have a chance to spend time there during the course of their education at the school.

Games. All the major team games are played. Badminton, cross-country, hockey, netball, squash and tennis are available throughout most of the year. Rugby and Girls Hockey are played in the Winter Term and Soccer and Netball in the Spring Term. In the summer, cricket, athletics and tennis are the major sports. The covered pool is heated.

Admissions. Truro School was once a Direct Grant Grammar School and most pupils join at the age of 11. There are vacancies for entry at other ages, particularly at 13 and 16.

Scholarships and Bursaries. Scholarships are available and the School offers a small number of means-tested bursaries up to the value of full fees. Truro School has recently linked with Truro Cathedral to offer scholarships for their new girl choristers from September 2015.

Fees per term (2016–2017). Senior School: Boarders £8,625; Weekly Boarders £7,410; Day Pupils (including lunch): £4,405. Prep (including lunch): £3,930 (Years 3–4), £4,075 (Years 5–6). Pre-Prep (including lunch): £2,850 (Nursery and Reception), £2,965 (Years 1 and 2).

Academic results. A number of pupils proceed to Oxbridge every year, along with overseas universities including, in 2016, MIT. Around 95% of the Sixth Form proceed to degree courses. The 2016 A Level pass rate was 99.7%, with nearly two-thirds at A* to B grades. At GCSE the 2016 pass rate was 97% with over 55% at grades A* and A.

Former Pupils' Association. There is a strong Former Pupils' Association with centres locally and in London and it has its own webalumnus. The "Friends of Truro School" involves parents, staff, old pupils and friends of the school in social events and fundraising.

Charitable status. Truro School is a Registered Charity, number 306576. It is a charitable foundation established for the purpose of education.

Visitor: The President of the Methodist Conference

Administrative Governors:
Chairman: K Conchie
R R Cowie, FCA
Mrs C Arter, BA Hons, RN, RNT, PGCE, FHEA, JP
N Ashcroft, MBE
T Daffern, BEng Hons, CEng, MBA, FIoMMM, FAusIMM
W Dexter, BSc, ACA
Dr S Evans, BSc, MB, ChB, PhD, FRCP
R S Funnell, MA
Mrs E Garner, BA Hons, MEd
C N Harding, BSc, FCMA, MIMgt
Revd Dr J Harrod, BSc, MA, PhD, FHEA
Mrs C Hogg, BSc, MBA
Mrs J Hosking, LLB Hons
P Kerkin, BSc Hons, FIFS
Dr R Kirby, PhD
P Rigby
P Stethridge, CEng, FICE, FIHT
Mrs H Sullivan, MA
R Thomas, BSc, MRICS
Revd S Wild, MA

Headmaster: A Gordon-Brown, BCom Hons, MSc, QTS

Deputy Heads:
N A Fisher, BSc, MSc, MA
Mrs E Ellison, BSc

Chaplain: A de Gruchy, MTheol

Boarding House Staff:
Mrs C Murphy, BA (*Malvern*)
T Copeland, BA (*Trennick*)
M A Nicholas, BEd (*Poltisco*)
Mrs S Mulready, BA (*Pentreve*)

Heads of Year:
Miss V J Gould, BA (*Co-Head of Sixth Form*)
Mrs J P Rainbow, MA (*Co-Head of Sixth Form*)
G D Hooper, PGCE (*5th Year*)
R T Picton, MPhys (*4th Year*)
Miss J R Egar BA (*3rd Year*)
Miss M E Macleod, BSc (*2nd Year*)
Mrs C McCabe, BSc (*1st Year*)

Heads of Department:
D Meads, BA (*Art*)
Miss S E Finnegan, BSc (*Biology*)
Dr A Brogden, MChem, PhD (*Chemistry*)
B Oldfield, BA (*Drama*)
C Baker, BSc (*Design and Technology*)
J Whatley, BSc (*Economics, Business Studies and Politics*)
Mrs A L Selvey BA, MA (*English*)
Mrs J Wormald, BSc (*Geography*)
Ms J Hope, BSc (*Geology*)
Dr M H Spring, MA, PhD (*History*)
S J McCabe, MA (*Mathematics*)
Mrs I Quaife, BA (*Modern Languages*)
M D Palmer, BMus, FRCO, LRAM (*Music*)
G C Whitmore, BEd (*PE and Games*)
A L Laity, BSc (*Physics*)
Mrs E L Mitchell, BA, MEd (*Religious Education*)

Truro School Preparatory School
(*see entry in IAPS section*)

Head: Ms S Patterson, BEd
Deputy Head: A MacQuarrie, BEd

Head of Pre-Prep Unit: Mrs S Hudson, BEd, MA

Bursar: Mrs A Robinson

University College School

Frognal, Hampstead, London NW3 6XH

Tel: 020 7435 2215
Fax: 020 7433 2111
email: seniorschool@ucs.org.uk
website: www.ucs.org.uk
Twitter: @UCSHampstead

University College School is a leading London day school providing places for approx 500 boys aged 11–16, with a co-educational Sixth Form of approx 300 places. UCS admitted its first cohort of girls into the Sixth Form in September 2008 and around 30–40 girls will join UCS each year.

University College School was founded in Gower Street in 1830 as part of University College, London and moved to its current location in Hampstead in 1907. The UCS Foundation comprises three separate schools offering education to children at each stage of their development from the ages of 3–18, founded to promote the Benthamite principles of liberal scholarship and education. Intellectual curiosity, breadth of study and independence of mind combine to achieve academic excellence; they are not subordinate to it.

Selecting children with no regard to race or creed, UCS fosters in them a sense of community alongside a tolerance of and a respect for the individual. By offering the fullest range of opportunities for personal and for group endeavour, it teaches the value of commitment and the joy of achievement. It is a place of study, but also of self-discovery and self-expression; a school that places equal value on learning with others as on learning from others.

Admission. UCS Pre-Prep accepts boys at the age of 4 to join Reception. Boys join the Junior Branch at the age of 7 and the Senior School at the ages of 11 and 13. We invite both boys and girls to apply at 16 for places in our Sixth Form. We always advise parents to check the admissions pages on the UCS website for the most up-to-date information. Please note that all applications, whether to the Pre-Prep, the Junior Branch or the Senior School, are now made online through the website.

Curriculum. The UCS curriculum is designed to match the educational needs of pupils at all stages of their development. At the Pre-Prep, the mix of formal and informal learning develops independent and enquiring thinkers. At the Junior Branch, whilst the emphasis is on breadth, boys are also prepared for Key Stage 2 Tests in English, Maths and Science.

The Lower School: In the first years at the Senior School boys aged 11–13 follow a common curriculum founded on the best features of the National Curriculum but enriched to develop a love of learning and positive study skills. These traits enable our pupils to develop their own academic specialisms as they go up through the school, whilst also ensuring that they receive a rounded academic education.

The subjects studied are Mathematics, PSHE, PE and Games. Mathematics is taught in banded groups related to boys' ability and progress. French is taught in sets to allow for those who have not studied the language previously. There is otherwise no streaming and subjects are studied within form groups. Homework is set each day, and usually takes between 45 minutes and one hour.

The Middle School. The curriculum is deliberately broad, in order to provide a suitable basis for further study leading to GCSE and Sixth Form courses. Pupils are divided into sets in Mathematics according to ability. More time is devoted to Science and boys may take up a further Classical or Modern Language (Greek, German, Spanish or Mandarin). In addition boys choose one option from Music, Drama and Computing. PSHE continues in Year 9 in the classroom and in the following two years, through a programme of presentations, discussions and visits from outside speakers. Homework tasks include a wider range of topics and activities than before.

For the two years leading to GCSE, boys continue with English and Mathematics. They may then choose freely a further seven subjects with the only proviso that, to maintain a sufficient breadth to their studies, they must include at least one Modern Language from those they have previously studied and at least one science subject. Boys in the top two Mathematics sets also take the Additional Mathematics qualification alongside their GCSE.

The GCSE subjects offered are: Biology, Physics, Chemistry, French, German, Spanish, Mandarin, Latin, Greek, History, Geography, Art, Design and Technology, Drama, Music, Computing and Physical Education.

The Sixth Form. Pupils may study any combination of four subjects in the Transitus (Year 12) and may freely mix Arts and Science subjects if they wish. Careful guidance is provided to ensure that the course upon which they embark will provide an appropriate basis for an application to the Higher Education course and institution of the individual pupil's choice. After one year of study, pupils may continue with three or four subjects in the Sixth Form (Year 13). Sixth Form sets normally include 8–10 pupils who, in preparation for Higher Education, are encouraged to take greater personal responsibility for study.

The A Level/Pre-U subjects available are: English, Mathematics, Further Mathematics, Biology, Physics, Chemistry, French, German, Spanish, Mandarin, Latin, Greek, History, Geography, Economics, Politics, Philosophy, Physical Education, Psychology, Drama and Theatre Studies, Computing, Design and Technology, Art, Music and History of Art.

Pastoral Care. We regard the personal, emotional and moral development of our pupils as a major priority at every single stage of the education that we offer. The aim of our pastoral system is to encourage pupils to develop their own identities and to express them with a proper regard for the feelings and sensitivities of others. Pupils are encouraged from an early age to develop a sense of responsibility for their own behaviour. Much stress is laid upon tolerance of and respect for one another. Considerable effort is made to build a sense of community within the school. To this end, three days a week the school starts with a whole school, deme or year assembly of a non-denominational character. Pupils and their parents know the identity and the responsibilities of the members of staff concerned for their care. Parents are involved as fully as possible in pastoral matters and will always be informed and consulted.

Careers. Pupils are guided by means of interviews and tests towards careers appropriate to their gifts and personalities. Pupils are given opportunities to attend holiday courses directed towards specific careers. Also, visiting speakers are invited to the School and there are frequent Careers events. There is a full Careers Library and a comprehensive programme of Work Experience. The Parents' Guild and Old Gowers' Club (alumni organisation) also provide advice and support.

Physical Education and Games. The state-of-the-art Sir Roger Bannister sports complex opened in December 2006. The pupils have periods of Physical Education within their normal timetable in the sports complex. The School playing fields cover 27 acres and are situated a mile away in West Hampstead. In addition to grass surfaces, there is a large all-weather pitch and two pavilions. The major sports for Lower and Middle school boys are Rugby, Football, Hockey and Cricket with increased choices from Year 9. The School has its own Tennis and Fives courts at Frognal, together with an indoor heated Swimming Pool. Other sports include Fencing, Athletics, Squash, Badminton, Basketball, Fives and outdoor pursuits. For sixth form boys and girls there is a wide choice of indoor and outdoor sports.

Music and Drama. There is a strong musical tradition at UCS and many pupils play in the Orchestras, Wind Band and a great variety of groups and ensembles. Choral music is equally strong and Jazz is a particular feature. Instrumental tuition is given in the Music School, opened in 1995, and this and Ensemble Groups are arranged by the Director of Music. The School's Lund Theatre, opened in 1974, is the venue for a range of Drama from major productions to experimental plays, mime and revue. An open-air theatre was completed in 1994. A regular programme of evening events is arranged for the Autumn and Spring terms.

Other School Societies. These cover a wide range of academic interests and leisure pursuits, including the Duke of Edinburgh's Award scheme. There is a very active Community Action Programme, which works in the local community and there are regular fundraising initiatives for both local and national charities.

Development Programme. The Foundation completed the final phase of an ambitious programme of redevelopment in 2008. A state-of-the-art Indoor Sports Centre opened in late 2006, comprising Sports Hall, Swimming Pool, Fitness Centre and Health Club. The new Jeremy Bentham Building houses Modern Languages and Art & Design Technology and opened in October 2007. There was extensive refurbishment and reorganisation of classrooms, indoor and outdoor play spaces, administrative areas of the School and Sixth Form Centre. A fundraising appeal helped to achieve these improvements and enabled the School to double the provision of fee assistance.

Fees per term (2016–2017). Senior School: £6,264; Junior Branch: £5,790. This excludes fees payable in respect of music and other private lessons, and books.

Scholarships and Bursaries. UCS is firmly committed to promoting and increasing access to our unique education through fee assistance. From its beginning in 1830 UCS has had at its core a commitment to access, with a pledge that religion should be no bar to entry. In the 21st century, we add a further commitment – that the education we provide will not be restricted solely to those who can afford it and each year we commit £1.2 million to bursary support. We offer bursaries of up to 100% and UCS consistently ranks at the top of independent schools in London for the number of 100% bursaries awarded each year. The School also offers music scholarships which award the holder a reduction in the annual school fees of between 10% and, in exceptional cases, 50%. The precise value will depend upon the standard of applicants and the competition in any one year. Music scholarships entitle the holder to free instrumental tuition at school on an instrument (including voice) of the candidate's choice, which will remain in place throughout a pupil's time at UCS Senior School.

Old Pupils' Society (Old Gowers). The School maintains an active register of former pupils and plans events throughout the year.

Charitable status. University College School, Hampstead is a Registered Charity, number 312748. Its aims and objectives are the provision of the widest opportunities for learning and development of students without the imposition of tests and doctrinal conformity but within a balanced and coherent view of educational needs and obligations.

Governors:
Chairman: Mr S D Lewis, OBE, MA
Dr Y Amin, BSc, MB ChB, DA, FRCAMs
Mr L Bard, MA, FCA, CTA
Ms L Bingham, OBE, MIPA, MABRP, DBA
¶Mr R Bondy
Ms S Bora BSc, MBA

Mr E Fordham, BA
¶Mr S Grodzinski, QC
Mr R Gullifer, MA
Ms J Hall, OBE, MA
¶Mr A G Hillier, MA, MBA
¶Professor P Sands, QC
Councillor G Spinella
Professor C Tyerman, MA, DPhil Oxford, FRHistS

¶ *Old Gower*

Senior School:

Headmaster: M J Beard, MA, MEd

Vice Master: C M Reynolds, BSc, MSc, FSS

Deputy Head (Academic): M T English, BA, MA
Deputy Head (Pastoral): A R Wilkes, BA

Assistant Head: R H Chapman, BSc
Assistant Head: L L Megaw, BSc, MA
Assistant Head: P S Miller, BSc
Assistant Head: S A P FitzGerald, BA

Deme Wardens:
Baxters: S C Walton, MusB
Black Hawkins: J R L Orchard, MA
Evans: T J Allen, BA
Flooks: J P Cooke, BA
Olders: M Foster, BSc
Underwoods: A H Isaac, BA, MA

Sixth Form:
Head of Sixth Form: R H Chapman, BSc
Deputy Heads of Sixth Form:
H A Levy, MA
A H Hon, MA

Lower School Wardens:
Head of Lower School: E A Barnish, BA, MA
Entry: E R Lodato, BA
Shell: O Bienias, BA

Senior School Heads of Departments/Subjects:

Art: Mr L A Farago, BA
Art History: Mr A M Mee, MA
Biology: Miss K R Sander, BSc
Chemistry: Mr E D Roberts, MSci
Classics: Mr D J Woodhead, BA
Director of Drama: Ms R H Baxter, BA, MA
Design & Technology: Mr M J Cloke, BA
Economics: Mr D G Hall, BA
English: Ms L C Birchenough, BA
Geography: Mr M B Murphy, BA
History & Politics:
Mr A G Vaughan, BA (*Head of History & Politics*)
Ms J L Heaton, BA, MA (*Head of Politics*)
Learning Support: Ms S K Thale, BA, MA
Mathematics & Computer Science:
Mr C K Blyth, BA, MA (*Acting Head of Mathematics*)
Mr S A Cork, BA (*Acting 2nd i/c Mathematics and Coordinator of Computer Science*)
Modern Languages:
Mr T P Underwood, BA (*Head of Modern Languages*)
Dr H L Laurenson, BA, PhD (*Head of Spanish*)
Mrs H Wiedermann, BA (*Head of French*)
Music:
Mr C R Dawe, BA, MA, MMus (*Director of Music*)
Mr I C Gibson, MA (*Head of Academic Music*)
Philosophy: Dr K S Viswanathan, BSc, MA, PhD
Physical Education: Mr E P Sawtell, BA (*Acting Director of Sport*)
Physics: Mr A Westwood, BSc
Psychology: Mrs C E Hawes, BSc, MSc

Junior Branch:
Headmaster: Mr L Hayward, MA
Deputy Head (Curriculum): Mr M A Albini, MA, BSc
Deputy Head (Pastoral): Mr D J Edwards, BA

Pre-Prep:
Headmistress: Dr Z Dunn, BEd, PhD, NPQH
Deputy Head (Head of EYFS): Miss N Watt

Uppingham School

Uppingham, Rutland LE15 9QE
Tel: 01572 822216
Fax: 01572 822332 (Headmaster)
        01572 821872 (Bursar)
email: admissions@uppingham.co.uk
website: www.uppingham.co.uk

Uppingham School's foundation dates from 1584, the year in which Archdeacon Robert Johnson, a local puritan rector, obtained a grant by Letters Patent from Queen Elizabeth I to found a free grammar school for the male children of poor parents. The boys were to learn Hebrew, Latin and Greek. In 1853 this small local school was transformed into one of the foremost public schools of its time by the remarkable educational thinker and headmaster, Edward Thring. His pioneering pastoral ideas and belief in the values of an all-round education shaped the School then and continue to define it now. Small, family-like boarding houses that offer children individual privacy; an all-round education that caters for a broad range of pupils, and inspiring surroundings in which children are happy and learn better – all of these lie at the heart of Uppingham's identity.

Uppingham is a fully boarding school for boys and girls aged 13–18. There are around 795 pupils in the School, of which some 350 are in the Sixth Form. Girls have been accepted into the Sixth Form since 1975, at 13+ since 2001, and now make up 41% of all pupils. Around 15% of the School's pupils are foreign nationals, mainly from the European Union, Eastern Europe and South East Asia.

Uppingham is a Christian Foundation, and the whole School meets in the Chapel five days a week. The quality and volume of the congregational singing is legendary. Some pupils are members of other faiths, and every consideration is given to their needs. Pupils are prepared for Confirmation every year.

Situation. Uppingham is a small market town set in the beautiful Rutland countryside. It is about 100 miles north of London, roughly equidistant from the M1 and A1/M11, and midway between Leicester and Peterborough on the A47. The A14 link road makes connections with the Midlands and East Anglia easier and faster. It is served by Kettering, Oakham, Corby, Peterborough and Leicester train stations, and by Stansted, Luton, Birmingham and East Midlands airports.

The Buildings. At the heart of the School are the impressive buildings of the main quadrangle: the Victorian School Room and Chapel designed by the architect of the Law Courts in the Strand, George Edmund Street, the Library housed in a beautiful building dating from 1592, the Memorial Hall and the fine classroom blocks where the Humanities are based. The three Music Schools on this campus reflect the vitality of a musical tradition dating back to 1855. Edward Thring appointed the first Director of Music in any English public school. Nearby are the central Buttery, the Language Centre and the Sixth Form Centre.

At the western end of the town lies the Western Quad, the School's inspiring architectural vision of a space that unites Arts, Sciences, Theatre and Sport, and winner of several Royal Institute of British Architects National Awards in

2015. The magnificent Science Centre contains 17 laboratories (including an environmental studies lab, outdoor classroom and project room), a lecture theatre, library, offices and meeting rooms. There is also a giant working model of Foucault's Pendulum, reminding pupils and staff that despite the burdens of prep and marking, the earth continues to rotate. The Leonardo Centre for Art and Design looks across an open space studded with contemporary sculpture, and to the east sits the 300-seat Theatre with adjoining Drama Studio, workshops and Theatre Studies classrooms. To the north, overlooking an expanse of playing fields, lies the Sports Centre, opened by Lord Coe in 2011, its contemporary design complementing the central quad.

Academic Matters. Whilst the School is noted for its strong commitment to all-round education, the depth of its pastoral care and wealth of facilities, academic study is the priority. Pupils move around the School campus during the working day, and the 55-minute lessons encourage detailed and developed learning. A staff : pupil ratio of almost 1:7 caters for a wide range and ensures all subjects enjoy small class sizes. 26 different A Level/Pre-U subjects and 20 GCSE/iGCSE subjects are offered.

Until GCSE, specialisation is minimal and pupils are taught in sets for most subjects. Most take a minimum of nine GCSE/iGCSE subjects. Most members of the Sixth Form study four or five subjects in the Lower Sixth and three or four subjects in the Upper Sixth, a curriculum enriched by lectures and a variety of extracurricular activities. Extended Project Qualifications (EPQ) are offered in addition to A Level subjects.

In 2016, 45% of all A Levels and 68% of all GCSEs were A*/A grades; 76% of A Levels were A*–B. Almost a quarter of A Level candidates achieved straight A*/A grades. At GCSE 52% of the year group gained at least 8 A*/A grades and the A*–C pass rate was 97%.

Each pupil's progress is monitored by a Tutor and the Housemaster or Housemistress, with regular reviews and reports from subject teachers.

At all stages of a pupil's career the Housemaster/Housemistress is in regular contact with parents. Parent-teacher meetings take place annually for all year groups, and additional meetings are held to discuss options and higher education.

Nearly all pupils go on to further education. Parents and pupils may call on the School's Higher Education and Careers advisers and the professional services of Cambridge Occupational Analysts. Visiting speakers from universities and careers are featured throughout the year, and the School offers advice on GAP year planning.

Pupils have access to a beautiful, well-stocked central Library, the Science Library and other specialist libraries for most subject departments. For those with learning difficulties the School has trained staff to help with special education needs.

Beyond the Curriculum. Around 40 clubs and societies flourish within the School with a further 30 areas of activity on offer. Pupils can take bronze, silver and gold Duke of Edinburgh's Award. After the first year pupils can opt to join the long-established CCF for 2–3 years, or undertake community service such as visiting the elderly, assisting in local primary schools, Riding for the Disabled, music, journalism and other charity work.

Music. Uppingham has always had a very distinguished reputation for music, being the first school to put music on its curriculum for all pupils. More than 50% of pupils learn an instrument, and a busy programme of weekly public recitals, house and year-group concerts, and performances in the UK and abroad offer pupils of all abilities regular chances to perform. 42 visiting staff and 9 full-time staff enable pupils to receive conservatoire-style tuition at the school.

The Paul David Music School is an inspirational centre for learning and rehearsal, with cutting-edge music technology suites and a 120-seat recital room. The School has an outstanding Chapel Choir, accomplished orchestras and national prize-winning chamber groups, a slick and polished Big Band, and a thriving Alternative Music Society promoting rock concerts.

The School has produced international opera singers, members of world renowned choral groups such as The Sixteen and rock bands such as Busted and McFly, several Oxbridge organ scholars and numerous choral scholars, and these distinguished results also extend to national Conservatoires.

Further enquiries may be made directly to the Director of Music (01572 820696).

Sports and Games. Uppingham has a strong tradition of sporting excellence, and pupils have gained international honours in a variety of sports. The major sports are Rugby, Hockey, Cricket, Tennis, Cross Country and Athletics for boys, and Hockey, Netball, Tennis, Cross Country and Athletics for girls, and there is a wide range of further options available, including Squash, Badminton, Swimming, Football (for boys and girls), Sailing, Aerobics and Dance.

There is a full programme of formal house matches across all sports, providing an opportunity for all pupils to contribute within a team environment. The able are stretched and the very able are offered a high level of coaching from experienced coaches/professionals in all major sports, often going on to represent club, academy, county, regional or national teams.

The magnificent Sports Centre includes a sports hall, six-lane 25m swimming pool, fitness studio, gym, squash courts and dance studios. There are more than 65 acres of playing fields, three Astroturf surfaces (one floodlit), Tennis, Netball and Fives courts, a shooting range and climbing wall. All these facilities are open seven days a week under the guidance of the Sports Centre manager and appointed staff.

The Leonardo Centre. The striking design of the Art, Design and Technology Centre by Piers Gough CBE (a past pupil of the School) allows the broad range of creative activities taking place in its single glass-fronted open-plan space to interact and stimulate each other. The Centre houses a Fine Art and Printing space (with 3D printing), studios for Design (including CAD design), Ceramics, Sculpture, Photography and workshops primarily for wood, metal and plastic, and teaching rooms. The Warwick Metcalfe Gallery displays the work of pupils, staff and visiting artists. The Centre is manned and open to all pupils seven days a week as a creative, inspiring environment.

Drama. Uppingham Theatre is a flourishing professionally equipped 300-seat theatre, with a stylish adjoining Drama complex with an 80-seat 'black box' studio, workshops, classrooms and offices. Major school productions open to all pupils are staged annually, ranging from big musicals such as *Guys and Dolls* and *Miss Saigon* to opera and plays such as *Amadeus*, *Pygmalion* and Shakespeare. There are Junior Drama Society productions, joint boarding-house productions, and pupils are an integral part of every aspect of the running of the theatre. The theatre presents a varied programme of professional productions, including drama, music, children's theatre and comedy, and plays a significant role in the cultural life of the school and the local community. Drama and Theatre Studies are also taught at GCSE and A Level.

Boarding and Pastoral. There are fifteen boarding houses dotted around the town and School estate: nine for boys, one for Sixth Form girls and five for 13–18 year old girls. Houses are small, most being home to around 50 children, 45 in the case of the Sixth Form girls' house. All pupils eat their meals in their own house dining room, and are joined at lunch by teaching and non-teaching staff.

All boys have their own private study upon arrival and, by their third year their own study-bedroom or share with one other. All girls entering at 13 share a room with up to 3 other girls and also have their own study area. In their second and third years girls have bed-sitting rooms, usually shared with one other. All Sixth Form girls have individual study-bedrooms.

Much of the non-teaching life of the School is organised around the houses and they inspire strong loyalties. In addition to excursions and social events, there is a long-standing tradition of inter-house competitions (House Challenge, singing, debating and sports), house concerts, and some ambitious drama productions.

Pupils are supported by a wide-ranging pastoral network. The Housemasters and Housemistresses are resident, and lead a team of at least five tutors, including a Resident Tutor. Assigned to particular pupils, tutors help to monitor academic progress and social development. Some male staff are tutors in girls' houses, and vice-versa. Each house is supported by an experienced matron providing medical support and supporting the pastoral care of the pupils. Any pupil may use the services of a professional psychologist or the School's qualified counsellor. The School's Medical Centre is open 24 hours a day, with qualified medical staff in attendance.

Technological Environment. Uppingham provides outstanding technology facilities for pupils in both academic and boarding areas. A complex infrastructure of more than 1400 networked computers is maintained by an in-house team of eight IT experts, who ensure a fruitful and safe relationship with Cyberspace. Each pupil has their own desktop modem, enabling them to use a vast array of educational software, email and 100Mbps filtered internet access to complement their academic studies. Resources include the online Encyclopedia Britannica and JSTOR, an online collection of over 1,000 academic journals and one of the most trusted sources of academic content on the world wide web. The School also generates a wide variety of course-specific online media.

In the classroom academic departments have the tools to ensure that technology complements teaching and learning, from the Modern Languages Laboratory to the Music Technology Department's digital music suite.

Admission. Most pupils are admitted to Uppingham in the September following their thirteenth birthday. Prospective pupils and their parents usually visit the School at least three years prior to entry. If not already registered, prospective pupils should register then. Two years before entry all registered pupils are given pre-tests and interviews at Uppingham. All applications must be supported by a satisfactory reference from their current school. The Headmaster offers places to successful candidates after this process has concluded. Parents then complete and return an Acceptance Form together with an entrance deposit. Receipt of the entrance deposit guarantees a place in the School subject to the pupil qualifying for admission. In completing the Acceptance Form parents also confirm that Uppingham is their first choice of school.

The final offer of a place in the School is conditional upon the pupil qualifying academically (see below), and on his or her record of conduct.

There are three possible ways of qualifying academically:
• via the Common Entrance Examination (for which the qualifying standard is an average of 55% in the compulsory papers);
• via the Common Academic Scholarship Examination;
• in the case of pupils who have not prepared for the Common Entrance Examination, by means of a report from the Head Teacher of their present school and further tests and interviews at Uppingham.

To continue into the Sixth Form pupils are expected to achieve six passes of grade B or above in academic subjects at GCSE, excluding short-course GCSEs.

There are a limited number of places available for boys and girls for entry into the Sixth Form. Pupils may register an interest in Sixth Form entry to Uppingham at any time and formal registration should be completed by the end of September, eleven months prior to entry. The test, interview and offer procedures take place in October and November ten months before entry. Admission at this level is dependent on tests and interviews at Uppingham, and then achieving at least six B grades at GCSE (or equivalent), excluding short course GCSEs.

Enquiries and requests for information about admissions should be addressed to the Assistant Registrar (01572 820611).

Scholarships and Bursaries. Boys and girls may apply for Academic (ISEB Common Scholarship), Art/Design & Technology, Music, Sport and Thring (All-Rounder) Scholarships for entry at 13+. Exams are held in the February/March preceding entry, the deadline for entry being typically the end of December.

At 16+, Academic, Science, Art/Design & Technology, Sport and Music Scholarships are awarded in the November preceding entry. The deadline for entry is typically the end of September.

A number of music exhibitions granting free tuition on all instruments may also be awarded.

Where a family's financial means leaves them unable to afford a place at Uppingham they may be eligible to receive support via a means-tested bursary. All candidates seeking a bursary should be registered with the School and need to fulfil the same entrance criteria as described above.

Details of all scholarships and bursaries may be obtained from the Admissions Office (01572 820611).

Fees per term (2016–2017). Boarding £11,673; Day £8,171. There is a scheme for paying fees in advance; further details may be obtained from the Deputy Bursar (01572 820627).

Former Pupils. The Uppingham Association was founded in 1911 to maintain the link between OUs and the School. All pupils may become life members when they leave and a database of their names, addresses, school and career details is maintained at the School by the OU Administrator. In addition to a range of OU events that are organised each year for members, a magazine is published annually, which contains news about OUs and activities at the School, and all members are encouraged to make full use of the OU Website. Enquiries may be made directly to the Secretary to the Uppingham Association (01572 820616).

Charitable status. Uppingham School is a charitable company limited by guarantee registered in England and Wales. Company Number 8013826. Registered Charity Number 1147280. Registered Office: High Street West, Uppingham, Rutland LE15 9QD.

The Governing Body:

Chairman: The Rt Hon Stephen J Dorrell, MP [OU]
Vice-Chairmen:
Dr P Chadwick, MA, MA, FRSA
C J Cazalet Esq, MA, FCA [OU]

The Rt Revd D Allister, MA, Bishop of Peterborough
The Very Revd C Taylor, MA, Dean of Peterborough
Dr L Howard, BSc, OBE, JP, Lord Lieutenant of Rutland
J C Hanson-Smith Esq
A G Hancock Esq, MA
R Peel Esq, BSc, FRSA
D P J Ross Esq [OU]
A J D Locke Esq, MA [OU]
Dr S Goss, MA, DPhil

Dr D Hill, Hon DMus, MA, Hon RAM, FRCO, Hon FGCM
R Landman Esq, MA
Professor Sir D Greenaway
Mrs S H Mason [OU]
R J S Tice Esq, BSc [OU]
A E P Smith Esq [OU]
Professor Dame Carol Black, DBE, FRCP, FMedSci
R N J S Price Esq
Ms B M Matthews, MBE, BSc, FRSA [OU]
Dr D Thornton, MA, PhD, FSA, FRHistSoc
Ms S A Humphrey, LLB
The Rt Hon Sir Alan Duncan, MP

[OU] *Old Uppinghamian*

Bursar/Finance Director, Clerk to the Trustees: S C Taylor, MA, ACA

Headmaster: Dr R J Maloney, MTheol St Andrews, MA, PhD King's College London

Senior Deputy Head: K M Wilding, BA
Deputy Head Academic: B Cooper, MA
Registrar: C S Bostock, MA, MSc
Chaplain: The Revd Dr J B J Saunders, BA, PhD

Assistant Staff:
* *Head of Department*
† *Housemaster/mistress*
§ *Part time*

Art, Design & Technology:
S N Jarvis, BA
J A Davison, BA, MEd
Miss K L Hallam
Miss E K Rieveley, MA
C I Silvester, BA
C P Simmons, BSc
A Wilson, BA, FRPS

Biology:
*Dr C L Pemberton, BSc, PhD
C R Birch, BSc
§P L Bodily, BSc, MEd, CBiol, MIBiol, AIB
†N K de Wet, BSc, CBiol, MIBiol
Miss L E Hourston, BSc
Miss A S Roebuck, BSc
J A D Wilson, MChem

Chemistry:
C R Birch, BSc
*Dr L F Dudin, MSc, PhD
C L Howe, HDE
A Kowhan, BSc
J A D Wilson, MChem

Classics:
*S P Broadbent, BA
Mrs A J Broadbent, MA
†S G Dewhurst, BA
§†Mrs A M Howe, MA, MPhil
†G S Tetlow, MA
Miss S J Whitehouse, BA

Economics & Business Studies:
*G R Matthews, BSc
T G Howe, MA
D P Lovering, BSc
T G MacCarthy, BA

English:
*Mrs J S Broughton, MA, Dip RSA SpLD
†A C Boyd-Williams, BA
Miss L E Gooderham, BA
Miss C Hayne, MA
Mrs M N L Hunting, MA
Miss C M Mungavin, BA
Mrs N L Reihill, MA

Geography:
*T P Davies, BSc
A N Huxter, BSc
§Mrs S J Kowhan, BA
R J O'Donoghue, BA
†Mrs K L Robinson BSc
M B Stevens, BA
K M Wilding, BA

History:
*T P Prior, BA, MA
†J S Birch, MA
S J Hosking, BA
B M Kirby, MA
J Leang, BA, MA
Miss S E Lynch, BA
†J A Reddy, BA

History of Art:
*D S R Kirk, BA
§Miss E E Wilce, MA

Information Technology:
*Miss S E L Webster, BSc
†Mrs L J Allen, BSc, MBCS

Learning Support:
*Mrs A N M Nunn BTEC, HND
Mrs J S Broughton, MA, DipRSA SpLD
Mrs M Cuccio, Dip SLD
§Mrs L Howe, BA

§Mrs A M Merrett, BA
§Mrs K L Tetlow, BA
§Mrs J A Wilding, BSc

Life Skills:
*Mrs M N L Hunting, MA

Mathematics:
*J R Farrelly, BA, BBA, MSc
†Mrs L J Allen, BSc, MBCS
P Gomm, BSc
Miss L C Gallagher, BEd
Mrs K F Hanrahan, BSc
Mrs M J Melville-Coman, BSc
A S M Moosajee, BSc
P J Nicholls, BSc
Q H Sayed, MPhys
Miss L E A Stuchfield, BA

Modern Languages:
*Miss M A Barefoot, BA (*Spanish)
C M Brown, BA (*French)
Miss E S Semper, MA (*German)
Miss C Zhang (*Mandarin)
†Mrs K S Boyd-Williams, MA
M R Broughton, MA
†Ms F C Buckley, BA, MA
†Mrs H M Johnstone, BA
Mrs J E Newcombe, BEd
R Salvador Noguera
P A Westgate, BA, MA
R M B Wilkinson, MA
T R Worthington, BA

Music:
*S J Williams, BA
*P M Clements, MA, FRCO
A A Ffrench, MA, AGSM, PG Dip GSMD

Visiting Music Staff:
S Andrews (*Drums*)
M Ashford, GRSM (*Guitar*)
A Ashwin, BMus, LRSM (*Singing*)
S Baker, BMus (*Trombone*)
T Birchall, BMus, LGSM (*Violin*)
Mrs T Boison, MA (*Piano*)
G Boynton, Dip RCM (*Percussion*)
Mrs M Braithwaite BA (*Singing*)
Mrs J Burgess, BMus, LGSM (*Oboe*)
Dr J T Byron, BA, MA, PhD (*Piano*)
Mrs L Clements, BA (*Flute*)
Mrs J A Dawson, GRSM, LRAM (*Piano*)
Mrs L H Ffrench, GRSM, LRAM (*Piano*)
N M France, GMus (*Drums*)
Mrs N J Gibbons, MMus, MPhil, LRAM, LRSM (*Piano*)
Miss N Giddens, BMus (*Creative Music Production*)
Mrs C J Gunningham, BA, MSTAT (*Alexander Technique*)
I Hildreth (*Bagpipes*)
Miss E S Hodgkinson Bmus, LRAM (*Piano*)
A Kennedy (*Singing*)
K Learmouth, ALCM, FRSA (*Classic Guitar*)
Ms R R E Leyton-Smith, MA, Adv PG Dip RCM (*Cello*)
Mrs C Li, BMus, LRAM(*Flute*)
G K Lumbers, BMus (*Saxophone*)
Miss J A Moffat, DipRCM (*Singing*)

Mrs C A Griffiths, GMus
A G Laing, BA, DipPSMP
S A Smith, BA, PPRNCM
Miss J Stevens, GGSM, MA
A P Webster, GGSM, PDOT
T C H Ward

Philosophy and Religious Studies:
*P M Shacklady, BA
B Cooper, MA
†R C Hegarty, MA
Dr R J Maloney, MTheol, MA, PhD
I J Knight, BA
The Revd Dr J B J Saunders, BA, PhD
J E Taylor

Physical Education:
*Mrs S M Singlehurst, BEd, MSc
†D J Bartley
§J M Baker, BSc
K G Johnstone, BEd
Mrs K L Maloney-Smith, BSc

Physics:
*Miss G T Barbour, BA
W S Allen, BEd
B P Fell, MA
C L Howe, HDE
G S Wright, BSc

Political Studies:
*†T Makhzangi, BA
R Hardman
†T G Howe, MA, MSt, MBA

Theatre Studies:
*Miss C J Rayner, BA
†A C Boyd-Williams, BA
J Holroyd, BA

S P Morris, BMus (*Clarinet, Saxophone*)
Mrs V F Morris, AGSM, LRAM (*Clarinet & Saxophone*)
Miss A Osman, BMus (*Double Bass*)
A Pike, BA (*Music Technology*)
D N Price, LRAM (*Trumpet*)
Mrs A M Reynolds, MusB, GRNCM (*Piano*)
S Roberts, BMus (*Tuba*)
C Rutherford (*Horn*)
Mrs Y S Sandison, PPRNCM (*Singing*)
N Scott-Burt, BA, MMus, PhD, LRAM, ARCO (*Piano, Organ & Composition*)
Miss C Tanner (*Bassoon*)
Mrs E Turner (*Harp*)
J P Turville, MA, MMus, LLCM (*Piano*)
Ms P Waterfield, ARCM, MSTAT (*Alexander Technique*)
T J Williams, MA (*Singing*)
Mrs V D Williamson, GMus, RNCM, PPRNCM, LRAM (*Singing*)
Miss R Woolley, BMus, MMus (*Violin*)

Houses and Housemasters/mistresses:
Brooklands: Nick de Wet
Constables (*Girls*): Tyrone and Alex Howe
Fairfield (*Girls*): Kate Robinson
Farleigh: James Birch
Fircroft: Jim Reddy
Highfield: Richard Hegarty
Johnson's (*Girls*): Lesley Allen
The Lodge (*Girls*): Alex and Kate Boyd-Williams
Lorne House: Andrew Huxter
Meadhurst: Sam Dewhurst
New House (*Girls*): Fiona Buckley
Samworths' (*Girls*): Helen Johnstone
School House: Simon Tetlow
West Bank: David Bartley
West Deyne: Toby Makhzangi

Victoria College
Jersey

Mont Millais, Jersey, Channel Islands JE1 4HT
Tel: 01534 638200
Fax: 01534 638216
email: admin@vcj.sch.je
website: www.victoriacollege.je

Motto: *Amat Victoria Curam*

The College was founded in commemoration of a visit of Her Majesty Queen Victoria to the Island and opened in 1852. It bears the Arms of Jersey.

There are currently 682 boys in College, 287 in the Preparatory School and 90 in the Pre-Prep.

The College is situated in extensive grounds above St Helier and looks south over the Bay of St Malo.

The fine building of 1852 with its Great Hall, libraries and administrative areas is set at the centre of new teaching accommodation including classrooms, a music centre, an extensive Science suite opened by Her Royal Highness The Princess Royal, a Sixth Form centre, Art and Design Technology suite, five computer suites and the Howard Davis Theatre refurbished in 1996. A suite of 4 new English classrooms were finished in 2014 along with a new modern Sixth Form Centre and new Houserooms in 2015.

College Field is adjacent to the main buildings and includes an all-weather hockey pitch.

Located in the grounds is a 25-yard shooting range, squash courts and CCF Headquarters. A multimillion pound sports complex with swimming pool was opened in 2003.

Education. There is an emphasis on academic success; nearly all boys go on to University in the UK. The curriculum conforms to the requirements of the National Curriculum. In the Junior School boys study Religious Education, English, Mathematics, French, Spanish, History, Drama, Geography, Biology, Chemistry, Physics, Music, Art and ICT.

Thereafter the basic curriculum includes Religious Education, English, Mathematics, a language, Sciences and ICT. In addition, boys select from optional subjects those which best suit their natural talents, the choice being guided by teaching staff in consultation with students and parents.

Boys may study four or five A Level subjects suited to their objectives and abilities. Enrichment skills are developed through the CCF, The Duke of Edinburgh's Award and wide-ranging co-curricular programmes.

At all Key Stages there is opportunity for voluntary work, Music and the Arts, and these, with other subjects, are also encouraged by numerous School Societies.

Prizes. Her Majesty The Queen gives three Gold Medals annually for Science, Modern Languages and Mathematics as well as two Prizes for English History. The States of Jersey offers a Gold Medal and a Silver Medal annually for French. There is an award given to the boy achieving the top score in Year 7 Entrance Examination called the St Mannelier et St Anastase Gold Medal.

Physical Education and Games. The College places strong emphasis on sport and each year there are sports tours to different countries, and to the United Kingdom. The College has been runner up in the Aviva Independent Sports School of the Year Award.

Winter games include Association Football, Rugby, Hockey, Squash; and in the summer Cricket, Swimming, Shooting, Tennis and Athletics.

Matches are played against Elizabeth College, Guernsey and College sides visit the mainland for matches against English Independent Senior Schools.

The College has an excellent CCF Contingent with an authorised establishment of 105 in the Army Section, 75 in the RAF Section and 75 in the RN Section. It is commanded by Wing Commander David Rotherham.

Admission. The age of admission is 11 years though boys are considered for entry at all ages. Entrants must pass the College Entrance Examination.

Fees per term (2016–2017). £1,770. A grant is payable by the States of Jersey to supplement fees.

Preparatory School. The College has its own Preparatory School which stands in the College grounds. Boys, on passing the Entrance procedure, progress to the College at the age of 11. (*For further details see entry in IAPS section.*)

Leaving Scholarships. There are a number of Scholarships (of varying amount). The Queen's Exhibition is tenable for three years at University; the Wimble Scholarship, the Sayers Scholarships and the Baron Dr Ver Heyden de Lancey Scholarship each of up to £750 a year, tenable at British Universities and the Rayner Exhibitions are recent additions to the rich endowment of Scholarships enjoyed by the College for its students.

Visitor: Her Majesty The Queen

Governing Body:
Chairman: B Watt

Vice Chairman: J Giles
A Watkins	D Evans
D Pateman	S Gibson
G Wright	G Burton
J Silvester	M Godel
P Le Brocq	W Adam
N Cawley	A Hossard

Headmaster: **Alun D Watkins**, BEd Hons, MEd Oxon

Assistant Staff:

Marianne Adams, BA Hons
Kieran Akers, BA Hons
Keith Baker, BSc Hons
Christopher Baughan, BA Hons
Gareth C Bloor, BD, MA
Heather Bougeard, BA Hons
Jacky Bryan, BA Hons
Gary Burton, BEd Hons
Brendan Carolan, BA Hons
Samuel Coe, BSc Hons
Steven Cooke, PhD, BEng
David Cox, BA, BEd
Joseph Crill, BSc Hons
Matthew Dixon, BA Hons
Nicole Edgecombe, MA, BA Hons
Thomas Fallon, BA Hons
Joshua Franco, BA Hons
Robert Gibbons, BEd Hons
Andrew Gilson, MA
William Gorman, BA Hons
Mark Gosling, BA Hons
Samuel Habin, MPharmacol
Cristina Herrera-Martin, BA Hons
Ian Hickling, BSc, MSc
Stephanie Humphries, BMus Hons
Andrew Lau, BSc Hons
Angela Matthews, BSc Hons
David McNally, BSc Hons
Denise Montgomery, BA Hons
Rebecca Moon, BSc Hons
Michel Morel, BSc Hons
Laura Navarro-Lopez, MA
Aaron O'Hare, BSc Hons
Emma O'Prey, BEd Hons
Lucy Ogg, BA Hons, LTCC
Karen Palfreyman, BA Hons, MA
David Payne, MA
Richard Picot, BSc
Orla Priestley, BSc, MSc
Majella Raindle, BSc Ed, MSc
Jefferson Randles, BA Hons
Steven Roberts, BA Hons, MA, PhD
Anna Robinson, BA Hons
David Rotherham, BEd, FRGS
Jennifer Roussel, BA Hons, M-ès-Lettres
Andrew Royle, BSc
Helen Ryan, BSc Hons, BA Hons
Rachel Smith, BA Hons
Matthew Smith, BA
Thomas Smith, BEng Hons
Julie Spencer, MA
Martyn Taylor, Cert Ed
Moira Taylor, BSc, MSc
Dierdre Twomey, BSc
Valerie Videt, Lic-ès-Lettres
Olivia Varney, BA Hons
Susan Watkins, BEd Hons
Robbie Webbe, MPhys
Matthew Widdop, MChem, MRSC
Graeme Wright, BA Hons, MA, FRCA

Preparatory School
Headmaster: Dan Pateman, BA Hons

Warminster School

Church Street, Warminster, Wiltshire BA12 8PJ

Tel: 01985 210100 (Senior School)
            01985 224800 (Prep School)
email: admissions@warminsterschool.org.uk
website: www.warminsterschool.org.uk
Twitter: @Warminster1707
Facebook: @WarminsterSchool
LinkedIn: /WarminsterSchool

The original boys' school was founded in 1707 by the first Viscount Weymouth, an ancestor of the present Marquess of Bath. It became an Independent Educational Trust in 1973 formed by the amalgamation of the Lord Weymouth School with the long-established local girls' school, St Monica's, founded in 1874. The School is a Limited Company whose Directors are Trustees elected by and from within the Board of Governors which is in membership of the Association of Governing Bodies of Independent Schools. The Headmaster is a member of both HMC (Headmasters' and Headmistresses' Conference) and The Society of Heads.

The School is a co-educational boarding and day school numbering some 550 pupils (140 in the Sixth Form) from 3 to 18, of whom around 200 are boarders. The Prep School of 140 pupils works in close cooperation with the Senior School and enjoys many of the same facilities. (*For further details see Warminster Prep School entry in IAPS section.*)

The School is situated along the western periphery of the town, looking out over open countryside, while its buildings are linked by extensive gardens and playing fields.

It is easily accessible by rail (via Warminster or Westbury) from London, Heathrow, the South Coast and the West, and by road (via the M3, M4 and M5).

Aims and Philosophy. The Warminster education aims to encourage each boy and girl to fulfil their academic potential and to promote intellectual curiosity and a love of learning. In addition, the School provides a secure and supportive pastoral environment, with an emphasis on character, values, leadership and service. The School believes in an all-round education and offers a wide range of co-curricular opportunities and experiences; it fosters a culture of enthusiasm, optimism and participation. A Warminster education prepares the pupils for life beyond school, at university and in the world of work. We are a community in which each boy and girl is valued and nurtured on the basis of who they are, whatever their year group, gender, natural gifts or background. *It is a preparation for life.*

Buildings. As befits a school with a long history, there is a wide variety of historic buildings. The History department, for example, teaches in the School's oldest building, School House, which was founded by Viscount Weymouth in 1707. The school boasts one of the oldest working Fives courts in England.

A multimillion pound development programme has taken place in recent years and has included completion of the Thomas Arnold Hall – a fantastic new multi-purpose space, a state-of-the-art science centre, new library, design technology centre as well as additional boarding facilities. Existing boarding accommodation has been extensively refurbished.

Boarders are cared for by Housemasters or Housemistresses, Resident Tutors and Matrons. Pupils typically enjoy single study-bedrooms in the Sixth Form.

Curriculum. In the first three years of the Senior School, all pupils follow a broad curriculum and GCSE pupils study a full and varied range of subjects. All pupils are involved in PE and Games, and Health and Social Education, as well as a comprehensive programme of Careers advice.

In the Sixth Form greater individual freedom and responsibility are encouraged. Sixth Formers are offered a choice between studying A Levels, the International Baccalaureate Diploma and the IB Career Related Programme, which is an increasingly popular choice for many of our pupils with others joining the Sixth Form from elsewhere to follow our successful IB programmes. The first school in the South-West to offer the IB Diploma, our IB results have placed us each year within the top thirty UK IB schools. Although the vast majority of pupils will be aiming for University, with over 95% winning places at leading institutions including Oxford and Cambridge, some will pursue gap years or enter business or the Armed Services directly. The overall pupil : staff ratio is under 10:1. Pupils receive an exceptional amount of individual attention and are encouraged to realise their full potential in as many areas as possible. There is an extensive tutorial system and a strong sense of the importance of the individual within the community. The school is at the forefront of developing 'personal, learning and thinking skills' both through the tutorial system but also via its academic and its rich co-curricular programme. A small learning support unit is staffed by expert and dedicated specialists.

Activities. A very wide range of activities is on offer, and pupils are encouraged to involve themselves fully. The School has a strong tradition of drama, and musical activities, including choir, orchestra and jazz band, are a real strength. There are currently over 40 hobby activities available and Forest School.

The School enjoys close links with the Armed Services, and the CCF, though voluntary, is traditionally strong. There is also a large involvement in The Duke of Edinburgh's Award scheme, whilst a number of pupils are actively engaged in Community Service in Warminster and the local area.

Games. Sports offered include Rugby, Hockey, Cricket, Tennis, Athletics, Netball, Rounders, Swimming, Cross-Country Running, Basketball, Squash, Badminton, and Volleyball.

There is a spacious Sports Hall with recently renovated squash courts, hard tennis courts, heated swimming pool, an Astroturf all-weather pitch and an indoor shooting range. Pupils have access to the local Golf Club and Riding Stables.

Admission. Pupils are admitted to the Preparatory School from the age of 3. Boarders are admitted from the age of 7. Pupils who enter after the age of 8 will be required to sit the Warminster School entrance examinations relative to the proposed year of entry. A report from the Head of a pupil's present school will always be requested. Older pupils who qualify by good GCSE results and school report may be admitted directly to the Sixth Form. Scholarships are available for entry at 7+, 9+, 11+, 13+ and 16+. Examinations for Scholarships are held annually. Details may be obtained from the Head of Admissions.

Progress throughout the School, including the transfer from the Prep to the Senior School, is not automatic but will be based on the School's assessment of each student's ability at key points and will always be dependent on the pupil's continued commitment and progress in all areas of activity.

Great care is taken to consider individual needs and circumstances. The School provides a Special Support Facility for pupils who are mildly dyslexic, or who have other similar needs. Parents of such pupils should ask to meet the Head of Learning Support.

Please telephone the School (01985 210160) to arrange a visit, and to meet the Headmaster or the Head of the Prep School.

A Registration Fee of £100 is payable and, upon the acceptance of a place, a guarantee fee of £500 for UK based parents and £1,000 for overseas based parents, credited to the final account, will be payable.

Fees per term (2016–2017). Day: Preparatory School £2,450–£3,920; Year 7 to Sixth Form £4,910. Boarding: Prep School £6,925; Years 7 to Sixth Form £9,555–£10,195.

Fees are as inclusive as possible, covering meals, stationery and textbooks. The Bursar welcomes consultation with parents over fees, insurance and capital payment schemes. As the School is an Independent Educational Trust, any financial surplus is used exclusively for the further improvement of the School. Fees are kept to the minimum required to run the School effectively, employ first-rate staff and keep the facilities and resources up to the level expected by parents.

Charitable status. Warminster School is a Registered Charity, number 1042204. It exists to promote the education of boys and girls.

Patrons:
The Revd Canon E J Townroe
Mrs D P Goodger
Mr R C Southwell, QC
The Rt Revd the Bishop of Salisbury
The Marquess of Bath

Chairman of Governors: The Right Hon Sir David Latham, QC

Staff:

Headmaster: Mark Mortimer, MBA, BA

Deputy Head: Rick Clarke, BA Hons, PGCE
Deputy Head (Academic): Mark Sully, BSc, PGCE
Head of Co-Curricular: Mrs Terri Wilcox, CertEd
Head of Sixth Form: Dr Thomas Horler-Underwood, BA, MPhil, PhD, PG Cert
Head of Middle School: Ms Nia Davies, BSc Hons, PGCE
Head of Lower School: Simon Rossiter, MSc, PGCE, CCRS
Examinations Officer: Dr Mark Martin, BSc Hons, PhD, PGCE, MIBiol

Heads of Department:
Art: Mrs Louisa Clayton, MA, PGCE
Business Studies & Economics: Adam Jacobs, BA, PGCE
D&T: Simon Rossiter, MSc, PGCE, CCRS
Drama: Mrs Emily Harris, MA, BA
EAL: Mrs Sarah Shanks, BA Hons, PGCE, RSA Dip TEFL
English: Miss Eleanor Mears, BA, PGCE
Geography: Harry Phillips, BSc
History: Mrs Juliette Walker, BA, QTS
Learning Support: Mrs Alison Hicks, BA Hons, Cert SpLD, Hornsby Cert
Mathematics: Austin Hill, BA, PGCE, CertEd
Modern Languages: Mrs Nicola Rogers, BA, PGCE
Director of Music: Mrs Caroline Robinson, BA, PGCE
Psychology: Mrs Felicity Beck, BSc Hons, PGCE
RS: Matthew Harris, MA Oxon, MPhil, MEd, PGCE
Science: Dr David Hankey, BSc, PhD, MRSC
Director of Sports: Christopher Knight, BEd Hons

There are 30 other full-time and part-time staff.

House Staff:
Mr and Mrs Jon Bonnell (*St Boniface*)
Mr and Mrs Geoffrey Knapman (*Stratton House*)
Mr and Mrs Malcolm Miller (*St Denys*)
Mr and Mrs Jonathan Mercer (*Old Vicarage*)
Mr and Mrs Damien Crinion (*Ivy*)
Mrs Hayley Arter, RGN (*School Nursing Sister*)

Bursar & Clerk to the Governors: Mrs Alison C Martin, MBA, FMAAT
Head of Admissions: Miss Fiona Beach-MacGeagh

Warwick School

Myton Road, Warwick CV34 6PP

Tel:	01926 776400
Fax:	01926 401259
email:	enquiries@warwickschool.org
website:	www.warwickschool.org
Twitter:	@warwickschool
Facebook:	/OfficialWarwickSchool

Motto: '*Altiora Peto*'

Warwick School is the oldest boys' school in the country and can produce documentary evidence that suggests its existence in the days of King Edward the Confessor; it probably dates from 914. In 1123 the School was granted to the Church of St Mary of Warwick. In 1545 King Henry VIII increased and re-organised the endowments. The School subsequently moved to the Lord Leycester Hospital. In 1571 it moved to another site within the boundaries of Warwick, and in 1879 to its present site south of the town on the banks of the Avon.

Warwick School is an independent day and boarding school for boys. There is a Senior School (approx 985 boys), age range 11 to 18 years, and a Junior School (approx 250 boys), age range 7 to 11 (*see also Junior School entry in IAPS section*). There is boarding accommodation for about 60 boys.

The School Buildings and Grounds. The school is situated on the outskirts of Warwick town with fine views over the River Avon and Warwick Castle. In 1879 the school moved into its present buildings designed in a rococo Tudor style with 50 acres of playing fields attached to the school. There is a programme of continuous development across the site including improved and extended boarding facilities, an ICT and Library building, Music Department, Science Centre, Bridge House Theatre, a new classroom block and the Halse Sports Pavilion. Most recently the new Warwick School Hall was completed Summer 2016, a state-of-the-art venue, which is now one of the largest and finest performance venues in the region.

Admission is by entrance examination set by the School. Entry to Junior School is at ages 7, 8, 9 and 10. Entry to Senior School is at 11, 12, 13 and 16. The assessment at 11+ includes Non-Verbal Reasoning, English and Mathematics. The assessment at 13+ includes English, Maths, MFL, Science and VR. Sixth Form entry requires a minimum of 5 B grades at GCSE.

Curriculum. The aim of the school is to provide a broadly based education which allows pupils to achieve academic excellence. All pupils are encouraged to develop their individual talents to the full and to accept responsibility for themselves and others.

In the Junior School the curriculum aims to give a firm grounding in the National Curriculum foundation subjects English, Mathematics and Science. A range of other subjects including History, Geography, Technology, French, IT and Religious Education are taught throughout the school by specialist subject teachers. French is taught throughout as is Art, Music and Physical Education.

In the Senior School the curriculum offers a range of options but there is a core curriculum of English, Mathematics, Physics, Chemistry, Biology and Languages up to GCSE. Virtually all boys continue into the Sixth Form where three subjects are studied, with a fourth subject for the academically more able. The curriculum is designed to give all boys a broad general education and to postpone any specialisation for as long as possible.

Games and other activities. Active interest in out of school activities is much encouraged. Winter games are rugby, hockey, cross-country and swimming. These are played in the Michaelmas and Lent terms and our national reputation is strong throughout. Summer games are cricket, tennis and athletics. Badminton, basketball, clay pigeon shooting, golf and squash are played throughout the year. There are fine sporting facilities in the Halse Sports Pavilion, including a 25m 6-lane pool, squash courts, state-of-the-art rock climbing wall, fitness suite and sports hall.

There are usually some 90 different clubs and societies active in school life. There is a CCF contingent (with Army and RAF sections) an outdoor activities group and a Voluntary Service Group linked with the local community. Other activities include drama, music, debating, and fencing.

Religious teaching. The Chapel Services and teaching are according to the Church of England, but there are always pupils of other denominations and race and for these other arrangements may be made. Pupils attend services during the week, and boarders and some day pupils the service on Sunday. The Chaplain prepares members of the school for Confirmation each year.

Boarding. Senior School boys may be weekly or full boarders. Flexi boarding can sometimes be arranged for day boys to accommodate short term requirements. There is also an opportunity for an extended day facility.

Fees per term (2016–2017). Senior School Tuition: £4,061; Boarding (in addition to Tuition): £4,738 (full); £4,178 (weekly). Junior School Tuition: £3,282–£3,977.

Scholarships. *Governors Scholarships* (11+, 12+, 13+, 16+) are available to reward academic excellence and talent. Scholarships are awarded up to the value of 20% of fees based on the results of the entrance examination and interview. For existing Sixth Formers, the scholarships are awarded based on GCSE results and school reports.

Sixth Form Science Scholarship: The Ogden Trust sponsors pupils of outstanding scientific ability to attend Warwick School in the Sixth Form. Awarded up to 100% of fees, funded jointly by Ogden Trust and Warwick School. For pupils educated entirely in a non-selective state school, achieving a minimum of 6 GCSEs at Grade A, including Physics and Mathematics. The successful candidate must study Mathematics and Physics at A Level and intend to read a Physics degree at university. Joint parental income should be less than £50K.

Governors Music Scholarships at 11+, 13+ and 16+ are awarded up to the value of 20% of fees based on musical ability and potential with a high level of achievement in the entrance examination.

Two *J M A Marshall Music Scholarships* are available to be awarded to boys entering Year 5 in the Junior School – 50% of the music tuition fees for two years for one instrument.

Two *Choral Scholarships*, each to the value of £1,500 per annum, may be awarded each year to boys aged between 7 and 11 years on 1st September, who are either entering or who are in attendance at Warwick Junior School and the Choir of St Mary's Church, Warwick.

Further details from the Admissions Registrar, Tel: 01926 776400, email: admissions@warwickschool.org.

Charitable status. Warwick Independent Schools Foundation is a Registered Charity, number 1088057. It exists to provide quality education for boys.

Governing Body:
Mrs M-B Ashe
Mrs S M Austin
Mr A N Bell
[1]Mr J P Cavanagh, QC
Dr A D Cocker
Mr T B Cox (*ex officio*)
[1]Mr A C Firth (*Chairman*)
[1]Mr C R Gibbons
Cllr Mrs M-A Grainger
Prof D Grammatopoulos

[1]Mr R M B Griffiths (*Vice Chairman*)
[1]Mr N F Keegan
[1]Mr T H Keyes
Mrs E J Lillyman
Mrs G Low (*Chair – King's High School/Warwick Preparatory School*)
[1]Miss K A Parr
Mrs C A I Sawdon
Mrs P A Snape
Mr D B Stevens (*Chairman – Warwick Independent Schools Foundation*)

[1] *Warwick School Committee*

Foundation Secretary: Mr S T Jones

Head Master: Mr A R Lock, MA Oxon

Deputy Headmaster: Mr D J Wickes, MA Oxon

Deputy Head, Co-Curricular: Mr J T Barker, BA
Deputy Head, Academic: Dr S R Chapman, BA, PhD
Deputy Head, Staff: Mr C G McNee, BA
Assistant Head, Academic: Mr D Seal, BSc

* *Head of Department*

Art:
*Mr J T Ramsay, BA, MA
Mrs G K Odling, BA
Mr D Snatt, BA

Careers:
*Mrs C Oates, BA

Classics:
*Mr D A Stephenson, BA, MA
Mr M G L Cooley, MA, MSt
Dr L D C Hopkins, BA, MPhil, DPhil
Mr R Hudson, MA
Mrs R E Morgan, MA, BA

Computing:
*Mr M J Colliver, BSc, MA
Mr J Peel, BSc
Mr D Seal, BSc (*Assistant Head, Academic*)

Design and Technology:
*Mr B V N Schalch, BA
*Mr C Riman, BA (*Acting Head of Department*)
Mr M J Alton, BA
Mr A R G Peck, BA
Mr J D Stone, BSc

Drama:
*Mr M C Perry, MA
Miss J E Gurnett, MA

Economics:
*Mr D A Williams, BA, MA, MBA, EdD
Mr W A C Deacon, BSc
Mr M D W Graham, BSc

English:
*Mrs K J Wyatt, BA, MA
Miss N J E Atkinson, BA
Mr C M Bond, MA
Mrs L M Haines, BA
Mrs L Hodge, BA
Miss G E Pearce, BA
Mrs A S Quinn, BA

Dr A T Shaw, BA, MA, PhD

Geography:
*Dr A Hodskinson, BSc, PhD
Miss H J Bowie, BSc
Dr S R Chapman, BA, PhD
Miss J C Lewis, BSc, PG Dip Ed
Mr R M H Thomson, BA
Mrs E Thornton, BA

History and Politics:
Mr C G J Gibbs, BA (*History)
Mr J N Jefferies, MA (*Politics)
Mr J E Delaney, MA
Mr E Hadley, MA
Mr O R O'Brien, BA
Mr J A Sutherland, BA, MSt
Mr P M Walker, BA
Mr D J Wickes, MA (*Deputy Headmaster*)

Mathematics:
*Mrs J K D'Arcy, BSc, MSc
Mrs V J Bell, BSc
Mr B Cuttell, MA
Mr K C Davenport, BEng
Mr B L Davies, BSc
Mr G Giudici, MA
Mr J D Lambdon, BSc
Mr E N Leaf, BSc
Mr W S Macro, BSc, MSc
Mr N A Martlew, BSc
Mr G D Milsom, BSc
Mr P J O'Grady, MA
Mr P M Titmas, BSc

Modern Languages:
*Mrs L A Slack, BA, MA Ed
Mrs J R Estill, BA (*German)
Mrs J E Goodbourn, BA (*Spanish)

Mrs E R Allin, MA
Mrs H V Brebner, MA
Mrs D M Hammond, BA, MA
Mrs K Ingram, BA
Mr C G McNee, BA
Mrs C Morel-Bedford, BA
Dr L M Syme, BSc, MSc, DPhil
Mrs O Thomas, Lic d'Anglais
Miss J A Wiltsher, BA

Music:
*Mrs E J Green, BMus, ARCM (*Director of Music – Academic & Choral*)
*Mr S Hogg, ARAM, LRAM, GRSM, ARCM, Dip RAM (*Director of Music – Performance*)
Mr C Druce, ABSM, GBSM, ARCM, ARCO, FRCO (*Head of Keyboard*)
Mr G Hopkin, BMus, GRNCM (*Head of Chamber Music*)
Mr P Montero, BMus (*Head of Woodwind*)
Mr D G Robertson, BMus (*Head of Brass*)
Mr J J Sampson, BMus, ARCM (*Head of Strings*)
Mr J Soper, BA
Mr D Storer, BMus (*Head of Jazz and Rock*)

Physical Education:
*Mr G A Tedstone, BEd (*Director of Sport*)
Mr S R G Francis, BA (*Director of Cricket*)
Mr M A Nasey, BEd, Masters SpL (*Director of Rugby*)
Mr C A Newby (*Assistant Director of Rugby*)

Mr T D Pierce, BSc (*Head of Tennis*)
Mr H Venter (*Rugby*)
Mr G M F Wade (*Head of Hockey/Athletics*)

Psychology:
*Miss N L Boyd, BSc

Religious & Philosophy:
*Revd A W Gough, BA
Revd M D Hewitt, BSc, BA
Mr J S Barker, BA (*Deputy Head Co-Curricular*)
Mr L D Eaton, BA, MA

Science:
Mr G B Callan, BSc (*Chemistry)
Mr I S Dee, BSc (*Biology)
Dr T D Munoz-Britton (*Physics)
Dr G Cafolla, BSc, PhD
Mr G J Field, MA
Miss B F M Gainford, BSc
Dr C Gane, MPhys, PhD
Dr B Gill, BSc, PhD
Mr C J Grant, BSc
Dr L M John, BSc, PhD
Mr M E Lucas, BEng, MSc
Mr H S N Moore, BSc
Dr C M L Nuttall, BSc, PhD
Dr D J Tchakhotine, BSc, PhD
Dr K Tudge, BSc, PhD
Mr A P M Whittle, BEd
Mrs M Yates, BSc
Miss Z J Yeldham, BSc

Curriculum Support:
*Mrs L E Allan, MBA
Mrs M F V Browne, BA
Miss H Cadman, BA
Mrs C M Fellows, BA, MEd
Ms M Harper, BA, MA
Mrs P J S Kitchen, BSc

Junior School

Headmaster: Mr A C Hymer, BA, MA Ed

Deputy Headmaster: Mr T C Lewis, Cert Ed

Mrs A J Appleyard, MA
Mrs C J Askwith, MA
Mrs H D Brotherton, BA
Mrs K Bull, BEd
Mrs G R Clark, BEd
Mrs R J Cowie, BEd
Mrs F J Goodrem, BEd
Mr T W Hancock, BSc
Mrs O R Hartwell, BA
Mr O R Herringshaw, BA
Mrs J P Jobburn, BA

Mrs A J Jones, BEd
Mrs J Kruze, BSc
Mr K Marshall, BEd
Miss H N Mellor, BA
Ms H D Sayers, BEd, MA Ed
Mrs J E Schalch, BA, MA
Miss L C Sharp, BA
Miss C F Townsend, BA
Miss K L Walton, BA
Mr J Williamson, Cert Ed, MSc

Librarian: Ms A Best
Medical Officer: Dr H Mulder
Headmaster's EA: Mrs S Pery
Admissions Registrar: Mrs V Tomblin
Marketing Manager: Mrs A Hartin
Alumni Relations Officer: Mrs A Douglas

Wellingborough School

London Road, Wellingborough, Northamptonshire NN8 2BX

Tel:	01933 222427
Fax:	01933 271986
email:	headmaster@wellingboroughschool.org
website:	www.wellingboroughschool.org
Twitter:	@WboroSnrSchool
Facebook:	/Wellingborough-School

Motto: *Salus in Arduis*

The endowment of this School was first set aside for charitable purposes in the year 1478. Further land, purchased from the Crown, was granted by Letters Patent in the reigns of Edward VI and Elizabeth I. The endowment was confirmed as being for educational purposes by an Order of the Lord Keeper of the Great Seal in 1595. The School moved to its present site in 1881 upon which new and improved buildings have from time to time been added.

The School offers day co-education for boys and girls from the age of 3 to 18. The School is firmly wedded to Christian principles, to equality of opportunity and the enrichment of individuals in the community. The School is divided into a Pre-Preparatory School (age 3–8: 169 pupils), the Preparatory School (age 8–13: 295 pupils) (*see also entry in IAPS section*), and the Senior School (age 13–18: 408 pupils).

Wellingborough is situated 63 miles from London, 10 miles east of Northampton. Close to the main railway line from St Pancras to Leicester and Sheffield, it is served by an excellent network of motorways and dual carriageways connecting the A1, A14 and the M1.

Buildings and Organisation. The School occupies a fine site on the south of the town, and stands in its own grounds of 45 acres. In the Senior School there are five boys' houses and three girls' houses, organised on boarding house lines. Each house has about 45 pupils. The Sixth Form numbers around 140 pupils, 90% of whom go directly to higher education.

Admission at 13+ for boys and girls is by means of entry tests and interview or the Common Entrance Examination from preparatory schools. Direct entry into the Sixth Form is on the basis of an interview, school report and likely GCSE results confirmed before entry. Please note that A Level courses begin in June after GCSE examinations.

The Preparatory School, while sharing some of the facilities of the Senior School, has its own buildings and classrooms on the east side of the campus. In recent years work has been completed on a large new library, incorporating a computer research area, fiction and non-fiction working areas, classroom and science laboratory, with up-to-date facilities and IT throughout. The Pre-Preparatory School occupies its own modern purpose-built buildings which have been substantially refurbished and extended.

The main school buildings include an ICT study centre, a library, assembly hall, careers room, chapel, and three classroom blocks including seven newly refurbished science laboratories and the information technology department. There is a design technology centre, music school, modern languages centre, sports hall, 2 art buildings and central dining hall.

Religion. Religious teaching is according to the Church of England. Pupils attend a mixture of morning prayers and longer services on weekdays, and a morning service on some Sundays during term. The Chaplain prepares members of the School for confirmation each year, the confirmation service taking place in the Lent Term.

Curriculum. In the Pre-Preparatory School and the Preparatory School the curriculum is an enriched version of the National Curriculum. French, Latin and Spanish are also taught in the Preparatory School.

In the first year of the Senior School, pupils follow a core curriculum in English, Mathematics, French, Physics, Chemistry, Biology, History, Geography, Design Technology, Art, Music, RE, Information Technology and PE. Spanish and Latin are both options in this year. GCSE courses are offered in English, English Literature, French, Mathematics and dual award sciences. Options include separate Sciences, Latin, Spanish, History, Geography, Art, Design Technology, Music, Drama, PE and Religious Studies.

The following subjects are offered for A Level examination: Art and Design, Biology, Business Studies, Chemistry, Design Technology, Economics, English Literature, French, Spanish, Geography, History, Mathematics and Further Mathematics, Music, PE, Physics, Politics and Psychology. Information Technology, Drama, English Language and Religious Studies are offered as freestanding AS Levels.

Music, Drama, Art, Design. The Music School contains a central teaching hall, a second newly refurbished teaching room and several practice rooms. Professional tuition is given on all instruments and there are chapel and concert choirs, junior and senior bands and a school orchestra.

Concerts, school and house drama productions and lectures are held in the School Hall, which has well-equipped stage facilities. The Richard Gent Design Centre offers workshops and studies for design technology and ceramics. The highly successful Two-Dimensional Art Department has its own dedicated building. Pupils are encouraged to make full use of these facilities in their spare time.

Sport. The playing fields, over 40 acres in extent, are used for the main boys' sports of rugby, soccer and cricket and hockey and netball for girls; cross country, athletics, and tennis are also highly popular. The school site also boasts a nine-hole golf course, astroturf pitch, five all-weather tennis courts, two squash courts, shooting range, gymnasium and sports hall. The latter has four badminton courts, indoor cricket nets and facilities for fencing, table tennis, basketball and dedicated fitness suite.

Other Activities. After their first term in the Senior School pupils join the Combined Cadet Force (RN, Army, Commando or RAF Section) until the end of Year 10 at least. Training is given in first aid, map reading and orienteering, and camping expeditions take place at weekends. There is an annual CCF camp and there are opportunities for band training, open range shooting, REME work, canoeing and sailing. The Duke of Edinburgh's Award scheme is also a very popular option for older pupils.

A wide range of extra-curricular interests is available through various societies and clubs. Pupils may also take part in local community service work.

Careers. Guidance is available to all pupils on further education and careers prospects through the Head of Careers and other members of staff. The School is a member of the Independent Schools Careers Organisation.

Scholarships and Bursaries. Foundation scholarships are offered to external candidates for entry to the Preparatory School at 11+. The examination is held in January and entries are required by the end of December.

At 13+ entrance scholarships are offered to pupils entering the Senior School. The examination is held in January.

At 16+ Sixth Form academic scholarships are offered.

Music, Drama, Art and Sports scholarships are available at 13+ and 16+. An All-Rounder Scholarship is also available at 13+.

The Nevill Trust Sixth Form Bursary is awarded to pupils currently attending a Northamptonshire state school.

Bursaries are available, on a means-tested basis (subject to annual review), to support those pupils who would benefit from a Wellingborough education but whose families are unable to afford the full fees. Means-tested Bursaries may also be available to augment Scholarships.

Further details and application forms for all the above awards may be obtained from the Registrar.

Fees per term (2016–2017). Senior School: £4,925 (Years 9–13); Preparatory School: £4,595 (Years 7 & 8), £4,395 (Years 4, 5 & 6); Pre-Preparatory School: £2,965 (Years 2 & 3), £2,840 (Nursery, Reception & Year 1). Reduced rates are offered for children in Nursery Class not attending all sessions and children from age 3–5 are eligible for the Government's Early Years Funding. Fees include most extras apart from instrumental lessons (termly payment), public examination fees and books.

Admission. Applications should be made to the Registrar for entry of boys and girls at 13+ and for direct entry into the Sixth Form. Enquiries concerning entries between the ages of 3 and 7 should be addressed to the Pre-Prep School Registrar, and entries between the ages of 8 and 12 to the Registrar of the Preparatory School.

Term of Entry. New pupils are accepted at the beginning of any term. The largest entry is in September each year.

Old Wellingburian Club. All former pupils who have spent at least one year in the School are eligible for membership. Correspondence should be addressed to the OW Club Secretary at the School.

Charitable status. Wellingborough School is a Registered Charity, number 1101485. It exists to provide education for boys and girls from the age of 3 to 18.

Governors:
Dr J Cox, MA Cantab, MB BChir, BA (*Chairman*)
Mrs A Coles, MA (*Deputy Chairman*)
T Baldry, FCA
D K Exham, MA, PGCE
J J H Higgins
G Jones
Mrs D A Line, BA, CA
N B Lyon, MA
S M Marriott (*Representative Governor of the OW Club*)
Mrs P Perkins, OBE
R H Thakrar, BSc Hons, MBCS
P R Tyldesley, BA, ARICS
D A Waller, MA
C A Westley

Bursar & Clerk to the Governors: C J P Evans, BA Durham

Senior School:

Headmaster: G R Bowe, BA Kent, PGCE Leeds (*History*)

Bursar & Head of Finance: C J P Evans, BA Durham
Deputy Head Academic: Mrs S M Barnhurst, BSc Salford, MA Northampton (*Physics*)
Deputy Head Pastoral: Q Wiseman, BA Newcastle, PGCE London, BSA Roehampton (*Geography*)
Master i/c Sixth Form Academic Progress: J R Gray, BSc Bangor (*Biology*)
Assistant Head Co-Curricular: Mrs L J McAuley, BSc Glasgow (*Mathematics*)
Director of Marketing & Communications: M Deoraj, BA Sheffield

Housemasters/Housemistresses:
Fryer's House: M Baddeley, BSc York (*Mathematics*)
Garne's House: *D A Coombes, BA, Liverpool John Moores (*Design Technology*)
Platt's House: T J Fourie, MSc Port Elizabeth SA · (*Mathematics*)
Cripps' House: *K C M Hargreaves, Rose Bruford College of Speech & Drama
Parker Steyne's: G E Houghton, BA Durham (*PE/Games*)

Marsh House: Miss C S Irvin, BSc Loughborough (*Head of Academic PE*)
Nevill House: Miss J M Livingstone, BA Queen's Belfast (*Geography*)
Weymouth House: Mrs H M Pattison, BSc King's College London (*Head of Biology*)

Teaching Staff:
Mrs H C Arimoro, BA Durham (*Psychology*)
Miss J H Austin, BSc Oxford Brookes (*PE and Geography*)
Mrs S Bailey, Technikon Pretoria – National Diploma, Language Diploma and Baccalaureus Technologiae – Language practice, Tshwane University of Technology – PGCE (*English as a Foreign Language*) [Maternity Leave]
Mrs S J Baxby, BA Northampton (*Head of Business Studies*)
J Blackmore, Jazz BMus, Teaching LRAM, Royal Academy of Music (*Musician in Residence*)
E Buck, BSc Worcester (*Sports Graduate Assistant*)
*Mrs F J Burgess, BEd Exeter (*Head of PSHCE*) (*PE/Games*)
J Burrows (*Sports Graduate Assistant*)
Mrs L Burton, BSc Lincoln (*Biology*)
K Cook, BSc Secondary Science PGCE and QTS Wolverhampton, PG Cert Staffordshire (*Biology*) [Maternity cover]
*Miss S M Curley, BA De Montfort (*English/Latin/EPQ*)
*S L Egan, BEng Leicester (*Head of Design Technology*)
*Mrs C Y Elwyn, Baccalaureat Lycee Nationalise Mixte, Diploma Languages I C, PGCE(*French/Latin*)
J Q Fargas (*Spanish Language Assistant*)
P J Farley, BA York, MA Liverpool (*History, Head of Politics*)
Mrs S E Fellows, BA Birmingham (*Head of Spanish, French*)
J M Furness-Gibbon, BA Worcester, MA, London (*English*)
A R Gamble, BA St Edmund Hall Oxford (*Head of English*)
Mrs S Gibson-Foy (*Politics*)
Mrs J C Hennessy, BA Leicester Polytechnic (*Head of Art*)
Dr A Higginson, PhD UMIST (*Head of Science, Head of Physics*)
S T Hill, BA JNC St John's College Nottingham (*Chaplaincy Youth Worker*)
L M Hilton, BSc Loughborough (*Director of Sport*)
Mrs H L Hodgson, BEng Liverpool (*Head of Mathematics*)
*Mrs A S Holley, BA Birmingham (*Head of Classics*)
Miss C E M Horry, BA Kent (*Art, Chair of Senior School Council*)
Mrs K R Kenney, BA Birmingham (*English*)
Mrs S J Kielty, BA Wales, MA Warwick (*Head of History*)
*Miss B Lavin Campo, Licenciado en Filosofia y Letras Valladolid, Spain (*Spanish*)
Mrs B Lawson, BSc Loughborough (*Mathematics*)
Mrs S D Lawson, BA, PGC-SEN Coordination Northampton, PGCE/QTS Leicester (*Head of Learning Support*)
Dr K M Loak-Chrisp, PhD Aston (*Chemistry*)
P J Lowe, BA Southampton (*Head of Geography*)
C Martin-Sims, BSc Sussex, MSc Reading, BA Open (*Head of Drama, Head of Psychology*)
*Ms J A Mason, BA Teesside (*Design Technology*)
K Meagan, FA Coaching Certificate, FA Coaching License and UEFA "B" Award (*PE*)
Dr A S Monaghan, BSc Dundee, PhD Cambridge (*Chemistry/Physics/Biology*)
A G Peacock, BA Trinity College Oxford, MA Lancaster (*History/RS*)
C Perret (*French Language Assistant*)
Mrs L Peters (*Games*)

Dr P J Phillips, BSc Portsmouth Polytechnic, PhD Warwick (*Physics*)

Mrs S S Rich, BSc Durham (*Head of Chemistry*)

Mrs G M Rodgers, MA Newnham College Cambridge (*English*)

*I Runnells, BA Northampton, LTCL, LLCM, ARCO (*Director of Music*)

Mrs G Scott, BA Leicester, PGCE Bedford (*Business Studies*)

Mrs J F Selby, BA Leicester, PGCE Oxford (*History*)

*Mrs C Stroud, Licence ès Lettres Sorbonne Nouvelle Paris (*Head of Modern Languages*)

*Miss C T H Thomas, BA Leicester (*French*)

*Revd M J Walker, BA Lincoln College Oxford, BA St John's College Durham, DipES Geneva (*Chaplain & Head of RS*)

P B Waugh, BEd Manchester Metropolitan (*Head of ICT*)

S J Whitby, BEng Kingston, PGCE Leicester (*Design & Technology, Art*)

A D Woodward, BSc City (*Head of Economics*)

Mrs C L Woodward, BA Surrey Institute of Art & Design (*Art, Photography*)

*also teaches in Preparatory School

Preparatory School:

Headmistress: Mrs Sue Knox, BA Hons UCNW, MBA Cranfield, GradDipEd & MEdLead Macquarie University Sydney

Deputy Head, Curriculum: Mrs K Owen, BSc Exeter

Deputy Head – Pastoral: Mrs C Petrie, BSc Loughborough

Pastoral Coordinator: Mrs J B Rowley-Burns, BSc Greenwich (*Head of Maths*)

Year 4 Coordinator: Mrs A J Simmons, BA Stirling, PGCE Sheffield Hallam (*Form Tutor 4AS, Maths, English, Science*)

Academic Progress and Reporting Coordinator: Dr A I Fordham, BSc Oxford Brookes, MRes Open, PhD Open (*Head of Geography*)

Club Presidents:

Tigers: Miss S C Allan, MA Cardiff (*Form Tutor 8SA, English, Games*)

Bears: P W Dennis, BA Oxford Brookes (*Form Tutor 8PD, English, Head of History, Spanish, Games*)

Panthers: W Richardson, BEd Leicester (*Form Tutor 8WR, Maths, Games*)

Wolves: B J Russell, Fd BSc Northampton (*Form Tutor 8BJR, Maths, Games*)

Jaguars: Mrs C L Whitaker, BA Brighton (*Form Tutor 8CLW, Geography, PE, Games*)

Lions: S J Whitby, BEng Kingston, PGCE Leicester (*Form Tutor 8SJW, DT, Games*)

Teaching Staff:

Mrs C Allen, Cert SpLD (*Learning Support*)

Mrs L A Barltrop, BA, Dip RSA, NASENCo Northampton (*Head of Learning Support*)

Miss H J Clark, BA Chester, PGCE Worcester (*Form Tutor 6HJC, French*)

C W Pickett, BCS Auckland University of Technology, PGCE Buckingham [Sabbatical]

Mrs F J Drye, BA Wales (*Form Tutor 5FD, Head of English*)

Mrs J Ferguson, BSc Northumbria, PGCE Sunderland (*Form Tutor 5JF, Science*)

S Groom, BA Northampton (*Form Tutor 7SG, Head of ICT*)

N R Grove, BA Lancaster, MA Liverpool (*Form Tutor 7NRG, English, History*)

L Irvine, BA Trinity College Carmarthen, PGCE Wales Institute Cardiff (*Head of Sport & Extra Curricular Activities*)

Miss A S Kingstone, BA Northampton (*Form Tutor 4AK, History, Games*)

K W Leutfeld, BMus Guildhall School of Music & Drama, MA Institute of Education, PGCE Nottingham Trent (*Head of Music*)

Ms H F Machin, BA King's College London, (*Form Tutor 7HM, Head of French and Spanish*)

Mrs C L McDougall, BSc Brighton (*Form Tutor 4CM, English, Maths, RS, Science, Games*)

Mrs L McMillan, BSc Leeds Polytechnic (*Science*)

Miss J Petrie, BA Hons Bournemouth (*Form Tutor 6JP, History and English*)

Mrs K J Reade, Cert In-Service Education (*Visual Impairment*)

Mrs R Roberts, BEd Chester, (*Form Tutor 5RR, Head of Art*)

Mrs A J Staughton, BA Leeds Polytechnic (*Form Tutor 7AJS, Head of Science*)

L Williams, BA Bath, MSc Brunel (*Form Tutor 6LW, Head of PE, Geography, Games*)

Pre-Preparatory School:

Headmistress: Miss J M Everett, MA, BEd London (*French*)

Assistant Head (Curriculum): D C Popplewell, BA Warwick (*Year 3 Teacher – Games/PE – Gifted & Talented*)

Assistant Head (Pastoral): Mrs R M Girling, BEd Cambridge (*Year 3 Teacher – Maths*)

Teaching Staff:

Mrs J A Askham, BEd Loughborough (*Years 2 & 3*)

Mrs J E M Espin, BA New Hall Cambridge (*Year 1 – Humanities*)

S Garfirth, Dip RCM, ALCM, Royal College of Music (*All Year Groups – Music*)

Mrs E Jakeman, BEd Worcester College (*Years Reception, Year 1, Year 3*)

Mrs S A Jamieson, BA Northampton (*Year 2 – Art/DT*)

Mrs J Mellor, BEd Kingston (*Reception – Early Years*)

Mrs K Wood, BA East Anglia (*Reception – Science*)

Mrs C H Waite, BEd Ripon & York St John (*Year 2 – Literacy*)

Mrs L Gillard, BA Northampton (*Year 1 – Library*)

*Ms M Mannion, HLTA Northampton (*Specialist Teacher of Computing (ICT Coordinator)*)

* also teaches in Preparatory and Senior School

Nursery Staff:

Mrs H Cockbill, NNEB West Bridgford College (*Nursery*)

Mrs M Gutteridge, NNEB Southfields College (*Nursery*)

Miss D Herbert, NVQ Early Years Care & Education Level 3 (*Nursery*)

Mrs S M Sandall, Adv Dip Early Years Education & NNEB, Solihull Technical College (*Nursery*)

Teaching Assistants:

Mrs S Barber, FDLT Northampton (*All Year Groups*)

Mrs M E Campbell, Art Diploma & BTEC, Tresham College (*Year 3*)

Miss B Gosling, NNEB Northampton College (*Nursery & Year 3*)

Mrs K Harris, NNEB Tresham Institute (*Years 1 & 3*)

Mrs A Martin, NNEB Stoke on Trent College (*Year 1*)

Mrs C Maher (*Nursery Assistant*)

Mrs A Mower, HLTA Level 4 Northampton (*Reception*)

Mrs Z Shah, NNEB Northampton College (*Year 2*)

Mrs C Ward, NNEB Northampton College (*Year 1*)

Miss A M Ystenes, NNEB Nene College (*Reception*)

Wellington College

Duke's Ride, Crowthorne, Berkshire RG45 7PU

Tel:	The Master: 01344 444101
	Director of Admissions: 01344 444013
	Group Finance Director & Bursar: 01344 444020
	Reception: 01344 444000
Fax:	01344 444002
email:	info@wellingtoncollege.org.uk
website:	www.wellingtoncollege.org.uk
Twitter:	@WellingtonUK
Facebook:	/WellingtonCollege

Wellington College was founded by public subscription as a memorial to the Great Duke. It was granted its Royal Charter in 1853 and took its first pupils in 1859. The school is set in a woodland estate of 400 acres.

The College builds upon its honourable past while adapting its values and traditions for the Twenty-First Century in a dynamic and sustainable way. Our fusion of originality and innovation with tradition and history produces a unique education. We seek to open the hearts and minds of all at Wellington thereby making it one of Britain's and the world's most inspiring co-educational schools for both boarding and day pupils. We want each and every one of our pupils to learn, to achieve and to be happy and by so doing to develop a recognisable Wellington identity. It is an identity built on intellectual curiosity, true independence, a generous and far-reaching inclusivity and the courage to be properly and unselfishly individual. It is, in short, the capacity to be inspired to become the very best you can be.

Our curriculum is challenging, ambitious and global. We offer the IB Diploma alongside A Level and GCSE.

Wellington has a Christian foundation, which celebrates and respects children from all religious faiths and backgrounds. A commitment to leadership, service and an international outlook lie at the heart of Wellington which has, at its core, values chosen by the whole community: *Courage – Integrity – Respect – Kindness – Responsibility*.

Organisation. There are approximately 1,045 pupils, with 640 boys and 405 girls, spread across all age groups.

All pupils belong to one of seventeen Houses, seven of which are located in the main College buildings and ten in the grounds. Fifteen of the Houses accommodate the 80%+ who board at Wellington as well as a handful of day pupils. There are also two specific day Houses, one each for girls and for boys. 13+ boarders share rooms in their first year, and may do so in a second or third year, but then move on to their own room. There is a central dining hall with modern kitchens and serveries. Meals are taken here on a cafeteria basis by most of the pupils although some Houses outside the main buildings have their own dining facilities. The V&A café is also open during school hours for drinks and snacks. The school has its own Medical Officer and a 9-bed Health Centre constantly staffed by fully-qualified nurses. All Houses have their own tutors, House Matrons and domestic team, which are led by the Housemaster or Housemistress.

Academic Work. Academic standards are higher than they have ever been in the College's history. In 2016, our sixth formers achieved over 92% A*–B grades at A Level or the IB equivalent, (73% A*/A). Over 85% of GCSE grades were A*/A. For the third year in a row its IB Diploma results made it one of the UK's highest achieving boarding schools to offer the IB Diploma, with the average score being 39: 49% of pupils secured 40 points or more and four candidates secured a perfect 45 points. Last year 95% of leavers secured places at their first or second choice university, 31

won places at Oxford or Cambridge with a further five receiving offers from Ivy League colleges.

The academic curriculum is designed to give pupils a broad and rounded education while allowing them maximum opportunity to develop their individual interests and strengths through their chosen fields of specialist study.

Pupils in the Third Form take a bespoke, Wellington-designed programme offering both breadth and depth in eight key learning areas: Mathematics, Science, English, Modern and Classical Languages, Humanities, the Arts, Technology and Physical Education. The curriculum accentuates personal enquiry, independent study, internationalism and social responsibility, with all courses emphasising the links between subjects and between school and the outside world. Following their initial experience of Wellington, pupils entering the Fourth Form choose a single curriculum combining the more traditional programme of GCSEs and IGCSEs with a number of bespoke Wellington-designed courses. This integrated approach ensures both breadth and rigour in the middle school curriculum.

On entering the Sixth Form, pupils may choose between A Levels and the International Baccalaureate Diploma Programme. While plenty of advice is offered, pupils are free to choose the kind of education they want for their future.

Facilities. Most work takes place in modern specialist blocks near to the main buildings. The Queen's Court building houses the Humanities and also contains a theatre. The Science laboratories are numerous and the Kent Building houses well-equipped Design & Technology and Information Technology centres. An architecturally stunning Art School, new Chemistry and Physics laboratories have been built. A flagship Modern Languages block is now open with our inspirational Mandarin Centre across the road. A state-of-the-art, digital library was recently opened and this is complemented by the learning and social areas of the Water Library and Selangor Court, bringing learning right into the heart of the school. The new Performing Arts Centre, currently being built, was voted "Best Building in Education" at the World Architecture Festival.

Enrichment Activities. Personal enrichment is an imperative at Wellington and each student takes part in a range of activities that broaden and refine their education. Such enrichment is structured within the eight aptitudes of learning with dedicated time on a Monday, Wednesday and Friday. There are some fifty-two clubs, societies and other enrichment activities which include Amnesty International, Classical Hebrew, Debating, Equality & Diversity, Field Gun, Mandarin, Mindfulness, Photography, Model United Nations, GeoVenture, Real Tennis, Food for Thought, Law Society, Dance Classes, Film Society, Creative Writing and even Channel Swimming. All pupils on arrival join the Junior Society which introduces them to a wide variety of activities. A Creative Writing Group meets regularly and a pupil editorial team produces The Wellingtonian, a news and features publication. There are a number of other pupil-led magazines specific to particular subject areas, and most importantly the student-run TV station provides media experience to pupils as well as providing weekly programmes recording College life. We have just launched Dukebox, a student-run radio station that links all members of the Wellington family of schools.

Art, Music, Dance and Drama are outstanding. There are regular visiting lecturers on a variety of topics, an Artist in Residence, and masterclasses in Art, Music/Drama and Literature. The range of performance, the ambition and the comprehensive nature of Wellington's artistic programme are particular features. Wellington is particularly proud of its Physical Theatre team – who perform a mixture of Street and acrobatic inspired dance, its excellent Chapel choir and its award-winning a cappella group. Each year the school stages a major musical as well as many serious plays and opportunities for student-run productions. There is a rich programme of classical concerts featuring a variety of orchestras and ensembles, while dance is well represented by an annual show and a House competition. Wellington also hosts an annual arts festival each autumn.

The school has built upon its historic legacy of leadership, dating back to the First Duke of Wellington, and has established programmes to offer each pupil training and opportunities in leadership throughout their time at the College. The College runs several annual inter-schools conferences on leadership and is currently working with the Government to develop a nationwide character-building, leadership training programme. This emphasis on building character and leadership skills is complemented by Wellington's well-being curriculum which teaches pupils how to flourish. In this, as in so many areas, Wellington is pioneering. Wellington has been a Round Square school since 1995; membership of the Round Square organisation is a fundamental part of Wellington's holistic approach to education. Partnership with over seventy schools worldwide allows us to pursue our aim to produce compassionate global citizens of the future.

Sport. At Wellington our aim is to provide a sports programme based on enjoyment, learning and performance. We believe in the development of the whole child, the fostering of an 'active life' philosophy and the promotion of a lifetime investment in sport and physical activity. We seek to establish a sporting ethos that is linked to the College's well-being and leadership programmes and the 'eight aptitudes'.

Wellington's sporting reputation continues to thrive. The school has a national reputation for prowess in a number of sports, particularly in rugby, hockey, cricket, netball, shooting, swimming, athletics, rackets, triathlon, squash, golf, riding and polo. There are numerous opportunities for pupils to represent the College in teams across a wide range of competitive sports as well as recreational activities, all of which are supported by the outstanding College facilities. These include over 80 acres of playing fields, two all-weather pitches for hockey and all-weather tennis courts. There is a sports complex which incorporates a rackets court, five squash courts, an indoor pool, a large sports hall, a spectacular sports pavilion, and a new real tennis court. The main sports centre caters for a wide variety of indoor games as well as specialist weight training and conditioning rooms, dance studios and a rock climbing area. An outstanding nine-hole golf course was opened in September 2001 and is enjoyed by many in the community. The traditional pattern of boys' sport is rugby (we regularly field up to 20 XVs) in the Michaelmas Term, hockey, football and cross country in the Lent Term and cricket, athletics, tennis and swimming in the Summer. For the girls, hockey has been the main sport in the Michaelmas Term, with netball in the Lent and cricket, rounders, athletics, tennis and swimming in the Summer. There is also the opportunity for girls to play lacrosse competitively. Recently sporting options throughout the school have been expanded and many other sports have been made available as a first or second choice option for pupils which include squash, basketball, tennis, sailing, football, rugby 7s, triathlon, fencing, karate, badminton, swimming, cross country and a variety of fitness and health-related activities. Wellington College's coaching philosophy is continuously evolving; however, it is based around some core principles that our staff firmly believe in. We aim to provide pupils with a transformative experience, using a variety of methods to help individuals to achieve their personal sporting aspirations. Our vision is to create the best possible "safe, friendly and challenging" environment for our pupils, which in turn promotes enjoyment, learning and performance. We believe in a player-centred approach to coaching which encourages pupils to think for themselves and helps to raise the individual's self-awareness. All of our staff are regarded as high quality "people coaches".

Admission to the School. Most pupils enter the school in September when they are between 13 and 14 years of age. There are occasionally places available for pupils at 14+. Around 40 pupils also join the College for the Sixth Form. Registrations (with £200 fee) should be addressed to the Registrar, or in the case of Foundationers, to the Bursar. Those registered for 13+ entry (by the end of Year 5) sit the ISEB Common Pre-Test in the Michaelmas term of Year 6 and, if sufficiently strong academically or in other areas (e.g. sport, music), are invited for an assessment day (usually in the Lent term of Year 6). Those who are successful are then offered a conditional place subject to satisfactory results in Scholarship, Common Entrance or other entry exams. A Waiting List also operates. Where appropriate, an overseas deposit is also payable.

Scholarships. Detailed information about the Scholarships available on entry at age 13+ or 16+ can be found on our website, and a booklet may be obtained from the Admissions Office. This detailed information explains aspects such as application, requirement, examinations, assessments, timetable and tenure. No Scholarships are awarded at 14+ entry.

Scholarships at 13+ and 16+ are available in a range of categories: Academic, Music, the Arts (Art, Design and Technology, Drama, Dance) and Sport. The College also offers All-Rounder awards to talented children who have displayed potential across a number of different areas.

Being awarded a Scholarship upon entrance to the College is considered a great accolade and award holders will partake in specialist extension programmes within their sphere of particular talent.

Scholarships do not, in themselves, provide any fee reduction, although Music Scholarships afford parents free tuition in two instruments and free composition and Alexander Technique lessons.

Bursaries. Widening access to Wellington is at the heart of the Governors' and Master's vision for the future of the College. All financial aid in terms of fee reduction is therefore awarded via a means-testing procedure (details from the Bursar's Office). Our aim is to enable an increasing number of families, who otherwise would not have been able to afford the fees at Wellington, to send their son or daughter to the College.

Means-tested bursaries are available to the families of children who have been successful in winning a Scholarship. The value of bursaries may be up to 95% of College fees, depending on individual family circumstances.

Foundation places: Very generous remission is available for the sons and daughters of deceased military servicemen and servicewomen and of others who have died in acts of selfless bravery, subject to entry requirement and according to the rules of the Foundation. Further details are available from the Bursar's Office.

The Prince Albert Foundation, founded in 2010, offers life-changing bursaries, up to full fees, for talented and deserving pupils who otherwise would be unable to access the quality of education and opportunities presented by attending Wellington College due to limited financial means. The College works closely with a number of educational charities to identify worthy candidates and also considers direct approaches from families.

Fees per term (2016–2017). Boarders £12,370, Day (in boarding House) £10,385, Day £9,040. Separate charges totalling £287.50 per instrument are made for musical tuition (10 lessons). The school runs an attractive fees in advance scheme for parents with capital sums available.

Old Wellingtonian Society. Much of our programme for Old Wellingtonians is centred around career networking and mentoring support for sixth formers and alumni of all ages. Currently we have over 20 career networking groups representing a wide range of sectors. The OW Society also has 26 branches in 19 countries, clubs representing 11 different sports, around 9,000 members, and an active and varied programme of social events. To find out more please email Emma Browne on elb@wellingtoncollege.org.uk or go to our website wellingtoncollege.org.uk.

The Wellington Group. A significant feature of Wellington is its outward-looking, expansive approach to education. Wellington College Shanghai, Wellington College Tianjin, the Wellington Academies in Wiltshire and Eagle House prep school all offer our pupils numerous opportunities to learn with others and to engage in partnership activities. This, combined with our Teaching School initiative, Leadership Institute, ISSP programme and extensive lectures and conference programme which culminates in the annual Daily Telegraph/Wellington College Education Festival, reflects our commitment to lifelong learning and to leading educational debate in the country.

Charitable status. Wellington College is a Registered Charity, number 309093. It exists to provide education for boys and girls aged 13–18.

Visitor: Her Majesty The Queen

President: HRH The Duke of Kent, KG, GCMG, GCVO, ADC, DL

Vice-President & Chairman of Governors: Mr Peter Mallinson, BA, MBA

Ex officio Governors:
The Archbishop of Canterbury, MA, BA, DipMin

Governors:
Arthur Charles Valerian Wellesley, 9th Duke of Wellington, OBE, DL
Dr Rosemary Groves, BA, PhD
Dr Peter Frankopan, MA, DPhil, FRSA
Tim Bunting, MA
Robert Perrins, BSc Hons, ACA
Howard Veary, BA, FCA
Mrs Margot Chaundler, OBE
The Rt Hon The Lord Strathclyde, CH
Ron Dennis, CBE
Thomas Cookson, MA
Edward Chaplin, CMG, OBE
Marshal of the Royal Air Force Lord Stirrup, KG, GCB, AFC
Roland Rudd, MA
Duncan Ritchie, FCA
Nigel Howard-Jones
Mrs Felicity Kirk, LLB
Ms Virginia Rhodes, BA Hons
Mrs Gabriela Galceran Ball

Master: **Julian Thomas**, BSc Hons, MBA, FRSA

Second Master: Robin Dyer, BA
Director of Admissions: James Dahl, MA, MA
Deputy Head (Academic): Matt Oakman, BA
Deputy Head (Co-curricular): Mrs Cressida Henderson, BA
Deputy Head (Educational Developments & Partnerships): Iain Henderson, BA
Deputy Head (Organisation): Dr Alastair Dunn, MA, DPhil
Interim Deputy Head (Pastoral & Wellbeing): Neill Lunnon, BSc

Assistant Staff:
* *Head of Department/Year*
† *Housemaster/mistress*

Art:
*Edward Twohig, BEd, MA
Miss Sally-Anne Burt, BA
Mrs Bethan Carr, BA
Ms Amy Flanagan, BA
Miss Rachel Humphries, BA

Adam Rattray, BA (*Art History*)
Mrs Harriet Thistlethwaite, BA
James Trundle, BSc, BFA
Miss Alice Wilson, BA (*Art Textiles*)

Biology:
*Dr Harry Wright, BSc, PhD
Miss Emma Bavin, BSc
Mrs Vanessa Giannikas, BSc
Sam Laing, MSc
Dr Elizabeth Lambert, BSc, PhD
†Miss Kate Larkin, BA
Svend Larsen, BSc, MEd
Nicholas Light, MA, MSc

Chemistry:
*Dr Caroline Evans, BA, PhD
Miss Charlotte Barrett Denonain, BA
Nicolas Casasanto, BA
Dr Elaine Hood, BSc, PhD
†Mrs Rachel Loaring, BSc
Jack McGarey, MChem
Mrs Kyley Mitchell, MSc
Dr Julian O'Loughlin, MSc, PhD (*Director of Digital Learning*)
David Wilson, MA

Classics:
*Simon Allcock, MA
Dr Robert Colborn, BA, MSt
Dr Robert Cromarty, MA, PhD
Ms Rowena Hewes, BA
Dr Matthew Johncock, MA, PhD
Miss Sarah Stuckey, BA

Dance:
*Mrs Caroline Kenworthy, BA

Design Technology:
*Mark Ellwood, BEd
Ben Attenborough, BA
Ms Stephanie Porrino, BEd
Greg Woodrow, MA

Drama:
*Ms Amelia Morse, BA
Mrs Katie Hamilton, BA (*LAMDA*)
Alexander Mancuso, BA
Mrs Kirsty Richardson, BA

Economics:
*Dushy Clarke, BA, MSc
Mrs Emmie Bidston, BA
Mrs Amanda Campion, MA
Chris Ewart, MA (*Careers)
†John Giannikas, BA
Simon Roundell, MA
†Iain J Sutcliffe, MA, MBA
Mrs Julia Sutcliffe, BA (**4th & 5th Forms*)
†Ed Venables, BA
David Wiltshire, BA

English:
*Mrs Estella Gutulan
Ms Eleanor Bradley, BA
James Breen, MA
Ms Denise Brown, MA
Miss Sarah Donarski, BA
†Gavin Franklin, BA
Tim Head, BA
Carl Hendrick, MA
†Tom Hicks, MA
Miss Rachael Kirby, BA
Dr Ruth Lexton, BA, MPhil, PhD
James Lugton, MA

Miss Kirsty Tyrrell, BA
†Mrs Jo C Wayman, BA
†Tom Wayman, BA, MPhil

Geography:
*Miss Rachel Trafford, MA
Jim Dewes, MA
Mrs Grace Elliott, BA (*Academic Support*)
Christopher Foyle, BA
Mrs Katy Granville-Chapman, BA, MSc
Jack Murray, BA
Miss Alice Taylor, BA

History:
*Ben Lewsley, BA
Dr Victoria Gardner, BA, MLitt, DPhil
Sam Gutteridge, MA
Tristan Macleod, BA
Robin Macpherson, BA, MSc
Matthew Pattie, MA
Miss Lucy Robb, MA

Mathematics:
*Aidan Sproat, MA
Richard Atherton, BSc, MPhil (*IB*)
Nick Carpenter, BSc
Mike Cawdron, BSc
Paul Cootes, MA, MSc
Miss Clare Edwards, BA
Miss Helen Gray, BSc
Jonathan Hooper, PGDip (*Computer Science*)
Bob Jones, BSc
Edward Jones, BA, MSc
Ilia Kurgansky, MSc
Kyle McDonald, BSc
John Rawlinson, BSc
George Wells, BA
Ben White, MEng
†Jonathan White, BA

Modern Languages:
*Dr Rachelle Kirkham, MA, PhD
Thierry Drot-Troha, MA
†David Edwards, BA
Ms Aurora Gomez, BA
Mrs Polly Gutteridge, MA
†Mrs Sophie Jobson, Lic d'Anglais, Dip d'Étude IFI
Miss Camilla Keep, BA
Simon Kirkham, BA (*German*)
Miss Charlotte Le Bihan, Double Licence, Provence (*French*)
Mrs Ningning Ma, MA
†Mrs Magali Ogilvie, Lic d'Anglais
†Charles Oliphant-Callum, MA
Sam Owen (*Spanish*)
Oliver Peat, BA
Mrs Hossa Skandary-Macpherson
Mrs Yunyun Tang, MA
†Andrew Wilkinson, BA, MSc
Miss Catherine Willis, BA
Alexander Young, BA

Music:
*Simon Williamson, MA, FRCO (*Director of Music & Arts*)
Sean Farrell, BA (*Academic*)
George de Voil, BA
†Mrs Libby Fisher, BA
Mrs Susanne Henwood, GRSM Hons, LRAM, ALCM
Xavier Iles, BA
Jeff Oakes, ARCM
Dylan Quinlivan-Brewer, BMus Hons, PGDip RCM

Philosophy & Religion:
*Tom Kirby, BA, MSt
Dr Guy Williams, MA, DPhil (*Theory of Knowledge*; *6th Form*)
James Ellis, BA
†Mrs Jessica Goves, BA
Peter Thistlethwaite, BA, MSt

Physical Education:
*Steve Shortland, BEd, MSc (*Director of Sport*)
Mrs Jane Grillo, BEd (*PE*)
Murray Barratt, BA
†Kevin Brennan, MSc
Miss Adele Brown, BEd
Miss Sophia Candappa, BSc
Gareth Carr
Miss Kate Murphy, BSc
Dan Pratt, MSc
Ryan Tulley, BA, BSc

Physics:
*Dr Jacqueline Chapman, BSc, PhD
†Alexis Christodoulou, MA
Mrs Tamara Christodoulou, BA
Dr Mark Farrington, MSc, PhD
Ian Frayne, BSc
Miss Amy Haddock, BEng
Dr Will Heathcote, MPhys, DPhil
†Chris Mitchell, BEng
Dr Dan Tice, BA, DPhil

Politics:
*Dibran Zeqiri, BA, MSc
Rob Murphy, BA (*3rd Form*)

Psychology:
Keith Reesby, MSc

Wellbeing:
*Ian Morris, BA
Mrs Delyth Lynch, BSc

Academic Support:
*Dan Clements (*Interim*)
Mrs Ellie Farrell, Grad Dip RCM
Mrs Debbie Hathaway, BSc
Mrs Ginette Vonchek, BEd, Cert TEFL, Cert IELTS (*EAL*)

plus 50 visiting instrumental teachers

Senior Chaplain: The Revd Tim Novis, BA, MDiv

Houses and Housemasters/mistresses:
Anglesey: Mrs Rachel Loaring
Apsley: Alexis Christodoulou
Benson: Tom Hicks
Beresford: Gavin Franklin
Blücher: Kevin Brennan
Combermere: Mrs Libby Fisher
Hardinge Boys: Charles Oliphant-Callum
Hardinge Girls: Mrs Sophie Jobson
Hill: John Giannikas
Hopetoun: Mrs Magali Ogilvie
Lynedoch: Chris Mitchell
Murray: Iain Sutcliffe
Orange: Mrs Jo Wayman and Tom Wayman
Picton: David Edwards
Raglan: Andrew Wilkinson
Stanley: Ed Venables
Talbot: Jonathan White
Wellesley: Miss Kate Larkin

CC CCF: Ian Frayne, BSc
Group Finance Director & Bursar: Stephen Crouch, BA, ACA
Director of Finance: Paul Thompson, MA, ACMA

Works & Estates Bursar: Malcolm Callender, MBA, FCMI, MCGI, MinstRE

Head of the Wellington Community: Murray Lindo, BA, MA, MSc, CIPD

International Business Director: Mrs Helen Kavanagh, BA Hons

Legal & Compliance Director: Mrs Katherine Baker, MA

Operations Manager: Brian Cannon, MSyl, MCGI

Medical Officer: Dr Anant Sachdev, MB ChB, CFP, D Pall Med

Health Centre Sister: Mrs Bev Gilbert

Registrar: Mrs Louise Peate, BSc

Head of Teaching School: Mrs Rachel Carter, BA

EA to the Master: Mrs Angela Reed

PA to the Second Master: Miss Su Taylor

Bursary Assistant: Mrs Lisa Thompson

Wellington School

South St, Wellington, Somerset TA21 8NT

Tel:	01823 668800
Fax:	01823 668844
email:	admissions@wellington-school.org.uk
website:	www.wellington-school.org.uk
Twitter:	@wellingtonsch1
Facebook:	/WellingtonSchool

Motto: *Nisi dominus frustra*

Founded in 1837, Wellington School is a co-educational, academically selective school providing a friendly, disciplined environment and a wide range of co-curricular opportunities.

Situation. Located on the southern edge of Wellington, at the foot of the Blackdown Hills, this fully co-educational School is equidistant from Tiverton Parkway and Taunton Railway Stations. The M5 approach road (Junction 26) is within a mile. Currently there are 600 pupils in the Lower and Upper Schools (11–18 years), of whom 20% board.

Buildings. The School has witnessed an extensive building programme over the last twenty years, the new buildings having been carefully and tastefully blended in with existing architecture.

The John Kendall-Carpenter Science Centre has state-of-the-art laboratories and lecture theatre, a multimillion pound sports complex, a purpose-built Prep School and a new classroom block and examination hall. Major improvements to Performing Arts facilities, including a new foyer and theatre space, were completed in 2010. Plans are under way to refurbish boarding houses, the School cafe, the all-weather hockey pitch and to create a new study hub.

Grounds. There are 29 acres of playing fields as well as a floodlit all-weather hockey pitch, squash courts, an indoor swimming pool and a climbing wall.

Houses. There are separate Houses for boys and girls in Upper and Lower School. All Houses have their own changing, work and recreational facilities.

There is a central Dining Hall and all meals are served on a cafeteria basis. The School also has its own well equipped laundry.

There is a fully equipped Health Centre, with a trained staff under the direction of the School Medical Officer.

Academic Organisation. The School is divided into the Upper School (Year 9–Sixth Form) and the Lower School (Years 7 and 8). The Prep School (Nursery–Year 6) is on a separate, adjoining campus.

Most pupils enter the School at Year 7, 9 or 12. The curriculum in Years 7, 8 and 9 is designed to allow pupils to develop the skills needed to succeed at GCSE and features a good range of practical and more academic subjects including Latin. At GCSE all pupils study English, English Literature, Mathematics and a Short Course in Religious Education as well as a Modern Foreign Language and a further five or six subjects. Pupils have a free choice of studying three sciences separately or as Dual Award Science. The Mathematics and Science courses lead to IGCSE qualifications. The most able mathematicians take IGCSE at the end of Year 10 before taking Additional Mathematics in Year 11. Students have a free choice from a wide range of subjects in the Sixth Form as well as the Extended Project Qualification. A system of grades every term and tutor groups ensure that academic monitoring of pupils is supportive and effective.

Religious Education is part of the curriculum throughout the School. The School is Christian in tradition and there is a short Act of Worship in the School Chapel on each weekday with a longer Sunday service. The content and form of these services are based on contemporary Anglican procedures. Attendance is expected although sensitivity is shown towards pupils of other faiths for whom alternative provision can be made.

Music. Tuition is available on all orchestral instruments, as well as piano, organ, drum kit and percussion, classical and electric guitars and voice. The department consists of 2 full-time, 1 part-time and 25 specialist instrumental staff. The School is an All Steinway School and facilities include a fine Steinway model D Concert Grand Piano. There is a large Rodgers Digital Organ in the Chapel. Some 30 ensembles rehearse each week, giving plentiful opportunities to performers of all ages and all instruments. The department currently runs 7 choirs of various kinds and styles from the renowned Chapel Choir to the lighter sounds of Girlforce9. Concerts of all kinds take place throughout each term and the Wellington Professional Concerts Series bring world class musicians to the School to give recitals and masterclasses. Pupils are entered for ABRSM, Trinity Guildhall and Rockschool exams each term.

Physical Education and Games. New Sport and Wellbeing Department in 2016 with all pupils playing games regularly, unless exempt for medical reasons. Wellbeing, which is also part of the curriculum for Years 7 to 11, takes place in the Sports Complex and includes nutrition, psychology and mental health alongside activities such as judo, zumba and body-pump with the aim of embedding physical activity as part of a healthy lifestyle. All pupils learn to swim and are given the opportunity to take part in as many sports as possible. In the winter term, rugby and hockey are the main sports; in the spring term hockey, netball and cross-country running; in the summer term athletics, girls and boys cricket, tennis and swimming. Team practices take place throughout the week with matches on Saturday afternoons. The Sports Complex houses a purpose-built fencing salle.

Out of School and CCF Activities. All pupils from the Year 10 upwards either join the large CCF contingent, with army, naval and RAF sections, or are engaged in volunteering activities on a weekly basis, ranging from community services and conservation, to music, art and creative activities such as producing school radio podcasts. Outdoor Education, both within the CCF, as part of the flourishing Duke of Edinburgh's Award scheme and climbing and caving clubs are very popular, with many trips organised for all year groups. The CCF also has a highly respected Corps of Drums, which frequently features in local ceremonial events. Societies, in addition to the above, include art, chess and drama at various levels, STEM, computing and others.

Careers. A complete careers guidance service is offered including visits to and from employers, a careers speed-dating event, careers talks, a careers networking dinner and careers fair with local schools.

Entry. Entrance exam for Year 7, 9 and Sixth Form. There is a registration fee of £50 for all pupils and a refundable deposit of £500.

Scholarships and Bursaries. A number of academic and sport, drama and art and design scholarships are offered each year for entry at 11+ and 13+. Music scholarships are awarded for entry at 11+, 13+ and above. Awards may be increased by an income-related bursary. A small number of awards are offered for the Sixth Form.

Fees per term (2016–2017). Boarders £8,750–£9,590, Weekly Boarders £7,200–£7,500, International Boarders £9,250–£9,870. Fees include tuition, board, laundry, medical attention and Health Centre and books. Day pupils £4,260–£4,785.

Extras. Apart from purely personal expenses, the termly extras are private music lessons from £235 to £290; EAL lessons at various rates depending on need.

Charitable status. Wellington School is a Registered Charity, number 1161447. It aims to provide a happy, caring co-educational day and boarding community, where pupils are provided with the opportunity of making best use of their academic experience and the School enrichment activities, in order to enhance their overall preparation for life after the age of eighteen.

Governing Body:

Chairman: A Govey, MSc
Joint Vice Chairmen: J Hester and Mrs A Wilson

L Dodds	Mrs K Schofield
Mrs T Humphreys	Cllr V Stock-Williams
J Knowles	Mr P Tait
Prof L la Velle	Reverend T Treanor
Dr D Lungley	Mrs S Vigus-Hollingsworth
B McDowell	Mrs L Wyeth
Mr R Palfrey	

Headmaster: **H W F Price**, MA Oxon

Academic Deputy Head: Dr H Barker, BA Hons, PhD
Deputy Head (Pastoral): R MacNeary, BA Hons, MA
Assistant Head (Co-curricular): A Anderson, BA, PGCE

Academic Staff:

A Anderson, BA, PGCE	G Durston, BSc Hons
C A Askew, BA, PGCE	T Fasham, BSc, PGCE
Mrs A E Bazley, BEd	Mrs C Foster, BA Hons
Mrs K Bishop, BA Hons, MA, PGCE	Dr P T Galley, BSc, DIC, PhD, PGCE
L Blain, BA Hons	A Garcia, CertEd
P J Buckingham, MA, PGCE	W Garrett, BA, PGCE
Mrs L Burton, BA, PGCE	Mr E Grey, BSc Hons, PGCE, Prof GCE
A R Carson, BSc, PGCE	Mr C Hamilton, MChem, ACA, PGCE
Mr J Caulfield, BA, QTS	
Mr M Charlton, MA, PGCE	Mrs I Hare, BA Hons, PGCE
Mrs N Clewes, BEng Hons, PGCE	Mrs C Harris, BA, PGCE, TEFL
D A Colclough, BSc, PGCE	Miss F E Hobday, MA
M Cole, BEng Hons, PGCE	Dr K A Hodson, BA, MA
Miss M Collins, BA, MA, PGCE	Mrs M Jago, BA
	S W James, BA
Mrs J Cooling, BSc Hons, PGCE	Dr A R Jolliffe, BA, MA, DPhil
S Costello, BA Hons, PGCE	S Jones, BSc, PGCE
	Mrs T Kaya, BA, TESOL
Mrs V Daley, BSc, PGCE	P Lawrence
Miss R Davies, BA, PGCE	J Leonard, BA
Mrs C Davies, BA Hons, PGCE	Mrs L E Leonard, BA
Mrs S A Dean, BA, PGCE	Mrs L MacAlister, BA Hons
M E Downes, BSc, PGCE	Miss R L Marsden, BA, PGCE
Mrs S D'Rozario BA, MA, PGCE	R Marsh, BA, PGCE

Miss S Middleton, BA, PGCE	Mrs T Robertson, BA Hons, MPhil, PGCE
D Millington, BA, MSc, PGCE	Mrs H J Salter, BA, PGCE
Miss A Moffat, MA Hons, PGCE	Miss K Sass, BA Hons, PGCE
Mr A Moy, BSc Hons, PGCE	A C Shaw, BA, MSci, PGCE
Mrs A D Musgrove, MA, MBA	Mrs R Shaw, LTCL
	N S Smith, BSc, PGCE
Mrs M Payne, BA Hons, BTEC, PGCE	R E Stevens, BSocSc, PGCE
A Phillips, BSc, PGCE	A W Stevenson, MA, PGCE
N Renyard, MSc, BA, PGCE	Mrs L Tabb, BSc, PGCE
Mrs V K Richardson, BSc	Miss S F L Toase, BSc, MSB, C Biol, PGCE
Miss H Richards, BSc Hons, QTS	A J Trewhella, BA, ARCO
	A Wilson, BA

Bursar: T D Williams, BA, FCCA
Registrar: Mrs R Debenham, BA, FCIPD
Medical Officer: Dr R Yates

Wells Cathedral School

The Liberty, Wells, Somerset BA5 2ST

Tel:	01749 834200
Fax:	01749 834201
email:	admissions@wells-cathedral-school.com
website:	www.wells-cathedral-school.com

In 909AD there was a Cathedral School in Wells providing education for choir boys. Today, Wells Cathedral School is fully co-educational. Its spirit is a passion for learning and life; its dream an inspiring education set in a musically alive and beautiful environment as a brilliant foundation for life; and its focus, inspiring success.

There is a senior and junior school with 660 boys and girls aged from 3 to 18. Boarders number 270, whilst the remainder are day pupils. Once accepted, a child normally remains in the school without further Entrance Examination until the age of 18+.

Fees per term (2016–2017). Sixth Form (Years 12–13): Boarders £9,983, Day £5,965. Upper School (Years 10–11): Boarders £9,761, Day £5,829. Lower School (Years 7–9): Boarders £9,398, Day £5,634. Junior School (Years 3–6): Boarders £7,956; Day £4,574; Pre-Prep £2,509; Reception £2,424. Nursery: Morning with lunch £19; Afternoon with lunch £23; Afternoon £19; All day with lunch £33.

Scholarships and Bursaries. Scholarships and academic awards are made at 11+, 13+ and 14+ to those who show outstanding ability in the Entrance Assessment Tests held in late January at the school. Specialist gifts or aptitudes (e.g. sport, drama, dance, art) are also considered. Sixth form academic, sporting, creative and all-rounder awards are made following the scholarship assessment day in November. Awards are given on the basis of performance in the assessment, rigorous interview, predicted GCSE results and a confidential reference from the applicant's current school. The value of the awards will depend on individual financial circumstances.

Means-tested specialist mathematics awards are available at 11+ for outstandingly gifted mathematicians.

A number of music awards are available depending upon the standard and quality of applicants and individual financial circumstances. Pre-auditions are held from September to December and successful candidates are invited to the main auditions held in January.

In addition, the school is one of only four in England designated by the Department for Education providing specialist musical education. The DfE therefore provides generous assistance (up to 100% of fees) with tuition, boarding and music fees for up to 78 gifted musicians, grants being linked to parental income, under the DfE Music & Dance Scheme.

Cathedral choristerships and bursaries, which can provide up to 25% of boarding and tuition fees, are awarded annually to boys between the ages of 8 and 10. Choral trials and academic entrance tests take place in January. Special arrangements can be made for children from overseas. School bursaries to the value of 10% of tuition fees are available for girl choristers. Supplementary means-tested bursaries are also available.

Ex-chorister bursaries: On ceasing to be a chorister, boys and girls are eligible for an ex-chorister bursary up to the value of 8% of tuition or boarding fees.

For further details of awards contact the Admissions Registrar, Tel: 01749 834213, email: admissions@wells-cathedral-school.com.

Situations and Buildings. The mediaeval city of Wells, with its famous Cathedral and a population of only 10,500, is the smallest city in England. It is just over 20 miles from Bath and Bristol where there is a good rail service, and easily accessed from the M4 and M5 motorways. Bristol International Airport is a 40-minute drive away. The school occupies all but one of the canonical houses in The Liberty. This fine group is planned to keep its mediaeval and 18th century atmosphere while providing for the needs of modern boarding education. There are modern classrooms and science laboratories built amongst walled gardens. A sports hall provides indoor facilities for tennis, badminton, cricket, basketball, volleyball, hockey, five-a-side football, climbing and multi-gym. There are theatrical and concert facilities, a music technology centre, a computer studies centre, art, design and technology department, drama studio, library, sixth form centre, 25-metre covered swimming pool, tennis and netball courts, astroTurf pitch, three sports fields and an all-weather hard play area.

There are two boarding Houses in the junior and lower school and a further seven in the senior school, three for boys and four for girls, the most senior pupils having study-bedrooms. The aim is to give security to the younger and to develop a sense of responsibility in the older.

Organisation and Curriculum. Despite its national and international reputation, the school has retained close links with the local community, and its fundamental aim is to provide all its pupils with an education consistent with the broad principles of Christianity. More specifically, the school aims to be a well-regulated community in which pupils may learn to live in harmony and mutual respect with each other and with the adults who care for them. The curriculum has been designed to enable all children who gain entry to the school to develop fully all their abilities, and to take their place in due course in tertiary education and the adult community of work and leisure. Forms are limited to a maximum of 25; average class sizes are typically less than this. Two years before GCSE a tutorial system is introduced whereby some ten boys and girls are the responsibility of one member of staff for academic progress to GCSE. Pupils then choose a subject faculty for sixth form tutoring in similar groups.

The emphasis is on setting by ability in particular subjects rather than streaming. There is every attempt to avoid early specialisation. All take IGCSE mathematics and English, as well as double science, plus a foreign language to GCSE. There is a sixth form of some 200 taking A Level courses in all major academic subjects.

The majority of pupils take up places at Russell Group Universities, with about 5–6 places regularly offered by Oxford and Cambridge; whilst musicians are regularly awarded scholarships to the top music colleges each year.

Societies. There is a wide range of indoor and outdoor activities in which pupils must participate, although the choice is theirs. Outdoor education is an important part of the curriculum. Besides a Combined Cadet Force with Army and RAF sections and a Duke of Edinburgh's Award scheme, activities as diverse as chess and kite making, photography, sailing and golf are also on offer. Ballet and riding lessons are also arranged.

Music. The school is one of four in England designated and grant-aided by the Department for Education (DfE) to provide special education for gifted young musicians, who are given substantial financial assistance. Wells is unique in that both specialist and non-specialist musicians are able to develop their aptitudes within a normal school environment. These talents are widely acknowledged by audiences at concerts given by pupils from Wells throughout the world.

There are over 200 talented pupils following specially devised timetables which combine advanced instrumental tuition and ensemble work with academic opportunity. More than half of the school learns at least one musical instrument. Violin and cello is taught to all children in the pre-prep as part of the curriculum. Pupils receive the highest quality teaching, often leading to music conservatoires and a career in music. Central to specialist music training are the opportunities to perform in public and there is a full concert diary. There are also regular concerts by the many ensembles in the school.

The Wellensian Association. Old Wellensians, Wells Cathedral School, Wells, Somerset BA5 2ST.

Charitable status. Wells Cathedral School Limited is a Registered Charity, number 310212. It is a charitable trust for the purpose of promoting the cause of education in accordance with the doctrine of the Church of England.

Patron: HRH The Prince of Wales

Governors:
Chairman: The Revd Canon Andrew Featherstone, MA
The Reverend Canon Nicholas Jepson-Biddle, BA, MA
Prebendary Helen Ball, OBE
Prebendary Barbara Bates, BA, MA, FRSA
Mr David Brown, OBE, MA
Mr Tim Lewis, BA, FCA
Mr Derek Pretty, BSc, MBA, LLD
Martin Smout, BSc, CEng, MICE
Robert Sommers, BA
Mr Jonathan Vaughan, Dip RCM Perf, Dip RCM Teach

Head: Elizabeth Cairncross, BA (*English, Latin*)

Deputy Head: Dr Andrew Kemp, BA, MA, PGCE (*Mathematics*)
Assistant Head (*Teaching & Learning*): Alex Battison, BSc, MSc Oxon (*Geography, Rugby, Hockey*)
Assistant Head (*Pastoral Care & Co-Curriculum*): Andrew Mayhew, BSc (*Mathematics, Football*)
Assistant Head for Digital Strategy: Simon Balderson (*Head of Computing*)
Director of Music: M Stringer

Senior School

Teaching Staff:
Claudia Alabiso (*Modern Foreign Languages*)
Alison Armstrong, BMus, LRAM, PGCE (*Head of Academic Music*)
Martin Ashton, BA, PGCE (*English, Media Studies, Housemaster Cedars*)
Jonathan Barnard, BSc Hons, PGCE (*Physics*)
Jeremy Boot, BA, FRGS (*Head Geography, Cricket*)
Neil Bowen, BA, PGCE (*Head of English Faculty*)
Anna Brown (*Head of Year 9, Head of PSHE*)
John Byrne, Dip Moscow Cons, GRNCM (*Head of Keyboard*)
Andrew Clements, BSc Hons, PGCE (*Head of Chemistry*)

Nicola Connock, BSc, PGCE (*Head of Mathematics Operations*)

Jack Coward (*Music*)

Sarah Cowell, BA Hons, CTEFLA (*EAL*)

Andrew Davies, BA, PGCE (*Religion, Philosophy & Ethics, Housemaster Ritchie, Cross country*)

Shelley Deans, MA (*Expressive Arts*)

Paul Denegri, FTCL, LTCL, Hon ARAM (*Head of Brass*)

Jules Desmarchelier, PGCE (*Head of Modern Foreign Languages*)

Christopher Eldridge (*Head of History*)

Mandy Fielding, BSc, PGCE, Cert SEN, Dip SpLD (*Head of Food Technology*)

Christopher Finch, MA, BMus Hons, LRSM, Dip ABRSM (*Head of Music Operations, Head of Vocal Studies*)

Philippa Garty, BSc, PGCE (*Biology*)

Janice Gearon, BA, MA, PGCE (*English*)

Penny Hall (*Religion, Philosophy & Ethics, Learning Support*)

Dominic Hansom, BMus, LRSM, ARCM (*Head of Accompaniment*)

Stephen Harvey (*Private Learning Coordinator*)

Revd Juliette Hulme, BEd Hons, Cert Theo & Min, Dip Christian Spirituality (*Chaplain*)

Ken Humphreys, BSc, PGCE (*Chemistry, Co-Curricular Director*)

Margaret Humphreys, BA, PGCE, AMBDA (*Modern languages French, German, Learning Support*)

Teresa Jarman, BA, QTS (*Economics & Business*)

Lisa Jarvis (*Head of Girls' Games, PE & Sport, Assistant Head of 6th Form, Assistant Houseparent Ritchie*)

Marcus Laing, MA, PGCE (*Head of Economics & Business*)

Ed Leaker (*Head of Woodwind*)

Catherine Lord, ARCM, Juilliard Diploma (*Senior Violin*)

Pippa Maple (*History, Housemistress Claver Morris*)

James Mayes (*History, Classics, Latin and Sports, Assistant Houseparent Cedars*)

Michael Meally, MA, BA, BEng, PGCE, Dip HSWW (*English*)

James Moretti (*Mathematics*)

Carina Morgan (*Dance*)

Robin Murdoch, BA, MA, PGCE (*Mathematics*)

Dr Hilary Murphy, MA, BMus, LRAM, PhD, PGCE (*Head of Creative Arts Faculty, Academic Music*)

Eliana Nelson, BA Hons, QTS, CertEd (*Graphics, Photography*)

Jayne Obradovic, LTCL (*Head of Percussion*)

Keith Orchard, BSc (*Science, Physics*)

Kenneth Padgett, BSc (*Head of Science Faculty, Head of Biology, Ten Tors*)

Elaine Paul (*History*)

Susie Petvin-Jameson, BSc, PGCE, CSci, FIMA, FCIEA (*Head of Mathematics Faculty, Director of Specialist Mathematics*)

Lawrence Plum, BA Hons, AKC, PGCE (*Head of Classics, Housemaster (De Salis), CCF*)

Gemma Pritchard, BSc, PGCE (*Director of Sport – whole school*)

Jenny Rintoul (*History of Arts*)

Jenna Rowland (*Head of Psychology, Assistant Houseparent Plumptre*)

Rebecca Redman (*Housemistress Haversham, Religion, Philosophy & Ethics, Geography, CCF*)

Christopher Rondel (*CCF Contingent Commander, Outdoor Education and Duke of Edinburgh's Award Scheme Coordinator, History, Houseparent De Salis*)

David Rowley, BSc, PGCE (*Geography, Geology, Head of Year 7 & 8*)

Sally Rowley, BA Hons, PGCE (*English, Head of 6th Form*)

Dr Janette Shepherd, BSc, PhD (*Biology, Housemistress Canon Grange*)

Ellie Smith (*Head of Religion, Philosophy and Ethics*)

Matthew Souter, AGSM, Hon ARAM (*Head of Strings*)

Linzi Stockdale Bridson, BA, PGCE (*Head of Art & Design, Graphics and Photography, Lower School skiing*)

Mark Stringer (*Director of Music*)

Martin Swarfield, BA, PGCE, PGC (*Academic PE, Rugby, Housemaster Shrewsbury*)

Jan Tapner, BA, ADT, PGCE (*Art*)

Steve Tapner, BSc, CertEd (*Mathematics, Boys' Hockey, Boys' Tennis*)

Ben Taylor, MA, PGCE (*Higher Education and Careers Advisor, French, Italian, NQT Supervisor*)

Damian Todres (*Head of Drama & Theatre Studies*)

Laurence Whitehead, BA, MA, GGSMD, PGCE (*Academic Music*)

John Williams, BA Hons, PGCE (*Academic Music, Music Technology*)

Lara Williams (*English*)

Junior School

Head of Junior School: Julie Barrow, BEd (*PSHE Coordinator*)

Deputy Head: Karl Gibson, Dip Teach, BEd (*Science Coordinator*)

Head of Pre-Prep: Janet Bennett, BA

Director of Studies: Amanda Clark, BEd

Rebecca Allen, BSc, QTS (*EYFS Teacher*)

Steve Bratt, BEd (*Head of Sport & PE*)

Kate Dennis, BEd (*KS2*)

Jill Edmonds, BSc, ALCM (*Head of Music*)

Stuart Elks (*Junior School Teacher*)

Kelly Fairey, BEd (*PP teacher*)

Valerie Hancock (*Early Years*)

Daisy Hunt (*Junior School teacher*)

Kateley Kinnersley (*KS1*)

Juliet Knollys (*Head of Learning Support*)

Charlotte Leatherby (*Junior School Teacher*)

Richael Mccloskey (*Nursery Manager*)

Emma Morley, BEd (*Teacher*)

Fiona Shaw (*KS1*)

Emily Spencer (*Junior School Teacher*)

Jane Tucker, DipEd (*Art Coordinator*)

Lesley Wanklyn (*Junior School Teacher*)

Jonathan Ward, BSc, PGCE (*Mathematics Coordinator*)

Rosie Warner, BA QTS (*History Coordinator*)

Bursar and Clerk to the Governors: P Knell

Assistant Clerk to the Governors: D Shortland-Ball

Admissions Registrar: J Prestige

Head's PA: Mrs C Edwards

Development Director: M Coote, BA, MA Ed

Publicity Manager: Mrs K Chantrey, BSc Hons

School Doctor: Dr C Bridson, MB BS, MRCGP, DipOCC, MED

West Buckland School

Barnstaple, Devon EX32 0SX

Tel:	01598 760281
Fax:	01598 760546
email:	headmaster@westbuckland.com
website:	www.westbuckland.com
Twitter:	@westbuckland
Facebook:	@wbsdevon

Motto: '*Read and Reap*'

West Buckland School is an independent day and boarding school set in 90 acres of beautiful North Devon countryside in the South West of England. Founded in 1858, the school has always stressed the importance of all-round character development alongside good academic achievement. Our size allows pupils to receive plenty of individual care and attention to their needs and talents.

West Buckland Preparatory School educates children between the ages of three and eleven. There is strong cooperation and support between the schools which share the same grounds, so making the transition as easy as possible.

West Buckland is fully co-educational.

Situation. The School stands in 90 acres of beautiful North Devon countryside on the edge of Exmoor. Barnstaple is 10 miles away and the M5 motorway can be reached in 35 minutes. Boarders arriving by train at Exeter station are met by coaches.

Buildings and Grounds. The central range of buildings, dating from 1861, still forms the focus of the school, and now includes a performing arts centre. Other developments include a Sixth Form Centre, Mathematics and Physics Centre, boarding houses for boys and girls, a Preparatory School classroom block and the ICT Centre. The campus offers outstanding sports facilities, including a 9-hole golf course, an indoor heated 25-metre swimming pool, and an Astroturf hockey pitch. The Jonathan Edwards Sports Centre opened in 2008 and the award-winning 150 Building for Art, Design Technology and a Theatre opened in 2010. A new study centre for all senior school pupils and a co-educational Sixth Form boarding house with single en-suite bedrooms are now open.

Admission. Boys and girls are admitted as boarders or day pupils. The present number of pupils is: 110 boarding, 483 day.

Entrance to the Preparatory School is by interview and assessment. Entry to the Senior School is by assessment at 11+ or to the Sixth Form upon interview and school report. Entry at other ages is usually possible and assessment arrangements are made to suit individual circumstances.

Fees per term (2016–2017). Senior: Boarding £7,770–£10,325 Day £4,710. Preparatory: Day £2,525–£3,830. Nursery: Government-funded places under Early Years Entitlement are available up to 15 hours per week during term time. £4.00 per hour thereafter.

Scholarships and Bursaries. A number of scholarships are awarded for entry at 11+, 13+ or 16+ (up to a value of 10% of the tuition fees). Candidates must be under 12, 14, or 17 years of age on 1st September following the examination, which will take place in late January or early February.

Music scholarships are available for entry at 13+ and Sports scholarships at 11+, 13+ and 16+.

With the support of the West Buckland School Foundation, means-tested bursaries are available for boarders and day students at all ages.

Curriculum. In the Preparatory School the main emphasis is upon well-founded confidence in English and Mathematics, within a broad balance of subjects that adds modern languages to the national curriculum. Particular attention is given to the development of sporting, artistic and musical talents.

In the Senior School breadth is complemented by specialisation. All students study the three separate sciences from Year 7, while both French and Spanish are the principal languages offered from Year 7. Our flexible options arrangements at GCSE respond to students' individual strengths and preferences. A wide range of A Level subjects is offered to sixth formers whose results uphold the high academic standards of the School.

Careers. The Careers Staff advise all pupils upon the openings and requirements for different careers. They make full use of the facilities offered by Connexions.

Games, The Performing Arts and other activities. One of the most impressive features of life at West Buckland is the quality and range of extracurricular activities, with a high level of involvement from pupils and staff.

The school has a strong sporting tradition. Rugby, hockey, cricket, netball, tennis, athletics, swimming, cross-country, squash, golf, shooting and many other sports offer opportunities for inter-school and inter-house competition and for recreation.

About a third of all pupils receive instrumental and singing tuition from specialist teachers. The wide range of choirs and instrumental groups give concerts at least once a week throughout the year. Drama is strength of the school with productions of many kinds throughout the year. The Performing Arts are complemented by the exceptional facilities provided by the school's award-winning 150 Building which houses an impressive studio theatre.

Music. Over 120 members of the school receive instrumental tuition on all instruments. They are encouraged to perform in concerts, in choirs and instrumental groups. Music Technology is also a strong feature of the department's work.

Outdoor Education. Much use is made of the proximity of Exmoor and the coast for climbing, kayaking, mountain biking, surfing and other adventurous activities. All pupils receive instruction in camp craft, first aid and map reading. The Combined Cadet Force has Army and Royal Air Force sections, and offers a range of challenging pursuits. Our students succeed at all levels in The Duke of Edinburgh's Award scheme each year, and there is a regular programme of expeditions in this country and overseas.

Religion. The tradition is Anglican but the school welcomes children from all denominations and faiths – or none. Services of worship are held throughout the week including many Sundays. A number of services are held at East Buckland Church. The Chaplain prepares boys and girls for confirmation every year.

Attitudes and values. The School sets out to be a friendly and purposeful community in which happiness and a sense of security are the foundation on which young lives are built. At all levels members of the school are asked to lead a disciplined way of life, to show consideration for others, to be willing to be challenged and to recognise that the success of the individual and the success of the group are inextricably linked.

Charitable status. West Buckland School is a Registered Charity, number 306710. Its purpose is the education of boys and girls from 3 to 18.

The Governing Body:

President: P D Orchard-Lisle, CBE, TD, DL LLD [hc], DSc [hc], MA, FRICS

Vice Presidents
R B W Aldiss, OBE, FRSL
H J Pedder
Lady Gass, JP, MA
W H G Geen

Chairman: J M H Light, LLB

Vice Chairmen:
S D Fox, BA
Mrs L Cairns, BA Joint Hons

Governors:
The Countess of Arran, MBE, DL
Dr R J Fisher-Smith, BA, MA, PGCE, PhD
R A Ingram, MA, PGCE
N Kingdon, BDS, MOrthRCS
A Boggis, MA, PGCE
Mrs M A Read, BA Hons
P Stucley, BA Hons

J Palk
A C B Browne, BSc Hons, FCA
Mrs S C E Salvidant, BEd Hons

Headmaster: **Mr Phillip Stapleton**, BSc, MA Durham, MBA, PGCE, MRSC

Deputy Head: D M Hymer, BSc University College London

Director of Studies: C J Burrows, MA Exeter College Oxford

Pastoral Deputy: A N Calder, BA/BSc Hons Brunel

Headmaster, Preparatory School: A D Moore, BEd

Chaplain: A Watkinson-Trim, BA Hons

Teaching Staff:

C J Allin, BA	Mrs Tracy Hill, MSc
Mrs T Anderson	A Jansen, BSc
Mrs J Beech	Ms S Johnson
C Block	Mrs E M Kent, BMus
Mrs B Joly-Bloodworth	A M Kimberley, BSc Hons
M Bohl, BA Hons	T Lutley, BA Hons
P J Brand, BSc Hons	C Main, BA Hons
M T Brimson, BA	J K McKerrow, PhD
Mrs J E Brock, MEd	W D Minns BEng
Miss A Brown, BA	G J Monk, MA
Mrs J F Bunclark, MA	Mrs L Napier, BEd
Ms C Campbell	T O'Brien, BSc
Mrs P Cartmell, BA Hons	Ms P Plummer
R D Clarke, BA, BEd	Miss A-S Prian
Mrs H C Clements, BA Hons	S J Prior, BSc
Miss N R Cordon, BA	Mrs A L Pugsley, BA
P H Davies, BSc	D Price Ed Ord
C H Dawson, BSc	N T Shawcross, BSc
Miss A Episkopos, BSc	Ms S Stoyanova
D R Ford, BA Hons	Mrs R L Thompson, BEd Hons
J E Freeman, BEng	G Turner
S Rodriguez Garcia	Miss K Venner, BSc Hons
Dr E N D Grew, PhD	D Vickery, BSc Hons
Mrs A Hart	A Watkinson-Trim, BA Hons
R Hathway, BA Hons	Mrs A J Willmott, BEd
Mrs Y Helicon, BA	

Bursar: B Login, MA, MBA, FCIS, MBIFM
Headmaster's Secretary: Mrs S Harris
Librarian: Miss L Warrillow
Medical Officer: Dr C A Gibb, BMed, BM, DA, MRCGP, DRCOG, DPD

Houses & Housemasters/mistresses:
Brereton House: Dr E N D Grew, PhD Exeter
Courtenay House: C J Allin, BA Leicester
Fortescue House: Mrs A L Pugsley, BA University College Chester
Grenville House: Mrs R L Thompson, BA Aberystwyth

Head of Boarding: D R Ford

Houseparents:

S Morrison	Mrs K Turner
Mrs A Booker	Mrs A Melchior
Mrs S Bailey	J Conlon
Mrs V A Ford	

Westminster School

17 Dean's Yard, Westminster, London SW1P 3PB

Tel:	020 7963 1042 (Head Master)
	020 7963 1003 (Registrar)
	020 7963 1000 (Other enquiries)
	020 7821 5788 (Westminster Under School)
Fax:	020 7963 1002
email:	registrar@westminster.org.uk
website:	www.westminster.org.uk
Twitter:	@wschool

Motto: '*Dat Deus Incrementum*'

Westminster School is a Boarding and Day School which is co-educational in the Sixth Form. The present number of boys and girls is 742.

The School traces its origins to the school that was attached to the Benedictine Abbey at Westminster. Queen Elizabeth I re-founded the School in 1560 as part of the College of St Peter at Westminster.

The Queen's Scholars. An examination (The Challenge) is held annually to elect The Queen's Scholars who board in College, one of our 6 boarding houses. There are a total of 48 Queen's Scholars, with 12 chosen every year: eight boys at age 13 and four girls at age 16. The fee for a Queen's Scholar is set at half way between 50% of the boarding fee and the day fee. Boys who do not wish to board may be candidates for the title of Honorary Scholar. Up to 5 exhibitions may be awarded each year to those who narrowly miss being offered a scholarship. Boys, who must be under 14 on 1st September of their year of entry, sit The Challenge at Westminster School in late April or early May. The examination consists of papers in Mathematics, English, French, Science, Latin, History, Geography and an optional Greek paper. A scholarship, which is not means-tested, is normally tenable for 5 years.

Application forms and past papers may be obtained from The Admissions Administrator (13+ Entry) (tel: 020 7963 1003, email: registrar@westminster.org.uk).

The value of a scholarship may be supplemented by a bursary (remission of the fees) up to a maximum of 100% if there is proven financial need. Parents who wish to apply for financial assistance should request a Bursary Application Form from the Registrar.

Music Scholarships. Up to eight 13+ and four 16+ music scholarships worth 10% of the day fee may be awarded annually These may be supplemented by additional means-tested bursaries to a maximum of the full fees. There are also several Music Exhibitions which provide for free music tuition on two instruments.

Applications for 13+ close on 1st December and the auditions take place in late January. Candidates, who must be under 14 years of age on the following 1st September, must subsequently take either the Common Entrance or gain admission through the Scholarship Examination, The Challenge.

Applications for 16+ close on 5 October and the auditions take place in late November at the same time as the academic entry interviews. The Dean and Chapter of Westminster Abbey also kindly support a 16+ Henry Purcell Organ Scholarship at Westminster School worth 10% of the current day fees.

The Director of Music is happy to give informal advice to potential candidates and it is recommended that an informal audition is arranged before submitting an application. Please contact the Music Administrator on 020 7963 1017.

Music Scholarships are also available at Westminster Under School at 11+.

For further information on all Scholarships, please contact the Registrar.

Bursaries. Westminster School has made it possible, since its first foundation, for academically able pupils to attend the School who would not otherwise have been able to do so without financial support. Bursaries (remission of fees) up to a maximum of 100% are available and are awarded according to individual need following a full financial assessment, which may include a home visit, to pupils who gain a place on academic merit. Bursaries are awarded at 13 + and 16+ entry to Westminster School and at 11+ entry to Westminster Under School. All bursaries continue until a pupil leaves the School at 18, although they may be adjusted up or down if financial circumstances change.

Parents who wish to apply for financial assistance should request a Bursary Application Form from the Registrar at Westminster School (tel: 020 7963 1003) or Westminster Under School (tel: 020 7821 5788).

Admission. The two main points of admission are 13+ (boys only) and 16+ (girls and boys). Parents should register their sons for 13+ entry by the start of Year 6 – the academic year of a child's 11th birthday. In the Autumn Term of Year 6, the boy will take the ISEB Common Pre-Tests in Mathematics, English and Verbal and Non-Verbal Reasoning. Selected boys will be invited to Westminster School for interview during the Spring Term. On the basis of the candidate's test results, the interview and a report from his present school a decision will be made whether to offer a conditional place. Boys with conditional places must still qualify for entry to the School by sitting the Common Entrance examinations or The Challenge (scholarship examinations) when they are 13, but failure at this stage is very rare. Candidates who are not offered a conditional place may be placed on a waiting list and they may sometimes be invited to sit further tests at the start of Year 8. Registration for 16+ entry opens in the summer a year before entry. Entry is by competitive examination and interview at the School in November. Candidates choose four entry examination subjects, usually the four subjects they plan to take for A Level. For further information about entry at 13+ or 16+ or to arrange a visit to the School please telephone 020 7963 1003. Please see the school's website www.westminster.org.uk for details of open days.

Fees per term (2016–2017). Boarding: £12,154, £6,077 (Queen's Scholars). Day Pupils (inclusive of lunch): £8,416, £9,200 (entry at Sixth Form).

Preparatory Department (Day Boys only). The Under School has 286 pupils; entry is at 7, 8 and 11. All enquiries should be addressed to the Master (Mr M O'Donnell), Westminster Under School, Adrian House, 27 Vincent Square, London SW1P 2NN (tel: 020 7821 5788).

(*For further details, see entry in IAPS section.*)

Charitable status. St Peter's College (otherwise known as Westminster School) is a Registered Charity, number 312728. The school was established under Royal Charter for the provision of education.

Visitor: Her Majesty The Queen

Governing Body:
Chairman: The Dean of Westminster, The Very Reverend Dr John Hall (*Chairman*)
The Dean of Christ Church, The Very Reverend Professor Martyn Percy
The Master of Trinity, Sir Gregory Winter, CBE, FRS
The Reverend Canon Jane Sinclair, MA, BA
The Reverend Canon David Stanton
Professor Stephen Elliott
Lord Julian Hunt of Chesterton, CB, FRS [OW]
Mr Michael Baughan [OW]
Mr Christopher Foster [OW]
Dr Priscilla Chadwick, MA, FRSA

Professor Sir Christopher Edwards, MD, FRCP, FRCPEd, FRSE, FMedSci, HonDSc
Dr Alan Borg, CBE, FSA [OW]
Sir Peter Ogden
Mr Richard Neville-Rolfe, MA [OW]
Dame Judith Mayhew Jonas DBE
Mr Mark Batten [OW]
Ms Joanna Reesby
Mrs Ina De [OW]
Mr Edward Cartwright [OW]
Mr Tony Little, FRSA
Ms Emily Reid [OW]

[OW] *Old Westminster*
* *Head of Department/Subject*

Secretary to the Governing Body and Bursar: C A J Silcock

Head Master: P S J Derham, MA (*History*)

Under Master: D A Smith, MA, PhD (*Mathematics*)

Director of Studies: R R Harris, MA (*Geography*)

Senior Master: K E Clanchy, MA, MBA (*French and Russian*)

Senior Tutor: J J Kemball, BSc (*Biology*)

Assistant Staff:
R Agyare-Kwabi, MSc, PhD (*Electronics)
E Alaluusua, MA (*Art*)
J L Allchin, BA MA (*Art*)
H A Aplin, BA, PhD (*Russian)
K Y Au, MMath (*Mathematics*)
S T Bailey, MA (*Theology and Philosophy*)
C J Barton, BA (*Drama*)
Miss H L Barton, BA (*History*)
S J Berg, BA (*Spanish)
S G Blache, PhD (*French)
R A Black, BA (*History*)
Ms M V Bustamante-Jenke, BSc (*Computer Science*)
P A Botton, BSc (*Chemistry*)
M R Bradshaw, MA (*Chemistry*)
G P A Brown, MA, DPhil (*History*)
J H Brown, BA (*Economics*)
Ms C M Buchanan, BA, MA, PhD (*History*)
I T Butler, BA (*Mathematics*)
Miss L Cappenberg (*German Assistant*)
P J Chequer, DipPA (**Director of Drama*)
Miss J L Chidgey, BA, MA (*Product Design)
Miss B Choraria, MPhys (*Physics*)
Ms S E Clarkson, MSt (*English; US University advisor*)
T R Cousins, BA, MMath (*Mathematics*)
E T A Coward, BA, MSci (*Chemistry)
A M L Crole, BA, MA (*English*)
S Crow, BA (*Art)
S N Curran, BA (*English*)
M C Davies, MA (*Mathematics)
T P Edlin, MA (*History*) [OW]
Miss R J Evans, PhD (*Biology)
N A Fair, MA (*Economics*)
Ms A E Farr, MA (*English)
M H Feltham, MA (*Master of The Queen's Scholars*; *Mathematics*)
Miss G M French, MSc, MRSC, LTCL, FRSA (*Chemistry*)
W D Galton, BA (*Mathematics*)
Miss A P Gandon, BA (*Classics*)
T D Garrard, BA (**Director of Music*)
Mrs R-E G Gibbons-Lejeune, BA, MA (*History of Art*)
B E J Gravell, BA (*Classics*)
Mrs A K Griffiths, BA, MA (*German and French*)
Miss V Guichard, BA, MA, PhD (*French Assistante*)
Mrs N C Hallam, MMath (*Mathematics*)
J Harding, MA (*Arabic*)

P A Hartley, BSc, PhD (*Biology*)
S C Hawken, MA (**Economics*)
G D Hayter, MMath (*Mathematics*)
D R Hemsley-Brown, BSc, MIEE (*Electronics and Product Design*)
U Hennig, BA (**German*)
R J Hindley, MA, CMath (**Director of IT*)
J N Hooper, BA (*Mathematics*)
G St J Hopkins, MA (*Registrar; Music*)
Miss J J Hughes, BSc, MA (**Geography*)
R M Huscroft, MA, PhD (*History*)
J A Ireland, MA (*Classics*)
Ms K E Ireland, MSc (*Study Skills Coordinator*)
D A Jones, BA (*Classics*)
G K Jones, MA (**Modern Languages; French, Russian and German*)
Ms S M Joyce, BSc (*Biology*)
N G Kalivas, BSc, DPhil (*Mathematics*)
Miss A Kebaier (*French Assistant*)
J D Kershen, BA, MA (**Sport and PE*) [OW]
C M C Kingcombe, BSc (*Biology and Chemistry*)
R A Kowenicki, MA, MSci, PhD (**Chemistry*)
Mr H Kwak (*Mathematics*)
D Larsson, MA (*Geography*)
A J Law, BA (**Keyboard; Piano*)
Miss C M Leech, MA (*Spanish*)
Mr E A Lewis, BA (*Classics*)
Dr J E D Lillington, MA, PhD (*Chemistry, Physics*)
Mrs F Lofts (*Italian*)
L A Lorimer, BA, MA (*Mathematics*)
Mrs L D MacMahon, BA (*German and French*)
G D Mann, BA, MSt (**History*)
Ms A Marquez, BA (*Spanish Assistant*)
Dr D J McCombie, BA, MSt, DPhil (*Classics*)
J Moore, BA (*Biology*)
Ms L C M Murphy, MA, LLM (*English*)
A E A Mylne, MA (**Classics*)
Mrs L J Newton, BSc (*Economics*)
Miss S Page, BA, MSc (*IT; *PSHE*)
T D Page, MA (*Religious Studies*)
B W Parker-Wright, BA (*Mathematics*)
Dr M R Parry, MA, PhD (*History*)
Dr H J Prentice, MSci, MA, PhD (*Physics*)
R J Pyatt, MA (*English*)
Mr S E Quintavalle, MA (*Physics*)
Mrs S A Ragaz, PhD (*English*)
C D Riches, BEd, MSc (**PE; Rowing; History*)
M N Robinson, BA (*Chemistry*)
Mrs J Rogers (*Japanese*)
S C Savaskan, BA, MMus, DPhil (*Deputy Director of Music*)
P Sharp, MA, MSc (*Physics*)
Mrs E D Shortland, BA (*Deputy Head of Sixth Form; Religious Studies*)
N J Simons, MMath, DPhil (*Head of Sixth Form; Mathematics*)
B J Smith, MA (**Well-being*)
K W Smith, BA, MA (*Study Skills*)
Mr W T Stockdale, MA (*Geography*)
M J A Sugden, MA (*French and German*)
L Tattersall, BSc, MA (*Mathematics*)
A Theodosiou, BA (*Modern Greek*)
A C Tolley, BA (*Mathematics*)
K D Tompkins, BA (*English*)
C J R Ullathorne, MA, MSci (**Physics*)
R C Wagner, BA, PhD (*Mathematics*)
Dr K A P Walsh, BSc, PhD (**Science and Technology; Physics*)
B D Walton, BA (*History of Art*)
Ms H Wang, BSc, MA (*Chinese*)
Mr G W Warner, BA (*Arabic*)

Miss G D Ward-Smith, MA, PhD (*History*)
The Revd G J Williams, MA (*Chaplain*)
Dr J C Witney, MA, MIL (**Modern Languages*)
J G Woodman, BA (*Art*)
T D W Woodrooffe, BA, BTh, MA (**Religious Studies*)
S D Wurr, BA (*Geography*)

Houses and Housemasters:

Boarding House for Queen's Scholars and Girls' Day House:
College: M H Feltham

Boys' Boarding and Mixed Day Houses
Grant's, 2 Little Dean's Yard: N A Fair
Rigaud's, 1 Little Dean's Yard: Dr P H Williams

Mixed Boarding and Mixed Day Houses:
Liddell's, 19 Dean's Yard: T D Page
Busby's, 26 Great College Street: P A Botton

Girls' Boarding and Mixed Day House:
Purcell's, 22 Great College Street: Dr G D Ward-Smith

Day Houses:
Ashburnham, 6 Dean's Yard: Dr S A Ragaz
Dryden's, 4 Little Dean's Yard: D R Hemsley-Brown
Hakluyt's, 19 Deans' Yard: Mrs L C M Murphy
Milne's, 5A Dean's Yard: Dr P A Hartley
Wren's, 4 Little Dean's Yard: S D Wurr

Librarian: Mrs C Goetzee
Archivist: Miss E Wells

Westminster Under School

Master: M O'Donnell, BA, MSc Arch, EdM, PGDE, FRSA
Deputy Master: D R Smith, MA (*History and RS*)
Assistant Master (Pastoral): D S C Bratt, BA (*Maths*)
Assistant Master (Academic): Miss S Wollam, BSc (*Science*)
Assistant Master (Extra-Curricular): M J Woodside, BSc (*Science and History*)

Mrs L Adams, BA, Dip Counselling (*School Counsellor*)
Mrs E-L Allison, BA, MA (*English Support*)
Mrs A C Apaloo, MA (**Religious Studies*)
I Baillie, ACTC, MBA, Pg Dip Adv Net (*ICT Consultant*)
Ms E Beauclerk, MA, BA (*Teaching Assistant*)
A J P Busk, Dip Fine Art (*Art, Games*)
O T Campbell Smith, MA, MSc (**Geography, Head of Year 8*)
C R Candy, MA (*French, English, 8C Form Teacher*)
Mrs L R Chacksfield, BA, MA (**PSHE, English*)
Ms R Collins, BA (*Study Skills*)
Miss S E K Corps, BSc (*Science*)
P Daly BA, MA (**Classics, Games, 7D Form Teacher*)
A J Downey, BA, MA (*Latin, Greek, Games*)
T Dumas, BSc (*Science, Games*)
Miss M E Ellis, BEd (**Mathematics, Games, 8E Form Teacher*)
G Gougay, BA (*French, Games, 6G Form Teacher*)
I D Hepburn, BA, MA (**Director of Sport, 6H Form Teacher*)
C H W Hill, MA (**Drama, English*)
G K Horridge, PhD (**History, Games, 8H Form Teacher*)
Ms F M Illingworth, BA (**Art & 3D Design*)
S R H James, BA (*Latin, Greek, Games, Vincent Editor*)
Mrs V James, BEd (*Librarian, Art*)
Mrs D L F Jones BA, MEd (**Learning Enrichment*)
Miss J Lawrence, BA (*Art Technician*)
C Magalhães, BBA (*Music Administrator*)
Miss E R Marr, BA (*English, 5M Form Teacher*)
E Matthews, M Eng (*Mathematics, 5M Form Teacher, Enterprise Coordinator*)

Mrs M Raikes, BEd, Dip Counselling (*Religious Studies*) [Maternity cover]

Miss H Roome, BSc (**Science, 7R Form Teacher*)

P A Rosenthal, BA (**English, Games, 8R Form Teacher*)

D Shaw, BSc (*Sport, Head of Year 7*)

Miss A Simpson, BA (*Art Technician*)

S Singh, BSc (**ICT, 7S Form Teacher*)

Ms H Tefera, BSc (*IT Technician*)

S Thébaud, BSc, MA (**French, Games, 7T Form Teacher*)

Mrs R Thorn, BMus, MMus (*Assistant Director of Music, Head of Years 5 and 6*)

Miss L Timms, BSc (*Mathematics, 5T Form Teacher*)

Miss H L Verney, BSc (*Head of Junior Forms, 3V Form Teacher*)

J S Walker, BEd, LRAM, FRSA (**Director of Music*)

Miss C Wheeler-Bennett, BSc (*4W Form Teacher, Geography*)

Miss H Wellman, BSc (*4H Form Teacher, PSHE, Geography, Drama*)

Administration:

PA to the Master: Mrs O Unterhalter, BA

Registrar: Ms A-M McCarthy

Receptionist and Admissions Assistant: Miss S Tindley, BA

Financial Secretary: Mrs M Waggett

School Matron: Miss L Blanchard, BA

Personnel Bursar: Mrs S Parsons, BA

Winchester College

College Street, Winchester, Hampshire SO23 9NA

Tel: 01962 621100 (Headmaster and Office)
          01962 621200 (Bursar)
          01962 621247 (Admissions)
email: admissions@wincoll.ac.uk
website: www.winchestercollege.org

Motto: '*Manners Makyth Man*'

Winchester College – 'the College of the Blessed Virgin Mary of Winchester near Winchester' – was founded in 1382 by William of Wykeham, Bishop of Winchester. Wykeham planned and created a double foundation consisting of two Colleges, one at Winchester and the other (New College) at Oxford. The two Colleges are still closely associated.

In Junior Part (Year 9) all boys study Biology, Chemistry, English, French or German, Geography, History, Latin, Mathematics, Physics and PE. A third foreign language is taken from Chinese, French or German, Ancient Greek, Russian and Spanish. Art, Design Technology and Music are studied by all boys on a rotating basis. At the end of Junior Part, boys make GCSE choices. Mathematics, English Language, Latin and French or German are mandatory subjects. Boys must additionally chose at least two sciences (Biology, Chemistry, Physics). They may take up to two further modern foreign languages and up to two creative subjects (Art, DT, Music). Ancient Greek and Geography are also options. Boys will normally take nine subjects to GCSE in V Book (Year 11). In VI Book (Years 12 and 13), almost any combination of arts and sciences can be studied. The School teaches the Cambridge Pre-U syllabus in all VI Book subjects. Division – a daily lesson encompassing many aspects of culture and civilisation – plays a central role throughout the curriculum at all levels.

Scholarships and Exhibitions. The Scholarship examination (Election) is held in May each year, and about 14 scholarships are awarded. All scholarships are means-tested. Bursaries are available. Scholars live together in College.

Based on performance in the Scholarship Examination, about six Exhibitions may also be awarded which ensure a place in a Commoner House. Applications for bursaries are encouraged.

Candidates must be over 12 and under 14 on 1st September following the examination.

Further particulars and copies of specimen papers can be obtained from: The Master in College, Winchester College, College Street, Winchester, Hampshire SO23 9NA.

Music Awards. Music scholarships are available annually; they are subject to means-testing and carry free instrumental tuition for up to two instruments and singing. There are also Music Exhibitions, which offer free tuition for one or more specified instruments. In cases of financial need additional bursary grants will be awarded. One or more awards may be reserved for Winchester College Quiristers and for Sixth Form entrants. Successful candidates are generally at the level of Grade VI–VIII distinction. Music award tests take place in late January/early February each year. Music can also be offered as an option in the academic scholarship examinations in May.

The award of all Music Scholarships is conditional upon candidates satisfying the academic requirements for entry into the School. Music Award candidates who are not taking the Scholarship Examination will be required to take the Entrance Examination. For 13+ entry, candidates must be under 14 on 1 September of the year they come into the School.

The Master of Music is pleased to answer queries and to see prospective candidates at any time. Full details available from: The Master of Music, Winchester College Music School, Culver Road, Winchester, Hampshire SO23 9JF.

Bursaries. In cases of financial hardship bursaries are available to support boys entering the school. All bursaries are awarded on a means-tested basis. Particulars of bursaries may be obtained from the Bursar. Please contact Mrs W A Neville (wan@wincoll.ac.uk).

Sixth Form entry. A number of places is offered each year to boys joining the Sixth Form from other schools. Examinations and interviews take place in Winchester in late January each year. Enquiries should be sent to the Deputy Registrar (admissions@wincoll.ac.uk).

Fees per term (2016–2017). Boarders £12,226 (£36,678 pa). There is an entrance fee of £500.

Commoners. There are about 60 Commoners in each House.

The Housemasters are:
Chernocke House (A): J R Fox
Moberly's (B): S E Hart
Du Boulay's (C): L N Taylor
Fearon's (D): M J Winter
Morshead's (E): Dr J McManus
Hawkins' (F): Dr J E Hodgins
Sergeant's (G): D E Yeomans
Bramston's (H): Dr J P Cullerne
Turner's (I): C J Good
Kingsgate House (K): Dr M Romans

Boys should be registered any time after their eighth birthday and before the end of Year 5 (9+ to 10+). They are usually at least 13, but under 14, on 31 August in the year of entry to the School but exceptions may be considered in special circumstances. Places are offered after tests and an interview in Year 6. The Registrar holds a Reserve List, which includes the names of late applicants, but it is essential to have a place at another school until a firm place at Winchester has been confirmed.

The entrance examination covers the normal subjects; particulars and copies of recent papers may be obtained from the Deputy Registrar.

Term of entry. Usually September.

Old Boys' Society, Wykehamist Society. *Secretary*: A F J Roe, Donovan's, 73 Kingsgate Street, Winchester SO23 9PE.

Charitable status. Winchester College is a Registered Charity, number 1139000. The objects of the charity are the advancement of education and activities connected therewith.

Visitor: The Bishop of Winchester

Warden: C J F Sinclair, CBE, BA, FCA

Sub-Warden: R H Sutton, BA

Fellows:
J B W Nightingale, MA, DPhil
The Rt Hon Sir Andrew Longmore, PC, MA
R B Woods, CBE, MA
Ms J H Ritchie, QC, LLM
Professor Sir Curtis Price, KBE, AM, PhD, Hon RAM, FKC, FRNCM, Hon FASC (*Warden of New College*)
Professor C T C Sachrajda, FRS, PhD, FInstP, CPhys
P Frith, MD, FRCP, FRCOphth
Major-General J D Shaw, CB, CBE, MA
C M Farr, MA
A N Joy, MA
N E H Ferguson CBE, BSc, MBA
W E J Holland, FCA, MA
W E Poole, MA, DPhil, FSA
M Young MA

Bursar and Secretary: S P Little, MA, FCA

Headmaster: T R Hands, BA, AKC, DPhil

Second Master: N P Wilks, MA, ARAM

Director of Studies: P M Herring, MA

Registrar: A C Shedden, BEd

Deputy Registrar: Mrs P C McComb

Assistant Masters:
C J Tolley, MA, DPhil, FRCO
L C Wolff, MA, FRSA (*Head of History of Art*)
C H J Hill, MA
M D Wallis, MA
A S Leigh, MA
N I P MacKinnon, BA
W E Billington, MA, MICE
P G Cornish, BA, MMus, FTCL, ARCM, PhD (*Head of Mathematics*)
D J Ceiriog-Hughes, MA, PhD, FRSA
Miss C J Ovenden, MA
A P McMaster, BSc
I E Fraser, BSc (*Master in College*)
L N Taylor, BA Ed (*Senior Housemaster*)
M D Hebron, BA, DPhil (*Director of Drama*)
J G Webster, MA, DPhil (*Director of External Affairs*)
C Cai, BA, MA, PhD
C J Good, BEd
J E Hodgins, BSc, PhD
G J Watson, BA (*Head of Economics*)
C G Yates, BA (*Head of Careers and Higher Education*)
J P Cullerne, BSc, DPhil (*Under Master*)
C S McCaw, BSc, DPhil, DES, CChem, MRSC (*Head of Science*)
A D Adlam, Dip Mus
A P Dakin, BA
M Romans, BA, MA, PhD
Mrs L J Quinault, MA
J McManus, MChem, PhD
N A Salwey, MA, MSc, DPhil, ARCM, LGSM (*Deputy Master of Music*)
D E Pounds, BSc

Mrs A M Lombardo, MA, BA (*Head of French*)
J J L Douglas, BA, MSc (*Head of Physics*)
D I Follows, MChem, MSc, DPhil (*Head of Chemistry*)
D E Yeomans, BA
M G Crossland, MPhys
M J Winter, MA
G E Munn, MSci
M D Archer, MA, FRCO, FGCM, FNMSM, ARCM (*Director of Chapel Music*)
S E Hart, MEng
S A Tarrant, MEng (*Head of Design Technology*)
J P Spencer, MA (*Head of Classics*)
T E Giddings, BA, MSt
P E Hepworth, BSc, PhD
S D Rich, BA (*Head of MFL*)
A P Savory, BSc, PhD (*Head of Biology*)
Mrs C L Talks, MA
A Vieilleville, BA
C N Berry, MA, PhD
L M Guymer, MA PhD (*Head of History*)
A P Jaffe, BSc
J J Sutton, BA, BMus, ARCO
E J Donovan, MSc
Dr A French, MA, MPhil, MSc, PhD
D J Leigh, MA (*Head of PSHE*)
Miss R Poole, MBioCHem, MSc
M J Rogers, BSc
O Tarney, BMus, MMus
Mrs C Crowther, MA
Miss C Cadoret, BA
Dr R E J Foster, MA, MSt, DPhil
R S Stillman, BA, MA (*Head of English*)
Mrs M Zampeta, BA, MSc, MA
R S Moore, BA
J A A Barron, BA, MSci, PhD
C P Barnes, BSc
J E de Bono, BA
L P F Dunne, MA, BPhil
J R Fox, BSc, ARCS
S J Harden, MA, MSt, DPhil
L J Ronaldson, MA, PhD
C Schofield, BA (*Head of Learning Support*)
O O'Neill, BA
M P Bruzon, BA (*Head of Art*)
M L Dedynski, BA
A M Humphreys, MMath
J J Pinnells, BA
Mrs E K M Wright, BA
Dr S A T Thorn, BSc, PhD (*Dean of Chapel*)
D S Thomas, MA (*Master of Music*)
T F K Bird, BA
A I Clayton, BSc Res, BSc
J W Cole BSc
D A Alizadeh, BA
Dr A A H Graham, BSc, MASt, PhD
P J Lambert, BA
A Kashlach
H J Podger, BSc
P F Lewthwaite, BA, FRBS
N R Baker, BSc
A J Sparkes, CMG, MA
S T Baddeley, BA, MSt
Mrs C A Webster, MA
J J J C Wright, BSc
M J Pawlowski, BA
D J R Rowland, MA
Dr E W Steer, MChem, DPhil
Dr N A Townson, MA, PhD
M J Weaver, BA
C Syrett, BA
Mrs E M Veal, BA

Wisbech Grammar School

North Brink, Wisbech, Cambs PE13 1JX

Tel:	01945 583631 Senior School
	01945 586780 Magdalene House
	01945 586750 Admissions
Fax:	01945 476746 Senior School
	01945 586781 Magdalene House
email:	Office@WisbechGrammar.com
website:	WisbechGrammar.com
Twitter:	@WisbechGrammar
Facebook:	/WisbechGrammar

Founded during the turbulent reign of Richard II in 1379, Wisbech Grammar School was established by a society of local merchants, the Guild of the Holy Trinity, to provide education for poor boys of the town. Now a fully co-educational day school, it draws around 500 pupils aged 4 to 18 from the three counties of Cambridgeshire, Norfolk and Lincolnshire.

Occupying a prime site on the North Brink, one of England's most handsome Georgian streets and a magnet for film makers, the School – the finest in Fenland – is set in 34 acres of magnificent grounds in a conservation area. Open, friendly and welcoming, the School is small enough for staff to know all the pupils individually, but large enough to provide an impressive range of opportunities. The traditional emphasis on the pursuit of academic success is complemented by a sensitive and highly effective pastoral care system. All members of the Senior School and Magdalene House Preparatory School are encouraged to develop their confidence and unlock their true potential, both inside and outside the classroom, as well as engaging with the wider community.

Development. The ongoing development programme has included a dedicated 6th Form centre and a floodlit, all-weather Astroturf pitch, as well as the refurbishment of the science laboratories and an upgrade of the information technology infrastructure. A new £2.5m refectory opened in 2015 and a major expansion of the on-site playing field provision has recently been completed. The old dining hall will soon house a state-of-the-art Learning Resource Centre and Library for the whole school community. Two more classrooms and a new hall have been constructed for the rapidly expanding preparatory school, which takes its name from Magdalene College. The Cambridge college has enjoyed a close connection with the Grammar School for over 350 years and the Master and Fellows appoint two of their number to the governing body.

Senior School admission. The main entry is at age 11 by a competitive entrance examination. The test, which consists of mathematics and English, is designed to discover potential. Pupils can also enter at 2nd, 3rd and 4th Form levels. Offers of 6th Form places are made on the basis of interview and a report from a pupil's current school.

Fees per term (2016–2017). Senior School £4,192; Magdalene House Preparatory School £2,932–£2,998.

Bursaries and Scholarships. Wisbech Grammar School offers a bursary programme which provides financial assistance to pupils who would not otherwise be able to take up the offer of a place, allowing them to achieve their full potential. Bursaries are means tested and will require the parents to make a detailed statement of their income and assets. Awards range from 5% to 85%. In exceptional cases an award of 100% may be granted. The School also offers Scholarships for children entering Year 7, Year 9 and Year 12. Scholarships are awarded to children who excel in a number of areas (Academic and All-Rounder); this includes financial support and may be awarded alongside a bursary. Application forms for Bursary Assisted Places are available from the Admissions Team: Admissions@WisbechGrammar.com.

Travel to School. The School's catchment area embraces King's Lynn, Hunstanton, Downham Market, March, Whittlesey, Peterborough and Long Sutton. School buses run from a number of these places, visiting villages en route, and there is a late bus for pupils involved in after-school activities. The School is also well served by local buses.

Teaching and learning. The School aims to foster a love of learning and to provide an environment which nurtures talent and breeds success. In recent years the expansion of the teaching staff has helped to reduce class size and foster more individual learning. There is a high regard for the traditional disciplines, but the School is also ready to open up exciting new fields of study. An extensive academic curriculum in the first three years of the Senior School includes opportunities to sample a broad range of subjects. One pupil has recently reached the national finals of the Foreign Language Spelling Bee competition. The option system at GCSE ensures a broad-based curriculum as well as allowing pupils to play to their strengths. In the 6th Form, the subject range is extensive and pupils have their first chance to take business studies, economics, government and politics, and graphics. The School also provides support which allows bright pupils with learning difficulties and disabilities to rise to the challenge of a rigorous academic education.

The 6th Form experience. The School has a first-class track record in enabling pupils to realize their university and career aspirations. Entrusted with a greater degree of independence, sixth formers are encouraged to make their mark and develop leadership qualities, both within the house system and at a wider level. The 6th Form centre provides a fine facility for the School's most senior pupils.

Creative and performing arts. The flourishing music department provides practical opportunities for pupils to develop their creative talents. Nine visiting instrumental and vocal tutors give individual tuition to nearly a fifth of the pupils, and there are numerous opportunities to join in choirs, wind and steel bands and perform in the annual concerts and community charity events.

A dynamic tradition of drama allows pupils to build their confidence and hone their acting skills, both in major productions on the main stage and in more intimate performances in the studio. Audiences have sampled everything from Renaissance drama to experimental twentieth century works, and ambitious recent productions have included *Amadeus, Oh what a lovely war, Twelfth night and Macbeth.*

The art and design department is a highly visible presence in the School, mounting exhibitions on-site and at the Reed Barn at the neighbouring National Trust property, Peckover House, and talented artists and designers regularly win places at the top art colleges.

A competitive spirit. The Director of Sport ensures that teams enjoy the challenge of a competitive fixture list against schools across the eastern counties and in the midlands, and Wisbech Grammar School takes pride in punching above its weight. An extensive inter-house programme also allows pupils of all abilities to develop their competitive spirit. The main games for boys are rugby in the Michaelmas term and hockey and rugby sevens in the Lent term, together with cricket, athletics and tennis in the Trinity term. Girls play hockey in the Michaelmas term and netball and rugby sevens in the Lent term and rounders, tennis, cricket and athletics in the Trinity term. For pupils above the 3rd Form who are not involved in a major team game, the options range from badminton and basketball to archery and spinning. The facilities include a recently refurbished, full-sized sports hall, a fitness suite and an extensive on-site floodlit Astroturf pitch, together with generous playing field provision. Pupils also enjoy access to a covered swimming pool, a sports hall, a dance studio and a fitness centre at a neighbouring leisure centre.

Beyond the classroom. Wisbech Grammar School believes in learning on location. The biology department has recently run a field class in Galapagos, and the 5th Form went on a recent expedition to Borneo with a Madagascar expedition in the pipeline. Geographers have explored the west coast of the United States and there are frequent art trips to New York. There is a flourishing exchange with the Willibrord Gymnasium in Emmerich, and the French department has added a GCSE study trip to Normandy and an A Level cross-curricular visit to Paris to the annual chateau trip. Pupils also criss-cross the country for hands-on learning, and excursions such as the 3rd Form trip to Shakespeare's Globe or the Royal Shakespeare Theatre run regularly. Around 130 pupils participate in the Duke of Edinburgh's Award, with those at the highest level mounting expeditions to the Lake District, Snowdonia and Mont Blanc. The Senior School adventure begins with an outdoor activity weekend for the 1st Form.

Closer to home, sixth formers hone their business skills in the Young Enterprise scheme, regularly reaching the regional finals. Clubs such as language leaders, riding and grow, cook, eat help to stretch the mind and develop life skills. Members of Caritas, the charity and community service team, reach out to those in need, both on their doorstep and across the globe, and the School hosts an annual party for local pensioners.

Magdalene House Preparatory School caters for pupils from Reception to Prep 6. (*For further details see entry in IAPS section.*)

Old Wisbechians Society. Further information about the society can be obtained from the Admissions Team at the School, to whom requests for the school magazine, *Riverline*, should be sent. News of past pupils is published on the School website, WisbechGrammar.com.

Charitable status. The Wisbech Grammar School Foundation is a Registered Charity, number 1087799. It exists to promote the education of boys and girls.

Governing Body:

Chairman: Dr D Barter, MB BS, MRCP, FRCPCH, DCH
Vice Chairman: J E Warren
R Calleja, MD, MSc Urol, FRCS Urol
C Goad, BSc, ACA
S King, MSc
The Venerable Hugh McCurdy, BA, Archdeacon of
    Huntingdon and Wisbech
I MacLachlan
Dr C Mair, BSc Hons, BVetMed, MRCVS
Mrs S Meekins
Mrs E Morris, LLB
Dr F Sconce, MB ChB, DFFP
Dr F P Treasure, MA, MSc, PhD, CStat

Nominated by the Master of Magdalene College,
    Cambridge:
Prof J Raven, MA, PhD Cantab, MA Oxon, LittD Cantab,
    FSA, FRHistS

Clerk to the Governors: Mrs K Massen (*Headmaster's PA*)

Teaching Staff:
* *Head of Department*
† *Head of House*
§ *Part-time*
¶ *Old Pupil*

Headmaster: C N Staley, BA, MBA

Bursar: Mrs N J Miller, BA
Registrar: Mrs K Barclay, BSc
Senior Deputy Head: T I McConnell-Wood, BSc (*Business Studies, Economics, Child Protection Officer*)
Deputy Head Academic: M L Forrest, MA
Deputy Head Operations: P G Logan, BSc (*Mathematics*)

Deputy Head Digital Learning: Mrs V Garment, BA, MA
    (*Economics, Business Studies*)
Head of Lower School: K J Mann, BA, PhD (*History*)
Head of Middle School: T W Calow BA (*German*)
Head of Upper School/Sixth Form: Mr P W Timmis BSc
    (*Physics, French*)

Mr M Arnold, BEng (*Computer Science, Maths*)
Mr K R Bergh (*PE & Sport*)
T D Chapman, MA (**History, Government & Politics*)
Miss A M Clayton, BA (*English*)
C I Cole, BSc (*Physics*)
¶Miss D C Cook, BSc (*Biology, Lower School Science, Sport*)
Mrs S D Cooper, BA (**Textiles, Art & Design, Deputy Head of Lower School*)
A Duncan, GTP (*Performing Arts)
Mrs S Duncan, BSc (*Technical Theatre Manager, Drama, Speech & Communication Skills*)
S Emmerson, BA (*History)
Mrs S C Fox, BA, MSc (†**Lower School Science*)
R D Frost, BEd (**Design Technology*)
¶D S Garfoot, BSc (†*Head of Outdoor Learning, Sport, Geography, D of E Coordinator, Deputy EVC*)
Dr J Garner, BSc, PhD (*Chemistry*)
¶Miss J M Gomm, BSc (**Psychology, Sport*)
Mrs S M Goodier, BSc (†, *PE and Sport*)
Mrs C Harding, GRSM, AMBDA (*SENCO*)
P J Harrison, BA (*Art and Design*)
P J Harrison, BA (†, *Art*)
G E Howes, BSc (*Mathematics)
A P Jarvis, MA, MEd, PhD (*English)
M A Jarvis (*Hockey Coach, Design & Technology*)
T Jestin, MA (**Lower School Modern Foreign Languages, French*)
R D Killick, BSc (**Geography, Professional Tutor*)
Miss J L Lasouska, BSc (*Biology*)
A C Laybourne, MSc (*PE & Sport, Psychology, Deputy Head of Upper School/6th Form*)
S J Miller, BSc, PhD (**Biology, Senior Tutor, Higher Education Adviser*)
Mrs J M Missin, BA (**Upper School Music, Oxbridge*)
Mrs N P Neighbour, MA (**Upper School Modern Foreign Languages, French*)
G H Nunnerley, BSc (*Geography, Careers Advice, EVC*)
Mrs A Ogston, BSc (*Mathematics, Deputy Head of Middle School, PSHCE Coordinator*)
G Paine, BSc, PhD (*Chemistry)
§Mrs J T Reavell, BEd (*PE and Sport*)
I Rodriguez, BA (*Spanish*)
A J L Shillings, MSc, PhD (**Upper School Science, Physics*)
Mrs M Skinner, BA (*German*)
¶Mrs A L Sloan, BSc, MA (**Food & Nutrition*)
M P Stump, BA (**Art & Design*)
Miss K Taylor, BA (*Geography, Deputy Director of Examinations, Deputy Head of Upper School/6th Form*)
C Thursby, BA, MA (*Mathematics, Director of Examinations*)
Mrs K Timmis, BA (*English, Internal Exams*)
¶Mrs M Tooke, BSc (*Food and Nutrition*)
P J A Webb, BA (**Director of Sport, History*)
¶J D Williams (*Sports Coach*)
Mrs B Wrigley-Pheasant, BA (*Textiles, Art and Design*)

Headmaster's PA: Mrs K Massen/Mrs T Gambell

Magdalene House Preparatory School
Acting Head: Mrs K Neaves

Withington Girls' School

Wellington Road, Fallowfield, Manchester M14 6BL

Tel: 0161 224 1077
Fax: 0161 248 5377
email: office@wgs.org
website: www.wgs.org
Twitter: @WGSManchester

Motto: *Ad Lucem*

Independent (formerly Direct Grant).

Since its foundation in 1890, Withington has remained relatively small with about 660 pupils, 123 of whom are in the Junior Department and 141 in the Sixth Form. This size allows a friendly, intimate environment together with a broad and balanced curriculum. Withington provides a wide range of opportunities for girls, helping them to achieve their potential, academically, socially and personally. Withington attracts pupils from a wide geographical area and from many different social and cultural backgrounds, producing a diversity in which the school rejoices.

The School's A Level and GCSE results have been consistently outstanding. Girls who gain a place as a result of the entrance examination normally take GCSE/IGCSE examinations in 10 subjects, followed by 4 AS Levels, and then 3 or 4 A Levels. In addition, they have the option to take AS or A Level General Studies and/or an Extended Project Qualification in a subject of their choice. In September 2016 an exciting and varied Enrichment programme has been introduced for Lower Sixth Formers which includes such core elements as financial, literacy, PSHE and professional skills plus a range of options from astronomy to mosaics and Eastern Philosophy. Studies are directed towards encouraging a love of learning for its own sake, as well as towards the ultimate goal of University entrance, including Oxford and Cambridge. All the girls go on to Higher Education.

The School enjoys excellent facilities and has an ongoing programme of major developments. Recent projects have included a new, purpose-built Junior School building, a central, enclosed "Hub" area at the heart of the school and an expanded and refurbished suite of university-standard Chemistry laboratories, all of which were completed in 2015.

Withington fosters all-round development and the girls' academic studies are complemented by an extensive range of extra-curricular activities. Music is strong and very popular; there is a comprehensive range of choirs and orchestras, involving all age groups. Drama also thrives with regular productions including original works. Girls play a variety of sports, including hockey, lacrosse, netball, tennis, athletics, cricket and football. Pupils are regularly selected for county and national squads and there are regular sports tours within Europe and further afield, such as to Australia and South Africa. In addition to fixtures with other schools, games players compete within the School's House system. The four Houses, named after Withington's founders, also provide a focus for dramatic, musical and other activities.

The Duke of Edinburgh's Award scheme and the Young Enterprise scheme, Model United Nations conferences, voluntary work in the local community, science and mathematics Olympiads, residential activity weekends, foreign trips and local fieldwork all feature prominently in the School's provision. Numerous extra-curricular clubs and societies include: Model United Nations, debating, zumba, yoga, robotics, film making, app development, dance and chess. Awareness of the wider world is encouraged, girls participate in many fundraising activities and the School has special links with a hospital and two schools in Kenya. Each year parties of girls give up their holiday time to participate in community projects in Uganda and The Gambia; others participate in an annual World Challenge expedition (to Malaysia and Borneo in 2016). Preparation for life after school starts early and involves a programme of careers advice, work experience and UCAS application guidance.

Visitors are warmly welcomed at any time. Open Days are held in November. A substantial number of means-tested Bursaries are awarded annually together with awards from various external Trusts. Entrance at age 7–11 is by Entrance Examination, held in January, together with interview and report from current school. Admission to the Sixth Form is by interview and is conditional upon GCSE results. For entry at other points, don't hesitate to contact the Registrar for more information.

The School engages in a number of projects with local State schools and has strong links with the local community. Withington was named as The Sunday Times Parent Power Top Independent Secondary School of the Year 2009/10 and the Financial Times Best Value Independent Day School in 2012. Consistently named as the top secondary school in the north west by the Sunday Times, The Tatler Schools Guide named Withington as a Runner-Up for Public School of the Year 2015.

Fees per term (2016–2017). Senior School £3,895, Junior School £2,895. LAMDA and individual instrumental music lessons are charged separately.

Charitable status. Withington Girls' School is a Registered Charity, number 1158226. It aims to provide an exceptional quality of opportunity, to encourage independence of mind and high aspirations for girls from seven to eighteen.

Board of Governors:
Chair: Mrs E Lee, LLB
Mr D Illingworth, BA, FCA (*Hon Treasurer*)
Mr M Adlestone, OBE, FGA
Dr J Allred, MB ChB, MRCGP, DRCOG, DFFP
Professor S B Furber, CBE, FRS, FREng, FBCS, CEng, MA, PhD
Mrs G Byrom, BSc, MA
Miss S Johnson-Manning, GRSM, LRAM, ARCM
Mrs J Kinney, FdSc, LLB
Dr A Kirkham, BSc, BA, MA, PhD, ACA
Mr A Pathak, BSc
Mr M Pike, LLB
Mrs L Sabbagh, BA
Mr H Sinclair

Headmistress: **Mrs S J Haslam**, BA Lancaster (*English*)

Deputy Head: Ms J M Baylis, MA Manchester (*English and Drama*)

Director of Studies: Mr I McKenna, BA Manchester (*Religious Studies*)

Assistant Head: Dr S E Madden, PhD Newcastle (*Biology*)

Bursar: Mrs S Senn, BSc Hull, ACA

Full-time Staff:
Mrs L Berry, BA Manchester (*Drama*)
Mrs J W Bowie, MA Dundee (*English*)
Mrs L Bradshaw, MA Cantab (*Physics*)
Miss K L Browning, BA London (*Geography*)
Miss D Bruce, BA Birmingham (*Religious Studies*)
Mrs J Buckley, BA Durham (*Geography*)
Miss M Cahill, BA Leeds (*History*)
Mrs H Carey, MChem Manchester (*Chemistry*)
Mrs A Collard, BSc Durham (*Mathematics*)
Miss A Collier, BA Liverpool (*Physical Education*)
Mrs J C Clark, BA Sheffield (*History*)
Ms C J Davies, BA Hull, MA Open University (*English*)
Mr K Eckersall, BSc Leicester, MA Durham (*Chemistry*)
Mrs C E Edge, MA Leeds (*English*)
Ms J E Ellis, BA Bath (*German*)

Mrs M Ferrol, BEd Dunfermline College (*Physical Education*)
Mrs S E Fletcher, BEd Brighton (*Mathematics*)
Mr C Forrest, MPhys Manchester (*Physics*)
Mr A Gooch, BSc Manchester (*Mathematics*)
Miss E Hall, MSc Durham (*Biology*)
Mrs S E Hamilton, MA Aberdeen (*Geography*)
Mrs J Healey, BSc Newcastle (*FTT*)
Miss A R H Holland, BMus Birmingham (*Music*)
Mrs J C Howling, MA Cantab (*Classics*)
Miss C McGregor, BSc Manchester (*Biology*)
Dr E A Maisey, PhD London (*Chemistry*)
Mrs Y T Menzies, MA Salford (*French, German*)
Ms C Morton, MA Sheffield (*Spanish*)
Mrs S I Mounteney, BSc London (*Mathematics*)
Miss B O'Neal, MSc MMU (*Psychology*)
Mrs C Ositelu, DEA-ès-L Nantes (*French*)
Mr A Parry, BSc Manchester (*Mathematics*)
Miss J Richards, BA Liverpool John Moores (*Physical Education*)
Mrs E K Robinson, MA Cantab (*Classics*)
Mrs G E Sargent, BMus London (*Music*)
Mr A Snowden, BSc Warwick (*ICT*)
Miss N Toubkin, BSc Manchester (*Economics*)
Dr C P G Vilela, PhD Lisbon (*Biology, Chemistry*)
Ms N A West, BA Manchester (*English*)

Junior School:
Head of Junior School: Mrs E S K Burrows, MA St Andrews (*Geography*)
Mrs D Odeyinde, BSc Queen's Belfast (*Year 6*)
Mrs S Roberts, MA Manchester (*Year 6*)
Mrs S J Rigby, BA Nottingham (*Learning Support*)
Mrs K Williams, BA Victoria, Canada (*Year 5*)
Miss H Dillon BA Manchester (*Year 5*)
Mrs H Stallard, BA Newcastle-upon-Tyne (*Year 4*)
Miss L Geoghegan, BA York (*Year 3*)
Mrs B Lowe, BSc Northumbria (*Year 3*)

Part-time Staff:
Mrs C Air, BA Oxon (*History*)
Mrs U Asim, BSc UMIST (*Science*)
Mrs S Birch, BEd Edge Hill (*FTT, Drama*)
Mrs N Cottam, BSc Durham (*Biology, Careers*)
Mrs F Cotton, BA Heriot-Watt (*Design & Technology*)
Miss K Easby, MA Manchester (*Ancient World*)
Mrs R Fildes, MA MMU (*Art*)
Ms A Furlong, MA St Mary's (*English*)
Ms A Godwin, BA Oxon (*Learning Support*)
Mrs Z Goldman, BA Manchester (*Design Technology*)
Mrs A Humblet, BA University of Dijon (*French, Spanish*)
Mrs J Johnston, BA MMU (*Art*)
Dr Z Kenny, PhD Edinburgh (*Biology*)
Mrs V Kochhar, BSc Exeter (*Mathematics*)
Mrs E Lee, BSc Manchester (*Physics and ICT*)
Miss S Lloyd, BSc Bangor (*Biology*)
Ms M Lopez, BSc Pennsylvania (*Spanish*)
Dr R Pavey, PhD Liverpool (*Science*)
Mrs V Scott, BSc Liverpool (*Mathematics*)
Mrs A Siddons, BA Bath (*German*)
Mrs J Stockton, BA Leeds (*English*)
Mrs Z Taylor, BA MMU (*Art*)
Dr E L Terrill, DPhil Oxon (*Mathematics*)
Dr D Verity, PhD Hull (*Physics*)
Mrs J C Wallis, BA Leeds (*Politics*)
Mrs N Watson, BA Leeds (*FTT, Careers*)
Mrs F Whitfield, MSc Manchester (*Mathematics*)

Librarians: Mrs D Sutton, MA MMU; Mrs H Brackenbury, MA Sheffield
Network Manager: Mr A Lockett, BSc Bradford

School Nurses: Mrs J Lees, RGN; Mrs V Proudley, PgDip Clinical Nursing
Examinations Officer: Mrs H Coubrough
Assistant Examinations Officer: Dr S E Madden, PhD Newcastle (*Biology*)
Development Director: Mrs T Leden, BSc Surrey
DofE Award Scheme Coordinator: Miss C McGregor, BSc Manchester (*Biology*)

Administration:
PA to Headmistress: Mrs A L Adams, BA Sheffield Hallam
Registrar: Mrs L Jefferies, BA Manchester
PA to Bursar: Mrs P A Willis
School Secretary: Mrs A Easton, MSc Birmingham

Wolverhampton Grammar School

Compton Road, Wolverhampton, West Midlands WV3 9RB

Tel: 01902 421326
email: wgs@wgs.org.uk
website: www.wgs.org.uk
Twitter: @WGS1512
Facebook: /Wolverhampton-Grammar-School-Official
LinkedIn: /WGS Old Wulfrunians and Friends

Wolverhampton Grammar School was founded in 1512 by Sir Stephen Jenyns – a Wolverhampton man who achieved success as a wool merchant, became a member of The Merchant Taylors' Company then Lord Mayor of London. He decided to benefit his home town by founding a school "for the instruction of youth in good manners and learning". The school retains close links with the Company.

Wolverhampton Grammar School is an independent, selective day school for boys and girls aged 7–18 from a wide catchment area throughout the West Midlands, Staffordshire and Shropshire.

In 2011, the school opened a junior school (Wolverhampton Grammar Junior School) for students aged 7–11. The Junior School has proved exceptionally popular with parents advised to apply early to avoid disappointment.

The school's mission is to deliver education that transforms lives as well as minds, as individual as every child, within an environment that's like no other. The school delivers a personalised curriculum to provide an education and learning experience that is unique. Students achieve excellent GCSE and A Level exam results alongside an experience that includes the largest range of co- and extra-curricular activities available in the area.

The school was inspected in April 2011 and was judged to be excellent in all areas. The report can be read on the ISI website: www.isi.net.

Buildings. The stunning 23-acre site includes a purpose-built Sixth Form Centre and a £3.8 million Arts & Drama Centre home to the Viner Gallery and Hutton Theatre. A Sports Centre and floodlit Astroturf pitches provide some of the best sporting facilities in the area, with a new Sports Pavilion unveiled in October 2012 providing panoramic views of the sports fields. The early 20th century Merridale and Caldicott buildings house laboratories that have been refurbished to the highest modern standards. State-of-the-art ICT facilities provide Wi-Fi internet access to all parts of the school and all teachers use iPads and app technology to enhance the learning experience.

Admission. The School accepts applications to the Junior, Senior and Sixth Form (Year 3 to Year 13) throughout the year, although new students usually join the school in September. The school's own Year 7 entrance tests are held in the preceding January. For the Sixth Form: offers of places are made subject to GCSE results and interview.

Fees per term (2016–2017). Junior School £3,274, Senior School and Sixth Form £4,313.

Entrance Scholarships. There are a number of options available which offer support with fees, including a range of Bursaries and Scholarships. The awards vary according to the level of family income and are reviewed annually so please contact Jane Morris, Admissions Registrar on 01902 421326 or email jam@wgs-sch.net for further details.

Assistance with Fees. The School offers a number of means-tested bursaries to children from less affluent families who can demonstrate that they will benefit from the opportunity of an education with Wolverhampton Grammar School. Bursaries are reviewed annually so please contact Jane Morris, Admissions Registrar on 01902 421326 or email jam@wgs-sch.net for further details.

Curriculum. The curriculum is delivered using a two-week timetable. Supported by a vast range of co-curricular activities, it covers a broad range of academic subjects that includes three language choices and Classics. Sixth Formers have a choice of 26 A Level subjects. Sixth Formers usually take 3 or 4 A Level subjects and this can also be supported by an Extended Project Qualification (EPQ) as well as structured work experience and HE/UCAS advice and guidance. Students go on to excellent universities including Oxford, Cambridge and other Russell Group institutions.

Games and Outdoor Activities. Wolverhampton Grammar School offers the largest range of extra-curricular activities, clubs, societies, trips, international expeditions and sport tours of any independent school in the area. Sport has a long tradition at the school and students compete at city, regional and national level. The 23-acre site includes rugby, cricket, hockey and football pitches, netball courts, an all-weather Astroturf and athletics track as well as a fully equipped sports centre with multi-gym and indoor courts for badminton, squash and nets. A 'sport for all' attitude exists in games and PE, where the staff endeavour to match the student to a sport or activity in which they can succeed. There is a commitment to the highest standards of skill and sportsmanship but the emphasis is also placed on enjoyment. The school participates in The Duke of Edinburgh's Award scheme and there are opportunities to undertake field trips and foreign exchanges. There is a rigorous outdoor education programme. The School also boasts Fives Courts as well as a purpose-built climbing wall and sports pavilion offering panoramic views of large outdoor sports fields.

Dyslexia. The School's OpAL (Opportunities through Assisted Learning) department is designed to allow bright children with Specific Learning Difficulties (Dyslexia) to enjoy the challenge of a first-rate academic education. OpAL students have consistently achieved exceptional GCSE and A Level grades – consistently above the national average.

Arts and Other Activities. Purpose-built facilities for art, music and drama provide the best venues possible for exhibitions and school productions. The school boasts a purpose-built art gallery known as the Viner Gallery, which is used by students and commercial artists alike. A large contemporary theatre known as the Hutton Theatre is home to exceptional performances by students from across the School. The location of the music department at the heart of the school ensures the sound of singing, ensemble and band music is always heard on campus. There is a wide variety of extra-curricular clubs and activities giving students the opportunity to discover and cultivate new interests, both inside and outside the classroom. A Community Service programme and an active student Charity Fundraising Committee ensure that all students are involved in working for the good of others.

Pastoral Care. The school is proud of the pastoral care and support it offers to its students. In the Junior and Middle Schools care is provided by a form tutor under the overall responsibility of the appropriate Heads of Schools. Regular consultations are held with parents supported by full and frequent reports. An important forum is the Student Parliament which consists of elected representatives from all year groups who are encouraged to voice concerns and suggest improvements to the running and organisation of the school. The weekly meetings, with the Head plus one other member of staff in attendance, are run by an elected Chair and Secretary.

Charitable status. Wolverhampton Grammar School Limited is a Registered Charity, number 1125268.

Council Members:
Chairman: Mr Philip Sims, ACIB
The Mayor of Wolverhampton (*ex officio*)
Mrs Anne-Marie Brennan
Mr Mervyn Brooker, BA
Revd Sarah Cawdell
Mr Robin Cooper [OW] (*ex officio USA*)
Dr Stephen Gower, MA, PhD [OW] (*Appointed by the University of Birmingham*)
Dr Carol Griffiths, MBChB, FRCGP, MMedEd, DCH, DRCOG, DPD
Mr Peter Hawthorne, CBE, MA [OW]
Professor Keith Madelin, OBE, MSc, CEng, FICE, FIHT
Mr Peter Magill (*Appointed by the Merchant Taylors' Company*)
Dr Mark Nicholls, BA, MA, PhD (*Appointed by St John's College Cambridge*)
Mr Tony Phillips [OW] (*Appointed by the Old Wulfrunians Association*)
Mr Jay Patel
Mr Robert Purshouse, LLB [OW]
Mr James Sage, BSc Hons
Mr Sathnam Sanghera, MA [OW]
Mr Eddie Sergeant, BSc, BTh [OW]
Mr Carl Tatton, BA, ACMA

[OW] *Old Wulfrunian*

Head: Mrs Kathy Crewe-Read, BSc Aberystwyth

Deputy Heads:
Mr Nic Anderson, BSc Leeds (*Academic & Pastoral Years 7–9, Mathematics*)
Mr Toby Hughes, MA, MPhil Queens' College Cambridge, PGCE Homerton College Cambridge (*Academic & Pastoral Years 10–13, Geography*)

Assistant Head Curriculum: Mr Alex Yarnely, BSc Hull (*Mathematics*)

Acting Head of Junior School: Mr Dan Peters, BMus Birmingham

Staff:
Mr Tom Baker, BSc Edinburgh (*Head of Geography*)
Mr Mark Benfield, BA Leeds, GCD Birmingham (*Head of English*)
Mrs Diane Birt, MA St Andrews (*Head of Classics*)
Miss Emma Bowater, BA Birmingham City (*Art*)
Dr Neil Bradley, BSc, PhD Nottingham (*Mathematics*)
Mrs Sarah Brentnall, BA Birmingham (*Modern Languages*)
Mr Andrew Carey, BSc London (*Head of Chemistry*)
Mrs Alison Causebrook, BSc Birmingham, MA Wolverhampton (*Head of Girls' Games*)
Mr Russell Charlesworth, BA Lady Margaret Hall Oxford (*Head of History*)
Mr Steven Clancy, BSc Loughborough (*Head of Year 8, Boys' PE & Games, English*)
Miss Victoria Clarke, BA Cambridge (*Geography*)
Mr Francis Cooney, BSc Brunel (*Physics*)
Mrs Clare Cooper, BA Royal Holloway London (*Junior School*)
Mr Truan Cothey, BSc Lancaster (*Junior School*)

Mr Nigel Crust, BA Bangor (*Deputy Head of Sixth Form, Head of Boys' Games*)

Mrs Lynn D'Arcy, BSc Wolverhampton (*Junior School*)

Mrs Anna Dalton, BA Nottingham Trent (*Junior School*)

Mr Joe David, BA Newcastle-upon-Tyne (*History*)

Mrs Helen David, MChem York (*Chemistry*)

Mrs Katherine Dyer, BSc Gloucestershire (*Psychology, Girls' Games*)

Mrs Katherine Finn, BA Manchester (*Head of Theology & Philosophy*)

Dr Karen Flavell, BSc, PhD Wolverhampton (*Biology*)

Mrs Diana Gibbs, BA Bristol (*Junior School*)

Miss Katie Gilchrist, BSc Birmingham (*NQT Girls' PE*)

Mrs Amelia Grant, BSc Open University (*Geography*)

Mr James Griffiths, BA Liverpool John Moore's (*Junior School*)

Mrs Petra Grigat-Bradley, Erstes und Zweites Staatsexamen, Ruhr-Universität Bochum (*German*)

Ms Nikki Guidotti, BA Anglia Polytechnic University (*Music, Music Technology*)

Mr Jonathan Hall, BA Newcastle upon Tyne (*Head of Year 11, English*)

Mr Edward Hamill, BSc Glasgow (*Science*)

Mrs Elizabeth Harris, BA Southampton (*Head of Modern Languages*)

Mrs Helen Hills, BSc Nottingham (*Head of Biology*)

Mr Peter Hills, BSc Nottingham (*Mathematics*)

Mrs Mary Howard, BA Leicester, Dip RSA (*OpAL*)

Mrs Jessica Howe, BA, MA Cambridge (*Junior School*)

Mrs Amy Hughes, BEd Cambridge (*Junior School*)

Mr Stephen Jackson-Turnbull, BA, MA Huddersfield (*Head of Year 9, Design & Technology*)

Mr Robert Jagger, BA Liverpool (*English*)

Mr Peter Johnstone, BA Hull (*Head of Psychology*)

Miss Claudine Jones, BA Nottingham Trent, Dip RSA (*Head of Year 7, OpAL*)

Mr Theo King, ICC, Senior Coach (*Games Coach i/c Cricket*)

Mr Ryan Lovatt, MA Liverpool (*Physics*)

Mrs Pav Mahey, BA Central England (*ICT, Economics, Business Studies*)

Mrs Patrizia Manzai, BA Turin (*Italian*)

Mr Robert Mason, BA Nottingham (*German*)

Mr James Millichamp, BA, MA Wolverhampton (*Head of Art*)

Mr Nick Munson, BSc Birmingham (*Head of Physics*)

Mrs Rachel Munson, BA Leeds (*Modern Foreign Languages*)

Mr Francis Murton, BMus Sheffield (*Director of Music*)

Dr Chris O'Brien, BSc, PhD Imperial College London (*Head of Mathematics*)

Mr Simon O'Malley, BA Wolverhampton (*Head of Design & Technology*)

Mr Simon Palmer, Senior Coach (*Girls' Hockey Coach*)

Mr Mark Payne, BA Warwick (*English*)

Mrs Noreen Perks, Diploma of Fellowship London College of Music (*Music*)

Miss Rhiannon Platt, BA Birmingham (*Deputy Head of Sixth Form, English, Careers*)

Dr Ryan Pounder, PhD, MChem Warwick (*Chemistry*)

Mrs Claire Ray, BA Luton (*Girls' PE*)

Mr Andrew Reddish, BA Sunderland (*Head of ICT*)

Mr Jim Ryan, BEd Crewe & Alsager College, MEd, Adv Dip SNE Open University, AMBDA, SpLD APC (*Head of Year 10, OpAL*)

Miss Arti Shukla, BA Wolverhampton (*Year 4 Teacher*)

Mr Gordon Smith, BEd Loughborough (*Design & Technology*)

Mr Tom Smith, BA Strathclyde (*Head of Economics & Business Studies*)

Mr Liam Taylor, BA Reading, MA Birmingham (*History*)

Mrs Ruth Taylor-Briggs, BA, PhD Birmingham (*Classics*)

Mr Ian Tyler, BA Saskatchewan, MEd Birmingham, Dip DA RADA (*Assistant Head, Head of Teaching & Learning, Director of OpAL, SENCO, English, Theatre Studies*)

Mr Callum Underwood, BA Christ's College Cambridge (*French*)

Mr Kartar Uppal, BA Wadham College Oxford, MPhil Birmingham (*Mathematics*)

Mrs Fran Wainwright, BSc Hertfordshire, PGCE Wolverhampton (*Mathematics*)

Mrs Diana Ward, BA, MA Birmingham (*Art*)

Miss Emily Watson, BSc Manchester (*Physics*)

Mr Jonathan Wood, BA Royal Holloway London, MA Ed Bangor (*OpAL, Peer Support, Exams*)

Miss Emma Yates, MA Leicester (*Junior School*)

Miss Rachel Young, BSc Warwick (*Biology*)

Mrs Beverley Young, BA Reading (*Religious Studies*)

Bursar: Mrs Penny Rudge

Head's PA: Mrs Caroline Harris

Woodbridge School

Burkitt Road, Woodbridge, Suffolk IP12 4JH

Tel:	01394 615000
	01394 382673 (The Abbey Prep)
Fax:	01394 380944
email:	admissions@woodbridgeschool.org.uk
website:	www.woodbridgeschool.org.uk

Motto: '*Pro Deo Rege Patria*'

Situation. Woodbridge is an attractive market town on the River Deben, opposite the site of the famous royal Saxon ship burial at Sutton Hoo. Timber-framed buildings dating from the Middle Ages, and Georgian facades draw many visitors to the town throughout the year as does the Aldeburgh Festival at the nearby international Snape Maltings Concert Hall. Excellent sailing facilities are available on the River Deben. Woodbridge is seven miles from the Suffolk coast and close to the continental ports of Felixstowe and Harwich. The rail journey to London takes a little over an hour.

History and Buildings. Woodbridge School was originally founded in 1662. The scholars were to be taught "both Latin and Greek until thereby they be made fit for the University (if it be desired), but in case of any of them be unapt to learn those languages … they should be taught only Arithmetic, and to Write, to be fitted for Trades or to go to Sea". They were also to be "instructed in the principles of the Christian Religion according to the Doctrine of the Church of England".

For 200 years, the School existed in cramped quarters in the town until its incorporation with the Seckford Trust. Endowment income then enabled it to move to its present undulating site overlooking the town and the River Deben and to begin the steady expansion and development which have accelerated over the last 25 years. The School has been fully co-educational for nearly four decades. The latest additions are the new state-of-the-art 350-seat Seckford Theatre and refurbished Britten-Pears Music School.

Woodbridge has had close links with the local community and, through its outstanding Music and Science, with Finland, France, Spain, The Netherlands, Hungary and Germany. Woodbridge has a British Council International School Award for its international links, pupils are able to go on cultural exchange to countries as diverse as Australia, Oman, South Africa, India and China.

The Abbey prep school is centred in a beautiful house dating from the 16th Century in the town, adjacent to which two large new buildings have been added. Taking pupils from 7–11, it has full use of the Senior School swimming pool, sports hall, tennis courts, etc. (*For further details, see entry in IAPS section.*) There are currently 160 pupils in the Abbey prep school.

Queen's House, the pre-prep department for 85 pupils aged 4–6, opened in 1993 in its own building on the Woodbridge School site.

Organisation. There are approximately 800 pupils. The Senior School (11–18) numbers 305 boys and 296 girls, with a Sixth Form of about 200. There is a co-educational Boarding House for pupils aged 13+. A Day House system exists with a Junior House for 11 year old entrants and four other Day Houses for those aged 12–16. All Sixth Form day pupils are based in the Sixth Form Centre.

Music, Games and Activities. Music is at the heart of much of the life of the School. Over 60 concerts every year, large and small, offer pupils opportunities to perform at all levels. Some 45% of pupils study at least one instrument. In recent years Woodbridge School has had more members of the National Youth Choirs of Great Britain than any other school in the UK.

Woodbridge is a chess centre of excellence, representing England at the world chess championships.

Sailing, riding, shooting and hockey are real strengths. Other main games are rugby and netball in the winter; cricket, also tennis, athletics, swimming and rounders in the summer. The Sports Hall has facilities for most indoor sports.

The first-class Combined Cadet Force embraces Army, RAF, and Royal Navy Sections. The large variety of clubs and societies includes The Duke of Edinburgh's Award scheme. All 11 and 12 year olds follow the Seckford Scheme which paves the way for these, and many other, activities.

Careers. The School offers comprehensive careers advice and there are close links with county and university careers departments.

Chapel and Religious Education. The School has a strong Christian ethos and pupils attend Chapel every week. There is an annual Confirmation Service.

Admission. The majority enter the Senior School at 11 through the School's own examination, interview and report. At age 13, entry is through the School's own or the Common Entrance examination. Entry to the Sixth Form is based on interview and GCSE results. Admission to The Abbey is at any stage from the age of four.

Registration Fee: £50 (day), £100 (boarding). Acceptance Fee: £300 (day), £500 (UK boarding), £9,167 (overseas boarding).

Fees per term (2016–2017). Day: Pre-Prep (Queen's House) £2,788; Prep (The Abbey) £4,299; Senior School: Years 7–9 £4,814; Years 10–13 £5,210. Boarding: £9,799.

Scholarships and Bursaries. Due to its generous endowment, the School is able to offer remission of up to 100% of fees to pupils whose parents have incomes in the lower and middle ranges through Awards and/or Means-Tested Bursaries.

Academic Scholarships, worth up to 50% of tuition fees, are available for entry at 11, 13 and 16. These are awarded on the results of the annual entrance examinations at 11+ and 13+ and on the basis of interview and GCSE results at 16+.

Music scholarships are available, worth up to 50% of fees plus free music tuition. Instrumental or Choral Awards, entitling pupils to free music tuition, may be offered.

Drama scholarships are available worth up 25% of fees including a free weekly LAMDA lesson.

Art scholarships, worth up to 10% of fees at 11+ and up to 25% of fees at 13+ and 16+, are available annually.

Sport scholarships are available annually, worth up to 10% of fees at 11+ and up to 25% of fees at 13+ and 16+.

All-round Awards can be offered at 11+, 13+ and 16+ to those who have good overall talent, but who have not reached the standard of Award in any specific area.

Chess Awards are available worth up to 10% of tuition fees and include free tuition for one chess lesson each week.

Charitable status. The Seckford Foundation is a Registered Charity, number 1110964. Its aims are to give education for "poor children" by the provision of scholarships and fee remissions out of charity funds, and to maintain "the elderly poor" by providing a subsidy out of the charity for the Almshouses and Jubilee House.

Governing Body: The Trustees of The Seckford Foundation

Chairman: R Finbow, MA Oxon

Headmaster: N P Tetley, MA

Deputy Head: M R Streat
Deputy Head (*Academic*): M J Jennings
Deputy Head (*Pastoral*): Miss S Norman
Curriculum Administrator: R F Broaderwick
Chaplain: The Revd N Cook

Assistant Staff:
Head of Music: J R Penny
Head of Science: S E Cottrell
Head of Geography: Miss J A Gill
Head of Computing: J A Hillman
Head of Art: H J Tebbutt
Head of MFL: Mrs L R Chandler
Head of Classics: G Gilbert
Head of Chemistry: Mrs A Hillman
Head of Biology: Dr L V Rickard
Head of History: N E Smith
Head of Drama: Miss G Mayes
Head of Mathematics: J M C Allen
Head of Academic PE: Miss N L Sanders
Director of Sport: I J Simpson
Head of Religious Studies: Miss E Tattoo
Head of Design: H J Tebbutt
Head of Economics: R E Fernley
Head of Business Studies: J M Percival
Head of English: Dr A E Renshaw
Head of Physics: J D Morcombe

Bursar: G E Watson
School Medical Officer: Dr J P W Lynch
Headmaster's Secretary: Miss C Shaw

The Abbey and Queen's House – Woodbridge Prep and Pre-Prep Schools

Head of Prep and Pre-Prep: J A Brett
Deputy Head of Prep: Mrs C M T Clubb
Deputy Head of Pre-Prep: Mrs S Lindsay-Smith

Assistant Staff:

Reception Class Teachers: Ms K Spalding and Mrs M N Kiley
Year 1 Class Teachers: Mrs H M Cory and Mrs L Ford
Year 2 Class Teachers: Mrs J K Duncan and Mrs H Forrest
Year 3 Class Teachers: Mrs S Griffiths and Mrs P A Martin
Year 4 Class Teachers: Mrs J O Chamberlain and Mrs S K Cox-Olliff
Year 5 Class Teachers: M R Fernley and L M Palin
Year 6 Class Teachers: Miss G R Ballam, C J French and C S Smith

Head of Spanish: Mrs L Verona
Head of Music: Mrs M M Williams
Director of Sport: I J Simpson

Woodhouse Grove School

Apperley Bridge, Bradford, West Yorkshire BD10 0NR

Tel:	0113 250 2477
Fax:	0113 250 5290
email:	enquiries@woodhousegrove.co.uk
website:	www.woodhousegrove.co.uk
Twitter:	@woodhouse_grove
Facebook:	/woodhousegroveschool

Motto: '*Bone et fidelis*'

Woodhouse Grove was founded in 1812 and is a co-educational day and boarding school for pupils aged from 3 to 18 years. Boarding pupils are taken from the age of 11 years.

At Woodhouse Grove, we appreciate that every child is a unique individual and this is at the heart of everything we do. We aim to motivate pupils academically and beyond the classroom and to provide an educational environment designed to allow students to fully participate in school life.

We offer a rich, challenging and dynamic curriculum and want our students to ask questions of the world around them with an open mind; to have the character to listen to others, but also to stand up for their beliefs. We encourage our pupils to 'give back' to their community and we believe that this well-rounded, diverse approach is the key to building academic and personal confidence. Ultimately, our objective is to provide our students with the drive and aspiration to become the very best version of themselves that they can be.

Set in idyllic grounds near Leeds, the school is opposite Apperley Bridge train station and within four miles of Leeds Bradford Airport. We have high standards and an all-encompassing approach to education and our outstanding facilities reflect this. A recording studio, 230-seater theatre, sports halls, swimming pool and climbing wall are all within our 70-acre campus.

Numbers. There are 700 pupils in the Senior School including 80 boarders and a Sixth Form of over 200 students. Brontë House (age 3–11 years) has around 300 pupils.

Buildings. Our facilities include a purpose-built sports centre with a multi-functional sports hall, a fitness suite, a dance studio, a 25m competition swimming pool, squash courts, floodlit outdoor courts, floodlit all-weather pitch, performing arts centre and climbing wall. We have fully equipped science laboratories, a new state-of-the-art DT and Art centre, a spacious music and drama block, language suite and fully-equipped IT rooms. We have a modern spacious Sixth Form centre and refurbished boarding houses to provide a separate sixth form annexe for boys.

Sport. We have approximately 40 acres of playing fields including grounds for Cricket, Rugby, Football and Athletics as well as indoor Squash, Basketball and Swimming facilities. There are several all-weather Tennis Courts, a floodlit outdoor court for Netball and Tennis and a floodlit all-weather pitch.

Music. 33% of pupils have instrumental or vocal tuition and pupils can perform in a wide variety of music, drama and dance groups. Accredited exams offered include ABRSM & Trinity Guildhall Speech and Drama. There are a number of high-profile annual performances taking advantage of the dedicated theatre and recording studio. Music tours take place every two years. Sixth form courses are available in Music and Music Technology.

Curriculum. Boys and girls can enter the Senior School at any age but mainly at the age of 11, 13 and 16 and the curriculum is arranged to provide a seamless transition through from Brontë House and upwards through the Sixth Form to University entrance. A wide range of GCSE (and IGCSE) courses are offered and in 2016/17 we are offering 28 subjects at A Level. Specialist support is offered to meet EAL, dyslexia and other learning needs. All students get the chance to study French, Spanish and German. The campus is served by full-site Wi-Fi.

Sixth Form Entry. Places are available for students who want to come into the School at the Sixth Form stage subject to entry requirements.

Scholarships and Bursaries. Scholarships can be applied for directly from the headmaster for academic, all-rounder, art, sport and music. In addition, bursaries can be awarded following the offer of a place, in cases of financial need (plus allowances for children of ministers and of service personnel). Extras include excursions and extra tuition, such as music.

Admission. Places are offered subject to availability and based on our own entrance exam, in-school interview and previous school report. Pupils are usually accepted in September, although arrangements can be made for entry throughout the school year.

Brontë House is our Preparatory School and takes boys and girls during the term that they turn three. Ashdown Lodge Nursery & Reception takes pupils on a day or part-day basis, all year round.

Fees per term (2016–2017). Main School: £8,640–£8,660 (full boarders), £8,085–£8,185 (weekly boarders), £4,155–£4,275 (day). Brontë House: £3,115–£3,740 (day). Ashdown Lodge Nursery and Reception: £2,835 (full day), £1,765 (half day). Fees include all meals, books, stationery, examination fees and careers tests.

Extra Subjects. There is a wide range of extra subjects available including individual music lessons, singing, speech and drama, dancing, extra sports coaching, debating, Duke of Edinburgh's Award, photography and fencing.

Old Grovians Association. *Secretary*: Mrs Heather Garner.

Charitable status. Woodhouse Grove School is a Registered Charity, number 529205. It exists to provide education for children.

Governors:
A Wintersgill, FCA (*Chairman*)
S Burnhill, BSc
R S Drake, LLB Hons, ACIArb
Mrs P M Essler, BSc
Dr G H Haslam, MBChB
R C Hemsley, FCA, MA
A S P Kassapian
F J McAleer, BA Arch, Dip Arch, RIBA
I M Small, BA, DipEd
Mrs V Snowden, BEd, MEd, FRSA
Revd Dr R L Walton
Revd P Whittaker, BA
G Wilson, CertEd

Staff:

Headmaster: **J A Lockwood**, MA

Deputy Head (*External Relations*): D N Wood, BA
Deputy Head (*Academic*): E J Wright, BSc
Deputy Head (*Pastoral*): A M Cadman, BA
Assistant Head (*Boarding and Compliance*): S P Vernon
Assistant Head (*Curriculum*): Mrs E Ainscoe
Assistant Head (*Organisation*): K D Eaglestone
Assistant Head (*Pupil Welfare*): Mrs F L Hughes
Assistant Head (*Teaching and Learning*): Mrs D L Shoesmith-Evans
Chaplain: Revd D H Bonny, BA, BD
Clerk to the Governors & Finance Director: D Ainsworth, BA, ACA
Operations Director: Mrs V Bates, ACA

* *Head of Department*
† *Head of House*

Mrs E Ainscoe, MA (*Biology*)
Miss F Alimundo, BSc (*Geography*)
J Allison, BA (**Design Technology, †Vinter*)
S Archdale (*Speech and Drama*)
Miss A Barron, BA (*German*)
E Bean, BSc (**Physics*)
A Cadman, BA (*PE*)
J Carter, BA (**History, RE*)
Mrs P N Charlton, MA (*Art & Design*)
J C Cockshott, CertEd (*Design Technology*)
Miss E Corson, BA (*Modern Foreign Languages*)
A N Crawford, BA, ARCO (*Music, Mathematics,*
    †Findlay)
Miss C Couper, BA (**Drama and Theatre Studies*)
Mrs C J Couzens, BA (*PE and Games*)
Mrs K Curtis, BSc (*PE and Games*)
T Davis, BA (**Chemistry*)
S Dillon, BA (*Mathematics*)
K Eaglestone, BSc (*Mathematics*)
Mrs J L Edger, BSc (*Physics*)
Mrs E Farley, BA (*English & Media Studies*)
Mrs H Fisher, MA (**Psychology*)
Miss L Follos, BA (*Design Technology*)
R I Frost, BEd (**PE and Games*)
Mrs C Gibson, BA (*Business Studies and Economics,*
    †Towlson)
Mrs K L Goodwin-Bates, MA (*English & Media Studies*)
C K Henderson, BSc (*Chemistry, Biology, †Southerns*)
D Hole, BSc (*Chemistry*)
Mrs A Howard, BA (*PSE, Physics*)
E R Howard, BA, BEd (**Sport*)
Mrs F L Hughes, BEd (*French*)
Miss L Hughes, BA (*English*)
A Jarvis, BA (*Modern Languages*)
Miss C D Jemmett, BA (*English*)
A Jennings, BA (**Religious Studies*)
Mrs K Jennings, BEd (**PE*)
R Johnson, BA (*English & Media Studies*)
Mrs A Kerr, BSc (*Mathematics*)
P Lambert, BA (*Modern Foreign Languages*)
Miss E Landy, BSc (*Chemistry, Biology*)
O Mantle, BA (*IT, *Business Studies and Economics,*
    †Atkinson)
Mrs H Mitchell, BA (**Modern Foreign Languages*)
P J Moffat, BA (*Geography*)
Miss B Monk, BA (**ESOL, *Learning Support*)
M F Munday, BA (*Geography*)
Mrs C Nott, MA (**Mathematics*)
Miss L Oakley, BA (**English*)
Miss C Pearce, BA (*PE and Games, Geography*)
A J Pickles, BA (**Art & Design*)
Mrs H Priestley (*Drama and Dance*)
Mrs L Richardson, BSc (**Biology*)
J B Robb, BA (**Religious Studies*)
Miss J Russell, BA (*IT*)
Mrs R Sharpe, BA (*English and Media Studies*)
Mrs D L Shoesmith-Evans, BA (**Humanities*)
Mrs L Smith, BA (*Modern Foreign Languages*)
Miss H Spiller, BA (*Art*)
C Softley, BA (*PE*)
D Sugden, BSc (*Mathematics*)
A Sweeney, BA (*History, †Stephenson*)
J P A Tedd, MA (**Music*)
Mrs R Vernon, BA (*PE*)
S Vernon, BA (*PE*)
Mrs R Warner, MA (*Politics, History*)
Mrs P L Watson, MA (*Business Studies, IT*)
Mrs R Wickens, BA (**Geography*)
Mrs L Watmough, BA (*Business Studies*)
G Williams, BSc (**Science*)
D N Wood, BA (*English and Media Studies*)

E Wright, BSc (*Mathematics*)

Headmaster's Secretary: Mrs T Gilks
Registrar: Mrs J Amos

Brontë House
Headmaster: S Dunn, BEd
Deputy Head: Mrs S Chatterton, BEd
Director of Studies: Mrs N Woodman, MPhil
KS1 Coordinator: Mrs H J Simpson, BA
Foundation Stage Coordinator: Mrs A Hinchliffe, BA

Worth School

**Paddockhurst Road, Turners Hill, West Sussex
RH10 4SD**

Tel: 01342 710200
Fax: 01342 710230
email: admissions@worth.org.uk
website: www.worthschool.org.uk
Twitter: @worthschool
Facebook: @worthschool
LinkedIn: /worth-school

Worth is a Catholic Benedictine boarding and day school for boys and girls aged 11–18. It is a truly distinctive school, known for its strong community values, friendly atmosphere and the excellence of its all-round education. The School has been under the leadership of Mr Stuart McPherson (formerly at Eton College) since September 2015 and in the Head Master's words is: "a place where we seek to uncover and ignite children's passions and talents. The path a life takes often begins at school, and this is why we do not just provide education, we offer learning with heart and soul, and this gives Worth a difference of kind that sets us apart."

This magnificent school is in the heart of the Sussex countryside, about halfway between London and Brighton, and less than 15 minutes from Gatwick airport. We are ideally placed to allow students to sample some of the cultural highlights that Britain has to offer, while providing a beautiful environment in which to learn.

In January 2011 we had a full Ofsted inspection on provision for Boarders at Worth. The school was found to be 'Outstanding' and no recommendations were made. In the words of one pupil quoted by Ofsted, "This school grows happy pupils, organically".

The school offers a broad curriculum, where students can opt for the International Baccalaureate Diploma or A Levels. The School has offered the IB since 2002 and a pre-IB course was introduced for non-UK students in Year 11 in 2015. Examination results are excellent and pupils enter the best universities in the UK and abroad, including Oxford, Cambridge, Russell Group universities and Ivy League institutions.

The wider curriculum is rich and varied with a huge range of activities, societies, lectures and trips from which to choose. There is also a lively sporting programme which has produced students of national and county standard, and the school's reputation for performing arts is outstanding.

History. Worth School is situated in the midst of the beautiful Worth Abbey estate where a monastery was founded in 1933 by a group of monks from the Benedictine community at Downside in Somerset. The monks bought a large country house called Paddockhurst and its 500-acre estate situated on a ridge of the Sussex Weald which had formerly been the property of the first Lord Cowdray and opened a prep school for boys. In 1957, the monastery became independent and Worth admitted the first boys to its own senior school in 1959.

Worth welcomed girls into Years 7 and 9 in September 2010. They joined other girls in an already thriving co-educational Sixth Form, and the School has been fully co-educational since 2012 with girls integrated into all aspects of school life.

Courses of study. At GCSE level, students usually take ten subjects. The compulsory core is: English, Mathematics, Sciences, French or Spanish or German (plus PE and SMSC). Two or three options are chosen from: Art, Drama, Economics, Classical Civilisation, French or Spanish or German as a second language, Geography, History, ICT, Latin, Music and Photography. Tuition is available (for an additional fee) in Greek, Italian and Chinese to GCSE and A Level.

There is a wide choice of subjects at A Level: Art, Biology, Business Studies, Chemistry, Drama, Economics, English, French, Geography, German, History, ICT, Maths and Further Maths, Music, Music Technology, Physics, Physical Education, Photography, Politics, Psychology and Spanish. There is also the opportunity to take the Extended Project Qualification (EPQ).

Alternatively, Sixth Form students may study the International Baccalaureate. This involves the study of six subjects, three at Higher Level and three at Standard Level. Students study one subject from each of the following groups:

Group 1: English, German, Italian

Group 2: English, French, German, Greek, Italian (ab initio), Latin, Spanish (also ab initio)

Group 3: Economics, Geography, History, Philosophy, Psychology

Group 4: Biology, Physics

Group 5: Mathematics (HL), Mathematics (SL), Mathematical Studies (SL)

Group 6: Music, Theatre Arts, Visual Arts, Chemistry, French, History, Economics, Greek

Sixth Form students may also choose to study for Oxbridge entrance and a number gain places at either Oxford or Cambridge.

A Benedictine school. Worth believes that each person is on a spiritual journey and that the school should support them wherever they are on that journey, and try to encourage a faith which will sustain pupils in later life. Over half of the 575 students at Worth are from Roman Catholic families, and there are a significant number of Christians from other denominations. Equal members of the community in every way, non-Catholic pupils have no difficulty integrating in the school and bring a different perspective which is most welcome. The School Chaplaincy team includes a part-time Anglican Chaplain, as well as Catholic Chaplains and lay members. Everyone is expected to subscribe to the School's Benedictine values which include Hospitality, Service, Worship and Community amongst others.

There are prayers each day in Houses, whole school worship each Thursday and Mass every Sunday for those boarding over the weekend and for local families.

Pastoral Care. Care of each student is of central importance throughout the School, as evidenced by our 'Outstanding' Ofsted grading for Boarder provision. Each pupil is a member of a House and has a personal tutor who monitors work progress and assists the Housemaster/Housemistress with overall care. The House support structure also includes a Chaplain and, for boarding houses, a matron. There is a counsellor who is available should pupils need him. The Benedictine tradition of community life underpins everything. Many staff families live on-site and parents are welcomed as integral to the school. There are regular points of contact, with parent-teacher consultations, meetings, social events and active support from the Friends of Worth (the parents' association).

Sport. Worth loves its sports. The main sports are: rugby, football, hockey, netball, cricket, tennis and athletics. Other sports played at competitive level include fencing, squash, golf and basketball and sports are also available through school clubs and activities (see below). There is a floodlit Astropitch, an eight-hole golf course, squash courts, tennis courts, fencing salle, dance studio and fitness suite. The school also makes use of the excellent athletics facility and 50m swimming pool at the new multi-sports centre nearby.

Performing Arts. Music is important at Worth. There is a flourishing choir that is involved in tours and recordings as well as regular appearances in the Abbey Church. Parents, local friends and students join the Choral Society for at least two concerts each year (performing such works as Requiems by Fauré and Duruflé). The School orchestra performs regularly, as does the Jazz Band. The annual House Music, Battle of the Bands and Worth Unplugged competitions provide all pupils with an opportunity to perform and encourage an interest in music.

Drama also flourishes with regular productions at all levels and the standard of performance is exceptional. There are three major productions a year, taking place in the purpose-built Performing Arts Centre which comprises a 250-seater theatre, box office, drama office and workshop, dressing rooms, recording studio, a sound-proofed 'rock room', rehearsal rooms, a recital room and music classrooms.

Extracurricular activity. On Wednesday afternoons every pupil participates in one or more activities, ranging from Age Concern and photography to sailing, clay pigeon shooting, and polo. Worth is also a centre of excellence for The Duke of Edinburgh's Award scheme. There are lectures by external speakers and a wide array of trips, visits and exchanges both at home and abroad.

Continuous investment. Worth is part way through a development programme as part of its vision for the next 10 years. The demolition of the Old Rutherford building has created space and light at the heart of the campus. A second girls' day House has opened, the House for Years 7 and 8 is now co-ed, there are extra classrooms, a state-of-the-art fitness suite and a magnificent art facility, building and gallery. There is a new chaplaincy with drop-in facilities in a central location which is proving highly popular.

The most striking and important 'new' building since 1933 is the modern Abbey Church which underwent an extensive refurbishment during 2010–11. It continues to be an inspiring place of prayer and retreat as well as an iconic building in its own right.

Admissions Policy. Entry at 11+: Entrance tests in English, Maths and Non-Verbal Reasoning are held in January each year. Offers are based on test results, a report from the student's current school and an interview with the Head Master. Annual promotion is subject to the pupil having shown satisfactory academic performance as determined by the Head Master, and a good disciplinary record.

Entry at 13+: Entrance tests in English, Maths and Non-Verbal Reasoning are held in January each year. Worth now also offers the entrance process one year earlier for those seeking entry into Year 9. Offers are based on test results, a report from the student's current school and an interview with the Head Master. Common Entrance examination results will be used for setting purposes only.

Entry at 16+: Entrance into the Sixth Form depends on the student's GCSE results or equivalent, an interview with the Head Master and a satisfactory reference from their current school. The normal requirement for students entering the Sixth Form at Worth is six GCSE passes at grades A to C, with at least three at grade B or above.

For further information on Admissions please contact the Registrar on 01342 710231.

Scholarships. Scholarships at Worth are highly prestigious awards available to students demonstrating outstanding talent and ability in the spheres of Academic Study, Art, Drama, Music or Sport.

Scholars are offered exciting programmes and opportunities to develop their skills to the maximum and are also expected to act as role models, promoting their area of excellence and encouraging others to follow their example. All scholarships are won in open competition and are awarded solely on merit. Candidates must be registered with the School prior to entering the scholarship process and applications for bursaries should be made at the same time as applications for scholarships.

For all types of scholarships, awards can range in value and a candidate may also hold one or more awards, so that Academic, Art, Drama, Music or Sport awards may be held concurrently, but the maximum fee remission that can be held through scholarships is 40%. Additionally, at the Head Master's discretion, exceptional awards with a fee concession which may be greater than 40% can be made where, during the assessment process, we identify exceptional potential or need. Tenure of any award depends upon continued satisfactory progress. The School reserves the right to vary the number of awards according to the strength of applications. The level of fee concession provided can be augmented by bursary support which is subject to means assessment.

St Benedict's Scholarships enable local Catholic children of real ability, whose parents' financial circumstances would normally preclude attendance at Worth, to benefit from the opportunities offered by the school. One day place is available for Year 7 and two day places for Year 12 are available each year.

For further information on scholarships and bursaries, please see the School website.

Fees per term (2016–2017). Years 9–13: Boarding £10,380, Day £7,350; Years 7 & 8: Boarding £6,630, Day £4,990, Flexi (boys only) £6,330.

Friends of Worth. The parents of children at Worth run their own programme of social events to which all parents are invited. Typical events are coffee mornings, drinks receptions and a bi-annual ball.

Worth Society. All Worthians are entitled to join the alumni society. Contact Mary Lou Burge at worthsociety.org.uk.

Charitable status. Worth School is a Registered Charity, number 1093914. Its aims and objectives are to promote religion and education.

The Abbot's Board of Governors comprises both monks and laity:
President: The Rt Revd Dom Luke Jolly, BA
Chairman: Mrs Alda Andreotti, FCILT
The Revd Dom Mark Barrett, MA, PhD
Mr David Buxton, BA, MTh, MA
Mr Benedict Elwes, BSc
Mr Jeremy Fletcher, BA
Mrs Henrietta Fudakowski, BA
Mr Peter Green, Cert RE, MA
Dom David Jarmy, Cert Theol, PGCE
Mr Gordon Moore, BA Econ, CA
Mrs Fiona Newton, BA, PGCE
Mrs Helen Parry, BSc, FCIS
Mr Tim Pethybridge, MA
Dr Ralph Townsend, MA

Head Master: Mr Stuart McPherson, MA

Second Master: Mr André Gushurst-Moore, MA
Deputy Head (Academic): Mr Simon Fisher, BA
Deputy Head (External): Mr Gordon Pearce, MA
Deputy Head (Pastoral): Mrs Maria Young, BA, MA
Assistant Head (Welfare)/Biology: Mrs Louise Chamberlain, BSc
Assistant Head (Co-Curricular): Mr Julian Williams, BSc, MA, Dip TESL

Senior School Chaplain: Dom Peter Williams
Director of Finance and Operations: Mr Robin Burdell, FCMA
Director of Development: Mr Edward Schneider, FRSA, Fidpe

Teaching Staff:
* Head of Department/Subject

Mr Paul Ambridge, BA (Physics, Austin & Rutherford Year 7&8 Housemaster)
Mrs Frances Baily, MSc (*Physics)
Miss Jo Barnes (Games & Physical Education)
Mrs Andrea Beadle, BA, MA (German Assistant)
Mr Jonathan Bindloss, BA (*Christian Theology and Philosophy, Theory of Knowledge)
Mr Stuart Blackhurst, HND (Head of Digital Strategy)
Mr John Brake (Games & Physical Education)
Mr Andrew Brinkley, MA (History)
Ms Amanda Brookfield, BA, MA (Head of Sixth Form, English)
Mrs Caroline A Brown, BA, MA (Religious Studies)
Mr Nathan Brown, Dip EFL, BA (English, SMSC Coordinator)
Mrs Sophie Bruton, BA (French)
Mrs Caroline Burton, MSC (Biology)
Mr David Burton, BEd (Director of Sport)
Mrs Lucinda Button, BA (Art & Design)
Mr Raj Chaudhuri, BCom, ECB Level 4 (Master in charge of Cricket)
Mrs Minakshi Chaudhuri, BA (Activities Manager)
Mrs Cheryl Cheeseman, RCN, Dip Paeds (Head Nurse, Medical Department)
Mr Philip Chorley, MA (*English)
Dr Stephanie Corlett, PhD (Physics)
Mr William Crénel, LLCE (French)
Miss Ainhoa Cruces, BA (Spanish)
Mr Damian Cummins, BA (Physical Education, Rutherford Housemaster)
Mr Simeon Dann, BA, MA (Religious Studies)
Mrs Jayne Dempster, BSc (*Mathematics)
Mr Stephen Doerr, BA (Learning Support, Mathematics)
Mr Matthew Doggett, MA, MSci (Mathematics, Science)
Mr Clement Donegan, BSc, MA (Chemistry, Butler Housemaster)
Mr Sebastien Donjon, BSc (Mathematics, Timetable)
Mr Jeremy Dowling, BEd (Mathematics)
Mrs Ursula Evans, BA (Spanish Language Assistant)
Mr John Everest, BA (Photography)
Mr Simon Faulkner, BA (Head of Hockey, Games & Physical Education)
Mrs Sarah Flint, BA (*French)
Mr Jonathan Fry, BA (Economics, Farwell Housemaster)
Mrs Andrea Fullalove, BA (Learning Support, St Catherine's Housemistress)
Mrs Theresa Gartland-Jones, MA (Art & Design)
Ms Joanne Geraghty, MA (*Spanish,)
Mr Kevan Goddard, BA (Mathematics)
Mr Benjamin Gray, MA, BSc (Religious Studies)
Mrs Joanna Gray, BA (Assistant Director of Music)
Dr Bruna Gushurst-Moore, BA, MSt, PhD (English, St Anne's Housemistress)
Mrs Joanna Hall-Palmer, BSc (Games & Physical Education)
Mr Edward Hall, BSc (Economics & Politics)
Mrs Karolina Hall, BA (English as an Additional Language)
Miss Juley Hudson, BA, MA (*Art)
Mrs Siobhan Isaacs, BA (Games & Physical Education)
Miss Diana Janus, MRSC, CChem (Chemistry)
Mrs Mia Kazi-Fornari, BSc, BA (Mathematics)
Ms Melanie Kendry, MA (English)

Mrs Emma Kenyon, BA (*French*)
Mrs Andrea Kirpalani, BSc (**Science*)
Mrs Kerrie-Anne Langendoen, BSc (*Learning Support*)
Mrs Catherine Latham, BSc, MSc (*Head of Learning Support and SENCO*)
Mr Andrew Lavis, BA (**Geography*)
Mrs Natalie Lynch, BA (*Director of Drama*)
Mr Mark Macdonald, BSc (*Geography, Chapman Housemaster*)
Mr David Marks, MA, BA (*English as an Additional Language*)
Mr Dominic Marshall, BA (*Religious Studies*)
Mr Mike Matthews, BA (*Music, St Bede's Housemaster*)
Mrs Gemma McCabe, BSc (*Mathematics*)
Mr Alan Mitchell, BSc (*Games & Physical Education*)
Mr Bruce Morrison, BEd (*Games & Physical Education*)
Mr Robin Moss, BSc (*Chemistry & Scicence*)
Mr Michael Oakley, BA, MA, MMus (*Director of Music*)
Mr Christopher Offler, BSc (*Geography*)
Mr Andrew Olle (*Games & Physical Education*)
Mr Andrew Oxley, BSc (*Science*)
Mr James Phillips, BA (*Head of Academic ICT*)
Mr Richard Phillips, BSc (**Economics and Business Studies*)
Mr Tom Phillips, BA, MA (**History & Politics*)
Ms Alessandra Pittoni, Laurea in Lingue (*Italian*)
Dr Duncan Pring, MA, PhD (*Economics & Business Studies, Head of Careers*)
Miss Kate Reynolds, BSc (*Biology*)
Ms Linda Rice, BA, MA (*Learning Support*)
Mr Thomas Richardson (*Head of Rugby*)
Mr Liam Richman, BSc (*Mathematics*)
Mr Philip Robinson, MA (*Classics*)
Ms Victoria Sadler, MA (*Geography*)
Dr Peter Scott, MA, PhD (**Biology*)
Mrs Sarah Smith, BA (*English*)
Mrs Rebecca Steinebach, BA (*Modern Languages, St Mary's Housemistress*)
Mr Stefan Steinebach, Staatsexamen (**Modern Languages, Director of IB*)
Mr Guy Teasdale, BEd (*Economics & Business Studies*)
Mr Philip Towler, BA (**Classics*)
Mr Giles Watson, BA (*History, Gervase Housemaster*)
Mrs Samantha Webster, MA (*Religious Studies & Drama*)
Mr James Williams, BSc (*Physics*)
Mrs Naomi Williams, BSc (**Psychology*)

Registrar: Mrs Lucy Garrard
Head Master's Secretary: Mrs Samantha Braund
Medical Officers: Dr R Harvey, Dr S Ferrier
Lead Nurse: Cheryl Cheeseman, SRN, Paediatric Dipl
Nurses:
Jo Doyle, RN
Julia Horner, RN
Lorna Lindo, RN
Helen Paine, RN
Angela Wheatley, RN

Wrekin College

Wellington, Shropshire TF1 3BH

Tel:	Main: 01952 265600	
	Headmaster's Office: 01952 265602	
	Admissions: 01952 265603	
Fax:	01952 415068	

email:	admissions@wrekincollege.com
website:	www.wrekincollege.com
Twitter:	@WrekinCol
Facebook:	/WrekinCollege

Motto: '*Aut vincere aut mori*'

Wrekin College was founded in 1880 by Sir John Bayley and in 1923 became one of the Allied Schools, a group of six independent schools including Canford, Harrogate Ladies' College, Stowe and Westonbirt.

The College is situated in an estate of 100 acres on the outskirts of the market town of Wellington. We pride ourselves on the excellent quality of our staff, as well as the excellent quality of our facilities, and we measure our achievements not only by our examination results, but also by the whole development of individuals within the school. Being a relatively small school, about 400 pupils, the quality of relationships is good and enables a purposeful atmosphere to prevail in which pupils can achieve their potential, both in academic and extra-curricular activities. Our facilities include a purpose-built Theatre, a double Sports Hall, Astroturf and 25m indoor swimming pool, together with all the expected classrooms, ICT facilities and a dedicated Sixth Form Centre. The new, purpose-built Business School will open in 2017 providing a unique combination of teaching and real-life engagement in an office-style setting. Teaching is expert and disciplined. Co-educational since 1975, there are 7 Houses, which cater for both day and boarding pupils, and these include dedicated junior Houses for the 11 to 13 intake. Everyone eats together in a central dining room and a Medical Centre is available to all pupils. The Chapel is central to the school both geographically and in the impact it makes on the ethos of the school.

Admission. Boarders and day pupils are admitted at 11+ or 13+ after passing the Entry Examination or Common Entrance. There is also a Sixth Form entry based on GCSE achievement. Entry into other years is dependant on places being available.

Term of entry. The normal term of entry is the Autumn Term but pupils may be accepted at other times of the academic year in special circumstances.

Academic Matters. The core purpose of the school is teaching and learning to support each child in reaching their academic potential. Wrekin is proud of its strong academic record, based on stimulating intellectual curiosity, providing excellent and inspiring teaching, and making learning exciting. Our guiding principle is to help every child achieve the most they are capable of, to prepare them for the competitive world they will enter, and to give them a lasting sense of the pleasure and value of learning that will enrich their future lives.

Classes are small, typically no more than twenty for the younger pupils and between eight and fifteen at A Level. Our teachers are experienced, expert and approachable, and give a great deal of time to pupils both inside and outside the classroom. Our tutoring system means each pupil has personalised academic support throughout the year. Our Support for Learning staff can help those with additional needs, and our enrichment programme stimulates and stretches our more able students.

Our curriculum is constantly reviewed in the light of changes in educational policy and philosophy, but we are committed to offering our pupils a solid and broad academic foundation. We offer a wide range of subjects for GCSE, AS and A2 exams, and guide pupils in choosing subjects that suit their interests, abilities and future plans. Our Head of Careers advises pupils throughout their time at school, and the Head of Sixth Form offers expert advice on university applications.

Sport. For a small school, our sporting prowess is remarkable. We aim for very high standards in our core sports and a very wide range of options – up to twelve different sports in any term. Our sporting philosophy is based on a pyramid, with elite athletes at the top (including our national level gymnasts, swimmers, athletes and cross-country runners) and minor sports to appeal to all at the base. We believe in excellence but also in participation – sport for all, and for life.

Educating the Whole Person. The outdoors is one of Wrekin's most valuable classrooms. The skills learned and adventures experienced during pupils' participation in the Combined Cadet Force and the Duke of Edinburgh's Award scheme stay with them for life. Both are enthusiastically supported by highly dedicated staff, and the take up among our middle year pupils is impressive. We are very proud that Wrekin's 'completion rate' at all levels of the scheme is substantially above the national average.

What happens on the sports pitch and in the music rooms, the theatre and the art studios is just as important a part of a Wrekin education. The range and quality of activities available to every pupil is outstanding, especially for a school of this size. Our pupils' development and achievements in these areas are supported by wonderful facilities and highly dedicated staff.

Scholarships and Bursaries. *Academic Scholarships* are awarded at our normal entry points of 11, 13 and 16. Candidates should be under 12, under 14 or under 17 on September 1st of the year in which they will enter the school. Age may be taken into account when comparing candidates, so that those who are young for their year are not disadvantaged.

Music and Art/Design Scholarships take place in November (11+/16+) and February (13+). As for all other scholarships, Music and Art Awards will not exceed twenty five per cent of the fees. However, Music Scholarships carry with them a specified amount of free instrumental and/or vocal tuition. Candidates must also satisfy the school's normal academic entry requirements.

Sports Awards: Sports Scholarships may be awarded to candidates with outstanding ability in Sport. Applicants must attend a sports assessment day and satisfy the school's normal academic entry requirements. Candidates should be capable of a very significant contribution to the sporting success of Wrekin College. Typically candidates will have representative success at regional or National level.

Pendle Awards may be offered to all-rounders who have high academic standards and excellence in other areas such as sport, music or art. Those seeking a Pendle Award must sit the academic Scholarship Examination, either at 11+, 13+ or 16+ level and meet scholarship standard in at least one other area.

Bursaries may be awarded on entry and can be awarded in addition to a scholarship. All bursaries are means tested and could in some circumstances cover the whole school fee.

For further information please visit our website www.wrekincollege.com.

Fees per term (2016–2017). First and Second Forms: £4,685 (day); £6,750 (weekly boarding); £8,550 (full boarding). Third-Sixth Forms: £5,675 (day); £7,990 (weekly boarding); £9,930 (full boarding).

Music lessons £22 per 35 minute session; Extra Tuition £22 per 35 minute session.

We offer a 10% discount to serving members of the Armed Forces; to children of Old Wrekinians; and for a second full-time boarder from the same family. When three siblings are enrolled in Wrekin College/The Old Hall School each child attracts a 20% remission in fees.

Old Wrekinian Association. A flourishing Wrekinian Association of over 3,500 members exists to make possible continuous contact between the School and its old pupils, for the benefit of both and to support the ideals and aims of the school. It is expected that pupils will become members of the Old Wrekinian Association when they leave Wrekin.

Charitable status. Wrekin Old Hall Trust Limited is a Registered Charity, number 528417. It exists to provide independent boarding and day co-education in accordance with the Articles of Association of Wrekin College.

Visitor: The Rt Revd The Lord Bishop of Lichfield

Governors:
R J Pearson, BSc (*Chairman*)
R D Bubbers, MA Oxon
A J Dixon, LLB
J A Grant, BSc [OW]
M Halewood, BEng, CEng, MICE, MAPM [OW]
P A T Hunt, BA
V L Hughes-Hines
A B Huxley [OW]
C Jones [OW]
A F Lock, MA Oxon, PGCE
R Mottram
J Richardson, MA Cantab, FRSA
T Shaw, BSc, MRICS [OW]
N A Wilkie, MA Cantab, MSc, FRSA [OW]

[OW] *Old Wrekinian*

Headmaster: T Firth, BA Hons

Senior Deputy Head: Mrs S E Clarke, BA, FRGS

Deputy Head (Teaching and Learning): Mrs A Wright, BSc

Director of Planning: Dr G Roberts, BSc, PhD

Director of External Relations: Mrs A Nicoll

Head of Sixth Form: T Southall, BSc

Chaplain: Revd M Horton, MA Cantab, MA Oxon, CertTh, DipTh

Assistant Staff:
† *Housemaster/mistress*

J Ballard, BSc	†Mrs J D Kotas, BA
Mrs H E Berry, CertEd	K B Livingstone, BA
P J Berry, BA	D McLagan, BA
†A J I Brennan, BA	J Mather, BSc
†H S R Brown, BA	R B Nayman, BA
Miss B Camargo Castillo, FyL	Mrs E M Perry, BSc
	J G Phillips, BA
Mrs F Coffey, BSc	Mrs C A Ritchie-Morgan
†Mrs M Crone, BA	T A Southall, BSc
Dr K Cusack, BSc, MSc, DIC, PhD	P M Stanway, BSc
	Mrs C Thust, BSc
†Mrs K Davies, BSc	P Trahearn, BA
Mrs D von Dongen, BSc	A J Ware, BSc
M Easter, BSc	Mrs M N J Warner, BSc
A Francis-Jones, BSc	Mrs A E Wedge, BSc
J C Frodsham, CertEd, Adv DipEd	Ms G T Whitehead, BA Oxon
Miss A V Gardener, BA	Dr A Whitton, BA, MA, PhD
H R Gray, BSc	
Miss J Harris, BSc	Miss A Williams, BSc
A R Hurd, BSc	†I Williamson, BA
Mrs A Jagger, BA	†D J Winterton, BA
A Knight, BSc	

Support for Learning:
Ms H Ingoldby, BA, TEFL
Mrs J M Lloyd, BSc, MEd, DupELS, AMBDA, TEFL, APC SpLD Patoss, TPC SpLD Patoss
Mrs A H Livingstone, MA, RSA CELTA
Mrs J Panchen, TEFL
Mrs J Roberts, BA, BSc, TEFL
French Assistante: Mrs F Kennedy

Visiting Music Staff:
Miss K Burningham, MA, Dip ABRSM (*Piano & Organ*)
M Buxton (*Piano*)
A Clark (*Piano*)
Ms N J Clifton-Griffith, BMus, PgDip (*Singing*)
Miss S Croxon, BMus (*Brass*)
M M Davy, MA, FRCO, LRAM, ARCM (*Organ*)
C Hickman, BMus (*Trombone & Lower Brass*)
C J Jones, BMus (*Piano, Clarinet and Saxophone*)
L Jones, BA, RNCM (*Violin*)
Miss Y Kagajo, MMus PGDip (*Piano*)
Miss S A Lane, ARCM (*Flute*)
Ms J Magee, MA, GRSM, LRAM, ARCM, ABSM (*Cello*)
T Mvula, BMus (*Singing*)
P Parker (*Guitar*)
G Santry (*Drums*)
Miss C S Sazanova, BMus (*Flute*)
Mrs F Stubbs, MA, GCLM (*Bassoon*)
M Svensson, BMus (*Head of Strings*)
Ms R Theobald (*Piano, Oboe & Singing*)
Miss A Tiffin (*Voice*)

Games:
J Mather (*Head of Boys' Games*)
Mrs C A Ritchie-Morgan (*Head of Girls' Games*)

Sports Coaches:
Mrs K Bennett (*Girls' Games*)
S Blount (*Boys' Games*)
D Clarke (*Swimming*)
G Davies (*Cricket*)
B Gleeson (*Cricket Umpire*)
K Holding (*Fencing*)
S Jenkins (*Basketball*)
R Oliver (*Cricket*)
Mrs R Reilly (*Swimming*)
A C Sammons (*Rugby*)
C J Sheperd (*Cricket*)
G Singh (*Cricket*)
Mrs C Still (*Gymnastics*)
Miss V Woodman (*Netball*)
M de Weymarn (*Cricket Umpire*)

Medical Officers: Dr J Middleton & Dr E Williams

CCF:
SSI & Outward Bound Activities Instructor: RQMS, E J Fanneran, late RA
Secretary OWA: M Joyner, BSc

Bursar: Mrs Y K Thomas, MBA, FCA

Deputy Bursars:
Facilities: B C Crone
Operations: P Rowles

Admissions Registrar: Ms R Curel
Headmaster's Personal Assistant: Mrs P Bottomley

Wycliffe College

Bath Road, Stonehouse, Gloucestershire GL10 2JQ

Tel:	01453 822432
Fax:	01453 827634
email:	senior@wycliffe.co.uk
website:	www.wycliffe.co.uk
Twitter:	@WycliffeCollege
Facebook:	@WycliffeCollege
LinkedIn:	/wycliffe-college

The School was founded in 1882 by G W Sibly and placed on a permanent foundation under a Council of Governors in 1931.

Location. Wycliffe College is a thriving day and boarding school set in a stunning 54-acre campus for over 719 girls and boys, including around 300 boarders across the Prep and Senior Schools. The elegant main house is surrounded by first-class teaching facilities, extensive sports pitches, state-of-the-art boarding accommodation and extensive social areas such as a café available for all pupils at the senior school.

The Preparatory School (under its own Headmaster) is on a separate, adjacent campus with extensive facilities including a university-style classroom block for Years 7 and 8 which features high-tech teaching resources and spacious classrooms.

Conveniently located in the South West of England midway between the famous cities of Bath and Cheltenham, Wycliffe is within easy reach of international airports such as Heathrow, Bristol and Birmingham as well as major road and rail connections. The school is under two hours from London by car (M4 motorway) or train (direct line to the local station).

Organisation. Senior School 13–18: 218 Boys, 182 Girls, 227 Boarders, Sixth Form 160. Class sizes vary from 3–15 pupils. Preparatory School 2–13: 162 Boys, 157 Girls.

Admission. Pupils are admitted at key entry points following interview and assessment, via CAT testing or Scholarship examinations at 13+ and via GCSE or Scholarship examinations into the Sixth Form. Application should be made to the Head who is whole-hearted in his desire for all pupils to achieve their full potential in every sphere of education and undertakes to be readily available to parents.

Religion. Christian interdenominational, all faiths welcome. Confirmation classes, Christian Fellowship group and daily worship in keeping with this generation are an integral part of College life.

Houses. Wycliffe's House system promotes a strong sense of community, building staunch friendships and promoting healthy competition, and ensuring high levels of personal and pastoral care. There are seven Houses with dedicated study areas for day pupils and three Sixth Form Halls of Residence, each with study-bedrooms and en-suite facilities. All boarding houses are refurbished on a rolling programme. Main meals are taken in Wycliffe Hall. In September 2017, we will be opening a brand new multimillion pound Boarding House with state-of-the-art boarding facilities and the latest security and safety systems.

Tutors. Each pupil has a House-based tutor in the Lower School and a specialist tutor in the Sixth Form. Supported by a Housemaster/Housemistress, Tutor, Chaplain and Head of Year, each pupil gains maximum advantage towards personal fulfilment in a community noted for its friendly and caring support.

Medical Centre. 24-hour attendance is provided by qualified staff in a state-of-the-art Centre. The Health Centre is nearby. Special dietary requirements for health or faith are met by first-class catering facilities.

One Year GCSE programme/Pre-A Level Development Year. Some international pupils choose to join the Development Year (DY) at Wycliffe before embarking on the full two year A Level programme. This is because they wish to improve their English and experience a range of subjects while living and working in a traditional British boarding school.

DY pupils study a broad range of subjects including English, Maths and the Sciences and many can take up to six GCSEs as well as a range of ESOL exams. During the year they also receive an introduction to some A Level subjects, in preparation for Sixth Form. The DY students are part of all the house, sports, and social activities in which they can build friendships and improve their language skills.

Included in the timetable, students benefit from expert tuition in English as a Second Language.

A Levels. As a general rule students choose four subjects to study in the Lower Sixth or one of two available BTEC courses. Most students then continue to study three subjects in the second year to A2 Level. Apart from the traditional subjects, the following are also on offer to A2 Level: Art and Design, Design and Technology, Japanese, Psychology, Business Studies, Film Studies, Government and Politics, Computer Science, Theatre Studies, Music Technology, Sociology and Physical Education to name but a few of the subjects on offer.

GCSEs are usually taken three years after 13+ entry. The School offers a wide range of subjects supported by outstanding tutorial practices. Four modern languages and four sciences are among those on offer to students who may make a free choice at age 14.

Scholarships and Bursaries. Thanks to the generosity of Trustees, Old Wycliffians and Friends of Wycliffe, awards are available offering a reduction of up to 40% of the fees. These may be supplemented in cases of financial need up to a maximum of 90%.

For 13+ entry a candidate must be under 14 on 1 September of year of entry and sit the examination in the Spring Term.

For 16+ entry, examinations are held in the Autumn prior to arrival or by arrangement.

At other ages, applications to be made to the Registrar.

Awards are made to candidates with academic talent or potential and also specifically in music, art, design technology, drama and excellence in sports (including cricket, rugby, football, girls' hockey, netball and squash).

Special awards are also available to (a) those with all round merit, (b) children of serving members of the Services school fees fixed at CEA + 10% of school fees, (c) vegetarians.

Physical Education. Our sports and physical education programme gives opportunities to develop talents and skills and to enjoy sport as a team member, individual or for recreation. We recognise and support gifted sports players and have the facilities to offer a wide range of sports such as rowing, rugby, hockey, fencing, football, netball, squash, badminton, basketball, swimming, cricket, tennis, athletics, health and fitness, yoga, shooting, and cross country.

Training for Service is available via the Combined Cadet Force, Duke of Edinburgh's Award Scheme, Leadership Courses, and the Wycliffe Charitable Organisation.

International Travel is regularly organised for varied groups; trips can enhance academic study, provide exchanges with our sister schools in America and Japan, be part of the Comenius partnership with schools in Europe or specific sporting or musical tours. Pupil trips and exchanges are arranged for those studying foreign languages.

School Societies. Among those available are Cookery, Chamber Choir, Music, Christian Union, Creative Writing, Photography, Drama Workshops, Theatre Trips, Voluntary Work, Philosophy, Language, Debating, Art, Computing, Scrabble, Squash, Shooting, Choral, Instrumental Music, First Aid, Investment Club, Bee Club, Sewing, Student Magazine, UKMT, MOOC and Equestrian.

Sunday Specials. Brunch is a highlight of Sunday morning and a variety of activities, both at the College and locally, are organised for boarders.

Music. A purpose-built music school including a dedicated Music Technology suite with enthusiastic staff enables high standards to be achieved. Music is taken at GCSE and A Level with Music Technology also offered at A Level; several pupils each year continue their music studies at the Conservatoires and universities. There are two choirs, numerous large ensembles and bespoke chamber ensembles developing a high level of performance in all styles of music. Associated Board Examinations are taken every term as well as Trinity and Rock school exams. The School hosts professional concerts and dramatic productions annually as well as the School's own artistic output.

Careers Guidance forms a vital department which is recognised as a centre of excellence. The College has its own experienced Careers Manager who is available to advise and support students throughout the school day. The Careers Library is well-equipped with information on careers and entrance to Higher Education. The school offers SAT preparation for American Universities.

Teacher Training. Wycliffe has been selected as a training centre for teachers, reflecting the high esteem in which the College is held.

Fees per term (2016–2017). Senior School: Boarders £10,180, new Sixth Form entrants £10,595, Development Year £11,385; Day pupils £5,810–£6,330 (Lunch £325). Preparatory School: Boarders £6,030–£8,500, Foundation Year £8,500, Residential Short English Course £725 per week; Day pupils: £2,200–£4,470 (Lunch £240).

It is the College's aim to keep extras to a minimum but may include expeditions, exam fees and certain Society subscriptions.

Alumni. Our thriving community supports OWs and parents through open communication, engagement and networking. We hold multiple events throughout the year from global drinks receptions to local dinner dances, sports events, plays and recitals.

For more information please use the following ways to make contact:

Facebook: https://www.facebook.com/WycliffeCollegeTWS
Website: http://www.wycliffe.co.uk/the-wycliffian-society
OW Registrar: Tel 01453 820439
Email: TWS@wycliffe.co.uk

Charitable status. Wycliffe College Incorporated is a Registered Charity, number 311714. It exists to provide education for boys and girls.

Council of Governors:

President: S P Etheridge, MBE, TD, JP, MBA, FIFP, CFP, FCII, ACIArb

Chair of Governors: Brigadier {Retd} R J Bacon, MBA, Chartered FCIPD, FCMI, CMILT

Vice Presidents:
Major General G B Fawcus CB, MA, MInstRE
Air Chief Marshal Sir Michael Graydon, GCB, CBE, FRAeS

Vice Chair: Mrs S J Lacey, MEng, BA

S K Collingridge, BA Hons, LLB
Mrs C Duckworth, MA
W R Garrard, MBA, BSc Hons
N J Hughes
S F Lloyd, BSc Hons, Est Man, MRICS
I H Paling, BMet, MMet
Mrs A L Palk, MBE, BA Hons
J C H Pritchard, DipM
Group Captain {Retd} Dr G E Reid, MB ChB, FRCPsych, RAF
J Slater, FRICS
J R E Williams, FCA

Financial Director and Company Secretary: A C Golding, ACA

Head: N J Gregory, BA, MEd

Senior Deputy Head: P Woolley, BA, PGCE (*Politics*)
Deputy Head (Academic): S V Dunne, BA, PGDipJ, PGCE (*Media Studies*)
Deputy Head (Pastoral): Mrs E A Buckley, BSc, PGCE (*Physical Education*)

Head of Sixth Form, Head of Higher Education and Careers: M J Archer, MA (*Chemistry*)
Head of Lower School: Mrs S V Collinson, BA, PGCE (*Business Studies*)
Director of ICT: B Ittyavirah, BSc, MSc, PGCE (*ICT*)
Chaplain: The Reverend J M McHale, BTh, BA, PGCE (*RS*)

House Staff:
Collingwood House: Mr K Patrick, BA Hons, PGCE (*History*)
Haywardsend: Mrs L Nicholls, BA, PGCE (*Geography*)
Haywardsfield: I Russell, BSc, PGCE (*Mathematics*)
Ivy Grove: Mrs E J Lunch, BSc, PGCE (*Mathematics*)
Lampeter House: Mrs L Knighton-Callister, BSc, PGCE (*Head of Applied Science and Coordinator of EPQ*)
Loosley Halls: T Larkman (*Geography*)
Robinson House: J S Mace, BSc, PGCE (*Head of Biology*)
Ward's House: A M Golightly, BA, MA, PGCE (*Head of Drama*)

Teaching Staff:
Mrs A Attwell (*English*)
R O Beamish, BA, PGCE (*Head of Media & Film Studies*)
J A S Beltrami, BA, PGCE (*Mathematics*)
Mrs M Bray (*Italian & Spanish*)
G C Brown, BSc, PGSE (*Computer Science*)
Miss C E Browne, BA, PGCE (*English*)
Mrs N Bryant (*Chemistry*)
J P Clements, BEng, PGCE (*Curriculum Leader Science and Head of Physics*)
Mrs A K Cobbs, BA, PGCE (*Head of Mathematics*)
G P Constable, BA, QTS (*Business Studies & Economics*)
Mrs C R L Conway, BA, MA, QTS (*History*)
Mrs B Cook, BA, PGCE (*ICT & Coaching, Mentoring Coordinator*)
S Costello (*Head of Psychology and Sociology*)
Mrs J Cottrell, BA, PGCE (*SEN*)
E M Crownshaw, BA, PGCE (*Physics*)
W H Day-Lewis, BA DiELTA, PGCE (*Head of Development Year*)
Mrs S M Dudley, BSc, PGCE (*Head of Girls' Games*)
Miss K F Elliott, BA, PGCE (*Head of ESOL*)
A J Finebaum, BEng, PGCE (*Mathematics*)
G G Flower, Cert Higher Ed Sports Coaching (*Head of Rowing*)
Mrs S Flye, BSc, PGCE (*Mathematics*)
B W Gannon, BSc, Level 3 Cert Cricket Coaching QCF (*Sport*)
S R Garley, BAF (*Fencing Coach and CCF*)
Mrs N Golightly, BEd (*Drama*)
Miss N Green, BA, PGCE (*Head of Art & Design*)
Ms L Goodwin (*International Universities Coordinator*)
A J J Hamilton (*Head of Physical Education*)
C J Hancock, BA, PGCE (*Head of RS*)
Mrs M Hardwick, MA, PGCE (*French & Spanish*)
J C Harford, Level 3 Coach Award Squash (*Director of Squash*)
T A Hayes, BA Hons, PGCE (*Design & Technology*)
W H Helsby, BA, RSA DipTEFL, PGCE (*ESOL*)
Mrs R Honeywill, BA, Cert Ed (*French & German*)
S J Hubbard, BA (*Art & Design*)
Mrs E J Hughes, BSc, PGCE (*Mathematics*)
W James (*Business Studies & Economics*)
M J Kimber, New Zealand Coaching Cert, ECB Level 1, RFU Levels I & II (*Head of Boys' Games*)
Ms S Knight, MChem, PGCE (*Chemistry*)
Mrs E S Lambert, BA, PGCE (*English*)
D Lester, BA Hons, MEd Applied Linguistics (*French Assistant*)
W Luecke (*Business Studies & Economics*)
J Lunch, BSc Hons, PGCE (*Head of Boys Training*)

Miss S L Madden, BA Hons, PGCE (*English*)
M Martinez, PGCE (*Spanish*)
Mrs C Moran, BA, Celta (*ESOL*)
Ms K Morgan, DipTEFLA (*ESOL*)
J S Murphy, BA (*Media Studies*)
A C Naish, BSc, PGCE (*Director of Sport*)
Mrs L Newton, BA, PGCE (*Head of Business Studies & Economics*)
Miss A P Norman-Walker (*Art & Design*)
J J O'Sullivan, PGCE (*Economics*)
R Pender, BSc, PGCE (*Head of Geography*)
Mrs H S Phelps, BA, BSc, MSc (*Psychology and Sociology*)
Mrs V Ralph, BSc, PGCE (*Biology & Chemistry*)
Miss S K Revie, BA, PGCE (*Head of Japanese*)
Dr R K Rose, MA, MSc, PhD, PGCE (*Head of Chemistry*)
Lt Col P N Rothwell (*OC CCF*)
Mrs G L Russell, BA, PGCE (*Director of Music*)
Mrs N J H Scott, BA, PGCE (*Head of History*)
P D Scott, MBioChem, PGCE (*Mathematics*)
Miss H Sherwood, Level 2 Cert Hockey Coaching QCF, Level 1 Cert Teaching Swimming (*Sport*)
Mrs N Stephens-Mikesch, PGCE (*Head of German*)
Dr J E Sullivan, BA, MA, PhD, PGCE (*English*)
Mrs S Suzui, BEd (*Head of Japanese*)
Mrs G Tavner, BA, PGCE (*English*)
J E Thomas, BSc, PGCE (*Mathematics*)
Mrs S L Trainor, HDipEd, PGCE (*Biology*)
W A Weaver, BMus, MMus, PGDE (*Assistant Director of Music*)
G J Wheeler, BEd (*Head of Design & Technology*)
Mrs J A White, BSc Hons, PG Dip SpLD, APC 0414/361, PG Cert Boarding Mgt, PG RSA DELTA (*Head of Learning Support & SEND*)
I L Williams, BSc, PGCE (*Science*)
Miss J Wilson, BA, PGCE (*English*)
Mrs L Wisbey, BA, PGCE (*Head of Spanish*)
Mrs L A Wong, BSc, RSA Dip TEFLA, PGCE (*ESOL*)
Ms L E Wood (*ESOL*)
Miss H Woodham (*School Staff Instructor/CCF*)
Mrs R A S Wordsworth, BA (*Art & Design*)
Mrs K Worsdell, BA Hons, PGCE (*English*)
Mrs J Wright, BA, PGCE (*PE, Games & Head of BTEC*)
Dr D York (*Physics*)

Teaching Support Staff:
R Feather, BA, PGCE (*Data & Exams Manager*)
Mrs S A Hodgkins (*Librarian*)
Mrs M Holden (*Careers Education Manager*)

Visiting Music Staff:
Mrs S Blewett, FTCL, LTCL, LWCMD (*Flute*)
Mr M Bucher, Dip Perc (*Percussion*)
Mrs M Cope, GMus, LTCL, Cert ABRSM (*Piano*)
Mr I Dollins, BMus, ARCM (*Voice & Piano*)
Mrs V Green, GRSM, ARCM, LRAM (*Piano & Double Bass*)
Mr N Nash (*Saxophone & Clarinet*)
Miss J Orsman, GBSM (*Violin & Viola*)
Mr G Rees, Dip Trpt (*Brass*)
Mr P Reynolds, BA Hons (*Guitar*)
Mr D Thompson, MA, BA Hons (*Piano*)
Mrs L Thompson, BMus Hons, ARCM, CertEd (*Cello*)

Medical Officers and Staff:
Mrs J Lewis (*School Nurse*)
Mrs P Norman (*School Nurse*)

Administration:
Director of Operations: Mrs A Bromley
Director of Marketing and Admissions: Mrs T Nichols
HR Manager: Mrs W Jenkins

Wycliffian Society and Foundation Manager: Mrs S Indranie
Admissions Manager: Miss C H Phillips
Head's PA: Mrs C J Philp

Preparatory School:
(*see also entry in IAPS section*)

Headmaster: A Palmer, BEd, MA
Headmaster's Wife: Mrs J Palmer, Cert Ed (*SENCo to Lower Prep, General Subjects Teacher*)
Deputy Head: Mrs V Jackson, BA, PGCE, TEFL (*Languages Teacher*)
Director of Pastoral Care: Mrs L Askew, LAMDA (*Head of Drama, Child Protection Officer*)

Teaching Staff:
S J Arman, BEd (*Chaplain, Head of Shaftesbury, Head of Humanities*)
Mrs B Bate, BSc, PGCE (*Year 4 Teacher*)
Mrs J Baylis, NVQ3 (*Lower Prep Assistant*)
Mrs K Bierer, BA, Support Teaching Cert Level 3 (*Lower Prep Assistant*)
Mr C Bish, BA (*Year 2 Teacher*)
Mr T Bloodworth, BSc, PGCE (*Year 4 Teacher, Head of Geography*)
Mrs S Bond, BEd (*Reception Teacher, EYFS Lead*)
Miss H Boswell, BA, PGCE (*Head of Swimming and Girls' Games*)
D Broadhead, BA, PGCE (*Languages Teacher*)
Mrs C Brown, BA, PGCE, TESOL (*Head of Lincoln, Head of Modern Foreign Languages*)
Miss S Carman, BA (*Lower Prep Assistant*)
Mrs A Cleere, BEd, ASA Level 2 (*General Subjects Teacher*)
Miss M Coughlan, BA (*Lower Prep Assistant*)
Mr L Darcy, BSc, PGCE (*Maths and Science Teacher*)
Mrs N Ely, BTEC National Diploma, BTEC First Diploma (*Middle Prep Assistant*)
Mrs E Flake, BEd (*Director of Studies Teaching; General Subjects Teacher*)
Miss J Florio, BSc, PGCE (*Maths and Science Teacher*)
Mrs N Gaunt, BEd, OCR Level 5 (*SEN Teacher, Games Teacher*)
R Gaunt, BA QTS (*Head of Mathematics*)
Mrs N Gidman BA, QTS (*Year 5 Teacher*)
C Guest, BSc, PGCE (*Head of Scott, Head of SEN*)
Mrs R Hanson, BA, PGCE (*Head of Grenfell, Year 5 Teacher*)
T Holroyde, BSc, PGCE (*Head of Science*)
A Jones, ECB Club Coach, BTEC Sports and Exercise Science (*Games Teacher*)
R Irwin, BSc, PGCE (*Director of Studies Learning, Year 5 Teacher*)
D Lester BEd, Med (*Languages Teacher*)
Miss C Lewis, BA (*Year 3 Teacher*)
Mrs Y Martin, BEd (*Year 1 Teacher*)
R Mein BA (*Middle Prep Assistant*)
Mrs E Muszasty, BA (*Head of English*)
Mrs M Perhirin, Bain MFL and European Studies, PGCE (*Lower Prep French Teacher and Lower Prep Assistant*)
Mrs S Poccard, TEFL, CELT (*ESOL Teacher*)
Miss M Potts, BA (*Head of ICT, Data and Exams Manager, Gifted and Talented Coordinator*)
Miss A Scammell BA (*Lower Prep Assistant*)
Mrs J Seyburn BA, MA, PGCE (*English and Humanities Teacher*)
A Sinclair, BA, PGCE (*Year 3 Teacher*)
Mrs C Stanley, BA, PGCE, Cert SpLD (*SEN Teacher*)
M Stopforth, BA, PGCE (*Head of Art & DT*)
Mrs R Taylor, BA, PGCE (*Director of Music*)
Mrs S Warren, BEd (*Games Teacher*)
S Wainwright, BA (*Head of PE and Boys' Games*)

Boarding House Staff:
Mrs L Field (*Housemistress*)
Mr A Jones (*Assistant Housemaster*)
Miss K Thomas (*Assistant Housemistress*)
Mrs J Porter (*Matron*)
Mrs J Swirski Matron)
Mrs K Yates (*Matron*)

Day Matrons:
Mrs N Murray, British Red Cross First Aid at Work Cert
Mrs S Phillips, British Red Cross First Aid at Work Cert, GCS Foundation to Counselling

Administration Staff:
Admissions Manager: Miss B Armstrong
School Secretary: Mrs J Fisk
Headmaster's PA: Mrs S Rogers
Lower Prep Administrator: Mrs L Sherwood

Nursery:
Mrs C Marsh, NNEB, C&G Child Care 0–7, Supervisory Management Educare Plus Cert, NVQ4, Foundation Degree in Early Years, Ofsted Registered Suitable Person (*Nursery Manager, Lower Nursery Teacher*)
Mrs A Hawes, BA Early Childhood Studies, EY Professional Status, Early Years Safeguarding Lead (*Deputy Nursery Manager, Upper Nursery Teacher*)
Miss K Holmes NVQ3 (*Lower Nursery Teacher*)
Mrs S Walker NVQ3 (*Upper Nursery Teacher*)
Mrs S Asquith BA, Cert EY Practice (*Nursery Assistant*)
Miss L Chapman, NVQ3 (*Nursery Assistant*)
Miss A Chivers, NVQ2 (*Nursery Assistant*)
Miss C Holmes, NVQ3 (*Nursery Assistant*)
Miss S Johnson, NVQ3 (*Nursery Assistant*)
Mrs C Pearse, NVQ3 (*Nursery Assistant*)

Out-of-School Care:
Mrs R Sampson, NVQ3 (*OSC Manager*)
Mrs L Summers, NVQ3 (*OSC Deputy Manager*)

Wycombe Abbey

High Wycombe, Buckinghamshire HP11 1PE
Tel: 01494 897008
email: registrar@wycombeabbey.com
website: www.wycombeabbey.com
Twitter: @wycombeabbey
Facebook: @wycombeabbey

Motto: *In Fide Vade*

Founded in 1896.
Numbers on roll. 601 Girls: 558 Boarding; 43 Day Girls.
Age range. 11–18.
Aims. Wycombe Abbey aims to provide an education in the widest sense and our pursuit of academic excellence goes hand in hand with our commitment to pastoral care. We believe the welfare and happiness of every girl to be paramount. Each individual is encouraged to achieve her full potential; she receives first-class academic teaching and has the opportunity to discover and develop her talents – artistic, creative, musical, sporting. She also learns to take responsibility for herself and to have respect for others. It is an intrinsic part of the School ethos that girls care for each other and offer service to the community.
Location. Near the centre of High Wycombe, five minutes' drive from the M40.
Buildings. The School buildings are all within the extensive grounds of 160 acres which include playing fields, woods, gardens and a lake.

Boarding Houses. There is a Junior House for UIII. At LIV, girls move to one of nine Houses where they remain until the end of the Lower Sixth. In the final year all girls move to the Upper Sixth House where they are encouraged to prepare for university life.

Religion. Wycombe Abbey is a Church of England foundation with its own Chapel. All girls attend morning prayers and a Sunday Service. (Roman Catholic girls can attend Mass and Jewish girls may receive instruction from a Rabbi.) Christian principles inform the whole ethos of the School and a resident Chaplain oversees spiritual matters and plays a central role in pastoral care.

Curriculum. The Lower School curriculum includes the study of English, English Literature, History, Geography, Religious Studies, French, German, Spanish, Latin, Greek, Mathematics, Biology, Chemistry, Physics, Information Technology, Design and Technology, Art, Cookery, Drama, Music, Singing, Personal, Social and Health Education and PE. In the Sixth Form, Economics, History of Art, Classical Civilisation, Government and Politics, Psychology and Physical Education are also available. Critical Thinking AS is compulsory. Girls are prepared for the IGCSE, GCSE, AS and A2 Level examinations, Pre-U and for university entrance. Girls proceed to leading universities in the UK with about 30–40% going to Oxbridge and a handful to America.

Teaching facilities are very good and have been extended and upgraded over recent years.

Physical Education. The School has excellent outdoor facilities, including five lacrosse pitches, a full-size multi-purpose floodlit Astroturf pitch, an athletics track and twenty tennis courts which can be used for netball in the winter. The Davies Sports Centre is a state-of-the-art sports complex including a six-lane 25m swimming pool, well-equipped fitness suite and four glass-backed squash courts. Girls are taught lacrosse, netball, tennis, athletics, swimming, gymnastics and dance. A huge range of extra-curricular sports and activities is also available.

Music. There is a strong tradition of music-making with outstanding facilities for tuition and for recitals. About three-quarters of the girls study at least one musical instrument and are taught by a large team of visiting specialists who provide tuition in a wide range of instruments, including voice. There are many opportunities for performing in orchestras and ensembles. In addition, there is a strong tradition of singing; the Chapel choir plays a central role in Chapel worship and undertakes biennial overseas tours.

Drama. As well as class Drama, GCSE and A Level Drama, extra-curricular Speech and Drama lessons are also available from Year 8 in groups of approximately six girls and from Year 10 in pairs or solo. LAMDA examinations take place in the fully-equipped 436-seater proscenium arch theatre and generally culminate in a Grade 8 Gold Medal in the final year. There are extra-curricular production opportunities at various points throughout the year, several girls annually get into the National Youth Theatre and alumnae include Naomi Frederick, Rachel Stirling and Polly Stenham.

Art, Craft, Design & Technology. Girls can pursue their interests in these subjects at weekends when the studios are open, as well as in curriculum time. Visiting artists provide workshops at weekends to give girls a broad experience in the subject.

Other Activities. A wide range of clubs and societies, usually led by girls, are very popular as are the numerous social events with leading boys' schools.

Fees per term (2016–2017). The fees for boarders are £12,250 (£9,188 for day boarders). They are inclusive and cover, in addition to the subjects and activities already mentioned, lectures, concerts, most textbooks and stationery.

Admission. Girls are admitted at the age of 11 or 13. Application should be made well in advance. The suggested procedure is given in the prospectus information booklet.

Sixth Form Entry: Competitive entry by examination for a limited number of places. Application must be received at least fifteen months prior to the proposed date of entry.

Scholarships and Bursaries. Lower School Entry: A variety of Scholarship and Exhibition awards are available for candidates under 12 and under 14 on 1 September of the proposed year of entry.

Some awards are also available for candidates entering the Sixth Form.

Music Scholarships and Exhibitions of varying value are available to candidates under the age of 14 on 1 September of the proposed year of entry. A Music Scholarship is also available to girls entering the Sixth Form.

Bursaries: A number of means-tested bursaries are available. Bursaries are held subject to the satisfactory conduct and progress of the recipient.

For further information, please contact the Director of Admissions.

Charitable status. The Girls' Education Company Limited is a Registered Charity, number 310638. Its aim is the provision of first class education for girls.

Governing Council:

President: The Rt Hon The Lord Carrington, KG, GCMG, CH, MC, JP, PC

Vice Presidents:
Mr A K Stewart-Roberts, MA
Mr A M D Willis, LLB, FCIArb
Mrs C M Archer, MA

Chairman:
Mr P P Sherrington, LLB, LLM, FCIArb

Council Members:
Lady Sassoon, MA
Mr Keith Oates, MSc, BSc Econ, LLD, DSc
Mrs Sue Singer, BA
The Hon Mrs Justice Carr, DBE
Mr D P Lillycrop, LLB, FCMI
The Rt Revd Dr Alan Wilson, MA, DPhil, Bishop of Buckingham
Mrs Diana Rose, MA
Dr Louise Fawcett, MA, DPhil
Mr Richard Ashby, MSc, BSc Eng, ARSM, FRICS
Mr Richard Winter, BA, FCA
Mr J W Bailey, ACA
Mr Patrick Lewis, MA, MBA

Staff:

Senior Leadership Team:

Headmistress: Mrs R Wilkinson, MA Oxon, PGCE, MEd, Dip SpLD

Bursar and Clerk to the Council: Mrs A Bolton, MA Cantab, MBA

Deputy Headmistress (Academic): Miss E Boswell, MA Oxon, PGCE Roehampton

Deputy Headmistress (Operational): Miss R A Keens, BEd Liverpool

Director of Sixth Form: Mr J Franks, MA Cantab, GTP e-Qualitas

Director of Digital Learning: Mr T Bennett, MA Cantab, PGCE Oxford Brookes

Director of International School(s): Ms S Brazendale, BA Durham, MBA INSEAD

Director of External Relations: Miss K Fox, MA Cantab

Director of Development and Communications: Mrs H Ison, BA Oxon

Director of Admissions: Mrs S Langdale, BA Dunelm

Head of Boarding: Mrs A Spillman, BA Open, BSc Exeter, PGCE Greenwich

Assistant Director of Studies: Mr M Welch, MEng, BA Cantab, PGCE Nottingham

Housemistresses (Pastoral):

Airlie: Mrs S McGeehan, BSc Glasgow, PGCE Jordanhill College

Barry: Mrs A Spillman, BA Open, BSc Exeter, PGCE Greenwich

Butler: Miss R Harris, BA Durham, PGCE Bristol

Campbell: Dr A Yuasa, BA Oxon, PhD Reading, PGCE Cantab

Cloister: Mrs S Harris, BTS Toulouse

Pitt: Miss H Allen, BA Hons, Cert Ed Brunel

Rubens: Miss C Perri, Licence de Litterature Université Aix-Marseille, PGCE Cambridge

Shelburne: Mrs S Jenkins, CertEd West Midlands, DipEd Reading, CPP Roehampton

Wendover: Ms E Watson, BEng UMIST, MSCi, PGCE Buckingham

Junior House: Miss V Fawkes, BA Swansea, GTP Reading

Deputy Head of Sixth Form (UVI): Miss C Hoyle, MA Edinburgh, PGCE Cantab

Deputy Head of Sixth Form (LVI): Ms J Kung, BA Sydney, BA DipEd Macquarie

Deputy Head of Sixth Form (Enrichment): Dr A Goddard, BA MA PhD KCL

Chaplain: The Revd J Chaffey, MA Oxon, BA Dunelm

Heads of Department:

English: Mr S Winchester, BA Hons Leeds, PGCE Institute of Education London

Mathematics: Mr R Tidbury, MPhys Warwick, PGCE Oxon

Science & STEM: Mrs S Jones, BSc Dunelm, PGCE Oxon

Physics: Mrs C Dowdall, BSc Warwick, PGCE Nottingham

Chemistry: Mrs Z Edwards, BSc St Andrews, PGCE Dunelm

Biology: Mr M Whiteley, BA Cantab, PGCE Canterbury

Modern Languages and French: Miss S Landsmann, Licence d'anglais La Sorbonne Nouvelle, PGCE Reading

German: Mrs M Dworkin, MA Cantab, PGCE King's College London

Spanish: Ms E Piqué, MA Langues Etrangères et Appliquées Droit et Commerce Montpellier, PGCE Cardiff

Classics: Mrs J Tidbury, MA Cantab, PGCE Cantab

Geography: Mr T Bennett, MA Cantab, PGCE Oxford Brookes

History: Dr S Tullis, BA DPhil PGCE Oxon, MLitt St Andrews

History of Art: Miss E Bowen, BA Oxon

Religious Studies: Mrs A Khan, MA, PGCE Oxon

Economics: Miss L Peden, BSc Queen's Belfast, PGCE Manchester

Computer Science: Mr A Porter, BSc, PGCE East Anglia, MA Reading, MBCS

Art, Design and Technology: Miss F Clark, BA Goldsmiths London, PGCE London

Drama: Miss C Livesey, BEd Cantab, AGSM Guildhall

Director of Music: Mr L Tubb, BA Oxon, ABRSM

Director of Sport: Miss L Taylor, BSc Hons Bath, PGCE Chichester

Wellbeing: Miss S Blunt, BA Kent

For a full staff list, please visit our website.

Yarm School

The Friarage, Yarm, Stockton-on-Tees TS15 9EJ

Tel: 01642 786023
Fax: 01642 789216
email: dmd@yarmschool.org
website: www.yarmschool.org

Yarm School, a co-educational day school, was founded in 1978. It has its own separate Preparatory School for pupils from 4 to 11 years of age and a nursery for 3 year olds. There are about 1,100 pupils in the School including 330 pupils in the Preparatory School (*see entry in IAPS section*). There are about 200 in the Sixth Form.

Situation and Buildings. Yarm School is situated in the attractive and historic town of Yarm on a beautiful site with the River Tees running through it.

The Senior School is set around The Friarage (an impressive eighteenth century mansion). There are outstanding facilities, including a first-rate science and design technology building, Sixth Form Centre, sports hall, fitness suite and two all-weather, floodlit pitches. A performing arts centre for music, dance and drama was added in 2012 which includes the stunning 800-seat Princess Alexandra Auditorium which has won several national design awards. A brand new Music School, Boathouse and full-size astro opened in September 2015.

The Preparatory School occupies an adjacent site and also has a range of first-class facilities, including a purpose-built Pre-Prep which was opened in 2012.

Admission. Pupils are admitted to the Senior School at 11 and 16 by means of the School's own Entrance Examination. The Preparatory School has its own entrance procedures.

Curriculum. The School's academic reputation both nationally and locally is high and virtually all leavers go on to take university degrees. In 2016 over 13% of the leavers went to Medical School and a further 10% to Oxbridge.

In the Preparatory School the curriculum is both wide ranging and demanding. Whilst the basics in English and Mathematics are given great emphasis, the Sciences, Technology and Modern Languages also form an important part of the timetable.

See website for full description of the School curriculum and further information.

Organisation. Pastoral care is based on both a year group and a House system. Every pupil belongs to one of four Houses for his/her whole school career. Houses exist to promote competitions, sports events, charity fundraising etc. Each pupil also has a personal Tutor and Head of Year whose task it is to look after all the pupils within a given year group. Sixth-formers have the opportunity to serve as House Officers, School Prefects and as Peer Support Mentors.

Games and Activities. The school believes firmly in "education for life" and has more sport and activities within its timetable than is offered in most day schools. Its sporting reputation is enviable, with success being achieved right up to national level (London 2012 Olympic gold medallist, Kat Copeland, learned to row at Yarm) and the wide range of sports offered caters for most tastes and both genders. There are many school societies. A great deal of extracurricular activity is centred on The Duke of Edinburgh's Award scheme. Rock climbing, canoeing and other aspects of outdoor education are given some prominence and residential weekends at an outdoor pursuits centre are a fixed part of the curriculum. There is a flourishing CCF contingent (membership, though popular, is entirely voluntary). School excursions are frequent and very varied. Expeditions in recent years have travelled as far as India, America and Guyana.

Drama (at least three major productions a year) and Music (several choir and orchestral concerts are given each year) are given every encouragement and have a strong following.

Religion. The School is an interdenominational community comprising pupils of both Christian and non-Christian backgrounds. There are regular assemblies and occasional services held in the local Parish Church.

Fees per term (2016–2017). Senior School £4,096; Preparatory School £3,090–£3,418; Pre-Prep and Nursery £2,427–£2,469; Pre-Prep and Nursery (with Nursery Grant): £1,663. Lunches: £196.

Scholarships and Bursaries. A range of scholarships and bursaries is available.

Several (usually six each year) Academic Scholarships, up to the value of 10% of the full fee, are awarded as a result of performance in the 11+ Entrance Examination (held late January).

Yarm School Sixth Form Science Scholarships and Yarm School Humanities Scholarships are available and awarded on academic merit (subject to other criteria being met) based on the January scholarship examination.

The school is affiliated to the Arkwright Scholarships Trust and offers Sixth Form Design and Technology Scholarships.

The school also offers Music Scholarships which provide some fee remission or instrumental tuition. Candidates for major awards are normally expected to offer a minimum of two instruments or one instrument plus voice. Music Scholarships can be awarded at any stage in the pupil's school career and modest awards can be upgraded in the light of further outstanding progress.

Means-tested bursaries are available to allow children who satisfy the entry criteria to be educated at Yarm School.

Please contact the School for further details.

Former Pupils. Past members of the School are eligible to join the Former Pupils' Society.

Charitable status. Yarm School is a Registered Charity, number 1093434. It exists to provide quality education for boys and girls.

Governing Body:
Chairman: A P Thomson, LLB, FCCA, FIDM
Vice-Chair: Mrs R M Langford, BDS
Mrs F Ajekigbe, BSc, PGCE, MEd, NPQH
Mrs S H Anderson, FCA, BSc
Dr P M Chapman, MA, PhD
S R Davidson, BSc, PGCE
L D Gamble, MA, VetMB, MRCVS
Dr P S A Jones, MA, PhD
Mrs L Longstaff, Cert Ed NPQH
I Lovat, BSc, PGCE
M Thompson, BA, ACMA
A M Turner, BSc, MB, ChB, FRCS Paeds, PhD

Headmaster: **D M Dunn**, BA

Deputy Headmaster: D G Woodward, BSc, CBiol, MIBiol
Director of Studies: D K Morton, MA
Head of Sixth Form: Dr A M Goodall, MA, PhD
Head of Middle School: Mrs K A Gratton, BEd
Head of Learning and Achievement: D Boddy, BA, MSc, FCIEA, FCollT, FRSA

School Manager: Ms C J Evans, MA, MBA, ARCM
Headmaster's PA: Mrs J L Herbert, BSc, Dip FLB

Preparatory School

Headmaster: W E C Sawyer, BA, PGCE

Deputy Headmaster: G N Stone, BEd, MA
Director of Studies: Mrs J E Pawluk, Dip RAM, LRAM, PGCE
Pre-Prep Coordinator: Mrs J Speight, BA Ed, QTS

Entrance Scholarships

Academic Scholarships

Abingdon School (p. 7)

Ackworth School (p. 9)

AKS Lytham (p. 11)

Aldenham School (p. 12)

Alleyn's School (p. 13)

Ampleforth College (p. 16)

Ardingly College (p. 18)

Ashford School (p. 19)

Ashville College (p. 20)

Bablake School (p. 22)

Bancroft's School (p. 23)

Barnard Castle School (p. 26)

Bedales School (p. 28)

Bede's Senior School (p. 30)

Bedford Modern School (p. 32)

Bedford School (p. 35)

Benenden School (p. 38)

Berkhamsted School (p. 41)

Birkdale School (p. 44)

Birkenhead School (p. 45)

Bishop's Stortford College (p. 47)

Bloxham School (p. 49)

Blundell's School (p. 51)

Bootham School (p. 55)

Bradfield College (p. 56)

Brentwood School (p. 62)

Brighton College (p. 64)

Bristol Grammar School (p. 66)

Bromley High School (p. 68)

Bromsgrove School (p. 70)

Bryanston School (p. 74)

Campbell College (p. 77)

Caterham School (p. 79)

Charterhouse (p. 82)

Cheltenham College (p. 85)

Cheltenham Ladies' College (p. 87)

Chigwell School (p. 90)

Christ College (p. 91)

Christ's Hospital (p. 94)

Churcher's College (p. 95)

City of London Freemen's School (p. 97)

City of London School (p. 101)

Clayesmore School (p. 104)

Clifton College (p. 106)

Cokethorpe School (p. 109)

Colfe's School (p. 110)

Colston's (p. 112)

Cranleigh School (p. 113)

Culford School (p. 116)

Dauntsey's School (p. 119)

Dean Close School (p. 120)

Denstone College (p. 122)

Downe House (p. 125)

Downside School (p. 127)

Dulwich College (p. 128)

Durham School (p. 132)

Eastbourne College (p. 134)

The Edinburgh Academy (p. 136)

Ellesmere College (p. 140)

Eltham College (p. 142)

Emanuel School (p. 145)

Epsom College (p. 147)

Eton College (p. 151)

Exeter School (p. 153)

Felsted School (p. 156)

Fettes College (p. 158)

Forest School (p. 160)

Framlingham College (p. 163)

Francis Holland School (p. 164)

Frensham Heights (p. 166)

George Heriot's School (p. 169)

Giggleswick School (p. 171)

Glenalmond College (p. 174)

Godolphin (p. 177)

Gordonstoun School (p. 181)

The Grange School (p. 183)

Gresham's School (p. 186)

Guildford High School (p. 189)

The Haberdashers' Aske's Boys' School (p. 192)

Haberdashers' Monmouth School for Girls (p. 195)

Halliford School (p. 197)

Hampton School (p. 199)

Harrow School (p. 203)

Hereford Cathedral School (p. 205)

Highgate School (p. 206)

Hurstpierpoint College (p. 210)

Immanuel College (p. 215)

Ipswich School (p. 217)

James Allen's Girls' School (JAGS) (p. 219)

Jerudong International School (p. 548)

The John Lyon School (p. 222)

Kent College (p. 226)

Kent College Pembury (p. 227)

Kimbolton School (p. 229)

King Edward VI School (p. 231)

King Edward's School (p. 233)

King Edward's School (p. 236)

King Edward's Witley (p. 237)

King Henry VIII School (p. 239)

King William's College (p. 241)

Winchester College (p. 507)

Wolverhampton Grammar School (p. 512)

Woodbridge School (p. 514)

Woodhouse Grove School (p. 516)

Worth School (p. 517)

Wrekin College (p. 520)

Wycliffe College (p. 522)

Wycombe Abbey (p. 525)

Yarm School (p. 527)

All-Rounder Scholarships

Abingdon School (p. 7)

Ampleforth College (p. 16)

Ardingly College (p. 18)

Bloxham School (p. 49)

Blundell's School (p. 51)

Bradfield College (p. 56)

Brighton College (p. 64)

Bryanston School (p. 74)

Caterham School (p. 79)

Charterhouse (p. 82)

Cheltenham College (p. 85)

Christ College (p. 91)

Clayesmore School (p. 104)

Cokethorpe School (p. 109)

Cranleigh School (p. 113)

Culford School (p. 116)

Dauntsey's School (p. 119)

Denstone College (p. 122)

Downe House (p. 125)

Downside School (p. 127)

Ellesmere College (p. 140)

Epsom College (p. 147)

Felsted School (p. 156)

Fettes College (p. 158)

Forest School (p. 160)

Framlingham College (p. 163)

Giggleswick School (p. 171)

Glenalmond College (p. 174)

Gordonstoun School (p. 181)

Hampton School (p. 199)

Hereford Cathedral School (p. 205)

Hurstpierpoint College (p. 210)

Ipswich School (p. 217)

King Edward's Witley (p. 237)

The King's School (p. 259)

Kingswood School (p. 264)

Lancing College (p. 268)

Leicester Grammar School (p. 273)

The Leys (p. 277)

Lord Wandsworth College (p. 283)

Malvern College (p. 294)

Marlborough College (p. 299)

Merchant Taylors' School (p. 303)

Merchiston Castle School (p. 306)

Millfield (p. 315)

Monmouth School (p. 319)

Mount Kelly (p. 322)

Mount St Mary's College (p. 323)

New Hall School (p. 325)

Oakham School (p. 332)

The Oratory School (p. 335)

Oundle School (p. 337)

Pangbourne College (p. 340)

Plymouth College (p. 343)

Princethorpe College (p. 349)

Prior Park College (p. 354)

Queen Anne's School (p. 356)

Queen's College (p. 358)

Radley College (p. 362)

Ratcliffe College (p. 364)

Reed's School (p. 368)

Repton School (p. 373)

Roedean School (p. 376)

Rossall School (p. 378)

The Royal Hospital School (p. 387)

The Royal Masonic School for Girls (p. 389)

St Edmund's College (p. 417)

St Edmund's School Canterbury (p. 420)

St Edward's, Oxford (p. 423)

St Lawrence College (p. 428)

St Mary's Calne (p. 431)

St Mary's School Ascot (p. 434)

Seaford College (p. 441)

Sherborne Girls (p. 445)

Sherborne School (p. 447)

Shrewsbury School (p. 452)

Silcoates School (p. 454)

Stamford School (p. 457)

Stonyhurst College (p. 464)

Stowe School (p. 467)

Uppingham School (p. 483)

Wellingborough School (p. 492)

Wellington College (p. 495)

Wells Cathedral School (p. 500)

Wolverhampton Grammar School (p. 512)

Woodbridge School (p. 514)

Wycliffe College (p. 522)

Art Scholarships

Dance Scholarships

Design Technology Scholarships

Drama Scholarships

Music Scholarships

Sport Scholarships

Other Scholarships

Arkwright Engineering

Boarding

Chess

Choral

Classics

Computing

Cricket

Design

Drumming

Economics
James Allen's Girls' School (JAGS) (p. 219)

Expressive Arts
George Heriot's School (p. 169)

Fencing
Truro School (p. 480)

Golf
Bedford School (p. 35)
Culford School (p. 116)
Ellesmere College (p. 140)
Loretto School (p. 285)
Queenswood School (p. 361)

Hockey
Culford School (p. 116)
Queenswood School (p. 361)

Humanities
Yarm School (p. 527)

ICT
Repton School (p. 373)

IT
Bedford Modern School (p. 32)
Gordonstoun School (p. 181)

Mathematics
Bristol Grammar School (p. 66)
Wells Cathedral School (p. 500)

Modern Languages
Bristol Grammar School (p. 66)
Wells Cathedral School (p. 500)

Ogden Trust Science
Birkdale School (p. 44)
Exeter School (p. 153)
Hereford Cathedral School (p. 205)
Ipswich School (p. 217)
Kirkham Grammar School (p. 266)
Norwich School (p. 328)
Oakham School (p. 332)
Warwick School (p. 490)

Organ
Bloxham School (p. 49)
Charterhouse (p. 82)
Cheltenham College (p. 85)
Clifton College (p. 106)
Dean Close School (p. 120)
Durham School (p. 132)
Ellesmere College (p. 140)
Glenalmond College (p. 174)
King's Ely (p. 253)
The King's School (p. 256)
King's Rochester (p. 257)
Lancing College (p. 268)
Princethorpe College (p. 349)

Queen's College (p. 358)
St Edmund's School Canterbury (p. 420)
Solihull School (p. 455)

Performing Arts
Bedford Modern School (p. 32)
Bradfield College (p. 56)
Caterham School (p. 79)
Dauntsey's School (p. 119)
Ellesmere College (p. 140)
Lord Wandsworth College (p. 283)
Plymouth College (p. 343)
Queen's College (p. 358)
Strathallan School (p. 469)
Wells Cathedral School (p. 500)

Photography
Frensham Heights (p. 166)

Piping
Fettes College (p. 158)
Glenalmond College (p. 174)
Merchiston Castle School (p. 306)
Strathallan School (p. 469)

Rugby
Culford School (p. 116)
Ellesmere College (p. 140)
Plymouth College (p. 343)

Sailing
The Royal Hospital School (p. 387)
Ryde School with Upper Chine (p. 399)

Science
Bedales School (p. 28)
Bristol Grammar School (p. 66)
Caterham School (p. 79)
Dauntsey's School (p. 119)
Eastbourne College (p. 134)
Ellesmere College (p. 140)
Framlingham College (p. 163)
Uppingham School (p. 483)
Yarm School (p. 527)

STEM
Wolverhampton Grammar School (p. 512)

Swimming
Culford School (p. 116)
Ellesmere College (p. 140)
Mount Kelly (p. 322)
Plymouth College (p. 343)

Tennis
Culford School (p. 116)
Ellesmere College (p. 140)
Queenswood School (p. 361)

Textiles
RGS Worcester (p. 385)

Bursaries

Abingdon School (p. 7)

Ackworth School (p. 9)

AKS Lytham (p. 11)

Aldenham School (p. 12)

Alleyn's School (p. 13)

Ampleforth College (p. 16)

Ardingly College (p. 18)

Ashford School (p. 19)

Ashville College (p. 20)

Bablake School (p. 22)

Barnard Castle School (p. 26)

Bedales School (p. 28)

Bedford School (p. 35)

Benenden School (p. 38)

Berkhamsted School (p. 41)

Birkdale School (p. 44)

Birkenhead School (p. 45)

Bishop's Stortford College (p. 47)

Bloxham School (p. 49)

Blundell's School (p. 51)

Bolton School Boys' Division (p. 53)

Bootham School (p. 55)

Bradfield College (p. 56)

Bradford Grammar School (p. 59)

Brentwood School (p. 62)

Brighton College (p. 64)

Bristol Grammar School (p. 66)

Bromley High School (p. 68)

Bromsgrove School (p. 70)

Bryanston School (p. 74)

Bury Grammar School Boys (p. 76)

Campbell College (p. 77)

Caterham School (p. 79)

Charterhouse (p. 82)

Cheltenham College (p. 85)

Cheltenham Ladies' College (p. 87)

Chetham's School of Music (p. 88)

Chigwell School (p. 90)

Christ College (p. 91)

Christ's Hospital (p. 94)

Churcher's College (p. 95)

City of London Freemen's School (p. 97)

City of London School (p. 101)

City of London School for Girls (p. 103)

Clayesmore School (p. 104)

Clifton College (p. 106)

Cokethorpe School (p. 109)

Colfe's School (p. 110)

Culford School (p. 116)

Dauntsey's School (p. 119)

Dean Close School (p. 120)

Denstone College (p. 122)

Dollar Academy (p. 124)

Downe House (p. 125)

Downside School (p. 127)

Dulwich College (p. 128)

The High School of Dundee (p. 130)

Durham School (p. 132)

Eastbourne College (p. 134)

The Edinburgh Academy (p. 136)

Ellesmere College (p. 140)

Eltham College (p. 142)

Emanuel School (p. 145)

Epsom College (p. 147)

Eton College (p. 151)

Exeter School (p. 153)

Felsted School (p. 156)

Fettes College (p. 158)

Forest School (p. 160)

Framlingham College (p. 163)

Francis Holland School (p. 164)

Frensham Heights (p. 166)

George Heriot's School (p. 169)

Giggleswick School (p. 171)

The High School of Glasgow (p. 173)

Glenalmond College (p. 174)

Godolphin (p. 177)

Gordonstoun School (p. 181)

The Grange School (p. 183)

Gresham's School (p. 186)

Guildford High School (p. 189)

The Haberdashers' Aske's Boys' School (p. 192)

Halliford School (p. 197)

Hampton School (p. 199)

Harrow School (p. 203)

Hereford Cathedral School (p. 205)

Highgate School (p. 206)

Hurstpierpoint College (p. 210)

Hutchesons' Grammar School (p. 212)

Hymers College (p. 214)

Immanuel College (p. 215)

Ipswich School (p. 217)

James Allen's Girls' School (JAGS) (p. 219)

Kelvinside Academy (p. 224)

Kent College (p. 226)

Kent College Pembury (p. 227)

Kimbolton School (p. 229)

King Edward VI School (p. 231)

King Edward's School (p. 233)

King Edward's School (p. 236)

King Edward's Witley (p. 237)

King Henry VIII School (p. 239)

King William's College (p. 241)

King's College School (p. 243)

The King's School (p. 249)

The King's School (p. 251)

Headmasters' and Headmistresses' Conference International Members

Schools in Europe

The British School of Brussels

Pater Dupierreuxlaan 1, 3080 Tervuren, Belgium

Tel: 00 32 2 766 04 30
Fax: 00 32 2 767 80 70
email: admissions@britishschool.be
website: www.britishschool.be
Twitter: @BSB_Brussels
Facebook: @britishschoolbrussels
LinkedIn: /the-british-school-of-brussels

Creation. The British School of Brussels (BSB) was founded in 1969 as a non-profit making organisation in Belgium and was opened in 1970 by HRH The Duke of Edinburgh. It is run by a Board of Governors, comprising distinguished British and Belgian citizens from both the professional and business worlds, together with parent and staff representatives.

Site. The school occupies a beautiful site of ten hectares, surrounded by woodlands and lakes near the Royal Museum of Central Africa in Tervuren, which is 20–25 minutes by car from the centre of Brussels. The site belongs to the Donation Royale, the Foundation which manages the estates left to the Belgian people at the beginning of the 20th century by King Leopold II.

Facilities. The school has excellent modern facilities, including a science and maths centre, networked IT suites, all with internet access and Wi-Fi. Students in most year groups are issued with either their own iPad or laptop computer. The school has dance and drama studios as well as nine science laboratories, four art studies and three technology workshops, including a state-of-the-art design & technology workshop and food & nutrition rooms, comprehensive modern languages and humanities suites and a self-service cafeteria. There is an Early Childhood Centre for children of 1–3 years also on campus. The school has developed its sporting facilities extensively and has a multi-purpose sports hall, gymnasium, fitness suite and dance studio. It is the only international school in Belgium to have its own swimming pool that opened in September 2016.

Organisation. The British School of Brussels is an independent, fee-paying, non profit-making international school. The School is a co-educational, non-selective day school for students from 1 to 18 years of age, with over 1,350 currently on roll. Approximately 34% of the students are British and there are 70 other nationalities represented. Our curriculum, both in the Primary and Secondary Schools, is a British-based curriculum, adapted to suit the needs of our European context and international students. In the Secondary School, students sit GCSE/IGCSE examinations at the end of Year 11 (aged 16). Senior students then have the choice of three pre-university qualifications: the International Baccalaureate (IB) Diploma (with English/French or English/Dutch bilingual options), GCE A Levels or BTEC courses in business, sports, applied science and hospitality prior to moving on to Higher Education in the UK, Belgium or beyond. Provision is also made for Oxbridge tuition. Our examination results, year on year, are very impressive for a non-selective school. In 2016 our students achieved 100% pass rate in IB and BTEC with a 99% pass rate in A Levels. Students successfully graduate to some of the top universities around the world.

BSB has an established French/English bilingual programme for children aged 4–14 years to complement its English-medium teaching. We introduce the teaching of Spanish, German or Dutch as optional additional languages in the Secondary School. We have developed programmes to help students with learning differences and to help students who join us with little or no English skills. The school also employs a counsellor.

Sports and Extracurricular Activities. Use of the extensive sports facilities (purpose-built sports centre with gym, sports hall, fitness suite, dance studio and 25m indoor swimming pool) together with all-weather artificial pitches, grass pitches, floodlit training area, four outdoor tennis courts and a 240-seat Brel Theatre. In addition to curricular sport, a wide range of competitive sports is offered: athletics, cricket, cross country, gymnastics, hockey, rugby, football, swimming and tennis, as well as recreational activities such as basketball and golf. The school participates very successfully in the International Schools Sports Tournaments (ISST) and ISGA (Gymnastics).

Music and Drama. The Music Department houses an extremely well-equipped music technology studio, a recording studio and a rehearsal studio for the School's orchestras, concert bands and instrumental ensembles. Individual instrument lessons are available from visiting specialist teachers, and take place in the suite of music practice rooms. The school is the largest Associated Board centre in Europe. Each year up to fifteen drama productions – including student-directed performances – are presented across the full student age range. The Theatre has its own workshop and Green Room, as well as a more intimate studio space that seats 80.

Careers. The school has the highest expectations of its student population and advice on careers, as well as higher and further education opportunities, is of vital importance to the further development of the students. The school takes part in many careers conventions and has its own international higher education and careers team.

Fees per annum (2016–2017). From €25,650 (Reception) to €32,800 (Years 10–13). Some assistance is offered as part of the school's Assisted Places Scheme.

Past Students' Association. The school has a growing association of Alumni and has its own official BSB Alumni Facebook page. Please visit the Alumni section of the school website: www.britishschool.be to see how to subscribe to the alumni newsletter and follow the school on Twitter and LinkedIn.

Patron:
Her Excellency the British Ambassador to the King of the Belgians

Chairman of the Board: Mr Ian Backhouse

***Principal*: Ms Melanie Warnes**

Vice Principal and Head of Primary School: Ms Pauline Markey

Vice Principal and Head of Secondary School: Mr Gary Minnitt

The British School in The Netherlands

BSN Junior School Leidschenveen (3–11 years)
Vrouw Avenweg 640, 2493 WZ, The Hague, The Netherlands
Tel: 00 31 (0)70 315 4040
Fax: 00 31 (0)70 444 7861

BSN Junior School Diamanthorst (3–11 years) (IAPS Member)
Diamanthorst 16, 2592 GH, The Hague
Tel: 00 31 (0)70 315 7620
Fax: 00 31 (0)70 444 7621

BSN Junior School Vlaskamp (3–11 years)
Vlaskamp 19, 2592 AA, The Hague
Tel: 00 31 (0)70 333 8111
Fax: 00 31 (0)70 333 8100

BSN Senior School (11–18 years)
Jan van Hooflaan 3, 2252 BG, Voorschoten
Tel: 00 31 (0)71 560 2222
Fax: 00 31 (0)71 560 2200

email: admissions@britishschool.nl
website: www.britishschool.nl
Twitter: @BSNetherlands
Facebook: /BSNetherlands
LinkedIn: /the-british-school-in-the-netherlands

The British School in The Netherlands (BSN) was founded in 1931 as an independent, non-denominational school. Since then, it has grown into a school of over 2,300 students from Foundation 1 (age 3) to Year 13 (age 18). The BSN prides itself on being 'Internationally British' with over 80 different nationalities enrolled across its four campuses around The Hague.

The School was inspected by The Independent Schools Inspectorate (ISI) in 2015 and was rated "excellent" in all criteria stating that *"The school is highly successful in achieving its aims for educating the students in an international environment of excellence. At all levels of the school, the achievement of students is excellent"*.

Aims. The School aims to develop the potential of its students by providing a caring environment, in which they are offered the greatest possible educational opportunities. Students are helped to develop their powers of reasoning, increase their knowledge and become aware of the importance of their individual contribution and responsibility to society. All are encouraged to aim for excellence and to respect one another. These aims are achieved in a happy school whose students join with high expectations and where they are encouraged in the belief of their fulfilment.

Junior School Diamanthorst. JSD opened in September 2003. The site boasts excellent resources including a new dance/drama studio, as well as a recently fully landscaped brand new outdoor learning/play area.

Junior School Leidschenveen. JSL opened in 2010 and offers superb landscaped grounds, the campus includes dedicated facilities for Out of School Care, a Day Care Centre for 0 to 3 year olds as well as a Sports and Community Centre.

Junior School Vlaskamp. JSV's award-winning building was opened in 1997 and provides a range of excellent resources, including notably extensive outside play and environmental areas.

Senior School. The Senior School, located in Voorschoten (a small town just north of The Hague), was completed in 2003 and offers enviable state-of-the-art facilities, including new science laboratories, information technology stations, library resources and much more. The school recently opened two all-purpose sports pitches and a newly renovated Art department, together with brand new events foyer, improved fitness facilities, and a remodelled Sixth Form area and Student Café. This investment represents a commitment to providing a modern and stimulating learning environment, to support the comprehensive educational programme.

Staff. Each school has a Headteacher, supported by a Deputy Headteacher. The Principal has overall responsibility for all schools in the BSN group. All teachers are fully qualified and are mostly recruited from the United Kingdom.

Transport. An independent school bus service links the schools and covers most of The Hague, Voorburg, Leidschendam, Wassenaar, Voorschoten, as well as parts of Rotterdam, Rijswijk, Leiden, Amsterdam and Zoetermeer.

Curriculum. Students follow challenging programmes of study based on the National Curriculum for England and Wales but with an added international dimension. All students study English, mathematics, science, technology, history, geography, music, art and physical education from the age of five years. Dutch is taught from the age of five and French from the age of ten. In the Senior School, Spanish and German are also taught from Year 7 at age 11. Students prepare for the GCSE (at 16+) and IB Diploma Programme or AS/A2 Level examinations at 17/18 years. The School has a long and proud record of success. In the past five years, our students have achieved places at 181 different universities in over 18 countries.

Sport. Facilities are available for indoor and outdoor games, including rugby, hockey, aerobics, tennis, athletics, judo, football, basketball, volleyball and gymnastics. At Senior School level, fixtures are arranged with local clubs and other schools, including annual tours and tournaments in the United Kingdom and elsewhere in Europe.

Activities and Trips. The School takes pride in its regular participation in the annual Model United Nations Conference in The Hague. It also operates a full programme of field and activity trips in The Netherlands, the United Kingdom, France, Switzerland, Spain and Germany, capitalising on its central location in Europe.

Pastoral System. To ensure that each pupil is known individually, and cared for, there is a pastoral system which begins with the form teacher, who is responsible to a year group leader. Together they work to care, support and guide the individual in all aspects of school life. Success is achieved only through close cooperation between home and school, a positive learning environment and high standards of discipline.

Special Needs & EAL. Special provision is made for students with learning difficulties. Any child with Special Needs will be considered according to the School's policy on Special Needs Provision, which is available on request. Specialist help is provided throughout the School for students requiring individual tuition in English as an Additional Language.

Admission. Admission is granted at any time in the school year, depending on availability and the School's ability to meet the academic needs of the child. Great care is taken to ensure the academic and social integration of each child.

Fees per annum (2016–2017). Foundation Stage Full Time €13,560, Years 1–2 €13,920, Years 3–6 €14,100, Years 7–9 €18,240, Years 10–11 €18,780, Years 12–13 €19,230.

Charitable status. The British School in The Netherlands is a Registered Charity, number V409055.

Principal: **Kieran Earley**
Principal's Office: Boerderij Rosenburgh,
Rosenburgherlaan 2, 2252 BA, Voorschoten
Tel: 00 31 [0]71 560 2251
Fax: 00 31 [0]71 560 2290

Headteachers:
Junior School Diamanthorst: Angela Parry-Davies (*IAPS Member*)
Junior School Leidschenveen: Karren van Zoest
Junior School Vlaskamp: Sue Aspinall
Senior School Voorschoten: James Oxlade (*Acting Headteacher*)

The British School of Paris

38 quai de l'Ecluse, 78290 Croissy sur Seine, France

Tel:	00 33 1 34 80 45 90
Fax:	00 33 1 39 76 12 69
email:	info@britishschool.fr
website:	www.britishschool.fr
Twitter:	@BritishSchParis
Facebook:	@BritishSchParis

Age Range. 3–18.
Number of Pupils. 800 (Boys and Girls)
Fees per annum (2016–2017). Senior School €25,844–€28,094; Junior School €17,381–€23,569.

The BSP provides, in a caring environment, a high-quality British-style education for international students, to enable them to become caring citizens and to lead fulfilling lives.

Located just 15 kilometres from Paris, the School caters for English-speaking children of over 50 nationalities (about 30% are British) from ages 3–18. It is a not-for-profit association in France and is presided over by a governing body under the patronage of His Excellency the British Ambassador to France.

The **Junior School** provides education for primary aged children from 3–11 years. The purpose-built Junior School is located very close to the Senior School along the leafy banks of the river Seine. There are 35 classrooms accommodating up to 500 pupils, as well as 4 bespoke classrooms and 2 activity areas that are dedicated to our foundation stage/ nursery section. Studies are based on the English National Curriculum with emphasis on English, Maths and Science, and of course, the French language. Being a holistic educator the BSP has a strong co-curricular base with a special focus on music and drama as well as a large variety of sports. (*For further information about the Junior School, see entry in IAPS section*).

The **Senior School**, which caters for pupils aged from 11–18 years, is situated beside a beautiful stretch of the Seine in Croissy sur Seine. The buildings, with the exception of two nineteenth century houses, have been built since 1990. The Science and Technology block provides excellent facilities for Science, Information Technology, Electronics and Design. There are six large, well equipped science laboratories. The other classroom blocks house Humanities, Art, Business Studies, Modern Languages, Music, English and Mathematics. Other facilities include a generously staffed and resourced student career guidance programme, a library, IT labs, a refectory, a large sports hall and fitness centre. Students enter at the age of 11 and for the first three years, a broad general education is maintained in line with the National Curriculum. Pupils are prepared for the GCSE and A Level examinations in a comprehensive range of subjects.

Music and drama are an integral part of school life; the music centre includes teaching and practice facilities as well as a well-equipped electronic studio. Specialist teachers visit the School to provide individual lessons in a wide range of instruments. Children take the Associated Board exams at regular intervals.

The School has had considerable sporting success over the years, winning the International Schools' Sports Tournament competition in girls' field hockey, and boys' rugby.

Our international fixture lists provide an incentive to gain a place in school teams. As well as local matches our teams travel regularly to Belgium, Holland and the UK.

Small overall numbers, modest class sizes and a supportive pastoral system all help new pupils integrate quickly. Our examination results are outstanding. At A Level almost 40% of all grades were A* and A and 93% of all grades at GCSE were between A* and C in 2016. These results compare very favourably with high-calibre schools in the UK. Most students continue their education at prestigious universities in the UK, USA, France and worldwide. BSP students have been successfully admitted to the Universities of Cambridge and Oxford, London School of Economics, University of Pennsylvania, Stanford University, McGill University, Universidad de Madrid, Seoul National University, L'Université de la Sorbonne, to mention but a few.

Chairman of Governors: Mr P Kett

Headmaster: Mr N Hammond

Head of Senior School: Dr J Batters

Head of the Junior School: Ms K Tuckwell

Registrar: Mrs V Joynes

King's College
The British School of Madrid

Paseo de los Andes 35, Soto de Viñuelas, Madrid 28761, Spain

Tel:	00 34 918 034 800
Fax:	00 34 918 036 557
email:	info@kingscollege.es
website:	www.kingscollegeschools.org
Twitter:	@Kings_Soto
LinkedIn:	/King's College, Soto de Viñuelas

King's College is a British co-educational day and boarding school founded in 1969. It is the largest British curriculum school in Spain and the first school to have had full UK accreditation through the Independent Schools Inspectorate. The Headteacher is an international member of HMC, while the school is a member of COBIS, NABSS and BSA.

The school is governed by the Board of Directors and School Council which is composed of distinguished members from the business and academic communities.

There are three separate schools in Madrid which cater for children of approximately 48 nationalities between the ages of 2 and 18 years. Pupil enrolment in 2013–14 was 2,125 –including 44 boarders. There are over 140 fully-qualified staff, most of whom are British.

The Vision of King's College, is "to be at the forefront of British education internationally" as well as to provide students with an excellent all-round education while fostering tolerance and understanding between young people of different nationalities and backgrounds.

King's College, Soto de Viñuelas caters for more than 1,500 pupils between the ages of 20 months and 18 years (Pre-Nursery to Year 13) and stands on a 12-acre site in a residential area about 25 km from the centre of Madrid near the Guadarrama mountains and surrounded by open countryside. It is well connected to the city centre by motorway and rail. There is an optional comprehensive bus service to the city of Madrid and its outlying residential areas and all routes are supervised by a bus monitor.

Facilities. There are extensive, purpose-built facilities which include 7 science laboratories, 2 libraries, an art studio, 3 computer centres with multimedia stations, and 2 music rooms. All classrooms are fitted with interactive whiteboards and there are computers in all Primary classrooms. The school offers a purpose-built Early Learning Centre, an Auditorium with seating for over 350 people and a Music School with 6 rooms for individual or small group tuition. The sports facilities include a 25-metre indoor heated swimming pool, a floodlit multi-purpose sports area, football pitches, basketball and tennis courts, a gymnasium with fitness centre and a horse riding school. Future development includes plans for a covered sports hall.

Tenbury House, the school boarding residence, opened in September 2011 and offers brand new purpose-built accommodation for up to 44 boarders. The residence is located in the school grounds and offers pupils a breakfast room, kitchen, laundry, work room, lounge, TV room, storage and easy access to the new AstroTurf pitch and sports facilities.

King's College School, La Moraleja. The school caters for more than 500 pupils aged 3 to 14 (Nursery to Year 9) and is located in a residential area just 16 kilometres from the centre of the city. The modern on-site facilities include a library, ICT centre, laboratory, music room, multi-purpose sports surface and gymnasium.

At the age of fourteen, at the end of National Curriculum Year 9, pupils transfer to King's College, Soto de Viñuelas to complete their final four years of study.

King's Infant School, Chamartín. Conveniently located in the Chamartín area of central Madrid, the school offers purpose-built facilities for boys and girls between the ages of 3 and 6 (Nursery to Year 2) and has a capacity of approximately 200 pupils. There are air-conditioned, spacious and well-equipped classrooms, complete with independent bathrooms for the Nursery pupils, a library and computer room and a playground area. At the age of seven, at the end of National Curriculum Year 2, pupils from King's Infant School automatically transfer either to King's College, Soto de Viñuelas or King's College School, La Moraleja.

Curriculum. Pupils at all three King's College schools in Madrid follow the English National Curriculum leading to (I)GCSE, GCSE, AS and A Level examinations. A wide range of subjects is available. All pupils learn Spanish. The school has a reputation for high academic standards and excellent examination results with students going on to top universities in Britain, USA and Spain amongst others.

An Oxbridge preparatory group works with the most able students to prepare university applications. There is a very experienced Careers and University Entrance Advisory Department for all students.

Activities. King's College has choirs, musical ensembles and drama groups, which participate in numerous events throughout the year. Pupils are encouraged to explore their capabilities in the areas of music and the arts from a very early age.

Sports play an important role at the school and pupils are encouraged to take part in tournaments and local competitive events, in addition to their normal PE classes. King's College currently has football, basketball and swimming teams participating in local leagues, and also takes part in inter-school championships in athletics and cross-country.

There is a programme of optional classes which includes horse riding, ballet, judo, Spanish dancing, swimming, tennis, tuition in various musical instruments, performing arts and craft workshops.

Admission. Pupils entering the school at the age of 7 or above are required to sit entrance tests in English and Mathematics and possibly other subjects, while younger candidates are offered a review by the Head of Admissions in each school. For those applying to the Sixth Form, admission depends on the results of the (I)GCSE examinations, or equivalent.

Fees per term (2016–2017). Tuition: €1,738–€3,566 excluding lunch and transport. Boarding (including tuition): Full €7,430–€8,104.

Scholarships. The school offers a small number of scholarships to Sixth Formers selected on academic merit.

Further information may be obtained from The Director of Admissions at the School: Rebecca Conlon, rebecca.conlon@kingsgroup.org.

Headteacher: **Matthew Taylor**, MA Oxon, MA London, PGCE, MRCIEA

Deputy Headteacher: Nicola Lambros, BSc Birmingham, MEd Roehampton, PGCE Brunel

Head of Secondary Department: Christopher T Parkinson, BEd Hons Crewe and Alsager

Director of Studies: James Slocombe, BSc Hons Bath, PGCE Bristol, MA OU

Head of Primary Department: Paula Parkinson, BA Hons Newcastle, PGCE Manchester

Deputy Head of Primary: Adele Dickson, LLB, PGDE

Head of Spanish Studies: Sara Fernández, Lic Filología Hispanica UCM

Head of Boarding: Hanan Nazha, BA QTS London

Head of Admissions: Rebecca Conlon, BSc Hons Kent, MSc London Metropolitan University

Other International Schools

Africa

Kenya

Peponi School
PO Box 236, Ruiru 00232, Kenya
email: info@peponischool.org
website: www.peponischool.org

Headmaster: Mark Durston

South Africa

Michaelhouse
Balgowan 3275, Kwazulu-Natal, South Africa
email: info@michaelhouse.org
website: www.michaelhouse.org

Rector: Greg Theron

Zimbabwe

Peterhouse
Private Bag 3741, Marondera, Zimbabwe
email: rector@peterhouse.co.zw
website: www.peterhouse.co.zw

Rector: Howard W Blackett

St George's College
Private Bag 7727, Causeway, Harare, Zimbabwe
email: headsec@stgeorges.co.zw
website: www.stgeorges.co.zw

Headmaster: G Kevin Atkinson

Asia

Brunei Darussalam

Jerudong International School
PO Box 1408, Bandar Seri Begawan BS8672, Negara
Brunei Darussalam
email: enrol@jis.edu.bn
website: www.jis.edu.bn

Principal: Barnaby Sandow, BSc Eng Durham, PGCE
Exeter

China

Dulwich College Beijing
89 Capital Airport Road, Shunyi District, Beijing
101300 PRC, China
email: info@dulwich-beijing.cn
website: www.dulwich-beijing.cn

Headmaster: Mr Simon Herbert

India

The British School, New Delhi
Dr Jose P Rizal Marg, Chanakyapuri, New Delhi 110021,
India
email: britishschool@british-school.org
website: www.british-school.org

Director: Vanita Uppal, OBE

The Cathedral & John Connon School
6 Purshottamdas Thakurdas Marg, Fort Mumbai 400
001, India
email: cajcs@mtnl.net.in
website: www.cathedral-school.com

Principal: Mrs Meera Isaacs

The Doon School
The Mall, Dehradun 248001, Uttaranchal, India
email: hm@doonschool.com
website: www.doonschool.com

Headmaster: Mr Matthew Raggett

The International School Bangalore
NAFL Valley, Whitefield-Sarajapur Road, Near
Dommasandra Circle, Bangalore –562 125, Karnataka
State, India
email: school@tisb.ac.in
website: www.tisb.org

Principal: Mr Peter Armstrong

Woodstock School
Tehri Road, Mussoorie, Uttarakhand 248179, India
email: communications@woodstockschool.ac.in
website: www.woodstockschool.in

Principal: Dr Jonathan Long

Indonesia

The British School Jakarta
Bintaro Jaya Sector 9, Jl Raya Jombang - Cileduk,
Pondok Aren, Tangerang 15227, Indonesia
email: principal@bsj.sch.id
website: www.bsj.sch.id

Principal: Mr Simon Dennis

Malaysia

Kolej Tuanku Ja'afar
Mantin, 71700 Negeri Sembilan, West Malaysia
email: principal@ktj.edu.my
website: www.ktj.edu.my

Principal: Dr Simon Watson

Singapore

Tanglin Trust School
95 Portsdown Road, Singapore 139299
email: admissions@tts.edu.sg
website: www.tts.edu.sg

Chief Executive Officer: Peter J Derby-Crook

Head of Junior School: Clair Harrington-Wilcox
(See Junior School entry in IAPS section)

Head of Infant School: Paula Craigie

Thailand

Shrewsbury International School
1922 Charoen Krung Road, Wat Prayakrai, Bang Kholame, Bangkok 10120, Thailand
email: enquiries@shrewsbury.ac.th
website: www.shrewsbury.ac.th

Principal: Stephen Holroyd

Australia and New Zealand

Australia

Anglican Church Grammar School
Oaklands Parade, East Brisbane, Queensland QLD 4169, Australia
email: reception@churchie.com.au
website: www.churchie.com.au

Headmaster: Dr Alan Campbell

Camberwell Grammar School
PO Box 151, Balwyn, VIC 3103, Australia
email: headmaster@cgs.vic.edu.au
website: www.cgs.vic.edu.au

Headmaster: Dr Paul Hicks

Geelong Grammar School
50 Biddlecombe Avenue, Corio, VIC 3214, Australia
email: principal@ggs.vic.edu.au
website: www.ggs.vic.edu.au

Principal: Stephen Meek

Haileybury
855 Springvale Road, Keysborough, VIC 3173, Australia
email: admissions@haileybury.vic.edu.au
website: www.haileybury.com.au

Principal: Derek Scott

Kincoppal-Rose Bay School of the Sacred Heart
New South Head Road, Rose Bay NSW 2029, Australia
email: reception@krb.nsw.edu.au
website: www.krb.nsw.edu.au

Principal: Mrs Hilary Johnston-Croke

The King's School
PO Box 1, Parramatta, NSW 2124, Australia
email: headmaster@kings.edu.au
website: www.kings.edu.au

Headmaster: Dr Tim F Hawkes

Knox Grammar School
7 Woodville Avenue, Wahroonga, NSW 2076, Australia
email: contact@knox.nsw.edu.au
website: www.knox.nsw.edu.au

Headmaster: John Weeks

Melbourne Grammar School
Domain Road, South Yarra, Melbourne, VIC 3004, Australia
email: mgs@mgs.vic.edu.au
website: www.mgs.vic.edu.au

Headmaster: Roy Kelley

Methodist Ladies' College
207 Barker Road, Kew, Victoria 3101, Australia
email: college@mlc.vic.edu.au
website: www.mlc.vic.edu.au

Principal: Miss Diana Vernon, BA, PGCE, MACE, MACEL

St Leonard's College
163 South Road, Brighton East, VIC 3187, Australia
email: stleonards@stleonards.vic.edu.au
website: www.stleonards.vic.edu.au

Principal: Mr Stuart Davis

Scotch College
1 Morrison Street, Hawthorn, VIC 3122, Australia
email: scotch@scotch.vic.edu.au
website: www.scotch.vic.edu.au

Principal: I Tom Batty

The Scots College
Victoria Road, Bellevue Hill, NSW 2023, Australia
email: reception@tsc.nsw.edu.au
website: www.tsc.nsw.edu.au

Principal: Dr Ian P M Lambert

Shore School
PO Box 1221, Blue Street, North Sydney, NSW 2059, Australia
email: headmaster@shore.nsw.edu.au
website: www.shore.nsw.edu.au

Head: Dr Timothy Wright

Trinity Grammar School
PO Box 174, 119 Prospect Road, Summer Hill, NSW 2130, Australia
email: mcujes@trinity.nsw.edu.au
website: www.trinity.nsw.edu.au

Head Master: G Milton Cujes

Wesley College
577 St Kilda Road, Melbourne, VIC 3004, Australia
email: principal@wesleycollege.net
website: www.wesleycollege.net
Principal: Dr Helen Drennan

Central, North and South America

Argentina

St Andrew's Scots School
Roque Saenz Peña 654, 1636 Olivos, Buenos Aires,
Argentina
email: administration@sanandres.esc.edu.ar
website: www.sanandres.esc.edu.ar
Head: Gabriel Rshaid

St George's College North
C. Rivadavia y Don Bosco, Los Polvorines 1613, Buenos
Aires, Argentina
email: informes@stgeorges.org.ar
website: www.stgeorges.edu.ar
Headmaster: Robin W Silk

Brazil

St Paul's School
Rua Juquiá 166, Jardim Paulistano, São Paulo SP 01440-
903, Brazil
email: spshead@stpauls.br
website: www.stpauls.br
Head: Ms Louise Simpson
(*See entry in IAPS section*)

Canada

Shawnigan Lake School
1975 Renfrew Road, Shawnigan Lake, BC
V0R 2W1, Canada
email: rtaylor@shawnigan.ca
website: www.shawnigan.ca
Head: David Robertson, MA, PGCE

Chile

The Grange School
Av Principe de Gales 6154, La Reina, 687067, Santiago,
Chile
email: rectoria@grange.cl
website: www.grange.cl
Rector: Rachid R Benammar
(*See Grange Preparatory School entry in IAPS section.*)

Europe

Cyprus

The English School
PO Box 23575, 1684 Nicosia, Cyprus
email: head@englishschool.ac.cy
website: www.englishschool.ac.cy
Headmaster: Graeme Garrett

Czech Republic

The English College in Prague
Sokolovska 320, 190-00 Praha 9, Czech Republic
email: office@englishcollege.cz
website: www.englishcollege.cz
Headmaster: Dr Nigel Brown

Greece

Campion School
PO Box 67484, Pallini, Athens 153 02, Greece
email: satherton@campion.edu.gr
website: www.campion.edu.gr
Headmaster: Stephen W Atherton

St Catherine's British School
PO Box 51019, Kifissia GR 145 10, Greece
email: headmaster@stcatherines.gr
website: www.stcatherines.gr
Headmaster: Mr Stuart Smith

Italy

The British School of Milan
Via Pisani Dossi 16, 20134 Milan, Italy
email: info@sjhschool.com
website: www.britishschoolmilan.com
Principal & CEO: Dr Chris Greenhalgh

St George's British International School
Via Cassia, La Storta, 00123 Rome, Italy
email: secretary@stgeorge.school.it
website: www.stgeorge.school.it
Principal: Martyn J Hales, BSc

Portugal

St Julian's School
Quinta Nova, 2776-601 Carcavelos Codex, Portugal
email: ccoelho@stjulians.com
website: www.stjulians.com
Headmaster: Craig Monaghan

Spain

The British School of Barcelona
Cognita Schools Group
Carrer de la Ginesta 26, 08860 Castelldefels, Barcelona, Spain
email: school@bsb.edu.es
website: www.britishschoolbarcelona.com

Executive Headteacher: **Mr John Bell**

Switzerland

Aiglon College
CH-1885 Chesières-Villars, Switzerland
email: info@aiglon.ch
website: www.aiglon.ch

Head Master: **Mr Richard McDonald**, MA Oxon, PGCE

Middle East

Bahrain

St Christopher's School
PO Box 32052, Isa Town, Kingdom of Bahrain
email: office.principal@st-chris.net
website: www.st-chris.net

Principal: **Mr Ed Goodwin**, BA, MA, MBA

(See entry in IAPS section)

Oman

British School Muscat
PO Box 1907, Ruwi, Muscat PC112, Sultanate of Oman
email: admissionsoffice@britishschoolmuscat.com
website: www.britishschoolmuscat.com

Principal: **Mr Kai Vacher**

Qatar

Doha College
PO Box 7506, Doha, State of Qatar
email: seniorexec@dohacollege.com
website: www.dohacollege.com

Principal: **Dr Steffen Sommer**

United Arab Emirates

The British School - Al Khubairat
P O Box 4001, Abu Dhabi, United Arab Emirates
email: head@britishschool.sch.ae
website: www.britishschool.sch.ae

Headmaster: **Mr Mark Leppard**, MBE

Dubai College
PO Box 837, Dubai, United Arab Emirates
email: dcadmin@dubaicollege.org
website: www.dubaicollege.org

Headmaster: **Mr Michael Lambert**

Jumeirah English Speaking School
PO Box 24942, Dubai, United Arab Emirates
email: jess@jess.sch.ae
website: www.jess.sch.ae

Director: **Mr Mark Steed**

Head Teacher, JESS Jumeirah Primary: **Mr Asa Firth**

Head Teacher, Arabian Ranches Primary: **Mr Darren Coulson**

Headmasters' and Headmistresses' Conference

Associates

In addition to Full membership (open to Heads of independent schools in the UK and Ireland) and International membership (open to Heads of independent schools overseas), HMC also elects a small number of Associates each year.

HMC Associates are either heads of high-performing maintained sector schools proposed and supported by HMC divisions or influential individuals in the world of education, including university vice-chancellors and academics, who endorse and support the work of HMC.

The following is a list of current HMC Associates:

BRIDGET TULLIE
Batley Grammar School, Batley, West Yorkshire
website: www.batleygrammar.co.uk

DR STUART D SMALLWOOD
Bishop Wordsworth's Grammar School, Salisbury, Wiltshire
website: www.bws.wilts.sch.uk

ROBERT J MASTERS
The Judd School, Tonbridge, Kent
website: www.judd.kent.sch.uk

DAVID HUMPRHEYS
Methodist Independent Schools Trust, London NW1
website: www.methodisteducation.co.uk

RUSSEL ELLICOTT
Pate's Grammar School, Cheltenham, Gloucestershire
website: www.pates.gloucs.sch.uk

PETER MIDDLETON
Welbeck – The Defence Sixth Form College, Loughborough, Leicestershire
website: www.dsfc.ac.uk

JILL BERRY
Educational Consultant

DR BRENDA DESPONTIN
Former Head

PART II
Schools whose Heads are members of the Girls' Schools Association

ALPHABETICAL LIST OF SCHOOLS

554

The following schools, whose Heads are members of both GSA and HMC, can be found in the HMC section:

Benenden School
Berkhamsted School
Bromley High School
Cheltenham Ladies' College
City of London School for Girls
Downe House
Francis Holland School, Regent's Park
The Godolphin and Latymer School
Haberdashers' Monmouth School for Girls
James Allen's Girls' School (JAGS)
Kent College Pembury
Queen Anne's School
Queenswood School
Roedean School
St Albans High School for Girls
St Mary's Calne
St Mary's School Ascot
Sherborne Girls
Withington Girls' School
Wycombe Abbey

GEOGRAPHICAL LIST OF GSA SCHOOLS

Individual School Entries

Abbots Bromley School
A Woodard School

High Street, Abbots Bromley, Staffordshire WS15 3BW

Tel:	01283 840232 (24 hrs)
email:	head@abbotsbromleyschool.com
website:	www.abbotsbromleyschool.com
Twitter:	@AbbotsBromley
Facebook:	/abbotsbromleyschool

Founded in 1874, the school is part of the Woodard Schools Corporation (Midland Division).

Abbots Bromley School is quite a remarkable school. Set in 53 acres of stunning grounds and adjoining beautiful countryside, Abbots Bromley was opened some 141 years ago as one of the first schools with Nathaniel Woodard's Christian ideals of 'Faith, Unity and Vision' to provide an education for young people in an environment which would cultivate pride and excellence in every aspect of life. The school finds inspiration from its heritage and gives both staff and students a very special pride and a sense of identity and the Woodard motto is as relevant today as it was almost two centuries ago. Our historic buildings create an ethos and environment which is truly inspiring.

We believe ourselves to be rich in resources with a stunningly beautiful chapel, incredible facilities for Dance (studios and staff to match the very best delivered to the highest standard through the Alkins School of Dance) and Drama and a superb set of sports facilities including a beautiful pool, wonderful gymnasium and a state-of-the-art astroturf pitch. Also, hidden in our grounds is an Equestrian Centre housing ponies and horses belonging both to our students as well as liveried to staff and local people that may be enjoyed by members of our community. We are fortunate indeed.

Our mission is to inspire excellence and fulfil potential and our vision is threefold:

1. To be parents' first-choice school.
2. To be a centre of academic excellence where every member of the Abbots Bromley community feels valued.
3. To be more than simply a school; more 'a way of life'

We aim for all students to be nurtured as uniquely talented individuals, finding fulfilment through their learning and the development of their intellectual, creative, physical and emotional capabilities and in this regard we welcome applications for anyone wishing to subscribe to this ethos. Should you wish to visit our splendid school, please do not feel that you need to wait to be invited to an Open Event, as every day is open day at Abbots Bromley. Indeed members of the student body, staff or myself would be happy to show you around. We are so very proud of what is on offer here.

We believe it is important for our students to develop the moral integrity to become responsible global citizens, so that they may take their place in society with confidence. We are confident that anyone associated with the Abbots Bromley learning community, pupil, student or adult, will leave the richer for their experience.

I am often asked who are our students and how do they learn? The answer is simple. We accept girls and boys (of all or no faith and all abilities) into our Kindergarten and Preparatory School & Sixth Form, where they are nurtured and flourish. The Senior School accepts girls (age 11–16) who are keen to learn, motivated to engage in both academic study and extracurricular activities and interested in learning about the world beyond the school. From September 2017 we will accept boys into Year 7 and the whole school will be fully coeducational by 2020.

Our Sixth Form became co-educational in September 2015, giving boys and girls (age 16–18) the opportunities to access courses which will give them a superb education. Young people are taught in small classes and with a personalised learning agenda and any who need additional support with either language or learning skills (including those who are Gifted and Able) are our focus. We also have AB International College on site, opened September 2015, and we will provide courses for overseas students wishing to improve their English whilst enjoying all that an English Boarding School can provide.

Our Boarding Houses are well equipped and senior students have their own study-bedrooms with wi-fi access. Students say that boarding here at AB is a 'home from home' and we believe our experienced, caring staff know our students very well and support them to gain independence and confidence in their own abilities, whilst always being supported. We offer full boarding, flexi boarding and occasional packages to suit all parents' requirements.

Fees per term (2016–2017). UK Students: Full Boarding £6,968–£8,575, Weekly Boarding £5,680–£7,184, Day £1,506–£5,119. International Students: Full Boarding £7,665–£9,435.

Exhibitions and Scholarships. Abbots Bromley is delighted to offer a variety of exhibitions and scholarships for entry into years 7, 8, 9, 10 and 12. Awards are available for academic, art, dance, music, equestrian and sport for our more able pupils enabling them to further challenge themselves at every opportunity. Values range from 10–20% of gross fees.

Charitable status. Abbots Bromley School Ltd is a Registered Charity, number 1103321.

Visitor: The Rt Revd The Bishop of Lichfield

Council:
Custos: Mrs P Norvall, Cert Ed
Vice Custos: Mr R Mansell, ACIB
Mr S Bourne
Miss E Carroll, BA Hons
Revd S Davis, BSc, MA, MIET
Mrs H Graham, BA Hons
Mr S James, LLB Hons
Mr R Knight, FRICS
Mr I Whyte, DO
Professor Dr R Luther

School Bursar and Clerk to the Council: Mr R van Driel

***Executive Head*: Mrs V Musgrave**, BA, MEd Mgt, FRSA

Head of Senior School: Mr R Udy, BSc Hons, PGCE
Head of AB International College: Mrs A Johnson, Hon BA, Cert Ed, Cert Prof St Ed
Head of Preparatory School: Mrs W Gordon, BEd Hons
Director of Staff and Student Support: Mrs E Ellis, BSc Hons, PGCE
Director of Academic Studies: Mrs K Rowlands, BA Hons, PGCE

Chaplain: The Revd P Conway, BA, Dip Min

Medical Centre:
Medical Nurse: Sister J Fox, RGN, Dip
Centre cover: Mrs L Shaw, NVQ3 Paediatric First Aid

Boarding Staff:
Head of Girls' Boarding: Miss R Francis, BA Hons, Dip RE
Deputy Head of Girls' Boarding: Mrs K Lomax, RGN

Residential:
Boarding Tutor: Miss R Vinter, BA Hons, ALCM, CertRCO; Miss H Sutton, BA Hons
Relief: Mrs J Turnbull
Senior Day Matron: Mrs L Woolley

Boarding Assistants:
Day: Mrs L Woolley
Evening: Mrs L Shaw, NVQ3, Miss G Norrington, NVQ3

GAP Assistants (2016):
Miss Catherine Burley
Miss Courtney Dudgeon
Miss Olivia Pearless
Miss Rose Wood

Head of Boys' Boarding: Mr I J Ravenhill
Deputy Head Boys' Boarding: Mrs J Harris, BSA Induction (appointment 1/9/2016)
Resident Boarding Tutors: Mr J Rayfield, BMus, PGCE, Mr R Armour, BA Hons, PGCE
Boarding Assistants:
Mrs S Ravenhill, DipM, Cert TESOL
Miss A Noya Martinez, CAP, BSpanish Studies, QTS

Designated Safeguarding Lead: Mrs A Johnson, Hon BA, Cert Ed, Cert Prof St Ed
Designated Safeguarding Person (EYFS): Mrs W Gordon, BEd Hons

International College Academic Staff:

Mrs A Johnson (*EYFS*) Hon BA, Cert Ed, Cert Prof St Ed

Art: Mr D Gleeson, MA, PGCE
English as a Foreign Language:
Mr I Williams, BA Hons, PGCE
Mrs S O'Brien, Childhood Level 2, CELTA
Mrs S Ravenhill, DipM, Chartered Marketer, Cert TESOL
Computer Science: Mr R Armour, BA Hons, PGCE
Mathematics: Mr A Coghlan, BSc Hons, PGCE
Modern Foreign Languages: Ms H Chadfield, BA Hons, PGCE
Science:
Miss J Merchant BSc Hons, PGCE
Miss R Davis, BEng Hons, PGCE

Senior School Academic Staff:

Head of Senior School: Mr R Udy, BSc Hons, PGCE

Heads of Faculty:
Languages: Mrs M Steer, BA Hons, PGCE, Dip SEN
Science: Mrs V Standing, MEng, PGCE
Mathematics: Mrs S Booth, BSc Hons PGCE
Humanities: Mrs S Towell, BA Hons, PGCE
Physical & Creative Arts: Mrs A Moore, BA Hons, PGCE

Heads of House:
St Mary and KS3: Mrs B Coulthard, BA Hons, PGCE
St Anne and KS4: Mrs J Preston, Licence d'anglais, PGCE, Dip Ed, Dip Translation
St Chad and KS5: Miss J Merchant, BSc Hons, PGCE
St Gregory & LES/Gifted & Talented: Mrs S Robertson, BA Hons

Head of Senior School: Mr R Udy, BSc Hons, PGCE
Director of Academic Studies: Mrs K Rowlands, BA Hons, PGCE
Director of Staff & Student Support: Mrs E Ellis, BSc Hons, PGCE
Head of Sixth Form: Mrs V Hawley, BA Hons
Oxbridge Mentor: Mr T Dobney, BMus Hons, PGCE

Librarian/Careers Advisor: Mrs J Wheeldon, BA Hons

* *Subject Lead*

Art:
*Mrs A Moore, BA Hons, PGCE
Mr D Gleeson, MA, PGCE
Miss N Gandy, BA Hons, PGCE, QTLS

Business Studies:
Mr R Armour, BA Hons, PGCE

English:
*Mrs M Steer, BA Hons, PGCE, Dip SEN
Ms E Godwin BA Hons, PGCE, MA
Mrs E Lampard, BA Hons, PGCE, CELTA OU Dip (*Mandarin, German*)
Mr I Williams, BA Hons, PGCE
Miss H Sutton, BA Hons
English as a Foreign Language:
Mrs E Lampard, BA Hons, PGCE, CELTA OU Dip (*Mandarin*)
Mrs S O'Brien, Childhood Level 2, CELTA
Mrs J Preston, Licence d'anglais PGCE, Dip Ed, Dip Translation
Mrs S Ravenhill, DipM, Chartered Marketer, Cert TESOL
Mr I Williams, BA Hons, PGCE

Food Technology:
Mrs A Moore, BA Hons, PGCE

Geography:
*Mrs S Hind, BSc Hons, PGCE
Mrs A Johnson, Hon BA, Cert Ed, Cert Prof St Ed
Mrs K Rowlands, BA Hons, PGCE
Mr R Udy, BSc Hons, PGCE

History:
*Mrs S Towell, BA Hons, PGCE
Mrs K Rowlands, BA Hons, PGCE

Information Technology:
*Mr R Armour, BA Hons, PGCE
Network Manager: Mr R Ellis

Learning Enrichment:
Mrs U Griffiths, BA Hons, Dip ELS, Dip SpLD AMBDA, Dip HCS MHS, Dip CP MNCS
Mrs J Turnbull, FdA DPP, NVQ Level 3 IPM
Learning Support Assistant:
Mrs A Henry, CACHE 3
Mrs V Peach, City & Guilds 3

Mathematics:
*Mr A Coghlan, BSc Hons, PGCE
Mrs S Booth, BSc Hons, PGCE
Mr G Johnson, BA, NPQH, PGCE
Mrs J Powner, BA Hons, PGCE

Modern Languages:
*Mrs B Coulthard, BA Hons, PGCE
Ms H Chadfield, BA Hons, PGCE
Mr J Redmond, BA Hons, PGCE
Mrs K Rowlands, BA Hons, PGCE
Mrs J Preston, Licence d'anglais PGCE, Dip Ed, Dip Translation

Music:
**Director of Music:* Mr T Dobney, BMus Hons PGCE
Miss R Vinter, BA Hons, ALCM, CertRCO
Visiting specialist vocal and instrumental staff

Photography:
*Miss N Gandy, BA Hons, PGCE, QTLS

Physical Education:
*Mr B Bullyment, BA Hons, PGCE
Mrs S Robertson, BA Hons

Visiting Specialist Coaches

Religious Studies:
Revd P Conway, BA, Dip Min

Sciences:
*Miss J Merchant, BSc Hons, PGCE
Mrs C Ashton, BSc Hons, PGCE
Mrs A Chester, BSc Hons
Miss R Davis, BEng Hons, PGCE
Mrs E Ellis, BSc Hons, PGCE
Mrs V Standing, MEng, PGCE

Science Technician: Mrs H Stephenson

Social Sciences:
*Mrs V Hawley, BA Hons

Educational Visits Coordinator:
Mrs A Johnson, Hon BA, Cert Ed, Cert Prof St Ed (*EYFS*)

Enrichment Coordinator:
Mr I Ravenhill

PSHCE Coordinator:
Miss J Merchant, BSc Hons, PGCE
Mrs M Swinnerton, BA Hons, PGCE, Cert SpLD (*for
    Preparatory Department*)

Preparatory Department Academic Staff:

Head: Mrs W Gordon, BEd Hons

Learning Enrichment & Support/Pastoral Leaders:
Mrs M Swinnerton, BA Hons, PGCE, Cert SpLD
Mrs U Griffiths, B Hons, Dip ELS, Dip SpLD, AMBDA,
    Dip HCS MHS, Dip CP MINCS

Early Years Lead: Mrs W Gordon, BEd Hons

Form Teachers:
Mrs W Gordon, BEd Hons
Mrs S Crout, Dip Ed
Mrs M Swinnerton, BA Hons, PGCE, Cert SpLD
Mrs J Hobbs, BA Hons, PGCE, CELTA
Miss K Shore, BEd Hons

Pastoral Classroom Assistants:
Mrs A Henry, CACHE 3
Miss G Norrington, NVQ3

Kindergarten Leader: Mrs A Dunmore, NVQ3

Extracurricular Departments:

Dance:
Artistic Directors:
Mr R Alkins, RAD Cert TC Dist
Mrs M Alkins, RAD Cert
Visiting Specialist Dance Staff: Ballet, Modern & Tap,
    Musical Theatre and BTEC

Duke of Edinburgh's Award Scheme Coordinator:
Manager: Mrs S Robertson, BA Hons

Riding (Abbots Bromley Equestrian Centre):
Director of Equitation: Miss S Vickers, BHSI, Snr BHS
    Assessor, Cert Ed
Instructor: Miss L Kilgallon, BHS Stage 4 Horse Care
Relief Instructor:
Mrs S Wilson, BSc, BSHII
Mrs D Atkin, BHSI, PTT, NVQ 3 Horse Care
Working Pupils: Miss G Madders, BHS 1, Miss H
    Silvester, BHS 1

Speech & Drama & Teacher of GSCE Drama:
Mrs A-M Morrell, LLAM, FRSA, HND Theatre Design,
    Dip Fashion & Design

Administration:
Registration & Admissions: Mrs A Johnson, Head of ABIC
PA to Head, Senior School: Mrs K Addy

PA to Head, Preparatory School: Mrs J Dale
Lettings & Accounts Administrator: (*to be appointed*)
School Finance Officer: Mrs V Carter
Finance Assistant: Mrs A Sangster
Guild Development Manager: Mrs J Cairns Smith
Secretary/PA to Head of ABIC: Mrs R Kirkland
Examinations Officer: Mrs J Simon
Personnel Secretary: Mrs H Meadows
Receptionist: Mrs M Mellor

Site:
Site Manager: Mr D Wallis, Dip Management
Maintenance Supervisor: Mr G Mottram
Caretaker: Mr A Stinchcombe
Relief Caretaker: Mr M Hydes
Domestic Supervisor: Mrs J Glennan
Relief Domestic Supervisor: Miss N McQuillan

Abbot's Hill School

Bunkers Lane, Hemel Hempstead, Herts HP3 8RP

Tel:	01442 240333
Fax:	01442 269981
email:	registrar@abbotshill.herts.sch.uk
website:	www.abbotshill.herts.sch.uk
Twitter:	@AbbotsHill
Facebook:	/AbbotsHillSchool
LinkedIn:	/abbot's-hill

Motto: *Vi et Virtute*

Founded 1912.

Abbot's Hill School is an Independent Day School for girls aged 4–16 years. Our Day Nursery and Pre-School caters for girls and boys from 6 months. The School is situated in 76 acres of parkland on the edge of Hemel Hempstead.

A great emphasis is placed on providing a complete and balanced education. We have a strong record of academic success. Throughout the school, pupils are taught in small classes in which excellent teaching and personalised support ensure that everyone is inspired to exceed their potential.

We pride ourselves on our pastoral care. The sense of being part of an extended family is frequently commented on by pupils, parents and staff alike. In such a nurturing environment, pupils grow naturally in confidence, are happy to embrace new challenges and eagerly take on increasing responsibilities. Pupils leave Abbot's Hill fully equipped to take on with passion the challenges and opportunities life has to offer.

With small classes and a high teacher-pupil ratio, the school aims to develop the academic and creative talents, social skills and confidence of each pupil. Every pupil benefits from being known personally by the Headmistress and teaching staff who seek to create a happy and caring environment.

Senior School. The Senior School is based in a spacious and comfortable 19th Century house, which, combined with purpose-built teaching blocks, Science, Sport, Performing Arts and ICT suites, provides our pupils with first-class facilities.

Curriculum. During the first three years, a broad programme based on the National Curriculum is followed, encompassing both academic and creative subjects. Each girl's potential and progress is carefully monitored by both teaching staff and a personal tutor. Subjects studied include English, Maths, Science, French, Spanish, Geography, History, Media Studies, Information and Communication Technology, Religious Studies, Music, Personal, Social, Health,

Economic and Citizenship Education, Art and Design, Drama, Food Technology and Physical Education.

In Years 10 and 11 a core GCSE curriculum of up to 8 subjects is followed with girls choosing up to three further subjects.

Music and Performing Arts. The School has very strong Music and Performing Arts Departments with excellent facilities. The Performing Arts building includes studios for dance, drama and music as well as a theatre. The School Choirs and Orchestra perform regularly in concerts, recitals, plays, musicals and various functions throughout the year and there is a school production each year.

Sports. The School has a strong sporting tradition. There is a well-equipped Sports Hall, lacrosse pitches, grass and hard tennis courts, and a heated outdoor swimming pool. The main sports played are Lacrosse, Netball, Athletics, Tennis, Rounders and Swimming. All girls are encouraged to participate in the sporting opportunities at Abbot's Hill and currently there are a number of girls who have reached County and National standard in selected sports.

Extracurricular Activities. Many activities and clubs are held outside of School and these vary in range from Dance, Art, The Duke of Edinburgh's Award scheme, Music, Speech and Drama and all sports.

Admission. Admission to Abbot's Hill is by Entrance Examination, interview, and a report from the previous school.

Scholarships and Bursaries. Academic, Art, Drama, Music and Sport scholarships are available giving 5–10% reduction in fees. Means-tested Bursaries are also available.

Fees per term (2016–2017). Senior School: £5,858 (Years 7–11); Prep School: £3,350–£4,167 (Reception to Year 6); Nursery: from £53 per day.

Prep School. Abbot's Hill Prep is situated in the same grounds as the Senior School. The Prep School provides Pre-Preparatory and Preparatory education for girls aged 4 and above. Abbot's Hill Nursery and Pre-School welcome boys and girls from 6 months of age. The Prep mixes the formal setting of the classroom with the wealth of opportunity provided by our physical surroundings. Children are given the freedom in which to grow, learn and play. Classrooms and corridors are bright and well decorated with children's work reflecting the diversity of the curriculum.

The Prep School plays a very important role within our school community and is an integral part of the school as a whole. It is our aim at Abbot's Hill to nurture the whole child, thus enabling our pupils to develop their talents whether they be academic, artistic or sporting. Specialist teaching is introduced from a child's earliest days; French, Music and PE are introduced in the pre-school year. This is added to as a child progresses to include Drama, Games, ICT and Geography. By the time a girl reaches Year 5 she is being completely subject taught and is able to adapt to moving around whilst being supported by a class teacher.

The small class sizes at Abbot's Hill Prep enable individual needs to be recognised and met early with the minimum disruption. For those who need extra support this is offered within the classroom setting or one-to-one as appropriate. Gifts or talents for a particular area of learning can be extended and developed to their potential.

The wider curriculum plays a key role. Educational visits are an integral part of the teaching programme and children are regularly taken on visits to galleries and museums to enhance their learning experience. Outside visitors lead workshops at school for year groups or the whole school as appropriate. The extracurricular programme is wide ranging and ever changing. It currently includes such wide-ranging pursuits as languages, trampolining, gardening and board games as well as a wealth of musical and sports clubs.

Further information. Abbot's Hill welcomes visits from prospective parents and pupils. If you would like to visit the School, please contact the Registrar for an appointment on 01442 240333 or email registrar@abbotshill.herts.sch.uk.

Charitable status. Abbot's Hill Charitable Trust is a Registered Charity, number 311053, which exists to provide high quality education for children.

Chairman of the Governing Body: Mrs J Mark, BA Hons, QTS

Headmistress: **Mrs E Thomas**, BA Hons, PGCE, NPQH

Head of Prep School: Miss K Twinn, BA Hons with QTS

Head of Senior School: Mrs S Doyle, BEd Hons

Bursar: Mr N Webb, MA, ACA

Registrar: Ms A Cooper

Adcote School

Little Ness, Shrewsbury, Shropshire SY4 2JY

Tel: 01939 260202
Fax: 01939 261300
email: admissions@adcoteschool.co.uk
           marketing@adcoteinternational.com
website: www.adcoteschool.org.uk
Twitter: @AdcoteSchool
LinkedIn: /Adcote-School-for-Girls

Age Range. 7–18.
Number in School. 240 Girls.

Adcote School is a thriving boarding and day school for around 240 girls currently. Despite its imposing exterior, we are proud of our welcoming, friendly and unpretentious reputation. We are fortunate to be located in a beautiful and safe rural setting with a magnificent Grade I listed building, with 30 acres of beautifully landscaped parkland surrounding the school. These wonderful gardens provide an incredibly safe, secure and idyllic backdrop to this historic school. Adcote has begun a multimillion pound project of modernisation and investment in the school – the most significant development in Adcote's 109 year history. New facilities completed by 2015 include new classrooms, four science labs, catering facilities, boarding accommodation, sports hall, art and textiles block.

Perhaps Adcote's greatest achievement is the variety and breadth of education that it provides for its pupils. Both day girls and boarders benefit from excellent tuition in a range of activities including tennis, horse riding, gymnastics and swimming as well as plenty of healthy competition with local schools in netball, hockey and other sports. Every year, as the GCSE and A Level examination results come in, we are proud of the achievements of each girl and of our school. The excellent results and high league table ranking reflect the hard work of the girls, excellent teaching and the support of parents and families.

Every girl at Adcote, when she leaves the school, should feel she has achieved all she can both academically and intellectually.

Curriculum. Adcote is committed to fostering the achievement of all our girls, without undue pressure. Self-confidence and poise distinguish our pupils whose teachers are dedicated to cultivating the strengths of each girl. Adcote produces confident, enquiring and well-rounded girls who are equipped to play full and constructive roles in an ever-changing society.

Years 7, 8, and 9 follow a broad curriculum which ensures that there is continuity and progression together with sufficient flexibility to respond to individual needs and interests.

The GCSE and IGCSE programme taught in Years 10 and 11, includes the core subjects of English Language, English Literature, Mathematics, ICT (Cambridge Nationals), PE (non-examined) and PSHE (non-examined), plus at least one Science and 7 other subjects from a range of 16 options choices. IGCSE qualifications are internationally recognised by schools, universities and employers as equivalent to, or even slightly more challenging than, UK GCSEs. They are an excellent preparation for A/AS Level courses.

Adcote's outstanding academic results at A Level, Oxbridge success, and entry to other top Universities, accounts for the recent and growing number of pupils in the Sixth Form. The Sixth Form requires each girl to follow her specialist subjects in depth. In Lower Sixth (Year 12), most girls choose to take four A Level subjects from a list of 21 options, in addition to PSHE and PE, which are compulsory but non-examined. In the Upper Sixth (Year 13) three subjects are usually continued to full A Level (A2). As part of ongoing investment in buildings and facilities, the school has recently created a dedicated Sixth Form Centre.

Performing Arts. The school places great emphasis on Music, Dance, and Drama as well as a range of other activities. All the performing arts are included in the core curriculum to age 14, and thereafter voluntarily. Instrumental playing is much encouraged, there are several choirs in the school which practice regularly and there are extracurricular workshops in dance and drama, and performances several times a year.

Activities. All girls participate in a wide range of activities, including rowing, fencing, Chinese, Russian, Yoga, gardening and horse riding. Sport plays an important part in the life of the school. The school regularly plays hockey, netball, rounders and tennis, with gymnastics being particularly strong. Outward bound programmes also play an important part of life at Adcote, as do interesting weekend activities, and trips away from school. There is an interesting programme of weekly activities for boarding students. A new sports hall was built in 2014 for use by all pupils.

Pastoral Care. The school's size means that the children, staff and parents really get to know each other. There is a tangible sense of community, creating a warm and enabling family atmosphere. Boarders are looked after by Housemistresses and the resident staff, and all girls have a personal tutor, responsible for individual welfare and academic progress. Great importance is attached to understanding the individual and developing personal abilities so that girls meet the demands of the modern world with confidence and good judgement. There is a range of full and weekly boarding options.

Fees per term (2016–2017). UK/Domestic Students: Day Girls £3,047–£4,946; Weekly Boarders £5,754–£8,251 Full Boarders £6,539–£9,032.

Reductions are made in fees of second and subsequent sisters. Bursaries are available for children from the clergy or from Forces families. There are scholarships for academic excellence. The school welcomes applications from girls whose parents cannot afford the fees in full or in part. In line with our aim as a Charity to provide public benefit the school offers means-tested bursaries to outstanding pupils who would not otherwise be able to benefit from the education we provide. The school offers a wide range of discretionary and means-tested bursaries each year to pupils.

A prospectus and further details may be obtained from the Admissions Assistant: admissions@adcoteschool.co.uk.

Charitable status. Adcote School Educational Trust Limited is a Registered Charity, number 528407.

Board of Governors:
Chairman: Mr Mark Fairbrother
Vice-Chairman: Lt Col [Retd] J Moody, OBE

Members:
Mrs T Heath-Campbell BA Hons
Mr J Leighton, BSc Hons, Dip Ed
Mr I Galliers
Mrs A Roberts

***Headmistress:* Mrs D Browne**, BA UC Wales, PGCE Exeter, MEd Gloucestershire, NPQH NCSL

Head of Academics: Mrs S Dale, BA Oxford Brookes, PGCE Edge Hill
Head of Student Wellbeing: Miss L Hudson, BEd Hons Bedford
Head of Lower School: Mrs J Greenwood, BA Hons Wales, PGCE Manchester

Head of Faculties:
Languages: Mr G Carter, BA Hons Leeds, PGCE Leeds
STEM: Mr N Aston-Smith, BSc Hons Southampton, PGCE Oxford
Humanities: Miss S Roberts, BA Hons Chester, PGCE Aberystwyth
Physical: Miss A Pugh, BSc Hons Loughborough, PGCE Birmingham
Creative: Mrs M Cooke, BPhil Hons Durham, PG Cert Canterbury

Bursar: Mr Richard Walker

Chaplain: Reverend L Burns

Academic Staff:
Mr N Aston-Smith, BSc Hons Southampton, PGCE Oxford (*Mathematics, RE*)
Mr D Barker, BSc Hons Manchester, Cert Ed Wolverhampton (*Physics*)
Mrs E Barnett, BSc Hons Glasgow, PGCE Bristol (*Science*)
Mrs C Besterman, BA Hons Cambridge, MA Hons Cambridge (*Classics*)
Miss N Bignall, BEng Hons Liverpool, PGCE Wolverhampton (*Science, Maths*)
Mrs A Brown, BSc Hons Nottingham, PGCE Lancaster, Dip SpLD OCR APC (*Learning Support*)
Mr C Bunn, BMus Hons Royal Academy, PGCE Edge Hill (*Junior School*)
Mrs N Candler, BA Hons Birmingham, PGCE Wolverhampton (*Junior School*)
Mr G Carter, BA Hons Leeds, PGCE Leeds (*EAL*)
Mr I Clark, MA Warwick, PGCE London (*Economics*)
Mrs M Cooke, BPhil Hons Durham, PGCert Canterbury (*Drama, Child Development, Dance*)
Mrs S Dale, BA Oxford Brookes, PGCE Edge Hill (*English*)
Mr J Davies (*Drama, English*)
Mr C Farmer, BEng Hons Coventry, PGCE (*Head of ICT, ICT Manager*)
Mrs K Gardner, BSc Hons Nottingham, PGCE Loughborough
Mrs G Heawood, BA Hons Wolverhampton, PGCE Glos (*Junior School*)
Miss G Hepper, BA Hons Wolverhampton, PGCE West Midlands (*Junior School*)
Miss S Jones, BSc Liverpool, MSc Manchester, PGCE Edge Hill (*Psychology*)
Miss A Kordas, Dip Ed Warsaw
Ms L Nixson (*Assistant Director of Sport*)
Mr A O'Connor, BA Middlesex, PGCE Carmarthen, Dip TEFL/ESP London (*SENCO*)
Miss J Owen-Evans (*Gymnastics Coach*)
Mr I Phillips, BSc Hons Leeds, PGCE Aberystwyth (*Head of Science*)
Mrs J Phillips, BSc Hons Leeds, PGCE Chester (*Science*)
Miss A Pugh, BSc Hons Loughborough, PGCE Birmingham (*Director of Sport*)

Mrs L Richards, BSc Hons Leicester, PGCE Leicester
(*Mathematics*)
Mrs K Rink, BA Hons Oxford (*English*)
Mrs R Roberts, BSc Hons Bath, PGCE Staffordshire (*Food Technology*)
Miss S Roberts, BA Hons Chester, PGCE Aberystwyth (*History*)
Miss M Warner, BSc Hons Huddersfield, PGCE Birmingham (*Textiles*)
Mrs C Wemyss, BA Hons Cardiff, PGCE Cardiff (*Junior School*)
Mrs H Wrobel, BA Hons NE Wales, PGCE Chester (*Art*)

Music Staff:
Mrs E Bouyac, BA Hons, MA, PGCE (*Singing*)
Mrs C Stone, BA Hons, MA (*Percussion*)
Mrs R Glossop, LRAM, LTCL, DipMus Huds, PGCE (*Piano*)
Mr D Heywood, ABRSM, Birmingham, QTS (*Brass*)
Mr A Jones, BA Hons Leeds (*Guitar*)
Mrs K Langdon (*Woodwind*)
Mrs A Lawrence, GMus, ALCM, PGCE (*Violin*)
Mrs O Lewis, Academy of Music, Moscow (*Piano*)
Mrs J Lumley, LLCM TD (*Woodwind*)

Sports/Extracurricular Staff:
Miss L Davies (*Dance*)
Miss E Gittins (*Yoga*)
Mr D Hiam (*Fencing*)
Mr M Markham, LTA Level 4 coach (*Tennis*)
Mrs A Moody (*Ballet*)
Mr B Strefford, LTA Level 2 coach (*Tennis*)

Support Staff:
Assistant Bursar: Mrs M Modebe
Financial Assistant: Mrs H Jones
School Secretary/Headmistress's PA: Miss E Brown
PA to Heads of Faculties: Mrs P Peplow-Freer
Head of UK Admissions: Mrs P Jones

Teaching Assistants:
Miss L Jones
Mrs V Healy
Mrs L Hughes

Head of Boarding: Ms N Jones
Enrichment Officer: Miss J Turvey
International Officer: Mrs P Wang
Boarding House Matrons: Mrs W Edwards, Mrs S Okell
School Nurse: Mrs B Evans
Science Technician: Mrs A Wright

Alderley Edge School for Girls

Wilmslow Road, Alderley Edge, Cheshire SK9 7QE

Tel:	01625 583028
Fax:	01625 590271
email:	jbedigan@aesg.co.uk
website:	www.aesg.co.uk
Twitter:	@schoolforgirls
Facebook:	@Alderley-Edge-School-For-Girls

Age Range. 2–18.
Number in School. Nursery, Pre-School and Reception 46; Junior School 150; Senior School 328; Sixth Form 64.
Fees per term (2016–2017). Nursery £2,490; Pre-School £2,106; Key Stage 1 £2,577; Key Stage 2 £3,039; Senior £3,316, Sixth Form £3,816.

Background. For many years the village of Alderley Edge was the location for two of the finest Independent Girls' Schools in the North West of England. In September

1999 the two schools became one. An independent, all girls, ecumenical school is unique in England and the merger of the two schools was welcomed and supported by the Anglican and Roman Catholic clergy and the founders of both schools.

The Sisters of St Joseph, a Roman Catholic Order, founded Mount Carmel School in 1945. St Hilary's was founded in 1817 and became part of the Woodard Corporation, a Church of England foundation, in 1955. Alderley Edge School for Girls is linked to the Woodard Corporation, the largest group of schools in England. Among them are independent and maintained schools in England, the United States and Australia.

General. This forward-looking girls' school offers a high level of personal attention. Respect for hard work, the development of the whole person and good discipline are the traditional principles on which our creative and innovative educational philosophy is based. We aim to provide a well-balanced education which celebrates achievement in all aspects of school life from Nursery to Sixth Form. In February 2015, the school was judged 'outstanding' and 'excellent' – the best possible outcomes – by the Independent Schools Inspectorate.

Location. The school is situated in a semi-rural area of Alderley Edge in Cheshire, 15 miles south of Manchester, with easy access to the motorway network and only minutes from Manchester Airport and two Intercity mainline stations. Transport is readily available throughout the area.

Admissions. The Early Years Department caters for girls from 2 years. Admission for girls to the Junior School is at 4/5 years old. Admission to the Senior School is at 11 years by Entrance Examination and interview.

Curriculum. *Senior School*: Students follow a broad and balanced curriculum based on the National Curriculum but with many additions. Subjects include: Mathematics, English Language, English Literature, Computer Science, Biology, Chemistry, Physics, French, German, Spanish, Latin, History, Geography, Music, Drama, Religious Studies, Food Technology, Art, Design Technology, Business Studies, PPE (Philosophy, Politics, Economics), PSHE (Personal, Social, Health Education) and Physical Education. At A Level the following subjects are offered in addition those listed above: Further Mathematics, Philosophy & Ethics, Economics, Psychology and Theatre Studies.

In addition to their normal academic studies, all Lower Sixth pupils study AS General Studies and high fliers are encouraged to do the Extended Project Qualification (EPQ).

Academic excellence is the school's main aim and attention is paid to meeting the individual needs and abilities of the students. Small classes and continuous assessment ensure high levels of pupil achievement.

Junior School: Creative and academic learning are at the heart of the Junior School. The work is based on the National Curriculum with English, Mathematics and Science providing the foundations for learning with History, Geography, RE, Art, Design, Computing, Music, PE, French, Dance/Drama and Spanish completing the curriculum. Latin is also taught from Year 5. There is considerable input into the specialist teaching from the Senior School staff.

Examination Results 2016. Junior school pupils undertake InCAS (Interactive Computerised Assessment System) assessments.

GCSE results: Overall pass rate (A*–C) 97%; 45% of all passes at A*/A.

A Level results: Pass rate 100%; 90% of all grades at A*–C.

The Arts. *Music*: A very large percentage of pupils learn a musical instrument and examinations may be taken. The school runs 4 choirs, 2 orchestras, a jazz band and numerous smaller instrumental ensembles including string groups, a brass group and 5 different woodwind groups. Many cups have been won in local festivals and pupils perform in local youth orchestras.

Drama and Dance: Both are offered. The majority of pupils are involved in school productions and all pupils participate in House and other productions. There are four dance squads which rehearse weekly and holiday courses in Dance and Drama are also on offer.

Sports and Clubs. *Sports*: tennis, rounders, hockey, athletics, netball, gymnastics, football, swimming, dance, cross country, badminton, volleyball, squash, fitness, self-defence. In the Sixth Form a huge variety of options are available for the girls including golf and aerobics.

Senior Clubs: language club, Biology/Chemistry/Physics workshops, Maths clinics, French club, book club, DT and Art clubs, magazine committee, dance, drama, poetry, public speaking, hockey, netball, tennis, rounders, athletics, Duke of Edinburgh's Award, Games, Comenius European Educational Project, Model United Nations, Young Enterprise, Youth Speaks and Mock Trial.

Junior Clubs: Contemporary Dance, Drama, Judo, Short Tennis, Brownies, Gardening, French, Netball, Spanish, Library, Cycling Proficiency and many more.

Facilities. In creating a new school we achieved our objective to remain small enough to care for every child's needs and yet the school enjoys all the benefits and resources of a much larger school. A multimillion pound investment programme has provided a new Senior School, and a completely refurbished Junior School. Facilities include six superbly equipped science laboratories, four ICT suites with online facilities throughout the school, Language Suite with language laboratory, Humanities block with Business Studies centre, competition-size Sports Hall, Gymnasium, Performing Arts Centre, Chapel and a Library with breathtaking views over the Cheshire Plain. In addition there is a modern and well-appointed Sixth Form centre – including a dedicated ICT suite – to accommodate the increasing number of girls in our Sixth Form.

Scholarships and Bursaries. Several Academic scholarships and scholarships for Music are awarded at 11+, 13+ and 16+. Art and Sport scholarships are available at 11+. Bursaries are also available (income linked).

Charitable status. Alderley Edge School for Girls is a Registered Charity, number 1006726. It exists to provide education for children.

Chair of Governors: Mrs S Herring

Headmistress: Mrs Helen Jeys, BA Durham

Deputy Headmistress: Mrs C Wood, BA Hons, PGCE Leicester
Director of Studies: Mrs C Millar
Head of Junior School: Ms B Howard, BEd Hons Exeter
Head of Lower School (Years 7–8): Mrs J Barker
Head of Year 9: Miss M Moss
Head of Upper School (Years 9–11): Mrs J Waterhouse
Head of Sixth Form: Mr J Russell
Bursar: Mr S Malkin
Registrar: Mrs J Bedigan

Heads of Department:

Art: Mrs C Latimer
Business Studies: Mrs S Balfour
Chemistry: Dr D Hughes
Classics: Mr P Tandler
Design Technology: Mrs K Boyland
Drama: Mrs C Foster
English: Ms L Telford
Food Technology: Mrs C Leigh
Geography: Miss N Johal
History: Mrs C Millar
ICT: Mr J Chadwick
Mathematics: Mr S Cunliffe

Modern Foreign Languages: Mrs I Jones
Music: Mrs A Pattrick
Physical Education: Mrs S Waite
Physics: Mrs K Torr
Psychology: Mrs A Raval
Religious Education: Ms A Laing
Science: Dr D Hughes

Badminton School

Westbury-on-Trym, Bristol BS9 3BA

Tel:	0117 905 5200
Fax:	0117 962 3049
email:	admissions@badmintonschool.co.uk
website:	www.badmintonschool.co.uk

Motto: *Pro Omnibus Quisque Pro Deo Omnes*

Founded 1858. Non denominational.

Badminton is an independent girls' boarding, weekly boarding and day school situated in a 15-acre site in Westbury-on-Trym on the outskirts of the university city of Bristol.

Age Range of Pupils. 3 to 18.

Number of Pupils. 450: Boarding 187; Day 263.

Number of Staff. Full-time teaching 37, Part-time teaching 16. Teacher Pupil ratio is currently 1:7.

Educational Philosophy. Whilst the school retains an outstanding academic record, its focus continues to be on nurturing the girls' natural curiosity and fuelling their passion for learning. The enduring excellence that Badminton girls achieve, stems from the positive atmosphere in the School and the holistic approach to education, as well as the exceptional relationships between staff and pupils, which are mature, friendly and based on principles of courtesy and mutual respect. Teachers are highly-qualified specialists in their field and encourage girls to develop academic confidence and to become independent learners by taking responsibility for their work and progress. The most important feature of academic life at Badminton is the resounding philosophy that it is the norm to ask questions, to seek help and, above all, to enjoy learning.

It is a characteristic of Badminton girls that they are thoughtful individuals, able to evaluate information and decide for themselves. This approach extends beyond their studies and into the day-to-day life of the School, where girls are given a wide range of opportunities to grow, develop and express themselves in an enormous range of activities. Staff also enjoy sharing their enthusiasm for their subject and often involve girls in projects and competitions in the local community and nationally.

The Badminton community gives girls a chance to develop an understanding of the viewpoints of others and to think about contributing to the world around them. Girls leave Badminton ready to face the changing and challenging wider world and, when they do, they take with them a strong network of lifelong friends developed through a wealth of shared experiences.

Boarding. The size of the campus and community at Badminton gives a homely and vibrant feel to the School. This, coupled with excellent pastoral care, leaves no scope for anonymity, but rather lends itself to strong mutually supportive relationships between girls as well as between girls and staff.

The boarding accommodation is split into three areas (junior, middle and Sixth Form) so girls get a good sense of progression and development as they move up through the school. Full-time, weekly or flexi boarding are offered and day girls are welcome to flexi board, allowing girls to easily combine their academic schedules with the many activities that are on offer after school and at weekends.

Bartlett House offers cosy bedrooms for boarders in Years 5–8 and easy access to gardens and play areas. Sanderson House, a modern boarding house opened in 2008, accommodates boarders in Years 9, 10 and 11. The Sixth Form Centre provides Years 12 and 13 with a more independent environment in double or single study-bedrooms. In each House, boarders have the support of a resident Housemistress, Assistant Housemistresses and Resident Tutors and there is a broad range of clubs and activities on offer every day as well as a full weekend programme.

The School's enrichment programme is extremely important in the overall development of the pupils and girls participate in many activities and are encouraged to do so. The activities offered vary depending on the interests of the girls; some have an academic bias, others let the girls explore their creative interests. Girls are very much encouraged to enjoy and value their own and their peers' successes and triumphs in every area of life.

Curriculum. The School's broad curriculum provides a rich and varied experience for the girls. Through Art, Drama and Music programmes, each girl has many opportunities to express her individuality and develop her own unique identity. In an increasingly global society, the importance of languages has never been greater and girls have the opportunity to study Mandarin and Greek in addition to more traditional languages such as French and Latin.

Small classes ensure that all the girls receive individual help and attention from their teachers. Badminton girls are proactive and independent learners; they are not afraid to take intellectual risks and are always happy to ask questions. The emphasis at Badminton is on a holistic education, not narrowly academic, and both the curriculum and the timetable are constructed to create a balance between academic achievement, personal development, life skills and other enterprising activity.

Academic Record. Badminton has a fine academic record at GCSE, AS and A Level. The GCSE and A Level pass rate is 100%. Sixth Form leavers go on to study at some of the top universities and Music Conservatories in the UK and overseas, including Oxford, Cambridge and the Royal Academy of Music and further afield.

Facilities. All the facilities of the school are on site and include a 25m indoor swimming pool, international-sized astro pitch, 7 tennis and 4 netball courts, gymnasium and fitness suite as well as a fully-equipped Science Centre, Creative Arts Centre and self-contained Sixth Form Centre. There are extensive fiction, careers, music and art libraries as well as a Music School.

Music, Drama and Creative Arts. All girls are involved in the Arts, both within the curriculum and as extracurricular activities, and the School attaches great importance to the development of musical and artistic talent.

Music is extremely popular at Badminton with over 85% of all pupils studying at least one musical instrument. There is a wide range of choral and instrumental groups to join including Junior and Senior Choir, Schola (choral group), orchestra, swing band, string ensembles, woodwind ensembles and other mixed musical groups. With visiting peripatetic teachers, all of whom are professional musicians, the students can study any instrument of their choice. There are a wide variety of performance opportunities including informal concerts and concerts for the local community.

There are several drama productions every year including plays directed and produced by the girls. Many girls take optional Speech and Drama lessons and LAMDA examinations.

There is an excellent Creative Arts department, with a wide choice of subjects for the girls to pursue including Fine Art, Pottery and Sculpture, Textiles, Design, Jewellery-making and Photography.

Clubs and Societies. A wide range is offered including: Extended Project Qualification, The Duke of Edinburgh's Award, Italian GCSE, Sports Leaders Award, Leith's Cookery Course, Modern Languages, Debating, Drama, Musical Theatre, Mandarin, Cookery, Art and Crafts, Science Outreach and The Prince's Trust.

Games and Activities. Specialist PE teachers and coaches offer timetabled and optional sport including Hockey, Tennis, Netball, Swimming, Athletics, Rounders, Gymnastics, Badminton, Basketball, Self-Defence and Judo.

Optional extras. All girls participate in activities which include the full choice of Games, Creative Arts and Clubs as above and boarders have the opportunity of additional activities at weekends.

Badminton is fortunate in being sited on the outskirts of the university city of Bristol; regular visits are arranged to concerts, lectures and theatres and there is considerable contact with Bristol University. Community and voluntary work is strongly encouraged, with girls assisting with Science Outreach and reading in local primary schools, volunteering in local hospitals and charity shops.

Admission. Girls sit the Senior School entrance assessments in the January prior to year of entry. Entrance assessments are taken in English, Mathematics as well as an online adaptive test. Girls are also interviewed by a senior member of staff and the girl's current school is asked to provide a reference.

Girls sit Sixth Form entrance papers in the November in the year prior to joining. They choose two academic subjects they are intending to study for A Level and also sit a General Paper. They too will be interviewed by a senior member of staff and the girl's current school is asked to provide a reference.

Prospective Junior School pupils are assessed by spending a day in the school during which they are observed and assessed informally by staff and the Junior School Headmistress, Mrs Emma Davies. This also helps them to make initial relationships with their prospective peers and gives them a real taste for life at Badminton. From Years 3–6 the tests are more formal and written papers in English, Maths, Reading and a Reasoning test are completed during the assessment day. Entry for Little Acorns (our pre-reception class) is by appointment with the Junior School Headmistress, Mrs Emma Davies, and girls will also have a short observation session in our Little Acorns class.

Prospective parents are encouraged to visit the school individually or attend one of our Open Mornings. To obtain a prospectus and arrange a visit, please contact the Admissions Department via email at admissions@badminton school.co.uk or call 0117 905 5271.

Scholarships. Academic, Music and All-Rounder scholarships are available for girls entering Badminton in Years 7, 9 and 12. A STEM Scholarship is also available in Years 7 and 9 and an Art Scholarship is available in Years 9 and Year 12. Scholarships for entry into the upper end of the Junior School are also available. Parents of girls who are awarded scholarships are also eligible to apply for a means-tested Bursary.

Scholarship application forms and more information can be obtained by emailing our Admissions Department at admissions@badmintonschool.co.uk.

Bursaries. Bursaries are means-tested and awarded on the basis of parents' financial circumstances. Application forms may be obtained by emailing admissions@badminton school.co.uk.

Fees per term (2016–2017). Day: Juniors £3,200–£3,600, Seniors £5,500–£5,950. Boarding: Juniors £7,100–£7,800, Seniors £10,500–£11,750.

Forces families in receipt of CEA or an equivalent civilian allowance receive 20% remission of fees.

Charitable status. Badminton School Limited is a Registered Charity, number 311738. It exists for the purpose of educating children.

Chairman of Governors: Mr Bill Ray

Clerk to the Governors, Secretary and Bursar: Ms E Sandberg, LLB Hons

Headmistress: Mrs R Tear, BSc Hons Exeter, MA London, PGCE London

Deputy Head: Mrs A Chapman, BA Hons Birmingham, PGCE Birmingham

Director of Studies: Mr S Dalley, BA Hons Exeter, MA Bristol

Director of Welfare: Mrs J Scarfe, BA Wales

Head of Junior School: Ms E Davies, BA Hons Cardiff, PGCE

Heads of Section:

Head of Creative Arts Section and Head of English: Mrs L Griffith, BA Oxon

Head of STEM Section and Head of Biology: Mrs N Warden, BSc Exeter, BA Oxon

Head of Languages Section and Head of French: Mrs N Walton, BA Durham

Head of Humanities and Head of Geography: Ms C Morgan, BA Hons Durham

Head of Physical Education: Mrs J Gunter

Director of Higher Education and Professional Guidance: Mrs A Proudman, BA, PGCE

Director of Academic and Pastoral Care (Sixth Form): Mrs Z Wheddon, BA, PGCE

Executive Assistant to the Headmistress: Mrs S Brown

Bedford Girls' School

Cardington Road, Bedford, Bedfordshire MK42 0BX

Tel:	01234 361918
email:	admissions@bedfordgirlsschool.co.uk
website:	www.bedfordgirlsschool.co.uk
Twitter:	@BedfordGirlsSch
Facebook:	@BedfordGirlsSch
LinkedIn:	/bedford-girls'-school

Foundation – The Harpur Trust.

"Let me keep an open mind so I understand as much as I can in my lifetime and not reach the limits of my imagination."

Bedford Girls' School is a dynamic, forward-thinking selective independent day school for girls aged 7–18. As an exceptional school, we value creativity and innovation highly. From Year 3 to Sixth Form, it is our belief that learning should be exciting and lifelong, so that girls leave us fully equipped academically, personally, emotionally and morally fulfilled individuals capable of achieving their full potential in every aspect and at every stage of their lives.

Part of the Harpur Trust, we are one of the few girls' schools in the UK to offer both the International Baccalaureate and A Level to Sixth Formers. Whichever course of study our pupils elect to take post-16 our philosophy lies in equipping them with critical thinking skills and the attributes of the IB learner profile from the moment they join us, whether in the Junior or Senior Schools. As such, we are one of a very small number of UK schools to offer Thinking Skills as a timetabled subject and creativity is valued across the curriculum and beyond. As a result, we find that the natural curiosity of the girls is heightened and sharpened and they are extremely engaged with their own learning. In con-

sequence, not only do they excel academically but also as well-rounded, capable young women equipped for compassionate leadership in the 21st century.

The atmosphere of our school is unique and exciting. Classrooms fizz with energy and enthusiasm and each day brings forth new discoveries and achievements. We would be delighted to welcome you to visit, either for one of our Open House events or a private tour, to experience at first hand a true flavour of life at Bedford Girls' School. Please visit www.bedfordgirlsschool.co.uk for further information or call our Admissions Team on: 01234 361918.

Admissions. Entry to the Junior School is on the basis of informal assessment and written tests in Mathematics, Reading and Writing. Entry to the Senior School is on the basis of interview, written tests in Mathematics, English and Verbal Reasoning, school report and reference. Sixth Form entry is on the basis of interviews, Verbal Reasoning, GCSE results, school report and reference.

Fees per term (2016–2017). Junior School (7–11 years) £3,012; Senior School (11–16 years) £4,233; Sixth Form (16–18 years) £4,233.

Bursaries. The Harpur Trust welcomes bursary applications from families of girls in the Senior School and Sixth Form who require financial assistance. All awards are means tested and subject to annual reassessment. Bursaries can be awarded from a value of 25% of fees up to a full bursary place at the discretion of the School and the Harpur Trust.

Charitable status. Bedford Girls' School is part of the Harpur Trust which is a Registered Charity, number 1066861.

Chair of Governors: Ms T Beddoes

Head: Miss J MacKenzie

Deputy Head: Mr T Hill

Assistant Head: Mrs K Jones
Assistant Head: Mrs N Keeler
Assistant Head: Mrs S Mason-Patel
Assistant Head: Ms E Teale
Director of Sixth Form: Dr J Walters

Head of Bedford Girls' School Junior School: Mrs C Howe

Blackheath High School
GDST

Vanbrugh Park, London SE3 7AG

Tel:	020 8853 2929
Fax:	020 8853 3663
email:	info@bla.gdst.net

Junior Department:
Wemyss Road, London SE3 0TF

Tel:	020 8852 1537
Fax:	020 8463 0040
email:	info@blj.gdst.net
website:	www.blackheathhighschool.gdst.net
Twitter:	@BlackheathHigh
Facebook:	@BlackheathHighSchool
LinkedIn:	/Blackheath-High-School

Founded 1880.

Blackheath High School is part of the Girls' Day School Trust (GDST), the UK's leading network of independent girls' schools. As a charity that owns and runs 24 schools and two academies, it reinvests all its income in its schools. For further information about the Trust, visit www.gdst.net.

Blackheath High School is a selective, independent day school for girls aged 3–18 situated in Blackheath, South East London. We enjoy an enviable 'village' like location, within the Royal Borough of Greenwich and have a long history of educating a rich social and cultural blend of students, that reflects the cosmopolitan character of London itself.

Rated 'excellent' in the latest ISI inspection, academic success is at the heart of what is offered at Blackheath High School. Fuelled by our aspirational culture, students make exceptional progress, with excellent public examination results and a range of ambitious and interesting university destinations. This is achieved through the provision of an innovative and interesting curriculum that challenges and inspires students and nurtures a love of learning. Alongside our core curriculum there are unique opportunities such as Astronomy GCSE at the Greenwich Planetarium and our bespoke academic enrichment programme – The Wollstonecraft. Optional courses are designed to engage and inspire, covering topics as diverse as: the culture and history of Tibet; an introduction to architecture and designing a radio programme for Radio 4 Woman's Hour.

Within the core curriculum, girls are able to choose two languages from Mandarin, German, French and Spanish and study these all through to year 13 and great value is placed upon the girls broadening their horizons beyond the school with a range of exciting trips and work experience opportunities. A strong focus on science and technology subjects ensures that our students defy the national trends in terms of numbers of girls applying for science and technology subjects. Strong role models and a curriculum that is well supported by the latest technology, including iPads, digital radio stations and 3D printing, inspire ever-growing numbers of girls to pursue ambitions related to computing, science and design. This is a school where girls are encouraged to discover their passions and teachers support and challenge girls in pursuing their aims.

Fortunately situated between beautiful Greenwich Park and stunning Blackheath, our school is located over three sites: separate Junior and Senior Schools and a dedicated sporting facility in Kidbrooke Grove that enables us to ring-fence curriculum time for the girls' sporting activity. With a multimillion pound investment in our Senior School facilities this year, the opportunities available to the girls will continue to grow. Adding to our recently refurbished dedicated Sixth Form Centre 'Westcombe House', the redevelopment will include a state-of-the-art library, creative arts centre, science labs and entrance building to enhance the opportunities already on offer through our theatre, dance and drama studios, language lab, science suite and teaching rooms.

Individuality is cherished and there is a culture of open-mindedness and harmony. Teachers pride themselves on their superb knowledge of the girls and the positive relationships that are fostered in the school. This is a community where older girls mix readily with younger and the atmosphere of open-mindedness and tolerance is genuine and tangible. These excellent relationships are founded upon the staff's willingness and desire to provide a superb and wide-ranging co-curricular programme. From overseas trips to exotic destinations like Peru and Beijing, to clubs designed to appeal to every girl, like 'crochet collective', 'Samba Band' or 'Iron Woman running club', the co-curricular programme builds vital life skills and cements positive and productive relationships. Our strong focus on 'putting girls first', as part of our founding mission, ensures that this is a school where girls take pride in their talents and ability and there is no truck with gender stereotypes.

As described in the ISI report, the school provides an educational experience that is "stimulating and extraordinarily supportive, conducive to the highest standards of teaching and learning".

Admission to the school is by examination and interview; scholarships and bursaries are available. Regular Open Days are held in the autumn and spring terms, but visitors are always welcome and the Headteacher likes to discuss each girl's particular needs individually with pupils and parents. Please telephone our Admissions Secretary on 020 8557 8409 for a prospectus and to arrange a visit.

Curriculum. We offer a broad choice of subjects at GCSE and an even wider choice at AS and A Level. An education at Blackheath High School inspires and equips girls to strive for personal excellence in all their endeavours: intellectual; physical; creative; cultural; social and moral. We prepare and empower girls for the future by providing an atmosphere in which academic curiosity is cultivated, confidence is built and a balanced, open-minded outlook is nurtured.

As an all-through 3–18 school, we have the luxury of being able to design a curriculum entirely tailored to these aims in every key stage.

Fees per term (2016–2017). Senior School £5,094, Junior Department £4,191, Nursery £3,262.

The fees cover the regular curriculum, school books, stationery and other materials, choral music, and games, but not optional extra subjects, school visits or lunch.

Bursaries. The GDST makes available to the school a number of scholarships and bursaries. The bursaries are means tested and are intended to ensure that the school remains accessible to bright girls who would profit from our education but who would be unable to enter the school without financial assistance.

Scholarships. A number of Scholarships are available to internal or external candidates for entry at 11+ or to the Sixth Form.

Several Academic scholarships are offered every year, awarded on academic merit as measured by the entrance examination. Particulars of the examination are available from the Admissions Secretary.

Up to 2 Music Scholarships may be offered annually. Auditions are held following the entrance examination.

One Art Scholarship may be offered annually. Art assessments are held following the entrance examination.

Charitable status. Blackheath High School is part of The Girls' Day School Trust, which is a Registered Charity, number 306983.

Chairman of Local Governors: Mr J Vennis, BSc, PGCE

Headteacher: **Mrs C Chandler-Thompson**, BA Exeter, PGCE

Deputy Head (*Pastoral*): Mrs C Maddison, BA Staffordshire, MSc Leicester, PGCE

Deputy Head (*Academic*): Miss P Dunn, MA Oxford, MA Essex, PGCE

Director of Finance & Operations: Mr R Ryan

Director of IT: Mr D Nott, BSc Reading

Assistant Head (*Co-Curricular & Enrichment*): Mrs C Pheiffer, BA London, QTS

Assistant Head (*Organisation & Communication*): Mrs N Argile, BSc Newcastle, MSc, PGCE

Head of Junior School: Mrs S Skevington, LLB Hons Sheffield, PGCE EYP

Head of Sixth Form: Mrs K Elliott, BSc Cardiff, PGCE

Admissions Secretary: Mrs F Nichols, BA London

Bolton School Girls' Division

Chorley New Road, Bolton, Lancs BL1 4PB

Tel: 01204 840201
Fax: 01204 434710
email: seniorgirls@boltonschool.org
website: www.boltonschool.org/seniorgirls
Twitter: @BoltonSchool
Facebook: /boltonschool.org
LinkedIn: /bolton-school

Bolton School Girls' Division was founded in 1877 as the High School for Girls and quickly gained a reputation for excellence. In 1913 the first Viscount Leverhulme gave a generous endowment to the High School for Girls and the Bolton Grammar School for Boys on condition that the two schools should be equal partners known as Bolton School (Girls' and Boys' Divisions).

Bolton School is a family of schools, where children can enjoy an all-through education, joining our co-educational Nursery for 3 and 4 year olds or Infant School before moving up to our single-sex Junior and Senior Schools with Sixth Forms. We are strong believers that girls and boys from 7+ perform best in a single-sex environment, but one where there are co-educational activities – the best of both worlds.

The School occupies a stunning 32-acre site and the Girls' Division Senior School contains over 770 day pupils. The co-educational infants' school, Beech House, offers an education for 225 pupils aged 4–7 and up to a further 200 girls are educated in the Girls' Division Junior School (age 7–11). In the Senior School over 210 girls are in the Sixth Form. The School also has its own nursery.

Bolton School Girls' Division seeks to realise the potential of each pupil. We provide challenge, encourage initiative, promote teamwork and develop leadership capabilities. It is our aim that students leave the School as self-confident young people equipped with the knowledge, skills and attributes that will allow them to lead happy and fulfilled lives and to make a difference for good in the wider community.

We do this through offering a rich and stimulating educational experience which encompasses academic, extracurricular and social activities. We provide a supportive and industrious learning environment for pupils selected on academic potential, irrespective of means and background.

Facilities. Housed in an attractive Grade II listed building the school has an impressive Great Hall which seats 900 people, spacious corridors, a theatre, two Resistant Materials workshops, two Textile studios, two Food Technology rooms, four computer rooms, seven laboratories, three Art studios and two fine libraries staffed by two qualified librarians and their staff. As of September 2013, the Sixth Form moved into the purpose-built £7m Riley Sixth Form Centre, where girls and boys share a Common Room, cafe and learning areas equipped with the very latest technology. The girls' dining room was completely redeveloped in the Summer of 2015.

Besides having its own fully-equipped gym, the Girls' Division shares the award-winning Careers Department, the Arts Complex and Sports Hall, a 25-metre swimming pool, extensive playing fields, the Leverhulme Sports Pavilion and an outdoor pursuits facility at Patterdale Hall in the Lake District. Pupils also have the option of spending a week undertaking sailing lessons in the Irish Sea on the School's boat, Tenacity of Bolton.

Beech House Infants' School. The curriculum, though based on the National Curriculum, extends far beyond it. Specialist teaching is provided for older pupils in Physical Education and Music and all children are taught French. The school has recently moved to purpose-built state-of-the-art

premises and in addition to its own resources, Beech House benefits from the use of Senior School facilities such as the swimming pool, playing fields and Arts Centre.

The Girls' Junior School. There are 2 classes in each of Years 3–6. In September 2010, the junior girls moved into their new £5m school which has its own hall, laboratory, art and design facility, IT suite and library, as well as large classrooms. Besides following the National Curriculum with Senior School specialists teaching PE, Music and French, pupils have additional opportunities. The many clubs and wide range of extracurricular activities ensure a full and well-balanced programme.

The Senior School. The curriculum encompasses all the National Curriculum but also offers the study of two modern languages, the classics and a wide range of modules in Technology. At age 11 all girls follow a similar weekly timetable. The twelve subjects offered are: Art, English, French, Geography, History, Classical Studies, Mathematics, Music, PE, Religion and Philosophy, Science and Technology. All pupils in Year 9 begin to study GCSE Biology, Chemistry and Physics. The above list does not fully show the great variety of opportunities available which also include: Athletics, Biology, Chemistry, Computer Graphics, Dance, Drama, Earth Science, Electronics, Food Technology, Gymnastics, Information Technology, Lacrosse, Netball, Physics, PSHE, Resistant Materials Technology, Rounders, Swimming, Tennis and Textiles Technology. This breadth is maintained to GCSE with a second language, German, Latin or Spanish, being offered in Year 8. In Years 10 and 11 we also offer Archery, Badminton, Basketball, Climbing, Fitness/Gym sessions, Football, Rounders, Unihoc and Volleyball.

GCSE. There is extensive choice at GCSE. All follow a common curriculum of English, English Literature, Mathematics, Biology, Chemistry and Physics (with an option to consolidate down to Dual Award Science at the end of Year 10) together with non-examined courses in Information Technology, PE, and Religion and Philosophy. Personal aptitude and inclination are fostered by allowing a maximum of 11 GCSEs: the core subjects plus options chosen from Art, Biology, Business and Communication Systems, Chemistry, Food Technology, French, Geography, German, Greek, History, Information Technology, Latin, Music, Physics, Religious Studies, Resistant Materials Technology, Spanish and Textile Technology. Essential balance is maintained by requiring all to include one Humanity and one Modern Language, but the choice is otherwise entirely free.

The Sixth Form. Flexibility is a key feature of the Sixth Form. Teaching in the Sixth Form is in smaller groups and single-sex teaching remains the norm, although in a very few subjects co-educational arrangements are in operation. Students choose from a list of approximately 30 AS courses. Breadth is promoted further by our complementary Curriculum Enrichment Programme. All students have the opportunity to follow a range of non-examined courses as well as Physical Education (sports include golf, football, life-saving, rugby, self-defence, tennis and yoga). Links beyond school include the Community Action Programme and Young Enterprise scheme, as well as opportunities with Business Awareness and Work Experience.

Students in the Sixth Form have greater freedom which includes wearing their own smart clothes, exeat periods and having their own Sixth Form Centre away from the Senior School. Joint social and extracurricular events are regularly organised with the Boys' Division. There are opportunities for students to assume a variety of responsibilities both within the school and in the wider community. Increasing personal freedom within a highly supportive environment helps students to make the transition to the independence of the adult world. Some students stretch themselves by taking the AQA Baccalaureate qualification.

Almost all students (95%) go on to Higher Education (10% to Oxford and Cambridge).

Music and Drama are popular and students achieve the highest standards in informal and public performances. The wide variety of concerts and productions may take place in the Arts Centre, the Great Hall or the fully-equipped Theatre, all of which make excellent venues for joint and Girls' Division performances. The School regularly performs at Manchester's Bridgewater Hall.

Personal, Social and Health Education, and Citizenship. PSHE and Citizenship are targeted in a variety of ways and coordinated centrally. Some issues may be covered within departmental schemes of work while others will be discussed in the informal atmosphere of form groups led by the form tutor. Those areas which require specialist input are fitted into longer sessions run by experts from outside school.

Careers. The Careers Department helps prepare students for adult life. It is staffed by two experienced assistants and has a resource centre giving access to all the latest information. The extensive programme starts at age 11 and includes communication skills, work sampling, and support in making choices at all stages of schooling. In addition, girls prepare their CVs and applications to Higher Education with the individual help of a trained tutor.

Extracurricular Activities. Patterdale Hall, our outdoor pursuits centre in the Lake District, offers many activities including abseiling, gorge walking, orienteering and sailing, both on Lake Ullswater and in the Irish Sea on the ketch, Tenacity of Bolton. Awards are regularly made to enable individuals to undertake a variety of challenging activities both at home and abroad while every year, the whole of Year 9 as well as many older girls embark on The Duke of Edinburgh's Award scheme. In addition to the annual exchanges for Modern Languages students, we also offer a wide range of educational and recreational trips both at home and abroad. All have the opportunity to follow a wide range of non-examined courses of their choice, including Physical Education.

Admission. Entrance to the school is by Headteacher's report, written examination and interview in the Spring term for girls aged 7 and 11. New girls are also welcomed into the Sixth Form. Applications to other year groups are welcomed and spaces may be available depending upon migration.

One in five Senior School pupils receives assistance with their fees through the School's own bursaries. Non-means-tested Scholarships are also awarded to those pupils who achieve highly in the Entrance Examination.

Fees per term (2016–2017). Senior School and Sixth Form £3,836; Infant and Junior Schools £3,068. Fees include lunches.

Charitable status. The Bolton School is a Registered Charity, number 1110703. Under the terms of the Charity it is administered as two separate Divisions providing for boys and girls under a separate Headmaster and Headmistress.

Chairman of Governors: M T Griffiths, BA, FCA

***Headmistress*: Miss S E Hincks**, MA

Deputy Head: Mrs L D Kyle, BSc
Assistant Head: P Linfitt, BSc, MEng
Assistant Head: Ms H Bradford-Keegan, MA

Head of Sixth Form: Mrs C Winder, MA
Head of Upper School: Mrs I Smalley, BSc
Head of Middle School: Mrs A Field, BA

Senior School:

Heads of Departments:

Art, Design & Technology: Miss J A Fazackerley, BA
Careers and Higher Education: Mrs E Lowe, BA
Classics: Mrs J Hone, BA
Economics & Business Studies: Miss L Jones, BA
English: Mrs R Worthington, BA

Food Technology: Mrs N James, BA
Geography: Ms S Noot, BA
History: C Owen, MA
ICT: Mrs S Brace, BSc
Learning Support Coordinator: Mrs A Elkin, BA
Mathematics: G Heppleston, BSc
Modern Languages: Mrs A Shafiq, BA
French: C Fico, BA
German: Mrs E Warburton, BA
Spanish: Mrs A Shafiq, BA
Music: Mrs A Price, MA
Physical Education: Mrs K A Heatherington, BA
Religion and Philosophy: Mrs K E Porter, BA
Resistant Materials: Miss R Langley
Science: Dr A Fielder, BA
Biology: Mrs A D Furey, BSc
Chemistry: Ms M Teichman, BSc
Physics: Mr R Ball, BSc
Psychology: Mrs J Sanders, BSc

Instrumental Music Staff:
Brass, Cello, Clarinet, Flute, Guitar, Oboe, Organ, Percussion, Piano, Saxophone, Singing, Violin.

Lower Schools:

Junior Department (Age 7–11):
Head: Mrs C Laverick, BSc
Deputy Head: Mrs H Holt, BEd

Beech House (Age 4–7):
Head: Mrs T Taylor, BEd
Deputy Head: Mrs J Mees, BSc

Brighton & Hove High School
GDST

The Temple, Montpelier Road, Brighton, East Sussex BN1 3AT

Tel:	01273 280280
Fax:	01273 280281
email:	enquiries@bhhs.gdst.net
website:	www.bhhs.gdst.net
Twitter:	@BHHSGDST
Facebook:	@BrightonHoveHighSchool

Founded 1876.

Brighton & Hove High School is part of the GDST (Girls' Day School Trust). The GDST is the leading network of independent girls' schools in the UK. As a charity that owns and runs 24 schools and two academies, it reinvests all its income in its schools. For further information about the Trust, see p. xxiii or visit www.gdst.net.

Additional information about the school may be found on the school's website and a detailed prospectus is available from the school.

See also Brighton & Hove Prep GDST entry in IAPS section.

Number of Pupils. 400 Girls in the Senior School (age 11–18), including 50 in the Sixth Form; 230 in the Prep School (age 3–11).

Location. The school stands in its own grounds in the centre of the city of Brighton and Hove. It is about half-a-mile from Brighton Railway Station and pupils come in from Lewes, Haywards Heath and Lancing by train. It is easily reached by bus from all parts of Brighton and Hove.

The Prep School is housed in premises in Radinden Manor Road. The Senior School is in the Temple, a gentleman's residence built by Thomas Kemp in 1819 which has been considerably altered and enlarged to offer all modern amenities, most recent of which is a Sports Hall and Dance

Studio. There is a self-contained Sixth Form Centre and the school owns a Field Centre on the River Wye in mid-Wales.

Curriculum. The school course is planned to provide a wide general education. Girls are prepared for GCSEs and in the Sixth Form a wide choice of A Level subjects is offered in preparation for universities and other forms of professional training.

The school has an all-weather hockey pitch at the Prep School site with facilities for hockey, rounders, netball and tennis. Gymnastics and dance are also taught with swimming for junior forms, and senior forms choose from activities including badminton, cricket, netball, water sports and dance.

Fees per term (2016–2017). Senior School £4,380–£4,510, Prep School £2,850–£3,200, Nursery £2,250.

The tuition fees cover the regular curriculum, school books, stationery and other materials, choral music and sport, but not optional subjects. There is compulsory catering up to year 10, invoiced termly.

The fees for extra subjects (instrumental music and speech and drama) are shown in the prospectus.

Admission at all ages is by interview and test/entrance examination, except at 16+ where GCSE qualifications are essential. The main entry points are 3+, 4+, 11+ and 16+, though occasional vacancies occur at all ages.

Scholarships and Bursaries. The GDST has made available to the school a number of scholarships and bursaries. The bursaries are means tested and are intended to ensure that the school remains accessible to bright girls who would profit from our education but who would be unable to enter the school without financial assistance.

Trust Scholarships are available on merit, irrespective of income, to internal or external candidates for entry at 11+ or to the Sixth Form.

Charitable status. Brighton & Hove High School is part of The Girls' Day School Trust, which is a Registered Charity, number 306983.

Chair of Local Governors: Mrs J Osler

Head: Jennifer Smith, MA Glasgow, MEd

Deputy Head (Pastoral): Ms W Fox, BA Durham

Deputy Head (Curriculum and School Evaluation) : Ms H Boyes, BSc King's College London, PGCE Hull

Head of Prep School: Mrs S Cattaneo, BA, Cert Ed Sussex

Head of Sixth Form: Mrs O Pianet, BA Hons QTS, PGCE Brighton

Registrar: Mrs E Manning, BSc

(Full staff list available on the school's website.)

Bruton School for Girls

Sunny Hill, Bruton, Somerset BA10 0NT

Tel:	01749 814400
Fax:	01749 812537
email:	admissions@brutonschool.co.uk
website:	www.brutonschool.co.uk
Twitter:	@BrutonSchool
Facebook:	@Bruton-School-for-Girls

Established in 1900 and set in beautiful English countryside in Somerset, overlooking Glastonbury Tor, Bruton School for Girls is a day school for girls and boys aged 3–7 and a day and boarding school for girls aged 7–18. It is a small school with approximately 250 pupils, of whom roughly 60 board. Full, weekly and flexi boarding options

are available. The teaching week is Monday to Friday with no Saturday lessons.

Sunny Hill Preparatory School comprises the Nursery School, Pre-Prep and Prep School. Boarding is available for girls from the age of 7 years old. Reception, Year 1 and Year 2 classes are co-educational until the age of 7. A low pupil-teacher ratio and good relationships enable creative and dedicated teachers to make the most of the inquisitive childhood years and ensures that every pupil receives quality individual attention. Pupils develop strong learning habits. In a broad curriculum, they explore the exciting world of science, information technology, humanities, French, music, design technology and creative arts. Mathematics and English programmes build firm foundations for purposeful learning. The Early Years Foundation (Nursery to Reception) has an 'Outstanding' Ofsted rating. (*See also entry in IAPS section.*)

The **Senior School** is a thriving community of girls age 11–16 years who are taught in separate year groups 1–5. Girls joining the Senior School come from a wide variety of local, national and international schools, as well as from Sunny Hill Prep School. At GCSE, 18 subjects are offered with an A* to C pass rate well above the national average, most girls taking 9 or 10 subjects. Pupils are set for Mathematics, English, Modern Languages and Sciences to maximise individual achievement. The curriculum offers three separate sciences and three foreign languages. Additional learning support is available from specialist Skills Development teachers where appropriate.

The **Sixth Form** offers excellent preparation for university, with tutorial support and individual study programmes. The school has a considerable reputation for academic achievement, "Oxbridge" and university entrance and is currently the second highest ranked school in Somerset for A Level results (DfE data). Cultural and social skills are developed to enhance independence and career ambitions. An extensive range of A Levels is complemented by cultural activities, extension studies and extracurricular activities which include public speaking and the Leiths Certificate in Food and Wine. Career and Higher Education advice feature prominently at this stage. Many girls entering the Sixth Form transfer from the Senior School but are joined by students from other schools.

Why choose BSG? We are passionate about, and experts in, girls' education. We believe in offering every girl a well-rounded education in an environment with the space to inspire, challenge, encourage and support her to develop her full potential to become the amazing person she can be in this fast-changing world. We want your child to grow with us, learn with us, make friends for life and enjoy her time with us. We encourage her to develop intellectual curiosity, self-esteem, respect and care for others, independence and excellence in all she does, with a real love for life.

Academic and Personal Expectations. Academically, the school has high expectations and many girls gain places at prestigious universities. The girls are encouraged to have self-belief, to set challenging goals, display independence of thought and enjoy learning for its own sake.

There are many opportunities for leadership and the development of personal and social skills, particularly in the Sixth Form, where students may take up the role of prefect or hall captain.

Location. Set on a 40-acre campus in beautiful countryside, the school is close to the Somerset, Wiltshire and Dorset borders, and has easy access to the M3/A303 corridor between London and the South West. Bristol, Bath, Salisbury and the south coast are all within approximately one hour's travel. Castle Cary station, served by London Paddington-Exeter express trains, is 4 miles away and Templecombe on the line to London Waterloo is 10 miles; the school offers minibus connections. Students are collected from London Heathrow, Bristol International and other airports. A network of daily buses serves the school from surrounding areas.

Boarding. Our boarding houses provide comfortable and well-appointed accommodation appropriate to the different age ranges of pupils. Facilities include common rooms, games rooms, kitchens and dining areas as well as access to computer facilities and telephones. Younger girls share dormitories while Fourth, Fifth and Sixth Form students have their own study-bedrooms or, in Form 4, may share with one other girl. Sixth formers enjoy an increased degree of independence that aims to bridge school and university. The boarding houses are situated on the school campus and girls are cared for by experienced Housemistresses and assistant house staff. A variety of activities is offered each weekend.

The school has its own medical centre with a qualified nursing Sister on duty every weekday during term time and comprehensive medical care available at Bruton Surgery.

A high standard of catering is provided, with a wide variety of choice. Specific dietary needs are catered for.

Extracurricular Activities. Art, Drama, Music and Sport feature strongly. The outstanding success of the Art department is reflected in work displayed around the school. The Hobhouse Studio Theatre provides a professional-standard performance space for productions and 'speech and drama' presentations. There is a wide range of opportunities for both instrumental and choral performance, with four choirs performing music across a range of styles and numerous instrumental groups, including two school orchestras and a wind band. The sports department offers a wide range of activities in which every girl can participate either competitively or for her own enjoyment. There is a full fixture list of competitive matches in the traditional sports of hockey, netball, rounders, swimming, athletics and tennis. Tennis coaching, horse riding, judo, trampolining, modern and classical dance, yoga and individual exercise regimes are available. There is also the popular Duke of Edinburgh's Award programme. Having been awarded the Eco-Schools Green Flag, many girls participate in the Eco Club and assist with the schools recycling programme. In the Preparatory School, all pupils from Reception to Prep 6 participate in Forest School.

Entry. There is open entry into the pre-prep and preparatory school from which pupils normally progress seamlessly into the senior school. The senior school entry process includes the school's own diagnostic assessments or Common Entrance. Entry into the Sixth Form is by interview and GCSE or equivalent qualifications.

Fees per term (2016–2017). Day: £5,300 (Senior School and Sixth Form), £3,800–£3,900 (Preparatory School), £1,900–£2,530 (Pre-Preparatory School), £20 per session (Nursery). Boarding: £6,935–£8,950 (full), £6,285–£8,175 (weekly boarding), £58.40 per night (occasional/flexi boarding).

Scholarships and Bursaries. Bruton School for Girls has a range of scholarships, which are offered on entry to the Senior School at 11+, 13+ and Sixth Form on the basis of aptitude and achievement in particular areas, including academic studies, music, art, sport and drama.

11+: Foundation Scholarships (Academic), Besly Music Scholarship.

13+: Chappell Scholarship (Sport), Golledge Scholarship (Art, Humanities or Languages), Knight Scholarship (Sciences or Mathematics), Hobhouse Scholarship (All-Rounder), Palmer Music Scholarship.

Sixth Form: Edith Radford Scholarship (Academic), Howard Music Scholarship, Zhou Guang-Ren Scholarship (Piano), Cumberlege Scholarships (Art, Drama or Sport).

Governors' Exhibitions (means-tested) exist to support those pupils whose families would find difficulty in meeting the full fees and are awarded on entry to the Senior School and Sixth Form.

Charitable status. Bruton School for Girls is a Registered Charity, number 1085577, and a Company Limited by Guarantee. It exists to provide education.

Governors:
Chairman: Mr D H C Batten

Headmistress: Mrs Nicola Botterill, BSc, MA, PGCE, NPQH, FRGS, FRSA

Deputy Head: Mrs Rachel Robbins, BA, PGCE

Director of Teaching and Learning: Mr Will Talbot-Ponsonby, BSc, MA, PGCE

Head of Preparatory School: Mrs Helen Snow, BEd

Bursar: Mr A H D Harvey-Kelly

Director of Admissions: Mrs Carrie Crook

Burgess Hill Girls

Keymer Road, Burgess Hill, West Sussex RH15 0EG

Tel:	01444 241050
Fax:	01444 870314
email:	registrar@burgesshillgirls.com
website:	www.burgesshillgirls.com
Twitter:	@BHillGirls
Facebook:	@BurgessHillGirls
LinkedIn:	/burgess-hill-girls

An independent day and boarding school or girls age 2½ to 18 years, founded in 1906 by Miss Beatrice Goode. Our school has a Nursery (accepts boys), Junior School, Senior School and Sixth Form. To fully appreciate our school come for a visit and talk to the students, they will be delighted to show you around. (*See also Burgess Hill Girls Junior School entry in the IAPS section.*)

General. The ethos of the School is to provide a caring, challenging and supportive atmosphere which encourages young people to use their initiative, be inquisitive and creative and develop responsibility and independence. Boys are welcome in the nursery. Our school is a community in which girls flourish; from age 4 the focus is firmly on girls and the way they learn. They develop self-esteem and confidence and go on to make a positive contribution in their chosen professions. We have small classes with fully qualified, professional staff dedicated to catering for the needs of each individual child. The School has established a reputation for excellence in Music, Sport, Art, Textiles and Drama and achieves impressive academic results. We are consistently highly ranked nationally and regularly lead the field in Sussex. We believe that education for life involves much more than academic success alone. Girls can, and do, strive for excellence wherever their talents lie.

School Facilities. The Senior School offers specialist teaching rooms including: a state-of-the-art language suite equipped with computers and specialist software for personalised listening and speaking; a Music room equipped with the latest Apple Mac composition software; Music practice rooms; two Art studios with an exhibition area, Art library and a kiln area; a Drama studio; a fully-equipped Media suite; two modern Chemistry labs; a specialist Textiles room and Technology workshop; a Learning Resource Centre and enhanced outdoor PE facilities with tennis courts and an Astroturf training area. The Performing Arts facilities have been extended with a glazed, curved entrance foyer.

The Junior School's facilities include a Learning Hub which incorporates a library, large learning space and access to iPads and interactive electronic screen. The Junior School also offers fully-equipped subject-specific classrooms rooms for Music, ICT, Art, Science and Technology and access to all the sports facilities on the main school campus. The Infants are based in a building with bright, open classrooms and have their own hall and library. The Infants and Juniors have an exciting playground with a wooden adventure trail and outdoor classroom.

The Sixth Form centre includes a seminar room, contemporary classrooms, a study room with ICT facilities, a higher education library, a music practice room, two common rooms and a new student kitchen. All curriculum areas are well served with appropriate specialist accommodation, either in the Sixth Form Centre or in the Senior School complex for Art, Drama, Music, Media, PE, Science, Technology and Textiles. All classrooms are equipped with interactive whiteboards, and suites of laptop computers ensure that technology is available when and where needed.

The school has three Edwardian boarding houses with bedrooms and common rooms which are spacious, light and pleasantly furnished.

Curriculum. The curriculum is broad and challenging and relevant to the needs of young people. There is a wide choice of subjects both at GCSE and A Level with many extracurricular activities.

ISI Inspection 2014. The Senior School report recognises the many strengths of the Senior School's provision. Each phase of the school is praised, with comments such as: *The quality of teaching is excellent. The achievements of all pupils, including those with SEND or EAL, are excellent. The curricular and extracurricular programme makes an excellent contribution to the pupils' success ... The personal development of the pupils is excellent. Pupils are confident and articulate, having high levels of self-esteem.*

The Senior and Junior Schools' Inspection reports can be viewed on www.isi.net.

Entrance Procedures. Entrance to either the Junior or Senior School is by examination and school reference. Senior girls are also interviewed by the Headmistress. Scholarships are awarded each year for academic and/or musical excellence into Years 3–6 inclusive, 7, 9 and the Lower Sixth. Sport/Creative scholarships are available for students entering Year 7, 9 and the Lower Sixth. The Margaret Morris All-Rounder Scholarship is available to girls entering Year 9.

Fees per term (2016–2017). Senior School: £4,600–£5,650 (day girls); £9,100–£10,150 (boarding). Junior School: £2,450–£4,350 (day girls).

Old Girls' Association. The Old Girls' Association is an association run by former students and the school. It helps everyone to keep in touch with each other and what is happening at the School. Please contact the School for further information.

Charitable status. Burgess Hill School for Girls is a Registered Charity, number 307001.

Chairman of Governors: Dr Alison Smith, MB ChB, MRCGP

Headmistress: Mrs Kathryn Bell, BSc Hons, PGCE

Deputy Headmistress: Mrs E Laybourn, BEd Hons
Bursar: Mr G Bond
Director of Academic Development: Mr R Tapping, BSc Hons, PGCE, NPQH, CGeog, FRGS
Head of Junior School: Mrs H Cavanagh, BA Hons QTS
Deputy Head of Junior School: Mrs T Pearson-Rujas, BSc Hons, PGCE, QTS, Cert Mgmt
Head of Sixth Form: Mr N Dyson, BA Hons, PGCE
Head of Upper School: Miss M Bramley, BSc Hons, PGCE
Head of Lower School: Miss E Webster, BA Hons, PGCE

Heads of Departments:
Art: Ms E Levett, BA Hons, PGCE
Biology: Miss M Bramley, BSc Hons, PGCE
Business Studies & Economics: Mrs J King, BEd

Chemistry: Mrs S Lympany, BSc Hons, MSc, PGCE
Classics & Latin: Mrs B Johns, BA Hons, PGCE
Computer Science: Mr R Stanway, BSc Hons, PGCE
Design & Technology: Mrs B Bradley, BEd Hons C&G
English/Media: Mr P Reynolds, BA Hons, PGCE
Speech & Drama: Mrs E Cassim, BA Hons, PGCE
French: Mrs I Martin, Licence Maîtrise, DDT
Geography: Mrs J Sharp, BSc Hons, MSc, PGCE
German: Mrs J Edey, MA Hons, PGCE
History: Mr T Clarke, BA Hons, PGCE
Learning Resource Centre: Ms Y Akehurst, BA
Mathematics: Mr R Stanway, BSc Hons, PGCE
Music: Mr P Newbold, BMus Hons, MMus, PGCE
Physical Education & Games: Miss S Clapp, BA Hons QTS
Physics: Mrs S Marsh, BSc Hons, MSc, PGCE
Psychology: Mrs G Humphrey, BSc Hons, PGCE, MBPsS
Religious Studies: Miss S Cull, BA Hons, PGCE
Spanish: Mr J Montesinos, BA Hons, PGCE

Head of Marketing & Events: Mrs Y Irvine, DipM ACIM
Registrar: Mrs M R Roach
Senior Housemistress: Ms C Trevor, BA Hons
Housemistresses:
Mrs L Bussell
Miss M Buckley
Mrs D Scott
School Nurse: Mrs S Ramanan, RGN
Careers Adviser: Mrs J Edey, MA Hons, PGCE

Bury Grammar School Girls

Bridge Road, Bury, Lancs BL9 0HH

Tel: 0161 696 8600
Fax: 0161 763 4658
email: girlsoffice@burygrammar.com
website: www.burygrammar.com
Twitter: @BuryGrammarSch
Facebook: /BuryGrammarSchoolGirls

Motto: *Sanctas Clavis Fores Aperit*

The Girls' School was founded in 1884 as the Bury High School for Girls and amalgamated, a few years later, with the Bury Grammar School (Boys). The school maintains high academic standards and traditional grammar school values whilst encouraging each girl to develop her individual talents and abilities as far as she can in a lively environment which responds to the challenge of change.

The numbers at present are 40 in the Pre-School, 140 in the Co-educational Infant Department, 150 in the Junior School and 420 in the Senior School.

The **Senior School** is housed in a distinctive Edwardian building which dates from 1906. The school is conveniently situated near the centre of the town and the bus-tram interchange. Facilities are regularly improved and updated; a major building project has led to the creation of an Arts Centre containing a modern library and work facility in the heart of the school surrounded by new classrooms for English, Art, Design and Technology, Textiles and Food Technology. This was followed by the opening of a dedicated sixth form pre-university centre which is used jointly by girls and boys. It contains work rooms with full access to interactive learning, private study areas which allows students to complement their lessons with independent learning and access to the library and internet and a Cafetorium with a central sixth form entrance.

The curriculum is broad and balanced in the first five years of the Senior School. At Key Stage Three all girls follow a core curriculum of Mathematics, English, the three

Sciences, PE, RS, History and Geography which is enhanced by courses in Art, ICT, Design Technology, Food and Nutrition, Latin, Classical Civilisation, Business Studies and two Modern Languages from a choice of French, German and Spanish. Traditional teaching methods are combined with pupil-centred learning work, group work, investigative work and a problem-solving approach. In a variety of cross curricular projects, pupils seek solutions to problems and take an ever-increasing responsibility for their own learning.

PE and Music are well established; in recent years the School has been represented in National Netball, Tennis and Swimming Championships and on County Netball, Hockey, Cross-Country, Swimming, Tennis, Athletics and Badminton teams. Each year the Festival Choir gives concerts internationally and in the UK. There are also two orchestras, string quartets, a flute choir and a jazz band.

The School works closely with Bury Grammar School (Boys) for dramatic and musical productions, and other extracurricular activities. The Sixth Form Centre is open to both boys and girls.

Public examinations are taken in Years 10, 11, 12 and 13, according to the requirements of individual pupils. There is a wide choice of subjects in the Sixth Form and each year all or virtually all students proceed to degree courses at prestigious universities, including Oxford and Cambridge. The School achieves high pass rates in public examinations.

These successes and initiatives, along with PSHE, careers advice and extracurricular activities, clubs, visits, holidays in England and abroad, charity work and school productions, offer wide educational opportunities and encourage links to be forged with industry and commerce and with the community in Bury and beyond.

The **Junior School** has its own purpose-built premises on the Senior School site, has shared use of the Roger Kay Hall, Gymnasium, Sports Hall, and Swimming Pool. The eight large and attractive classrooms, Music Room and large Library/Computer suite provide a comfortable and very pleasant environment in which the girls aged 7–11 learn and work.

The Junior School curriculum is based on the National Curriculum but with enhancements. The curriculum includes the three core subjects and Design/Technology, ICT, History, Geography, Religious Education, Art and Craft, Music and Physical Education. Particular emphasis is placed on the teaching of skills in reading, writing and mathematics. The aim is to provide a broad and balanced education and to give each girl the opportunity to develop her full potential. The combination of a dedicated staff and excellent facilities allows girls to maintain the high academic standard enriched by many extracurricular activities with particular strengths in music and sport.

The School has a purpose-built **Co-educational Infant School** situated on the school campus which includes a preschool taking pupils who will become 3 during the academic year. In lively and stimulating surroundings the children progress rapidly in all six areas of learning. They make use of the Senior School pool and have specialist PE instruction, their own dedicated gymnasium and tuition in music in a specially designed music room. The focal point of the new building is the central octagonal hall used for assemblies and performances. Pupils also have access to a unique and exciting rooftop play area and a Learning Resource Area with supervised computer access. There is a Breakfast Club before school and an After-School Club.

Bursaries and Scholarships. At 11+ the Governors offer a number of means-tested bursaries and non-means tested scholarships based on academic excellence.

Fees per term (2016–2017). Pre-School, Infant and Junior School £2,586; Senior School £3,480.

Charitable status. Bury Grammar Schools Charity is a Registered Charity, number 526622.

Chair of Governors: Mr L A Goldberg

Bursar and Clerk to the Governors: Mrs J Stevens

Headmistress: **Mrs J Anderson**, BA, MEd, PGCE

Deputy Headmistress: Mrs J A Buttery, BA Lancaster

Second Deputy Headmistress: Miss V White, BA MA Manchester

Assistant Heads:
Mrs S Fielden, BSc London
Mrs V Leaver, BSc Hull
Mrs Y Hanham, BSc Salford

Senior Teacher: Mr J Southworth, BA Liverpool

Heads of Departments:
Art and Design: Mrs J Southworth, BA Liverpool
Careers: Mrs S Taylor, BSc Manchester
Chemistry: Dr J Yates, BSc Durham, PhD Bristol
Classics: Mrs C Kilshaw Walster, BA London, MA Manchester
Economics and Business Studies: Mrs M Whitlow, BA York
English: Mrs C Woodhouse, BA MA St Andrews
Geography: Ms J Tomkinson, BSc Hull
History: Mrs C Bevis, BA Bolton
ICT: Mr D Ashworth, BA Manchester Metropolitan
Mathematics: Mrs Y G Hanham, BSc Salford
Modern Languages: Mrs C Banks, Licence Bordeaux
Music: Miss R Britton, BMus Manchester
PE: Mrs J Slade, BSc Loughborough
Physics: Mr D Lehan, BEng Liverpool, BA Oxon
Politics: Mrs S Thorpe, BA Salford
Psychology: Ms C McDermott, BA Sheffield
RS: Mrs J Rumboldt, BA Cambridge
Science and Biology: Mrs S Fielden, BSc London
Theatre Studies: Mrs H Hammond, BA Liverpool

Head of Sixth Form: Miss V White, BA MA Manchester
Head of Upper School: Mrs R Newbold, BSc Loughborough
Head of Middle School: Mrs J Haworth, BA Keele
Head of Year 7: Mrs S C Banfield, BA Bangor

Co-educational Infant and Girls' Junior School: Mrs V Hall, BSc Cardiff

Registrar: Mrs S Lewis

Channing School

The Bank, Highgate, London N6 5HF

Tel:	020 8340 2328 (School Office)
	020 8340 2719 (Bursar)
Fax:	020 8341 5698
email:	info@channing.co.uk
website:	www.channing.co.uk
Twitter:	@ChanningSchool
Facebook:	@ChanningSchool

At Channing everything is possible!

Channing School values the individuality of every girl and their unique system of Personalised Education ensures that girls will be understood, respected, supported and empowered.

Founded in 1885, Channing is a day school for girls aged 4 to 18, with 600+ in the Senior School including the Sixth Form and 240 in the Junior School. The School has been a centre of academic excellence in North London for more than 130 years and its results consistently place it in the top 50 schools in the country. The stimulating and vibrant educational experience nurtures and sustains independent thinking, confidence and creativity. Channing upholds its Unitarian heritage and encourage girls to develop respect, tolerance and understanding of all faiths as well as individual and social responsibility.

The School is situated in Highgate Village, in attractive grounds, and offers a balanced education combining a traditional academic curriculum with modern educational developments. The complex of old and new buildings has been constantly adapted to provide up-to-date facilities, and there are strong links with the local community and local schools.

Girls usually take nine or ten subjects to GCSE and there is a wide range of A Level choices, including Physics, Further Maths, Government and Politics and Drama and Theatre Studies. The Junior School has its own building – the elegant family home of Sir Sydney Waterlow, one-time Lord Mayor of London – set in spacious gardens, and is notable for its happy and secure atmosphere.

Most girls learn at least one musical instrument and there are frequent concerts and theatrical productions. The school is fortunate in its gardens, open space and its facilities. The school is currently further investing in new facilities including a Sixth Form Centre with bespoke study facilities and a state-of-the-art Sports Centre, both of which opened in December 2014, and a modern Performing Arts Theatre, due to open in Spring 2017.

Entry is by assessment at 4+, an examination and interview at 11+ and predicted GCSE results and interview at 16+. In addition, entry is subject to a satisfactory report from the applicant's current school. Entry assessments for occasional vacancies that arise for other years are age appropriate.

Further information can be obtained from the School prospectus and the Sixth Form prospectus available from the Registrar and the school website (www.channing.co.uk).

Scholarships and Bursaries. Academic Scholarships are offered at 11+. Academic awards are also offered to Sixth Form entrants, based on predicted GCSE grades and contribution to the school or as a result of interview and predicted GCSE grades for external candidates. Music Scholarships are offered at 11+ and 16+. These cover up to 50% of the tuition fees and lessons in school on one instrument for a year (renewable). Art Scholarships are offered to Sixth Form entrants based on submission of a portfolio of work. Bursaries are offered at 11+ and 16+. Please see the school website for further details.

Fees per term (2016–2017). Junior School (Reception to Year 6) £5,350; Senior School (Years 7–13) £5,860.

Charitable status. Channing House Incorporated is a Registered Charity, number 312766.

Governors:

Ms C Leslie, LLB (*Chair*)

Mr J Alexander, FCA
Mr A Appleyard, BSc (*Vice Chair*)
Mrs J Burns, BA
Revd D Costley, BA
Mrs J De Swiet, MA
Ms M Jayaweera, MA
Miss D Patman, FRICS, ACIArb, FRSA
Ms B Rentoul, MA Yale

Mrs C Richards, BSc
Mr W Spears, MBA, FRGS
Mrs C Stephenson, Cert Ed
Dr A Sutton, MB ChB, DRCOG, MRCGP, DFSRH
Dr R Williams, BSc, MSc, PhD
Mr C Underhill, FPCS
Mrs I Wassenaar, MA, DPhil

Bursar & Clerk to the Governors: Mr R Hill

Headmistress: Mrs B M Elliott, MA Cantab Modern & Medieval Languages

Deputy Head: Mr A J Underwood, MEd Cantab Theology

Director of Studies: Mrs K Thonemann, MA Oxon Mathematics

Ms S Beenstock, BA Leeds (*English*)
Mrs G Bhamra Burgess, BA London (*Economics, Assistant Head of Middle School Year 9*)
Mr T Bigglestone, BA Durham (*Head of Religious Education, Humanities*)
Mr A Boardman, BA Durham (*Geography, Assistant Director of Studies*)
Mr P Boxall, GRSM, ARCO Royal Academy of Music (*Director of Music*)
Miss J Bramhall, BA Oxon (*Head of Geography*)
Dr M Bremser, DPhil Oxon (*English & Critical Thinking, Oxbridge Programme Coordinator part-time*)
Miss E Burns, MA Cantab (*History of Art part-time*)
Mr D Coram, BA Dunelm, MA London (*Classics*)
Mr P Daurat, BEd Huddersfield (*Mathematics*)
Ms S Della-Porta, BEd Australia (*Head of Physical Education*)
Ms A Derbyshire, MA Goldsmiths (*Art part-time*)
Mrs W Devine, BA Reading (*Head of Politics, Publications Manager*)
Dr N Devlin, MA, DPhil Oxon (*Classics part-time*)
Mrs S Elliot, BA Cantab (*Head of Classics*)
Miss P Evernden, MA Cantab (*Head of English*)
Miss L Feilden, BA Brighton College of Art (*Art part-time*)
Mr S Frank, BSc Birmingham (*Head of Biology*)
Miss S-L Fung, BSc Coventry (*Physics*)
Ms A Gill Carey, BA Canterbury (*Head of Drama*)
Mr P Gittins, BA Wolverhampton (*Art, Head of PSHE, Assistant Head of Middle School*)
Mrs S Gorrie, MA Glasgow (*Spanish, French*)
Mrs G Hannan, MA Cantab, MTeach London (*Head of History, Gifted & Talented Coordinator*)
Mrs R Harper, BA Kent, ALAM (*English, Head of Middle School*)
Mr A Haworth, MA RCA (*Head of Art*)
Mrs B Hernandez, BA Alicante (*Spanish, French*)
Mr M Holmes, BSc City of London Polytechnic (*Head of Information and Communication Technology*)
Miss A Hosseini, BSc London (*Head of Chemistry*)
Mr R Jacobs, BA Oxon (*Head of Physics, Head of Science*)
Mrs H Kanmwaa, BA Oxon (*English*)
Mrs A Kennedy, MSc London (*Chemistry*)
Miss C Long, MA London (*French*)
Ms T MacCarthy, BSc Edinburgh (*Mathematics part-time*)
Mrs S Mahmood, BSc Alberta (*Chemistry part-time*)
Mrs L Marshall, BSc Edinburgh (*Chemistry*)
Ms J Newman, BA Leicester (*Head of Economics, Head of Sixth Form*)
Mrs H Nissinen-Lee, BSc London (*Geography part-time*)
Mrs J Ogidan, BSc Liverpool (*Biology, Head of Careers, Head of Upper School*)
Miss H O'Sullivan, BSc Birmingham (*Physical Education*)
Miss V Penglase, BA London (*Drama and Theatre Studies part-time*)
Ms Y Rabet, BA UHB France (*Head of Modern Foreign Languages, Head of Spanish*)
Mr D Riggs-Long, BSc London (*Mathematics part-time*)
Miss S Salmon, MA London (*Geography*)
Ms M Sharma-Yun, BSc London (*Mathematics part-time*)
Mrs D Shoham, BSc Birmingham (*Biology part-time*)
Dr C Spinks, PhD Manchester (*Chemistry*)
Miss H Stacey, BA Nottingham (*English part-time*)
Ms A Stöckmann, MA Westfaelische Wilhelms (*Head of German*)
Mr P Thompson, MA Oxon (*History and RE part-time*)
Miss M Wilkes, BA London (*Spanish and French*)
Miss A Wilkinson, MA London (*History*)
Ms K Wilkinson, BA East Anglia (*English, Assistant Head of Upper School*)

Mrs R Williams, BSc London (*Mathematics part-time*)
Mr P Williamson, BEd Huddersfield (*Head of Mathematics*)
Miss A Yasamee, MA Manchester (*Librarian*)
Miss L Zanardo, BA Mus Australia (*Assistant Director of Music*)
Ms N Zekan, BEd Australia (*Physical Education*)
Mrs D Zuluaga de la Cruz, MA France (*French part-time*)

Junior School:

Head: Mrs L Lawrance, BPrimEd Hons Port Elizabeth, South Africa

Deputy Head: Mrs C Constant, MA Greenwich (*Year 6*)

Mrs P Gibson, MEd London (*Classroom Teacher*)
Miss E Glennon, BA Manchester (*Classroom Teacher Year 1*)
Miss K Goldstein, BA Birmingham (*Classroom Teacher Year 2*)
Mrs I Hawkins, BEd London (*Classroom Teacher Year 3 part-time*)
Mrs T Luxford, BA Middlesex (*Classroom Teacher Year 3 part-time*)
Ms R McGinnety, BA Cantab (*Classroom Teacher Year 4*)
Miss A McLennan, BA Leeds (*Classroom Teacher Reception*)
Miss L Panton, BA Southampton (*DT & Drama, Art, ICT*)
Miss M Pepper, LTCL (*Head of Music – Junior School*)
Miss A Phipps, BEd Middx Polytechnic (*Classroom Teacher Year 2*)
Mrs C Rand, CertEd (*Classroom Teacher part-time*)
Mrs B Rayner, BA Twickenham (*Classroom Teacher Reception*)
Miss S Snowdowne, BEd Plymouth (*Classroom Teacher Year 5*)
Ms S Unsworth, BA Bath Spa (*Classroom Teacher Year 1*)
Ms H Younger, BA Oxon (*Director of Studies – Junior School & Classroom Teacher Year 6*)
Mrs S Ahmed (*Teaching Assistant Year 3 part-time*)
Ms A Beasley (*Teaching Assistant Years 4–5 part-time*)
Mrs C Brierley (*Teaching Assistant Year 2*)
Mrs A Done (*Teaching Assistant Year 2 part-time*)
Mrs D Galli (*Teaching Assistant Year 2 part-time*)
Mrs K Hadjipateras (*Teaching Assistant Reception part-time*)
Miss Z Hira (*Teaching Assistant Reception*)
Miss M Holmes (*Teaching Assistant Year 6 part-time*)
Miss J Hudson (*Teaching Assistant Year 1*)
Ms S Ibrekic (*Teaching Assistant Reception part-time*)
Miss E Krajewski (*Teaching Assistant Year 1*)
Miss S Litiu (*Teaching Assistant Reception*)
Mrs R Pieri (*Teaching Assistant Year 3 part-time*)

Visiting Music Teachers:
Mr S Allen, ARCM (*Clarinet*)
Miss J Bacon, BA, PG Dip (*Voice*)
Mrs H Bennett, BMus Hons (*Trumpet*)
Miss S Bircumshaw, GRSM Hons (*Violin Junior*)
Mrs M Bradbury-Rance, MA (*Voice*)
Mr A Brown, Dip TCL (*Percussion*)
Mrs P Capone, AGSM (*Piano*)
Miss M Carroll, BMus (*Double Bass*)
Mr N Harrison, GRSM, SRCM (*Bassoon*)
Miss J Herbert, BA (*Cello*)
Mrs H Jolly, GRSM (*Flute*)
Ms M Keogh, ARAM (*Harp*)
Mr A Khan, LTCL (*Guitar*)
Mrs L Knight, MA (*Singing*)
Mrs P Malloy, LRAM, ABRSM (*Violin/Viola*)
Miss N Myerscough, ARAM (*Violin*)
Miss C Philpot, LRAM (*Oboe*)
Miss J Rayner, BA (*LAMDA*)

Miss E Rossiter, PG Dip, MMus (*Piano*)
Miss L Seddon, Dip ABRSM, BMus Hons (*Cello*)
Miss H Shimizu, BMus (*Piano*)
Miss A Szreter, BA (*Singing*)
Ms A Thomas, BMus (*Flute*)
Miss C Thompson, LRAM (*Violin*)
Mr T Travis, BMus (*Saxophone*)
Miss S Vivian, LTCL, Dip (*Singing*)
Miss J Watts, FRCO, GRSM, LRAM (*Piano*)
Mr A White, MMus, MA (*Lower Brass*)

Assistant to Bursar & Clerk to the Governors: Miss E Lismore-Burns
Headmistress's Secretary: Ms L Carreras
Development Director: Ms H Tranter
Director of Marketing: Mrs H Gething
Registrar: Mrs M McHarg
Senior School Secretary: Mrs E Ingram
Junior School Secretary: Mrs L McInerney
Development Assistant: Miss G Greco
School Counsellor: Miss W Jones (*part-time*)
SENCO: Ms C Dodsworth (*part-time*)
Nurses: Mrs C Cooper & Mrs T Franklin

Cobham Hall

Brewers Road, Cobham, Kent DA12 3BL

Tel:	01474 823371
Fax:	01474 825906
email:	enquiries@cobhamhall.com
website:	www.cobhamhall.com
Twitter:	@CobhamHall
Facebook:	/CobhamHall

Cobham Hall is an international boarding and day school for 180 girls aged between 11 and 18. Founded in 1962, Cobham Hall is the only all-girls Round Square school with both boarding and day pupils in the United Kingdom. It is an IBO World School and offers the International Baccalaureate Diploma or International Baccalaureate Diploma Courses in the Sixth Form.

Situation. The School is set in 150 acres of parkland. Situated in North Kent, close to the M25 and adjacent to the M2/A2. Thirty minutes from London, 60 minutes Heathrow, 45 minutes Gatwick and Stansted, 60 minutes Dover and Channel Tunnel, 10 minutes Ebbsfleet International Eurostar Railway Station (17 minutes to St Pancras, 2 hours Paris).

School Buildings. This beautiful 16th century historic house was the former home of the Earls of Darnley. There are many modern buildings providing comfortable accommodation for study and relaxation. Brooke and Bligh Houses are separate buildings within the school grounds offering Sixth Form accommodation in single or twin studybedrooms, many with en-suite facilities. Both Houses have common rooms with a kitchen and computer room.

Curriculum. An IBO World School, Cobham Hall offers the IB Diploma or IB Diploma Courses in the Sixth Form, with a wide range of subjects across Languages, Social and Experimental Sciences, Mathematics and the Arts.

Sixth Form. The Sixth Form numbers 55–60 students. Academic tutorial groups are spread across the two years and facilitate interaction between students. There are exceptional leadership opportunities, including election to the Student Leadership Team which plays a significant part in the management of the school. University destinations include Aston, Central St Martins, Durham, Exeter, University College London, Leeds, Loughborough, Lancaster, LSE, Manchester and Nottingham Trent, as well as Oxford and Cambridge.

Sporting and other activities. The School's main sports are Tennis, Swimming, Hockey, Athletics and Netball. There are seven hard tennis courts, six netball courts, a large, indoor multi-sports complex, including fitness centre, dance studio and a heated indoor swimming pool, which is in use throughout the year. Horse riding and golf may be taken as 'extras'. A wide variety of extracurricular activities is available.

Careers. High-quality Careers Guidance and personal support is offered across Lower and Middle School and in the Sixth Form by School staff. Activities in partnership with external providers include Futurewise Profiling, Interview Training and an annual "Dragons Den" Day.

Round Square. The School is a member of this international group of schools, which subscribes to the philosophy of educationalist Dr Kurt Hahn. Annual conferences are attended by a school delegation including Sixth Formers. In recent years these have been held in Australia, America, India, Singapore, South Africa, Transylvania and Germany. Younger students attend Round Square conferences in the UK and Europe. Students have the opportunity to visit other member schools on an exchange programme as well as visit other countries by taking part in service projects and relief work organised by the Round Square.

Health. Residential trained nursing staff providing 24-hour medical care.

All Terms. Two Exeat Weekends and a Half Term break.

Admission. Admission is by the School's own entrance assessments which can be taken on Entrance Assessment Days in October (Lower/Middle School) and November (Sixth Form) or at a girl's own school. Girls normally enter the School between the ages of 11+ and 13+ and follow a course leading to GCSE level at the end of the fifth year and to the International Baccalaureate Diploma at the end of the seventh. Girls wishing to enter the Sixth Form should achieve at least five GCSE or equivalent examination passes at Grade C or above.

Scholarships. Scholarships are available for 11+, 13+ and Sixth Form entry.

11+: Academic, Art, Drama, Music and Sport.

Candidates for Academic Scholarships who demonstrate outstanding potential at Entrance Assessment Day will be invited back to sit a General Scholarship paper. Candidates for other scholarships will have an audition/assessment on Entrance Assessment Day.

13+: Academic, Art, Drama, Music and Sport.

Candidates for Academic Scholarships who demonstrate outstanding potential at Entrance Assessment Day will be invited back to sit scholarship papers. Candidates for other scholarships will have an audition/assessment on Entrance Assessment Day.

Sixth Form: Academic, Art, Music, Theatre and Physical Education.

Scholarship examinations and interviews usually take place in the second half of the Autumn term. Candidates sit entrance papers in English, Mathematics, and a scholarship paper in one other subject, which must be one which the candidate intends to study as part of her IB Diploma Programme. Candidates for other scholarships will have an audition/assessment.

All Scholarships are subject to annual review by the Headmaster.

For further information contact Admissions on 01474 823371.

Bursaries. Special bursaries are available for boarders from British Services families, diplomats and those families working for UK Charitable Trusts overseas and charitable bursaries for very able children from certain areas. For further information, contact Admissions.

Fees per term (2016–2017). Day girls: £5,571–£7,052. Boarders: £8,416–£10,607.

Old Girls' Association. Known as Elders. There is a representative committee which meets regularly in London or at the School. The Chairman is Mrs Tracey Balch, email: tracey.balch@outlook.com or elders@cobhamhall.com.

Charitable status. Cobham Hall is a Registered Charity, number 313650. It exists to provide high quality education for girls aged 11–18 years.

Governing Body:
Mr M Pennell (*Chairman*)

Mr C Sykes	Mrs P Tebbitt
Mr C Balch	Mrs S McRitchie
Mr M Frost	Dr K O'Neill-Byrne
Mrs L Ellis	Mrs S Webb
Mr J Dick	

Staff:

Headmaster: **Mr P Mitchell**, BSc Newcastle

Deputy Headmistress, Director of Studies: Dr S Coates-Smith, BSc, PhD London
Bursar: Mr D Standen, BSc Bradford
Assistant Headmistress and Head of Boarding: Mrs W Barrett, BSc London
Head of Sixth Form: Mrs M Thompson, BSc London (*Biology*)
Senior Tutor for Middle School: Mrs S Carney, BEd Exeter
Senior Tutor for Lower School: Mrs R Keys, BA Plymouth

* *Head of Faculty*

English:
*Miss J West, BA Oxford, MA Oxford
Miss J Stevens, BA Hull
Mrs F West-Lindsay, BA Reading

Mathematics:
*Ms Danielle Deacon, BA Greenwich, GDPP Greenwich, PGCE Canterbury Christchurch
Mrs W Barrett, BSc London
Mrs M Martin, BSc Loughborough
Mr M Pattison, BSc NE London, MA London

Science:
*Mr J Fryer, BSc Leicester, MA Kent (*Biology*)
Dr S Coates-Smith, BSc, PhD London (*Physics*)
Mrs M Thompson, BSc London (*Biology*)
Mr P Hosford, BSc Thames Polytechnic (*Physics*)
Mr A Kirkaldy, BSc Wales, PGCE Southampton (*Chemistry*)

Art:
*Mrs K Walsh, BA Kent Institute of Art & Design
Mrs A Lockheart, BA Illinois State University, PGCE London

Drama:
Miss S Boyle, MA Kent
Mrs P Gough, BEd London

Economics:
Mr M Pattison, BSc NE London, MA London

Film Studies:
Mrs F West-Lindsay, BA Reading

Geography:
Mrs R Keys, BA Plymouth
Mrs S Carney, BEd Exeter
Miss K Lambert, BSc Gloucestershire

History:
*Miss A Williams, BA Brasenose College Oxford
Mr N Bushell, BA York

IB Coordinator:
Mrs A Jakso, BA Perth, BEd Tasmania (*IB Coordinator*)

Computer Science/ICT:
Mr K Eyers, Teaching Diploma Canterbury Christ Church

Latin:
Dr P Marin, BA, MA USA, PhD Dublin

Modern Foreign Languages:
Mrs B Tismer, BA London
Mrs E Wilkinson, BA London
Miss J Caro Quintana, Licenciada en Filologica Inglesa, Valencia, Spain
Mrs M Gutierrez, Licenciada en Lenguas Extranjeras Columbia, GTP Christ Church
Mrs X-W McArthur, BA China, PGCE Canterbury
Mrs T Russell, BA La Sorbonne, PGCE Lancaster

Music:
Miss P Clements, BA London
Mr M Haas, BA Michigan, MMus London

Physical Education:
Mrs K Hooper, BA Greenwich
Mrs S Carney, BEd Exeter
Miss K Lambert, BSc Gloucestershire

Religious Studies:
Miss A Williams, BA Brasenose College Oxford

PSHE:
Mrs M Thompson, BSc London
Miss K Lambert, BSc Gloucestershire
Mrs R Hillier, BA Exeter
Mrs B Tismer, BA London
Mrs E Wilkinson, BA London

Psychology:
Mrs K-A Hickmott, BSc Middlesex

Theory of Knowledge:
Miss K Lambert, BSc Gloucestershire

EFL:
*Mrs C M von Bredow, BA Hons Birmingham, MA Exeter, PGCE Open University, RSA Dip TEFL
Ms C Abbaticola, BA London

Student Support Department:
*Ms J Konec, BA London, PGCE London, OCR Level 7 Diploma
Mrs J Balson, BTEC Level 3 (*Teaching Assistant*)
Mrs R Hillier, BA Exeter

Careers:
Sixth Form: Mrs W Barrett, BSc London
Middle School: Mrs S Carney, BEd Exeter
Lower School: Miss A Williams, BA Brasenose College Oxford

Librarian:
Mrs A Jakso, BA Perth, BEd Tasmania

Laboratory Technicians:
Mrs B Reed
Mrs D Weaver

Art Technician:
Mrs L Hunt

Computer Support:
Mr D Wright (*Network Manager*)

Boarding Staff:
Mrs W Barrett, BSc London (*Head of Boarding*)
Mrs D Didzinskiene, BA Šiauliai Univ Lithuania, MS Vytautas Magnus Univ Lithuania (*Day Housemistress*)
Mrs D Jackson, RGN/RSCN (*Resident Nurse/Housemistress*)
Mrs C Fenice (*Housemistress*)
Miss K Ebun-Cole (*Assistant Housemistress*)

Miss N Shipton (*Graduate Housemistress*)
Miss J Richards (*Graduate Housemistress*)

Visiting Staff for:
Cello, Clarinet, Double Bass, Drums, Flute, French Horn, Guitar, Keyboard, Oboe, Percussion, Piano, Recorder, Saxophone, Trombone, Trumpet, Tuba, Viola, Violin, Drama, Voice and Communication, Ballet, Self-Defence and Tennis.

Administration:
Registrar: Mrs J Shelley
Assistant Registrar: Mrs H Standen
Marketing Assistant: Mrs J Booth
Marketing Assistant: Mrs T Reid
Receptionists: Mrs N Chaplin, Mrs C Coster
Headmaster's PA: Mrs C Blackwell
Deputy Head's PA: Mrs K Theobald
Assistant Head's PA: Mrs S Slater
School Secretary: Mrs J Webster
Bursar's Secretary: Mrs J Brace
Accounts Administrator: Mrs K Pinder, MAAT
Accounts Assistant: Mrs S Thompson
Maintenance Foreman: Mr J Best
Grounds Foreman: Mr T Gilbert

Cranford House

Moulsford, Wallingford, Oxfordshire OX10 9HT

Tel:	01491 651218
Fax:	01491 652557
email:	admissions@cranfordhouse.net
website:	www.cranfordhouse.net
Twitter:	@CHSMoulsford

Cranford House is a non-selective independent day school for girls aged 3–16 years and boys 3–11 years. It has an excellent reputation for providing its 400 pupils with a balanced, all-round education within a warmly nurturing environment. Set in over 14 acres of rural South Oxfordshire the small class sizes, close community and committed staff ensure each pupil is ably supported and challenged to achieve their full potential. The school was rated as 'Excellent' in all categories in its ISI Inspection of November 2014. The Early Years Foundation Stage was rated as 'Outstanding'.

The Early Years Foundation Stage (EYFS) encompasses Nursery and Reception, catering for boys and girls aged 3–5 years. Pupils benefit from a large, off-site Nursery School in a beautiful setting with plenty of green space for free-flow activities and learning. There are many links to the main school site for integration with Reception, swimming lessons and whole-school productions and activities.

The Junior School comprises Years 1 to 6. Juniors benefit from Senior School facilities and specialist subject teachers are used in a variety of disciplines. The school's all-inclusive approach sees all pupils taking part in competitive sports matches from Year 3 upwards. Lesson content is based on the National Curriculum, but supplemented to ensure pupils develop their own collaborative, reflective and reasoning skills and abilities. Results are excellent. Responsibility is offered at a young age through posts such as Junior Head Girl and team captains.

In the Senior School, girls follow a common core curriculum. In the 2016 Sunday Times Parent Power league tables, Cranford House was rated 3rd nationally for its GCSE results in the small schools, no sixth form category.

Key to the excellent pastoral offering is a vibrant House system which encourages both a sense of community and leadership. On reaching Year 11, pupils enjoy further positions of responsibility. The school has extensive recreational facilities and games fields. In winter, hockey, football and netball are played, and in summer, tennis, rounders, cricket and athletics. Swimming takes place on site. Dramatic, musical and dance productions are an important aspect of school life and all are encouraged to take part.

In addition to the extensive range of enrichment activities offered throughout the school, all pupils have the opportunity to join educational trips and excursions. For Senior pupils, Bronze and Silver levels of The Duke of Edinburgh's Award scheme are offered, in addition to far-flung expeditions with World Challenge. Opportunities for overseas travel are also offered through exchanges, ski and sports trips and choir tours. School transport operates over a wide area.

Scholarships and awards are offered for Year 7 entry into Senior School.

Our aim is to encourage pupils to achieve their full potential, becoming motivated, confident and happy individuals, recognising the importance of respect and support for others, but ready to seize life's opportunities.

Fees per term (2016–2017). £3,500–£5,350.

Charitable status. Cranford House School Trust Limited is a Registered Charity, number 280883.

Board of Governors:
Mrs N Scott-Ely (*Chair*)
Mr R Fisher (*Chair Finance Committee*)
Mrs H Gittins (*Education Committee, SEN*)
Mrs G Moody (*Chair of Bursaries Committee*)
Mrs L Kilroy (*Bursaries & Scholarships Committee, Legal*)
Mr P Thomas (*Education Committee*)
Mrs M Flower (*Safeguarding*)
Mr R Fisher
Mr P Tollett

Head: Dr James Raymond, PhD, BA Hons, PGCE, NPQH

Deputy Head: Mrs L Lawson, BA Hons, PGCE
Assistant Head (*Academic*): Mr C Ellis, MA, MEd, BA Hons, PGCE
Assistant Head (*Junior School*): Mrs A Stewart, BA Hons, PGCE
Director Finance & Operations: Mrs E Taylor, MA
Director of Studies: Mr R Barker, BSc Hons, PGCE
Director of Music: Mrs J Powell, BA Hons, Dip Adv Studies RAM
Head of Pastoral Care: Mrs C Smythe, BA Hons, Dip Ed

Senior School Teaching Staff:
Mrs N Butler, BA Hons, CAPES
Dr N Carr, MA, PhD, PGCE
Mrs L Rafferty, BA Hons, PGCE
Mr S Cowley, BA Hons, PGCE
Mrs S Day, BA Hons, PGCE
Mrs L Gifford-Guy, BMus Hons
Mrs K Heard, BA Hons, PGCE
Miss A Holbrook, BSc Hons, PGCE
Mrs R Lanyon, MSc, PGCE
Mrs A Macmillan, PGCE MFL
Mrs J McCallum, MA, PGCE
Mr K McIntyre, BSc
Mrs E Mean, BA, PGCE
Mrs G Mitcham, MA, PGCE
Miss A Robson, MA, PGCE
Mrs V Senior, BA, PGCE
Mrs S Stegeman, BSc, PGCE
Mrs F Stone, BA Hons, PGCE
Mrs J Turner, BA Hons, PGCE
Mrs N Tiedeman, BA Hons, PGCE
Mrs A Watkins-Cooke, BEd
Mrs D Cranton, BA Hons, PGCE

Miss S Carrington, BA Hons, PGCE

Junior School Teaching Staff:
Head of EYFS: Mrs K Knight, BA Hons, EYPS
Head of Key Stage 1: Mrs A Diamond, BEd Hons
Head of Key Stage 2: Miss H Stanley BA Hons; Mrs L Morris, MSc, BA Hons
Mrs C Bennett, BA Hons, EYPS
Miss R Carpenter, BA Hons, PGCE
Mrs K Dubuisson, BA Hons QTS
Mrs B Graham, BSc Hons, PGCE
Mrs A Greedy, BEd Hons
Mrs N I'Anson, BEd Hons
Mrs J Morris, BA Hons, PGCE
Miss C Oliver, BA Hons, PGCE
Mrs N O'Loughlin, BA Hons, PGCE
Miss A Slade, BA
Miss V de Trense, BA Hons, PGCE
Mrs S Wagstaff, BA Hons, PGCE

Nursery Teaching Staff:
Head of EYFS: Mrs K Knight
Deputy Head of Nursery: Mrs K Walters, BA Hons, CACHE L3
Mrs L Burrows, NVQ3
Mrs A John, NVQ3
Miss S Swift, NVQ3

Learning Support:
Miss D Smale, BA Hons, BSc Hons

Croydon High School
GDST

Old Farleigh Road, Selsdon, South Croydon, Surrey CR2 8YB

Tel: 020 8260 7500
Fax: 020 8657 5413
email: info2@cry.gdst.net
            admissions@cry.gdst.net
website: www.croydonhigh.gdst.net
Twitter: @CroydonHigh
Facebook: @CroydonHighSchoolGDST

Founded in 1874, the school's original site was in Wellesley Road Croydon but is now situated in the leafy suburb of Selsdon.

Croydon High School is part of the GDST (Girls' Day School Trust). The GDST is the leading network of independent girls' schools in the UK. As a charity that owns and runs 24 schools and two academies, it reinvests all its income in its schools. For further information about the Trust, see p. xxiii or visit www.gdst.net.

For over 140 years, Croydon High School has provided a superb all-round education for girls, around the Croydon area and further afield. The school combines tradition with a forward-looking, supportive and nurturing atmosphere where every girl is encouraged and supported to achieve her personal best. The school welcomes girls from a wide range of backgrounds; excellent pastoral care ensures that each girl is known as an individual.

Croydon High offers girls a wide range of extracurricular opportunities ensuring that each can find something she enjoys. The school regularly achieves local, regional and national success in Sport; its Arts are also outstanding, with a vibrant Music department offering opportunities to musicians at varying ability levels to develop their talents in all musical genres. Termly productions involve students across all year groups and young artists are motivated and inspired to develop their creative talents in different media.

The school aims to develop confident young women with wide ranging interests and abilities who have also achieved excellent academic results. Emphasis is placed on ensuring that girls are happy and fulfilled in whatever career path they choose for the future.

Number of Pupils. Senior School (aged 11–18): 380 girls (including 110 in the Sixth Form). Junior School (aged 3–11): 215 girls (including 17 in the Nursery).

Facilities. The purpose-built school has outstanding facilities; including specialist music rooms, a drama studio, a language laboratory, 5 computer suites, 10 science laboratories, design technology room and a recently refurbished sports block incorporating sports hall, gym, indoor swimming pool, fitness room and dance studio. The school is surrounded by spacious playing fields with netball/tennis courts, athletics track and an all-weather hockey pitch.

The Junior School, which has its own Nursery, is in an adjacent building on the same site, sharing many of the excellent facilities. It also boasts a state-of-the-art 4D immersive learning room, where girls can experience sound and sights that inspire them to produce highly imaginative written and verbal work.

The Sixth Form have their own suite of rooms, including a common room and quiet study area, adjacent to the school library and excellent Further Education and Careers resources are available on site.

Curriculum. Most girls take 10 GCSE subjects with the aim of providing a broad and balanced core curriculum which keeps career choices open. Over 23 subjects are offered at AS and A Level including Government & Politics, Economics, Latin and Physical Education. Almost all girls proceed to University, and, each year, a number are offered places at Oxbridge or to read Medicine

Admission. A whole school Open Day is held annually in October and a Sixth Form Open Evening in November. An Open Event for both Junior and Senior Schools is held in May. Tours and private visits are welcome and can be arranged at any time through the Admissions Registrar.

The school admits girls to the Junior School on the basis of either individual assessment (younger girls) or written tests (girls of 7+ and above). Selection procedures are held early in January for Juniors and assessments for Infants are held during the Autumn and Spring Terms for entry in the following September.

For entrance to the Senior School in Year 7, the school holds Entrance Tests in November for entry in the following September. All applicants are interviewed by the Headmistress and references are taken up.

Entrance Tests are held in January for Year 9 entry in the following September.

For the Sixth Form, the school interviews applicants and requests reports from the present school. A Sixth Form Open Evening is held in November and Scholarship and Bursary applicants sit an examination later that month.

Further details on the admissions process are available on the website or via the Registrar, admissions@cry.gdst.net.

Fees per term (2016–2017). Senior School: Years 7–9 £4,986, Years 10–13 £5,172; Junior School: Nursery (full time) £3,115, Reception–Year 2 £3,917, Years 3–6 £4,073.

Scholarships and Bursaries. Following the ending of the Government Assisted Places Scheme, the GDST has made available to the school a number of scholarships and bursaries.

Academic scholarships are available for entry at 11+ or to the Sixth Form. Music, art & design, drama and sports scholarships are also available at 11+ and 16+.

For entrance at Year 9, the school offers two Academic Plus scholarships to applicants joining from other schools, who have chosen to be assessed academically and in one of the following subjects; art, music, drama or sport.

Bursaries are means tested and are intended to ensure that the school remains accessible to bright girls who could not otherwise benefit from the education we offer. These are available to Senior School girls only.

The school has a vibrant and active Old Girls Network – The Ivy Link – which supports the school in numerous ways, including offering careers and mentoring connections.

Charitable status. Croydon High School is part of The Girls' Day School Trust, which is a Registered Charity, number 306983.

Chairman of Local Governors: Mr A Spiro

Headmistress: Mrs E L Pattison, BA

Deputy Head: Mrs P Clark, MA London

Director of Sixth Form, Sixth Form: Mr J Haidar, Licence LLCE Paris

Assistant Head, Curriculum: Mr M Pickering, BA, MSc Manchester

Head of Junior School: Mrs S Bradshaw, BA Bristol

School Business Manager: Mrs A Hinkson, MBA Kingston

Director of Marketing: Mrs F Cook, BSc Southampton

Derby High School

Hillsway, Littleover, Derby DE23 3DT

Tel:	01332 514267
Fax:	01332 516085
email:	headsecretary@derbyhigh.derby.sch.uk
website:	www.derbyhigh.derby.sch.uk
Twitter:	@DerbyHighSchool
Facebook:	/derbyhighUK
LinkedIn:	/DerbyHighSchool

Derby High School is an independent day school conveniently situated in the Derby suburb of Littleover which educates boys and girls aged 3 to 11 and girls only from 11 to 18.

Academically, the school regularly achieves the best results in the county, however a Derby High education is about much more than academic results. Whether your child is musical, creative, analytical or sporty, at Derby High each student's individual strengths are identified to help them achieve their potential in a fun, friendly and supportive atmosphere.

There are 570 pupils in school of whom 310 are in the Senior School, which is for girls only, and 260 are in the Infants and Juniors which are both co-educational.

The Primary Department follows an enhanced national curriculum course. KS1 and KS2 take internal assessments. ASPECTS are used for pre-school and INCAS for Year 5. There is considerable enrichment in the curriculum with a wide variety of sports, music, drama and other activities available both within the curriculum and at club time.

The Senior School offers courses in Art and Design, Biology, Chemistry, Design Technology, Drama, Business, English Language and Literature, French, General Studies, Geography, German, History, Home Economics, ICT, Mathematics, Further Maths, Music, Physical Education, Psychology, Physics, Religious Studies, Spanish and Theatre Studies. The curriculum is enhanced by activities such as Young Enterprise, The Duke of Edinburgh's Award and World Challenge. Sports, drama and music are also strengths, with pupils gaining recognition at county and national level.

The main points of entrance are at pre-school, Reception, Year 3, 11+ and 16+ where Scholarships and Assisted Places are available. Entrance is by examination and interview. Entrance at other ages is by assessment and takes place by arrangement.

The school has an active Christian ethos and broadly follows the teaching of the Church of England, but pupils of all faiths are welcomed and valued.

Examinations. Pupils are entered for ASPECTS, INCAS, GCSE and GCE AS and A Level examinations, some Sixth Form pupils take the EPQ. The school takes part in INCAS and MidYIS testing. Short course GCSE ICT is taken by all pupils. Many pupils have individual music lessons and take music examinations through the Associated Board of the RCM. LAMDA is offered in the Junior School, leading to examinations. The Young Enterprise examination may be taken by Company members.

Games. Hockey, Netball, Rounders, Tennis, Swimming, Athletics, Short Tennis, Tag Rugby, Football and Trampolining are major sports.

Fees per term (2016–2017). £2,745–£3,999.

Charitable status. Derby High School Trust Limited is a Registered Charity, number 1007348. It exists to provide education for children.

Governors and Foundation Governors:
Chairman: Dr R Faleiro
Mr B Bailey
Ms H Barton
Mrs J Bullivant
Dr V Churchhouse
Mrs S Clover
[1]Mr M R Hall, DL, Hon D Univ, FCA, FCMA, FCT
Mrs R Hughes, BA, ACIB
Mrs F Lazenby
Mr T Ousley
Mrs R Williams
Reverend Alicia Dring (*Bishop's representative*)

[1] *Foundation Governor*

Head: Mrs D Gould, BA Comb Hons Birmingham, PGCE Birmingham, NPQH

Deputy Head: Mrs A Chapman, MA Open University, BA Hons Nottingham, PGCE Warwick

Head of Sixth Form & Assistant Head: Mr A Lee, BA Hons Salford, PGCE Leicester

Assistant Head: Miss A Jordan, BA Hons Wolverhampton, PGCE Newcastle

Assistant Head: Mr A Maddox, MMath Oxford, PGCE Oxford, PGDES Oxford

Chaplain: Ms J Whitehead, MA Sheffield, BA Hons Nottingham

Bursar: Mrs M Mitchell, BA Hons, ACA, ICAEW

* *Head of Department*

Miss A Allum, BSc Hons Brunel, PGCE Brunel (*Physical Education*, **PSHE*)
Mrs A Arthey, BA Comb Hons Birmingham, PGCE Nottingham (*French*)
Mrs K Aydi, BSc Aberdeen, PGCE Bath (**Biology*)
Mrs A Bodycombe, BA Hons Central St Martin's College of Art & Design, MA Coventry, PGCE OU (*Art, Design Technology*)
Mr J Buckley, BSc Hons York, PGCE York (*Mathematics*)
Mrs S Bussey, BSc Econ Hons Aberystwyth (*Information Resources Manager*)
Miss C Danac, BA Hons Nice, PG DipEd Birmingham (*French, Spanish*)
Mr R Dodson, MEng Hons Bristol (**Mathematics*)
Mrs S Dowling, BSc Hons Aston, PGCE Kingston (*Physics, Mathematics*)

Mrs N Driver, BEd Hons Lancaster (**Religious Education, PSHE, Head of Years 7–9*)
Mrs J Fraser, BSc Hons Derby, PGCE Nottingham Trent (*Psychology*)
Mr J Gallagher, BA Hons Durham, PGCE Nottingham (**Geography*)
Mrs S Goodman, BSc Hons Sheffield, PGCE Sheffield (*Physical Education, Deputy Head Sixth Form*)
Mrs J Hancock, BEd Hons Manchester Metropolitan (**Physical Education*)
Mrs K Hewitt, BSc Hons Birmingham, PGCE Leeds (*Biology, Food & Nutrition*)
Mrs R Hill, BSc Hons Liverpool, PGCE (*Liverpool*) (*Biology*)
Mrs S Hilton, BA Hons Brighton, PGCE Brighton (**Business, ICT*)
Mrs L Hough, BSc Hons Brunel, CertEd (**Design Technology, Art & Design Graphics*)
Miss A Jordan, BA Hons Wolverhampton, PGCE Newcastle (*History, EPQ, T4L, Assistant Head*)
Miss S Kelliher, BA Hons Dublin, PGCE Birmingham (**German, *French, *MFL*)
Mrs R Lesley, BMus Hons Birmingham, PGCE Birmingham, LTCL
Mrs N Ley, BSc Hons Loughborough, PGCE Loughborough (*Mathematics*)
Mr A Maddox, MMath Oxford, PGCE Oxford, PGDES Oxford (*Mathematics, Assistant Head*)
Mrs M Martinez Hernandez, BA Salamanca, PGCE Madrid (**Spanish*)
Mrs S Martin-Smith, HND Swansea, BA Hons Swansea, PGCE Swansea (**Art, Textiles*)
Dr S Mathews, BA Hons Sheffield Hallam, MSc Manchester, PhD Manchester (**History*)
Mrs C McDonald, BSc Hons Manchester, PGCE Manchester (**Home Economics*)
Dr J Myers, BSc York, PGCE Leics, PhD Edinburgh (**Chemistry*)
Dr J A Nelmes, BSc Hons London, PGCE Nottingham, PhD Loughborough (*Physics, Chemistry*)
Mrs J Orr, BSc Hons Ulster, PGCE Nottingham Trent (**Physics*)
Mrs C E Read, BA Hons Reading, PGCE London (*English, *General Studies*)
Miss M Render, BA Hons Hull, PGCE Hull (*English, SENCO*)
Miss C V Riley, BSc Hons Leeds, PGCE Leeds (*Chemistry, Head of Years 10 & 11, DofE Award*)
Mrs M Roe, BA Hons Nottingham (*Geography, DofE Award*)
Mrs L Seymour, BA Hons, PGCE Notts (*German*)
Mrs E Smith, BA Hons Loughborough, PGCE Loughborough (*Drama, English*)
Mrs F Supran, BA Hons Manchester, PGCE Oxford, Cert TEFLA Oxford Brookes (*English, *Drama*)
Mr E Temple, MusB Hons Manchester, PGCE Manchester (**Director of Music*)
Mrs J Webster, MA Hons Cambridge (**English & Psychology*)
Mr S Williams, BSc Hons Birmingham, PGCE Nottingham (*Mathematics, *ICT*)
Miss L Wilson, BA Hons Manchester, PGCE Manchester (*Religious Education, History*)
Mrs C Wood, BSc Hons Manchester, PGCE Nottingham (*Biology*)

Primary School:
Head of Primary: Mrs M Hannaford, BEd Hons Derby, MA Ed OU, NPQH
Mrs K Hopkinson, BEd Hons QTS Derby, MA (*Primary Assistant Head*)
Miss L Baker, BA Hons Derby, PGCE Derby

Mrs K M E Carey, BEd Liverpool Chester College
Mrs C Courtney-Hale, BA Ed Hons Wales, MA Ed
  Loughborough (*EYFS Coordinator*)
Mrs A Dowell, BSc Hons, QTS Newman Coll of HE
Mrs S Evans-Bolger, BA Hons QTS, MA Ed BG
  University College Lincoln
Miss R Ford, BA Hons Leeds, PGCE Primary Bradford
Mrs J Foster, BEd Hons Derby
Mr R Gould, BA Hons Wolverhampton, PGCE
  Birmingham City
Mrs M Higham, BA Oxford, PGCE Birmingham City
Mr C Horne, BEd Primary Hons Derby
Miss D Hyland, BA Hons Birmingham, PGCE
  Birmingham
Miss H Law, BA Hons Nottingham, Primary PGCE
  Manchester
Mrs C Lodge, BEd Hons Derby
Miss L Pitt, BA PrimEd Birmingham
Mrs L Soutar, BA Hons Nottingham, PGCE Music Leeds
Mrs J Swainston, BEd Hons Sheffield
Mrs A Trindell, BSc Hons QTS BG University College
  Lincoln
Mrs R Youngman, BEd Hons Derby, NPQML

Dodderhill School

Droitwich Spa, Worcestershire WR9 0BE
Tel: 01905 778290
email: enquiries@dodderhill.co.uk
website: www.dodderhill.co.uk

Introduction. Founded in 1945, Dodderhill School is an independent, non-denominational, day school administered by a Board of Governors. The school provides a seamless education for girls aged 3 to 16 years and welcomes boys from 3 to 7 years. Small classes and experienced, motivated staff mean that pupils can achieve their academic and personal potential. Excellent pastoral care and a friendly, family atmosphere help pupils to build the confidence, self-esteem and maturity that will help them to continue to achieve in the world of post-16 and higher education.

Location. The school is set in its own grounds on the outskirts of Droitwich Spa and only minutes from the M5/M42 interchange. It serves families from Droitwich Spa, Bromsgrove and a wide area of North Worcestershire. Minibus transport is provided between school and Droitwich Spa station and many pupils take advantage of the excellent local rail network.

Facilities. A superbly designed foundation stage and junior block incorporating a spacious multi-purpose school hall complements the newly refurbished original Georgian buildings. An ongoing development programme instituted by the governors in 1998, included in March 2004 an exciting new Nursery providing babies and toddlers (6 weeks to 3 years) with the same warm, happy, caring and family friendly atmosphere enjoyed throughout the school. In 2008 a new building was opened providing further classroom accommodation and a new food technology room. During 2009 a second ICT room for use by teaching staff was completed and in October the redesigned and enlarged outside area for the Early Years Foundation Stage was opened. In 2009 and 2010 science laboratories were refurbished to provide the latest up-to-date facilities for girls in Years 4–11. In 2013 the old gymnasium was converted to a Performing Arts Centre.

Curriculum and Teaching. From the Early Years until Year 3 emphasis is on literacy and numeracy and children are class taught with specialist input in ICT, French, Music, PE and, from Year 3, DT. From Year 4 all subjects are specialist taught and in Years 5 and 6 increasing use is made of senior facilities to ease transition and enhance learning opportunities. In Years 7, 8 and 9 in addition to the core subjects of English, mathematics, science, RE and PE, all girls learn French, German, Spanish, geography, history, classic civilisation, philosophy, art, catering, ICT, music and textiles. For GCSE all girls take English, mathematics, science, RE, a modern foreign language, history or geography and two additional subjects from a choice of a second foreign language, a second humanity and the creative subjects. Class sizes are small, expectations are high, teachers are well qualified and experienced and the individual is paramount. Results are excellent. Dodderhill is regularly at or near the top of the Government GCSE performance tables for Worcestershire. In 2011 the School topped the tables for the third successive year.

Extra-Curricular Activities. The school offers a stimulating and diverse range of extra-curricular opportunities. Creative arts, music, outdoor activities, including the Duke of Edinburgh's Award and sport are all catered for. Pre-school care is available at no charge from 8.00 am. There is an after-school club until 6 pm – a charge is made for this service.

Admissions and Scholarships. Formal entrance examinations are held in January each year for entry at 9+, 11+ and 13+. Two 11+ academic scholarships and an 11+ music scholarship are available at this time. Children may transfer from other schools at any time during the year and admission is then by taster day, examination and school reference. Entrance for younger children is by taster day and individual assessment.

Bursaries. The Board of Governors has set up a Bursarial Fund to widen access to Dodderhill by providing assistance to girls entering the school at Year 5 or later.

Fees per term (2016–2017). Tuition fees are from £2,100 in Kindergarten to £3,590 in the senior school, inclusive of lunches and textbooks. There is a 5% reduction for siblings.

Charitable status. Dodderhill School is a Registered Charity, number 527599. It exists to provide education for girls and boys.

Governors:

Mr D Allchin	Mr P Martin
Revd L Handy	Mr A Robinson (*Chairman*)
Mrs W Haines	Mr Ricketts
Mrs A Hines	Mrs K Wormington
Mrs J E Lowe	

Headmistress: **Mrs C Mawston**, BA Hons

Academic Staff:

Mrs J Allen Griffiths, BA Hons	Mrs R Hatfield, BA Hons
	Miss C Hawkley, BA Hons
Mrs E R Barnett, BA Hons	Mrs J Hodges, BEd Hons
Mrs A Benigno-Thomas, BA Hons	Mrs S C Johnson, MEng Hons
Miss S Berwick, BA Hons	Mrs S G R Loveday-Fuller, BEd Hons
Mrs R Bradley, BA Hons	
Mrs A Cartwright, BSc Hons	Mrs A L Macrae, BA Hons
	Mrs T Palmeri, BEd Hons
Miss L Cassidy, BEd Hons	Mrs S Richards, BSc Hons
Mrs C Churchill, BA Hons	Mr J Rudge, BSc Hons
Miss L Crane, BA Hons	Mrs C A Salter, BSc Hons
Mr P D Cross, BSc	Mrs C Vinson, BMus Hons
Mrs M Finnikin, BA Hons	Miss C Williams, BA Hons
Mr N Giffin, BA Hons	

Administrative Staff:
Bursar: Mrs S Howell
Headmistress's PA: Mrs Y Wood
HR: Mrs R Brown

Finance: Mrs A Lane
School Receptionist: Mrs R Patel
Matron: Mrs J Cameron-Price

Durham High School for Girls

Farewell Hall, Durham DH1 3TB

Tel:	0191 384 3226
Fax:	0191 386 7381
email:	enquiries@dhsfg.org.uk
website:	www.dhsfg.org.uk

Durham High School for Girls aims to create, within the context of a Christian ethos, a secure, happy and friendly environment within which pupils can develop personal and social skills, strive for excellence in academic work and achieve their full potential in all aspects of school life.

- Highly qualified, specialist staff.
- Excellent examination results.
- Continuity of education from 3 to 18 years.
- Entry at 3, 4, 7, 10, 11 and 16.
- Superb modern facilities include state-of-the-art Science/ICT/Library Block and Performing Arts Suite.
- Academic, Music, Performing Arts, Art, Drama and Sports Scholarships.
- Financial assistance available at all stages.

Number on roll. 421 day pupils.

Age range. Seniors 11–18; Juniors 7–11; Infants 4–7; Nursery from age 3.

Entry requirements. Assessment, formal testing and interview if age is applicable. Sixth form entry is dependent on the level of achievement at GCSE.

Junior House (age range 3–11). A purpose-built Nursery provides a stimulating environment for children aged 3–4 years. Children may start the day after their 3rd birthday. Early Years Funding available. Superb Outdoor Learning environment.

Junior House follows a topic-based curriculum linked to the National Curriculum which enables girls to enjoy every aspect of learning and discovery. Form teachers encourage and support a high standard of achievement in all areas of the curriculum and promote a feeling of warmth and security.

Extra-curricular activities include: Choirs, Instrumental Tuition, Debating, Textiles Group, Drama, Hockey, Rounders, Netball, Tennis, Ballet, Karate, Amnesty Club, Dance and Drama. A range of sports fixtures are made with other schools.

The immediate environment plays an important role in stimulating learning and regular visits are made to the theatre, museums and places of educational interest.

Senior House Curriculum. The curriculum is designed to be enjoyable, stimulating and exciting, providing breadth and depth in learning.

- Wide choice of options at GCSE and Advanced Levels.
- Languages: French, Spanish, Latin and Classical Greek.
- Separate Sciences.
- Personal and Social Education programme.
- Careers Education and Guidance.

Extra-curricular activities include regular visits abroad, foreign exchanges, visits to the theatre, art galleries, museums and concerts. There is also a thriving programme of Music, Drama and Sport, as well as a flourishing Duke of Edinburgh's Award scheme and debating clubs.

The Sixth Form. The Sixth Form of 67 girls takes a full and responsible part in the life and organisation of the school. A wide range of A and AS Level subjects is available. Girls usually take 3 or 4 subjects in L6 and 3 in U6, with an option of an EPQ.

Fees per term (2016–2017). Nursery £1,300*, Infants (Reception–Year 2) £2,120**–£2,790, Juniors (Years 3–6) £3,080, Seniors (Years 7–13) £4,120.

*Fees for hours above the 15 hours per week provided by the Early Years Funding.

**Fees for 4 year olds qualifying for Early Years Funding.

Extra subjects. Greek, Speech and Drama, Astronomy and Music (piano, strings, brass, woodwind, singing).

Scholarships and Bursaries. Means-tested Scholarships are available at at 7+, 11+, 14+ and 16+.

At 11+ a number of academic Open Scholarships are offered and bursaries are available in cases of financial need. There is also the Barbara Priestman award of £600 per annum for daughters of practising Christians. Scholarships (Academic, Performing Arts, Sport and Music) are awarded at 11+ and financial help is available at all stages from age 11.

At 13+ Academic, Music, Performing Arts and Sport Scholarships are available.

At 16+ there are a number of academic scholarships available to external and internal candidates. Music scholarships are also available at 16+, as well as Performing Arts, Sports and an Art Scholarship.

Transport. Transport is available from most local areas and the school is also accessible by public transport.

After School Care. After School Care is available until 5.30 pm and is free of charge (there is a charge for Nursery children).

Further information. The Head is always pleased to welcome parents who wish to visit the school. For further information and a full prospectus please contact the School on: tel: 0191 384 3226; fax: 0191 386 7381; website: www.dhsfg.org.uk; email: enquiries@dhsfg.org.uk.

Charitable status. Durham High School for Girls is a Registered Charity, number 1119995. Its aim is to create a friendly, caring community based on Christian values and to encourage academic excellence.

Governors:
Mrs M Cummings, BA (*Chairman*)
Mr S Cheffings (*Vice Chairman*)
Miss L Clark, BEd, MA
Revd Dr H Cleugh
Mr K Delanoy, FCCA
Dr C English
Dr M Gilmore, MA, PhD
Miss M Green
Dr M Hyder
Revd P Kashouris
Mr A Lake
Mr I Meston, BTh Min
Mr A Ribchester, MBE, FCA
Mrs P Walker

Headmistress: Mrs L Renwick, BEd, NPQH

Deputy Head: Mrs J Tomlinson, BSc Newcastle (*Biology*)

Assistant Head: Mr L Fox, MA Rostock, Germany (*Modern Languages and Physical Education*)
Assistant Head: Mrs L Ibbott, BA Cardiff (*English; Marketing and Development*)

Head of Junior House: Mrs K Anderson, BEd Neville's Cross

Bursar: Mr D Payne, BSc London, ACA

Senior House:
* *Head of Department*
Dr N Alvey, MPhys, PhD Kent (*Physics*)
Mrs Armitage, BA Newcastle (*Geography*)
Mrs C Baring, Oxon (*Classics*)

Mr A Cartmell, BA OU, BSc Southampton (*Mathematics*)
Miss G Casey, BA Cantab (*Modern Languages*)
Mr R Coates, BA Dunelm (*History*)
Mrs P G Clarke, BSc Cork (*Physics*)
Miss G Colon, BA Hons London (*Modern Languages*)
Mrs C I Creasey, BA Dunelm (**Geography*)
Mrs D L Elliott, BSc Dunelm (**Biology*)
Mrs A Jenkinson (*Physical Education*)
Mrs J Flavell, MA Cambridge (*Chemistry*)
Mrs E Gentry, BSc St Andrews (*Science*)
Dr S Grant, BSc Newcastle (**Science, *Chemistry*)
Mrs A Hawkins, BA London (*English, Sociology*)
Miss N Hill, BA Leeds (**Modern Languages*)
Mr P Hitchcock, BA Sunderland (**Art & Design*)
Mrs A Jenkinson, BEd Leeds Metropolitan (*Physical
    Education*)
Mrs M Kenyon, BSc York (*Chemistry*)
Mrs C Kelly, BSc York, MSc Sunderland, MA Dunelm
    (*Mathematics*)
Mrs C Lawrence-Wills, BA Cantab (**Music*)
Mrs A Lee, BA Manchester (*Learning Support*)
Mrs J Lonsdale, BA, MA Leeds (**Drama*)
Mr T Lonsdale, BA Leicester (*French, German*)
Mrs L Lowes, MA Newcastle (**Director of Sport*)
Mrs K Measor, BA Sunderland, MA OU (*Business Studies
    and Economics*)
Mrs L Middleton, BA Dunelm (**Religious Education*)
Mr J Neeson, MA Manchester (*Art*)
Mrs J Newby, BSc Warwick (*Biology*)
Mrs H O'Neill, BA Hons Dunelm (*Modern Languages*)
Mr J Priest, MSc Bath (**Mathematics*)
Mrs D Rabot, MA Ed Sunderland (*ICT*)
Mrs K Ridley, BSc Liverpool (*Careers Coordinator*)
Revd Dr S Ridley, MA Oxon, EdD Dunelm (*Classics*)
Miss A Scholfield, BSc Northumbria (*Physical Education*)
Mrs J Shaw, BA Manchester (*Mathematics*)
Mrs J V Slane, BSc Surrey (*Physical Education*)
Mr D Smith, MA Oxon, CertTh York (**History and
    Politics*)
Miss J Sneddon, BA Hons, MA Edinburgh (*Art Textiles*)
Mrs R Stephenson, BA Newcastle (*English*)
Ms K Sullivan, BSc London, MSc Liverpool
    (*Mathematics*)
Ms D Todd, BA Hons Sunderland (*English*)
Revd B Vallis, BA Cambridge, BA Theology Dunelm
    (*Chaplain and Religious Education*)
Mrs C Wheeler, BA Dunelm (*Psychology; Head of Sixth
    Form*)
Mrs I Woodland, MA Cantab (*Geography*)

Junior House:
Mr P Allaker, BA Hons Dunelm
Mrs R Booth, BMus Manchester
Mrs E Brothers, BSc Sheffield (*Deputy Head*)
Miss S Cook, BSc York
Mrs J A Coxon, BEd Liverpool (*Physical Education*)
Mrs P Everett, BEd Hons Cambridge
Mrs K A Hall, BA Central Lancashire
Mrs C M Hopper, BA Nottingham
Mrs L Mock, BA Dunelm
Miss S Rose, BSc Wales, MSc London, MA Durham
Mr G Wright, BA Hons Sunderland

Junior House Support Staff:
Mrs A Maddison, NNEB Durham
Mrs C Gorman
Mrs M Harrison
Mrs Moorcroft, BA Dunelm
Mrs J Tipple, MEng Sheffield Hallam (*After School Care*)

Visiting Staff:
Mrs R Barton-Gray (*Cello*)

Miss V Bojkova, Diplomas in Conducting & Piano
    Performance (*Singing and Piano*)
Mr Bovill (*Drum Kit and Percussion*)
Mrs K Gkatziou, (*Drama*)
Miss S Innes, BMus, LRAM (*Violin & Viola*)
Mrs F Preston (*Woodwind*)
Mr G Ritson, GRNCM, PPRNCM (*Brass*)
Ms H Saunders (*School Counsellor*)
Miss R J Shuttler, BA, MMus, LTCL (*Piano*)
Miss C Smith, BA, FRSA (*Clarinet & Saxophone*)
Miss B Walker (*Violin*)
Mrs E Walker, BSc Newcastle, MSc Sheffield (*Educational
    Psychologist*)

Administrative Staff:
Head's PA: Mrs A Thompson
Administrator: Mrs J Ridley
Marketing/Publicity: Mrs A Wright
Librarian: Mrs J Durcan, ALA
Assistant Bursar: Mr P Atkinson
Accountant: Mrs C McAdams
ICT Systems Manager: Mr J Kerton
ICT Technician: Mr P Cass
Reception: Mrs P Steele, Mrs C Gillham
Catering Manager: Mrs A Hibbart
Laboratory Manager: Mrs L Foskett, MChem York
Laboratory Technician: Mr T Rabot, MSc Bishop Burton
Laboratory Assistants: Miss J Cummings, Mrs L Deveaux-
    Robinson, Miss L Tinnion
Performing Arts/Art Technician: Mr N Raine, BSc
    Newcastle, BEd Sunderland
Caretaker: Mr K Riding
Assistant Caretakers: Mr D Wilson, Mr P Tennant, Mr A
    Brack

Edgbaston High School

**Westbourne Road, Birmingham, West Midlands
B15 3TS**

Tel: 0121 454 5831
Fax: 0121 454 2363
email: admissions@edgbastonhigh.co.uk
website: www.edgbastonhigh.co.uk

This independent day school, founded in 1876, attracts
girls both from the immediate neighbourhood and all over
the West Midlands. They come for the academic curriculum,
the lively programme of sporting, creative and cultural
activities, and for the individual attention and flexibility of
approach.

Personal relationships at EHS are of paramount importance. Parents, both individually and through their association, give generously of their time to support our activities;
while staff, through their hard work and good relationship
with the girls, create an atmosphere at once orderly and
friendly.

Organisation and Curriculum. There are three departments working together on one site which caters for over
950 day girls aged two and a half to eighteen. One of the features of EHS is the continuity of education it offers. However, girls can be admitted at most stages. Staff take special
care to help girls settle quickly and easily. Pupils enjoy a
broadly based programme which substantially fulfils the
requirements of the National Curriculum and much more.

**The Pre-Preparatory Department, known as
Westbourne,** offers facilities for about 100 girls aged two
and a half to five in a spacious, purpose-built, detached
house. The staff aim to create an environment in which they
can promote every aspect of a girl's development. A brand

new Nursery (part of the £4 million Octagon building) was opened in February 2005.

The Preparatory School accommodates over 350 girls from 5+ to 11 in up-to-date facilities, among them a new IT suite, Science Laboratory, Library and Design Technology Centre. A full curriculum, including English, Mathematics, Science and Technology, is taught throughout the department.

The Senior School caters for about 500 girls aged 11+ to 18. Girls follow a well-balanced curriculum which prepares them for a wide range of subjects at GCSE and A Level.

Examination results are very good with high grades distributed across both Arts and Science subjects. The vast majority of girls in the Sixth Form of over 100 proceed to Higher Education. Every year girls obtain places at Oxbridge and Russell Group Universities.

Extra Curricular Activities. Girls can take part in a broad range of activities including art, ceramics, Mandarin, drama, Duke of Edinburgh's Award, music, sport and Young Enterprise. There are clubs during the lunch hour and after school. Instrumental music lessons are available. There is a strong music tradition in the school. Girls go on visits, expeditions and work experience in this country and abroad. We encourage girls to think of the needs of others.

Accommodation. There is a regular programme of improvements to the buildings. An exciting new multi-purpose hall, The Octagon, was opened in February 2005. A floodlit all-weather surface was opened in Summer 2006. The school has its own indoor swimming pool, 12 tennis courts and 8 acres of playing fields. Work on extended Sixth Form accommodation, a new library and fitness suite, at a cost of £3.5m, was completed in January 2011. In August 2016 the school completed a building development designed to enhance the Preparatory School. At a cost of £1.6 million, the project has resulted in a newly extended library, Art room and large welcoming Reception space.

Location. The school is pleasantly situated next to the Botanical Gardens in a residential area, 1½ miles south-west of the city centre. It is easily accessible by public transport and also has its own privately run coaches.

Fees per term (2016–2017). Pre-Prep £1,744 (mornings to 1.00 pm), £2,596 (5 days); Prep £2,686–£3,774; Senior £3,994.

Scholarships and Bursaries. Academic Scholarships are available at 11+, awarded on the basis of performance in the entrance examination. Sixth Form Academic Scholarships are awarded based on examination and interview.

Two external scholarships of up to 20% are offered to suitable candidates for entry into Year 3, following assessments in Mathematics, Reading Skills and Creative Writing. Assessments take place in January.

Two Music Scholarships are also offered annually: one at 11+ and one at 16+. 11+ candidates must sit the main entrance examination in October and then have written, aural and practical tests. Candidates at 16+ attend an audition and interview in January.

At 16+ there are further scholarships for Art, Performing Arts and Sport awarded to girls of outstanding ability. Assessments take place in January.

A Bursary fund exists to help girls of good academic ability in financial need to enter at 11+ and the Sixth Form and to assist those whose financial circumstances have changed since they entered the Senior School. Bursaries may cover part or full fees. All scholarships can be combined with means-tested bursaries in cases of need.

Further information. Full details may be obtained from the school. Parents and girls are welcome to visit the school by appointment.

Charitable status. Edgbaston High School for Girls is a Registered Charity, number 504011. Founded in 1876, it exists to provide an education for girls.

President: Sir Dominic Cadbury, BA, MBA

Vice-Presidents:
Mr Duncan Cadbury, MSc
Mr I Marshall, BA
Her Honour Judge Sybil Thomas, LLB

Council:
Chairman: Mr J D Payne, BSc, MRICS
Deputy Chairman: Mrs C Fatah, RGN

Ms H J Arnold, BSc Hons
Lord Bhattacharyya, KB, CBE, FREng
Mrs S A England Kerr
Mr I Griffiths, MA, MA, PGCE
Mrs A E S Howarth, CertEd, DipEd
Dr J Leadbetter, PhD, BSc, PGCE, BSc Hons, MEd Ed Psych, AFBPs, CPsychol
Mrs V Nicholls, Chartered MCIPD
Mr G I Scott, MA Oxon
Mrs S Shirley-Priest, MA, MRICS
Mrs J Tozer, LLB Hons, Solicitor, BD

Representing the Old Girls' Association:
Mrs A Stanley, BA

School Staff:

Headmistress: Dr Ruth A Weeks, BSc, PhD Birmingham

Deputy Head Academic: Mrs S-E Rees, MA Oxford
Deputy Head Pastoral: Mrs J Coley, BA Reading
Director of Studies: Miss J Rance, BSc Manchester, MEd Birmingham

School Management Team:
Mrs C Cardellino, BA Leicester (*Head of Sixth Form*)
Mrs A Lacey, BSc East Anglia (*Senior Teacher*)
Mr J Sabotig, BSc Birmingham (*Common Room Representative*)

* *Head of Department/Subject Leader*

Ms G Ajmal, BA Wolverhampton (*English, Head of Year 8*)
Miss Maria Aznar-López, BA Birmingham (*Spanish, French, DofE Bronze Coordinator*)
Miss M Barbet, Licence d'Anglais Université de Clermont-Ferrand, France (*French, Spanish*)
Mrs L Batchelor, BSc Birmingham (**Physical Education, Head of Year 7, Outreach Coordinator*)
Mr G Bateman, BMus Sunderland, Dip ABRSM (*Music*)
Mr D Berman, MA Oxford (*Science; Octagon Technician*)
Miss A G Bosc, BSc Birmingham (*Biology*)
Mrs A M Brookes, BSc Brunel (**Chemistry*)
Mrs C Cardellino, BA Leicester (*Head of Sixth Form, *German*)
Mrs J Chalmers, BA York (*Mathematics*)
Mrs A Cirillo-Campbell, BA Birmingham (**ICT, Head of Year 11*)
Miss J Cox, BA Newcastle upon Tyne (*RS and History*)
Dr E Cruice, BSc Sussex, PhD Birmingham (*Science*)
Miss A Cummings, BA Northampton (*Food & Nutrition and Textiles*)
Mr N Day, BA Huddersfield (*History*)
Mr M Dukes, BA Wolverhampton (**Art, Director of Visual Communications*)
Mrs Z Ehiogu, BA University East London (*Physical Education, PSHEE and Study Skills Coordinator*)
Mrs C A Evans, Cert Ed Anstey College of Physical Education (*Physical Education*)
Mrs S Flitter, MA Oxford (*Classics*)
Mr A Flox-Nieva, Licenciado en Filología Inglesa, Castilla, Spain (**Spanish*)
Mrs J Forrest, BSc Open University (*Biology*)
Miss S Glover, BA Nottingham (*History*)

Ms D Graham, BSocSc Birmingham, Grad Dip Psych Aston (*Psychology and Sociology, Deputy Head of Sixth Form*)

Miss J P Harrison, BA Southampton, MA Birmingham (*English, *Critical Thinking, Higher Education Advisor, Examinations Secretary*)

Miss M Hayday, BA Hull (*Religious Studies, Head of Year 9*)

Mrs J Hayward, BSc Newcastle-upon-Tyne (*Mathematics*)

Mrs S Hewison, BA Ed Exeter (*Physical Education*)

Mrs H Howell, GBSM, ABSM, Birmingham (*Music*)

Mrs K Hughes, BA Durham (*Geography*)

Miss K Jacks, BA Durham (*Physical Education*)

Mr M James, BA Northumbria (*Art*)

Mrs J Johnson, BA Aberystwyth (*MFL, Gifted & Talented Coordinator*)

Miss N Jones-Owen, BA Manchester Metropolitan (*English, *Media Studies*)

Mrs M Khuttan, BSc Keele (*Mathematics*)

Mrs A Lacey, BSc East Anglia (*Senior Teacher, *Science*)

Mr S Lane, BA Plymouth (*Drama*)

Mrs A Lee, BSc Birmingham (*Mathematics*)

Mrs S Lynch, BSc Sheffield, MA Sheffield (*Science*)

Mr P Malone, BA Sheffield (*ICT, Business Studies*)

Miss K Massey, BSc Reading (*Geography, Charities Coordinator*)

Mrs R J Matthews, BSc Aberystwyth (*Science, Biology, Head of Careers*)

Miss M P Monet-Rossetti, BA Open University (*French, German*)

Mrs L Mooney, BA Wolverhampton (*Food & Nutrition, *Textiles*)

Miss S H Mullett, BA Nottingham (*Art*)

Mrs K E Newling, BSc Birmingham (*Mathematics*)

Mrs R Norman, BSc Liverpool (*Mathematics*)

Miss S O'Hare, MA St Andrews (*English*)

Mrs S Park, BA Cardiff, MPhil Cardiff (*English*)

Mrs G Parsons, BSc University of Wales Institute, Cardiff (*Physical Education, Head of Year 10*)

Mrs L Parsons, BSc Coventry, MSc Coventry (*Psychology*)

Mr C J Proctor, BA Swansea (*English*)

Miss K Rankin, MA Oxford (*Classics*)

Miss F M Richards, BSc Bristol, BA Birmingham (*Art*)

Miss R Richardson, BA Reading (*History, *Critical Thinking, Extended Project, Higher Education Advisor*)

Mr K Robson, BMus Conservatoire Birmingham, MA Huddersfield (*Music*)

Mrs S Rowntree, BA Salford (*Drama*)

Dr D Royal, BSc UCL, PhD UCL (*Physics*)

Miss C Roye, BSc Loughborough (*Physical Education*)

Mr J Sabotig, BSc Birmingham (*Physics, Head of Houses*)

Mrs D Saddington, Cert Ed Nottingham Trent (*Food & Nutrition and Textiles*)

Dr Y Shang, BSc Peking, China, MSc Beijing, China, PhD Loughborough, BA Jinan, China (*Mandarin*)

Mrs J Shutt, BA Keele (*Business and Economics, Head of Careers*)

Mr P Smith, BA Staffordshire (*Religious Studies, Outreach Coordinator*)

Mrs K J Stocks, BMus Birmingham, ARCM (*Music*)

Mrs C Syer, BSc Oxford Polytechnic (*Food & Nutrition and Textiles*)

Mr S Thomas, BA Cambridge, MPhil Cambridge, MA Cambridge (*Mathematics*)

Mr M Tomaszewicz, BSc Birmingham (*Science*)

Miss S E Vann, BEd De Montfort (*Physical Education*)

Miss H Welsh, BSc Portsmouth (*History, English, PSHEE and Academic Support*)

Mr M Wiggins, BA Birmingham (*Religious Studies, *Sociology*)

Mr D Wilkins, BA Birmingham (*English*)

Miss E Wood, MA Edinburgh (*Classics*)

Librarian: Mrs S E Sansom, BA Bangor, MCLIP

Library Assistant/Examinations Officer: Mrs J Hall, BSc Surrey

Network Manager: Mrs S Srinivas, MSc Coventry

Language Assistants:
French: Ms M Romero
German: Miss S Krickl
Spanish: Miss C Gonzáles

Technicians:
Art: Miss A Birch, BA Southampton
Food & Nutrition and Textiles: Mrs C Harris
ICT: Mr A Ijaz
Science:
Mr J Coley, BSc Northampton
Mrs A Duvnjak, BSc Coventry, MSc Birmingham
Miss V Gutzmore, BSc OU, HND

D of E Silver and Gold Coordinator: Mrs S Griffiths

Visiting Staff:

Music:
Pianoforte:
Ms E Cockbill, MA, LLCM, ALCM
Mrs L Kitto, GBSM, ABSM, LTCL
Miss M Morris, MMus, Birmingham; LRSM
Mrs C J Purkis, GBSM, ABSM, LRAM
Flute:
Miss H Jones, BA
Mrs S Wilson, BA
Recorder:
Mrs K J Stocks, BMus Birmingham, ARCM
Clarinet/Saxophone:
Miss M Harper, GRNCM, ARMCM
Mr J Meadows, BA, ABSM
Horn:
Mrs C Butler, BMus Birmingham
Violin/Viola:
Miss A Chippendale, BMus
Mr M Owen, LRAM
Cello:
Miss J Carey, GRSM, ARCM
Guitar:
Miss L Larner, BMus
Brass:
Mrs M Brookes, DRSAMD
Percussion:
Mr J Groom, BMus
Singing:
Mrs S Allsop, ARCM, ABRSM
Miss S Purkis, BMus
Miss S Vango, BMus
Theory:
Mrs K Stocks, BMus, ARCM
Miss M Harper, GRNCM, ARMCM

Fencing:
Professor P Northam, BAF

LAMDA Teachers:
Mrs T Bolt
Ms C Fidler, BA, LRAM, FETC, IPA
Mrs J Foley

Life Saving: Rose Link

Gym Club: Mrs S Hewison

Administrative Staff:
Headmistress's P.A: Ms G Franchi
Finance Director: Mrs D Johnson, BCom Acc, FCA
Head of Marketing & Development: Mrs A Rowlands, BSc Lancaster
Senior School Admissions Secretary: Mrs H Head

Nurses:
Mrs M Al-Ani
Mrs H Heyes
Mrs J Irving, RGN, SCM

Facilities Manager: Mr S Watson, MHCIMA

Preparatory School:

Head: Mrs S Hartley, BEd Bristol

Deputy Heads:
Mrs S Alderson, CertEd City of Birmingham College of
  Education
Miss C Robinson, BA Exeter

Mrs A Aston, BSc Birmingham
Mrs A M Collins, BEd Birmingham
Mrs S Crompton, BSc Leeds
Mrs A Dawes, BSc Cardiff
Miss S Dawes, BSc Leeds
Miss R Deacon, BSc Newman College
Mrs S Draper, BSc Swansea
Miss C Dugdale, BSc Leeds Metropolitan
Mrs C Eveleigh, BSc Bath
Mrs S Flitter, MA Oxford
Mrs J Goodyear, BA Ed Worcester College of Higher
  Education
Mrs L Hobbs, BSc Birmingham
Miss S Howarth, BSc Worcester College of Higher
  Education
Mrs L Humble, BA Swansea
Mrs H Jones, BA Swansea
Mrs J Knott, BA Birmingham
Miss K McKee, BA Sussex
Miss V Nelsey, BA Hull
Miss F O'Connor, BEd Wolverhampton
Mrs M Poade, BA Reading
Mrs F Scott Dickins, BA London
Mrs G Villiers Cundy, BEd Bath
Mrs K Waterworth, BSc Aston
Mrs F Watson, BA Leeds
Mrs V Woodfield, BEd UCE Birmingham

Librarian: Mrs N Ash

Teaching Assistants:
Mrs D Audley
Mrs M Bracey
Mrs G Draysey
Mrs N Mohamed
Mrs J Russon

Preparatory School Nurse: Mrs H Heyes
Preparatory School Technician: Mr P Flynn
Preparatory School ICT Coordinator: Mr N Hartley

Before School Care Supervisor: Mrs C Harris
School Support and After School Care Supervisor: Mrs M
  Henry
School Support and After School Care Assistants:
Miss E Clinton
Mrs J Eyres
After School Care Assistants:
Miss L Osborne
Mrs M Rees

Administration Staff:
Prep School Secretary: Mrs N Gough
Prep School Office Assistant: Mrs K Williams

Pre-Preparatory Department:
Mrs L Bowler, BA Leicester
Miss V Brenner, BA St Martin's College, Lancaster
Mrs J Goodman, BA Birmingham
Mrs D A Kennedy, BEd West Midlands College of Higher
  Education

Mrs H Robinson, BEd University of Wales
Mrs H Skidmore, BA Trinity College, Carmarthen

Teaching Assistants:

Mrs R Aulak	Mrs F Green
Miss S Collins	Mrs C Holliday
Mrs J Corbett	Mrs A Knight
Mrs E Cornelius	Mrs J Redden
Mrs H Coulson	Miss A Sanzari
Mrs D Deakin	Mrs P Varma

Before School Care Supervisor: Mrs H Coulson
Before School Care Assistant: Mrs C Holliday

After School Care Supervisor: Mrs R Aulak
After School Care Assistants:
Miss E Clinton
Mrs M Hart
Mrs P Varma

Visiting Staff:

Ballet: Miss D Todd

Farlington School

Strood Park, Horsham, West Sussex RH12 3PN
Tel: 01403 254967
Fax: 01403 272258
email: office@farlingtonschool.net
website: www.farlingtonschool.net
Twitter: @Farlington_Sch
Facebook: /FarlingtonSchool

Motto: *Vive ut Vivas*

The School. The official foundation of Farlington School
(then Farlington House) was in 1896 at Haywards Heath.
The School moved to its present site in 1955. It is situated in
33 acres of beautiful parkland on the Sussex-Surrey border.
It has two lakes, sports and recreational facilities.

Farlington has approximately 350 girls aged from 3 to 18.
Girls can board from the age of 8, on a full, weekly or
occasional basis, or attend as day girls. All are equally
important members of the School community. In September
2008 the Courtyard Building opened, designed to complement the existing Prep School building which opened in
1997. This offers facilities for our co-educational Nursery
Class for children aged 3–4 years. The building also
includes further classrooms, a multi-purpose hall, a kitchen,
a library and administration offices. Girls at Farlington also
enjoy a purpose-built Science Building, a Sports Hall with
facilities for badminton, volleyball, netball and basketball, a
floodlit all-weather hockey pitch, and a modern Sixth Form
Centre. The new junior boarding house, "Fishponds" provides a home-away-from-home environment for girls in
Years 4 to 8, and the Mansion House boarding facilities provide excellent accommodation for the older girls.

*See also Farlington Preparatory School entry in IAPS
section.*

Farlington was last inspected by the Independent Schools
Inspectorate in 2010. Farlington was rated excellent/out-
standing in every standard. The report included the following two quotes: "*An overall excellent curriculum and
outstanding teaching enable preparatory and senior school
pupils to achieve excellent all-round standards.*" "*As a
result of excellent guidance pupils exhibit outstanding personal development. The school is successful in fostering
individuality, pupils are happy, succeed and flourish, and
relationships are very positive. It is a very friendly, welcoming school.*"

Curriculum. We aim to provide a broad and balanced curriculum for all age groups. Our academic standards are high, and we encourage girls to raise their own expectations of achievement. Our approach involves good teaching practice coupled with clearly set targets and positive encouragement throughout every girl's school life. The rewards are excellent examination results: in 2016 a 98% pass rate at A Level with 77% at grades A*–C, and 95% overall pass rate at grades A*–C at GCSE. Our sixth formers go on to study the subject of their choice at universities including Oxbridge and the Russell Group.

Important though academic standards are, Farlington is about more than examination results: we aim to educate the whole child.

Spiritual awareness, care for others, tolerance and compassion are the basis of our religious education. We are a Church of England foundation, but we welcome all faiths. There is an assembly most weekday mornings, and boarders are given the opportunity to attend a service at a church of their choice on Sundays. Work for charity and service to the community are part of the ethos at Farlington.

Farlington's emphasis on care and guidance in personal development is underlined in our tutorial system. Each girl is placed in a tutor group where she is given individual attention. Tutors liaise with other members of the teaching staff, boarding staff (where appropriate) and parents. They monitor academic progress and extra-curricular activities. Each week a tutor period is devoted to the discussion of a wide range of topics within our Life Skills (PSHE) programme, including moral issues, personal relationships, health education and study skills.

Extra-Curricular Activities. Opportunities for pursuing activities of all sorts exist after school and during lunch hours. Some are physical activities, such as The Duke of Edinburgh's Award Scheme, trampolining, fencing; others are more creative, such as Art or Drama club. Musical activities are popular with numerous choirs, ensembles, orchestras and bands on offer. There is a strong drama and music tradition within the School, and three major productions are staged each year. A wide range of sporting activities is available and the School enjoys considerable success at county and national level in many sports. Other activities include Debating, Chess Club and Ballet. All girls are encouraged to take at least one activity, and there is also supervised prep until 5.45 pm. Extended day provision is available at a charge until 7.00 pm.

Admission. Admission is by the School's own entrance examination and interview. *Entrance Examination Day in 2017*: Wednesday 4th January.

Scholarships are awarded on merit. Scholarships will be held for the duration of the girl's time at Farlington, subject to annual review. There will be an enrichment programme for, and public recognition of, Scholars, and all girls who maintain their scholarships until they leave after A Levels will be further acknowledged at their final Prize Giving.

Scholarships are available at three points of entry in the Senior School:

Entry into Year 7: Examination in January.

Academic, Music, Sport, Drama and Art Scholarships are available. Both internal and external candidates need to apply for all subject Scholarships. Candidates should be registered and entered by Friday 18th November 2016. All girls who sit the Entrance Examination in January will automatically be considered for Academic Scholarships so there is no need to apply for these.

The Vive Scholarship offers a 50% reduction in the annual tuition fee to girls entering Year 7 who can demonstrate academic excellence and expertise in at least one other extra-curricular area. Closing date for applications is Friday 18th November 2016.

Entry into Year 9: Examination in January.

Academic, Music, Drama, Sport and Art Scholarships are available to both internal and external candidates who will need to apply in all cases. Candidates should be registered and entered by Friday 18th November 2016.

Entry into the Sixth Form: Examination in November.

Academic, Music, Drama, Sport and Art Scholarships are available to both internal and external candidates who will need to apply in all cases. Candidates should be registered and entered by Friday 14th October 2016, with assessments taking place on Tuesday 8th November 2016.

Scholarship application forms may be obtained from the Registrar.

Bursaries. The School offers means-tested Bursaries for all prospective and current pupils from Year 5 upwards. Bursaries are not available when one or more parent is resident outside of the UK, with the exception of serving members of the UK Armed Forces and members of the UK Diplomatic Corps.

The main bursary award process is carried out in the first half of the Spring Term and applications, therefore, should be made in the second half of the preceding Autumn Term.

Subject to available funds, applications for bursaries will be considered at other times of the year, on a half-termly basis if parental circumstances change unexpectedly.

Fees per term (2016–2017). Prep School: Day £2,350–£4,750; Boarding from age 8: £7,550–£8,260 (weekly), £7,980–£8,690 (full).

Senior School: Day £5,660; Boarding: £9,170 (weekly), £9,600 (full).

Charitable status. Farlington School is a Registered Charity, number 307048. It exists to provide education for girls.

Governing Body:
Council of twelve members
Chairman: Mrs S Mitchell, BA, MA, PGCE

Headmistress: Ms L Higson, BSc, PGCE

Assistant Head (*Academic*): Mrs A Binns, BA, PGCE

Assistant Head (*Pastoral*): Mrs A Higgs, BEd

Head of Prep School: Mrs F Mwale, BSc, PGCE, MSc

Deputy Head of Prep School: Mrs S E Povey, BEd, CertEd

Bursar: Mr R Bosshardt, FCIPD, BSc, MSc

Registrar: Mrs S Apps, MBA

Boarding Staff:
Mrs D Roberts-Barter
Mrs V Kelly, BA
Mrs Wragg
Mrs Colson
Mrs Y Crook
Mrs J Humphreys

Nurses:
Mrs D Hartnell
Mrs J Cooper

Farnborough Hill

Farnborough Road, Farnborough, Hampshire GU14 8AT

Tel:	01252 545197/529811
Fax:	01252 513037
email:	admissions@farnborough-hill.org.uk
website:	www.farnborough-hill.org.uk

Twitter: @FarnboroughHill
Facebook: /Farnborough-Hill

Motto: *In Domino Labor Vester Non Est Inanis*

Farnborough Hill is a leading independent Roman Catholic day school for 550 girls aged 11 to 18. The school was established in Farnborough in 1889 by The Religious of Christian Education and is now an educational trust. It welcomes girls of all Christian denominations, other faiths or no faith, who are supportive of the ethos. Farnborough Hill is committed to the education of the whole person in a happy, caring Christian community in which each individual is valued.

Academic standards are high with students usually taking ten GCSE subjects. In the Sixth Form most students take four AS subjects in the Lower Sixth and three A Levels in the Upper Sixth. The vast majority then go on to Higher Education. The school is a member of ISCO and there is a well-equipped Careers department and a specialist Careers teacher.

Farnborough Hill offers a wide range of extracurricular activities and is especially renowned for its reputation in music, sport, drama and art.

The school's impressive main house, once the home of Empress Eugenie, has had modern purpose-built facilities added. These include a sports hall, indoor swimming pool, newly refurbished laboratories, drama studio, IT suites, art and design technology centre, a music suite, a chapel and extensive playing fields.

Although within a few minutes' walk of both Farnborough Main and Farnborough North railway stations, the school is situated in 65 acres of parkland and woodland with magnificent views over the Hampshire countryside. Girls come from Hampshire, Surrey and Berkshire with many travelling by train or by school coach.

Admission. Entry is by examination taken in January for the following September.

Scholarships and Bursaries. The school offers academic, music and sports scholarships and also bursaries for parents who are in need of financial assistance. Academic scholarships are offered for entry at 11+. One of these is reserved for a Roman Catholic student. In addition music, sport and art and design scholarships are awarded at 11+. Sixth Form scholarships are awarded for academic achievement, excellence in the performing arts, the creative arts and sports. An additional scholarship is awarded by Farnborough Hill Old Girls' Association.

Fees per term (2016–2017). Tuition: £4,569.

Further information. The prospectus is available from the Director of Admissions. The Headmistress is pleased to meet prospective parents by appointment.

Charitable status. The Farnborough Hill Trust is a Registered Charity, number 1039443.

Board of Governors:
Mrs C E Hamilton (*Chair*)
Mrs J Windeatt (*Deputy Chair*)
Mrs A Berry
Dr C Chadwick
Mr T J Flesher
Mrs M Welford
Mrs D O'Leary
Mr S Nelson
Mrs G Rivers

Headmistress: **Mrs A Neil**, BA Soton, PGCE Canterbury, MEd Oxford Brookes

Deputy Head: Mrs A Griffiths, BEd Roehampton, MA Surrey, NPQH
Deputy Head (Pastoral): Miss P Sexton, BA Swansea, PGCE Oxon, MA Herts

Assistant Head: Mr J Hoar, BA Hull, PGCE Soton
Assistant Head: Mr C McCready, BSc PGCE Queen's Belfast

Teaching Staff:
Mrs E Aitchison, BA QTS Chichester (*Physical Education*)
Miss D Andrews, BSc Cardiff, PGCE Homerton (*Biology, Chemistry*)
Mrs A Barker, BSc Bath, PGCE Kingston (*Mathematics*)
Miss P Bartlett, BA, PGCE Oxon (*Mathematics*)
Mrs S Batt, BSc Glasgow, QTS GTP (*Computing and ICT*)
Mrs K Bell, BA Bristol, PGCE Southampton (*History*)
Mrs S Bond, BA Soton, CertEd Sheffield Hallam (*Art and Design*)
Mrs J Brereton, BA Soton, PGCE Reading (*Geography*)
Dr M Bright, BSc Sierra Leone, MSc PhD Birmingham (*Chemistry*)
Mrs G Brocklehurst, BSc UWIST, PGCE OU (*Mathematics*)
Mr P Butler, BA, PGCE Reading (*French, Classics*)
Mrs R Byrne, BA South Glamorgan Inst, Art TCert Goldsmiths College (*Art and Design*)
Mrs S Campbell, BA Dunelm, PGCE Oxon (*English*)
Mrs S Camprubi-Reches, BA Barcelona, MEd Cardiff, PGCE Barcelona (*Spanish*)
Mrs K Cappleman, BSc Exeter, QTS GTP (*Mathematics*)
Miss E Casey, BA Exeter, PGCE Roehampton (*French, Spanish*)
Miss H Clutterbuck, BSc, PGCE Warwick (*Biology, Chemistry, Physics*)
Mrs J Cornelius-Green, BSc PGCE Brunel (*Physical Education*)
Mrs M Davy, BA Surrey, PGCE St Mary's (*RE, Philosophy and Ethics*)
Mrs H de Mattos, BA, PGCE Roehampton, MA Royal Central School of Speech and Drama (*Drama*)
Mrs B Dunnage, BA Birmingham, PGCE Southampton (*Geography*)
Miss V Ellender, BSc St Mary's Twickenham, PGCE Brunel (*Physical Education*)
Mrs L J Evans-Jones, BA Royal Holloway, PGCE Roehampton (*English*)
Mrs L Fitzwater, Licence Valenciennes, QTS GTP (*French*)
Mr P Forrest-Biggs, MA London, QTS CfBT (*Classics*)
Mrs L Fowles, MA UCL, PGCE Institute of Education (*Classics, History*)
Mrs L Gildea, BA PGCE York, MSc Edinburgh (*History*)
Mr P Gillingham, BA Reading, PGCE Bath (*History, Government and Politics*)
Mrs A Goddard, BEd Bath (*Design and Technology*)
Mrs M Greene Lally, BA MSc UCL (*English*)
Mr S Haddock, BSc UEA, PGCE Institute of Education (*Psychology*)
Mrs E-J Harrison, BA QTS Brighton (*Physical Education*)
Mrs S Hayes, BSc Leicester, PGCE Ripon and York St John (*Biology*)
Mrs S Haynes, BSc Imperial College, PGCE Reading (*Chemistry, Physics*)
Mrs L Hooper, BSc Liverpool, GTP Reading (*Mathematics*)
Mrs R Inman, BA UCL (*English*)
Mrs K Jackson, BEd Bedford (*Physical Education*)
Mr A Johnson, BA UCA (*Graphics*)
Mr K Johnson, MA Cantab, DipEd Oxon (*Greek*)
Miss F Kelsey, BA QTS St Mary's Twickenham (*Physical Education*)
Mr T Kurian, BComm Mahatma Gandhi, AdvDip Cantab, PGCE Canterbury (*Mathematics*)
Miss C Lawson, BA W Surrey College of Art and Design (*Art and Design*)
Mr E Maccherini, BA MA Sienna (*Classics*)

Mrs S Macey, BSc UMIST, PGCE Cantab (*Chemistry*)

Mrs V McCarthy, BA UCC, PGCE Oxon (*RE, Philosophy and Ethics, History*)

Mr M McCarthy-Brown, BSc, PGCE Exeter (*Computing and ICT*)

Mr S McSweeney, BA Liverpool, PGCE Liverpool Hope (*Music*)

Miss L Miller, BA Reading, PGCE UWE (*Economics*)

Mrs J Nash, BSocSc Birmingham (*Economics*)

Mrs J Nix, BEd Winchester (*Design & Technology, Information Technology*)

Miss D O'Laoire, MA Nottingham, PGCE King's College (*Classics*)

Mrs A Payne, BSc BCHE, PGCE Bristol (*Geography*)

Miss K Pengelley, BA Nottingham, MA, PGCE Institute of Education (*Classics and History*)

Miss R Peters, BSc Cardiff, PGCE Institute of Education (*Mathematics*)

Mrs C Peilow, BA Exeter, QTS GTP (*Drama*)

Mrs J Quinlan, BA Luton, PGCE Manchester Met (*Spanish, German and French*)

Mr J Quinnell, BA Winchester, MA Durham, PGCE Lancaster (*English*)

Dr S Rawle, MA, DPhil Oxon (*Physics*)

Miss H Rowsell, BA Exeter, PGCE Oxon (*Geography*)

Mrs A Smith, MA Cantab, PGCE Cantab (*Mathematics and ICT*)

Mrs L Storrie, BSc Salford, PGCE Manchester (*Biology*)

Mrs C Swire, BEd St Mary's Belfast (*Religious Education*)

Dr I Taylor, BA, MSt, DPhil Oxon (*Music and Music Technology*)

Mr S Temple, MChem PGCE Sussex (*Chemistry*)

Dr A Tytko, BSc, PhD Leeds, MBA Dunelm, PGCE Kingston (*Economics and Business Studies*)

Miss L Warwick, BMus, DipABRSM Manchester, PGCE (*Music and Music Technology*)

Mr R Wellington, BA Exeter, PGCE Birmingham (*Theology*)

Miss P White, BA UCL, PGCE King's College London (*French and Spanish*)

Mr N White, MA Cranfield (*Business Studies*)

Mrs L Winch-Johnson, BA Hertfordshire, MSc, PGCE Surrey, CCRS Dip Perf Coach Newcastle (*English, Drama, Learning Support Coordinator*)

Dr C Wood, BSc Dunelm, DPhil Oxon, GTP Reading (*Physics*)

Mrs T Zimmermann, BA Leeds, PGCE Manchester (*German and Spanish*)

Librarian and Website Manager: Mrs J Wood, MA Cantab, DipLIS London

Matron: Mrs N Walker, RGN and Mrs F Clark, RGN

Bursar: Cmdr M G Robertson, BSc Hons, ACIPD

Director of Admissions: Mrs C Duffin, BA Hons, FCIM Chartered Marketer

Chaplain: Miss S Farmer, BA Hons, Dip Counselling UEA, MBACP, Spiritual Director, Dip Spiritual Accompaniment

ICT Coordinator: Mr A Labuschagné

Examinations Officer: Mrs C Barlow, BA Hons

Francis Holland School
Sloane Square

39 Graham Terrace, London SW1W 8JF

Tel: 020 7730 2971
Fax: 020 7823 4066

email: office@fhs-sw1.org.uk
website: www.fhs-sw1.org.uk
Twitter: @FHSSloaneSquare
Facebook: /FHSSloaneSquare

Founded 1881.

Numbers and age of entry. There are 520 Day Girls in the School and entry by the School's own examination is at 4+ for the Junior School (ages 4–11), 11+ for the Senior School (ages 11–18) (member of The North London Independent Girls Schools' Consortium) and 16+ for Sixth Form.

Curriculum and Aims. Excellent academic standards are achieved through the provision of a challenging academic curriculum and talented staff who encourage an enthusiasm for learning, intellectual curiosity and creativity. This allows our girls to thrive in a relaxed and happy environment where they are respected as individuals and able to fulfil their unique potential.

Junior School. There is a Junior Department attached to the school.

Religious Education. The school's foundation is Anglican but girls of other faiths are welcomed.

Physical Education. Hockey, Netball, Volleyball, Rounders, Health-related Fitness, Gymnastics, Athletics, Tennis and Swimming are taken. Senior girls have a choice of other activities as well including Squash, Step Aerobics, Boot Camp Fitness, Golf, Pilates, Yoga and Rowing.

Fees per term (2016–2017). £5,650–£6,390.

Scholarships and Bursaries. There are the following competitive awards each year:

11+ Academic scholarships and Music scholarships are available to the value of 5% of fees. 1 Art award is also available.

Sixth Form: Academic scholarships (internal and external) up to the value of 25% of fees, Music scholarships up to the value of 25% of fees, Drama scholarships up to the value of 25% of fees.

We will consider awarding a bursary to girls who demonstrate the ability to succeed at Francis Holland, but whose parents might not have sufficient financial resources. The level of assistance provided will depend on individual circumstances, which will be reviewed annually. The number of bursaries awarded each year is at the discretion of the Governors and may vary.

Remission of a third of the fees is available for places offered to daughters of the clergy.

Charitable status. The Francis Holland (Church of England) Schools Trust Limited is a Registered Charity, number 312745. It exists to provide high quality education for girls.

Patron: The Right Revd and Right Hon The Lord Bishop of London

Council of Governors:

Chairman: Mrs M Winckler, MA
Vice Chairman: Mrs A Edelshain, BA, MBA, MCIPD
Mr P Ashton, BSc, ACA
Mr A Beevor, BA, MBE
Ms C Black, MCSI
Rev Dr M Bowie, BA, DPhil
Ms J Briggs, BA, MA, PGCE, Adv Dip CIPFA
Mr D Dowley, MA, QC
Mrs S Graham-Campbell
Dr M Harrison, BA
Mr J Hawkins, BA
Mrs S Honey, BSc, MRICS
Mr R Owen, BA, FRICS
Professor J Parry, MA, PhD
Mr S Pitchford, MA

Lady R Robathan, BSc
Miss S Ross, BSc, FInstP (*Safeguarding*)
Dr H Spoudeas, MBBS, DRCOG, FRCPCH, FRCP, MD
Mr G Stead
Professor J Yeomans, MA, DPhil, FRS

Bursar Mr G Wilmot, BA, ACA
Clerk to the Governors Mrs G Shaw, BSc

Senior Leadership Team:

Headmistress: Mrs L Elphinstone, MA Cantab, FRSA
(*English*)

Deputy Head Pastoral: Mrs C Remy-Miller, BSc MSc
France (*French*)
Senior Mistress: Miss A Stevenson, BA Durham, BA
Open, MA Open (*French/Spanish*)
Assistant Head: Dr P Bennett, BSc Durham, MA Durham,
MEd Buckingham, PhD Bristol (*Mathematics*)
Director of Sixth Form: Mrs R Sawyer, MA Cantab
(*History*)
Head of Junior School: Ms C Spencer, BSc Leeds, MSc
Sheffield
Director of Communications: Mrs V McKinley, BA
London
Director of Information Systems: Mr T Oladuti, BA
Winchester, MBCS

Senior School – Full time:
* Head of Department

Mr D Agathoklis, MSc Athens (*Mathematics*)
Miss A Allen, BA Chichester (*Assistant Head of Lower
School, Physical Education*)
Miss J Arlington, BA Surrey (**Photography, Art*)
Mr C Bartram, BA Portsmouth (**Biology*)
Mrs M Bloor-Black, MA Middlesex, BA Brighton
(**Drama [Acting Head]*)
Ms M Bonnaud, Licence Montpellier (**Modern Foreign
Languages, French*)
Miss E Boon, MA Oxon (**History*)
Mrs R Bridges, BA Chichester (**Physical Education*)
[Maternity Leave]
M. F Calvet, MPhil Grenoble, MA Perpignan, Diploma
Toulouse (*Second in-charge of MFL, French*)
Mr L Dare, BA Cantab (*Physics*)
Miss H Davidson, BA Newcastle (*Music*)
Mr D Edes, BA Exeter (**Art*)
Miss R Flower, BA UCL (*Drama*)
Ms H Ford, MA Cantab (**Mathematics, Timetabler*)
Mr W Galloway, BA Nottingham (*English, Head of
Charity Fundraising*)
Ms C Georgulas, BA London, AMBDA (*Learning
Support*)
Miss C Graham, MA Oxon (*Director of Co-curriculum,
Religious Studies*)
Ms W Grimshaw, BA Manchester (*Head of Upper School
Years 10–11, History*)
Miss M Geussens, BA Cantab (*English, History, EPQ
Coordinator*)
Mrs G Hammond, BA Sheffield (**Psychology,
Mindfulness*)
Mrs N Hogg, BA Bath (**Physical Education*)
Mrs S Hyde, BA London (**Economics*)
Miss D Kaleja, I and II Staatsexamen Hanover, BA London
(**German*)
Father M Kenny, BA Leeds, MA London (*Religious
Studies and Spiritual Enrichment, *Debating*)
Mme A Lenec'h, Licence Rouen, MA Connecticut USA
(*Head of Lower School Years 7–9, French*)
Mr T-S Li, BA London, MPhil Cantab, MTeach London
(**English*)
Miss S Macrae, BMus Leeds (*Music*)

Dr T Marshall, BA Cantab, PhD Edinburgh (*Biology,
Chemistry, Examinations Officer*)
Miss M McLaren, BSc Glasgow (**Chemistry, *Science*)
Miss G Newsome, BA Bath (*Physical Education*)
Miss D Ortega, MA London (**Spanish*)
Mrs C Price, BSc Durham (*Mathematics, Assistant
Examinations Officer*)
Miss A Rinck, BA Cantab, MEd Manchester (*Biology,
Chemistry, Physics, Stretch and Challenge Coordinator*)
Mrs R Smith, MA Cantab (**Classics, *PSHE*)
Mr S Taylor, BSc Leeds (*Second-in-charge of
Mathematics*)
Dr N Upcott, BSc, PhD Leeds (**Physics, Expedition
Coordinator*)
Miss H Vickery, MA Cantab, LRAM, Dip RAM (**Music*)
Mrs R Williams, BSc Birmingham (**Geography*)

Junior Staff – Full time:
Miss J Anand, BPA Northern School of Contemporary
Dance
Miss B Collins, MSc Leicester
Miss N Hackett, BSc Oxford Brookes
Mr M Hamilton-Foyn, BSc Aberystwyth (*Assistant Head of
Junior School*)
Miss Y Jeevanjee, Advanced Montessori Diploma
Miss V Kay, BA Sheffield
Miss R Merolla, BA UCL
Ms N Mikac
Miss H Poyer, BSc Bath
Miss M Rao, LLB Exeter
Mr W Russell, MSc Bristol
Ms J Schott, BA Open
Miss C Smith, BA Oxford Brookes
Miss N Van Kamp, MA Central Saint Martins

Staff – Part time:
Miss D Adams, BA Wellesley College USA (*History*)
Mr R Allan, BA UCL (*Geography*)
Mrs L Alexander, BA London (*Geography*)
Mrs M Arnaud, MA Grenoble (*French*)
Mrs J Banks, BA Durham, MA London (*English, Debating,
Head of School Partnerships*)
Dr L Bourne, BA Oxon, MRCPath (*Chemistry*)
Mrs L Carr, BA Leeds French
Ms S Carr-Gomm, BA UEA, MA London (**History of Art*)
Miss J de Rome, BEd London, Cert Ed Homerton (*Art*)
Ms P Edgeley, MA London (*Art*)
Mrs R Floyd, BA Durham (*Music*)
Mrs K Francis, BEd Hertfordshire College (**Learning
Support*)
Ms G Gishen, BA Goldsmiths (*Religious Studies*)
Ms T Jensen, MA Bristol (*Classics*)
Ms H Lambert, BA London (*Classics*)
Mrs V Marshall, MA London, BSc Newcastle (*Learning
Support, Science*)
Mr D Mathews, BSc York (*Music Technology Sound and
Lighting Engineer*)
Mrs J Mesrie, BSc Leeds (*Art*)
Miss S Pope, BSc City University
Ms R Reynolds, BA Guildhall School of Music and Drama
(*Actor in Residence, Drama*)
Ms P Scott, BSc Thames Valley (*Senior Learning Skills
Coordinator*)

Visiting Staff:
Mrs G Bailey-Smith (*Jazz Dance*)
Miss A Barlow, BA Bath (*Pottery*)
Ms L Barry, BA, MMus Canterbury (*Singing*)
Ms J Benson, BA (*Singing*)
Miss C Constable, MMus, BMus, PGPerf, Cert RCM,
ABSM (*Cello and Piano*)
Miss B Corsi, LTCL, FTCL (*Clarinet, Recorder, Piano*)
Miss A Cviic, BA, PG Dip RCM (*Singing*)

Mr P Dalle (*French Club*)
Mr J Godfrey, BMus, PG Dip RCM (*Percussion*)
Ms D Halpin, MMus, PG Dip Guildhall (*Singing*)
Ms J Hamola (*Fencing*)
Mrs V Hitchen, Dip RBS TTC (*Classical Ballet*)
Mr H Lamb (*Tennis*)
Ms M Leaf, BA London (*Speech & Drama*)
Miss J Lister, MA Cantab (*Harp*)
Mr S Mantas (*Chess*)
Mr M Mason (*Cricket*)
Miss E Mazzon, MA Trieste (*Italian*)
Mr P Moore, BMus LRAM, LGSMD (*Piano*)
Miss V Puttock, BMus (*Saxophone*)
Mr D Schroyens, FTCL (*Piano*)
Mrs R Smallshaw, MA Estonia (*Accompanist Classical Ballet*)
Miss V Smith, BMus RCM (*Violin*)
Mr J Sparks, BA, MA, FCCM (*Guitar*)
Mrs L Sparks, MMus, BMus, LRAM (*Flute*)
Mrs S Stewart, BMus, LRSM, PG Dip RCM (*Singing*)
Mr C Weale, BMus, PG Dip RCM (*Piano*)
Mr Y-S Yeo, BMus (*Piano*)

Mrs T Bannister (*Reprographics & Resources Manager*)
Mrs C Bradshaw (*Lab Technician*)
Mr A Brown, MA (*Alumni Relations Officer*)
Mr P da Costa, BSc (*Information Systems Manager*)
Miss E Devane (*Receptionist*)
Miss R Gillam, BA (*LSA and Trips Coordinator*)
Mrs F Holland (*Registrar*)
Miss L Ivison, BA (*Librarian*)
Miss L Payn, BA (*Marketing Assistant*)
Miss V Phillips (*PA to the Headmistress*)
Dr P Richards, PhD, BA (*ICT Support Technician*)
Mrs L Richmond (*Development Manager*)
Mrs C Robinson, BA (*Office Administrator*)
Miss G Sorrell, BA (*School Secretary*)
Mrs D Streatfield, BA (*Head of Careers*)
Mrs L Taylor-Mitchinson, BA (*Marketing Executive*)
Ms J Zhang, MSc (*Lab Technician*)
Dr S Rankine, MBBS, DCH, DRCOG, DFFP, MRCGP (*School Doctor*)

Gateways School

Harewood, Leeds LS17 9LE

Tel: 0113 288 6345
Fax: 0113 288 6148
email: info@gatewaysschool.co.uk
website: www.gatewaysschool.co.uk
Twitter: @Gatewaysschool
Facebook: /gatewaysschool

Gateways School is an independent school, founded in 1941, located in a delightful rural area on a 20-acre site in Harewood village between Leeds and Harrogate. It currently welcomes girls from age 2 to 18 and boys aged 2 to 11.

The school has international status in recognition of its work in promoting multiculturalism, global issues and internationalism. The school has an active Community Outreach programme which organises several events throughout the year to raise funds for charities supported by the school, while the proactive Environment club, and its commitment to green issues, has contributed to Gateways' ongoing status as a Green Flag school.

The ethos and objectives of Gateways School are to provide, within a structured framework, the opportunities and encouragement for every pupil to achieve his or her personal best. The environment is safe and caring, with outstanding pastoral care. Pupils develop self-confidence, self-discipline and a breadth of interests.

Teaching and Learning. Gateways consistently achieves excellent academic results – 98% of GCSE grades were A*–C in 2016 and 90% of all entries achieved A*/A; first in Maths and Science for value added in the country as published in the 2016 CEM study; at A Level 96% of pupils got their first or second choice university and 100% A*–B grades in Classics, Economics, Geography, Further Maths and Physics. All this while encouraging students to make the most of the wide range of extra-curricular and enrichment activities on offer. Smaller class sizes allow pupils to develop academically through high-quality teaching from dedicated staff in a supportive environment.

The curriculum at Gateways is broad and challenging and pupils are always encouraged to think for themselves, and to become inquiring and independent learners. A wide range of subjects is offered at AS and A2 Level.

The Stella programme ensures that the most able pupils are challenged and support is available to help individuals with specific learning needs.

Pupils participate in a variety of extra-curricular activities including Drama, Music, Sport, the Duke of Edinburgh's Award Scheme, Leeds Young Enterprise and Community Outreach.

Facilities. The school has an ongoing programme of development to renew and enhance its facilities. Recent projects include The Terrace Music Suite with recording studio. There is a state-of-the-art Performing Arts Centre, extensive playing fields, tennis courts, well-equipped Sports Hall and Dance Studio, the Cox-Simpson Library and specialist facilities for Science, Mathematics, Languages and Business Studies.

The Gateways Community. The Friends of Gateways (PTA) and The Old Gatewegians Association both play an active role within the school community.

Location and Transport. Gateways School is set in 22 acres of beautiful parkland in the village of Harewood, just north of Leeds. The former Dower House of the Harewood Estate forms the heart of the School. Gateways is within easy reach of Harrogate, Wetherby, Leeds, Ilkley, Otley and the surrounding villages. A comprehensive school transport service is available. The school also has a mini-bus.

Scholarships and Bursaries. The school has a programme of Scholarships which are awarded through examination or assessment and interview depending on the type of scholarship applied for. Academic, Sports and Arts (including Music, Drama, Dance and Art and Design) Scholarships are awarded to pupils who demonstrate exceptional ability. In addition, an Exhibition Scholarship is awarded for all-round contribution to school life, high standards across the curriculum and in extra-curricular areas. The value of the Scholarships will be up to a maximum of 25% of the tuition fee. A foundation scholarship can be awarded at the Head's discretion to a candidate who performs at a high academic level but could not otherwise access education in an independent school. It holds up to 100% fee remission.

A limited number of means-tested bursaries are available.

Fees per term (2016–2017). Sixth Form £4,240; High School (Years 10–11) £4,240, (Years 7–9) £4,208; Prep School (Years 4–6) £3,178, (Year 3) £3,124, (Years 1–2) £2,646, (Reception) £2,625; (Pre-Reception) £2,540 (school day), £3,167 (extended day); Nursery: £25.25 (morning/afternoon), £48.00 (extended day). Lunch: Reception to Lower 1 £247.50 per term, Upper 1 to Sixth Form £262.50 per term.

Charitable status. Gateways Educational Trust Limited is a Registered Charity, number 529206. It exists to offer a broad education to girls aged 2–18 and boys aged 2–11, where they are encouraged to strive for excellence to the best of their ability.

Governing Body:
Chairman: Mr R Barr
Professor D Hogg, BSc Hons, MSc Hons, DPhil
Dr R H Taylor, BEd, MA, PhD
Mr S Watson
Mr R Webster, BSc Hons, MRICS
Mrs J Wrench

Staff:

Headmistress: Dr Tracy Johnson, BSc, PhD, PGCE

Deputy Head: Mrs K Titman, BEng, PGCE (*ICT*)
Head of Preparatory School: Mrs S A Wilcox, BEd Hons
Head of Sixth Form: Mr M Davison, BA Hons, PGCE

Miss K Ashurst, BSc Hons, PGCE (*Head of Science, Physics*)
Mrs C Bartle, NNEB (*Head of Early Years*)
Mrs L Braithwaite, BA Hons, PGCE (*Subject Leader of PE*)
Mrs L Brown, BA Hons, PGCE (*Head of German*)
Mrs M Burns, BA Hons, PGCE (*Head of English*)
Mr S Scholfield, BA Hons (*Head of Prep Games & PE*)
Mrs S Crawshaw, BA Hons, PGCE (*Subject Leader of Art*)
Mr J Dunford, BA Hons, LTCL, ARCO, AMusTCL, ALCM (*Director of Music*)
Mrs J Emerick, BA Hons, Dip Dramatic Art (*LAMDA*)
Miss F Feeney, BA Hons, PGCE (*SENCO*)
Mrs A Ingham, BA Hons, MPhil, CertEd (*Subject Leader of Religious Studies*)
Mrs D Kennedy, BSc, PGCE (*Head of Mathematics, Mathematics*)
Mrs F Wilson, BA Hons, PGCE (*Head of MFL*)
Mrs L Wood, BSc Hons, PGCE (*Head of Pupil Development, Science*)

Finance Director: Mr J Halliday, ACA
Registrar: Mrs S Parker
School Nurse: Mrs D White, RGN

Haberdashers' Aske's School for Girls

Aldenham Road, Elstree, Herts WD6 3BT
Tel: 020 8266 2300
Fax: 020 8266 2303
email: theschool@habsgirls.org.uk
website: www.habsgirls.org.uk

Motto: *Serve and Obey*

This School forms part of the ancient foundation of Robert Aske and is governed by members of the Worshipful Company of Haberdashers, together with certain representatives of other bodies.

Haberdashers' Aske's School for Girls is situated on a site of over 50 acres, and has an excellent reputation for academic, sporting and musical achievements. Entry to the Junior School is at 4+ or at 7+; and to the Senior School, at 11+ and Sixth Form. The academic results are outstanding, a reflection of able pupils who enjoy learning and thrive on a full and challenging curriculum.

Facilities are first-class with a brand new Dining Room and Learning Resources Centre opening in the autumn term and a very wide range of extra-curricular activities. Sport, music, drama, art and debating thrive and there are many other opportunities for leadership within the school community including the Duke of Edinburgh's Award scheme, the Community Sports Leadership Award and a very active community service programme. Life at Habs is busy and challenging, embracing new technology, for example, digital language labs, touchscreen interactive whiteboards and remote access to all electronic work areas via the intranet, alongside old traditions, which include the celebration of St Catherine's Day as patron of the Haberdashers' Company.

Over 110 coach routes, shared with the Haberdashers' Aske's Boys' School next door, bring pupils to school from a thirty-mile radius covering north London, Hertfordshire and Middlesex. The provision of a late coach service ensures that pupils can take part safely in the wide range of the many clubs and societies organised after school. The St Catherine Parents' Guild, the school's parents' association, provides enormous support to the school through fundraising and social events.

Junior School. There are approximately 300 day girls aged 4–11 in the Junior School, with two parallel classes from Reception to Year 6.

Pastoral Care: Class teachers and Learning Support assistants maintain close contact with girls and their parents. It is very important that the girls feel happy and comfortable. Every adult has a responsibility for the girls' welfare and security and there are many layers of care in place. From the outset, through the behaviour code, girls are encouraged to be friendly, polite and caring to everyone else in the community, whether adults or children, and there is strong peer support among the girls. There are two nurses, a counsellor and two individual needs specialists, all of whom are able to provide support and to ensure each girl understands her unique importance in the school community. Where appropriate, older girls have responsibility for younger ones and Senior School Sixth Formers regularly help Juniors in the classroom. A programme of PSHCE (personal, social, health & citizenship education lessons) covers important issues of self-development and allows girls to reflect on their responsibilities to each other and the wider community. Many parents are involved in the classroom, clubs and outings.

Spiritual and Moral Education: Haberdashers' is a school with a Christian tradition which welcomes the rich diversity of faiths within the community. Assemblies are held for the whole school twice a week and on other days are separate for Key Stage One and Key Stage Two. Themes, stories and reflections are drawn from a range of cultures, traditions and faiths. Once a year, each class performs an assembly to which their parents are invited. Parents are also very welcome to attend our assemblies on major occasions such as St Catherine's Day and are often invited to speak to the girls in assemblies on an area of their expertise or experience relevant to the children. Girls take part in many charitable ventures throughout the year, raising money and enhancing their awareness of lives in the wider world.

Enrichment: There is a wide range of over 30 clubs covering the girls' interests in sport, music, arts and crafts, languages, science, maths, creative writing, reading, games and puzzles, cookery and gardening. Visits linked to the curriculum are arranged for every class and there are regular visitors to school such as theatre companies, historical recreations, authors, illustrators, musicians and scientists. Joint events with the Boys' School occur at intervals throughout the year for the different age groups.

Sport and Performance Arts: We have first-class sports facilities, including a sports hall, gymnasia, netball and tennis courts, a swimming pool and ample playing fields. The curriculum provides a core of gymnastics, dance, swimming, netball, tennis, athletics and rounders. Teams in netball, cricket, football, gymnastics, rounders and pop lacrosse compete against other schools.

Concerts and drama productions are a major part of school life, showcasing the wide range of creative talent among the girls. Our Performance Space gives girls many opportunities to explore and extend their interests in the performance arts. There are two major drama productions annually: an Infant production for all girls in Reception and Key Stage One, and a dramatic production for Year 6. The annual Spring Concert showcases all the musical groups and ensembles as well as a massed choir of all Key Stage Two girls. The summer Chamber Concert features ensembles of girls who learn a musical instrument. Informal lunchtime concerts occur at least once a term for Year 4 to 6 soloists or duets. The girls' own art and design work is displayed around the school.

Curriculum: There is a broad and challenging curriculum with the provision of opportunities for active and independent learning, with plenty of practical tasks and problem solving, to enable girls to develop their bright young minds. Fun is a vital ingredient. There are curriculum evenings for parents to learn about the school's approach to particular subject areas and how they can best support the girls at home and work in true partnership with the school.

The Early Learning Goals of the Foundation Stage are met through a balance of child-initiated opportunities and teacher-led activities. There is a daily range of stimulating, play-based activities which prompts girls to ask questions, to discover, to wonder and to learn new skills. No homework is set in Reception or Year 1 so that girls can enjoy the precious childhood pleasures of imaginative play and being read to by a parent when they get home. Music and daily PE lessons are taught by specialist teachers. Phonics teaching enables girls to make rapid progress with reading and to gain an easy independence in their writing while the foundations of mathematical thinking are laid through carefully selected practical tasks.

Extensive use is made of IT throughout the Junior School, with a dedicated IT Suite enabling an exciting Computing curriculum, including coding and robotics. In addition, from September 2016, each pupil has an iPad which she can use in class under the supervision of the teacher. The use of mobile technology is not meant to replace traditional learning but to supplement and enhance it and, in some cases, to open up whole new ways of learning for the pupils.

Creativity is fostered in music and dance, in art, design technology, literacy activities, drama and role play. The school grounds provide a rich environment for building knowledge about the world of nature as well as space to develop physical skills.

At Key Stage One, curriculum subjects are English, mathematics, science, history, geography, religious studies, French, Spanish, ICT, art, design technology, music, PSHCE and physical education, including swimming. Fostering a love of reading is paramount. A little homework is introduced in Year 2.

As girls progress through Key Stage Two they encounter more subject specialists. Science lessons, which are taught in the well-equipped laboratory, strongly feature practical and investigative work. The Art Room is a magnificent space for the creation of stunning works of art, while girls can feel transported to another culture as soon as they step into the Languages Room and they are introduced to German for the first time.

Senior School. There are approximately 870 day girls aged 11–18 in the Senior School.

Pastoral Care: In such a big and busy school, care for each individual girl is deeply important so that all girls flourish and fulfil themselves in every way. Looking after them is a pastoral team consisting of the Deputy Head, Heads of Section, Form Tutors, a School Nurse, a Counsellor and an Individual Needs Specialist. The provision of pastoral care is designed to help girls make decisions and to care about others within the framework of a very diverse community. There is an outstanding range of opportunities for the girls' personal development and to help them consolidate a system of spiritual beliefs and a moral code. The welfare of the girls is of paramount importance and it is the responsibility of all members of staff, teaching and support

staff, to safeguard and promote it. From the moment a girl joins the school, emphasis is placed on the partnership with parents so that, hand-in-hand, school and parents can support each child, operating on a basis of trust and with people she knows from the start.

Spiritual and Moral Education: Haberdashers' is a school with a Christian tradition which welcomes the rich diversity of faiths within the community. Every day begins with the whole school meeting in an assembly or House meeting to reinforce the school's values and its sense of community. These meetings are often led by the girls themselves. Once a week there are separate faith assemblies: Christian, Hindu, Jain and Sikh, Humanist, Jewish or Muslim. Girls can choose which one they attend. Holy Communion takes place twice a term. Roman Catholic Mass is celebrated each half term, either in the Girls' or the Boys' School. Girls may pray at lunchtime in a room set aside for them to do so. Girls organize and run many charitable events within their Houses throughout the year. This enhances their awareness of the wider world as well as raising funds for charities small and large, at home and abroad.

Enrichment: There is a wide range of clubs on offer in the Senior School, including art, creative writing, cricket, dance, debating, design technology, drama, football, maths, philosophy, science, and swimming; there are also campaigning groups such as Amnesty International and the Animal Welfare Society. Trips and visits include a Year 7 adventure holiday and various trips abroad, with language exchanges, work experience, and study visits. Subject specific trips in the UK and abroad include field trips, theatre visits, trips to sites of historical importance, museums and art galleries, music and sports tours.

Sport and Performance Arts: The core curriculum includes gymnastics, dance, swimming, lacrosse, netball, tennis, athletics and rounders. For older girls, there are additional options in self-defence, basketball, volleyball, football, step-aerobics, trampolining, badminton, weight-training, judo, life-saving, synchronised swimming, water polo, golf and squash. There are clubs in a range of sports for recreational enjoyment as well as for the teams. There are major drama productions in all sections of the school and symphonic concerts showcasing a variety of ensembles including three orchestras, wind and jazz bands, percussion groups, flute choirs, and rock bands as well as recitals and chamber concerts. There are annual Drama and Music Festivals; occasionally, there are joint productions and orchestral concerts with the Boys' School. Girls' painting, sculpture and design installations are displayed around the school.

Opportunities for leadership and challenge are valued and encouraged. Activities include: The Duke of Edinburgh's Award; Tall Ships; Community Service; Community Sports Leader's Award; European Youth Parliament; Model United Nations; English Speaking Union; and the Oxford Union.

Curriculum: The school follows its own wide-ranging academic curriculum tailored to the needs of its very able pupils. It preserves the best of a traditional education whilst responding positively to curricular developments. Much emphasis is placed on developing the girls' ability to think and learn independently, nurturing an intellectual resilience and self confidence which will prepare them for the world beyond school. In all subjects, the curriculum aims to be something that inspires the girls and stimulates discussion and ideas. A high value is placed upon creativity, imagination and the opportunity to pursue topics beyond the confines of the exam specifications. The school is not required to follow the National Curriculum but draws upon the best practice of what is happening nationally and in other schools. In the first three years of the Senior School, girls follow a set curriculum, studying French, Spanish and German on a carousel and then choosing two to continue with into Year 8. As they progress through the school they are given greater choice and the opportunity to personalise their curriculum to suit their needs and interests. Thus the GCSE curriculum has space for up to four optional subjects. In the Sixth Form the girls have a free choice of subjects from the 23 subjects on offer. At each level, the curriculum is designed to prepare them for the opportunities, responsibilities and experiences of the next stage of their education and their lives.

Fees per term (2016–2017). Senior School £5,482; Junior School £4,982. A number of scholarships are awarded annually and means-tested financial assistance (up to full fees) is also available.

Charitable status. The Haberdashers' Aske's Charity is a Registered Charity, number 313996. It exists to promote education.

Clerk to the School Governors: Mr C M Bremner

Headmistress: Miss B A O'Connor, MA Oxon

Personal Assistant to the Headmistress: Mrs B Cohen

Senior Deputy Head, and Executive Head of the Junior School: Mr R James-Robbins, BA London
Deputy Head (Pastoral): Miss G Mellor, BA Exeter
Deputy Head (Academic): Dr F Miles, BA Cantab

Bursar: Mr D Thompson, BA Manchester, ACIB

Assistant Heads:
Mrs R Davies, BA Cardiff (*Head of Sixth Form*)
Mrs L Winton, BA Manchester (*Head of Middle School*)
Mrs S Wright, MA Cantab (*Deputy Head, Junior School*)
Mrs S Ashton, BSc Keele (*Staff Development*)
Mr D Sabato, BA Nottingham (*Pupil Experience, Teaching & Learning*)
Mr T Scott, MA Cantab (*Development & Marketing*)
Mr S Turner, BSc Brunel (*Pupil Experience, Extracurricular*)

Head of Careers and Higher Education: Mrs L Mee, BSc London

Director of IT: Mrs N Verma, BSc Westminster

Library: Miss F Hackett, BA Loughborough

Teaching Staff:
* Head of Department

Art:
*Mrs P White, BA Sheffield School of Art & Design
Mrs S Deamer, BA Manchester
Mrs D Hobbs, BA Lancaster
Mrs S Wiseman, MA London

Classics:
*Mr A Doe, BA Oxon
Dr G Brunetta, MA Udine
Mrs R Pittard, MA Cantab
Miss E Tesh, BA Cantab

Design and Technology:
*Mr M Squire, BSc South Bank
Miss C Marshall, BA Portsmouth
Mr J Oliver, BA Warwick
Mr S Turner, BSc Brunel

Drama:
*Ms L Wallace, BA London
Ms E Bridgeman-Williams, BA Middlesex

Economics:
*Mrs S Hopkin, BA Reading
Mrs K Healer, MEd Cantab
Mrs S Hender, BA Leeds

English:
*Miss I Condon, BA Manchester
Miss Z Bowie, MA London

Mrs F Graves, MA Leicester
Mrs A Leifer, BA Birmingham
Dr F Miles, BA Cantab
Mrs K Nash, MA Cantab
Mr D Thakerar, BA London
Ms S Walton, BA Oxon
Mrs L Winton, BA Manchester (*Head of Middle School*)

Geography:
*Miss S Nanji, BA London
Mrs S Ashton, BSc Keele
Mrs C Gilbert, BA Nottingham
Mrs C Needham, BSc Loughborough
Miss H Wakefield, MSc Lougborough

History:
*Mr R Yarlett, BA Leicester
Mr K Davies, MA London
Mrs R Davies, BA Cardiff (*Head of Sixth Form*)
Mrs C De Groot, BSc Loughborough
Mr P Harper, MA Oxon
Mr D Heyman, BA Oxon
Ms L Mesrie, BA Birmingham
Mr D Sabato, BA Nottingham
Mrs C Wilding, BA Bristol (*Government and Politics*)

Individual Educational Needs:
Ms A Baker, BA Oxford Brookes

Mathematics:
*Mrs A Svoboda, ARCS London
Miss L Chelliah, BSc Kent
Mrs C Godfrey, BSc Leicester
Mrs N Gohil, BEng Aston
Mr C Howlett, BSc Dunelm
Mr J Kinoulty, MSc Dublin
Mrs S Lee, BSc Manchester
Mrs V Lees, BSc Cardiff
Mrs L Mee, BSC London (*Head of Careers and Higher Education*)
Mrs R Patel, BSc LSE
Mrs S Patel, BSc City
Mrs L Woodville, BSc York

Modern Languages:
*Sr J Carbonell, MA London (*Spanish*)
Mme A Bass, MA Le Mans, France
M M Fouilleul, Licence, Caen (*French*)
Fr E Green, BA Oxon
Miss G Mellor, BA Exeter
Mme K Osmond, BA Bristol
Mme H Robinson, BA Cantab
Sra M Salvatierra-Romero, BA Seville
M M Smeaton, BA Leeds
Frl A Tebb, BA Oxon (*German*)
Ms K Ting, BA Taiwan
Srta A Villarejo-Carrion, BA Portsmouth

Music:
*Mr A Phillips, MMus London
Mr D Davies, BA Keele
Mr T Scott, MA Cantab
Ms A Turnbull, LRAM
Miss C Turner, BMus Manchester (*Assistant Director of Music*)
and 25 visiting teachers

Physical Education:
*Miss C Hill, BSc Birmingham
Miss N Burns, BSc Exeter
Miss E Daly, BEd Plymouth
Miss N Haw, BA Leeds
Miss K Roberts, BSc Loughborough
Miss G Turnham, BEd Plymouth Marjon

Politics:
*Mrs C Wilding, BA Bristol

PSHCE:
*Mr D Davies, BA Keele

Religion and Philosophy:
*Mrs K Opie, MA London (*Deputy Head of Sixth Form*)
Ms L Childs, BA Manchester
Mrs S Evans, MA Oxon

Science:
Mrs V Leigh, BSc London (*Biology*)
Miss S Adat, BSc Nottingham
Dr K Bridge, BSc Loughborough
Dr H Burgess, MA Cantab
Mrs J Dabby-Joory, BSc Southampton
Miss E Dinsey, BSc London
Mr P Duddles, BEng Warwick
Miss E Frankel, BSc Nottingham
Mrs N Ghinn, BSc Nottingham
Mrs L Gupta, LLB Keele
Dr J Harvey-Barrett, BSc Newcastle
Mr G Jervis, MA London
Miss R Lane, BA Cantab
Miss L Lilley, BSc Durham
Mrs Z Makepeace-Welsh, MA Oxon
Dr M Mirza, BSc Brunel
Miss N Percy, BSc Leeds (**Physics*)
Dr C Ruddick, BSc Exeter
Mrs A Sharif, BSc London
Mr C Shaw, BSc London (**Chemistry*)
Mr R Shopland, BA Exeter
Ms M Smith, MPhil Nottingham
Mr E Stock, MPhys Oxon

Junior School:
Executive Head: Mr R James-Robbins, BA London
Deputy Head: Mrs S Wright, MA Cantab
Assistant Head: Mrs L Patel, BSc Middlesex
Miss C Chapman, BA East Anglia
Mrs S Collins, MA Kingston (*ICT Specialist*)
Mrs E Davies, BA Brighton (*Individual Needs*)
Mrs R Desbois, BSc London
Mrs K Ede, BA Bournemouth
Mrs S Fishburn, BA Middlesex (*Individual Needs*)
Mrs L Flynn, BSc Southampton
Miss E Galvin, BA Warwick
Mrs C Gibson, BSc Worcester
Mrs J Harrington, BA Leeds Met
Mrs S Hayes, BA Durham
Ms M Hirsch, BMus London
Mr N Hobley, BSc Oxford Brookes
Miss K Keith, BA Bournemouth
Mrs J Kirk, ARCM, Dip RAM
Mrs L Liddelow, BEd Exeter
Mrs A Mack, BEd Brighton
Mrs E Miller, BA Hertfordshire
Mrs J Millman, BEd Leeds
Mr M Mitcham, BA London (*MFL Specialist*)
Mrs J Nicholas, BA Newcastle
Miss R Nutkins, BA Exeter
Mrs C Prendergast, BA Brighton
Miss L Ryan, BA Brighton
Mrs C Sawkins, BA Surrey
Mrs M Tatman, BA Hertfordshire
Ms S Tersigni, BA Middlesex

Harrogate Ladies' College

Clarence Drive, Harrogate, North Yorkshire HG1 2QG
Tel: 01423 504543
email: enquire@hlc.org.uk
website: www.hlc.org.uk

Harrogate Ladies' College is a Boarding and Day school for 342 girls aged 11–18. Situated within the College campus, Bankfield Nursery and Pre-Prep is a Day Nursery and Pre-Prep for over 70 boys and girls between the ages of 2–4. Highfield Prep School, which opened in 1999, is a Day Prep school for over 240 boys and girls between the ages of 4–11.

Location. The College is situated in a quiet residential area on the Duchy Estate about 5 minutes' walk from the town centre and is easily accessible by road and rail networks. Leeds/Bradford airport is 20 minutes' drive away. Harrogate itself is surrounded by areas of natural interest and beauty.

Accommodation. Approximately half of the pupils are full boarders. Houses are arranged vertically from Upper Three (Year 7) to Lower Sixth. Upper Sixth Formers enjoy a greater sense of freedom in their own accommodation called Tower House. This contains a large, modern kitchen, comfortable lounges and relaxation areas and girls have individual study-bedrooms. Each house has a Housemistress and Assistant Housemistress who are responsible for the well-being of the girls. There is a well-equipped Health Centre with qualified nurses.

Curriculum and Examinations. The College aims to provide a broad-based curriculum for the first three years in line with National Curriculum requirements. This leads to a choice of over 28 subjects at GCSE, IGCSE, Applied, AS and A Level. Each girl has a form tutor who continuously monitors and assesses her development.

Facilities. The central building contains the principal classrooms, hall, library, and dining rooms, and a Sixth Form Centre with studies, seminar rooms, kitchens and leisure facilities. The College Chapel is nearby. An extension provides 8 laboratories for Physics, Chemistry, Biology and Computer Studies. Three dedicated computer suites, provision in the boarding houses and throughout the school, form an extensive computer network. Sixth Formers have network access using their own laptops from studies and bedrooms. Additional facilities for specialised teaching include Art, Textiles, Photography, Design and Technology, Drama and Home Economics/Food Technology.

Our award winning HLC Business School is where girls are able to enjoy the academic study of Economics, Accounting, Business Studies and Psychology in a state-of-the-art business-like environment which helps prepare young women of today for the global world of tomorrow.

Sport. The College has its own sports hall, a full size indoor swimming pool, gymnasium, fitness centre, playing field, 9 tennis courts and 2 squash courts. Girls are taught a wide range of sports and may participate in sporting activities outside the school day. Lacrosse and netball are played in winter, and tennis, swimming and athletics are the main summer physical activities. Extra-curricular sports include badminton, basketball, fencing, golf, horse riding and gymnastics.

Sixth Form. The College has a thriving Sixth Form Community of 140 pupils. Girls have a choice of 26 courses at AS/A Level. There is a broad range of general cultural study. In preparation for adult life, Sixth Formers are expected to make a mature contribution to the running of the school and many hold formal positions of responsibility. Personal guidance is given to each girl with regard to her future plans and most pupils choose to continue their education at University.

Religious Affiliation. The College is Anglican although pupils of other religious denominations are welcomed. We focus on inclusion, mutual respect and understanding of people of all faiths and of no faith.

Music. A special feature is the interest given to music and choral work both in concerts and in the College Chapel, and the girls attend frequent concerts and dramatic performances in Harrogate. There are Junior and Senior choirs, orchestra, string, wind and brass groups.

Scholarships. Academic, All Rounder, Art, Textiles, Music, Choral, Drama and Sport scholarships are available.

Fees per term (2016–2017). Boarding £9,145–£11,470; Day £5,240–£7,920. Fee remissions are available for girls with a sibling at Harrogate Ladies' College or at Highfield Prep School.

Entry. Entry is usually at age 11, 13 or at Sixth Form level. Entry is based on the College's own entrance examination and a school report. Sixth Form entry is conditional upon GCSE achievement and an interview with the Principal.

Charitable status. Harrogate Ladies' College Limited is a Registered Charity, number 529579. It exists to provide high-quality education for girls.

Chair of Governors: Dr Angela Fahy

Principal: **Mrs Sylvia Brett**, MA London, BA Dunelm

Director of Finance: Miss Rebecca Henriksen, MA Edinburgh, ACA
Director of Admissions and Marketing: Mrs Sarah Bowman, BA UWE, MSc Stirling
Senior Deputy Head: Mr Richard Tillett, MA Cantab
Head of Highfield: Mr James Savile, BEd Southampton
Deputy Head Academic, Senior Resident: Miss Claire Preece, BSc Manchester, MA OU
Assistant Head, Head of Lower School: Mrs Judith Grazier, BEd Warwick, ACA
Assistant Head, Head of Middle School: Mrs Fran Irvine, BEd Bedford
Assistant Head, Head of Sixth Form: Dr Rebecca Ashcroft, BA PhD Huddersfield
Assistant Head, Sixth Form (Temporary Joint Head) and Boarding: Mrs Sarah Parker, MA Oxon
Estates Manager: Mr Chris Briscoe, BSc Northumbria
HR Manager: Mrs Lucy Condon, BSc Leicester, MSc Nottingham, CIPD
Chaplain: Ms Joanne Wright, BA Leeds

Headington School

Oxford, Oxfordshire OX3 7TD

Tel: 01865 759100
           Admissions: 01865 759 861/113
Fax: 01865 760268
email: admissions@headington.org
website: www.headington.org
Twitter: @HeadingtonSch
Facebook: /HeadingtonSchool

Headington is a highly successful day and boarding school in Oxford for 828 girls aged 11–18 with a Preparatory School for 254 girls aged 3–11 occupying its own site just across the road. (*See Headington Preparatory School entry in IAPS section.*)

The school offers girls from Nursery to Sixth Form an unrivalled opportunity to pursue academic, sporting and artistic excellence in a caring and nurturing environment.

Founded in 1915 and set in 23 acres of playing fields and gardens, our superb facilities provide the perfect backdrop for teaching and learning that extends way beyond the classroom and curriculum. We encourage participation in all aspects of sport and culture, teamwork and leadership, challenging girls to discover and explore their own potential and achieve more than they thought possible.

Consistently in the premier league of academic schools in the UK, life at Headington is about much more than exam results. Through the sheer breadth of subjects and activities at Headington – and the option to study for the International Baccalaureate – we aim to educate the complete individual, giving girls the confidence and self-awareness to compete, contribute and succeed at school, university and in their adult lives.

Facilities. Headington offers a superb range of facilities to day girls and boarders to support and enhance their learning. Our state-of-the-art Music School is a worthy addition to the school's arts complex and has superb acoustics that inspire musicians of all abilities. As well as its teaching rooms it includes a recording studio and electronics studio. The 240-seat Theatre, run by a professional team who provide expertise in set design, lighting and sound design, is home to the school's drama department. The Art School provides a fitting environment to display our students' work, complemented by four art studios and a photography darkroom. In April 2015 a multimillion pound Dance and Fitness Centre was completed including a fully equipped gym, training rooms and a large dance studio equipped with a Harlequin dance floor. Other sports facilities include a floodlit all-weather pitch, sports hall and light and airy 25m indoor swimming pool. In 2016, the School opened its new state-of-the-art Library, complete with 'sonic chairs' where girls can listen to music, lectures or vocabulary without speakers and without disturbing their neighbours and interactive tables capable of ten 'touches' at a time for group working.

Curriculum. In Years U3 and L4 in the Lower School girls are taught in four classes of around 20 each, which increases to six slightly smaller classes in U4 after 13+ entry. They learn English Language and Literature, Mathematics, three sciences, French, Latin, Geography, History and Religious Studies, with a choice of German or Spanish added in L4. The inclusion of Art, DT, Textiles, Food and Nutrition, Drama, Music, ICT and PE in the timetable from U3 means all girls can benefit from the widest possible curriculum. Girls choose their GCSE options in U4, usually taking a maximum 10 subjects in years L5 and U5. We offer a mix of IGCSE and GCSE, with seven core subjects and a free choice from a further 14 subjects. The majority of students move into the Sixth Form from the Middle School and many new girls, both day and boarders, also join us at this stage. Headington offers both A Levels and the International Baccalaureate Diploma in the Sixth Form (our Diamond Jubilee building, opened in 2012, has 13 full-size classrooms and includes two Sixth Form teaching rooms fitted out as IT suites).

Physical Education. From Olympic rowers to recreational dancers, Headington offers a genuinely inclusive approach to PE and extracurricular sport and encourages each girl to enjoy sport at the level that suits her. PE is taught throughout the school and many girls choose to study PE to GCSE. They can choose from more than 30 different sporting activities, from dance and fencing to equestrian and trampolining. Games such as hockey, netball and athletics are played competitively against other schools and girls have the chance to represent the school across a range of abilities. More than 70 girls currently compete at county level and beyond and the school enjoys national success in a wide range of sports including swimming, cheerleading and rowing. Our rowers compete at the very highest level, with the school consistently triumphing at the National Schools' Regatta and earning its spot at the top of the sport. More than 150 of our girls row and regularly go on to represent Great Britain at international competitions.

Music. At Headington every girl has the opportunity to enjoy music at the level that is right for her, both within the curriculum and beyond. Musical opportunities in our state-of-the-art Music School are impressive. Five hundred individual music lessons take place each week and 28 visiting teachers offer girls the opportunity to learn a wide range of instruments. The Senior School has three orchestras and three choirs, varying in style from the Second Orchestra and Third and Fourth Form Choir, for which there are no auditions, to the exceptional Chamber Choir, which has made numerous recordings and toured overseas.

Drama. The 240-seat Theatre is home to a thriving drama department. There is a busy programme of productions each year and girls of all ages become involved in all aspects of theatre, from writing and producing their own plays, to lighting, costume and make-up. Girls progress from a weekly class in the Lower School to choosing drama at GCSE and A Level, or as part of the International Baccalaureate. Many girls also elect to take private Guildhall Speech and Drama exams in school.

Dance. At Headington the state-of-the-art Dance facilities provide a multitude of opportunities for every girl. Dance is part of the curriculum in the Lower School and a Games option throughout the School. The Dance Department was established in 2015 and outside the classroom there is a huge range of dance options, from Ballet and Ballroom to Street Dance and Contemporary. As well as annual Dance Shows, the Headington Dance Company competes in local and national competitions.

Extracurricular activities. More than 50 extracurricular activities take place every week during lunchtime, before and after school. A wide choice of subjects, sports, interests and hobbies ranges from The Duke of Edinburgh's Award and Drama to Astronomy and Run Your Own Company and includes such diverse pastimes as debating and fencing, cheerleading and quilting. Headington has a very successful Combined Cadet Force, with around 60 cadets from L5 and above in our Army detachment. Success at CCF and The Duke of Edinburgh's Award gives girls a huge sense of personal achievement, increased confidence, leadership and teamwork.

Higher Education and Careers. Whether they have chosen to study for A Levels or the International Baccalaureate Diploma, all girls continue to higher education, heading to leading universities in the UK and abroad. A significant number of girls choose Oxbridge each year; some head for medical or veterinary college and others take up Art Foundation courses. Girls graduate from a wide range of arts and science degrees in subjects as diverse as civil engineering, architecture, classics and natural sciences. Detailed assistance on choice of universities is given in the Sixth Form through specialist computer programmes and careers tutors. A careers programme is in place throughout the school, with plenty of individual help as girls reach their GCSE years.

Boarding. Headington has always been a boarding school and just over a quarter of the school – around 200 girls – board with us today. The five boarding houses provide the girls with a 'home from home' where, supported by a team of highly experienced staff, they learn to develop into mature and independent young people. Many of our boarders come from the UK and we are also very proud of our international boarding community, made up of more than 30 nationalities from all over the world. Girls can choose between full boarding, weekly boarding or half-weekly boarding.

Uniform. The blue-checked skirt, light blue shirt, jumper and blazer are smart, comfortable and easy to care for. Girls in the Sixth Form wear their own smart-casual clothes.

Entrance. Entry to the Prep School is in order of application from nursery to 6+, with priority given to girls with siblings already at Headington, and by examination from 7+. The main entry points to the Senior School are at 11+, 13+ or, for the Sixth Form, 16+. Girls are occasionally able to join at other ages if places become available. Girls enter the school at 11+ via our own examination day and interview in December and, at 13+, through the spring Common Entrance Examination. Girls can sometimes enter into Upper 4 by taking our own papers that we write/set. Sixth Form entrance examinations and interviews are held in the November before the proposed year of entry.

Our registration fees for the Prep School are £95 (UK) and £150 (overseas based families) and for the Senior School are £125 (UK) and £250 (overseas based families). For information about admissions, please check our website, www.headington.org, or contact our friendly admissions team who will be happy to help.

Fees per term (2016–2017). Senior School: Full Boarders: £10,700–£11,750; Weekly Boarders: £9,450–£10,350; Half-Weekly Boarders: £7,470–£8,170; Day Girls: £5,485–£5,990.

Scholarships and Bursaries. Scholarships are awarded for academic achievement, art, dance, drama, music and sport. These awards recognise talent and achievement and carry only a nominal financial benefit – our scholars are highly respected and enjoy a special status in the school. The Headington Access Programme (HAP) supports talented girls who would benefit from all that the school has to offer but who may not be able to access a Headington education without some form of financial assistance. Means-tested bursaries of up to 100 per cent of fees are available for local day girls who achieve high marks in our entrance examinations and are awarded at 11+, 13+ and in the Sixth Form.

Charitable status. Headington School Oxford Limited is a Registered Charity, number 309678. It exists to provide quality education for girls.

Governing Council:
Chair of Governors: Mrs Sandra Phipkin, ACA
Vice Chair of Governors: Miss Margaret Rudland, BSc
Dr Susan Burge, OBE, BSc, BM, DM, FRCP
Professor Katya Drummond, MA Oxon, PhD
Mr Christopher Harris
Mr Steven Harris, BSc, ACA
Lady Nancy Kenny, BA, PGCE
Mrs Penelope Lenon, BA Hons
The Revd Darren McFarland, BA Hons, BTh
Miss Bryony Moore, MBA
Dr Kate Ringham, BA Hons, PhD
Mrs Sallie Salvidant, Cert Ed London, BEd Hons London
Mr Stephen Shipperley

Company Secretary: Mr John Clarke, BA of Stone King LLP

Clerk to the Council: Mr Richard Couzens, MBE, MA Cranfield

Headmistress: Mrs C Jordan, MA Oxon

Executive Committee:
Headmistress: Mrs C Jordan, MA Oxon
Head, Prep School: Mrs J Crouch, BA Keele, MA London
First Deputy Head (Academic): Dr J Jefferies, BSc, PhD Exeter
Second Deputy Head (Staff, Admissions & Marketing): Mrs C Knight, BSc Strathclyde
Deputy Head (Pastoral): Mr S Miller, BA Hons Kent
Bursar: Mr R Couzens, MBE, MA Cranfield

Senior Leadership Team:
Headmistress: Mrs C Jordan, MA Oxon

First Deputy Head (Academic): Dr J Jefferies, BSc, PhD Exeter

Second Deputy Head (Staff, Admissions & Marketing): Mrs C Knight, BSc Strathclyde

Deputy Head (Pastoral): Mr S Miller, BA Hons Kent

Deputy Head (Co-curricular): Mr S Hawkes, BA Brunel

Bursar: Mr R Couzens, MBE, MA Cranfield

Senior Management Group:

Assistant Bursar (Finance): Mrs K Hoy, BSc Birmingham

Assistant Head (IB): Mr J Stephenson, BSc Nottingham

Assistant Head (Pupil Development): Mr J Kelly, MChem Oxon

Assistant Head (Staff): Mrs V Sinclair, Cert Ed London, CELTA

Assistant Head (Digital Strategy): Mrs R Bowen, MA Oxon

Acting Academic Director of Sixth Form: Dr A Stanton-Ife, MA Cantab, MA UCL, PhD UCL

Acting Pastoral Director of Sixth Form: Miss Sarah Patterson, BSc Edinburgh

Head of Lower School: Mrs D Bates-Brownsword, BEd University of South Australia

Head of Middle School: Ms B Dyer, BEd Central School of Speech & Drama

Admissions Registrar: Mrs J Mullen, BSc Keele

Marketing Manager: Ms N O'Shea, MA Cantab, CIM

Director of Development: Mr T Edge, BA London

Estates Manager (Clerk of Works): Mr P Mulvany, CIOB

HR Manager: Mrs J Seetaram, CIPD Oxford Brookes

Head of Boarding: Mrs K Olliver, BA Dublin

Chaplain: Mr T Howell, MBiochem Oxon

Heads of Year:

Deputy Head Sixth Form: Mr S Drew, BA, MA Lancaster

Deputy Head Sixth Form: Mrs S Young, BSc Bristol, MA Cantab

Head of U5: Mrs R Schwarz, BSc Manchester

Head of L5: Miss C Hatt, BA Bristol

Head of U4: Miss R Hudson, BA Hons Oxon, PGCSE Oxon

Head of L4: Mrs J Hamilton, BA Leicester, MPhil Sheffield

Head of U3: Mrs J Reid, BA Oxon

Boarding:

Head of Boarding: Mrs K Olliver BA Dublin

Celia Marsh Housemistress: Mrs M Rahmatallah, LLB Durham

Davenport Housemistress: Mrs E Layfield

Hillstow Housemistress: Mme C Preston, Licence Orléans

MacGregor Housemistress: Miss H Leigh, BSc Sussex

Napier Housemistress: Miss L Holloway, BA Oxon

IB Team:

Director of IB: Mr J Stephenson, BSc Nottingham

Creativity Action Service Coordinator: Mrs V Sinclair, Cert Ed London, CELTA

Theory of Knowledge Coordinator: Mr M Wilson, MusB Manchester

Heads of Departments:

Art and Design and Art History: Mr M Taylor, BA Coventry

Classics: Mrs A Barrett, BA Oxon

Drama and Theatre Studies: Mrs Imogen Neale, BA Hull

Economics and Business Studies: Mrs H Waywell, BSc Loughborough

English: Dr S Burley, BA UCL, MPhil Oxon, PhD London

English as an Additional Language: Mrs V Sinclair, Cert Ed London, CELTA

Environmental Science: Mrs J Quirk, BSc Birmingham

Geography: Mr D Cunningham, BSc Glasgow

History: Mrs S Wilkinson, BA Newcastle

Home Economics: Mrs M Colquhoun, BEd Bath

Information and Communication Technology: Mr M Howe, BA East Anglia

Law: Mrs C Shepherd, LLB Birmingham

Learning Development: Dr J Leadbeater, BA, PhD Dunelm

Mathematics: Mrs M Clarke, BSc Portsmouth

Modern Languages: Mr J Marshall, MA Oxon

French: Mme V Crépeau, Licence Caen

German: Mr T Kendall, BA London

Italian: Mrs D Bonifaci, MA Rome

Spanish: Mrs P Wood, BA Dunelm

Music: Mr J Hutchings, BMus London

Philosophy and Religious Studies: Mr C Fox, BA Sheffield, MA Warwick

Physical Education:

Director of Sport and Rowing: Mr R Demaine, BA Rhodes University

Head of Academic Physical Education: Mrs N Burton, BSc Brunel

Head of Games: Mr D Bridle, BSc Oxford Brookes, UKCC

Politics: Mrs N Wilson, BA Oxford Brookes

Psychology: Mrs K Pigott, BA Cape Town, MA Oxford Brookes

Science: Mr J Morris, BSc Sussex, MSc Imperial College

Biology: Mrs J Quirk, BSc Birmingham

Chemistry: Dr E Regardsoe, BSc UCL, MPhil and DPhil Oxon

Physics: Mr G Skym, MSc Dunelm

Admissions Registrar: Mrs J Mullen, BSc Keele

Heathfield School
Ascot

London Road, Ascot, Berkshire SL5 8BQ

Tel:	01344 898343
Fax:	01344 890689
email:	registrar@heathfieldschool.net
website:	www.heathfieldschool.net
Twitter:	@HeathfieldAscot
Facebook:	/HeathfieldSchool
LinkedIn:	/heathfield-school

Introduction. Pioneering high standards in girls' education since 1899, Heathfield School in Ascot was named in the Top Ten of Small Schools in the UK by the Telegraph in 2016. The boarding and day school provides outstanding education for girls in beautiful surroundings less than an hour from London in the heart of Berkshire near the world-famous Ascot Racecourse.

The school combines exemplary standards of pastoral care with a personalised academic curriculum which adds value to every girl's achievements to provide a holistic education for girls aged 11–18. In 2016, more than six in ten Heathfield girls choosing a university in the UK secured places at the elite Russell Group of universities including Oxford, University College London and Warwick, after record A level results at the school. Over four in ten (42%) of the exams taken were awarded the top A*–A grades with 91% of the exams taken scoring an A*–C grade. At GCSE, 47% of all the exams taken were awarded the top A*–A grades (47%) while one in three of the candidates scored an impressive 3 A* grades and above each in their string of GCSEs.

Not only is Heathfield firmly on the academic map but it also produces county and national sportswomen and talented artists, photographers, actors, musicians and dancers.

Heathfield is headed by Oxford English Language and Literature graduate Marina Gardiner Legge, previously the school's Director of Studies, who is dedicated to excellence in all areas of the school under her leadership. Mrs Gardiner Legge was appointed Head in September 2016.

In 2016, the school also boosted its growing reputation for the STEM (Science Technology Engineering and Maths) subjects with the completion of a state of the art STEM facility, officially opened by Lord Robert Winston.

The school will offer weekly boarding from September 2017 with registrations now being taken.

Atmosphere and Ethos. The school's aim is to help every student get the most out of life by providing the very best intellectual stimulation, physical challenges and pastoral care. The school is founded on Church of England principles but welcomes all faiths.

Pastoral Care. Heathfield's strength is in its size meaning each girl is supported throughout her school career and can never slip under the radar. Pupils are overseen by a team of academic staff, Housemistresses, Heads of House and prefects. They work together to provide the highest level of pastoral care. Teachers will meet with your daughter regularly to discuss her particular needs and to ensure she is achieving her maximum potential.

Curriculum. Heathfield offers variety in terms of the subjects on offer as well as fundamental excellence in all the traditional subjects. At AS and A Level, girls can choose from over twenty subjects. Academic results are consistently impressive and all girls go on to higher education. Extras such as the Leiths Basic Certificate in Food and Wine and the Duke of Edinburgh Awards are also offered. The school is famous for its excellence in the creative arts and launched a unique progression partnership with the University of the Arts, London, in September 2014. It has also won a record five Good Schools Guide awards Art and Design Photography at A Level.

Activities. The St Mary's Theatre and the Sports Hall are always hives of activity and there are many other extra-curricular activities: frequent museum and theatre trips, field trips and overseas visits.

Sport. Heathfield's outstanding facilities include a large multi-purpose gym, two squash courts, a dance studio, five lacrosse pitches, tennis courts and an indoor swimming pool. The school competes successfully at lacrosse, netball, swimming, rounders, athletics, polo, and show jumping. Girls have represented the school regionally, nationally and internationally in a variety of sports.

Boarding Accommodation. Boarding accommodation is first-class. From Form IV onwards, all girls have single rooms. For more freedom and independence, the Upper Sixth live in Wyatt House – known as the Sixth Form Bungalow – which contains two fully-equipped kitchens and areas in which to study and socialise.

Medical Welfare. Three nursing sisters and the school doctor are in charge of the girls' medical welfare, supported by Heads of House, Housemistresses and Tutors. The Heads of House or Housemistresses are available at all times for any parental concerns.

New Facilities. A state-of-the-art STEM (Science, Technology, Engineering and Maths) block opened in January 2016.

Admission. Admission points are 11+, 13+ and Sixth Form. Places may be available in other year groups on enquiry. Junior entrants are assessed at the school on 'invitation days' which involve examinations, workshops and interviews. Common Entrance examinations are also used as a guide if they are taken. Entry into the Lower Sixth Form is via predicted GCSE grades and interview. Deferred entry is also available and international students wishing to apply are guided through the procedure step by step by our Admissions team. For further information see: www.heathfield school.net

Scholarships and Bursaries are awarded. Scholarships are worth £750 per annum. Bursaries are available varying between 10% and 40% reduction in fees. Bursaries are awarded at the Headmistress's discretion and are financially means tested. Armed Forces discounts are also available.

Fees per term (2016–2017). Senior (Forms III–UVI): Boarding £11,400, Day £7,092. Lower (Forms I–II): Boarding £11,125, Day £6,900.

Charitable status. Heathfield School is a Registered Charity, number 309086. It exists to provide a caring boarding education leading to higher education for girls aged between 11 and 18.

Board of Governors:
Chairman: Mr Tom Cross Brown, MA Oxon, MBA Insead
The Rt Revd Dr Jonathan Baker, Bishop of Fulham, MA Oxon, MPhil, Dip Theol
Mrs Sally-Anne Barrett
Mr Charlie Caminada
Mr Roger Drage
Mr Guy Egerton-Smith, FRICS
Mr Robert Gregory, BSc Hons Sussex
Miss Caroline Slettengren, BSc Hons Southampton, CPE/ Grad Dip Law, LPC College of Law
Mrs Sally Tulk-Hart
The Revd Canon Dr Philip Ursell, BA Wales, MA Oxon

Senior Leadership Team:

Headmistress: Mrs M Gardiner Legge, MA Oxon, PGCE Hong Kong

Bursar: Mrs R Frier, BSc Hons Bristol, FCA
Director of Studies [Acting]: Mr D Mitchell, MA Hull, MSc York, BA Hons Warwick, PGCE UWE
Director of Pastoral and Co-Curricular Activities: Mrs K de Ferrer, MA Leeds, BA Hons USA, PGCE London
Director of Sixth Form: Mr J Hart, MA London, BA Hons London
Director of Boarding: Mrs L Curtis
Director of IT: Mr M Taylor, BSc Eng London, PGCE Greenwich, MBCS, CITP
Director of Marketing & Admissions: Ms A Morgan, MCIM, MIDM
Chaplain: Fr D Clues, BD Hons London, Cert Theol Oxon, PGCE London

Academic Staff:
+ *Head of Faculty*
* *Subject Leader/Coordinator*

Art & Textiles:
*Mrs E Feilen, MA Goldsmiths, BA Hons ECA, PGCE Cambridge (*Art & Textiles*)
Miss H Smith, BA Hons Aberystwyth, PGCE Bath Spa (*Art*)
Mr S Myers (*Illustration*)
Miss N James, BA Manchester School of Art (*Fashion Designer in Residence*)
Mrs M Butler, BA Hons TVU (*Art & Photography Technician*)

Business:
*Mrs G Kendall, BA Hons Reading, PGCE London, D&B Dip Credit and Finanical Analysis (*Business Studies, Economics & Accounting*)

Cookery:
*Mrs M Blackburn, BEd Hons Cardiff
Miss P Fairclough, BA Hons Oxford Brookes, Adv Cert Leiths Food & Wine

Dance:
Mrs N Shaw, BA West Sussex, ALAM, RAD TC, AISTD

Drama:
*Mrs S O'Connor, MA Ed Chichester, BA Hons Surrey, QTS Reading, NPQH (*Director of Drama*)
Mrs K de Ferrer, MA Leeds, BA Hons USA, PGCE London, Drama
Mrs N Shaw, BA West Sussex, ALAM, RAD TC, AISTD (*also Dance*)

English:
*Mr A Grey, MA Oxon, PGCE Ambleside
Mrs M Gardiner Legge, MA Oxon, PGCE Hong Kong
Mrs S Shirwani, MA Oxon, BA, MA London, GTP Reading (*Highly Able Coordinator*)
Miss C Jackson
Mrs S O'Connor, MA Ed Chichester, PGCE Reading, QTS, NPQH

Geography:
+*Mrs B Mason, BA Hons Nottingham, PGCE London, SpLD Level 5
Mrs L Worrall, BSc Hons Kingston, PGCE Kingston

History & Politics:
*Mr D Mitchell, MA Hull, MSc York, BA Hons Warwick, PGCE UWE
Mr J Hart, MA London, BA Hons London
Ms L Worrall, BSc Hons Kingston, PGCE Kingston

History of Art:
*Ms J Meeson, BA Hons East Anglia

ICT:
*Mrs R Millns, BA Joint Hons Wales, PG Mgt Cert Wales, GTP RBWM

Latin & Classical Civilisation:
+*Mr A Valner, MA Nottingham, BA Nottingham, PGCE London
Dr D Stobart, PhD Cambridge, PGCE Utrecht

Mathematics:
*Mrs Z Benjamin, BSc Hons Reading, PGCE Bath
Mr G Benjamin, MSc Bath, PGCE Bath
Mr J Doyle, BA Canberra, Dip Ed Canberra
Miss K Johnson

Modern Foreign Languages:
*Mrs F Rayner, MA Strasbourg, PGCE Oxford Brookes
Miss J Menon, MA France, PGCE Oxford Brookes (*French*)
Mrs A Pullen, BA Hons Cordoba (*Spanish*)
Ms E Bibet, Master France (*French Assistant*)
Mr T Chatzivadaris, MA London, BA Athens (*Greek*)
Ms K Davies, PGCE Oxford Brookes, Dip Teaching (*German*)
Mr K Forrester, BA Tokyo (*Japanese*)
Ms A Khoursheen, MA Surrey, BA Aleppo, Dip Translation Aleppo (*Arabic*)
Mrs M Strain, Dip Foreign Languages Moscow (*Russian*)
Ms S Zhou, BA Birmingham, BA Beijing (*Chinese*)

Music:
*Mrs J Dance, BA Hons Birmingham, PGCE Birmingham, LRAM (*Director of Music*)
Miss S M Kong, MA Birmingham City, BA Hons UCSI University Malaysia, PGCE Buckingham, Advanced Piano Studies Franz Liszt Academy of Music, FTCL (*Assistant Director of Music*)
Mrs J Minns (*Flute/Piano*)
Mr S Ash (*Drums*)
Mrs Z Phillips, BMus Hons Surrey, PG Dip TCM (*Clarinet/Flute/Saxophone*)
Miss L Turner (*Singing*)
Miss M Bentley, BMus Surrey, PG Dip Birmingham Conservatoire (*Violin*)
Mr K Bulford, BA Hons Swansea (*Drums*)

Mr N Charlton, BA Hons Mus Ed, LTCL (*Cello*)
Mr M Davies, BMus Cardiff, LRAM, ARCM, LWCMD (*Singing*)
Ms A Liokoura, Dip Piano Thessaloniki, PG Dip TCM, PGA Dip Dist TCM, MMus Performance Studies Dist TCM (*Piano*)
Ms L Head, LTCL, FTCL (*Brass*)

Photography:
*Miss K White, BA Hons Oxford Brookes, ABIPP
Mrs M Butler, BA Hons TVU (*Photography Technician*)

Physical Education:
+*Miss W Reynolds, BEd Hons Liverpool (*Director of Sport*)
Miss J Talbot, BPhysEd Otago, NZ
Miss N Livanis, BA Hons ITT St Mary's Twickenham
Miss D Adlington, BSc Adelaide, BEd Adelaide
Mrs S Bettison, DipEd London (*Games*)
Mrs G Glimmerveen (*Equestrian*)
Mr A Turner, LTA, CCA, BTCA (*Tennis Coach*)
Mr A Moir, LTA Registered, Registered Professional BTCA (*Tennis Coach*)

Psychology:
Mrs R Oakley, MSc Bristol, BA Hons Swansea, PGCE West England

PSHE:
*Mrs A Diaz, BA Hons Open, Cert Ed Cambridge

Religious Studies:
*Mrs V Homewood, Subject Leader Religious Studies
Ms K Oster, Fil Mag Linkoping, PGCE Cambridge
Fr D Clues, BD Hons London, Cert Theol Oxon, PGCE London

Science:
+*Miss C Wells, BSc Hons Bath, PGCE Exeter
Mrs J Kemp, BSc Hons London, PGCE (*Biology*, *Physics*)
Mr S Moore, MEng, BSc Hons UMIST, PGCE Reading, MInstP, MBCS (*Physics*)
Mrs C Donner, MSc Aberystwyth, BSc Hons Reading, PGCE Open, FRSB (*Biology*)
Mr J O'Brien (*Chemistry*)
Mrs A Milner, HND Applied Biology Ulster, Bsc Biology/Ecology Ulster (*Senior Science Technician*)
Mr I Whitehurst, BA Surrey (*Science Technician*)

Teaching & Learning Support:

Spectrum Learning Support & EFL:
*Mrs R Colley, BA Hons Oxford Brookes, PGCE Roehampton, SpLD Level 5, CPT3A, TEFL London (*SEN & EFL*)
Mrs S Simpson, BEd Birmingham, PG Dip Dyslexia & Literacy York (*SEN*)
Mrs M Battleday, HLTA Maths, NOCN Speech and Language, ADHD, Dyspraxia, Dyslexia (*SEN*)
Mrs A Jones, HLTA Maths, Diplome de Langues Paris (*SEN*)
Dr M Snow, PhD London, MA Hons Aberdeen, MSc Robert Gordon, PGDip Aberdeen, CELTA, FHEA (*EFL*)

Teaching Support & Coordinators:
Mrs N Tenorio (*Examinations Officer*)
Mrs H Fernandes, MSc Sheffield, BA Hons Brighton (*Librarian*)
Ms D Hunt (*Duke of Edinburgh's Award Coordinator*)
Mrs G Glimmerveen (*Equestrian Coordinator*)
Mrs M Butler, BA Hons TVU (*Art & Photography Technician*)
Mrs A Milner, HND Applied Biology Ulster, BSc Biology/Ecology Ulster (*Senior Science Technician*)
Mr I Whitehurst, BA Surrey (*Science Technician*)

Miss S M Kong, MA Birmingham City, BA Hons UCSI University Malaysia (*Assistant Director of Music*)

Pastoral:

Pastoral & Boarding:

Mrs K de Ferrer, MA Leeds, BA Hons USA, PGCE London (*Director of Pastoral and Co-Curricular Activities*)

Mrs L Curtis (*Director of Boarding*)

Mr J Hart, MA London, BA Hons London (*Director of Sixth Form*)

Mrs R Oakley, MSc Bristol, BA Hons Swansea, PGCE West England (*Deputy Director of Sixth Form*)

Miss K White, BA Hons Oxford Brookes, ABIPP (*Head of House, Austen*)

Miss J Talbot, BPhys Ed Otago, NZ (*Head of House, de Valois*)

Mrs M Battleday, HLTA Maths, NOCN Speech and Language, ADHD, Dyspraxia, Dyslexia (*Deputy Head of House, de Valois*)

Mrs J Kemp, BSc Hons London, PGCE (*Head of House, Seacole*)

Mrs L Worrall, BSc Hons Kingston, PGCE Kingston, Geography (*Deputy Head of House, Seacole*)

Mr J Doyle, BA Canberra, Dip Ed Canberra (*Head of House, Somerville*)

Mr G Benjamin, MSc Bath, PGCE Bath (*Deputy Head of House, Somerville*)

Mrs C Beresford (*Housemistress, Form I*)

Miss S Crafer, NNEB, RSH (*Housemistress, Form II*)

Miss L Champion, BA Hons Derby (*Housemistress, Form III*)

Ms A Brooks (*Deputy Head of Boarding; Housemistress, Form IV*)

Mrs J Liepa, BA Hons London, PGCE Middlesex (*Housemistress, Form V*)

Miss S Broomfield (*Housemistress, LVI Form*)

Mrs P Munro, BSA Boarding Diploma (*Housemistress, UVI Form*)

Mrs P Kerley (*Housemistress, UVI Form*)

Mrs A Diaz, Cert Ed Cambridge, BA Hons Open (*Assistant Housemistress, Forms III & IV*)

Mrs S Jackson (*Evening Assistant Housemistress*)

Miss J Paterson (*Evening Assistant Housemistress*)

Ms A Sidat (*Evening Assistant Housemistress*)

Surgery:

Sister M Couzens, RGN (*Senior Nursing Sister*)

Sister E Warrington, RNC (*Nursing Sister*)

Sister L Brazel, RGN, BSc Hons London (*Nursing Sister Weekends*)

Miss S Lambert, BSc, PGDip, MSc, HCPC, MCSP, AACP (*Physiotherapist*)

Ms M Jemmett, BSc Hons London, HE Dip Counselling Bucks (*School Counsellor*)

Support Staff:

Administration:

Ms P Lavender, BA Hons Open (*Headmistress's PA & Marketing & PR Coordinator*)

Mrs C Bradberry (*Administration Supervisor & PA to the Director of Studies*)

Mrs P von Sachsen-Altenburg (*PA to the Director of Pastoral and Co-Curricular Activities*)

Mrs V Williams, BA Hons Dunelm, CPRS (*School Administrator*)

Miss K O'Brien (*Receptionist & School Administrator*)

Mrs D Chapman (*Receptionist & School Administrator*)

Mrs M McNamara (*Evening Receptionist & Administrator*)

Admissions:

Mrs I Hutchings (*Registrar*)

Mrs N Clarke (*Administrator*)

Bursary:

Mrs R Frier, BSc Hons Bristol, FCA (*Bursar*)

Mrs L Farrin (*Deputy Bursar*)

Mrs D Davies (*Accounts Administrator*)

Mrs H Hill (*Accounts Assistant*)

Facilities:

Mr I Parham, C&G London (*Facilities Manager*)

Mr P Brown (*Foreman*)

Mr A Lata (*Facilities*)

Mr R Ruffle (*Facilities*)

Mr D Brown (*Groundsman*)

Mr S McDonagh (*Apprentice Groundsman*)

Fellowship:

Mrs R Farha (*Fellowship Coordinator*)

Housekeeping:

Mrs R Tatum, NVQ Business Mgmt, Dip Music Ukraine (*Housekeeping Manager*)

IT Systems:

Mr M Taylor, BSc Eng London, PGCE Greenwich, MBCS, CITP (*Director of IT*)

Mr T Lodder (*Senior IT Administrator*)

Mr G Lewis (*IT Technician in Residence*)

Marketing:

Ms A Morgan, MCIM, MIDM (*Director of Marketing & Admissions*)

Miss L Ivens, MA Hons Oxon, NCTJ (*Director of Communications*)

Miss I Cumming, BA Hons Newcastle (*Marketing Executive*)

Swimming Pool:

Mr D O'Toole (*Swimming Pool Manager*)

Hethersett Old Hall School

Norwich Road, Hethersett, Norwich, Norfolk NR9 3DW

Tel:	01603 810390
Fax:	01603 812094
email:	enquiries@hohs.co.uk
website:	www.hohs.co.uk
	www.hohs_blog.com
Twitter:	@HOHS_tweets
Facebook:	/HethersettOldHallSchool

Hethersett Old Hall School, founded in 1938, is located in 16 acres of beautiful Norfolk countryside in the heart of East Anglia, just minutes from Norwich city centre.

The school is a charitable trust administered by a Board of Governors, which is in membership of AGBIS. The Headmaster is a member of GSA and the school is also in membership of BSA.

The school provides education for around 180 pupils aged between 3 and 18 years old. The school is co-educational from age 3–11 and girls only from age 11 (Year 7). Full, weekly and flexi boarding is available for girls from age 9 (Year 5). The school welcomes international students. Younger boarders live in the historic main house and sixth formers have their own separate building. All girls are cared for by resident house staff who organise an exciting programme of evening and weekend activities.

Aims. Hethersett offers a friendly, supportive community in which each child is encouraged to develop their academic, creative and practical skills and to become self-reliant, tolerant and concerned for others.

Curriculum. Classes are small and teaching staff are well qualified, well informed and enthusiastic.

The Preparatory School is situated in modern, purpose-built accommodation with a dedicated play area. In Lower Prep (pupils age 3–7) the key skills of reading, writing and numeracy are developed in a stimulating atmosphere that builds on children's natural inquisitiveness and enthusiasm for learning.

The Upper Prep department (pupils age 7–11) provides a thorough grounding in the core curriculum. Sport, drama and music feature strongly in each year's programme of study. There are many opportunities for pupils to compete against other schools in swimming galas and games fixtures.

Pupils in the Senior School are offered a broad range of academic, technological and creative subjects. Their achievements at GCSE are consistently high and in 2016 85% achieved 5+ grades A*–C. Support, advice and individual care throughout the senior school enables pupils to be confident in planning their future education and careers.

Sixth Form. Over 20 AS and A Level subjects are offered, from the unusually creative combination of art, photography and art textiles to a range of highly academic subjects; Maths, Biology, Chemistry and Physics. The majority of sixth formers choose to go on to university after benefiting from dedicated personal guidance from staff in choosing courses, completing their UCAS form and composing their personal statement. In 2016 girls achieved a pass rate of 97% at A Level and once again all applicants gained entry to their first-choice university to study subjects as diverse as clergy training, astrophysics and interior design.

The EPQ (Extended Project Qualification) is now well established at the school and has proved popular with universities as it fosters research skills. In 2016 86% of the passes in this A Level standard qualification were at A or A* grades. Most Sixth Formers also achieve the Gold Duke of Edinburgh's Award.

Buildings and Facilities. The school has excellent teaching facilities with bright, modern, purpose-built teaching blocks. The senior school teaching blocks feature an ICT suite, science laboratories, an art and technology suite with photography dark room, design technology and food and nutrition rooms. Pupils also benefit from the dedicated music rooms, 'The Barn' for drama, an indoor heated swimming pool, tennis courts, sports fields, gardens, woodland and an orchard. Sixth formers have their own common room, kitchen, study room and careers library. The boarding facilities include bright, attractive accommodation for younger girls with en-suite bathrooms. Older girls move onto single study-rooms and sixth formers are housed in their own separate building.

Recreational Activities. The school offers a wide range of recreational activities and optional extras which includes drama, dance, choir, orchestra, rock band and individual musical instrument tuition, sport clubs – swimming, tennis, football, rugby, badminton, tae kwon do, trampolining, kayaking, shooting, rounders, hockey and netball. The majority of senior school girls successfully take part in The Duke of Edinburgh's Award scheme, achieving their Bronze, Silver and Gold awards. There is also a wide range of clubs pupils can join, including Rock Band, Maths, Art, Drama, Bird Club and Green Club,

Entrance. Entry is by the school's own assessment designed to give staff an indication of the child's stage of development, and to ensure they are able to meet the demands of the curriculum. The assessment focuses on maths, English and a reasoning test. Entry to the Sixth Form is by interview, school record and assessment. For further information or to obtain a prospectus please contact the Registrar.

Scholarships are open to internal or external candidates.

Year 7 and Year 9 Scholarships. Three types available: academic – day and boarding, creative and sporting. Academic Scholarships are awarded on the basis of examination and interview. Creative Scholarships are awarded on the basis of audition or practical test plus interview with the head of subject and the Headmaster. They can be taken in art, music or drama. Sporting Scholarships are awarded on the basis of ability trials held by the PE Department plus interview with the Head of PE and Headmaster. Applications and assessments are made in the January preceding September entry.

Sixth Form Scholarships. Two types are available: academic – day and boarding and citizenship – day and boarding. Academic Scholarships are awarded on the basis of examination and interview with a panel of senior staff and the Headmaster. Citizenship Scholarships are awarded on the basis of a letter outlining the contribution a candidate could make to school life and an interview with a panel of senior staff and the Headmaster. Applications and assessments are made in the November preceding September entry.

Bursaries. Means-tested bursaries are available to enable pupils to attend the school who meet the entry criteria but who cannot afford the fees. These awards may be up to 100% of fees. They are limited in number and their award is discretionary.

Fees per term (2016–2017). Nursery fees (age 3–4) vary according to the length of the term and are charged at £29.05 for a morning session and £45.55 for a full day. Lower Prep Department (age 4–7) £3,075; Upper Prep Department (age 7–11): £3,595 (day), £6,180 (weekly boarding from age 9); £7,780 (full boarding from age 9); Senior School: £4,795 (day), £7,380 (weekly boarding); £8,980 (full boarding). All day fees include a cooked lunch.

Charitable status. Hethersett Old Hall School is a Registered Charity, number 311273. It exists to provide a high quality education.

Chairman of Governors: Mr Martin Matthews

***Headmaster*: Mr Stephen G Crump**, MA

Deputy Headmistress: Mrs Joanna Collin

Senior Housemistress: Miss Anna Cushing

Financial Administrator: Mrs Helen Eastwood

Head's Secretary: Mrs Susan Brown

Registrar: Mrs Linda Jones

Howell's School Llandaff
GDST

Cardiff Road, Llandaff, Cardiff CF5 2YD

Tel:	029 2056 2019
Fax:	029 2057 8879
email:	admissions@how.gdst.net
website:	www.howells-cardiff.gdst.net
Twitter:	@HowellsSchool
Facebook:	/Officialhowells

Founded in 1860 as a school for girls, the school was built by the Drapers' Company from the endowment left in 1537 by Thomas Howell, son of a Welshman, merchant of London, Bristol and Seville and a Draper.

Howell's School Llandaff is part of the Girls' Day School Trust (GDST). The GDST is the leading network of independent girls' schools in the UK. As a charity that owns and runs 24 schools and two academies, it reinvests all its income in its schools. For further information about the Trust, see p. xxiii or visit www.gdst.net.

Student numbers. 794: Nursery 30; Junior School 228; Senior School 315; Co-Educational College 221.

Howell's School, Llandaff (GDST) is Wales' leading non-denominational school for girls aged 3–18 and boys aged 16–18, and has a proven track record of success in public examinations. In August 2016, GCSE results topped the league tables, coming in first place in Wales with 74% of girls achieving an A* or A, and in the co-education Sixth Form College, the students scored 81% A*–B at A Level. In February 2015, the whole school had a full Estyn inspection and was awarded the acclaimed double excellent mark for its current provision and prospects for improvement.

From the moment you enter Howell's, you are greeted by beautiful buildings; glorious grounds; friendly staff and a happy and positive environment. The excellent facilities include an indoor swimming pool, an outdoor classroom in the Junior School; and most recently an extensive refurbishment of the Art department. Modern laboratories provide students with the best science teaching facilities in the area.

Howell's School puts great value on a rich and varied life outside of the classroom, and the list of extra-curricular activities that students take part in is seemingly endless, as well as endlessly diverse, running from Archery to Zumba. The extensive Enrichment Programmes, together with impressive Wellbeing and Laureate Programmes, make Howell's a special place to learn and develop in an exciting, creative and thriving environment. The school's strong Leadership Team; talented and dedicated teaching and support staff; wonderful young people and committed and interested parents are what make Howell's unique.

The Nursery @ Howell's is situated in Roald Dahl's childhood home and takes inspiration from its famous former occupant. Girls who enter the nursery experience a safe, family atmosphere, making the transition from home to nursery a relaxed and happy one. The Junior School radiates an atmosphere in which every child is valued and nurtured. Great emphasis is placed on developing the self-identity, self-esteem and self-confidence of every girl.

When entering the Senior School, girls are encouraged to develop skills of self-analysis and reflection, and choose the learning methods that suit them best, whilst teachers challenge and motivate them towards an appetite for lifelong learning. Howell's aims to help students acquire skills essential to tackling a competitive and rapidly changing world. The established co-educational college has a proven track record for excellence in and out of the classroom, and offers students an exceptional learning experience with flexible teaching styles designed to manage the transition between school and university.

Curriculum. All National Curriculum subjects including Welsh are taught at Key Stages 1, 2 and 3. In Year 7, French, Spanish and Welsh are on offer. Latin is introduced in Year 8. First language Welsh (throughout) and Greek (A Level) are taught on demand. There is a broad range of AS and A2 subjects available in the College. Examinations in a number of AS subjects are taken at the end of Year 12. Active learning styles are an essential part of the classroom experience, and the curriculum is made more diverse by:

- Educational visits, locally and abroad;
- Visiting authors, poets, musicians, artists and lecturers;
- Special activity weeks focusing on particular areas of the curriculum.

Extra-curricular activities. Howell's aim is to fulfil the potential of all the students in all areas, which it achieves through a rich extra-curricular programme. Extra-curricular opportunities include:

- Orchestras, choirs, chamber and jazz groups;
- Reading and reviewing, eco, science, mathematics, history, geography, language and religious and cultural clubs;
- Concerts, plays, a drama festival and eisteddfodau;
- Tennis, hockey, rounders, swimming, athletics, cross-country, netball, rugby and football teams;

- The Duke of Edinburgh's Award, Envision and Interact;
- Quiz, public speaking and debating teams;
- Community service and fundraising for charities.

The school seeks to support the widest range of students' needs through specialist dyslexia teaching at our on-site Dyslexia Institute satellite, and through an extensive and comprehensive careers programme.

Admission. A selection process operates for all points of entry. Contact Admissions for further details.

Fees per term (2016–2017). Sixth Form College: £4,439; Senior School: £4,389; Junior School (Years 3–6): £3,393; Junior School: (Rec–Year 2): £3,330; Nursery: £2,610. Fees quoted are inclusive of non-residential school trips. Lunch is included in full-time Nursery to Senior School fees.

Scholarships and Bursaries. Bursaries, which are means-tested, are available in the Senior School and in the Sixth Form College; these are intended to ensure that the school remains accessible to bright students who would benefit from our education, but who would be unable to enter the school without financial assistance.

Details of scholarships and bursaries are available, on request, from the school.

Charitable status. Howell's School Llandaff is part of The Girls' Day School Trust, which is a Registered Charity, number 306983.

Chairman of Governors: Miss K Powell

***Principal*: Mrs S Davis**, BSc London

Deputy Principal: Mrs N Chyba, BA London

Deputy Principal: Dr S Southern, BSc PhD Durham

Deputy Principal: Mrs J Ashill, BEd Swansea

Director of Finance and Operations: Mr R C Read, OBE, CDir

Director of Development and Communications: Mrs V Yilmaz, BA

Ipswich High School
GDST

Woolverstone, Ipswich, Suffolk 1P9 1AZ

Tel:	01473 780201
Fax:	01473 780985
email:	admissions@ihs.gdst.net
website:	www.ipswichhighschool.co.uk
Twitter:	@IHSforGirls
Facebook:	/ipswichhighschool

Ipswich High School is a leading independent day school in Suffolk for girls aged 3–18. Founded in 1878, Ipswich High School has a longstanding reputation for offering an exceptional education and experience to girls. The school tailors its curriculum and approach for each individual, challenging students and encouraging growth, enthusiasm and self-development.

The school's beautiful 84-acre campus is located in Woolverstone, just outside Ipswich. The spacious site has superb facilities including a theatre, ICT suites, a 25m swimming pool, a recently refurbished Sixth Form suite, cookery rooms and a floodlit AstroTurf pitch. It also capitalises on its outstanding natural surroundings with the woodland providing an outdoor learning area for the Junior School, whilst the pond and parkland are used for scientific research.

Girls are welcomed from across Suffolk, Essex and South Norfolk, many of whom travel to school using the extensive coach network.

Ipswich High School is proud to develop girls who are inspirational, respectful, courageous, ambitious and have real integrity. Its passion and proficiency for offering girls-only education is unique to the Suffolk region. The girls follow a tailored, balanced curriculum with a comprehensive enrichment programme offering extensive extracurricular activities within the school day.

The 2016 GCSE A*/C pass rate was 98.40% with 69.6% of all entries at A*or A grade. The A Level pass rate was 100% with 39.1% A* or A grades awarded in 2016. The girls progress to degree courses in a wide variety of subjects and receive offers at their first-choice (often Russell Group) universities. The school has a well-deserved reputation for art, sport, drama and music with scholarships offered to high achievers in these areas.

Ipswich High School is one of the 26 schools and academies within The Girls' Day School Trust. As part of the GDST family the school can draw on a wealth of expertise and resources from professional development and training through to access to the GDST Alumnae network, the 67,000-strong association of former GDST pupils nationwide.

Admissions. Admission to the Nursery School is on the basis of informal assessment in a play situation. Entry to the Junior School is on the basis of informal assessment or written test. Entry to the Senior School is on the basis of interviews, written tests and school report. Sixth Form entry is on the basis of interviews, GCSE results and school report.

Fees per term (2016–2017). Junior School: Woodland Pre-Prep including Reception £2,730, Years 1–2 £2,892, Years 3–6 £3,216; Senior School & Sixth Form: Year 7–9 £4,396, Years 10–13 £4,458.

Bursaries & Scholarships. The Girls' Day School Trust allocates over £10.5 million worth of funds to scholarships and bursaries each year in order to enable the brightest and most deserving girls the opportunity to receive a GDST education.

Scholarships are highly sought after and are reserved for those candidates believed to be of an exceptional standard. Scholars are expected to continuously raise the standard in their chosen field and to provide inspiration to others. For entry at Senior School Academic, Art, Drama, Music and Sports scholarships are offered and at Sixth Form an All-Rounder scholarship.

Charitable status. Ipswich High School is part of The Girls' Day School Trust, which is a Registered Charity, Number 306983.

Chairman of Local Governors: John Pickering

Headmistress: **Ms Oona Carlin**

Head of Junior School: Mrs Eileen Fisher

Registrar: Ms Rebecca Geoghegan

Kilgraston School

Bridge of Earn, Perthshire PH2 9BQ

Tel:	01738 812257
Fax:	01738 813410
email:	headspa@kilgraston.com
website:	www.kilgraston.com
Twitter:	@kilgraston
Facebook:	@kilgrastonschool

Kilgraston is an independent boarding and day school for girls aged 5 to 18 years. It is an all-through school comprising Junior Years, Senior School and Sixth Form.

The Independent School Awards named Kilgraston UK Independent School of the Year in 2011, making it Scotland's first school to be awarded this accolade. In 2014, Kilgraston received the Sunday Times Scottish Independent School of the Year award. Most recently the school has been named the Sunday Times top-performing independent school in Scotland for Intermediate 2, Highers and Advanced Highers and won the best-schools.co.uk award for the top-performing independent school for Highers in Scotland.

Kilgraston is set in a Georgian mansion house located in 54 acres of stunning parkland three miles from the centre of Perth with Edinburgh and Glasgow only an hour away. The school has benefited from extensive recent investment in facilities including a state-of-the-art science centre, a sixth form study centre, a 25m indoor swimming pool complex, and floodlit astroturf hockey pitch and tennis courts. Kilgraston is also the only school in Scotland with an on-site equestrian centre incorporating a 60m x 40m floodlit arena with show jumps.

Visitors to Kilgraston are struck by its warm and welcoming atmosphere, and the sense of community and friendship across the year groups. Staff know each pupil individually, and are proud of the well-rounded girls who thrive in a range of curricular and co-curricular activities. Kilgraston's Sacred Heart ethos is central to school life, providing a firm foundation for personal growth and individual contribution, whilst welcoming girls of all faiths and none.

The Curriculum. Kilgraston follows the Scottish educational system with all the girls studying a broad curriculum before selecting subjects to continue at National 5 (GCSE equivalent). Over 18 subjects are offered at Higher/Advanced Higher (A Level equivalent). Kilgraston has a record of high academic achievement and the girls gain entrance to top UK and international universities including Oxbridge. In 2015, Kilgraston was named the Sunday Times top-performing Independent School in Scotland for Intermediate 2, Highers and Advanced Highers.

Music, Art and Drama play an important part of life at Kilgraston. The Music Department alone has 14 individual teaching rooms, a recording studio and two large music rooms designed to suit all needs. There are also many opportunities for pupils to perform throughout the year by participating in orchestra, string orchestra, fiddle, woodwind and brass groups or one of several choirs.

The Art Department is housed in the top of the mansion with superb views across the Ochil Hills and the school boasts an impressive number of past pupils who are practising artists.

Sports and recreation are catered for within a superb sports hall including a climbing wall and fitness gym. The extensive grounds incorporate the indoor 25m swimming pool, nine floodlit all-weather courts, playing fields and athletics track. Whilst the main sports are hockey, netball, tennis, rounders, swimming and athletics other sports include football, touch rugby, skiing, cricket, badminton, yoga, karate, fencing, aerobics, ballet, modern dance and highland dancing. Fixtures and competitions are also arranged against other schools throughout the year. Kilgraston also hosts the Scottish Schools' Equestrian Championships every Spring.

Kilgraston is divided into houses which compete against each other in games, music and debating. The girls can also take part in The Duke of Edinburgh's Award scheme and are encouraged to use all the facilities not only for curriculum lessons but also for leisure activities.

Kilgraston Junior Years is for pupils aged 5–12. The boarders live in the newly refurbished Butterstone House. All of the pupils benefit from the many facilities of the Senior School. (*See separate entry in IAPS section.*)

Admission is normally interview and school report. Entry to the Junior Years is by interview and assessment.

Means-tested bursaries are available on application. Scholarship Examinations are held in early February and awards are also offered each year as a result of outstanding performance in the Academic Scholarship Examinations. Scholarships are also offered in Art, Music, Drama and Sport.

Fees per term (2016–2017). Senior: Day £5,490 Boarding £9,380, Junior Years: Day £3,385–£4,295, Boarding £7,165.

Charitable status. Kilgraston School Trust is a Registered Charity, number SC029664.

Chair of Governors: Mr Timothy Hall
Senior Leadership Team:

Headmistress: Mrs D MacGinty, BEd Hons, NPQH, DipMonEd

Bursar: Mr B Farrell, BCom, HDE, ACIS
Deputy Head: Mrs C A Lund, BA Hons, MA, MA Ed Man, PGCE
Head of Pastoral Care & Boarding: Mrs G McFadden

Academic & Pastoral Staff:
Miss E Bain, BEd Hons (*Physical Education*)
Mrs J Baird (*Classroom Assistant, Playground Supervisor*)
Ms C Blackler, BSc Hons (*Science Technician*)
Mrs S Birrell, MSc, BAA Hons, PGCE Primary (*Head of Support for Learning*)
Mrs A Bluett, BA Hons, PGCE (*Latin*)
Miss J Buchholz (*Gap Student*)
Mrs A Caldwell, BSc Hons, PGDE (*Mathematics*)
Miss L Cameron (*Residential Assistant*)
Mr C Campbell, MA, PGDE (*Head of History and Modern Studies, Year Head L6*)
Mr E Connolly, BSc Hons, PGDE (*Director of Science*)
Ms D Cooper, MA Hons (*Junior Form Teacher*)
Mme I Dépreux, BA Hons, Maitrise, PGCE (*French*)
Mrs A Dunphie, BSc Hons, PGCE (*Maths*)
Miss R Elliot, BHSAI (*Equestrian Instructor*)
Mrs P Ferguson, MA Hons, PGCE (*Junior Form Teacher, Early Years Coordinator*)
Mrs H Ferry, BEd Hons (*Head of Physical Education*)
Mr A Fynn, MA Hons, PGDE (*Head of Modern Languages*)
Miss A Gates (*Residential Assistant*)
Mrs K Guthrie, MA Hons, PGCE, CELTA (*ESOL*)
Mrs S Hewett, MSc, BSc, PGCE (*Physics*)
Mrs S Hewitt, BA (*Swimming Development Manager*)
Miss S Howett (*Assistant Residential Mistress, Mater*)
Mr S Johnston, MA, BA, PGDE (*Religious Studies*)
Mr T Kearns, MA Ed, Dip Lit, PGCE, BA Hons (*Head of English, Head of UCAS*)
Mrs C Kirkpatrick, BEd, MEd (*Junior Support for Learning, Form Teacher*)
Miss C Laidlaw, MA Hons (*Chaplain*)
Mr D Laird (*Duke of Edinburgh's Award Coordinator*)
Mrs E Lyle, BA Hons, PGDE (*Spanish and French*)
Miss G Macleod, BA Hons, PGCE Moray House (*Head of Art & Design*)
Miss R Martinez (*Gap Student*)
Dr J Mathers, BSc Hons, PhD (*Science Technician*)
Mr J McAuley, BA Hons (*Director of Music*)
Mrs D McCormick, BSc Ed Hons (*Science, Year Head U6 & Head of Kinnoull*)
Miss M McKenzie (*Residential Assistant*)
Miss R McLean, BHSPI (*Equestrian Manager/Riding Instructor*)
Mrs M Malloch (*Junior Learning Assistant*)
Ms P Martin, BA Hons (*Art*)

Mrs K Megahy, NVQ Early Years Care and Education (*Classroom Assistant*)
Miss S Muller, Bachelor of Social Work, PGCE (*Residential Mistress, Mater*)
Mrs L A Murray, RGN, SCM (*Matron*)
Mrs D Neville, MA Hons, PGDE (*Head of ESOL*)
Mrs A O'Hear, BSc Hons, PGCE (*Biology, Year Head U5 & Head of Moncreiffe*)
Mrs L Oswald, BEd Hons (*Maths, History, Year Head U4 & Head of Arran*)
Miss M Patton, MA Hons, BA Hons (*Assistant Residential Mistress*)
Dr C Phillips, BA Hons, MA, PhD, PGCE (*Head of Geography*)
Mrs R Reid, MA, BEd (*Support for Learning*)
Mrs E Rodger, BEd Hons (*Physical Education*)
Mrs M Saunders, BA Hons (*English*)
Mrs K Scott, BHSPI (*Equestrian Instructor/Assistant*)
Mrs L Scott, BA (*Head of Drama*)
Mrs L Sidey, BA (*Classroom Assistant*)
Mrs L Smith (*Assistant Residential Mistress*)
Mrs S Speed, BSc Hons (*Head of Maths & Computer Science, Co-Curricular Coordinator*)
Miss B Spurgin, MA Hons (*Librarian*)
Mr A Stewart, MTheol, PG Dip OEd, PGDE (*Head of Junior Years, Head of International Development*)
Mrs E Stewart, Dip Ed (*Junior Form Teacher*)
Mrs S Stewart, BA Hons, PG Dip, PGDE (*Business Studies, Year Head L5 & Head of Inchcolm*)
Mrs P Stott (*Director of Sport, Year Head L4*)
Miss L Watt (*Equestrian Assistant*)

Administration and ICT Staff:
Mrs S Harrison (*School Secretary*)
Mrs J Kennedy (*Receptionist*)
Mrs A Macdonald, LLB, Dip LP, HNC (*Data Manager and Examinations Officer*)
Mrs A McHugh, BEd Hons (*Receptionist*)
Mr G Muirhead, BSc Hons (*ICT Manager*)
Mrs L Sidey (*Receptionist*)
Ms T Stack (*School Secretary*)
Mr D Macdonald (*Catering Manager*)
Mr M Richmond, BSc, MSc (*Facilities Manager*)
Mrs A Roger (*Assistant Bursar*)
Mrs K Mackie (*Finance Assistant*)
Ms S Littlejohn, Marketing & Communications Hons (*Language and Activities Manager*)
Mr D Milner, BA Hons (*Marketing Manager*)
Mrs A Johnstone, BA Hons (*Head of Admissions*)

King Edward VI High School for Girls
Birmingham

Edgbaston Park Road, Birmingham B15 2UB

Tel: 0121 472 1834
Fax: 0121 471 3808
email: enquiries@kehs.co.uk
website: www.kehs.org.uk

Independent, formerly Direct Grant.

Founded in 1883, the School moved in 1940 to its present buildings and extensive grounds adjacent to King Edward's School for Boys. There are 577 girls from 11 to 18 years of age, all day pupils.

Curriculum. The curriculum is distinctive in its strong academic emphasis and aims to inspire a love of learning. The purpose of the curriculum is to help girls realise their full potential. Excellence is sought in aesthetic, practical and physical activities as well as in academic study. Our aim is to achieve a balance of breadth and depth, with dropping of subjects postponed as long as possible so that girls may make informed choices and have access to a wide range of possible careers.

In **Year One** all girls take English, Mathematics, separate Sciences, Religious Studies, French, Latin, History, Geography, Music, Art and Design, Drama, Information Technology, Games, Swimming, Dance and Creative Skills.

In **Years Two and Three** all girls take English, Mathematics, separate Sciences, Religious Studies, French, Latin, German or Spanish, History, Geography, Music, Art and Design, Information Technology, Physical Education, Creative Skills.

Core subjects in **Years Four and Five** are English Language, English Literature, Mathematics, at least two Sciences, but they can take three, Latin, French. Girls then choose from 3 option blocks their other GCSE subjects. Another modern language can be taken as a two-year GCSE course.

In the **Sixth Form** girls choose four A Levels from a wide range of subjects, all Arts, or all Sciences or a mixture of the two. Stress is placed on breadth at this level. The school also offers Critical Thinking in the Upper Sixth as well as the Extended Project Qualification. Various philosophical, scientific and practical topics are explored in short courses.

All girls follow a course in personal decision-making in which they explore and discuss a wide range of issues which call for personal choice and which helps develop life skills.

Religious and moral education are considered important. Academic study of them is designed to enable girls to be informed and questioning. There is no denominational teaching in the school in lessons or morning assembly. Girls of all faiths or of none are equally welcome.

Girls take part in Physical Education, until the Upper Sixth Form where it is voluntary, with increasing choice from gymnastics, hockey, netball, tennis, rounders, dance, fencing, badminton, squash, fives, swimming, athletics, basketball, volleyball, self-defence, aerobics, archery, health related fitness. We have our own swimming pool, sports hall and extensive pitches, including two artificial hockey areas.

In addition to the music in the curriculum, there are choirs and orchestras which reach a high standard. These are mostly joint with King Edward's School. Individual (or shared) instrumental lessons, at an extra fee, are arranged in school in a great variety of instruments. Some instruments can be hired. Individual singing lessons can also be arranged.

A large number of clubs (many joint with King Edward's School) are run by pupils themselves with help and encouragement from staff. Others (eg Drama, Music, Sport) are directed by staff. Help is given with activities relating to the Duke of Edinburgh's Award scheme. Some activities take place in lunch hours, others after school and at weekends.

As part of the school's commitment to developing an awareness of the needs of society and a sense of duty towards meeting those needs, girls are encouraged to plan and take part in various community service projects as well as organising activities in school to raise money to support causes of their choice.

A spacious careers room is well stocked with up-to-date information. Individual advice and aptitude testing is given at stages where choices have to be made. The Careers Advisor has overall responsibility but many others are involved with various aspects. Girls are encouraged to attend conferences, gain work experience, make personal visits and enquiries. Old Edwardians and others visit school to talk about their careers. There is good liaison with universities and colleges of all kinds. Virtually all girls go on to higher education. A wide range of courses is being taken by Old Edwardians.

Admission of Pupils. Entry is normally for girls of 11 into the first year of the school in September. Applications must be made by September the year before they are due to start secondary school. The entrance examination is held early October. Girls should have reached the age of 11 years by 31st August following the examination. Girls are examined at the school in English and Mathematics. The syllabus is such as would be normally covered by girls of good ability and no special preparation is advised.

Girls from 12 to 15 are normally considered only if they move from another part of the country, or in some special circumstances. Applications should be made to the Registrar. Such girls can be admitted at any time if there is a vacancy.

There is an entry into the Sixth Form for girls wishing to study four main A Level subjects. Application should be made to the Principal as early as possible in the preceding academic year.

Fees per term (2016–2017). £4,014.

Scholarships and Bursaries. The equivalent of up to a total of two full-fee scholarships may be awarded on the results of the Governors' Admission Examination to girls entering the first year, with a maximum of 50% for any individual scholarship. These are independent of parental income and are normally tenable for 7 years.

Means-tested Bursaries are available for girls entering the school at 11+ and 16+.

Charitable status. The Schools of King Edward VI in Birmingham is a Registered Charity, number 529051. The purpose of the Foundation is to educate children and young persons living in or around the city of Birmingham mainly by provision of, or assistance to its schools.

Governing Body: The Governors of the Schools of King Edward VI in Birmingham

Principal: **Mrs A Clark**, MA Cantab, PGCE

Vice Principal: Ms Susan Pallister, BA Birmingham, MA York, NPQH, PGCE
Vice Principal: Mrs Neelam Varma, BSc & MA Warwick, PGCE
Vice Principal: Mr Martin Lea, BSc Sheffield, PGCE
Assistant Head: Mrs Kam Sangha, MBA UCE, PGCE Warwick
Head of Lower School and 3rds Coordinator: Mrs Sarah Shore-Nye, BA Swansea, PGCE

Teaching Staff:
Mrs Rachel Arnold, MA Cantab, PGCE
Mrs Marcia Atkins, MA Reading, QTS
Mrs Nishat P Azmat, BA Hons Acc & Fin Lon, ACCA, PGCE
Dr Victoria Bailey, BSc Cardiff, PhD Cardiff, PGCE
Mr Nicholas Bassett, BA, MA Kingston, PGCE
Mrs Marion Bellshaw, BSc Westfield College London, PGCE
Mrs Susan Bhagi, BSc Birmingham, PGCE
Dr Sheila Blain, BA, MA Cantab, PGCE
Mrs Sophie Blake, BA Oxon
Miss Sarah Blanks, BA Birmingham, GTP, QTS
Mrs M Cas Britton, BA London, PGCE
Miss Catherine A Brown, MA/MMath Cantab, PGCE, BSc Mol Sci Open
Mrs Gemma Buck, BSc Nottingham, PGCE
Miss Angela L Buckley, BA Oxon, GTP, QTS
Mrs Gillian K Chapman, BEd Chelsea School of Human Movement
Dr Jonathan Chatwin, BA Hull, MA Hull, PhD Exeter, PGCE
Mrs Rebecca M Coetzee, MA Cantab, PGCE

Mr Timothy O Cooper, BA Bristol, PGCE
Mrs Kate Cowan, BSc Glasgow, MRes Glasgow, MA Ed OU, PGCE
Mrs Rita D'Aquila, Master Cert Ed Catania
Mrs Jennifer Douglas, BA Hons Sheffield, PGCE
Mr Andrew E Duncombe, MA Cantab, PGCE
Miss Penny Evans, BA Hons Exeter, PGCE
Mme Laurence D Franco, Maîtrise LLCE Montpellier III, PGCE
Dr Claire E Gruzelier, BA, MA Auckland, DPhil Oxon, PGCE
Mrs Fiona Hall, MA Oxon, PGCE
Mrs Gemma Hargreaves, BSc Cardiff, PG DipEd
Dr Stephanie J T Hayton, BSc, PhD Newcastle, PGCE
Mr James Heather, BSc Birmingham, PG DipEd
Mr Simon Holland, BA Warwick, PGCE
Mr R Mel Hopkinson, BSc Hull, MSc London, PGCE
Mrs Christine M Hosty, BA York, PGCE
Mrs Sally A Huxley, BEd Bradford
Ms Sara Huxley-Edwards, BA Birmingham, PGCE
Dr Rachel M Jackson-Royal, BA King's College London, MA London, PGCE, PhD Birmingham
Mr Tom Jarvis, MusB Manchester, PGCE
Mr Harry J Kavanagh, MA Cantab, PGCE
Mrs Helen D Kavanagh, BA Bristol, PGCE
Miss Georgina King, BSc Warwick, PGCE
Miss Roselyne R Laurent, Diplome de technicientrilingue Haute Alsace, PGCE
Mrs Victoria J Law, BA Hons Oxon, PGCE
Dr Andrew Limm, BA, PhD Birmingham, PGCE
Mr Findlay Mackinnon, BA Strathclyde, PGCE
Mrs Jaspal K Mahon, BSc London, PGCE
Mrs Aurore Marquette, BA, MA France, MPhil, PGCE
Mrs J E Moule, BA Durham, PGCE
Mrs Elena Norman, BA Hons USSR, QTS Wolverhampton
Miss Jill Oldfield, BSc Durham, PGCE
Miss Sarah Platt, BSc Manchester, PGCE
Mrs Christine Pollard, BSc Nottingham, PGCE
Dr Manish Popat-Szabries, BSc City, MA Warwick, PhD Warwick, PGCE
Miss Rebecca Priest, BA Aberystwyth, PGCE
Miss Hannah Proops, BA Central School of Speech & Drama, GTP, QTS
Ms Michelle N Sanders, GRSM, ARCM Royal College of Music, PGCE
Mr Richard T Sheppard, BEng Manchester, PGCE
Dr Daljit Suemul, BSc Hons Polytechnic of North London, PhD Polytechnic of North London, PGCE
Dr Bernard L Tedd, BSc London, MA Mgt Ed, PhD Leicester, PGCE, AKC
Mrs Beverley Thompson, BSc Sheffield Polytechnic, PGCE
Dr Astrid Voigt, BA Cologne, DPhil Oxon
Mrs Adele Waites, BA Hull, MA Birmingham, PGCE
Mr Andrew Wager, BA Birmingham, PGCE
Mrs Joanna Whitehead, BSc Birmingham, PGCE
Miss Catrin E Woods, BA Warwick, QTS
Miss Katherine Williams, BA Cantab, PG DipEd

Librarian: Miss S Alan [maternity leave]
Principal's PA: Mrs B Overton
Admissions Registrar: Mrs C Oakes
Matron: Miss T Norman

King's High School

Smith Street, Warwick CV34 4HJ
Tel: 01926 494485
Fax: 01926 403089
email: enquiries@kingshighwarwick.co.uk
website: www.kingshighwarwick.co.uk

King's High School is an independent day school for girls aged 11 to 18. From our beginning in 1879, our expertise has been girls; providing an exceptional educational environment tailored to their needs in which they may thrive and become well-rounded, well-educated and compassionate young women. The school is part of the Warwick Independent Schools Foundation, alongside Warwick School and Warwick Preparatory School, and we enjoy our strong links with our Prep and brother schools. Located in the heart of Warwick, the listed 18th century Landor House is complemented by superb ultra-modern additions: the Sixth Form Centre and St Mary's Building opened by Dame Judi Dench, DBE in 2006, the Creative Arts Centre opened by Miss Catherine Bott in 2009 and the Dining Room opened by Miss Prue Leith in 2011.

The curriculum aims to give pupils as broad, engaging and rigorous an education as possible. All pupils study two modern languages and Latin and may choose three separate sciences for the IGCSE. There is an exceptionally wide choice of A Level subjects.

Our pupils' outstanding success at GCSE and A Level and in gaining places at prestigious universities of their first choice was remarked on in our 2011 Inspection Report, which especially noted that our A Level exam performance exceeded that of pupils in selective maintained schools. This success continues today with our 2016 A*-B A Level results having been the best of any girls' school in Warwickshire.

Extra-curricular and community activities flourish. Most girls achieve the Duke of Edinburgh's Bronze Award and many continue to Silver and Gold. Girls distinguish themselves in sport, music, drama and the countless other activities on offer. We offer a unique, bespoke qualification, The King's High Baccalaureate, which reflects the depth and breadth of our supra-curricular and extra-curricular opportunities. The school organises many day, evening and residential trips to destinations at home and abroad and invites prestigious women, such as Dame Judi Dench, DBE and Professor Germaine Greer, to visit and speak.

King's High provides an enjoyable, safe and stimulating experience in which girls can grow into confident and secure young women, equipped to make choices as they progress through their education and enter the world, prepared for change and able to make a positive and generous contribution to society.

Admission. Girls are required to take an entrance examination and attend an interview.

Fees per term (2016–2017). Tuition £3,956. Music: Brass, Pianoforte, Strings, Woodwind, Guitar, Drums, Singing £250 for 10 lessons.

Financial Assistance. Academic and subject scholarships in Art, Drama, Music and Sport are available on entry at age 11. Application for a range of Sixth Form Scholarships is open to internal and external candidates for the Sixth Form. Means-tested Warwick Foundation Awards, up to the value of full fees, are also available on entry at 11+ and at Sixth Form.

Charitable status. King's High School is a part of the Warwick Independent Schools Foundation which is a Registered Charity, number 1088057. The aim of the charity is "to provide for children (3–18) of parents of all financial means – a high proportion of whom shall come from Warwick and its immediate surroundings, but subject to satisfying academic standards where required – education of academic, cultural and sporting standards which are the highest within their peer groups".

Chairman of the Warwick Independent Schools Foundation:
Mr D B Stevens BA

Chairman of King's High School Committee:
Mrs G Low, MA Oxon

Foundation Governors:
Mrs M B Ashe, CA SA
Mrs S M Austin, BA, PgDPM, MCiPD
Mr A Bell, ACIB, PIIA, ACOR
Dr A D Cocker, BA, DPhil, MBA
Professor D Grammatopoulos, PhD, FRCPath
Mrs E J Lillyman, Cert Ed, NFF
Mrs C Sawdon, BSc, JP
Mrs P A Snape, FCIPD

Foundation Secretary: Mr S Jones

Senior Management Team:

Head Master: Mr R Nicholson, MA Pembroke College Oxford, ARCO, PG Cert Ed Man (*Deputy Child Protection Officer*)

Deputy to the Head Master, Deputy Head (Pastoral)/Child Protection Officer: Mrs C Renton, BSc Leicester, MSc London
Deputy Head (Academic)/Director of Studies: Mr S Bethel, BSc Birmingham
Acting Deputy Head (Academic)/Director of Studies: Dr R Cheetham, BSc London, PhD
Director of Co-curricular Activities: Mrs S Didlick, BEd CNAA
Director of Educational Innovation: Mrs J Parkinson-Mills, MSc Cantab
Head of Sixth Form: Miss E Carney, BA Manchester
Head of Key Stage 4 (Years 10–11): Mrs K Hewitt, BA Bristol
Head of Key Stage 3 (Years 7–9): Mrs S Watson, MA Oxon

Teaching Staff:

* *Head of Department*
§ *Part-time*

Art:
*Ms S Jordan BA Wolverhampton
Mrs E Ashby BA Kent
§Mrs J Knight, BA Portsmouth

Business Studies:
§Mrs E A Thornton, BA Nottingham (*Teacher in Charge*)
§Mrs A E Browning, BA London
Careers & Higher Education:
*Mrs J A Coplestone-Crow BA Durham
Miss R Bradbury, BA York, MA Leeds (*Oxbridge Coordinator*)
§Mrs A E Browning, BA London (*Work Experience Coordinator*)
Dr G Gifford MSc MA PhD Edinburgh (*Careers Advisor*)
Dr R Lidgett BA PhD Birmingham (*Careers Advisor*)
Mr J W Wood BA Nottingham MSc Leicester (*Careers Advisor*)

Classics:
*Mrs J A Coplestone-Crow, BA Durham
§Mrs R Morgan, BA Bristol, MA UCL

Design Technology:
*Mr N C Walker, BSc Brunel (*Duke of Edinburgh's Award Coordinator*)
§Mrs J Knight, BA Portsmouth

Drama:
*Miss C Price, BA Manchester (*Head of House*)
§Mrs J Wild, BA UEA
Mrs S Marshall, BA Schol of GSMD, ADB Theatre Studies (*Head of LAMDA*)
§Mrs M Mackenzie, BA Sheffield, MA Derby, RADA Dip (*Teacher of LAMDA*)
§Mrs F Mills, BA Leeds (*Teacher of LAMDA*)

English:
*Miss R Bradbury, BA York, MA Leeds (*Assistant to the Deputy Head Academic*)
§Mrs F Hill, BA Surrey
Miss P James MA Warwick
Miss J Mimms, MA Glasgow
§Mrs C Richards, BA Exeter
Mrs L Shaw, BA Warwick, MA UWE (*Assistant Head of Key Stage 5 – Year 12 & Coordinator of KHS Baccalaureate*)

Economics:
Mr J W Wood, BA Nottingham, MSc Leicester (*Teacher in Charge*)
§Mrs J Roberts, BA Leeds

Food Technology:
*Mrs S Didlick, BEd, CNAA
Mrs D Gregory, BSc Birmingham

Geography:
*Mrs K White, BA Exeter, MEd Cantab
§Mrs A E Browning, BA London
Mrs R Cresswell, BA Georgia (*Assistant Head of Key Stage 3*)
§Mrs E A Thornton, BA Nottingham
§Mrs C Walker, BEd Chelsea School of Movement
Mrs S Watson, MA Oxon (*Head of Key Stage 3*)

History & Politics:
*Mrs C Wellman, BA Warwick (*Head of House*)
Miss E Carney, BA Manchester
Dr G Gifford, MSc MA PhD Edinburgh
§Mrs I Gillett, German teaching degree Johann Wolfgang Goethe, Frankfurt

Information Technology:
*Mrs E Powell, BSc Anglia Ruskin
§Mrs N Russell, BSc Loughborough

Mathematics:
*Mr A Wild, BSc Wales
Mr H Ashby, BEng CNAA (*Examinations Officer Assistant*)
Mr S Bethel, BSc Birmingham
Miss U Birbeck, BA Warwick
§Mrs B Molesworth, BSc Birmingham
Mr R Sharpe, BEd Bristol Polytechnic, Dip DA New College of Speech & Drama
Mrs L Y Sherren, BSc Sheffield (*Examinations Officer*)
Mrs C Topping, BSc Wales, MSc Warwick

Modern Languages:
*Mrs C Murphy BA Royal Holloway (*Head of French*)
Mrs N Lopez BA Madrid (*Head of Spanish*)
Ms K Gibson, BA Salford
§Mrs V McRoberts, Licence MA University of Saint Etienne
§Mrs E Montiel, Licenciatura en Educación
§Miss D Pearce, BA London
Mrs R Wickes, MA Cantab (*Head of German & Coordinator of Personal Development*)
§Mrs K Bartel (*German Assistant*)
§Mrs M Esteban-Stephenson (*Spanish Assistant*)
§Mrs M H Quinney, DEUG Nantes & Chartres (*French Assistant*)

Music:
*Mr M Smallwood, BA Mus Anglia Polytechnic University
Mrs D Wallace, BMus London, LRAM, LTCL (*Assistant Director of Music*)

PSHEE & Personal Development:
Mrs R Wickes, MA Cantab (*Personal Development Coordinator*)
Mrs C Renton, BSc Leicester MSc London
Mr S Cleaver, BSc Manchester
Mrs R Cresswell, BA Georgia
Mrs S Didlick, BEd CNAA
Miss C E A Gilbert, BA Liverpool John Moores
Miss L Grant, BA Cardiff
Mrs K Hewitt, BA Bristol
Miss J Kneeland, MPhys Durham, MA Warwick
Mr R Nicholson, MA Oxon
Mrs S Watson, MA Oxon

Physical Education:
*Miss C E A Gilbert BA Liverpool John Moores (*Assistant Head of KS4 & Educational Visits Coordinator*)
§Mrs K Bryce, BSc Brunel
§Mrs K Riley, BA Exeter, MSc Chester
Mrs L Steinhaus, BSc Sheffield Hallam (*Second in Department & Head of Year 7*)
§Mrs C Walker, BEd Chelsea School of Movement

Psychology:
Ms J Griffiths, BSc Open University (*Teacher in Charge & Assistant Head of Key Stage 5 – Year 13*)

Religion & Philosophy:
*Dr R Lidgett, BA PhD Birmingham
Dr G Gifford, MSc MA PhD Edinburgh
Miss L Grant, BA Cardiff
Mrs K Hewitt, BA Bristol

Science:
*Mrs R Chapman, MA Oxon
Mrs S Didlick, BEd CNAA

Biology:
*Mrs A Sims, MA Cantab [Maternity Leave]
*§Dr P Boulton, BSc London, PhD Birmingham [Maternity Cover]
Mr R Henderson, BSc Durham (*Dual Award Coordinator*)
Mr P McCorquodale, BSc Imperial College London
Dr C M Pickup, BSc Manchester, DPhil Oxon, AMBDA (*Head of House*)
§Mrs K Pitchford, BSc Southampton

Chemistry:
*Dr A Grist, BSc PhD Leicester
Mrs R Chapman, MA Oxon
Mr S Cleaver, BSc Manchester
§Mrs S Kavaliauskas, BPhil Ed Warwick
Miss J Kneeland, MPhys Durham, MA Warwick
Mr P McCorquodale, BSc Imperial College London
Mrs J Parkinson-Mills, MSc Cantab
Dr C M Pickup, BSc Manchester, DPhil Oxon, AMBDA (*Head of House*)
§Mrs K Pitchford, BSc Southampton

Physics:
*Miss J Kneeland, MPhys Durham, MA Warwick (*Engineering Coordinator*)
Dr A Chamberlain, BSc PhD Warwick (*Academic Administrator*)
§Mrs K Clarke, BSc MSc Birmingham
Mr S Cleaver, BSc Manchester

Special Educational Needs Coordinator:
§Mrs A Thomas, Dip Ed Strathclyde Jordanhill, Dip SpLD Dyslexia Warwick, PG Cert ASD Worcester

Able, Gifted & Talented Coordinator:
Dr A Chamberlain, BSc PhD Warwick

Visiting Staff for Music:
Miss F Barsby, BMus
Mrs D Harriss, BA, LTCL, ABRSM
Mrs C Herbert, BMus
Mrs S M Irving, BEd Cantab, MMus
Mrs R Jefferies, BA, MMus, ARCM
Mr N Jones
Mr T Lindsay, BSc Grad Dip Birmingham Conservatoire
Mr C E Matthews, BA, MA
Mr R B Meteyard, AGSM
Mrs S Meteyard, GBSM, ABSM
Ms C Mills, BMus, LTCL, ABRSM, LRSM, ARCM
Miss B Morley, BA Coll
Mrs R Pepper, BMus, LRSM
Mr G Prosser, HND
Miss S Saunders, BA
Mrs M Todd, Diploma Lucerne Conservatoire
Miss A H Whelan, DRSAMD
Mrs A Williams, LRAM, ARCM

Visiting Coaches/Teachers for Activities:
Mr M Beckett (*Duke of Edinburgh's Award*)
Mr D Bryce (*Hockey/Football*)
Mrs S Cartwright-Randle (*Badminton*)
Mr N Chapman [Warwick School] (*Fencing*)
Mrs S Cleaver (*Netball*)
Mrs A Cooke SRN (*First Aid*)
Mrs J Curry & Miss C Curry (*Gymnastics*)
Mrs L England (*Dance/Hip Hop*)
Mr P Fox (*Clay Pigeon Shooting*)
Miss I Gray (*Ballet*)
Mr P Helps [Warwick School] (*Clay Pigeon Shooting*)
Mr G Henderson (*Tennis*)
Mrs J Ho (*Mandarin*)
Mr A Hodskinson [Warwick School] (*Climbing Club*)
Mrs E Holding (*Hockey*)
Mrs L McQuade (*Yoga*)
Mrs D Monnington (*PE & Junior Badminton/Rounders*)
Miss R O'Donnell (*Contemporary Dance*)
Mr C Osborne (*Badminton*)
Mr P Pardoe (*Clay Pigeon Shooting*)
Mrs P Quinn (*Fitness*)
Mrs L Rodriguez (*Martial Arts*)
Mrs A Stanley (*Zumba*)
Mr A Wilson (*Duke of Edinburgh's Award*)
Mrs C Wilson (*Duke of Edinburgh's Award*)
Mrs M Yeates [Warwick School] (*Lifesaving*)

Admissions, Marketing & Alumnae Relations Manager: Mrs J Horton
Marketing Assistant: Mrs H Leighton [Maternity Leave]
Marketing Assistant: Mrs D Shields [Maternity Cover]
Registrar: Mrs G Worrall
Head Master's PA: Mrs D E Ralphs
PA to Deputy Heads & Cover Manager: Mrs S Norton
Administration Manager: Miss H Shawcross
Office Receptionist/Administrator: Mrs F Eddy
Office Receptionist/Administrator: Miss K Lewis
Data & Exams Administrator: Mr A Sherren
Matron: Mrs T Rutter
Well-being Mentor: Ms E Williams
Administrative Assistant, Music Dept: Mrs A Williams
Librarian: Mrs C Burman
Alumnae Relations Assistant & Administrative Marketing Assistant: Mrs E Guest
Head Caretaker: Mrs R Cox
Secretary of Old Girls' Association: Mrs P Beidas

The Kingsley School

Beauchamp Hall, Beauchamp Avenue, Royal Leamington Spa, Warwickshire CV32 5RD

Tel: 01926 425127
Fax: 01926 831691
email: schooloffice@kingsleyschool.co.uk
website: www.thekingsleyschool.com

Independent Day School for Girls aged 3 to 18, and boys up to 11 years, founded in 1884.

For over 130 years this School has had an excellent reputation for high academic standards and first class pastoral care. What sets The Kingsley School apart from other schools is its distinctive family ethos and friendly atmosphere. We are immensely proud of the fact that everyone who visits us remarks on the happy staff-student relationships and the sense of community it fosters. At Kingsley, pupils have a positive and purposeful approach to learning. The atmosphere is unique; enthusiastic and approachable teachers inspire pupils to learn; behaviour is excellent and pupils are challenged and supported according to individual need. Where practical, we aim to personalise the curriculum so that pupils can reach their potential whatever their gifts and talents.

The Kingsley **Preparatory School** is friendly and purposeful and offers a rich, vibrant and creative curriculum for girls and boys aged 3–11. Outstanding teaching encourages a love of learning by providing a balance between the sound foundations for academic progress with character-building creativity. Kingsley has a well-established core curriculum in which the focus is on excellence within English, mathematics and science, supported by bespoke teaching in music, drama, modern foreign languages and physical education. In support of the core curriculum we have developed an exciting creative curriculum which sets our pupils a challenge; to explore and discover the real world. Most girls progress to The Kingsley Senior School, and boys move on to the next stage with self-assurance, some having been awarded scholarships for entry into local schools.

The **Senior School** provides continuity of academic and pastoral care. We offer a broad, balanced and stimulating academic experience. The curriculum at Kingsley is structured to maximise progress, building on girls' prior learning to encourage creativity, intellectual curiosity and independence. Our GCSE results are excellent, with high attainment year on year. At GCSE our curriculum provides opportunities for girls to study examinations in the core subjects of English, mathematics and the three separate sciences, as well as in the humanities subjects, the performing arts, physical education and modern foreign languages. The school delivers an academically rigorous timetable, yet has the flexibility and scope to offer additional subjects such as Latin and classical civilisation. Girls also experience a range of design subjects, for example food technology and textiles. Academic standards are high, with the 2016 GCSE results showing a 98% pass rate at grades A* to C in at least 5 subjects, of which 81% of passes were at grades A* to B, and 96% of students achieved A* to C in 5 subjects including Maths, English and Science.

The Kingsley School's **Sixth Form** provides a wide range of opportunities for all students. We offer a high-quality A Level curriculum and cater for a wide range of interests and post-16 aspirations. Students' academic achievements are outstanding and the diversity of their goals is embraced, with most progressing to their first-choice university, choosing to take apprenticeships within prestigious commercial organisations or studying further Higher Education courses. In the 2016 A Level exams 23% achieved A* to A grades. Recent leavers' destinations include Medicine at UEA, Law at Liverpool, Medieval and Modern Languages at Cambridge, Nursing at King's College London, Music at Birmingham Conservatoire and a Fashion and Retail Apprenticeship at Harrods, London.

Kingsley offers many enrichment activities which both extend and enhance the curriculum. The inclusive programme is designed to engage each pupil allowing them to enjoy new experiences in addition to developing essential life skills. There is a diverse selection of clubs and activities on offer. Opportunities include The Duke of Edinburgh's Award, Young Enterprise and World Challenge schemes. There are a variety of trips and visits, both local and international, for example theatre trips, an art and Spanish visit to Barcelona, geography trips to Iceland and the West Coast of the USA and a choir tour of Tuscany.

Sport and physical education are a vital part of life at Kingsley; each child is encouraged to achieve their personal best. We recognise that mental and physical fitness go hand in hand to develop wellbeing and academic potential. Sport helps to develop resilience, teamwork and leadership skills and lifelong health and fitness. Each week there is an inclusive programme of extracurricular sports offered before school, during lunchtimes and at after-school clubs. We compete regularly against local and regional opposition, with thriving sports teams. Kingsley also runs its own competitive riding squad, and is currently the only school in Warwickshire with a ski team.

We offer tuition in the performing arts leading to national music and drama qualifications. There are Kingsley choirs and musical ensembles and bands with regular opportunities to perform and showcase talent; both Prep and Senior School have annual musical theatre and drama productions.

Fees per term (2016–2017). Preparatory School: £3,345 (Reception to Year 2), £3,895 (Years 3–6). Senior School & Sixth Form: £4,185.

Scholarships and Bursaries. Academic, art, music, drama, sport and performing arts scholarships are available at 7+, 11+, and 16+.

Bursaries are available.

Our fleet of school minibuses serves a wide area and before and after-school care is available.

Charitable status. The Kingsley School is a Registered Charity, number 528774. It exists to provide high-quality education for girls aged 3 to 18 and boys up to 11 years.

Governors:
Chair: Mrs J Burns

Dame Y Buckland	Mrs S Hill
Mr N Button	Mr A Maher
Mr A Bye	Mr D Muldoon
Mr D Cleary	Mrs C Rigby
Mrs C Ellis	Mr J Strain
Mrs M P Hicks	Mrs E Smith

Clerk to the Governors: Mrs M Griffin

Head Teacher: Ms H Owens, BA Hons, PGCE, NPQH

Deputy Head (Pastoral): Mrs J Bailey, BA, MEd, CertEd

Assistant Headteacher (Curriculum): Ms R Dyson, BA, PGCE

Head of Preparatory School: Mrs R Whiting, BA, MA, PGCE, NPQSL

Head of Sixth Form: Mrs D Morgan, BA, PGCE

Staff:
* Head of Department

Art:
*Mr E Lax, BA PGCE

Classics:
*Ms I Peace, BA, PGCE

Design & Technology:
*Mrs C Dempsey, BEd
Mrs K Hughes-O'Sullivan, BEd, MA
Miss C Shephard, BSc, PGCE

Economics & Business Studies:
*Mrs M Bennett, BEd, MA

English:
*Mrs A Hamilton, BA, PGCE
Mrs P Doubleday, BA Phil, BA, CertEd
Mrs D Morgan, BA, PGCE
Miss J Roche, BA, PGCE, MA

Geography:
*Mrs R Rogers, BSc, PGCE
Mrs J Bailey, BA, MEd, CertEd

History:
*Miss C Parry, BSc Econ, PGCE
Ms R Dyson, BA, PGCE

Information Technology:
*Mrs M Bennett, BEd, MA
Mrs C Dempsey, BEd
Mrs S Mace, BA, PGCE
Mrs M Roberts, BEd, MA

Mathematics:
*Mr T Spillane, BSc, PGCE
Mrs P Davies, BSc, PGCE
Mrs L Laubscher, HED [SA], QTS
Dr A Smith, BA, PhD, PGCE

Modern Languages:
*Mr I Stickels, BA, PGCE
Mrs C Cocksworth, BA
Mrs T Connor, BA
Mrs M Gawthorpe, BA, MA
Miss M Mahé, Mâitrise de Littératures et Langues, Licence
de Langues

Performing Arts:
Miss J Roche, BA, MA, PGCE
Mrs J Rhodes, BA, QTS
Mr J Smith, BMus, PGCE
Mrs A Vallance, BA QTS (*Dance*)

Personal & Social Education:
Mrs S Mace, BA, PGCE
Mrs K Hughes-O'Sullivan, BEd, MA

Physical Education:
*Miss S Windsor, BEd
Mrs S Bates, BA, CertEd
Mrs K Close
Mrs J Davies, BEd

Psychology:
*Mrs S Mace, BA, PGCE
Mrs K MacLeod, BSc, Cert Teach

Religious Studies:
*Miss R Bubb, BA, PGCE
Mrs S Mace, BA, PGCE
Mrs J Rhodes, BA QTS

Science:
*Dr C Robertson, BSc, PhD, PGCE
Mrs S Bains, MSc, PGCE
Mrs S Baker, BSc, PGCE
Mrs A Hawthorn, BEng, MSc, PGCE
Mrs H Woodbourne, BSc, PGCE

Preparatory School:
Head: Mrs R Whiting, BA, MA, PGCE, NPQSL
Mrs G Adair, BN, PGCE
Miss J Clark, BA, PGCE

Mrs C Divers, BA QTS
Miss C Harris, BSc, PGCE
Mrs S Holmes, BA QTS
Miss M Knight-Adams, BSc, PGCE
Mrs C Lopez, BA, MA (*Spanish*)
Miss L Miller, BA QTS
Miss E Smith, BA (*Drama*)

Careers:
Mrs S Bennett

Academic Learning Support:
*Mrs L Payne, BA
Mrs R Athwal, BSc, MEd, PGCE
Mrs C Cocksworth, BA
Ms J Harper, BA
Mrs Y Raja
Mrs S Smith, BA, PGCE

Learning Resources Centre:
Miss E Smith, BA

Finance Office:
Mr B Cheney, ACMA (*Head of Finance*)

Administration:
Mrs J Bostock (*PA to Headteacher*)
Miss J Prosser (*Premises Manager*)
Mrs S Tsang (*Exam Secretary/Cover Administrator*)

Marketing:
Mrs S Scaysbrook (*School Registrar*)
Mr J Farrington-Smith, BA (*PR & Marketing Assistant*)
Mrs A Wheals, BA CIMD (*Head of Marketing & Admin*)

Duke of Edinburgh's Award:
Mrs K Hughes-O'Sullivan, MA, BEd

Speech, Drama and Dance:
Mrs K Buckingham, LAMDA
Ms N Shurvinton (*Modern Dance Tutor*)
Mrs A Vallance, BA QTS (*Dance*)

School Nurse: Mrs T Ball, SRN, BSc Hons

The Lady Eleanor Holles School

Hanworth Road, Hampton, Middlesex TW12 3HF

Tel:	020 8979 1601
Fax:	020 8941 8291
email:	office@lehs.org.uk
website:	www.lehs.org.uk
Twitter:	@LEHSchool

This Independent Girls' School is one of the oldest in the country, founded in 1710 in Cripplegate under the Will of the Lady Eleanor Holles. In 1937, the school moved to purpose-built premises in Hampton. Numerous additions to the building, and the acquisition of more land, have enabled the school to increase to some 880 girls, aged from 7 to 18 years, who enjoy a wealth of specialist facilities and the use of 24 acres of playing fields and gardens. Nine science laboratories, Learning Resources Centre, Sixth Form Library, a Design and Technology suite, extensive IT and multimedia language facilities and a dedicated Careers area are complemented by grass and hard tennis courts, netball courts, 5 lacrosse pitches, track and field areas and a full-sized, indoor heated swimming pool. A Boat House, shared with Hampton School, was opened in October 2000 and a large Sports Hall, adjacent to the swimming pool, in September 2001.

September 2012 saw the opening of a new Arts Centre consisting of a 300-seat theatre, new Music and Art Departments, Sixth Form Common Rooms, followed in September

2013 by a new dining room, a new suite of classrooms, two dedicated Drama Studios, a Conference Room and The Friends' Courtyard.

At the time of writing, a further building project is under way to provide enhanced student social facilities as well as state-of-the-art computing and design laboratories and several new classrooms. This building will open in September 2017.

Both the Junior and Senior Schools are equipped with a lift for the disabled.

The School's Statement of Purpose embodies the original aim, to encourage every girl to develop her personality to the full so that she may become a woman of integrity and a responsible member of society. It also emphasises the value of a broad, balanced education which gives due importance to sport, music and the creative arts in general, whilst providing the opportunities for girls to achieve high academic standards within a framework of disciplined, independent study.

The Curriculum. In Years 7–9, girls take two modern foreign languages, Latin, separate sciences, dedicated computing lessons and a PSHE programme which continues throughout the school. Selection rather than specialisation for GCSE allows girls to respond to individual abilities and attributes, and every girl continues to experience a broad education in which as few doors as possible are closed. A large sixth form of about 180 girls means that a wide choice of Advanced Level subjects is offered. Most girls will study four or five subjects in L6th, proceeding to A Level with three or four. The girls have the option of taking the Extended Project Qualification, and a great deal of emphasis is placed on leadership roles and extra-curricular activities. All sixth form students move on to further training, the majority to universities, and there is a sizeable Oxbridge contingent annually. The formal Careers programme, which begins in Year 9, continues throughout the school and uses external specialists, parents, past pupils, ECCTIS and other computer programmes, as well as the School's own, trained staff.

Extra-Curricular Activity. A key strength of the school is the range and diversity of its flourishing extra-curricular provision. Some 120 clubs run each week ranging from Music, Drama and Sports to Outward Bound and subject clubs, all aiming to stimulate further and inculcate a love of learning outside the classroom: 'The Other Half'. Sixth Formers lead a number of groups which focus on various political, environmental and ethical issues, including 'Model United Nations', 'Amnesty' and 'Make Poverty History'. Girls are encouraged to take the initiative to form their own clubs with a Medic Group, Law Society and Book Club formed in the recent past. The school is very much at the heart of the educational community and has developed a wide range of activities to ensure that students are aware of their social responsibilities, including Service Volunteers which works with disadvantaged students and the elderly, and running numerous activities in local primary schools, including language and drama clubs. Pupils are strongly encouraged to participate in extra-curricular activities.

The Junior School (190 pupils aged 7–11) is accommodated in a separate building in the grounds which was very extensively renovated and refurbished in 2003. It is an integral part of the whole school community and uses many of the specialist facilities available for Seniors.

(*See entry in the IAPS section for more details.*)

Entrance. Pupils may enter the Junior School from the age of 7, and the Senior School at 11 years. LEH Junior School pupils are guaranteed places in the Senior School (other than in exceptional circumstances). Girls with good academic ability may apply for direct entry to the Sixth Form. All external applicants must sit the School's competitive entrance examinations, which are held in November for Sixth Form entry and January (7+ and 11+) each year, for admission in the following September. There are no internal hurdles for entry to Sixth Form. Registration and Entrance Examination Fee: £100.

Scholarships and Bursaries.

11+ Entry Academic Scholarships: On average ten awards are offered each year. These are expressed as percentages of the full fee and will thus keep pace with any fee increases. Awards are non-means-tested and usually 10%. The awards are based on performance in the school's own Entrance Examinations and subsequent interview.

Governors' Bursaries: Candidates who sit entrance papers at any stage from 11+ onwards may be considered for a bursary award. These are available for up to 100% of fees, plus extras, and are means tested and subject to annual review.

Sixth Form Academic Scholarships: A maximum of ten Scholarships worth 10% of fees over the two years of Sixth Form study are offered to internal and external candidates who sit the Sixth Form Entrance and Scholarship Examination in November before the year of proposed entry.

Music Scholarships: Both Major and Minor Awards for Music are available at 11+ and 16+. These are for 10% and 7.5% of fees respectively, plus free tuition on one instrument. Candidates must satisfy academic requirements in entrance papers before being invited to a music audition. Full details are available from the school.

At 16+ only, Scholarships are also available in Art and Drama (one in each) for girls who propose to take A Level in the subject.

Fees per term (2016–2017). £5,231 in the Junior School; £6,315 in the Senior School. Fees are inclusive of books and stationery and exclusive of Public Examination fees.

Former Pupils' Association. The Holly Club address for communications: Alumnae Administrator c/o The Lady Eleanor Holles School; email: nnolan@lehs.org.uk.

The Cripplegate Schools Foundation

Chairman of the Foundation: Mr C S Stokes

Governors:
Mr G Cox, ACE, CA SA
Mrs E de Vise, BA
Mr P Gray, BSc, FRICS
Mr S R Kamat, BE, MS, MBA
Mr N D Lewis, LLB, DipLP
Dr S McCormick, MA Oxon, PhD, CBiol, FIBiol
Ms A Meyric Hughes, BA, PGCE, MA
Ms C Millis
Mrs L Stacey, LLB
Mr R T Welch, FCA
Mrs W J Wildman, BA, PGCE, Dip Counselling

Clerk to the Governors: Mrs S Whitehouse, BA

Head Mistress: Mrs Heather G Hanbury, MA Edinburgh, MSc Wolfson College Cambridge

Deputy Head: Mrs L D Hughes, BA Warwick

Director of Finance: Mr M Berkowitch, BSc, JD

Senior Assistant Head: Miss A Proctor, BA Jesus College Oxford, MSc Durham {maternity leave}
Miss S J Ferro, MA St Anne's College Oxford, MA University College London

Senior Assistant Head: Mr M J Williams, BA City of London Polytechnic

Assistant Head (Pastoral): Mr M Tompsett, MA Selwyn College Cambridge

Assistant Head (Pastoral): Mrs H Ndongong, MA St Edmund Hall Oxford

Assistant Head (Pastoral): Miss M J Waters, BEd Bedford College of HE

Assistant Head – Director of Studies: Mr D M Piper, BA King's College London

Director of Development and Communications: Mrs J Blaiklock, MA St Hilda's College Oxford

Senior School

Art:
Miss S Pauffley, BA Goldsmiths University of London
Mr L Curtis, BA Slade School of Art, MA Royal College of Art
Mrs E Knight, BA Wimbledon School of Art
Miss A Lindsey, BA Manchester (*History of Art*)
Miss H Peat, BA Loughborough College of Art and Design (*Deputy Head of Middle School*)
Ms A E Seaborn, BA Winchester School of Art
Miss S White, BA University of the Arts

Classics:
Miss F Ellison, MA Girton College Cambridge (*Head of Lower Sixth*)
Mrs R Brown, BA Durham (*Head of Upper Fifth*)
Miss K C Eltis, BA Balliol College Oxford
Miss M Hart, BA Exeter (*Head of Lower Fifth*)
Mr D Piper, BA King's College London (*Assistant Head – Director of Studies*)

Design Technology:
Miss A M Travers, BEd Surrey
Mrs A Angliss, BEd Trinity College Dublin
Mr S G Bicknell, BSc Brunel, PG Dip

Drama:
Dr B J Tait, BA CSSD, PhD Royal Holloway University of London
Miss G Guttner, BA Kent
Mrs P Tate (*Music and Drama Administrator*)

Economics:
Miss A J Matthews, BA Leicester (*Head of Careers*)
Miss D A Self, BSc Brunel

English:
Mr T-S Li, BA University College London, MPhil St Edmund's College Cambridge
Miss H Barnett, BA Durham
Miss E Evans, MA Durham
Mrs H M Ndongong, MA St Edmund Hall Oxford
Ms J Parry, MA St Andrew's
Mrs U Renton, MA Aberdeen
Mrs C Richardson, BA Reading
Miss A-M Wright, MA Aberdeen

Geography:
Mr C Tracey, BSc Lancaster
Mrs A R Lloyds, BSc Exeter
Mrs R Lockett, BA Southampton
Mr L M Tresserras, BA Southampton (*Examinations Officer*)

History and Politics:
Miss N Randall, BA York
Mrs A M Bradshaw, MA St Andrews
Ms J FitzGerald, BA Newcastle, MA Central School of Speech & Drama
Mrs L Harding-Anderson, BA Warwick
Mrs L D Hughes, BA Warwick (*Deputy Head*)

Information Technology:
Mr M Britland, BSc Gloucestershire (*Director of ICT*)
Mrs P M Stewart, BSc Bath

Mathematics:
Mrs J Manns, BSc Sheffield

Mrs N Banerjee, BA Delhi
Mrs S Leigh, BSc Edinburgh
Mr S Maloney, BA York, MSc Open
Mr S Mitchell, BSc Reading
Mrs M Najjar, BSc University College London
Miss R Nicholl, BSc King's College London
Mrs M Read, BSc Durham
Mrs K Sinnett, BA Peterhouse Cambridge (*Head of Thirds*)
Miss C Swainston, BSc Surrey
Mr M J Williams, BA City of London Polytechnic (*Senior Assistant Head*)

Modern Languages:
Mrs Y Wiggins, BA Staatsexamen Universität Würzburg (*Head of MFL and German*) {maternity leave}
Mrs A Buck, Licenciada en Filología Anglogermanica Universidad de Valencia (*Spanish and German*)
Mrs V M Kean, BA Leeds (*Head of French*)
Ms N Murray, BA Leeds, MA Leeds
Mrs U Arrieta, BA Deusto, Bilbao (*Head of Spanish and Acting Head of MFL*)
Mrs N J Rees, MA New Hall Cambridge (*Spanish and Special Educational Needs*)
Mrs K Reid, MA University of Trier, Germany
Miss D L Robbins, MA St Andrews (*French*)
Mrs A Rowe, BA Nottingham
Mr M Russell, BA St Catherine's College Oxford
Mr M Tompsett, MA Selwyn College Cambridge (*German, Assistant Head Pastoral*)

Music:
Director of Music: Mrs M Ashe, MA St Catherine's College Oxford
Miss N Redman, BMus Manchester, MMus GSMD
Miss C Sheppard-Vine, BMus Birmingham, MMus (*Clarinet*)
Mrs P Tate (*Music and Drama Administrator*)

Natural Sciences:
Mrs J Barwise, BSc Manchester, MA London (*Physics*)
Mrs P R Bond, BSc Leeds (*Biology*) {maternity leave}
Mrs H Bull, BSc St Andrews (*Biology*)
Mrs N C Camilleri, BSc Manchester (*Physics*)
Mrs J Crook, BSc Nottingham (*Chemistry*)
Mrs P Earl, BSc Swansea (*Biology*)
Mrs K M Ellis, BSc Durham (*Physics*)
Ms C Dyson, BA Durham, MSc University College London (*Psychology*)
Mr A Hayter, BSc Durham (*Head of Chemistry*)
Mr R Ives, BSc Sheffield Hallam (*Head of Physics*)
Mrs S Jansz, BSc Bangor (*Chemistry*)
Mrs A Jeffery, BSc Southampton (*Chemistry, STEM Coordinator*)
Mrs H Lenox-Smith, BSc University College London (*Biology*)
Miss F Mably, BSc Bath (*Head of Biology*)
Ms L Monteil, BSc Manchester (*Psychology*)
Mrs C R Nicholls, BSc Cardiff (*Biology*)
Mr J Noton, MEng Keble College Oxford
Miss S S Ostrander, BSc Bristol (*Head of Psychology, Biology*)
Ms C Packer, BSc University College London (*Chemistry*)
Miss R Parker, BSc Manchester (*Chemistry*)

Physical Education:
Mrs N Budd, BSc Brighton (*Director of Sport and Outward Bound Activities*)
Miss H Bovaird, BEd Otago
Mr J Cheesman (*Head of Rowing*)
Mrs R Crane, BA St Mary's Twickenham
Miss A Cutteridge, BA Durham
Miss L Marsom, BA Waikato New Zealand

Miss M J Waters, BEd Bedford College of HE (*Assistant Head Pastoral*)

Miss C Williams, BSc Leeds Metropolitan

Mrs E Harding, BSc St Mary's Twickenham (*Duke of Edinburgh's Award and CCF Coordinator*) {maternity leave}

Mrs N Crowther (*Duke of Edinburgh's Award and CCF Coordinator*)

Philosophy and Religious Studies

Dr P Gibbons, BA Surrey, MA Surrey, DPhil Regent's Park College Oxford

Miss L Prothero, BA Harvest Bible College, Melbourne, Australia, MA University College London

Mrs S Sinclair, BA Sunderland Polytechnic

Careers Advice:

Miss A J Matthews, BA Leicester Polytechnic (*Economics*)

Mrs R Brown, BA Durham (*Classics*)

Miss M Hart, BA Exeter (*Classics*)

Mr A Hayter, BSc Durham (*Chemistry*)

Mrs N Murray, BA Leeds, MA Leeds (*French*)

Mrs H M Ndongong, MA St Edmund Hall Oxford (*English, Assistant Head Pastoral*)

Mrs C R Nicholls, BSc Cardiff (*Biology*)

Miss S S Ostrander, BSc Bristol (*Psychology and Biology*)

Miss R E Parker, BSc Manchester (*Chemistry*)

Miss L Prothero, BA Melbourne, MA UCL (*Philosophy and RS*)

Mr M Tompsett, MA Selwyn College Cambridge (*German, Assistant Head Pastoral*)

Mr L M Tresserras, BA Southampton (*Geography*)

Learning Support:

Miss M Christodoulou, BA Middlesex, MA Durham, PGCert Dyslexia and Literacy

Mrs N Rees, MA New Hall Cambridge

Manager LRC: Mrs L Payne, BA University of California [Davis], MA California State University San Francisco, MCLIP

Junior School

Head of Junior School: Mrs P Mortimer, BEd Westminster College Oxford

Teaching Staff:

Mrs J E Allden, BSc London, MSc Kingston

Miss V M Barnes, BA Kingston

Mrs M M Bass, BEd Natal

Mrs J Deverson, BEd Oxford Brookes

Mrs J Dilworth, BSc UCL, MPhil Cambridge

Miss L Evans, BA Kingston

Mrs M Frampton, BEd Exeter

Miss S L Gain, BSc St Mary's Twickenham

Mrs S Grant-Sturgis, BA Exeter

Mrs S Harding, BEd De Montfort

Mrs K Hide, BEd La Sainte Union College of Education

Mrs L Kent-Skorsepova, MA Comenius University Bratislava

Mrs C Lyne, Dartford College of Physical Education, BA OU

Miss J Mackay, BEd Westminster College, Oxford (*Deputy Head of Junior School*)

Miss S Newbold, BEd West of England

Mrs K Sehgal, BA St Mary's

Mrs M Walker, BA Canterbury Christchurch {maternity leave}

Mrs V Wood, BEd College of St Mark & St John, Plymouth

Mrs L Cowin (*Teaching Assistant*)

Mrs L Hovsepian (*Teaching Assistant*)

Administration:

Estates Manager: Mr M Walburn, MRICS, CBuild E FCABE

HR Manager: Mrs G Hopkins, MCIPD

Personal Assistant to the Head Mistress: Mrs C E Dinsdale

Registrar: Ms A Stark, BSc

School Office Manager (*Senior School*): Mrs S Austyn

Senior School Nurse: Sister S Brew, RGN

Alumnae Administrator: Mrs N Nolan, BA

Personal Assistant to the Head of Junior School: Miss J Chudleigh

School Secretary (*Junior School*): Mrs J Rees, BA

Junior School Nurse: Nurse L Parker, RCN

Leicester High School for Girls

454 London Road, Leicester LE2 2PP

Tel: 0116 270 5338
Fax: 0116 270 2493
email: enquiries@leicesterhigh.co.uk
website: www.leicesterhigh.co.uk
Twitter: @LeicesterHigh
Facebook: /Leicester-High-School-For-Girls

The school is a Trust with a Board of Governors in membership of AGBIS and the Headmaster belongs to the GSA.

Leicester High School is a well established day school for girls situated in lovely grounds on the south side of the city. Founded in 1906 as Portland House School, it now comprises a Junior Department of 110 girls (3–9 years) and a Senior School of 250 girls (10–18) sited on the same campus.

The school offers an academic education of a high standard, and the Sixth Formers almost invariably go on to Higher Education. It is a friendly community where an emphasis is placed on honesty, integrity and respect for the views of others. Class size is kept small so that there is every opportunity for each girl to achieve her full potential whilst developing the self-confidence and self-discipline to help in her future.

The Headmaster is responsible for both the Junior Department and Senior School. The staff are well-qualified specialists and the school is renowned for both its academic excellence and extra-curricular programme. At present 17 subjects are offered at GCSE Level and 21 subjects at A Level.

Facilities. The premises are a combination of modern purpose-built units and the original Victorian house, skilfully adapted to its present purpose. The facilities of the school have been systematically improved. A purpose-built library and resource centre and new sixth form centre was opened in September 2001. The Junior Department benefited from new buildings opened in January 2002. The extension and improvement includes a computer suite and new library, enlarged hall, dining facilities and new classrooms. The EYFU was extensively redesigned in 2009. In September 2010, the school completed new facilities for Science, Art & Design and Modern Languages, and in 2014, a new Drama Studio was opened.

Religion. The school has a Christian foundation but welcomes girls of other faiths or of none.

Admission. All candidates over the age of 7 are required to pass an entrance examination for admission into the Junior and Senior sections. Entry into the Senior School would normally be at Year 6 or Year 7, but entry at other ages is considered. There is also direct entry into the Sixth Form dependent on GCSE results. Entrance into the Foundation Unit is by assessment. A registration fee of £85 is payable for all applicants.

Fees per term (2016–2017). £2,835–£3,870.

Extras. Individual Music lessons, Speech and Drama, and Ballet are offered.

Scholarships and Bursaries. Bishop Williams Scholarships for outstanding academic ability are awarded annually to girls entering Year 7 on the basis of performance in the January Entrance Examination. In 2014 a Maud Elkington Scholarship and a Sir Thomas White Scholarship and in 2015 The Headmaster's Scholarship were also introduced for Year 7 pupils. Music scholarships are also available throughout the school, and Bursaries are available from Year 6 onwards. The Ogden Trust sponsors a fully-funded scholarship covering 100% of the fees, subject to a means test, which is on offer to any Sixth Form candidate who is planning to study Physics and Maths at A Level.

The Headmaster is always pleased to meet parents of prospective pupils and to show them around the school. All communications should be addressed to the Registrar from whom prospectuses, application forms and details of fees may be obtained.

Charitable status. Leicester High School Charitable Trust Limited is a Registered Charity, number 503982. The Trust exists to promote and provide for the advancement of education based on Christian principles according to the doctrines of the Church of England.

Board of Governors:
Chairman: Mrs M Bowler, JP, BA Hons
Vice-Chairman: Mr J Jethwa, BSc
Mr J Allen, FCA
Mr M Dunkley, LLB, TEP
Mr J Gregory
Mr T Leah, BA, NPQH
Mrs K Mayes, BSc, FCA
Mrs M Neilson, BEd
Mr J Tomlinson, FCA, MA
Mrs S Webb, BA, PGCE, MBA, NPQH

Clerk to the Governors: Mrs E Mackay, AAT

Headmaster: Mr A R Whelpdale, BA, NPQH

Deputy Head: Miss D E J Wassell, BA

Assistant Head: Mrs N O'Brien, BSc

Head of Sixth Form: Mrs D Solly, MSc, BSc

Head of Year 6: Nurse Abby Cox

Teaching Staff:
* *Head of Department*

Careers:
*Miss E Tyler, BSc

English:
*Mrs K Penney, BA
Mrs E Brookes, BA
Mrs H Rees, BA
Miss D Wassell, BA

Expressive Arts:
Mrs E Bott, BA (*Art and Design)
Mrs J Rose, BEd (*Drama)
Mr M Haynes, MMus (*Music)

Food Studies:
*Mrs J Whalley, BSc
Mrs H Rai, BSc

Geography:
*Mrs K Haresign, BA
Mrs N Pulham, BA
Mrs J Whalley, BSc

History and Politics:
*Miss A Paul, MA

Mrs S Smith, BA

Information Technology:
Mr S Norbury, BSc (*ICT Coordinator, Head of KS4 Years 10–11*)

Mathematics:
*Dr S Hills, BSc, MSc, PhD
Mr A Stewart, BEng
Mrs D Solly, MSc
Mr J Stoeter, BSc

Modern Languages:
*Mrs L Soto, MA
Mrs M Buxton-Thomas, BA
Mrs C Dwyer, BA
Mrs G Wheeler, BA

Personal, Social, Health and Citizenship Education:
*Mrs D Morgan, BSc (*Head of KS3 Years 7–9*)

Physical Education:
*Mrs J Davison, BEd
Miss S Watson, BA

Religious Studies:
*Miss C Teal, BTh
Mrs E Brookes, BA

Science:
Mr A Chappell, BSc (*Physics)
Mrs N O'Brien
Mrs H Rai, BSc, MSc (*Biology)
Dr N Singleton, BSc, PhD (*Chemistry)
Miss E Tyler, BSc

Social Science:
Mrs K Haresign, BA (*Economics)
Miss N Perveen, BSc (**Psychology and Sociology*)
Miss C Teal, BTh

Sixth Form Enrichment Programme:
Mrs C Dwyer, BA
Mrs D Morgan, BSc

Special Educational Needs and Disabilities Coordinator:
Miss C Teal, BTh

More Able Coordinator:
Mrs M Buxton-Thomas, BA

Heads of Houses:
Mrs E Bott, BA
Mrs J Rose, BEd

Duke of Edinburgh's Award/Adventure Service Challenge/ Outdoor Education:
Miss S Watson, BA

School Bursar: Mrs E J Mackay, AAT
Accountant: Mrs K Allen, BA, FCA
Headmaster's PA: Ms S Davies
Registrar: Mrs J Harbage
Receptionist: Mrs K Clark, BTec
Examinations Officer: Mrs A Wall
Marketing Manager: Mrs A Whitlock, BSc
Librarian: Mrs S Timms
ICT Network Manager: Mr A Collins
IT Technician: Mr R Rai
School Nurse: Mrs A Cox, Dip HE, RN
Laboratory Technicians: Mrs M Cupac, Mrs M Atter
Art Technician: Miss R Winder
Caretakers: Mr M Hopkins, Mr G Neary

Visiting Staff:
Mr N Bott, BA (*Percussion*)
Mrs J Bound, GBSM (*Piano*)
Mr A Chandrasingh (*Piano*)
Mr J Cloke (*Tennis*)

Mrs L Davis (*Woodwind*)
Mrs C Lee, LRAM (*Violin*)
Mrs K Loomes, FIDTA (*Ballet*)
Mrs R Odari (*Piano*)
Mrs R Pells, GSMD, LAMDA, EMPA, IDTA (*Speech and Drama*)
Mr B Siddall, BA (*Guitar*)
Miss C Sullivan, BA (*Speech & Drama*)
Miss A Summerfield, BA (*Voice*)

Junior Department:

Head of Department: Mrs S J Davies, BA Ed
Early Years Coordinator: Miss C Pow, BA

Class Teachers:
Y5: Mrs S Davies, BA Ed
Y4: Mrs S Wayman, BEd
Y3: Mrs S Hague, BA and Mrs P Gascoigne, BA (*and Junior PE Coordinator*)
Y2: Mrs J Woodcock, BEd
Y1: Miss E Stell, BA
EYFS:
Miss C Pow, BA
Mrs S Moffatt, BSc

Foundation Unit:
Mrs L Boyer, NNEB
Mrs J Hunter, NNEB
Mrs J Jethwa, NVQ5
Miss S Gray, NNEB
Mrs N Sturmey, NVQ5

Administrator: Mrs M Singh, NVQ

Classroom Assistants:
Mrs A Cobley
Mrs L Dunn
Mrs P Jackson, NNEB

Leweston School

Sherborne, Dorset DT9 6EN

Tel: 01963 210691
Fax: 01963 210786
email: admin@leweston.dorset.sch.uk
website: www.leweston.co.uk
Twitter: @LewestonSchool
Facebook: @Leweston

Leweston School is an Independent Boarding (full, weekly and flexi) and Day school which is co-educational in the Nursery and Junior Department and all-girls in the Senior School and Sixth Form. Roman Catholic foundation but all denominations welcome. Excellent academic reputation and strong Sixth Form.

Situated in 46 acres of beautiful Dorset parkland, 3 miles south of Sherborne, the school offers all the advantages of both the traditional and modern in education with excellent facilities, particularly in the Sciences, Design & Technology and Sport. The school is also a Pentathlon GB Modern Pentathlon Training Academy, and one of only 8 in the country, thanks to its impressive record in the field of multisport disciplines. The school runs dedicated training programmes for these disciplines and hosts a number of popular training camps and competitions throughout the year. Leweston pupils are achieving outstanding results in these sports as representatives of the school, the county and even Team GB.

Founded by the Sisters of Christian Instruction in 1891, the school is a Catholic school but has a large percentage of pupils from other denominations. There are approximately 290 girls in the school of whom around 100 are boarders.

The ethos of the school is based on a wide social mix with a spread of talents, firm but friendly discipline and a keen sense of Christian and moral values. The Head is forward looking with a strong sense of leadership and vision. The school has a Visiting Chaplain and girls are expected to attend Chapel once a week. Preparation for confirmation is available for both Catholic and Anglican pupils.

The academic standard of the school is high. At both GCSE and A Level pass rates are consistently over 95% and the school's reputation for excellence in Music and Drama runs parallel with academic achievement in Sciences and the Arts. Each year girls gain places at leading universities and go on to read a wide range of degrees. The real success of the school, however, is achieved by realising the full potential of each individual pupil; much emphasis is placed upon the rich extracurricular offering, which helps to discover and nurture a wide range of talents.

Teachers are dedicated and imaginative, including specialist teachers for Dyslexia and EAL. The school's special quality is its ability to encourage in each pupil a sense of her own worth and ability. Girls are outgoing, well-mannered and unstuffy. While Leweston has a high proportion of day girls, the school is fully committed to boarding, offering a wide programme of activities in the evenings and at the weekends. Riding is especially popular.

The school has close links with the Sherborne Schools and there are many combined social, recreational, musical and cultural activities between the schools. Sherborne is an attractive historic abbey town with few of the distractions of a large city but at the same time, it is served by regular Network Express trains to and from London and good road links to Salisbury, Exeter and Bath. The school's facilities are among the best in the West Country. There is a fine floodlit all-weather sports pitch, Art and Design Centre, modern Senior Science Centre, Health Centre, Home Economics and Cookery Suite, large Library, heated indoor swimming pool, sports hall, multi-gym, squash courts, tennis courts and extensive well-maintained grounds and playing fields.

Leweston Junior Department (IAPS) for girls and boys aged 3 months to 11 years, with boarding provision for girls from age 8, is situated on the same campus, thus offering continuity of education for girls to age 18. Excellent early years provision including French and weekly swimming lessons from 3 years, beautifully situated Nursery and weekly Parent and Toddler Group. (*For further details, see entry in IAPS section.*)

Scholarships are awarded at 11+, 13+ and Sixth Form entry. Academic scholarships are available as well as Music, Art/Design, Drama, Sport and a limited number of all-rounder awards. Dates of examinations: Late November for Sixth Form scholarships, late January for others. Further details and entry forms can be obtained from the Registrar or found on the school website.

Fees per term (2016–2017). Full Boarding £8,096–£10,407; Weekly Boarding (4 nights) £7,013–£8,371; Weekly Boarding (5 nights) £7,318–£8,676; Day £5,740–£6,165. Flexi Boarding (including supper): £40–£48 per night.

Charitable status. Leweston School Trust is a Registered Charity, number 295175. It is a charitable foundation set up for educational purposes.

Governing Body:
Canon Richard Meyer (*Chair*)
Mr C Fenton (*Deputy Chair*)

Mr N Bathurst   Mr E Newton
Mr C Comyn   Mr I Stanton
Mrs S Gordon Wild   Mrs E Treichl

Head: **Mrs K Reynolds**, LLB Bristol, PGCE Bath

Deputy Head Academic: Mr G Smith, BSc Hons Open University, PGCE (*Mathematics*)

Deputy Head Pastoral: Mr L Beecham, MA, PGCE, MEd Cantab (*English and Drama*)

Head of Sixth Form: Mrs E Massey, BSc Hons Oxford Brookes, PGCE Chichester (*Mathematics, EPQ*)

Bursar: Lt Col Gus Scott-Masson

Visiting Chaplain: Fr Jean-Patrice Coulon

Teaching Staff:

Classics:
Miss L Flannery, BA Hons Warwick (*Head of Classics, Head of Years 10 and 11*)

English and Drama:
Miss S Evans, BA Hons Sheffield, PGCE London (*Head of English and Drama*)
Miss J Ateyo (*English, Head of Years 8 and 9*)
Mr L Beecham, MA, PGCE, MEd Cantab (*English and Drama*)
Mrs K Pankhurst, HND Theatre and Performing Arts, PGCE (*Speech and Drama*)
Mrs J Ogilvie, PG Dip Dyslexia & Literacy York (*Head of Individual Needs*)
Mrs A Croy, BA Hons Newcastle, PGCE Edinburgh (*Individual Needs Teacher*)

Modern Languages:
Mrs L Bryson, BSc Hons Bournemouth, CertEd Exeter (*Head of Modern Languages, Spanish*)
Mrs G Gotke, BA Hons London, PGCE Kent (*Spanish, French and Italian*)
Mrs L Maynard, MA Hons University of Liberec (*French*)
Mrs L Vandyck, BA Hons Ealing (*German*)

Geography:
Mrs A Dencher, BA, MA, PGCE Cantab. (*Head of Geography*)
Mr D Barlow, BSc Hons Nottingham, MSc London, PGCE Birmingham (*Geography, Physical Education*)

Home Economics, Health & Social Care:
Mrs S Larkin, Dip Naturopathy, Sydney, PGCE Exeter (*Home Economics, Health and Social Care*)

Mathematics:
Miss L Cozens, BSc Bristol, PGCE Oxford Brookes (*Head of Mathematics*)
Mrs E Massey, BSc Hons Oxford Brookes, PGCE Chichester (*Mathematics, EPQ, Head of Sixth Form*)
Mr G Smith, BSc Hons Open University, PGCE (*Mathematics, Deputy Head Academic*)
Mr A Okai, MSc, PGCE Portsmouth (*Mathematics*)

Religious Studies:
Ms C O'Toole, BA Hons London, PGCE, Catholic TCert Liverpool (*Head of Religious Studies, PSHE Coordinator*)
Mrs E Littlechild, BA Hons York, PGCE Twickenham (*Religious Studies*)

Psychology:
Mrs S Hunt, BA Hons Bournemouth, PGCE Exeter (*Head of Year 7*)

Science:
Mrs A Harwood, BSc Hons London, PGCE Oxon (*Head of Science & Biology*)
Mr P Ainsworth, BSc Hons, PGCE (*Physics*)
Mrs R Dawson, BSc Hons Bristol, PGCE Cambridge (*Biology*)
Dr O Kemal, BSc Hons, PhD London, PGCE Surrey, MRSC (*Head of Chemistry*)
Dr C Maunder, BSc Hons London, PhD Bristol, PGCE Open University (*Chemistry, Biology*)

Mrs A Valentine, BSc Hons Swansea, PGCE London (*Head of Physics*)
Dr R Whale, BSc, PhD Birmingham, PGCE Exeter, CChem, MRSC (*Chemistry*)

Economics and Business Studies:
Mrs L Bruller (*Head of Economics and Business, Senior Academic Boarding Tutor*)

ICT:
Mrs L Christy-Clover, BSc Hons CITM Open University (*ICT*)

History:
Mr M Hayward, BA Hons Oxon (*Head of History, History of Art*)
Mrs J Gregory, BA Hons Worcester, MA Hons Exeter, PGCE (*Head of Government and Politics, History*)

Art, Design and Technology:
Miss J Lacey, BA Hons Winchester School of Art (*Head of Art and Design*)
Mr F Bush, BTEC Nat Dip Plymouth, BA Hons St Martins (*Art*)
Mrs A Wright, MA Royal Academy of Art (*Art and Design*)

English as an Additional Language:
Mrs J Taylor, BA Hons Bath Spa, CELTA (*Head of EAL*)

Physical Education:
Mrs S Guy, BA Hons Keele, PGCE Hull (*Director of Sport*)
Miss G Phipps, CertEd Chelsea (*Housemistress Years 10–13*)
Mr M Flaherty, NVQ Management Level 4 (*Head of Swimming and Pentathlon*)
Ms A Parnell (*Swimming Pool Manager*)
Mr M Long, LTA Coach (*Tennis*)
Mr T Prideaux-Brun (*Tennis*)

Music:
Dr R Milestone, MMus, BA Hons Wales, PhD Leeds, LRSM (*Director of Music*)
Mrs K Gannon (*Singing*)
Mr R Hill (*Guitar*)
Mr P Huddleston, BTech (*Percussion*)
Mr D Price, LRAM (*Violin, Viola*)
Mrs N Price, GRSM Hons, ARCM, LRAM (*Pianoforte, Bassoon*)
Mrs M Riquelme Toomey (*Piano*)
Mr A Serna (*Violoncello*)
Mrs A Slogrove, BA Hons, LRSM, PGCE (*Piano*)
Ms K Whatley (*Harp*)
Ms A Whittlesea (*Recorder*)

Marketing & Admissions Manager: Miss L Cox
Registrar: Mrs C Damant
Librarian: Ms S Day
Academic Administrator: Mrs J Wells

Loughborough High School

Burton Walks, Loughborough, Leicestershire LE11 2DU
Tel: 01509 212348
Fax: 01509 215720
email: reception@leshigh.org
website: www.leshigh.org
Twitter: @LboroHighSchool
Facebook: /LoughboroughHighSchool

Loughborough High School is part of Loughborough Endowed Schools. Loughborough Grammar School (*see*

HMC entry) is the brother school and the co-educational junior school is known as Fairfield (*see IAPS entry*). Our Lady's Convent School, Loughborough, joined Loughborough Endowed Schools on 1 September 2015. We enjoy a very old foundation, established in 1850 as one of the oldest girls' grammar schools in England. The High School is located on a delightful 46-acre site close to the town centre with many first-rate facilities, which are being added to and improved continuously.

Loughborough High School is an 11 to 18 school of approximately 570 day girls with a large Sixth Form numbering around 160. At the High School we aim to provide an excellent academic education in a caring atmosphere. Since we are a comparatively small school, we are able to know our pupils as individuals and this leads to a strong community spirit. In providing a strong academic education in a disciplined atmosphere we hope to enable each girl ultimately to enter the career of her choice. The school offers a wide range of cultural, recreational and sporting activities and there are clubs and societies for virtually all tastes and interests (many in the senior school are run jointly with Loughborough Grammar School). We believe that our academic curriculum and extra-curricular activities nurture our pupils and encourage them to become active citizens of a modern world.

Further details about the school can be obtained by contacting the school's Registrar.

School Curriculum. Art and Design, Biology, Business, Chemistry, Classical Civilisation, Computer Studies, Drama, Economics, English, French, Games (hockey, netball, tennis, rounders and athletics), Geography, German, Greek, Gymnastics, History, Latin, Mathematics, Modern Dance, Music, Physical Education, Physics, Politics, Religious Studies, Spanish, Food, ICT, Psychology and Theatre Studies. Careful note is taken of the National Curriculum with additional subjects included within the curriculum to provide breadth and depth.

Fees per term (2016–2017). £3,824. Music (individual instrumental lessons): £220 (for 10 lessons).

Scholarships and Bursaries.

Academic Awards: The Governors offer a number of scholarships at 11+ which are awarded on academic merit. All candidates are considered for these awards without the need for any further application.

Music Awards: Music Scholarships are available to musically promising and talented pupils who are successful in the Entrance Examinations. Auditions are held around the time of the Entrance Examinations.

Bursaries: Means-tested Foundation Bursaries of up to 100% remission of tuition fees are available. These awards are normally made only to those entering at 11+ and 16+.

Further details of all these awards are available from the School.

Charitable status. Loughborough Endowed Schools is a Registered Charity, number 1081765, and a Company Limited by Guarantee, registered in England, number 4038033. Registered Office: 3 Burton Walks, Loughborough, Leics LE11 2DU.

Governing Body:
Chairman: Mr G P Fothergill, BA
Deputy Chairman: Mr H M Pearson, DL, DUniv Hon, BA Econ

Vice-Chairs:
Mrs M Gershlick
Professor J Feather, MA, PhD, FRSA
Dr P Cannon, MA Cantab, BM BCh Oxon, FRCS, MRCGP
Professor A Dodson, BSc Hons, PhD, DSc

Co-optative Governors:
Professor R Allison, BA PhD

Mrs E K Critchley MA Oxon
The Lady Gretton, JP, Lord-Lieutenant of Leicestershire, LLD Hon, D Uni Hon, Hon DLitt
Mr R Harrison, MA Cantab, Dip Arch RIBA
Mr P M Jackson, FIMI
Mr A D Jones, BA FCA
Professor J Ketley, BSc Hons, PhD Bham, CBiol, MSB
Mrs R J E Limb MA Cantab
M Mulla, BSc, MSc, MIM
Mrs P O'Neill, MA Cantab
Mrs G Richards, BA Hons, MEd, Hon EdD
Admiral Sir Trevor Soar, KCB, OBE, DEng Hon, FCMI
Mr J Stone

Nominated Governor:
Sister C Leydon

Ex-Officio Governors:
Dr A de Bono, MA, MB, FRCGP, FFOM (*Bursary Committee member*)
Dr P J B Hubner, MB, FRCP, DCH, FACC, FESC (*Bursary Committee member*)

Foundation Secretary & Treasurer: J Doherty

Headmistress: Mrs G M Byrom, BSc Manchester, MA Ed Open

Deputy Head: Mrs W Kempster, BSc Reading

Director of Studies: Dr S Jackson, BSc PhD UMIST, CChem, MRSC

Assistant Head Curriculum: Miss C Hitchen, MEng Newcastle

Assistant Head Pastoral: Miss C E Nelson BSc Manchester

Joint Head of Sixth Form:
Mrs R E F Burn, MA Cambridge
Dr C Burnett, BEng, EngD Swansea
Head of Year 11: Mrs G Nightingale, BSc Sheffield
Head of Year 10: Miss H Latham, BSc Sheffield
Head of Year 9: Miss V Standring, BSc MSc Chester
Head of Year 8: Miss E Rees, BSc Leeds
Head of Year 7: Mrs J Day, BSc Manchester

Staff:

Art and Design:
Mrs S R O Henson, BA Loughborough
Miss S Budzik, BA Leeds, MA Surrey

Artist in Residence Ceramics:
Miss C Collins, BA Hons Leicester

Careers:
Dr C Burnett, BEng, EngD Swansea
Mrs R E F Burn, MA Cambridge
Dr D Cladingboel, BSc, PhD Southampton

Classics:
Mrs R E F Burn, MA Cambridge
Mr K Lomax, MA Cambridge
Mr G C Stevens, BA Liverpool

Drama:
Ms S E Boon, BA Plymouth Dartington
Miss R Hooper, BA Hons Leicester

Economics and Business:
Mr R J L Needs, BA Nottingham, IMS Cert, ACCA, Dip Ed Mgmt Leicester
Mr P Lodhia, BA Hons Nottingham

English:
Miss E Bancroft, BA Oxford
Mrs L Harrison, BA Leeds Met
Mrs H Jones, BA King's College London
Miss C Longe, BA Leicester

Mr J Martin, BA Hons Wales
Mrs A Palmer, BA Chester

Food:
Mrs M A Reilly, BSc Surrey
Mrs J A Squire, CertEd Nottingham

Geography:
Mr A Moreton, BA Manchester
Mrs H Chamberlain, MSc Loughborough
Mrs J Day, BSc Manchester
Miss V Standring, BSc MSc Chester

History:
Dr E C Eadie, BA Birmingham, DPhil Oxford
Mrs J Bower-Gormley, BA Hull
Dr D Cornell, BA PhD Durham

Information & Communications Technology:
Mr J Singh, BA Coventry
Mrs C Winship, BSc Reading

Mathematics:
Mrs J Beardsley, BEng Surrey
Miss C Hitchen, MEng Newcastle
Mrs W Kempster, BSc Reading
Miss R Mistry, BSc Warwick
Mr G Needham, MA Liverpool
Miss C I Shawcross, BSc Loughborough
Mrs R Slade, BSc Surrey
Mrs A Smith, BA Oxford

Modern Languages:
Mr R W Tomblin, MA Oxford
Miss J Anguiano Gomez, BSc, MRes MEd Granada
Mr D Gough, BA Sheffield
Mrs A Lee, BA Nottingham
Mrs E Raouf, BA Salford
Mrs M West, MA Swansea

Language Assistants:
Miss J Bavencoff (*French Assistant*)
Miss M Garcia (*Spanish Assistant*)

LES Music School:
Mr R J West, BA Durham, MSc Herts, LGSMD, LRSM
Mrs N Adkinson, BA Durham
Mr N Ellum, BA Keele
Miss C Revell, BMus Huddersfield
Dr P J Underwood, MA Cambridge, MMus London, PhD Birmingham

Personal, Social, Health & Citizenship Education:
Mrs J Conway, BA MA Ulster

Physical Education:
Miss S Cockayne, BA Birmingham
Miss J Carter, BSc Leeds
Miss S Griffin, BSc Loughborough
Mrs F Moore, BEd De Montfort Bedford
Miss V Standring, BSc MSc Chester

Psychology:
Mrs A Kenyon, BA Hull
Miss E Rees, BSc Leeds

Religious Studies:
Mrs J A Lewis, BA Nottingham
Mrs A Justice, BEd Warwick
Mrs R Gacs, MA Nottingham

Science:
Mrs J E Stubbs, BSc Nottingham
Mrs M Ghaly, BSc Teesside
Mrs J Pellereau, MSc Loughborough, MA Cambridge
Dr D Cladingboel, BSc PhD Southampton
Dr J Downing, BSc PhD Bristol
Dr S Jackson, BSc PhD UMIST, CChem, MRSC

Miss H Latham, BSc Sheffield
Miss C E Nelson, BSc Manchester
Mrs G Nightingale, BSc Sheffield
Mrs J Peart, Grad Dip Phys Guy's
Dr N Simmonds, BSc PhD Leicester
Miss C E Todd, BSc Manchester
Dr A Williamson, BSc PhD Imperial College London

Learning Support:
Ms E Johanson, BA Bradford

Librarian:
Mrs G Burton, BLS Loughborough

Matron:
Mrs A Cannon, RGN
Mrs S Chad Smith, RGN

Examinations Officer: Mrs S English, Level 4 Prof Cert Managing Examinations
E-Learning Coordinator: Mrs C Winship, BSc Reading
PR, Communications & Events Manager: Ms L E Shipman
PA to the Headmistress: Miss C Hughes, BA Leicester
Registrar and Data Manager: Miss A M Anderson, BSc Aston
School Secretary: Mrs A Cox
Receptionist: Ms J Calow
Administrative Assistant and Reprographics Technician: Miss A Burrows, MA Bangor
Charity Coordinator: Ms L E Shipman
Voluntary Service Unit Coordinator: Dr A Williamson, BSc PhD Imperial College London

Art/Food Technician: Mrs J Pheby
Modern Languages & Humanities Technician: Mrs T Hicks
Laboratory Technicians:
Mrs E Fraser, BSc DMU
Mrs K Bedwell, BSc De Montfort, MSc Loughborough
Mrs L Deamer, BSc Loughborough
Mrs L Hirst

LHS Duke of Edinburgh's Award Scheme Coordinator: Mr M House, BSc Lancashire

ICT Support: Mr T Simpson

Bursary:
Foundation Secretary and Treasurer: Mr J Doherty, ISBA
Foundation and Schools' Accountant: Mr R Harker, BA Coventry, FCA
Estates Manager: Mr T Allardice, MCIOB, MBEng
Compliance Officer: Mr G Leeson, BA Northumbria
Commercial Manager: Mrs G Collicutt, BA Nottingham

Development Office:
Mrs J Harker (*Head of Development and External Relations*)
Mrs E Parry, MCIPR (*Marketing Manager*)

Catering:
Mrs J L Johnstone (*Operations Manager – Catering & Events*)
Mrs F Coltman (*Catering Manager, Fairfield Kitchen*)

Manchester High School for Girls

Grangethorpe Road, Manchester M14 6HS

Tel:	0161 224 0447
Fax:	0161 224 6192
email:	administration@mhsg.manchester.sch.uk
website:	www.manchesterhigh.co.uk

Twitter: @mhsg
Facebook: /ManHighSG

Manchester High School for Girls (MHSG) offers students a vibrant atmosphere and a strong sense of community. In such a supportive environment, each girl feels happy, cared for and valued as an individual. Its academic record is outstanding; in GCSE, A Level and the IB Diploma girls are taught not just how to achieve excellent examination results, but are encouraged to enjoy learning.

MHSG was founded in 1874 and has a long and successful history. The School offers a seamless education from age 4 to 18 and has extensive experience of helping girls to achieve their best. All members of the school community have a strong sense of the School's traditions, but MHSG is forward looking and keen to embrace new educational developments. Since September 2010, girls entering the Sixth Form have been able to choose to study the International Baccalaureate (IB) Diploma.

At MHSG, artistic and sporting talents are nurtured and students enjoy a diverse range of extra-curricular activities. These are complemented by superb modern facilities which include a state-of-the-art Sixth Form Centre with lecture theatre, common room and study area, a sports complex, a fitness suite, a dance studio, all-weather sports pitches, a multi-purpose auditorium, a drama studio and a purpose-built Music House. Instrumental and Speech & Drama lessons are optional extras.

Students at Manchester High come from a wide range of backgrounds and this rich social and cultural mix gives the School a warm and friendly feel. The girls learn about the importance of social responsibility with charity, voluntary and community work strongly encouraged.

Highly skilled and committed staff strive to ensure that every MHSG student leaves the School a well-educated young woman, with highly-developed interpersonal skills and a broad range of interests. Our girls are confident in their own worth, prepared for an independent life and capable of making a positive contribution to society. It is from this cornerstone that they go on to pursue varied and fulfilling careers.

Entry to the Reception class is by assessment while an entrance examination is set for the Juniors and Year 7. From time to time vacancies in other year groups can become available, but the main entry levels are at ages 4, 11 and 16. Sixth Form assessment is by interview and GCSE qualifications.

MHSG is committed to providing education to academically gifted girls regardless of circumstance. In the Senior School financial assistance is offered through a limited number of part or full means-tested bursaries. One or more scholarships may be awarded for excellence in performance in the entrance tests taken at the age of 10 or 11 for admission to the Senior School in September. Such scholarships will be awarded on merit only, not on the basis of parental income, and will provide part remission of fees. Music, Sports and Dance scholarships are also available.

Further details and a prospectus are available from the Registrar.

The Report of the ISI Inspection in October 2010 can be viewed on the School's website.

Fees per term (2016–2017). Seniors £3,751, Juniors £2,754, Infants £2,711.

Charitable status. Manchester High School for Girls Foundation is a Registered Charity, number 532295. The aim of the charity is the provision and conduct in Manchester of a day school for girls.

Board of Governors:
Chairman: Mrs S E Spencer, BA
Dr A Ahmed, DCH, DRCOG, DFFP, MRCGP
Mrs S Beales, MA

Mr A Clarke, FCA
Lady R Cooper, OBE
Dr J Dwek, CBE, BSc, BA, DSc
Mrs M Grant, Cert Ed
Mrs S Klass, MA Oxon
Mrs D Kloss, MBE, LLB, LLM, Hon FFOM
Her Honour Judge L Kushner, LLB, QC
Ms M Lowther, BSc Hons, MBA, CIMGT, FCIB, LLD
Professor R W Munn, PhD, DSc, FRSC
Mr S Ruia, BSc
Mrs C V F Sargent, BSc
Mr C J Saunders, OBE, MA, FSI
Mr F R Shackleton, MA, LLM
Mr K S Yeung, MBE

Hon Treasurer: Mr A Clarke, FCA

Head Mistress: Mrs A C Hewitt, BSc, NPQH

Deputy Heads:
Ms J L Hodson, MA Cambridge, BA Cambridge (*Biology*)
Mrs A P Goddard, BA Thames (*Theological Studies*)

Assistant Heads:
Mr W Perry, BSc Warwick, PG Cert Educational Leadership, Leicester (*Director of Co-Curriculum, Physics*)
Mrs S Norton, BA UC Berkeley USA, MA Mills College USA (*Director of Sixth Form Studies, English*)

Staff:
* *Head of Department*
§ *Part-time*

Mr S Banks, BA Salford (*Modern Languages*)
§Mrs P Bell, BA Leeds Polytechnic (*Art & Design Technology*)
Mrs C Bennett, BSc Staffordshire (*Physics*)
Mr A Bradley, BMus Birmingham (*Music)
Mrs D Brown (*Dance & PE*)
Ms J Burley, BA Liverpool (*English*)
Mrs A G T Chambers, BA West Surrey College of Art & Design, ATC (**Art & Design Technology*)
Mr J Clarke, BA, MPhil Manchester (*History)
§ Miss E Compton, BSc Nottingham (*Psychology*)
Miss L Cooke, BSc Wales (**Careers, Biology*)
Mrs E S Counsell, BA Leeds, MSc Birmingham (*French, German*)
§Mrs R E Crowley, BSc Manchester (*Mathematics*)
Mrs R Daly, BA Durham (*Geography)
§Mrs T Davey, BA University of Wales (*English*)
Mrs E A Diamond, BA Birmingham (*Religion & Philosophy*)
Mr B Eaton, BSc Manchester (*Physics*)
Ms T Fitzgibbon, BSc Hull (*Psychology*)
Mrs J L Fordham, Cert Ed Manchester (*Art & Design Technology*)
Mr K Gilkes, BSc Bolton (*ICT*)
Miss S Hadley, BA Liverpool (*Psychology*)
§Miss C Hannan, MA Cantab (*Classics*)
§Mrs J Haves, BA De Montfort Leicester, PGCE (*Drama*)
Mrs J R Heydecker, BA Leicester (*History*)
Mr F Heywood, BSc Nottingham, MSc UMIST (*Mathematics*)
§Mr C Hilton, BA, MA Cambridge, Dip TEO QTS Manchester (*Mandarin*)
Dr R E Hoban, BSc, PhD Newcastle (*Chemistry)
Mr S P Holmes, BSc Nottingham (*Mathematics*)
Ms E Hudson, BA Hull (*English*)
Mrs P Inglis, BSc Manchester (*Chemistry*)
Mr D L Jones, BSc Manchester (*Mathematics*)
Miss K Large, BSc Leeds (*Chemistry*)
Dr M Leach, BA Oxford, PhD Durham (*Physics)
Mrs K Loughrey-Davies, BA Warwick (*English*)

§Miss K Martin, BA Birmingham, MPhil Birmingham
(*History*)
Dr F Menon, MSc Padova, PhD Manchester (*Biology*)
§Mrs C Mills, MChem Oxford, PGCE (*Chemistry*)
Dr L Moore, BSc Lebanon, MSc UMIST, PhD (*Chemistry*)
Mrs S A Moores, BA Cardiff (*Modern Languages*)
Mrs N Morgan, BMus Lancaster (*Music*)
Mrs S Newman, BEd Leeds Metropolitan (**Physical
Education*)
Mr B Norris, BSc Cardiff (*Mathematics*)
Mr P J O'Brien, BA Hull (*German*, **Modern Foreign
Languages*)
§Mrs E Othen, MA, MPhil, Cambridge (*Classics*)
§Mrs C J Ousey, BA Southampton (*English*)
§Miss J Parker, BSc Imperial College London (*Biology*)
Mrs C Pattison, BSc Newcastle (*Mathematics*)
Dr C M Poucher, BSc, PhD Leeds (*Biology*)
Mrs M Price, BA Manchester (*English*)
Ms A N Protheroe, BSc Swansea (*Mathematics)
§Mrs C Purvis, BA Lancaster (**Religious Studies*)
Mr M Randall, BA CNAA, MA Leicester (**Business
Economics IT*)
Miss C Rennox, BSc Leeds Metropolitan (*Physical
Education*)
§Mrs S Reynolds, BA UCL, MSc Kingston (*Geography*)
Mr D Rose, BA, MA Kent (*English*)
Miss S C Rowley, BA Staffordshire (*Physical Education*)
Mrs P Scott, BA Duncan of Jordanstone College of Art (*Art
& Design Technology*)
§Mrs T Slack, BA Manchester (*Modern Languages*)
Dr R Smither, BSc Bath, MPhil, PhD Cambridge (*Biology*)
§Mrs J Taylor, BA Manchester (*Philosophy & Literary
Studies*)
Mrs R Thompson, BA, MPhil Birmingham (*Spanish)
§Mrs D E Troth, BA Exeter (*History*)
§Mrs C M Tynan, BA York (*Physics*)
Mr S R F Vance, BA Manchester (*Art & Design
Technology*)
§Dr A Walker-Taylor, MSc Warwick, PhD UCL
(*Biology)
Miss L Warwick, BSc Manchester Metropolitan (*Physical
Education*)
§Mrs J Watson, BSc Newcastle-upon-Tyne (*Geography*)
Miss J Welsby, BA Manchester (*Classics)
Mrs K A Whelan, BSc Bradford (*Business Economics and
IT*)
Mrs C Wilkes, BA Sorbonne, MA Rennes (*Modern
Languages*)
Mrs C Zakaria, BA King's College London (*Spanish,
French*)

Preparatory Department Staff:

Head of Preparatory Department: Mrs E Nash, BEd
Cambridge

Mrs K Adam, BSc Sheffield Hallam
Mrs R A Anderson, BEd Glasgow
Mrs V Baird, BSc Lancaster
Mrs C Callanan, BA MMU
Miss S Diamond, BEd Cantab
Mrs S Edale, BA Derby
Miss J H Floyd, BA Charlotte Mason College
Mrs M R Heggie, BMus, BEd New South Wales
§Mrs R James, Cert Ed, PG Dip SpLD, CCET
Mrs E Mason, BA Nottingham
Mrs J Newton, BA UMIST
Mrs J C Philip, BA Manchester
Miss A Pritchard, LLB Manchester
Miss F Sanderson, BA Manchester Metropolitan
Miss C Taylor, BSc UMIST
Mrs C Westall, BA Huddersfield

Bursar: Mr J P Moran, FCCA
Registrar: Mrs P Percival
PA to Head Mistress: Mrs K Joynes
Librarian: Miss Z Hawker, BA Liverpool, MSc
Northumbria
Archivist: Dr C Joy, BA, PhD Leeds
School Medical Officer: Dr J Herd, BM BS, DFFP,
DRCOG, MRCGP

Manor House School, Bookham

Manor House Lane, LIttle Bookham, Surrey KT23 4EN

Tel: 01372 457077
Fax: 01372 450514
email: admissions@manorhouseschool.org
            admin@manorhouseschool.org
website: www.manorhouseschool.org
Twitter: @ManorHseSchool
Facebook: @manorhousesch

Motto: "An individual approach to academic success."

Manor House School, Bookham is a selective independent day school for girls aged 4–16 with an award-winning
co-educational nursery.

Founded in 1920, the school is a charitable trust located
partly in a Georgian building and set in seventeen acres of
parkland within easy distance of London in the Surrey com-
muter belt. A range of local minibus routes operate before
and after school each day. The day boarding system operates
from 8.00 am to 6.00 pm.

Manor House School provides a nurturing yet challenging environment with an extensive enrichment programme
that develops a confidence in students to seek new experiences and instils the qualities of courage, kindness and
integrity.

The school maxim 'An individual approach to academic
success' is brought to life by ensuring that every girl can fulfil her potential in whichever subject areas or activities it
lies.

Girls learn together at their own pace, develop the confidence to take risks, choose any field of study without stereotypical influence, grow in emotional intelligence and show
compassion for others while honing life and leadership
skills for the future. But most importantly, develop into
happy, confident and successful young women.

The excellent facilities include a purpose-built spacious
Art/Textiles studio, Music and Drama Room and Home
Economics facility, a recently refurbished ICT suite, language laboratory, fit-for-purpose Science block, and Sports/
Theatre/Assembly Hall in addition to a further main hall in
the Manor House itself. The School has excellent sports
facilities which include an open-air heated swimming pool,
five floodlit tennis and netball courts, hockey and rounders
pitches, and an athletics track.

Manor House girls follow a wide curriculum throughout
their school career and generally take 9.5 or 10.5 GCSE subjects achieving consistently strong academic results and
being highly sought after by sixth form and college destinations. There are typically over fifty extracurricular clubs and
activities taking place during any one term and these are an
important part of school life.

Pastoral care is a particular strength of the school. Senior
girls are caring role models for younger pupils and we have
a flourishing peer support group. A Manor House girl is academically successful, confident and outgoing with a strong
sense of values and the ability to succeed in her chosen
career.

Admission to the Senior Department is at 11+ is by the
School's own Entrance Examinations, which are held in the

second week of January prior to the September entry. Other main entry points are at Reception Class and Year 3 although the school welcomes mid-year applications and applications to other entry years. Entry is subject to availability of places and the selection criteria is determined by a visit to the school followed by successful completion of an age-appropriate taster and assessment day. Offers are made following the outcome of this process at the discretion of the Headteacher.

Scholarships and Bursaries. There are two major academic scholarships offered at age 11+ valued at 50% of the basic annual fee. Plus a sport scholarship valued at 30% of the basic annual fee and a scholarship/s in the Creative and Expressive Arts valued at 30% of the basic annual fee. The awards are awarded based on performance in the Entrance Examinations and attendance at Scholarships Day in November. To apply please contact: admissions@manorhouseschool.org.

Means-tested bursaries may also be applied for and further details are available from Mr C Burton, Director of Finance and Operations at cburton@manorhouseschool.org.

Fees per term (2016–2017). Tuition: From £1,314 (Nursery, 3 sessions) to £5,447 (Seniors).

Charitable status. Manor House School is a Registered Charity, number 312063. It exists for the promotion of children's education according to their academic, social, sporting and musical abilities.

Governors:
Chair of Governors: Mr M Parkhouse, BA Hons, MA, MSc
Miss S Clare
Mr J Compton, LLB Hons, LLM
Mr C Heath-Taylor
Dr M J Richardson
Mr M Ruscoe
Mrs G Sims-Brassett

Senior Leadership Team:

Headteacher: Ms T Fantham, BA Hons, MA, NPQH

Deputy Head: Mr M Gates, BMedSc Hons, MEd
Director of Finance & Operations: Mr C Burton, Hons BCompt, Prof Accountant SA
Head of Key Stage 4 (Seniors): Miss K Gall, BEng Hons, PGCE
Head of Key Stage 3 (Seniors): Miss J Ward, BA Hons, PGCE
Head of Key Stage 2 (Juniors): Mrs T Hilleard, MA, BEd Hons
Head of Key Stage 1 & EYFS (Pre-Prep): Mr D Ayling, MA Cantab, PGCE
Admissions and Marketing: Ms M Fowell, Higher Dip Marketing, CIAM Dist

Heads of Department
Art: Mrs T Williams, BA Hons, PGCE
Drama: Mrs T Williams, BA Hons, PGCE
English: Mrs E Mayes, BA Hons
Geography: Miss C Grindrod, BSc Hons, PGCE
History: Miss R St Johnston, MA Hons, PGCE
Home Economics: Mrs K Tercan, BEd Hons
Latin and Classical Civilisation:
Mrs V Diprose, BA Hons, PGCE
Mrs L Stephens, BA Hons, PGCE
Academic Advancement: Ms S Howes, NPQH, Adv Dip Ed Mgt, BSc Hons, PGCE, BDA SpLD
Mathematics and ICT: Mr D Pelham, BSc Eng Hons, CEng, MBCS, CITP
Modern Foreign Languages: Mrs C Peel, MA, PGCE
Music: Miss J Ward, BA Hons, PGCE
Physical Education: Miss C Poultney, BEd Hons
Religious Studies:
Mr C Perceval, BA Hons, Dip Law, PGCE

Mrs L Pillar, BEd Hons
Science: Mrs S Brodie, BSc Hons, PGCE

Admissions Officer: Mrs A Clark

The Marist School

Kings Road, Sunninghill, Ascot, Berkshire SL5 7PS
Tel: 01344 624291
Fax: 01344 874963
email: officesenior@themarist.com
website: www.themarist.com
Twitter: @Marist_School

Independent Catholic Day School for Girls aged 11–18 founded in 1870 by the Marist Sisters. The school has been at the current site since 1947 and is set in 55 acres of attractive woodland in the village of Sunninghill near Ascot.

Number of Pupils. 320 girls.

Mission Statement. To be a centre of excellent education where outstanding teaching and pastoral care underpins academic success; this combined with the development of the whole person equipping children and young adults with the capacity to succeed in their life's journey.

Strengths.
- Strong reputation for academic excellence as well as sport, drama, music and creative arts.
- Able to offer a wide range of both academic and extra-curricular activities.
- Strong emphasis on pastoral care, spiritual and personal development; care and consideration for others.
- Small class sizes to enhance individual progression and recognition.
- The school is renowned for its high standards regarding moral values, community spirit, respect and care. This is in line with the overall ethos of the Marist order which has a worldwide presence, providing a truly international dimension to a girl's education.

Facilities. Indoor swimming pool, Sports Hall, dedicated Sixth Form suite, comprehensive ICT suite, Music and Drama block, Language Laboratory, Ceramics Studio & Darkroom, AstroTurf Multi-Sports Surface and Learning Resource Centre.

Academic Curriculum. Art, Biology, Business Studies, Classical Civilisation, Chemistry, Drama/Theatre Studies, Economics, English, French, Geography, German, History, ICT, Italian, Latin, Mathematics (also Pure & Mechanics, Pure, Statistics, Pure & Statistics), Music, Personal, Social & Health Education, PE, RE, Religious Studies: Philosophy & Ethics, Science, Spanish, Sports Studies, Textiles, Food Science, Psychology, Photography and Government & Politics.

Sixth Form. The school offers a total of 26 subjects at A Level. Year 12 students will study 4 four subjects in their first year (in certain circumstances some students can take 5). Girls will decide which 3/4 subjects they wish to continue on to final exam.

Extra-Curricular Activities. Art, Athletics, Choir, Clarinet & Saxophone Ensemble, Drama Club, Duke of Edinburgh's Award, Flute Group, French Films, Greek (Ancient), Guitar Group, History Films, Hockey, Human Rights, ICT, Latin, Library Club, Literacy, Netball, Orchestra, Prayer Group, Public Speaking/Debating, Rock Band, Science, Strategy/Numeracy, Swimming, Swing Band, Textiles, Tennis, Young Enterprise.

Results. 2016: 66% of all grades were A*–B. GCSE students achieved 61% A*–A. Each student averaged 11 GCSEs A* to C.

Admission. Entrance examination tests in (1) English, (2) Mathematics and (3) cognitive abilities, (4) Portfolio, (5)

Compulsory Interview with the Principal and (6) Reference from Primary/Preparatory Headteacher.

Sixth Form Entry. A minimum of 7 GCSEs A*-C grade or above, preferably B grade in subjects to be studied.

Fees per term (2016–2017). £4,500. Extra benefits: Generous sibling discount scheme (4th and any subsequent children free), after school care provided.

Scholarships. Year 7 and Sixth Form Academic, Art, Drama, Music and Sport scholarships are available.

Preparatory School. We also have a Preparatory school on the same campus which is for girls aged 2½–11. This allows girls to continue their education with their friends in the happy and secure environment they are used to. (*For further details, see the Marist Preparatory School entry in the IAPS section.*)

Affiliations. Girls' Schools Association (GSA), Catholic Independent Schools Conference (CISC), Silver Artsmark, Eco-Schools award and Healthy School.

Charitable status. The Marist Schools is a Registered Charity, number 225485. The principal aims and activities of the Marist Schools are religious and charitable and specifically to provide education by way of an independent day school for girls between the ages of 3 and 18.

Chair of Governors: Mrs A Nash

Principal: **Mr K McCloskey**, BA Hons, PGCE, MA

Senior Vice Principal: Mrs W Reed, BA Hons, PGCE

Heads of Department:
Art: Mrs R Ellwood
Classics: Mrs A Osmon
Drama: Ms E White
Economics/Business Studies: Ms Clare Knox
English: Mrs L Lutton
Food Science: Mrs G White
Geography: Mr E de Grande
History: Mr A Baker
ICT: Mrs J Shill
Mathematics: Mrs A Hynds
Modern Foreign Languages: Mrs R Beckh
Music: Mrs L Karakurt
Psychology: Mrs J Cope
Physical Education: Mrs J Bishopp
Religious Education: Miss L Vaughan Neil
Science: Mrs A Costello
Textiles: Ms S Bowley

Head of Sixth Form: Ms N Fenning

The Mary Erskine School

Ravelston, Edinburgh EH4 3NT
Tel: 0131 347 5700
Fax: 0131 347 5799
email: admissions@esms.org.uk
website: www.esms.org.uk
Twitter: @esmsedinburgh
Facebook: /esmsedinburgh
LinkedIn: /erskine-stewart's-melville-schools

The Mary Erskine School was founded by Mary Erskine and the Company of Merchants of the City of Edinburgh in 1694. It is therefore one of the oldest schools in the UK endowed specifically for girls. Known in its early years as 'The Merchant Maiden Hospital', its aims were to educate and care for the daughters of City Burgesses who found themselves in reduced circumstances. Throughout its history, the school has been administered by the Edinburgh Merchant Company. In November 1989 this authority was devolved to the Erskine Stewart's Melville Governing Council.

The school, named The Mary Erskine School in 1944 to mark the 250th anniversary of its foundation, has been housed on various sites in the city – the Cowgate, Bristo, Lauriston and Queen Street – and the buildings are depicted on the engraved glass panels in the Sports Centre and on murals in the Assembly Hall. The current school buildings, at Ravelston, command splendid views of the nearby city and castle.

Since 1978 the school has been twinned with Stewart's Melville College (*see entry in HMC section*). This includes a fully co-educational Junior School for children between the ages of 3 and 12, single-sex but very closely twinned secondary schools between the ages of 12 and 17 and a fully co-educational pre-university Sixth Form which provides the ideal bridge between school and university. The girls and boys from The Mary Erskine School and Stewart's Melville College come together in the Combined Cadet Force, in orchestras, choirs, drama and musicals and in numerous outdoor education projects.

The Senior School (733 Girls). The school curriculum corresponds predominantly with practice in Scotland. Girls generally sit the public examinations prescribed by the Scottish Qualifications Authority.

S1 and S2 follow a broad curriculum, whereby girls are equipped to pursue all routes to National 5. In S3 girls commence eight courses, including English, Mathematics, at least one modern language, at least one science, and a "humanities" subject. In S5 the majority of girls take five subjects at Higher level. Girls are expected to achieve their full potential. The majority will continue their studies for a Sixth Year, usually at Advanced Higher level, to provide a firm foundation for degree courses in Scotland and England. Most girls proceed to such courses.

The playing fields at Ravelston underpin a fine tradition in hockey and tennis. Physical Education facilities include grass hockey pitches, two floodlit astroturf hockey pitches, a running track and twelve tennis courts. A Games Hall and Fitness Suite complement the other sporting facilities. The Pavilion, which provides the Sixth Form girls and boys with a Common Room and Study area during the week, is available to parents and friends as a coffee area on Saturday mornings and other times when sports events take place.

Staff from the well-equipped Technology Centre work closely with those in the bright, modern Home Economics Department. The attractive Library is next to one of the computer rooms, forming a combined resource centre which is accessed by all departments.

In the Art Department the girls enjoy first class facilities which help them develop diverse artistic talents. There is a specially designated area for Sixth Form girls, many of whom proceed to Art colleges, as well as darkroom facilities for keen photographers.

The Music Department possesses fine facilities in Ravelston House and the school enjoys a notable reputation for the quality and range of its musical activities. The attractive School Hall and designated Studio offer good facilities for drama and there are frequent productions involving girls and boys of all ages.

The Combined Cadet Force comprises Army and RAF sections. The combined Pipe Band has an international reputation and girls in the Highland Dancing team also achieve frequent success in competition. Many girls participate in The Duke of Edinburgh's Award scheme, as well as in hill-walking and other forms of outdoor recreation. Each week the school offers to girls a wide variety of extra-curricular clubs and societies ranging from curling to drama.

The school has a sophisticated system of Guidance. S1 tutors, led by the Head of S1, help girls to make the transition from Junior School to Senior School a smooth and happy experience. During the next four years girls belong to one of six houses. The Heads of House, led by the Head of Upper School, liaise closely with colleagues on each girl's academic progress, teach the personal and social education programme in house groups and encourage each girl to derive maximum benefit from the school's extra-curricular programme.

The Sixth Form is co-educational with the Sixth Formers of Stewart's Melville College. While girls sustain their loyalty and commitment to The Mary Erskine School, they are equally at home in the Sixth Form Centre of the boys' school. We see the Sixth Form as a preparation for university, when girls and boys assume greater responsibility for their academic programme and their career aspirations. All girls in the school receive guidance and help from the staff of a well-established careers department.

Boarding. There is a boarding house (Erskine House) with accommodation for approximately 28 girls in brightly decorated study-bedrooms. The girls share dining and recreational facilities with the Stewart's Melville boarders in Dean Park House. Both Houses have a friendly, family atmosphere and provide an ideal "home from home" for brothers and sisters.

Fees per term (2016–2017). Day: Nursery to Primary 7 £2,546–£2,853; Secondary £3,639. Full Boarding: Primary 6 and 7 £6,515; Secondary £7,301. Weekly Boarding: Primary 6 and 7 £6,333; Secondary £7,119.

Scholarships and Bursaries. Means-tested Bursaries worth up to 100% of the tuition fee may be available to parents of children entering any year group in the Senior Schools and at P7 in the Junior School. Academic scholarships worth £300 annually are offered to girls applying to enter S1, following a competitive selection process. These are known as Merchant Company Scholarships. The top scholarship holder at The Mary Erskine School receives the Mackay Scholarship, worth £1,250 annually. Scholarships are paid to the pupil and are held in trust by the school until completion of their Sixth Form year. Music Scholarships of £300 per annum are offered from S3.

ESMS Junior School. In The Junior School (1,254 pupils), girls and boys are educated together from age 3 to 11. Children in Nursery to Primary 3 are based on The Mary Erskine School site at Ravelston, while boys and girls in Primary 4–7 are taught on the Stewart's Melville College site. Normal entry points are Nursery (age 3 or 4), Primary 1, Primary 4, Primary 6 and Primary 7. The school is remarkable for the breadth of its educational programme and the quality of its sporting and cultural activities, in particular the professional standards attained in Music and Drama.

The Mary Erskine School Former Pupils' Guild. Contact: MES Guild Office, The Mary Erskine School, Ravelston, Edinburgh, EH4 3NT. Tel: 0131 347 5722.

Charitable status. The Merchant Company Education Board is a Registered Charity, number SC009747. It is a leading charitable school in the field of Junior and Secondary education.

Governing Council:
Chairman: Mr Mike Sims

Clerk to the Governors: Mr D Wright, LLB

Principal: Mr J N D Gray, BA

Bursar: Mr J B Molloy, MA Hons

Vice Principal and Deputy Head: Mrs L A Moule, BA Hons, PGCE

Director of Studies: Mr A P McDiarmid, BA Hons PGCE
Staff Development Coordinator: Ms V Thomson, BEd Hons, BSc
Head of Upper School: Dr E A Murray, BSc Hons, MEd, PhD, PGCE

Head of S1/Admissions: Ms K S S Nicholson, MA Hons, PGCE
Director of Sixth Form: Dr I R Scott, MA Hons, PhD, FRSA, CertEd

* *Head of Department*
† *Head of House*

Art:
*Mrs F J MacGregor, BDes Hons, PGCE
Mrs C Burns, BA Hons, PGCE

Biology:
*Dr C Turnbull, PhD, BSc Hons, MRes, PGDE
Dr S Corbet, BSc Hons, MSc, PhD, PGCE
Miss K Davies, BSc Hons, Dip Ed
Mrs S Horrix, BSc, PGCE
Dr C Turnbull, BSc, MSc, PhD
Miss J Burgess, BSc Hons, PGCE

Business Studies:
*Mrs E Proudfoot, BA Hons, PGCE, PG Dip
Mrs F K McCrudden, BA Hons, PGCE
Mrs M Thorniley-Walker, MA Hons, MCIPS, PGCE
Mrs C Forrester, BA Hons, PGCE

Careers:
Mrs F K McCrudden, BA Hons, PGCE

Chemistry:
*Dr C J Spracklin, BSc Hons, PhD, PGCE
Mrs S Ferrington, BSc Hons, PGDE (†*Appin*)
Mrs C Murdie, BSc Hons, PGCE
Dr E A Murray, BSc Hons, MEd, PhD, PGCE (*Head of Upper School*)
Dr F Neave, BSc Hons, PhD, PGCE

Classics:
*Mr T E McBratney, MA Hons, PGCE
Mrs J R Brown, BA, MA, GTP
Miss R Newland
Miss E Shackleton, BA Hons, PGDE

Drama:
*Miss J R Flockhart, BA Hons, PGCE
Mrs L Howarth, MA Hons, PGCE

English:
*Mrs K A J Yip, BA Hons, MA, PGCE
Ms D Esland, BA Hons, PGCE
Mrs N Ramirez, MA Hons, PGCE (†*Kintyre*)
Mrs R Connet, BA Hons, PGCE
Mrs A Holt, BA Hons, PGCE, ALCM (†*Lochaber*)
Mrs C S Park, MA Hons, PGCE (†*Torridon*)
Mrs M Tetley, BA Hons, MSc, QTS
Mrs E Smith

Geography:
*Dr M Davies, BA Hons, PGCE, PhD
Ms K S S Nicholson, MA Hons, PGCE (*Head of S1/Admissions*)
Miss J F Pollitt, MA Hons, PGCE
Mr J Talbot, BA Hons, MEd, PGCE
Miss M Wilkinson, MA Hons, PGDE

History:
*Mrs A J Ferguson, MA Hons, MEd, PGCE, PGCE
Mrs L F Alexander, MA Hons, PGDE
Mrs L J Allan, MA Hons, PGCE (*Deputy Head, Sixth Form*)
Mr R Robertson, MA Hons, PGCE
Mr A P McDiarmid, BA Hons, PGCE

Home Economics:
*Mrs J Campbell, BA, PGDE
Mrs N L Murray, BA, PGCE, PGC

Mathematics:
*Mrs F J Houbert, BEd Hons
Dr B Duncan, MPhys, PhD, PGCE
Mr J D Hamilton, BSc Hons, MSc, PGCE
Mrs S Jack
Mrs C A Morrison, BSc, Dip Ed
Mrs J Smart, BSc Hons, FFA, PGDE
Mrs M Grant, MA Hons, PGCE
Mrs M Clarkson

Modern Languages:
*Mr M G Chittleburgh, MA Hons, Dip Ed, PGCE
Ms J H Bremner, MA Hons, PGCE
Mrs J Fitzgerald, MA Hons, PGCE
Mrs V McBratney, BA, PGCE
Miss L McGuinness, MA, PGCE
Mr R Million, BA, PGDE
Miss C Watson, MA Hons, PGDE
Ms C Wolsley, MA Hons, PGCE

Modern Studies:
Mrs R Molloy, MA Hons, PGCE
Mrs L Allan, BA Hons, PGCE

Music:
Mr S Cheney, Director of Music
*Mr J Matthews, BMus, PGDE
Pipe Major Robert Burns
Mr Tim Paxton
Mr J Smith, BA Hons
Ms D Smith
Mr S Walsh (*Drumming*)
Mrs J Wilson, BA, PGCE

Philosophy:
*Dr I R Scott, MA Hons, PhD, FRSA, CertEd (*Director of Sixth Form*)
Mr D Kemp, MTheol, PGCE

Physical Education:
*Mrs N Aitcheson, BEd Hons
Mrs P Johnston
Mrs V G Thomson, BEd Hons, BSc
Miss C Lampard, BEd Hons (†*Appin*)
Ms L Lanigan, BEd Hons
Miss S McHard, BA Hons, PGDE
Mrs G Longmuir, BEd Hons
Mrs J L Miller, BEd Hons
Mrs K A Mundell, BEd Hons
Miss K J Henderson, BA Hons, PGCE
Miss C MacLean, BEd Hons

Physics:
*Dr T Hely, MSc, PhD, PGCE
Mrs J McLaren, MEng Hons, PGDE
Mrs J Paterson, BSc Hons, MPhil, PGCE
Mr C Templeton, BA Hons, MA Cantab, PGCE

Product Design:
*Mr D K Bowen, BA Hons, ATC, Dip SIAD
Mrs C A Hemmati, BSc Hons, PGCE, MSc
Mr R Strachan, B Des Hons, PGDE

Religious Moral and Philosophical Studies:
*Mr D Kemp, MTheol, PGCE
Ms J Shepherd, BA Hons, PGCE
Mrs F Levitt Muir, BA Hons, PGCE, MEd

Support for Learning:
*Mrs C Maxwell, BA, Dip Ed
Mr S Hollins, BA Hons, PGCE
Miss R Meredith, BSc, PGCE, PG Dip
Mrs J Miller, BEd Hons
Mrs L A Moule, BA Hons, PGCE (*Deputy Head*)

Junior School:
Head Master: Mr M Kane, MA Hons
Senior Deputy Head: Mrs G Lyon, DCE, Dip RSA
Deputy Head (*Early Education*): Miss S Mackay, ALCM, LLCM, BMus Hons, PGCE
Assistant Head (*Primary 4–7*): Mr D McLeish, DCE
Assistant Head (*Primary 4–7*): Mrs J Hewitt, BSc, PGCE
Assistant Head (*Early Education*): Ms C Macpherson, BEd

Marymount International School

George Road, Kingston-upon-Thames, Surrey KT2 7PE

Tel: 020 8949 0571
Fax: 020 8336 2485
email: admissions@marymountlondon.com
website: www.marymountlondon.com

An Independent boarding and day school for girls aged 11–18. A member of GSA, CIS and MSA (USA).

Number of Pupils. 250, including 100 boarders.

Established in 1955 by the Sisters of the Religious of the Sacred Heart of Mary, Marymount International School is an independent day and boarding school for girls, aged 11–18 (grades 6–12), welcoming girls of all faiths and traditions.

A small school with 250 students (of which 100 are boarders), the overall student : teacher ratio is 6:1 and the average class size numbers 11 students. Teaching is relevant, topical and flexible, enabling students to remain motivated and achieve their full potential.

The school aims to provide an intellectually stimulating and emotionally secure environment in which the academic, social and personal needs of each individual student may be met. Education is seen as a continuous process of growth in awareness and development towards maturity in preparation for participation in the world community. Each student's schedule is individually tailored to the subjects she wishes to follow. The language of tuition is English (fluency is essential) but additional languages on offer for native speakers include German, Spanish, French, Japanese, Chinese, Korean, Italian and Arabic.

With over 40 nationalities in the School, students are fully prepared for life in a global setting and develop an instinctive cultural fluency so sought after by today's employers.

Facilities in the beautiful seven-acre campus include a Fab Lab (the first in a UK School), newly refurbished Library, Sports Hall, Auditorium, Art Studio, Science Centre, Music Centre and tennis courts. New classrooms have been recently added and e-learning has been introduced across the entire school with Mac TVs (to be used in combination with iPads) planned for all classrooms. The Dining Hall and boarding facilities have also been updated recently.

Curriculum. Students are prepared for the International Baccalaureate Diploma (ages 17–18, grades 11–12) by the IB Middle Years Programme (ages 11–16, grades 6–10). Marymount was the first British school to be accepted to teach the MYP, which stretches students without the need for incessant testing.

The School has taught the IB Diploma since 1979 and has unparalleled experience in its delivery. The IB diploma syllabus leads to UK university admission and US college credit. Student go on to the top universities in the world. In 2015 82% of students applying in the UK gained places at Russell Group Universities, including Oxford and Cambridge. Perfect scores of 45 are achieved regularly and 25% of Class of 2015 scored above 40 points, which is achieved by only 5% worldwide.

The school programme also includes the option to visit a variety of foreign locations designed as educational trips and closely aligned to the curriculum.

The school is within a half-hour drive of Heathrow Airport and conveniently located for M25/A3 road links to Gatwick Airport.

Admission. Previous reports, teachers' recommendations, placement testing in English and Mathematics and interview.

Fees per annum (2016–2017). Tuition: £19,290 (Grades 6–8); £22,035 (Grades 9–12). Boarding Supplement: Grades 6–12: £13,730 (5-day), £15,325 (7-day).

Charitable status. Marymount International School is a Registered Charity, number 1117786. It exists for the promotion of education.

Executive Headmistress: **Ms Sarah Gallagher**, BA Hons, HDipEd, MA Hons Ireland

PA to Headmistress: Ms Sue Palmer-Simmons
Executive Headmistress Assistant, Theory of Knowledge:
  Ms Annah Langan, MA Hons Glasgow, MA St Mary's
  Twickenham, PGCE Roehampton
Deputy Head, IB Coordinator: Mr Nicholas Marcou, BA
  Hons York, PGCE Roehampton, MA St Mary's
  Twickenham
*Assistant Head, Deputy Designated Child Protection
  Officer, English*: Ms Anna-Louise Simpson, BA Hons
  Southampton, MSc Southampton, QTS
Bursar: Mr Alan Fernandes, MBA, BSc Surrey
*Middle School Coordinator, Pastoral Life Coordinator,
  Designated Person for Child Protection*: Mrs Geraldine
  Donnelly, BA Barry (*English*)
Director of Admissions: Mrs Cheryl Eysele, BA Hons
  South Africa, Cert Further Professional Study
  Cambridge
*Chair of Theory of Knowledge, English, College
  Counsellor*: Mr Matthew Harvey, BA Hons Warwick,
  MA Hons St Mary's Twickenham, QTS Reading
Head of Boarding: Ms Tammy Parks, BA Rhodes, USA,
  MA New York, USA
Director of Development & Communications: Mrs Karin
  Purcell, BA Hons Stellenbosch South Africa

Faculty:
Mr João Barroca, BSc Hons Portugal, MBA Spain
Mr Malcolm Blake, BSc Sheffield, PGCE Reading
Dr Eamon Byers, BA Hons Belfast, MA Hons Belfast, PhD
  Belfast
Ms Raquel Cagigas, BA Spain, QTS
Ms Lorraine Clancy, BA Ireland, MSc Ireland, QTS
Mr Stephen Clarke, MA Hons Glasgow, PGCE Glasgow,
  TESOL
Ms Christiana Davidson, BA Hons South Africa, PGCE
  London
Dr Alexandre Delin, BA Brittany, MA Brittany, PGCE
  Wales, PhD Paris
Mr Joe Dodd, BA Hons UCL, MA Hons UCL
Mr James Elden, BSc Kent, PGCE Canterbury Christ
  Church Kent
Ms Sandra Forrest, BA Denison University, US, MA NYU,
  PGCPSE Open University
Ms Dolores Garcia Suarez, BA Spain, MA King's College
  London
Ms Lauren Gregory, BA Mississippi USA, MEd North
  Texas USA
Ms Linda Holland, BSc Hons QMC London, MSc
  Birkbeck, PGCE Chelsea, CBiol, MSB, FRES
Ms Kristina Hucke, BA Diplom Germany, MA London,
  PGCE Kingston, QTS Kingston
Ms Christina John, BSc Kerala, MSc Kerala, MPhil
Mr Damian Kell, MA Oxford
Ms Linda Kelly, BA Hons Bradford, PGCE Nottingham

Ms Anna Kossakowska, BSc Poland, QTS Poland
Mr Jin Seok Lee, BSc Imperial London, MPhil Cambridge
Mrs Jung Soon Lee Park, MA Ed Cheon Nan University,
  Korea
Ms Kate Martin, MA Cambridge, PGCE Roehampton
Ms Victoria Mast, BA Hons Durham, PGCE Buckingham
Ms Ana Maria Navarro, BA Spain, DipEd Spain
Ms Amy O'Brien, BSc Hons Cardiff, PGCE Roehampton
Mr John O'Farrell, BRE Dublin, MMus Dublin, MA
  London
Ms Sarah Openshaw, BA Hons Bristol, TEFL Cambridge,
  PGDip South Bank
Ms Alicia Paddon, BA Hons Cambridge, PGCE
  Roehampton
Mrs Nathalie Pengilly, BA Hons Lyon, France, MA Hons
  Lyon, France, PGCE Thames
Ms Ulrike Richter, BA Hons Sussex, MA Sussex, QTS
Mr Jerome Ripp, BA, MA Oxford, BSc Open
Mr Jim Robertson, BA Hons Kingston, QTS
Mrs Helena Sansome, BA Hons, HDipEd Dublin, BPhil
  Liverpool, MLitt Oxford
Mr Jon Santiago, BSc MIT USA
Ms Katrina Schieber, BA Queensland, Dip Ed Queensland
Mr Mitsuo Shima, BA Meiji Gakuin, Cert Japanese as a
  Foreign Language
Ms Bethany Sims, MA Cambridge, PGCE, CELTA, MA
  Sheffield, QTS
Ms Rebecca Sprowl, BA Shippenburg US, MA Boston,
  PTC, ATC, QTS
Ms Helen Szymczak, BA Dramatic Art Hons AFDA South
  Africa, ATCL, MA London
Mr Alexis White, BA Hons Oxford, PGCE St Mary's
  University
Dr Alwyn Williams, BA, MSc Hons UEL, PhD Sydney
Ms Huiping Wu, BA Liaoning, China, MA Liaoning,
  China, PGCE Westminster

Residential Houseparents:
Mrs Paula Horton, CELTA (*Assistant Head of Boarding*)
Ms Katrina Brown
Ms Jolly Chou, BSc, MSc Lancs
Ms Catherine Marshall, BPhoto, Dip Ed Griffith,
  Queensland, QTS
Ms Dervila McMorrow, BA Ireland, MA Dublin
Ms Martina Michalcova, BSc OU

Admin/Support Staff:
Mr Robert Edwards, MATT
Ms Ingrid Renshawe, BA Hons Leeds
Mrs Alison Young
Mrs Sandee Roberts
Miss Nadia Al-Akhal, BA Hons Southampton Solent
Miss Ella Tukana, BSc Hons Kent
Mr Matthew Pearce
Mr George Johnston
Mrs Maria Cardoso
Ms Christina Abreu
Ms Mina Eyarhono
Ms Celina Kwiatkowska
Ms Angelika Luciow
Ms Bozena Malinowska
Mrs Zaneta Vozarikova
Ms Celina Kwiatkowska
Mr Alberto Butcher
Mr Saleque Begh
Ms Yvonne Francis
Dr Orsolya Bellovits, PhD Eotvos Lorand Hungary
Mr Adrian Botau, BA Romania
Mr Jose Cardoso
Mr Peter Dickinson, HND Landscape & Horticultural
  Technology, BTEC Cert Management Studies
Mrs Natalja Dolman, BSc Latvia

Ms Helga Kadarne-Kalmar
Fr Christopher McAneny, MA Pittsburg
Ms Shirley Mujico, HCIMA, CIM London
Ms Sara Wilson, BSc Brunel
Ms Sarah Ross
Ms Francesca Powell, BA Hons Sussex

Mayfield School
(formerly St Leonards-Mayfield School)

The Old Palace, Mayfield, East Sussex TN20 6PH

Tel: 01435 874623 (Headmistress and Secretary)
          01435 874600 (School)
          01435 874642 (Admissions)
Fax: 01435 872627
email: enquiry@mayfieldgirls.org
website: www.mayfieldgirls.org
Twitter: @mayfieldgirls
Facebook: /mayfieldgirls

Mayfield is a lively, happy and successful School. It offers amazing opportunities, helping girls to challenge stereotypical views of what they can and should achieve. Mathematics and Science are among its most popular and successful subjects; results are consistently high at GCSE and A Level. Equally successful are subjects as diverse as Geography and Music. Mayfield also excels in creative areas: with an internationally-renowned Ceramics Department, innovative Drama and an enviable sporting tradition. Creativity is important in everything that goes on inside and outside the classroom. Girls are challenged and encouraged to look for links between subjects, and individual talents are nurtured. This leads to girls choosing an eclectic range of option choices: Chemistry and Ceramics or Physics and History of Art are not unusual A Level/Pre-U combinations. Most go on to Russell Group, Oxbridge or, increasingly, American and overseas universities, to study all manner of subjects from Architecture to Zoology, with a regular stream of Engineers, Medics and Vets, Lawyers and Economists.

Mayfield instils in each girl the confidence to find her strengths – wherever they may lie – and build on them. Staff who are experts in their field and passionate about their subjects help provide the challenge, support and inspiration each girl needs to flourish. A Mayfield girl is challenged to set herself demanding targets and helped to find strategies to achieve them. Girls are expected to think independently, to question their own and other people's ideas, and to learn to make informed decisions; mindful of the impact their actions have on the society in which they live.

The Mayfield community dates back to 1872, when Cornelia Connelly and her Society of the Holy Child Jesus opened the School, although the first School opened in 1846 and the network reaches as far afield as its sister schools in Africa, America and Europe. Traditionally it has attracted pupils from around the world, as well as locally. Such a cosmopolitan ethos helps the girls to understand and appreciate different cultures and perspectives, and to value diversity. Friendships forged at Mayfield continue not only through School, but into the future, and Mayfield proudly welcomes successive generations back.

Curriculum. The curriculum at Mayfield is designed to reflect the Catholic foundation of the School and is rooted in the convictions of its founder, Cornelia Connelly. As such, the curriculum aims to provide breadth and depth of opportunity: it is wide and varied, and all subjects within it are granted equal value within School.

Our curriculum meets the individual needs of each girl. It is designed to challenge all pupils and to extend the most able, but also support those with weaknesses in certain areas and those for whom English is a second language.

In Years 7, 8 and 9 (Key Stage 3) a rigorous curriculum is in place offering a breadth of subjects from languages such as Spanish and Mandarin, to Textiles and Ceramics; encompassing Humanities and Sciences, all taught by subject specialists. Most girls study eleven subjects at GCSE, comprising a compulsory core of eight subjects and three optional subjects chosen from a substantial list. Options blocks for both GCSE and A Level are structured around the choices of current students. The guiding principles of the A Level course at Mayfield (Years 12 and 13) continue to offer breadth and depth. Pupils choose up to five subjects at AS Level, three or four of which are then pursued at A2 Level, from a list of 31 possible options. This leads to students accepting offers from Oxbridge, American and European Universities as well as from the Russell Group.

Extra-Curricular Activities. A wide-ranging extra-curricular provision complements learning in the classroom and girls are encouraged to try new activities ranging from riding, fencing and zumba to textiles, debating and dissection. We also have a burgeoning exchange scheme with sister schools in the USA.

Our 'Actions not Words' programme, linked with our involvement in The Duke of Edinburgh's Award scheme, provides opportunities to be involved in service, both in the local community and further afield, ensuring that faith in action continues to be an important part of Mayfield life. Girls travel overseas, working with the elderly and infirm pilgrims in Lourdes, teaching English and working with disadvantaged children in Thailand and Cambodia, among other activities. We want actions to be inspired by a sense of justice and integrity, sustained by faith and respect for others.

Admission. At 11+ via the School Entrance Examination; at 13+ via the School Entrance and Scholarship Examination or Common Entrance Examination; at 14 (exceptionally) on assessment and school report; at 16+ (for Sixth Form Course) via assessment. An offer is normally conditional upon the pupil achieving at least nine GCSEs at grades A* to C, with grades A* or A in the subjects she wishes to study at A Level.

Registration fee: £125.

Fees per term (2016–2017). Full Boarders £10,600, Day girls £6,550.

Scholarships and Bursaries. Academic Scholarships and Gifted & Talented Scholarships are available for entry at 11+, 13+ and 16+. Scholars are identified through a programme of examination and assessment and are expected to show a high degree of academic aptitude, or considerable talent in one or more of Art, Dance, Drama, Music, Organ and Sport (including Riding). Scholarships are offered on merit and bring a discount of up to 25% on school fees and may be supplemented by a Means-Tested Bursary up to 100% of a day or boarding place.

Examinations and assessment for 11+, 13+ and 16+ Scholarship assessments take place in November.

Charitable status. Mayfield School is a Registered Charity, number 1047503. It exists to provide education for girls in keeping with its Catholic foundation.

Governors:
Lady Davies of Stamford, MA Oxon, MBA (*Chairman*)
Mrs Elizabeth Byrne Hill, BA, MA, PGCE (*Deputy Chairman & Chairman of Education Committee*)
Dr Christopher J Storr, KSG, MA, PhD, FRSA (*Deputy Chairman and Chairman of Governance Committee*)
Mr Chris Buxton, BA, ACA (*Chairman of Finance Committee*)
Miss Julia Bowden, BA, PGCE, MBA
Sister Maria Dinnendahl, SHCJ, BA, MA Oxon, BA, Lic Phil
Mrs Sara Hulbert-Powell, BA
Mrs Rhona Lewis, MA
Mrs Maureen Martin, BA, PGCE
Mrs Marion McGovern, BA, Cert Ed

Mrs Cloe Moody, BA
Sr Paula Thomas, SHCJ, BEd, MA
Mr Eddie Walshe, OBE, PhD, BSc

Headmistress: Miss A M Beary, MA, MPhil Cantab, PGCE

Deputy Head: Deputy Head (Pastoral & Boarding): Mrs S M Ryan, MA Oxon, MA

Senior Managers:
Director of Studies: Mrs A R Bunce, BSc, PGCE
Bursar: Lt Col {ret} A H Bayliss, MA Cantab, CEng, MICE
Head of Sixth Form: Mr J G Filkin, BA Oxon, MA, PGCE
Head of Middle School: Mrs J Stone, BSc, MSc, GTTP
Head of Lower School: Mr P F G Christian, BA Dunelm, MA, PGCE
Director of Organisation: Mrs L R Varley, MA Oxon, PGCE
Director of External Relations: Mrs T C Howard-Vyse

Teaching staff:

Art:
Miss J Thackray, BA, PGCE (*Head of Department*)
Mrs A Sivyour, BA, PGCE

Ceramics:
Mr T Rees-Moorlah, BA, PGCE, QTS (*Head of Department*)
Mrs Y McFadyean, BA
Miss J Thorn, BA (*Artist in Residence*)

Classics:
Mrs D Downing, BA, MA (*Head of Department*)
Mrs E Aherne, MA, BA Oxon
Mrs M Bushell, BA, PGCE
Mrs S Ryan, MA Oxon, MA
Dr A Towey, MA Cantab

Drama & Theatre Studies:
Mrs S Gerstmeyer, BA, GTP, QTS (*Head of Department*)
Miss J Caldwell, BA, PGCE
Miss Sophie Watkiss, BA, MA (*LAMDA*)

Economics & Business Studies:
Mrs A Cox, BSc, PGCE (*Head of Department*)
Mrs C Bryan, BA, MA, PGCE

English:
Mrs N Evans, BA, PGCE (*Head of Department*)
Mrs L Parrett, BA, PGCE, MSc (*Deputy Head of Department*)
Mrs E Aherne, MA, BA Oxon
Mrs C Cox, BA Oxon, PGCE
Mrs E Crawley, BA, PGCE, Cert SpLD, EYPS
Mr J Filkin, BA Oxon, MA, PGCE
Mrs J Foley, BA, PG Dip Ed
Mrs J Leslie, BA, PGCE

ESOL:
Mrs J D Sandoval, MA, DipTEFLA (*Head of Department*)
Mrs A Maimi, BA, CELTA, QTS
Mrs K Kilvington, BA, MA Oxon, MSc, DipTEFLA

Food & Nutrition:
Mrs C Davies, CNAA, BEd, PGCE (*Head of Department*)
Mrs S Rothero, BEd, CertEd

Geography:
Mr S Gough, BSc, PGCE (*Head of Department*)
Mrs V Williams, BA, MA, MSc, PGCE, QTS
Mrs F Morris, BEd

History:
Mr D Warren, BA, PGCE (*Head of Department*)
Mrs M Bushell, BA, PGCE

History of Art:
Mrs J Weddell, BA Arch, MA (*Head of Department*)
Mr J Davis, ARHistS, PGCE, Dip Counselling, MBACP

Information Technology:
Miss L Jackson, BA, QTS, Dip RSA (*Years 7–11 Head of Department*) {maternity leave from Nov 2016}
Mr J Ashby, BEng QTS {maternity cover from Nov 2016}
Mr S Gough, BSc, PGCE (*Years 12 and 13 Head of Department*)

Learning Support:
Mrs J Foley, BA, PG, DipEd (*Head of Department*)
Miss S Benson, BA, PGCE, PGCiPP, MA
Mrs P Bryer, HLTA
Mrs D Colebeck, BA
Mrs Z Sargent, BA Oxon, PGCE

Librarian:
Mrs J Gabriel, BA, MA

Mathematics:
Mrs A Pullinger, BSc, PGCE (*Head of Department*)
Miss A Demetriou, BSc, PGCE (*Deputy Head of Department*)
Mr W Clarke, BSc, PGCE
Mrs S Howie, BSc, PGCE
Dr E Keyman, BSc, MSc, DPhil, QTS
Mrs L Motoc, BSc, PGCE
Mrs J Stone, BSc, MSc, PGCE

Modern Languages:
Mrs R Boumediene, BA PGCE (*Head of French*)
Ms M Criado, BA, PGCE (*Head of Spanish*)
Mrs A von Wulffen, MA Oxon, PGCE (*Head of German*)
Mrs A Boyle, BA
Mrs A Fernandez, BA, CAP
Mrs A Maimi, BA, CELTA, QTS
Mlle C Richard, BA, MA, MA, PGCE
Mrs B Santini, Dip di Laurea Pisa
Mrs C Smith, BA, PGCE

Music:
Mr P Collins, GRSM, LRAM, ARCM, PGCE (*Director of Music*)
Miss L Barrett, BA, PGCE
plus c.20 visiting music teachers

Physical Education:
Mrs G Fletcher, BA, MA, PGCE (*Head of Department*)
Miss S Evans, BA, QTS, Dip RSA (*Deputy Head of Department*)
Miss S Auer, BA, PGCE
Mrs J Jones, BA, QTS, Dip RSA
Mrs H Miller, BA, PGCE
Mrs F Morris, BEd
Miss C Povey, BA, QTS
Mrs P Whitby, BA, QTS

Politics:
Ms C Bryan, BA, MA, PGCE (*Head of Department*)

Psychology:
Mrs D Buchner, BA, HDE, BA, CBT Diploma (*Head of Department*)
Mrs P Tysh, BA, PGCE

Religious Studies:
Dr D Coughlan, MSt Oxon, MA PhD Cantab (*Head of Department*)
Mr S Cahill, BTh Oxon, PGCE
Mr P Christian, BA Dunelm, MA, PGCE
Miss T A Rakowska, BSc, PGCE
Mrs C Smith, BA, PGCE
Mrs E Warnett, BA, MA, PGCE

Riding:
Miss J Barker, BEd, BHSII J, CertEd (*Director of Riding*)

Sciences:
Mrs J Mahon, BSc, PGCE (*Head of Biology and overall Head of Science*)
Ms A Mistry, BSc, PGCE, MA (*Head of Chemistry*)
Mr J Ashby, BEng QTS
Mr D Bullock, BSc, MA, PGCE
Mrs S Buckle, BSc, GCE
Mrs A R Bunce, BSc PGCE
Mrs R Davies, BSc, PGCE
Mrs J Gradon, BA Cantab, PGCE
Miss R Jackson, BSc Dunelm, PGCE
Miss T A Rakowska, BSc, PGCE
Mrs L Varley, MA Oxon, PGCE

Textiles:
Mrs T Budden, Dip Fashion Design & Construction (*Head of Department*)
Mrs H Robertson

Technicians:
Mrs E Brown, MI Biology (*Biology*)
Mrs S Chapman (*Food & Nutrition*)
Mr J Fuggle (*Ceramics*)
Mrs J Mackenzie HNC Medical Microbiology (*Chemistry*)
Miss H Oliver (*Art*)
Mrs J Pyett (*Physics*)

Careers Coordinator: Mrs G Fletcher, BA, MA, PGCE
Examinations Officer: Mr A Welford
Gifted & Talented Coordinator: Mrs K Kilvington, BA, MA Oxon, MSc, DipTEFLA

Housemistresses, Pastoral & Medical staff:

Leeds House (Years 7 and 8):
Mrs Elizabeth Crawley, BA, PGCE, Cert SpLD, EYPS (*Housemistress*)
Miss P Kotesovska (*House Matron*)

Connelly House (Years 9 and 10):
Mrs J Roberts, HND, CertEd (*Housemistress*)
Mrs C Jones (*House Matron*)

Gresham House (Year 11):
Mrs S Buckle, BSc, GCE (*Housemistress*)
Mrs J Mead (*House Matron shared with St Dunstan's*)
Miss C Povey, BA (*Assistant Housemistress*)

St Dunstan's House (Years 12 and 13):
Mrs C Smith, BA, PGCE (*Housemistress*)
Mrs J Mead (*House Matron shared with Gresham*)
Miss S Benson (*Assistant Housemistress*)

Graduate Assistants:
Miss L Allinson, BSc
Miss R Bennion, BA, MRes

School Doctor:
Dr A Fyfe, Woodhill Surgery, Mayfield

Senior Nurses:
Mrs D Streeter, RGN
Ms A Winter, RGN, RSCN
Mrs C Slade, RCN

Sixth Form:
Head: Mr J Filkin, BA Oxon, MA, PGCE
Deputy Head: Ms C Bryan, BA, MA, PGCE
Senior Tutor: Mrs V Williams, BA, MA, MSc, PGCE, QTS

Middle School:
Head: Mrs J Stone, BSc, MSc, PGCE
Year 9 Senior Tutor: Miss L Jackson, BA, QTS, Dip RSA
  [Mrs R Testa, BA, PGCE from Nov 2016]

Year 10 Senior Tutor: Mrs K Kilvington, BA, MA Oxon, MSc, DipTEFLA
Year 11 Senior Tutor: Mrs A Maimi, BA, CELTA, QTS

Lower School:
Head: Mr P Christian, BA Dunelm, MA, PGCE
Senior Tutor: Mrs P Whitby, BA, QTS

Chaplaincy:
Lay Chaplain: Miss P Cronin, MA
Resident Priest: (*to be appointed*)

Society of the Holy Child Jesus (at Mayfield):
Sr Teresa Joseph Barret
Sr Maria Dinnendahl
Sr Jean Sinclair

The Maynard School
(Sir John Maynard's Foundation)

Denmark Road, Exeter, Devon EX1 1SJ
Tel: 01392 355998
Fax: 01392 355999
email: admissions@maynard.co.uk
website: www.maynard.co.uk
Twitter: @MaynardSchool
Facebook: @The-Maynard-School
LinkedIn: /the-maynard-school

The Maynard is a selective independent day school in Exeter, for girls aged 4–18. We are the third oldest girls' school in the country, founded in 1658 by Sir John Maynard. Girls and boys learn differently and we are experts in educating girls; our long history is testament to our ability to bring out the best in each and every one of them.

Ethos. A dynamic and supportive community, The Maynard is committed to excellence in providing learning opportunities that inspire and challenge. Students will demonstrate creativity, be socially responsible and through their shared experience, become independent and reflective learners. A wide-ranging extra-curricular programme enables students to achieve in all aspects of school life. Pastoral care is a vital component to ensure every student is valued. Students achieve highly in all public examinations.

Numbers. There are approximately 370 day girls in the School, of whom 80 are in the Junior School and 80 in the Sixth Form.

School Buildings. The School is situated in an attractive conservation area five minutes from the centre of the city. The extensive buildings include a separate Sixth Form Centre; a purpose-built block for Science, Mathematics, and Computing; well-equipped Food & Nutrition and Textiles Rooms; Music and Art Rooms, a large Gymnasium, and an impressive Sports Hall which provides full-scale indoor facilities. The Junior School and Pre-Prep is situated within the grounds and is fully equipped for the education of girls aged 4–11 years.

Curriculum. The curriculum is academically rigorous and maintains a good balance between Arts and Science subjects. English, Mathematics, the Sciences and Sport are particular strengths; full scope is given to creative and practical activities, as well as ICT skills. The School prepares all girls for University, including Oxford and Cambridge. A carefully developed programme of careers advice, begun at 11+ and continuing through to the Sixth Form, ensures that all pupils are individually guided in subject options with their long-term career interests at heart. The Maynard Aspire programme is an enrichment initiative for high achieving students in Upper 5 (Year 11) and the Sixth Form who are ready to develop their skills in a wider context as they make decisions about their future career paths.

Examinations. Candidates normally take 10 subjects at GCSE and 3 at A Level. Students are fully prepared for Oxford and Cambridge University Entrance.

Physical Education. Hockey (outdoor and indoor), Netball, Badminton, Basketball, Volleyball, Fencing, Dance and Gymnastics are offered in the winter terms; Tennis and Rounders are played in the Summer Term. Training is given in Athletics and Swimming is part of the normal timetable for all girls during the Summer Term. Besides its excellent indoor facilities and the three hard courts in its own grounds, the School has access to a playing field a short walk away and is close to three swimming pools and an Astroturf playing area. The school has an extensive fixture programme in Netball, Hockey, Indoor Hockey, Badminton, Basketball, Tennis, Swimming, Athletics and Rounders. Teams have regularly reached national standard. In addition, The Maynard has a strong extra-curricular programme of outdoor pursuits including the Ten Tors, the Duke of Edinburgh's Award and Exmoor Challenge.

Admission. All admissions, except sixth form, are subject to an Entrance Assessment graduated according to age and held in January each year for entry in the following September.

Fees per term (2016–2017). Pre-Prep: Reception £1,800, Years 1–2 £2,200; Junior School: Year 3 £3,200, Years 4–5 £3,400; Senior School: Years 6–13 £4,195. Fees include wrap-around care 8.00 am to 5.30 pm.

There is a generous Sibling Discount Scheme.

Scholarships and the Maynard Award Programme. A range of Academic, Sport, Music and Creative Arts Scholarships are available for senior school entry at 11+ and 13+. Sixth Form Scholarships are available: for Academic, Sport, Creative Arts and Music. In addition the Maynard Award Programme is a new initiative which offers opportunities to girls from all sectors of the community. A total of 19 Maynard Awards are available for students joining the school in September 2017 at any age from Year 7 to Lower Sixth.

Further Information. The Prospectus and Scholarship and Maynard Awards information are available from the Admissions Office. Visitors are very welcome by appointment, and tours and taster days can be arranged for girls considering the school.

Old Maynardians. Email: RachaelBoard@maynard.co.uk.

Charitable status. The Maynard School is a Registered Charity, number 1099027. It exists to provide quality education for girls.

Governors:

Appointed by the Governing Body of St John's Hospital:
Mr Simon Gregory
Mr Henry Luce
Lady Jan Stanhope
Ms Sarah Witheridge

Co-opted by the Governors:
Lady Jan Stanhope (*Chair*)
Ms Mandy Pearse
Mrs Sarah Pritchard
Mrs Lynn Turner

Appointed by Devon County Council:
Mr Peter Bowden

Appointed by Exeter City Council:
Mr Norman Shiel

Appointed by the University of Exeter:
Ms Jilly Court
Prof Robin Mason

Staff Governors:
Mrs Sian Fanous
Mrs Cathy Gabbitass

Parent Governors:
Lt Col Nick Bruce-Jones
Mr Paul Morrish

Ex officio:
The Right Worshipful, The Lord Mayor of Exeter

Headmistress: Miss S Dunn, BSc Exeter

Deputy Head: Mrs P Wilks, MA Oxford (*History*)
Head of Sixth Form: Mr T Hibberd, MA Cambridge
Director of Studies: Dr P Rudling, MA Cambridge, MSc, PhD Exeter
Head of Junior School: Mr S Smerdon, BEd Exeter
Bursar & Clerk to the Governors: Mr P Hammond, BSc Warwick

Teaching Staff:

Full-time:
Mr Barry Anderson, BSc Hons Birmingham, QTS Hertfordshire (*Science*)
Ms J Bellamy, BA Manchester (*Drama*)
Miss A Blackwell, BA, MA Durham, LTCL (*Director of Music & Performing Arts*)
Mrs A Briscoe, BA Hons Sussex (*English*) [Maternity Leave]
Mrs L Burt, BA Hons Plymouth (*Head of Computing*)
Mrs A Cox, MA Bristol (*Classics*)
Mrs W Dersley, BSc Open University (*Mathematics*)
Mrs Ria Fabian, BSc Exeter, PGCE Exeter (*Physical Education*)
Mrs S Fanous, BEd Keele (*Food & Nutrition/Textiles*)
Miss K Gwynne, MTheol St Andrews, ThM Princeton (*Religious Studies*)
Mrs R Halse, BA University of Arizona (*Spanish*)
Mr S Hardes, BSc Hons Essex, MA Bath (*Chemistry*)
Mrs K Harvey, BSc Bristol, MEd Exeter (*Geography*)
Dr L Hawtree, MA, PhD Exeter, MA St Andrews (*Classics*)
Mrs A J Horton, BSc Exeter (*Mathematics*)
Dr L Keen, MA, PhD Exeter, MA St Andrews (*Classics*)
Mrs S Kerrane, BSc Swansea (*Biology*)
Mrs R Khreisheh, BA Oxford (*Junior School*)
Ms Katy Lavelle, BSc Birmingham, PG DipEd Birmingham (*Physical Education*)
Mr Matt Loosemore, BA Southampton, PGCE Exeter (*English*)
Mr I Macdonals, BSc Sussex (*Chemistry & Physics*)
Mrs A Meaton, BA Ed, Southampton (*Pre-Prep*)
Dr P Merisi, MPhil, PhD Exeter (*Mathematics*)
Mr D O'Neill, BA York (*German & French*)
Mrs I Powell, BSc, MSc Rennes (*French*)
Mrs H Reynolds, BSc Open University (*Junior School*)
Mr P Richards, LLB Southampton (*Lead Teacher of Economics*)
Mr C Ridler, MA Hons Warwick (*Physics*)
Mrs C Rowe, DipEd Edinburgh (*Junior School*)
Mr J Tabb, BA London (*History & Geography*)
Mrs S Thorne, BSc Nottingham (*Chemistry, Biology*)
Miss N Wintle , BA Ed Hons Exeter, National SENCO Masters Level Qualification (*SENCO*)
Mrs S Wood, BA Ed Exeter (*Physical Education & Mathematics*)
Mrs Z Vingoe, BA Manchester Metropolitan (*Art*)

Part-time:
Mrs C L Austin, GRSM, LRAM (*Music*)
Mrs C Finnegan, BA Central Saint Martins (*Food & Nutrition/Textiles*)
Mrs C Flavelle, BA, MA Cambridge (*History*)
Mrs K Fry, BEd Exeter (*Junior School*)
Mrs C M Gabbitass, BSc Loughborough (*Physical Education*)

Mr A Ganley, BA Nottingham (*Drama*)
Mrs C Gorrod, BA Surrey (*Junior School*)
Ms A M Hurley, MA London (*Art*)
Mrs E Kilkelly, BA Exeter (*Religious Studies*)
Mrs R Khreisheh, BA Oxford (*Junior School*)
Mrs B Knight, BEd Cambridge Institution of Education (*SENCO*)
Mrs D Lewis, BA Cheltenham (*Geography, Examinations Officer*)
Miss T Lothingland, MA Exeter (*EFL*)
Mrs V Martin, BA Hull (*English*)
Mr P Pienkowski, BSc London (*Economics*)
Mrs A Rowley, BA Liverpool (*English*)
Mrs C Smith, MA Tours (*French/Spanish*)
Mrs A Weeks, BSc Loughborough (*Physics*)
Mrs S Woolley, MA Oxford (*Study Skills & Learning Support*)
Mrs V Woulfe, BSc Keele (*Mathematics*)

Non-Teaching Staff:
Mrs S Arnold (*Assistant Chef*)
Mr A Ayre (*Chef Manager*)
Mrs G Baker (*Kitchen Assistant*)
Ms M Beach (*Junior School Teaching Assistant*)
Mr D Bratt (*Gardener*)
Mrs E Bremner (*Marketing and Development Assistant*)
Mrs R Board, BA Warwick (*Press and Alumnae Relations*)
Mrs J Burston (*Kitchen Assistant*)
Mrs J Conway, BSc Southampton (*Marketing and Development Manager*)
Mrs J Crowley (*Assistant Secretary*)
Mrs M Davey (*Junior Department Support Assistant*)
Mrs Rusha El-Nashar, MA Edinburgh (*PA to Deputy Head & Director of Studies*)
Mr M Everhard (*Estate Dept*)
Mrs A Farndell (*Bursar's Assistant*)
Mrs S Gardner (*Senior Finance Manager*)
Mrs M Green (*Bursar's Assistant*)
Mrs H Halpin, BSc Surrey (*Resources Manager*)
Mrs W Holt, BEng Plymouth (*Science Technician*)
Mrs J Hourihan, BSc Birmingham, BA Hons Open University, PG Dip Information & Library Studies Robert Gordon University (*Assistant Librarian*)
Mrs J Jephson (*Art Technician*)
Mrs K Jones (*Kitchen Assistant*)
Miss Lora Jones (*Head's PA*)
Miss K Kovacova (*Cleaner*)
Mrs D Lees (*Pastoral Secretary*)
Mrs M Jones, BA Derby (*Registrar*)
Mrs S McLoughlin (*Reception*)
Mrs L Mitchell (*Chemistry Technician*)
Mrs Lisa Oldfield (*School Administrator*)
Mrs W Parker (*Admissions Administrator*)
Mrs J Piatkowska (*Cleaner*)
Mr K Pomeroy (*Estates Manager*)
Mrs F Prior-Palmer (*School Nurse*)
Mr B Pugh (*Cleaning Supervisor*)
Mrs J Pugh (*Assistant Cleaning Supervisor*)
Mr M Reid (*Multimedia Creative Manager*)
Mrs J Ridehalgh, BA Warwick (*Marketing & Development Assistant*)
Mrs K Sanders (*Resources Assistant*)
Mrs J Slade (*Kitchen Assistant*)
Mrs A Tancock (*Reception & Office*)
Mrs J Thomas (*Strategic Development Manager*)
Mrs A Trevallion (*Pre-Prep & Junior School Teaching Assistant*)
Mrs J Wallis (*Kitchen Assistant*)
Miss J Watson (*Pre-Prep & Junior School Teaching Assistant*)
Mr J Wicksteed, BSc St Andrews (*IT Systems Manager*)

Mrs H Wright (*Science Technician*)

Visiting Staff:
Mrs F Austen (*Harp*)
Mrs C Austin, GRSM, LRAM (*Oboe*)
Mrs R Allsop, BEd (*Clarinet*)
Ms A Baker (*Head Hockey Coach*)
Mrs S Barlow (*Ballet*)
Miss C Bradley (*Cello*)
Mrs D Broomfield (*Choirs*)
Mrs E Bucci (*Netball Coach*)
Dr H Catterick (*Kick-Boxing/Martial Arts Instructor*)
Mr J Childs (*Hockey Coach*)
Mr D Cottam, AGSM (*Guitar*)
Mrs A Cox (*Street Dance Instructor*)
Mrs H Edwards (*Netball Coach*)
Mrs N Fitzgerald (*Badminton Coach*)
Miss N Fowler (*Zumba Instructor*)
Dr E Grier (*Harp*)
Mr J Hamilton (*Tennis Coach*)
Mrs J Hannah, LGSM (*Flute*)
Mrs A Higgins, ARCM (*Piano, Bassoon*)
Ms E Highton, BA, ALCM, LTCL (*Piano, Flute*)
Mrs S Hill, BMus Hons Cardiff (*Singing and Flute*)
Miss M Hiley, Dip RCM (*Percussion*)
Miss A Kettlewell (*Singing*)
Mr N Lawrence (*Voice*)
Mrs P Leonard, NCSD, LUD (*Speech & Drama*)
Mrs F Maclean-Buechel (*Violin, Viola*)
Mr A Nuthall (*Brass*)
Mr T Parker (*Badminton Coach*)
Mr C Pettet (*Singing*)
Mr R Porch (*Piano Tuner*)
Mr J Rycroft (*Lead Tennis Coach*)
Mr R Taverner, ARCM (*Piano*)
Mrs A Tillson-Hawke, BA, LTCL (*Violin, Viola*)
Miss C Warren, BA Hons, PG Dip, LRSM (*Cello*)
Ms I Woollcott (*Double Bass*)
Mr C Worcester (*Basketball Coach*)

Merchant Taylors' Girls' School Crosby

80 Liverpool Road, Crosby, Liverpool L23 5SP

Tel: 0151 924 3140
Fax: 0151 932 1461
email: admissionsmtgs@merchanttaylors.com
website: www.merchanttaylors.com
Twitter: @MerchantsCrosby
Facebook: /merchanttaylorscrosby

Motto: *Concordia Parvae Res Crescunt*

The Senior Girls' School was opened in 1888 on the site which had been occupied by the Boys' School for over 350 years. The original grey stone building, erected in 1620, is still in daily use as the Library. Over the years extensions have been made to include a Fitness Suite, Science Laboratories and a Sixth Form Centre. The Centenary Hall provides ample accommodation for concerts, plays and sports. The School is beautifully situated approximately 8 miles from Liverpool and within 10 minutes' walk of the Sefton coastline. There are netball and tennis courts on the premises with a playing field and the joint schools' multimillion pound sports centre, opened in 2011, is situated further down the road on the Boys' School site. The Centre incorporates a Sports Hall suitable for a variety of indoor sports, dance and fitness studios, a refreshment area and classrooms.

A new entrance was built in 2009 to include a new reception area and an art gallery space called The Vitreum. This gallery has been used to showcase pupils' work as well as exhibitions from local, national and international artists.

Merchant Taylors' is a family of Schools. There is a separate Primary School, 'Stanfield', situated in a self-contained building near to the Main School with girls aged 4–11 and boys aged 4–7. This recently underwent a £5.5 million redevelopment which was completed in December 2014. The Senior Girls' School age range is 11–18. There are at present 944 pupils at both schools.

The girls receive a broad academic education. Subjects included in the curriculum are Art, Biology, Chemistry, Classics, Drama and Theatre Studies, Economics, English Language and English Literature, French, Geography, German, Government and Politics, History, Home Economics, Information Technology, Latin, Mathematics, Music, Physical Education, Physics, Psychology, Religious Studies and Spanish.

Fees per term (2016–2017). Tuition: Senior School £3,650; Junior School £2,728, Infant School (ages 4–7) £2,701.

Examinations. Pupils are prepared for their GCSE and A Level examinations.

The Music Examinations taken are those of the Associated Board of the Royal Schools of Music, The London College of Music, Trinity Guildhall.

Parent Teachers' Association. *Chairperson:* Helen Ashton, c/o The School.

Old Girls' Association. *Hon Secretary:* Mrs S Duncan, 'Fairhaven', The Serpentine South, Liverpool L23 6UQ.

Charitable status. The Merchant Taylors' Schools Crosby is a Registered Charity, number 1125485, and a Company Limited by Guarantee, registered in England, number 6654276. Registered Office: Liverpool Road, Crosby, Liverpool L23 0QP.

Governors:
Chair: Mrs B Bell, LLB Hons FCILT FRSA FSOE FIRTE
Mr P G Magill, MSc, FCIPD
Miss A M Dobie, BA Hons
Mr S A Wilkinson, BA Hons, FCA
Mr D S Evans, MA Oxon
Ms L C Martin Wright
Dr J Fox, MBCh Birm, DRCOG, MRCGP
Mr J Sutcliffe, BEng Hons, CEng, MICE, MRICS, MCIOB
Mr C Williams, FCA FIMC

Clerk to the Governors: Mrs Jan Baccino
Accounts: Mr David Norton

Headmistress: Mrs L A Robinson, BA Hons York, PGCE, NPQH, MEd Liverpool

First Deputy Headmistress: Miss J Tyndall, BD Hons/AKC King's College London, PGCE

Deputy Headmistress: Mrs M L Bush, MA Liverpool, BMus Hons Wales, FRSA, NPQH, PGCE

School Staff:

Art & Craft:
Mr M Gill, BA Hons Newcastle upon Tyne, MA Royal Academy, PGCE, RA Schools PG Dip Painting
Miss L McWatt, BA Hons UWE Bristol, PGCE

Biology:
Mrs J Johnson, MA Oxon, BSc OU, PGCE, FSB
Ms N Houghton, BSc Hons, PGCE
Mr J S Jones, BSc Hons Liverpool, PGCE
Miss J Burns, BSc Hons, PGCE

Business Studies:
Mrs A H Irwin, BA Hons UCLAN Preston, PGCE
Mr F Lawell, MA Hons, PGCE

Careers Coordinator:
Mrs V Mee, BA Hons

Chemistry:
Mrs B Miller, BSc Hons Bristol, PGCE
Dr M McWatt, PhD Birmingham, BSc Hons Birmingham
Mrs L Syms, BSc Hons Central Lancashire, PGCE
Mrs V Copley, MChem Hons Manchester, PGCE

Classics:
Mr D Lamb, MA Liverpool, BA Hons Liverpool, PGCE
Mrs A Wadsworth, BA Hons Durham, PGCE
Miss J Johnson, MA, BA Hons, PGCE

Drama & Theatre Studies:
Ms S Tickle, BA ORD Manchester, PGCE

English:
Mrs J Cecil, BA Joint Hons Aberystwyth, DipEd Liverpool, PGCE
Mrs M Myring, MPhil Bangor, BA Hons UCNW, MA SDUC
Mrs E Neophytou, BA Birmingham, PGCE
Mrs A Hickey, MEd, BA Hons, PGCE

Geography:
Mrs C Mason, BSc Hons Manchester, PGCE
Mrs H M Peppin, BSc Hons Leeds, PGCE
Mrs R Hames, BSc Hons Leeds, PGCE

Gifted and Talented Coordinators:
Mrs R Hames, BSc Hons Leeds, PGCE (*Years 7–10*)
Mrs S Heywood, MA Oxon, PGCE (*Years 11–13*)

History & Politics:
Mrs C Grindley, BA Hons Leeds, PGCE
Mr G Evans, BA Hons Hull, PGCE
Mrs S Heywood, MA Oxon, PGCE

Home Economics:
Ms M Hutchins, BA Hons Newcastle-Upon-Tyne, PGCE
Mrs B Jones, BEd Liverpool

Information Technology:
Mr J Power, BEd Hons, PGCE

Librarian:
Mrs A Barry, BLib Aberystwyth, MCLIP, Dip Arc, Trinity Cert TESOL

LDD Coordinator:
Miss L Rimmer, BSc Hons Lancaster

Mathematics:
Mr M Wood, BSc Hons Aberystwyth, MSc Dundee, PGCE
Mrs H F Hurst, BSc Joint Hons Keele, PGCE
Mrs E Tickle, MEng Durham, PGCE
Miss C Hampson, BSc Hons, PGCE
Mrs R Fisher, MMath Hons, BSc Hons, PGCE

Modern Languages:
Mrs C Y Whalley, BA Hons Leeds, PGCE
Mrs J Doyle, BA Hons Nottingham, PGCE
Mme P Mistry, Licence Lettres University of Metz, PGCE
Mr F Rubia, BA Hons
Mrs C Southworth, BA Joint Hons Bristol, PGCE
Miss E Hutchinson, MA, BA Hons, PGCE
Mrs Y Blagbrough, MA
Mlle E Batardiere, Masters FLE

Music:
Mr S Newlove, BA Hons, MMus, PGCE
Mrs M L Bush, MA Liverpool, BMus Hons Wales, FRSA, NPQH, PGCE

Visiting and Part-time Music Staff:
Miss J A Carr (*Voice*)
Miss S Hayes (*Voice*)
Mr S Lock (*Clarinet, Saxophone*)

Mr B Johnson (*Flute, Oboe*)
Mr D Bridge (*Guitar*)
Miss L Gregg (*Percussion*)
Mr D Byles (*Percussion*)
Miss D O'Hara (*Piano*)
Mrs J Richards (*Cello, Double Bass*)
Mrs L Mycock (*Violin, Viola, Flute*)
Mr C Jones (*Clarinet, Saxophone*)
Mr M Palmer (*Brass*)

Physical Education:
Mrs E Moore, BEd Hons Liverpool
Miss L Taylor, BSc Hons, PGCE
Mrs L Barker, BA Hons

Physics:
Mrs H Heaton, BSc Hons Durham, PGCE
Mr P Price, BSc Hons Leeds, PGCE
Mrs J Lynch, BSc Hons, PGCE

PSHE Coordinator:
Mrs N Houghton, BSc Hons Liverpool John Moores, PGCE

Psychology:
Miss S Ladbrook, BSc Hons Central Lancashire
Mr B Wilson, BA Hons St David's Lampeter, PGCE

Religious Studies:
Mrs G Vaughan, BA Hons Manchester, PGCE
Mr B Wilson, BA Hons St David's Lampeter, PGCE
Miss J Tyndall, BD Hons/AKC London, PGCE

Marketing and Admissions:
Marketing & Development Director: Miss M J Riches, BA Hons
Admissions Officer: Mrs S Barrington

Administration:
PA to Headmistress: Mrs J Baccino
School Secretary: Mrs A Regan
Receptionist: Mrs J Price
Examinations: Mrs M Surridge
Examinations Secretary: Mrs G Hurst
Computer Network Manager: Mr S Coughlan, BSc Hons
New Media and ICT Technician: Mr A Heighway-Sephton
Central Reprographics Manager: Miss L Tickle MA, BA Hons Liverpool
Central Reprographics Assistants: Mrs A Bramhall, Mr A Best, Mr D Crompton
Lab Technicians: Mrs S Lacy (*Senior Lab Technician*), Mr D Borrows, Mrs L Wynne
School Nurse: Miss A Dalton, RGN, RSCN, Dip Child Health

Merchant Taylors' Primary School, 'Stanfield':
Head of School: Miss J E Yardley, BA Hons Liverpool, PGCE, NPQH
Deputy Head: Miss E Lynan, BA Hons, PGCE, MAST Maths Specialist Teacher

Mrs L Baker, BA Hons
Miss V Beckerleg, BA Hons Leeds
Mrs J Birtwistle, BA Hons Loughborough
Mrs K Bonner, BA Hons London, MA Brighton
Mr L Crewe
Mrs L Cunningham
Mrs S Curwen, BEd Hons Lancaster
Mrs C Darbyshire, BTech Child Ed (*Nursery Nurse*)
Mrs A Dunne, BSc Hons Coventry, MBA Open University (*Teaching Assistant*)
Mrs C Evans (*Netball Coach*)
Mrs S Garforth, BEd Hons Lancaster
Mrs K Higham, BA Hons
Mrs A-L Hodkinson (*Swimming Coach*)
Miss H Jack

Mrs R Loan, BA Hons Nottingham
Mrs S McEvoy, BA Hons
Mrs A Nagy, BEd Liverpool
Mrs C Oakes, BA Hons Manchester
Mrs J O'Mahony, BA, CertEd Lancaster
Mrs L Ramsdale, BA Hons
Mrs B Richardson, BEd London
Miss E Riding, BA Hons QTS
Mr T Roberts, BA Hons Dunelm, ATCL
Mrs M Silverman, BA Hons Liverpool
Mrs S Taylor, BEd Leeds
Miss C Watkin, BA Hons Lancaster (*Head of EYFS*)
Mrs S Ryan, NNEB (*Nursery Nurse*)
Mrs A Saunders, Teaching Degree (*Nursery Nurse*)
Miss E Williams (*Nursery Nurse*)
Miss H Callaway

Admissions Officer and Head's PA: Mrs M Langham
Receptionist: Mrs N McKie-Thomson
ICT Coordinator: Mrs A Coughlan, HNC Computing
Activities Manager: Miss L Harper
Kitchen Manager: Mrs M Hughes

Visiting Music Staff:
Miss H Burgoyne (*Piano*)
Mr T Evans (*Flute, Clarinet, Saxophone, Oboe*)
Mrs J Richards (*Cello and Double Bass*)
Mrs S Rookyard (*Singing*)
Mr D Elliott (*Guitar*)

Moira House Girls School

Upper Carlisle Road, Eastbourne, East Sussex BN20 7TE

Tel: 01323 644144
Fax: 01323 649720
email: admissions@moirahouse.co.uk
website: www.moirahouse.co.uk
Twitter: @moirahouse1875
Facebook: @moirahouse

Motto: *Nemo A Me Alienus*

Foundation. Moira House was founded in 1875 in Surrey. The School moved to its present site in 1887. The founders, Mr and Mrs Charles Ingham, were regarded in their time as gifted pioneers in the field of female education. In 1947 the School became an Educational Trust.

Situation and Facilities. Situated on high ground in Eastbourne with views over the sea, the grounds open directly onto the Downs which provide magnificent walking country and offer opportunities for expedition work and field studies. There are extensive playing fields with facilities for Tennis, Cricket, Soccer, Hockey, Netball and Athletics, a 25-metre indoor heated swimming pool and an excellent all-weather sports hall. Each subject has its own resource base. Eastbourne is a thriving cultural centre containing 3 theatres, an art gallery and a concert hall.

Faith. The School is interdenominational.

Organisation. *Prep & Pre-Prep Departments* (IAPS): The Prep & Pre-Prep Departments have provision for 120 day girls. We offer boarding starting from the age of 9. (*See Prep & Pre-Prep Departments entry in IAPS section.*) Our Nursery welcomes boys and girls and we also have a Baby Unit.

Senior School: The Senior School has provision for 140 boarders and 150 day girls.

Boarding Houses: There are two boarding houses, one of which is dedicated to Sixth Form students with single and twin study-bedrooms. Each house has a team combining resident staff and house mothers. Emphasis is placed upon a full range of extracurricular activities, both in the evenings and at weekends.

Curriculum. *Prep & Pre-Prep Departments*: We offer a wide curriculum, whilst preparing for transfer to the Senior School.

Senior School: The formal academic courses follow a broad curriculum offering 22 subjects leading to GCSE, AS and A Level and University Entrance. At GCSE we offer English Language, English Literature, Mathematics, Business Studies, Biology, Chemistry, Physics, Computing, French, German, Spanish, Latin, History, Geography, Religious Studies, Music, Economics, Mandarin, Photography, Drama, Art and Design, Design/Technology, Physical Education and Food Technology.

Sixth Form: A Levels are offered in Art, Craft and Design, Biology, Business Studies, Chemistry, Theatre Studies, Economics, English Literature, Further Mathematics, Geography, History, ICT (Applied), French, German, Spanish, Latin, Mathematics, Music, Photography, Physical Education, Physics, Psychology, and Religious Studies.

Careers Counselling. We have a strong programme of Careers Counselling, led by our Careers Counsellor.

Drama and Music. Drama and Music have always been strengths of Moira House. We are aware of the part Speech and Drama play in the development of clear communication and creative expression. There are a number of School productions and concerts each year, and school choirs take part in performances throughout Sussex. We also enter the local festival of Music and Drama and proximity to Glyndebourne gives girls a chance to have their first taste of opera at an early age. As well as regular class music lessons, there is every opportunity to learn a musical instrument, and the exams of the various musical examining bodies are taken. There is also a state-of-the-art recording studio. There are also overseas tours, most recently a Paris music tour.

Physical Education and Sport. We provide excellent new facilities. The main sports are Swimming, Netball, Tennis, Athletics and Hockey, and teams represent the School in these and in cricket and football. In addition, coaching is given in Sailing, Riding, Squash, Dance, Golf and Badminton, to name a few.

Activities. Activities are considered an essential part of the curriculum. Many activities are offered, including: Drama, Music, Trampolining, Pottery, Chess, Local History, Sailing, Down-walking, Environmental Studies, Poetry/Play Reading, Table Tennis, Duke of Edinburgh's Award, Mandarin, Japanese, and Debating. Girls are also encouraged to be aware of the needs of others. Senior girls work regularly with local charities. There are annual expeditions both within this country and to Europe and the School has links with French, German and international schools of a similar nature to ours.

Health. The school doctor holds regular surgeries at the School and there are Sisters in charge of the health centre.

Entry. Entry is by interview and review of previous school reports and references. Admission to the Prep & Pre-Prep Departments at any age; to the Senior School usually at 11–13+ and 16+.

Scholarships and Bursaries. Academic Scholarships are awarded annually for admission to Years 3 to 12. Prep Department candidates have assessments in the Prep Department and are also interviewed by the Principal.

In addition, the School offers Music, Art, Drama and Sport Exhibitions to candidates who are especially gifted in these disciplines, and these are awarded on the basis of an audition or practical assessment. Where appropriate, these awards may be supplemented with a Bursary.

Fees per term (2016–2017). Senior School: £5,005–£5,760 (Day Pupils); £7,840–£9,405 (Weekly Boarders); £8,300–£10,355 (Boarders). Prep & Pre-Prep Department: £2,980–£4,180 (Day Pupils); £6,985 (Weekly Boarders); £7,505 (Boarders).

Charitable status. Moira House Girls School is a Registered Charity, number 307072. It exists to provide quality education for young women.

The Council:
Chairman: Ms Jill A Jackson-Hill, BA Hons, FRSA
  (*Company Director and former pupil*)
Dr Debbie Davison, MBBS, DRCOG (*parent of pupil*)
Mr Peter Hawley, FIH (*Hotelier, parent of former pupil*)
Mr Patrick Henshaw, BSc Hons, MRICS, MaPS
Mrs Jenny Herold, BDS, FDSRCPS, MSc, MOrthRCS
  (*Consultant Orthodontist, parent of former pupil*)
Mr Chris Manville, BA, Mont Dip (*parent of pupil*)
Mrs Elizabeth Mullaney, Dip Res EA (*Solicitor*)
Mr Michael Ogilvie, FCA, CPC
Mr Eric Reynolds, BA Hons, PGCE

The Common Room:
Mrs Karen Best (*Active Chair of the Common Room Committee, Faculty Head, Head of Science and Physics*)

Senior Leadership Team:

***Acting Principal*: Mrs Elodie Vallantine**, BA Hons, PGCE

Deputy Principals:
Mr Kevin Ashby, MA, BA Hons QTS
[Mrs Elodie Vallantine, BA Hons, PGCE]

School Management Team:
Mrs Theresa Bees, BSc QTS (*Head of Pre-Prep and KS1, Year 2*)
Mr Adrian Cooper, BA Hons (*Digital Learning and IT Network Manager, Exams Officer, Staff Cover, DT*)
Mr Stephen Crum, BA Hons, PGCE (*Mathematics KS3 Pastoral Coordinator*)
Mr James Harding (*Director of Admissions*)
Mrs Ruth Harris-Moss, BA Hons, PGCE (*Faculty Head, Head of Modern Foreign Languages, Head of Sixth Form*)
Ms Hannah Holland, CIM (*Director of Marketing, Communications & Development*)
Mrs Sarah Hughes, BA Hons Early Years (*Head of Nursery*)
Mr Graham James, MIH (*Operations Manager*)
Miss Katherine James, BA Hons PE QTS (*Faculty Head, Head of Physical Education, KS4 Pastoral Coordinator*)
Mrs Cecy Kemp, BSc, Dip RE (*Director of Studies – Prep, Year 6*)
Mrs Carol Richards, BA, HDE (*Director of Pastoral and Boarding*)
Mrs Nicola Langford (*Principal's PA & Administration and Personnel Manager*)

Senior School Academic Staff:

Art, Design Technology, Food Technology, ICT and Special Educational Needs (SEN):
Mrs Emma-Jayne Haining, BA Hons, PGCE (*Faculty Head, Head of Art, DT & Photography, Residential Housemistress*)
Miss Georgina Bates, BA Hons, PGCE, BIPP (*Photography*)
Mr Adrian Cooper, BA Hons (*DT*)
Mr Oscar de la Torre-Martin (*CDT Technician*)
Mrs Judith Kneen, Cert Ed (*Art Technician*)
Mrs Christine Mcmahon, Cert Ed (*GCSE Food Technology*)
Mrs Barbara Power, PG Dip, Cert Ed (*Head of ICT*)
Mrs Moira Reid, BA Hons, PGCE (*Junior and Senior School Art*)
Mrs Suzanne Teear, BA Ed Hons, QTS (*SENCO*)
Mrs Karen Williames, BA Hons, PGCE (*Art*)

Drama and Music:
Mr Robert Cousins, BMus Hons, PGCE (*Faculty Head, Director of Music & Public Performance*)
Mrs Barbara Ashby, GGSM, PGCE (*Music, Music Coordinator KS4 & 5*)
Mrs Natasha Jordan, Dip Professional Acting Hons (*Director of Drama Junior and Senior School*)
Dr Rebecca Swingle-Putland, DMA, MM, BM, BA (*Director of Outreach & Assistant to the Director of Public Performance*)
Mr Frank Schulmeyer (*Audio Visual Technician*)

English, Geography, History, Library, PSE and Religious Studies:
Mr John Brennan, BA Hons, PGCE (*Faculty Head, Head of History*)
Mrs Olivia Barber, BA, BSc Hons, PGCE (*Religious Studies Subject Leader*)
Mrs Alison Gamester, BA Hons, PGCE (*RE, Geography & History*)
Mrs Ella Lewis, BA Hons (*Assistant Librarian*)
Ms Linda Rosson, MA, BA Hons, PGCE (*English*)
Mrs Alison Standen, BA Hons (*Senior Librarian*)
Ms Tamara Stevens, BSc Ed (*Head of English, Academic Enrichment Coordinator*)
Mrs Jacqueline Wood, BSc Hons, PGCE (*Head of Geography*)

English as Additional Language (EAL) and Modern Foreign Languages (MFL):
Mrs Ruth Harris-Moss, BA Hons, PGCE (*Faculty Head, Head of Modern Foreign Languages, Head of Sixth Form*)
Miss Gabrielle Bonner, MA, BA (*Head of EAL*)
Mme Nathalie Couture, BA Hons, MBA, PGCE (*Junior and Senior School French*)
Ms Hong Deng, MA, PGCE (*Mandarin*)
Mrs Rosie Horsnell (*Mandarin*)
Mr Duncan Martin, BA Hons, PGCE, CELTA (*EAL*)
Mrs Bernardine Mcnamara, BA Hons, PGCE (*French*)
Mr Christopher O'Reilly, BA Hons, PGCE, TEFL (*Spanish, Latin*)
Miss Camilla Venditti (*Assistant Teacher*)
Mrs Lucinda Westwood, BA Hons, PGCE, CTEFLA (*EAL, Spanish*)

Psychology and Science:
Mrs Karen Best, BA (*Faculty Head, Head of Science and Physics*)
Mrs Dorinda Dodd, BSc Hons, PGCE (*Subject Leader Chemistry*)
Ms Cheryl Lloyd, BEd Hons (*Science Technician*)
Dr Fiona Mansfield, BSc, PhD, QTS (*Subject Leader Biology*)
Miss Hannah Savage, BSc (*Subject Leader Psychology, English*)
Miss Eleni Symeon (*Science Technician*)
Mrs Sandra Twaites, BA Hons, QTS (*Science*)

Business Studies, Economics and Mathematics:
Mrs Jane Lambert, BA Hons (*Faculty Head, Head of Mathematics*)
Mr Kevin Ashby, MA, BA Hons QTS (*Mathematics*)
Mr Stephen Crum, BA Hons, PGCE (*Mathematics KS3 Pastoral Coordinator*)
Mrs Christine Hamilton, BA Hons, PGCE (*Mathematics*)
Mr Colin Mcmahon, BSc, PGCE (*Mathematics*)
Mr David, Pollard, BA Hons, QTS (*Mathematics*)
Mr Stephen Wood, MA Ed, BA Hons, PGCE, FCIEA (*Head of Business Studies & Economics*)

Physical Education:
Miss Katherine James, BA Hons PE QTS (*Faculty Head, Head of Physical Education, KS4 Pastoral Coordinator*)

Miss Dawn Cook, BEd (*Physical Education*)
Mrs Lesley Pyle, BEd Hons (*Physical Education*)
Miss Alison Rowsell, BA Hons, PE QTS, PGDPSE (*Physical Education*)
Mrs Wendy Pritchard, FIST Level 1 Coach (*Swimming Teacher*)
Ms Gillian Burt, IOS, ASA, STA (*Swimming Teacher/ Rookie Instructor*)
Mrs Renee Harris (*Assistant Swimming Teacher*)
Ms Catherine Hook (*Swimming Teacher*)
Mr William Dodd (*Lifeguard*)
Miss Debra Miller (*Swimming Teacher*)

Teaching Assistants:
Ms Gill Burt (*Teaching Assistant*)
Mrs Helen Deane (*Teaching Assistant*)
Miss Veronica Fernandez del Villar Lledo (*Language Assistant*)
Miss Maria Gomez Berrocal (*Language Assistant*)
Miss Romy Martin, BSc Hons (*Teaching Assistant*)

Administration:
Mrs Nicola Langford (*Principal's PA & Administration and Personnel Manager*)
Miss Nicola Difrancesco (*School Office Administrator*)
Mrs Jenny Hafernik (*Junior School Office Administrator*)
Mrs Judith Langford (*School Administrator*)
Mrs Jane Mole (*Database Administrator*)
Mrs Elizabeth Powell (*School Office Receptionist/ Administrator*)
Mrs Miriam Ripley (*School Office Receptionist/ Administrator*)

Admissions and Marketing:
Ms S Graham (*Head of Communications*)
Mr James Harding (*Director of Admissions*)
Mrs Elaine Allen (*Admissions & Marketing Administrator*)
Mr Giles Carrington (*Market Development Manager*)

Operations:
Mr Graham James, MIH (*Operations Manager*)
Mrs Jane Stutter, NVQ2 in Team Leading (*Domestic Bursar*)

Finance:
Mrs Jayne Hollister-Sheppard (*Accountant*)
Mrs Jayne Ring, MAAT (*Accountant*)

Information Technology:
Mr Adrian Cooper, BA Hons (*Digital Learning and IT Network Manager*)
Mr Ryan Dray (*IT Technician*)

Examinations Officer:
Mr Adrian Cooper, BA Hons (*Examinations Officer*)

Extracurricular Activities:
Miss Alison Rowsell, BA Hons PE QTS, PGDPSE (*Extra-Curricular Activities Coordinator*)

Prep & Pre-Prep Academic Staff:
Mrs Theresa Bees, BSc QTS (*Head of Pre-Prep and KS1, Year 2*)
Mr James Collins, BA Hons (*Year 4*)
Mme Nathalie Couture, BA Hons, MBA, PGCE (*Junior and Senior School French*)
Mrs Cecy Kemp, BSc, Dip RE (*Director of Studies – Prep, Year 6*)
Mr Christopher Kerswell, BA Hons QTS (*Year 3*)
Mrs Wendy Lambert, BA Hons, PGCE (*Physical Education*)
Mrs Fiona Martirossian, BA Hons, PGCE (*Year 1*)
Mr Martin Neill, Dip Mus, BMus Hons, PGCE (*Head of Junior School Music*)
Mrs Karon Pont, NVQ Level 3 (*Teaching Assistant*)
Miss Jacqueline Sheridan, BA, PGCE (*Year 5*)

Miss Gemma Wood, BA Hons, Primary EYPS (*Reception*)
Mrs Linda Whicker (*Lunch time and After-School Club Coordinator*)

Mini Nursery Moho / Baby MoHo:
Mrs Sarah Hughes, BA Hons Early Years (*Head of Nursery*)
Mrs Carly Cornford, BA Learning & Development, EYP Early Years Professional (*Deputy Nursery Manager*)
Miss Margaret Diaper, NNEB (*Nursery Nurse*)
Miss Hannah Evenden, NVQ Level 3 Childcare (*Nursery Nurse*)
Mrs Jane Keen, Dip Level 3 (*Nursery Nurse*)
Mrs Danielle Legg, Dip Level 3 Early Years Care and Ed (*Nursery Nurse*)
Miss Courtney Neate, NVQ Level 2 (*Nursery Nurse*)
Miss Lisa Tomasetti (*Nursery Nurse*)
Miss Helen Wallis, NVQ Level 3 Childcare (*Nursery Nurse*)
Miss Carly Winter, NVQ Level 3 (*Nursery Nurse, Acting Deputy*)
Mrs Loraine Worrall, NVQ Level 3 Playgroup Practice (*Nursery Nurse*)

Boarding House Staff:

Director of Pastoral Care and Boarding (*Residential*): Mrs Carol Richards (*School House*)

Senior Housemistresses (*Residential*):
Mrs Helen Deane (*Senior Housemistress, Boston House*)
Mrs Emma-Jayne Haining (*Senior Housemistress, Boston House*)
Miss Alison Rowsell (*Senior Housemistress, School House*)
Housemistresses:
Mrs Jennifer Shuman (*School House*)
Mrs Samia Slim (*Boston House*)
Mrs Christine Armstrong (*School House & Boston House – Residential*)

Graduate Assistants (*Residential*):
Miss Camilla Venditti
Miss Maria Gomez Berrocal
Miss Veronica Fernandez del Villar Lledo

Housemothers:
Mrs Judith Kneen
Ms Anna Romnaki
Mrs Lynda Sorrell-Fleet
Mrs Julie Summers
Miss Deborah Walton

Visiting Staff:
Mrs Yvonne Burrell, BA Hons Humanities with Music (*Piano*)
Miss Alison Barnard, FISTD, Imperial Ballet Grades Examiner (*Dance Teacher*)
Mr Paul Beasley, BA, EPEE L1 (*Fencing Coach*)
Mr Paul Bridge, GNAS L1 (*Archery Coach*)
Mrs Maeve Cooper, Dip RCM Perf, Dip RCM Ten (*Violin*)
Mr Dave Cottrell (*Percussion*)
Mr Peter Cousins, FRCO, ARCM (*Accompaniment*)
Mr James Cruttenden, BA Hons, ABSM (*Double Bass*)
Mr Alun Francis, Professional Cert RCM (*Clarinet, Saxophone*)
Miss Natalie Golding, Law Society
Ms Susan Gregg, BA LTCL (*Flute*)
Mrs Rachel Grimes, BA Mus (*Cello*)
Mrs Franciska Laursen, DRS (*Piano*)
Mr Ben Lucas, Youth Worker, All Saints Church
Miss Lydia Hammond, Youth Worker, All Saints Church
Mr Kevin Pallister (*LAMDA*)
Mr Marcus Plant, BA Hons, LRAM, Dip RAM, PGCE (*Brass*)

Mrs Paula Pout (*Singing*)
Mr Jeremy Taylor, OBE (*Drama*)
Mrs Claire Walker, DIP L3 (*Dance Teacher*)

Medical Centre:
Dr Alice Sharma, MB ChB (*School Doctor*)
Dr Jenny Rowe, MBBS, BSc, DFSRH, DRCOG, MRCGP (*School Doctor, Cover in Dr Sharma's absence*)
Mrs Audrey Bushnell, RGN (*Nursing Sister*)
Mrs Nicola Freeborn, RGN (*Nursing Sister*)

More House School

22–24 Pont Street, London SW1X 0AA

Tel: 020 7235 2855; Bursar: 020 7235 4162
Fax: 020 7259 6782
email: office@morehouse.org.uk
website: www.morehouse.org.uk

More House is an Independent Day School of up to 220 girls between the ages of eleven and eighteen. It occupies two adjoining houses, conveniently situated in Knightsbridge, retaining many of the original architectural features, but modernised to include four laboratories, two computer rooms, common rooms, study rooms, a chapel, a library and a drama and dance studio. Our newly refurbished Sixth Form Centre consists of two study rooms, a common room and kitchen. More House is a small and happy community in which a generous teacher: pupil ratio allows the talents of each girl to flourish with all the stimulus and encouragement that she needs. The maximum class size is normally sixteen, streamed where necessary in mathematics, science and languages. All girls leaving the Sixth Form proceed to Higher Education, including Oxbridge, and then to careers in every field. Girls are given full advice about careers and Higher Education.

A Catholic Foundation, More House was opened in 1953 by the Canonesses of St Augustine; since 1969 it has been under lay management as a charitable trust and with a Board of Governors. More House celebrated its Diamond Jubilee in the academic year 2013–2014. The School attracts pupils from a wide area of London. More House warmly welcomes girls of all faiths.

Places at the school are usually awarded on the basis of an interview, a report from the candidate's previous school, and the North London Consortium examination held in January each year. Girls who join us in the Sixth Form are required to have achieved grades A–C in at least five subjects at GCSE level.

Our level of pastoral care is very high indeed, supporting the girls in all aspects of their lives.

Instrumental tuition is available in school and in recent years the School Choir has given performances in Portugal, Spain, Paris, Rome, Malta and the USA. Full advantage is taken of the school's position in Central London and regular visits to lectures, galleries and exhibitions are organised.

Extra-curricular activities before, during and after school include Music, Drama, Sport, Dance, Art, and the Duke of Edinburgh's Award Scheme and World Challenge Expeditions. Our extra-curricular sports programme is extensive and includes netball, hockey, athletics, swimming, climbing, rowing, football, cricket and rounders. The latest school drama production was *Guys and Dolls*.

The Curriculum. The school curriculum offers a wide range of subjects at all levels. In the first two years all girls study Mathematics, Science, English, French, German, Latin, History, Geography, History of Art, Religious Studies, Information Technology, Drama, Art, Physical Education, Dance and Music. Spanish is added in Year 9, giving the possibility of taking two modern languages at GCSE, where the core curriculum of Mathematics, Science, English Language and Literature and Religious Studies is supplemented by four further options.

The Advanced Level courses offered are structured around each girl's choice of subjects, new options available at this stage being Business Studies, Classical Civilisation, Economics, Textiles and Theatre Studies; further breadth of study is achieved through an Enrichment programme. Each subject has its own specialist rooms and for Physical Education the excellent sport and leisure facilities available in the neighbourhood are used, such as those found in Battersea Park and at Imperial College.

Fees per term (2016–2017). £5,950 including lunch, stationery and some educational visits. Academic and Music Scholarships are available on merit.

Charitable status. More House Trust is a Registered Charity, number 312737. It exists to provide an academic education for girls aged 11 to 18 within the framework of a Catholic Day School.

Governing Body:
Chairman: Mr J J Fyfe, BSc Birmingham
Mrs S Shale, BA Birmingham, FCA (*Vice-Chairman*)
Mr P I Ewings, BA Belfast, Solicitor of the Supreme Court in England and Wales
Ms W Fisher, BSc Hertfordshire, MSc Hertfordshire, SRN, SCM
Mrs J Kafati
Ms N Patel, BA Nottingham, MCIPD, CQSW
Mrs S Sturrock, BMus London, ARCM

Clerk to the Governors: Mrs A Barker, BA UCLAN

Head: Mrs A Leach, BSc Liverpool

Deputy Head: Mr M R Keeley, BMus London

Director of Studies: Mr L Garwood, BA Brunel, MA Hertfordshire

Senior Teachers:
Ms S Brown, BA Bristol
Ms K Devine, BA Bristol
Mr T Robertson, BSc Leeds

Bursar: Ms J Forsyth, AAT

Chaplain: Father Michael Doyle

PA to the Headmaster and Registrar: Mrs J Barnwell
Marketing and Communications: Ms N Burley, BA London, MA London

Academic Departments:
* *Head of Department*

Art:
*Ms L Beatty, BA London
Ms K Devine, BA Bristol
Ms D Rigby, MA Chelsea

Business Studies and Economics:
*Mrs P Revell, BA Wellington

Classics:
*Mrs R Gilbertson, MA St Andrews
Mrs R Tunnicliffe, BA London, MA London
Ms S Buck, MPhil Cantab

English and Drama:
*Mrs J Boulter, BA London
Miss H Travers, BA Bristol
Mr P Hegarty, BA London
Mrs L Garwood, BA Durham

History of Art:
Mrs B Hunt, BA Scotland, MBA Scotland

Humanities:
*Ms G Collins, BA Birmingham and Santa Barbara
Ms B Owen, BA Lancaster
Mr J La Frenais, BA Leeds
Mrs P Revell, BA Wellington
Mrs R Tunnicliffe, BA London, MA London

Information Technology:
Mrs A Leach, BSc Liverpool

Support for Learning:
Ms J Jones, Dip Theatre, Cert Ed, Cert SpLD, CELTA
Mrs A Williams, MA Cambridge
Miss S Gunner, BA Roehampton
Mrs M Tomlinson

Mathematics:
*Mr M Ginever, BSc Exeter
Mrs J Mullins, MSc Cape Town
Mr T Robertson, BSc Leeds
Ms O Soltani, BA Ternopil

Modern Foreign Languages:
*Ms S Brown, BA Bristol
Ms C Gremillet, BA Barcelona, MA Bristol
Mr M Caroll, BA Belfast
Ms N Stojanovic, MA Paris

Music:
Mr D Anstice, MA London (*Director of Music*)
Mr M Keeley, BMus London
Ms G Dale, BA Sydney, MA Sydney

Physical Education:
*Miss S Minto, BSc Brunel, QTS
Mr L Garwood, BA Brunel, MA Hertfordshire
Miss K Dennis, BSc Exeter

Religious Studies:
*Mr S Green, BA Dublin, MA Dublin
Ms S Buck, MPhil Cantab
Ms K Gulin, MA Sweden

Sciences:
*Mrs A Scott, BSc Norwich
Ms B Clench, BSc Pennstate
Ms S Tahhan. BEng London
Ms J Seconi, BSc Massey, MSc Massey
Ms I Wijewardana, BSc London

Mr S Keeley (*Network Manager*)
Miss B Hollobon (*Science Technician*)

Peripatetic staff:
Ms D Matthews Forth, RAD TC, BBO TD, IDTA T, IDTA M
plus various instrumental teachers

Moreton Hall

Weston Rhyn, Oswestry, Shropshire SY11 3EW
Tel: 01691 773671
Fax: 01691 778552
email: admin@moretonhall.com
website: www.moretonhall.org
Twitter: @moretonhall
Facebook: /moretonhall

One of the UK's highest achieving schools, Moreton Hall was founded in 1913 by Ellen Lloyd-Williams (Aunt Lil) in Oswestry and moved to its present location in 1920. In 1964, the school became an educational trust. Although the school is predominantly boarding, a number of day pupils are admitted each year.

Member of GSA, The Society of Heads, IAPS, AGBIS, ISCO.

Admission. Moreton First is the preparatory school of Moreton Hall, sharing not only its extensive facilities but also a commitment to nurture and celebrate the talents of each child. Moreton First takes girls and boys from Transition (age 3) to Year 6 and offers a unique start to their education, ensuring academic rigour goes hand in hand with encouragement to achieve success in all creative and sporting fields.

Girls are admitted to Moreton Hall, normally in September at age 11 and 13, either by Common Entrance or by the School's entrance examination which is held at the end of January each year. This examination requires no knowledge of foreign languages and is designed to test potential ability rather than factual recall. This examination can be taken by pupils at 10+, with supplementary papers at 12 and 13. Candidates from preparatory schools may enter through Common Entrance if they so choose at ages 11, 12 and 13. Sixth Form entrance is by current school report and interview, and numbers are limited. All applications should be addressed to the Principal.

Though predominantly boarding, day girls are welcomed. Boys may board from the age of 8–11.

Scholarships and Bursaries. A number of Academic scholarships worth up to 10% of fees will be awarded to pupils at ages 11+, 12+, 13+ and 16+. Scholarships for Music, Drama, Art and for outstanding sporting talent are also available. Students may apply for more than one scholarship. Means-tested bursaries may be awarded up to the value of 100% of fees. The Bronwen Scholarship is available to girls entering the school in Years 5–8.

Fees per term (2016–2017). Boarders: £7,090 (Moreton First), £10,320 (Years 7 and 8), £10,900 (Years 9–13). Day pupils: £3,075–£4,340 (Moreton First), £8,300 (Years 7 and 8), £8,980 (Years 9–13).

Curriculum. Going well beyond the National Curriculum, some 20 subjects are available at GCSE, varying from traditional academic subjects such as Latin and the Sciences, to practical subjects such as Drama, Dance and Physical Education. Modern Languages available include French, German, Spanish, Mandarin Chinese and Russian. A Levels in History of Art, Social Biology, Business Studies and Theatre Studies extend the range of the curriculum. Information Technology is a compulsory subject up to Sixth Form, optional thereafter.

Examinations offered. GCSE, A Level, ABRSM, ESB (English Speaking Board). Over 95% of Upper Sixth go on to University.

Religious activities. Non-denominational. Weekday service, longer service on Sunday, visiting preacher.

Academic, Sporting and Extra-Curricular facilities. Moreton Hall is engaged in an ambitious development programme and has facilities of the highest quality designed to provide the right environment for the education of girls in the twenty-first century.

Younger girls are housed in the Stables building under the supervision of resident houseparents, assistants and matrons. The building is designed to create a family atmosphere with dormitories split into smaller units, close to common rooms, washrooms and staff accommodation.

As pupils progress up the school, the dormitories are gradually replaced by double and finally single study-bedrooms. The Sixth Form Houses provide single and double en-suite facilities. Here, within the structure of a boarding school, senior girls are given the necessary freedom to prepare for the next stage in their careers.

A Centenary Science Centre was completed in 2013 with a unique Medical Science Faculty. The Science Centre, Information Technology rooms and Art and Design Centre are housed within a short distance of the central classroom, careers and library complexes.

All classrooms, libraries and boarding houses are networked and all Sixth Formers have internet access from their study-bedrooms.

An exceptionally well-equipped Sports Centre comprising a sports hall and floodlit tennis courts along with a heated indoor swimming pool, nine-hole golf course, an all-weather surface, and playing fields are set in one hundred acres of beautiful parkland at the foot of the Berwyn hills. The school offers a wide range of sporting options including Lacrosse, Netball, Hockey, Cricket, Tennis and Athletics. Sailing and Riding are also popular.

The Musgrave Theatre, Outdoor Theatre and Music School stimulate theatrical and musical activities ranging from house plays, lunchtime shows and jazz evenings through to ambitious school plays and orchestral concerts. Great emphasis is placed on girls taking part in as wide a range of extra-curricular interests as possible.

The nationally acclaimed Moreton Enterprises offers the girls real business experience. Supervised by professional advisers but all run by the girls themselves, Moreton Enterprises consists of 7 retail businesses on site with a turnover of £50,000.

Old Moretonian Association. Katy Tanner, c/o Moreton Hall.

Charitable status. Moreton Hall Educational Trust Limited is a Registered Charity, number 528409. It exists to provide a high quality education for girls.

Governing Body:
Chair: Mrs J G France-Hayhurst, LLB Hons (*Barrister-at-Law*)
Vice-Chair: Dr L V Boon, MB BS, LRCP, MRCS
S Baynes, MA
Dr J Dixey
Mrs S Fisher, BEd Hons
Ms E J Flynn, MA Ed
Dr M Grant
M Heath
Mrs C M Neilson
C N H Pursglove
S Roberts, MA
A Stockdale
Mrs S Tunstall
Mrs L Yule, BSc

Principal: J Forster, BA, FRSA

Vice Principal: Mrs C Tilley, GRNCM, PPRNCM
Head of Senior School: Miss S Hughes, MTheol
Head of Moreton First: Mrs C Ford, MA, BSc
Director of Studies: I Fitton, BSc
Director of International Recruitment: Mrs V Eastman, MA

Mathematics:
*S Lang, BEng Cranfield, MSc Cranfield, MA King's College London, MBA Open, CEng, FIMechE
I Fitton, BSc Bangor
Miss F Cummins, BSc Durham, PGCE Worcester
T Quantrell, BSc Southampton, PGCE Worcester (*Subject Coordinator*)
Mrs J Counter, BSc Nottingham, PGCE Chester
Mrs H Powers, BA Hons Oxon Literae Humaniores, PGCE The Marches Consortium SCITT
Mrs R Turnbull, BSc Hons Leicester, MSc Southampton, PGCE Kingston
I Wood, BEd Keele [part-time]
Mrs P Fitton, BSc Open University [part-time]

English and Drama:
*A Macdonald-Brown, BA Oxon
Mrs C Lang, BA Warwick, MA University College London
Mrs S Thomas, BA Cardiff

M Dennison, MA Oxon, MPhil Glasgow [part-time]
Mrs V A Lewis, BA Durham, Cert SpLD
Mrs K Howells BA Hons Acting Guildford School of
Acting (*Drama*)
M Jenkins, BA Hons Music Theatre Central Lancashire
(*Drama*)

Learning Support:
Mrs A Wray, SENCO, BSc Staffordshire, PGCE, CELTA,
OCR Dip SpLD, APC, AMBDA
Mrs V A Lewis, BA Durham, Cert SpLD

Modern Languages:
Ms G Slater, BA Lancaster (**French*) [part-time]
Mrs L J Eyre, BA Exeter (*French*) [part-time]
Mrs A G Greaney, BA, MA Sheffield (*French*)
Miss L Kennedy, BA Bristol, MSc UCL (*Greek*)
M Edmunds, BA, MA Cardiff, PhD Bangor (*German*)
[part-time]
Ms S Evans, BA Leeds (*Spanish and French*) [part-time]
R Rhodes, BA Manchester, Foundation Degree Mandarin
Leeds Metropolitan (*Mandarin*)
Miss S Lee, BA Derby (*Mandarin*) [part-time]
Mrs M Jorge Teraga (*Spanish*) [part-time]

Classics:
Miss L Kennedy, BA Bristol, MSc UCL (*Latin, Classical
Civilization*)
Mrs H Powers, BA Hons Oxon Literae Humaniores, PGCE
The Marches Consortium SCITT
C Symons, BA University College London [part-time]

Science:
S Lang, BEng Cranfield, MSc Cranfield, MA King's
College, London, MBA Open,CEng, FIMechE (**STEM,
Physics*)
M Long, BSc Durham, PGCE Birmingham (*Physics*)
Mrs H Peel, MA Cantab, MSc University College London,
PGCE (**Biology and Ecology*)
Mrs J Counter, BSc Nottingham, PGCE Chester (*Physics*)
M Firth, BSc Liverpool, PGCE Chester (*Subject
Coordinator Chemistry*)
Miss L Stanley, BA Hons, MA Oxford, PGCE, Dip
Environmental Policy, MEd Open (*Chemistry*)
Mrs S Champion, MSc Manchester, BSc Loughborough
(*Psychology, Chemistry and Biology*)
T Keeley, BSc Manchester, CBiol, MSB (*Biology*)
Mrs R Turnbull, BSc Hons Leicester, MSc Southampton,
PGCE Kingston (*Junior and Senior Science*)
Mrs P Fitton, BSc Open (*Biology*) [part-time]
R Rhodes, BA Manchester (*Junior Science*)

Geography:
*Mrs A Plowden, BA UWE
J Hindson, PhD, BA, PGCE Aberystwyth

History:
*D Reffell, BA Royal Holloway London
M Dennison, MA Oxon, MPhil Glasgow [part-time]
Mrs G Dennison, BA Durham

Art and History of Art:
*Mrs R Mills, BA Central St Martin's London, PGCE
Birmingham City
Mrs J Miller, BA Kingston, PGCE London
I Edwards, BA Sussex, MA Reading [part-time]

Religious Studies:
Miss J Blanchard, BA Open (*Head of Subject*)
Miss S Hughes, MTheol St Andrews

Business Studies and Economics:
*Mrs C Ashworth, BEd North East Wales Institute
(*Business Studies, Careers*)
Mrs K Booth, HND Lancashire (*Business Studies*)
Mrs A Matthews, BSc Wales, MSc London (*Economics*)

Food Technology:
Miss C Sheffield, BSc Sheffield Hallam, PGCE
Manchester Metropolitan (*Head of Subject*)
Mrs J A P Field, BEd Bristol [part-time]

ICT:
Mrs S Champion, MSc Manchester, BSc Loughborough
B Sutcliffe, BA Glyndwr
R Briggs, BSc Manchester Metropolitan
I Monro, GRSC Kingston (*Computer Science*) [part-time]

Physical Education:
*Mrs K Simlett-Groves, BCom Johannesburg, MSc
Loughborough
Miss C Barnardo, PGCE Sports Science Cambridge, ESOL,
CELTA
Mrs C Dilks, BA De Montfort
Mrs J Sanderson, BEd Bedford College of Higher
Education (**Lacrosse*)
Mrs L Lewin, BEd Bedford College of Higher Education
(*Senior Lacrosse Coach*)
S Taylor, BA Derby
Miss H Harrington, BSc Birmingham (*Lacrosse Coach*)
Ms A Macdonald, BSc Hons Northumbria, UKCC Level 5
LTA Master Coach (**Moreton First Sport*)
Mrs L Jones, ASA Level 2 and NPLQ Lifeguard

Music:
*Mrs H Rayner, BMus Hons Bangor (*Director of Music*)
Mrs C Tilley, GRNCM, PPRNCM
Mrs A Lott, BA Bangor
Miss S Chakravarty, BMus Hons Trinity College of Music
Mrs C Lapage, BMus University College Cardiff, MA
University College Cardiff, ARCO [part-time]

Moreton First:
Mrs C Ford, MA, BSc Leicester (*Head of Moreton First*)
Mrs G Dennison, BA Durham
Mrs N Perry, BEd Crewe and Alsager College, Foundation/
Key Stage 1 Coordinator
Mrs J Sheppard, Cert Ed Lady Spencer Churchill College
Oxford
Miss M Davies, BA Glyndwr
Mrs M Roberts, BA Wolverhampton
B Sutcliffe, BA Glyndwr
I Wood, BEd Keele [part-time]
Mrs C Swain, BA Wales, Cardiff
Mrs J Eaton, HLTA, STAC Open (*Learning Support in
Moreton First*)
Mrs S Phillips (*Classroom Assistant*)
Miss J Brown (*Resident Moreton First Matron*)
Ms K Longland (*Teaching Assistant*)
Mrs J Bromage, BA Sweet Briar College, MA
Manhattanville
Mrs J Firkins, BA Bangor
Ms A Macdonald, BSc Hons Northumbria, UKCC Level 5
LTA Master Coach (*Head of Moreton First Sport*)
Mrs S Davies (*Moreton First Administrator*)

Spoken English:
Miss M Halsall-Williams, BA, LGSM, ALAM, North West
School of Speech and Drama, FESB
Mrs M Jones [part-time]

Careers:
Mrs C Ashworth, BEd North East Wales Institute

Librarians:
Mrs E M Nolan, BA Open
Mrs P Forster, BA Manchester, Dip Lib & IT Studies [part-
time]

Science Technicians:
Mrs J Stonier, NVQ3
S Ferrington, BSc Open

ICT Technicians:
J Ryan
G Woodcock

Health Centre:
Contact: 01691 776032
School Medical Officers:
Dr J Roberts, BA, MA, BMBCH, MRCP, DRCOG, MRCGP, DFFP
Dr E Thompson, MB ChB

House Staff (resident and non-resident):

The Stables:
Mrs C Dilks (*Housemistress*)
Mrs R Lloyd (*Assistant*)

Pilkington:
Mrs I Parry (*Housemistress*)
Mrs S Phillips (*Assistant*)

Gem:
Mrs P Fitton (*Housemistress*)
I Fitton (*House Parent*)
Mrs C Tilley (*Resident Tutor*)
Mrs S Penrose (*Assistant*)

Lloyd-Williams:
Mrs K Davenport (*Senior Housemistress*)
Mrs S Cheetham (*Housemistress*)

Rylands:
Miss F Cummins (*Housemistress*)
Miss G Jones (*Assistant*)
Mrs L Williams (*Assistant*)
Mrs N Hughes (*Assistant*)

Charlesworth:
Mrs A Wray (*Senior Housemistress*)
Miss L Kennedy (*Assistant*)
Mrs J Hughes (*Assistant*)

Administration:

Bursary:
I Davies (*Financial Controller*)
Mrs R Watkinson (*Finance Office Manager*)
Mrs L Cobb (*Accounts Assistant*)
Ms S Janes (*Accounts Assistant*)

School:
Mrs R Brown (*Principal's PA and Admissions*)
Miss H Gingell (*Examinations and Transport Secretary*)
Mrs P Willis (*Reception*)
Miss R Stafford (*Reception and School Secretary*)

Foundation and Marketing:
Mrs K Tanner (*Foundation and Development Director*)
R Briggs (*Communications Development Manager*)
Miss M Evans (*Marketing Development Manager*)

Business Development:
Ms A Griffith (*Business Development Director*)
R Watkinson (*Facilities Manager*)
M Couch (*International Recruitment Consultant*)

International Study Centre:
Victoria Eastman, MA Swansea, PGCE, CELTA (*Director of International Recruitment*)
Emma Williams, BA Hons Lincoln, TOEIC (*Head of ISC*)
Elyse Conlon, BA Hons Liverpool, PGCE, DELTA (*Director of Studies*)
Carike Barnardo (*Housemistress*)
John Davies, BSc, PhD Leicester (*Mathematics, Physics, Chemistry*)
Delfino Taboada, CELTA (*EAL*)
Emma Taboada, BA Hons Bristol, CELTA (*EAL*)
Jenifer Chippett-Williams, Cert Ed (*EAL*)

Dale Abram, BSc (*EAL*)
G Jones, BA Lancaster, CELTA (*EAL*)
Sally White, BA Hons, CELTA (*EAL*)
Joan King (*House Staff*)

The Mount School
York

Dalton Terrace, York, North Yorkshire YO24 4DD
Tel: 01904 667500
01904 232323
email: admissions@mountschoolyork.co.uk
website: www.mountschoolyork.co.uk
Twitter: @MountSchoolYork
Facebook: /mountschoolyork

Motto: Fidelis in Parvo

"Yes, The Mount gets good grades and students get into good universities, but there's so much more to The Mount than that. The people here, students and staff alike, are among the kindest I've met in my life, and that's largely due to the nature of the School; it fosters goodwill. That, to me, is what sets The Mount apart." – Mary Fulford, Headgirl of The Mount, 2014–15.

The Good Schools Guide describes The Mount's pastoral care as "an absolute strength of the school".

"The strong Quaker ethos creates an environment in which everyone appreciates and values each other, fostering both independence and equality. The pupils thrive in this atmosphere of safety, confidence and trust." – ISI Report, 2012.

Age Range. Senior: Girls 11–18. (Junior: Girls 2–11, Boys 2–10.)

Numbers. 55 Boarding, including Weekly boarding, 205 Day.

Values. The Mount is the UK's only Quaker school for girls aged 11–18 years.

The Mount School encourages everyone to:
• respect and value every individual
• have the freedom to flourish in a calm and caring community
• strive for personal excellence
• think and live adventurously
• make a positive contribution to our changing world.

Facilities. Set in sixteen acres of magnificent grounds a convenient ten-minute walk from York's historic city centre, The Mount has exceptional purpose-built facilities for Science, Art and Design, Music, Drama and Sport. With on-site pitches, tennis courts, our own 25-metre indoor pool, multi-purpose sports hall, gymnasium and outdoor Forest School, students enjoys a wide range of sporting activities and outdoor pursuits.

Organisation. After Year 6 at The Mount Junior School girls gain automatic entry to The Mount Senior School and transfer into Year 7. Boarding and day pupils mix well throughout the school, and flexible boarding arrangements cater for all family situations.

Curriculum. GCSE, AS and A Levels plus AQA BACC, incorporating Extended Project Qualification (EPQ). 20 AS/A Level subjects.

Sixth Form: Most sixth formers take 4 or 5 subjects at AS Level (mix of arts and sciences), 3 at A Level; in addition, some take AS and A Level General Studies.

Vocational: Work experience is available and encouraged in Year 11.

Special provision: Specialist learning support teacher and Qualified EAL provision.

Languages: French, German and Latin offered to GCSE, AS and A Level (French or German compulsory to GCSE); also GCSE Spanish in Sixth Form and clubs in other languages, e.g. Russian and Japanese. Regular visits to Europe; classical trips to Italy biennially.

ICT: computers with internet access (at all times) in computer suites and all departments; pupils have their own school email addresses; wireless networked throughout school; OCR Nationals in ICT offered.

Extra-Curricular. Girls can participate in their choice of 50 extra-curricular activities covering Crafts, Languages, Music ensembles, Performance Arts, and a wide range of individual and team Sports. Boarders enjoy a bustling programme of weekend activities that make the most of Yorkshire's unique attractions and exquisite countryside.

Entrance. The Mount School Scholarship Examinations for Years 7 and 9 take place in January. Entrance Examinations can be arranged to be taken at other times of the year. Sixth Form Scholarship Examinations take place in November.

Entry at age 11 and above (into Years 7–10): Girls sit The Mount's own entrance exam and take papers in English, Mathematics and Verbal Reasoning (for entry to Years 7–9 only). The English paper comprises a reading comprehension exercise and a piece of writing; the Mathematics paper (one part to be completed with the use of a calculator and one without) includes a wide variety of questions. Year 10 candidates take papers in English and Mathematics only. Girls are invited to attend a Taster Day and meet the Principal. School references and the interview are given weight alongside exam performance.

Entry at 16+ (A Level study): Prospective entrants are invited for interview. There is no examination if the entrants are studying for GCSE or IGCSE. The offer of a place will usually be conditional upon gaining at least 6 GCSEs at Grade C or above and at least Grade B in the subjects the student wishes to pursue at A Level. School references and the interview are given weight alongside exam performance. Prospective pupils who are not studying for GCSE or IGCSE will be expected to take papers in English and Mathematics.

Scholarships and Bursaries. Academic and Music scholarships are available for Year 7 entry; also Academic, Music, Drama, Art, and Sport scholarships in Year 9 and Sixth Form. A Scholarship is awarded for the duration of a girl's school career at The Mount up to and including Sixth Form. The value of awards is 5% of the current day fee, to which a means-tested bursary may be added which can be worth up to 100% of fees. Scholarships of up to 100% of fees are available for girls entering the Sixth Form with 7 or more A*s at GCSE.

Members of the Society of Friends are assessed under the Joint Bursaries Scheme for Friends' Schools and according to need may be helped by other Friends' funds in addition to School funds.

Means-tested bursaries are also available for other candidates.

Fees per term (2016–2017). Senior School: Years 9–13: Full UK Boarders £9,438, Weekly Boarders £8,403, Day Pupils £5,694; Years 7–8: Full or Weekly Boarders £6,568, Day Pupils £5,845.

Additional charges are made for private lessons, craft materials, external examination fees, outside lectures and concerts. Parents not expected to buy textbooks. Further details about registration, offers of places and Awards may be obtained from the Registrar.

Junior School: Juniors (Years 3–6) £3,586; Infants (Years 1–2) £2,702; Reception £2,392; Pre-School: £6 per hour (7.30 am to 6 pm). Government Nursery Vouchers are accepted in part payment.

The Junior School, for day children aged 2 to 11 years, shares the ethos of the Senior School, to encourage and develop the potential of the individual. There is a creative and stimulating learning environment which promotes the exploration of skills and the development of confidence. Academic standards are high and progress is carefully observed.

See The Mount Junior School entry in IAPS section.

Composition Fees Scheme. Parents are encouraged to consider paying School Fees by lump sum in advance. This can generate considerable reductions in the overall cost. The acceptance of a Composition Fee Payment is not a guarantee that a place can be offered at the appropriate time, but such payments are normally transferable between schools. Composition Fees may be accepted at any time prior to the probable date of entry and may be supplemented by additional payments either prior to or during the child's schooling. Further particulars are available from the Bursar.

Mount Old Scholars' Association. Hon Secretary: Susan Croft, via mosafriends.co.uk

Charitable status. The Mount School (York) is a Registered Charity, number 513646. It exists to provide education for girls from 2 to 18 and junior boys.

Management Committee (Board of Governors):
Clerk: Timothy Phillips

***Principal:* Adrienne Richmond,** BSc, MA, NPQH

Deputy Principal: Bridget Perks, BSc, PGCE

Head of Junior School: Rachel Capper, BEd Hons

Admissions Manager: Fiona Ward MA, PGCE

Newcastle High School for Girls GDST

Senior School:
Tankerville Terrace, Jesmond, Newcastle-upon-Tyne NE2 3BA

Tel: 0191 281 1768
email: seniorschooloffice@ncl.gdst.net

Junior School:
Chapman House, Sandyford, Newcastle-upon-Tyne NE2 1TA

Tel: 0191 285 1956

website: www.newcastlehigh.gdst.net
Twitter: @NewcastleHigh

Newcastle High School for Girls offers an unrivalled educational opportunity for girls of the North East of England. It provides an outstanding academic education, always putting girls first to make sure that every single one of them grows into a bold and independent young woman, ready to take on the world.

Newcastle High is part of the GDST (Girls' Day School Trust), the leading network of independent girls' schools in the UK which educates around 20,000 girls across the country. Its mission is to deliver an outstanding, forward-looking education, rooted in traditional values. As a charity that owns and runs 24 schools and two academies, it reinvests all its income in its schools. For further information about the Trust, see p. xxiii or visit www.gdst.net.

Pupil Numbers. 870: Senior School 570 (aged 11–18 years) of whom 200 are in the Sixth Form; Junior School 300 (aged 3–11 years).

Launched in September 2014, Newcastle High was formed by the merger of Central High and Church High and has quickly established itself as a leading School in the North East and among one of the best in the country; not surprisingly so with the combined 250 years of experience brought from its two founding schools.

In keeping with its proud history, Newcastle High School for Girls is exciting and innovative. The ethos, environment and curriculum have all been designed to meet the demands of the 21st Century. It aims to develop outward looking and socially responsible girls who are equipped with the confidence and ability to be the person they want to be and to embrace the opportunities and challenges of adult life. At Newcastle High, girls excel academically, develop skills, build character and participate in a wide range of co-curricular and enrichment activities.

With academic rigour and excellence at its heart, the school curriculum benefits from cross-curricular planning and a focus on deep learning that spans the subject disciplines through open ended enquiry and independent research. Creativity flourishes across the whole curriculum and the pupils at the School are motivated and full of energy. There is outstanding provision for Sport, Music, Art, Dance and Drama and the girls have the opportunity to develop many new interests and skills through the varied co-curricular programme.

The School strongly believes that one of the main reasons why girls succeed is its impressive pastoral care system underpinned by strong pupil teacher relationships and a supportive and caring school community.

The facilities across the whole School are excellent and all girls are able to take full advantage of them. Situated at Chapman House, Sandyford Park, Newcastle upon Tyne, the Junior School has undergone a major refurbishment to provide the very best learning environment for girls. Set in five acres of grounds, and including a John Dobson designed mansion, Chapman House offers a piece of the countryside right in the heart of the city centre. New classrooms have been furnished with excellent resources to support teaching and learning and the Early Years have direct access to a specific open-air learning environment. There is ample indoor and outdoor space to explore ideas, discover and think creatively. The grounds have recently been landscaped to include all-weather surfaces, outdoor classrooms, a story telling area, kitchen garden and bog garden – just some of the exciting features designed to bring learning to life.

Senior girls moved to brand new state-of-the-art Senior School facilities in September 2016. The multimillion pound development in Jesmond included the remodelling of a beautiful Victorian building and the construction of a new three-storey building to create an outstanding school for the 21st Century. New facilities include an impressive Performing Arts venue with professional-standard lighting and sound equipment; up-to-the-minute Science laboratories, Science Demonstration Area, and Rooftop Terrace; and a Learning Resources Centre. Every teaching room includes a large interactive touch screen to enable truly flexible and seamless teaching and learning to take place. A brand new all-weather pitch and track has been in use from January 2017.

Curriculum. The Junior School follows an innovative and creative curriculum which is focused on extending the girls' learning by allowing them to explore topics and subjects in greater depth. It is enriched with Music Art, Drama and Dance to give the girls ample opportunity to express their creativity. Outdoor leaning is an important part of the curriculum and the Junior School is an accredited Forest School.

The Senior School curriculum is designed to provide girls with the skills, knowledge and understanding that they will need in the years to come. The curriculum is rich in the Arts and strong in Humanities, Sciences and Languages. Sport is for all. The breadth and depth of intellectual challenge is a strong feature. As well as subject specific lessons, the Newcastle High curriculum promotes a cross-curricular approach that enables girls to make more sense of their learning. Knowledge and skills in one subject area are used to reinforce learning in another.

In Sixth Form, intellectual challenge and a love of learning are at the centre and the girls can choose from a wide range of A Levels. In addition to their A Level studies, the girls take part in an enrichment programme designed to extend their studies and broaden their understanding. All girls take an Extended Project Qualification on a topic of their choice.

Admissions. Junior School: by assessment and interview. Senior School: by entrance examination, interview and school report.

Sixth Form: by GCSE results, interview and school report.

Fees per term (2016–2017). Senior School £4,072, Junior School £3,217, Nursery £2,629.

The fees cover the regular curriculum, non-residential curriculum trips, school books, games and swimming but not optional extra subjects or school meals.

Bursaries. The GDST Bursaries Fund provides financial assistance in the Senior School to suitably qualified girls whose parents could not otherwise afford the fees to enter or remain in the School. Bursaries are available for girls entering Year 7 and Year 12.

Charitable status. Newcastle High School for Girls is part of The Girls' Day School Trust, which is a Registered Charity, number 306983.

Chair of Local Governors: Mr P Buchan, BSc Hons, Dip Arch, RIBA, FRFA

Headmistress: **Mrs H J French**, MA Oxon, MEd Newcastle, PGCE Durham, NPQH

Deputy Head (*Development and Well-being*): Mr M Tippett, MA Oxon, PGCE Cantab, NPQH

Deputy Head (*Academic*): Mrs A Hardie, MA Oxon, MEd Newcastle, PGCE Durham

Director of Sixth Form: Mrs H Harrison, BA Hons Huddersfield, PGCE Newcastle

Head of Junior School: Miss A Charlton, BA Hons, PGCE Newcastle, NPQH

Director of Finance and Operations: Mr J Crosby, MEng Nottingham, Adv Dip Durham, FCA

Director of Marketing: Mrs J Graves, BA Hons Northumbria

North London Collegiate School

Canons, Canons Drive, Edgware, Middlesex HA8 7RJ

Tel: Senior School: 020 8952 0912
            Junior School: 020 8952 1276
Fax: 020 8951 1391
email: office@nlcs.org.uk
website: www.nlcs.org.uk
Twitter: @NLCS1850
Facebook: @nlcs1850

North London Collegiate School was founded by Miss Frances Mary Buss in 1850 to provide an education for girls that would equal that of boys and it produced many of the first women graduates. Since its foundation the school has continued to provide an outstanding education for girls.

It is a unique school that combines academic excellence with a vibrant extracurricular life, an international outlook, glorious facilities and a warm community. We are proud of our tradition of producing independent, often pioneering, young women with the drive and confidence to make the most of opportunities and a difference in the world. That was the vision of the school's founder and it remains true of the school today. Although steeped in tradition, the school has always helped to pioneer women's education and constantly looks to improve the education offered. That is why we have enjoyed the accolade of being named the leading Independent Secondary School of the Year twice in the last decade.

Examination success is only part of the picture. Art, music, drama, dance, sport, community service projects and over 30 clubs and societies create a vibrant atmosphere and help girls to flourish and enjoy their time at North London. Every girl matters and the pastoral care at the school ensures pupils feel supported and valued throughout their time here.

North London Collegiate School enjoys the beauty, space and safety of a parkland setting within London. The school provides an ambitious education for girls from a wide range of social backgrounds. The very best of academic teaching is coupled with the widest range of extracurricular activities to help the pupils fulfil their potential.

There are approximately 1,080 girls at North London Collegiate School: 120 in the First School aged from 4+ to 7, 190 Juniors aged 7–11, and 770 in the Senior School aged 11–18, of whom 235 are in the Sixth Form.

The school's academic record is outstanding. It has twice been named as *The Sunday Times* "Independent School of the Year" and *The Daily Telegraph* has described it as the most consistently successful academic girls' school in the country. Results in 2016 were again consistent with the school's academic profile. Over 96% of A Level entries in principle subjects were A*–B grades, with 87% of students gaining straight A* or A grades in all subjects taken.

For the eleventh year running the International Baccalaureate results placed our students in the top 4% of candidates worldwide. Five girls gained the maximum score of 45 points, something achieved by approximately 150 students out of 60,000 internationally. 57% of entries in Higher Level subjects were graded 7, the equivalent of an A* grade at A Level.

39 students secured places at Oxford or Cambridge Universities. This reinforces the Sutton Trust's report published in 2011, which placed North London first nationally for the proportion of students gaining places to highly selective universities.

The GCSE 2016 results were equally outstanding, with over 98% of grades at A*/A.

The facilities at the school are first class, designed to offer the girls every opportunity to develop themselves both academically and socially. These facilities include lacrosse pitches, all-weather tennis courts and a Sports Centre with indoor swimming pool and fitness centre.

The Performing Arts Centre, with a 350-seat auditorium, orchestra pit, galleries and rehearsal rooms, hosts over 35 productions a year. Music and Drama are strong, with opportunity for all to take part in productions, choirs and orchestras. The music programme includes challenging pieces for the most able, with such events as the National Chamber Group competition where the school has won the Founder's Trophy as the most successful competing school on several occasions. On the campus are a Music School, Drawing School and Design Technology Block, all situated around the lake, where waterlilies in the summer make it the ideal place to relax during the long lunch interval. Alternatively, girls may visit the beautifully light and spacious four-floor library.

There is an extensive school coach scheme.

Full details of Open Days and "Taster Afternoons" are on the school's website. Midweek visits can be arranged by appointment. Please contact 020 8952 0912 to arrange a visit.

Bursaries. Enabling bright girls from all backgrounds is central to the ethos of the school. Many bursaries are offered to girls who do well in the 11+ test and those entering the Sixth Form, whose parents can demonstrate financial need.

Scholarships. A number of Academic Scholarships, up to the value of 50% fees, are awarded each year based on the results of the 11+ and 16+ entrance examinations and interviews.

A number of Music Scholarships, up to the value of 25% fees, are awarded at 11+ each year.

Fees per term (2016–2017). Senior School: £6,354; Junior School: £5,370.

Charitable status. The North London Collegiate School is a Registered Charity, number 1115843. It exists to provide an academic education for girls.

The Governing Body:
Mr T Suter, MA (*Chairman*)
Ms S Aminossehe, FRICS, RIBA
Mr K M Breslauer, BSc, MBA
Mrs S Carter, BSc Hons, Associate CFA
Mrs E Davis, BA, Dip ONL
Mr A Emmanuel, BSc, MD, FRCP, FRCPE
Mr A Fox, MA, MD, MSc, MB BS, DCH, FRCPCH, FHEA, Dip Allergy
Mr J Herlihy, MA, FCCA
Mr S Jaffe, BSc Hons, FCA
Mr P Linthwaite, MA
Mr P Needleman, MA, FIA
Ms J Quinn, LLB Hons, BCL
Mr L Rabinowitz, QC, BA, LLB, BCL
Mrs E A Raperport, BA, FCT
Professor Brian Young, BA, MA, DPhil

Chief Operating Officer: Mr I Callender

Headmistress: Mrs Bernice McCabe, BA, MBA, FRSA

Deputy Head – Academic: Mr P Dwyer, BA Oxon

Deputy Head – Pastoral: Mrs A Wilson, BA Surrey, MA London

Director of Studies and Administration: Mr M Burke, BA Newcastle, MA Durham

Head of Junior School: Mrs J M Newman, BEd Cantab

Director of Development: Mrs D Sobel

Assistant Heads:
Teaching and Learning: Mr S Foster, BA Oxon, MA Warwick
Curriculum: Mrs M Fotheringham, MA Oxon
Extra-Curricular: Mr F Hitchcock, BA Bristol
Staff Development: Mr R Sykes, BA Manchester
Head of Sixth Form: Ms D Picton, BA Oxon
Head of Upper School: Mr C Carter, MSc London
Head of Middle School: Dr H Bagworth-Mann, BA Brunel, PhD Brunel

Director of University Admissions: Mrs K Hedges, MA Cantab

SEN Advisor: Ms L. Timm, MChem Oxon

Director of IB: Mr D James-Williams, BA London, MA Open

Careers Advisor: Mr H Linscott, BA London, MA London

Heads of Academic Departments:
Art and Design: Mr J Robinson, BA Nottingham Trent
Classics: Mrs D O'Sullivan, BA Cantab
Economics: Mr S Foster, BA Oxon, MA Warwick
English: Mr D James-Williams, BA London, MA Open
Drama: Miss D Gibbs, BA Surrey
Geography: Miss M Wheatley, BSc London

History and Government & Politics: Dr S Goward, BA Surrey, MA London, MSc Aberystwyth, PhD Oxford Brookes

Information Technology: Dr A P Cripps, PhD London

Mathematics: Ms M Copin, MA Cantab

Modern Languages and Spanish: Mr R Sykes, BA Manchester

French: Miss K Bonnal, Maîtrise Avignon

Italian: Mr P Langdale, MA Oxon

Russian: Mr N Massey, MRes London, BA Cantab

German: Dr J Baughan, BA Bristol, MLitt Bristol, PhD Exeter

Music: Mr L D Haigh, BMus Edin

Physical Education: Mrs L Cooper, BSc Loughborough

Religious Studies & Philosophy: Mr J Holt, BA Durham, MA Open

Science and Biology: Mr R McMillan, BSc Southampton

Chemistry: Dr T Thomas, BSc Durham, PhD Bristol

Physics: Mrs N Timoshina, MSc Moscow

PA to the Headmistress: Mrs D Daum

The pupil teacher ratio is 11:1

Northampton High School
GDST

Newport Pagnell Road, Hardingstone, Northampton NN4 6UU

Tel:	01604 765765
	01604 667979 Junior School
Fax:	01604 709418
email:	nhsadmin@nhs.gdst.net
website:	www.northamptonhigh.gdst.net
Twitter:	@NorthamptonHigh
Facebook:	@NorthamptonHigh
LinkedIn:	/northampton-high-school-gdst

Northampton High School is part of the GDST (Girls' Day School Trust). The GDST is the leading network of independent girls' schools in the UK. As a charity that owns and runs 24 schools and two academies, it reinvests all its income in its schools. For further information about the Trust, see p. xxiii or visit www.gdst.net.

Our school, which opened in 1878, is an independent day school for girls. We encourage our pupils to develop values which will provide them with a constant base in an ever-changing world and aim to respond to the individual needs of every girl. In 1992 we moved to a 27-acre site on the southern edge of town. Our extensive purpose-built accommodation includes 8 well-equipped laboratories, Art, Textiles, Information Technology, Music, Design Technology, Home Economics, Modern Languages and other specialist rooms for all curriculum areas. A large library with computer facilities for independent study is also provided.

The Junior School, which takes girls from the age of three, adjoins the main buildings and has its own hall, dining facilities, library, practical room and IT suite. At the age of 11 the majority of girls transfer to the Senior School.

There are splendid sports facilities on the site. These include a 25m swimming pool, all-weather pitch, a fitness suite, badminton, squash, netball and tennis courts and hockey pitches.

Girls are prepared for GCSE and Advanced Level examinations and go on to universities and other institutions of higher education.

Scholarships are offered at 11+, 13+ and in the Sixth Form. Means-tested bursaries are available in the Senior School.

Fees per term (2016–2017). Senior School (Years 7–13): £4,665. Junior School: £3,517 (Rec–Year 2), £3,609 (Years 3–6). Fees include Lunch.

Old Girls and Associates. *Secretary*: Mrs C White, Northampton High School, Newport Pagnell Road, Hardingstone, Northampton NN4 6UU.

Charitable status. Northampton High School is part of The Girls' Day School Trust, which is a Registered Charity, number 306983.

Local Governing Body:
Mrs D Newham (*Chairman*)
Mr S Chown (*Vice Chairman*)
Mr J Church
Mr J Griffiths-Elsden
Mr J Lane
Mrs K Holland
Mrs A Rowe
Dr T Crawford

Staff:
* *Head of Department*
‡ *Holder of Teacher's Certificate or Diploma*
§ *Part-Time*

Senior Leadership Team:

Head Mistress: ‡**Dr H M Stringer**, BA Hons Bristol, MA, DPhil Sussex, PGCE Institute of Education London

Deputy Head (Pastoral Care & Guidance): ‡Mrs A O'Doherty, MA University College London, BA Hons Birmingham City, QTS Wolverhampton

Deputy Head (Academic): Mr H Rickman, MBA Leicester, BA Hons Kent (*French*)

Head of Junior School: Mr R Urquhart, BSc Hons Brunel, QTS

Director of Finance and Operations: Mrs A Morris, BA Hons Manchester, ACMA

Development Director: Mrs J Fitzroy-Ezzy, BA Hons Nottingham

Director of Sixth Form: Mrs J Cantwell, BSc Hons Durham (*Science, Chemistry, Director of Sixth Form*)

Assistant Head: ‡Mrs M Langhorn, BSc Hons Coventry (*Business Studies & Economics*)

Senior School Teaching Staff:
‡Mr R Attwood, BSc Hons Leeds, PGCE Leeds (*Biology)
‡Mrs E Arkell, BA Hons Cambridge, PGCE Huddersfield (*Music*)
‡Mr A Ball, BEng Hons Coventry, PGCE Bedford College of HE (*Mathematics)
‡§Mrs S Battams, BSc Hons Nottingham, MPhil Loughborough, PGCE Nottingham (*Physics*)
‡Mrs M Beacroft, BA Hons Northumbria, PGCE Manchester Metropolitan, (*Art)
Miss A Buxton, BA Hons Wolverhampton, PG Dip Lib Northumbria (*Librarian*)
‡Mrs C Care, BA Hons Nene College PG Dip, CertEd, MA Northampton (*Theatre)
‡Dr N Carr, BSc, PhD Hull (*Chemistry*)
‡Mrs J Carr, BSc Hons Lancaster, PGCE Roehampton (*Chemistry*)
‡Miss A Chapman, BSc York, PGCE London (*Psychology)
‡Mrs D Curtis, BA Hons Nottingham, PGCE Leicester (*History*)
‡Mr A Donaldson, BA Hons Warwick, PGCE Keele (*History)
‡Mrs A Down, BSc Hons London, PGCE Cambridge (*Mathematics*)

‡Mr J Earp, BA Hons PGCE Nottingham (*Geography*)

‡Mrs R Fenn, BA Hons, MA Cambridge, QTS Hertfordshire (*Chemistry*)

Ms S Fernandes, BA Hons Northwest Univ, South Africa (*Physical Education*)

‡Mrs E Ford, Business Studies Dip, Teaching Cert Northampton (*Physical Education*)

‡Mrs W Forsyth, BEng Cambridge, PGCE Northampton (*Mathematics*)

‡Miss S Fraser, BA Hons QTS De Montfort (*Physical Education*)

‡§Mrs G M Gray, BA Hons, MA London (*History*) PGCE London

Mrs J Hackett, BEd De Montfort (*Physical Education*)

‡Mrs A Halstead, BA Hons UCL, PGCE Southampton (*English*)

‡Mrs K Harrison, BA Hons Lancaster, PGCE Warwick (*Mathematics*)

‡Mrs L Heimfeld, BA Hons Wales, MA PGCE Leeds (*Film Studies*)

‡Mrs D Hill, BA Hons PGCE Leeds (*Modern Languages, French*)

‡Mr J Holland, BA Leicester, MA Hertford, MSc PGCE Cambridge (*Classics*)

‡Mrs S Holland, MA Oxford, PGCE Bedford College (*Classics*)

‡Mrs C Hopley, BA Hons Liverpool (*English*)

‡Mrs S L Holland, MA Oxford (*Classics*)

‡Mrs R Hymers, BSc Hons Bradford, PGCE Wolverhampton (*Business Studies and Economics*)

‡Miss C Hurst, BA Hons Brighton, QTS Chelsea School of PE (*Physical Education*)

‡Mrs J James, BA Hons PGCE Belfast (*Spanish*)

‡Miss R Kneen, BSc Hons PGCE Exeter (*Geography, Deputy Director of Sixth Form*)

‡Mrs S Knight, BSc QTS Nottingham Trent (*Food*)

‡Mr D Laubscher, BA BEd Stellenbosch South Africa (*Art*)

‡Mrs R Laubscher, BSc HDE Stellenbosch South Africa (*Mathematics*)

‡Mrs Li-Lakkappa, MA Institute of Education London, PGCE Durham (*Chemistry*)

‡Mrs R Littlewood, BEd Liverpool (*Physical Education*)

‡Mrs E Morgan, BA Hons Bristol, PGCE Oxford (*Spanish*)

‡Ms S Margareto, BA, DipEd Macquarie, Sydney, Dip Special Needs/Dyslexia Northampton (*Special Education Needs*)

‡Mr J Martin, MA Belfast, PGCE Homerton College Cambridge (*Computing and eLearning*)

‡Mrs K Maskell (*EAL Coordinator*)

‡Mrs A Maslen, MSc Staffordshire, Maîtrise Univ of International Affairs, France (*Spanish*)

‡Miss K Mason, BA Hons Newcastle, PGSCE Durham (*Classics*)

‡Mr P Nathan, BA Hons Sheffield, MGTP East London (*Music*)

‡Miss S Orvoen, BA Hons Université de Bretagne Sud, PGCE Oxford Brookes (*French*)

‡Miss C Parboteeah, MA Hons, PGCE Leicester (*Chemistry*)

‡§Mrs E Pearson, BSc Hons, MSc Birmingham, PGCE Homerton College Cambridge (*Biology*)

‡Mrs L Peck, BA Hons Oxford, QTS Buckingham (*Theology and Philosophy*)

‡Miss T Robinson, BA Manchester, PGCE Liverpool Hope (*Theology and Philosophy*)

‡Mrs A Scanlan, BA Hons PGCE Durham (*Geography*)

‡Mrs I Tansley, BA Hons Kingston, PGCE University College Worcester (*Economics and Business*)

‡Mrs L Taylor, BA Hons Loughborough, PGCE De Montford (*Art*)

‡Mr A Viesel, MA University College London, BA PGCE St Hugh's College Oxford

‡Mrs A Vizor, BA Hons Cambridge, PGCE Bristol (*Physics*)

‡Mr M Watson, BA Hons Liverpool, PGCE Liverpool John Moores (*Spanish*)

‡Mrs J Webb, BA QTS De Montfort (*Physical Education*)

‡Mr J Williams, BA Hons Manchester, PGCE Leicester (*English*)

Junior School:

Deputy Head: Mrs J Purvey-Tyrer, BEd Hons Leeds

‡Mrs C Bleech, BSc Bristol

‡Miss N Brandon-Jones, BA Hons Wales

‡Mrs S Dadge, BA Hons Warwick

‡Mrs S Dale, BA Hons Bedfordshire

§Mrs A Davis, OGCE Ripon and York St John

‡Ms F Duck, BA Hons Cardiff

‡Mrs K Farrar, BEd Hons Northampton

‡Mrs K Fordham, BA Hons Exeter

‡Mrs L Green, BA Hons Manchester Polytechnic

‡Mrs H Greenbank, BEd Hons Plymouth

Miss S Mayes, BA Hons Surrey

‡Mrs C Miller, GTCL Trinity College of Music, London

‡Mrs E Shaw, BEd Hons Newman College, Birmingham

‡Mrs S Shaw, BA Hons Northampton

‡Mrs J Stock, BEd Hons Newland Park College

‡Miss N Taylor, BSc Hons Bristol

‡Mrs E Andrew, NVQ Level 4 Northampton College

‡Mrs S Waters, BA Northampton

Headmistress's Secretary: Mrs D Brown

Peripatetic Instrumental Staff:

Miss F Brannon, BMus Hons, MA (*Flute, Recorder*)

Miss J Coventry, LGSM Hons (*Brass*)

Mr M Dezelu, BSc Hons (*Guitar and Bass Guitar*)

Mrs C Jones, BMus Hons, MTC (*Cello and Double Bass*)

Mrs E Leutfeld (*Piano*)

Mrs S Liddiard (*Oboe and Bassoon*)

Ms V Murby, ARCM (*Violin and Viola*)

Mr S O'Gorman, BMus (*Clarinet and Saxophone*)

Ms J Partridge, AGSM, LRAM (*Piano, Jazz Piano and Theory*)

Mr I Riley, GLSM (*Piano*)

Ms R Sherry, BA Comb Hons, MA, LRAM (*Singing*)

Mr P Slane, AGSM, DipEd, ARCM (*Singing*)

Ms A Sparks, BA Hons (*Singing*)

Mrs N Taylor (*Violin and Viola*)

Mr M Thomas, LGSM (*Guitar*)

Mr M Wild (*Drum Kit*)

Northwood College for Girls GDST

Maxwell Road, Northwood, Middlesex HA6 2YE

Tel: 01923 825446
Fax: 01923 836526
email: admissions@nwc.gdst.net
            office@nwc.gdst.net
website: www.northwoodcollege.gdst.net
Twitter: @NorthwoodGDST
Facebook: @NorthwoodGDST
LinkedIn: /northwood-college

Creating exceptional futures

Northwood College for Girls is part of the Girls' Day School Trust (GDST), the UK's leading network of independent girls' schools. As a charity that owns and runs 24 schools and two academies, the GDST reinvests all its income in its schools. For further information about the Trust, see p. xxiii or visit www.gdst.net.

Combining academic excellence with strong pastoral support and a focus on moral development we inspire, challenge and support each individual girl. The education of girls lies at the heart of our vision. Academic rigour and excellent exam preparation are a given – girls deserve the opportunity to grow as individuals, assume leadership roles, develop lasting friendships, take risks and excel in an environment that caters for their needs.

Foundation. An independent day school for girls, Northwood College for Girls was founded in 1873 as one of the first girls' schools in London and now educates 926 girls aged 3 to 18 years.

Ethos. Our aim is to raise young women who know their own minds and are creative and flexible thinkers, as well as being able to achieve outstanding exam results.

We are academically selective, but not narrowly exclusive. We value girls for more than simple academic performance, because our unique approach to advanced thinking skills means that we can develop, stretch and challenge every single one of them. We think that makes for an interesting and vibrant school community – and it's what makes Northwood College for Girls special.

Thinking Skills. Our approach to thinking skills sets Northwood College for Girls apart and gives our girls an edge in the way they approach any task or challenge. Through the programme, we ensure our girls start to understand and develop how they think from the day they join Nursery through to the end of the Sixth Form. Over the years, they build up their reasoning skills, improve their creativity and acquire strategies for tackling complex problems and decisions. It gives them a life skill that will be as useful at university and in the workplace as it is at school.

Location. The school is 14 miles from Central London and a 5 minute walk from Northwood tube station on the Metropolitan Line. There are several good local bus services and 6 different supervised school coach routes.

Single Site. All parts of the school share a single site, divided into distinct areas. The Junior School occupies its own self-contained buildings and our youngest girls have a purpose-built Early Years Centre. (*See also Junior School entry in IAPS section.*)

Facilities. We have enviable facilities for all subject areas in both the Junior and Senior Schools. Highlights include three art rooms, ten science laboratories, four ICT Suites and specialist centres for Technology and Modern Languages. We also have a fabulous Performing Arts Centre, with sophisticated sound-recording and music technology suites.

Sports facilities include a sports hall and 25-metre six-lane indoor swimming pool, as well as three hard tennis/netball courts, a hockey/rounders pitch and an all-weather pitch.

Examinations. Pupils are prepared for GCSEs, A Levels and for University Entrance.

Curriculum. We offer all National Curriculum subjects. In addition, French is taught from Year 3, Spanish from Reception, German from Year 7, and Latin from Year 4. Drama is taught throughout the school. A very wide range of A Level subjects is available in the Sixth Form, including Psychology, Economics, Politics, and Music Technology.

Music and Drama are real strengths at Northwood College for Girls with a fantastic range of opportunities for young musicians and budding thespians. The school has a wide range of orchestras, bands and choirs and we hold concerts each term, as well as music competitions and fully staged musical productions. Instrumental tuition is extensive and girls are prepared for the Associated Board examinations.

There is one major school play or musical every year in both Junior and Senior Schools that is always a highlight in the school calendar and often elicits rave reviews in the local papers. A number of smaller productions take place year round and girls may take individual drama lessons with visiting teachers.

Physical Education. We recognise the importance of encouraging girls to stay physically fit and active. Trained staff teach a wide variety of sports such as Hockey, Netball and Gymnastics during the winter months and Tennis, Rounders, and Athletics in the summer. Swimming is taken all year round and senior girls are able to explore other sports such as Golf, Self-Defence and Fitness Training.

Entry Requirements. Entry to the College is by examination and interview, except for Nursery, which uses a play-based assessment. At 11+ we use the North London Girls Schools' Consortium exam. Entry to the Sixth Form is by GCSE results and interview.

Scholarships and Bursaries. For details, please contact the Admissions Office.

Fees per term (2016–2017). Sixth Form £5,360–£5,370; Senior School: Years 7–11 £5,360–£5,407; Junior School: Years 3–6 £4,516–£4,521, Reception–Year 2 £3,846–£3,854, Nursery (full-time) £3,451. Fees include lunch, loan of text books, stationery and certain school trips.

Charitable status. Northwood College for Girls is part of The Girls' Day School Trust, which is a Registered Charity, number 306983.

Governors:
Chair: Mr Geoff Hudson
Mr Ken Wild
Mr David Tidmarsh
Mr Tony Patteson
Mrs Catherine Pain
Professor Ashley Braganza
Mr John Orchard
Mr Dipesh Patel

Head Mistress: **Ms Jacqualyn Pain**, MA, MA, MBA, NPQH

Director of Finance & Operations: Mr Tim Brown, BA, MBA

Deputy Head Mistress (Academic): Ms Claire Adby, BSc Hons, PGCE

Deputy Head Mistress (Learning Innovation, E-Learning and Staff Development): Ms Jane Jackman, BA Hons, PGCE, MBA

Director of Marketing and Development: Ms Claudine Moyle

Deputy Head Mistress (Pastoral Development and Well-Being): Mrs Elizabeth Skelton, MA, DipEd, NPQH

Director of Sixth Form: Mrs Rebecca Brown, BA Hons, MSt Oxon, MA Oxon

Head of Junior School: Mrs Zara Hubble, BA Hons, PGCE

Heads of Faculty:
Performing, Creative Arts & Design: Mrs Leanne Brown, BSc Hons, PGCE
Maths, Science & IT: Miss Caroline Hinchliffe, MA, PGCE
English & Humanities: Miss Natasha Shirman, BA Hons, PGCE
Learning Outside the Classroom/Co-curriculum: Miss Jo Simpson, BA Hons
Learning Enrichment & Personal Development: Mrs Tara Smith, BA Hons, MA, PGCE

Registrar: Mrs Jemma Davidson

Norwich High School
GDST

95 Newmarket Road, Norwich, Norfolk NR2 2HU
Tel: 01603 453265
Fax: 01603 259891
email: admissions@nor.gdst.net
website: www.norwichhigh.gdst.net

Founded 1875.

Norwich High School is part of the GDST (Girls' Day School Trust). The GDST is the leading network of independent girls' schools in the UK. As a charity that owns and runs 24 schools and two academies, it reinvests all its income in its schools. For further information about the Trust, see p. xxiii or visit www.gdst.net.

Number of pupils. Senior School: about 500, aged 11–18 years, of whom about 130 are in the sixth form. Junior School: about 160, aged 3–10 years.

Norwich High School draws its pupils in almost equal numbers from the city of Norwich and the county of Norfolk. It stands in 13 acres of grounds on the main Newmarket Road, a mile-and-a-half from the city centre. The main buildings are attached to a distinguished Regency house, built in 1820. In addition, there is a junior school with many specialist rooms, a recently extended sixth form centre, music school, spacious sports hall, 25m indoor heated pool and a performing arts centre. There are playing fields around the school with an additional astroturf a short walk away, and a wide range of indoor and outdoor physical activities is offered, including netball, hockey, lacrosse, athletics, tennis, rounders, badminton, gymnastics and dance. The school holds the International Schools' Award, the Sportsmark Gold Award for its sporting achievements and Artsmark for creative subjects.

The school is a caring community and parent-friendly. We are open early for breakfast and late for tea. Girls may use the ICT and library facilities after school in the senior school; the junior school has its own after-school club. There is a minibus service from the surrounding areas in all directions, both before and after school.

Admission. All girls are assessed prior to entry. The normal ages of admission are 3, 7, 11 and 16. Occasional vacancies may occur at other ages.

Curriculum. The school has always been proud to provide a broad and rich education, preparing girls for admission to universities, professions, commerce and industry. A wide range of subjects is available, currently 25 at A Level and 22 at GCSE.

Information systems. A computer network is shared by all departments, including the laboratories, library, all teaching rooms, two computerised language laboratories, the sixth form IT suite as well as the two senior and two junior IT suites. All girls work towards the European Computer Driving Licence qualification in Years 8–9.

Careers education and advice. A carefully planned Careers Information Education and Guidance programme commences in Year 7. Virtually all sixth formers continue on to higher education and the school ensures that they have received comprehensive guidance and preparation. The school has initiated an Inspiring Females programme which draws a wide variety of successful women into school to share their experiences and mentor the girls.

Co-curricular Activities. These are extensive, for infants through to seniors. Music, Sport and Drama are all strong features of the school. Girls also participate in both the Duke of Edinburgh's Award and Young Enterprise schemes, rowing, equestrian, debating and chess clubs, Amnesty International, Christian Union, fencing and life saving, and over 40 other clubs and societies.

Many excellent residential and day trips are arranged each year, by various departments. These are finely tuned to the curriculum and cover a full range of activities.

Fees per term (2016–2017). Senior School £4,514, Junior School £3,430, Nursery £2,852.

The fees cover the regular curriculum, school books, stationery and other materials, games fixtures and swimming lessons, but not optional extra subjects or school meals. The fees for extra subjects, including individual music tuition, are shown in the prospectus.

Financial Assistance. The GDST has made available to the school a substantial number of scholarships and bursaries.

Bursaries are available on or after entry to the senior school and applications should be made to the Head in cases of financial need. All requests are considered in confidence. Bursaries are means tested and are intended to ensure the school remains accessible to bright girls who would profit from a GDST education, but who would be unable to enter the school without financial assistance.

Various **Scholarships**, including music scholarships, are available to internal or external candidates for entry at 11+ or to the sixth form.

Charitable status. Norwich High School is part of The Girls' Day School Trust, which is a Registered Charity, number 306983.

School Governors:
Chairman: Mrs R Randle, LLB Hons

Headmistress: Mrs K von Malaisé, MA Cantab

Deputy Head (Academic): Dr B Ashfield, MA Oxon, PhD

Deputy Head (Pastoral): Mrs H P Dolding, BEd De Montfort

Head of Junior School: Mr N Tiley-Nunn, BEd Canterbury

Director of Communications and Admissions: Mr R Nobes

Director of Finance and Operations: Mrs J C Thompson, ADSBM

Registrar: Miss A Ready

Notre Dame School

Burwood House, Cobham, Surrey KT11 1HA
Tel: 01932 869990
email: office@notredame.co.uk
website: www.notredame.co.uk
Twitter: @NotreDameCobham
Facebook: /notredamecobham
LinkedIn: /notredamecobham

Set in 17 acres of beautiful parkland in Cobham, Notre Dame School nestles in a picturesque 18th century mansion beside the River Mole. Despite the tranquil setting Notre Dame School is a hive of activity, with approaching a thousand children and teachers working hard in the important business of education. The school has an enviable reputation for the highest academic standards underpinned by over 400 years of international educational tradition in 30 countries. Recent A Level students gained the highest percentage of A*–B grades (84%) in over ten years and girls went on to study at prestigious Russell Group universities in a wide range of disciplines. At GCSE over half the grades awarded were A and A*. Twin aims of academic success and building self-confidence create rounded, compassionate, highly qualified and wise young women. Past pupils proliferate the professional sphere, many of whom enthusiastically retain links to Notre Dame.

Notre Dame School is an independent Roman Catholic day school for approximately 600 girls aged 2–18. Our school is part of a worldwide educational organisation, founded in Bordeaux in the 17th century by Saint Jeanne de Lestonnac. The Company of Mary Our Lady is the oldest recognised educational order, devoted to the teaching of girls. We welcome families of all faiths, who wish their daughters to grow spiritually, academically and socially in a dynamic, challenging yet caring environment.

Our objective is to give every girl a balanced education, based on motivation, achievement, enjoyment and high personal expectations. We recognise and nurture strengths and encourage individuality and independence.

From their first day in the Senior School, well-motivated girls are challenged by a wide-ranging curriculum, delivered by highly qualified subject specialists. Enthusiasm is the hallmark of lessons at Notre Dame, whether for science or arts subjects, technology, humanities or mathematics. Confidence is fostered by small teaching groups, so that academic rigour can be encouraged and enjoyed by all.

We give as much focus to sport, art, music, design and drama as we do to science, languages, maths, the humanities and English, and as we do to leadership opportunities, community service, supporting others and building confidence.

It is our mission to recognise and nurture individual potential in all areas of endeavour. Inherent in all we do is our ethos; that we are all important, special, and valued. We are a community, and we are, together, accompanying our young women in their efforts to build their lives for today and tomorrow.

By providing opportunities for pupils to grow intellectually, spiritually and socially, Notre Dame aims to enhance talents, develop interests and enable the fulfilment of ambitions. It is our firm belief that by respecting the best traditions of the past and meeting the rigorous requirements of the modern world through the provision of extensive, high-quality facilities and effective teaching and learning, we will prepare young women for their role as responsible citizens of the wider world.

Sixth Form. Notre Dame Sixth Form is superb: an exciting community where exam results are excellent, facilities are modern and the culture of opportunity and responsibility thrives. It is a vibrant learning environment with an exciting range of extra-curricular opportunities, all of which are designed to complement academic study.

Girls who make the decision to join Notre Dame Sixth Form can expect to leave us as independent learners, and active members of the community, confident in the pursuit of their chosen goals. Whether the girls leave us for university, further education or employment, they will be empowered with choices and will be able to fulfil any role with purpose, direction and a sense of fun.

Developments. Notre Dame has embarked on a multi-million pound investment programme in recent years, not only in attracting top-quality teaching staff, but also in capital expenditure to ensure that the school keeps well ahead of the demands of a thoroughly modern education programme. Our pupils are fully prepared to go out into the world and able to take their place in society, thanks to the opportunities and facilities they enjoyed during their treasured, formative years at Notre Dame. In recent years, this investment programme has seen the completion of:

- Fantastic Multi-Space Learning Resources Centre
- Senior School Library and Networked IT Suites
- Fully Equipped Six-lab Science Block
- Self-Contained BlueBelles Nursery
- Complete Classroom Refurbishment
- Professionally Equipped 380-Seat Theatre
- Specialist Dance and Drama Studios
- 25m Indoor Swimming Pool
- Forest School and Adventure Tree House
- Dining Hub and Coffee Bar
- Dedicated Sixth Form Centre
- All-Weather Sports Facilities

Transport: We run a comprehensive selection of coach and minibus routes covering all the local area along with routes on the A3 from/to Guildford, Wimbledon and Putney, and can offer flexible single/return journeys. Private coaches from: Ashford, Barnes, Byfleet, Chertsey, Claygate, Cobham, Esher, Fulham, Hampton, Kingston, Molesey, Mortlake, Oxshott, Putney Bridge, Putney Heath, Richmond, Raynes Park, Sheen, Surbiton, Teddington, Thames Ditton, Twickenham, Walton, Wandsworth, Wimbledon, Woking and all over Surrey.

Admission. Admission to the Senior School is normally at 11+, although girls may be admitted at other ages subject to an entrance examination and the availability of places. Academic scholarships are awarded at 11+ based on the entrance examination. Scholarships are also awarded to girls entering the Sixth Form. A number of means-tested assisted places are available on entry to the school. Short-term bursaries may be made available to assist parents in times of personal financial hardship. Approximately half our intake at 11+ comes from Notre Dame Prep.

Preparatory School. For further information about the Prep School, please see entry in IAPS section.

Fees per term (2016–2017). Senior School £5,205; Prep School £1,260–£4,225.

Charitable status. Notre Dame School Cobham is a Registered Charity, number 1081875. It exists to provide education for girls.

Governors:
Mr Gerald Russell (*Chair of Governors*)
Sr Ernestine Velarde ODN
Sr Anne Gill ODN
Sr Nieves Escalada ODN
Fr Mervyn Williams SDB (*Chair of Finance Committee*)
Sr Inmaculada Naranjo Cruces ODN
Sr Maria Quinn ODN (*Chair of Lestonnac Committee*)
Mrs Wanda Nash (*Chair of Education Committee*)
Mrs Mary-Claire Travers (*Health & Safety Committee*)
Mrs Suzanne Ware [Practising as Suzanne Ornsby QC] (*Building Committee*)
Mrs Susan Bailes (*Education Committee*)

Executive Team:

Head Teacher (*Senior School*): Mrs Anna King, MEd, MA Cantab, PGCE, FRGS

Head Teacher (*Prep School*): Ms Merinda D'Aprano, BEd Hons, MA, CTC, FRSA, ISI Team Inspector

Bursar: Mr Phillip Brown, BA Hons, MA Oxon

Senior Leadership Team:
Executive Team (*as above*)
Assistant Head – Curriculum: Ms Sarah Badger, BSc Hons, PGCE
Assistant Head – Teaching and Learning: Mr Michael Coackley, BA Hons, PGCE
Assistant Head – Sixth Form: Miss Janine Harber, BA Hons PGCE
Assistant Head – Pastoral: Mrs Jan Slade, BA Hons, PGCE
Assistant Head – Prep: Mrs Clare Barber, BSc Hons, PGCE
Head of EYFS: Miss Melanie Lehmann, BA Hons, EYPS
Head of Infants: Miss Geraldine Deen, BA Hons QTS
Pastoral Director – Prep: Miss Rebecca Golding, BA Hons, PGCE
Estates Manager: Mr Anthony Madigan

Pastoral:
Assistant Head – Pastoral: Mrs Jan Slade, BA Hons, PGCE
Year 7: Miss Sophie Dudgeon, BEd Hons
Year 8: Mr Kim McClenaghan, BA Hons, MSc

Year 9: Mrs Mary Turner, BA Hons, PGCE, Cert Counselling Skills
Year 10: Mrs Anita Ingram, BSc, PGCE
Year 11: Mrs Ellie Ha, BA Hons, PGCE and Mrs Candice Chislett, BA, HDE
Sixth Form: Miss Janine Harber, BA Hons, PGCE

Art:
*Mrs Su Avizius, BA Hons
Mrs Deborah Howorth, BA, PGCE

Design and Technology:
*Mrs Emma Fahy, BA Hons, PGCE

Drama:
*Miss Christina Graham, BA Hons, PGCE
Mrs Sherna Treherne, LAMDA

Economics/Business Studies:
Mrs Karen Franco, BA, PGCE

English:
*Mrs Christine Johnson, BA Hons
Mrs Sapna Bedia, BA Hons, PG Dip Ed
Mrs Candice Chislett, BA, HDE
Ms Bianca Hendicott, PhD, BA Hons, MSc
Mr Kim McClenaghan, PhD, BA Hons, MSc
Mrs Mary Turner, BA Hons, PGCE, Cert Counselling Skills
Mrs Lex Franklin, BSc Hons, PGCE
Mrs Catherine Coles, BA Hons, PGCE

Food and Nutrition:
Mrs Carly Anderson, BSc, PGCE

Geography:
*Mrs Andrea Griffiths, BA Hons
Mr Brendan Conway, MA, BSc Hons, PGCE
Miss Janine Harber, BA Hons PGCE

History, Classical Civilisation, Politics, Sociology:
*Mrs Ellie Ha, BA Hons, PGCE
Mrs Vanessa Brown, BA Hons, BPS Teacher Education Canada
Miss Lucy Evans, PhD, BA Jt Hons, PGCE
Mr Michael Coackley, BA Hons, PGCE
Miss Janine Harber, BA Hons PGCE
Mrs Anna King, MEd, MA, PGCE

Information Technology:
*Mrs Catherine Archer, MSc, BA Hons, PGCE
Mr David Colpus, BSc, PGCE

MFL:
*Miss Christèle Claveau, Tours University, PGCE
Mrs Juliana Costa-Veysey, MA, BA Hons, PGCE
Mrs Maria Edwards, BA Hons, TEFL
Mrs Marie-Claire McGreevy, MA, BA Hons, PGCE
Mr Alberto De Anca Fernandez, BA
Mrs Sapna Bedia, BA Hons, PGCE

Mathematics:
*Mrs Sarah Breame, BSc Hons, PGCE
Ms Sarah Badger, BSc Hons, PGCE
Mrs Anita Ingram, BSc, PGCE
Mrs Alice Nield, MSc and BSc
Mrs Alison Paige, BA Hons, PGCE
Mrs Susan Wallace, BSc, PGCE

Music:
*Mr David Black BEd Hons, BMus, MMus

Physical Education:
*Mrs Heather Marsh, BA Hons, PGCE
Miss Sophie Dudgeon, BEd Hons
Ms Clare Mason, BSc Hons, PGCE
Miss Jade Mulcahy, BA, PGCE

Psychology:
Mrs Candice Chislett, BA, HDE
Mrs Lex Franklin, BSc Hons, PGCE
Miss Fiona Foskett, BSc, PGCE [Maternity Cover]

Science:
*Mr Elliot Lee, BSc Hons, PGCE
Mrs Rachael Bantin, MA, BA Hons, PGCE
Dr John Brooke, PhD, BSc, QTS
Mr Luke Howse, MSc, MPhys, PGCE
Ms Carmel O'Keeffe, BSc, HDipEd
Dr Heather Prideaux King, PhD, BA, PGCE
Mrs Jan Slade, BA Hons, PGCE

Theology:
Mr Thomas Newman, MA, BA, PGCE
Miss Lucy Evans, BA Jt Hons, PGCE
Mrs Sally Carter-Esdale, BA Hons, PGCE

Technicians:
Science:
Mrs Vanessa Catalano
Mrs Judy Matkin
Art and D&T:
Ms Deborah Duffy, BA Hons, PGCE
Mrs Rosie Rees

Librarian: Mrs Sharon Finch, BA Hons

Examinations Officer: Mrs Anita Ingram BSc, PGCE

Learning Support – Senior:
*Mrs Mary Akarslan, BA Hons, QTS
Mrs Kate St John, BA Hons, SpLD, TESOL
Mrs Helen Brittain, BSc Hons, PGCE (*Maths tutor*)
Mrs Lynda Shore, BSc Hons, MSc, C&G TCert Adult Education (*Maths tutor*)
Ms Clare Mason, BSc Hons, PGCE

Prep School Subject Leaders/Teaching Staff:

Art: Miss Geraldine Deen, BA Hons, QTS
Dance: Mrs Rachel Thomas, RAD Teaching Dip
Drama: Ms Lucy Fletcher
English: Mrs Clare Barber, BSc Hons, PGCE
Humanities (TASK): Mrs Carole West, BA Hons, PGCE
Information Technology: Mrs Louise Plummer, BSc Hons, Dip M, PGCE, Cert IT
LAMDA: Mrs Collette Wighton, Dip Ed, LTCL
MFL: Mrs Nerea MacDonald, BA, PGCE
Mathematics: Ms Jenn Caverhill, BA PGCE
Music:
*Mrs Julie Shaw, BA Hons PGCE
Mrs Toni Bryant, LTCL, Dip Perf
Physical Education: Mrs Terry-Lee Purgavie, BA Hons, QTS
Sports Assistant: Mr Robert Parsons, BSc
Swimming: Mrs Elaine Jones, IOS, RSA
Science: Mrs Rachel Hunt, BA Hons, QTS

Form and Subject Teachers:
Ms Jenn Caverhill, BA, PGCE
Mrs Rachel Hunt, BA Hons, QTS
Mrs Irene May, BA Hons, Dip Ed, CEPC
Mrs Jane Pollard, BEd, CTC
Mr Matthew Power, BA Hons, PGCE
Mrs Caroline Singleton, BSc, PGCE, CTC
Mrs Oksana Stolcere, BSc Hons
Mrs Christiana Wilcox, Cert Ed, CTC
Mrs Carole West, BA Hons, PGCE
Miss Rebecca Golding, BA Hons, PGCE
Ms Sarah Shaaban, BMus Hons, PGCE
Dance: Mrs Rachel Thomas, RAD
LAMDA: Mrs Collette Wighton, Dip Ed, LTCL

Learning Support – Prep:
*Mrs Anna Biggs-Davison, BEd Hons, Hornsby Dip
Mrs Catherine Bremner, BSc Hons, SLT, SpLD
Mrs Susan Ward, SpLD
Mrs Carol Teunon, SpLD
Mrs Samantha Rice, NVQ2, LSA
Mrs Helen Smith (*EAL Support*)

Teaching Assistants:
Mrs Tracy Davies, BSc Hons, Cache Level 3 Childcare and
  Education
Mrs Virginia Martin, City & Guilds TA Cert, DPP Pre
  School Practice 3
Mrs Heather Fletcher, Cert Ed Internal & External
  Assessor, Level 3 HLTA
Mrs Karyn Skuse, City & Guilds TA Cert Level 2

Early Years Educators:
Mrs Caroline Moffatt, NNEB, ADCE
Mrs Jane Holt, Dip Pre-School Practice
Mrs Eleonora Ferguson, NVQ 3
Miss Rachel Martin, CACHE 3
Mrs Marzena Wajnert, BSc, NVQ 6
Mrs Pauline Irving, NVQ 3
Miss Tara Nicholls, NVQ2 EYFS
Mrs Yuko Salisbury, City & Guilds Level 3 Supporting
  Teaching & Learning

Librarian: Mrs Anne Thompson, BSc Hons

School Support Services:

After School Club Supervisor: Mrs Pauline Irving, NVQ3

Bursary:
Bursar: Mr Phillip Brown, BA Hons, MA Oxon
PA to Bursar: Mrs Natalie Foreman

Finance:
Mrs Maxine Burgess
Mrs Beckie Purkiss
Mrs Preeti Madan

Human Resources: Mrs Paula Clifton, MCIPD

Estates Department: Mr Anthony Madigan
Estates Assistant: Ms Michèle Appadoo

Maintenance:
Mr A Fletcher
Mr C Green

Grounds:
Mr R Nicholls
Mr R Johnson

Caretakers:
Mr M Willoughby
Mr Paul Ashborn
Minibus Driver:
Mr Adrian Witherley

ICT Department:
Director: Mr David Colpus, BSc, PGCE
Mr Lawrence Hepworth, BSc
Mrs Judy Gillett, LRQA [Maternity Leave]
Mrs Mary Randall, BSc Hons

Admissions Manager: Mrs Beccy Johnson, MA Oxon, Dip
  Stat
Marketing and Events Manager: Sara Pittman, BA Hons
Digital Marketing & Publicity: Mrs Louise Plummer, BSc
  Hons, Dip M, PGCE, Cert IT
Alumnae Officer: Mrs Ros Roberts, NUJ, IoIC, IoD

School Nurse:
Mrs Jennifer Simpkin, RGN, Dip Midwifery
Mrs Anne-Marie Sykes, Early Years Paediatric First Aid

School Visits Coordinator: Mrs Carole West, BA Hons,
  PGCE

PA to Heads: Mrs M Hart

School Office Manager: Mrs Shirleen Keane, BTEC Credit
  Management

School Secretary/Administrators:
Mrs N Hallala
Mrs J Russell
Mrs J Clay

Theatre Manager: Ms S Gilhespie, BA Hons

Notting Hill and Ealing High School
GDST

2 Cleveland Road, Ealing, London W13 8AX

Tel:	020 8799 8400
email:	enquiries@nhehs.gdst.net
website:	www.nhehs.gdst.net
Twitter:	@nhehs

Founded 1873.

Notting Hill and Ealing High School is part of the GDST (Girls' Day School Trust). The GDST is the leading network of independent girls' schools in the UK. As a charity that owns and runs 24 schools and two academies, it reinvests all its income in its schools. For further information about the Trust, see p. xxiii or visit www.gdst.net.

An academically selective, independent day school for girls aged 4 to 18. Separately housed and run Junior Department (ages 4+–11) and Senior Department (ages 11+–18) on the same site.

Pupils and Location. Approximately 900 pupils. 590 in the Senior School (153 in the Sixth Form) and 310 in the Junior Department. Transport links are excellent (Ealing Broadway station is nearby and several buses stop outside the school). Girls come from Ealing and all over west London.

Ethos. This is a school with a long tradition of academic excellence and creativity within an exceptionally warm and supportive environment. Notting Hill and Ealing girls are well grounded, confident and independent. They are proud of their school and value kindness and laughter, fun and friendship. This is a place where tolerance and mutual respect are nurtured; where you can be yourself. With a wide variety of activities and opportunities, and a strong emphasis on charitable giving, everyone can enjoy being part of a vibrant community and express their passion for learning, and for life.

Pastoral Care. The system of pastoral care is overseen by the Deputy Head – Pastoral working through the Heads of Year and Form Tutors. The Head also takes a personal interest in all pupils. The result is a well structured system that is sufficiently flexible to support every girl and to ensure that she is treated as a whole person with individual strengths and needs. In the Sixth Form the tutor team is led by the Head of Sixth Form and her deputy.

Curriculum. Throughout the Junior and Senior Schools our curriculum is broad and balanced and encourages independence of learning and thought. In Years 7–9 everyone follows courses in English, History, Geography, Mathematics, Physics, Chemistry, Biology, Design Technology, ICT, Religious Studies, Art, Music, and Drama. In Year 7 and 8 all girls study Mandarin plus a second modern language (French, German or Spanish). In Year 8 Latin also becomes available. Girls usually take ten subjects at GCSE, including a compulsory core of English Language and Literature, Mathematics, 3 Sciences (IGCSE) and a Modern Language. 26 subjects are offered at A Level. Most girls take 4 or 5 subjects. Those who wish may also take the Extended Project Qualification which is highly regarded by university admissions tutors. Each department runs a special programme to support UCAS applications and there is additional support for those applying to Oxbridge or particularly competitive universities. There are also lessons in personal health, ethical and social issues appropriate to each age and stage. Physical Education is taught throughout the school.

The Sixth Form. Our sixth formers play an important role in the school. They enjoy the independence of their own new Sixth Form Centre with common rooms, outdoor space for relaxing, café and fitness centre. They take responsibility for many extra-curricular activities such as organising clubs and act as mentors for girls in the lower years. Additional leadership opportunities are offered by the House system, and voluntary and charity work. All go on to Higher Education and, with excellent results (90% achieving grades A*, A or B in 2016, with 72% of grades being A*/A and 32% of grades being A*), successfully secure places at their choice of university (including Oxford and Cambridge).

Extra-Curricular Activities. As well as covering a wide variety of sports and activities connected with art, drama and music these range from computer animation to competing in the London-wide Hans Woyda Maths competition and from debating to The Duke of Edinburgh's Award scheme.

We take full advantage of everything London offers, with visits to theatres, museums, galleries, performances, and conferences incorporated into the curriculum. Trips abroad are arranged for modern languages, geography, history, art and art history, politics and economics. There is an annual ski trip.

Careers Advice. All girls are offered the Morrisby test free of charge in Year 10 and the school is a member of ISCO (the Independent Schools Careers Organisation) which entitles all students to careers help and advice until the age of 23. Sixth formers receive extensive support with university applications, including mock interviews. The GDST Alumnae Network, the unique resource from the GDST, offers each student access to a database of former GDST students, who will give advice and support on careers (including helping with work experience) and universities. An annual Careers Evening typically featuring senior representatives from almost 70 different professions and occupations is organised by the Parents' Guild.

Creative Arts. There are three orchestras, three choirs, and many chamber and ensemble groups. School productions offer opportunities either to perform or to work with production, lighting, sound, costume and staging. Art thrives within the curriculum and through various art clubs. It also contributes to work in design technology and various aspects of ICT, such as web design and animation projects.

Sport. Sport is taken seriously with success in local fixtures and championships, and we encourage participation and enjoyment at all standards. On site facilities include all-weather pitch, four-court sports hall, dance studio and indoor swimming pool. Lifeguard training is available for sixth formers. Aerobics, self-defence, kick boxing and football are among the extra-curricular sports clubs currently available.

Fees per term (2016-2017). Junior School £4,475, Senior School £5,754.

The fees cover the regular curriculum, necessary school books, normal public examination fees, membership of the FUTUREWISE scheme including the Morrisby careers aptitude test, stationery and other materials, but not optional extra subjects or school meals. Fees for extra subjects including instrumental music, speech and drama, are shown in the prospectus. Certain off-site sports are charged for separately, as are school trips.

Scholarships and Bursaries. Academic and music scholarships are available at 11+. At 16+ there are academic awards as well as awards for Physical Education, Drama, Art, and an All-Rounder scholarship.

Means tested bursaries are available in the Senior Department only. Application should be made via the school.

Admission. Usually at 4+, 7+, 11+ and 16+, by appropriate test and/or interview.

Occasionally, vacancies may become available in other year groups.

Charitable status. Notting Hill and Ealing High School is part of The Girls' Day School Trust, which is a Registered Charity, number 306983.

Chairman of Local Governing Board: Ms Sue Blyth

Head: **Mr Matthew Shoults**, MA Oxon

Deputy Head – Pastoral: Mrs Katie Swift, MA, PGCE
Deputy Head – Academic: Mr Alex Smith, MA, MEd, PGCE

Head of Junior Department: Mrs Silvana Silva, BEd Hons

Nottingham Girls' High School
GDST

9 Arboretum Street, Nottingham NG1 4JB

Tel: 0115 941 7663
Fax: 0115 924 0757
email: enquiries@not.gdst.net
            admissions@not.gdst.net
website: www.nottinghamgirlshigh.gdst.net
Twitter: @NottmGirlsHigh
Facebook: @FriendsofNGHS
LinkedIn: /Friends of Nottingham Girls High School

Founded 1875.

Nottingham Girls' High School is part of the GDST (Girls' Day School Trust). The GDST is the leading network of independent girls' schools in the UK. As a charity that owns and runs 24 schools and two academies, it reinvests all its income in its schools. For further information about the Trust, see p. xxiii or visit www.gdst.net.

Additional information about the school may be found on the school's website and a detailed information pack may be obtained from Central Admissions at the school.

Number of Pupils. Senior School 581 (including 143 in the Sixth Form); Junior School 250.

A selective day school, NGHS is on a single site adjacent to a park in the middle of Nottingham. The original Victorian houses have been modernised and there have been extensive additions to create a well-resourced school. The Junior School is housed in separate buildings on the same campus as the Senior School, and has been extended to include a library and ICT learning resources centre as well four additional classrooms. A major programme of refurbishment in the Senior School has included refitting the science laboratories, food technology and design technology. A state-of-the-art performing arts centre is due to be completed in 2016.

There is a self-contained Sixth Form Centre providing a large coffee shop-style common room and recreational area. The tutorial rooms are light and airy, and fully equipped with the latest technology.

The school grounds include an all-weather sports pitch, climbing wall, outdoor learning area, gymnasium, sports hall and fitness suite. There is also a sizeable sports field close to the school. The modern dining hall has excellent facilities for providing a wide choice of snacks and meals throughout the day.

Although examination results are among the best in the country, the school believes that education for life involves much more. Leadership, confidence, teamwork, flexibility and reliability are among the qualities increasingly demanded in today's ever changing society. Everyone is encouraged to take the opportunity to participate fully in a wide range of enrichment activities to develop skills and qualities that will lead to a happy, successful and fulfilling life.

At all ages, it is hoped that the girls will enjoy their studies. The school provides a lively, stimulating learning environment to encourage girls to discover the excitement and satisfaction of high academic achievement coupled with growing knowledge and understanding.

Curriculum. The curriculum is designed to give a broad academic education and due regard is paid to the National Curriculum. In the Junior School as well as following a pattern of work designed to help develop a confident grasp of core skills, the girls benefit from a stimulating and challenging integrated creative curriculum with enrichment experiences firmly embedded into teaching and learning. Girls take complete internal assessments in Year 6 and results are consistently very high. There is liaison with the Senior School staff, helping to ensure continuity for pupils at 11+. In the Senior School girls are prepared for GCSE, AS and A2 Levels, with almost all girls proceeding to university.

Girls at all ages follow a comprehensive programme of personal and social development including aspects of careers, citizenship, health and sex education, current affairs and environmental issues.

Throughout the school girls are encouraged to develop their physical skills and the school has an excellent sports record; teams regularly win trophies at City and County level with many being selected to compete at regional or national level.

Admissions. At 4+ entry, small groups of girls are invited to come into school and take part in a number of activities together to see if they are ready for school. Entry at 11+ is by interview and a written test which includes English, mathematics and verbal reasoning and is designed to determine potential and understanding. Most of the existing students stay on at 16+ and a number of students are admitted into the Sixth Form from other schools. The entry requirement is 8 GCSE subjects at an average of grade B, with grades A or B in any subject to be studied in the Sixth Form as specified by the department. This is supported by individual interviews and a report from the current school. The school will consider applications for admission into most year groups if there are available places.

Fees per term (2016–2017). Seniors (excluding lunch): Years 7–13 £4,227; Juniors: Rec–Year 6 (inc lunch) £3,243. The fees cover non-residential curriculum trips, school books, stationery and other materials, games and swimming, but not optional extra subjects.

Scholarships and Bursaries. The GDST makes available a substantial number of bursaries. These are means tested and intended to ensure that the school remains accessible to bright girls who would profit from our education but who would be unable to enter the school without financial assistance. Up to 100% of the tuition fee may be awarded. Bursary application forms are available through Central Admissions at the school.

A limited number of scholarships are available each year for entry to the Senior School at both 11+ and direct into the Sixth Form. The value of a scholarship is to a maximum of 10% of the current tuition fee. Scholarships are awarded solely on the basis of academic merit and no financial means test is involved. Music scholarships are available from Year 10.

Charitable status. Nottingham Girls' High School is part of The Girls' Day School Trust, which is a Registered Charity, number 306983.

Chairman of Local Governors: Mrs Jean Pardoe, OBE, DL

Headmistress: Miss J Keller, BA

Deputy Head: Ms K Handford-Smith, MEd

Assistant Heads:
Mrs R A Halse, BSc
Mrs L M Wharton-Howett, BA

Head of Junior School: Mrs L Fowler, BA Ed

Director of Finance and Operations: Mr J C Dunn, ACA

Central Admissions:
Mrs S M Webb-Bowen
Mrs C L Haddow

Oxford High School
GDST

Belbroughton Road, Oxford OX2 6XA

Tel: 01865 559888
Fax: 01865 552343
email: oxfordhigh@oxf.gdst.net
website: www.oxfordhigh.gdst.net
Twitter: @OxfordHighSch
Facebook: @OxfordHighGDST

Motto: *Ad Lucem.*

Oxford High School is an independent day school for girls founded in 1875. It is Oxford's oldest girls' school and is located in the heart of Oxford. It is part of the Girls' Day School Trust (GDST) which is at the forefront of educational innovation, teaching over 20,000 girls across the UK in 26 schools and is the leading network of independent girls' schools in the UK.

Tatler describes OHS girls as 'fearless and independent' and with outstanding results, record numbers entering Sixth Form and a 'have a go' attitude, it remains true to its heritage of pioneering girls' education, in its 140th anniversary year.

Pupil numbers. 900: Junior School 300, Senior School 600.

The school is on three sites in North Oxford. New buildings at the Senior School include the School Hall, Lecture Theatre, Dining Hall, Library, Drama Studio and Language Suite. Already extremely well resourced, the Senior School has a sports hall, indoor swimming pool, The Mary Warnock School of Music, and separate purpose-built centres for all other subjects and the Sixth Form. The school is networked with well-equipped ICT areas.

Curriculum. Girls are prepared for GCSE and AS/A Level. Sixth-formers choose from 26 subjects and their timetable is individually tailored around their choice of subjects. Mandarin is a compulsory language for Year 7 along with French. The school offers 8 languages including Latin and Ancient Greek. Approximately 30% proceed to Oxbridge annually. Many girls take examinations in Music, and Speech and Drama, as well as belonging to the Duke of Edinburgh's Award Scheme, Young Enterprise and the Combined Cadet Force. 2016 sees a new innovative Sixth Form programme called The 360 Programme.

A strong co-curricular programme offers about 100 clubs at any one time, with everything from rock bands to gardening.

Admission. The main points of entry are at Reception, Year 3, Year 7, Year 9 and Year 12. Contact Mrs Teresa Hobbs, Admissions Registrar for details.

Fees per term (2016–2017). Reception to Year 2: £3,291 (plus lunch £215); Years 3–6: £3,617 (plus lunch £256);

Senior School (Years 7–13): £4,808 (plus lunch £256 for Years 7–11). Lunch is compulsory for girls from Reception to Year 11 and optional for Sixth Form girls only.

The fees cover the regular curriculum textbooks, stationery and other materials, educational visits, choral music, games and swimming, but not optional extra subjects or school meals.

Bursaries. The School offers bursaries. These are means tested and ensure that the school remains accessible to bright girls who would be unable to profit from the education provided but who would be unable to enter the school without financial assistance. Bursaries are available at Year 7, Year 9 and Year 12 entry to the Senior School and confidential application can be made to the GDST.

Scholarships. Scholarships for Year 7 and Year 9 entry in Art, Drama, Sport, Music, Academic and the Head's Scholarship. Year 12 scholarships in Art, Academic, Drama, Music and Sports and the Head's Scholarship.

Charitable status. Oxford High School is part of The Girls' Day School Trust, which is a Registered Charity, number 306983.

Chairman of School Governing Board: Mrs L Ansdell

Head: Mrs J Carlisle

Deputy Head – Students and Staff: Dr S Squire

Deputy Head – Academic: Dr P Secker

Assistant Head – Curriculum: Mr J Nicholl

Head of Junior School: Mrs K Gater

Director of Finance and Operations: Ms J Hasnip

Head of Sixth Form: Miss R Pallas-Brown

Admissions Registrar: Mrs Teresa Hobbs
Assistant Registrar: Miss Dani Kecojevic

Palmers Green High School

Hoppers Road, London N21 3LJ

Tel:	020 8886 1135
Fax:	020 8882 9473
email:	office@pghs.co.uk
website:	www.pghs.co.uk
Twitter:	@PGHSGirls
Facebook:	@palmersgreenhighschool
LinkedIn:	/palmers-green-high-school

Motto: *By Love Serve One Another*

Founded 1905.

Palmers Green High School is an independent day school for approximately 300 girls aged 3–16. Located in the pleasant suburb of the London Borough of Enfield, the school has good transport links by car, bus rail and tube. It is close to British Rail Stations in Winchmore Hill and Palmers Green. Southgate on the Piccadilly Line is the nearest Tube Station.

Palmers Green High School is celebrating 111 years of educating girls, challenging them to aim for the stars whilst enjoying its happy family atmosphere. The school welcomes back alumnae from the different generations to share their memories, present experiences and future plans. The school motto, 'By Love, Serve One Another' was carefully chosen by its founder, Miss Alice Hum, and it still epitomises the school's special ethos where each individual is nurtured, successes are celebrated and contribution to the community is greatly valued.

Palmers Green High School is an academically selective school and caters for girls in the Pre-Prep, Prep, Junior and Senior years and is proud of the fact that all aspects of the

school attained the top grading of "outstanding/excellent" in its most recent inspection report.

Lower School classes benefit hugely from the encouragement and expertise of their class teachers and teaching assistants. Favourable teaching group sizes, light and airy classrooms and access to senior school facilities all lead to an inspirational learning environment. This is enriched by specialist teaching in Art, Design & Technology, Drama, French, German, Latin, Music, PE and Russian – frequently in half-class groups.

In Senior School small class sizes (an average of only 10 at GCSE) and a broad range of extra-curricular activities enrich the girls' experience. New Year 7s enjoy a three-day residential PGL trip and friendships are formed quickly and easily. Excellent teamwork helped our Year 10 pupils to win the 2014 London Schools Hydrogen Challenge, in a world record-breaking time. Over the last five years 72% of GCSE/IGCSE grades were A* or A, placing pupils amongst the top performers in the country.

Ranked 4th in The Sunday Times league table for Small Schools in 2016, parents can be reassured that Palmers Green High School girls not only attain excellent results in relation to their abilities and aptitudes, but also grow in confidence and poise as members of this very special school community. Here a plethora of opportunities ensures that girls have freedom to flourish.

In 2008 the school opened a new nursery for 3–4 year olds – The Alice Nursery – in Bush Hill Park which can accommodate up to 24 children. The Alice Nursery is situated approximately 10 minutes' drive from the main school and is open from 8.45 am until 3.45 pm. The day is divided into morning and afternoon sessions with a break in the middle of the day for lunch. Girls may attend Nursery for the whole day or morning with lunch only. Being an academic nursery, pupils follow a stimulating but demanding curriculum in preparation for Reception at the main school.

The curriculum, embracing the National Curriculum, is designed to give a broad education in which the active acquisition of skills, as well as knowledge, is encouraged. Children are familiarised with computers from the Preparatory Department upwards. The performing arts are encouraged in the school and each term sees a large number of pupils taking part in plays, musicals and concerts. Careers education is an integral part of the timetabled curriculum from 11–16 and all pupils participate in careers lectures, exhibitions and work experience placements. Pupils are prepared for up to 10 GCSE subjects, with a view to continuing their studies to A Level and beyond.

Fees per term (2016–2017). Nursery: £2,995 (Full time), £1,795 (Part time); Reception–Year 2 £3,460; Years 3–6 £3,710; Years 7–11 £4,920.

Scholarships. Academic scholarships and bursaries of up to 100% of fees and Music awards are available to candidates aged 11+ for entry in September.

Entrance. Admission to all forms is by test and interview, the main intakes being at 3+, 4+ and 7+ and 11+.

Charitable status. Palmers Green High School Limited is a Registered Charity, number 312629. It exists for the education of girls.

School Council:
Chairman: Mr Dermot Lewis, FCIB IAC, Banker
Mr John Atkinson, Chair of Buildings Committee, Special interest in Health & Safety
Miss Anna Averkiou, Chair of Risk Mitigation Committee
Mrs Melanie Curtis, Vice Chair of Governors, Chair of Education Committee
Miss Alexia Eliades
Mrs Bronwen Goulding, Special interest in Safeguarding
Mrs Gay Kettle, MBE
Mr Robert Keys
Mr Jeremy Piggott

Mrs Karen Tidmarsh, Special interest in Safeguarding
Mr Jeffrey Zinkin, Chair of Finance & General Purposes Committee

Headmistress: **Mrs Wendy Kempster**, BSc Reading, PGCE

Bursar: Mrs Angela Monty, MAAT
Deputy Head KS2 and Head of ICT: Mrs Karen Thompson, BA Denver, Colorado
Assistant Head (Prep Department Coordinator, Lower School Class Teacher): Miss Hannah Lucas, BSc Sussex, MSc, PGCE

* Head of Department

Mrs L Aghassi, CertEd Middlesex (**Computing*)
Miss R Begum, MA Cantab (**English*)
Mrs H Bhundia, Dip Playgroup Practice (*First Aid Coordinator, Teaching Assistant*)
Mrs M Brent, MA Cantab, GTP London Institute (**Geography*)
Mrs B Broad, BEd Leeds (**Physical Education*)
Miss T Fan Cho, MSc London, PGCE (*Science*)
Miss T Fong Cho, MSc London, PGCE (*Science*)
Mrs E Christodoulou, BA Middlesex, PGCE (*Lower School Class Teacher*)
Mrs K Conlon, MSc London, BSc London (*Librarian*)
Mrs A Davey, BA Leeds, PGCE (*English*)
Mrs A Deans, BSc London Metropolitan, PGCE (*Lower School Class Teacher*)
Mr A Desai, BEng, BEd India, OTTP, PGCE (*Mathematics*)
Mrs C Doe, BA East Anglia, MA Ed Open, PGCE (**English, Careers*)
Dr J English, BA Southampton, MMus London, PhD Cantab, PGCE Manchester (*Music*)
Mrs H Eve, BA Bristol, PGCE (**Drama*)
Miss L Gelsthorpe, BA Manchester, MSc Salford, PGCE (*Lower School Class Teacher*)
Mrs K Gil, CACHE Level 3 (*Nursery Assistant*)
Miss S Govani, BA London School of Economics, PGCE Oxford (**History*)
Mrs S Hagi-Savva (*Assistant School Secretary, Teaching Assistant*)
Mrs S Harney, BEd Cantab (*Head of Nursery*)
Mrs E Hassan, NVQ3 (*Lower School Teaching Assistant*)
Miss J Henry, BA Newcastle, MA, PGCE (**Art*)
Mrs S Kazim, BSc Middlesex PGCE (**Science*)
Senora M Laratonda, MA London, BEd Buenos Aires, PGCE (*Spanish*)
Mr J Matthews, BMus Cardiff, LTCL (**Music*)
Mrs M Mehran, BSc North London (*Science Technician*)
Ms L Meltzer, MA Oxon, PGCE (*Individual Needs*)
Mrs A Michael, NNEB (*Nursery Assistant*)
Miss S Mitchell, BA Liverpool, PGCE (*Art*)
Miss J Newman, BA London, PGCE (*French*)
Mrs M Nicolaou, NVQ3 (*Teaching Assistant*)
Mme K Parry-Garnaud, Licence Anglais Tours/France, BA Sunderland (**Modern Foreign Languages*)
Mrs J Pauk, BA Aberystwyth, PGCE (*Lower School Class Teacher*)
Mr A J Pepper, BSc Loughborough, CertEd (**Design and Technology*)
Mrs H Pestaille, BA Middlesex, PGCE (*Geography*)
Miss V Rich, BSc Bedfordshire, PGCE (*Lower School Class Teacher*)
Miss K Robinson, BA London, PGCE (*Lower School Class Teacher*)
Miss L Selley, BA Brighton (*Physical Education*)
Ms A Singh, BA London (*Examinations Officer & Individual Needs Teaching Assistant*)
Mrs C Shaw, BSc Warwick, PGCE (**Mathematics*)
Mrs M Suleyman, NVQ3 Childcare (*Reception Teaching Assistant*)

Mrs S Turanli, BSc London, PGCE (*Physical Education*)
Mrs K Woods-Shelley, BA Middlesex, PGCE, LLAM (*Drama*)

Visiting Staff – Instrumental Tuition:
Clarinet/Saxophone: Mr J Matthews, BMus, LTCL
Flute: Ms K Bircher, BA, FTCL
Piano: Miss S Pope, LRAM
Singing: Miss M Taylor, AGSM, PGCE, ATCL
Violin/Viola: Miss V David, AGSM
Violin/Viola: Miss M Pound, FTCL, LTCL

Administrative Staff:
PA to the Headmistress: Mrs L Mount
Admissions Officer/Office Manager: Miss V Bennett
School Secretaries: Mrs A Dudley and Mrs S Hagi-Savva
Assistant Bursar: Mrs D Hadjicostas, MICM
Assistant to the Bursary Department: Mrs M Soudah
Marketing Officer: Mrs D Simmons, BA Bournemouth, Dip Marketing CIM
Caretaker: Mr G Munian
Caretaker: Mr D Singh

Pipers Corner School
High Wycombe

Great Kingshill, High Wycombe, Bucks HP15 6LP

Tel:	01494 718255
Fax:	01494 719806
email:	theschool@piperscorner.co.uk
website:	www.piperscorner.co.uk
Twitter:	@PipersCornerSch
Facebook:	/PipersCornerSchool

Pipers Corner is an independent day school for girls aged 4–18. From Pre-Prep through to Sixth Form there is a focus on academic excellence as girls are supported and challenged to achieve their full potential. Academically successful, our girls progress to further study at Oxbridge and other top universities or specialist dance, drama and music colleges.

Set in 96 acres of beautiful Chiltern countryside, the school is less than one hour from central London (40 minute rail links to Marylebone Station in London) and 45 minutes from Heathrow airport, 4 miles north of High Wycombe and 2 miles from Great Missenden.

The standard and extent of our excellent facilities along with our commitment to a programme of continual improvement means that our girls have all the space and equipment they need to enable them to excel. Sport is popular at Pipers and from the 25 metre indoor swimming pool, to the sports hall and outdoor pitches we can accommodate a wide range of activities. Similarly those with creative interests benefit from the use of dance, drama, textiles, art, ceramics, design and technology studios, as well as a large music department.

In addition to providing a stimulating learning environment we also encourage the girls to cultivate any sporting or creative talents they have through a wide range of lunchtime and after school clubs and activities. Girls are able to develop their own interests in areas including: sport, music, dance, drama, technology, languages and outdoor pursuits. Team spirit is developed through a regular programme of sports fixtures.

The Pipers Corner environment allows girls to thrive. Whatever their strengths, the girls are challenged and supported as they pursue their own unique learning journeys. This approach enables them to fulfil their academic and personal potential and emerge as mature, confident and independent young women.

Fees per term (2016–2017). £2,750–£5,570.

Scholarships and Bursaries. Pipers Corner girls are extremely successful in many areas of achievement. In recognition of this success, the Governors are keen to encourage girls' potential and to widen access to ensure that as many talented girls as possible are able to take advantage of the excellent education that Pipers Corner can provide.

Girls from any primary school, as well as girls from Pipers Corner Prep Department may apply for an 11+ Scholarship for entry into the Senior School in any one of the following areas: Academic, Art, Drama, Music and PE.

Means-tested Bursaries are also available up to a maximum of 100% of fees (including any Scholarship award).

The Jessie Cross Award – for an all-rounder at 11+ – is a means-tested award of up to 100% of fees, available to a deserving student currently educated in a maintained primary school and who shows promise in a number of areas. Students applying for the award would need the recommendation of their Headteacher and would also need to provide supporting evidence of their achievements and involvement in their school, church or community. Girls applying for the Jessie Cross Award may not also apply for a scholarship.

Applications for Scholarships and Bursaries must be received by early December of the year preceding the intended entry to the School. Entrance Assessments are held early in January and potential scholars will be invited back shortly afterwards for further interview and assessment. Prior to this girls will also be invited in to school for an entrance interview with the Headmistress.

Sixth Form Academic Major and Minor Scholarships: Girls from any secondary school as well as girls from Pipers Corner may apply for a Sixth Form Scholarship. Girls who apply for a Scholarship may be awarded either a Major or Minor Scholarship for study in the Pipers' Sixth Form. Neither of these Awards is means-tested. The entry process is the same for both Awards. Please contact the school for further details.

Charitable status. Pipers Corner School is a Registered Charity, number 310635. It exists to provide high quality education for girls.

Visitor: The Rt Revd The Lord Bishop of Buckingham

Chair of Governors: Lady Allison, MA
Mr A Cannon, BA Hons
Ms E Carrighan, MBA, MA
Mr M F T Harborne, CBII
Mrs J B Ingram, BA, JD
Professor P B Mogford
Ms H F Morton, MA, MSc, CEng
Mr H B P Roberts, BSc Eng, FCA
Mrs J E Smith, BEd, MSc, DipM, MCIM, Chartered Marketer
Mr P B Wayne, MusB, NPQH

Headmistress: **Mrs H J Ness-Gifford**, BA Hons, PGCE

Deputy Head: Mr N Walker, BSc, PGCE, MA

Assistant Head: Mrs E Cresswell, BA Hons, PGCE

Assistant Head: Mrs C Derbyshire, BSc Hons, PGCE

Head of Prep and Pre-Prep Department: Mrs C Etchegoyen, BEd Hons

Bursar and Clerk to the Governors: Mr P R Forrester, MA, FCA

Director of Admissions & Marketing: Mrs F Knight, BA Hons

Director of Digital Strategy: Mr A Rees, BSc Hons, PG Dip

Portsmouth High School
GDST

25 Kent Road, Southsea, Hampshire PO5 3EQ
Tel: 023 9282 6714
email: admissions@por.gdst.net
website: www.portsmouthhigh.co.uk
Twitter: @portsmouthhigh
Facebook: /PortsmouthHigh

Founded 1882.

Portsmouth High School is part of the GDST (Girls' Day School Trust). The GDST is the leading network of independent girls' schools in the UK. As a charity that owns and runs 24 schools and two academies, it reinvests all its income in its schools. For further information about the Trust, see p. xxiii or visit www.gdst.net.

Additional information about the school may be found on the school's website and a prospectus pack is available from the Admissions Officer at the school.

Number of Pupils. 350 are in the Senior School (11–18), 150 in the Junior School (rising 3–11).

Portsmouth High School is a community of learning committed to academic excellence and preparing girls to be the leaders of tomorrow. Each girl is encouraged to develop her own voice and her own views and to understand and build on her strengths. A broad based education encourages each girl's talents and potential to the full in an atmosphere of achievement and excellence. Characteristic of the GDST philosophy, Portsmouth High School has a profile of sustained academic achievement, strong relationships with the local community and outstanding pastoral care. Situated close to the sea, the school draws pupils from an extensive area of Hampshire, West Sussex and the Isle of Wight. All major transport providers serve the area. The school recently received the highest category in each section of the Independent Schools Inspectorate Report 2015. The school underwent a four-day inspection in April 2015 which looked at the following criteria: the success of the school, the quality of academic and other achievements, the quality of the pupils' personal development and the effectiveness of governance, leadership and management. In each section the school was ranked "excellent".

The Senior School provides a broad and balanced education that prepares girls to specialise at A Level and the Sixth Form provides a perfect bridge to higher study. The Senior School is accommodated in the original building; a capital investment programme has seen the development of a Sport, Design Technology and Geography building on the senior school site.

A partnership with the University of Portsmouth means the school has joint use of the Langstone sports ground facilities, including a floodlit synthetic turf pitch and a multi-use games area; the site is just 2 miles from the school. In addition, the school site facilities include a Sport England standard sports hall, 4 hard tennis courts and 6 netball courts. Sixth Form students do not wear uniform, but have a 'Dress for Work' code. Sixth Formers have a recently refurbished Sixth Form Centre with a large common room, kitchen, study rooms and IT room.

The Junior School, through the provision of our innovative and challenging curriculum, develops curious, confident and collaborative learners. The Junior School is located 2 minutes' walk away in a wonderful period house with extensive gardens including 4 netball courts, and a range of indoor and outdoor facilities. Major investment in the Junior School saw the completion of an award-winning Pre-Prep building and science discovery lab. With the addition of a Nursery class which, along with Reception, was judged "Excellent" in all categories in the school's ISI inspection

(2015), the school is able to offer continuity of education throughout the Foundation Stage.

The Curriculum. The aim at Portsmouth High School is to foster in each girl the confidence to take risks and tackle new challenges within an atmosphere of ambition and enterprise, by providing appropriate teaching, advice and support. The focus on girls' learning is reflected in the design of learning spaces; the use of digital technology; a challenging and rewarding curriculum and a focus on pupils taking responsibility for their learning and having the confidence to take intellectual risks.

Co-Curricular Activities. There is an extensive programme of co-curricular activities in both the Junior and Senior schools. The lunchtime and after-school clubs range from dance to public speaking. There is an enthusiastic involvement in music, art, sport and drama with many performances and fixtures throughout the School calendar for Junior and Senior girls. Senior Girls have the opportunity to become involved in The Duke of Edinburgh's Award scheme as well as a Sixth Form Seminar Group and Enrichment Programme. There are regular overseas music, and other, tours.

Admission Procedures/Entrance Examinations. At 11+ and 13+ entry the examinations in mathematics and English are designed to test potential rather than knowledge. Prior to the 11+ examinations all girls take part in a series of team activities in school. At 13+ girls take part in a Shadowing Day and are interviewed by the Headmistress. Sixth Form entry is based on having at least 7 GCSEs at grade B or above. Most subjects will require at least grade A as a prerequisite for A Level study and applicants are invited for interview. Entry into the Junior School is based on assessments and examinations dependent on age.

Fees per term (2016–2017). Senior School £4,396, Junior School £3,185, Nursery £2,630.

The fees this year cover the regular curriculum, school books, non-residential curriculum trips, stationery and other materials, public examinations, choral music, games and swimming. The fees for extra subjects, including individual lessons in instrumental music and speech training, are shown in the Admissions Handbook.

Scholarships and Bursaries. The GDST makes available to the school a number of scholarships and bursaries. Bursaries are means tested and are intended to ensure that the school remains accessible to bright girls who would be unable to enter the school without financial assistance.

Academic and Music Scholarships are available for 11+, 13+ and Sixth Form, with Art, Drama and Sport Scholarships available in the Sixth Form. HSBC scholarships are also available for Sixth Formers.

Charitable status. Portsmouth High School is part of The Girls' Day School Trust, which is a Registered Charity, number 306983.

Chair of the School Governing Board: Mrs A McMeehan Roberts, BA

Headmistress: Mrs J Prescott, BSc Cardiff, PGCE, NPQH

Deputy Head (Pastoral): Mrs H Trim, MSc Leicester, BSc Southampton

Deputy Head (Academic): Mr J Paget-Tomlinson, BA Reading, MA King's College

Headmaster, Junior School: Mr P Marshallsay, BA Education

Admissions Registrar: Miss L Nunan

Princess Helena College

School Lane, Preston, Hitchin, Hertfordshire SG4 7RT

Tel: 01462 432100
Fax: 01462 443871
email: office@princesshelenacollege.co.uk
website: www.princesshelenacollege.co.uk
Twitter: @PHCPreston
Facebook: @PHCPreston
LinkedIn: /Princess Helena College

Motto: *Fortis qui se vincit*

Princess Helena College is a day and boarding school for girls aged between 11 and 18. The College is located in Hertfordshire and set in 180 acres of rolling hills, fields and beautiful woodland. This, combined with its close proximity to London, enriches the girls' educational experience.

History. Founded in 1820 we are one of England's oldest academic girls' schools. We are extremely proud of our heritage and aim to maintain high academic standards and respect for traditional values. The school was founded for daughters of officers who had served in the Napoleonic Wars and daughters of Anglican priests. We now encourage this tradition by offering bursaries to daughters from families that are in the forces and the clergy.

Ethos. At Princess Helena College, we believe every girl is an individual and aim to inspire her to achieve both her academic and personal goals. We choose to remain a small school because we strongly believe this unique approach provides many benefits in academic, extracurricular and pastoral areas. The educational benefits include a flexible curriculum and small classes. Both result in individual attention and excellent value-added attainment. A smaller school allows teachers to understand girls' individual learning styles, to recognise their particular strengths and weaknesses and to set individual learning targets. Pastoral care is strengthened by excellent relations between pupils and staff, which result in a strong family atmosphere. Knowing our girls well allows us to encourage them to take risks safe in the knowledge that we will support them. This allows every girl to be challenged, to achieve and to grow. Within a small school your daughter's chances of being selected for a team, a place in the orchestra, a part in a play or a position of responsibility are far higher. Having the opportunity to take part or perform in these activities will increase her confidence and self-belief. The value of this should not be underestimated.

Facilities. As well as an idyllic and safe learning environment, Princess Helena College has excellent educational facilities. The main building is a beautiful Queen Anne mansion that lies in fine Gertrude Jekyll gardens and 183 acres of parkland. Over the past 5 years the school has invested heavily in developing the facilities for all girls: a Sixth Form area has been added, the boarding house has been renovated and there are plans for a Performing Arts Centre. Other developments include a new science centre, art and design studios, a fitness suite and a refurbished learning resources centre.

Curriculum. We offer every girl the opportunity to excel within a varied and stimulating curriculum. Taught in small classes by highly-qualified and enthusiastic teachers who are dedicated to supporting each girl's talents and interests, our girls attain high levels of academic excellence and confidence. Girls are taught in sets that rarely exceed 18 and their potential and progress is carefully monitored.

The lower school curriculum (Years 7–9) consists of English, French, Spanish, Mathematics, Computing, Biology, Physics, Chemistry, History, Geography, Religious Education, Music, Drama, Physical Education, Art and Design. There are also programmes in PCC (PSHEE, Citizenship and Careers) and general studies.

In Years 10–11, girls study their chosen GCSE subjects, following much consultation with staff and parents. On average, girls study between 8 and 10 GCSE subjects.

In the Sixth Form, A Level courses are available in all the traditional academic subjects, as well as Economics, Dance, Media Studies and Photography. Extensive career and Higher Education support and advice is provided; in addition our one-to-one mentor scheme monitors the girls' academic progress and welfare.

In 2016, 37% of girls received A* at A Level, 65% A*–A and 95% A*–C.

A flexible approach to boarding. Princess Helena College is a vibrant community made up of boarders and day girls. We offer a very flexible approach to boarding and full, weekly, and flexible boarding are well established. Day girls can choose to stay into the early evening to make full use of the optional extended school day, participating in supervised prep or one of the numerous after school activities.

The Arts. Princess Helena College is particularly strong in Art & Design, Dance, Drama, Music and Speech & Drama. Girls may enter examinations in all these areas. Dance is a hugely popular activity, with girls learning jazz, modern, ballet, Irish and tap. Most of the College is involved in some form of musical activity, with many girls choosing to take part in one of the many different music groups or ensembles. Plays are staged throughout the year and there are regular joint productions with neighbouring boys' and co-educational schools.

Sport. In addition to timetabled lessons, there are sports activities on weekdays after school and on some Saturdays. Girls participate in a wide range of sports including lacrosse, netball, tennis, athletics, badminton, cross-country, rounders and swimming. Girls are given the opportunity to participate in competitive sport, recreational sport and fitness – we aim to encourage all girls to find an activity they will enjoy at school and in the future.

Co-curricular activities. Life is busy at Princess Helena College – there is an exciting array of extracurricular activities and clubs, which form part of our exciting SCITLLE (Serve, Create, Inspire, Thrive, Lead, Learn, Explore) programme. Girls can choose to join in with these activities either during their extended lunch break or after school. From photography to public speaking, from language club to life saving and from touch typing to trampolining, there is an activity for everyone. The Duke of Edinburgh's Award scheme is also a popular activity, with girls attaining Gold, Silver and Bronze awards each year.

Religion. Girls attend the nearby village church of St Martin's in Preston, which is also used for the school's Confirmation Services. Although the school's affiliation is to the Church of England, girls of other denominations and religions are welcomed.

Location. Set in 180 acres of rural parkland the College offers an easily accessible location within a safe and beautiful environment. The College is situated 30 minutes north of London between the A1 and the M1, just 5 minutes from the market town of Hitchin. Our excellent transport links include rail access (35 minutes to King's Cross) and proximity to several airports (Luton 15 mins, Stansted 45 mins and Heathrow 60 mins). There is an extensive network of school bus routes to Ashwell, Brookmans Park, Cottered, Cuffley, Digswell, Enfield, Gustard Wood, Hadley Wood, Harpenden, Hertford, Hitchin, Kimpton, Little Wymondley, London Colney, Luton, Potters Bar, St Albans, Stevenage, Stotfold, Welwyn and Wheathampstead.

Admission. We welcome girls aged 11–18. Most girls join the school at age 11 (Year 7), but there are also entrants at age 13 (Year 9) and the Sixth Form (Year 12). Please contact Melanie Harper, Registrar (01462 443888) for a prospectus or to find out the date of our next Open Day. All girls must sit either the College's own Entrance Exam or the Common Entrance Exam. Sixth Form places are conditional on GCSE results.

Fees per term (2016–2017). Day Girls: Years 7 and 8 £5,195; Years 9–Sixth Form £6,325. Weekly Boarding or Full Boarding: Years 7 and 8 £7,395; Years 9–Sixth Form £9,195. Flexible Boarding: Year 7–8 £60 per night, Years 9–Sixth Form £70 per night. Overseas Boarders additional fees: £750 for weekend activities and £750 for EAL lessons. Fees include break, lunch, afternoon tea and supervised prep but exclude some books.

Scholarships and Bursaries. Scholarships are awarded for excellent potential. Scholarships (worth up to 15% of annual fees) are available for academically able pupils. Art, Dance, Drama, Music and Sport scholarships are also available. Bursaries of 10% of fees are available for daughters of the clergy and of members of the armed forces. Sibling bursaries are 5% of fees.

Charitable status. Princess Helena College is a Registered Charity, number 311064. It was founded in 1820 for the purposes of education.

Patron: Her Majesty the Queen

President: HRH The Duchess of Gloucester

Governing Body:
Chairman: Mr David Prosser, BSc, FCA, MSt Cantab
Vice-Chairman: Mrs Louise Smith, BSc Hons
Treasurer: Mr Ian Chambers, BSc, FCA

Clerk to the Governors and Bursar: Dr James Bentall, MA, MBA, PhD, ACII, ACMI

Headmistress: Mrs Susan Wallace-Woodroffe, BSc

Deputy Head: Ms Rachel Poston, BSc, PGCE

Registrar: Ms Melanie Harper

Head's PA: Mrs Heather Baim

Putney High School
GDST

---

35 Putney Hill, London SW15 6BH

Tel: 020 8788 4886
Fax: 020 8789 8068
email: putneyhigh@put.gdst.net
website: www.putneyhigh.gdst.net

Founded 1893, Putney High School is part of the GDST (Girls' Day School Trust). The GDST is the leading network of independent girls' schools in the UK. As a charity that owns and runs 24 schools and two academies, it reinvests all its income in its schools. For further information about the Trust, see p. xxiii or visit www.gdst.net.

Putney High School is one of the UK's leading schools for bright girls aged 4–18, with a reputation for academic excellence alongside outstanding opportunity. Wellbeing is paramount.

We develop a culture of intellectual agility, with girls stretched, challenged and supported by staff keen to nurture the same sense of academic curiosity that they themselves enjoy. Students have fun and can take risks, secure in the knowledge they are in a safe environment. We lead in digital innovation – all girls have their own iPads, for example.

We want girls to have a voice, to take ownership in all aspects of their school life.

Students go on to some of the best universities around the world, from Stanford in the USA to Oxford, Cambridge, LSE and Durham amongst others, as well as to music conservatoires and art colleges.

"A spirit of innovation, openness and creativity" pervades Putney High School concluded the most recent Independent Schools Inspectorate report, which awarded the school the highest possible grading in every category.

Facilities. A Performing Arts Centre with professional sound and lighting showcases the wealth of talent in Drama, Music and Dance. A boathouse on Putney embankment builds on the growing success and popularity of our rowing. Our £5 million state-of-the-art Sixth Form Centre incorporates cutting-edge technology as well as offering cafés, a rooftop terrace and a professionally-equipped fitness centre only for Sixth Form use.

Curriculum. Well-qualified, specialist staff provide continuity of education from Reception through to A Levels at 18. Girls are welcome to enter the school at 4+, 11+ and 16+ or in other years if an occasional vacancy arises.

In the Senior School, the girls follow a broad and balanced curriculum, which includes Latin with Greek, French, Chinese (Mandarin), German, Spanish and Design Technology. On entering the GCSE years, all girls study the core subjects plus Biology, Physics and Chemistry and at least one modern language. They are also able to choose from a wide list including Art, Computing, DT-Textiles, DT-Resistant Materials, Drama, Geography, History, Latin, Music, PE and RS. At A Level these subjects may be supplemented by others such as Business, Economics, Government & Politics, History of Art, Further Mathematics and Psychology. Students can also complete an Extended Project on a topic of their choice.

Music. Putney is renowned for its musical excellence. A huge number of pupils learn a musical instrument; many are accomplished musicians, studying at the junior conservatoires and/or are members of nationally auditioned choirs and orchestras. Private tuition is available in all instruments and voice. Girls have many opportunities to participate in music – three orchestras; four Senior Choirs and a Junior Choir and many smaller ensembles.

Sport. Putney High School has earned a national reputation in sport. We also promote a 'sport for all' policy, encouraging all pupils to participate for enjoyment and fun. As well as facilities on site, the school uses off-site grounds at Wimbledon Rugby Football Club. All girls have lessons in netball, lacrosse, gymnastics, tennis and athletics. Rowing is introduced in Year 9 and is a popular extracurricular club from Year 7. Other clubs include dance, badminton, trampolining, cross country and fencing. Tennis, lacrosse, netball, rowing, cross country, gymnastics, athletics and sports acrobatics teams compete successfully nationally.

The Junior School promotes a love of learning through active, exciting experiences within and outside the classroom. We aim to develop mental agility through high quality inspirational teaching. Every pupil from Year 1–6 has a timetabled thinking and learning lesson to teach learning dispositions which will help her to thrive – resilience, resourcefulness, creativity, perseverance and tenacity. Philosophy and debating develop critical thinking skills.

There are 976 pupils, of whom about 660 are in the Senior School (ages 11–18), which includes a Sixth Form of 150, with 315 in the Junior School (ages 4–11).

Fees per term (2016–2017). Senior School £5,803, Junior School £4,801.

The fees cover the regular curriculum, school books, stationery and other materials, choral music, games and swimming, but not optional extra subjects or special sports. All pupils below the Sixth Form take school meals for which the charge is £179 per term (Reception–Year 2) and £212 per term (Years 3–11). The fees for instrumental tuition are shown in the Prospectus.

Financial Assistance. We are committed to offering opportunities to bright girls whose parents would not be able to afford the fees. The GDST has its own means-tested Bursary Scheme. Bursaries are available in Senior School and Sixth Form.

Scholarships. Academic, music and sports scholarships are available to internal or external candidates (up to 50% of fees) for entry at 11+. At 16+ we provide academic, art, design, drama, music, and sports scholarships, as well as travel scholarships in modern languages and science.

Charitable status. Putney High School is part of The Girls' Day School Trust, which is a Registered Charity, number 306983.

Local Governing Body:
Mr P Wake, OBE, MSc City (*Chairman*)
Mrs R Bell, BSc UCL, MSc Stirling
Mrs C Boardman, MA Cantab, MBA City
Mr J David, BA Keele
Ms A Di Marco, MA Cantab, MBBS King's, Guy's and St Thomas', MRCS Eng, AKC
Ms C Lux, MA Oxon
Mrs M Matley, MA Oxon
Prof C Ozanne, BA, MA Oxon, DPhil
Ms A Scott-Bayfield, MA, Solicitor of the Supreme Court
Mr M Wright, FCSI

Headmistress: **Mrs S Longstaff**, BA Dunelm, MA Bath

Senior Leadership Team:
Deputy Head (*Academic*): Ms J Lowson, MA Cantab
Deputy Head (*Pastoral*): Mrs H Armstrong, BA Nottingham
Director of Curriculum Studies: Mr M Finnemore, BSc Imperial, ARCS
Head of Junior School: Mrs J Wallace, BMus Manchester, MA Bath
Director of Sixth Form: Miss B Britten, BA Sheffield
Director of Co-curricular Activities: Dr J Brandon, BMus, PhD London
Director of Assessment: Mr G Oliver, MA Cantab
Lead Teacher: Ms S Norman, BA Brunel
Director of Finance and Operations: Mr A Gray, BSc Aberdeen, MA Cranfield
Director of Communications & Development: Mrs S Fearon

Senior School:

Heads of Department:
Art: Mrs I Vickers, BA Oxon
Business and Economics: Mr A Ross, BCom Edinburgh
Classics: Mrs A Nicoll, MA Oxon
Design Technology: Miss S Norman, BA Brunel
Drama: Miss E Burford, BA London
English: Miss M Slesser, BA Reading
Geography: Mrs E Matthews, BA Exeter
History/Government & Politics: Miss P Bradley, BA Oxon
History of Art: Mrs I Vickers, BA Oxon
Mathematics: Mrs S Fairlamb, BSc Birmingham
Modern Languages: Miss J Morgan, MA Cantab
Music: Mr A Meryon, BMus Dip, ARCM
Physical Education: Mrs E Fraser, BA Brighton
Psychology: Miss E Keeble, BSc Cardiff
Religious Studies: Mrs S Tyler, BD King's College
Science: Dr W Dixon, MA, DPhil Oxon
Biology: Mr R Cameron, BSc Deakin
Chemistry: Ms V Filsell, BSc London
Physics: Mr M Ogretme, BSc Istanbul, MSc Istanbul

Junior School:

Head of Junior School: Mrs J Wallace, BMus, MA, PGCE
Deputy Head of Junior School (*Academic*): Mrs B Matthews, BEng Wales
Deputy Head of Junior School (*Pastoral*): Mrs W Archibald, BA OU, LTCM

Visiting Instrumental Staff: Bassoon, Cello, Clarinet, Clarinet, Double Bass, Flute, Guitar, Horn, Oboe, Organ,

Percussion, Piano, Recorder, Saxophone, Trumpet, Violin, Voice.

PA to the Headmistress: Mrs H Gordon-Smith, BA Exeter

Queen Mary's School
A Woodard School

Baldersby Park, Topcliffe, Thirsk, North Yorkshire YO7 3BZ

Tel: 01845 575000
email: admin@queenmarys.org
website: www.queenmarys.org
Twitter: @QueenMarysSch
Facebook: @Queen-Marys-School

Queen Mary's is an all-girls boarding and day school for pupils aged 7 to 16. It has a co-educational Early Years and Pre-Prep department for day pupils aged 2 to 7. The total school roll is currently 230.

Queen Mary's has a unique family atmosphere with friendliness and concern for others being an important part of the school's ethos. The country setting provides a safe haven for girls to thrive and develop self-confidence.

Location. Queen Mary's is situated at Baldersby Park in a beautiful Grade 1 Palladian mansion, with 50 acres of grounds, including formal gardens, playing fields, and riding stables. Despite its idyllic surroundings, it is only 2 miles from Junction 49 of the A1 and within ten minutes of Thirsk railway station. York and Harrogate are within easy reach and so are Leeds/Bradford and Teesside airports. Minibuses, each covering a twenty-five mile radius, transport girls to and from home on a daily basis.

The Curriculum. The National Curriculum forms the basis of what is taught, and all pupils sit Key Stage tests at the appropriate age. However, pupils are offered much more in terms of breadth and depth of learning. Generous time is given to core subjects, English, mathematics, science and modern languages, but strong emphasis is also placed on the supporting subjects – geography, history, religious education, classics, ICT, design technology, music, art and a varied programme of physical education. Classes are kept deliberately small, which means that every girl can receive plenty of support from her teachers. The school has an excellent learning support department for those pupils who have specific learning difficulties. The two years leading up to GCSE are full and focused, with most girls taking ten subjects at GCSE. The public examination results are outstandingly good and the school is one of the highest achieving non-selective schools in the country.

Pastoral care. All girls in school have personal tutors who oversee the academic, social and emotional development of each of their tutees. Building self-confidence and developing the individual talents of each pupil is seen as a vital aspect of the education offered. Each girl is encouraged to be self-reliant from an early age and pupils are taught a real concern for the needs of others. Girls in their final year at Queen Mary's undertake a number of important responsibilities to help the school community function smoothly.

Boarding. Queen Mary's offers a number of boarding options to suit the needs of parents and their daughters. Those who choose to board may be weekly or full boarders. The experience of boarding is considered to be valuable for all girls and, when space permits, day girls may board on a nightly basis to fit in with extracurricular commitments or parental need. The boarding accommodation is all within the main building and the girls find their dormitories cheerful and comfortable. The full boarders, who stay at weekends, enjoy a broad range of activities and trips, often much to the envy of those who go home. The Housemistress, together with her colleagues, looks after the general health of the girls, while the school nurse and the school doctor oversee all medical care.

Extracurricular Activities. An impressive range of extracurricular activities is available to all members of the school community. Choral and orchestral music are both huge strengths of the school; sport is good too with hockey, lacrosse and netball being played in the winter terms and tennis, rounders and athletics in the summer. Facilities include a modern indoor swimming pool and AstroTurf pitch. Drama, debating and The Duke of Edinburgh's Award at bronze level are highly popular choices and the all-weather outdoor riding manège allows more than 90 girls to ride each week. Children enjoy the opportunity to tackle the climbing wall, canoe on the adjacent River Swale or participate in very popular pheasant-plucking club.

Religious Affiliation. The school is part of the Woodard Corporation, an Anglican foundation which promotes Christian education and high academic and pastoral standards within all its schools. The school has its own Church of England chapel. The school Chaplain prepares girls for confirmation. Girls of other denominations are welcome.

What happens after GCSE? Queen Mary's has no Sixth Form and this is seen as a real strength of the school. Specialist careers advice is offered throughout the senior school and well informed staff support the girls as they seek to make application to their new schools and colleges. Each senior girl is able to choose a school or Sixth Form college which can offer her exactly the courses and educational environment she requires for her Sixth Form studies. A healthy proportion of the girls join their new schools as scholars. A few girls will embark on GNVQs or vocational training. Queen Mary's girls can be found in the Sixth Forms of over 30 different schools and colleges.

Scholarships. Scholarships are offered at 11+, 12+ and 13+ to those candidates who show particular academic flair or have special talent in Music, Sport or Art. Examinations are held during the Spring Term.

Entrance. By interview with the Head. Entry can be at most stages, subject to availability. An up-to-date prospectus will be dispatched immediately on request. The school's website also provides useful information.

Fees per term (2016–2017). Day: Nursery £28.50 per half-day session; Reception £2,430; Years 1–2 £2,910; Year 3 £4,560; Years 4–6 £4,820; Years 7–8 £5,225; Years 9–11 £5,930.

Boarding: Years 3–6 £6,530; Years 7–8 £6,925; Years 9–11 £7,710.

Extra subjects per term: Music £220, Speech and Drama £60–£105, Riding £230 (group).

Charitable status. Queen Mary's School (Baldersby) Ltd is a Registered Charity, number 1098410. It exists to educate children in a Christian environment.

Chairman of Governors: Mr H R V Morgan Williams, OBE, BA

Head: **Mrs C Cameron**, MA, PGCE, NPQH, FRGS

Deputy Head: Mrs D Hannam Walpole, BEd Hons

Miss E Abrahams, Mont Dip (*Year 1*)
Mrs R Askew, BA Hons, PGCE (*Head of Classics*)
Mr P Bailey, BA Hons, PGCE (*Mathematics*)
Miss S Booth, BA Hons, PGCE (*Modern Languages*)
Mrs J Coles, BEd Hons (*KS2 Science*)
Mrs D Coull, BA Hons, PGCE (*English*)
Mr A Cowey, BEd Hons (*Year 2, KS1 Coordinator*)
Mrs C Donnelley, BA Hons (*Language and Teaching Assistant*)
Mr S Dunkley (*Music*)
Miss F Edwards, BA Hons, PCGE (*Head of Modern Languages*)

Mrs S Elliston (*Teaching Assistant & After School Care*)
Miss C Fitzgerald, BSc Hons, PGCE (*Head of PE*)
Mrs R Foster, BSc Hons, PGCE (*Year 4*)
Mrs M Grant, MA, PGCE (*Learning Support*)
Mr N Hanysz, BSc Hons, PGCE (*Science*)
Mrs K Henderson, BA Hons, PCGE (*Head of Design Technology*)
Mrs E Hopkins, CertEd (*Head of Modular Science, Learning Support Coordinator*)
Mrs A Howard, BA Hons (*Drama*)
Mrs S Hughes, BMus, MA, PGCE (*KS2 Music*)
Mr R Knox, BEd Hons (*Geography Supply*)
Miss A Kopp, BA Hons, MA, PGCE (*Art*)
Miss C Larvin, MA Hons, PGCE (*English*)
Mrs E Lindsley, BSc Hons, PGCE (*Physical Education*)
Mrs J Nuttall, BEd Hons (*Year 6 KS2 English*)
Mrs L Nuttall, BSc Hons, PGCE (*Mathematics*)
Mr P Nuttall, BSc Hons, PGCE (*Head of Science*)
Miss A Pearson, BA Hons, PGCE (*Head of History*)
Miss D Pegg, BA Hons, PGCE (*Physical Education*)
Mrs A Petty, CertEd (*Special Needs*)
Mrs V Potter (*Head of PSHE, Physical Education*)
Mrs M Redmond, PGCE (*German, Spanish*)
Mr S Rudsdale, BSc Hons, PGCE QTS (*Head of Mathematics*)
Mr A Sebestyen, BSc, PGCE (*Head of IT/Computing*)
Mrs D Sheppard (*Key Stage Two*)
Mr J Singh, BA Hons, PGCE (*Head of Religious Studies*)
Mrs M Smerdon, BA Hons, QTS (*Head of KS3/4 and Religious Studies*)
Mr A Smith (*Outdoor Education*)
Mrs L Thomson, MA, BEd Hons, PGCE (*Key Stage Two*)
Miss K Vaughan, BEd Hons, ALAM, UCPD (*Head of Drama*)
Mrs L Weston (*Classroom Assistant*)
Mrs V Wild, BA Hons, PGCE (*KS2*)
Mrs C Wiggins, BSc Hons, PGCE (*Head of Geography*)
Mr A Would, BA Hons, PGCE (*Key Stage Two*)

Early Years Department:
Head of Early Years: Mrs M-J Foster, BA, PGCE
Early Years Practitioner: Mrs R Bowsher, BSc Hons, PGCE
Early Years Practitioner: Mrs P Bruce, DPP3
Early Years: Miss C Myers

Careers and Work Experience: Mrs M Smerdon, BA Hons, QTS

Head of Boarding: Mrs A Hickling
School Nurse: Mrs S Beaumont

School Chaplain: Reverend Graham Wright

Riding: Mrs E Swinburn

School Secretary: Miss F Rose
Head's PA: Mrs A Stringer
Finance and Estate Manager: Mrs J Wright
Admissions: Mrs V Potter

Queen's College, London

43–49 Harley Street, London W1G 8BT
Tel: 020 7291 7070
Fax: 020 7291 7090
email: queens@qcl.org.uk
website: www.qcl.org.uk

Queen's College was the first institution to provide an academic education and qualifications for young women. It was founded in 1848 by F D Maurice, Professor of Modern History at King's College, and was housed originally at 45 Harley Street.

Today it is a thriving school of 375 girls aged from 11–18, of whom 80 are in the Sixth Form. Queen's College Preparatory School (020 7291 0660), which opened in 2002 at 61 Portland Place, takes girls from age 4–11.

Queen's College is situated in Harley Street, combining the beauty of four eighteenth century houses with modern facilities for science, languages, art, drama, music and ICT, as a well as a Hall and gymnasium. Two libraries, in the care of a graduate librarian, offer the students some 17,000 books, and we also preserve a unique archive recording the history of the College.

Curriculum. Class sizes rarely exceed twenty and the normal size of a year group is 55–60, divided into three forms. The year group is streamed for mathematics and French during the first year and at a later stage for English, Latin and science.

The curriculum is wide, including five modern languages, as well as Latin, Greek and classical civilisation. Girls usually take nine or ten subjects at GCSE, and the three sciences are taught separately. At A Level it is possible to study history of art, economics, or government and politics as well as the subjects already taken at GCSE.

There is a very full programme of sport offered, with the traditional team games taking place in Regent's Park. Girls play netball, lacrosse, rounders, and tennis; there are thriving clubs before and after school for swimming, cross-country running and other leisure pursuits. Dance and PE are offered at GCSE. Regular sports fixtures are arranged against local schools. The Duke of Edinburgh's Award is organised at bronze, silver and gold levels. Individual music lessons are offered in all instruments including voice, and the musical or dramatic productions and jazz concert are highlights of each year.

The location of the College means that theatre and other educational visits in London are an integral part of the curriculum, complemented by opportunities to travel abroad or to other parts of the country. Every summer Year 7 visit Northumberland for a week and in recent years groups of girls have visited France, Greece, Germany, Italy and China. There is at least one ski trip each year, usually run jointly with Queen's College Preparatory School.

Almost all girls leaving Queen's proceed to university, including Oxford or Cambridge; and several students each year choose to take an Art Foundation course at one of the London colleges. Former students are prominent in medicine, education, writing and the media; they retain contact with each other and the college through the Old Queen's Society, which also gives bursaries to families in financial need.

Pastoral Care. Queen's College prides itself on its friendly and informal atmosphere, highly valued by girls, parents and staff. Pastoral care is strong and we have a full-time nurse to support the work of form tutors and pastoral staff. A specialist in various special educational needs works individually with pupils once the need has been identified. We send reports to parents every half-term and hold regular Parents' Evenings; contact with parents benefits from the use of email by all members of staff. Parents also support the College through membership of the Parents' Association, giving practical and some financial assistance to College functions.

Admission. The College is a member of the North London Independent Girls Schools' Consortium for entry at 11+ and all candidates are interviewed individually. As well as high academic standards we value enthusiasm and creativity, and academic, music and art awards are available to 11+ entrants.

If vacancies arise we also welcome applicants at other ages, particularly after GCSE, where there is a long-standing tradition of accepting students to undertake their A

Level education at Queen's. Some scholarships are available on entry at this stage. Means-tested bursaries are available at all points of entry.

Fees per term (2016–2017). £5,900.

Charitable status. Queen's College, London is a Registered Charity, number 312726. It exists to provide education for girls. It is an Anglican foundation, open to those of all faiths or none who are prepared to subscribe to its ethos.

Patron: Her Majesty The Queen

Visitor: The Rt Revd and Rt Hon the Lord Bishop of London

Council:
Chairman: Michael Sharman, BSc Southampton
The Revd Charlotte Bannister-Parker, BA MA Durham
David Gallagher, ACA
Matthew Hanslip Ward, MA Cantab
John Jacob, BSc Southampton
Mrs Danielle Salem, BA Farnham
Professor Alison While, BSc MSc PhD London, RGN RHV
Mrs Rhiannon Wilkinson, MA Oxon, MEd Manchester

Bursar and Secretary to the Council: S N Turner

Principal: Dr F M R Ramsey, MA DPhil Oxon

Headmistress of Queen's College Preparatory School: Mrs E Webb, BA London

Senior Tutor: Mrs K C Woodcock, BA Bristol

Director of Studies: M J Wardrop, MChem Oxon

Registrar: Miss F A Murdoch, BSc Portsmouth

Queen's Gate School

133 Queen's Gate, London SW7 5LE
Tel: 020 7589 3587
email: registrar@queensgate.org.uk
website: www.queensgate.org.uk
Twitter: @Queens_Gate
Facebook: @133queensgate

Queen's Gate School is an independent day school for girls between the ages of 4 and 18 years. Established in 1891, the school is an Educational Trust situated in five large Victorian Houses within easy walking distance of Kensington Gardens, Hyde Park, Stanhope Gardens and the Museums of South Kensington.

The aim of the school is to create a secure and happy environment in which the girls can realise their academic potential and make full use of their individual interests and talents. The School encourages the development of self-discipline and creates an atmosphere where freedom of thought and ideas can flourish.

Close cooperation with parents is welcomed at every stage.

There is no school uniform except for PE and for the Junior girls, a top coat in winter and blazer and boater in summer. There is a dress code and girls are expected to wear clothing and footwear suitable for attending school and taking part in school activities.

Curriculum. Girls follow as wide a curriculum as possible and generally take GCSE in ten subjects that must include English, Mathematics, Science and a modern language.

An extensive range of AS/A Level subjects is offered. Four AS Levels are studied in the first year and three of these are taken at A2 Level.

Games. Netball, Hockey, Tennis, Swimming, Rowing, Athletics, Basketball, Horse Riding, Cross-Country, Biathlon and Dance.

Admission. By test and interview in the Junior School; by the North London Independent Girls' Schools' Consortium entrance examination at 11+; by the School's own entrance examinations for entry to other years in the Senior School. Applicants for the Sixth Form are expected to have passed a minimum of six GCSEs at A Grade with A grades required in those subjects they wish to pursue to A Level.

Registration fee: £100.

Fees per term (2016–2017). £5,500–£6,300.

Governors:
Mr Michael Cumming (*Chairman*)
Mrs Laura Marani (*Deputy Chairman*)
Mr Jonathan Dobson
Mr William Gillen
Mrs Reica Gray
Dr Jill Harling
Mr Gary Li
Mr Jospeh McNeila
Mr Peter Trueman
Mrs Manina Weldon

Staff:

Principal: Mrs R M Kamaryc, BA Hons, MSc, PGCE

Deputy Principal: Mr M Alter, BSc Hons, MSc, PGCE
Director of Pastoral Care: Ms C A Yates, BEd, MA
Director of Academic Admin & Compliance: Miss B Ward, BEd Hons
Director of Teaching & Assessment and Head of Upper School: Mr M Crundwell, BSc Hons, MPhil London, MEd Dist, QTS
Director of Academic Development: Miss Z Chidoub, BA, MA Oxon, PGCE
Head of Sixth Form: Dr M Lee, BSc, PhD London
Head of IVth Form: Mr R Moss, BA Hons, PGCE
Head Lower School: Mr J Denchfield, BA Hons, PGCE

Art & Design:
Mr S Mataja, BA, PGCE
Mrs K Bonnington, BA Hons, PGCE
Miss N Sitko, Master of Fine Arts Poznan Academy of Fine Arts

Art, History of:
Ms I Cornwall-Jones, MA Hons, PGCE

Biology:
Miss J Miller, BSc, MA, PGCE
Miss L Coulton, BSc Hons, PGCE
Mr I Gallagher, BSc Hons, PGCE

Careers Education & Guidance:
Ms I Cornwall-Jones, MA Hons, PGCE
Mrs S Sexon, BA, MA, QTS

Chemistry:
Mrs C Mayne, BSc, PGCE
Mr A Selkirk, BSc, BComm, PG Dip Teaching Secondary
Mrs V Manson, MChem, PGCE

Classics:
Dr T Bell, MA, PhD
Mr R Moss, BA Hons, PGCE
Miss C Fox, BA Hons, PGCE
Mrs N J Clear, BA Hons, PGCE
Mrs S Sexon, BA, MA, QTS

Computing:
Ms E Adler, MA, PGCE
Mr G Booth, BA, QTS

Design & Technology:
Mrs V Thompson, BSc, PGCE
Mr J Francis, BA Hons, PGCE
Miss E Oppong, BA Hons, PGCE

Drama & Theatre Studies:
Ms L Arthur, MA Hons, MA RADA/London, Dip
    Teaching NZ
Miss F Sutherland, BDiv Hons, MA RADA/London,
    PGCE, LGSM

LAMDA:
Ms J Doolan, MA

Economics:
Mr M Smith, MA, PGCE

English:
Mrs E Burnside, MA, BA, PGCE
Mr J Denchfield, BA Hons, PGCE
Ms C A Yates, MA, BEd
Miss F Clarke-Williams, BA Hons, PGCE
Mrs S Sexon, BA, MA, QTS
Mrs H Hutton, BA, PGCE
Mr M Spicer, BA, BEd
Mrs N J Clear, BA Hons, PGCE

French:
Mme F Collombon, Maîtrise Langues Etrangères
    Appliquées, Licence Anglais Langues et Civilization,
    PGCE
Mlle C Manier, MA, PGCE [Maternity Leave]
Mme S Riglet, BA Hons, CAPES IUFM Paris, PGCE
M P Solomons, BA, MA, LLP
Mlle M Van Zuijam, Licence Langue, Littérature et
    Civilisation Etrangère [Maternity Cover]

Geography:
Mr M Crundwell, BSc Hons, MPhil London, MEd Dist,
    QTS
Dr M Lee, BSc, PhD London
Miss Z Chidoub, BA, MA Oxon, PGCE
Miss S Scott, BSc Hons, PGCE, PCET, MEd

German:
Frau I Atufe-Kreuth, MA Mag Phil, Cert Ed

History:
Mrs J S Ditchfield, MA Hons, PGCE
Mrs S Sexon, BA, MA, QTS
Mrs H Hutton, BA, PGCE
Ms E Heseltine, BA Hons, BSc Hons, MA Ed, MSc, PGCE

ICT Network Manager:
Mr H Hirani

ICT Assistant:
Mr S Siktar

Italian:
Mr S Mocci, MA, PGCE

Mathematics:
Mr J Toby, BSc, PGCE
Ms P Howe, BA Hons Oxon
Mrs R Kamaryc, BA Hons, MSc, PGCE
Mr M Alter, BSc, MSc, PGCE
Ms A Helm, BSc, PGCE
Mr A Chaudhry, BSc, PGCE, MEd
Mr I Maclean, BSc, PGCE

Music:
Mr E Liepa, BMus Hons
Ms L Sansun, MA, LRAM, MTC

Physical Education:
Miss C Hurlbatt, BA Hons, PGCE
Miss A Allen, BSc Hons

Miss B Ward, BEd Hons BEd Hons
Miss A Molineaux, BA, BSc, PGCE
Miss E Pillow, BA Hons
Mr A Labourt
Ms J Marshall, BSc, PGCE
Miss M Mealiff, BHPE
Mr G Marton (*Rowing*)
Mr V Meshkov (*Fencing*)

Philosophy:
Mr R Stevens, BA Hons, PGCE

Physics:
Dr J Mercer, PhD, BSc Hons, ARCS, PGCE
Miss C Wise, MPhys, QTS

PSCHE:
Miss Z Chidoub, BA, MA Oxon, PGCE
Miss S Palframan, BSc, PGCE

Psychology:
Miss S Palframan, BSc, PGCE

Religious Studies:
Mr R Stevens, BA Hons, PGCE
Mrs N J Clear, BA Hons, PGCE
Mrs H Hutton, BA, PGCE

Sociology:
Mrs H Hutton, BA, PGCE

Spanish:
Sta S Gomez, Licenciada en Filología

Laboratory Technicians:
Mr D I Swan, BSc Hons, MRSC
Mr M Sell, MSc

Art & DT Technician:
Mr K Lynn, BA Hons

Librarian: Mrs E Scott, BA, MSCLIS, US Teaching
    Certificate
Assistant Librarian: Miss C Podavitte, Dottoressa in
    Archeologia, Milano

SEN Coordinator: Ms S Robertson-Glasgow, BEd Hons,
    MA Ed, Adv Dip Ed
Debating: Mr T Barclay

Junior School:
Director of the Junior School: Mrs S Neale, BEd, ARCM,
    LTCL

Form Tutors:
Miss E Allan, BA, BEd, PGCE (*EYFS Coordinator*)
Miss C Askem, BA Hons
Miss S Bradnick, BEd
Miss K Jonczyk, BA, MA
Mrs C Makhlouf, BEd Hons (*English Coordinator*)
Mrs L Shanley, BA Hons, GTP (*11+ Coordinator*)
Miss E Smith, BA, MA, PGCE (*KS1 Coordinator*)
Miss J Hasler, BEd Hons (*KS2 Coordinator & Children's
    Literacy Advisor*)
Mrs C Makhlouf BEd Hons (*Curriculum Coordinator*)

Teaching Assistants:
Mrs M Kolnikaj, Mrs S Leigh, Mrs McDonnell, Mrs Y
    Meneely, Mrs L Menez

Head of Music (*Juniors*): Ms S Hörcsög, BA Hons
History & RS: Mrs C White-da Cruz, BA Hons, PCSE,
    MLitt
Art & Design Coordinator: Miss N Sitko, Master of Fine
    Arts Poznan Academy of Fine Arts
Science Coordinator: Mrs C Mayne, BSc, PGCE
LAMDA (*Juniors*): Ms J Doolan, MA
Learning Support: Ms S Robertson-Glasgow, BEd Hons,
    MA Ed, Adv Dip Ed

KS2 & 3 Computing Coordinator: Mr G Booth, BA, QTS
Librarian: Miss C Podavitte, Dottoressa in Archeologia,
    Milano

Administration Staff:
Bursar: Mr J Cubitt, ACCA
Finance Manager: Ms O Lynn, BCom, ACCA
Bursar's Assistant: Lady Wilkinson
*PA to the Director of the Junior School & Junior School
    Secretary*: Miss P Jackson
School Archivist: Miss C Podavitte Dottoressa in
    Archeologia, Milano
Registrar: Miss I Carey, MA
Principal's PA: Mrs S Evans, BA Hons
Principal's Assistant: Mrs C Bickford
Senior School Secretary: *Miss L Pearson*: BSc Hons
Alumni Fundraising & Events Officer: Mrs H Thackwray,
    BA Hons
Communications Officer: Miss A Hinds, MA

Redmaids' High School

Westbury Road, Westbury-on-Trym, Bristol BS9 3AW

Tel:	0117 962 2641
Fax:	0117 962 1687
email:	admissions@redmaids.bristol.sch.uk
website:	www.redmaidshigh.co.uk
Twitter:	@RedMaidsSchool
Facebook:	@The-Red-Maids-School

Redmaids' High is the country's oldest surviving girls' school, founded in 1634 by John Whitson, former Mayor and MP for Bristol. Whitson's vision for the school – to provide for "40 poor women children" who would be "kept and maintained and taught to read English and to sew" – is remembered each year on Founder's Day. It is a proud day for students, staff, parents and governors as the school processes through the centre of Bristol to a service of thanksgiving at Bristol Cathedral. The school still benefits from Whitson's financial legacy, allowing the provision of scholarships and bursaries to girls from many backgrounds.

In 2016 two of Bristol's most successful girls' schools, Red Maids' and Redland High, merged. The two schools have been educating girls in Bristol for a combined total of over 600 years so the future of girls' education in this major city can be assured for this generation and many more to come.

Character. Redmaids' High is a friendly, purposeful school; intellectual curiosity, energy and enthusiasm are characteristic of students and teachers alike. The students are encouraged to discover and develop their own abilities, to think for themselves and strive for success whether academic, in sport, in creative arts or practical technologies.

Facilities. Set in 12 acres of green parkland, on-site sports facilities include an international standard astroturf and two competition standard grade 1 netball courts. The additional facility at nearby Golden Hill enables even more sports lessons and matches to be played. An award-winning extension to the Junior School in 2008 has since been followed by the opening of two further classrooms, allowing two-form entry into Year 3. Other investment includes the refurbishment of the Senior School science laboratories, the re-development of the Sixth Form Centre and in 2014 the building of a two-storey library, refurbished dining hall, and a new visitor reception. A new state-of-the-art performing arts space including extra classrooms is currently under construction, due to be open in autumn 2017.

Extended Day. Girls can arrive from 7.45 am and stay until 6.00 pm, at no extra charge. Breakfast can be bought on an ad-hoc basis and supervised homework and extra-curricular activities take place until 5.30 pm. Clubs and societies include: current affairs, choirs, orchestras, Duke of Edinburgh's Award, film production, drama and many sports clubs and societies.

School Life. The School Council and Sixth Form leadership positions encourage students to take responsibility for others. Peer support systems, clubs run by older students and staff, and charitable fundraising demonstrate the pupils' involvement in their community. Assemblies celebrate pupils' all-round achievements, examine topical issues and offer opportunities for thought, reflection and spiritual exploration.

Curriculum. For the first three years, all Redmaids' High students shadow Key Stage 3 of the National Curriculum. Mathematics is taught in sets from Year 7 and separate Sciences from Year 9. From Year 7, the girls each learn two languages from a choice of French, German, Russian and Spanish. In Years 10 and 11, they study IGCSEs in English, Science, Mathematics and Modern Languages. GCSE subjects include Religious Studies, History, Geography, Latin, Food Technology, Textiles Technology, Art, Music, Drama, Physical Education, Business Studies and Classical Civilisation.

Sixth Form. Redmaids' High is the only school in Bristol that offers the choice of studying A Levels or the International Baccalaureate (IB) Diploma. At A Level, additional subjects include Further Maths, History of Art, Philosophy and Ethics, Government and Politics, Psychology, Photography, Computing, and Theatre Studies. Many A Level students also study for the EPQ (Extended Project Qualification). IB Diploma students select six subjects, one each from English, Mathematics, Science, Humanities, Languages and one other. These subjects, together with Theory of Knowledge, Creativity Action Service and the Extended Essay, form the Diploma programme over two years.

Redmaids' High sixth formers enjoy excellent teacher relationships and the independence of a modern, purpose-built Sixth Form Centre with dedicated teaching, seminar and common rooms, café, an ICT suite and careers library. Students achieve their full academic potential through high-quality teaching and developing habits of independent study and academic rigour. Almost all students go on to study at University, including Oxbridge. Sixth formers take on many leadership roles within the school and develop a broader understanding of the wider world through a varied community service programme. They also follow a Life Skills course and receive individual careers advice.

Fees per term (2016–2017). Senior School £4,440, Junior School £3,020. Curricular school trips are included in this fee. Lunch is compulsory for Years 7–9 and is invoiced termly. Other extras are individual Music lessons, Speech and Drama lessons, optional non-academic trips, and any one-to-one tuition for those with individual needs.

Admission to Senior School. All students are admitted on the basis of an entrance examination, interview and headteacher's report. Key points of entry are at Year 7, 9 and 12. The entrance exam for Years 7 and 9 is held in January for admission the following September. Entry can take place into other years, subject to availability. For further information about admission procedures, contact the Admissions Registrar.

Scholarships and Bursaries. Scholarships are available to new entrants at 11+, 13+ and in the Sixth Form. Non-means-tested academic scholarships worth up to 50% each can be awarded annually for outstanding performance in the 11+ Entrance Examination. A Sports Scholarship and two Music Scholarships are also available.

In addition two 100% places are awarded to girls on the basis of their performance in the 11+ entrance examination and taking financial need into consideration.

Academic, music and sports scholarships can also be considered for students joining at Year 9.

Entrance scholarships are available for students joining at Sixth Form, awarded on academic merit, interview and examination. The Sixth Form Scholars' programme provides added stretch and responsibility for existing Red Maid scholars and those joining at Year 12 with scholar status.

A number of means-tested bursaries are available to students joining the school at Year 7. These also take the student's academic ability into account and are likely to be valued at up to a maximum of 50% of full fees.

Junior School. *See Junior School entry in IAPS section.*

Charitable status. Redmaids' High School is a Registered Charity, number 1105017. It has existed since 1634 to provide an education for girls.

Governing Body:
Chairman: Mrs Jane MacFarlane
Vice-Chairman: Mr Michael Davies

Mrs Elizabeth Clarson	Dr John Littler
Mrs Yvonne Craggs	Mr Christopher Martin
Mrs Val Dixon	Mr Richard Page
Mrs Sally Dore	Mrs Susan Perry
Mrs Anne Ebery	Mr Timothy Phillips
Mrs Judith Egerton	Mrs Lucy Pollock
Mr James Fox	Mrs Phyllida Pyper
Mr Andrew Hardwick	Mrs Gilly Rowcliffe
Mrs Rosemary Heald	Mr Stephen Ryan
Mr Michael Henry	Mrs Anne Taylor
Mr Andrew Hillman	Mr David Taylor
Mrs Thelma Howell	Mrs Jeannie Whatmough

Senior School:

Headmistress: Mrs Isabel Tobias, BA Hons New Hall Cambridge

Deputy Head – Co-Curricular and Operations: Mrs Kate Doarks, BSc Hons Bristol
Deputy Head – Academic: Mrs Laura Beynon, MA Durham
Deputy Head: Mrs Perdita Davidson, BA Bristol, PGCE Bristol
Director of Sixth Form: Miss Kate Fleming, BSc Hons Manchester
Senior Teacher – Pastoral: Mrs Jacklyn Turner, BSc Hons Aston
Senior Teacher – Staff: Mr Tom Johnston, BA Hons Bath College of Higher Education
Acting Senior Teacher – IB Coordinator: Mr Jon Cooper, MA Hons St Andrews
Bursar: Mr Peter Taylor, BA Hons UWE, ACMA, CGMA

Junior School:
Headteacher: Mrs Lisa Brown, BSc Hons Leicester

Headmistress's PA: Mrs Jenny Bell
Bursar's PA: Mrs Susannah Wooldridge
Admissions Registrar: Miss Sarah Patch

The Royal High School Bath
GDST

Lansdown Road, Bath BA1 5SZ

Tel: 01225 313877
Fax: 01225 465446
email: royalhigh@rhsb.gdst.net
website: www.royalhighbath.gdst.net
Twitter: @royalhighbath
Facebook: /The-Royal-High-School-Bath

The Royal High School Bath is part of the GDST (Girls' Day School Trust). The GDST is the leading network of independent girls' schools in the UK. As a charity that owns

and runs 24 schools and two academies, the GDST reinvests all of its income into its schools. For further information about the Trust, please visit www.gdst.net.

Uniquely, The Royal High School Bath is the only school in the GDST to offer boarding in addition to day provision, and the only school to offer the highly challenging, rewarding and globally recognised International Baccalaureate at Sixth Form.

The Royal High School Bath is a leading independent day and boarding school. We provide an outstanding, contemporary, girl-centred education for girls aged 3 to 18, providing a happy, seamless experience that transforms and adds value at every level. Time and again, we have seen the added value of our all-through education translate into tangible academic success, with those girls proceeding from our Junior School to our Senior School achieving higher exam results at GCSE and A Level.

Number of Pupils. 615, including 126 in our Junior School and 157 in the Sixth Form.

Boarding. The Royal High School is unique among schools in the GDST in offering the enriching experience of boarding at Senior School and Sixth Form College. This gives parents the flexibility to choose the type of education best suited to their daughter's needs. If family circumstances change, so too can school arrangements. Our boarding accommodation is comfortable, spacious and well-equipped. The school enjoys a splendid location in beautiful grounds in the World Heritage City of Bath.

The School – Nursery, Junior, Senior, Sixth Form College. Laughter and a lifelong love of learning, collaboration and camaraderie, drive and determination, inspiration and involvement, aspiration and achievement – those are the qualities that form the heart of our school. From a group of giggling three-year-old girls holding hands in the playground of our 'outstanding' Ofsted rated Nursery, to a revitalised Junior School where lifelong friendships are forged and sporting and academic triumphs shared, to a passion for continued discovery and exploring new horizons at our exceptionally high-achieving Senior School and on to our dynamic Sixth Form College buzzing with mature, confident, gregarious young women, the RHS journey is a seamless one, with four life-enhancing experiences along the way.

This all-through, all-girls education is unique in Bath. We embrace all-round excellence and help every single girl to be happy and to be who she wants to be. We do this with a rich and exciting curriculum, with every opportunity for girls to focus on their strengths but also to develop their skills and talents across the broadest academic, social and personal spectrum. The school develops the confidence, capabilities and character needed to underpin success at university, throughout careers and in achieving ambitions in every aspect of life.

Our doors are always open to welcome girls from across the UK and across the world, who come here to achieve their very best academically, socially and personally, have fun, make friends, live, develop a global perspective in education, enjoy life and learn how to fly.

The Junior School. The Junior School is based at Cranwell House in Weston Park, Bath. It is a beacon of academic excellence for girls aged 3 to 11 set in its own 11 acres of stunning grounds. With the Cranwell Curriculum, anything and everything is possible. It is a rich, diverse, unique, girl-centred and enabling curriculum that provides the girls throughout the Junior School with extraordinary opportunities to seek out irresistible challenges and support incredible learning adventures. The Cranwell Curriculum uses initial explorations to help the girls develop a sound understanding of all the subjects they are studying, develop a rich vocabulary relating to the subject and to understand it in terms of scientific, linguistic and creative possibilities. It means more traditional ways of working within the curriculum are considerably enhanced and become even more valuable.

The Royal High Junior School was the top performing independent Junior School in the area in a recent Sunday Times Parent Power guide. The school recently gained the Arts Council's Artsmark Gold award for its extensive provision in the expressive and performing arts. Many girls have individual drama or music lessons. Extra-curricular activities include judo, theatre club and pottery. We have an after-school care programme which enables pupils to stay in school until 6.00 pm and a breakfast club starting at 7.30 am. The Junior School also offers holiday clubs for girls and boys aged 3–11, which prove very popular and girls have the opportunity to excel at Modern Foreign Languages studying French, Spanish and Mandarin.

The Senior School. We are a dynamic, warm, friendly, culturally cosmopolitan school that values the special spark in each girl and gives her the confidence, character and self-esteem to explore her unique talents. We watch that spark of passion ignite into The Royal High School spirit.

Great exam results and impressive statistics are one thing (and we certainly have those), but it's your daughter's happiness, well-being and personal development that matter most to us. We want her to be comfortable with who she is and what she is good at, while supporting her to positively challenge herself inside and outside the classroom. We are proud of our holistic approach towards developing accomplished young women and we work as a team to help each girl find her own place in the school. Here, your daughter will become the very best that she can be, in whatever fields she chooses.

Wisdom, leadership, teamwork, energy, courage, self-knowledge, confidence, compassion, courtesy, integrity and a sense of humour are part of the school's DNA and run through everything that we do. In common with all GDST schools, academic standards are excellent. The broad curriculum includes a choice of four modern European languages plus Mandarin. Most students study three sciences separately at GCSE. Girls can also take Latin or Classical Greek.

GCSE Results 2016. The GCSE class of 2016 celebrated a fantastic set of results with 76% of grades either A* or A. Amazingly a third of the girls achieved a clean sweep of A* and A grades in ALL their exams – an outstanding achievement. These results are the best for five years at The Royal High School with the A*–A percentage of 76% being the best in Bath. Overall, a remarkable 98% of the grades this year were A*–C.

In a year of outstanding performances particular mention goes to one student who achieved 10 x A* grades as well as being awarded the Arkwright Scholarship (a national scholarship) for her Design & Technology work, and another who achieved 9 x A* and 1 x A whilst balancing her study with training and competing as a swimmer, reaching British Championship and English National level.

Languages continue to thrive at The Royal High School, going against the national trend, with students excelling in French, German, Spanish, Italian, Russian, Dutch and Chinese (where 100% of the students, all non-native speakers, achieved an A* or A). In English the school achieved a superb 100% A* to B grades whilst in Mathematics this figure was a fantastic 94%.

Sixth Form College. The Royal High Sixth Form College offers girls the opportunity to take either A Levels or the International Baccalaureate Diploma Programme, a unique provision in the Bath area. We are one of a growing number of approved IB World Schools, which share a commitment to high-quality, challenging, internationally-focused education. Whatever choice our girls take, our talented staff ensure they are continually developing the academic credentials and an outlook on life that will shape their future. In addition to this choice of academic pathways, the college offers a real alternative to the traditional Sixth Form experience, with a greater measure of responsibility and a clear understanding that these two years are the preface to the next step of Higher Education and employment. All students are provided with a laptop to enhance learning. Results are excellent and the majority of students move on to Russell Group Universities and leading international institutions. Support for the UCAS process is superlative with tailored programmes to support applicants to particular disciplines, and our newly launched 'Aspire' scheme provides a dedicated programme of extension studies for high achievers, specially designed to support those seeking entrance to Oxford or Cambridge University.

A Level and IB Results 2016. This was another exceptional year for our A Level and IB students, with both cohorts achieving outstanding results and succeeding in being accepted onto courses at a wide range of top-class further education establishments, both in the UK and overseas.

A Level: Our students achieved a 100% pass rate and, against the national average, our percentage of A* grades rose, and 82% achieving A*–B grades overall.

Rising from last year, 19% of our grades were awarded the coveted A* grade with 14 girls achieving a full set of A*/A grades within their results. The EPQ (Extended Project Qualification) results were also very pleasing with an increase in candidates this year, achieving an impressive 4 A*, 9 A and 4 B grades between them.

IB: The average score achieved by our girls was an exceptional 37 out of a possible 45, which is 7 points above the global average. Four of our girls scored 40+ points, an incredible achievement, and one of the two highest scorers, both of whom finished with 43 points, deserves particular credit given that she is a year young.

Extra-Curricular Activities. Girls are encouraged to participate in our rich extra-curricular programme, including weekend activities. We have a strong tradition in music and drama; we stage a number of major performances each year, in addition to informal lunchtime concerts. Our students regularly win prizes in the local annual performing arts festivals. We currently have record numbers of students participating in The Duke of Edinburgh's Award scheme and Ten Tors Expedition.

Sport. Pride, passion and performance. We believe in nurturing all sporting talent, both in individual and team sports and in recent years a number of our students have represented their country in a range of sports including swimming, diving, gymnastics, rowing, fencing and badminton. A large number of teams are fielded for weekend and evening fixtures. Girls who prefer non-competitive sport are encouraged to join in other fitness activities, such as one of our many dance groups. Opportunities for sport and exercise are available every day at lunch times and after school and, as we are a boarding school, at weekends too. The school holds the prestigious Sportsmark awarded by the Sport England Foundation for its extensive provision and commitment to sport.

Our elite sportswomen also benefit from using the wonderful facilities at the University of Bath nearby, the training ground for world champions.

Entry Procedures. In the Junior School, admission is by informal assessment. In the Senior School, entry at Year 7 is by examination and personal interview in January. For pupils currently in our Junior School, transfer to the Senior School is automatic, unless parents have been informed in writing (by the end of Year 5) that the transfer cannot be guaranteed. We have students who join later, subject to availability of places. Admission in these years is by entrance examination. While Y11 students automatically transfer to the college, a substantial number of new students also join us for the Sixth Form. All students entering the Sixth Form College are expected to have passes in at least 6 subjects at grades A*–B, with grade A/A* in any subject they intend to study, together with a minimum of a C in Maths and English.

Fees per term (2016–2017). Full Boarding £8,999–£9,458; Weekly Boarding £8,045–£8,502; Day £3,083–£4,372. 10% discount on full boarding fees for serving members of HM Forces. Flexi boarding is available.

Scholarships and Bursaries. Scholarships are awarded at entry to Years 7, 9 and 12 for the Sixth Form College for all-round academic excellence or for outstanding promise in specialist areas such as art, music, sport and drama. A Scholars' Programme ensures additional enrichment opportunities for the most able students.

Our bursary scheme ensures that the school is accessible to bright and talented students from families who require financial assistance towards the fees. Bursaries up to 100% (means-tested) are awarded at Years 7, 9 and 12 to girls who demonstrate outstanding all-round academic excellence or exceptional promise in a specialist area.

Charitable status. The Royal High School Bath is part of The Girls' Day School Trust, which is a Registered Charity, number 306983.

Head: **Mrs Jo Duncan**, BA Hons, MA

Senior Deputy Head – Curriculum: Mr Hadrian Briggs, MA, PGCE

Deputy Head – Pastoral: Mrs Debbie Dellar, BEd Hons

Head of Sixth Form: Mr Nicholas Hayward, BA Oxon, PGCE

Head of Junior School: Miss Heidi Hughes, BSc, PGCE, MA Ed Mgt

Senior Resident Housemistress: Mrs E Custodio, BA, PGCE

Registrar: Miss Lynda Bevan, BA Hons

Rye St Antony

Pullen's Lane, Oxford OX3 0BY

Tel:	01865 762802
email:	enquiries@ryestantony.co.uk
website:	www.ryestantony.co.uk
Twitter:	@RyeStAntony
Facebook:	/RyeStAntony

Motto: *Vocatus Obedivi*

Big enough to challenge; small enough to care

First-class teaching, unrivalled facilities and a wide programme of extra-curricular opportunities support Rye St Antony pupils in discovering who they are and who they have it in them to become.

Recent inspections have given the school top rankings: 'Outstanding' by Ofsted and 'Excellent' by the Independent Schools Inspectorate. Set in a beautiful twelve-acre site only one mile from the centre of Oxford, Rye helps pupils seek excellence in the recognition that every pupil is an individual with talents to be developed. Academic standards are high, and we never forget that wider life skills are also important to prepare our pupils for a happy, fulfilling and successful life.

Rye St Antony is a school of 350 pupils that provides an environment both safe and stimulating in which every individual is considered a valued member of the community. Everyone is encouraged to respect others and to consider their opinions; no one is overlooked. Pupils have access to the best and most varied opportunities for enrichment which challenge them, develop their characters and help them to be independent, determined and resilient. Each year almost

every member of Sixth Form achieves her preferred university place, and destinations range from Natural Sciences at Cambridge, to English at York, to Law and Criminology at Sheffield, to Theatre Dance at London Studio Centre, to Mechanical Engineering at Cardiff. The school really does bring out the best in each pupil, helping all pupils discover the subjects about which they are passionate and enabling them to take their first steps towards a rewarding future.

We have day places for girls aged 3–18 years and boys aged 3–11 years. Rye St Antony offers full, weekly and flexible boarding options, including occasional boarding days to help each pupil to fully participate in all that the school has to offer.

Of the 350 pupils, 100 are in the Prep School (ages 3–11) and 250 are in the Senior School (ages 11–18). Of the 60 members of Sixth Form, all prepare to continue their studies at university. In recent years the average UCAS points score per candidate has been 350; two-thirds A Level grades have been A*, A or B. GCSE results each year give almost everyone grade C or above in at least five subjects, 70%+ with grade C or above in at least ten subjects.

The school is highly regarded for its happy and purposeful atmosphere and its strong sense of community. The school's aim is to help each pupil develop the intellectual curiosity and skills, the emotional understanding and resources, the ability to work independently and with others, and the personal, social and spiritual values that will lead to personal fulfilment and the ability to contribute something of value to the world.

Religious Life. The school's sacramental life is of central importance, the Eucharist uniting the school with Christ and his church. Several Oxford priests act as the school chaplains and celebrate school masses at the beginning of each term and on Sundays in term-time. Religious education is an integral part of the school curriculum.

Senior School Curriculum. Academic standards and expectations are high, pupils are offered many opportunities in music, art, drama and sport, and there is a busy programme of evening and weekend activities.

In the Senior School all pupils follow a broad and balanced common course for the first three years, comprising English, Mathematics, Physics, Chemistry, Biology, Religious Education, French, History, Geography, Technology, Information and Communications Technology, Art, Music, Drama and Physical Education. Latin and Spanish are optional subjects. There is a cross-curricular Health Education programme.

Twenty plus subjects are offered as GCSE subjects. For the two-year GCSE course pupils usually study 10 subjects, a mixture of options and core subjects (including Coordinated Science, a double award subject).

In Sixth Form three or four A Level subjects are chosen from a range of twenty or more options.

Careers Guidance. The school's careers advisory service provides help and guidance for all pupils, and there is a formal programme of careers advice throughout Years 9, 10 and 11 and Sixth Form. Almost all pupils go on to university and are helped to investigate thoroughly the Higher Education and careers options open to them, careful guidance being given concerning their applications and interviews. The support of the Head, the Head of Sixth Form and other senior staff is available at all stages. Work experience placements are organised, and pupils are encouraged to make particular use of this option at the end of their GCSE courses. Visiting speakers give lectures on various higher education and careers topics and visits to appropriate conferences and exhibitions are arranged regularly.

Prep School Curriculum. The Prep School and Senior School are closely linked, and Prep School pupils are steadily introduced to the specialist teaching and facilities of the Senior School. In the early years the teaching of most subjects is undertaken by the class teachers. In Years 5 and 6 pupils are taught by subject teachers, some of whom also teach in the Senior School, and this arrangement gives them the benefit of specialist teaching and encourages them to develop a feeling of confidence and continuity when the time comes for them to move into the Senior School. Use of the Senior School facilities is particularly valuable in Science, Art, Music, Physical Education and Drama. There is a Prep School Library in Langley Lodge, and older Prep School pupils may also use the King Library in the Senior School.

Performing Arts. The school has a strong tradition of debating and public speaking, and pupils have many successes to their credit in city, county and regional competitions. A major drama production each year, and various smaller presentations give pupils the opportunity to develop their skills in performing, directing, lighting, sound, stage design, costume design and make-up. There are frequent visits to Stratford, London and regional theatres including the Oxford Playhouse. The majority of pupils learn one musical instrument and some learn two or more; there are two choirs, one orchestra and several smaller ensembles, and some pupils are members of the Oxford Girls' Choir, the Oxford Youth Chamber Choir, the Oxford Schools' Symphony Orchestra, the Oxfordshire Youth Orchestra and the Thames Vale Orchestra. Instruments learnt include piano, violin, viola, 'cello, flute, oboe, clarinet, trumpet, bassoon, saxophone, French horn, guitar and percussion. Through musical productions, concerts and the liturgy there are many opportunities for pupils to contribute to the musical life of the school. In Drama pupils prepare for the examinations of the London Academy of Music and Dramatic Art (LAMDA), and in Music, they prepare for the examinations of the Associated Board of the Royal Schools of Music (ABRSM).

Sport. The school has an indoor sports centre, good playing fields, all-weather hard courts and an outdoor heated swimming pool. The principal winter sports are netball and hockey; the principal summer sports are tennis, swimming, athletics and rounders. Girls compete regularly in local, county and regional tournaments.

Duke of Edinburgh's Award. The school has an outstanding record in The Duke of Edinburgh's Award, each year about 20 girls achieving the Bronze Award, 10 girls or so achieving the Silver Award and several more girls achieving the Gold Award. The purpose of the Award is to give challenge, responsibility and adventure to young people, thus encouraging them to develop initiative and team skills.

Visits. Fieldwork, conferences, lectures, art exhibitions, plays and concerts give girls an interesting programme of visits within the UK. Visits abroad include study courses, exchanges, sports tours and skiing holidays, and the school regularly hosts visiting groups from schools overseas.

Health. The School Nurses work closely with the School Medical Adviser who sees girls at the nearby Health Centre. Dental and orthodontic treatment can be arranged locally, and the John Radcliffe Hospital is five minutes away.

Admissions. Admission to the Prep School is by interview and the school's own entrance tests. Admission to the Senior School is by interview and entrance examination. Admission to the Sixth Form is by interview, school report and GCSE results.

Scholarships. Scholarships are available at 11+, 13+ and 16+.

Fees per term (2016–2017). Senior School: Full Boarders £7,995; Weekly Boarders £7,610; Day Pupils £4,725. Prep School: Full Boarders £6,850; Weekly Boarders £6,470; Day Pupils £3,120–£3,760.

Charitable status. Rye St Antony School Limited is a Registered Charity, number 309685, to provide for the education and welfare of pupils, in accordance with the school's aims.

Board of Governors:
Mr Ian Callaghan (*Trustee*)
Mr Sean Calnan (*Trustee*)
Dr Tom Czepiel, BMus, DPhil, PG Dip LATHE
Mr Simon Detre, BA, QTS
Mrs Sue Hampshire
Revd Dr John Jackson, DPhil
Dr Eleanor Lowe, BA, MA, PhD
Mrs Shuna McGregor, MSc, BA, CQSW
Mr Paul Mitchell
Mr Tim Morton (*Vice-Chairman*)
Mr David Parke (*Trustee*)
Mr Ray Potts
Mrs Margaret Shinkwin, BA, MA, NPQH (*Trustee*)
Mrs Hilary Stafford Northcote, BA (*Trustee and Chairman*)

Headmistress: **Miss Alison Jones**, BA, PGCE

Deputy Head: Mr Philip Humphreys, BSc PGCE
Curriculum Director: Mrs Jenny Owens, BSc, PGCE, CBiol, MIBiol
Head of Sixth Form: Miss Jo Croft, Maîtrise, BA, QTS
Head of Prep: Mrs Emma Coode, BA, PGCE
Bursar & Clerk to the Governors: Mrs Teresa Hudson, MBA MP, DMS, MAAT
Head of Boarding and Activities Director: Miss Helen Tomlinson, BEd
Head of Pre-Prep: Ms Jo Reed, BEd
Lay Chaplain: Dr Sean Willis, BA, MA, QTS, PhD

Heads of Departments:
Art and Design: Miss Jenny White, BA, PGCE
Director of Music: Mr Chris Gill, BA, PGCE
English and Drama: Ms Jo Creber, BA, PGCE
Geography: Mrs Sarah Oscroft, BSc, MSc, PGCE
Humanities, History: Mrs Zoe Ireland, BA, PGCE
ICT and Computing: Mrs Fiona Mullaney, BSc, MSc, PGCE
Languages: Miss Jo Croft, Maîtrise, BA, QTS
Mathematics: Mr Paul Moylan, BA, PGCE
Physical Education: Miss Kate Mackenzie, BSc, PGCE
Science: Mr David Williams, BSc, Cert Ed
SEN Coordinator: Miss Nicole DeRushie, MA, PGDE

Administrative Staff:
Headmistress's PA: Mrs Elizabeth Cheeseman
Registrar: Mrs Fern Williams
Human Resources Manager: Miss Ellen Phelips, BA
Marketing and Communications Manager: Mrs Samantha Eaves, BA

St Augustine's Priory School

Hillcrest Road, Ealing, London W5 2JL

Tel:	020 8997 2022
Fax:	020 8810 6501
email:	admissions@sapriory.com
website:	www.sapriory.com
Twitter:	@staugustinesp
Facebook:	@St-Augustines-Priory
LinkedIn:	/St-Augustines-Priory-School

Motto: *Veritas*

St Augustine's Priory was founded in France in 1634 by Lady Mary Tredway to provide a haven where young English women could be provided with an Independent Education. Moving to Ealing in 1914–15, at its current location, the School follows the philosophy expounded by its Patron, St Augustine of Hippo, and known to every parent that is that children (and for that matter adults) achieve their best when they are happy. Pressurising girls yields very short term dividends. Our excellent results are achieved by stimulating the girls and passing on to them a joy in learning. This is far more effective and indeed much more fun for the teachers.

The School's success is firmly rooted in its readiness to adapt to change while retaining its unique identity and, by adhering to these ideals, we provide our girls with those skills which will enable them to face the future with confidence.

Our academic achievement is only part of our success and we firmly believe in equipping girls with a range of important skills to be effective in the workplace and beyond.

Number of Pupils. There are approximately 460 girls aged from 3–18 (63 in the Sixth Form).

Location. The School is well served by public transport, with Hanger Lane, North Ealing and Park Royal Underground stations all within a ten minute stroll and Ealing Broadway Underground and main line station approximately 20 minutes' walk away. The School sits on top of Hanger Hill in an idyllic setting of thirteen acres, with views across to the South Downs. Buses stop near the entrance.

Admission. St Augustine's Priory is a unique and vibrant community, and the best way to understand it is to come and look around the school and importantly to meet our pupils, Headteacher and staff. During the application process we invite Parents to visit us on Open Day during the Michaelmas and Lent Term and you are also warmly invited to visit the school for a private appointment at other times. Admission to the Preps is via interview in the Michaelmas Term. Girls from St Augustine's Junior School transfer automatically into the Senior School. External candidates for 11+, 13+ and 16+ sit examinations in Lent Term. We make offers based on academic performance, personality and an assessment of what the girl and her family want from the school and can offer to it. We hold an Open Evening for prospective Sixth Formers and their parents during the Michaelmas Term, which is followed up by a Taster Day. The Taster Day allows prospective Augustinians to experience a day in the life of our School and get a feel for how they would fit in. Interviews are then conducted by the appropriate Heads of Department along with the Headteacher, and offers are sent out with conditional GCSE pass requirements. Occasionally places arise in other years. Once a completed Application Form is received, your daughter's name will be placed on the Applications Register appropriate for her age, and will be considered should a vacancy arise.

Religion. St Augustine's Priory is a Catholic Independent Day School for Girls. The Chapel is at the heart of school life and is used for assemblies, weekly Masses and as a place for moments of quiet reflection and prayer. Whilst most students are Catholic, we welcome girls from other religions and faiths and learn from them.

Pastoral Care. Children from all backgrounds and all races, with a wide range of gifts, make up the vibrant community which is St Augustine's. From their first day, girls become part of a family which respects the beliefs and customs of its members and learns to work together. When problems arise and questions need to be asked, we encourage a very personal approach. The Form Teacher has a special relationship with pupils, looking after their day-to-day needs and encouraging them to get the very best out of their time at school. It is to the Form Teacher that pupils and parents can look in the first instance for help and guidance.

Curriculum. We offer an extensive and balanced curriculum including PSHE, and offer 20 subjects at GCSE and IGCSE and 23 subjects at AS and A2 Level. Girls can take a number of subjects as part of a fast-tracking programme. Girls are expected to take ten or more subjects at GCSE.

The Sixth Form and Careers. The Sixth Form facilities include a common room, kitchen and balcony overlooking the South Downs. The Head Girl and Deputy Head girls have their own offices.

Sixth Form students have the chance to take part in a range of additional activities to try out new sports or skills and meet people from other schools.

We encourage girls to think about their next step and to make informed decisions at every stage of their development. The Sixth Form is supported by the Careers team providing advice and guidance. The team works with the students to consider their many future options, assisting with university and course selection, preparation for Oxbridge and other university applications and subsequent interviews. This process is supplemented by an annual Careers Conference with guest speakers, mentors and experts in key fields invited in to speak and to offer advice and insight.

Working with the Directors of Sixth Form, every girl is encouraged to examine her own strengths and to explore possibilities suitable for her interests and personal abilities. Talks, conferences, seminars and courses, a visit to a Careers Fair and University Open Days, career profiling, as well as a well-stocked, up-to-date Careers library and the Internet, allow all our students to keep abreast of opportunities on offer. The school is a member of ISCO.

All of this support builds on the guidance received throughout the school. When our girls leave here for university, they take with them not only impressive qualifications but also kindness, an understanding of, and the ability to adapt to, the world in which they live, the confidence to succeed in whatever they choose to do and above all, friendships which will last them through life.

Extracurricular Activities. Apart from Physical Education in the curriculum, the school also excels in its extremely popular after-school sports activities fielding winning teams in hockey, netball, swimming and cross country. Tennis, karate, football, ballet and gymnastics are all catered for after school.

Whilst Drama forms a part of the curriculum and is very strong here at St Augustine's we also stage an annual major production in the Spring which allows involvement by the whole Senior School.

Music is a particular strength with girls from Prep III to the Sixth Form being given the opportunity and encouragement to take any instrument they choose, from violin, cello and flute to harp, drums and guitar. If a girl is interested in a particular instrument we will try to find a teacher for her. As a result music flourishes throughout the school with girls taking part in lunchtime and after-school orchestras, music groups and choirs, and music tours abroad.

The Art is outstanding with the girls' work displayed throughout the school. An annual Art Exhibition is held each summer, and the department makes use of visits to the many theatres, museums and galleries in London.

The School is licensed as a Centre for The Duke of Edinburgh's Bronze, Silver and Gold Awards. Trips to Nepal, Borneo and China are recent examples of the girls' visits into the far-flung reaches of the world with skiing trips for Juniors and Seniors, French student visits and Husky Sledging in Norway forming the basis of our recent European travels.

Facilities. St Augustine's Priory offers superb amenities including a full-size floodlit all-weather astroturf pitch and floodlit competition-sized netball court set in stunning 13-acre grounds.

In addition to sporting facilities, our 13 acres include a dedicated Prep meadow, orchards, Sixth Form rose garden and croquet lawn. The state-of-the-art Science Wing opened in 2007 with four laboratories and dedicated Senior and Junior music and drama rooms. A new Nursery block was completed in March 2011. To complement this there are two IT suites, music practice rooms, Senior and Junior Art rooms, a Sixth Form Art studio, Modern Languages Academy, dedicated Sixth Form areas and private studies, and

Scriptorium. Kitchens are on site and the Chef and catering staff serve fresh cooked lunches daily.

Fees per term (2016–2017). Nursery Department £1,500–£3,320, Preparatory Department £3,524, Junior Department £3,944, Senior Department £4,723.

Additional information may be found on the school's website and a more detailed prospectus may be obtained from the School.

Charitable status. St Augustine's Priory School Limited is a Registered Charity, number 1097781.

Board of Governors:
Mrs S Kirby, BA (*Chair*)
Mrs C Philips, LLB (*Vice Chair*)
Mrs J Austin, BA (*Chair of Academic Committee*)
Mrs F Baker, MA (*Chair of Capital Planning Committee*)
Ms J Burbury (*Marketing Governor*)
Deacon A Clarke, BA, BD (*Chair of Safeguarding Committee*)
Mrs S Collis, BA, ACA (*Chair of Finance Committee*)
Mr P D'Arcy, BSc, MRICS (*Capital Planning Governor*)
Mr F Steadman, BA (*Academic Governor*)

Mr J Powell (*Bursar & Clerk to the Governors*)

Headteacher: Mrs S Raffray, MA, NPQH (*Designated Safeguarding Officer – Seniors*)

Deputy Head – Seniors: Mrs M-H Collins, MA Oxon (*Designated Safeguarding Officer – Seniors*)
Deputy Head – Seniors: Mrs K Cotton [Maternity Cover]
Head of Preps and Pre-Preps: Miss E Keane, BA (*Designated Safeguarding Officer – Preps and Pre-Preps*)
Deputy Head – Juniors: Mrs N Tippen, BA (*Designated Safeguarding Officer – Juniors*)

Heads of Subject Departments:
Art: Miss C Eng, BSc, MRS
Science: Mrs L Harley, BSc
Science: Mr M Kane [Maternity Cover]
Chemistry: Mr P Thomas, BSc, MEd, MCIEA (*Examinations Officer*)
Classics: Dr G Carleton, MA, PhD
Drama: Ms C Brown, BA
English: Mrs M Eaton, BA
Geography: Mr I Chappory, BA
History: Miss P Trybuchowska, MA Oxon
IT: Mr M Dellow
Key Stage 1: Miss E Keane, BA
Key Stage 2: Miss A L Gambrill, BEd
Mathematics: Mrs J Bennett, MA Oxon
Modern Languages: Mr A Alejandro, BA
Director of Music: Dr G Higgins, MA
Physical Education: Mrs H Gosling, BSc
Religious Studies: Mrs L Mcdermott, BA
Social Sciences: Mr P Murphy, BSc, MEd (*Director of Sixth Form – UCAS*)

Teaching Staff:
Ms F Assemat, MA (*Modern Foreign Languages*)
Miss A Burrell (*Head of Biology*) [Maternity Cover]
Mrs C Costello, BEd (*Prep*)
Miss A Cross (*PE*)
Mrs L Cvetkova (*EYFS Practitioner and Teaching Assistant*)
Miss N Daya, BA (*Junior School*)
Mrs H Eccleston, BA
Mr N Elder, BA (*English*)
Mrs D Farmer, BA, QTS (*English*)
Miss A Gambrill, BEd (*Juniors*)
Ms A Gandi, MA (*Faculty Leader Arts*)
Mrs L Griffiths, BA (*Classics*)
Miss L Hales, BA (*PE*)

Miss L Halton, NNEB (*Teaching Assistant*)
Mr N Harnett (*Maths*)
Mrs A Islam (*Level 3 Teaching Assistant*)
Miss F Johnson, MA, ALCM (*Music/Senco*)
Miss M Keep, BA (*Geography*)
Miss A Kloc, MA (*Russian*)
Ms M De Lahitte, BA (*Learning Support*)
Mrs T Lakomy, BSc (*Mathematics*)
Miss V Lee (*Mandarin*)
Mrs C Lindsay (*PE*)
Mrs L Lubowieska, BA (*Prep*)
Mrs C Lunn, BA (*History*)
Ms C Macallister, ALCM, BA, ACA (*Humanities*)
Ms K Mackay, BA (*Art*)
Mrs H Moore (*Learning Support*)
Mrs N Morris, NNEB (*Nursery Practitioner*)
Mrs H Nikolova (*EYFS Practitioner*)
Miss C O'Brien, BA
Miss L O'Connell, BA
Mrs P O'Connell, DPP (*Teaching Assistant*)
Mr M Pereira, BCom (*Mathematics*)
Mrs G Pugh (*Biology*)
Mrs C Racadio, BSc (*Mathematics*)
Miss A Rai (*Teaching Assistant*)
Mrs H Round, BA (*Juniors*)
Mr J Salmon (*Physics*)
Mrs H Sandhu, MA, QTS (*Juniors*)
Ms C Slight (*Nursery*)
Ms G Taher, BSc (*Psychology*)
Mrs Z Thackray, BA (*Learning Support*)
Mr P Thomas, BSc, MEd, MCIEA (*Science, Examinations Officer*)
Mrs K Toynton, BA (*Modern Foreign Languages*)
Mrs R van der Merwe, PGCE, BA, QTS (*Juniors*)
Ms F Verne (*Chemistry*)
Mrs A Wright, BA, QTS (*Art*)
Mrs C Young, Mont Cert (*Support in Learning Assistant*)

Welfare Staff:
Mrs R Good, BSc, Dip Counselling (*Counsellor*)
Ms J Roberts (*School Health Practitioner*)

Peripatetic Staff:
Ms R Aspinall, BMus TCM (*Harp*)
Miss E Balaam (*Cheer leading Coach*)
Mrs J Bull (*Maths*)
Mrs E Curran, MGR (*Piano*)
Mr F Deguzman (*Martial Arts*)
Mrs E Ellis, Life Member RAD (*Ballet*)
Miss V Ellis, MRAD (*Ballet*)
Miss E Ferrari, ALCM (*Singing*)
Miss E Jackson, MA, GMus, ARCM (*Violin, Viola*)
Mr I Judson, LWCMD, ALCM (*Flute*)
Ms L McMullin (*LAMDA*)
Mr M Rose, BMus (*Guitar*)
Mr C Smith, BMus, LRAM (*Brass*)
Miss E Tingey, LWCMD, ACC (*Oboe*)
Mrs J Warren, GTCL (*Cello*)
Mrs S Watson (*Clarinet, Saxophone*)

Technicians:
Mr S Wood (*ICT Technician*)
Ms P Morrison, BSc (*Laboratory Technician*)

Administration:
Miss D Aiton (*School Office Manager*)
Mrs K Bhatti (*Librarian*)
Mrs C Cox, BSc Econ (*Design Manager*)
Miss K Daly (*Saturday Receptionist*)
Mrs M Eaton (*Receptionist*)
Miss C Goulding, BA (*Operations Manager*)
Ms M King, BA (*Communications Administrator*)
Mrs J Lanek (*Domestic*)

Mr P Martin, BA (*ICT & Data Services Manager*)
Miss L Naylor (*Finance Assistant*)
Mrs G Savic (*Registrar & Marketing Manager*)
Mrs R Sharma (*Domestic*)
Mrs C Sumpter (*PA to the Headteacher*)
Miss C Sumpter, BA (*Communications Officer*)
Mrs G Vymeris, MA (*Assistant Bursar*)

Estate Staff:
Mr C Mortimer, BSc (*Head Groundsman*)
Mrs M Gelderblom (*Minibus Driver*)
Mr Marc Raffray (*Part-time Premises Officer*)
Mr I Smith (*Groundsman*)

St Catherine's School
Bramley

Station Road, Bramley, Guildford, Surrey GU5 0DF

Tel:	01483 893363
Fax:	01483 899608
email:	schooloffice@stcatherines.info
	admissions@stcatherines.info
website:	www.stcatherines.info
Twitter:	@stcatsbramley

Founded as a Church of England School for Girls in 1885, welcoming both day girls and boarders, St Catherine's is one of the UK's premier girls' schools. The location, just three miles south of Guildford and surrounded by miles of countryside offers space and green vistas and yet is within one hour of central London and Heathrow Airport.

In a recent Sutton Trust report, St Catherine's was positioned in the top 5 schools in the country sending students to the UK's most highly selective universities. Superb examination results are testament to the quality of teaching and learning, where students are not afraid to show enthusiasm and ambition. Lessons are taught in well-appointed classrooms by subject specialists. in 2016 92% of girls achieved A*–B at A level and 92% achieved A*/A at GCSE.

With extensive playing fields, superb sports facilities and an auditorium which boasts better acoustics than many London venues, it is no surprise that St Catherine's is always buzzing with life after the teaching day is over.

A well-established House system underpins the whole School, allowing new girls to feel at home very quickly, encouraging an ethos of care and concern for others as well as a friendly competitive spirit.

The outstanding results gained by our students in public examinations secure them places at the top universities, in competitive disciplines like medicine and veterinary science, law and languages. This success comes not only as a result of the fine quality of the teaching, but is also due to the individual attention received by every girl. St Catherine's places great emphasis on creating a happy environment where every girl is encouraged to work hard to maximise her talents. The atmosphere is friendly and one in which children can develop and grow in a very stimulating environment.

Pivotal to the life of St Catherine's are the six school Houses. The girls' loyalty and affection for their Houses is impressive with memories of inter-house plays, competitions and matches enduring long after School days have ended.

A broad and varied curriculum allows all pupils to participate in many challenging and rewarding extracurricular activities. As a Church of England School girls are encouraged to think of others and impressive sums of money are raised for charity each year. The School has its own beautiful chapel which is used by the girls on a daily basis.

The School's flexible approach to boarding is making it increasingly attractive to busy, professional families; the ISI team picked out boarding as one of the outstanding features of St Catherine's. The School welcomes both weekly and full boarders who enjoy a busy and exciting programme.

There are exceptional on-site facilities including 3 lacrosse pitches, a multi-purpose sports hall, fitness suite and indoor pool. The auditorium provides superb acoustics for our musical and theatrical productions, better than many London venues. The Sixth Form girls have their own Library which provides a perfect study environment right at the heart of the School. These facilities i.e. the Anniversary Halls and the Speech Hall Library were officially opened by HRH the Duchess of Cornwall in February 2014. The first Baron Ashcombe, the Duchess's Great-Great Grandfather was one of the original founders and benefactors of St Catherine's.

Activities Week is held each year in the Summer Term when every girl in the School participates in a variety of programmes organised to both support the curriculum and offer challenges not normally met in the classroom. Pupils participate in outward bound ventures, an industrial heritage tour to the north and midlands, modern language courses in France, Germany and Spain, whilst Sixth Formers focus on university choices. Activities Week costs are included in the fees.

International links are also very important. St Catherine's has an exchange programme with St Catherine's Melbourne, Australia and there are also links with schools in Kenya, South Africa and Afghanistan.

St Catherine's has an unrivalled reputation in art, music, sport and drama; photography and textiles are popular options amongst the Sixth Form, and younger girls are encouraged by an enthusiastic Art and Design department to take advantage of the superb facilities, and join many after-school clubs.

Music is an important feature of school life, with numerous choirs, orchestras and concert bands rehearsing each week and performing regularly. There are in excess of 600 individual music lessons taking place each week where over half the girls learn to play a musical instrument. There are flute choirs, string quartets, recorder groups and ensembles to cater for all levels of ability. Concerts and recitals are held regularly. An exciting venture has been the Organ Academy and the Jennifer Bate Organ Scholarship in conjunction with Guildford Cathedral and the Andrew Lloyd Webber Foundation. The School boasts two organs, one in the School Chapel and a second in the Preparatory School.

Many girls go on to represent their county in netball, lacrosse, swimming, squash and athletics. Every girl is encouraged to take part in sport at school, whatever her level of expertise. The PE Department regularly fields four or five teams for lacrosse and netball, allowing every girl who wishes to play competitively the opportunity to do so.

Drama and Theatre Studies are extremely popular options and all girls are encouraged to audition for the annual middle and senior school plays. As well as acting opportunities, pupils are also offered the opportunity to help backstage and front of house and learn many valuable skills as a result. LAMDA classes are offered to all year groups. With the opening of the impressive new performance halls including state-of-the-art lighting and acoustics, facilities for Theatre are second to none. St Catherine's also has its own very popular School of Dance.

The Preparatory School: most girls join at 4 with a limited number of places available in other years. It aims to support families in helping younger pupils develop a strong sense of values, high standards of behaviour and consideration to others, as well as achieving excellent academic success. The girls benefit from specialist teaching, combining the best of traditional methods with modern technology to prepare them for the Entrance Examinations to all Senior Schools at 11+, including St Catherine's.

St Catherine's is situated in extensive grounds, in the heart of the attractive Surrey village of Bramley, three miles south of Guildford which has a main line station (Waterloo 35 minutes). The school operates a return bus service to Guildford Station Monday to Friday and there is a Friday evening bus service to London for weekly boarders. There is easy access to Heathrow and Gatwick and travel arrangements are made for overseas boarders. Close proximity to London allows frequent visits to theatres and galleries and the miles of countryside on our doorstep is an asset to the many girls who take part in The Duke of Edinburgh's Award scheme.

Fees per term (from January 2017). Day Girls (including lunch): £2,860 (Pre-Prep 1), £3,465 (Pre-Prep 2), £4,090 (Pre-Prep 3), £4,830 (Prep School), £5,850 (Senior School).

Boarders: Middle and Senior Boarding and Tuition £9,635.

Fees include the Activities Week programme for Senior School girls and lunches for all pupils aged 4–18.

Entry. This is by Entrance Examination held in January. The Preparatory School also holds its entrance assessments in January.

Scholarships and Bursaries.

11+: There are four Academic Entrance Scholarships available for pupils at age 11. These are awarded on the results of the Entrance Examination. Two scholarships are for 20% of the fees payable and the other two are for 10% of the fees. These run through the Middle School and can be extended through the Sixth Form at the discretion of the Headmistress and in consultation with the teaching staff.

Upper 5 and Sixth Form (Year 11): The following scholarships are awarded during the Summer Term of the girls' Lower Fifth (Year 10). Selection for the awards is based on the results of the June examinations at the end of the Lower Fifth, performance throughout the Lower Five year, a Scholarship Examination paper, and an interview.

There are several internal academic Sixth Form Scholarships: these are scholarships of 20% of the fees payable to run for three years (through Upper 5 and the Sixth Form).

Sixth Form Scholarships: These are scholarships of 20% of fees. However, this group can be extended by a mix of additional 20% or 10% awards depending on the performance of the candidates and the recommendations of the awarding panel.

The Clare Gregory Memorial Sports Scholarship: This is awarded for sporting prowess and is for 20% of the day fees in the Sixth Form.

The Sixth Form Art and Textiles Scholarship: There is an Art and Textiles Scholarship to the value of 20% of the School Fees, awarded during the Autumn Term of Upper 5.

The Sixth Form Drama Scholarship: There is a Drama Scholarship to the value of 20% of the School Fees, awarded during the Autumn Term of Upper 5.

Scholarships for New Entrants to the Sixth Form: There are up to three external academic scholarships of up to 20% of fees and these are awarded at the discretion of the Headmistress, to new pupils joining the School in the Sixth Form. N.B. The Sixth Form Art and Music Scholarships may be applied for by external applicants by the end of October each year.

Music Scholarships and Awards:

An *11+ Music Scholarship* of 20% of the fees and tuition on one instrument may be awarded annually upon entry to an 11+ candidate adjudged by the Director of Music and the independent adjudicator to have strong musical talent. A second Music Scholarship of 10% of fees and tuition on one instrument can be awarded in years where the field of applicants is particularly strong. Applications should be made by November and auditions are in January. A *Sixth Form Music*

Scholarship is awarded to a pupil entering the Sixth Form – from within the School or as an external applicant – to the value of 20% of the School Fees.

The Jennifer Bate Organ Scholarship, offered in conjunction with Guildford Cathedral, is awarded in alternate years to a girl who is already a good organist or shows potential. This award is typically for 20% of fees payable, but may involve means-tested bursary assistance if appropriate.

Further Music Awards which cover music tuition, exam fees and sheet music on a range of musical instruments from chapel organ to piccolo and voice are available to pupils in the Senior School. Some are specifically for those wanting to take up less 'popular' instruments. Auditions for Awards take place at the same time as Music Scholarship auditions

Bursaries: Means-tested bursaries are available to external applicants which may cover up to 100% of the fees payable. For further details please contact the Business Manager.

Prospectus and School Visits. Please apply to the Registrar. The Headmistress will be pleased to see parents by appointment.

Charitable status. St Catherine's School Bramley is a Registered Charity, number 1070858. It exists to provide education for girls in accordance with the principles of the Church of England.

Governing Body:
Chairman: Mr P J Martin, BA, FRGS, FCCA
Dr Helen Bowcock, DL
A Carruthers, BCom Hons
Prof Finbarr Cotter MB, BS, FRCP[UK], FRCPath, FRCP[I],PhD
Mrs P Crouch, LLB
Professor Andrea Dlaska, DPhil, Mag Phil
Mrs M Greenway, LLB, QTS
Mrs C Johnstone [Dr Clare Higgens], MRCS, LRCP, MBBS, MD, FRCP
Dr M Jordan, MA, MB BChir, FRCA
T W Kendall, FRICS
Dr Janet McGowan, MBBS, FRCA
Mrs S E Shipway
J C M Tippett, BSc, FCA, TEP
B M Way, D Arch RIBA

Headmistress: **Mrs Alice Phillips**, MA Cantab

Business Manager: Mrs Christine Silver, BSc Durham, PGCE
Head of Boarding: Mrs Lorinda Munro-Faure, MA Oxon, PGCE
Director of Studies: Mrs Jacki Deakin, BSc UCL, PGCE
Senior Housemistress: Mrs Kirsty Meredith, BA Hons London, AKC, PGCE
Director of Staff: Mrs Claire Wyllie, MA Dunelm, PGCE
Head of Sixth Form: Mrs Kate Hawtin, BA Dunelm, PGCE
School Administrator: Mrs Sheila Kelsall, MA Open, BSc Hons Open, PGCE
Head of Prep School: Miss Naomi Bartholomew, MA London, BEd Cantab, QTS, MA London
Deputy Head – Curriculum: Mrs Julie Micklethwaite, BEd Hons Roehampton
Deputy Head – Pre-Prep: Mrs Jill Cochrane, BEd, CertEd Leicester, PGCPSE Open
Deputy Head – Staff: Mrs Wendy Gibbs, BEd Hons Winchester

Marketing: Mrs Gill David, BA Manchester, PGCE
Development Director: Ms Pippa Carte, BD, MA
Association Director: Mrs Dawn Pilkington, BA

Chaplain: Revd Dr Benjamin McNair Scott, BA, MA, PGCE, CELTA, PhD

School Housemistresses:
Ashcombe: Mrs Amanda White
Merriman: Mrs Rosa McQuade
Midleton: Mrs Kirsty Meredith
Musgrave: Mrs Penny Harris
Russell-Baker: Mrs Izzy McLean
Stoner: Mrs Simone Berry

Boarding Housemistresses:
Bronte: Mrs Lucinda Norman
Symes: Miss Helen Wilson
Keller: Mrs Charlotte George
Sixth Form: Mrs Vic Alexander

Heads of Departments:
Art: Mr Alexander Perry-Adlam, BA Hons Liverpool John Moores, Cert Ed
Biology: Mrs Claerwen Patterson, MA Oxon, PGCE
Careers: Mrs Sue Weighell, BA Hons Birmingham, QTS Business Studies
Chemistry: Mrs Nicola Austin, MChem Oxon, QTS
Classics: Mrs Jessica Ashby, BA Cantab, PGCE
Drama: Mrs Sally Gallis, BA Ed Plymouth, QTS
Design Technology: Mr Alastair White, BA Hons Winchester
Economics/Business Studies: Mr Nigel Watson, BA Hons Ealing College of Higher Education, PGCE
English: Mr Jonathan Worthen, MA Oxon, PGCE
Examinations Coordinator: Mr Carl Gladwell, BA London
French: Mrs Lucy Strong, BA Hons Bristol, PGCE
Food and Nutrition: Mrs Nicola Genzel, BA Hons Roehampton, PGCE
Geography: Mrs Sophie Mackness, BSc Hons London, PGCE
German Dr Elodie Nevin, MA Oxon, PhD, QTS
History: Mrs Gill David, BA Manchester, PGCE
History of Art: Mrs Sarah Phillips, BA Open, QTS
ICT: Mrs Catherine Lamb, BA and DipE Central Queensland University, QTS
Librarian: Mrs Kathryn Bainbridge, MA Loughborough, BA Hons, CILIP
Study Skills Coordinator: Mrs Caroline Warren, BA Hons, Lancaster, PGCE
Mathematics: Mr Alasdair Wright, BSc Hertfordshire, PGCE
Director of Music: Mr Matthew Greenfield, MEng Oxon, QTS
Physical Education: Mrs Nancy Moore, BA Wales, PGCE
Physics: Dr Kathleen Puech, BSc PhD Dublin, PGCE
Politics: Mr Carl Gladwell, BA Hons London, PGCE
Psychology: Mrs Jean Arrick, BSc Hons Liverpool, PGCE
PSHE: Mrs Amanda White, BSc Hons Wales, PGCE
Religious Studies: Mrs Cecilia Townley, MA London, BA Sheffield, PGCE
Sixth Form General Studies: Mr Carl Gladwell, BA Hons London, PGCE
Spanish: Mrs Margarita Perez-Garcia,Maîtrise, Diplôme d'Etudes Montpellier III, PGCE
Textiles: Mrs Lorna Crispin, BA Hons Manchester
Timetable: Mrs Heather Bryn-Thomas, BSc Kent, PGCE

Administration:
Senior School Registrar: Mrs Clare Woodgates
Prep School Registrar: Mrs Sally Manhire
PA to the Business Manager: Mrs Diane Haeffele
PA to the Headmistress: Miss Toppy Wharton
Office Manager: Miss Sally Marshall

St Catherine's School
Twickenham

Cross Deep, Twickenham, Middlesex TW1 4QJ

Tel:	020 8891 2898
Fax:	020 8744 9629
email:	admissions@stcatherineschool.co.uk
website:	www.stcatherineschool.co.uk

Motto: 'Not Words But Deeds'

Age Range. Girls 3–18 years.
Number in School. 416 Day Girls.
Founded in 1914 by the Sisters of Mercy, St Catherine's moved from its original site to its current location in 1919. Today the school is under lay management. St Catherine's is a Catholic School in the ecumenical tradition, and pupils of all denominations are welcome.

Aims. Our aim is to provide a broad and balanced education within a stimulating and supportive environment which encourages and challenges girls to strive to be the best they can be in all areas of the curriculum. Success is achieved through personal responsibility, high expectations and a close partnership between parents and school. Emphasis is placed on self-discipline, responsibility and the importance of respect for others. Since we are a relatively small school with small class sizes the staff know the pupils as individuals and there is a strong sense of community which promotes academic success.

Situation. The school enjoys an enviable position, located next to the River Thames. It is a short distance from the centre of Twickenham and approximately 10–15 minutes' walk from Strawberry Hill and Twickenham Stations. Both have regular services to London (Waterloo), Surrey, Berkshire and Middlesex. There are also a number of local bus routes.

Entrance. Main points of entry are at 3, 5, 7, 11 and 16 but girls are accepted at any stage subject to availability. Places at the school are usually awarded on the basis of an interview, a report from the candidate's previous school and an assessment (examination in the Senior School).

Scholarships and Bursaries. Academic Scholarships, up to the value of 50% of the fees, are awarded annually at 11+ and 16+. At 11+ girls are invited to sit scholarship papers on the basis of their entrance examination results. At 16+ students are required to sit three examination papers in the subjects they plan to study at A Level. Art, Drama, Music and Sport scholarships are also awarded annually following an audition/assessment and are conditional on the applicant achieving the school's academic requirement for entry.

A limited number of means-tested Bursaries are offered depending on need and funds available.

Curriculum. In the Senior School pupils follow courses in English, Mathematics, Biology, Chemistry, Physics, Religious Education, French, German, Spanish, History, Geography, Drama, Music, Art, Food Technology, ICT and Physical Education. All of these subjects are offered at GCSE with the addition of Economics, Psychology, Textiles and Photography. Most pupils study ten subjects to GCSE level. All of the above subjects are available at A Level, with the addition of Business Studies, Classical Civilization, Government and Politics, Graphics, History of Art, Law, Further Mathematics, Music Technology and Sociology.

There is a strong commitment to Sport, Music, Drama and extracurricular activities. The school has its own hockey pitch and indoor swimming pool as well as tennis and netball courts. Sports include swimming, netball, athletics, hockey, tennis, gymnastics, trampolining and rounders and our pupils achieve considerable success at county, regional and national level.

Music plays an important part in the life of the school; all pupils are encouraged to participate in choirs, orchestras and ensembles, and there is a varied programme of concerts and informal performances each term.

Drama is popular and, as well as opportunities to perform in school productions, regular theatre visits take place during the year.

Buildings. The Preparatory and Senior departments are on one site. The buildings include a large multi-purpose hall as well as a smaller assembly hall, well-stocked Prep and Senior Libraries, three ICT Suites, a spacious Art and Photography Suite and a Food Technology Room. The Music Centre has class and individual practice rooms. There are fully-equipped laboratories for Physics, Chemistry and Biology. A large programme of new building has recently added extra teaching blocks, a Sixth Form Centre, Drama Studio and Fitness Suite.

Extracurricular Activities. These play a significant role in the life of the school. Activities include the Duke of Edinburgh's Award scheme, Badminton, Science Club, Football, Rugby, Rowing, Cross-Country Running, Zumba, Chess and Photography. Trips, both locally and abroad, add to the extensive range of activities on offer. Pupils also take part in community service and fundraising activities.

Fees per term (2016–2017). Inclusive of lunch: Nursery £3,385, Reception £3,618, Years 1 and 2 £3,715, Years 3 to 6 £3,905, Years 7 to 13 £4,674 (excluding examination fees).

Charitable status. St Catherine's School, Twickenham is a Registered Charity, number 1014651. It aims to provide for children seeking education in a Christian environment.

Chair of Governors: Mr Edward Sparrow

Headmistress: **Sister Paula Thomas**, BEd Hons, MA

Deputy Head: Miss A Wallace, MA, BA, PGCE

Bursar & Clerk to the Governors: Mr I G Stewart, BAcc, CA

Admissions Secretary: Mrs A Faulkner, FAPA, PAFSA

St Dominic's Brewood

Bargate Street, Brewood, Staffordshire ST19 9BA

Tel: 01902 850248
Fax: 01902 851154
email: enquiries@stdominicsbrewood.co.uk
website: www.stdominicsbrewood.co.uk
Twitter: @StDomsBrewood
Facebook: /DominicansBrewood

St Dominic's Brewood provides education for over 200 pupils – girls from 3 to 18 and boys from 3 to 11. Development of the 'whole person' is at the heart of our school. We believe each child has special talents and we work to enable them to achieve their full potential within a caring environment. We nurture the pupils academically, socially, creatively and spiritually. We are pleased to have introduced overseas students to our Sixth Form.

Teaching & Learning. Small class sizes facilitates individual attention so strengths and weaknesses are diagnosed and all work is tailored to match individual's needs. We believe in close partnership with parents, keeping you informed about your child's progress.

Curriculum. We offer a broad and balanced curriculum with enhancement and enrichment. The National Curriculum is taught throughout the school. This is enhanced with additional subjects including performing arts, dance, drama

and singing which are integrated into the weekly timetable. We offer a comprehensive range of subjects at AS and A Level.

Expressive Arts. We are renowned for our musical and dramatic excellence. Our contemporary Performing Arts Centre houses a Drama and Dance Studio, a Music Suite and a Recording Studio. Pupils are encouraged to join the choirs, play an instrument, take up dance, singing or tread the boards. Throughout the year there are a variety of performances ranging from the Pre-Preparatory Christmas play, to productions such as *Oklahoma* and *Annie*. The pupils participate in many local and regional competitions, take part in local festivals and public speaking events. Many do LAMDA examinations and all Year 7s take English Speaking Board examinations.

Sports. We offer a broad curriculum including netball, hockey, dance, gymnastics, aerobics, football, volleyball, basketball, badminton, rounders, tennis, golf, athletics and cross-country. Our all-inclusive extracurricular programmes provide further sporting variety including Zumba, gymnastics, trampolining, modern dance and ballet, with all abilities encouraged to attend.

There is a comprehensive fixtures programme incorporating inter-house events and annual Junior and Senior Sports Days. We take part in ISA sporting events at local, regional and national level.

The facilities include newly-resurfaced netball and tennis courts, hockey, football and rounders pitches and athletics track. We also have an excellent fully-equipped sports hall with new cricket nets and electronic basketball hoops.

Extracurricular Activities. Four days a week there is an all-inclusive after-school programme where pupils can undertake a variety of activities ranging from The Duke of Edinburgh's Award scheme to street dancing, debating, cooking, Young Enterprise, STEM Club and gardening.

Throughout the year, pupils are encouraged to become involved in fundraising for local and national charities. These activities help each girl develop a good community spirit with respect and consideration for others.

Pastoral Care. Our outstanding pastoral care system and Christian ethos create an atmosphere which fosters trust and mutual respect between pupils and teachers. Pupils feel relaxed and secure and develop their self-respect, self-confidence, personal discipline and consideration for others.

Examination Results. Our pupils achieve outstanding exam results year on year outperforming the national averages of both comprehensive and independent schools at Key Stage 2, GCSE and A Level.

Facilities. We have a purpose-built Kindergarten and Junior building, which encompasses a Junior Hall, IT room, DT and Art room, Home Economics room and library. The Senior building has fully-equipped science laboratories, IT room and library. All classrooms have networked computers and interactive whiteboards. The Sixth Form and Performing Arts Centre is a modern, state-of-the-art facility housing the latest technology in music, IT and the Performing Arts. It has a common room with terraces and a well-equipped Library with Wi-Fi technology.

Admissions. Although selective, we draw our pupils from a wide ability range, which makes our record of results outstanding. Assessment is made during trial days at school. Entry into the Senior Department is through entrance assessment in November and a place in the Sixth Form is conditional upon GCSE results.

Fees per term (2016–2017). Transition 5 mornings including lunch £1,118, Reception including lunch £2,086, Year 1 including lunch £2,512, Year 2 including lunch £2,737, Years 3–6 £3,173, Years 7–9 £3,850, Years 10–13 £4,032, Sixth Form 'Homestay' Boarding: £21,500 per annum.

Scholarships and Bursaries. Scholarships may be available for Preparatory. Academic, Sport and Performing Arts scholarships may be awarded for entry into Year 7, Art scholarships in Year 8 and a range of scholarships awarded in Year 12. Means-tested Bursaries are available.

Chairman of Governors: Mr Rob Turton

Head of School: **Mr Peter McNabb**, BSc Hons, PGCE

Bursar: Mr Paul Tudor
Assistant Head (Pastoral): Miss Louise Hovland, BEd Hons
Assistant Head (Curriculum and Safeguarding): Mrs Nicola Hastings Smith, BA Hons, PGCE, NPQH
Head of Preparatory School: Mrs Samantha Kirwan, BA QTS, RSA Cert SpLD
Head of Sixth Form: Mrs Coriarna Morris-Smith, BSc Hons, PGCE

Heads of Faculty:
Mathematics: Mrs Rosemary Cowley, BA, Cert Ed
Science and Technology: Mr Ian Henderson, BSc Hons, MRSC, PGCE, QTS
Expressive Arts: Mrs Carol Molin, BA Hons, PGCE, LGSM
Communications: Mrs Nicola Hastings Smith, BA Hons, PGCE, NPQH
Humanities: Mrs Kathryn Simmonds-Vaughan, BA Hons, PG Dip Ed

Finance Manager: Mrs C Goodridge
Finance Officer: Mrs S Tillett
Admissions Officer: Mrs S Molloy

St Gabriel's

Sandleford Priory, Newbury, Berkshire RG20 9BD

Tel: 01635 555680
Fax: 01635 555698
email: info@stgabriels.co.uk
website: www.stgabriels.co.uk
Twitter: @StGabrielsNews
Facebook: @stgabrielsnewbury

Independent Day School for Girls, in membership of GSA and IAPS.
Number of Pupils. 450.
Academic excellence, high expectation, intellectual challenge and a fulfilling co-curricular life are all vital elements of St Gabriel's. Securing the very best possible results and university places for students is the bedrock of this successful school.
Visitors to St Gabriel's quickly recognise that this is no ordinary school. From Nursery to Sixth Form they are struck by the enthusiasm and sense of purpose of both staff and pupils. Some parents choose St Gabriel's because of its reputation for achieving exceptional academic standards; others welcome the individual attention which is given to all pupils.
Curriculum. The formal curriculum is broad and well-balanced, providing an education that is both traditional and forward-thinking. Small class sizes, an outstanding system of pastoral care and dynamic teaching assist pupils to achieve their full potential both academically and holistically. To ensure connectivity to the real world and to prepare the students to meet the challenges of the 21st Century workplace, the school has forged strong links with high-tech industry and multi-national businesses.
A choice of 28 subjects is offered at GCSE of which English, English Literature, Mathematics, all three Sciences, a Modern Foreign Language, a Humanity and Religious Studies are compulsory.

At Sixth Form, students choose three subjects to study to A Level from the 28 offered. All students also study for the Extended Project Qualification.
Extra-Curricular Activities. As well as offering a thorough academic education, the school provides a wide range of opportunities outside of the classroom. Numerous activities and visits extend and enrich the girls' learning experience throughout the school. The performing and creative arts, sport and a wide range of clubs and societies ensure that the girls progress to the next stage of their education with confidence. Whether it is through The Duke of Edinburgh's Award or World Challenge, the girls constantly rise to meet new challenges.
Music. There are two orchestras, four choirs a wide range of ensembles including two string quartets, jazz and rock bands and several woodwind ensembles. Most orchestral instruments may be learned.
Sport. Netball, Hockey, Swimming, Rounders, Athletics, Cross-Country, Dance, Gym and Tennis.
Facilities. Specialist IT suites, science laboratories and MFL rooms, multi-disciplinary sports hall, theatre and dance studio.
Christian Community & Ethos. St Gabriel's has a Church of England foundation but girls of other faiths are welcome. A strong moral code and Christian values ensure the girls leave the school as well-balanced, unpretentious, spirited individuals with the confidence to be assertive and decisive with warmth and without arrogance. The girls are always encouraged and supported to resist pressures and to have the confidence to make the right choices.
Supervised Prep. This is provided on a daily basis between 4.00 pm and 6.30 pm.
Scholarships & Bursaries. Academic, Sport, Art, Dance, Drama and Music scholarships are awarded at 11+ and 13+. Sixth Form scholarships are also awarded at 16+. Bursaries covering up to 100% of fees are available through the Montagu Award scheme, which aims to ensure that St Gabriel's is accessible to girls who would otherwise not be able to enjoy the unique education the school offers.
Admission. Entry to the Junior School for children aged 6–10 years is by assessment. An entrance exam is held in November for entry at 11+ and 13+ and girls are accepted in to the Sixth Form on the basis of their GCSE results and an interview.
Fees per term (2016–2017). £5,230–£5,420.
Junior School. (*See entry in IAPS section*).
Charitable status. The St Gabriel Schools Foundation is a Registered Charity, number 1062748. It exists to provide education for girls.

Governing Body:
Chairman: Mr N Garland, BSc Hons

Mr S Barrett	Mr S Ryan
Mrs S Bowen	Mr M Scholl
Mr D McAllan	Mr J Toogood
Mr D Peaple	Mrs J Whitehead
Mrs A Rowse	

Principal: **Mr R Smith**, MEd, MA, PGCE

Vice-Principal: Mrs A Chapman, BA Hons, PGCE (*Spanish*)
Bursar & Clerk to Governors: Mrs J Bond, BSc Hons
Director of Teaching & Learning: Mrs H Trevis, BSocSc Hons, PGCE (**Religion, Philosophy & Ethics*)
Director of Curriculum: Mrs A Chicken, BA Hons, PGCE (*Mathematics*)
Head of Sixth Form: Mrs C Reseigh, BA Hons, PGCE (*French*)
Head of Upper School (Years 9, 10 & 11): Mrs E Hammons, LLB, PGCE (*History & Politics*)

Head of Lower School (Years 7 & 8): Mrs R Wright, BSc Hons, PGCE (*Physical Education*)

Head of Junior School: Mr P Dove, BA Hons, PGCE (**Thinking Skills*)

Deputy Head of Junior School: Miss A Smith, BEd Hons (*Form Tutor Year 2, *Computing*)

Sandleford Curriculum Manager: Mrs C Lawrence, BA Ed, PGCE (*Form Tutor Reception*)

Sandleford Manager: Mrs K Noonan, BA Hons

Sandleford Deputy Manager: Mrs M Bullock, NVQ Level 3

Director of Education Partnerships: Mrs W Rumbol, BA Hons, PGCE, DMS (*French, Spanish*)

Compliance Coordinator: Mrs V Vaughan, BSc Hons (*Mathematics*)

Challenge & Extension (Senior School): Mrs A Chicken, BA Hons, PGCE (*Mathematics*)

Challenge & Extension (Junior School): Miss A Smith, BEd Hons, QTS (*Form Tutor Year 2, *Computing*)

Senior School Teaching Staff:
* Head of Department
Mrs N Archer, BA Hons, PGCE (*English*)
Mrs N Bailey, BA Hons, QTS (*Mathematics*)
Mrs A Beake (*Science Technician*)
Mrs K Cook (*Art Technician*)
Mrs S Court (*Science Technician*)
Mrs R Dadds, BSc Hons, PGCE (**Psychology*)
Mrs D Evans, BSc Hons, PGCE (*Business Studies*)
Miss S Ferretti, BA Hons, PGCE (**Modern Foreign Languages, Italian, French*)
Mrs S George, MA, BA Hons, QTS (*Art*)
Miss M Gu, MSc, BSc Hons, PGCE (*Mandarin Chinese*)
Ms M Gunn, BA Hons (*Music*)
Ms S Hall, BA Hons, PGCE (**English*)
Miss E Halstead, BA Hons (*Classics*)
Mrs K Hastings, BA Hons, PGCE (**Dance*)
Mr R Havercroft, MEng, QTS (*Biology, Physics*)
Mrs S Haywood Smith, BSc Hons, JEB (*Computer Science*)
Mrs R Heveron, MMath Hons, PGCE (*Mathematics*)
Ms M Hunter, BA Hons (*Art, Textiles, Photography*)
Mr M Ives, MA, BA Hons, PGCE (**Classics, Latin, Greek*)
Mrs P Joseph, MEd (*Physical Education*)
Miss A Keenleyside, BEd Hons (*Art, Textiles, Photography*)
Mrs J Knott, BSc Hons, PGCE (**Design Technology*)
Miss R Lawson, BSc, Hons, PGCE (**Geography*)
Mr B Lewis, MA Cantab, PGCE (**History, *Politics*)
Mr J Mannion, BA Hons, PGCE (**Computer Science, History*)
Miss T Matthews, CertEd (*Religion, Philosophy & Ethics*)
Mr G May, BA Hons, QTS (*Physical Education*)
Mrs D McLaughlin, BSc Hons QTS (*Physics*)
Mrs H Porter, BSc Hons, PGCE (*Biology, KS3 Science Coordinator*)
Miss V Rajkumar, MA (*Chemistry*)
Ms H Rayner, BA Hons, PGCE (*Physics*)
Mrs N Rogers, BA Hons, PGCE (*French, Italian*)
Mr T Saville, MA, BA Hons, PGCE (*Art*)
Mr J Scobie, MA Ed, BSc Hons, PGCE (**Science*)
Mrs L Sharman, BA Hons, PGCE, QTS (*Drama*)
Mrs S Sim, BSc Hons, PGCE (**Mathematics*)
Miss L Smith, BSc Hons, QTS (**Physical Education*)
Dr P Tebbs, DPhil Oxon (**Music*)
Mrs A Thayer, MA Cantab, BA Hons, QTS (*English*)
Mrs L Tyler, BA Hons, PGCE (*Spanish*)
Mr C White, BSc Hons, PGCE (*Chemistry*)
Mrs P Willetts, BA Hons, PGCE (*Geography, *Economics*)
Mrs S Yeoman (*Technology Technician*)
Miss L Zhu, MSc, BA Hons, PGCE, QTS (*Mandarin Chinese*)

Mrs T Zogaj, MA, BA Hons, PGCE (*HE – Food & Nutrition*)

Junior School Teaching Staff:
* Subject Leader
Miss S Black, BEd Hons Cantab (*Form Tutor Year 4*)
Mrs S Bloxsom, BA Hons (*Form Tutor Reception & Year 2*)
Mrs M Davidson, BEd Hons (*Form Tutor Year 5, *English, MFL*)
Miss M Gu, MSc, BSc Hons, PGCE (*Mandarin Chinese*)
Ms M Gunn, BA Hons (**Music*)
Mrs K Hastings, BA Hons, PGCE (**Dance*)
Mr R Havercroft, MEng, QTS (*Form Tutor Year 5, *Science*)
Mrs L Hayes, BA Hons, PGCE (*Year 4, French*)
Mrs S Haywood Smith, BSc Hons, JEB (*Computing*)
Mrs P Joseph, MEd (*Physical Education*)
Mrs J Knott, BSc Hons, PGCE (**Design Technology*)
Mr J Mannion, BA Hons, PGCE (*Computing*)
Mr G May, BA Hons, QTS (*Physical Education*)
Miss H Moth, BA Hons (*Form Tutor Year 3, *Art*)
Mrs A Pasternakiewicz, BEd Hons (**Physical Education*)
Miss J Pearmine, BA Hons, PGCE (*Year 6 Form Tutor, *Humanities*)
Mrs N Rogers, BA Hons, PGCE (*French, Italian*)
Mrs L Sharman, BA Hons, PGCE, QTS (*Drama*)
Mrs S Webb, BSc Hons, PGCE (*Form Tutor Year 1, *PSHE*)
Mrs T Zogaj, MA, BA Hons, PGCE (*HE – Food & Nutrition*)

Teaching Assistants:
Mrs C Arblaster
Mrs C Cockar
Mrs S Ducker
Mrs H Martin
Mrs S Morris
Mrs T Stoyanova

Mrs A Borzoni, BA Hons, PG Dip (*Librarian*)
Mrs H Corkhill, BEd Hons (*Examinations Officer*)
Mrs M Goodhead, Cert SpLD (*Individual Needs*)
Mrs C Oxley, BSc Ed Hons, Dip SpLD (**Individual Needs*)
Mrs S Porter-Scott (*Matron*)

Visiting Music Staff:
Mrs K Addis (*Double Bass*)
Mr D Birnie, BMus Hons (*Guitar*)
Mr T Bott, BMus Hons, PG Dip (*Violin*)
Mr N Cope (*Piano, Singing*)
Mrs J Frith, CT ABRSM (*Flute*)
Miss E Gregory, BMus Hons (*Voice*)
Mr M Lijinsky, CT ABRSM (*Piano*)
Miss S Monaghan, BA Hons (*Drum Kit*)
Mr S Parker, ALCM, LLCM, CT ABRSM (*Clarinet, Saxophone*)
Mrs H Rawstron, BA, LTCL (*Oboe*)
Mrs S Riddex, BA Hons, PECE, LTCHM, LESMD (*Cello*)
Mr P Tarrant, ARCM, CertEd (*Brass*)
Mrs V Toll, LRAM, CertEd (*Piano*)

Administrative Staff:
Mrs J Benney (*Registrar*)
Mrs J Goodman-Mills (*Transport Coordinator*)
Miss C Jackson (*Executive Secretary*)
Mrs A Kail (*Data Manager*)
Mrs T Robinson (*School Secretary*)
Mrs A Williams (*Assistant Accountant*)
Mrs S Willson (*Accountant*)
Mrs A Morris (*HR Advisor*)

St George's, Ascot

St George's School, Wells Lane, Ascot, Berks SL5 7DZ

Tel:	01344 629920
Fax:	01344 629901
email:	admissions@stgeorges-ascot.org.uk
website:	www.stgeorges-ascot.org.uk
Twitter:	@stgeorgesascot
Facebook:	@stgeorgesascot

Member of GSA, AGBIS, BSA.

St George's Ascot, is a vibrant Boarding and Day school for girls aged 11–18 providing an excellent academic education in a supportive and caring environment.

The school is set in 30 acres of stunning grounds, only 30 minutes from central London and located just off the High Street in Ascot. The school is in the top 5% in the country for added value, helping the girls achieve at least a grade higher at both GCSE and A Level.

Our results are excellent. We aim to add at least one grade higher at GCSE and A Level than their baseline prediction, and to enable girls to achieve their ambitions. However we are not a narrowly academic school – academics matter but this alone is not what makes a great education. St George's prides itself on offering a much more in-depth approach to learning; preparing our pupils beyond school by developing good communication skills, a love of learning and a willingness to get involved.

Friendly atmosphere, small classes, strong pastoral care and opportunities for individual development make St George's stand out from the crowd.

St George's is a boarding and day school for girls aged 11 to 18. The school is set in 30 acres of beautiful grounds with magnificent views. We are just a stone's throw from the world-famous Ascot racecourse and Windsor Great Park, and less than 25 miles from London.

Curriculum. Our small class sizes ensure that every girl is given the right balance of academic challenge and support by our inspirational teaching staff, who deliver a wide-ranging and varied curriculum. Girls are given opportunities to excel, not only in traditional subjects but also in Art, Drama, Music and Sport. Team sports are offered in Lacrosse, Netball, Swimming, Tennis, Rounders, Athletics, Squash and Polo.

Academic results at St George's are strong, with the majority of the girls going on to Russell Group universities. All Sixth Form girls take the Extended Project Qualifications in addition to A Levels, and typically one third of the candidates achieve three or more A grades.

Entrance. Entry at 11+ is by our own assessment, reference from the current school, examinations in English, Mathematics and Verbal Reasoning and a short presentation to a senior member of staff. For entry at 13+, testing takes place in the February preceding entry.

Students considering an application to the Sixth Form will be invited for an interview with the Head of Sixth Form or another senior member of staff. Any offer of a place made will be contingent on meeting our minimum admissions criteria of achieving at least six, A*–C grades at GCSE (or equivalent), with at least a B grade in any subject to be taken at A Level. A wide range of scholarships are available at 11+, 13+ and 16+.

Fees per term (2016–2017). £11,020 Boarding, £7,040 Day.

Scholarships. Scholarships are available at 11+, 13+ and 16+ for outstanding potential, as evidenced by examination results. Academic, Art, Performing Arts, Sport, Music and All Round scholarships and instrumental awards are available at 11+ and Academic Art, Music, Drama, Performing Arts, All Round and Sport scholarships at 13+ and 16+.

Extra Subjects. Other languages (including Mandarin), Music (most instruments), Speech and Drama, Ballet, Modern Stage and Tap Dancing, Individual Tennis, Polo, Riding, Zumba, and Pilates.

Charitable status. St George's School Ascot Trust Limited is a Registered Charity, number 309088. It exists to provide independent secondary girls' education.

Governors:
[1]Mr E Luker, FRICS (*Chairman*)
[2]Mr G W P Barber, MA Oxon, LVO
[2]Mrs D R Brown, MBE
[2]Mrs A Hems, MA Oxon, PGCE
[1]Mr P James
[1]Mrs A Laurie-Walker, BSc MSc Provence
[1]Mr A Mackintosh, BSc Aberdeen, MBA City
[2]Mr A Miles, BSc Durham, PGCE
[1]Mrs R E S Niven Hirst, BArch Newcastle, RIBA
[1]Mr P Sedgwick, MCSI

[1] *Member of Finance and Marketing sub-committee*
[2] *Member of Education sub-committee*

Staff:

Headmistress: Mrs E Hewer, MA Cantab, PGCE

Bursar and Clerk to Governors: Mrs J M Wood, JP, BA Hons, DipFM

Deputy Head (Pastoral): Mrs H L Simpson, BEd Hons Exeter (*Head of Boarding, Head of PSHE, Designated Safeguarding Lead, Physical Education*)

Assistant Head (Head of Sixth Form): Mr A Wright, BA Oxford, MA London, PGCE (*Deputy Designated Safeguarding Lead*)

Teaching Staff:
* *Head of Department*

Art, Textiles, Photography and Cookery:
*Mrs C Fidler, BA Wolverhampton, PGCE
Ms E Townsend, BA East Anglia, PGCE
Mrs A Morgan, BA Dundee, PGCE
Ms K Gilbert, BA Chichester, PGCE
Ms A Magee, BA Connecticut, MA Vermont, GDE Melbourne

Business and Economics:
*Mrs J Obaditch, BEd Wales, MA London

Classics:
*Miss L Fontes, BA Leeds, PGCE
Mrs R Belkacem, BSc London, PGCE
Mrs C Phipps, BA Nottingham, PGCE
Mrs J Condliffe, MA BA Leeds, PGCE

Computing:
*Mrs R Belkacem, BSc London, PGCE
Mr Naeem Mohammad, MA Punjab, BSc Punjab, HDipE Dublin
Dr C Alsop, PhD Durham, PGCE

Drama:
*Mr A Carroll, BA St Mary's, PGCE
Mrs E Gregan, BA Liverpool, PGCE
Mrs J Condliffe, MA BA Leeds, PGCE

English:
*Mr N Lee, BD BA MA London, PGCE
Mrs L Jones, BEd Durham
Mrs H Dorey, BA Wales
Ms M Johnston, BA East Anglia, MA London, PGCE
Mrs J Condliffe, MA BA Leeds, PGCE

EAL:
*Mrs N Anderson, MA East Anglia, PGCE
Mrs S Davies, CTESOL Trinity

Mrs D Ractliffe, CertEd Homerton, CTEFLA DTESOL Trinity

Dr A Tieanu, PhD Babes-Bolyai, Romania

Film Studies:
*Mrs E Gregan, BA Liverpool, PGCE

Geography:
*Mrs S Johnson, BSc Exeter, PGCE [Maternity leave]
*Mrs J Addison, BSc Durham, PGCE [Maternity cover]
Mr K Fraser, BA Hons Leeds, PGCE

History and Politics:
*Mrs D Kratt, BA Reading, PGCE
Miss L Jackson, BA Aberystwyth, MTL Canterbury, PGCE
Mr A Wright, MA Oxford, MA London, PGCE
Mrs M Soni, BA, MA Oxford Brookes

History of Art:
*Ms E Collyer, MA BA Courtauld, PGCE

Languages:
*Mrs F Burrows, Maîtrise Toulouse, GTP
Miss A Figueira, Licence Paris, PGCE
Mrs R Martinez, BA Portsmouth, PGCE
Mrs S Cope, Licence Orléans, PGCE

Learning Support:
*Ms M Johnston, BA East Anglia, MA London, PGCE

Mathematics:
*Mr P Wilson, BEng Nottingham, PGCE
Mrs S Scolefield, BSc London, PGCE
Mrs C Lilley, BSc London, PGCE
Mr Naeem Mohammad, MA Punjab, BSc Punjab, HDipE Dublin

Music:
*Mr I G Hillier, GLCM, FLCM, FCSM, FGMS, PGCE
Miss C Mason, LLB Bristol, PGCE

Physical Education:
*Mrs M Lowe, BEd Sheffield Hallam
Miss K Lofthouse, PTI Cert Army
Miss K Spencer, BA Chichester
Mr N Greenall, HNC, DTLLS, PTLLS Gloucestershire
Mrs R Tune, BSc Hons Loughborough, PGCE

SMSC:
*Mrs H Simpson, BEd Exeter
Mr K Fraser, BA Hons Leeds, PGCE
Miss L Jackson, BA Aberystwyth, MTL Canterbury, PGCE

Psychology:
*Mrs E Shingles, BSc Brunel, GTP

Philosophy, Ethics and Religion:
*Mrs M Magill, BA Bristol, PGCE
Mrs R Graham, BA London

Science:
*Mr S Rhodes, BSc Canterbury, New Zealand, PGCE
Miss D Schmidt, MSc BEd Pretoria, South Africa
Dr C Alsop, PhD Durham, PGCE
Mr Naeem Mohammad, MA Punjab, BSc Punjab, HDipE
Mrs F Radley, BSc Bristol, PGCE
Mrs E Shingles, BSc Brunel, GTP
Mrs S Gibbins, BSc Liverpool, PGCE

Residential Staff:
Markham Housemistress: Mrs M Soni, BA, MA (*First to Fourth Year*)
Knatchbull Housemistress: Mrs H Dorey (*Fifth Year and Sixth Year*)
Loveday Housemistress: Mrs J Condliffe (*Seventh Year*)
Assistant Housemistress (*Markham*): Miss O Kellaris, BA Durban

Tutor in Residence (*Markham*): Miss E Crawley, BSc Hons Leeds
Tutor in Residence (*Knatchbull*): Miss A Figueira, License Paris, PGCE
Assistant Housemistress: Dr A Tieanu, PhD Babes-Bolyai, Romania
Director in Residence: Miss R Johnson, BA Hons Warwick
Artist in Residence: Miss R Spencer Jolly, BA Oxford

Co-Curricular Staff:
Director of Learning: Mr S Rhodes, BSc
Director of Co-curriculum: Miss K Lofthouse, PTI
Assistant Head of Sixth Form: Mr A Carroll, BA
Head of Alexander House: Miss L Jackson, BA, MTL
Head of Becket House: Miss K Spencer, BA
Head of Churchill House: Mrs C Fidler, BA
Head of Darwin House: Miss A Kennedy, BA, MSc
Careers: Mr D Moran, BA
Charities: Revd J Sistig, BTh, MTh
Duke of Edinburgh's Award: Mr D Moran, BA

Visiting Staff:
Arabic: Mrs A Surridge, BA, MA
French: Mrs A Langlois, Maîtrise
Spanish: Mrs T Bello, BA
Chinese: Mrs K Baldwin
Japanese: Mrs K Forrester, BA
Italian: Mr G Galli, BA PhD
Russian: Mrs M Strain, MA
Greek: Mr D Vaxevanakis
German: Mrs K Davies, BA, PGCE
Learning Support: Mrs R Baxter, BA; Mrs J Hooper, BComm
Flute: Mrs D Burt
Percussion: Mr R Smith
Violin: Mr S Perkins, BMus
Guitar: Mr P Williams, BA
Clarinet and Saxophone: Mrs D Head
Singing: Mr T Carleston, BMus; Mr A Thompson, BA; Mrs C Lloyd-Griffiths, BA, MA
Piano: Miss E Krivenko, MMus; Mrs K Stanley, BMus; Mr M Stanley, BMus
LAMDA: Mrs M Fitzgerald, Miss A Rooke, BA GTP
Tennis: Mr N Ingham
Ballet & Pilates: Ms E Haigh/Miss L Willey
Modern & Zumba: Ms A White
Squash: Mrs N Leader, BSc

Support Staff:
Marketing and Admissions Manager: Mrs K Bertram, OG
Admissions Officer: Miss M Harding
Admissions Assistant: Mrs L Bird
Marketing and Design Assistant: Mrs K Elliott, BA Hons
Deputy Bursar: Mr M Heather, ACIB
Finance Manager: Mrs E Foster, FCMA
Resources Officer: Mrs T Barber
Accounts Assistant: Mrs T Vickers
PA to Headmistress: Mrs J Witt
Administrator: Mrs C Reader
Secretary (*Mon and Tue*): Mrs S Davies
Secretary (*Thu and Fri*): Mrs D Macro, BA
Administrative Assistant: Mrs S Berry, BA
Data Manager: Ms A Shevills
Alumnae Officer: Mrs S van der Veen, MA
Domestic Bursar: Mr S Cornish
Deputy Domestic Bursar: Mrs J Burns
Chef: Mr J Eddyvean
Network Manager: Mr J Skinner
IT Technician: Mr M Bettridge
Theatre Technician: Mr R Pearn, BA
Science Technicians: Mr P Goldsborough, BSc; Mr B Nguessan

Doctor: Dr L Gardner, BM BS
Nurse: Mrs N Tomsett, NMC
Counsellor: Ms S Byrne
Listener: Ms E Manners
Chaplain: Revd J Sistig, BTh, MTh
Head Librarian: Ms A Kennedy, BA, MSc
Librarian: Mr D Moran, BA PGD
Clerk of Works: Mr R Cotterell
Groundsman: Mr P Thompson
Carpenter: Mr H Bowyer
General Maintenance: Mr F Baldwin
Electrician: Mr C Smith

St Helen & St Katharine

Faringdon Road, Abingdon, Oxon OX14 1BE

Tel: 01235 520173
Fax: 01235 532934
email: admission@shsk.org.uk
website: www.shsk.org.uk
Twitter: @SHSKSchool
Facebook: /StHelenStKatharine

Founded on Christian values, our goal is to enable every girl to discover and develop her own strengths. St Helen & St Katharine is a school where success is celebrated but not revered. Our pupils achieve excellent academic results and our goal is to ensure that every girl achieves success as she defines it, so that she can believe in herself, her talents and abilities.

A culture of kindness. We are one of the leading girls' schools in the country and the whole community is justifiably proud of a tradition of high aspiration and academic achievement (our students have just achieved record-breaking GCSE results with 77% A*). We take just as much pleasure in the warmth and fun of the atmosphere here and the inspiring range of extracurricular opportunities available to students. We also celebrate the importance of values, social responsibility and reflection.

This is a happy place and an environment in which relationships built on kindness and respect are made for life. Our ambitions for our students are wide-ranging but we know that the most lasting future successes will be based upon them developing confidence and an open-minded and creative approach to life and learning.

22 acres surround an Edwardian campus. New additions include a brand new Sports Centre (detailed below), Performing Arts Centre, a state-of-the-art library facility, a refurbished refectory, and an extended and revamped Sixth Form Centre. In September 2014 the new Science Centre opened providing 12 new laboratories, break-out spaces and a 200sqm science-themed glass atrium and in September 2015 a new 3D Design Centre opened with space for Ceramics and Design Technology.

Extraordinary Extracurricular. At St Helen and St Katharine we go the extra mile to provide exciting extracurricular activities to meet the needs of every student. From Minecraft to Mandarin, Silversmithing to Sailing, Board Games to Big Band and much more besides, we believe in emphasising the 'extra' in extracurricular. With a vibrant life beyond the classroom, students can choose from a wide range of sports, clubs and societies, music, arts, drama, educational visits and expeditions including Young Enterprise and The Duke of Edinburgh's Award scheme. Activities for all year groups are designed to spark a new interest or develop an existing passion. We aim to inspire girls to develop their learning and experiences, to enjoy all that is on offer and provide them with the space and opportunity to make their own choices and find their own niche.

Drama is a thriving part of school life. Productions take place throughout the year that allow pupils the opportunity to take part in technical support, design, stage management and front of house, as well as acting. Productions, where possible, join forces with Abingdon School. Original play writing is encouraged and supported through an annual play writing competition, the winning entry being staged as a lunchtime performance. A busy calendar of theatre trips to London, Stratford and other regional theatres support those studying GCSE drama and A Level theatre studies, including the Shakespeare Institute where pupils research original performance conditions.

Music. Musical activities lie at the heart of the school, with hundreds of pupils involved in individual music lessons. The Music department aims to provide opportunities for all pupils to participate in and perform music, whatever their level of experience and expertise. Everyone who learns a musical instrument or has singing lessons in school or outside is strongly encouraged to join a group, ensemble or school choir.

Sport. The wellbeing benefits (having fun, making new friends and feeling good) of extracurricular activities are linked to higher academic performance and involvement in sport is an excellent example. We offer great clubs and activities ranging from badminton and basketball, to dance and dressage, fencing and football that enable us to inspire girls positively in a way that suits them. Covered in glory at an international championship or just covered in mud on the lacrosse pitch, we celebrate involvement, effort and progress at all levels.

Our new leading-edge 6-court Sports Centre, opened in October 2016, will impact every student and reinforce our reputation as one of the leading independent girls' schools for sport in the UK. Over the past 5 years, we have restructured the PE curriculum entirely to include a broad range of activities through which the girls learn physical skills, but also many other aspects. Health benefits, personal and social benefits, and links to academic performance are all well documented and understood but not inevitable. Our systematic and measurable programme, including but not limited to traditional team games, aims to be motivating, beneficial and most importantly, fun! We aim to engage and inspire pupils in their PE lessons – this is the core of our provision, every girl in every year group has PE lessons and this is where we have the opportunity to reach every pupil encouraging them to participate in sport and develop a lifelong love of physical activity.

Expeditions. First-hand experience is an essential part of developing lifelong interests. We therefore provide a range of expeditions both in length and scope which offer opportunities for personal development for all ages, aptitudes and interests.

Learning beyond the Classroom. We recognise the importance of broadening and enriching pupils' understanding of subjects beyond the curriculum. We encourage exploration beyond the classroom in a number ways, some organised in school and others for girls to pursue independently.

St Helen and St Katharine Sixth Form. St Helen's 6 is an exciting and formative experience, a point of transition in an environment which will spark your intellectual spirit and imagination. We foster a curiosity about ideas and a willingness to take risks within a culture that nurtures self-esteem and recognised endeavour alongside outcome.

It is of huge social importance that young women have the personal and intellectual confidence to play a leading role in today's and tomorrow's complex world, where opportunities and possibilities abound, yet determination, self-reliance and resilience are a prerequisite, Our expertise is in working with aspirational young women, enabling them to excel and develop the skills, self-assurance and networks to prepare them for life beyond school.

Small class sizes provide the opportunity for personal attention, discussion and independent learning across 20+ A Level subjects: Art and Design, Biology, Chemistry, Drama and Theatre, Economics, English Literature, French, Further Mathematics, Geography, German, Government and Politics, Greek, History, Italian, Latin, Mathematics, Music, Physical Education, Physics, Psychology, Religion Philosophy and Ethics and Spanish – with additional AS and A Levels including Further Mathematics. There is also a study programme to develop knowledge and experience in non-European languages (Arabic, Mandarin), computer coding and information technology. Our 2016 A Level highlights include 67% A*/A, 92% A*–B and 47% obtained 3 or more A* or A grades

St Katharine's Study is an independent research project on a subject of particular personal interest with tutorial support from a research specialist. Students may undertake an extramural course, through providers such as Coursera or Future Learn, or pursue an external qualification, like an EPQ, as part of their St Katharine's Study, or the Cambridge Pre-U Global Perspectives.

We look forward to talking to you about our exciting new Sixth Form offer for 2017.

Fees per term (2016–2017). £4,915.

Charitable status. The School of St Helen and St Katharine Trust is a Registered Charity, number 286892. The Trust was established to promote and provide for the advancement of education of children in the United Kingdom and elsewhere; such education to be designed to give a sound Christian and moral basis to all pupils.

Governors:
Chair of Governors: Miss Jane Cranston

Mrs Alison Allden	Prof Susan Lea
Mrs Pauline Cakebread	Mr Kevan Leggett
Ms Sally Dicketts	Mrs Joanne Loveridge
Mr Adrian Dray	Mr Ian Mason
Mr Jon Gabitass	Mrs Diana May
Mrs Rebecca Kashti	Prof Steven Parissien
Mrs Hazel Knott	Mr Ian Todd
Mr Dave Lea	Mr Jeremy Wormell

Clerk to the Governors: Mrs Sarah Boulton-Jones

Staff:

Headmistress: Mrs R Dougall, MA London, QTS

Deputy Headmistress: Mrs B Stubley, MA Greenwich, PGCE
Bursar: Mr D Eley, BSc London, ACA
Assistant Head, Director of Students: Mrs E Bedford, MA, BA Durham, PGCE
Assistant Head, Director of Staff & IT: Mr J Hunt, MA St Andrews, QTS
Head of Sixth Form: Mrs J Armstrong, BSc Leeds, PGCE
Director of Studies: Mr C Morris, MA Oxon, PGCE
Head of Middle School: Mrs H Nash, BA Southampton, PGCE
Head of Lower School: Mrs K Taylor, BA Wales, PGCE
Head of Junior Department (*Year 5 & 6*): Miss N Talbot, BSc Nottingham, PGCE
Head of Year Upper Sixth: Mrs S Hughes-Morgan, BA Exeter, PGCE
Head of Year Lower Sixth: Mrs S Wilson, MA OU, BSc Brunel, QTS
Deputy Heads of Middle School:
Mrs H Hanratty, MA Oxon, PGCE
Dr C Holyoak, BSc Manchester, DPhil Manchester Metropolitan, QTS
Deputy Head of Lower School: Mrs D Jackson, MSc OU, BSc Keele, PGCE
Chaplain: Revd K Windle, MTheol OU, PGCE

Art, Design and Technology:
Ms J McDonald, MA RCA, ATC London
Mr W Cotterill, BA Central Saint Martins
Mr B Drew, BA London, QTS
Mrs C Langston, BA Middlesex, PGCE
Miss H McCague, BA West of England, PGCE
Miss A Wardell, MA London

Careers and Higher Education:
Mrs J Armstrong, BSc Leeds, PGCE, Adv Cert CEG
Miss S Comerford, BSc Aston, PGDip
Mrs J Bridge, BA Liverpool, Grad CIPD

Classics:
Mr D Hodgkinson, MA Oxon, MLitt Dublin
Miss L Simon, BA Oxon, PGCE
Mrs J Twaits, MA Cantab, PGCE

Computer Science:
Mrs L Stringer, BSc East Anglia, PGCE, PG Dip
Mrs R Green, MA Oxon, PGCE
Dr R Strong, MPhys Bath, PhD Cantab, QTS

Drama:
Miss J Watt, BA Durham, PGCE
Miss E Jewitt, BA London, PGCE
Miss L Lee, BSc Durham
Miss R Pearmain, BA London
Ms S Pullen-Campbell, BA Loughborough
Mr A Verjee, MA Oxford Brookes

The Duke of Edinburgh's Award:
Mrs G Wilson, BEd Lancaster

English:
Dr F Macdonald, BA, MSc, DPhil Oxon, PGCE
Ms A Fogg, MA Maryland, QTS
Mrs E Haines, BA Oxon, PGCE
Mrs S Hughes-Morgan, BA Exeter, PGCE
Mrs C Nash, MA Oxon, PGCE
Mrs H Nash, BA Southampton, PGCE
Ms T Nixon, MA London, PGCE
Ms F Tierney, MA Cantab, PGCE

Examinations Officer:
Mrs J Andrews

General Studies:
Ms S Hayward, BA Durham, PGCE

Geography:
Miss H Spencer, MA Cantab, PGCE
Mrs E Bedford, MA, BA Durham, PGCE
Ms L Snowdon, BA London, PGCE
Mrs A Tate, BA Leeds, PGCE

History:
Miss D Smith, BA Durham, PGCE
Dr L Gribble, MA Münster, DPhil Oxon, PGCE
Mrs S Scott-Malden, BA London, PGCE
Mr J Smart, BA Exeter, PGCE

Home Economics:
Mrs G Grant-Ross, BEd Liverpool, CertEd

Junior Department:
Miss N Talbot, BSc Nottingham, PGCE
Mrs R Green, MA Oxon, PGCE
Miss D O'Brien, MA Cantab, PGCE

Learning Support:
Mrs D Cobbing, BA Birmingham, APC SpLD [PATOSS]

Library:
Mrs D Pocock-Bell, BA Wales, MA London
Mrs K Gray, BSc Manchester, Dip IPM
Mrs B Mallett, MA Université Francois Rabelais, Tours, France

Mathematics:
Mrs C Buffham, BSc Warwick, PGCE
Mrs S Allwright, BA Cantab, PGCE
Miss C Clarke, MSc, Exeter, PGCE
Mrs H Hanratty, MA Oxon, PGCE
Miss R Herbert, BSc Oxford Brookes, QTS
Dr A Hull, BA, PhD Nottingham, PGCE
Mr D Ireland, BSc Leicester, QTS
Mrs M Moore, BSc Lancaster, PGCE
Mr C Morris, MA Oxon, PGCE
Mrs C Russell, BSc London, PGCE
Mrs S Sharp, MA Cantab, PGCE
Dr R Strong, MPhys Bath, PhD Cantab, QTS

Medical:
Senior Nurse: Mrs J Tollemache, RGN
Nurse: Mrs C Berry, RGN
Nurse: Mrs A Gibb, RGN

School Counsellor: Mrs J Leahy, BA Open University,
PCert Reading

Modern Languages:
Mrs L Probert, BA Bath, PGCE
Mrs Y Anderson, MEd, PGCE
Mrs N Botherel, Licence/BA Nantes
Mrs M Diaz-Smith, BA Rafael Urdaneta, PGCE
Mr J Earnshaw-Crofts, MA London, PGCE
Mrs C Fisher, BA Milan, PGCE
Mr C Gonzalez-Valdes, MA Universidad de Chile
Mrs I Hichens, Licence/BA, Paris La Sorbonne, PGCE
Mrs L Littlejohn, MA Cantab, PGCE
Mrs F Shannon, MA St Andrews, DPhil
Mrs K Taylor, BA Wales, PGCE
Mr H Thomson, BA Exeter, PGCE

Music:
Miss H Rakowski, BA, MA Oxon, PGCE (*Director of Music*)
Miss H Coad, MSc Edinburgh, PGCE (*Assistant Director of Music*)
Mrs E Dickens, Dip RCM, CTABRSM (*Head of Keyboard*)
Mr P Foster, LTCL (*Head of Wind and Brass*)
Miss P Grant, BA, MA Oxon (*Head of Singing*)
Revd Dr E Pitkethly, MLitt Oxon, BPhil Warwick, PGCE
Mrs M Walton, BA York, PG Dip, LGSM (*Head of Strings*)
Mr C Ayres, BMus London (*Electric Guitar*)
Miss J Broome, MA Cantab (*Harp*)
Mr R Burley, ALCM, LLCM (*Guitar*)
Mr M Cooke, PPRNCM, GRNCM (*French Horn*)
Mrs J Craven, MA, BA, GTCL, LTCL, LRAM (*Piano*)
Mr R Cutting, RMSM Kneller Hall (*Brass*)
Mr W Dutta, BMus, LTCL (*Piano*)
Mr S Fawbert (*Percussion*)
Miss R Gladstone, BA, MA Cantab, Dip TCM (*Cello*)
Mr M Heighway, BMus LRAM (*Double Bass and Bass Guitar*)
Dr E Hodson BA, DPhil Oxon, PGDip (*Violin and Viola*)
Mrs L Howarth, MA Cantab, MMus, MMP (*Singing*)
Dr R Manasse, BSc London, DPhil Cantab (*Flute*)
Mr D McNaughton, BA Oxon (*Brass*)
Mrs S Mears, MA Oxon, LRAM, PGCE, Dip HSW OU (*Piano*)
Mrs A Phillips, BMus RCM, ARCM (*Singing*)
Miss J Rhind-Tutt, BA Oxford Brookes, QTS, CTABRSM (*Oboe*)
Miss C Scott, MA Oxon, MMus Perf, PPRNCM (*Clarinet*)
Miss A Strevens, BSc, London (*Flute*)
Miss J Thomas, BMus Birmingham, PGCE (*Singing*)
Mr R Thorne, BMus, AMusA (*Flute*)
Ms R Van Der Berg, MMus Perf, BMus (*Singing*)

Mr G Williams, LRAM, ARCM, FTCL, FLCM, MSTAT, PGCE (*Bassoon, Clarinet, Saxophone*)
Mr S Wilson, BA Oxon (*Cello*)
Mrs S Windsor-Lewis, BMus Surrey, PG Dip, Art Dip (*Singing*)
Mr J Wood, MSc London, LRSM, Dip ABRSM (*Singing*)

Personal Development:
Ms K Meuleman, BEd Eeklo, Belgium, PG Worcester

Physical Education:
Mrs S Wilson, MA OU, BSc Brunel, QTS
Miss E Aston, BSc Loughborough, PGCE
Mrs J Chilvers, FTI
Mrs S Keogh, BSc Birmingham, QTS
Miss N Lydall, BSc Bath, PGCE
Mrs L Trumper, BEd Liverpool
Mrs M Uezzell, BA Winchester, QTS
Mrs A Wilson, BEd Brunel

Politics, Economics and Business:
Dr L Gribble, MA Münster, DPhil Oxon, PGCE
Dr A Hull, BA, PhD Nottingham, PGCE
Mrs R Kitto, MA OU, QTS
Mrs S Scott-Malden, BA London, PGCE
Mr J Smart, BA Exeter, PGCE
Mrs B Stubley, MA Greenwich, PGCE

Psychology:
Mrs K Collett, BSc Worcester, PGCE
Mrs R Watson, BSc Warwick, PGCE

Religion, Philosophy and Ethics:
Ms S Hayward, BA Durham, PGCE
Mrs E Bedford, MA, BA Durham, PGCE
Ms K Meuleman, BEd Eeklo, Belgium, PG Worcester
Mr T Bownass, BA Bristol, PGCE
Mrs A Tate, BA Leeds, PGCE

Science:
Biology:
Mrs R James, BSc Bristol, MSc Oxon, PGCE
Dr T Bainbridge, BSc Leeds, PhD London, PGCE
Miss A Bourne, MSc Bristol, PGCE
Mrs K Homann, MA Cantab, PGCE
Dr M Wait, Phd Nelson Mandela Metropolitan, MSc Port Elizabeth, PGCE
Mrs K Wright, BSc London, PGCE
Chemistry:
Mrs G Lydford, BSc UEA, QTS
Mrs J Armstrong, BSc Leeds, PGCE
Dr C Holyoak, BSc Manchester, DPhil Manchester Metropolitan, QTS
Mrs C Lomax, MChem Oxon, PGCE
Dr J Saba, BSc Aberdeen, DPhil Leeds, PGCE
Mrs T Lewis, BSc Reading, PGCE
Physics:
Mrs J Edwards, BSc Nottingham, PGCE
Mrs K Brudenell, MEng Durham, PGCE
Dr Z Chater, MPhys, PhD Birmingham, PGCE
Mrs D Jackson, MSc OU, BSc Keele, PGCE

St Helen's School

Eastbury Road, Northwood, Middlesex HA6 3AS
Tel: 01923 843210
Fax: 01923 843211
email: enquiries@sthelens.london
          admissions@sthelens.london

website: www.sthelens.london
Twitter: @StHelensSchool
Facebook: /sthelensnorthwood

Independent Day School for Girls founded in 1899.

St Helen's School has a commitment to academic excellence that has given us an enviable reputation for over 100 years. To build on this tradition, the school is also embarking on an exciting and creative long-term plan to become the 'exceptional' choice for girls' day schools in North London, including the building of a state-of-the-art new Junior School, which opened in September 2016, and is enabling exciting learning via the creation of flexible 'break-out spaces' and ICT zones, along with specialist facilities for Science, Design & Technology, Music, Computer Science, Drama and Art. The Junior School's 'living roof' also offers an innovative outdoor learning environment. We provide a complete academic education for able girls, developing personal integrity alongside intellectual, creative and sporting talents. The staff are highly qualified and enthusiastic, the facilities are excellent, and we pride ourselves on knowing, valuing and nurturing every pupil as an individual. Above all we encourage all the girls at St Helen's to pursue their dreams and develop the academic, social and transferable skills which will enable them to become leaders in their fields, professions and communities.

The school is divided into three departments: Little St Helen's (3+ to 7), Junior School (7+ to 11) and Senior School (11+ to 18), enabling continuity and progression in the education of every pupil. Main entry points are at 3+, 4+, 7+, 11+ and 16+.

St Helen's has an excellent academic record and girls achieve outstanding results in public examinations at all levels. In our flourishing Sixth Form there are approximately 160 girls. A Levels are offered in the Sixth Form, with girls able to choose from 30 subjects and going on to prestigious universities, including Oxford and Cambridge, after comprehensive support through the university applications and preparation process.

The St Helen's Portfolio records and celebrates the full and impressive range of skills, qualifications and co-curricular experiences of each girl throughout her time in the Sixth Form. These are invaluable to success at university and in professional life. Students are able to complement their A Level programme with additional qualifications such as the European Computer Driving Licence (ECDL), the Extended Project Qualification (EPQ), a Post-16 Diploma in Spanish (DELE) or study Further Mathematics. All students also follow a programme in core skills to help them hone their study techniques. This will ensure that they maximise their academic potential in the Sixth Form and beyond, and will provide them with those professional and life skills which will give them the confidence to compete at the highest levels. In addition, the Portfolio recognises the skills acquired through participation in national schemes such as Young Enterprise and the Duke of Edinburgh's Award, through their leadership of teams, orchestras, CCF, societies and clubs at school, and through their contribution to community service. As well as the core skills programme and optional courses, all members of Year 12 and 13 participate in a lecture series which aims to broaden horizons and encourage debate and discussion of a wide range of topics.

The curriculum is designed to enable every girl to achieve intellectual and personal fulfilment and to develop her talents to the full. We support the aims of the National Curriculum, but offer a wider range of subjects and teach to greater depth, so enabling the girls to explore their interests and talents. The staff are subject specialists whose aim is to inspire a love of their subjects. They help the girls to learn how to study independently and develop good study habits, through stimulating and rigorous teaching. On entry to the Senior School in Year 7, all girls study two modern foreign languages together with Latin. Science subjects are popular at all levels of the Senior School. We expect the girls to study with commitment and to develop qualities of intellectual curiosity and resilience. Music, Art, Drama and Sport are all an integral part of the life of the school and involve every girl. Many also take extra Music, Ballet, Speech & Drama lessons and Sports coaching.

Girls take a full part in the broader life of the school and, through co-curricular activities, discover new interests to complement their academic achievements. Clubs and societies abound, catering for the widest possible range of interests and hobbies, and we have a flourishing programme of optional outdoor and adventurous activities. We have recently been recognised as an independent licensing authority for the Duke of Edinburgh's Award Scheme, and many girls successfully complete their Bronze, Silver and Gold Awards; in the Summer of 2016 a cohort of 25 girls participated in a memorable Gold Award Expedition to Morocco. A full range of CCF activities is offered in partnership with Merchant Taylors' School, with whom we also organise 'Phab Week', an annual residential activity week for disabled children. Further co-curricular opportunities include Model United Nations and Young Enterprise, and we are proud that one of our Young Enterprise teams was crowned UK Company of the Year for 2015, going on to represent the UK in the pan-European Young Enterprise Finals. We have a thriving vertical House system which girls actively help to run, and competition between the Houses is characterised by universal participation and friendly rivalry.

St Helen's is located on a spacious 21-acre greenfield site and is easily accessible on the London Underground Metropolitan Line. Northwood Station is less than five minutes' walk from the school. The School also runs extensive and flexible coach services from the surrounding areas, including Beaconsfield, Watford, Stanmore, Finchley and Ealing.

Our popular Breakfast Club and after-school care programme allow girls to extend their day in the safety of the school environment, where they are provided with refreshments and their activities are supervised by our qualified staff. The Mint Café, a sixth form facility during the school day, is available to all Senior School pupils from 7.30 am and after 4 pm.

Fees per term (2016–2017). Senior School: £5,326. Junior School (including Speech & Drama): £4,225. Little St Helen's: Reception, Year 1 and Year 2 (including Lunch, Ballet, Speech & Drama) £4,016; Nursery (including Lunch, Ballet, Speech & Drama) £3,807.

Registration Fee: UK £100; Overseas £150.

Scholarships. Academic entry scholarships to Senior School are awarded annually at 11+ and 16+; Music Scholarships and Exhibitions are available at 11+ and 16+ for applicants of exceptional musical ability. Sport Scholarships are available at 11+ and 16+, and Sixth Form Art Scholarships are also awarded. St Helen's is committed to increasing access to girls who would thrive in our environment irrespective of their families' ability to pay the fees by expanding our Bursary provision; an academic Scholarship is awarded each year to a pupil at 14+.

St Helen's Alumnae Relations. Development Director: Ms Zoe Baines, email: zoe.baines@sthelens.london.

St Helen's Old Girls' Club. Secretary: Mrs Sally Fleming, email: secretary.ogclubs@sthelens.london.

Charitable status. St Helen's School for Girls is a Registered Charity, number 312762. It exists to provide quality education for girls.

Council of Governors:
Chairman & Safeguarding Governor: Ms S Woolfson, BSc, FCA
Mrs M Bhandari, LLB, LLM, LPC
Mr N Boghani, BSc Hons, CA
Ms P Mongia, MA MEng Cantab, CEng, MRAeS, MBA
Mrs A Phillipson, MA Cantab, MBA, PGCE
Dr S M Pitts, MSc, MA, PhD

Mrs E Radice, MA Oxon, Cert Ed
Mr V Sapra, SFA, MBA, CEng, BEng, MICE
Mrs M Weerasekera, Mont Dip, LLB

Headmistress: Dr M Short, BA London, PhD Cantab

Deputy Head Pastoral: Mrs J Parker, BA Liverpool
Deputy Head Academic: Mr P Tiley, BSc Bristol
Deputy Head Development: Dr P Arnold, MA DPhil Oxon
Business Director and Clerk to the Council: Mr M
    Mackenzie Crooks, BSc Oxford Brookes, MSc, MBA
    Cranfield

Pastoral Head of Sixth Form: Mr H Dymock, BA Durham,
    MA London
Head of Upper School: Mrs D Sinclair, MA London
Head of Middle School: Mrs C Hill, BA Newcastle
Head of Junior School: Mrs K Serinturk, BEd London
Head of Little St Helen's: Miss K Cooper, BA Canterbury

Director of Drama: Mrs M Connell, BA Manchester
Director of Futures: Miss E McKinley, BA Heriot-Watt
Director of Music: Mr P Martin, MA Cantab, LRSM
Director of Sport: Miss J Hurt, BA Brunel

Development Director: Ms Z Baines, BA Birmingham,
    MSc LSE
Head of Marketing & Communications: Miss H Openshaw,
    BA MEd Durham, AMDIS Dip

Senior School Staff:
* *Head of Department*

Art:
*Mrs N Smith, BA Sunderland, MA London
Mrs J George, BA Solent, MA London
Mr V Hazeldine, Diploma AD UAL
Mrs J Tibbs (*Technician*)

Classics:
*Dr A Berriman, BA Bristol, PhD Nottingham Trent
Dr P Arnold, MA DPhil Oxon
Mr H Dymock, BA Durham, MA London
Mrs N O'Hagan, CertEd Westminster, BA Calabria, Italy
Miss S Wu, BA Warwick

Computer Science:
*Mr M Hoffman, BA South Africa
Mr J Firestone, MA Brighton
Mr R Shaikh, BA Brighton

Design & Technology:
*Mr B Gee, MA Open
Mr S Binning, BA Greenwich
Mrs L Hallam, BA Middlesex
Mr R Shaikh, BA Brighton
Mrs A Flash, BA Loughborough (*Technician*)

Drama:
*Mrs M Connell, BA Manchester (*Director of Drama*)
Mrs J Barton, BA Oxford Brookes
Mrs K Newby, BA Loughborough
Mrs D Sinclair, MA London
Mrs H McGreal, BA Salford (*Speech & Drama teacher*)

Economics & Business Studies:
*Mr M Khan, BSc Wollongong Dubai, MSc London
Mr L Casey, BA Wales, MA Middlesex

English:
*Mr R Johnston, BA Liverpool
Ms S Ahmed, BA Essex, MA London
Mrs K Douglas, MA St Andrews
Ms B Fidder, MA St Andrews
Mr T Gerig, BA Illinois
Mr A Williams, MA Cantab

Geography:
*Miss E Rynne, MA London
Mr D Froggatt, BSc Cardiff
Mr R Pimlott, MA Middlesex

History, Government & Politics and History of Art:
*Mr B Nemko, BA Birmingham, MSc City, MA London
Mrs L Hatchard, MA Manchester, MA St Andrews
Mrs C Hill, BA Newcastle
Dr N Marx, BA Amherst, MA London, PhD Harvard
Mrs R Reidel-Fry, MPhil, MA Columbia USA, MA
    London [maternity leave]
Mr A Reynolds, BA Birmingham
Miss H Sinclair, MA St Andrews [maternity leave]
Mr P Whalley, BA Portsmouth

Individual Needs:
*Ms J Halmagyi, MA Debrecen Hungary, NASCO
    Middlesex
Mrs R Bird, BA London
Ms P Vine, BA Exeter
Mrs C Craigie-Williams

Mathematics:
*Miss C Kerry, BEng London
Miss G Day, BSc Durham
Dr J Donovan, MEd MSc PhD London
Mrs J Hurley, BSc Sheffield
Mrs S King, BEng Bristol
Mr B Manivannan, BSc Eng Sri Lanka
Mrs S Michaels, BSc Manchester
Mrs T Onac, BSc London
Mr P Tiley, BSc Bristol
Dr C Yu, BSc Southampton, MSc PhD Kent

Modern Foreign Languages:
Mrs E Serrano, Filologia Inglesa Degree Madrid (*Modern
    Foreign Languages and Spanish*)
Mr P Vines, BA UEA (*French*)
Mrs E Davis, BA Birmingham, MA Westminster (*Subject
    Leader German, Deputy Head of Middle School*)
Ms J Lee, MSc London (*Subject Leader Mandarin*)
Mrs G Chuykov, BA Yaroslavl Russia, MA London
Mrs M Ishikawa, MA London
Miss L Louiset, BA MA Antilles
Miss E McKinley, BA Heriot-Watt
Mrs N O'Hagan, CertEd Westminster, BA Calabria Italy
Mrs J Orme, BA Durham
Mrs J Parker, BA Liverpool
Miss A Shepherd, BA Cantab
Mrs N Wright, BA Manchester
Miss J Lepka (*German Assistant*)
Mrs C Gauci, BA Mexico (*Spanish Assistant*)
Mrs B Lee (*Mandarin Assistant*)
Miss A Morin (*French Assistant*)
Dr Y O'Connor, BSc MSc Kyoto Japan, PhD Tokyo Japan
    (*Japanese Assistant*)

Music:
*Mr P Martin, MA Cantab LRSM (*Director of Music*)
Ms A Stobart, BA Nottingham, MEd Cantab LRSM
    (*Assistant Director of Music*)
Mrs J Taylor, BSc Northumbria, Prince 2 (*Music
    Administrator*)

Music – Visiting:
Miss A-M Andritoiu, BMus Birmingham Conservatoire,
    MMus Trinity Laban
Ms C Barry, BA Mod Trinity College Dublin, LTCL
Miss J Chen, BMus PGDip Royal Academy of Music
Mrs E Coleman-Boyle, BA MA Chichester
Mrs D Ellin, BMus Royal Scottish Academy of Music,
    PGDip, LRAM

Mr A Gathercole, GGSM, ALCM Guildhall School of Music and Drama
Mrs S Gregory, LRAM, LTCL
Mr R Halford, GNVQ St Albans
Mr D Hester, DipTCL, LTCL, PDOT Guildhall School of Music and Drama
Mr C Hooker, ARAM, LRAM, DipRAM
Miss D Kemp, MA Oxon, Dip RCM, ARCM
Miss R Krbilkova, DiS Pardubice Conservatory Czech Republic
Miss E Kyte, BMus MMus Guildhall
Mrs J Maclean, BSc City, LTCL
Mr I Marcus, LTCL
Mr N Martin, Cert NLP
Mr A McAfee, BA Nottingham Trent, PGCert Trinity College of Music
Miss E Tsampa, MA Royal Academy of Music, BMus Athens, LRAM

Physical Education:
*Miss J Hurt, BA Brunel (*Director of Sport*)
*Miss S Chadburn, BSc Sheffield Hallam (*Head of Curriculum PE, Senior School*)
*Mrs D Macey, BSc Brunel (*Head of Co-Curricular PE, Senior School*)
*Miss K Pickering, BA Chichester (*Head of PE, LSH & Junior School*)
Mrs A Arnot, BEd Bedford
Mrs J Barton, BA Oxford Brookes
Mrs N Barton, BSc Loughborough
Miss H Harding, PTTLS Award
Miss S Heath, BEd Bedford, MA Brunel
Miss N Miller, BSc Leeds Met
Miss B Roberts, BA Brighton

Psychology:
*Mrs L Winter, BSc Plymouth
Mrs A Hussain, BSc MSc Brunel

Religious Studies, Philosophy & Ethics:
*Mr G Bezalel, MSc LSE, MA London
Mr H Dymock, BA Durham, MA London
Miss S Hussey, BA Cantab
Mr E McCartney, BSc London
Mrs A Saunders, MA Cantab (*Head of Academic Extension & Oxbridge Coordinator*)
Miss H Williams, MA Edinburgh

Science:
Dr J Schofield, BSc PhD London (**Science*)
Mrs A Adlam, BSc Southampton, MSc Imperial, MInstP (**Physics*)
Mr M Reynish, BSc York (**Chemistry*)
Dr C Ryan, MChem Southampton PhD London (**Biology*)
Mrs J Arthur, BSc Reading
Miss K Baker, BSc Southampton, MA London (*Deputy Head of Middle School*)
Mrs C Jenkins, BSc Cardiff
Dr C Jones, BSc Nottingham Trent, PhD London
Mr C Le Bas, BSc Edinburgh
Dr S Sayed-Marikar, BSc MSc PhD London
Mrs S Thomas, MSci London [maternity leave]
Mr P Tiley, BSc Bristol
Mrs S Wardley, BSc Southampton
Mrs S Williams, BSc Exeter
Mrs Z Alidina, City & Guilds Pharmacy (*Technician*)
Mrs A Ghosh, BSc Calcutta (*Technician*)
Mrs B Lee, BEng China (*Technician*)
Dr Y O'Connor, BSc MSc Kyoto Japan, PhD Tokyo, Japan (*Technician*)

Library:
*Ms E Howard, BA Leicester, MA Roehampton, DipLib Metropolitan

Mrs S Gleave
Mrs R Serbos, BA Sheffield Hallam, MA London

Junior School Staff:
Head of Junior School: Mrs K Serinturk, BEd London
Deputy Head of Junior School: Miss E Sami, MEd Herts
Mrs I Cane, BA Birmingham
Miss E Carey, BA Durham
Mrs H Casingena, LLAM LAMDA
Mrs A Cawthorne, BSc Surrey, MA Middlesex
Mrs E Coleman-Boyle, BA MA Chichester
Mrs G Collins, BEd Queen's University Ontario, MA Calgary [maternity leave]
Miss S English, BA Portsmouth
Miss Z Farrell, MA St Andrews
Miss N Gavigan, BSc Birmingham
Mrs A Groves, BA Brunel
Miss S Gupta, BA Roehampton
Mrs L Lasky, BSc Liverpool
Mrs N Lawson, BA Bath
Miss R Moore, BA UEA
Mrs M Parry, BA Warwick, MTeach London
Mrs M Pratt, BA Griffith, PDipEd Queensland
Mrs P Prosser, BEd Durham
Mrs H Sansom, BEd Herts
Ms D Sarnat, BA Tel Aviv (*Head of Music, LSH & Junior School*)
Mr T Senkalski, BA Newcastle Australia

Pre-Preparatory Staff –Little St Helen's:
Head of Little St Helen's: Miss K Cooper, BA Canterbury
Deputy Head of Little St Helen's: Mrs S Begley, BSc Bangor, MPhil Pontypridd
Deputy Head of Little St Helen's: Ms D Smith, BEd Warwick
Mrs D Allsopp, MontDip London
Mrs L Baldwin, BEd Cantab [maternity leave]
Mrs H Casingena, LLAM LAMDA
Miss R Cox, BA Ryerson BEd Queen's University Ontario
Mrs R Garton, BA Surrey
Mrs N Johar, BA Brunel
Miss R Kansagra, BA Leeds
Mrs A Lam, BA Essex
Mrs D Moody, BEd Oxon
Mrs H Morris, BA Winchester
Mrs D Roberts, BA Surrey
Ms D Sarnat, BA Tel Aviv (*Head of Music, LSH & Junior School*)
Mrs H Scherbel-Ball, BA Birmingham
Mrs R Sirera, BA MA Manchester
Mrs T Wood, BA Surrey

Administrative Staff:
PA to the Headmistress: Miss D Quane
PA to the Business Director: Mrs K Campbell
Secretary to the Deputy Heads: Mrs A Bedin
Examinations Officer: Mrs D Dobson
Compliance Officer: Mrs N Choudhry, LLB Hons London
Catering Manager: Mr I Folwell
Senior School Secretary: Mrs J Steadman
Junior School Secretary: Mrs P Robbins
Little St Helen's Secretary: Mrs F Kahan
Senior School Office Manager: Mrs S Page
Admissions Officer: Ms L Hailey
Registrar: Miss S Heath, BEd Bedford, MA Brunel
Human Resources Manager: Mrs S Hart, BSc, MIPD
Accountant: Mr D Dhrona, FCCA
Head of IT Systems: Mr D Nanton, MCSE, MCP, CISCO ITIL Prince 2
Facilities & Lettings Manager: Mrs L Toms
Estates Manager: Ms A Steele, BA Manchester
Maintenance Manager: Mr D Shaw
Head of Grounds: Mr I Thom
Sports Centre Manager: Mr M Jones

St James Senior Girls' School

Earsby Street, London W14 8SH

Tel:	020 7348 1777; Admissions: 020 7348 1748
Fax:	020 7348 1717
email:	admissions@sjsg.org.uk
website:	www.stjamesgirls.co.uk

Motto: *Speak the truth. Live generously. Aim for the best.*

Founded in 1975, St James Senior Girls' School is a day school for 295 pupils aged from 11–18. We are situated on a spacious site in Olympia, West Kensington, shared with our own Junior School.

We offer an education which nurtures and enriches the physical, intellectual, emotional and spiritual development of our pupils. Our happy, united atmosphere provides the ideal environment for every girl to discover her own unique combination of strengths and talents and to 'be the best she can'.

St James girls are industrious, open-hearted and courageous; they work together, enjoying others' successes as well as their own. They achieve the highest academic standards and are also encouraged to develop strength through self-discipline and an ability to live according to an intelligent understanding of what is wise and true. Regular opportunities for stillness and quiet enable pupils to learn to be at ease with themselves, to appreciate the value of being fully present and to develop their ability to concentrate.

Our teachers have excellent subject knowledge and give their time generously to support the well-being and development of their pupils. Relationships throughout the school are extremely positive and are characterised by a spirit of love, trust and mutual respect.

Whilst admission to the school is through a selective procedure, the school seeks to admit those candidates who are able and willing to make good use of the education offered. We aim to foster creativity and intellectual curiosity, challenging our pupils to achieve excellence. Standards in public examinations are high: nearly all leavers proceed to Higher Education degree courses either at university, a specialist music college or to pursue an art foundation course.

The Curriculum offers appropriate education in PSHEE, SMSC, citizenship, philosophy and religious studies as well as leadership training, public speaking and debating. Community Service runs throughout the school. Careers Guidance is offered to all pupils from Years 7–13. All pupils engage in sports, performing arts and ICT.

Subjects available to GCSE/IGCSE: art, biology, chemistry, classical Greek, computer science, drama, English language, English literature, French, geography, history, Latin, mathematics, music, physical education, physics, religious studies, Sanskrit and Spanish. Year 7 are taught General Science prior to commencing the three separate sciences in Year 8. Year 7 also receive lessons in needlework and the Art of Hospitality.

Subjects offered at A Level: art and design, biology, chemistry, drama and theatre studies, economics, English, French, geography, Greek, history, history of art, Latin, mathematics, further mathematics, music, physics, religious studies, Sanskrit and Spanish. Students also take the Extended Project Qualification, a project which develops research and independent learning skills.

The Sixth Form. Most pupils stay on to complete their education in the Sixth Form. This is treated as a very distinct stage and pupils' growth in initiative and responsibility is supported and encouraged. The PSHEE and SMSC programme is continued in order to provide support for personal development through a series of talks, debates and workshops. Emphasis is given to academic excellence and the cultivation of social awareness and, in particular, leadership skills are developed through assuming responsibility for younger pupils in the school. In Year 12 students are offered a community service project abroad (currently each year a group travels to Kolkata, India to help orphaned children and another group travels to South Africa to trek in the wilderness and do volunteer work in a Zulu village).

Creative Arts. Music, drama and dance are strong features of the school. There is a tradition of choral and solo singing, as well as instrumental music making. Most of our productions take place in our assembly hall, fully equipped with lighting and sound. There are several choirs, orchestras and instrumental ensembles and girls are strongly encouraged to take up individual instruction with one of our visiting instrumental and/or vocal teachers. There are performance opportunities for all pupils every year: the Lower School (Years 7–9) perform a play one year, a musical the following year and vice versa for the Upper School (Years 10–13). Recent Lower School productions include: *Arabian Nights* (2016), *Barnum* (2015) and *Into the Woods* (2014). Recent Upper School productions include: *The Wizard of Oz* (2015) and *The Beggar's Opera* (2014). The dance programme introduces pupils to a variety of dance forms: ballet, modern dance, ballroom and choreography. As well as extra-curricular lessons, pupils also have the opportunity to perform in the school's Youth Dance Company and music, speech, debating, dance and other artistic competitions. There is also an annual Arts Week during which pupils have the opportunity to take part in various workshops.

Physical Education. Sports and PE is an important part of school life. Athletics, gymnastics, health related fitness, lacrosse, netball, rounders, basketball, football, handball, indoor hockey, kwik cricket, tag rugby, team building, tchoukball and tennis are all offered. We have a playground and gymnasium on site and use the facilities at Barn Elms Sports Centre and King's House Sports Ground which are a 15 minute coach journey from the school.

Extra-Curricular Activities. Pupils are offered a wide range of clubs including art, classics, cookery, dance, drama, lacrosse, netball, football, karate, politics, rounders, science, The Duke of Edinburgh's Award, ICT, choirs and orchestras. Years 7–11 attend the annual Activity Week with their own class at a variety of locations within and outside the UK.

Admission. For entry at 11+ girls sit the North London Independent Girls' Schools Consortium Entrance examination; at Sixth Form candidates are required to sit an entrance exam and to attain the necessary GCSE grades for A Level study. For occasional vacancies in Years 8, 9 and 10 candidates will need to take an entrance examination.

Fees per term (2016–2017). £6,110.

Bursaries. There are limited funds available for Bursary assistance. Awards are discretionary and based on a full financial enquiry into parents' means by the Bursary Fund Committee. The funds are primarily to assist children already attending St James, but some help may be available to new parents in specific circumstances. Enquiries should be made in the first instance to the Bursar.

Charitable status. The Independent Educational Association Limited is a Registered Charity, number 270156. It exists to provide education for children.

Governors:
Mr Jeremy Sinclair (*Chairman*)
Mrs Koula Ansell, BA Hons
Mrs Jennie Buchanan, Mont Dip
Mr George Cselko, BA Hons
Mr Aatif Hassan, BSc Hons, CA (*Joint Deputy Chairman*)
Mrs Miranda Munden, BA Hons, PGCE
Mr Jon Pickles BA, ACMA
Mr John Story, FRICS (*Joint Deputy Chairman*)
Mr Hugh Venables, BSc, MBA
Mr Jerome Webb, MA, MRICS
Dr Fenella Willis, BSc, MBBS, MD, FRCP, FRCPath

Headmistress: **Mrs Sarah Labram**, BA

Deputy Heads:
Mr Bertie Cairns, MA Oxon, QTS (*Academic*)
Mr Christian Kendall-Daw, BA, BPh, STB, QTS, FRSA (*Pastoral*)

Director of Studies: Dr Jane MacRae, MSc, PhD, QTS

Head of Sixth Form: Mrs Yolanda Saunders, BA, PGCE
Assistant Head of Sixth Form: Mr Stephen Allen, MA Cantab, MSci, PGCE

Senior Teachers:
Mrs Melissa George, MA, PGCE
Miss Anna Holliss, BA, QTS

Head of Lower School (Year 7): Mrs Sarah Forrester, BA
Head of PSHE / Middle School (Years 8 & 9): Mrs Annabel Lubikowski, BA, MPhil, PGCE
Head of Upper School (Years 10 & 11): Miss Lorraine Razzell, BA, LRAD

Teaching Staff:
Miss Joanna Adamkiewicz, MSc, PGCE (*Teacher of Mathematics*)
Ms Rupinder Ahluwalia, MEd, QTS (*SENCO*)
Mr Stephen Allen, MA Cantab, MSci, PGCE (*Teacher of Chemistry*)
Mrs Edel-Anne Bailey, MA Cantab, QTS (*Head of English*) Miss Hannah Capron, BA, MA, PGCE (*Teacher of Art*)
Mlle Mylène Chaudagne, Licence, MA, PGCE (*Head of Modern Foreign Languages*)
Mrs Sue Cooper, BA Art & Design Assoc RSA (*Head of Art*)
Dr Josef Craven, BA, MPhil, PhD (*Head of History; Citizenship*)
Mr Jonathan Crowe, BA, PGCE (*Teacher of History*)
Mr Nicholas de Mattos, BA, PGCE (*Teacher of Classics*)
Mrs Danniella Downs, MA, DipRS, AMI, PGCE (*Head of Religious Studies*)
Ms Pauline Flannery, MA, PGCE (*Head of Drama*)
Mrs Sarah Forrester, BA (*Head of Careers, Teacher of French*)
Miss Stephanie Furneaux, BSc, PGCE (*Teacher of PE, in charge of Lacrosse*)
Mrs Melissa George, MA, PGCE (*Teacher of English; Academic Enrichment Coordinator*)
Ms Ioanna Georgiou, MSc, MPhil, QTS (*Second in Mathematics Department*)
Miss Lisa Hayat, MA, PGCE (*Head of History of Art*)
Miss Anna Holliss, BA, QTS (*Head of PE*)
Mr Peter Holloway, BA, PGCE (*Head of Music*)
Mr Alastair Horsford, BA, QTS (*Head of Geography*)
Mrs Elena Jessup, BSc, MA (*Teacher of Sanskrit*)
Mr Warwick Jessup, BA Oxon, MA, MPhil (*Head of Sanskrit*)
Mr Mark Kerrigan, PGCE, MTL (*Head of ICT and Computer Science*)
Mrs Rachel Knox, BA, PGCE (*Teacher of English*)
Mrs Sally Kuhrt, BA (*Head of Art of Hospitality*)
Mrs Annabel Lubikowski, BA, MPhil, PGCE (*Head of Economics*)
Mrs Jane Mason, MA Oxon, PGCE (*Head of Classics*)
Mrs Helena McDowell, BA, QTS (*Teacher of Geography*)
Ms Karen McLoughlin, BSc, PGCE (*Teacher of Science*)
Mr Ben Mohammed, BSc, PGCE (*Head of Mathematics*)
Miss Annette Morgan, Sanskrit Dip EAL, Cambridge Cert (*Teacher of Sanskrit*)
Mrs Sylvie Piegelin-Coles, Maître, MA, PGCE, BLT (*Teacher of French*)
Miss Lorraine Razzell, BA, LRAD (*Head of Dance*)
Mrs Yolanda Saunders, BA, PGCE (*Teacher of Classics*)

Mrs Gordana Tarundzioska, BEd, BSc (*Teacher of Mathematics*)
Dr Clare van der Willigen, MSc, DPhil, PGCE (*Head of Science & Biology*)
Mrs Lynsey Walters, BA, QTS (*Teacher of PE; Head of Outdoor Pursuits*)
Mr Tomas White, BSc, PGCE (*Head of Chemistry*)
Mrs Montserrat Wight-Rahona, BA, QTS (*Head of Spanish*)
Mr Stuart Young, BSc, QTS (*Head of Physics; Head of ICT Strategy*)
Mr Henryk Zdzienski, BSc, MPhil, PGCE (*Teacher of Science*)

Support Staff:
Mrs Anna Bhowmick (*Teaching Assistant*)
Mrs Alison Buchanan (*Examinations Officer*)
Mrs Selina Coleman RSciTech (*Senior Laboratory Technician*)
Mrs Clare Featherby, RGN (*School Nurse*)
Ms Eleanor Parker, MA (*Librarian*)
Mrs Fern Roberts, PGDip, MA (*Library Assistant*)
Ms Mikyla Taylor (*Assistant Laboratory Technician*)

Administrative Staff:
Mrs Sue Allen (*Registrar & School Uniform*)
Miss Tricia D'Sa, BSc (*PA to Headmistress*)
Miss Abigail Davies, BA (*School Secretary & PA to Director of Education*)
Mrs Lindsey Kavanagh, BA, MCIM (*Marketing Manager*)
Ms Leah Murray (*Events Manager*)
Ms Olivia Palmarozza, BA, MA (*Secretary to Deputy Heads*)

Bursary:
Mr William Wyatt (*Bursar*)
Ms Kat Moult (*Assistant Bursar*)
Ms Hermione Fricker (*PA to Bursar*)

Property Management:
Mr Gyorgy Simon (*Estates Manager*)
Mr Alex Bekvalac
Mr Salah Chebiouni
Mr Tulio Ferreira

St Margaret's School for Girls
Aberdeen

17 Albyn Place, Aberdeen AB10 1RU
Tel: 01224 584466
Fax: 01224 585600
email: info@st-margaret.aberdeen.sch.uk
website: www.st-margaret.aberdeen.sch.uk

Founded in 1846, St Margaret's School is the oldest all-through girls' school in Scotland and the Head is a member of the Girls' Schools Association, Scottish Girls' Schools Group and SLS. Education is provided for around 400 girls from Nursery to Sixth Year. The Nursery is within the main building, and boys and girls are admitted from the age of 3 years.

St Margaret's School is conveniently situated in the west end of Aberdeen. The school's excellent facilities include spacious, well-equipped science laboratories, dining room, art studio, an attractive music suite, a fine gymnasium, playing fields and a pavilion at Summerhill. The school has three computer suites, and the whole school is networked.

Aims. We aim to provide a stimulating education for girls in an all-through school where each girl is encouraged to realise her potential in a friendly, caring atmosphere. The school also aims to provide public benefit through the advancement of education. We encourage staff and girls to contribute to the development of Scottish education.

Curriculum. Girls are prepared for National 4, National 5, Intermediate 2, Higher and Advanced Higher examinations of the Scottish Qualifications Authority. National examinations can be taken for awards in music and drama.

The curriculum includes Art and Design, Biology, Business Management, Chemistry, Classical Studies, Computer Studies, Drama, Economics, English (language and literature), Food Technology, French, Geography, German, History, Information Systems, Latin, Mathematics, Modern Studies, Music, Personal and Social Education, Philosophy, Physical Education, Physics, Religious and Moral Education and Spanish.

Girls are encouraged to take part in extracurricular activities which include dance, swimming, drama, debating, computer club, science club, Scripture Union, junior and senior orchestra, woodwind ensemble, junior, senior and chamber choir, The Duke of Edinburgh's Award, Young Enterprise, highland dancing, chess and Choi Kwang Do.

Admission. Girls are admitted to the School by informal or formal assessment.

Fees per term (2016–2017). Nursery (10 half day sessions) £2,105–£3,367; 1 Junior £1,921–£3,074; 2 Junior £1,921–£3,269; 3 Junior £2,528–£4,045; 4 Junior £2,590–£4,144; 5, 6 and 7 Junior £2,698–£4,316; I to VI Senior £3,043–£4,870.

These fees include SQA examination fees and all books and materials for nursery and early years classes; they are payable termly with an option to pay monthly. A reduction is made when three or more siblings attend at the same time.

Means-tested bursaries are available for entry to 6 and 7 Junior, I Senior, V and VI Senior.

Charitable status. St Margaret's School for Girls is a Registered Charity, number SC016265. It exists to provide a high quality education for girls.

School Council:
Councillor J Gifford (*Chair*)
Mr J M Baillie, BSc Hons, MEng
Mr A Bannister, BA, CA
Prof E Gammie, Dip M, BA, CA, PhD
Mrs J Craik, BSc Hons, PGCE
Mr M Grattidge, BSc Hons Arch, Dip Adv Arch, ARIAS, ARB
Dr J M House, MBBS, MRCGP
Mr D Wood
Dr A Bruce
Mrs F Littlejohn
Mrs A Everest

Clerk to the Council: Squadron Leader [Ret'd] A R Mountain

Head: Miss Anna Tomlinson, MTheol Hons, PGCE

Deputy Head: Mrs S Lynch, MA Hons, PGCE (*Modern Languages*)

Senior Staff:
* *Head of Department*
§ *Part-time or Visiting*

Mr R Adair, BSc Hons, PGCE Sec (**Chemistry*)
§Miss J Aitken, BEd (*Physical Education*)
Mrs L Arthur, BSc Hons, MSc, PGCE (*ICT*)
Ms S Brown, BEd, ATCL (*Music*)
Mrs A Bryce, BSc Hons, PGCE (*Mathematics*)
Ms L Chellal, Licence d'Anglais Pau, Licence FLE Grenoble, PGCE (**Modern Languages*)
Mrs S Cooper Weber (*English*)
Mrs L Counsell (*Music*)
Miss K Cowie, BA Hons, PGCE (**Art and Design*)

Mrs E Crisp, BA Hons, CGeog, FRGS, PGCE (**Geography*)
Mr G Cunningham, MA Hons, PGCE Sec (**Economics and *History*)
Mrs D Dale, MA, PGCE S (*English*)
Miss S Forgie, BA Hons, PGCE (*Modern Languages*)
Mrs K Fowler, BEd Hons (*Physical Education*)
Mrs L Goodwin, BEd (**Speech and Drama*)
Mrs L Gurney, LTCL (*Music –Woodwind*)
Mrs L Howitt, BSc Hons, PGDE (*Biology and Chemistry*)
Mrs H Jennings, BD, PGCE (*History, *Philosophy and *RMPE*)
Mrs J Johnson, DipDomSc, DipSEN (**Food Technology*)
Mrs S Lynch, MA Hons, PGCE (*Modern Languages*)
Ms E MacDonald (*English*)
Mrs S MacFadyen, BSc, PGCE (*Mathematics*)
Miss W Main, BA Hons, PGCE (**Classics*)
§Mrs A Miller, BSc Hons, PGCE (**Biology*)
Miss E Moore, BSc Hons Physics, BSc Medical Physics, PGDE (**Physics*)
§Mrs H Nehring, BA, PGCE (*Modern Languages*)
Mrs K Norval, BEd Hons (**Physical Education*)
§Miss S Orr, MA Hons, PGDE (*History*)
Mr P Parfitt, BA Hons, MMus (**Music*)
Mrs J Reid, BEd Hons (*Physical Education*)
Mr G Rennet (*Geography and Modern Studies*)
§Mrs J Richardson, BA Hons, PGCE (*Art and Design*)
§Mrs J Robson, GRSC pt11, PGCE (*Chemistry*)
Mrs J Slater, Dip Comm (**Business Mgt, Word Processing, Guidance and PSE*)
Mrs S Smith, BA Hons, PGCE (**Mathematics*)
§Mrs S Hendry, BSc Hons, PGDE (*Biology, Physics*)
§Mrs L Tapper, BSc Hons, PGCE (*Mathematics*)
Mrs S Torrie (**English*)
Mrs M Wiedermann, ATCL, AMusTCL (*Head of Strings*)

Junior Department:
§Mrs C Bradbury, DPE
Ms A Dressel, BSc, PGCE
Mrs J Garden, BEd Primary
Mrs S Lowe, MA Hons, PGCE (*Junior French*)
Mrs E McDonald, BEd Hons Primary Education
Mrs N Murray, BSc Hons PGCE (**Head of Junior School*)
Miss R Parley, BA Music, PGDE Primary
§Mrs L Reilly, MA, CertEd
Mrs M Smith, BEd, PGC Inclusive Practice
Mrs P Twigg, BA Hons, PGDE (*Principal Teacher*)
Mrs S Wightman, BEd Hons, PGCE Autism and Learning
Mrs A Wilson, BEd Hons

Classroom Assistants:
Mrs C Duncan, HNC
Miss G Gray, SVG4 Playwork
Mrs D Gregory, SVQ2 in Care

Nursery at St Margaret's:
Mrs L Dredge
Miss W Fraser, HNC Childcare & Education SVQ Level 3
Mrs V Gerbrandy
Miss A Milne
Miss J Minett, BA Hons Childhood and Youth Studies (**Early Years Coordinator*)
Miss K Thomson, CCLD Level 3 [maternity leave]

Support for Learning:
*Ms L Hawthorn
Mrs I Laing, BSAc Hons Speech and Language Therapy
§Mrs J Robson, GRSC pt11, PGCE

Administrative Staff:
Bursar: Squadron Leader [Ret'd] A R Mountain
Assistant Bursar: Mrs D Brody
PA to Head: Mrs G Smith

Head of Development: Mrs L Taylor
Admissions: Mrs K Schmitz
Marketing Officer: Mrs F Littlejohn
Sports Coordinator: Mrs S Lowe, MA Hons, PGCE
School Administrator/Receptionist: Miss A Fraser
ICT Technician: Mr C Morris, BSc Hons
Laboratory Technician: Miss K Mackie, ONC, HNC, Bio Sci
Sports Coordinator: Mrs S Lowe, MA Hons, PGCE
Payroll & HR: Ms Z Spalding
Facilities Manager: Mr D Cordiner
Art Technician: Mr P Henry
Janitors: Mr B Henderson & Mr J Son

After-School Care and Playground Supervision:
Mrs S Crabb
Miss W Fraser, HNC Childcare & Education SVQ Level 3 (*After-School Care*)
Ms M Hussain, BA, MSc, Cert Primary Education
Mrs S Ingram (*Playground Supervisor*)
Mrs I Laing, BSAc Hons Speech and Language Therapy
Miss J Minett, BA Hons Childhood and Youth Studies (*Early Years Coordinator*)
Miss K Thomson, CCLD Level 3 (*After-School Care*)
Mrs S Flores

There are also visiting instrumental teachers for strings, brass and percussion and three modern language assistants for French, German and Spanish.

St Margaret's School
Bushey

Merry Hill Road, Bushey, Herts WD23 1DT

Tel:	020 8416 4400
Fax:	020 8416 4401
email:	schooloffice@stmargarets.herts.sch.uk
website:	www.stmargaretsbushey.co.uk
Twitter:	@StMargsBushey
Facebook:	@StMargaretsBushey
LinkedIn:	/St-Margaret's-School-Bushey

Motto: *Sursum corda Habemus ad Dominum*

Founded 1749.

St Margaret's School in Hertfordshire is among the oldest girls' schools in the UK. It has an excellent record of academic success, which is attributed to its emphasis upon providing the very best pastoral care, which has been a continuous hallmark of the school since it was established for the orphans of Church of England clergy in 1749. The School is set within 74 acres of stunning Hertfordshire countryside, which offers girls abundant space to grow and be inspired in safety. St Margaret's educates girls all the way through from age 4 to 18. It is predominantly a day school; however, boarding facilities are available to a limited number of 90 girls, from the age of 11.

St Margaret's Senior School consistently performs at the highest of academic standards. In 2016, 100% of EPQ grades were A* or A, 85% of girls went on to attend their first-choice university, 86% of A Level grades were A* to C, 25% of AS Level students received straight As.

St Margaret's has evolved into a thriving multi-cultural community, ideally located in rural surroundings, yet within easy reach of London and the country's best national and international transport links. The school's facilities boast the best of old and new. The main school building (including its chapel) was designed by the celebrated Victorian architect Sir Alfred Waterhouse, who also designed London's Natural History Museum and Manchester Town Hall. Modern buildings have been added to the campus over the past century and the School is presently in the process of a multimillion pound development which will see it become one of the best resourced schools in the UK.

St Margaret's offers a wide range of sporting and cultural activities, for example, the Duke of Edinburgh's Award and the Young Enterprise Scheme as well as charitable fundraising drives. The school has close links with fellow Comenius project partners in Germany, Hungary, Portugal, Italy, Belgium, Poland and Norway, and there are regular field trips, outings and theatre visits. Other activities include choir, orchestra, speech and drama, drama, ballet and fencing.

St Margaret's has a full school open day each year, as well as a sixth form open evening and a variety of 'school at work' mornings, which allow parents to see classes in action. The School's website contains the most up-to-date information: www.stmargaretsbushey.co.uk

Fees per term (2016–2017). Junior School: Years 4–6 £4,389, Transition (Year 3) £3,996, Reception, Years 1 & 2 £3,333. Senior School (Years 7–13): Day £5,259; Full Boarding £9,855; Weekly Boarding: £7,224 (up to 3 nights), £8,457 (up to 5 nights).

Means-tested bursaries are available and discounts for members of the Forces, Clergy and Old Girls.

Scholarships. Academic, Art, Drama, Music, Sport and STEM Scholarships are awarded at 11+, 13+ and 16+.

St Margaret's Guild (Old Girls' Association). *Secretary*: Mrs J Wilson, 43 Chase Ridings, Enfield, Middx EN2 7QE. Guild Membership available to any old girl of St Margaret's School.

Charitable status. St Margaret's School Bushey is a Registered Charity, number 1056228.

Trustees:
Chairman: Margaret Rudland
Chairman, F&GP Committee: Philip Walton

Headmistress: Mrs Rose Hardy, MA Oxon, MEd, FRSA

Academic Deputy: Mrs G Erdil, BSc Hons
Pastoral Deputy Head: Miss J Chatkiewicz, BA, PGCE
Bursar: Dr K Young, ARSM, DIC
Examinations Officer: Mr R Aniolkowski, BSc, PGCE

Heads of Departments:

Art:
Mrs K O'Hanlon, BA Hons, PGCE

Careers:
Mrs A Griffiths, BA Hons

Classics:
Mrs C Jessop, BA Hons, PGCE

Drama:
Mr S Borril, BA Hons, PGCE

English:
Mrs P Metcalfe, BA London, TEFL Dip

Food Technology:
Ms S Poulter, BSc, PGCE

Geography:
Mrs Sheila Wills, BA, PGCE

History:
Mrs E Clarke, BA, PGCE

Information Technology:
Ms D Soulsby
Mr M A Hammond, MA Cantab, PGCE, FRCO, LRAM

Mathematics:
Mr S Moore, CEng, MA Cantab, PGCE

Modern Languages:
Ms A Corbach, MA, BA Cologne, PGCE

Music:
Mr I Hope, BMus, PGCE, LTCL

Psychology:
Dr L D'Souza, BSc Hons

Physical Education:
Mrs D Pimlott, BEd Hons

Religious Studies:
Ms K Roberts, BA, MA London, PGCE

Science:
Mr D Anderson, BSc, BEd, PGCE

Social Studies:
Mrs E Chaudhri, BA, PGCE

Learning Support:
Ms J Collier, BEd Hons

Junior School:
Head: Mrs C Aisthorpe, BEd Hons, LRAM

Senior Housemistress:
Miss R Price

The Duke of Edinburgh's Award:
Mrs A Ribton, BA Hons

St Martha's

**Camlet Way, Hadley Wood, Barnet, Hertfordshire
EN4 0NJ**

Tel: 020 8449 6889
Fax: 020 8441 5632
email: admissions@saint-marthas.org.uk
website: www.st-marthas.co.uk
Twitter: @stmarthas
Facebook: /StMarthasEN4

Age Range. 11–18 Girls.
Number in School. 220 Day Girls.
Fees per term (2016–2017). £4,625.

St Martha's was founded in Barnet as a Catholic girls' school in 1903. As the school's popularity grew, a senior school was established in 1947 at its current location, The Mount House, in the leafy environs of Monken Hadley Common and Hadley Wood. St Martha's still follows the Catholic tradition but has evolved to accept girls of all beliefs and faiths into our community. We treasure our picturesque, rural surroundings yet benefit from close public transport links by tube and rail to central London.

The Headmaster, Matthew Burke, and his staff pride themselves on the supportive family atmosphere at St Martha's, where Sisters still teach and have been instrumental in the success of the school, and the girls who attended, since the school's establishment. We are renowned as a warm and friendly school that believes a demanding and challenging ethos can go hand in hand with a caring and supportive atmosphere.

St Martha's is in the top 10 of Independent Catholic Day schools for girls and places great emphasis on high academic standards, with our GCSE and A Level results placing us in the top 5% of schools in the UK for added value. The school has excellent academic results – in 2016 we again secured 100% pass rates at both GCSE and A Level with 42% of grades at A Level being A*–B 44% with every one of our Upper Sixth students gaining entry to their first-choice university.

Additionally, St Martha's Value Added Score places the school in the top 10 of Independent Girls' Catholic Schools nationally.

The school has responded to the recent declaration on the value of student applications with scientific qualifications from leading universities, by investing in the refurbishment and creation of three new laboratories –one for each subject. Accordingly more students at St Martha's are choosing to study Biology, Physics and Chemistry at GCSE and A Level, with GCSE results in sciences being 100% A*–C in Chemistry, Biology and Physics over the last 2 years!

St Martha's calm and supportive environment motivates its pupils and students to develop individuality and become independent learners, encouraging creativity, initiative and a deep love of learning. Each pupil and student is allowed to develop her own unique talents and is encouraged to become involved in the local community through a wide breadth of social projects. St Martha's is an exceptional day school in that it is small enough to nurture and value each girl and large enough to provide her with a diverse and rich range of learning opportunities.

Sports are an important part of life at St Martha's with girls competing in school, county, national and international fixtures and competitions. The school recognizes that competition and sport develop self-esteem, confidence and leadership skills, so encourages the girls to participate in a wide variety of sports including hockey, football, athletics, gymnastics, netball, swimming, golf, basketball, sailing, rounders and badminton. St Martha's running and swimming athletes have shown particular promise in the last 12 months competing and placing gold and silver for the county and UK at events.

An integral part of St Martha's pastoral provision is the Tutorial System, with each girl matched to a Personal Tutor who provides one-on-one personal support from the day she starts at the school. Tutors meet weekly with their tutees and are a link between parents and their daughter's subject teachers; they monitor the pupils' academic progress, advising on their choice of subjects as they progress through the school and advising on career possibilities on the strength of the close bond and relationship they develop.

St Martha's provides daily school bus and shuttle services to and from local rail and underground stations. The routes available on the bus service are extensive and we are accommodating in trying to add new pick up points on routes which currently cover Arkley, Canons Park, Cockfosters, Cricklewood, East Barnet, Edgware, Enfield, Finchley, Friern Barnet, Hadley Wood, Hampstead, Hendon, High Barnet, Mill Hill, New Barnet, Palmers Green, Southgate, Totteridge, Whetstone, Winchmore Hill and Woodside Park.

Choosing a school for your daughter for the vital years of secondary education is an important and often difficult task, and so we want to provide you with every opportunity to visit and be welcomed by us. Please come along to see just what makes us so special and experience at first hand why so many parents are choosing St Martha's to educate their daughters. We have numerous Open Mornings for entry at First Form and a dedicated Open Evening for entry into Sixth Form. The Admissions team are happy to organise individual visits and tours of the school. Please contact them on 0208 449 6889 or admissions@saint-marthas.org.uk.

Governors and Trustees:

Chair of Governors: Mr Les Edgar
Mr Michael McCann
Mr Seamus O'Sullivan
Sr Irene Brogan
Mr Joseph Medayil
Mr Sean Heaney
Mrs Genia Moccia
Mrs Maria Strauss
Mrs Pina Griffin

Trustees:
Sister Cécile Archer

Sister Christina O'Dwyer
Sister Teresa Roseingrave

School Staff:

Headmaster: Mr Matthew Burke, BA Hons, PGCE, Adv Dip Ed, NPQH

Deputy Head: Sr T Roseingrave, CertEd, CTC
Director of Studies: Dr M Wall, BSc Hons, PhD, PGSE
Head of Sixth Form: Ms R McGonagle, BA Hons, PGCE, NPQSL [maternity leave] / Mr C McCormick, BA Hons, MA, PGCE [maternity cover]
Bursar: Mr S Rayner
Assistant Bursar: Mrs R Nagevadia
Admissions & Marketing: Mrs M Naismith

House Mistresses:
Avila: Mrs M Walmsley, BSc Hons, PGCE
Siena: Mrs C Carpenter, BA Hons, PGCE
Liseaux: Miss P Smyth, BSc Hons, PGCE

* *Head of Faculty*

Art:
*Mrs C Carpenter, BA Hons, PGCE
Mr A Halliday, BA Hons, PGCE
Ms E Somerville, BA, PGCE

Business, Mathematics & Technology:
*Mr J Boonzaier, BCom, HDE

Classics:
Mrs K Fallon, BA Hons, MLDP, PGCE

Drama:
Miss R McGonagle, BA Hons, PGCE, NPQSL [maternity leave] / Ms F Dawson

Economics:
Mr L Spence

English:
*Mrs R MacDonald, MA Hons, PGCE
Ms D Harris, BA Hons, PGCE
Mr E Whitmore, BA, MLS, PGCE

Food Technology:
Mrs B Rodgers, BA Hons, GTP
Sr T Roseingrave, CertEd, CTC

History:
Mr C McCormick, BA Hons, MA, PGCE

Humanities:
*Mr C McCormick, BA Hons, MA, PGCE

IT:
Mrs M Walmsley, BSc Hons, PGCE

Latin:
Mrs E Stamidou, BA, MA

Mathematics:
*Mr P Gallagher, BSc Hons, MSc
Ms M Platona, BSc, PGCE
Mr A Hosseinian

Mandarin:
Miss Y Li, MSc, BA Hons, HND

Music:
Mrs C Butterworth, BA Hons, PGCE

Modern Foreign Languages:
*Mrs M Lazouras, BA Hons, PGCE
Ms W Manni-Saada

Photography:
Mr A Halliday, BA Hons, PGCE

Politics/Economics:
Mr L Spence

Ms Clancy, BA, PGCE

Psychology:
Mr T Klidzia, GMus Hons, BSc Hons, PGCE

Physical Education:
*Miss S Wilkins, MS Hons, PGDE
Miss P Smyth, BSc Hons, PGCE

Religious Education:
*Ms H Baly
Mrs D Mela, GLCM, ALCM
Mr M Burke, BA Hons, PGCE, Ad Dip Ed, NPQH

Science:
Mrs D Martin, BSc Hons, MSc, PGCE (*Chemistry*)
Mrs R Stern (*Biology*)
Dr M Wall, BSc, PhD, PGCE (*Biology*)

Sociology:
Mr P Allman
Mrs S Allman
Mrs A Melekis, BA Hons, PGCE

Textiles:
Mrs K Woollard, BA Hons, GTP
Mrs T Agyepong

Inclusion Manager: Mrs A Melekis, BA Hons, PGCE

Catering:
Mr G Stubbs (*Catering Manager*)
Mr J Young (*Brookwood Chef*)
Mrs A Patel (*Brookwood Kitchen Assistant*)
Mrs E Bray (*Brookwood Kitchen Assistant*)
Mr I Fernando (*Brookwood Kitchen Assistant*)

Site Team:
Mr C Heaney (*Site Manager*)
Mr M Robinson (*Groundskeeper*)
Mrs P Meally (*Housekeeping*)

Support Staff:
Mrs M Naismith (*Headmaster's Personal Assistant [interim]*)
Mrs A Swynnerton (*International Admissions*)
Miss N Tasou (*School Secretary*)
Mrs A Bavisha (*Examinations Officer*)
Mrs E Rayner & Mrs C Millitello (*Receptionists*)
Mrs J Waldon (*Communications Coordinator*)
Mr A Erotocritou (*Information Technology Manager*)

Learning Support:
Ms T Meyrick (*Learning Support Assistant*)

Technicians:
Mrs M Dixon (*Art Technician*)
Ms R Panak (*Science Technician*)

Visiting Teachers:
Mr N Barnes (*Football coach*)
Mr E Flores (*Piano*)
Ms F Hammacott (*Singing*)
Mr J Lee (*Drums*)
Mr R Richards (*Violin*)
Mrs K Sherry (*LAMDA*)
Mrs M Tomas (*Singing*)
Miss J Prestifilippo (*Cheerleading/Dance*)

Saint Martin's School
Solihull

Malvern Hall, Brueton Avenue, Solihull, West Midlands B91 3EN

Tel:	0121 705 1265
Fax:	0121 711 4529
email:	mail@saintmartins-school.com
website:	www.saintmartins-school.com

Motto: *The Grace of God is in Courtesy*

Welcome to Saint Martin's School. We are an exceptional independent day school for girls that has the tradition of providing the best education from Nursery to Sixth Form. We are proud of being a school that educates girls and only girls.

Location. Saint Martin's is a well-established day school for approximately 415 girls situated in a beautiful twenty-acre site in the south of Solihull. Solihull is about 8 miles from Birmingham and is on the edge of a rural district within very easy reach of Warwick, Coventry, Leamington Spa and the M42.

Buildings and Facilities. In addition to the main school buildings which are attached to the very fine Grade II listed Malvern Hall, there are separate, self-contained buildings for the Nursery, Preparatory and Junior Departments; the Sixth Form is housed in renovated and extended listed buildings near to the main school. The school has its own 25-metre indoor swimming pool and an all-weather floodlit astro pitch. All playing fields, including tennis and netball courts, are on the premises and an exceptionally wide range of indoor and outdoor activities is offered.

The school enjoys well-resourced, specialist accommodation for teaching science, music, art, ICT and technology. A Performing Arts Building (SMArt) was completed in Summer 2012 and offers specialist facilities in drama and dance with a 130-seat theatre and state-of-the-art lighting and sound systems. The Discovery Hub, an exciting new music, art, design and technology and science zone, was opened in September 2015 for girls in Nursery to Year 6.

Curriculum. Girls receive a broad academic education with considerable opportunities for the development of individual interests and good academic standards are maintained. Emphasis is placed on hard work and independent learning. Courses leading to GCSE examinations are offered in all the usual subjects as well as ICT, Spanish, German, Latin, Classical Civilisation, Art and Music and all girls are required to continue with Mathematics, English Language, English Literature, a modern language and all three sciences. Classes are not streamed, but some subjects are taught in ability sets. In the Sixth Form, the majority of girls will study four Advanced Subsidiary subjects in the first year and complete three Advanced Level courses in the second year chosen from the same range as is offered at GCSE, with the addition of Economics, Business Studies and Psychology. The Extended Project Qualification is offered to the Upper Sixth. Virtually all Sixth Form students go on to higher education and all senior pupils receive extensive careers education and advice and all take part in work experience in Year 11 and the Lower Sixth.

Extra-Curricular Activities. Sport, music and drama are all strong in school: plays and concerts are held throughout the year at all ages and a very large proportion of girls study at least one instrument. A large selection of other extra-curricular interests is catered for, such as Young Enterprise and the Duke of Edinburgh's Award Scheme. Clubs and societies are encouraged. There are many visits to enrich the curriculum, including regular field trips, and trips abroad to Merville, Iceland, Geneva, Italy, China and New York among others.

Admission is by assessment for girls aged 5–10 and by interview and examination for older pupils. Girls are admitted to the Sixth Form on the basis of GCSE results and interview.

Fees per term (2016–2017). Reception–Year 2 £3,100; Junior School £3,640; Senior School £4,230, Sixth Form £3,900. Nursery: £44 per full day.

Scholarships. A number of Academic scholarships are offered each year for entry to the Senior School at 11+. Awards are made to candidates who show outstanding ability in the entrance examination and interview. Music, Performing Arts and Sports scholarships are also available at 11+.

Scholarships are also awarded annually to pupils entering the Sixth Form. Candidates are required to sit papers assessing a variety of skills and their potential for further study. Those who are shortlisted are interviewed by the Head and the Head of Sixth Form.

Charitable status. Saint Martin's (Solihull) Limited is a Registered Charity, number 528967. It exists to provide education for girls.

Board of Governors:
Patron: Baroness Joan Secombe, JP
President: Mrs P Harbour, MA
Vice President: Revd J Bradford, BA, MEd, AdvCertEd, FRSA
Vice President: Mrs N S Bridgewater, JP
Chair: Mrs C McNidder, BSc
Revd D Ballard, BSc, CertD, DipD, MTh
Mrs F de Minckwitz
Mrs H Ellis, BA, PGCE, MIHM
Mr V Hallan, MSc, JP
Mr K Lewis
Dr N Manley, LDS, RCS, DPDS
Mr I Ralph
Mr J Shepherd, FRICS
Mr S Skakel
Mr P Tegg
Mrs G Tillman, BSc

Head: **Miss N Edgar**, BA Hons Liverpool, PGCE, NPQH

Deputy Head: Mrs J Parker, BSc Reading, MA Nottingham, PGCE
Deputy Head: Miss L Mountford, BSc Warwick, PGCE
Assistant Head (Head of Sixth Form): Mrs R Speirs, BA Nottingham, PGCE
Assistant Head (Head of Years 7 to 11): Mrs F Fowles, BA Dunelm, MSc Reading
Assistant Head of Year: Miss E Harlock, BA Hons Sheffield, PGCE

Staff:

Art:
Mrs M Terry, BA University of Wales Newport, PGCE
Technician: Mrs R Parkes

Business Studies and Economics:
Mr C B Mason, BA Lancaster, MSc Lancaster, PGCE

Careers:
Miss E Harlock, BA Hons Sheffield, PGCE

Classics:
Miss E Hodgkiss, BA Hons Birmingham. MA Birmingham, PGCE
Ms I Simmons, BA Oxon, QTS

Dance:
Ms J Felix

Drama:
Mrs K Stafford, BA Hull, MA Birmingham, PGCE
Mr J Brown, BA Exeter, PGCE

Technician: Mrs R Parkes

English:
Mrs C Inns, BA Kent, PGCE
Mr J Brown, BA Exeter, PGCE
Miss E Hodgkiss, BA Hons Birmingham. MA
  Birmingham, PGCE
Ms I Simmons, BA Oxon, QTS
Mrs R Speirs, BA Nottingham, PGCE
Mrs S Watton, BA Hull, PGCE

Food and Textiles:
Mrs J Massarella, BEd Bath College

Geography:
Mrs F Fowles, BA Dunelm, MSc Reading, PGCE
Miss C Bednall, BSc Cheltenham, MSc London, PGCE
Miss N Edgar, BA Hons Liverpool, PGCE, NPQH

History:
Mr M van Alderwegen, BA Leeds, MA Nottingham, PGCE
Miss E Harlock, BA Hons Sheffield, PGCE

Information Technology:
Mrs C Dance, BSc Keele, PGCE
Mrs S A King, BSc Portsmouth, PGCE
Network Manager: Mr P Carlson, BS St Paul TVI
Technician: Mr D Johnson

Learning Support:
Mrs F Franklin, BA Hons Leeds, QTS, OCR Dip SpLD
Mrs C Knight, BSs Birmingham, PGCE

Mathematics:
Mrs E Linford, BSc Salford, MSc Southampton, PGCE
Mrs H Barber, BA York, PGCE
Mrs L Gunn, MEng Warwick PGCE
Mrs S A King, BSc Portsmouth, PGCE
Mrs R Lawson, BEd Warwick
Mrs A Short, BSc London, PGCE

Modern Languages:
Mr P Delaney, BA Exeter, PGCE
Mrs C Gibney, DUT Nancy, MIL, PGCE
Ms K Harris, BA Leeds, MA Birmingham
Mrs I Jardon, DipIl, PGCE, MA Warwick
Miss S Timson, BA Nottingham, PGCE

Music:
Mr P Allen, BA Liverpool, PGCE, ALCM
Mrs J Bamford, PGCE, GLCM (*Piano*)
Mr R Bull, GLCM, PGCE (*Brass*)
Mrs G Kirby, G Mus, PGCE, ALCM, LTCL (*Violin, Viola*)
Ms L Hands, ATCL (*Piano*)
Mrs G Hattley, GBSM, ABSM (*Piano, Keyboard, Singing*)
Mrs K Moore (*Clarinet, Saxophone*)
Miss C Slominska, BMus Wales (*Percussion*)
Mr M Sharpe, BA Music Oxford Brookes (*Brass*)
Mr O Srba, Masters in Music (*Piano*)
Dr A Thompson, BA, MA, PhD, PGCE (*Flute*)
Mr M Whittaker, BMus (*Guitar*)

Physical Education:
Mrs H Burgess, BA Birmingham, PGCE
Mrs T Farnell, BSc Bedfordshire, PGCE
Mrs T Gallagher, BEd Leeds Metropolitan
Mrs J Green, BSc Cheltenham and Gloucester, PGCE

Psychology:
Mrs M E Thompson, BSc Nottingham, PGCE

Religious Studies:
Mrs I Igoe, BEd Newman
Miss E Harlock, BA Hons Sheffield, PGCE

Science:
Mr A Swift, MSci Birmingham, PGCE
Mr D Whiting, BSc Dunelm

Miss L Mountford, BSc Warwick, PGCE
Mrs J Parker, BSc Reading, MA Nottingham, PGCE
Mrs S Parker, BSc Leicester, PGCE
Dr F Ryland, BSc Warwick, MPhil Birmingham, PhD
  Birmingham, PGCE
Mrs A Short, BSc London, PGCE
Mrs R Trainor, BSc Warwick, PGCE
Mrs J Waters, BSc Birmingham, PGCE
Senior Science Technician: Miss R Morris, BSc
Science Technician: Mr D Wade

Technology:
Mr J Hands, BA Northampton
Technician: Mrs R Parkes

Head of Nursery to Year 6: Mrs H Kirby, BA Lancaster

Junior School (Years 3–6):
Deputy of Junior School: Mrs E Inglis, BEd Westminster
  College Oxford
Mr J Brown, BA Exeter, PGCE
Mr S Cordelle, BEd Derby
Mrs J Creaton, BMe University of Western Australia
Mrs T Dacombe, BEd Leeds
Mrs V Higley, BEd Christ's & Notre Dame
Miss G Hull, BA Sheffield, PGCE
Miss A R Parry, BA Oxford Brookes, PGCE
Miss C Rich, BA & MSCi Education D'Youville College
Miss H Winn, LLB Manchester Metropolitan, PGCE
Teaching Assistant: Miss P Wheeldon

Alice House (Nursery–Year 2):
Deputy of Alice House: Mrs McArthur, BA East London,
  PGCE
Mr J Brown, BA Exeter, PGCE
Miss J Chatwin, BEd UCE
Mrs J Creaton, BMe University of Western Australia
Mrs L Harper, BA Oxford Brookes
Mrs E Pimlott, BSc Portsmouth, PGCE

Teaching Assistants:

Mrs P Annandale	Mrs A Garside
Mrs N Byrne	Mrs J Green
Mrs K Duffy	Mrs M Lee
Miss W Evans	Mrs S Sargent
Miss M Field	

St Mary's School
Colchester

Lexden Road, Colchester, Essex CO3 3RB
Tel:	01206 572544 (Office)
	01206 216420 (Registrar)
Fax:	01206 576437
email:	info@stmaryscolchester.org.uk
website:	www.stmaryscolchester.org.uk
Twitter:	@stmaryscolch
Facebook:	/stmarycolchester

Motto: *Scientia et Veritas*

St Mary's –a happy, high achieving school
At St Mary's the emphasis is on encouraging pupils to be happy and to make the most of all the opportunities school life brings. When they feel secure and supported, pupils are able to do their best academically and also to develop as individuals, finding confidence, talents and interests that will bring them pleasure and fulfilment throughout their lives.

Lessons at St Mary's are lively and designed to encourage a real enthusiasm for learning among girls aged 3 to 16 (and boys aged 3 to 4 in the Kindergarten). Art, drama, music, sport and all manner of other activities are also entered into with great energy and our pupils' achievements across the board never cease to amaze.

St Mary's has a happy and caring atmosphere. In this very positive culture, pupils are keen to achieve, and this leads to success. St Mary's pupils' GCSE results are consistently among the best in the area –in 2016, 92% of all GCSE entries at St Mary's were graded A* to C –and SATs results are well above the national expectations, with many pupils achieving grammar school places and St Mary's Senior School scholarships. All this, despite the fact that St Mary's is not an academically selective school.

"I am always delighted to see our pupils' hard work pay off," says St Mary's Principal Mrs Hilary Vipond, "but what makes me most proud is meeting former pupils who tell me that without the happy and focused education they received at St Mary's they wouldn't be the positive and successful individuals that they are today. They look back on their school days with fondness –'once a St Mary's girl, always a St Mary's girl'!"

Fees per term (2016–2017). Senior School: £4,355–£4,575; Lower School: £2,990–£3,750; Kindergarten: from £45.50 per day. Fees are inclusive of accident insurance, lunch and drinks (including milk in the Lower School), as well as extra tuition and learning support if required.

Charitable status. St Mary's School (Colchester) Limited is a Registered Charity, number 309266.

Chair of Governors: Mrs M Haddrell

Principal: **Mrs H Vipond**, BSc Hons, MEd, CertEd, DipEd, NPQH

Director of Senior School: Miss A Jones, BEd, NPQH

Director of Lower School: Mrs E Stanhope, GMus, NPQH

Bursar: Mr S Cooke

Registrar: Mrs J Tierney

St Mary's School
Gerrards Cross

Gerrards Cross, Buckinghamshire SL9 8JQ

Tel: 01753 883370
Fax: 01753 890966
email: registrar@st-marys.bucks.sch.uk
website: www.stmarysschool.co.uk
Twitter: @StMarysSchoolGX
Facebook: /St-Marys-School-Gerrards-Cross

Badge: *Ecce Ancilla Domini*
Founded by Dean Butler in 1872. Formerly at Lancaster Gate. Established in Gerrards Cross in 1937 as an Independent Day School catering for 330 day girls.

The School is situated in the attractive residential area of Gerrards Cross which is surrounded by beautiful countryside, 20 miles from London, close to the M25 and A40/M40, on the main bus routes and 10 minutes from the Railway Station.

The aim of the School is to provide an excellent academic and rounded education leading on to University for day girls between the ages of 4 and 18 and to enable each of them to develop their own talents and personalities in a happy, caring and purposeful environment, and to become successful, fulfilled adults.

Curriculum. Subjects offered include English Language and Literature, History, Geography, RE, Drama, French, German, Spanish, Business Studies, Economics, Information Technology, Mathematics, Psychology, Chemistry,

Biology, Physics, Music, Art & Design, Food & Nutrition, Gymnastics, Hockey, Netball, Tennis, Rounders, Football, Rugby, Swimming, Media, Personal, Social, Cultural and Health Care, Dancing and other sporting activities. Regular trips are made to places of educational interest, field courses are undertaken, foreign visits including a ski trip to the USA are arranged, and there is highly successful participation in The Duke of Edinburgh's Award scheme and Young Enterprise. There is an excellent staff/pupil ratio.

Examinations: Girls are prepared for Entrance to the Universities and Colleges in all subjects; for the General Certificate of Education at AS, A2 and GCSE/IGCSE Level; Associated Board Examinations in Music and examinations in Speech and Drama (LAMDA). The School is an 11+ centre.

The Buildings are an attractive mixture of old and new and include two Libraries, Dining Hall, a Science Block with Laboratories, a Geography Room, a large open-plan Art Studio, a Home Economics Room, Textiles Room, two Computer Suites, a modern Sixth Form Centre, two Music Rooms, Drama Studio, Chapel and two Assembly Halls/Gymnasiums equipped to the highest standards. The Prep Department, in the grounds of the Senior House, comprises a Nursery and two modern purpose-built blocks, with a Science Laboratory, Hall, Gymnasium, Textiles/Art room and ICT suite. The lovely grounds include tennis and netball courts, a hockey pitch and an athletics lawn. A new Sport England full-size Sports Hall opened in 2009.

School Hours. The hours are 8.30 am –3.40 pm. The School year is divided into 3 terms.

Reports are sent to Parents at the end of each term and there are regular Parent/Staff meetings. The School also communicates with Parents via ParentMail.

Fees per term (2016–2017). £1,750–£5,232.

Scholarships and Bursaries. Academic scholarships are available at 7+, 11+ and at 16+ in the Sixth Form. There are also Music and Art scholarships at 11+. A means-tested Bursary scheme is in operation.

Charitable status. St Mary's School (Gerrards Cross) Limited is a Registered Charity, number 310634. It provides education for girls from Nursery to A Level in a well-structured, academic and caring environment.

Governors:
Chairman: Mr D R Wilson, BA, FCA
Mrs C Bayliss, CertEd
Mr D Campkin, ACA, BSc Hons
Mrs C Eilerts de Haan, MSc, ChemTech Ingenieur, PGCE
Mrs M Hall, MA Cantab, CPA, EPA
Mr N Hallchurch, LLB Hons
Prof S Machin, MBChB, FRCP, FRCPath
Mrs R Martin, MEd, NPQH, FRSA
Mr N Moss, MNAEA
Mr A Rahman

Senior Leadership Team:

Headmistress: **Mrs J A Ross**, BA Hons Manchester, NPQH (*French*)

Bursar: Mr D Martin, BSc Hons London
Deputy Head: Mrs J Kingston, BSc Hons Cardiff, MPhil Bath (*Chemistry*)
Assistant Head Sixth Form: Ms J Ambrose, BA Hons Swansea (*English*)
Head of Preparatory Department: Mrs M Carney, BA Hons Galway (*Year 6 Class teacher*)
Director of Studies, Preparatory Department: Dr H Creber, PhD Cardiff (*Year 5 Class teacher*)

Senior House:
Mr A Adams, BSc Hons London (*Physics*, *Chemistry*)
Mrs E Beasley, BA Hons Cambridge (*Geography*)

Miss S Betteridge, BA Hons York (*French, Spanish, Housemistress Latham*)

Mr P Boland, BEng Hons Mc Gill (*Head of Science, Physics*)

Mrs J Cannon, BA Hons Newcastle (*Head of Modern Foreign Languages, Housemistress Butler*)

Mrs M Christensen (*French*)

Mrs J Davison, BA Hons Leicester (*Acting Head of History*)

Mrs J Deadman, BEd Hons Exeter (*Head of KS3, Physical Education*)

Mr J Dodd, BSc Hons Lancaster (*Head of Business and Economics*)

Mrs N Douglass, BA Hons Plymouth (*Head of Art*)

Mrs W Fox, MA Cambridge (*Biology*)

Mr A Gibb, BA Hons Queens (*English, Teacher in Charge of Professional Studies*)

Mrs Z Glenister, BA Hons Newcastle upon Tyne (*German, French, Acting Head KS4*)

Mr J Heath, BSc Hons Loughborough (*Acting Head of Humanities*)

Miss R Hillier, BA Hons Sussex (*Head of Religious Studies, Senior House Mistress*)

Mr R Khumra, BA Hons Liverpool (*Mathematics*)

Mr A Levai, Ministry of Education, Hungary (*History*)

Mr P Macken, BA Hons Essex (*Head of Drama, Head of Co-curricular Learning, Housemaster Temple West*)

Mrs I Martin, MA Cambridge (*Biology*)

Mrs E McNally, BA Hons UWE (*Head of English*)

Miss R Mulchrone, BSc Hons St Mary's Twickenham (*Head of Psychology, Head of Charities*)

Miss R Perry, BA Leeds (*Head of Physical Education*)

Mrs J Phillips, MA Beds (*Head of Expressive Arts and Director of Music*)

Mrs F Qureshi, BSc London (*Head of Mathematics*)

Mrs J Rayat, MA Hons Hertfordshire (*Art*)

Mrs E Roberts, BEd Hons Sheffield (*Food & Nutrition, Textiles, Housemistress Kirk*)

Mrs B Sivaramalingam, MA London (*Mathematics*)

Miss H Snaith, MA Canterbury Christ Church (*Director of ICT and Systems Management*)

Mrs K Stansfield, MA York (*Head of Humanities, History*)

Mrs G Sugrue, BA Hons Northampton (*Support for Learning*)

Mrs G Swart, BA Hons Durham (*French/Spanish*)

Mrs B Taylor, PGD Leeds BA Hons de Montfort (*Head of Support for Learning*)

Miss E Warburton, BSc Hons Warwick (*Chemistry*)

Miss C Wilkins, BA Hons St Mary's Twickenham (*Physical Education, Duke of Edinburgh's Award Coordinator*)

Mrs H Williams, BA Hons Cardiff (*Head of Media Studies, English, UCAS Coordinator*)

Mrs T Wingfield, MA Oxford Brookes (*Chemistry*)

Preparatory Department:

Mrs A Bishop, LLB Liverpool Polytechnic School of Law (*Music Coordinator*)

Mrs S Brereton, BA Hons Leicester (*Y3 Class Teacher, Science*)

Mrs S Burton, BA Leeds (*Teacher of English*)

Mrs M Carney, BA Hons Galway (*Y6 Class Teacher, Head of Prep Department*)

Miss G Connell, BA Hull (*Y1 Class Teacher*)

Dr H Creber, PhD Cardiff (*Y5 Class Teacher, Director of Studies*)

Mrs C Fell, BA Hons Sheffield (*Y2 Class Teacher*)

Mrs L Gibson, NVQ Level 3 (*Teaching Assistant*)

Mrs K Hemsworth, BEd de Montfort (*Physical Education, 11+ Coordinator*)

Mrs M Keal, Level 4 Dyslexia Cert (*Learning Support Assistant*)

Mrs J Kraushar, BSc Bristol (*Science Coordinator*)

Mrs L Louth, BA Hons Kingston (*Y1 Class Teacher*)

Mrs E Roche, BSc Hons Leeds (*KS2 Art/Design Technology Specialist*)

Miss R Rose, BA Hons Plymouth (*EYFS Teacher, Pre Prep Coordinator*)

Mrs C Stuart-Lee, MA Oxon (*French*)

Miss K Sweeney, BA Hons Plymouth (*Y4 Class Teacher*)

Visiting Staff:

Mrs C Cohen, MSc London (*Educational Psychologist*)

Mr P Bresnen (*Tennis*)

Mr M Collins (*Martial Arts*)

Mr R Corden (*Flute, Clarinet, Saxophone*)

Mrs S Firman, British Gymnastics Level 2 Coach (*Gymnastics*)

Mrs P Goldie, Proficiency in Yoga, 200 hour Teacher Training (*Yoga*)

Mrs J Gresham, BA Hons (*Piano*)

Miss K Harding, BA Hons, MPhil Cantab, LTCL (*Cello, Double Bass*)

Mr S Jordan, BA Hons Bristol (*Violin*)

Mr P Mallyon (*Drums*)

Mr J Martin, LTA Licensed Coach (*Tennis*)

Mrs S McPherson, Dip Children & Young People's Work Force (*LAMDA*)

Mrs G Pierozynski, GRNCM, ARNCM (*Piano, Singing*)

Mr A Rodgers, BA Huddersfield (*Brass*)

Mr A Schofield (*Tennis*)

Miss J Stevenson, AGSM (*Singing*)

Miss C Wells (*Classical guitar*)

Mrs R Wheeler, ALCM, CTABRSM, MA (*Piano*)

Mrs K Williamson, BMus (*Voice*)

Non-Teaching Staff:

Mrs Z Arcari, BA Hons (*Head of Marketing*)

Mrs S Chapman, MSc King's College London (*Science Technician*)

Mrs L Chorley (*Administration Assistant*)

Mrs L Dimmock (*Attendance Officer/Receptionist*)

Mr C Gutteridge (*Assistant Caretaker*)

Mrs S Jenkins (*Administration Assistant, First Aid Officer*)

Mrs H Kelly (*Assistant to the Bursar*)

Mr D Long (*Site Manager*)

Mrs S Murray (*Librarian*)

Mrs M Nemec, AAT (*Assistant to the Bursar*)

Mrs C Panayiotou, BA Hons Kent (*Marketing Assistant*)

Mr R Petersen (*Caretaker*)

Mrs Y Rogers (*Examinations Officer*)

Mrs C Sylvester (*PA to the Headmistress*)

Mrs E Szczerbiak (*Registrar*)

St Mary's School
Shaftesbury

Shaftesbury, Dorset SP7 9LP

Tel: 01747 852416 (General Enquiries)
          01747 857111 (Admissions)
Fax: 01747 851557
email: enquiries@stmarys.eu
website: www.stmarys.eu

St Mary's School, Shaftesbury is an outstanding Independent Catholic Boarding and Day School for girls aged 9–18. Situated in the heart of the Dorset countryside, St Mary's offers a very special environment in which girls thrive academically and socially. A strong commitment to traditional values is fostered and girls are inspired to achieve a fulfilling all-round education.

Girls achieve their first-choice University offers as well as Oxbridge success. Inspired to have the courage to face the unexpected and challenge the ordinary girls are encouraged to think globally and work collaboratively with other Mary Ward and CJ schools around the world.

A very happy and friendly school; two-thirds of the school is boarding and everyone here enjoys a real sense of community, staff and pupils alike. Girls are welcomed to the main school from age nine, and at sixteen into the Sixth Form.

Situated in 55 acres of beautiful parkland, St Mary's offers a secure learning environment with excellent facilities and a forward thinking approach. St Mary's is less than two hours by train from London; on the A30 just outside Shaftesbury, it is very accessible for visits and school trips to Salisbury, Bath and the surrounding area.

Houses. There is a junior boarding house and 3 main boarding houses with a modern Upper Sixth Form house. Excellent modern facilities include Rookwood –the academic facility for English, History and Geography and Learning Support and a new art building completed in 2014, complete with a conference centre. This is home to Fine Art, Photography, History of Art, Textiles and Ceramics and is an inspiring and creative work space for the students here.

Admission. The School has its own Entrance Examination held in January for 9+, 11+ and 13+ entry. Sixth Form entry is by testimonial and interview and is then conditional on 5 GCSE passes.

Scholarships and Bursaries. 9+, 11+, 13+ and Sixth Form Scholarships are available in: Academic, Sport, Music, and Art. Catholic Local Primary School scholarships are also awarded.

Additional Head's Scholarships can also be awarded at 9+, 11+, 13+ and 16+.

All Scholarships offer up to 10% remission of day or boarding fees with a further 40% available by a means-tested bursary.

Scholarship Examinations take place in January.

Fees per term (2016–2017). Boarders £6,500–£9,840, Day Girls £5,250–£6,650.

Aims and Curriculum. The School aims to give girls as broad an education as possible, combining academic, personal, spiritual and extra-curricular elements, to foster independent thinking and the opportunity for each girl to realise her own strengths and potential. Girls achieve outstanding results year on year.

In Years 5–9 all girls follow a common curriculum which includes, English, History, Geography, French, Latin, Mathematics, Information Technology, Religious Education, Science, Art, Textiles, Music, Singing, PSE and PE. From Year 10 both the core curriculum: English Language and Literature, Mathematics, One Modern Foreign Language, Religious Education and either Triple or Double Award Science; options are arranged to ensure that each girl follows a balanced course suitable to her ability and interests.

We offer a choice of 22 subjects at A Level in addition to General Studies, General RE, and PE and the Leiths Basic Certificate in Food and Wine as a professional qualification. Some also go on to more vocational forms of Higher Education or pursue their studies in the Creative Arts.

The School is a member of ISCO (Independent Schools Careers Organisation) and all girls receive individual careers advice from the Head of Careers and Guidance.

Music. With a thriving Music Department any orchestral instrument may be learned. In addition there are two school choirs, an orchestra and various instrumental ensembles. Recent bi-annual choir trips have been to Vienna, Rome, Budapest and Venice.

Sport. Winter: Hockey, netball, cross country, swimming and water polo teams with a wide range of additional activities also available such as dance, badminton, volleyball; tag-rugby and football. Summer: Swimming, tennis, rounders, athletics & water polo and also a range of other activities available to choose from. The School has its own Sports Hall, Fitness Suite, floodlit Astroturf and a 25m six-lane indoor swimming pool.

Extra subjects or activities. Speech and drama, ballet, riding, polo, tennis coaching, Duke of Edinburgh's Award, photography, and a wide range of other clubs and societies including book groups, debating, Politics, Science club and many more.

Charitable status. St Mary's School Shaftesbury Trust is a Registered Charity, number 292845. Its aims and objectives are to administer an independent Roman Catholic school for the education of children of any denomination.

Governors:
Major General Sir Sebastian Roberts (*Chair*)
Mr M Farmer
Mr R T Moulding
Dr K Mounde
Mrs B Quest-Ritson
Sister G Simmonds, CJ
Mrs J Watts
Mrs V Younghusband

Senior Management Team:

Headmistress: Mrs M Arnal

Deputy Head: Miss J Walker
Bursar: Mr M Doran
Director of Studies: Dr C Enos
Senior Housemistress: Mrs D Webb

Chaplain:
Miss A Eddy

Resident Priest:
Father Andrew Moore

Leadership Team:
Deputy Head: Miss J Walker
Director of Studies: Dr C Enos
Head of School: Mrs G Cork
Senior Housemistress: Mrs D Webb

Heads of School:
Head of Upper VI: Mr P Daley
Head of Lower VI: Mrs R Vita
Head of Senior School: Mrs S Pugh
Head of Middle School: Mrs G Cork
Head of Lower School: Mrs K Le Poidevin

School Departments:

Administration:
Mrs S Awdry (*Assistant Registrar*)
Mr C Bent (*Head Groundsman*)
Mrs K Bevan (*Reception –Morning*)
Miss L Coffin (*School Office*)
Ms T Goodbody (*Bursar's Assistant*)
Mrs M Gordon (*Accounts & Human Resources Bursar*)
Mrs L Gardiner (*Domestic Bursar*)
Mr C Hedger (*Assistant Caretaker*)
Mr A Watford (*Accounts Assistant*)
Mr R A Pitman (*Caretaker*)
Mrs J Sampson (*Head's PA*)
Mrs J Waterton (*Reception –Afternoon/evenings/weekends*)
Miss D Williams (*Accounts Assistant*)

Art & Design:
*Miss M Bridger
Mrs J Hodge (*Art, Design, Textiles*)
Mrs D Sudlow (*Art, Design*)
Mrs K Banneel (*Art Technician*)

Business Studies:
Mrs E Wimhurst

Careers:
Mrs R Vita

Classics:
*Mr P Daley
Mrs D Clark

Critical Thinking:
Mrs J Bowe

Drama:
*Mr C J Sykes (*MAG&T Coordinator*)
Mrs S Holman

Duke of Edinburgh's Award Scheme:
Mr R Wiltshire
Mr P Daley

Economics:
Mrs G Hurl

English:
*Ms R M R Brand
Mrs H Key
Mr C Sykes

English for Speakers of Other Languages:
Mrs C Waddington

Examinations Officer:
Dr C Enos
Mrs D Whitehead (*Assistant*)

Geography:
*Mrs S Bramble
Mrs D Philips

History:
*Mr T Goodwin
Mrs M Harland

History of Art:
Mrs O Karamenova

House Staff:

Senior Housemistress:
Mrs D Webb

Harewell House:
Mrs S Holman (*Housemistress*)
Mrs S Shutler (*Assistant*)
Mrs J Watts (*Assistant*)

Hewarth House:
Mrs S R Hill (*Housemistress*)
Mrs M Tomlinson (*Assistant*)
Mrs B Wakefield (*Assistant*)

Mary Ward House:
Mrs D Webb (*Housemistress*)
Mrs E Boote (*Assistant*)
Mrs T Richards (*Assistant*)

York House:
Mrs B Roberts (*Housemistress*)
Mrs G Bent (*Assistant*)
Mrs K Bull (*Assistant*)

Newby House:
Mrs D Whitehead (*Housemistress*)
Mrs H Sanger (*Assistant*)
Mrs D Healey (*Assistant*)

ICT:
*Mrs K Le Poidevin

Information and Communication Support:
Mr C Norman (*Head of Information Services*)

Mr A Barnes (*ICT Technician*)
Mr J Davies (*Database Manager*)
Mr C Davis (*ICT Technician*)

Learning Support:
Mrs R Kerby (*Coordinator*)
Mrs Y Atkinson
Mrs R Dixon
Mrs J Kaskow
Mr J O'Hare

Library:
Miss A Edmonds (*Librarian*)

Marketing Manager:
Mrs L Cowan
Ms M Tibbs

Mathematics:
*Mrs L Philips
Mr I Philips
Mr R Wiltshire

Modern Languages:
*Mr J Giblin (*Spanish, French, Italian*)
Mrs G Cork (*French*)
Mrs A Lodder (*French, German*)
Mrs D Webb (*French, Spanish*)

Additional Languages Offered:
Mrs C Waddington (*Portuguese*)

Language Assistants:
Mrs S Abraham (*German*)
Mrs O Green (*Spanish*)
Miss V Raffenne (*French*)

Music:
Mr D Harris (*Director of Music, Piano, Singing*)
Mrs S Pugh (*Head of Instrumental Music, Oboe, Recorder*)
Miss S Williams (*Flute*)

Peripatetic Music:
Mrs K Alder (*Piano, Aural Classes*)
Mrs J Brookfield (*Piano*)
Mrs A Caunce (*Piano*)
Mr P Caunce (*Violin and Viola*)
Miss T Seligman (*Singing*)
Mr J Gilbert (*Percussion*)
Mr R Hill (*Guitar*)
Miss S Lockyer (*Clarinet, Saxophone*)
Mr S Lockyer (*Cello, Double Bass*)
Miss L Lowndes-Northcott (*Harp, Viola, Violin*)
Mrs J Lucas (*Violin and Ukelele*)
Mr C Mahon (*Pipe Organ*)
Miss M Marton (*Singing*)
Mr D Mayo (*Acoustic, Electric Guitar*)
Mr M Newman-Wren (*Brass*)
Mrs J Vivienne (*Singing*)
Miss E Tolfree (*Clarinet, Bassoon, Saxophone*)

Nursing Staff:
Mrs S Savage (*Registered Nurse, Senior Nurse*)
Mrs E Crossley (*Senior Health Care Worker*)
Mrs L Fish (*Registered Nurse*)
Mrs A Horak (*Health Care Worker*)

Personal and Social Education:
*Miss J Walker

Physical Education:
Mrs N Boyer-Castle (*Director of Sport*)
Mrs K Booth
Mrs E James
Mrs B Roberts (*Pool Manager*)
Miss J Walker

PE Coaching:
Mr I Griffin (*Tennis*)
Mrs V Peck (*Tennis*)

Psychology:
Miss S Williams

Religious Education:
*Mrs J Bowe
Miss A Le Guevel
Mrs C Watson

Science:
Dr G Caunt (*Biology*)
Dr C Enos (*Chemistry*)
Mrs A Fearnley (*Chemistry*)
Miss S Flower (*Biology*)
Mrs K Le Poidevin (*Biology*)
Mrs D Kok (*Physics*)
Mrs Y Leece (*Science Technician*)
Mrs C Gray (*Science Technician*)

Speech and Drama:
Mrs S Holman
Mrs H Earle
Mr S Earle

St Nicholas' School

Redfields House, Redfields Lane, Church Crookham, Fleet, Hampshire GU52 0RF

Tel: 01252 850121
Fax: 01252 850718
email: headspa@st-nicholas.hants.sch.uk
website: www.st-nicholas.hants.sch.uk

Motto: *Confirma Domine Serviendo*

St Nicholas' School is a small independent day school for girls aged 3–16 and boys 3–7. Founded in 1935 in Branksomewood Road, Fleet, the school moved to Redfields House, Redfields Lane, Church Crookham in 1996. Redfields House, a Victorian Mansion, is set in 27 acres of glorious parkland and playing fields.

Branksomewood, the Nursery and Infant department, retains the original name of the road where the school was founded. Being built of natural wood with a wonderful airy atmosphere this building gives light and space to our younger children, creating a calming environment in which they thrive. With an adventure playground set in the woods, a large hall fitted with PE equipment, overlooking the grounds and our experienced teaching staff, it is no wonder the children are so happy.

St Nicholas' Junior department is based in Redfields House itself which keeps the charm of the old family house with its oak panelling and the senior department is located in the newer part of the school behind. All three departments have benefited from several building projects.

In December 2000 an Olympic-size sports hall opened with netball and tennis courts, showers, changing rooms and a viewing gallery. This has enhanced the sports lessons and enabled even more sports competitions as well as extra-curricular activities. Badminton, tennis, netball, volleyball and basketball may be played throughout the year.

Spring 2006 saw yet another addition with the opening of the art, design technology and textiles centre, offering three spacious rooms with large work benches, and a kiln for pottery. By having this wonderful new building it opened an opportunity for the school to adapt the old art centre into several music practice rooms. Tuition in the violin, piano, guitar, harp, drums as well singing, woodwind and brass is offered.

In November 2009 The Pritchard Hall, named after the school's founder, was unveiled. The performing arts centre has raked seating for over 330, in the semi round, with an orchestra pit, concerts and plays are staged regularly. The drama department has in addition two studios.

September 2013 welcomed the opening of state-of-the-art laboratories for juniors and seniors. The classrooms include teaching areas as well as practical learning spaces in a bright and welcoming environment.

2016 will see the development of an all-weather pitch and two new tennis courts. The new sand-based AstroTurf will be floodlit and provide pupils with a multi-use sports facility including hockey, tennis and netball. The tennis courts will also be floodlit. Hockey, athletics and rounders take place on the games field and the floodlit courts are used all year round.

Pupils come to St Nicholas' from Hampshire, Surrey and Berkshire. School buses operate from Farnham, Odiham, Fleet, Basingstoke, Camberley, Yateley, Aldershot and Farnborough. Situated just off the A287, Hook to Farnham road, junction 5 of the M3 is approximately 4 miles short away.

Religion. The school is a Christian foundation but children of other faiths are welcomed. Assemblies are held each morning. Children are encouraged to show tolerance, compassion and care for others.

Curriculum. St Nicholas' offers an extended day, from 8 am to 6 pm. Academic standards are high and a balanced curriculum is offered. Small classes place greater emphasis on the individual and pupils are encouraged to achieve their full potential in every area of school life. The curriculum is kept as broad as possible until the age of fourteen when choices are made for GCSE. The option choices vary year by year depending upon the girls' abilities and talents. On average each girl sits ten subjects at GCSE. More than twenty subjects are offered at this level. A carefully structured personal development course incorporates a Careers programme. Our girls move confidently on to enter sixth form colleges or scholarships to senior independent schools. Choir, drama and music thrive within the school and there are frequent performances which enable the girls to develop self-confidence.

Physical Education. Pupils take part in inter-school and local district sports matches: hockey, netball and cross-country in winter; and tennis, athletics and swimming in summer. Rounders and lacrosse are also played.

Entry. Children may enter at any stage subject to interview, school report and waiting list. Scholarships and Bursaries are available. For 11+ candidates there is an entrance examination.

Fees per term (2016–2017). Infants Reception & Year 1 £3,300, Year 2 £3,380; Juniors (Years 3 to 4) £3,775; Juniors (Years 5 to 6) £3,850; Senior School £4,510. Nursery: £9.00 per hour.

Further Information. The prospectus is available upon request from the Registrar. The Headmistress is pleased to meet parents by appointment.

Charitable status. St Nicholas' School is a Registered Charity, number 307341. It exists to provide high quality education for children.

Chair of Governors: Mr G Cockayne

Headmistress: **Annette V Whatmough**, BA Hons Bristol, CertEd

Deputy Head –Pastoral: Caroline Egginton, BEd Hons London

Deputy Head –Academic: Christine Moorby, BSc Hons Southampton, CertEd

Teaching Staff:
Josephine Allen, BA Hons QTS West of England (*Key Stage 2*)

Alison Audino, BEd Hons Bath (*Food Technology*)

Florence Ayache, BA Hons Glamorgan, QTS (*Spanish & French*)

Helen Barnes, BA Ed Hons Exeter (*Key Stage 2*)

Jenny Brackstone, BA Hons Nottingham, PGCE (*Key Stages 3 & 4*)

Nicky Brooks, BA Hons Exeter, PGCE (*Key Stage 2*)

Sarah Carter, BEd Hons Southampton (*Key Stage 2*)

Janet Coombe, BA Hons Manchester, PGCE (*Geography*)

Isabel Cook, BA Hons Southampton, PGCE (*Head of History*)

Nicola Dale, BA Hons Surrey, PGCE (*Key Stage 2*)

Deborah Di Carlo, BA Hons Central Saint Martins, PGCE

Josie Downer, BA Hons Leeds, MA King's (*Head of Drama*)

Barbara Edwards, BA Hons Sheffield, PGCE (*English*)

Amy Franke, BMus Hons Surrey, MMus (*Music*)

Brenda Green, CertEd, CNAA (*Director of Sport*)

Edwina Grosse, BA Hons Trent (*Head of Art*)

Rosalie Hague, BA Hons Lancaster, PGCE (*Head of English*)

Valerie Helliwell, BEng Hons Liverpool, PGCE (*Head of Mathematics, Examinations Officer*)

Laura Homer, BA Hons Wales, PGCE (*Key Stage 1*)

Pilar Kimber, MA Reading (*Latin & Classical Civilisation*)

Janice R King, BSc Hons London, PGCE (*Head of Biology*)

Alexandra Lawrence, MA Oxon, PGCE (*Head of Modern Languages*)

Deborah Martin, BA Hons Surrey (*Mathematics*)

Julie Merker, BA OU, CertEd (*PE*)

Michelle Morgan, NNEB (*Nursery*)

Paul Nicholls, BA Hons London (*Key Stage 2*)

Virginia Pearson, Perf Cert RAM, LTCL, ARCM (*Part-time music*)

Tracy Perrett, BEd Sussex (*Head of Juniors*)

Benjamin Pont, BMus Hons (*Director of Music*)

Joanna Pont, BMus Hons (*String Tutor*)

Lee Render, BA Hons QTS Surrey (*Head of Infants*)

Lisa Ruffell, BA Hons QTS Surrey (*Key Stage 2*)

Jane Stansbury, BEd Cambridge, PG SpLD Kingston (*Curriculum Support*)

Michelle Strevens, BEd, CNAA (*Foundation Stage*)

Julia Tiley, BA Hons QTS Kingston (*Head of Foundation Stage*)

Jane Tomlinson, BA Hons London, PGCE (*Modern Languages*)

Frances van Heerden, BSc Natal, UED (*Science*)

Suzanne Walch, BA Hons OU (*Head of Curriculum Support*)

Catherine Williams, BA Hons Salford (*Head of IT*)

Xinsheng Zhang, MEd Johannesburg SA (*Chinese Mandarin*)

Peripatetic Music:

Wendy Busby, BMus Hons (*Voice*)

Tamasin Cline, BMus Hons (*Violin*)

Rebekah Duncalfe, BMus (*Violin*)

Sylvia Ellison, BA Hons, PG Dip RCM (*Oboe*)

Susan Gillis, PG Dip Mtpp, ALCM, LLCM (*Piano*)

Claire Hickling, BMus Hons (*Piano, Flute*)

Claire Hasted, BMus Hons (*Violin*)

Melanie Hornsby, BMus Royal Academy of Music, London (*Violin*)

Oksana Maxwell, LTCL, (*Piano*)

Valerie Mitchell, LRAM (*Piano, Cello*)

Austin Pepper, ALCM (*Brass*)

Rachel Riordan, Adv Teaching RSM (*Saxophone, Clarinet*)

Administration:

Teaching Assistant: Tania Negus

School Nurse: Sarah Watkins, RGN, NNEB

Bursar: Tarn Canning, ACCA

Payroll & Pensions Administration: Debbie Smitherman

Headmistress's PA: Dawn Brown, FInstAM, FGPA

Marketing & Admissions Registrar: Tammi Townley, BA Hons Greenwich

School Secretary: Sarah Watkins

Laboratory Technician: Michele Axton, BA OU

Catering: Chartwells, Compass Group PLC

Maintenance: Marurice Readman, Paul Rippingale, Joseph Carrig, Peter White

Caretaker: Robert Crail

Bus Driver: Timothy Hunt, Glenn Shearer

Second Hand Uniform Shop: Maureen Mullins

Librarian: Sarah Stokes

St Paul's Girls' School

Brook Green, Hammersmith, London W6 7BS

Tel:	School Office: 020 7603 2288
	Admissions: 020 7605 4882
	Business Director: 020 7605 4881
Fax:	020 7602 9932
email:	admissions@spgs.org
website:	www.spgs.org

Founded in 1904 as one of the first purpose-built schools for girls, St Paul's embraces both tradition and innovation. The emphasis on liberal learning established by the first High Mistress, Frances Gray, and Director of Music, Gustav Holst, finds expression today in an academically challenging curriculum, which encourages intellectual freedom, discovery and the joy of scholarship.

St Paul's is committed to providing an outstanding academic education within a highly supportive environment. Girls regularly achieve exceptional results (over 57% A* at A Level and 93% at GCSE in 2016), but the school aims to teach far beyond the prescribed curriculum, endowing girls with a lifelong love of learning and the necessary tools of scholarship and enterprise. It is also the opportunities outside the classroom which make a St Paul's education distinctive. Most of the 100+ clubs and societies are run by pupils –for pupils –and new ones are created every year to reflect passion and demand. Girls are given leadership opportunities and an environment in which to experiment, innovate and push boundaries. Girls follow a traditional liberal education and are prepared for GCSE and IGCSE in Year 11; alternative school directed courses in art, drama and music are also offered for this age group. Sixth form students are offered 23 subjects at A Level or Pre-U, and are prepared for university entrance by our specialist higher education and careers advisory team. Virtually all students go on to study at major universities in the UK and the USA, with about 40 per cent going to Oxbridge annually. The creative and performing arts are at the heart of school life. Since its foundation music has always been a particularly strong feature with well over half the student body taking instrumental lessons; there are also multiple orchestras, choirs and ensembles on offer. Art and design benefit from studio and workshop facilities and there are several major exhibitions of students' work every year. Drama enjoys a purpose-built theatre and drama studio and any girl can direct her own production. Indeed, facilities are some of the best offered by a central London school with extensive sporting facilities on site. All girls from Year 7 are placed in small tutor groups of no more than 12 girls to ensure the highest standards of pastoral care. The main ages of admission are 11 and 16. There are currently 747 girls on the roll. The school is committed to making a St Paul's education available to the brightest girls whatever their means and has an active development campaign dedicated to raising funds for that purpose.

Scholarships. *The Ogden Trust Science Scholarship* (16+) is a means-tested award which may be available to a successful senior candidate who is entering the school and who wishes to study Physics and Mathematics. The Ogden Trust has specific criteria and applications for the scholarship are made via the school.

Junior Music Scholarships (11+) to the value of lessons in two instruments/voice, currently worth £1,560 per annum, tenable for five years when scholars will be able to apply for a 16+ scholarship in Year 11 for their final two years at St Paul's

Senior Music Scholarships (16+) to the value of lessons in two instruments/voice, currently worth £1,560 per annum, tenable for two years *(choral awards up to the value of one lesson in voice may be available)*. External candidates must be successful in the Senior School entrance examination.

Senior Art Scholarships (16+) of the value of £250 per annum are offered to up to two internal and two external candidates who are currently in their final GCSE year and who, if applying from another school, have previously been successful in the Senior School entrance examination. Candidates take part in a workshop and are also required to submit a portfolio.

Bursaries. *Junior Bursaries* (11+) to a value of up to full fee remission based on proven financial need subject to annual review are available. Candidates must be successful in the 11+ entrance examination. The number of Junior bursaries available each year will vary.

Senior Bursaries (16+) to a value of up to full fee remission based on proven financial need subject to annual review are available for candidates who have been successful in the Senior School entrance examination and who are currently in their final GCSE year at another school.

Fees per term (2016–2017). £7,671, including lunches and personal accident insurance, and excluding textbooks. The fees per term for new entrants entering at 16+ are £8,247.

Registration & Examination Fee £125.

Charitable status. St Paul's Girls' School is a Registered Charity, number 1119613, and a Company Limited by Guarantee, registered in England, number 6142007 and is governed by its Memorandum and Articles of Association. It exists to promote the education of girls in Greater London. The sole member of the charitable company is the Mercers' Company.

Governors:
Chairman: The Hon Timothy Palmer
Deputy Chairman: Ms Kate Bingham
Mr Mark Aspinall
Mrs Zeina Bain
Mr Nicolas Chisholm MBE
Professor Henrietta Harrison
Mrs Gillian Low
Mrs Dervilla Mitchell CBE
Miss Cally Palmer CBE
Miss Judith Portrait OBE
Professor Jane Ridley
Dr Julia Riley

Clerk to the Governors: Mrs Nicola Goodfellow

High Mistress: Ms Clarissa Farr, MA Exeter

Deputy Head, Director of School:
Mr Paul Vanni, MA London (*Modern Languages*)

Deputy Head, Director of Studies:
Mr Andrew Ellams, MA Oxon (*Economics*)

Deputy Head, Director of Senior School:
Mr Will le Fleming, BA Cantab (*English*)

Deputy Head, Director of Pastoral Care:
Mrs Su Wijeratna, BA Birmingham (*Geography*)

Mrs Gillian Abbott, MA St Andrews (*Geography*)
Ms Kathryn Arblaster, BA Oxon, MSc MPhil Imperial (*Biology*)
Miss Elizabeth Armstrong, BSc Exeter, MRes Lancaster (*Geography*)
Mr Tim Askew, BA Oxon (*History*)
Miss Helen Barff, BA Goldsmiths College, MA Camberwell (*Art and Design*)
Revd Mrs Vanessa Baron, MA Cantab, BSc City (*Religious Studies*)
Mr Wayne Barron, BA Cantab (*Classics*)
Miss Sandra Barth, BA Martin-Luther-Universität Halle-Wittenberg (*Modern Languages*)
Miss Mekhla Barua, BSc Warwick (*Mathematics*)
Miss Jessica Basch, BA Eastern MA Eastern (*Physical Education*)
Mrs Paola Bianchi, MEng Cagliari (*Mathematics*)
Mr Allyn Blake, BSc Imperial (*Mathematics*)
Mrs Lucy Bond, BSc Exeter (*Biology*)
Miss Clare Brashaw, MA Leeds (*Art and Design*)
Mr Jonathan Bromley, BA Oxon (*History*)
Mr Spencer Buksh, BSc London (*Mathematics*)
Mr Matthew Bunning, BA Cantab (*Art and Design*)
Mrs Birgit Cassens, MA Christian Albrechts Universitaet Kiel (*Modern Languages*)
Mrs Rachel Chamberlin, BSc Durham (*Geography*)
Ms Mathilde Ciais, BA Toulouse (*Modern Languages*)
Miss Sophie Corthine, BA Durham (*Physical Education*)
Ms Liza Coutts, MA Oxon, MA London (*History*)
Mr Ian Crane, BSc Durham (*Mathematics*)
Miss Gill D'Lima, BSc St Andrews (*Mathematics*)
Mr Alexander Daglish, BA Plymouth (*Art and Design*)
Ms Suzanne Debney, BA Rose Bruford (*Drama*)
Miss Marjorie Delage, BA Limoges (*Modern Languages*)
Dr Phoebe Dickerson, BA, MPhil, PhD Cantab (*English*)
Mrs Marianna Doria, MChem Oxon, MSc Imperial (*Chemistry*)
Ms Alice Dvorakova (*Modern Languages*)
Mr Anthony Ellison, BSc Nottingham (*Chemistry*)
Miss Katherine Evans, BA London (*History of Art*)
Miss Emilie Eymin, BA Toulouse, MA Toulouse/London (*Modern Languages*)
Mrs Danu Fenton, BA Oxon, MA Courtauld (*History*)
Mrs Hannah Filippi, BA Edinburgh (*Religious Studies*)
Miss Isabel Foley, BA London (*Drama*)
Miss Megan Folley, BA Edinburgh (*Physical Education*)
Miss Kate Frank, BA London, MA London (*Modern Languages*)
Mrs Hannah Fussner, BA Oxon, MA Stanford, USA (*Learning Support*)
Miss Penelope Garcia-Rodriguez, BA Oviedo, Spain, MA London (*Modern Languages*)
Miss Anna Gibbs, BA Oxon (*Economics*)
Ms Blanche Girouard, BA Oxon (*Religious Studies*)
Mr Roger Green, MA Kent (*Mathematics*)
Miss Emily Hardy, BA Cantab (*English*)
Miss Elizabeth Hodges, BA Wolverhampton Polytechnic, MA Royal College of Art (*Art and Design*)
Dr Anna Holland, BA Oxon, DPhil (*Classics*)
Dr Philip Jackson, BSc Sussex, PhD London (*Chemistry*)
Mrs Amy Kember, MChem Oxon (*Chemistry*)
Mrs Manuela Knight, BA Milan (*Modern Languages*)
Dr Kingston Koo, BSc Warwick, PhD London (*Physics*)
Mrs Nina Lau, BSc London (*Biology*)
Mr John Lee, BA Oxon, BA London (*Mathematics*)
Dr Kate Lee, BSc Witwatersrand, MSc Cape Town, PhD London (*Physics*)
Miss Hsiang-Ju Lin, BA Soochow, MA London (*Modern Languages*)

Miss Gill MacMillan, BSc Nottingham Trent (*Physical Education*)

Ms Paula Mahoney-Velez, MA Cordoba (*Modern Languages*)

Mr Rory Malone, BA Harvard (*Economics*)

Ms Silvana Marconini, BA Turin (*Modern Languages*)

Miss Daniella Mardell, MA Cantab, MEd Cantab (*Modern Languages*)

Mrs Hélène May, MA aggregation Sorbonne (*Modern Languages*)

Mr Paul McDonald, BA Oxon, MSc LSE (*Mathematics*)

Mr Richard Michell, BA Bristol, MA Chelsea School of Art (*Art and Design*)

Mrs Jo Moran, BA London (*Information Technology*)

Dr Joanna Moriarty, BSc Birmingham, PhD Reading (*Biology*)

Dr Joshua Newton, BA Reed, PhD Cantab (*History*)

Mrs Irina Ninnis, BA Moscow and London (*Modern Languages*)

Miss Narelle O'Byrne, BPhysEd Otago, NZ (*Physical Education*)

Miss Sarah O'Connor, BA Cantab (*Chemistry*)

Mr Dipesh Patel, BSc Bristol (*Mathematics*)

Dr Jonathan Patrick, BA, DPhil Oxon (*English*)

Mr Roger Paul, BA Norwich, ARCO (*Music*)

Miss Emma Payler, BSc London (*Biology*)

Mr Tom Peck, BA Manchester (*History and Politics*)

Dr Alexandra Randolph, MA Oxon, PhD Nottingham (*Mathematics*)

Mrs Jocelyne Rapinac, MA Aix-Marseille (*Modern Languages*)

Mr Matthew Reeve, BSc Newcastle (*Biology*)

Miss Jessamy Reynolds, MA St Andrews (*Classics*)

Mrs Julie Runacres, MA Cantab, MA London (*English*)

Ms Leonie Rushforth, BA Cantab (*English*)

Ms Kaarin Scanlan, BA Bristol (*Physical Education*)

Dr Jemma Senczyszyn, MChem York, PhD Manchester (*Chemistry*)

Mrs Alexandra Shamloll, MA Cantab (*Mathematics*)

Mrs Holly Shao, BSc Hunan, China (*Modern Languages*)

Dr Clare Sharp, MA, DPhil Oxon (*Classics*)

Dr Marcin Slaski, BSc Krakow, PhD Krakow (*Physics*)

Mrs Kate Snook, MA, MPhil St Andrews (*History*)

Ms Claire Suthren, BA Cantab (*Classics*)

Miss Jessica Tipton, BA Bristol, MA London (*Modern Languages*)

Miss Faith Turner, BA York (*English and Drama*)

Dr Damon Vosper Singleton, MMath Oxon, PhD London (*Mathematics*)

Dr Sarah Wah, MA Leeds, DPhil Cantab (*English*)

Mrs Victoria Watkins, BA Lancaster (*Drama*)

Miss Mary Wenham, BA Oxon (*Modern Languages*)

Miss Sydne Wick, BA Queen's University of Charlotte (*Physical Education*)

Mrs Victoria Whiffin, MEng Southampton (*Physics*)

Mr Gregory Wilsdon, MA Oxon, MBA Stanford (*Classics*)

Ms Kirsten Wilson, BA Oxon (*Geography*)

Ms Jane Zeng, BSc Guangzhan, China (*Modern Languages*)

Director of Music:
Mr Leigh O'Hara, BA York, MMus London

Deputy Director of Music and Head of Singing:
Miss Heidi Pegler, BA Cardiff, LTCL

Head of Keyboard:
Miss Alexis White, BMus RNCM, MMus Eastman School of Music, NY

Head of Strings:
Miss Hilary Sturt, AGSM, ARCM (*Viola and Violin*)

Head of Wind & Brass:
Mr Matthew Dickinson, BA Nottingham, GSMD Guildhall (*Percussion, Drum Kit*)

Composer in Residence:
Dr Bernard Hughes, MA Oxon, MMus London, PhD London

Music Department Manager:
Miss Gabbi Freemantle, BA Durham, MMus London

Miss Charlotte Ansbergs, LRAM, Dip RAM (*Violin*)

Mr Edward Barry, Dip Mus, LTCL (*Violin*)

Mrs Emily Bates, BA, MSTAT (*Alexander Technique*)

Ms Lisa Beckley, MA Oxon (*Singing*)

Ms Anna Boucher, BA Durham (*Singing*)

Ms Emma Brain-Gabbott, BA Cantab (*Singing*)

Mr Andrew Brownell, DMusA Guildhall, FRCO (*Piano*)

Ms Alexia Cammish, MA Cantab, MA GSMD, LGSMDT (*Horn*)

Mrs Jane Clark-Maxwell, BMus London, AKC, LTCL (*Singing*)

Mr Adam Cooke, MusB Manchester, MMus GSMD (*Brass*)

Miss Jane Fisher, LTCL, PGCE (*Flute*)

Mr John Flinders, BA York, LGSM (*Piano*)

Miss Carolyn Foulkes, GRSM, LRAM, ARAM, Dip Adv Studies (*Singing*)

Ms Gill Hopkin, GRNCM, ARNCM, PGCE (*Violin*)

Mr John Langley, BA (*Theory*)

Mr Mornington Lockett, BA (*Saxophone*)

Miss Naadia Manington, BMus, LGSM (*Jazz Piano, Piano*)

Miss Hannah Marcinowicz (*Saxophone, Clarinet*)

Ms Bridget Mermikides, LRAM (*Singing*)

Mr Alexander Mobbs, BMus (*Double Bass*)

Miss Amanda Morrison, BA (*Singing*)

Miss Helen Neilson, BSc, PG Dip Adv RCM, MMus (*Cello*)

Ms Jessica O'Leary, BMus, Dip CSM, LTCL, LRAM (*Violin, Viola*)

Ms Emma Ramsdale, GRSM, LRAM, Dip RAM, ARAM (*Harp*)

Mr Daniel Roberts (*Strings*)

Mr Mark Rose, BMus London, MMus London (*Guitar*)

Mr Neil Roxburgh, Dip RCM, ARCM, ARCT (*Piano*)

Miss Julie Ryan, ARCM (*Trumpet*)

Miss Rachel Shannon, MA Cantab, RAM (*Singing*)

Mr Nicholas Shaw, BA Oxon, Diploma RCO, MMus London (*Organ*)

Ms Janet Shell, BEd Lancaster, AGSM

Miss Erica Simpson, ARAM, ARCM (*Cello*)

Mr James Sleigh, ARCM, Hon ARAM (*Viola*)

Ms Louise Strickland, BMus, MMus, LGSMD (*Recorder*)

Mrs Sarah Stroh, BMus, Dip Dist RAM, LRAM (*Singing*)

Ms Shelagh Sutherland, ARAM, LRAM, STAT (*Piano, Alexander Technique*)

Ms Sarah Thurlow, MMus, Dip RCM (*Clarinet*)

Miss Emma Tingey, LWCMD, ACC PG Dip (*Harp*)

Ms Seaming To, BMus RNCM (*Singing*)

Miss Judith Treggor, BMus Connecticut (*Flute*)

Ms Frith Trezevant, ARCM, LTCL (*Music Education and Speech & Drama*)

Ms Joanne Turner, Dip RCM, ARCM (*Bassoon, Flute*)

Miss Enloc Wu, ARCM, LRSM (*Piano*)

Ms Masumi Yamamoto, MMus QCGU Brisbane, PG Dip RAM, PG Dip TCM, LRAM (*Harpsichord*)

Mrs Fiona York, AGSM (*Piano*)

Director of Operations: Ms Barbara Sussex, BA, MPhil Birmingham

Assistant to the High Mistress: Mrs Lindy Hayward, BA Open

Admissions Officer: Miss Claire Richardson, BA Cantab

Librarian: Mrs Linda Kelley, BA Manchester, MSc UCE

St Swithun's School

Alresford Road, Winchester, Hampshire SO21 1HA

Tel: 01962 835700
Fax: 01962 835779
email: office@stswithuns.com
website: www.stswithuns.com
Twitter: @st_swithuns
Facebook: /StSwithunsSchool

St Swithun's is a modern and flourishing educational organisation. The school is set on an impressive and attractive campus of 45 acres in the South Downs National Park on the outskirts of Winchester. It offers girls excellent teaching, sporting and recreational facilities.

The school offers weekly boarding and full boarding and day options for girls aged 11–18. At present the senior school (girls aged 11–18) has 294 day girls and 216 boarders. There is an adjoining Junior School for girls aged 3–11 and boys from 3–7 years (*see Junior School entry in IAPS section*).

Ethos. St Swithun's is an 'appropriately academic' school which means that we celebrate intellectual curiosity and the life of the mind, but not to the exclusion of all else. We expect our pupils to develop individual passions and through them to acquire a range of skills and characteristics. These characteristics will include a willingness to take risks, to question and to debate, and to persevere in the face of difficulty. In the words of Samuel Beckett: "Ever tried. Ever failed. No matter. Try again. Fail again. Fail better." If a girl can immediately excel at everything we ask of her, we as educators must set the bar higher.

We want all girls to learn about life beyond the school gates, to appreciate the rich variety of our world, to develop an understanding of compassion and to value justice. We encourage all pupils to become involved in fundraising and community work. They should appreciate how their decisions and their actions can affect those around them.

St Swithun's was founded by Anna Bramston, daughter of the Dean of Winchester, and Christian values underpin our approach to education. We provide a civilised and caring environment in which all girls and staff are valued for their individual gifts and encouraged to develop a sense of spirituality and of kindness. We believe that kindness and tolerance are at the heart of any fully functioning community.

Location. The school is on a rural site in Winchester's 'green belt' but only a short distance from the city centre. It is easily accessible from Heathrow and Gatwick airports and is one hour from London by car (via the M3 motorway). There is a frequent train service to London Waterloo (one hour). We also offer a popular London taxi service from St Swithun's School to London on a Friday evening and a return journey on Sunday.

Curriculum. Girls at St Swithun's benefit from a broad and balanced curriculum that promotes individual choice and achievement. The timetable is designed to enable each pupil to fulfil her intellectual, physical and creative potential through a dynamic range of purposeful lessons and activities.

From their first years here girls are taught to examine social, cultural and moral issues so that they can make informed decisions about their own way of living as well as respecting the values of each individual. The PSHEE & citizenship programme is tailored for each year group and is delivered through a range of school activities and specialist speakers.

All girls follow an enrichment programme known as Stretch. This consists of taught short courses and lectures from visiting speakers. Courses are wide-ranging and topics such as magic and mathematics, biblical Hebrew, cryptic crosswords and French cinema. M5 girls will use Stretch to undertake community service.

Games and PE are taught throughout the school so that girls can participate in a wide range of team and individual sports. Both in lessons and as recreational activities, the emphasis is on personal enjoyment and the development of a healthy, active life, but all pupils receive expert coaching and the most talented individuals and teams are entered into county, regional and national competitions.

Learning support provides bespoke support for individual girls who may be experiencing difficulties in aspects of their academic studies.

Girls take 9 or 10 GCSE exams to allow time for other interests and activities. Everyone takes English language, English literature, mathematics, at least two sciences and one modern foreign language. The girls then choose a further three or four subjects from a choice of 13. Girls are encouraged to take at least one humanity or social science to ensure a breadth of knowledge and skills.

In the sixth form girls are offered 22 subjects from which they choose four at A Level (five if maths and further maths are chosen). Advice is given about the implications for their choice of university, degree course and career to ensure sensible combinations. Some girls choose to follow courses in subjects which are not offered at GCSE. Over half the sixth form study at least one science subject at A Level. Girls normally continue with three of their lower sixth subjects to complete three full A Levels.

In addition, all sixth-formers may choose to do the Extended Project Qualification (EPQ). This is worth half an A Level and is graded from A*–E. The qualification gives girls the opportunity to research an area of personal interest. Universities recognise the value of the skills required for the qualification and it attracts UCAS tariff points. Italian GCSE is also available in the sixth form.

Religion. The school is a Church of England foundation. There are close ties with Winchester Cathedral, where termly services and the annual confirmation and carol services are held. A full-time chaplain prepares girls for confirmation. There is a newly converted chapel at the heart of the school.

Music. From the first hymn in the morning to the final applause on concert nights every day is enriched by music and the school enjoys a fine reputation for the excellence and variety that girls achieve. Through lessons, practice, rehearsals, exams, competitions, performances and cathedral services, the girls are drawn together to make the most of a busy and ambitious musical life: 75% have instrumental lessons and there is a choice of twenty-two instruments to study. Twenty flourishing school ensembles create a wealth of music and everyone is welcome to join in. Our most accomplished musicians are also cathedral choristers or play in county and national groups. There are endless possibilities at St Swithun's whether it is Renaissance church music, African drumming or 21st century pop music that girls wish to study, listen to, compose or perform. They are taught to appreciate many different styles of music from all over the world and from different historical eras. Learning to compose enables some to express themselves through music and we encourage performing as an integral part of what we offer. Learning a musical instrument and sharing this with an audience requires a high standard of creativity, commitment, technique and courage.

Sports. All girls are encouraged to be involved in sport throughout their time at the school. Sport at St Swithun's has so much to offer, emphasising cooperation, leadership, teamwork, competition and respect. Our girls learn how to deal with success and failure, how to be self-disciplined and how to communicate with each other. We expect every girl to try her best in every area of school life and sport is no exception. Many girls represent their county, region or even country in sports as diverse as lacrosse, fencing, diving, athletics and tennis and we are naturally very proud of these individuals. However, whilst we celebrate success and our teams aspire to excellence, we value effort and sportsmanship as much as winning and we are proud to run first, second and sometimes third teams for all age groups.

Of supreme importance to us is identifying at least one sport to suit each girl so that she will acquire a lifelong enjoyment of exercise.

Facilities. The original school building contains the main teaching rooms and libraries and has been extended and developed to provide specialist areas for languages, information technology, food and textiles and careers. The science wing contains eight fully equipped modern laboratories and project rooms. In addition, there is an art, design and technology centre and a performing arts building was opened in 2003. This has a 600-seat main auditorium and two smaller performance spaces. A new library, careers and ICT facility was opened in 2007.

School Houses. There are 6 boarding houses and 4 day girl houses, each staffed by a housemistress and assistant who take pride in the high level of pastoral care offered to each girl. The junior house is for girls aged 11 who are then transferred to one of the senior houses after a year. They remain in the senior house until they have completed one year in the sixth form. The upper sixth house is for boarders and day girls together, with study-bedrooms for boarders, study facilities for day girls and common rooms and kitchen for all.

Careers. Most girls continue to university, including Oxford and Cambridge, and all continue to some form of higher education and training. Each girl is counselled by one of the team of careers staff in a well-resourced department. Lectures and video presentations are organised frequently and a careers fair held annually.

Leisure Activities. There is an extensive range of co-curricular activities and an organised programme of visits and activities at the weekend. Girls participate in the Duke of Edinburgh's Award scheme, Young Enterprise and local community service work. The sixth form are able to assist with Stretch activities and this can count towards their UCAS tariff. Each year there are drama productions as well as regular drama activities. There are many overseas study and activity trips which include visits to Uganda to meet pupils from St Katherine's, our sister school, volunteer work, language trips, ski trips and watersports holidays.

Health. The school health centre forms part of the main buildings. It is staffed by qualified RGNs and visited by the school doctor twice a week.

Entrance. Entry is by means of a pre-test and the Common Entrance examination for Independent Schools. The majority of girls enter the senior school at the age of 11 or 13 years, but girls are accepted at other ages, including the sixth form, subject to satisfactory tests.

Scholarships and Bursaries. Academic scholarships, carrying a fee subsidy of up to 20%, are available for day girls and boarders entering the school at 11+, at 13+ and to the sixth form.

Music scholarships carry a subsidy of up to 20% and provide free tuition on two instruments; exhibitions provide free tuition on one instrument. Music scholars can apply for a means-tested award of up to 100% of school fees.

Sports scholarships may be awarded each year to suitable applicants at 11+ and 13+. These scholarships will have a maximum value of 20% fee remission.

Bursaries of up to 100% of school fees are available for girls who meet the school's entrance criteria. All bursaries are subject to means-testing.

Fees per term (2016–2017). Senior School: Boarders £10,456; Day Girls £6,525. Junior School: £1,655–£4,265.

Charitable status. St Swithun's School Winchester is a Registered Charity, number 307335. It exists to provide education for girls aged 11–18 years.

Visitor: The Bishop of Winchester, The Right Reverend Tim Dakin

School Council:
Chairman: Professor Natalie Lee, LLB
The Right Worshipful, the Mayor of Winchester Cllr Jane Rutter (*ex officio*)
The Dean of Winchester (*ex officio*)
The Headmaster of Winchester College (*ex officio*)
Mr Tom Bremridge
Mr Luke Meynell, MA
Mrs Sarah Parrish, MA Cantab, FIET, FBCS, CITP
Mrs Anna-Louise Peters, BSc, ACA
Mr Martin Reid, MA, FCA (*Treasurer, ex officio*)
Ms Margaret Rudland, BSc, PGCE
Mr Mike Wilson, BA
Mrs Frances Robinson, LLB Hons
Mr Jonathan Russell, BSc Hons, MSc
Dr Claire Thorne, BA Hons, MSc, PhD
Andrew Lilley, LLB
Mrs Julia Eager, BEd, MSc
Prof R Adam, DipArch, RIBA, FRSA
Mrs Emma Clancey, BA Hons

Headmistress: Ms Jane Gandee, MA Cantab

Deputy Headmistress: Mrs Alison Burns-Cox, BSc London
Deputy Head Academic: Mr Charlie Hammel, AB Princeton, MLitt St Andrews
Head of Professional Practice: Miss Alison Oliver, BA Warwick
Bursar and Clerk to the Council: Mr Matthew Carter, FCMI
Director of Marketing and Development: Mr Simon Mayes, BA Newcastle
Head of Professional Practice: Miss Alison Oliver, BA Warwick, MSc Southampton
Chaplain: Revd Paul Wallington, BA Trinity College Bristol

Senior School Teaching Staff:

Art:
Mrs Kim Ross, BA Surrey
Miss Geraldine Harris, BA Kent
Miss Katie Lintott, BA Warwick, MA The Courtauld Institute of Art
Miss Sally Wright, BA Hons, MFA Slade School of Art
Miss Charlotte Wirdnam, BA Wimbledon School of Art

Classics:
Dr Liza Martin, MA, PhD Cantab
Mrs Pippa Giles, BA Birmingham
Mr Charlie Hammel, AB Princeton, MLitt St Andrews
Mrs Alex Komar, BA Cantab
Miss Rebekah Smith, BA Birmingham

Design and Technology:
Mrs Hilary Mitchener, BEng Exeter

Drama and Theatre Studies:
Ms Tracy Spring, BA Hertfordshire, MA Middlesex, CertEd
Mrs Tamzin Mason, BA Winchester
Miss Leah Hanmore, BA Winchester

Visiting Staff:
Ms Judith Wilson, BA North London, MA Winchester
Mrs Marie Armstrong, BA Bretton Hall
Ms L Tait, MA London

Economics:
Mrs Jacqueline Campbell, BSc Plymouth State University USA

English:
Mrs Naomi Anson, MA, Mtcg London
Miss Claire Goymour, BA London
Miss Caroline Howard, BA Leicester
Mr Sam Lenton, BA Cambridge, MA Cantab
Miss Alison Oliver, BA Warwick
Miss Laura Stewart, BA Wheaton College USA
Mrs Sophie Toland, MA Cantab
Mrs Sally Walmsley, BA Oxford

English as an additional language:
Mrs Nicola Young, BA Birmingham
Miss Nicola Thomas, BA Cantab
Ms Karen Butler

Food Technology and Textiles:
Mrs Nicola Sanvoisin, BSc Cardiff
Mrs Rachel Curry, BA Manchester
Miss Heather Jones, BA Liverpool

Geography:
Mr Jonathan Brown, BA Birmingham
Miss Emily Farrell, BA Nottingham, MA Institute of
  Education, London
Ms Emily Hartley, BA Leeds

History and Politics:
Ms Georgina Manville, BA Bristol, MA Bristol
Mrs Kathryn Batten, BA West of England
Mrs Jenny Dixon-Clarke, BA Reading, MA London
Mr Charles Hammel, AB Princeton, MLitt St Andrews
Miss Emily Tait, BA Cardiff

ICT:
Mrs Anne Walker, BEd Leeds

Mathematics:
Mr Stephen Power, BA Oxon, MSc Colorado
Mrs Corinna Bolger, BEng Exeter, CEng, MIMechE
Mr Paul Debont, BSc Warwick, MSc Essex
Mrs Helen Greene, BSc London, MA OU
Mr John Gillespie, BSc Dunelm
Mrs Jill Meekums, BSc Portsmouth, MSc Southampton
Mrs Hannah Savory, MEng UMIST
Mrs Cindy Thompson, BSc Ed Exeter

Modern Languages:
Mr Anton Kendall, BA Exeter
Miss Fiona Bolton, MA Oxon
Mrs Laura Camba-Robinson, BA OU
Dr Catherine Dey, BA Birmingham, PhD Birmingham
Ms Jane Gandee, MA Cantab
Mrs Manu Grice, BA Southampton
Mrs Nelly Porter, Maîtrise Strasbourg
Ms Stephanie Stratford, BA Warwick
Mrs Anne Steer, MA Ed Frankfurt

Music:
Mrs YiRu Hall, MA Cantab
Ms Judy Martin, BA Cambridge, MA Cambridge
  [maternity cover]
Ms Natasha Wright, BMus Hons, PPRNCM, MMus,
  PGDipGSMD
Mr Clive Watkiss, GRSM, LRAM

Visiting Music Staff:
Mrs Katie Alder (*voice*)
Mrs Michelle Allen, BMus, Dip LRAM (*voice*)
Mrs Sally Bartholomew, BMus (*bassoon*)
Mrs Suzanne Bevis (*harp*)
Mr Martin Davis (*french horn*)
Mrs Kate L Field, PPRNCM, BMus, RNCM (*voice*)
Mr Mark Frampton (*double bass*)
Mr Simon Gallear (*voice*)
Mr Brian Gordon, LRAM, DipRAM (*voice*)
Mrs Kate Ham, BMus Hons (*harp*)

Mrs Helen King (*piano*)
Mrs Anna Leyland (*voice*)
Mrs Jane Lloyd, ARCM, LGSM (*piano*)
Ms Claire Lowe, GRSM, LRAM (*voice*)
Mr Fraser MacAuley (*oboe*)
Mr Michael Mace, Dip RAM (*violoncello*)
Ms Rebecca Miles, LTCL (*recorder*)
Mr Richard Morrow (*guitar*)
Miss Kate Murrelli, BA, MMus (*piano*)
Miss Helen Paskins, MA Cantab, Dip RCM (*clarinet*)
Mr Todor Nikolaev, MMus, BMus Hons GSMD (*violin*)
Mr Jason O'Kane, LWCMD (*guitar*)
Mr Donal O'Neill, PG Cert Perf, BA Mus (*percussion*)
Mrs Jo Paterson-Neild, BA (*saxophone*)
Mrs Angela Roberts, BA London Dundee (*flute*)
Mrs Gilly Slot, BMus, ALCM, LTCL (*piano*)
Mrs Judith Turner, MSTAT (*Alexander Technique*)
Miss Salvita Vysniauskiene, MMus, LMTA (*piano*)
Mr Alastair Warren, BMus Hons RCM, MMus RCM
  (*trombone, tuba*)
Dr Nigel Wilkinson, MMus, ARCM, Hon ARAM (*piano*)
Miss Karen Wills, GTCL, LTCL, DipRAM (*flute*)

Physical Education:
Mrs Justine Mackenzie, BSc Temple University USA
Mr Paul Boyd-Leslie
Mrs Leonie Campbell, BA Chichester
Miss Kelly Drew, BSc Brunel
Mrs Zoe Enticknap, BSc Chichester
Miss Emily Harris, BA Bedfordshire
Mrs Dot Hogg, BSc Swansea
Mrs Sara Heffernan, BA Chichester
Miss Kate Nelson-Lee, BA Swarthmore College USA

Visiting Staff:
Mrs Natalie Potter (*aerobics*)
Mrs Fredricka Brooks (*Pilates*)
Miss Caroline Pont (*judo*)
Mr Simon Budden (*karate*)
Mr Allen Cooke (*fencing*)
Mrs Patricia Francis, BA National Teaching University,
  Colombia (*gym*)

Duke of Edinburgh's Award Coordinator:
Mr Andrew Parker, BA Newcastle, MBA Manchester

Psychology:
Dr Julia Adlam, BSc, MSc, PhD Hamburg

Religious Studies:
Miss Antigone Storey, BA Dunelm, MA Dunelm
Mrs Anna Campbell, BA Dunelm, DipRE Nottingham,
  CFRS Portsmouth, RSA Dip TEFLA
Dr Elizabeth Mackintosh, BA Durham, MA Durham, PhD
  Durham
Miss Emily Tait, BA Cardiff

Science:
Mrs Susanna Wilkinson, BSc Southampton
Mrs Laura Bream, MSc, DipM
Mrs Penny Burley, BSc Swansea
Mrs Alison Burns-Cox, BSc London
Mrs Catherine Elkins, BSc Reading
Mrs Sarah Evans, BSc London, MA OU
Mr Bruce Hansen, BSc, MSc Canterbury New Zealand,
  Grad Dip TchLn Christchurch New Zealand
Dr Hilary Otter, BA, PhD Cantab, FSB, CBiol
Mr Ravi Shah, BSc East Anglia
Dr Jemma Savillewood, BM Southampton
Dr Susan Sturton, BA Oxon, PhD Leeds
Mr Michael Tanner, BSc Loughborough
Dr Rebecca Topley, BSc King's College London, PhD
  University of the West Indies
Mrs Sally Walmsley MA Oxon

Higher Education & Student Guidance:
Mrs Anna Campbell, BA Dunelm, DipRE Nottingham,
CFPS Portsmouth, RSA DipTEFLA

Learning Support:
Mrs Ruth Horner, BEd Bulmershe, Diploma SpLD

IT:
Mr Andy Healy (*IT Systems Manager*)
Mr Laurence Moon (*Data Manager*)
Mr Nick Morland (*Senior IT Systems Administrator*)
Mr Lewis Humphries (*IT Systems Administrator*)

Boarding House Staff:
Head of boarding: Miss Jayne Webber
Assistant Head of Boarding: Mrs Sophie Toland
Finlay:
Housemistress: Mr Bruce Hansen and Mrs Rachel Hansen
Assistant: Miss Nicola Thomas
High House:
Housemistress: Miss Helen Carruthers
Assistant: Ms Judy Martin
Hyde Abbey:
Housemistress: Miss Heather Jones
Assistant: Miss Philippa Sutton
Earlsdown:
Housemistress: Miss Geraldine Harris
Assistant: Miss Abbey Connor
Hillcroft:
Housemistress: Mrs Tamzin Mason
Assistant: Miss Laura Duncan
Le Roy:
Housemistress: Miss Emily Tait
Assistant: Miss Jo Parsons

Day House Staff:
Caer Gwent:
Housemistress: Mrs Anna Campbell
Assistant: Mrs Nicola Sanvoisin
Venta:
Housemistress: Mrs Hilary Mitchener
Assistant: Mrs Hannah Savory
Davies:
Housemaster: Mr Ravi Shah
Assistant: Ms Tracy Spring
Mowbray:
Mrs Pippa Giles
Miss Emily Tait

Library:
Mrs Alice Kelly (*librarian*)

Medical Staff:
Dr Hannah Ingram Evans, MBChB, MRCS, MRCGP Dist,
DFFP
Mrs Paulette May, RGN
Mrs Eleanor Oakley, RGN
Ms Nicola Smith, RGN

Clinical Counselling Psychologist:
Dr Helen O'Connor, PhD London, BA Wales

Technicians:
Miss Charlotte Wirdnam (*art*)
Mrs Jennifer Dickinson, Mrs Ewa Kerth, Mr Ian Newton,
Mrs Gill Quelch (*science*)
Mr Niall Burke (*technology*)
Mr Simon Freakley (*performing arts technical manager*)
Mrs Polly Perry (*performing arts technical assistant*)

Admissions:
Registrar: Mrs Kate Cairns
Assistant Registrar: Mrs Liz Turner

Administrative Staff:
PA to the Headmistress: Mrs Rachel Nicholls

Examinations Administrator: Mr Jonathan Nelson
School Secretary: Mrs Barbara Tyler-Smith
Assistant School Secretary: Mrs Laura Slaney-Sharpe (*job share*)
Assistant School Secretary: Mrs Debbie Wassell (*job share*)
General Office Administrator: Miss Beth Knight
Music Administrative Assistant: Mrs Karis Grover
Head of Development: Mrs Emma Boryer
Communications Officer: Mrs Mel Kinder
Old Girls Association Manager: Mrs Kim Lampard
Swimming Pool Manager: Mrs Louise Greenway

Bursary:
Accountant: Mrs Jan Bollard
Domestic Bursar: Ms Sarah Draycott
Lettings Administrator: Mrs Sandra Kelly
Bursary Supervisor: Mrs Lorna Gale
Bursary Assistant: Mrs Pam Eynon
Bursary Assistant: Mr Curtis Gale
Bursary Assistant: Mrs Sally Warden
HR Officer: Mrs Helen Wentworth
HR Administrator: Mrs Kate Lyall
Estates Manager: Mr Jim Ewing

Junior School

Acting Headmistress: Ms Jane Gandee, MA Cantab

Deputy Head: Mrs Katherine Grosscurth, BSc Plymouth,
PGCE

Deputy Head Academic: Mrs Haylie Saunders, BA
Winchester

Teaching staff:
Miss Caroline Albin, BA Leeds, PGCE
Mrs Karen Brown, BSc Reading
Mrs Louise Caldwell, BA Cardiff, PGCE
Mrs Allison Greenfield, BA Bristol, PGCE
Mrs Iona Gunner, BEd Cambridge
Mrs Lottie Harding, BSc Hull, PGCE
Mrs Rebecca Hay, BEd Bedford College of Higher
Education
Mrs Jenny Hayden, BSc Open University, NNEB, Cert
NatSc
Mrs Judith Heinrich, Cert Ed Oxford
Miss Katie Iliffe, BA Surrey
Miss Jo James, BA Ed Reading
Miss Kathryn Jones, BEd St Martin's College, Lancaster
Mrs Marian Mallindar
Mr Roger Marshall, BEd Wales
Miss Victoria Meinel, BA Kent
Mrs Y Murray BEd Exeter
Mrs Juliette Nicholson, BEd London
Mrs Sue Phillips, BA Warwick, PGCE
Miss H Povey, BA Middlesex
Mrs Angela Roberts, BA London
Mrs Sarah Romero, BEd Northumbria
Miss Stephanie Robinson, MA Glasgow, PGCE
Miss Caroline Silvester, BMus RCM, PGCE Reading, Dip
RCM, LTCL, ALCM
Miss Karen Sprunt, BEd Cambridge
Miss Sharon Taylor, MA, PGCE Edinburgh, MCIL
Miss Freya Webb, BA Hull, PGCE

School Office and Senior Management team administrator:
Mr Adam Marshall
Office Administrator: Mrs Claire Hardwick
Registrar: Mrs Sara Mathieson

Sheffield High School for Girls
GDST

10 Rutland Park, Sheffield, South Yorkshire S10 2PE

Tel: 0114 266 0324
email: enquiries@she.gdst.net
website: www.sheffieldhighschool.org.uk
Twitter: @SheffieldHigh
Facebook: /sheffieldhighschool
LinkedIn: /Sheffield-High-School

Sheffield High School for Girls is part of the GDST (Girls' Day School Trust). The GDST is the leading network of independent girls' schools in the UK. As a charity that owns and runs 24 schools and two academies, it reinvests all its income in its schools. For further information about the Trust, see p. xxiii or visit www.gdst.net.

Number of Pupils. 880: 200 (Junior School), 498 (Senior School), 182 (Sixth Form).

The school was opened in 1878 and has occupied its pleasant site in the suburb of Broomhill since 1884. It draws its pupils from all parts of the city and from more distant rural and urban areas of Nottinghamshire, Derbyshire and Yorkshire, many travelling on special coaches organised by parents.

The Junior School, Senior School buildings and Sixth Form Centre are adjacent and share gardens, sports hall, hockey/rounders pitch, netball/tennis courts and a gymnasium on the site. An additional hockey and athletics field is situated a short bus ride from the school.

The infants and juniors have their own purpose-built libraries, a science room and art and music studios. The Junior School also provides a breakfast club from 7.45 am and supervised after-school care is available until 6.15 pm.

Recent additions to the Senior School include a new Cookery Room, an IT suite, Science laboratories, additional Art & Design studios, Music facilities, a Drama studio, two new libraries, a language media suite and a large extension to the Sixth Form Centre with refurbished common rooms, teaching rooms and tutorial bases as well as a new Learning Resource Centre which provides access to key study materials, laptop computers and a wealth of careers resources. There is a modern and bright café-diner as well as a decked outside eating area for the students. In 2012 the School opened a Year 11 common room with kitchen facilities in the Year 11 base in the Moor Lodge building. A multimillion pound refurbishment of the Old Gym and School House to enhance the school's facilities for Sport and Drama has begun and is due for completion in early 2017.

Curriculum. The usual Junior subjects are taught plus French, German, Spanish, Art, Computer Studies, Art/Technology, Drama, Music and PE. Most lessons are with form teachers, but specialist staff teach older girls. In the Senior School, girls generally take 10 GCSE subjects from the range of usual options plus German, Greek, Latin, Drama, Spanish, Art and Design, Business Studies, Geology, Music and PE. Over 75% stay on to the Sixth Form and nearly all go on to Higher Education.

The school attaches great importance to the wide range of opportunities it offers and has received a string of prestigious national awards for the exceptional quality of its extra-curricular provision such as PE Quality Mark with Distinction, Arts Mark (Gold), GO4it, ICT Quality Mark, Eco-Schools Award and Career Mark, making it the only school in South Yorkshire to be so accredited for the quality of its careers provision. The school's sporting provision has also been commended nationally for its outstanding quality with teams regularly competing in national finals in addition to fielding national finals teams in film-making and debating. The School has almost 100 lunchtime and after school clubs, which encourage excellence in sport, music, drama and art and offers the full Duke of Edinburgh's Award Scheme. A varied programme of residential trips and expeditions at home and abroad is offered, including Sport, Music, Foreign Language and Art tours. The School has strong community links and has received four Independent School Awards as well as being shortlisted in two further years. Awards have been for: Best Independent-Maintained School Collaboration, Outstanding Community Initiative and Best Leadership Team.

Fees per term (2016–2017). Senior School £4,030, Junior Department £2,857–£2,963.

The fees cover the regular curriculum, school books, stationery and other materials, most extra-curricular activities, but not school lunches. Girls are required to stay for school lunches up to Year 7 and these are charged separately per term.

Scholarships and Bursaries. The GDST makes available to the School a substantial number of scholarships and bursaries. The bursaries are means-tested and are intended to ensure that the School remains accessible to bright girls who would profit from the education offered but who would be unable to enter the School without financial assistance.

A large range of scholarships and bursary support is provided at Sheffield High School. From Year 7, a number of prestigious Academic Scholarships are provided each year with an additional four means-tested HSBC Scholarships also available. In the Sixth Form, a range of Scholarships, as well as a further four HSBC Scholarships, are also made available to suitably talented girls.

Charitable status. Sheffield High School is part of The Girls' Day School Trust, which is a Registered Charity, number 306983.

Chair of Local Governors: Mr M Greenshields, FCA

***Headmistress*: Mrs V A Dunsford**, BA Manchester, NPQH

Deputy Head: Mrs S White, BA Sheffield

Senior Teacher, Assistant Head (*Examinations, Assessment and Learning*): Mrs K Boulton-Pratt, MSc Leicester

Director of Sixth Form: Ms Cathy Walker, BA Sheffield

Assistant Head (*PR, Marketing and Communications*): Mrs A Bouchier, BA Sheffield

Assistant Head (*Pastoral*): Mrs A Reed, BA Sheffield Hallam

Head of Junior School: Mr C Hald, MA York

Director of Finance and Operations: Mr I Kane, BSc Open

South Hampstead High School
GDST

3 Maresfield Gardens, London NW3 5SS

Tel: 020 7435 2899
Fax: 020 7431 8022
email: senior@shhs.gdst.net
            junior@shhs.gdst.net
website: www.shhs.gdst.net
Twitter: @SHHSforgirls
Facebook: @SouthHampsteadHighSchool
LinkedIn: /SouthHampsteadHighSchool

Founded 1876.

South Hampstead High School is part of the GDST (Girls' Day School Trust). The GDST is the leading network of independent girls' schools in the UK. As a charity that owns and runs 24 schools and two academies, it reinvests all its income in its schools. For further information about the Trust, see p. xxiii or visit www.gdst.net.

The school is situated close to the Finchley Road and Swiss Cottage underground stations and to Finchley Road and Frognal railway station. It is also easily reached by bus from central, north and north-west London.

In the Senior School there are 640 pupils, including 144 in the Sixth Form. There are 260 girls in the Junior School. Entry to the Junior School is at 4 and 7; entry to the Senior School is at 11; occasional vacancies arise at other ages and new girls are welcomed into the Sixth Form if they achieve the necessary entrance qualifications. Full details of the admission procedures are available from the school website: www.shhs.gdst.net

The Junior School occupies two large houses with gardens about 5 minutes' walk from the main Senior School site. The Senior School is in a brand new purpose-built premises which was opened in November 2014. Sixth Form students occupy the Oakwood Centre, a large house which is interconnected to the Senior School. Their common room has its own café and kitchen; they have dedicated classrooms and workspaces as well as full use of facilities in the Senior School building.

At SHHS, the curriculum is designed to provide a secure and imaginative basis for academic progress at each key stage of a pupil's development. Our intention is that all our girls will develop their own enthusiasms and initiative within a broad educational framework. The curriculum aims to provide our pupils with a rich experience in linguistic, mathematical, scientific, technological, human and social, physical, and aesthetic and creative education. In the Junior School we have a clear focus on developing literacy and numeracy skills and have established an integrated approach to our curriculum whereby we focus the learning across several subjects around a theme. In this way girls develop real depth of knowledge, as well as confidence in key skills such as research, analysing results and interpreting and presenting information. In the Senior School our curriculum has a strong academic spine. English, Mathematics, Biology, Chemistry and Physics are studied from Year 7 to Year 11 by all students; at least one modern foreign language must be studied to GCSE level; History and Geography are studied from Year 7 and at least one of the humanities must be taken through to GCSE. Alongside these students also study Art, Drama, Music, Theology & Religion, Latin, Design Technology and Computing, all of which are available as option choices for GCSE. Most students study for 10 subjects at GCSE of which 2 are their free options. A few choose to study for 11 subjects, taking a third free option. In the Lower Sixth, pupils choose 4 subjects to study at AS level. Many will continue to A2 with four subjects into the Upper Sixth and others will drop a subject and concentrate on 3. Classical Civilisation, Economics, History of Art, Politics and Psychology are offered in the Sixth Form.

Pupils participate enthusiastically in an enormous number of extra-curricular clubs, societies and courses. Creativity in art, writing, music and drama is strongly encouraged at all stages. There are many orchestras, ensembles and choirs. Tuition in almost any instrument and singing can be arranged and girls are prepared for the examinations of the Associated Board of the Royal School of Music. Large numbers of pupils participate in the Duke of Edinburgh's Award scheme and Young Enterprise business scheme.

Fees per term (2016–2017). Senior School £5,641, Junior School £4,613.

The fees cover the regular curriculum, games and swimming, but not school meals or instrumental/singing lessons. The fees for instrumental/singing lessons are detailed in the prospectus.

Scholarships and Bursaries. A number of scholarships and bursaries are available through the GDST to internal or external candidates for entry at 11+ or to the Sixth Form. The bursaries are means tested to ensure that the school remains accessible to bright girls who would benefit from our education but who would be unable to enter the school without financial assistance.

Charitable status. South Hampstead High School is part of The Girls' Day School Trust, which is a Registered Charity, number 306983.

Local Governors:
Chairman: Mrs H Strange, GRSM, PGCE, RGN
Miss E Clements, BA, BArch, RIBA, FRSA
Miss D Navanayagam
Mrs K Fear
Mrs L Frank
Prof R Jackman, MA Cantab
Mrs J Solomon
Mrs M Trehearne, MA, BEd

Headmistress: Miss Vicky Bingham, BA Oxon

Deputy Heads:
Mr D Bradbury, MSc Keele University, MA Open, MInstP, CPhys (*Mathematics and Physics*)
Mrs Z Brass, BA Queen's University, Canada (*Economics*)
Ms S Paillasse, BA Guildhall, MSc Bath (*French*)

Head of Sixth Form: Mr J Waller, BA Oxon (*Economics*)

Director of Finance and Operations: Mr G Collins-Down, BSc Cardiff

Senior School Teaching Staff:
Mr D Adams, MA King's College London (*Science*)
Miss A Aneja, MSc King's College London (*Mathematics*)
Mrs J Arundale, BSc Lancaster (*Physics*)
Mr P Arundale, BSc Manchester (*Chemistry*)
Mr K Baker, MSc Imperial College London (*Mathematics*)
Miss P Baker, BA Greenwich (*Religious Studies*)
Mrs R J Banfield, BA Brighton (*Physical Education*)
Mrs A Bartnicka, CLM Granada (*German*)
Mr C Beecroft, BMuS Trinity Laban (*Music*)
Mrs S Bernstein, BSc London (*Physics*)
Ms A Bokkerink, MA Cambridge (*English*)
Mrs V Boyarsky, BA Cantab, MPhil London (*History*)
Miss L Bush, BA Oxford Brookes (*Sport*)
Ms R Buttigieg, BSc Malta (*Biology*)
Mr E Cabezas, BA Seville (*Spanish*)
Ms E Chandler-Thompson, MA London (*History*)
Ms M Cohen Christofidis (*Philosophy*)
Dr S Collisson, BMus Manchester (*Music*)
Ms A Coogan, BA Dublin (*Geography*)
Mrs G Cooke, BA Brighton (*Physical Education*)
Mrs O Crossley-Holland, BA Oxon (*English*)
Dr M Egan, BA University College London, MA Essex, PhD University College London (*Politics, History and Critical Thinking*)
Ms N Elliot, BA, Manhattanville College (*Biology*)
Miss S Ellis, BMus Cardiff (*Music*)
Ms K Etheridge, BA Oxford (*English*)
Miss M Fajardo Duran, QTS, CILT (*Spanish*)
Mrs S Fanning, BSc London, Dip Arch RIBA (*Design Technology*)
Mrs C Finley, CAPES Toulouse (*French and Spanish*)
Mr M Gadgil, BSc OU (*Chemistry*)
Mrs C Gallagher, BSc Leeds (*Biology, Geography and Physics*)
Miss K Garnett, BA Exeter (*Physical Education*)
Mr N Garrard, MA Cantab, MA Manchester (*English*)
Mr C Gerstrom, BA Oxon (*Economics*)
Ms R Goodman, BA University College London (*Art*)
Miss M Greenland, BSc London (*Computing*)
Mr J Hansford, BA York (*Mathematics*)
Mr B Harkins, MA Cantab, MA London (*English*)

Mrs D F Hugh, BA Manchester, MBA (*Modern Languages*)
Miss J Humphreys, BSc Birmingham (*Geography*)
Mr N Hunter, BA Liverpool, MA Goldsmiths London (*Art*)
Mrs A Johnson, BA Birmingham (*Religious Studies*)
Mr T Jones, BA Cambridge (*Mathematics*)
Mr A Keiler, BA Leicester (*English*)
Ms N Kennedy, BA St Patrick's
Ms A Khoursheed, MA Surrey (*Arabic*)
Miss L Knowles, BA Sheffield (*History and Theology and Religion*)
Miss A Knox, MSci Durham (*Chemistry*)
Mr P Larochelle, BA Massachusetts (*Drama and English*)
Mrs N Liston, MA Oxon (*Geography*)
Mrs A Logan, BSc Wales (*Science*)
Miss S G Lopez, BEd Edinburgh (*Physical Education*)
Miss S-L Lui, BA Oxon (*Classics*)
Dr A Maldjian, PhD Glasgow (*French and Italian*)
Miss N Marchant, BA Cantab (*Classics*)
Mrs E Marriott, BA Oxon (*Classics*)
Ms K Martin, BA De Montfort (*Drama*)
Miss J Matthews, BSc Loughborough (*Netball*)
Miss H McDougall, BA Oxon (*History*)
Mrs J Meyer, BSc, MA London (*German*)
Dr E Morewood, MA Cantab (*Biology*)
Mrs P Morgan, MA Cantab (*History*)
Miss S Morgan, BA, MA Norwich (*Art*)
Mr M Morley, BA Lancaster (*French and History*)
Mr W Moss, BA Cardiff, MDes Edinburgh College of Art (*Art*)
Mrs G Nwoko, MA Roehampton (*Spanish and French*)
Dr R Osborne, PhD Imperial College London (*Physics*)
Mrs J Patel, BA York (*Mathematics*)
Mr L Poza, BSc London (*Chemistry*)
Mrs L Raitz, MA Cantab (*French*)
Mrs E J Sanders, BSc Miami (*Geography*)
Mr K Sarrafan-Chaharsoughi, BA Cambridge (*Physics*)
Mrs P Shah, BA Oxford (*Mathematics*)
Ms C Simpson, BA Oxford (*Classics*)
Ms V M Spawls, BSc Westminster (*Biology*)
Miss R Stern, BA London (*Drama*)
Mr D Suarez, BSc London (*Mathematics*)
Mr C Tanfield, MA Oxon (*Classics and Universities Officer*)
Ms V Teles, MA Institute of Education (*Mathematics*)
Miss C Waghorn, BA Exeter (*Psychology*)
Miss Y Wang, BSc ICL (*Mathematics*)
Mr M Willett, BA Cambridge (*Mathematics*)
Mr G Willson, BA Bath (*Design Technology*)
Ms Z Wing-Davey, BA Cambridge (*Classics*)
Dr C J Woodward, BSc, PhD London (*Biology*)
Ms E Wren, BSc Sussex (*Biology*)
Ms A Wrigglesworth, BA Loughborough, MA Cambridge (*Design Technology*)

Science Technicians:
Mrs C I Ezike, BSc
Mrs A Weekes, HND
Mrs T Zabergja, BA/BSc
Art Technician:
Mr A Hennessey, BA
Ms B Wilson, BA
DT Technician:
Miss S Uddin, BA
Language Assistants:
Mrs B Arnold
Miss D Cobo Montes
Mrs I Rush-Canevet
Librarians:
Miss M Ravetto-Wood

Dr M Brainard, PhD Universität Osnabrück, MSLIS, Pratt Institute

Junior School:
Head of Junior School: Mrs Gabrielle Solti, BA Oxon

Deputy Head of Junior School: Miss L Szemerenyi, BSc Sussex

Junior School Staff:
Mrs C Atkinson, MA Cantab
Mrs H Blackford, BSc Durham
Ms C Doyle, BA Manchester
Mrs S Elian, BA Strathclyde
Miss N Evans, BSc University College London
Ms K Gosling, BA Portsmouth
Mrs A Hendry, BA Queen Mary London
Ms B Lagaay, BSc Sheffield Hallam
Mrs S-J Lewis, BA London
Miss C MacSwiney, BSc Sussex
Miss S Prevezer, BA Manchester
Ms K Rattenbury, BMus Manchester
Mrs A Ruffini, MA Milan
Ms J Stewart, BA Oxford Brookes
Miss R Tropp, BA Birmingham
Mrs L Young, BEd Bath
Mr M Weddell, BEng Brunel
Junior School Librarian:
Ms T Volhard, BA

Junior School Teachers' Assistants:
Ms E Bartunekova, NVQ Level 3
Mrs M Shakil, NVQ Level 3
Mrs S Suganthan, NVQ Level 4
Ms T Volhard, BA

Visiting Music Staff:
Piano:
Ms G Cracknell, LRAM
Mr I Laks, BMus
Mr P Moore, ARAM, DipRAM, BMus, LRAM, LGSMD
Miss S Warwick, BMus RCM
Mr S Wybrew, BMus RCM
Strings:
Ms C Barry, BA (*Cello*)
MsC Cohen, BMus, LRAM (*Violin*)
Mr R Fogg, BA (*Guitar*)
Mrs K Laks, BMus (*Violin*)
Mrs E Menenzes, BA (*Violin*)
Ms L Moore, BMus, LRAM, PPRAM (*Cello*)
Ms G Murray, BA (*Double Bass*)
Mr S Perkins, BMus, DipNCOS (*Violin, Viola*)
Wind:
Ms D Calland, BMus, LRAM (*Brass*)
Ms F Carpos, MMus, FTCL (*Bassoon*)
Ms S J Clarke, GGSM (*Clarinet, Saxophone, Theory*)
Mr D Clewlow, BA (*Brass*)
Ms K Corrigan, BA Dunelm, MMus (*Recorder*)
Mrs G Jones (*Horn*)
Mr I Judson, LRWCMD (*Flute*)
Mr A McNeil, BMus (*Saxophone*)
Mr M Onissi, LTCL (*Saxophone*)
Miss E Tingey, LWCMD, ACC WCMD, TCM (*Oboe, Theory*)
Percussion:
Mr T Marsden, BMus, MMus
Singing:
Ms C Barnett-Jones, MA
Mr J Clarkson, MA
Ms L Dyke, BA
Mr V Kirk BMus
Ms M Phillips, BA
Ms D Thomas, Dip Degree

Support Staff:
Admissions Registrar: Ms P Karavla
Alumnae Manager: Ms F Hurst, BA Hons
Director of IT: Mr R Bailey, BSc
Exams Officer: Mrs D Greengrass, BSocSc, PgDip
Music Administrator: Miss J Chorley
Finance Manager: Mr Y Essinki, BSc, AdDip
Finance Officer: Ms J Williams
Finance Assistant: Ms J Douch
Marketing and Communications Manager: Ms M
   Springate, MSc, MSc
Headmistress's PA and Administrative and HR Manager:
   Mrs L Cripps, AssocCIPD
ICT Technician: Mr L Pagurschi, BSc
Junior ICT Technician: Miss H Spilsbury
*Junior School Headmistress's PA and Admissions
   Registrar*: Ms N Flack
Junior School Secretary: Mrs S Denton
Teacher Resources Officer: Mrs S Bell
Receptionist: Miss L Dunne
School Counsellor: Mrs R Shock
School Life Coach: Ms R Leonello
School Nurse: Mrs L Mullins
Site Managers: Mr R Clarke, Mr B Clulow, Mr D Lacey,
   Mr J Murray
Caretaker and Security: Mr A Adamou
SMT Secretary: Ms H Jolley

Stamford High School

St Martin's, Stamford, Lincolnshire PE9 2LL

Tel:	01780 484200
Fax:	01780 484201
email:	headshs@ses.lincs.sch.uk
website:	www.ses.lincs.sch.uk
Twitter:	@SpedeNews
Facebook:	@stamfordendowedschools

Motto: *Christe me spede*

Founded by Browne's Hospital Foundation, of Stamford, 1876.

Introduction. Stamford High School is one of three schools within the overall Stamford Endowed Schools Educational Charity, along with Stamford School (boys) and Stamford Junior School, the co-educational junior school.

Numbers and Boarding Houses. There are 633 girls aged 11–18 years including boarders. The main point of entry is at age 11 though applications are welcomed at any stage up to the Sixth Form. Girls who enter through the Junior School progress automatically on to the High School without further competitive entrance testing. Boarders are received from the age of 8 (in the Junior School). There are two Boarding Houses for girls including a Sixth Form Boarding House where the girls have single or shared study bedrooms. The School accepts full, weekly and three-night boarders.

Fees per term (2016–2017). Day £4,755; Full Boarding £8,809; Weekly Boarding £7,680; 3-Night Boarding £6,674.

These fees include all stationery, textbooks and games. School lunches for day girls are at additional charge.

Registration Fee £75. Acceptance Fee £250.

Extras. Individual music lessons, Speech and Drama, Dancing (Riding for boarders only).

Curriculum. The curriculum is designed to ensure all girls have a balanced educational programme up to age 16 thus avoiding premature specialisation. The National Curriculum is broadly followed but much more is added to the curriculum to make it stimulating and rewarding. Most girls are entered for at least 9 GCSE examinations and continue

on to A Level examinations leading to university entry. In partnership with Stamford School, all Sixth Form girls have access to the full range of A Level subjects offered across the two schools providing an exceptionally wide choice of 25 subjects.

Throughout their time in the school girls are prepared for the examinations of the Associated Board of the Royal Schools of Music in music and The London Academy of Music and Dramatic Art for speech and drama. There is much scope for creative activities in Music, Art and Drama and state-of-the-art facilities for Information & Communication Technology, including access to the Internet. The Director of Music for the Stamford Endowed Schools ensures that the Music Department works very closely with Stamford School providing access to a wide range of activities for orchestras, bands, Chapel Choir and choirs. There are joint drama productions and a Performing Arts Studio.

Sport and Physical Education include Hockey, Netball, Tennis, Swimming, Golf, Judo, Athletics, Volleyball, Basketball, Badminton, Trampoline, Gymnastics and Squash. There is a very full programme of extracurricular activities including Olympic Gymnastics, Athletics and Taekwondo. There is a heated, indoor swimming pool, a Sports Hall and a floodlit artificial hockey pitch. The Duke of Edinburgh's Award Scheme operates at Bronze, Silver and Gold levels with a considerable number of girls taking part each year. There is a thriving, mixed CCF offering RN, Army and RAF sections. There are many school clubs and societies and a thriving weekend activity programme.

Entrance Examinations are held in January.

Scholarships and Bursaries. The Schools offer a range of scholarships for pupils entering into years 7, 9 and 12 (Sixth Form). Scholarships are less common for pupils entering into other years but may at times be available. There are scholarships for Academic, Music, Art, Sports and All-Rounder performance. Means-tested bursaries can be applied for by families of pupils who would otherwise not be able to benefit from a Stamford education. Please see our website for full details.

Charitable status. As part of the Stamford Endowed Schools, Stamford High School is a Registered Charity, number 527618.

Chairman of the Governing Body: Dr Michael Dronfield

***Principal of the Stamford Endowed Schools*: William Phelan**

***Vice-Principal, Head*: Victoria Buckman**

Deputy Head: Andrew Murphy
Director of Studies: Lorraine Johnson
SLT –Pastoral Care: Dominique Evans
SLT –PSD, Events and Trips: Denise Smith
Head of Sixth Form: Christine Hawkins
SES Chaplain: The Revd Mark Goodman

Teaching Staff:
Kirsten Allen (*Geography*)
Diana Ashley (*Art*)
Tessa Bennie (*Head of 6th Form Enrichment*)
Maria Bewers (*PE*)
Michael Blissett (*Head of Classics*)
Caroline Boyfield (*DT*)
Aimee Brock (*Maths*)
Daniel Burke (*Head of Maths*)
Lucy Cade-Stewart (*Classics*)
Elida Calleja Rubio (*Head of Spanish*)
Rachael Carter (*Maths*)
Nicholas Clift (*Spanish*)
Christian Collett (*History*)
Andrew Cox (*Head of Religious Studies*)
Andrew Crookell (*Head of Chemistry*)
Anneke Davies (*Head of Drama*)

Sarah Davies (*Head of History*)
Katie Dexter (*English*)
Yvonne Dias (*Art*)
Jillian Dickson (*Maths*)
Kate Docherty (*Religious Studies*)
Charlotte Echezarreta (*English*)
Alison Gossel (*Home Economics*)
Jennifer Hamflett (*Biology*)
Lynette Harte (*Psychology*)
Annabelle Holland (*Head of Art*)
Julia Husbands (*Physics*)
Nicola Jeffs (*English*)
Anna Johnson (*Maths*)
Anne Johnstone (*Head of Biology*)
Luke Jones (*Religious Studies*)
Emmanuelle Kerbrat (*MFL*)
Rachel Kersey (*Psychology*)
Amy Lewin (*Home Economics*)
Jacqueline Lewis-Gorman (*MFL*)
Alexandra Marsden (*Maths*)
Victoria Maskell (*Head of Psychology*)
Holly McCullough (*English*)
Lucy Meadows (*PE*)
Brenda Murphy (*Coach –Fitness*)
Holly Naismith (*Head of PE*)
Adam Patchett (*Head of Physics*)
Ruth Peterson (*Science*)
Amanda Rackham (*History*)
Catherine Raitt (*PE*)
Elizabeth Salt (*Head of Careers and UCAS*)
Victoria Saunders (*History*)
Kiren Sekhar (*Chemistry*)
Michael Smith (*Head of Geography*)
David Tuck (*Head of Politics*)
Catherine Vié (*Head of French*)
Emma Ware (*Psychology*)
Nicola Watson (*Drama*)
Nigel Webster (*Chemistry*)
Grant Weeks (*Biology*)
Elizabeth Wenban (*Physics*)
Gary Whitehouse (*Head of Learning Support*)
Hazel Williams (*Maths*)
Christopher Williamson (*Maths*)
Karen Wilson (*Head of Food and Nutrition*)
Vivienne Wilson (*Classics*)
Mark Zacharias (*Head of English*)

Music Department:
Giles Turner (*Director of Music*)
Duncan McIlrae (*Assistant Director of Music*)
Stephen Chandley (*Head of Brass*)
Daniel Leetch (*Head of Strings*)

Visiting Music Staff:
Steven Andrews (*Drum Kit, Percussion*)
Jonathan Aughton (*Flute*)
Margaret Bennett (*Singing*)
Karen Bentley (*Cello, Double Bass*)
Tatiana Boison (*Pianoforte*)
Susan Bond (*Singing*)
David Brown (*Clarinet*)
Alexander Crutchley (*Lower Brass*)
Julie Dustan (*Flute*)
Frances Gill (*Saxophone*)
Nicholas Gray (*Electric Guitar*)
Nan Ingrams
Sarah Latham (*Violin, Viola*)
Alexander MacDonald (*Classic Pianoforte*)
Margaret Maclennan (*Pianoforte*)
Anne McCrae (*Bassoon, Pianoforte*)
Elizabeth Murphy (*Violin, Pianoforte*)
Janet Roberts (*Cello*)

Kieran O'Riordan (*Percussion*)
Elizabeth Taylor, BA (*Violin, Viola*)
Nicholas Taylor
Eleanor Turner (*Harp*)
Lynn Williamson, LTCC (*Pianoforte*)

Boarding:

Welland House:
Miss E Kerbrat (*Resident Housemistress*)
Mrs M Tyers (*Assistant Housemistress*)

Park House:
Mrs C Vié (*Resident Housemistress*)
Mrs S Johnson, Mrs W Hartley
Mrs S Kavanagh (*Deputy Housemistress*)

Medical Officer: Dr J Barney, MBChB, DAvMed, DOccMED, MRCGP

Streatham & Clapham High School GDST

42 Abbotswood Road, London SW16 1AW
Tel: 020 8677 8400 (Senior School)
          020 8674 6912 (Prep School & Nursery)
Fax: 020 8677 2001
email: senior@schs.gdst.net
          prep@schs.gdst.net
website: www.schs.gdst.net
Twitter: @schs_gdst

Motto: *ad sapientiam sine metu*

Streatham & Clapham High School is a distinguished historical foundation. It was founded, as Brixton High School, in 1887 by the Girls' Public Day School Trust as one of its earliest member schools. HRH Princess Louise, Duchess of Argyll opened its buildings in Wavertree Road, London SW2, in 1895, now the site of the Prep School. In 1994 the Senior School moved to Abbotswood Road, London SW16, into the imposing buildings of the former Battersea Grammar School.

The School offers an inspiring, enlightened and intellectually challenging education for its pupils in a lively, vibrant and warmly supportive environment. The family ethos of Streatham & Clapham High School enables its masters and mistresses to know, value and nurture each pupil as an individual. The School celebrates diversity and draws strength from its rich social and cultural mix.

The School's core belief is that all members of its community should be inspired to outperform expectations on a daily basis. The pursuit of excellence is thus the School's defining feature. It nurtures pupils to attain success across the widest spectrum of activity, extending far beyond the conventional 'academic' horizon. In so doing, they learn the beauty of reason, the allure of the aesthetic, and the vitality of the physical. The School's pupils thus learn to navigate the landscape of the human spirit and achieve beyond the realms of expectation.

General information. Streatham & Clapham High School is an independent, academically selective school for girls aged 3–18, with 700 pupils on the roll. Girls aged 3–11 attend the Nursery and Prep School, located in spacious buildings with outstanding facilities in Wavertree Road in Streatham Hill. The Senior School inhabits a four-acre site focused on a symmetrical 1930s building designed by J E K Harrison, FRIBA in a delightfully tranquil and leafy oasis of south London, next to Tooting Bec Common, where the soundscape is dominated by birdsong.

Many girls live locally and an increasing number walk or cycle to School, encouraged by the School's commitment to sustainable travel. The Senior School is ten minutes' walk from Streatham Hill National Rail station and seventeen minutes from Balham National Rail and Underground. Other pupils come from further afield, including Battersea, Clapham, Wandsworth, Dulwich, Tooting and Brixton. The School is also within easy reach of the theatres, museums and galleries of central London.

Facilities. The School enjoys first-class facilities for learning, providing an environment that enables girls to develop their interests and strengths both inside and outside the classroom. The School keeps up-to-date with teaching methods and innovative techniques, such as interactive online learning, and use them to engage and extend its pupils. The senior-school facilities include two ICT suites, a music suite including a dedicated music technology suite, a recital hall, two design and technology workshops, a magnificent full-size indoor sports hall, dance, art and pottery studios, and sports pitches and tennis courts. The Sixth Form is housed in the Millennium Building, which comprises several study areas, a common room, a kitchen area and a dedicated, state-of-the-art café. The Prep School and Nursery have large and well-equipped premises, including a new library and a spacious indoor and outdoor area built specifically around the needs of the Nursery children. The School has recently embarked on a £15m building development project, which will provide for a new sixth form centre, a creative arts faculty, new dining facilities, and freshly landscaped grounds.

Academic matters. The ability profile of the School is significantly above the national average, with a proportion of pupils being far above the national average. In recent years, the School has been in the top 20% of independent schools in terms of its public examination results: for instance, in 2016 over 70% of grades awarded at GCSE or IGCSE were A* or A, and the number of A*s achieved by A Level students was almost double the national average. Virtually all sixth-form students proceed to the most competitive Russell Group universities, including Oxbridge.

Curriculum. Pupils in the Upper Third, Lower Fourth and Upper Fourth (Years 7 to 9) study the core disciplines of English, Mathematics, and Science. Other subjects offered include Art, Classics, Computing, Design & Technology, Drama, French, Geography, History, Italian, Latin and Ancient Greek, Music, Physical Education, Religious Studies, and Spanish. All these subjects (except Classics) are available in the Fifth Form (Years 10 and 11); pupils follow the GCSE or IGCSE courses depending on the subjects they have chosen.

The School offers a range of subjects for study at AS and A Level, including Art and Design, Biology, Chemistry, Classical Civilisation, Latin, Critical Thinking, Design and Technology, Drama and Theatre Studies, Economics, English Literature, Geography, Government and Politics, History, French, Italian, Spanish, Mathematics, Further Mathematics, Music, Physical Education, Physics, Psychology and Religious Studies. Sixth-form students also have the opportunity of pursuing the Extended Project Qualification to extend their interests and knowledge.

The timetable is organised into 80 teaching periods over a two-week cycle. Each period is of 40 minutes' duration, except for the 'Kinza' period, which is 55 minutes in length (see below).

Enrichment programme ('Kinza'). Kinza, an Arabic term meaning 'hidden treasure', is the unique enrichment programme of timetabled weekly sessions throughout the year. Every Kinza activity is designed to encourage a love and respect for learning for its own sake, utilising the interests and expertise of staff. The activities provide a wide spectrum of choice for each pupil, covering an extremely broad range of activities, including Mandarin, Anthropology, Robotics, Chess, Law, Meditation, Model United Nations, Podcast Production, Urban Wildlife, Magic, and much more. Opportunities to deepen aspects of the broad knowledge acquired through Kinza are afforded through co-curricular trips, individual research, and collaborative working processes in a vertical tutoring system, with younger pupils learning side-by-side with older girls. Each participates in several different activities during the course of the year.

Activities. The School has a thriving co-curricular life, with societies and clubs in the fields of Art, Design and Technology, Classics, English, Geography, History, ICT, Mathematics, Modern Foreign Languages, Science and Religious Studies, as well as more specialised activities such as Young Enterprise. There are a very large number of performing arts activities, pupils having the opportunity to perform in a number of dramatic productions during the school year or to belong to around 15 music ensembles, including choirs and orchestras, which annually lead the School's Carol Service at Southwark Cathedral. Pupils may belong to a legion of sporting clubs (including hockey, netball, rounders, rowing, tag rugby, athletics and much more) and fixtures, and have the opportunity to participate in a number of outdoor educational activities, such as the Duke of Edinburgh's Award. A busy programme of trips and expeditions is scheduled, for instance Classics and Languages trips to Greece and Italy, a History trip to discover the Paris of Henri IV, an annual flagship sixth-form trip to Cambodia, and Music tours of the Continent. Pupils have trekked across the Atlas Mountains in Morocco and reached the Base Camp of Mount Everest. The School's proximity to central London makes possible many excursions to concerts, museums, art galleries and theatres.

Pastoral care. The School does not view outstanding pastoral care as an 'add-on' to its academic programme. Neither does it believe that a 'hothouse' atmosphere is desirable or healthy. The School's core belief is that girls achieve best if they are happy and settled in their social relationships. Hence the 'family' ethos of the School, which holds that the way in which individuals are nurtured and valued is intrinsic to the pupils' progress and success. All members of staff, up to the Head Master, are easily accessible to pupils, and to ensure that the School's social and emotional care is comprehensive and alert, the School has a Deputy Head Mistress with oversight of pastoral matters. In conjunction with the work of the Heads of Year and the sixth-form mentoring scheme, this enables the School to identify challenges or problems early and then work with pupils and where necessary their parents to overcome them. It also helps the School to encourage and celebrate real progress and achievement every day. The strong prefectorial system and school council under the leadership of the Head Girl ensure that the pupil voice has suitable influence in shaping the life and work of the School.

Admission. There are six principal admission stages: by assessment for the Nursery (3+ years), 4+ and 7+, and by competitive entrance examination at 11+ and 13+ and at Sixth Form level. Occasional places sometimes arise at any age; interested parents are advised to contact the Registrar. All candidates for 11+ entry are called for interview in the Michaelmas Term. Applicants for 13+ entry will have individual interviews after the 13+ entrance examination.

All senior-school applicants sit the School's entrance examination. The 11+ examination comprises papers in English and Mathematics. Applicants for 13+ entry sit papers in English, Mathematics and Science.

The transfer of a pupil from the Prep to the Senior School is contingent on the School's assessment of the pupil's suitability for admission into the Upper Third Form (Year 7).

Fees per term (2016–2017). Senior School £5,463, Prep School £4,244, Nursery £3,234.

The fees are inclusive of non-residential trips and extras, but exclude the cost of lunch.

Academic scholarships. A number of academic scholarships, worth up to a maximum of 50% of fees, are available for 11+ entrance. They are not means-tested. Awards are made on the basis of individual candidates' performance in the entrance examination and interview. A number of sixth-form academic scholarships are also available, on the basis of a written assessment and interview.

Specialist scholarships. Specialist scholarships are awarded at 11+ in the fields of Art, Drama, Music and Sport. Further details are available on the school website.

Bursaries. A small number of means-tested bursaries are available at 11+. All requests are considered in confidence and application forms are available from the Registrar.

Charitable status. Streatham & Clapham High School is a member of The Girls' Day School Trust, which is a Registered Charity, number 306983.

The Board of Local Governors:
Mrs S Wrixon, BA, PGDip Journalism (*Chairman*)
Mrs R Bailey Packard, BA
Mrs K Eldred
Mrs F Smith, BA Dunelm, PGCE
Mr P Wright, ACA, BSc

Head Master: **Dr Millan Sachania**, MA Cantab, MPhil, PhD, FRSA

Second Master: R Hinton, BSc, PGCE (*Mathematics*)

Deputy Head Mistress: Mrs G Cross, BA, MA. PGCE (*English*)

Assistant Head Mistress (Sixth Form): Mrs S Ridley, BA, PGCE (*Classics*)

Director of Studies: Mrs N Snelgrove, BSc, PGCE (*Mathematics*)

Director of Co-Curricular Studies and Outreach: A Christie, MA Oxon, PGCE (*Classics*)

Head of Prep School: T Mylne, BA, PGCE

Bursar: J Gibson, GIPM, MCIPD

Assistant Masters and Mistresses (Senior School):
* *Head of Department*
¹ *Head of Year*

¹Mrs C Ainsworth, BEd, PGCE (*Physical Education*)
Mrs S Akintunde, BSc, MSc, GTP (**Chemistry*)
Mrs C Baker, LLB, QTS (*English*)
Ms R Baker, BA, PGCE (*Art*)
Mrs C Barry, BA, Dip SLD (**Learning Support*)
Mrs E Basson, BA, PGCE (**Academic Physical Education*)
¹Mrs K Birtwistle, BSc (*Biology*)
Mrs F Brent, BA, PGCE (*Art*)
Mrs Jane Cameron (*LAMDA*)
¹Madame C Casset, BA, MA, PGCE (*French*)
Mr K Chaudery, BSc, MSc, PGCE (*Mathematics*)
Mr Ian Chiew, BSc, MA, QTS (*Mathematics*)
Dr S Choudhry, MEng, PhD, PGCE (*Science*)
Mrs J Cobain, BA, PGCE (*English*)
Mrs C Copeman, BA Cantab, PGCE (*Mathematics*)
Mr A Doddridge, BSc, PGCE (**Geography*)
Miss M Durello, BA, PGCE (*Italian*)
Ms B Elton, BA, PG Dip D&T, PGCE (**Design and Technology*)
Ms Chiara Eves, BA, QTS (**Sport and Physical Education*)
Mrs M Evans, BA, PGCE (**Drama*)
Miss S Fitzgibbon, BSc (**Physics,*Science*)
Mrs E Fitzsimons, BA, PGCE (**English*)
Miss C Forber, MMath, PGCE (*Mathematics*)
Mr P Frost, BA, ACMA, PGCE (**Computing and Digital Learning*)
Miss C Garcia-Gomez, BA, PGCE (*Spanish*)

¹Miss H Gibbons, BA, MA, PGCE (*History*)
Mr B Goakes, BA Ed (*Duke of Edinburgh's Award Leader, Design and Technology*)
Mrs C Goetz, BSc, PGCE (*Chemistry*)
Miss A Gunga, BA, PGCE (*Religious Studies*)
Mr T Heaton, BA, QTS (*Design and Technology*)
Ms F Helszajn, BA (*Spanish*)
Mrs A James, BSc, PGCE (**Biology*)
Mr C Johnston, BA, MEd, PGCE (**Economics,*Careers*)
Miss L Kay, BA, MA, QTS (**History, *Government and Politics*)
Miss G Kennedy, BSocSc, PGCE (*Geography*)
Mrs J Kirby, BA, PGCE (**Mathematics*)
Ms L Kressly, BA (*Drama*)
Dr C Laverick, BA, MA, PhD, NPQH (*Computer Science*)
Miss Lucy MacPhee, BA, PGCE (*Classics*)
Ms P May, BMus (**Music*)
Mr W Nolan, BA, PGCE (**Classics*)
Mrs Rebecca Oliver, BMus, PGCE (*Music*)
Miss A Sillitoe, BA, PGCE (**Art, Lead in Extended Learning, Innovation and Research*)
¹Mr M Spooner, BSc, MA, PGCE (*Physics*)
Dr E van Heerden, BA, BA, BEd, MSocSci, DPhil, PGCE (**Psychology*)
Ms J Watts, BD, PGCE (**Religious Studies, Critical Thinking*)
Mrs A Weymes-McElderry, BA, PGCE (**Modern Foreign Languages, Oxbridge Coordinator*)
Mrs E Wheeler, BSc, PGCE (*Biology*)
Mrs K Wheeler, BEd (*Physical Education*)
Ms D Zoromba, BA, PGCE (*English*)
Mr C Whyld, BSc, MA, PGCE (**Drama*) {Acting Head}

Head Master's PA: Mrs B Wheeler, BMus, BSc, PGDip Ed Mgmt
Registrar: Mrs P Warner

Sydenham High School
GDST

19 Westwood Hill, London SE26 6BL
Tel: 020 8557 7000
email: info@syd.gdst.net
website: www.sydenhamhighschool.gdst.net
Twitter: @sydenhamhigh

Founded in 1887, Sydenham High School is part of the GDST (Girls' Day School Trust). The GDST is the leading network of independent girls' schools in the UK. As a charity that owns and runs 24 schools and two academies, it reinvests all its income in its schools. For further information about the Trust, see p. xxiii or visit www.gdst.net.

Pupil numbers. Senior School 380, Junior School 200.

For 130 years, Sydenham High School has been committed to the fundamental aim of providing a first-class education for girls –grounded in a tradition of academic excellence and focused on developing in our pupils the skills and confidence to face the challenges and enjoy the opportunities of life both in and beyond school.

Occupying the grounds of a Victorian mansion, we enjoy an open, leafy setting in a location that is easily accessible by public transport. Our Junior School has its own facilities with ready access to those of the Senior School. The School has a distinctive blend of Victorian buildings and purpose-built accommodation refurbished to a high standard. Our facilities are impressive and include an extensive library with online facilities, several ICT suites and a design technology centre. We have seven science laboratories and a Performing Arts Centre, featuring a Theatre and Recital

Hall. New dining facilities, including a café area, opened early in 2015.

Excellent on-site sports facilities comprise a Sports Hall and all-weather pitch, supplemented by extensive sports fields close by in Lower Sydenham. We produce fine sportswomen who compete in a variety of sports at national level and our elite athlete support programme helps girls who train outside school to balance their school and sporting commitments.

Curriculum. The School offers a broad curriculum, ensuring all our pupils are stimulated and excited by learning. English and Maths provide a solid foundation while languages offered include French, German, Spanish, Italian and Latin. All students study biology, chemistry and physics. Creative and practical subjects include design technology, art, PE, music and drama. Humanities include History, Geography, Religious Studies and Classical Civilisation. All pupils receive a thorough grounding in ICT, taught as a discrete subject and confidently used as a cross-curricular tool.

In the Sixth Form, further mathematics, business studies, government & politics, computer science, theatre studies, PE and sociology are offered in addition to the normal range of AS and A Level courses. Specifically-focused preparation is provided for entry to prestigious universities, including Oxford and Cambridge. Our co-curricular and careers programmes bring in speakers and take students out to visit exhibitions and industry. Huge opportunities are available for leadership across the school including SydApprentice (Year 8), Young Enterprise (Year 12), sports teams, administering clubs, and an extended prefect system.

Students make informed choices of GCSE, AS and A Level subjects, supported throughout by specialist staff. Work in Careers and PSHE also informs the decision making process. Our students are offered places at top universities, while some take gap years abroad. The breadth of extra-curricular opportunities encourages all pupils to broaden their interests and develop personal skills. Drama is popular with numerous clubs and productions at the Junior and Senior Schools. A diversity of opportunity for making music is available to pupils whatever their instrument or level of expertise. Highly-qualified peripatetic staff teach instrumental lessons. Specialist music staff train school ensembles, concert band and choirs which perform in, and beyond, the School on a regular basis. Involvement in the wider community is encouraged through our successful involvement in the Duke of Edinburgh's Award scheme and charity work.

Fees per term (2016–2017). Senior School £5,234, Junior School £4,116.

School fees include examination fees, textbooks, stationery and other materials, choral music, PE and swimming, ISCO and Careers counselling. They do not include instrumental music, speech and drama, and after-school clubs.

Scholarships and Bursaries. *Entrance Scholarships*: The Girls' Day School Trust provides a number of scholarships each year for entry to the Senior School at 11+ and directly into the Sixth Form. Scholarships are awarded on academic merit and no financial means test is involved.

Bursaries: The GDST provides bursaries which are means-tested and intended to ensure that the School remains accessible to bright girls who would benefit from our education, but who would be unable to enter the School without financial assistance. Bursaries are awarded on the basis of financial need and academic merit. Details can be obtained from the Admissions Secretary. It is recognised that occasions will arise when some form of short-term assistance is required –a small fund exists to help pupils taking public examinations in such cases.

Sydenham High School Scholarships: Art, music, drama and sports scholarships may be awarded on entry at 11+ in addition to our academic scholarships.

Charitable status. Sydenham High School is part of The Girls' Day School Trust, which is a Registered Charity, number 306983.

Chair of Local Governors: Ms G Evans

***Acting Head [Jan-Apr 2017]*: Mr K Guest**, MA St Mary's Twickenham, PGCE

Headmistress [from Apr 2017]: Mrs K C Woodcock, BA Bristol

Deputy Head (*Academic*): Mr C Batty, BSc Bangor, Wales, PGCE

Deputy Head (*Student Development*): [Mr K Guest, MA St Mary's Twickenham, PGCE]

Head of Junior School: Ms C Boyd, BA London, PGCE

Head of Sixth Form: Ms R Parrish, BA Southampton, PGCE

Talbot Heath

Rothesay Road, Bournemouth, Dorset BH4 9NJ

Tel: 01202 761881 Senior School Admissions
            01202 763360 Junior School Admissions
            01202 755410 Finance
Fax: 01202 768155
email: office@talbotheath.org
website: www.talbotheath.org
Twitter: @TalbotHeathSch
Facebook: @TalbotHeathSch
LinkedIn: /Talbot-Heath-School

Motto: *Honour before Honours*

The School is an Independent School, founded in 1886 by private effort and transferred to Trustees in 1898 and is administered under a scheme drawn up by the Ministry of Education in 1903. It is a Church of England Foundation and pupils of all denominations are welcome. This School is committed to safeguarding and promoting the welfare of children and young people. The School is also committed to a policy of equal opportunity.

There are some 327 girls in the Main School, of whom 80 are in the Sixth Forms and 40 are Boarders. There is a Junior Department for about 147 girls between the ages of 7 and 11. The Pre-Preparatory department caters for 120 girls aged 3+ to 7.

Talbot Heath is among the longest-established schools in the Bournemouth area, with over a century of success. The school enjoys an attractive wooded site and outstanding facilities for Art, Drama, Music and the Sciences (new Art and Drama studios opened in September 2000, new Science Centre opened in March 1999) together with good ICT provision and extensive modern accommodation for a wide range of sports activities.

The school follows the best practice of the National Curriculum but does not undertake Key Stage testing at levels 1, 2 and 3.

Examinations. 21 subjects are offered to GCSE (including Core Subjects) and A Level, and girls gain places at a variety of universities, including Oxford and Cambridge, or go on to other forms of higher education or professional training.

Admission. Girls are admitted into the Junior School by examination at 7 and above and into the Main School by examination at 11+, 12+ and 13+. The Entrance Examination is held annually in January and girls must be capable of working with those of their own age. Entry to the Pre-preparatory Department requires no examination.

Boarding Houses. St Mary's Boarding House is located in the School grounds, Miss Scarr being in overall charge.

Fees per term (2016–2017). Tuition: Senior School: £4,444; Junior School: £2,037–£3,626; Kindergarten according to sessions. Boarding (in addition to Tuition Fees): £3,428 (full); £3,059 (weekly); flexi: £61 per night or £150 for a 3-night package.

Scholarships and bursaries are available and there is also a discount for daughters of Service families and the clergy.

Charitable status. Talbot Heath is a Registered Charity, number 283708. It exists to provide high quality education for children.

Governing Body:
Chairman: Mr G Exon
Vice Chair: Mrs C Norman
Dr T Battcock
Mrs D Leadbetter
Dr A Main
Mr R Peak
Revd Canon Dr C Rutledge
Mrs R Small
Mrs S Thomas, LLB
Mr D Townend
Mrs C Sutcliffe
Mrs C Edwards

Head: **Mrs A Holloway**, MA Oxon

Deputy Head, Pastoral: Mrs C Stone, BSc Hons Royal Holloway London
Head of Junior School: Mrs S Weber-Spokes
Deputy Head of Junior School: Mrs E Pugh

Heads of Faculty Senior School:
Mrs T Magrath, MA York (*English*)
Mrs J Maynard, BSc Hons Nottingham (*Mathematics*)
Mr A Hill, BMus Hons, FTCL (*Creative Arts & Technology*)
Mr M Gibson, BSc Hons Hull (*Science*)
Mrs H Chapleo, BSc Hons Kingston (*Humanities*)
Miss L Marks, BSc Hons Loughborough (*Physical Education*)
Miss A Klemz, PGCE Liverpool

Visiting teachers also attend for Piano, Violin, Violoncello, Double Bass, Flute, Clarinet, Oboe, Bassoon, Horn, Saxophone, Trumpet, Trombone, Tuba, Percussion, Singing, Dancing, Speech Training and Voice Production, English for foreign students, French, Spanish and German Conversation.

Director of Support Services: Mr C Evans
Medical Officer: Dr M Shaw
Director of Finance: Mr G Ives
Head of Admissions: Mrs K Wills
Head's PA/Office Manager/HR Manager: Mrs D Flynn

Tormead School

Cranley Road, Guildford, Surrey GU1 2JD

Tel: 01483 575101
Fax: 01483 450592
email: registrar@tormeadschool.org.uk
website: www.tormeadschool.org.uk
Twitter: @TormeadSchool

Tormead is an academically selective independent day school for around 760 girls from 4 to 18 years of age. Founded in 1905, it stands in pleasant grounds, close to the centre of Guildford. The atmosphere is lively and the teaching stimulating and challenging. Standards and expectations are high and girls leave the school as confident, articulate and self-reliant young women, ready to meet the challenges of university and beyond. Almost all girls leave Tormead to read for degrees at the university of their choice. On average, 10% gain an Oxford or Cambridge place.

An extensive extracurricular programme provides further challenge and opportunity. We believe that a breadth of interests, skills and initiative are an essential complement to academic success for the future lives of our pupils.

The school has a lively and active musical life with orchestras, various chamber groups, ensembles and choirs as well as a highly popular and talented Jazz Band which has undertaken tours to various European countries. Drama, dance, public speaking and debating, Young Enterprise, The Wings of Hope Achievement Award, and Duke of Edinburgh's Award are all very well supported and sixth form girls have the opportunity to travel to Vietnam and Zambia.

A wide range of sports is on offer and there is a busy programme of fixtures in Hockey, Netball, Rounders, Athletics and Swimming in all of which we compete with great success. Gymnastics has been a particular strength for some years with our teams competing successfully at national level.

Fees per term (2016–2017). Reception £2,527, Years 1–2 £2,787, Years 3–4 £4,150, Years 5–6 £4,212, Years 7–13 £4,818.

Scholarships and Bursaries. Academic, Music, Art and Sport Scholarships are offered at 11+ and 16+. Bursaries are available at 11+ and 16+ entry and are dependent on the level of parental income.

Tormead Old Girls' Association. Email: toga@tormeadschool.org.uk.

Charitable status. Tormead Limited is a Registered Charity, number 312057. It exists to provide education for able girls.

Board of Governors:
Chairman: Mrs R Harris, BA Hons, ACA
Mr R Jewkes, BEng
Dr C Kissin, MBChB, MRCP, FRCR
Prof G Nicholls
Mr P J O'Keefe, RIBA, MCIOB, MIMgt
Dr J Page, LLM, BSc, MB BS, MRCP, FRCR, MFFLM
Miss A Spender
Cllr J Wicks
Mr D M Williams, BA, FCA

Bursar and Clerk to the Governors: Mr M O'Donovan, BA Canterbury

Headmistress: **Mrs Christina Foord**, BA, MPhil, PGCE Birmingham

Deputy Head Academic: Mr J Coles, BA Swansea, PGCE UEA (*Geography and IT*)
Deputy Head Pastoral: Miss T King, BA Cambridge, PGCE Oxford (*English*)

Senior School Staff:
* *Head of Department*

Mrs A Arnold, BA, PGCE Keele (*French/German*)
Mr S Baird, BSc Edinburgh, PGCE Brunel (*Geography)
Miss K Banks, MA Edinburgh (*English, Drama*)
Miss D Bell, BA, PGCE Greenwich (*Physical Education*)
Mrs H Boczkowski, BSc Bath Spa (*Head of Food Technology*)
Mr T Breslin, BA Sussex, PGCE Buckingham (*History*)
Miss S Buchan, BA & MEng Cambridge, PGCE Oxford (*Physics*)
Mrs E A Burton, BA, PGCE Birmingham (*Mathematics, Physical Education*)
Dr V Campbell (*English, German*)

Mrs N Chaffe, MA Open University (*English*)

Mrs S Clarke, MA Cantab, DipLib, MCLIP (*Senior Librarian*)

Mrs S Culhane, BA Washington USA, PGCE Goldsmiths London (*English*)

Mrs K Dabill, BSc Bangor, PGCE Surrey (*Mathematics*)

Mrs C Don, MA Oxford, PGCE Surrey (*Mathematics*)

Mrs T A Dyer, BA Swansea, PGCE London (*Spanish, French*)

Mrs S Elmes, BA King's College London, PGCE Cardiff (*Religious Studies*)

Mr R Ewbank, BA, PGCE Goldsmiths London (*Art, Technology, ICT*)

Mrs A Ferns MA Cantab (*Assistant Librarian*)

Miss K Finch (*Physical Education*)

Mrs K Fletcher, BA UCL, CTEL, PGCE Trinity College London (*Classics*)

Ms A Franchot, MA Paris (*French Language Assistante*)

Mrs S M Gibbs, BSc Bangor, PGCE Nottingham (*Science*)

Mrs E Gil Rivas, BA Southampton, MA Surrey, PGCE King's College London (*MFL*)

Mrs J Glazier, BSc Exeter, PGCE Gloucs (*Mathematics*)

Mrs S Harrod Booth, MA Kingston, PGCE Cambridge (**Mathematics*)

Mr P Heap, BA Hull, PGCE Manchester Metropolitan (*Teacher i/c Drama*)

Ms T Hetherington, BA Westminster, MA St Martin's College, PGCE Roehampton (*Art, 3D Studies*)

Mr M Holford, BMus Surrey, PGCE Roehampton, ARCO, LTCL (*Assistant Director of Music*)

Mr R Isaacs, BSc Hons St Andrews, PGCE Reading (**Biology*)

Mr C Ives, BA Warwick, PGCE Reading (**German*)

Mrs S Jones, BSc Surrey, PGCE St Mary's College (*Geography*)

Mrs T Kaminska-Moult (*German*)

Mrs F Khan-Evans, BA London, MA Surrey Institute, PGCE London (**Art*)

Mr J Keey, MA St Andrews, PGCE St Mary's College (*Religious Studies*)

Mrs C Kennedy, BA Cambridge, MA Twickenham, PGCE GTC (**RS*)

Mrs R Landon, BSc UEA, PGCE Kingston (*Science*)

Mrs E Lange, MA ESCP Europe, BA North Carolina USA (*MFL*)

Miss M Langlet, MA Toulouse le Mirail, PGCE Oxon (*Teacher i/c French, Spanish*)

Mrs D Ledgerwood, MA Oxon, PGCE Reading (**Chemistry*)

Miss N Lloyd, BA Boston (**Hockey*)

Mrs G M Mackay, BA, UED Rhodes (*English*)

Mr A Merryweather, BA East Anglia, PGCE Buckingham (*Director of Music*)

Miss S Michalopoulou, BA Leeds, MSc Edinburgh (*Classics*)

Mrs P Moodie, BA Manchester Metropolitan, PGCE Manchester (*Teacher i/c Spanish, French*)

Miss M Morlang, MChem Surrey (*Chemistry*)

Miss E Murray, MA St Andrews, Dip Law, Manchester, PGCE Cumbria (**History*)

Mrs M O'Brien, BEd Chichester (*Director of Sport*)

Mr J Parsons, BA & MA Lancaster, PGCE Reading (*Head of English*)

Miss I Painter, BA Durham (*Classics*)

Mrs K Perkins, BA Surrey (*Physical Education*)

Mr G Press, BSc, CertEd Brunel (*Teacher i/c Design and Technology*)

Mrs E Robinson, MA Oxon, PGCE York (*Spanish*)

Dr S Smedley, MPhys Lancaster, PhD Cantab (*Physics*)

Mr J South, BA & MA London, PGCE London (*History*)

Mr J E Sykes, BA Westminster, MSc LSE (*Government & Politics*)

Mrs C Tee, BA South Bank, CertEd South Bank (*Food Technology*)

Mrs L Tidy, BA Chichester (*Physical Education*)

Ms S Travis, MA, PGCE Cantab (*Chemistry*)

Miss M Uezzell, BA Southampton (*Physical Education*)

Miss E Walshe, BSc Greenwich, PGCE Surrey (*Science*)

Mrs S Wightman (**PE*)

Mr D Wilkinson, BMus Huddersfield, PGCE Durham, DipPsych Open University (**Psychology*)

Mrs C Williams, BA Cambridge (**Careers, *Economics*)

Mr P Wilkinson, MA Cantab, MSc UCL, MBA Brunel, CEng, CSci, MIChemE (**Physics*)

Mrs L Whitaker, BSc Manchester, PGCE Exeter (*Geography*)

Mr O Wright, BA Hons Durham, MA Durham (*English, Drama*)

Mrs C Wyatt (*Mathematics*)

Mrs A Woodfine, MEng Oxford, PGCE Chichester (*Mathematics*)

Junior School Staff:

Head: Mrs L Salmond Smith, BA East Anglia, MMus Hull, PGCE Gloucestershire, MBA Keele

Deputy Head: Mrs K Moulder, MA Kingston, BEd Avery Hill

Mrs E Alderman, BSc Leeds (*Class Teacher*)

Mrs G Blackburn, BSc Sussex, RSA Dip Helen Arkell Dyslexia Centre (*Special Educational Needs, Dyslexia*)

Mrs C Boyd, BA UWE (*Class Teacher*)

Mrs C Broadway, BSc, PGCE Roehampton (*Design Technology Teacher*)

Mrs P Butler, BA Liverpool, PGCE Oxford Brookes, GradDip RE Sydney

Miss M Colyer, BSc York, PGCE Cantab (*Class Teacher*)

Mrs N Fry (*Class Teacher*)

Miss S Insch (*Class Teacher*)

Mrs J Johnson, BA Durham (*Key Stage 2*)

Mrs J L Norman, MPhil Reading, BSc Nottingham (*Teaching Assistant*)

Miss L Payne (*Teaching Assistant*)

Mrs K Perkins, BA Surrey (*Physical Education*)

Miss H Rees, BA York, PGCE Birmingham (*Class Teacher*)

Mrs K Richards, BEd De Montfort (*Class Teacher*)

Mrs S Vega, BA, PGCE Durham (*Music*)

Miss L Warden, BEd Hons Kingston (*Pre-Prep Class Teacher*)

Registrar: Mrs C Scott

Headmistress's PA: Mrs Y Nixon

Junior School Secretary: Mrs T Kelly/Mrs N Overgaard

Truro High School for Girls

Falmouth Road, Truro, Cornwall TR1 2HU

Tel:	01872 272830
email:	registrar@trurohigh.co.uk
website:	www.trurohigh.co.uk
Twitter:	@TruroHigh
Facebook:	/TruroHighSchoolForGirls

Founded 1880. Independent, formerly Direct Grant.

Truro High School combines a Pre-Prep and Preparatory Department of approximately 80 girls aged 4–11 and a Senior School of approximately 240 girls (aged 11–18). Boarding accommodation is provided from the age of 7. Entry is based on the school's own selection procedure. Academic, Music, Sport, Drama and Art Scholarships are offered on entry to Years 7, 9 and 12. Means-tested Bursaries are available.

A broadly based curriculum is provided to GCSE including Art, Religious Philosophy & Ethics, English, History, Geography, Latin, French, Spanish, Mathematics, Physics, Chemistry, Biology, Music, Art, Food and Nutrition, Textiles, Theatre Studies and Physical Education. Further subjects at AS/A2 in the Sixth Form are Business Studies/Economics, Classical Civilisation, History of Art and Psychology alongside an Extended Project Qualification. A Careers Department exists to advise girls and parents on openings available over a wide field including entrance to Universities and other institutions of Higher Education. Music forms an important part of the curriculum and there are two orchestras, two strong choirs, jazz band and numerous ensembles. The school has good facilities: six well-equipped Science laboratories, a Modern Languages block with digital laboratory, a new Studio Theatre, Textiles and Cookery rooms, three Information Technology suites, indoor heated swimming pool, tennis and netball courts and an all-weather hockey/athletics pitch. Pupils in the Sixth Form have their own Sixth Form Centre with individual cubicles for private study and a wi-fi Study Zone. Two outstanding boarding houses are located in the centre of the campus.

There is a wide range of extra-curricular activities and all pupils are encouraged to participate. The school enjoys good relationships with other schools in the neighbourhood.

Fees per term (2016–2017). Tuition: Pre-Prep £1,780–£2,104; Prep £3,940; Senior School £4,201.

Boarding (in addition to Tuition fees): £3,381 (weekly), £4,004 (full), £4,004 (overseas).

Charitable status. Truro High School for Girls is a Registered Charity, number 306577.

Governors:
President: The Rt Revd Tim Thornton, BA, Bishop of Truro
Chair: Mrs Anna Corbett
Revd Canon Dr Lynda Barley
Mrs Suzanne Bennet
The Very Revd Roger Bush
Mrs Sarah Hall, BVet Med, MRCVS
Mr N Trefusis, RN, DL
Mr David Humphreys
Mr John Keast

Headmaster: Dr G Moodie, BA, MA, Dip Arts, PhD

Senior Deputy Head: Mrs M Smith, BA Hons
Deputy Head: Miss D Freeman, BEd Hons
Head of Sixth Form: Mrs M Sharp and Miss A Whitney
Head of Preparatory School: Miss A Ramsey, BEd Hons

Assistant Staff:
* *Head of Department*

Art, Design Technology and Food:
*Mrs J Tutin, MA
*Mrs W Williams, BA Hons
Mrs L van der Lem, BSc Hons
Mrs S G Weiringa, BSc, MBA (*Textiles*)
Miss C Rowe, MA (*Art Technician*)

Business Studies/Economics:
*Mr T Elliott, BA Hons

Careers & Work Experience:
Mr P Crump, BA Hons, NPQH
Miss C Rowe, MA

Classics:
*Mrs S J Brown, MA Oxon

English and Drama:
*Mrs J A Holland, BA Hons

Miss A Whitney, BA Hons
Mr I Tutin, BA Hons
Mr P Crump, BA Hons, NPQH
Mrs J Trewellard, BA Hons

Geography:
Miss S Miles, BA Hons, PGCE
Miss S Morris, BA Hons

History:
*Mr G Ford, BA Hons

ICT:
Mr H Wardle, BSc Hons
Mr C Kellow (*ICT Manager*)
Mrs B Clark, BSc Hons (*Data Manager*)

Mathematics:
*Miss C Harding, BSc Hons
*Mrs C Goodright, BSc Hons
Mrs S Robins, BSc Hons
Mr T Wells, BSc Hons

Modern Languages:
*Mrs K Cox, BA Hons
Mrs S Murley, BA Hons
Mrs M Smith, BA Hons
Mrs A Simmonds, MA
Mrs F Ferris, BA Hons

Music:
*Mr R Norman, BMus Hons, PGCE

Peripatetic Music Staff:
Miss K Allen (*Singing*)
Mrs R Brenton (*Clarinet, Saxophone*)
Ms J Courtenay (*Piano, Theory*)
Mrs J Edwards (*Violin, Viola*)
Mr M Edwards (*Piano*)
Mr G Graham (*Guitar*)
Ms F Hooper (*Flute*)
Ms J Kershaw (*Brass*)
Mrs M Hoadley (*Singing*)
Ms H Robinson (*Cello*)
Mrs N Williams (*Guitar*)

Physical Education:
*Mrs K Barbary-Redd, BEd Hons
Mrs J Barnfield, BEd Hons
Miss D Freeman, BEd Hons
Mrs G Tregay, CertEd
Miss A Veall, BSc, PGCE

Psychology:
Mrs K Pooley, BSc Hons

Preparatory Department:
Head: Miss A Ramsey, BEd Hons
Mrs Y Simpson, BEd Hons
Mrs R Bateson, BA Hons
Miss H Mills, BEd Hons, MEd
Mrs K A Roberts, BEd Hons
Mrs E Symons, BA Hons
Mrs J Dick
Miss K Cameron

Religious Philosophy & Ethics:
*Mr P J Mothersole, BA Hons, MA
Mrs R Westley, BA Hons
Mr I Tutin, BA Hons

Science:
*Mr J Dean, BSc Hons, NPQH
Mrs M Sharp, BSc Hons
Mr G Bennett, BSc Hons
Mrs C Hallam, BSc Hons
Mr S Loosley, BSc Hons

Learning Support Centre:
*Mrs K Wood, SpLD, CCET Level A
Mrs J Hood, BA Hons, PGCE
Mrs R Westley, BA Hons

Librarian: Mrs K Pooley, BSc Hons

Medical:
Dr C Newton, MB, ChB, MRCGP, DRCOG, DFFP, DCH
Mrs D Kingston

Finance Manager: Miss C Beacham, BA Hons, ACA
Marketing and Business Development Director: Mrs Sarah Lillicrap
Estates Supervisor: Mr G Williams
HR Manager: Mrs H Andrew, BA Hons, MCIPD
Assistant Accountant: Miss S Trevena
Billing Ledger Clerk: Mrs F Knight
Payroll Assistant: Mrs S Talbot
Registrar: Miss C Shaw
Headmaster's PA: Mrs J Norriss
Development Officer: Mrs F Osman, BA Hons
Marketing Assistant: Miss G Kennard, BA Hons
School Receptionists: Mrs J Jenkins, Mrs G Gray
Reprographics: Mrs H Martin

Tudor Hall

Wykham Park, Banbury, Oxon OX16 9UR

Tel: 01295 263434
Fax: 01295 253264
email: admissions@tudorhallschool.com
           admin@tudorhallschool.com
website: www.tudorhallschool.com
Twitter: @TudorHallSchool
Facebook: /TudorHallSchool

Motto: *Habeo Ut Dem*

Tudor Hall is an Independent Boarding School for Girls aged 11–18 years. The school was originally founded in 1850 and moved to Wykham Park in 1946. It is situated in spacious grounds 1½ miles from Banbury Station and is within easy access of London, Oxford and Stratford-upon-Avon –M40, Junction 11. This enables the girls to enjoy a wide range of cultural and educational activities.

The school accommodates approximately 258 boarders and 78 day girls. Its buildings comprise a 17th century and an 18th century manor with a modern purpose-built house for 96 Sixth Formers and extensive new facilities. These include laboratories for biology, chemistry, physics and general science; CDT workshop; 2 information technology rooms; language laboratory; modern languages and domestic science rooms; drama studio; music school; studios for art and pottery; textiles room; gym and sports hall. There are tennis and netball courts, a swimming pool, squash courts, astroturf and pitches for hockey, lacrosse and rounders. An extension to the Sixth Form block has been completed, with the original rooms undergoing extensive refurbishment. The Year 10 House has recently undergone extensive refurbishment and plans are in place to build a purpose-built drama studio and sports complex.

The curriculum includes a full range of academic subjects and, where possible, outings and fieldwork are arranged. All girls begin Latin and French with Spanish or German. Italian, Ancient Greek, Mandarin and Russian are also available. Music and Drama are strongly encouraged. Girls are prepared for GCSE and Advanced Level GCE, and appropriate certificates in optional extra subjects. Girls may also take riding and dancing lessons. There is a library and a careers room where advice is given about university entrance and further training.

Admission is by internal examinations at 11+ and internal examinations and Common Entrance at 13+. Entry may also be made to the Sixth Form where all girls pursue courses leading to higher education or vocational training and they are treated as students. Those entering at 11 are accustomed to being away from home by being housed separately in a smaller environment. Girls are divided into four competitive Houses but residence is with their own age group.

Tudor Hall places great importance on having a friendly atmosphere, a lively and united spirit and high standards. Girls are expected to take an interest in a wide range of activities as well as following a broad educational programme. Involvement in the local community through the Duke of Edinburgh's Award and social service, and participation in events with other schools are encouraged. Debating and public speaking are strong and there is keen involvement in the Young Enterprise Scheme, Model United Nations and European Youth Parliament. Tudor Hall is an Anglican school but members of other religious groups are welcomed. There is a small chapel.

Scholarships and Bursaries. *Academic* 11+/13+ and 16+. These are awarded to candidates entering at 11+ or 13+ on the basis of their performance at Common Entrance and interviews. At 16+ awards are offered on the basis of interview, school report and examination. The value of the award is up to £1,000 per annum. These awards are intended for the support of the pupil's academic interests.

Music 11+/13+ and 16+. These are awarded on the basis of ability and potential at 11+, 13+ and 16+. The value of the award is up to £1,000 per annum to entrants who show outstanding musical ability. Music awards exist in the form of free tuition in one or more instruments for the duration of the student's time at the school.

Art 13+/16+. These are awarded on the basis of ability and potential either at 13+ or 16+. The value of the award is up to £1,000 per annum. These awards are intended for the support of the pupil's Art interests.

Dance 16+. These are awarded on the basis of ability and potential at 16+. The value of the award is up to £1,000 per annum. These awards are intended for the support of the pupil's Dance interests.

Drama 13+/16+. These are awarded on the basis of ability and potential either at 13+ or 16+. The value of the award is up to £1,000 per annum. These awards are intended for the support of the pupil's Dramatic interests.

Sport 13+/16+. These are awarded on the basis of ability and potential either at 13+ or 16+. The value of the award is up to £1,000 per annum. These awards are intended for the support of the pupil's Sporting interests.

Textiles 16+. These are awarded on the basis of ability and potential at 16+. The value of the award is up to £1,000 per annum. These awards are intended for the support of the pupil's Textiles interests.

Bursaries are awarded to new and current parents who are in financial need.

Fees per term (2016–2017). £10,870 for boarders; £6,915 for day pupils.

Board of Governors:
Chairman: Mr John Gloag
Chairman of Finance & General Purpose Committee: Mr Barry Gamble
Chairman of Education Committee: Mr Joe Davies
Chairman of Carrdus School Committee: Mrs Rosalind Hayes

Mr Simon Biggart
Mr Duncan Bailey
Mrs Sally Bowie

Mr Adrian Brett
Miss Charlotte Duncombe
Mr John Elliot

Mrs Kathy Fidgeon
Mrs Victoria Harley
Mrs Rosalind Hayes
Miss Mary Kinnear

Mr Bob Lari
Mrs Sez Maxted
Mr Mark Wiggin

Senior Management Team:

Headmistress: Wendy Griffiths, BSc Wales, PGCE London

Bursar: Bruno Delacave
Deputy Head: Clare Macro, MA Oxon, PGCE Oxon
Deputy Head (Pastoral): Rani Tandon, BA Birmingham, PGCE Manchester Met
Assistant Head (Sixth Form): Ian Edwards, BSc Newcastle, PGCE UEA
Senior Teacher: Lucy Keyte, BA Nottingham, PGCE Warwick
Senior Teacher: Julia Thorn, BA Reading, MSt Oxon
Director of Operations: Lesley Evans
Director of Digital Learning: John Field, MA Oxon, PGCE Oxon
Director of Co-Curriculum: Pippa Duncan-Jones, BSc Loughborough, PGCE Leeds

Teaching Staff:
Sarah Allitt, BSc Oxford Brookes (*Learning Support*)
Carola Beecham, BA Exeter QTS (*English*)
Jo Benlalam, BMus, AKC, PGCE London (*Head of Careers, Academic Music*)
Amanda Brauer, BA Kent, PGCE Bedford (*Physical Education*)
Elizabeth Buckner-Rowley, BA Portsmouth, PGCE Leeds (*Spanish*)
Lucinda Burton, BA Leeds, PGDipEd QTS Birmingham (*Religious Studies*)
Alan Christopher, MA Essex, BTEC Kingshurst, HND Coventry (*Drama*)
Struan Cockcroft, BSc Science, BSc Physics Free State, MSc KwaZulu-Natal, PGCE SA (*Physics*)
Sheila Craske, BA Oxon, PGCE Manchester Poly (*Head of Art*)
Lindsey Cullen, MA Oxon (*Head of Classics*)
Gerard Duncan, PGDSST, BPE University of Otago, New Zealand (*Physical Education*)
Pippa Duncan-Jones, BSc Loughborough, PGCE Leeds (*Physical Education*)
Ian Edwards, BSc Newcastle, PGCE UEA (*Mathematics*)
John Field, MA, PGCE Oxon (*English*)
Sara Fordy, BA Winchester, PGCE Oxon (*Head of Textiles*)
Elizabeth Fulton, BA Reading, MA Warwick (*Head of History of Art*)
Jonathan Galloway, BA Middx, PGCE London (*Head of Religious Studies*)
Alison Gamble, MA London, CPE Law (*Head of Senior History & Politics*)
Peter Garratt, BA Nottingham, PGCE Oxon (*Maths*)
Marie Genot, MA Provence, France, PGCE UWE (*French/Spanish*)
Florence Gifford-Cagnol, MSc Paris, PhD Paris (*Learning Support*)
Shazia Gleadall, BA Birmingham, PGCE Chester (*Head of KS3 Religious Education*)
Wendy Griffiths, BSc Aberystwyth, PGCE Portsmouth (*Biology*)
Elizabeth Gulliver, BA Oxon (*Head of Learning Support*)
Kerri Hadfield, BA Leeds, PGCE Canterbury (*Head of Geography*)
Jane Haggarty, CertEd Bedford (*Head of Home Economics*)
Sarah Hammond, BA Worcester (*Dance*)
Louise Harper, BA Durham, PGCE Oxon (*Head of KS3 Geography*)

Matthew Harper, BA Oxon (*French/Spanish*)
Marilyn Harris, BA London, PGCE Bulmershe (*French*)
Kate Hart, BA Manchester Metropolitan, PGCE Birmingham (*Head of PSHE*)
Susie Jeffreys, BSc Plymouth, PGCE Exeter (*Geography*) [maternity leave]
Monica Jimenez, BA Spain, PGCE Canterbury (*Head of Spanish*)
Kathryn Joel, BA Warwick, DELTA, TESOL (*EAL Coordinator*)
Christine Jolliffe, BSc, PGCE Leicester (*Head of ICT, Business Studies*)
Nicola Jones, BA, MA Dunelm, MA Arts & Musical Theatre London (*RS/Drama*)
Joanna Kelly, LTA Level 2 Coach, Netball Level 2 Coach (*Physical Education*)
Matthew Kent, BA Keele, MA, PGDip Ed Birmingham (*Head of KS3 English*)
Kate Kettlewell, BVSc Bristol, PGCE Oxon (*Biology/Chemistry*)
Lucy Keyte, BA Nottingham, PGCE Warwick (*French*)
Holly Kidman, BA Portsmouth, QTS (*Textiles*)
Rachael Knapman, Netball Level 1 Coach UKCC (*Physical Education*)
Sadie Lapper, BSc Worcester, PGCert Gloucester, MSc Oxford Brookes (*Director of Sport*)
Lindsey Lea-James, BMus, LTCL, ALCM, PGCE Huddersfield (*Director of Music*)
Caroline Ledger, BEd Plymouth (*Physical Education*)
James Long, BA, PGCE Liverpool (*Physical Education*)
Clare Macro, MA, PGCE Oxon (*Religious Studies*)
Victoria Marsh, BSc Keele, PGCE Exeter (*Head of Mathematics*)
Sarah Malpass, BSc Sheffield, MSc Dunelm, PGCE London (*Head of Junior Science & Biology*)
Harriet Millar-Mills, BSc Loughborough, PGCE MMU (*Mathematics support*)
Richard Moody, BSc PGCE Southampton (*Mathematics*)
Bev Murphy, BA Wales, MA, PhD, PGCE UEA (*Head of Junior History*)
Pervin Özkan, Licence Tours, France, PGCE Exeter (*Head of French*)
Charlotte Pemble, BSc, PGCE Worcester (*2 i/c Physical Education*)
Jonitha Peterpillai, BSc Warwick, MSc, PGCE Oxon (*2 i/c Maths*)
Ryan Pickering, NPLQ, NUCO, DEFIB TA (*Sporting Facilities & PE*)
Cherylin Preston, BSc Leicester, PGCE Exeter (*Head of Chemistry*)
Florence Ravenhall, BSc Galway, PGDip Ireland, QTS Warwick (*ICT*)
Verity Redrup, BA London, PGCE Canterbury (*Biology*)
Bob Roberts, BA, MA Warwick, PGCE Lancaster (*Head of English*)
Bronwen Robinson, BEd Worcester, Dip PE (*Dance*)
Ian Robinson, BEng PGCE Lancaster (*Head of Science*)
Anne-Marie Sanderson, BMus King's London (*Music*)
Virginia Seckerson, BA Loughborough, PGCE Brighton (*Head of CDT*)
Catherine Simpson, BA, GDL, MPhil Cantab, PGCE Belfast (*English*)
Elizabeth Smith, QTS (*Learning Support*)
Rachel Smith, BA Wales, PGCE Leicester (*Head of Psychology*)
Elizabeth Snoddon, BA Portsmouth, PGCE Portsmouth (*Head of Photography*)
Rhea Stafford-Smith, BA York (*History/Politics*)
James Stead, BA Cumbria, PGCE Wales (*Art*)
Erin Stephens, BA Ball State, MEd Portland State (*German*)

Justine Stephens, BA London, PGCE Middx (*Head of Drama*)

Rani Tandon, BA Birmingham, PGCE Manchester Met, PGDip Warwick (*History, PSHE, Politics*)

Holly Thomas, BA Bath, PGCE Coventry (*Head of Modern Languages*)

Richard Thompson, MA Oxon, PGCE London (*Head of Economics & Business Studies*)

Julia Thorn, BA Reading, MSt Oxon (*Classics*)

Kelly Thornton, BA, QTS De Montfort (*Physical Education*) [maternity leave]

Nicole Thurgur, BA South Africa, MA Hertfordshire, QTS (*Textiles*)

Henry Vigne, BA London, MA Kent (*History, PGCE Trainee*)

Kitty Wells, BA London, QTS (*Head of Outdoor Education*)

Helen Wilks, PhD Bristol, PGCE Warwick (*Chemistry, EPQ Coordinator*)

Layla Williams, BA London, PGCE De Montfort (*Dance*)

James Woodward, BSc Wales, PGCE Exeter (*Head of Biology*)

Health Centre:
School Doctor: Dr Nicola Elliott
Sister in Charge: Janet Bonham, RGN
Sister: Caroline Hutchison, RGN
Sister: Lindsay Pickering, RGN
Sister: Virginia Rayner, RGN

Registrar: Philippa Drinkwater
Director of Marketing: Shanna Wells
Headmistress's PA: Jenny Lewis
PA to Bursar: Penny Ranken
Senior Administrative Secretary: Helen Mascall
Examinations Officer: Richard Moody
Head of Communication and Alumnae Relations: Emma McGowan
Data Manager: Laura Pountney
Financial Controller: Harriet Stapleton
Librarian: Alison Falconer Hall

Walthamstow Hall

Senior School:
Holly Bush Lane, Sevenoaks, Kent TN13 3UL

Tel: 01732 451334
Fax: 01732 740439

Junior School:
Bradbourne Park Road, Sevenoaks, Kent TN13 3LD

email: registrar@whall.school
website: www.walthamstow-hall.co.uk
Facebook: /Walthamstow-Hall

Walthamstow Hall is an Independent girls' day school based on two separate sites in Sevenoaks. Founded in 1838, the school celebrated its 175th anniversary in 2013. The Junior School in Bradbourne Park Road takes pupils from age 3–11 years and the Senior School in Holly Bush Lane takes pupils from 11–18 years.

The school has a long established history of preparing academically-able girls for stimulating, purposeful and happy lives within and beyond school. The belief that every student given the right opportunities, encouragement and inspiring teaching can develop an incredible range of skills and talents, is central to the everyday life of the school.

The Headmistress is a member of the GSA (Girls' Schools Association).

The school was judged to be 'Excellent' by the ISI in 2013, excellent being the highest category awarded.

Facilities. Walthamstow Hall is set in its own grounds within the town of Sevenoaks. Girls are taught in light and airy classrooms in buildings specifically designed for learning. The original 1882 Arts and Crafts school building still lies at the heart of the school. Recent campus developments have included: swimming pool complex opened in 2008, Maths Suite and Drama Studio opened in 2009, Music and Design Technology rooms opened in September 2010, additional IT room and Student Entrance and Art Gallery opened in 2012. The school's Ship Theatre was refurbished in 2014 and a gym created for students in Year 10 upwards. A new Dining Hall opened at the Junior School in 2014. A new Sports Centre opened at the Senior School in September 2015 and work commenced on a new Sixth Form Centre in July 2016.

Curriculum. Walthamstow Hall delivers an enriched curriculum which is innovative and flexible, facilitating breadth and individual choice, without sacrificing depth of study. This is brought to life with inspirational teaching.

All girls in their first three Senior School years (7, 8 and 9) follow a core curriculum of 17 subjects, with a second language being added in Year 8. As they progress through to public examinations the flexibility of the curriculum enables girls to study a wide breadth of subjects rather than being shackled by restrictive subject blocks.

Subjects taught include: Art, Biology, Business, Chemistry, Classical Civilisation, Computer Studies, Design and Technology, Drama, Economics, English, Fine Art, French, History, Geography, German, Government and Politics, ICT and Computing, Latin, Mathematics, Music, the Global Perspectives and Research Project, Physical Education, Physics, Religious Studies, Sociology, Spanish, Creative Textiles and Theatre Studies.

Girls are prepared for GCSE, IGCSE, A Levels and Cambridge Pre-U. The record of success in public examinations is excellent. In 2016 83% of Pre-U and A Level examinations were passed at grades A*–B, and 92% of I/GCSEs were passed at grades A*–B.

The breadth and flexibility of the curriculum, combined with expert teaching and encouragement to be ambitious, enables students to be highly successful in their post-Sixth Form choices. In 2016 over 80% of university destinations were to Russell Group universities, and 71% secured their first-choice place.

Religious Teaching is interdenominational.

Extra-Curricular Activities. The high profile of Drama, Music, Sports, trips, careers and study skills and personal development, together with an excellent pastoral system, provides further opportunity and support for every girl.

An active policy of 'sport for all' enables both team players and individuals to find the sporting activities that suit them best. Lacrosse, netball, swimming, athletics, badminton, judo, curling and tennis teams achieve highly at local, county and national levels.

A high proportion of students participate in the Duke of Edinburgh's Award scheme, Business enterprise, the school choirs and orchestra and Trinity Drama.

Girls undertake voluntary service within the local community and abroad.

Admission. Admission to the Junior School is by interview and tests suitable to the age group. Admission to the Senior School for Year 7, 9 and Sixth Form is through the School's own entrance examinations and interview. Parents are warmly invited to visit the School at Open Mornings or on a personal visit.

Fees per term (2016–2017). Senior School and Sixth Form £6,270.

Scholarships. Academic scholarships are awarded annually to the candidates who show the greatest academic potential in the school's own Year 7, 9 and Sixth Form scholarship examinations.

Music and Sport scholarships are also available for Year 7 and Year 9 entry. Drama and Art Awards are offered for Year 9 entry.

Academic scholarships and Art Awards are offered in Sixth Form.

All awards are available to both internal and external candidates.

In addition, a means-tested bursary scheme in the Senior School provides financial help with school fees based on a family's financial circumstances. The scheme includes our Founders' Bursary, which pays nearly 100% of a pupil's school fees throughout their time at the school.

Charitable status. Walthamstow Hall is a Registered Charity, number 1058439. It exists to provide education for girls.

Chair of Governors: Mrs J Adams, BA Joint Hons
There are 16 school governors.

Headmistress: Mrs J Milner, MA Hons English Oxford, PGCE Oxford

Deputy Head: P Howson Esq, BA Hons Plymouth, QTS Kent, AST London (*English*)

Deputy Head: C Hughes Esq, BSc Hons, Cert Ed Loughborough, NPQH (*Mathematics*)

Director of Studies: S Ledsham Esq, MA Oxford, PGCE Sussex (*Physics*)

Head of the Junior School: Mrs D Wood, BSc Hons, PGCE Durham

Senior Teacher, Head of Sixth Form & Careers: Ms E Ancrum, MA Oxford, MPhil Hong Kong, PGCE London (*Economics/Business*)

Senior School:
* *Head of Department/Teacher in Charge of Subject*

Ms J Bisset, BSc Hons Heriot-Watt, PGTC Edinburgh (*Chemistry*)

Mrs F Boorman, BA Hons, PGCE Kent (*Business, Assistant Head of Lower School*)

Mrs V Bower-Morris, BA Hons Surrey, PGCE Goldsmiths (**Drama/Trinity Guildhall Drama*)

Mrs E Brown, BA Hons Leeds, PGCE Brighton (*Art and Textiles*)

N Buckingham Esq, BA Hons, MA Reading, PGCE London (**Classics, Examinations Officer*)

Miss K Burtenshaw, BEd Westminster College Oxford, Cert Ed (**Geography, Assistant Head of Careers*)

N Castell Esq, BMus Hons, PGCE Manchester (**Director of Music*)

J Christian Esq (*Lacrosse Coach*)

Mrs J Cox, MA Cambridge, PGCE Open, ATCL (**Biology*)

T Dakin Esq, BSc Hons Bristol, PGCE Sussex (*Mathematics, Able, Gifted and Talented Coordinator*)

Mrs S Dalton, BSc Hons Keele, PGCE Canterbury, Dip SpLD Dyslexia (**Learning Support*)

Dr R Davies, BSc Hons, PhD Imperial College, PGCE King's College (*Mathematics/Physics*)

Mrs P Durrant, BSc Hons Southampton (*Mathematics, Head of Middle School*)

Mrs C Evans, BA Hons Greenwich, QTS (**Technology –D&T, Food*)

Mrs S Fitzmaurice, BSc Hons Manchester, PGCE Manchester (*Biology, Food Technology*)

Miss M Fournier, Licence, Masters Lille (*MFL*)

Mrs E Garcia, BA Hons Seville, PGCE Sheffield (*MFL*)

Mrs K Hofmann, MA St Andrews, QTS MFL

Mrs H Hook, BA Hons Aberystwyth, PGCE Cambridge (*English*)

Miss L Hope, BSc Hons Imperial, PGCE King's (*Science*)

Mrs K Howlett, BEd Hons Sussex (**PE, Head of Lower School, i/c Swimming, Acting Head of Lacrosse*)

Mrs C Hughes, BA Hons West Surrey College of Art and Design, BSc Hons Middlesex, PGCE London (**Art and Textiles*)

Mrs R Hunt, BA Hons Exeter (**MFL*)

Mrs S Isted, BA Hons Warwick, PGCE King's College (*Classics*)

Mrs R Jennings, BSc Hons Southampton, PGCE Open, ACA (**Mathematics*)

Mrs V Jones (**Theology & Philosophy*)

Miss C Kevis, BA Hons Durham, PGCE King's College (*RS/Phliosophy, History*)

Ms M Knight, BA Hons London, PGCE Canterbury (*English*)

Dr P Le Bas, MA Cambridge, DPhil Oxford, STB/STL Rome, PGCE St Mary's College (**Physics*)

Miss R Leggett (**Director of Sport*)

Miss S Mehaffey, MA, PGCE Edinburgh (**English, Assistant Head of Sixth Form*)

Mrs C Mulcahy, BA Hons Surrey, PGCE London (*Design & Technology, Art*)

Ms A Murphy, MA Oxford, PGCE East Anglia (*History/Politics, Oxbridge Coordinator*)

Mrs E Peters, BSc Hons, PGCE Southampton (*Mathematics*)

Miss A Philip (*Lacrosse Coach*)

Mrs A Phillips, BA Hons Bristol (*Drama, Charities Coordinator*)

Mrs C Platt, BA Hons London, QTS (*French/Spanish*)

Mrs L Rowell, BA Hons Surrey, PGCE King's College (**Computer Science and ICT*)

Miss C Scholey (*Lacrosse Coach*)

Mrs A Sherwen, BSc Hons London, PGCE Leeds (*Biology*)

Mrs C Solan, BA Hons London, PGCE Canterbury (*Art and Textiles*)

D Swann Esq, BSc Hons, PGCE Canterbury (*Mathematics, Computing, Examinations Manager*)

Mrs B Tanner, BA Hons Wales, PGCE Southampton (*Spanish, French*)

Mrs C Taylor (*Classics*)

Mrs L Thomas, MA Open, BA Hons Wales, PGCE Bristol (*History, GPR Coordinator*)

Mrs L von Kaufmann, MA, BA Hons Oxford, PGCE Bristol (*Geography, RS*)

P Walker Esq, BSc Hons Loughborough, ACA, PGCE London (*Mathematics*)

Mrs S Walker, BSc Hons London, QTS Greenwich (*Chemistry*)

J Ward Esq, MMus, BMus Hons RCM, PG Dip London (*Music, RS*)

Mrs S Whawell (*Mathematics*)

Mrs R White, BA Hons, PGCE Bristol, MA Hons New York, PGCE Canterbury (*English, Assistant Head of Middle School*)

Dr S Willcox, MA Cambridge, DPhil Oxford, SCITT/QTS Bromley (*Science*)

S Wilson Esq, BA Hons Sunderland, PGCE London (**Sociology*)

Ms O Windle, MA, BA Hons Edgewood College USA (**History, Politics*)

Mrs M Wood, BSc Hons Aberdeen, PGCE London (**Chemistry, *Science*)

Mrs Z Wood, MA Hons St Andrews, PGCE London (*RS/Philosophy*)

Mrs N Yates (*Art*)

Junior School:
Head of the Junior School: Mrs D Wood, BSc, PGCE Durham
Deputy Head Teacher: Mrs A J Rotchell, BEd Hons Westminster College Oxford, Dip SpLD York
Director of Studies: Mrs P I Potter, BEd Southampton, Dip MEd Roehampton Institute
Senior Teacher: Mrs C Conway, BA Hons First Class, MA Johannesburg, PGCE Canterbury Christ Church
Head of Pre-Prep Department: Mrs G Watts, MA Hons St Andrews, EYPS, QTS

H Andrews Esq, BA First Class Hons, AKC King's College
Mrs N Armitage, BA Hons Nottingham GTP (*Nursery Coordinator*)
Mrs G Cameron, Foundation Degree
Mrs A Carr, BEd Hons Cheltenham
Mrs L Carter, BSc Hons Durham
Mrs K Ellerby, NVQ3 (*After-School SOCS Supervisor*)
Mrs L Everitt, Cert Ed North Worcestershire College of Education
Mrs K Fassnidge, BA Hons Cardiff, TEFL, QTS
Mrs M Fewster, BSc Hons, PGCE Bath
Mrs L Ireland, BA/QTS Roehampton, Dip RSA (*Head of Learning Support*)
Mrs H Malcolm, Dip Ed Aberdeen College of Education
Miss S Millington, BA Hons, Cert Ed Kent, QTS (*Head of Junior School Music*)
Miss E Mogan, BSc Hons, PGCE Brunel (*Head of Junior School PE*)
Miss M Murphy, BA Hons Swansea, PGCE Liverpool Institute of Higher Education
Dr C Parr, MBChB, PGCE Leeds
Mrs K Pattison, BA Hons Keele, MEd Open, PGCE Durham
Miss A Philip, BEd Hons Nottingham Trent, PG Dip Open

Visiting Staff:
Mrs C Baker, MBACP (*Senior School Counsellor*)
Miss C Brand, MMus London, GTCL, ARCM, LRAM (*Piano*)
B Brooker Esq (*Percussion*)
Miss S Burkett (*Judo*)
Mrs G Cameron, Foundation Degree (*Netball Coach*)
Miss A Carroll (*Gymnastics Coach*)
Mrs V Christophers, BMus Hons London (*Drama*)
Miss J Collis (*Dance*)
R Connell Esq, BA Hons Canterbury, PGCE, ATCL (*Guitar*)
Mrs A Da Costa, BSc Hons, PGCE UCL, Cert Maths Open, MA King's College (*Maths Learning Support*)
Mrs J Dammers, LRAM (*Violoncello, Music Administrator*)
Dr R Davies, BSc Hons, PhD Imperial College, PGCE King's College (*Numeracy/Maths Learning Support*)
R Dilks Esq, Dip Ed Rose Bruford College of Speech and Drama (*Speech and Drama*)
Miss N Dobie, BA Hons, 1st class City University, LTCL, NCDT, Dip Opera Performance London (*Singing*)
Mrs D Gaskell, Cert Ed Leeds (*Literacy Support*)
Mrs A Goff, BSc Leicester, QTS (*Numeracy Learning Support*)
Ms S Graham, LRAM, GRSM Hons, Dip RAM (*Singing*)
Mrs H Greenfield, BMus Hons Birmingham Conservatoire, LRAM, DPP RAM, Dip CESMD (*Clarinet, Saxophone*)
Mrs J Hamlet, Chelsea Ballet School (*Dance*)
Mrs G Hayward, Dip Music Newcastle, LTCL, ALCM, PG Dip Orchestral Studies London (*Singing, Piano*)
P Hill Esq (*Squash Coach*)
Mrs F Hillyar, BMus Hons Royal College of Music, PGCE Reading (*Piano*)

Mrs H Houghton-Berry, BA Hons Oxford, PGCE Cambridge (*Literacy Support*)
Mrs C Howell, BA Hons Bristol, ARCM, LRSM, ARCM (*Piano, Flute*)
Miss L Jeffery, BMus Trinity College of Music, PG Dip Royal Academy of Music (*Flute*)
Miss S Kisilevsky (*Drama*)
Ms E Leather, BA Hons Leeds, PGDipMus Guildhall School of Music, Artist Diploma Cincinnati (*Music Coach*)
P Leresche Esq, Master of Performance Guildhall School of Music, Master of Piano Pedagogy Switzerland (*Piano*)
Miss V Longhurst, BMus Trinity College of Music (*Harp*)
Mrs J Muggeridge, Badminton England Qualified Coach, Double Olympian and Double Gold Medallist Commonwealth Games (*Badminton*)
Miss A Murray, ATCL, LTCL Trinity College of Music (*Recorder*)
Mrs V Newman, BA Hons Oxford, PGCE Wales, BSc Hons Open, Dip SpLD (*Learning Support*)
Ms S Oakley, BA Hons Surrey (*Speech and Drama*)
Mrs S Purton, LRAM Royal Academy of Music (*Oboe*)
Mrs J Rhind, GRSM Hons, LTCL, LRAM (*Saxophone, Clarinet*)
Mrs M Rice (*Dance*)
D Smith Esq, BA Iowa, USA (*Cross Country Coach*)
R Smith Esq, ASA Level 2 Coaching/Swimming, NPLQ (*Swimming Coach*)
I Snape Esq, BSc FCA (*Chess Coach*)
Mrs A Steynor, BA Hons Durham, PGCDM Open, ABRSM Dip (*Piano*)
Miss L Tunnah, MA Royal Academy of Music, BA Mus Hons Royal College of Music, Dip RAM London, GRCM, GRAM (*Violin*)
Miss E Wiggins (*Brass*)
T Williams Esq, BA Fine Art First Class Oxford, Art & Design Foundation (*Songwriting*)
Miss A Wood, BSc Hons Manchester (*Singing*)
Miss A Wynne, BA Hons Birmingham, MMus Leeds (*Harp*)

Technicians & Assistants:
Mrs L Clarke, Dip Natural Sciences, BSc Hons (*Biology Technician*)
Mrs A Ford (*Art Technician*)
Mrs R Gardner, BSc Hons Manchester, RPharmSGB Bath, PGCE Oxford Senior (*Science Laboratory Technician*)
C Hayward Esq, TEC, BTEC, MIBiol, PGCE (*Science Laboratory & DT/3DD Technician, D of E Coordinator*)
J Mitchell Esq, BEng Hons Surrey (*Drama/Performing Arts Technician*)
Sta A Perez Barona (*Spanish Assistant*)
Mlle A Radiere (*French Assistant*)
T Stevens Esq, BSc Hons Staffordshire (*Senior ICT Technician*)
E Thompson Esq (*ICT Technician*)

Medical Centre:
Mrs E Leisinger, Dip Nursing Brighton
Mrs L J Mottram, Dip Nursing Studies City University

Administrative Staff:
Mrs J Alcock, BSc Greenwich (*Facilities Manager*)
Ms R Boardman, Management Diploma Canada (*Assistant Librarian, Archives*)
Mrs R Boughton, BSc Hons Manchester (*School Secretary*)
Mrs J Butler, BA Hons Sheffield (*Marketing and Admissions Assistant*)
Mrs C Buxton, BSc Hons King's College (*Receptionist*)
Mrs S Cockett, BA (*Bursar's Assistant*)
P Cole Esq, Network and Data Manager
Mrs C Croft, BA Hons Birmingham, PGCE Greenwich (*Administrative Assistant, Junior School*)

Mrs C Eames (*Domestic Bursar*)
Mrs W Fahy (*Junior School Secretary*)
A Horner Esq, MBA, CMgr, FCMI (*Bursar*)
Mrs A Knight (*Admissions Registrar*)
Miss K Lippiatt (*PA to the Headmistress*)
Mrs P Lowton, BSc Hons Keele, ACMA (*Finance Manager*)
Mrs H Manning (*Receptionist*)
Mrs A Parkin (*Clerk*)
Mrs S Pelling, BA Hons Keele (*Head of Marketing*)
Mrs S Seeds (*Staff Secretary*)
Mrs L White, MA Brighton, MCLIP (*Lead Librarian, i/c School Archive*)

Westfield School

Oakfield Road, Gosforth, Newcastle-upon-Tyne NE3 4HS

Tel: 0191 255 3980
email: westfield@westfield.newcastle.sch.uk
website: www.westfield.newcastle.sch.uk
Twitter: @Westfieldschool
Facebook: /WestfieldSchool
LinkedIn: /westfield-independent-day-school-for-girls

Westfield is a day school for 380 girls aged 3+ to 18, in Junior and Senior Houses situated on one campus in a very pleasant wooded site of over 6 acres. The School's aim is an uninterrupted education, a high academic standard and a wide curriculum offering scope and stimulus for individual development. There is a vast range of extra-curricular activities with particular emphasis on Sport, Outdoor Pursuits, Music, Art and Drama. The Duke of Edinburgh's Award scheme has a high profile and all senior girls are encouraged to participate. In addition to a sound grounding in basic skills, Junior House (3–11) offers specialist teaching in Art, Craft, PE, French and Music. So that every child may be assured of individual attention class sizes are restricted to a maximum of 20. Frequently, classes are further divided into smaller units.

Senior house (11–18), has first rate classroom and laboratory facilities with excellent specialist accommodation for Home Economics and Music. A wide range of subjects is taught by specialists. Initially all girls have lessons in the traditional academic core subjects, in English, Mathematics, Geography, History, Science (taught as 3 separate subjects) and French, as well as in Music, Drama, PE, Food and Nutrition, ICT and Design. German and Spanish are introduced in the second year. Girls are encouraged to aim for breadth in their choice of subjects at GCSE. Most girls achieve 9 passes in the A–C range of the GCSE, a number with straight A and A* passes. There is a carefully structured programme of Careers and Personal and Social Education and a well developed pastoral system.

The Sixth Form occupies a cottage block in the grounds and is under the direction of the Head of the Sixth Form.

There is a full range of AS, A2 and other courses and girls are prepared for University and other Higher Education courses, including Oxbridge, as well as for other courses and for employment. The A level pass rate is always over 90%, ensuring for most girls a place in their first choice of institute of higher education.

Sixth Formers have considerable responsibility within the School in addition to their own thriving academic and cultural life.

Westfield is a member of Round Square, a worldwide association of schools which share a commitment, beyond academic excellence, to personal development and responsibility through service, challenge, adventure and international understanding. Girls from Westfield have the opportunity to attend the Annual International Conference and to participate in exchanges with member schools from all over the world, and in the Round Square International Service Projects in developing countries.

Westfield is totally committed to producing happy, self-confident, well-balanced young women who are international in their outlook and fully prepared to face life in the 21st Century.

Admission to Westfield is by interview and examination. While children of all faiths are accepted, the religious life of the school is based on Christian principles.

Fees per term (2016–2017). In Junior House fees range from £2,990 to £3,310 and in Senior House are £4,185.

Scholarships are available at 9+, 11+, 13+ and Sixth Form, including Academic, Art, Music and PE. Some bursaries are also available in cases of financial need.

Charitable status. Westfield School is owned and administered by the Northumbrian Educational Trust Ltd, which is a Registered Charity, number 528143. It exists for the purpose of education.

Governors:
Chairman: Mrs J Keep, MSCP, SRP
K Bainbridge, BA Hons
A L Dowie, MA Cantab
I Greenshields, LLB
I Henderson, BA Hons
Mrs L Keightley, BA Hons
Dr K Manzo, PhD
Mrs J Robson
Mrs I Smales, MA

Headmistress: Mrs C Jawaheer, BA Hons Liverpool, PGCE, Dip Ed, NPQH

Deputy Headteacher: Mrs K Quinn, BA Hons Leeds, PGCE

Assistant Head: S Ratcliffe, LLB Newcastle, BA Hons Wimbledon School of Art, MFA Cranbrook Academy of Art, Michigan

Assistant Head: Mrs W Wise, BA Hons Newcastle, PGCE

Head of Sixth Form: Mrs E Wise, BA Hons Newcastle, PGCE

Art/Design:
S Ratcliffe, LLB Newcastle, BA Hons Wimbledon School of Art, MFA Cranbrook Academy of Art, Michigan
D Stone, BA Hons Kingston, PGCE

Biology:
Mrs S Vallance, BSc Hons London, PGCE

Business Studies:
Mrs C Gaynor, BEd Hons Warwick, PG DMS

Chemistry:
P Russell, BSc Hons Bath, PGCE

Drama/Theatre Studies:
Mrs E Forster, MA Hons Cantab, PGCE

English:
Dr A Leng, BA Hons Reading, MA Reading, PhD
Mrs E Forster, MA Hons Cantab, PGCE

Food & Nutrition:
Mrs L Hender, BA Hons Northumbria

French:
Mrs F Boyce, BA Hons Salford, PGCE
Mrs S Dodds, BA Hons Dunelm, PGCE
Mrs E Wise, BA Hons Newcastle, PGCE

Geography:
C Dunn, MA Hons Cantab
Mrs E Gardner, MA Hons Cantab, BA Hons Cantab, PGCE

German: Mrs E Wise, BA Hons Newcastle, PGCE

History:
Mrs J Harris, BA Hons Northumbria, PGCE

Information Communication Technology:
Mrs C Lloyd, BA Hons, PGCE Liverpool

Mathematics:
Dr C Barnett, MMath Newcastle, PhD Dunelm
Mrs L Marshall, BEng Hons, PGCE

Music:
Dr L Hardy, BA Hons Keele, PhD

Physical Education:
Miss N Baguley, BSc Lancaster, PGCE
Miss M Lamb, BSc Sheffield, PGCE

Physics:
Dr E Corbin, BA Oxon, MSc Newcastle, PhD Newcastle

Religious Studies:
S Shieber, BA Hons Durham, PGCE, MA

Science:
Miss H Fraser, BSc Columbia, New York
Mrs J Dudley, BSc Hons Newcastle, PGCE

Spanish:
Mrs S Dodds, BA Hons Durham, PGCE

Additional Learning Support:
Mrs E Thompson, BSc, PGCE
Mrs N McGowan, BA Hons East Anglia, PGCE

Junior House:
Assistant Head: Mrs C Baines, BSc Hons UMIST, PGCE

Teachers/Teaching Assistants:
Mrs N Alexanders, BA Hons Newcastle, PGCE
Miss J N Brown, BSc Hons Huddersfield, PGCE
Mrs F Collier, BA Hons Keele, PGCE
Mrs H Dean, BEd Hons Newcastle
Mrs S Hann, BA Hons Hull, PGCE
Mrs N Kyle, BA Hons Durham, PGCE
Mrs M Johnson, CertEd Eastbourne
Mrs K Meeson, BSc Hons Northumbria, PGCE
Miss G McKeating, BEd Hons York
Mrs L McNaught, BA Hons Staffs, NCFE2
Mrs T McQuade, NCFE Level ONC Dyslexia Level 3
Mrs A Rabey-Wilson, BA Hons London, PGCE
Mrs J Slack, BA Hons Hull, PGCE

Visiting Staff:
Music:
B Alimohamadi, BA OU, LGSM, CertEd Newcastle
Mrs M A Huntingdon, BSc, FTCL, LRAM
Mrs P Green, BA Hons Newcastle, CT ABRSM
Mrs Alison Northey
Miss S Harrison, LTCL
Bursar: Mrs S Duffey
Domestic Bursar: Mrs D Oldroyd
Headmistress's Secretary: Mrs J Jokelson
Junior House Secretary: Mrs A Dryden, BA Northumbria
Laboratory Technician: Mr D Wiles
Examinations Officer: Miss H Fraser
Assistant Examinations Officer: Mrs S Vallance
Marketing Coordinator: Mrs D Clark
School Librarian: Dr A Leng

Westonbirt School

Tetbury, Gloucestershire GL8 8QG
Tel: 01666 880333
email: admissions@westonbirt.org
            enquiries@westonbirt.org
website: www.westonbirt.org
Twitter: @WestonbirtSch
Facebook: @Westonbirt-School
LinkedIn: /Westonbirt-Schools

Location. Westonbirt School is a Senior all-girls Day and Boarding School and Westonbirt Prep is a mixed Prep School –both are set in 210 acres of magnificent parkland in the heart of the Cotswolds, close to the cultural cities of Bath, Bristol and Cheltenham and only 90 minutes from London.

Philosophy. Westonbirt School encourages every girl to achieve her full potential, instilling confidence in a safe, secure yet stimulating environment. Pupils experience exceptional pastoral care and outstanding educational opportunities in a 'greenhouse, not a hothouse' environment. This is achieved through our boarding ethos, which is shared by day pupils, and delivered through a unique educational environment where pupils thrive in a vibrant community with small classes, magnificent grounds and inspiring teachers

We are a Church of England School, with our own Chapel and Chaplain and our Christian ethos underpins all that we do. Strong friendships are formed across year groups and every girl is guided by nurturing academic and pastoral staff.

Curriculum. All pupils follow the national curriculum and are offered a full sporting timetable with a wide range of extra-curricular opportunities to provide each girl with an outstanding rounded education. The exceptionally able are stretched and challenged and individual help and support is tailored by specialists for those who need Learning Support or English Language Training.

The school has performed consistently well in both GCSE and A Level results –69% of pupils achieved A–B* at GCSE in 2016 and 50% A*–B at A Level. Westonbirt is in the top 5% of schools in the UK for value added. This objectively assessed measure conducted by the University of Durham calculates pupils' academic improvement between the ages of 11 and 16. Analysis shows that girls at Westonbirt achieve almost a grade higher than expected in each subject at GCSE. Westonbirt is a non-selective school which consistently delivers strong results.

Each girl has her own personal tutor, helping her manage her time and acquire effective study skills from the moment she joins until securing her place at university.

Headmistress Natasha Dangerfield has implemented a robust 'Skills for Life' program designed to compliment academic success and prepare young women for the challenges facing them in a global society. The program explores the diversity of the workplace, promotes career achievement and offers practical and financial training for life beyond school.

Music, Drama and Art and Design. The state-of-the-art Music Technology Centre boasts a rehearsal room, fully-equipped Apple technology suite and recording studio. As well as individual lessons, girls have many opportunities to perform regularly in choirs, orchestras or ensembles.

Art and design is a key strength and has its own fully-equipped design studios. Pupils regularly achieve places at prestigious design and art institutions.

Drama is thriving at the school with outstanding productions every year and our talented pupils performing at the Edinburgh Festival to great acclaim. The Orangery Theatre, with adjacent Green Room and Rehearsal Studio, provides a versatile venue for the performing arts. Individual speech and drama lessons are popular with many pupils successfully performing at competition level.

Sports and Leisure. Westonbirt has extensive grounds and sports facilities, including a £3m modern Sports Centre, 25m indoor swimming pool, full fitness suite, nine-hole golf course, tennis courts, lacrosse pitches, netball, and athletics facilities. The school has an ambitious equestrian team and those keen on equestrian sports may take riding lessons at nearby stables and polo at the neighbouring Beaufort Polo Club. Our sports teachers are experts in their fields and many of the girls go on to compete at county and national level.

Extracurricular Activities. Girls are inspired to participate in the broad range of extra-curricular activities on offer. Drama, music and dance are particularly popular, but there are many other varied and rewarding options. Older girls participate in The Duke of Edinburgh's Award scheme, World Challenge, Leiths cookery school or demonstrate their business acumen in the Young Enterprise scheme. Planned activities are offered every weekend including cultural, fun and shopping trips, which are open to day girls as well as boarders. Overseas cultural and world challenge trips broaden pupils' horizons and have recently taken students to France, Italy, Spain, the USA and Peru. Community and fundraising projects are strongly supported at the school.

Learning Support. The Learning Support Department at Westonbirt School prides itself on a personalised approach to learning. We are a small specialist team that works closely with pupils and all members of staff to provide support and guidance to pupils with learning support needs so that they approach their studies with confidence.

The department is passionate about nurturing the talents of all our students identifying their unique qualities, supporting them in developing skills and becoming successful independent learners

ELT (English Language Training). Our English Language Training department offers specialist individual and group lessons. All pupils are assessed on entry to ensure they have the requisite amount of support needed and are taught in mainstream lessons for all other subjects. International girls appreciate the supportive and professional ELT department who work closely with all academic staff.

Entrance Requirements. Girls normally join the school at 11, 13 or 16, though they may do so at other ages in special circumstances. At 11+ and 13+ they must sit either the Common Entrance Examination or take the school's own entrance papers, attend an interview with the Headmistress, and provide a reference from their current school. Sixth Form entrants must have a minimum of 5 GCSEs at grades A*–C, attend an interview and sit tests in the subjects they intend to study at A Level.

Fees per term (2016–2017). Boarding (full & weekly) £8,850–£11,430; Day £5,850–£7,195. The fee is inclusive of tuition, board, lodging, stationery and laundry. Day girls may stay one night per week free of charge and on additional nights for a small fee. The school is renowned for its flexible approach to boarding and girls can stay up to 3 nights per week on a flexi-boarding basis, space permitting. [*In October 2016 Westonbirt announced a significant reduction in the senior day and boarding fees, effective from September 2017. Years 7–13: Boarding £9,750; Day £4,995.*]

Scholarships and Bursaries. Scholarships are available for those entering Years 7 (11+), 9 (13+) and 12 (16+) and these are given for Academic Excellence, Art, Drama, Music, Sport, Organ and Choral. We also offer the Mary Henderson Performing Arts Scholarship, for all-round excellence in Music, Drama and Dance. These can be each worth up to a maximum of 10% of the current tuition (day) fees. Scholarships may be topped up with bursaries. Bursary application forms are available on request from the Director of Admissions.

Charitable status. Westonbirt School Limited is a Registered Charity, number 311715. It exists for the education of girls in mind, body and spirit.

Governing Body:
Chairman: Mr D McMeekin, MBA
Vice-Chairman: Miss J Greenwood, BSc, FRICS
Mr M Barrow, CBE
Mr D Battishill, BA Hons
Mrs K Broomhead
Mr T Gaffney, MBA
Mrs P Leggate, BA, MEd, PGCE
Mrs H Metters, BSc Hons, PGCE
Mr M Pyper, OBE
Mrs S Whitfield, MA
Mr C Wyld, MA
Mr S Smith
Mrs T Luggar

Head: **Mrs N Dangerfield**, BA Brighton

Deputy Head –Academic: Mrs J Barlow, BSc Birmingham, PGCE Open
Deputy Head –Pastoral: Mrs J Price, BA Durham, PGCE Cambridge
Chief Operating Officer: Mr S Kenny
Director of Admissions: Mrs P Stevenson
Director of Marketing & Digital Communications: Mrs L Brook, BSc Hons, CIM Dip
Chaplain: Revd A Monaghan, BA Cambridge, MA Edinburgh

Heads of Department:
Art: Ms M Stockton, BA Hull, MA Reading, PGATC S Glam
Business Studies: Mrs J Edwards, BA Exeter
Classics: Mr P Holland, BA Oxford
Design Technology: Mr J Sproule, CertEd London
Drama: Mr A English, BA Winchester, PGCE Bath
ELT: Miss C Lloyd, BA, MA Coventry, Cert TESOL London
English: Mrs D Browne, BA UC Wales, PGCE Exeter, MEd Gloucestershire, NPQH
Food & Textiles Technology: Mrs J Bell, BEd Bath
Geography: Mrs N Gill, BA Hons Manchester, PGCE Cambridge
History: Mr I Ahmed, BA Gloucestershire, PGCE Bath, MEd UWE
Digital Learning & Computing: Mr D Thompson, BSc Hons Exeter, PGCE Exeter
Learning Support: Mrs P Reuter, BA London
Mathematics: Mrs J Barlow, BSc Birmingham, PGCE Open
Modern Languages: Mrs C Rock, L-ès-L Université de Metz
Music: Ms N Kendall, BA, PGCE Bath Spa
Physical Education: Mrs L Johnson, BEd Brighton
Psychology & Religious Education: Miss A Douglas, BA Winchester, PGCE Bristol
Science: Miss H Rogerson, MPhys Southampton, PGCE Edinburgh
Physics: Dr J Stimpson, PhD Leicester, BSc Leicester, PGCE Leicester
Biology: Mrs S Barr, BSc, PGCE Leeds
Chemistry: Mr M Gluning, BSc, PGCE Aberystwyth, MA Kingston

Health & Well-being Centre: Mrs R Etherington, RCN Staffordshire

Housemistresses:
Badminton House: Mrs J Price, BA Durham, PGCE
   Cambridge
Beaufort House: Miss C Crowley
Dorchester House: Miss S Gould
Sixth Form: Mrs L Bradbury, BA Hons Loughborough,
   MA Camberwell, PGCE Plymouth

Wimbledon High School
GDST

Mansel Road, London SW19 4AB

Tel: 020 8971 0900 (Senior School)
          020 8971 0902 (Junior School)
email: info@wim.gdst.net
website: www.wimbledonhigh.gdst.net
Twitter: @WimbledonHigh
Facebook: @WimbledonHighSchoolGDST

Founded 1880.

Wimbledon High School is part of the GDST (Girls' Day School Trust). The GDST is the leading network of independent girls' schools in the UK. As a charity that owns and runs 24 schools and two academies, it reinvests all its income in its schools. For further information about the Trust, see p. xxiii or visit www.gdst.net.

Pupil numbers. Junior School: 324 aged 4–11; Senior School: 580, including 150 in the Sixth Form.

Wimbledon High School combines academic strength with a firm belief that learning should be fun. Jane Lunnon took up the Headship in September 2014 and says she has been "struck by the natural, unaffectedness of the students, their scholarship and their willingness to get involved in all aspects of school life". Results at A Level and GCSE are consistently extremely high, music and drama are a vibrant part of school life and a Director of Sport and new Director of Rowing have rejuvenated PE at the school. Activities include World Challenge, Model United Nations and The Duke of Edinburgh's Award, alongside many smaller clubs and societies, from Mah Jong to Coding. The older girls often run these themselves.

A secure framework of pastoral care supports students through what can sometimes be difficult teenage years. They increasingly gain more responsibility as they move up through the school. Sixth Formers practise leadership through the School Council and by mentoring younger girls; there is a peer counselling service and older students help with Easter revision classes at local schools.

Junior and Senior Schools share one central Wimbledon site, with excellent facilities: a swimming pool and sports hall, Performing Arts Centre and a centre for design and technology. The playing fields are ten minutes' walk away at Nursery Road (the site of the original All England Lawn Tennis and Croquet Club) providing a full-size, all-weather hockey pitch and five netball/tennis courts. The school believes in nurturing all sporting talent and a fit and active lifestyle is encouraged.

The **Junior School** provides a creative and academic education in a happy and stimulating environment –bright, purpose-built accommodation, with specialist rooms for art, ICT and science. There is a balance of class and specialist subject teaching and girls are set clear and challenging targets for their learning. An enriched and extended National Curriculum is the foundation, with the school embracing the 'creative curriculum' encompassing various areas of learning at the same time; Spanish, Italian and French are taught at various times, as well as Latin. An after-school care programme offers flexibility to working parents.

The **Senior School** curriculum runs over a two week timetable. In Key Stage 3, girls study English, Mathematics and Sciences, taught distinctly but with the emphasis on the links between them; they learn German or Spanish alongside French (Latin is added in Year 8) as well as Geography, History, Religious Studies, PE, Music, Drama, Art, Design & Technology (textiles, product design and cookery and nutrition, on rotation), Computer Science, Study Skills and PSHE (Personal, Social and Health Education).

At Key Stage 4 all girls study English (Language and Literature), Mathematics and three separate sciences. The girls have a free choice of four other subjects, of which one must be a Modern Foreign Language, with the possibility of adding Classical Greek as an 11th GCSE. PE and PHSE continue. A Global Perspectives course in Year 10 brings breadth beyond the curriculum, and Mind Matters is a series of thought-provoking talks held for Year 10 and above. The school also holds regular Roswell Lectures for older girls, parents and staff.

In the **Sixth Form,** students may choose from the same subjects on offer at GCSE (except PE –compulsory in Year 12 but non-examined), plus Further Mathematics, Economics, Psychology. Politics and Classical Civilisation. The school has moved to a linear programme, with students taking 3 or 4 A Levels (not AS –with the exception of AS Mathematics). There is a high uptake of science subjects and in recent years the Extended Project Qualification has been popular. An extensive programme of enrichment (starting in Year 11 and continuing in Years 12 and 13) offers short courses in scores of subjects from dissection to Zumba, as well as the opportunity to participate in Community Service or the Young Enterprise scheme. PSHE continues and a comprehensive programme of careers and university entrance advice is offered.

Admissions. 4+ girls are assessed in groups in a nursery-style environment; indication of a girl's potential is the key at this stage, rather than evidence of what has already been learnt.

7+ girls have a small group interview following formal assessments in English including comprehension and a story, mathematics and reasoning.

For 11+ entry, applicants have group assessments in the autumn term, prior to the January entrance examination (in verbal and non-verbal reasoning, plus a creative problem-solving task). The occasional entry examination for other years tests Maths and English (plus Science for Year 10 and above).

16+ assessment comprises entrance exam and interviews. Offers of places are conditional upon GCSE A* grades in candidates' chosen A Level subjects (7+ under the new system), and a minimum of nine B grades (or eight grades 6–9) overall.

Fees per term (2016–2017). Senior School £5,776, Junior School £4,490.

The fees cover the regular curriculum, school books, choral music, games and swimming, but not optional extra subjects.

Scholarships and Bursaries. Academic scholarships are awarded to girls who do exceptionally well in the 11+ exam, worth 5% of the fees. There are also music and sport scholarships at 11+. At 16+ there are scholarships in Art, Drama, Music and PE, worth up to 10%. A 16+ science scholarship is worth up to 50%. Details and application forms available on request.

Bursaries take account of academic merit, but all are means tested. The maximum value is the full fee.

Charitable status. Wimbledon High School is part of The Girls' Day School Trust, which is a Registered Charity, number 306983.

Chairman of the Local Governors: Mr G Williams, BA
   Econ Manchester

Head: **Mrs J Lunnon**, BA Bristol

Deputy Head, Academic: Mr P Murphy, BSc Hons Cantab, BA Hons London

Deputy Head, Pastoral: Miss F Kennedy, MA Oxon

Head of Junior School: Miss K Mitchell, BEd Warwick, MA York

Director of Finance & Operations: Mrs S Lawton, AInstAM Dip

Director of Sixth Form: Dr J Parsons, BMus, MA, PhD Cardiff

Director of Studies: Mr B Haythorne, MA Oxon

Assistant Head (Co-curricular): Miss J Cox, BSc Brunel

Assistant Head (Performance): Mrs C Duncan, BSc Sheffield

Deputy Head, Junior School: Miss G Peacock, BA Nottingham Trent

Director of Marketing: Mrs R Brewster, BA Oxon, MA Leeds

Director of Technology and eLearning: Mr C Thackray, BSc Hons Cardiff

Woldingham School

Marden Park, Woldingham, Surrey CR3 7YA

Tel: 01883 349431
Fax: 01883 348653
email: registrar@woldinghamschool.co.uk
website: www.woldinghamschool.co.uk
Twitter: @WoldinghamSch
Facebook: @woldinghamschool.co.uk

Independent School for Girls aged 11–18.

Woldingham is a leading independent Catholic boarding and day school for girls. It is a happy and successful school and develops confident and compassionate young women. Woldingham's approach to religious instruction is 'all-inclusive', welcoming girls from all faiths.

Foundation. The school was founded in 1842 by the Society of the Sacred Heart and has been sited at Woldingham since 1946. Today, under lay management, Woldingham is part of the international network of over 200 Sacred Heart schools in 44 countries.

Situation and Buildings. Woldingham is situated south east of London, just inside the M25 near Junction 6. The school is set within 700 acres in the Surrey countryside, with its own train station in the grounds that offers easy access to Clapham Junction (25 minutes) and London Victoria (35 minutes). Journey times to Gatwick and Heathrow airports are 25 and 45 minutes respectively. A stunning Jacobean house is the centre piece of the idyllic setting in a designated Area of Outstanding Natural Beauty. An intensive yet sympathetic buildings programme has now furnished the school with some impressive facilities.

The Millennium Centre for the Performing Arts includes a 600-seat auditorium with orchestra pit, industry standard sound and lighting control rooms, scenery construction dock, wardrobe room for costume and prop construction and a fully-equipped studio theatre. In addition, the Centre hosts a Recital room, a Mac Suite, keyboard studio, String and Woodwind rooms, numerous practice rooms and an exceptional eight-track digital recording studio. The purpose-built Art department comprises two large 2D studios, facilities for printmaking and a superb 3D area equipped with a range of power tools and two kilns. Design Technology is taught in a fully-equipped workshop and studio, using state-of-the-art computer-controlled machinery. The Sports Centre includes a Sports Hall, 2 squash courts, fully-equipped Fitness Suite and a Dance/Gymnastics studio. In addition there are extensive outdoor playing areas, an indoor tennis dome, an indoor swimming pool and an all-weather floodlit pitch. "The grounds are stunning and sports facilities are excellent" (Tatler).

Boarding accommodation is impressive, "more like home than home" (Good Schools Guide), "almost boutique-hotel standard" (Tatler). Shanley House, the Upper Sixth centre, is a modern block with en-suite accommodation. Berwick House is the Lower Sixth centre and provides single room accommodation. All girls from Year 10 upwards have single study-bedrooms in Main House. Marden House is a small, friendly junior house with welcoming accommodation for the first two years.

Developments over the past five years include the completion of a new whole school dining area with state-of-the-art food preparation facilities and serveries. The Year 11 boarding area has been entirely refurbished to bring it up to date and in line with the newly redecorated and refurnished junior boarding house, Marden, for Years 7 and 8. Four new, airy and modern classrooms were built for the History and Politics Department within the junior boarding house development and January 2013 saw the inauguration of an entirely new building –the Examination Centre. This centre includes spacious, contemporary testing rooms, individual examination suites and additional classroom space. In summer 2014, two new Biology laboratories were entirely refurbished and modernised in the Science Centre with a major refurbishment of a further four labs, staff and prep rooms, central hall, rooftop greenhouse and external cladding in summer 2015. 2016 saw the final three labs and second prep room refurbished, completing the project.

Size. The school accommodates 550 girls within the 11–18 age range, some 300 of whom are boarders. 60% of boarders are from families living in London and Home Counties and 25% come from overseas. Approximately 25% of the intake are of nationalities other than British; these students enrich the school by bringing to it an international dimension and outlook.

Pastoral Care. This is a key strength of the school and the teaching is "adorned with dollops of TLC" (Good Schools Guide). In each year care of the boarding side of the school life is the responsibility of the Head of Year, who acts in loco parentis and ensures that each girl is known and cared for as an individual. The Head of Year is assisted by a team of Tutors, each of whom is responsible for the girls' individual guidance. Buddy schemes ensure that girls provide support for each other. The boarders in each year are cared for by two House Mistresses.

Curriculum. All girls take a common course for the first two years. Year 7 students take Latin and two of French, German or Spanish. In Year 9 the creative subjects and languages are optional, with the majority of girls choosing to continue with two languages (of which Latin can be one) and three creative subjects (from Art, Drama, Design Technology, Computer Science and Music). The more able linguists may choose three languages and only two creative subjects at this time, while others may choose to only study one language and the four creative subjects instead. Health Education is studied by all students in Years 7–9, but is not examined.

It is expected that the majority of Years 10 and 11 girls will follow a total of 10 (occasionally 9) GCSE courses. The aim is to provide a broad and balanced curriculum for all up to the age of 16. All students take GCSE courses in English Language and Literature, Mathematics, Theology and at least one Modern Foreign Language. Science is also compulsory; most girls take it as an IGCSE double award, although a sizeable minority sit separate papers in Biology,

Chemistry and Physics. For their options, girls are recommended to choose an overall combination of subjects which includes Geography or History, plus one creative or practical subject, including Computer Science and Physical Education. In 2016 74% of GCSEs were A*–A grade and 93% were A*–B.

Students in all year groups have regular PSHEE sessions, which includes the Thrive programme, developing healthy study skills and focusing on the importance of reaching their goals through a balanced, healthy and mindful approach. There is also an annual Thrive Day, on which all students are off-timetable and take part in various activities including time spent on reflection and helping the closer and wider communities.

In the Sixth Form, girls will choose to follow three or four linear A Levels, taking all formal examinations at the end of the Upper Sixth. Selected students in Sixth Form are invited to take the EPQ (Extended Project Qualification), Financial Studies Certificate, Level 3 Certificate in Higher Sports Leadership, Level 3 Mathematical Studies or MOOCs. All Sixth Formers have Physical Education lessons.

A Level results in 2016 were 55% at A*–A and 81% A*–B grades. The school bucks the national trend in uptake of Science, Economics and Mathematics. Girls also achieve outstanding results in Humanities, Languages and Art. The School also has a Gifted and Talented programme, a challenging Oxbridge programme providing specialist support and guidance, as well as specialist programmes for those students seeking to apply for courses in medicine, veterinary science or dentistry.

Careers Guidance and University Application. The School encourages students to begin thinking early in their education about their future careers and the skills and qualifications required through a variety of software programmes and career talks. An annual careers fair and a universities fair are open to all students from Year 9 upwards as well as a diverse programme of invited speakers and workshops. In the GCSE years students participate in the ISCO Futurewise programme and receive a detailed skills analysis supported by professional careers guidance to assist in choosing A Level subjects and higher education options. Over 80% of Sixth Form leavers attend Russell Group universities and the school prides itself on the range of subjects students pursue in both the Sciences and the Arts. The School also sends several students to top USA and overseas universities and to both Art Foundation courses and Drama colleges.

Music. Woldingham is well known for its strong and lively tradition of music. Over half the students play a musical instrument; there is a full school orchestra, a string orchestra, two wind bands, a jazz band, Scholars ensemble, and three choirs. School musical productions, public concerts, international tours, and the Church's liturgical celebrations provide scope for a variety of talent and performance. A Mac suite provides for Music Technology learning, as well as composition using Sibelius and Logic.

Drama. Drama is run by dedicated professionals and is very impressive here providing high standards of both curricular and extracurricular Drama. Girls are involved in local and professional theatre and may go on to become specialists in their chosen field of Drama.

Art. Everyone takes Art for the first two years, developing creative and imaginative powers and acquiring a visual language, with the option to specialise at GCSE or A Level. On offer are drawing, painting, sculpture, ceramics, textile design, printmaking and photography. Our Year 11 students visit St Ives and this provides an excellent opportunity for working with local artists in their studios, and also the Tate and Hepworth Museums there.

Sport. The School has good sporting facilities, supporting an extensive range of team/individual games/activities to cater for a wide range of interests. It organises competitive matches in the sports of hockey, netball, swimming, cross country, rounders, tennis, and athletics. There are also fixtures for badminton, fencing, football, lacrosse and squash. Although not formally part of the curriculum, the School is able to provide girls with polo, sailing, skiing and fencing instruction. All girls are encouraged to attend extracurricular activities and sessions are run across the ability range. Elite athletes are guided towards the county pathways for their chosen sport. Certain evenings are dedicated to sports matches and training so girls can pursue music and drama options as well.

International Exchanges. Close links exist with Sacred Heart schools abroad. There is an excellent exchange programme to France, Spain and Germany.

Extracurricular Activities. These are not optional extras; they are considered an essential part of a girl's education at Woldingham. The programme of regular weekly activities includes a priority schedule to enable girls to make manageable choices.

The extensive programme of activities, in addition to traditional sports and clubs, offers something for everyone and includes: fencing, archery, taekwondo, polo, jazz band, close harmony singing, backstage drama, life drawing, Chinese and Russian, community service and mountain biking.

The 'Saturday Active' programme is available to girls in Years 7–10, running until noon. The girls can choose from a wide range of high-quality activities, delivered by visiting specialists in their fields.

The Duke of Edinburgh's Award scheme has become well established at Woldingham. The majority of Year 10 girls are involved at Bronze level and a large number go on in the Sixth form to achieve their Gold Award.

Community. The School is involved with many community projects, including volunteering at local nursing homes and a hospice shop, running reading groups at primary schools and helping out at a sports club for adults with learning difficulties, as well as year-round fundraising for several charities both at a local level and internationally.

Exeats. A weekly boarding arrangement is in place for Year 7 and sixth form boarding students and flexi boarding is an option for Years 7 and 8. All boarders are allowed home most weekends from Saturday midday. There are two long weekends (from Friday evening) each term with an additional two optional exeats each term.

Health. There is an excellent Health Centre which has two resident nurses. Two doctors attend regularly. There is a Health Education programme which emphasises healthy living. Our Wellness Centre provides support and a positive approach to matters of health.

Admissions. Main entry to Woldingham is via the Woldingham School examination in the autumn prior to the year of entry for 11+, 13+ and 16+ candidates. Students wishing to join the Sixth Form should be capable of taking three or four A Level courses and should have achieved nine or 10 subjects at level 6 (B grade) at GCSE, including Maths and English (grade A in Sixth Form options).

Applicants for occasional vacant places in other year groups are also required to sit the school's own entrance examination.

Scholarships. Academic, Art, Music, Drama, Sport and All Rounder scholarships are offered at 11+, 13+ and 16+. A Science Scholarship is also offered at 16+

Fees per term (2016–2017). Boarders: £10,444–£11,371; Day £6,532–£7,119. Sixth Form Direct Entry carries a premium for Boarders of £500, Day £250.

Charitable status. Woldingham School is a Registered Charity, number 1125376. It exists for the education of girls.

Chairman of Governors: Mr Ian Tyler, BCom, ACA, FICE

Headmistress: **Mrs A Hutchinson**, MA Oxon

Senior Deputy Head: Mrs M Giblin, BA Maynooth

Deputy Head Academic: Ms N Weatherston, BSc Hons Newcastle
Deputy Head Pastoral: Mrs J Brown, BEd CNAA
Head of Sixth Form: Ms J Lane, BA Leeds
Head of Marden: Ms C Owen, BA Royal Holloway London
Bursar: Mr N T Campbell, MBA, DEF

Registrar: Mrs L Underwood

Heads of Departments:
Art: Miss C Reay, BA Manchester Metropolitan
Careers and Higher Education: Mr R Peachey, BA Oxon, BA Open, MA SOAS
Classics & Latin: Mr T Hayward, MA SOAS
Design & Technology: Mr D Wahab, BA Brighton
Drama: Mrs L Mann, Dip Drama Middlesex
EAL: Miss H Smith, BEd Swansea, MEd Bath
Economics & Business: Mr W Bohanna, BA UEA
English: Mrs J Vivian, BA Wales, MEd Newcastle
French: Mrs C Maillot, BA equiv France
Geography: Mr D Lock, BA London
German: Mr V Ceska, BA Czech, MA France
Government & Politics: Mrs K Payne, BA Dunelm
History: Miss G Noble BA Exeter, MEd Cantab
History of Art: Mr A Cullen, BA SOAS
Computer Science: Mr M Underwood, BSc Liverpool, MA IOE
Learning Enhancement: Ms K Moorvan, BA S Africa, MEd OU, BEd S Africa
Mathematics: Mrs C Sinclair, MA Oxon
Media Studies: Mr S Maunder, BA Sheffield
Music: Mr J Hargreaves, BA York
Personal, Social & Health Education: Miss A O'Neill, BEd London
Physical Education: Mrs C Treacy, BSc Gloucestershire
Theology: Mr T Oulton, MA Oxon, MSt Oxon
Biology: Mrs S Baldwin, BSc London
Chemistry: Dr R Yu, BA, MSc Cantab, Dr rer nat Dresden, Germany
Physics: Mrs K Connor, BSc East Anglia
Psychology: Miss R Collinson, BMus, PG Dip RCM
Spanish: Mr A Lopez, BA Oviedo

Wychwood School

74 Banbury Road, Oxford, Oxfordshire OX2 6JR

Tel:	01865 557976
Fax:	01865 556806
email:	reception@wychwoodschool.org
website:	www.wychwoodschool.org
Twitter:	@wychwoodschool

Wychwood is a unique and friendly day and boarding school for girls, with excellent academic grades and outstanding pastoral care. Situated in the heart of Oxford, the school offers an exceptional education for pupils of all abilities through its small class sizes which allow for extensive individual attention without intense pressure. Established in 1897, individuality has always been more important than conformity at Wychwood and the girls have opportunities for success in many directions.

Curriculum. All girls are expected to take up to 10 subjects at GCSE; most go on to work for AS and A2 and University entrance. The lower school curriculum includes: Religious Education, English, History, Geography, Mathematics, Biology, Physics, Chemistry, French, ICT, Textiles, Singing, Art, Photography, Music, Computing, PSE, Gymnastics, Spanish (from Year 8), Drama, Swimming and Games. Visiting staff teach other optional foreign languages

and musical instruments; there is a school choir and chamber groups.

School Council. Day-to-day life is largely controlled by the School Council which meets weekly and consists of staff, seniors (elected by the school) and form representatives. This is a type of cooperative government, the matured result of a long series of experiments, which trains the girls to deal with the problems of community life and gives everyone, in greater or lesser degree according to her age and status, an understanding of, and a voice in, the rules necessary for a sensibly disciplined life.

Sixth Form. Members of Wychwood Sixth have considerable freedom yet play an active part in the life of the school. The choice of subjects at AS and A2 is wide, and classes are small and stimulating. Individual help with university applications and careers is a key feature of the Sixth Form. There are regular outside speakers and girls attend a variety of lectures, conferences, exhibitions and meetings. Their participation in school plays and concerts as well as School Council is greatly valued. Sixth Form girls may spend approximately 2 hours per week on community service. Optional computer courses are run after school. Sixth Form boarders have individual study bedrooms.

Entrance. A personal interview is usually essential between the Headmistress and both a parent and the pupil, though this may be waived where circumstances make it impossible. There is an entrance test to satisfy the staff that the girl will benefit from an education of this kind; the opinion of the girl's former school is also taken into account, particularly in relation to non-academic qualities.

Scholarships and Bursaries. Scholarships are offered in creative arts, art, music, science and academic areas.

Academic: At 11+ one Scholarship worth £1,200 pa and two Scholarships worth £600 pa are offered. Academic Scholarships are awarded on the results of the general entrance paper.

Academic: At 16+ one Scholarship worth £1,800 pa and one Scholarship worth £900 pa are offered, and one Science Scholarship worth £1,800 pa.

Two Music Scholarships are offered at ages 11+ or 16+ to cover instrumental tuition on up to 3 instruments. Candidates will be expected to play two prepared pieces on their instrument(s) and to do some sight reading and aural tests.

Two Creative Arts Scholarships, each worth £1,200 pa, are offered at age 11+ to candidates with outstanding ability in Art or Creative Writing.

Creative Writing: Candidates are asked to bring six different pieces of writing, including poetry, a story and a description. These will be discussed with the Head of English. A piece of creative writing will be set on the afternoon of the test day.

Art: Candidates are asked to bring six artistic compositions or craft items which will be discussed with the Head of Art. A short unprepared task will be undertaken on the afternoon of the test day.

Bursaries: There are means-tested bursary funds available for a limited number of pupils in particular financial need.

Fees per term (2016–2017). Boarders £7,800, Weekly Boarders £7,400, Day Girls £4,900.

Charitable status. Wychwood School is a Registered Charity, number 309684. It exists for the education of girls from the ages of 11 to 18.

Trustees:
[1]Mr P Hall, BA (*Chairman*)
Mrs D Pluck, BA, FCA
[1]Mr R Briant

Board Members:
¶Mrs D Pluck, BA, FCA (*Chairman*)
[1]Ms A Stewart, MA, ACA (*Deputy Chairman*)

[1]Mr R Briant, MA
Miss M Crawford, BA Hons, PGCE
[1]Mr P Hall, BA
Mrs R Hayes, BA Hons, MA, PGCE, FRGS
[1]Mrs A Hunter, Cert SpLD
Mrs N King, BA Hons
[1]Dr K Rogers, BM BChir
[1]Dr A Sharpley, BSc Hons, PhD

¶ *Old Pupil*
[1] *Parent or Past Parent*

Staff List:

***Headmistress*: Mrs A Johnson**, BSc Dunelm, PGCE

Deputy Head: Ms B Sherlock, BA, MEd (*English*)
Director of Studies: Dr A Pringle, BA Hons, MSc Oxon, DPhil Oxon
Head of Wychwood Sixth: Mrs J Sherbrooke, BSc Hons, MSc, PGCE

Miss H Barnes, BSc Hons, MSc Hons, PGCE (*Physical Education*)
Mrs A Bennett-Jones, BSc, PGCE (*Mathematics*)
Miss J Bettridge, TESOL Cert (*EAL*)
Ms M Bridgman, LDS (*Textiles*)
Mrs C Crossley, BA Hons, PGCE (*RS, SENCo*)
Mrs C Collcutt, DEUG (*French, Examinations Officer*)
Mrs E Dean, MA Oxon, PGCE (*English*)
Mrs L Doughton, BSc Hons, MA (*Biology*)
Mrs S Gauden, BA Hons, PGCE
Mr P Ilott, BEng (*Physics*)
Mr L Jimenez, LLB, MA (*Spanish*)
Ms A Jones, BA Hons, PGCE (*Art & Design*)
Ms S Jones, BA Hons, PGCE (*Drama*)
Mrs H Kirby, BA Hons, PGCE (*English*)
Mr M Pennington, BA Hons, MA (*Photography*)
Dr A Pringle, BA Hons, MSc Oxon, DPhil Oxon (*Psychology*)
Ms L Reece, BA Hons, Dip CG (*Careers*)
Mrs F Roitt, BSc Hons, PGCE (*Geography*)
Mrs J Sherbrooke, BSc Hons, MSc, PGCE (*History*)
Mrs A Stacey, BA Hons, PGCE (*Chemistry*)
Mrs M Stephenson, BSc Hons, PGCE (*ICT, Careers, SENDCo*) [maternity cover]
Mrs B Stevens, BSc Hons, PGCE (*Mathematics*)
Mrs G Troth, BSc Hons (*Economics & Business Studies*)
Mrs B Walster, BMus Hons, PGCE (*Music*)
Dr J Williams, BA Hons, PGCE, SRN, RSCN (*History of Art*)

Reception /Office Assistant Miss P Sayers
Head's PA: Mrs S Grainger
Marketing & Admissions: Miss N Jones, BEd Hons
Bursar: Mr I Williams
Senior Housemistress, Head of Boarding: Mrs L Henk
Junior Housemistress: Miss J Tyers
School Doctor: Dr C Hornby, MB BChir, MRCGP
School Counsellor: Mrs M Davis
Librarian: Ms V Evans, BA Hons, MA, QTS

Entrance Scholarships

Academic Scholarships

Abbots Bromley School (p. 557)
Abbot's Hill School (p. 559)
Alderley Edge School for Girls (p. 562)
Badminton School (p. 563)
Blackheath High School (p. 565)
Brighton & Hove High School (p. 568)
Bruton School for Girls (p. 569)
Burgess Hill Girls (p. 570)
Bury Grammar School Girls (p. 571)
Channing School (p. 572)
Cobham Hall (p. 574)
Cranford House (p. 576)
Croydon High School (p. 577)
Derby High School (p. 578)
Durham High School for Girls (p. 581)
Edgbaston High School (p. 582)
Farlington School (p. 585)
Farnborough Hill (p. 586)
Francis Holland School (p. 588)
Gateways School (p. 590)
Haberdashers' Aske's School for Girls (p. 591)
Harrogate Ladies' College (p. 594)
Headington School (p. 595)
Heathfield School (p. 597)
Hethersett Old Hall School (p. 600)
Howell's School Llandaff (p. 601)
Ipswich High School (p. 602)
Kilgraston School (p. 603)
King Edward VI High School for Girls (p. 604)
King's High School (p. 606)
The Kingsley School (p. 609)
The Lady Eleanor Holles School (p. 610)
Leicester High School for Girls (p. 613)
Leweston School (p. 615)
Loughborough High School (p. 616)
Manchester High School for Girls (p. 618)
Manor House School, Bookham (p. 620)
The Mary Erskine School (p. 622)
Marymount International School (p. 624)
Mayfield School (p. 626)
The Maynard School (p. 628)
Moira House Girls School (p. 632)
More House School (p. 635)
Moreton Hall (p. 636)
The Mount School (p. 639)
North London Collegiate School (p. 641)
Northampton High School (p. 643)

Northwood College for Girls (p. 644)
Norwich High School (p. 646)
Notre Dame School (p. 646)
Notting Hill and Ealing High School (p. 649)
Nottingham Girls' High School (p. 650)
Oxford High School (p. 651)
Palmers Green High School (p. 652)
Pipers Corner School (p. 653)
Portsmouth High School (p. 654)
Princess Helena College (p. 655)
Putney High School (p. 656)
Queen Mary's School (p. 658)
Queen's College, London (p. 659)
Queen's Gate School (p. 660)
Redmaids' High School (p. 662)
The Royal High School Bath (p. 663)
Rye St Antony (p. 665)
St Catherine's School (p. 669)
St Catherine's School (p. 671)
St Dominic's Brewood (p. 672)
St Gabriel's (p. 673)
St George's, Ascot (p. 675)
St Helen & St Katharine (p. 677)
St Helen's School (p. 679)
St Margaret's School (p. 686)
St Martha's (p. 687)
Saint Martin's School (p. 689)
St Mary's School (p. 691)
St Mary's School (p. 692)
St Nicholas' School (p. 695)
St Swithun's School (p. 699)
Sheffield High School for Girls (p. 703)
South Hampstead High School (p. 703)
Stamford High School (p. 706)
Streatham & Clapham High School (p. 707)
Sydenham High School (p. 709)
Talbot Heath (p. 710)
Tormead School (p. 711)
Truro High School for Girls (p. 712)
Tudor Hall (p. 714)
Walthamstow Hall (p. 716)
Westfield School (p. 719)
Westonbirt School (p. 720)
Wimbledon High School (p. 722)
Woldingham School (p. 723)
Wychwood School (p. 725)

All-Rounder Scholarships

Badminton School (p. 563)

Bruton School for Girls (p. 569)

Burgess Hill Girls (p. 570)

Cobham Hall (p. 574)

Croydon High School (p. 577)

Derby High School (p. 578)

Gateways School (p. 590)

Harrogate Ladies' College (p. 594)

Leweston School (p. 615)

Manor House School, Bookham (p. 620)

Marymount International School (p. 624)

Moreton Hall (p. 636)

The Mount School (p. 639)

Notting Hill and Ealing High School (p. 649)

Pipers Corner School (p. 653)

St Gabriel's (p. 673)

St George's, Ascot (p. 675)

Stamford High School (p. 706)

Talbot Heath (p. 710)

Tudor Hall (p. 714)

Woldingham School (p. 723)

Art Scholarships

Abbots Bromley School (p. 557)

Abbot's Hill School (p. 559)

Alderley Edge School for Girls (p. 562)

Badminton School (p. 563)

Blackheath High School (p. 565)

Brighton & Hove High School (p. 568)

Bruton School for Girls (p. 569)

Burgess Hill Girls (p. 570)

Channing School (p. 572)

Cobham Hall (p. 574)

Cranford House (p. 576)

Croydon High School (p. 577)

Derby High School (p. 578)

Durham High School for Girls (p. 581)

Edgbaston High School (p. 582)

Farlington School (p. 585)

Farnborough Hill (p. 586)

Francis Holland School (p. 588)

Gateways School (p. 590)

Harrogate Ladies' College (p. 594)

Headington School (p. 595)

Heathfield School (p. 597)

Hethersett Old Hall School (p. 600)

Howell's School Llandaff (p. 601)

Ipswich High School (p. 602)

Kilgraston School (p. 603)

The Kingsley School (p. 609)

The Lady Eleanor Holles School (p. 610)

Leweston School (p. 615)

Manor House School, Bookham (p. 620)

Marymount International School (p. 624)

Mayfield School (p. 626)

The Maynard School (p. 628)

Moira House Girls School (p. 632)

More House School (p. 635)

Moreton Hall (p. 636)

The Mount School (p. 639)

Northampton High School (p. 643)

Northwood College for Girls (p. 644)

Notting Hill and Ealing High School (p. 649)

Oxford High School (p. 651)

Pipers Corner School (p. 653)

Portsmouth High School (p. 654)

Princess Helena College (p. 655)

Putney High School (p. 656)

Queen Mary's School (p. 658)

Queen's College, London (p. 659)

Queen's Gate School (p. 660)

The Royal High School Bath (p. 663)

Rye St Antony (p. 665)

St Catherine's School (p. 669)

St Catherine's School (p. 671)

St Dominic's Brewood (p. 672)

St Gabriel's (p. 673)

St George's, Ascot (p. 675)

St Helen & St Katharine (p. 677)

St Helen's School (p. 679)

St Margaret's School (p. 686)

St Martha's (p. 687)

St Mary's School (p. 692)

St Nicholas' School (p. 695)

St Paul's Girls' School (p. 696)

Sheffield High School for Girls (p. 703)

Stamford High School (p. 706)

Streatham & Clapham High School (p. 707)

Sydenham High School (p. 709)

Tormead School (p. 711)

Truro High School for Girls (p. 712)

Tudor Hall (p. 714)

Walthamstow Hall (p. 716)

Westfield School (p. 719)

Westonbirt School (p. 720)

Wimbledon High School (p. 722)

Woldingham School (p. 723)

Wychwood School (p. 725)

Dance Scholarships

Abbots Bromley School (p. 557)
Edgbaston High School (p. 582)
Gateways School (p. 590)
Headington School (p. 595)
Manchester High School for Girls (p. 618)

Mayfield School (p. 626)
Princess Helena College (p. 655)
St Gabriel's (p. 673)
Tudor Hall (p. 714)

Drama Scholarships

Abbot's Hill School (p. 559)
Bruton School for Girls (p. 569)
Burgess Hill Girls (p. 570)
Cobham Hall (p. 574)
Cranford House (p. 576)
Derby High School (p. 578)
Durham High School for Girls (p. 581)
Edgbaston High School (p. 582)
Farlington School (p. 585)
Francis Holland School (p. 588)
Gateways School (p. 590)
Harrogate Ladies' College (p. 594)
Headington School (p. 595)
Heathfield School (p. 597)
Hethersett Old Hall School (p. 600)
Howell's School Llandaff (p. 601)
Ipswich High School (p. 602)
Kilgraston School (p. 603)
The Kingsley School (p. 609)
The Lady Eleanor Holles School (p. 610)
Leweston School (p. 615)
Manor House School, Bookham (p. 620)
Marymount International School (p. 624)
Mayfield School (p. 626)
Moira House Girls School (p. 632)
More House School (p. 635)
Moreton Hall (p. 636)

The Mount School (p. 639)
Notting Hill and Ealing High School (p. 649)
Oxford High School (p. 651)
Pipers Corner School (p. 653)
Portsmouth High School (p. 654)
Princess Helena College (p. 655)
Putney High School (p. 656)
Queen's Gate School (p. 660)
The Royal High School Bath (p. 663)
Rye St Antony (p. 665)
St Catherine's School (p. 669)
St Dominic's Brewood (p. 672)
St Gabriel's (p. 673)
St George's, Ascot (p. 675)
St Helen & St Katharine (p. 677)
St Helen's School (p. 679)
St Margaret's School (p. 686)
St Paul's Girls' School (p. 696)
Sheffield High School for Girls (p. 703)
Streatham & Clapham High School (p. 707)
Sydenham High School (p. 709)
Truro High School for Girls (p. 712)
Tudor Hall (p. 714)
Walthamstow Hall (p. 716)
Westonbirt School (p. 720)
Wimbledon High School (p. 722)
Woldingham School (p. 723)

Music Scholarships

Abbots Bromley School (p. 557)
Abbot's Hill School (p. 559)
Alderley Edge School for Girls (p. 562)
Badminton School (p. 563)
Blackheath High School (p. 565)
Brighton & Hove High School (p. 568)
Bruton School for Girls (p. 569)
Burgess Hill Girls (p. 570)
Channing School (p. 572)
Cobham Hall (p. 574)
Cranford House (p. 576)
Croydon High School (p. 577)
Derby High School (p. 578)

Durham High School for Girls (p. 581)
Edgbaston High School (p. 582)
Farlington School (p. 585)
Farnborough Hill (p. 586)
Francis Holland School (p. 588)
Gateways School (p. 590)
Haberdashers' Aske's School for Girls (p. 591)
Harrogate Ladies' College (p. 594)
Headington School (p. 595)
Heathfield School (p. 597)
Hethersett Old Hall School (p. 600)
Howell's School Llandaff (p. 601)
Ipswich High School (p. 602)

Sport Scholarships

Oxford High School (p. 651)
Pipers Corner School (p. 653)
Portsmouth High School (p. 654)
Princess Helena College (p. 655)
Putney High School (p. 656)
Queen Mary's School (p. 658)
Queen's Gate School (p. 660)
Redmaids' High School (p. 662)
The Royal High School Bath (p. 663)
Rye St Antony (p. 665)
St Catherine's School (p. 669)
St Catherine's School (p. 671)
St Dominic's Brewood (p. 672)
St Gabriel's (p. 673)
St George's, Ascot (p. 675)
St Helen & St Katharine (p. 677)
St Helen's School (p. 679)
St Margaret's School (p. 686)

St Martha's (p. 687)
Saint Martin's School (p. 689)
St Mary's School (p. 692)
St Nicholas' School (p. 695)
St Swithun's School (p. 699)
Sheffield High School for Girls (p. 703)
Stamford High School (p. 706)
Streatham & Clapham High School (p. 707)
Sydenham High School (p. 709)
Talbot Heath (p. 710)
Truro High School for Girls (p. 712)
Tudor Hall (p. 714)
Walthamstow Hall (p. 716)
Westfield School (p. 719)
Westonbirt School (p. 720)
Wimbledon High School (p. 722)
Woldingham School (p. 723)

Other Scholarships

Arkwright Engineering
St Paul's Girls' School (p. 696)

Boarding
Hethersett Old Hall School (p. 600)

Choral
Harrogate Ladies' College (p. 594)
St Paul's Girls' School (p. 696)
Westonbirt School (p. 720)

Design
Putney High School (p. 656)

Equestrian
Abbots Bromley School (p. 557)
Mayfield School (p. 626)

Ogden Trust Science
The Maynard School (p. 628)
St Paul's Girls' School (p. 696)

Organ
Mayfield School (p. 626)
St Catherine's School (p. 669)
Westonbirt School (p. 720)

Performing Arts
The Kingsley School (p. 609)
St Dominic's Brewood (p. 672)
St George's, Ascot (p. 675)
Saint Martin's School (p. 689)
Westonbirt School (p. 720)

Science
Putney High School (p. 656)
Wimbledon High School (p. 722)
Woldingham School (p. 723)
Wychwood School (p. 725)

STEM
Badminton School (p. 563)
St Margaret's School (p. 686)

Textiles
Harrogate Ladies' College (p. 594)
St Catherine's School (p. 669)
Tudor Hall (p. 714)

Bursaries

PART III
Schools whose Heads are members of
The Society of Heads

ALPHABETICAL LIST OF SCHOOLS

The following schools, whose Heads are members of both The Society of Heads and HMC, can be found in the HMC section:

Ackworth School
Bedales School
Bristol Grammar School
City of London Freemen's School
Clayesmore School
Cokethorpe School
Halliford School
Kirkham Grammar School
Leighton Park School
Lincoln Minster School

Reading Blue Coat School
Reed's School
Rendcomb College
Rydal Penrhos School
St Columba's College
Seaford College
Shiplake College
Warminster School
Wisbech Grammar School

The following schools, whose Heads are members of both The Society of Heads and GSA, can be found in the GSA section:

Burgess Hill Girls
Moreton Hall
St Augustine's Priory School

THE SOCIETY OF HEADS
GEOGRAPHICAL LIST OF SCHOOLS

Individual School Entries

Abbey Gate College

Saighton Grange, Saighton, Chester CH3 6EN

Tel: 01244 332077
Fax: 01244 335510
email: admin@abbeygatecollege.co.uk
website: www.abbeygatecollege.co.uk
Twitter: @AbbeyGateColl
Facebook: @AbbeyGateCollege

Motto: *Audentior Ito*

Founded in 1977, Abbey Gate College is a co-educational day school for boys and girls from 4–18 years of age.

Location and Facilities. The senior school is set in beautiful grounds at Saighton Grange some three miles south of the City of Chester. The history of Saighton Grange goes back long before the Norman Conquest, although most of the present building is Victorian. From 1853 the Grange was a residence of the Grosvenor family. Additional facilities include a large Sports Hall, playing fields and an Arts and Media Centre opened in March 2004 by HRH the Duchess of Gloucester. A purpose-built Art and Design & Technology Centre and new science laboratory were completed in Spring 2008 and opened by His Grace the Duke of Westminster. The completion of a modern Sixth Form Centre with purpose-built ICT, Careers, Social and Study facilities marked the culmination of the 30th Anniversary celebration in 2008. In 2013 developments included a new multi-purpose classroom and drama studio and the next scheduled developments include a Sports and Teaching Pavilion with a fitness room and an all-weather pitch. The Infant and Junior Departments are sited in Aldford, a picturesque village only two miles from Saighton. Facilities here include excellent playing fields, an ecology and wildlife area plus a number of other outdoor learning spaces. The Juniors and Infants benefit from shared use of the senior site facilities and specialist staff that teach throughout the age range.

Aims. The College encourages its pupils to aim to achieve their academic and personal potential. Outside the world of academia our objective is also to introduce our boys and girls to a wide range of extracurricular activities. In addition much emphasis is placed on good manners and discipline; this is a friendly, family school particularly aware of the values of moulding character in conjunction with the search for excellence in the classroom. We provide a caring environment; we are proud of the relationship between the teaching staff and their pupils; we encourage a love of learning and ensure that children feel safe, happy and eager to do their best.

Academic Programme. The College aims to provide children with a broad general education through GCSE and A Levels to university or other forms of higher education. In Years 7 and 8 pupils study Art, Drama, English, French, German, Spanish, Home Economics, Geography, History, Mathematics, Music, Physical Education, PSHE, Textiles, Religious Studies, Science, Spoken English, Design & Technology, Information and Communication Technology.

In Years 10 and 11 an option scheme takes effect: within the core, all pupils study English, English Literature and Mathematics, a modern foreign language and at least two Sciences. Study skills are developed and all pupils participate in sport and a rolling PSHE programme. To support their academic curriculum, Year 10 undertake a week's work experience and participate in a Development Course

designed to build teamwork, self-confidence, leadership skills and peer mentoring.

Option subjects for GCSE are taken from the following: Art, Biology, Chemistry, Design and Technology, Drama, French, Geography, German, History, Music, Physics, ICT, Spanish and PE.

In the Sixth Form A Level subjects available (according to demand) are: Mathematics, Further Mathematics, English Literature, English Language, History, Government and Politics, Geography, Geology, Economics, Business Studies, Physics, Chemistry, Biology, French, German, Art, Music, Product Design, PE, ICT, Psychology and Theatre Studies. Sixth Form students follow a comprehensive PSHE programme, have the opportunity to study AS Citizenship, complete an EPQ (Extended Project Qualification), the AQA Baccalaureate and participate in a range of sports, music and drama at the College.

In the Lower Sixth students may also join the Young Enterprise scheme which gives theoretical and practical knowledge of the business world. They enjoy an active community service programme. A number of outside speakers visit the school and regular trips to theatres, conferences or galleries are arranged. All the Lower Sixth students also attend a study skills and team building course in the Lake District in their first term which supports the transition from GCSE to A Level.

Music. The College is well known throughout Chester and North Wales for the outstanding quality of its music. The Chapel Choir has for several years undertaken week-long summer visits to Cathedrals in various parts of the country including Ely, Gloucester, St Albans, Ripon, Tewkesbury, Hereford, Winchester, Durham, York, Bath, Norwich and Hereford, as well as touring overseas: the USA in 2003; more recently, Italy in 2009, Belgium in 2010 and Poland in 2013. Annually, the Chapel Choir sings Evensong at St Paul's Cathedral or St George's Chapel, Windsor. The College also has a Concert Band, The Saighton Syncopators dance band, a modern Funk Band and a Barber Shop Group.

Many pupils of all ages take music lessons and with visiting staff are prepared for the Associated Board Examinations.

Drama. There are two major drama productions each year and these can be drama and musical. There is a whole-school production, a Key Stage 3 performance and GCSE and A Level plays. Pupils are also prepared for examinations in Speech and Drama and regularly enter local competitions with great success. All pupils in Years 7–9 participate in the English Speaking Board scheme within the English and Drama curriculum, helping to develop their confidence and public speaking skills. Year 6 Junior pupils also present a summer performance in their final term before moving into Year 7.

Sport. The College has extensive playing fields, tennis courts and a sports hall, with plans for a new Sports and Teaching Pavilion, fitness room and state-of-the-art all-weather surface. The Sports Hall offers four badminton courts, five-a-side soccer, volleyball, basketball, netball, indoor hockey, tennis and cricket nets.

All pupils participate in physical education and games. Boys play rugby, soccer, cricket and tennis; girls play hockey, netball, tennis and rounders. Athletics is popular for both boys and girls and all sports provide full fixture lists for the various College teams. The local swimming pool is reserved each week for sessions with a fully-qualified instructor for the younger pupils.

The College competes in both Regional and National Independent Schools sports events, and has enjoyed great success in athletics and swimming. Pupils are regularly sent for trials for Chester and District and County teams with players selected to represent Cheshire in handball, football, hockey, cricket and rugby. There have been soccer tours to Malta and Spain and recent Hockey tours to South Africa, Germany and Spain. The school's Ski Racing team trains weekly and is involved in many competitions including the annual British Championships in France where individual and team performances have been impressive. A number of pupils already train with the English Schools Ski Squad. The equestrian team has achieved national honours, with riders being selected to represent their country and the college organises a local competition and sponsors a number of pony club or equestrian competitions.

Junior Department. Our Infant & Junior School provides excellence in education with a broad based curriculum supported by a diverse extracurricular programme that gives children aged 4–11 a wide range of opportunities. These include choir, gymnastics, team games, Spanish, Belleplates, Ju-Jitsu, creative arts and drama to name but a few. There are frequent school trips and excursions that support the school experience, including a Year 6 residential outdoor and adventurous week at Glaramara in the Lake District.

Other activities. The College has a remarkable record of giving generously to Charities and the three Houses serve to raise money through sponsorship; Sixth Formers take a leading role in this. At weekends and during holidays many pupils take advantage of outdoor pursuits and many choose to follow The Duke of Edinburgh's Award scheme; there are over 70 participants at all levels from Bronze to Gold Award.

Admission. *Senior School*: Most pupils enter the College at age 11 following an Entrance Examination held in the Spring Term, although where occasional places occur in other year groups, assessments can be made mid year. Each pupil is allocated to one of the Senior School Houses; the house system encourages competition, community and positive attitudes through the allocation of home points.

Junior Department: Pupils are admitted to the Junior Department by means of short assessment and interview at ages 7, 8, 9 and 10 dependent on spaces being available. It is expected that children already in this part of the school will move directly into the College at age 11.

Infant Department: Entry at ages 4, 5 and 6 is also available. Reception places are limited and assessments run on separate occasions throughout the year.

Sixth Form: Priority is given to existing pupils but places are offered to others and are conditional on good results at GCSE.

Scholarships. A number of academic scholarships are available following the results of the Entrance Examination. A comprehensive Bursary Scheme also operates at 11+ and Sixth Form entry offering places to pupils with proven ability or talents who would normally not be able to afford the school fees.

For musical talent awards are offered including Music Exhibitions at Year 7 and Sixth Form level and the Daphne Herbert Choral Scholarship. In addition there are sports awards available at 11+.

Fees per term (2016–2017). Tuition: Infant and Junior Departments £2,803; Senior School £4,019.

Old Saightonians. All pupils are encouraged to join the Old Saightonians' Association. Further details of the Association can be obtained from the Registrar at the College.

Charitable status. Deeside House Educational Trust is a Registered Charity. number 273586. It exists to provide co-education for children in the Cheshire, Wirral and North Wales areas.

Visitor: His Grace The Duke of Westminster

Chairman of Governors: Mr D Weir, CA

Head: Mrs T Pollard, BEd Hons, NPQH, MA

Deputy Heads:
Mr D P H Meadows, BA Hons, PGCE (*History*)
Mr G Allmand, BSc Hons, PGCE (*Geography*)

Academic Staff:
Mr A Austen, BSc Hons, PGCE (*Geography*)
Mr S Ball, PhD, MPhys (*Physics*)
Mrs C Bennett, BA Hons, PGCE (*Modern Foreign Languages*)
Miss K Burdon, BSc PGCE (*Mathematics*)
Mrs N Burton, MA, BA Hons PGCE (*Art*)
Mr M Cavallini, BSc Hons, GTP (*Mathematics, Head of Sixth Form*)
Mr C Cutler, BSc Hons (*PE*)
Mrs S Dolan, BSc Hons, PGCE (*Biology*)
Mr M Dickins, BA, PGCE (*History*)
Mrs R Fitzhugh, BA Hons, PGCE (*Geography*)
Mrs V Goodwin, MusB Hons, PGCE (*ICT*)
Mr A P Green, BEd (*PE & Mathematics*)
Mrs S Hall, BA Hons, History, QTS, AMBDA, PGCE (*Learning Enrichment*)
Mrs C Houghton, BA Hons, PGCE (*History*)
Mrs C House, BA Hons, PGCE (*Drama*)
Mrs K Jackson, HDE, GTP (*English*)
Miss E Jones, BA Hons, (*Physical Education*)
Mrs J Jones, CertEd (*Home Economics and Religious Studies*)
Mrs S J Kay, BSc Hons (*Mathematics*)
Mrs C Kingsley, BSc Hons, PGCE (*Mathematics*)
Mrs H Kitchin, BSc Hons, PGCE (*Economics & Business Studies*)
Dr E Leatherbarrow, PhD, BSc Hons PGCE (*Science*)
Mrs Z Leonard, BA Hons, PGCE (*English*)
Mrs N Moses, BA Hons, PGCE (*English*)
Mrs S Parker, MSc, PGCE (*Geography*)
Mrs L Poyser, BSc, PGCE (*Chemistry*)
Mrs A Prestwich, Maîtrise FLE, PGCE (*Modern Foreign Languages*)
Mr D Rowett, BSc Hons, PGCE (*PE*)
Mrs C Russell, PGCE, MA (*English*)
Mrs E Sanders, BEd Hons (*PE*) (*Maternity*)
Mr S F Smith, BA, CertEd, ARCM, LMusLCM (*Music*)
Mr D I Stockley, MSc, PGCE (*Design & Technology*)
Mrs S Storrar, BSc (*PE*)
Mr M Tempest, BEng Hons, PGCE (*Physics/Chemistry*)
Mrs Z Walker BA Hons PGCE (*Art*)

Part-time Staff:
Mrs J Ashurst, BSc Hons, PGCE (*Science*)
Mrs C Ayton, BA Hons, PGCE, PGC SpLD, AMBDA, APC (*Learning Enrichment*)
Mrs K Baty, MA, PGCE (*English*)
Mrs J Dukes, BEd (*Music*)
Mrs C Garratt, BA Hons (*Modern Foreign Languages*)
Mr K Gray, BSc Hons, PGCE (*Geography*)
Mr T L C Griffiths, BEd Hons PGCE (*History*)
Mrs A Hall, BSc Hons (*Mathematics*)
Miss A Heaps, BA Hons (*Art*)
Mrs J Heaton, BEd Hons (*Learning Support*)
Mrs F Kay, BSc Hons, PGCE (*Biology & Psychology*)
Mrs J Lewis, BA Hons, PGCE (*Modern Foreign Languages*)
Mrs E Sanders BEd Hons (*PE*)
Mrs N Stammers, HND, BA Hons, PGCE (*ICT*)
Mrs J Townsend, CertEd (*PE*)
Mrs J Walker, BSc, PGCE (*Mathematics*)

Junior Department:
Head of Junior Department: Mrs A M Hickey, BSc Hons, PGCE (*Mathematics*)
Assistant Head: Dr J Gallagher, PhD, BSc Hons, PGCE
Mr P Butcher, BEd Hons
Mrs H Courtney, BEd Hons
Mrs W Richards, BEd Hons
Mrs S Tomlins, BA Hons, PGCE
Mrs C Travis, BA Hons, PGCE
Mrs A Williams, BEd Hons
Miss E Williams, BEd Hons
Miss M Webley, BSc Hons, PGCE, MA
Teaching Assistant: Mrs C Spreyer
After School Care Coordinator: Mrs G Foulkes

Musical Instruments Teaching:
Miss K Banerjee (*Piano*)
Mr E Hartwell-Jones, BMus (*Singing*)
Mr A Bowen-Lewis, CT ABRSM, Adv Dip MusTech (*Brass*)
Mr G Macey (*Woodwind*)
Mrs M Parsonage (*Violin*)
Mr J Rowlands, LLB (*Drums*)
Miss R Owen (*Woodwind*)

Speech and Drama:
Mrs C Faithfull, LRAM, FNEA

Bursar: Mrs H Barnes, MEng
Finance Manager: Mrs P Rees, FCCA
Marketing Manager: Miss C Evans, BA Hons
Director of ICT: Mr D Stewart
Network System Admin Manager: Mr P Rowlands, BSc Hons
ICT Assistant: Mr J Shenyagwa
Finance Manager's Assistant: Mrs K Campion
Examination Officer: Mrs J Moulton, BA Hons
Registrar: Mrs S Boyd
PA to Head: Mrs K Simons
PA to Aldford Head and Data Manager: Mrs J Rawlinson-Smith
PA to SLT & Clerk to the Governors: Mrs S Knowles
School Secretary: Mrs D Roxborough
School Reception: Mrs A McCleary
School Administrator: Mrs D Humphreys
School Nurse: Miss P Sheckley
Librarian: Mrs J Littler
School Helper: Mrs W Jones
After School Care Assistant: Mrs L Greenwood
After School Care Assistant: Mrs R Leach
Technicians: S Huxley, J Jones, Mrs J Leach, B Shaughnessy, R Slater

Abbotsholme School

Derbyshire

Rocester, Uttoxeter ST14 5BS
Tel: 01889 594265 (admissions)
             01889 590217 (main number)
Fax: 01889 591001
email: admissions@abbotsholme.co.uk
website: www.abbotsholme.co.uk
Twitter: @AbbotsholmeSch
Facebook: @abbotsholmeschool
LinkedIn: /abbotsholme-school

Abbotsholme School is an independent co-educational boarding and day school from ages 2–18 in a rural setting on the border of Derbyshire and Staffordshire, in the United Kingdom.

Abbotsholme School Aims. Abbotsholme aims to prepare its pupils for the whole of life, by giving them a balanced education through a strong academic curriculum and an extensive range of extracurricular activities. We give academic, personal and social development equal standing, recognise the diversity of talent in each pupil and encourage pupils and staff to do their best.

Abbotsholme aims to provide:
• Knowledge to help everyone achieve and succeed to the best of their individual academic ability
• An understanding of the natural environment and the importance of protecting it
• Challenges which build strength and test courage, as well as providing a stimulating and enjoyable experience
• Cultural enrichment to widen perspective and to develop awareness of our responsibilities to others.

Our Vision. It is our firm belief that a good, balanced education is an essential preparation for the whole of life. An education at Abbotsholme provides not only the starting blocks but also propels each individual through the start of life outside Abbotsholme. Abbotsholme wants all of its pupils not only to succeed – whatever their individual talents or abilities may be – but also to feel successful. The Abbotsholme ethos encourages a sense of self-worth and of pride in their own achievements, whilst, in equal measure, celebrating the success of others. Although we are committed to helping all Abbotsholmians fulfil their academic potential, the measure of our success cannot be judged by scholarly achievements alone. Indeed, it is their development as people that must be seen as the ultimate test. Our vision is that pupils leave Abbotsholme as responsible and socially aware young men and women, able to face an increasingly demanding world with confidence and a zest for life. In years to come, we would wish to know that they were happy with themselves and with their lives; we also would want them to be successful in their personal and professional endeavours whilst remaining sensitive to the needs of others.

Pupils are encouraged to take advantage of all aspects of School life for a rounded and grounded educational experience.

ISI Inspection. Following its latest inspection in May 2011 by the Independent Schools Inspectorate, Abbotsholme received another excellent report with many comments of "outstanding" and "excellent". The report stated that: "*Abbotsholme is exceptionally successful in achieving its aims. Pupils are empowered to find success ... Achievement is excellent. The pupils' personal development is exemplary. Pupils embrace wholeheartedly the school's aspirations of courage, honesty, humility, integrity and respect.*"

Location. Abbotsholme is located on the Staffordshire/Derbyshire border in a beautiful estate of some 140 acres on the banks of the River Dove in rural Derbyshire, close to the magnificent Peak District, easily accessible by road and rail and less than an hour away from three international airports.

Special Characteristics. Membership of the *Round Square* organisation (www.roundsquare.org) provides a strong international perspective. A worldwide and unique association of schools committed to personal growth and responsibility through service, challenge, adventure and international understanding, members share one aim – the full and individual development of every pupil into a whole person.

Our *outdoor education* programme is both well known and well regarded. Its pioneering principles inspired such organisations as the Outward Bound movement, the United World Colleges and The Duke of Edinburgh's Award scheme. With adventures both close to home and internationally, it presents pupils with personal challenges, both physical and mental, and teaches them the importance of taking responsibility for themselves and others. Many pupils are involved in The Duke of Edinburgh's Award scheme and all participate in summer camps and autumn hikes each year.

Abbotsholme is one of the very few schools in England to have a working *farm* upon which pupils are able to learn about animal husbandry and crop management and gain a healthy respect for the environment. In addition to the 70-acre farm, our British Horse Society approved *Equestrian Centre* is a popular place to be for our horse enthusiasts, who happily involve themselves in the upkeep of the stables and yard and can study for NVQ or BHS exams.

All pupils are encouraged to appreciate *Music* in some way, either by learning to play an instrument or taking singing lessons or by simply attending some of the performances that are frequently organised. Both the orchestra and the choir comprise a mixture of staff and pupils, which fosters the special atmosphere so typical of Abbotsholme.

Drama flourishes, in and out of the classroom, with performances in the 120-seat theatre that always oversubscribed. All pupils who are keen to be involved, whether on stage or behind the scenes, find regular opportunities to experience the fun and self-discipline characteristic of performance and improvised theatre.

The influence of the *Art* department is evident throughout school, where pupils' painting, drawing, pottery, ceramic, graphic design and 3D creations are permanently on display. In addition many pupils enjoy the facilities of the *Design and Technology* department, which provides excellent opportunities for developing creative design into quality manufacture. Photography is a real strength of the Art department and pupils have access to a traditional darkroom as well as cutting-edge editing equipment.

We believe that the physical and mental disciplines of working together in a team are very important. *Sport* teaches the art of winning and losing with equally good grace, self-reliance and leadership, and the opportunities to compete are grasped by many of our pupils. Sports at Abbotsholme include: rugby, football, hockey, netball, tennis, swimming, athletics, squash, skiing, cross-country, horse riding, badminton and basketball.

Curriculum. Abbotsholme caters for a broad ability range. Academic standards are high with the majority of sixth formers going on to their first-choice university. Breadth and balance shape the curriculum, which aims to develop critical and creative thinking and self-discipline across a wide range of subjects at GCSE and A Level.

Activities. Abbotsholme firmly believes that a school should have a greater purpose beyond preparing students for College or University. As a result we seek not only to help all pupils realise their individual academic potential but also to develop in everyone a sense of responsibility for themselves and others through active participation within the community as well as a sense of adventure through challenges in and beyond the classroom. A comprehensive range of compulsory activities is integral to the curriculum, taking place on four afternoons a week. Each week's activities alternately include Outdoor Education and Farm/Conservation work, commitments to team sports, music and drama.

Home from Home. The boarding experience at Abbotsholme is a happy one, where staff and pupils know each other well and where every individual shares equal responsibility for the community's well being and progress. Small, friendly homes are run by resident houseparents as family units. Younger boarders share bright and comfortable dormitories in threes and fours whilst older pupils have single or shared study-bedrooms. A log cabin village has been added for sixth formers giving them opportunities to experience a greater degree of independence and privacy. Weekly boarding has become a popular option for families with busy lives and for our full boarders, a full programme of weekend activities provides plenty of choice and lots of fun, balancing academic work with social time. Our modern approach

to boarding means that sleepover and flexi boarding are also options.

Facilities. These include: dedicated classroom areas for each subject, including specialist science laboratories, art, music, design and IT centres (two suites), a purpose-built studio theatre for drama, sixth form centre, log cabin complex, indoor climbing wall, 70-acre working farm, equestrian centre and manège, film studies and films, a modern, multi-purpose sports hall, extensive playing fields and swimming pool, and a chapel, which combines as the venue for morning assembly as well as concerts.

Fees per term (2016–2017). Day £2,900–£7,080; Weekly Boarding £5,650–£8,700; Full Boarding £7,735–£10,395; Occasional Boarding: £37 per night.

The Abbotsholmians' Club. The Club currently has some 2000 members and is run by a Committee of Old Abbotsholmians, elected yearly. Members receive regular mail-outs, which give contact addresses and details of the adventures of OAs, young and old. There are also regular invitations to events, to help them keep in touch with each other and with current developments at the school. An enormous amount of networking takes place between OAs, often facilitated by the Club, ensuring that friendships are sustained and memories are relived.

The Club operates a small Bursary fund specifically aimed at helping to educate sons and daughters of OAs at Abbotsholme.

Abbotsholme Arts Society. The School is host to one of the most respected concert presenters in the country. Although embracing jazz, poetry and drama performances, its core programme of chamber music has brought a Who's Who of big-name musicians to the school over the years – Ashkenazy, Brendel, Galway, Hough, the Amadeus Quartet to name just a few. Pupils are able to attend any of the Arts Society concerts free of charge.

Abbotsholme Parents' Association. Run by parents, for the benefit of parents, children and school, the Parents' Association (APA) aims to help new families settle in and become quickly familiar with Abbotsholme and all that it has to offer. Keen to promote active parental involvement in the school, members regularly organise social activities and fundraising events.

Charitable status. Abbotsholme School is a Registered Charity, number 528612. It exists to advance education and in particular to provide for children and young persons a broad, general education in accordance with the principles, traditions and aims developed since the school's foundation in 1889 by Dr Cecil Reddie.

Chair of Governors: Dr Paul Kirtley

Headmaster: Mr Steve Fairclough, MSc

Headmaster's PA: Mrs Julie Noon

Head of Marketing & Admissions: Katharine Brookes, BA Hons, PGCE

Admissions Manager: Michele Archer, CIM

Austin Friars

Etterby Scaur, Carlisle, Cumbria CA3 9PB

Tel:	01228 528042
Fax:	01228 810327
email:	office@austinfriars.cumbria.sch.uk
	admissions@austinfriars.cumbria.sch.uk
website:	www.austinfriars.co.uk
Twitter:	@AFSMSchool
Facebook:	/AFSMSchool
LinkedIn:	/Austin Friars St Monica's School

Motto: *"In Omnibus Caritas"*

Austin Friars is a co-educational day school, founded by members of the Order of St Augustine in 1951. It is the UK's only Augustinian school and pupils of all denominations are welcome into the School which provides education for 450 boys and girls aged 3–18. (*For Junior School details see entry in IAPS section.*)

Standing in its own grounds of 25 acres, Austin Friars aims to foster the personal development of all its pupils spiritually, academically, socially and physically, to enable them to take their place creatively in society. The School has high expectations of its pupils and encourages them to develop their potential in a happy, positive, productive and disciplined atmosphere. Consequently, Austin Friars has established an enviable reputation for bringing out the best in each of its pupils.

The curriculum is broad and balanced in keeping with the School's philosophy to provide an all-round education. Class sizes are small and high standards are expected and achieved through careful monitoring of progress and a commitment by all to outstanding teaching and learning. Pupils are encouraged to become increasingly independent learners as they progress towards public examinations with excellent support mechanisms available, on an individual or small group basis, for those pupils with specific learning difficulties who require specialised provision.

The quality of pastoral care is one of the School's greatest strengths. All pupils belong to a tutor group, and the tutor is the first point of contact for the students and parents. The Senior School is divided in to three Houses. A key feature and strength of the school, the House is central to the strong sense of a community which older and younger pupils mix freely; kindness, self-respect and respect for others are instantly evident.

Studies. The following subjects are available to GCSE and/or A Level: English, Latin, French, Spanish, History, Geography, Economics, Business Studies, Mathematics, Further Mathematics, Physics, Chemistry, Biology, Art, Music, Classical Civilisation, Religious Studies, Design Technology, ICT, PE, Drama, Philosophy and Ethics, Psychology and Photography.

Activities. The Junior and Senior Schools Choirs perform regularly and there is a musical performed every other year. The School Orchestra and Swing Band are also very active. Extra music tuition is provided by peripatetic teachers, who also run ensemble classes for groups of wind, brass, strings and guitar.

Both staff and pupils appreciate that school extends beyond the classroom and extracurricular activities are a strong facet of Austin Friars. The School is an excellent centre for developing new and existing interests and talents. Some 40 extracurricular activities are available to pupils including Chess, Fell Walking, Manadrin, Italian, Photography, Duke of Edinburgh's Award, Young Enterprise and a Debating Society.

Sport. The school has a full-sized astroturf which is utilised throughout the year. The range of sporting options available is vast: Rugby, Hockey, Netball, Cross-Country in winter; Athletics, Rounders, Cricket, Tennis in summer. Football, badminton, dance and fitness are all offered within the activities programme. The pupils regularly achieve county status in their various sports. Qualified and enthusiastic staff provide coaching in team sports, and the School's record in inter-school competition is acknowledged far beyond Cumbria. Annual skiing trips take place.

Admissions. The Senior School adopts a three-form entry policy. The majority of places are offered at 11+ with a further entry at Sixth Form. Admissions at other ages are considered, subject to availability of places.

All pupils at 11+ sit the Senior School's entrance examination; entry to the Sixth Form is on the basis of performance at GCSE. The 11+ entrance examination takes place in November prior to entry the following September.

Fees per term (2016–2017). £4,556 (Years 7–11), £4,656 (Years 12–13). Fees are inclusive of lunches.

There is a reduction of 5% for brothers/sisters in the School at the same time. Bursaries are available at all levels.

Junior School. *For information about Austin Friars Junior School, see entry in IAPS section.*

An invitation to see the School and meet the Headmaster is extended to all those who write for information.

Charitable status. Austin Friars is a Registered Charity, number 516289. It exists for the purpose of educating boys and girls.

Chairman of Trustees: Revd Dr Peter Tiplady, MB BS, MRCGP, FFPHM, FRIPH

Headmaster: Mr M F Harris, BSc, PGCE

Deputy Head: Mrs J Thornborrow, BSc, PGCE
Deputy Head (Academic): Mr M C F Fielder, MA, PGCE
Head of VI Form: Mr S Parry, MEd, BSc, PGCE, Dip RSA
Head of Junior School: Mr J Slingsby, BEd
Bursar: Mr E Swinton, ACIBS
Admissions Registrar: Miss A Burns, BA

Heads of Department:
Art and Photography: Miss K Quinn, BA, PGCE
Science and Biology: Mr D Harte, BSc, PGCE
Design Technology: Mr M Turnbull, BSc, PGCE, NPQH
Chemistry: Mrs R Fielder, BSc
Classical Civilisation: Mr P Thornton, BA, PGCE
Drama: Mr M Judge, BA, PGCE
Economics and Business Studies: Mr N Brady, BA
English: Mrs K Smith, BA, PGCE
Geography: Mr S Parry, BSc, PGCE
History: Mr S Wright, MA, BA, PGCE
Mathematics: Mr N Barraclough, BSc, PGCE
Modern Languages: Mrs S Green, BA, PGCE
Music: Mr C W J Hattrell, MA
Physical Education: Mr J Tiffen, BA, PGCE
Physics: Mr N Edmondson, BEd
Religious Studies: Mr J Finn, BA, PGCE

Bedstone College

Bucknell, Shropshire SY7 0BG

Tel:	01547 530303
Fax:	01547 530740
email:	admissions@bedstone.org
	headmaster@bedstone.org
	reception@bedstone.org
website:	www.bedstone.org
Twitter:	@BedstoneCollege
Facebook:	/Bedstone-College

Motto: *Caritas*

Bedstone College, founded in 1948, is a fully co-educational, independent, boarding and day school catering for children between the ages of 4 and 18 years. The school enjoys a beautiful 40-acre campus within an idyllic setting amongst the south Shropshire hills, close to the ancient and beautiful market town of Ludlow, and within 40 minutes' drive of both Shrewsbury and Hereford.

The school comprises the Junior School (for children aged 4 to 11 years) and the Senior College (for ages 11 to 18 years), all integrated within one campus. Over 50% of the students in the senior school are full boarders and students from age 9 are welcome to board.

Bedstone offers a broad and balanced curriculum with some 18 subjects available at GCSE, AS and A2 Levels. Despite being non-selective and catering to those of all ability levels, Bedstone is proud to boast that over 90% of its Upper Sixth leavers secure places at University with a large majority (80% in 2015) being at their first-choice institution. In the DfE performance tables of 2015, Bedstone was named as the top ranked school for GCSE Ebacc subjects in both Shropshire and Herefordshire.

The College aims to fulfil the potential of every child wherever that potential may lie and, with an average teacher/pupil ratio of 1:8, the smaller class sizes allow individual needs to be catered for. The well-qualified and highly-motivated staff believe that each child has a unique talent which it is their job to find and to nurture.

Bedstone is very aware of the problems that learning difficulties, such as dyslexia, can cause and the nationally recognised Learning Support Department, led by its full-time director with the aid of fully-qualified staff, is central to the help provided. Bedstone is one of just 37 schools (both state and independent) in the UK to be accredited by CReSTeD as a Specialist Dyslexia Unit.

Character of the College. Many children who join Bedstone have done so because their parents feel that the individual strengths of their child have become lost within their current school; that the challenges and opportunities for fulfilling their child's unique talents do not exist, or that they wish for greater pastoral support and guidance for their child. Every parent knows that what they want is the education of the whole child – mind, body and spirit – and Bedstone provides that with its academic and extracurricular programme coupled with its outstanding pastoral care and boarding ethos.

Family Education. There is a guarantee that once any member of a family is accepted at Bedstone, brothers and sisters will gain automatic entry by interview only provided that we can cater for any special needs. This is of immense value to parents who wish for all their children to be educated at the same school.

Accommodation. The main house, Bedstone Court, is a listed building of fine architectural merit and accommodates the Junior and Senior boys' houses. In addition, it houses the administration offices, library, dining hall and sixth form cellar club. The two girls' boarding houses are on the opposite side of the campus with the senior girls accommodated within a purpose-built boarding house and the junior girls within the homely surroundings of a 19th century manor house. All boarding houses have been completely refurbished. All boarding houses have resident staff and their families as houseparents. There is seating for 300 people in the Rees Hall Theatre with full AV facilities. There is a modern well-equipped Sports Hall, Design Technology and Art Centre, Music School, a Medical Centre staffed by RGNs, Fitness Suite, Performing Arts Studio, Learning Support and Counselling facility, a heated swimming pool and a wide range of additional facilities. There is also a social club for the Sixth Form with a weekend bar manned and carefully controlled by teaching staff. The College has a campus-wide wireless LAN.

Religious Education. The formal classroom teaching of Religious Studies follows the National Curriculum which covers all the major world religions. More broadly, the college follows the teachings of the Church of England though other denominations, and children without any religious affiliation, are most warmly welcomed. Children, whose parents wish it, are also prepared for Confirmation by the Chaplain. The College enjoys a strong choral tradition and the Choir enjoys an excellent reputation.

Senior College Curriculum. From the First Form (Y7) to the Third Form (Y9) (when a number join from other Preparatory and Primary Schools) the subjects taught are: Religious Education, English Language and Literature, History, Geography, French, Spanish, Mathematics, Biology, Physics, Chemistry, Design Technology, Art, Music, Physical Education and ICT.

In the Fourth and Fifth Forms, in addition to the Core Curriculum of English, English Literature, Mathematics, one modern foreign language (French or Spanish), the three Sciences, Religious Studies, (and non-examination Physical Education), options are: History, Geography, Art, Business Studies, Music, French, Spanish, Design Technology and Sports Studies. Latin and German tuition are also available off timetable.

Throughout the College, in all classes, we help students achieve the very best that they are capable of and surpass their own expectations. There is no "cramming" at Bedstone and we are not an academic hothouse. However, with the aid of close tutorial support, a well-qualified staff, an excellent staff/pupil ratio, plus, of course, determined effort on the part of the students, good progress and examination success are assured. AS/A2 courses are offered in English, History, Geography, French, Spanish, Business Studies, Art, Design Technology, Mathematics, Further Mathematics, Music, Physics, Chemistry, Biology, Psychology and Sports Studies. The Extended Project Qualification (EPQ) is on offer to all Sixth Form students and provision can be made for preparation in languages such as German, Polish, Chinese and Russian.

The College has its own Learning Support Department. Excellent EAL provision is available for those who require it in addition to pre-sessional intensive English courses, three-year A Level programme, IELTS, IGCSE and subject-specific language support.

Careers. There are specific careers staff and a well-resourced Careers Room. Bedstone makes full use of the Independent Schools' Careers Organisation and all members of the Fifth Form take the ISCO Psychometric tests and have the opportunity to undertake work experience. Our individual guidance means that, typically, 90% or more of Sixth Former leavers gain entrance to their university of first choice.

Games and Physical Education. There are 15 acres of playing fields, with an excellent Sports Hall, fitness suite, performing arts studio and netball & tennis courts plus an astroturf. The success of the boys and girls in physical activity at school, county and district level has been nothing short of remarkable. The school holds several ISA National Championships in various disciplines including Rugby 7s, Cross Country, Tennis and Hockey.

Rugby, Football, Athletics, Cross-Country and Cricket are the main sports for the boys and Hockey, Netball, Rounders, Cross-Country and Athletics for the girls but they can join in many more. A rotation system ensures that all students, to a greater or lesser degree, have their share of such activities as Basketball, Swimming, Badminton and Tennis. Nor are the individualists forgotten. Horse riding is popular, teams in Biathlon and Triathlon have been successful both regionally and nationally, and there are facilities for Table Tennis and Mountain Biking, whilst the South Shropshire and Powys hills provide excellent opportunities for Duke of Edinburgh's Award activities.

Clubs and Activities. The Duke of Edinburgh's Award scheme flourishes and there is a wide range of out-of-class activity, including splendid dramatic and musical productions, debating, individual music tuition. There are twice weekly 'activities' sessions which offer some 40–50 different clubs over the course of any one year. Pupils are expected to know and observe all College rules and parents to cooperate in seeing that this is done. Prefects play an important part in the pastoral system of the College. There are also a number of trips and visits that take place throughout the year, including visits to some of the most beautiful cities in Europe. Every two years there are major international sports tours for both the boys and the girls.

Bedstone Junior School is for boys and girls aged 4 to 11 years. The school is housed in its own separate accommodation and yet shares all the facilities of the senior school. Science, Modern Foreign Languages, Sport, Art and Music are all taught by senior school subject specialists within specialist areas. There is a specialist gifted and talented mathematics programme for the most able junior school students and talented sports players are developed through specialist coaching from the teachers in the senior college and entry into regional and national competitions.

The Junior School is an integral part of the College and children find the transition to the Senior College seamless. Any child accepted within the Junior School is automatically accepted into the Senior College.

Scholarships. For entry to the Senior College, there is a scholarship examination, held at the College on a Saturday in the early Spring Term. Bedstone offers Academic, Sport, Music, Art, DT and All-Rounder scholarships at 11+, 13+, 14+ and 16+ with the maximum award being up to 25% remission of fees. For local children from maintained schools, who might not be realistically considered Bedstone as an option, there is also the 'Four Counties' Scholarship which is worth up to 50% remission of fees. The school is also able to provide separate means-tested bursaries.

Forces fees discounts available upon request. We also offer scholarships in the Junior School to mirror what is done in the Senior College.

Fees per term (2016–2017). Junior School: Day: Reception to Year 2 (age 4–7) £1,660, Years 3–6 (age 7–11) £3,500; Boarding (Years 5–6, age 9–11) £5,765. Senior School (Years 7–13, age 11–18): Day £4,835, Boarding £8,755.

Old Bedstonian Society. Hon Secretary: Ms Hannah Croft.

Charitable status. Bedstone College is a Registered Charity, number 528405. It is established for the education of young people.

Governors:
Chairman: Grp Capt [Retd] J P S Fynes
Vice Chairman: Mr B Meldrum

Mrs Y Thomas, BSc	Mr D Owens
Mr J Smith	Mr S Stringer
Mr E Dunphy	Mr J Jones
Dr M Lawton	Mrs S Phillips

Headmaster: Mr D Gajadharsingh, BSc, PGCE, CPhys, MInstP, NPQH

Deputy Headmaster: Mr J Lynch, BA, PGCE, MA Ed
Director of Studies: Mr A A Whittall, BA, PGCE
Head of Junior School: Mr J Forster, BSc, MSc
Bursar: Mr A R Gore, AFA, FIAB, AIMgt

Houseparents:

Boys Boarding:
Pearson House: Mr & Mrs A Whittall
Rutter House: Mr and Mrs O Downing

Girls Boarding:
Bedstone House: Mr & Mrs P Singh
Wilson House: Mr & Mrs M Rozée

Members of Common Room:
Ms J Bartley, BA, PGCE (*Head of Modern Foreign Languages*)
Ms J Bird, BA, Dip TEFL (*Head of EAL*)
Mr C Braden, BEd QTS, PG Dip Man (*Head of Design Technology, Head of UCAS & Careers*)
Mrs E Bryden, BA, PG Dip Perf RCM, MMus, PGCE (*Head of Music*)
Miss L Bullock, BA, PGCE (*Head of History & PHSE*)
Mr E Olive, BSc, PGCE (*Head of Physics*)

Mr D Foreman, BSc, PhD, PGCE (*Head of Biology*)
Mrs S Simmons, MA, PGCE (*Mathematics*)
Mrs C Hunter, CDMVA La Sorbonne (*Modern Foreign Languages*)
Miss C Jenkins, BA, MPhil, PGCE, Adv Cert TEFL (*Head of English*)
Mr J Lowe, MA, PGD Inclusion & SEN, PGCE (*Head of Learning Support*)
Mrs N Newman, BA, MA, PGCE (*English*)
Mrs S Morris, BA, PGCE, Cert TEFL (*Head of Religious Education*)
Mr D P Marsh, BSc, PGCE (*Head of Geography*)
Mr D M Rawlinson, BSc, PhD, PGCE (*Head of Mathematics*)
Mr D M Rozée, BSc, PGCE, MSRC (*Head of Science*)
Mr J P Smith, BA (*Head of Art*)
Mr J R Simpson, BA, QTS (*Sports Studies, Head of Boys' PE & Games*)
Mrs N Williams, BSc, PGCE (*Head of Business Studies*)
Mrs E Coyle, BSc, PGCE Science)
Miss M Wilson, BA QTS (*Sports Studies, Head of Girls' PE & Games*)

Junior Department:
Mrs J Richards, BA, PGCE, MA Ed
Mrs S Crabtree, BA, QTS
Mrs R Rawlinson, BSc, MSc, PGCE
Mrs J Marriott, BA
Mrs J Williams, BEd
Mrs L Meredith, NNEB

Learning Support:
Mr J Lowe, PGD Inclusion & SEN, PGCE
Mrs T Chilles, BSc, PGCE, PGD SpLD Dyslexia, AMBDA

EAL:
Ms G Kindermann
Mr C Morris, BA, CELTA

Lay Chaplain: Mr A C Dyball, MA Cantab, Dip Ed

School Medical Team: Mrs N Stead, RGN & Mrs T Chave, RGN
School Counsellor: Mrs C Hall
School Doctors: Dr M L Kiff & Dr A Lempert

Visiting Music Staff:
Mr D Kirk (*Drums*)
Mr D Luke (*Guitar*)
Mrs S Freeman (*Brass*)
Mr J Hymas (*Violin*)
Mrs K Norton (*Piano*)
Mr M Buxton (*Singing*)

Competitive Houses:
Hopton: Mrs E Bryden
Stokesay: Ms J Bird
Wigmore: Mr J Lowe

Headmaster's PA: Mrs Paula Davis
Accounts Administrator: Mr Paul Downes
Director of Admissions, Marketing & Development: Mr Gary Wright, BA, MA, PGCE, NPQH
Admissions Marketing & Enterprise Assistant: Ms Beckie Broadbent
IT Manager: Mr S Davis, BSc
Drama: Mrs E Bryden
Receptionist: Miss J Court
Accounts Clerk: Mrs S Gore, BSc
Science Laboratory Technician & Librarian: Mrs R Shenton
Catering & Domestic Manager: Mr T Campbell
School Shop: Mrs A Forster
Transport Manager: Mr P Singh

Beechwood Sacred Heart School

Pembury Road, Tunbridge Wells, Kent TN2 3QD

Tel: 01892 532747
Fax: 01892 536164
email: bsh@beechwood.org.uk
website: www.beechwood.org.uk

Beechwood is an independent co-educational day and boarding school for pupils aged 3–18. Founded in 1915 by the Society of the Sacred Heart. As a Sacred Heart School, it retains sound Catholic values, whilst welcoming pupils from all nations and beliefs.

The Nursery School (age 3–5), Preparatory School (age 5–11) and Senior School (age 11–18) are located in 23 acres of landscaped grounds overlooking open countryside, close to the centre of the historic town of Royal Tunbridge Wells. The Main School is based in a Victorian villa with all facilities located on a single campus. There are 400 pupils on roll.

Boarding is offered for seventy boys and girls in modern and comfortable accommodation on the school campus. Junior boarders share in two or three bedded rooms whilst all sixth-form boarders are allocated single study-bedrooms. We receive a large number of applications for boarding places each year, so an early application is advised. The School does not operate 'Exeat' weekends.

Beechwood is noted for its genuine family atmosphere. Consideration for others underpins the code of behaviour for all pupils, making Beechwood a happy school with high academic standards being achieved through expectation and challenge, rather than prescription. We are an ambitious, caring school and that sense of confidence and generosity of spirit permeates throughout the school. At Beechwood we prepare our pupils for the future but encourage them to enjoy the present.

Curriculum. In our small classes, teachers stimulate pupils to excel in what they are good at and build confidence in areas they find difficult, from the youngest child in the Preparatory School through to our oldest Senior School pupils. Our Learning Development department supports the individual needs of those pupils who require extra support.

Beechwood provides a broad education. At Key Stage 3 all pupils study a range of subjects including our innovative COGS+ (Thinking Skills) programme in Year 7. Most subjects are taught in mixed-ability classes of boys and girls. Mathematics is setted from Year 7. French is studied in Year 7, with options to study Spanish and German from Year 8. Academic standards are important and we challenge our pupils to achieve their best. We also encourage our pupils to participate in a wide range of extracurricular activities, trips, and visits.

At GCSE pupils can study ten GCSEs from a wide range of subjects. Biology, Chemistry and Physics ('triple Science') are offered as single subjects and we offer French, German, and Spanish as Modern Foreign Language options. Mathematics, English Language, and English Literature are compulsory at GCSE as well as at least one science subject. This also enables pupils to select from a wider range of options when they construct their GCSE portfolio. Additional English language lessons are provided for international pupils. Pupils participate in a diverse PE curriculum and study PHSCE as part of their personal development.

At A Level, more than twenty subjects are offered including three Sciences, Theatre Studies, Further Mathematics, Business Studies, Photography, Product Design, Psychology, Law, Media Studies, History and Textiles. The Sixth Form curriculum is enhanced by an enrichment course that includes Life Skills and comprehensive Careers and University application advice.

Sixth Formers are encouraged to show initiative and take responsibility. They have opportunities for leadership as prefects and in organising activities for younger pupils. All leavers successfully gain places at university on a wide range of courses.

Examination Results. Beechwood's record in public examinations is particularly impressive for a non-selective school, with a pass rate (A*–C) of around 90% at GCSE and 100% at A Level, and is in the top 25% of schools for value-added performance at A Level.

Sports. Pupils are encouraged to experience a wide variety of sports, the emphasis being on fun and participation. Recent successes include being Kent County Basketball Champions. Sports facilities include hockey and football pitches, netball, basketball and tennis courts, cricket nets, gymnasium, badminton and volleyball courts. We also take advantage of local all-weather pitches. Construction of a new Sports Hall is planned to commence is 2017.

Preparatory School and Nursery. Adjacent to the Senior School, the Preparatory School and Nursery provide an excellent beginning for every child in a supportive, family atmosphere. The curriculum stimulates enquiry, academic standards being maintained through regular monitoring and assessment. French is studied from Year 1 and all pupils also enjoy cookery lessons. In addition, by sharing the facilities of the Senior School, pupils participate in a wide variety of sports and can represent the school in matches. Extracurricular activities include chess, crafts, gardening and keyboard music making, and many pupils have instrumental music lessons.

Entry Requirements. The school is non-selective academically, selection being based on interview with the Headmaster, previous school report, performance in entrance assessments and confidential reference. All enquiries and applications should be addressed to the Registrar.

Fees per term (2016–2017). Full boarders £9,250; Weekly boarders £8,250; Day pupils £3,100–£5,550.

Scholarships. Academic, Music, Art, Sport and Drama scholarships are available at 11+, 13+ and 16+. Entrance and Scholarship Days take place in January for 13+ and in November for 11+ and 16+ prior to entry the following September.

Charitable status. The Sacred Heart School Beechwood Trust Ltd is a Registered Charity, number 325104.

Governors:
Mrs Marie-France Mason (*Chairman*)
Dr David Findley, BSc, PhD (*Vice-Chairman*)
Mrs Gillian Hill
Mr Robert Park
Mrs Constance Williams
Sister Moira O'Sullivan
Mr Michael Southern
Mr Michael Stevens
Dr Amanda Turner

Company Secretary and Clerk to the Governors: Mr Andrew Harvey

Head: Mr Aaron Lennon, BA Hons, NPQH

Deputy Head: Mrs Helen Rowe, BA Hons, PGCE
Director of Studies: Mrs Kim Allen, BSc Hons, PGCE
Chaplain: Miss Victoria Gillespie

Staff:

Heads of Division:
Mr Joshua Rowe, BSc, PGCE (*Junior Division*)
Mrs Carol Mitchell, BA, PGCE (*Middle Division*)
Mr Michael Awdry, BA Hons, PGCE (*Senior Division*)

Heads of Department:
Mrs Olga Clarke, PGCE, Maîtrise MA, Licence/Deug BA (*Modern Languages*)

Mr Gary Hatter, MEd, PGCE (*Art*)
Mrs Louise Neill, BSc Hons, PGCE (*Geography*)
Mrs Gwen Goodley, MBA, BA Hons, BSc Hons (*History*)
Mr Daniel Sumner, MA, BA Hons, DELTA (*EAL*)
Mr Jonathan Millward, BSc Hons, PGCE (*Science*)
Mrs Sarah Kershaw, BA Hons, PGCE (*Music*)
Mrs Kim Cook, BEd Hons, Dip Ed, AMBDA (*Learning Development*)
Mrs Carol Mitchell, BA, PGCE (*Physical Education*)
Mrs Candy Prodrick, BD, PGCE (*Religious Education, PSHE*)
Mrs Diana Ringer, BSc Hons, PGCE, MSc (*Mathematics*)
Mr Mark Thomas, BSc Hons, PGCE (*ICT*)
Ms Nicola Phipps, BA Hons, PGCE (*English*)
Mr Sumair Hussain, BA Hons, PGCE (*Drama*)
Mr James Walters, BSc Hons, PGCE (*Design Technology*)

Preparatory School:
Head: Mr Patrick Gush, BEd Hons
Director of Studies: Mrs Teresa Cutts, MA Cantab, PGCE

Head's Secretary: Miss Liz Milner
Registrar: Mrs Sue Dyke

Bethany School

Curtisden Green, Goudhurst, Cranbrook, Kent TN17 1LB

Tel:	01580 211273
Fax:	01580 211151
email:	registrar@bethanyschool.org.uk
website:	www.bethanyschool.org.uk
Twitter:	@bethanyschkent
Facebook:	@bethanyschkent
LinkedIn:	/Bethany-School-Kent

The School was founded in 1866 by the Revd J J Kendon. It is a Charitable Trust administered by a Board of Governors, a member of the Association of Governing Bodies of Independent Schools.

Bethany has 345 pupils, aged 11 to 18. Approximately 30% board on either a weekly or termly basis, with a varied weekend programme of activities available for termly boarders. A generous staff to pupil ratio of 1:8 ensures small classes and high quality pastoral care. Individuals are encouraged to develop their potential to the full in academic and all other respects. Most teaching takes place in modern classroom blocks, the result of an ongoing building development programme. Development in ICT has been a priority at Bethany: a wireless network enables pupils from Year 8 upwards to use laptops across the curriculum, and our Year 7 pupils are gifted an iPad by our Alumni to use for their studies.

The Sixth Form house offers single study-bedrooms with en-suite facilities for the Upper Sixth boarders, study rooms for day pupils and communal facilities for both Upper and Lower Sixth Form pupils. Recent additions to the School include a brand new six-lane, 25m indoor swimming pool, a state-of-the-art fitness suite and a new Sixth Form centre as an extension of our dedicated Sixth Form Boarding House. Our next major project will be a Digital Performing Arts Centre.

Situation. The School occupies a scenic, 60-acre, rural campus in the heart of the Weald of Kent, easily accessible from most parts of South East England: an hour from Charing Cross (Marden Station) and easy access to Gatwick and Heathrow Airports, the Channel ports and Ashford and Ebbsfleet International railway stations.

Admission. The normal age of entry is at 11 or 13 by the School's Entrance Assessment and at Sixth Form level based on predicted GCSE grades, but the school welcomes pupils to the Bethany community at other stages if places are available.

Fees per term (2016–2017). Full boarders £8,780–£9,915, weekly boarders £8,140–£9,015, day pupils £5,265–£5,830. Learning Support and English as an Additional Language, if required, incur an additional fee of up to £598 per term.

Scholarships and Bursaries. Academic Scholarships are awarded based on performance in the Entrance Examination. Scholarships are also available in Art, Design & Technology, Drama, Dance, Music and Sport at the main points of entry, which are Years 7 and 9 and into the Sixth Form. The Christopher Jackson Scholarship is available for pupils who attend state primary schools local to Bethany, are particularly able and have a capacity for academic excellence. This award is for boys and girls entering Bethany at Year 9 who are aged 14 years or under at the start of the academic year of entry. Means-tested bursaries are also available. Children of members of HM Forces and the Clergy receive a 10% fee discount.

Curriculum. The broad curriculum is based on the National Curriculum. The full range of subjects is taught including Information Technology from 11+ and Spanish from 13+. We have also introduced Mandarin at Year 7, and GCSE Dance. There are 26 GCE A Level subjects, including Economics, Business Studies, Food & Nutrition Studies, Government and Politics, Music, Photography, Politics, Textiles, Theatre Studies and Media Studies. Almost all Sixth Form leavers proceed to degree courses at University.

Dyslexia. The Dyslexia and Learning Support department, which enjoys an international reputation, has been supporting pupils at Bethany for over 30 years.

Games and Activities. The School offers a wide range of sporting opportunities and enjoys an extensive fixture list, having established a long tradition of inter-school Sport. Facilities include a Sports Centre, climbing wall, fitness room, three squash courts, tennis courts, an indoor swimming pool and a floodlit AstroTurf. There is a also wide range of clubs and activities. The Duke of Edinburgh's Award scheme is well established at Gold, Silver and Bronze levels.

Music. There are wide-ranging opportunities for instrumental tuition. There are sectional instrumental groups including: a Symphony Orchestra, Rock School, Jazz Band, Concert Band, Brass Consort and a Choir, all making use of the fine Music School with its recording studio and music technology area.

Careers. The School is a member of ISCO (Independent Schools Careers Organisation) and Careers Education is an important part of the Curriculum. Sixth Form pupils take part in the Coursefinder Analysis Scheme and receive detailed advice regarding Higher Education and Gap Year opportunities.

Chapel. The Chapel, built in 1878, is the focal point of School life and all pupils are expected to attend services. Confirmation classes are offered for those who wish to participate.

Charitable status. Bethany School Limited is a Registered Charity, number 307937.

Governors:
Mr R J Stubbs, BSocSc, MMRS (*Chairman*)

Mr D Boniface, MA, MSc	Mr M L Hammerton, BSc, MBA
Mrs A Carboni, MA Cantab	
Mr M Clark, BSc, CEng, MICE, MIStructE	Dr R Hangartner, BSc, MB BS, MBA, FRCPath
Mr R C Clark	Mrs W Kent
Mrs A Culley, CertEd	Mr N P Kimber, BSc, FCA
Mr A Cunningham	Mr R J Pilbeam
Mr J M Fenn, LLB	Mr R Walden

Bursar and Clerk to the Governors: Mr S J Douglass

Staff:

Headmaster: Mr M F Healy, BSc, HDipEd, NPQH

Deputy Headmaster: Mr S Winter, BA Hons

Assistant Head Academic: Mrs E Hill, BA Hons, PGCE

Assistant Head Pastoral: Mr A Sturrock, BA Ed Hons

Lay Chaplain: Mrs C Turvey

Staff:
Mrs Rachel Antikatzidis, BA Hons
Mr Alex Bolton
Mr Jonathan Booth
Miss Nicola Brown, BDes, PGDE
Ms Liz Bryant
Ms Fen Burley
Mr Ryan Bing
Ms Dilys Coley
Mr Cliff Cooper, MSc
Mr Simon Cuthbert, BA Hons, PGCE
Mr Simon Davies, BA Hons
Mrs Karen Dawson, BA, PGCE
Mrs Jo Digby, BSc, PGCE, Dip SpLD
Mr Simon Duff, BEd, TEFL, NPQML
Mrs Kate Harper, BSc Hons QTS, PG Cert SpLD
Mr Tim Hart Dyke, BA Hons
Mrs Frances Healy, BA, SpLD
Mr Jay Holland, BSc Hons, PGCE
Mr Phil Hughes, BA Hons, PGCE
Ms Ann Hurst
Mr Anthony Khan, BA Hons, PGCE
Miss Sam King, BA
Mr Adam Manktelow
Dr John Marks, BSc, PhD, PGCE
Mrs Rossy McGovern, BA Hons
Mrs Cathy Miles
Miss Claire Mills, BEd Hons, PG Cert SpLD
Mr Marcus Norman, BEd Hons
Mrs Claire Pack, BA Hons
Mr Suresh Parmar, BSc Hons, MBA, PGCE
Mr Matt Payne, BSc Hons PGCE
Mrs Rachael Payne, BA Hons, PGCE
Mr Devin Reilly, BSc Hons
Mrs Carly Shapland, BA Hons
Mr Dan Smith, BA Hons
Miss Fleur-Estelle Shaw, MA, PGCE
Mr Gareth Stubberfield, BA Hons, PGCE
Mrs Anne-Marie Sturrock, BEd Hons
Mr Mike Thomas, MSc, PhD
Mrs Sue Thorpe, BA Hons
Mrs Becky Tinson, BSc, PGCE, CELTA
Mr Mike Turner, BA Hons
Mr James Vickerman, BSc Hons, PGCE
Mrs Jules Wareham, BEd Hons
Mrs Caron Wickham, BA Hons, PGCE
Mrs Katy Williams, BSc

Medical Officer: Dr J N Watson, MBBS, MRCGP

Marketing & Admissions Manager: Mrs G Corbett

Registrar: Mrs S Martorell

Headmaster's Secretary: Mrs A Discombe

Bournemouth Collegiate School
United Learning

Senior School:
College Road, Southbourne, Bournemouth, Dorset BH5 2DY
Tel: 01202 436550
email: registrar@bcschool.co.uk

Prep School:
40 St Osmund's Road, Poole, Dorset BH14 9JY
Tel: 01202 714110
email: prep-admin@bcschool.co.uk

Twitter: @BCSPrep; @BCSHeadmaster
website: www.bournemouthcollegiateschool.co.uk

The Best in Everyone

Bournemouth Collegiate School is a popular and successful independent, non-selective, co-ed Senior School (day and boarding, 11–18), situated in an inspiring location next to Bournemouth's golden beaches, and Preparatory School (day, 2–11) in a spacious woodland setting in Lower Parkstone, Poole.

Parents and pupils are attracted by the small classes, excellent results and outstanding facilities across both sites including indoor swimming pools at both schools.

BCS is an extraordinary place to learn. We are part of a country-wide educational group, United Learning, that seeks 'the best in everyone', and we take that mission very seriously.

We offer an exhaustive extracurricular, sporting and music programme and run a successful Sports Academy for talented athletes. BCS really believes in developing the potential of every pupil and is determined to get the best out of everyone.

The caring, supportive ethos of the school is based on a policy of mutual respect. We encourage independent learning and intellectual curiosity and enable pupils to experience a broad range of experiences which includes numerous trips, seminars, talks by guest speakers and the opportunity for fun, expression and friendship in the many school events on offer.

Fees per term (2016–2017). Prep School: £2,300–£3,535. Senior School: Day Students £4,665; Weekly Boarders £8,800; Full Boarders £9,100.

Scholarships and Bursaries. Scholarships may be offered to pupils who join the school into Year 7 to Year 12. They are awarded to students with all-round excellence or special ability in academia, music, performing arts, art or sport.

Assisted Place Bursaries are available for those entering Year 7, Year 9 and Year 12.

The 'BCS Award' combines academic excellence and the Assisted Place, effectively offering a means-tested academic scholarship, awarding up to a 100% discount on the School fees.

Charitable status. Bournemouth Collegiate School is part of United Learning which comprises: UCST (a Company Limited by Guarantee, Registered in England, number 2780748, and a Registered Charity, number 1016538) and ULT (a Company Limited by Guarantee, Registered in England, number 4439859, and an Exempt Charity).

Headmaster: Mr Russell Slatford, BSc, MA Cantab

Senior Deputy Head: Mrs Maria Coulter, BSc Hons, PGCE, NPQH, Dip Ed

Head of Prep School: Miss Kay Smith, BEd, NPQH

Admissions Registrar: Miss Rhiann Bowden

Box Hill School

Mickleham, Dorking, Surrey RH5 6EA

Tel: 01372 373382
            01372 385002 (Registrar)
Fax: 01372 363942
email: enquiries@boxhillschool.com
website: www.boxhillschool.com

Affiliations: The Society of Heads, Round Square, BSA, AGBIS, ISBA, BAISC, IBO, DofE, NAGC.

Box Hill School is a co-educational school set in forty acres of grounds in the heart of the Surrey countryside, offering day and boarding places for 11–18 year olds. We have a strong educational, artistic and sporting tradition; however, what makes us stand out is that we discover and nurture the talents and abilities of every student, so that they all unlock their potential. Box Hill School is proud of its academic attainment and broad curriculum. Standards, recognised as outstanding by inspectors in the 2012 Inspection, are consistently high, and the school is always above national averages in exam performance.

The Sixth Form curriculum focuses on the IB Diploma programme and A Levels were reintroduced from 2013 as an exciting curriculum expansion initiative. Subject combinations are flexible within the constraints of our options timetable system, and we aim to cater for as wide a range of choices as possible.

Box Hill School is a proud founder member of the Round Square, an international organization of over 90 schools united by a set of 'IDEALS': Internationalism, Democracy, Environmental concern, Adventure, Leadership and Service.

All the Houses at Box Hill School are small and friendly, and students never feel lost or overlooked. The six single-sex Boarding Houses each board around 20–35 pupils with the majority of boarders' rooms being doubles, particularly at Key Stage 4 and above. First-time Boarders are reassured by the family structure of our Houses and find them easy to settle into. To strengthen the bond between students even further, a central school dining room is provided and students are allocated to competitive group teams for school-wide competitions. Full-time Boarders also enjoy a variety of outings at the weekend. An on-site medical centre is provided, staffed by qualified nurses with two non-resident school doctors on call. Boarders may stay in school during term time, except at half terms. There are no 'exeat' weekends.

We provide strong pastoral support for each student, each one being assigned to a House, complete with common room and kitchen. The Houses are run by teaching House staff and each student is assigned to a personal tutor within their house – a member of teaching staff who supports their academic and pastoral development.

We believe that activities outside the classroom form an important part of education, and all students take part in the extensive timetabled activities programme. As well as this regular programme, younger students take part in expeditions around the UK twice a year. The Duke of Edinburgh's Award is particularly strong in the school. Students have the opportunity to participate in Round Square expeditions, carrying out community based projects in locations including Peru and South Africa. They also have the opportunity to go on an exchange to another Round Square school overseas.

The school has an active Parents Association, comprised of supportive parents and friends of the school who maintain links with the local community as well as running social functions and fundraising events. Parents are strongly encouraged to join.

Special features of the School.
- International opportunities through Round Square membership
- IB World School
- Small classes and a high level of academic support
- Outstanding pastoral care
- Weekly and termly activities for all students from an exciting and wide range of options
- International Study Centre

Courses offered. GCSE: Mathematics, English Language, English Literature, Biology, Chemistry, Physics, Geography, History, Business Studies, ICT, French, German, Spanish, Mandarin, Music, Art, Textiles, Drama, Physical Education, Design Technology.

IB: Biology, Environmental Systems, Business Management, Chemistry, Psychology, Theatre Arts, Economics, English, Visual Art, Geography, History, Mathematics, German, Russian, Japanese, Mandarin, French, Spanish, Music, Physics, Design Technology.

A Level: Art, Biology, Business Studies, CDT, Chemistry, Drama, English, Fashion and Textiles, Further Mathematics, Geography, History of Art, ICT, Mathematics, Music, Music Technology, Physics, Psychology, Spanish, Sport Studies.

Sports. Athletics, basketball, cricket, football, hockey, netball, rounders, rugby and tennis as competitive sports but many others as part of the activities programme. Horse riding, Taekwondo, pilates, golf and mountain biking are available by arrangement.

Drama, Music and Art. Art students gain excellent examination grades each year, with many going on to be accepted at major art schools. Our purpose-built Music School has greatly enhanced the already wide range of musical opportunities within school, including a choir, chamber choir, wind ensemble, string ensemble, jazz band, funk band and numerous rock/pop bands. The school stages senior and junior plays each year and has performed *The Crucible* and *Bugsy Malone* in the last academic year. LAMDA coaching is available and the school has an excellent record in these examinations.

Fees per term (2016–2017). Years 7–11: Boarders £10,350; Weekly Boarders £8,500; Day Pupils £5,570–£5,840. Sixth Form: Boarders £10,800; Weekly Boarders £8,900; Day Pupils £6,100. ISC Fee: £12,250.

A fee discount of 20% is offered to students who have a parent who is a serving member of HM Armed Forces.

Scholarships. A variety of awards are offered for entry to Box Hill School; the latest information can be found on the school's website. Scholarships are available for those entering Years 7, 9 and the Sixth Form, under the following categories: Academic, Art, Expressive/Performing Arts, and Sport.

Bursaries are available on application following registration and are subject to means testing and are offered on the basis of a formula laid out in the school's Scholarships and Bursaries Policy which is available on request from the Bursar. All bursaries are reviewed annually.

Method of Entry. Entry is based on an interview, the two most recent reports from the pupil's present school, and written tests in Maths and English. Sixth Form entry is based on report, interview and GCSE predictions. For overseas pupils a personal interview on site is desirable but we are happy to conduct a Skype interview if necessary. Main school entrance ages are 11, 13 and 16 years. Under normal circumstances, we like to meet prospective pupils and their parents or guardians – this also gives you an opportunity to have a look around our campus facilities and meet key staff and students.

Charitable status. Box Hill School Trust Limited is a Registered Charity, number 312082. It exists to promote the advancement of education.

Warden: Vice-Admiral Sir James Weatherall, KCVO, KBE

Chairman of Governors: Mr John Banfield

Headmaster: Mr Cory Lowde

Bursar: Mr John Pratten

Registrar: Mrs Kirstie Hammond

Headmaster's PA: Ms Samantha Jepp-Panteli

Bredon School

Pull Court, Bushley, Tewkesbury, Gloucestershire GL20 6AH

Tel: 01684 293156
Fax: 01684 298008
email: enquiries@bredonschool.co.uk
website: www.bredonschool.org
Twitter: @BredonSchool
Facebook: /Bredon-School

Age Range. 5–18.
Number of Pupils. 249. Boarders: 81 Boys, 22 Girls. Day: 99 Boys, 47 Girls.

Bredon School is situated in a magnificent 84-acre rural estate and delivers a broad-based education centring upon individual attention and personal recognition. Since the school was founded 53 years ago, it has set out to discover and nurture children's strengths and talents and to support them in overcoming any weaknesses.

Ethos. Bredon educates the whole child through sound, realistic, academic provision, sympathetic pastoral care, regular leadership challenges and a varied sports programme. The small and friendly environment allows children of all ages to thrive and achieve more than they thought possible.

Learning Support. The school is internationally-renowned for its expertise in supporting children with specific learning difficulties, such as dyslexia and dyspraxia. It is also CReSTeD-accredited, holding Dyslexia Specialist Provision (DSP) status. Within the dedicated Access Centre, an extensive range of specialist software and specialist tuition allows pupils to organise their thoughts, practice their skills and use voice-activation to enhance their individual progress.

Curriculum. Bredon provides a broad academic curriculum at all Key Stages through to GCSE and A Level. In addition Bredon offers extensive vocational programmes at Foundation, Intermediate and Advanced levels. The School Farm offers a vocational route for those interested in pursuing a career in agriculture. or land-based studies. Class sizes across the school average 10 in number and the teacher/pupil ratio is 1:7.

Physical & Outdoor Education. In addition to the many sporting opportunities on offer; including frequent competitive fixtures with local schools, there is a fully-equipped gymnasium, a 30-metre sports hall, a climbing wall and bouldering course, a clay shooting ground, plus numerous outdoor sports pitches and cross country running trails. Bredon also has a swimming pool, a canoe launch onto the River Severn, a forest school and thriving School Farm with pigs, ponies, cattle and small animals, which add to the amount of time children spend learning outdoors and engaged in practical activity. The school also organises an extensive range of trips and expeditions through the Duke of Edinburgh's Award scheme, and dedicated overnight outdoor education activities.

Clubs and Activities. There are many thriving lunchtime clubs including model making and music activities. In addition, once a week, the afternoon lessons are given over to activities and the children can choose from activities as varied as sailing, cycling, dancing, music, art, cookery, magic club, fencing, engineering, farming and clay pigeon/air rifle shooting.

Boarders. There is provision for full-time, weekly or flexi boarders from age nine and they are cared for by house parents, creating a real home from home environment. Accommodation is in dormitory-style rooms until Year 11 when boys move into individual study-bedrooms. Girls from Year 11 can choose to have a small individual room or share with a friend. Boarders have an extensive range of after school activities to participate in and there is a lively schedule of weekend events too.

Admissions. Admission is by potential not just attainment, and specialist support is available to pupils with learning difficulties. There is no entrance examination, instead school reports and any specialist reports will be requested and assessed, followed by a 3-day guest visit to the school to assess suitability. A place is usually offered upon completion of a satisfactory guest stay.

Fees per term (2016–2017). Day £2,260–£6,145; Weekly Boarding £6,632–£9,450; Full Boarding £6,806–£9,630.

Chairman of Local Governing Body: Mr Aatif Hassan

Principal: **Mr David A T Ward**, MA, BEd

Deputy Head: Mr B Ferrari, MA, PG Cert, BA Hons, DipEdPsy, FIFL
Deputy Head: Mr N S Allison, BSc, Dip SW, PGCE
Deputy Head: Mrs G Hamilton, PCGE
Head of SEN: Mrs D Jones, BA Hons, Cert SpLD
Head of Junior School: Mrs J Merchant, MEd Hons, PGCE, SENCO KS 1 & 2
Bursar: Mrs H Archer-Smith, FCA, DChA
Registrar: Mrs J Graham

The Cathedral School Llandaff
A Woodard School

Llandaff, Cardiff CF5 2YH

Tel: 029 2056 3179
Fax: 029 2056 7752
email: registrar@cathedral-school.co.uk
website: www.cathedral-school.co.uk
Twitter: @cslcardiff

Set in 15 acres of parkland and playing fields within minutes of Cardiff city centre, the Cathedral School was founded in 1880. Acknowledged by Estyn as an "excellent" school (2012), there are currently almost 800 pupils at the co-educational school between the ages of 3 and 18 years. The Cathedral School is a member of the Woodard Corporation and adheres to a firmly Christian ethos.

Building on Strong Foundations. First-class academic teaching, excellent facilities and an extensive co-curricular programme, underpinned by high quality pastoral care and the school's Christian ethos, give Cathedral School pupils and students the opportunity to reach their full potential, both academically and personally, in a vibrant and supportive environment. The school is small enough to ensure that everyone is known and cared for, yet large enough to offer a real breadth of challenge and opportunity. Pupils of all denominations and faiths are welcomed.

Nursery, Infants & Juniors. A positive experience of learning in our earliest years at school sets the foundations for being an engaged and successful learner later in life. The classroom is a place of energy and creativity, a place of high expectations within an atmosphere of nurture and encouragement.

Beyond the classroom walls there are extensive opportunities to enjoy competitive sport, especially team games which have busy and challenging fixture lists; opportunities to perform music at an excellent standard including opportunities for boys and girls to join choirs and to sing in Llandaff Cathedral, along with drama, dance and elocution; opportunities to enjoy the outdoors, wildlife, outward bound activities; opportunities to get involved in action for good causes, including environmental awareness and charity work. There are also plenty of inter-house activities to get involved with which create a vibrant atmosphere.

Nearly all pupils transfer into the Senior Section to continue their educational journey through to 18.

The Seniors. At this school we pride ourselves upon being a strong learning community. It is important that everyone feels valued and that they have a meaningful part to play. From the initial Year 7 bonding weekend creating new friendships, to the competitive house system, a mutually supportive environment means that every pupil's skill, interest, talent and potential are nurtured.

Regularly recognised, whether by the schools inspectorate Estyn, or in newspaper league tables, as one of the highest achieving schools in Wales academically, a great emphasis is also placed upon the "co-curricular". For Years 10–13 the Duke of Edinburgh's Award is followed, which is hugely popular and delivered by our own dedicated staff and for Years 7–9, the Head's Award, a junior and anticipatory version of D of E.

The quality of music at the Cathedral School is outstanding. It is our boys and girls who sing in Llandaff Cathedral's choral services day by day, and the same excellence of musicianship rubs off in school within a wide range of genres, from the classical to rock and pop, chamber music to jazz. On the sports field a similar appetite for excellence pervades all we do. With a very high coach to player ratio and a busy, competitive fixture list, rugby, football, sevens, cricket, hockey, netball, rounders, rowing, kayaking, climbing and gym all thrive here. Equally, ambitious participation in public speaking and debating competitions, challenging drama productions and various genres of fine art all add to the opportunities for all pupils to achieve standards which help them grow in confidence.

Sixth Form. Following the introduction of Sixth Form teaching in 2013, we have been delighted with the outstanding results gained by our sixth form cohorts in both 2015 and 2016. With a 100% overall pass rate, 82% of all grades were A*–B in 2016, with a third of the cohort achieving exclusively A*/A grades. Our students are progressing to the most selective and sought-after universities, including Oxford, Cambridge, Imperial College London, Bath, Warwick and Maastricht.

The Cathedral School Sixth Form offers very small classes, highly experienced staff with close university links and a culture which is ambitious and supportive in equal measure. The Sixth Form Centre provides dedicated social and study space for students. Every sixth former is invited to engage in the school's professional mentoring programme, which pairs students with leading professional figures in the areas of working life which most appeal to them, for advice and guidance.

Beyond their A Level studies, students have many opportunities to broaden their interests and abilities through initiatives including outward bound expeditions, the Duke of Edinburgh's Award at Gold Level, competitive sport, outstanding musical performances, debating and public speaking and the Extended Project Qualification.

A Level Subjects: Art, Psychology, Chemistry, Computing, Economics, Biology, Drama, English Literature, Spanish, Geography, Mathematics, Further Mathematics, Religious Studies, Latin, History, Design & Technology, Physics, French, German, Music and Physical Education.

Scholarships & Bursaries. Financial support is available for bright pupils at Year 7 and Year 12 entry, with scholarships for especially gifted children – academic, music, all-rounder, sport – and means-tested bursaries worth up to 100% of fees.

School Transport. School transport is available with bus routes from Castleton, Cowbridge, Caerphilly, Colwinston, Llantrisant and Lisvane.

Fees per term (2016–2017). Year 7 & above £4,015, Years 5 & 6 £3,678, Years 3 & 4 £3,265, Reception, Years 1 & 2 £2,862, Nursery £2,458.

Charitable status. The Cathedral School Llandaff Limited is a Registered Charity, number 1103522. It exists to provide a high standard of education for girls and boys with a caring Christian ethos.

Chairman of the Council: G C Lloyd

Senior Management Team:

Head: **Mrs Clare Sherwood**, MA

Deputy Head Pastoral: Mr Lawrence Moon, BA, MA, GTP

Deputy Head Academic: Dr Nathan Horleston, PhD, MSci

Head of Sixth Form: Mrs Catrin Ellis-Owen, BA

Deputy Head Juniors: Mr Bret Garland, CertEd, BEd

Director of Infants: Mrs Sally Walsh, BEd, NPQH

Bursar: Mr Robert Leek

Claremont Fan Court School

Claremont Drive, Esher, Surrey KT10 9LY

Tel: 01372 467841
email: info@claremont.surrey.sch.uk
website: www.claremont-school.co.uk

Situation. Claremont Estate is one of the premier historic sites in the country. The original house and the famous Landscape Garden were first laid out by Sir John Vanbrugh for the Duke of Newcastle early in the eighteenth century. Later Capability Brown built the present Palladian Mansion for Clive of India. For over a century Claremont was a royal residence and played an important part in Queen Victoria's early years. In 1930 the School acquired the Mansion and now owns 100 acres of peaceful parkland. Esher is only 16 miles from London and almost equidistant from Heathrow and Gatwick airports with access points onto the M25 within 3 miles.

General Information. Claremont Fan Court School is a co-educational school for pupils from 2½–18 years. The School consists of the Pre-Preparatory and Nursery School for pupils aged 2½–7 years, the Preparatory School for pupils aged 7–11 years and the Senior School for pupils from 11–18 years. Claremont Fan Court is a school with strong Christian values and welcomes pupils from all faiths and none

Aims. To care for and value the potential of every child. With this recognition comes the expectation of high academic achievement and participation in sporting and cultural activities.

Curriculum. The core curriculum provides all pupils with the opportunity to learn the skills and understandings required to continue learning throughout their lives. Emphasis is placed on the acquisition and development of skills in numeracy and literacy while providing a wide and varied range of subjects to stimulate the joy and wonder of learning. These curriculum ideals are delivered in a manner appropriate to the ages of the pupils throughout the Pre-Preparatory, Preparatory and Senior School.

An important element in our teaching philosophy is to understand the link between academic rigour and the value of good character. The academic curriculum ensures that all pupils attain the highest qualifications of which they are capable for entry into university or college.

Many pupils excel in the sporting arena where they develop talents through fixtures against other schools as well as in county or national school championships. Annual tours, both nationally and overseas, give an added dimension to pupils' sporting education.

Music, art and drama are also important aspects of the daily curriculum. All contributions are valued, whether they be leading, supporting or backstage roles, in order for the participants to be given every opportunity for creative thought and individual expression and to develop an awareness of self-worth.

Sixth Form. The Sixth Form is a vibrant and vital part of the School, focusing on 26 A Level courses. It forms a bridge between the years of compulsory schooling and the more independent years of Higher Education. Students take on many responsibilities including leadership and organisational roles which provide an all-round experience of special value to universities, colleges and employers.

At Sixth Form, Claremont Fan Court also welcomes external students, who meet our entry requirements. The Sixth Form Centre provides recreation and study facilities and is housed in the historic surroundings of White Cottage, designed by John Vanburgh in 1715.

Careers. Pupils receive careers advice from Year 8 onwards. All sixth form students have a weekly dedicated Careers lesson, delivered by a specialist Careers teacher. This ensures that all students receive detailed personalised guidance, leading them to courses and career choices that are appropriate for their individual preferences. Interviews are organised for pupils and conducted by external advisors.

Co-Curricular Activities. Making individual choices in the learning programme and developing a wide range of interests are both necessary preparations for lifelong learning. All pupils are actively encouraged to participate in a wide variety of clubs and enrichment activities, including The Duke of Edinburgh's Award scheme, offshore sailing and international trips.

Admissions. The main intake of pupils occurs at 2½, 3, 7+, 11+, 13+ and Sixth Form. Places are offered subject to a pupil reaching the School's entry requirements. Applications for entry at other levels are welcome subject to a place becoming available.

Fees per term (2016–2017). Pre-Preparatory and Nursery: Nursery £1,665; Reception–Year 2 £3,325. Preparatory School: Years 3–6 £4,190. Senior School: Years 7–8 £5,160; Years 9–11 & Sixth Form £5,510.

Scholarships. Academic Scholarships are offered at Year 3, to continue through to the end of Year 6, and at Year 7 and Year 9 to continue through to the end of Year 11. Offers are based on a written examination and interview. Sixth Form Academic Scholarships are also available.

All-Round Scholarships are offered at Year 7.

Music Scholarships are available for Senior School applicants. As a guide, scholarship candidates should be working at the following levels before applying: Year 7 – Grade 4, Year 9 – Grade 5, Sixth Form – Grade 6. Sixth Form Scholarships will be awarded for the two-year course. Year 7 and Year 9 Scholarships will be awarded through to the end of Year 11.

Sports Scholarships are awarded for pupils of exceptional sporting ability. Sixth Form Scholarships are awarded for the two years of the course. Year 9 Scholarships are awarded through to the end of Year 11. Tennis Scholarships are also available.

Art and Drama Scholarships are available to candidates applying for a Sixth Form place and are awarded for the duration of their two-year course.

Full details about scholarships are available on the school website.

Charitable status. The School is owned and run by an educational foundation with charitable status, Registered Charity number 274664.

Head of Senior School: **Mr Jonathan Insall-Reid**, BSc Waikato, NZ, BArch Hons VUW, NZ, Teaching Dip

Head of Preparatory School: Mr Duncan Murphy, BA Hons Sheffield, MEd Buckingham, FRSA, FCMI, FCollT

Head of Pre-Preparatory and Nursery School: Mrs Louise Fox, BEd Hons Sussex

Clifton High School

College Road, Clifton, Bristol BS8 3JD

Tel:	0117 973 0201 (School Office)
	0117 933 9087 (Admissions)
	0117 973 3853 (Finance)
Fax:	0117 923 8962
email:	admissions@cliftonhigh.bristol.sch.uk
website:	www.cliftonhigh.bristol.sch.uk
Facebook:	/CliftonHighSchoolBristol

Clifton High School, founded in 1877, is a co-educational independent school offering a first-class education to around 570 pupils from nursery school (rising 3s) to Sixth Form. Host family boarders are accepted from the age of 16 years. Unique in Bristol, the school has adopted a Diamond Edge model where boys and girls are taught separately in core subjects in Years 7–9 before becoming fully re-integrated in Year 10 and above.

Aims. The school is a community that places importance on knowing each and every member – students, parents, staff and old friends. High value is placed on the importance of the individual. The school aims to inspire, support and challenge the individual, enabling pupils to achieve their full potential and excel at their particular talents. The school believes that each and every student has a brilliance; within an environment of high expectations, excellent teaching, supportive staff and outstanding pastoral care the school aims to give pupils a rich and varied educational experience where they can realise that brilliance. The school believes that with the privilege of an excellent education comes responsibility, and they aim to send students out into the world who not only have a lifelong passion for learning but who are ready to make a real and positive contribution to society.

Facilities. The school occupies a splendid site in Clifton, near the Downs and Suspension Bridge. The facilities and accommodation are excellent and include a science department with seven laboratories, well stocked libraries and over 250 networked workstations, a multimedia language laboratory, Sixth Form centre and a performing arts theatre and cinema. Sports facilities include a heated 25m indoor swimming pool with spectators gallery, gymnasium and floodlit multi-games courts on site. Professional grade off-site sports facilities, in partnership with the University of Bristol, include an indoor tennis centre (with four courts), ten outdoor courts, two artificial turf hockey pitches and grass pitches for football, rugby and cricket.

Curriculum. Class sizes average 15 in the Early Years and Junior School and 17 in the Senior School.

The *Nursery to Junior Schools* offer an excellent academic, social and moral foundation:

The *Early Years* follow the Foundation Stage curriculum, focusing upon: personal, social and emotional development; communication; language and literacy; problem solving, reasoning and numeracy; knowledge and understanding of the world; physical development and creative development. The children enjoy a myriad of experiences in a safe and stimulating environment. 'By the end of their time in Reception, children's high levels of personal development show that they are extremely well prepared for the next stage of their education.' (ISI Inspection report 2016)

Years 1 and 2, working in an informal atmosphere within a structured framework, focus on high standards of literacy and numeracy, stimulating the children's minds through creative work and challenging projects. The curriculum also includes English, Mathematics, French, IT, Science, History, Geography, Art, Music, Swimming and Games. Pupils in Years 1 and 2 enjoy regular visits to a nearby Forest School throughout the year.

The *Junior Department* gives children a strong grounding in English, Mathematics, Science, IT, History, Geography, Modern Languages, Music, Art, Drama, Design Technology, Religious Studies, Gymnastics, Athletics and Games (Netball, Hockey, Rugby, Football, Tennis, Rounders and Cricket). As pupils progress through the school a greater number of subjects are taught by specialist teachers, for example French, Art, Mathematics, Science, Music, Swimming and PE. Over 40 extracurricular activities are on offer including Choirs, Orchestra, IT, Speech and Drama, Dance and Art and Craft, together with a wide range of sports clubs providing opportunities for individual and team sports. Visiting speakers and regular trips to the local area and further afield enhance the curriculum in all departments. Children in the Junior Department also have the opportunity to enjoy an overnight residential trip each year.

The *Senior School* is fully co-educational throughout. Boys and girls are taught separately for English, Mathematics, IT, Physics, Chemistry and Biology in Years 7–9 together in all other subjects before moving back into fully mixed classes for their chosen examination subjects when they reach Year 10. This is the pioneering Diamond Edge Model of education and Clifton High School is the only school in the Bristol area to adopt this approach. 'Pupils benefit greatly from the small class sizes enabled by the Diamond Edge model in Years 7 to 9 and from the way that teaching is adapted to meet the differing needs of boys and girls.' (ISI Inspection 2016). Year 7–9 pupils study a broad and balanced curriculum including English, Mathematics, Physics, Chemistry, Biology, IT, History, Geography, Religious Studies, modern languages (French, German, Spanish), Latin, Drama, Music, Art & Design, Design & Innovation, Food & Nutrition, Creative Technology and Textiles, PE and Personal, Social, Health and Economic Education (PSHE). In Years 10 and 11, Physical Education and PSHE form part of the general programme. For study at GCSE there is a common and balanced core of English, Mathematics, separate sciences, humanities and a modern foreign language, in addition to which pupils may select subjects based on their interests and career plans. There is also a newly introduced programme of Life Skills and Competencies which runs alongside the GCSE courses and provides further opportunities for pupils to develop and identify extra skills, qualifications and interests. The school has an excellent academic record at GCSE, AS and A Level. In 2016, 100% of GCSE pupils achieved at least 6 A*–C Grades including Mathematics, English and the separate Sciences. Throughout the Senior School and Sixth Form pupils have a personal tutor who monitors their academic and social welfare. 'Throughout the school, pupils' personal development is excellent, in line with the school's conviction that promoting their individuality, as well as their achievement is fundamental.' (ISI Inspection 2016)

The co-educational *Sixth Form* is a thriving centre of excellence within the school. The students play an important part in the whole school community, developing their leadership skills with the younger pupils through a peer support scheme, the House system, the Pupil Council, the Head's Team, the Eco Club Committee and many other opportunities. Students have a wide choice of A Level subjects. Almost all students progress to university or higher education. The most able are encouraged to apply for Oxbridge entrance and the vast majority of those who apply gain the offer of a place. All Sixth Form students take part in Futures and Skills which is an enrichment programme designed to offer a range of experiences and also have individual careers guidance sessions. All students have regular one-to-one tutorials. Sixth formers holding scholarships are encouraged to manage a scholars' *Forum* by producing an annual programme of debates and current affairs discussions with other pupils and for inviting speakers in to the school to talk on specific topics of interest.

Host Family Boarding. Clifton High School offers a unique opportunity for students over 16 (especially those from overseas) to board, full-time or weekly, with families with a very close link to the school. All host families are carefully vetted by the school. The Host Family Boarding Coordinator continuously supports the student and the host family, and oversees the welfare and progress of the student during his or her stay at Clifton High School. The 2009 Ofsted Inspection of the School's Family Boarding Facilities awarded the school "outstanding" in all areas and a very positive interim ISI inspection in 2013 confirmed compliance with all National Minimum Standards.

Physical Education is a key part of the curriculum, not only for competitive sport, but for promoting a healthy lifestyle through the enjoyment of sport and exercise. In addition to the school's traditional sports of hockey, netball, football, rugby, swimming, athletics, rounders, cricket, tennis and gymnastics, specialist staff also teach a wide variety of other activities including squash, badminton, volleyball, basketball, water polo and trampolining. Boys and girls regularly gain county and national honours and both boys and girls sports teams perform strongly in their relevant leagues and tournaments.

Music and Drama. Virtually any instrument, including voice, may be studied, with some 50 per cent of pupils having individual lessons. Associated Board examinations are taken. There are opportunities to belong to orchestras, wind bands, drama groups and choirs who perform in a variety of concerts and productions throughout the year including some of the highest profile events in the school calendar. In Speech and Drama, a large number of pupils enter LAMDA examinations.

Charitable and Extracurricular Activities. Pupils have a strong sense of social responsibility and are actively involved in various local and national charity fundraising events throughout their school careers. Annual collections amount to several thousand pounds. There is a lively extracurricular activities programme throughout the school, responding to pupils' interests. There are well over 100 clubs running at any time, including Robotics Club, Sewing Craft Club, Tennis Club, Mixed Cross Country, Circus Skills, Judo Club, Art Club, Orchestra, Yoga Club, Ancient Greek Club and Eco Club. Pupils regularly take part in the Duke of Edinburgh's Award and World Challenge programmes. There is a rich programme of trips both home and overseas.

Admission and Scholarships. Entry to the Nursery class is not selective. Entry to Early Years and Junior School is by in-class assessment and taster session with the relevant class. Entry to the Senior School is dependent on the results of an entrance examination, Head's interview and school report. Pupils in Clifton High School Year 6 also sit the entrance exam to Senior School. Some academic scholarships are awarded for Year 7, 9 and Sixth Form entry level but there is sometimes flexibility. Some school-assisted places are available in the Senior School as are Music and Sports awards. Sports, performing arts and creative arts awards are also available in the Sixth Form. Further details are available from the School Admissions Registrar.

Fees per term (2016–2017). Tuition: Nursery School – details on request from the Admissions Registrar; Early Years: Reception £3,245, Years 1–2 £3,265; Junior School (Years 3–6) £3,285; Senior School (Years 7–11) £4,710; Sixth Form (Years 12–13) £4,720. Lunch: Reception–Year 6 £233, Years 7–13 £244. Family Boarding (exclusive of Tuition): £3,735. EAL: details on request from the Home Boarding Coordinator. From September 2016 termly fees across the school are inclusive of all compulsory educational visits.

Reductions for siblings concurrently in the school (except where fees are paid by an authority or bursary): 2nd – 7%; 3rd – 15%; 4th – 25%.

Charitable status. Clifton High School is a Registered Charity, number 311736. It exists to provide first-class education for pupils aged 3 to 18 years.

The Governing Body – School Council of Governors:

Patron: Dr Richard Gliddon, BSc Hons, PhD, FIBiol
Chair: Mr James Caddy, BSc Hons
Vice Chair: Ms Lise E Seager, BA Hons, MBA (*Designate for Health and Safety*)
Dr Peter Bodkin, BSc St Andrews, PhD St Andrews (*Designate for Education*)
Prof Selena Gray, BSc, MBClB, MD, FRCP, FFPH (*Designate for NQT and Academic Matters*)
Mr David Marval, BArch Hons, DipArch, RIBA (*Designate for Buildings and Facilities*)
Mr John Smith, MA (*Designate for Human Resources and Equality and Diversity*)
Mr Richard Storey–Walker BSc Hons, CChem, CSci, FRSC (*Designate for Education*)
Mrs Hilary Vaughan, BEng, CEng, MICE (*Designate for Child Protection, Safeguarding, Pupil Welfare and Host Family Boarding*)
Mr Richard Whitburn, BA Hons (*Designate for EYFS and Education*)

Head of School: Dr Alison M Neill, BSc Hons UCW Aberystwyth, PhD UCW Aberystwyth, PGCE

Senior Leadership:
Dr Alison M Neill, BSc Hons UCW Aberystwyth, PhD UCW Aberystwyth, PGCE
Mr Guy Cowper, BA Hons Warwick, MSc Sheffield (*Director of Operations*)
Dr Mark Caddy, BSc Hons Warwick, PhD Warwick (*Deputy Head of School, Years 3–6 and Years 10–11*)
Dr Helen Pascoe, BSc Hons Reading, MSc Leicester, PhD Reading, PGCE (*Deputy Head of School, Nursery School–Year 2 and Years 7–9*)

Leadership:
Mr Manolis Psarros, BA Hons Wales, MA Bristol, MEd Bristol (*Assistant Head, Sixth Form*)
Mr Chris Collins, BA Hons UWIC, MA Bath, PGCE (*Assistant to Deputy Heads, Senior Pastoral Lead Years 7–11*)

Child Protection and Safeguarding:
Ms Alison Taylor, BSc Hons Reading, MEd Bristol, PGCE (*Designated Safeguarding Lead Years 7–13*)
Miss Claudia Mulholland (*Designated Safeguarding Lead Support Nursery School–Year 6 including EYFS*)

Senior Management Team – Assistant to Deputy Head:
Mrs Alice Bagnall, BSc Hons UCW, Cardiff, PGCE (*Years 3–6*)
Mrs Sarah Barker, BEd Hons UWE (*Nursery School–Year 2*)
Mr Samuel Goldsmith, BSc Hons Birmingham, GTP (*Years 10–11*)

Lead Support – Assistant to Deputy Head:
Mrs Julia Sutcliffe, BA Hons Warwick, PGCE (*Nursery School–Year 2*)
Mrs Helen Tabb, BA Hons Surrey, QTS (*Years 3–6*)

Senior School Teachers:
* *Head of Department*

Art and Design:
*Mr Paul Ayers, BA Hons Cornwall, MA Falmouth, PGCE
Ms Claire Jaques, BA Hons Plymouth, PGCE

Business Studies:
*Mr Peter Jackson, BA Hons Westminster, PGCE

Classics:
*Mrs Jade Alexander, BA Hons Bristol, PGCE
Mr Manolis Psarros, BA Hons Wales, MA Bristol, MEd Bristol

Design and Technology:
*Mr Samuel Goldsmith, BSc Hons Birmingham, GTP (**Food and Nutrition*)
Mr Bryan Murphy, MA Cambridge, PGCE (**Design and Innovation*)
Mr Justin Noyce, BA Hons Manchester, PGCE (**Creative Technology*)
Mrs Donia Pieters, BA Hons Brunel, MMus Goldsmiths, QTS (*Music Technology)
Mrs Emma Warwood–Smith, BSc Hons Bolton, PGCE (**Textiles Technology*)
Dr Helen Pascoe, BSc Hons Reading, MSc Leicester, PhD Reading, PGCE (*Food and Nutrition*)

Drama:
*Mr Craig Pullen, BA Hons Manchester Metropolitan, MA Leeds Metropolitan, PGCE
Mrs Susan Johnson–Martin, BA Hons Royal Holloway College London, PGCE

English:
*Mrs Philippa Lyons–White, BA Hons Bristol, PGCE
Mrs Jade Alexander, BA Hons Bristol, PGCE
Mr Christopher Hope, BA Hons Hull, MA Birmingham, PGCE
Mrs Siobhan Hosty, MA Kingston
Mr Manolis Psarros, BA Hons Wales, MA Bristol, MEd Bristol

Geography:
*Mrs Laura Giles, BSc Hons Loughborough, PGCE
Mrs Helen Ellerton, BSc Hons Manchester, PGCE
Mrs Mary Gliddon, BSc Hons Reading, PGCE

History, Government and Politics:
*Mrs Alexandra Baker, BA Hons Manchester, PGCE
Mr Oliver Mullins, BA Hons Birmingham

Information Technology:
*Mr Justin Noyce, BA Hons Manchester, PGCE
Mr Oliver Mullins, BA Hons Birmingham
Mr Richard Shelswell, MEng Hons Bath, PGCE

Mathematics:
*Mr Christopher Collins, MMath Oxford, PGCE
Dr Mark Caddy, BSc Hons Warwick, PhD Warwick
Mr Andrew Harkin, MSc Dublin Institute of Technology, PGCE
Miss Emily Lyons, BEng Hons Swansea University, PGCE
Mr Richard Shelswell, MEng Hons Bath, PGCE
Ms Alison Taylor, BSc Hons Reading, MEd Bristol, PGCE
Mr Stuart Trutch, BSc Hons Exeter, PGCE

Modern Languages – French, German and Spanish:
Miss Helen McKenna, BA Hons York, PGCE (*French)
Mrs Tara Harris, BA Hons Newcastle upon Tyne, PGCE (*German)

Miss Louise Sobey, BA Hons Portsmouth/Murcia, PGCE (*Spanish*)
Miss Natasha Widdison, BA Joint Hons Nottingham, PGCE (*Modern Foreign Languages*)

Music:
*Mr Andrew Cleaver, BA Hons Lincoln and Hull, QTS (*Head of School Music*)
*Mrs Donia Pieters, BA Hons Brunel, MMus Goldsmiths, QTS (*Head of Senior School Music, Academic*)

Physical Education:
*Mr Christopher Collins, BA Hons UWIC, MA Bath, PGCE (*Head of School Games, Boys*)
*Miss Julia Bowkett, BSc Hons UWIC, PGCE (*Head of School Games, Girls*) [maternity cover for Mrs Lynne Reid]
*Mrs Lynne Reid, BSc Hons Cardiff, PGCE (*Head of School Games, Girls*) [maternity leave]
Mr Max Bitterlin, BSc Hons Gloucestershire, PGCE
Dr Mark Caddy, BSc Hons Warwick, PhD Warwick
Mr James Taylor, BSc Hons Sheffield Hallam
Miss Alice Woodyatt, BSc Hons Brunel, PGCE

Science – Biology, Chemistry, Physics:
Mrs Kate Greenslade, BSc Hons Southampton, PGCE (*Biology*) [maternity cover for Dr Alice England]
Dr Alice England, BSc Hons Sheffield, PhD Sheffield, PGCE (*Biology*) [maternity leave]
Miss Rebecca Cole, BSc Hons Bath, PGCE (*Biology*)
Mr Gareth Phillips, MSc Bristol, PGCE (*Chemistry*)
Mrs Louise Brackenbury, BSc Hons UWIC, PGCE (*Chemistry*)
Dr Alison Camacho, BSc Hons Bristol, PhD Cardiff, PGCE (*Physics*)
Mr Bryan Murphy, MA Cambridge, PGCE (*Physics*)
Mr Paul Griffin, BSc Hons Birmingham, PGCE (*Physics*)

Religious Studies:
*Miss Jacinth Awolola–McNab, CertEd Birmingham, BEd

Enhanced Learning Department:
*Mrs Gabrielle Pilgrim BA Hons Reading, PGCE, BDA ATS, SpLD APC Patoss
Mr Frank Allen, BA Hons Nottingham Trent, MEd Queensland, PGCE
Mr Tracy Kemp, BEd, Bristol Polytechnic
Mrs Amanda Swannell, BA Hons, Hull, MA UWE, PGCE, PG Dip Dyslexia
Ms Vivienne Swarbrick, BSc UEA, PGCE

Life Skills and Competencies:
*Mr Samuel Goldsmith, BSc Hons Birmingham, GTP
Mrs Alexandra Baker, BA Hons Manchester, PGCE
Mr Paul Griffin, BSc Hons Birmingham, PGCE
Miss Louise Sobey, BA Hons Portsmouth, PGCE
Mrs Susan Johnson–Martin, BA Hons Royal Holloway College London, PGCE
Mr Bryan Murphy, MA Cambridge, PGCE

Extra–Curricular Lead:
Mr James Taylor, BSc Hons Sheffield Hallam

Futures and Skills:
*Mrs Laura Giles, BSc Hons Loughborough, PGCE
Mr Manolis Psarros, BA Hons Wales, MA Bristol, MEd Bristol
Mr Christopher Collins, MMath Oxford, PGCE

Nursery School to Year 2 Teachers including EYFS:
*Mrs Sarah Barker, BEd Hons UWE
Mrs Donna Andrews, BSc Hons Bath, QTS, EYPS
Mrs Jo Denyer–Warr, BA Hons UWE, QTS
Mrs Linda Mitchell, BSc Hons Edinburgh, PGCE
Miss Claudia Mulholland, BSc Hons Swindon, PGCE
Mrs Caroline Pope, BA Hons London, PGCE

Mrs Clare Shaw, BA Hons King Alfred's College, QTS
Mrs Julia Sutcliffe, BA Hons Warwick, PGCE
Mrs Sarah Willerton, BA Hons Bath Spa, PGCE

Year 3 to Year 6 Teachers:
*Mrs Alice Bagnall, BSc Hons UCW, Cardiff, PGCE (*Years 3–6*)
Mrs Hannah Crofts, BEd Hons Winchester
Miss Jesse Dyer, BA Hons Exeter, MSc Bristol
Ms Claire Jaques, BA Hons Plymouth, PGCE
Mr Charles Lowe, BA/Ed Joint Hons Goldsmiths
Miss Elizabeth Poustie, BSc Hons Gloucester, PGCE
Mr David Pye, BA Hons West London Inst of HE, PGCE
Mr Samuel Rimmer, BSc Hons Leeds, MSc Brock Ontario, PGCE
Mrs Helen Tabb, BA Hons Surrey, QTS

Teaching Assistants:
Mrs Lindsey Burch, NNEB, NVQ Level 3
Mrs Amanda Clancy, NNEB
Miss Debbie Clements, NNEB
Ms Karen Collins, Level 3 Supporting Teaching and Learning
Mrs Amanda Godshaw, NNEB
Mrs Viviane Owen, CertEd Bristol
Mrs Emma Takle, NNEB
Miss Selena Wilcox, NNEB

Pupil Welfare Counsellors:
Mrs Jackie Brangwyn, BEd Hons Sussex, MSc Bristol, Diploma
Mrs Jodie Sheward, Dip City of Bristol College

School Nurse:
Ms Joy Whitehead, RGN Leeds General Infirmary

Business Support Staff:

Head's Office:
Mrs Trudy Scales (*PA to Head of School*)
Mrs Jane Evans (*Head's Office Communications Manager*)

Compliance:
Mrs Joanne Rosser (*Compliance Officer and School Projects*)

Admissions:
Mrs Melanie Johnson (*Admissions Registrar*)
Mrs Sarah Maidment (*Administrator – Admissions and Reception*)

Examination Administration Support:
Mrs Emily Freire–Baños

School Office:
*Ms Sophie Smith (*School Office Manager*)
Miss Feona Horrex (*School Office Administrator and Events Coordinator*)
Mrs Punam Kaur (*School Office Administrator*)

Librarian:
Mrs Sarah Cuthill

Catering Manager:
Mr Tim Fletcher

Modern Language Assistants:
Mme Marie Boehler (*French*)
Frau Ev Milker (*German*)
Srta Sara Roman de la Peña (*Spanish*)

After School Activities Club:
*Mrs Sarah Barker BEd Hons, UWE (*Senior Manager responsible for ASAC*)
Mrs Jane Doubleday
Mrs Emma Takle
Miss Selena Wilcox

Miss Elizabeth Williams
Miss Kirsty Wills

Lunchtime Supervisors:
Mrs Jane Doubleday
Mrs Patricia Doubleday
Miss Kamlesh Kaur
Miss Alicia Martinez–Fernandez
Miss Niru Patel
Miss Sophie Price
Mrs Emma Takle
Miss Cleo Vasey
Miss Selena Wilcox
Miss Elizabeth Williams
Miss Kirsty Wills

Visiting Music Staff and Sports Coaches:

Visiting Music Teachers:
Miss Melanie Baker, GTCL, LRAM, ALCM (*Clarinet and Piano*)
Miss Lucy Beveridge, BMus Hons, Dip ABSRM (*Flute*)
Mr Timothy Bowman, BA Hons, PGCE (*Orchestral percussion*)
Mrs Rozanne Carpenter, BMus (*Piano*)
Mr Adam Chetland (*Electric Guitar*)
Miss Ethel–Jane Cormack, BA Hons (*Singing/Piano*)
Mr Philip Gittings ARCM, Dip RCM (*Oboe*)
Mrs Becky Hall, BMus Hons PGDip (*Violin & Viola*)
Mrs Maria Johnson, MA, MEd, PGCE (*Piano*)
Miss Christine Johnstone, BA Hons, Dip NCOS (*Cello*)
Mr Matthew Jones, BA Hons (*Percussion*)
Mr Alex Stewart, BMus Hons (*Junior Brass*)
Mr Robert Webb, BMus Hons PGCE (*Senior Brass*)
Mrs Rachel Whitworth, BSc Hons (*Violin*)

Sports Coaches:
Mr Jim Buck (*Rugby*)
Mr Richard Conway (*Tennis*)
Mr Andy Martin (*Fencing*)
Miss Heidi Postlethwaite (*Dance*)
Mr David Rees (*Rugby*)
Mr Neil Warburton (*Taekwondo*)

Swimming Coaches:
Mr Jez Birds (*Swim Coach*)
Miss Annie Brown (*Swim Coach*)
Mr Jon Falco (*Swim Coach*)

Concord College

Acton Burnell Hall, Shrewsbury, Shropshire SY5 7PF
Tel: 01694 731631
Fax: 01694 731389
email: enquiries@concordcollege.org.uk
website: www.concordcollegeuk.com

Concord College is a highly successful international boarding college providing GCSE and A Level courses. Set in 80 acres of Shropshire parkland, the College combines outstanding facilities with first-rate academic performance. The College is regularly rated in the top 20 schools in the UK. Students are cared for by a dedicated staff in a safe and beautiful environment. UK day and boarding students are also welcome at the College. Concord is a community that celebrates national and cultural diversity while students and staff are united by the wish to set high standards. The result is a happy and open community in which students are polite, articulate and conscientious without ever losing their sense of fun.

The College dates back to 1949 and moved to its present site in 1973. In 1983 it became a charitable trust. Over the years, students from over eighty countries have attended Concord.

The College is a co-educational day and boarding school for students aged 13–19.

Number of students: 520 (approximately equal numbers of boys and girls) of whom over 440 are boarders.

Facilities. Facilities at Concord College are superb. Based around an historic Main Building, there are many new additions as well as medieval ruins within the grounds. There is a stunning Theatre and Music School, an excellent Sports complex, indoor swimming pool as well as an outstanding Science facility. Students eat their meals in the College Dining Room and select from a variety of international cuisine. Most students have individual study-bedrooms on campus, some with en-suite bathrooms. Students have a wide variety of facilities including a sports hall, social centre and student kitchen.

Education. Teaching at Concord is undertaken in groups that average 16 at GCSE and 14 at A Level. Teachers are experts in their subjects.

At GCSE Biology, Chemistry and Physics are taught as separate subjects and emphasis is placed upon laboratory experience. Other compulsory subjects are Mathematics, English, Religious Studies and Physical Education. Optional subjects include Art, Economics, Geography, History, IT, Music, Spanish, French and German.

At AS and A Level students normally study at least three A Levels and at least one further AS Level. Subjects include Art, Accounting, Biology, Chemistry, Chinese, Economics, English Language, English Literature, Geography, History, Law, Mathematics, Further Mathematics, Music, Photography, Physics and Spanish. All students who do not have GCSE English are expected to study English.

Lessons are taught in a variety of excellent classroom facilities. The new classroom block, The Jubilee Building, which opened in September 2010 houses the English and Mathematics departments in state-of-the-art classrooms.

In addition to their teachers, students have an individual tutor with whom they meet daily and who monitors their academic progress. Students also have a House Parent who is responsible for their well-being. Support is available to all students to develop their oral and discursive skills to ensure that they are able to express their ideas confidently especially at university interview.

Examination Results and University Entry. The College achieves excellent examination results with 95% A*/A/B at A Level in 2016, placing Concord within the top 10 schools in the UK according to The Times league tables. The College is highly successful in placing students into UK medical schools and other top UK universities. In 2016, 25 students won places at Oxford or Cambridge University, 18 at Imperial College London and 12 at the LSE. 29 students went on to read Medicine at medical schools.

Selection for Entry. The college selects applicants upon the basis of interviews, school record and entry tests. Online tests are arranged for overseas applicants. Students can be accepted for entry at all ages.

Fees per annum (2016–2017). Full Boarding £36,000, Day £13,500. (Boarding fees are payable in 2 instalments.)

Scholarships and Bursaries. A fee reduction of up to 10% of full fees may be available to students who have a particularly strong academic background. For entrants to GCSE classes, scholarship entry tests are administered. General bursaries are also available on request: indeed the College has a 'needs blind' admissions policy for its day students.

Holidays. Half term holidays involve only a long weekend. The Christmas holiday is one month and Easter is only two and a half weeks. There is a long summer vacation from the end of June until early September.

The college remains open at half term and during the Easter holiday (for students over the age of 16) and there is no additional charge for holiday accommodation and meals.

The School Day. Lessons run from 9 am to 4 pm Monday to Friday with Wednesday afternoon allocated to sport and to a trip to Shrewsbury for senior students. There is compulsory supervised study (prep) for two hours each evening Monday to Friday.

Saturday morning is used for whole-college testing. The public examination rooms are used for this purpose so that the rooms hold no fear for the students when the final public examinations are taken.

Reports to Parents. These are sent at half term in the first term and subsequently at the end of each term.

Clubs, Sports and Extracurricular Activities. Students at Concord can choose from a multitude of activities. Sports, music, dance and drama are all available in our own facilities. There is a Sports Hall, squash courts and gymnasium as well as outdoor facilities including football, athletics and tennis. A wealth of sporting activities is on offer ranging from archery to fencing and badminton to Taekwondo. For dancers, there is a purpose-built dance studio where ballet, modern, latin and ballroom and streetdance clubs take place. Musicians can join the orchestra, wind or string groups. Choir and singing club can develop all levels of vocal talent. Many other activities are also offered ranging from bridge and chess to horse riding and mountain-biking. Students take part in Concord's outdoor education programme and the Duke of Edinburgh's Award scheme is also available. Whatever their talents, students are able develop them at Concord.

Charitable status. Concord College is a Registered Charity, number 326279. It exists to provide high quality education for secondary age students.

Chair of the Governors: Dr Iain M Bride

Clerk to the Governors and Bursar: Mrs Barbara Belfield-Dean

Principal: **Neil G Hawkins**, MA Cantab, PGCE

Vice-Principal (Academic): Tom Lawrence, BA, PGCE
Vice-Principal (Pastoral): Jeremy Kerslake, MA
Head of Lower School: Mrs Rachel Coward, MEd, BEd
Assistant Principal: Phil Outram, PhD, BSc
Assistant Principal: Daniel Wilson, MA
Assistant Principal: Rob Pugh, PhD, BA

Principal's Personal Assistant & Admissions Registrar: Mrs Wendy Hartshorne

---

Derby Grammar School

Rykneld Road, Littleover, Derby DE23 4BX
Tel: 01332 523027
email: headmaster@derbygrammar.co.uk
           admissions@derbygrammar.co.uk
website: www.derbygrammar.co.uk

Derby Grammar School is a boys' school with a co-educational Sixth Form which was founded in 1995 to provide a high quality education for able pupils in Derbyshire, Staffordshire and Nottinghamshire. It has 270 pupils from the age of 7 (Year 3) to 18 (Year 13). Whilst pupils perform extremely well academically, the School places great emphasis on developing character and leadership skills across and beyond the curriculum. There is a full competitive sports programme and a wide ranging and flourishing music scene. There is an extremely strong tradition of charity work and fundraising, featuring ongoing links with a community in Tanzania. The School has a broad programme of outdoor education, including The Duke of Edinburgh's Award, as well as numerous trips and visits both at home and overseas.

Location and Facilities. The School is set in a superb Victorian parkland site on the edge of the city of Derby, near to the arterial A38 and A50 routes. The original manor house has been converted and extended with a purpose-built teaching block, Chemistry and Design Technology building. The buildings also house specialist Biology and Physics laboratories and Music and Music Technology rooms and a recording studio. The School has recently acquired sports facilities that will provide an AstroTurf for hockey, rugby and cricket pitches and a sports hall.

Curriculum. The Junior School follows an enhanced curriculum, providing a strong grounding in all subject areas. In addition, the pupils have specialist teaching in Music, French and Latin. In the Senior School, all pupils follow a broad common curriculum at Key Stage 3 which includes teaching in each of the separate sciences and two modern foreign languages up to the end of Year 9. Pupils will study 9 or 10 GCSEs, including at least one modern foreign language and the three separate sciences. Pupils in the Sixth Form can choose from over twenty different A Level subjects and the options process is based around pupil choice rather than being in fixed blocks. In recent years nearly 75% of students have studied at least one science at A Level and over 25% have gone on to study biomedical, science or engineering degrees at university.

Admissions. Admission to both the Junior and Senior School is through assessment in English, Mathematics and reasoning papers. The main Entrance Examinations are held in January but are available throughout the year.

Open days are held each term, but visits and taster days are welcomed at any time by prior appointment. For further information contact Admissions Secretary, Louise Slater Blackwall, on 01332 510030 or visit the school website.

Scholarships and Bursaries. There is a full range of Scholarships and Bursaries available for entry into the Senior School. Specialist Sports, Music and Choral Scholarships are available and are awarded after successful trials or auditions.

Fees per term (2016–2017). £2,766 (Years 3–4), £3,373 (Years 5–6), £4,215 (Years 7–13).

Charitable status. Derby Grammar School is a Registered Charity, number 1015449.

Chair of Governors: Mr Tim Wilson

Vice Chair of Governors: Mr Simon Richardson

Headmaster: **Mr Richard Paine**, BA Hons, PGCE

Deputy Headmaster: Mrs L C Reynolds, BSc Hons
Senior Master: Mr P D Hilliam, BA Hons
Head of Lower School: Mr K Clark, BA Hons
Head of Upper School: Mrs V Charnock, BAHons
Head of Sixth Form: Mrs C Bramall, BA Hons
Chaplain: Revd P Taylor, BA Hons
School Bursar: Miss J Jameson, MAAT
Registrar: Mrs L Slater Blackwall

Senior School Teaching Staff (principal subjects):

Art:
Ms E Sellors, BA Hons

Classics:
Mr S Fletcher, BA Hons

Biology:
Mrs L C Reynolds, BSc Hons
Mr I Lowden, BSc Hons

Design Technology:
Mr R Smith, BEd
Mr P Lakritz, BSc Hons

Chemistry:
Mr R Edge, BSc Hons
Mrs S Burton, BSc Hons
Mr T Fearn, BSc Hons

Economics:
Mrs K Cowgill, BSc Hons

English:
Mrs C Bramall, BA Hons
Miss J Rowe, BA Hons

Mr S Penny, MA
Mrs K Watson, BA Hons

Geography:
Mr C Critchlow, MA

History:
Mr R Paine, BA Hons
Mr J Taylor, BA Hons

Mathematics:
Mr M R Allen, BSc Hons
Miss C Bruce, BSc Hons
Mrs V Charnock, BSc Hons
Mr C D Whitworth, BA
Hons

Modern Languages:
French:
Miss K Stebbings, BA
Hons
Mrs J Lathbury, BA Hons,
MBA

Junior School Staff:
Head of Junior School: Mrs A Sly, BEd Hons
Mrs K Genders, BSc Hons
Mrs R Hamilton BSc Hons
Mrs E Jackson, BSc Hons
Mrs H Monk, BEd Hons

German:
Mrs K Schwarz Caswell,
MLitt, BA Hons
Mr I Watson, BA Hons

Spanish:
Miss K Stebbings, BA
Hons

Music:
Mr N Coley, BA Hons

Physical Education:
Mr K Clark, BA Hons
Mr C D Whitworth, BA
Hons
Mr J Smyth, BA Hons

Physics:
Mr D Hills, BSc Hons, BEd
Mr K Lambert, BSc Hons

Religious Studies:
Mr P D Hilliam, BA Hons
Mrs K Lacey, LLb Hons

Dover College

Effingham Crescent, Dover, Kent CT17 9RH

Tel: 01304 205969
Fax: 01304 242854
email: admissions@dovercollege.org.uk
website: www.dovercollege.org.uk
Twitter: @DoverCollege
Facebook: @DoverCollege
LinkedIn: /Dover-College

Dover College was founded in 1871 and occupies the grounds of the Priory of St Martin, a 24-acre site in the heart of Dover on the southeast coast of Kent. The site has been occupied for nearly 900 years and the College Close is surrounded by a number of impressive medieval buildings. Pupils still use the original Refectory, and the School Chapel is a fine 12th Century building. Another 20 acres of playing fields are nearby.

The College was granted a Royal Charter by His Majesty King George V in 1923 and the Patron of the College is the Lord Warden of the Cinque Ports.

We are the closest school to continental Europe, with easy access by Eurostar, Tunnel or Ferry. Dover Priory Station with its High Speed Link and good road links are within easy reach of the School making London about an hour away. London Heathrow and Gatwick airports are convenient by car.

Co-education. Dover College (3–18) has been fully co-educational since 1975 and the 307 boys and girls are integrated at all levels. There are 100 boarders.

Organisation. The school divides into four parts: the Infants and Juniors from age 3–11, Priory from 11–13, Lower College from 13–16, and the Sixth Form from 16–18. For Lower College and the Sixth Form there are four Houses, all situated on the College Close, two for boys and two for girls, all incorporating both day pupils and boarders.

Dover College's Infant and Junior School is housed in a spacious self-contained building within the beautiful grounds of Dover College and Priory has its own House accommodation.

Catering. The catering team provides delicious, healthy, well-balanced homemade food and meals are taken in the 'Harry Potter' style Refectory.

Curriculum. Infants and Juniors study a wide range of subjects. Great importance is placed upon literacy, numeracy, information technology, science and key skills. Pre-Reception children follow the Early Years "learn through play" curriculum. French, Spanish and Music are taught by specialist teachers. Fourth and fifth form pupils study between six and ten GCSE subjects, depending on their level of ability. The curriculum at this level is flexible, enabling pupils to have an academic curriculum designed to suit individual needs.

All pupils are given very careful guidance when making their GCSE level choices, by their Academic Tutor, Housemaster/Housemistress, the Careers Department and by the Director of Studies.

At all stages of a pupil's time at Dover College, progress is carefully monitored. Assessment periods occur regularly, during which pupils are graded for achievement and effort. A merit/demerit system operates for pupils up to 16 years. Classes at Dover College are kept as small as possible. Class sizes up to GCSE are generally 15–20 and at A Level 10–15. Some A Level sets are smaller.

Considerable emphasis is placed upon the breadth of education offered: music, art and drama are an integral part of the curriculum. All pupils participate in a variety of sports, with prominence placed upon the development of leadership skills and confidence.

Sixth Form. The Sixth Form is overseen by a Head of Sixth Form and pupils are able to choose AS and A Levels from a list of over 20 subjects. Some BTEC subjects are also available (Sports, Health and Social Care, Travel and Tourism). Traditional academic subjects are provided, as are the practical subjects of art, design and technology, textiles, photography, drama and music.

Sixth Formers wear business attire and are given more choice and freedom than junior pupils, being expected to respond positively to their treatment as young adults. A well-equipped Sixth Form Centre is used as a meeting place and social club.

The School's Careers Adviser works in liaison with external agencies to plan, deliver and evaluate an integrated careers education and guidance programme. This enables pupils to gain the necessary knowledge, skills and understanding in order to make informed career plans before attending the universities of their choice.

International Study Centre (ISC). The International Department was started in 1957 and backed at the time by members of NATO, although international boarding has a far longer history than this starting point. The International Study Centre provides intensive English courses for pupils whose first language is not English. These courses vary in length and the aim is to enable all pupils to integrate fully into the life of Dover College as soon as possible after their arrival.

Individual Support. There is an Individual Needs Department in which pupils with learning difficulties (e.g. Dyslexia) receive 1:1 tuition. Each pupil has a member of staff as a personal tutor. The tutor supervises his/her pupils' general academic progress.

Art and Technology. The Art Department is situated in purpose-built accommodation. Fine Art, pottery, textiles and photography are all available. Examination results are always excellent both at GCSE and A Level.

The Technology Department shares the building with Art and is situated in a large, well-equipped, open-plan workshop. Pupils are encouraged to work with a range of materials (wood, plastic etc) and use CAD software. Design Technology is available at GCSE and A Level. There are many opportunities for the students to use the workshop outside curriculum time. Design and Technology also thrives as an activity.

Music and Drama. Music plays a particularly important part in the life of the School. The well-equipped Music School was relocated on site in January 2011 and opened by Julian Lloyd Webber. It comprises high-tech soundproof pods of various sizes for practice, classrooms and recital room. Extracurricular activities are numerous. The Chapel Choir meets three times a week and is the backbone of the many concerts and services, but there are weekly rehearsals for the Choral Society, String group, Windband, Jazz band, and Madrigal group. There is a concert at the end of each term, held in the Refectory, and numerous informal concerts in a variety of locations. A House Music competition takes place annually.

Drama is a very active part of the cultural life of the School, as well as part of the Lower School curriculum; there is a major school production each year together with additional House productions. Drama is offered at A Level and GCSE.

Learning Resources Centre. It provides cutting-edge facilities and resources to all pupils, including Careers information.

Sport. The School's main playing fields are a short distance away; on site are tennis courts, an astroturf, basketball court and an excellent Sports Hall with a fitness suite. Sports include Athletics, Badminton, Basketball, Cricket, Cross Country, Running, Football, Hockey, Netball, Rugby, Sailing, Tennis, Volleyball and various PE activities. Swimming takes place at the indoor swimming pool in the local leisure centre. Golf may be played on local courses and horse riding is also offered locally through the School.

Extracurricular Activities. In addition to sport, pupils have the opportunity of taking part in a wide range of over 50 activities including Adventure Training, Art, Car Mechanic, Chess, Computing, Debating, Duke of Edinburgh's Award, Dancing, Fencing, First Aid, Horse Riding, Language Clubs, Music, Photography, Wine Tasting, Stage Management and Technology. The London West End theatres are within easy reach and regular trips to a variety of productions are made.

Pastoral Care. All pupils benefit from a carefully designed system of outstanding pastoral care. Every Dover College student belongs to a House and Boarders are provided with comfortable accommodation in one of four boarding houses. All Sixth Formers have single study-bedrooms. A Housemaster or Housemistress, supported by a team of tutors, runs each House; it is their role to give pastoral support as well as supervising the pupils' academic progress.

Pupils have access to a fully equipped and professionally staffed Medical Centre, which can accommodate pupils overnight.

Religious Life. College has its own Chapel and is a Church of England school. All pupils are encouraged to respect each other's beliefs and faiths from a position of tolerance and understanding.

Entry. Pupils are typically admitted into the Senior School at 11, 13 or 16 years old, but may come at any age. Most pupils join the College in September, but entry in January and April is possible.

Entry into the Infants and Juniors is by interview and an informal assessment carried out during a "Taster Day" at the school. The School has its own 11+ examination. 13+ pupils normally sit the Common Entrance at their own Preparatory School. Provision is made for direct entry into the Sixth Form for boys and girls. This is normally conditional upon GCSE results. Further information can be obtained from Admissions.

Fees per term (2016–2017). Junior Day £2,335–£3,420; Senior Day £4,040–£5,075; Senior Weekly Boarding (up to 6 nights per week) £6,530–£7,855; Full Boarding £7,140–£9,640.

Scholarships. Academic Scholarships are awarded by competitive examinations.

Scholarships for Music, Drama, Art, Design Technology, Sport and All-Rounder are available by competitive interview.

Scholarships are available to pupils at 11+, 13+ and 16+ entry. Scholarships are not awarded to pupils in the Infant and Junior School.

Sibling Bursaries (10%) and Service Bursaries are automatically awarded. Members of HM Armed Forces and the Diplomatic Service who are eligible for the boarding allowance only pay a parental contribution of 10% of the full boarding fee.

Further details may be obtained on application to Admissions.

Old Dovorian Club. President: Mr Roger Hovell, c/o Dover College.

Friends of Dover College (PTA). Chairman: Mrs Jessica Doodes, c/o Dover College.

Charitable status. Dover College is a Registered Charity, number 307856. The School exists to develop confidence and individual talents.

Members of Council (Governors):
Chairman: Mr Joe Sullivan
Vice Chairman: Mr Anthony P D Lancaster [OD]
Mr Paul Brown
Mr Graham Alan Conlon [OD]
Mr Michael John Dakers [OD]
Mr John Evans
Mr Michael Goodridge [OD]
Ms Karen Rogers [OD]
Mr David Rolls
Mr Michael Rutherford
Mr James Gregory Ryeland [OD]
Mr Paul Richard Tapsell
Mr William Terence 'Terry' Westwater

Visitor: The Right Reverend Trevor Willmott, The Bishop of Dover in Canterbury

[OD] *Old Dovorian*

Senior Management Team:

Headmaster: Mr Gareth Doodes, MA

Bursar & Clerk to the Governors: Mr Steve Bartlett, BA
Deputy Head (Academic): Mr Duncan Ellerington, BSc, BA, MA
Deputy Head (Pastoral): Mr Simon Kibler, BA
Director of Admissions and Marketing: Mr Chris Townend, BA, ACIM

Teaching Staff:
Mrs Abena Akuffo-Kelly (*Head of ICT; iSAMS Administrator*)
Miss Sarah Allen (*Teacher of Maths*)
Mr Haydn Annakie (*Junior School Teacher – Year 4*)
Mrs Eva Aylward (*Director of Teaching & Learning; Head of MFL*)
Mr Edward Breeze (*Teacher of English; 2ic of Leamington House*)
Mr David Brooks (*Director of Teaching & Learning; Head of Maths, Economics and Business Studies*)
Mr Keith Cox (*Head of LRC; Teacher of English*)
Mr Julian Dewick (*Head of Art*)
Mr Gareth Doodes (*Headmaster; Teacher of History*)
Mrs Nina Dougall (*Junior School, Individual Needs*)
Mr Duncan Ellerington (*Deputy Head (Academic), Head of Physics*)
Mrs Joy Ellerington (*Individual Needs*)

Mr Brett Fairclough (*Deputy Head Academic of Junior School; Curriculum Coordinator of Junior School; Junior School Teacher – Year 5*)

Miss Lauren Geddes (*Teacher of Business Studies, Travel and Tourism; 2ic of St Martin's House*)

Ms Julie Green (*Head of English*)

Mrs Sarah Groombridge (*Junior School Teacher – Year 6*)

Mr Carl Hadler (*Housemaster of Leamington House; Teacher of Maths*)

Mrs Sara-Jane Hardy (*Teacher of Textiles and Art*)

Miss Henrietta Harper (*Gap Student*)

Mr George Rupert Hill (*Senior Master; Head of Geography*)

Mrs Leonie Hodson (*Teacher of EAL*)

Mrs Pamela Hopkins (*Teacher of Maths, Economics and Business*)

Miss Paula Huertas Lopez (*Spanish Assistante*)

Mr Lee Irwin (*Housemaster of School House; Teacher of DT*)

Mr Kieron Ives (*Junior School Teacher – Year 2*)

Mrs Sarah Kennett (*Head of Science*)

Mr Simon Kibler (*Deputy Head (Pastoral); Teacher of Geography and Sport*)

Mr Chris Lockyer (*Deputy Director of Music; Junior School Teacher*)

Miss Charline Marie (*Teacher of MFL*)

Miss Stephanie Marriott (*Junior School Teacher – Year 1*)

Mr George Mees (*Faculty Head; Head of DT*)

Mrs Emma Miller (*Junior School Teacher – Reception*)

Mrs Tracey Mills (*Deputy Head Pastoral of Junior School; Junior School Teacher – Early Learners; EYFS Coordinator*)

Mr Neville Pattison (*Teacher of Maths and Economics*)

Mr Jack Payne (*Teacher of Sport*)

Mrs Charlotte Pearson-Miles (*Housemistress of St Martin's House; Teacher of History, English and French*)

Miss Amy Perry (*Teacher of Science, Head of Key Stage 3*)

Mr Martyn Prince (*Teacher of History*)

Miss Sara Richardson (*Junior School Teacher*)

Mrs Lindsey Shefford (*Teacher of EAL*)

Miss Jude Single (*Acting Housemistress of Duckworth House; Head of Sixth Form; Head of Drama*)

Miss Elodie Stafford (*Head of Faculty; Head of French; Teacher of Spanish*)

Madame Therese Taylor (*Staff Tutor; Housemistress of Priory House; Teacher of French*)

Mrs Ludmilla Waitt (*Teacher of Russian*)

Miss Laura Walters (*Teacher of Art & Photography*)

Mr Peter Wharton (*Teacher of Chemistry*)

Mr Paul Young (*Director of Music*)

Support Staff:

Accounts Manager: Mrs Justine Laws

Admissions Registrar: Miss Wendy Parkins

IT Manager: Mr Chris Judd

Estates Manager: Mr Rik Sullivan

PA to the Headmaster: Ms Kay Anderson

PA to the Bursar: Mrs Deborah Wheeler

Medical Centre: Mrs Claire Hunt, Mrs Sarah May-Bradshaw

d'Overbroeck's

The Swan Building, 111 Banbury Road, Oxford OX2 6JX

Tel: 01865 310000
email: mail@doverbroecks.com
website: www.doverbroecks.com

Age Range. 11–18 (11–16: day only; 16–18: day and boarding).

Number in School. 485.

Fees per term (2016–2017). Tuition: £5,355 (Years 7–11); £7,450 (Years 12–13). Boarding: £2,350–£4,200.

d'Overbroeck's is a co-educational school in Oxford for pupils aged 11–18. We are fairly evenly divided between residential and day students in the Sixth Form; but are day only up to the age of 16.

Our academic approach is characterised by small classes (maximum of 10 students per class in the Sixth Form and 15 up to GCSE) and a highly supportive and encouraging approach that builds on each student's strengths and enables outstanding academic achievements.

Teaching is highly interactive and seeks to generate enthusiasm for the subject, sound academic skills and effective working habits – while at the same time providing a thorough preparation for public examinations and ensuring that the learning experience is motivating and fun. The environment is friendly, stimulating and engaging with staff and students working together to achieve the best possible results.

A wide range of sporting and other extra-curricular activities is available to complement the learning in the classroom. Students can take part in numerous school events and performances as well as benefit from the wide range of educational, cultural and social activities which Oxford has to offer. We believe that happiness and success go hand in hand – and throughout the school we do our utmost to ensure that every student is given new opportunities to develop and is encouraged and rewarded – whether in the classroom, on stage or on the sports field.

The Sixth Form is based on a different site from Years 7 to 11 and the value of this is that it allows us to provide a clear sense of progression as students start their A Level studies and begin to make the transition towards university. Many students from other schools also join us for direct entry into our Sixth Form.

We expect high standards of commitment and effort from our students and have a track record of strong GCSE and A Level results, both in absolute terms and on a value-added basis. Students benefit from excellent teaching and a positive approach which enables them to maximise their potential. In 2016, for example, our students achieved 59% grade A*–A at GCSE and 54% grade A*–A at A Level. The overwhelming majority of students go on to university and we have an excellent record of success with entry including Oxford and Cambridge as well as medical, law, veterinary and art schools.

Main Entry Points: at 11+, 13+ and directly into the Sixth Form, post GCSE.

Scholarships: Academic, Science, Art, Music and Drama.

Principal: **Sami Cohen**, BSc

Administrative Principal: Richard Knowles, MA, DPhil (*Philosophy**)

Bursar: Peter Talbot, BEd

Head of Years 7–11: Mark Olejnik, BA, PGCE (*History*)

Head of Sixth Form: Alasdair MacPherson, MA (*English**)

Head of Lower Sixth: Kate Palmer, BSc, PGCE, SDes (*Geography**)

Head of International Section: Helen Wood, MA, PhD, DTEFLA (*EAP*)

Academic Coordinator: Alastair Barnett, BA, PGCE (*History**)

Teaching Staff:
* *Head of Department or Departmental Coordinator*

Katie Amiri, BA, DELTA (*EAP*)
Louise Arnould, BA, PGCE (*Art, Textiles*)
Rosie Astley, Froebel Dip RSA SpLD (*Learning Support*)
Daniel Austin, BA DELTA (*EAP**)
Michelle Barton, MSc, PGCE (*Chemistry*)
Rebecca Bates (*Biology*)
Franziska Becker, MA, PhD (*German*)
Shanti Bharatan, MSc, PhD (*Biology*)
Joe Bibby, BSc, PGCE (*Physics*)
Ursula Boughton, BSc, PGCE (*Mathematics, Independent Learning**)
Jennifer Bowden, BSc (*Chemistry, Science*)
Christophe Brinster, M-ès-L (*French*, Film Studies**)
Kelly Bristow, MSc, PGCE, CPsychol (*Psychology**)
John Butler, BA, PGCE (*Sociology**)
Evelyn Campbell, BA, PGCE (*Mathematics*)
Chiara Carpita (*Italian*)
Francesca Centamore, BSc, PGCE (*Physical Education*)
Jennifer Clark, BSc, PGCE (*Chemistry, Science*)
Jane Cockerill, BA, MEd, PGCE (*Music*)
Andrew Colclough, BA, MA (*Politics**)
Claire Coltellini, MA, PGCE (*French*)
Francesco Corbetta, BSc, PGCE (*Physics, Science*)
Margaret Craig, BA, MA, FAETC (*History of Art*)
Stephen Creamer, MEng, PGCE (*Chemistry, Physics*)
Charles Currie, MPhys, PGCE (*Physics**)
Jon-Paul Davies, BSc, MA, PGCE (*Geography*)
Jonathan Doering BA, MA, PGCE, TESOL (*English, EAP*)
Robyn Eaton, BSc, PGCE (*Psychology*)
Andrew Gillespie, MA (*Business Studies**)
Laurence Goodwin, MA (*Classics*)
Anita Goriely, MS, PhD (*Mathematics*)
Nick Haines, MMathPhil (*Mathematics**)
Robert Harris, BA, MSc (*Sociology*)
Simon Harrison, BA (*Economics**)
Christopher Holland, BA, MPhil (*English*)
Graham Hope, MA, DPhil (*Mathematics*)
Clare Horne, BSc, PhD, PGDip (*Mathematics*)
Fizza Hussain, BA, PGCE (*Drama*)
Anna Irvine, BA, DELTA (*EAP*)
Laura Johnson (*Computing, ICT*)
Adam Johnstone, MA, MSt (*EPQ*, Biology*)
Anne-Marie Jones, BSc, PhD (*Biology*)
Susanne Kreitz, PhD (*German**)
Andrew Latcham, BA, DPhil (*History, Politics*)
Cheryl Linton, BSc, PGCE (*Physics*)
Dearbhla Loughran (*Spanish, French*)
Chelsey Lovell-Smith, BA (*History, Politics*)
Kate MacDonald, BA, DSpLD (*Learning Support*)
David Mackie, BA, MA, DPhil, CPE, PGDL (*Classical Civilisation, Latin, Philosophy*)
Christine Martelloni, MSc (*French*)
Susan McKendrick, BA, PGCE (*Music*)
Sarah McSwiggan, BA (*English*)
Elina Medley, BA, MA, PGCE (*Photography*)
Matthew Meyer, BSc, PGCE (*Mathematics*)
Sandra Monger, BA, DELTA (*EAP*)
Jane Nimmo-Smith, BA (*Classics*, Ancient History**)
James O'Connor, BTEC HND (*Music Technology*)
Stephen O'Keeffe, MA (*Mathematics*)
Max Parsonage, BSc, PGCE (*Chemistry**)
Jill Partridge, BSc, PGCE (*Biology*)
Mark Piesing, BA, PGCE (*Communication and Culture**)
Robert Pollard, BA, TESOL, PGCE (*History, Politics*)
Steven Pool (*Computing*)
Martin Procter, BA, PGCE (*Physical Education**)
Philip Purvis, MMus, PhD, PGCE, FRSA (*Music**)
Wendy Rawding, BA, PGCE (*Art*)
Nick Reeves, MA, PGCE (*Art*, History of Art*, Photography**)
Jonathan Richards, BSc, PGCE (*Physical Education**)

Sara Roberts, BA, MA (*English*)
Ana Rodriguez Nodal, BA (*Spanish*)
Emily Saddler, BA, PGCE (*English, Drama*)
Mark Schofield (*Politics*)
Aleksandra Selkovaja (*Maths*)
Joan Shaw, BSc (*Physics*)
Sarah Shekleton, BA, MA, PGCE (*Mathematics**)
Amy Smith, BA (*Economics, Business*)
Janey Su (*Mandarin*)
Joe Swarbrick, BA, PGCE (*Drama**)
Ben Symington, BA, MMath (*Mathematics*)
Jaimie Tarrell, BEd (*Biology**)
Rachel Thanassoulis, MA, PGCE (*English**)
Emma Tinker (*Film Studies*)
George Vlachonikolis, BA, MA, PGCE (*Economics*)
Rie Wakayama (*Japanese*)
David Wareham, BA, MA, DELTA (*EAP*)
Rebecca Watkins (*English, Drama*)
Natasha Wertheim, BA, PGCE (*Religious Studies and Critical Thinking*)
Louise Wheaton, BSc, PGCE (*Geography*)
Paul Wheeler, BSc, PGCE (*Geography*)
Clare Wildish, BA (*Business Studies*)
Helen Wilson, BA, PGCE (*Art*)
Henry Winney, MA, PGCE (*Chemistry, Biology*)
Sharon Wyper, BA, PGATC, MA (*Art*)
Jonathan Young, BA, BSc (*Business Studies*)

Sport & Extra-Curricular Activities:
Jonathan Richards, BSc (*Physical Education**)

Registry:
Years 7–11: Rob Barker
Sixth Form: Lynne Berry and Sarah Jex

Boarding Office:
Felisa Deas
Emma Brett

School Counsellor: Charlie Morse-Brown

Higher Education & Careers Coordinator: Philip Purvis, MMus, PhD, PGCE, FRSA

Principal's PA: Tracy Roslyn, BA, DipRSA

Dunottar School
United Learning

High Trees Road, Reigate, Surrey RH2 7EL
Tel: 01737 761945
email: info@dunottarschool.com
website: www.dunottarschool.com
Twitter: @dunottarschool
Facebook: /Dunottar

The aim of Dunottar is to offer an outstanding education to boys and girls and, through excellent teaching and high levels of individual support, to enable pupils to achieve added value which is amongst the top 10% of schools in the UK. Dunottar is a vibrant, co-educational secondary school which, as part of United Learning's family of schools, shares the group's core values of ambition, confidence, determination, creativity, respect and enthusiasm along with the objective of bringing out the "Best in Everyone". Dunottar celebrates achievement in its broadest sense resulting in a community of happy, confident pupils who achieve their first choice ambition for their future education and employment.

The School was founded in 1926 and joined United Learning in 2014. It is situated in 15 acres of gardens and playing fields on the outskirts of Reigate, convenient to mainline stations and bus routes. The main building is a handsome Palladian mansion and purpose-built wings include additional classrooms, art and design suites, the main hall, Sixth Form common room, a 25-metre heated indoor swimming pool and large sports hall. Outdoor space includes a sports field, several courts and woodland trail and an arrangement with Reigate Rugby Club further extends the sporting facilities.

Religion. The School holds the Christian ethos paramount and welcomes children from any denomination or none.

Curriculum. The school offers a broad education and preserves a balance between arts and science subjects. Early specialisation is avoided, though some subject options become necessary from the beginning of the GCSE year. Subjects include English Language and Literature, Mathematics, French, Spanish, History, Geography, Religious Studies, Biology, Physics and Chemistry, Business and Economics, Design and Technology, Computer Science, Physical Education, Drama, Food and Nutrition, Music and Art and Design. Dunottar has strong sporting and music traditions. Teaching is given in a wide range of musical instruments and pupils are encouraged to join the orchestras, music groups and choirs. A busy fixtures list offers many opportunities for competitive sport and 'sport for all' is encouraged within school and through the co-curricular programme. Rugby, football, athletics, netball, lacrosse, swimming, cricket and rounders are amongst the sports on offer. Co-curricular clubs are designed to broaden horizons and encourage new skills, hobbies and interests and range from current affairs debating to science based groups such as 'dissection club' and sports including badminton and swimming. Students also participate in The Duke of Edinburgh's Award scheme at Bronze, Silver and Gold levels.

Careers. Advice is provided at each key stage of education. Pupils are encouraged to research and discuss career plans and opportunities with staff and work experience is offered in a variety of careers.

Examinations taken. GCSE and A Levels, Associated Board of the Royal School of Music, London Academy of Music and Dramatic Art, Imperial School of Dancing, Royal Society of Arts.

Admissions. The admissions process at Dunottar is designed to identify those pupils who will thrive at the school. The admissions process is as friendly and relaxed as possible. The main entry points for Dunottar School are at 11+, 13+ and 16+. Deferred 13+ entry (e.g. assessment taken at 11+ and deferred for two years) is also offered. Entry into other year groups will be considered where places are available and families who are relocating to the area will be considered at any time. Prospective pupils can be registered at any time prior to the registration deadline. For 11+ entry pupils should be registered before 30th November of the year prior to entry and assessments take place in January of the year of entry. For 13+ pupils should be registered by the end of October and are assessed in November proper to the year of entry. Applications for entry to Sixth Form are usually required by 31st January in the year of entry. The Admissions Department are happy to answer any questions about the admissions process.

Fees per term (2016–2017). £5,013 (Year 7 to Upper Sixth).

Scholarships. Academic Scholarships are awarded annually at 11+ and 13+ to those who reach the highest standard in the entrance tests. 16+ scholarships will be awarded to those who reach a high standard in the scholarship papers. The 16+ scholarship examinations take place in November. Scholarships are also available at 11+, 13+ and 16+ for those who show exceptional promise and talent in Music, Art and Design, Performing Arts and Sport. All candidates are automatically considered for the Headteacher's Award, which is based upon the interview and potential to contrib-

ute to school life. At 16+ there are two specialist programmes for budding entrepreneurs and future medics which offer fee discount and specialist support and work experience. Further particulars may be obtained from the Admissions Department.

Charitable status. Dunottar School is part of United Learning which comprises: UCST (a Company Limited by Guarantee, Registered in England, number 2780748, and a Registered Charity, number 1016538) and ULT (a Company Limited by Guarantee, Registered in England, number 4439859, and an Exempt Charity).

Chair of Board of Governors: Dr R Given-Wilson

Head Teacher: Mrs R Cole, BSc Hons Exeter, MBA

Senior Management:
Deputy Head (*Pastoral*): Mr M Broughton, BA Hons Worcester
Deputy Head (*Teaching & Learning*): Mrs P Smithson, BA Combined Hons Exeter, PGCE, MEd

* *Head of Department*

English:
Ms T Ariyanayagam, BA Hons Hull, PGCE (*Head of Performing Arts*)
Mr M Broughton, BA Hons Worcester
*Ms K Lewis, MBA De Montfort, BEd Hons Sunderland
Mrs P Smithson, BA Combined Hons Exeter, PGCE, MEd
Mrs C Turner, BA Hons London, PGCE

Mathematics:
Ms N Budgen, BComm Durban, PGCE
Miss E Carr, BSc Hons Edinburgh, PGCE
*Mrs R McTavish, BSc Hons York, ACMA, CSBM, PGCE
Mrs J Pardoe, MA Cantab, PGCE

Science:
Mrs R Cole, BSc Hons Exeter, MBA
Miss C Davies, BSc Imperial College, PGCE
Miss K Evans, BSc Hons Durham
Mrs C Hammond, BSc UCL, PGCE, MEd Cantab
*Mrs R Pope, BSc Hons Nottingham, PGCE
Mrs J O'Dwyer, BSc Hons Durham, PGCE
Mrs S Sagar, MSc Coventry, BSc Hons Birmingham, PGCE

Foreign Languages:
Mrs S Bartlett-Rawlings, BA Hons Open University, PGCE
Mrs A Boyd, BA Hons Swansea, PGCE
*Ms M Hurriaga, MEd Cantab, PGCE, LLb Complutense
Mrs A Robertson, BA Hons Bristol, PGCE

Information and Communications Technology:
*Mr I Richardson, BSc Hons Greenwich, PGCE (*Asst Head of Upper School, Director of Co-Curricular*)

Design and Technology:
*Miss F L Exley, BSc Hons Brighton, PGCE

Geography:
*Mrs S Thorne, BA Hons Leicester, PGCE
Mrs N Jackson, BSc Hons Sheffield, PGCE (*Head of Upper School*)

Economics and Business Studies & Government and Politics:
*Mrs N Wintle, MA Oxon, PGCE

History:
*Mrs J Boden, MA St Andrews, PGCE
Miss S Colman, BA Hons Exeter
Mrs R Stringer, BA Hons Warwick, PGCE

Art and Design:
*Mrs S Emblem, BA Hons Wimbledon, PGCE
Mrs M Baker, BA Hons Bath Academy, PGCE

Music:
*Miss E Pettet, BMus Surrey, PGCE (*Director of Music*)

Physical Education:
Mrs E Pieters, BA Hons Brighton, QTS (*Head of Girls' Sport*)
Miss H Field (*PE Assistant*)
Mr S Manning, BA Hons Exeter, PGCE (*Head of Boys' Sport, Asst Head of Lower School*)
Mr J Myers, BA Chichester, PGCE

Psychology:
*Mrs H Cowie, BPsych, BA Hons Goldsmiths College London, PGCE
Mrs S Williams, BSc Kingston, PGCE

Religious Studies and Philosophy:
*Mr P Cooper, BA Nottingham, PGCE

Food Technology:
*Mrs R Macintyre, BA Hons East London, PGCE

Careers:
Mrs S Thorne, BA Hons Leicester, PGCE

Special Educational Needs:
*Mrs A Aylwin, RSA Dip SpLD (*Special Needs Coordinator*)
Mrs S King (*SEN Support*)
Ms S Saward, BA Hons London, PG Dip Dyslexia & Literacy, AMBDA, LTCL, QTS, CELTA (*Gifted and Talented Coordinator, Deputy SENCo*)
Ms S Wilson (*SEN Assistant*)

Support Staff:
Mrs C Allison (*School Nurse*)
Mrs S Ameen, BSc Hons Southampton, AIET (*MIS Manager*)
Mr R Ashworth (*Senior Science Technician*)
Mrs P Crosthwaite, BA Hons Bournemouth (*Director of Marketing*)
Mr G Davies (*Finance Officer*)
Mrs M Denton, BSc Hons Aston (*Admissions and Marketing Assistant*)
Mrs S Edwards (*Headteacher's PA/Admissions Secretary*)
Mrs S Fribbance (*Finance and Admin Manager*)
Mrs J Hyden (*Maintenance*)
Mrs J Jones (*School Secretary*)
Mrs L Longstaff (*Examinations Officer*)
Mrs S Machacek (*Laboratory/Art and DT Technician*)
Mrs L Moon (*Accounts Assistant*)
Mr A Morris (*Premises Officer*)
Mr M Thomas, BSc Hons Kingston (*Network Manager*)
Mr E Thomas (*Operations Manager*)

Ewell Castle School

Church Street, Ewell, Surrey KT17 2AW

Tel: 020 8394 3561 (admissions)
           020 8393 1413 (main office)
Fax: 020 8786 8218
email: admissions@ewellcastle.co.uk
website: www.ewellcastle.co.uk
Twitter: @EwellCastleUK

Ewell Castle is an independent, co-educational day school in Surrey, twenty minutes from London. It was built as a castellated mansion in 1814. It offers a Nursery, Pre-Preparatory School, Preparatory School, Senior School and a Sixth Form.

The gardens and playing fields of the Senior School cover some fifteen acres and were once part of Nonsuch Park. The Senior School is accommodated at The Castle.

The Preparatory School occupies two other premises in Ewell village: Chessington Lodge, a Georgian house minutes from The Castle; and Glyn House, the former Rectory to the parish church, opposite the Senior School. The School, which was founded in 1926, is registered as an educational charity and is administered by a Board of Governors, which is in membership of AGBIS (Association of Governing Bodies of Independent Schools). The Principal is a member of The Society of Heads and the Head of the Preparatory School is a member of IAPS (Independent Association of Prep Schools).

The school comprises approximately 550 pupils in total with 350 pupils in the Senior School and 200 pupils in the Preparatory School.

Buildings. The school is located on three sites within the village of Ewell, accommodating The Preparatory School (Chessington Lodge: co-educational 3–7 years; Glyn House: co-educational 7–11 years) and the Senior School (The Castle: co-educational 11–16 years and the Sixth Form co-educational 16–18 years). Academic departments are well resourced and accommodated. A new building on The Castle site (completed August 2011) provides six new classrooms, purpose-built kitchen and dining/assembly area, Sixth Form cafeteria, cloakrooms and office accommodation. Other recent developments include: major refurbishment of the Library (The Castle), new hard play area (Glyn House), the building of a new Nursery building and establishment of new garden area (Chessington Lodge). The new Music Pavilion, which will incorporate classrooms, a recording studio and a recital room (The Castle) will be completed in the Spring of 2017.

Vision. The vision of our School is to **Inspire** and **Nurture** our pupils to **Achieve**, within a happy, family friendly atmosphere.

Ethos. Ewell Castle is a happy school with an atmosphere of purposeful, academic work. Care, consideration, honesty, integrity, fairness and tolerance are valued. Self esteem is enhanced and all aspects of personal development are fostered. With an ethos in which each child's achievements are acknowledged, valued and celebrated, students thrive academically as a result of the small class sizes, a varied and stimulating curriculum, an extensive extracurricular programme and strong support systems.

Values. Integrity, Trust, Respect, Responsibility, Determination

Organisation. The Preparatory School is co-educational and accepts pupils from three years. Most pupils transfer to the Senior School, whilst others go to a range of Independent and selective/non-selective schools at 11+. The Sixth Form has been co-educational since September 2013 and the Senior School became fully co-educational in September 2015.

Curriculum. National Curriculum requirements are incorporated into Senior and Preparatory School schemes, although the broad and flexible curriculum extends beyond such criteria. Breadth at KS3 (11–13 years) is replaced at KS4 (14–16 years) by a core of Mathematics, English, Science and Religious Studies, supplemented by a wide ranging option scheme covering the languages, arts, humanities and technologies. There is an increased range of subjects available at AS and A Level in the Sixth Form

Work experience is undertaken by pupils in Year 11. Specialist HE/Careers guidance is available from Year 9 within the Senior School.

After the Sixth Form the majority of pupils proceed to universities and colleges, with most pupils achieving their first choice of institution.

Extracurricular Activities. The principal sports are rugby, football, hockey, netball and cricket. In addition there are numerous pursuits which include: athletics, badminton, basketball, table tennis, skiing, and tennis. There is an extensive music and drama programme and other activities such as The Duke of Edinburgh's Award scheme. Regular language, sports and field trips embarked for America, Austria, Belgium, France, Germany, Iceland, Ireland, Italy and Spain in recent years.

The school benefits from an active PTA known as the PSFA.

Admissions. Boys and girls are admitted to the Preparatory School at the age of three. There are no entry requirements at this stage. Older children are invited to attend the school for a day's assessment within a class, during which time they may undertake tests in English & Mathematics.

At the Senior School the standard points of entry are at 11+, 13+ and 16+. Subject to availability, there may be places at other levels. Entry requirements include interview, report from previous school, written assessments and a Taster Session. At 13+ and 16+ the assessments may take the form of Common Entrance or GCSE respectively.

Visitors are welcome to the school on scheduled Open Days or by appointment. Individual assessments are held by arrangement. Scholarship assessments are undertaken in January each year.

Scholarships. Scholarships are available for pupils entering the school at 11+, 13+ and 16+. At 11+ awards are made on the basis of competitive examination/assessment in the designated category. In the case of 13+ and 16+ awards are likely to be made on the basis of Common Entrance and GCSE performance respectively. Awards are made for Academic excellence and also in the categories of Art, Design and Technology, Drama, Music, and Sport.

Fees per term (2016–2017). Senior School £5,075, Pre-Preparatory School £2,630, Preparatory School £3,480.

Preparatory School. *For further information, see Ewell Castle Preparatory School entry in IAPS section.*

Charitable status. Ewell Castle School is a Registered Charity, number 312079. The aim of the charity is to achieve potential and excellence over a broad field: in academic, in sport, in the arts, and in numerous other extracurricular activities and aspects of school life.

Chairman of the Governing Body: Mr P Durnford-Smith, BA, MCIM

Principal: Mr P Harris, MSc, BSc, PGCE, NPQH

Head of Preparatory School & Vice Principal: Ms S Bradshaw, BEd

Deputy Head of Senior School & Vice Principal: Mr S Bromley, BA, PGCE

Director of Studies & Assistant Principal: Mr S Leigh, BA, PGCE

Deputy Head of Preparatory School & Assistant Principal: Mr A Robson, BEd, NPQH

Head of Pre-Preparatory School & Assistant Principal: Mrs S Fowler, BSc, PGCE

Bursar: Mr G Holland, BSc, ACA

Marketing, Development & Alumni Manager: Ms C Hernandez, BA, CIM Grad Dip

Heads of Department:
Art & Design & Photography: Ms D Carrick, BA, QTS
Business Studies, Economics, & Politics: Mr M Carragher, MPhil, BSc, PGCE
Design Technology: Mr S Getty, BA, QTS
Drama: Mr L Bader-Clynes, BA, RADA
English: Ms K Wallace, BA, PGCE
History & Classics: Mr J C W Blencowe, BA, PGCE
Information Technology: Mr J Bernardo, MEd, BSc
Learning Support, SENCo: Mrs C Buckley, BA, PGCE
Mathematics: Mr D Vijapura, BSc, PGCE
Modern Foreign Languages: Miss P Hernandez, Licence LLC, PGCE (*Deputy DSL*)
Music: Mr B Essenhigh, BA, QTS
Physical Education: Mr P Bilsby, BEd

Science: Mr K Hungsraz, BSc, QTS
PSHCE: Mr K Peto, BA, PGCE
Psychology: Mr J D'Souza, BSc, PGCE
Religious Studies: Mrs D Hillman, MA, BEd

Principal's PA: Mrs K El-Dahshan, BA
Registrar: Mrs T Wilkins

Farringtons School

Perry Street, Chislehurst, Kent BR7 6LR
Tel: 020 8467 0256
Fax: 020 8467 5442
email: fvail@farringtons.kent.sch.uk
website: www.farringtons.org.uk
Twitter: @FarringtonsSch
Facebook: @Farringtons-School

Methodist Independent Schools Trust.

Farringtons School is situated in 25 acres of green belt land in Chislehurst, which provide attractive surroundings while still being within easy reach of London (25 minutes to Charing Cross), the South Coast and Gatwick (45 minutes) and Heathrow airport via the M25 (1 hour).

The School is committed to providing a first-class education for pupils of all ages in a caring community which supports all its members and helps each pupil to achieve his or her full potential both academically and personally. After school care is available until 6.00 pm.

The curriculum offered is that of the National Curriculum, with a wide range of GCSE and A Level subjects available. Nearly 100% of Sixth Form leavers customarily go on to degree courses at Universities or Higher Education Colleges. Academic standards are high from a comprehensive intake of pupils and in 2016 a 96% pass rate was achieved at A Level.

The excellent facilities include a Technology building, a large Sports Hall with Dance Studio and Fitness Suite, splendidly-equipped Science and Modern Language departments, well-stocked libraries, Careers Room, new indoor heated swimming pool and extensive playing fields, as well as a School Chapel, where the School regularly comes together.

The main sports are netball, tennis, football, rugby, swimming and athletics, but badminton, volleyball and table tennis are also undertaken and other extracurricular activities available include The Duke of Edinburgh's Award scheme, Business Enterprise, various choirs and instrumental ensembles, gymnastics, jazz-dance, ballet, drama club, fencing, etc.

To obtain a prospectus and further information or to arrange a visit, contact the Registrar.

Fees per term (2016–2017). Day: £3,030 (Pre-Reception full time), £3,740 (Junior), £4,700 (Senior); Weekly Boarding £8,940; Full Boarding £9,490.

Charitable status. Farringtons School is a Registered Charity, number 307916. It exists solely to provide a high-quality, caring education.

Governing Body:
Chairman: Mr D Chaundler, OBE
Vice-Chairman: Mrs R L Howard

Members:

Ms K Davies	Ms C Morgan
Miss M Faulkner	Mr A Raby
Mr T Harris	Mr S Richardson
Mr R Hinton	Mr W Skinner
The Reverend J Impey	Dr A Squires
Mrs J King	Mr M Vinales

Bursar and Clerk to the Governors: Mrs Sally-Anne Eldridge

Headmistress: Mrs Dorothy Nancekievill, MA, BMus, PGCE, HonARAM

Deputy Head: Mr N Young
Head of Junior School: Mr J Charlton
Assistant Head Senior School: Mrs R Frances
Assistant Head Senior School: Mr L Garwood
Chaplain: Reverend Dr J Quarmby
Registrar: Miss R Copeland (*Day*), Mrs F Vail (*Boarding*)

* *Head of Department*

English:
*Mrs V Denman
Miss S Bliss
Mrs L Bowdery
Mr B Coultard
Mrs S Freeston
Ms L Hirsh
Mrs M Kershaw
Ms K MacMahon
Mrs E Russell
Mrs D Scott-White
Mrs A Wigley

*Miss R Azulay
Miss N Lubrani
Mrs K Matthews
Mr L Smith
Miss Z Tynan-Campbell
Mrs S Watson

Music
*Mr N Rayner
Mrs P White

Mathematics:
Mr F Gray
Mrs I Haider
Mrs Z Hanson
Mrs E Lovell
Revd Dr J Quarmby
Mrs E Stenning
Mr N Varley
*Mrs D York

Learning Support:
Mrs J Maynard
Mrs J Pyle
Mrs A Vinales

Sport:
Mr A Doherty
*Mr C Doyle
Mrs G Ody
Mrs J Sherwood
Mr B Suverkrop
Miss E Whitehead

Science:
Mrs J Daws
*Mrs P Garton
Dr N Haughey
Mr C Jarvis
Mrs A Maunder
Mrs V Owen
Miss L Paton
Mrs L Sriram

Modern Languages:
*Mlle I Mosqueron
Miss R Frances
Mrs H Razii-Rydall
Mr P Scowen
Miss C Argibay
Mrs G Bastos

Humanities:
Mr C Catling
*Mr G Curran
Mr A Essex
Mrs L Mortimer
Mrs H Rowett
Miss C Sivvery
Mrs J Spencer

Business, Finance & Technology
Mr Earl Case
Mr John Gardner
*Miss Kat Ootim
Mr Sarvesh Sundaram
Mrs Liria Williamson

Creative Arts
Mrs G Allen

Junior School:
Ms F Alexander
Ms S Austin, BEd Hons
Mrs G Bastos, BA
Mrs L Benjamin
Mrs P Brookman
Mrs S Carter
Miss A Cox
Miss S Cox
Mrs C Crouser
Mrs J Cryan
Ms C Curtis
Mrs T Devaux
Mrs C Dolding-Smith
Mrs V Fox
Ms C Franklyn
Ms C Frisby
Mrs A Johnson
Ms H Kearns
Mrs L Long
Miss F Ody
Ms N Pasquie
Miss K Randall
Mr T Ruffle
Miss S Seager
Mr J Shimmin
Ms K Streeter
Mr B Suverkrop
Mrs A Vinales
Mrs S Walker
Ms S Watts
Ms T Waterman
Mrs C Williams
Miss H White
Ms J Wilkins

Boarding Staff:
Mr S Dillow
Mrs S Medcraft
Mrs V Suverkrop
Mrs E Gilby

Mr R Fuller
Miss Z Tynan-Campbell
Miss L Paton
Mrs J Holmes

Fulneck School

Pudsey, Leeds, West Yorkshire LS28 8DS
Tel: 0113 257 0235
Fax: 0113 255 7316
email: enquiries@fulneckschool.co.uk
website: www.fulneckschool.co.uk
Twitter: @FulneckSchool
Facebook: @FulneckSchool

Fulneck School was established on 1 September 1994 by the merger of Fulneck Boys' School and Fulneck Girls' School, both originally founded in 1753, by the Moravian Church (a very early Protestant Church which has two schools in England and many more abroad) as part of a settlement on the slopes of a valley within the Green Belt on the outskirts of Pudsey. Leeds and Bradford are both nearby and the School has easy access to the motorway network and airports.

The School is a registered charity and the Provincial Board of the Moravian Church is the Trustee of the School. The Governing Body provides a range of professional expertise and is in membership of AGBIS (Association of Governing Bodies of Independent Schools). The Principal is a member of The Society of Heads and the Head of the Junior School is a member of IAPS (Independent Association of Prep Schools).

Originally founded for the education of the sons and daughters of ministers and missionaries, the school nowadays provides an education for just under 400 pupils from all backgrounds. Most of the pupils live in West Yorkshire and travel daily to School, but approximately 75 of them are boarders including some who board weekly and return home from Friday evening to Monday morning.

The School is co-educational and provides a modern, academic curriculum based on Christian principles. Fulneck Sixth Form offers 20 A Level subjects and the school has an outstanding record of success in public examinations. Class sizes rarely exceed 20 and most teaching groups are smaller; in the Sixth Form groups seldom exceed 10.

Buildings. The main buildings of the School are part of the original settlement, yet other buildings on the campus have been added over the years. Most recently these include a new Junior Library with ICT facilities, a new self-contained Sixth Form Centre, performing arts building and a totally refurbished teaching block. The boys' boarding accommodation was extended in the summer of 2008 with further extensions under way in 2012 involving both boarding houses. Extensive playing fields and tennis courts are located on the site, which adjoins Fulneck Golf Club, and looks over to the Domesday village of Tong.

Pastoral Care. The staff work closely and effectively together, sharing in the duties and recreational needs of the School. A senior Pastoral Tutor and two assistants look after the pupils' welfare. The School Nurse, who is medically qualified, and other house staff take care of the boarders in conjunction with the resident teaching staff and the Principal, who also lives on the campus. Weekly and flexi boarding are offered in addition to full boarding.

Sport. Netball, Hockey, Football, Rugby, Cricket and Tennis are the main games of the School, but Athletics, Basketball, Badminton, Cross-Country running, Golf, Rounders, Swimming, Table Tennis and Martial Arts are all available to the pupils as part of a rapidly expanding programme of outdoor pursuits. Teams of various ages, in most sports, have full fixture lists with neighbouring schools. Dance classes are also run.

Activities. Music education is very strong with choirs, bands, a jazz group, a flute group, a rock band, and other orchestral groups. The Senior Choir performs often to the public. Drama is actively pursued with pupils involved in both lessons and Theatre Workshop productions.

There are a number of clubs and societies such as Art, Computer, Cooking, Golf, Orienteering, Hockey, Netball, Table Tennis, Forensic Club, Theatre Workshop, Science, Gardening, Eco Friends, Dance and Martial Arts.

The Duke of Edinburgh's Award scheme is available to pupils over the age of 14, together with a wide range of trips and residential visits, walking and skiing. The school has regularly participated in World Challenge expeditions.

Careers. The Careers teacher is on hand to advise, and the Library stocks most of the available literature on the whole range of courses and careers. All pupils complete a period of work experience at the end of Year 10.

Foundation Stage/Key Stage 1. This is housed within the main building and caters for children from the ages of 3 to 7.

Junior School (Key Stage 2). The Junior School is self-contained and caters for pupils from the ages of 7–11. Once a pupil is admitted he or she will usually progress into the Senior School, after examination at age 11. The Junior School has access to many of its own specialist facilities for Science, Art, Technology, Music, IT and Library, as well as to the Senior School sports facilities.

Learning Support Unit. Specialist staff provide help on an individual or small group basis to children with dyslexia or other learning differences. The Unit is CReSTeD approved and has repeatedly confirmed its 'DU' status, the highest grade awarded to mainstream schools.

Parents and Friends Association. There is a flourishing organization which acts as a fundraising body, and also supports the School in a variety of other ways. This is a living example of the belief that education is a partnership between home and school.

Admission. Admission to the school is welcomed at any age depending on the availability of places, although the main intake is at the ages of 3, 7 and 11. Direct entry to the Sixth Form is also possible. Means-tested academic bursaries and other scholarships are available.

Fees per term (2016–2017). Junior School Day: Nursery (mornings only) £1,430; Foundation Stage (full day) £2,320; Years 1 & 2 £2,520; Years 3–6 £3,120; Weekly Boarding: £5,795; Full Boarding £6,295; Flexi Boarding £30 per night. Senior School: Day £4,120; Weekly Boarding £7,230; Full Boarding £7,995; Flexi Boarding £30 per night.

Fulneck Former Pupils' Association. Mr D Robbins, Fulneck School, Pudsey, West Yorkshire LS28 8DS.

Charitable status. Fulneck School is a Registered Charity, number 251211. It exists to provide a traditional, Christian education for boys and girls between the ages of 3 and 18.

The Governing Body:
Mrs L Sharp (*Chair*)
C J Stern (*Vice-Chairman*)

C Robinson	Mrs A Roberts
Revd M Newman	Mrs L Johnson
D Scott	Mr C Smith
Miss C Kernohan	Mr B El-Haddadeh

Principal: Mrs D M Newman, BEd Bedford

Vice-Principal, Head of Senior School: D Newman, MA Oxford, BA, PGCE

Head of Junior School: C Bouckley, BEd

Bursar: G Blackstone

Hampshire Collegiate School
United Learning

Embley Park, Romsey, Hampshire SO51 6ZE
Tel: 01794 512206 (Senior School)
            01794 515737 (Prep School)
Fax: 01794 518737
email: info@hampshirecs.org.uk
website: www.hampshirecs.org.uk
Twitter: @hampshireschool
Facebook: /hampshireschool

Hampshire Collegiate School (HCS) is a warm and welcoming independent day and boarding school for boys and girls aged 2–18. There is a collective energy about the school's 130-acre campus which provides a beautiful space in which students can learn, play, compete and achieve. HCS continues to go from strength to strength and visitors to the school will witness a dynamic Sixth Form as well as a thriving boarding community that attracts both UK and international students.

At HCS our aim is to focus on each individual child, creating an environment where they will flourish, whatever their ability and talent. Our vision is that our students have the enthusiasm to learn and the ambition to succeed. It is important to us that they have the confidence and determination to explore their interests and that they have the opportunity to develop creatively as well as academically. We are a truly international community where a fundamental value is respect for all, regardless of nationality, interest or ability. Academic excellence continues to be a key priority and we strive to help your child achieve to the very best of their ability.

Constitution. There are about 558 pupils, with approximately 90 in the Sixth Form and 181 in the Prep School. Boys and girls are admitted at 11 and 13 by examination; and into the Sixth Form, at age 16, on GCSE results.

There are boarding places available for both boys and girls (11–18), and the whole School is divided into four houses. Day pupils and boarders are members of the same houses, thus obviating any feeling of division between boarding and day.

All senior pupils attend Assembly, often with Chapel and then commence six 55-minute lessons (with a twenty-minute morning break and an hour lunch break). Following the academic routine, every afternoon and at lunchtime, games or activities are organized allowing day pupils to depart between 4.00 pm and 5.00 pm having experienced the daily routine and ethos of a boarding school. Many day pupils opt to board in their senior years.

Prep School lessons are from 8.45 am to 3.15 pm for Nursery, with staggered finishes, then to 3.35 pm for KS2, followed, again, by voluntary activities every afternoon.

Curriculum. The Prep School follows the National Curriculum in the main and as a basis but seeks to go beyond this in many areas using imaginative teaching and innovative cross-curricular projects. The use of ICT is increasingly embedded throughout the curriculum. In addition French is taught together with Spanish in the older age groups. There is a wide range of after-school clubs including sport, art, performance and music activities.

The GCSE curriculum offers a choice of many subjects (including separate subject sciences) and careful note has been taken of those elements of the National Curriculum considered vital to personal development. All pupils study Spanish in Year 7, and continue with Spanish and French from Year 8. Each pupil must study a minimum of 1 foreign language to GCSE level. There is a wide range of subjects on offer. Most pupils take a minimum of 9 GCSE examinations.

More than 20 AS and A Level subjects are available.

Careers guidance is given by tutors from the earliest days, and is backed up by professional advice. Work experience is undertaken in the summer of Year 10.

Games and Activities. Rugby, Football, Cricket, Hockey, Rounders and Netball are the main games, with Cross Country, Basketball, Swimming, Tennis, Athletics, Lacrosse and Golf among others in a supporting role.

The School has a strong games tradition, achieving representation at County level, and beyond, a reputation for drama and art and a thriving musical life.

The School has its own practice golf course, floodlit pitch, lake, and 7,000 sq ft Sports Hall, dance studio, all-weather playing areas, tennis courts under lights and swimming pool.

All Senior School pupils are encouraged to attempt The Duke of Edinburgh's Award scheme; there are several expeditions each year in the neighbouring New Forest National Park, or in Wales; and abroad, including two ski trips.

In the Prep School Year 6 take part in a residential activity week in Normandy.

Admission Procedures. Admission to the Prep School is by informal assessment and a 'taster day' for younger pupils and, for the older pupils, interview with the Head Teacher, satisfactory reports and assessments in English and Mathematics.

An examination is set at 11 + and an interview expected, plus report from present school (often a State Primary School).

At 13+ HCS Entrance examination and an interview and report.

At 16+ an interview and report including details of GCSE success are expected.

Places are occasionally available in other age groups.

Examination and interviews may take place at any time during the twelve months preceding entry.

Details from the Registrar.

Scholarships and Assisted Places. Scholarships and Assisted Places are available to both internal and external candidates at 11+, 13+ and 16+. An assessment morning and takes place in January.

Scholarships may be awarded for Academic, Music, Art, Design Technology, Drama, Sport or All-Round ability. Assisted Places may also be awarded.

Sixth Form Scholarships are awarded to internal and external candidates on the basis of GCSE and contribution (both actual and potential) to wider school life.

Fees per term (2016–2017). Nursery: £2,740 (full time). Payment by Termly Direct Debit: Prep School £3,080–£3,530; Senior School: £4,980 (day), £8,435 (UK boarding), £9,370 (International Boarding).

There is a reduction for brother/sister and children of the Clergy, HM Forces and Teachers.

Location. Easily accessible from Southampton Airport (20 minutes), Southampton Parkway Railway Station (20 minutes) and M27 (5 minutes), HCS is 1½ miles North West of Romsey, on the Salisbury (A27) road. There is a railway station in Romsey.

Former Pupils. email: HCSSociety@hampshirecs.org.uk.

Charitable status. Hampshire Collegiate School is part of United Learning which comprises: UCST (a Company Limited by Guarantee, Registered in England, number 2780748, and a Registered Charity, number 1016538) and ULT (a Company Limited by Guarantee, Registered in England, number 4439859, and an Exempt Charity).

Local Governing Body:
Dr S Allen
Mr R Butler
Ms C Levy
Mr R Mancey

Mrs D Moody, AILAM
Mr S Neilson
Revd T Sledge
Professor T Thomas (*Chairman*)

***Principal*: Mrs E-K Henry**, BA

Senior School:

Deputy Head Academic: Mr G Yates, MA
Deputy Head Pastoral: Mr J D Cuff, MSc
Senior Housemistress: Mrs K Cuff, BA
Head of Sixth Form: Mr J Hillier, BA
Director of Studies: Mr S Bowyer, MA

Heads of Years:
Mrs L Goodey, BA
Mrs A Fernandez-Garcia, BA
Miss E Boutcher-West, BA
Mr J Schofield, BSc

Head of Design & Technology & Art Faculty: Mr M Lambert, MA
Head of Drama: Ms S Clarke, BA
Head of English: Mrs E Driver, MA
Head of Geography: Mrs N Spurr, BA
Head of History, Government and Politics: Mr D Harris, MA
Head of Mathematics: Mr R Clare, BSc
Head of Modern Language: Mrs S O'Leary, BA
Head of Music: Miss Z Boyle, BMus
Head of Science: Mrs L Miller, BSc
Director of Sport: Mr A Egford, BSc
SENCO: Ms J Hodge, BA

Teaching Staff:
Mr A Barbor, MEng, PGCE (*Mathematics, Maths Challenge Coordinator, Head of Nightingale House*)
Mrs W Bonney, CertEd (*Psychology*)
Miss E Boutcher-West, BA, QTS (*PE, Head of Core PE, Professional Mentor, Head of Year 10*)
Mr S Bowyer, MA, PGCE (*Director of Studies*)
Miss Z Boyle, BMus (*Head of Music*)
Mr J Churchill, BSc, PGCE (*Chemistry*)
Mr R Clare, BSc, QTS (*Head of Mathematics*)
Ms S Clarke, BA, QTS (*Head of Drama*)
Mrs R Clayton, BSc, PGCE (*Geography*)
Mrs S Cornforth, BSc, PGCE (*Mathematics, DoE Award Silver Level Supervisor*)
Miss G Cornick (*Girls' Sport, i/c Hockey, Textiles*)
Mrs K Cuff, BA, PGCE (*Senior Housemistress, Head of Careers, Head of PSHE*)
Mrs E Driver, BA, PGCE (*Head of English*)
Mr A Egford, BSc, PGCE (*Director of Sport*)
Mr S Fenlon, BSc, PGCE (*Mathematics*)
Mrs A Fernandez Garcia, BA, QTS (*Spanish, French, Head of Year 9*)
Mrs L Goodey, BA, PGCE (*Spanish, French, Head of Lower Seniors, DoE Award Gold Level Supervisor*)
Mr D Harris, BA, MA, PGCE (*Head of History*)
Mr J Hillier, BA, PGCE (*Head of Sixth Form, English*)
Mr P Hilton, BSc, PGCE (*Head of ICT, Business Studies, Deputy Head of Boarding*)
Ms J Hodge, BA, PGCE (*SENCO*)
Mrs T Johnson, BA (*French*)
Mrs J Kennedy, MSc, QTS (*Biology, Science, DoE Award Resources Coordinator*)
Mr S Kent-Davies, BA, PGCE (*Music*)
Mr M Lambert, MA, PGCE (*Head of Design Technology & Art Faculty*)
Mr A Leathem, BA, QTS (*PE, Head of Academic PE, Head of Palmerston House*)
Mrs B Luxton, BA, PGCE (*Art*)
Mrs M Matlock, BA (*English*)

Miss A McLean, MA, PGCE (*History*)
Mrs L Miller, BSc, PGCE (*Head of Science*)
Mrs E Mills, BA, PGCE (*Mathematics, Deputy Head of Sixth Form*)
Mr P Nelson, BA, PGCE (*Drama, LAMDA*)
Mrs L Newhall, BA, MA, LPC (*Law, Government & Politics*)
Mr J Nurse, MA (*Music*)
Mrs S O'Leary, BA, PGCE (*Head of Modern Language, Spanish, French, University & College Placements*)
Mr C O'Sullivan, BA, QTS (*English*)
Mrs J Penfold, BA, PGCE (*French, German, Spanish*)
Mrs S Platt, BA, PGCE (*Spanish, French*)
Mrs M Raymond, BSc, PGCE (*Head of Physics, DoE Award Coordinator & Bronze Level Supervisor*)
Mr B Robinson, BSc, PGCE (*Economics, Business Studies*)
Mrs S Rowe, BA, QTS (*Learning Support*)
Mr J Schofield, BSc, PGCE (*Business Studies, Head of Year 10, Head of Austen House*)
Mrs N Spurr, BA, PGCE (*Head of Geography*)
Miss K Stewart, BTh (*Head of Religious Studies, Able, Gifted & Talented Coordinator*)
Mr I Stuart, BEd (*English, Director of Activities, i/c Cricket*)
Mr R Summerson Watson, BEd (*Design and Technology, Head of Chichester House*)
Mr D Swan, BEng, PGCE (*Physics*)
Mr A Thickbroom, MA, PGCE (*Head of Chemistry, Mathematics*)
Ms C Troke, BSc, PGCE (*Head of Economics & Business Studies*)
Ms C Walker, BA (*Learning Support*)
Mrs A Wolfe, MA (*Learning Support*)

Prep School:
Head of Prep School: Mrs H Donnelly, BA, BEd
Deputy Head of Prep School: Mr P Brady, BEd (*Palmerston House Tutor*)

Teaching Staff & Learning Assistants:
Mrs F Adams, BA Ed (*Class Teacher*)
Miss R Alford, Level 3 CACHE (*Teaching Assistant*)
Miss L Barnes, BA, QTS (*Deputy Nursery Manager*)
Mr A Bown, BSc, PGCE (*Head of Subject Science*)
Miss Z Boyle, BMus (*Head of Music*)
Mr T Brittan, BSc, QTS (*Head of Subject Design Technology, House Tutor – Nightingale*)
Mrs K Brown, NVQ3 (*Teaching Assistant*)
Mrs T Collins, NVQ2 (*Teaching Assistant*)
Mrs M Corlass, Teachers Cert (*Teaching Assistant & Lunchtime Supervisor*)
Mrs M Coveney, BA, QTS (*Head of Subject Art*)
Mrs H Dobson, BA, QTS (*Class Teacher i/c KS1*)
Miss A Fitzpatrick, BA, PGCE (*Class Teacher*)
Miss C Fletcher, BA, PGCE (*Head of Subject Drama*)
Mrs J Hammond, BEd (*SENCO*)
Miss S Hardy, BA, EYPS (*Class Teacher*)
Mrs C Harvey, NVQ3 (*Teaching Assistant*)
Mr P Meaden, BA, PGCE (*Educational Visits Coordinator*)
Miss R Medd, BSc, PGCE (*Class Teacher*)
Miss C Paget-Lowe, Level 3 CACHE (*Nursery Assistant*)
Mrs L Phillips, NVQ3 (*Teaching Assistant*)
Mrs K Ross, MA, QTS (*Head of Subject Maths, House Tutor – Chichester*)
Mrs T Sacree, NVQ3 (*Nursery Manager*)
Miss S Smith, BSc, PGCE (*Head of Prep School Sport*)
Mrs W Speirs, BEd (*Head of Subject English*)
Mrs K Tibble, NNEB (*Deputy Nursery Manager*)
Mrs F Walker, BEd (*Class Teacher, Head of Subject LOC*)
Mrs V Worden, MA (*Head of Subject Modern Foreign Languages*)

Visiting Tutors:
Mr R Armstrong, RMSM (*Percussion*)
Mrs M Forrest (*Russian*)
Mrs R Gao (*Chinese*)
Mr R Garrard-Abrahams, BEd, LTCL (*Piano*)
Mrs J Gover, ATCL, LTCL (*Flute*)
Mr D M Halford, PGA Advanced Professional (*Golf*)
Mrs G Kuznicki, ALCM, LLCM (*Singing*)
Mrs R McDonald, BMus (*Violin, Viola & Piano*)
Mr P Nelson, BA, PGCE (*LAMDA*)
Mr D Phaure, Dip Level 6 (*Acting and Coaching*)
Mr G Richford, BA (*Prep School Choir Master*)
Mrs E Ruggles (*German*)
Mrs E Sharrock, BMus (*Cello*)
Mrs M Shearer, GTCL, LCTL (*Clarinet & Piano*)
Mr A West, Dip Level 6 (*Guitar*)
Miss C Williams, BA Hons, CertEd (*Piano & Brass*)
Miss M Williams (*Woodwind*)
Mr P Wray (*Kit Percussion*)

Principal's EA: Mrs R Wells, BA
Registrar: Mrs J Baird
Principal's PA: Mrs M Boterhoek
Prep School Head's PA: Mrs J Piper
Bursar: Mr P Dawson, CIMA, DipM
Finance & Transport Officer: Mr A Peters
Examinations Officer: Mrs T Crookes
Senior Matron: Mrs D Jarvis, RGNII
Assistant Matron: Mrs E Appleton, RGNII
Housemother: Mrs K Lelean

Highclare School

10 Sutton Road, Erdington, Birmingham B23 6QL
Tel: 0121 373 7400
Fax: 0121 373 7445
email: enquiries@highclareschool.co.uk
website: www.highclareschool.co.uk

Founded 1932.
Age Range. 15 months to 18 years. Co-educational throughout.
Number of Pupils. 700.
Fees per term (2016–2017). £2,195–£3,950.
Location. The School is situated on three sites on the main road (A5127) between Four Oaks, Sutton Coldfield and Birmingham. The Senior Department and Sixth Form, is on direct train and bus routes from Birmingham City Centre, Tamworth, Lichfield and Walsall as well as being serviced by our own buses. There are two Primary Schools, known as Highclare Woodfield and Highclare St Paul's. Wrap-around care operates from 7.30 am until 6.00 pm for the parents who require it, including holiday cover. The ethos of the school lies in the encouragement of individual excellence for each pupil, outstanding pastoral care and a belief in the education of the 'whole person'.
Organisation. Four departments:
Nursery and Preparatory Department (age 18 months to 7 years, Girls and Boys). The Nursery caters for children from 18 months to 3 years and although an independent unit it has the support of facilities and resources of the Preparatory Department. French is taught from Reception.
Junior Departments (age 7+ to 11 years, Two co-educational Departments). The Junior Departments, with classes of up to a maximum of 22 pupils, follow National Curriculum guidelines. Pupils also have the benefit of specialist tuition in French, PE and Music. Other foundation subjects are taught by subject and by class teachers. Entry by School's own assessment procedure.

Senior Department (age 11 to 16, co-educational). The full curriculum is covered at KS3. At GCSE all students study English Language and English Literature, Mathematics, Science and Additional Science, with the opportunity to study separate sciences, and a modern foreign language, either French, German or Spanish with a wide choice of options. In addition pupils also study PSHCE and take the ECDL qualification in Information Technology. Physical Education, Music and Performing Arts also form important parts of the curriculum. Through a wide programme of enrichment activities every child has the opportunity to enjoy activities beyond the academic. Entry by School's own assessment procedure.

Sixth Form (age 16+). The Sixth Form is co-educational and accepts external candidates as well as pupils transferring from Highclare Senior School. A wide range of A Level subjects is available for study with excellent pastoral, higher education and careers guidance available. The timetable is structured to meet the individual requirements of each student.

All parts of the School participate in extensive lunchtime and after-school activities.

The School is multi-denominational. Further information may be obtained from the School or the website and prospective parents are always welcome to visit. Open mornings are held throughout the year.

Charitable status. Highclare School is a Registered Charity, number 528940.

Chair of Governors: Mrs L Flowith

School Leadership Team:

Headmaster: Dr R Luker, PhD Sheffield Hallam, MA, BA Hons, PGCE Madeley

Head of Senior School: Mrs A Moore, BA Hons UCE, PGCE Birmingham

Head of Junior Schools: Mrs P Bennett, BA Hons Liverpool, PGCE Liverpool

Business Manager: Mrs M P A McGoldrick, MSc Manchester, BA Hons Manchester, MAAT, AInstAM Dip

Deputy Head of Senior School: Mrs A Healey, BSc Hons Durham, PGCE Durham

Senior School Staff:

Head of Senior School: Mrs A Moore, BA Hons UCE, PGCE Birmingham

Heads of Departments:

Art: Mrs V Hughes, BA Hons Birmingham, PGCE Birmingham
Design & Technology: Mrs H Good, BEd Hons Worcester
English: Mrs K J Dawson, BA Hons Exeter, PGCE Oxford
Geography: Mrs S Cassell, BA Hons Oxford, PGCE Keele
History: Miss M Watson, BA Hons Durham, MA Warwick, PGCE Glos
Home Economics: Mrs A Cobbold, BEd Bath
Information Technology/Computing/Business: Mrs V Patel, BA Hons Brighton QTS
Law: Mrs L J Embury, LLB Hons Wolverhampton, City & Guilds Teacher's Cert
Mathematics: Mr S Parkinson, BSc Hons Southampton, PGCE Birmingham
Modern Languages: Mrs J Lightfoot, BA Hons Newcastle, PGCE Warwick
Music: Miss R Mosley, MA, BA Hons Oxford
Drama: Miss M Sharman, BA Hons Birmingham QTS
Psychology: Mrs A Thorpe, BSc Hons Aston, PGCE Wolverhampton
Physical Education: Mrs A de Sousa-Bartlett, BEd Hons St Mary's College

Religious Studies: Mrs J Palmer, BSc Hons Open, PGCE Birmingham
Science: Mrs R Trotter, BSc Hons York, PGCE Nottingham
Sociology: Dr D Edwards, BA Hons Liverpool, PGCE Leics, MA, PhD Manchester

Posts of Additional Responsibility (Senior):

Assistant Head of Senior School (Operational): Mrs S Cassell, BA Hons Oxford, PGCE Keele
KS5 Coordinator/Head of Sixth Form: Mr S Parkinson, BSc Hons Southampton, PGCE Birmingham
KS4 Coordinator/Gifted & Talented Coordinator: Mrs A de Sousa-Bartlett, BEd Hons St Mary's College
KS3 Coordinator/Gifted & Talented Coordinator: Mrs H Good, BEd Hons Worcester
Learning Support – KS3, 4, & 5: Mrs K Johnson, BEd Hons Leeds

Junior School Staff:

Head of Junior Schools: Mrs P Bennett, BA Hons Liverpool, PGCE Liverpool

Highclare St Paul's:
Site Head: Highclare St Paul's: Mrs J Booker, DipEd Edinburgh, MEd Birmingham
KS2 Coordinator: Mrs J Griffiths, BA Hons, QTS York, MA Wolverhampton
KS1 Coordinator: Mrs J Newman, BEd Hons Cheltenham & Gloucester
EYFS Coordinator: Mrs J Harris, MA, PSC, BA Hons ECS Birmingham EYPS

Highclare Woodfield:
Site Head: Highclare Woodfield: Mrs L Morgan, BEd Hons Wales, PGCE Wolverhampton
KS2 Coordinator: Mrs G White, BA Hons, PGCE Birmingham
KS1 Coordinator: Mrs K S Tidman, BA Hons UCE, PGCE Birmingham
EYFS Coordinator: Mrs L Bayliss, BA Hons Liverpool, MARCA, PGCE Birmingham QTS
Nursery Manager: Mrs S Pointon, NNEB, Early Years, BA Hons Birmingham

Support Staff:
Business Manager: Mrs M P A McGoldrick, MSc Manchester, BA Hons Manchester, MAAT, AInstAM Dip
Marketing Manager: Mrs J Baden
Admissions Registrar: Mrs L Madden
Facilities Manager: Mr D Underwood
ICT Systems Manager: Mrs S Robinson

Hill House School

Fifth/Sixth Avenue, Auckley, Near Robin Hood Airport, Doncaster, South Yorkshire DN9 3GG

Tel:	01302 776300
Fax:	01302 776334
email:	info@hillhouse.doncaster.sch.uk
website:	www.hillhouse.doncaster.sch.uk
Twitter:	@HillHouseSchool

Hill House was founded in 1912 and now occupies the site of the former RAF Officers' Quarters of RAF Finningley. The school provides a seamless, fully co-educational day education from age 3 to 18, and aims to provide a top-class holistic education where extra-curricular success and personal development stand alongside academic excellence. Hill House was named Independent School of the Year 2012–13.

Number of Students. There are 700 pupils, with an equal number of boys and girls.

Education. Children enter the School at 3 years of age via Nursery where structured play and learning are the order of the day. As children progress through the School there is a gradual change to subject based teaching in specialist rooms, in preparation for GCSEs at 16 and A Levels at 18. Upon leaving the Junior School children enter a full house system for pastoral care. All main school subjects are offered, including individual Sciences, French, Spanish, German, Mandarin and Latin.

Facilities. The whole school is based in a historic building with new, purposely renovated classrooms. The site includes a large hall, dining room and theatre. In 2011 Hill House Sixth Form was launched, housed in its own new Sixth Form Centre, including classrooms, coffee shop and large common room. A new Music School contains practice rooms, a recording studio and a performing studio. 2013 saw the opening of the school's new sports grounds at Blaxton. In 2015, the blue Astroturf Paver Hockey Pitch was opened.

Extra-Curricular Activities. Music, Drama, Art and Sport play an important part in the life of the School. Throughout the year over 100 academic, recreational, musical and sporting activities per week are also offered in extra-curricular time. The major sports undertaken include rugby, netball, hockey, cricket, tennis, athletics and rounders. There is a competitive fixture list including a number of overseas tours. There are two orchestras and five choirs within the school, who enjoy the newly-built Music School. Drama productions and concerts are undertaken on a regular basis. Residential trips and sports tours are undertaken at most age levels.

The School Day. School opens at 8.00 am, with lessons from 9.00 am to 4.00 pm. Activities run from 4.00 pm, and a before and after school club operates from 7.30 am and until 6.00 pm. The school operates a five-day week, with a full games afternoon for all ages above 7. There are some activities and fixtures at weekends. Sixth Formers also have an Internship Afternoon, where they spend time at local businesses, hospitals etc.

Fees per term (2016–2017). £2,800–£4,10 according to age. Fees include lunch and most extras.

Scholarships. Scholarships are available at 11+ for Academic, Sport, Art, Music and Performing Arts, and at 16+ for Academic and Leadership.

Charitable status. Hill House School Limited is a Registered Charity, number 529420.

Governors:
Mrs E Paver (*Chair*)
R De Mulder (*Deputy Chairman*)
S Colbear
Mrs V Cusworth (*Chair Designate*)
N Ebdon
R Fennell
M Gutowski
P Iqbal
Mrs J Jameson
R Leggott
J Sprenger
M Wilson-MacCormack

Headmaster: **David Holland**, MA Cantab

Deputy Head: Mrs Belinda McCrea, MA Cantab
Head of Junior School: Mr Jonathan Hall, BEd Hons
Senior Master: Mr Simon Hopkinson, BA Hons
Head of Sixth Form: Mrs Caroline Rogerson, BSc Hons
Deputy Head of Junior School: Mrs Charlotte Leach, BA Ed Hons
Bursar and Clerk to the Governors: Mrs Karen Kidney, ACMA Hons

Heads of Departments:
Mr Mark Cadman, BA Hons (*Director of Music*)
Mr Richard Dorman, BA Hons (*Head of History*)
Mrs Rachel Frisby, BA Hons (*Head of Geography*)
Mr Chris Keyworth, BEd Hons (*Head of Physical Education*)
Mrs Julia Major, BEd (*Head of Modern Languages*)
Mrs Wendy Parkhurst, BA, MA (*Head of Art*)
Dr Carole Boynton, PhD (*Head of Science*)
Mrs Mahjabeen Thomas, BSc Hons (*Head of Mathematics*)
Mr Martin Webdale, BSc Hons (*Director of Sport*)
Dr Kurt Johnson, PhD (*Head of English*)

Housemistress (*Field House*): Mrs Mahjabeen Thomas, BSc
Housemaster (*Master House*): Mr Peter Shipston, BA, MA
Housemaster (*School House*): Mrs Christine Havard, BA Hons

Kingham Hill School

Kingham, Chipping Norton, Oxfordshire OX7 6TH

Tel: 01608 658999
Fax: 01608 658658
email: registrar@kinghamhill.org
website: www.kinghamhill.org.uk
Twitter: @kinghamhillsch
Facebook: @Kingham-Hill-School
LinkedIn: /kingham-hill-school

Motto: *In virum perfectum.*

Kingham Hill School is in the heart of the glorious Cotswold countryside, just 80 minutes from London Paddington, in a 100-acre estate where pupils have a safe place to learn, explore and make their home. With just over 300 pupils Kingham Hill remains small to allow the school to sustain its caring, home-from-home community where every child is nurtured, challenged and inspired to succeed academically and within their personal lives.

Highly qualified, specialist staff offer a broad and challenging curriculum (27+ courses at A Level) to ensure every pupil has opportunities to learn, excel and realise their potential. Top-class facilities, including a new £4m Maths and Science building and a new £1.5m library, ensure pupils have the best amenities to enhance their learning. Small class sizes deliver a bespoke learning experience that can be tailored to individual needs to help discover the talent in every child.

The school has an extensive range of team and individual sports available, including water polo, mountain biking and fencing so that every pupil can find something to enjoy and succeed in. Facilities include floodlit astro pitches, tennis courts and a leisure centre with a gym and indoor pool. Professional coaches, including Rugby Union Lifetime Award Winners & Oxford University players, nurture high achievers and deliver excellent support so all pupils can maximise their potential.

Creative arts are a strength of the school and there are opportunities for every pupil to find and express their creativity. All Year 7 and 8 joiners are given a musical instrument to learn and music events held throughout the year range from regular concerts to the annual Burns Night Ceildh! There are two annual drama productions, recently including Great Expectations and Peter Pan. The art department offers painting and sculpting as well as photography & product design courses.

An American Program, the first of its kind in the UK, allows US students to study at Kingham Hill and was developed in conjunction with the US Department of State.

Our record for enabling significant improvement in grades, achievement on the sports field and stage, and growth in all-round confidence, is superb. '*The strength of the school community is remarkable. Students receive a high quality education in a supportive, warm and beautiful environment.*' NEASC 2015.

Our pastoral care is a real strength of the school and we provide small (average 35 pupils) boarding houses with modern, comfortable facilities to provide a homely feel. There is a real sense of community amongst both the day and boarding students. '*The spiritual, moral, social and cultural development of the pupils is excellent.*' ISI 2014.

We run an academic society – Octagon. The seven most able pupils from each year group sit with the master in charge and are challenged with extended studies, visits to public lectures, involvement in debates, etc. These pupils are expected to achieve outstanding results and go on to top universities.

Open Days: 4 February 2017, 17 June 2017, 7 October 2017, 3 February 2018, 16 June 2018

Assessment Days: Monthly Assessment Days

Fees per term (2016–2017). Full Boarding: £7,885 (Years 7 & 8), £9,750 (Years 9–11), £10,200 (Sixth Form). Weekly Boarding: £7,595 (Years 7 & 8), £8,895 (Years 9–11), £9,290 (Sixth Form). Day: £5,320 (Years 7 & 8), £6,075 (Years 9–13).

SEND tuition: £1,290 (variable rate depending on age and level of support). ESOL tuition: £1,325. American Studies: £2,050.

Scholarships and Bursaries. The School is able to offer several categories of Scholarship. Generous Bursaries for sons and daughters of HM Forces personnel.

Charitable status. The Kingham Hill Trust is a Registered Charity, number 1076618, and a Company Limited by Guarantee, registered in England, number 365812. The school exists to provide education for girls and boys from 11 to 18.

Governors:
John Richardson (*Chair*)

Carol Anelay	Dr Angela Netherwood
Kenji Batchelor	Rhett Parkinson
Debbie Buggs	Caroline Pellereau
Revd Richard Cunningham	Colin Townsend
Revd Johnny Juckes	Jeremy Welch
Col John Lewis	

Headmaster: Revd Nick Seward, BEng, MA (*Economics*)

Deputy Headmaster: Andrew Evans, BA, BSc, MBA (*Head of Business*)
Bursar: Catriona Thompson, BEng Hons
Second Deputy: Rob Jones, BMus, MMus (*Head of Drama*)
Assistant Head – Curriculum: Timothy Bostwick , BA, MA (*History*)
Head of Conduct: Mark Buckler, BA Hons (*Head of Art*)
Chaplain: Andrew Savage, BTh, BSc Hons, MSc (*Theology*)

Teaching Staff:

Douglas Ansley, BEng Hons (*DT Technician, Maintenance*)
Christopher Ashton, BSc Hons (*Extra-Curricular Assistant, Norwich Houseparent*)
Janet Balinski BA, MA (*Head of ESOL*)
Dominic Beasant, BA, MA (*Mathematics, Greenwich Houseparent*)
Helena Berkeley, BA (*Latin & English, Head of Octagon*)
Scott Birnie (*Head of Hospitality & Leisure*)
Michael Cartwright, BSc Hons (*PE*)
Daniel Chambers, BA, MA (*Head of Music*)

Jessica Chapman, BA Hons (*Head of Sixth Form and Destinations*)
Jeffrey Elliott, BA (*English*)
Helen Evans, BA (*SpLD*)
Magnus Eyles, BSc (*Mathematics, Sports Coaching, Sheffield Houseparent*)
Andrew Ferrero, BA (*History*)
Justine Fowler, BEng Hons (*Mathematics*)
Nick Fox, BA (*Head of History & Politics*)
Louanne Gill, BA (*Mathematics*)
Rachel Gruber, BSc, PhD (*Science Technician part-time*)
Athena Harper (*Lettings Assistant, Latimer Day Houseparent*)
Dani Heywood-Lonsdale, BA, MA, MSc (*Head of American Program*)
Holly Hiscox, BA, MA (*History & Politics, Professional Tutor*)
Alan Hutchings, BEd (*Head of DT/ICT*)
Sara Hutchings, BEd (*Head of Mathematics*)
Graham Lane, BSc Hons (*Science*)
Chris Larner, BA (*Geography & Economics*)
Susie Lowe, CertEd, AGSM (*Speech & Drama part-time*)
Rebecca Lund, BA Hons (*Director of Sports, Head of PE*)
Adam Marks, BSecEd (*Mathematics, Plymouth Houseparent*)
Timothy Martin, BA (*Head of SpLD, Bradford Houseparent*)
Jane McFarlane, BSc Hons, MSc (*Science*)
Kyle McFarlane, BA (*Head of Geography*)
Murray Metcalfe, BA (*MFL, Clyde Day Houseparent*)
Stephen Miller, BSc, HDE (*Head of Science*)
William Osborne, BA Hons (*Theology*)
Karen Parkin (*School Counsellor*)
Linda Petra, MA TESOL (*ESOL part-time, Bradford Deputy Houseparent*)
Stephen Petra, BSc (*Science*)
Pippa Phillips, BA (*Speech & Drama part-time*)
Antonia Rankine, BA (*SpLD*)
George Rees, BA Hons (*English*)
Cathy Rogers, BSc (*Science Technician part-time*)
Lucy Savage, BA Hons (*Animal Club Coordinator*)
Donna Saxby, BSc Hons (*Librarian, Digital Literacy Coordinator*)
Edward Scates, MA (*Head of English*)
Basil Strang, BSc (*Science*)
Lilly Tigwell, BA (*Art/Art Technician*)
Gareth Williams, BA Hons (*Head of MFL*)
Mary Williams, BSc (*SpLD*)

Headmaster's PA & Registrar: Jo Cavan
Marketing & Communications Manager: Jessica Cotton

Kingsley School
Methodist Independent Schools Trust

Northdown Road, Bideford, Devon EX39 3LY

Tel:	01237 426200
Fax:	01237 425981
email:	admissions@kingsleyschoolbideford.co.uk
website:	www.kingsleyschoolbideford.co.uk
Twitter:	@KSBideford
Facebook:	@KingsleySchoolBideford

Kingsley School Bideford, a single campus co-educational Boarding and Day school for pupils aged 3 to 18, is committed to discovering, nurturing and celebrating the talents and achievements of each and every one of its pupils. This commitment makes it the ideal school for families, from the UK and overseas, who believe that every child is an individual, worthy of individual attention and encouragement.

As a relatively small school of around 400 boys and girls from nursery to Sixth Form, Kingsley's atmosphere is like that of a large family where everybody knows each other well. The school's philosophy encourages personal qualities such as courage, generosity, honesty, imagination, tolerance and kindness. In addition we develop the students' wider interests and skills in sport, music, art, and drama. Overall, a Kingsley education develops the individual character and talents of each and every student both inside and outside the classroom.

Location. Kingsley School is situated in the beautiful North Devon market town of Bideford, an historic port beside the estuary of the River Torridge. The spectacular scenery of the North Devon coast and beautiful beaches are on our doorstep and there is easy access to the National Parks of Exmoor and Dartmoor. The North Devon link road, which passes close to Bideford, provides a direct route to the M5 motorway.

Organisation. Kingsley School is entirely co-educational and comprises a Senior School with approximately 200 pupils, aged 11 to 18 years and a Junior School with approximately 130 pupils aged 2½ to 11 years, as well as 50 in our Nursery which offers wrap-around care for children from 8 weeks to 3 years old. The Grenville Dyslexia Centre, with a nationwide reputation for outstanding dyslexia provision, serves around 25% of the school's pupils.

Site and Buildings. Situated on a beautiful 25-acre site, the School has two Boarding Houses for boys and one for girls, all of which have immediate access to extensive playing fields, an all-weather hockey pitch, netball and tennis courts.

In recent years an ambitious programme of building has led to the provision of first-class facilities for science, ICT, drama, gymnastics, art and science. The Library provides an excellent environment for study, research and career guidance.

Curriculum. Senior School pupils study a core of subjects, including English, Mathematics, Biology, Chemistry, Physics, Modern Languages and Religious Studies. Subjects such as Geography, History, Art, ICT, Food & Nutrition, Design & Technology, Drama, Music, Sport and PSE complete the programme of study for Years 7–9.

For GCSE, in addition to the core subjects, other courses include Design & Technology, Food & Nutrition, Computer Science, Physical Education, Art, Engineering, Statistics, Drama, Geography, History and Music.

In the Sixth Form there is a wide choice of AS, A Level and vocational subjects including English Literature, Mathematics, Biology, Chemistry, Physics, Geography, History, Art, Modern Foreign Languages, Hospitality, Psychology, Business Studies, Performance Arts, Photography, Sport and Music. Tuition in English for speakers of other languages is also available.

Sport and Physical Education. All pupils, girls and boys, are encouraged to participate in a large variety of sports including: rugby, hockey, netball, cross-country, handball, cricket, gymnastics, badminton, basketball, football, rounders, tennis, judo, swimming and health-related fitness. The Judo Academy has a unique link with the elite Team Bath, and the School's gymnasts compete at a local, regional and national level. Kingsley School is also home to the Devon Handball Squad – recently the girls' handball team came second in the Handball Nationals. A number of our students are on the England and GB squad path for handball.

Clubs and Activities. There is an extensive range extra-curricular activities which are organised and supervised by staff. Among the most popular are The Duke of Edinburgh's Award scheme, choir, orchestra, judo, computing, art, music, climbing and surfing. Numerous expeditions and field trips, both in the UK and abroad, are organised each year. Musicals, plays and concerts are regularly presented in the school's purpose-designed theatre.

Careers. From Year 9 onwards, pupils are offered a planned programme of careers education and guidance as part of the tutorial programme. This is complemented by presentations from visiting professionals, visits to careers events and close contact with Careers advisers from Connexions Cornwall and Devon. All pupils have access to the latest careers information in the School Library.

Religion and Pastoral Care. In common with every Methodist Group School, Kingsley has a Christian ethos, and welcomes children of all religious denominations, as well as those without religious affiliation. In addition to their Year Heads, all pupils have a personal Tutor who is responsible for monitoring their academic progress and personal well-being. For Boarders, care is also the responsibility of the Housemaster or Housemistress.

Admission. Boys and girls are admitted to the Nursery from the age of 3 months. Entry to the Junior and Senior Schools is by interview and taster day. Assessment for academic scholarships is made through written tests in Mathematics, English and Science, as well as a verbal reasoning test. For pupils with recognised learning difficulties entry is by interview together with an up-to-date educational psychologist's report. 13+ admission is through our own Entrance Examination or Scholarship Examination. For older pupils, an interview together with a report from their present school is required.

Prospectus. The Kingsley School prospectus is available from the Registrar, Mrs Caroline Bailey, email: admissions@kingsleyschoolbideford.co.uk, tel: 01237 426200 or online via the school's website: www.kingsley schoolbideford.co.uk. Visitors are most welcome to tour the School by appointment.

Scholarships. Entrance Scholarships are offered annually for pupils joining Year 7 and Year 9 on the basis of the results of entrance tests held in the preceding January. Awards are also available where candidates show outstanding ability in Music, Art, Drama, and Sport. Sixth Form Academic Scholarships are awarded on the basis of GCSE performance.

Fees per term (2016–2017). Junior School: Day (including lunch): £1,895 (Reception), £1,995 (Years 1 and 2), £2,495 (Years 3 and 4), £3,240 (Years 5 and 6); Boarding (from Year 4): £5,495 (weekly), £7,070 (full). Senior School: Day (including lunch) £4,055–£4,300; Boarding: £8,340 (full), £6,855 (weekly),

Charitable status. Kingsley School, Bideford is a Registered Charity, number 306709.

Governors:
Chairman: Mr David Pinney

Dr Mike Cracknell	Mr Michael Portman
Mrs Sue Fishleigh	Mr John Tomalin
Mrs Jane Hellier	Mrs Jane Woodhams
Mr Richard Holwill	Mr Ian Huggett
Mr Andrew Laugharne	Mt Patrick Hamilton

Ex officio:
Mr Peter Rigby, Senior Executive Officer and Director of Finance, Methodist Independent Schools Trust
The Revd Canon Graham Thompson, Chairman of Plymouth and Exeter District of the Methodist Church

Head: **Mr Pete Last**, BA Hons Cantab, Ad Dip Ed London, MEd Buckingham

Junior Head: Mr Matthew Lovett, BA

Deputy Head & Director of Studies: Dr Susan Ley, BSc, PhD

Deputy Head and Head of Pastoral Care: Mr Joe Knight, BA

Senior School Teaching Staff:
* *Head of Department/Subject*

Mr Chris Beechey, BA, MA, ACIEA (*Head of History, Religious Studies*)
Mrs Michele Borsten, BA, MA (*Head of Drama, English*)
Miss Gemma Braunton (*PE & Games, Gymnastics Coach*)
Mrs Judith Brock, BA, MEd (*Information Technology*)
Mr Matt Child, MEng (*Head of 6th Form, Head of Engineering*)
Mr Simon Cannon, MA (*Chemistry*)
Mrs Christine Hamilton, MA (*Head of Maths*)
Mr Leigh Crossman, BA (*Head of Music, Drama, Theatre Technician*)
Ms Stephanie Loftahouse, BSc (*Psychology, Science*)
Mr Jon Dickinson, BA (*Head of Art & Photography, Applied Art & Design, Head of Upper School*)
Miss Rosalyn Dyer, BSc (*Mathematics, ICT*)
Miss Sarah Gosai, BA (*Food Science*)
Mr Ian Holleran, BSc (*Head of Science, Physics*)
Miss Helen Luca, BA (*Head of Girls Games, EAL*)
Miss Kathryn Makepeace, BA (*Head of English*)
Mr Simon Mathers, BSc (*Head of Boys' PE & Games, Science*)
Miss Sarah Parsons, BSc (*Mathematics, Careers Coordinator, Head of Lower School*)
Ms Diana Percy, BA, MEd (*Head of EAL*)
Mrs Hilary Roome, BEd Cambridge (*Technical Sport*)
Mrs Barbara Sochon, BEd, Adv Dip SEN (*Dyslexia Centre, EAL*)
Mrs Linda Stella, BA (*Geography, Outdoor Ed, DoE, Head of Boarding*)
Miss Kat Timms, BA (*Art & Photography, PE, Applied Art & Design*)
Mrs Sandrine Toubin-Whale, DEUG Licence, BA (*Head of French, EAL, Houseparent Belvoir*)
Mr Simon Ward (*PE & Games, Judo Coach*)
Mr Steve Whaley, BSc (*Head of Geography*)
Miss Caroline Williams, BA (*Head of Spanish, EAL*)
Mrs Louise Wivell, BA (*Head of Business Studies*)

Junior School and Pre-School Teaching Staff:
Mr Matthew Lovett, BA (*Junior Head*)
Miss Gemma Braunton (*PE and Games*)
Dr Jennie Cousins, BA, MA, PhD (*MFL*)
Miss Emma Ford, BA (*Class Teacher*)
Miss Sarah Gosai, BA (*Food Technology*)
Miss Helen Luca, BA (*PE and Games*)
Mr Simon Mathers, BSc (*PE and Games*)
Mrs Melanie Smithson, BEd (*Class Teacher*)
Mrs Linda Stella, BA (*Geography*)
Mrs Elaine Thorne, BA (*Class Teacher*)
Mr Simon Ward (*PE and Games*)
Mrs Emma Wilson, BA Ed (*Class Teacher*)
Mr Paul Wilson, BSc (*Class Teacher, Forest Schools*)
Miss Rachel Wilson, BA (*Class Teacher*)
Mrs Fiona Woolcott, BEd, Dip SpLD, Cert Inclusive Ed, Cert TEFL (*Class Teacher, SENCO*)
Mrs Meda Maynard, Montessori Cert Teaching
Mrs Elaine Henry, Montessori Cert Teaching
Mrs Kim Curtis BTEC Nat Diploma
Mrs Mary Lock, Montessori Cert Teaching
Miss Catherine Smith, NVQ, Children's Nursing, Level C
Miss Alison Sunman, Foundation Degree Early Childhoood Studies
Miss Sian Wade, BTEC Level 3 Childcare & Learning Development

Nursery Staff:
Miss Harriet Dare, Nat Dip Children's Care Learning & Development Level 3 (*Acting Nursery Manager*)
Miss Chloe Elliott, Nat Dip Children's Care Learning & Development Level 3 (*Deputy Nursery Manager*)
Miss Sophie Baglow, BA Early Childhood Studies Level 6
Miss Loren Braund, BA Early Childhood Studies Level 6
Miss Emma Cunneen, CACHE Dip Children and Young People's Workforce (*Level 3*)
Miss Alice Davey, Nat Dip Children's Care Learning & Development Level 3
Miss Clare Heard, Level 3 BTEC Nat Dip Children's Care Learning and Development
Miss Eilish Hodgson, Nat Dip Children's Care Learning & Development Level 3
Miss Samantha Loates, BTEC Nat Cert Children's Care Learning and Development Level 3
Miss Eloise McPake, BTEC Childcare Learning & Development Level 3
Miss Chelsea Rockey (*Trainee Nursery Nurse*)
Mrs Naomi Russell, NVQ Level 3 Children's Care Learning & Development
Miss Saskia Scott, BTEC Nat Dip Children's Care Learning & Development
Miss Becki Westlake, BTEC Nat Dip Health and Social Care Level 3

Head of Marketing: Mrs Lucy Goaman, BA, MA
Director of Finance: Mr Andy Stevenson
Registrar: Mrs Caroline Bailey, BSc
ICT Technician: Mr Jon Hector
Exams Officer & Data Systems/Web Manager: Mrs Fo Edmonds, BA
Head's PA: Ms Sandie Hall
Logistics Administrator: Mrs Ann Neale
Acting Junior Departments Secretary: Mr Frank Watson
Student Support Services & Stationery Manager: Mrs Wendy Flint
Food Technology Technician: Mrs Katharine Stone
Senior Science Laboratory Technician: Mrs Philippa Veillet
Matron/School Uniform: Mrs Sarah Glover

Langley School

Langley Park, Loddon, Norwich, Norfolk NR14 6BJ

Tel: 01508 520210
Fax: 01508 528058
email: admissions@langleyschool.co.uk
website: www.langleyschool.co.uk
Twitter: @Langley_School
Facebook: @LangleySchool

Langley School, formerly the Norwich High School for Boys, was founded in 1910. The School relocated from Norwich to Langley Park in 1946 and was renamed. It is the Senior School to Langley Preparatory School at Taverham Hall in Norwich and the business affairs of both schools are managed by a Council of Management as a non-profit making educational charity.

Langley admits boys and girls between the ages of 10 and 18 years to day, weekly boarding, flexi boarding or full boarding status. There are 560 pupils in the School, of whom around 100 are boarders.

Langley School aims to provide a framework within which each pupil will develop effective learning skills and will achieve their maximum academic potential. A happy, secure and well-ordered environment is maintained in a beautiful Grade 1 listed country house setting with 110 acres of extensive grounds and playing fields, where individuals are encouraged to set their sights high. Their progress is monitored by a strong tutorial system to ensure that they follow a course of study that best suits their individual skills and needs. Langley pupils are encouraged to identify their talents and to use and develop them whilst contributing to a wide variety of new experiences that will help them acquire the values of honesty, enterprise, independence and social awareness. Small classes and a well organised House system help our children to sample these new experiences with confidence. They will learn to take personal and social responsibility and will get ample opportunities to develop leadership qualities. We hope to produce young people who will be prepared to meet the demands of a rapidly changing and demanding world which will require versatile, adaptable, receptive and confident citizens of the future.

Langley School is passionate about sport and serious about education; we are very proud to have partnerships with five sporting clubs including Norwich City Football Club and Leicester Tigers. This enables us to offer the very best opportunities, training and experience to our students on the sports field.

Location and Facilities. Situated in over 100 acres of playing fields and wooded parkland south of Norwich, Langley benefits from good accessibility by road, rail, air and sea.

In recent years the school has been steadily expanding and its facilities have been substantially enhanced. Recent developments include a complete refurbishment programme for boarding facilities, a new floodlit Astroturf pitch, a multimedia suite for Modern Languages, a fully refurbished and extended Mathematics block and a multi-gym with fitness centre. In September 2010, a new state-of-the-art block of fifteen classrooms and four ICT rooms was opened, alongside the refurbishment of two other blocks. In September 2012 a brand new medical centre was opened and an excellent state-of-the-art Sixth Form Centre and Performance Hall opened in January 2014.

Academic Curriculum. Syllabuses and schemes of work are designed to complement the National Curriculum and the Common Entrance Examination Syllabuses up to Year 9.

Lower School (10–13 years): All pupils in these years study English, Mathematics, Geography, History, Biology, Chemistry, Physics, Design and Technology, Drama, Art, Information Technology, Music, Physical Education, Religious Studies and a choice of two modern languages from French, German, Mandarin or Spanish. A programme of Personal and Social Education includes study skills and careers guidance. Pupils are setted on ability in the core subjects while in other subjects streaming applies.

Middle School (14–16 years): All pupils are prepared for the GCSE examinations. The School is an examining centre for a number of Boards, and this enables staff to select those syllabuses which they believe are most appropriate to the needs of their pupils. All pupils study English, Mathematics and the Sciences. A variable number of additional subjects are selected which enables the most able pupil to study up to eleven subjects. A brochure on GCSE courses is available on request.

Most students in the Sixth Form will study 4 AS Levels in the Lower Sixth from a choice of 28 subjects and continue with three of these to A Level in the Upper Sixth. Other permutations of AS and A Levels are possible to suit students of varying ability.

Monitoring Academic Progress. High priority is given to the monitoring of each pupil's progress and is the specific responsibility of the Heads of Year with a team of tutors. A combination of complementary short, medium and long-term recording systems are in use. This permits effective communication between teachers, and between the School and the parent.

Extracurricular Activities. The school offers a wide choice of sports, artistic, musical, dramatic, scientific, technical and literary activities to enhance students' lifelong learning. In total there are more than 80 such activities operating throughout the week. All staff and students are required to contribute to this programme. The major sports are rugby, football, cricket, tennis, athletics, hockey and netball. Sailing, fencing, judo, squash, basketball, climbing, shooting, polo and golf are but a few of the other options.

The School has a thriving CCF (Army, RAF and Navy sections) and encourages participation in The Duke of Edinburgh's Award scheme.

The self-confidence which can be acquired through participation in music and drama is immeasurable. Consequently, the school promotes participation by all in dramatic and musical events at a class, house and school level. An Arts Umbrella programme offers the opportunity for pupils to experience the theatrical and musical productions in London and other centres.

Admission. Pupils will be considered for admission to Langley at 10+, 11+, 13+ and into the Sixth Form. Entry may be possible at other levels when vacancies permit and is conditional on an interview followed by detailed and satisfactory school reports. At Sixth Form level, satisfactory performance in GCSE is required.

Scholarships. Scholarships may be awarded in each of the following categories: Academic, Art, Drama, Music, Sport and Design & Technology. We also offer an All Rounder Scholarship Award for academically bright students, who also have a flair in one or more of the non-academic areas – in Years 6, 7, 9 or 12.

Further details and a Scholarships application form may be obtained from the Headmaster's PA.

Fees per term (2016–2017). Years 6–13: Boarders £9,845, Weekly Boarders £8,213, Day Pupils £4,845.

Generous family and Forces discounts are offered.

Further Information is available on the school's website. Please contact the Admissions Department with any enquiries or to receive a school prospectus – admissions @langleyschool.co.uk or 01508 520210.

Charitable status. Langley School is a Registered Charity, number 311270. It exists to provide a sound education for boys and girls.

Council of Management:
Mrs Margaret Alston (*Chair of Governors*)
Mr P Sheppard (*Deputy Chairman*)

Lady Bacon	Mrs P Parker
Mr S Brown	Mr C Self, FRICS, IRRV
Mr D Coventry, CA Z	Mrs C Smith
Mr J Fuller	Mrs J Timmins
Mr A Harmer	Mr C Townsend
Mr R Hewitt	Mr P Foster

Headmaster: Mr Dominic Findlay, BA Ed, NPQH

Senior Deputy Headmaster: Mr Frank Butt, BEng Hons Dundee, PGCE Swansea

Deputy Headmaster (Years 10–11, Sport and Partnerships): Mr Andrew Walker, BA Hons QTS Brunel

Deputy Headmaster (Years 6–9): Mr Philip Oldroyd, BA, PGCE

Assistant Head, Student Welfare: Mr Jamie McRobert, BA Joint Hons, PGCE Swansea

Joint Heads of Sixth Form:
Mr Jon Kempton, BA Hons Bristol, PGCE Bristol
Mrs Leslie McRobert, BSc Hons

Mr Kai Barron, BA Hons, PGCE (*Head of Drama*)
Mr Tim Batchelor, BA Hons Nottingham, PGCE Homerton (*Head of Modern Languages*)
Ms Nikola Bodmer-Tripp, BA Hons UEA, PGCE (*Humanities*)

Mrs Joanna Butt, BA Hons Wolverhampton, Cert TEFL (*Head of EAL*)

Mr Frank Butt, BEng Hons Bath, PGCE Roehampton (*Deputy Head Academic, Design Technology*)

Mrs Alison Clark, MA Hons Dundee, PGCE Swansea (*2nd i/c English & KS4*)

Mr Paul Clark, BA Hons Northumbria, PGCE Sunderland (*Head of Yrs 6/7, Head of Business Studies, Economics*)

Mr Jamie Clegg, BSc Hons, PGCE Hull (*Head of Science*)

Dr Sarah Clegg, PhD Hull, PGCE UEA (*Science & Mathematics*)

Mr Chris Cooper, MGCI (*Pastoral Head of Yrs 8/9, Contingent Commander CCF*)

Ms Jenny Corser, BA Hons Elmira College, USA, PGCE (*KS3 English*)

Mrs Sarah Cossey, BA Hons PGCE, MA (*English, Literacy Coordinator*)

Mrs Clare Cracknell, BSc Hons, PGCE (*Head of Psychology*)

Mrs Angela Dain, Cert Ed, BEd Cambridge, MA, PhD UEA (*History, Philosophy & Ethics*)

Ms Laura Daniel, BSc, PGCE (*Mathematics*)

Mrs Mary Ellwood, BA Hons, PGCE (*Spanish, French*)

Mrs Chris Feakes, BEd Worcester (*Pastoral Head of Yrs 10/11, Mathematics*)

Mr Iain Felton, BA Hons Portsmouth, PGCE UEA (*Head of History, Government & Politics*)

Mr Tim Goodge, BSc Hons East London, PGCE (*Geography, Games*)

Mr Stuart Goodhew, MEng Hons, PGCE (*Head of Mathematics*)

Miss Andrea Hanzelyova, MA Preston QTS (*Duke of Edinburgh's Award Coordinator, KS3 Mathematics*)

Mrs Diana Harrington, BA Joint Hons, PGCE, RSA Dip TEFL (*French, i/c Spanish*)

Mr Derek Haysom, BSc Hons City University, Cert Ed (*Head of Computer Science*)

Mrs Laura Holmes, BA Hons, PGCEUEA (*French, Spanish*)

Mr Matt Holmes, BA, Cert Ed Brunel (*Design Technology, i/c Cricket, Games*)

Mr Stuart Hughes, BA Hons, QTS Nottingham Trent (*Design Technology*)

Mr David Innes, BA Hons Falmouth (*Head of ICT*)

Mr Jon Kempton, BA Hons Bristol, PGCE Bristol (*History, Joint Head of Sixth Form*)

Mrs Karen Lambert, BA Hons Sussex, PGCE Nottingham (*Head of Geography*)

Mr Mattthew Lutkins, BSc UEA, PGCE UEA (*Physics*)

Miss Louise Madeley, BSc Hons Hull Science (*Science*)

Mrs Tanya Martin, BA Hons, PGCE UEA (*English*)

Dr Aysin Mason, BSc, MSc, PhD, MET University, PGCE UEA (*Science, Head of Chemistry*)

Mr Craig McAllister, BA Hons, PGCE (*Head of Media Studies, English*)

Mr Philip McComish, BSc, PGCE (*Academic Head of Yrs 10/11, Head of Physics*)

Mrs Victoria McComish, BA Hons, DELTA Bath (*English as an Additional Language*)

Mrs Leslie McRobert, BSc Hons (*Biology, Joint Head of Sixth Form*)

Mr Jamie McRobert, BA Joint Hons, PGCE Swansea (*English, Head of PSHE, Boarding Master*)

Dr Craig Munday, BSc Hons, MMedSci, PhD (*Science, Head of Biology*)

Mr John Norton, BA Hons, MA (*Head of Design Technology*)

Mrs Gillian Ogden, PGCE, MA University of Western Ontario (*English as an Additional Language, English*)

Mr John Ogden, BA Hons, PGCE Lancashire (*Head of Art*)

Mrs Sam Oldfield, BSc Hons, PGCE (*Geography, Careers & Work Experience Coordinator*)

Mr Philip Parker, BSc Hons UEA, PGCE Cambridge Institute of Education (*Chemistry*)

Mr Stephen Read, LLB Cardiff (*Head of Law, Psychology, Head of Mancroft*)

Mrs Rebecca Robinson, BA Hons, MA (*i/c Photography, Art*)

Miss Emma Rowley, BSc Hons Durham, PGCE (*Deputy Head Yrs 6 & 7, Science, Biology*)

Mr John Schofield, PhD, PGCE, UEA (*Mathematics*)

Mr Leigh Sitch, BSc, MEd, PGCE (*Academic Head of Years 8/9, Chemistry*)

Mrs Jenni Skelton, BA Hons Oxford Brookes, PGCE Leeds (*i/c German, French*)

Mrs Angela Smith, BA Hons Aberystwyth, PGCE Cert TEFL (*English as an Additional Language*)

Mr Matt Vanston, BSc Hons Sheffield, PGCE UEA (*T&L Coordinator, 2nd i/c Geography*)

Mr Andrew Walker, BA Hons Bruncl, QTS (*Head of RE, Philosophy & Ethics*)

Mr Mike Webb, BA Hons Leeds, QTS (*Resident Tutor, Cover Teacher, MFL*)

Mr Rufus Wood, BA Hons, MPhil PGCE Liverpool (*Head of English*)

Mrs Moira Woolsey, Cert Ed Bath College of Educ (*Home Economics, PSHE*)

Mrs Abigail Yandell, BA Hons Newnham College Cambridge, PGCE, Cert TEFL (*English as an Additional Language*)

Mrs Helen Yates, BA Hons, PGCE (*Business Studies*)

Music:

Mrs Rebecca George-Broom, BA Hons, GTP (*Head of Music*)

Mr Rob White (*Head of St Giles, Music*)

Games:

Mr Tim Malone, BA Hons Lancaster, PGCE UEA (*Director of Sport, Head of Crome*)

Miss Sam Tea, BEd Hons (*Director of Physical Education, Head of Girls' Games*)

Mr Chris Cooper, MCGI (*Pastoral Head Years 8 & 9, BTEC Public Services, Games*)

Miss Emily Creed, BA Hons, PGCE (*Girls Games, Girls Ambassador Coordinator, Sport BTEc*)

Mr Chris Greenhall, BA, PGCE UC Wales (*Games, Head of Beauchamp*)

Mr Ryan Oakes, BSc (*Head of Strength, Conditioning and Performance Analysis*)

Mrs Claire Vinsen, BSc, PGCE M (*Girls Games, Sport BTEC*)

Lichfield Cathedral School

The Palace, The Close, Lichfield, Staffordshire WS13 7LH

Tel:	01543 306170
Fax:	01543 306176
email:	thepalace@lichfieldcathedralschool.com
website:	www.lichfieldcathedralschool.com

Age Range. 3–18.

Number of Pupils. 420 including 39 Cathedral chorister.

Fees per term (2016–2017). Pupils £1,660–£4,910; Instrumental Music Tuition: £245 per instrument per term.

Our mission is to be an internationally recognised school that serves its local area by creating an inclusive school community devoted to Christian ideals of learning, raising the aspirations of each of its members and fulfilling their potential in body, mind and spirit. Founded in 1942 principally as a boarding school for the choristers of Lichfield Cathedral, the school has since grown considerably and now provides all through education for boys and girls aged 3 to 18.

The ethos of the school is that of a community where Christian values are upheld and, whilst most pupils are members of the Church of England, children of other denominations and religions are welcomed.

The school occupies two main sites: the Junior Years are located 3½ miles north of Lichfield city centre in six acres of countryside at Longdon Green, while the Middle and Senior Years occupy several buildings in the Cathedral Close, one being the magnificent 17th century Palace, the home of the Bishops of Lichfield until 1952.

The link with the Cathedral remains strong with a twice-weekly school service, as well as concerts and services throughout the year. The 22 boy choristers (aged 7–13) and 17 girl choristers (aged 10–15) are supported by scholarships provided by the Cathedral Chapter and the school. Former choristers continue their choral training in Cantorum, the scholarship-based youth choir. Academic, art, drama, sport and music scholarships are available to internal and external students entering Year 7 (11+), Year 9 (13+) and Sixth Form.

Learning in the Early Years Foundation Stage is planned around half-termly topics and the children take part in a range of activities which are balanced between adult-led and child-initiated opportunities. Activities are carefully structured to challenge children, encouraging them to develop confidence and the skills needed to solve problems. The outdoor facilities offer children an exciting environment in which to explore and investigate, and we ensure children have the time for free play. Forest School is a popular element of the Junior Years curriculum that provides a holistic, individualised approach to outdoor learning, with a strong focus on developing self-esteem, confidence, communication skills and social and emotional awareness.

The spirit of intellectual enquiry is at the heart of teaching and learning at the school. Academic results are strong, particularly at GCSE and A Level. Throughout Key Stages 1 to 3, pupils follow a broad and balanced curriculum of English, Mathematics, Science, French, Spanish, German, Latin, History, Geography, Religious Studies, Art, Design, Music, Drama, Physical Education and Games and Personal, Social and Health Education. ICT skills are developed across every subject.

We offer a wide range of GCSE subjects, including Art and Design, Biology, Business Studies, Chemistry, Design Technology, Drama Studies, English Literature, English Language, French, Geography, German, History, Information and Communication Technology, Mathematics, Music, Physical Education, Physics, Product Design, Religious Studies and Spanish. The same subjects are offered at A Level with the addition of Computer Science, Economics, Further Mathematics, Government & Politics, Music Technology, Philosophy and Ethics, Psychology and Theatre Studies.

A co-curriculum of 'Beyond the Classroom' activities ensures students are well-rounded and gain valuable skills for higher education, employment and life outside school. Extra-curricular activities every day after school cover a wide range of subjects from chess to cooking and from Taekwondo to tennis. Several orchestras and ensembles are extremely active, as are the five main school choirs. The whole school ethical leadership programme helps pupils and students to develop both the life skills and the strength of character to succeed in the world beyond education.

All pupils have access to a rich variety of both residential and day trips as well as pupil exchanges, overseas expeditions and cultural immersion opportunities. Many are directly linked to the curriculum, but the benefits to pupils go far beyond the purely educational. The Duke of Edinburgh's Award scheme is thriving, along with Young Enterprise.

The school has a long-term association with the Waterloo Schools Project in Sierra Leone; Sixth Form students lead the fundraising efforts as well as visiting the project annually to help with the restoration and rebuilding of primary and secondary schools and the improvement of facilities in the neighbouring refugee camp.

Parents are welcome to contact the school for a tour and a meeting with the Head or to attend the any of the school Open Events held throughout the year.

Charitable status. Lichfield Cathedral School is a Registered Charity, number 1137481. It exists to provide education for boys and girls.

Governors:
Chairman: Mr C Hopkins, BA, MBA
Mrs C Abbott, BA
Mr H Bishop
The Very Revd A Dorber, BA, MTh, Dean of Lichfield
Mrs N Dawes, OBE
The Revd Canon P Hawkins
The Revd Canon P Holliday, BCom, MA, FCA
Mrs J Mason, PGCE
The Revd Canon Dr A M Moore, MA Cantab, PhD
Mr C Rickart, BA Hons, PGCE
Mrs C Tonks, BA

Head Teacher: **Mrs Susan Hannam**, BA Hons, MA, PGCE

Deputy Head: Mr A Harrison, BEd Hons QTS
Assistant Head, Pupil Support & Guidance: Mrs J Reynolds, BSc Hons, PGCE
Head of Early Years Foundation Stage: Mrs A M Stevens, BEd
Head of Junior Years: Mrs J M Churton, BSc Hons, PGCE
Key Stage 2 Coordinator: Mrs A Lomas, BEd Hons
Head of Years 7–9: Mr S Lane, BEd Hons
Head of Years 10–11: Mrs M Godwin, BA Hons, PGCE
Head of Sixth Form: Mr A Sherrington, LLB, PGCE

Mr S Daykin, BMus Hons, PG Dip Music (*Director of Music*)
Mr M Turner, BSc Hons, PGCE (*Head of Sport*)
Mrs J M Sedgley, BA Hons, PGCE (*Head of English*)
Mrs H Ghazireh, BSc Hons, MSc, PGCE (*Head of Mathematics*)
Mrs M Gardner, BSc Hons, PGCE (*Head of Science*)
Mrs C Farrell, Licence d'Anglais, PGCE (*Head of Modern Foreign Languages*)
Mrs I Johnson, BA Hons, PGCE (*Head of Religious Studies*)
Mrs B A Dunne, BA, PGCE (*Head of Drama*)
Mrs S E Whatley, BA Hons, PGCE (*Head of Art and Design*)
Mr J Gardiner, BA Hons, PGCE (*Head of Computing*)
Miss E Davies, BA Hons, PGCE (*Head of History*)
Mrs S Black, BSc Hons, PGCE (*Head of Geography*)

Residentiary Canon and School Chaplain: Canon A M Stead, BA, MA

Longridge Towers School

Longridge, Berwick-upon-Tweed, Northumberland TD15 2XQ

Tel: 01289 307584
Fax: 01289 302581

email: enquiries@lts.org.uk
website: www.lts.org.uk
Twitter: @LongridgeTowers

Motto: *Carpe Diem*

The school occupies a Victorian Mansion set in 80 acres of woodland in the beautiful Tweed Valley and enjoys excellent road and rail links with England and Scotland. Daily school bus services operate within a radius of 30 miles from the school.

Longridge Towers, refounded in 1983 under its founder and President, the late Lord Home of the Hirsel, has grown from 113 pupils to nearly 300 pupils. It is probably unique in offering the close personal relationships between pupils, staff and parents which creates a genuine 'family atmosphere'. The school has a reputation for turning out well-rounded and confident young people, the vast majority of whom continue their education at university.

Alongside the excellent academic results, the school offers many opportunities through its sporting and extra-curricular enrichment activities. All of these combine to give all pupils the chance to participate and acquire a variety of skills.

Sport figures strongly in the life of the pupils and many gain representative honours at county and national level in a variety of sports, such as rugby, hockey, cross-country running, athletics, tennis and cricket. Art, Music and Drama are also very popular and successful activities.

Entry. The school caters for a wide spectrum of abilities among its pupils who are taught in small classes. Special provision is made for the needs of pupils with mild dyslexia and for the small proportion of pupils for whom English is their second language.

Assessments upon entry to the Junior and Senior Departments in Mathematics and English are diagnostic and have no fixed pass mark.

The school is divided into 2 departments, Junior and Senior, and caters for pupils throughout their school career, from three to eighteen years. Pupils may enter at any age provided that a vacancy exists. Classes are small with less than 20 pupils per teaching set, reducing to about half this in the Sixth Form.

Activities. Longridge Towers is a school where the development of the pupils outside the academic sphere is considered to be vital. Every afternoon there is an extensive Enrichment programme offering a wide range of activities including: archery, rocket making, lacrosse, football, computer construction, dance, karate, judo, drama, kick boxing, creative writing, wildlife and gardening, young engineers, science club, debating, along with many others. The major team games are rugby, hockey, tennis, cross-country running, athletics and cricket. Many senior pupils participate in the Duke of Edinburgh's Award Scheme. The musical activities within the school are varied and numerous. There are five Choirs, two Orchestras and various instrumental groups. Almost half of the pupils take private instrumental lessons and the taking of grade examinations is encouraged. No visitor to the school could fail to be aware of the variety and excellence of the artwork on display which includes clay modelling and photography.

Public Examinations. Sixteen subjects are offered at GCSE level, including Physics, Chemistry and Biology and 19, including Economics, Psychology, Sports Studies and Drama, are offered in the Sixth Form at A or AS Level.

Parents receive reports half-yearly and three-weekly Grade Cards ensure that they are kept up to date about their children's progress.

Boarding. The Boarding House and pastoral care are in the hands of resident non-teaching house parents. There is medical and dental care. Pupils have access to telephones and email and may send or receive fax messages using the facilities in the school office. Boarders may attend on a weekly or termly basis from age 8 years onwards. At weekends the boarders participate in a wide range of activities.

Scholarships and Bursaries. Academic awards at various levels are available annually to pupils aged 9–14 and 16 (into Sixth Form). Music, Sports and All-Rounder Scholarships are also available to pupils aged 11–14 and 16.

Bursaries are available to children of serving members of the Armed Forces.

Bursaries are also available to pupils; the value of these is determined after consideration of a statement of parental income.

Fees per term (2016–2017). Full Boarders: £8,182 (Junior), £8,636 (Senior). Weekly Boarders: £6,238 (Junior), £6,706 (Senior). Day pupils: Government funded Nursery with charges for extra hours, £2,708 (Junior age 4–7), £3,776 (Junior age 7–11), £4,241 (Senior age 11–18).

Charitable status. Longridge Towers School is a Registered Charity, number 513534. It exists to provide an academic education for boys and girls.

Board of Governors:
Chairman: Mr J Smithson

Mr A Bell	Mr J A Houston
Mr A Birkett	Dr E Miller
Mr T Bramald	Mrs J McGregor
Mrs J Coats	Mr J Robertson
Mrs C Davies	

Headmaster: **Mr J C E Lee**, MA Hons, ACA, QTS

Deputy Head: Mr P Whitcombe, BSc, PGCE

Head of Junior Department: Mrs S Maddock, BEd

Senior Teachers:
Mrs I Cheer, BA, BSc, Cert HSC, Dip HSW (*Music, Pastoral, SENCO*)
Mr I Dempster, BEd (*History, Games, Examinations*)
Mr P Dodd, BEng, DIS, PGCE (*Mathematics, Operations*)

Teaching Staff:
Mr P Brooke, BA, PGCE (*English*)
Ms D Bryden, BEd (*Junior Department*)
Mrs S Bullen, BA, HLTA, FDEYP, QTS (*Reception/EYFS*)
Mr M Caddick, BA, PGCE (*German*)
Dr N Dalrymple, PhD, MLitt, BA, PGCE
Mr R Davie, BSc, PGCE (*Mathematics, Computing*)
Mrs A Gettins, BA (*Librarian, English*)
Mr R Glenn, BSc, PGCE (*ICT Coordinator*)
Mrs N Green, BA, PGCE (*EFL*)
Mr R Johnson, BA, MA, PGCE (*English*)
Mrs J Masey, BSc, PGCE (*Science*)
Mrs B Mayhew, BA, PGCE (*French/Spanish*)
Miss J McCalvey, BSc, PGCE (*Science*)
Mrs E McCorquodale, BA (*Art*)
Mr P McParland, BSc, MSc, PGCE (*Geography, Mathematics*)
Mrs L Monkman, BA, QTS (*Junior Department*)
Mr R Moscrop, BA, QTS (*Junior Department*)
Mrs L Peters, BEd (*Girls Games, Sports Studies*)
Miss K Phillips, BA (*Drama/Speech & Drama*)
Mr E Roney, BSc, MSc, PGCE
Mr P Rowett, BA (*RE, History, Geography*)
Mrs E Shaw, BA, PGCE (*Girls Games, Sports Studies*)
Mr A Skeen, BA, QTS (*Economics, Games*)
Mrs G Skeen, BSc, QTS (*Junior Department*)
Mr A Skipper, BSc, PGCE (*Physics*)
Mrs M Soutter, BEd
Mr A Westthorp, BEng, PGCE (*CDT, Computing*)
Mrs K Westthorp, MA, PGCE (*French*)
Mrs A Young (*Teaching Assistant Sport*)

Boarding Staff:
Mr G Hattle (*House Parent*)
Mrs L Patterson (*House Parent*)
Mrs M Robson (*Senior House Parent/Resident Matron*)
Mr M Short (*House Parent*)

Visiting Music Staff:
Mrs C Robb
Mr D Dougall
Mr G Kennedy
Mr R Cheer
Mrs M Rowland
Mrs J Warren
Mrs H Cattanach

Matron: Mrs M Hattle, RGN

Administration:
Bursar: Mr S Bankier, BA, FCMA
Assistant: Mrs L Mason
Head's Secretary: Mrs J Higgins
Marketing Manager: Mrs M Burns
Reception: Mrs C Jobson
Site Manager: Mr E Sutherland
Catering Manager: Mrs C Krause

Luckley House School

Luckley Road, Wokingham, Berkshire RG40 3EU
Tel: +44 (0)118 978 4175
Fax: +44 (0)118 977 0305
email: registrar@luckleyhouseschool.org
website: www.luckleyhouseschool.org
Twitter: @LuckleyHouse
Facebook: /LuckleyHouseSchool
LinkedIn: /Luckley House School

Luckley House School is a co-educational day and boarding school located in beautiful Berkshire. The current numbers are 225 pupils aged 11 to 18. The majority are day pupils, but approximately 30 are either full or weekly boarders. Pupils are selected on the basis of an entrance examination and interview. The main age of entry is at 11 years, 13 years and into the Sixth Form. Our in-house transport service covers a wide area, with late drop-offs for students wishing to stay for prep or after-class activities. We will be offering a transport service to West London from Sept 16, to provide an excellent option for families looking for weekly boarding away from the city.

Luckley was founded on its present site in 1918. In 1959 it amalgamated with Oakfield School, established in 1895 in the Lake District. Initially the school was administered by the Church Society but in 1969 it became an independent educational trust. A gracious Grade II listed Edwardian country house forms the centre of the school, which is on a 14-acre site with views of the countryside and woodlands.

We have high expectations for all our pupils, achieving excellent academic results and we are proud of our exceptional added-value record.

Luckley boasts fantastic facilities: the school is set in beautiful, safe and secure grounds, with modern classrooms, new science laboratories, contemporary boarding accommodation, a state-of-the-art music centre and stunning performing arts centre and conference theatre, well-equipped art studios and a large sports centre with extensive playing fields, tennis courts, fitness suite, climbing wall and fully-sprung dance floor.

Curriculum. The curriculum is broad and challenging with pupils taking 9.5 subjects for GCSE. A wide variety of A Level courses is offered and almost every student goes on to higher education as a preparation for careers in, for example, languages, medicine, engineering, law, business and design.

The school has a well-deserved reputation for Art, Drama, Music and Sport and offers a range of other activities including computing, debating, riding, The Duke of Edinburgh's Award scheme, Combined Cadet Force and Young Enterprise. Boarders and Day students are encouraged to join in this extensive programme of extra-curricular activities during the extended day slot from 4.00–5.30 pm. Instrumental lessons, Singing, Speech and Drama and Latin are offered as additional subjects.

Boarding. Weekly and flexi boarding offer the opportunity to experience the fun of boarding while keeping close links with home and avoiding long daily journeys. Full boarding, with an extensive weekend activity programme, can provide a stable and secure education for pupils whose schooling would otherwise be interrupted. Living accommodation for all boarders is situated in the Main House and Cornish House.

Ethos. Luckley House School is built on the Christian foundations of love and service. We enable our students to thrive in a secure and encouraging environment, thereby equipping each pupil to be resourceful and resilient, and ready to take on the challenges and opportunities that lie ahead.

Fees per term (2016–2017). Full Boarders £9,318; Weekly Boarders £8,636; Day Pupils £5,325.

Scholarships and Bursaries. Scholarships are awarded at 11+ on the results of the Entrance Examination and on entry to the Sixth Form. Music, Drama, Art and Sports scholarships are also available.

Means-tested Bursaries offering a reduction of up to 80% of fees are offered at Year 7 and Sixth Form entry. Forces Bursaries are also available.

Charitable status. Luckley House School Limited is a Registered Charity, number 309099. It offers day and boarding education for pupils on the basis of Christian values.

Governing Body:
Ms L Moor (*Chair*)

Reverend G Curry	Dr J Ledger
The Lady Farmer	Mr A Imlay
Dr V Houghton	Mr R Scurlock
Mr B Gardiner	Mrs C Tao

Head: **Mrs J Tudor**, BSc Hons UCL, MA Ed Open University

Bursar: Mr N Patterson, MSc
Deputy Head Pastoral (*Lower School*): Mrs S Hills, MSc London, BEd Hons Leeds
Deputy Head Academic: Mr I Vallance, BEd Bristol, MA Ed London South Bank
Deputy Head Pastoral (*Upper School*) *and Head of Sixth Form*: Mrs C Gilding-Brant, BA Brighton

Staff:
* *Head of Department/Subject*

English:
*Mrs C Rees, BA Hons Queen's Belfast, MA York, PGCE Bristol, MEd Bath
Mrs M Kempton, MA, BA Hons Reading, BEd Hons London, Cert TESOL, Dip RSA (*also EAL*)
Mrs E Simpson, BA Hons Portsmouth, PGCE Sussex

Mathematics:
*Miss R Duncan, BSc Hons Surrey
Mrs N Dawson, Higher Diploma Univ of Natal, South Africa
Mr I Vallance, BEd Bristol, MA Ed London South Bank
Miss J Warren, BSc Bath, PGCE, Dip LCM

Science:
Mr R Everatt, BSc Hons York (**Chemistry*, **Science*)
Mr S Bond, MA Oxon (**Physics*)
Dr R Jones, PhD Aberdeen (**Biology*)
Mrs J Tudor, BSc Hons UCL, MA Ed Open University
Mrs H Buck, BSc Hons York
Dr W Ross, PhD Imperial College London

Modern Languages:
*Mrs S Berns, BA Hons Reading
*Mrs E Samnée-O'Brien, BA Cologne University, Germany
Mrs M Lewin, BA Hons Institute of Linguists London
Miss H Ryan, BA Hons Southampton, MEd Exeter

Economics & Business Studies:
*Ms L Stephens, BA Hons York

Classics:
*Mrs D Gummery, BA Hons Southampton

Geography:
*Mr G Cromb, BSc Hons London
Miss A Caldwell, BSc Hons Hull, MSc London (*also Religious Studies & Careers*)

History:
Mr P Maynard, BA Hons Portsmouth

Psychology:
Mrs E Kermode, BA Hons University of South Africa

Religious Studies:
*Mrs K Matsuya, BA Hons Durham
Miss A Caldwell, BSc Hons Hull, MSc London

Information & Communication Technology:
Mrs C Bennett, BEd Hons Plymouth

Design & Technology (*Food & Nutrition & Textiles Technology*):
*Mrs S Gibson, BSc Home Economics
Mrs C McCafferty, HND CertEd MlfL QTLS

Art:
*Mr R Battrick
Mrs J Fogarty, BA Hons London
Mrs A Venables

Drama & Theatre Studies:
*Mrs J Cordery, Dip Musical Theatre
Mrs J Harris
Mr I Cullen (*Speech & Drama*)

Music:
Mrs J Ellwood, GRSM Hons, Dip RCM, PGCA Perf RCM, QTS Reading

Physical Education:
*Miss K Dobney, BA Hons Brighton
Miss C Edgerley, BA Brighton
Mrs S Hills, MSc London, BEd Hons Leeds Polytechnic (*also SEN*)
Miss J Cumming, BA Hons Carmarthen

Finance Bursar: Mrs R Stevens, BA Hons, ACA
Registrar: Mrs Claire Bell
School Secretary: Mrs J Leatherby
Headmistress's PA: Mrs N Hall, CIPD
School Nursing Sister: Mrs J Craven
Marketing, Admissions & Development Manager: Mrs D Ennis, Dip CIM
ICT Manager: Mr B Clarke

LVS Ascot

London Road, Ascot, Berkshire SL5 8DR
Tel: 01344 882770
email: registrar@lvs.ascot.sch.uk
website: www.lvs.ascot.sch.uk
Twitter: @lvsascot
Facebook: /LVSAscot

LVS Ascot is a non-selective, co-educational day and boarding school of around 870 pupils aged 4–18. It is an all-through school so pupils can begin their school career at LVS Ascot at age 4 and remain there until they complete Sixth Form.

In 2016 LVS Ascot recorded its highest ever A Level pass rate (99.2%), and achieved an increase in GCSE A*–C grades to 83.8% as nationally the figure saw its sharpest ever drop to 66.9%.

Numbers. Junior School 170, Senior School 650 (including 170 in Sixth Form), boarding approx 165.

Organisation. Pupils aged 4 to 11 (Years R to 6) are taught in the Junior School, in separate classes each with a class teacher. Houses are used for sports and other competitions. Junior School pupils may board from Year 3 (age 7) and join a mixed House (Bass House), which is an integral part of the Junior School buildings.

Senior School pupils, aged 11 to 18 (Years 7 to 13), are placed in tutor groups and a school House, with a tutor who monitors their pastoral care and oversees their academic performance. Students are taught in ability groups with a maximum class size of 20. Boarders are accommodated in four separate boarding Houses, each supervised by Housemasters/mistresses: Bass (Junior House) is mixed for pupils from Year 3 to Year 7; Carlsberg (girls' House) for pupils from Year 8 to Year 11; Guinness (boys' House) for pupils from Year 8 to Year 11; Gilbey (mixed Sixth Form House) for pupils in Years 12 and 13.

Location. LVS Ascot is north of the A329, close to Ascot Racecourse and Royal Windsor. The school is easily accessible from the M3, M4 and M25 motorways as well as Heathrow and Gatwick airports. The school bus service connects with trains at Ascot Station, as well many surrounding towns within a 20 miles radius.

Facilities. LVS Ascot is a modern day and boarding school in the UK. The purpose-built facilities, set in 26 acres of landscaped grounds, include: boarding accommodation and classroom blocks, a sports centre, all-weather pitch, indoor swimming pool, fully-equipped theatre and a music technology suite. LVS Ascot hosts over five-hundred networked computer workstations, with every classroom equipped with ICT resources for digital and interactive learning. Wireless networking provides additional facilities for centrally-managed student laptops, eBooks and other devices in a secure environment. There is a dedicated Sixth Form Centre, and a Learning Resource Centre, that has an extensive range of books and journals.

Curriculum. The curriculum is broad and based on the national curriculum "plus". Pupils follow a common core curriculum of English, Mathematics, Science, one/two foreign languages, plus PE and PSHE. Science is taught as separate subjects. At GCSE, students select their choices from: Business Studies, Technology, Art & Design, Geography, History, Food Technology, Music, Drama, Media Studies, Economics, Physical Education, Computer Science, Spanish, German or French.

A wide range of A Level and vocational options are provided, including Mathematics, Physics, Chemistry, Biology, Music, Geography, History, Economics, Business Studies, English, Art & Design, Theatre Studies, Design & Technology, Media Studies, Photography, Psychology, French, Spanish, German, ICT, Computer Studies, Engineering and Physical Education.

Sport. The school has superb indoor and outdoor facilities with a large Sports Hall, dance studio with ballet bars, a 25-metre swimming pool and a well-equipped gym as well as rugby, football and hockey pitches, tennis courts and an all-weather pitch. The school has achieved considerable success in providing County, Regional and National standard players in a wide range of sports. Whilst all pupils play team games such as Rugby, Football, Cricket, Hockey, Tennis, Netball, Basketball or Athletics in their early years, the range of options widens as pupils become older to encourage fitness for life, with opportunities such as skiing, skating, polo, fencing and playing squash.

Clubs and Activities. LVS Ascot is an accredited Duke of Edinburgh's Award training centre and runs a vibrant and popular award scheme. Alongside this there is a range of co-curricular activities such as music ensembles, newspaper club, riding, canoeing, rowing, climbing, cookery, animation and film club. In September 2015 LVS Ascot Junior School introduced a range of 25 co-curricular after-school clubs.

Admissions. There is no entrance examination; reports are requested from a student's current school. All students are interviewed prior to acceptance. Prospective students and their families are welcome to visit the school. Personal tours can also be arranged by appointment.

Open Days 2016–2017.
Saturday 5th November 2016: Sixth Form Tour
Saturday 19th November 2016: Reception Class Tour
Wednesday 8th February 2017: Junior School & Senior School Open Morning
Saturday 18th March 2017: Senior School & Sixth Form Tour
Saturday 22nd April 2017: Junior School Tour
Tuesday 9th May 2017: Junior School & Senior School Open Morning

Fees per term (2016–2017). Infants £3,176; Junior: £3,804 (Day), £8,128 (Boarding); Senior: £5,395 (Day), £9,610 (Full/Weekly Boarding); Sixth Form: £5,693 (Day), £10,002 (Full/Weekly Boarding).

Scholarships and Bursaries. Academic, Music, Art, Drama, Sport Scholarships are available at Year 7 entry and various Scholarships are available for entry to the Sixth Form (Year 12).

Fee discounts and Bursaries are available to assist parents working in the Licensed Drinks Trade, MoD and British Diplomats. Third child discount is also available.

Charitable status. The Society of Licensed Victuallers is a Registered Charity, number 230011. It exists to provide education for boys and girls.

Patron: Her Majesty The Queen

Director of Education: Mr I Mullins, BEd Hons, MSc, MBIM

School Principal: Mrs C Cunniffe, BA Hons, MMus, MBA

Deputy Head/Academic: Mr C Davis, BSc Hons, PGCE

Deputy Head/Pastoral: Mr C Bingham, BA Hons, PGCE

Deputy Head/Head of Sixth Form: Dr P Hodges, PhD, BSc, MSc, PGCE

Deputy Head Academic/Development & Co-curricular: Mr C Jenkins, BA Hons, PGCE

Deputy Head/Teaching & Learning: Mr B Padrick, BA, MTS Hons

Housemasters/mistresses:

Boarding Houses:
Housemaster of Bass: Mr J Rudkin, MEd, BA, PGCE
Assistant HM of Bass: Mr T Wyndham-Smith
Housemistress of Carlsberg: Mrs S Alder, HLTA
Assistant HM of Carlsberg: Miss J Atkinson, BSc
Housemaster of Gilbey: Mr T Jarrett, MA, PGCE
Assistant HM of Gilbey: Mr W Truter, BSc, PGCE
Housemasters of Guinness: Mr J Wilder, FASC, BMus Hons, PGCE & Mr B Hunt, BSc Hons, PGCE
Assistant HM of Guinness: Mr D Bury, BA, MEd

Day Houses:
Housemaster of Bell's: Mr B McMurray, BSc Hons, PGCE
Housemistress of Courage: Mrs T Bason, BA, PGCE
Housemistress of Whitbread: Mrs C Robinson, MA

Designated Safeguarding Leads:
Mr C Bingham, BA Hons, PGCE (*Senior School*)
Mrs L Rawlinson, BEd Hons (*Junior School*)

Child Protection Officers:
Mrs R Sandford, BA Hons
Mrs S Litherland, BA Hons, PGCE

Heads of Departments:

Art and Design: Mrs S Litherland, BA Hons, PGCE
Business Studies: Mr P Doyle, MA
Head of Design Technology: Mrs C Robinson, MA
Drama: Mrs G Windsor, BA Hons, PGCE
English and Media Studies: Ms S Quant, BA Hons, MA, PGCE
Additional Learning Needs (ALN): Mrs J Pearce, BA Hons, PGCE
Geography: Mrs D Finch, BA Hons
History: Mr A Kydd, BA Hons, PGCE
Information Technology: Mrs S Featherstone-Clark, BA Hons
Law: Mr K Towl, LLB, PGCE
Mathematics: Mr R Bignell, MBA, BSc Hons
Modern Foreign Languages: Mr J Nye, BSc, PGCE, MA
Director of Music: Mr D Gravett, BSc Hons
Director of Sport: Mr J Percy, BSc
Psychology: Mr J Paterson, BSc Hons
Philosophy and Religion: Mr B Padrick, BA
Science: Mrs S Catlin, BSc, PGCE (*also Head of Biology*)
Learning Resource Centre: Mrs E Keeler, MA Hons, PG Cert, MCLIP

Junior School:
Senior Master: Mr E Dennis, BA, PGCE
Assistant Head of Junior School: Mrs L Rawlinson, BEd Hons

Administrative Staff:
Examinations Officer: Mrs L Ingles, BEng Hons
Principal's PA: Mrs L Humphreys
Marketing: Mrs P Smith
Registrar: Mrs M Buttimer
Senior School Secretaries: Miss H Austin, Mrs L Reddy
Senior School Reception: Mrs A Davies
Senior Master of Junior School's PA: Mrs D Pearce

Milton Abbey School

Blandford Forum, Dorset DT11 0BZ
Tel: 01258 880484
email: admissions@miltonabbey.co.uk
website: www.miltonabbey.co.uk
Twitter: @MiltonAbbey
Facebook: @MiltonAbbeySchool

Foundation. Milton Abbey was founded in 1954 and comprises 240 pupils. From September 2012 the School became fully co-educational.

Milton Abbey has a unique ability to deliver a bespoke education. We tailor each pupil's education to make the most of their individual skills and talents in a way which nurtures and cultivates their natural abilities so that they can achieve the best possible results, both inside and outside the classroom.

Our School promotes individuality and the pursuit of personal strengths and preferences; care, guidance and carefully targeted support in learning is available wherever required, resulting in greater confidence and enhanced self-esteem. We inspire pride in pupils' individual work, whether in sport, academia, the creative arts or in our range of outdoor and practical subjects. Milton Abbey offers parallel learning pathways to a common destination, giving pupils the opportunity to study GCSEs and A Levels alongside the widest range of vocational subjects in the independent schools sector.

Our small size allows for a great involvement in School life and greater opportunity for pupils to represent the School and to master a chosen subject or activity. Lasting and fulfilling friendships are forged, and everyone has the chance to get to know one another. Class sizes are small (averaging eight for the Sixth Form and twelve for the Lower School) so no one is overlooked or left behind.

Situation. Our picturesque grounds and stunning surroundings offer space yet safety and security, and provide an inspirational countryside setting for our pupils. The Dorset towns of Blandford and Dorchester are located nearby and are conveniently situated for weekend outings and activities, along with the coastal towns of Weymouth, Poole and Bournemouth.

Buildings. The two remaining buildings of the Monastery are the Great Abbey, which is now the School Chapel, and the Abbot's Hall around which a Georgian mansion was built by the Earl of Dorchester in 1770. Outside the mansion house, the modern facilities which are on a par with those of a much larger school including contemporary boarding houses, a Music school, Art Studio, Pottery, Technology/ Computer building, 370-seat theatre, IT suite, School Farm, all-weather pitch, indoor heated 25-metre pool, cricket pavilion, Design Technology centre and Library.

Organisation. Milton Abbey is proud of its full-boarding status and of the comprehensive academic and extracurricular provision, including a full weekend programme. Boarding pupils live at the School throughout the week and over weekends during term time, and go home for a long weekend (or exeat) twice a term, half term and holidays. The School runs a comprehensive transport service to London, Hampshire, Sussex, Kent, Wiltshire, Gloucestershire, Shropshire, Somerset and Devon, as well as to major airports and train stations.

On joining the School, every boarding pupil is assigned to a House; a close-knit community where year groups are fully integrated and where every pupil is inspired to feel that they belong. Each House has a team of resident staff and matrons to help provide a home-from-home environment. Milton Abbey has five boarding Houses: Athelstan, Damer, Hambro, Hodgkinson, and Tregonwell.

Our provision is all-encompassing and centers around encouraging every pupil to lead a fulfilling and rewarding life during their time at Milton Abbey. Hard work and academic determination are balanced with a comprehensive programme of activities and social events. Pupils are encouraged to take an active role in School life; our Heads of School and Heads of Houses provide role models and guidance to younger pupils, and have a key role in the running of the School.

Curriculum. All pupils follow a broad and balanced curriculum up to GCSE. A pupil is setted separately in most subjects, enabling him or her to work towards academic goals at a comfortable pace. Most GCSE subjects are taken over Years 10 and 11. New Pupils wishing to enter the Sixth Form must have an interview with the Headmaster. The Sixth Form offers a range of academic courses which incorporates traditional A Levels, vocational BTECs and top-up GCSEs.

Music. A wide variety of individual tuition is available and in singing. With five choirs, singing is a strong and popular part of school life.

Clubs and Societies. We run a comprehensive programme of engaging and rewarding extracurricular activities which enhance pupils' experience of living and learning at Milton Abbey. Activities for both Lower School and Sixth Form pupils take place twice a week on Tuesday and Thursday afternoons and cater for a wide range of interests. From Leith's cookery courses to mechanics, and textiles to School Farm Club, there is something for all year groups to enjoy. In addition, there is a termly programme of fun and competitive inter-House activities for pupils to take part in, including sports matches, debating tournaments, music and drama competitions, quiz nights and pizza making.

The School's thriving CCF contingent has Royal Navy, Army and Royal Air Force sections, and enjoys close links with service establishments in the area. There are regular camps in the holidays, as well as expeditions at home and abroad. Most weekends offer an opportunity for a pupil to choose from caving, climbing, sailing, windsurfing and canoeing. In their first year in school, pupils undertake a range of activities every Wednesday afternoon, designed to broaden their spectrum of interest. These and many other activities positively support our aspiration to become a member of the Round Square organisation and form the pillars of the Round Square IDEALS (Internationalism, Democracy, Environment, Adventure, Leadership, Service).

Games. Michaelmas Term: Rugby, Football and Hockey. Lent Term: Hockey, Netball, Lacrosse and Cross Country. Summer Term: Cricket, Athletics, Dinghy Sailing and Racing in Portland Harbour, Tennis and Rounders. All year round: Swimming, Squash, Rifle Shooting, Basketball, Golf, Polo, Riding, Canoeing and Clay Pigeon Shooting.

Admission. Most pupils join the School at 13+ in the Third Form/Year 9, having passed Common Entrance exams in the Summer Term before entry. Level 1 papers at Common Entrance are accepted but pupils may be asked to come for a pre-assessment during Year 8. Milton Abbey welcomes those who have not been prepared for Common Entrance, asking pupils to sit our own entry papers in English and Maths. A satisfactory report from the pupil's current school will also be required.

Those with Special Educational Needs will be asked to come for pre-assessment with the Head of Learning Support three to four terms before entry, to make sure that the School can offer them the correct level of support.

If space is available, it may be possible to join Year 10 following an interview with the Headmaster, the completion of the School's entrance papers and a satisfactory report from the pupil's current school.

For entry into the Sixth Form, candidates attend an assessment day where they will be interviewed by the Headmaster, a Housemaster/Housemistress and the Director of Studies, as well as completing an assessment paper. Candidates should have a good GCSE pass in each of the subjects he or she is intending to take for A Level and a satisfactory report from their current school.

Fees per term (2016–2017). Boarding £11,780, Day £5,965.

Scholarships. Several Scholarships are awarded annually: Academic scholarships (held during the Lent Term); Music, Drama, Art, DT, Sailing and Sport scholarships (held during the Lent Term). Candidates must be under 14 on 1 September. Scholarships also awarded at Sixth Form entry level. Full particulars from the Admissions Office. Bursaries may also be considered in cases of need.

Charitable status. The Council of Milton Abbey School Limited is a Registered Charity, number 306318. It is a charitable Trust for secondary education.

Visitor: Revd C W Mitchell-Innes, MA

Governors:
Chairman: P W McGrath, MA, MW [OM]
C Bigham, BA Hons
K Butler, MA Hons
Col O J H Chamberlain, QVRM, TD, DL [OM]
A Harvey, BA Hons, PGCE [OM]
Mrs S Russell, LLB
M P Sherwin, BSc
J H Simm, MA, FCA, JP
Mrs L J F Sunnucks, BA
S J Young, MC, JP, FRICS, DL

[OM] *Old Miltonian*

Bursar and Clerk to the Governors: Julian Litchfield, FCIPD

Headmaster: Magnus Bashaarat, MA

Deputy Head: Matthew Way, BSc Hons, MEd
Assistant Head (*Teaching and Learning*): Natalie Perry, BSc Hons, MSc
Assistant Head (*Tutoring*): Chris Barnes, BA Hons
Assistant Head (*Pupil Welfare*): Ruth Butler, BA Hons
Assistant Head (*Round Square*): Matthew Porter, BA Hons
Bursar: Julian Litchfield, FCIPD
Head of Admissions: Claire Low

Housemasters:
Athelstan: Will Fraser, MA
Damer: Matthew Porter, BA Hons
Hambro: Henry Stoot, BA Hons
Hodgkinson: Liz Alway, BA Hons
Tregonwell: Fergus Wilson, BSc

Head of Upper School Studies, Director of UCAS & Careers: Joshua Bradbury, BA, MA, PhD, PGCE
Examinations Officer: Rachael McNulty, HND
SENCO: Ruth Dal Din, BSc
Head of PSHE: Ruth Butler, BA Hons
Gifted & Talented Coordinator: Philip Morrow, MA, CELTA
Chaplain: Jo Davis, BA Hons, MTh, PG Cert
Library Manager: Maggie Butler, BA Hons, TEFL
Director of Sport, Ben Lawes, BSc Hons

* *Head of Department*

Art & Photography:
*Sara Burton, BA Hons
Kate Clarkson, BA Hons
Sarah Church, BA Hons, PGCE (*History of Art*)
Elizabeth Barnes, BA Hons

Business Studies/Economics:
*Rebecca Barton, BSc Hons
Chris Barnes, BA Hons

Communication Studies:
Joshua Bradbury, BA, MA, PhD, PGCE

Design & Technology:
*James Ratcliffe, BA (*Director of Design*)
Simon Power, BA Hons
Sukey Fenwick, BA Hons

Drama:
Liz Bemment, BA (*Director of Drama*)
Suzanne Barker, BA Hons
Louisa Thompson (*Theatre Manager*)

English & Communication Studies:
Kelly Lawrence, BA Hons (*Head of Department*)
Craig Lucas, BA Hons
Joshua Bradbury, BA, MA, PhD, PGCE
Will Fraser, MA
Victoria Bendall, BA Hons

Enrichment:
Ruth Butler, BA Hons (*Head of PSHE*)

Geography:
*Henry Stoot, BA Hons
Nick Batchelor, BSc Hons

History & Politics:
*Chris Barnes, BA Hons
Matthew Porter, BA Hons
Matthew Way, BSc Hons, MEd

Information Technology:
Angela Giesens, BSc Hons (*Director of ICT*)
James Ratcliffe, BA

Learning Support:
*Ruth Dal Din, BSc
David Baney, BEd Hons
James Burlton, MA
Hayley Chipman, BA Hons
Helen Ashwell, BA Hons, TESOL
Ginny Catarinella
Sally Dean
Sarah Isard, HND
Catherine Molland, HND
Liz Pope
Polly Hughes

Mathematics:
*Michael Sharp, BA, MA, Cert Ed
Nicola Burg, BSc Hons
Richard Curren, BSc Hons, MSc
Andrew Watson, BA

Modern Languages:
*Christophe Douchet, Maîtrise, DP, LPC, PGCE
Hugo Mieville, BA, MA, Dip EdMan
Philip Morrow, MA, CELTA (*Able, Gifted and Talented Coordinator*)

Music:
*Shaun Pirttijarvi, BA Hons, PGCE, FMAOS
Darren Jones (*Music Technology*)
Faye Eldret, BMus Hons
Alana Brook, BA (*Organ Scholar*)
Dan Baker, BSc (*Bass Guitar, Jazz Piano*)
Paul Beavis (*Percussion*)
Martin Ings, MA, ARCM (*Trumpet, Horn*)
Bob Walker (*Bagpipes*)
Richard Hall, BA, PhD (*Piano*)
Jackie Hayer (*Woodwind*)

Religious Studies:
*Gabriella Burchell, BA Hons
Jo Davis, BA Hons, MTh, PG Cert

Science:
*Natalie Perry, BSc Hons, MSc
Daniel Roberts, BSc (*Applied Science, Biology*)
Giles Vigar BEng Hons (*Physics*)
Lizzie Barnes, BSc (*Biology, Chemistry*)
Fergus Wilson, BSc (*Biology*)
Robert Pay (*Laboratory Technician*)
Janet Collins (*Laboratory Technician*)

Vocational Studies:

Countryside Management and Equine Management:
Elisabeth Carr, BSc Hons (*Director of Land Based Studies*)

Jordan Williams, FdScm, BSc
Lydia Lee, DTLLS
Kevin Hurst (*Countryside Management Technician*)
Gail Marsh (*Equine Technician*)

Creative Media:
Angela Giesens, BSc Hons, MA
Joshua Bradby, BA, MA, PhD
James Ratcliffe

Enterprise and Entrepreneurship:
Rebecca Barton, BSc Hons, MA
Chris Barnes, BA Hons
Emma Hack, BA Hons

Hospitality:
*Leionie Monaghan, BA
Elka Charlton
Elizabeth Askew

BTEC Sport:
*Fran Porter, BSc
Ben Alway, BSc
Erin Clare Cassidy, BA
Sam Green, MSc
Ben Lawes, BSc Hons
Charlotte Ogle, BA Hons
Josh Ovey, BSc Hons
Sam Drewitt, BA Hons
Chris Hill

Myddelton College

Peakes Lane, Denbigh, North Wales LL16 3EN
Tel: +44 (0)1745 472201
email: admissions@myddeltoncollege.com
website: www.myddeltoncollege.com
Twitter: @MyddeltonCol
Facebook: /MyddeltonCollege

Age Range. 11–18.
Number in School. 83 pupils.
More than just an Education. "Being a great school requires more than just providing the best possible education, it requires a different view of what education is". At Myddelton College, we take the broadest possible view of education and our students, whether boarders or day students, are exposed to a wide range of activities that encompass the whole experience of what it means to be human. Yes, there are the academic subjects there, with high standards and even higher expectations of success (because a strong academic background is a necessity in today's global community), but beyond that, a Myddelton College student will be expected to develop interests in sporting, creative, aesthetic and cultural areas. But alongside that, there is the need for breadth and balance – which is why the education provided at Myddelton includes the extra activities, and why every student is expected to be involved in all aspects of College life.

Myddelton College is about providing a pastoral care structure that goes beyond basic welfare. At Myddelton we focus on developing and maturing the individual, both emotionally and intellectually. Myddelton College students will have an international perspective as members of the global village. Vitally, it is about preparing young people for life beyond College: helping them gain access to their chosen university, helping them to be fully prepared for the life they will lead beyond, and then equipping them to become suitably qualified and confident to lead, to serve, to be a good influence – wherever life takes them.

21st Century Learning. Upon joining us, all students at Myddelton College will be provided with a Microsoft Win-

dows touch screen device. Using these devices as part of their everyday work and learning will become second nature to our students, as we help to prepare them for life after school. We place a huge importance on the use of technology in order to offer a richer and more realistic 21st century experience for our students.

As a Microsoft Global Showcase school, we are proud to be innovators in education, building a 21st century curriculum, so that our students leave with the skills required to be successful, whatever the future holds. With 5 Microsoft Innovative Educator Experts on staff, we know that the use of technology is the very best it can be. The fact that our curriculum is seen as an example of the very best use of technology, globally, is a real strength.

Learning through the Outdoors. Our 'Learning through the Outdoors Programme' will enable all students to undertake a wide range of activities designed to help them develop the leadership skills that collaboration and teamwork in the physical environment provide. Whether that's through joining our Cadet Force, the Duke of Edinburgh's Award programme or training with our triathlon team, our students will learn the skills that will see them through their lives.

Physical sports should encourage a young person to extend themselves and see themselves as a physical being – by building a programme that includes climbing, caving, orienteering and triathlon sports, young people have a wider exposure to what they are capable of. Alongside this, a broad, general and inclusive fitness programme, supported by measurable, observable and repeatable results, is a core part of our provision. This programme prepares the young people for any physical contingency – not only for the unknown but for the unknowable, too.

Tailored University Preparation. Our Researcher in Residence, Richard Crowther, is currently undertaking a PhD at Cambridge University, having obtained a Masters at Oxford. He will be ensuring that all the teachers at Myddelton have access to the very latest global research in terms of what works best in education, working alongside them to ensure that the students get taught in the very best way possible.

He will primarily bridge the gap between classroom practice and academic research but will also be working on collaborating with universities, forming strategic partnerships and strengthening the school's links to Oxbridge and Russell Group Universities.

Sixth Form. Our rigorous Sixth Form curriculum will provide the opportunity to study a wide variety of Cambridge International A Levels subjects valued by high performing universities and employers alike. All taught by a highly qualified and experienced team of subject specialist in small class sizes. Believing it is important for students to present more than a suite of examination results, we offer a broad range of enrichment courses, enhanced by our extensive facilities.

There is a range of full and weekly boarding options.

Fees per term (2016–2017). UK/Domestic Students: Day Pupils £1,700–£3,333 (£4,000 for Upper School); Weekly Boarders £5,150–£9,366; Full Boarders £5,950–£10,700.

Reductions are made in fees of second and subsequent siblings. Bursaries are available for children whose parents or guardians are key workers or from Forces families. There are scholarships for academic, sporting, music, drama, artistic or technological excellence. The college welcomes applications from pupils whose parents cannot afford the fees in full or in part. The college offers a wide range of discretionary and means-tested bursaries each year to pupils.

A prospectus and further details may be obtained from the UK Admissions Manager: admissions@myddelton college.com.

CEO/Executive Headmaster: **Andy Howard**, BSc, MA, NPQH

Strategic Planning Group:
Head of Academic: Mark Roberts, BSc, PGCE
Head of Student Wellbeing: (*to be appointed*)
Head of 21st Century Technology: Stuart Ayres, BSc, MSc
Operations Manager: Paul Gibson

Operational Group:
Head of English: (*to be appointed*)
Head of Mathematics: Daniel Napper, BSc Hons, PGCE
Head of Science: David Kynes, MSc, PGCE
Head of Outdoor Learning: Natalie Churchill, BSc Hons, PGCE
Researcher in Residence/University Admissions Tutor: Richard Crowther, BA Hons, QTS, MSc Oxon
UK Admissions Manager: Rebecca Davies
Head of Student Support: Joanna Davies

Teaching Staff:
English: Ruby Rehan-Williams, BA, PGCE
Art/Technology: Gail Jones, PGCE
Religious Studies/Philosophy: Fiona Williamson MA, PGDE
History: Joanne Orchard, BA Hons, PGCE
Physics: (*to appointed*)
Biology: Alicia Davies, MSc, PGCE
Maths: Peter English
Spanish: Laura Harrhy, BA Hons, PGCE
Business Studies/Economics: Edie Shemilt-Griffiths, BA Hons, PGCE

Support Staff:
Finance Assistant: Sue Downes
Alumni Liaison Officer: Wendy Grey-Lloyd
College Secretary: Nicola Evans

Grounds & Maintenance Staff:
Mark Pierce
Phil Jones
Johnny White

Newcastle School for Boys

Senior School:
34 The Grove, Gosforth, Newcastle-upon-Tyne NE3 1NH
Tel: 0191 255 9300
Fax: 0191 213 0973
email: enquiries@newcastleschool.co.uk

Junior School:
30 West Avenue, Gosforth, Newcastle-upon-Tyne NE3 4ES
Tel: 0191 255 9300
Fax: 0191 213 1105
email: info@newcastleschool.co.uk

website: www.newcastleschool.co.uk

Age Range. 3–18.
Number of Boys. 400.
Fees per term (2016–2017). £2,870 (Reception), £3,380 (Years 1–2), £3,485 (Years 3–6), £4,270 (Year 7 and above).

Newcastle School for Boys is now established as the only independent school in the north east providing continuous education for boys from ages 3 to 18. Situated on three sites in Gosforth, Newcastle-upon-Tyne, the Senior School site on The Grove covers 5 acres of playing fields and buildings that currently house Years 7 to 13. Our Junior School is housed on nearby sites on West Avenue (Juniors) and North Avenue (Infants). The School currently has 393 pupils on role from Nursery to Year 13.

The academic curriculum starts in the Infants and provides boys with opportunities for stretch and challenge from the outset. This leads through the Juniors to GCSE and A Level qualifications in a wide range of disciplines at the Senior School.

Pastoral care is outstanding throughout the school and boys receive plenty of individual attention so that they grow in confidence and independence.

Newcastle School for Boys believes strongly in enhancing learning beyond the classroom and runs an extensive trips and visits programme with great emphasis being placed on this in the junior and infant departments. Residential and day visits are offered to all pupils from age 5 onwards and culminate in major overseas trips and Duke of Edinburgh's Gold Award expeditions in the Sixth Form.

Senior School. The Senior School starts at Year 7 (11+) and runs through to Year 13 (18+).

We generally run two classes per year group and offer an enhanced curriculum leading up to GCSE, where most boys sit 10 subjects. The Senior School provides an extensive co-curricular programme of music, drama and a wide range of sports, including a number of major overseas trips. The School enhances its sporting provision through the use of a number of excellent local facilities including at South Northumberland Cricket Club and Northern Rugby Club.

Sixth Form. The School has established a successful and growing Sixth Form offering students a wide choice from a traditional AS and A Level structure. The Sixth Form provides the learning and support the boys need to achieve their best possible academic and personal outcomes.

Entrance and Scholarship Examinations are offered in January for boys entering Year 7 (11+), Year 9 (13+) and Year 12 (16+). Entry at other points is possible following a full academic assessment and interview.

Junior School. The well-established Nursery and Infant Department is housed in spacious accommodation to the west of Gosforth High Street and lays the foundations for everything which is to follow. A happy and safe environment is provided, where self-esteem and self-confidence are paramount. Throughout the Foundation Stage and Key Stage 1, the curriculum is a blend of the traditional and the innovative, and is designed to balance the need for adventure and fun, while maintaining progress in numeracy and literacy.

Breakfast club and after-school clubs and activities provide full 'wrap-around' care,

In the Junior Department (Years 3–6), the learning environment is tailored to the needs of the younger boys, taking into account their energy and enthusiasm for challenge and discovery. The boys are provided with opportunities to develop their individual academic talents and to pursue their creative goals. Excellence is also pursued in the sporting arena where boys have opportunities including soccer, rugby, cricket, golf and fencing.

Regular drama performances and musical productions encourage teamwork and build confidence from an early age.

Charitable status. Newcastle School for Boys is a Registered Charity, number 503975.

Chairman of Governors: Dr N Lloyd-Jones, MBBS, MRCGP, LLB, LLM

Headmaster: **D J Tickner**, BA, MEd

Deputy Head: G Hallam, BSc

Deputy Head: A Newman, BA

Head of Sixth Form: Mrs S Rourke

Head of Juniors: S Asker, BA

Head of Infants: Mrs S G P Woosnam, BEd

Bursar: Mrs C Dobson, FCCA

Ockbrook School
Derby

The Settlement, Ockbrook, Derbyshire DE72 3RJ

Tel: 01332 673532
email: enquiries@ockbrooksch.co.uk
website: www.ockbrooksch.co.uk
Twitter: @ockbrookschool
Facebook: @Ockbrook-School

Motto: *In Christo Omnia Possum*

Founded in 1799.

Independent Day and Boarding School for boys and girls aged 2–18. Member of The Society of Heads, IAPS and AGBIS.

Situation. Situated in the heart of the Midlands, Ockbrook School lies equidistant between the historic towns of Derby and Nottingham and is easily accessible from the motorway network, rail and air transport. The School is set in a superb rural position overlooking the Trent Valley and it is surrounded by its own estate including landscaped gardens, grounds, playing fields and farmland. This setting, and the high standard of facilities within it, provides an excellent environment for learning … free from urban noise and distractions.

Pupils. There are c400 pupils, who are divided between the Primary School (age 2–11) and Senior School (age 11–18). Boarders are accepted from the age of 11 years for entry into Year 7 or above.

Ethos. We aim to develop individual potential and self worth through stimulating and positive relationships and through an understanding of Christian values so that our pupils are prepared for the changes they will face in their future lives. We believe that education should be a partnership between School, pupils and parents. To this end we provide comprehensive feedback on progress in the classroom and welcome family and friends at our extracurricular drama productions, concerts, sports events, open door days and acts of worship.

Curriculum.

Primary School:

Early Years (Ages 2–5). A dynamic programme of language, numeracy and scientific activities provide a secure foundation for later conceptual development.

Key Stage 1 (Years 1 & 2). The core subjects of Mathematics, Science and English are covered in addition to nine other subject areas including French and Information Communications Technology.

Key Stage 2 (Years 3–6). Study for the core of subjects continues with additional experience in nine other subjects including Dance, Drama and Gymnastics.

Teachers' assessments are carried out throughout both Key Stages and form the basis of internal assessment procedures for progression through to the Senior School at 11+.

Senior School:

Lower School (Years 7–9). Pupils study the core subjects and a broad range of additional subjects including ICT, French, Spanish, German, Drama and PSHCE (Personal, Social, Health & Citizenship Education). From Year 9 students follow IGCSE courses in Mathematics and the three sciences.

Upper School (Years 10–11). At GCSE level all pupils study Mathematics, English Language and English Literature, plus additional subjects; there is a wide range of options.

Sixth Form. Students usually study for 4 AS Levels in the Lower Sixth and proceed to 3 A2 subjects in the Upper Sixth. A wide range of subjects is available and students can opt to do an additional EPQ. Great emphasis is placed on the development of Life Skills which help to develop the competencies so necessary for adult life, whilst adding to the breadth of study. The vast majority of pupils leaving the Sixth Form proceed to higher education, including Oxbridge.

Sport. As well as the core PE subjects the school has a strong tradition in sport, i.e. athletics, cross country, netball, swimming and rounders etc. Teams of various ages, in most sports, have full fixture lists with neighbouring schools and the School is proud of its County and National representatives. We are also a member of the Sports Leaders Award Scheme.

Activities. The Duke of Edinburgh's Award scheme is available to pupils over the age of 14, together with a wide range of trips and outdoor holidays, walking, canoeing and skiing. Other activities include Young Enterprise, Wilderness Expertise, Community Service, chess, debating, and numerous other clubs or societies. A School Holiday Club also operates from the School.

Music and Drama. Many pupils learn musical instruments and a large number play to a high standard. Opportunities are provided by the Primary and Senior choirs, orchestras, chamber choir, strings group, and wind band. Performance venues include Westminster Abbey, Manchester, Derby and Barcelona Cathedrals, Ojab-Haus Aigen, Salzburg, Salzburg Cathedral, Pfarrkirche Bad Ischl Salzburg and Chatsworth House, Derbyshire. There is a wide range of dramatic productions each year providing as many pupils as possible with the chance of developing their dramatic talents.

Art and Design & Technology. Great emphasis is given to the development of creative talent both as academic subjects and interests. Out-of-class involvement is strongly encouraged.

Fees per term (2016–2017). Tuition £2,760–£4,060; Full Boarding £8,230–£8,405; Weekly Boarding £6,455–£6,790.

Admission. *Primary School*: Entry is decided as a result of a combination of interview, assessment day and school report (if applicable).

Senior School: Entry is decided as a result of a combination of interview, assessment, school report and if necessary an entrance examination held throughout the year and in January for Year 7 and Year 12.

Sixth Form: Entry is decided as a result of a combination of interview, school report, predicted GCSE grades and ultimately a good performance in the GCSE examinations.

Scholarships and Bursaries. Scholarships are available for Academia, Sport, Art, Drama and Music (including voice) for Year 7 and Sixth Form entry. A Head Teacher's Award is also available for all-round achievement. Bursary applications are considered by way of a full means test which may also include a home visit assessment. Full details are available from the Registrar, Mrs J Sheldon, email: enquiries@ockbrooksch.co.uk.

School Prospectus. A prospectus and registration details may be obtained from the Registrar, details as above, or on the school website: www.ockbrooksch.co.uk. Parents are encouraged to visit the School and appointments may be made by contacting the Registrar.

Charitable status. Ockbrook School is a Registered Charity, number 251211.

Governing Body:
Chair of Governors: Mrs A Redgate, LLB
Deputy Chair: Mr J Luke
Mr J Barley
Revd J Kreusel
Dr G Lamming, FRCOG
Dr V Poultney, MEd
Mr C Purcell, BA Hons, MCIPR
Mrs M Ralph, MEd, MCollP
Mrs G Taylor, FCA

Clerk to the Governors: Mrs J Buckley

Leadership Team:

Headmaster: Mr T Brooksby, BEd Crewe & Alsager, NPQH

Head of Primary & Music Coordinator: Mrs S Worthington, BA Exeter
Deputy Head: Mrs H Springall, BA Newcastle, MA Open, NPQH
Deputy Head of Primary & ICT Coordinator: Mr R Beach, BA Sussex
Head of Lower (Years 7–10): Mrs S Wood, BA Hull
Head of Upper (Years 11–13) : Mr N Gupta, BSc MAPSE Leicester
Head of Achievement and Progress: Mr A Walsh, BA Huddersfield

Early Years:
Mrs S Taylor, BA Scarborough (*Head of Early Years, EY SpLD*)
Mrs N Felstead, BA Loughborough

Primary Department:
Mrs S Breedon, BA Nottingham (*English Coordinator*)
Mrs J Cresswell, BEd College of St Mark & St John
Mrs L Ireland, BEd Derby (*PSHCE Coordinator*)
Mrs M Lamell, BA Newcastle (*Drama*)
Mrs H Marsden , BEd Derby (*History, Geography & RS Coordinator*)
Mrs K Morris, BA Norwich School of Art & Design (*Art, DT Coordinator*)
Mrs J Mullineux, BEd Bedford College (*Physical Education, Dance, Humanities*)
Mrs S Shooter, BSc Royal Holloway
Mrs B Thornton, BEd Derby (*Science Coordinator*)
Mr D Williams, BEd Bangor (*PE Coordinator*)
Mrs P Ward, CertEd Kesteven

Senior Department:
Mrs L Archibald, BA Leeds (*Food Technology & Head of Careers*)
Mrs J Bacall, BA Sheffield Hallam (*English*)
Mrs F Birkbeck, BA Edinburgh, MEd (*Psychology*)
Dr E Burguin, BSc Sheffield, PhD York (*Languages*)
Ms K Chetwin, BSc London, BA Nottingham (*Science & Business Studies*)
Ms K Cleland, MA Glasgow (*English*)
Mrs L Coggle, BSc Sheffield (*Mathematics & Head of Boarding*)
Mrs F Faulkner, BSc Newcastle (*ICT*)
Mr R Finch, BA Leicester (*Humanities*)
Mrs C Fletcher-Eton, BSc Loughborough (*Religious Studies*)
Mr S Gilbert, BSc Sheffield (*Mathematics & Duke of Edinburgh's Award*)
Mr P Kinsella, B Ed Liverpool (*Physical Education*)
Mrs M Lamell, BA Newcastle (*Drama*)
Mrs C McBeth, BEd MSc Loughborough
Mrs J McGahey, BA Leeds (*Fine Art, Art & Design, Art Textiles*)
Mr J McNaughton, MA Cambridge (*Geography*)
Mrs E Marsh, BSc Leeds (*Physics, Sciences*)
Mrs J Moses, BA Nottingham (*Modern Languages*)
Mrs S Mitchell, BA Hull (*English*)
Mrs K Moorhouse, BSc Loughborough (*Physical Education, Dance*)
Mr R Moorhouse, BSc Loughborough (*Physical Education*)
Mrs A M Newton, BSc Essex (*Mathematics*)
Mrs R O'Reilly, BA Liverpool (*Physical Education, Dance*)
Mrs S Price, BSc York (*Chemistry/Sciences*)

Miss A Renow, BA Leicester, MEd Nottingham (*History*)
Mr T Sands, BA Sheffield Hallam (*Product Design*)
Mrs S Scott, BSc Hertfordshire (*Biology*)
Mrs A Sidery, BEd Nottingham (*English*)
Mr E Swindell, BMus, MMus Manchester (*Director of Music*)
Mrs P Theaker, BSc Nottingham (*Mathematics*)
Mrs M Watkins, BA Leeds (*Modern Languages*)
Mrs S West, BA Birmingham (*Drama*)

Support Staff:
Head Teacher's PA: Mrs C Derbyshire
Business Manager: Mrs E Green
Operations Manager: Mrs J Buckley
Registrar: Mrs J Sheldon
Finance and HR Assistant: Mrs N Brierley
Administrator: Miss L Lambord
Administrator: Mrs S Everill
Network Manager: Mr A Crowter

Boarding Houses Staff:

Mrs M Cooper	Mrs C Horspool
Mrs S Cooper	Miss A McComb
Mrs K Fisher	Mrs C Rigby
Mrs R Gascoigne	Miss M Truman
Nurse W Holmes, EN	

Classroom Assistants:

Mrs C Bowers	Mrs A Kenyon, NNEB
Mrs S Cooper, Cert EYP	Mrs J Leighton, NNEB
Mrs J Federici	Mrs C Newby, BSc
Mrs S Hawksworth, NNEB	Mrs Nutty
Mrs A-M Heaps	Mrs Payne
Mrs L Holmes, BTEC	Mrs M Shawcross

Nurse: Mrs L Tanser, RN

Grounds & Maintenance:
Mr D Bailey
Mr P Davis-Wells
Mr A White

Technicians:
Mrs S Cullen, BSc (*Combined Science*)
Miss V Betesta

Librarian: Mrs C Purcell, BSc, MSc

Oswestry School

Upper Brook Street, Oswestry, Shropshire SY11 2TL
Tel: 01691 655711
Fax: 01691 671194
email: enquiries@oswestryschool.org.uk
website: www.oswestryschool.org.uk
Twitter: @oswestryschool
Facebook: @oswestryschool

Motto: '*We learn not for school but for life.*'

Oswestry School, founded in 1407, is one of the oldest non-denominational schools in England. The School is registered as a Charitable Trust and administered by a Board of Governors which is in membership of the Association of Governing Bodies of Independent Schools.

Oswestry School is a co-educational day and boarding school for pupils aged 4 to 18. Pupils are taught on two closely situated sites. The Prep Department, Bellan House, is situated in the town centre a short walk from the Senior School. The Senior School, located on the outskirts of the town, caters for First Form to Upper Sixth, ages 11 to 18, both day and boarding. Oswestry School moved to its present site in 1776, and its beautiful grounds and playing fields now occupy a site of 50 acres.

Curriculum. The School aims to provide a broad general education up to GCSE with more specialised subjects in the Sixth Form. At present, the following subjects are taught to A Level: Art, Biology, Business Studies, Chemistry, Design Technology, English Literature, Economics, French, Geography, History, ICT, Mathematics and Further Mathematics, Music, Physics, Psychology, Religious Studies, Spanish, Sports and Physical Education. All pupils, supported and encouraged by an excellent team of staff, are expected to make the most of their abilities. The size of the School helps Oswestry achieve its ethos and pupils are bright, energetic, confident and, above all, happy. The School is large enough to grant pupils a feeling of independence and to house many superb facilities, but small enough for each pupil to be well known and make a significant contribution to the School. A combination of the School's size and a high teacher-per-student ratio allows Oswestry to give personalised and consistent care and attention, and to monitor and motivate pupils as they make academic and personal progress.

Boarders. Boarders are accommodated in three comfortable boarding houses on the School site, and are cared for by attentive and dedicated house staff. Each boarding house has a resident Houseparent and Assistant Houseparents, and every pupil benefits from a high level of pastoral care. Wi-Fi throughout the School site makes it easy for pupils to stay in touch with home. The spacious, modern dining hall provides three hot meals a day; food is served as a buffet selection and includes fresh vegetables, fruit and desserts and there is plenty of variety to ensure all diets are catered for. In addition to the academic programme, a wide range of weekend activities is arranged for the boarding pupils by members of the teaching staff.

School Chapel. The School Chapel plays an important part in the life of the School and the Chaplain is central to the pastoral structure of the School.

Games. The School has a strong tradition of participation in sports. Extensive playing fields, an all-weather pitch, gymnasium, netball/tennis courts and a twenty-metre heated indoor swimming pool are some of the sporting environments at Oswestry.

Out of School Activities. There is a wide range of extracurricular activities and all pupils are encouraged to join at least two clubs. The clubs and extracurricular activities on offer are designed to appeal to pupils of various ages and interests. The inclusion of such a programme serves to further personal development and leadership skills. Included are such diverse activities as sailing, chess, photography, horse riding, rock climbing, self-defence, personal fitness, badminton and mountain biking. After-School activities and clubs vary each term but there is always a wide variety of activities to choose from.

CCF and Community Service. There is an active CCF contingent, membership of which is voluntary after two years' service; pupils may also pursue The Duke of Edinburgh's Award scheme. Both schemes offer opportunities to develop leadership skills, self-reliance and responsibility.

Admissions. Pupils from 4+ are welcome to apply for entry to the Prep Department at any time, however, as places are limited, early registration is advised. Boys and girls are accepted into the Senior School from the age of 11, although applications are always considered for entry up to Fourth Form and for Sixth Form.

Registration fee: £50.

Fees per term (2016–2017). Day Pupils: £2,720 (Reception), £2,810 (Years 1 & 2), £2,890 (Years 3 & 4), £3,310 (Years 5 & 6), £4,610 (First and Second Form), £4,900 (Third Form–Upper Sixth). Full Boarding: £8,190 (First and Second Form), £10,250 (Third Form–Upper Sixth); Weekly Boarding: £7,130 (First and Second Form), £8,640 (Third–Upper Sixth).

Scholarships. Academic, Art, Music and Sport scholarships are available at 7+ 11+, 13+ and 16+.

Further details of all these Scholarships are available from the Headmaster.

Reductions for Services Families. Generous awards are available for school age children of Services personnel.

Charitable status. Oswestry School is a Registered Charity, number 1079822.

Governing Board:
Chairman: Mr P T Wilcox-Jones
Vice-Chairman: Mr T Moore-Bridger

The Rt Hon The Earl of Powis, Patron
Mr E Bowen
Mr J Edwards
Mr D Evison
Mr J Hancock
Miss B Y Gull
Mr A Moss
Mr M Symonds
The Revd S G Thorburn
Mrs R Warner
Mr B Welti
Mr C Schofield

Headmaster: **Mr J P Noad**, BEng

Deputy Head (Academic): Dr T Jefferis, MSc, BSc, EdD, PGCE

Deputy Head (Pastoral): Ms S Nancini, BA Manchester, PGCE, FAHE

Our Lady's Abingdon Senior School

Radley Road, Abingdon, Oxfordshire OX14 3PS

Tel:	01235 524658
Fax:	01235 535829
email:	office@olab.org.uk
website:	www.olab.org.uk
Twitter:	@OLAabingdon
Facebook:	@OLAabingdon

Motto: *Age Quod Agis – Whatever you do, do it well*

Founded in 1860 by Sister Clare Moore of the Sisters of Mercy, Our Lady's Abingdon (OLA) is an independent, Catholic day school, for boys and girls aged 3–18.

OLA offers outstanding pastoral care and a wide range of academic and extra-curricular activities, ensuring that pupils are confident, engaged and excited about their next steps in life.

Small class sizes allow staff to get to know every single pupil, giving them the support and encouragement they need to fulfil their academic and personal potential.

The school encourages independence of thought and responsibility for one's own learning and behaviour. OLA, a Christian school in the Catholic tradition, welcomes pupils of all faiths and none, who wish to share its ideals and expectations.

The school received an excellent Inspection Report in 2010, which noted in particular that:

"Pupils achieve excellent results in a range of extracurricular activities, especially in sport.

Pupils make exceptional progress in their academic studies in relation to their ability profile.

Pupils' spiritual, moral, social and cultural development is excellent.

The outstanding pastoral care does much to ensure their safeguarding, and to foster their personal development and academic achievement."

Numbers. There are 384 pupils aged 11–18 in the Senior school and 120 pupils aged 3–11 in the Junior section, which is on the same site under its own headteacher, Erika Kirwan. (*See Junior School entry in IAPS section.*)

Facilities and Buildings. Bright, spacious classrooms and an excellent library provide a pleasant ambience conducive to study and learning. The grounds surround both buildings, an attractive setting of lawns, flowerbeds and trees in which the pupils can relax during breaks. Sports facilities include a number of tennis courts, a sports hall with fitness room, hockey and athletics provision and a 25-metre indoor swimming pool. It has benefited recently from the creation of a new Design & Technology Centre, with other recent building projects including an auditorium and library, the latest in ICT equipment, an extended Art department and additional Science laboratories. The Music department benefits from new facilities to aid composition and to support the wide variety of instruments taught in the school.

Curriculum. The school teaches a balanced range of subjects both academic and practical during the first three years. Latin is a core subject. Pupils take 9 or 10 subjects at GCSE, including English, Mathematics, Science, Religious Studies and two modern languages. Options are chosen from the Humanities to Classics and Physical Education. Four subjects are studied in the Lower Sixth at AS, continuing with three at A2. The great majority of the Sixth Form go on to Higher Education, but some have also succeeded in gaining places on highly competitive professional placement programmes. There is also support for Special Educational Needs, and for pupils for whom English is not their mother tongue.

Extra-curricular activities. The school provides a wide programme of extra-curricular activities including drama, music, art, debating and many forms of sport. Rowing and sailing are particularly popular. Buses run later on three evenings of the week to accommodate these activities and to allow for supervised homework. There is also a strong commitment to local community schemes and an impressive record in The Duke of Edinburgh's Award scheme and Young Enterprise. In both 2011 and 2012 the OLA Young Enterprise group won the award for Best Business Plan.

In 2008 and 2011 OLA was one of only 508 schools to be accredited with the Department for Education's International School Award for the "outstanding work done by the staff and pupils". The school has gained the Eco-Schools Silver Award and is working towards the "Green Flag".

Fees per term (2016–2017). £4,785.

Admission. Through the school's own Entrance Examination at 11 and 13; Pupils require at least 5 GCSEs Grade B for entry at Sixth Form level. Pupils interested in entering the Sixth Form for whom English is a second language must in addition have achieved a minimum level of 6.5 in IELTS for each category. Pupils may join in any year if a place is available.

Pupils may apply for Scholarships for entry to Year 7, Year 9 and the Sixth Form. Candidates may also apply for Bursaries which are awarded at the discretion of the Governors.

Charitable status. Our Lady's Abingdon Trustees Limited is a Registered Charity, number 1120372, and a Company Limited by Guarantee, registered in England and Wales, number 6269288.

Board of Governors:
Chairman: Mr E McCabe, MA Oxon, MBA

Governors:
Mr T Ayling MA Oxon
Mr M Barber, MA Oxon, MSc

Dr A Colbrook, BSc, PhD
Mr J Cunliffe, MA Oxon
Mrs A Freeman, BEd
Mr D Heavens
Father J McGrath, STB, MA
Mr T Prosser, BSc, MSc, MBA, FIFireE
Mrs H Ronaldson
Ms J Shillaker, MA, LIM
Mrs M Shinkwin, BA, MA Ed, NPQH
Mr A Sullivan
Mr I Yorston, MA

Bursar & Clerk to the Governors: Mr S Hughes, BA Hons

Principal: **Mr Stephen Oliver**, BA, MLitt

Deputy Head: Mr N Hathaway, BA Hons, PGCE, PGDipEd

Assistant Head (*Teaching & Learning*): Susan Robson, BSc Hons, NPQSL, PGCE

Director of Studies: Mrs S Wales, BA Oxon, PGCE

Sixth Form Tutor: Mr D Willcock, MA Oxon
Year 11 Tutor: Mrs A Okeke, BSc Hons, MSc, PGCE
Year 10 Tutor: Mr R Ford, BSc, PGCE
Year 9 Tutor: Mr L Allen, BSc, PGCE
Year 8 Tutor: Mr P Hudson, BSc Hons, PGCE
Year 7 Tutor: Miss F Gunn, LLB Hons, PGCE, MA

Heads of Departments:
Art: Mrs H Holden, BA Hons, MSt, PGCE
Business Studies: Mrs J Acutt, BA Hons, PGCE
Careers: Mrs A Varney, BEd, CertEd
Classics: Miss P Smith, BA Hons Oxon
Design & Technology: Mr C Sephton, MSc, PGCE
Drama: Dr E Lawson, BA Hons, MA, PhD Loughborough
Economics: Mrs W Meigh, BEd
English: Miss M Hemingway, BA Hons, PGCE
Food Technology: Mrs H Black, BA Hons, PGCE
Geography: Mr A Jackson, BA, MSc, PGCE
History: Mrs J Mead, BA Hons, PGCE, MA
Information Technology: Miss B Habayeb, MSc, PGCE
Learning Support: Mrs L Barr, MSt, MA, BA, PGCE
Mathematics: Mr R Ford, BSc, PGCE
Modern Languages: Mrs C Friend, MA Hons Oxon, MA, PGCE
Music: Dr P Foster, BA Hons, MMus, PhD Reading, PGCE
Physical Education: Mrs M Barnett, BA Hons, QTS & Mr E Barnett, BA Hons, QTS
PSHE: Mr T Carroll, BSc, SSTQ
Psychology: Mrs A Beasley, MA Hons, PGCE
Religious Studies: Mr D Willcock, MA Oxon
Science: Mr P Hudson, BSc Hons, PGCE
Textiles: Mrs K Rowe, CertEd

Communications and Marketing Manager: Mrs C Wareing
Admissions Registrar: Mrs F Russell

The Peterborough School
A Woodard School

Thorpe Road, Peterborough PE3 6AP
Tel: 01733 343357
           Bursar: 01733 355720
Fax: 01733 355710
email: office@tpsch.co.uk
website: www.thepeterboroughschool.co.uk
Twitter: @PeterboroughSch

The Peterborough School is the City's only independent day school for boys and girls from Nursery to Sixth Form. Situated in beautiful surroundings in the heart of Peterborough, the School enjoys excellent road and rail links. The School is a member of the Woodard Corporation, the largest group of Church of England Schools in England and Wales.

Situation and Buildings. The School is located in beautiful secluded grounds, near the centre of Peterborough, 50 minutes by fast train from King's Cross and easily accessible by road from the A1, A14 and A47. The elegant Victorian house is the centre of a modern purpose-built complex of classrooms, laboratories, Music School, Art Block, Sixth Form Centre, Library and a modern Computing Suite. The new Sports Facility was completed in September 2012.

The Preparatory School. Boys and girls are admitted into the Reception Class from the age of 4+. The National Tests are taken at Key Stage One and Two. The whole range of Key Stage subjects is covered in addition to a variety of other subjects and activities, e.g. Latin, Reasoning, French and other languages. Some subjects are taught by specialist staff from the Senior School. There is emphasis on academic standards, good manners, Physical Education, Music and Drama.

The Senior School. The curriculum of the Senior School is characterised by small classes and an emphasis on individual guidance and target-setting. A balanced programme leads to high achievement at GCSE. English, Mathematics, Sciences, Religious Education, Games and PE remain compulsory throughout; Languages, Computer Science, Food Tech, History and Geography, Art, Art Textiles and Graphic Products, Music, Drama, Latin and Physical Education form the matrix of options. Unusually, German and French are studied from Year 7.

External candidates are selected from the entrance examination and opportunities for Scholarships exist at Year 7 and Sixth Form entry.

The School has a modern Computing Suite with state-of-the-art equipment, including iPads and laptops. All classrooms are networked.

There are specialist laboratories for all sciences and a new Sixth Form science lab.

In the Sixth Form students usually take three A Level subjects but may in some circumstances undertake four. These are linear qualifications, with examination at the end of the two-year course of study: there are no AS examinations available at the end of the Lower Sixth other than in Mathematics. In addition to their academic studies, Sixth Formers undertake a significant enrichment programme that includes volunteering, the Extended Project Qualification (EPQ) and an electives programme.

As a School with pupils from Reception and children in the Nursery from 6 weeks and above, older pupils have many opportunities to develop a sense of involvement and responsibility, and carry out valuable service in the wider School community. Business sense is developed through the Young Enterprise scheme, in which the School is very successful. The Duke of Edinburgh's Award Scheme is also prioritised.

The Nursery. The Peterborough School Nursery offers daycare for children aged from 6 weeks to 4 years. Optional lessons include French, Ballet and Key Sports.

Religion. Weekly Communion Services are held and attendance is compulsory.

Music and Drama. The music of the School, in particular its choral tradition, is renowned and the School benefits from holding its own Music Festival. Tuition in singing, piano and all orchestral instruments is available. Major theatrical and musical productions take place several times a year, and the School presents an Art & Design Exhibition each summer.

Games and Physical Education. The pupils achieve outstanding success in team and individual sports and athletics. Many pupils have represented the county, the region, and even England. The School estate is spacious with several pitches and all-weather courts. The many and varied sporting facilities of the city are within easy reach for swimming, rowing and athletics. The School is benefiting from the major development of its Sports Facility, including a Fitness Suite and Climbing Wall.

Extra-curricular Activities. Many clubs and societies operate in extra-curricular time, and field visits and excursions illuminate classroom work. Many pupils undertake the Duke of Edinburgh's Award Scheme at both Bronze and Gold levels, with outstanding success.

Fees per term (2016–2017). Reception/Infants £3,333; Years 3–6 £4,040; Years 7–13 £4,848.

Lunches, breaktime snacks and all UK based educational trips and visits are included.

Scholarships. Academic, Art, Music and Sport are the main scholarships available to those entering Year 7. Sixth Form Academic Scholarships are also available. Please apply to the Registrar for more information.

The Peterborough School Alumni (Westwoodians' Association). Secretary: Mrs Ivana Zizza who is based at the School.

Charitable status. The Peterborough School Limited is a Registered Charity, number 269667. It is an independent school which exists to promote the education of children.

School Council:
Chairman: Ms L Ayres, LLB
Mrs A Arculus, MA Hons
Mrs P Dalgliesh
Mrs L Frisby
Mrs K Hart, BA Hons
Mr P Hayes
The Revd R Hemingray, LLB
Prof C J Howe, MA, DPhil, FLS
The Rt Revd R Ladds, SSC, Provost of Woodard Schools
Mrs H Milligan-Smith, LLB Hons
Mrs E Payne
The Revd Canon B Ruddock
Mr D Sandbach, BA, FCA, D Ch A
Mr P Simmons
Mr P Southern, FRICS
Dr J S Thompson, LMSSA, MBBS, DRCOG

Head: Mr A Meadows, BSc Hons Manchester, NPQH

Deputy Headmaster: Mr R Cameron, BA Hons Southampton
Head of the Preparatory School: Mrs A-M Elding, MA OU, BEd Hons Derby
Head of Pastoral Care: Mrs E Rivers, BSc Hons London
Chaplain: Revd T Sherring, MTh Oxon, BA Exeter

Staff:
Miss H Adams, BSc Hons (*Mathematics*)
Mrs L Andrew, BEd Hons (*Preparatory*)
Mr P Baldwin, BA Hons (*Preparatory*)
Mr K Banyard, MA (*English*)
Mrs R Bierton, BA Hons (*Head of Individual Learning*)
Mr K Bingham, BA Hons (*Preparatory*)
Mr C Brocklesby, BA Hons (*Geography*)
Mrs K Brocklesby, BSc Nottingham (*Mathematics*)
Miss Z Chappell, BA Hons Cantab (*Preparatory*)
Miss S M Clarkson, BA Hons Cantab (*History*)
Mr G Cloke, BSc Hons (*Preparatory*)
Mrs L Coles, BA Hons (*French, Head of Sixth Form*)
Mrs K Davis, BSc Hons (*Chemistry, Head of Key Stage 3*)
Mrs R Ditcher, BSc Hons (*Preparatory*)
Ms T Doyle, MNATD (*Director of Creative Arts*)
Mr S Dyer, BA Hons (*Economics, Business Studies, Careers*)
Mrs A Elffers, BA (*Latin*)
Mrs J Evans, Licence (*French*)
Dr L Fox-Clipsham, PhD, BSc (*Science*)
Mrs L Grinyer, BA Hons (*English*)

Mrs R Hampson, BA Hons (*Art, Textiles*)
Mr A Harwin, BA Hons (*Art*)
Mr S Holbird, BA Hons, MSc (*Graphic Products*)
Mr A Jackson, BA Hons (*German*)
Miss C Johnson, BSc Hons (*Biology*)
Mrs E Kay, BSc Hons (*Physical Education*)
Mr C King, BSc Hons, CMath, MIMA (*Mathematics*)
Mrs L Lane, BSc Hons (*Physical Education*)
Mr S Law, BSc Hons (*Physics*)
Miss A Loffman, BA Hons (*Religious Education*)
Miss L McChlery, BEd (*Preparatory*)
Mrs L McClarnon, BEd Hons (*Preparatory*)
Mrs H McKillop, BA Hons (*Music*)
Mr C McManus, MA Ulster (*History*)
Mr J Marsden, BSc Hons (*Physical Education*)
Mrs G Mason, OND Hotel & Catering (*Food Technology & Preparatory Classroom Assistant*)
Miss R Mayle, BA Hons (*Geography*)
Mr D Moxon, BSc Hons, MSc (*Psychology*)
Mrs S Noone, BEd (*Preparatory*)
Mrs E Porsz, BA Hons (*Physical Education*)
Ms E Potbury, BA Hons (*French*)
Mrs A Quy, BSc Hons (*Preparatory*)
Mrs J Roberts, BA Hons (*English*)
Mr S Roberts, BA Hons (*Director of Sport*)
Ms S Robinson, BEd Hons (*Preparatory*)
Mr P Schavier, Masters Degree (*German*)
Mrs R Shang, BA Hons (*Drama*)
Mrs M Silvester, BSc Hons (*Mathematics*)
Mrs A Skelton, BA Hons (*Preparatory*)
Miss C Steward, BA Hons (*Preparatory*)
Mrs S Ward, BSc Hons, PGCE (*Biology*)
Mr M Webb, BSc Hons (*Computing & Digital Strategy*)
Mrs J Young, BSc Hons (*Head of PE and Girls' Games*)

Instrumental Music/Speech & Drama :
Miss K Birtles, BMus Hons (*Flute & Oboe*)
Mr J Cranfield, BA Hons (*Guitar*)
Mr S Hamper, Army School of Music (*Percussion*)
Mr R Haylett, BA Hons Cantab (*Singing*)
Mr G Haynes, BA Hons (*Choral Music*)
Mr M Jewkes (*Jazz Piano & Saxophone*)
Mr A Kershaw, BMus Hons (*Brass*)
Mrs M McAuliffe, Dip ABRSM (*Violin*)
Mr G Pooley, BMus (*Singing*)
Mrs L Reid, MA Hons Oxon (*Choral Director/Singing*)
Mrs P Samuels, LGSM Cert Acting GSMD (*Speech & Drama*)
Miss E Smith BMus Hons (*Lower Strings*)

Administrative Officers:
Bursar: Mr N A Johnson, MA, FCMI
Head's PA: Mrs J Farrow
Marketing Manager/Registrar: Mrs L Pengelly
Development Manager/Assistant Registrar: Mrs I Zizza
Administration/HR Assistant: Mrs Z Vickers
Administrative Assistant: Miss E Nicholson
Accounts: Mrs J House BA Hons, Mrs R Forman
Domestic Bursar: Mrs Z Clark
Estate Manager: Mr D Thornton
Laboratory Technician: Mrs A Albon, BSc
Art Technician: Miss H Senior, BA Hons
Computing: Mr L Taylor, Mr S Crier, Mr J Smart
Food Technology Technician: Mrs V Tobin
LRC Manager: Mrs C Thomson
Receptionist: Mrs R Adcock

Teaching Assistants & Supervisors:
Mrs S Browne
Ms E Drew, BA Hons
Mrs Z Green
Miss L Henry
Mr L Jacobs

Mrs W Langford
Mrs E Penniston, BA Hons
Mrs J Reade
Mr R Westbrook

Medical Staff:
Mrs M Doust, RGN (*Senior Matron*)
Mrs F Aylmore, BSc Hons (*Matron*)
Mrs M Lay, BSc Hons (*School Counsellor*)

Pitsford School

Pitsford Hall, Pitsford, Northamptonshire NN6 9AX
Tel: 01604 880306
Fax: 01604 882212
email: office@pitsfordschool.com
website: www.pitsfordschool.com
Twitter: @pitsford_school

Age Range. 4–18 Co-educational.
Number of Pupils. 300 boys and girls.
Fees per term (2016–2017). Kits (Pre-School): £2,661; Junior School: £2,843–£4,316; Senior School: £4,620. Lunches: £263.

The School was founded in 1989 to offer a traditional Grammar School standard education to boys in Northamptonshire. Today, the School still offers the same high standards of education but to boys and girls from 4–18 years of age.

In April 2016 the school opened its brand new £2 million sports centre, complete with large sports hall, café and state-of-the-art fitness suite.

Pastoral Care. The School's academic success is complemented by effective pastoral support. By keeping class sizes small, a friendly, family atmosphere is evident, allowing pupils to grow and develop in confidence as they progress through the School.

Admissions. Nursery, Year 7 and Sixth Form are the most common years of entry to the School, although pupils may be admitted in other years when required, if space is available.

Entry to Key Stage 1: pupils are invited to spend a day with their current year group to ensure they are happy in their future surroundings.

Entry to Key Stage 2: pupils are invited in for an Assessment.

Entry to the Senior School: Prospective pupils are invited to sit the School's own entrance test.

It is expected all pupils will take 10 GCSEs before transferring to the Sixth Form at the end of Year 11.

The Sixth Form is structured to provide a stepping stone from the discipline of Senior School to the demands of Higher Education. Sixth Formers take a full part in the life of the School and have many positions of responsibility.

Sport and Extracurricular Activities. Rugby, netball, cricket and tennis are played throughout the School. In addition, the School's Cross Country Team enjoys ongoing success when competing against other Schools. The Pitsford Run is a well known local event.

Numerous Extracurricular Activities are on offer to pupils throughout the School:

Junior School activities range from School Council to English Speaking Board (ESB) and from Rugby and Netball to Art and Craft.

Senior School pupils have over 60 activities to choose from. Most Activities take place on site, however the School's excellent location means that a number of activities such as Sailing, Kayaking, Horse Riding and Fishing are available just a short distance from the School. All are extremely popular.

Music and Drama. Music and Drama are integral elements of school life at Pitsford School.

Musical Recitals are held in Pitsford Hall every Thursday lunchtime and in addition, the School holds Four Evening Concerts per year. As well as individual music lessons in a wide range of instruments, group participation and performance opportunities include woodwind, guitar, percussion, strings, sax and flute ensembles and also two choirs.

A number of Junior and Senior plays take place throughout the year, ranging from Shakespeare to Musicals.

Charitable status. Northamptonshire Independent Grammar School Charity Trust Limited is a Registered Charity, number 298910.

Governing Body:
Chairman: Mr A Tait

Mr M Adams	Mr A Moodie
Mr J Brown	Mrs J Tice**
Mr S Coleman	Reverend S Trott
Mrs J Harrop	Mr J Wilmer
Mrs F McGill	Mr T Young
Mr K Mason	

** *Foundation Governor*

Headmaster: Mr N R Toone, BSc, MInstP, FRSA

Deputy Head: Mrs F M Kirk, BA, MEd

* *Head of Department*

Mr O Auckland, BA Hons (*Junior School*)
Mrs C Ball (*Junior School*)
Mrs C Cabrera-Alvarez (*Modern Languages*)
Mrs F L Care, MA (*Mathematics*)
Mrs L A Chacksfield, BEd (*PE and Games**)
Mme M H Conroy, BA (*Junior School*)
Mrs J Cowie, BA (*Junior School*)
Mrs A Cowling, BSc Hons (*Biology and Chemistry*)
Mrs J M Drakeford, BSc (*Chemistry and Biology**)
Dr J Ewington, BSc Hons, MSc, PhD (*Physics**)
Mrs S E Goode, BSc Econ (*Junior School*)
Mr Harrison, MA, PGCE (*History**)
Miss S M Jackson, BSc (*Head of Sixth Form, Chemistry*)
Mrs F Jeffrey, BA Hons (*Asst Head EYFS/KS1, Junior School*)
Mrs L Jones, BA (*Junior School*)
Mr M Kefford, BA (*PE and Games*)
Mrs C King, BA (*EFL*)
Mrs F M Kirk, BA, MEd (*English, General Studies*)
Mrs J M Leeke, BSc (*Mathematics*)
Mr M J Lewis, BSc, FRGS, FRMetS, CGeog (*Geography**, Careers & Higher Education*)
Mrs L M Lyon, BEd (*Modern Languages*)
Ms M F McQuilkin, BA (*Art**)
Mrs M McNally, BSc (*Geography and Games*)
Mrs J Middlewood, BA (*Spanish*)
Mr J Smorfitt, BA (*Economics**)
Mr C L Stoner, BSc, MSc, Dip CEG (*Mathematics**)
Dr A Templeton, BSc, MSc, PhD (*Physics*)
Mrs H Thorne, BA, PGCE, CTABRSM (*Junior School Music*)
Mr R P Tickle, BA, DipTh (*History and Religious Studies*)
Mr F B Vié, Licence d'histoire, PGCE (*Modern Languages**)
Miss E Walsh, BMus Hons (*Director of Music**)
Mr J A White, BA, DipTh (*English**)
Mrs C Whiting, MA (*ICT**)
Mrs J Willmott, BEd (*Head of Junior School*)
Dr J Wood, BA, MA, PhD (*English*)

Bursar: Mr C Bellamy
Admissions: Miss J Pullin

Portland Place School
Alpha Plus Group

56–58 Portland Place, London W1B 1NJ

Tel:	020 7307 8700
Fax:	020 7436 2676
email:	admin@portland-place.co.uk
website:	www.portland-place.co.uk
Twitter:	@PortlandPlaceHd

Portland Place School was founded in 1996 in response to demand in central London for a mixed school that provided for pupils from a broad range of backgrounds and abilities.

Age Range. 8–18 Co-educational.
Number of Day Pupils. 263 Boys, 176 Girls.
Fees per term (2016–2017). £6,665.

Aims and Philosophy. Portland Place is an inclusive and non-elitist school. We encourage pupils to excel in the arts, sport and in their academic studies. Discipline is firm, but compassionate. Our uniform is simple and functional. Teaching is structured. All teachers are not only specialists in their subjects, but are chosen for their ability to enthuse and draw out the best in all students at all levels. The relationship between teachers and pupils is courteously informal. We teach in small classes to offer every child individual attention. While we always strive for academic excellence, we never allow this to overshadow our dedication to nurturing natural intelligence or true potential. Each child's progress is followed through tests, homework and up to six reports a year. Parents are also encouraged to meet our staff to discuss any concerns at any time, as well as at a Parents' Evening every term. We are also a school in touch with the real world. The future of the children in our care comes first in all our decisions and the education every child receives is a journey to a successful later life.

Location and Buildings. Portland Place is ideally located right in the centre of the capital, less than five minutes' walk from Regent's Park (where much of the outdoor sporting activities take place) and ten minutes' walk from Oxford Circus. The school is housed in two magnificent Grade II* listed James Adam houses in Portland Place with a separate Art, Drama and Science building and a separate Senior School building close by in Great Portland Street. The buildings have been refurbished to an exceptionally high standard. Classrooms are supplemented by specialist rooms for drama, photography and computing.

Curriculum. The curriculum at Portland Place is developed from the English National Curriculum and offers a flexibility that puts the pupil first. Homework is supervised until 5.00 pm for those who want or require it and each pupil has a homework diary that details the homework programme for each week. Each child takes part in a comprehensive programme of physical education. Pupils in Years 4–9 have four PE sessions per week. Full advantage is taken of its central London location and excellent local facilities available. The outdoor programme takes place in neighbouring Regent's Park and includes athletics, hockey, football, rugby, tennis and cross-country. Indoor sports include basketball and fencing. Pupils represent the school in numerous matches against other London schools and in national tournaments. Class music is a compulsory part of the curriculum in Years 4–9 and all pupils are encouraged, if they do not already play one, to take up a musical instrument and take advantage of the team of visiting instrumental teachers.

Sport and Extracurricular Activities. Our central London position means that we have easy access to world-class facilities. All children are encouraged to participate in an interesting and varied physical education programme. Portland Place School offers a wide range of popular sport including: Athletics, Basketball, Cricket, Cross Country, Fencing, Football, Hockey, Netball, Rounders, Swimming, Tennis and Rugby. Outdoor sports such as football, netball, tennis, cricket and athletics take place in Regent's Park less than a ten minute walk from the school. Indoor activities including basketball and fencing take place at the University of Westminster gym just minutes away in Regent Street. Swimming is at the Seymour Centre, and in the summer we have nets at Lords indoor school. Optional after-school sport activities abound with senior and junior clubs for matches held with schools across London and the UK.

There is a wide and expanding range of extracurricular activities that are offered at the end of afternoon school. Whole school productions, concerts, chamber groups and small dramatic workshops take place throughout the year and clubs ranging from politics and debating to games and Christianity all thrive throughout the year. During the last week of the summer term all pupils take part in an Activities Week that includes outdoor adventure centres and overseas trips.

Admission. Entry to the school (usually at 8+, 9+, 10+, 11+, 13+ and Sixth Form) is by examinations in English and Mathematics and interview. Interviews for September entry are held in the Autumn term prior to entry and the school's entrance examination is in January.

Governance. Portland Place School is part of the Alpha Plus Group of schools.

Senior Management Team:

Headmaster: Mr David Hyman, BSc London, PGCE, NPQH (*Mathematics*)

Deputy Head (*Academic*): Ms Julia Findlater, MEd St Mary's Twickenham, BA Hons Sussex, PGCE (*English*)
Deputy Head (*Pastoral*): Ms Elayn O'Neill, MEd Edinburgh, BEd, PG Dip Counselling
Director of Studies: Mr Matthew Fowler, BSc Hons Manchester, PGCE (*Mathematics*)
Bursar: Mrs Jane Monk, BA Hons Anglia Ruskin, Cert Acct Open

Teaching Staff:
Dr Abhilasha Aggarwal, BSc Hons London, PhD, PGCE (*Mathematics*)
Mr Kamran Akhtar, BSc Hons, MSc London, PGCE (*Mathematics*)
Mr Thomas Barnes, MA Cantab, PGCE (*English*)
Miss Sarah Birtles, BA Hons UAL, PGCE (*DT*)
Mr Leonardo Blonda, PhD Bari Italy, MA London, BA Bari Italy (*Film Studies*)
Miss Christina Boyle, BA Hons York, PGCE RNCM, MMU (*Music*)
Miss Hannah Bridge, BSc Hons Manchester, PGCE UCL (*Business Studies*)
Mr Richard Brightwell, BA York, PGCE (*Music*)
Mr Colin Bryce, BSc Glasgow (*Physical Education*)
Miss Charlotte Butler, BA Hons Leeds, PGCE (*History*)
Ms Maeve Byrne, BComm Hons Dublin, PGCE (*Business Studies & Economics*)
Mr Juan J Caballero, BA, CAP Seville, PGCE IoE London, MA IoE London, MEd Barcelona (*ICT*)
Mr Charles Chambers, BSc Hons Oxford Brookes, PGCE (*Teacher of KS2*)
Mr David Chivers, BA Cumbria, PGCE (*Drama*)
Miss Lydia Coles, BA Hons Oxford Brookes, PGCE (*KS2*)
Miss Danielle English, MSc Queen Mary London, MRSC, PGCE (*Chemistry*)
Miss Daciana Florea, BEd Oradea Romania (*Teacher of EAL*)
Dr Konstantinos Foskolos, BA Hons, MSc Oxon, MA, MSc, DPhil Oxon (*Psychology*)

Mrs Emily Galvin, BA UCL, MA Royal Holloway, PGCE (*Teacher of SEN*)
Ms Kirin Gill, BA Brunel, PGCE (*English*)
Miss Patricia Halcakova, BA Hons London, MA London (*Head of Learning Support*)
Miss Elise Hartopp, BA Hons York, PGCE (*English*)
Ms Lisa Hunt, BA Hons, MA MPhil London, PGCE (*History*)
Miss Hannah Johnston, BSc Hons St Andrews, PGCE (*Geography*)
Mrs Audrey Jones, BA Calvin College, USA, PGCE (*KS2*)
Mr Matthew Jones, BA London, PGCE (*Art*)
Mr Paul Jones, BA Leeds, PGCE (*Media and Film Studies*)
Mrs Natalie Keen, BA Hons Manchester, PGCE (*English*)
Mr Daniel Kemp, BSc Hons London, PG Cert (*Science*)
Dr Charlotte Knox-Williams, BA Hons Falmouth, PGCE Brighton, MA Winchester, PhD (*SENDCo*)
Mr Joe Kubik, BA Hons St Mary's Twickenham (*Physical Education*)
Mr Thomas Lalande, BA Bordeaux, PGCE (*French and Spanish*)
Mrs Caroline Lambert, BA Lancaster, PGCE (*Drama*)
Ms Christine Linton, BA Hons University of the Arts London, PGCE (*DesignTechnology*)
Mr Chad Macfarlane, BA Ed Goldsmiths London (*Design with Technology*)
Miss Charlotte Magniez, BA and MA Boulogne-sur-Mer, GTP (*French and Spanish*)
Mr Adrian Martjiono, BSc London, PGCE (*Chemistry*)
Mr Jamie McLoughlin, BSc Hons Brunel, PGCE (*Physical Education*)
Mr Ebrahim Naemi, BSc Hons University College Cardiff, PGCE Institute of Education (*Maths*)
Ms Sarah Nelson, MA London, BA Cardiff, PGCE (*English*)
Ms Tanya Nicholas, BA, BSc Hon Monash Australia, GDE OTTP (*Science*)
Miss Lauren O'Donnell, BA Hons Queen Mary London, PGCE (*English*)
Miss Teffany Osborne, BA Hons Slade (*Art*)
Ms Anita Philipovszky, BA Hons Universita di Roma La Sapienza, PGCE UCL (*Modern Languages*)
Ms Ruth Picado, BA Coruña Spain, PGCE (*Spanish*)
Ms Lucy Price, MA Edinburgh, PGCE (*Classical Civilisation and History*)
Dr Anthony Purcell, BEng, MEng, PhD, Grad Dip Teaching Melbourne (*Physics*)
Miss Sophie Pym, BSc Hons Brunel (*Physical Education*)
Mrs Julie Rider, BSc London, GTP (*Physical Education*)
Mr Scott Rider, BA Hons Brunel, PGCE (*Physical Education*)
Miss Imogen Riley, BA Oxon, PGCE (*Geography*)
Mr Pardeep Sagoo, MSci Imperial College London, GTP (*Biology/Chemistry*)
Miss Sara Segerstrom, BEd Kalmar Sweden, PGCE (*Mathematics*)
Mr Phillip Stanway, BA Manchester Metropolitan, PGCE (*Physical Education*)
Ms Alison Stringell, PG Slade, PGCE Goldsmiths (*Art*)
Mr Toni Tasic, BA Hons UCL, PGCE (*English*)
Mr Steve Thompson, BSc Plymouth, PGCE (*Physics*)
Dr Klaus Wehner, BA, MA, LCP, PhD (*Fine Art*)
Miss Natalie Whittle, BA Hons Chichester, PGCE (*Physical Education and KS2*)
Dr Nader Yazdi, MSc Leeds, PhD UCL, MBA Imperial (*Computing and ICT*)

Visiting Music Teachers:
Mr Nick Bentley (*Brass*)
Mr Adam Blake (*Guitar*)
Miss Zrinka Bottrill (*Classical Piano*)
Ms Rhonda Browne (*Voice*)

Miss Christine Cunnold (*Voice*)
Mr Dan Ezard (*Bass*)
Mr Jay Jenkinson (*Strings*)
Mr Sam Jesson (*Drums*)
Mr Siobhan Lavin (*Voice & Flute*)
Mr Darren McCarthy (*Guitar*)
Mr Mike O'Neill (*Jazz Piano*)
Mr Balint Szekely (*Violin*)
Miss Naomi Thomas (*Clarinet*)

Administration and Support Staff:
Miss Michelle Botha (*Admissions Registrar*)
Mrs Belinda Carvalho (*Librarian*)
Mrs Jane Monk (*Bursar – SMT*)
Mrs Amanda Tom-Dollar (*School Buildings Manager*)
Mrs Sharon Norman (*SIMS/DATA Manager*)
Ms Gill O'Brien (*Examinations Officer*)
Mrs Penny Ritchie (*Assistant Science Lab Technician*)
Mr Dom Scozzaro (*Finance Assistant*)
Miss Clemmie Studd (*School Secretary*)
Mrs Magaly Trigalet-Dombasi (*DT Technician*)
Ms Sharon Wood (*Headmaster's Secretary*)
Mr Kim Wykes (*Laboratory Technician*)

Caretaking Staff:
Mr Joseph Akyeampong (*Caretaker*)
Mr John Himana (*Maintenance*)
Mr Jay El Mouden (*Assistant Caretaker*)

The Purcell School

Aldenham Road, Bushey, Hertfordshire WD23 2TS

Tel: 01923 331100
Fax: 01923 331166
email: info@purcell-school.org
website: www.purcell-school.org
Twitter: @PurcellSchool
Facebook: @PurcellSchool

The Purcell School is one of the world's leading specialist centres of excellence and has a national and international reputation in the education and training of exceptional young musicians. It is the oldest specialist music school in the UK, having been founded as the Central Tutorial School for Young Musicians in 1962. It moved to its current site in Bushey, on the outskirts of London, in 1997.

There are over 180 pupils, boys and girls, aged from 10 to 18, with around 90 in the Sixth Form. All pupils are meanstested on entry to the School and receive Scholarships under the Government's Music and Dance Scheme or from the School's own Scholarship Fund.

The Purcell School exists to provide young musicians of exceptional promise and talent with the best possible teaching and environment in which to fulfil their potential, irrespective of their background. It has consistent success in national and international competitions and has an extensive programme of outreach and community work. The majority of pupils progress to music conservatoires although a small number each year elect to go to University to study both music and non-musical subjects.

The Music Department at The Purcell School aims to provide:

• A stimulating and challenging musical environment, at the heart of which is an individually tailored programme for every pupil. We try to ensure that both the balance of musical studies and the balance between musical and academic work are fine-tuned to suit each pupil.

• A flexible timetable, designed to enable pupils to practise. Pupils in Years 5 to 8 are able to put in up to 3 hours each day on their first study. In Years 9 and 10 that rises to 3–4 hours and sixth formers are able to do 4–5 hours or even more depending on their academic commitments. We provide practice supervisors, themselves graduate musicians, who work with pupils up to Year 9 to ensure they use their practice time effectively. Our experienced and expert instrumental teachers set practice goals and teach practice strategies.

• Twice-weekly contact with the pupil's first study instrumental teacher for a total of up to 2 hours' tuition. All our instrumental teachers have considerable experience of working with motivated young musicians and have proven their ability to enable their students to succeed. Many of them also teach at the London conservatoires.

• An enriched musical programme that includes chamber music, orchestras, piano classes, choirs and aural and theory training. Frequent performing opportunities range from daily lunchtime concerts at school and in the surrounding area to formal recitals around the UK and in the capital's leading venues. Pupils can audition for the chance to play concertos with the school's orchestras, to give solo and chamber music recitals at the Royal Festival Hall, Wigmore Hall, Purcell Room and other prestigious venues.

• The work of our regular teachers is enhanced by visits from the world's leading musicians for masterclasses, recitals, courses and collaborative projects.

• An academic programme which (as far as possible) is organised around each pupil's musical commitments, whilst still enabling pupils to achieve the necessary examination grades and all-round education to pursue a musical career if they choose, or to otherwise enjoy a successful future.

• Pastoral care which is provided by professionals who understand the demands on and needs of performing musicians. This includes dedicated boarding staff, a school nurse, physiotherapist and independent counsellor.

• A supportive and sympathetic peer group, keen to help each other to achieve their potential. We are well aware of the benefits of being embedded in a musical environment in which all students understand and support each other, and this is an approach which we actively foster.

Academic Studies. The school aims to achieve a balance between musical studies and an all-round general academic education. Music comprises a significant proportion of the timetable time depending on age and needs. The remainder of time is spent studying a range of subjects including mathematics, English, sciences, modern languages and humanities.

The size of the school ensures that classes are generally small. This allows for a great deal of individual attention from an experienced and dedicated staff of teachers.

All pupils are set homework each day and time is allocated in the boarding houses each evening for this to be completed. Pupils' academic progress is closely monitored and parents receive frequent progress reports.

Boarding. The Purcell School is international in its outlook and welcomes pupils from all over Britain and from all over the world. Over 75% are boarders, all of whom live on the School campus. The needs of overseas pupils are cared for by a dedicated member of staff.

The youngest pupils, aged between 10 and 12, live in Avison House. Sunley House (girls) Graham Smallbone House (girls) and Gardner House (boys) are all superb new or recently refurbished boarding facilities. Members of the Sixth Form can use their rooms for practice as well as for study. In addition to the Houseparents, resident practice supervisors help the pupils to maintain their busy musical schedules.

In each half of the term there is an Exeat weekend when all pupils go home or to their guardian or to friends. There is also an extended half-term period in each of the three terms.

Admission. Entrance is by musical audition and interview – please see the school website for further details. The

Registrar, Mrs Karen Gumustekin, will be pleased to answer queries.

Fees per term (2016–2017). Day £8,484; Boarding £10,833.

Bursary funding is available, for those pupils who meet the eligibility criteria, under the Department for Education Music and Dance Scheme, and there is the possibility of means-tested financial support from the school for those who do not. Parents are welcome to consult the Bursar for guidance.

Charitable status. The Purcell School is a Registered Charity, number 312855. It aims to offer specialist musical training, combined with an excellent general academic education, to children of exceptional musical ability.

Royal Patron: HRH The Prince of Wales

Patrons:
Sir Simon Rattle, CBE (*President*)
Baroness Warnock, DBE (*Vice-President*)
Vladimir Ashkenazy, CBE
Sir Andrew Davis, CBE
Donatella Flick
Dame Kiri Te Kanawa, DBE
Yevgeny Kissin
Dame Fanny Waterman, DBE

Governing Body:
Sir Roger Jackling, KCB, CBE (*Chairman*)
Peter van de Geest (*Deputy Chairman*)
Charles Beer, MA (*Chairman of Finance and General Purposes Committee*)
Professor Timothy Blinko, BMus Hons, MMus, Dip RCM
Dr Xanthe Cross, BMed Sci, MBBS, MRCGP, DFSRH
Jonathan Eley, MA
James Fowler, MA (*Chairman of Education Committee*)
Janice Graham, ARCM, AGSMD, ACT
Professor Colin Lawson, CBE, MA, MA, PhD, DMus, FRCM, FRNCM, FLCM, RAM
Julie Nicholls, BA, ACA
Ian Odgers, MA
Mark Racz, BA, MFA Hon, FBC, Hon RAM
Julia Somerville, OBE, BA
Joanna Van Heyningen, OBE, MA, MA, Dip Arch, RIBA

Headmaster: **Stephen Yeo**, BMus Hons, LTCL MusEd, NPQH

Deputy Head (*Students & Innovation*): Christine Rayfield, BA Hons, PGCE
Deputy Head (*Staff and Communications*): James Harding, MA, PGCE
Bursar: Aideen McNamara, BA Hons

Head of Sixth Form: Elizabeth Willan, BA Hons, PGCE

Music Department:

Head of Strings: Charles Sewart
Tony Cucchiara (*Violin*)
Alda Dizdari (*Violin*)
Sadagat Mamedova-Rashidova (*Violin*)
Nathaniel Vallois (*Violin*)
Tanja Goldberg, PhD (*Violin*)
Felicity Lipman (*Violin*)
Ben Wragg (*Violin*)
Sarah-Jane Bradley (*Viola*)
Pal Banda (*Cello*)
Alexander Boyarsky (*Cello*)
Ben Wragg (*Cello*)
Tim Lowe (*Cello*)
Neil Tarlton (*Double Bass*)
Francesco Mariani (*Guitar*)
Tony Cross (*Alexander Technique*)
Jean Mercer (*Alexander Technique*)

Head of Keyboard: William Fong
Lidia Amorelli (*Piano*)
Andrew Ball (*Piano*)
David Gordon (*Harpsichord & Improvisation*)
Caterina Grewe (*Piano*)
Gareth Hunt (*Piano*)
Jianing Kong (*Piano*)
Alla Kravchenko (*Piano*)
Ching-Ching Lim (*Piano*)
Pascal Nemirovski (*Piano*)
Tessa Nicholson (*Piano*)
Danielle Salamon (*Piano*)
Tatiana Sarkissova (*Piano*)
Deborah Shah (*Piano/Accompanist*)
Daniel Swain (*Accompanist*)
Patsy Toh (*Piano*)

Head of Brass, Percussion, Voice & Harp: Kevin Hathway
Tony Cross (Trumpet)
Rob Workman (Trombone)
Stephen Wick (*Tuba*)
Beth Randell (Horn)
Daphne Boden (Harp)
Charlotte Seale (Harp)
Tom Marandola (Voice)
Daniella Ganeva (Percussion)

Head of Wind, Clarinet: Joy Farrall
Hannah Grayson (*Flute*)
Anna Pope (*Flute*)
Amy Green (*Saxophone*)
Graham Hobbs (*Bassoon*)
Izzie Couch (*Clarinet*)
Melanie Ragge (*Oboe*)
Barbara Law (*Recorder*)

Head of Jazz: Simon Allen
Ross Anderson (*Jazz Trombone*)
George Hogg (*Jazz Trumpet*)
Steve Waterman (*Jazz Trumpet*)
Oliver Hayhurst (*Jazz Bass*)
Chris Montague (*Jazz Guitar*)
Tom Challenger (*Jazz Piano*)
Kit Downes (*Jazz Piano*)
David Gordon (*Jazz Piano*)
Darren Altman (*Jazz Drums*)
Jacqui Hicks (*Jazz Voice*)

Head of Composition: Alison Cox, OBE, GRNCM, DipAdvStdMus Comp, PGCE
Joseph Phibbs, BMus, MMus
Simon Speare, MA, ARCM
Jacques Cohen, BA Hons, ARCM

Head of Academic Music: Mary-Kate Gill, BA Hons, Adv Cert GSMD, PGCE
Alison Cox
Edward Longstaff
Christine Rayfield
Andrew Williams
Stephen Yeo

Head of Music Technology: Aidan Goetzee, MSc, GRSM, ARCM

Academic Staff:
* *Head of Department*
§ *Part-time*

Peter Banks, BSc Hons, PGCE (*Chemistry*)
Alison Cox, OBE, GRNCM, DipAdvStdMus Comp, PGCE (§*Academic Music*, *Composition)
Paul Elliott, MA Hons, PGCE (*German, *Drama)
Panos Fellas, BSc, MA Sc Ed (*Science, *Physics)

Mary-Kate Gill, BA, AdvCert, GSMD, PGCE (*Academic Music)
Aidan Goetzee, MSc, GRSM, ARCM (*Music Technology)
James Harding, MA Hons, PGCE (Deputy Head Staff & Communications, English)
Deborah Harris, BMus, PGCE (§Juniors)
Jocelyne Hazan, BA, MA (§French, Overseas pupils Guardian Coordinator)
Katherine Higgins, BEd, MA TEFL, MSc (*EFL)
Saleem Izhar, BSc, MSc UCL, PGCE (§Mathematics)
Christopher Lehane, BA Hons, PGCE (*Sports)
Andrew Leverton, BA, Dip Ed (*English)
Edward Longstaff, BMus Hons, MMus, LRSM, PGCE (Music)
Monica Lowenberg, BA Hons, MA (§German)
Darrell Pigott, BSc, PGCE (*History)
Christine Rayfield, BA Hons, PGCE (Deputy Head Students & Innovation, Music)
Nadine Sender, BA Hons (*Art)
Alexandra Stone, BSc (*Maths)
Jan Szafranski, BA Hons (Drama)
Martin Whitfield, BSc, MSc, PGCE (Mathematics)
Dorothy Withers, BA, PGCE (Biology)
Sally-Ann Whitty, BA (*Learning Support)
Elizabeth Willan, BA Hons, PGCE (*Modern Languages, *French)
Andrew Williams, BA, MA, PCGE (§Academic Music)

Resident Graduate Sports Assistant:
Andy Ingram, BSc (Sports)

Boarding Houses:
Avison: Jane Malan
Gardner: Mary Pitkin
Graham Smallbone: Rachel Branch
Sunley: Sally Pearson

Administration Staff:
PA to Headmaster: Judy Rollinson
Deputy Bursar: Jo Wallis
School Office: Antonia Holmes, Jannice Raw, Caroline Fletcher
Administrator & Overseas Pupil Coordinator: Louise Wigodsky
Music Department Secretary & Registrar: Karen Gumustekin
Music Timetabler: Fiona Duce
Librarian: Harriet Rayfield
Concerts Manager: Jane Hunt
Concerts Administrator: Abigail Willer
Fundraising Manager: Ruth Blake
Development Department Assistant: Emma McGrath
Fundraising Assistant: Celia Crowne
PR & Communications Manager: Susannah Curran
Marketing Intern: Aimee-Deborah Peters
Finance Officer: Susan Pickard
ICT Network Manager: Simon Kingsbury
Art Technician: Joshua Radburn
Science Technician: Hawreen Osman
Technology Technician: Tom Bell
Estates: Tina Little
Catering: Holroyd Howe Independent Limited
School Nurse: Hilary Austin
Physiotherapist: Sarah Upjohn

The Read School
Drax

Drax, Selby, North Yorkshire YO8 8NL

Tel:	01757 618248
Fax:	01757 617432
email:	enquiries@readschool.co.uk
website:	www.readschool.co.uk

Age Range. Co-educational 2–18 (Boarding 8–18).

Number in School. Total 210: Day 175, Boarding 35; Boys 130, Girls 80.

The school is pleasantly situated in the rural village of Drax and is very convenient for main rail (Doncaster, York, Leeds) and road access (M62, M18, A1). Manchester is the nearest international airport (1½ hours distant). It is a relatively small school where children are well known to each other and to the staff.

The school has been a focal point for education in the Selby-Goole area since the 17th century and will celebrate its 350th anniversary in 2017. There has been a school on the same site since 1667 and it is proud to be one of the oldest educational establishments in the UK. The school has been co-educational since 1992 and offers a wide range of academic studies at GCSE and A Level, together with a full programme of Sports, Drama, Music, CCF and recreational activity. There is one class in each Prep School year from Pre-School to Year 6. There are two classes in each of the Senior years (7–11). There is a small Sixth Form (40 pupils) following AS and A Level courses. High standards are expected in all aspects of endeavour, and in behaviour and manners.

Facilities. In addition to the refurbished Edwardian buildings there continued to be steady developments in the facilities and accommodation throughout the 1980s and 1990s. These include the fine Moloney Hall, Ramsker classrooms, Sports Hall, Coggrave Building for the Prep School (Years 3–6), in addition to internal developments, especially in the provision of IT. The Pre-Prep has recently moved into the Shipley building on the main school campus and enjoys more up-to-date facilities. In 2009 a new Creative Arts Centre was provided for Art, Design Technology and Food. More recently, the biology and physics labs have been fully refurbished, as has the Memorial Library. In the summer of 2011 a stunning upgrade of the Sports Hall was implemented. The girls' boarding accommodation was moved onto the main school site in 2015 and underwent a complete renovation with new bathrooms, common room and improved facilities. Over the summer of 2016 the MUGA was completely relaid and refurbished and a new building to house the music department was begun; it is expected to open in the spring of 2017.

Fees per term (2016–2017). Boarders: £7,220–£9,030; Day: £2,685–£3,935.

Admission. An offer of a place in the school is made after interview (and verbal reasoning and mathematics tests for admission to the Senior School) and satisfactory report from the pupil's current school.

Charitable status. The Read School is a Registered Charity, number 529675. It exists to provide a proper education for boys and girls aged 2–18.

Chairman of Governors: Peter Watt

Head: J A Sweetman, BSc, PhD, FRSB

Deputy Head: M A Voisey, BA (Head of English)

Assistant Head (Curriculum): Ms C M Palmer, BSc, MSc (Mathematics)

Teaching Staff:
§N J Borthwick, BSc (*Psychology*)
P J Budd, BSc (*Physics*)
Miss J Bullock, BSc, MSc (*Head of Science, English Additional Language*)
§Ms S L Campbell, BSc (*Pre-Prep School*)
Mrs S Chambonnet, BA (*Latin, French*)
Mrs J Clark (*Head of Music, brass instruments, piano, CCF*)
Miss C Cross, BA (*Head of Sixth Form, English*)
M Dell, BSc (*Head of Mathematics*)
Mrs L Fairhurst, BA (*Prep School*)
B Garrard, BSc (*Head of PE and Games*)
§D I Gisbourne, BSc (*Director of ICT, Mathematics*)
§Mrs H Hewson, BA (*English*)
Mr G Hill, BA (*Prep School*)
§Mrs K Ives, BA (*French, Spanish*)
§Mrs E Jackson, BSc (*Mathematics*)
§Mrs P Kavanagh, BA (*Business Studies*)
Mrs K Limbert (*Pre-School Manager*)
§Mrs B J Maunsell, BA (*Drama*)
Mrs S Morrell, BEd (*History, Religious Studies, PSHE Coordinator*)
Miss F M Newman, BA (*Prep School, KS3 Art, Dance*)
Mrs K E Patrick, PGDip Counselling, PGDip SEN, MA (*Head of Inclusive Learning*)
C S Patrick, BSc (*Specialist Tutor*)
§Mrs S Prosser, BA (*PE and Games*)
Mrs S Rothwell-Wood, BEd (*Design Technology, Food*)
Mrs S Scholefield, BSc (*Head of Humanities*)
§R P Stark, BSc, DipEd (*Physics*)
§J Staves, BSc, PhD (*Chemistry*)
Mrs R M Wake, BA (*Key Stage 2 Coordinator*)
Mrs A L Watson, BA (*Key Stage 1 Coordinator*)
§Miss A J Williamson, MA (*Art*)
Mrs C M Wynne, BEd (*Pre-Prep School*)

Reddam House Berkshire
Formerly Bearwood College

Wokingham, Berkshire RG41 5BG
Tel: 0118 974 8300
Fax: 0118 977 3186
email: headmaster@reddamhouse.org.uk
           registrar@reddamhouse.org.uk
website: www.reddamhouse.org.uk
           www.reddamschools.com

Reddam House Berkshire (the former Bearwood College) is a co-educational independent day and boarding school, which inspires excellence in education for pupils from three months to 18 years old. This newly restructured through-school, which has been divided into three sections – an Early Learning School, a Junior School and a Senior School – is set in a majestic parkland of 120 hectares comprising extensive playing fields, woodland and a lake.

While its historic buildings are situated in a beautiful and secure rural estate, the school is conveniently located between Reading and Wokingham in the royal county of Berkshire, a vibrant location with very easy access to the M3, M4, Heathrow and London.

The recent change to the school's name came about on the acquisition of Bearwood College by the Reddam House group of schools (see further below) in September 2014; and under its new banner it has been selected as the group's flagship school among its expanding network in the UK and Europe.

Bearwood had a proud history, originally as a school for children of merchant seamen. A strong culture has emerged

over the years – closely aligned to the existing Reddam culture – in which pupils are acknowledged as individuals and their distinct personality traits, attributes and special strengths are celebrated and optimised.

The Reddam House philosophy and formula for success are based on the quality and depth of their schools' curricular, cultural and sporting activities and – above all – on the uncompromising selection of outstanding teaching staff, in full recognition that the rapport between teacher and pupil is the strongest influence on an individual child's development and on the overall success of a school.

The Reddam House Group has its origin in South Africa and has opened other schools in Sydney, Australia. In both countries the schools have achieved singular success – both in terms of the well-rounded quality of person introduced to the world and in academic ranking: they top the league tables in South Africa and are among the top ten schools in New South Wales. They are also extremely successful in the diversity and quality of their co-curricular activities: music, dance, drama, public speaking and a wide range of sports. They are also true to their motto 'We Shall Give Back', instilling a strong sense of civic engagement, which holds a special appeal to pupils and parents.

Academic Structure. At Reddam House we expect each child to achieve his or her best. Each pupil works to an academic programme which is individually targeted and permanently monitored. It provides a structured, supported and demanding academic challenge appropriate to each pupil's capacity. The academic curriculum is based on and exceeds the guidelines of the National Curriculum. In the years up to GCSE, we provide a programme which offers choice, breadth of experience and the opportunity to develop particular academic skills, which are then further developed in greater depth at A Level. The individual attention and specialised teaching that continues into the Sixth Form enables an enviable success rate of entry into first-choice universities.

Pastoral and Boarding Arrangements. Day care and education is available for children from 3 months to 18 years with boarding from 11–18. Once joining the Senior School the following day/boarding arrangements are available:

- Full boarding with continuous care and involvement for seven days a week.
- Weekly boarding with the chance to go home at weekends once school commitments have been fulfilled.
- Occasional or flexible boarding for limited or irregular periods to help busy parents.

Sport and Activities. All pupils take part in a wide range of games and activities outside the classroom. They enjoy a breadth of experience as well as being expected to discover specific areas in which to excel.

Everyone takes part in physical activities on most days. Sports and games give the pupils physical fitness, personal and team skills and recreation. They offer many opportunities to find a sense of achievement. On-site sports and activities on the extensive array of playing fields and facilities include all the usual field sports together with additional opportunities for: golf, equestrian sports, cycling and mountain biking, sailing, shooting, and canoeing.

Extracurricular activities: Outdoor pursuits are encouraged to balance the pursuit of academic excellence. The extensive grounds and lake are used for sailing, canoeing, mountain biking, camping, cross country and many other activities. Few schools can boast such a varied estate.

Combined Cadet Force: All pupils in the third and fourth forms of the Senior School join the Combined Cadet Force (CCF). Cadets learn self-reliance and teamwork, and develop their own leadership skills. The CCF also provides an unrivalled opportunity to experience outdoor pursuits. Two camps are held during holiday periods each year. The annual adventure training expedition provides boys and girls with the opportunity to experience environments that test and challenge their characters whilst under the supervision of highly qualified staff. Many cadets choose to continue their service in the cadet force during their fifth and sixth form years. At this time they take on the extra responsibilities of being senior cadets. The experience they gain from taking an active role in teaching and helping younger cadets provides a valuable insight into the qualities required from leaders.

The Duke of Edinburgh's Award: All pupils in the fourth form are encouraged to start The Duke of Edinburgh's Award at bronze level. This is organised partly in conjunction with the cadet force who help with the training for the expedition section. Senior pupils are encouraged to continue with both silver and gold awards. The scheme provides pupils with an ideal opportunity to develop their own skills, fitness and commitment to others whilst fostering self-confidence and personal esteem.

Music: Music is part of the life of every pupil, non-specialist and specialist alike. Everyone participates in music events including the House Singing Competition and the Choral Society. There are regular informal and formal concerts given by instrumentalists and singers. All pupils are encouraged to take up instrumental and vocal lessons with professional peripatetic musicians. Regular visits to concerts and other musical outings take place.

Theatre and Drama: Our Theatre represents the very best that is available for the pursuance of music and dramatic arts. A busy programme of concerts, recitals and plays ensure that this 350-seat auditorium is continually in use. All pupils are encouraged to make a contribution to these productions. Pupil performers are supported by their peers as theatre technicians, lighting and sound engineers, stage crew and scenery builders. Drama is for all, and all have their part to play in the many productions.

Specialist tuition leading to LAMDA Speech and Drama grades and awards is available. These help to develop confidence and competence in acting, public speaking and general communication.

Dance: Dance is an exciting and vibrant part of everyday life. Whether pupils decide to study GCSE or A Level Dance, or enjoy dance outside the curriculum, there is a class for everyone. A variety of dance styles are taught outside the curriculum, including, Ballet, Contemporary, Jazz and Street Dance allowing the truly passionate to share their commitment and flair through performance.

Facilities. The splendid Mansion House is the centre of the school, around which all our other buildings are located. Historic rooms house modern facilities.

The Cook Library is situated in the former drawing room, one of the most beautiful rooms in the Mansion. It has a collection of both fiction and non-fiction books for loan and reference use. The library resource is further enhanced by networked computers with internet access. Pupils are encouraged to read daily quality broad sheet newspapers to keep abreast of current affairs, politics and news. This learning resource is run by a full-time Librarian and supports all areas of the curriculum as well as providing for recreational reading.

The need for modern technology is supported by an excellent IT backbone. All departments in the College have Apple TVs and wireless is available throughout the school, and ongoing investment in digital technology for teaching and learning is integral to the restructuring process undertaken by Reddam House.

The range of further facilities for pupils at Reddam House is extensive. A fully-equipped photographic suite, extensive sports pitches, netball courts, a swimming pool, tennis courts, weights-training room and rifle range are all found immediately adjacent to the main building.

The Early Learning School and Junior Schools are located close to the main Victorian Mansion House, in a thoughtfully converted, listed Coach House. The splendid surroundings of the wider campus combined with the intimate security of the Coach House allow children safely to explore, discover and learn. The Reggio Emilia approach to teaching young children introduced by Reddam House puts the natural development of children as well as the close relationships that they share with their environment at the centre of its philosophy – something which is uniquely enabled by the school's parkland setting.

Admission. Entry is normally 0+, 3+, 5+, 11+, 13+ and the Sixth Form, but applications at other ages are accepted, subject to vacancies. Assessment is by interview, assessment and by Common Entrance where appropriate. Entry to the Sixth Form is normally conditional upon the achievement of a minimum of 5 GCSEs at B grade or above.

Fees per term (2016–2017). Early Learning School: From £55 (short day), £68 (full day) to £3,165 (full time Reception); Junior School (Years 1–6): £3,315–£4,085; Senior School: Tuition: £5,515 (Years 7–13); Weekly Boarding: £8,515 (Years 7–9), £9,815 (Years 10–13); Full Boarding: £9,015 (Years 7–9), £10,315 (Years 10–13).

Scholarships. A significant number of Academic, Dance, Drama, Music, Art and Sport Scholarships are offered each year for entry at 11+.

Board of Governors:
Dr Stephen Spurr (*Chairman*)
Mr Graeme Crawford
Mr Nadim M Nsouli
Mr David Brickell
Mr Graham Able
Mrs Jenny Aviss

Headmaster: **Mr Toby Mullins**, BA Hons, MBA

Headmistress Junior School: Mrs T Howard, BSc, Cert Ed

Deputy Head Senior: W A Webster, BA Hons, HDE
Director Teaching & Learning: Mrs K Dain, MEd Cantab, PG Dip, AMBDA
Deputy Head Junior: Mrs S Whitcher, BA, BSc, PGCE, Cert Ed
Deputy Head ELS: Mrs B Lancaster, BA Hons, PGCE
Business Manager: Mrs P Horwood, BA Hons, MBA

Heads of Faculty:
Science: Mrs Sarah Nichol, BSc, PGCE
Sport, Dance & Team Gym: Mr Jason Dance, BA Ed Hons
Business Studies, Modern Foreign Languages & Art: Mr James Day, BA, BEd
English: Mrs Nicky Phillips, BA Hons, DipEd
Humanities, Music and Drama: Natalie Holsgrove-Jones, BA Hons, PGCE
Maths & ICT: Mr Scott Nichol, BSc, BEd
Study Support: Mrs S Pooley, BEd Hons

Boarding House Parents: Mr & Mrs Paxton

Rishworth School

Rishworth, West Yorkshire HX6 4QA
Tel: 01422 822217 (Main School)
Fax: 01422 820911
email: admissions@rishworth-school.co.uk
website: www.rishworth-school.co.uk
Twitter: @RishworthS
Facebook: /RishworthSchool

Rishworth is an exceptionally friendly, caring community, in which pupils are as strongly encouraged to rejoice in each other's achievements as to take pride in their own. The School succeeds in combining a disciplined environment with a relaxed and welcoming atmosphere.

While pupils are at Rishworth, we try to ensure that, in addition to the knowledge and skills acquired through academic study, they develop:

- A love of learning and the will to succeed.
- A sense of responsibility, self-discipline, purpose and fulfilment.
- A capacity for both self-reliance and cooperation.
- An appreciation of certain personal virtues and spiritual values, such as honesty, dependability, perseverance, commitment, humility and respect for others.

General organisation. Founded in 1724, Rishworth is a co-educational day and boarding school comprising a nursery for children from age 3, a Junior School, Heathfield, which has its own separate site where children are taught up to the age of 11, and the Senior School up to age 18. Rishworth is a Church of England foundation, but welcomes children of all faiths, or of none. Numbers stand at about 500 pupils, of whom over 100 are boarders.

Facilities and Location. Superbly located in 130 acres of a beautiful Pennine valley, the School has a mix of elegant older buildings and excellent modern facilities including a capacious sports hall with fitness suite, a separate, newly-redeveloped Sports Club with 25-metre indoor swimming pool and squash courts, a large expanse of games pitches, a music block, 3 modern ICT suites, wireless (and cabled) Internet and Intranet connection across the whole site, a Performing Arts Theatre, a centre dedicated to sixth-form study, freshly-refurbished boarding houses and newly-installed, state-of-the-art science laboratories.

Access to the School by road is easy, with the M62 within five minutes' drive. School buses run to the Halifax, Todmorden, Rochdale, Oldham and Huddersfield areas.

Welfare and Pastoral. The unusually high degree of attention afforded to pupils by small teaching groups, the careful monitoring of progress, coordinated pastoral support and a close working partnership with parents enables pupils to build on their strengths and allows specific needs to be addressed. Each boarding pupil is under the direct care of a Housemaster or Housemistress, who is ably supported by assistant staff in each boarding house.

Teaching. Taught by a dedicated staff of qualified specialists, the curriculum, both academic and non-academic, is broad and stimulating, and offers every pupil the chance to be challenged and to excel. A general curriculum, broadly in line with the National Curriculum, is followed until Year 9, after which pupils select GCSE options in consultation with their parents, tutors and subject teachers. AS and A2 options are also selected via consultation.

Support is given by qualified specialists for certain special needs including dyslexia and English where this is not the pupil's first language.

Broader Education. In order to help our pupils to become the confident, balanced and considerate young men and women we wish them to be, we encourage participation in a wide range of activities outside the classroom.

Sports are well appointed and well taught, and each term boys and girls enjoy excellent results. The School also has a justly high reputation in music and drama.

Other activities range from The Duke of Edinburgh's Award to golf, skiing, and many others.

Boarding. We have no dormitories. Boarders (from age 10 or 11, and sometimes age 9) are accommodated in individual study-bedrooms, almost all single or double occupancy, which allow pupils their personal space. These are located in spacious houses, overseen by house staff. The boarding houses have recently undergone major refurbishment which has ensured that the character of the historic buildings has been retained alongside the provision of top-rate modern amenities. A full programme of activities is arranged for the evenings and weekends, and there are good recreational facilities reserved for the boarders, including dedicated social areas.

Admission. Places in the Junior School, Heathfield, are given, subject to availability, on individual assessments appropriate to each applicant's age and previous education. Entrants for Rishworth at Year 7 are asked to sit the School's own entrance assessment, which also forms the basis for the award of scholarships.

Those who wish to join the School at other stages are assessed individually.

Fees per term (from April 2016). Reception to Year 2 £2,050; Years 3 to 6 £3,010; Years 7 & 8: £3,690 day, £8,160 full boarding, £7,405 weekly boarding; Years 9 to 13: £4,020 day, £8,895 full boarding, £8,100 weekly boarding. The School operates a number of schemes, including monthly payments, to ease the financial burden on parents.

Scholarships and Bursaries. Scholarships & Bursaries are available, the former on merit, the latter for demonstrable financial need. The extent to which these awards can be offered will also be determined by other factors, such as the School's own circumstances and the nature of a given cohort of applicants.

Scholarships may be awarded, up to a value of 50% of Tuition fees, for excellence in academic work, sport, music or drama. For Year 7 entry scholarships, applicants are formally assessed. For Year 12 entry, awards are made on the basis of an individual's past record (including examination results).

Most awards are made to applicants at these entry levels. However, suitable candidates at any stage will be considered.

Substantial discounts are available for siblings of pupils in the School, for children of serving members of the Armed Forces and of ordained members of the Church of England. Bursaries may also be available in cases of financial need.

The Old Rishworthian Club maintains a fund for the grant of scholarships to children of ORs.

For more information contact the Admissions Officer.

Charitable status. Rishworth School is a Registered Charity, number 1115562. It exists to provide education for boys and girls.

Visitor: The Most Reverend The Lord Archbishop of York

Honorary Governor: A J Morsley, Esq

The Governing Body:
Dr C A G Brooks (*Chairman*)
G C W Allan, Esq
Mrs J C Slim
J G Wheelwright, Esq
T M Wheelwright, Esq
Mrs D M Whitaker, JP (*Vice Chair*)
Revd T L Swinhoe
W P Hodgson, Esq

Advisor to the Board: Revd Canon Hilary Barber

Bursar and Clerk to the Board of Governors: J Clague, BA Hons, FCA, CTA

Teaching Staff:
* *Head of Department*

Headmaster: **A S Gloag**, BA (*RS*)

Deputy Headmaster: P Seery, BSc MEd (*Chemistry*)
Director of Marketing: Mrs S J Stamp, BSc (*Geography*)
Director of Studies: S Ogden, BSc (*Geography*)
Director of Teaching and Learning: Dr J Ladds, MChem, PhD, MEd (*Science, Assistant Head of Sixth Form*)
Head of Lower & Middle School: Ms J Sheldrick, BSc (*DSL, Science, Food & Nutrition*)
Head of Heathfield: A M Wilkins, BA, MA Lit, MA Hist

Mrs E Allison BSc (*Head of Early Years, Key Stage 1, Heathfield*)

T Anderson (*Sports and Games Coach, Rishworth and Heathfield*)

Mrs M T Arbelo-Dolan, BA (*Spanish*)

Mrs R Aujla BA (**Geography*)

D Baker, BEd (*Deputy Head, Key Stage 2 Teacher, ICT & Mathematics Coordinator, Heathfield*)

S Barrott, B Ed (*Key Stage 2 Teacher, Heathfield*)

R A Beecher, BA (**Economics, Business Studies, EPQ Coordinator*)

P Bell, BA, MSc (**ICT & Computing*)

Mrs H Bower, BSc (**PE & Sport, Mathematics; PE, Heathfield*)

Mrs J Bradley, LTCL, GTCL, CKME (*Music Coordinator, Heathfield*)

C Brass, BSc (*Science Coordinator, Key Stage 1 Teacher, Heathfield*)

Mrs J Bridges NVQ3 (*Teaching Assistant, Heathfield*)

M Brown, NVQ2 (*Teaching Assistant, Heathfield*)

Ms V Callagher, NVQ 3 (*Foundation Stage Key Person, Heathfield*)

G Davies, BSc (*Mathematics*)

Mrs C Devney, BA, BSc (**Learning Support*)

Mrs C Ellis, MA, BSc, MCLIP (*Librarian*)

Mrs K Fraser, BA (**Art, Assistant Head Lower & Middle School*)

Mrs S Gaynor, BTEC (*Out of School Care Deputy Manager, Teaching Assistant, Heathfield*)

Miss S Greenwood, BEd (*Key Stage 1 Teacher, Heathfield*)

Mrs E Gregory, BA (*History*)

Mrs C Hall, BA, DipEd (**Food & Nutrition, Assistant Housemistress Wheelwright, Careers Coordinator*)

S Haslam, PhD (*Science, Teacher i/c Chemistry*)

P Heap, BA (**Drama*)

Mrs J Higgins, NNEB (*Teaching Assistant, Learning Support, Heathfield*)

C D Holmes-Roe, BA, MA (*History, Resident Housemaster of Slitheroe*)

D I Horsfall, BSc (*Mathematics*)

Mrs J Howcroft, BSc, MSc (*Mathematics*)

Mrs H Hoyle, NVQ3 (*Teaching Assistant, Heathfield*)

Mrs J Hudson, BA (*Key Stage 2 Teacher, Learning Support, English Coordinator, Heathfield*)

Mrs V Hutchinson, BA (*RE Coordinator, Key Stage 2 Teacher, Heathfield*)

Mrs N I'Anson, BA (*Nursery Teacher, Heathfield*)

Ms K A James, LLB (*EFL, Resident Housemistress Wheelwright, i/c Girls' Boarding*)

Mrs K Jones, BSc (**Mathematics*)

P W Jones, MA Cantab (*Science Advisor, Teacher i/c Biology*)

Mrs A M Kellett-End, BA, PGCLD (*Learning Support*)

Mrs S Kiy, BA (*French Coordinator, Key Stage 1 Teacher, Heathfield*)

C Lewis, BA, LRAM, LGSM (**Director of Music*)

Ms J Marsden, BA (*English, Drama*)

Miss B Martin, BSc (**Psychology*)

Mrs R C McGarry, BA (*English, RS*)

S H J McGarry, BEng, MSc (*Science, Teacher i/c Physics*)

Mrs L Meredith, BA, ARCM (*Music, English, Teacher i/c Provision for Academically Most Able*)

Mrs R Millington, MA Cantab (*Science*)

Mrs S Moore, BA (*English*)

Miss M Needham, BA (*Art, Design Technology*)

D Newby, BTech (**Design Technology, Day House Area Master for Hanson House Years 9 & 10*)

Mrs R Ogden, BEng (*Mathematics*)

Mrs P Pritchard (*Out-of-School Care Manager, Teaching Assistant, Heathfield*)

Mrs G Putnam (*Teaching Support, Heathfield*)

E Redmond, BEd (*Key Stage 2 Teacher, Heathfield*)

Mrs C Robinson, BA (*Teaching Assistant, Learning Support*)

Miss E P Robinson, BA (*Art & Library Coordinator, Heathfield*)

P I M Robinson, BEd (**Business Studies, Head of Sixth Form, UCAS & HE Coordinator, Enhanced Curriculum, EPQ*)

Mrs J Roe, BA (*EFL*)

Mrs K Rose, BA (*Key Stage 2 Teacher, Heathfield*)

M Schlag, BA (*EFL*)

Mrs S Senkuviene, BEd (*Nursery Teacher, Heathfield*)

M E Siggins, BA (**English, General Studies*)

G M Smith, BA (**Modern Languages*)

Mrs M Smith, BA (*PE Coordinator, Heathfield*)

Mrs J Stanley (*Teaching Assistant, Heathfield*)

Miss H E A Stembridge, BEd (*Key Stage 1 Teacher, Humanities Coordinator, Heathfield*)

C Stone, BA (*Games Coach, Assistant Resident Housemaster of Calder*)

Mrs G Sunderland, SRN (*Senior Teaching Assistant, Marketing, Heathfield*)

A J Thomas, BSc (**Director of Physical Education and Sport, Resident Housemaster of Calder, i/c Boys' Boarding*)

Mrs J Thompson, BA (**EFL*)

Miss L V Turner, BA, MA (*French, EFL*)

Mrs F A Wagstaff, BA (*Design Technology, ICT & Computing*)

Ms L Watkins, BA, MA (*English*)

Ms A Wilson, BA, RGN (*Housemistress of Goathouse Barn*)

*M Wilson, BA (**History*)

Mrs L E Wood, BSc (*Physical Education & Sport, PSHCE Coordinator*)

Instrumental Music Teachers:
Mrs R K Burbidge
C D Wood
Miss H Bywater
P Brown
N Darwent
Ms H Grieg
Ms C Bishop
M Wagstaff
C Pulleyn

Administrative Staff:

Bursar: J Clague, BA Hons, FCA, CTA
Assistant Bursar: Mrs V Wheeler
Admissions Officer: Mrs J Sutherland
Headmaster's PA: Mrs S Billington
Matron: Mrs D K Robinson

Ruthin School

Mold Road, Ruthin, Denbighshire LL15 1EE

Tel:	01824 702543
Fax:	01824 707141
email:	registrar@ruthinschool.co.uk
website:	www.ruthinschool.co.uk

Motto: *Dei gratia sum quod sum*

Ruthin School was originally founded in 1284. Refounded in 1574 by Gabriel Goodman, Dean of Westminster, the School was a centre of academic excellence in North Wales, and was granted a Royal Charter.

The School is co-educational with over 330 pupils, comprising 220 boarders and 110 day pupils. The emphasis is on academic excellence and providing an environment to gain our students entry to the very best universities in the UK. Good manners, personal discipline and respect for others are of supreme importance, as is a thorough grounding in central subjects of the curriculum. We believe that social responsibility can be developed in a small community with a family atmosphere, comprising a wide range of academic and other talents. This is reflected in our entry policy. Ruthin School is committed to providing an education of the highest quality, endeavouring to develop the potential of all its pupils in all spheres of education. The pupils develop self-confidence through recognising and building upon their strengths as well as identifying and striving to improve their weaknesses. They are thus prepared to face the challenges of the changing world beyond school.

Organisation. Places (both day and full boarding) are offered to boys and girls from the age of 11.

The five boarding houses – Archbishop Williams, Ellis, Goodman, Russell and Wynne – have their own House system under the guidance of resident Housemasters.

Admission. The normal method of entry to the School is by interview, examination and reports.

Activities. A wide range of non-curricular activities is provided and has included fitness training, basketball, swimming, yoga, judo, Taekwondo, drama, rock climbing, sailing and canoeing, mountain biking, stage management, shooting, weight training, table tennis, badminton, conservation, gardening and tennis. Boys and girls are encouraged to participate in the Duke of Edinburgh's Award Scheme at the age of 14 until they have completed the Bronze Award; several go on to complete the Silver and a few aspire to the Gold Awards. A lively mix of traditional and contemporary musical and dramatic productions is a feature of the school year and half the pupils receive individual instrumental tuition from the professional music staff. A programme of excursions is organised for boarders in the evenings and at weekends and these are open to all pupils.

Bursaries and Awards. In addition to academic awards, remissions are available for siblings, children of members of the armed forces, and of Old Ruthinians.

Curriculum. A wide curriculum is offered and includes English, Mathematics, History, Geography, Latin, separate Biology, Physics and Chemistry, Art, Music, Information Technology, French, Mandarin and Spanish. PE and Economics are added at GCSE level. Further Mathematics is taught in the Sixth Form.

An option scheme operates for Form 4, but English, Mathematics, Physics, Chemistry, Biology, Geography and Economics are compulsory.

Careers. Guidance begins in the Senior School and a comprehensive programme evolves through Forms 4 and 5 and the whole of the Lower Sixth is devoted to research and visits before university applications are made. All members of the Sixth Form who wish to enter university are successful. Work experience is undertaken in Form 4 and the Lower Sixth.

Games. Rugby, basketball, football, cross-country, netball, tennis and athletics all feature in the coaching programme. A new Sports Hall was opened in January 2004.

Fees per annum (2016–2017). Day £10,000–£13,000; Boarding £28,500. Fees are payable twice yearly, at beginning of August and February. British parents have the option to pay monthly by Direct Debit.

Transport. The School provides daily transport to and from the North Wales coast, the Chester area and the Wroxham area. Transport is provided for boarders from Manchester airport to the School, at the beginning and end of each term.

The Old Ruthinian Association fosters close links between past and present pupils of the School.

Charitable status. Ruthin School is a Registered Charity, number 525754. It exists to provide education for boys and girls.

Visitor: Her Majesty The Queen

Patron: Sir William Gladstone, Bt, KG, MA

Council of Management:
Chairman: Mrs J Oldbury
C W Conway
Revd J S Evans
Mrs T Kerrigan
Dr G H Roberts
J E Sharples
His Honour Judge I J C Trigger

Principal: **T J Belfield**, MA Cantab

Vice-Principal: I Welsby, BSc, MIBiol, PGCE, DipEd

Assistant Principal – Teaching & Learning: Mrs J K Higham, MA, PGCE, CPE
Assistant Principal – Lower School: I M Rimmer, BSc, PGCE
Assistant Principal – Sixth Form: Miss K A Goodey, MEd, TESOL, BEd, CETFLA
Assistant Principal – Exams & Assessment: P J French, BSc, PGCE

Teaching Staff:
N J R Blandford, BA, MA, PGCE
Miss C Boffey, BSc, PGCE
Miss G Bonner, MA Hons, PGCE, DELTA
Mrs E T Brodzinska, LLB, MA, DELTA
Mrs E M Brown, BA, MA Ed, PGCE, TEFL, AMBDA
B Cribb, BA, PGCE, MEd
Mrs R Crowther, BA, PGCE
Dr D G Edwards, BA Hons, DPhil
Mrs S J Eve, BSc, PGCE
Dr N Fairbank, PhD
Miss P Foster, BA, PGCE, DELTA
Dr I Franjic, BSc, MSc, PhD
Mrs S Frencham, BSc, PGCE
Dr G H Green, BSc, MA, PhD
J P Hamer, BA, PGCE
Dr M D Hannant, PhD, PGCE
Mrs I Haywood, BSc, MBA, PGCE
J R Henry, BA, PGCE
M H L Hewer, MA Oxon, DipEd
D J Heywood, BA, PGCE
L Hogan, BSc, PGCE
Miss R Howlett, BSc, PGCE
Dr A W Hughes, BEng, PhD
Mrs K Hughes, BA, PGCE
Dr M L Leatherbarrow, BSc, DPhil, PGCE
Mrs M Kenworthy, BSc, PGCE
Mrs S Morley, BEd, CELTA
Mrs J I Morton, BSc, PGCE
M A Orchard, BSc, PGDE
D A Owen Booth, MGCI, BEd, DipHE
C Perry, BSc, PGCE
M S Robinson, BA, MA Oxon, PGCE
C Sennett, DRSAMD, PGCE
R A Wadon, BSc, PGCE
Miss J Warriner, BSc, MEng, MA, PGCE
Miss H Webb, BSc, PGCE
Miss D A Williams, BSc, PGCE
Dr M Wilton, PhD, PGCE
K Whiting, BSc, PGCE
Miss L Zhao, BA, PGCE

Registrar and PA to the Principal: Mrs S E Williams
Finance Administrator: Mrs S Weaver
School Medical Officer: Dr T Kneale
School Nurse: Mrs C Bland, RGN
School Nurse: Mrs S Fitzsimmons, BSc, RSCN

St Christopher School

**Barrington Road, Letchworth Garden City, Herts
SG6 3JZ**

Tel: 01462 650850
Fax: 01462 481578
email: school.admin@stchris.co.uk
            admissions@stchris.co.uk
website: www.stchris.co.uk
Twitter: @StChris_School
Facebook: @StChrisLetchworth
LinkedIn: /st-christopher-school-letchworth-garden-city

Fully co-educational from its foundation in 1915, St Christopher has always been noted for its friendly informality, breadth of educational vision, good academic standards and success in developing lifelong self-confidence. There are over 500 pupils from rising 3 to 18. Boarders can start from age 10. Weekly Boarding is available for pupils in Years 6–11. Full Boarding is available in Years 7–11 and for Sixth Formers. We aim for our young people to develop competence and resourcefulness, social conscience and moral courage, a capacity for friendship and a true zest for life.

When the School was founded in 1915 the Daily Herald reported that the School was based 'not on the sameness of children, their conformity to type, but on their differences'. This concept of treating children as individuals was revolutionary at the time and continues to be one of the distinctive characteristics of a St Chris education. We do things differently because they work. We allow children to decide what they wear to school because it teaches them to be self-reliant and to make informed choices. Everyone is called by their first names (pupils and teaching staff alike) because we have found that this promotes better relationships between children and teachers, based on mutual trust. Parents also tell us that the use of first names makes conversations with teachers easier and more productive.

The School provides for children of average to outstanding ability. All who are admitted to the Junior School (for 3 to 11 year olds) may continue through the Senior School, subject to performance. Entry to the Sixth Form is dependent on GCSE results and the ability to cope with the A Level programme.

Academic Programme. The Nursery dovetails the National Early Years Curriculum (EYFS) with the very best of Montessori Practice to provide a real educational experience within a caring and nurturing environment in the Early Years Centre.

Close attention is given to the transition to the Junior School which follows a programme that includes extensive enrichment built around the core elements of the National Curriculum. The Junior School offers small classes and a wide range of opportunities. Subject specialists teach modern languages, music and sport and the children at the top of the Junior School spend one afternoon a week in the Senior School to prepare them for their onwards move.

In the Senior School a wide-ranging programme continues to the age of 16, including the study of sciences to Double Award GCSE or GCSE in all three Sciences. In Modern Languages there are exchanges with schools in France or Spain. The creative and expressive arts are particularly encouraged and the School has been awarded the Arts Council Artsmark Gold award.

The Sixth Form. Although St Christopher is not a large school, the Sixth Form is a good size (generally numbering around 100) with excellent facilities in its Sixth Form Centre. Over 20 A Level courses are on offer with all the usual Arts and Science subjects and, in addition, Theatre Studies, Psychology, Economics, Media Studies and Design Technology. There is a lively extracurricular programme.

Learning through experience. There is an emphasis on learning through experience both with regard to academic subjects and more generally. There are many opportunities for practical and community work and for outdoor pursuits. At the end of the Summer Term the timetable is suspended for all pupils to undertake an extended project, generally away from the School campus. Each year two groups of Sixth Formers visit development projects in the Indian desert province of Rajasthan. There are also long-standing international projects in Ladakh. As a result of these the School was awarded the International School Award by the Department for Education through the British Council. The Vege Centre, the School's cookery centre, opened in 2011 and cooking is an important part of life at St Chris.

A humane and global outlook. There is no uniform (except for games). All children and adults are called by their first names. Internationalist and green values are encouraged and the School was re-awarded the Eco-Schools Award in 2010. People of different religions and of none feel equally at home; there is a significant period of silence in every assembly.

Self-Government. The School is founded on democratic principles and every voice is valued. Everyone, child and adult, is represented on the School Council which is chaired by an elected senior pupil. The elected Major Officials and Committees look after different aspects of community life. The informality of the School encourages openness: children speak up for themselves – and for others.

Treating children as individuals. From the outset the School has sought to treat children as individuals. In consequence, the ethos is an encouraging one and suits children who enjoy a broad education and who will thrive in a non-competitive academic environment where each child is asked to do their best, rather than being compared to their peers. In our Learning Centre individual and group help is available. We also deal individually with those of very high ability and children are placed "a year ahead" or "a year behind" according to their needs.

Creative and Performing Arts. The School has an excellent tradition in these areas and has fine purpose-built facilities that reflect this. There are several productions a year in the Theatre which has tiered seating and full technical resources. Similarly there are regular concerts and recitals in the Music Centre. A Music Technology Suite opened in 2007. In the Arts Centre there are studios for fine art, for design and for ceramics, together with individual Sixth Form work areas and a lecture theatre.

Technology and Computing. The School benefits from a modern ICT Centre and online resources for teaching and learning are standard.

Clubs and Societies. There are plentiful activities for pupils to join in with, taking place after School and at weekends. Staff share their enthusiasms and pupils too can take the lead in their own areas of interest.

Health, Fitness and Physical Education. The diet is broad and healthy and considerable pride is taken in the catering. There is a full-time nurse with relief staff on call. The PE programme is full and varied, making use of the extensive playing grounds including playing fields, gym, sports hall, all-weather surface and a 25m indoor swimming pool. Matches take place against many other schools.

Full collaboration with parents. The Parents' Circle was founded in 1921 and the School has, throughout, valued the close involvement of parents who are welcome in the School, not just for consultation about their children but also to take part in evening classes and in sharing the many performances, events and information evenings. We want parents to share in the education of their children and in the School community.

Boarders. There are up to 50 boarders living in 2 boarding houses. Flexible boarding is available from Year 6 upwards. The provision for younger pupils is in cosy, traditional rooms in the heart of the School. Year 11 and 12 students are in a modern, light extension which has recently been renovated. Year 13 students are in a separate house on the School grounds. Boarding at St Chris has a family feel with all students under the supervision of resident House Parents, with most pupils in single rooms. Weekly evening activities available include movie night, cookery, games nights. Weekend activities almost always involve a trip away from school. Cooking facilities for snacks are available to students, though older students have a good kitchen and cook for a weekly supper club.

Day Pupils. Day pupils benefit from the residential nature of the community, sharing in the evening and weekend life and taking meals in the School when they wish. Sixth Formers have their own study areas in the Sixth Form Centre.

Fees per term (2016–2017). Day Pupils £1,180–£5,785, Full Boarding £9,890, Weekly Boarding £6,320–£7,825. There are discounts for second and subsequent children, so long as they have an older sibling in the School. A range of financial assistance is available through a Bursary Scheme. Fees for International students on application.

Admission Procedure. The most usual ages of admission are "rising 3", 4, 7, 8 or 9 into the Junior School, and at 11 or 13 into the Senior School. A number also enter at Sixth Form level. Our assessment procedure includes diagnostic tests and interview. Assessment for Years 7 and 9 entry takes place in January. Art and Academic Scholarships are available for entry into Years 7, 9 and 12.

Situation and Travel. The School has an attractive 35-acre campus on the edge of Letchworth Garden City with excellent transport links. The A1(M) is a mile away and there are direct train lines to London (King's Cross, 35 minutes) and Cambridge (25 minutes). Stansted Airport is 35 minutes and Heathrow 60 minutes by car. The School runs bus services to surrounding areas including North London and Cambridge.

Old Scholars. The Membership Secretary of the St Christopher Club is David Cursons who can be reached c/o The School. The Annual Reunion is held over a weekend each July.

Charitable status. St Christopher School is a Registered Charity, number 311062. It exists to provide education for boys and girls, aiming to treat all as individuals and to develop their proper self-confidence.

Board of Governors:
Bertie Leigh (*Chair*)
Sarah Kilcoyne (*Vice-Chair*)
Emma-Kate Henry
Peter McMeekin
Sophie Nolan
John Simmonds
Rabinder Singh
Ben Walker

Head: Richard Palmer, BEd, FRSA

Deputy Head: Cliff Canning, BD, BA, HDipEd
Second Deputy (Academic Director): Andy Selkirk, MBA, BSc, DipPhy, PGCE
Director of Pastoral System: Gavin Fraser-Williams, BA, MA
Director of Activities: Byron Lewis, BSc
Head of Junior School and Early Years: Katie Wright, BA

Teaching Staff:
Lizzie Anstice-Brown, BA, MA (*Art, Artist in Residence*)
Alison Bagg, MA (*Head of Mathematics*)

Sylvester Beecroft, BA, PGCE (*French, Careers, Head of Examinations*)
Michael Collins, BA, MA, PGCE (*History, Politics*)
Wendy Cottenden, Cert Ed (*Head of PSHE, Cookery*)
Sarah Davies, BSc (*Mathematics*)
Chris Drayton, BSc (*Mathematics, Outdoor Pursuits*)
Denise Eades, BA (*Head of Geography*)
Gemma Fernandez, Licence University of A Coruna (*French, Spanish*)
Gavin Fraser Williams, BA, MA (*Craft, Design & Technology*)
Martin Goodchild, GRSM, LRAM, PGCE (*Director of Music*)
Janine Hall, BA (*Art, Art Technician*)
Ian Hughes, BA (*Head of PE & Games*)
Helen Hunt, BSc (*Biology*)
David Ilott, BA, DipEd (*Head of English, Head of EFL*)
Richard Jones, BEd (*Drama*)
Anne-Marie Knight, BA, MA (*Music, PSHE*)
Kate Kreyenborg-Nichols, BSc (*Biology*)
Andrew Lambie, MA, PGCE (*Chemistry*)
Charlotte Leeke, BSc (*Geography*)
Byron Lewis, BSc (*ICT, Director of Activities*)
Kate Kreyenborg-Nicols (*Biology*)
Penny Main, BA, MA, PGCE (*History, English, Head of Year 12*)
Mario May, BA, MA, PhD, PGCE (*Head of History & Politics, Humanities Faculty Coordinator*)
Isabelle Mills, Licence d'Anglais, PGCE (*French, Spanish*)
Helen Ogilvie, PhD, MSc, PGCE (*Chemistry*)
Angeles Ojeda, Licendiada (*Spanish, German*)
Susanne Okulitch (*English, Media Studies*)
Andy Owen, BSc, PGCE (*Physics, Head of Science Faculty*)
Jennifer Petit, BSc (*Physics*)
James Robertson, BA (*CDT*)
Emma Roskilly BA, PGCE (*English, Head of Media Studies*)
Jennifer Savage, BA, MA (*Geography, Music, Drama*)
Andy Selkirk, MBA, BSc, DipPhy, PGCE (*Second Deputy – Academic Director, Biology*)
Emma Semple, BA, MA, PGCE (*Head of Arts Faculty*)
Cyrille Simon, Maîtrise (*Head of MFL, Faculty Coordinator*)
Allan Simpson, BA (*Music Technology*)
Claire Slater, BEng (*Maths*)
Rebecca Sweeney, BA, MA (*English*)
Maria Walker, BSc (*Mathematics*)
Ben Wall, BSc, PGCE (*Head of Craft, Design & Technology*)
Sarah Waller, BSc (*Biology*)
Jeremy Wallis, BSc, MA (*Economics*)
Donald Walmsley (*Biology*)
Jenny White, BEd (*Head of Girls' PE and Games*)
Rebecca Wilson, BA, PGCE (*English, ICT*)
Susan Woollard, BSc, MSc (*Psychology, Science*)
Jonathan Wright, BSc (*PE, Games*)
Naz Yeni, BA, MA (*Drama*)

Junior School and Early Years Centre:
Head of Junior School and Early Years: Katie Wright, BA
Secretary: Jean Benjamin
Bryan Anderson, BEd
Sarah Brown, Maria Montessori Diploma
Lesley Farrell, HNC, AMI Asst Cert (*Deputy Head of Early Years Centre*)
Christine Hawkes, BEd
Emma Hughes, BA Ed
Clare McComb, BA (*Deputy Head of Junior School*)
Lyn McGregor, BEd (*PE & Games*)
Carly Ougham, BA, PGCE

Claire Plain, BA
Rebecca Simon, BSc
Coralie Skerman-Gray, BEd
Lydia Somerville, BA
Jennifer Whale, BA (*Junior School Resources*)
Avril Harker, BA (*After School Care Organiser*)
Teaching Assistants: Corrine Toller, Sarah Gardener, Anita
Moore, Chloe Palmer, Natasha Paxton, Lucy Pinkstone,
Roxanne Jackson, Denise Sheelan,

Librarian: Linda Aird, BA, Dip Lib, MCLIP
Performing Arts Technician: Mike Li
School Doctor: Carole Brookes, MBChB, DRCOG
School Nurse: Caroline Dorrington
Assistant School Nurse: Vivien Morse

Individual Needs:
Karen Hoyle, BA, Cert Dyslexia and Literacy (*Joint Head
of Individual Needs*)
Elizabeth Miller, BEd, DipRSA SpLD (*Joint Head of
Individual Needs*)
Tracey Martin, BSc (*Junior School Individual Needs
Coordinator*)
Cordelia Lewis, BSc, MA
Jessica Maddams
Jane Miller
Sue McMillan
Maria Overhill
Tessa Palfreyman
Joanna Pitts
Sally Smyth
Jayne Thomas, BA

Bursar, Company Secretary & Clerk to the Governors:
William Hawkes, MA
Assistant Bursar: Nicola Payne

Marketing and Admissions:
Marketing and Communications Manager: Rhiannon
Butlin, BA, MSc
Registrar: Michelle Gahan

Boarding Staff:
Arundale: Chris and Cecilia Drayton
Arunside: Malcolm and Pippa Hodgson

St Edward's School

**Cirencester Road, Charlton Kings, Cheltenham, Glos
GL53 8EY**
Tel: 01242 538600
Fax: 01242 538610
email: headmistress@stedwards.co.uk
website: www.stedwards.co.uk
Twitter: @StEdwardsChelt
Facebook: /StEdwardsSchoolCheltenham

Motto: *Quantum Potes Aude*

St Edward's is a lay-run, co-educational Catholic day
school for 11–18 year olds of all denominations. Awarded
'Excellent' in all 8 categories in their recent ISI inspection,
St Edward's prides itself in offering a full curricular and
extra-curricular programme to all its pupils, to enable them
to succeed in whatever field they choose. A broad range of
subjects is offered at GCSE, together with some 20 subjects
at A Level. The broad range of subjects ensures that pupils
are taught in small class sizes, enabling each pupil to receive
individual attention.

Admission. The main entry to the Senior School is at age
11. Pupils can also join the School at age 13 and into the

Sixth Form and entry is by exam. Scholarships are available
for entry into Year 7, 9 and 12.

Fees per term (2016–2017). £4,225–£5,145. Discounts
are offered for the third, fourth and subsequent children.

The Senior School offers means-tested Bursary-Scholar-
ships for entry at age 11, scholarships for academic excellence, art, music, drama and sport. For entry into Year 9
scholarships are available for academic excellence, art,
music, drama, sport and design and technology. Scholarships for entry into Sixth Form are available for academic
excellence, art, music, drama and sport.

Old Edwardians' Association. Secretary: Mrs P Hem-
ming, St Edward's School, Cirencester Road, Charlton
Kings, Cheltenham, Gloucestershire GL53 8EY.

Further information is available on the School's website, www.stedwards.co.uk. A School prospectus is available
on request from the Headmistress's PA & Registrar. You are
warmly invited to arrange a visit to the School by telephoning her on 01242 538600.

Charitable status. St Edward's School is a Registered
Charity, number 293360.

Chairman of Trustees: Dr Sue Honeywill

Headmistress: **Mrs Pat Clayfield**, BSc, PGCE

Saint Felix School

Halesworth Road, Reydon, Southwold, Suffolk IP18 6SD
Tel: 01502 722175
email: schooladmin@stfelix.co.uk
website: www.stfelix.co.uk
Twitter: @StFelixSch
Facebook: /Saint-Felix-School

Motto: *Felix Quia Fortis*

Age Range. 2–18.
Number of Pupils. 350.

Saint Felix School was founded in 1897 and is set in 75
acres overlooking the Blyth Estuary near the picturesque
town of Southwold in Suffolk. The extensive buildings are
purpose built and well equipped.

As a co-educational day and boarding school Saint Felix
offers boys and girls a broad and balanced curriculum from
the age of 1 to 18. A through school from the Nursery, Pre-
Prep & Prep Departments (ages 1–10) through to the Senior
Department (ages 11–16) and then into the Sixth Form.

Academic. A well-structured timetable, and a broad and
balanced curriculum, encourages children in the Pre-Prep
and Prep Departments to achieve their personal best, both
academically and socially. Small class sizes and specialist
teaching staff ensure excellent results together with happy,
well-mannered and confident pupils.

In the Senior Department, each individual child is
encouraged to achieve the highest grade attainable, made
possible by the expertise of committed, skilled and motivated teachers working in small class groups. A wide and
distinctive range of subjects can be studied at GCSE, AS
and A Level. Sixth Form students this year achieved 100%
pass rate at A Level, enabling entry into many of the country's finest Art, Drama and Music colleges, and universities.
In addition the school's system of pastoral care ensures that
children have continuous support and mentoring throughout
their time at Saint Felix.

Music. Music is popular with over half taking peripatetic
lessons. There is a variety of musical groups including
chapel and chamber choirs, choral societies, orchestras as
well as several chamber ensembles, eg piano trio, string
quartets, jazz group and a rock band with electric guitar and

drums especially popular. All pupils are encouraged to learn an instrument and Pre-Prep pupils learn the recorder. A 'Music in Residence' group encourages pupils to take up instruments. Music can be studied at GCSE and A Level. The department has 18 practice rooms and a performance area.

Sport. Facilities include a 25m indoor swimming pool, sports hall complex, squash courts, fitness suite and a 25-acre equestrian cross-country course.

A wide variety of sports are on offer including tennis, rugby, cricket, football, netball, hockey and rounders. Swimming is particularly strong throughout the school resulting in pupils competing in county, regional and national championships and achieving national recognition. An extensive range of other sports is available including squash, sailing, basketball, fencing, table tennis, wall climbing and horse riding.

Arts. The school promotes the Arts with regular exhibitions and displays and eagerly-awaited school productions throughout the year. The combination of Art, Music and Drama is actively encouraged through an Arts Week. Photography and Art throughout the school is of a very high standard with excellent results at both GCSE and A Level. The Silcox Theatre with a 200-seat capacity and state-of-the-art lighting and sound system further enhances the creative arts, one of the great strengths of Saint Felix.

Extra Curricular Activities. There is an extensive list of activities available. All pupils are actively encouraged to take part in the Duke of Edinburgh's Award Scheme. A similar scheme runs in the Prep Department. The school day is extended to include activities.

Community. The school actively encourages the local community to get involved in school life and various clubs are closely linked to the school (Norwich City Football Club, Guides, Brownies, The Choral Society, Southwold Rugby, Netball and Tennis Clubs) enabling pupils to be involved in groups outside school.

Fees per term (2016–2017). Day: £2,400–£5,150; Boarding: £5,650–£7,150 (weekly), £7,375–£8,995 (full).

Forces Boarding School Allowance available.

Scholarships. Saint Felix School seeks high-calibre candidates, who will contribute very positively and proactively to the life of the school community. The maximum award for an academic scholarship is 50% and for an exhibition 25% of the fees.

Academic awards at 11+ and 13+. All applicants will sit competitive academic examination papers. Awards will be made to high flying candidates, who demonstrate flair and the potential to excel in their academic studies. Exhibitions are awards given for candidates who show promise but do not attain the exacting standards demanded of scholars.

Examinations. Applicants for academic awards at 11+ and 13+ will sit examination papers in English, Mathematics, Science and Aptitude. Topics will be closely linked to those covered in Key Stages 2 and 3.

Music Scholarships at 9+ through to 14+. These will be awarded on the basis of an audition, voice test and interview with the Director of Music and members of the Scholarship Selection Committee. Candidates will be asked to offer two instruments, one of which should be an orchestral instrument.

Margaret Isabella Gardiner Scholarship for candidates aged 11+ and 13+. Outstanding candidates may be eligible for this highly prestigious award, worth up to 75% of the fees. This scholarship will be awarded only to a candidate of sufficiently high calibre and not necessarily on an annual basis.

Performing Arts awards at 13+ and 14+. Open to applicants who excel in at least two of the following disciplines: Drama, Dance, Music (including singing).

Sports Scholarships at 9+, 11+, 13+& 14+. Candidates should offer a range of sporting talents. Pupils at 11+ should be playing at club level in at least one sport. Pupils at 13+ should have been selected for county/regional level sport and be playing at club level in at least one sport. There should be evidence of success in competitions and events for both age groups.

Swimming Scholarships at 9+ through to 14+. These are awarded to candidates who swim at county, regional and national level and are currently dependent on the level of times gained.

Sixth Form Scholarships and Exhibitions. Scholarships and exhibitions for Academic Studies, Design & Technology (Phipps Award), Drama, Music, Sport and Visual Arts (Art & Photography) are available for talented Sixth Form applicants, as the result of a competitive examination, trial or audition.

Full details of all awards, including Founder's Scholarships, Remissions and Swimming Scholarships may be obtained from the Registrar. Further information on Bursaries (available to current parents only) are available from the Bursar.

Charitable status. Saint Felix School is a Registered Charity, number 310482. It exists to promote and advance education.

Board of Governors:
Chairman: Dr J Kelly
Vice-Chairman: [1]Mr N Johnson, BA
Chairman (F&G): Mr J Whyte
Mrs H Anthony, BA
Miss R Booth
Dr L Dawson, OBE
Mr K Dobson
Mrs L Le Versha
Revd B Slatter
Mr R Turvill
Mr S Hill (*Parent Governor*)
Mr R Stephens(*Parent Governor*)
Mr R Wise (*Parent Governor*)

Head: [1]**Mr J Harrison**, BA Hons Durham

[1] *PGCE/DipEd qualification*

Deputy Head: [1]Ms A Hardcastle, BA Hons Huddersfield

Head of Sixth Form: Mrs J Harlock, BA Hons Nottingham, MA De Montfort

Head of Fifth Form: Mrs C Gallagher, BA Hons De Montfort

Head of Prep Department: [1]Mr T O'Connell, BSc Hons Exeter

Head of Pre-Prep Department: Mrs S Duckett, NNEB, CertEd

Senior School:

Art, Photography & Textiles:
Mrs S Bassett, BA Hons East London
[1]Mrs H Cole, BA Hons Norwich, MA NUA
[1]Mr C Dunn, BA Hons Cardiff
[1]Ms L Roberts, BA Hons Leicester
[1]Mrs S Whyte, BA Hons Leeds

Business Studies/Economics:
Mrs J Harlock, BA Hons Nottingham, MA De Montfort
[1]Mr A Williams, BA Exeter, MA Hons Keele

Classics:
Miss C Ayres, BA Hons, MRes Roehampton
[1]Mr J Harrison, BA Hons Durham

Design Technology:
Mr R Kay, BEd Hons, DipEd Nottingham
[1]Mr D Kirby, BSc Loughborough

Drama and Performing Arts:
Mrs R Barrett BA
Mrs Charles Saker, BA Hons Essex
[1]Ms A Hardcastle, BA Hons Huddersfield
Mrs T Marriott, MIDA, SIPBE

English:
[1]Mr P Currie, BA Hons Bolton Institute of Higher
   Education
[1]Ms A Hardcastle, BA Hons Huddersfield
[1]Mr R Lynch, BA Hons Birmingham, MA London

English as an Additional Language (*EAL*):
[1]Mrs K Dunn, BSc Hons Wales
[1]Mrs A Eastaugh, MA Hons Edinburgh, TEFL

Geography:
[1]Mrs K Dunn, BSc Hons Wales
[1]Mr I McLean, BSc Hons UEA

History:
Mrs K Bland, BA Hons Open, OCR Level 5 SpLD
   Dyslexia
[1]Mr R Farrands, BA Hons Kent

History of Art:
[1]Ms L Roberts, BA Hons Leicester, CTEF

Home Economics:
Mrs J Anderson, BA Hons OU, CertEd Wales

ICT:
Mr C Barlow
[1]Mr D Kirby, BSc Loughborough

Learning Support:
Mrs K Bland, BA Hons Open, OCR Level 5 SpLD
   Dyslexia
Mrs B Every, LSA
Mrs T Fitzgerald
Mrs A Grimsey, Fd UCS
Mrs A Horne, NVQ3

Mathematics:
Mrs K Bland, BA Hons Open, OCR Level 5 SpLD
   Dyslexia
Mr J Cowan BSc Hons Sheffield Hallam
[1]Miss S Fenwick, BA Hons Warwick
Mr C Smith, BEd Nottingham Trent
Mrs M Westlake, BSc Hons UEA

Modern Languages:
Mr A Adady, BA Hons Essex, MA Essex
Miss Y Picton, BA Hons UEA
[1]Mrs J Rogers, BA Hons Nottingham

Music:
[1]Mr L Allen, BMus Huddersfield
Miss R Knight
Mr N Vine

Pastoral:
Mrs C Gallagher, BA Hons De Montfort
Mrs J Harlock, BA Hons Nottingham, MA De Montfort
[1]Mr I McLean, BSc Hons UEA

PSHE:
Mrs H Meldrum, BA Hons London

Psychology:
Mr R Kearney, BSc Hons St Andrews

Science:
[1]Mrs N Cowan, BSc Hons OU (*Biology*)
[1]Mr M Colville, BSc Leeds (*Chemistry*)
[1]Mr A Hill, BSc Wales, MA OU (*Physics*)
Mr R Kearney, BSc Hons St Andrews
Mrs M Westlake, BSc Queen Mary College London

Sports:
Mr B Collis, LTA Tennis Coach
[1]Miss S Fenwick, BA Hons Warwick
Mrs C Gallagher, BA Hons De Montfort
Mrs T Marriott, MIDA, SIPBE
Mrs G Nash, CertEd Sussex
[1]Mr T O'Connell, BSc Hons Exeter
Miss E Rushmere, BSc Hons Kingston

Swimming:
Mrs J Greenacre, BEd Hons W Sussex, MA UEA
Mrs L O'Connell, ASA Swimming Assistant, BSc Hons
   Exeter
Ms S Purchase, ASA Swimming Coach
Miss E Rushmere, BSc Hons Kingston
Mr N Thompson
Miss A Watling

Technicians:
Mr C Cowan
Miss B Laybourne

Careers & Sixth Form:
Mrs J Harlock, BA Hons Nottingham, MA De Montfort

Chaplain: Mrs H Meldrum, BA Hons London

Librarian: Mrs C Thomas, BA Hons London, PG Dip,
   MCLIP

House Staff:

Head of Boarding: [1]Mr T O'Connell, BSc Hons Exeter

House Parents:
[1]Mrs D Colville, HND Buckinghamshire
[1]Mr M Colville, BSc Leeds
[1]Mr C Dunn, BSc Hons Wales
Mr R Kearney, BSc Hons St Andrews
[1]Mr D Kirby, BSc Loughborough
Mr R Kearney, BSc Hons St Andrews
Mrs G Nash, CertEd Sussex
[1]Mr T O'Connell, BSc Hons Exeter
Miss Y Picton, BA UEA
Ms G Poulter

Medical Centre:
Sister P Canham, RGN
Sister A Carr, RGN
Sister N Linkin

Medical Officer: Dr M Niemeijer

Management Support:
Office Manager: Ms G Poulter
Receptionist/School Secretaries: Mrs D Colville & Ms G
   Poulter
Headmaster's PA: Mrs E Foskett
Registrar/Database Administrator: Miss M Bridgman
Finance Assistants: Mrs L Davison, Mr D Rees, Mrs J
   Tracey

Pre-Prep, Prep Departments and Nursery:
Mrs K Barbrook, BA Hons (*Nursery Assistant*)
Mrs K Bland, BA Hons Open, OCR Level 5 SpLD
   Dyslexia (*Year Teacher, Learning Support*)
Miss C Bridle, BA Hons Hertfordshire Campus (*Nursery
   Assistant*)
[1]Mrs R Crane, BA Hons (*French*)
Mrs A Evans, BA Hons (*Year Teacher*)
Mrs S Duckett, NNEB, CertEd (*Head of Pre-Prep
   Department, Class Teacher, Key Stage 1 Curriculum
   Coordinator*)
Mrs A Forward, NNEB (*Teaching Assistant*)
Miss N Foster (*Apprentice Assistant*)
Ms C Fisher (*Learning Support Assistant*)
Mrs T Grimmer, HLTA (*Teaching Assistant*)

Mrs J Greenacre, MA UEA, BEd Hons W Sussex (*PE, Games, Swimming*)

Miss S Greenfield, BEd (*Year Teacher, English Co-ordinator*)

Mrs J Heal, Cert EYP Open FD Open (*Year Teacher*)

Mr R Kearney, BSc Hons St Andrews (*Science*)

¹Mrs P Kinsella, BA Hons (*Year Teacher, Key Stage 1 English Coordinator*)

¹Mrs L Knights, BA Hons

Mrs L Laughland, CCE, DNN (*EYFS Coordinator*)

Mrs G Nash, CertEd Sussex (*Girls' Games*)

Mrs A Nunn, BA Hons (*Year Teacher, Art*)

¹Mr T O'Connell, BSc Hons Exeter (*Head of Prep Department*)

Miss C Oldman, Dip LCM (*Music*)

Mrs J Proctor, NVQ3 (*Learning Support Assistant*)

Mrs J Rogers, BA Hons Nottingham (*French*)

Miss E Rushmere, BSc Hons Kingston (*Games*)

Mrs A Stephens, NNEB (*Learning Support Assistant*)

Miss A Watling (*Swimming*)

St James Senior Boys' School

Church Road, Ashford, Surrey TW15 3DZ

Tel:	01784 266 930
	01784 266 933 (Admissions)
Fax:	01784 266 938
email:	admissions@stjamesboys.co.uk
website:	www.stjamesboys.co.uk

St James Senior Boys' School, founded in 1975, is registered as an educational charity and is administered by a Board of Governors. The Headmaster is a member of The Society of Heads and the Independent Schools Association. The school is a member of the International Boys' Schools Coalition (IBSC). These Associations require that excellence is assured by regular inspections by the Independent Schools Inspectorate which is itself monitored by Ofsted.

The school has 390 students – all boys, aged between 11 and 18.

The school relocated from its site in Twickenham in 2010 and now resides in the magnificent Victorian/Gothic building which once housed St David's School in Ashford, Surrey, set in 32 acres of grounds. This move has provided the physical space necessary for every boy to develop his sporting, artistic and dramatic talents in addition to working in high-quality classrooms and state-of-the-art laboratories.

Aims and Values. St James Senior Boys' School offers a distinctive education that unites a unique philosophical ethos with academic excellence and outstanding skills for life.

At St James we believe that every child is a pure and perfect being; it is our job as educators to help the pupils in our care to discover and express their individual talents and reveal their brilliance. With this room to grow and blossom each boy develops in body, mind and spirit.

Although academic potential is important to us, pupils at St James are not selected solely on their examination performance; we are also interested in strength of character, future potential and emotional intelligence. We are looking for a boy with a spark, who gives freely of themselves whether in the classroom, on the stage or the sports field.

We are known internationally for our championing of Meditation and Mindfulness, something we have been successfully practising for 40 years. Each boy has the opportunity to connect with their inner being in periods of Quiet Time each day. This makes an enormous difference to pupil development and academic achievement.

We also like to offer the pupils in our care the opportunity to push themselves beyond any self-imposed limits, and our beautiful 32-acre site certainly enables a wealth of sports, drama, music and other extracurricular activities to flourish. Activities offered include: Cadets, The Duke of Edinburgh's Award, Sailing Club, Mountain Biking, Kayaking and even Open Water swimming in our lake!

At St James we wish to produce young men who can question with sharp minds, who can contemplate in quietude, who can find their way ahead with wisdom and moral discrimination and who can meet others with open-hearted compassion.

St James is ideally located with easy access from Central London and the South West London Suburbs through to the Thames Valley.

Academic Standards and Successes. Academic standards are high, but we also measure success to the extent that boys surpass their own expectations. 2016 results were: GCSE 100% pass rate; A*AB 73%; A*ABC 93%; A Level Pass Rate 100%, A*ABC 90%.

Extracurricular Activities. Boys are offered an adventure pursuits programme designed to challenge the young men in terms of fitness, endurance, courage, leadership skills, service, self-esteem and confidence. Cadets (239 Para detachment), The Duke of Edinburgh's Award, Skiing, Sailing Club, Climbing Club, Community Service and Task force are among the activities offered.

Educational Trips. These are fairly regular and frequent for the Lower School, but there is an Activities Week in March when Year 7 enjoy an adventure break in the UK; Year 8 go to Greece to further their studies of Classical Civilisation; Year 9 spend a week devoted to Shakespeare, and Year 10 spend some time in Lucca in Italy for leadership training and aspects of teamworking, then move on to Florence to study Renaissance art and architecture.

Philosophy. Each class throughout the school has one period of Philosophy per week. The boys are opened up to the great ideas relating to human values and relationships. Broadly, the themes prepare boys through different stages of development – Years 7 to 8: the correct use of mind, the power of attention; Years 9 to 11: aspiring to a great vision of Man and exploring human relationships and personal mastery; Years 12 to 13: living the philosophical life, making it practical, the importance of service.

Meditation and Quiet Time. The importance of inner stillness is recognised in the school, with two 5 minute periods of Quiet Time every day. During this time, boys can meditate, pray, read something of value or just be still. Every lesson begins and ends in a quiet moment of stillness and rest.

Admissions. The standard entry is at 11+, 13+ and 16+. Boys applying for entry to Year 7 take an Entrance Exam in January and also are all interviewed by a member of the Senior Management Team shortly afterwards. Boys are not judged solely on their exam results for the Headmaster favours selection by character and their ability to express themselves. At 13+, students are required to pre-test at either 11+ or 12+ level (in Y6 or Y7). We welcome applications to our Sixth Form at 16+. Very good GCSE performance and satisfactory interviews will be the basis of selection.

Fees per term (2016–2017). £5,760.

Open Days and Visits. Every year we hold two Open Days in October. We also encourage parents to come and see the school in action at one of the monthly tours. Please book by telephoning the admissions office.

Charitable status. The Independent Educational Association Limited is a Registered Charity, number 270156.

Chairman of Governors: Jeremy Sinclair

Headmaster: David Brazier, BA Hons, PGCE, MSc

Deputy Headmaster: Koen Claeys, BA, GLSE Belgium (*French, German*)

Deputy Headmaster Academic: Charles Neave, BA, Grad Dip Ed, Grad Dip Mus, QTS (*English*)

Assistant Headmaster: David Hipshon, BA Hons, MPhil Cantab, PhD, PGCE (*History*)
Head of Sixth Form: David Beezadhur, BA Hons, MA, GTTP (*Ancient History*)
Head of Upper School (*Years 9–11*): James Johnson, BSc Hons, PGCE (*Science*)
Head of Lower School (*Years 7 & 8*): Richard Fletcher, BSc Hons, GTTP (*Mathematics*)

Academic Staff:
Charlotte Atkinson, BA Hons, PGCE (*English*)
Paul Bahia, BSc Hons, PGCE (*Mathematics, Economics*)
Kevan Bell, MA, MSc, BEd (*Sports Performance Director*)
Gillian Bloor, MA (*English*)
Helen Brennan, BSc Hons, PGCE (*Head of Geography*)
Stuart Bridge, BA Hons, PGCE (*German, French, Drama*)
Frank Byrne, BEng Hons, PGCE (*Physics*)
Anne-Helene Choimet, BA France, PGCE MFL (*French, German*)
Laurence Doroumain, BA, PGCE (*Spanish, French*)
Sarah Ford, BSc Hons, PGCE (*Chemistry*) [Maternity Leave]
Rishi Handa, MA, BSc Hons, PhD (*Sanskrit, Classical Greek, Religious Studies*)
Claudia Hindle, MA Hons (*Classics*)
Adam Hooper, BEng (*Physics*)
Anisah Hussain, BA Hons, MA, PGCE (*Classics*)
William Jeffreys, BA (*Physical Education*)
Nic Lempriere, MA, PGCE (*Head of English*)
Oliver Lomberg, BA Hons Cambridge (*Acting Head of Classics*)
Keith Lovell, Cert Ed (*Head of Design Technology*)
Neil MacKichan, BSc Hons GTTP (*Head of ICT, Computing*)
Rowan Mangion, BSc Hons, PGCE (*Chemistry*) [Maternity Cover]
Pardeep Marway, BSc Hons, PGCE (*Head of Science, Designated Safeguarding Lead*)
Nicola Michael, BA Hons, PGCE (*Geography*)
Stevie Mitchell, BA Hons, PGCE (*Mathematics*)
Rubel Molla, MSc, BSc Hons, Dip (*Mathematics*)
Nathaniel Palmer, BA Hons, PGCE (*Geography, PE*)
Marco Piotti, MSc, PGCE (*History*)
Caroline Pugh, BA Hons, PGCE (*Head of Drama*) [Maternity Leave]
Virginie Quartier, BA, GLSE Belgium (*Head of Languages*)
Peter Rogers, BSc, PGCE (*PE*)
Adam Rood, BA (*Drama*) [Maternity Cover]
Antonia Ruppel, BA, MPhil, PhD Cambridge (*Acting Head of Sanskrit, Classics*)
Julia Russell, BA Hons, GTTP (*Art, Art of Science Coordinator*)
Derek Saunders, BA Mus, PGCE (*Director of Music*)
Oliver Saunders, BA Hons, GTTP (*Head of History*)
Mark Saunders, BA, HND Art & Design (*Head of Art*)
Lorraine Soares, MSc Hons, PGCE (*Chemistry Academic Director*)
Tammy Taylor, BA (*Librarian*)
Joanna Thorn, BSc Hons (*English*)
Ben Wassell, BSc Hons, GTTP (*Head of PE*)
Michaela Weiserova, MSc (*Head of Mathematics*)
Steven Whitehouse, BSc, PhD, PGCE (*Mathematics*)
Sandra Williams, BEd (*Head of Business Studies, Careers Coordinator*)
Alice Wood, BA Hons, PGCE (*English*)

Learning Support:
Jayne Chandler
Christine Davies
Angela Hall
Sarah-Jane Hipshon, BA Hons Lit Open

Caroline Moir, BSc Hons Psychology, Dip SpLD (*SENCO*)
Carola Robinson-Tait (*Learning Support Specialist Teacher*)
Cora Wren, Cert Ed, BA Hons, OCR Level 5 Dip SpLD (*SENCO*)

Headmaster's PA: Nina Patel
Assistant to the Deputy Head: Cecilia Leggett
Receptionists: Sindy Bahia, Monica Lacey
Matron: Alison Jefferies RSCN
Estates Manager: Branimir Karavla
Caretakers: Nicholas Freddino, Mark Freddino, Tim Prendergast
Groundsman: Stephen Fidler
Registrar & Marketing Manager: Lauren McCready BSc Dip
Examinations Officer: Reshma Kanani
Lab Technicians: Anil Sud, Lorraine Hayson
Health & Safety Officer: Nathaniel Palmer
Designated Safeguarding Lead: Pardeep Marway
Events Manager: Lisa Canderton
Sixth Form Cover Supervisor / School Staff Instructor (*CCF*): Timothy Paul
Bursar: William Wyatt
PA to the Bursar: Hermoine Fricker

St John's College

Grove Road South, Southsea, Hampshire PO5 3QW
Tel: 023 9281 5118
Fax: 023 9287 3603
email: info@stjohnscollege.co.uk
website: www.stjohnscollege.co.uk

Founded in 1908 by the De La Salle Brothers, St John's seeks to provide an excellent all-round day and boarding education to boys and girls of all abilities. Children of all Christian denominations, those of other faiths and those with no formal religious affiliation but who are in sympathy with the values of the school are welcome. The College became fully independent and decoupled from the De la Salle Trust in September 2015, but continues to provide an academic education based on the spiritual and moral ethos of the Founder John Baptist De La Salle.

St John's is a thriving co-educational day and boarding school for pupils aged 2 to 18 (boarding from Year 5). Number of Pupils: 581 including 90 Boarders.

Situation. St John's day and boarding campus is located in the heart of Southsea, an attractive and thriving seaside suburb of Portsmouth. The College's 40 acres of sports fields are located on the outskirts of the city, with transport provided to and from that site.

Approach and Ethos. Academically, St John's is a non-selective school, its aim being excellence for every pupil according to their personal potential. All children who are able and willing to benefit from the curriculum provided are welcome to join the school community. The school's academic record – by all measures – is outstanding.

The pastoral care offered to boarders and day pupils is of very high quality. The commitment of the staff to the welfare and progress of each pupil is second to none. In return, honest effort and application is expected from the children – in order to meet the challenging standards set in academic work, sporting endeavour, behaviour and self-discipline.

Nursery. The Nursery (Little St John's) is located within the Junior School. It has its own entrance and secure playground. The Nursery caters for children aged from two to four years. The children are actively involved in a carefully constructed pre-school programme. Great emphasis is placed on creative artwork, outdoor play and educational visits – as well as on acquiring foundation skills and concepts relating to numeracy and literacy.

Junior School. The Junior School is also located within the main College campus. This enables younger children to make daily use of all the College's excellent facilities and to benefit in some areas from specialist tuition by Senior School staff. The broadly-based curriculum incorporates and extends the National Curriculum. Great emphasis is placed on English, mathematics and science – which is taught in well-equipped laboratories. Musical talent is also carefully nurtured, with all pupils learning a musical instrument from the age of seven. The Junior School Choir and Orchestra provide opportunities for ensemble playing and performance.

Senior School. The Senior School curriculum again incorporates and extends the National Curriculum. All subjects are taught by appropriately qualified specialists in well-resourced subject areas. A wide range of GCSE subjects is offered alongside IGCSE Maths, English and Science. Instrumental tuition is encouraged and the Senior School Choir and Orchestra are open to all pupils. Sport – principally rugby, cricket, hockey and netball – is strong at all levels. Pupils' progress in all areas is assessed formally each half-term, with formal examinations being held twice yearly.

Sixth Form. As they progress into the Sixth Form, older students are enabled and encouraged to become independent and self-motivated learners – in preparation for Higher Education. The teaching and pastoral staff continue to work closely with parents, who are kept fully informed of progress and achievement. A wide range of AS and A2 Level subjects is offered. The College ensures a good student/teacher ratio, allowing for close and constant monitoring of the performance and effort of each student. Preparation for Oxbridge entry is available, and students are also offered practice interviews for university and job applications and a full careers service.

Beyond the formal curriculum, a wide range of sporting, academic, dramatic, cultural and social activities is available. The Politics Society, administered predominantly by Sixth Form students, enjoys a national reputation.

Admission. Pupils are accepted and placed on the basis of a formal assessment and previous reports.

Fees per term (2016–2017). Junior School: Day £2,880–£3,075, Years 5 & 6 UK Boarding £8,150. Senior School: Day £3,780, UK Boarding £8,150, Overseas Boarding £8,765.

Occasional Boarding (including bed, breakfast, evening meal): £38 per day.

Music fees are extra.

Scholarships and Bursaries. Academic and other scholarships and bursary awards are available.

Charitable status. St John's College, Southsea is a Registered Charity, number 1162915.

Chairman of Governors: Mr T Forer, BA

Head of College: Mr T Bayley, BSc, MA

Deputy Head: Mrs M Maguire, BSc, PGCE
Head of the Junior School: Mr T Shrubsall, MA Ed, BH
Assistant Head Academic: Mr A Martin, MEng, ACGI, Fri, PGCE
Assistant Head Pastoral: Mr M Round, BSc, PGCE
Senior Master: Mr M Renahan, BA, HDE, MEd
Bursar: Mr S Merriam, BSc
Estates Manager: Mr R Phillips
Head of Marketing and Development: Miss C Young, BA
Admissions Registrar: Mrs J Mengham

Heads of Department:
Art and Design: Mrs K Brown, BA
Design and Technology: Mr R Kirby, BA, QTS

Economics & Business Studies: Ms M Faulkner, BSc
English: Mr D Celestine, BA
Geography: Mr McBeath, BSc
Government & Political Studies: Dr G D Goodlad, PhD, BA
History: Mrs K Audsley, BA, MA
ICT & Computing: Mr T Harris, BSc, QTS
Learning Support: Mrs L Gorham, BA, DipSpLD
Mathematics: Mr M Renahan, BA, HDE, MEd
Modern Languages: Mr A Jackson
Music: Mr D Jones
Physical Education: Mr K Long
Religious Studies: Mrs J Turner, BA, MA
Sciences: Mr A Martin, BSc

Head's PA/Admissions: Mrs H Williams

St Joseph's College

Belstead Road, Ipswich, Suffolk IP2 9DR

Tel:	01473 690281
Fax:	01473 602409
email:	admissions@stjos.co.uk
website:	www.stjos.co.uk
Twitter:	@MyStJos
Facebook:	/StJosephsCollegeIpswich
LinkedIn:	/St-Joseph's-College-Ipswich

St Joseph's College is a vibrant day and boarding school, for girls and boys aged 3 to 18. Its Nursery, Prep, Senior and Sixth Form provision offers a broad, well-rounded and seamless education.

Located on a 60-acre parkland site near to the centre of Ipswich, the College is situated just ten minutes' walk from Ipswich train station or alternately just a five-minute drive from the A12/A14 interchange.

Traditional values are at the heart of the school community which, at the same time, is forward-thinking as it meets the challenges of an ever-changing world. Pupils are provided with every opportunity to develop their talents to the full, growing up in a happy and fulfilling Christian environment where all are valued and encouraged.

Ethos. St Joseph's feels different. And that's the way we like it. Our uniqueness is shaped by our ethos, which combines strong Christian values with a distinctive approach to supporting and nurturing children individually within a friendly, family environment. Along with the pursuit of excellence, this approach is reflected in all aspects of life at the College, academic, sporting and cultural.

Developments. The second phase of the College's ambitious Building for the Future plans came to fruition in September 2016 with the opening of a state-of-the-art Sixth Form Centre, combining 21st century technology with light, space, serenity and colour.

Eight years earlier, the innovative Prep School building was formally opened. This fascinating curved building with its Maltings-style wind-catcher towers provides a highly stimulating environment for pupils between 3 and 11 years of age and is equipped with the latest technological and physical resources.

In September 2015 a new Technology Centre opened and in March 2014 a floodlit Astroturf, new changing rooms, a spectators viewing facility and function suite were added to the school's facilities within its 60 acres.

ISI Inspection. In March 2013, the College received an excellent ISI inspection report.

All areas of EYFS were judged to be outstanding. The quality of pupils' spiritual, moral, social and cultural development; pastoral care and quality of teaching; the curriculum and extra-curricular provision; and pupils' achievement were all excellent. ISI judged that '*all children make excellent progress and achieve better than age-related expectations in all areas of learning.*'

The arrangements for pastoral care and boarding were also judged to be excellent. '*A well-developed network of support, with clear lines of communication, provides the basis for pastoral care throughout the school and supports the pupils' excellent personal development. The family community is an obvious strength of the college. Pupils value the kindness and support that staff show them and enjoy positive relationships with all.*'

Judgements on achievement and teaching and learning included: '*Standards in the EYFS are high and pupils continue to make good progress towards their GCSE exams, where results are good. Pupils' personal and social development are excellent, in accordance with the Christian values which permeate the life of the college. Teachers have good subject knowledge and the most successful teaching promotes academic rigour and uses a variety of methods and resources. The pupils' performance in extra-curricular activities is frequently outstanding. They have had significant successes in sport, particularly rugby and cricket, but also in drama, music and art.*'

The most recent Inspection of Boarding in 2016 confirmed it was fully compliant and found no action points – in line with the most recent quantitative inspection in 2013, which deemed it excellent.

Boarding. Although primarily a day school, we also offer flexible, weekly and full boarding in family-run, spacious and warm boarding houses. The College has two boarding houses which provide both single and shared rooms, with kitchen, study and recreational facilities.

Curriculum. The curriculum is designed to provide a broad and balanced education for all pupils from 3 to 18. Strong foundations in the core skills of reading, writing and numeracy are laid down in the Infant Department through innovative programmes such as Read Write Inc and Singapore Mathematics. The Junior section continues the process of preparing the children for their secondary education by concentrating further on the core skills. In addition to these subjects, Science, French, Music and PE are taught and the children are introduced to a wider curriculum, including Design & Technology, Art, History, Geography, RE, IT and Games.

The Senior School prepares pupils for entrance to universities, other forms of higher education and the professions. Pupils are set according to ability in certain subjects. In Years 7 to 9, the emphasis continues to be placed on the core subjects whilst developing knowledge, skills and experiences necessary for the GCSE courses. Languages studied at the College include French and Spanish.

GCSE studies maintain a broad and balanced curriculum, but with the introduction of a degree of specialisation. Mathematics, English Language & Literature, Double Science Award and RE are compulsory. Once again core subjects continue to be set by ability. To cater for developing interests and abilities, there is a wide range of further choices from Food Technology and Photography to History, Spanish and Business Studies.

The majority of our pupils continue into the Sixth Form to complete their A Level courses before going on to university. There is a wide range of subjects available in the Sixth Form and students choose 4 AS Level subjects for examination in the Lower Sixth, reducing to 3 A2s for completion in the Upper Sixth. The post-16 curriculum at the College also includes EPQ and BTEC in Sport (single, double and triple), together with a wide range of sporting and other leisure and cultural opportunities.

A Learning Support department operates throughout the College to provide support individually or in small groups for students of all abilities with specific learning needs and differences.

There is comprehensive careers guidance from Year 9 and extensive help with university admission in the Sixth Form.

Extra-Curricular Activities. Sport, Art, Music, Dance and Drama are strongly encouraged, together with participation in The Duke of Edinburgh's Award scheme. A large number of extra-curricular clubs meets weekly. Regular ski trips, activity holidays and language exchanges are organised throughout the College.

Admission. Entry to the College is normally at 3+, 7+, 11+, 13+ and the Sixth Form, with applications for vacancies at other ages, subject to spaces being available. The entry process includes an interview, a Taster Day in the school, a formal assessment and a report from the applicant's previous school. For the Sixth Form, the academic assessment is replaced by GCSE results.

Fees per term (2016–2017). Nursery: £48.75 (per full session); Infants (Reception to Year 2): £2,840; Juniors (Years 3 to 6): £3,690 (day). Senior School (Year 7–8): £4,360 (day); £7,645 (weekly boarder); £8,000 (full boarder/EEA); £8,000 (overseas boarder). Year 9: £4,635 (day); £7,645 (weekly boarder); £8,000 (full boarder/EEA); £10,635 (overseas boarder). Year 10–11: £4,635 (day); £7,825 (weekly boarder); £10,340 (full boarder/EEA); £10,635 (overseas boarder). Sixth Form: £4,635 (day); £8,360 (weekly boarder); £10,340 (full boarder/EEA); £10,635 (overseas boarder).

Scholarships and Bursaries. The College offers a number of Academic Scholarships each year for different points of entry, as well as Scholarships for Music, Art, Drama, Dance and Sport. Bursaries are also available in cases of need. Please contact the Admissions team for further information.

Charitable status. St Joseph's College is a Registered Charity, number 1051688. It exists to provide high quality education for children.

Governing Body:
Chair: Mr Paul Clement, BSc Hons, MA
Vice Chair: Mr Richard Stace, LLB

Mr John Button	Mr Malcolm Earl
Ms Joanna Carrick	Mr Perry Glading
Mrs Penny Cavenagh	Mr Andrew Goulborn
Mrs Renata Chester	Mrs Josephine Lea
Mr Joseph Cook	Mr Anthony Newman
Mr Philip Dennis	Mr Matthew Potter

Special Responsibilities:
Prep & EYFS: Mrs Josephine Lea
Safeguarding: Mr Richard Stace
Boarding: Mr Anthony Newman
Finance: Mr Perry Glading, Mrs Renata Chester
Health & Safety: Mr Malcolm Earl, Mr Perry Glading

Senior Leadership Team:

Principal: Mrs Danielle Clarke, BA Hons, NPQH

Vice Principal and Head of the Prep School: Dr M Hine, BEd Hons, PhD, NPQH, FRSA
Director of Studies: Mr S Phaup
Bursar: Mrs D Baber

Senior School Heads of Faculty and Pastoral Leads:
Mr A Bloore (*Head of Technology*)
Miss L Cunningham (*Head of Learning Support*)
Mrs S Daley and Mr C Branch (*Co-Directors of Sport*)
Mrs K Drake (*Head of English*)
Mrs A Hall (*Head of Upper School*)
Mrs V Harvey (*Head of Creative & Performing Arts*)
Miss L Hassell (*Head of Science*)
Mr C McNicholas (*Head of Humanities*)
Mr L Ball (*Head of MFL/EAL*)
Mrs S Medhurst (*Head of PSHEE*)

Mr S Cinnamond (*Head of Sixth Form*)
Mrs G Rowlands (*Head of Boarding*)
Mrs M Simmonds (*Head of Lower School*)
Mr N Walkinshaw (*Head of Mathematics*)

Prep School:
Mrs V Wood (*Deputy Head of the Prep School*)
Mrs L Wright (*Head of EYFS & Infants, Nursery to Year 2*)
Mrs D Searle (*Head of Juniors, Years 3 to 6 & Director of Studies*)

Scarborough College

Filey Road, Scarborough, North Yorkshire YO11 3BA

Tel: 01723 360620
Fax: 01723 377265
email: admin@scarboroughcollege.co.uk
website: www.scarboroughcollege.co.uk
Twitter: @ScarboroughCol1
Facebook: /ScarboroughCollege

Motto: *Pensez Fort*

Scarborough College, founded in 1896, is a thriving co-educational day and boarding school for children aged 3–18 with an exceptional academic pedigree and an unrivalled reputation for making the most of every child's potential. The College and its Junior School, Bramcote, share the same site. Our beautiful campus overlooks the spectacular North Yorkshire coast and is ten minutes' walk from the centre of the stunning seaside town of Scarborough. The boarding houses are merely a 15 minute walk from the beach. The College has fine views overlooking the South Bay of the town and Scarborough Castle.

Although the ethos of the College is firmly based upon wholesome traditional principles we have a progressive approach to education, which has led to us offering the International Baccalaureate in our Sixth Form for the past ten years, a qualification that is highly prized throughout the world. Our average staff to student ratio of 1:8 ensures we develop the full potential of every child.

Superb facilities including 20 acres of sports pitches, a fully floodlit AstroTurf, a performing arts centre with 400-seater theatre, sports hall and neighbouring 18-hole golf course all ensure a truly first-class education can be delivered to nurture the talents of all.

Scholarships for academic performance, sport, music and as an 'all-rounder' are awarded at all entry points. Means-tested bursaries are also available.

Admission. *Junior School*: Admission is by visit to the school and an interview with the Head of Junior School. Taster days can be arranged.

Senior School: Admission at age 11 is following an Entrance Assessment and interview. Admission at all other ages is subject to recommendation from the previous school, an interview and satisfactory performance in a general assessment.

Sixth Form: Admissions are subject to the achievement of a minimum of five GCSEs at Grades A* to C and an interview with the headmaster. *Overseas Students* are required to submit: school reports for the previous two years; academic certificates, if appropriate (GCSE or equivalent and any other exams taken); written reference from the Head of current/previous school. They are also required to sit our English and maths assessments and undergo an interview either during a visit to the school or via Skype. Scholarships and bursaries are available.

Senior School. Students join us in all year groups with especially high numbers of new arrivals in Years 7, 9 and 10

for GCSE, Year 11 for our bespoke Pre-IB course and the Lower Sixth for the IB Diploma.

Students in Years 7, 8 and 9 study three modern languages and three sciences, providing them with a firm foundation for further study. Along with English and maths, they also study traditional subjects including history, geography, music, art, religious education, classics, ICT, drama, and design and technology. Further options appear as GCSE subject choices in Year 10.

A dedicated Learning Support and English as an Additional Language team of staff ensures all individual needs are fully met.

Sport, music, and drama are very important parts of the daily College life with over 50 clubs and societies on offer every year. Horse riding is particularly popular and the College has both a Surf Academy and Golf Academy.

Bramcote Junior School.
Our educational vision is simple: the pursuit of excellence in every aspect of school life in an environment which will develop active, questioning, confident, thinking children.

At the core of our school is a traditional academic approach and a challenging curriculum. We provide the best pastoral care and support for every child. We also pride ourselves on the breadth of our education inside and outside the classroom. Dedicated subject specialists deliver a stimulating programme including art, drama, design technology, French and music, as well as daily games and outdoor pursuits. The enrichment programme is rich and varied.

In addition we offer free wrap-around care before and after school for our busy working parents plus a fun and caring Holiday Club for those who need additional child care support.

Sixth Form and the IB Diploma. The International Baccalaureate Diploma programme provides our Sixth Form students with a stimulating and challenging post-16 curriculum. Our experience has shown that the IB encourages the development of inquisitive, critical and reflective thinkers who engage fully in the learning process to acquire knowledge. 29 separate subject course options are available.

In our Sixth Form, students develop a new relationship with their teachers within a university-style tuition setting. They have many opportunities to show and develop their leadership skills and become very involved in the School Council, hosting and organising school, house and social events as well as prefect duties and helping younger students in roles such as mentors and sports coaches. There is a rich programme of visiting speakers and exchange visits, and they have their own dedicated Study Centre, Café and Common Room. This is a caring, friendly and warm environment which is a great place to develop and grow into inquisitive and confident young adults.

Boarding. There are three traditional and charming boarding houses at Scarborough College, offering boarding accommodation for pupils aged 11–18 years from all around the world. These really do provide a warm family environment with a home-from-home feeling for all our students, both British and foreign.

A busy programme of weekend entertainment is planned each term to keep the students active. More spontaneous events also include house barbecues, impromptu sports, trips to the beach, go karting, mountain biking, surfing and cinema trips, just to name a few.

Our boarding staff are all experienced members of staff with families of their own, so know how challenging and demanding teenagers can be from time to time, but also are very caring, understanding and sympathetic to the needs of each and every individual child.

Day Pupils benefit from all of the extras that being part of a boarding school brings, including the opportunity for occasional boarding. The school bus service operates daily to Bridlington, Whitby, Driffield, Malton and Pickering.

For further up-to-date information on the school, please visit the College's website.

Fees per term (2016–2017). Senior School: £4,122–£4,595 (day), £6,892–£7,755 (UK and MOD boarding), £7,460–£8,258 (EU boarding), £8,036–£8,899 (Overseas boarding). Junior School: £2,341–£3,762 (day).

Charitable status. Scarborough College is a Registered Charity, number 529686.

Governors:
Dr J Renshaw (*Chairman*)
A S Green (*Deputy Chairman*)
M Baines
Mrs G Braithwaite
J M Green
R Marshall
Dr I G H Renwick
J Rowlands
R Guthrie
S Fairbank
Mrs V Gillingham
N Gardner

Senior Management Team:

Headmaster: Mr Charles Ellison

Head of the Junior School: Mr Chris Barker

Deputy Head: Miss Kate Tipton

Director of Studies: Mr Simon Harvey

Assistant Head – Academic Administration: Mr James Fraser

Business Manager & Clerk to the Governors: Mr Tim Fenton, MBE

Shebbear College

Shebbear, North Devon EX21 5HJ
Tel: 01409 282000
Fax: 01409 281784
email: registrar@shebbearcollege.co.uk
website: www.shebbearcollege.co.uk

Shebbear College is a day and boarding school for boys and girls between the ages of 3 to 18 years. Set in 85 acres of beautiful Devon countryside, the school, which was founded in 1841, offers superb facilities and plenty of room to run around in a very safe and healthy environment. The school is part of the Methodist Independent Schools Trust and embraces all faiths as it welcomes pupils from all over the world. The secure, happy family atmosphere at Shebbear, free from urban distractions, offers pupils full, weekly, or occasional boarding and day education. We aim to instil self-confidence in all our pupils, we teach them to be self-disciplined and they leave the College with excellent qualifications, many of our Sixth Form leavers achieving places at their chosen universities. Shebbear College offers all our pupils "A foundation for life".

Number in College. In the Senior School there are around 280 pupils, of whom around 80 are boarders, and around 80 pupils in our Prep School.

Situation and Location. Shebbear College borders on Dartmoor National Park and stands in 85 acres of unspoilt countryside. It can be easily reached by main road and rail links; only 40 miles west of Exeter and 40 miles north of Plymouth. Both cities have their own regional and international airport.

Buildings. The main College buildings include Prospect House, Lake Chapel, Beckly Wing, Shebbear College Prep School, Science Department, Music School, Sixth Form Centre, Language Centre and Sports Hall. All classrooms have interactive whiteboards. There are 2 Senior boarding houses and 1 Junior boys boarding house. The Junior girls have a separate area within the Senior girls house.

In recent years there has been an impressive record of school building projects. The latest work has been to build a full-size all-weather pitch and multi-gym. A new Prep School extension houses new classrooms and Assembly Hall. Two new buildings have now been completed – a new Music Centre and a new Sixth Form Centre.

Admission. The Kindergarten accepts children from the age of 2½ where boys and girls are admitted to the Prep School from the age of 5. Entrance to the College at 11 years from other schools is by examination in January for entry in September. Pupils are also admitted at 13 or 14 after submitting Common Entrance Examination papers, but if they wish they may sit our own entrance papers instead. Entry into the Sixth Form is conditional upon GCSE performance.

Houses. Every pupil belongs to a House – Ruddle, Thorne or Way. These Houses organise activities and games competitions throughout the year. Our boarders also belong to an additional boarding house – Pollard House for Senior boy boarders, Pyke House for Junior boy boarders and Ruddle House for girl boarders – each having a Senior Houseparent and two assistants who live in. The House Tutors watch each child's progress academically as well as their general development.

Curriculum. All pupils at Shebbear College follow the National Curriculum until the age of 14. A wide choice of subjects is available in the following two years, leading to GCSE, but everyone is obliged to take English, Mathematics, Science and, usually, a foreign language. In the Sixth Form there is not only a wide choice of A2 and AS levels, but there is particularly flexible timetabling which enables students to mix Arts and Science subjects.

Sport. With more than 25 acres of playing fields, modern sports hall with multi-gym, dance studio, cricket nets, all-weather pitch, tennis and netball courts, pupils have the security to exercise within the school grounds confidently. The main games covered for the boys are rugby, football, hockey and cricket, in which we have fixtures with most of the major schools in the South West of England. For the girls, we have teams in netball, hockey, rounders and tennis. All pupils are also offered tennis, basketball, athletics, cross-country, badminton and table tennis. All pupils up to the 4th Form have one afternoon of games plus an additional one period of PE every week.

Music and Drama. Pupils are strongly encouraged to participate in music and drama. Our choir has over 40 members and our orchestra, which represents most instruments, also has over 40 members. Players perform regularly in concerts and instrumental ensembles. Every term candidates proudly achieve Honours and Distinctions with The Associated Board of the Royal School for Music. Also, every term, a theatrical production is performed to a very high standard.

Societies and Activities. All pupils participate in at least 4 afternoons a week of extra-curricular activities. This widens their interests and develops their self-confidence. The list of activities is endless and includes the usual and unusual. Many pupils enjoy getting involved with Ten Tors training, hillwalking, camping, sailing, canoeing, and surfing. The Army-run Ten Tors Challenge is proving to be very popular and many pupils are involved in the Duke of Edinburgh's Award scheme.

Careers. Careers advice is taken very seriously. Staff help our students prepare for their chosen career. The College is a member of ISCO. Individual attention is given at appropriate levels and a team of Old Shebbearians covering many professions visits the school regularly and helps with work experience and placement.

Scholarships and Bursaries. On application, scholarships and bursaries are awarded at the discretion of the Headmaster.

At 11+: All candidates take the Entrance and Scholarship Examination in January.

At 13+: The Scholarship Examination is held in the Spring Term. Awards are also made following Common Entrance Examination results.

For Sixth Form candidates, scholarships are awarded on the basis of interview, school report and GCSE performance.

Further details may be obtained from the Registrar.

Fees per term (2016–2017) Pre-Prep Years 1 and 2 £2,080. Preparatory School: Day £2,660–£3,070, Weekly Boarding £4,425–£4,850, Full Boarding £5,850–£6,290. Senior School: Day £4,175, Weekly Boarding £6,130, Full Boarding £8,250.

Charitable status. Shebbear College is a Registered Charity, number 306945. It exists to provide high quality education for children.

Chairman of the Governors: Mr M J Saltmarsh

Headmaster: Mr S D Weale, MA Oxon

Deputy Head Pastoral/Head of Boarding/Designated
  Safeguarding Lead: Mr M Newitt, BSc Hons, PGCE
Deputy Head Academic: Mrs E Bearpark, LLB
Head of Upper School: Mr J Sanders, BSc Hons GTP
Head of Lower School: Mrs F Lovett, BA Hons
Head of Prep School: Mr M Furber, BEd Hons
Bursar & Clerk to the Governors: Mr B Horn, ACMA,
  ACIS, CGMA

Heads of Departments:
Art: Mr A Barlow, BA Hons, SIAD Dip AD, LSDC, PGCE
Business Studies & Economics: Mr L Oxenham, BA Hons,
  PGCE, MSc
Biology: Mr M Greig, BSc, PGCE
Chemistry: Mr G Drake, BSc
English & Drama: Mr R Wolverson, BA Hons, PGCE
Media: Mrs F Lovett, BA Hons
English as a Second Language: Mrs A Vassilaki, BA Hons
Geography: Mrs L Douglas, BA HMS, UDE
History: Mr M Rogers, MA Hons, BA Hons, PGCE
ICT: Ms M Davies, BSc Hons, MSc
Learning Support: Miss L Body, BA Hons, PGCE
Mathematics: Mr S Trask, BEng Hons, PGCE
Music: Mr K Parker, GRSM
Modern Languages: Mrs C Fanet, BA, MA, PGCE
Physics: Mr M Palmer, BEng Hons, PGCE
Psychology: Dr F Gillies, BSc, PsyD, MSc
Religious Studies: Mr M Rogers, MA Hons, BA Hons,
  PGCE
Director of Sport: Mr A Steel, BSc Hons GTP

Headmaster's PA/Registrar: Miss N Giddy

Sibford School

Sibford Ferris, Banbury, Oxon OX15 5QL

Tel: 01295 781200
Fax: 01295 781204
email: admissions@sibfordschool.co.uk
website: www.sibfordschool.co.uk
Twitter: @SibfordSchOxon
Facebook: /Sibford-School

Founded 1842. A Co-educational Independent Boarding (full/weekly) and Day School. Membership of The Society of Heads, BSA, AGBIS.

There are 392 pupils in the school aged between 3 and 18: 332 pupils in the Senior School and 60 pupils in the Junior School. There are 85 teachers plus visiting staff.

Curriculum. Broad and balanced curriculum which reflects our view that while some may have talent for maths or history others may be gifted in the arts or horticulture. Renowned dyslexia tuition and support for a small number of pupils with other learning difficulties.

Junior School (age 3–11): a wide-ranging curriculum with an emphasis on outdoor education is provided to children in small groups. Literacy, numeracy, science and technology skills are emphasised alongside art, music, drama and PE. Enriched Curriculum in Year 6 with Senior School Staff. Specialist teachers help individual children with specific learning difficulties.

Senior School (age 11–16): all pupils follow courses leading to GCSE, in a curriculum expanding on the National Curriculum. Information Technology is introduced at an early age and the use of laptop computers is widespread.

Dyslexic pupils have special tuition in small groups on a daily basis. Highly regarded Specific Learning Difficulties (Dyslexic) Department provides specialised support within the timetable. Personal and Social Development runs through the school.

Sixth Form (age 16–18) students take A Levels and/or BTEC Diplomas. The Sixth Form curriculum leads to higher education, and offers a particularly wide range of opportunities for further study.

Overseas pupils are welcomed into the school community. English as an additional language is taught by ESOL qualified teachers.

Entry requirements. Admission to the Junior School, Senior School and Sixth Form is by interview and internal tests. Where applicable a report from the candidate's current school is required. No religious requirements.

Examinations offered. A Level, GCSE, BTEC Diploma, Associated Board Music Examinations, Oxford and Cambridge IELTS Examinations.

Academic and leisure facilities. Exceptional Performing & Creative Arts in purpose-built facilities, multi-purpose Sports Centre, squash courts, 25m indoor swimming pool, well-equipped Library and Information Technology Centres, Design Technology Centre, separate Sixth Form Centre, wide range of indoor and outdoor activities, 50 plus-acre campus set in beautiful North Oxfordshire countryside. Three boarding houses (for girls, boys and sixth form). Easy access to Stratford, Oxford, Cheltenham, Birmingham, London.

Religion. The School has a distinctive Quaker ethos. It welcomes pupils of all faiths, backgrounds and nationalities, encouraging in each of them genuine self-esteem in a purposeful, caring and challenging environment.

Fees per term (2016–2017). Full Boarders £8,856–£9,035, Weekly Boarders £8,249–£8,412, Flexi Boarding £58 per night, Day Pupils £4,559–£4,650. Junior School: Day Pupils £2,896–£3,504. The fee for a full term of learning support is £1,615.

Scholarships and Bursaries. The School offers general Academic scholarships and specific scholarships in Art, Music and Sport. A limited number of bursaries is offered to both Quaker and non Quaker children. Limited bursary support is available for UK boarders in Years 7–8.

Charitable status. Sibford School is a Registered Charity, number 1068256. It is a company limited by guarantee under number 3487651. It aims to give all pupils a vehicle to educational and personal success.

Chair of School Committee: Seren Wildwood

Head: Toby Spence, BA, MEd

Deputy Head: Maggie Guy, BA (*English*, *Child Protection*,
  Head of Boarding)

Senior School:
* *Head of Department*
§ *Part-time*
† *House Parent*
LSA *Learning Support Assistant*

Charles Atkinson (§*English*)
Simon Baker, BSc (**Geography, Enrichment Week Coordinator, EcoSchools Coordinator, Head of Houses*)
Katie Bertie (§*Dyslexia Teacher*)
Derek Bottomley, BSc, Cert TEFL (*Mathematics)
Angela Bovill, BEd, CertEd (§*Countryside & Environmental Sciences & Horticulture*)
†David Brassett (§*Assistant to PE Department*)
Matthew Brock, BSc (*PE)
Simon Chard, BA (*PE, Vocational Education*)
John Charlesworth MSc (*Assistant Head Curriculum*)
Hannah Copping, BSc (§*Geography*)
Emma Crocker, BA (§*Design Technology,* *Home Economics)
Tamsin Cygal, BSc (*Science*)
Melanie Deans, BSc, Cert Ed (*Mathematics, PSHE Coordinator KS3/4*)
Darren de Bruyn, B Bus Admin (**Business Studies, Head of House, PSHE Coordinator KS5*)
Christopher Dudley, BA, MEd (§*Economics*)
Frances Eason, Dip Theatre Design/Craft, Cert Ed Post 16 (*Teaching Assistant*)
Helen Earle, BSc (§*Maths*)
James Elliot, BSc (*Science*)
Debby Evans, Cert Ed PCE, Cert SpLD (**ICT, BTEC Quality Nominee, Holiday Club Coordinator*)
†Claire Ferley, BSc (§*PE*)
†Richard Ferley, BSc (§*PE*)
Jenny Fisher, DTEFLA (§*ESOL*)
Rebecca Flynn, BA, MA, CTEFL (§*Psychology, ESOL, Dyslexia*)
Andrew Foakes, BA, MA (**Media, English, Head of House*)
Andrew Glover, Dip SpLD, BA, Dip TEFL (§*ESOL*)
Victoria Hall, BA (§*English, Assistant Head of Boarding*)
Cath Harding, BSc (§*Science)
Jane Harper, BSc (*Teaching Assistant*)
Deborah Holroyd, BSc, MA Ed (§*Science*)
Adam Hosler, BSc, QTLS (*Maths*)
Fiona Hudson, BA, Licenciate Trinity College Music (*Music)
Gillian Hughes, BA, Cert SpLD (§*Teaching Assistant*)
John James, BA (§*Ceramics*)
Pippa Jones (§*Teaching Assistant*)
Jane Kenehan (*Teaching Assistant, Dyslexia*)
Tracy Knowles, BA Ed (*Assistant Head Pastoral, English*)
Anna Jo Lawrence, BA (*Director of Studies, NQT Mentor, G&T, History*)
Tracey Leigh, MA (*Art)
Victoria Macaulay, MSc (*2nd in Science, Head of House*)
Neil Madden BA (*Drama)
Michael Maguire (*Teaching Assistant*)
Cate Mallalieu-Needle, MA, NQPH (*Head of Sixth Form, English/Drama*)
Joanna Mayes, BA, Cert TEFL, Cert Ed (§*ESOL*)
Christian Mineeff, BA (§*Teaching Assistant*)
Isabelle Murphy (§*Teaching Assistant*)
Ingar Noble, Dip Clinical & Pathological Psychology (§*LSA*)
Moira Oliver (§*Teaching Assistant*)
Dolores Papin, Licence Anglais, Maitrise Anglais (**Modern Foreign Languages, Head of House*)
Caroline Perry, Licence Anglais (§*Modern Foreign Languages*)
Linda Phillips, BSc, MA (*Mathematics, Joint Coordinator Duke of Edinburgh's Award*)

Sally Pickering, BA, Dip TEFL (*ESOL)
Barney Porter (*Assistant to Music department, Teaching Assistant*)
Jeremy Ross, MA (*History, Joint Coordinator Duke of Edinburgh's Award*)
Lois Self, BA (*Careers Coordinator*)
Jessica Shalders, QTS (§*PE*)
Zoë Simms, BA, MA, AKC (**RS, Philosophy & Ethics, Charities Coordinator, Quaker Outreach*)
Deborah Simpkins, BA (*Modern Foreign Languages*)
Annie Smith, BSc, Cert Dyslexia & Literacy (*Assistant Head of Support for Learning*)
Penelope Spring, BA (**English, PGCE mentor*)
Victor Stannard, BA (**Design Technology*)
Catherine Stockdale, MA SEN (**Support for Learning*)
Emma Sutcliffe, BA (*Textiles*)
Allison Warrillow, BA (*Assistant Head of PE*)
Jayne Woolley, BA, Cert Ed (§*Dyscalculia*)
Sibford Junior School:
Edward Rossiter, BSc, PG Dip Social Sciences, MEd (*Assistant Head Junior School*)
Rebecca Edwards, BSc, MA Ed (*Years 1 & 2*)
Helen Hoy, BA (*Head of Early Years Foundation Stage*)
Margaret Allen, BA (*Year 4*)
Helen Arnold, BA (*Year 3*)
Rachel Bee, BMus (§*Music*)
Nicholas Hadley, BA (*Year 6*)
Jason Harris (*Outdoor Environment Facilitator*)
Jane Kenehan (*Teaching Assistant, Dyslexia*)
Nicola Key, BA Education (*Senior Early Years Assistant*)
Amanda Levett, BA (§*Junior School Dyslexia teacher*)
Alice Pennell, BEd (*Year 5*)
Lois Self, BA (*LSA, Senior School Careers Coordinator*)
Helen Sinton, BSc (*Early Years Assistant*)
Claire Solesbury (§*LSA*)
Susan Spillett, BA (*LSA*)
Katy Stotesbury, BA (*Year 5*)
Hazel Sykes, BA (§*Year 6, Dyslexia*)
Jayne Woolley, BA, Cert Ed (§*Dyscalculia*)

Business Manager: Peter Robinson, Health and Safety, Estate & Business Management
Admissions: Elspeth Dyer
Marketing: Ali Bromhall

Stafford Grammar School

Burton Manor, Stafford, Staffordshire ST18 9AT
Tel: 01785 249752
Fax: 01785 255005
email: headsec@staffordgrammar.co.uk
website: www.staffordgrammar.co.uk

Motto: *Quod tibi hoc alteri*

Number in School. There are 329 pupils (11–18 years) of whom 155 are boys and 174 girls. There is a Sixth Form of 98. Stafford Preparatory School has just over 100 pupils.

Stafford Grammar School is housed in a fine Victorian manor house, designed by Augustus Pugin, standing in 47 acres of grounds with sports pitches, tennis courts and extensive additional specialist accommodation. Sixteen acres of sports land have recently been developed to further enhance outside sport provision.

Curriculum. In Year 7 and Year 8 all pupils follow a common course consisting of English, Mathematics, Science, French, German, Geography, History, Music, Art, Drama, Computing, Design, Technology, Religious Education and Physical Education. Year 9 sees Science divide into separate subjects.

Pupils in Years 10 and 11 study nine or ten subjects at GCSE: English (2), Mathematics, Science (IGCSE dual or triple award) and a language, together with three further subjects chosen from a whole range including humanities and practical subjects. Physical Education continues and Careers and Life Skills are introduced.

There is setting in Mathematics from Year 8, Science from Year 9 and English from Year 10. Other subjects are taught in mixed ability groups. Classes are kept small so that pupils can receive individual attention.

In the Lower Sixth Form students study three or four A Level subjects (AS) leading to three or four A Level subjects (A2) in the Upper Sixth Form. Approximately 20 A Level subjects are available.

Creativity and the Arts. The School has an extensive Art and Design Department. Pupils' powers of observation and awareness are developed through practical skills and theoretical studies involving areas as varied as painting, printing, 3-D work, photography and textiles. There are frequent competitions and exhibitions of work as well as projects linked with other departments.

Music plays an important part in the life of the School. There is an orchestra, a concert band and choirs which perform on many occasions in musicals, church services and concerts. Ensembles, both instrumental and vocal, are encouraged. Pupils have the opportunity to learn to play a wide range of musical instruments with tuition provided by peripatetic teachers. The bi-annual music trips abroad are well supported.

Drama enables pupils to gain confidence and self-understanding. It is particularly effective in the early years in the School. Two annual School Plays are major productions on the School's excellent stage and involve a large number of pupils. Recent productions include *Les Misérables, West Side Story and Fame.*

Art and Drama are available at both GCSE and A Level. Peripatetic LAMDA tuition is available from Grade 1 to Gold Medal (Grade 8). LAMDA students also attend local drama festivals.

Sport and Activities. Whilst competitive sport plays a prominent part in School life, the emphasis is also on preparation for future leisure time.

The School has outstanding sports facilities and the following sports are available: Soccer, Hockey, Rugby, Cricket, Tennis, Badminton, Basketball, Netball, Volleyball, Athletics, Gymnastics, Rounders, Table Tennis, and Health-related Fitness, as well as Swimming. The School has an extensive fitness suite.

The School plays a large number of matches against other schools, both state and independent, and is fully involved in local leagues. Individuals regularly secure places in Staffordshire and Midlands teams.

Our range of activities is deliberately wide since we believe that every child is good at something and that it is our job to discover and develop talent in any direction.

There are many Clubs and Societies of widely differing kinds and a large number of pupils are working for The Duke of Edinburgh's Award scheme.

At present there are 15 inter-House competitions. These range from Technology to Public Speaking and from Football to Hobbies, and include some which are specifically for younger pupils.

The intention of these is not only to enable as many pupils as possible to represent their Houses, but also to stress that we value excellence in any area.

Pastoral Care. In its pastoral organisation, the School seeks to nurture the potential of every child giving both support and encouragement in an overt and practical way. The School is divided into three houses, the Head of House being the key figure in the academic and personal development of each child. Tutor groups are kept small and are based on the House to maintain continuity and to strengthen communal bonds. Tutors maintain strong links with each pupil using a programme of active tutoring which includes

scheduled interviews. We place great emphasis on close contact with parents, believing that lack of progress and other problems are best addressed jointly and as early as possible.

In the Sixth Form a slightly different system operates. Although retaining the same House Tutor, the pupil will have a Form Tutor from a specialist team of Sixth Form Tutors. Additionally one of the Senior Teachers is attached to this team. Further to this is the opportunity for each pupil to choose a Personal Tutor with whom to build a special rapport.

Sixth Form. The Sixth Form is the ideal environment in which to foster confidence, responsibility, leadership, initiative and self-discipline.

The keynote of the Sixth Form is freedom with responsibility. At this stage pupils still need help in planning their time and in establishing good working habits, and the guidance of an understanding tutor can mean the difference between success and failure. There is an extensive UCAS programme which includes Oxbridge preparation.

Careers. Considerable attention is paid to career advice, and there are frequent visits by speakers from industry and the professions. From Year 10 onwards, individual advice is given by our own careers staff, and pupils are also encouraged to consult the County Careers Service.

Religion. Although we welcome pupils of all faiths, or none, the School is a Christian foundation.

The School seeks to live by the Christian ideal, in particular by being a community in which members genuinely care about each other.

Admission. Entrance is by examination and interview in order to ensure that pupils have sufficient reasoning ability to be able to attempt GCSE in a reasonable range of subjects.

Entrance to the Sixth Form is by GCSE results and interview.

Scholarships and Bursaries. The Governors have allocated funds to enable pupils of exceptional ability or limited means to join the school.

Fees per term (from January 2017). Grammar School: £4,039 excluding lunch; Preparatory School (including lunch): Reception–Year 2 £3,303, Years 3 & 4 £3,483, Years 5 & 6 £3,621.

Stafford Preparatory School opened, in purpose-built accommodation, in September 2007 admitting pupils into Years 5 and 6. A Year 4 class was admitted in September 2008, a Year 3 class in 2009, Years 1 and 2 in September 2012, and a Reception class in 2014. Stafford Preparatory School provides exciting opportunities for pupils to prepare for selective senior school education at Stafford Grammar School or elsewhere.

Charitable status. Stafford Independent Grammar School Limited is a Registered Charity, number 513031. It exists to provide education for children.

Patrons:
The Right Hon The Earl of Shrewsbury
The Lord Stafford
The Right Hon The Earl of Lichfield

Governing Body:

B Baggott (*Chairman*)	R Nicholls
Mrs J Causer	D Pearsall
Mrs J Colman	Mrs P Pearsall
Revd J Davis	C Sproston
B Hodges	Mrs H Watson Jones
J Lotz	A Wright

Headmaster: M R Darley, BA

Deputy Head: M P Robinson, BA, Dip Ed Man
Director of Studies: Dr P A Johnson, BSc, PhD
Senior Teacher: R C Green, BA
Senior Teacher: Mrs A Saxon, MA, BEd
Senior Teacher: L Thomas, BA

Assistant Staff:

C Anderson, BSc	Mrs K Horsley, BA
Mrs E Ayirebi, BA	A C Johnson, BSc
D R Beauchamp, BSc	T Kirsch, BSc
Mrs R Beauchamp, BA	G R Lamplough, BMus
G Beckett, BSc	D Mole, BA
Miss K Butler, BA, MA	Mrs E M Neville, BA
C Cooke, BA	Mrs K Owen-Reece, BA
Ms K Farmer, BA	Mrs E L Paton, BA
Mrs K Fletcher, BA	Mrs P H Patrick, BSc
Dr R Foster, BSc, PhD	Mrs F F Shakesheave, BSc,
S Godwin, MSc, BA	BA
Mrs R Godwin-Bratt, BSc	Mrs D Shaughnessy, BA,
Mrs L J Griffiths, BA	MA
Miss H Hackett, BSc	Mrs C Slater, BA
Miss G Hague-Jones, BA	Mrs S Smith, BA
J. Hamilton, BSc	Ms C Taig, BSc
L J Harwood, BEd	Mrs A L Weetman LAES
Mrs T A Hollinshead, BSc,	
MSc	

Chaplain:
Prebendary R Sargent, MA
Revd J Davis, MBE, KStJ, BA, MA

Bursar: J Downes

Headmaster's Secretary: Mrs S M Pickavance

Stonar

Cottles Park, Atworth, Wiltshire SN12 8NT

Tel:	01225 701740
Fax:	01225 790830
email:	office@stonarschool.com
website:	www.stonarschool.com
Twitter:	@StonarSchool
Facebook:	/StonarSchool

Co-educational Day and Boarding School from Nursery to Sixth Form.

Ethos. Stonar combines an impressive all-round education, with a wide-ranging curriculum and a wealth of extracurricular activities. Pupils go on to achieve outstanding academic results, with almost all pupils gaining their first choice of university course in 2015/16. Stonar develops the talents of every individual, enabling pupils of all abilities to achieve their potential across and beyond the formal curriculum. There is a positive work ethic and excellent pastoral care. Curiosity, confidence and independence are encouraged so that pupils leave school well-equipped for the challenges of adult life and keen to contribute to the wider community.

Curriculum. A talented and committed staff offers pupils a broad and flexible curriculum, with literacy and numeracy firmly at the centre of the Prep school timetable and an individual choice from wide ranging options in addition to the core of Science, Maths, English, a foreign language and ICT at GCSE. AS and A2 courses can include Psychology, Photography, Business Studies, PE and IT. 'Gifted and Talented' pupils are identified throughout school and opportunities to extend their learning exist both within the curriculum and in extracurricular activities.

Considering the wide range of academic ability, Stonar's results are outstanding and pupils go on to university courses ranging from Medicine, Law and Accountancy to Geology, Veterinary Science and Music. Talented artists proceed to a variety of Art Foundation Courses. Young riders take up careers in eventing or go for the Equine Studies

option. The BHS, EQL and UK CC courses are available to pupils in Year 11 and the Sixth Form.

Extracurricular Activities. The school's internationally renowned Equestrian Centre provides tuition for all ages and abilities. Facilities include indoor and outdoor arenas, cross country training fields and a hacking track. The Equestrian Centre has the top level of BHS accreditation and is also a Pony Club centre.

The Sports Hall, indoor Swimming Pool, AstroTurf, Theatre, Music, Sixth Form & Arts Centre offer first-class opportunities for sport, music and drama. A timetabled tutorial period provides a rolling programme of careers advice, health education, study skills, first aid, self-defence, citizenship and industrial awareness. An extensive programme of after-school activities includes academic, sporting and life skills options which challenge and extend pupils' development. In the Sixth Form, girls enjoy debating, dance, film studies, aerobics and a Cookery Course including the Leiths Toolkit. The Duke of Edinburgh's Award scheme flourishes at Stonar.

Boarding. Boarders live in comfortable, family-style houses, each with internet access. Pupils of any religion and of all nationalities are welcomed and can work towards IGCSE English, if this is not their first language.

Admission. Straightforward entrance procedures via Stonar entrance examinations in early January and school report at appropriate ages.

Fees per term (2016–2017). Prep Day £2,710–£3,655; Senior Day £4,875–£5,265; Prep Boarding £6,485; Senior Boarding £9,500.

Scholarships and Bursaries. Year 7 & Year 9 Entry: Academic, Art, Drama, Sport, Music and Riding Scholarships are offered. Scholarship assessments take place in January following the Entrance Examination.

Sixth Form Entry: Academic, Art, Drama, Sport, Music and Riding Scholarships are available. Scholarship examinations, assessments and interviews held in November.

Means-tested Bursaries are available. A Forces Bursary is available to Senior School boarders whose parents are current serving members of HM Forces.

Governance. Stonar is a part of NACE Educational Services Limited, Company Registration No. 8441252, Registered Address: 17 Hanover Square, London, United Kingdom W1S 1HU.

Board of Directors:
Mr A McEwen, NACE UK Ltd (*Chairman*)

Head: Dr Sally Divall, MA, PhD, PGCE

Bursar: Mrs Claire Sparrow, BA Hons MBA ACMA

Deputy Head: Mrs Nicola Hawkins, MSc, BSc Hons, PGCE

Director of Studies: Mrs Alison Rivers, BSc Hons, PGCE

Senior Staff:
§ *Part-time*

Mrs S Aikman, BA Hons, PGCE (*Head of Modern Foreign Languages*)
Mrs C Bennett, BA Hons, PGCE (*Head of Sixth Form, Geography, RS*)
Mrs K Bouchard, BSc Hons, PGCE (*Science*)
§Mrs H Brain, BA Hons, PGCE (*Learning Support*)
§Mrs T Brain, BA Ed Hons (*English*)
§Mrs J Brighouse, BA Hons, PGCE (*French, EAL*)
Miss A Catt, BA Hons, GTP (*EAL*)
Miss S Cholmondeley, MEng Hons, PGCE (*Subject Leader of Maths*)
Mrs R Cross, BEd (*Maths, ICT*)
Mrs S Crouch, NNEB (*Teaching Assistant*)
Miss H Culverhouse, BSc Hons, PGCE (*PE and Games*)

Mr A Curtis, MSc, BSc Hons, PhD (*Head of Careers, Psychology*)
Mrs C Deans, MA, TEFL Dip (*Head of EAL*)
Mr J Dyde, BA Hons, PGCE (*Head of English*)
Ms N Gardiner, BFA Hons, PGCE (*Art and Photography*)
§Mrs T Gates, BA Hons, PGCE, PGDip (*Learning Support*)
Miss S Gomersall, BA Hons, PGCE (*PE and Games*)
Mr N Goodall, BA Hons, MMus, PGCE (*Director of Music, ICT*)
§Mrs D Harding, BEd (*Learning Support*)
Miss L Havranek, BA Hons, PGCE (*French, Spanish, Houseparent of Hart*)
Mrs M-P Jones, BA Hons (*French*)
Miss P Kirby, BSc Hons, PGCE (*Subject Leader of Biology*)
§Dr F Martinelli, BSc Hons, PhD, PGCE (*Science*)
§Mrs S McQueen, BA Hons PGCE (*EAL*)
§Mrs L Medworth, MA, PGCE (*Maths, Learning Support*)
Miss S Meehan, BA Hons, PGCE (*Assistant Director of Music, English*)
Mr R Miller, BA Hons (*Director of Sport and PE*)
Ms P Nix, BSc Hons, PGCE (*Head of Chemistry*)
Mrs L Noad, BA Hons (*RS, Assistant Houseparent*)
Mr A O'Hanlon, BA Hons, PGCE, PGDip (*Head of Art & Photography*)
Mr N Proud, MA, BA Hons, PGCE (*Head of Drama*)
Mrs L Ross, BA Hons, PGCE (*Subject Leader of History*)
Mrs G Sherman, BSc, MCLIP, MBCS (*Head of ICT, Latin*)
Mrs L Smith, BSc Hons, PGCE (*Head of Geography*)
Mrs T Tilley, BSc Hons, PGCE (*PE, Biology, Houseparent of Curnow*)
Mr D Wicks, MSc, BSc Hons, PGCE (*Head of Science, Physics*)
Mrs J Wigley, BLib Hons, MCLIP (*Learning Resources Supervisor*)
Mrs P Willcox, BA Hons, PGCE (*Learning Support*)
Ms N Wills, BArch, PGCE (*Subject Leader of Food and Nutrition*)

Prep School:

Head of Prep: Mr M Brain, BA Ed Hons
Deputy Head of Prep: Mrs A Thethy, BEd (*Year 6 Tutor*)
Mrs T Attwell, BA Ed Hons (*Reception Class Tutor*)
Mr G James, BA Hons PGCE (*Year 2 Tutor*)
Miss K Fielding, BA Ed Hons (*Year 3 Tutor*)
Mrs H Mittra, BSc Hons, PGCE (*Year 4 Tutor*)
Mrs J Skinner, BA Hons, PGCE (*Year 5 Tutor*)
Mrs M Tober, MEd (*Year 1 Tutor*)
Mrs Sandra Crouch, NNEB, EYFS (*Reception Class Teaching Assistant*)

Nursery:
Nursery Manager: Miss M Urbieta Irastorza, QTS
Mrs I Alexander-Gunn, Level 6, FdA Early Years and Childhood Studies (*Deputy EYFS Nursery Lead*)
Mrs J Redsull, NNEB (*Forest School Leader*)
Miss E Fiducia-Brookes, Level 4 Diploma (*EYFS Assistant*)

Equestrian Centre:
Mr D Scaife, FBHSI, BE AcCoach UKCC Level 3 (*Director of Riding*)
Miss J Chilcott, BHSII (*Senior School Instructor*)
Miss J Foster, BHSAI (*Prep School Instructor*)
Miss E Halsey, BHSII (*Prep School Instructor*)
Miss J Edge (*Centre Manager*)
Miss R Hogg (*Yard Manager*)
Mr T Passmore (*Yard Manager*)
Miss J Cockin (*Head Groom*)
Mrs E Sowels (*Equine Secretary*)

Registrar: Mrs K Ibbott

Stover School

Newton Abbot, South Devon TQ12 6QG
Tel: 01626 354505 (Main switchboard)
            01626 331451 (Preparatory School)
            01626 359911 (Registrar)
            01626 335240 (Finance Office)
Fax: 01626 361475
email: mail@stover.co.uk
website: www.stover.co.uk

Stover School is a leading independent, co-educational, non-selective, day and boarding school for pupils aged 3 to 18. It is set in 64 acres of beautiful and historical grounds in the heart of Devon's glorious countryside between the foothills of Dartmoor and the South West Coastline. In the last Independent Schools Inspection the School was judged as excellent in teaching, pastoral care, welfare, health and safety, quality of leadership and management and governance.

Stover School delivers a cutting edge Research Based Learning Curriculum across the entire age range while retaining a healthy focus on traditional Christian morals, values and manners. Happy children are at the very centre of the school's ethos, reflecting the robust system of pastoral care. Children who feel safe, valued, respected and who trust those around them are free to focus on learning to their maximum potential.

Pupils are encouraged, motivated and supported in achieving their aspirations in all areas of the academic and broader curriculum. Successes are celebrated wherever they occur, be that in Bushcraft, French, Hockey, Science, Judo, Art or Computer Programming.

The extensive activities and enrichment programmes ensure that everyone can enjoy, develop and challenge themselves. In this relatively small school every pupil is well known. The strong House system provides a framework for pupils to develop a sense of collectiveness within the supportive environment. Pupils learn respect for themselves and others through the teaching of moral values and good standards of behaviour.

The aim is to ensure that every child enjoys their experience at Stover School having achieved the best they are capable of in the broadest education sense and having equipped themselves with the qualifications and skills required for future success and fulfilment.

Recent developments include a refurbished Art Studio and Sixth Form Centre, a newly established tennis academy, creation of a music ensemble practice suite and recording studio and the arrival of the first vegetable beds, chickens and beehives which will develop into the Stover School Farm.

Examinations. Public examinations set by all examination boards include GCSE, BTEC and A Level. Music examinations are set by the Associated Board of the Royal Schools of Music. Speech and Drama examinations are set by LAMDA. Sixth Form pupils can also take CoPE and CSL/HSL qualifications, set by ASDAN and Sports Leaders UK respectively.

Physical Education. Hockey, rugby, netball, table tennis, football, rounders and cricket are the core team games. Individual sports include athletics, gymnastics, golf, tennis, badminton and cross country. Other sports throughout the year include adventure development, orienteering and dance.

The school has extensive grass pitches, six tennis courts (3 floodlit), a 9-hole golf course, cross-country tracks, clay pigeon range and cricket nets. We run a full range of school sports activities, clubs and fixture lists for both Senior and Prep.

Optional subjects. In addition to a wide variety of activities organised by Stover's own staff there are specialist peripatetic staff for instrumental and voice tuition, speech and drama, riding, fencing, judo, golf, clay pigeon shooting and tennis coaching.

Fees per term (2016–2017). Preparatory School: Day: Reception–Year 2 £2,560, Year 3 £2,780, Years 4–5 £3,160, Year 6 £3,440. Weekly Boarding: Year 3 £5,430, Years 4–5 £5,820, Year 6 £6,100. Full Boarding: Year 3 £6,290, Years 4–5 £6,670, Year 6 £6,950.

Senior School: Years 7–11: £4,030 (day), £7,040 (weekly boarding), £8,310 (full boarding);

Years 12–13: £4,140 (day), £7,190 (weekly boarding), £8,480 (full boarding).

Entrance and Scholarships. Compatibility of new pupils is assessed through a Head's interview, school tours, a series of taster days and submission of previous school's full written report. Academic, Music, Sport and Arts Scholarships are available and can be sat on point of entry or on our Scholarship Assessment Day in January. In addition means-tested bursaries are available. Stover School, in association with Plymouth University, also offers the Excellence in Mathematics Scholarships to International students. This attracts a 10% remission of fees at Plymouth University for the duration of the Undergraduate Degree course (3 years).

Health. Nursing care is provided by our on-site Matron who is a Registered General Nurse. All boarders are registered with the school's GP.

Old Stoverites. c/o Stover School.

Charitable status. Stover School Association is a Registered Charity, number 306712. Stover School is a charitable foundation for education.

Board of Governors:

Chairman: Mr S Killick, ND, ARB
Vice Chair:
Vice Admiral B J Key, BSc, FCMI, RN
Mr D Wilson, ACIB, MBA

Members:
Ms B Atkinson, MSc, BSc, RGN, RSCN, Dip N Lond
Mrs V Bamsey, BSc
Mrs K Bann, BSc, MRICS, FNAEA, MARLA
Mrs M Batten, BSc RHC
Lt Col D Hourahane
Mrs L Jones MA
Mrs J Milstead, BSc
Mr C Oliver, LLB, MBA
Mr M Roberts, BA, MRTPI
Mr T Synge, BA, FCA
Dr E J Wolstenholme, BSc, PhD

Honorary Members:
Dr P J Key, OBE, MB BS
Mrs C Walliker, BSc, MBA

Clerk to the Governors: Mr P Jenkins

Executive Head Teacher: Mr Richard Notman, BCom Hons

Deputy Head Teacher: Dr J Stone, BSc, MEd Open, PhD, HDipEd
Head of Preparatory School: Mr D Burt, BA, PGCE
Head of Sixth Form: Mr C Baillie, BSc, PGCE
Bursar: Mr P Jenkins
Senior Teacher (Pastoral): Mrs H Notman, BSc

Chaplain: Mrs F Wimsett, BA, PGCE
PA to the Executive Head Teacher: Mrs A Warren
Examinations Officer /Academic Secretary: Mrs H Cleaton, BSc, BTEC
Senior School Secretary: Mrs H Symons
Registrar: Mrs E Schramm
Communications Manager: Mrs R Robinson
IT Manager: Mr S Condict
Preparatory School Administrator: Mrs F Martin

Academic Staff:
Ms P Absalom, BA, PGCE (*Head of Drama*)
Dr D Allway, BSc, MSc, PhD, PGCE (*Head of Science*)
Mrs M Ayela, DEUG, Licence ES (*Head of Modern Foreign Languages*)
Mr C Baillie, BSc, PGCE (*Head of Sixth Form*)
Mrs E Barnes, BEd
Mr P Barter, BA, PGCE (*Head of Humanities*)
Mr S Cocker, BSc, QTS (*Head of Mathematics*)
Miss T Craven, BA, QTS (*Head of Sport*)
Mrs E Creates, BA, MA, PGCE (*Geography*)
Miss E Evans, BA, PGCE (*French*)
Mrs S Farleigh, BA (*Music*)
Mrs R Fenton, BA, PGCE (*Head of English, Teacher of Media*)
Mr G Forsyth, BA, PGCE (*English*), TEFL
Mrs K Gardner, BA, PGCE (*History*)
Mrs S Griffin, BEd (*Head of Years 7, 8 & 9*)
Mr J Haigh, BA, MA, PGCE (*Mathematics, Sixth Form Tutor*)
Mr M Halse, BA, PGCE (*Head of Boys Sport*)
Miss J Henwood, BSc, PGCE (*Mathematics*)
Mrs C Howard, BA, PGCE (*Head of Art & Photography*)
Dr L Le Tissier, BA, BSc, PhD, PGCE (*Head of Psychology*)
Mrs E Machin, BA, PGCE (*Director of ICT, Head of D&T Graphics, Head of Years 10 & 11*)
Miss A Morgan, BSc, PGCE (*Biology*)
Mrs A Richards, BSc Ed, PGCE (*Head of Physics*)
Mrs D Robinson, BA, QTS (*Sport*)
Mrs B Seward, BA, PGCE (*Philosophy & Ethics*)
Mrs C Sewell, BA, MA, PGCE (*German*)
Ms C Simmons, BA, Ed, PGCE (*Mathematics & Science*)
Mrs A Stone, BA, HDipEd, CELTA (*Head of English as an Additional Language*)
Mr J Tizzard, BMus, Dip Ed, PGCE (*Head of Music*)
Mr L Turnbull, BA, PGCE (*Business Studies*)
Mrs F Waring, Cert Ed, DELE, TEFL (*Spanish, Drama & History*)
Mrs C Wightman, BA, PGCE (*Art*)
Mrs F Wimsett, BA, PGCE (*RE, Chaplain*)

Learning Support Staff (Special Educational Needs):
Mrs K Sorensen-Parkes, Dip Bus Mgt (*Head of Learning Support*)
Mrs T Dodd, NVQ3 Child Care
Mrs J Ford, NCFE Level 2
Mrs S Hunt, NVQ3 Child Care
Mrs M Roberts, NVQ3 Child Care
Mrs S Tanner, BA, PGCE, CPT3A
Mrs G Thompson, NVQ3 EYCE
Mrs M Hind, NVQ3 EYCE

Support Staff:
Mr R Camilleri, BSc, PGCE
Mrs M Luczak

Visiting Staff:
Mr P Adcock BA, ARCO (*Accompanist*)
Mrs J Baldwin, ATCL, CTABRSM, Dip ABRSM (*Keyboard, Piano*)
Mr N Burns
Mrs M Downs, Dip (*Acting*), PCert LAM (*LAMDA*)
Mrs S Durant, GLCM, ALM, PGCE (*Brass*)
Mrs S Farleigh, BA (*Voice and Flute*)
Mrs C Hayek, LRAM, Prof Cert RAM (*Violin and Viola*)
Mr P Hill (*Guitar*)
Mrs A O'Donovan, BEd, ACCM (*Woodwind, Piano, Keyboard*)
Mr S Smith, LTCL, GTCL, PGCE (*Woodwind*)
Mr T Unwin (*Jazz Piano*)
Mrs H Wills, ALCM (*Cello, Piano*)

Stover Preparatory School:

Head of Preparatory School: Mr D Burt, BEd, MA, PGCE

Leadership Team:
Mr D Burt, BEd, MA, PGCE
Mr M Appleby, BEd, MA, MEd, PG Dip Psych (*Director of Teaching & Learning*)

Teachers:
Miss J Attwood, BA,PGCE
Mr M Ayer, BSc (*Ed*), PGCE
Mrs A Coster, BA, PGCE
Ms D Fallshaw, BA, PGCE
Mrs C Harrison, BA, PGCE
Mrs M Pallister, BEd
Mr L Ryan, BSc, TEFL, PGCE
Mrs F Waring, Cert Ed, DELE, TEFL
Mr B Watt, BA, PGCE
Mrs K Wilson, BA, PGCE
Mrs S Yonge, BA Ed

Assistants:
Mrs K Freeman, NNEB
Mrs J Sanders, NNEB

Nursery:
Mrs A Cattell, BA, NNEB, HND (*Nursery Manager*)
Miss N Carey, NVQ3 (*Nursery Group Leader*)
Mrs I McIntosh, NNEB (*Nursery Group Leader*)

Residential Staff:
Mr R Notman (*Executive Head Teacher*)
Mrs H Notman (*Senior Teacher Pastoral*)
Mrs J Coughlin (*House Parent*)
Mrs F Martin (*House Tutor*)
Mr L Ryan (*House Parent*)
Mr T Sherwood (*House Tutor*)
Boarding Assistants:
Mr J Bristow
Miss E Ettridge

School Medical Officer: Dr D Milburn, MB BS
School Nurse: Miss S Edworthy, RGN

Tettenhall College

Wood Road, Tettenhall, Wolverhampton, West Midlands WV6 8QX

Tel: 01902 751119
Fax: 01902 793000
email: head@tettcoll.co.uk
website: www.tettenhallcollege.co.uk
Twitter: @TettColl
Facebook: @TettColl

Motto: '*Timor Domini Initium Sapientiae*'

Tettenhall College offers a remarkable opportunity for your child's education in the UK; set in a stunning location with outstanding facilities our boarders live as part of a true family community where your child will be happy, safe and cared for. This really is "home from home" and family is at the heart of all we do.

We place emphasis on developing individual strengths in pupils of all abilities and our caring staff create a nurturing environment, with small class sizes and excellent pastoral care. Boarders are a diverse mix of British and international pupils and all enjoy a close relationship with the staff that live on site to look after them.

Outside the classroom, there are many opportunities for extracurricular activities, such as music, drama, sport and charity work. Boarders benefit from weekend activities and cultural visits which makes leisure time enjoyable and enriching and staff are always there to share our pupils' successes and help them with any problems.

Tettenhall is a thriving school where pupils in all years exceed expectations whether that be their reading levels in Preparatory School, GCSE examinations or A Levels in Sixth Form. Leavers' destinations include some of the most prestigious names in the educational world – Oxford, Cambridge and RADA to name a few. Alongside academic achievement pupils are involved in a full programme of exciting extracurricular activities and opportunities which we believe develops the whole individual.

Situation and Buildings. Set in acres of 33 acres of beautiful woodland grounds, with outstanding sporting facilities, Tettenhall College is a blend of historic buildings and modern amenities where pupils thrive within a caring family atmosphere. Located in the historic village of Tettenhall, yet only 40 minutes from Birmingham International Airport, the School is one of the leading independent day and boarding schools in the region catering for girls and boys from 2 to 18 years.

Amenities include a Sixth Form Centre, a campus-wide Information Technology Network, Library and Resources Centre, indoor heated Swimming Pool, Sports Hall, Squash Courts, Sports Pavilion and floodlit courts for Netball and Tennis. There are two Cricket squares and playing fields for Rugby, Football and Athletics.

The College is embarking on an ambitious development plan to bring all the facilities at the School up to the highest standard. Following the updating of the Girls' Boarding House last year, the Boys' Boarding House is to be completely refurbished this year as are the classrooms and theatre in the Towers. A full-size floodlit artificial pitch for hockey is to be installed, together with two smaller floodlit artificial pitches for Tennis, Netball and 5-a-side Football. Wi-Fi will also be installed across the site.

There are also plans to further develop the Woodlands with a mountain bike trail and a high ropes course. This will enhance their use in many aspects of the School's educational offering where its exceptional setting is often used to promote pupils' learning experience.

Religion. Services in the College Chapel are interdenominational.

Entry. The school accepts girls and boys. Entry to the Senior School (age 11–18) is normally by way of assessment in Mathematics, English and Non Verbal Reasoning. By arrangement with the Headmaster, pupils may be interviewed and tested according to their individual needs. Assessments are set by the Head of Preparatory School for pupils between the ages of 7 and 11. These can be taken in any term by appointment.

Organisation. Senior School (Years 7 to 11 and the Sixth Form) and the Preparatory School (Reception to Year 6) are divided into four Houses which compete in activities, work and games. The Nursery comprises Day Nursery and Pre-School from the age of 2 to 4.

Senior School Curriculum. GCSEs may be taken in the following subjects: Art, Biology, Business Studies, Chemistry, Drama, Electronics, English, French, Spanish, Geography, History, Information Technology, Mathematics, Music, Physics, Physical Education and Religious Studies.

In the Sixth Form numerous combinations of subjects are possible, and AS and A Level courses offered include Art, Biology, Business Studies, Chemistry, Drama and Theatre Studies, Economics, Electronics, English, French, Geography, German, History, Mathematics, Further Mathematics, Music, Photography, Physics, Physical Education and Psychology.

Careers. Extensive advice is given by the Head of Careers and every Sixth Former is assigned a Personal Tutor to guide and support them over the two years. This is enhanced by many visits and seminars throughout the year from external organisations such as universities and local companies. In addition the School is supported by Old Tettenhallians who will come in to host career talks and seminars.

Societies and Activities. All pupils are encouraged to become fully involved in the life of the community and to play a part in the social and cultural organisations.

Pupils take part in The Duke of Edinburgh's Award scheme, working for Bronze, Silver and Gold Awards. In addition to the sporting opportunities already mentioned, there is a full range of other sports activities available at lunchtime or after school, including Archery, Badminton, Basketball, Cross Country, Table Tennis and Fencing. There are numerous clubs and societies that meet regularly, for example Chess, Cookery, Classical Civilisation, Photography, Debating, Drama, Dance, Latin, Mandarin, Spanish, Pottery and Business Enterprise. Excursions are frequently arranged by all subjects, and foreign excursions have, in recent years, regularly included music tours, science trips, sports tours, art and business studies trips, as well as foreign exchanges. School plays and musicals are produced each year; there is a house festival of Performing Arts and the Music Department has a deservedly strong reputation for its quality of performance and opportunities. All senior pupils take part in the extended day programme where activities range from climbing and mountain biking to the Extended Project Qualification for our older pupils

Preparatory School. The Preparatory School is housed separately in a purpose-designed building opened in 2002. It shares a number of the facilities with Senior School and Senior School Staff help with games and specialist teaching.

The curriculum goes far beyond the confines of the national curriculum. Younger pupils are taught by a form teacher with an emphasis on the acquisition of key skills in Literacy and Numeracy. As children move through the years they are introduced to teaching from subject specialists.

Athletics, Cricket, Netball, Hockey, Rounders, Rugby, Soccer, Swimming and Tennis are the main sports and all pupils have PE and two afternoons of games each week. Extracurricular activities change regularly but include clubs in all the previously mentioned sports plus Art and Craft, Chess, Computing, Dance, Drama, Latin and Table Tennis. Drama, Music and the playing of musical instruments are strongly encouraged.

Fees per term (2016–2017). Senior School: Full Boarders: £6,888 (Years 7–9), £9,555 (Years 10–12), £9,100 (Year 13); Weekly Boarders: £6,311 (Years 7–9), £7,392 (Years 10–12), £7,040 (Year 13); Day Pupils: £4,404 (Years 7–12), £4,330 (Year 13).

Preparatory School: Full Boarders £6,888, Weekly Boarders £6,311, Day Pupils £3,310

Scholarships and Bursaries. Senior School Academic Scholarships may be offered to outstanding boys and girls from either state or independent schools. Scholarships are also awarded for Music, Art, Drama, Performing Arts and Sport.

Means-tested Bursaries are available. There is a reduction in fees for the children of the Clergy and members of HM Forces as well as children of former pupils.

The Old Tettenhallians' Club. Membership is automatic on reaching 18 years of age.

Charitable status. Tettenhall College Incorporated is a Registered Charity, number 528617. It exists to provide a quality education for boys and girls.

Governors:
Chairman: J F Woolridge, CBE, DL, BSc Hons
Vice-Chairman: Revd Prebendary G Wynne, DLitt, MTh, BSc Soc, BD, AKC
K Bruerton, BA Hons, FCCA
Mrs L Cook, BA
Mrs C Hammond, BA

Mrs S Isbister
Mr S Jones, BSc Hons
S C P Maddox, AB Eng, ICIOB
Mrs D Margetts
Mrs J Parker, SRP, MCSP, JP
G D H Sower, BA

Clerk to the Governors: R Ennis

Senior Leadership Team:

Headmaster: **D C Williams**, BA Hons, MSc

Bursar: C Way, BSc Hons
Deputy Head (Academic): Mrs R Samra-Bagry, BSc Hons, PGCE
Deputy Head (Pastoral): J Shipway, BSc, MA Hons
Head of Preparatory School: S Wrafter, BA Hons

Teaching Staff:

Miss C Belcher, BTEC, FDE	S L Lawrence, BSc Hons, Cert Ed
J Bullock, BSc	R M Leighton, BA, MA
P J Bullough, BA	Mrs M Lofting, BA, MA
T Clark, BEng, MSc	Miss N Minaker, BSc
Mrs N Claxton, BTEC Level 3	Mrs A Nash, ACIB
R Ellmore, BSc	Miss N Parkes, BTEC
P G Evans, BSc	Mrs S Patchett, PGCE
A T Foster, BA	Miss N Pike, BA, BTEC
Miss J Griffin, BA, GRTP	Mrs R Kay, BA
D Groom, BA, BEd	Mrs R Samra-Bagry, BSc Hons, PGCE
Mrs L Hall, BA	T Seston, BA, MA
J Higgs, BA	Mrs D E Spencer, BEd
M T Jackson, BEd	Miss J Turner, NNEB
Miss S Jassal, NVQ3	Miss M D Uttley, BA, PGCE
Mrs P Jones, Cert Ed, Dip RSA SpLD	Mrs K Ziolkowski, BA, CACHE

Visiting Teachers:
11 staff provide Music tuition, 3 take pupils for individual learning support and 2 provide additional sports coaching.

Personal Assistant to the Headmaster: Mrs N Phelps

Medical Officers:
Dr J Bright
Dr A Williams

School Nurse: Mrs C Wagstaff

Thetford Grammar School

Bridge Street, Thetford, Norfolk IP24 3AF
Tel: 01842 752840
Fax: 01842 750220
email: hmsec@thetgram.norfolk.sch.uk
website: www.thetgram.norfolk.sch.uk

Refounded in the 17th century by Sir Richard Fulmerston, Thetford Grammar School can however show an unbroken roll of Headmasters from 1114 and traces its origins to the 7th century. In more recent times it was voluntarily controlled until, augmented by the adjacent girls' grammar school, it returned to independence in 1981. Today it is a two-form entry 3½–18 co-educational day school with 220 pupils drawn from a radius of 30 miles across the Norfolk/Suffolk border. We seek to combine worthwhile academic standards with a tradition of care and support for the individual and commitment to the breadth of educational experience. A member of The Society of Heads (elected 1996), Association of Governing Bodies of Independent

Schools and the Independent Schools Bursars' Association the school is administered by the Governors of the Thetford Grammar School Foundation, acting as Trustees on behalf of the Charity Commission.

Buildings and Situation. Situated close to the centre of Thetford, the school occupies a well-established site graced by several buildings of architectural interest and the ruins of a medieval priory. There are extensive playing fields with a refurbished pavilion within walking distance of the main buildings, as well as an award-winning, eco-friendly Sixth Form Centre built around the original Cloisters.

Organisation. Prep Department pupils (to age 11) are taught primarily in their own premises with independent facilities. Older Prep pupils, however, have contact with specialist teachers in several subject areas and benefit from similar integration into many other aspects of school life. Main School education from 11 follows a two-form entry pattern with setting in core subjects to GCSE. Sixth Form students, who have their own Common Room, play a full part in the life of the school.

Curriculum. Prep Department teaching follows National Curriculum lines with strong emphasis on the English/Mathematics core and the range of specialist subjects in support. Music and Drama are important, while a full programme of PE and Games allows for the development of team sports and individual fitness.

Main School education through to GCSE is based on a common core of English, English Literature, Mathematics, a Modern Language (French or German) and the Sciences. Options allow students to develop skills and interests in History, Geography, RS, Business Studies, Languages, the Expressive Arts, Physical Education and Technology. IT is strongly represented across the curriculum. AS and A2 courses are offered in all these subjects. Mathematics and Science lead a strong pattern of results at this level and sixth form students proceed to university degree courses.

Sport and Extracurricular Activities. The life of the school extends widely from the classroom into sport, community service, dramatic and musical presentation; the lessons taught by the pursuit of excellence through individual commitment and teamwork are greatly valued.

Winter sports are Rugby, Soccer, Hockey, Netball and Cross-Country with Cricket, Tennis, Rounders and Athletics in the Summer. Popular indoor sports such as Basketball, Aerobics, Badminton, Volleyball and Gymnastics are also followed.

A majority of pupils take part in training for The Duke of Edinburgh Award scheme. Musically, a lively concert programme supports individual instrumental tuition and choral rehearsal while opportunities for theatre are provided termly by House and School productions.

There is a varied programme of curricular and extracurricular trips including expeditions and foreign visits.

Admission. Admission into the Prep Department follows a day in school with the appropriate year group during which an assessment is made. Admission into Main School is by formal examination with interview and school report. Sixth Form entrance is on the basis of interview and school report, with subsequent performance at GCSE taken into consideration. The main Entrance Examination is held in January but supplementary testing continues through the year. Full details from the Headmaster's Secretary.

Fees per term (2016–2017). Prep Department: Reception–Year 2 £3,397, Years 3–6 £3,908; Main School £4,424, including books and tuition, but excluding uniform, lunches, transport, examination entry fees and some specialised teaching such as instrumental music lessons.

Scholarships and Bursaries. Within the limits of available funds the Governors are able to provide financial support with the fees in case of need. Such bursaries are based on a declaration of family income and can be up to 75% of the fees. They can be available from Year 3 upwards. They are dependent of course on the pupil fulfilling the entrance requirements of the school. Scholarships of an honorary nature may be awarded to the top performers in the entrance examinations. Music scholarships are available on entry in Year 7 or 9 which will provide free instrumental or voice tuition. Scholarships are also available into the Sixth Form for both internal and external candidates. These can provide a reduction in fees for two years and are awarded as the result of a scholarship paper sat in December or in recognition of outstanding GCSE performance in the summer.

Details of all awards may be obtained from the Headmaster.

Charitable status. Thetford Grammar School is a Registered Charity, number 311263. It exists to provide education for boys and girls.

The Governing Body:

Chair of Governors: Mrs M Eade
Vice-Chair: Mrs K Colborn
Cllr R Brame (*Breckland District Council Representative*)
J Brown
Cllr B J Canham (*Thetford Town Council Representative*)
Mrs J Chamberlin
I M Clark
Mrs B Garrard, MA, BSc, Cert Ed
T J Lamb, BSc
S McGrath
J Pearson, MCIWM
Mrs J M Sinclair
R Spink
R Walden, BSc, FRICS

Clerk to the Governors: Ms A Ryan
School Business Manager: Mrs T Godden, FCCA

Headmaster: M S Bedford, BA Wales, PGCE Oxon, MPhil Cam, NPQH

Deputy Head: Mrs K Elders, MA Nottingham
Head of Sixth Form: Ms L Pearson, BA Oxford Brookes, Cert Ed
Head of Preparatory Department: Mrs N Peace, BA Bishop Grosseteste

Academic Staff:
Mrs A Alecock, BA Manchester
Miss E Bailey, MEd Cambridge, PGCE
Mrs T Beukes, BSc Stellenbosch SA
Mrs J Boyce, BA Bristol PGCE
S Braden, BSc RMCS Shrivenham
Mrs H Butler-Hand, BA, MEd Cantab
Mrs S Collins
Mrs R Dimminger, Dip Ed Bulawayo
Miss D Dunsmore, BSc Cambridge, PGCE
A M Durling, BA UEA, MCIL
M Foreman, BEd Nottingham
Mrs J Foreman, BA Warwick
Miss F Foster, BA Warwick
M Glassbrook, BSc Northumbria, PGCE
Mrs T E Granger, BSc Wolverhampton, PGCE
Miss C Griffiths, BA LCC, PGCE
M Hill, BA Bedfordshire
J A Law, BEd Loughborough
R Maringue, MA Grenoble, PGCE
Mrs H Pringle, BA Teesside Polytechnic
Mrs C Salt, BEd Exeter
Miss A Sherring, BA Camberwell School of Art
S R Simpson, BSc Birmingham, PGCE
J Snipe, BSc Bristol, PGCE
Miss F Travers, BA Nottingham Trent
A Ward, BSc London, PGCE
Mrs P Weyers, MMus Wales, PGCE
Miss M Wharton, BA Bristol, PGCE

Mrs L Wingham, BA London, PGCE
B Young, MA UWCC, PGCE

LAMDA:
Ms G Irving, MA Lancaster, PGCE

Teaching Assistants:
Mrs M Bedford, BA Wales, ACoT Dyslexia PG Dip Brunel
Miss J Blakemore, FdA UEA & Essex
Mrs S Bradfield, BSc UEA, Dip PFS, AC11, F10S
O El Oakley
Miss K Fitch

Learning Support:
Mrs K Jones, BSc QTS, Dip SpLD, AMBDA, SpLD APC
Patoss
Mrs P Ballard, BEd Southampton
Mrs V S Webber, BA Open University

Visiting Music Staff:
Mrs N Absolum (*Piano*)
Mrs S Brotherhood (*Woodwind*)
M B Clarke, BA Sussex, MA Illinois (*Clarinet, Saxophone*)
Ms F Levy, LLCM TD, ALCM (*Violin*)
J Rowland, (*Drum Kit and Jazz Piano*)
A H Salazar, GSMD, PGC, PG Adv Dip TCM (*Voice*)
D Scragg (*Brass*)
G Griffiths (*Guitar*)
Mrs J G Weeks, GRSM, ARMCM (*Piano*)

Administrative Staff:
Mrs E Brooks (*Headmaster's Secretary*)
Mrs C Huggins (*Accounts Secretary*)
Mrs C Reynolds (*Senior School Secretary*)
Mrs S Roochove (*Marketing Officer*)
Mrs J Settle (*Librarian*)

Technicians:
Mrs S Grimwood (*Art*)
A Jenkinson (*DT*)
Mrs A Kingsnorth, BSc London, PGCE (*Science*)
D Simpleman, BSc Southampton (*ICT*)

Tring Park School for the Performing Arts

Tring Park, Tring, Hertfordshire HP23 5LX

Tel:	01442 824255
Fax:	01442 891069
email:	info@tringpark.com
website:	www.tringpark.com

Tring Park School for the Performing Arts is a co-educational boarding and day school for pupils aged 8–19.

Number in School. Boarders: Boys 37, Girls 168. Day: 64.

Tring Park School for the Performing Arts stands at the forefront of specialist performing arts education in the UK. At Tring Park talented young people from 8–19 specialise in Dance, Acting, Musical Theatre or Commercial Music and receive a full academic education to GCSE, BTEC and A Level where Tring Park offers up to 21 A Level subjects. Entrance is via audition and scholarships are available for Dance via the Government's Music and Dance Scheme and Dance and Drama Awards. School scholarships and bursaries are available for Drama and Musical Theatre.

Pupils perform in Tring Park's Markova Theatre as well as in London, throughout the UK and Europe. Performances have included *To Dance with the Gods, Jesus Christ Superstar, Guys and Dolls* and *Cabaret*. Tring Park provides ballet dancers for the Christmas productions of *Nutcracker* and *Le Corsaire* with English National Ballet and for ENB's production of *Swan Lake* at the Royal Albert Hall. Several pupils have played the part of Billy in *Billy Elliot* in London and on tour, others have joined the cast of *Matilda* and performed the role of Gavroche in the London production of *Les Misérables*.

Alumni success.
Daisy Ridley – Rey in *Stars Wars The Force Awakens*; **Lily James** – *Cinderella, War and Peace* and *Romeo and Juliet*; **Lily James** and **Jessica Brown Findlay** – *Downton Abbey*; **Bryony Hannah** and **Helen George** – BBC's *Call the Midwife*. **Drew McOnie** – awarded an Olivier Award for Best Theatre Choreography; **Caroline Finn** – Artistic Director of National Dance Company Wales; **Max Westwell** – Principal with English National Ballet; **Tyrone Singleton** – Principal with Birmingham Royal Ballet. Tring Park also celebrates considerable academic success with students entering Russell Group universities and another who was awarded a Scholarship to study English at Churchill College, Cambridge.

Fees per term (2016–2017). Prep School: Boarders £7,905, Day £4,690. Age 11–16: Boarders £10.445, Day £6,745. Sixth Form Entry: Boarders £11,180, Day £7,470. Sibling discount 10% of termly fees. Forces discount available on request.

Aided places for Dance are available under the Government's Music and Dance Scheme and Post 16 Dance and Drama Awards. School scholarships are available for Drama and Musical Theatre.

Charitable status. The AES Tring Park School Trust is a Registered Charity, number 1040330. It exists to provide vocational and academic education.

Board of Governors:
Chairman: Mr Michael Geddes
Mrs Carol Atkinson
Mrs Mary Bonar
Ms Alice Cave
Mr John Clark
Mr Michael Harper
Mr Mark Hewitt
Mrs Juliet Murray
Mrs Angela Odell
Mr Eric Pillinger
Mrs June Taylor
Mr Daniel Zammit

Principal: **Stefan Anderson**, MA Cantab, ARCM, ARCT

Deputy Principal: Anselm Barker, MSt Oxon, BA Harvard

Director of Dance: Rachel Rist, MA, FRSA
Deputy Director of Dance: Teresa Wright, ARAD Adv, FISTD Cecchetti Branch Dip

Director of Drama: Edward Applewhite, BA Hons
Deputy Director of Drama: Heather Loomes, BA Hons
Deputy Director of Drama: Dominic Yeates

Director of Music: Elizabeth Norriss, BMus Hons, PGCE, ALCM
Head of Commercial Music Course: Harmesh Gharu, MA, BMus Hons, PGCE

Director of Musical Theatre Course: Donna Hayward, FISTD
Deputy Director of Musical Theatre Course: Simon Sharp, BA Hons, PGCE

Head of Performance Foundation Course: Louisa Shaw
Head of Theatre Arts: Elizabeth Odell, BA, AVCM, AISTD, FDI, QTS

Director of Academic Studies: Brian Liddle, MEd, PGCE, BSc Hons

Deputy Director of Academic Studies: Anu Mahesh, PhD, MSc Hons, PGCE

Head of Sixth Form: Edward Hawkins

Bursar: Nick Edwards, MA

Marketing Director: Miriam Juviler, ARAM, LRAM
Fundraising Director: Lynne Misner

Head of Learning Support: Suzanne Kennedy, BA Hons, PGCE, MA, NPQH, SpLD, SENCOs

Trinity School

Buckeridge Road, Teignmouth, Devon TQ14 8LY

Tel:	01626 774138
Fax:	01626 771541
email:	enquiries@trinityschool.co.uk
website:	www.trinityschool.co.uk

Foundation and Ethos. With a joint Anglican/Catholic foundation, Trinity School's Christian ethos and family atmosphere are complemented by a commitment to excellence in both academic and personal development. With recent inspections by both ISI and Ofsted rating the School as 'Outstanding' in many areas, the School has successfully demonstrated a determination to deliver the best education possible for the pupils in its care.

Pupil Body. 450 pupils from Nursery to 19 years: 80 boarders. 65%: 35% boy to girl ratio. Full ability range with about 15–20% receiving targeted support through the Learning Success Department.

Location and Facilities. The School offers excellent facilities in a very attractive environment with panoramic views of Lyme Bay. Facilities include a purpose-built Design Technology building, IT laboratories, a Music Centre, a Science block, a Food Technology Centre, en-suite boarding accommodation for Sixth Formers, indoor and outdoor tennis facilities, a 25m heated swimming pool, and an Art Centre. The School is very well connected by road and rail, with the nearest railway station being under a mile away and on the London main line.

Academic Record. At the upper end of our ability profile, we have a proven track record of sending pupils to Russell Group universities. We have gained 6 Good School Guide Awards for performance in English, Business Studies and Science. Prep pupils' performance considerably exceeds expectations at KS1 and KS2. ISI rated all aspects of EYFS provision to be 'Outstanding' (2014). 95% of Sixth Form students in recent years have progressed to university or apprenticeships. A mix of BTEC and A Level subjects are taught (inc all facilitating subjects) in the Sixth Form.

Pastoral Care and Welfare. The quality of the School's pastoral care is an established and considerable strength as proven by the recent inspections. Our Anglican/Catholic ethos permeates all that we do. We believe that for care to be effective, it is essential that school and family work closely together – the relationship needs to be dynamic, honest and built on mutual trust and understanding. This approach, and the fact that Trinity provides education for girls and boys of all ages, helps to generate the School's warm, 'family' atmosphere.

Personal Development. Extensive sporting, cultural, charitable and leadership opportunities are available at all ages: rich musical life with yearly musical productions involving Prep and Senior department pupils; South West Junior Choir of the Year 2011 and 2012; one of the most active CCF sections in the country; Ten Tors and DofE regulars; Lawn Tennis Association centre of excellence with one national LTA champion and 4 Independent Schools Association (ISA) champions; over 40 pupils have won medals at ISA national sports finals (swimming, athletics, cross country, tennis – Prep and Senior).

Admissions. Entry to the School is by assessment and interview of the younger pupils, and entrance test and interview for the older pupils. Scholarships are by open competition at 11+, 13+ and 16+, for academic, music, art, drama, sport and all-rounder Notre Dame Awards (selection in January). Bursaries and HM Forces Bursaries.

Fees per term (2016–2017). Tuition: £2,455–£3,905. Boarding (in addition to Tuition): Preparatory: £3,235 (weekly), £3,760 (full); Senior: £4,115 (weekly), £4,800 (full). No compulsory extras.

Charitable status. Trinity School is a Registered Charity, number 276960.

Patrons:
Rt Revd Mark O'Toole, Bishop of Plymouth
Rt Revd Robert Atwell, Bishop of Exeter

Chairman of Governors: Mr Simon Brookman

Headmaster: Mr Lawrence Coen, BSc Hons Aberystwyth

Deputy Head: Mrs Wendy Martin, BSc Hons Kent, PGCE Kent

Senior Department:
Mr Mark Acher, BSc Hons Sheffield, PGCE Nottingham (*Senior Tutor*)
Mrs Rachael Arkell, BA Hons Coventry, PGCE Birmingham (*Director of Learning, Int and Performance Studies*)
Mrs Lucy Atkins (*Subject Leader English*)
Mrs Anna Brown, BA Hons Glamorgan, PGCE Bristol (*Deputy Head of 6th Form, Subject Leader Business*)
Mrs Julia Bryant, MEd Open, BSc Hons London, PGCE Exon, ADSNEd, PGDPD (*Director of Studies, Subject Leader Psychology*)
Mr Patrick Cairns, BEd Liverpool (*Subject Leader Art*)
Mrs Fenella Cooke, BA Hons Worcester, PGCE Surrey (*Subject Leader Drama & Performing Arts*)
Mrs Sheridan Couch, BA Ed Hons Exeter (*Subject Leader Physical Education*)
Mrs Kathryn Crook, Dip TEFL, LTCL Trinity (*Subject Leader EAL*)
Mrs Geraldine Davis, BA Hons UWE Bristol, QTS (*Head of Key Stage 3*)
Ms Sarah Evans, MA Oxon, PGCE Oxon (*Subject Leader History*)
Mrs Wendy Grant, BSc Hons ACIB, MEC Plymouth, PGCE Exeter (*Subject Leader Mathematics*)
Mme Sandrine Haytread, Dip Travel & Tourism Ecole Cadre Paris, Cert Ed (*Subject Leader Modern Languages, Boarding Tutor*)
Mr Darrel Jones, BSc Hons Liverpool, PGCE Liverpool (*Director of Learning Science Faculty*)
Mr Robert Larkman, BEd Hons Plymouth (*Head of Key Stage 4*)
Mr Mike Milne, BA Hons West of England, PCGE West of England (*Head of Sixth Form and Head of House MD*)
Mrs Joan Potts, BA Hons Central Lancashire, PGCE Wolverhampton (*Subject Leader English*)
Mrs Giulietta Swift, BA Hons Bristol, PGCE Bath (*Subject Leader ICT*)
Mrs Fiona Tamlyn, BEd Hons Cambridge (*Subject Leader Learning Support*)
Mr Ben Whittles, BSc Hons East Anglia, PGCE Canterbury Christ Church (*Subject Leader Geography*)

Preparatory Department:
Mrs Rachel Eaton-Jones, BSc Hons Bristol, NPQH (*Head of Preparatory Department*)

Mr Michael Burdett, BEd Hons Oxon (*Deputy Head of Preparatory Department, Year 6, Assessment Coordinator*)

Mr Sean Lovett, BEd Primary Physical Education Plymouth (*EYFS/KS1 Coordinator, PE, Thrive, Forest School*)

Miss Elizabeth Parker, BA Ed Hons Exeter (*KS2 Coordinator*)

Mr Simon Fisher, BSc Hons Wales, PGCE Wales (*Sports Coordinator*)

Nursery Department:
Mrs Liz Saunders, NNEB (*Nursery Manager*)
Mrs Claire Savva, Montessori Dip Level 4 (*Assistant Nursery Manager*)

Administration:
Bursar: Mr Shaun Dyer, BA Portsmouth
Registrar: Ms Fleur Rogers
Headmaster's PA: Mrs Alison Miles
Academic Administrator: Mr John Turner
Head of Prep's PA: Mrs Lisa Paget

Walden School (formerly Friends' School)

Mount Pleasant Road, Saffron Walden, Essex CB11 3EB

Tel:	01799 525351
Fax:	01799 523808
email:	admissions@waldenschool.co.uk
website:	www.waldenschool.co.uk

Walden School is a school with a difference. Small, diverse, vibrant, and located in the heart of Saffron Walden. Located on a beautiful 37-acre site, with a tradition of more than three hundred years of enlightened education for both boys and girls, the school offers education for students aged 3–18 with boarding from age 11. High standards of teaching and academic attainment are enriched by a broader framework of personal development.

At Year 6, pupils finish Walden Prep School well prepared for their transition into the Senior School. Walden School currently delivers almost a grade higher in value added scores, improving the achievement between age 11 and GCSE. We achieve this through small teaching groups with excellent, committed staff and a focus on academic progress and achievement within a framework of all-round development. Our supportive environment results in secure, happy students who succeed academically with internationally recognised qualifications and go onto a range of good British Universities.

Pastoral care is excellent and staff get to know each pupil well, making the most of our small class sizes. Pupils at every age receive plenty of individual attention and support in their studies.

We offer a wide-ranging extracurricular programme of clubs and activities; we have a strong creative tradition in the performing arts, while our extensive playing fields, heated swimming pool and modern sports hall offer a broad range of sporting opportunities for all children.

We offer day places, or flexi, weekly or full boarding options. House staff provide supportive and friendly environments where boarders are encouraged to take increasing amounts of responsibility and to contribute to the life of the Boarding House.

With excellent road and rail connections to London, Cambridge and Stansted Airport, access is easy both locally and nationally.

Admissions. By interview, entrance test and school report.

Fees per term (2016–2017). Day £2,875–£5,575; Weekly boarding £6,820–£8,130; Full boarding £7,435–£9,095.

Scholarships and Bursaries. Scholarships are available to internal and external candidates.

Academic scholarships are available to applicants wishing to join Years 7, 9 and Sixth Form. In addition, there are awards made for Art, Drama, Music and Sport.

Further details are available from the Admissions Registrar.

Walden School is able to offer some assistance with fees in some cases. No application for a child who would benefit from the education that Walden School provides should be discouraged solely on the grounds of financial need. Please contact the Bursar for further information.

Charitable status. Walden School Limited is a Registered Charity, number 1000981.

Clerk to the Board of Governors: Susan Garratt

Head: **Anna Chaudhri**, BA, MA Cantab, PGCE

Bursar: Stephen Welch, FCA
Deputy Head: Eleanor Mackenzie Lambert, MEd Cantab, BSc, Dip Env Sc

Teaching Staff:
‡ *Holder of PGCE*

Art:
‡Serena O'Connor, BA
‡Matthew Miller, BA, BTEC

Business Studies:
Carolyn White, MEd, BEd

Careers:
Julie Anderson, BEd

Design Technology – Product Design:
‡Jessica Armitage, BA
‡Richard Twinn, BA

Design Technology – Food:
Sophie Ward, BSc

Drama:
‡Richard Smith, BA
Shelley Dowsett, BSc, GTP

Economics:
Mark Munsen, MA

English:
‡Gillian Kinnear, BA
§Joanna Matthews, BEd
Adrian Lockwood, BA, MA

ESOL:
‡Lynda Langford Powell, MA
‡Rebecca Auty

Film Studies:
‡John Searle-Barnes, BA, MA

Geography:
‡Oliver Staines
‡Hannah Sargent, MSc, BSc

History:
‡John Searle-Barnes, BA, MA
‡Charlotte O'Neill, BA
Jennifer Allwood, BEd

Computing:
§Carolyn White, BEd
Jessica Armitage, BA

Library:
Jennifer Mizen

Mathematics:
Adrian Clarke, BEd
Bernadette Gilbert, BSc
Antonia Everett, BSc
‡Geoffrey Curtis, BSc
Carolyn White, MEd, BEd

Modern Languages:
‡Peter Fasching, BA
§‡Jane Pearce, BA
‡Anna Chaudhri, MA
Joanne Sherriff, BA

Music:
‡Gavin Greenaway, BA
Mary Richardson, BA

Peripatetic Music Teachers:
Mary Richardson, BA, PGCE, DipABRSM
Jason Meyrick, FTCL, LRAM, LTCL, Prof Cert
Alison Townend, BA, LLCM, LGSM, LTCL
Nicky Ogden, BA, PGCE, LRAM
Edward Dodge, MA, GRSM, ARMCM, PGCE
Steven Hynes, BTEC
Louis Thorne, BSc
Sarah Clark, BTEC
Angela Leslie, BMus, PGCE
Amy Klohr, BA, LRAM
Richard Partridge, BMus
Iain Mann, MA, BA

Physical Education:
Nicholas Batcheler, BEd, DipT
Jennifer Allwood, BEd
Raymond Mordini, BPHE
Shelley Dowsett, BSc, GTP
Grant Ward, BA

Psychology:
Jonathan Slinger, BA, BEd, MEd

Religious Studies & PSHE:
§‡Helen Golden, BA
‡Biddy Vousden, BA, MPhil

Science:
Wayne Steel
‡Philip Dant, BSc
§Julie Anderson, BEd
‡Eleanor Mackenzie Lambert, MEd, BSc, Dip Env Sc
Raymond Mordini, BPHE
Genevieve Millard, PhD, MA, BSc
Christine Proudfoot, BSc

Speech & Drama:
Sonia Lindsey-Scripps, BA

Study Centre – Specialist Teaching:
Caryn Pepper
Heather Douglas, MSc
Fiona Glickman
Louise Plant
Joy Wheeler
Virginia Elam
Jane Bull
Jacqui Parnham

House Staff:
‡Matt Kiely, BSc
Judy Camp
Sonia Hood, BSc

Head of Junior School: Sally Meyrick, BA

Junior Class Teachers:
‡Kate Richardson, BSc
Elizabeth Brimer, MPhil
Deborah Ballingall, BEd
‡Sally Meyrick, BA
Lucy Nicholson, MA, PGCE
Sarah Kiely, BEd
Chris Clayton-Smith, BA
Iain Mann, MA, BA

Infant Department & Early Years:
Sally Manser, CertEd (*Head*)
Tiffany Johnson, NNEB

Learning Support:
Judith Langton, BE

Nursery Coordinator:
Catherine Armstrong, NNEB

Welbeck – The Defence Sixth Form College

Forest Road, Woodhouse, Loughborough, Leicestershire LE12 8WD

Tel:	01509 891700
Fax:	01509 891701
email:	helpdesk@dsfc.ac.uk
website:	www.dsfc.ac.uk

Welbeck Defence Sixth Form College aims to provide an environment in which young people from all backgrounds can reach the very highest academic and personal standards in pursuit of a career as a Technical Officer within the Armed Services and the Civil Service. Welbeck's history began in September 1953 at Welbeck Abbey, near Worksop in Nottinghamshire, as a Sixth Form College for potential Engineering Officers for the British Army. The Defence Training Review of 2002 resulted in the decision to expand the College across all three Armed Services as well as the Defence Engineering and Science Group (DESG), and in September 2005 Welbeck – The Defence Sixth Form College opened at its new purpose-built site in Woodhouse, Loughborough. Welbeck is the first stage of the Defence Technical Officer and Engineer Entry Scheme (DTOEES) which sponsors students to study their A Levels at Welbeck and then move on to partner Universities to study Technical or Engineering degrees. Students receive an annual bursary of £4,000 whilst at University, and once they have graduated they will enter Initial Officer Training with the service that has sponsored them through the scheme or, in the case of DESG, they will enter the Graduate Training Programme.

Welbeck is a full boarding establishment offering a technically focused A Level education. There are approximately 175 places available for Year 12 students who have passed the selection for sponsorship by one of the three Armed Forces or the Defence Engineering and Science Group. The College will also accept a limited number of applications from private students.

Situation. Welbeck College is situated on a 36-acre site in the charming rural setting of Charnwood Forest in Leicestershire. Welbeck has a spacious campus with state-of-the-art facilities and amenities.

Approach and Ethos. Our aim is to provide all students with an outstanding education that will enable them to achieve A Level results that will qualify them to continue to the next stage of the DTOEES scheme – an engineering or technical degree at a top university.

Welbeck educates its students in the broadest sense of the word; it offers a programme of intellectual, personal and physical development specifically designed to meet the needs of today's modern Armed Forces. Pupils will have innumerable opportunities to develop their understanding of leadership and of success, and in doing so will leave the College better equipped for life in the Armed Forces. As you would expect, there is a strong emphasis on core military skills and values. Additionally, sport plays a prominent role for all students with College teams regularly securing regional, and occasionally national, honours. At Welbeck, such an education is founded on moral integrity, responsibility and a genuine sense of service, which together lead to inculcating the core skills of leadership which are not only strong in our community but enduring.

Our students come from all over the United Kingdom and from a variety of backgrounds. The vast majority of them have never boarded before, but find themselves surrounded by others who are in the same position. Pastoral care at Welbeck is outstanding, and through House Staff and personal Tutors all individual students are supported throughout their time at the College. Welbexians are ambitious and motivated, and thrive in an environment with other like-minded individuals who have the same drive and determination to succeed and make the most of each and every opportunity. Students leave the College resolute, skilled in communication and with their ambitions extended, having shared excellence and involvement in the many and varied experiences offered by the College.

Admission. To apply to Welbeck, and subsequently the Armed Services, candidates should be medically fit UK, Commonwealth or Irish citizens aged between 15 and 17 years and six months on 1st September in the year of entry to the College. Commonwealth citizens are required to have 5 years residency in the UK prior to application. Certain other single-service conditions may apply and will be outlined at the time of application. To join Welbeck as a DESG Civil Service student candidates must be British citizens or hold dual nationality, one of which must be British. To join the Welbeck Private Scheme (WPS), applicants must show a strong commitment to develop themselves both personally and academically at Welbeck, and are also required to meet the academic, medical and fitness criteria of the MOD Sponsored students.

Requirements for successful candidates will include an A in Maths, B in Physics or BB in Dual Award Science and C in English Language at GCSE or the equivalent qualifications.

All MoD candidates are required to attend a Service Selection Board prior to entrance to Welbeck. Welbeck Private Scheme (WPS) candidates undergo a similar selection process at Welbeck.

Fees. *MoD students*: Tuition is paid for by the Ministry of Defence. Parents or guardians are required to make a contribution towards the cost of their child's maintenance which covers board, lodging and the value of clothing and services provided. *Welbeck Private Scheme*: Fees per term £6,333.

Chair of Governors: Vice-Admiral D L Potts CB Royal Navy – Director General Joint Force Development & Defence Academy of the United Kingdom

Principal: **Mr J P Middleton**, MA Oxon

Westholme School

Meins Road, Blackburn, Lancashire BB2 6QU

Tel:	01254 506070
Fax:	01254 506080
email:	secretary@westholmeschool.com
website:	www.westholmeschool.com

Westholme School comprises: Nursery (Boys and Girls from the age of 3 months), Infant School (Boys and Girls aged 3–7), Junior School (Boys and Girls aged 7–11), Senior School (Boys and Girls aged 11–16) and Sixth Form (Boys and Girls aged 16–18).

There are currently 750 day pupils at Westholme: 450 girls in the Senior School and Sixth Form, 370 in the Infant and Junior Departments, and 30 boys and girls in the Nursery.

Westholme School is administered by a Board of Governors which includes three nominated Governors representing current parents. Although the school is non-denominational, its Christian foundation is regarded as important, the emphasis being placed on the moral aspect of Christian teaching.

Senior School, Sixth Form. The aim of the Senior School is to provide an atmosphere in which each pupil can develop his or her abilities to the full and can excel in some field of activity. There is constant effort to widen interests and to instil a strong sense of individual responsibility. Most students continue to the Sixth Form and then move on to Higher Education. Most pursue degree courses, a significant number at Oxford and Cambridge.

The Senior School offers an academic curriculum in English Language and Literature, Mathematics, Biology, Chemistry, Physics, Geography, History, French, German, Mandarin, Spanish, Design Technology, Food, ICT, Textiles, Art, Physical Education, Business Studies, Classical Civilisation, Drama, Latin, Music, Ethics, Philosophy & Religion (EPR), Psychology, Sociology and Theatre Studies. Most of these subjects can be taken for the GCSE examination and at AS and A Levels; Oxbridge tuition is also offered.

Set in the countryside to the west of Blackburn, Westholme School offers excellent facilities. The premises have been regularly upgraded to give purpose-built accommodation for specialist subjects such as Art, Design and Information Technology and Music; seven modern laboratories support the three separate sciences. Sporting facilities include a sports hall, indoor swimming pool, brand new all-weather pitch and tennis courts and a large playing field with running circuit. The full-sized professional theatre opened in 1997, seats 700 and offers students outstanding production resources. The library has open-access multimedia giving students full research facilities. The Sixth Form wing opened in September 2003 complete with lecture theatre, common room, café and classrooms.

The Performing Arts are a special feature of the school. There are several school choirs and girls have the opportunity to learn a string, brass or wind instrument and to play in the school orchestras or wind ensembles. Co-curricular drama includes the full-scale spectacular musical, in the round productions, club and house competitions, while make-up and costume design are popular options at GCSE.

School societies and house teams meet on most days during midday break and girls are encouraged to participate in a variety of activities and in their house competitions. These provide younger girls with opportunities beyond the curriculum and older students with the chance to assume a leadership role.

Westholme Infant School, Westholme Junior School. There is close cooperation between these schools and with the Senior School. A family atmosphere allows children to learn in a supportive and happy environment. Firm academic foundations are laid with the emphasis upon the basic skills of literacy and numeracy. Excellent facilities afford ample teaching space and resource areas; the Junior School has three halls, music rooms and specialist provision for Information Technology. Co-curricular activities include public speaking, orchestra, choir, sports, societies and school visits. Music and sport are taught by specialists and all Departments use the swimming pool, sports hall, athletics track and outdoor pitches at the Senior School.

Admission. Pupils usually enter the school in September. Entry to the Junior and Senior Schools is by examination, and to the Infant School by interview. The normal ages of entry are at 2, 3, 4, 7, 11 and 16.

In view of the demand for places, parents are advised to make an early application.

The Principal is happy for prospective parents to visit the school during normal working hours; appointments may be arranged through the Registrar, from whom application forms are available. Annual Open Days are held in October and other open days are held in the spring and summer terms.

Private coaches run from Accrington, Blackburn, Bolton, Burnley, Colne, Chorley, Clitheroe, Darwen, Leyland, Preston, Standish, Ribble Valley, South Ribble, the Rossendale Valley and Wigan.

Fees per term (from January 2017). Senior School £3,550; Junior School £2,775; Infant School: £2,575; Pre-School: £2,740; Nursery (age 2–3 years) £200 pw; Nursery (age 3 months–2 years) £220 pw.

Scholarships are available at the Senior School for students who show good academic ability and various Bursaries are available (means-tested).

Charitable status. Westholme School is a Registered Charity, number 526615. It exists for the education of children between the ages of 3 months and 18.

Governing Body:
Chairman: Mr B C Marsden, FCA
Vice Chairman: Mr P Forrest, MRICS, FCIOB
Mr M Abraham, BEd
Mr K J Ainsworth, FGA
Mr S Anderson, BA Hons, FCA
Mr J Backhouse, LLB Hons
Mr D J Berry, BA, FCMA, MIBM
Mrs A Booth
Mrs J Meadows, BSc Hons, ACA
His Honour E Slinger, BA
Mr J R Yates, BSc

Clerk to the Governors: Mr J Backhouse, LLB Hons

Principal: Mrs Lynne Horner, BA Hons, PGCE

Commercial Director: Mrs Vivienne Davenport, MA Oxon

Deputy Headteacher, Curriculum: Miss Francine Smith, FRSA, BSc Hons Brunel, PGCE

Deputy Headteacher, Pastoral: Mrs Jude Gough, BA Hons Wolverhampton, PGCE, MISTC

Assistant Headteacher: Mr James Dumbill, BA Hons Bristol, PGCE

Windermere School – Browhead

Patterdale Road, Windermere, The Lake District, Cumbria LA23 1NW

Tel: 015394 46164
            International +44 15394 46164
Fax: 015394 88414
email: admissions@windermereschool.co.uk
website: www.windermereschool.co.uk
Twitter: @windermeresc
Facebook: /Windermere-School

A small and friendly school, with an emphasis on challenge through adventure and academic excellence.

Windermere School, is an independent co-educational boarding and day school, founded in 1863, and is an Educational Trust administered by a Board of Governors. It is divided into the Senior School (ages 11 to 18) and the Infant and Junior School (ages 2 to 11).

Located in the heart of the English Lake District National Park, our school offers a rich environment in which pupils can achieve academic and personal excellence. It has the beauty and tranquillity of a wooded campus overlooking the mountains and lake, along with a lakefront boathouse, beach and watersports centre. The amenities of the vibrant resort of Windermere are within minutes of the school. Even with its breathtaking location, the school has easy access to the motorway network, main rail lines and major airports.

Adventure activities and watersports opportunities are provided for each pupil with nationally recognised certificates from organisations including the Royal Yachting Association and the British Canoe Union. This combined with the rich literary and cultural heritage of the Lake District provides a unique setting for academic study and self-development; thus the motto Vincit qui se Vincit, *One conquers, who conquers oneself*.

The Senior School and Sixth Form is located on a mountainside campus overlooking the lake, with the Infant and Junior School campus and watersports centre nearby. The school owns over 100 acres in the Lake District National Park. There is a modern Sixth Form Boarding House with single and double study-bedrooms, plus a lodge-style Boys Boarding House with magnificent views south and west over Lake Windermere and the mountains, and a traditional girls dormitory in Browhead, formerly a private estate.

Numbers. There are approximately 355 pupils in total. The Senior School has approximately 256 pupils, of whom 50% are boarders. The size of the community has the advantage of providing a friendly atmosphere of understanding and fosters good staff-pupil relationships. Many members of the teaching staff hold additional qualifications in outdoor adventure. There is a 4-house system for competitions and games.

Curriculum. The curriculum offered at Windermere School reflects the belief that students should be exposed to as many opportunities as possible and leave the school as well-rounded individuals. It is tailored to the needs of each child, with small class sizes. Each pupil is provided with a personal tutor that stays with them throughout their years at the school, to oversee work on a daily basis and act as an advocate. One year and two year GCSEs and IGCSEs are taken in Years 10 and 11. Sixth Form students undertake the internationally recognised International Baccalaureate Diploma.

There are qualified staff and programmes in place for Special Educational Needs, English as an Additional Language, and Gifted and Talented pupils.

Music, Art, and Drama play an important part in the life of the school. There are two choirs, and individual instruction leading to chamber groups and orchestra. Students are prepared for the written and practical music exams of the Associated Board of the Royal Schools of Music. The school participates in regional Music Festivals. The Central School of Speech and Drama and LAMDA's examinations are also taken in Speech and Drama. Art, Pottery and Design Technology provide considerable scope and opportunity. The Art Studios contain facilities for History of Art and an Art History Library. Drama classes are included in the curriculum, and there are several productions staged each year.

Extra-Curricular Activities. Windermere School's watersports centre, Hodge Howe with over 160 metres of lakefront on the shores of Windermere, hosts a wide range of activities during the school's timetabled curriculum, and as part of the extra-curricular activity programme. The centre has accreditation from the British Canoeing Union and the Adventure Activities Licensing Authority, as well as being a Royal Yachting Association Teaching Centre. In 2014, the School was announced as a RYA Champion Club for its race training. Windermere is the only school in the UK to be awarded this status.

There are traditional competitive sports teams in hockey, netball, tennis, athletics and more. Many students play for regional and national teams, as well as for the school.

Service. Windermere School has a strong tradition of Community Service where pupils are active participants. The most high profile is Life Change South Africa with many staff and pupils travelling to South Africa each year to contribute to projects. The school supports many other charities including local Hospices, Young Carers, NSPCC, Save The Children Fund and works with regional Rotary Clubs.

Religion. The school is Christian in outlook and welcomes other denominations.

Medical. The health of the pupils is under the care of appointed school Doctors and a School nurse. There is a regular clinic, and dispensary twice daily.

Societies. More than 40 Clubs and Societies provide a variety of interests for out-of-school hours.

Uniform. Senior School – Girls wear blue kilt and striped blazer plus light blue blouses and optional navy jumper. Boys wear dark grey trousers, navy blue blazer, white shirt and school tie with optional navy jumper. Home clothes may be worn at weekends. The Sixth Form wear dark suits and they may wear home clothes in the evenings and at weekends.

Infant and Junior School – Girls wear blue kilt and striped blazer plus light blue blouses in the winter. In the summer the kilt is worn with a blue and white flowered short-sleeved blouse and blue sleeveless slipover. Boys wear grey trousers, pale blue shirts and sweater, the school tie and blazer.

Boarding. There is a strong boarding tradition at Windermere School that benefits the whole school community. Each Boarding House has live-in staff supervised by a House Mistress or House Master. Each evening, academic staff oversee prep and are available for extra tuition and advice. There are weekend activities both on campus and with staff-led excursions throughout the Lake District and beyond. It is a safe and caring extended family environment where pupils can excel both academically and personally.

Round Square. The School is a member of the international Round Square group of schools. Exchanges and Overseas Service Projects are regularly arranged between the schools involved in Australia, Canada, Germany, India, Switzerland, South Africa and USA and Brunei.

Infant and Junior School. The nearby Infant and Junior School is in the care of a Head, and takes boarders from age 8, along with day children up to Year 6. The Infant and Junior School is fully integrated with the Senior School giving continuity of teaching programmes and use of joint facilities.

Entry. Pupils are accepted into the Senior School from Prep and Junior schools at age 11+, or by direct entry into the Sixth Form. In other circumstances students may be accepted at other times. In the Infant and Junior School, pupils are taken at various stages from Nursery onwards. Visitors are welcome at anytime during the year, and Open Days are held once a term.

Fees per term (2016–2017). *Average* Day Fees (including lunch): Reception £2,485, Years 1–2 £3,326, Years 3–6 £4,912, Years 7–8 £4,980, Years 9–11 £5,540, Years 12–13 £5,640.

Average Weekly Boarding Fees: Years 3–6 £7,880, Years 7–8 £8,390, Years 9–11 £9,480, Years 12–13 £9,580.

Average Full Boarding Fees: Years 3–6 £8,330, Years 7–8 £8,880, Years 9–11 £9,970, Years 12–13 £9,990.

Average International Students: Years 3–6 £8,330, Years 7–8 £8,880, Years 9–11 £9,970, Years 12–13 £9,990.

Discounts are available for Forces families eligible for the MOD Continuity of Education Allowance (CEA).

Scholarships. Scholarships are available for entry in Years 7, 9 and 12. For more information please visit the school's website or contact Admissions.

Charitable status. Windermere Educational Trust Limited is a Registered Charity, number 526973, with a mission to provide education of the highest quality.

Chairman of Governors: Mr Michael Dwan

Head: **Mr Ian Lavender**, MA Oxford, BA Hons Oxford, NPQH

Deputy Head Pastoral: Miss J Parry, MPhil, BSc Hons Liverpool, PGCE Manchester

Deputy Head Academic: Mr S King, MA Aberdeen, MSc Oxford, PGCE Northern College of Education

Administrative Staff:
School Business Manager: Mrs S Ross
Head's PA: Mrs J Jones
School Secretary: Mrs S Dougherty
Admissions Manager: Mrs R Akistter

The Yehudi Menuhin School

Stoke d'Abernon, Cobham, Surrey KT11 3QQ
Tel: 01932 864739
Fax: 01932 864633
email: admin@yehudimenuhinschool.co.uk
website: www.yehudimenuhinschool.co.uk
Twitter: @menuhinschool

The Yehudi Menuhin School was founded in 1963 by Lord Menuhin and is situated in beautiful grounds in the Surrey countryside, close to London and within easy reach of both Gatwick and Heathrow.

The School provides specialist music tuition in stringed instruments, piano and classical guitar to 80 musically-gifted boys and girls aged between 7 and 19 and aims to enable them to pursue their love of music, develop their musical potential and achieve standards of performance at the highest level. The School also provides a broad education within a relaxed open community in which each individual can fully develop intellectual, artistic and social skills. We are proud that our pupils develop into dedicated and excellent musicians who will use their music to inspire and enrich the lives of others and into friendly, thinking individuals well equipped to contribute fully to the international community.

Music. At least half of each day is devoted to musical studies. Pupils receive a minimum of two one-hour lessons each week on their first study instrument and at least half an hour on their second study instrument. Supervised practice is incorporated into the daily programme ensuring that successful habits of work are formed. All pupils receive guidance in composition and take part in regular composers' workshops and concerts. Aural training and general musicianship studies are included in the music curriculum. To awaken feeling for good posture, training in Alexander Technique is provided. GCSE and A Level Music are compulsory core subjects for all pupils.

Regular opportunity for solo performance is of central importance to the musical activity of the School, and pupils also perform chamber music and with the String Orchestra. Concerts are given several times each week within the School and at a wide variety of venues throughout the United Kingdom and overseas. The most distinguished musicians have taught at the school, including Boulanger, Perlemuter, Rostropovich and Perlman. Lord Menuhin visited the school regularly. Selection of pupils is by stringent audition which seeks to assess musical ability and identify potential. Special arrangements are made for applicants from overseas, who account for almost half of the School's pupils.

The School opened a state-of-the-art Concert Hall in 2006 seating 315 with outstanding acoustics. Concerts and outreach programmes are now presented in this new facility. New purpose-built Music Studios opened in September 2016.

Academic Studies and Sport. The curriculum is designed to be balanced and to do full justice to both the musical and the general education of each pupil. Academic studies including the understanding of art, literature and science are considered vital to the development of creative, intelligent and sensitive musicians. All classes are small with excellent opportunities for individual attention, and as a result GCSE and A Level examination grades are high. To broaden their artistic and creative talents, all pupils work in a wide variety of artistic media including painting, ceramics, jewellery and textiles. Pupils from overseas with limited English receive an intensive course in the English Language from specialist teachers.

The extensive grounds allow plenty of scope for relaxation and sport, including tennis, dance, badminton, football, running, swimming and yoga. An indoor swimming pool was opened in 2010.

An International Family. The international reputation of the School brings pupils from all over the world who find a happy atmosphere in a large musical family. Pupils live in single or shared rooms and are cared for by the resident House Staff and Nurse. New en-suite single rooms for senior pupils were provided in the girls' house in September 2015; similar facilities in an extension for the boys' house opened in September 2016. Special attention is paid to diet with the emphasis on whole and fresh food.

Fees and Bursaries. All pupils fully resident in the UK are eligible for an Aided Place through the Music and Dance Scheme which is subsidised by the Department for Education (DfE). Parents pay a means-tested contribution to the school fees based on their gross income assessed on a scale issued by the DfE. Pupils from overseas pay full fees for two full calendar years until they acquire the residence qualification needed for support through the Music and Dance Scheme. The school has some bursary funds available to assist with fees for pupils until they become eligible for the Music and Dance Scheme.

Admission. Entry to the School is by rigorous music audition, and prospective pupils are auditioned at any time during the year. Candidates may audition at any age between 7 and 16.

Charitable status. The Yehudi Menuhin School is a Registered Charity, number 312010. It exists to provide musical and academic education for boys and girls.

President: Daniel Barenboim

Vice-Presidents:
Barbara R-D Fisher, OBE
Sir Alan Traill, GBE, QSO

Governor Emeritus:
Daniel Hodson
Anne Simor

Music Patrons:
Sir András Schiff
Heinrich Schiff
Steven Isserlis, CBE
Tasmin Little, OBE

Governors:
Chairman: Richard Morris, MA Oxon, Hon FRAM, RCM, RNCM
Vice-Chairman: Peter Willan, BSc Hons, MBA, FCMA

Noël Annesley
The Hon Zamira Menuhin Benthall
Lord Norman Blackwell
John Everett
Prof Sebastian Forbes
Andrew Hunter Johnston
Oscar Lewisohn

Stuart Mitchell
John Pagella
Alice Phillips
Geoffrey Richards
Vanessa Richards
Dr John Scadding
Veronica Wadley

Staff:

Headmaster: Dr Richard Hillier, MA Cantab, PhD

Director of Music: Malcolm Singer, MA Cantab

Director of Studies: Richard Tanner, MA Oxon

Finance Director: Melanie Smith, FCA

Development Director: Dr Anthony Medhurst, PhD, MPhil, BA Hons

Academic Staff:

Art and Craft: Patsy Belmonte, BA Hons
Biology and Science:
Karen Lyle, BSc Hons, PGCE
Jenny Dexter, BSc Hons, PGCE
English & Drama:
Alan Humm, BA Hons QTS
Kendra Shute, MA Ed, MA Mus, BA Mus
French & German: Didier Descamps, MA
German & Russian: Petra Young, MA MSc London
History: Sarah Howell, BA Hons, PGCE
Junior Subjects:
Janet Poppe, BA Hons, PGCE
Philippa Brown (*Teaching Assistant*)
Mathematics:
Richard Tanner, MA Oxon
Sarah Lee, BSc Hons, PGCE
English as an Additional Language: Naomi Roberts, BSc Hons, BA Hons, MA, PGCE, RSA TEFLA Cert & Dip
Japanese: Akiko Kubo, BA
Chinese: Xiang Yun Bishop, BA, MA, TCAFL
Spanish: Nuria Lopez-Costa
Turkish: Ayla Turacli
PE and Fitness: Fraser Dewar, BSc Hons, PGCE
Yoga: Jennifer Garcia, BMus Hons
Dance: Katie Brewer

Music Staff:

Violin:
Natalia Boyarsky, Dip Solo Performance & Teaching
Lutsia Ibragimova, Dip Solo Performance Baroque Violin, Teaching
Akiko Ono, 1st Cert Dip Mus & Perf Arts Vienna
Diana Galvydyte, MMus RCM, BMus

Violin/Viola:
Boris Kucharsky, MMus

Violin Assistants:
Akerke Ospan
Elliott Perks, BMus Hons
Oscar Perks, BA Hons Cantab
Jenna Sherry, BM Violin Perf, MPerf
Anna Ziman, BMus Hons

Cello:
Thomas Carroll, ARCM
Bartholomew LaFollette, BMus, MMus

Cello Assistant: Steffan Morris

Double Bass:
Caroline Emery, LTCL, GTCL, Cert Ed

Guitar:
Richard Wright, GRSM Man, ARMCM

Guitar Assistant:
Laura Snowden, MMus, MPerf

Piano:
Ruth Nye, MBE, Dip Mus Perf Melbourne Conservatory
Marcel Baudet, Groningen Conservatory

Piano Deputy:
Mariana Izman, BMus Conservatorium van Amsterdam

Piano Assistant:
Miho Kawashima BMus Hons MA

Piano Supporting Study:
Mariko Brown, BMus Hons, LGSM (*Piano 1st Study*)
Alexis White, MMus Piano Perf and Literature, BMus

Harpsichord:
Carole Cerasi Hon ARAM

Staff Pianists:
Nigel Hutchison, B Mus Hons
Svitlana Kosenko, Baccalaureate Diploma
Nathan Williamson, BMus, Master Mus [Dist], Master
    Musical Arts Yale

Chamber Music:
Dr Ioan Davies, PhD MA Cantab

Senior Orchestra:
Malcolm Singer, MA Cantab

Junior Orchestra:
Dr Oscar Colomina I Bosch, PhD RAM, MMus, BMus
    Hons GSMD

Chance to Play:
Elliott Perks, BMus Hons

Choir:
David Young, MA Choral Conducting, BMus

Interpretation through Improvisation:
David Dolan, BMus, MMus

Composition:
John Cooney, BMus Hons, Cert Adv St RCM & GSMD,
    Hon ARAM

General Music:
Oscar Colomina I Bosch, BMus, MMus
Damian leGassick, PG Dip Surrey

Voice Coach:
Jenevora Williams, PhD BA Hons Bristol, ARCM

Alexander Technique:
Hannah Walton, NNEB, MSTAT

Pastoral Staff:
Housemistress, Music House & Senior School Nurse: Ann
    Sweeney, MSc, RN, SN, QN
Housemaster, Harris House: Fraser Dewar, BSc Hons,
    PGCE
Assistant Housemistress, Music House: Kendra Shute, MA
    Ed, MA Mus, BA Mus
House Tutor, Harris House: Graham Sweeney, MBA
Assistant School Nurse: Chris Owen, RN, SN Cert

Support Staff:
Headmaster's PA: Donna Trout
Music Administrator: Catharine Whitnall, MA Cantab,
    LTCL
Receptionist: Poppy Telling
Examinations and Alumni Officer: Elaine Hillier, BA Hons
Music Admin Assistant: Dave Greenwood
Science Lab Technician: Delphine Wellington

Bursary:
Accountant: Mark Armstrong, ACCA, BSc Hons
Bookkeeper: Kate Hylands

Development:
Communications Coordinator: Julie Sperring, BMus Hons

Estates:
Estates Manager: Brian Harris
Assistant Estates Manager: Ben Wyithe

Catering:
Catering Manager: Jean Labourg
Senior Chef: Jo Busby
Commis Chef: Samuel Bartlett
Kitchen Porter: Paulo Trindade Fernandes

Menuhin Hall:
Menuhin Hall Manager: Alice Benzing, BA Hons
Menuhin Hall Admin Assistant: Sian Gandhi, BA Hons,
    PGCE
Menuhin Hall Box Office Manager: Penny Wright
Menuhin Hall Box Office Assistants:
Katherine Peat, BA
Clive Stevens
Menuhin Hall Technical Manager: Brian Fifield
Part-Time Assistant Technical Managers:
Luke Brough, BSc Hons
Jamie Gamache, BTech Mus
Al Forbes
Dominic Mackie
Menuhin Hall Bar and Holiday Course Supervisor: Jon
    Griffin
Menuhin Hall Bar Staff:
Suzie Bliss
Alex Chamberlain
Wendy Gabriel
Kate Hylands
Anna Larson
Ben Pattison
Adrian Whyte

Entrance Scholarships

Academic Scholarships

Abbey Gate College (p. 735)

Austin Friars (p. 738)

Bedstone College (p. 739)

Beechwood Sacred Heart School (p. 742)

Bethany School (p. 743)

Bournemouth Collegiate School (p. 744)

Box Hill School (p. 745)

Bredon School (p. 746)

The Cathedral School Llandaff (p. 746)

Claremont Fan Court School (p. 747)

Clifton High School (p. 748)

Derby Grammar School (p. 753)

Dover College (p. 754)

d'Overbroeck's (p. 756)

Dunottar School (p. 757)

Ewell Castle School (p. 759)

Hampshire Collegiate School (p. 762)

Hill House School (p. 765)

Kingham Hill School (p. 766)

Kingsley School (p. 767)

Langley School (p. 769)

Longridge Towers School (p. 772)

Luckley House School (p. 774)

LVS Ascot (p. 775)

Milton Abbey School (p. 776)

Newcastle School for Boys (p. 780)

Ockbrook School (p. 781)

Oswestry School (p. 782)

Our Lady's Abingdon Senior School (p. 783)

The Peterborough School (p. 784)

Pitsford School (p. 786)

Portland Place School (p. 787)

The Purcell School (p. 789)

The Read School (p. 791)

Reddam House Berkshire (p. 792)

Rishworth School (p. 793)

Ruthin School (p. 795)

St Christopher School (p. 797)

St Edward's School (p. 799)

Saint Felix School (p. 799)

St Joseph's College (p. 804)

Scarborough College (p. 806)

Shebbear College (p. 807)

Sibford School (p. 808)

Stafford Grammar School (p. 809)

Stonar (p. 811)

Stover School (p. 812)

Tettenhall College (p. 814)

Thetford Grammar School (p. 815)

Trinity School (p. 818)

Walden School (formerly Friends' School) (p. 819)

Westholme School (p. 821)

Windermere School – Browhead (p. 822)

All-Rounder Scholarships

Austin Friars (p. 738)

Bedstone College (p. 739)

Bredon School (p. 746)

The Cathedral School Llandaff (p. 746)

Dover College (p. 754)

Dunottar School (p. 757)

Hampshire Collegiate School (p. 762)

Langley School (p. 769)

Longridge Towers School (p. 772)

Newcastle School for Boys (p. 780)

Ockbrook School (p. 781)

Saint Felix School (p. 799)

Scarborough College (p. 806)

Shebbear College (p. 807)

Stonar (p. 811)

Trinity School (p. 818)

Art Scholarships

Austin Friars (p. 738)

Bedstone College (p. 739)

Beechwood Sacred Heart School (p. 742)

Bethany School (p. 743)

Bournemouth Collegiate School (p. 744)

Box Hill School (p. 745)

Bredon School (p. 746)

Claremont Fan Court School (p. 747)

Dover College (p. 754)

d'Overbroeck's (p. 756)

Dunottar School (p. 757)

Ewell Castle School (p. 759)

Hampshire Collegiate School (p. 762)

Hill House School (p. 765)

Kingham Hill School (p. 766)

Kingsley School (p. 767)

Langley School (p. 769)

Luckley House School (p. 774)

LVS Ascot (p. 775)

Milton Abbey School (p. 776)

Newcastle School for Boys (p. 780)

Ockbrook School (p. 781)

Oswestry School (p. 782)

Our Lady's Abingdon Senior School (p. 783)

The Peterborough School (p. 784)

Portland Place School (p. 787)

Reddam House Berkshire (p. 792)

St Christopher School (p. 797)

St Edward's School (p. 799)

Saint Felix School (p. 799)

St Joseph's College (p. 804)

Scarborough College (p. 806)

Shebbear College (p. 807)

Sibford School (p. 808)

Stonar (p. 811)

Stover School (p. 812)

Tettenhall College (p. 814)

Trinity School (p. 818)

Walden School (formerly Friends' School) (p. 819)

Windermere School – Browhead (p. 822)

Dance Scholarships

Bethany School (p. 743)

Kingham Hill School (p. 766)

Ockbrook School (p. 781)

Reddam House Berkshire (p. 792)

Saint Felix School (p. 799)

St Joseph's College (p. 804)

Design Technology Scholarships

Bedstone College (p. 739)

Bethany School (p. 743)

Bredon School (p. 746)

Dunottar School (p. 757)

Ewell Castle School (p. 759)

Hampshire Collegiate School (p. 762)

Kingsley School (p. 767)

Langley School (p. 769)

Milton Abbey School (p. 776)

St Edward's School (p. 799)

Saint Felix School (p. 799)

Drama Scholarships

Austin Friars (p. 738)

Beechwood Sacred Heart School (p. 742)

Bethany School (p. 743)

Bournemouth Collegiate School (p. 744)

Box Hill School (p. 745)

Bredon School (p. 746)

Claremont Fan Court School (p. 747)

d'Overbroeck's (p. 756)

Ewell Castle School (p. 759)

Hampshire Collegiate School (p. 762)

Kingham Hill School (p. 766)

Kingsley School (p. 767)

Langley School (p. 769)

Luckley House School (p. 774)

LVS Ascot (p. 775)

Milton Abbey School (p. 776)

Newcastle School for Boys (p. 780)

Ockbrook School (p. 781)

Portland Place School (p. 787)

Reddam House Berkshire (p. 792)

Rishworth School (p. 793)

St Edward's School (p. 799)

Saint Felix School (p. 799)

St Joseph's College (p. 804)

Shebbear College (p. 807)

Stonar (p. 811)

Tettenhall College (p. 814)

Trinity School (p. 818)

Walden School (formerly Friends' School) (p. 819)

Windermere School – Browhead (p. 822)

Music Scholarships

Abbey Gate College (p. 735)

Austin Friars (p. 738)

Bedstone College (p. 739)

Beechwood Sacred Heart School (p. 742)

Bethany School (p. 743)

Bournemouth Collegiate School (p. 744)

Box Hill School (p. 745)

Bredon School (p. 746)

The Cathedral School Llandaff (p. 746)

Claremont Fan Court School (p. 747)

Clifton High School (p. 748)

Derby Grammar School (p. 753)

Dover College (p. 754)

d'Overbroeck's (p. 756)

Dunottar School (p. 757)

Ewell Castle School (p. 759)

Hampshire Collegiate School (p. 762)

Hill House School (p. 765)

Kingham Hill School (p. 766)

Kingsley School (p. 767)

Langley School (p. 769)

Longridge Towers School (p. 772)

Luckley House School (p. 774)

LVS Ascot (p. 775)

Milton Abbey School (p. 776)

Newcastle School for Boys (p. 780)

Ockbrook School (p. 781)

Oswestry School (p. 782)

Our Lady's Abingdon Senior School (p. 783)

The Peterborough School (p. 784)

Portland Place School (p. 787)

The Purcell School (p. 789)

The Read School (p. 791)

Reddam House Berkshire (p. 792)

Rishworth School (p. 793)

St Edward's School (p. 799)

Saint Felix School (p. 799)

St Joseph's College (p. 804)

Scarborough College (p. 806)

Shebbear College (p. 807)

Sibford School (p. 808)

Stafford Grammar School (p. 809)

Stonar (p. 811)

Stover School (p. 812)

Tettenhall College (p. 814)

Thetford Grammar School (p. 815)

Trinity School (p. 818)

Walden School (formerly Friends' School) (p. 819)

Westholme School (p. 821)

Windermere School – Browhead (p. 822)

Sport Scholarships

Abbey Gate College (p. 735)

Austin Friars (p. 738)

Bedstone College (p. 739)

Beechwood Sacred Heart School (p. 742)

Bethany School (p. 743)

Bournemouth Collegiate School (p. 744)

Box Hill School (p. 745)

Bredon School (p. 746)

Claremont Fan Court School (p. 747)

Clifton High School (p. 748)

Derby Grammar School (p. 753)

Dover College (p. 754)

Dunottar School (p. 757)

Ewell Castle School (p. 759)

Hampshire Collegiate School (p. 762)

Hill House School (p. 765)

Kingham Hill School (p. 766)

Kingsley School (p. 767)

Langley School (p. 769)

Longridge Towers School (p. 772)

Luckley House School (p. 774)

LVS Ascot (p. 775)

Milton Abbey School (p. 776)

Newcastle School for Boys (p. 780)

Ockbrook School (p. 781)

Oswestry School (p. 782)

Our Lady's Abingdon Senior School (p. 783)

The Peterborough School (p. 784)

Portland Place School (p. 787)

The Read School (p. 791)

Reddam House Berkshire (p. 792)

Rishworth School (p. 793)

St Edward's School (p. 799)

Saint Felix School (p. 799)

St Joseph's College (p. 804)

Shebbear College (p. 807)

Sibford School (p. 808)

Stafford Grammar School (p. 809)

Stonar (p. 811)

Stover School (p. 812)

Tettenhall College (p. 814)

Trinity School (p. 818)

Walden School (formerly Friends' School) (p. 819)

Windermere School – Browhead (p. 822)

Other Scholarships

Choral

Abbey Gate College (p. 735)

Derby Grammar School (p. 753)

Newcastle School for Boys (p. 780)

Design

Saint Felix School (p. 799)

Environmental Awareness

d'Overbroeck's (p. 756)

Equestrian

Saint Felix School (p. 799)

Stonar (p. 811)

Organ

Kingham Hill School (p. 766)

Performing Arts

Hill House School (p. 765)

Kingham Hill School (p. 766)

Saint Felix School (p. 799)

Tettenhall College (p. 814)

Photography

Saint Felix School (p. 799)

Rugby

Hill House School (p. 765)

Sailing

Milton Abbey School (p. 776)

Science

d'Overbroeck's (p. 756)

Swimming

Saint Felix School (p. 799)

Textiles

Saint Felix School (p. 799)

Bursaries

Abbey Gate College (p. 735)

Austin Friars (p. 738)

Bedstone College (p. 739)

Bethany School (p. 743)

Bournemouth Collegiate School (p. 744)

Box Hill School (p. 745)

The Cathedral School Llandaff (p. 746)

Clifton High School (p. 748)

Concord College (p. 752)

Derby Grammar School (p. 753)

Dover College (p. 754)

Dunottar School (p. 757)

Ewell Castle School (p. 759)

Fulneck School (p. 761)

Hampshire Collegiate School (p. 762)

Kingham Hill School (p. 766)

Longridge Towers School (p. 772)

Luckley House School (p. 774)

LVS Ascot (p. 775)

Newcastle School for Boys (p. 780)

Ockbrook School (p. 781)

Our Lady's Abingdon Senior School (p. 783)

Pitsford School (p. 786)

The Purcell School (p. 789)

The Read School (p. 791)

Reddam House Berkshire (p. 792)

Rishworth School (p. 793)

Ruthin School (p. 795)

St Christopher School (p. 797)

St Edward's School (p. 799)

Saint Felix School (p. 799)

St James Senior Boys' School (p. 802)

St Joseph's College (p. 804)

Scarborough College (p. 806)

Shebbear College (p. 807)

Sibford School (p. 808)

Stafford Grammar School (p. 809)

Stonar (p. 811)

Stover School (p. 812)

Tettenhall College (p. 814)

Thetford Grammar School (p. 815)

Trinity School (p. 818)

Walden School (formerly Friends' School) (p. 819)

Westholme School (p. 821)

Windermere School – Browhead (p. 822)

The Yehudi Menuhin School (p. 823)

The Society of Heads

Additional Members Overseas

MATTHEW FARTHING
Principal
The British International School Bratislava, Bratislava, Slovakia
email: info@bisb.sk
website: www.bisb.sk

DR WALID EL-KHOURY
Principal
Brummana High School, Brummana, Lebanon
email: info@bhs.edu.lb
website: www.bhs.edu.lb

JON MURRAY-WALKER
Headmaster
Greensteds International School, Nakuru, Kenya
email: office@greenstedsschool.com
website: www.greenstedsschool.com

DEBORAH DUNCAN
Principal
The Junior and Senior School, Nicosia, Cyprus
email: contact@theseniorschool.com; contact@thejuniorschool.com
website: www.thejuniorandseniorschool.com

KOEN RINGOOT
Head
Leerwijzer School, Oostduinkerke, Belgium
email: info@leerwijzer.be
website: www.leerwijzer.be

MARK DURSTON
Headmaster
Peponi School, Ruiru, Kenya
email: info@peponischool.org
website: www.peponischool.org

JONATHAN HUGHES D'AETH
Headmaster
Repton School Dubai, Dubai, UAE
email: info@reptondubai.org
website: www. reptondubai.org

VALERIE MAINOO
Principal
The Roman Ridge School, Accra, Ghana
email: enquiries@theromanridgeschool.com
website: www.theromanridgeschool.com

ANDREW BOULLE
Headmaster
St Andrew's Senior School, Turi, Molo, Kenya
email: officesenior@turimail.co.ke
website: www.standrews-turi.com

DR CHRISTIAN BARKEI
Principal
St George's International School, Luxembourg
email: info@st-georges.lu
website: www.st-georges.lu

PART IV

Schools whose Heads are members of the Independent Association of Prep Schools

ALPHABETICAL LIST OF SCHOOLS
UK

The following school, whose Head is a member of both IAPS and ISA, can be found in the ISA section:
Ballard School

GEOGRAPHICAL LIST OF IAPS SCHOOLS

IAPS Member Heads and Deputy Heads

Individual School Entries

Abberley Hall

Worcester WR6 6DD

Tel: 01299 896275
Fax: 01299 896875
email: victoria.beswick@abberleyhall.co.uk
website: www.abberleyhall.co.uk
Twitter: @abberleyhallsch

Chairman of Governors: The Hon David Legh

Headmaster: **W J Lockett**, BA, PGCE

Deputy Headmaster: N Richardson, BSc Hons

Age Range. 2–13.
Number of Pupils. Prep School: 177 (103 Boys, 74 Girls; 96 Boarders, 81 Day Pupils). Pre-Prep & Nursery: 63 (33 Boys, 30 Girls).
Fees per term (2016–2017). Prep: Boarders £7,545, Day Pupils £3,565–£6,010. Pre-Prep & Nursery: £1,700–£3,025.

Abberley Hall is co-educational. It is situated 12 miles north-west of Worcester, with easy access to the M5. It is a boarding and day school and nursery for boys and girls aged 2–13 years (boarding from 8 years), and is set in 100 acres of gardens and wooded grounds amid magnificent countryside.

Pupils are prepared for all Independent Senior Schools. Although there is no entry examination, the school has a strong academic tradition with consistently good results in scholarships and Common Entrance, thanks to a highly-qualified staff, favourable teacher/pupil ratios and small classes. This also helps encourage the slower learners, for whom individual attention is available.

The school's facilities include an indoor swimming pool, chapel, library, music school and concert studio, two science laboratories, technology room, DT centre and extensively equipped computer centre, art studio and pottery rooms, multi-purpose hall with permanent stage, rifle range and climbing wall, sports hall, hard tennis courts, Ricochet court and ample playing fields for the major games and athletics, including a large Astroturf pitch. The school also owns its own French chalet where children go on three-week blocks for total immersion into the French language and way of life.

The pupils are also encouraged to take part in a wide range of hobbies and activities including archery, chess, fishing, golf, horse riding, fencing, model-making, printing, ballet, mountain-biking, woodwork and many more.

The school aims to combine a friendly atmosphere with the discipline which enables pupils to achieve their full potential and learn to feel responsibility for themselves and others.

Charitable status. Abberley Hall is a Registered Charity, number 527598. Its aim is to further good education.

Abercorn School

Early Years:
28 Abercorn Place, London NW8 9XP
Tel: 020 7286 4785
email: admin@abercornschool.com

Pre Prep:
The Old Grammar School, 248 Marylebone Road, London NW1 6JF
Tel: 020 7723 8700
email: togs@abercornschool.com

Prep:
38 Portland Place, London W1B 1LS
Tel: 020 7100 4335
email: portland@abercornschool.com

website: www.abercornschool.com

High Mistress: **Mrs Andrea Greystoke**, BA Hons

Headmaster: **Mr Benedict Dunhill**, BA Hons

Age Range. 2½ to 13+ Co-educational.
Number of Pupils. 400.
Fees per term (2016–2017). £3,050–£6,085. Fees include all extras, apart from lunch and school transport.

Abercorn School aims to offer its pupils the best start in education by providing a friendly, caring and inspiring academic atmosphere where a true love of learning is nurtured.

At Abercorn, children are continuously evaluated, supported and challenged in order to foster individual talents and skills.

The school has gained an enviable record of excellence and achievement for boys and girls from 2½ to 13 years of age. We guide both pupils and parents through the education process to ensure our pupils attain the highest standards and meet their potential.

We are firm believers in traditional values and standards, including excellent pastoral care. However, we are committed to embracing the best of what the 21st century will offer and preparing your child to face the challenges of the modern world with confidence and competence.

Happiness is an essential prerequisite to the acquisition of knowledge. At Abercorn learning is serious but fun!

Aberdour School

Brighton Road, Burgh Heath, Tadworth, Surrey KT20 6AJ
Tel: 01737 354119
email: enquiries@aberdourschool.co.uk
website: www.aberdourschool.co.uk

The School is an Educational Trust run by a Board of Governors.

Chairman of the Governors: Mr R C Nicol, FCA

Headmaster: **Mr S D Collins**, CertEd

Senior Deputy Headmistress: Mrs T Thomas, BEd Hons
Deputy Headmaster: Mr C Hoy, BA Ed
Head of Pre-Prep: Mrs A Terry, BA Hons

Age Range. 2–13.
Number of Pupils. 347 Day Boys and Girls.
Fees per term (2016–2017). £1,220–£4,495 inclusive.
Children are taken at 2 years old into the Pre-Preparatory department and transfer to the Preparatory school at age 7. Children are prepared for all the major Senior Schools and many scholarships have been won. There is a school orches-

tra and a concert band as well as a large school choir. There are ample playing fields, two all-weather areas, a large sports hall and indoor heated swimming pool. There are two science laboratories, a design technology room and a brand new Arts & Innovation wing with a STEM room, classrooms, music rooms and dance studios. All the usual games are coached and the general character of the children is developed by many interests and activities. Aberdour offers a uniquely personalised education.

Charitable status. Aberdour School Educational Trust Limited is a Registered Charity, number 312033. Its aim is to promote education.

Abingdon Preparatory School

Josca's House, Kingston Road, Frilford, Abingdon, Oxon OX13 5NX

Tel: 01865 391570
Fax: 01865 391042
email: admissions.manager@abingdonprep.org.uk
website: www.abingdon.org.uk/prep

The School was founded in 1956. In 1998 it merged with Abingdon School to become part of one charitable foundation with a single Board of Governors.

Chairman of the Governors: Adrian Burn

Headmaster: **Crispin Hyde-Dunn**, MA Oxon, PGCE, MA Ed, NPQH

Age Range. Boys 4–13.
Number of Pupils. 250 Day.
Fees per term (2016–2017). £3,755–£5,160.

Main entry points are at age four and seven, although entry into other years is sometimes available. The majority of boys move on to the senior school, Abingdon. At the end of Year 5 (age 9/10) of the Prep School, the great majority of Abingdon Prep boys will be offered a place at Abingdon School for Year 9 (age 13 entry). For these boys there is no Pre-Test and the 13+ Common Entrance exams at the end of Year 8 are sat internally. This offer of a place at Abingdon is conditional on the pupil maintaining his profile of achievement in Years 6 to 8 at Abingdon Prep. Boys not moving on to Abingdon are prepared for other senior school entrance examinations.

Abingdon Preparatory School is a thinking and learning school – as well as a teaching school. Pupils' needs are served by providing a happy and stimulating environment where the children are encouraged to develop self-reliance and a sense of responsibility. Considerable emphasis is placed on helping pupils to develop good working patterns together with sound organisational and learning skills.

The school enjoys extensive facilities including dedicated art, drama, ICT, music, CDT and science suites and a multipurpose sports hall. There has been substantial refurbishment of many of the existing facilities including the swimming pool, library and classrooms. The School benefits from extensive grounds with woodland, gardens, adventure play areas and acres of sports fields.

The extracurricular activities are a major strength of the school outside the classroom. The splendid amenities enable every child to participate in a wide range of sports and activities. There are regular fixtures against local schools in the main school sports of rugby, football, cricket, tennis and athletics. All pupils swim at least once a week. There is a range of after-school clubs, which includes amongst many others, orchestra, choir, art, science, judo, golf, fencing, gardening, chess and drama.

A regular number of academic, music, drama and all-rounder awards are gained every year to senior schools – the majority to the senior school, Abingdon.

A large number of trips are organised for all year groups during the year and the oldest boys go abroad for a week on completing their Common Entrance examinations.

Charitable status. Abingdon School is a Registered Charity, number 1071298. It exists to provide for the education of children aged 4–18.

Aldenham Preparatory School

Aldenham Road, Elstree, Herts WD6 3AJ

Tel: 01923 851664
email: prepschool@aldenham.com
website: www.aldenhamprep.com

Chairman of Board of Governors: Mr J T Barton

Head of Preparatory School: **Mrs V Gocher**, MA

Age Range. 3–11.
Number of Pupils. Total 171: 89 Boys, 82 Girls.
Fees per term (2016–2017). Prep: £4,367; Pre-Prep: £3,944; Nursery: £28.30 per morning or afternoon session, £57.50 per day, £3,010 per term (five full days).

At Aldenham Preparatory School, we provide a warm, happy and nurturing environment where quality learning takes place and the needs of each individual child are fulfilled.

The Preparatory School is a co-educational day school encompassing the Nursery (3–4 years), the Pre-Prep Department (4–7 years) and the Prep Department (7–11 years). It forms an integral part of the main school which was established in 1597 and remains on the same glorious site, set in over 110 acres of countryside yet only 13 miles from the centre of London.

Our primary aim is to provide an excellent all-round education, presenting all of our pupils with exceptional opportunities. The school is dedicated to ensuring the flexibility for each child to develop their own individual abilities, whether they are academic, creative or sporting. We offer high-quality teaching from enthusiastic, motivated and caring staff.

An inspection commissioned by the Independent Schools Inspectorate (ISI) praised the school for being "... *a lively, happy community in which young children thrive. They benefit from a high standard of education and very good care in all year groups. Children's attitude to learning and their behaviour are exemplary. Relationships between children and staff are friendly and courteous.*"

Small class sizes (a maximum of 23 in the Pre-Prep and Prep) and expert teaching from an early age ensure that academic attainment is high. The requirements of the National Curriculum and preparation for 11+ entrance exams are blended into a broad based curriculum. This along with an excellent staff/pupil ratio enriches our children's learning and encourages them to work to the very best of their ability.

Extensive extracurricular provision including Cookery, Fencing, Chess, Choir and Karate and specialist teachers in French, Drama, Music and Sport enrich the children's education.

The accommodation for both Pre-Prep and Prep Departments is first class with pupils having access to their own DT and art room, library, music and drama suite, computer room and three-acre playing field. We are also able to share the Aldenham School campus as a whole, enabling us to enjoy use of the extensive grounds and facilities, including the sports complex, artificial turf pitch, chapel, dining hall, and theatre. (For further information about the senior school, see Aldenham School entry in HMC section.)

We have high expectations of all our pupils and encourage initiative, independence and self-confidence. We also insist on good manners and consideration for others, as a result there is a strong sense of community at Aldenham.

Entry is primarily at rising 3 and 4+, although there are also a number of places available at 7+.

Our excellent established Nursery facilities provide a structured lively and stimulating introduction to Aldenham School with morning and afternoon classes or full days.

All our children find themselves well equipped and prepared for the next stage of their education with many moving on to Aldenham Senior School.

Charitable status. The Aldenham School Company is a Registered Charity, number 298140. It exists to provide high quality education and pastoral care to enable children to achieve their full potential in later life.

Aldro

Lombard Street, Shackleford, Godalming, Surrey GU8 6AS

Tel:	01483 813530 (Headmaster)
	01483 813535 (Admissions)
	01483 810266 (School Office)
email:	hmsec@aldro.org
website:	www.aldro.org
Twitter:	@AldroSchool
Facebook:	@AldroSchool

Chairman of the Governors: Philip Robinson

Headmaster: **Mr James Hanson**, MMath Oxon, MSc Oxon, MPhil, PGCE, CMath, FIMA

Age Range. 7–13.
Number of Boys. 220: 50 boarders, 170 day boys.
Fees per term (2016–2017). Boarding: Form 3 £7,110, Forms 4–8 £7,695. Day: Form 3 £5,305, Forms 4–8 £5,890.

Aldro is a boys' independent day and boarding prep school set in a beautiful rural location yet within a mile of the A3 and 45 minutes of central London, Gatwick and Heathrow airports.

Aldro aims to offer boys an exceptional all-round education in a happy, purposeful community. It has a Christian foundation and this underpins the values and ethos of the school. Each school day starts with a short service in the lovely Chapel, beautifully converted from an eighteenth century barn.

The school is fortunate in having a spacious site including a lake and about 20 acres of playing fields. We have our rowing lake, the new sports centre, four all-weather tennis courts, two shooting ranges, swimming pool and a croquet lawn. The Centenary Building opened in 2000 and houses most of the classrooms, the ICT centre, an outstanding library and, in the basement, changing rooms and a large common room. The Crispin Hill Centre incorporates a Music School and theatre. Two science laboratories and the Art and Design Technology Centre have been developed in eighteenth century buildings either side of the Chapel. The Argyle Building including a new dining hall and kitchen was opened in late 2003. The dormitories in the main building have recently been refurbished. The boarders enjoy high-quality pastoral care and a varied programme of activities in the evenings and at weekends.

In the classroom, there is a balance between the best traditional and modern approaches, whilst firm and friendly encouragement of each individual has led to an outstanding academic record of success at Common Entrance and Scholarship level. Forty academic awards have been won in the last four years (2016 being a record breaking year) to leading schools such as Charterhouse, Eton, Sherborne, Winchester, Radley, Tonbridge and Wellington College.

Aldro is committed to giving boys real breadth to their education and much emphasis is placed on extracurricular activities. There are many opportunities for the arts, with a good record of success in Art and Music scholarships – 20 awards have been won in the past four years. An astounding 200 boys learn musical instruments and there are three choirs, brass group, and numerous more ensembles. Drama also features prominently with several productions each year.

The major sports are rugby, soccer and hockey in the winter, with cricket in the summer. Athletics, tennis, swimming, cross-country running, polo, sailing and shooting are secondary sports and high standards are achieved. A huge range of activities are available including badminton, dodge ball, pioneers, bottle digging, fly fishing and pétanque. The school has an enviable record for Chess with 9 teams winning National championships in the past five years.

Boys at Aldro are treated as individuals with talents to develop. They lead cheerful and purposeful lives, and are well-prepared for a wide range of leading senior schools.

'Bringing out the best in boys' is what Aldro has been achieving through the generations. There is a focus on excellence and achievement, whether that is in the classroom, music room or on the sports field. Aldro prepares boys for the rest of their lives.

Charitable status. Aldro School Educational Trust Limited is a Registered Charity, number 312072. It exists to provide education for boys.

Aldwickbury School

Wheathampstead Road, Harpenden, Herts AL5 1AD

Tel:	01582 713022
Fax:	01582 767696
email:	secretary@aldwickbury.org.uk
	registrar@aldwickbury.org.uk
website:	www.aldwickbury.org.uk

Chairman of Governors: S A Westley, MA

Headmaster: **V W Hales**, BEd Hons Exeter

Age Range. 4–13.
Number of Boys. Prep School: 250 (including up to 34 weekly boarders). Pre-Prep: 120.
Fees per term (2016–2017). Day Boys: Pre-Prep £4,090–£4,227, Years 3–8 £4,520–£5,060. Weekly Boarding Fee: £29.90–£36.40 per night.

Aldwickbury is a day and boarding school set in 20 acres on the outskirts of Harpenden. Aldwickbury is a boys' school that focuses on boys' education, their growth and development. We allow them to flourish in an environment that challenges and stimulates them whatever their interests, passions or talents. Our teaching mixes traditional approaches together with modern ideas and methods; interactive whiteboards have been installed in all departments.

The school provides an extensive extracurricular programme for the boys. Music, art and drama are well catered for with an emphasis on involvement as well as the desire for excellence. There are plays and concerts providing performance opportunities for all age groups, both formally and informally. A games session is held every day for all boys in Years 3–8 and teams in all the major sports at every level. The school has an excellent reputation at all sports and has had national recognition in skiing, swimming, athletics, tennis and soccer in recent years.

The school has excellent facilities based around a large Victorian House. Purpose-built teaching blocks, including a modern pre-prep department, ensure that the education is of a high standard. Other facilities include an indoor swimming pool, tennis courts, gymnasium and playing fields. Recent additions to the buildings have been a library, dining room and changing rooms. A new hall complex including a new music department, performance space and classrooms was completed in 2014; in 2016 the science labs were refurbished and the Coach House renovation providing a new Art and DT department was finished.

The boys move onto a wide range of senior schools, both day and boarding. The recent results at Common Entrance, entry tests and scholarships have been a reflection on the good teaching that the boys receive.

The Pre-Preparatory Department is accommodated in a building opened in 2001.

Charitable status. Aldwickbury School Trust Ltd is a Registered Charity, number 311059. It exists to provide education for children.

All Hallows School

Cranmore Hall, East Cranmore, Somerset BA4 4SF

Tel: 01749 881600
Fax: 01749 880709
email: info@allhallowsschool.co.uk
website: www.allhallowsschool.co.uk
Twitter: @AllHallowsSch
Facebook: @allhallowssch

Headmistress: **Ms Annie Lee**, BA, PGCE, MA

Age Range. 3–13 Co-educational.
Number of Pupils. 284: 134 Boys, 150 Girls.
Fees per term (2016–2017). Boarding £7,260; Day: £2,560 (Rec–Year 2), £4,815 (Years 3 & 4), £4,865 (Year 5–8). There are no compulsory extras.

The all-round personal development of children has long been at the heart of the vision and ethos at All Hallows. The school passionately promotes an individualised and holistic approach to learning that seeks to inspire each child to fulfil their potential. The dedicated and experienced team at All Hallows works in partnership with parents to truly prepare children for the ever changing world they are growing up in and for the lives they will lead, nurturing and encouraging them to live responsibly and compassionately and to embrace with energy and enthusiasm the fantastic opportunities that lie ahead.

All Hallows pioneered Catholic boarding co-education for preparatory school age children and the school continues to be very innovative and quite distinct being rated '*Excellent*' in all areas by ISI in 2014, '*Outstanding*' in all categories by Ofsted in 2009, and in 2010 for Boarding and pastoral care – the latter finding no recommendations for improvement. In their latest report ISI recognised the school in all areas as "*of exceptionally high quality*" noting that "*children are exceptionally well cared for*".

Christian principles are integrated into daily life so that all faiths are welcomed into the life of this Roman Catholic foundation. Professionally qualified, energetic and family-orientated staff, many of whom reside in the school, provide for the academic and pastoral welfare of the children.

The school has a happy and deliberate mix of boarders and day pupils. Attractive flexibility exists between boarding and day arrangements. There is an extensive and innovative Activities Programme for all children each evening after school, with weekend and holiday highlights as well as an innovative Saturday enrichment programme for years 6, 7 and 8 comprising an ever broader range of extracurricular activities.

The school enjoys regional and national sporting success in rugby, hockey, cricket, tennis, trampolining and athletics, as well as regular competitive fixtures for children of all abilities against local opposition in the traditional team sports. Excellence within a framework of sport for all is our aim. Our Tennis Academy carries an LTA Clubmark for excellence and is available to every child in the school as well as siblings and parents. It also has strong links with the Tennis Performance Centre in Bath.

Music and the Arts thrive, ranging from the grace of the Chapel Choir to the creativity and performance of dance and drama. Exceptional facilities throughout the campus allow the children and staff to discover talent and develop potential. A new state-of-the-art Creative Centre opened in 2014 offering the children fantastic design facilities including 2D and 3D design packages, 3D printing, laser cutting, animation, digital photography and fantastic 'making' opportunities. All Hallows also enjoys Forest School status, this fresh learning approach brings immense benefits and the outdoor environs are an integral part of the curriculum at the school, helping to foster the skills and wider perspective that truly encourage innovation, risk-judging and positive risk-taking, self-belief, ambition and a genuine sense of optimism.

All Hallows' independent status from any one particular senior school enables parents and the Head to select the most appropriate senior school to suit a particular child's needs and talents. In the last few years we have sent pupils to over forty different schools. In 2016 60% of the leavers gained an Award to their Senior School. We offer a range of scholarships and bursaries.

Charitable status. All Hallows is a Registered Charity, number 310281. The school is a Charitable Trust, the raison d'être of which is the integration of Christian principles with daily life.

Alleyn Court Preparatory School

Wakering Road, Southend-on-Sea, Essex SS3 0PW

Tel: 01702 582553
Fax: 01702 584574
email: office@alleyn-court.co.uk
           admissions@alleyn-court.co.uk
           head@alleyn-court.co.uk
website: www.alleyn-court.co.uk
Twitter: @AlleynCourt; @AlleynCourtPE

Headmaster: **Mr Rupert Snow**

Age Range. 2½–11.
Number of Pupils. 302 Boys and Girls.
Fees per term (from April 2016). £970–£3,923 according to age.

Alleyn Court was founded in 1904 by Theodore Wilcox and is a non-selective, co-educational day school, for children aged 2½–11. The school is situated in beautiful grounds within the Thorpe Bay area of Southend and has an excellent reputation for its breadth of curriculum, academic achievement, sporting success, art, music, French and general all-round pastoral care. A happy and relaxed atmosphere, family ethos and strong sense of community underpin the purposeful approach to school life and activities.

The school is split into three sections: two parallel Pre-Preparatory departments, located on the main school site in Thorpe Bay and on the original school site in Westcliff, offer an education based on Montessori principles for children aged 2½–5 years in the EYFS. The Junior School offers class-based teaching and a solid academic grounding to Years 1–3 and the Senior School offers largely subject specialist teaching and preparation for entrance exams and 11+ to Years 4–6. All year groups have parallel classes, which rarely rise above 20 children. Children are accepted for entry into any year group, providing that spaces are available.

Children are prepared for 11+ entry to the local selective grammar schools and for senior independent schools, with some successfully gaining scholarships. French is taught from age 4, with specialist teaching for Art, French, Music and PE from Year 1 upwards. All lessons in Years 5 and 6 are taught by subject specialists in dedicated subject rooms.

Academic facilities on the main school site include a library, fully-equipped science laboratory, music department, modern computer suite and network with 21 workstations, an additional support unit (ASU) and an art and design technology studio. Part of the school site has recently been developed to create a Woodland School and outdoor classroom to offer more practical and skill-based learning. A lifeskills programme also encourages and develops study skills, critical and lateral thinking, problem-solving and philosophy for children. Independent learning is widely encouraged and children also use iPads for research projects and learning enrichment.

The school offers extensive provision for sport and extra-curricular activities, with a variety of clubs being offered whenever children aren't in the classroom – these occur and are well attended before and after school, as well as during morning and lunch breaks. The school offers the following sports: athletics, badminton, basketball, cricket, cross-country, dodgeball, football, gymnastics, hockey, orienteering, rounders, rugby and table tennis.

Sports facilities include: large, picturesque, on-site playing fields, sports hall, cricket nets, refurbished netball and tennis courts, a woodland cross-country course and a smart pavilion with changing rooms, kitchen and function room.

The performing arts are also well provided for with a dedicated music block which houses a classroom and music practice rooms. Additionally, an indoor and outdoor stage provide space for drama and LAMDA activities, where children prepare for productions, exams and local festivals and competitions.

Non-sporting clubs include: art, ballet, chess, debating, drama, DT, French, G&T core subjects, IT, jewellery, karate, VR.

Scholarships and means-tested bursaries are available annually for pupils with academic, sporting, musical, dramatic or artistic talent.

Alleyn's Junior School

Townley Road, Dulwich, London SE22 8SU
Tel: 020 8557 1519
email: juniorschool@alleyns.org.uk
website: www.alleyns.org.uk

Chairman of Governors: Mr Iain Barbour

Head: Mr Simon Severino, MA Hons, PGCE

Registrar: Mrs Felicity Thomas

Age Range. 4–11.
Number of Pupils. 240 boys and girls.
Fees per term (2016–2017). Reception to Year 2 £5,217; Years 3–6 £5,433 including lunches, out of school visits and one residential trip per year for Years 3–6.

The school is part of the foundation known as 'Alleyn's College of God's Gift' which was founded by Edward Alleyn, the Elizabethan actor, in 1619.

Opened in 1992 to provide a co-educational Junior School for Alleyn's School and sharing the same excellent green site, Alleyn's Junior School provides a happy and lively environment in which well-motivated boys and girls follow a broad and academic education. Boys and girls work together with their teachers in a calm and structured way to develop their potential and self-confidence as they pursue the highest standards across a curriculum which embraces many opportunities for art, MFL, drama, music, ICT and a wide range of sports. Entry to the school is at 4+, 7+ and 9+. The overwhelming majority of children move on to Alleyn's senior school at 11+.

Within small classes and with a balance of class and specialist subject teaching, children are set clear and challenging targets for their learning. Children perform at above average level in KS1 and KS2 tests. The school enjoys a strong extracurricular life offering children varied and exciting opportunities to extend their learning beyond the classroom.

Progress is carefully monitored and individual differences appropriately met. Competition has its place in the encouragement of the highest academic, artistic and sporting standards, but it is always tempered by an emphasis on values of thoughtfulness, courtesy and tolerance. All members of the school community are expected to maintain high standards in their behaviour, manners and appearance, showing pride in themselves and their school.

The school enjoys excellent support from its parent body. Regular meetings and reports keep parents informed of academic progress and pastoral matters and The Alleyn's Junior School Association works tirelessly to promote social cohesion within the school and to support the charity, sporting, dramatic and extracurricular programmes. It also organises an After School Care scheme through which children can be supervised at school each day during term time until 6 pm.

Charitable status. Alleyn's College of God's Gift is a Registered Charity, number 1057971. Its purpose is to provide independent education for boys and girls.

Alpha Preparatory School

21 Hindes Road, Harrow, Middlesex HA1 1SH
Tel: 020 8427 1471
email: sec@alpha.harrow.sch.uk
website: www.alpha.harrow.sch.uk

Chairman of the Board of Governors: I Nunn

Headmaster: C J W Trinidad, BSc Hons, PGCE

Age Range. 3–11.
Number of Pupils. 165 boys and girls (day only).
Fees per term (2016–2017). Inclusive of lunch, with no compulsory extras: Nursery £1,100–£2,275; Pre-Preparatory £3,200; Main school £3,530.

The School, situated in a residential area of Harrow, was founded in 1895, and in 1950 was reorganised as a non-profit-making Educational Charity, with a Board of Governors elected by members of the Company; parents of pupils in the School are eligible for membership.

The majority of children enter the Main School at the age of 4 by interview and assessment but there can also be a few vacancies for older pupils and here entry is by interview and/or written tests, dependent upon age.

There is a full-time staff of 16 experienced and qualified teachers, with additional part-time teachers in instrumental Music. The main games are Football and Cricket, with cross-country, athletics, tennis and netball. Extracurricular activities include Piano and Violin instruction.

Religious education, which is considered important, is non-sectarian in nature, but follows upon the School's Christian foundation and tradition; children of all faiths are accepted.

Outside visits to theatres, concerts and museums form an integral part of the curriculum and during the Lent Term pupils in Year 6 visit the Isle of Wight.

Regular successes are obtained in Entrance and Scholarship examinations, with many Scholarships having been won in recent years.

The School has its own Nursery (Alphabets) for children aged 3 in the term of entry. Further details can be obtained from the Registration Secretary.

Charitable status. Alpha Preparatory School is a Registered Charity, number 312640. It exists to carry on the undertaking of a boys and/or girls preparatory school in Harrow in the County of Middlesex.

Altrincham Preparatory School

Marlborough Road, Bowdon, Altrincham, Cheshire WA14 2RR

Tel: 0161 928 3366
email: admin@altprep.co.uk
website: www.altprep.co.uk

Headmaster: **Mr A C Potts**, BSc

Age Range. 2+–11.
Number in School. 320 Day Boys.
Fees per term (2016–2017). £2,010–£2,685.

With an engaging curriculum designed to capture the imaginations of its boys and a reputation for outstanding academic, musical and sporting achievements, Altrincham Preparatory School is widely regarded as one of the very best schools for 2–11 year olds in the North-West.

Altrincham Preparatory School believes in delivering academic excellence and its boys go on to some of the best selective grammar schools in the region, including Altrincham Grammar School and The Manchester Grammar School. Yet while recent examination results are hugely impressive – 92 per cent of Year 6 boys have an offer for a Grammar School place in September 2016 – Altrincham Preparatory School is also a music school, an arts and technology school and a sports school. The culture of participation means the boys want to be part of everything and two full-time specialist PE teachers have guided the boys to national finals in a range of sports.

Altrincham Preparatory School is described as "excellent" in the latest ISI report (February 2016) with the broad overall provision "enriching the pupils' educational and personal experience, enabling them to develop their talents happily and fruitfully." The ISI was also impressed by the boys' positive approach to their studies, while the "high quality teaching" was reflected in "good and often rapid progress and significant academic achievement". Pastoral care is at the centre of everything it does.

Altrincham Preparatory School is committed to providing such high-quality education in a happy, safe and state-of-the-art environment. The brand-new Early Years Foundation Stage Centre at Bank Place opened in 2015 with a beautiful 16-place Nursery for boys aged 2 and above feeding into the Pre-School. Boys there are able to access the adjacent Bell Field for outdoor exploration, while the use of Bowdon Cricket, Hockey and Squash club's facilities means games can take place on high-quality artificial and grass surfaces. With bright, well-equipped and attractive classrooms, Altrincham Preparatory School is welcoming, nurturing, and most important of all, happy.

Amesbury

Hazel Grove, Hindhead, Surrey GU26 6BL

Tel: 01428 604322
email: l.wright@amesburyschool.co.uk
website: www.amesburyschool.co.uk

Chairman of the Governors: Tarquin Henderson

Headmaster: **Nigel Taylor**, MA

Age Range. 2–13.
Number of Pupils. 360.
Fees per term (2016–2017). Prep School: £4,570–£4,950; Pre-Prep: £3,235; Early Years (Pre-Nursery to Reception): from £30.75 per session.

Amesbury is a co-educational day school founded in 1870 and is the only co-educational Prep school in the Hindhead/Haslemere area. The main building is unique, as the only school to be designed by Sir Edwin Lutyens, and stands in its own 34-acre estate in the heart of the Surrey countryside.

We are a family school, keen for siblings to study together and to feel equally valued irrespective of their aptitudes and abilities. There is no competitive entry. Entry is based on registration plus a visit – not a formal assessment but the opportunity for child and school to get acquainted.

Classes are small guaranteeing individual attention. Study programmes currently lead to senior school entrance and scholarship examinations at 11+ and at 13+. We have a proud tradition of academic, sporting and artistic achievement. The school has excellent purpose-built facilities with a new Visual Arts Facility opened in September 2015.

We pride ourselves on sending children to the best senior schools in the country at both 11+ and 13+. Amesbury's academic record is excellent with an average of 20% of pupils receiving senior school scholarships. "Many a school may claim to be 'academically rigorous'. Not all would also make such a virtue out of also being 'relaxed' … this one does." (Good Schools Guide 2013).

In addition to a compelling academic record, Amesbury has a thriving Performing Arts Department: "Music embraces everything from formal chapel choir to semi-secret bands formed each year, strutting stuff at annual concert. There's plentiful dance and drama including ambitious takes on Shakespeare" (Good Schools Guide 2013). As for sport, the site is 34 acres, with an all-weather astro, indoor sports hall and an all-school tennis programme. Our Extra Curricular programme runs a whole host of activities including Mandarin Chinese, Judo, Golf, Chess, Music Technology, Drama and many more.

Amesbury understands its role as part of your family life. We believe weekends should be your time; there is no Saturday school and prep can be done at school. We offer Breakfast Club and After School Care. Our Pre-Nursery and Nursery offer early drop-offs, late pick-ups and holiday care.

Open Mornings take place in October, February and May.

Charitable status. Amesbury School is a Registered Charity, number 312058. It exists to provide education for boys and girls. It is administered by a Board of Governors.

Ardingly College Prep & Pre-Prep Schools
A Woodard School

Ardingly, Haywards Heath, West Sussex RH17 6SQ

Tel: 01444 893200 (Prep)
           01444 893300 (Pre-Prep)
email: registrar@ardingly.com
website: www.ardingly.com

Chairman of School Council: Mr J Sloane, BSc

Headmaster: Mr C B Calvey, BEd Hons

Deputy Head: Mr J Castle, BEd

Head of Pre-Prep: Mrs H Nawrocka, MSc, PGCE

Age Range. Pre-Prep 2–7, Prep 7–13.
Number of Pupils. Pre-Prep 120, Prep 265.
Fees per term (2016–2017). Day Pupils: Nursery & Pre-Nursery: £2,800 (5 full days), £2,150 (5 half days); Additional sessions: £23.00–£39.00 per session or £51.00 per full day; Reception, Years 1 & 2: £2,800; Years 3–4 £4,020 Years 5–6 £4,930, Years 7–8 £5,050 including meals. Weekly Boarding (in addition to Day Fees): £250–£1,000 (1–5 nights). Casual boarding: £40 per night.

Ardingly College Prep School is the Preparatory School for Ardingly College Senior School (*see entry in HMC section*).

Ardingly College Prep School is set within 250 acres of glorious Sussex countryside, which it shares with the Senior School and Pre-Prep. The School is co-educational and has over 360 pupils from Pre-Nursery to Year 8 (ages 2–13). The Prep School benefits from the College's Chapel, Music School, Dining Hall, Gymnasium, Sports Hall, Indoor Swimming Pool, Astro Pitch, Medical Centre and School Shop. The Prep School has recently moved into a refurbished teaching block which provides bright and modern classrooms in a building which has retained its original character. Girls and boys are admitted into the Pre-Prep from the age of 2, and into the Prep School from the age of 7. The Prep School offers weekly boarding to children from Year 3 with pupils taking an option of anything from one to five nights a week. There is an extensive after-school care provision which includes activities that run until 7 pm for all pupils.

The extracurricular activities include Riding, Drama Club, Fencing, Lego Club, Dance, Swimming Clubs, Orchestra, Jazz Club, Greek Club, as well as numerous Sports Clubs.

Children are prepared for Common Entrance in the core subjects, but follow our own Humanities curriculum which links with the programmes of study in the Senior School.

Girls play hockey, netball and rounders. Boys play football, hockey and cricket. In the summer both girls and boys enjoy athletics, cross country and swimming.

Religious Education is in accordance with the teaching of the Church of England.

Details of Scholarships available may be obtained from the Registrar.

The Farmhouse Pre-Prep provides children with the perfect introduction to their education. Safely yet idyllically situated within the College estate, our Pre-Preparatory is housed within carefully restored Grade 2 listed Victorian farm buildings. We have full use of the College facilities, including the swimming pool, sports hall, playing fields, chapel and full medical on-site care. The school grounds provide us with a wealth of resources for many different purposes including Forest School.

We aim to lay the basic foundations – academic, social, physical and spiritual – upon which every child can build a sound education, all within a vibrant, caring and yet challenging atmosphere.

The Farmhouse caters for children from 2 to 3 years in our Pre-Nursery, 3 to 4 years in our Nursery and from 4 to 7 in the Pre-Preparatory classes. The Pre-Preparatory children are taught in classes of about 16 pupils, whilst the Nursery may cater for up to 25 children (full day available).

The Farmhouse has its own highly qualified staff and access to a range of specialist staff. French is taught from the age of 4 years and a wide variety of sport is included in the curriculum.

After-school activities include Hockey, Ballet, Football, Zumba, Chess, Tennis, Modern & Tap dance, ArdinGlee and Lego Clubs.

Our school is run from Monday to Friday. There are no boarding facilities at this age but a Before-School (from 8 am) and After-School (to 6 pm) Care service is available.

Charitable status. Ardingly College Limited is a Registered Charity, number 1076456. It exists to provide high quality education for boys and girls aged 2–18 in a Christian context.

Ardvreck School

Crieff, Perthshire PH7 4EX

Tel: 01764 653112
Fax: 01764 654920
email: office@ardvreck.org.uk
           admissions@ardvreck.org.uk
website: www.ardvreckschool.co.uk
Twitter: @ArdvreckSchool
Facebook: /Ardvreck-School

Chairman of the Governors: Michael Riddell-Webster

Headmaster: Dan Davey, BEd Hons

Age Range. Co-educational 3–13.
Number of Pupils. Main School: 62 Boarding, 43 day. Little Ardvreck 11.
Fees per term (2016–2017). Main School: £6,997 (boarders), £4,655 (day); Little Ardvreck £2,180.

Ardvreck School is an independent boarding and day preparatory school for boys and girls aged 3–13.

Ardvreck stands in 42 acres of Perthshire countryside on the edge of Crieff having been purpose built and founded in 1883. The School has a long tradition of providing academic excellence as well as outstanding achievement in sport and music. There are 17 full-time and 3 part-time members of the teaching staff and classes are no larger than 16. Health and domestic arrangements are under the personal supervision of the Head of Pastoral Care who is assisted by four full-time Matrons (two resident) and one qualified school Nurse. The School Doctor visits regularly.

Boys and girls are prepared for senior schools throughout Britain. In recent years, all have passed the Common Entrance to their schools of first choice both North and South of the border and over 35 scholarships have been awarded in the past four years.

Children aged 3–7 join Little Ardvreck before joining Junior House at the age of 8. Montessori mornings run every morning for 3–4 year olds and after-school care until 6.00 pm is provided.

Rugby, Netball, Hockey, Cricket, Rounders and Athletics are the main games and on several Saturdays in the summer, pupils are provided with picnic lunches enabling them to explore the surrounding countryside, accompanied by members of staff, where they can study the wildlife, fish in one of the rivers or lochs, climb, sail or canoe. Other activities include Golf, Riding, Tennis, mountain biking and Shooting, a sport for which the School has a national reputation for excellence having won the UK Prep Schools Championship for the last fifteen years. Outdoor Pursuits are a regular fixture on the Ardvreck calendar with a range of activities on offer from munro bagging and mountain biking on offer. Inside and Out – it's all academic.

A modern and well-equipped Music School provides the best possible opportunities for music-making. There is an orchestra and choir both of which regularly achieve distinction at music festivals. Visiting music specialists teach a wide range of instruments including the bagpipes. Music and Drama play an important part in the life of the School and a major production is staged annually with several smaller productions and numerous concerts taking place throughout the year. Ardvreck boasts the largest prep school pipe band in Scotland.

There is a heated, indoor swimming pool (all children are taught to swim), an Astroturf surface for hockey, tennis and netball, and a superb sports hall.

Most full-time staff live within the School grounds and a special feature of Ardvreck is that there are three houses – one for the Juniors, one for the senior girls and one for the senior boys. The senior houses are where pupils gain a little more independence and are encouraged to show greater personal responsibility in readiness for the transition to senior schools.

Many boarders live overseas (forces and expat) and they are escorted to and from Scottish Airports; all necessary documentation can be handled by the School if required. Overseas pupils are required to have a guardian in the UK with whom they can stay during exeats.

Admission is by a meeting with the Headmaster and an overnight or day 'taster'. Financial assistance is available. Means-tested bursaries.

Charitable status. Ardvreck School is a Registered Charity, number SC009886. Its aim is to provide education for boys and girls.

Arnold House School

1 Loudoun Road, St John's Wood, London NW8 0LH
Tel: 020 7266 4840
email: office@arnoldhouse.co.uk
website: www.arnoldhouse.co.uk

Chairman of the Board of Governors: B O'Brien Esq

Headmaster: V W P Thomas, BEd, MA

Age Range. 5–13.
Number of Boys. 270 (Day Boys only).
Fees per term (2016–2017). £5,878 including Lunch.
Arnold House is an independent day school for boys founded in 1905.

Most boys join the school after their fifth birthday. A few join at other ages.

The Arnold House website gives full details of recent developments in the school's curriculum and facilities. These include the complete refurbishment and extension of the main teaching facilities at Loudoun Road. At the school's 7 acres of playing fields at Canons Park, Edgware, the existing pavilion hall has been adapted to become an auditorium seating 150 with a fully-equipped stage and associated facilities. The Canons Park Activity Centre has become an important addition to the excellent facilities at Loudoun Road.

Boys transfer to their chosen independent senior schools at the age of 13. Arnold House has an enviable record of success in placing each boy in the school that is right for him. More than half of the boys move on to the most sought-after London day schools: City of London, Highgate, Mill Hill, St Paul's, UCS and Westminster. Others transfer to renowned boarding schools: Bradfield, Eton, Harrow, Marlborough, Radley, Rugby, Tonbridge, Wellington and Winchester have been popular destinations in recent years. Arnold House takes a long view of a boy's education. Academic breadth, a balance between study, sport, music, the arts and activities together with excellent pastoral care constitute the foundations of the school's philosophy and success.

Charitable status. Arnold House School is a Registered Charity, number 312725. It exists to provide education for boys in preparation for transfer to senior independent schools at 13.

Ashdown House

Forest Row, East Sussex RH18 5JY
Tel: 01342 822574
Fax: 01342 824380
email: secretary@ashdownhouse.com
website: www.ashdownhouse.co.uk

The School is part of The Cothill Educational Trust.

Headmaster: Haydon J S Moore, BTh Oxon, PGCE

Age Range. 4–13 Co-educational.
Number of Pupils. 125.
Fees per term (2016–2017). Boarding: £8,690 (Years 3–8); Day: £6,350 (Years 7–8), Day: £5,800 (Years 5–6), £4,680 (Years 3–4), £2,670 (Reception, Years 1–2).
The School (mainly full boarding in Years 6–8) with most day pupils begging to board by Year 5 or 6) is a Latrobe house situated in its own grounds of 40 acres, on the edge of the Ashdown Forest. We have an indoor sports hall, theatre and music centre, new Science Block and well-equipped ICT provision. There is an indoor swimming pool, three tennis courts, a golf course and open countryside surrounding us for field studies and adventure.

An escorted train to London and back on exeat weekends and half terms and easy access to Gatwick & Heathrow airports make us a popular choice for London parents and families living abroad.

Every child in Year 7 spends a full term in the Château de Sauveterre and there are residential trips, often to the Old Malthouse in Dorset for Geography/Science/outward bound based trips – both the Château and The Old Malthouse are owned by the Trust.

There are 26 full-time members of teaching staff, most of whom live within the grounds. Music of all kinds is studied under resident and peripatetic teachers and Art, DT and ICT are part of every child's curriculum. Scholarships are regularly won in all disciplines.

Games. Major sports for boys are cricket, soccer, rugby; the girls play netball and rounders, and hockey and athletics are played by both girls and boys. In addition there are huge numbers of other sporting opportunities, including swimming, tennis, riding, golf, squash, archery and cross-country.

The Headmaster and his wife, supported by houseparents, matrons and a State Registered Nurse look after all pastoral and domestic arrangements.

Charitable status. The Cothill Educational Trust is a Registered Charity, number 309639.

Ashfold School

Dorton House, Dorton, Bucks HP18 9NG
Tel: 01844 238237
Fax: 01844 238505
email: registrar@ashfoldschool.co.uk
website: www.ashfoldschool.co.uk
Twitter: @AshfoldSchool

Chairman of Governors: Mr H Taylor

Headmaster: **Mr M Chitty**, BSc

Age Range. 3–13 Co-educational.
Number of Pupils. 161 boys, 109 girls (day pupils and weekly boarders).
Fees per term (2016–2017). Weekly boarders £6,345; Day £5,020–£5,295; Pre-Prep £2,305–£3,595.

Ashfold is an independent day, weekly and flexi boarding school for boys and girls aged three to thirteen years. Set in thirty acres of stunning grounds in rural Buckinghamshire, the School is located within easy reach of Thame, Princes Risborough, Oxford, Bicester and Aylesbury. The nearest mainline station with regular connections to London Marylebone and Birmingham is just 15 minutes away. Ashfold is a busy and vibrant place with a reputation as a friendly, family-orientated school.

Founded in 1927, Ashfold is a country prep school offering the very best in both traditional and innovative teaching. The School's extensive facilities include a purpose-built Pre-Prep Building, sports hall, full-sized astroturf and a heated outdoor pool. A new Art & Design Centre opened in January 2016 with state-of-the-art facilities for design technology, cookery & nutrition, art, ceramics and textiles.

Most children join the School in the Pre-Prep Department and move on to top independent senior schools at 13+. Ashfold has a strong academic record with, on average, more than 40% of the Sixth Form achieving scholarships or awards to their chosen schools over the last nine years.

The School offers an excellent all-round education with outstanding opportunities for sport, art, music and drama as well as a wide-ranging programme of extracurricular activities.

In the School's latest inspection by the Independent Schools Inspectorate in 2015, the following areas of the School's provision were all rated 'excellent': pupils' achievements and learning; curricular and non-curricular provision; teaching; the spiritual, moral, social and cultural development of pupils; pastoral care; boarding; governance; and leadership and management.

Charitable status. Ashfold School Trust is a Registered Charity, number 272663. It exists to provide a quality preparatory school education, academically and in other respects, for all the children entrusted to its care.

Ashford Prep School
United Learning

Great Chart, Ashford, Kent TN23 3DJ
Tel: 01233 620493
Fax: 01233 636579
email: ashfordprep@ashfordschool.co.uk
website: www.ashfordschool.co.uk
Twitter: @AshfordSchool
Facebook: @AshfordSchool

Co-educational Day School with Boarding from Year 6.

Chairman of School Council: Mr W Peppitt, MRICS
Head: **Mr R Yeates**, BA Hons

Age Range. 3–11.
Number of Pupils. 416: 202 Boys, 214 Girls.
Fees per term (2016–2017). Day: Nursery: £640 (one full day per week), £2,975 (full-time); Reception £3,100, Years 1 and 2 £3,300, Years 3–6 £4,600.

Ashford Prep School is part of United Learning and as such has benefited from significant recent investment, including extensive refurbishment and new facilities. The school believes in the importance of focusing on the development of the individual through a broad education in which every child can find success whilst developing confidence, motivation, self-esteem and emotional intelligence.

A focus on pastoral care and the pursuit of excellence go together with high standards of discipline and a strong Christian ethos.

Situated in a rural setting, Ashford Prep School lies in some 25 very attractive acres. The School enjoys both class-room-based and excellent specialist teaching with well-designed facilities for science, art, music, PE, ICT and design technology and has recently undergone a large investment development. These new buildings provide 18 new classrooms, new kitchens, reception area, library facilities and a new hall. The School is fully networked and has exceptional provision for ICT with ACTIVboards in all classrooms, a computer room capable of accommodating entire classes and broadband access to the Internet throughout. We have recently celebrated the opening of our new floodlit all-weather pitch and work is continuing on our cricket grounds and running tracks.

The thriving Nursery operates on a flexible basis and the school offers full, wrap-around care from 7.30 am to 6.30 pm for all our children. The school operates Mondays to Fridays. Holiday Clubs operate during school breaks.

Throughout the school, team sports include rugby, hockey, netball, football, rounders, athletics and cricket. Regular fixtures are held with other local schools. Children also participate in PE and swimming as part of their curricular programme.

An extensive range of co-curricular activities is provided, both at lunchtime and after school. Individual music tuition with a wide range of instruments is available. Music, drama, dance and public speaking are all important opportunities; productions and presentations are performed by all age groups to a high standard and take place throughout the year. The choir and orchestra meet regularly.

A programme of educational trips and visits provides a stimulating and important addition to the all-round education and development of the 'whole' child and the costs of these are included in the fees.

An inspection by the Independent Schools Inspectorate in March 2014 declared the whole school 'outstanding' or 'excellent' in every category.

Children normally progress to Ashford Senior School (*see HMC entry*) without the need to take an entrance test unless they wish to sit scholarship exams. The Prep School has had considerable success in preparing children for scholarships to leading independent schools as well as other entrance tests including the 11+.

Charitable status. Ashford Prep School is part of United Learning which comprises: UCST (a Company Limited by Guarantee, Registered in England, number 2780748, and a Registered Charity, number 1016538) and ULT (a Company Limited by Guarantee, Registered in England, number 4439859, and an Exempt Charity).

Ashville College Junior School

Green Lane, Harrogate, North Yorkshire HG2 9JP

Tel: 01423 724800
Fax: 01423 505142
email: ashville@ashville.co.uk
website: www.ashville.co.uk
Twitter: @AshvilleCollege
Facebook: /AshvilleCollegeHarrogate

Chairman of Governors: Mr P Whiteley, BSc, FCA

Headmaster: Mr S Bailey, BA

Age Range. 7–11 Co-educational.
Number of Pupils. 150.
Fees per term (2016–2017). Tuition: £3,175–£3,830.
Boarding (in addition to tuition fees): Full £2,590. Lunch for
Day Pupils: £270.

Ashville College Junior School, located on the South side
of Harrogate, has gone from strength to strength in recent
years and can now legitimately claim to be one of the leading Independent Junior Schools in the North. In 2011 the ISI
(Independent Schools Inspectorate) rated the Junior School
"outstanding" in all areas. The majority of pupils are day
pupils, however a number of pupils board in a thriving,
newly refurbished co-educational boarding house.

Academically, children are taught in form groups of no
more than 22 pupils and additional learning support is available for those who need it. Pupils have excellent attitudes
towards learning and are proud of their achievements. Academic standards are high and the most able children are well
catered for through an excellent Gifted & Talented programme. Consequently, national test results are well above
average.

Sporting facilities are outstanding, with all children using
the full size swimming pool weekly for lessons. Recently in
competitive sport the school has had some notable successes. In Rugby, the U11 boys recently won the Westville
Festival and Lyndhurst Invitational Sevens. In Cricket, the
U11 team reached the National Finals, the U10 Netball were
runners up in the HMC North East Tournament and the
Swimming team are ranked 8th nationally.

Music is a strong feature of the school. There are two
choirs, an orchestra, and over 100 children taking individual
exams. Concerts are performed throughout the year. Drama
also features, with an annual full-scale production in addition to individual speech and drama lessons for children
working towards their LAMDA exams.

There are over fifty extracurricular clubs and activities
available to the children to ensure that pupils find their
niche, whatever it may be. Ashville College Junior School
Pupils are confident and caring with a purposeful approach
to school life.

Charitable status. Ashville College is a Registered
Charity, number 529577.

Ashville College Pre-Prep School

Green Lane, Harrogate, North Yorkshire HG2 9JP

Tel: 01423 724815
Fax: 01423 505142
email: ashville@ashville.co.uk
website: www.ashville.co.uk
Twitter: @AshvilleCollege
Facebook: /AshvilleCollegeHarrogate

Chairman of Governors: Mr P Whiteley, BSc, FCA

Headteacher: Mr S Bailey, BA

Age Range. 3–7 (Pre-School to Year 2) Co-educational.
Number of Pupils. 100.
Fees per term (2016–2017). Pre-Prep Tuition: £2,650.
Lunch: £243. Pre-School Tuition: Sessions vary.

Ashville Pre-Prep School is part of Ashville College. It
is a warm and friendly school which focuses on the individual child, with class sizes of no more than sixteen in Reception and eighteen in Year 2. The school is housed in a
modern, purpose-built building which benefits from a
library, a spacious school hall, a baking and technology area
and a well equipped playground and garden. The children
also have access to the facilities of the Senior School; for
example all children partake in weekly swimming lessons in
the College pool, and also have use of the Sports Hall where
the children in Year 2 have their Games lesson. These children also benefit from the expertise of a tennis coach who
comes in to teach them on a weekly basis. The extracurricular opportunities are outstanding; during the school day children all participate in a dance lesson and many also have
Speech and Drama lessons; they are encouraged to play a
musical instrument and many learn the violin or cello and
have piano lessons, whilst all the children in Year 2 learn to
play the recorder. Spanish is also taught throughout the Pre-
Prep School. After-school activities include ballet, tap,
street dancing, ICT and judo and the Pre-Prep School also
has its own Rainbow pack.

Learning to read and all aspects of Literacy are a priority
in the Pre-Prep School and attainment in reading is high. A
love of books is fostered from the very beginning and consequently the children's enthusiasm for reading and their thirst
for knowledge permeate the rest of the curriculum. They
read aloud willingly and confidently and are keen to participate in class and school assemblies and concerts. These
skills acquired at such an early age equip the children to
move through the school with confidence.

The small class sizes enable the teachers to differentiate
in numeracy also, ensuring all children are challenged and
reaching their full potential. There are dedicated teachers in
charge of all the foundation subjects, which are taught
around topic work. This creative curriculum is organised on
a three year cycle so that the topics are always new and
exciting, indeed they are inspirational In addition specialist
teachers from Senior School also contribute to the curriculum programme, particularly with MFL, PE, music and RE.

The children display good relationships with each other
and also with their teachers. This enables them to ask for
assistance and explore new ideas confidently. Motivation is
high in lessons; they are keen to answer questions and share
their ideas, which mean they make considerable progress.
Learning is promoted by the children's willingness, eagerness and enthusiasm to cooperate and focus on their work.

The Pre-Prep provides children with the best start in life,
offering a safe environment where they are encouraged to
enjoy all aspects of life, from helping in the garden, to learning Spanish, to taking part in the annual school play. In addition there is a wide range of trips which link with their topic
work, an annual highlight being the Year Two trip in the
summer term, which last year took the children to Edinburgh; the previous year the children had travelled to London. Children leave with a strong sense of community and
respect, which enables them to move on to Junior School as
happy confident children who have enjoyed a rich and varied programme in their early years of schooling.

In September 2015 **Ashville College Pre-School** opened,
extending the Pre-Prep School to include children from age
three. The Pre-School class is situated in a new, purpose-
built classroom and is very much part of the Pre-Prep School
and the Ashville Community. The class follows the Early

Years Foundation Stage Curriculum. The focus for the EYFS is learning through play and the Pre-School offers the very best in play-based learning experiences for your child. Day-to-day experiences on offer include role-play, mark making and small world play.

The Pre-School building has been designed specifically with young children in mind, to provide a safe environment in which they can learn and play. The classroom offers a spacious indoor learning environment which benefits from lots of natural light and links seamlessly to a covered veranda area and well-resourced play area beyond. Being part of the Ashville family also means that the Pre-School has access to additional facilities on the Ashville campus which includes a spacious hall for sports, dance and musical activities, and the swimming pool.

Children build social and independent skills through carefully planned activities and topics, designed to help the children discover a lifelong love of learning.

Charitable status. Ashville College is a Registered Charity, number 529577.

Austin Friars Junior School

Etterby Scaur, Carlisle, Cumbria CA3 9PB

Tel:	01228 528042
Fax:	01228 810327
email:	office@austinfriars.cumbria.sch.uk
	admissions@austinfriars.cumbria.sch.uk
website:	www.austinfriars.co.uk
Twitter:	@AFSMSchool

Chairman of Trustees: Revd Dr Peter Tiplady, MB BS, MRCGP, FFPHM, FRIPH

Headmaster: Mr M F Harris, BSc, PGCE

Head of Junior School: **Mr J Slingsby**

Age Range. 3–11.
Number of Pupils. 150.
Fees per term (2016–2017). Junior School: £2,310 (R–Year 2), £2,563 (Years 3–4), £3,303 (Years 5–6). Pre-School: £5.75 per hour, plus £1.90 for lunch.

Austin Friars Junior School offers a wide and varied curriculum, which encourages academic achievement alongside sporting, musical, cultural and creative development, thus allowing each child's talents and potential to be fully pursued.

The teaching staff form a capable and highly motivated team totally dedicated to the aims and ethos of the School.

Pupils benefit from specialist teaching in subjects such as ICT, music, drama, maths, modern languages and sports and games. Learning support is an integral part of the curriculum for those who will benefit.

Academically, the school has a fine reputation within the City of Carlisle and beyond, with a record of many scholarship successes at age 11.

Music, speech and drama have a high profile. Annually Junior 1 (Year 3) pupils are given a musical instrument to learn and enjoy specialist tuition. Juniors take LAMDA Verse and Prose Speaking Examination achieving consistently high grades.

Good use is made of the extensive grounds surrounding the school, including Astroturf, providing ample scope for PE lessons as well as hosting matches against local school teams.

A wide range of extracurricular activities is offered from 4.00–6.00 pm, including history, chess, hockey, art, science, computing, young engineers, French, football and netball.

Due to the expansion of pupil numbers, a £3.1 million state-of-the-art Junior School was completed in February 2008.

The Junior School is an Ofsted-registered provider of Free Nursery Education Entitlement for three and four year olds. Reception follows the Early Years Foundation Stage curriculum.

The Early Years Foundation Stage Pre-School occupies a spacious detached two-storey house, adjacent to the main School.

Set within its own grounds and bordered by a mature garden, the Pre-School provides pupils with excellent facilities, including an interesting garden bordered by mature trees and all-weather safe play area. The secure building and grounds offer parents an opportunity to educate children within a natural and comfortable setting.

The main aim of the Pre-School is to provide a caring and stimulating environment, endowing children with a positive attitude to learning which will serve them through their formative years. The Early Years Foundation Stage curriculum covers the six areas of learning. Through carefully-structured and well-planned, play-based activities pupils are encouraged to develop their own ideas and to learn sound spiritual and social values by being cooperative and aware of others. Pre-School pupils are taught to listen carefully, to make friends, share, take turns and be polite and to use good manners.

The 3–18 profile of the Austin Friars allows pupils more time to respond to the core Augustinian values of Unity, Truth and Love which are enshrined in the way the School goes about its business on a daily basis. The three-phase, 3–18, model also facilitates a seamless transition from Pre-School to VI Form and presents our younger pupils with access to facilities usually the preserve of secondary pupils, such as science laboratories, music suites, specialist sports facilities and design technology workshops.

Admission. Children are admitted into the Pre-School in the three to four age range.

Entry into the Junior School at all levels, except Kindergarten, is by formal assessment of English, mathematics and non-verbal reasoning; prospective pupils spend a taster day in School. All prospective pupils are screened for specific learning difficulties. Entry into Kindergarten is by interview and a taster afternoon.

Senior School. *For information about Austin Friars Senior School, see entry in The Society of Heads section.*

Charitable status. Austin Friars School is a Registered Charity, number 516289.

Avenue House School

70 The Avenue, Ealing, London W13 8LS

Tel:	020 8998 9981
Fax:	020 8991 1533
email:	school@avenuehouse.org
website:	www.avenuehouse.org

Co-educational Day School.

Proprietor: Mr David Immanuel

Headteacher: **Mr Justin Sheppard**, BA Hons, PGCE

Age Range. 3–11.
Number of Pupils. 100.
Fees per term (2016–2017). £1,920–£3,560.

Avenue House School provides a small, caring environment where children gain the confidence to flourish in all areas of the curriculum. Good manners, mutual respect and a caring community are prevalent at all times.

Children are taught in small classes conducive to the development of an excellent work ethos and achieve high standards in academic subjects as well as an appreciation and understanding of Drama, Art, Music and Sport.

Avenue House School does not test children on entry to Reception as we feel that each child develops at their own individual rate. All pupils are monitored and assessed individually throughout the year and meetings between parents and school are frequent as we believe a positive approach leads to excellence.

Children have access to our own small library and small hall for the younger children. The school has laptop computers with wireless broadband internet connection and whiteboards are installed throughout.

Pupils are prepared for the competitive entrance examinations to the London Independent Day Schools.

Avenue House School is proud of the many high standard musical and drama productions that are performed throughout the year from Nursery children to Year 6.

Physical Education is an important part of our curriculum and all pupils go swimming every week. Children in the Nursery, Reception and Year 1 have Physical Education in our Gymnasium and small playground. From Year 2 the children have weekly sports lessons at Trailfinders Sports and Leisure Club. The traditional annual sports day for the whole school is also held. The children are also involved in inter-House matches.

Extra curriculum activities form a valuable and key part of our education. Apart from the daily homework club other activities include football, drama, guitar, Junior & Senior choir, Junior & Senior ICT, art, ballet, Mad Science, French and gardening (Summer Term). For Years 5 and 6 we also have lunch-time clubs which include Debating, School Magazine and Mathematics Club.

Educational visits play an important role in helping children relate their class work to the real world. For this reason pupils are taken on outings each term where they can benefit from having first-hand knowledge of London and its surrounding areas. Children have the opportunity to go on residential trips which include Dorchester, France, the Isle of Wight and Black Mountain in Wales.

Avenue Nursery & Pre-Preparatory School

2 Highgate Avenue, Highgate, London N6 5RX
Tel: 020 8348 6815
email: office@avenuenursery.com
website: www.avenuenursery.com

Principal: **Mrs Mary Fysh**

Head: **Mrs Sarah Tapp**

Age Range. 3–7 Co-educational.
Number of Pupils. 75.
Fees per term (2016–2017). £2,500–£4,400.

The ethos of the School is the happiness of every child through a secure, friendly and exciting environment. The provision of a wide and different extracurricular programme of activities from pottery to ice skating contributes considerably towards achieving this aim. The high staff/child ratios enable children to learn and achieve in small groups thus progressing successfully throughout the curriculum. External assessments (PIPS) are introduced in the Nursery and continued through Reception, Year 1 and 2. The results are collated and provide a useful means of tracking the progress of each child: it also aids the planning and learning needs of different children. The School is non-denominational and

children of all denominations or none are welcome. Children are made aware of major religious festivals including Christmas.

Pre-Nursery children enter the School when rising 3. The staff ratio is 1:6 and the children enjoy participating in many different activities designed to promote speech and language skills, hand/eye coordination and learning to interact with peers and adults. The large garden provides many opportunities for physical activities, role play and social interaction.

The Nursery takes children from the age of 3+ for five mornings a week and the staff ratio remains at 1:6. The children build on the skills they have learned in Pre-Nursery and are also introduced to letters and numbers. Pottery is added to the curriculum plus visits off site to places of interest.

The Reception Class is divided into two groups according to age. These groups are taught Literacy and Maths in groups of 9 and the work is differentiated so that each child is able to achieve at the level appropriate to them. French and trampolining are added to the curriculum. Children remain at school until 3 pm and bring a packed lunch.

The Year 1 and 2 children's respective class teacher remains with them throughout Key Stage 1 to ensure a seamless transition from Year 1 to 2 greatly benefiting the children's preparations for their future 7+ assessments. The classes follow a curriculum based on the National Curriculum but designed to enable each child to progress towards a successful outcome at 7+. Ice skating is added to the extracurricular timetable.

Children leave the School at varying stages. Some of the girls leave at 4+ and others at 7+. Boys generally stay until 7+. We have built up good relationships with other schools in the area and as members of the IAPS (since November 2009) enjoy meeting and visiting member schools.

Aysgarth School

Bedale, North Yorkshire DL8 1TF
Tel: 01677 450240
Fax: 01677 450736
email: enquiries@aysgarthschool.co.uk
website: www.aysgarthschool.com
Twitter: @AysgarthSchool
Facebook: /aysgarthschool

Chairman of Governors: J M P D Stroyan

Headmaster: **Mr Rob Morse**, BEd Hons De Montfort

Assistant Headmaster: Mr Philip Southall, BA Hull, PGCE St Mary's Twickenham

Age Range. 3–13.
Number of Pupils. 225. Pre-Prep Department: 68 boys and girls aged 3–8. Prep School: 157 boys aged 8–13.
Fees per term (2016–2017). Boarders (full and weekly) £7,940, Day £6,100, Pre-Prep £2,485–£3,300.

The Prep School is a boarding school for boys set in 50 acres of grounds in North Yorkshire about 6 miles from the A1. It attracts boys from all over the UK, and boys go on to the country's leading independent senior schools, many of them in southern England. Some boys start as day boys or weekly boarders to enable them to adjust to boarding gently. For exeats, boys can be escorted on trains from Darlington to the north and south and there are coaches to and from Cumbria and Lancashire.

Boys of all abilities are welcomed and academic standards are high. All boys are prepared for Common Entrance and several gain scholarships. Before entry, each boy is assessed to ensure that any special needs are identified early and given fully integrated specialist help where necessary.

Class sizes are typically around 12. There is a newly equipped computer centre and every teacher has a laptop to link to digital projectors and interactive whiteboards in most classrooms.

The activities in which boys can participate are enormously varied. The facilities include a new heated indoor swimming pool, a modern sports hall, tennis, fives and squash courts, 17 acres of excellent playing fields and a floodlit all-weather pitch. Cricket, Soccer and Rugby Football are the main school sports, and there are opportunities to participate in a wide range of other sports. Music is one of the strengths of the school with more than 75% of boys playing a musical instrument and several boys have been awarded music scholarships. There are three choirs and the school musicians have regular opportunities to perform both in the school and locally. Each term different year groups produce a play or musical. Art and Craft and Design & Technology are taught by specialist teachers.

The school has a fine Victorian chapel, and boys are encouraged to develop Christian faith and values in a positive, caring environment. Pastoral care is the first priority for all staff. The headmaster and his wife, a housemaster and his wife and three matrons, are all resident in the main building. A wide range of exciting activities in the evenings and at weekends ensure that boys are keen to board, and they are encouraged to do so particularly in their last two years as preparation for their next schools.

The school aims to encourage boys to be well mannered and courteous with a cheerful enthusiasm for learning and for life and a determination to make the most of their abilities.

There is also a flourishing Pre-Prep Department including a Nursery for day boys and girls aged 3 to 8.

Charitable status. Aysgarth School Trust Limited is a Registered Charity, number 529538. Its purpose is to provide a high standard of boarding and day education.

Babington House School – Preparatory Department

Grange Drive, Chislehurst, Kent BR7 5ES

Tel: 020 8467 5537
Fax: 020 8295 1175
email: enquiries@babingtonhouse.com
website: www.babingtonhouse.com

Chairman of Governors: Mr C Turner

Headmaster: **Mr T Lello**, MA, FRSA, NPQH, PGCE

Head of Preparatory Department: **Mrs C Sherwood**, BA Hons, PGCE

Age Range. 3–11 Co-educational.
Number of Pupils. 254: 152 Girls, 102 Boys.
Fees per term (2016–2017). £4,082 (Reception to Year 6).

At Babington House Preparatory we provide a happy, family atmosphere, where children can flourish, develop their academic potential and enjoy success in a wide range of other activities.

We believe that children learn best in a caring, friendly environment, where they feel valued as individuals and confident in themselves.

Our expectations are high, encouraging good behaviour, a strong work ethic and an awareness of the wider community. Pupils engage with each other with respect and an appreciation of diversity, following a curriculum designed to promote curiosity and stimulate a desire to learn about the world in which they live.

High-quality teaching effectively supports pupils to become creative and critical thinkers, who can employ different learning styles to improve their understanding.

We recognise that every child is unique and we greatly value the contribution they each have to make to our school. Babington House School pupils have a reputation for being articulate, enthusiastic and well-mannered.

The Preparatory Department is housed in new purpose-built accommodation linked to the Senior School, thus ensuring close liaison and smooth transition between the two. We are proud of the exciting series of developments providing facilities to enhance the impressive standards for which our pupils have become known.

At each Key Stage our pupils achieve results far above the National Standards and are well prepared for the next stage of their education.

Babington Early Years top of Bromley Early school league tables in 2016 with score of 98%.

Charitable status. Babington House School is a Registered Charity, number 307914.

Bablake Junior School and Pre Prep

Junior School:
Coundon Road, Coventry, West Midlands CV1 4AU

Tel: 024 7627 1260
Fax: 024 7627 1294
email: jhmsec@bablakejs.co.uk
website: www.bablake.com/junior
Twitter: @BablakeJunior
Facebook: @BablakeJunior

Pre Prep:
8 Park Road, Coventry, West Midlands CV1 2LH

Tel: 024 7622 1677
Fax: 024 7623 1630
email: bablakepreprep@bablakejs.co.uk
website: www.bablake.com/pre-prep

Chairman of Governors: Mrs J McNaney

Headmaster: **N A Price**, BA Hons, PGCE

Deputy Head: Mr L Holder, BEd
Head of Pre Prep: Mrs T Horton, BEd Hons Cantab

Age Range. 3–11.
Number of Pupils. 360 Day Pupils.
Fees per term (2016–2017). £2,218–£2,778.

Bablake Junior School offers an outstanding educational experience that allows children to thrive. Pupils enjoy coming to school and are given broad opportunities to develop and learn. They acquire skills and interests that will equip them for their future learning and for life.

We are a school where children are nurtured as individuals. This helps them to achieve all that they are capable of academically, creatively and on the games field. Excellent learning support is offered to those who may not be achieving their potential. Most of our pupils continue their education at Bablake until they complete their A Levels. (*See Bablake School entry in HMC section.*) Throughout the school, we help our pupils make the most of their abilities and the outstanding opportunities that exist here for them.

We follow a broad and balanced curriculum – lessons are interesting and our academic results excellent. Our teachers' commitment to helping everyone achieve their potential is reflected in the support of our parents and the hard work our pupils put into their studies. All achievement – academic, creative or sporting – is recognised and celebrated. The support and respect of the community helps all children achieve their best.

Pupils receive expert coaching in a wide variety of sports and have the opportunity to take part in many activities. We believe in participation and the pursuit of excellence and all children have the opportunity to represent the school in fixtures. We share the swimming pool, fields, sports hall and astroturf with our Senior School and make use of Bablake's fantastic theatre and other specialist facilities. Taking part in a wide variety of activities builds confidence and reinforces positive child development.

Children may join Bablake Pre Prep in the September after they turn 3. The Pre Prep offers a happy, homely and stimulating environment where thorough and considered preparation takes place for the challenges ahead. Later admission to the Pre Prep and Junior School is available at any time should space exist. An assessment of a pupil's potential takes place before entry.

Charitable status. Coventry School Foundation is a Registered Charity, number 528961. It exists to provide education for boys and girls.

Badminton Junior School

Westbury-on-Trym, Bristol BS9 3BA

Tel:	0117 905 5271
Fax:	0117 962 3049
email:	admissions@badmintonschool.co.uk
website:	www.badmintonschool.co.uk

Chairman of Governors: Mr Bill Ray

Headmistress: Mrs Emma Davies, BA, PGCE

Age Range. 3–11.
Number of Girls. 132.
Fees per term (2016–2017). Day: £3,200–£3,600 inclusive of lunch and extended day. Boarding (from Year 5): £7,100–£7,800.

Educational Philosophy. Children learn best when they are interested, happy and supported in their work. Our girls thrive in a stimulating environment where high standards of work and behaviour are expected. All subjects in the Junior School are taught by enthusiastic subject specialists in classes of up to sixteen pupils. We provide a welcoming and friendly atmosphere so that all of our girls feel emotionally secure and we encourage them to develop their own particular talents and interests. Key notes in our philosophy are the development of self-confidence, a healthy respect for one another and the nurturing of curious, critical minds.

We believe children enjoy being kept busy and acquiring new skills and so we try to create a balance between academic work in the classroom, plenty of physical exercise, a range of extra-curricular activities and opportunities for recreational and creative play. The girls are given the opportunity to explore and develop their language skills and study French, Latin, German and Spanish whilst additional languages, such as Mandarin and Italian, are offered in after-school clubs.

Facilities. The Junior School is well appointed with light airy classrooms, dedicated rooms for Art and Music, a Science laboratory, and an ICT suite. We have a well-stocked library and an Assembly Hall in which various activities including ballet, drama and musical concerts take place. There is a wonderful, secure adventure playground which the girls make the most of during break and lunch times.

Being on the same campus as the Senior School, the girls make use of all the facilities on site which include the 25m indoor swimming pool, gymnasium and the all-purpose sports pitch. There are excellent facilities for music, which plays an important part both inside and outside the curriculum.

With our extended day facilities we aim to provide a warm and caring environment to suit the needs of all our pupils and their parents. Every day clubs such as gardening, chess, drama, art or playground games take place after school and girls are welcome to stay on for prep or late stay until 5:45 pm, at no additional cost

For further information on Badminton School, see entry in GSA section. A prospectus is available on request from our Admissions Department (admissions@badminton school.co.uk).

Charitable status. Badminton School Limited is a Registered Charity, number 311738. It exists to provide education for children.

Bancroft's Preparatory School

High Road, Woodford Green, Essex IG8 0RF

Tel:	020 8506 6751
	020 8506 6774 (Admissions)
Fax:	020 8506 6752
email:	prep.office@bancrofts.org
website:	www.bancrofts.org

Chairman of the Governors: Prof P Ogden, BA, DPhil, AcSS

Head: **J P Layburn**, MA

Assistant Head: M Piper, BA
Director of Studies: N Thomas, BCom, MA

Age Range. 7–11.
Number of Pupils. 123 girls, 136 boys.
Fees per term (2016–2017). £4,430.

Bancroft's Preparatory School was established in September 1990 in the attractive grounds of Bancroft's School in Woodford Green (*see entry in HMC section*) and became a member of IAPS in 2000. Academic results are excellent and places are much sought after – the school is heavily oversubscribed with numbers of registrations rising year by year.

The Prep School has its own distinct character within the Bancroft's community and has the advantage of being able to use the excellent Senior School facilities including the sports hall, music facilities, Chapel, catering facility and hard play area. The School has recently expanded with an impressive new wing providing a further three classrooms, a performing arts studio for drama, music and dance, a science/design & technology room, a new front entrance and reception area as well as a children's adventure play area. This expansion has enabled the school to reduce its class sizes; the School now has three forms in each of its four year groups.

The school seeks to provide an education enriched by a vibrant, multicultural environment. Pastoral care is seen as key and the happiness of all the children is fundamental. Assemblies link with PSHE and focus on key values – such as treating others as you would like to be treated and going "the extra mile". The school constantly seeks to encourage children to feel part of a happy and caring community.

Regular charity work is seen as very important and through it children gain an appreciation of the advantages on offer to them and so develop a sense of compassion for the world beyond Bancroft's.

The class teacher has a central role to play and there is an emphasis on specialised teaching in the top two years, so that staff can pursue their subject passions to the benefit of the children. Academic standards are high with a broad, structured curriculum including French, Humanities, Creative Thinking, PSHE, Drama, Music, Games, Swimming, PE and Art. The Prep School wants its bright pupils to have fun and "to sparkle" while they learn so that they will derive a lifelong love of learning.

As well as establishing a strong academic base, the school is very much concerned with an holistic approach for each child – encouraging good manners, respect for others and a keen sense of humour. Children take part in a great variety of extracurricular activities at lunch times, after school and at weekends. Older children are given the opportunity to take on responsibilities around the school – every child becomes a Monitor at some stage in their final year. The school hopes that the children will in time become successful adults who will make a difference in the 21st century.

Children are assessed for entry at the age of six/seven, visiting the school in small groups and testing by the Head and Head of Transition is friendly and low key. Once accepted, pupils have guaranteed transfer to Bancroft's Senior School (on the same site) at the age of eleven. Bancroft's Prep School offers up to two Francis Bancroft's means-tested awards for pupils entering the School at the age of 7 each year. These are awarded based on disclosure of family finances and performance in the entrance tests; these only cover Prep School fees.

The administration of the Prep School and Senior School are closely linked and the Head and Assistant Head of the Prep School are members of the Senior Management Team of Bancroft's School.

In 2013 the Prep School was inspected and the school was delighted with the excellent report in which they were awarded the top grade in most areas. The full report can be read by visiting the ISI website: www.isi.net.

Charitable status. Bancroft's School is a Registered Charity, number 1068532. It exists to provide a rounded academic education for able children.

Barfield School & Nursery

Guildford Road, Farnham, Surrey GU10 1PB
Tel: 01252 782271
Fax: 01252 781480
email: admin@barfieldschool.com
website: www.barfieldschool.com

Barfield School is part of the Cothill Educational Trust.

Chairman of Governors: Sir Henry Aubrey-Fletcher Bt

Headmaster: **Mr James Reid**, BEd Hons

Age Range. 2+–13 Co-educational.
Number of Children. 165.
Fees per term (from Jan 2017). Prep £4,400–£4,540, Pre-Prep £3,055–£3,220, Nursery £1,056–£3,055.

Barfield School, set in 12 acres of beautiful grounds, was awarded "Excellent" in all eight areas of inspection by the ISI in 2016. The school is co-educational and takes children from the age of 2–13 years.

The Nursery is an integral part of the school and is bright and airy, with plenty of green space. Open 50 weeks of the year from 8.00 am to 6.15 pm, experienced and qualified staff nurture, encourage and support all the children, ensuring they feel both happy and secure in our care. The children have use of all the school facilities and access to specialist teachers for swimming and music.

Barfield School has an excellent reputation for high academic standards and caring staff. Facilities include a Cook House, Library, Auditorium, Music and Music practice rooms, ICT suite, Art and DT rooms. The school has a flourishing PE and Outdoor Pursuits Department, with most major and minor sports covered. There is a magnificent indoor heated swimming pool and children are encouraged to participate in a wide range of extracurricular activities. Activity courses are run throughout the school holidays and are enjoyed by children from Reception to Year 8.

Children are taught in small classes and are prepared for Common Entrance and Scholarship examinations, as well as Grammar School entry.

Visitors are always welcome – please contact the school.

Charitable status. Barfield School is part of the Cothill Educational Trust, which is a Registered Charity, number 309639.

Barlborough Hall School
Preparatory School to Mount St Mary's College

Barlborough, Chesterfield, Derbyshire S43 4TJ
Tel: 01246 810511
email: headteacher@barlboroughhallschool.com
website: www.barlboroughhallschool.com

Chair of Governors: Fr Adrian Porter SJ

Headteacher: **N Boys**, BA

Age Range. 3–11 Co-educational.
Number of Pupils. 177.
Fees per term (2016–2017). £2,487–£3,315.

Barlborough Hall School is a co-educational preparatory school in the Jesuit Catholic tradition, welcoming pupils aged 3–11 of all denominations. The preparatory school to nearby Mount St Mary's College (11–18), Barlborough is set in over 300 acres of parkland.

Barlborough became a school in 1939 and is built around an Elizabethan manor house which now houses many of the teaching rooms. The school encourages children to develop their talents in many different areas: academic, social, spiritual and physical with a strong focus on the individual. Academically, pupils achieve success through small classes, low pupil to teacher ratios and setting from Year 3 onwards. Teaching facilities ensure that children receive a traditional preparatory school education and include a science laboratory, technology lab and ICT suite. Pupils learn French from Nursery and most pupils learn Latin in Years 5 and 6.

All pupils receive pastoral care and academic tutoring through their form teachers, under the leadership of the Key Stage Coordinators. There is a clear sense of progression from Pre-Prep, situated in its own distinct area with its own playground, to the Upper School, which allows pupils to develop greater independence but still within a nurturing environment. There is a Jesuit chaplain who works closely with the teachers on the Chaplaincy team.

Emphasis is placed on developing the whole person, and the school enjoys an impressive reputation for its sport and music. There is an indoor heated swimming pool, dance studio and extensive games fields, and pupils enjoy a wide range of sports. Barlborough Hall is well-established on the rugby, football, hockey and netball circuit and plays regularly against other schools. Many pupils learn instruments from skilled peripatetic teachers and the school's music teacher leads prize-winning choirs and an orchestra. Drama also flourishes, with a major production every year in the school's theatre.

There are many extracurricular activities, allowing pupils to develop their interests in a wide range of fields. Pupils are encouraged to take part in at least two activities a week and have the option to attend Saturday school, where they are able to enjoy hobbies in a more relaxed environment or practise for team sports. The wide range of activities available includes Chess, Ballroom Dancing, Art, Drama and Touch Typing. Pupils can also stay after school every evening to do homework under teacher supervision.

Admission to Barlborough Hall is by interview. Further details and a prospectus can be obtained from the Head-teacher's Secretary.

Barlborough Hall pupils can automatically transfer at age 11 to Mount St Mary's College (*see entry HMC section*).

Charitable status. Mount St Mary's is a Registered Charity, number 1117998.

Barnard Castle Preparatory School

Westwick Road, Barnard Castle, County Durham DL12 8UW

Tel: 01833 696032
Fax: 01833 696034
email: prep@barneyschool.org.uk
website: www.barnardcastleschool.org.uk

Chairman of Governors: Mr A Fielder

Head: Mrs Laura Turner, MA

Age Range. 4–11 years.
Number of Pupils. 182 girls and boys, including 8 boarders.
Fees per term (2016–2017). Prep: £5,925 (Boarders), £6,814 (International Boarders), £3,055 (Day). Pre-Prep: £2,015.

Barnard Castle Preparatory School is the junior school of Barnard Castle School and offers an all round, high quality education for boys and girls aged between 4 and 11 years. The School offers both day and boarding places and is situated in a beautiful setting on the edge of a traditional English market town.

The campuses of the two schools are adjoining, allowing shared use of many excellent facilities. At the same time the Preparatory School is able to provide a separate, stimulating environment, with small classes, a wide range of extracurricular activities and an exciting school excursion programme. The school has recently benefited from an extensive building and refurbishment programme. This has included the construction of 3 new classrooms and a Science Laboratory.

The School is well served by a bus network system and a breakfast club and after school supervision is readily available. The boarders reside in a newly developed boarding house, which creates a warm and friendly environment supported by a full range of facilities including the School's medical centre. Flexi-boarding from 2–4 nights is also available.

Our Director of Studies oversees a carefully designed, broad and balanced curriculum. Sport, drama and music occupy important places in the life of the School. All children have numerous opportunities to participate in each of these, as well as in an extensive co-curricular programme. The School also offers a qualified learning support service to those children who require further assistance.

Charitable status. Barnard Castle School is a Registered Charity, number 1125375. Its aim is the education of boys and girls.

Barnardiston Hall Preparatory School

Barnardiston, Nr Haverhill, Suffolk CB9 7TG

Tel: 01440 786316
Fax: 01440 786355
email: registrar@barnardiston-hall.co.uk
website: www.barnardiston-hall.co.uk

Principal: K A Boulter, MA Cantab, PGCE

Headmaster: T W T Dodgson, BA Hons, PGCE

Registrar: Mrs L P Gundersen

Bursar: Mrs A Gregory

Age Range. Co-educational 6 months –13 years.
Number of Pupils. Day 180, Boarding (full and weekly) 27.
Fees per term (2016–2017). Day Pupils £1,365–£4,350; Weekly Boarders £6,015; Full Boarders £6,525.

Barnardiston Hall, set in 29 acres of grounds on the borders of Suffolk, Essex and Cambridge, offers an individual all-round education for boys and girls, both day and boarding. High standards are achieved by small classes taught by graduate and teacher-trained staff, a caring approach and close liaison with parents.

The School has good facilities, including a Nursery, a Pre-Preparatory Block and Art Room / CDT complex, a very modern and well-equipped computer room, assembly hall, music room, science laboratory, library, tennis/netball courts, astroturf and extensive sports fields. For the boarders, the dormitories are bright, uncluttered and home-like.

The curriculum is designed to allow pupils to reach Common Entrance standards in the appropriate subjects. The best of traditional methods are mixed with modern ideas to provide an enjoyable and productive learning environment. French and computers are taught from the age of 3; Latin from age 7. The School is CReSTeD registered. It has received outstanding gradings in ISI reports for both welfare and education. Pupils go on to a wide range of secondary schools.

Sports in the Michaelmas and Lent Terms are hockey, swimming (Pre-Prep only) and cross-country/orienteering for all pupils, rugby for the boys and netball for the girls. During the Summer, all do athletics, cricket/rounders, and tennis/short tennis. The School has won the National Orienteering Championships for the last six years.

There is a wide range of clubs and societies including 3 choirs, an orchestra, recorders, chess, painting, drama, carpentry, air rifle, cookery and pottery. Ballet, speech and drama, piano, guitar, woodwind, violin, brass, string and singing lessons are also offered.

Throughout the term, there are weekend activities for boarders (optional for day pupils) which include mountain walking. Derbyshire Dales at 6, Ben Nevis at 8, camping, visits to museums/historic buildings and other places of interest and theatre trips. There is an annual trip to Europe. Some pupils aged 7+ have reached Everest Base Camp.

Barrow Hills School

Roke Lane, Witley, Godalming, Surrey GU8 5NY

Tel: 01428 683639
email: info@barrowhills.org
website: www.barrowhills.org.uk

Twitter: @BarrowHills
Facebook: @BarrowHillsSchool

Chairman of the Governors: Mrs Justine Voisin

Headmaster: Mr Sean Skehan, BA, PGCE, MA, NPQH

Age Range. 2–13.
Number of Pupils. 230.
Fees per term (2016–2017). Tuition: £3,215–£4,995 (including meals). Nursery and Kindergarten according to sessions.

Barrow Hills School is a prep school that believes having a long and happy childhood is integral to being a successful person in later life. This demands the highest standards of pastoral care and academics, underpinned by core values. Our ethos is the Catholic ethos of education: educate the whole child, find out what they are good at and celebrate this in the school community. To achieve this aim we have a broad and deep curriculum, increasingly specialist taught, as children progress through the school. Ability in specific subject areas is identified and supported. There is a Hebrew proverb, 'Do not confine children to your own learning for they were born in another time'. Embracing this, we are a 'totally connected' school and have provided Samsung tablets with digital s-pens for each and every child from Year 3 upwards. Access to tablet devices is also provided for younger pupils along with Wi-Fi, large screen digital displays and air printers across the entire school. Resources are cloud based and we have our own encrypted site on Google, running Google apps for education. You also need to know that our children have a full childhood; they are encouraged to be themselves and take risks with their learning. All we do is underpinned by our values of kindness, honesty, empathy, fortitude and charitable works. Music and theatre is in our DNA and our children are part of a culture that sees everyone, every year, perform. Sport matters too, and by Year 3 all children have five hours of sport a week including, whenever possible, competitive matches against rival schools. The major team sports are: hockey, netball, rounders, tennis and some lacrosse for girls; football, rugby, hockey and cricket for boys. We offer an 11+ scholarship programme with scholarships in Art, Music, Drama, Sport, Academic and All-Rounder for exceptional candidates worth up to 30% of fees. We have strong links with excellent senior schools, in particular with King Edward's Witley, our partner school, and many of our children are awarded scholarships. We are proud of our 100% success at Common Entrance with all children gaining entry to their chosen senior school at 13+. We offer broad range of extracurricular activities and a comprehensive programme of educational and residential visits.

Barrow Hills School is an independent co-educational Catholic day school for children of all denominations aged 2 to 13 years. Our main building is an attractive Arts and Crafts house, and we have 33 acres of beautiful gardens, playing fields and woods in the Surrey Hills countryside. We are close to Guildford, Godalming and Haslemere. Key entry points: Nursery, Kindy, Reception, Year 3 and Year 7.

Charitable status. Barrow Hills School Witley is a Registered Charity, number 311997.

Bassett House School

60 Bassett Road, London W10 6JP
Tel: 020 8969 0313
email: info@bassetths.org.uk
website: www.bassetths.org.uk
Twitter: @bassetths
Facebook: /Bassett-House-School

Motto: *Quisque pro sua parte* (From each to the best of his or her ability).

Chairman of Governors: Mr Anthony Rentoul

Head: Mrs Philippa Cawthorne

Age Range. 3–11 Co-educational.
Number of Pupils. 190.
Fees per term (2016–2017). Nursery (5 mornings) £2,735, Pre-Prep £5,470, Prep £5,700.

Bassett House School was founded in 1947 and takes both boys and girls from the age of 3 or 4 until age 11. Entry is, in the younger years, non-selective and the school has some 195 pupils in thirteen classes.

Philippa Cawthorne, the headmistress, believes she has "yet to meet a child who isn't naturally curious. It's our job to develop this curiosity so it becomes a lifelong love of learning." The school believes in a regime of creativity, encouragement and reward, but firstly ensures every child feels secure and welcome. Children blossom when they feel happy and valued, and nurturing individuality is at the heart of the school's teaching philosophy – this leads to outstanding results.

Bassett House School also teaches the value of endeavour and of staying power, of developing social skills and forming respectful relationships. It has an extensive programme of extra-curricular activities and clubs, day outings and residential trips, as well as a lively schedule of music, drama and sports.

Bassett House provides a thorough and broad educational grounding following the national curriculum and embracing different teaching techniques (including Montessori). The school has invested heavily in the latest classroom technology to give teachers additional tools to make learning lively, fun and effective. It has specialist teachers in maths, English, science, computing, French, music, physical education, art/design technology, eurhythmics, Latin and dance.

The school was built towards the end of the 19th century and what was originally designed as a large family house now provides modern spacious and airy classrooms. The school premises include use of a separate annex comprising an assembly hall with a stage and gymnasium, three classrooms, a kitchen and a garden. The main school building has a playground and the school also uses excellent local play and sports facilities.

Beachborough

Westbury, Nr Brackley, Northants NN13 5LB
Tel: 01280 700071
Fax: 01280 704839
email: office@beachborough.com
website: www.beachborough.com

The School is administered as a non-profit-making Educational Trust by a Board of Governors.

Chairman of Governors: C Dudgeon, BA Oxon

Headmaster: J M Banks, BA, MEd Buckingham

Age Range. 2½–13.
Number of Children. Main School 200 (40% flexi boarding), Pre-Prep 100.
Fees per term (2016–2017). Prep School: Years 5–8 £5,358, Years 3–4 £4,914, Reception, Years 1 & 2 £3,412. Nursery £287 per session per term. Flexi boarding from £28 per night.

Beachborough is a friendly and energetic Independent Prep School ideally situated on the borders of Buckinghamshire, Oxfordshire and Northamptonshire. We provide an outstanding all-round education for around 300 boys and girls, a quarter of whom take advantage of our flexible boarding provision. We are large enough to have a diverse and lively community, yet small enough for each individual to be known and nurtured.

We believe that a good prep school education will give children opportunities that will equip them intellectually, physically, culturally and emotionally for the challenges of the twenty-first century. At whatever stage your child joins us, be it Early Years (pupils aged 2½ to 5), Pre-Prep (pupils aged 6 to 7) or Prep School (pupils aged 8 to 13) they will be warmly welcomed into the school. We are not obsessed with reflecting on past glories or the latest headline-grabbing news, but have an active desire to find each child's individual talent and help them surpass their personal best. Our parents use words such as inclusive, nurturing and rounded to define our school, so if you share in our belief that happy children thrive, please come and visit.

Charitable status. Beachborough is a Registered Charity, number 309910.

The Beacon

Chesham Bois, Amersham, Bucks HP6 5PF

Tel: 01494 433654
Fax: 01494 727849
email: office@beaconschool.co.uk
website: www.beaconschool.co.uk
Twitter: @Beacon_School
Facebook: /beaconschoolamersham

Chairman of the Governors: David M Hollander

Headmaster: **William T Phelps**, MA New York, BA, AKC

Age Range. 4–13.
Number of Boys. 525.
Fees per term (2016–2017). Upper School (Years 7 & 8) £5,400, Middle School (Years 5 & 6) £5,100–£5,360, Lower School (Years 3 & 4) £4,950, Years 1 & 2 £3,950, Reception £3,600.

The Beacon is an independent day school for boys aged 4 to 13 years. The Beacon prepares boys for secondary education through a curriculum that offers both richness and diversity of opportunity. From the earliest steps in initial learning, to independent success in competitive examinations; the priority is to ensure sound academic development, within a happy and stimulating environment.

The ethos of The Beacon is encapsulated in the words: *Traditional Values, Contemporary Education*. Over 500 boys are educated in extremely well-resourced buildings; a blend of old: 17th century farmstead and barns; and new: including a 250-seat theatre, a Design and Technology Suite, Food Technology room, Science suite, Drama Studio, Modern Languages Laboratory, Music Technology Suite, two Libraries, a large Sports Hall and an AstroTurf, set in attractive surroundings, with sixteen acres of playing fields.

There are three Reception classes with a maximum of 18 boys in each. Each class teacher has an assistant.

There is a second entry point in Year 3 at age 7 when boys join the Lower School. Class sizes are a maximum of 18. Boys study a broad range of subjects, including international studies from Year 2 to Year 5. They look at nine of the most spoken languages in the world examining their cultures, practices and languages, including Mandarin and Russian as well as Spanish and French.

The school's attitude to sport is all-inclusive and exemplifies teamwork, emphasising the school ethos that everybody matters. Boys regularly compete at County level in cricket, hockey, tennis, swimming and rugby. The Beacon have an excellent record of success in the many national and regional competitions.

The music department has twelve instrumental ensembles, five choirs, individual music scholarship mentoring, music technology work on Cubase and a 'Rock Band' Club. There are 24 visiting music teachers with over 300 weekly music lessons taking place. Beacon choirs compete and tour to countries around the world.

The third entry point is in Year 7 at age 11 where boys are prepared for the Beacon Certificate of Achievement, Common Entrance and Scholarship examinations to many leading independent senior schools. In Year 8 boys take on leadership roles and demonstrate greater responsibility and independence.

The School's examination record is excellent, both at 11+ into Buckinghamshire Grammar Schools and at 13+ to senior independent day and boarding schools, with a variety of academic, music, art and sports scholarships being won each year.

Charitable status. The Beacon Educational Trust Limited is a Registered Charity, number 309911. It exists to provide education for boys.

Beaudesert Park

Minchinhampton, Stroud, Gloucestershire GL6 9AF

Tel: 01453 832072
email: office@bps.school
website: www.beaudesert.gloucs.sch.uk

Chairman of Governors: M C S-R Pyper, OBE, BA

Headmaster: **J P R Womersley**, BA, PGCE

Age Range. 3–13.
Number of Pupils. Weekly and Flexi Boarders 149, Day Boys and Girls 150, Pre-Prep Department 130.
Fees per term (2016–2017). Nursery from £1,750 (5 mornings or 3 days); Reception £2,832; Years 1 & 2: £2,947; Year 3 £3,864; Year 4 £4,592; Years 5–8 £5,496. Boarders (Years 5–8) £7,142.

The School was founded in 1908 and became an educational trust in 1968.

Beaudesert Park is a preparatory school for boys and girls from 3–13. There is a strong academic tradition and all pupils are encouraged to work to the best of their ability. There is great emphasis on effort and all children are praised for their individual performance. Pupils are prepared for Common Entrance and Scholarship examinations. They are given individual attention in classes which are mostly setted not streamed. Over the last five years an average of 16 scholarships a year – academic, art, music, sport and technology – have been awarded to leading independent senior schools. The staff consists of 48 full time teaching staff and 18 music teachers, all of whom take a personal interest in the children's welfare.

Good manners and consideration for others are a priority. Beaudesert strives to create a happy and purposeful atmosphere, providing for the talents of each child in a wide range of activities – cultural, sporting and recreational. There are thriving drama, art, pottery and music departments. Sporting activities include cricket, football, rugby, hockey, netball, rounders, tennis, swimming, athletics, golf, badminton, fencing, dance, judo, riding and sailing. A wide number of societies and clubs meet each week.

The school is very well equipped with a brand new Performing Arts Centre and Library, indoor and outdoor swimming pools, sports hall, art studio and design technology department. There are also astroturf tennis courts and hard courts which are situated in beautiful wooded grounds. The school stands high up in the Cotswolds adjoining 500 acres of common land and golf course. Despite its rural location, the school is within half an hour of the M4 and M5 motorways and within easy reach of the surrounding towns of Gloucester, Cheltenham, Cirencester, Swindon, Bath and Bristol.

Charitable status. Beaudesert Park is a Registered Charity, number 311711. It exists to provide education for boys and girls in a caring atmosphere.

Bede's Preparatory School

Duke's Drive, Eastbourne, East Sussex BN20 7XL

Tel: 01323 734222
email: prep.school@bedes.org
website: www.bedes.org

Co-educational day and boarding school with Nursery and Pre-Prep departments.

Chairman of Governors: Anthony Meier, CB, OBE

Headmaster: **Giles Entwisle**, BA Hons

Deputy Head: Ben Purkiss, BSc Hons

Age Range. 3 months–13 years Co-educational.
Number of Pupils. 380: Prep 239 (160 boys, 79 girls), Pre-Prep 55, Nursery 86. Boarders: 20.
Fees per term (2016–2017). Boarding £2,550 (in addition to Tuition); Tuition: Prep £4,425–£5,485, Pre-Prep £3,225. Nursery Prices per session.

Bede's Prep School, founded in 1895, is situated in Eastbourne, on the South Coast with spectacular views of the sea. It takes a couple of minutes to reach the beach from the school and the principal playing fields are in a wide natural hollow nestling in the South Downs.

Boarders sleep in cosy bedrooms in a house that has a real family feel and are looked after by dedicated and caring staff. Both winter and summer weekends are filled with an exciting variety of activities and special celebrations take place on the children's birthdays.

Pupils are prepared for Common Entrance and the more able are tutored to sit scholarships to independent senior schools. Last year 95% of pupils chose to continue their education at Bede's Senior School (*see HMC section entry*).

Bede's offers academic, sport, music, dance, art and drama scholarships and bursaries for children from the ages of 7 to 12 years.

Pupils from the age of 4 are given Information Technology lessons at least once a week in a Computer Centre which is constantly updated to keep at the forefront of educational technology. French and Music, Short Tennis and other Sports are also introduced to children in this age group.

New science laboratories and classrooms were opened five years ago. In September 2009 a beautiful new building overlooking the sea and housing new kitchens and dining room and eight new classrooms opened.

In January 2016, a newly expanded nursery facility opened with a state-of-the-art baby unit for babies from 3 months upwards and expanded provision for toddlers. This was followed by the launch of the school's Pre School Scheme with two classrooms, a messy activity area and free flow access to a new outside play area.

The Art and Design and Technology Departments are both very strong, opening for after-school activities to encourage young talent. Music also plays an important role at Bede's. There is a thriving orchestra and the majority of pupils learn one or more instruments, with children as young as six playing in recorder groups. Informal concerts take place during the school year and there are also several choirs.

Drama forms an integral part of the school. The Pre-Prep produces a Christmas play and there are frequent productions throughout the year for older children to take part in.

Sport at Bede's is taken seriously. Boys play soccer, rugby, hockey, cricket, tennis and athletics and the major sports for girls are netball, hockey, rounders, athletics, cricket and tennis. All the pupils use the indoor 20-metre swimming pool. The fixture list is very comprehensive and, whilst the top teams enjoy a high standard of coaching and performance, special emphasis is placed on ensuring that the other teams also have the opportunity to play matches against other schools. The Sports Hall covers two indoor tennis courts and is used to house a huge variety of sports. Wet weather activities include badminton, basketball, climbing and table tennis. Children also regularly use facilities at the Senior School nearby.

There is a Learning Enhancement department staffed by qualified learning support staff which can cater for pupils who require additional or particular support. The school also has an EAL centre which is run by highly trained and experienced staff. Gifted children are placed on a Curriculum Enhancement Programme to maximise their potential.

The School operates a comprehensive programme of activities after lessons which children are encouraged to participate in ranging from fencing to cookery and basketball to art masterclasses.

The school runs a comprehensive coach and minibus service locally and transport to and from Gatwick and Heathrow airports is arranged by the transport department.

Entry to Bede's Prep School is by interview.

Charitable status. St Bede's School Trust Sussex is a Registered Charity, number 278950. It exists to provide education for boys and girls.

Bedford Girls' School Junior School

Cardington Road, Bedford, Bedfordshire MK42 0BX

Tel: 01234 361918
email: admissions@bedfordgirlsschool.co.uk
website: www.bedfordgirlsschool.co.uk
Twitter: @BedfordGirlsSch
Facebook: @BedfordGirlsSch

Foundation – The Harpur Trust.

"Let me keep an open mind so I understand as much as I can in my lifetime and not reach the limits of my imagination."

Chair of Governors: Ms T Beddoes

Head of Bedford Girls' School: Miss J MacKenzie

Head of Bedford Girls' School Junior School: **Mrs C Howe**

Age Range. 7–11.
Number of Pupils. 230 Girls.
Fees per term (2016–2017). £3,012.
Bedford Girls' School is a dynamic, forward thinking selective independent day school for girls aged 7–18. As an exceptional school, we value creativity and innovation

highly. It is our belief that learning should be exciting and lifelong, so that girls flourish academically, personally, emotionally and morally fulfilled individuals capable of achieving their full potential in every aspect and at every stage of their lives.

This journey begins in the Junior School where our expert teachers recognise and ignite the curiosity of each individual girl, harnessing her natural curiosity and fuelling her confidence to develop her own thoughts, opinions and talents. In consequence, pupils not only excel academically but also as well-rounded, insightful, caring girls with a joy and passion for life and learning.

The atmosphere of our school is unique and exciting. Classrooms fizz with energy and enthusiasm and each day brings forth new discoveries and achievements. We would be delighted to welcome you to visit, either for one of our Open House events or a private tour, to experience at first hand a true flavour of life at Bedford Girls' School Junior School. Please visit www.bedfordgirlsschool.co.uk for further information or call our Admissions Team on: 01234 361918.

Admissions. Entry to the Junior School is on the basis of informal assessment and written tests in Mathematics, Reading and Writing.

Charitable status. Bedford Girls' School is part of the Harpur Trust which is a Registered Charity, number 1066861.

Bedford Modern Junior School

Manton Lane, Bedford, Bedfordshire MK41 7NT

Tel: 01234 332513
email: info@bedmod.co.uk
website: www.bedmod.co.uk
Twitter: @BedfordModern
Facebook: @BedfordModernSchool

Chairman of the School Committee: I McEwen, BPhil, MA, DPhil

Head of Junior School: **Mrs J C Rex**, BA Hons, PGCE

Age Range. 7–11 Co-educational.
Number of Pupils. 258 (M: 55%; F: 45%).
Fees per term (2016–2017). £3,091.

The Junior School is housed in its own separate buildings adjacent to the Senior School. Facilities include specialist rooms for Art and Science, ICT, Design Technology and a newly refurbished Library, with designated Year 3 classrooms and play area and a superb state-of-the-art School Hall.

The whole site overlooks the School playing fields and the Junior School has extensive views over the Ouse Valley. Many of the Senior School facilities are available to the Junior School, including full use of the playing fields, Sports Hall, Gymnasium, covered and heated Swimming Pool and all-weather pitches. The Howard Hall provides facilities for full-scale drama productions and use is made of the Music School.

There is a strong musical, dramatic and sporting tradition.

Students are admitted to the Junior School at ages 7, 8, 9 and 10, after taking tests, some of them on computer, in January each year in English, Maths and non-verbal reasoning. Students proceed to the Senior School at 11, unless special circumstances prevent this.

(*See Bedford Modern School entry in HMC section.*)

Charitable status. Bedford Modern School is part of the Harpur Trust which is a Registered Charity, number 1066861. It includes in its aims the provision of high quality education for boys and girls.

Bedford Preparatory School

De Parys Avenue, Bedford MK40 2TU

Tel: 01234 362216
email: prepadmissions@bedfordschool.org.uk
website: www.bedfordschool.org.uk
Twitter: @bedfordschool
Facebook: @Bedford-School

Chairman of Governors: Professor Stephen Mayson, LLB, LLM, PhD, Barrister, FRSA

Headmaster: **Mr Ian Silk**

Deputy Head (Academic): Mr Jonathan Egan

Age Range. 7–13.
Number of Boys. Day Boys 363, Boarders 20, Weekly Boarders 2.
Fees per term (2016–2017). Day £3,894–£5,102, Full Boarding £6,930–£8,230, Weekly Boarding £6,605–£7,905.

Bedford Prep School is a thriving and vibrant independent day and boarding school for boys aged 7–13.

We believe that boys learn best when they're happy, confident, and their curiosity is stimulated, so we feel it's paramount that learning is fun, creative, inspirational and active. We also recognise boys learn differently from girls and this informs our teaching.

Whether it's music and the arts, science and technology, language and literature, or sports and games, boys are encouraged to learn new skills and embrace new experiences.

Visit our classes and you'll find boys thoroughly engaged in their learning, inspired by challenge, competition, high expectations and risk within a safe environment. Our expectations are high, but achievable, and our curriculum encompasses and transcends the National Curriculum, uniting traditional practice with innovative teaching and the best of the creative and academic.

Our extensive campus offers boys outstanding academic, sporting, music, drama and art facilities. We share the swimming pool, recreation centre, playing fields, astro and tennis courts with the Upper School and make use of the school's fantastic theatre and other specialist facilities.

Working with each and every boy, we help them to develop their sporting talents. We provide expert coaching in a wide variety of sports, including rugby, hockey, cricket, golf, skiing, horse riding, cross country, swimming, badminton and rowing.

Creative arts are a big part of school life, with boys taking part in concerts, exhibitions and performances throughout the year. In our dedicated music building, with a state-of-the-art music technology suite and well-equipped practice rooms, many of our boys learn to play one or more instruments.

Boys can also get involved in a broad range of extracurricular activities: from cookery to steel band, chess to canoe building – there is something for every boy.

A full range of wrap-around care options is available to working parents. Boys can stay at school, free of charge, until 5.45 pm in our Late Room or join one of our before and after school 'Day Plus' sessions.

Eagle House, our purpose-built junior boarding house, is a real home from home for our boarders, who flourish in its warm, family atmosphere. Full, weekly, flexi and occasional boarding are available, enabling boys and their parents to find an option that is just right.

Admissions. Entrance assessments for the Prep School are held during the Spring Term and all boys are assessed in

English, Maths and underlying ability. We will also request a report from your son's current school.

We recommend that families come and visit us to see the school in action, and meet the boys and staff. Please call admissions on 01234 362216 or email: prepadmissions@ bedfordschool.org.uk to arrange a visit or request a prospectus.

Charitable status. Bedford Preparatory School is part of the Harpur Trust, which is a Registered Charity, number 1066861.

Beechwood Park

Markyate, St Albans, Hertfordshire AL3 8AW
Tel: 01582 840333
Fax: 01582 842372
email: admissions@beechwoodpark.com
website: www.beechwoodpark.com
Twitter: @BWPSchool
Facebook: /BWPSchool

Chairman of Governors: Mr G Freer

Headmaster: **Mr Edward Balfour**, BA Hons, PGCE

Age Range. 3–13.

Number of Pupils. 524: 55 boarders (aged 9–13), 245 day boys and 179 day girls (aged 4–13). In addition there are 45 pre-school children at the Woodlands Nursery which is housed in new purpose-built premises on the main school site.

Fees per term (2016–2017). Day pupils: Senior £5,075, Middle £4,105, Junior £4,000, Reception £3,385. Boarders (up to 4 nights per week in addition to day fees) £1,206. No compulsory extras. Fees are inclusive of lunches, most trips and visits.

Beechwood Park occupies a large mansion, with a fine Regency Library and Great Hall, in 37 acres of surrounding grounds, which provide ample space for the Forest School. Modernisation has added Science laboratories, computer suites, Design Technology workshop, gymnasium and sports facilities, including a large sports hall and two squash courts, hard tennis courts, an all-weather pitch and two heated indoor swimming pools. Boarding House with modern facilities and spacious common rooms. Two purpose-built classroom blocks house the Middle and Junior Departments. The Music Department has a song room, 14 practice rooms and a Music Technology Suite. A large Performance Hall provides space for assemblies and the many music and drama productions.

Day pupils use private buses serving Harpenden, St Albans, Dunstable and the surrounding villages. Many subsequently convert to boarding under the care of the Houseparents, Mr and Mrs R Humphreys.

Class size is around 20 (15 in Reception); major subjects are setted from Year 5 onwards. There is a resident Chaplain. The Director of Music has a staff of visiting instrumentalists in a flourishing Music Department.

The number of scholarships gained each year and Common Entrance results affirm a high standard of work, against a background of wide ranging extracurricular activities.

Football, Rugby, Cricket, Rounders, Netball, Hockey, Swimming, Athletics and a Sport for All programme, which includes an unusually wide range of minor sports, are all coached by well-qualified PE Staff.

Charitable status. Beechwood Park School is a Registered Charity, number 311068. It exists to provide education for boys and girls from 3–13.

Beeston Hall School

West Runton, Cromer, Norfolk NR27 9NQ
Tel: 01263 837324
Fax: 01263 838177
email: office@beestonhall.co.uk
website: www.beestonhall.co.uk

Chairman of Governors: T E Leicester

Headmaster: **W F de Falbe**, BA Hons, PGCE

Business Manager: Mrs S Lubbock

Age Range. Co-educational 7–13 years.

Number of Pupils. 124: 65 Boarding, 59 Day Pupils. 66 Boys, 58 Girls.

Fees per term (2016–2017). Boarding: £6,250 (Year 3), £7,700 (Years 4–8); Day Pupils: £2,500 (Pre-Prep), £3,890 (Year 3), £5,650 (Years 4–8).

Beeston Hall was established in 1948 in a Regency house set in 30 acres in North Norfolk, close to the sea and surrounded by 700 acres of National Trust land. Beeston's reputation for being a happy, caring family school is in no small part due to the real sense of community which pervades throughout. The strength of the Pastoral Care system ensures that every child is closely watched over and cared for. Beeston is a Boarding and Day School offering Full, Weekly and Flexi boarding; most of the children experience boarding before they leave, the majority moving on to boarding schools such as Ampleforth, Eton, Gresham's, Harrow, Oakham, Oundle, Queen Margaret's York, Radley, Repton, Rugby, Stowe, Tudor Hall and Uppingham. In addition to the usual examinable subjects, Art, Music, DT, Computing and Theatre Studies are all timetabled, providing the children with a wide curriculum and the opportunity to find an activity in which they can excel. The school enjoys great success at scholarship level, with over 50 scholarships won in the last 5 years. Extra help is given on a one-to-one basis in English, Mathematics and French; a dedicated, professionally run Learning Support department emphasises the importance of the learning support work being carried into the classroom. There is a positive emphasis on values such as courtesy, kindness, hard work and awareness of others, and at every stage of their education the children are encouraged to maximise their potential and think and act for themselves. Drama and Music are considered important for every child: each takes part in at least one play production each year. Three choirs and ten different music groups meet every week and over 90% of the school learn a musical instrument. The school is equally proud of its record on the sports field where all children are coached regardless of ability by a dedicated team of staff, and where all are, at some stage, given the opportunity to represent the school. In addition to the usual major sports, others offered include Cross Country, Athletics, Swimming, Tennis and Shooting, whilst a comprehensive activities programme provides opportunities to suit all tastes: Modern Martial Arts, Fencing, Sailing, Golf, Chess and Cooking, to name but a few.

The 2010 ISI Inspection Report comments on: "*the rich educational experience provided ... the excellent pastoral care and support ... the excellent relationships between staff and pupils ... and the overall excellent curricular and co-curricular provision.*"

Religious denomination: Mainly Church of England; 15% Roman Catholic.

Charitable status. Beeston Hall School Trust Limited is a Registered Charity, number 311274. It exists to provide preparatory education for boarding and day boys and girls.

Belhaven Hill

Belhaven Road, Dunbar, East Lothian EH42 1NN

Tel:	01368 862785
Fax:	01368 865225
email:	secretary@belhavenhill.com
website:	www.belhavenhill.com
Facebook:	/BelhavenHill

Chairman of Governors: Angus Macpherson

Headmaster: Henry Knight, BA, PGCE, MEd

Age Range. 7–13 Co-educational.
Number of Pupils. 65 boys, 59 girls. Boarders 72, Day 52.
Fees per term (2016–2017). Boarding £7,359. Day: £5,150 (Form 6: £3,580).
Religion. Non-denominational.

Overlooking the sea in an idyllic East Lothian parkland setting, Belhaven is an independent boarding and day school for boys and girls from 7 to 13 years. Since its establishment in 1923, the school has focused on developing well-rounded, happy, confident children through a strong academic curriculum, lots of sport and a broad extracurricular programme. Ideally placed just off the A1, it is close to both a mainline London-Edinburgh railway station and less than an hour to Edinburgh airport.

A full boarding and day school, Belhaven Hill has a long tradition of providing a first class all-round education before sending its pupils far and wide to all the leading public schools in both England and Scotland. These include Ampleforth, Downe House, Eton, Fettes, Glenalmond, Harrow, Loretto, Merchiston, Oundle, Queen Margaret's York, Radley, Rugby, Shrewsbury, Stowe and Uppingham. Committed and enthusiastic members of staff work with small classes of between 10–16 pupils. There is ample opportunity for scholarship and extended work, resulting in an excellent number of awards being gained every year. A strong learning support department with four dedicated, trained staff provides one-to-one and small group tuition.

Belhaven Hill pupils are renowned for being happy children and this is in no small part due to the excellent pastoral care provided. The majority of staff live on site and the policy of the governors has been to keep the school comparatively small in order to retain a family atmosphere. The boys are housed in the original main building and the girls in a separate, purpose-built house. The pastoral system revolves around the six patrols, with each pupil being looked after by their form teacher in the junior years and a personal tutor, higher up the school. Six matrons take care of the children's health. The Headmaster's Wife is in overall charge of the pastoral care.

The school has an excellent reputation for sport with rugby, netball, hockey, cricket, rounders, tennis and athletics, making up the main part of the sporting programme. Swimming takes place all year round either in the school's heated outdoor pool or at a local indoor pool. In addition many opportunities abound for a wide variety of other recreational activities: skiing, surfing, horse riding, fencing, golf on the adjacent links course and gardening for those who want to grow their own produce in the school's walled garden. An extensive Activity Programme offers something for everyone to discover and enjoy such as bridge, debating, 'mastermind', fly-tying, model-making, computer programming, cookery, crafts, chess, Mandarin, fencing, modern dance and reeling to name but a few.

Music and Drama flourish at Belhaven and every child has ample opportunity to perform in regular concerts and productions throughout the year. A state-of-the-art music building houses a vibrant department which caters for a wide range of instrumental ensembles and choirs. Over 90% of the children play one or more instruments, with specialist tuition provided by a team of peripatetic music staff.

The school is well resourced with purpose-built facilities, including an outdoor heated swimming pool, floodlit all-weather pitch, playing fields, sports hall, specialist music and art schools, attractive teaching rooms, two ICT suites and a new library.

Belhaven begins with the belief that every child is an individual who has a talent and that it is their mission to foster both their individuality and abilities. To achieve these aims it places the child at the core of everything it does. By providing an environment that promotes enjoyment, exploration and nurturing of curiosity, each child grows to understand that they too are responsible for their learning, alongside staff and parents. As a result they grow to value and respect those around them, delighting in the achievements of others as well as their own. Qualities such as courtesy, tolerance, honesty and perseverance are all encouraged and celebrated, with the children understanding that it is better to have had a go and fail, than never to have tried at all. Whether they are day pupils or boarders, all our children benefit from a boarding school ethos of community and friendship, where challenges are plenty, but where a sense of fun and enjoyment pervades all school life.

The school now welcomes a seven year-old entry and has introduced an outdoor education element into its junior curriculum where children can learn more about their environment through practical, hands-on learning experiences.

Means-tested bursary support is available. Fee concessions are available for children of members of the armed forces. For a prospectus and more information please see our website www.belhavenhill.com or contact Tessa Coleman at secretary@belhavenhill.com.

Charitable status. Belhaven Hill School Trust Ltd is a Registered Charity, number SC007118. Its aim is to educate children in the full sense of the word.

Belmont
Mill Hill Preparatory School

The Ridgeway, Mill Hill, London NW7 4ED

Tel:	020 8906 7270
Fax:	020 8906 3519
email:	office@belmontschool.com
website:	www.belmontschool.com

Chairman of the Court of Governors: Dr R G Chapman, BSc, MB BS, FRCGP

Head: Mr Leon Roberts, MA, PGCE

Senior Deputy Head (Pastoral): Mr P Symes, BSc, PGCE
Deputy Head (Academic): Mrs R Alford, BEd
Deputy Head (Operations): Mr J Fleet, BSc, PGSE
Head of Lower School: Mrs R Sutherns, MA, SESI
Assistant Head (Teaching & Learning): Miss J Harrison, BSc, PGCE
Head of Upper School: Mr J Pym, MA, PGCE
Assistant Head (Marketing, Communications and Admissions): Mr J Pym, MEd, PGCE

Age Range. 7–13.
Number of Pupils. Day: 264 Boys, 230 Girls.
Fees per term (2016–2017). £5,605 including lunch.

Belmont Mill Hill Prep is situated in the Green Belt on the borders of Hertfordshire and Middlesex, yet is only ten miles from central London. It stands in about 35 acres of its own woods and grounds and enjoys the advantages of a truly rural environment, but at the same time the capital's cultural facilities are easily accessible.

Belmont is part of the Mill Hill School Foundation; the Pre-Prep Grimsdell and Mill Hill School are situated less than a quarter of a mile away. Opened in 1912, Belmont takes its name from the original mansion built on the Ridgeway about the middle of the eighteenth century. Successive alterations and additions have provided a chapel, a gymnasium, music-rooms, science laboratories and a fully resourced ICT room, ample games fields, five all-weather cricket nets, two all-weather cricket pitches, and six hard tennis courts. A major building and refurbishment programme has recently been undertaken and provides a large new multi-purpose hall, junior classroom block, extra science labs, a new resources centre, design technology room, additional music teaching space and catering facilities.

Use is made of the Fives courts and the indoor heated swimming pool at Mill Hill School.

The School became co-educational in 1995 and 47% of the pupils are girls.

The usual age of entry is at 7 or 11 years, but 8, 9 and 10-year-olds are considered as vacancies occur. It is expected that most children will pass to Mill Hill at the end of Year 8, but some may be prepared for entry to other senior schools.

There is a permanent teaching staff of 55, with 20 visiting teachers for Instrumental Music, supportive English and Mathematics, Ballet and Fencing. There is a full-time Matron and a visiting counsellor while the school's catering is all in-house.

The main games are Rugby, Soccer, Cricket, Hockey, Netball and Rounders, but minor sports also flourish, as do instrumental and choral music, drama, and many out-of-school activities. There are French exchanges with Belmont's 'twin' school in Rouen, and all the children take part in the Summer Activities Programme, which includes for senior children a Geography field trip and an outward bound week.

Charitable status. The Mill Hill School Foundation is a Registered Charity, number 1064758. It exists to provide education for boys and girls.

Belmont Grosvenor School

Swarcliffe Hall, Birstwith, Harrogate, North Yorkshire HG3 2JG

Tel:	01423 771029
Fax:	01423 772600
email:	admin@belmontgrosvenor.co.uk
website:	www.belmontgrosvenor.co.uk
Twitter:	@BelmontGrosveno
Facebook:	/BelmontGrosvenor

Chair of Governors: Mrs Frances Trowell

Head: **Mrs Jane Merriman**, BEd, MA, NPQH

Age Range. 3 months–11 years Co-educational.
Number of Pupils. 175.
Fees per term (2016–2017). Prep £3,322 Pre-Prep £2,808, Pre-Reception £323–£2,808. Nursery: Under 2s £28.50–£56.50 per session; Over 2s £26.50–£49.50 per session.

Belmont Grosvenor School is a magical place – a caring, friendly school where every child is nurtured and made to feel special.

Along with its Magic Tree Nursery, Belmont Grosvenor caters for boys and girls from three months to 11 years and is set in 20 acres of beautiful countryside just three miles from the centre of Harrogate, North Yorkshire.

One of our greatest strengths is the continuity of education we offer. We provide a rich, diverse, happy, and supportive learning environment, fostering each child's intellectual, creative, sporting, and personal development.

We encourage our children to enjoy and respect learning, to develop as effective communicators and as independent, critical thinkers and decision-makers, accept challenges, and appreciate and respect differences.

Each child at Belmont Grosvenor is valued both as an individual and as a member of the school community, and we offer them a range of educational opportunities to fulfil their ambitions and potential.

It is our goal that Belmont Grosvenor School children learn to live as informed, concerned and responsible members of society.

Our 20 acres of grounds ensure our children learn both inside and outside the classroom – our Forest Schools area is well used with weekly lessons on the timetable for Nursery youngsters to Year 2 and we are a member of the National Eco Schools programme and the recipient of a prestigious Green Flag for our environmental work.

Belmont School

Feldemore, Holmbury St Mary, Dorking, Surrey RH5 6LQ

Tel:	01306 730852
Fax:	01306 731220
email:	admissions@belmont-school.org
website:	www.belmont-school.org
Twitter:	@BelmontPrep
Facebook:	/BelmontPreparatorySchool

Chairman of the Governors: Mr N Butcher

Headmistress: **Mrs H Skrine**, BA Hons Exeter, PGCE London, NPQH, FRSA

Age Range. 2–13.
Number of Pupils. 229 Boys and Girls: Day, Weekly and Flexible Boarding.
Fees per term (2016–2017). Day Pupils: Kindergarten, Transition & Pre-Reception (per morning/afternoon) £287, Reception £2,870, Years 1–2 £3,310, Years 3–4 £4,730, Years 5–8 £4,780 per term. Boarding: £500 (1 night per week), £1,000 (2 nights per week), £1,460 (3 nights per week), £1,895 (4 nights per week, Monday to Thursday), £2,105 (5 nights per week, Sunday to Thursday).

Founded in London in 1880, the School is now established in 65 acres of wooded parkland overlooking the picturesque village of Holmbury St Mary, between Guildford and Dorking. The main house, Feldemore, was completely refurbished in the early 1990s so that the school now boasts an historic building with a purpose-built interior. Outstanding facilities include a brand new Early Years building, impressive sports hall, a well-equipped theatre, two state-of-the-art computer suites, newly-refurbished Science lab and woodland adventure courses. These, together with our friendly, talented staff and confident, happy boys and girls, make Belmont the very best choice you could make for your child.

We offer co-educational day education for boys and girls aged 2 to 13, and optional weekly boarding or flexible boarding arrangements. We prepare children for Common Entrance and Scholarship examinations to a wide range of schools, and will assist children in preparing for other Senior Schools that have their own admissions procedures.

Here, every child matters and we look to develop children as individuals, seeking to inspire and to unfurl the hidden strengths of every boy or girl. There is a happy, industrious atmosphere and high expectations pervade throughout all aspects of school life. In addition, we have a challenging curriculum and an extensive array of extracurricular opportunities which together are designed to captivate the imagination. Creativity is a particular strength of the school. The teaching staff is well qualified and healthy pupil: staff ratios have enabled us to develop a flexible setting system within a relatively small school.

The curriculum covers all the required Common Entrance subjects plus Drama, Art, DT, IT, Music, PSHCE, PE and Games. Sports include Netball, Rugby, Football, Cross-Country, Hockey, Tennis, Swimming, Cricket, Athletics and Rounders.

Children in Year 1 and above attend for a half day or full day visit prior to entry. Further details can be obtained from the Registrar, Mrs Nikola Meaney.

Charitable status. Belmont School (Feldemore) Educational Trust Limited is a Registered Charity, number 312077.

Berkhampstead School, Cheltenham

Pittville Circus Road, Cheltenham, Glos GL52 2QA

Tel: 01242 523263
email: office@berkhampsteadschool.co.uk
website: www.berkhampsteadschool.co.uk

Chairman of Governors: Mrs J Kent

Headmaster: **R P Cross**, BSc Hons, PGCE

Age Range. 3 months–11 years co-educational.
Number of Pupils. 250 day pupils plus 60 in Day Nursery.
Fees per term (2016–2017). Kindergarten: £1,233 (5 mornings), £2,267 (5 full days); Pre-Prep: £2,170 (Reception), £2,300 (Year 1), £2,475 (Year 2); Prep: £2,685 (Year 3), £2,895 (Year 4), £3,060 (Years 5), £3,205 (Year 6). Lunches: £212.

Children are capable of remarkable things and achieve these at Berkhampstead, Cheltenham.

Enthusiastic and imaginative teaching of small classes allows our pupils to gain skills and confidence – they emerge with the characteristic 'can-do' attitude of the Berkhampstead pupil. Our outstanding record of Independent School Scholarships and Grammar School places speaks for itself – it is second to none. Berkhampstead equips children to thrive at their chosen next school.

Our academic record is impressive – children have huge opportunities to achieve – but there is much more than this to Berkhampstead. From the very youngest age, children are engaged in a happy and positive environment, surrounded by supportive adults and they embrace all that's on offer. Specialist staff in French, Music and PE enrich the Early Years curriculum; specialists teach throughout Prep. Creative teaching is the norm and it inspires – our superb staff write and produce musicals and plays, devise experiments and plan experiences to make lessons memorable and fun.

Our bright Day Nursery is a place of play and creativity for the very smallest – from 3 months – a fun-filled preparation for more formal learning to come. Moving on, the qualified teachers in our School Nursery support and stretch, stimulate and inspire. Their collaborative approach pays dividends and the children are really involved in their learning.

Berkhampstead's non-pressurised yet purposeful environment allows children to flourish academically. Art and Drama are impressive. Pupils excel in music – most play an instrument, from the popular double bass to the trombone – regular Recitals, Concerts and ensemble groups give all the opportunity to perform.

Sport is excellent, with specialist coaching from the earliest age. Every child will represent the school in competitive fixtures, children play sportingly and the Berkhampstead team spirit often shines through to give victory against larger opponents.

Berkhampstead is a purposeful place crammed with opportunities where each pupil's talents are celebrated. Our outstanding Pastoral Care and respectful staff/pupil relationships ensure that we have happy children – a real priority. Our talented staff, with many male teachers, help the individual to move on to senior school; secure, confident and having achieved remarkable things.

Small classes. Happy children. Excellent results.

Berkhamsted Pre-Preparatory School

Chesham Road, Berkhamsted, Herts HP4 2SZ

Tel: 01442 358188
            01442 358276 (Berkhamsted Day Nursery)
email: preprepoffice@berkhamstedschool.org
website: www.berkhamstedschool.org
            www.berkhamsteddaynursery.org
Twitter: @BerkoPrePrep
Facebook: /berkhamstedschool

Chairman of Governors: Mr G C Laws

Principal: Mr Richard Backhouse, MA Cantab

Head: **Ms Karen O'Connor**, BA, PGCE, NPQH

Age Range. 3–7 years Co-educational. Day Nursery: 5 months–3 years.
Number in School. 114 Boys, 106 Girls.
Fees per term (2016–2017). £3,355–£3,455 (including lunch).

Berkhamsted School's Pre-Preparatory School caters for children from the ages of three to seven. The School is set in a tastefully converted Georgian coach house and stables in eight acres of grass and woodland, conveniently located on the Herts-Bucks border, 10 kms from the M25 and M1 motorways, at the Chesham exit of the A41. It has a walled garden, a woodland trail, an outdoor classroom and a large Sports Hall. The site provides a beautiful, safe environment – the ideal place for children to start their educational journey.

Berkhamsted Pre-Prep is a caring, vibrant community. It endeavours to create an extended family atmosphere where happy children enjoy learning and each child is encouraged to reach his or her full potential. The school offers a broad-based, stimulating education, including Spanish and French, Music, Drama, Dance, Sport, Sciences and Art. Children progress to the next stage of their education and into the world beyond, making the most of their strengths and achieving at the highest possible levels across the curriculum. Because of our small numbers, adults have time to listen and appreciate each child as a unique person. The children learn to communicate confidently with people of all ages.

There is a wide variety of after-school clubs and children participate in outings and trips. Before- and after-school clubs provide wrap-around care from 7.30 am to 6.30 pm, with homework supervision where required. Mini BASE-CAMP, our holiday activities camp at the school designed for 3–5 year olds, is also available every holiday from 7.30 am to 6.30 pm.

Berkhamsted Day Nursery (0–3+ years) is open 50 weeks per year from 7.30 am to 6.30 pm, and is situated on the school site. Children can join Berkhamsted Day Nursery from five months of age and can move on to Berkhamsted Pre-Prep, which is just next door. Berkhamsted Day Nursery caters for children up to the September that they begin in the Nursery class at Berkhamsted Pre-Prep (when they can use the school's out-of-hours clubs).

In June 2016, the Independent Schools Inspectorate found the quality and standards of the early years provision at Berkhamsted Day Nursery and Berkhamsted Pre-Prep to be '*outstanding*' across all five key areas. The ISI also concluded that "*All children make excellent, continuous progress in relation to their individual starting points and capabilities due to the nurturing and supportive environment that recognises each child as an individual*".

Berkhamsted Preparatory School

Doctors Commons Road, Berkhamsted, Hertfordshire HP4 3DW

Tel: 01442 358201/2
Fax: 01442 358203
email: prepadmin@berkhamstedschool.org
website: www.berkhamstedschool.org
Twitter: @berkhamstedprep
Facebook: /berkhamstedschool

Chairman of Governors: Mr G C Laws

Principal: Mr R P Backhouse, MA Cantab

Head: Mr J Hornshaw, BEd, MEd, NPQH

Deputy Head: Mr P D Whitby, BA, MA

Age Range. 7–11.
Number of Pupils. 161 boys, 172 girls.
Fees per term (2016–2017). £4,470–£4,755.

Berkhamsted Preparatory School is part of Berkhamsted School, a school with a 'Diamond' structure that combines single-sex and co-educational teaching. Boys and girls are taught together at the Pre-Preparatory (Haresfoot site) from age 3 to 7, and at the Preparatory (Doctors Commons Road site) from age 7 to 11. They are then taught separately from age 11 to 16 (Berkhamsted Boys and Berkhamsted Girls), before coming back together again in a joint Sixth Form.

Berkhamsted Preparatory School offers first-class facilities for the 7 to 11 age group, in conjunction with the highest standards of teaching and educational development. All classes offer a happy, caring environment where children are encouraged to investigate and explore the world around them. Classes at all levels have access to computers. Key features include a multi-purpose hall, modern dining facilities and a full range of specialist classrooms (e.g. Science laboratory, a DT and an ICT suite with mobile device accessibility for all year groups, Drama Studio, new Food Technology and Art classrooms). Within the last two years, the school has also added a netball court, fives courts and an outdoor learning area. The Preparatory School also has use of Senior School facilities including extensive playing fields, tennis and netball courts, a Sports Centre, a swimming pool and a 500-seat theatre.

All children are encouraged to develop to their full potential and grow in confidence and independence. The School's general approach is progressive, while retaining traditional values and standards; courtesy and politeness towards others are expected at all times. Academic achievement is of great importance, but the emphasis on other activities such as sports and music ensures that pupils receive a well-rounded education.

The most recent ISI Inspection Report (November 2012) noted that the school offers a high quality educational experience to its pupils, whose achievement was excellent because of their highly positive attitude to learning. Personal development of pupils was also found to be excellent, exemplified in the pupils' high levels of interpersonal skills, confidence and self-esteem. It was also reported that the pupils feel happy, secure and well cared for due to the school's exemplary pastoral care.

A wide range of voluntary extracurricular activities is offered at lunch-time, the end of the school day, including art, drama, music and sport. Choirs and orchestras perform in concerts and services throughout the year and school teams compete successfully in a variety of sports.

Berkhamsted Schools Group is committed to supporting working parents and offers wrap-around care from 7.30 am to 6.30 pm each day. In addition, the school operates a holiday care facility, BASECAMP, which offers a variety of courses from multi-activity to specialist sports and cookery each holiday with extended care available from 7.30 am and to 6.30 pm each day.

Charitable status. Berkhamsted Schools Group is a Registered Charity, number 310630. It is a leading Charitable School in the field of Junior and Secondary Education.

Bickley Park School

24 Page Heath Lane, Bickley, Bromley, Kent BR1 2DS

Tel: 020 8467 2195
Fax: 020 8325 5511
email: info@bickleyparkschool.co.uk
website: www.bickleyparkschool.co.uk
Twitter: @bickleyparksch
Facebook: @bickleyparksch

Chairman of Governors: Mr M Hansra

Headmaster: **P Wenham**, MA Cantab, PGCE

Age Range. Boys 2½–13, Girls 2½–4.
Number of Pupils. 320 Boys, 20 Girls.
Fees per term (2016–2017). From £2,000 (Nursery) to £4,765 (Boys in Years 7 & 8). There are no compulsory extras.

Bickley Park School, founded in 1918, occupies two sites in Bickley, the Prep Department at 24 Page Heath Lane and the Pre-Prep Department at 14 Page Heath Lane. The school has excellent modern facilities to complement the original Victorian buildings. Both sites are extremely attractive and the school's sports field is on the opposite side of the road.

The EYFS Department (recently rated as outstanding) provides a very caring and stimulating environment for children to start their school lives. At Key Stage 1, the children are cared for by a class teacher with the addition of specialist teaching for Music and Games. Classes are kept small with none exceeding 18 in total.

In the Prep Department, the children are introduced to more specialist teaching and setting for Mathematics, English, Science and French is introduced. The curriculum is broad with the emphasis being placed on encouraging the children to develop their potential to the full in a very caring environment. There is a wide range of extracurricular activities and a full sports programme. The major sports played are football, rugby and cricket, whilst athletics and tennis are also offered.

The majority of children leave at 13+ through the Common Entrance or Scholarship examinations whilst a small number leave at 11 to join local Grammar Schools.

The Parents Association, run by parents and staff, arrange events, both social and fundraising, during the year.

Visitors are made very welcome.

Charitable status. Bickley Park School Limited is a Registered Charity, number 307915. It exists to provide a broad curriculum for boys aged 2½–13 and girls aged 2½–4.

Bilton Grange

Dunchurch, Rugby, Warwickshire CV22 6QU

Tel:	01788 810217
Fax:	01788 816922
email:	admissions@biltongrange.co.uk
website:	www.biltongrange.co.uk
Twitter:	@biltongrange
Facebook:	/biltongrangeschool

The school is registered as an Educational Trust under the Charities Act and is controlled by a Board of Governors.

Chairman of Governors: Charles Barwell OBE

Headmaster: Alex Osiatynski, MA Oxon, PGCE

Deputy Headmaster: Paul Nicholson, BA Hons, PGCE
Bursar: Laura Howard, ACA
Assistant Head Pastoral: Sue Warner, BA Hons
Assistant Head Academic: Greg Das Gupta, BSc, BCom, PGCE
Head of Pre Prep: Adrian Brindley, BSc, MA, PGCE
Registrar: Liz Graham, BSc Hons
International Admissions Registrar: Caroline Morgan, MA Oxon

Age Range. 4–13.

Number of Pupils. 295 boys and girls of whom 93 are full, weekly, or flexi boarders. Preparatory (8–13 year olds): 193 pupils; Pre-Preparatory (4–8 year olds): 102 pupils.

Bilton Grange School was established in 1887 and is one of the foremost co-educational prep schools in the country. Set in 90 acres of heritage parkland, woods and sports fields, dominated by a 19th Century Pugin mansion, the school prides itself on bringing out the very best in every child. Children are extremely happy, and in a nurturing, inspiring and caring environment, confidently find their true potential.

Bilton Grange offers a diverse range of opportunities all designed to support individual accomplishments. Here, children share common values of respect, awareness of others and courtesy. They are usually 'all-rounders', willing to take advantage of all the opportunities open to them – be it on the sports field, in the classroom or on an adventure weekend. The school builds on the proven advantages of the traditional prep school curriculum – small class sizes, a broad range of subjects, and specialist teaching staff – with innovative approaches to teaching and learning, using technology as appropriate, but also the magnificent 90-acre site to the fullest extent to enhance pupils' education.

The school is very proud of its pupils' accomplishments. Bilton Grange is non-selective and yet maintains the highest standards in every arena, all with a remarkable sense of relaxed informality. Children are entered for the Common Entrance Examination and go on to top senior schools across the UK including Rugby, Oundle, Eton, Repton, Oakham, Bloxham and Uppingham. Every year a large number of pupils win awards and scholarships to senior schools and, in recent years, all Year 8 leavers have gone on to the senior school of their choice.

Full, weekly and flexible boarding are offered with over 50 boys and girls boarding on a full and weekly basis. Together the team of House Parents and Matrons create a nurturing environment where children can feel comfortable, safe and secure, whether they are staying for an occasional night a week or full boarding.

The School offers unrivalled facilities, as well as fully resourced classrooms, Science laboratories and a Design Technology workshop. Bilton Grange maintains a theatre, library, Music School, chapel, sports hall, 25-metre indoor heated swimming pool, nine-hole golf course, shooting range and a floodlit artificial grass hockey pitch situated within Pugin's walled garden. The school has seen great sporting success in recent years at a regional and national level. The creative arts are a big part of school life with scholarship successes and creative achievement across Music, Art, Drama and Design Technology.

Fees per term (from April 2016). Preparatory: Full Boarding £8,330, Weekly Boarding £7,730, Day £5,395–£6,115. Pre-Preparatory: £3,170–£3,800.

There are fee discounts for Services children and third child.

Bursaries and academic scholarships are awarded annually, with the scholarship competition open to internal and external candidates in Year 6 to commence in Year 7. Bursaries are awarded on the basis of financial need to those in Year 3 and above. This annual application process gets under way in January and details are available on the school website.

We encourage all prospective parents and children to visit the school to see and experience teaching and learning of the highest standards in an inspiring setting.

Charitable status. Bilton Grange Trust is a Registered Charity, number 528771. It exists to provide education for boys and girls.

Birchfield School

Albrighton, Wolverhampton, Shropshire WV7 3AF

Tel:	01902 372534
Fax:	01902 373516
email:	office@birchfieldschool.co.uk
website:	www.birchfieldschool.co.uk
Twitter:	@BirchfieldSch
Facebook:	@Birchfield-School

Acting Chairman of the Governors: T Carver

Headmaster: Hugh Myott, BA Hons, PGCE

Age Range. 4–13.

Number of Pupils. 155: Pre-Prep (age 4–7) 58, Prep (age 8–10) 68, Senior (age 11–13) 29.

Fees per term (2016–2017). Under 5s £2,210; Reception & Year 1 £2,840; Year 2 £3,805; Years 3 to 8 £4,615.

Birchfield School is now fully co-educational with 60 girls and 80 boys. The last Independent Schools Inspectorate report in March 2012 highlighted the first-class education delivered by the School. The School obtained the highest descriptor 'excellent' in the following key areas: Boarding; Extracurricular provision; Pastoral Care; Leadership and Management; Overall Achievements of the Pupils; Pupils' Personal Development; and Quality of the Pupils' Achievements and Learning.

Birchfield's academic staff consists of many subject specialists who operate from well-equipped classrooms and modern facilities such as a Lego Innovation Centre, music suite, science laboratory, design and technology workshop and art studio, library and food technology room. There are two ICT suites with networked PCs. iPads are used throughout the School.

Sport is a fundamental part of school life and with superb playing fields and a recently refurbished outdoor swimming pool, Birchfield enjoys an excellent sporting reputation.

Birchfield also has a floodlit synthetic sports surface which is used for a variety of sports and by all age groups.

Birchfield also encourages self-expression through music, drama, art and design technology. Art is a considerable strength of the School. The Music Department holds regular concerts and our musicians have performed with professional bodies in major productions. The pupils are also involved in a wide range of extracurricular activities.

The School has a well-resourced Learning Enhancement department with two members of staff who provide excellent support for pupils with special educational needs. For those demonstrating strong academic prowess a scholarship form is in place during the final years.

In recent years senior pupils have achieved numerous scholarships and awards. One in three leavers at 13+ leaves with an award. There is a rich and challenging programme for pupils up to the age of 13, including the opportunity to board in the final years. When the time comes to say goodbye, senior pupils are prepared for entry into a wide range of independent senior schools and local grammar schools which best suit the individual's needs.

The Headmaster's wife is actively involved in school life and there is a full-time school nurse. Birchfield has a fine reputation for its all-round holistic education.

Set in 20 acres of attractive grounds and playing fields, Birchfield School is close to Wolverhampton and Telford and boasts excellent transport links.

Co-educational nursery Prepcare (managed by Prepcare LLP) operates on the Birchfield School site and welcomes children from 6 weeks to 4 years old, all year round (except weekends and Bank Holidays) from 8.00 am until 6.00 pm.

Charitable status. Birchfield School is a Registered Charity, number 528420.

Birkdale Prep School

Clarke House, Clarke Drive, Sheffield S10 2NS

Tel: 0114 267 0407
Fax: 0114 268 2929
email: prepschool@birkdaleschool.org.uk
website: www.birkdaleschool.org.uk
Twitter: @BirkdalePrep
Facebook: /BirkdaleSchool

Chairman of Governors: P Houghton, FCA

Head of Prep School: **C J Burch**, BA, PGCE

Age Range. 4–11.
Number of Boys. 250 day boys.
Fees per term (2016–2017). Pre-Prep Department £2,725; Prep Department £3,325. Lunch included.

Birkdale Prep School is Sheffield's only school specialising in quality education and care exclusively for boys. Continuous education is offered from 11–18 at Birkdale Senior School (Co-educational Sixth Form).

Birkdale Prep School is based at Clarke House, situated in a pleasant residential area near the University and close to the Senior School. The school has a firm Christian tradition and this, coupled with the size of the school, ensures that the boys develop their own abilities, whether academic or otherwise, to the full.

The Pre-Prep Department is based in a new building, Belmayne House. The facilities are outstanding and designed specifically to meet the needs of 4–7 year olds. Specialist subject teaching across the curriculum starts at the age of 7 and setting in the core subjects in the final two years enhances, still further, the pupil/teacher ratio.

The school has its own Matron and pastoral care is given high priority. Boys are encouraged to join a wide variety of clubs and societies in their leisure time. Music plays a significant part in school life, both in and out of the timetable. There is a large choir, brass band and orchestra and there are strong choral links with Sheffield Cathedral where many of the choristers are Birkdalians.

Cricket, Association and Rugby Football are played on the School's own substantial playing fields, which are within easy reach of the school. A broad range of activities is available as part of the extensive extracurricular programme.

The majority of boys pass into the Senior School.

Charitable status. Birkdale School is a Registered Charity, number 1018973, and a Company Limited by Guarantee, registered in England, number 2792166. It exists to provide education for boys.

Bishop's Stortford College Prep School

Maze Green Road, Bishop's Stortford, Hertfordshire CM23 2PH

Tel: 01279 838607
Fax: 01279 306110
email: psadmissions@bishopsstortfordcollege.org
website: www.bishopsstortfordcollege.org
Twitter: @BSCollege
Facebook: /bishopsstortfordcollege

Chairman of Governors: Dr P J Hargrave, BSc, PhD, FREng

Head: **W J Toleman**, BA

Age Range. 4–13.
Typical Number of Pupils. 50 boarders and 410 day pupils.
Fees per term (2016–2017). Full Boarders £6,394–£6,937; Overseas Boarders £6,680–£7,225; Weekly Boarders £6,325–£6,868; Day £4,329–£4,852; Pre-Prep £2,804–£2,859. There are no compulsory extras.

Bishop's Stortford College is a friendly, co-educational, day and boarding community providing high academic standards, good discipline and an excellent all-round education.

There are 50 full-time members of staff, and a number of Senior School staff also teach in the Prep School. As the Prep and Senior Schools share the same campus, many College facilities (design and technology centre, music school, sports hall, swimming pool, all-weather pitches, dining hall, medical centre) are shared. The Prep School also has its own buildings containing a multi-purpose Hall, laboratories, IT centre, library, art room and classrooms. In 2013 the Dawson Building was opened, enhancing and extending the Prep School facilities.

The Prep School routine and curriculum are appropriate to the 7–13 age range, with pupils being prepared for Common Entrance and Senior Schools' Scholarships, although most children proceed to the College Senior School. There are 23 forms streamed by general ability and setted for Maths. High standards of work and behaviour are expected and the full development, within a happy and friendly atmosphere, of each child's abilities in sport and the Arts is actively encouraged. A strong swimming tradition exists and many of the Staff are expert coaches of the major games (rugby, hockey, cricket, netball, rounders, tennis and swimming). The choirs and orchestra flourish throughout the year, and two afternoons of Activities provide opportunities for pupils to participate in many minor sports, outdoor pursuits, crafts, computing and chess. Six major dramatic productions occur every year.

A Pre-Prep for 4–6 year olds was opened in 1995 and new purpose-built accommodation was opened in September 2005.

The Prep School is run on boarding lines with a six-day week and a 5.00 pm finish on four days with Wednesdays ending at 4.00 pm and Saturdays at 3.00 pm. The 7 and 8 year olds have a slightly shorter day and their own dedicated building.

Entry tests for 7, 8, 9, 10, 11 year olds are held each January. Scholarships are available at 10+ (Academic and Music) and 11+ (Academic, Music, Art and Sport), as is Financial Assistance.

Charitable status. The Incorporated Bishop's Stortford College Association is a Registered Charity, number 311057. Its aims and objectives are to provide high quality Independent Day and Boarding education for boys and girls from age 4 to 18.

Bishopsgate School

Englefield Green, Surrey TW20 0YJ

Tel: 01784 480222 (Admissions)
          01784 432109 (School Office)
email: headmaster@bishopsgatesch.uk
          office@bishopsgatesch.uk
          admissions@bishopsgatesch.uk
website: www.bishopsgate-school.co.uk

Chairman of Governors: Mr T Eddis

Headmaster: **Mr Rob Williams**, MA Hons Edinburgh, PGCE Bedford

Age Range. 3–13.
Number of Pupils. 346.
Fees per term (2016–2017). £4,832 (Years 5–8), £4,213 (Years 3–4), £3,526 (Years 1–2), £3,108 (Reception), Nursery: £1,668 (5 mornings), £1,339 (5 afternoons).

Set in 20 acres of beautiful woodland, close to Windsor Great Park, Bishopsgate is blessed with a glorious learning environment. The heart of the school remains as a large, Victorian house, but many additional modern buildings have been added over the past 15 years with the creation of dedicated Upper and Lower School building offering parents outstanding on site facilities for their children.

In 2013, the School completed the development of a four-lane 25 metre swimming pool and swimming is included in the curriculum from Nursery. During the same year, additional new classrooms were added in the Windsor Lower School Building along with a state-of-the-art Design & Technology suite. In addition, a major investment to upgrade the IT Suite included touch screen computers and the procurement of laptops and Chromebook for our pupils. In 2014, the School completed an extension to the Dining Room followed by a major refurbishment of the Science Classroom. Most recently, the completion of a major upgrade of the School All Weather Facility, the Performing Arts Studio, the building of a new cricket square, and the redevelopment of the current all-weather surface has vastly enhanced the facilities.

In early summer this year, an extension to the Music House has increased the number individual teaching rooms and the music classroom. At the same time, major improvements were made to the School Kitchen, the administrative offices in Main Building, and a significant improvement to the School's IT equipment and infrastructure. These developments and other future projects are part of the Governors long term plan to ensure Bishopgate continues to offer excellence in teaching along with progressive facilities.

Children may enter Bishopsgate from the age of rising 3 into our Nursery. Some children may already be 4 when they join in September if their birthday falls in the Michaelmas term. Our trained staff and well-equipped Nursery ensure that each child is given the best possible start to life. There is a warm family atmosphere as we recognise how important it is for children to feel happy and secure. We place great emphasis on building a solid foundation of social skills and a love of learning, which will enable each child to settle confidently into school life. A wide variety of activities is on offer with plenty of opportunities for healthy outdoor learning, including Forest School.

Beyond Nursery, a class teacher remains at the core of each child's learning. Emphasis is placed on establishing a firm foundation in literacy and numeracy, but the curriculum is broad with a range of educational visits planned to enrich and extend the children's learning. The teaching of French, Music, PE, Singing and Dance is provided by specialist teachers. Good use is made of our glorious grounds as a learning resource.

Form-based teaching continues in Years 3 and 4, but by Year 5 all teaching is by subject specialists. Programmes of study in Upper School are full and varied, covering the traditional academic subjects as well as Art, Design, Music, Computer Studies, PSHE and Physical Education. The children are prepared carefully for entrance to a range of senior schools and we are proud of our record of success. We prepare children for 11+ entry to senior schools, but we hope our children will remain with us to 13 and participate in the exciting Prep School Baccalaureate.

In Upper School, opportunities to represent the school in sports teams, plays, choirs and instrumental groups are all part of the 'Bishopsgate Experience'. In addition, a busy programme of extracurricular activities ensures that all children have the opportunity to shine at something.

Music plays an essential part in the life of the school with many of our pupils enjoying individual music lessons. There are choirs and ensembles. Participation by children of all abilities, with ample opportunities to perform, is our aim. Drama productions, dance and public speaking events all provide additional occasions when the children can develop their presentation skills.

Our vibrant Art and Design Department occupies a spacious studio equipped with a kiln for ceramics and a printing press for design projects. There is an annual art exhibition for both Lower and Upper School and the children's work is displayed proudly around the school and in our annual School magazine. There is a popular after-school Art club for children and regular weekend workshops with professional artists.

Team Games, Rowing, Athletics, Dance, Tennis, Gymnastics, Judo, Taekwondo, Swimming and much more are all included in a varied and exciting sporting programme within the school day. An extensive programme of inter-school fixtures is arranged each term and we like to see as many parents in support as possible! We like to win, but our priorities are participation, enjoyment and teamwork.

A prospectus and further details can be obtained from the Admissions Office.

Charitable status. Bishopsgate School is a Registered Charity, number 1060511. It aims to provide a broad and sound education for its pupils with thorough and personal pastoral care.

Blackheath Preparatory School

4 St German's Place, Blackheath, London SE3 0NJ

Tel: 020 8858 0692
Fax: 020 8858 7778

email: contact.us@blackheathprepschool.com
website: www.blackheathprepschool.com

Co-educational Day School.

Chairman of Governors: Mr Hugh Stallard

Headmistress: Mrs P J Thompson, BA Hons, PGCE, BDA Dip

   Age Range. 3–11.
   Number of Pupils. 172 Boys, 206 Girls.
   Fees per term (2016–2017). Nursery: £2,340–£3,785; Reception–Year 2 £3,595; Years 3–6 £3,915.

   The school is located in an attractive residential area close to Blackheath village, overlooking the heath itself and borders of Greenwich Park. The five-acre site includes attractive playing fields, cricket nets, tennis courts and two playgrounds, providing enviable sporting opportunities and room for children to play.

   A most attractive learning environment includes specialist rooms for Science, ICT, Art, DT, Maths and Music. A spacious multi-purpose hall and music suite enhance the opportunities for Music, Drama, Sport and extracurricular activities. Over 40 activities are offered in a wide-ranging extracurricular programme.

   Most children join the school in the nursery at the age of three and progress through the Pre-Prep (4–7) and Prep (7–11) before leaving to transfer to selective senior schools. Academic standards are high and pupils are well prepared for selection at 11 and achieve consistent success in obtaining places at their first choice of grammar or independent senior school. On average over the last five years more than 50% of Year 6 pupils have been awarded academic scholarships each year and a plethora of pupils are awarded scholarships in Art, Music, Drama and Sport.

   The form teacher of every class is responsible for the pastoral welfare of each child. In the Nursery and the Pre-Prep the key worker and the form teacher are primarily responsible for teaching the children. However, there is a strong emphasis on specialist teaching from the very beginning. Music, French, PE, Drama and Dance are introduced in the Nursery. As the children progress through the school, more specialist teachers are responsible for Art, ICT, Design Technology, Maths, English and Science. The quality of teaching has been recognised as one of the many strengths of the school and pupils display real pleasure in their learning.

   The school positively encourages parental involvement in the daily life of the school. The strong ethos and vision of the school is underpinned by the vibrant enthusiasm of all involved and by the very strong sense of community.

The Blue Coat School

Somerset Road, Edgbaston, Birmingham B17 0HR
Tel: 0121 410 6800
Fax: 0121 454 7757
email: admissions@thebluecoatschool.com
website: www.thebluecoatschool.com
Twitter: @bcsbirmingham

Founded 1722. Co-educational Day Preparatory School.

Chairman of Governors: Mr B H Singleton

Headmaster: Mr N G Neeson, BEd Hons, NPQH

   Age Range. 2–11.

   Number of Pupils. The total enrolment is 570 children. Buttons Nursery and Pre-Prep have 268 girls and boys from 2–7 years, while Prep has 302 from 7–11 years.
   There is a graduate and qualified full-time teaching staff of 46, and 9 part-time teachers.
   Fees per term (2016–2017). Pre-Prep: £2,579–£3,246; Prep: £3,829–£3,966. The fees quoted include lunches and morning and afternoon breaks. Over 50 extracurricular activities are available, some of which are charged as extras.
   Assisted Places are available to children with a demonstrable need, entering Years 3 and 4.
   Scholarships are offered for academic and musical excellence at age 7 (entry to Year 3).
   The School is set in 15 acres of grounds and playing fields just 2 miles from the centre of Birmingham. Its well-designed buildings and facilities comprise the Chapel, the Administrative Building, the Prep Teaching Centre, the Pre-Prep Department, the Pre-School (Buttons Nursery), sports pitches, short tennis courts and a superb multi-purpose Sports Centre with a heated 25m swimming pool. After-school care is available. In Prep this is provided in two spacious, purpose-designed Houses.
   Additional features include the Library Resource Centre and specialist facilities for Science, Art, Design and Technology, Music, Media Studies and ICT. All the classrooms have an IWB, and the school is very well equipped with Apple and Windows computers including desktops, laptops and tablets.
   Children are prepared for scholarships and examinations to prestigious local schools. The school enjoys particular success in the 11+ examinations to Birmingham's grammar schools and the schools of the King Edward VI Foundation. The Statutory Framework for the Early Years Foundation Stage is followed for children aged 2 to 5, and the National Curriculum is incorporated at Key Stages 1 and 2 as part of a wider academic structure.
   The school places great emphasis on Music. The robed Chapel Choir is affiliated to the RSCM, and there are five further choirs and a significant number of instrumental groups and ensembles. The school benefits from Sibelius software, used in the teaching of composition, and from a Steinway concert grand housed in the spacious auditorium. Musicals, concerts and recitals feature in abundance, involving the great majority of the children. Over 250 instrumental lessons are given weekly.
   The main sports are Hockey, Netball, Rounders, Rugby, Soccer, Cricket, Athletics and Swimming. The teams enjoy considerable success in inter-school competitions and all children have the opportunity to develop their skills.
   Co-curricular activities include Gymnastics, Judo, Ballet, Drama, LAMDA, Science and Chess. A Ski Trip, French Trip, Outward Bound activity, as well as excursions and field courses are available each year.
   Charitable status. The Blue Coat School Birmingham Limited is a Registered Charity, number 1152244, and a Company Limited by Guarantee, registered in England, number 8502615.

Blundell's Preparatory School

Milestones House, Blundell's Road, Tiverton, Devon EX16 4NA
Tel: 01884 252393
Fax: 01884 232333
email: prep@blundells.org
website: www.blundells.org

Chairman of Governors: Mr C M Clapp, FCA

Headmaster: Mr A D Southgate, BA Ed Hons

Age Range. 2½–11 years.

Numbers of Pupils. Boys and Girls: Prep (aged 7–11) 137; Pre-Prep (aged 2½–7) 76.

Fees per term (2016–2017). Prep: £3,750–£3,830 (Lunch £295); Pre-Prep: £2,090–£2,665 (Lunch £260); Nursery: £17.35 per session (Lunch £5.20 per day).

Blundell's Preparatory School is a family school and all the staff adopt a personal interest in every child and work in partnership with the parents. The school places great emphasis on children being happy, secure and confident, thus offering individuals every opportunity to achieve their full potential within a caring family atmosphere.

The School has been established for over seventy years and is part of the Blundell's Charitable Trust. It enjoys its own separate site within the very extensive Blundell's campus. This rural setting is within easy reach of the market town of Tiverton and is conveniently placed less than ten minutes from the M5 motorway and Tiverton Parkway Station.

The School has an excellent reputation for providing the essentials. Sound academic standards are based on providing the core subjects of Maths, English and Science taught to an extremely high standard. Added to this is the bonus of a wide range of supplementary subjects, well taught by specialist teachers. The School has recently had a major redevelopment and a significant extension. This includes a fully-equipped Art & Design Centre and a new Food Technology Suite.

Drama, music and art flourish at Blundell's Preparatory School with all the children participating fully both in lessons and as part of extracurricular activities. Specialist music teachers offer an extensive variety of different instruments. The Drama and Music department have their own dedicated facility.

The sports department has an enviable reputation of producing good all-round sporting pupils, as well as nurturing and extending those with talent. Amongst the sports offered are rugby, football, netball, hockey and cross-country in the winter and cricket, rounders, tennis, athletics and swimming in the summer. The Preparatory School has access to the extensive sporting facilities within Blundell's campus.

There is an comprehensive choice of extracurricular activities offered to the pupils which includes ballet, chess, fencing, golf, art, judo, bushcraft club and woodwork.

Priority entrance to Blundell's is given to its Preparatory School pupils but the school's autonomous position ensures that, if wished for, the pupils are prepared for entrance, including scholarships, to a variety of other senior schools.

(*See also Blundell's School entry in HMC section.*)

Charitable status. Blundell's School is a Registered Charity, number 1081249. It exists to provide education for children.

Bootham Junior School stands apart by treating each member of its community, in a practical application of Quaker principles, as equally important. We welcome all faiths or none, encouraging our children to develop their own convictions while learning to respect those of others. The Independent Schools Inspectorate reports '*A sense of calm and a quiet pace to the working of the school that enables individuals to flourish*'. Although our children are as boisterous as any others, and, indeed, enjoy a tolerance to behave as children, quietness is important. The values of cooperation, community, and quietness grow from the Quaker tradition, but they resonate with the modern world of work, where teams find solutions individuals can't, where knowledge is seen as interrelated and not separate, and where values-driven responses earn our respect.

At Bootham Junior School, we aim to encourage a lifelong love of learning and inspirational teaching is a good place to start. Equally important is the mutual high regard and understanding that children and teachers enjoy. This relationship provides the very best environment for learning to take place. High standards are achieved because children feel happy, confident, motivated and respected. Education is more than examination preparation; it is about unlocking potential skills and aptitudes. We want our children to find their particular strengths: through sport, through music, through the Arts, through outdoor education, through social debate and action.

Bootham Junior School has a beautiful sports field, a swimming pool at the senior school dating from 1912 and hard courts for tennis and netball. The range of sports taught include: gymnastics, dance, athletics, netball, tennis, swimming, football, basketball, cricket and rounders. Our Director of Music has a range of musical groups including: two choirs, orchestra, flute group, string group, clarinet group and recorder group. Individual music lessons are also available in all instruments should parents wish it. Engagement with the community is in line with a Quaker sense of responsibility and extends to children's activities too. Drama flourishes both within and beyond the formal curriculum. Regular productions of plays and musicals cater for different age groups and allow talents to be explored, nurtured and showcased. Children also take part in LAMDA schemes for recital and public speaking. Our Outdoor Classroom is an extremely well-used resource and all children have the opportunity to take part in residential experiences, from nursery age onwards. We believe in building adaptable, resilient young people who can respond to the world around them. Whatever their interests, this is the place where all our children can find inspiration and where they will be inspired. The small size of our school means that everyone has the chance to try something new. The result is a sense of personal achievement both in and outside the classroom.

Charitable status. Bootham School is a Registered Charity, number 513645.

Bootham Junior School

Rawcliffe Lane, York YO30 6NP

Tel: 01904 655021
email: junior@boothamschool.com
website: www.boothamschool.com

Clerk to the School Committee: Stephen Sayers

Head: **Helen Todd**, BA Hons, MA Ed, QTS

Age Range. 3–11 Co-educational.
Number of Pupils. 140.
Fees per term (2016–2017). £2,665–£3,390 inc lunch for full-time pupils.

Boundary Oak School

Roche Court, Wickham Road, Fareham, Hampshire PO17 5BL

Tel: 01329 280955
email: registrar@boundaryoak.co.uk
            office@boundaryoak.co.uk
website: www.boundaryoakschool.co.uk
Twitter: @boundaryoak
Facebook: @boundaryoak

Headmistress: **Mrs Hazel Kellett**, BSc Hons, PGCE

Age Range. 2–16.
Number of Pupils. 24 Boarders, 183 Day Pupils.

Fees per term (2016–2017). Full Boarder £5,475–£7,090; Weekly Boarders £4,883–£6,498. Day Pupils: £2,805–£4,654 (Reception–Year 11), Pre-School: £2,805 (full time). Sessions available.

The school was founded in 1918 and moved to Roche Court in 1960. A new 99 year lease was secured in 1994. The school is set in 22 acres of pleasant, self-contained grounds between Fareham and Wickham in Hampshire and enjoys extensive views of the countryside around.

The Pre-School takes children from the age of 2 to rising 5 and this group is housed in a purpose-built centre offering the most up-to-date facilities. This department is structured to the needs of this age group and the day can extend from 8.00 am to 5.30 pm.

The Pre-Prep Department has its own purpose-built buildings and other facilities within the school, and caters for children from rising 5 to 8 years of age (Reception to Year 3).

At 8 years the children move to the Preparatory Department where they remain until they are 13 (Year 8). From here they move to Seniors in Year 9 where they are introduced to our GCSE subjects. Full, weekly and flexi boarding are offered to all from the age of 7 years and the school has a policy of admitting boarders in a flexible system that is of great benefit to all. Pupils are prepared for a wide number of independent schools throughout the United Kingdom in a friendly and caring environment.

Apart from the historic main house of Roche Court where the boarders live, there is the Jubilee Block of classrooms, two laboratories, the Widley Block, Library and the Music Centre. The School has an ICT Suite and a purpose-built Art and Design Technology Centre that incorporates work areas for Photography, Pottery and Carpentry. The school has a fine Assembly Hall that is also used for Drama and Physical Education.

As well as extensive playing fields with woods beyond for cross country and an all-weather AstroTurf pitch which incorporates football, hockey, netball and tennis courts, there is an outdoor swimming pool and the indoor Fareham Pool is within very easy reach.

Most sports are taught and there is a wide selection of clubs and activities run in the school for both day and boarding pupils including judo, horse riding, art, camp craft, chess, shooting and many more.

For a copy of the prospectus and details of scholarships and bursaries, please apply to the Registrar, email: registrar@boundaryoak.co.uk or look at our website www.boundaryoakschool.co.uk.

Bradford Grammar Junior School

Keighley Road, Bradford, West Yorkshire BD9 4JP

Tel: 01274 553742
Fax: 01274 553745
email: chsec@bradfordgrammar.com
website: www.bradfordgrammar.com
Twitter: @juniorschoolCH
            @bradfordgrammar
Facebook: /bradfordgrammarschool
LinkedIn: /bradfordgrammar

Chairman of the Board of Governors: Lady L Morrison, LLB

Interim Head: **Miss K L Howes**, BSc, MSc

Age Range. 6–11.
Number of Pupils. 97 boys, 89 girls.
Fees per annum (2016–2017). £9,645.

Bradford Grammar Junior School is a selective school for boys and girls aged 6–11, holding no catchment boundaries and a strong reputation for specialist teaching.

The school seeks to inspire happy, respectful and grounded children, who are ready for the transition to Senior School. The school's aim is to provide exceptional care in a relaxed atmosphere so that each child can thrive.

Location. Bradford Grammar Junior School is located at the same site as the Senior School at Keighley Road, Bradford. It is housed in an original seventeenth century manor house called Clock House.

Specialist facilities. The school offers pupils a wide range of specialist facilities, including a swimming pool, theatre, instrumental music tuition and dedicated Computer Science and Design Technology rooms. Full use is made of the Senior School facilities including Science laboratories, Sports facilities and Art rooms.

Specialist teaching. In Years 2, 3 and 4 (age 6–9) pupils are taught the majority of subjects by form teachers and are based in their classrooms, with specialist teaching for Art, Modern Foreign Languages, Music Computing, and Games. In Years 5 and 6 pupils have increasing input from specialist teachers utilising the extensive facilities throughout the whole school.

Co-curricular Activities. There is a long tradition of excellence in sport, music and drama. Co-curricular activities take place during lunchtimes. Sports include rugby, netball, hockey, swimming, cross-country, cricket, rounders and athletics. Societies and clubs include dance, gymnastics, animation and Design Technology.

Pastoral Care. The school's aim is to provide young boys and girls with a wide range of educational experiences and to develop the right attitude to learning so that they fulfil their potential. The school is a safe, friendly, tolerant and caring environment.

After Care. Bradford Grammar Junior School provides before and after school care from 7.45 am to 6 pm.

Transport Links. The school organises private coach transport for pupils travelling to and from Huddersfield, Halifax, Bramhope, Horsforth, Rawdon, Wharfedale and Oxenhope. It is situated a short walk from Frizinghall Railway Station, which is on the Airedale and Wharfedale lines. There are half hourly rail services, taking approximately 30 minutes, to Leeds, Skipton, Ilkley and Apperley Bridge.

Entry. The school is selective and takes a number of pupils each year for entry from Year 2 (age 6–7) through to Year 6 (age 10–11).

Entry to Years 2, 3 and 4 (age 6, 7 and 8) is by assessment. Entry to Years 5 and 6 (age 9 and 10) is by entrance examination and involves tests in Maths and English.

Pupils who progress from Bradford Grammar School Junior School to the Senior School are not required to sit the 11+ entrance exam. The close relationship between the two schools enables a smooth transition from Junior to Senior School.

Charitable status. Bradford Grammar School (The Free Grammar School of King Charles II at Bradford) is a Registered Charity, number 529113. It exists to provide education for children.

Brambletye

East Grinstead, West Sussex RH19 3PD

Tel: 01342 321004
Fax: 01342 770197
email: schooloffice@brambletye.com
website: www.brambletye.co.uk

Chairman of Governors: Mr P J Lough, MA, PGCE

Headmaster: **Mr Will Brooks**, BA, PGCE, MBA Ed

Age Range. 2½–13 Co-educational.
Number of Pupils. 272 day/boarding pupils.
Fees per term (2016–2017). Boarders £7,800–£7,980; Day Pupils £5,880–£6,545, Pre-Prep (Years 1 & 2) £3,160. Nursery £2,625 (5 full days).

Brambletye is an independent day and boarding Preparatory School for boys and girls aged 7–13 years, situated in beautiful grounds in rural Sussex. There is a Pre-Preparatory/Nursery department which takes boys and girls from the age of 2½ years to the age of 7 years.

Brambletye is a large country house in its own wooded estate of 140 acres, overlooking Ashdown Forest and Weir Wood Reservoir. The school stands one mile south of East Grinstead. Gatwick Airport is only 20 minutes by car and Heathrow is an hour away. London is 30 miles by road and 50 minutes by rail. There is escorted travel to and from London at the beginning and end of all exeat weekends and half-term holidays.

The school has outstanding academic, sporting, music, drama and arts facilities. These include a new modern classroom block, 2 redeveloped science laboratories, an up-to-date Arts Room and Design Technology workshop, an extensive Library, an ICT room, a large theatre and music rooms. There is also a Sports Hall, tennis and netball courts, two squash courts, a swimming pool, a golf course and several playing fields. We aim to produce happy, confident, well-rounded children who work hard, enjoy drama, games and music, play a part in some of the numerous societies and hobbies, and take a full share in the daily life of the school. These facilities in conjunction with high quality teaching staff, generate regular awards for the children from the schools that inherit them.

Brambletye has always been run along family lines, with a distinctive warm and friendly atmosphere. Traditional values such as high standards of manners and good behaviour provide a platform for academic and personal development. As a co-educational day and boarding school, pupils enjoy and benefit from living and working in a community. At weekends, there is a full programme of activities for the boarders and children are encouraged to make constructive use of their spare time. The environment is inspirational and pupils develop a love of learning which creates a positive interaction with the staff and a curiosity about the world around us.

The Nursery and Pre-Preparatory Department is situated in a self-contained purpose-built state-of-the-art building. The main aim of the Department is to provide a secure, friendly and structured environment in which all children are encouraged to achieve their full potential and to develop at their own rate.

Children may join the Nursery class at the age of two and a half before progressing to Reception at four. Boys and girls transfer to the Preparatory Department at the age of seven. All children acquire the basic skills, while following the breadth of the National Curriculum. Religious Studies, Physical Education, Art, Music, Science and Technology are all integrated into the weekly timetable. Children have swimming lessons throughout the year in the indoor pool, and teachers from the Preparatory Department visit regularly to teach Music and to coach games. The Pre-Prep has an exciting School in the Woods project.

Enquiries about admissions, our scholarships and bursary programme are welcomed throughout the year. Brambletye offers generous discounts for Armed Services Families. Please contact the Headmaster's Secretary for a prospectus.

Charitable status. Brambletye School Trust Limited is a Registered Charity, number 307003. It aims to provide an all-round education for the children in its care.

Bramcote Junior School
Junior School to Scarborough College

Filey Road, Scarborough, North Yorkshire YO11 3BA

Tel: 01723 380606
email: juniorschool@scarboroughcollege.co.uk
website: www.scarboroughcollege.co.uk
Twitter: @ScarboroughCol1
Facebook: /Scarborough College

Chairman of the Governors: Dr John Renshaw

Head of School: **Mr Chris Barker**

Age Range. 3–11 Co-educational.
Number of Pupils. 90.
Fees per term (2016–2017). Tuition: Years 5–6 £3,762, Years 3–4 £3,499, Years 1–2 £2,951, Reception £2,341. Pre-School: £19.50 (per half-day session), £38.00 (full day with lunch).

Wrap-around School Care (3–7 year olds) comes at no extra charge. Holiday Clubs (8.00 am to 6.00 pm) operate throughout the main school holidays (closed for Christmas and Easter): £16 per half day, £29 per full day.

Bramcote Junior School was formed from the merger of Bramcote Preparatory School with Scarborough College Junior School in 2012. The origins of both schools date back to the 19th Century.

The Junior School occupies superb purpose-built premises on the Scarborough College site with an outlook over Oliver's Mount, the South Bay and Scarborough Castle. Facilities include a self-contained pre-school, early years and junior suites, an administration unit together with a school hall and a fully dedicated design and technology/art workshop. Classrooms are well equipped including many with interactive whiteboards and all classroom computers are networked to the schools' two ICT suites with intranet and internet facilities. The Junior School shares many impressive resources and amenities with the Senior School: science laboratories, drama studio, main sports/drama hall, music school, sports fields, a full-size all-weather pitch, swimming pool and school minibuses.

The breadth of opportunity on offer does not detract from the solid grounding pupils receive in the core subjects. Class teaching – with thoughtfully introduced specialist support where this is advantageous – is the pattern until Year 4. This is then advanced by full subject specialist teaching in the last two years, in readiness for transfer to the Senior School. The full complement of well-qualified staff ensures a generous teacher-pupil ratio. Provision is further enhanced by a Special Educational Needs Coordinator who oversees the school's learning support unit.

The standard of pastoral care at the school is very high. The Junior School seeks to nurture well-rounded, confident and competent pupils who are ready for the challenges of secondary education at Scarborough College.

Bramley School

Chequers Lane, Walton-on-the-Hill, Tadworth, Surrey KT20 7ST

Tel: 01737 812004
Fax: 01737 819945
email: office@bramleyschool.co.uk
website: www.bramleyschool.co.uk
Twitter: @BramleySchool
Facebook: /Bramley-School

Chairman of Governors: Mr Mike Webb

Headmistress: Ms P Burgess, MA, BEd Hons, NPQH, IAPS

Age Range. 3–11.
Number in School. 90 Girls.
Fees per term (2016–2017). £1,785 (mornings only) to £4,095.

Bramley was founded in 1945 as an independent pre-preparatory and preparatory day school and became an Educational Trust in 1972. A registered charity, the school is administered by a Trust Council and all income is used for educational purposes.

The strength of Bramley School lies in its commitment to developing happy, confident, self-motivated pupils with a lifelong love of learning. An excellent teacher/pupil ratio; a caring friendly atmosphere; highly qualified, specialised and enthusiastic staff, and a genuine concern for each child's welfare contribute to academic success. Bramley achieves excellent examination results at 11+ and many girls gain places and scholarships to prestigious senior schools within both the independent and maintained sectors. Alongside this, children are encouraged to develop their own interests and talents and a wide range of extracurricular activities are offered.

Throughout the school girls work in small classes, according to their age group, with particular attention being paid to meeting the specific needs of individuals. All children in the Pre-Preparatory Department are taught by dedicated class teachers who have full responsibility for their classes, whilst older children benefit from specialised teaching staff, for example in Mathematics, English, Science, Computing, Music, PE and Art. A specialist teacher teaches French from the age of 5. The Preparatory Curriculum is constantly being developed to keep abreast of educational changes in the National Curriculum, whilst retaining the excellence of well-tried methods.

The Little Bramley Nursery Department is an ideal starting point for school life with literacy and numeracy skills fostered through play in a safe and nurturing environment. Children from three years of age settle quickly and happily and the impressive outdoor facilities allow the early curriculum to take place outdoors as well as indoors.

Open Mornings take place twice in the academic year – details can be found on the school website.

Charitable status. Bramley Educational Trust Limited is a Registered Charity, number 270046. Its aim is to provide an excellent educational establishment for 3–11 year old girls.

Brentwood Preparatory School

Middleton Hall, Middleton Hall Lane, Brentwood, Essex CM15 8EQ
Tel: 01277 243239 (ages 3–7)
          01277 243333 (ages 7–11)
Fax: 01277 243340
email: prepadmissions@brentwood.essex.sch.uk
          prep3–7@brentwood.essex.sch.uk
          prep7–11@brentwood.essex.sch.uk
website: www.brentwoodschool.co.uk

Chairman of Governors: Sir Michael Snyder, DSc, FCA, FRSA [OB]

Headmaster: Mr K J Whiskerd, BA, PGCE

Head of Early Years and Key Stage 1: Mrs V Audas, BEd

Age Range. 3–11.

Number of Children. Prep 411.

Fees per term (2016–2017). Nursery £2,230, Prep £4,460.

Brentwood Preparatory School has its own buildings and grounds quite distinct from Brentwood School (qv) but close enough to share the use of its chapel, indoor swimming pool, Sports Centre and world-class athletics track.

The co-educational Preparatory School, which opened in 1892, educates children from age 3 to 7 in the spacious Higgs Building with very well-equipped classrooms. Entrance is by an informal assessment at age 3.

Older children, aged 7 to 11, are based in Middleton Hall, an elegant building which has its own extensive grounds, sports pitches and all-weather Astroturf. Entrance is at age 7 by an academically-selective test and candidates come from a wide range of schools. Small class sizes and a team of well-qualified teachers provide a caring and challenging environment. Specialist rooms for art, design technology, drama, French, ICT, music and science provide outstanding facilities and a stimulating environment in which children can thrive.

There is an extensive programme of house and inter-school sports matches. Three choirs, two orchestras and a variety of ensembles perform regularly both in and out of school. Every child has the opportunity to take part in a major drama production. There is a wide range of lunchtime and after-school clubs, and a late stay scheme for children to complete homework at school. Many day visits to museums and places of interest complement school-based work and children enjoy annual residential trips in the holidays.

The Preparatory School has a strong academic tradition and a reputation for providing an excellent all-round education. The vast majority of pupils transfer to the Senior School (founded in 1557) at age 11.

The Preparatory School was last inspected in 2013 by the ISI and received a superb report with inspectors giving 'excellent' findings in every category of school life. Inspectors reported that "*the School is successful in meeting its aims and offers a high quality educational experience to its pupils ... The pupils' achievements are particularly notable in mathematics, literacy, music, art and drama*". The School fulfils its aims "*to encourage pupils to develop a lifelong love of learning and to strive for the highest academic standards in the classroom ... Teaching is well planned with a high degree of awareness of the differing needs of all the pupils ... Extremely well planned, lively lessons ensure pupils of all ages thoroughly enjoy their learning and provide stimulus and challenge*".

The report continued: "*The teachers' subject knowledge is excellent in all subjects and pupils benefit from specialised teaching in a wide range of subjects. Teachers have very high expectations for pupils, and praise and encouragement are used to good effect. All staff know their pupils well and the excellent relationships are marked by mutual respect, creating an environment conducive to learning and exemplary behaviour from pupils in class.*"

Charitable status. Brentwood School (part of Sir Antony Browne's School Trust, Brentwood) is a Registered Charity, number 1153605. It exists for the purpose of educating children.

Brighton & Hove Prep
GDST

Radinden Manor Road, Hove, East Sussex BN3 6NH
Tel: 01273 280200
Fax: 01273 280201

email: juniorenquiries@bhhs.gdst.net
website: www.bhhs.gdst.net
Twitter: @BHPrep
Facebook: @BrightonAndHovePrep

Chair of Local Governors: Mrs J Smith

Head: **Mrs S Cattaneo**

Age Range. Girls 3–11.
Number of Pupils. 245.
Fees per term (2016–2017). £2,850–£3,200, Nursery £2,250.

The Prep School of Brighton & Hove High School stands on a large site in Hove. It benefits from an extensive purpose-built site which provides many specialist areas such as a new well-equipped IT suite, a large refurbished science lab, bright and airy art studio, and a spacious music room with several practice rooms. Despite our urban site we make the most of our green areas with an extensive all-weather play area and pond and our new large astroturf and netball courts are great additions to the PE opportunities.

Our Nursery, which takes girls from age three, is very much part of the BHHS community and almost all girls transfer to the Reception class. We have a significant intake at Year Three and girls are then prepared for transfer to our Senior School at the end of Year Six. (*See Senior School entry in GSA section.*)

The ethos of the school is firmly centred on the benefits of a girls-only education. We believe that girls are more independent, focused and self-motivated and that relationships are more positive in a girl-centred setting. We put a strong emphasis on a rounded education and believe that the confidence built at an early age with a range of opportunities and experiences provides a great platform for girls for the future. We currently run several choirs, an orchestra and other musical opportunities. We offer a wide PE curriculum which includes the opportunity to be involved in inter-school matches. Drama and Art are also well resourced and girls often get involved in local events such as the Brighton Festival.

We pride ourselves on having a strong relationship with parents and readily involve them in the life of the school. We continue to build positive links with the community with a number of outreach projects. We are the holder of the prestigious Green Flag which reflects our eco work and commitment to energy saving and eco awareness. Despite the short distance between the sites we often use the opportunity to have whole-school events, such as an annual dance show for Years 3–13.

Charitable status. Brighton & Hove High School is part of The Girls' Day School Trust, which is a Registered Charity, number 306983.

Brighton College Prep School

Walpole Lodge, Walpole Road, Brighton, East Sussex BN2 0EU

Tel: 01273 704210
email: paprep@brightoncollege.net
website: www.brightoncollege.net

Chairman of Governors: Professor Lord Skidelsky, FBA

Headmaster: **Harry Hastings**, BA, MEd

Deputy Heads:
Jane Ashfold, BSc, PGCE
Lois Griffiths, BPharm, PGCE

Headmistress of Pre-Prep: Jo Williams, BEd

Head of Admissions, Prep and Pre-Prep: Jo Wergan, BA Hons, PGCE

Age Range. 3–13.
Number of Pupils. Prep 300, Pre-Prep 211.
Fees per term (2016–2017). From £3,140 (Reception) to £6,070 (Year 8).

Brighton College Prep School is a co-educational school, which offers a broad curriculum taught to high standards by dedicated and energetic staff. The Pre-Prep School cares for children from 3–7 years in a nearby purpose-built building with playing fields, overlooking the sea. The Prep School is situated adjacent to the Senior School on its own site. The site is urban, but enjoys close proximity to the sea, the Downs and the vibrant sports and culture of Brighton, where an annual arts festival is held in May.

The excellent facilities provided by Brighton College are shared by the Prep School. These include the Chapel, swimming pool, a sports hall (new building due 2019), two areas of playing fields, a purpose-built Performing Arts Centre and The Great Hall, which doubles as a large theatre for the Prep School's annual senior musical. The Prep School itself has many specialist rooms including a well-equipped ICT suite, a large design technology room, art room, science laboratories, home economics room, library and hall. Art and DT are both key subjects on the timetable for all year groups. The Pre-Prep School offers specialist lessons in art, music, French, Mandarin, PE and games on its own well-equipped site.

Pastoral care is very strong and a culture of kindness is commonplace and reinforced in assemblies, form time and tutor meetings. Year 8 are split into tutor groups of four or five. The motto is 'Be Good. Be Kind. Be Honest. Be the Best You'.

Academic standards are high and are one of the foundations upon which school life is built, along with the broad range of subjects and activities. A variety of teaching methods is used – the key principle being that children enjoy their lessons and thus develop a love for learning.

The school caters for able dyslexic pupils who are fully integrated into classes. The Learning Support Centre attached to the school provides specialist teaching; dyslexic pupils are given extra support in small groups during their English and French lessons. They learn conversational Spanish.

Sport is a very important part of the life at the school. Major girls' games are netball, hockey, athletics and rounders. Major boys' games are football, rugby, cricket and athletics. Swimming is on the curriculum for all pupils.

The Prep School is well known for its musical strength with a suite of specially designed music rooms and practice areas. Two orchestras, a concert band and three choirs are organised by the Director of Music and thirty-five visiting music teachers provide tuition for the large number of pupils who learn a wide variety of instruments including piano, violin, harp, saxophone, clarinet and drums.

Drama clubs and coaching are available for every year group and there are opportunities for children to perform during the academic year through assemblies, recitals, chapel services and also through annual drama productions and musicals. Drama is on the curriculum in Years 4 and 5.

The Brighton College School of Dance, based in the Performing Arts Centre, is thriving and many pupils attend classes on Saturdays and after school during the week.

The Prep School runs a large number of clubs and activities (over 70) after school and at lunchtimes. There is a range of school bus routes. For details of assessment procedures, scholarships available at 13+ and bus routes, please contact the Director of Admissions.

Charitable status. Brighton College is a Registered Charity, number 307061. It exists to provide high quality education for boys and girls aged 3–18.

BGS Infants and Juniors

Elton Road, Bristol BS8 1SR

Tel:	0117 973 6109
Fax:	0117 974 1941
email:	recruitment@bgs.bristol.sch.uk
website:	www.bristolgrammarschool.co.uk

Chairman of Governors: Mr N Reeve, FCA

Headmaster: **Mr Peter R Huckle**, BA, MEd

Age Range. 4–11.

Number of Pupils. 327: 206 Boys, 121 Girls (all day children).

Fees per term (2016–2017). Juniors: Years 3–6 £3,150. Infants: Years 1 & 2 £2,930, Reception £2,590. Fees include Lunch.

BGS Infants and Juniors is an independent co-educational day school. It was founded in 1900 and since 2010 has offered Infant as well as Junior provision. The school occupies self-contained buildings on the same site as the Senior School, Bristol Grammar School (*see entry in HMC section*). Its own facilities include a Hall, Library, Music, Art, Science and technology rooms. Some facilities are shared with the Senior School, particularly the Sports Hall, Theatre and Dining Hall. The school now thrives on the happy and purposeful demands of approximately 320 girls and boys aged 4–11 years.

Entry into BGS Infants is by an informal assessment session. Entry for the Junior School is by test and is normally at seven or nine years old (entry to other age groups is subject to the availability of places). Peloquin bursaries are awarded annually and are means tested. Children who have been members of the School since the start of Year 5 or earlier are offered places in the Senior School following continuous assessment of their progress. Other children take the normal Senior School entrance test.

The school aims to provide a rich, broad and balanced curriculum while also maintaining a nurturing environment for children to flourish. BGS Infants and Juniors encourages all students to develop their own ideas, giving support so they gain skills and confidence, and offering challenges to stretch their thinking. Many subjects are taught by subject specialists, including specialists from the Senior School. Music, Art, Dance and Drama are particularly encouraged with the annual MADD Evening a particular highlight. There are many clubs and activities including Craft, Lego, Gardening, Fencing, Orchestra, Chess, Ukelele and extra sports. In addition all children in the Infant School, and many Juniors, take part in Forest School and have violin tuition. The children have many opportunities to develop leadership and responsibility. The Infant and Junior School Councils meet regularly with the Headmaster and there is a Charity Committee.

A wide range of sports is offered to the pupils at the School's superb playing fields at Failand with its state-of-the-art sports pavilion. The impressive purpose-built sports hall on the main campus provides facilities for indoor PE. Pastoral care is provided by the Form Tutors and Assistant Heads, supported by all teaching staff and the Headmaster. Form Tutors take a lead in ensuring that children are learning and progressing well. A prosperous House system produces many friendships between age groups, with mentors and buddies showing new pupils the ropes, making sure that things are running smoothly for them. This leads to a strong sense of family and community within the school owing much to the warm and trusting relationships between children with each other and with their teachers.

Charitable status. Bristol Grammar School is a Registered Charity, number 1104425. The object of the Charity is the provision and conduct in or near the City of Bristol of a day school for boys and girls.

Brockhurst School

Hermitage, Newbury, Berkshire RG18 9UL

Tel:	01635 200293
email:	registrar@brockmarl.org
website:	www.brockmarl.org.uk

Headmaster: **D J W Fleming**, MA Oxon, MSc

Age Range. 3 to 13.

Number of Boys. 154 Boys (including 74 Boarders).

Fees per term (2016–2017). Boarding £7,373, Day £5,161–£5,490. Pre-Prep School (Ridge House): £3,278 (full-time). Temporary Overseas Boarders £7,957.

Established in 1884, Brockhurst is situated in 500 acres of its own grounds in countryside of outstanding beauty, but is only four miles from access to the M4. The school is located on the same site as Marlston House Girls' Preparatory School which occupies separate, listed buildings. Boys and Girls are educated separately, but the two schools join forces for drama, music and many hobbies. In this way, Brockhurst and Marlston House aim to combine the best features of the single-sex and co-educational systems: academic excellence and social mixing. The schools have built up a fine reputation for high standards of pastoral care given to each pupil within a caring, family establishment. (*See also entry for Marlston House School.*)

The Pre-Prep School, Ridge House, is a co-educational department for 75 children aged 3 to 6½.

Boys are prepared for entry to all Independent Senior Schools and there is an excellent scholarship record.

All boys play Soccer, Rugby, Hockey and Cricket and take part in Athletics, Cross Country and Swimming (25m indoor heated pool). Additional activities include Riding (own ponies), Fencing, Judo, Shooting (indoor rifle range) and Tennis (indoor court and three hard courts). Facilities for gymnastics and other sporting activities are provided in a purpose-built Sports Hall. Year 7 pupils make a week-long visit to a Château in France as part of their French language studies.

The school is currently building a new dedicated Music School and Theatre to open in the Summer Term 2014. Music and art are important features of the curriculum and a good number of pupils have won scholarships to senior schools in recent years.

Where appropriate, pupils can be transported by members of staff to and from airports if parents are serving in the armed forces or otherwise working overseas.

Bromsgrove Preparatory & Pre-Preparatory School

Prep:
Old Station Road, Bromsgrove, Worcs B60 2BU
Tel: 01527 579679

Pre-Preparatory:
Avoncroft House, Hanbury Road, Bromsgrove, Worcs B60 4JS
Tel: 01527 579679

email: admissions@bromsgrove-school.co.uk
website: www.bromsgrove-school.co.uk
Twitter: @BromsSchool
Facebook: /BromsgroveSchool

Chairman of Governors: Paul West

Headmistress: **Mrs Jacquelyne Deval-Reed**, BEd

Age Range. 3–13.
Number of Pupils. Prep School (7–13): 223 day boys, 213 day girls, 40 boy boarders, 25 girl boarders. Pre-Preparatory & Nursery (3–7): 98 boys, 102 girls.
Fees per term (2016–2017). Nursery: £2,680 full-time; Pre-Prep: £2,390–£2,760; Prep: £3,585–£4,665 day, £7,400–£9,125 full boarding, £5,400–£6,530 weekly boarding.
Forces Bursaries and, from 11+, scholarships are available.

Bromsgrove Preparatory School feeds the adjacent 900-strong Senior School. (*See Bromsgrove School entry in HMC section.*) The sites covering 100 acres offer exclusive and shared facilities, with a combined Prep and Senior Performing Arts Centre currently being built, which will give outstanding performance and rehearsal facilities to the school. A new purpose-converted boarding house for 70 boys and girls was opened in 2012. This allows the school's youngest boarders to live together in modern and comfortable surroundings. Other recent improvements include a new suite of classrooms, an upgrading of the dining hall, a new science laboratory, refurbishment of the library, main hall and sports hall. Pupils have access to a flourishing Forest School. Teachers working in both Senior and Preparatory Schools ensure continuity of ethos and expectation.

Academic, sporting and cultural facilities are extensive and outstanding.

Pupils are admitted at the age of 7+ with another substantial intake at 11+, but pupils, including boarders, are admitted throughout the age range up to 13. Admission to the school is by Entrance Test (English and Maths) supported by a report from the current school. Year 5 and 6 pupils are assessed during the course of the year; the outcome of these assessments allow them to be guaranteed a place in Bromsgrove Senior School two years later. Pupils admitted at age 11 are also guaranteed entry to the Senior School.

Prep School boarding is flourishing and the junior boarding house is a lively, homely environment where pupils are cared for by resident houseparents and a team of tutors. The school aims to make a boarder's first experience of life away from home enjoyable and absorbing.

Parents can choose either a five or six day week for their children. All academic lessons are timetabled from Monday to Friday with Saturdays offering an optional and flexible programme of activities and sports fixtures. The school has a national reputation in a number of sports.

The aim of the school is to provide a first-class education, which identifies and develops the potential of individual pupils, academically, culturally and socially. It prepares them to enter the Senior School with confidence.

In the Preparatory School there is a purposeful and lively atmosphere. Mutual trust, respect and friendship exist between staff and pupils. The high-quality and dedication of the teaching staff, favourable teacher/pupil ratio and regular monitoring of performance ensure that the natural spontaneity and inquisitiveness of this age group are directed purposefully. The 2016 ISI Inspection found the school to be excellent in every category. The pastoral care system is rooted in the school's Christian heritage and firmly founded on the form tutor. It is designed to ensure that every pupil is recognised as an important individual and that their development is nurtured.

The School has its own feeder Pre-Preparatory School which takes children from the age of 3. The clear majority of children transfer to the Prep School at the end of Year 2. Situated just a mile away in the spacious tree-lined grounds of an old manor house, the Pre-Preparatory School has spacious and light classrooms, equipped with interactive whiteboards. High teacher to pupil ratios and small class sizes ensure each pupil's individual needs are met.

Charitable status. Bromsgrove School is a Registered Charity, number 1098740. It exists to provide education for boys and girls.

Brontë House
The Junior School of Woodhouse Grove

Apperley Bridge, Bradford, West Yorkshire BD10 0PQ
Tel: 0113 250 2811
Fax: 0113 250 0666
email: enquiries@brontehouse.co.uk
website: www.woodhousegrove.co.uk
Twitter: @woodhouse_grove

Chairman of Governors: A Wintersgill, FCA

Headmaster: **S W Dunn**, BEd

Headmaster's Secretary and Admissions: Mrs C Richardson
Deputy Head: Mrs S Chatterton
Director of Studies/Key Stage Two Coordinator: Mrs N S Woodman
Key Stage One Coordinator: Mrs H J Simpson
Foundation Stage Coordinator: Mrs A Hinchliffe

Age Range. 3–11 Co-educational.
Number of Pupils. 336 Boys and Girls.
Fees per term (2016–2017). £3,115–£3,740 (day). Ashdown Lodge Nursery and Reception: £2,835 (full day), £1,765 (half day). Fees are graduated according to age. The day fee covers an extended day from 7.30 am to 6.00 pm; there are no extra charges for breakfast, tea or the majority of supervised activities after lessons.

The School is situated in its own grounds, a short distance from the Senior School, close to both Leeds and Bradford and within easy access to Leeds/Bradford Airport and the Yorkshire Dales National Park.

At Brontë House we welcome children to Ashdown Lodge, our Early Years setting, during the term that they turn three.

During their time in Foundation Stage, we aim to develop a child's ability and self-confidence, encouraging good behaviour and consideration for others. Children are provided with a stimulating programme of learning and play within a calm and relaxed atmosphere, providing a framework for every individual to fulfil their potential ready for the next stage of their education.

The EYFS curriculum is followed, beginning in Nursery and lasting for two years. Language and literacy, mathematics, knowledge and understanding of the world, physical and creative development are promoted in preparation for the transfer to Key Stage One.

By encouraging a child's intellectual, creative, sporting and personal development, we aim to get the best from our children in the classroom, on the games field, in music, drama and all other activities. We also offer bushcraft lessons to all pupils, appropriate to their age, where they learn about the outdoors, nature and survival skills. The broad academic curriculum covers a wide range of subjects, including foreign languages, but with particular emphasis on ensuring a strong foundation in reading, writing, mathematics and science.

As children progress through the school they are encouraged to take increasing responsibility and to show consideration for others. Friendship, trust and courtesy are promoted so our children have a sound foundation as they move up to Woodhouse Grove at the end of Year Six.

We aim to encourage every pupil to develop his or her potential by participating in a variety of activities both as part of the curriculum and extracurricular. As they progress through the school, sport plays an increasingly significant role in the life of the children and there are plenty of opportunities for pupils to be involved in team games and individual sports, which encourage not only physical achievement but also a healthy outlook for enjoying school life to the full.

As with sports, music and drama also play an important part of life at Brontë House. All children are encouraged to learn an instrument. The music curriculum is a mixture of traditional and modern with opportunities for composing and performing. There are many choirs and ensembles and the children are regularly offered the chance to take part in concerts and festivals. Housed in spacious rooms on the top floor of Brontë House, our children are given excellent opportunities to develop musically and creatively.

Charitable status. Woodhouse Grove School is a Registered Charity, number 529205. It exists to provide education for children.

Brooke Priory School

Station Approach, Oakham, Rutland LE15 6QW
Tel: 01572 724778
email: registrar@brooke.rutland.sch.uk
website: www.brooke.rutland.sch.uk
Twitter: @BrookePrioryS

Headmistress: **Mrs E S Bell**, BEd Hons

Age Range. 2 to 11 years (co-educational).
Number of Pupils. 192: 163 (age 4+ to 11); 29 (Nursery, age 2 to 4).
Fees per term (2016–2017). £2,381–£2,961.
Staff. There are 20 graduate and qualified members of the teaching staff.

Brooke Priory is a day Preparatory School for boys and girls. The school was founded in 1989 and moved into its own purpose-built building in February 1995. Since then it has doubled its classroom provision, established a Nursery, fully-networked Computer Suite, well-resourced Library, Theatre, Art & DT Studios, individual Music Practice Rooms and Sports Changing Rooms.

Brooke Priory provides a stimulating, caring environment in which children are encouraged to attain their highest potential. Class sizes are optimally 16, in parallel forms, and children are grouped according to ability in Mathematics and English.

The school delivers a broad and varied curriculum, where every child will participate in Art, Drama, French and Music. Over 60% of children in the Prep Department enjoy individual music lessons and are encouraged to join the Choir and Ensemble.

Brooke Priory enjoys a high success rate at Common Entrance and Senior Independent School Entry Examinations, with many children being awarded scholarships. With this solid foundation pupils move confidently on to their chosen senior schools.

Sport is an important part of the curriculum. Children swim weekly throughout the year and are coached in a wide variety of games by specialist staff. The main sports are Soccer, Rugby, Hockey, Netball, Cricket, Rounders, Tennis and Athletics.

The original Brooke Priory, which is situated just 1 mile outside Oakham, is set in 30 undulating acres and everyone, from the Nursery to Year VI, visits regularly for Welly Days.

The school offers a wide choice of extracurricular activities.

Before and after school care is available and holiday clubs are enjoyed by many children at the end of every term.

Broughton Manor Preparatory School

Newport Road, Broughton, Milton Keynes, Buckinghamshire MK10 9AA
Tel: 01908 665234
Fax: 01908 692501
email: info@bmprep.co.uk
website: www.bmprep.co.uk

Chairman of the Governors: Mr David Pye, BA Hons, Cert Ed, MA Ed Dist, HETC, SEDA III, FRSA

Headmaster: **Mr James Canwell**, BA Hons, PGCE

Deputy Head: Mrs Rachel Smith, BA Hons PGCE

Age Range. Nursery 2 months–2½ years. Pre-Prep 2½–7 years. Preparatory Department 7+–11 years.
Number of Pupils. 350 Day Pupils.
Fees per term (2016–2017). Nursery (per week): £265 (babies under 1 year), £275 (1–2½ years). Pre-Preparatory: £3,735 (2½–5 years), £3,900 (6–7 years). Preparatory £4,290 (8–11 years).

Broughton Manor Preparatory School is a well-established, family-owned school, with two sister Pre-Preparatory and Preparatory schools based across Milton Keynes.

Opening hours are 7.30 am to 6.30 pm for a 35-week academic year and a total of 46 weeks per year, enabling children of working parents to join playschemes in school holidays and to be cared for outside normal daily school hours.

Staff are highly qualified and committed to delivering the very best teaching and levels of care. Academic standards are "excellent", as rated in the most recent ISI Inspection, with pupils being prepared for entry to senior independent schools locally and nationally and to grammar schools. Teaching is structured to take into account the requirements of the National Curriculum, with constant evaluation and assessment for each pupil. Scholarships are offered for those with all-round academic and sporting abilities from the ages of 7+.

Housed in a modern purpose-built building, all departments also have their own outside soft play and extensive playground areas; there is a multi-purpose sports hall and Astroturf court.

State-of-the-art facilities include an Art workshop, high-tech CTS Suite and Science laboratory.

Additional facilities at The Farm, the school's Environmental Studies Centre, include a fully-equipped fitness room, dance and music studio, arts and craft room and CTS suite. Outside there are a weather station, large pond and poly-tunnels.

Music and Sport play an important part in the life of the school. Concerts are held, and a wide variety of sport is played, with teams competing regularly against other schools, and additional clubs are held for those wanting to learn specialist activities such as karate and ballet.

The school aims to incorporate the best of modern teaching methods and traditional values in a friendly, caring and busy environment, where good work habits and a concern for the needs of others are paramount.

Bruern Abbey School

Chesterton House, Chesterton, Oxfordshire OX26 1UY

Tel:	01869 242448
Fax:	01869 243949
email:	secretary@bruernabbey.org
website:	www.bruernabbey.org

Chair of Governors: Mrs Sarah Austen, BA Hons

Headmaster: **Mr J Floyd**, MA, PGCE

Age Range. Boys 7–13.
Number of Pupils. 140.
Fees per term (2016–2017). Day £7,654, Boarding £9,209, Flexi Boarding £54 per night.

Bruern Abbey School is unique in the marketplace because it is the only school in the country that caters exclusively for children diagnosed with learning difficulties and prepares them for Common Entrance to mainstream public schools; learning difficulties should not preclude academic success. ISI has stated that 'pupils are successfully educated in a secure and nurturing environment where they are given every possible help and encouragement to overcome the challenges presented by their specific learning difficulties'. Bruern provides a tailored education in beautiful surroundings and maintains high expectations for the academic future. We aim to enhance boys' self-esteem, in the firm belief that confidence is the key to academic success. A recent Crested report stated that 'Bruern Abbey is a unique school with its own special way of delivering an all-round education for its pupils. It successfully prepares boys for the Common Entrance Examination whilst at the same time developing each boy into a happy and confident individual'.

In most other respects, Bruern models itself on traditional preparatory schools, with breadth to the curriculum, including French to Common Entrance, full and varied sports, activities and cultural programmes, and the adherence to good manners, self-discipline and common courtesy. We encourage boys to share their aspirations and their anxieties. Ofsted has stated that 'the school has an incredibly warm and compassionate approach to all the boys' and also that 'pastoral care is exceptional – very understanding and caring staff'.

At Bruern we place great emphasis on experiencing all that prep school life has to offer; specialist teaching should not mean missing out on all the fun. We also make every effort, despite our somewhat diminutive size, to give the boys an action-packed time – be it musical, theatrical, cultural or sporting.

Bruern differs from traditional preparatory schools in many ways which allow our boys to succeed at Common Entrance and be ready for life beyond. These are regarded as the 'pillars' upon which the School's ethos and reputation, founded by the Principal in 1989, still stand, not to be compromised under any circumstances, and ingrained within the mission statement. They are not necessarily in any order of priority, but are:

- a clear focus on literacy and numeracy, with nine periods each of English and Mathematics a week. We have approximately twice as many English and Maths lessons as standard prep schools for all our Junior School boys, and there are two teachers in each class for these key subjects;
- small classes (eleven pupils or fewer) which allows boys more individual attention in class;
- limited withdrawal for remedial support, as boys needs are met in class;
- the extensive use of IT as a tool with which to deliver the curriculum;
- the use of laptops in lessons. For those who have difficulty in expressing themselves as swiftly or as coherently on paper as they do in speech, this is an absolute godsend;
- the teaching of reading as a distinct curriculum subject and
- the importance attached to good food and to finding the time for children within their busy schedule to eat, talk, play and relax together without the distraction of television or electronic games.

The Buchan School

Castletown, Isle of Man IM9 1RD

Tel:	01624 820481
Fax:	01624 820403
email:	admissions@kwc.im
website:	www.kwc.im

Chairman of the Governors: N H Wood, ACA, TEP

Acting Headteacher: **Mrs Janet Billingsley-Evans**, BSc

Age Range. 4–11.
Number of Pupils. 168 (91 boys, 77 girls).
Fees per term (2016–2017). Day only: £3,156 (P1–P3), £3,963 (Forms 1–2), £4,116 (Forms 3–4).

After more than a century of independence, mainly as a Girls' School, The Buchan School amalgamated, in 1991, with King William's College to form a single continuous provision of Independent Education on the Isle of Man.

As the Preparatory School to King William's College (*see entry in HMC section*), The Buchan School provides an education of all-round quality for boys and girls until the age of 11 when most pupils proceed naturally to the Senior School although the curriculum meets the needs of Common Entrance, Scholarship and Entrance Examinations to other Independent Senior Schools.

The school buildings are clustered round Westhill House, the centre of the original estate, in fourteen acres of partly wooded grounds. The whole environment, close to the attractive harbour of Castletown, is ideally suited to the needs of younger children. They are able to work and play safely and develop their potential in every direction.

Classes are small throughout, providing considerable individual attention. A well-equipped Nursery provides Pre-School education for up to 65 children. At the age of 5, boys and girls are accepted into the Pre-Preparatory Department. They work largely in their own building in bright, modern classrooms and also make use of the specialist Preparatory School facilities where they proceed three years later.

The School is particularly well-equipped with ICT facilities extending down to the Pre-Prep Department. There is a Pavilion with fields marked out for a variety of team games and a multi-purpose area which is used for Netball, Tennis and Hockey.

There is emphasis on traditional standards in and out of the classroom, with an enterprising range of activities outside normal lessons. Music is strong – both choral and instrumental – and there is energetic involvement in Art, Drama, Sport.

The school strives for high academic standards, aiming to ensure that all pupils enjoy the benefits of a rounded education, giving children every opportunity to develop their individual talents from an early age.

Entry is usually by Interview and School report and the children may join The Buchan School at any time, providing there is space. The School is a happy, friendly community where new pupils integrate quickly socially and academically.

Charitable status. King William's College is a Registered Charity, number 615. It exists for the provision of high quality education for boys and girls.

Buckingham Preparatory School

458 Rayners Lane, Pinner, Middlesex HA5 5DT
Tel: 020 8866 2737
email: office@buckprep.org
website: www.buckprep.org

Chairman of Governors: Mrs Lynn Grimes

Headmistress: **Mrs Sarah Hollis**

Age Range. Boys 2–11.
Number of Pupils. 92.
Fees per term (2016–2017). £2,959–£3,794 (includes lunches)

Buckingham Preparatory School (BPS) is a small school which offers its pupils an extremely high level of pastoral care. This was confirmed by the Independent Schools Inspection in June 2011 which found that '*the standard of pastoral care provided and support for pupils is excellent*'. In the EYFS Inspection of 2014, the provision was judged to be 'outstanding' overall.

With a maximum class size of 18 throughout the school, individual attention is guaranteed.

BPS pupils consistently achieve excellent academic results, due to the inspirational teaching, commitment and professionalism of its highly qualified teaching staff. Each year, Year 6 pupils gain offers to the major Independent and Grammar schools in the area and beyond. In the majority of cases, this is to the boys' first-choice schools, often with scholarships.

BPS also prides itself in its results in other areas of the curriculum; areas which are vital in building confidence and self-esteem. Achievement in sport, music and drama is excellent. The pupils regularly take part in local fixtures, often winning inter-school tournaments in cricket, unihoc, football, rugby swimming and cross-country, and other sports. A thriving choir and orchestra, school concerts and plays allow the pupils plentiful opportunities for performance. Many pupils play an orchestral instrument.

The Expressive Arts Week, when pupils have the opportunity of participating in approximately 14 categories of events, is also a focal point of the academic year allowing all boys from the very youngest to demonstrate their individual talents.

The School also believes in forging a strong Parent/ Teacher partnership so that parents feel they have a vital role to play in the education of their child. The Inspectors found that '*the School has excellent relationships with parents*'. A thriving Parent/Teacher Association also organises as many as three major fundraising events during the academic year which are always well supported and are highlights of the year.

Charitable status. The E Ivor Hughes Educational Foundation is a Registered Charity, number 293623.

Burgess Hill Girls – Junior School

Keymer Road, Burgess Hill, West Sussex RH15 0EG
Tel: 01444 241050
email: registrar@burgesshillgirls.com
website: www.burgesshillgirls.com
Twitter: @BHillGirls
Facebook: @BurgessHillGirls
LinkedIn: /burgess-hill-girls

Chairman of Governors: Dr Alison Smith MB, ChB, MRCGP

Headmistress: **Mrs K Bell**, BSc Hons, PGCE

Head of Junior School: **Mrs H Cavanagh**, BA Hons

Deputy Head of Junior School: Mrs S Collins BA Hons PGCE

Age Range. Girls 2½–11.
Number of Pupils. 172.
Fees per term (2016–2017). £2,450–£4,350.

Burgess Hill Girls is a day and boarding school for girls between 2½ and 18 years. We welcome boys into our Nursery (2½ to 4 years).

The school stands in 14 acres of beautiful grounds close to the centre of Burgess Hill town. It is a five minute walk from Burgess Hill railway station and coaches and minibuses collect girls from outlying areas of East and West Sussex.

It is small enough that pupils are known as individuals yet large enough to offer breadth, choice and opportunity. Girls are able to strive for excellence wherever their talents lie and the mix of ages, working together on the same site, gives the school a special character. The aim of the school is to provide each girl with the opportunity to realise her potential and the focus is firmly on girls and the way they learn.

The Junior School provides a broad, varied and stimulating curriculum within a warm and caring environment. Every girl is helped to reach her full potential socially, physically, emotionally and intellectually. Whilst academic achievement is important, the school aims to educate young people for life, providing education in the broadest sense.

The Junior School offers small classes and specialist teachers for music, sport and languages. It has an excellent reputation for Music and the Junior School Choir has been invited to sing at St Paul's and Chichester Cathedrals and their recording of 'Ding Dong Merrily on High' was broadcast on Christmas Day on BBC Sussex and BBC Surrey radio stations.

All Junior pupils take part in sports, with PE lessons most days of the week. There are many opportunities to play against other schools in a range of sports and many pupils achieve sports success at local, county and national level.

The Junior School offers fully-equipped subject-specific classrooms for Music, ICT, Art, Science and Technology and access to all the sports facilities on the school campus plus a Learning Hub incorporating a library – a large learning space with access to iPads and an interactive electronic screen.

The Infants are based in the Little Oaks building with bright, open classrooms and have their own hall and library.

The Infants and Juniors have an exciting playground with a wooden adventure trail and outdoor classroom.

Entrance to the Junior School is by examination and school reference. Scholarships are awarded each year for academic and/or musical excellence into Years 3–6 inclusive.

ISI Inspection 2014. The inspection team reported that:

"Pupils achieve high levels of knowledge, understanding and skills in curriculum subjects and extracurricular activities. Pupils come happily to learn in an environment where they feel safe and secure and where they are valued for their unique personalities and qualities."

"Pupils are well-educated and their levels of achievement are excellent ... pupils of all abilities make good progress. Pupils' attainment ... is judged to be high in relation to national age-related expectations. They achieve excellent learning skills ... effectively equipping them for the next stage of their education."

"Excellent arrangements are in place for the pastoral care of the pupils. Tolerance and understanding are at the heart of their daily interactions. The curriculum is highly effective ... making a significant contribution to pupils' achievements ... supported by an excellent range of extracurricular activities."

The inspectors also commented on our parents *"who are overwhelmingly supportive of all aspects of the school ... overwhelmingly positive about the school and the support their children are given"*.

The inspectors found that *"strong dynamic leadership"* with clear *"vision and determination"*, coupled with *"excellent strategic planning and high levels of self-evaluation are key elements to ensure success"*.

The full report can be viewed on www.isi.net.

Charitable status. Burgess Hill Girls is a Registered Charity, number 307001 (formerly known as Burgess Hill School for Girls).

Bute House Preparatory School for Girls

Bute House, Luxemburg Gardens, Hammersmith, London W6 7EA

Tel: 020 7603 7381
Fax: 020 7371 3446
email: mail@butehouse.co.uk
website: www.butehouse.co.uk

Chairman of Governors: Mr S Wathen

Head: Mrs Helen Lowe, BA, LGSM

Age Range. 4–11.
Number of Pupils. 310 Day Girls.
Fees per term (2016–2017). £4,875 inclusive of lunches.

Bute House overlooks extensive playing fields and is housed in a large bright modern building. Facilities include a science laboratory, art room, technology room, music hall, 2 drama studios, multi-purpose hall and a large well-stocked library. A well-qualified, enthusiastic and experienced staff teach a broad curriculum which emphasises both the academic and the aesthetic. Information Technology is an integral part of the curriculum and the school has a wireless network. The classrooms are all equipped with multimedia machines. Laptops are also widely used for individual or class work. Monitored access to the internet is available. French and Spanish are taught from Year 1.

Sports include swimming, gymnastics, dance, tennis, lacrosse, netball and athletics which are taught on excellent on-site facilities. Full use is made of all that London has to offer and residential trips further afield are also offered to older girls.

Girls are encouraged to take full part in the school life from an early age. There is a democratically elected School Council and regular school meetings run by the girls when all pupils are able to put forward their views as well as to volunteer for duties around the school. A wide variety of extracurricular activities is available.

The school aims at academic excellence in a non competitive, happy environment where girls are encouraged to be confident, articulate and independent and where courtesy and consideration are expected. There is a flourishing Parents Association. Entry is by ballot at age 4 and by assessment at age 7.

Caldicott

Crown Lane, Farnham Royal, Bucks SL2 3SL

Tel: 01753 649300
email: registrar@caldicott.com
website: www.caldicott.com

Chairman of the Board of Governors: M S Swift

Headmaster: **Simon Doggart**, BA

Age Range. 7–13.
Number of Boys. 125 Boarders and 168 Day Boys.
Fees per term (2016–2017). Boarders £8,451; Day Boys: Middle School £5,732, Junior School £5,238.

Caldicott, founded in 1904, is an educational trust. The school is situated in over 40 acres of grounds and playing fields and is adjacent to more than five hundred acres of Burnham Beeches. It is conveniently placed close to London, between the M4 and M40 motorways and is within 20 minutes of Heathrow Airport.

The school's ethos is based on traditional values with a modern outlook. These are underpinned by an excellent teaching and pastoral staff, many of whom live on-site, support staff and a governing body which is both highly valued and supportive.

The school's buildings and extensive sports grounds are constantly maintained and upgraded. Classrooms are spacious, well-planned and light and these have been enhanced recently by a modernised art and design technology department and music department as well as a new science block. The latest IT technology is used in all classrooms.

The new performing arts centre, with its very good acoustics, provides a drama, music and entertaining space and the indoor sports centre houses two squash courts, a climbing wall, indoor cricket nets, basketball and other sports facilities next to the outdoor swimming pool.

All boys board at school in the last two years (some may choose to board a year earlier) in preparation for boarding at their senior schools. They are prepared for the Common Entrance and Scholarship examinations to the top UK independent senior schools.

The school has a Christian foundation. The day begins with a short chapel service on most weekdays and on Sundays parents are welcome to join in the evening services. There is a strong tutorial system and much emphasis is placed on extracurricular education. Each boy is encouraged to learn how to use his leisure time sensibly.

The principal games are rugby, football and cricket. Other sporting activities include athletics, golf, swimming, tennis, cross-country, basketball, squash, martial arts, as well as rowing, sailing and fencing for smaller groups. All boys get the option to represent the school in sporting competition.

The prospectus is available online or on application to the Registrar. The Headmaster is always pleased to meet parents and to show them round the school.

Charitable status. Caldicott is a Registered Charity, number 310631. Its purpose is to provide education for the young.

Cameron House

4 The Vale, London SW3 6AH
Tel: 020 7352 4040
Fax: 020 7352 2349
email: info@cameronhouseschool.org
website: www.cameronhouseschool.org

Founded in 1980.

Principal: **Miss Josie Cameron Ashcroft**, BSc, DipEd

Headmaster: Mr Padraic Fahy, BA Hons, PGCE

Age Range. 4–11 Co-educational.
Number of Pupils. 118.
Fees per term (2016–2017). £5,845.

Based in a beautifully designed Edwardian building, just steps from London King's Road, Cameron House School prides itself on sending pupils to some of the most sought-after schools in the country.

At 11, boys go on to Latymer, Emanuel, Alleyn's, City of London, Colet Court, Westminster Under and other day and boarding schools, and girls leave for St Paul's, Godolphin and Latymer, Queen's Gate, Francis Holland and City of London, as well as a number of other day and boarding schools.

The school is designed to be completely child-centred, modern and warm, creating the right atmosphere for learning. Yet it is not a hot house: its programme is designed to develop each child's personality and to stretch his or her individual talents. A high teacher/pupil ratio is essential to Cameron House's success. Excellent provision is made for children of exceptionally high IQ, or unusual ability, eg a Native French Speakers' Club, and Artists' Group.

The aim is to instil a firm sense of self, a passion for exploration and a freedom to express creativity, balanced by good manners, kindness and a selfless interest in others.

One of the first tasks is to foster a joy of reading, which Cameron House believes is the best foundation in each class. All pupils can access the school's own intranet, interactive whiteboards, class sets of laptops and the extensive computer suite.

From their earliest years, music, art, drama and sport form an integral part of the children's school life and excellent local facilities allow the pupils to engage in a wide variety of sports. Unusually, a large majority of children learn karate, which builds physical confidence. Verbal communication skills are also developed, leading to English Speaking Board Examinations or Guildhall Examinations. Other popular clubs are Lunchtime Latin, Touch Typing, Tennis, Chess, Ballet, Tap and Fencing, to name just a few.

Three active choirs, as well as singing and percussion classes, composition and musical appreciation classes, and individual instrument lessons, lead to grade examinations of the Association Board of the Royal Schools of Music.

There is a genuinely open dialogue between parents and teachers, also fostered by The Friends of Cameron House. This contributes to the welcoming feel of the school. The Headmistress of Cameron House is always delighted to give parents a tour of the school so that they can experience its special qualities for themselves.

Cargilfield School

45 Gamekeeper's Road, Edinburgh EH4 6HU
Tel: 0131 336 2207
Fax: 0131 336 3179
email: admin@cargilfield.com
website: www.cargilfield.com
Twitter: @cargilfield

Chairman of the Board of Governors: Mr David Nisbet, BA Hons

Headmaster: **Mr Rob Taylor**, BA, PGCE

Assistant Headmaster: Mr David Walker, BA Hons

Deputy Heads:
Mrs Emma Buchanan, MEd, BEd
Mr Ross Murdoch, BEd Hons

Age Range. 3–13.
Number of Children. 300.
Fees per term (2016–2017). Boarding: £6,185 (weekly). Day Pupils: £4,900–£5,040, Pre-Prep £3,270, Nursery £1,925–£3,270.

Cargilfield is the oldest independent boarding and day prep school in Scotland, for more than 300 boys and girls, aged 3–13 years. Each child has an extensive range of opportunities to learn, explore and discover before they leave Cargilfield to join leading senior schools across the UK. Children leave with confident, lively minds, secure values and a sense of identity and community spirit that serves them well for their future lives. We achieve this by delivering a broad and challenging education in a supportive and caring family-led environment.

A small prep school means that your child feels secure and valued within the community. We get to know our pupils well so that we can guide them towards a senior school that will best suit their needs and reflect your priorities for their education. This year we will send pupils to fifteen different senior schools across Edinburgh, Scotland and the UK with over twenty scholarships earned for academic, sporting, creative and all-round excellence.

Small classes, good teaching and high expectations mean that we can achieve high standards for a range of abilities. In addition, a broad curriculum, both inside and outside the classroom, will develop your child's all-round abilities. We play sport every day from age 8 onwards and offer regular opportunities for music, art, design and drama. This is supported by over 50 different clubs, looking to inspire new talents and a wide range of interests. Try fly-tying or snowboarding, highland dance or computer coding.

As your child grows through the school, there are opportunities to challenge and stretch them further with opportunities to join evening activities, to board on a weekly or flexible basis or to join us on weekend camps or school-based activity weekends.

Charitable status. Cargilfield School is a Registered Charity, number SC005757.

Carrdus School

Overthorpe Hall, Nr Banbury, Oxfordshire OX17 2BS
Tel: 01295 263733
Fax: 01295 254644
email: office@carrdusschool.co.uk
website: www.carrdusschool.co.uk

Chairman of Governors: Mr John Gloag

Headmaster: **Mr Edward Way**, BSc Hons

Deputy Head: Mr Mark Tetley, BA Hons

Age Range. Boys 3–8, Girls 3–11, Nursery Class for children 3–4½.

Number of Day Pupils. 115 (94 girls, 21 boys).

Fees per term (2016–2017). £225–£3,575. Compulsory extras: Insurance £5; PTA membership £5. Sibling discount: £75 per term.

Carrdus School is a day school for girls and a pre-preparatory school for boys. The large house stands in 11 acres of beautiful grounds.

The teaching staff consists of nine full-time qualified teachers and fifteen part-time specialists. Boys are given a good grounding for their preparatory schools and 7+ or 8+ entry exams. Girls take 11+ Common Entrance and all other 11 year old transitional tests. The school has an excellent record of success in examinations, regularly sending girls to many well-known independent senior schools.

There is a heated outdoor swimming pool, two tennis courts and a purpose-built Sports Hall. Sport, music, drama and art are highly valued in the curriculum.

The aim of the school is to produce confident, well-disciplined and happy children, who have the satisfaction of reaching their own highest academic and personal standards. This is possible for an organisation run by teachers for children, flexible enough to achieve a balance between new methods of teaching and sound traditional disciplines.

Charitable status. Carrdus School is part of Tudor Hall School, which is a Registered Charity, number 1042783.

Casterton, Sedbergh Preparatory School

Kirkby Lonsdale, Cumbria LA6 2SG

Tel:	015242 79200
email:	hm@sedberghprep.org
website:	www.sedberghprep.org
Twitter:	@Sedbergh_Prep
Facebook:	/SedberghPrep
LinkedIn:	/casterton-sedbergh-preparatory-school

Chairman of Governors: Hugh M Blair

Headmaster: **Mr Scott G Carnochan**, BEd

Age Range. 6 months – 13 years Co-educational.

Number of Pupils. 200.

Fees per term (2016–2017). Day £2,542–£5,100, Full Boarding £6,314–£7,483, Weekly Boarding £5,947–£7,117.

Casterton, Sedbergh Preparatory School is situated in the spectacular rural location of the Lune Valley. There is no rush to grow up here but, the foundations are laid for nurturing the resilience our children need as young adults and the tenacity essential for achieving high standards. This is evident in the unrivalled activities' programme and around the clock personal care which is offered to our children. Breadth of opportunity and depth of involvement is what sets us apart. Maths competitions, explosions and dissections in Science lessons, pony care at our stables and collecting eggs from the School chickens will, create outstanding prep school memories for the young people in our care. Above all, we incubate a sense of success in each and every one of our pupils.

Facilities at our Prep School are first class and include a new Design and Manufacturing Department, 7 Science specific laboratories, flood lit astro and tennis courts, a theatre, a heated pool, an equestrian centre and an iMAC and iPad

suite. Our three boarding houses – Beale, Thornfield and Cressbrook – are very much 'home from home' environments with all houses having space for music practice and a kitchen for preparing those all-important snacks! Very few prep schools dovetail their educational lectures and activities in the way we do here at Sedbergh Prep. Likewise we balance our academics with outdoor learning, we are creating a School farm and pupils already consult with the School Chef about growing vegetables and herbs in the new Secret Garden. We are excited by the curiosity and thirst for learning that each child, regardless of their academic ability, naturally displays. We work hard to allow each child the time to question and develop their thoughts independently, leading to fresh discoveries in an innovative learning environment. Each child is actively taught to 'own' their learning because all our teachers plan their lessons using three strands – discovering, applying and communicating. To support this, we have recently introduced a Digital Enhanced Learning strategy, including SOLE (self organised learning environment) lessons. This encourages our children to use what they have learnt, to create their own ideas which are then communicated to their peers. The end result is the celebration of learning – a reward in its own right! One of our strengths is a focus on the individual. We are not a School of rote and regurgitation. Rather, we understand that a child's future success is dependant upon their ability to use what they know and to use it in a variety of creative ways, most of which we, as teachers could never have imagined. Every area of School life provides fantastic opportunities for creativity of all kinds. Day in, day out, we encourage our pupils to give their best in all that they do. Our ethos is 'give it a go and try your best' in order to help them develop a level of resilience and determination which will give them the best chance of overcoming challenges, in all areas of their schooling and beyond. We are responsible for making memories and we are determined to make them special.

Castle Court Preparatory School

The Knoll House, Knoll Lane, Corfe Mullen, Wimborne, Dorset BH21 3RF

Tel:	01202 694438
Fax:	01202 659063
email:	office@castlecourt.com
website:	www.castlecourt.com
Facebook:	/Castle-Court-School
LinkedIn:	/Castle-Court-School

Chairman of the Governors: David W N Aston

Headmaster: **Richard D P Stevenson**, BA Hons, PGCE

Deputy Head: Luke Gollings, BA Hons, PGCE

Age Range. 2–13.

Number of Pupils. 363 (210 boys, 153 girls) including Pre-Prep, Reception and Badgers (Nursery).

Teaching Staff. 25 full time, 31 part time.

Fees per term (2016–2017). £2,775 (Reception to Year 2), £4,995 (Years 3 to 8). Nursery fees on application.

Castle Court is a day prep school for girls and boys aged 2 to 13, situated in over 40 acres of beautiful grounds and woodlands within easy reach of Bournemouth, Poole, Blandford, Dorchester and the Isle of Purbeck. A gracious Regency house forms the heart of the school and contains the reception rooms, dining rooms, offices and some of the junior classrooms, as well as the formal rooms used for entertaining parents and visiting school teams. The Badgers, Reception and Pre-Prep departments (for 2 to 7 year olds) are all self-contained and, like the senior classrooms, are all purpose-built. There is a spacious hall for school plays, concerts, drama and gymnastics, as well as school assemblies. Adjacent to the hall is the music department, which includes classrooms and practice rooms, as well as a dance and drama studio. A science and art complex provides laboratories, art studios, design and technology room and the central IT centre (although all classrooms are networked, plus there is Wi-Fi across the site and the junior part of the school has their own banks of computers). From September 2015, all children in Years 3 to 8 have their own iPad provided by the school. The library is situated in the heart of the school and offers the children from all age groups the opportunity to explore and expand their reading. Other facilities include poolside sports changing rooms, an academic block with four classrooms, and office space, as well as smaller quieter rooms where individual learning support can be provided. There is an outdoor heated swimming pool and extensive playing fields including an all-weather astro hockey pitch, which is also used for tennis in the summer, as well as cricket practice. Planning permission has just been received to build a new sports hall; the building will be completed by Easter 2017.

To take full advantage of the fabulous site the school has become an accredited Forest School, to ensure that the outdoor space is used fully in all the children's learning. The Forest School has just been given a tipi by the Parents and Friends to enable them to make full use of the woods throughout the year. The teaching programme is used across all areas of the school.

While Castle Court is a day school, children are able to stay on for tea and prep or explore various activities before going home at 5.45 pm. This is totally voluntary. The younger children (Badger Cubs to Year 2) have a very relaxed programme of child care, more of a home-from-home environment, with activities dependent on weather, tiredness of the children etc. Activities for children from Year 3 upwards vary from term to term but include athletics, lego robotics, Ancient Greek, swimming, drama, dance, cookery, cross-country, chess, orchestra, band, choir, squash, rugby and reasoning. There is also a breakfast club, which is open from 7.45 am each day for children from Badger Cubs upwards. From Year 3, there is no extra charge for the breakfast and the majority of the after-school clubs. There is a small charge for the younger children for pre- and post-school care. Please contact our Admissions Registrar for more information.

The normal curriculum includes English, mathematics, science, French, Latin, history, geography, religious studies, information technology, design and technology, art, music, and sport, drama and dance. All the children are prepared for the Common Entrance or Scholarship exams to senior independent schools, as well as for entry to local grammar schools. The school has a strong musical tradition with its own Orchestra, Band, Choir and various ensembles. Sport also forms an important part in the life of the children with rugby, soccer, hockey and cricket for the boys, and netball, rounders and hockey for the girls, with athletics, cross-country, gymnastics, dance, swimming and tennis for all. There are opportunities for sailing instruction, riding and golf. Trips include visits to local places of interest, camping weekends, and expeditions to the continent.

Our goal at Castle Court is to provide an outstanding day education based upon strong Christian values, and ensure that all the children here do the best they can and find their natural talents. The children have one childhood, it has to be the best.

A prospectus (with details of the school bus service if required) will be sent on application to the Admissions Registrar; further information may be found on our school website, Facebook page, Instagram or You Tube channel.

Charitable status. Castle Court School Educational Trust Limited is a Registered Charity, number 325028. It aims to provide a first class education for local children.

Caterham Preparatory School

Harestone Valley Road, Caterham, Surrey CR3 6YB
Tel: 01883 342097
email: prep.reception@caterhamschool.co.uk
website: www.caterhamprepschool.co.uk

Chairman of Governors: J E K Smith, CBE

Headmaster: **H W G Tuckett**, MA Ed

Age Range. 3–11 years.
Number of Pupils. 288: 160 Boys, 128 Girls.
Fees per term (2016–2017). Pre-Preparatory £1,818–£3,049, Preparatory £3,892–£4,679. Lunch: £200 (Nursery), £210 (Pre-Preparatory and Preparatory).

The School stands in 200 acres of grounds in the green belt on the slopes of the North Downs, approximately 1 mile outside Caterham.

The curriculum offers the normal range of subjects, including Technology and Science, in well-equipped laboratories. In addition, French is taught from age 4. There is a full PE programme including Soccer, Netball, Cricket, Rounders, Athletics, Tennis, Swimming and Gymnastics. Regular use is made of the sports hall, astroturf and 25m indoor swimming pool. Drama is taught in a purpose-built drama studio.

Over 30 clubs and co-curricular activities take place each week including Computer Club, Sailing, Drama, Short Tennis, Taekwondo, Needlework, Choir, Orchestra and facilities for instrumental tuition.

All classrooms are equipped with their own multimedia computers and are fully networked with screened internet access. There are also separate ICT Suites in both Prep and Pre Prep with 20 computers each.

The Preparatory School enjoys close liaison with Caterham School, to which pupils normally proceed at age 11. In 1995 Caterham School became fully co-educational and a member of United Learning. This heralded an exciting series of developments providing the facilities for all pupils to continue achieving the high standards for which the School is well known.

Charitable status. Caterham School is an Associate School of United Learning and is a Registered Charity, number 1109508.

The Cavendish School

31 Inverness Street, London NW1 7HB
Tel: 020 7485 1958
email: admissions@cavendish-school.co.uk
website: www.cavendishschool.co.uk
Twitter: @CavendishSchool
Facebook: /The-Cavendish-School

Chairman of Governors: Mrs M Robey

Head: **Mrs Teresa Dunbar**, BSc Hons, PGCE, NPQH

Age Range. 3–11.
Number of Children. 229 Day Pupils.
Fees per term (2016–2017). Reception–Year 6: £4,550; Nursery £2,520–£4,350 depending upon number of sessions. Fees include lunch.

The Cavendish School is a small, friendly IAPS school for girls aged three to eleven and boys aged three to seven. The school is situated near Regent's Park in the heart of Camden Town with its excellent public transport links. The

Cavendish has a Christian ethos and welcomes pupils of all faiths and none.

The school is non-selective at entry. We provide manageable class sizes and high teacher-pupil ratios so that the foundations of a good education and effective study habits are laid from the beginning.

Through a broad and balanced curriculum we provide personalised learning and much specialised teaching which allows our pupils to flourish. Many gain entry and scholarships to top senior schools at 11+.

There is an extensive programme of extracurricular activities, after-school care services and flexible arrangements for nursery-age pupils.

Our strengths in music, drama and art are reflected in the renewal of our Artsmark Gold in 2012 by Arts Council England. Class music is taught by specialists; instruction is available in a wide variety of instruments and we have a thriving orchestra and choirs.

The school is housed in well maintained Victorian buildings and a modern wing with purpose-built ICT facilities. It has recently expanded into a new building which contains a further five classrooms and a 230-seater multi-use auditorium.

The school maintains close links with the local community in a variety of ways both charitable and educational.

Our most recent inspection report by the Independent Schools Inspectorate awarded us 'excellent' in all areas and is available to read via our website.

Charitable status. The Cavendish School is a Registered Charity, number 312727.

Chafyn Grove School

33 Bourne Avenue, Salisbury, Wiltshire SP1 1LR
Tel: 01722 333423
Fax: 01722 323114
email: office@chafyngrove.co.uk
website: www.chafyngrove.co.uk
Twitter: @chafyngrove
Facebook: /chafyngrove

Chairman of Governors: Lady Congleton

Headmaster: **Simon Head**, MA Cantab

Age Range. 3–13.
Number of Pupils. 292: 180 Boys, 112 Girls.
Fees per term (2016–2017). Day Children: Reception £2,250, Pre-Prep (Years 1–2) £2,765, Transition (Year 3) £4,095, Main School (Years 4–8) £5,430. Boarding supplement £2,070. Nursery: £19.90 per session.

Chafyn Grove is set in 14 acres of grounds on the edge of the historic city of Salisbury – just an hour and a half from London by road, with easy access to air and rail links. The children thrive in an ambitious academic environment, where good sports facilities; extensive Art, Music and Drama opportunities and a commitment to extracurricular activities encourage your child to discover their interests and their strengths.

Chafyn Grove has a happy family atmosphere that is created by a caring pastoral system and a team of talented and committed teachers. Pupils at Chafyn Grove School enjoy a good relationship with our staff; there is mutual friendship and a healthy respect. Our children also develop good relationships with other pupils, whether younger or older. Assemblies, chapel and tutor time all foster an understanding of how people should treat one another.

We have a mix of day and boarding pupils. Our boarding enhances the sense of community and is all about making the most of your time at school, developing independence

and making friends for life – our aim is to provide a caring and happy environment in which children thrive and grow. Our boarders benefit from a secure and homely atmosphere and are accommodated in cosy, brightly decorated dormitories, often creatively decorated with their own pictures and posters, their own bedding and of course a teddy or two! There is a full weekly activity programme for boarders as well as a full weekend programme where both boarding and teaching staff are fully involved with the children creating a strong bond between staff and pupils.

Small class sizes and a commitment to high standards allow our pupils to perform impressively in the classroom. In 2016 all pupils achieved entry to the senior school of their choice and 10 Scholarships to King's Bruton, Bryanston, Warminster, Marlborough, Sherborne, Candford and Dauntsey's were awarded.

Pupils are also prepared for the 11+ entrance exam to the two Grammar Schools in Salisbury with many children winning places there, although some still opt to stay at Chafyn!

Scholarships to Chafyn are awarded in Years 2, 4, and 6, and take place in at the end of January or early February for admission the following September.

Our facilities include five acres of playing fields, a large astroturf pitch, 25-metre heated swimming pool, 2 tennis courts, 2 squash courts, sports hall, music school, creative arts centre, two science laboratories and a computer centre. A library block with a computerised resource centre and 8 classrooms and a modern Pre-Prep building.

Please go to our website to read the latest 'Excellent' ISI Inspection Report.

Charitable status. Chafyn Grove School is a Registered Charity, number 1119907. It exists to provide an excellent education for children.

Charlotte House Preparatory School
Nursery, Pre-Prep & Preparatory School for Girls

88 The Drive, Rickmansworth, Herts WD3 4DU
Tel: 01923 772101
email: office@chpschool.co.uk
website: www.charlottehouseprepschool.co.uk
Facebook: /CharlotteHousePrepSchool

Chairman of Governors: Mr Paul McGlone

Headmistress: **Miss P Woodcock**, BA Hons QTS

Age Range. 3–11.
Number of Pupils. 140 Girls.
Fees per term (2016–2017). £1,080–£3,875.

Charlotte House is a forward-thinking dynamic school built on traditional values. This winning combination means we instill in our girls all the social and academic tools they need to become independent, successful, confident and caring women.

Our pupils aspire to be the best. We help them discover their talents and encourage them to persevere when they meet challenges. To aid this we teach them a varied curriculum and they are fortunate to have specialist teachers right the way through the school commencing in Nursery.

We are passionate about the learning that goes on outside the classroom walls, whether it is their manners as they move around the school, discovering mini beasts in our beautiful garden or meeting up with their French pen pals in France; we provide the girls with a wealth of experiences to learn more about themselves and the world around them.

Charlotte House encourages the girls to be confident so that they meet challenges head on. We enter many academic and sporting inter-school competitions. We were delighted to win the prestigious Haileybury Science Challenge in 2015 and reached the Prep School Finals Swimming Championships in Sheffield for the third year running. We also encourage the girls to be confident on stage with termly class assemblies and each girl is involved in an annual play.

At Charlotte House, we recognise the importance of strong links between home and school and provide many opportunities for parents to visit us and find out more about their daughter's progress.

Charlotte House has an excellent record at Secondary Transfer and we have a thorough programme in place to ensure both the girls and their parents feel supported and ready for the challenges secondary transfer poses. Our girls go on to a wide range of schools including state and private schools and the secondary schools often comment on how pleased they are to welcome our girls as they know they will be of a high calibre.

We are a dynamic school whose girls achieve great things!

Charitable status. Charlotte House School Limited is a Registered Charity, number 311075.

Cheam School

Headley, Newbury, Berkshire RG19 8LD
Tel: 01635 268381
               Registrar: 01635 267822
Fax: 01635 269345
email: registrar@cheamschool.co.uk
website: www.cheamschool.com
Twitter: @CheamSchool

The School, originally founded in 1645, is a charitable trust controlled by a Board of Governors.

Chairman of Governors: R Boycott

Headmaster: **M J S Harris**, BSc Loughborough, PGCE

Assistant Headmaster: T C Haigh, BA Birmingham, PGCE

Age Range. 3–13.
Number of Pupils. 90 boarders, 425 day children.
Fees per term (2016–2017). £8,995 Boarders; £3,805–£6,655 Day children.

The School became co-educational in September 1997. A merger with Inhurst House School, formerly situated at Baughurst, and which relocated to the Headley site in 1999, offers parents the opportunity for education from 3–13+ for their sons and daughters.

Bursaries are offered annually for 8 year olds.

Classes are small (maximum 18) and pupils are prepared for the major senior independent schools with Eton, Harrow, Radley, Marlborough, Sherborne, Wellington, Downe House, St Mary's Ascot, St Mary's Calne and Sherborne Girls' featuring frequently. Recent improvements include excellent facilities for Design Technology and Information Technology, a dedicated Science Building, a refurbished Chapel and Teaching Block, a Music School, a Sports Hall and much improved boarding facilities. Dormitories are comfortable, carpeted and curtained. A new Art & Design Centre and Pre-Prep classrooms and Assembly Hall opened in September 2012.

Rugby, Soccer and Cricket are the major team games for boys; Netball, Rounders, Tennis and Hockey for girls. A heated outdoor swimming pool, 6 all-weather tennis courts and a 9-hole golf course in the extensive 80-acre grounds

allow a wide range of other sports and pastimes to be enjoyed.

The School is situated half way between Newbury and Basingstoke on the A339 and is within easy reach of the M3 and M4 motorways and the A34 trunk route from Portsmouth, Southampton and Winchester to Oxford and the Midlands. London Heathrow Airport is within an hour's drive.

Charitable status. Cheam School Educational Trust is a Registered Charity, number 290143. It provides high-class education for boarding and day pupils; traditional values; modern thinking; education for the 21st century.

Cheltenham College Preparatory School

Thirlestaine Road, Cheltenham, Gloucestershire GL53 7AB
Tel: 01242 522697
Fax: 01242 265620
email: prepadmissions@cheltenhamcollege.org
website: www.cheltenhamcollege.org
Twitter: @cheltprep
Facebook: @cheltenham.prep

President of Council: Mr Bill Straker Nesbit

Headmaster: **Mr J F Whybrow**, BEd Exeter

Age Range. 3–13.
Number of Pupils. 400 (40 boarders, 360 day boys and girls).
Fees per term (2016–2017). Boarders £5,725–£7,470; Day Boys and Girls £2,560–£5,750.

Cheltenham College Preparatory School is a co-educational preparatory school from 3 to 13. The Pre-Prep Department, Kingfishers, is located in a separate purpose-built wing.

The school stands in a beautiful 15-acre site near the centre of Regency Cheltenham; the town itself being well served by both motorway and rail networks. Pupils enjoy a brand new, dedicated Science and Technology Centre with university grade Science labs and state-of-the-art technology equipment including a laser cutter and 3D printer. Around the school, other excellent facilities include: an art studio, extensive ICT suites, music school, large multi-purpose Assembly Hall, and woodland Forest School. It also benefits from the College's amenities including the stunning College Chapel, spacious sports complex with a 25m indoor swimming pool, floodlit astroturf all-weather pitches, athletics track, squash courts, tennis courts, and fully-equipped Science laboratories.

The curriculum is wide and stimulating with all pupils being prepared for 13+ Common Entrance and Scholarship examinations. In addition to the normal academic subjects, all pupils study Art, Music, PE, Information Technology, and Design & Technology, all led by a team of professional and dedicated teachers.

A wide range of sports are available including: rugby, cricket, hockey, cross country, netball, badminton, athletics, golf, gymnastics, squash, ballet, sailing, skiing, horse riding, fencing, archery, swimming, tennis and orienteering. Sporting skills are taught from an early age and include swimming for the whole school.

The Boarding House aims to provide a 'home from home', with excellent pastoral care and a wide range of extracurricular activities under the supervision of the House Parents. The boarding facilities themselves are large and airy, with plenty of pictures, toys and colourful duvets making the place warm and homely. Regular contact with parents is encouraged with frequent exeat weekends, with flexi boarding being a popular option for children from Year 3 up. Progress reports are issued three times a term and either formal parent/teacher meetings are held or full reports issued at the end of each term.

Visitors are warmly welcomed and further information is available from the Prep Admissions team, who arranges school tours, Taster Days, entry assessments and meetings with the Headmaster, Jonathan Whybrow.

Charitable status. Cheltenham College is a Registered Charity, number 311720. It exists to provide education for boys and girls.

Chesham Preparatory School

Two Dells Lane, Chesham, Bucks HP5 3QF
Tel: 01494 782619
Fax: 01494 791645
email: secretary@cheshamprep.co.uk
            registrar@cheshamprep.co.uk
website: www.cheshamprep.co.uk

Chairman of Governors: Mr Nick Baker, BA Hons, PGCE

Headmaster: Mr Michael Davies, BA, PGCE

Age Range. 3–13.
Numbers of Pupils. 400 boys and girls.
Fees per term (2016–2017). £2,950–£4,550 (inc lunch).
Chesham Preparatory School has a well justified reputation for being an incredibly friendly school where boys and girls work hard, behave well and achieve wonderful things. The most recent ISI report (2016) is glowing in its praise for a school in which, "The quality of the pupils' achievements and learning is excellent. The pupils' attitude to their work and learning is exemplary."

Founded in 1938, Chesham Prep has developed into a flourishing co-educational school. As a non-selective school which educates pupils from 3 to 13 years of age, it champions the strong belief that boys and girls of Prep school age should be educated together. They thrive in the holistic, caring environment and there is a real emphasis on ensuring that every child fulfils his or her potential whatever their varied strengths.

In September 2011 the school was delighted to announce the opening of its nursery – extending the provision offered to children rising 3 years old. From that early age, the children are well prepared for a smooth transition into their Reception class and, very importantly, they feel part of the Chesham Prep family.

The school boasts excellent success rates at 11+ Grammar school entry, as well as 13+ Common Entrance to senior independent schools. All pupils benefit enormously from the wonderful years of personal development at Chesham Prep.

Sports teams are highly skilled and competitive, while there is a fabulous choir and orchestra, as well as a wide range of opportunities for involvement in the creative arts. Children are encouraged to express themselves with joy and passion!

Above all, it is the aim of Chesham Preparatory School to inspire children with a love of learning and a confidence to make the most of their abilities.

To find out more or to arrange to visit the school, please visit our website: www.cheshamprep.co.uk.

Charitable status. Chesham Preparatory School is a Registered Charity, number 310642. It exists to provide education for boys and girls.

Chigwell Junior School

Chigwell, Essex IG7 6QF
Tel: 020 8501 5721
Fax: 020 8501 5723
email: admissions@chigwell-school.org
website: www.chigwell-school.org

Chairman of the Governors: Mrs S Aliker, BA, MBA, ACMA

Head of the Junior School: Mr A Stubbs, BA, PGCE

Age Range. 4–13.
Number of Pupils. 560 Day Pupils.
Fees per term (2016–2017). £3,590–£5,500 inc Lunch/Tea.
The Junior School is housed in a purpose-built building on the same site as the Senior School only 7 miles from the heart of London. It shares the use of a wide range of activities and facilities including Chapel, Science laboratories, Music School, Arts and Technology Centre, Theatre, Gymnasium, Swimming Pool, Sports Hall and 100 acres of playing fields.

The curriculum and administration of the Senior and Junior Schools are very closely linked and are overseen by the Headmaster.

Pupils sit a written test for entry to the Junior School and are normally admitted to the Senior School without further examination. (*See Chigwell School entry in HMC section.*)

A Pre-Prep opened in September 2013 for 4–7 year old children in a purpose-built building. Entry is by assessment.

Charitable status. Chigwell School is a Registered Charity, number 1115098. It exists to provide a rounded education of the highest quality for its pupils.

Chinthurst School

Tadworth, Surrey KT20 5QZ
Tel: 01737 812011
Fax: 01737 814835
email: info@chinthurstschool.co.uk
website: www.chinthurstschool.co.uk
Twitter: @ChintSchool

The School is an Educational Trust, administered by a Board of Governors.

Chairman of Governors: Mr Andrew Bisset

Headmaster: Mr Tim Button, BEd

Age Range. Rising 3–13.
Number of Pupils. 152.
Fees per term (2016–2017). Nursery: £330 per session, £3,125 (full-time); Pre-Prep £3,125 (Lunch £280); Preparatory £4,350 (Lunch £290).
The School is set in modern and attractive rural surroundings with spacious games facilities including a swimming pool and astroturf area.

Pupils are prepared for all Senior Independent Schools, by way of the Common Entrance or Scholarships. A very experienced and well-qualified staff ensures a high standard is achieved both academically and on the games field. Chinthurst has a 'family' ethos, aimed at the achievement of high academic standards allied to a purposeful and active school life within a happy environment.

Charitable status. Chinthurst School is a Registered Charity, number 271160 A/1.

The Chorister School

Durham DH1 3EL

Tel: 0191 384 2935
Fax: 0191 383 1275
email: secretary@thechoristerschool.com
website: www.thechoristerschool.com

Chairman of Governors: The Dean of Durham, The Very
Revd Michael Sadgrove

Headteacher: **Mrs Y F S Day**, BMus Cape Town, MMus
London, GDL College of Law

Age Range. 3–13.

Number of Pupils. 220 (40 Boarders, 180 day pupils,
including 69 in the Nursery and the Pre-Prep.) The school
became co-educational in 1995 and there are girls in every
year group.

Fees per term (2016–2017). Choristers (including piano
lessons) £3,585, Full/Weekly Boarders £6,840, Day Pupils
£3,995, Pre-Prep £2,935, Nursery £22.95 per half day session. Reductions are available for children of CofE clergy,
serving members of the armed forces, children of Durham
University staff, children of former pupils and for younger
siblings. Scholarships available at entry to Year 7. Fees are
inclusive of all normal requirements; there are no compulsory extras.

The Chorister School is in an outstanding situation in a
World Heritage Site tucked behind Durham Cathedral. Quiet
and secluded it is a haven in the centre of Durham City.
Whilst it is the school for the choristers who sing in the
renowned Cathedral Choir, over eighty per cent of pupils are
not choristers.

Pastoral care is the responsibility of all members of staff.
The needs of the boarders are attended to by a dedicated
team led by the Housemistress, Housemaster and Headmistress. Before and After School Care is available from the
Nursery onwards and there is a wide range of after-school
activities including: Art, Ancient Greek, Textiles, Rowing,
Gardening, Choirs, Dance, Film Club, Sports, Speech and
Drama, Music Ensembles and World Challenge. Flexible
boarding is also available.

Our curriculum introduces French from Pre-Prep level,
where each of the classes has its own class teacher. In the
Prep School class-teaching of the core curriculum is gradually replaced by subject-specialist teaching as children are
prepared for Common Entrance and Scholarship examinations to senior schools. The school has a reputation for academic success, but cherishes all its pupils, whatever their
academic attainment. The curriculum, which includes RE,
PE, swimming, Art, Technology and Music, is designed to
ensure that academic edge does not lead to academic nar-
rowness.

Games are an important element in the curriculum. The
Chorister School competes at various levels with other
schools in athletics, cricket, netball, hockey, rounders,
rugby, football and swimming. Badminton, volleyball, basketball, tennis, indoor football and netball (in our large
Sports Hall) are also played. The Chorister School has its
own sports fields, tennis court and play areas, and uses the
indoor swimming pool at Durham Cathedral.

Individual instrumental music lessons are available in
almost all instruments, and all pupils take class music in
which they sing and learn about musical history, musical
instruments, simple analysis and some famous pieces.

Entry is by English and Maths test graded according to
age or by informal assessment during a 'taster' day, as
seems best for the age of the individual child. Competitive
auditions for aspiring Choristers are held regularly, with pre-
audition training sessions offered by appointment.

Next School. Children move from The Chorister School
to a wide range of maintained and independent secondary
schools throughout the North East and further afield. The
school advises and guides parents in the appropriate choice
of next school and aims to secure a successful transition for
every pupil. In the past ten years every child has won a place
to the senior school of choice, with an average of 60% winning an academic or subject scholarship or a competitive
entry place.

Charitable status. The Chorister School and Durham
Cathedral enjoy charitable status (exempt from registration)
and the school exists to provide boarding education for the
choristers of Durham Cathedral and day or boarding education for other children aged 3–13.

Christ Church Cathedral School

3 Brewer Street, Oxford OX1 1QW

Tel: 01865 242561
Fax: 01865 202945
email: schooloffice@cccs.org.uk
website: www.cccs.org.uk

Chairman of Governors: The Very Reverend Professor
Martyn Percy, Dean of Christ Church

Headmaster: **Mr Richard Murray**, BA, MA

Age Range. 3–13 (Co-ed Nursery).
Number of Boys. 20 boarders, all of whom are Cathedral
Choristers (who must board), and 135 day pupils.

Fees per term (2016–2017). Day boys (including lunch)
£5,059; Pre-Prep £3,525 (including lunch); Cathedral Choristers £3,188; Probationer Choristers: £3,526 (Chorister
fees are subsidised by the Cathedral); Nursery £938–£2,308.

Christ Church Cathedral School is a day Preparatory and
Pre-Preparatory School for Boys with a Co-ed Nursery.

The School provides Choristers for the choirs of Christ
Church Cathedral and Worcester College, and is governed
by the Dean and Canons of Christ Church, with the assistance of lay members drawn from the city's professional
community, some of whom are past or current parents.

It was founded in 1546 when provision was made for the
education of eight Choristers in King Henry VIII's foundation of Christ Church on the site of Cardinal Wolsey's earlier
foundation of Cardinal College. In the latter half of the nineteenth century, at the initiative of Dean Liddell, father of
Alice Liddell, the inspiration for 'Alice in Wonderland', the
boarding house was established at No 1 Brewer Street, and
in 1892, during the Headship of the Reverend Henry Sayers,
father of Dorothy L Sayers, the Italian Mediaeval scholar
and creator of Lord Peter Wimsey, the present building was
erected.

The School is centrally situated off St Aldates, two hundred yards from Christ Church. It therefore enjoys the
unique cultural background provided by Oxford itself as
well as beautiful playing fields on Christ Church Meadow.
Buildings include a former residence of Cardinal Wolsey
and the Sir William Walton Centre, which contains a recital
hall and spacious classrooms.

Charitable status. Christ Church Cathedral School Education Trust is a Registered Charity, number 1114828.

Churcher's College Junior School

Midhurst Road, Liphook, Hampshire GU30 7HT

Tel: 01730 236870
Fax: 01428 722550
email: ccjsoffice@churcherscollege.com
website: www.churcherscollege.com

Chairman of Governors: M J Gallagher, Dip Arch Hons,
RIBA, MIoD, FIMgt

Head: **Mrs F Robinson**, BA, MA

Age Range. 2¾–11 Co-educational.
Number of Pupils. 230.
Fees per term (2016–2017). £3,020–£3,225 excluding
lunch.

Churcher's College Junior School provides a happy, stimulating, safe and secure environment in which every child feels valued and is able to develop personally, socially and academically. Each child is nurtured and taught to hold a high regard for others and themselves.

We view education as a joint partnership between teachers, parents and pupils, and strive to develop a team spirit in which every member gives of their best. We hold high expectations of staff and pupils and aim to create an environment that values individuals, applauds success, strives to encourage questioning, lets pupils explore, be controversial and be special.

The Junior School is sited in Liphook approximately 8 miles from the College, but continues to have strong links with the Senior School in Petersfield.

The school is set in beautiful rural surroundings providing extensive grounds for sports practices, three separate playing areas and a nature garden. Latest computer technology, networked classroom computers and interactive whiteboards are all used by staff and pupils to enhance curriculum studies. The school has a fully-equipped computing suite, science laboratory, dedicated music and art rooms and a Performing Arts wing.

The wider curriculum is valued, offering additional depth and scope in all subjects and pupils are encouraged to take part in a broad range of experiences both in and out of the classroom. The Sensory Garden and external Education and Activity Trail enhance the quality of outdoor learning.

Churcher's College Junior School provides pupils with:

- a broad-based and challenging curriculum that enables all pupils to achieve their individual potential in all areas and caters for their individual abilities, needs and interests.
- a functional education in which pupils are able to develop transferable skills and a love of learning that will enable them to succeed in the ever-changing world.
- experiences of an aesthetic, creative and spiritual nature, with an emphasis on Learning Outside the Classroom

Teaching and learning activities cater for the varying needs of our pupils and allow all to achieve their full potential in a wide variety of areas – academic, creative, sporting, outdoor learning etc.

We maintain a broad and balanced curriculum in which pupils experience a wide range of activities to maximise their learning opportunities. Teaching is grounded in pupils past experiences and they are helped to see the importance of each area of study.

The school is seen as a continually evolving organisation and we constantly reflect upon practice as a means of self-improvement.

Charitable status. Churcher's College is a Registered Charity, number 307320.

City of London Freemen's Junior School

Ashtead Park, Surrey KT21 1ET

Tel: 01372 822474 (PA)
            01372 822423 (Admissions)
Fax: 01372 822415
            01372 822416 (Admissions)
email: admissions@clfs.surrey.sch.uk
website: www.clfs.surrey.sch.uk

Co-educational day school.

Chairman of Governors: Mr Roger Chadwick
Head: **Mr Matt Robinson**, BA Hons, MA, MEd

Age Range. 7–13.
Number of Pupils. 397.
Fees per term (2016–2017). Tuition £4,229–£4,588.

The City of London Freemen's Junior School was established formally in 1988 as an integral part of CLFS and it prepares girls and boys for entry to the Senior School in Year 9. The School is located on a magnificent 57-acre site in Ashtead Park, Surrey, where the many outstanding facilities are available to all pupils (*see separate entry in HMC section*).

With its broad based curriculum and modern purpose-built facilities, the Junior School offers a challenging and unique atmosphere for all. There is a Junior School Head with specialist teaching staff and a clearly defined academic and pastoral structure to ensure that all pupils know what is expected of them. The Junior School encourages young pupils to develop their strengths and discover new skills and passions in an environment of kindness, honesty and fun. There are usually 20 pupils in each of the three parallel classes in each year group. In Year 7 the year groups rises to four classes. Junior pupils benefit greatly from seeing their Form Prefects, who are Sixth Formers from the Senior School, on a daily basis.

For the first four years, in Key Stage 2, Heads of Year work in liaison with the subject coordinators and the Heads of Senior School Departments to ensure that the programmes of work are compatible and progressive. The aim is to establish a secure foundation in traditional core subjects within a curriculum which will broaden experience and excite the imagination of each child. In Years 7 and 8 the teaching programme is managed by the Heads of the Senior School Departments using specialist teachers for all of the subjects. Whilst academic excellence throughout the Junior School is still a major aim, there is also an enrichment programme and a very full programme of extracurricular activities including drama, music and sports.

Fully integrated into whole school routines, the Junior School takes full advantage of Ashtead Park's facilities. Extensive playing fields, the floodlit all-weather pitch and the sports hall ensure that the sports facilities available are second to none.

There are three Houses in the School providing pastoral care and supervision whilst also promoting healthy competition in many activities. In both the Senior and the Junior School outstanding work and good progress, inside and outside the classroom, are recognised by the award of appropriate merits and distinctions.

Admission to the Junior School is through entrance examination, interview and feeder school report. Progression to the Senior School is based on continuous assessment with no separate qualifying entrance test and as such is almost always automatic for Junior School pupils. Pupils are constantly reviewed and can be assured that they will move through to the Senior School with many familiar faces around them.

Claremont Fan Court Pre-Preparatory and Nursery School

Claremont Drive, Esher, Surrey KT10 9LY
Tel: 01372 463695
email: preprepschool@claremont.surrey.sch.uk
           info@claremont.surrey.sch.uk
website: www.claremont-school.co.uk

Chair of Governors: Mr Gordon Hunt, MA Kingston, Adv Dip Ed Exeter, Cert Ed Belfast

Head: Mrs Louise Fox, BEd Hons

Age Range. 2½–7 Co-educational.
Number of Pupils. 145.
The Pre-Preparatory and Nursery School ensures that the beginning of each child's education is a happy and fulfilling experience. We combine enthusiasm for learning in a stimulating, creative environment with dedicated teachers and assistants. Values for life are taught in a supportive, caring atmosphere with shared aims and aspirations between home and School.

The School is situated in wooded parkland where children have the freedom to grow and develop in a secure and healthy environment. Here we care for the needs of Claremont Fan Court's youngest children in spacious classrooms with excellent facilities and resources.

We place a strong emphasis on the children acquiring sound knowledge and skills in literacy and numeracy, whilst providing every opportunity to explore and develop each child's potential in creative, sporting and musical activities.

Fees per term (2016–2017). Pre-Nursery (per morning) £355; Nursery (5 mornings per week) £1,665; Nursery (per afternoon) £333; Reception, Years 1 & 2 £3,325.

Charitable status. The Claremont Fan Court Foundation Limited is Registered Charity, number 274664.

Claremont Fan Court Preparatory School

Claremont Drive, Esher, Surrey KT10 9LY
Tel: 01372 465380
email: prepschool@claremont.surrey.sch.uk
           info@claremont.surrey.sch.uk
website: www.claremont-school.co.uk

Chair of Governors: Mr Gordon Hunt, MA Kingston, Adv Dip Ed Exeter, Cert Ed Belfast

Head: Mr Duncan Murphy, BA Hons, MEd, FRSA, FCMI, FCollT

Age Range. 7–11 Co-educational.
Number of Pupils. 200.
The Preparatory School is housed in the historic Stable Court and backs onto an idyllic Walled Garden, originally built by Sir John Vanbrugh in 1708. Whilst there is a rich cultural and historical heritage that permeates every aspect of their day-to-day life, pupils also benefit from a progressive educational philosophy which incorporates the very best of contemporary practice.

Life here is busy, engaging and fulfilling. An atmosphere of conviviality underpins our dynamic curriculum, which offers each child the opportunity to develop their unlimited potential in and out of the classroom. The ethos of our school promotes tolerance, respect and friendship; children

settle in and become a valued member of our tight-knit community very quickly.

We are fortunate to be situated within a hundred acres of beautiful Grade One listed landscape; this spectacular setting provides the backdrop to a hive of industry where children thrive in a stimulating environment. No two days are ever the same! Friendships flourish and confidence is nurtured by a rich educational experience which overflows with energy and excitement.

There is a forward-thinking curriculum which incorporates the latest ICT thinking, careful pastoral care and a broad range of co-curricular activities. A keenly contested House system with points available for effort, academic performance and a range of competitions throughout the school year captures the imagination of the children and provides an additional sense of camaraderie.

Each child is closely monitored by a vigilant team of staff; the form teacher is initially responsible for the academic development and general well-being of the children in their class whilst the Director of Studies oversees the academic and pastoral implementation of the curriculum. The Head plays an active role in the day-to-day life of the pupils and maintains a keen interest in, as well as overall responsibility for, their academic progress and pastoral well-being.

Fees per term (2016–2017). £4,190.

Charitable status. The Claremont Fan Court Foundation Limited is Registered Charity, number 274664.

Clayesmore Preparatory School

Iwerne Minster, Blandford Forum, Dorset DT11 8PH
Tel: 01747 813155
email: prepadmissions@clayesmore.com
website: www.clayesmore.com
Twitter: @clayesmoreprep

Chairman of Governors: Mr J Andrews, LLB

Headmaster: Mr W G Dunlop, BA

Age Range. Rising 3–13 years.
Number of Pupils. 217 (Boarders 56, Day 161).
Fees per term (2016–2017). Boarders: £5,620 (Year 3), £7,990 (Years 4–8). Day Pupils: £2,450 (Pre-Prep), £4,210 (Year 3), £5,970 (Years 4–8).

Filled with a warm, friendly atmosphere, Clayesmore Prep offers excitement and opportunity at every turn with the aim of developing the unique gifts of every pupil. Founded in 1929 at Charlton Marshall House by R A L Everett, the Prep School moved to Iwerne Minster in 1974 and now nestles side by side with the thriving Senior School. There is also a Nursery and Pre-Prep, with their own snug self-contained home, where little ones learn and develop through play and via a host of activities led by specialist teachers.

An ongoing development programme has provided this fully co-educational school with outstanding facilities for sport, music, drama and the arts, while the 62-acre parkland campus, in beautiful rural Dorset, is the ideal environment for young ones to experience a true childhood as they grow. A state-of-the-art building was opened in 2008 comprising five classrooms and two Science laboratories. An adventure playground, complete with pirate ship, has recently been built, and the ballpark has been updated.

The 'all through' provision means there is a comfortable transition between schools and Prep pupils can make a worry-free step up to Senior School accompanied by a soothing sense of familiarity.

Day children can join Pre-Prep at the start of the term in which they are 3 and the youngest boarders usually arrive at age 7/8. The boarders enjoy welcoming boarding facilities with nurturing pastoral care, friendly staff and a real family feel.

Admission is normally by interview and a report from a child's previous school. Academic, Art, Music, Sporting and All-Rounder Scholarships are offered each year, together with 11+ Continuity Scholarships for candidates intending to go on to the dynamic Clayesmore Sixth Form in the Senior School.

The school is proud of its long association with HM Forces and offers a number of service bursaries. There are also children from expatriate families and the school is well versed in handling overseas travel arrangements.

Small classes and individual attention ensure speedy progress and each day at Clayesmore is further enriched by the superb facilities and exciting activities. Younger children spend most of their time with their Form Teacher but by age 10, children are taught by specialist subject teachers. In the upper school the children are put in sets for Mathematics and English, with some streaming taking place in Science, Humanities and Languages, to allow them to proceed at their own pace. Though the pressure of academic work increases as examinations approach, every child experiences a full range of Art, Music, ICT, Design Technology and Games as well as vital play and relaxation time.

There is a strong sporting life at Clayesmore with the main games for boys being rugby, hockey, football and cricket and for girls: netball, hockey, tennis and rounders. A well-equipped Sports Centre with a 25-metre heated pool, a floodlit all-weather hockey pitch and extensive playing fields provide every opportunity for pupils to reach the highest standards. The school also enjoys considerable success at athletics, swimming and orienteering, and numerous other sports are also available.

Music is highly regarded and many children are encouraged to learn an instrument. The Chapel Choir has toured in Italy, France, Germany, USA, Spain, South Africa and Prague. As well as Prep School orchestras there are several instrumental ensembles and the Concert Band that draws the best instrumentalists from both schools, is in hot demand locally, as well having toured abroad. There is also excellent Art provision and the Prep School has its own dedicated Art Department with separate pottery.

Clayesmore has an outstanding reputation for supporting pupils with dyslexia. Regular staff training means that the work of the Learning Support specialists is understood and reinforced by subject staff and form teachers.

When they are ready to move on to the next stage of their education, pupils are prepared for Common Entrance and Senior School Scholarship examinations.

Charitable status. Clayesmore School Limited is a Registered Charity, number 306214. It exists for the purpose of educating children.

Clifton College Pre-Preparatory School

Guthrie Road, Clifton, Bristol BS8 3EZ

Tel:	0117 405 8470
Fax:	0117 315 7592
email:	prepadmissions@cliftoncollege.com
website:	www.cliftoncollege.com
Twitter:	@Clifton_College
Facebook:	/CliftonCollegeUK
LinkedIn:	/clifton-college

Chairman of College Council: Mr Richard Morgan, MA

Headmistress: **Joanne Newman**, BSc, MSc, PGCE

Age Range. 2–8.

Number of Pupils. 187.

Fees per term (2016–2017). 2 year olds (3–5 full days) £2,150–£3,500; 3–4 year olds (3–5 full days) £2,000–£3,150; Reception (5 full days) £3,150; Year 1 £3,350; Years 2–3 £3,200.

Clifton College Pre-Preparatory School, part of the main Preparatory School, is independent of Clifton College in terms of running and organisation. However, it benefits from being governed by the same Council and enjoys the considerable advantages of sharing many of the College's extensive facilities. These include the swimming pool, sports hall, gymnasium, multi-activity hall, Chapel and Theatre. The School is situated in two buildings either side of a superb playground with a variety of play equipment.

The School caters for children in the Foundation Stage (Nursery and Reception), Key Stage 1 (Years 1 and 2) and Year 3, the first year of Key Stage 2. The Nursery has up to 50 children on roll, with a staff-pupil ratio of 1–8. Attendance in the Nursery may be either five mornings, three days or full-time. Morning sessions include lunch at no extra cost. The Nursery staff are either qualified teachers or Early Years practitioners.

There are two classes in Reception and in Years 1, 2 and three in Year 3. Each with a class teacher and teaching assistant. In all there are 22 full-time and 15 part-time staff. Qualified specialist class teachers deliver a topic-based curriculum, with specialist teachers for Music, Dance (Ballet, Jazz Dance, Tap), Sport, French, Mandarin and IT. Piano and instrumental lessons are available from Year 2, and all children in Years 2 and 3 learn the recorder, strings and sing in the choir. Some sports activity takes place every day.

Life at the Pre-Preparatory is busy and challenging. Year 2 and 3 pupils may take part in a range of co-curricular activities at lunchtimes or after school, when around sixteen clubs and societies are held. These change termly and include a variety of sports, sewing, puppet-making, junior detectives, zoo club, chess etc. Termly services and concerts are held in the Chapel, and an annual musical is performed in the Redgrave Theatre. There is a full programme of visits and outings for all ages, including a youth hosteling trip for Year 3.

Recent investment has seen the creation of an outdoor area leading from the reception classrooms. This is designed to give reception classes easy access to an outdoor space which they can use to extend and enhance their learning.

Another exciting provision is the Forest School at our Beggar's Bush Sports Ground. All year groups, from Nursery to Year 3, visit the School and it provides a range of stimulating outdoor experiences for the children, enabling them to learn, achieve and develop confidence through curriculum-linked activities and free exploration of the natural woodland.

Charitable status. Clifton College is a Registered Charity, number 311735. It provides boarding and day education for boys and girls aged 2–18.

Clifton College Preparatory School

The Avenue, Clifton, Bristol BS8 3HE

Tel:	+44 (0)117 405 8396
Fax:	+44 (0)117 315 7504
email:	prepadmissions@cliftoncollege.com
website:	www.cliftoncollege.com
Twitter:	@Clifton_College
Facebook:	/CliftonCollegeUK
LinkedIn:	/clifton-college

Chairman of College Council: Mr Richard Morgan, MA

Headmaster: J Milne, BA, MBA

Age Range. 8–13.
Number of Pupils. 307.
Fees per term (2016–2017). Boarders (from Year 4) £7,140–£9,080; Flexi Boarders (3 nights from Year 4) £5,155–£6,495; Day Pupils £4,155–£5,495.

There is a full time teaching staff of 58, all of whom are qualified. A wide range of subjects is included in the normal curriculum.

The majority of pupils go on to the Upper School with whom there is cooperation on curriculum matters, but a number are prepared for and win scholarships to other schools. Over 60 awards have been won in the past three years. Pupils can be prepared for the Common Entrance examination to other schools.

The administration of the School is entirely separate from the Upper School, but some facilities are shared, including the Chapel, Theatre, Sports Complex, Indoor Swimming Pool, Gymnasium, Squash and Rackets Courts and 90 acres of playing fields. This includes an Olympic-standard water-based Hockey pitch, a 3G pitch, and an indoor Tennis and Net-ball Centre and a new Activity Centre. The School has its own Art & Design Centre and possesses one of the most advanced Information Technology Centres in the West of England.

The single-sex system operates for both boarders and day pupils. Two Houses cater for the boarders, each under the supervision of a Housemaster or Housemistress assisted by wife or husband, Tutors and Matrons. The remaining six Houses cater specifically for day pupils. In September 2012 a new substantial building opened, purpose-built and in keeping within the local Conservation area containing two Houses, with a whole level having a dance studio with light-rigging and sprung-floor. All other Houses are fully renovated.

Out-of-school activities supplementing the main School games are many and varied, the aim being to give every child an opportunity to participate in an activity from which he or she gains confidence and a sense of achievement.

The youngest boys and girls (aged 2–8) work separately in the Pre-Preparatory School next door, under the care of their own Head and teachers. (*See separate IAPS entry for Clifton College Pre-Preparatory School.*)

Charitable status. Clifton College is a Registered Charity, number 311735. It provides boarding and day education for boys and girls aged 2–18 years.

Fees per term (2016–2017). Nursery (full time) £2,490; Reception, Years 1 & 2: £2,690; Year 3: £2,885. Nursery Education Grant accepted for 3 and 4 year olds.

Clifton School and Nursery is the Pre-prep of St Peter's School, York. The school has large modern buildings on the St Peter's School site which occupies 47 acres in the centre of York. There are new outdoor play surfaces and 25m swimming pool.

Curriculum. An exciting and dynamic thematic skills based curriculum is covered, which offers breath and challenge to all of its pupils. There is a Thinking Skills lesson each week where children are encouraged to be independent. Small classes, individual attention and after-school activities enable high standards to be achieved. French is offered to all children from Nursery upwards.

Music and Drama. Nursery children have a session of music and movement, and all other classes have weekly lessons with a specialist teacher. From Year 2, children have the opportunity to learn to play the recorder, piano, violin or guitar at school. Each year there are opportunities for children to participate in performances to a wider audience. All classes have weekly drama lessons, and there is the opportunity for Y2 and Y3 to do speech and drama as an after school activity.

Sport and Co-Curricular Activities. Physical Education starts in the Nursery. As children grow older, games and swimming are added. The pupils at Clifton School and Nursery have access to the sports facilities at St Peter's School. Co-curricular activities include Board Games, Chess, Swim Squad, Badminton, Team Games, Football and Tag Rugby, Tennis, Choir, Speech and Drama, Art Clubs, Explorers Club, Library Club, K'Nex & Lego Clubs and Cookery.

Assessments. Throughout Nursery and Reception children work towards achieving the Early Learning Goals, culminating in the completion of the Foundation Stage Profile. Work is assessed continuously and children's progress is discussed at monthly staff meetings. Incas is used in Years 1 to 3 for assessment purposes which informs future planning. There is ongoing communication between parents and staff through a reports system, invitations to visit the school and parent evenings.

At the last ISI inspection, the inspectors reported that: "The School provides a high-quality education, which is outstanding in several important respects".

Charitable status. St Peter's School, York, is a Registered Charity, number 1141329. It exists to provide education for boys and girls.

Clifton School and Nursery
The Pre-prep School of St Peter's School, York

Clifton, York YO30 6AB
Tel: 01904 527361
Fax: 01904 527304
email: enquiries@cliftonyork.org.uk
website: www.cliftonyork.org.uk
Twitter: @PhilHardyCPS
Facebook: /clifton.school.and.nursery

Chairman of the Governors: Mr W Woolley

Head: Mr Philip Hardy, BA Northumbria, PGCE

Deputy Head: Mrs Antonia Clarke

Age Range. 3–8 co-educational.
Number of Pupils. 115 boys, 94 girls.

Cokethorpe Junior School

Witney, Oxfordshire OX29 7PU
Tel: 01993 703921
Fax: 01993 773499
email: admin@cokethorpe.org
website: www.cokethorpe.org.uk
Twitter: @cokethorpe

Chairman of Governors: Sir John Allison, KCB, CBE, FRAeS

Headmaster: D J Ettinger, BA, FRSA, MA, PGCE

Head of Junior School: Mrs C A Cook, BEd Hons

Age Range. 4–11 Co-educational.
Number of Pupils. 133.
Fees per term (2016–2017). £4,050 Reception–Year 2, £4,150 Years 3–6. Fees include lunch.

Staff. 17 full-time and 4 part-time qualified and enthusiastic staff teach the 10 classes.

Location. Cokethorpe Junior School is set in 150 acres of beautiful Oxfordshire parkland, two miles from Witney and ten from Oxford. It was established in 1994 and occupies the elegant Queen Anne Mansion House that is at the heart of Cokethorpe School. The Junior School retains its own identity, independence and distinct character, allowing the children to flourish, develop confidence and feel valued, whilst having the advantage of being part of a wider community with the Senior School.

Facilities. Whilst self-sufficient in most respects, the Junior School benefits from having access to the Senior School facilities, especially the all-weather pitches, Sports Hall and other sports facilities, performing arts, science laboratories, ICT resources and the splendid Dining Hall. There is also a dedicated play area, library, art room and music room.

Aims. Excellence is at the heart of Cokethorpe School with success measured by the progress of the individual. Teaching and learning extends beyond the classroom and participation is encouraged across all aspects of school life, challenging each child to aim higher, try harder and discover their own potential. Children in the Junior School are excellent company, great fun, hardworking and eager to be involved in all the School has to offer. It is a firm belief at Cokethorpe that children have individual talents, and providing a range of opportunities for them to discover new skills and passions is essential. Whether it is an appetite for academic challenge, a creative flair, a musical ear or natural athleticism, the variety provided by the academic and extra-curricular programme ensures that children experience a host of new activities and are inspired to pursue those they enjoy.

Curriculum. The Junior School offers a fully balanced curriculum with the focus on developing high standards and providing intellectual challenges. Children receive vital foundations for study in small classes and in a positive and purposeful learning environment. Whilst the National Curriculum is followed, the freedom to offer breadth is fully embraced. Trips and events support work done in the classroom and also help children meet the School's high academic, behavioural and social expectations.

Enrichment. Sport and The Arts play a strong part in the Junior School. Children participate in team sports on two afternoons a week, including competitive fixtures, and time is also found for other sports such as swimming, tennis, judo, golf, modern dance and ballet. There are drama productions each year and it is often the case that every child has a speaking or singing role. In addition they have the opportunity to take part in concerts and recitals throughout the year. The dedicated art room is a riot of colour and creativity with displays decorating the corridors and classroom walls.

The School enjoys a particularly close relationship with parents and there is a strong Parents' Association.

Entry. There is no formal assessment for entry to the Reception although children will be invited to spend either the day or half day in School. For entry to Years 1 to 6, children are invited to an Assessment Day, during which they will complete an assessment appropriate to their age. Individual arrangements for assessment can be made throughout the academic year. Reports are also requested from the child's current school or nursery. Early registration is recommended as places are limited. The majority of pupils continue to Cokethorpe Senior School, with many going on to achieve scholarships in the Senior School. (*See Cokethorpe School entry in HMC section.*)

Charitable status. Cokethorpe Educational Trust Limited is a Registered Charity, number 309650.

Colfe's Junior School

Horn Park Lane, London SE12 8AW

Tel: 020 8463 8240 Junior Head
           020 8463 8266 Junior Office
Fax: 020 8297 2941
email: junioroffice@colfes.com
website: www.colfes.com

Chairman of the Governors: Mr Matthew Pellereau, BSc, FRICS

Head of the Junior School: Miss C Macleod, MSc

Head of KS2: Mrs V Welch, BA, Cert Ed
Head of KS1/EYFS: Mrs S Gurr, BEd Hons
Director of Studies: Mr M Heil, BEd

Age Range. 3–11.
Number of Pupils. 420 boys and girls.
Fees per term (2016–2017). Junior School, KS2 £4,395 (excluding lunch); KS1 £4,155 (including lunch); EYFS £3,978 (including lunch).

Colfe's Junior School is a co-educational day school under the general direction of the Governors and Headmaster of Colfe's School (founded in 1652). It is academically selective, offers a broad curriculum and aims to provide an excellent all-round education. Children normally enter at the ages of 3, or 4 although the occasional vacancy arises at other times.

The Junior School is housed in modern purpose-built accommodation with spacious and well-equipped classrooms. Small class sizes and a team of well-qualified teachers provide a caring and vibrant environment. Excellent library facilities and specialist accommodation for art and design, ICT and science provide boys and girls with a stimulating environment in which to learn. Full use is made of the school's swimming pool, sports centre, visual and performing arts centre and extensive on-site playing fields including a MUGA sports pitch. The school also holds the freehold of the Old Colfeians' ground at Horn Park.

PE specialists teach a wide range of sports. There is an extensive programme of house and inter-school sports matches. A school choir, orchestra, strings group and numerous ensembles perform frequently both in and out of school. Drama productions normally take place each term. There is a wide range of after-school clubs on offer (over 50 each week for the 7–11 year olds) and a late school scheme until 6 pm. A very successful Breakfast Club is in operation from 7.30 am until 8.00 am each day.

The school has a strong reputation in the local area for excellence within a friendly and caring atmosphere.

Recent developments include the Performing Arts centre and the Pre-prep and Nursery expansion. The opening of the Stewart Building in 2015, comprising a purpose-built Sixth Form suite and eight hi-tech classrooms, marked the end of a £10 million phase of site improvement.

Charitable status. Colfe's School is a Registered Charity, number 1109650. It exists to provide education for children.

Collingwood School

3 Springfield Road, Wallington, Surrey SM6 0BD

Tel: 020 8647 4607
email: secretary@collingwoodschool.org.uk
website: www.collingwoodschool.org.uk

Headteacher: Mrs Dee Heron, BEd

Age Range. 3–11 Co-educational.

Number in School. Day: 100.

Fees per term (2016–2017). £1,530–£2,750 (reduction for siblings).

Collingwood was founded in 1928 and became an Educational Trust in 1978.

It is a school that has deliberately remained small in order to foster a very friendly and caring environment.

Our aim is to give children a first-class academic and sporting education while at the same time instilling the virtues of courtesy, respect and consideration for others. These traditional values, coupled with a modern, relevant education, make Collingwood the happy, purposeful and unique place that it is.

We offer an exciting range of subjects including ICT, French and Spanish. Currently we have over twelve extra-curricular activities taking place each week including street dance, drama, football, gardening, gymnastics and Latin. Children are also able to learn to play a musical instrument such as piano, keyboard, drums, violin, cello, guitar or recorder. We also offer a breakfast, after-school and holiday club.

Although we are a non-selective school, many of our children over the years have gained entry into the local Grammar or Independent Selective Schools.

For a prospectus or to arrange a visit, call Mrs King, the Headmaster's PA, on 020 8647 4607.

Charitable status. Collingwood School Educational Trust Ltd is a Registered Charity, number 277682. It exists to promote and foster a sound education for boys and girls aged 3–11 years.

Colston's Lower School

Park Road, Stapleton, Bristol BS16 1BA

Tel: 0117 965 5297
Fax: 0117 965 6330
email: admissions@colstons.org
website: www.colstons.org
Twitter: @colstonsschool
Facebook: /Colstons-School

Chair of Governors: Mr T Kenny

Head of Lower School: Mr D A H Edwards, BEd, MA

Deputy Head: Mr M Weavers, BEd Hons
Head of Juniors: Mr O Barwell, BA Hons
Head of Pre-Prep: Mrs S Howlett, Cert Ed

Age Range. 3–11.

Number of Pupils. 220 Day Pupils.

Fees per term (2016–2017). Reception, Year 1 and 2 £2,410; Years 3 and 4 £2,995; Years 5 and 6 £3,290. Lunch: £200. Nursery: £31.00 per morning (8.30 am–12.30 pm inc lunch); £21.50 per afternoon (12.30–3.30 pm). Scholarships are offered from 7+.

Colston's Lower School is located in Stapleton village which is within the city of Bristol. It is less than one mile from Junction 2 of the M32 and therefore easily accessible from north Bristol and South Gloucestershire. In addition to its own specialist facilities for Science, ICT, Music, Design & Technology, Art and Games, the Lower School has full use of facilities at the neighbouring Upper School including 30 acres of playing fields, theatre, concert hall and sports centre.

At the end of Year 6 pupils move from the Lower to the Upper School (see entry in HMC section). They work in small classes on a broad and engaging curriculum that extends and enthuses a community of highly active learners.

It incorporates the full range of academic subjects together with French, Design and Technology, ICT, Art, Music, Forest School and competitive sports. A wide range of co-curricular activities such as climbing, golf and ballet are also available. The School benefits from a highly efficient Learning Support Unit for those needing additional support and a Gifted and Talented program for those who show particular strengths.

The creative arts flourish in the Lower School, with a choir and orchestra, regular concerts, school plays and music competitions. A large number of children also play musical instruments, with specialist teachers providing weekly tuition.

In addition to PE lessons there are two afternoons of junior games each week. The boys principally play rugby, hockey and cricket, and the girls play hockey, netball and rounders. Pupils also enjoy opportunities to take part in football, tennis, swimming, athletics and badminton. All juniors are encouraged to take part in competitive sports fixtures, and sports tours are also arranged.

The school also has its own excellent Forest School site which is used every week for outdoor learning.

Colston's Lower School offers a wide range of clubs and activities, and pupils are able to stay on at school under supervision for an extended day or start with Breakfast Club. There are numerous visits and trips including skiing and adventure activities.

Charitable status. Colston's School is a Registered Charity, number 1079552. Its aims and objectives are the provision of education.

Copthorne School

Effingham Lane, Copthorne, West Sussex RH10 3HR

Tel: 01342 712311
Fax: 01342 714014
email: office@copthorneprep.co.uk
website: www.copthorneprep.co.uk

Chairman of Governors: James Abdool

Headmaster: C J Jones, BEd Hons

Deputy Head: S King

Age Range. 2–13.

Number of Boys and Girls. 359 (20 Boarders).

Fees per term (2016–2017). Day: Reception £2,860, Year 1 £2,945, Year 2 £3,000, Year 3 £3,960, Year 4 £4,340, Years 5–8 £4,980. Weekly Boarding £5,650. Occasional Boarding £25 per night.

Copthorne is a flourishing IAPS Prep School with approximately 359 boys and girls aged from 2 to 13. The school has grown by over 75% within the last 5 years. Children are prepared for Independent School Scholarships or Common Entrance. In the last 5 years Copthorne children have been awarded 48 Scholarships or Awards to a variety of Senior Schools.

We believe that, in order to learn, children must be happy and feel secure in their environment. Copthorne Prep School is full of happy children and the environment is caring but still allows children the freedom to develop as individuals.

The school helps to develop each child's confidence, to raise self-esteem and to make children feel good about themselves. Nothing does this more than children enjoying success in all areas of school life. This is why Art, Music, ICT, DT, Drama and Sport are all just as important as the pursuit of academic excellence.

We provide opportunities for children to achieve success in all areas of the curriculum and we always celebrate their achievements.

We recognise that all children have talents, and every child is encouraged to realise their true potential, whatever that may be, in whatever area of school life.

We demand and set high standards, and our children respond by always giving of their best.

Put simply, our mission is to:

Develop **C**onfidence – Provide **O**pportunity – Realise **P**otential – in every single child.

The school is very proud of its history of over 100 years, and retains all the important traditions of the past whilst developing a very forward thinking approach. The children receive a "child-centred" education, where their individual needs come first, in an environment that is "parent-friendly", with very high levels of communication and pastoral care.

Charitable status. Copthorne School Trust Limited is a Registered Charity, number 270757. It exists to provide education to boys and girls.

Cottesmore School

Buchan Hill, Pease Pottage, West Sussex RH11 9AU

Tel:	01293 520648
Fax:	01293 614784
email:	office@cottesmoreschool.com
website:	www.cottesmoreschool.com
Twitter:	@cottesmoreprep

Independent Co-educational Preparatory Day and Boarding School.

Headmaster: **T F Rogerson**, BA, PGCE

Age Range. 4–13.
Number of Pupils. 100 Boys, 50 Girls.
Fees per term (2016–2017). Prep: £5,708 (Day), £7,802 (Boarding); Pre-Prep: £3,048–£4,065.

Cottesmore is a preparatory school offering Day and Full Boarding. In September 2009 the school opened a Pre-prep Department.

Cottesmore is situated a mile from Exit 11 of the M23, ten minutes from Gatwick Airport and one hour from Central London and Heathrow Airport.

Curriculum. Boys and girls are taught together in classes averaging 14 in number. The teacher/pupil ratio is 1:9. Children are fully prepared for Common Entrance and Scholarship examinations.

Music. The musical tradition is strong – more than 80% of children learn a variety of instruments; there are three Choirs, a School Orchestra and several musical ensembles.

Sport. The major games are Association and Rugby Football, Cricket, Hockey, Netball and Rounders. Numerous other sports are taught and encouraged. They include Tennis, Squash, Golf, Riding, Athletics, Cross-Country Running, Swimming, Windsurfing, Fishing, Boating, Gymnastics, Shooting, Judo and Archery. The School competes at a national level in several of these sports.

Recent Developments. Our Technology Centre houses a constantly developing Information Technology Suite, a Design Technology room for metal, woodwork, plastic and pneumatics, a Craft room, Kiln, two Science laboratories and Art Studio.

Hobbies and Activities. These include Pottery, Photography, Stamp Collecting, Chess, Bridge, Model-Making, Model Railway, Tenpin Bowling, Gardening, Rollerblading, Ballet, Modern Dancing, Drama, Craft, Carpentry, Printing, Cooking and Debating.

The boys and girls lead a full and varied life and are all encouraged to take part in as wide a variety of activities as possible. Weekends are a vital part of the school life and are made busy and fun for all.

Entry requirements. Entry is by Headmaster's interview and a report from the previous school. For a prospectus and more information, please write or telephone the Registrar, Lottie Rogerson.

Coworth Flexlands School

Chertsey Road, Chobham, Woking, Surrey GU24 8TE

Tel:	01276 855707
email:	secretary@coworthflexlands.co.uk
	registrar@coworthflexlands.co.uk
website:	www.coworthflexlands.co.uk
Twitter:	@CoworthFlexSch
Facebook:	@CoworthFlexSch

Chairman of Governors: Mr Gordon Hague

Headmistress: **Mrs Anne Sweeney**, MA, DipEd

Age Range. Girls 3–11 years; Boys 3–7.
Number of Pupils. 135.
Fees per term (2016–2017). £930–£4,275.

Welcome to Coworth Flexlands School & Nursery, a caring and happy independent preparatory school for girls aged 3 to 11 with a mixed pre-prep for boys to 7 years. Nestled in 13 acres between Chobham, Windlesham and Sunningdale and close to Virginia Water we offer quick and easy access to the M3 yet are in the heart of the countryside. The grounds combined with our spacious, light-filled classrooms with specialist teachers and small teaching groups provide an excellent academic learning environment.

Our foremost priority is to provide a secure and happy school life enabling our pupils to obtain skills to achieve heights in every discipline. This success is a result of our philosophy that all pupils deserve the best and so are given high-quality, specialist teaching across a broad curriculum. Threading through this central pillar of academic schooling the children are encouraged to develop social and emotional skills and good manners, all within a strong Christian & pastoral ethos that will serve them well throughout their lives.

We proudly hand our boys on to their chosen preparatory school at the age of seven knowing that they are skilled in academics, performance arts and sports and can bring much to their new schools. We are delighted to receive feedback that our boys continue with a strong work ethic and a maturity and confidence that gives them a robust platform from which to leap forward in the next stage of their educational journey.

New girls join us in Prep, aged seven, to take up all the advantages of a single-sex education at this impressionable time in their lives. All-girl form classes mean greater diversification of talent, sports teams within each year group and wider friendship circles all of which enhance development. We split the forms for academic subjects knowing smaller groups can improve pupil attainment with the girls coming together for sport, Forest School, and performing arts.

We are immensely proud of our girls when they leave us having secured places at a wide range of top senior schools, many with scholarships or exhibitions. The polite confidence and self-assurance the girls take with them bear witness to the success of the educational experience we provide, with its focus on supporting the individual to take a full and active part in every aspect of our broad and varied curriculum.

The best way to measure us is to talk to our pupils. We warmly invite you for a tour of Coworth Flexlands School to see how "It all Adds Up".

"Coworth Flexlands School is successful in meeting its aims and this is reflected in the excellent achievements of its pupils." ISI Inspection Report October 2014.

Charitable status. Coworth Flexlands School is a Registered Charity, number 309109 and Christian Foundation school, which welcomes pupils from all faiths. It exists to provide an excellent education and preparation for the next stage of schooling for all our pupils.

Crackley Hall School

St Joseph's Park, Kenilworth, Warwickshire CV8 2FT

Tel: 01926 514444
Fax: 01926 514455
email: post@crackleyhall.co.uk
website: www.crackleyhall.co.uk
Twitter: @CrackleyHallSch
Facebook: /crackleyhallandlittlecrackersofficial

Co-educational Nursery and Junior School.

Headmaster: **Mr Robert Duigan**, BComEd, MEd

Deputy Head: Mr Duncan Cottrill, BSc, PGCE
Assistant Head – Co-Curricular Activities: Mr James Ferris, BA, QTS
Assistant Head – Early Years: Mrs Julie Habaoui, BEd, QTS, CCRS

Age Range. 2–11 years.
Number of Pupils. 285 (163 boys, 122 girls).
Fees per term (2016–2017). Junior School: £2,869–£3,038. Nursery: £237.00 per week (full time, term time only), £231.50 per week (full time, all year).

Crackley Hall is a co-educational independent Catholic day school which welcomes pupils of all denominations. The school is part of The Princethorpe Foundation comprising Little Crackers Nursery, Crackley Hall School, Crescent School and Princethorpe College.

Crackley Hall continues to go from strength to strength following the merger with Abbotsford School in September 2010. Under the leadership of Headmaster, Robert Duigan, pupil numbers have risen considerably and we are now well known for our high academic standards, sporting provision and excellence in the performing arts.

Building work to provide more classrooms, specialist teaching rooms for Art and Music, greatly enhanced IT, Science and Technology suites, and improved sports changing rooms was completed in 2013, and the second phase of major development, a new multi-purpose hall with additional teaching space, was completed in Spring 2016.

Situated on the outskirts of Kenilworth, Crackley Hall occupies a pleasant and safe setting with playing fields a short distance across the road. An extended day facility is offered; pupils may be dropped off from 7.50 am and can stay at school until 6.00 pm. Nursery attendance times are flexible, with term time and year round places available.

Crackley Hall bases its care for individuals on the sound Christian principles of love and forgiveness; children become strong in the understanding of themselves and others. There is a keen sense of community between pupils, staff and parents. We encourage fairness, freedom, friendship and fun.

Small class sizes promote individual attention. The curriculum is based on national guidelines, but pupils are encouraged to achieve well beyond these targets. During the early years, great emphasis is placed on developing key skills in reading, writing, speaking, listening, mathematics and science. The learning of tables and spellings is actively developed through simple homework tasks. Specialists teach Art, Design Technology, French, Music, Games, ICT and RE. Recent investment has resulted in specialist teaching rooms for Art and Music, greatly enhanced IT, Science and Technology suites and improved sports changing facilities.

Football, rugby, cricket, hockey, netball, tennis, athletics, swimming, rounders, trampolining and judo are all available. There is a strong and thriving music department and all pupils together with members of the choir, choral group and orchestra participate in concerts and stage productions to enrich their learning and to build confidence and self-esteem. Pupils have the opportunity to study a wide range of individual instruments under the guidance of a team of peripatetic staff and specialist teachers offer classes in music theatre, speech and drama and dance. Other activities are offered before and after school as well as during lunch breaks including art, chess, craft, ICT, gardening, steel band, food and textiles.

Admission is through interview with the Head, assessments in English and Mathematics, and a taster day at the school. We also ask for a reference from the child's current school. The admission information is considered as a whole so that as accurate a picture as possible of the child can be obtained. The pastoral elements are as important to us as academic ability.

Parents are welcomed into school for Friday morning assembly when the children's good work is celebrated. An active Parent Teacher Association organises social and fundraising events. Pupils are encouraged to maintain their links with the school by joining the Past Pupils' Association.

Charitable status. The Princethorpe Foundation is a Registered Charity, number 1087124. It exists solely for the purpose of educating children.

Craigclowan Prep School

Edinburgh Road, Perth PH2 8PS

Tel: 01738 626310
Fax: 01738 440349
email: head@craigclowan-school.co.uk
website: www.craigclowan-school.co.uk

Chairman of Governors: Bill Farrar

Headmaster: **John Gilmour**

Bursar: Iain MacDonald
Admissions & Marketing: Jennifer Trueland

Age Range. 3–13.
Number of Pupils. 237: 119 boys, 118 girls.
Fees per term (2016–2017). £3,940.

Craigclowan provides a warm and nurturing environment for boys and girls aged 3–13. Set in stunning grounds with magnificent views over Perthshire, the school has a distinguished history and a reputation for the highest standards and expectations.

Our learning environment delivers a modern and distinctive education within a framework of proven traditional values, effectively balancing the best of old and new in education. Grant funding is available for Pre-school pupils and particular attention is paid to the transition period as our Pre-school children begin their primary education. Every pupil is encouraged to achieve their all-round potential, both academically, on the sports field and in more than 50 extra-curricular activities on offer. These range from skiing, on the school's own dry ski slope, to judo, metafit, bushcraft skills, mountain biking and fencing. The school is a hive of activity and our outdoor classroom, all-weather training ground, sports fields, Forest School and new trim trail are in daily use. With an average class size of 12 pupils, and a friendly, caring and supportive ethos, staff are able to get to know the children closely and treat them as individuals in all they do. When it comes to moving on to senior school, all our children secure places to their first-choice school, many having been awarded scholarships.

Minibuses collect children from Kinross, Alyth, Blairgowrie, Meikleour and Cargill in the mornings and the latest addition to our minibus fleet operates our new bus route from Cupar in Fife. To assist working parents, our Breakfast Club is open from 0730 and free after-school care is available for all children until 1800 daily. We also operate a number of holiday activity camps throughout the year including multi-activity camps and hockey, cricket and tennis coaching.

Charitable status. Craigclowan School Limited is a Registered Charity, number SC010817. It exists to promote education generally and for that purpose to establish, carry on and maintain a school within Scotland.

Cranford House Junior School

Moulsford, Wallingford, Oxfordshire OX10 9HT
Tel: 01491 651218
Fax: 01491 652557
email: admissions@cranfordhouse.net
website: www.cranfordhouse.net
Twitter: @CHSMoulsford

The School is a Charitable Trust run by a Board of Governors.

Chair of Governors: Mrs Natalie Scott-Ely

Headmaster: **Dr James Raymond**

Head of Junior School: Mrs Alison Stewart

Head of Nursery & EYFS: Mrs Kim Knight

Age Range. 3–11 Co-educational.
Number of Pupils. 205.
Fees per term (2016–2017). £3,500–£4,450.

Cranford House's co-educational Junior School has a reputation for excellence, as well as a unique approach to education that is modern and progressive. Our innovative curriculum is delivered in a stimulating environment, underpinned by traditional values, within a warmly nurturing community.

We have a strong set of values that underpins everything we do here at Cranford House. We believe in caring for the development of the whole person and ensuring every child reaches their fullest potential whilst ensuring that the education we provide enables our boys and girls to become well-adjusted young adults in the future.

Children are admitted from the age of 3 into the Cranford House Nursery School. The large, spacious purpose-built Nursery offers plenty of green space for free-flow play and learning. With an on-site Forest School, weekly swimming lessons and specialist coaches for sports, the children thrive and make great progress in their learning. In the September of the year they turn five years old, children move into Reception on the main school site. Nursery and Reception children follow the Early Years Foundation Stage curriculum.

The curriculum in Years 1 to 6 is founded on the National Curriculum, but supplemented to ensure children learn to develop resilience, independence, collaborative, reasoning and reflective skills. Junior pupils benefit from Senior School facilities and specialist subject teachers are used in a variety of subjects, including Sport, Music and Languages. Results in the Junior School are excellent.

With an all-inclusive emphasis very much in evidence throughout the school, all Junior pupils take part in school drama productions, learn a wide variety of musical instruments and benefit from a full choir, chamber choir and orchestra. Sport is equally inclusive at Cranford House, with competitive sport being provided for all, regardless of ability, and an incredible array of sports and activities on offer. In addition, an extensive programme of extracurricular clubs and activities ensures the widest possible range of opportunities and the all-round development of our pupils.

Responsibility is offered at a young age through posts such as Junior Head Girl, House Captains and team captains.

Charitable status. Cranford House School Trust Limited is a Registered Charity, number 280883.

Cranleigh Preparatory School

Horseshoe Lane, Cranleigh, Surrey GU6 8QH
Tel: 01483 542058
Fax: 01483 277136
email: fmjb@cranprep.org
website: www.cranprep.org
Twitter: @CranleighPrep
Facebook: /CranPrep

Chairman of Governors: J A V Townsend, MA

Head: **M T Wilson**, BSc

Age Range. 7–13.
Number of Pupils. 338 (48 Boarders, 290 Day).
Fees per term (2016–2017). Boarders £7,550; Day Pupils: £4,815 (Forms 1 & 2), £6,245 (Forms 3–6). These are genuinely inclusive and there are no hidden or compulsory extras.

The school stands in its own beautiful and spacious grounds of 35 acres. Cranleigh Preparatory School is a co-educational boarding and day school. A teaching staff of 46 enables classes to be small. The Head and his wife live in the school, as do the boys' boarding master and his family and the girls' housemistress and her family. They are fully involved with the health and happiness of the boys and girls, together with pastoral staff, including matrons. A great source of strength is the close partnership with Cranleigh School 'across the road'. The Preparatory School has use of Senior School sports facilities, including an indoor pool, artificial pitches, the stables and golf course.

The boys and girls are prepared for Common Entrance and many Scholarships are won. Through these exams about three quarters of the children move on to Cranleigh School and the remaining one quarter to a wide variety of other independent senior schools.

Boarding life is busy and fun. Pupils return home every weekend. There is also the opportunity to flexi board for two or more nights during the week.

The curriculum is broad, balanced and covers all and more than that laid down by the National Curriculum. The school teaches computing, and technological problem solving is encouraged. Art (including design, pottery, woodwork and various craft skills) and Music are included in the curriculum at all level. Individual instrumental lessons are available and peripatetic music staff teach at both schools. There are choirs, orchestras, a band and several ensembles. Boys and girls are given every incentive to develop spare time interests and a choice of activities is built into the timetable.

The school is fortunate to have excellent facilities including a full-sized artificial pitch, a large sports and drama hall, a dance studio, a music school, very light airy classrooms and laboratories. The school has recently undergone a very large refurbishment programme and all facilities are extensive and modern. Boarding accommodation is bright and cheerful and fully modernised. Additions and improvements to the facilities are ongoing.

Rugby, football, hockey, netball, cricket, athletics, tennis, swimming, rounders, squash, cross country, basketball, fencing, riding, golf, Eton Fives, archery and badminton, are among the sports.

Normal entry age is at seven or eleven. Places are sometimes available in the intervening year groups.

Charitable status. Cranleigh School is a Registered Charity, number 1070856, whose Preparatory School exists to provide education for boys and girls aged 7–13.

Cranmore School

Epsom Road, West Horsley, Surrey KT24 6AT

Tel: 01483 280340
Fax: 01483 280341
email: admissions@cranmoreprep.co.uk
website: www.cranmoreprep.co.uk

Chairman of Governors: M J G Henderson, FCA

Headmaster: **M P Connolly**, BSc, BA, MA, MEd

Age Range. 2½–13 Co-educational.
Number of Pupils. 475 Day Pupils.
Fees per term (from January 2017). Nursery (term time) from £1,395; Junior Department £3,950; Senior Department £4,725.

The School is equidistant between Leatherhead and Guildford and is easily accessible from Cobham, Esher, Weybridge, Dorking and Woking with school transport available. Normal entry points are Nursery, Reception and Year 3 (7+); entry is non-selective in the early years and assessments are held for 7+ entry. There is a Scholarship programme for 7+ entry offering Academic, Sport and Music Scholarships. The most recent Inspection awarded the school top grades in every category including 'Outstanding' for the Early Years (Nursery and Reception).

Bright Stars Nursery (from age 2½) offers both term-time and all-year-round attendance. It has its own dedicated accommodation which includes several rooms and outdoor learning area. The Junior Department (4–8 years) offers all children access to tremendous resources including the sports hall, gymnasium, swimming pool and music facilities. Pupils enter the Senior Department at 8+ years and are taught by specialist subject teachers. For National Curriculum Year 7 we create a Scholarship class and two parallel Common Entrance classes. Cranmore's academic standards are high and pupil development enables all pupils to fulfil their individual potential.

Children are prepared for entry to a wide range of senior schools. We have an impressive track record in Common Entrance and in our pupils gaining Scholarships to a wide variety of prestigious schools. Pupils at the upper end of the school (Years 7 and 8) are given significant additional opportunities culminating in an impressive post-Common Entrance programme.

An ongoing programme of investment over several years has given the school many outstanding facilities based on the extensive 25-acre site. These include a £250,000 redevelopment of the Bright Stars Nursery outdoor learning area, a forest school, refurb of 25m swimming pool, new hospitality suite, teaching block with 3 large well-equipped science labs, and 2 ICT suites. The sports facilities include: a sports hall; gymnasium; 25m swimming pool; 4 astro tennis courts; 5-a-side astro, 9-hole golf course, large playground with rubberised surface; 3 squash courts and fitness room plus extensive playing fields.

Sports teams compete in galas, tournaments at local and national level, Inter-School and Inter-House competitions to allow all pupils to take part. All children have the opportunity to represent the school at one of the main sports. Rowing, golf, tennis, ski and many other sporting clubs operate. There is a thriving extracurricular programme ranging from Archery to Science Technology. Many other out-of-school activities are offered including annual PGL and skiing trips.

The Drama, Speech and Music school offers every pupil the opportunity to learn an instrument, sing in a choir and play in a wide variety of ensembles and orchestras.

Cranmore is a Catholic school with children of all denominations warmly welcomed.

Charitable status. Cranmore School is a Registered Charity, number 1138636. It exists to provide education for children.

Crescent School

Bawnmore Road, Bilton, Rugby, Warwickshire CV22 7QH

Tel: 01788 521595
Fax: 01788 816185
email: admin@crescentschool.co.uk
website: www.crescentschool.co.uk
Twitter: @CrescentSchRug
Facebook: /cres.school

Chair of Governors: Mrs Mary O'Farrell, BEd, QTS, CTC

Headmaster: **Mr R Huw Marshall**, BSc Hons Wales, PGCE

Deputy Head: Mrs Bryony Forth, BSc Hons, PGCE
Assistant Head: Mr Alan Webb, BEd Hons
Senior Teacher: Mrs Sarah Lowe, BEd Hons
Finance Manager and Registrar: Mrs Helen Morley, ACIB

Age Range. 4–11.
Number of Pupils. 133 Day Boys and Girls (70 boys, 63 girls).
Fees per term (2016–2017). £2,750–£3,000.

The Crescent School is an independent co-educational preparatory school for day pupils aged 4–11 years. It merged with the Princethorpe Foundation in September 2016; the other schools in the foundation are Little Crackers Nursery, Crackley Hall School and Princethorpe College. In addition, there is a Nursery on site for children from the age of 6 months to pre-school run by Nature Trails for 51 weeks of the year.

The school was founded in 1947, originally to provide a place of education for the young children of the masters of Rugby School. Over the years the school has steadily expanded, admitting children from Rugby and the surrounding area. In 1988, having outgrown its original premises, the school moved into modern, purpose-built accommodation in Bilton, about a mile to the south of Rugby town centre. The buildings provide large and bright teaching areas, with a separate annexe housing the Nursery and Reception classes. There are specialist rooms for Science, Art, Design Technology, ICT and the Performing Arts. In addition, there is also a spacious Library and Resource Area. The multi-purpose hall provides a venue for daily assemblies, large-scale music-making, is fully equipped for physical education and has all the necessary equipment to turn it into a theatre for school productions. The school is surrounded by its own gardens, play areas and sports field.

The requirements of the National Curriculum are fully encompassed by the academic programme and particular emphasis is placed on English and mathematics in the early years. All pupils receive specialist tuition in Information and Communication Technology, Music and Physical Education. Specialist teaching in other subjects is introduced as children move upwards through the school. Spanish is introduced in Reception, followed by French in Year 4 and Latin in Year 5. The pupils are prepared for the local 11+ examination for entry to maintained secondary schools, including local grammar schools, and specific entrance examinations also at 11+ for independent senior schools.

The performing arts are a particular strength of the school and lessons are given in speech and drama, singing, percussion, musical theory and appreciation and recorder playing. Instrumental lessons (piano, brass, woodwind and strings) are offered as an optional extra. There is a school choir, orchestra, brass, string and wind ensembles and recorder groups.

Charitable status. The Princethorpe Foundation is a Registered Charity, number 1087124. It exists solely for the purpose of educating children.

The Croft Preparatory School

Alveston Hill, Loxley Road, Stratford-upon-Avon, Warwickshire CV37 7RL
Tel: 01789 293795
email: office@croftschool.co.uk
website: www.croftschool.co.uk

Principal: Mrs L K M Thornton, CertEd London

Chairman of the School's Governing Committee: Mrs Vanessa Aris, MBE, MSc

Headmaster: Mr M Cook, BSc Hons, PGCE

Deputy Headmaster: Mr E Bolderston, BSc Hons, PGCE
Head of Pre-Prep: Mrs N Badger, BEd Hons

Age Range. 2–11.
Number of Pupils. 403: 215 boys, 188 girls.
Fees per term (2016–2017). £560–£3,838.

The Croft is a co-educational day school for children from 2 to 11 years old, situated on the outskirts of Stratford upon Avon. Founded in 1933, the School occupies a large rural site with superb facilities and extensive playing fields, offering children some of the most exciting educational opportunities in the area. There is also a nature conservation area with lake.

A family-based school, The Croft provides specialist teaching in small groups, where good discipline and a wider knowledge of the world around us, both spiritual and geographical, is encouraged. Music, Sport and Drama each play an important part in the curriculum. The resulting high educational standards provide the all-round excellence which is at the heart of the School.

In 2012, the School opened its 600-seat Theatre and fully-equipped 400m² Sports Hall. Mundell Court was completed in 2009 – a two-storey building providing additional, spacious teaching areas for ICT, DT and Mathematics. It also incorporates a small-scale performance space.

Children are prepared for 11+ entry either to the local Grammar Schools or Senior Independent Day Schools, or to go on to Boarding Schools.

Entrance requirements. Children can be accepted in the Nursery from the age of 2 years. Children above Reception age are assessed.

Crosfields School

Shinfield Road, Reading, Berks RG2 9BL
Tel: 0118 9871810
email: office@crosfields.com
website: www.crosfields.com

Chairman of Governors: Mr C Bradfield

Headmaster: Mr Craig Watson, BEd, MA

Deputy Headmaster: Mr Simon Dinsdale, MA Ed Open, BA Hons Chichester, FLCM, LTCL, LLCM, FISM, PGCE Open

Age Range. 3–13.
Number of Pupils. 535.
Fees per term (2016–2017). £3,038–£4,653 including lunches, school visits and after-school care for Years 1–8. There is an additional charge for children in Nursery and Reception who remain in school after 4.15 pm.

Crosfields School is a co-educational day preparatory school based in Shinfield, Reading. It offers a first-class education with opportunities for all for boys and girls aged 3–13 years. Academically the school is excellent. Pupils progress quickly in small class sizes where they receive individual attention from dedicated teaching staff. Pupils move on to a range of senior schools and there have been a good number of scholarships and exhibitions in recent years and also an excellent record of entry to Reading School.

Facilities within the 40 acres of grounds are unrivalled at prep school level in the area, with a modern library, ICT suite, theatre and music complex, sports hall, indoor swimming pool, cricket nets and even a 6-hole golf course. The main sports for boys are Football, Rugby and Cricket with Netball, Hockey and Rounders for girls. Mixed football and tag rugby are played by both girls and boys and there is a wide range of extracurricular hobbies and clubs from Year 3 upwards including Cookery, Golf, Drama, Judo, Dance and Fencing. A new Food Technology room opened in May 2009.

The school offers bursary awards of up to 100% of the fees at 11+ entry.

Charitable status. Crosfields School Trust Limited is a Registered Charity, number 584278. The aim of the School is solely to provide education for children between the ages of 3 and 13.

Culford Preparatory School

Bury St Edmunds, Suffolk IP28 6TX
Tel: 01284 728615
Fax: 01284 728631
email: admissions@culford.co.uk
website: www.culford.co.uk
Twitter: @CulfordSchool

Chairman of Governors: Air Vice Marshall S Abbott, CBE, MPhil, BA

Headmaster: M Schofield, BEd

(For a full list of staff, please see Culford School entry in HMC section.)

Age Range. Co-educational 7–13.
Number of Pupils. 181 (Day), 45 (Boarders).
Fees per term (2016–2017). Day £3,660–£4,820, Boarding £7,195–£7,365.

Admission is by entrance examination at all ages, though the majority of pupils enter at age 7 or 11 and scholarships are available at 11+.

Culford Prep School has its own staff and Headmaster, but remains closely linked to the Senior School. This allows the School to enjoy a significant degree of independence and the ability to focus on the particular needs of prep school age children while benefiting from the outstanding facilities and community spirit of Culford.

Facilities. Culford Prep is situated in its own grounds, within Culford Park. The heart of the School is the impressive quadrangle at the centre of which lies the Jubilee Library. Other facilities include two science laboratories and two state-of-the-art ICT suites which, in common with the rest of the Prep School's classrooms, have networked interactive whiteboards.

Outside Prep have a mix of playing fields for all the major sports and the perennially-popular adventure playground. Prep School pupils also have free access to Culford's magnificent Sports and Tennis Centre with its 25m indoor pool, indoor tennis courts, artificial turf pitches, fitness suite and sports hall.

Teaching & Learning. Prep School pupils are given a thorough grounding in the essential learning skills of Mathematics and English and the curriculum broadens beyond the confines of the National Curriculum. Work in the classrooms is augmented by an extensive Activities Programme which offers pupils a wide range of opportunities and experiences, including trips out and visits from guest authors and experts in their field.

Music and drama play a significant part in Culford Prep School life, and a variety of theatrical performances, choirs and ensembles are performed each year, either in Prep's own hall or in Culford's purpose-built Studio Theatre. Specialist speech and drama lessons are also offered.

Boarding. Prep School boarders live in Cadogan House, a mixed boarding house located next to the School overlooking the playing fields. Boarders are able to take advantage of a comprehensive programme of weekend activities and are looked after by a team of dedicated staff under the direction of the Housemaster. Recent trips have included visiting Harry Potter World, the Oasis Camel Park and the North Norfolk Coast.

Religious affiliation. Methodist: pupils from all faiths, and those of none, are welcome.

Charitable status. Culford School is a Registered Charity, number 310486. It exists to provide education for boys and girls.

Cumnor House School
Cognita Schools Group

Boys School:
168 Pampisford Road, South Croydon, Surrey CR2 6DA
Tel: 020 8660 3445
Fax: 020 8645 2619
email: admin@cumnorhouse.com

Girls School:
1 Woodcote Lane, Purley, Surrey CR8 3HB
Tel: 020 8660 3445
Fax: 020 8660 9687

email: registrar@cumnorhouse.com
website: www.cumnorhouse.com
Twitter: @WeAreCumnor
Facebook: /WeAreCumnor

Headmaster – Boys School: **Mr Floyd Steadman**, MEd

Headteacher – Girls School: **Mrs D Mallett**, BA Ed Hons

Nursery Managers: Mrs C White @ Pampisford Road, South Croydon and Mrs I Cheshire @ Woodcote Lane, Purley

Age Range. Boys 4–13, Girls 4–11. Co-educational Nursery 2–4 years.

Number of Pupils. Prep & Pre-Prep: 380 Boys, 185 Girls. Nursery: 170.

Fees per term (2016–2017). £3,165–£4,030 (including lunch and school trips).

Cumnor House School for Boys is one of Surrey's leading Preparatory Schools. Pleasantly and conveniently situated, the School prepares boys for scholarships and common entrance examinations to leading senior independent schools and local grammar schools.

Scholarships have been won recently to Dulwich, Epsom, Westminster, Charterhouse, Tonbridge and the local senior independent schools, Whitgift, Trinity and Caterham.

Music, Sports, Art and Drama play a large part in the life of the School and all contribute to the busy, happy atmosphere.

Choir, sports tours and matches, ski trips, regular stage productions and a broad spectrum of clubs and options, give the boys the opportunity to pursue a wide range of interests.

Entry requirements: Assessment test and interview.

At **Cumnor House School for Girls** our main aim is to give parents and their daughters as much choice as possible when selecting their senior schools in Year 6. This journey starts in the Early Years; by developing confidence and a positive attitude to learning, we lay vital foundations for the future.

Practical experiences complement the curriculum and encourage the love of learning needed to embrace the academic, cultural, sporting and musical opportunities that Cumnor House School for Girls provides. The girls are encouraged to develop all their interests and talents, both within the extensive curriculum and through involvement in a wide range of clubs and activities.

Cumnor House School

Danehill, Haywards Heath, West Sussex RH17 7HT
Tel: 01825 790347
Fax: 01825 790910
email: office@cumnor.co.uk
website: www.cumnor.co.uk

Chairman of Governors: Niall FitzGerald

Headmaster: **C St J S Heinrich**, BA Hons, PGCE

Deputy Headmaster: M N P Mockridge, BSc Hons, PGCE

Age Range. 3–13.

Number of Pupils. 373: 197 boys, 176 girls; 90 in the Pre-Prep; 60 boarders.

Fees per term (2016–2017). Boarding £7,455, Day £6,265, Pre-Preparatory £3,315, Nursery £420–£2,550 (depending on number of sessions attended, i.e. from 2 mornings to 5 full days).

We aim to provide a happy and purposeful atmosphere in which children learn to set themselves high standards. Individuality is encouraged and equal esteem is given to achievements in and out of class.

The School has a strong tradition of scholarship, and many awards have been won at a wide range of senior schools, primarily academic but also in art, music, sport, drama and technology.

Out of school we offer children many opportunities for sports and cultural activities. Girls and boys in the Prep school all play sport every day. Each term children are given a choice of 20 or so supervised hobbies, from which they choose three. Much music and drama takes place: 95% of pupils in the Prep school learn an individual instrument and the choirs perform regularly. There are two orchestras and a wind band, as well as much singing and ensemble work. Each Summer term 50 or more children are involved in the annual production of a Shakespearean play in our open air theatre. Our rebuilt Sussex barn is used as a Music School. A purpose-built theatre complex operates as a local arts centre for concerts, lectures, exhibitions and winter term plays. Set in 50 acres of fields and woodland, the school has a Sports Hall, four tennis courts and a heated outdoor pool, as well as a 25m indoor pool. Football, Rugby, Cricket, Netball, Hockey, Rounders and Athletics are all part of the sporting mix with 20 or so teams involved every Wednesday and/or Saturday. Old farm buildings have been converted into blocks for science, music, art, ICT and home economics whilst additions of new boarding wings, new kitchens and laundry are all recent. A new barn conversion in 2006 has provided 6 additional classrooms and a design technology centre and all classrooms have interactive whiteboards. The boarding staff includes a full-time qualified nurse. Boarding, entirely elective, is on a bi-weekly basis, allowing time for full weekends both at home and at school.

Charitable status. Cumnor House School Trust is a Registered Charity, number 801924. It exists for the advancement of education.

Dair House School

Bishop's Blake, Beaconsfield Road, Farnham Royal, Buckinghamshire SL2 3BY

Tel: 01753 643964
Fax: 01753 642376
email: info@dairhouse.co.uk
website: www.dairhouse.org.uk

Chairman of Governors: Mr J O'Brien

Headmaster: **Mr Terence Wintle**, BEd Hons

Age Range. 3–11 Co-educational.
Number in School. 114 Day pupils.
Fees per term (2016–2017). £1,620–£4,100.

Located on the A355 at Farnham Royal we are conveniently placed for the Farnhams, Gerrards Cross, Beaconsfield, Stoke Poges and surrounding villages.

Dair House offers an exciting and personalised education to boys and girls from 3–11. We take pride in our warm, friendly, individual care, catering for each child's abilities. We provide our children with a firm sense of belonging and a sure foundation from the start in classes which are no larger than 16. The school has excellent facilities with a new ICT suite, a new dining room, new office, a recently updated library and Learning Support Department. Each class is fully resourced with interactive whiteboards and computers.

Dair House is situated in wonderful tree lined grounds with a large sports field, multi-purpose gym and all-weather sports surface.

We offer a breakfast club from 8.00 am and an after-school tea club until 5.00 pm, as well as a plethora of lunch-time and after-school activities.

Charitable status. Dair House School Trust Limited is a Registered Charity, number 270719. Its aim is to provide 'a sure foundation from the start'.

Dame Bradbury's School

Ashdon Road, Saffron Walden, Essex CB10 2AL

Tel: 01799 522348
email: office@damebradburys.com
website: www.damebradburys.com
Twitter: @DameBradburys

Dame Bradbury's is a co-educational day school, founded in 1525. It is a member school of the Stephen Perse Foundation, Cambridge.

Chairman of Governors of the Stephen Perse Foundation: Dr G Sutherland

Head: **Mrs Tracy Handford**, MA

Age Range. 3–11.
Number of Pupils. 214 Day Boys and Girls.
Fees per term (2016–2017). Kindergarten: Full day £2,480. A minimum of 3 morning sessions a week is required. Reception: £3,460; Years 1–2: £3,750; Years 3–4: £4,095; Years 5–6: £4,275. Lunch is included for all children in Kindergarten to Year 6.

Dame Bradbury's is co-educational, teaching children from the term they turn 3 to 11 in the beautiful town of Saffron Walden. At Dame B's, each child is taken on an individual journey so they are inspired to achieve their dreams. Each will leave with an exceptional skill set and will be ready and confident to take on the next step in their education.

We are non-selective but that doesn't mean we're not academic. Our children perform well above the national average. Over their time, pupils will enjoy a rich intellectual, cultural and social mix and a love of learning. Small classes mean we can get to know our children and their families to really understand their strengths, interests and personalities.

Dame Bradbury's has a history dating back to 1317 which houses our 21st century facilities from an ultra-modern sports hall, theatre, creative room and inspirational library. It's a perfect marriage of tradition and innovation. In our Forest School, pupils learn about taking risks, exploring and working together as they search for the best wood to make a bow and arrow or cook up a feast in the mud kitchen. Digital technology is integral to learning for all our pupils providing them with tools to learn in a way that suits them as an individual.

As part of the Stephen Perse Foundation, we can offer a natural route into the senior school in Cambridge and our children are already used to visiting for joint activities, trips and projects. The Independent Schools Inspectorate describes Dame B's as "outstanding" and says that Years 1 and 2 and the Prep "provide an outstanding education that challenges and motivates pupils in equal measure".

Danes Hill

Leatherhead Road, Oxshott, Surrey KT22 0JG

Tel: 01372 842509
Fax: 01372 844452
email: registrar@daneshill.surrey.sch.uk
website: www.daneshillschool.co.uk

Chair of Governors: Mr Hugh Monro

Headmaster: **Mr William Murdock**, BA, PGCE

Age Range. 3–13 co-educational.
Number of Children. 880.

Fees per term (2016–2017). £2,135–£5,915.

As a co-educational school, Danes Hill prepares boys and girls for Scholarship and Common Entrance examinations to senior schools. A high academic record (67 scholarships to senior schools awarded in 2016) combines happily with a strong tradition of sporting prowess, to ensure that all children are exposed to a kaleidoscope of opportunity on a peaceful 55-acre site set well back from the main Esher-Leatherhead road. The Pre-Preparatory Department takes children from 3 to 6 years and is situated separately, but within easy walking distance of the Main School. There is a transport system available to take children both to and from Main School.

Extensive facilities include 2 state-of-the-art IT suites, a science block with 5 fully-equipped laboratories, a high-tech Art and DT centre, and new studio theatre. Both Pre-Prep and Main School sites have covered swimming pools.

The curriculum is broad and a wide range of extra-curricular activity is encouraged. Languages are a particular strength of the school. All children learn French and Spanish from age 3. All scholars and some Common Entrance pupils also study Latin. Scholars are encouraged to sit one or more modern foreign languages at GCSE in their final year.

Pastoral care and pupil welfare are closely monitored. The school's Learning Support Centre provides a high level of support both for those with specific learning difficulties as well as running a programme for the exceptionally gifted and talented.

Residential and day trips are seen as an essential part of the school experience. The school operates language trips to centres in Spain and France. The annual Trips Week is a very special feature of the school calendar with over 500 children leaving the site to a range of residential destinations in the UK and abroad. There are also annual ski trips, as well as choir, rugby, netball and hockey tours.

Sport is a major strength and specialist games staff ensure that all the major sports are expertly coached. A floodlit astroturf pitch allows all-weather training and team spirit is valued alongside ability. There are extensive programmes of inter-school fixtures for all age groups. Every child is encouraged to participate. We also arrange annual games dinners for the senior teams and their parents to celebrate the end of each season. In-house Easter and Summer holiday activity courses are also very popular options with the pupils.

Charitable status. Danes Hill School (administered by The Vernon Educational Trust Ltd) is a Registered Charity, number 269433. It exists to provide high-quality education for boys and girls.

Daneshill School

Stratfield Turgis, Hook, Hampshire RG27 0AR

Tel: 01256 882707
Fax: 01256 882007
email: office@daneshillprepschool.com
website: www.daneshillprepschool.com

Headmaster & Proprietor: **Simon V Spencer**, Cert Ed, Dip PhysEd

Age Range. 3–13.
Number of Pupils. Day Boys 124, Day Girls 139.
Fees per term (2016–2017). Nursery on application; Reception £3,550, Year 1 £3,650, Year 2 & Year 3 £3,950, Years 4–8 £4,580. Lunch included. There are no compulsory extras.

Founded in 1950, Daneshill has always prided itself on the collective qualities of its teaching staff and their ability to interact with pupils and deliver a stimulating learning experience.

Set in a beautiful, rural location close to the Hampshire-Berkshire border the School provides the perfect environment and atmosphere for each pupil to grow and prosper as an individual with a strong set of core values.

Academically the Daneshill curriculum has always maintained the expectations of the national curriculum while also offering so much more in respect of what we would regard as real education. Traditional values form the basis of a learning experience that engenders an enthusiasm for knowledge and encourages hard work as a means to academic success. This broadly-based curriculum also allows the development of high academic achievement to sit comfortably alongside our enthusiasm for pupils to become actively involved in all areas of the performing arts as well as the pursuit of sporting excellence.

Our aim has always been to develop enthusiastic learners who will make a strong contribution to their senior schools as good citizens and as pupils who are prepared to work hard in order to achieve success. This is certainly made easier by the children at Daneshill who possess a self-confidence and natural carefree joy which makes them a pleasure to teach. Each of them is a living testament to our belief that self-esteem is crucial to their development and success. We are also justifiably proud of the way our pupils exude courtesy, honesty, warmth and respect for others. They develop responsible attitudes to learning and life, and are a credit to themselves and their families.

Visitors to the School will be made very welcome and straight away they will experience the atmosphere that makes Daneshill unique.

Davenies School

Beaconsfield, Bucks HP9 1AA

Tel: 01494 685400
Fax: 01494 685408
email: office@davenies.co.uk
website: www.davenies.co.uk

Chairman: Mr S Dodds

Headmaster: **Mr Carl Rycroft**, BEd Hons

Age Range. 4–13.
Number of Boys. 330 (Day Boys only).
Fees per term (2016–2017). £3,995–£5,400.

Davenies is situated in the heart of Beaconsfield, a Georgian town on the edge of the Chiltern Hills, close to the M40 and only thirty minutes from the centre of London by rail and car. Founded in 1940, the school aims to provide a broad education for day boys between the ages of 4 and 13. It enjoys a 'family' atmosphere, confident and courteous pupils and enthusiastic and committed staff.

The large site includes modern, airy classrooms, a purpose-built Science Laboratory, DT facility and Art Studio and a fully modernised IT Suite and Music Wing. A state-of-the-art Sports Complex incorporates an indoor swimming pool, Sports Hall and Performing Arts Centre. Boys are taught Rugby, Football, Cricket, Hockey, Athletics and Swimming and compete regularly against other schools. A new Pre-Prep and Junior School building opened September 2015.

Davenies follows a broad curriculum and there is a strong emphasis on numeracy and literacy from an early age. Specialist subject teaching begins in Year 3. French is taught from Year 1 and Latin from Year 6. There is an exciting array of over fifty extra-curricular activities each week which cater for individual interests; these include jazz band, mountain biking, rock climbing, snowboarding, photography, electronics, cookery and media. The school also has its own Cub Pack.

Once they leave the Pre-Prep Department, the academic and pastoral welfare of the boys is undertaken by a network of form teachers. The Deputy Head and two of the Assistant Heads oversee the management of this care and ensure that regular, detailed communication with parents takes place, both formally and informally.

Some pupils move on to local Grammar Schools at the end of Year 6, although many choose to stay on to enjoy the hugely popular programme that Davenies offers its senior pupils before they move on to Senior Independent Schools at 13. As well as individual attention in the classroom, senior boys take part in the Davenies Award Scheme (DAS) which introduces them to challenging, often unusual activities, whilst promoting team building and character development. DAS activities include paintballing, go-karting, sailing, skiing, water skiing and golf. Senior boys also have opportunities to go on skiing and adventure holidays, outward bound weekend and a wide variety of education trips. They also have the opportunity to participate in various sports tours, both at home and abroad.

Developing the whole individual is paramount at Davenies, where great emphasis is placed on the value of courtesy, good manners and consideration for others, encapsulated in the school's motto: 'singulus pro fraternitate laborans' (one working for the good of all).

Charitable status. Beaconsfield Educational Trust Ltd is a Registered Charity, number 313120. It exists to provide high standards and the fulfilment of each child's potential.

Dean Close Pre-Preparatory School

Lansdown Road, Cheltenham, Gloucestershire GL51 6QS
Tel: 01242 258079
Fax: 01242 258005
email: squirrels@deanclose.org.uk
website: www.deanclose.org.uk
Twitter: @DeanCloseSchool
Facebook: /DeanCloseSchool

Chairman of Governors: Mrs K Carden

Headmistress: Dr C A Shelley, BEd, PhD

Age Range. 2–7 Co-educational.
Number of Pupils. 119.
Fees per term (2016–2017). £2,596–£2,685.

Dean Close Pre-Preparatory School is a co-educational, Christian family school which occupies the same campus as Dean Close Preparatory and Dean Close School and is, therefore, able to share their outstanding facilities including the swimming pool, sports hall, tennis courts, theatre and art block.

The Pre-Preparatory School is based in a purpose-built school building opened by Lord Robert Winston in June 2004. The School has a large hall surrounded by classrooms on two floors. There are two playgrounds – one for the Nursery and Kindergarten and one for Reception and Years 1 and 2.

The curriculum within the Pre-Preparatory School offers a wide range of learning opportunities aimed at stimulating and nurturing children's development and interests in an intellectual, physical, spiritual, social and emotional sense. Speech and Drama, Dance, Tennis, Music, Orchestra and Choir are some of the extra-curricular activities available.

All children participate in Forest School, which inspires creativity, thinking skills and cooperation, together with a love of the natural world.

Charitable status. Dean Close School is a Registered Charity, number 1086829.

Dean Close Preparatory School

Lansdown Road, Cheltenham, Gloucestershire GL51 6QS
Tel: 01242 258000
email: dcpsoffice@deanclose.org.uk
website: www.deanclose.org.uk
Twitter: @DeanCloseSchool
Facebook: /DeanCloseSchool

Chairman of Governors: Mrs K Carden

Headmaster: Mr Paddy Moss

Age Range. 7–13.
Number of Pupils. 310: Boarding Boys 38, Boarding Girls 36, Day Boys 137, Day Girls 99.
Fees per term (2016–2017). Boarders £6,294–£7,970, Day Boarders £4,305–£6,139, Day Pupils £3,588–£5,422.

Dean Close Preparatory School is a co-educational, Christian, family school which occupies the same campus as Dean Close School and is, therefore, able to share the outstanding facilities. These facilities include: 25m swimming pool, amphitheatre, shooting range, performance hall, 550-seat theatre and chapel. There are also extensive playing fields and sports facilities including hard tennis courts, floodlit astroturf hockey pitches and the new sports hall, which houses indoor tennis and cricket nets, as well as a large gymnasium and dance studio.

The Prep School also has its own teaching blocks and Music School, and a new £4.5m building which opened in autumn 2013. This contains an additional 360-seat theatre and 8 teaching areas located over two floors, with a dedicated IT suite and drama rooms.

The new building also contains a music suite, which links to the existing Music School, and comprises 6 music practice rooms including a dedicated guitar room. The building has a formal reception area where parents and visitors are welcomed into the School.

There are two additional classroom blocks. One consists of 10 specialist teaching rooms including 2 laboratories and a computer centre. The other has 7 purpose-built classrooms, together with day house facilities, a staff Common Room, a new Library and an Art and Technology block. There is also a separate dining hall and kitchens.

Although the Preparatory School is administered by the same Board of Governors as the Pre-Prep and the Senior School, it has its own Headmaster and staff. There are 48 teaching staff who either hold degrees or diplomas in education. As well as a dedicated Director of Music, Director of Sport and Director of Drama. The music department is also supported by a team of excellent peripatetic music teachers specialising in a variety of instruments.

The School has three boarding houses one for girls, one for boys and a mixed boarding house for the younger children. Each boarding house has a team of resident Houseparents, 2 House Tutors and a resident matron.

The day pupils are accommodated in three purpose-built houses. Each is run by a Housemaster/Housemistress, assisted by House Tutors.

The School follows a curriculum which embraces the National Curriculum and Common Entrance, preparing boys and girls for entry to the Senior School at 13+ by CE and internal transfer procedures. A few transfer to other independent senior schools.

The main games for boys are rugby, hockey and cricket, and for girls, hockey, netball, cricket, rounders and tennis. Swimming, athletics and cross-country running are also taught and use is made of the School's covered playing area. Golf and horse riding are available nearby.

A wide range of additional activities is also available: camping, canoeing, hillwalking, orienteering, judo, climbing, cooking, watercolour painting and all forms of dance, to name but a few.

Finally, the Prep School provides the Choristers for Tewkesbury Abbey – the Schola Cantorum. Boys can apply to join the Schola Cantorum from age 7.

Charitable status. Dean Close School is a Registered Charity, number 1086829. It exists to provide education for children.

Denstone College Preparatory School at Smallwood Manor

A Woodard School

Uttoxeter, Staffs ST14 8NS

Tel:	01889 562083
Fax:	01889 568682
email:	enquiries@denstoneprep.co.uk
website:	www.denstoneprep.co.uk
Twitter:	@Denstone_Prep
Facebook:	/denstonecollegeprep

Custos: Pamela Yianni

Headmaster: Jeremy Gear, BEd Hons

Age Range. 2–11.
Number of Pupils. 79 Boys, 75 Girls.
Fees per term (2016–2017). £3,115–£3,995.

Denstone College Preparatory School at Smallwood Manor is a co-educational Nursery and Day School for children aged 2 to 11, set in 50 acres of beautiful woods and parkland just south of Uttoxeter on the Staffordshire/Derbyshire border.

The aims of the school are:

• To ensure that every child enjoys coming to school and that each individual's potential is fully realised.

• To educate the whole child so that academic achievement goes hand in hand with developing spiritual, cultural and physical maturity.

• To emphasise traditional Christian values of good manners and responsible behaviour.

• To provide a stimulating programme of activities to encourage children to develop skills and interests which will make their school careers successful and rewarding.

• To lay a firm foundation for further education.

As a Woodard School, Denstone College Preparatory School has strong ties with Denstone College and has enjoyed an excellent reputation for preparing children for 11+ Entrance Examinations and Scholarships. Our pupils enjoy excellent sports facilities which include: a covered heated swimming pool, a gymnasium, superb sports pitches and two hard tennis courts. Rugby, Hockey, Football and Netball are the main winter games; Cricket and Rounders are the main summer games.

Denstone College Preparatory School has a fine modern Chapel and our award-winning choir sings regularly in Music Festivals and local churches. Each child learns the violin for a year and a large percentage of our pupils learn at least one musical instrument to a high standard. Our peripatetic music team provide opportunities for pupils to learn brass, woodwind, strings, piano and voice. The school has a string group, wind band and various musical ensembles. Many of our pupils, past and present, sing in the National Children's Choir of Great Britain. Last year 20% of the NCC were our current pupils. Eighteen scholarships or exhibitions were awarded by senior schools to last year's leavers and 58 awards have been given over the past five years.

We offer an exciting range of clubs and activities after school including: Forest School, Clay Pigeon Shooting, LAMDA, Beginners Spanish (for adults and children together), Table Tennis, Cookery, Art and Crafts, Playball, Board Games, Hockey, Dodge Ball and Computers. Our after-school care extends from 8 am until 6 pm.

Charitable status. Smallwood Manor Preparatory School Limited is a Registered Charity, number 1102929. It aims to provide a Christian education for boys and girls aged 2 to 11.

Devonshire House Preparatory School

2 Arkwright Road, Hampstead, London NW3 6AE

Tel:	020 7435 1916
Fax:	020 7431 4787
email:	enquiries@devonshirehouseprepschool.co.uk
website:	www.devonshirehouseschool.co.uk
Twitter:	@DHSPrep

Headmistress: Mrs S Piper, BA Hons

Age Range. Boys 2½–13, Girls 2½–11.
Number in School. 650: 340 Boys, 310 Girls.
Fees per term (2016–2017). £3,135–£5,740.

Devonshire House School is for boys and girls from three to thirteen years of age and the School's nursery department, the Oak Tree Nursery, takes children from two and a half. The academic subjects form the core curriculum and the teaching of music, art, drama, computer studies, design technology and games helps to give each child a chance to excel. At the age of eleven for girls and thirteen for boys the children go on to their next schools, particularly the main independent London day schools.

Devonshire House pursues high academic standards whilst developing enthusiasm and initiative. It is considered important to encourage pupils to develop their own individual personalities and a good sense of personal responsibility. A wide variety of clubs and tuition are available in ballet, judo, yoga, Mandarin, chess, speech and communication and in a range of musical instruments. High standards and individual attention for each child are of particular importance.

The School is located on the crest of the hill running into Hampstead Village and has fine Victorian premises with charming grounds and walled gardens.

Dolphin School

Waltham Road, Hurst, Berkshire RG10 0FR

Tel:	0118 934 1277
Fax:	0118 934 4110
email:	omnes@dolphinschool.com
website:	www.dolphinschool.com
Twitter:	@DolphinSch
Facebook:	/dolphinschoolhurst

Founded in 1970.

Head: Tom Lewis, BA, PGCE

Registrar: Helen Waneis

Age Range. 3–13.
Number of Pupils. 203: 112 Day Boys, 91 Day Girls.
Fees per term (2016–2017). Nursery £3,180 (9 am to 3 pm, 5 days); Reception £3,385; Years 1 and 2 £3,745; Years 3–8 £4,405.

We believe that children have special gifts and talents, which too often remain hidden forever. Dolphin School offers an environment which encourages these gifts to flourish. Children leave Dolphin with confidence in themselves, a strong sense of individualism, the ability to adjust well in school and social situations, at least one area in which they can feel pride in their own achievement and a strong sense of curiosity and enjoyment in learning. Throughout life, in an ever more quickly changing world, they will have the skills and the confidence successfully to pursue their ambitions and interests and to lead happy and fulfilled lives.

Dolphin children are allowed to develop as individuals and encouraged to fulfil their various potentials in small classes under the careful guidance of specialist teachers. Abundant academic, artistic, social and sporting stimulation is provided through an extremely broad, well-rounded programme. We encourage lateral thinking and the ability to cross reference. Expectations for all children are high and academic rigour is a key component in all lessons.

Dolphin School provides the friendly, family atmosphere of a small school. All members of staff are actively concerned with the pastoral care of all the children, but each form teacher assumes special responsibility for the daily well-being and the overall progress of a very small group of children. In addition children in their final three years have a personal mentor. Class sizes average twelve to sixteen. Children learn both to talk and listen to each other, to evaluate and tolerate the opinions of others and to take pride in each other's achievements. They are also encouraged to accept responsibility and to develop their leadership abilities.

Courses offered. Children are taught by graduate specialists from age seven in most subjects. In the early years we provide a firm grounding in English-based skills throughout all humanities subjects. French begins in Nursery, Mandarin in Year Five, Latin in Year Six and Spanish and Greek in Year Seven. Laboratory science is taught from age seven. Mathematics, geography, history, ICT, classical studies, art, design technology, drama, music and PE are taught throughout the upper school. Architecture, astronomy, philosophy, thinking skills, religious education, current affairs and earth studies are also on the curriculum.

Activities. A unique strength of Dolphin School is our residential field trip programme in which all children participate from age seven. The work related to these trips forms major sections of all departmental syllabuses. Principal annual field trips visit East Sussex, Dorset, Ironbridge, North Wales, Northumbria, Normandy and Italy, while departments organise residential trips to Boulogne and Stratford. We also offer an extensive mountain-walking programme. We have a large number of trained British Mountain Leaders. Staff and children participate in a graded fell walking programme. Locations range from the Lake District and Brecon Beacons to Snowdonia and the Alps. We also organise sports tours and a "custom made" adventure week in North Wales.

We believe in 'hands-on' learning, whether in or outside the classroom, and children participate in a very wide range of day trips to museums, theatres, archaeological sites and many other venues.

Almost all costs associated with field, walking and day trips are included in the fees, as are lunch-time and after-school clubs which include: athletics, tennis, short tennis, judo, rounders, cricket, embroidery, computing, swimming, football, netball, gymnastics, craft, hockey, chess, cross-country, rugby, art, table tennis, orchestra, windband, string group, choir, orienteering, gardening, cookery and drama.

We field teams at all levels in football, rugby, cricket, chess, netball, rounders, tennis, swimming, cross-country, athletics, hockey and judo. We are well represented at county level.

Facilities. Our hall offers a splendid venue for school concerts and plays. We stage several major productions each year. Grounds include a swimming pool, all-weather tennis, hockey and netball courts, and playing fields. Cricket matches are played at Hurst, a neighbouring county standard ground.

Entry. Nursery at age 3+, Reception at age 4+, and throughout the Upper School as places become available.

Internal and external scholarships are available to children aged 12–13 in the performing arts, art, creative writing and sport. Academic bursaries are also available.

Examination results. Our examination results are very strong and we regularly win scholarships (academic, drama and sport) to senior independent schools, including Abingdon, The Abbey, Queen Anne's and Leighton Park. We have a thriving Old Delphinian organisation. Most past pupils gain good degrees with several going on to Oxbridge.

The Downs Malvern

Colwall, Malvern, Worcs WR13 6EY
Tel: 01684 544 108
Fax: 01684 544 105
email: registrar@thedownsmalvern.org.uk
website: www.thedownsmalvern.org.uk
Twitter: @DownsMalvern
Facebook: /The-Downs-Malvern-Prep-School

Chairman of Governors: Reverend Kenneth E Madden, BA, PGCE

Headmaster: **Alastair S Cook**, BEd Hons, FRGS, IAPS

Age Range. 3–13 years Co-educational.
Number of Pupils. 256 children.
Fees per term (2016–2017). Full Boarding £4,636–£7,157; Weekly boarding £4,079–£6,298; Flexi boarding £37.08 per night; Day £3,841–£5,407; Pre-Preparatory £2,251–£3,047; Early Years: £23.03 per am/pm session, £46.06 per day (8.30–3.30), £50.38 per day (8.30–5.00).

The Downs Malvern is a busy, vibrant and successful co-educational preparatory school for boarding and day children aged between 3 and 13 years, offering an outstanding education.

Located 3 miles west of Malvern, 4 miles east of Ledbury, 15 miles from the M5 motorway, on the main line from Paddington and served by Malvern College transport, the Downs is situated on the Herefordshire side of the Malvern Hills on a striking rural 55-acre campus in Colwall.

The Downs Malvern strives to exceed the confines of the National Curriculum in academic, as well as cultural, sporting and social accomplishments. The school offers a broad curriculum challenging the academically gifted and supporting those with special needs. The School was subjected to an Independent Schools Inspectorate (ISI) inspection in 2015 and was considered to be "*an excellent School*". The full inspection report is available on the School website.

The Early Years and Pre-Prep have now settled into their newly refurbished building and, after a seamless move over to the Prep Department at 7 years old, pupils will move on to

Malvern College, or to their preferred senior school at 13 to complete their school education.

Year 8 pupils have moved on to a variety of independent senior schools on the basis of scholarship or Common Entrance examinations and, whilst the option to go on to a wide variety of independent schools is still there, the direction has changed. The Downs is the main feeder school for Malvern College and the emphasis in Years 7 and 8 is not only a preparation for scholarships and Common Entrance, but also to allow a smooth transition to the College academically and socially.

Sports, especially team games, are a significant part of the curriculum, as are Music and Art. 80% of the pupils learn to play a musical instrument. There is also a wide and expanding Hobbies programme that includes Railway Engineering as well as Speech and Drama, Dance, Design Technology and Art.

Boarding. The newly refurbished Boarding House provides a home for up to 60 boarders. Boarding can be full, flexi or a one-off experience with a published programme of evening and weekend activities. All boarders are looked after by a caring staff, dedicated to their welfare. A boarding inspection carried out by the ISI in November 2015 found the provision of boarding care at The Downs to be "*excellent*".

Facilities. There is a wide range of facilities including a 300-seat capacity Concert Hall, self-contained Music and Art buildings; new Science laboratories; a new Design and Technology suite, Pottery studio and wired computer network with whiteboards. A new sports complex is supplemented by an astroturf Hockey pitch, 3 Netball/Tennis courts and 55 acres of grounds set aside for games pitches, Forest School lessons and relaxation. The school has its own narrow gauge steam railway!

11+ Scholarships and Exhibitions, as well as being awarded to pupils who show academic excellence, are also awarded to pupils who show academic competence as well as having a particular talent in Art, Music, Drama or Sport.

Bursaries are available offering assistance to parents subject to completion of a means test form.

Charitable status. The Downs, Malvern College Prep School, trading as The Downs Malvern, is a Registered Charity, number 1120616. It exists to provide education for girls and boys from 3–13 years.

The Downs School

Wraxall, Bristol BS48 1PF

Tel: 01275 852008
email: office@thedownsschool.co.uk
website: www.thedownsschool.co.uk
Twitter: @TheDownsSchool

Chairman of Governors: A M J Currie

Head Master: **Marcus Gunn**, MA Ed, BA, PGCE, IAPS

Age Range. 4–13.
Number of Pupils. 279: 173 boys, 106 girls.
Fees per term (2016–2017). £3,420–£5,185 including lunch.

The Downs was founded in 1894 on the parklands of Bristol, otherwise known as the Downs. The school moved to the estate of Charlton House, its present site, in 1927. The Headmaster at the time, Mr Wilfred Harrison, stated that the relocation was because of the "incessant roar of traffic" and the "nerve-racking turmoil of the city". As a consequence of his vision, today at the end of a long meandering drive, three miles from the turmoil of a busy city, approximately two hundred and eighty children excel in the stunning rural environment of The Downs School.

Our children enjoy a vibrant all-round education that is stimulating, challenging and exciting. Academic study is important and we expect all our pupils to adopt a healthy work ethic and achieve high standards, but we believe that to truly educate it is essential to embrace the creative, the physical and the spiritual as much as the intellectual.

At The Downs we embrace a strong set of traditional values and expectations. Childhood is cherished; our young children wear wellies, climb trees and make dens. They make elaborate daisy chains, delight in playing conkers and relish bushcraft cooking. The sophisticated world of mobile devices and adolescence remains at the front entrance for later life. Within this healthy, happy and wholesome environment we seek to nurture unaffected good manners, we embrace grace and humility, and we applaud the qualities of friendship, excellence and respect. We encourage and have high regard for individuality, we endorse aspiration and we celebrate success. Essentially, however, quality of character is considered equally as important as achievement.

Class sizes are small (ideally 18). Pupils are prepared for the major independent senior schools with Badminton, Clifton College, Bristol Grammar School, Queen Elizabeth's Hospital, Millfield, Marlborough, Sherborne, King's College Taunton and Winchester featuring regularly. The pupils follow the Common Entrance Syllabus, a programme that enables the school to make the most of its independence to the benefit of the pupils. The traditional disciplines of English, Maths, Science and French form the core studies. The Foundation subjects of History, Geography and Religious Education are taught independently. These are complemented by a range of contemporary subjects such as Computer Science, Spanish, (Latin optional) and the Theory of Music and Etiquette.

Sport is of an exceptional standard, but there is a team for everyone; it is not unusual to field twenty teams or more at one time. All the major team sports are played. The Performing Arts are valued highly and standards are impressive: 85% of pupils play instruments, choir is compulsory in the Prep School, over 50% of the school attend Speech and Drama lessons, productions are continual, Dance in its many forms is popular and the vibrant Art Department provides for all styles.

Excellent facilities include a purpose-built Pre-Prep, new classroom block, theatre, two IT suites, woodwork centre, extensive playing fields, Forest School, huge Sports Hall, 2 astroturf pitches, and outdoor swimming pool. Significant work to extend the facilities for the Performing Arts is under way.

An independent Prep School, The Downs does not feed any particular senior school. Over the last decade our children have moved on to numerous schools including the best and most demanding in the country. Considerable time is taken to get to know these schools in order that we can provide constructive and objective advice to interested parents. This consultative process is evidently successful, as it is extremely unusual for a child not to gain entry to a school of their first choice, indeed many of our pupils are awarded scholarships.

Visitors are warmly welcomed. The School Registrar, Caroline Crew, is very happy to assist interested parents at their convenience.

For further information or to arrange a visit to see the children at work and play, please contact The School Office on 01275 852008.

Charitable Status. The Downs School is a Registered Charity, number 310279. It was established for the education of boys and girls aged 4–13.

Downsend

Cognita Schools Group

1 Leatherhead Road, Leatherhead, Surrey KT22 8TJ

Tel: 01372 372311
Fax: 01372 363367
email: admissions@downsend.co.uk
website: www.downsend.co.uk
Twitter: @DownsendSchool
Facebook: @DownsendSchool
LinkedIn: /downsend-school

Headmaster: **Mr I Thorpe**, BA Ed Hons Exeter, MA Ed
Open

Deputy Head: Mr G S Watts, BA Hons London, PGCE
Head of Upper School: Mr K Newland, BSc Hons Surrey, PGCE
Acting Head of Lower School: Miss H Black, BA Hons London, PGCE
Assistant Head (External Relations): Mr J Albert, BSc Hons Kingston, MA Ed, QTS

Age Range. 2–13 co-educational.
Number of Pupils. Day: 435 (aged 6–13), 305 (aged 2–6).
Fees per term (2016–2017). Pre-Preparatory £935–£3,490, including lunch for full-time pupils and 'Early Bird' and 'Little Lates' facilities. Preparatory: £3,845 (Year 2), £4,655 (Years 3–8), including lunch. Sibling discounts apply for more than one child in Reception or above.

Downsend is a co-educational day school for children aged between 2 and 13 years.

The preparatory school stands on a pleasant, open site just outside the town, surrounded by its own playing fields, tennis courts, all-weather pitch and sports pavilion. The Sports Complex includes a large indoor swimming pool and sports hall. The comfortable and vibrant library, expanded networked ICT provision, bespoke facilities for Design Technology, Textiles and Food Technology, a new Music Suite (complete with sound proof practice rooms) and Drama Room extend the curriculum to support children's learning and development.

Pre-Preparatory (age 2 to 6). There are three co-educational pre-preparatory school sites in Ashtead, Epsom and Leatherhead. Pupils work in a welcoming and stimulating environment, in small classes, where a strong focus on education builds solid foundations in Numeracy and Literacy. Dance and Drama, French, Music and Swimming are all taught by specialists and enhance the curriculum across all year groups. An enhanced afternoon programme, further supported by a wide range of after school clubs including Spanish, is also on offer. An extended day facility provides complimentary 'Early Bird' and 'Little Lates' facilities each day from 8.00 am to 5.30 pm (6.00 pm at Epsom & Leatherhead Pre-Prep), which is especially useful for working parents. Leatherhead Pre-Prep also offers a breakfast club from 7.30 am for a small charge (includes breakfast). At the age of 6 the children move up to Downsend Preparatory School where they are joined by children from other local independent and state schools.

Preparatory (age 6 to 13). Founded in 1891, Downsend is an established academic prep school preparing children for Common Entrance, Scholarship and Senior School examinations. The school is a thriving community where children are encouraged to develop their talents both in and outside the classroom. A huge variety of extracurricular opportunities are offered to allow children to try new activities during and after school.

The standard of work is high and the school is particularly proud of its scholarship record with 49 being achieved in 2016 to some of the top senior schools in the area.

There is a broad and engaging curriculum. Our approach to learning sees English, Science, Maths, Languages, Humanities, Art and Technology being lifted off the pages of textbooks and worksheets though creativity and enthusiasm. In addition to the normal Common Entrance subjects children study Art, Drama, Food Technology, ICT, Music, Design Technology, Textiles and PSHE. Parents are kept informed of their children's progress through regular parents' evenings and termly reports and are welcome at all times to communicate with teaching staff and the management team.

The school has a strong reputation for music, with regular and varied concerts throughout the year, as well as orchestras and choirs for the Lower and Upper School. A large number of children learn musical instruments and all pupils in Year 3 enjoy the instrumental scheme where they try different instruments before choosing which one to learn for the rest of the school year. Drama is equally important and there is a production at the end of each term. Pupils can take part in a full range of sports not only in school but also at local, regional and national level. Regular visits occur outside school and trips abroad are also offered.

The holiday care activity scheme, Downsend+, gives pupils access to exciting and absorbing workshops, courses, themed days and thrilling days out. Run by qualified Downsend staff, this provision is available to children aged 4–13 from 8.00 am to 5.30 pm, including breakfast, lunch and tea as appropriate. Downsend Pre-Prep+ is also available as a dedicated facility for children aged 2–5 at Leatherhead Pre-Prep.

Dragon School

Bardwell Road, Oxford OX2 6SS

Tel: 01865 315400
Fax: 01865 311664
email: admissions@dragonschool.org
website: www.dragonschool.org
Twitter: @thedragonschool
Facebook: @DragonSchoolOxford

Chairman of Governors: Professor R W Ainsworth

Headmaster: **John Baugh**, BEd

Age Range. 4–8 (Lynams Pre-Prep), 8–13 (Dragon).
Number of Pupils. Total: 845. Lynams (Pre-Prep): 212 (120 boys, 92 girls); Bardwell Road (Prep): Day 391(224 boys, 167 girls), Boarders 242 (163 boys, 79 girls).
Fees per term (2016–2017). Day £3,750–£6,610; Boarding £9,530.

The Dragon School, just north of Oxford city centre, enjoys a leafy setting on the banks of the River Cherwell. Traditional buildings, contemporary facilities and extensive playing fields are the setting for an exceptional all-round academic education for boarding and day pupils. Dragons are noted for a spirited informality and a confident, enthusiast approach to all they do. A culture of learning how to learn and the appreciation of effort of every kind, result in all-round academic, sporting and cultural excellence. A nonselective school, the Dragon regularly achieves an impressive list of scholarships and awards (44 in 2012) and children go on to the country's finest Independent Senior Schools.

The Dragon is composed of small, friendly communities. A dedicated building for Year 4 (E block) with its own playground offers children a gentle introduction to a preparatory school that is large enough to grow with them. Boarding is the heart of the school where warm support and a caring ethos are enjoyed by boarders from the local community and around the world. Homely boarding houses of varying sizes provide a gradual transition to life at senior schools; an additional house for girls opened in 2009/10.

The extensive curriculum is taught by highly qualified and individual staff whose innovative lessons and high standards led to the Dragon being deemed 'outstanding' on many fronts in its 2011 Inspection. A very strong sporting tradition is mirrored by rich creativity in drama, music and art.

Extracurricular activities encompass games, languages, sports, debates, drama, music and much more. Dragons are seasoned travellers and many expeditions and trips are made to destinations ranging from local woodlands to Brazil and including Sri Lanka, Switzerland, South Africa and Morocco. There is a regular exchange programme with schools in New York and Tokyo.

The Dragon Pre-Prep Lynams is a short distance away in Summertown with its own staff and facilities for Reception and Years 1, 2 and 3. The Ofsted report for Reception was 'Outstanding'.

Bursaries of up to 100% of fees are offered for boarding or day places. Academic awards worth up to 50% of fees are also offered.

For further information or to arrange a visit please contact the Registrar on 01865 315405.

Charitable status. The Dragon School Trust Ltd is a Registered Charity, number 309676. It aims to provide education for boys and girls between the ages of 4 and 13.

Duke of Kent School

Peaslake Road, Ewhurst, Surrey GU6 7NS

Tel: 01483 277313
Fax: 01483 273862
email: office@dokschool.org
website: www.dukeofkentschool.org.uk

Chairman of the Governing Body: Mr Richard Brocksom

Head: **Mrs J Fremont-Barnes**, MA Oxon, MEd

Age Range. 3–16.
Number of Pupils. 301.

Set in inspirational grounds high in the Surrey Hills, surrounded by forest land, Duke of Kent School provides an excellent co-educational option for pupils from 3 to 16 years. Coming from Guildford, Horsham, Dorking and surrounding local villages, many pupils use the School minibus service.

Extended day arrangements for those pupils who wish to arrive before or stay beyond the end of lessons (7.30 am to 7.30 pm) provide families with exceptional flexibility. At the end of the School day, pupils can choose to complete their Prep at school under supervision or at home, and can also choose from a varied programme of sport, academic and social activities.

The small size of the School enables us to know our pupils very well and to ensure that all pupils can reach their potential. All pupils receive the appropriate combination of academic challenge and support to enable them to achieve. A Duke of Kent School pupil is expected to contribute and participate to the very best of his or her ability, take an active role in community life and take responsibility for his or her learning. Our able and committed teaching and support staff work in partnership with pupils and their families. The expectation is that each pupil will strive to achieve a string of 'personal bests': in the classroom, on the sports field, in

personal development, in exploring the arts and in a wide range of activities. We focus on each child's attitude to learning in order to ensure that they are fully equipped to make maximum progress. Teaching and learning is supported by a well established 1–1 iPad programme and supported by our dedicated fibre optic line.

Pupils are prepared for GCSE/IGCSE examinations in the context of a curriculum which aims to take pupils above and beyond exam preparation. There is a focus throughout the School of encouraging pupils to adopt a growth mindset in order to become successful learners. Building on the work of our Prep School in which Creative Curriculum provides excellent stretch and challenge for pupils, our rigorous GCSE programme prepares pupils for A Level and university study and sparks what may be lifelong intellectual passions. Learning beyond the classroom, whether on educational visits or through outdoor learning on site, is a crucial aspect of our pupils' experience. Personal development receives close attention. Our pupils develop confidence and self-esteem from opportunities to lead and to serve. Kindness is expected and encouraged from pupils of all ages.

The School maintains a busy fixtures calendar at all ages. We have extensive playing fields, a swimming pool, all-weather tennis courts and a full-sized sports hall. More than half of our pupils are learning a musical instrument. Music and Drama activities take place in a purpose-built Performing Arts Hall with facilities for Music Technology. The quality of Art on display and in production is a particular strength of the School.

In 2016 52% of all grades at GCSE were awarded at A*/A. All our pupils achieved the benchmark of 5 A* to C passes including IGCSE English Language (69% A* to A) and Mathematics (58% A* to A). Highlights include fantastic results in Physics, English Literature and Spanish (all at 61% A* to A). In recent years our pupils have gone on to successful courses of further study at day and boarding schools and colleges, both locally and further afield.

Prospective pupils are invited to attend a visit day during which they will be interviewed by the Head or another senior member of staff, and will take a range of cognitive tests (CAT4). Scholarships and bursaries are available on admission.

Fees per term (2016–2017). £2,165–£5,625.

Charitable status. The Duke of Kent School is a Registered Charity, number 1064183.

Dulwich Prep London

42 Alleyn Park, Dulwich, London SE21 7AA

Tel: 020 8766 5500
Fax: 020 8766 7586
email: admissions@dulwichpreplondon.org
website: www.dulwichpreplondon.org

The School was founded in 1885 and became a charitable trust in 1957 with a board of governors.

Chairman of Governors: Mr R F Maidment

Headmaster: **M Roulston**, MBE, MEd

Age Range. Boys 3–13, Girls 3–5.
Number of Boys. 847 day boys, 18 girls, 7 weekly boarders (aged 8–13).

Fees per term (2016–2017). Tuition: Day boys £3,950–£5,840 inclusive of lunch (there are no compulsory extras). 13 flexi-boarders: £165 per week in addition to tuition fee.

Dulwich Prep London (formerly known as DCPS) is an independent prep school with a national reputation for excellence.

While we are essentially a boys' school, with about 850 pupils aged between 3 and 13, we start with the Early Years Department which also caters for girls. There are four other sections to the school: the Pre-Prep (Years 1 & 2), the Lower School (Years 3 & 4) and the Middle & Upper Schools (Years 5 & 6 and 7 & 8). In addition we have a well-equipped boarding house set in 13 acres of grounds with tennis courts and playing fields. We are delighted to offer weekly boarding.

At 13+ our boys go on to more than fifty excellent day and boarding schools throughout the country. Alleyn's, Charterhouse, Dulwich College, Eton College, Marlborough College, Tonbridge, St Paul's, Wellington College, Westminster and Winchester College are just a selection of our leavers' destination schools. In the 2015–16 academic year our leavers gained more than 40 academic, musical, artistic and sporting scholarships and awards.

Situated in SE21, we have the very best in educational facilities. These include very spacious classrooms, science block containing 3 labs, DT suite, cookery suite and an observatory, a dedicated music school, a large sports hall, a studio theatre, 3 ICT suites, a superb art studio, a six-lane 25m swimming pool and more than 25 acres of playing fields, quite unique given our privileged location.

Some of the opportunities available to our pupils are:

- We run more than 25 sports teams each term with the top teams regularly doing well in national competitions. Recent sports tours include cricket to South Africa, football to Italy, swimming in the USA and rugby to Portugal and Ireland.
- More than 700 individual music lessons take place every week and boys have opportunity to perform regularly in a range of groups and ensembles.
- Approaching 30 groups perform regularly in our own 300 seat concert hall. Many also appear on the programme for our gala concerts at prestigious venues such as St John's, Smith Square and Southwark Cathedral.
- We provide more than 100 clubs and extra-curricular activities, stimulating boys' intellectual and sporting interests.
- We run residential trips for pupils in Years 4–8 within the curriculum that are built in to the fee structure. 15 more trips, ranging from cultural visits to skiing, are offered during the holidays.
- Drama productions are staged by forms and year groups from Reception to Year 8.

Charitable status. Dulwich College Preparatory School Trust is a Registered Charity, number 312715. It exists to provide education for boys.

Dulwich Preparatory School

Coursehorn, Cranbrook, Kent TN17 3NP

Tel:	01580 712179
Fax:	01580 715322
email:	registrar@dcpskent.org
website:	www.dcpskent.org
Twitter:	@DPS_Cranbrook
Facebook:	@DPSCranbrook

Chairman of Governors: Mr R Maidment

Headmaster: **Mr Paul David**, BEd Hons

Age Range. 3–13.

Number of Boys and Girls. Day and Boarding: 279 (Upper School), 191 (Little Stream), 64 (Pre-Prep).

Fees per term (2016–2017). Day: £5,535 (Years 5–8), £4,710 (Years 2–4), £3,555 (Year 1), £3,455 (Reception), Nursery: £2,905 (full day), £1,815 (mornings). Boarders: £32–£36 per night.

The School, which is one mile from the country town of Cranbrook, has extensive grounds (50 acres) and offers a broad and varied education to boys and girls from 3 to 13+. To ensure that children receive the personal attention that is vital for this age range the School is divided up into three separate, self-contained, departments. These are Nash House (3–5 year olds), Little Stream (5–9 year olds) and Upper School (9–13 year olds). Each department has its own staff, teaching equipment, sports facilities, playgrounds, swimming pools, etc. Pupils are prepared for Common Entrance or Scholarship examinations to any school of their parents' choice, and there is a strong emphasis on up-to-date teaching methods. The wide scope for sporting activities – Football, Rugby, Cricket, Hockey, Netball, Rounders, Athletics, Cross Country, Swimming, Tennis – is balanced by the importance attached to Art, DT, Drama, ICT and Music. Over 200 pupils learn the full range of orchestral instruments. There are two Orchestras, Wind and Brass Bands, Jazz Band, and four Choirs. The boarders are divided into two houses, boys and girls, each under the care of House staff. The happiness of the boarders is a particular concern and every effort is made to establish close and friendly contact between the School and the parents. There is a flourishing Parents Association, and regular meetings are held between staff and parents.

The School is a Charitable Trust, under the same Governing Body as Dulwich College Preparatory School, London, although in other respects the two schools are quite separate. The link with Dulwich College is historical only.

Charitable status. Dulwich College Preparatory School Trust is a Registered Charity, number 312715. It exists for the provision of high quality education in a Christian environment.

Dumpton School

Deans Grove House, Deans Grove, Wimborne, Dorset BH21 7AF

Tel:	01202 883818
Fax:	01202 848760
email:	secretary@dumpton.com
website:	www.dumpton.com
Twitter:	@dumpton
LinkedIn:	/dumpton-school

Chairman of Governors: Mr B Davies

Headmaster: **A W Browning**, BSc, PGCE, MA Ed, CChem, MRSC

Age Range. 2–13.

Number of Pupils. Girls and Boys: 220 aged 7–13 and 116 aged 2–7.

Fees per term (2016–2017). £4,936 for the Prep School (Years 3–8) and £2,755 for the Pre-Prep (Reception, Years 1 & 2). Nursery on application. The school week is from Monday to Friday with some Saturday fixtures. All fees include meals and there are no compulsory extras.

Dumpton School is a co-educational day school for pupils aged 2 to 13 years. The school is set in a beautiful rural setting with 26 acres of grounds, but is nevertheless only one mile from Wimborne and school buses run daily to and from the nearby towns of Bournemouth, Poole, Wareham, Ringwood and Blandford.

Despite record numbers in the school, class sizes are small. Children enjoy excellent teaching as well as incomparable opportunities for Music, Art, Drama and Sport in which the school excels. Dumpton is renowned for its caring approach in which every child is encouraged to identify and develop his or her abilities and personal qualities as fully as possible. This safe and supportive environment sees the children thrive and reach their full potential. The framework of family and Christian values emphasises the importance of teamwork and mutual respect that pervades the school. It is a very happy and successful school and children regularly win scholarships to their Senior Schools or places at the local Grammar Schools. Over the past seven years Dumpton pupils have been awarded over 168 scholarships to schools such as Bryanston, Canford, Clayesmore, Millfield, Talbot Heath and Sherborne.

Recent developments have included a new multi-purpose Performing Arts venue complete with music recital room, a new outdoor adventure playground for the Prep School, a new Science and Maths Block, a full-size floodlit Astroturf, a covered swimming pool, a new Art, Design and Food Technology Centre, an outdoor classroom, climbing wall and environmental area, complete with ponds, pontoons, beehives and pupil allotments. In addition the school has recently been awarded Green Flag status by Eco Schools.

The school motto 'You can because you think you can', lies at the cornerstone of teaching at Dumpton and our aim is for pupils to leave us having reached their full potential, as confident communicators and appreciating good manners and tolerance.

For a copy of the prospectus, please apply to the Headmaster's Secretary.

Charitable status. Dumpton School is a Registered Charity, number 306222. It exists to provide education for boys and girls.

Dunhurst
Bedales Prep School

Alton Road, Steep, Petersfield, Hampshire GU32 2DR

Tel: 01730 300200
Fax: 01730 711820
email: jjarman@bedales.org.uk
website: www.bedales.org.uk

Chairman of Governors: M Rice, BA

Head: **Mrs J Grubb**, BA

Deputy Head, Pastoral and Head of Blocks: Nick Robinson, MSc, PGCE Portsmouth
Director of Teaching & Learning: Andy Wiggins, BA Kent, PGCE Portsmouth

Age Range. 8–13.
Number of Pupils. Currently 160 pupils (80 boys and 80 girls, 105 day, 31 boarders, 24 flexi-boarding).

Fees per term (2016–2017). Boarders £7,908; Half Boarding (3 nights) £7,047; Day: £6,319 (Year 4), £6,207 (Years 5 and 6), £6,107 (Years 7 and 8); Flexi Boarding: £43.05 per night.

John Badley founded Bedales School in 1893 to educate through head, heart and hand. When Dunhurst was added in 1902 as the prep school, Badley's philosophy on education continued. It is apparent from the moment you enter Dunhurst that it is a unique school. This ethos spearheads thinking in education today and is distinctive because of the following key elements:

Inquisitiveness –We recognise that key to opening a child's joy for learning is to encourage them to question.

Relationships –Children are confident in their learning and have the support to develop because relationships between pupils and teachers at Dunhurst are built on trust and mutual respect.

Informality –A friendly and inclusive atmosphere helps every individual to thrive with room for their personality to grow. Our approach is underpinned by a clear structure which channels young people to flourish with guidance.

Choice –Our environment celebrates individuality by encouraging pupils to make choices about who they are and how they shape their learning in and out of the classroom.

Preparation for life –We produce young people with a determination to keep learning, happy in their own skins, and equipped with the skills to succeed.

We are proud of our environment at Dunhurst, our teachers and our academic results. Most important to the school is how to ensure children's learning thrives. Children respond to lessons that challenge their thinking. Dunhurst engenders inquisitiveness in pupils so they are prepared for the academic rigour of IGCSEs, Bedales Assessed Courses (BACs), A Levels and beyond. It isn't all about getting results; there is depth to pupils' learning because of Dunhurst's diverse curriculum. The creative and performing arts, sport, the outdoor work programme and the wealth of activities on offer ensure that every pupil can develop new interests and skills.

Matches against other schools take place regularly in Athletics, Cricket, Football, Hockey, Netball, Rounders, Rugby and occasionally Swimming and Tennis. A wide range of other sports and outdoor activities is also offered, including Judo and Golf.

Dunhurst makes full use of the first-rate facilities at Bedales which include the Bedales Olivier Theatre, a Sports Hall, floodlit netball and tennis courts, an all-weather pitch and covered swimming pool. This and the similarity of ethos, makes for an easy transition for pupils moving from Dunhurst to the Senior School at the age of thirteen.

There is a strong boarding community at Dunhurst. Many of the older pupils are full boarders and provision is made for flexible boarding for day pupils.

Applicants for both boarder and day places sit residential entrance tests. The main points of entry are at 8+ and 11+. Entry at other ages is dependent on the availability of places.

For information about Dunannie, the Pre-Prep (3–8 years), see the Bedales entry in HMC section.

Charitable status. Bedales School is a Registered Charity, number 307332. It exists to provide a sound education and training for children and young persons of both sexes.

Durlston Court

Becton Lane, Barton-on-Sea, New Milton, Hampshire BH25 7AQ

Tel: 01425 610010
Fax: 01425 622731
email: secretary@durlstoncourt.co.uk
website: www.durlstoncourt.co.uk
Facebook: /DurlstonCourt

Chairman of Governors: Mr Chandra Ashfield

Headmaster: **Mr Richard May**, BA, PGCE

Age Range. 2–13 Co-educational.
Number of Pupils. 300 Day Pupils.
Fees per term (2016–2017). Kindergarten £26.60 per morning or afternoon session, £49.40 a day, £2,830 (Reception–Year 2), £4,215 (Year 3), £5,130 (Years 4–8).

Durlston Court Preparatory School, founded in 1903, is a happy and successful day school set in a beautiful campus with impressive facilities.

Durlston Court Prep School prides itself on preparing its pupils fully for Senior School and enabling pupils to reach their potential in all areas. This is demonstrated in the range of recent Scholarships awarded to pupils who transferred to senior schools. In addition to academic performance, scholarships were awarded to pupils excelling in Sports, Performing Arts and as All-rounders. Results also included a 100% pass rate to King Edward V1 School, Southampton.

Durlston offers:

- Over 50 extra-curricular clubs such as STEM (Science, Technology, Engineering and Maths), Golf, Sailing and Den Activities providing unlimited opportunity.
- Purpose-built facilities, such as the Art Centre, Music School and a new Design Technology Centre teaching CAD, CAM.
- Daily sports coaching and regular opportunities to compete in sporting fixtures to help instil team spirit and confidence.

This exciting environment combined with a focus on traditional values makes Durlston Court Prep School an extremely happy place where pupils truly thrive!

Bus services cover routes from the Beaulieu, Bournemouth, Brockenhurst, Burley, Christchurch, Ringwood, Lymington, Lyndhurst and Sway.

Parents are most welcome to visit the school by making an appointment or by attending an Open Morning.

Further details of the school are available by visiting the school's website or by contacting the Headmaster's Secretary by phone or email, as above.

Charitable status. Durlston Court School is a Registered Charity, number 307325, which exists to provide quality education for children from 2–13 years.

Durston House

12 Castlebar Road, Ealing, London W5 2DR

Tel:	020 8991 6532
Fax:	020 8991 6547
email:	info@durstonhouse.org
website:	www.durstonhouse.org

Chairman of Governors: A J Allen, MA, FCA

Headmaster: N I Kendrick, MA, BEd Hons

Deputy Head: W J Murphy, BA, DipTch
Director of Studies: Ms J Sparks, Diplom-Kaufmann, PGCE
Head of Junior School: S W Perkins, BEd Hons
Head of Pre-Prep: Mrs N Sharma, BA Hons, PGCE

Age Range. 4–13.
Number of Boys. 412 Day Boys.
Fees per term (2016–2017). £3,880–£4,720.

Durston House is an Educational Trust with charitable status. The school has a long history of academic success reflected in Scholarships won at many of the leading senior schools. The emphasis is on high standards of work and targets that are commensurate with each pupil's personal development.

Pre-Prep and Junior School (boys aged 4–8) cater for three classes of about sixteen boys in each year group. There is generous ancillary staffing and learning support for specific needs.

In Middle and Upper School (boys aged 9–13) the Headmaster is helped by a Deputy Head, a Director of Studies and a team comprising graduate specialist Heads of Department for English, Classics, Mathematics, Modern Languages, Science, ICT, History, Geography, Music, Art, Physical Education and Religious Studies.

Throughout the school there are Activities Programmes offering a wide range of cultural, recreational and sporting pursuits. Both playing field complexes have floodlit all-weather facilities and there has been much sporting success in recent years. Extensive use is made of local facilities, especially for drama and swimming. There are fixtures with other prep schools, full participation in IAPS events, and regular expeditions at home and abroad.

Entry into the Reception year is in order of registration. For all other years entry assessment procedures take place some six months before boys are due to enter, which is usually in November, or later if there are vacancies. Durston House is currently seeking to increase its provision of bursaries for boys who would benefit from an education at the school.

Charitable status. Durston House School Educational Trust Limited is a Registered Charity, number 294670. Its aim is the provision and promotion of education.

Eagle House

Crowthorne Road, Sandhurst, Berkshire GU47 8PH

Tel:	01344 772134
email:	info@eaglehouseschool.com
website:	www.eaglehouseschool.com
Twitter:	@EagleHouseSch
Facebook:	/EagleHouse

Chairman of Governors: H W Veary, Esq

Headmaster: A P N Barnard, BA Hons, PGCE

Age Range. 3–13.
Number of Children. 400: 60 Boarders, 340 Day Children.
Fees per term (2016–2017). Prep School: £7,640 (boarders), £5,595–£5,690 (day pupils). Pre-Prep: £3,635. Nursery: £2,190 (5 mornings including lunch).

Eagle House was founded in 1820, and has been on its present site since 1886. The School is administered by a board of governors under the overall control of Wellington College.

Children are prepared for Scholarship and Common Entrance examinations to senior Independent Schools. There are 65 members of staff and two matrons. The average class size is 16.

The school is situated between Sandhurst and Crowthorne in over 30 acres of playing fields which include a large all-weather sports area, a Sports Hall, an indoor heated swimming pool, extensive woodlands, adventure playground and a small lake. The principal games are rugby, netball, hockey, soccer, rounders and cricket. Other sports include athletics, swimming, tennis, cross country, squash, judo, basketball, archery, golf, riding and badminton.

Much emphasis is placed on the Arts and there are excellent facilities for music, art, design and drama. Music scholarships are available for outstanding young musicians.

The school has its own chapel.

Recent major building works have provided a new Sports and Performing Arts Centre, Design and Food Technology facilities, a Science Laboratory and Library.

Charitable status. Wellington College is a Registered Charity, number 309093. Eagle House School is owned by Wellington College and is part of the same charity registration.

Eaton House The Manor Girls' School

58 Clapham Common Northside, London SW4 9RU

Tel: 020 7924 6000
Fax: 020 7924 1530
email: admin@eatonhouseschools.com
website: www.eatonhouseschools.com

Headmaster: **Mr Oliver Snowball**

Deputy Head: Mrs Nicola Borthwick

Age Range. 4–11.
Number of Pupils. 192 Girls.
Fees per term (2016–2017). £4,915.

Eaton House The Manor Girls' School is a single-sex school, conveniently situated on Clapham Common, which offers an excellent education to girls aged 4–11. The Headmaster, Mr Snowball, has a distinguished career as an educator with some years experience as a Headmaster.

Our girls are encouraged to achieve their full potential in the academic, sporting and artistic fields. They are taught good manners and respect for others and themselves.

Each girl is treated as an individual; Eaton House The Manor Girls' School is intimate and nurturing, and offers state-of-the-art facilities in its new buildings, including a large gymnasium, library, ICT laboratory, art studio and new theatre.

All pupils at schools in the Eaton House Group enter Reception (or Kindergarten) on a first-come, first-served basis, and for many years all have achieved entry to their first choice of Senior Day or Boarding school.

Eaton House The Manor Pre-Preparatory School

58 Clapham Common Northside, London SW4 9RU

Tel: 020 7924 6000
Fax: 020 7924 1530
email: admin@eatonhouseschools.com
website: www.eatonhouseschools.com

Headmaster: **Mr Huw May**, LWCMD, ADWCMD, PGCE, MA Ed, NPQH

Age Range. 4–8.
Number of Pupils. 214 Boys.
Fees per term (2016–2017). £4,915.

The quality of an Eaton House The Manor education means that all of the boys leaving the Pre-Prep and Preparatory Schools go on to their first choice of senior school with several winning scholarships. Our approach, which teaches according to ability in small groups, means that we succeed in bringing out the best in each child, fostering a lifelong enthusiasm for learning and attaining the highest academic results. Pupils go on to the most prestigious independent schools including Eaton House The Manor Prep, Westminster Under School, Colet Court, Dulwich College Prep, Westminster Cathedral School, The Dragon School, Ludgrove and Summer Fields.

The curriculum at Eaton House The Manor Pre-Prep is traditional. Strong moral values and a concern for others are emphasised in the classroom and through the House system. Care is taken to develop each child's confidence, and instil a

healthy pride in achieving personal goals as well as participating in team games and competitions.

Pupils are taught in a vibrant environment on an exceptionally large site opposite Clapham Common. A recent multimillion pound investment to extend and improve facilities means they benefit from the latest computer technology in the new ICT lab, lavish art and design rooms, a new theatre, an extended library and extremely good music facilities.

The children enjoy many day and weekend trips as part of the curriculum and are encouraged to take part in a host of extra-curricular activities. Displays, concerts and dramatic performances in the new school theatre and gym always prove popular, as do the many parent vs pupils sporting events. Parents are encouraged to be closely involved in their children's education, and to take part in many of the children's activities.

Admission to Eaton House The Manor Pre-Preparatory School is non-selective and on a first-come, first-served basis into the Reception (Kindergarten) Year. Parents wishing to enrol their children in the School are advised to register them at birth.

Eaton House The Manor Preparatory School

58 Clapham Common Northside, London SW4 9RU

Tel: 020 7924 6000
Fax: 020 7924 1530
email: admin@eatonhouseschools.com
website: www.eatonhouseschools.com

Headmistress: **Mrs Sarah Segrave**

Deputy Head: Mr Peter Rixham

Age Range. 8–13.
Number of Pupils. 215 Boys.
Fees per term (2016–2017). £6,030.

The quality of an Eaton House The Manor education means that all of the boys leaving the Prep School go on to their first choice of senior school, with several winning scholarships. Our approach, which teaches according to ability in small groups, means that we succeed in bringing out the best in each child, fostering a lifelong enthusiasm for learning and attaining the highest academic results. Pupils go on to the most prestigious independent schools including Westminster, St Paul's, Eton, Harrow, Radley, Charterhouse, Marlborough, King's Wimbledon and Dulwich College.

The curriculum at Eaton House The Manor Prep is traditional. Strong moral values and a concern for others are emphasised in the classroom and through the House system. Care is taken to develop each child's confidence, and instil a healthy pride in achieving personal goals as well as participating in team games and competitions. Every day, children at the Prep School enjoy a reading period after lunch and can attend a supervised homework club at the end of the day.

Pupils are taught in a vibrant environment on an exceptionally large site opposite Clapham Common. A recent multimillion pound investment to extend and improve facilities means they benefit from the latest computer technology in the new ICT lab, lavish art and design rooms, new theatre, an extended library and extremely good music facilities.

The children enjoy many day and weekend trips as part of the curriculum and are encouraged to take part in a host of extra-curricular activities. Displays, concerts and dramatic performances in the new school theatre and gym always prove popular, as do the many parent vs pupils sporting events. Parents are encouraged to be closely involved in their children's education, and to take part in many of the children's activities.

Entry to the Preparatory School is at 8 years of age by examination and interview. Places are offered at 7+ and 8+. 8+ assessments will occur in the academic year before the child's projected start date, backed up by a report from their current Pre-Preparatory School.

Eaton Square School

79 Eccleston Square, London SW1V 1PP

Tel:	020 7931 9469
Fax:	020 7828 0164
email:	registrar@eatonsquareschool.com
website:	www.eatonsquareschool.com

Headmaster: **Mr S Hepher**

Age Range. 2½–13 Co-educational. Senior School (age 11–18) opening September 2017.

Number of Pupils. 530.

Fees per term (2016–2017). Nursery £1,605–£5,625, Pre-Prep £6,645, Prep £6,850.

Contact. *Pre-Prep & Prep*: Penelope Stitcher, Registrar, email: registrar@eatonsquareschool.com.

Nursery: Lyndsay Salaman, Nursery Registrar, email: nursery@eatonsquareschool.com.

Ethos. Eaton Square School is one of the few co-educational day schools in the heart of London offering nursery, pre-preparatory and preparatory education. The School maintains high standards and encourages in every child an enthusiasm for learning, good manners, self-discipline and, in all things, a determination to do their best and realise their potential. The 2010 ISI inspection report indicated that the "pupils' personal development is outstanding". The School offers a stretching, challenging approach to learning that emphasises achievement and builds confidence. Great emphasis is placed on experiential learning including ski trips, classical tours of Rome and Pompeii, survival skills in the mountains of Scotland and a week's French immersion spent in a French château in Normandy in Year Seven.

Academic Life. The Class Teachers teach general subjects to their classes up to the age of 10. Thereafter, specialist subject teachers continue the curriculum in preparation for the Common Entrance Examinations for senior English Independent Schools, for girls at age 11 and for both boys and girls at age 13. A wide range of subjects are encompassed in the curriculum. ICT is introduced from the age of 3 and it is an integral part of the syllabus. In addition, all Prep School classrooms are equipped with interactive whiteboards and data projectors.

Pupils are prepared for entry into both selective London Day schools and leading Boarding schools through London Day School examinations at 11+ and Common Entrance examinations at 13+.

Sport & the Arts. Sport and Physical Education include Swimming, Fencing, Gymnastics, Football, Rugby, Cricket, Hockey, Sailing, Skiing and Tennis and the School has successful teams competing against other London and national schools. Music is a flourishing department within the School. Appreciation of music, singing, composition, music theory and recorder tuition are taught by specialists at all ages. There are active School Choirs, an orchestra and a variety of ensembles that rehearse throughout the week. Instruction in Music, Art and Design Technology is included for all children from Nursery School upwards, as part of the Curriculum. Drama is integrated within the curriculum and each child takes part in at least two public productions every year. The Prep School production for children in Years 5–8 is held at a West End Theatre during the Summer Term.

Upper School. We are delighted to announce that in September 2017 we will open our first London Senior School. This exciting development will allow our families a seamless progression from Nursery into Eaton Square Upper School, Mayfair. In a superb location, 106 Piccadilly is a beautiful Grade I listed building, with views over Green Park in the heart of London.

Eaton Square Upper School, Mayfair will be co-educational, with entry points into Years 7, 8 and 9. It will be academically inclusive, with the same family-focused ethos which permeates all of our schools. We aim to create a nurturing environment in which well-rounded, considerate, confident and resilient children will prosper, allowing all of our students to reach their full potential, both personally and academically.

Eaton Square School is part of the Minerva Education group which owns a number of private schools in London, East and South East England. Through Minerva's "Inspiring Learning" programme, we seek to share best practice and ensure the continuing improvement in every child's education.

Edge Grove

Aldenham Village, Radlett, Herts WD25 8NL

Tel:	01923 855724
Fax:	01923 859920
email:	office@edgegrove.com
website:	www.edgegrove.com
Twitter:	@EdgeGrove

Chair of Governors: Mrs Jean Scott

Headmaster: **Mr Ben Evans**, BA Hons

Age Range. 3–13.

Number of Pupils. Day: 151 (Pre Prep), 298 (Prep); Boarders 50.

Fees per term (2016–2017). Day: Pre Prep £2,190–£3,945; Prep £4,535–£5,275; Boarding supplements: Weekly Boarding £1,990; Flexi Boarding: £495–£1,825.

Edge Grove is a vibrant and successful day and boarding school for boys and girls aged 3–13 years. It is set in 28 acres of parkland, only 15 miles from central London and conveniently located close to the M1 and M25 motorways. Our wonderful setting and facilities ensure our children are exposed to a wide range of experiences and develop confidence in a challenging, fun and inspirational environment. The school was inspected by the Independent Schools Inspectorate (ISI) in September 2015 who rated it 'excellent' in all areas. The ISI stated that at all stages of the school "the quality of pupils' academic and other achievements is excellent. Key factors supporting high achievement are the extensive and innovative curriculum, pupils' understanding attitudes towards their learning and excellent teaching." They observed that pupils are "articulate and highly effective listeners. They are diligent in their approach to lessons and their behaviour is exemplary."

The Pre Prep at Edge Grove caters for children between the ages of 3 and 7 and is situated within the grounds, close to the main Preparatory school. Classes sizes are no more than 20, supervised by a teacher and teaching assistant. A broad curriculum is offered with French, Music, Sport and Forest School taught by specialist teachers.

Edge Grove follows the Independent Curriculum and pupils are consequently encouraged to discover, apply and communicate their learning and understanding, to become independent thinkers, to grow in confidence whilst enjoying inspirational and creative teaching. As Ben Evans, Headmaster, explains: "As a school we must preserve tradition but also be forward-thinking and embrace the new – new teaching methods, new technologies and new habits. But without forgetting our values and the most basic and common-sense approach to education – happy children and inspirational teaching will ensure good progress by all."

Pupils move on to a wide variety of senior independent schools across the country and the school has an excellent record of Scholarship and Common Entrance success. Music and Art are also particularly strong and Edge Grove is a leading player in the world of prep school sport. There is a great range of after-school activities on offer every day until 6.00 pm.

Facilities include an outdoor learning hub with a gazebo and stage; two Forest School sites; an adventure playground; a language classroom with a dedicated 'virtual language lab'; iPads throughout the school and 1:1 from Year 5; iMacs for music technology; a fully-equipped textiles room and two science laboratories; and purpose-built and state of the art facilities for Home Economics. Sports facilities include a 20-metre heated swimming pool; vast playing fields with ten junior football fields; a 3-court badminton Sports Hall; an AstroTurf hockey pitch; two tennis/netball courts and six outdoor/four indoor cricket nets.

Weekly and flexi boarding is available at Edge Grove to children in Years 3–8. The boarding community is housed in the original building of the school in contemporary, comfortable dormitories organised by age. The Headmaster and his family live in the main building as do the Housemaster, Housemistress and Gap Students, all of whom work to maintain the smooth running of the boarding community and to enhance the quality of life of the boarding pupils.

Charitable status. Edge Grove School Trust Ltd is a Registered Charity, number 311054.

Edgeborough

Frensham, Farnham, Surrey GU10 3AH

Tel:	01252 792495
Fax:	01252 795156
email:	office@edgeborough.co.uk
website:	www.edgeborough.co.uk

Chairman of Governors: P Fulker

Headmaster: **C J Davies**, BA, PGCE

Age Range. 2–13.
Number of Children. Boarders 64, Day 174, Pre Prep 77, Nursery 46.
Fees per term (2016–2017). Years 5–8 £5,535, Years 3–4 £4,965, Pre Prep Years R–2 £3,390. Weekly Boarding (4 nights): £30.00 per night.

Edgeborough is a co-educational IAPS School, for 2–13 year olds, situated on a 50-acre estate in Frensham, near Farnham, Surrey.

The school offers an excellent all-round education to our girls and boys based upon outstanding teaching, wonderful facilities, space and fun. One of the main strengths is the 'value added' input to all children which means that high standards can be achieved by pupils of all abilities. Subsequently, pupils are prepared for entry and scholarships to the country's best senior schools.

The strong boarding community gives the school its family atmosphere. In addition to weekly boarding, flexi boarding is offered so that girls and boys can enjoy their first experiences of boarding at an early age with their friends. Breakfast and After School care offer logistical help to parents.

Edgeborough enjoys equally proud records of achievement in sports and in the expressive and performing arts. Scholarships to Senior Schools are frequently awarded for academic work, sports, art, drama music and all round leadership skills.

Day and residential trips both at home and abroad are a regular feature of the school term as is an active, healthy lifestyle.

As well as the spacious grounds and playing fields, the range of facilities is a strength of the school. They include well-equipped and spacious classrooms, a stunning science and technology building, large state-of-the-art ICT and music suites, an art and pottery centre, a fully-equipped theatre, separate dance and drama studios, a generous sports hall, floodlit astroturf fields, a swimming pool, woodlands, an excellently resourced library, an athletics track and an outdoor amphitheatre.

These facilities enable the school to provide a wide and varied programme of extracurricular activities. In addition to the main sports of rugby, football, cricket, hockey, netball, rounders, lacrosse and athletics, pupils can enjoy golf, badminton, tennis, swimming, climbing, gymnastics and judo. There are numerous school visits organised for the pupils, including a residential week in France, an annual ski trip, and sporting tours to Spain.

Charitable status. Edgeborough Educational Trust is a Registered Charity, number 312051.

Elm Green Preparatory School

Parsonage Lane, Little Baddow, Chelmsford, Essex CM3 4SU

Tel:	01245 225230
Fax:	01245 226008
email:	admin@elmgreen.essex.sch.uk
website:	www.elmgreen.essex.sch.uk

Principal: **Mrs A E Milner**, BTech Hons, MSc, PGCE

Age Range. Co-educational 4–11 years.
Number of Day Pupils. 220.
Fees per term (from April 2016). £2,685.
Religious affiliation. Non-denominational.

Elm Green was founded in 1944 and enjoys a lovely rural setting, surrounded by National Trust woodland.

Children enter in the September after their fourth birthday and in their final year are prepared for scholarships, entry to other independent schools and for entry to maintained schools. Many of the pupils take the Essex 11+ and the school has an excellent record of success in this examination.

The school maintains a high standard of academic education giving great emphasis to a secure foundation in the basic subjects whilst offering a wide curriculum with specialist teaching in many areas.

Information technology and design technology form an integral part of the curriculum and there are flourishing art, music and PE departments. The school competes successfully in a wide range of sports – football, rugby, netball, swimming, cricket, gymnastics, athletics, rounders and tennis.

There are many extra-curricular activities and all the children are encouraged to work and to play hard in order to fulfil their potential.

The school aims to foster intellectual curiosity and to encourage individual and corporate work. Kindness and thought for others are given a high priority.

The Elms

Colwall, Malvern, Worcestershire WR13 6EF
Tel: 01684 540344
email: office@elmsschool.co.uk
website: www.elmsschool.co.uk

Founded 1614.

Chairman of the Governors: T N Hone, MA, MBA

Head Master: **A Thomas**, BA Hons, PGCE

Age Range. 3–13.
Number of Pupils. Main School: 128: 64 Boys, 64 Girls.
50 boarders. Pre-Prep: 38.
Fees per term (2016-2017). Full board £7,650; Day board £6,550; Pre-Prep (3–7) £2,560–£4,295. Fees are payable termly. There are no compulsory extras.

The Elms is run as a charitable, non-profit making company with a Board of Governors. Children are taken in the Main School from the age of rising 8 and there is a Pre-Preparatory Department for 3–7 year olds.

An experienced staff and small classes ensure attention to each pupil's special needs and a high academic standard is maintained to CE and Scholarship levels. Small numbers help to create a family atmosphere with comfortable accommodation and a resident Headmaster and staff.

Gardens, fields and woodland with stream in 150 acres surround the school, beautifully set at the foot of the Malvern Hills, and include fine playing fields for Rugby, Association Football, Hockey, Cricket, Athletics, Netball and Rounders. Facilities include a Floodlit AstroTurf, Theatre, Sports Hall, Tennis Courts, Laboratory, Computer Rooms, new teaching block, DT Centre and an Art Room with facilities for Pottery. There is also a heated indoor swimming pool. The children manage a small farming enterprise and many ride on school ponies or bring their own.

Bursaries available for sons and daughters of Services personnel, the Clergy and Teachers; there are also competitive awards.

Charitable status. The Elms (Colwall) Limited is a Registered Charity, number 527252. It exists to provide education for boys and girls.

Eton End School

35 Eton Road, Datchet, Slough, Berkshire SL3 9AX
Tel: 01753 541075
email: admin@etonend.org
website: www.etonend.org

Chairman of Board of Governors: J Clark, Esq

Headmistress: **Mrs S Stokes**, BA Hons, PGCE

Age Range. Girls 3–11, Boys 3–7.
Number of Pupils. 210: 165 girls, 45 boys.
Fees per term (2016–2017). Nursery: £1,850–£2,975; Pre-Prep £3,030–£3,260; Prep £3,595–£3,880. Fees exclude lunch.

The school is a day school set within six acres of spacious grounds. All the classrooms are purpose built and modern, offering excellent facilities, including specialist rooms, e.g. Art & Craft, Music, Science Laboratory, School Library and IT Suite with touch-screen computers. There is a large well-equipped gymnasium, two hard tennis/netball courts, a football and sports field. Boys are prepared for all preparatory

schools in the area. Girls leave after the 11+ Entrance Examination often gaining Scholarships. Small classes allow each child to reach their maximum potential in a happy caring environment.

The school's origins lie in the traditions inspired by educationalist, Charlotte Mason, who founded the PNEU movement.

Charitable status. Eton End School Trust (Datchet) Limited is a Registered Charity, number 310644. The aim of the charity is to provide a well-balanced education for children whose parents wish them to attend Eton End School.

Eversfield Preparatory School

Warwick Road, Solihull, West Midlands B91 1AT
Tel: 0121 705 0354
Fax: 0121 709 0168
email: enquiries@eversfield.co.uk
website: www.eversfield.co.uk

Chairman of Governors: Mr D Adamson

Headmaster: **Mr R Yates**, BA, PGCE, LPSH

Age Range. 2¾–11 Co-educational.
Number of Pupils. 326.
Fees per term (2016–2017). £1,818–£3,422 according to age and inclusive of lunch, books and swimming lessons.

Eversfield is a Day Preparatory School on an attractive five-acre site in the centre of Solihull preparing boys and girls for entry to the leading Independent Senior Schools in the Midlands. The school was founded in 1931 and its mission is to provide an outstanding, broad education within a safe, caring, happy, family atmosphere where the talents of every child are valued and nurtured.

The curriculum focuses on academic excellence whilst also retaining the breadth which nurtures the creative, sporting, technical and social skills and potential of each child. There is a wide and varied range of lunchtime and after-school extra-curricular and holiday activities. Eversfield promotes high moral standards and responsible attitudes based upon clear and relevant Christian teaching. A strong sense of community exists where small classes, a well-ordered routine and good pastoral support help pupils to feel secure and develop their self-confidence.

On-site facilities include specialist rooms for art, design & technology, science, food technology, music and computing. Sporting facilities comprise a gymnasium, extensive playing fields and all-weather courts. In addition September 2015 saw the opening of a brand new Sports and Performing Arts Centre with an indoor heated pool. This state-of-the-art building has three badminton courts, indoor cricket nets and is also marked for netball. The customised lighting and sound system, theatre curtains, modular staging and retractable seating for over 200 make it the perfect venue for performances.

Charitable status. Eversfield Preparatory School Trust Limited is a Registered Charity, number 528966. It is under the direction of a Board of Governors and exists to carry out the work of an Independent Preparatory School.

Ewell Castle Preparatory School

Glyn House, Church Street, Ewell, Surrey KT17 2AP
Tel: 020 8394 3579
Fax: 020 8394 2220

email: enquiries@ewellcastle.co.uk
website: www.ewellcastle.co.uk
Twitter: @EwellCastleUK

Chairman of Governors: Mr P Durnford-Smith, BA,
MCIM

Principal: Mr P Harris, MSc, BSc, PGCE, NPQH

Head: Ms S Bradshaw, BEd Hons

Deputy Head of Preparatory School & Assistant Principal:
Mr A Robson, BEd, NPQH

Head of Pre-Preparatory School & Assistant Principal:
Mrs S Fowler, BSc, PGCE

Age Range. 3–11.
Number of Pupils. 200 Boys and Girls.
Fees per term (2016–2017). £2,630–£3,480.
Vision. The vision of the School is to **Inspire** and
Nurture our pupils to **Achieve**, within a happy, family
friendly atmosphere.
Ethos. Ewell Castle is a happy school with an atmosphere of purposeful, academic work. Care, consideration,
honesty, integrity, fairness and tolerance are valued. Self-
esteem is enhanced and all aspects of personal development
are fostered. With an ethos in which each child's achievements are acknowledged, valued and celebrated, students
thrive academically as a result of the small class sizes, a varied and stimulating curriculum, an extensive extracurricular
programme and strong support systems.
Values. Integrity, Trust, Respect, Responsibility, Determination.
Ewell Castle Preparatory School is an independent co-
educational day school, located on two sites in the heart of
Ewell Village. Nursery to Year 2 pupils (3–7 years) are
based at Chessington Lodge in Spring Street, while Years 3
to 6 (7–11 years) are based at Glyn House in Church Street,
opposite the Senior School (co-educational 11–18 years),
with which a close liaison is maintained.
Those entering the Nursery may attend for a half-day
(minimum three sessions per week) until they are ready for
full-time education. There are no entry requirements for
Nursery children, but older pupils attend the school for a
day's assessment, which will include tests in Mathematics
and English. The majority of pupils at Glyn House proceed
to the Senior School and a number of aided places and
scholarships are available at 11+, 13+ and 16+ entry. All
pupils are prepared for entry at 11+ to selective state
schools. The National Curriculum is incorporated within a
broad curriculum.
The creative arts play an important part in school life.
Apart from the timetabled music lessons, there is the opportunity for pupils to learn a variety of instruments under professional teachers. Drama productions take place regularly.
Pupils' art work can be seen on display in the local community and is always to be found decorating the school walls.
All pupils join in various sporting activities as part of the
weekly curriculum. In addition, a wide variety of activities
are available after school and during the holidays.
All pupils use the five acres of attractive gardens and
playing fields at Glyn House for outdoor play and games
lessons. In addition, Preparatory School pupils benefit from
full access to the excellent sporting facilities, including a
sports hall and playing fields, on the 15-acre site at The Castle. The main games are football, netball, hockey, cricket
and tennis. There are also athletics and cross country events,
including a school sports day. All pupils receive swimming
instruction.
Outside speakers include police liaison officers and
actors and authors who conduct workshops with pupils. A
number of visits occur to places of interest which are rele-

vant to a particular area of study. There are regular school
visits abroad.
The school also enjoys close links with St Mary's
Church, where regular assemblies are held throughout the
year.
The Preparatory School aims to provide a caring, responsive and stimulating environment in which pupils are able to
fulfil their potential. Hard work and high standards together
with courtesy and consideration to others are of prime
importance.
Charitable status. Ewell Castle School is a Registered
Charity, number 312079. It exists to provide education for
boys and girls.

Exeter Cathedral School

The Chantry, Palace Gate, Exeter, Devon EX1 1HX
Tel: 01392 255298
Fax: 01392 422718
email: reception@exetercs.org
website: www.exetercs.org

Chairman of Governors: The Dean of Exeter

Headmaster: James Featherstone, BA Hons, PGCE

Age Range. 3–13.
Number of Pupils. 18 full/weekly boarders, 35 regular
flexi boarders, 263 day pupils.
Fees per term (2016–2017). Day Pupils (excluding
lunches): £2,238–£3,733. Boarding (in addition to Day
fees): £2,330 (full). Flexi boarding is also available.
Founded in 1159, the Cathedral School provides 36 Boy
and Girl Choristers for Exeter Cathedral and educates 267
other pupils to the same high standard.
Entry is normally at age 3 into the Nursery (the School is
a member of the Government's Early Years Funding
Scheme) or at age 7 or 8 years into the Prep School, though
pupils may join the school at any stage, subject to place
availability.
Voice Trials for Cathedral Choristers are usually held in
February each year, or by arrangement. There are 18 scholarships available for Boy Choristers and 18 for Girl Choristers to the value of 25% of the tuition fee.
Pupils are prepared for senior school entry to both independent and maintained schools and the School has a proven
track record of academic, music, art, drama and sports
scholarship success.
There are no Saturday lessons, though day pupils sometimes join boarders in weekend or after school activities.
The curriculum encompasses all National Curriculum and
Common Entrance subjects, including Modern Foreign Languages and Latin.
In the Michaelmas Term, rugby and netball are the team
sports. Netball, soccer and hockey are played in the Lent
Term. During the Trinity Term, cricket, rounders, athletics
and swimming are all pursued competitively. Swimming
takes place all year round.
Musical activities, including school choir, orchestra and
ensembles for string, woodwind, brass and jazz instrumen-
talists are available to all pupils in the prep school.
Daily morning worship takes place in the Cathedral or in
The Chapter House led by the Headmaster, School Chaplain
or a member of the Cathedral Clergy.
The buildings are located around the Close and include a
Science Laboratory, a gym, music and drama school, as well
as a large portion of the 14th Century Deanery. There is a
Food Technology Centre, Design and Technology Department and Computer Centre.

For games, use is made of first-class facilities at Exeter University as well as other playing fields and swimming baths situated short distances away in the city.

Charitable status. Exeter Cathedral School is a Registered Charity, number 1151444.

Exeter Junior School

Victoria Park Road, Exeter, Devon EX2 4NS
Tel: 01392 258738 Headmistress
           01392 273679 Registrar
Fax: 01392 498144
email: admissions@exeterschool.org.uk
website: www.exeterschool.org.uk
Twitter: @ExeterSchoolUK

Co-educational Day School.

Chairman of Board of Governors: Mr A C W King

Headmistress: Mrs Sue Marks, BSc, PGCE

Age Range. 7–11.
Number of Pupils. 194: 121 Boys, 73 Girls.
Fees per term (2016–2017). £3,700 (includes lunch which is compulsory).

Exeter Junior School is housed in a spacious, Victorian building in the grounds of Exeter School. The close proximity of the Junior School to the Senior School enables the pupils to take full advantage of the facilities on site, which include a chapel, music centre, science laboratories, sports hall with dance studio, fitness suite and squash courts, outdoor heated swimming pool, playing fields, all-weather astroturf arena and tennis courts.

In addition to this the Junior School retains its own playground and green space, therefore giving the School a separate and clearly recognisable identity.

Liaison between Junior and Senior staff is a positive feature of this thriving Junior School.

The School aims to offer, in academic, cultural and sporting terms, the widest possible range of opportunities thus helping each pupil to identify the activities which will give the greatest scope for development and fulfilment in years to come. Music, drama, art, sport and expeditions all have an important part to play in the life of the school.

The majority of pupils enter the school at age 7 or 9, and entrance is by informal assessment in January. This includes a report from the child's previous school, classroom sessions in the company of other prospective pupils, and literacy, numeracy and general intelligence tasks. Pupils may enter the school at other ages where space is available.

Pupils are offered an academic programme which incorporates the National Curriculum model with the addition of French which is introduced from Year 3.

Specialist teaching is offered from the outset, with the additional support of Senior School staff in Science, French, Music and ICT.

A wide variety of clubs are available during the week including art & craft, dance, modern languages, calligraphy, sewing, football, hockey, netball, rugby, chess and drama. After-school care is available until 5.30pm.

(*For further information about the Senior School, see Exeter School entry in HMC section.*)

Charitable status. Exeter School is a Registered Charity, number 1093080. It exists to provide education for children.

Fairfield Preparatory School

Leicester Road, Loughborough, Leics LE11 2AE
Tel: 01509 215172
Fax: 01509 238648
email: admin@lesfairfield.org
website: www.lesfairfield.org
Twitter: @ffdheadmaster

Chairman of the Governors: Mr G P Fothergill, BA

Head: Mr A Earnshaw, BA Lancaster, NPQH

Age Range. 3–11.
Number of Pupils. 252 Boys, 234 Girls (all day)
Fees per term (2016–2017). Pre-Prep £3,226, Upper Prep £3,272. Lunches and individual music lessons extra.

Fairfield is the preparatory school of Loughborough Endowed Schools, a foundation of four schools comprising Loughborough Grammar School (boys, 10–18, day and boarding – *see HMC entry*), Loughborough High School (girls, 11–18 – *see GSA entry*) and Our Lady's Convent School (co-educational 3–11, girls 11–18 – *see ISA entry*), which became the foundation's fourth school on 1st September 2015. The schools operate under one governing body and are situated on two neighbouring campuses in the town.

In 2014, the school embarked on an ambitious new building project to provide pupils with additional space and improved accommodation, including new classrooms for pupils in Reception and Years 1–3, an extended gymnasium with spacious changing rooms for pupils and staff, a specialist arts and craft room, an additional performance hall, designated main entrance and essential office space. It will also house a brand new purpose-built Kindergarten unit for children aged 3+ during term time from January 2016.

Fairfield's partnership with pupils, parents and the wider community ensures every child is given the ability to reach their full potential through a combination of academic, cultural, sporting and artistic opportunities.

Learning is extended through a wide range of activities, utilising iPads and other technologies, along with specialist teaching in science, ICT, modern foreign languages, PE, and music. Music is a vital part of the school's culture and the facilities available to pupils are second to none. All Year 2 pupils follow a course in instrumental playing, and children in the Upper Prep have the opportunity to have individual instrumental lessons with one of the LES Music School's peripatetic staff. In September 2015, the LES Music School became the only All-Steinway School in the Midlands, demonstrating the foundation's commitment to providing pupils with the very best instruments on which to learn, practise and perform.

Fairfield provides access to an extensive range of extra-curricular activities. There are a greater number of sports, and more teams, clubs and opportunities for extracurricular music on offer than ever before. Practically every single member of staff at the school runs at least one extracurricular session, ensuring that our programme of activities meets the diverse and ever-changing interests of our pupils.

In a nurturing, happy atmosphere, children are guided along their educational journey through purposeful, academic work and are constantly encouraged to succeed. Staff help develop each child's confidence, courtesy and self-worth so they grow stronger, not only as individuals, but also as members of their local community. By taking individual differences into account, the successful Fairfield Preparatory School pupil of today acquires the skills and values which allow them to make a valuable contribution to the success of the senior schools, and through their lives, to the society of tomorrow.

The Headmaster is happy to show prospective parents around the school by appointment. Further information can be found on the school website at www.lesfairfield.org.

Charitable status. Loughborough Endowed Schools is a Registered Charity, number 1081765, and a Company Limited by Guarantee, registered in England, number 4038033. Registered Office: 3 Burton Walks, Loughborough, Leics LE11 2DU.

Fairstead House School

Fordham Road, Newmarket, Suffolk CB8 7AA
Tel: 01638 662318
email: registrar@fairsteadhouse.co.uk
website: www.fairsteadhouse.co.uk

Chair of Governors: Dr Patrick Round

Head: **Dr Lynda Brereton**, BSc, PhD, PGCE

Age Range. Co-educational 9 months – 11 years.
Number of Children. 110.
Fees per term (2016–2017). Nursery: £29.50 per morning session (including lunch) and £22.50 per afternoon session. Main School (including lunches): Reception & Year 1 £3,070, Years 2 & 3 £3,255, Years 4, 5 & 6 £3,310.

Fairstead House is situated in the heart of Newmarket and offers a combination of an excellent academic education with an emphasis on creativity and imagination in a caring, happy community with a unique family ethos, closely linked to the local community.

From Nursery onwards, we offer a broad and stimulating curriculum which provides the children with a solid foundation for their onward journeys to senior schools in both Independent and State sectors. The curriculum is complemented by Art, DT, Music, Drama and Sports.

Pupils take part in a variety of sports such as rugby, football and cricket for boys and hockey and netball for girls. All children play rounders and take part in cross country running and athletics.

Extracurricular Speech & Drama lessons are available, as is private tuition in a wide selection of musical instruments. Children may join the Fairstead House Orchestra or Choir and take part in the many theatrical productions that are held at School.

A programme of development has ensured the provision of first-class facilities throughout the School including a state-of-the-art Music & Drama Centre with specialist facilities, an ICT suite, iPads, interactive whiteboards in every classroom and a dedicated Science & DT area.

As well as a breakfast club and after-school care club providing wrap-around care, there is a diverse range of after-school activity clubs available offering such activities as yoga, aikido, pottery and strategy games together with the major sports. A Holiday Club is also available for all children out of term time.

Throughout the year, pupils go on a variety of trips and excursions, both day and residential. The residential trips to Norfolk and Snowdonia for the older pupils are designed to encourage independence and cultivate a spirit of adventure as well as personal responsibility and development.

Charitable Status: Fairstead House School Trust Limited is a Registered Charity, number 276787. It exists to provide education for boys and girls.

The Falcons Schools
Alpha Plus Group

Boys Nursery and Pre-Prep:
2 Burnaby Gardens, London W4 3DT
Tel: 020 8747 8393
Fax: 020 8995 3903
email: admin@falconschool.com
website: www.falconsboys.co.uk

Boys Prep:
41 Kew Foot Road, Richmond, Surrey TW9 2SS
Tel: 020 8948 9490
Fax: 020 8948 9491
email: admin@falconsprep.co.uk
website: www.falconsboys.co.uk

Girls School:
11 Woodborough Road, Putney, London SW15 6PY
Tel: 020 8992 5189
Fax: 020 8752 1635
email: admin@falconsgirls.co.uk
website: www.falconsgirls.co.uk

Head Teacher, Girls School: **Mrs Sophia Ashworth Jones**

Head Teacher, Pre-Prep Boys School: **Mr Andrew Forbes**, BA Hons, DipEd
Head Teacher, Prep Boys School: **Mr Deon Etzinger**, BA, HDipEd

Age Range. Boys School: 3–7 (Pre-Prep), 8–13 (Prep); Girls School 3–11.
Number of Pupils. 355 Boys; 85 Girls.
Fees per term (2016–2017). Boys School: £2,772–£5,665. Girls School: £2,730–£4,990.

The Falcons Schools enjoy a well-deserved reputation for excellence. Results to the leading London Day Schools are impressive, as too is the specialist teaching on offer throughout the schools. The schools provide a safe outdoor space for play and sport and a school hall for gym, assemblies and lunch. Nearby sports facilities are used to enhance an exciting sports program. There are well-equipped libraries, music rooms, ICT suites, with a much-admired art and science facility. Our overriding emphasis is on achieving excellence in numeracy and literacy whilst offering a broad and creative curriculum. The Falcons is a uniquely caring and stimulating environment, where learning is seen as fun and the pursuit of excellence is embraced by all.

Farleigh School

Red Rice, Andover, Hampshire SP11 7PW
Tel: 01264 710766
Fax: 01264 710070
email: office@farleighschool.com
website: www.farleighschool.com
Twitter: @FarleighSchool

Chairman of Governors: Mr Tim Syder

Headmaster: **Fr Simon Everson**

Age Range. 3–13. Boarding from age 7.
Number of Pupils. 90 boarders (53 boys, 37 girls), 357 day, including 23 flexi boarders; 103 in Kindergarten and Pre-Prep.

Fees per term (2016–2017). Senior boarders (Years 7 and 8) £7,985; Junior boarders (Years 3–6) £7,195; HM Forces boarders (Years 3–8) £6,785; Day pupils £1,685–£6,135.

Celebrating its Diamond Jubilee in 2013, Farleigh was originally founded in 1953 as a Roman Catholic boys' boarding school. Today, it is a fully co-educational boarding and day school, welcoming children of all faiths. Situated in a stunning Georgian country house standing in 60 acres of magnificent parkland and landscaped woodland in the Test Valley of Hampshire, Farleigh is just over an hour from London and within easy reach of Southampton and London airports.

High standards are achieved both in and out of the classroom and excellent academic results are the norm, with leavers going to a large number of leading senior schools and many obtaining scholarships.

Farleigh has outstanding facilities, including spacious and light Art and Design Technology building, computer rooms with state-of-the-art Apple Macs and mobile technology, a theatre with tiered seating, music suite, spacious recreation rooms, a fine Chapel, gymnasium, 22-metre heated indoor swimming pool, five tennis courts, squash courts and purpose-built Pre-Prep and Kindergarten. Opened in September 2012 were two new buildings, which accommodate four new classrooms, three new science laboratories and a food technology room, as well as additional circulation space with a well-lit ball play area and a small amphitheatre to the rear of the existing Farleigh theatre. In 2016 an all-weather pitch was built and a new music school with 12 practice rooms, a concert hall, rehearsal room, rock room and recording studio is due for completion by the end of the year.

The teaching staff is complemented by a committed pastoral team including Year Heads, House Parents and three matrons who are qualified nurses. Many staff are resident, giving the school a welcoming family atmosphere, often commented upon by visitors. The latest Ofsted inspection (2010) of the school's boarding provision was "Outstanding" in all six areas inspected, "with no recommendations". The inspectors added, "This is a very caring school that is child-centred and achieves high standards throughout."

The school provides a vibrant and active evening and weekend activity programme for boarders. Regular dinner nights, barbecue parties, X-Factor competitions, theatre trips, quiz nights, bowling are just some of the weekend events organised for pupils. Weekday activities include building dens in the woods, cycling, judo, winter cricket nets, community service, swimming, water polo, tennis, football, unihockey, jewellery making, art and craft.

Drama, music and art have important places in school life with two-thirds of the school learning at least one musical instrument and a third of the school taking up LAMDA drama lessons. A programme of major musical productions and informal concerts take place throughout the year and the children's artwork is displayed around the school.

The major sports for boys are rugby, football, cricket, athletics and cross country; for girls they are netball, hockey, rounders, athletics and cross country. Swimming lessons and extra tennis coaching are offered throughout the year.

Charitable status. Farleigh School is a Registered Charity, number 1157842. It exists for the purpose of educating children.

Farlington Preparatory School

Strood Park, Horsham, West Sussex RH12 3PN

Tel: 01403 282566
Fax: 01403 272258

email: prepheadmistress@farlingtonschool.net
website: www.farlingtonschool.net
Twitter: @Farlington_Sch
          @FarlingtonPH
Facebook: /FarlingtonSchool

Chairman of Governors: Mrs Sue Mitchell, BA, MA, PGCE

Headmistress: **Mrs Frances Mwale**, BSc, PGCE, MSc

Registrar: Mrs Sue Apps, MBA

Age Range. 3–11.
Number of Girls. 150.
Fees per term (2016–2017). Day: £2,350–£4,750. Boarding from age 8: £7,550–£8,260 (weekly), £7,980–£8,690 (full).

The Early Years Foundation Stage and Pre-Prep Departments at Farlington are housed in an impressive courtyard building opened in September 2008. This purpose-built accommodation comprises nursery, large Pre-prep classrooms, a Pre-prep library, a separate Prep library, and two innovative play areas. The spacious hall and dining facilities are enjoyed by all of our Prep Pupils. The Prep School girls are also housed in purpose-built classrooms that mirror the architecture of the Pre-prep buildings. Younger children quickly feel at home in this close-knit community, and the older girls have the opportunity to learn responsibility and have status in "their" school by becoming Prefects, Librarians, Sports or House Captains.

Early school days that are happy and secure, provide a sound basis for learning and for life. At Farlington, we aim to achieve high academic standards in our Preparatory School, with the emphasis on encouragement: we educate for confidence! The philosophy of the School is based on Christian ethics, but we welcome girls from a wide range of religious and cultural backgrounds.

We have a staff of well-qualified and dedicated teachers. They form a wonderfully good-humoured team, who support fully the ethos of the School. Literacy and numeracy are the building blocks of education, and these form the foundation of our curriculum in the Pre-Prep Department.

We follow the National Curriculum, but offer much more in terms of subject content, and, of course, individual attention. As girls become older, they are taught most subjects by specialist teachers (for example, English, Mathematics, Science, French, Spanish, Latin, PE/Games, Drama, Music and Art). Science skills are developed in a challenging way, using exploration and experiment, as well as practice and problem-solving. Science is taught in the well-equipped laboratories in the Senior School. There is also a strong emphasis on Music and individual tuition can be arranged for most instruments. Girls can progress from the Training Orchestra to the Concert Orchestra.

All girls enjoy the beautiful 33-acre parkland setting for recreation and for learning. Farlington embraces the Forest School Initiatives and we enjoy the benefits of having our own trained instructor on the staff. We run weekly sessions using our wonderful outdoor environment, opening up the amazing natural world through the seasons, giving the children a programme filled with discovery and difference.

The Prep School offers a wide range of extra-curricular activities which take place at lunchtimes and after school. These range from sporting clubs such as tennis, trampolining, golf and judo to musical activities which include choir, orchestra, recorder ensembles and a samba band. We offer chess tuition, ballet, jazz dance, fencing and much more. Although school finishes at 3.20 pm for girls in Reception to Prep 2, they can stay on at school until 4.30 pm supervised by members of staff. There is no charge for this after-school care. Extended day care (chargeable) is provided until 5.45 pm or 7.00 pm. A breakfast club is also available.

At Farlington we believe that education is a partnership between home and school, and we hope that parents will take an active part in their daughter's education. Farlington has a very active PTA and a Parents' Round Table (a focus group to develop ideas throughout the school).

Boarding is available to girls from the age of 8. Our new Prep Boarding House, "Fishponds", is small and friendly and run on family lines, providing a home-away-from-home atmosphere.

Prospective parents are always welcome to come to meet the Headmistress and have a tour of the School. Please telephone for an appointment and we shall be delighted to send you our prospectus and current information booklet.

For further information on the Senior School, see Farlington School entry in the GSA section.

Charitable status. Farlington Preparatory School is a Registered Charity, number 307048. It exists solely for the purpose of educating girls.

Felsted Preparatory School

Felsted, Essex CM6 3JL

Tel:	01371 822610
Fax:	01371 822617
email:	senioradmissions@felsted.org
website:	www.felsted.org
Twitter:	@felstedprep
Facebook:	@felstedschool
LinkedIn:	/Felsted School

Chairman of the Governors: Mr J H Davies

Head: **Mr S C James**, BA Hons, PGCE

Deputy Head: T J Searle, BSc Loughborough, PGCE

Age Range. 4–13 Co-educational.

Number of Pupils. 513 pupils (of which 5 are full-time boarders, 15 weekly and 61 flexi boarders).

Fees per term (2016–2017). Day: Preparatory £4,220–£5,550, Pre-Preparatory £2,925. Weekly Boarding £7,195, Full Boarding £7,540, Flexi Boarding (1–4 nights) £49.50–£114.00 per week.

The staff, excluding the Headmaster, consists of over 50 full-time qualified teachers and there are additional part-time teachers for instrumental music and games. There are six matrons and two sisters in charge of the Medical Centre.

The School was rated 'excellent' in every category by the Independent School Inspectorate at its latest inspection, in addition to a legacy rating of 'Outstanding' by Ofsted for EYFS and Boarding.

The Preparatory School, set in its own grounds, is separate from Felsted School itself, with all its own facilities, including a modern well-equipped library, an excellent theatre/assembly hall, music practice rooms, a new multi-purpose sports hall, open-air heated swimming pool and floodlit, multi-purpose, hard play/games area. Use is made of Felsted School's extra amenities at regular times so that indoor swimming, two Astroturf hockey pitches, small-bore rifle shooting, squash courts, a new state-of-the-art Music School and another indoor sports hall are also available to the pupils. Pupils in Years 7 and 8 also lunch at the senior school every day.

Rugby, football, netball, hockey, cricket, tennis, swimming, athletics and cross country are the major sports. Music plays an important part in the School's life, and there is an excellent Chapel Choir. Regular instrumental, orchestral and rock concerts are given. The School has a deserved reputation for its drama productions, while Art, Design and Technology, PSHE, and Computing are part of the weekly timetable. Out-of-class activities include public speaking and debating opportunities, horse riding, chess, fencing, golf, public speaking, aerobics, cookery and dance/ballet, among others.

Pupils joining at 11+ can be guaranteed assured transfer to Felsted School at 13, as can pupils of a similar age already at the Preparatory School, following successful completion of assessment tests. The majority of pupils proceed to Felsted School itself, but a number regularly move on to other major independent senior schools, having taken Common Entrance, and there is an excellent record of academic, art, music, sport, drama and Design & Technology scholarships. (*For further information about Felsted, see entry in HMC section.*)

Academic and Music Scholarships and Mary Skill Awards are open to pupils joining Felsted Preparatory School at ages of 11+ in the September of the year of entry. Top-up bursaries may also be available on a means-tested basis. One 100% bursary is available each year to a child who meets the right criteria and is given at the discretion of the Head.

Charitable status. Felsted School is a Registered Charity, number 310870. It exists to provide education for boys and girls.

Feltonfleet School

Byfleet Road, Cobham, Surrey KT11 1DR

Tel:	01932 862264
Fax:	01932 860280
email:	office@feltonfleet.co.uk
	admissions@feltonfleet.co.uk
website:	www.feltonfleet.co.uk

Chair of Governors: Mrs M Jenner, MBE, JP

Headmaster: **Mr A G Morrison**, BA, PGCE

Deputy Head: Ms M Guest, BD, PGCE

Registrar: Mrs Jackie Williams, BA Hons

Age Range. 3–13.

Number of Pupils. Nursery/Pre-Prep 80, Years 3–8 319, of whom 48 are Boarders.

Fees per term (2016–2017). Boarders £7,490, Day Pupils £3,760–£5,445; Nursery £1,985.

Feltonfleet School was founded in 1903 and became an Educational Trust in 1967. The School is situated in 25 acres of scenic grounds close to the M25 between Heathrow and Gatwick Airports. There are 56 full-time and 4 Gap Year members of the teaching staff. The School became fully co-educational in September 1994 and offers both weekly boarding (Monday to Friday) and day education, as well as a flexible boarding option. There is a flourishing, purpose-built Pre-Preparatory Department called Calvi House.

Academics. In 2016 academic results were the best in Feltonfleet's history – the best CE results the school has ever seen including 19 Senior School Scholarships. Headmaster, Alastair Morrison and his staff are 100% committed to drawing out the best in each and every child and this is really shining through in Feltonfleet's results.

Ethos. It is the School's strongly held belief that, if children are happy, they will fulfill their potential and, by recognising the individual in a child, this is more likely to happen, which is why it is committed to fostering a small school atmosphere centred on family values, but also keeping academic achievement at its heart. The School places the children first, meets each child's needs on an individual basis, encourages and nurtures the positive aspects of 'self': self-discipline, self-confidence, self-motivation, self-reliance and self-esteem. High-achieving children, irrespective of their real potential, are those who have a high self-esteem – without it very little can be achieved.

Pastoral. Caring for each other matters at Feltonfleet. From a child's first day, the adult community provides care, direction and confidence. The form tutor is the welcoming face on a daily basis and a secure link with daily routine, a familiar and reassuring presence, a trusted confidant and role model. Small classes make quality pastoral care much more certain. Once pupils join the Main School, the Head of Year provides further direction and guidance. The boarding house is run by two house parents, seven boarding house tutors and two matrons who promote the personal, family atmosphere on which Feltonfleet prides itself.

Entry. Children are admitted from the age of three into the Nursery in the Pre-Preparatory Department and, having moved into the Main School at the age of seven, are prepared for Common Entrance or Scholarship examinations to a wide range of independent senior schools. In the Main School there is a staff : pupil ratio of 9.5:1, with the average class size of 18.

For entry into the Main School pupils are required to sit an entrance assessment and interview. Academic, Art, Music, Drama, DT, All-Rounder and Sports Scholarships are offered at 11+.

Facilities. A brand new, state-of-the-art, 200-seater Performing Arts Centre opened in May 2015, where dramatic productions, dance shows and music are performed by all year groups. Well-equipped Science, Art, DT and Digital Learning Departments and Library. The Pre-Prep, Calvi House, has its own hall, gardens and ICT suite. There are landscaped play areas throughout the school and a stunning tree house, pond and wildlife area with bird hide.

Sport. The Sports Department prides itself on its ability to encompass both excellence and sport-for-all within a very busy prep school environment. All pupils receive high quality teaching and coaching in a variety of sports and activities in a positive and safe learning environment. Facilities include a magnificent sports hall, sports fields, a 15m indoor swimming pool, a shooting range for air and .22 rifles, a large floodlit Astro pitch and a climbing wall.

Games played are rugby, football, hockey, netball, lacrosse, athletics and cricket.

Extra-Curricular Activities. The School has an active policy of preparing children for the challenges of today's world and an exceptional activities programme is offered to all pupils during the school day as often as possible. Pupils in the main school are offered the opportunity to attend residential activity courses as well as subject-related overseas trips. In the final two years pupils attend residential leadership courses. After Common Entrance examinations, Year 8 pupils take part in a varied programme of activities, lectures and trips in preparation for leaving Feltonfleet and moving on to their senior schools.

In recent years sporting teams have visited Barbados, Dubai, Belgium, Spain and Qatar.

Charitable status. Feltonfleet School Trust Limited is a Registered Charity, number 312070.

Fettes College Preparatory School

East Fettes Avenue, Edinburgh EH4 1QZ

Tel:	+44 (0)131 332 2976
Fax:	+44 (0)131 332 4724
email:	prepschool@fettes.com
website:	www.fettes.com
Twitter:	@Fettes_College

Chairman of Governors: Lord C Tyre

Chairman of Preparatory School Committee: H Bruce-Watt

Headmaster: **A A Edwards**, BA Hons, PGCE

Age Range. 7–13.
Number of Pupils. 205: 45 boarders, 160 day pupils; 106 boys, 99 girls.
Fees per term (2016–2017). Boarders £7,795, Day Pupils £4,990, including all meals and textbooks.

Fettes Prep School lies within the Fettes College grounds – 80 acres of parkland in the heart of Edinburgh. Although housed in separate buildings about 200m away from the main Fettes College building, the Prep School has all the advantages of the excellent facilities of Fettes College but with the ability to be a complete campus in its own right. Due to expansion in the school roll, William House was completed in 2009 – a state-of-the-art teaching block with superb eco credentials.

Their HMIe inspection had superb results with both Fettes Prep and Fettes College deemed as 'sector-leading'.

The Boarding houses of Iona (girls) and Arran (boys) offer a safe, secure and happy environment. The pastoral staff; housemaster, housemistress, matron and resident tutor, are of the highest calibre and dedicate themselves to creating a secure and happy home.

The curriculum is structured to reflect the strengths of the Curriculum for Excellence, the National Curriculum of England and Wales and IAPS guidance. A strong emphasis is placed on a sound and thorough grounding in the traditionally important subjects of Maths and English as well as specialists subjects such as Science, Art and Languages being taught by specialist teachers. Class sizes remain small to allowing individual attention for each child.

Formal coaching is given to boys in rugby, hockey, athletics and cricket and to girls in hockey, netball, rounders, athletics and tennis. Each year pupils from the school represent their district in these sports and others. Swimming is also taught as are judo, fencing, squash and shooting (the vast majority taking place on campus). There are over 30 activities and clubs ranging from climbing to origami.

Music and Drama flourish. The School Choir and School Orchestra give concerts each term, and choirs and instrumental groups participate successfully in musical competitions. Year group concerts, too, are regularly held. Each year there is a large-production School Play, younger pupils produce their own pantomime, and shorter plays are performed in French and Latin. The art department continues to excel and every pupil within the school has their work displayed.

There are annual trips abroad to bring learning to life and other tours are regularly organised. All twelve year olds receive leadership training and the top two year groups are involved in a programme designed at the school to increase and improve skills in various areas including resourcefulness, initiative and personal challenge.

Entrance. Entrance at the age of seven, eight or nine is by assessment tests and at 10+, 11+ and 12+ by the Entrance Examinations, taken in late Jan/early Feb. All applicants can apply for a means-tested bursary which can cover up to 100% of the fees. There is a finite amount of funding available each year and therefore not all applicants will be successful. Bursaries are awarded independently of any Scholarship or Award.

All candidates who are applying for entry into the 1st Form at 11+ years of age, will automatically be considered for a Junior Scholarship. The results of the Entrance Examinations will determine who receives a Junior Scholarship.

These Scholarships are awarded for academic or all-round excellence and there is great kudos associated with being a scholar of The College. They can also attract reductions of up to 5% of the fees and these reductions are not related to parents' financial circumstances. A Music award can also be applied for at 11+ and 12+ entry.

Further information and a prospectus can be obtained from the Registrar (Tel: +44 (0)131 311 6744, email: admissions@fettes.com) who will be very happy to arrange a visit.

Charitable status. The Fettes Trust is a Registered Charity, number SC017489.

Finton House

171 Trinity Road, London SW17 7HL
Tel: 020 8682 0921
email: admissions@fintonhouse.org.uk
website: www.fintonhouse.org.uk
Twitter: @FintonHouseSch
Facebook: /Finton.House.School

Co-Founders: Terry O'Neill and Finola Stack founded Finton House in 1987.

Chair of Governors: Mr Mark Chilton

Headmaster: **Mr Ben Freeman**

Age Range. 4–11.
Number of Pupils. 140 Boys, 180 Girls.
Fees per term (2016–2017). £4,630–£4,850.
Entrance. No testing – first come/first served.
Exit. Boys and Girls at 11 for London Day, Prep or Boarding.

Aims to give an all-round education, developing the whole child with individual teaching to fulfil each child's potential. Academic subjects, Music, Art and Sports are all taught to a very high standard. A third of leavers win scholarships and awards to their senior schools. Strong policy of inclusion with a percentage of children with Special Needs. Employs a full-time Speech and Language Therapist, an Occupational Therapist and Special Needs Assistants. A stimulating environment which encourages all children to learn and gain confidence in their own abilities. Non-denominational but teaches a moral belief encouraging respect and self-discipline.

Charitable status. Finton House is a Registered Charity, number 296588. It exists to provide an broad, inclusive education for children.

Foremarke Hall
Repton Preparatory School

Milton, Derbyshire DE65 6EJ
Tel: 01283 707100
email: registrar@foremarke.org.uk
website: www.foremarke.org.uk
Twitter: @foremarkehall

Chairman of Governors: Sir Henry Every

Head: **R P Merriman**, MA, BSc Hons, FCollP

Age Range. 3–13.
Number of Pupils. 458: Boys: 44 boarders, 193 day; Girls: 22 boarders, 199 day.
Fees per term (2016–2017).
Prep Day: Y3 & Y4 £5,048, Y5 & Y6 £5,678, Y7 & Y8 £6,307.
Prep Boarding: Y3 & Y4 £6,910, Y5 & Y6 £7,538, Y7 & Y8 £8,168. Flexi Boarding prices available on request.
Pre-Prep: Y1 & Y2 £3,422, Reception £3,087, Nursery £2,935 (full-time), £293 per session.

Foremarke Hall is under the control of the Governors of Repton School. Boys and girls are prepared for all Independent Schools but most choose to continue to Repton.

The school is situated in a fine Georgian mansion surrounded by 55 acres of woods, playing fields and a lake. The facilities include all that the school requires including a new classroom building to house mathematics, three science laboratories, sophisticated computer technology with full-time IT specialist, an extensive library run by a chartered librarian, an indoor competition-sized swimming pool, a sports hall and a floodlit sports artificial turf surface.

The £6m Quad Development houses a contemporary music facility, a new language laboratory, many new classrooms, a new art block complete with kiln, a designated ICT suite for design and technology and a Greenpower garage for Foremarke's award-winning electric cars.

Great importance is attached to pastoral care where boarders have their own dedicated staff and space for themselves. There is an imaginative and varied programme of activities making most use of the grounds including outdoor pursuits. The games programme is extensive and includes athletics, cricket, football, hockey, rounders, netball, swimming and tennis. We also have an extensive and varied after-school activities programme.

We seek to bring out the most in every pupil, to provide a rounded education and a range of experience and skills that will be a preparation for life. We value our 'family atmosphere' and strong sense of community, the spacious grounds and happy environment.

Foremarke is situated in undisturbed countryside on a 55-acre site in the centre of England. It is easily reached by road from the M1/M6/M5 via the A50, by rail to East Midlands Parkway, or from nearby Birmingham and East Midlands airports.

Charitable status. Repton Preparatory School is a Registered Charity, number 1093165. It exists to provide high quality education for boys and girls.

Forest Preparatory School

College Place, Snaresbrook, London E17 3PY
Tel: 020 8520 1744
Fax: 020 8520 3656
email: prep@forest.org.uk
website: www.forest.org.uk
Twitter: @ForestSchoolE17
Facebook: /ForestSchoolE17

Co-educational Day School.

Chairman of Governors: David Wilson, LLB

Head: **Mr A Noakes**, BA Hons De Montfort, MA Ed Open University

Age Range. 4–11.
Number of Pupils. 272.
Fees per term (2016–2017). £3,869–£4,487.

Forest Preparatory School is part of Forest School (HMC), with which it shares a 30-acre site at the foot of Epping Forest on the east London/Essex border. Its aims are to offer an education of high quality, and to encourage and develop each child academically, physically and creatively. In the Pre-Prep, pupils are taught in small co-educational classes. From the age of 7, pupils are taught in single-sex classes, and at age 11 they proceed to the Senior Section of Forest School (*see separate entry in HMC section*).

Entry to the school is by selection at age 4 by means of an informal assessment and, at age 7, by entrance examination.

The Pre-Prep Department is co-educational, with forms of 16 pupils who are taught predominantly by form teachers and supported by classroom assistants. ICT, music, drama, swimming and PE are taught by specialist teachers. From the age of 7, forms become single-sex with 22 pupils in each. Form teachers teach the main curriculum subjects, while specialists teach modern foreign languages – Mandarin, Spanish and German – ICT, art, music, drama, dance, design and technology, physical education, swimming and games.

Academic standards, sport and music are all strengths of the school in equal measure. The main sports played are football, cricket, netball and rounders, and teams compete locally and regionally. Athletics, swimming and cross-country are all coached to a high standard. The musical life of the school is enriched by its choirs, orchestra and several chamber groups, and all pupils in Years 3 and 4 are provided with free tuition in a musical instrument. There are endless opportunities for pupils to perform in concerts or recitals throughout the year, and Chapel services, form assemblies and school competitions provide occasions for public speaking and performance. Activities take place at lunchtime, before school and after school, with a wide variety of extra-curricular clubs on offer. Breakfast club commences at 7.30 am and after-school care is available until 6.00 pm each day. Forest School also has an extensive school bus service in operation.

Charitable status. Forest School, Essex is a Registered Charity, number 312677. The objective of the school is education.

Forres Sandle Manor

Sandleheath, Fordingbridge, Hampshire SP6 1NS

Tel: 01425 653181
email: office@fsmschool.com
website: www.fsmschool.com
Twitter: @FSMSchool
Facebook: @FSMSchool

Headmaster: **M N Hartley**, BSc Hons, PGCE

Age Range. 3–13.
Number of Pupils. Prep: 168 (100 boarders, 100 boys, 68 girls). Pre-Prep: 49 (all are day children, 32 boys, 17 girls).
Fees per term (2016–2017). Boarders: £7,695 (Years 5–8), £7,400 (Year 4), £6,315 (Year 3); Day pupils: £5,635 (Years 7 & 8), £5,430 (Years 5 & 6), £5,145 (Year 4), £4,585 (Year 3), £2,885 (Years 1 & 2), £2,750 (Reception). Early Years Education Entitlement provider.

At Forres Sandle Manor, we believe that "Happy Children Succeed".

You may imagine, with a line like that, Forres Sandle Manor (or FSM as we are known) is some kind of holiday club dedicated to keep the children smiling and entertained. However, this is a surface sort of happiness. The sort of happiness FSM means comes from knowing that you are liked and respected by your peers and your teachers. It comes from knowing that no matter what your skills and talents, or indeed your lack of them, you will be helped and supported to do the best that you can in order to reach your own particular star.

From the Nursery all the way up to Year 8 there are many stars at FSM. Naturally there are those who excel in particular areas of the curriculum or indeed one of the many extra-curricular activities, and these children are enrolled into our Gifted and Talented Programme. Some of these children may also attend the fabulous, nationally renowned, Learning Support Centre which also provides essential support for those who learn differently when and where required. Not all children are all-rounders after all.

At FSM each and every child is supported by our skills based, creative curriculum which allows every single child to contribute to the plans of what they will be learning as a class. We believe that it is only when children have some ownership of their learning that they are able to fully engage with it so that it is meaningful and relevant to them

None of this happens by accident. FSM have exceptional resources; at the heart of the school is the manor house, which is surrounded by 35 acres of playing fields, woods and streams. Our facilities are the same as you would expect to find at a leading prep school; an astro pitch, a multi-purpose sports and performance hall, our Forest School, a 25-metre heated swimming pool as well as much more! Our most important resource, however, is our staff. The teachers at FSM are passionate about what they do and in all areas they actively seek out and nurture raw talent in whatever field that may be.

Life at FSM starts at the Pre-Prep, where children can join the Nursery during the half-term when they turn 3. The first years of school are vital and it's fundamental that they are of the very highest standard. It is at this time that children learn how to learn; that their curiosity is harnessed through meaningful and purposeful play and that they develop the neural pathways that will serve them for the rest of their lives. It is in these valuable years that a child's dispositions and attitudes to learning are developed and that children learn to take risks, to persevere, to explore and to ask questions, as well as the social and communication skills which can only develop through being with others.

FSM provides an environment which nurtures and encourages the developing child at this special time in their lives. We don't believe in hot-housing. We feel that's the way to produce rapid, but weak growth. Instead we allow children the most precious thing of all – time. It is only through sustained, active learning, that a child is able to become absorbed, make connections to past experiences, develop higher order thinking skills and truly learn.

The Music school produces amazing results and every child is encouraged to try an instrument and experience performance in many different areas. Drama is timetabled for all children from Year 3 and above. We encourage all the children to get up and perform as often as they can. It's a fantastic way of building up their self-confidence and by the time they get to Year 8, standing up in front of an audience becomes second nature.

Sport is played everyday, apart from Thursdays and there is always a full fixture list on Wednesday and Saturday afternoons. Every child has the opportunity to represent the school at some point, with our best sportsmen and women competing at County and National level.

Academically, FSM leads the way in its innovative approach to teaching. Many of the techniques used here have now been adopted by Prep Schools across the country and we are justifiably proud of the fact that every Year 8 has always been successful in achieving their first choice senior school. Always! Not only that, but the children win more than their fair share of scholarships and awards. We spend much time liaising with senior schools, children and parents to ensure that we match the child to the senior school, academically, pastorally, creatively, on the sports field and socially. As we are not a feeder school, we have the freedom to do just that – the children come first.

Much of the family atmosphere surrounding the school comes from the fact that at its heart, FSM is a boarding school; almost two thirds of the children in Years 3 to 8 are full or weekly boarders, and we have a waiting list of children eager to try! The recent Ofsted report supports our claim to have 'the Best Boarding House in the World' by grading it as "outstanding". The level of care shown by the pastoral team isn't just saved for the boarders though. The Senior Houseparent, and her team, extend their support not only to all the children but their parents as well. There is no segmentation between day children and boarders. Day children can also take part in the numerous hobbies and activities on offer at the end of the school day and we often invite our day children in to join in our legendary Wednesday nights; our boarders also get invited out to stay with day children at the weekends.

FSM excels in their care of children from HM Forces families as well as other overseas based families and have done for many, many years. We always have a large number of children staying in at the weekend who look forward to the planned activities as well as having a bit of "chill time"! The school office is excellent at, and very used to, handling any overseas travel arrangements.

FSM now offer several scholarships each year for children entering the school at Year 3 and Year 7 as well as a number of means-tested bursaries.

It is difficult to single out any one particular area and be able to say that FSM excels in this or that; perhaps this is where the uniqueness of FSM lies. We hope that to really get a feel for the school, you will come and visit us and as you walk around the beautiful manor house and amazing grounds you will also think that, actually, "Happy Children Succeed" isn't a clever advertising gimmick after all. It really is at the heart of everything we do.

Charitable status. Forres Sandle Manor Education Trust Ltd is a Registered Charity, number 284260. It exists to provide first-class education for boys and girls.

Fosse Bank School

Mountains Country House, Noble Tree Road, Hildenborough, Kent TN11 8ND

Tel: 01732 834212
email: admissions@fossebankschool.co.uk
             headteacher@fossebankschool.co.uk
website: www.fossebankschool.co.uk
Twitter: @FosseBankSchool
Facebook: /FosseBankSchool

Chair of Governors: Mr Mark Waddington

Headmistress: **Miss Alison Cordingley**, LTCL, PGCE, NPQH

Admissions Officer: Mrs Louise Taylor

Age Range. 2–11 Co-educational.
Number of Pupils. 88.
Fees per term (2016–2017). £588–£4,020.

Founded in 1892, Fosse Bank School and Kindergarten (available from the term in which the child turns 2 years old) offers an excellent academic education combined with a truly supportive, friendly and stimulating environment in which your child can learn, grow and flourish. Parents and children appreciate the excellent pastoral care. We celebrate each success and encourage every child to be the best that they can be. The importance of good manners is emphasised and our children have a reputation for being confident, articulate and well-behaved. The school has a strong family community and is located in a beautiful Grade II listed building with 26 acres of parkland and boasting a range of wonderful facilities including a computer suite, indoor heated swimming pool, tennis courts, sports hall and extremely well-resourced Kindergarten. There are extensive playing fields and wooded areas with a pond for field-studies, and ample, safe parking. With wrap-around care from 7.30 am to 6.00 pm, some working parents choose to park at

school and walk to Hildenborough railway station (ten minutes).

Academic Studies. In the Kindergarten and Foundation Stage we give the children a solid foundation based on the Early Years Foundations Stage Profile. Further up the school, we follow and extend the National Curriculum, offering broad, enriched learning experiences. Music, PE and French are taught by specialists so that high standards are achieved in all subject areas and the children are given frequent opportunities to perform and share their talents. Our children achieve excellent academic results accepting offers of places at selective state and independent schools every year. Our Kent 11+ results are excellent.

Extra-Curricular. A wealth of activities are available after school for all children, such as chess, cross-country running, ballet, football, choir, iPad Club, Lego and construction and many others. We also have a dynamic afterschool care facility, the Phoenix Club which provides lively activities from 3.30 to 6.00 pm.

Entry Procedure. Fosse Bank is not academically selective at entry, although the Headmistress reserves the right to make a decision as to whether the applicant's learning needs can be managed within the School's normal provision. All children are required to attend a Taster Day before an offer may be made.

Charitable status. Fosse Bank New School is a Registered Charity, number 1045435.

Framlingham College Prep School (formerly known as Brandeston Hall)

Brandeston Hall, Brandeston, Woodbridge, Suffolk IP13 7AH

Tel: 01728 685331
Fax: 01728 685437
email: admissions@framcollege.co.uk
website: www.framcollege.co.uk
Twitter: @FramPrep
Facebook: @framcollege
LinkedIn: /framlingham-college

Chairman of Governors: A W M Fane, MA, FCA

Headmaster: **M J King**, BA Hons

Deputy Head: R Sampson, BA Hons, PGCE

Senior Team:
Head of Junior Prep: J Loveridge, BA Hons, PGCE
Head of Pre-Prep & Nursery: Mrs R Steggles, BA Hons, EYPS
Head of Pastoral Care/Tutor: Ms S Thomson, BEd Hons
Head of Co-Curricular: B Wilson, BEd Hons

Age Range. 2–13 Co-educational.
Number of Pupils. 260.
Fees per term (2016–2017). Full Boarding £35 per night, Day £4,739.50 (inc lunch), Pre-Prep: Day £2,724 (inc lunch), Nursery: £35 (full day session inc lunch), £17 (half day session exc lunch).

All Framlingham College Prep School pupils are prepared for the ISEB Common Entrance Examination at 13 and it is worth noting that in the past 5 years all leavers have gained entry to the senior school of their choice, with a significant number choosing to make the transition to Framlingham College (*see HMC entry*)

A recent ISI Inspection Report described the children at the Prep School as *unfailingly polite to visitors* and pupils' social, moral, spiritual and cultural development was described as *outstanding*.

The ISI Inspection Report also recognised the *excellent standard* of boarding at the Prep School, which was recently backed up with an Ofsted Inspection that described the provision of boarding and pastoral care as *outstanding*. The girls and boys boarding accommodation is warm and welcoming and found on separate floors of the old manor house. The school has a core of full-time boarders and an increasing number of children who board on a flexible and occasional basis. All boarders enjoy a wide range of exciting evening and weekend activities.

Facilities include a library, sports hall, a Centre for Music and The Performing Arts, an Art and Design Centre, as well as two full-size floodlit all-weather pitches (hockey/tennis/netball courts) and a nine-hole golf course. In addition the parish church is enclosed in the grounds providing a focus for community activities, as well as a shooting range and covered swimming pool. Pupils also have use of all of the facilities at Framlingham College including the 20m indoor swimming pool, theatre, artificial pitches and castle.

Major games include boys rugby, girls and boys hockey, girls and boys cricket, girls netball, girls and boys tennis, and athletics. Skilled coaching is given and a full programme of matches is arranged at all levels in major and minor sports.

Music and Drama provide the perfect opportunity to star in a number of productions as well as performing in music recitals and attending drama workshops with visiting artists.

Pupils also enjoy many residential opportunities including camping trips throughout the UK, sports tours, adventure training camps and a biennial expedition to the Atlas Mountains. In addition the Prep School has the use of a European Education Centre, Château de la Baudonnière, in Normandy, France. Senior pupils are encouraged to develop their French language skills as well as understanding and appreciating another culture.

Various scholarships are available for 11+ and 13+ entrants.

Charitable status. Albert Memorial College is a Registered Charity, number 1114383. It exists for the purpose of educating children.

The Froebelian School

Clarence Road, Horsforth, Leeds LS18 4LB

Tel: 0113 258 3047
Fax: 0113 258 0173
email: office@froebelian.co.uk
website: www.froebelian.com

Chair of Governors: Mr R Naru, BSc, MCOptom

Head: **Mrs Catherine Dodds**

Age Range. 3+ to 11+ years (3–4 years half days, optional afternoons).

Number of Pupils. 183 (83 boys, 100 girls).

Fees per term (2016–2017). £1,595–£2,380. Compulsory extras for full-time pupils, such as lunches and swimming, amount to approximately £249 per term.

Bursaries (income-related fee reduction) may be available.

Religious Affiliation: Christian, non-denominational.

Entry Requirements: Interview and assessment; written tests for older children.

Entry is usually at 3+, but limited places are sometimes available throughout the school.

Every child is respected as an individual and pupils are encouraged to reach their full potential in the purposeful atmosphere of this caring, disciplined school. High standards are achieved in all areas of the school – academic work, creative arts, music, sport, behaviour and manners. Early progress in language and mathematics is sustained and broadened in the junior curriculum, which includes French, information and design technology, drama and outdoor pursuits.

The school enjoys an envied reputation for success in entrance and scholarship examinations at 11+. Froebelian is the only school in Leeds to appear consistently in The Sunday Times list of 'Top 100' schools. A flourishing Parent Teacher Association supports the school and a growing database helps to keep former pupils in touch.

Situated to the north-west of Leeds, and close to Bradford, the school is well served by major transport links. 'Wrap-around' care is available from 7.30 am to 6.00 pm in the form of Breakfast Club, Little Acorns and Homework and Activities Club and there is a holiday club during the summer break.

Charitable status. The Froebelian School is a Registered Charity, number 529111. It exists to provide education of the highest quality at affordable fee levels.

Garden House School

Turk's Row, London SW3 4TW

Tel: 020 7730 1652 (Girls)
           020 7730 6652 (Boys)
email: info@gardenhouseschool.co.uk
website: www.gardenhouseschool.co.uk

Principal: Mrs J K Oddy, BA Hons

Headmistress – Upper School: **Mrs Charlotte Crofton**, BA Hons, PGCE
Headmistress – Lower School: **Mrs Julia Adlard**, BA Hons, Dip Montessori
Headmaster – Boys' School: **Mr Christian Warland**, BA Hons

Age Range. 3–11 Girls, 3–11 Boys.

Number of Pupils. 290 girls, 208 boys, taught in single-sex classes.

Fees per term (2016–2017). Kindergarten £4,500, Reception–Year 6 £7,000–£7,200. There is a 10% reduction for siblings.

Buildings and facilities. The School is housed in a charming, light and airy listed building in Chelsea. Original artwork hangs in every classroom and facilities include libraries for different age groups, a ballet/performance/drama hall and dedicated science and art rooms.

The school has its own garden within the grounds of the Royal Hospital where children enjoy science lessons and attend a Gardening Club. Sport is played in various locations close to the School.

School drama productions are ambitiously staged at the Royal Court Theatre in Sloane Square.

Aims, ethos and values. Garden House provides a thorough and balanced education in a lively and purposeful environment. Our children achieve strong academic results in a calm and constructive manner, being encouraged to have inquiring and independent minds. Emphasis is placed not only on academic, sporting and artistic ability but on manners and consideration to others. Our Kindness Code is adhered to and constantly re-emphasised.

Curriculum. English, Mathematics, Science, History, Geography, Religious Education, French (from Kindergarten), Latin, Computing, Current Affairs and Study Skills,

Art, Drama, Singing and Music, Dancing, Fencing and Physical Education (netball, tennis, rounders, gymnastics, swimming, athletics, cricket, hockey, pop lacrosse, rugby and football). We have many sports squads, sports clubs and matches. The Learning Support Department helps both children with special needs and those who are able learners, catered for in small groups, taught by two full-time and many visiting specialist teachers. 80% of children learn at least one musical instrument. The School runs four choirs and a chamber orchestra.

A diverse range of early morning and after-school clubs include Chess, Debating, Mandarin, Sculpture, Taekwondo and Touch-Typing.

Benefiting from our central London location, visits to museums, galleries and churches form an essential part of the Curriculum, as do annual field study and outward bound trips. Girls and boys spend a week in France after CE and boys enjoy a camping expedition among others including Outpost trip, a geography and science trip, a Bushcraft trip. The choir sings around the country; this year in Edinburgh Cathedral.

School Successes. Girls are prepared for the Common Entrance, with the majority leaving for the premier girls' Schools, 60% to leading London senior Schools, 40% to major boarding schools. Some boys leave us at 8, having been well prepared for entrance to leading London Prep Schools and 10% to top boarding Preps. Other boys remain at Garden House, being educated to the age of 11. Our children achieve several scholarships each year.

Entrance. We encourage you to visit the School. Girls and boys join Garden House in September after they reach 3 or 4 years of age. A Registration Form can be obtained from the School Office and once completed and returned with the relevant fee, your child's name is placed on the Waiting List. Entry interviews are held one year before entry. We look forward to welcoming you and your children to Garden House School.

Gatehouse School

Sewardstone Road, Victoria Park, London E2 9JG

Tel: 020 8980 2978
Fax: 020 8983 1642
email: admin@gatehouseschool.co.uk
website: www.gatehouseschool.co.uk

Headmaster: **Mr Robert Francis**

Age Range. 3–11 Co-educational.
Number in School. 378 Day Pupils.
Fees per term (2016–2017). £3,485–£3,670.

Gatehouse School is an Independent Co-educational School for girls and boys aged 3 to 11.

Founded by Phyllis Wallbank, in May 1948, in the gatehouse of St Bartholomew, the Great Priory Church near Smithfield London, the School was a pioneer of much that is now generally accepted in education. Gatehouse is based on the Wallbank plan whose guiding principle is that children of any race, colour, creed, background and intellect shall be accepted as pupils and work side by side without streaming or any kind of segregation with the aim that each child shall get to know and love God, and develop their own uniqueness of personality, to enable them to appreciate the world and the world to appreciate them.

Gatehouse is now located in Sewardstone Road close to Victoria Park and continues to follow this philosophy.

The Nursery is accommodated in a large sunny space with an outdoor play area. They follow a balanced curriculum of child-initiated and teacher-led activities.

Lower Juniors are taught most subjects by their own qualified teacher and assistant, but have French, PE and Music with a specialist teacher.

In Upper Juniors from the age of 7, teaching is by subject and is conducted by a highly qualified specialist staff. This is a special feature of Gatehouse and gives children from an early age, contact with subject specialists, not available to many children until secondary school.

Our classes average around 23 pupils.

We send children to schools such as City of London boys and girls, Forest, Bancroft's and Highgate, often with scholarships.

Charitable status. Gatehouse Educational Trust Limited is a Registered Charity, number 282558.

Gayhurst School

Bull Lane, Gerrards Cross, Bucks SL9 8RJ

Tel: 01753 882690
Fax: 01753 887451
email: enquiries@gayhurstschool.co.uk
website: www.gayhurstschool.co.uk

Chair of Governors: Mrs C Shorten Conn

Headmaster: **Mr G R A Davies**, BA Hons, PGCE, MEd

Age Range. 3–11 Co-educational.
Number of Children. 340.
Fees per term (2016–2017). £3,820–£4,850 (inclusive of lunch). Nursery: £24–£72 per session.

Gayhurst is a happy, thriving and vibrant independent preparatory school for girls and boys aged 3–11. For over 100 years the school has endeavoured to bring out the best in every child in its care by focusing on individual talents and supporting children to achieve their full potential. Since becoming co-educational in 2008, Gayhurst has built a reputation as a family school, providing first-class co-education in Gerrards Cross.

Life at Gayhurst is engaging and exciting with regular activities organised to enrich the education of its pupils. Children are encouraged to participate in sport, with a busy programme of fixtures against other schools. Creativity is evident throughout the school with opportunities to learn an instrument, become a member of one of the many musical ensembles or take part in the annual year group drama productions. There are also numerous visits to places of interest on both day and residential trips.

Gayhurst strives to ensure that pupils are given every opportunity to achieve the best start in life. The school's commitment to continual improvement and development means that the children benefit greatly from the facilities offered on the school's five acre site, including IT rooms, Science laboratories, woodland adventure playground and an all-weather AstroTurf.

Pupils consistently achieve strong academic results progressing to both local Grammar Schools and to Senior Schools, day and boarding, in the Independent sector.

"Our aims are clear," explains Headmaster Andrew Sims, "we provide a wide range of opportunities in music, drama, art and on the playing fields as well as through the curriculum. We want every girl and boy to discover and develop their particular talents and support them wholeheartedly in their aspirations for the future."

For more information about the school, or to arrange a visit, please contact the Registrar on 01753 279140 or email registrar@gayhurstschool.co.uk.

Charitable status. Gayhurst School Trust is a Registered Charity, number 298869.

Giggleswick Junior School

Giggleswick, Settle, North Yorkshire BD24 0DG

Tel:	01729 893100
Fax:	01729 893150
email:	juniorschool@giggleswick.org.uk
website:	www.giggleswick.org.uk
Twitter:	@GiggJunior
Facebook:	/GiggleswickJuniorSchool

Chairman of Governors: Mrs H J Hancock, LVO, MA

Head: **Mr James Mundell**, LLB, PGCE University of Wales Cardiff

Head of Early Years: Mrs Julie Middleton, BA Hons QTS Lancaster
Head of Boarding: Mrs C Gemmell, BEd Manchester Polytechnic
Headmaster's Secretary: Mrs S E Driver

Age Range. 3–11 Co-educational.
Number of Pupils. 80.
Fees per term (2016–2017). Boarders (Years 5–6): £6,678 (full), £5,152 (3-night flexi). Day Pupils: £4,010 (Years 3–6), £2,506 (R–Y2).

Boys and girls from the age of three up to eleven flourish in the busy, vibrant and supportive community of Giggleswick Junior School, where the happiness and progress of every child is an absolute priority. Our idyllic setting in the Yorkshire Dales gives life at the School a real sense of adventure and discovery, giving children the space and freedom to grow as individuals and develop a lifelong love of learning.

We welcome day pupils across all years and full and flexi boarders in Years 5 and 6. The boarding ethos of the wider school creates a unique homely atmosphere and the extended day allows children the time to develop their individual talents with 19 clubs and activities a week including 70 specialist music lessons, 40 dance sessions, 40 French sessions and 136 sports fixtures each year.

All pupils in Years 1 and 2 learn a stringed instrument as part of the Foundation Strings Scheme. In Years 3 to 6 over 75% of pupils take lessons on at least one instrument.

We set high academic standards to nurture all levels of ability, with a strong focus on personal and social development and helping young children to become independent learners. Our pupils benefit from small classes, specialist teaching and excellent IT provision, allowing us to provide a tailored learning programme for each child.

In Year 6 our pupils study 15 different subjects a week and everyone learns two modern languages. 100% of pupils achieved or exceeded national expectations in English in Year 3 and 88% achieved or exceeded national expectations in Key Stage 1 Maths.

Children have plenty of opportunity to learn outdoors in our forest school, to grow food and plants in our garden and to learn a respect for nature by taking care of our pets in school. The Junior School shares its campus with the Senior School, providing access to some of the best school facilities in the region including an indoor swimming pool, a mountain bike trail, floodlit astro-turf, two indoor sports halls, an Observatory, The Richard Whiteley Theatre and Giggleswick School Chapel.

We were delighted to be voted 'One of the UK's Top 10 Best Value Prep Schools' by the Daily Telegraph, acknowledging our outstanding teaching and learning facilities alongside highly affordable fees.

To help busy, working parents and families travelling from across the region, we provide daily bus services on seven routes covering a 45 minute radius of the School.

Areas include Kirkby Lonsdale, Grassington, Skipton, Ilkley, Colne, Clitheroe and the Lune Valley.

"Team spirit and trust thrive within the school's friendly community. Pupils were keen to report that theirs is a trusting and friendly school. Courtesy and kindness prevail throughout the setting and behaviour is exemplary." Independent Schools Inspectorate (ISI) 2015

Charitable status. Giggleswick School is a Registered Charity, number 1109826.

Glebe House School

Cromer Road, Hunstanton, Norfolk PE36 6HW

Tel:	01485 532809
Fax:	01485 533900
email:	ghsoffice@glebehouseschool.co.uk
website:	www.glebehouseschool.co.uk
Twitter:	@GlebeHS

Chairman of the Governors: Mr Adam Poulter

Headmaster: **Mr John Crofts**, BA, PGCE

Age Range. 6 months to 13 years.
Number of Children. 47 Boys, 58 Girls, Nursery 79.
Fees per term (2016–2017). Prep £4,160; Pre-Prep £2,600. Weekly boarding: £300–£745 (1–4 nights).

Glebe House School and Nursery was founded in 1874 as a preparatory school and is surrounded by 12 acres of playing fields with a stunning new Nursery building.

The Junior School children are accommodated in a purpose-built building. The Senior School has specialist areas for all academic subjects and music, sport and drama are a significant part of a child's life at Glebe House. Our 25-metre indoor heated swimming pool, astroturf pitch for hockey, tennis and netball, adventure playground, gym, music school and performance hall all help to ensure that the core academic subjects are supported by a balanced and stimulating curriculum. Lessons finish at 3.30 pm (Pre-Prep), 4.10 pm (Prep) but breakfast club, after-school activities, cooked tea and supervised prep provide day care from 7.30 am to 6.30 pm.

Aims and Values. At the heart of Glebe House is our emphasis on supporting and valuing the individual. We encourage the traditional values of courtesy, consideration for others, self discipline and a desire to contribute to society.

Academic Life. We are committed to high academic standards, harnessing the best of modern educational practice. Class sizes remain small and every child is encouraged to achieve their full potential. Close supervision, with one-to-one support where necessary, is maintained and progress is carefully monitored through regular standardised testing and classroom assessments. The broad curriculum both incorporates and exceed national requirements, including offering a second modern language in addition to French from year six. Glebe House enjoys a high success rate at Common Entrance and in Independent Scholarship Examinations and with this solid foundation our pupils move confidently on to a wide range of senior schools.

Sport and Activities. We offer a wide sporting programme aimed to encourage fitness and a healthy enjoyment of sport that will remain with the children for life. Rugby, hockey and cricket are the main sports for boys and hockey, netball and rounders for girls. We also encourage involvement in many activities including athletics, cross country, football, golf, swimming and tennis. The lunchtime and after-school activity programme is varied and includes sporting, dramatic, artistic and musical groups as well as others such as Mandarin Chinese. We offer a wide range of activities during the summer holidays, including ball sports, swimming, craft, music and drama workshops, tennis, and sailing.

Pastoral Care and Boarding. Relations between children and staff are respectful but relaxed and the children know they are free to talk to all staff, one of the great advantages of a school this size. All pupils belong to one of three houses and have a tutor who sees them each morning and is the first point of contact for parents. Good communication is crucial and we operate an open door policy to parents. The school offers 35 weekly boarding places and flexibility in choosing from one to four nights.

Travel. Our minibus picks up in the morning and takes home at 4.15 pm and 6 pm to Kings Lynn and surrounding areas.

Further Information. Prospective parents and children are most welcome to contact the School Administrator to meet the Headmaster and tour the school.

Charitable status. Glebe House School Trust Limited is a Registered Charity, number 1018815.

The Gleddings Preparatory School

Birdcage Lane, Savile Park, Halifax, West Yorkshire HX3 0JB

Tel: 01422 354605
Fax: 01422 356263
email: TheGleddings@aol.com
website: www.TheGleddings.co.uk

Headmistress: **Mrs P J Wilson**, CBE

Age Range. 3–11 Co-educational.
Number of Pupils. 193.
Fees per term (2016–2017). £2,660.

"The Gleddings is very special. It is precious to several generations of families in the locality and beyond. We are now educating the children of our past pupils. We consider it a great privilege to do so.

The staff and I remember, all of the time, the trust that parents bestow in us. We promise our best efforts for every child.

Our academic results speak for themselves but The Gleddings is about much more. We develop self-discipline, self-respect and confidence within The Gleddings' unique "YOU CHOOSE" ethos. We encourage children to THINK! and to learn how to learn."

Jill Wilson, Headteacher.

Godolphin Prep

Laverstock Road, Salisbury, Wiltshire SP1 2RB

Tel: 01722 430652
Fax: 01722 430651
email: prep@godolphin.wilts.sch.uk
website: www.godolphin.org

Chairman of the Governors: M J Nicholson, Esq

Headmistress: **Miss J Miller**, BA, MEd

Age Range. 3–11.
Number of Pupils. 85 Day Girls.
Fees per term (2016–2017). Boarding: £7,637 (Full), £6,522 (5-day), £5,667 (3-day), £8,134 (International). Day: £4,210 (Years 4–6), £3,350 (Year 3), £2,186 (Years 1–2), £2,179 (Reception).

Godolphin Prep is a purpose-built, compact school for girls aged from three to eleven. It is a mainstream academic school which focuses on the strengths of its pupils, values their potential as individuals and nurtures the girls to become caring members of society.

Many of the varied visitors to the school comment on the friendly atmosphere which they encounter. It is within such an environment that the girls are encouraged to have high expectations, good work habits and an active desire to take advantage of all that is on offer to them. Early specialist teaching across the curriculum is available from the age of 7, taught by people who are both dedicated and enthusiastic about their subjects. The high standard of teaching is reflected in the National Curriculum assessment results, as well as the scholarship awards gained by a significant number of pupils at eleven. There is an ambience of learning which comes from the 'work hard–play hard' ethic.

Courtesy and good manners are an implicit part of daily life at Godolphin; the basic precept is *'Never be the cause of another's unhappiness'*.

The school opened in 1993 as a part of the development plan of Godolphin. Following an inspection in 1996, which resulted in IAPS accreditation and then Department for Education registration two years later, the Prep has continued to thrive.

Godolphin Prep is a day school where outside interests are encouraged and weekends are perceived as family time, however, there is a programme of after-school activities which creates opportunities for those who travel considerable distances to school by bus. This arrangement offers an element of choice which ensures that the girls develop as well-balanced individuals. Godolphin Prep introduced boarding for Years five and six in September 2011. Girls are accommodated in bright and cheerful rooms and benefit from a tailor-made enrichment programme. There is also be a Breakfast club for day girls.

About 60% of the pupils move to Godolphin following Common Entrance. Others move to boarding schools slightly farther afield or transfer to the local girls' grammar school.

Charitable status. The Godolphin School is a Registered Charity, number 309488. Its object is to provide and conduct in or near Salisbury a boarding and day school for girls.

Godstowe Preparatory School

Shrubbery Road, High Wycombe, Bucks HP13 6PR

Tel: 01494 529273
           01494 429006 Registrar
Fax: 01494 429009
email: schooloffice@godstowe.org
website: www.godstowe.org
Twitter: @GodstoweSchool
Facebook: /GodstoweSchool

Motto: *Finem Respice*
Founded 1900.

Chairman of the Governors: K Allner, BA Econ

Headmaster: **Mr David Gainer**, BEd Hons London

Age Range. Girls 3–13, Boys 3–7.
Number of Pupils. Preparatory: 320 (boarding and day). Pre-Preparatory: 118.
Fees per term (2016–2017). Boarders £7,533, Day Children £3,335–£5,127. Nursery: £1,508–£3,015.

The School. Since its foundation in 1900, Godstowe Preparatory School has been at the forefront of education. It has a distinguished tradition as the first British boarding preparatory school for girls, in a foundation that includes Wycombe Abbey, Benenden and St Leonards.

Today, Godstowe is a flourishing boarding and day school with 416 pupils, enjoying an unparalleled academic reputation. It has a Pre-Prep department for boys and girls aged between three and seven, and a Preparatory School for girls from seven to thirteen years old. Class sizes are small allowing children to benefit from individual attention.

A new multi-purpose sports hall as well as a theatre and drama suite have recently been completed. The school recently underwent an independent inspection and was regarded as outstanding in every respect.

Academic Record. Godstowe enjoys an excellent and unparalleled academic reputation amongst British independent schools. Despite its non-selective entry policy, Godstowe consistently achieves unrivalled academic results. In 2016, 54 scholarships and distinctions were awarded. By the age of nine, pupils are taught by specialists in 16 subjects across the curriculum. Language teaching includes French, Spanish and Latin. Sport, ICT, art and music are all outstandingly taught within first-rate facilities.

Boarding. Girls' boarding life is focused within three houses in the grounds, one of which is a dedicated junior house. Each has three resident staff and a warm and supportive atmosphere. A combination of professional and caring staff and beautifully refurbished accommodation ensures a safe and relaxing environment. Each house has its own garden and tennis court, reinforcing the feeling of 'going home' at the end of the school day. Weekends are packed full of activity and fun, with many weekly boarders often choosing to stay at School for the weekend.

The **Enrichment Curriculum** is an extended school day from 7.30 am to 7.00 pm, with some 50 after-school activities scheduled each week. The 'E-Curriculum' gives children the chance to try many exciting and challenging new pursuits including poetry writing, rock climbing, watersports, football and debating. In addition, supervised homework sessions are offered every evening. Day children may join the boarders for breakfast and supper. Other than those sessions supervised by outside instructors all activities are offered free of charge. An Enrichment programme is also in place for Pre-Prep children.

Charitable status. The Godstowe Preparatory School Company Limited is a Registered Charity, number 310637. It exists to provide education and training for young girls and boys.

Grace Dieu Manor School

Grace Dieu, Thringstone, Leicestershire LE67 5UG

Tel:	01530 222276
Fax:	01530 223184
email:	registrar@gracedieu.com
website:	www.gracedieu.com

Chairman of Governors: Mr R Gamble

Headmaster: **Mr P S Fisher**, MA Ed Res, MA Ed Mgt, BA Hons, PGCE Cantab

Age Range. 0–11 Co-educational.
Number of Pupils. 156.
Fees per term (2016–2017). £3,327–£3,502.

Grace Dieu is a modern, vibrant, Catholic, co-educational day school for pupils aged 0 to 11; a happy school where children are encouraged to work hard, play hard and care for each other. Working parents will be delighted to know that children may be cared for from 8 am until 6 pm and that there is no additional charge for this service. We also have a daily morning minibus service operating routes from local villages.

The purpose-built area designed specifically for our 3–7 year olds provides an inspiring, fun and safe environment. Classrooms are bright and colourful and provide easy access to a spacious and secure outdoor area. Small class sizes and a team of qualified teachers and nursery nurses ensure that children have an outstanding start to their education.

A warm, family atmosphere based upon Christian values and traditions welcomes families, whatever their denomination or faith. Staff share a close interest and involvement in the development of every child and experience shows pupils and parents very quickly become part of the school family.

The academic life of the school is central and outstanding results in Key Stage tests and senior school entry exams and Scholarships are evidence of this. A broad range of natural ability is welcomed and celebrated at Grace Dieu.

Pupils find many opportunities for fun and friendship. Grace Dieu offers ample space for pupils to participate in the full range of team games on our sports fields, in our indoor heated swimming pool and in our sports hall Weekly sporting fixtures give pupils opportunity to compete locally and nationally. Situated in 120 acres of beautiful grounds in the heart of the Leicestershire countryside we make the most of our surroundings and all classes have a timetabled Forest School session every week.

The arts are a key part to Grace Dieu life, and regular music and drama performances feature in the termly diary.

After-school activities are offered and these greatly enrich the lives of the children.

Charitable status. Grace Dieu Manor School is a Registered Charity, number 1115976.

The Grange
Monmouth Preparatory School

Hadnock Road, Monmouth NP25 3NG

Tel:	01600 715930
email:	thegrange@monmouthschool.org
website:	www.habs-monmouth.org
Twitter:	@GrangeMonmouth

Acting Chairman of Governors: A W Twiston-Davies

Head: **N Shaw**, MA

Age Range. 7–11.
Number of Pupils. 130 boys.
Fees per term (2016–2017). Day £3,484, Boarding (from age 9) £6,333.

The Grange provides the friendliness and close pastoral care of a small school together with the outstanding resources of a large school through its association with Monmouth School, a Haberdashers' school for boys aged 11 to 18. There are also strong links with the other schools in the area belonging to the family of Haberdashers' Monmouth Schools – Haberdashers' Agincourt School (for boys and girls aged 3 to 7), Inglefield House (for girls aged 7 to 11) and Haberdashers' Monmouth School for Girls (for girls aged 11 to 18). In their final year at The Grange boys take the General Entry Assessment for Monmouth School. Almost without exception there is a 100% pass rate and a significant number of boys gain scholarships and other awards – academic, music and sport. A wide and very popular extra-curricular programme combines with high academic achievement to provide a vibrant and stimulating educational experience. In 2011 independent research carried out by RSAcademics showed that the school was one of the very best they had surveyed in terms of how highly the parents regarded the school. Details are on the website. In 2014 a full school inspection by ESTYN (Her Majesty's Inspectorate for Education and Training in Wales) graded the school as "Excellent" (the top grade) in every key question and every quality indicator – the first School to have achieved that grading since the new regulations came into place in 2010. Details are on the website.

Aims. The aims of The Grange are to provide an excellent education as the foundation for future achievement and to develop personal qualities of confidence, independence and social conscience.

Location. In February 2009 The Grange moved into brand new purpose-built premises on a Monmouth School site, situated next to Monmouth School Sports Complex with its own 25-metre swimming pool.

Facilities. Its new building has light, spacious, well-equipped classrooms, each of which opens out onto the play area, as well as a large hall, library, art studio, science laboratory, computer suite, music room and music studios. The Grange also has its own newly-equipped kitchens. The grounds provide a safe, spacious area for recreation, games and outdoor projects. In addition, The Grange shares the facilities of Monmouth School which include the School Chapel, large playing fields (25 acres), Sports Complex, new Sports Pavilion, Drama Studio and Performing Arts Centre – the Blake Theatre.

Staffing. 8 full-time and 9 part-time staff teach the 8 classes, in addition to peripatetic teachers and specialist coaches for extra-curricular activities.

Curriculum. The curriculum is broad and varied and takes account of, though is not constrained by, the National Curriculum. Subjects include English, Mathematics, Science, Information and Communication Technology and Computing, History, Geography, Religious Education, Art, Design Technology, Music, Physical Education, Games, Drama and French. There is subject specialist teaching throughout. A part-time learning support teacher provides extra help on an individual or small group basis for boys who would benefit from it.

Extra-Curricular Activities. There is a full programme of activities which take place both in the lunch break and after school. These vary slightly according to the season though in any one year would normally include rugby, football, cricket, tennis, swimming, golf, karate, cross-country running, string orchestra, wind band, choir, fencing, art, gardening, modern foreign languages, computing and chess. There is a good record of boys playing at county and national level in rugby, cricket, fencing and chess.

Entry. Entry is usually at 7+ following assessment, though due to the larger new premises recruitment is currently across all year groups.

Charitable status. William Jones's Schools Foundation is a Registered Charity, number 525616. Its aims and objectives are to provide an all-round education for boys and girls at reasonable fees.

Age Range. 3–11
Number of Girls. 90.
Fees per term (2016–2017). £3,300–£3,325.

Grange Park Preparatory School is a long established, happy and successful school that provides a broad and stimulating education. It is situated in the pleasant residential area of Grange Park. Hidden behind what was once a residential house lies a purpose-built school with excellent facilities for the modern curriculum, including a fully-equipped ICT suite and excellent facilities for science, art and design technology. There are two libraries, one for KS1 and the other for KS2. Whilst younger children are taught PE and games within the school grounds, from Year 3 we make use of off-site facilities for netball and rounders/athletics and swimming.

We remain committed to educating girls in a small school with small class sizes, thus allowing every child to be known as an individual. The girls enjoy a broad curriculum taught by experienced staff who encourage excellence in all areas of school life.

In September 2015 GPPS opened a Nursery class for boys and girls aged 3 and 4. Nursery staff and children have access to the excellent resources available at GPPS, including outside space, the gym and a cooked lunch for those children staying the whole day. The children follow the Early Years Curriculum with additional specialist teaching in French, Dance, Drama and Music.

In KS1 the children are taught mostly by form teachers with specialist teaching being introduced gradually in KS2. From Reception specialist teachers teach games, French, music, dance and drama. Individual music tuition is available from Year 1.

In Key Stage 2 preparation for 11+ state selective and independent secondary schools starts from as early as Year 3, where girls undertake verbal and non-verbal reasoning as part of the curriculum. In addition in Year 5, girls wishing to sit for selective schools attend extra prep classes, thus equipping them with the tools to achieve their maximum potential in terms of academic attainment.

Girls enjoy a very busy school life and benefit from an excellent variety of extra-curricular activities, including LAMDA, horse riding and chess, further enriching their experience and creating lifetime memories.

The school has a healthy eating policy. Lunches are cooked in school using only fresh ingredients; no processed food is used. There is always a vegetarian option and salads and fresh fruit are available daily.

Places for Reception are offered after the Headteacher has met with parents and their daughter. Children taking up chance vacancies in other classes will be invited to spend a day in school to ensure they will fit into the class successfully.

Charitable status. Grange Park Preparatory School is a Registered Charity, number 268328.

Grange Park Preparatory School

13 The Chine, Grange Park, London N21 2EA
Tel: 020 8360 1469
Fax: 020 8360 4869
email: office@gpps.org.uk
website: www.gpps.org.uk

Day School for Girls.

Chair of Governors: Mr Nigel Barnes

Head: **Miss Flavia Rizzo**, MA Ed Hons

The Granville School

2 Bradbourne Park Road, Sevenoaks, Kent TN13 3LJ
Tel: 01732 453039
email: secretary@granvilleschool.org
website: www.granvilleschool.org

Chairman of Governors: Mr J Sorrell

Headmistress: **Mrs Jane Scott**, BEd Hons Cantab

Age Range. Girls 3–11, Boys 3–5.
Number of Pupils. 200.
Fees per term (2016–2017). Nursery (mornings only) £1,815, Transition (all day) £3,118, Reception, Years 1 & 2

£3,673, Years 3 £4,154, Years 4, 5 & 6 £4,680. Lunch included for Transition to Year 6.

Extras: Private Lessons: Singing, Pianoforte, Violin, Cello, Oboe, Clarinet, Flute £211 per term. Shared Lessons: Recorder £34, Ballet £66.50 per term.

The Granville School was founded on VE Day, 8th May 1945, with the Dove of Peace and Churchill's victory sign chosen to form the school crest.

The Granville is an exceptional school which combines the very best of a Prep school tradition with a vibrant, forward-looking outlook where change is embraced and innovation celebrated. Girls aged three to eleven, and boys aged three to four, thrive on individual attention and achieve their best in a happy, secure and stimulating environment. Our highly-qualified, specialist teachers make learning enjoyable, develop enquiring minds and raise levels of expectation.

The school maintains Christian principles and traditional values within a broad and stimulating curriculum. The Granville has a strong record of academic achievement and children are prepared for 11+ entry into independent schools and state grammar schools. Granville pupils excel in music, art, drama and sport. There is a wide range of extra-curricular activities available for all age groups and the school runs an early morning breakfast club and after-school care until 6 pm.

The school is set in five acres of garden and woodland close to Sevenoaks Station. The original house and new buildings enable pupils to enjoy a high-quality learning environment with light and airy classrooms. The Granville has its own indoor heated Swimming Pool, a Sports Hall, Science Lab, Studio for Music and Drama, French room, ICT Suite, individual teaching rooms and Junior and Senior Libraries. A new building, opened in January 2014, provides high-quality Early Years facilities together with a large Art and DT room. Outside facilities include three netball/tennis courts, sports/playing field, junior activity playgrounds and a woodland classroom.

Means-tested bursaries are available on request.

Charitable status. The Ena Makin Educational Trust Limited is a Registered Charity, number 307931. Its aim is to run any school as an educational charity for the promotion of education generally.

Great Ballard

Eartham, Chichester, West Sussex PO18 0LR

Tel: 01243 814236
Fax: 01243 814586
email: office@greatballard.co.uk
website: www.greatballard.co.uk
Twitter: @GreatBallard
Facebook: /GreatBallardSchool

Headmaster: **Mr Richard Evans**, BEd Hons, Adv Dip Ed Mgt, IAPS

Age Range. 2–13 co-educational.

Number of Children. 138: 80 Boys, 58 Girls (including 59 in Pre-Prep and approx 35 flexi boarders).

Fees per term (2016–2017). Day: Prep School £4,250–£ 4,850, Pre-Prep £2,600–£2,950. Boarding: Weekly (4 nights) £5,150, Full (7 nights) £7,150–£7,725. Nursery: £32.50–£34.50 (morning or afternoon), £37.50–£39.50 (including lunch), £48–£52 (all day including lunch). Boarding fee discounts for HM Forces. The school offers a limited number of Scholarships for children with exceptional abilities. These awards can be supplemented by a means-tested bursary.

The school is located in 30 acres of wonderful countryside in the South Downs National Park between Chichester and Arundel. The school itself is based around a stunning eighteenth century house surrounded by glorious woodlands which are a feature of the impressive school grounds, which the children are allowed to explore and love building dens in the woods.

Children are prepared for Senior School entrance exams, as well as for 13+ Common Entrance and Scholarship examinations to a wide range of Independent Senior Schools. The emphasis is on providing children with numerous opportunities to identify their talents and ensure that they all achieve their potential both inside and out of the classroom. The average number of children in a teaching group in the prep school is 12. A small number of International Students are welcomed who benefit from our family-centred community and are able to enjoy their first overseas boarding experience in a small, friendly, family atmosphere.

Outdoor activities include: Soccer, Rugby, Hockey, Cricket, Netball, Rounders, Tennis, Athletics, Swimming, Golf, Mountain Biking, Trampolining, Volleyball and Forest School. In addition, there is a growing outdoor education and country pursuits programme.

Facilities include: multi-purpose gym and hall, libraries, a computerised science laboratory, dance/drama studio, indoor heated pool, extensive sports fields, tennis courts, cricket nets and an astro practice area. In addition, there is a fantastic Forest school. ICT facilities are in the main ICT suite and tablet computers are increasingly used throughout the school. A very wide range of extra-curricular clubs are enjoyed which give all children the opportunity to experience a wide variety of activities. There are also visits to France for intensive language studies as well as exciting outdoor education residential trips for most year groups in the Prep school.

Children showing real potential in Art, Drama or Music are able to take advantage of excellence classes, a range of instruments are taught and with choirs and various ensemble groups, many children participate in festivals, sit musical exams and enjoy performing in concerts.

Drama is a timetabled subject and every child appears in a form and school play at some time during the year. LAMDA classes are also offered. Cookery is also on the timetable as well as a popular after-school activity.

Art is a significant strength of the school; many children build up quality portfolios to take to their next school and scholarships are won regularly. The constantly changing displays throughout the school show both the quality of work and the children's enthusiasm for Art.

The Pre-Prep Department, for children aged 2–7, is housed in a walled garden area with plenty of space for play activities. The curriculum is delivered by well-qualified, enthusiastic form teachers with extra input from Prep School specialists in PE, music, swimming and drama. The school also offers a Holiday club for Pre-Prep children which operates for 48 weeks a year.

The 'After-hours' club, for children from Nursery age upwards, enables parents to work a full day. This involves both a breakfast club from 7.45 am and after school supervision to 6.00 pm.

Boarding remains popular and many children take advantage of the very flexible arrangements the school offers. Boarding facilities are in the Grade II listed House in small cosy dormitories. The Headmaster and his family together with other members of staff live in the House, giving the boarding community a very homely feeling.

The happiness and safety of our children remain priorities. This is supported by the ISI Inspection report that states that "*the quality of relationships between the pupils and staff is outstanding*".

Great Ballard is a traditional, but forward-looking Prep school where proven values and high standards and expectations of behaviour are the norm; it is undoubtedly a hidden gem and well worth a visit!

Great Walstead School

East Mascalls Lane, Lindfield, Haywards Heath, West Sussex RH16 2QL

Tel: 01444 483528
Fax: 01444 482122
email: admin@greatwalstead.co.uk
website: www.greatwalstead.co.uk
Twitter: @greatwalstead

Chairman of the Board of Governors: M Searle

Headmaster: **C Baty**, BEd, DipT, CPP Boarding Hons, NPQH

Deputy Head: J Sutherland, BEd
Acting Director of Studies: Graham Floyd, BA Hons, PGCE

Age Range. 2½–13.
Number of Pupils. 465: Main School 309; Pre-Prep 72; Nursery and Reception (EYFS) 84.
Fees per term (2016–2017). Tuition: EYFS £646–£2,565, Pre-Prep £3,075–£3,590, Main School £4,545–£4,945. Boarding (in addition to Tuition): £280–£970 (1–4 nights).
Founded in 1925 by Mr R J Mowll in Enfield, the school moved to its present location in the heart of Sussex two years later. Staff and pupils came to a large country house set in over 260 acres of fields and woodland, where children could learn and play in unspoiled surroundings.

From these beginnings, Great Walstead has developed into a thriving co-educational prep school, catering for children from 2½ to 13 years of age. It is a school which values children as individuals and regards it as vital that each child develops his or her potential – academically, creatively, socially and spiritually. Above all, the school is built on the strong values of Christian Faith, Success, Communication, Environment and Dedication, creating an essential foundation for the whole of a pupil's education and life.

The Early Years Foundation Stage incorporates Nursery and Reception classes, welcoming children from the age of 2½ until it is time to enter the Pre-Prep at 5. It provides a full, rich and varied Early Years education, laying firm foundations in basic skills and understanding for future learning. They share a dedicated outdoor learning and play space with a giant covered sandpit, mud kitchen and music area.

The Pre-Prep covers the ages from 5 to 7 within its own section of the school. It has its own library, ICT suite and play area. The aim here is to ensure that the foundation skills of reading, writing and maths are taught while, at the same time, teachers add a breadth of interest through specialist lead classes in French, computer skills, PE and Music.

Children enter the Junior School at 7. For the next two years they will have a class teacher who supervises them closely for a good proportion of the day, but have specialist teachers for French, Music, ICT, Art, Craft, Design & Technology, Sport and PE. They have games or outdoor activities each day and gradually learn to become more independent.

Children in the senior age group, from 9 to 13 years of age, are taught by graduate specialist teachers in preparation for the Common Entrance examination and senior school scholarships at 13. In the past ten years, Great Walstead pupils have won over 200 scholarships or awards to senior schools and in the last four years over 50% of pupils gained

such success. Facilities in the Senior School include two computer rooms with 21 linked PCs, a well-equipped science laboratory, and a fine Library.

The 269 acres of farmland, playing fields and woodland make many outdoor activities possible. The woods host learning activities in Eco-School and Forest School and fun exercises in camp-building, as well as teddy bear picnics for the younger children. In the summer, the older children camp out overnight. In addition, the purpose-built challenge course gives enormous pleasure all year round for all ages.

The Art, Craft and Design Technology department is housed in old farm buildings, which have been adapted to make workshops and studios; the lessons form an integral part of the curriculum for all children. New in 2016, the Great Walstead Farm is a wonderful addition to the curriculum, providing insight and hands-on experience of both horticultural and agricultural farming methods.

The school's extensive grounds allow a wide range of major sports. Swimming is possible all year round in our own heated pool. We have a superbly equipped sports hall and facilities including a wonderful new AstroTurf. Match Day on Wednesdays is a central weekly event with emphasis on sportsmanship, healthy competition and sport for all. All children (Years 3–8) have the opportunity to be involved in competitive sport at least once per season. Those children not involved in match fixtures on a particular week are able to access a carousel of indoor and outdoor activities, including: cookery, pottery, archery, art, ICT, woods games, gardening and a variety of sports.

The school has a Learning Development department where specialist staff are able to give the extra support required. The department helps children with all their learning needs whether helping with a specific difficulty or extending those children who are gifted and talented.

Music has long been a strength at Great Walstead, with a high proportion of the children learning instruments and playing in groups, bands and orchestras. Singing is encouraged from Nursery upwards. Drama is also an important part of the Arts here. All children are given the opportunity to act, with both major productions and form performances.

Great Walstead offers weekly boarding on a flexible basis (Monday to Thursday). The boarding areas provide a comfortable home under the care of a boarding family and assisted by other boarding staff. Matron, the school nurse, tends to the health of the children in the whole school. The school, through the Keep, provides flexible holiday, pre- and after-school care, as well as other holiday activities to meet the needs of today's parents.

Parents are always made most welcome at the school. There is a thriving parents' organisation called FOGWA (Friends of Great Walstead Association) which provides a number of successful social events and raises substantial sums for the benefit of the school.

Academic, Music and Sports Awards are offered at 9+, and Academic, All-Rounder, Art, Drama, Music, Performing Arts and Sport Scholarships at 11+.

Charitable status. Great Walstead School is a Registered Charity, number 307002. It exists to provide a good education on Christian foundations.

Greenfield

Brooklyn Road, Woking, Surrey GU22 7TP

Tel: 01483 772525
email: schooloffice@greenfield.surrey.sch.uk
website: www.greenfield.surrey.sch.uk

Chairman of Governors: Mrs Janet Day

Headteacher: **Mrs Tania Botting**, BEd, MEd

Age Range. 3–11 years.

Number of Pupils. 83 day girls, 112 day boys.

Fees per term (2016–2017). £1,821–£4,266.

Greenfield is a non-selective co-educational school for children aged from rising 3 to 11 years. We aim to offer every possible opportunity for children to reach their full potential and recognise that all children have talents and strengths in many different areas. We are proud of our academic and non-academic successes and have a strong track record of achieving scholarships to a wide range of senior schools for music, art, sport, and academic excellence.

At Greenfield we believe that a happy child will learn. Therefore, we provide a secure and caring environment working closely with our parents, to enable the children to develop their confidence and self-esteem and prepare them for the next stage of their education and future.

We attach importance to traditional values, promoting courtesy, respect, tolerance, empathy, humility and consideration for others.

Greenfield has high standards but we also appreciate the need to strike a happy balance between work and play and the formal and informal. There is an excellent ratio of adults to children throughout the school enabling children to receive individual attention and children are often taught in small groups. Visitors are welcome to visit the school at any time and appointments can be made by calling the school office. To request a copy of the prospectus, please visit the school website or call the school office.

Charitable status. Greenfield is a Registered Charity, number 295145. It aims to offer an excellent all-round education to children of all abilities.

Gresham's Prep School

Holt, Norfolk NR25 6EY

Tel: 01263 714600
        01263 714575 (Nursery and Pre-Prep School)
Fax: 01263 714060
email: prep@greshams.com
website: www.greshams.com
Twitter: @Greshams_School
Facebook: @greshamsschool

Chairman of Governors: A Martin Smith

Headmaster: **J H W Quick**, BA Hons Durham, PGCE

(For a full list of governors and staff, please refer to Gresham's Senior School entry in the HMC section.)

Age Range. 3–13.

Number of Pupils. 332: 53 Boarders, 279 Day pupils.

Fees per term (2016–2017). Boarders £8,050, Day £5,720, Day (Years 3 and 4) £4,610. Pre-Prep School: £3,075–£3,385.

Gresham's Prep School is part of the family of Gresham's Schools, which are located in the busy market town of Holt in a beautiful and tranquil part of North Norfolk. Some pupils enter the school from the Pre-Prep School, which is based in the pretty Georgian town of Holt, a quarter of a mile from the Prep School, but many others enter the school from elsewhere. Most pupils move on to Gresham's Senior School, but the school has a very good record of winning scholarships and gaining entry to other major Independent Schools.

The school has excellent facilities including extensive playing fields, an Art and Technology Centre, a Drama Hall, a modern and well-equipped Music School and Science labs. Use of the Theatre, Chapel, Astroturf pitches, swim-ming pool, sports hall and other excellent sports facilities is shared with the Senior School.

Boarders are accommodated in modern, comfortable bedrooms in Crossways House (girls) or Kenwyn House (boys). Flexible boarding is available and is extremely popular.

The school prides itself on the breadth of its curriculum. Sport, Performing Arts and Drama and Music play an important part in the lives of all pupils. The school has built up a considerable reputation in these areas in recent years. There is a wide range of extra-curricular activities available in the evenings which changes on a termly basis.

Above all the school wants children to enjoy the process of growing up and developing their talents to the full and to establish the strong roots that will help them become self-assured and well-balanced adults.

Entry Requirements. Entry is by assessment in Mathematics and English and a reference from the child's previous school. Entry is possible into all year groups.

Scholarships are available for entry into Year 7. Art, Drama and Performing Arts, Music and Sport are worth up to 10% of the fees. Academic Scholarships are worth up to 50% of the fees. All scholarships may be supplemented by a means-tested bursary. Headmaster's Awards are occasionally awarded to those entering other year groups.

Nursery and Pre-Prep School. Co-educational, age 3–7, day pupils only.

Headmistress: Mrs S Hollingsworth.

The Nursery and Pre-Prep School is housed in the beautiful setting of Old School House within the town of Holt and within walking distance of the Prep School. It is a vibrant and dynamic school which works to create an environment where happy, relaxed, calm, courteous and curious children can flourish and be their best. Children benefit from a broad and balanced curriculum which also includes music, drama, languages and sport within the school day.

Charitable status. Gresham's School is a Registered Charity, number 1105500. It exists for the purpose of educating children.

Grimsdell
Mill Hill Pre-Preparatory School

Winterstoke House, Wills Grove, Mill Hill, London NW7 1QR

Tel: 020 8959 6884
Fax: 020 8959 4626
email: office@grimsdell.org.uk
website: www.grimsdell.org.uk

Co-educational Pre-Preparatory Day School.

Chairman of Court of Governors: Dr R G Chapman, BSc, MB BS, FRCGP

Head: **Mrs Kate Simon**, BA, PGCE

Age Range. 3–7.

Number of Pupils. 189: 97 Boys, 92 Girls.

Fees per term (2016–2017). £4,612 (full day), Nursery: £2,501 (mornings only), £2,122 (afternoons only).

Grimsdell is situated in the Green Belt on the borders of Hertfordshire and Middlesex but only ten miles from central London. It stands adjacent to Mill Hill School's 120 acres of land, enjoying the advantages of a rural environment. Grimsdell is part of the Mill Hill School Foundation. It provides a happy, secure and rich learning environment for boys and girls aged 3 to 7. Belmont, Mill Hill Preparatory School, is less than a quarter of a mile away and educates pupils from 7 to 13, the majority of whom move on to the senior school, Mill Hill.

The boys and girls at Grimsdell learn through hands-on experience. With the support and guidance of professional, caring staff and excellent resources and equipment, each child is encouraged to reach their full potential. Our approach combines traditional skills of reading, writing and mathematics with the breadth and balance offered by an enhanced Early Years Foundation Stage and KS1 Curriculum. Every pupil can enjoy many opportunities offered by learning through Science, Technology and Computing. They also gain much from Art, Drama, Music, PE and French lessons.

The school is housed in a large Victorian building with its own secure play areas and adventure playgrounds, taking advantage of further facilities on the Mill Hill site including a Forest School area, sports fields, swimming pool and the-atre.

The usual age of entry is at 3 and 4 years, but 5 and 6 year olds are considered as vacancies occur. It is expected that most children will pass to Belmont at the end of Year 2.

Charitable status. The Mill Hill School Foundation is a Registered Charity, number 1064758. It exists to provide education for boys and girls.

Guildford High School Junior School
United Learning

London Road, Guildford, Surrey GU1 1SJ
Tel: 01483 561440
Fax: 01483 306516
email: guildford-admissions@guildfordhigh.co.uk
website: www.guildfordhigh.surrey.sch.uk
Twitter: @GuildfordHigh

Chairman of Local Governing Body: Mr D Perrett

Head of Junior School: Mr Michael D Gibb, BA Hons London

Age Range. Girls 4–11.
Number of Pupils. 285.
Fees per term (2016–2017). Reception, Years 1 and 2 £3,293, Years 3–6 £4,322.

Awarded the Sunday Times Independent Prep School of the Year 2015–16, the Junior School at Guildford High School is situated on the same site as the Senior School. It is a modern, bright, self-contained school with the third floor especially designed for art, music, science, IT and the Library.

The girls normally start in the Reception classes (4 years) or at Year 3 (7 years), however, they are welcome in any year group depending on spaces available, and work their way through the Junior School with natural progression on to the Senior School at Year 7 (11 years).

The breadth and depth of the curriculum encompasses 15 fast paced subjects, with an embedded thinking skills pro-gramme. Three modern foreign languages are included, with Spanish starting in Year 1 for the five year olds. Music, drama and sport play an important part in the curricular and co-curricular programmes. Specialist teachers and resources are employed throughout the Junior School. Parents and teachers work closely together to ensure excellent differenti-ation and a nurturing environment with strong pastoral care.

Guildford High Junior School girls of all abilities and temperaments are confident, happy and well-prepared for entry to the Senior School. (*See Guildford High School entry in HMC section.*)

Charitable status. Guildford High Junior School is part of United Learning which comprises: UCST (a Company Limited by Guarantee, Registered in England, number 2780748, and a Registered Charity, number 1016538) and ULT (a Company Limited by Guarantee, Registered in England, number 4439859, and an Exempt Charity).

The Haberdashers' Aske's Boys' Preparatory & Pre-Preparatory School

Butterfly Lane, Elstree, Hertfordshire WD6 3AF
Tel: 020 8266 1779
email: jones_d@habsboys.org.uk
website: www.habsboys.org.uk
Twitter: @habsboys
Facebook: /habsboys

Chairman of Governors: Sir Robert Fulton, KBE

Executive Head: Mr M L S Judd, BA Swansea

Deputy Head: Mr J J Evans, MA Homerton College Cambridge

Age Range. Prep 7–11; Pre-Prep 5–7.
Number of Boys. Prep 217, Pre-Prep 70.
Fees per term (2016–2017). Pre-Prep £4,638 (including lunch); Prep £6,152.

The Preparatory School is vibrant with the energy and curiosity of over two hundred boys aged 7–11 from a wide range of local schools and communities. It is a very special place to work and play.

It is housed in a purpose-designed building, opened by HRH The Princess Margaret, Citizen and Haberdasher, in 1983, on the same campus as the Senior School. The bright, cheerful classrooms provide a welcoming and stimulating environment. The Prep enjoys a unique mix of family atmo-sphere and close links with the Senior School. The boys are able to share the wonderful facilities and grounds of the Senior School, including the Sports Centre, the heated indoor Swimming Pool, the Music School and the Dining Room. The Pre-Prep School is located 6 miles north of the school at How Wood, near St Albans.

The relationship between the Preparatory staff and their forms is close and friendly, within a context of firm disci-pline. In this environment, brimming with opportunities, the school ensures an education of breadth and depth extending well beyond national guidelines.

Sport and games play a major role in the boys' week, offering fitness and fun to all. Indeed the sporting ethos of team spirit and fair play underpins the whole structure of Prep School life.

The arts spring to life in a wealth of musical, dramatic and artistic activity, guided by specialists whose passion for their subject is matched by the enthusiasm of their pupils.

Every boy is a musician for at least one year when he studies an orchestral instrument of his choice, free of charge, through the Music Scheme; many of these fledgling musi-cians eventually make their way into the Senior School's First Orchestra.

There are many clubs and societies; however boys with some special interest often start their own, supported by staff, and eagerly attended by those of like mind. Some boys also stay on to enjoy extra play time with their friends or to do their homework and to have tea. The After School Care Facility is equipped with bean bags, games and sports equip-ment.

Boys are admitted each September after assessments to the Pre-Prep at the age of 5+ and to the Prep at 7+. Boys are expected to move into the Senior School at 11. Most boys will flourish in the Senior School as they have in the Prep, and the transition is made as natural as possible. A qualifying examination assures candidates that the Senior School is right for them and they are given help preparing for the different pace and rhythms they will find there. (*For further details, please see entry in HMC section.*)

Charitable status. The Haberdashers' Aske's Charity is a Registered Charity, number 313996. It exists to promote education.

The Hall

23 Crossfield Road, Hampstead, London NW3 4NU

Tel:	020 7722 1700
Fax:	020 7483 0181
email:	office@hallschool.co.uk
website:	www.hallschool.co.uk
Twitter:	@the_hallschool

Chairman of Governors: P Mullins, Esq

Headmaster: **C Godwin**, BSc, MA

Age Range. 4–13.
Number of Pupils. 464 Day Boys.
Fees per term (2016–2017). £5,262–£5,983 (inclusive of lunch).

Founded in 1889, the school is on three sites within close proximity. The majority of boys join Reception or Year 1 at the age of 4 or 5, but a few places are occasionally available in later years. The average class size is 18.

The school's buildings are spacious and well-appointed, and resources are good. There has been considerable investment over the last ten years in the school's fabric and facilities, and there is a continuing programme of improvements planned, including a well-advanced programme of ICT development. The Junior School (Years 1–3) is undergoing a programme of continuous refurbishment and provides up-to-date computing, science and music facilities. The Senior School boasts a modern library, spacious music, DT, pottery, computing facilities and changing rooms. Boys in the Junior School use the sports hall, located in the Senior School, and have lunch in the dining hall which serves the whole school.

From the Junior School, boys transfer to the Middle School for Years 4 and 5. During that time they make the transition from classroom based teaching to subject based teaching. Boys are taught by subject specialists from Year 5.

The Hall prides itself on the breadth of education it offers. Senior School boys study Life Skills, Art, Drama, Music, Pottery, ICT, Design Technology and Current Affairs within the timetable and there is a broad range of after-school activities. Music and Drama are considerable strengths within the school. Team games, soccer, rugby and cricket are played mainly at the Wilf Slack Memorial Ground, and in recent years fencing and skiing have developed as sporting strengths. A major development of the Wilf Slack Playing Fields has recently been completed, including the installation of two all–weather surfaces, the upgrading of all the pitches and a significant refurbishment of the pavilion to provide a high-quality facility. Hockey, squash, athletics, golf and other sports are also offered.

The school is not linked with any particular senior school. Two-thirds of the boys proceed to London day schools, such as Westminster, St Paul's, Highgate, City of London and UCS, and others proceed to leading boarding schools such as Eton, Harrow, Winchester and Tonbridge. In recent years numerous academic scholarships have been won at these and other schools. Other awards have been won in areas such as music and sport.

Means-tested bursaries are available at 8+ to 11+, and a number of boys apply at these entry points from London primary schools.

The school was last inspected in 2016 and the report may be found on the school's website.

Charitable status. The Hall School Charitable Trust is a Registered Charity, number 312722. It exists entirely for the purposes of education.

Hall Grove

London Road, Bagshot, Surrey GU19 5HZ

Tel:	01276 473059
Fax:	01276 452003
email:	office@hallgrove.co.uk
website:	www.hallgrove.co.uk

Headmaster: **A R Graham**, BSc, PGCE

Age Range. 3–13.
Number of Children. Pre-Preparatory (age 4–7) 102. Preparatory (age 7–13) 301.
Fees per term (2016–2017). Day fees: Pre-School (mornings) £1,905, Reception–Year 2 £3,400, Pre-Preparatory (Years 3–5) £4,150, Preparatory (Years 6–8) £4,445. Weekly Boarding: £1,290 supplement per term. Pre-Paid Flexi Boarding: £30 per night. Casual boarding: £40 per night. Sibling discount.

Hall Grove is a happy, vibrant school of over 430 boys and girls aged 3–13 with a separate pre-school in its grounds for those aged 3 and 4. Weekly/Flexi boarding is offered for up to 12 pupils. The main entry ages are 4, 7 and 11.

The school was founded in 1957 by the parents of the current Headmaster. At its centre is a most attractive Georgian house set in beautiful gardens and parkland. Recent additions have provided some modern rooms and specialist teaching areas, an impressive computer facility and new classroom blocks. Despite this building programme, the character and atmosphere of a family home has been retained.

The academic standards are high and there is a very strong emphasis on Sport and Music. A wide range of activities flourish; woodwork, ceramics, food technology, drama and a host of major and minor sports including soccer, rugby, hockey, netball, rounders, cricket, tennis, athletics, swimming, golf, judo, basketball, badminton and dance. Riding and stable management is an added attraction.

The school day continues until 5.40 pm for Years 7 and 8 and older children may stay overnight on a regular basis. There is also provision for after-school care and a full programme of evening activities.

Hall Grove has its own residential field study centre situated on the South Devon coast called Battisborough House and there are many field trips and expeditions both in Devon and overseas. Battisborough is available for hire by other schools and can accommodate up to 30 in comfort.

Hallfield School

Church Road, Edgbaston, Birmingham B15 3SJ

Tel:	0121 454 1496
Fax:	0121 454 9182
email:	office@hallfieldschool.co.uk
website:	www.hallfieldschool.co.uk
Twitter:	@HallfieldSchool

Founded 1879.

Governing Body: The Hallfield School Trust

Chairman of Governors: K Uff, MA, BCL of Gray's Inn, Barrister

Headmaster: **R Outwin-Flinders**, BEd Hons

Deputy Head: J P Thackway, BA Hons, PGCE

Age Range. 3 months to 11 years.
Number of Pupils. 570 Day Boys and Girls.
Fees per term (2016–2017). Pre-Prep: Transition £2,864 (5 days per week), Foundation to Year 2 £3,375; Upper School: £4,012 (Years 3–6). Lunches are included in the fees.

Since 1879, Hallfield School has offered an exceptional education for boys (and since 1995, boys and girls) which makes it the leading preparatory school in the Midlands and possibly the country. It is now a flourishing and highly successful co-educational day school.

However, the success of a school should not be judged simply on academic results. To the contrary, the School has always nurtured a strong 'hidden curriculum' which cannot be measured by league tables – where courtesy, manners, self-discipline and respect are valued and reinforced. It is this strong hidden curriculum which underpins everything that takes place at the School: 'happy children are successful children'.

The School's aims are clear and concise:
- To provide a safe, caring, happy and high achieving inclusive environment based on Christian principles, whilst welcoming children of all faiths to the School.
- To develop each child's full potential in academic, social, emotional, cultural and sporting areas.

Since becoming Headmaster of Hallfield in 2012, Roger Outwin-Flinders has steered the School through a successful inspection in January 2013, but he still continues to 'raise the bar' with his expectations for the children and staff.

In the last 3 years, 95 scholarships to the leading Independent Schools in the Midlands have been awarded to the Year 6 Leavers and in 2015–2016, 75% of Leavers were successfully offered places at selective Local Authority Grammar Schools. 85% of children who sat the entrance examinations to KES and KEHS were offered places.

However, Hallfield is more than just successful results at 11+ Examinations. In 2013 and 2015 the boys reached the National Finals of the Independent Schools Football Association U11 Seven-a-Side Tournament at St George's Park – the National Training Centre in Burton-upon-Trent. In 2013, the chess team became National IAPS champions for the third time in four years and in 2016 they became County Champions. In recent years, the Young Shakespeare Company has spent a week during the summer term working with Year 6 children to produce an exceptional interpretation of one of Shakespeare's classic plays, most recently "Hamlet" and, this year, a Year 6 girl became a member of the National Children's Choir.

There is something for everyone at Hallfield, but high standards are expected in everything the children take part in. Excellence and success are celebrated at every opportunity through Year group or School assemblies and, of course, the end of year School Prize Giving.

Hallfield strives for children to become happy, confident, independent learners and prepares them for their secondary education in an ever changing world.

Charitable status. Hallfield School Trust is a Registered Charity, number 528956. It exists for the purpose of providing education for children.

Halstead Preparatory School for Girls

Woodham Rise, Woking, Surrey GU21 4EE
Tel: 01483 772682
email: registrar@halstead-school.org.uk
website: www.halstead-school.org.uk

Chairman of Governors: Mr J Olsen

Headmistress: **Mrs P A Austin**, BA Hons London, LTCL Trinity College of Music, PGCE, NPQH

Age Range. Nursery–11.
Number of Pupils. 220 Girls.
Fees per term (2016–2017). Nursery (flexible) from £924; Reception (Kindergarten) and Year 1 £3,591; Year 2 £3,672; Years 3 to 6 £4,351.

Girls thrive in the calm, purposeful and happy atmosphere at Halstead with a good balance of study and fun and the opportunities to establish friends and many happy memories.

Halstead is delighted to have been recognised as 'excellent' in every aspect by the Independent Schools Inspectorate in 2014:

"The school meets its aims very successfully, providing a comfortable and homely environment where pupils are well known, treated as individuals and gain the confidence to thrive and fulfil their potential. From the Early Years Foundation Stage onwards, they achieve highly both in their academic work and in their activities outside the classroom, and have a great appetite for learning. This is thanks to the relevant and interesting curriculum and enthusiasm and expertise of teachers."

"Relationships throughout the school are excellent, and both pupils and their parents say it feels like a happy family."

"The school has a strong track record of success in entrance exams for prestigious local schools. Almost all pupils consistently gain places at their first choice of (senior) schools, with a considerable number being awarded scholarships."

Established in 1927 Halstead is situated in a leafy part of residential Woking. The main school building is a large Edwardian house to which modern facilities have been added including a purpose-built Food Technology, Design Technology and Art Room.

Prospective parents are very welcome to attend an Open Morning or, if more convenient, please make an appointment to meet Mrs Austin and see our happy, nurturing and secure school in action.

Charitable status. Halstead (Educational Trust) Limited is a Registered Charity, number 270525. It exists to provide a high quality all-round education for girls aged 2+–11.

Hampshire Collegiate Prep School
United Learning

Embley Park, Romsey, Hampshire SO51 6ZA
Tel: 01794 515737
email: info@hampshirecs.org.uk
website: www.hampshirecs.org.uk
Twitter: @hampshireschool
Facebook: /hampshireschool

Chairman of the Governors: Professor T Thomas

Principal: Mrs E-K Henry, BA

Head of Prep School: **Mrs H Donnelly**, BA, BEd

Deputy Head of Prep School: Mr P Brady, BEd

Age Range. 2–11 Co-educational.
Number of Pupils. 181 Day Pupils: 93 Boys, 88 Girls.
Fees per term (2016–2017). Nursery: £2,740 (full time). Payment by Termly Direct Debit: Prep School £3,080–£3,530.

The school operates an extended day from 8.00 am to 6.00 pm offering comprehensive care to support busy, modern family living.

The school has its own nursery (The Nightingale Nursery) taking children from age 2 and is very flexible in session bookings to suit parents' working patterns and family life. The nursery operates for 48 weeks of the year and there is also holiday cover for Reception Class, which can extend to Year 2 pupils if there is sufficient interest.

Reception to Year 2 pupils enjoy small class sizes with an emphasis on careful monitoring of progress in the core subjects and early intervention in the event of any identified learning needs. A broad curriculum is offered, including French, Music, IT, DT and PE taught by specialists.

Within Years 3 to 6 the focus is on careful monitoring of progress and the development of potential in each child alongside preparation senior schooling and associated scholarships. The school seeks to provide, through small class sizes, teaching expertise and support staff, a broad education tailored to the individual needs of the children in the school. There is both a clear and effective learning support structure and policy to help children experiencing difficulties, as well as challenge those who are our most able children. The school has three clear aims:

• At HCS we focus on the individual
• We believe that every child has special qualities – it is our responsibility to define and refine these
• We support a broad vision of excellence for our children and our teachers

Throughout the school the children take part in Learning Outside the Classroom (LOC). This is part of the curriculum and introduces the children to learning experiences that engage them in finding out more about their environment, making use of the school orchards, allotments, an outdoor classroom and an amphitheatre, all within our 130 parkland grounds.

There is a strong tradition of musical achievement in the school with choir, an orchestra, and a rock band. Children compete in a wide range of sports within curriculum time and as part of the busy House and fixture programme. Drama is promoted via its inclusion within the weekly timetable for all children, annual LAMDA preparation and regular productions. Our annual art exhibition showcases artistic talent in the school and regular linked work with local artists encourages enthusiasm for the visual arts. Each year our 10 and 11 year olds undertake residential visits. Year 5 experience geographical studies and outdoor pursuits on the Isle of Wight, whilst Year 6 travel to a Normandy château to experience a week's immersion in a wide variety of activities, all enjoyed in French.

The school seeks to achieve a high standard of academic achievement and to encourage attitudes of tolerance, adaptability, invention, persistence, responsibility, confidence, compassion, flexibility and creativity coupled with a life-long love of learning and endeavour. Our last ISI inspection highlighted the personal development of pupils as 'outstanding'.

Charitable status. Hampshire Collegiate Prep School is part of United Learning which comprises: UCST (a Company Limited by Guarantee, Registered in England, number 2780748, and a Registered Charity, number 1016538) and ULT (a Company Limited by Guarantee, Registered in England, number 4439859, and an Exempt Charity).

Hampton Pre-Prep & Prep School (formerly Denmead School)

Gloucester Road, Hampton, Middlesex TW12 2UQ

Tel: 020 8979 1844
email: admissions@hamptonprep.org.uk
website: hamptonprep.org.uk
Twitter: @Hampton_Prep

Chairman of Governors: N J Spooner, BA

Headmaster: **Mr Tim Smith**, BA, NZ Dip Tchg, MBA

Age Range. Boys 3–11, Girls 3–7.
Number of Pupils. 224.
Fees per term (2016–2016). Kindergarten (3–4 years): £1,815 (mornings), £3,630 (all day). Pre-Prep (4–7 years): £3,895. Prep (7–11 years): £4,200 including lunch for full day pupils.

The Prep School moved into its new state-of-the-art building in March 2016. The School is situated in a quiet, leafy part of Hampton and is easily accessible by road and rail. The School merged with Hampton School in September 1999 to become the Hampton School Trust's preparatory school. Although there is still no expectation for pupils to select Hampton as their first-choice secondary school, at least 50 per cent on average each year transfer there. Both schools are served by the same Board of Governors and the Headmaster of Hampton Prep reports to the Headmaster of Hampton School. The amalgamation produces economies of scale from which Hampton Prep benefits.

Boys transfer to senior schools at 11+. The Prep School is a two-form entry with 18 pupils per class, who are set for English and Maths. Since September 2004 Hampton has been offering Assured Places for 11+ entry. This is done from Year 2 through an ongoing programme of assessment of the boys and is also open to those starting in the Preparatory Department. In addition, those boys who perform very well in the 11+ Hampton entry exams, but who do not gain an award from Hampton, will be considered for the W D James Award made by Hampton Prep, which will be in the form of a reduction in the child's first term's fees at Hampton.

The Pre-Prep is housed on its own site in the homely atmosphere of two linked residential houses offering space and security. Rooms are well-appointed and there is one class per year group of 22 pupils. The Preparatory section, which backs onto an attractive public park, has undergone significant redevelopment and in February 2016 moved into a brand new, two-storey building. The old buildings have been demolished and the remainder of the site re-landscaped. The new state-of-the-art facilities will play a major part in the transformation of the School, its academic life included. Major school sports are Football, Rugby, Cricket and Athletics. An extensive programme of co-curricular activities includes: art club, chess, drama, judo, computing, Warhammer/Lego and a variety of minor sports. There is a School choir, an orchestra, and a flourishing tradition of drama. Individual music tuition is also provided.

Parents share in the life of the School as fully as possible and there exists a very active Parents' Association.

Please contact the School Office for a prospectus.

Charitable status. Hampton Pre-Prep & Prep School is part of the Hampton School Trust, which is a Registered Charity, number 1120005. It exists to provide a school in Hampton.

Handcross Park School

London Road, Handcross, West Sussex RH17 6HF
Tel: 01444 400526
email: info@handxpark.com
website: www.handcrossparkschool.co.uk
Twitter: @HandcrossPark
Facebook: /handcrosspark

Where potential is nurtured and success is celebrated in a friendly learning environment.

Chairman of Governors: L Tomlinson

Headmaster: R C M Brown, BA Hons, MA, PGCE

Head of Nursery & Pre-Prep: Mr J Gayler, BSc Hons QTS
Senior Deputy Head (*Pastoral*): Ms E Lyle, BSc USA, QTS UK
Deputy Head (*Academic*): Mr A Falkus, BSc Hons QTS

Age Range. 2–13 Co-educational.
Number of Pupils. 369: Boys 198, Girls 171.
Fees per term (2016–2017) Nursery according to number of sessions; Pre-Prep £3,060–£3,280; Prep £4,050–£6,040; Weekly boarding £5,090–£7,090; Full boarding (EU) £5,720–£7,720; Full boarding (non-EU) £10,480–£11,950.

Handcross Park is one of the Brighton College family of schools offering a pre-preparatory and preparatory school education, set in beautiful surroundings but conveniently located just off the A23 and close to Haywards Heath, Horsham, Gatwick and Crawley. The School provides a first-class education for children from 2 to 13 in a happy family atmosphere within a caring Christian framework.

The School unashamedly takes pride in the pursuit of excellence for all its pupils. Alongside academic endeavour staff believe ardently in educating children to become well-rounded, compassionate and articulate citizens.

The modern Nursery, situated in the Pre-Prep and accommodated in well-designed and purpose-built classrooms, offers a wonderful environment in which to begin the exciting adventure of a child's school career. Activities are specially designed to help young minds investigate and find solutions for themselves and the cleverly planned classrooms allow children the opportunity to pursue interests both inside and outdoors. With an excellent staff to pupil ratio throughout the Early Years and small class sizes right the way through the school, the emphasis is on helping the individual to flourish as part of a supportive, vibrant and happy community.

Handcross Park has a proven academic record with many Year 8 pupils gaining scholarships to Brighton College and other top Senior Schools both locally and further afield. We are proud of our 100% pass rate at Common Entrance and our excellent scholarship success over the years. But as well as a deep and broad knowledge of the curriculum, pupils also develop an understanding of the role they can play in society as informed and caring citizens.

Alongside the provision of a high quality academic education for all children, the School's well-qualified, friendly staff focus on nourishing the creative, musical and sporting aptitudes of the pupils. New for 2016 the School now has an all-weather pitch alongside a recently refurbished, vibrant Music Department, inspiring Art Studio, excellent sports coaching and facilities and well-equipped Science, IT and Design Technology Rooms, pupils are offered the best opportunities to foster and showcase their talents.

The 'home away from home' accommodation at Handcross Park has been refurbished, revamped and rejuvenated resulting in growing boarding numbers and a necessary extension to the Boarding House to cater for these additional numbers. With a variety of activities to choose from the focus is on having fun in a structured environment. Both weekly (Monday–Friday) and full boarding options are available and flexible pre and after school care offered to day parents.

Handcross Park was inspected in June 2014 and in the resulting inspection report achieved top rating across every area.

Charitable status. Newells School Trust is a Registered Charity, number 307038. Handcross Park School exists to provide a high-quality education to children aged 2 to 13.

Hanford School

Child Okeford, Blandford Forum, Dorset DT11 8HN
Tel: 01258 860219
Fax: 01258 861255
email: office@hanford.dorset.sch.uk
website: www.hanfordschool.co.uk
Twitter: @HanfordDorset
Facebook: @HanfordSchool

Chairman of Governors: Mrs L Sunnucks

Headmaster: Mr R Johnston, BA

Age Range. 7–13.
Number of Girls. 100.
Fees per term (2016–2017). Boarders £7,050, Day Girls £5,800.

Hanford School, located between Blandford and Shaftesbury in Dorset, was founded in 1947 by the Revd and Mrs C B Canning. It is housed in a beautiful 17th Century Jacobean manor house set in 45 acres of land in the Stour valley. The amenities include a Chapel, Laboratories, a Computer Room, a Music School, an Art School, a Gymnasium, a Swimming Pool, a Handwork Room, two Netball/Tennis Courts (hard) and an indoor covered Riding School.

Girls arrive from the age of seven onwards and leave at 13 after taking Common Entrance. Hanford is non-selective and prides itself on bringing out the best in each and every girl. Pupils are prepared for entry to Independent Senior Schools including: Marlborough, Bryanston, St Mary's Shaftesbury and Sherborne Girls.

Hanford believes children should be children for as long as possible, climbing trees, building dens, riding ponies and playing in the garden. Giving girls free time is something Hanford has always believed in as it encourages girls to become lost in their own imagination and develop creatively. Hanford recently took the decision to switch off all 'Smart devices', iPhones, tablets etc. during term time. Unplugging the girls from social media, games and communications was not done to protect them but to encourage them to make their own fun; they will have plenty of time to use social media but a relatively short time in which to be silly, fun-loving children. The girls use their free time to play games such as British Bulldog, riding the Hanford ponies, tending the chickens, gardening or climbing trees.

Hanford teaches girls to combine having fun with working hard. A strong and committed teaching staff seeks to bring out the best in each and every girl. This combination of fun and hard work pays dividends when it comes to Common Entrance and Scholarships. There have been 21 scholarships awarded in the past three years – evidence of this successful formula. Class sizes are small, normally 10–12, and there is learning support available if required. Alongside the core curriculum girls are taught handwork, where they make their own school uniform skirt, and Art Appreciation (Art Apre) where they can begin to understand and appreciate the cultural world around them. Music has always been central to life at Hanford with almost all girls learning at least one instrument or joining one of the choirs or folk group; music composition is also offered as an activity.

Sport is also strong at Hanford. Last summer term the rounders, tennis and athletics teams were all county champions. Hanford is perhaps most famous for its ponies and stables with most girls choosing to have riding lessons and some testing their equestrian skills at local and national events including tetrathlons.

Hawkesdown House School

27 Edge Street, Kensington, London W8 7PN

Tel:	020 7727 9090
email:	admin@hawkesdown.co.uk
website:	www.hawkesdown.co.uk

Pre-Preparatory Day School for Boys.

Acting Head: **Mrs L Quilter**, BEd

Admissions Secretary: Miss V Bailey-King

Age Range. 3–8.
Number of Pupils. 130 Boys.
Fees per term (2015–2016). £5,090 (age 3), £5,530 (age 4), £5,855 (age 5–8).

Early literacy and numeracy are of prime importance and the traditional academic subjects form the core curriculum. A balanced education helps all aspects of learning and a wide range of interests is encouraged. The School finds and fosters individual talents in each pupil. Boys are prepared for entry at eight to the main London and other preparatory schools. The School places the greatest importance on matching boys happily and successfully to potential schools and spends time with parents ensuring that the transition is smooth and free of stress.

Sound and thorough early education is important for success and also for self-confidence. The thoughtful and inspirational teaching and care at Hawkesdown House ensure high academic standards and promote initiative, kindness and courtesy.

The School provides an excellent traditional education, with the benefits of modern technology, in a safe, happy and caring atmosphere. Many of the boys coming to the School live within walking distance and the School is an important part of the Kensington community.

There are clear expectations and the boys are encouraged by positive motivation and by the recognition and praise of their achievements, progress and effort. Individual attention and pastoral care for each of the boys is of great importance.

Hawkesdown House has a fine building in Edge Street, off Kensington Church Street.

Religious Denomination: Non-denominational; Christian ethos.

Parents who would like further information or to visit the School and meet the Acting Head, should contact the School Office for a prospectus or an appointment.

The Hawthorns

Pendell Court, Bletchingley, Surrey RH1 4QJ

Tel:	01883 743048 (Prep); 01883 743718 (Pre-Prep)
Fax:	01883 744256
email:	admissions@hawthorns.com
website:	www.hawthorns.com
Twitter:	@HawthornsSchool
Facebook:	/hawthornsschoolbletchingley

Chair of Governors: Mrs Z S Creighton

Headmaster: **A E Floyd**, BSc, PGCE

Head of Pre-Prep: Mrs E Forsyth, Cert Ed

Age Range. 2–13.
Number of Pupils. 530 Day Pupils.
Fees per term (2016–2017). From £680 (Nursery 2 mornings) to £4,480.

In a wonderfully diverse friendly, family setting, girls and boys from 2 to 13 years are nurtured under the motto 'Love God, love thy neighbour'. They develop the confidence and skills to take ownership for their learning, with habits of minds which help them to care and work through life's challenges. Dynamic and energetic leadership together with an open parental partnership makes The Hawthorns a vibrant, exciting and forward looking community. Set in 35 beautiful acres with fabulous facilities, we blend all roundedness with excellence.

In a wonderful setting, The Hawthorns is a remarkable School where children enjoy their childhood developing their characters and the skills for life. The warmth and atmosphere of Pendell Court immediately appeal. As an outstanding day School for 2 to 13 year olds, we offer an exceptional breadth and vision for the whole child.

Underpinning an outstanding record of academic achievement at senior schools, The Hawthorns' academic curriculum is broad and balanced. Developing the talents of each child is at the heart of our work. Excellent teachers create high expectations and, as a result, boys and girls achieve success in a wide variety of areas. A wonderful programme of sport and the extraordinary output of art, music, drama and design and technology mean that every child has the opportunity to be challenged and to excel. A healthy balance of tradition and modernity, which has been embraced over several decades at The Hawthorns, ensures that happy children learn and strive for excellence.

Children are loved, feel secure and learn from both their mistakes and their endeavours. Laughter and energy abound as boys and girls, teachers and staff create this wonderful School. Come and visit The Hawthorns and we shall be pleased to share our School and more of its work with you and your child.

Charitable status. The Hawthorns Educational Trust Limited is a Registered Charity, number 312067. It exists to provide education for girls and boys of 2 to 13 years.

Hazelwood School

Wolfs Hill, Limpsfield, Oxted, Surrey RH8 0QU

Tel:	01883 712194
Fax:	01883 716135
email:	bursar@hazelwoodschool.com
website:	www.hazelwoodschool.co.uk

Chair of Governors: Mrs Annabel Lark

Head: **Mrs Lindie Louw**

Age Range. 6 months–13 years.
Number of Pupils. 570 co-educational.
Fees per term (2016–2017). Day Pupils from £3,070 (Reception) to £5,040.

Founded in 1890, Hazelwood stands in superb grounds, commanding a magnificent view over the Kent and Sussex Weald.

Pupils enter at age 4 into the Pre-Prep or at 7+ to the Prep School, joining those pupils transferring from the Pre-Prep to the Prep School. Entry at other ages is possible if space permits. Hazelwood School's Nursery and Early Years, open all year round for children from 3 months to 4 years, opened in September 2009 on the Laverock site which offers unrivalled accommodation and facilities.

A gradual transition is made towards subject specialist tuition in the middle and upper forms. Pupils are prepared for the Common Entrance examinations at 11+ and 13+, and also for Scholarships to Senior Schools. Over 200 academic, all-rounder, sporting, music and art awards have been gained since 1995. The school has recently introduced Philosophy for Children and Forest Schools into the curriculum.

Extracurricular activity is an important part of every pupil's education. Excellent sports facilities, which include games fields, heated indoor swimming pool, gymnasium and many games pitches, tennis courts and other hard surfaces, allow preparation of school teams at various age and ability levels in a wide range of sports. A fully-equipped Sports Hall was completed in May 2004. Our aim is that every pupil has an opportunity to represent the School. In September 2016 the new Baily Building was opened containing 14 classrooms, a Recital Room, a Food Tech Kitchen, a Lower School Art Room and a 450-seat auditorium, The Bawtree Hall.

Art, Technology, Music and Drama are on the curriculum as well as being lively extramural activities. Our Centenary Theatre incorporates a 200-seat theatre, music school and Chapel. All our pupils are encouraged to play an instrument and join one of the music groups catering for all interests and abilities. Further extracurricular activities include tap, ballet and jazz dance, judo, art, gymnastics, scuba, debating, fantasy football, Forest Skills, computing, Lego modelling and chess.

Our pupils develop a curiosity about the world in which they live and a real passion for learning. Most importantly of all they become confident learners, mature and articulate individuals who love coming to school each day.

Charitable status. Hazelwood School Limited is a Registered Charity, number 312081. It exists to provide excellent preparatory school education for girls and boys in Oxted, Surrey.

Hazlegrove

Sparkford, Yeovil, Somerset BA22 7JA

Tel: 01963 440314
Fax: 01963 440569
email: office@hazlegrove.co.uk
website: www.hazlegrove.co.uk
Twitter: @HazlegrovePrep
Facebook: @HazlegrovePrep

Senior Warden: Lt General [Ret'd] A M D Palmer CB CBE

Headmaster: Richard Fenwick, BEd, MA

Deputy Headmaster: Vincent Holden, BSc Hons, MEd

Head of Pre-Preparatory Department: Eleanor Lee, BEd

Age Range. 2½–13.
Number of Pupils. 363 boys and girls of whom 93 are boarders. Preparatory (7–13 year olds) 297 pupils; Pre-Preparatory (2½–7 year olds) 50 pupils.

Fees per term (2016–2017). Preparatory: Boarders £6,429–£8,203 (fees are inclusive, with few compulsory extras); Day pupils £4,387–£5,596. Pre-Preparatory: £2,760. Nursery: on application.

Scholarships and Bursaries. Academic Scholarships are available for entry at 7+ and 11+. Armed Forces Bursaries are also available to serving members.

Hazlegrove is located within a 200 acre park and is based around a country house built by Carew Hervey Mildmay in 1730. The entrance to the school is situated on the A303 roundabout at Sparkford. The Preparatory School has a strong boarding ethos. This is reflected in the full days, Saturday morning lessons from Year Four and the full range of activities for boarders, and those day pupils who wish to join in, during the evenings and at weekends. The school was awarded "Excellent" in all nine areas of judgement in the last ISI Inspection in the autumn, 2015

Hazlegrove is a happy and purposeful school with a strong tutor system. The curriculum provides a varied and exciting experience for pupils as they progress through the school and includes Art, Food Technology, Design and Technology, Drama, Music and Outdoor Education. Latin and Mandarin are introduced in Year 5. The main sports are Rugby, Hockey, Cricket, Netball, Rounders, Tennis, Athletics and Swimming. Squash, Golf, Horse Riding, Judo and Karate are also available among other activities.

Streaming and setting is introduced as pupils progress through the school with a scholarship stream in the top two years. Pupils are entered for Common Entrance or Scholarship Examinations. About half go to the senior school, King's School Bruton (*see entry in HMC section*). Others move on to major secondary schools such as Bryanston, Eton, Sherborne, Sherborne Girls, Millfield, King's College Taunton, Marlborough and Winchester. Between 25 and 30 scholarships and awards are gained by pupils each year. Extra support is available to those pupils who have specific learning difficulties or who are gifted.

Pupils have achieved considerable success at regional and national level in recent years through sport, in team and individual performances, in drama and in music.

Hazlegrove has outstanding facilities. These include a state-of-the-art new Teaching and Learning Centre, a Theatre, a Sports Hall, a 25m Indoor Heated Pool, two Squash Courts, the Design Centre, three award-winning Libraries, an extensive Music School a comprehensive wi-fi network. Outside, the extensive playing fields are complemented by two synthetic pitches, tennis courts, eight all-weather cricket nets and for golf, a 6-hole course, a putting green and driving nets. A full-time tennis coach ensures best use of the hard tennis courts and the second synthetic playing surface – both with flood lighting. The mini-farm now has pigs, chickens and raised vegetable beds and the adventure playground is equipped with a timing device so pupils can compete for the Tarzan award.

Pastoral care for Boarders, which is overseen by the Headmaster's wife, is provided by three sets of House Parents, four Matrons and a Nurse. Other resident staff provide additional support. The school has considerable experience of meeting the needs of pupils whose parents are in the Services or who live in expat communities working overseas. Flexible boarding can also be arranged to meet individual needs.

The school shop, which is on site, provides most necessary clothing and games kit.

Pre-Preparatory Department. Located in a purpose-built facility within the grounds, the Pre-Prep provides a carefully structured curriculum which encourages the development of the basic skills within a balanced programme of learning and play. The innovative curriculum includes Forest School and specialist taught French, drama, music, games and tennis. In addition to making full use of the Prep School facilities, the Pre-Prep enjoys its own Rainbow

Room dedicated to Science, Art and Investigation, an adjacent gardening area and extensive climbing equipment in the playground. After school care is available.

Charitable status. King's School, Bruton is a Registered Charity, number 1071997. It exists to provide education for children.

Headington Preparatory School

26 London Road, Headington, Oxford, Oxfordshire OX3 7PB

Tel:	01865 759400
Fax:	01865 761774
email:	prepadmissions@headington.org
website:	www.headington.org
Twitter:	@HeadingtonPrep
Facebook:	/HeadingtonSchool

Chairman of Board of Governors: Mrs Sandra Phipkin, ACA

Headmistress: **Mrs J Crouch**, BA Hons Keele, MA Hons London, NPQH

Age Range. Girls 3–11.
Number of Pupils. 280.
Fees per term (2016–2017). Day: £1,235–£4,295.

Headington Preparatory School occupies its own three-acre site just two minutes' walk from Headington School and one mile from the centre of Oxford.

The Prep School's friendly, family atmosphere means girls develop as happy individuals with a sense of responsibility and self-awareness, enjoying a wealth of experiences inside and out of the classroom as part of an outstanding education.

In September 2016, a brand new outdoor play area was created for the Early Years and Foundation Stage department. It includes a mound with a tunnel, extended climbing equipment with climbing wall, cargo nets and bridges and new all-weather flooring. This Centenary Campaign project also included a revamp of the nursery classrooms with new flooring, new lighting, redecoration and a two-storey role play area.

We have a wide range of extracurricular facilities including a gym and specialist art and design facilities, as well as a substantial performance space for music and drama, and a refurbished library. Our adventurous art and design curriculum allows girls to explore their imaginations through painting, drawing, clay-work and model-building and there are many exciting opportunities for girls in drama and music. We want all our girls to enjoy a variety of musical activities and we are quick to spot and nurture talent. From the age of seven, girls have the chance to learn at least one musical instrument and many of our girls play at a very high standard. All girls are taught to read music in both treble and bass clef through our keyboard scheme which is for Reception and Year 1. Theory clubs are offered to continue and support their learning.

In sport, specialist staff deliver a broad and balanced programme with a total of 12 different sports on offer. Girls are encouraged to try new activities and discover new talents to achieve their full potential, with many taking part in county level tournaments.

The school day runs from 8.30 am to 3.30 pm, with an extended day from 7.45 am to 6.00 pm. There are a large number of after-school clubs and activities from Fencing to Touch Typing and Trampolining and aftercare runs every day incorporating a range of activities, tea and prep.

Entry to the Prep School is in order of application from nursery to 6+, with priority given to girls with siblings already at Headington, and by examination from 7+. The majority of pupils continue to Headington School, with a number of girls awarded scholarships every year. (*See Headington School entry in GSA section.*)

Charitable status. Headington School Oxford Limited is a Registered Charity, number 309678. It exists to provide quality education for girls.

Heath Mount School

Woodhall Park, Watton-at-Stone, Hertford, Hertfordshire SG14 3NG

Tel:	01920 830230
Fax:	01920 830357
email:	registrar@heathmount.org
website:	www.heathmount.org

The school became a Trust in September 1970, with a Board of Governors.

Chairman of Governors: Mrs J Hodson

Headmaster: **Mr C Gillam**, BEd Hons

Senior Deputy Head: Mr M Dawes

Age Range. 3–13.
Number of Pupils. 249 Boys, 184 Girls. Flexi/Sleepover boarding offered.
Fees per term (2016–2017). Boarding (1–4 nights): £480–£1,970. Tuition: Nursery £2,160–£3,610, Pre-Prep £4,166, Years 3–6 £5,385, Years 7–8 £5,565.

There is a reduction in fees for the second and subsequent children attending the School at the same time.

Heath Mount School is situated five miles from Hertford, Ware and Knebworth, at Woodhall Park – a beautiful Georgian mansion with 40 acres of grounds set in a large private park. A dedicated Nursery and Pre-Prep and a new Lower School are situated a short walk from the main house. The fabulous facilities are inspiring – excellent sports facilities include a sports hall, covered swimming pool, an all-weather pitch for hockey and tennis, netball courts and cricket nets. The main house contains an imaginatively developed lower ground floor housing modern science laboratories and rooms for art, pottery, textiles, film making, food technology and design technology. There is a further information technology room and well-stocked research and fiction libraries. The boys board in a wing of the main house and the girls in a dedicated house in the adjoining park. Resident boarding house parents provide a welcoming environment for both the boys and girls.

The School has an excellent academic record, as well as outstanding art and sport and some of the finest school music in the Country. Illustrating this, in 2016, twenty-four of the 13+ leavers achieved scholarships to their senior schools across a range of areas.

Charitable status. Heath Mount School is a Registered Charity, number 311069.

Heatherton House School

Copperkins Lane, Amersham, Bucks HP6 5QB

Tel:	01494 726433
email:	enquiries@heathertonhouse.co.uk
website:	www.heathertonhouse.co.uk
Twitter:	@HeathertonHouse
Facebook:	/HeathertonHouse

Chairman of the Governors: Mr G C Laws (Chairman of Berkhamsted Schools Group)

Principal: Mr R P Backhouse, MA Cantab

Head: Mrs D Isaachsen, MEd

Age Range. Girls 3–11, Boys in Nursery only.
Number of Pupils. 136 Girls, 11 Boys.
Fees per term (2016–2017). £1,914–£4,235 inclusive of all but optional subjects.

Founded in 1912, Heatherton is set in an attractive green and leafy location on the outskirts of Amersham.

Heatherton provides an excellent all-round education. An experienced staff of specialist teachers encourage each child's individual academic and emotional development. High standards are achieved across a broad curriculum with small classes (max 20), a caring ethos and a close relationship with parents.

At 11 pupils progress to both local independent girls' senior schools and Buckinghamshire grammar schools. Excellent results are produced at all stages of school performance tests and the girls are tracked from an early age, both pastorally and academically.

Musical, artistic and sporting talents flourish at Heatherton. A thriving orchestra, individual instrument lessons and many drama, ballet and music productions are an important part of life in a school year. Art and design skills are celebrated in display and exhibitions, both internally and externally. Each pupil is offered a wide range of sporting activities – swimming, netball, gymnastics, dance, athletics, tennis, lacrosse and cross country with opportunities for yoga and unihoc.

An extensive range of educational visits and activities in the UK and Europe are organised each year. The school has recently introduced an additional Enrichment Curriculum to its pupils' timetables, offering the girls exciting opportunities to expand their knowledge, with topics as diverse as mindfulness, team-building and Tudor cooking.

In September 2015, the Heatherton Nursery became Co-Educational, providing for both boys and girls. Heatherton has been recognised for its '*outstanding quality of provision*' in the Early Years Foundation Stage. Its '*calm, purposeful environment*' and '*a host of stimulating learning opportunities*', were just some of the features highlighted by the Independent Schools Inspectorate who are now citing Heatherton's EYFS as an example of very best practice. Heatherton remains a girls' school from Reception class to Year 6.

Following a merger with Berkhamsted School in 2011, Heatherton pupils are increasingly enjoying the benefits of initiatives such as joint curriculum days, music and drama workshops, sports coaching and residential trips in partnership with Berkhamsted Prep, as well as access to the significant resources and infrastructure of the Berkhamsted Schools Group.

Charitable status. Heatherton House School is a member of the Berkhamsted Schools Group, which is a Registered Charity, number 310630.

Heathfield
The Junior School to Rishworth School

Rishworth, West Yorkshire HX6 4QF
Tel: 01422 823564
Fax: 01422 820880
email: admin@heathfieldjunior.co.uk
website: www.rishworth-school.co.uk

Motto: *Deeds Not Words*

Chairman of the Board of Governors: Dr C A G Brooks

Head: Mr A M Wilkins, BA, MA, MA

Age Range. 3–11 co-educational.
Number of Pupils. 120 day boys/girls and 50-place Foundation Stage Unit.
Fees per term (from April 2016). Reception–Year 2 £2,050; Years 3–6 £3,010.

Staffing. 10 full-time teaching and 5 part-time teaching; 2 NNEB staff and 6 teaching assistants; additional teaching support in physical education and specialist teaching in music, art, PE, dance, ICT and drama; specialist peripatetic staff provide expert individual tuition in Music and the Arts.

Location. Heathfield stands in its own grounds and enjoys an outstanding rural position in a beautiful Pennine location with easy access via the motorways to Manchester and Leeds.

Facilities. Well-equipped classrooms; Foundation Stage Unit and purpose-built Infant classes; designated teaching rooms for Music, Science, Art and Design Technology; modern ICT Suite; Library; a multi-purpose Hall for assemblies and productions; heated indoor swimming pool; netball court and football/rugby pitch; Pre/After School Care and Holiday School available. The extensive grounds are used for a wide variety of academic and other purposes.

Aims. To provide a stimulating and challenging environment in which individual attainment is nurtured, recognised and celebrated.

To ensure each child receives their full entitlement to a broad, balanced curriculum which builds on a solid foundation in literacy and numeracy.

Curriculum. An extensive programme of study which incorporates the Foundation Stage, Key Stage 1 and Key Stage 2. An emphasis on developing an independence in learning and analytical thinking through Literacy, Numeracy, Science, French, History, Geography, Religious Studies, Design Technology, Information and Communications Technology, Music, Art and Physical Education.

Extra-Curricular Activities. Drama, Choir, Orchestra, Baking, Brass, Recorder and String Groups, Steel Pans, Art, Board Games; Sports include Swimming, Rounders, Netball, Football, Rugby, Cross-Country, Cricket, Fencing, Athletics, Gymnastics, Hockey and Biathlon.

Extensive fixtures list of sports for boys and girls.

Each term there are plays and musical concerts incorporating most children in the School. Residentials include Outdoor Pursuits, Camping and Environmental Studies.

Charitable status. Rishworth School is a Registered Charity, number 1115562. It exists to provide education for boys and girls.

Hereford Cathedral Junior School

28 Castle Street, Hereford HR1 2NW
Tel: 01432 363511
email: enquiry@herefordcs.com
website: www.herefordcs.com
Twitter: @Herefordcs1
Facebook: /HerefordCathedralSchool

Established 1898.

Chairman of Governors: R Haydn Jones, BSc, MRICS

Headmaster: C Wright, BSc, MSc, PGCE

Age Range. 3–11.
Number of children. 238: 143 boys and 95 girls.

Fees per term (2016–2017). £1,455–£2,085 (Nursery), £2,624 (Reception–Year 2), £3,307 (Years 3–6).

The school is the Junior School for Hereford Cathedral School and has the same board of Governors. Games facilities, including the new sports hall opened in 2009, are shared and there is close cooperation between the two sections of the school, although the Junior School has its own specialist teaching staff.

Entry is generally via the Nursery or Reception but a number of children also enter at 7+ and above. Almost all children continue through to the senior school.

The School occupies listed Georgian and Medieval buildings in Castle Street at the East End of the Cathedral with facilities including specialist music rooms, a new Art and DT centre, an ICT suite and an extensive library. The Moat, a nine-classroom building to house the Pre-Prep, opened in 2003.

The quality of relationships between staff and children is a great strength and a positive and friendly atmosphere characterises the whole school. There is a full and broad curriculum with the School noted for the strength of its music, drama and games. French is taught from the age of 4.

The staff are well qualified and the maximum class size is 18. In the junior forms all subjects are taught by specialists.

Music plays an important part in the life of the school with the Cathedral Choristers being educated at the school and a team of over twenty peripatetic music teachers. There are two school choirs and an orchestra.

An extensive programme of clubs and activities is offered during lunchtime and after school aimed at giving all children opportunities to develop their talents. After school care is also available.

The games fields are on the banks of the River Wye with expert coaching being given in the main sports of cricket, football, rugby, hockey, netball, rounders, athletics and swimming.

There is an active PTA organising a wide programme of social and fundraising activities.

The Little Princess Trust founded in memory of former pupil, Hannah Tarplee, is based at the school and provides hair pieces for children who lose their hair through cancer treatment.

Charitable status. Hereford Cathedral School is a Registered Charity, number 518889. Its aims and objectives are to promote the advancement of education.

Hereward House School

14 Strathray Gardens, London NW3 4NY
Tel: 020 7794 4820
email: office@herewardhouse.co.uk
website: www.herewardhouse.co.uk

Headmaster: **Mr P J E V Evans**, MA

Age Range. 4–13.
Number of Pupils. 171 Day Boys.
Fees per term (2016–2017). £5,205–£5,355.

Hereward House provides a warm and welcoming atmosphere in which every child feels valued, secure and thrives. The school works hard to create a stimulating, purposeful and happy community, within which boys are encouraged and assisted to develop academically, morally, emotionally, culturally and physically. The school's aim is for boys to enjoy their school days yet at the same time be well prepared for the demands of Common Entrance and Scholarship examinations.

The school's academic success is built upon excellent teaching and the highly individual educational teaching programmes created to meet individual boy's needs. Great care is taken to ensure that a boy gains a place at the school which is right for him.

Boys are prepared for the Common Entrance and Scholarship examinations to highly sought after independent schools, both day and boarding. Two-thirds of boys proceed to top London Day Schools, such as City of London, Highgate, St Paul's, UCS and Westminster, others to leading boarding schools such as Eton, Harrow and Winchester. Scholarships and Awards have been won by our boys to several of the above schools.

The school takes pride in the breadth of education it offers. Music plays a major role in the boys' education. Almost all boys learn at least one instrument, most of them two or even three. There is a full school orchestra which gives a performance each term. Weekly concerts are held throughout the year.

Team Games play an integral part in the sports syllabus. We regularly field teams against other schools and have an enviable record of success in cricket, football and cross-country running. Swimming, tennis, hockey and athletics are included in our sports programme.

Art, pottery and drama have a valued place in the syllabus. Chess, judo, ICT and music theory are among the clubs available to the boys.

Herries Preparatory School

Dean Lane, Cookham Dean, Berks SL6 9BD
Tel: 01628 483350
Fax: 01628 483329
email: office@herries.org.uk
website: www.herries.org.uk

Chair of Governors: Miss N Coombs

Headmistress: **Ms S Green**, BSc Econ, PGCE

Age Range. 3–11 Co-educational.
Number of Pupils. 110 Day Boys and Girls.
Fees per term (2016–2017). £2,795–£3,280.

Herries has a delightful location alongside National Trust land and is close to Maidenhead and Marlow. Small class sizes enable each child to receive individual attention and to flourish in a secure environment. The curriculum is broad and balanced and there is a wide range of extracurricular clubs including football coaching with Wycombe Wanderers, Gymnastics, Judo, Cookery, Table Tennis and ICT programming. Instrumental Music lessons are available. Extended Day is available to all pupils from 7.30 am to 6.00 pm Monday to Friday. Herries has a distinctive family atmosphere and happy pupils who progress to the grammar and independent secondary schools of their choice.

Curriculum. The National Curriculum is covered and we teach beyond the levels expected of children in each age group. Class teachers deliver the core and foundation subjects in Key Stage 1 while there is subject specialist teaching in all subjects in KS2.

Examinations. Children are assessed through the NFER testing scheme and a variety of standardised tests. Emphasis is placed on preparing pupils for their next school of choice and the timetable includes 'Thinking Skills' which helps pupils learn to cope with a variety of different tests and exams.

Facilities. Set in a beautiful building which was the house in which Kenneth Grahame wrote 'The Wind in the Willows', the Nursery occupies a purpose-built and spacious suite of rooms. ICT is taught in a specialist room with the latest computers and software. Class rooms are equipped with interactive Smart Boards and there is an excellent library. Games are played at the National Sports Centre at Bisham Abbey, only a few minutes away by coach. Swimming and tennis are based at Court Garden in Marlow. Athletics events are held at Braywick Sports Centre.

High March School

23 Ledborough Lane, Beaconsfield, Bucks HP9 2PZ
Tel: 01494 675186
Fax: 01494 675377
email: office@highmarch.bucks.sch.uk
           admissions@highmarch.bucks.sch.uk
website: www.highmarch.co.uk

Established 1926.

Chairman of the Governing Board: Mr C Hayfield, BSc, FCA

Headmistress: Mrs S J Clifford, BEd Hons Oxon, MA London

   Age Range. Girls 3–11, Boys 3–4.
   Number of Pupils. 306 day pupils.
   Fees per term (2016–2017). £1,755–£4,530 inclusive of books, stationery and lunches, but excluding optional subjects.
   High March consists of 3 school houses set in pleasant grounds. Junior House comprises Nursery and Key Stage 1 classes, ages 3–7 years, whilst Upper School covers Key Stage 2, ages 7–11 years. Class sizes are limited. Facilities include a state-of-the-art 20-metre indoor heated swimming pool opened in September 2009, a well-equipped Gymnasium, as well as Science, Music, Art, Poetry, Design Technology, Drama, Information Technology rooms and a Library. Recent refurbishments include large extensions to the Art Room and Science Laboratory and re-landscaping of all the Upper School's outside space to include a new Adventure Playground, new Netball courts and an outdoor learning classroom. The playground at Junior House was re-landscaped in Summer 2015 and Summer 2016 and now includes a Sensory Garden as well as new play equipment.
   High March is within easy reach of London, High Wycombe, Windsor and within a few minutes' walk of Beaconsfield Station.
   Under a large and highly-qualified staff and within a happy atmosphere, the children are prepared for Common Entrance and Scholarships to Independent Senior Schools and for the 11+ County Selection process. All subjects including French, Latin, Music, Art, Technology, Speech and Drama, Dancing, Gymnastics, Games and Swimming are in the hands of specialists. The academic record is high but each child is nevertheless encouraged to develop individual talents.
   There is an Annual Open Scholarship to the value of one-third of the annual fee tenable for 3 years.

Highfield & Brookham Schools

Highfield Lane, Liphook, Hampshire GU30 7LQ
Tel: 01428 728000 (Highfield Prep)
           01428 722005 (Brookham Pre-Prep)
email: headspa@highfieldschool.org.uk
           office@brookhamschool.co.uk
website: www.highfieldschool.org.uk
Twitter: @HighfieldSch

Chairman of Directors: W S Mills, Esq

Headteacher, Highfield (Prep): **Mr Phillip Evitt**

Headteacher, Brookham (Pre-Prep): **Mrs Sophie Baber**

   Age Range. 3–13.
   Number of Children. 480.
   Fees per term (2016–2017). Day Pupils £3,500–£6,765; Boarders £7,470–£8,200.
   Discounts are available for siblings and Forces families.
   Highfield and Brookham are purpose-built, co-educational day and boarding schools set in 175 acres of superb grounds on the Hampshire/Sussex border, 15 miles south of Guildford with easy access (under an hour) to London and Heathrow Airport.
   The aim of the schools is to provide children with a keen sense of their own individual identity and to help them to develop a sense of responsibility towards others and fulfil their potential in a happy and caring environment. Highfield and Brookham children are encouraged to have high expectations, good work habits and a desire to benefit from all that the school offers.
   The curriculum is broad, stimulating and highly creative. Strong emphasis is placed on cross-curricular and outdoor learning, including Forest School, providing for all styles of learner. Sport, Drama, Music, Design Technology and Art all enjoy generous provision in the Timetable, providing every pupil with the opportunity to explore and develop their talents and interests. The aim is to develop enthusiastic, enquiring, rounded and adaptable independent thinkers who recognise that learning is both a joy and lifelong.
   The major sports on offer are rugby, soccer, hockey and cricket for the boys, whilst girls play netball, lacrosse, hockey and rounders. All the children take part in athletics, swimming, tennis and cross country. Activities take place in the evenings and weekends and include judo, ballet, chess, golf, drama, modelling, pottery, sewing and story telling.
   Highfield children have a distinguished record of success at Common Entrance and Scholarships to all the major senior schools including Eton, Winchester, Marlborough, Bryanston, Canford, Wycombe Abbey, St Swithun's and Downe House to name but a few.

Highfield Prep School

West Road, Maidenhead, Berkshire SL6 1PD
Tel: 01628 624918
Fax: 01628 635747
email: office@highfieldprep.org
website: www.highfieldprep.org

We are an Educational Charitable Trust Primary Day School with Nursery.

Chairman of Governors: Mr W Bradley

Head: Mrs Joanna Leach, BEd, NPQH

   Age Range. 3–11.
   Number of Pupils. Approximately 160 Girls (brothers in Nursery). Class sizes: average 19, maximum 22.
   Highfield Preparatory School is the leading independent girls' school in Maidenhead. It offers a great start to the life of learning in a safe, secure and stimulating environment. In the Nursery (3 and 4 year olds) and Reception classes (5 year olds) right through to Year 6 (11 year olds) the girls are taught to love learning and are inspired to achieve their very best. We provide every girl with the opportunity to shine and be proud, to learn who they are, and have the confidence to have a go with the belief that they can succeed.

We believe, that in the important primary years, girls learn best in girls' schools. They learn by doing, listening, exploring and experimenting. The girls are given daily opportunities to explore, question, try, investigate, discover, apply and have fun! This all starts in the Nursery, which was graded Excellent at inspection in 2013, where the girls learn to develop confidence and independence.

Our girls achieve well beyond national expectations and move on to some of the best schools in the area at 11+, often achieving academic, sports and music scholarships. We also offer a wide range of after-school clubs ranging from water-colours to cookery.

We offer wonderful resources in a happy, secure and stimulating environment where all girls learn and develop at their own pace. Highfield Prep School is a local school, 5 minutes' walk from the town centre, on the same site since 1918, and really is Maidenhead's best kept secret!

From Nursery to Year 6, we offer extended day care from 7.45 am to 6.00 pm, have an all-year round holiday club, serve hot lunches every day and our fees are highly competitive.

The entry process is non-selective.

Come and see for yourself why Highfield Prep is first for girls. A prospectus is available on request from the School Secretary.

Fees per term (2016–2017). Reception to Year 6: £2,635–£3,420; Lunch £320. Nursery: £2,750* (full-time inc lunch), £305 per morning session, £246 per afternoon session (inc lunch).

*Nursery Education Funding (NEF) is currently available for all 3 and 4 year olds attending a setting registered within the RBWM. Highfield Preparatory School is a registered setting. We offer the free entitlement NEF in 3 hour morning and afternoon sessions (maximum 15 hours per week)

New Nursery Package (from September 2016). In this changing world we recognise that working parents need childcare that fits with their busy lives, but still provides the best possible start for their daughter, and that's why we go that extra mile to support our Highfield Families.

For girls in the nursery we offer a free Breakfast club and free after-school care in The Den for each full day they attend school. That means we can care for your daughter from 7.45 am until 6 pm.

Your daughter will receive a nutritional breakfast on arrival and a sandwich tea is served at 4.30 pm as part of our after-school club. This is in addition to the cooked lunch that she will receive when she attends a full day in Nursery.

Terms and conditions:
• This package is only available to children in the nursery, it does not extend beyond this stage.
• This package is only available on the days where children attend a morning and an afternoon session combined.

Charitable status. Highfield School is a Registered Charity, number 309103. It exists to provide an all-round education for girls.

Highgate Junior School

Cholmeley House, 3 Bishopswood Road, London N6 4PL
Tel: 020 8340 9193
Fax: 020 8342 7273
email: jsoffice@highgateschool.org.uk
pre-prep@highgateschool.org.uk
website: www.highgateschool.org.uk

Chairman of Governors: J F Mills, CBE, MA, BLitt

Principal of Junior School: S M James, BA, MA

Principal of Pre-Preparatory School: Mrs D Hecht, PDCE

Age Range. 3–11 Co-educational.
Number of Day Pupils. Junior (age 7–11): 320 boys and girls; Pre-Prep (age 3–7): 130 boys and girls.
Fees per term (2016–2017). Junior School: £5,990; Pre-Preparatory School: £5,655 (Reception–Year 2), £2,825 (Nursery). Fees are inclusive of lunch (exc Nursery) and the use of books.

Pupils are prepared for Highgate School only. (*See entry in HMC section.*)

Entry to the Pre-Preparatory School is by individual assessment for entry at 3+. Entry to the Junior School is by test and interview at the age of 7. Transfer to the Senior School is at 11+.

The Pre-Preparatory School and the Junior School are both housed in self-contained buildings, located in Bishopswood Road, N6.

The School is well situated close to Hampstead Heath and has excellent facilities as the result of an ongoing development programme. There are several acres of playing fields attached; the Mallinson Sports Centre (which includes a 25-metre indoor pool) is shared with the Senior School, and a newly completed all-weather sports pitch.

A broad and balanced curriculum is followed with art, drama, music, games, ICT and design technology all playing an important part.

Charitable status. Sir Roger Cholmeley's School at Highgate is a Registered Charity, number 312765. The aims and objectives of the charity are educational, namely the maintenance of a school.

Hilden Grange School
Alpha Plus Group

Dry Hill Park Road, Tonbridge, Kent TN10 3BX
Tel: 01732 351169 / 01732 352706
Fax: 01732 377950 / 01732 773360
email: office@hildengrange.co.uk
website: www.hildengrange.co.uk
Twitter: @HildenGrange
Facebook: /HildenGrange

Headmaster: **J Withers**, BA Hons

Deputy Head: Mrs R Jubber, BSc, HDE

Age Range. 3–13 Co-educational.
Number of Pupils. 340: 240 Boys and 100 Girls.
Fees per term (2016–2017). Prep School £4,740, Pre-Prep £3,565, Nursery: £47.60 per day, £30.60 per morning, £23.80 per afternoon. Lunches are provided at £220–£250 per term.

Hilden Grange provides a friendly, secure and stimulating environment where children enjoy learning and participating in all aspects of school life.

We offer high standards of teaching and learning, excellent pastoral care and outstanding opportunities in art, music, drama and sport. Both inside and outside the classroom we strive to help each child achieve their own level of excellence – to do their best.

Though links are especially strong with Tonbridge and Sevenoaks boys and girls are prepared for all Independent Senior Schools and Grammar Schools at 11+ and 13+. We have an impressive record of success in this area. Examination results rank among the highest in Kent, and in the past ten years, all pupils gained entry to their chosen school at 13. Boys and girls who show special promise sit for scholarships to the school of their choice, and our track record in this area is excellent. 121 scholarships have been gained in the past ten years in areas as diverse as music, drama, technology and sport as well as traditional academic scholarships. Pupils benefit from specialist teaching in all subjects from Year 3, dedicated staff, and class sizes that average 16.

The School stands in about eight acres of attractive grounds in the residential area of North Tonbridge. Boys and girls are accepted into the Nursery at 3+ or at 4+ into the Pre-Preparatory Department within the school grounds, and at 7 into the main school. Tonbridge School Chorister awards may be gained; at present there are ten Choristers.

There is an outdoor heated swimming pool, a dedicated Sports Hall, all-weather tennis courts, Science Laboratories, Music Rooms, an Art and Design area, a Library, a Learning Support Area, a dining hall and two Information Technology Rooms, with networks of personal computers. An extensive building program was completed in September 2012 providing new education and communal facilities which are enjoyed by the whole school.

The Headmaster, staff and children welcome visitors and are pleased to show them around the School.

Hilden Oaks School & Nursery

38 Dry Hill Park Road, Tonbridge, Kent TN10 3BU
Tel: 01732 353941
Fax: 01732 353942
email: secretary@hildenoaks.co.uk
website: www.hildenoaks.co.uk
Twitter: @HildenOaks

Chair of Governors: Mr D Walker

Headmistress: **Mrs Katy Joiner**, NNEB, BEd Hons, QTS, MEd

Age Range. 3 months–11 years Co-educational.
Number of Children. 194.
Fees per term (2016–2017). Nursery (5 mornings per week inc lunch 8.15–12.30): Under 2s £2,275, Over 2s £2,135, Over 3s £2,030. Reception £2,995, Years 1 & 2 £3,350, Years 3 & 4 £3,770, Years 5 & 6 £3,996.

Hilden Oaks School, founded in 1919, became an Educational Trust in 1965. It is located in a residential area of north Tonbridge and the Trust owns all the land and buildings.

Hilden Oaks prides itself on being a happy, family school where every child is helped and encouraged to develop their potential and independent learning in a caring, stimulating and purposeful environment. We maintain high academic standards while expecting good manners and consideration to others at all times. This is reflected in the active parents' association, close liaison between parents and staff and the school's close involvement with the local community.

In the Pre-School and Pre-Prep, children are given a solid foundation upon which they can build, with additional specialist teachers for Computing, French, Music and PE. The Prep school has specialist teachers for Science, Computing, French, Music and PE. All forms are taught by form teachers for the core subjects.

Our pupils enjoy taking part in Music and Drama with regular opportunities to perform. They also enjoy competitive sport in house matches and against other schools. Extra-curricular activities include Choir, Drama, Art, Computing and Games. A late room operates where children are provided with tea. Prep is supervised for the older children while the younger children can relax and play.

All pupils are prepared for both the Common Entrance examination at 11 and the 11+ examination for entry to grammar schools. Our results in these examinations put us among the top prep schools in Kent.

Hilden Oaks offers a challenging and supportive environment designed to inspire children to life-long learning.

Charitable status. Hilden Oaks School is a Registered Charity, number 307935. It exists to provide education for children.

Hoe Bridge School

Hoe Place, Old Woking, Surrey GU22 8JE
Tel: Prep School: 01483 760018/760065
            Pre-Prep: 01483 772194
Fax: 01483 757560
email: enquiriesprep@hoebridgeschool.co.uk
            enquiriespreprep@hoebridgeschool.co.uk
website: www.hoebridgeschool.co.uk

Co-educational Preparatory and Pre-Preparatory School.

Chairman of Governors: Ian Katté

Headmaster: **N Arkell**, BSc

Deputy Headmaster: G D P Scott, BEd Exeter

Head of Pre-Prep: **Mrs Linda Renfrew**, MA, PGCE

Age Range. 2½–14.
Number of Children. Prep 285, Pre-Prep 214.
Fees per term (2016–2017). Day: Prep £4,290–£4,870 (including lunch); Pre-Prep £1,880–£3,420 (including lunch).

Hoe Bridge School is set in a perfect location on the outskirts of Woking surrounded by 22 acres of beautiful grounds and woodland and is only 20 minutes from London.

At the heart of Hoe Bridge stands the stunning 17th century mansion, Hoe Place. Hoe Place is steeped in history and was once the favourite retreat for Lady Castlemaine, one of the mistresses of King Charles II. Major development has taken place over the past few years and the school now boasts outstanding 21st century facilities. These facilities are second to none and we are immensely proud of the successes and achievements of our children as they take full advantage of all that is available to them here. The children are equally proud to call Hoe Bridge their school.

The Pre-Prep department is located in its own purpose-built building and achieved 'Outstanding' throughout at our last inspection. From Nursery to Year 2 the creative curriculum followed at the Pre-Prep enables the children to learn through play, adventure, discovery and experience.

Transition to the Prep Department is seamless and as children mature they become increasingly independent learners in preparation for the move to senior school. The results achieved by the children across the ability range are outstanding leading to success at some of the country's leading schools. The pupils are inspired by dedicated staff, lessons are rigorous and interactive and achievement is excellent.

Alongside the academics sport, music, art and drama play a major part throughout the school and children excel in many areas: end-of-year productions; sporting excellence achieving national success in netball and hockey, county success in cricket and football; individual musical success in national youth orchestras and choirs and a spectacular annual art exhibition. Scholarships in all these areas are won every year to a variety of schools across the country. "The pupils' successes in academic work, sport and music, both individually and in groups, are due to their excellent attitudes to learning." Latest ISI Inspection Report.

Senior pupils in Years 7 and 8 take part in regular extra-curricular activities such as Bush Craft weekends, French trips, cricket and netball tours and are challenged by preparing and presenting a gourmet meal to their parents. It is at this stage of their time at Hoe Bridge that they take on extra responsibility becoming prefects and role models to the younger children.

The atmosphere of every school is unique and we consider the strength and attraction of Hoe Bridge to lie in the atmosphere here. Created by the staff and children it combines warmth, care, good relations and pride in achievement. The children spend ten years at Hoe Bridge. These are formative years and they should be ten happy and rewarding ones and our aim is to do the very best for each child. Standards and targets are realistic, though set as high as possible. The bright are challenged and the less able supported; we endeavour to instil confidence in all our children. Visitors are amazed how happy the children are, how determined they are to succeed and how much they care about each other.

The School has an extremely good reputation and we are constantly striving to preserve the atmosphere, improve our results and explore all possibilities for enriching both the School and the children.

Charitable status. Hoe Bridge School is a Registered Charity, number 295808. It exists to provide a rounded education for children aged 2½–14.

Holme Grange School

Heathlands Road, Wokingham, Berkshire RG40 3AL

Tel: 0118 9781566
Fax: 0118 9770810
email: school@holmegrange.org
website: www.holmegrange.org
Twitter: @HolmeGrangeHead
Facebook: /holmegrange

Chairman of Governors: A Finch, Former Company Director

Head: **Mrs Claire Robinson**, BA, PGCE, NPQH

Age Range. 3–16 Co-educational. Admission to Year 9 commenced September 2015.

Number of Pupils. 394: 223 boys, 171 girls.

Fees per term (2016–2017). Little Grange Nursery £1,855–£3,230; Pre-Preparatory: £3,450 (Reception), £3,510 (Years 1–2); Prep: £4,420 (Years 3–4), £4,530 (Years 5–10), with an option to pay over 10 months. Reductions for second and subsequent children.

The School is a Day School receiving pupils from a wide catchment area and holiday care is available throughout the school holidays.

The School occupies a large country mansion, to which many additional facilities have been added, including an outdoor classroom, and most recently an additional science laboratory, food technology room, common room and additional classrooms. September sees the completion of a 300-seat Performing Arts Theatre, Music School and Drama Suite and a new block housing a dining room, kitchens and eight additional classrooms. An extension to the Sports Hall has also been completed.

The School is set in just over 20 acres of grounds comprising grass pitches, all-weather surfaces and woodland walks for the children to explore. Specialist teaching and facilities for Music, Art and Technology, Dance, Performing Arts, Science, ICT and Sport enhance our provision and support the individual development of all our pupils. Holme Grange is one of the first schools in the area to have gained Forest School status and has three qualified Forest Leaders on the Staff, thus allowing opportunities for children to achieve and develop confidence through hands-on learning

in a woodland environment. The recently erected Polytunnel provides opportunities for pupils to learn about sustainable education while the chickens and ducks not only supply to the school kitchens but also enable the pupils to learn about lifecycles in a very hands-on manner.

Little Grange is an established Nursery for 3 and 4 year olds in its own safe, secure environment within the School grounds, providing flexible education either part or full day including lunch and tea. All children may stay to 5.55 pm.

We are non-selective and both welcome and cater for pupils of a wide range of ability. We aim to foster confidence and a love of learning across the age range. Pupils are accepted from the start of the term in which they turn 3 providing continuous education until they take the Common Entrance or Scholarship examinations (Academic, Art, Music) for Senior Independent Schools. At both there is an enviable record of success. In September 2015, we successfully admitted our first Year 9 pupils and will be preparing students for their GCSE examinations in Year 11.

The Headteacher is assisted by a highly qualified and experienced teaching staff with classroom assistants in the Pre-Prep and NNEB assistants in Little Grange. There is an Accelerated Learning Centre giving help to those children with special needs.

The School's policy is to set high standards, to establish good all-round personalities and to give inspiration for each pupil's life. Our aim is to create an environment where every child can thrive. We appreciate children's differences and respond to their individual needs. In 2013 we were awarded the prestigious NACE Challenge Award for More Able, Gifted and Talented Pupils in recognition of the high quality work by the whole school in challenging all pupils to achieve their best.

At Holme Grange we offer excellence in personalised learning – a rare school that caters equally well for pupils at both ends of the academic continuum. We believe in our pupils and instil a belief in themselves.

We develop intellectual character through our learning habits and the ethos throughout the school is one of warmth and friendliness – questioning; divergent thinking and the freedom to learn from mistakes are all encouraged. Pupils are inspired to take responsibility for their own learning, develop good work habits and gain a sense that learning can thrill and invigorate.

We deliver a rounded education by providing opportunities in sport, the arts, languages, technology and a wide range of activities, maximising opportunities for success for all. We hope to inspire your child both in and outside of the classroom. At Holme Grange School, we foster self-reliance, self-discipline and self-confidence in a caring community where children gain interests and characteristics that give them a head start for life.

At Holme Grange we will not only unlock your child's potential but will also foster within them, a passion for learning. Our pupils are prepared to succeed in an ever changing, competitive world. We offer challenge, we strive to inspire, develop confidence, provide opportunity and realise potential in every child – and now up to the age of 16.

We are committed to providing the very best education. Academic standards are excellent. We provide our pupils with a toolkit to live their lives and when they eventually enter the adult world, we can be confident they will do so well prepared with a real life foundation for every challenge they will face.

Life in our school is a journey of exploration, and discovery. We are a holistic school offering an all-round education, bursting with life and vitality.

The School is a Trust, administered by a board of Governors who have considerable experience in education and business.

Charitable status. Holme Grange Limited is a Registered Charity, number 309105. It exists to serve the local community in providing an all-round education for boys and girls.

Holmewood House

Barrow Lane, Langton Green, Tunbridge Wells, Kent TN3 0EB

Tel: 01892 860006
Fax: 01892 863970
email: welcome@holmewoodhouse.co.uk
            registrar@holmewoodhouse.co.uk
website: www.holmewoodhouse.co.uk

Chairman of the Governors: J J Thompson, BSc

Headmaster: **J D B Marjoribanks**, BEd Hons, Dip d'Et Fr

Deputy Headmaster: J Wyld, BA Hons, PGCE

Age Range. 3–13.
Number of Pupils. 440 Boys and Girls.
Fees per term (2016–2017). Day Pupils: Years 5–8 £5,935, Years 3 & 4 £5,815, Pre-Prep £3,365–£3,880, Nursery £1,835–£2,710. Boarders: £7,020. There are reductions for third and fourth siblings, and children of Old Holmewoodians. Scholarships are available for entry into Years 3–7; sports, art and music awards are also available for children showing talent in these areas and entering Years 5–8.

The school was founded in 1945. The school is a Charitable Educational Trust with a Board of Governors. Holmewood stands in over 30 acres of beautiful grounds on the Kent/Sussex border, just outside Tunbridge Wells, which is one hour by rail from London.

A £4.4 million project to create a unique 'Learning Hub' will be completed in January 2017. This multi-functioning space will enhance the school with a digital IT suite, library and additional classrooms providing a light, spacious environment for students and staff. Cloisters lead the way through the building towards the South Lawns.

ISI Inspectors have described our pastoral care as *exemplary. The family atmosphere of the school is outstanding. Pupils have a strong sense of well-being and security.*

The breadth and quality of pupils' achievements are outstanding. Thanks to our highly qualified, dedicated and enthusiastic staff, Holmewood has an outstanding scholastic record in Common Entrance and Scholarship examinations. Despite being essentially a non-selective school, every year our Year 8 pupils gain a large number of scholarships (Academic, Music, Art, DT, Drama and Sport) to senior schools, with 21 proudly achieved in 2016.

A strong Learning Support Department (ISI Inspection: *a strength of the school*) provides additional support for less able pupils and we are proud of the achievements of those children who may require some additional support.

Children follow a broad curriculum throughout the school. For example, French is taught from the Nursery; pupils have separate teaching of Physics, Chemistry and Biology from Year 6; all children learn Latin for two years and Ancient Greek is also available. Year 7 and 8 have the opportunity to study Mandarin, Philosophy, Reasoning, Critical Thinking and Debating.

Holmewood leads the way in the use of educational ICT. The school has 350 networked computers and three networked computer rooms. All classrooms have interactive whiteboards; laptops and tablets are available for use in class.

ISI Inspection: *Outstanding creative development is promoted in Art, Design Technology and Music. A wealth of extra-curricular activities enriches the experience of pupils.*

Our Jubilee Theatre provides a showcase for the many concerts and stunning productions staged by our excellent music and drama departments. Children are encouraged to start learning an instrument in Year 1 (the instrument they most like the sound of!) and the Pre-Prep Orchestra produces a sound to be proud of. From these first musical notes, each year a number of our pupils progress on to win music scholarships to their senior schools.

The Art Department consists of one large studio classroom and a pottery, equipped with kiln, potter's wheel and slab roller. There are after-school Art activities available; and the Community Art Project runs for two terms of the year, involving pupils from five local primary schools and culminating in an exciting final exhibition. Pupils wishing to apply for an art scholarship are encouraged and supported.

In DT, children undertake a range of exciting projects and acquire skills which enable them to produce pieces of practical work way beyond their age. Several pupils have won DT scholarships to senior schools in recent years.

Expert coaching is given in a wide variety of sports and these include rugby, soccer, hockey, gymnastics, netball, cricket, rounders, tennis and table tennis, athletics, shooting, squash, swimming, cross-country, climbing, judo, basketball and dance. We regularly play at national level in most sports. There is a large Sports Hall, an indoor swimming pool, hard tennis courts, three squash courts, an artificial grass surface hockey/football pitch and running track, and an indoor .22 shooting range.

An extensive activity programme which is part of every school day in the Prep School provides all children with the opportunity to 'have a go' at a wide range of activities.

Weekly and flexi boarding are becoming increasingly popular.

Holmewood is an inspiring place for children. ISI Inspection: *Pupils clearly enjoy coming to school and revel in the opportunities the school provides.*

Charitable status. Holmewood House is a Registered Charity, number 279267.

Holmwood House Preparatory School

Chitts Hill, Lexden, Colchester, Essex CO3 9ST

Tel: 01206 574305
Fax: 01206 768269
email: headmaster@holmwood.house
website: www.holmwood.essex.sch.uk

Headmaster: **Alexander Mitchell**, BA Hons, LLCM, PGCE

Age Range. 4–13 Co-educational. Nursery: 6 months to 4 years.
Number of Pupils. 300.
Fees per term (2016–2017). Day Pupils £3,150–£5,565; Boarding: £33 per night. 5 nights boarding for the price of 4. All fees are inclusive; there are no compulsory extras. Nursery fees dependent on hours attended.

Holmwood House was founded in 1922 and stands in 30 acres of grounds only 2 kms from Colchester town centre. Children of all abilities are welcomed and are prepared for the Common Entrance examination and for scholarships to senior independent schools both locally and nationally.

The principal aim of the school is genuine all-round education with high academic standards at its core. Small class sizes, well-qualified staff, superb facilities and high-quality leadership ensure pupils at all levels make excellent progress. The Pre-Prep department enjoys spacious and modern accommodation and with *Forest School*, the children benefit even more from the beautiful grounds through a programme of outdoor learning. Specialist teaching starts in Reception (languages, music, PE, games, swimming) and this increases by age 6/7 (art, science, sports teams). In the Prep school, specialist teaching in all subjects offers pupils an outstanding range and depth of curriculum. Children are increasingly encouraged to take personal ownership of their learning through creative, collaborative and independent activities in all subjects. Pupils' progress is carefully monitored and the relationship between parents and school is an important partnership. Excellent Learning Support is available when required and all teachers have a highly developed understanding of learning needs, ability levels and strategies to enhance progress.

Facilities include 15 acres of sports fields; vibrant, well-equipped classrooms; five squash courts; indoor heated swimming pool; state-of-the-art sports hall; six tennis courts (two covered); floodlit tarmac play area; 2 adventure playgrounds; a permanent stage with sound and lighting systems; superb Art and Design facilities incorporating print and ceramic workshop; separate music facilities. The majority of pupils study at least one musical instrument. There are four well-equipped science laboratories. The ICT facilities, networked to all classrooms including two ICT suites a mobile suite of 130 chromebooks, 40 tablets and various display equipment, also supports pupils' learning.

The extensive sports programme in which every child takes part from age 7, is delivered through generous scheduled sessions of instruction in afternoons and evenings and weekly matches against other schools are a strong feature of the week. Classes and compulsory games are all timetabled conventionally; as are 'preps' –supervised homework. An impressive activities programme provides opportunities for pupils to experience a wide range of options; e.g. archery, fencing, kung-fu, design technology, cookery, knitting, jewellery design, athletics, squash, tennis, badminton, dance and much more. Music and drama flourish particularly, ranging from the large-scale productions to the smaller ensembles.

Flexi boarding is a popular option open to all pupils from Year 5 upwards and is a great start for those children who plan to go on to a senior boarding school, where they can gain a boarding experience in familiar surroundings with their friends, to develop the necessary confidence. There is a wide range of opportunities and activities for boarders to explore and during boarding time, pupils have use of all of the school's facilities, as well as a large cinema-style TV screen for special sports events and lectures, pool tables, table football, air hockey and table tennis.

Pastoral care is excellent and the family atmosphere is palpable. Pupils enjoy exceptionally good relationships with their teachers and the supportive atmosphere encourages them to make the most of their abilities and the abundance of opportunities on offer. Children at Holmwood House are comfortably confident, display excellent manners and have a thirst for learning. The school's guiding principles of care, courtesy and consideration provide a framework in which children can develop their values, emotional intelligence and sense of citizenship within this and the wider community.

Wrap-around care is offered as an option for children from Reception to Year 3 from 7.30 am, up until 6.00 pm, with one member of staff for every 8 children. Pupils in Year 4 upwards also have the option to be dropped off at 7.30 am and all Prep pupils stay until 6.10 pm at no extra cost; this is mandatory for Years 6–8.

Holmwood House Nursery caters for children from 6 months to 4 years. A flexible service is offered so that children can attend either during Holmwood House term only, or for any number of different sessions and options. The Nursery is open for 48 weeks in the year.

We would be pleased to send our prospectus and to welcome visitors to the school.

Holy Cross Preparatory School

George Road, Kingston-upon-Thames, Surrey KT2 7NU
Tel: 020 8942 0729
Fax: 020 8336 0764
email: admissions@holycrossprep.com
website: www.holycrossprepschool.co.uk

Headmistress: **Mrs S Hair**

Age Range. 4–11.
Number of Girls. 250.
Fees per term (2016–2017). £3,960.
Location. The school is situated on a private estate in an attractive area of Kingston Hill.

Facilities. The building, the former home of John Galsworthy, is of both historical and literary interest and provides excellent accommodation for two classes in each year group through the school from Reception to Year Six. The school contains a state-of-the-art sports and performing arts hall, library, Design and Technology facility, Music suite, ICT suite, science and cookery room, art room and 14 classrooms all with computers.

The 8 acres of stunning grounds include two tennis/netball courts, hockey pitch, running track and three large playing areas which have play equipment, including adventure climbing frames. There is a nature trail and ecology area, together with a fountain within the ornamental lawns and a pond which is well used in science lessons.

Educational Philosophy. The school was founded by the Sisters of the Holy Cross, an international teaching order who have been engaged in the work of education since 1844. A sound Christian education is given in an Ecumenical framework. The children are happy, cared for and well disciplined. The emphasis is on developing the God-given gifts of each child to their fullest potential, in a stimulating, friendly atmosphere where high standards of work, behaviour and contribution to the well being of the school community are expected.

Curriculum. There is a broad and relevant curriculum providing a high standard of education. Specialist teaching in French, Music, Physical Education, drama, art and Information Technology. The school has a first rate record of success in Common Entrance and in preparing pupils for top Senior Independent, High and Grammar Schools. The varied extra-curricular activities include ballet and dance, drama, pottery, art and design, music (including cello, piano, flute, clarinet, violin and guitar), sports, technology, languages, debating, judo, tennis, and chess.

Charitable status. Holy Cross Preparatory School is a Registered Charity, number 238426. It is a Roman Catholic School providing excellence in Christian education to local children.

Homefield Preparatory School

Western Road, Sutton, Surrey SM1 2TE

Tel:	020 8642 0965
Fax:	020 8642 0965
email:	registrar@homefield.sutton.sch.uk
website:	www.homefieldprep.school
Twitter:	@HomefieldSchool
Facebook:	/homefield.school

"I don't believe we could have found a better school in the country to bring out the best in both our sons."

Chairman of Governors: Dr Inderpreet Dhingra, BSc Hons, PhD, MBA, FSI

Head: **Mr John Towers**, MA, PGCE, NPQH, FRSA

Age Range. 3–13.
Number of Boys. 400.
Fees per term (2016–2017). Senior Department £4,275; Junior Department: 2nd Year £3,630, 1st Year £3,500; Early Years Department: Reception £2,885, Nursery: £2,785 (full day), £1,855 (mornings only). Lunches: £320 (Seniors and Juniors), £280 (Nursery and Reception).

Homefield is a preparatory school for 400 boys aged 3 to 13, and 50 staff, housed in an extensive purpose-built complex with well-equipped science laboratories, large Art, DT and Music suites, complemented by a spacious Early Years Department, a well-resourced Computing Department and a two-acre adjoining playing field.

Founded in 1870, Homefield has its roots in the 19th century and its branches in the twenty-first. The School has cemented its powerful academic reputation by continuing to achieve a 100% pass rate at Common Entrance to 46 senior schools over the last 10 years. 50 scholarships have been won to senior independent schools for academic, musical, sporting, artistic and all-round accomplishment in the last two years.

Throughout the School's development it has been very careful to preserve the original family ethos and intimacy, together with its reputation for academic excellence, the breadth of extra-curricular sporting, musical and artistic provision and first-class pastoral care. We pride ourselves on achieving fulfilment of individual potential, the openness of communication, the provision of specialist teaching at the earliest appropriate opportunity (French, ICT, Music and Sport from the Foundation Stage), our commitment to best practice and all-round academic, musical, dramatic, sporting and artistic achievements. *"Pupils make a strong contribution to their learning through their highly motivated and enthusiastic attitudes. The quality of pupils' achievements and learning is excellent."* (ISI Inspection, March 2013.)

The school has county or national representatives in table tennis, squash, tennis, athletics, swimming, soccer, rugby, cricket and chess.

Awareness of others is encouraged and the pupils are involved in many fundraising charity events. A wide range of opportunities are available to extend gifted pupils and learning support is available for children with special needs.

We offer academic, sporting, art and music scholarships as well as occasional bursaries.

Daily minibuses run to and from Wimbledon and other areas.

Breakfast and after school clubs are available.

Charitable status. Homefield Preparatory School Trust Limited is a Registered Charity, number 312753. It exists to provide education for boys.

Hornsby House School

Hearnville Road, London SW12 8RS

Tel:	020 8673 7573
Fax:	020 8673 6722
email:	school@hornsbyhouse.org.uk
website:	www.hornsbyhouse.org.uk

Chair of Governors: Mr Huw Davies

Headmaster: **Mr Edward Rees**, BA Ed Hons

Age Range. 4–11.
Number of Pupils. 209 Girls, 208 Boys.
Fees per term (2016–2017). £4,415 (Reception to Year 2), £4,745 (Years 3 to 6). Lunch: £235.

Hornsby House is a thriving IAPS co-educational prep school in Wandsworth, southwest London. At their most recent inspection in November 2010, the Independent Schools Inspectorate judged Hornsby House pupils' overall achievement as "excellent" and found that "pupils achieve high academic standards within a wide and creative curriculum". Pupils' personal development was described as "excellent and a strength of the school". Hornsby House provides a nurturing environment where attainment and happiness are key aims and the children achieve outstanding educational outcomes as a result. In 2016 our Year 6 children won 40 scholarships and awards between them. There are three classes in each year group, a generous staff : pupil ratio and around 430 pupils in the school. Entry into Reception classes is unassessed and is on a first-come, first-served basis with priority being given to siblings. Children wishing to enter the school in year groups above Reception are required to attend an assessment.

There is an extensive co-curricular programme with over 50 clubs, as well as before and after school care. Over half the children in the school play a musical instrument and a third sing in one of the three choirs. Sport is a central part of the curriculum, the staffing level is excellent and the benefits of teamwork are seen clearly in school life as a whole. The school has an outstanding ICT infrastructure, with four classrooms set up as e-learning suites and 120 iPads used to support the children's learning. The majority of leavers go to one of six London day schools: Dulwich College, JAGS, Alleyn's, Emanuel, Streatham & Clapham High School and Whitgift. The remainder move on to other day or boarding schools.

To arrange a visit to see the children at work, please contact the Registrar.

Charitable status. Hornsby House Educational Trust is a Registered Charity, number 800284.

Horris Hill

Newtown, Newbury, Berks RG20 9DJ

Tel:	01635 40594
email:	registrar@horrishill.com
website:	www.horrishill.com
Twitter:	@HorrisHill

Chairman of Governors: Ms M B Lund

Headmaster: **G F Tollit**, BA Hons

Deputy Headmasters:
A W Rendall, BA Hons, PGCE
F J Beardmore-Gray, BA Hons, PGCE

Age Range. 7–13.

Number of Boys. Boarders 100, Day 20.

Fees per term (2016–2017). Boarders £8,610; Day £6,390. (No compulsory Extras)

Horris Hill is one of the leading boys' prep schools in the UK. 120 boys learn in 85 acres of spectacular grounds just south of Newbury; most are boarders, but we enjoy having our few dayboys. Small means that we know the boys and their parents very well and our latest Inspection Reports (see www.horrishill.com) emphasise the fact that pastoral care is outstanding. High expectations in everything ensure a first-class prep school education with confident, charming boys going on to the top independent schools. Most Horris Hill parents choose boys-only schools for the next stage and over half our boys go on to Winchester, Radley and Eton; the remainder going to Sherborne, Harrow, Milton Abbey, Shrewsbury, Bradfield, Marlborough and many others.

Busy weekends, high academic standards, superb music and art, brilliant sport make this a wonderful school to work in for both boys and staff. Come and see for yourselves.

Charitable status. Horris Hill Preparatory School Trust Limited is a Registered Charity, number 307331. It exists to prepare boys for the Senior Independent Schools.

Hunter Hall School

Frenchfield, Penrith, Cumbria CA11 8UA

Tel:	01768 891291
Fax:	01768 899161
email:	office@hunterhall.cumbria.sch.uk
website:	www.hunterhall.co.uk

Chairman of Governors: Mr Peter Kirk

Head: Mrs Donna Vinsome, BEd Hons, MA

Deputy Head: Mrs Antonia Taylor, BA Hons QTS
Foundation Stage Manager and KS1 Coordinator: Mrs Georgina Griffiths, BEd Hons
Bursar: Mrs Joanne Airey

Age Range. 3–11 co-educational.
Number of Pupils. 95.
Fees per term (2016–2017). £2,367 Lower School (Reception to Year 2) £2,742 Upper School (Year 3 to Year 6) including after-school activities. Nursery paid per hour.

Hunter Hall School has grown rapidly from its inception 30 years ago into a thriving and vibrant community, providing high quality education for children aged 3 to 11. Its location is idyllic, in imaginatively converted farm buildings on the outskirts of Penrith and only 2 km from the M6, providing easy access to the attractions of the Lake District and the north of England generally.

It is providing a range of experiences that is important at Hunter Hall and staff recognise that effective learning can take place in a variety of situations. Within the classroom, creativity and independence is emphasised, and the objective is to provide the children with the knowledge, skills and confidence to prosper, not only whilst at Hunter Hall, but also in the schools that they will subsequently join. In the Foundation Stage, the activities that are undertaken are determined by the children, originating from their own interests and needs, then facilitated by the staff. The aim is to stimulate curiosity, interest and excitement in learning, and to encourage self-discipline and develop confidence. These qualities extend as the children move through the school, with the emphasis on providing them with a range of skills to help them to recognise that they have the ability (and courage) to think for themselves. In addition, perseverance and cooperation are especially valued, creating a warm,

friendly and almost tangible sense of community within the school.

The curriculum is broad, and specialist subject teaching is provided from Year 3. Class sizes are small. Teaching facilities are very good, with ICT featuring prominently in learning. Pupils are encouraged to take responsibility for their own progress and to set themselves challenging targets.

Children at Hunter Hall spend a great deal of time outdoors and, indeed, beyond the school boundaries. The environment in the local area lends itself admirably to geographical and historical investigation, as well as providing an unrivalled stage for exploration and adventure as part of our outdoor learning sessions. Participation in Art, Drama and Music is extremely active, with extensive representation at local festivals. The variety and quality of sport that is on offer is equally remarkable, and Hunter Hall children have received wide-ranging recognition at local and national level in recent years.

This is a happy school, in which a Christian ethos of tolerance and respect for each other is dominant. Children (their parents) and staff enjoy spending time here and contributing to the development of the community.

Charitable status. Hunter Hall School Ltd is a Registered Charity, number 1059098.

Hurlingham School

122 Putney Bridge Road, Putney, London SW15 2NQ

Tel:	020 8874 7186
Fax:	020 8875 0372
email:	office@hurlinghamschool.co.uk
website:	www.hurlinghamschool.co.uk

Headmaster: Mr Jonathan Brough, BEd Hons Cantab, NPQH, FCollT

Age Range. 4–11 Co-educational.
Number of Pupils. 326.
Fees per term (2016–2017). £4,985–£5,195.
Location and Facilities. Hurlingham is a non-selective independent preparatory school in Putney, in very close proximity to Wandsworth Park. The modern and spacious building provides excellent facilities which include bright classrooms, a large gym and a dance and drama studio, as well as a science laboratory, art studio, two ICT suites and several music rooms. Recreational space includes a large playground with climbing wall and a nature garden.

Ethos. The School's ethos is to provide a happy, secure atmosphere in which children flourish both academically and personally. Experienced and enthusiastic teachers provide opportunities for the children that strongly promote creativity and independence of thought, essential attributes for a child growing up in the 21st Century. Self-confidence, self-discipline, self-motivation, self-esteem and above all a thirst and enjoyment for learning are nurtured.

Academic. The curriculum is broad, with the aim of providing a balanced and rounded education in which every child is treated as an individual and is encouraged to make the most of their particular talents. The important skills of reading, writing and numeracy are given a high priority in everyday teaching; these are delivered through many exciting cross-curricular topics which bring the children's learning alive and allow them to make sense of the world around them. All children learn French and Spanish in Reception, then choose one for the remainder of their time in school. Latin is taught from Form IV; Thinking Skills and many aspects of Design Technology, including Ceramics, are also greatly enjoyed across the school.

Sport. Hurlingham children are fit and healthy, and all boys and girls participate enthusiastically. Seasonal team games skills are taught in football, rugby, hockey, netball, cricket, gym and athletics. Numerous matches are organised with other local schools throughout the sporting year. Every Summer Term the whole school joins in the traditional Sports Day activities, and a family picnic lunch.

Music. Hurlingham has an excellent music department. The youngest children are encouraged to sing, play simple instruments and enjoy performing. For older pupils there are many opportunities to learn individual instruments, play in ensembles and participate in music concerts. There are several, very popular and talented, choirs and ensemble groups.

Pastoral Care. Strong pastoral care is a very important feature of life at Hurlingham. All staff foster an intimate and welcoming environment centred on family values, with a clear focus on good manners and respect for one another. The House System, School Council and various pupil committees provide the children with wonderful opportunities to support each other and express their views about their own school.

Clubs. Children are encouraged to participate in a wide range of clubs which include: art, ballet, chess, drama, Japanese, karate, music, modern dance, pottery and science. Older children are able to do their homework in school at homework club.

Starting Out. Children begin their life at Hurlingham in Reception which, although contained within the school building, is a separate area allowing children to feel part of the whole school but not overwhelmed by it. The three parallel classrooms (divided according to the children's age) all have direct access on to the playground, thus enabling the teaching of the curriculum to extend outside. There is also a cosy dedicated Hall which provides space for all three forms to join together for group activities, regular access to computers and a quiet place for reading.

Entry. For entry to Reception there is no entrance test or interview. Places are offered in order of registration, although siblings, and those living within 1.2 km of the school, are given priority. Older children are invited to spend a day at Hurlingham and take part in lessons in order to assess their academic ability. Scholarships are available for children joining from 7+ onwards.

School Visits. Appointments should be arranged with the School Office. There is an underground car park which visitors are welcome to use.

Hurstpierpoint College Preparatory School
A Woodard School

Chalker's Lane, Hurstpierpoint, West Sussex BN6 9JS

Tel:	01273 834975 (Prep and Pre-Prep)
Fax:	01273 836900
email:	prepadmissions@hppc.co.uk
website:	www.hppc.co.uk
Twitter:	@Hurst_Prep
Facebook:	/HurstCollege

Chairman of Governors: Mr A Jarvis, BEd, MA, FRSA

Head of Prep School: I D Pattison, BSc Southampton

Deputy Head of Prep School: N J Oakden, BA Wales, NPQH, MEd Buckingham

Heads of Years:
Reception–Year 2: Mrs D Ross, BEd Brighton
Years 3–4: Mrs Z C Taylor-West, BA London

Years 5–6: Mr N J Oakden, BA Wales, MEd Buckingham, NPQH
Year 7: Mrs T Ann Preen, BSc Southampton
Year 8: Ms K A Pattison, BA Wales

Admissions Officer: Mrs C Treadaway

Age Range. 4–13 Co-educational.
Number of Pupils. Prep 280; Pre-Prep 57.
Fees per term (2016–2017). £2,223–£5,180. There are no compulsory extras.

The Prep and Pre-Prep Schools of Hurstpierpoint College (*see entry in HMC section*) share a beautiful 140-acre campus with the College. Although both Schools operate independently of the Senior School, having their own timetable, staff, buildings and Heads, the schools work closely together to offer a first-class programme of education for boys and girls from the age of 4 to 18.

Hurst's Pre-Prep School for children aged 4–7 opened in 2001. It occupies a self-contained unit with well-equipped classrooms and a new outdoor play area, built in 2016. There is one class for each year group.

The Prep School has joint use of many of the College's superb facilities, including a 25m heated indoor swimming pool, theatre, drama and dance studios, music school, large sports hall, tennis courts and full-size AstroTurf hockey pitches.

The aim of the Prep and Pre-Prep is to provide an outstanding education in a secure and happy environment.

The academic programme is exciting and innovative, with independent learning and mobile technology at the heart of our teaching and learning. The children are provided with an excellent grounding in the more traditional subjects and, as they progress through the school, they are encouraged to take more responsibility for their learning in order to develop the qualities and skills required for academic success in the Senior School.

The Sports programme is extensive with Netball, Hockey, Rugby, Football, Rounders, Cricket, Swimming, Tennis and Athletics on offer. In addition there is a wide-ranging activity programme which caters for the interests of all pupils.

The Music, Drama and Dance Departments are also very strong; about half the pupils learn musical instruments. The Preparatory School choir performs at the weekly Chapel service. There are at least three musicals or plays each year involving many children throughout the School.

The College has a dedicated Medical Centre with fully-qualified staff.

Each year a number of scholarship awards are available for entry into Year 7 (11+).

Charitable status. Hurstpierpoint College is a Registered Charity, number 1076498. The College provides a Christian education to boys and girls between the ages of four and eighteen.

Inglefield House
Haberdashers' Monmouth School for Girls Preparatory School

Hereford Road, Monmouth NP25 5XT

Tel:	01600 711205
	01600 711104 (Admissions)
Fax:	01600 711118 (Admissions)
email:	admissions@hmsg.co.uk
website:	www.inglefieldhouse.org
	www.habs-monmouth.org

Chairman of Governors: Mr A W Twiston-Davies

Head: **Mrs H Phillips**, BA Hons, BEd

Age Range. Girls 7–11. Boarding from age 7.
Number of Pupils. 130.
Fees per term (2016–2017). Day £3,484, Boarding £6,333.

Entrance to Inglefield House is selective, but great care is taken to look for potential, not just test performance.

A love of learning and an inquisitive, enthusiastic attitude to life are the cornerstones of our ethos, producing independent, confident girls who also have a very strong sense of responsibility and consideration of others. Girls at Inglefield House are happy and fulfilled, with a sense of fun and a sense of purpose.

A broad but balanced curriculum captures the imagination and allows girls to thrive in a variety of disciplines. Teaching is broadly class based in Years 3 and 4 but is supplemented by specialist teaching in humanities, physical education, modern foreign languages, music and drama. In Years 5 and 6, there is a wider range of subject specialist teaching, ensuring that the girls receive the finest tuition, grow in independence and by fully accessing the excellent senior school facilities, prepare smoothly for the transition into the senior school. This includes use of the science laboratories, the ICT suites, the Home Economics facilities and the Design Technology studios.

With encouragement and a high degree of personal attention, girls are given every opportunity to maximise their potential and achieve academic excellence. This forms just part of a school life which is vibrant, exciting and outward looking. Our location in the Wye Valley allows us to make educational trips to both Cardiff and Bristol with ease, as well as going further afield. Residential trips both in the UK and abroad are highly effective in broadening horizons and increasing a sense of independence as girls move into Years 5 and 6.

The performing arts are a wonderful method of building self-confidence in the young girls at school. Individual music lessons, the school orchestra, choir and string sections offer a chance to flourish at music, with a wide range of dance being taught as part of PE and within the extended curriculum.

Bringing enjoyment and enthusiasm to sport is another of our central aims. Sport plays a big part in school life, with specialist PE teaching and a large number of extracurricular clubs each week. We aim to nurture a love of team sports and to balance this with other activities which the girls can continue to enjoy into their adult lives. Making the most of our membership of IAPS, teams compete on a national level in a variety of sports, including hockey, netball, gymnastics and fencing. Inglefield girls have the advantage of using the senior school facilities including the 25-metre swimming pool, the gymnasium, a full-size sports hall and astroturf pitches.

There is a relaxed, warm relationship between children and staff, whether boarders or day girls. Boarding creates a real sense of community throughout Inglefield, where girls thrive in a safe, friendly environment which produces thoughtful, intelligent, compassionate girls who are well equipped for senior school life.

A number of scholarships are awarded each year to girls moving on to the senior school. (*For further details see Haberdashers' Monmouth School for Girls entry in the GSA section.*)

Inglefield House enjoys a close relationship with its brother school, The Grange, Monmouth Preparatory School and various joint events take place during the year.

Charitable status. William Jones's Schools Foundation is a Registered Charity, number 525616.

Ipswich Preparatory School

3 Ivry Street, Ipswich, Suffolk IP1 3QW
Tel: 01473 282800
Fax: 01473 400067
email: prepadmissions@ipswich.school
website: www.ipswich.school

Chairman of Governors: Mr H E Staunton, BA, FCA

Headteacher: **Mrs A H Childs**, BA QTS, PGC PSE, Dip Ed, MA

Age Range. 2–11.
Number of Pupils. 293.
Fees per term (2016–2017). Years 4–6 £3,805; Year 3 (inc lunch) £4,002; Reception, Years 1 & 2 (inc lunch) £3,652; Nursery (inc lunch): £31.95 per am/pm session, £60.43 per whole day.

The Preparatory School has its own staff and Headteacher. It is located just across the road from the senior school (*see Ipswich School entry in HMC section*).

The school seeks to provide a learning environment which allows pupils to develop skills and personal qualities. The curriculum is planned to encourage the children to develop lively, enquiring minds and appropriate emphasis is placed on securing for each child a firm foundation of skills in literacy and numeracy. The broad, balanced curriculum offered provides a breadth of experience which is suitable for children of primary age. High academic standards are reached by the pupils, but in addition, they are encouraged to develop skills in music, art, drama and sport.

Children's happiness is considered essential and the School works closely with parents to ensure a partnership which provides the best possible care for all girls and boys.

The school enjoys the advantage of sharing Senior School facilities such as playing fields, sports hall, swimming pool, theatre/concert hall and the Chapel. The Prep School has its own Art, Design Technology, ICT and Science facilities.

Charitable status. Ipswich Preparatory School is part of Ipswich School, which is a Registered Charity, number 310493. It exists for the purpose of educating children.

James Allen's Preparatory School

East Dulwich Grove, London SE22 8TE
Tel: 020 8693 0374
email: kate.garmeson@jags.org.uk
website: www.jags.org.uk
Twitter: @JAGS_Prep
Facebook: /JAGSschool

Chair of Governors: Mrs Frances Read, MA Cantab, FCA, MSI

Head: **Miss Finola Stack**, BA Hons, MA Ed Open, PGCE, Mont Dip

Age Range. Girls 4–11.
Number of Pupils. Day: 300 Girls.
Fees per term (2016–2017). £4,985.

James Allen's Preparatory School (JAPS) is an independent day school for girls aged between 4 and 11.

We see primary education as vital to the success of any child's education. We plan for the children to progress at their own pace, benefiting from working together in small groups. With a well-devised and balanced curriculum, the children reach high standards without the stress of blatant competition and are able to enjoy the many and varied opportunities which we offer, particularly in sport, drama, music and art.

The school has an excellent staff/pupil ratio of approximately 1:10 and provides specialist teachers in Art, DT, ICT, Music, PE and Science. In French the children are taught from 4 years onwards using the immersion method.

The Pre-Prep School (for pupils aged 4–6) is housed in a beautiful Edwardian building. The Middle School (for pupils aged 7–11) is a large, modern building with a first-class Hall and Library, as well as specialist rooms for Science, ICT, DT and Art. Some facilities (the theatre, swimming pool and games fields) are shared with our senior school, James Allen's Girls' School.

JASSPA is the James Allen's Saturday School for the Performing Arts for pupils and siblings and other non-JAPS pupils. This is entirely voluntary and complements the week's activities: music lessons, dance and drama are all offered.

Pupils normally enter the school in the year in which they are 4 or 7 on 1 September. Assessments take place the preceding January. 36 places are available for 4+ entry and up to 15 places available for 7+ entry. At 11, girls normally progress to JAGS by means of an open competitive examination, where JAPS girls regularly win many scholarships. (*See JAGS entry in GSA section.*)

Charitable status. James Allen's Girls' School is a Registered Charity, number 1124853. The purpose of the charity is the conduct at Dulwich of a day school in which there shall be provided a practical, liberal and religious education for girls.

Keble School

Wades Hill, Winchmore Hill, London N21 1BG

Tel: 020 8360 3359
Fax: 020 8360 4000
email: office@kebleprep.co.uk
website: www.kebleprep.co.uk

Chairman of Governors: Mr P Ruocco, MBA, BA Hons, D Inst M

Headmaster: **Mr G P McCarthy**, BSc Hons

Deputy Head: Mr P Gill, BA Hons

Age Range. 4–13.
Number of Boys. 220 Day Boys.
Fees per term (2016–2017). £3,760–£4,760.

As confirmed by the ISI Inspectors in September 2011, the warm and friendly atmosphere that exists at Keble ensures that the boys are well-motivated, keen to learn and able to mature at their own pace. Strong pastoral care is regarded as a key element in the boys' overall development and well-being, along with the encouragement of courteous and considerate behaviour.

The academic staff comprises 23 qualified graduate teachers, 5 classroom assistants and 2 Learning Support teachers. The buildings are well maintained and facilities are regularly updated. The school has an ambitious ICT development programme.

The average class size in the school is 15, although many classes are taught in half-groups and sets as the boys progress through the school. Boys follow the Foundation Stage in Reception. General subject teachers cover the academic curriculum in Years 1 to 4, with subject specialists following on from Year 5 onwards. The National Curriculum is used as a guide to curriculum development. Art, Music, PE, ICT,

PSHE and Games are introduced at appropriate stages and are included within the timetable. Boys are encouraged to learn a musical instrument, sing in the choir, perform in plays and concerts, and play an active part in the wide range of sports on offer.

Football, rugby and cricket are the major team games. Further opportunities exist to participate in hockey, swimming, basketball, athletics, cross country and tennis. There is a wide range of lunchtime and after-school activities and clubs, including drama, gardening and chess. There are also numerous educational outings and four residential trips.

Boys are not required to pass an assessment to gain entry into the school at Reception. Boys wishing to join the school at a later stage in Year 1 or above are assessed in order to ensure that they will fit comfortably into their new surroundings.

Boys are prepared for entry to senior independent schools through Common Entrance and Scholarship examinations at 13+. The school has a strong record of success in placing boys in the senior school which is right for them. In recent years, these schools include Aldenham, City of London, Haberdashers' Aske's, Highgate, Haileybury, Mill Hill, St Albans, St Columba's, University College and Westminster.

Charitable status. Keble Preparatory School (1968) Limited is a Registered Charity, number 312979. It exists to provide education for boys.

Kensington Prep School
GDST

596 Fulham Road, London SW6 5PA

Tel: 020 7731 9300
email: enquiries@kenprep.gdst.net
website: www.kensingtonprep.gdst.net

Founded in 1873.

Kensington Prep School is part of the GDST (Girls' Day School Trust). The GDST is the leading network of independent girls' schools in the UK. As a charity that owns and runs 24 schools and two academies, it reinvests all its income in its schools. For further information about the Trust, see p. xxiii or visit www.gdst.net.

Head: **Mrs P J F Lynch**, MA, PGCE

Age Range. 4–11 years.
Number of Girls. 295.
Fees per term (2016–2017). £5,299.

Since 1997 the School has been based in Fulham. The school is set in an acre of grounds and has large bright classrooms with specialist rooms for ICT, Art, Drama, Music, Science and Design Technology. The large playground provides fantastic play facilities, netball and tennis courts and a pond for environmental studies.

We have just completed an innovative £2.7m building project 'Creating Spaces for Growing Minds' transforming the school, providing ground-breaking facilities for independent exploration, self-directed learning and collaborative work. These include spacious classroom breakout areas with retractable doors, a high-tech 'Explore Floor', multi-media recording studio, and an Eco-Greenhouse. The specialist Drama, Art, Science and ICT suites have also been refurbished and the school is fully accessible throughout for pupils with two new lifts.

The school aims to provide an excellent, broadly-based but strongly academic curriculum. Independence, individuality and questioning thinkers are encouraged. Girls enjoy challenging and interesting work in a stimulating and caring environment, whilst being prepared for entry to leading boarding and day schools at 11+.

The School achieved the highest possible grades across the board in the recent Inspection by the Independent Schools Inspectorate and the quality of pupils' achievements and learning was rated 'exceptional'. Kensington Prep was named 'Independent Prep School of the Year' by the Sunday Times Parent Power for 2009–10 in recognition of its "consistently strong academic results, inspiring leadership and innovative curriculum".

Entry to the School is selective and the main entry points are at 4+ with a small intake at 7+. Occasional places do occur throughout the School from time to time.

Charitable status. Kensington Prep School is part of The Girls' Day School Trust, which is a Registered Charity, number 306983.

Kent College Junior School

Harbledown, Canterbury, Kent CT2 9AQ

Tel:	01227 762436
Fax:	01227 763880
email:	prepenquiries@kentcollege.co.uk
website:	www.kentcollege.com
Twitter:	@AndyCarterKentC
Facebook:	@kentcollege
LinkedIn:	/kent-college-canterbury

Chair of Governors: Lorna Cocking

Head Master: A J Carter, BEd Hons

(Full staff list can be found on the Kent College website.)

Age Range. 3–11 Co-educational.
Number of Pupils. Juniors (Day and Boarding) 156.
Fees per term (2016–2017). Juniors: Boarders £8,125; Day Pupils (including lunch): Year 6 £5,130, Year 5 £5,098, Year 4 £4,986, Year 3 £4,494, Year 2 £3,608, Year 1 £3,587, Reception £3,313, Nursery: £2,740 (5 full days).

GREAT – the foundation stones to educational success.

The GREAT programme (which stands for Gifted, Really Enthusiastic, Able and Talented) offered by the unrestricted curriculum structure at the Nursery, Infant and Junior School at Kent College is key to early success. Setting in core subjects is designed to accelerate progress and gives children the option to develop particular skills, be they academic, art, drama, music or sport. All children are on individualised programmes to maximise their academic potential and are set for English and Maths according to their needs and talents rather than their chronological age.

Parents can also choose for their child to enjoy more focus in a particular area: academic challenge; Kent Test preparation; art; design technology; drama; music or sport. Students do not have to sit the Kent Test, however, those that do enjoy excellent results. Scholarships to senior schools are targeted and in recent years there has been a success rate of over 50%.

Whilst the school day finishes at 4 pm there is a full range of after-school clubs and activities, which all the children can enjoy until 6 pm each evening. There are also holiday activity weeks meaning the school is open for at least 47 weeks a year.

Boarding places are available on a full, weekly or occasional basis and accompanied travel home is available to London's St Pancras station.

All in all a win-win situation resulting in the students being well equipped for senior school education and parents given the peace of mind so that they can focus on their busy working lives.

Charitable status. Kent College, Canterbury is a Registered Charity, number 307844. The School was founded to provide education within a supportive Christian environment and is a member of the Methodist Independent Schools Trust.

Kent College Preparatory School
Pembury

Old Church Road, Pembury, Tunbridge Wells, Kent TN2 4AX

Tel:	01892 820218
Fax:	01892 820214
email:	prepschool@kentcollege.kent.sch.uk
website:	www.kent-college.co.uk
Twitter:	@KentCollegePemb
Facebook:	@KentCollegePemb
LinkedIn:	/kent-college-pembury

Chairman of Governors: Mr E Waterhouse

Head: **Mr Nik Pears**, BEd Hons Cantab

Age Range. Girls 3–11.
Number of Girls. 200.
Fees per term (2016–2017). Day Girls £2,943–£4,390. Full Boarders £8,000. Weekly Boarders £8,000. Flexi-boarding £48 per night. All fees include lunches. There are no compulsory extras.

The school has its own purpose-built accommodation on a beautiful 75-acre site, shared with Kent College Pembury (Senior School), and benefits from facilities such as a 300-seater state-of-the-art theatre, specialist Library & Arts Centre, two large sports hall, indoor heated swimming pool with small learners pool, dining hall and dance studio.

The school believes that happy, confident children are successful ones and the girls love coming to school. Academic standards are high, but it is never forgotten that there is more to childhood and learning than examinations. Girls are successfully prepared in small classes (average 16) for a wide range of senior schools at age 11, but the school is not a crammer.

The curriculum is broad and balanced, based on the National Curriculum. All pupils benefit from specialist teaching in swimming, dance, drama, ICT, PE and music, with specialist French teaching from Nursery class.

Main intakes are in to the Early Years Department which incorporates the Nursery and Reception classes for girls rising 3 to 5. The department has its own wing of the School with light, colourful and well-resourced classrooms and its own outside playground areas. The Foundation Stage Curriculum is followed and by the end of the Reception year some of the pupils will be working at the lower stages of Key Stage One.

Performing arts is an important part of the curriculum with opportunities for music, drama and dance at all ages. The youngest pupils, aged 3, can do optional ballet lessons and girls enjoy specialist workshops at the recently launched Kent College Theatre Academy. The school has a choir and an orchestra and there are regular concerts and drama productions. There is a good range of sporting opportunities including The Kent College Gymnastics Academy, netball, hockey, tennis, rounders, cross-country, swimming, trampolining and athletics.

The school prides itself on providing an exciting and varied programme of over 35 clubs and activities and there is a good ethos of participation. The curriculum is supported with interesting trips and days out, and residential holidays for Years 5 and 6. A variety of well-known authors have visited the school to run workshops.

An After School Care facility is available for girls in Nursery upwards and is extremely popular for our working families. Full and weekly boarders are accepted from age 10, with flexi boarders accepted from age 8. All are part of a small, family-run Junior boarding house in which girls have a secure, happy and homely environment. Prospective boarders are invited to spend a day and overnight stay with us to give them a feel for the school. There is a 20% discount for Forces families.

Entry to Nursery, Reception, Years 1 and 2 are based on availability of places. Pupils in Years 3–6 are required to sit entry tests in English and mathematics. The Head is pleased to welcome visitors and to show them around the school.

Charitable status. Kent College Pembury is a Registered Charity, number 307920. It is a Christian school specialising in girls' education.

Kew College

24–26 Cumberland Road, Kew, Surrey TW9 3HQ

Tel: 020 8940 2039
Fax: 020 8332 9945
email: enquiries@kewcollege.com
website: www.kewcollege.com

Chairman of Governors: Mrs Sue Ouseley

Head: **Mrs Marianne Austin**, BSc Hons, MA Hons, ACA, PGCE

Age Range. 3–11 Co-educational.
Number of Pupils. 296.
Fees per term (2016–2017). £2,350–£3,675.

Kew College was established in 1953 and was made into a charitable trust in 1985 by its founder, Elizabeth Hamilton-Spry, to ensure the long-term continuity of the school. The school's ethos is to ensure all pupils have an excellent grounding in the basics, but with a strong emphasis on areas such as art, music, drama and sport to develop the whole child.

Kew College's style is described as traditional, yet imaginative and the atmosphere is happy and lively with a team of enthusiastic, caring and dedicated staff to help fulfil each child's potential. Pupils enjoy excellent facilities including specialist ICT and science labs. The ISI inspection in October 2010 concluded that '*Pupils achieve well across the curriculum and extra-curricular activities, and standards are exceptionally high in all aspects of English and Mathematics. The quality of their reading, writing and mathematical skills is in advance of their years. Pupils also exhibit great creativity, particularly in art work. Pupils display enthusiasm for their lessons and good learning skills. Pupils' personal development and the school's arrangements for welfare, health and safety are outstanding. Pupils develop into exceptionally moral beings. Pupils leave the school as well-balanced personalities. The school is a caring community where pupils are thoughtfully and skilfully looked after by the pastoral care of the whole staff, which contributes strongly to their personal development.*' In the Early Years Foundation Stage the inspectors commented that '*Children are happy and secure and their needs are met well. Careful attention is given to children's welfare and safety; their exemplary behaviour and excellent personal development are strengths.*'

Beyond the core curriculum pupils enjoy participating in lively mixed-year clubs within school on Friday afternoons including graphic design, origami, Sudoku and table tennis. A wide range of weekly after-school clubs includes chess, computer, debating, fencing, Spanish and jazz dance, with arts and crafts and little golfers for the younger pupils. There

are also school choirs, a wind band and string orchestra. The school takes full advantage of its London location for educational visits. There are residential field trips in Years 3, 4, 5 and 6. In their final term, Year 6 pupils enjoy a week-long stay at a château in France improving their language skills, cultural knowledge and doing outward bound team activities.

At 11+ pupils not only achieve places through competitive entrance examinations to selective London day schools but also win a good number of awards.

Charitable status. Kew College is a Registered Charity, number 286059.

Kew Green Preparatory School

Layton House, Ferry Lane, Kew Green, Richmond, Surrey TW9 3AF

Tel: 020 8948 5999
Fax: 020 8948 4774
email: secretary@kgps.co.uk
website: www.kgps.co.uk

Chairman of Governors: Dr Helen Ireland

Headmaster: **Mr Jem Peck**

Age Range. 4–11 Co-educational.
Number of Pupils. 260.
Fees per term (2016–2017). £5,405.

This non-selective school is housed in an attractive building and grounds directly next door to the Royal Botanical Gardens. The front of the school overlooks Kew Green, which is used for games, and the back of the school has a good-sized playground which looks onto the River Thames.

In a non-pressurised, caring environment, KGPS produces excellent academic results, sending its pupils to London's best independent senior schools.

The children are encouraged to use philosophy and ethical thinking throughout the curriculum, which includes English, maths, science, French, RE, music, design & technology, art, games/PE and computer studies. All Upper School children attend a summer term Residential Week where cross-curricular studies are applied in a non-urban environment.

There are many after-school clubs and sports activities including three choirs, an orchestra and rock band. Individual tuition is offered in piano, violin, brass, woodwind, cello, saxophone, guitar, drums and singing.

An 8.00 am to 6.00 pm All-Day Care service is offered to parents at an extra charge.

The school is noted for its warm, happy atmosphere where parents play a full part in enriching the curriculum and social life. Off-site visits and guest workshops presented by noted visitors are a regular feature of education at Kew Green.

The school is always heavily over-subscribed and registration is recommended from birth. A prospectus and registration form may be obtained from the school secretary.

Kilgraston Junior Years

Bridge of Earn, Perthshire PH2 9BQ

Tel: 01738 812257
Fax: 01738 813410
email: junioryears@kilgraston.com

website: www.kilgraston.com
Twitter: @kilgraston
Facebook: @kilgrastonschool

Chairman of Board of Governors: Mr Timothy Hall

Head of Kilgraston School: Mrs Dorothy MacGinty

Head of Junior Years: **Mr Andrew Stewart**

Age Range. Girls 5–12.
Number of Pupils. 49 Girls
Fees per term (2016–2017). Day £3,385–£4,295, Boarding £7,165.

Kilgraston Junior Years is the junior school for Kilgraston, a leading boarding and day school for girls aged 5–18 in Scotland. Located in its own building, the Junior Years is surrounded by 54 acres of stunning parkland in Bridge of Earn, three miles from the centre of Perth, 45 minutes from Edinburgh and an hour's drive from Glasgow.

Admission to Kilgraston Junior Years is by interview. Girls are able to progress to Kilgraston Senior School, or prepare for scholarship exams for Kilgraston and Common Entrance exams for other schools. The academic standard is high with all pupils completing the Junior Years and achieving a place in their senior school of choice.

Pupils are taught by class teachers until the age of nine, with specialist teachers for PE, French, music and drama. Form teachers hold pastoral responsibility for the pupils and classes are small with provision for additional support needs. From age ten, the curriculum becomes more specialised with increasing input from specialised subject staff and use of the facilities in the Senior School. Pastoral care is the responsibility of a tutor.

The core academic curriculum is enhanced by a wide range of co-curricular subjects. While academic excellence is a priority, art, drama and music flourish and are an important feature of life at Kilgraston. Classrooms are well equipped and modern IT facilities are spread throughout the school. Opportunities are provided throughout the year for pupils to perform in groups or as soloists and they compete successfully in local festivals and events. The girls have the opportunity to take LAMDA, Associated Board and Trinity examinations. There is an annual production involving all pupils.

Sports and recreation thrive within the superb Sports Hall, which includes a climbing wall and gym. Pupils benefit from a 25m outdoor swimming pool, 9 floodlit all-weather courts, playing fields and athletics track. Kilgraston is the only school in Scotland with an equestrian facility on campus and it also hosts the Scottish Schools Equestrian Championships each year.

The school's main sports are: hockey, netball, tennis, rounders, swimming and athletics, and fixtures are regularly played against other preparatory schools. The school has an excellent skiing record.

Kilgraston Junior Years has a pastoral House system. Inter-House competitions and challenges in games, music and debating provide an opportunity for friendly competition and fun. The family atmosphere in the newly refurbished boarding area, Butterstone, is enhanced by the wide range of weekend activities that make use of the superb local facilities in and around Perthshire.

Charitable status. Kilgraston School Trust is a Registered Charity, number SC029664. It exists to develop a love of learning, a spirit of adventure and openness of heart.

Kimbolton Preparatory School

Kimbolton, Huntingdon, Cambs PE28 0EA

Tel: 01480 860281
Fax: 01480 861874
email: prep@kimbolton.cambs.sch.uk
website: www.kimbolton.cambs.sch.uk
Twitter: @KimboltonSchool
Facebook: @KimboltonSchool

Motto: Spes Durat Avorum

Chair of Governors: C A Paull, MPhil, FCA

Headmaster: J P Foley, BA, NPQH

Age Range. 4–11 Co-educational.
Number of Children. Approximately 300.
Fees per term (2016–2017). £3,185–£4,035 (including lunch). A 2% discount is applied if fees paid by termly direct debit.

Mission Statement. Kimbolton School creates a caring, challenging environment in which pupils are encouraged to fulfil their potential and are given opportunities to flourish in a wide variety of curricular and extra-curricular interests.

We provide a close family environment where young people are educated to be tolerant, socially responsible and independent of mind, equipping them for our changing world. We are a community that challenges pupils to discover their talents, develop socially and excel.

Our Preparatory School is located at the western end of Kimbolton village in a mix of modern and Victorian buildings, while our Senior School is based at the opposite end of the village in Kimbolton Castle in 120 acres of parkland and playing fields. We are very much one school: the curricula of the Prep and Senior Schools are aligned; our warm, caring ethos starts at the Reception Year and continues through to the Upper Sixth; and some of our staff teach at both the Prep and Senior Schools.

Our normal entry points for the Prep School are 4+, 7+ and 9+, but we accept pupils into other year groups and/or at times other than September when space permits, subject to passing an appropriate assessment.

Reception, Year 1 and Year 2 have two classes per year group and Years 3–6 have three classes. Each has its own class teacher and pupils throughout the Upper Prep also benefit from a good deal of specialist teaching. We have provision for academically gifted children and provide one-to-one and small group tuition as needed.

We offer an extensive range of trips, visits and competitions to complement the curriculum, as well as regularly welcoming visiting speakers. From Year 4 onwards, children have the option of participating in residential trips.

There is a vibrant musical scene throughout Kimbolton School. The majority of children in Years 3–6 take individual music lessons in addition to class music; those in Years 1 and 2 may opt for small group string sessions. Performance opportunities abound, with formal and informal concerts plus an annual orchestral afternoon.

Lower Prep is located in Aragon House, a purpose-built facility for 4–7 year olds, which provides a safe, welcoming and happy environment. Children in Lower Prep also use the facilities on offer throughout the Prep School. Children automatically progress to the Upper Prep, with the expectation that at age 11 pupils will continue to the Senior School. (*See entry in HMC section*).

The Prep School has, on its own site, a dining hall, library, digital suite, assembly hall, music teaching and practice rooms, science laboratory, art and design technology room and sports hall, as well as large, light and airy classrooms. There is a full-time nurse on site.

Our outdoor facilities include tennis and netball courts, 400m grass athletics track, rounders fields, floodlit all-weather pitches, plus football, hockey and cricket pitches. Pupils also enjoy regular access to the first-class facilities at the Senior School, including a 25-metre swimming pool. We have a full programme of sports fixtures and tournaments and have achieved notable successes across a range of sports.

Out of hours options provide high-quality support to working parents. Children may arrive for breakfast at 7.45 am and our 'Kim Club' facility is available after school until 6.00 pm. There is also an extensive range of extra-curricular activities, clubs, and supervised prep to extend the school day. Many of our children use our daily bus service to travel to and from school.

Kimbolton Preparatory School was inspected by ISI in 2011.

Charitable status. Kimbolton School Foundation is a Registered Charity, number 1098586.

King Edward's Junior School
Bath

North Road, Bath BA2 6JA

Tel: 01225 463218
Fax: 01225 442178
email: junior@kesbath.com
website: www.kesbath.com
Twitter: @KESBath
Facebook: /kesbath

Chair of Governors: Mrs W Thomson, MEd, BEd Hons, LLCM TD

Head Teacher: **Mr G Taylor**, BA Ed, NPQH

Age Range. 7–11 Co-educational.
Number of Pupils. 182.
Fees per term (2016–2017). £3,520.

Our award-winning, purpose-built Junior School on the same North Road site as the Senior School is extremely well equipped for learning, with dedicated specialist teaching rooms for Science, Art, Design Technology and Music and a state-of-the-art ICT Suite and Technology Centre, all housed around a lovely central library. The School also includes a large multi-purpose hall and dining room.

Externally, the Junior School has its own adventure playground, pond, wildflower garden and multi-sport play area, as well as access to the Meadow, a delightful and spacious area with beautiful views over Bath.

The Junior School is an integral part of the King Edward's foundation and is governed by the same Board. It joins with the Senior School in major events, such as the Founder's Day Service in Bath Abbey, and shares various games facilities and specialist teaching staff.

All children learn the strings (violin, viola, cello and double bass) in Year 3, recorder in Year 4, whole class orchestra/band and Gamelan in Year 5 and Steel Pans in Year 6. Well over half of the children learn additional instruments under the tutelage of a strong peripatetic music team. A mixture of French, German and Spanish is taught throughout the School while purpose-built facilities in Art, Science, Technology and IT, coupled with specialist teaching, ensure high standards of achievement in those areas. The School is a very busy one renowned for its co-curricular programme. The wide variety of activities on offer include table tennis, gymnastics, fencing, judo, Lego, chess, newshounds and craft club. This is not to mention the various musical and instrumental groups and the many opportunities to play rugby, football, hockey, netball, cricket, basketball, tennis, rounders, cross country and athletics. Frequent educational trips are arranged in and around the local area and during the summer Activities Week; residential trips for Years 3–6, include destinations such as France and Devon. Sporting tours also take place each year.

The House system plays a central role in the life of the School. All children belong to one of four Houses and take part in many events and competitions during the year.

Pre-Prep & Nursery and Senior School. For details of the Pre-Prep and Nursery please see separate IAPS entry and for Senior School details please see King Edward's School's entry under HMC.

Charitable status. King Edward's Junior School is part of King Edward's School Bath which is a Registered Charity, number 1115875.

King Edward's School Pre-Prep and Nursery
Bath

Weston Lane, Bath BA1 4AQ

Tel: 01225 421681
Fax: 01225 428006
email: pre-prep@kesbath.com
website: www.kesbath.com
Twitter: @KESBath
Facebook: /kesbath

Chair of Governors: Mrs W Thomson, MEd, BEd Hons, LLCM TD

Head Teacher: **Ms J Gilbert**, BEd Hons, NPQH

Age Range. 3–7.
Number of Pupils. 98.
Fees per term (2016–2017). £2,615–£3,175.

King Edward's Pre-Prep and Nursery offers an exciting and stimulating world in which to start school life. A desire to make learning 'irresistible' in a nurturing environment is at the heart of everything we do. Personalised learning, combined with academic rigour, ensures that every child thrives and is provided with the extension and support that they need. New initiatives, fresh challenges, concerts, trips, visiting experts and inspiring projects all help to enrich our broad and creative curriculum.

Ethos. *Child focused* – First and foremost we want every child to feel safe, encouraged and happy in school. We place children at the centre of learning, creating a close match between your child and the curriculum. This helps to increase a child's eagerness to learn, builds self-esteem and encourages positive attitudes.

Family focused – Visitors to the Pre-Prep often remark on the wonderful 'family feel' that they sense in the school. We work very hard to be as family-focused as possible and are very fortunate to have such supportive parents; we are never short of volunteers for the many school trips that the children enjoy and for all the varied events that take place. It is lovely to see not only parents but grandparents taking an active role in the school.

Outdoor focused – At King Edward's the outdoor environment is a natural extension of the classroom and we are proud of our status as a Forest School. As well as allowing children to engage directly with the environment, outdoor learning also brings together many different elements of the curriculum and enriches school life.

Facilities. Our Pre-Prep and Nursery is situated in a beautiful Victorian house close to Royal Victoria Park, Bath. In addition to the light and airy classrooms, we have a well-equipped gymnasium and school hall with stage. There is also a specialist music room, ICT suite, Teddy's Lodge for pre and after school care, a newly enhanced art room and library. Children make full use of the spacious and safe grounds to the rear of the main house, with a dedicated outdoor cedar lodge classroom, storytelling corner, surfaced playground, wooden fort, wooded area and climbing frame. There is also a wilderness area and pond, used for lots of environmental. A magical sensory garden, playing field for team games and an area where the children cultivate their own garden complete our outdoor space.

Junior School and Senior School. For details of the Junior School please see separate IAPS entry and for the Senior School please see King Edward's School's entry under HMC.

Charitable status. King Edward's Pre-Prep and Nursery is part of King Edward's School Bath which is a Registered Charity, number 1115875.

King Henry VIII Preparatory School

Kenilworth Road, Coventry CV3 6PT

Tel: 024 7627 1307
Fax: 024 7627 1308
email: headteacher@khps.co.uk
website: www.khps.co.uk

Chairman of Governors: Mrs Julia McNaney

Head: **Mrs Gill Bowser**

Age Range. 3–11 Co-educational.
Number of Pupils. 500 Day Boys and Girls.
Fees per term (2016–2017). Reception–Year 2 £2,896 (inc lunch); Year 3 £2,960 (inc lunch); Years 4–6 £2,778 (exc lunch).

King Henry VIII Preparatory School is part of Coventry School Foundation, which includes King Henry VIII Senior School and Bablake School (3–18).

The School is situated on two campuses a short distance from each other on the south side of Coventry.

The Swallows Campus, opposite Coventry Memorial Park, educates children aged 3–8 in classes of 16 (from Reception onwards). The campus occupies a beautiful 3½ acre site and has a wealth of facilities, including its own Swimming Pool, Sports Hall, Music Department, Art & Design Centre, All-weather surface and Adventure Playground. Its main building dates to the 17th century. Most teaching is provided by class teachers, giving young children a continuity of approach and providing them with a key individual with whom to build a strong relationship and who will guide them through their daily studies. An increasing number of specialist teachers are provided as children progress through the infant years: Music from age 3, Games and Swimming from age 4 and Art & Design Technology from age 6. There is a strong family atmosphere and the aim is to provide children with a wonderful start to their education.

The Hales Campus is situated just down the road from Swallows and occupies a portion of the main King Henry VIII School site. The main building was purpose-built in 1997 and provides an excellent range of modern facilities for children aged 8–11. From Year 5 at this site children are taught by specialist teachers for all subjects in classes of 20. The Hales Campus has its own Sports Hall, Music Depart-ment, Library, Art & Design Room, Science Laboratory and playing areas. Some facilities are shared with the senior school, including games fields and a 25-metre indoor swimming pool.

The School seeks to help its pupils to be happy, confident 'all-rounders'. Academic standards are high and entrance to the School, from the age of 5, is through academic assessment (ages 5–6) and examination (ages 7–10). Children joining the School at the ages of 3 or 4 are not academically selected and names may be registered from birth. The majority of children continue from King Henry VIII Preparatory School to King Henry VIII Senior School at age 11; however, children may sit entrance to a variety of other schools.

The Arts and Sport are very important aspects within the curriculum. The visual and performance Arts are specialist taught from the infant years. Music is strong, with children being able to learn a wide variety of musical instruments from an early age. Drama and performance are aspects of school life which flourish, with all children taking part in a variety of performances during their time at the School. A large number of performance opportunities are available each year.

Games are taught within the timetable from Reception onwards and competitive matches against other schools start in Year 2. The main sports for boys are Rugby, Football and Cricket; for girls Netball, Hockey and Rounders. Beyond the main team sports, there is a range of other sports that may be experienced, both within the timetable and as extra-curricular activities.

Scholarships are awarded from the age of 8, for academic subjects as well as the Arts and All-Rounder awards. Bursaries are available at entrance from Year 3 onwards (7+).

The School has a vibrant extra-curricular activities programme which may be accessed by pupils from Reception onwards, this includes both lunchtime and after school clubs. Before school care (from 7.45 am) and after school care (up to 6.00 pm) are available daily during term time, as well as voluntary Saturday morning sports. There is a full programme of care for children aged from 3–11, starting at 8.30 am and continuing until 5.30 pm, during every school holiday.

School trips and educational visits are regarded as an important aspect of each child's experience at the School. These include visits to local places of interest, usually associated with programmes of study, but also residential trips for each year group from the age of 7 onwards, one of which will be to France in Year 5.

The School's motto *Confide Recte Agens* –have the courage to do what is right – lies at the heart of the School's ethos which encourages children to have the courage of their convictions. The School is a member of the Community of the Cross of Nails, thus having an association with Coventry Cathedral. This stresses tolerance and understanding between people of different creeds and faiths. The School happily accepts children from various faiths and looks to build genuine understanding and tolerance between its pupils.

Overall the School seeks to help its children to be happy, confident people who enjoy learning.

Charitable status. Coventry School Foundation is a Registered Charity, number 528961. Its aim is to advance the education of boys and girls by the provision of a school or schools in or near the City of Coventry.

King's College School

West Road, Cambridge CB3 9DN

Tel: 01223 365814
email: office@kcs.cambs.sch.uk
website: www.kcs.cambs.sch.uk

The School is part of King's College and is administered by a Board of Governors.

Chairman of Governors: Professor R Foley

Headmaster: N J Robinson, BA

Deputy Heads:
Mrs K Richardson, BEd Hons
Mr T Hales, BA Hons

Age Range. 4–13 Co-educational.
Number of Pupils. 388 day pupils, 32 boy boarders including 24 choristers.
Fees per term (2016–2017). Weekly Boarders £7,590; Choristers £2,550; Day Pupils £4,875; Pre-Prep £3,835.

The School is administered by Governors appointed by the Council of King's College. King Henry VI's charter founding King's College in 1441 provided for Choristers and their education. In 1878 the School moved to its present site near the University library, across the river from the College. Over the years the facilities have been greatly improved. The main house accommodates the catering facilities and boarding accommodation. A new Wiles Centre for Technology opened in June 1999 with first class facilities for ICT and DT. The Performing Arts Centre includes 16 new music rooms (opened in 2001) and a multi-purpose hall used for plays and concerts and also a fully-equipped gym. In 2010 an impressive new music wing was added to the department. A new classroom block called the Briggs Building was opened in May 2004 by the Duchess of Kent and it contains two very well equipped science labs, two maths classrooms, three modern language classrooms, two English classrooms and a new library. Sports facilities on site include two large playing fields, tennis courts and a heated outdoor swimming pool. A new floodlit astroturf field was laid in May 2005. Two new squash courts were built in 2010. The School also has the use of other nearby sports fields. The Pre-Prep has been expanded to accommodate two-form entry starting from September 2008.

The Headmaster is assisted by 50 full-time and 10 part-time teachers. There are 2 Matrons and a Day Nurse and a full-time Bursar and Assistant Bursar. There are 40 full- or part-time music staff. In 1976 girls were admitted as day pupils and the ratio of boys to girls is approximately 50:50. In September 1981 the School started a small special centre for dyslexic children of good intelligence which has now become an excellent Learning Support Centre. Pupils are prepared for the Scholarship and Common Entrance examinations of the boys' and girls' Independent Senior Schools. The school broadly follows the National Curriculum subjects, but also teaches French from the age of 4, Latin from 9, and Greek to some older children. The School has a tradition of winning numerous academic, art, music, drama and sports awards annually.

Apart from choral and instrumental music (there are 2 orchestras of some 80 players in each and about 40 chamber groups), activities include Drama, Art, Computing, Touch-typing, Spelling, Gardening, DT, Gymnastics, PE, Chess, Science, Wildlife Explorers, Library, Orienteering, Yoga, Ballet, Spanish, and Mandarin Chinese. Games include Rugby, Football, Hockey, Cricket, Girls' Cricket, Netball, Rounders, Athletics, Tennis, Squash, and Swimming.

Bursaries. King's is pleased to offer a place at the School to a child at a Primary School on a means-tested bursary worth up to 100% of the school fees. The place will usually start from Year 3 or Year 4 and continue until the child leaves King's.

Further information about the School may be obtained from the Headmaster. Enquiries concerning Choristerships should also be addressed to him. Choristership Auditions take place annually, usually in September and January.

Charitable status. King's College School is part of King's College Cambridge, which is a Registered Charity, number 1139422. Its aim is to provide an excellent education for girls and boys of mixed ability aged 4 to 13.

King's College Junior School

Wimbledon Common, London SW19 4TT

Tel: 020 8255 5335
Fax: 020 8255 5339
email: jsadmissions@kcs.org.uk
          HMJSsec@kcs.org.uk
website: www.kcs.org.uk
Twitter: @KCJSWimbledon

Chairman of the Governing Body: Mrs P L Hughes, CBE

Headmaster: Dr G A Silverlock, BEd Hons, MLitt, PhD

Age Range. 7–13.
Number of Boys. 460 (day boys only).
Fees per term (2016–2017). £5,530 (Years 3–4), £6,125 (Years 5–8).

The Junior School was established in 1912 as an integral part of KCS, to prepare boys for the Senior School. It shares with it a common site and many facilities, in particular the Music School, the Art, Design and Technology School, the Dining Hall, the Sports Hall, the swimming pool and extensive playing fields. For the rest, Junior School boys are housed in their own buildings. The Priory, rebuilt in 1980, contains twenty-three classrooms, including specialist rooms for languages, mathematics, history, geography, information technology and multimedia work. The youngest age groups have their own special accommodation in Rushmere, a spacious Georgian house whose grounds adjoin the Junior School. The School also has its own purpose-built library, science laboratories and well-equipped theatre and assembly hall.

The School is separately administered in matters relating to admission, curriculum, discipline and day to day activities. There are thirty-six members of staff in addition to those teaching in specialist departments common to both Schools.

The work and overall programme are organised in close consultation with the Senior School to ensure that boys are educated in a structured and progressive way from 7 to 18, having the benefit of continuity, while enjoying the range and style of learning that are best suited to their age.

Boys come from both maintained and pre-preparatory schools and are admitted at the age of 7, 8, 9 or 10. Entry is by interview and examination.

Charitable status. King's College School is a Registered Charity, number 310024. It exists to provide education for children.

King's Hall School
A Woodard School

Kingston Road, Taunton, Somerset TA2 8AA
Tel: 01823 285920
Fax: 01823 285922
email: schooloffice@kingshalltaunton.co.uk
          admissions@kingshalltaunton.co.uk
website: www.kingshalltaunton.co.uk
Twitter: @KingsHallSchool
Facebook: /Kings-Hall-School

Chairman of Governors: Roger Knight, OBE, MA, DipEd

Head: **Justin Chippendale**, BSc Joint Hons

Age Range. 2–13, Co-educational.
Number of Pupils. Preparatory (Years 3–8): 110 boys, 100 girls; including 40 boarders. Pre-Prep (Nursery–Year 2): 40 boys, 45 girls.
Fees per term (2016–2017). Preparatory Day £3,050–£5,225, Full/Weekly Boarding £5,810–£7,555, Pre-Prep £2,445–£2,540.

King's Hall School is a leading Pre-Prep and Prep school with around 300 girls and boys. Set in a beautiful countryside location surrounded by farmland, the school is only a couple of minutes' drive from the centre of Taunton. The school respects traditional values and boarding is a strong feature, which contributes to the tangible family atmosphere that exists in the school. Children enjoy a challenging all-round education in a progressive and stimulating environment. King's Hall has a partner senior school, King's College, Taunton, and the two schools benefit from having their own independent sites, furnished with excellent age-appropriate facilities and attitudes to maximise the opportunities for the children in our care. There is a close working relationship between King's Hall and King's College and the vast majority of pupils move on there at age 13. Scholarships are available for pupils with exceptional ability. These are awarded at 11+ and continue at King's College, Taunton up to age 18.

King's Hawford

Hawford Lock Lane, Claines, Worcester WR3 7SD
Tel: 01905 451292
Fax: 01905 756502
email: hawford@ksw.org.uk
website: www.ksw.org.uk

Chairman of the Governors: H B Carslake, BA, LLB

Headmaster: **J M Turner**, BEd Hons, DipEd, ACP

Age Range. 2–11.
Number of Pupils. 179 Boys, 131 Girls.
Fees per term (2016–2017). £2,288–£4,120 (excluding lunch).

King's Hawford is a junior school to the historic King's School, Worcester, and is set in twenty-three acres of parkland situated on the northern outskirts of Worcester. The school is accommodated within an elegant and recently refurbished Georgian house surrounded by well-maintained playing fields, with tennis courts, a heated enclosed swimming pool, a multi-purpose sports hall and performance space and secure play area for younger children. Academic results are excellent. The school has a strong focus on outdoor learning, with an outdoor classroom, a traversing wall, a forest school and trees that children can climb. Children are taught to navigate the adjacent canal in the school's katakanus. The childrens' weekly radio show is posted on the website.

There are extensive opportunities for a wide range of extra-curricular activities and there is a busy calendar of music, drama, sport, dance and many other clubs. Sports include Rugby, Association Football, Cricket, Hockey, Netball, Rounders, Athletics, Tennis, Cross-Country and Swimming. The school has been awarded the prestigious Artsmark Gold.

The Pre-Prep department accepts children from age 2–6 and the Junior department from age 7–11.

Charitable status. The King's School Worcester is a Registered Charity, number 1098236. It exists to provide a broad education for a wide range of children from 2–11 years.

King's House School

68 King's Road, Richmond, Surrey TW10 6ES
Tel: 020 8940 1878
Fax: 020 8939 2501
email: schooloffice@kingshouseschool.org
website: www.kingshouseschool.org

Established in 1946, the School was constituted as an Educational Trust with a Board of Governors in 1957.

Chairman of the Governors: Mr Graham Corbishley

Head: **Mr Mark Turner**, BA, PGCE, NPQH

Age Range. Boys 3–13 (Co-educational Nursery).
Number of Pupils. 450.
Fees per term (2016–2017). Nursery Department £2,165–£2,395; Junior Department £3,930–£4,590; Senior Department £5,120 (all fees inclusive of lunch excluding Nursery).

We believe the King's House School is a very special place and are very proud of what we have on offer here and what we do.

We are a lively, busy, happy School and one where we feel that the boys (and girls in our wonderful Nursery) thrive. Our aim is to offer a broad education to all our pupils, enabling them to develop their academic, social, sporting and artistic attributes. This breadth and balance on offer is we believe one of the strengths of the School.

The academic side underpins the education here with the emphasis on the core areas in the early years spreading to an increasing range of subjects by the top end of the School. The destination schools of our leavers show that the boys are achieving well academically.

We believe very much that King's House is a community; we pride ourselves on strong pastoral care and an environment where the children feel happy. The positive relationships that we enjoy with our parents and the local community and our links to Rwanda are all key to our sense of responsibility.

The School is based on three sites on Richmond Hill and also benefits from its own extensive playing fields in Chiswick. The three main School sites have spacious state-of-the-art facilities. The School also enjoys the advantages of having close access to London with all the educational opportunities that affords.

King's House is a friendly, caring and supportive School. We have a strong sense of community both within the School and with our parents but we are also keen to play a role in the local and global community and to develop our pupils' sense of awareness of the world around them.

King's House is a lively, busy and happy School and we aim to give each child a broad academic and balanced education. We provide an environment in which the children feel secure and are able to flourish; offering opportunities to take part and develop in all areas, so that the needs of each individual are catered for.

King's House is non-selective at our two main entry points, Nursery and Reception, and this means we have a range of pupils and abilities. We believe that boys benefit from staying in the prep environment until they are 13 years old before moving on. Their final two years here allow them to grow up and develop a sense of responsibility, taking on roles around the school. The boys are well-prepared for the transition to their senior schools.

King's House is proud of its traditions and history. Its principles and standards are founded on Christian values although the school is not aligned to any particular religion, and welcomes pupils of all religions and backgrounds.

For more information visit the school's website or contact our Registrar, Sally Bass, on 020 8940 1878 or bass.s@kingshouseschool.org.

Charitable status. Kings House School Trust (Richmond) Limited is a Registered Charity, number 312669. It exists for the education of children.

King's St Alban's School

Mill Street, Worcester WR1 2NJ

Tel:	01905 354906
Fax:	01905 763075
email:	ksa@ksw.org.uk
website:	www.ksw.org.uk

Chairman of the Governors: H B Carslake, BA, LLB

Head: **R A Chapman**, BSc

Age Range. 4–11 Co-educational.
Number of Pupils. 200.
Fees per term (2016–2017). Pre-Prep Dept £2,184–£2,511, Junior School £2,691–£3,951 excluding lunch.

Education is about far more than academic learning, although that is still our primary purpose. At King's St Alban's we aim to develop the whole child, encouraging each girl and boy to explore their capabilities, find fresh challenges and discover spheres in which they can excel.

King's St Alban's, an established school with a purpose-built Pre-Preparatory Department, is located near to Worcester Cathedral on a separate site adjacent to the Senior School. In the grounds stand the Chapel, the main buildings of the Junior School with the Pre-Preparatory Department on an adjacent, self contained site. The school has a large hall, a dedicated Science Laboratory, an IT suite, an Art and Technology Room, well-stocked Libraries and Music Rooms, all of which supplement the usual amenities of a preparatory school. In addition, use is made of Senior School facilities, which include an indoor Swimming Pool, a fully equipped Sports Hall, Dance Studio, Fitness Centre, the Music School, Playing Fields, and a purpose-built Theatre.

We work hard to discover talent and develop it to the full. Music, Art, Dance and Drama play an important part in the life of the school. King's St Alban's supports an Orchestra, Wind Band, Flute Choir and String and Recorder groups with most children playing at least one musical instrument. In the Junior School nearly all children are involved in the school's Choir and there is a smaller Chamber Choir. The annual Carol Service is held in the Cathedral with concerts and musical evenings held each term in the Theatre and Chapel. A major whole-school production is staged annually

in the Theatre with several smaller workshop productions taking place during the year.

The staff comprises a mix of men and women, all of whom are experienced and well qualified. In addition there are various visiting music and sport specialists.

The main sports are Rugby, Netball, Soccer, Hockey, Cricket and Rounders with Swimming, Cross-Country, Orienteering and Tennis also featured. Matches are arranged with other schools and excellence is sought, but participation of all girls and boys is the main objective. A thriving inter-House competition provides further opportunities for all to enjoy competition.

Beyond the classroom an extensive programme of after-school activities is available with opportunities varying each term, examples are Art & Craft, Science, Fencing, Ball Skills, Latin, Chess and Swimming. Children from across the school spend time each year at the school's Outdoor Activity Centre in the Black Mountains.

King's St Alban's is academically selective and pupils are expected to progress to the Senior School, subject to a satisfactory performance in their examinations at the age of 11. The main assessment of candidates for the Junior School takes place in early February for entry the following September, but assessments can be arranged on an individual basis throughout the year, when required. The tests cover English, Mathematics and Verbal Reasoning.

There are a small number of Scholarships and Bursaries available from the age of 7, as are Choral Scholarships for Cathedral Choristers.

Charitable status. The King's School, Worcester is a Registered Charity, number 1098236. It exists to provide high quality education for girls and boys.

Junior King's School

Milner Court, Sturry, Canterbury, Kent CT2 0AY

Tel:	01227 714000
email:	registrar@junior-kings.co.uk
website:	www.junior-kings.co.uk
Twitter:	@JuniorKingsSch

Chairman of Governors: The Very Revd Dr R A Willis, BA, Dip Th, FRSA, Dean of Canterbury Cathedral

Headmaster: **Mr P M Wells**, BEd Hons

Age Range. 3–13.
Number of Pupils. 359 (81 Boarders; 278 Day Pupils, including 91 Pre-Prep).
Fees per term (2016–2017). Boarders £8,080; Day Pupils £5,295–£5,890; Pre-Prep £3,500 (including meals).

Junior King's was founded in 1879 as the preparatory school to The King's School Canterbury, which can trace its roots back to the sixth century when St Augustine established a monastery in Kent.

Set in eighty acres of attractive countryside, just two miles from Canterbury city centre, Junior King's pupils enjoy a calm, happy and purposeful atmosphere drawing upon a rich Christian heritage. Girls and boys from the ages of three to thirteen years achieve their potential, both inside and beyond the classroom, whatever their ability.

The school has an outstanding reputation for academic excellence and scholarship due to a varied and stimulating curriculum. This is supported by first class teaching and opportunities to enjoy a wide range of sports, music, drama and extra-curricular activities.

The school is in the grounds of Milner Court, a 16th century Manor House This historic building, along with a Kentish Oast House used by the Pre-Prep, a newly-refurbished Tithe Barn used for theatre and musical productions, and a flint stoned church for services and assemblies has been sensitively augmented over the years. Other impressive facilities include specialist art, science, ICT and design suites.

Spacious and comfortable boarding accommodation for around 80 boarders with social rooms, kitchens and games rooms are at the heart of the school in the main building.

The school has a fine reputation for music, both instrumental and choral, as well as for art, design and drama. The school year includes a programme of concerts, recitals and exhibitions involving children of all ages.

In 2013, Mr Hugh Robertson, MP and Minister of State for Sport, Olympic Legacy and Tourism opened a stunning new all-weather sports pitch and tennis courts. In 2016, a magnificent new music school was officially opened by Dr Harry Christophers, CBE, OKS.

A large and modern sports hall is used for PE lessons, basketball, volleyball, badminton, and netball, as well as indoor hockey, soccer and tennis. Rowing and sailing take place on nearby lakes. Pupils make use of the large indoor swimming pool at the senior school.

For boys, cricket, soccer hockey and rugby are the main team games, while girls play netball, hockey and rounders. Athletics, tennis and fencing are joint pursuits.

Children can join the Nursery from the age of three in our impressive purpose-built 'Little Barn'. In its delightful Kentish Oast House setting, the Pre-Prep has its own spacious hall, library and seven bright classrooms complete with the latest ICT facilities. Outside, pupils have their own extensive adventure playground as well as sharing the main school facilities such as the sports hall, tithe barn, sports fields and dining hall.

Junior King's pupils progress at 13+ to The King's School Canterbury and other leading public schools, with a sense of achievement, maturity and self-confidence. Academic standards are high and the record of success in Scholarships and Common Entrance is outstanding.

(See entry for The King's School Canterbury in the HMC section.)

Charitable status. The King's School of the Cathedral Church of Canterbury is a Registered Charity, number 307942. It exists to provide education for boys and girls.

King's Ely Junior

Ely, Cambridgeshire CB7 4DB
Tel: 01353 660732
Fax: 01353 665281
email: admissions@kingsely.org
website: www.kingsely.org/Junior
Twitter: @kings_ely

Chairman of the Governors: Mr J Hayes

Head: Mr R J Whymark, BA Ed Hons

Age Range. 7–13.
Number of Pupils. Boarders: 25 Boys, 8 Girls; Day: 184 Boys, 132 Girls.
Fees per term (2016–2017). Boarding £7,004–£7,394; Day £4,393–£4,794.

King's Ely Junior has its own staff and its own buildings are part of the main school campus. The facilities of King's Ely Senior are freely available to King's Ely Junior boys and girls.

There is a family boarding house for boys and girls up to the age of 13 and a separate boarding house for the boy choristers of Ely Cathedral who are all pupils at King's Ely Junior. Each has its own Housemaster or Housemistress, assisted by House Tutors and experienced Matrons. Both

Houses have recently been refurbished and offer excellent boarding facilities.

During the school day all children are divided into four equal-sized co-educational 'Houses' for pastoral and competitive purposes. Each of these 'Houses' is staffed by a Housemaster or Housemistress and several House Tutors.

Entry to King's Ely Junior for boys and girls is through assessment tests and interview. The main two entry points are Year 3 (age 7) and Year 7 (age 11) but pupils may start in any year providing there is space. The main assessment weeks are in January, although it is common to assess for entry at other times of the year. Exceptional children for Year 7 entry may be invited to take the King's Ely Junior Scholarship examination. A broad preparatory school curriculum is followed and all pupils are prepared for the relevant transfer examination. While the great majority proceed to King's Ely Senior in Year 9, pupils can also be prepared for other Independent Schools.

The main games for boys are Rugby, Football, Cricket and Tennis, and for girls they are Hockey, Netball, Cricket and Tennis. Both boys and girls are involved in Athletics and Cross-Country Running. There is a Swimming Pool, a well-equipped Sports Hall, a full-size all-weather hockey/tennis area, and excellent playing fields. Rowing is offered throughout the academic year from Year 7 onwards. A wide-ranging programme of extra-curricular activities is also offered. All pupils have the opportunity to learn one or more of a wide variety of musical instruments. There are several Junior School Orchestras, and choral and ensemble music are taught. The Junior School musicians regularly tour abroad. The School has its own Music School and Technology Centre, and access to the Senior School's new £1 million Recital Hall and Music School. Years 7 and 8 enjoy a new £1.2m block of seven classrooms and a science laboratory, plus recreational and study facilities.

The School is also justly proud of its art and drama, which are taught in their own studios, and of its excellent computer facilities.

Charitable status. The King's School, Ely is a Registered Charity, number 802427. It exists for the provision of education.

King's Rochester Preparatory School

King Edward Road, Rochester, Kent ME1 1UB
Tel: 01634 888577
Fax: 01634 888507
email: prep@kings-rochester.co.uk
website: www.kings-rochester.co.uk
Twitter: @Kings_Rochester

Chairman of Governors: R W Hoile, MS, FRCS

Headmaster: R P Overend, BA, FTCL, ARCM, FRSA

Age Range. 8–13.
Number of Pupils. 250.
Fees per term (2016–2017). Boarders £6,860, Day Pupils £4,140–£4,700 (including lunches).

Admission between 8+ to 12+ is by interview and report from present school as well as Entrance Examinations in English, Mathematics and Verbal or Non-Verbal Reasoning. Many children also join at 11+ and sit either our November or March 11+ Assessment Tests in English, Mathematics and Non-Verbal Reasoning.

Scholarships are awarded (partly from the Cathedral, partly from the School) to Cathedral Choristers (boys only)

and King's (30%) or Governors' Exhibitions (means-tested up to 100%) to those whose performance in the Entrance Examination merits it.

The Preparatory School is an integral part of King's Rochester, founded in 604 AD by Justus, a Benedictine monk, the first Bishop of Rochester. The Cathedral is at the heart of the School's life with a weekly School service and every day the Choristers maintain the tradition of choral singing at the world's oldest Choir School. When the School is not in the Cathedral a religious assembly is held at the Preparatory School.

The School is a member of the Choir Schools' Association.

The School has been fully co-educational since 1993 and 40% are girls.

Set in Rochester Town Centre, the Preparatory School building overlooks the beautiful Paddock, one of the School's large playing fields. The teaching block consists of 12 classrooms, 2 Science Laboratories, a Computer Suite, Language Laboratory and a Library with over 6,000 volumes. Other facilities such as the Design and Technology Centre, Art Centre, Music School, Indoor Swimming Pool and Sports Halls are shared with the Senior School which virtually all pupils join following the internal Entrance Examination. Chadlington House, the purpose-built Pre-Preparatory School which educates pupils from age 3–8, and a Conference Centre are recent additions to the campus. In September 2012, sport benefited from the acquisition of the King's Rochester Sports Centre adding nine external tennis/netball courts, a large gymnasium, a fitness gym, physio suite and changing rooms to the indoor swimming pool and playing fields already on the 1400 year-old school's town centre site.

The Preparatory School has a small number of boarders who are housed either in School House for boys, or St Margaret's House for girls. Boarding, both full and weekly, is available for boys and girls from 11+.

The curriculum is broad and balanced. In Year 8 science is taught as three separate subjects, French and German are the modern languages, and Latin is taught to the A stream from Year 7. A full programme of CPSHE is given to all pupils. Individual educational support tuition and EFL is available if required.

All pupils enjoy the benefit of two full afternoons a week of Games in addition to a PE lesson for most year groups. Major sports include Rugby, Hockey, Cricket, Netball, Athletics, Rounders and Swimming. There is a wide range of extra-curricular activities at the end of the school day.

Choral and instrumental music is strong throughout the School. Many of our pupils learn one or more musical instruments and strong results are achieved in Associated Board examinations. Each year the Drama Club presents a play or musical held over three nights. Recently productions have required casts in excess of fifty and have been wonderful opportunities for pupils to show their dramatic and musical skills. Amongst latest productions have been *The Roman Invasion of Ramsbottom, Honk!, The Caucasian Chalk Circle, Olivia, Bendigo Boswell, Homer's Odyssey, Under Milk Wood, Bugsy Malone, In Holland stands a House* and *Little Shop of Horrors*.

Charitable status. King's School, Rochester is a Registered Charity, number 1084266. It is a Charitable Trust for the purpose of educating children.

Kingshott

St Ippolyts, Hitchin, Hertfordshire SG4 7JX

Tel:	01462 432009
Fax:	01462 421652
email:	pa2head@kingshottschool.com
website:	www.kingshottschool.com
Twitter:	@Kingshottsch
Facebook:	@KingshottSchool

Chairman of Governors: Mr Gavin Hill, MA, FIA

Headmaster: **Mr Mark Seymour**, BA, BSc, CertEd

Age Range. 3–13.

Number of Pupils. (All Day) Prep (7–13): 150 Boys, 92 Girls; Pre-Prep (4–7): 90 Boys, 72 Girls; Nursery (3–4): 17 Boys, 11 Girls.

Fees per term (2016–2017). (including Lunch) Nursery £1,880–£2,580, Pre-Prep £3,310, Prep £4,040.

Kingshott, founded in 1930, occupies a large Victorian building, with major recent classroom additions, in 23 acres of attractive grounds on the outskirts of Hitchin. Luton, Letchworth, Baldock, Stevenage, Welwyn and the A1(M) Motorway are all within a 10 mile radius. The school has continued to invest in new facilities including a stand-alone Nursery building, Pre-Prep, Middle School (for Years 3–5) and most recently a purpose-built Prep School.

Kingshott, a Charitable Educational Trust, with a Board of Governors, welcomes all denominations. Children are encouraged to work towards and realise their individual potential – academic, creative, sporting – and to this end there is a happy friendly atmosphere, with strong emphasis on manners and being part of the wider community.

Kingshott offers a wide range of academic subjects including Latin, French, DT, Drama and ample curriculum time for PE and Games. This is complemented by a full and varied after-school programme.

There is a strong and successful sporting tradition which includes Football, Rugby, Cricket, Hockey, Netball, Rounders, Tennis, Swimming, Cross Country and Athletics. The School has its own covered, heated swimming pool, astro-turf pitch, hard play areas and extensive playing fields. Many pupils stay for Prep each evening, and there is opportunity for involvement in a wide variety of After-School Hobby activities. The School also offers a Breakfast Club and After-School Care is also available until 5.30 pm for Pre-Prep pupils.

Academic, Music, Art and Sports Scholarships to Senior Independent Schools are gained each year, and Common Entrance results are very sound, with virtually all children accepted by their first-choice schools.

Entry for Reception and beyond is by assessment, appropriate to age.

Registration for Nursery and Pre-Prep is advisable several years before required admission.

Charitable status. Kingshott School Trust Limited is a Registered Charity, number 280626. It exists to provide education for boys and girls.

Kingsmead School

Bertram Drive, Hoylake, Wirral CH47 0LL

Tel:	0151 632 3156
Fax:	0151 632 0302
email:	enquiries@kingsmeadschool.com
website:	www.kingsmeadschool.com

Chairman of Governors: Mr T J Turvey

Headmaster: Mr M G Gibbons, BComm, MSc, QTS

Age Range. 2–16.
Number of Pupils. 97 boys, 60 girls.
Fees per term (2016–2017). £2,095–£3,550.

Academic, Music and Sports Scholarships are available. Scholarship and entrance examinations for Year 7 are held in January each year. Substantial Bursaries are available to the children of Clergy.

Kingsmead School was founded in 1904. It is in a rural setting with extensive playing fields on site, yet is easily accessible by road and rail, and the school provides a bus service. It has a strong Christian tradition, dedicated staff, a reputation for academic rigour, and a happy atmosphere.

There is provision for pupils to go on to Grammar Schools at 11+, although the majority remain at Kingsmead until GCSE (age 16).

Facilities include three Computer Rooms, two well-equipped Science Laboratories, a Food and Nutrition kitchen, a large Gymnasium, a lecture theatre and an indoor heated swimming pool available throughout the year. There is a strong Choir and facilities are available to those wishing to learn a musical instrument. All children have the opportunity to perform in plays, musicals and concerts. The Centenary Building was opened on the campus in February 2003, containing state-of-the-art classrooms for History, Geography, Design Technology (DT), Information and Communications Technology (ICT), Art and French.

Up to the end of Key Stage 1 (Year 2), pupils are taught in their own rooms by Class Teachers. In the Junior Department (Key Stage 2) there is specialist teaching of certain subjects at the appropriate level. Thereafter pupils are based in a Form Room under the care of a Form Teacher but move to the different subject rooms for lessons. For spoken English and Drama, the School has enjoyed excellent results in the English Speaking Board and other examinations. At any level in the school, intelligent children with specific learning difficulties can be given a structured programme of remedial help by a specialist teacher at an extra charge.

Games offered include Football, Rugby, Cricket, Netball, Rounders, Hockey, Athletics, Tennis, and Golf.

Clubs include Ballet, Chess, Gymnastics, Scripture Union, Swimming, Bushcraft, Homework Club, The Duke of Edinburgh's Award (Silver and Bronze), Shooting and Dance.

Charitable status. Kingsmead School is a Registered Charity, number 525920.

Kingswood House School

56 West Hill, Epsom, Surrey KT19 8LG

Tel:	01372 723590
Fax:	01372 749081
email:	office@kingswoodhouse.org
website:	www.kingswoodhouse.org

Founded in 1899, the school moved to its current site, a large Edwardian house in West Hill, Epsom, just outside the town centre in 1920. The school is an educational trust, overseen by a board of governors.

Chairman of Governors: Christopher Shipley, LLB Hons, MBA

Headmaster: Peter R Brooks, MA, BEd Hons, CertEd, IAPS

Age Range. Boys 3–16, Girls 3–7.

Number of Pupils. 200 day pupils.
Fees per term (2016–2017). Pre-Prep £3,375 (part-time Nursery payable by session). Junior 7+ upwards £4,395. Free after-school care provided until 5 pm.

Kingswood House is a thriving day preparatory school for boys aged 3–13 and girls aged 3–7. The school's reputation is based on a friendly and welcoming atmosphere, a positive and supportive ethos and successfully meeting the educational needs of all its pupils. Small classes facilitate individual attention from well-qualified teachers and allow pupils to learn in a relaxed, but stimulating and concentrated environment.

The broad aim of the school is to prepare boys for Common Entrance and Scholarships to senior school at age 13. Development of literacy and numeracy skills is the foundation of the curriculum. English, Maths, Science, History, Geography, French, Religious Education, PE, Music, Art, Design Technology and Information Technology make up the timetable. Study Skills and PSHE courses help prepare boys for senior school life and there is a Study Centre to supplement learning, with excellent provision for children with special educational needs. Kingswood House School is a member of CReSTeD (Council for the Registration of Schools Teaching Dyslexic Pupils) and NAGC (The National Association for Gifted Children).

The senior curriculum is determined by the Common Entrance syllabus with boys being prepared for a wide variety of local senior independent schools, including Epsom College, St John's, Ewell Castle, City of London Freemen's, Reed's, Box Hill and King's College, Wimbledon. Placing boys in the right senior school is of paramount importance and the teachers have wide experience in preparing boys for Common Entrance. There is an excellent success rate at 13+ Common Entrance, with a good proportion obtaining scholarships and awards.

The school prides itself on the quality of teaching, dedicated classrooms and resources provided for Art, Design Technology, Information Technology, Music and Science, all of which have been completely refurbished in the last few years. There are sporting facilities on site, with a playing field, astroturf surface, all-weather cricket nets, adventure playground and climbing wall. Pitches at Ashtead Cricket Club and Epsom College are also used.

Academic Scholarships are awarded at 7+ and there are fee reductions for siblings. The school is registered for the Nursery Education Grant.

Charitable status. Kingswood House School is a Registered Charity, number 312044. It exists to provide educational support in the form of bursaries for the parents of children in need.

Kingswood Preparatory School

College Road, Lansdown, Bath BA1 5SD

Tel:	01225 734460
Fax:	01225 734470
email:	kpsreception@kingswood.bath.sch.uk
website:	www.kingswood.bath.sch.uk

Chairman of Governors: Mr T Westbrook

Headmaster: Mr Mark Brearey, BA Hons, PGCE

Age Range. 3–11.
Number of Pupils. 323: Prep: 113 boys, 94 girls; Pre-Prep: 66 boys, 50 girls. 10 Boarders.
Fees per term (2016–2017). Nursery, Reception, Years 1 and 2: £3,157 (Nursery part-day pro rata); Years 3–4: £3,721; Years 5–6: £3,781. Boarding: £7,446–£7,820 (full), £6,254 (weekly).

Kingswood Preparatory School is the Preparatory School for Kingswood School, Bath. It is part of the Kingswood Foundation and each year over 95% of pupils move on to Kingswood School, through examination in January, at the end of Year 6.

Kingswood School is the oldest Methodist educational institution in the world, having been founded by John Wesley in 1748. Both Preparatory and the Senior Schools have extensive linked sites on Lansdown hill overlooking the world-famous city of Bath.

At Kingswood Preparatory School we are passionate about children's learning and combine high academic standards with a core of kindness that permeates every corner of our school. Our aim is to create a happy, caring community based upon Christian principles in which all individuals can develop respect for themselves and for others.

We provide for the children a rich variety of academic, sporting, creative and social experiences. By doing so we hope to give them the opportunity to develop their personalities and potential in an atmosphere of enthusiasm, enjoyment, security and care for fellow pupils.

As well as our regular Extra-Curricular Programme which currently contains over eighty weekly options, the school offers regular opportunities to participate in Music, Drama and Sport. We are able to use certain senior school facilities such as: the swimming pool, the astroturf hockey pitch and the theatre. The Prep School shares 56 acres of playing fields with the seniors.

The Prep School is situated in the splendid parkland setting of the Summerhill estate. Children of Pre-Preparatory age are educated in the modern, award-winning, purpose-built accommodation and the senior years in the main house, Summerhill. This fine mansion was designed by John Wood the Younger. Before it came into the school's possession in the 1950s it was the home of Ernest Cook, founder of the Ernest Cook Trust. The boarders live in High Vinnalls which offers all types of boarding to boys and girls aged between 7 and 11. Adjacent to the school and superbly situated in large gardens surrounded by woods and parkland, it has been acclaimed as a model for what boarding houses for young children should be like, in terms of its homely atmosphere and facilities. The school enjoys magnificent views over the City of Bath, and is situated only one and half miles from the centre.

Charitable status. Kingswood Preparatory School is a Registered Charity, number 309148. It exists for the purpose of educating children.

Knighton House

Durweston, Blandford, Dorset DT11 0PY

Tel:	01258 452065
Fax:	01258 450744
email:	admissions@knightonhouse.co.uk
website:	www.knightonhouse.com
Twitter:	@RedDungarees
Facebook:	@knighton.house.school

Chairman of the Governors: Mrs Camilla Masters

Headmistress: Mrs S Wicks, BEd

Age Range. Girls 3–13, Boys 3–7.
Number of Pupils. Prep School: 80; The Orchard, Pre-Prep and Nursery (co-educational): 41.
Fees per term (2016–2017). Boarders £7,380; Day: Prep £4,324–£5,596, Pre-Prep £2,325–£2,829, Nursery: £2,325 (full time but excluding Early Years funding). There are no compulsory extras.

Established in 1950, Knighton House is an exceptional friendly day and boarding school for girls aged 7–13 with an 'outstanding' co-ed pre-prep for children aged 3–7.

Knighton House keeps pace with the expectations of the 21st Century, whilst nurturing its unique traditional values. As one of the few remaining all-girls prep schools, we pride ourselves on our pastoral care and the opportunities we offer girls through a crucial developmental stage of their life. We encourage independent thinking and learning and outdoor play is a key part of the school day. In a delightful country setting, the school provides a safe but challenging environment in which children can discover their strengths, take risks and make friends. Boarding is entirely flexible and ponies and pets are all welcome.

The small classes and high staff/pupil ratio ensures individual attention. The scholarships and awards won from Knighton House reflect academic, musical, artistic and all-rounder prowess; there is a strong artistic and musical tradition. Team sports and swimming have an all-year-round place in the timetable. There are many extracurricular activities including riding from our own stables, triathlon, tetrathlon, dance, drama and outdoor environmental pursuits.

This careful balance of academic subjects and extracurricular activities encourages all aspects of personal growth. The size of Knighton House ensures that each pupil is known by everyone; each girl has an identity and is respected for her individuality.

Knighton House feeds a wide range of senior schools, both co-ed and single-sex.

Charitable status. Knighton House School Limited is a Registered Charity, number 306316.

Lady Eleanor Holles Junior School

Burlington House, 177 Uxbridge Road, Hampton, Middlesex TW12 1BD

Tel:	020 8979 2173
	Registrar & Senior School: 020 8979 1601
Fax:	020 8783 1962
email:	junior-office@lehs.org.uk
website:	www.lehs.org.uk
Twitter:	@LEHSchool

Chairman of Governors: Mr C S Stokes

Head Mistress: Mrs H G Hanbury, MA, MSc

Head of Junior School: **Mrs Paula Mortimer**, BEd

Age Range. 7–11.
Number of Pupils. 188 day girls.
Fees per term (2016–2017). £5,231.

Lady Eleanor Holles Junior School is housed in its own separate building in one corner of the school's spacious twenty-four-acre grounds. Junior School pupils make full use of the school's extensive facilities, such as a heated indoor 25m pool, Sports Hall and floodlit netball courts. (*See The Lady Eleanor Holles School's entry in the GSA section for more details.*) They also take advantage of a fleet of school coaches serving most of West London and Surrey.

The school is academically selective, with most girls joining in Year 3. Entrance exams in English and Maths are held the January before entry. The vast majority of Junior School pupils are given guaranteed places in the Senior School.

The school's teaching is firmly based on the National Curriculum and there are specialist teachers for Science, Art, French, IT, Music and PE from the beginning. The school is very well resourced and staff use a wide variety of teaching styles and activities to ensure pace, stimulation and progression.

There is a wide range of extra-curricular activities so girls can develop their own interests and abilities, and all achievements and progress are valued and praised.

Extra-curricular clubs include Drama, Chess, Gardening and various Art, Music and Sports activities.

Whilst LEH is a broadly Christian foundation, it welcomes girls of all faiths, and none. School Assemblies, some of which are performed by the girls for their parents, may feature Hindu, Islamic Sikh or Jewish festivals and stories, as well as Christian.

In 2003, Burlington House, the home of the Junior School, was the subject of a very extensive programme of extension and renovation, and now boasts superb facilities for a 21st-century education. Amongst the main improvements were four spacious new Practical Rooms for Art, DT and Science; two new Computer suites; a well-stocked and welcoming Library; and larger, brighter classrooms.

The staff work hard to establish and maintain a caring, supportive atmosphere in which girls feel confident to be themselves, to respect and care for everyone in the community, to be proud of their achievements and to persevere with things they find challenging. Pastoral care is a priority and we are proud of the happy, lively, hard-working pupils of the Junior School.

Charitable status. The Lady Eleanor Holles School is a Registered Charity, number 1130254.

Lambrook

Winkfield Row, Nr Ascot, Berkshire RG42 6LU

Tel: 01344 882717
email: registrar@lambrookschool.co.uk
info@lambrookschool.co.uk
website: www.lambrookschool.co.uk
Twitter: @lambrookschool
Facebook: /lambrook

Chairman of Governors: Tom Beardmore-Gray, MA, FCA

Headmaster: **J F Perry**, BA Hons, PGCE Cantab

Deputy Headmaster: P P Thacker, BA Hons, PGCE, FRGS

Age Range. 3–13.
Number of Children. 530.
Fees per term (2016–2017). Prep: Weekly Boarding £6,926–£7,417; Day £5,695–£6,186. Pre-Prep: Day £3,859. Nursery: £1,763–£3,526.

Lambrook is a co-educational day and flexi boarding preparatory school where girls and boys aged 3–13 are immersed in a world of opportunities. Our aim is to develop our children's feathers to fly by instilling the skills, attitudes and interests that will enable them to flourish at senior school and beyond; to be intellectually curious, multi-talented, caring and confident and happily unique. We are proud of our rich history of success and to have received an 'excellent' rating across the board from the Independent Schools Inspectorate.

Founded in 1860, we are one of the oldest preparatory schools in the country, with consistently high academic standards and success at Common Entrance. Our children progress to a diverse range of leading senior schools, often with scholarships awarded in recognition of their talents.

Nestled in the heart of Berkshire countryside, we combine the breathtaking expansive grounds of a country school with outstanding modern facilities. Our 50-acre site includes a professional Performing Arts Centre with a stunning auditorium where dancers, actors, instrumentalists and singers take to the stage in numerous concerts and performances. A number of our children have also gone on to thrill audiences in the West End, TV and movie productions and through performances at Windsor Castle, Eton College, The Edinburgh Fringe and Notre Dame, Paris.

Our sector-leading sports facilities include a cedar-clad indoor 25m pool and 9-hole golf course, all set within a vast campus combining pristine cricket pitches and wild campsites. The children's skills in the traditional senior sports of Rugby, Cricket, Football, Hockey, Lacrosse and Netball are developed to a high level, with a good number going on to perform at county and regional level. Our alumni have represented their country in sports ranging from Rugby to Rowing. A diverse range of additional sports are also on offer from polo to fencing and scuba diving to skiing.

On any day, the School is awash with activity on the academic, sporting and artistic fronts, whilst also offering opportunities for inspiration, risk and challenge through our enviable Activities Programme. Survival skills, leadership, team building and even etiquette are offered as part of our extensive extra-curricular sessions.

The development of each individual child is at the heart of everything we do allowing them to grow and thrive in a stimulating and rewarding environment. Through working, playing, learning, living, serving and sharing together our children grow mentally, physically, spiritually and in so doing, appreciate the gifts they have.

The School is situated near Ascot and is easily accessible from central London, the M4, M3 and M40 motorways. We provide transport services across the local area and also to and from West London. We are also close to international transport links with Heathrow a mere 30 minutes away by road.

Charitable status. Lambrook School Trust Limited is a Registered Charity, number 309098. Its purpose is to provide an excellent education for boys and girls.

Lancing College Preparatory School at Hove
A Woodard School

The Droveway, Hove, East Sussex BN3 6LU

Tel: 01273 503452
Fax: 01273 503457
email: hove@lancing.org.uk
website: www.lancingcollege.co.uk

Chairman of Governors: Dr H O Brünjes, BSc, MBBS, DRCOG, FEWI

Head: **Mrs K Keep**, BEd Hons

Age Range. 3–13.
Number of Pupils. 253.
Fees per term (2016–2017). £1,255–£5,065 (including lunch).

Lancing College Preparatory School is situated in an enviable position in Hove overlooking the English Channel.

Much of our ethos is drawn from the fact that we are a Christian based school and central to this is the belief that children must feel happy and secure in their surroundings if they are to succeed. The school is run on family lines, each child being given a sense of their true worth as an individual but also as part of the family.

The school offers an excellent academic education with a modern curriculum preparing for the Common Entrance and Scholarship Examinations at the end of academic year eight. Central to our curriculum beliefs is the idea that all pupils have an area in which they can excel, and to that end we place huge importance on the teaching of Art, Drama, Music and Sport as well as all the subjects that you would expect to find in the National Curriculum.

We have a fully qualified staff of twenty five full and part time teachers who enjoy facilities including a fully equipped science laboratory, an art design and technology room, gymnasium, ICT suite and library. As well as extensive grounds there is an all-weather area for the coaching of our main sports, cricket, football, rugby, hockey, netball, rounders and tennis.

Charitable status. Lancing College is a Registered Charity, number 1076483. It exists to provide education for boys and girls.

Lanesborough School

Maori Road, Guildford, Surrey GU1 2EL
Tel: 01483 880650
Fax: 01483 880651
email: office@lanesborough.surrey.sch.uk
website: www.lanesborough.surrey.sch.uk
Twitter: @lanesboroughSch
Facebook: /Lanesboroughschool

Chairman of Governors: Mrs S K Creedy, MA Cantab

Head: **Mrs C Turnbull**, BA Hons, MEd

Age Range. 3–13.
Number of Boys. 360 day boys.
Fees per term (2016–2017). Nursery £3,349 (Surrey County Council Early Years Free Entitlement offsets 3 hours per day for eligible pupils), Reception and Year 1 and Year 2 £4,046, Years 3–5 £4,547, Years 6–8 £4,694.

Lanesborough is the Preparatory School of the Royal Grammar School and the choir school for Guildford Cathedral. Cathedral choristers qualify for choral scholarships.

The main entry points are Nursery, Reception and Year 3. Many of the pupils gain entry to the Royal Grammar School at age 11 or 13, whilst others are prepared for Scholarship and Common Entrance examination to senior Independent schools at 13.

The School is divided into four Houses for House competitions. Pastoral care and supervision of academic progress are shared by the Head, Housemasters, Form and subject teachers. Extra-curricular activities include music, art, chess, drama, computer club, judo, fencing, tennis, basketball, science and general knowledge.

Music is a strong feature of the life of the school, which is a member of the Choir Schools Association. In addition to the Cathedral Choir, there are senior and junior choirs, an orchestra, wind and string groups. Private tuition by qualified peripatetic teachers is available in most instruments. There are music concerts and the school Carol Service at the Cathedral has achieved wide acclaim. Music scholarships to Independent senior schools are gained each year.

Art plays an important part in the curriculum also, with boys receiving tuition throughout the school.

A new performance space is due for completion in 2017 which will further enhance drama productions.

Games are: association football, rugby football, cricket, athletics, swimming, basketball, hockey and badminton. There is a school field, gym and astroturf. A brand new, purpose-built Sports Hall opened in September 2016.

Regular school visits are undertaken to local places of interest. School parties also go abroad, e.g. for skiing, watersports, football and on cultural visits.

The Pre-Preparatory department (for boys aged 3–7 and including a Nursery unit) is housed in a separate building

(Braganza House), but shares many of the facilities of the main Prep School.

There is an active and very supportive Parents' Association.

Charitable status. Lanesborough is governed by the trustees of The Royal Grammar School of King Edward VI, Guildford which is a Registered Charity, number 312028. It exists for the purpose of educating boys in or near Guildford.

Langley Preparatory School at Taverham Hall

Taverham, Norwich, Norfolk NR8 6HU
Tel: 01603 868206
Fax: 01603 861061
email: admissions@taverhamhall.co.uk
website: www.taverhamhall.co.uk
Twitter: @TaverhamHall
Facebook: /LangleyPrepTH
LinkedIn: /taverham-hall-preparatory-school

Motto: *Conanti Dabitur ~ through effort we succeed*

Chair of Governors: Mrs S Turner

Headmaster: **M A Crossley**, BEd Hons, NPQH

Deputy Heads:
J Hyatt, BA Hons
D Sowry, BSc Ed

Age Range. 2–13.
Number of Pupils. 368: Prep 195, Pre-Prep 108, Nursery 65.
Fees per term (2016–2017). Weekly Boarding £5,925; Day: Prep £3,800–£4,585 (inc lunch); Pre-Prep £3,325 (inc lunch). Nursery (per session): £33.20 (morning), £46.50 (all day).

Langley Preparatory School at Taverham Hall, originally founded in 1921, is a co-educational IAPS and ISA day and flexi/weekly boarding school set in 100 acres of beautiful woodland conveniently situated near Norwich whilst also offering extensive school transport covering Norfolk and Suffolk for those living further afield. Scholarships are available for children aged 7 to 11 in the areas of music, sport, academic and art and open mornings take place in each term.

The school was recently awarded the NACE Challenge Award for its outstanding provision for more able pupils. The high standards achieved by pupils are recognised by both senior schools and inspection teams. Since 2010 the school has received four outstanding inspection reports. There is a firm educational focus on the individual and personalised learning along with a commitment to small class sizes. Pupils are offered exciting performance opportunities in music and drama as well as 4–5 hours each week of PE and Games lessons including weekly sporting fixtures, termly tournaments and competitions at local, regional and national level.

The school's Gold Schools Games Mark, Healthy Schools Award and Good Diabetes Care in School Award all demonstrate the importance the school places on emotional health and well-being.

The school is dedicated to providing outstanding pastoral care combined with personalised, academic learning programmes and investigative hands-on Forest School experiences. The school offers a breadth of opportunities together with a focus on how children learn rather than simply what they learn. Inspiring teaching staff identify learning styles, set personalised targets and tailor teaching to the individual, ensuring that each child has every opportunity to achieve their personal best. Through small classes and individual academic guidance and a carefully thought out PSHEE program, pupils are encouraged to analyse their strengths and target their weaknesses.

Specialist teachers throughout the school ensure children flourish in the school's vibrant, warm and friendly atmosphere. Pupils are heard to read every day in the Pre-Prep department whilst pupils in the Nursery and Reception classes follow a bespoke curriculum which draws on the strengths of the Early Years curriculum whilst crucially offering children, who are ready, the opportunity to read and write at a younger age and to develop their mathematical skills beyond the current levels of expectation. The introduction of this bespoke curriculum has only been possible as a result of the school's excellent inspections including an 'outstanding' grading from Ofsted – the basis on which the school has been allowed to exit the EYFS framework whilst maintaining the funding. This is a fabulous time for the school to build on such solid foundations.

High pupil achievements contribute to the school's excellent record for when Year 8 pupils move to senior school as well as obtaining senior school scholarships each year.

As pupils approach Year 8 and Scholarship examinations, there is a greater move towards independence. Pupils take increased responsibility for their learning and conduct, as well as obtaining leadership roles within the school, including Prefect status and mentoring Year 3 pupils when in Year 8. Both the school's Council and Boarders' Forum provide pupils with a voice and an opportunity to play an active role in the school's community as well as enhancing ways in which pupils can communicate with staff and the school in general. In their top two years pupils are taught life skills which culminate in an exciting post-Common Entrance programme with a clear focus on fun, adventure and teamwork.

Inspection Reports and Awards can be viewed via the school's website: www.taverhamhall.co.uk.

Langley Preparatory School at Taverham Hall's Open Mornings take place in September/October, January and May.

Charitable status. Taverham Hall Educational Trust Ltd exists for the purpose of educating children and is a Registered Charity, number 311272. Registered Office: Taverham, Norwich, Norfolk NR8 6HU. Company Registration No. 910504.

Lathallan School

Brotherton Castle, Johnshaven, Angus DD10 0HN
Tel: 01561 362220
Fax: 01561 361695
email: admissions@lathallan.org.uk
website: www.lathallan.org.uk
Twitter: @lathallanschool
Facebook: /Lathallan-School

Chairman of Board of Directors: Professor Sir Graeme Catto

Headmaster: **Mr Richard Toley**, BA Hons, MPhil, PGCE, FRSA

Age Range. 6 weeks to 18 years.
Number of Pupils. 228, plus 58 in Nursery.
Fees per term (2016–2017). Tuition: J1–J2 £3,410, J3–J4 £4,310, J5–7 £4,884, S1 £5,575, S2–S6 £5,890. Weekly Boarding (in addition to Tuition): £1,412. Full Boarding (in addition to tuition): £2,185. Reductions for sib-

lings and Services children. Scholarships and Bursaries available.

Class sizes averaged at 12 pupils, bespoke academic staff and an unique environment are all contributors to fulfilling the claim that every child has the opportunity to develop to their own full potential. Being non-selective, there are no entrance exams; the school assesses each child on his or her own merit.

Recently the school saw pupils reaching national finals in a variety of fields such as drama, science and sports. The diversity of these achievements underpin the Lathallan School ethos that every child deserves to enjoy the success of their individual abilities in whatever field they lie – on the sports field, in the classroom, in the arts, in personal achievement. The school is also capitalizing on its stunning rural coastal location by widening its focus on Outdoor Learning and Environmental Studies, hosting a variety of conferences in this field.

Lathallan School is a place in which challenge, industriousness and maximising individual potential is pivotal in the pupils' educational development. Every individual is made to feel an integral and special part of the school.

Lathallan School, situated in a baronial castle in 62 acres of spectacular grounds overlooking the North Sea and is easily accessible. Daily coach runs serve Lathallan School's wide catchment area from Aberdeen and Stonehaven, to Aboyne in the west, as well as Forfar and Montrose to the south. Full, weekly and flexi boarding is available; the only school in the region to offer such a service.

Charitable status. Lathallan School is a Registered Charity, number SC018423. It exists to provide education of the highest standard for boys and girls.

Latymer Prep School

36 Upper Mall, Hammersmith, London W6 9TA
Tel: 020 7993 0061
email: registrar@latymerprep.org
            admin@latymerprep.org
website: www.latymerprep.org
Twitter: @LatymerPrep

Chairman of Governors: Mr James Graham, MA, FRSA

Principal: **Mr Stuart P Dorrian**, BA

Age Range. 7–11 Co-educational.
Number of Pupils. 165 Day Pupils.
Fees per term (2016–2017). £5,620.

Latymer Prep School, led by its own Principal, was granted independence by the Governors of the Latymer Foundation in 1995 – the Centenary Year of Latymer Upper School on its present site. Previously the Prep School had been run as a very successful department of the Upper School and the relationship remains an extremely close one with all children usually expected to proceed to the Upper School.

The school is academically selective and pupils are taught the full range of subjects following National Curriculum guidelines, but to an advanced standard. Classes are kept small (20) which allows for close monitoring and evaluation of each pupil's progress and well-being. Means-tested academic scholarships are available.

The school is well resourced and has attractive facilities in two elegant period houses adjacent to the River Thames. Catering, sports and theatre facilities are shared with the Upper School.

A main feature of the school is its friendly and caring atmosphere which offers close pastoral support to each individual pupil. Academic achievement is strong, but in addition, all staff and pupils contribute to an extensive range of activities featuring Sport, Music, Art and Drama. The school has 3 large choirs and its own orchestra. Opportunities exist for all pupils to participate in concerts, plays and inter-school sporting events.

The major sports are soccer, rugby, cricket, tennis, athletics, hockey and netball. There is also a thriving swimming club (the school has its own pool). Karate chess, drama and bridge are just some of the clubs which take place after school. There is an Arts Week, plus a residential to Norfolk for Y5 and a residential to Italy for Y6 pupils.

There is a Parents' Gild and opportunities occur frequently to meet with staff socially. Visits for prospective parents occur throughout the year and can be arranged by telephoning for an appointment.

Charitable status. The Latymer Foundation is a Registered Charity, number 312714. It exists to provide an opportunity for able pupils from all walks of life to develop their talents to the full.

Laxton Junior School

East Road, Oundle, Peterborough PE8 4BX
Tel: 01832 277275
email: info@laxtonjunior.org.uk
website: www.laxtonjunior.org.uk
Twitter: @Head_LJS
Facebook: @LaxtonJunior

Governors: The Worshipful Company of Grocers

Chairman: Mr Julian Tregoning

Headmaster: **Mr Mark Potter**, BEd Hons, MEd

Deputy Head: Miss Janet Bass, BA Hons, Dip TEFL, PGDPSE

Age Range. 4–11.
Number of Children. 255.
Fees per term (2016–2017). £3,510–£3,850 (including lunches).

Opened in 1973 and part of Oundle School, Laxton Junior is a co-educational day school for children aged 4–11 years. In September 2002 Laxton Junior moved into a new building which caters for 280 pupils. The school has 14 forms of no more than 20 pupils, each with a fully qualified Form Teacher. The curriculum includes Art & Design, Computer Skills, MFL, Music, PE and Performing Arts as well as the major academic subjects. Emphasis has always been placed on the individual child and the importance of each doing their best at all times, according to their ability. Children are prepared for entrance examinations for Independent Senior Schools in the area; Kimbolton, Oundle, Oakham and Stamford Schools being the key schools.

The new building has a large multi-purpose hall which is used for PE, Music and Performing Arts as well as concerts, school plays and social events The school has its own games fields and netball courts plus all children receive swimming instruction each week in the Oundle School Pool. The main games are football, rugby, cricket, netball, rounders, hockey and athletics plus coaching in tennis.

In Year 2 all pupils have the opportunity to play the violin or cello as part of the curriculum. From Year 3 the recorder is introduced, plus additional time is given for choir, orchestra and learning other musical instruments. The school also has an Education Support Unit which monitors all pupils' development and helps individuals with specific difficulties.

The aims of the school are to encourage the formation of good work habits and good manners, to lay the foundations for the development of self-discipline, self-confidence and self-motivation and to offer the children the opportunity of experiencing the satisfaction of achievement.

The partnership of home and school in the education of the child is strongly emphasises and all parents are members of the Parents' & Friends' Association.

Laxton Junior School was inspected in February 2014. The report is available on the school website.

Charitable status. Oundle School is a Registered Charity, number 309921. It exists to provide education for boys and girls.

Leehurst Swan School

19 Campbell Road, Salisbury SP1 3BQ
Tel: 01722 333094
Fax: 01722 330868
email: registrar@leehurstswan.org.uk
           reception@leehurstswan.org.uk
website: www.leehurstswan.org.uk

Chairman of Governors: Mr Christopher Walker

Headmaster: **Mr R N S Leake**, BSc, PGCE, CBiol, MIBiol

Age Range. 0–16 Co-educational.
Number of Children. 308.
Fees per term (2016–2017). Senior School £4,590; Prep School £2,730–£3,560; Pre-School £3,070 (Full time).

Leehurst Swan is an Independent Day School, just 10 minutes' walk from Salisbury city centre, which has been inspiring and educating pupils for 100 years. We are the only independent day school in Salisbury offering education for girls and boys from age 0–16. The benefits of an all-through education are widely recognised, eliminating the problems of transfer between the stages of education. A co-educational environment also encourages the development of excellent social skills. We celebrate the best of the old while embracing the latest innovations and technology.

The school is fully co-educational with over 300 children in the School: 150 children in the Prep School, 110 in the Senior School and 48 in the Pre-Prep. The School has small classes, a family atmosphere, and an environment that inspires and motivates pupils to achieve their best. The individual attention pupils receive reflects the ethos of Christian values and respect for the individual.

We have recently invested in a substantial building project to provide a new Prep school to give state-of-the-art teaching facilities which reflects the thriving and highly successful development of the school in recent years.

Leehurst Swan Pre-Prep was inspected in March 2014 and was graded as "outstanding" in every aspect. Recently opened due to parental demand 'The Nest' provides quality care for babies and toddlers from six weeks old. The Pre-Prep provides exciting activities and prepares the children fully for formal education. The Pre-Prep welcomes children from the age of 6 weeks. Set in a purpose-built building, nestling in a wooded glade, the Pre-Prep provides outstanding quality early years education and care in a safe and secure environment. The ethos is one of inclusion with parents as equal partners.

The Nest operates to the most rigorous standards offering bespoke childcare for children aged 6 weeks to 2 years. ensuring that parents can leave their child in the safest of hands.

Pupils in the Prep School have specialist teaching in key subjects and use dedicated school facilities in ICT, Science, Music, Art, and Design Technology. The children are prepared for 11+ examinations for entry into the local grammar schools and for entry into the Senior School.

In the Senior School the pupils normally pursue studies in ten GCSE subjects and academic results are excellent. The school equally values and nurtures creative and sporting talent awarding scholarships in these areas in addition to academic scholarships.

Individual lessons are arranged in a wide range of musical instruments leading to Associated Board examinations.

Leehurst Swan welcomes visitors to the school to come and see them at work and play.

Charitable status. Leehurst Swan Limited is a Registered Charity, number 800158. It exists to provide education for children.

Leicester Grammar Junior School

London Road, Great Glen, Leicester, Leicestershire LE8 9FL

Tel: 0116 259 1950
Fax: 0116 259 1951
email: friell@leicestergrammar.org.uk
website: www.leicestergrammar.org.uk/junior-school-home
Twitter: @LGS_Junior
Facebook: /LeicesterGrammarJuniorSchool

Chair of Governors: Dr Sarah M Dauncey, MRCGP

Headmistress: **Mrs C Rigby**, BA

Age Range. 3–11 Co-educational.
Number of Pupils. 385.
Fees per term (2016–2017). Years 3–6 £3,496; Kinders to Year 2 £3,312.

Leicester Grammar Junior School was founded in 1992 when Leicester Grammar School Trust took over educational responsibility for Evington Hall, an independent school run by the Sisters of Charity of St Paul.

The school is a selective, co-educational day school with a Christian Foundation. It acts as the junior school to Leicester Grammar School and is the first stage in a continuous education from 3 years through to A Level. In September 2008 both the Junior and Senior schools relocated to a new purpose-built campus SW of the city of Leicester. Thus, the school now encompasses the full 3–18 age range on the one site.

The school provides a stimulating, disciplined, happy environment where each child is encouraged to aim for the highest standards in everything they do and take a full and active part in all aspects of school life. It operates as an extension of the family unit within which the staff act with firmness and fairness. Respect and consideration underpin school life. Pupils are encouraged to develop a caring and responsible attitude to others, leading to good manners and acceptable behaviour.

The children benefit from not only academic success and development but also from excellent musical, sporting and dramatic involvement within a broad and well balanced curriculum.

Music is a particular strength of the school and plays an important part in the life of every child. From the beginning as 3 year olds, children are taught by a music specialist. Pupils have the opportunity to learn a variety of instruments and there is a particularly strong Infant String Scheme; children as young as five or six years of age learn to play the violin or cello. The school orchestra and ensembles perform at festivals, concerts and assemblies. There are also many choral opportunities within the Junior and Infant choir which are often linked with Drama. A number of boys and girls are also members of the Leicester Cathedral choir and enjoy weekly training sessions with the Cathedral Master of Music.

In 2004 the school received the Sportsmark Gold Award in recognition of the quality of sport within the curriculum and extracurricular. The PE and Games provision aims to develop skills in team and individual games, gymnastics, dance, swimming and athletics. The main team games are rugby, football and cricket for the boys and netball, hockey and rounders for the girls. After-school clubs offer additional sporting opportunities such as tennis, badminton, table tennis and cross country.

Admissions. Pupils are admitted at all ages between 3+ and 10+ although the vast majority enter in the September following their third or fourth birthday (Kinders or Reception). Following a visit to the school an Application Form is offered. When the form is returned a date for assessment is set. Parents wishing their children to be admitted to the Infant Department at times other than in September are invited to bring their child to school to spend part of a day with the class he or she would join. Class teachers then carry out an assessment to determine whether or not the child will be able to integrate into the year group.

Charitable status. Leicester Grammar School Trust is a Registered Charity, number 510809.

Leweston Junior Department

Sherborne, Dorset DT9 6EN

Tel: 01963 210790
Fax: 01963 210648
email: enquiries@leweston.dorset.sch.uk
website: www.leweston.co.uk
Twitter: @LewestonSchool
Facebook: /Leweston

Chair of Board of Governors: Fr Richard Meyer

Head: **Mrs Kate Reynolds**, LLB Bristol, PGCE Bath

Senior Teacher: Mrs V Bridgeman-Sutton, BA Hons Sheffield, MPhil Sheffield, QTS Dorset, PCES SpLD Southampton

Age Range. 3 months–11 years Co-educational.
Number of Pupils. 104: 72 Girls, 32 Boys.
Fees per term (2016–2017). Nursery (per day): £47.50–£50.00 (all day 08.00–18.00 including food); £25–£27.50 (1 x 5 hr session 08.00–13.00 or 13.00–18.00); Breakfast Club 07.30–08.00: £4.50.

Day (per term): Reception–Year 1 £1,900; Years 2–3 £2,500; Years 4–5 £3,100; Year 6 £3,700. Boarding (per term): Weekly £5,554–£5,859, Full £6,645.

Setting. Leweston Junior Department is an independent Catholic school for boys and girls with boarding provision for girls from Year 4 and above. The school is situated in forty-six acres of Dorset parkland three miles south of Sherborne and occupies an enviable setting in a skilfully converted former Coach House providing a unique range of bright spacious classrooms. The beautiful rural site is shared with Leweston School (girls 11–18 years), offering continuity of education for girls right through to A Level. The Junior Department enjoys the benefit of many excellent facilities including a modern, well-equipped Art and Design Centre, an all-weather sports pitch, a heated swimming pool, a large sports hall, tennis courts and extensive playing fields. As a result of the integration with Leweston School in 2014, Junior pupils now take advantage of the specialist teaching in Languages, Art, Maths, Domestic Science, Music and Sport that is provided by the Senior School. The parkland setting offers many opportunities for study and recreation.

Ethos. Traditional excellence in teaching is combined with modern facilities and resources in a stimulating, happy and purposeful Christian environment. The school motto 'Gaudere et Bene Facere' (Rejoice and Do Well) exactly reflects the importance of high academic standards together with artistic, musical and sporting excellence achieved in an atmosphere of joy and vibrancy. Each child is encouraged to develop individual talents within the caring and supportive school community. Small class sizes, a friendly family ethos, and traditional values of work and behaviour are appreciated by parents. Full and flexi boarding options provide flexibility for pupils to enjoy a wide variety of extra-curricular activities, whilst no Saturday morning school allows for rest and relaxation.

Curriculum. Programmes of study encompass the National Curriculum without being constrained by it. Basic subjects are taught to a high standard concentrating on literacy and numeracy acquisition in the early years before expanding into a broader curriculum in Years 3–6. Well-qualified class teachers and specialist subject teachers foster independent learning and encourage the development of problem solving and investigative skills in all areas of the curriculum. Academic standards are high and many pupils gain awards to senior school.

There is a strong tradition in the performing arts. Music, Drama and Performing Arts are taught within the curriculum. A high percentage of pupils learn to play musical instruments and take additional Drama. There is a school orchestra and choir and many opportunities throughout the year for performance and grade examinations in both Music and Drama. All pupils in Years 4–6 undertake English Speaking Board assessments. Individual and team sports are considered important as part of the healthy, active lifestyle and the school enjoys a particular reputation for hockey and cross-country. Art, Ceramics and Design Technology are taught by specialist teachers using the exceptional facilities in the Art and Design Centre.

Charitable status. Leweston School Trust is a Registered Charity, number 295175. It exists to provide for children a contemporary education in the Catholic tradition.

Littlegarth School

Horkesley Park, Nayland, Colchester, Essex CO6 4JR

Tel: 01206 262332
Fax: 01206 263101
email: office@littlegarth.essex.sch.uk
website: www.littlegarth.essex.sch.uk

Chairman of Governors: Mrs E Mimpriss, Cert Ed

Headmaster: Mr Peter Jones, BEd Hons

Deputy Head: Mrs Lynda Turner, BA Hons

Age Range. 2½–11.
Number of Pupils. Day: approx 180 Boys, 135 Girls.
Fees per term (2016–2017). £745–£3,380.

Littlegarth has grown steadily and in September 1994, we moved to our current premises of Horkesley Park. The Grade II listed Georgian house is situated in delightful Stour Valley countryside, designated as an Area of Outstanding Natural Beauty. The 30 acres of School land boast a number of purpose-built teaching rooms, including a multi-purpose Sports Hall, Science Laboratory, Music Room and numerous classrooms. A new development due to start in October 2016 will provide the children with increased opportunities to develop a range of skills, supported by our broad curriculum.

Outdoors, we make good use of our sports field with up to eight pitches and four outdoor cricket nets. Our outdoor play area has climbing and activity structures and a vegetable garden with a recent extension to the green area enhancing the natural space around our covered outdoor reading areas. Our innovative adventure woodland provides an excellent environment for nature walks and Forest School activities, which run from Nursery through to Year 4. This area has been enriched by the planting of wildflower meadows and the erection of an outdoor stage which will allow for productions and concerts by the children.

Starting in Nursery, children are provided with excellent specialist teaching in Drama, French, Music and Sport. Small class sizes ensure that children receive a high level of individual attention and the Early Years Foundation Stage (EYFS) framework provides a springboard for individualised learning which continues throughout the school. Pre-Prep teachers provide a firm foundation in the core subjects, supported by caring teaching assistants and learning support staff. In Year 3, the number of lessons taught by subject specialist teachers increases and from Year 4 all timetabled lessons are taught by subject specialists.

Pastoral care is one of the key strengths of Littlegarth, as highlighted in our inspection report. Year 6 children are given considerable opportunities to take on responsibilities, and further develop their self-confidence as Prefects, supporting children and staff in a variety of ways.

The school produces many plays each year and strong drama links with the local community are being forged. As well as running the school library, parents are also actively involved in running a wardrobe department and there is a flourishing 'Friends of Littlegarth' parent body.

A wide variety of clubs, extra-curricular activity and pre and after school care are offered.

Charitable status. Littlegarth School Limited is a Registered Charity, number 325064. It exists to provide education for children.

Lochinver House School

Heath Road, Little Heath, Potters Bar, Herts EN6 1LW

Tel: 01707 653064
Fax: 01707 663828
email: registrar@lochinverhouse.com
website: www.lochinverhouse.com
Twitter: @LHSPrep

Chairman of the Governors: William Moores

Headmaster: Ben Walker, BA Hons

Age Range. 4–13.
Number of Boys. 350 Day Boys.
Fees per term (2016–2017). £3,440–£4,525 with no compulsory extras.

The academic staff consists of 36 qualified and graduate teachers, Laboratory, ICT, DT technicians, Teaching Assistants and a Matron.

The school, founded in 1947, is situated in a pleasant residential area on the edge of green belt land in South Hertfordshire, and yet is conveniently placed for access to London. At the heart of the school is a late Victorian house. Facilities on our 8½ acre site are extensive and include a purpose-built Pre Prep Department, separate Sports Hall, Gymnasium & Theatre, Music Centre, two Science Laboratories and specialist IT, DT, and Art rooms. Lochinver is fully advanced with IT including an exciting project which provides iPads to older boys.

Boys are prepared for Common Entrance and Scholarship examinations to a wide range of top day and boarding Independent Schools.

The school has its own extensive playing fields on site, including an all-weather, Astro pitch. The major sports: Football, Rugby, Cricket, Athletics and Basketball are complemented by opportunities to take part in a very wide range of further sports and physical activity. All boys learn to swim whilst they are at the School. Residential trips take place both within the UK and overseas, such as skiing in Europe, a Classics trip to Italy and a Rugby Tour to South Africa. During their time at the school each boy will spend some time in France as this is an important and much valued part of the French Curriculum. There are opportunities for the boys to also study Spanish, Latin and Russian.

Music, Art, Drama, Design Technology and PE are part of the timetabled curriculum for all boys. The school encourages boys to learn at least one musical instrument and currently 75% of the children are doing so. There is a School Orchestra, Junior and Senior Choir, together with a variety of instrumental Groups. Parents appreciate our provision of extended care at both ends of the day.

The school is a non-profit making Educational Trust administered by a Board of Governors.

Charitable status. Lochinver House School is a Registered Charity, number 1091045. It aims to provide a quality education.

Lockers Park

Lockers Park Lane, Hemel Hempstead, Hertfordshire HP1 1TL

Tel:	01442 251712
Fax:	01442 234150
email:	secretary@lockerspark.herts.sch.uk
website:	www.lockerspark.herts.sch.uk

Chairman of Governors: C Lister, BSc Hons, MBA

Headmaster: **C Wilson**, BA Cantab, PGCE

Admissions: Mrs S Johnson

Age Range. 4–13. The Pre-Prep is co-educational and the Prep is boys only.

Number of Pupils. 157 children, of whom 70 are boarders or flexi boarders.

Fees per term (2016–2017). Boarders £7,720, Day Boys £3,350–£5,510. Day fees include the option to have breakfast, stay for supper and participate in evening activities at no extra cost.

Further details are outlined in the prospectus, available on application.

Lockers Park is located in 23 acres of parkland above the town of Hemel Hempstead, only five miles from both the M1 and M25 motorways. It lies within easy access of London (Euston 30 minutes) and all four of its airports; consequently the School is well accustomed to providing the necessary help and support to parents living both in Britain and abroad.

The main school building, purpose-built in 1874, is situated in grounds which are perfect for children, with well-maintained playing fields surrounded by woodland areas which easily occupy even the most active. There has been a steady process of modernisation over the past two decades and the School boasts first-class, all-round facilities: the Mountbatten Centre, which provides eight excellent specialist classrooms including a well-equipped ICT centre; an attached Science and Technology Building, containing two spacious laboratories, technology classroom and fully-fitted workshop; an exceptional art and pottery centre and a well-resourced library.

A purpose-built Pre-Preparatory School opened in September 2015 and admits both boys and girls while the main Prep School remains firmly committed to a boys-only education.

Sports facilities are of a high calibre and include a fully-fitted sports hall, two squash courts, a recently refurbished heated swimming pool, two tennis courts, an all-weather sports surface and cricket nets, a shooting range and a nine-hole golf course.

Lockers is proud of its academic and musical records; its success in both scholarships and Common Entrance examinations to 45 different schools in the past ten years reflects this well. The average class size is 14 and the pupil : teacher ratio a very healthy 1:7. The Music Department is well known; encouragement is given to every boy to find an instrument which he will enjoy and most gain proficiency in at least one. There is a full orchestra, wind, brass and jazz bands, a string ensemble and two choirs. The number of senior school scholarships of all types awarded to Lockers Park is considered high.

Drama plays a large part in school life with at least two major productions each year together with junior plays, school assembly productions, charades and public speaking debates.

At Lockers, there is a real family atmosphere, there is always someone to whom a boy can turn and great care is taken to ensure the happiness of every child. Boys are safe, happy, fit and well looked after. While day boys enjoy all the facilities and opportunities of a boarding school, boarding is fun; dormitories are warm and friendly rooms and opportunities for a variety of enjoyable weekend activities are immense. With day boys and boarders alike, great care is taken over the personal development of each individual.

Bursaries. Lockers Park is committed to offering financial help to deserving candidates, subject to financial resources. Bursarial help may be available up to 100% of fees in some circumstances.

Charitable status. Lockers Park School Trust Ltd is a Registered Charity, number 311061. It aims to provide an all round, high quality education on a non-profit making basis.

Longacre School

Shamley Green, Guildford, Surrey GU5 0NQ

Tel:	01483 893225
email:	office@longacreschool.co.uk
website:	www.longacreschool.co.uk
Twitter:	@longacreschool
Facebook:	/longacreschool

Headmistress: **Mrs Alexia Bolton**, BA Hons, QTS, PCPSE

Age Range. 2½–11.
Number of Pupils. 250+ boys and girls.
Fees per term (from January 2017). £1,560–£4,705.

Are school days really the happiest days of your life? Many Longacre pupils would answer "Yes!" The cheerful and purposeful atmosphere at Longacre is apparent as soon as you enter the school. Here, children are valued as individuals and are encouraged to fulfil their potential in every facet of school life. Personal and social development is highly valued, enabling pupils to grow in confidence as they mature.

The Headmistress and her staff believe that children learn more effectively when they are happy, and that excellent academic results can be achieved without subjecting pupils to hothouse pressure. The fact that Longacre pupils gain a range of scholarships, and that they transfer successfully to senior schools of parental choice, shows that this approach is definitely working.

Academic progress is closely monitored and regularly tested. Small classes (maximum eighteen) enable pupils to be taught at an individual level, with increasing subject specialist tuition as children progress through the school. Alongside the core curriculum, Longacre offers a wide range of sporting opportunities, LAMDA lessons, stimulating off-site visits and exciting workshops. There are after school clubs every evening, ranging from Spanish to judo, and regular masterclasses for able pupils.

Set in a beautiful rural location on the outskirts of the picturesque village of Shamley Green, between Guildford and Cranleigh, the school offers a wonderful environment for young children. The school buildings comprise the original large 1902 house plus modern, purpose-built classrooms standing in nine acres of grounds. Facilities include a brand new sports hall and astroturf, sports fields, gardens, woodland and an adventure playground.

Longacre is a community where parents are welcome. The school has a thriving and supportive PTA and parents are kept well informed about school events and their children's progress through a weekly newsletter, formal and informal meetings and written reports. The Headmistress and staff work closely with parents to ensure that their children are happy, successful and fulfilled.

To arrange a visit, please call 01483 893225. The Headmistress and her staff look forward to welcoming you to Longacre.

Lorenden Preparatory School

Painter's Forstal, Faversham, Kent ME13 0EN

Tel:	01795 590030
email:	office@lorenden.org
website:	www.lorenden.org
Twitter:	@LorendenSchool
Facebook:	/lorendenschool

Chairman of Governors: R Boyd-Howell

Headteacher: **Mrs K Uttley**, BA Hons, PGCE

Age Range. 3–11 Co-educational.
Number of Pupils. 120.
Fees per term (2016–2017). £2,695–£3,898.
Lorenden is situated in the village of Painter's Forstal between Faversham and the North Downs and within easy driving distance of Canterbury, Whitstable, Ashford and Sittingbourne; an idyllic position in the heart of the Kent countryside.

The school's avowed aim is to develop self-disciplined thoughtful children with a cheerful 'can do' attitude to life and a strong sense of fair play, exemplified through the motto 'We Care. We Share. We Strive. We Succeed'.

All round expectations are high and academic results are excellent. At eleven children either transfer to local grammar schools, or continue in independent education. The school places great emphasis in ensuring each individual is nurtured according to their strengths, and advice to parents on senior school choice is carefully tailored to each child, with parents then able to make the best decision. Able children are awarded major academic, sports or art scholarships annually to a range of senior schools.

Music is a great strength of the school and sports results are remarkably good. Every child 'gets a go' and resilience is the name of the game.

This is a school that needs to be experienced to be truly appreciated: a friendly, family environment where visitors are always delighted by what they find.

Enquiries concerning places and admissions should be made to the Secretary.

Charitable status. Lorenden School is a Registered Charity, number 1048805.

Loretto Junior School

North Esk Lodge, 1 North High Street, Musselburgh, East Lothian EH21 6JA

Tel:	0131 653 4570
Fax:	0131 653 4571
email:	juniorschool@loretto.com
website:	www.loretto.com
Twitter:	@lorettohead
Facebook:	/lorettoschool

Chairman of Governors: Lt Col S J M Graham

Headmaster: **P Meadows**, MA Cantab, CertEd

Age Range. 5–12.
Number of Pupils. 176.
Fees per term (2016–2017). Day Pupils £2,850–£4,950; Year 7 Full Boarding £6,950; Flexi Boarding (3 nights per week) £5,900; Overnighting £50 per night. Bursaries up to 105% of fees are available.

Pupils can enter the Nippers at 5 and are prepared for entrance and scholarship assessments, mostly to Loretto at 12+. A range of Bursaries are available for entry to the Nippers, usually at 10+ and 11+. Occasional and Flexi Boarding are possible for pupils aged 11 and over. The School has excellent facilities of its own in a safe, secure and leafy campus. The Nippers also enjoy access to the Sports Hall, Theatre, Chapel and Music School on the Senior School site. Specialist teaching is provided in Science (in a brand new laboratory), IT, French, Music, Art, Drama and PE; all pupils in Years 6 and 7 have their own iPad provided by the School. The school enjoys a fine reputation for Music, Drama, Art, Rugby, Hockey, Cricket and Golf Tuition. A wide range of different individual sports is also offered including Tennis, Squash, Skiing; all pupils now receive Golf Tuition in the School's new state-of-the-art indoor golf coaching facility. The staff are all University Graduates and each of the thirteen classes can accommodate up to 16 pupils; the average class size is currently 14. Pastoral care is of the highest quality. Catering is in the hands of an experienced Steward.

From an early age children are encouraged to use their initiative and accept responsibility.

A prospectus can be requested from the School.

Charitable status. Loretto School is a Registered Charity, number SC013978. It exists in order to educate young people in mind, body and spirit.

Loyola Preparatory School

103 Palmerston Road, Buckhurst Hill, Essex IG9 5NH

Tel:	020 8504 7372
Fax:	020 8505 5361
email:	office@loyola.essex.sch.uk
website:	www.loyola.essex.sch.uk

Chair of Governors: Mrs A M Fox

Headmaster: **P G M Nicholson**, BEd London

Age Range. 3–11.
Number of Boys. 184.
Fees per term (2016–2017). £3,005 (inc lunch).

Loyola Preparatory School is a long established school educating boys for over a century, originally as part of St Ignatius College. As a caring Catholic School it welcomes boys of all denominations offering a weekly mass to celebrate faith, ethos and values.

As a boys-only school, Loyola focuses its teaching techniques to harness the attention of boys by applying the extensive studies made into 'the ways boys learn best'. These practices encourage greater stimulation and enjoyment which is demonstrated by their overall behaviour and results.

Loyola has a high teacher to pupil ratio, facilitated by enthusiastic and committed teachers, supported by a generous quota of quality teaching assistants.

Loyola boys are encouraged to be kind and respect each other, with the older boys acting as role models for the younger boys. Year 6 boys are given Prefect responsibilities as well as the opportunity to be elected to the position of Head Boy and Deputy Head Boy. All boys regularly take part in community events including fund raising for national and local charities.

Loyola supports their boy's progression for the next step in their learning journey by preparing them for entrance and scholarship exams with English and Maths being taught in small ability sets from Year 3 upwards.

The curriculum covers all the normal primary subjects and includes German, science and computer studies. There are schola, choir and orchestra opportunities available in school, with additional tuition for piano, strings, woodwind, brass and guitar.

Loyola is proud of its range of sporting activities for the boys, aided by a large all-weather pitch on site. Sporting activities include soccer, cricket, rugby, swimming, athletics and sailing (Year 6) of which many are available during the school day and others offered as an after-school club.

During their time at the school, Loyola boys experience a wide range of trips and activities including a 5-day trip to Normandy (Year 6), a 3-day trip to Kingswood in Norfolk (Year 4), together with many day trips across the school years selected to stimulate and enrich their learning experience.

The school prospectus is available on the school website and prospective parents are welcome to telephone for an appointment to be given a personal tour of the school.

Charitable status. Loyola Preparatory School is a Registered Charity, number 1085079. The school is established in support of Roman Catholic principles of education.

Lucton Prep School

Lucton, Leominster, Herefordshire HR6 9PN

Tel: 01568 782000
Fax: 01568 782001
email: admissions@luctonschool.org
website: www.luctonschool.org
Twitter: @LuctonSchool
Facebook: @Lucton-School
LinkedIn: /lucton-school

Headmistress of Lucton School: Mrs Gill Thorne, MA, BA Hons, PGCE, LLAM

Head of Prep School: **Mr David Bicker-Caarten**, MBA

Age Range. 6 months–11 years.
Number in School. 135.
Fees per term (2016–2017). Day £2,215–£3,115, Weekly Boarding £6,990, Full Boarding £9,295.

Lucton Prep School is on the same site as Lucton School, which was founded in 1708. Lucton provides pupils with an excellent all-round education which aims to bring out their full potential. Pupils benefit from small classes, a friendly atmosphere and an idyllic rural location. The Prep School pupils benefit from the Senior School's extensive facilities, including a modern indoor swimming pool, sports hall and an equestrian centre. Lucton accepts boarders from Year 3 and has a good mix of day pupils, weekly boarders and full boarders.

Taught in small classes, with no combined year-groups, the pupils benefit from a very high degree of individual attention.

The Lucton Nursery accepts babies from the age of 6 months and with the extra early and late sessions, nursery children may be dropped off from 8.00 am and collected as late as 6.00 pm.

The vast majority of Lucton Prep School pupils continue through to the senior part of the school. (*See full details in Lucton School's entry in the ISA section.*)

School Facilities. The school is set in 55 acres of beautiful Herefordshire countryside. Facilities on site include:

• Separate junior and senior libraries
• Science laboratories
• ICT rooms
• Design and technology workshop
• Tennis courts
• Indoor swimming pool
• Indoor sports hall
• Games fields
• Equestrian centre.

Boarding pupils are housed in modern buildings and the Prep School boarders are all in dormitories in their own junior house. They have the opportunity to move into their own rooms in the Senior School.

Admissions. Admission can take place at any time of the year by interview and assessment. Prospective pupils are always invited to spend a taster day in the school without obligation. Examinations for academic scholarships are held in January each year.

Affiliations. The Head of Lucton Prep School, part of Lucton School, is a member of the The Independent Association of Prep Schools (IAPS); the Headmistress of Lucton School is a member of the Independent Schools Association (ISA); and Lucton School is in membership of the Boarding Schools' Association (BSA).

Charitable status. Lucton School is a Registered Charity, number 518076.

Ludgrove

Wokingham, Berks RG40 3AB

Tel: 0118 978 9881
Fax: 0118 979 2973
email: office@ludgroveschool.co.uk
website: www.ludgrove.net

Chairman of Governors: P D Edey, QC

Head: **S W T Barber**, BA Durham, PGCE

Registrar: Mrs J Austen

Age Range. 8–13.

Number of Boys. 190 Boarders.

Fees per term (2016–2017). £8,650.

Ludgrove is a thriving full boarding boys prep school situated in 130 acres of beautiful grounds in Berkshire. It is a magical place to spend five years of childhood, where outstanding pastoral care lies at the heart of everything.

The principal aims of the school are for boys to grow and develop in a happy caring environment, to explore and expand their potential and to learn to develop an awareness and concern for others around them. We aim to prepare our boys to meet the demanding challenges they will experience at the next stage of their education with confidence and good humour.

We are unashamedly ambitious for every boy and are proud of our strong academic record. In recent years we have sent over 70% of boys on to Eton, Harrow and Radley, in addition to other distinguished public schools. The boys have a wealth of opportunities: a stimulating curriculum, exceptional facilities and a vibrant extra-curricular programme with exposure to music, drama, sport and art.

Our extensive facilities include a stunning new 350-seat theatre, purpose-built science laboratories, art, pottery and CDT department, a large sports hall and well-stocked library, in addition to the impressive 120 acres of grounds incorporating numerous games pitches, a 9-hole golf course, squash courts, fives courts, an astroturf, tennis courts, a 20m indoor pool and adventure playground.

Charitable status. Ludgrove School Trust Limited is a Registered Charity, number 309100.

Lyndhurst House Preparatory School

24 Lyndhurst Gardens, Hampstead, London NW3 5NW

Tel:　020 7435 4936

email:　pmg@lyndhursthouse.co.uk

website:　www.lyndhursthouse.co.uk

Headmaster: **Andrew Reid**, MA Oxon

Age Range. 4–13.

Number of Day Boys. 168.

Fees per term (2016–2017) £5,735–£6,410 (including lunch and outings).

There is a full-time teaching staff of 20, with classroom assistants for the first four years and learning support across the year-groups. Entry is at 4+, or 7+ following interviews and assessment. All boys stay to 13+, and sit the Common Entrance Exam or Scholarship to the Independent Senior Schools. Lyndhurst is a friendly and lively traditional boys' school, with its own special atmosphere and character. The environment is warm and friendly, small and familiar in feel, yet full of bustle, activity and purpose. Strong foundations laid in the early years are followed by small sets in the top three years to provide the School's excellent record of success in transfers to London day schools and major public schools further afield. In addition to high academic expectations, there is a strong emphasis on sporting activity and achievement, as well as art, music, drama and computing. Lyndhurst House – a full, rich life in a personal, individual and friendly environment.

Magdalene House Preparatory School
Wisbech Grammar School

North Brink, Wisbech, Cambs PE13 1JX

Tel:　01945 586780

　　　01945 586750 Admissions

Fax:　01945 586781

email:　Office@MagdaleneHousePrep.com

website:　MagdaleneHousePrep.com

Facebook:　/MagdaleneHouse

Chair of Governors: Dr D Barter, MBBS, FRCP, FRCPCH, DCH

Acting Head: **Mrs K Neaves**, BEd, TDip

Age Range. 4–11 co-educational.

Number of Pupils. 155 day pupils.

Fees per term (2016–2017). £2,932–£2,998. Means-tested bursary support is available.

Magdalene House Preparatory School, caters for pupils from Reception to Prep 6. Great emphasis is placed on reading, writing and numeracy, and the pupils follow a broad-based curriculum. The pupils have access to many of the excellent senior school facilities, including the science laboratory, sports hall and theatre. They also have their own library, a dedicated computer room and a light and spacious hall. Specialist teaching is offered in science, music, design technology, physical education and games, information technology and drama. Many children receive peripatetic music lessons and there are three choirs. Opportunities for performance in drama and music, including class plays, assemblies and informal concerts, are regular features. In October the Prep 6 pupils sit an entrance examination for the senior school. (*See Wisbech Grammar School entry in HMC section.*)

Sporting opportunities abound and a full timetable of fixtures against other schools is arranged. The main boys' team sports are rugby, hockey and cricket, whilst the girls play hockey, netball and cricket. Members of the under 11 rugby and hockey teams enjoy an annual long weekend tour.

A varied after-school programme for both juniors and infants provides the opportunity to develop sports and leisure skills, as well as artistic and musical talents. A supervised homework club also runs each day.

Field trips, activity days at local museums and visits by theatre groups and outside speakers lie at the heart of the curriculum. Prep 4, 5 and 6 enjoy an annual residential visit to an educational activity centre.

Generally children are admitted to the Reception class at the beginning of the school year in which they reach the age of 5, but entry into all year groups is possible throughout the year. All children registering are invited to spend a day in school when they are assessed in a manner appropriate to their age. Candidates for entry are also welcomed at all other stages of the prep school age range.

All enquiries should be made to the Secretary at Magdalene House Preparatory School.

Charitable status. The Wisbech Grammar School Foundation is a Registered Charity, number 1087799. It exists to promote the education of boys and girls.

Maidwell Hall

Maidwell, Northampton, Northamptonshire NN6 9JG

Tel: 01604 686234
Fax: 01604 686659
email: thesecretary@maidwellhall.co.uk
website: www.maidwellhall.co.uk
Twitter: @maidwellhall
Facebook: /Maidwell Hall

Chairman of the Governors: R H Cunningham, Esq

Headmaster: **R A Lankester**, MA Cantab, PGCE

Age Range. 7–13.
Number of Pupils. 123: 109 Boarders, 14 Day pupils.
Fees per term (2016–2017). £8,450 Boarding, £5,500 Day.

Maidwell Hall is a co-educational boarding school with some day pupils. Occupying a substantial 17th Century hall the school is situated in beautiful countryside and is characterized by its rural location and by 44 acres of grounds. It is a Christian school and the teachings of Jesus Christ are central to the moral and spiritual education of the children. Every Sunday morning the school worships in the parish church on the edge of the school grounds. The school aims to encourage all the children to discover and develop all their talents through the academic curriculum, the games programme, Music, Art, Drama and an impressive range of hobbies and activities. The school's happy atmosphere is based on a clear framework of rules and conventions with strong emphasis placed on good manners and a traditional code of behaviour and courtesy.

The school is organized as a 7 day-a-week boarding school with a comprehensive programme of club activities in the evenings supplemented by a choice of outings or school based free-time activities on Sundays. There is a weekly boarding option for Year 4. The children benefit greatly from the freedom and security of the school's spectacular grounds including its famous arboretum (wilderness) and its large lake for fishing and boating. Leave-outs occur every 2 or 3 weeks and run from Friday midday until Monday evening and each term contains a long half-term break. Pastoral care for the boarders is the direct responsibility of the Headmaster and his wife, the Housemaster and the team of Matrons and other residential staff. In addition each pupil has an individual tutor.

Pupils are prepared for Common Entrance to the major independent senior schools (typically Eton, Harrow, Oundle, Radley, Rugby, Shrewsbury, Stowe, Uppingham and Winchester) and every year several sit scholarships. In addition to core subjects all pupils study Art, Design, ICT, Latin, Music and Religious Studies and there are also timetabled lessons in PE, Swimming, PSHE, and Drama. There is a specialist carpentry shop which operates as a club activity.

The school has a strong reputation for sport. The major games for the boys are rugby, football, hockey and cricket and there are also matches against other schools in athletics, cross-country running, golf, squash, swimming and tennis. The major games for girls are hockey, netball, tennis and rounders. Teams are entered for riding events and the Pytchley hunt meets at the school every year. There is a successful school shooting team. In the Summer and Autumn there is sailing once or twice a week. In addition to impressive games pitches, sporting facilities include a multi-purpose sports hall with climbing wall, a squash court, a 6-hole golf course, astroturf, hockey pitch, tennis courts and a heated indoor swimming pool. There is particular emphasis on outward bound activities and leadership. There is a strong musical tradition and most pupils play one or two musical instruments; there is a thriving church choir and strings, wind and guitar groups. There are regular concerts throughout the year and each year there is a major school play.

Charitable status. Maidwell Hall is a Registered Charity, number 309917. It exists for the purpose of educating children.

Maldon Court Preparatory School

Silver Street, Maldon, Essex CM9 4QE

Tel: 01621 853529
Fax: 01621 853529
email: enquiries@maldoncourtschool.org
website: www.maldoncourtschool.org

Principal: **Mrs L F Guest**, BEd Hons

Headteacher: Mrs E Mason

Assistant Headteacher: Mrs C Saggs

Age Range. 1–11 co-educational.
Number of Pupils. 152 Day Pupils.
Fees per term (2016–2017). £2,968 for the first child, with sibling discounts.

The school, founded in 1956, is a co-educational day school of nine classes. The school day begins at 8.45 am and finishes at 3.30 pm. Wrap-around care from 7.30 am until 6.00 pm is available which incorporates homework classes and a variety of clubs. The Pre-Prep department welcomes children from the age of 1. Nursery Education Grants are available and the Pre-Prep is Ofsted registered. The school has the reputation of being a happy, friendly community with a family atmosphere.

Maldon Court's premises comprise the larger part of an eighteenth century town house, a separate four-classroom block and a brand new assembly hall and nursery. The grounds consist of playgrounds, gardens and adventure play areas. The premises are very convenient for the town centre. Sports grounds for rugby, athletics, hockey, netball and tennis are leased locally. There is a wide variety of after-school clubs including netball, cricket, gymnastics, rounders, athletics, and 11+ preparations. Swimming is undertaken throughout the year at a nearby sports centre. The school's sporting standard is high; over recent years it has won both national and regional awards in netball, swimming, athletics, cross country and cricket.

Approximately half the children leave the school for independent secondary schools, half enter the maintained sector. Maldon Court's scholarship and entrance record to the independent schools is excellent as is its eleven-plus success rate to Essex grammar schools. Close contact is maintained with both systems of education. Its curriculum covers and goes far beyond the National Curriculum.

There is an active and energetic 'Friends of Maldon Court School' association, through which current and former parents play a vital role.

The school had its most recent ISI Inspection in May 2013 and achieved the highest possible rating of "Excellent" in every area.

Within the school motto of "Do it with thy might", the aims of Maldon Court are: to foster a love of learning in which the varied talents and life experiences of each pupil are recognised and valued; to provide a broad and stimulating curriculum through which pupils can flourish and become enthusiastic and independent learners, enabling them to reach their full potential; to promote the traditional values of kindness, respect and courtesy within a happy, nurturing atmosphere; to encourage a social awareness and respect for others through involvement in the local community; and to create confident and happy pupils, ready to face the challenges of the wider world.

The Mall School

185 Hampton Road, Twickenham, Middlesex TW2 5NQ
Tel: 020 8977 2523
Fax: 020 8977 8771
email: admissions@themallschool.org.uk
website: www.themallschool.org.uk

Chairman of Governors: R J H Walker, BSc

Headmaster: D Price, BSc, MA, PGCE

Deputy Head: J Fair, BA

Age Range. 4–13.
Number of Boys. 304 day boys.
Fees per term (2016–2017). Reception–Year 2 £3,750, Years 3–8 £4,210.

Founded in 1872, for over 140 years we have been preparing boys for a range of the leading independent London day and boarding senior schools. Many boys have secured scholarships (37 in the last 5 years) in a wide range of disciplines including Academic, Sport, Art, Drama, Choral, Allrounder and the highly coveted John Colet Award for St Paul's.

Boys are welcomed at 4+, as well as at 7+, and are taught by a well-qualified staff consisting of 29 full-time and 3 part-time members, in an average class size of 18–20. We teach a broad curriculum based on the Common Entrance syllabus, including Art, DT, Music, and Drama, in addition to sport and PE.

Cricket, Rugby, Football, Swimming and Athletics are the main sports played at the school. We have our own outstanding 25m indoor swimming pool and a state-of-the-art Sports Hall which opened in January 2014.

Music and Drama are warmly encouraged at the Mall School. There are 2 choirs and 2 orchestras with a large variety of ensembles and visiting teachers for piano, strings, guitar, woodwind and brass.

To help working parents, we provide an extensive range of after-school clubs, such as Chess, Judo and Art Clubs, as well as a homework club until 6.00 pm and a summer holiday club.

In addition to bright modern classrooms, facilities include Science Laboratories, Music practice rooms, IT suite, Library and a new Creative and Performing Arts Centre which provides a 160-seat theatre and large-sized Art and Design Technology studios. A morning minibus service is in operation which brings boys to school from the Teddingtion, Kingston, Richmond, St Margarets, Twickenham and Isleworth areas.

The Pre Prep is housed in an old Victorian Vicarage, a five-minute walk from the Prep school. This building was refurbished in 2015 and a new outdoor interactive play area was opened in September 2016.

The Mall School prospectus is available via the website or the Headmaster's PA. Early application is advisable as the school is non-selective for entry into Year R and there are only limited places available via assessment at 7+.

Charitable status. The Mall School Trust is a Registered Charity, number 295003. It exists to promote and provide for the advancement of the education of children.

Maltman's Green

Maltmans Lane, Gerrards Cross, Bucks SL9 8RR
Tel: 01753 883022
Fax: 01753 891237
email: office@maltmansgreen.com
website: www.maltmansgreen.com
Twitter: @MaltmansGreen
Facebook: @MaltmansGreenSchool

Preparatory School for Girls.

Chairman of Governors: Mr H Mann, OBE, FCIM

Headmistress: Mrs J Pardon, MA, BSc Hons, PGCE

Age Range. 2–11.
Number of Girls. 420.
Fees per term (2016–2017). £1,735 (5 mornings Nursery) rising to £4,680 in the Senior part of the school.

Maltman's Green is a non-selective girl's prep school. Currently taking girls from 3 to 11, however, from January 2017 we are delighted to announce we will be opening our new pre-school 'Little Malties' for girls aged two. Our girls thrive, working hard and having fun. We believe in the pursuit of excellence whilst maintaining a sense of fun. Our girls are encouraged to take risks in all aspects of school life and are well known for their enthusiasm and confidence. We also nurture old-fashioned values such as courtesy, doing one's best, and respect for others.

Maltman's Green has exceptional facilities including two libraries, specialist teaching classrooms for science, ICT, design and art, music practice rooms, a sports hall and gym and safe and secure traditional playgrounds and a state-of-the-art six-lane indoor swimming pool as well as a Discovery Garden.

There is plenty of open green space around the School. Sustainability is at the heart of the School Development Plan and the school has been awarded Green Flag Eco-School status for the second time.

Inside, the classrooms are all bright and spacious, with colourful, ever-changing displays. The atmosphere is lively, challenging and happy.

Although we are a non-selective school, our girls have an outstanding track record of winning scholarships to top independent schools and of gaining entrance to the local grammar schools.

The creative and performing arts flourish at Maltman's. The school strongly believes that all children should be given the opportunity to develop their creativity and express themselves.

From Nursery, all girls enjoy specialist Music lessons twice a week and from Reception upwards have weekly drama lessons. All the girls take part in a dramatic production every year.

In addition to the weekly lessons in Art and Design Technology, there are also numerous clubs.

All girls have a lesson of sport every day. Our girls are frequently local, regional and national champions in swimming, gymnastics, tennis and several team sports.

We provide specialist learning support for girls with learning difficulties, such as dyslexia, and make time to help any girl who might slip behind. Specialist support is also provided for the very able and gifted girls.

Finally, the partnership with parents is not a cliché at Maltman's, but is a genuine joint approach to education. If your daughter knows what is expected of her and is given the expert support and care, and if you are kept informed and involved, the girls have every opportunity to achieve their best.

Charitable status. Maltman's Green School Trust Limited is a Registered Charity, number 310633. It exists to provide a high standard of education for young girls.

Manor Lodge School

Rectory Lane, Ridge Hill, Shenley, Hertfordshire WD7 9BG

Tel:	01707 642424
Fax:	01707 645206
email:	enquiries@manorlodgeschool.com
website:	www.manorlodgeschool.com

Chair of Governors: Mr D Arnold, MBE

Head: **Mr G Dunn**, Cert Ed

Age Range. 3–11.

Number of Pupils. Nursery (age 3) 17; Infants (age 4–7) 179; Juniors (age 7–11) 221.

Fees per term (2016–2017). Nursery £3,215; Infants £3,425; Juniors £3,845.

There are three forms of 18–20 children in Reception to Year 6 inclusive. We have specialist teachers for French, PE, IT, DT, Art, Drama, Science (Years 5 & 6), and Music, as well as numerous instrumental teachers for piano, brass, woodwind, percussion and strings. All staff are fully qualified.

The main school building consists of an 18th century manor house and extension which offers classrooms, French, Science, Art, IT, DT and a hall. A magnificent new building housing further classrooms and a sports hall/theatre provides additional space for sports, music and the performing arts.

The cottage at the end of the drive houses our Nursery. The children must be siblings of pupils in the main school and are eligible to attend from the term in which they turn three.

Our classrooms are bright and well-equipped and the standard of work displayed is very high. We aim to provide excellent teaching and learning opportunities within a caring environment in which high standards of behaviour and good manners are encouraged and expected. We thus ensure that all pupils achieve their full potential and are prepared for entry to senior schools, both independent and state.

The twelve acres of grounds include woodland, pitches, an all-weather court and play areas with climbing activity equipment and other outdoor toys. The children are offered a wide range of sporting activities including football, rugby, hockey, cricket, netball, rounders, swimming and athletics.

Music plays an important part in the life of the school. There are several choirs, an orchestra, jazz band and various ensembles and almost half the children in school learn an instrument. Music is of course linked to our Drama activities. Reception to Year 5 children take part in at least two performances a year, and in Year 6 the children have a theatre experience in our brand new hall. Art is of a particularly high standard and the children use a variety of media, producing excellent original work.

Our caterers provide a delicious selection of fresh, healthy lunches and cater for a number of dietary requirements.

Extra activities available at the school include chess, drama and ju-jitsu. There are numerous clubs run by the staff after school until 4.30 pm, for example, cooking, football, rugby, cricket, netball, dance, athletics and choir.

Charitable status. Manor Lodge School is a Registered Charity, number 1048874. The school exists to provide an education which will maximise the potential of the girls and boys in our care.

The Manor Preparatory School

Faringdon Road, Abingdon, Oxon OX13 6LN

Tel:	01235 858462
Fax:	01235 559593
email:	admissions@manorprep.org
website:	www.manorprep.org
Twitter:	@ManorPrep

Chair of Board of Governors: Mr Shaun Forrestal

Headmaster: **Mr Piers Heyworth**, MA Oxon, PGCE

Age Range. Girls 2–11, Boys 2–7.

Number of Pupils. 363 Day: 315 Girls, 48 Boys.

Fees per term (2016–2017). £526–£4,800.

The Manor is a Charitable Trust.

A well-qualified staff teaches a full range of subjects. Boys are prepared for entry to preparatory schools and girls for the Common Entrance Examination for Girls' Schools, or for entrance examinations to other senior schools.

The curriculum is broad. Science, Information Communication Technology, Art, Design, Music, Physical Education and Modern Languages are all taught by specialists. All subjects have specialist teaching in the final two years of the preparatory department.

Computers are used throughout the school to supplement the curriculum and ICT skills are taught in three specialist ICT suites.

A vibrant music department of 18 visiting and 2 full-time and 2 part-time members of staff provides tuition in a full range of instruments; all orchestral instruments including harp are available. In addition tuition in singing, drums & guitar bring the total of pupils receiving instrumental lessons to around 60%. There are two school orchestras, four choirs, three string ensembles, a wind group, brass group, guitar band and harp ensemble. Regular performance opportunities include the annual Carol Service, Music Afternoons and the spring Manor Concert.

A highly skilled and dedicated PE Department teaches a wide variety of sport including Swimming, Netball, Hockey, Cross Country, Football, Tag Rugby, Rounders and Athletics. Specialist Tennis Coaches provide year-round lessons. The Manor competes at IAPS in Netball, Hockey, Tennis, Cross Country and Swimming, regularly reaching National Finals. The Manor teams have been finalists at the Schools' Biathlon at Crystal Palace and the British Biathlon Championships. A substantial range of "sport for all" clubs take place before school, after school and at lunchtimes. Sports Clubs range from Judo, Gymnastics, Archery and Golf to our more traditional sports.

The extra-curricular provision at The Manor is extremely broad with over 100 clubs taking place before school, at lunchtime and after school on a weekly basis. Clubs include musical groups and ensembles, sports, arts and crafts, computing and even Lego. These challenging and exciting activities support the curriculum in a way that makes our children happy to learn whilst enabling them to make the most of their abilities.

A free Early Birds Club where children can be dropped off at school at 8.00 am is offered. A Breakfast Club operates from 7.30 am to 8.00 am and there is an Extended Day service until 6.00 pm. There is a charge for these services. Flexible Nursery and Pre-Nursery sessions from the age of 2 are offered.

Bus transport is arranged for pupils travelling from surrounding areas including three of our own minibuses.

The school promotes close cooperation between parents and teachers. Parents' Evenings are a regular feature. "The

Friends of The Manor" association is run by parents to welcome new families and to support the school.

Charitable status. The Manor Preparatory School is a Registered Charity, number 900347. It exists to provide education for girls and boys.

The Marist Preparatory School

Kings Road, Sunninghill, Ascot, Berkshire SL5 7PS

Tel:	01344 626137
Fax:	01344 621566
email:	admissionsprep@themaristschools.com
website:	www.themaristschools.com
Twitter:	@Marist_School

Independent Catholic Day School for Girls.

Chair of Governors: Mrs A Nash

Principal: Mr Karl McCloskey, BA Hons, PGCE, MA

Vice Principal (*Prep*): **Mrs Jane Gow**, BEd Hons

Age Range. 2½–11.
Number of Pupils. 200 girls.
Fees per term (2016–2017). £3,015–£3,675.
Mission Statement. The aim of the school is to:

• provide a caring community where learning is guided by strong Christian values;
• promote excellence where all are encouraged to reach their full potential.

Strengths of the school:

• Early Years, infant and junior departments tailored to the specific needs of the girls at each stage of their education.
• Caring, well qualified and professional staff dedicated to developing happy, secure and stimulated girls.
• Curriculum designed to achieve all the foundation/early year learning goals.
• Able to offer a wide range of both academic and extra-curricular activities.
• High achievement in gym, ballet, art, judo, drama, choir and music.
• Strong emphasis on pastoral care, spiritual and personal development; care and consideration for others.
• Small class sizes to enhance individual progression and recognition.
• The school is renowned for its high standards regarding moral values, community spirit, respect and care. This is in line with the overall ethos of the Marist order which has a worldwide presence, providing a truly international dimension to a girl's education.
• Girls are taught to consider and help those less fortunate than themselves through involvement in a wide range of local, national and international charity projects.

The Marist Preparatory School is able to offer your daughter a complete and fulfilling education in the security of a single sex environment, from the age of 2½ to 11. We welcome all Christians and those supporting its ethos. We are renowned for our happy and caring ethos, where pastoral care is considered paramount. Your daughter will be treated as an individual and encouraged to achieve her full potential in every area. We have a strong academic record but we also place a strong emphasis on extra-curricular activities which help to develop important qualities such as self confidence, individual creativity and teamwork.

We also have a Senior School and Sixth Form on the same campus for girls aged 11–18. *For further details, please see The Marist School entry in the GSA section.*

Charitable status. The Marist School is a Registered Charity, number 225485. The principal aims and activities of the Marist Schools are religious and charitable and specifically to provide education by way of an independent day school for girls between the ages of 2½ and 18.

Marlborough House School

High Street, Hawkhurst, Cranbrook, Kent TN18 4PY

Tel:	01580 753555
Fax:	01580 754281
email:	registrar@marlboroughhouseschool.co.uk
	frontoffice@marlboroughhouseschool.co.uk
website:	www.marlboroughhouseschool.co.uk
Facebook:	@Marlborough-House-School

Marlborough House was founded in 1874 and is registered as an Educational Trust with a Board of Governors.

Chairman of Governors: H Somerset

Headmaster: M Ward, BEd

Deputy Head: P Tooze, BA, PGCE
Assistant Head (*Academic*): Mrs A Stables, BEd
Head of Senior School: Mrs K Atkins, BEd
Head of Middle School: Mrs C Walker, BA, PGCE
Head of Nursery & Pre-Prep: Ms V Coatz, BEd
Head's PA: Mrs M McTrusty

Age Range. 2¾–13 Co-educational.
Number of Pupils. 320
Fees per term (2016–2017). Prep £5,645, Pre-Prep £2,730–£3,335, Nursery according to number of sessions. Flexi boarding: from £31 per night. No compulsory extras.

Marlborough House School is an independent Preparatory School for boys and girls. The School is fully co-educational creating a friendly, family atmosphere for children between the ages of 2¾ and 13. We are a community where our values, with mutual respect at their core, are at the heart of everything we do. Happy, confident children are keen to learn, to push themselves and to achieve more. It is our job to help children achieve academically but, much more than this, we also want to nurture children to become well-rounded, enthusiastic, self-confident and fulfilled young people. We believe in high expectations, the value of knowing each child as an individual and providing a breadth of experiences but above all this is our commitment to making sure children here are happy – because we know that only then will they achieve their goals.

Marlborough House is situated in the village of Hawkhurst in beautiful countryside on the Kent/Sussex border, near the town of Cranbrook. The fine Georgian house is set in 35 acres of superb gardens, playing fields, lawns and woodland. The School has a Chapel, Computer Centre, large Sports Hall, 2 Performance/Dance Halls, superbly equipped Science Laboratory, Art, Pottery and Design Technology Department, Music Rooms, Swimming Pool, a .22 Rifle Shooting Range and 2 large all-weather games surfaces.

With our 50+ qualified teaching staff we aim to produce well motivated, balanced, confident children who know the value of hard work, and who will thrive in their next schools and the modern world beyond. Our classes are small and the children are prepared for all major Senior Schools, whilst those showing special promise sit scholarships.

Encouragement is given to each child to experience a wide variety of activities. In addition to the traditional sports of Cricket, Rugby, Soccer, Hockey, Athletics, Tennis, Netball and Rounders, opportunities are provided for Music (with around 12 peripatetic music teachers visiting the school each week, children can learn a wide range of instruments and join the many groups and choirs), Art (in many different media), Pottery, Drama, Ballet, Technology, Computing, Shooting, Sailing, Golf, Swimming, Fencing and Judo. The club programme is extensive with over 70 clubs offered in the course of a year.

The website is detailed and informative and the school also has a very active Facebook page.

Charitable status. Marlborough House School is a Registered Charity, number 307793. It exists to provide education for children.

Marlston House School

Hermitage, Newbury, Berkshire RG18 9UL

Tel:	01635 200293
email:	registrar@brockmarl.org
website:	www.brockmarl.org.uk

Headmistress: **Mrs C E Riley**, MA, BEd, CertEd

Age Range. 3–13.
Number of Girls. 169 Girls (including 65 Boarders).
Fees per term (2016–2017). Boarding £7,373, Day £5,161–£5,490. Pre-Prep School (Ridge House): £3,278 (full-time). Temporary Overseas Boarders £7,957.

Established in 1995, Marlston House is situated in 500 acres of its own grounds in countryside of outstanding beauty, only four miles from access to the M4. The school is situated beside Brockhurst Boys' Preparatory school and occupies separate listed buildings. Boys and girls are taught separately, but the two schools join together for drama music and activities. In this way Brockhurst and Marlston House combine the best features of the single-sex and co-educational systems: academic excellence and social interaction. The schools are proud of the high standard of pastoral care established within a family atmosphere. (*See also entry for Brockhurst School.*)

The Pre-Prep School, Ridge House, is a co-educational department of Brockhurst and Marlston House Schools for 75 children aged 3–6 years, and is situated on the same site in new self-contained, purpose-designed accommodation.

Girls are prepared for entry to a variety of leading Independent Senior Schools through the ISEB Common Entrance and Scholarship Papers at 11+ and 13+.

All girls play Netball (outdoor and indoor courts), Hockey, Rounders and Tennis (outdoor and indoor courts) and take part in Athletics, Cross Country and Swimming (25m indoor heated pool). Additional activities include riding (own equestrian centre), fencing, judo, shooting (indoor rifle range), dance and ballet. Facilities for gymnastics and other sporting activities are provided in a purpose-built Sports Hall. Year 7 pupils make a week-long visit to a Château in France as part of their French studies.

Music and Art are important features of the curriculum and a number of girls have won scholarships and awards to senior schools in these subjects recently. The school is currently building a new dedicated Music School and Theatre to open in the Summer Term 2014.

Transport is provided by the school to and from airports and between Newbury and Paddington stations. Pupils are accompanied by school staff to their destinations.

Mayfield Preparatory School

Sutton Road, Walsall, West Midlands WS1 2PD

Tel:	01922 624107
email:	info@mayfieldprep.co.uk
website:	www.mayfieldprep.co.uk

Administered by the Governors of Queen Mary's Schools.

Chair of Governors: Mrs J Aubrook

Headmaster: **Mr Matthew Draper**, BA, PGCE

Age Range. 2–11 Co-educational.
Number of Pupils. Day: 118 Boys, 94 Girls.
Fees per term (2016–2017). Main School £2,700; Pre-Nursery £1,620

A co-educational day school for children aged 2 to 11+, set in a listed building with beautiful surroundings and playing fields. A purpose-built Science/Art building opened in November 2000.

The self-contained Nursery Department accepts children at 2+.

A fully qualified Staff with full-time ancillary support throughout KS1 ensures that the individual child receives maximum attention.

The main aim at Mayfield is to encourage intellectual excellence. Children experience a thorough grounding in literacy and numeracy skills.

Through stimulating courses of correctly-paced work the school specialises in the preparation of the children for Grammar and Independent School entrance examinations at 11+.

Our children achieve excellent results, but it is always borne in mind that the individual child's needs are met by matching achievement to potential. All children are expected and encouraged to develop daily in confidence and security.

We believe in a balanced curriculum, and at Mayfield practical and non-academic activities additionally provide interest and varied experiences in Sports, Art, Music, ICT, DT, Dance, Drama and Public Speaking.

Good manners are expected at all times, as well as a happy and whole-hearted participation in the life and studies offered by the school.

Merchant Taylors' Prep (formerly Northwood Prep)

Moor Farm, Sandy Lodge Road, Rickmansworth, Herts WD3 1LW

Tel:	01923 825648
Fax:	01923 835802
email:	office@mtpn.org.uk
website:	www.mtpn.org.uk
Twitter:	@MTSPrep
Facebook:	/MerchantTaylorsPrep

Chair of Governors: Mr C P Hare

Head of School: **Dr Karen McNerney**, BSc Hons, PGCE, MSc, EdD

Assistant Head of School: Mr Michael Hibbert, BEd QTS
Deputy Head: Mr Andrew Crook, BA Hons, PGCE

Age Range. 3–13.
Number of Pupils. 300+ Day Boys.
Fees per term (2016–2017). £3,354 (Nursery full-time), £4,792 (Reception, Years 1 and 2), £5,030 (Years 3–8).

The School is located amidst 14 acres on a former farm in an ideal park and woodland setting. The Grade II listed buildings have been skilfully converted to provide a complete and unique range of classrooms and ancillary facilities. The mediaeval Manor of the More, once owned by King Henry VIII and used as a palace by Cardinal Wolsey, was originally located within the grounds and provides some interesting and historical associations.

The School is divided as follows: an off-site Nursery & Reception School for children aged 3+ and 4 + based at Merchant Taylors' School; then on the Merchant Taylors' Prep School site, there is the Pre-Prep (Year 1 to Year 2) and the Prep Department (Year 3 to Year 8).

Boys are admitted to the school after an assessment by Heads of Section. The main entry is into Nursery at 3+ when boys are admitted in the September after their third birthday. We also have a 4 plus and 7 plus entry. Boys are expected to remain until the age of thirteen. Parents of pupils at the Prep School will be given an assurance at the end of Year 5 as to whether their son will be able to progress to Merchant Taylors' School at the end of Year 8. Continuity scholarships will be awarded to some pupils in the Prep School in Year 6.

Work of a traditionally high standard is expected of all boys. The curriculum is interpreted as richly as possible and includes Technology, Music, Art, Drama, Physical Education and Games. We focus on an holistic education that emphasises that focuses on values and dispositions as much as academic skills. The School has modern teaching facilities and the fully qualified and experienced staff is generously resourced. The Sir Christopher Harding Building for Science and Technology, comprising two state-of-the-art laboratories, an ICT Suite and technology workshop was opened in November 2000. A Learning Resource Centre was created in September 2001. A centre for the Performing Arts was commissioned by Mr Kevin Spacey in April 2008 and a music school was opened in May 2008. A nursery school was opened in the grounds of Merchant Taylors' School in April 2008 now known as the Manor. Additional sports changing facilities were opened in February 2008. Additional classrooms have been added as part of our centenary celebrations in 2010. A new Centenary Trail accommodates a range of outdoor learning activities. In 2014 a new kitchen, dining hall and common room were added. In September 2016, the Reception Year moved over to the Manor where the Nursery is situated.

Swift access to London by train from nearby Moor Park Station means that staff often arrange for boys to visit places of historical and cultural interest and attend concerts and lectures.

While the Christian tradition on which the life of the School is based is that of the Church of England, boys from all Christian denominations and other faiths are welcomed.

There is an extensive programme of extra-curricular activities in which all boys are encouraged to take part. A key feature of the School's ethos is a strong tradition of caring, both for those within the community of the school, and those whom the boys can help through regular charitable activities.

Rugby Football, Association Football and Cricket are the principal team games. Tennis, Athletics, Judo and other sports are also coached. A fully equipped Sports Hall was opened in November 1996. The School has the benefit of a floodlit Astroturf facility.

The School has a flourishing Parents' Association which arranges social and fundraising activities, and an active association for former pupils, The Old Terryers.

Charitable status. Merchant Taylors' School is a Registered Charity, number 1063740.

Micklefield School

10 Somers Road, Reigate, Surrey RH2 9DU

Tel: 01737 224212
email: office@micklefieldschool.co.uk

website: www.micklefieldschool.co.uk
Facebook: /MicklefieldSchoolReigate

Chairman of the Council: Mr A B de M Hunter, FCA, FIPA

Headmistress: **Mrs L Rose**, BEd Hons, Cert Ed, Dip PC

Age Range. Rising 3–11.
Number of Pupils. 292 (149 boys, 143 girls).
Fees per term (2016–2017). £1,040–£3,695. Lunches £185–£190.

'*Micklefield recognised the individuality in my twins and helped them realise their potential socially and academically.*'

'*Micklefield has helped my boys build confidence and self-esteem in a friendly and secure environment.*'

'*My children have flourished at Micklefield.*'

These quotes from current and former parents sum up the very special education offered at Micklefield School. Established in Reigate over 105 years ago, we offer small classes, taught by qualified staff and qualified subject specialists. We cater for boys and girls from the age of rising 3 up to the age of eleven, preparing them for Common Entrance and other examinations. The children enjoy academic success and have an excellent record in examinations for entrance to senior schools including Scholarship Awards.

After-school care is available for children from Reception age.

In addition to the normal academic subjects, the curriculum includes design technology, computing, dancing, drama, French, netball, tennis, athletics, swimming, football, rugby and cricket.

The children take an active part in a variety of musical and theatrical activities and excel in sports. Dramatic productions and concerts provide opportunities for everyone to display their talents. We encourage participation in drama festivals, sports fixtures, the School's orchestra and choirs. Visits to concerts, theatres and museums are organised together with residential activity holidays for the older children.

The most recent building project provides an excellent art room and music suite with the added benefit of a walkway to our Preparatory Department building. There is a dining room where professional caterers serve high-quality, healthy lunches. The school also has its own sports field within 250 yards in St Albans Road.

Visit the website or telephone for a prospectus on 01737 224212. Mrs Rose, the Headmistress, is always pleased to show prospective parents around by appointment.

Charitable status. Micklefield School (Reigate) Limited is a Registered Charity, number 312069. It exists to provide a first-class education for its pupils.

Millfield Prep School

Edgarley Hall, Glastonbury, Somerset BA6 8LD

Tel: 01458 832446
Fax: 01458 833679
email: office@millfieldprep.com
website: millfieldschool.com
Twitter: @millfieldprep
Facebook: /millfieldprep

Chair of Governors: Sir J G Reith, KCB, CBE

Head: **Mrs Shirley Shayler**, MA, BSc Hons, PGCE

Tutor for Admissions: Ms Sally Garland-Jones

Age Range. 2–13.

Number of Boys and Girls. 133 Boarders, 296 Day Pupils.

Fees per term (2016–2017). Prep: Full and Weekly Boarding £8,880, Day £3,500–£5,850. Pre-Prep: Day £2,750. Flexi Boarding: £1,020 (2 nights), £1,535 (3 nights), £2,045 (4 nights). Occasional boarding: £55 per night.

The school is administered by the same Board of Governors and on the same principles of small-group teaching as Millfield (made possible by a staffing ratio of approximately 1 to 8) which ensures breadth and flexibility of timetable. It has its own attractive grounds of 185 acres some four miles from the Senior School, and its extensive facilities include games fields, art, design and technology centre, drama hall, music school, science laboratories, sports hall, AstroTurf, gymnasium, golf course, tennis courts, squash courts, sport pavilion, equestrian centre on campus, 25 metre indoor swimming pool, three IT laboratories and chapel. The pupils also have access to some of the specialist facilities at Millfield including water-based astro, Olympic-sized swimming pool, tartan athletics track and indoor tennis centre.

The Pre-Prep department, taking children from 2–7, moved onto the Prep school site in 2004 so that the school now offers an education for children from ages 2–13, after which the majority of pupils transfer to Millfield. The small class sizes allow the individual pupil to be taught at his or her most appropriate pace. The range of ability within the school is comprehensive and setting caters for both the academically gifted and those requiring additional learning support.

The curriculum is broadly based and provides a balance between the usual academic subjects and the aesthetic, musical and artistic fields. Junior pupils study French and in Year 6 there is a choice of Spanish or French plus a taster in Latin for more able pupils. In Years 7 and 8 there is a choice of French, Spanish and Latin. Children may choose either one or two foreign languages, dependent on ability. Pupils are also given a choice of extra-curricular languages: we are currently offering Mandarin and Russian (these languages vary depending on demand). Science is taught throughout the school and as three separate subjects from the age of 10.

There is a full games programme organised by qualified teachers of physical education, with the help of other staff. The programme includes Athletics, Canoeing, Caving, Climbing, Cross Country, Cricket, Fencing, Football, Golf, Gymnastics, Hockey, Netball, Riding, Rounders, Rugby, Sailing, Squash, Swimming, Tennis, Outdoor Pursuits and Multi-Sports to name but a few. Over 80 different clubs are available.

Within Music we offer two Choirs, an Orchestra, Wind Band and 19 different music ensembles ranging from rock bands and brass bands to cello club. Over 250 pupils learn at least one musical instrument. There are regular opportunities for performance and all pupils are coached in performance and presentation skills. Highlight events include themed large ensemble evenings such as the last Night of the Proms, Millfield at the Movies complete with cinema screen, Saturday morning breakfast masterclasses with visiting international artists and the traditional annual whole school House Singing competition.

Boys and girls can start from the age of 2 and up to the age of 12 and they come from over 20 different nationalities and widely differing backgrounds. Admission usually depends on interview, assessment and reports from the previous school. We award a number of Academic, Art, Chess, Music and Sports Scholarships each year for entry into Years 6, 7 and 8. We also welcome applications for scholarships from good all-rounders: boys and girls who have reached a good standard academically and show promise in specific areas such as Art, Music or Sport.

There are five boarding houses for pupils aged 7 years and above (three for boys and two for girls). Each house is under the care of resident houseparents and assistant house-

parents. The Medical Centre is staffed by 3 qualified nurses, a physiotherapist, and the School Doctor attends daily.

Charitable status. Millfield is a Registered Charity, number 310283. The Millfield Schools provide a broad and balanced education to boys and girls from widely differing backgrounds, including a significant number with learning difficulties, and many for whom boarding is necessary.

Milton Keynes Preparatory School

Tattenhoe Lane, Milton Keynes, Buckinghamshire MK3 7EG

Tel:	01908 642111
Fax:	01908 366365
email:	info@mkps.co.uk
website:	www.mkps.co.uk

Chairman of the Governors: Mr David Pye, BA Hons, Cert Ed, MA Ed Dist, HETC, SEDA III, FRSA

Principal: Hilary Pauley, BEd

Joint Heads:
Carl Bates, BA Hons
Simon Driver, BA, PGCE

Deputy Heads:
Patricia Cave, BEd
Olivia Quirke, BEd Hons, PGCE

Age Range. Nursery 2 months–2½ years. Pre-Prep Department 2½–7 years. Preparatory Department 7+–11 years.

Number of Pupils. 450 Day Pupils.

Fees per term (2016–2017). Nursery (per week): £270 (babies under 1 year), £280 (1–2½ years). Pre-Preparatory: £3,800 (2½–5 years), £3,940 (6–7 years). Preparatory £4,320 (8–11 years).

Milton Keynes Preparatory School is a well-established family-owned school, with two sister Pre-Prep and Preparatory schools based across Milton Keynes.

Opening hours are 7.30 am to 6.30 pm for a 35-week academic year and a total of 46 weeks per year, enabling children of working parents to join play schemes in school holidays and to be cared for outside normal daily school hours.

Staff are highly qualified and committed to delivering the very best teaching and levels of care. Academic standards are "excellent", as awarded by the recent Inspections, with pupils being prepared for entry to senior independent schools locally and nationally and to grammar schools. Teaching is structured to take into account the requirements of the National Curriculum, with constant evaluation and assessment for each pupil. Scholarships are offered for those with all-round, academic and sporting abilities, from the ages of 7–11.

Housed in a modern purpose-built building, all departments also have their own outside soft play and extensive playground areas and there is a large multi-purpose sports hall. The newly developed Nursery and Little Prep-Prep departments, with extended artificial grass terraces for year-round activities and learning, are a beautiful addition to the school.

State-of-the-art facilities include a Music Technology studio, CTS suite, Science laboratory, interactive DT and Art workshops and a superb Astroturf pitch.

Additional facilities at The Farm, the school's Environmental Studies Centre, provide a fitness room, music and dance studio, arts and crafts and computer room, plus an outdoor learning resource centre, weather station, large pond and polytunnels.

Music and Sport play an important part in the life of the school. Concerts are held, and a wide variety of sport is played, with teams competing regularly against other schools. Additional clubs are held in specialist activities such as judo and ballet.

The school aims to incorporate the best of modern teaching methods and traditional values in a friendly, caring and busy environment, where good work habits and a concern for the needs of others are paramount.

The Minster School
York

Deangate, York YO1 7JA

Tel: 0844 939 0000
Fax: 0844 939 0001
email: school@yorkminster.org
website: www.minsterschoolyork.co.uk

Chair of Governors: The Very Revd Vivienne Faull, Dean of York Minster

Head Master: **Alex Donaldson**, MA St John's College Cambridge, PGCE King's College London, Cert ICT Cambridge

Age Range. 3–13 Co-educational.
Number of Pupils. Preparatory 115; Pre-Prep Department 65.
Fees per term (2016–2017). Prep £3,265, Pre-Prep £2,135 (full day). Choristers receive substantial Scholarships, ranging between 60%–100%.

The Minster School was originally founded in 627 AD to educate singing boys. It is now a fully co-educational preparatory and pre-preparatory school, which includes a Nursery department. Its most recent ISI inspection report highlighted the Nursery teaching and provision as 'Outstanding' and the school overall was judged to be 'Excellent'. Teaching throughout the whole school was singled out as a particular strength and the achievement, attitude and behaviour of the pupils were warmly praised.

The Nursery and Pre-Prep departments are housed in their own accommodation with gardens, playgrounds and an ICT suite for junior pupils' use. French is taught from Year 2 upwards. In the prep school, teaching is delivered by well-qualified subject specialists. With computers in all classrooms, an IT suite, science lab, art room and DT suite the school is well equipped to deliver a broad curriculum. On our 8-acre sports fields, games are taught by school staff and professional coaches. Regular fixtures for boys and girls teams are arranged throughout the year. The major sports are football, hockey, netball, cricket and athletics. In addition to the normal academic curriculum, there is a flourishing music department and all orchestral instruments are taught. Pupils' levels of musical achievement are very high though there are no academic or musical tests to join the school.

Lunch and after-school care are not charged as extras and a wide variety of extracurricular activities is available, e.g. sewing, chess, ballet, fencing, judo, art and craft, model-making, drama and sports clubs etc.

Of the 180 children in the School, 20 boys and 20 girls are choristers who sing the services in York Minster in return for a substantial scholarship. Pupils are prepared for Common Entrance and Senior Independent School Scholarships. Many children gain music, art and academic scholarships to their senior schools.

Moira House Girls School Prep & Pre-Prep Departments

Upper Carlisle Road, Eastbourne, East Sussex BN20 7TE

Tel: 01323 636800
email: admissions@moirahouse.co.uk
website: www.moirahouse.co.uk
Twitter: @moirahouse1875
Facebook: /moirahouse

Chairman of School Council: Ms Jill Jackson-Hill, BA Hons, FRSA

Acting Principal: **Mrs Elodie Vallantine**, BA Hons, PGCE

Head of Key Stage 1: Mrs Tracy Bees
Director of Studies – Prep: Mrs Cecy Kemp

Age Range. Girls 0–11, Boys 0–4.
Number of Pupils. 115.
Fees per term (2016–2017). £2,980–£5,760 (Day Pupils); £6,985 (Weekly Boarders); £7,505 (Boarders).

Moira House is set within 15 acres of attractively landscaped grounds, on the outskirts of the historic town of Eastbourne on the South Coast of England. Founded in 1875, Moira House welcomes girls from the age of six months to eleven in the Pre-Prep and Prep Departments and boys in the Nursery, with full, weekly or flexi boarding offered from the age of 9. The Prep and Pre-Prep Departments share the site with the Senior School for girls aged eleven to eighteen. (*See entry in GSA section.*)

The Prep and Pre-Prep aim to provide a broad and balanced curriculum and activity programme, ensuring equal access and opportunity so that children can celebrate and strive for excellence. We believe that children will learn if they feel happy and secure, and if their natural curiosity is aroused. They learn best when they are actively involved in the learning, with skilled teachers to guide them. As a school our aim is to provide an atmosphere and a richness of experience within which each child's unique qualities can flourish. Our emphasis is on the importance of individual development, helping each child to realise her maximum potential. We aim, therefore, to set high standards for each child so that they are constantly challenged to develop further their skills and understanding.

Curriculum. The Foundation Stage and National Curriculum form the basis of what is taught but with the flexibility of specialist teachers and creative learning and teaching strategies. The curriculum aims to develop critical and creative thinking and self-discipline. Education at this stage is a foundation for the future and as broad as possible, combining the modern technology of interactive whiteboards and an ICT suite with all areas of the curriculum. Teaching is in small groups and is strong throughout. The girls enjoy mixed-ability classes but are grouped according to ability in Maths.

EAL, SEN, Sport, Drama, French, Swimming and Music are all taught or supported to an exceptional level by specialists. The Prep Department has three choirs and all the children are involved in productions, concerts and creative arts presentations across the year. Most of the children take individual music lessons on a variety of instruments.

PE and Swimming form part of the curriculum and the girls have been particularly successful in competitive challenges. The girls enjoy the facilities of a 25m heated indoor swimming pool, a sports hall and extensive playing fields and netball and tennis courts.

The school has recently created a wonderful outdoor classroom with a pond and large greenhouse where the children begin to understand how important their role is in looking after the natural environment in a more sustainable world.

Extracurricular. The school offers daily care from 8 am until Afternoon Activity Club at 6.00 pm. There is a fleet of buses which can transport children to and from home each day.

A wealth of extracurricular activities enriches the experience of the pupils. The activity programme includes Dance, Short tennis, Trampolining, Gymnastics, ICT club, Environmental Studies club, Sewing club, String ensemble and a wide variety of sporting clubs.

Charitable status. Moira House Girls School is a Registered Charity, number 307072.

Monkton Prep School

Combe Down, Bath BA2 7ET

Tel:	01225 831202
Fax:	01225 840312
email:	admin@monktonprep.org.uk
website:	www.monktonprep.com
Twitter:	@monktonprep
Facebook:	@MonktonCombeSchool

Chairman of Governors: Professor H Langton, RGN, RSCN, RCNT, RNT, BA Hons, MSc

Headmaster: **Mr M Davis**, BEd

Deputy Head Pastoral: Mr R J Lloyd Williams, BSocSc
Deputy Head Academic: Mrs H M Grant, BEd

Age Range. 2–13.
Number of Pupils. Boarders 27, Day 207, Pre-Prep 99.
Fees per term (2016–2017). Reception £3,104; Years 1 and 2 £3,194; Years 3 to 6 £3,750–£3,860; Years 7 and 8 £5,460. Boarding: Years 3 to 6 £7,300–£7,870; Years 7 and 8 £7,870.

There are no extra charges except for learning a musical instrument and specialist activities. There are reductions in fees for the children of clergy and HM Forces.

The School became fully co-educational in September 1993 and has full flexi boarding arrangements that cater for both boys and girls from the age of 8. It stands in its own grounds on a magnificent site with the city of Bath on one side and the Midford valley on the other. The buildings include a modern classroom block, a theatre for drama and music with 12 music practice rooms, a sports hall, an indoor 25-metre pool, 2 science laboratories and dance studio. The Coates Building incorporates an art studio, design technology workshop, a learning resource centre, seminar room and ICT suite. There are 20 acres of grounds, 3 all-weather netball courts, extensive playing fields as well as an all-weather hockey pitch.

The School has a strong musical tradition and flourishing Art and DT Departments. There are two choirs, an orchestra, a band and various other instrumental groups. Drama also plays an important part in school life.

Rugby, Hockey, and Cricket are the major boys' games; Netball, Hockey and Rounders are the major girls' games. All pupils take part in Gymnastics, Swimming, Athletics and Cross-Country. Squash, Badminton, Dance, Judo and Basketball are also available. There is a full programme of matches. All pupils take part in a variety of hobbies and activities sessions which include gardening, animation,

cookery, gymnastics (run by external professionals Baskervilles Gym) and fun science to name but a few.

Boys and Girls are prepared for Common Entrance and Scholarship exams to Independent Senior Schools. At least three-quarters of them proceed to the Senior School and a quarter to a wide range of other Independent Senior Schools. 90 Scholarships have been won in the past five years.

Over the years Monkton has educated many children from families who are working overseas, especially HM Forces families. We make special arrangements for them and are well used to meeting their various needs.

The School finds its central inspiration and purpose in its Christian tradition. The caring, family ethos is underpinned by a large number of resident staff, including the Headmaster and his wife.

Charitable status. Monkton School is a Registered Charity, number 1057185. Its aim is to provide education for girls and boys aged 2 to 18, in accordance with the doctrine and principles of the Church of England.

Moor Park School

Richard's Castle, Ludlow, Shropshire SY8 4DZ

Tel:	01584 876061
Fax:	01584 877311
email:	head@moorpark.org.uk
website:	www.moorpark.org.uk
Twitter:	@moorparkludlow
Facebook:	/MoorParkSchool

Founded in 1964, Moor Park is an IAPS, Catholic, co-educational boarding and day school accepting children from 3 months to 13 years of age. A family atmosphere pervades, resulting in happy, rounded and grounded children.

Chairman of Governors: Maj General A Denaro, CBE, DL

Headmaster: **Mr Charlie Minogue**, BSc Hons, PGCE

Deputy Head: Mrs J M Morris, Cert Ed

Age Range. 3–13.
Number of Pupils. 266.
Fees per term (2016–2017). Boarding £6,520–£7,825, Day £2,380–£5,310.

Children often start in the Tick Tock Nursery at Moor Park which provides a secure environment for our very youngest children. They then transfer to the Lower School Nursery and Kindergarten in the term that they turn 3. Children are then carefully prepared to start more formal schooling by a team of well-qualified and caring staff. Our Early Years provision was graded as 'Outstanding' by ISI in May 2016. All our children make full use of the 85 acres of stunning grounds but Moor Park is not just about getting muddy and exploring. Our children gain entry to the full range of schools nationally and have been awarded an extraordinary number of scholarships in recent years. These include academic and extra-curricular awards to some of the top senior schools in the country. It is also worth saying that Moor Park is emphatically not simply an academic hothouse and is a school where children of all abilities thrive. All of this is underpinned by a carefully maintained culture of kindness which ensures that all children are valued for who they are. Passionate teachers and an average class size of around 14 also make a difference.

Not every child can be good at everything but every child can be good at something and finding something for every child is something that we take seriously. Moor Park's facilities and, more importantly, enthusiastic and dedicated staff ensure that the school is well placed to get the best out of every child. A highlight of each term is the Big Weekend, for which we were shortlisted in the 2014 Independent Schools Awards.

Charitable status. Moor Park School is a Registered Charity, number 511800, which exists to provide education for young people.

Moorfield School

Wharfedale Lodge, 11 Ben Rhydding Road, Ilkley, West Yorkshire LS29 8RL
Tel: 01943 607285
email: enquiries@moorfieldschool.co.uk
website: www.moorfieldschool.co.uk
Twitter: @MoorfieldIlkley
Facebook: /Moorfield-School

Moorfield is an Education Charitable Trust and the Headmistress is a member of IAPS.

Chairman of Governors: Mr Simon Crebbin

Headmistress: Jessica Crossley

Age Range. 2–11 Co-educational.
Number of Pupils 120 Girls and Boys.
Fees per term (2016–2017). Nursery £25.95 per session; Main School £2,960 including lunch.
Staff: 10 full-time, 8 part-time.
Religious affiliation: Interdenominational.
Excellence in Education inspiring Kindness, Confidence & Creativity
Accommodated in a large house, Moorfield School is situated in a beautiful setting on the edge of Ilkley Moor. It prides itself in providing inspirational teaching within a giving and caring school. Independence and individuality are encouraged and confidence nurtured. The whole child is important and we work together to grow hearts, minds and intellectual strength of character.

High standards in English and Maths are the academic bedrock enabling all our pupils to get into their secondary school of choice. Outstanding teaching from a vibrant staff, gives pupils confidence to succeed in all subjects. With specialist teaching in many subjects, pupils are given the opportunity to develop skills and interests in Drama, Music and Sport, Art, Cookery and Bushcraft. Our Bushcraft programme covers a variety of traditional survival skills and techniques such as fire lighting, shelter construction, foraging and tree and plant lore. Extracurricular clubs offer a large range of activities at lunchtime and after school.

The school has spacious accommodation including a purpose-built EYFS, music department, subject teaching rooms, a large hall and dining room. A recent acquisition is a new astroturf and Forest School.

Support for working parents is provided by offering wrap-around care from 7.45 am to 6.15 pm and our 'Home from Home' holiday care is offered for 10 weeks a year.

Pupils leave Moorfield with a very secure foundation of learning, a strong work ethic and the confidence to be successful.

Moorfield is recommended by The Good Schools Guide.
Charitable status. Moorfield School Ltd is a Registered Charity, number 529112.

Moorlands School

Foxhill Drive, Weetwood Lane, Leeds LS16 5PF
Tel: 0113 278 5286
email: info@moorlands-school.co.uk
website: www.moorlands-school.co.uk
Twitter: @MoorlandsHead
Facebook: /MoorlandsLeeds

Acting Headmaster: **Mark Langley**, BSc Hons, MPhil, PGCE

Age Range. 2–11 Co-educational.
Number of Pupils. 148 Day Boys and Girls.
Founded in 1898, Moorlands School is dedicated to providing a first-class education for girls and boys aged 2 to 11 years in a warm, friendly environment.

The school is conveniently located off the Ring Road at Weetwood Lane, yet sat in beautiful grounds providing all the outdoor space (and off-road parking) required for children to play in a safe and secure environment. The school boasts fantastic wrap-around care facilities, excellent teaching standards, on-site swimming pool and small class sizes.

In 2012 Moorlands became a full member of the Methodist Independent Schools Trust (MIST) securing its long-term future and bringing with it the benefits of membership of a large network of independent schools.

The aim of the school is to develop the full potential of every child within a happy and caring environment fostered by small classes and the professional skills of a highly qualified staff. Strong links between the parents and the school are encouraged to facilitate the provision of an effective education.

Admission is by assessment and observation. Pupils are accepted at 2 years old for entry into the Nursery and are expected to progress through the school in preparation for entry to senior independent day and boarding schools. The school has a well-developed specialist facility to provide assistance to pupils with any learning issue such as dyslexia or to gifted children.

Blended with this traditional core of academic work is offered a comprehensive range of sporting activities and a wide range of musical and extracurricular pursuits.

At Moorlands, we have a simple yet beautiful motto, 'Intrepide', or 'be brave'! In school, we talk about how being brave or intrepid takes many forms. Being brave isn't always a grand gesture; sometimes it simply means 'having a go', such as attempting that difficult question, offering an answer in class when you're not quite sure or trying something new. This culture of intrepidness allows children to be brave and try new things in a safe, nurturing and stimulating environment.

Religious affiliation: Methodist.
Fees per term (2016–2017). Early Years £2,795; Reception £2,907, Years 1 and 2 £2,917, Lunch £190; Years 3 to 6 £3,272–£3,297, Lunch £210.
Charitable status. Moorlands School is a Registered Charity, number 529216. It exists to provide children with the finest education possible, using the best resources in an environment of care.

Moreton Hall Preparatory School

Mount Road, Bury St Edmunds, Suffolk IP32 7BJ
Tel: 01284 753532
email: office@moretonhallprep.org
website: www.moretonhallprep.org

Chairman of the Board of Governors: Neil Smith

Headmaster: C E Moxon, BA, PGCE

Age Range. 4–13.
Number of Pupils. Boys 52, Girls 67.
Fees per term (2016–2017). Boarding: £6,795 (full), £6,065 (weekly). Day: £2,715–£4,440.

Moreton Hall is a warm and welcoming school, set in an impressive historic building with 30 acres of attractive grounds. Its last inspection (2011) assessed both the personal development of the children and their pastoral care as excellent. Sporting standards are high with daily games sessions. Rugby, soccer, hockey, cricket, netball, rounders and swimming form the major sports. There is an outdoor, heated swimming pool and a large sports hall. A second, indoor swimming pool and squash courts are available for use at the adjacent health club.

The staff to pupil ratio is high with an average class size of 14 pupils. Some classes are setted, including all Maths lessons, in senior years to improve this ratio still further. Pupils are prepared for Year 9 Scholarship or Common Entrance examination to the full range of Senior schools; prestigious Academic, Music and Sporting awards are all achieved regularly. High importance is also placed upon Music and Drama. The majority of pupils learn a musical instrument and perform regularly in concerts; there are plays in each section of the school and weekly lessons in Speech and Drama are available.

The school accepts boarders from the age of 8 and day pupils from the year in which they turn 5. Weekly and flexible boarding arrangements are also popular. The Headmaster and his wife are also the resident Houseparents and they are supported by other staff and gap students. Bury St Edmunds is five minutes away, Cambridge just under an hour away and London is two hours by road or rail. The School can arrange transport to and from airports.

Moreton Hall has a Catholic tradition and welcomes children of all denominations. Financial support is available through means-tested bursaries.

For further information, please access our website or ring the office to arrange a visit or taster day.

The school is a member of CISC.

Charitable status. Moreton Hall School Trust Limited is a Registered Charity, number 280927. It exists to provide high quality education for boys and girls.

Moulsford Preparatory School

Moulsford-on-Thames, Wallingford, Oxfordshire OX10 9HR
Tel: 01491 651438
email: pa.registrar@moulsford.com
website: www.moulsford.com
Twitter: @Moulsford
Facebook: /Moulsford

The School is a Charitable Trust controlled by a Board of Governors.

Chairman of the Board of Governors: Mr E L A Boddington

Headmaster: B Beardmore-Gray, BA Hons, QTS

Age Range. 4–13.
Number of Boys. 34 Weekly Boarders, 290 Day Boys.
Fees per term (2016–2017). Day Boys £3,550–£5,300, Weekly Boarders £6,650. These fees are all inclusive but

individual coaching in music, judo, golf and fencing is charged as an extra.

The School has its own river frontage on the Thames, spacious games fields and lawns and is situated between Wallingford and Reading.

Boys are prepared for the Common Entrance and Scholarship examinations to the top independent schools in the country. An experienced and well qualified staff ensures that a high standard is achieved academically, musically, artistically and on the games field.

The principal games are rugby football, soccer, tennis and cricket. Other sporting activities include athletics, swimming, sailing, judo, golf and gymnastics. The school is proud of its fine academic and sporting reputation which has been built up over many years.

Charitable status. Moulsford Preparatory School is a Registered Charity, number 309643.

The Mount Junior School

Dalton Terrace, York YO24 4DD
Tel: 01904 667500
email: admissions@mountschoolyork.co.uk
website: www.mountschoolyork.co.uk
Twitter: @MountSchoolYork
Facebook: /mountschoolyork

Management Committee (*Board of Governors*):
Clerk: Timothy Phillips

Principal of The Mount School: Adrienne Richmond, BSc, MA, NQPH

Head of Junior School: **Rachel Capper**, BEd Hons

Admissions Manager: Fiona Ward, MA, PGCE

Age Range. Girls 2–11; Boys 2–10.
Number of Pupils. 106.
Fees per term (2016–2017). Juniors (Years 3–6) £3,586; Infants (Years 1–2) £2,702; Reception £2,392. Pre-School (2–4 years): 51 weeks per year (5 days per week, 7.30 am – 6.00 pm options) based on £6 per hour; Term Time only: £950 (afternoon sessions only), £1,267 (morning sessions only), £2,217 (8.30 am – 3.30 pm). Before/After School Care: £3 per half hour. Flexi boarding from age 10: £46 per night.

The Mount Junior School and Pre-School in York, for girls and boys aged 2 and above, offers a genuinely remarkable education in an environment which fosters self-belief, independent thought and sensitivity to others. Pupils know their views are listened to and they are able to contribute positively to make a difference to the School.

This co-educational Quaker School shares the same grounds and educational, recreational, medical, catering and security facilities as the prestigious Senior School on an exclusive 16-acre campus in the heart of York with impressive facilities, a wide range of music disciplines, sports, extracurricular activities and creative media. Pupils are encouraged to make the most of every opportunity, both inside and outside the classroom.

Academically, the Junior School is admired for its dedicated teaching staff who nurture in the children a love of learning and creative, independent thought. The stimulating curriculum produces results at critically important stages of a child's education. Even the smallest children enjoy the School's on-site Forest School and Enchanted Garden weekly where, through free play and structured activities, they learn to be adventurous, inquisitive and proud of their successes.

In 2012, 2014 and 2015 the Junior School achieved 100% Distinctions in the national London Academy of Music and Dramatic Arts (LAMDA) examinations.

For further details about the Senior School, see entry in GSA section.

Charitable status. The Mount School (York) is a Registered Charity, number 513646.

Mylnhurst Preparatory School & Nursery

Button Hill, Woodholm Road, Ecclesall, Sheffield S11 9HJ

Tel: 0114 236 1411
Fax: 0114 236 1411
email: enquiries@mylnhurst.co.uk
website: www.mylnhurst.co.uk

A Catholic Foundation Welcoming Families of All Faiths – maximising the potential of your children through partnership within a challenging and supportive Catholic Christian Community.

Headmaster: **Mr C P Emmott**, BSc Hons, MEd, MBA

Age Range. 3–11 Co-educational.
Number of Pupils. 179.
Fees per term (2016–2017). £3,030.

Situated in extensive private grounds, Mylnhurst provides a state-of-the-art teaching environment supported by our outstanding school facilities, which include a 25m pool, dance studio, sports hall and Apple Mac suite.

With a strong emphasis on school-parent partnership, Mylnhurst embraces your high expectations and ensures each child benefits from an exciting and stimulating curriculum.

Be assured of a very warm welcome and the opportunity to work closely with our committed and talented staff. So, whether it be an informal chat or a school open day, we look forward to sharing our vision with you and discussing the exciting future of your children.

Charitable status. Mylnhurst Limited is a Registered Charity, number 1056683.

Naima JPS

21 Andover Place, London NW6 5ED

Tel: 020 7328 2802
Fax: 020 7624 0161
email: secretary@naimajps.org.uk
website: www.naimajps.co.uk

Chair of Governors: Mrs Sabine Howard

Headmaster: **Mr J W Pratt**, GRSM Hons, CertEd

Age Range. 2–11 Co-educational.
Number of Pupils. 175 girls and boys.
Fees per term (2016–2017). £2,535–£4,235.

Naima JPS is centred on the belief that an excellent secular education and strong Jewish grounding are mutually attainable. As such, our twin goals merge as we aspire to prepare our children for a successful life in society imbued with Torah values. We aim to provide a secular education on a par with the top national private schools with a curriculum that extends beyond the minimum guidelines provided by the National Curriculum. As a private school, we provide both the environment and teaching resources to monitor each individual, and to help children of all abilities to reach their full potential.

Naima JPS challenges all children, together with their parents, no matter what their level of religious observance, to pursue ongoing spiritual growth as individuals. We encourage children on their journey to spiritual maturity in a harmonious and nurturing community environment of tolerance, respect and care for one another.

The school has a one-form entry. Given that class sizes seldom exceed 22 and the favourable ratio of teachers and assistants to children – as little as 1:5 depending on the age and need – programmes of learning have the flexibility for differentiation. The school has a high number of particularly able children with specific intellectual gifts.

During the crucial early years at school it is important that children define themselves by things they can do well. Self-esteem, that essential by-product of success, empowers strength and gifts. Once children understand how their minds work, as they learn in many different ways, they can feel comfortable about entering any environment and mastering it. Children who truly understand, value and like themselves are better equipped to flourish and embrace fresh challenges. Confidence through success contributes to strong identities that welcome new horizons. Resiliency, discovery, independence and spiritual maturity are nurtured at all levels. At Naima JPS education is not about coveting garlands for the few, but ensuring that all children reach their full potential.

Charitable status. Naima JPS is a Registered Charity, number 289066.

The New Beacon

Brittains Lane, Sevenoaks, Kent TN13 2PB

Tel: 01732 452131
Fax: 01732 459509
email: admin@newbeacon.org.uk
website: www.newbeacon.org.uk

Chairman of the Governors: Mr James Thorne

Headmaster: **Michael Piercy**, BA Hons

Age Range. 4–13.
Number of Boys. 400. Predominantly Day Pupils, but a small element of flexi boarding is retained from Monday to Thursday.
Fees per term (2016–2017). £3,635–£4,915. Fees include lunches.

Boys are prepared for both grammar and senior independent schools, and enjoy considerable success at 11+ and 13+, with many achieving scholarships (including music, sport, art and drama) to a wide range of first-class senior schools.

The School divides into Senior, Middle and Junior sections in which boys are placed according to age and ability. Initiative is encouraged by organising the School into 4 houses or 'companies'. The well-equipped main School building is complemented by several modern, purpose-built facilities: separate Pre-Prep and Junior School buildings for boys aged 4–9; a Sports Hall with modern changing facilities; a multi-purpose, astroturf sports pitch; a Theatre; a heated indoor Swimming Pool; a centre for Art and Music; and modern facilities for Science and Technology. Soccer, Rugby Union and Cricket are the major games. During the summer months Tennis and Athletics are available. Swimming and Shooting are available all year round. A very extensive range of extra-curricular activities is offered (including many interesting and exciting trips) together with a programme of Pre and After School care. Music, sport, art and drama at the School are highly regarded.

A limited number of music and academic bursaries are offered subject to means testing.

Charitable status. The New Beacon is a Registered Charity, number 307925. It exists to provide an all-round education for boys aged 4–13.

New College School

Savile Road, Oxford OX1 3UA

Tel:	01865 285560
Fax:	01865 210277
email:	office@newcollegeschool.org
website:	www.newcollegeschool.org

Governors: The Warden & Fellows of New College Oxford

Headmaster: **N R Gullifer**, MA, FRSA

Age Range. 4–13 years.

Number of Boys. 162 Day Boys, including 22 Choristers.

Fees per term (2016–2017). Reception £3,082, Year 1 £3,711, Years 2–4 £4,557, Years 5–8 £4,983, Choristers £1,773.

New College School was founded in 1379 when William of Wykeham made provision for the education of 16 Choristers to sing daily services in New College Chapel. Situated in the heart of the city, a few minutes' walk from the College, the school is fortunate in having the use of New College playing fields for sport and New College Chapel for school services.

The staff consists of some 22 full-time teachers and a full complement of visiting music teachers. Boys are prepared for the Common Entrance and Scholarship Examinations for transfer to independent senior schools at age 13. In the final year there is a scholarship form and a common entrance form. The school broadly follows the national curriculum subjects, but also teaches French, Latin, Design Technology and Greek.

Sports, played on New College Sports Ground, include soccer, hockey, cricket, rounders, athletics and rugby. Activities include archery, art, craft, pottery, design, chess, sport, computer, drama, and science clubs. There is a Choral Society for parents.

Music plays a major part in school life with orchestra, ensembles, concert and junior choirs and form concerts, in addition to individual tuition in a wide range of instruments. A optional Saturday morning music education programme is followed by boys from Year 5 upwards.

Boys are admitted by gentle assessment to the Pre-Prep Department at 4 years and to the Prep School at 7 years. Potential Choristers are tested between the ages of 6 and 7 at annual voice trials.

New Hall Preparatory School

The Avenue, Boreham, Chelmsford, Essex CM3 3HS

Tel:	01245 236192
Fax:	01245 451671
email:	prep@newhallschool.co.uk
website:	www.newhallschool.co.uk
Twitter:	@NewHallSchool
Facebook:	/newhallschool

Chair of Governors: Mrs Clare Kershaw, LLB Hons, MCMI

Principal: **Mrs K Jeffrey**, MA Oxon, PGCE Surrey, BA Div PUM, MA EdMg OU, NPQH

Head of Preparatory Division: **Mrs Carole Goodwin**, BA Hons QTS, MEd, NPQH

Age Range. 3–11 Co-educational.

Number of Pupils. 334.

Fees per term (2016–2017). Day: £1,817.40–£4,572; Boarding (from age 7): £6,114 (weekly), £6,754 (full).

New Hall Preparatory School is a Catholic boarding and day school which welcomes all who are in sympathy with its ethos. The school caters for boys and girls aged 3–11 with boarding available from the age of 7. The school is located in the beautiful, spacious and historic grounds of New Hall School, Chelmsford.

At New Hall you will find a welcoming and friendly atmosphere, a nurturing environment and a curriculum designed to stimulate imagination and develop young enquiring minds. Pastoral care is a significant strength of New Hall Preparatory School. Classes of around 20 pupils are taught by teachers who nurture the all-round development of every child.

We know that children excel academically when they are inspired to learn. Our curriculum is delivered through a range of exciting and engaging topics and built upon a progressive ladder of skills. We pride ourselves on teaching lessons which aim for academic excellence at all times.

From Pre-Reception onwards, our curriculum is enriched by specialist subject teachers for Mathematics, French, Information Technology, Latin, Drama, Music, Physical Education and Dance. Their expert knowledge and passion for their subjects greatly enhance the children's learning experience.

The extensive co-curricular activities on offer set New Hall Preparatory School apart; from Philosophy and Latin, to Mandarin and Poetry, there is always something to do.

Creative subjects including Music, Drama, Dance, Art and Design Technology all form part of the mainstream academic curriculum, and also feature in activities offered outside normal lessons. We have three choirs, infant, junior and chamber, as well as a Preparatory School orchestra. Our pupils regularly perform at prestigious venues, which include the O2 Arena and the Royal Albert Hall.

Sports such as rugby, swimming, tennis, netball, hockey and cricket form part of the core curriculum and pupils also have opportunities to pursue an array of activities after school and at weekends. They benefit from the use of state-of-the-art sports facilities, including our 25-metre indoor swimming pool, floodlit courts, AstroTurf pitch, and national standard running track.

We know that flexibility is important. Our wrap-around care offers flexibility for families, and provides opportunities for pupils to make new friends and develop new interests through the wide range of activities available. In the morning, there is an early drop-off option and breakfast club is available.

We also provide an After School Care service in a spacious, purpose-built facility within the Preparatory School. Once the school day finishes, pupils are able to enjoy a full programme of supervised activities until 6.00 pm. There is no additional charge for After School Care and no booking is necessary.

Charitable status. New Hall School Trust is a Registered Charity, number 1110286.

Newbridge Preparatory School

51 Newbridge Crescent, Wolverhampton, West Midlands WV6 0LH

Tel: 01902 751088
Fax: 01902 751333
email: office@newbridge.wolverhampton.sch.uk
website: www.newbridgeprepschool.org.uk

Chairman of Board: Mrs H M Hughes

Headmistress: **Mrs S Fisher**, BEd Hons

Age Range. Girls 2–11. Boys 2–7.
Number of Pupils. 147.
Fees per term (2016–2017). £1,720–£2,640 including dance, recorder, drama, gym, netball, singing for various year groups.

Newbridge Preparatory School, founded in 1937, occupies a super site on the outskirts of Wolverhampton, convenient for parents travelling from Telford, Bridgnorth, Shropshire, and Stafford.

The school is divided into Lower School (Pre-Nursery–Year 2) and Upper School (Years 3–6). Upper School is housed in the main building which is a substantial house set in huge, beautiful mature gardens. There are specialist facilities in Art and Design, ICT, Science, Music and PE. The school also has netball and tennis courts.

Staff : pupil ratio is high. Specialist teaching takes place in Key Stage Two in English, Mathematics, Music, Science, French, PE, Dance and Drama. In Key Stage One: Dance, PE, Music and French.

Lower School enjoys a separate Nursery and a new building for Pre-Nursery to Year 2. There is a sports hall.

Children with Special Needs are well supported and nurtured.

Upper School girls take drama and dance and enter examinations. They also enter the annual local festival for Music and Drama.

The school offers a Breakfast Club (7.30–8.00 am), an Early Club (8.00–8.30 am), an After-School Club (3.15–6.00 pm) and a Holiday Club (8.00 am – 5.30 pm).

Standards are high in all areas of the curriculum. Senior School results are excellent. Places are gained at local selective Independent and Maintained Schools but also Boarding Schools. Sporting, Academic and Speech and Drama Scholarships are attained for entrance into Senior School. Once examinations are complete, Year 6 follow an exciting STAR (Summer Term Activities Refreshed) curriculum and developing skills previously taught. Girls leave Newbridge well equipped to face the challenges of a Senior School.

Educational visits take place each term. Nursery children enjoy a Forest School experience. Residential visits occur in Years 3–6. The visits vary from outdoor activities and challenges and cultural visits to London and France.

Emphasis is placed on traditional values, personal development and responsibility. The curriculum is very broad, including many opportunities in Sport, Dance, Drama and Music.

Our school mission statement is: Aiming High, Building Bridges and Preparing for Life.

Children are taught to do their best in all areas, strive for a challenge and succeed at their own level.

Emphasis is placed on self-discipline, inclusion, equal opportunity and respect.

Charitable status. Newbridge Preparatory School is a Registered Charity, number 1019682. It exists to advance the education of children by conducting the school known as Newbridge Preparatory School.

Newcastle Preparatory School

6 Eslington Road, Jesmond, Newcastle-upon-Tyne NE2 4RH

Tel: 0191 281 1769
Fax: 0191 281 5668
email: enquiries@newcastleprepschool.org.uk
website: www.newcastleprepschool.org.uk

The School was founded in 1885 and is now a Charitable Trust with a Board of Governors.

Chair of Governors: Mrs C Wood

Head: **Margaret Coates**, BEd Oxon

Age Range. 3–11.
Number of Pupils. 280 Day Pupils (180 boys, 100 girls).
Fees per term (2016–2017). Reception & Year 1: £3,370, Years 2 & 3: £3,425, Years 4–6: £3,485.

The School is situated in a residential part of Newcastle with easy access from all round the area.

Newcastle Preparatory School is a fully co-educational day school for children aged 3 to 11 years. It is a warm, caring environment in which all pupils are encouraged to reach their full potential.

Children may join 'First Steps' at NPS from the age of 3 years. 'First Steps' is an exciting and colourful nursery with excellent resources and well qualified staff who look after the needs of each individual.

At age 4, children make the easy step into School where they experience many 'steps to success'.

The curriculum offered throughout school is broad and balanced so that children enjoy learning in a variety of ways. French is taught from the age of 4 with music and PE being taught by specialist teachers. As children progress through School they become independent learners, following a varied timetable and class sizes are small to provide individual attention.

Music is an important part of life at NPS. There is a choir and a lively swing band.

Sporting achievements too are very good. There is a purpose-built Sports Hall and a wide range of sport is offered with extracurricular activities including rugby, football, cricket, hockey, netball, athletics, tennis and swimming.

Also there are many clubs and activities to enrich the curriculum, eg Drama, Dance, Chess, Philosophy, Art, ICT, Design, Food Technology and there is an effective School Council as well as a Buddy System.

The variety of opportunities ensures that the children leave NPS well equipped for an easy transition to senior school. The academic results are very good and the children receive an all-round education, so that they are confident, eager learners.

Charitable status. Newcastle Preparatory School is a Registered Charity, number 528152. It exists to provide education for boys and girls.

Newland House School

Waldegrave Park, Twickenham TW1 4TQ

Tel: 020 8865 1234
Fax: 020 8744 0399
email: admissions@newlandhouse.net
website: www.newlandhouse.net
Twitter: @newlandhouse

Founded in 1897, the school was privately owned until 1971 when the Newland House School Trust was formed. It is a charitable Educational Trust with a Board of Governors.

Chairman of Governors: D Ridgeon

Headmaster: **D A Alexander**, BMus, Dip NCOS

Deputy Headmaster: D S Arnold, BA

Age Range. 4–13.
Number of Pupils. 245 Boys, 178 Girls.
Fees per term (2016–2017). Pre-Prep £3,625, Prep £4,055. Lunch is included in the Fees.

Newland House School is a co-educational day preparatory school set in a residential area on the Twickenham-Teddington border. The school is ideally situated for parents in the Richmond, Kingston and Hampton areas and is very close to the river Thames.

The school currently occupies approximately 5 acres with grounds that provide sports facilities, including an all-weather pitch. The school is also fortunate to have daily access to the nearby National Physical Laboratory Sports Ground.

The school is divided into Pre-Prep, which provides for children in Reception (EYFS) to Year 2, and Prep for children in Years 3 to 8. A new Pre-Prep school was opened in autumn 2016 immediately adjacent to the Prep School providing an innovative and unique learning environment for pupils using leading sustainable design and the latest technology. Following the move to the new premises, the additional space has enabled the school to offer a three-form intake, with an additional 20 places available in Reception from September 2016.

The school's main intakes are at the age of 4 (Reception) which is non-selective and Year 3 via a 7+ assessment (note the last intake via 7+ will be in 2018). Places may also become available in other age groups throughout the school year.

The Prep School has well-appointed, airy classrooms with a traditional feel, a large gymnasium/assembly hall, dining room, separate senior and junior libraries and two well-equipped science laboratories. There is an Art and Design Technology block, as well as a purpose-built Music block. The school has a substantial computer network, including a state-of-the-art computer suite.

The staff currently consists of 33 full-time teachers, and 10 classroom assistants, mostly in the Pre-Prep School. Children are well prepared for the Common Entrance and Scholarship examinations to Independent Schools. During the ISI Inspection in 2013, the school was found to be 'excellent' in many areas. In particular, the opportunities which the school provides for academic achievement and learning, as well as pastoral care and pupils' personal development, were clearly recognised.

There is a strong music department staffed by 19 visiting music staff who teach a variety of instruments. There are 5 choirs, several wind and brass ensembles, 2 orchestras and a jazz band who have the opportunity to perform at a variety of external venues.

The main games for boys are Rugby, Football and Cricket with Netball, Hockey and Rounders for girls. All children from the age of 7 have the opportunity to swim throughout the year. The teams take part in a range of leagues and competitions and there is an annual cricket tour to South Africa.

The school is committed to providing a broad and balanced curriculum and an environment that fosters enquiring minds. A wide variety of extra-curricular activities is available including, fencing, golf, chess, and badminton. The school also provides a Breakfast Club from 7.30 am each morning and an After-School Club until 6 pm.

Charitable status. The Newland House School Trust Limited is a Registered Charity, number 312670. It exists to promote and provide for the advancement of education for children of either sex or both sexes.

Newton Prep

149 Battersea Park Road, London SW8 4BX
Tel: 020 7720 4091
Fax: 020 7498 9052
email: admin@newtonprep.co.uk
website: www.newtonprepschool.co.uk
Twitter: @newtonprep

Chairman of Council: Dr Farouk Walji

Head: **Mrs A E Fleming**, BA, MA
head@newtonprep.co.uk

Administration & Finance Manager: Mr P Farrelly
bursar@newtonprep.co.uk

Admissions Registrar: Mrs Susan Symes
registrar@newtonprep.co.uk

Age Range. 3–13.
Number of Pupils. 650+: 50% Boys, 50% Girls.
Fees per term (2016–2017). £2,855–£6,050.
Average size of class: <20.
The current teacher/pupil ratio is 1:11.
Religious denomination: Non-denominational.

Newton Prep is a vibrant school which offers a challenging education for inquisitive children who are eager to engage fully with the world in which they are growing up. The school aims to:

- inspire children to be adventurous and committed in their learning;
- provide balance and breadth in all aspects of a child's education: intellectual, aesthetic, physical, moral and spiritual;
- encourage initiative, individuality, independence, creativity and enquiry;
- promote responsible behaviour and respect for others in a happy, safe and caring environment.

Entry requirements: Siblings are given priority when allocating nursery places; other nursery places are awarded by lottery, while ensuring an even balance of boys and girls; children joining Reception are assessed individually: a gentle process, with offers made by October half term in the year before entry. Older children come to an assessment morning in the Spring Term (on a case-by-case basis at other times) during which they will be assessed in reading, maths and some diagnostic, age-appropriate reasoning tests. Scholarships and means-tested top-up bursaries are available in and after Year 3.

Examinations offered: All entrance examinations to senior schools, Common Entrance and scholarships at 11, 12 and 13. Most children leave to go to London day schools though a significant minority leave to go boarding. We pride ourselves on the quality of guidance offered and, every 2 years, we organise a Senior Schools Fair attended by over 75 schools.

First-time visitors to the school are invariably impressed by the scale and range of our secondary-school-level facilities and by the wide open outdoor spaces enjoyed by the children on a large site so close to the centre of London.

Newton Prep occupies an early 20th-century elementary school building, which has been extensively remodelled internally, and behind which stands large modern extensions containing classrooms, the dining hall and kitchen, two gymnasiums, a 300-seat auditorium and a state-of-the-art recital hall (along with a recording studio and a music technology suite). The top floor of the Edwardian building provides one large general-purpose space as well as two art studios. Below are two floors of classrooms, including three collegiate-style science labs, three ICT suites and a library that is the envy of the many visiting authors, who all say it is one of the most vibrant and popular reading spaces they have come across in a school.

Newton Prep has two huge outdoor spaces for PE/Games and free play: behind the school, an all-weather pitch and, in front, a large playground for the littler children. The school also has a large garden with a wildlife area and an activity area with a pirate boat.

Despite the excellence of their education, Newton Prep children are notable for their lack of arrogance and entitlement. The kindness and generosity shown by the pupils towards their peers is remarkable and the engagement between the older children and the little ones is heartwarming.

Newton is not a blazers and boaters kind of school. As one current parent put it, "Newton combines a quirky nature and knowledge of families with great space and facilities … All the teachers understand my (very different) children, the management is open to fresh ideas and the school is large enough to accommodate variety."

Norland Place School

162/166 Holland Park Avenue, London W11 4UH
Tel: 020 7603 9103
Fax: 020 7603 0648
email: office@norlandplace.com
website: www.norlandplace.com

Headmaster: **Mr P Mattar**

Age Range. Girls 4–11, Boys 4–8.
Number of Children. 240.
Fees per term (2016–2017). £4,790–£5,594.

A Preparatory school founded in 1876 and still standing on the original site in Holland Park Avenue. Children are prepared for competitive London day schools and top rate boarding schools. The curriculum is well balanced with an emphasis on English, Mathematics and Science. Music, Art and Games are strong. The school contains a Library in addition to specialist Music, IT, Science and Art Rooms.

Early registration is essential.

Northbourne Park

Betteshanger, Deal, Kent CT14 0NW
Tel: 01304 611215
Fax: 01304 619020
email: admissions@northbournepark.com
website: www.northbournepark.com
Twitter: @northbournepark
Facebook: /Northbourne-Park-School

Chairman of Governors: Mr Brian Semple, OBE, MA, MSc

Headmaster: **Sebastian Rees**, BA Hons, PGCE, NPQH

Age Range. 3–13 Co-educational.
Number of Pupils. 146 boys and girls, including 40 boarders.

Northbourne Park is a co-educational day and boarding school set in 100 acres of beautiful park and woodland in rural Kent, close to Canterbury and within easy reach of central London, Eurostar and Gatwick Airport.

We provide children with a first-class education focusing on the individual needs of every child, inspiring them to succeed across a wide range of learning experiences. We offer each child the freedom and space, together with countless opportunities, to grow in confidence and succeed.

Academic. From the Nursery and Pre-Prep through to the Prep School all our pupils gain confidence in their learning, and through inspirational teaching from dedicated staff, the pupils adapt well to an engaging and stimulating curriculum with a real sense of achievement. Although non-selective, we consistently achieve 100% pass rate in examinations – entry to top Independent Senior and local Grammar schools, LAMDA and the Associated Board of the Royal Schools of Music. Many of our pupils gain scholarships to prestigious Senior Schools.

Northbourne Park's unique Language Programme helps every child develop foreign languages in an integrated learning environment. French is introduced at 3 years and we have a unique Bilingual programme for French pupils joining Years 7 and 8 who study the French academic curriculum. The result is a clear advantage when they move on to Senior Schools.

Sport. We are passionate about sport and through an excellent sports programme the pupils develop key skills and learn the importance of teamwork and leadership. There are many opportunities to try a variety of sports from the traditional to the more diverse such as archery and trampolining.

Creative Arts. We nurture a love for all the Arts. Many pupils learn one or more instrument in our purpose-built Music suite. They have the opportunity to take part in the choir, band, orchestra, string and brass groups performing regularly within the school and the local area. Other opportunities include LAMDA lessons, regular drama productions and Public Speaking that ensure pupils are articulate and confident in their performances. Artistic talents are encouraged through a range of media including sculpture, costume design, film-making on iMacs and pottery.

Community. Pupils are provided with a first-rate level of pastoral care in safe and nurturing surroundings with a real family atmosphere. Our welcoming boarding community provides a home-from-home environment and a continuous boarding service at weekends throughout the term. Boarders enjoy regular excursions and activities, and the accompanied services to London and Paris provide opportunities for weekends at home.

Extra Curricular. We provide the pupils with a fun and extensive programme of clubs that help develop their interests and skills in hobbies that can endure long into adult life. Love of the outdoors and respect for the environment begins in the Pre-Prep and develops through into the Prep School with fun physical adventures. Whether they are playing in the woods, camping out overnight or following our pioneering Outdoor Education Programme, children love Northbourne Park life.

Fees per term (2016–2017). Boarders: £6,610 (weekly), £7,680 (full); French Programme £8,340. Day Pupils: £2,866–£3,410 (Pre-Prep), £3,996–£5,335 (Years 3–8). Sleepover £39 per night. Fees include customary extras and many extra-curricular activities. We offer bursaries and a wide range of scholarships. Sibling, HM Forces and Clergy discounts are generous and popular.

Charitable status. Northbourne Park is a Registered Charity, number 280048.

Northwood College for Girls – Junior School

GDST

Maxwell Road, Northwood, Middlesex HA6 2YE

Tel:	01923 845067
Fax:	01923 836526
email:	juniorschool@nwc.gdst.net
	c.kelly@nwc.gdst.net
website:	www.northwoodcollege.gdst.net

Northwood College for Girls is part of the Girls' Day School Trust (GDST), the UK's leading network of independent girls' schools. As a charity that owns and runs 24 schools and two academies, the GDST reinvests all its income in its schools. For further information about the Trust, see p. xxiii or visit www.gdst.net.

Chairman of Governing Council: Mr G Hudson

Head of Junior School: **Mrs Zara Hubble**, BEd Hons

Age Range. Girls 3–11.
Number of Pupils. 356 Girls.
Fees per term (2016–2017). £3,451–£4,521. Fees include lunch, loan of text books, stationery and certain school trips.

Ethos. Our aim is to raise young women who know their own minds and are creative and flexible thinkers, as well as being able to achieve outstanding exam results. We are academically selective, but not narrowly exclusive. We value girls for more than simple academic performance, because our unique approach to advanced thinking skills means that we can develop, stretch and challenge every single one of them. We think that makes for an interesting and vibrant school community – and it's what makes Northwood College for Girls special.

Results show that Junior School girls reach standards far above national norms. All National Curriculum subjects are taught, plus Latin, Ballet and Drama. In addition, girls in Years 3–5 study French and girls in Year 6 study Spanish, Mandarin and German.

Thinking Skills. Our approach to thinking skills sets Northwood College for Girls apart and gives our girls an edge in the way they approach any task or challenge. Through the programme, we ensure our girls start to understand and develop how they think from the day they join Nursery through to the end of the Sixth Form. Over the years, they build up their reasoning skills, improve their creativity and acquire strategies for tackling complex problems and decisions. It gives them a life skill that will be as useful at university and in the workplace as it is at school.

Pupil Well-being. We take the challenge of turning out happy, confident and generous young women very seriously. Northwood College for Girls creates an atmosphere in which courtesy, respect and self-respect thrive. Girls are taught to understand the other person's point of view and to show good manners at all times. In keeping with this ethos, the Junior School operates a system of recognition and reward for good behaviour and attitude, as well as work.

Come and visit us. The Junior School is housed in three separate buildings, including an innovative Early Years Centre which has been designed to allow for both indoor and outdoor learning to take place in an exciting and challenging environment.

We enjoy showing parents and girls around Northwood College for Girls. *For more information please see our entry in the GSA section.*

Charitable status. Northwood College for Girls is part of The Girls' Day School Trust, which is a Registered Charity, number 306983.

Norwich School, The Lower School

Bishopgate, Norwich NR1 4AA

Tel:	01603 728439
email:	lsadmin@norwich-school.org.uk
website:	www.norwich-school.org.uk

Chairman of Governors: P J E Smith, MA, FIA

Master of the Lower School: **J K Ingham**, BA

Principal Deputy Head: A Wilson, BSc, MSc

Deputy Head (Academic): C M W Parsons, BSc

Age Range. 7–11.
Number of Pupils. 197.
Fees per term (2016–2017). £4,575.

The Lower School is the Junior Day School for Norwich School (*see entry in HMC section*). It is delightfully located in the Cathedral Close, between the East End of the Cathedral and the River Wensum. The Cathedral Choristers are educated at Norwich School, which is a member of the Choir Schools' Association.

The Lower School provides depth and breadth of education through a challenging curriculum. It seeks to recognise, nurture and develop each pupil's potential within an environment which encourages all-round emotional, physical, social and spiritual growth and to foster positive relations between pupils, teachers and parents. The dedicated teaching staff is committed to providing a stimulating programme of active learning which has rigour and discipline but avoids unnecessary pressure.

With two forms in each of its four year groups, the Lower School is the ideal size for ensuring a lively environment within a warm family atmosphere. The main building has bright, spacious areas for activities and lessons. As well as the library, there are specialised facilities for science, art, technology and ICT. There is an excellent play area in addition to the adjacent, extensive playing fields. A £750,000 extension for Science and Music opened in January 2014.

A wide range of extra-curricular activities and school trips is offered. Music is a strong feature of school life. Many pupils choose to learn a musical instrument and participate in the various instrumental music groups. Rugby, netball, hockey, cricket, rounders and tennis are taught and the games programme is designed to encourage pupils of all abilities to enjoy games and physical activity.

The School aims to attract pupils who will thrive in a challenging academic environment and is therefore selective. Prospective pupils are assessed in English, mathematics and non-verbal reasoning. There is a two-form entry at 7+ and a small number of places is available each year at 8+, 9+ and 10+. The prospectus and application forms are available from the Admissions Registrar, Tel: 01603 728442.

The vast majority of pupils from the Lower School progress to the Senior School at age eleven, and the curriculum is designed to prepare the pupils effectively for the next stage of their Norwich School education.

Charitable status. Norwich School is a Registered Charity, number 311280.

Notre Dame School
Preparatory School

Burwood House, Cobham, Surrey KT11 1HA

Tel: 01932 869990
email: office@notredame.co.uk
website: www.notredame.co.uk
Twitter: @NotreDameCobham
Facebook: /notredamecobham
LinkedIn: /notredamecobham

Chair of Governors: Mr Gerald Russell

Head of Prep: **Miss Merinda D'Aprano**, BEd Hons, MA, FRSA

Assistant Head: Mrs Clare Barber, BSc Hons, PGCE
Head of EYFS: Miss Melanie Lehmann, BA Hons, EYPS
Head of Infants: Miss Geraldine Deen, BA Hons QTS
Pastoral Director: Miss Rebecca Golding, BA Hons, PGCE

(*For full list of Preparatory School staff, see Notre Dame School GSA entry.*)

Age Range. Girls 2–11, Boys 2–7.
Number of Pupils. 250 Girls, 18 boys.
Fees per term (2016–2017). Nursery £1,260–£3,000 Reception £3,325, Prep 1 & 2 £3,805, Prep 3–6 £4,225.
Bursaries. A limited number of assisted places and bursaries are offered subject to income and asset tests.

Notre Dame School is an independent Roman Catholic day school for approximately 650 girls aged 2–18. Set in 17 acres of beautiful, rural parkland, our school is part of a worldwide educational organisation, founded in Bordeaux in the 17th century by Saint Jeanne de Lestonnac. The Company of Mary Our Lady is the oldest recognised educational order, devoted to the teaching of girls and a belief in the unique contribution they make to society. We welcome families, of all faiths, who wish their daughters to grow spiritually, academically and socially in a dynamic, challenging yet caring environment.

Notre Dame School has:

• An environment which educates, including 17 acres of park lands, sports pitches, swimming pool, forest school area, treehouse, and dedicated specialist teaching rooms.
• A vibrant, bespoke humanities curriculum to develop thinking skills, moral foundation and knowledge.
• A wide range of co-curricular activities to enhance the educational experience.
• Highly-qualified teaching staff including subject specialists for music, PE, drama, Spanish, swimming, upper junior science, and dance.
• A friendly, vibrant, mixed-ability community of happy girls.

The discovery of self is especially important during the Prep years. We draw out individual talents, develop personal strengths and positively address weaknesses. This is undertaken both in class and in a wide range of internal clubs and workshops. The Prep at Notre Dame explores every facet of academic life and the school is especially proud of its strengths in drama, art, music, sport and languages. These are subjects at the very core of self-expression and you will find them enthusiastically carried through to the Senior, where they are taken to an even higher level.

Curriculum. The curriculum has breadth, depth and relevance. It is an enhanced version of the National Curriculum, strong in literacy and numeracy, and designed to provide a truly rounded, challenging preparatory education. The girls learn how to get the best from themselves and grow in motivation to excel, enjoy and achieve. The development of learning skills continues to be an important theme, as pupils tackle more advanced work. Knowing how to learn will forever remain one of life's most valuable lessons. Social, sporting and leisure interests are also encouraged to blossom in an atmosphere of mutual cooperation. A comprehensive range of extra-curricular activities is offered, including: ballet, golf, Spanish, badminton, enthusiasts' swimming, orchestra, jazz, dance, yoga, fencing, Scrabble, chess, choirs, speech and drama, craft, tennis and art appreciation.

Notre Dame girls enjoy high levels of success in all areas of Sport, including swimming, while the professional, 370-seat bespoke Theatre gives pupils a really unique opportunity to tread the boards from a very young age: in drama, singing, ballet and dance or playing their individual instrument of choice.

Transport. Notre Dame is really easy to get to – just two minutes from the A3, less than 10 minutes from Walton, Weybridge, Cobham or Esher, and rarely more than 20 minutes from Guildford. Private coaches from: Barnes, Fulwell, Mortlake, Putney Bridge, Putney Heath, Richmond, Sheen, Teddington, Twickenham, Wandsworth, Wimbledon and all over Surrey offering flexible single/return journeys.

ISI Inspection 2011. Following an outstanding report in 2007, Notre Dame Preparatory School has continued to excel in all areas. '*The pupils' overall achievement from the EYFS onwards is outstanding and represents the successful fulfilment of the school's aim to strive for personal academic excellence.*'

Every aspect of the school from learning and teaching to extra-curricular events was scrutinised and evidence confirmed that: '*Pupils follow a demanding and imaginative curriculum and are successful in entry to the senior schools of their choice, including the award of scholarships*' and '*Their personal development benefits from a carefully planned programme of personal, social and health education. Parents and pupils commend the wide range of clubs and opportunities outside the classroom*'.

Teaching was again praised as being of the highest quality: '*Teachers know their pupils well and care is taken to ensure that they build on what they have already learnt. The pupils' successes are due, in large part, to the excellent teaching.*'

The school was particularly proud that the ethos of the school was reflected in the Inspectors' findings: '*Relationships between staff and pupils, and amongst the pupils themselves, are excellent. Parents appreciate the care provided for their children. Pupils are confident, caring and keen to celebrate the success of others. Pupils of all ages have outstandingly well-developed personal qualities. Excellent leadership and management are reflected in the pupils' outstanding overall achievement and personal development. The hallmark of the management is that nothing is left to chance, with meticulous attention to detail. Teamwork is of a high order.*'

In the words of the Chair of Governors: "*This report is a credit to all and recognition of the effort everyone puts in. To be rated so highly in every area is an important external validation*".

Admission. The usual entry points in the Preparatory School are at Early Years (age 2), Reception (age 4) and Year 3 (age 7) although pupils may be accepted at other points as occasional places often become available in other year groups and throughout the year. Children attend an observation/assessment day at the School. During this day they will be assessed in mathematics, English and reading at the appropriate age level, and have a chance to meet new friends.

Senior School. For further information about the Senior School, please see entry in GSA section.

Charitable status. Notre Dame School Cobham is a Registered Charity, number 1081875. It exists to provide education for girls.

Notting Hill Preparatory School

95 Lancaster Road, London W11 1QQ
Tel: 020 7221 0727
Fax: 020 7221 0332
email: admin@nottinghillprep.com
           l.tate@nottinghillprep.com
website: www.nottinghillprep.com

Co-Chairs of Governing Body:
Mr John Mackay
Mr John Morton Morris

Headmistress: **Mrs Jane Cameron**, BEd Hons

Age Range. 4–13 Co-educational.
Number of Pupils. 346.
Fees per term (2016–2017). £6,100.

NHP is a co-ed Prep School in the heart of Notting Hill, West London. It was created through the cooperation of parents and teachers and this partnership with parents is a cornerstone of the philosophy of the school. It operates on a split site, Reception to Year 3 being housed in a fine Victorian School House and Years 4–8 in a magnificent new building providing, in addition, school hall/dining room, music room and music practice rooms, Science lab and ICT suite.

Our aim is to educate children in the truest sense of the word – to light a fire, not simply fill the bucket. Driven by our Thinking School approach, and delivered by dynamic and inspiring teaching, we strive to develop a passion for learning that will carry our pupils through their school years and beyond.

We create an environment where children's views and ideas are respected and encouraged. We believe that the classroom should be a place where pupils feel safe to challenge and be challenged.

When children do not fear being wrong, they are ready to express their own views, test out new ideas and take risks. At NHP, we celebrate making mistakes, and learning from them, as the path to deeper learning. We nurture the hardy attitudes and habits that will serve our children now and in later life. We develop in our pupils the ability to problem solve and become independent learners. We focus on their ability to cooperate, to think and act collaboratively and to show consideration for the feelings and needs of others.

We are a preparatory school and believe in academic rigour, preparing our pupils comprehensively for entrance exams to all the major London day schools at 11+ or 13+, as well as boarding schools at 13.

Alongside academic achievement, we also believe in the innate joy of childhood and we encourage children to follow their passions inside and outside of the classroom.

Music and performance are particular features at the school, with creative staff producing original material for plays and concerts. There are four choirs, an orchestra, chamber groups and bands and over two-thirds of the pupils learn a musical instrument.

A wide and varied sports programme using local facilities as well as our own on site gym ensures that children develop and perfect skills in the major sports (football, netball, hockey, rugby, cricket, athletics and swimming). Opportunities for displaying these skills are provided by frequent fixtures arranged with local schools.

Regular school trips enhance all aspects of the curriculum. Full use is made of the many and varied opportunities

London offers to extend children's knowledge of their environment, their culture and their history.

NHP is noted for its open, friendly and happy atmosphere and its strong sense of being part of a wider community. Courtesy, kindness and appreciation of a diversity of talents, abilities and needs are defining values of the school's ethos.

The school is heavily oversubscribed and places are offered following a ballot. The School Secretary tries to keep waiting lists within reasonable limits.

Nottingham High Infant and Junior School

Waverley Mount, Nottingham NG7 4ED
Tel: 0115 845 2214
email: juniorinfo@nottinghamhigh.co.uk

Lovell House Infant School:
13 Waverley Street, Nottingham NG7 4DX
Tel: 0115 845 2222
email: lovellinfo@nottinghamhigh.co.uk

website: www.nottinghamhigh.co.uk

Chairman of Governors: David Wild

Head: **Mrs C Bruce**, MA

Age Range. 4–11 Co-educational.
Number of Pupils. 252 Day pupils.
Fees per term (2016–2017). Infant School £3,155; Junior School £3,670.

Nottingham High Infant and Junior School is now co-educational, welcoming girls into all year groups from September 2016.

The **Junior School** is housed in purpose-built premises on the main school site, having its own Classrooms, ICT Suite, Library, Art Room, Science Laboratory, Dining Hall and Assembly Hall.

Entrance Assessments are held in January, based around the core subjects of Mathematics and English, including reading, along with some measures of general ability. The tests are all set at National Curriculum ability levels appropriate for each age group.

The Junior School has an experienced and well-qualified staff. The curriculum is designed for those who expect to complete their education at Nottingham High School. The subjects taught are Religious Education, English, Mathematics, History, Geography, Science, French and PSHE. Full provision is made for Music, Art, Design Technology, Information Communication Technology, Swimming, Physical Education and Games.

The Junior School has its own Orchestra and about 100 pupils receive instrumental tuition. All Year 3 pupils play an instrument of their choice. A Concert and School Plays are performed annually. A wide range of supervised activities and hobbies takes place during every lunch time.

School games are Association Football, Netball and Rugby with some Hockey and Cross Country in the winter, Cricket and Tennis in the summer.

Lovell House Infant School opened in September 2008 for children in Reception, Year 1 and Year 2. Lovell House is situated across the road from the main High School in its own secure and self-contained grounds. The school has been completely refurbished and upgraded recently to provide state-of-the-art classrooms and facilities, and extensive play areas, all in a friendly, home-from-home surrounding. In fact, the main school building is very much like a large house, making the transition between nursery and the early stages of a formal school education so much easier.

Classes are deliberately kept small (a maximum class size of 18), so that our teachers are able to devote time to the children as individuals. The majority of subjects are taught by class teachers, although specialist teachers are used for ICT, Swimming, Music, French and Spanish. All subjects are taught in an integrated curriculum to allow time for play and problem-solving activities to take place.

Beyond the classroom we offer an excellent range of extra-curricular activities giving real breadth to our curriculum. We make full use of some of the Nottingham High School facilities, such as the swimming pool, the extensive games fields and both the music and drama facilities. Thus whilst Lovell House is largely self-contained we are also able to use the High School's wider facilities to expand the horizons of the children in our care.

Entry to Lovell House is by assessment; the admissions process is designed to assess the numeracy and literacy skills of the children applying for a place in Years 1 and 2, and a range of activities are used to assess the potential for learning for those applying for a place in Reception. In addition, all children are invited to school for a final classroom-based assessment where they are observed completing practical activities.

In the January of Year 2 all pupils sit the entrance assessment for Nottingham High Junior School, with the vast majority transferring not only through to the Junior School at Year 3, but also later to the Senior School at Year 7.

As part of Nottingham High School, Lovell House not only benefits from the continuity of education and community from entry at age 4 right through to A Level at age 18, but also from the extensive recreational and cultural facilities provided by the High School.

Charitable status. Nottingham High School is a Registered Charity, number 1104251. It exists to provide education for boys and girls between the ages of 4 and 18 years.

Oakwood Preparatory School

Chichester, West Sussex PO18 9AN
Tel: 01243 575209
email: office@oakwoodschool.co.uk
website: www.oakwoodschool.co.uk
Twitter: @Oakwood_School
Facebook: /Oakwood-School-Chichester

Headteacher: **Mrs Clare Bradbury**, BSc Hons, PGCE

Age Range. Co-educational 2½ to 11.
Number of Pupils. 250 Day boys and girls.
Fees per term (2016–2017). Pre-Prep £1,820–£3,275; Prep School £4,275–£4,565.

Oakwood was founded in 1912 and has grown into a thriving co-educational preparatory school.

Set in 160 acres of glorious park and woodland between the South Downs and the coast, Oakwood's home is a large Georgian country house.

The children learn in a wonderfully safe and spacious environment in the heart of beautiful Sussex countryside only three miles from Chichester. The school prides itself on its family atmosphere and the happiness of its children.

Oakwood is well-equipped with spacious classrooms, Science and Design Technology Studio, Art Room, Library, Music and Theatre Complex and ICT Centre. There is a Gymnasium and 3 floodlit tennis courts. The playing fields extend over nine acres, there is an indoor heated swimming pool and two adventure playgrounds.

The Pre-Prep, though fully integrated into the Oakwood community, enjoys its own spacious site with a safe and enclosed play area. The setting is particularly cosy and attractive, the classrooms having been sympathetically converted from a stable block.

There is a warm family atmosphere, as the school recognises the importance of children feeling happy and secure. Great emphasis is placed on building a solid foundation of social skills and a love of learning, thus enabling each child to settle confidently to school life.

There is a strong academic curriculum with small class sizes, ensuring that each child receives the closest possible attention. In the Prep School, children are set for English and Mathematics. The curriculum is broad with each child's timetable including Design Technology, Science, Humanities, French, Computing, PE, Drama and Music.

Form tutoring is of prime importance, the form teacher overseeing the development of each child – academically, socially and emotionally. Contact with parents is frequent and encouraged.

Opportunities to represent the school in sports teams, plays, choirs and academic workshops and competitions are all part of the "Oakwood Experience".

Music is very much a part of Oakwood life. The children enjoy music lessons each week and there is every opportunity to learn an instrument. The school has three choirs, guitar groups and a whole year group will often learn an instrument (e.g. clarinet) for a term, with each pupil receiving their own practice instrument on loan for the period. Each term there are music assemblies and there are concerts every year for both Prep School and Pre-Prep children. The summer term ends with a musical production by the departing Year 6 pupils. In addition, children are encouraged to perform in Assembly.

The Physical Education and Sports programme has an exciting mix to offer every child. Games are played three times each week and are coached by members of staff with an expertise and enthusiasm for their sport or by outside coaches.

In winter the boys enjoy a taste of all the major sports – Soccer, Rugby and Hockey, while the girls play netball and hockey. Judo, fencing, yoga, modern dance and ballet are also on offer to the boys and girls. In summer the boys play cricket and the girls play rounders, but the school also offers swimming, lacrosse, athletics and tennis. An extensive programme of inter-school fixtures is arranged each term for all sports teams.

Early arrivals care, after school clubs and activities all ensure that busy parents can benefit from a flexible school day.

There is an excellent record of examination, scholarship and academic award success to a variety of senior schools.

Oakwood School

59 Godstone Road, Purley, Surrey CR8 2AN
Tel: 020 8668 8080
email: enquiries@oakwoodschool.org.uk
website: www.oakwoodschool.org.uk

Chair of Governors: Ella Leonard

Headmaster: **Mr Ciro Candia**, BA Hons, PGCE

Age Range. 3–11 Co-educational.
Number of Pupils. 170.
Fees per term (2016–2017). £1,460–£3,060.
Charitable status. PACT Educational Trust Limited is a Registered Charity, number 1053810.

Old Buckenham Hall School

Brettenham Park, Ipswich, Suffolk IP7 7PH
Tel: 01449 740252
Fax: 01449 740955
email: admissions@obh.co.uk
website: www.obh.co.uk
Twitter: @OBHSchool

Chairman of Governors: N Bullen, BA Hons

Headmaster: T O'Sullivan, LLB Hons Durham, PGCE Cambridge

Deputy Head: Mrs J A Campbell, Adv Dip CSN, CertEd

Age Range. 3–13.
Number of Pupils. 92 Boarders; 59 Day Pupils; 46 Pre-Prep; 14 Nursery.
Fees per term (2016–2017). Full and Weekly Boarders £6,896–£7,851; Transitional Boarding: £5,166–£7,596; Day £4,774–£6,026; Pre-Prep inc Nursery £127–£2,971.

The School, founded in Lowestoft as South Lodge in 1862, moved in 1937 to Old Buckenham, Norfolk and in 1956 to Brettenham Park, Suffolk, 4 miles from Lavenham and 18 from Ipswich. It became an Educational Trust in 1967.

The pupils go on to a wide range of Senior Independent Schools via Common Entrance and Scholarship Examinations.

The Staff/Pupil ratio is approximately 1:8, giving an average class size of 14. All members of Staff, including part-time Staff, contribute to the provision of a wide range of extra-curricular activities in which every child has a chance to participate. The major sports are for boys: Rugby, Hockey, Soccer and Cricket and for girls: Hockey Netball, Rounders and introduced in summer 2015 girls' Cricket, but all pupils take part in Athletics and Swimming (heated open air pool and off-site swimming facilities). In addition there are opportunities for Tennis (6 courts including 3 astro courts), Golf (9-hole course), Squash (2 courts) and a wide range of activities including: Table Tennis, Woodwork & Metalwork, Pets, Arts & Craft, Cookery, Clay Pigeon Shooting, Orienteering, Bushcraft, Fencing, Archery. Art, Music and Drama particularly flourish. A full-size Astroturf has recently been installed enhancing the school's sports provision.

The 11-day boarding model established in September 2013 is proving to be a successful model, making more effective use of the school day with the boarding children going home every other weekend. The re-drafting of the school day has given the school the ability to focus on what is fundamental – delivering a high-quality curriculum where every pupil has the best possible opportunity to succeed.

Boarding continues to be popular with refurbished dormitories including separate boys' and girls' boarding common rooms, a separate common room for Year 8 and recently introduced Junior Common Room. An enhanced evening and weekend activity programme has been devised together with a new Enrichment programme exposing the children to a wide range of Life Skills. Outdoor classrooms have recently been introduced which are particularly popular at weekends together with a specially designed play area. The Science Department has been completely refurbished and was re-opened in 2010.

A School Prospectus can be obtained on application to the Registrar.

Charitable status. Old Buckenham Hall (Brettenham) Educational Trust Limited is a Registered Charity, number 310490. It exists to provide education for boarding and day pupils.

The Old Hall School

Stanley Road, Wellington, Shropshire TF1 3LB
Tel: 01952 223117
Fax: 01952 222674
email: admissions@oldhall.co.uk
          enq@oldhall.co.uk
website: www.oldhall.co.uk
Twitter: @oldhallschool
Facebook: /The-Old-Hall-School

Chairman of the Governors: Mr R J Pearson, BSc

Headmaster: Mr Martin C Stott, BEd Hons

Age Range. 4–11.
Number of Pupils. 241: 138 boys, 103 girls.
Fees per term (2016–2017). Lower School: £2,610 (Reception), £2,680 (Years 1–2); Upper School (Years 3–6): £4,060.

Founded in 1845, The Old Hall School is a co-educational day school (4–11 years), which is housed in spectacular premises, located alongside Wrekin College. The school offers first-class facilities; a double sports hall, 25-metre indoor swimming pool, Astroturf and grass pitches offer an excellent sports and games environment, whilst specialist music and drama areas help to promote high standards in the performing arts. A suite of specialist learning support rooms reflects the School's commitment to the needs of the individual. First-class facilities have also been created for pre-school care and the education of children from the age of three months.

The broad curriculum is enriched by a dedicated team of professionals who encourage pupils to fulfil their potential in a happy and secure environment.

Through the academic curriculum and caring pastoral system, the school aims to lay solid foundations in the development of well-motivated, confident and happy individuals who are always willing to give of their best on the road to high achievement.

Charitable status. Wrekin Old Hall Trust Limited is a Registered Charity, number 528417.

The Old School Henstead

Toad Row, Henstead, Nr Beccles, Suffolk NR34 7LG
Tel: 01502 741150
email: office@theoldschoolhenstead.co.uk
website: www.theoldschoolhenstead.co.uk

Headmaster: Mr W J McKinney, MA Hons, PG Dip, MA Ed

Age Range. 2½–11.
Number in School. 100 Day Boys and Girls.
Fees per term (2016–2017). £2,200–£3,170.

The Old School Henstead is committed to realising the immense potential of all its pupils, creating a place of learning that inspires children to excel in and make their own special contribution to the global environment that awaits them. Henstead children know not just what to learn, but how to learn it; they are interested and interesting and they have the words to prove it.

Whilst focusing on the core subjects, the teaching at The Old School Henstead ensures that every pupil maximises their potential through inspiring, motivating and enriching learning opportunities. The curriculum is designed to inspire and challenge all pupils, with teaching adapted to meet the varying needs of the pupils. The school's aim is to teach children how to grow into positive, responsible people, who can work and co-operate with others, whilst developing knowledge and skills in order to achieve their true potential. Above all, the school believes in making learning fun, to engender a love of lifelong learning in every child that passes through the school. Small class sizes, excellent teaching and an insistence on traditional values of hard work and good manners help all pupils at The Old School Henstead to achieve high academic standards. The school caters for pupils of all abilities, offering specialist support where needed at both ends of the ability spectrum. In Early Years (Reception) and the Lower School (Years 1 and 2), the children are taught in their class base by their class teacher for the majority of subjects. In the Upper School, from Year 3 onwards, the majority of subjects are taught by subject teachers. Assessment for learning plays a vital role in ensuring that every pupil makes excellent progress. Pupils are encouraged to take responsibility for their own learning, to be involved as far as possible in reviewing the way they learn, and to reflect on how they learn – what helps them learn and what makes it difficult for them to learn. Children learn French from Reception up.

After School Clubs take place after school from Monday to Thursday, for children in Reception upwards. The activities on offer vary from term to term.

The school has an active house system that encourages pupils to interact and collaborate with pupils outside their own year group. The School Council has two representatives from every year from Year 1 to Year 6, with Reception joining in the Summer Term.

Music-making is a very important part of life at The Old School Henstead. The School Choirs rehearse every week and lead the singing in the daily assembly and at regular services at St Mary's Church. In addition to this the school has, over the years, been very proud of the achievements of the choir at local, regional and national music festivals.

The school believes passionately in sport for all. At The Old School Henstead all pupils are expected to take part in competitive sport, representing the school in a range of sports. Outdoor Education is an important part of the curriculum, for it is inclusive, builds confidence and encourages supervised, sensible risk-taking and learning opportunities that are as varied and challenging as those enjoyed indoors. In sport, teams and individuals compete against local schools and further afield in both regional and national competitions.

In keeping with The Old School Henstead's focus on building our pupils' confidence, social skills and awareness of others, the Drama syllabus provides an approach which is both structured and adventurous. With drama games, improvisations, role play and practice of specific elements of Drama, the children are equipped to meet not only the challenges of regular performance and presentation within the broader curriculum of the school, but also in their ensuing educational experience. The Junior and Senior Summer Shows, the traditional climax to the year, are produced at an exceptional level of professionalism by talented and dedicated staff and include every child from Nursery to the top of the Senior School, at an appropriate level of performance. LAMDA tuition is also offered in the Upper School.

In the Early Years Foundation Stage the school aims to give each child a happy, positive and fun start to their time at The Old School Henstead, so that he or she can establish solid foundations on which to expand and foster a deep love of learning.

Religious affiliation: The school is underpinned by a Christian ethos, but accepts children of all faiths and none.

Charitable status. The Old School Henstead Educational Trust Limited is a Registered Charity, number 279265. It exists to provide education for boys and girls.

Old Vicarage School

48 Richmond Hill, Richmond, Surrey TW10 6QX

Tel:	020 8940 0922
Fax:	020 8948 6834
email:	office@oldvicarageschool.com
website:	www.oldvicarageschool.com

Chairman of Governors: Mr G Caplan

Headmistress: **Mrs G Linthwaite**, MA Oxon, PGCE

Age Range. 4–11.
Number of Pupils. 200 girls.
Fees per term (2016–2017). £4,380.

The Old Vicarage school is a non-selective girls' prep school based in a beautiful Grade 2* listed "castle" on Richmond Hill. The School was established in 1881 and became a Charitable Educational Trust in 1973. Whilst retaining traditional values, there is a clear vision for the future and teaching and facilities combine the very best of the old and the new. Girls are admitted to the school into one of the two Reception forms in September following their fourth birthday. Older girls may be admitted further up the school if a vacancy arises, following a day spent at the school to ensure it is a good fit for them. Girls are expected to remain until the age of 11, being prepared for Common Entrance Examinations at 11+ and for entry to the London Day Schools. A good range of academic, sporting, drama and arts scholarships to senior schools has been awarded to girls over the years.

Work of a traditionally high standard is expected of the girls and they are challenged and supported in classes of up to 15 girls, encouraging self esteem and enabling them to fulfil their potential. Girls in the Lower School are taught by a Form Teacher, with some specialist input. Girls in the Upper School are taught by subject specialists who impart a real enthusiasm and love for their subject areas. They will also have a form tutor to provide the pastoral support the school is known for. A system of older buddies, prefects and the Student Council ensures that all girls feel an integral part of the school from the beginning.

Music and drama are active throughout the school. Individual music tuition is provided in a wide range of instruments in purpose-built facilities and active choirs sing at numerous competitions and collaborations. All girls take part in at least one dramatic production a year, as well as in assemblies to which parents are invited.

The major sports are netball, hockey, rounders, athletics and swimming and the school has close access to state-of-the-art facilities in the surrounding area as well as our own gym and playground. Girls compete in fixtures against other schools from Year 3 and have had notable successes in recent years in borough-wide championships.

Extra-curricular activities cater to a range of interests and include art, photography, sports, Adventure Service Challenge, computing, cooking, craft and drama clubs. All girls in the Upper School attend a residential trip to Sussex, Dorset, Oxfordshire or France and up to fifty join the biennial ski trip to Italy.

Charitable status. The Old Vicarage School is a Registered Charity, number 312671.

The Oratory Preparatory School

Goring Heath, Reading, South Oxfordshire RG8 7SF

Tel: 0118 9844511
Fax: 0118 9844806
email: office@oratoryprep.co.uk
website: www.oratoryprep.co.uk
Twitter: @OPS_OratoryPrep
Facebook: @oratoryprepschool

Chairman of the Board of Governors: Dr C B T Hill
   Williams, DL, MA, FRGS, FRSA

Headmaster: R Stewart, BA, MA

   Age Range. 2–13.
   Number of Pupils. 400 (250 boys and 150 girls), including 50 full-time, weekly or flexi-boarders and 125 in the Pre-Prep department.
   Fees per term (2016–2017). Boarders: £6,500 (weekly boarders), £7,540 (full boarders); Day £5,045; Pre-Prep: £3,145 (all day), Kindergarten (5 sessions) £1,555; 'Little Oaks' Nursery £66.00 per day, £34.00 per pre-booked morning session.
   A Roman Catholic preparatory school, founded by John Henry Cardinal Newman, which prepares boys for The Oratory School and boys and girls for other independent senior schools. The OPS welcomes children of all denominations and faiths and aims to identify and develop their individual talents and gifts in all aspects of their school lives.
   The well-qualified and experienced staff of 56 full-time and 65 part-time and visiting teachers and teaching assistants form a strong and supportive team who deliver a broad curriculum characterised by an unusually wide range of subjects, activities and sports. A friendly and secure environment fosters the welfare of every child. Spiritual and pastoral needs are met by the chaplain, a nursing sister, three matrons, and a large and dedicated team of boarding and day staff operating a comprehensive pastoral and academic tutorial system.
   The school has an excellent record of achievement, with pupils gaining many academic, art, music, sports and all-rounder awards to The Oratory School and other major schools. Choral and instrumental music, drama and art play a major part in school life. The school is also very proud of its competitive success in rugby, rugby sevens, football, cricket, cross-country, hockey, netball and rounders as well as tennis, swimming, archery, squash, golf, badminton, basketball and table tennis. In addition there is an extensive range of activities to suit and stretch every child. The school also organises frequent educational, cultural and sporting tours, both within this country and overseas, to widen further pupils' horizons.
   The school's facilities have been extensively developed, with a large theatre, sports hall, indoor swimming pool and trainer pool, all-weather tennis and hockey surfaces, as well as well-equipped science and art departments and a well-stocked library. The music school contains two large spaces for performance and class teaching and seven smaller practice rooms for individual tuition. ICT provision is considerable and forms an integral part of the educational experience offered. The thriving Pre-Prep department is housed in an attractive courtyard setting on the same site and includes the purpose-built 'Little Oaks' Nursery that was opened in 2014 and takes children from 2 years upwards.
   The school stands in its own 65-acre estate, high above the Thames and easily accessible by train and road (via the M4 from London and Heathrow airport).

   Charitable status. The Oratory Schools Association is a Registered Charity, number 309112. It exists to provide general, physical, moral and religious education for boys and girls.

Orchard House School

16 Newton Grove, London W4 1LB

Tel: 020 8742 8544
email: info@orchardhs.org.uk
website: www.orchardhs.org.uk
Twitter: @orchardhs

Chairman of Governors: Mr Anthony Rentoul

Headmistress: **Mrs Maria Edwards**

   Age Range. Girls and Boys 3–11.
   Number of Pupils. 278: 159 Girls, 119 Boys.
   Fees per term (2016–2017). Nursery (5 mornings) £2,790, Pre-Prep £5,580, Prep £5,815.
   Orchard House School, with Bassett House and Prospect House, is part of the House Schools Group. It provides an excellent all-round education for boys and girls from 3 to 11, preparing them for the competitive entry examinations for the London day and country boarding schools whilst maintaining a happy, purposeful atmosphere.
   There is an emphasis on teaching traditional values tailored for children growing up in the 21st century. Uniform is worn and good manners are expected at all times. Children shake hands with the staff at the end of each day and are encouraged to take part, with the deputy head or headmistress, in describing the school to prospective parents and other visitors. Appetising lunches are provided and children are involved in growing vegetables and salad in the school garden.
   The main premises were designed by the well-known architect Norman Shaw and built around 1880; the building is Grade 2 listed. The school enjoys a corner site in Bedford Park and the classrooms have good natural lighting as well as overlooking a large playground/garden. Additional classrooms and associated study areas have been gained through the acquisition of another attractive building within 5 minutes' walk of the main school.
   Children aged 3 or 4 are admitted on a first come, first served basis. Occasional places higher up are filled following assessment. The Montessori method is used to deliver the Early Years Foundation Stage curriculum; at KS1 and KS2 the curriculum is based on the National Curriculum and the demands of the future schools. Specialist teachers are employed for many subjects and support teachers provide on-one or small group tuition where necessary. Staff turnover is low.
   Orchard House is proud of the excellent results the children achieve at their future schools which include many of the most academic schools in this country. The school is within easy reach of St Paul's schools, Latymer Upper, Hampton School, Notting Hill & Ealing High School and Godolphin & Latymer and many pupils have taken up places at one of these schools.
   The school boasts state-of-the-art ICT resources and attractive playgrounds/garden with all-weather surfaces. The children make good use of additional local facilities to enhance their Sport and Drama lessons.
   Orchard House participates in the Nursery Education Grant. There are occasional academic scholarships, through the House Schools Trust, and a bursary scheme for children entering Year 4. See www.houseschoolstrust.org.

Orchard School

Higham Road, Barton-le-Clay, Bedfordshire MK45 4RB

Tel: 01582 882054
email: admin@orchardschool.org.uk
website: www.orchardschool.org.uk

Chair of Friends: Mrs Jenny Devile

Head Teacher: Mrs Anne Burton, MEd Cantab, Cert Ed, HV SRN

Deputy Head: Miss Louise Burton, BEd Hons Cantab, QTS

Co-educational Day School.

Age Range. 4–9 years; Nursery for children aged 0–4.

Number of Pupils. Preparatory School 65; Nursery 30.

Fees per term (2016–2017). Tuition (inc lunch) £2,538. Breakfast Club £3.70 per day. After School Club (inc tea) £7.94 per day.

Location. Orchard School is a Preparatory School for boys and girls, ideally situated on the outskirts of a large village in south Bedfordshire.

The School has been established for 14 years, and the Nursery for 25 years. Located in a beautiful setting and backed by the Barton Hills (thought to be The Delectable Mountains in Pilgrim's Progress) both School and Nursery are surrounded by rolling countryside that hosts an abundance of wildlife.

Ethos. The school's motto – "to be the best that you can be" is reflected in all areas of school life. Orchard's aim is to enable each child to value and strive for the highest levels of achievement, and to nurture a pride in success. Praise and encouragement are the primary motivational tools employed, tempered by the recognition that every child develops at their own pace. Skillful and careful observations are undertaken by the teaching team to help the children meet and surpass key learning targets. The school also encourages an 'esprit de corps' and a sense of true belonging. Emphasis is placed on the moral, social and personal development of all pupils in order to expand their confidence and self-esteem.

100% academic success. The school boasts an exemplary academic record with (for example) a 100% pass rate into the nearby Harpur Trust schools in Bedford.

The combination of a progressive, structured, yet genuinely friendly family atmosphere creates an ideal environment for the children to thrive both academically and in other activities that they pursue.

Activities. We encourage each child to experience as wide a range of activities as possible; for example, music lessons, choir, ballet, dance and philosophy.

A comprehensive sporting programme including swimming and rugby is also included within the well-rounded curriculum. Further opportunities include craftwork, running, lacrosse, badminton and recorder are offered via lunchtime and after-school clubs. There are several visits a term across all year groups to complement topic learning and to provide a real-life context to the subjects being studied. Years 3 and 4 also enjoy residential trips to specialist adventure-based facilities where activities such as abseiling, kayaking and raft building help increase fun, team spirit and pupil confidence.

Friends of Orchard. Orchard is proud of its strong and supportive parent base and there is a well-established 'Friends of Orchard School' group which organises social gatherings and fundraising events, further enhancing the friendly and family inclusive atmosphere at the school.

Bursaries. Bursaries are available for year 3 and above.

Summary. Our aim is to develop well-motivated and confident children who are considerate to others, well-mannered, who know the value of hard work.

We are happy to say that virtually all Orchard School pupils have been proven to excel at their subsequent schools and seats of learning.

Orley Farm School

South Hill Avenue, Harrow on the Hill, Middlesex HA1 3NU

Tel: 020 8869 7600
Fax: 020 8869 7601
email: office@orleyfarm.harrow.sch.uk
website: www.orleyfarm.harrow.sch.uk

The school is a Charitable Trust administered by a Board of Governors.

Chairman of Governors: Mr C J Hayfield

Headmaster: Mr T Calvey, BA Ed Hons

Age Range. 4–13 Co-educational.

Number of Pupils. 493 Day pupils, including 183 in Pre-Prep (age 4 to 7).

Fees per term (2016–2017). Pre-Prep £4,428; Years 3–4 £4,707; Year 5 £5,108 Years 6–8 £5,108 (inclusive of lunch).

At Orley Farm School we are in the fortunate position of being a London day school blessed with boarding school acreage and facilities. Founded in 1850, the school has grown and developed to become one of the leading and largest co-educational prep schools in Greater London. Entry is by assessment at 4+ and at 11+. The academic journey of the children begins in Reception and ends when pupils transfer successfully to their senior schools – at the end of Year 6 for some of our girls and Year 8 for both girls and boys attending more traditional senior schools. Pupils enter a range of very impressive senior schools, including Eton, Godolphin and Latymer, Haberdashers' Aske's Boys and Girls, Harrow, John Lyon, Merchant Taylors', Northwood College, North London Collegiate, Notting Hill and Ealing, St Helen's, St Paul's, Westminster and Wycombe Abbey to name but a few. However, most impressively, Orley Farm has served over 41 senior schools over the past 5 years. We pride ourselves in finding the right future step for every child. Scholarships are regularly awarded to our senior pupils – 46 awards were offered in 2015–2016.

Success, happiness and future fulfilment start with a deep love of learning. So firmly do we believe in this philosophy, that we have invested £9 million in our facilities (a Music and Drama School, three state of the art Science Laboratories, a new Humanities department, a new Dining Hall and at the very heart, a cutting edge Library). Whilst some schools are binning books, we are buying more, and investing heavily in our environment to accompany a focused drive on study skills for life. Solid foundations are setting, not only in our new buildings, but also in the hearts and minds of a generation of young learners.

'Breadth, Balance & Excellence … The Orley Farm Way!'

Alongside academic excellence, we pride ourselves on giving pupils experiences and opportunities that foster a lifetime and love of learning. All pupils are expected to contribute to the broader curriculum and a packed programme of Drama, Art and Music and Design & Technology. Over 200 individual music lessons take place each week and are supported by many musical groups and choirs. Productions, concerts and competitions offer all pupils the chance to showcase their talents and dedication in a variety of different settings.

Sport plays a very large part in our school life. We have over thirty six acres of land and full use is made of this in providing a venue for training and matches. Pupils will compete internally and externally in athletics, cricket, football, hockey, netball, rounders and rugby. In addition basketball, cross-country, fencing, fives, gymnastics and tennis also thrive through activities, clubs and matches. A Gym, Sports Hall and full-sized AstroTurf pitch enable our strong PE and Games Department to help our pupils develop their sporting talents.

This rich blend of curricular and co-curricular education is exemplified by our Expeditions Week. All pupils and staff from Year 4 and above travel to a variety of venues to spend a week extending their curriculum in a host of new challenges and adventures.

Orley Farm School is located in North West London close to Harrow on the Hill and is only twenty minutes on the Metropolitan Line from Baker Street Station.

Entry to this exciting place of learning is by assessment. For further details contact the Registrar, Mrs Julie Jago, on 0208 869 7634.

Charitable status. Orley Farm School is a Registered Charity, number 312637.

Orwell Park

Nacton, Ipswich, Suffolk IP10 0ER

Tel:	01473 659225
Fax:	01473 659822
email:	headmaster@orwellpark.org
website:	www.orwellpark.co.uk

Chairman of Governors: James Davison, BA

Headmaster: **Adrian Brown**, MA Cantab

Age Range. 2½–13.

Number of Pupils. Prep: 273: 121 Boarders (52 girls, 69 boys); 131 Day Pupils (51 girls, 80 boys). Pre-Prep: 61 (21 girls, 40 boys).

Fees per term (2016–2017). Prep School: Full and Weekly Boarders: £6,860 (Year 3), £7,620 (Years 4–8); Day Pupils: £5,350 (Year 3), £5,930 (Years 4–8). Pre-Prep Day Pupils: £28.25 per session (Nursery), £2,370 (Reception), £2,785 (Year 1), £3,655 (Year 2).

Flexible Boarding (i.e. 1–3 nights a week) is also possible –£42.50 per night.

Pupils are prepared for all Independent Senior Schools (local day and national boarding) via the Scholarship or Common Entrance Examinations (37 awards in 2016). The school has a thriving Pre-Prep School, which is housed in a new, state-of-the-art building containing a large hall, six classrooms and music and ICT rooms.

The timetable is especially designed to be very flexible, with setting in most subjects, a potential scholars' set in Year 7 and a scholarship set in Year 8. The curriculum, both in and out of the classroom, is unusually broad. Children are encouraged to enjoy their learning and good learning support is offered. Thinking Skills and other opportunities for academic enrichment are also offered, including a weekly evening lecture programme to challenge the older children. There is a host of extracurricular activities (just under 100) run by permanent or visiting staff.

About 90% of the school learn a musical instrument and the school has a number of orchestral and ensemble groups. Drama is strong and all children have opportunities to perform regularly in school productions. All children take part in annual Reading and Public Speaking Competitions.

The very large Georgian style building and 110 acres of grounds (sandy soil) on the banks of the River Orwell have the following special features: 21 recently refurbished themed dormitories, 22 bright classrooms with modern audio-visual equipment, beautiful Orangery used as an Assembly and Lecture Hall, 2 ICT suites, large Design Centre including metal, wood and plastic workshop plus electronics, mechanics, home economics, radio and model-making areas, Music Technology Room, Music Room and 40 Practice rooms, 2 Laboratories plus associated areas, brand new Library, Art Room including large pottery area and kiln, Observatory with 10' Refractor Telescope, Photographic Room, 17 Games pitches and one Astroturf pitch, one Multi-Use Games Area, large Sports Hall with permanent stage, Climbing Wall, Games Room, large heated Swimming Pool, 3 Squash Courts, 5 Hard Tennis Courts, Nine-hole Golf Course (approx 1,800 yds) and a purpose-built Assault Course.

Good sports coaching is given and fixtures are arranged in the following sports: Rugby, Hockey, Cricket, Netball, Rounders, Tennis, Athletics, Squash, Sailing, Swimming and Cross-Country Running. Emphasis is also placed on individual physical activities and we offer a wide range including Gymnastics, Fencing, Ballet, Canoeing, Sailing, Modern Dance, Karate, Riding and Clay Pigeon Shooting. The school owns its own canoes and dinghies.

The School aims to introduce the pupils to a broad and varied set of experiences and opportunities. It tries to see that every activity, whether academic, sporting, social or character building, is properly taught using the best possible facilities and that each is conducted in an atmosphere which is friendly but disciplined. Core values include courage, compassion, commitment, compromise and courtesy. Children are encouraged to feel comfortable taking risks and to be confident without being arrogant.

Charitable status. Orwell Park School is a Registered Charity, number 310481. It exists to provide education for boys and girls.

Our Lady's Abingdon Junior School

St John's Road, Abingdon, Oxfordshire OX14 2HB

Tel:	01235 523147
Fax:	01235 530387
email:	officejs@olab.org.uk
website:	www.olab.org.uk
Twitter:	@OLAabingdon
Facebook:	@OLAabingdon

Chairman of Governors: Mr Edward McCabe, MA Oxon, MBA

Headteacher: **Ms Erika Kirwan**

Deputy Headteacher: Miss Brigid Meadows, GTCL Hons, PGCE

Age Range. 3–11 Co-educational.

Number of Pupils. 130.

Fees per term (2016–2017). Years 5 and 6 £3,738 Year 3 and 4 £3,115, Years 1 and 2 £2,693. Early Years (Nursery/Reception) £2,693 or £269.30 per session per term.

Staff: 16 full time and 5 part time. Specialist teaching in Mathematics, English, Science, French, PE, Art and Music.

Our Lady's Abingdon Junior School is a 'family' school with relationships firmly based on an ethos of care and dedication to the teaching of Christian values through which we aim to develop and foster a loving, caring and welcoming community. Children are at the very centre of all that we do at OLA and we encourage them to be confident, articulate members of the school community. The children are given an excellent all-round education and high academic standards are achieved. A love of learning and a positive attitude are both important elements of the way they are prepared for their future lives.

The 2010 Inspection Report was most complimentary, noting in particular that:

Pupils achieve excellent results in a range of extracurricular activities, especially in sport.

Pupils make exceptional progress in their academic studies in relation to their ability profile.

Pupils' spiritual, moral, social and cultural development is excellent.

The outstanding pastoral care does much to ensure their safeguarding, and to foster their personal development and academic achievement.

In the EYFS Inspection of 2010 it was noted that:

Good provision enables the achievement of the aim to develop a loving, caring and welcoming community.

Teachers provide very well for the acquisition of essential skills and have forged very strong links with parents and carers.

The leadership and management of the setting are outstanding.

Children's achievements are considerable.

Location. Our Lady's Abingdon Junior School is part of the larger Our Lady's Abingdon, which is a 3–18 school located in the market town of Abingdon. The school occupies its own buildings adjacent to the Senior School and has the advantage of maintaining its own distinct character and ethos, whilst being able to share the extensive facilities and specialist staff on offer in the Senior School. (*See also Senior School entry in The Society of Heads section.*)

Facilities. Bright, spacious classrooms, a well-equipped library, a recently refurbished ICT suite and other specialist rooms provide a stimulating environment conducive to the teaching and learning of our pupils. Sports facilities include a number of tennis courts, a Junior School gymnasium, a sports field and a recently-refurbished 25-metre indoor swimming pool. The Junior School has the advantage of sharing a number of the Senior School facilities, including science laboratories and D&T rooms, as well as benefiting from shared teaching by Senior School staff. The Nursery area is a well-resourced provision on two floors – a peaceful and relaxed classroom area on the first floor and a purpose-built kitchen and "wet" area on the ground floor leading to a large and excitingly resourced outdoor garden area. This provides a gentle yet exciting introduction to school where the children learn through play and discovery to develop their social and learning skills.

Curriculum. Throughout the school we believe that all children have the right to experience a broad and balanced programme of subjects, which provides continuity and progression, and takes into account pupils' individual differences and needs. Planning is based on the requirements of the Primary Framework and encompasses all the core subjects of Mathematics, English and Science as well as a wide range of others, including MFL (French), RE, Music, History and Geography, PE/Games/Swimming, Art/Craft, PSHE and ICT. In the older year groups, much of this teaching is done by specialist staff. We also provide support for those children who have Special Educational Needs or for whom English is not the mother tongue.

Children in the EYFS setting follow the Early Years Foundation Stage curriculum and are assessed according to the EYFS profiles. We are members of the Local Authority Early Years Partnership which enables parents to receive a grant that can be offset against school fees.

Extracurricular activities. The Junior School provides a wide programme of extracurricular activities including drama, music, art, many forms of sport, ICT, D&T, cooking, creative play and Thinking Skills to name but a few. These clubs operate from 3.20 pm until 4.00 pm each evening and are available to all children from Reception through to Year Six. A supervised homework session is also available for those who require it. The School Council, which meets regularly each term, is an integral part of the way in which we involve the pupils in the decision making process in the school and the Eco-Council works very hard to ensure we have an awareness of our local environment and how we should care for it. The school has gained the Eco-Schools Silver Award and is working towards the "Green Flag".

Admissions. Our Lady's Abingdon Junior School considers for admission any pupil for whom it is able to provide an appropriate education. The main intake is at the age of 3 or 4, although pupils may be accepted into any Year Group where there are vacancies, at the discretion of the Headteacher. Pupils are selected on the basis of application, previous reports (where applicable) and parents' interview. Pupils may also be asked to visit the school on one or more days prior to the term in which the place is required. The school will wish to ascertain the previous attainment of pupils entering years Four, Five and Six and this is done by formal testing in Mathematics, English and Verbal Reasoning.

Charitable status. Our Lady's Abingdon Trustees Limited is a Registered Charity, number 1120372, and a Company Limited by Guarantee, registered in England and Wales, number 6269288.

Packwood Haugh

Ruyton XI Towns, Shrewsbury, Shropshire SY4 1HX

Tel:	01939 260217
Fax:	01939 262077
email:	hm@packwood-haugh.co.uk
website:	www.packwood-haugh.co.uk
Twitter:	@packwoodhaugh

Chairman of Governors: Mrs E Lewis

Headmaster: **C N Smith-Langridge**, BA Hons, QTS

Deputy Heads
N R Jones, BEd, CertEd
Mrs S Rigby, BA Hons, PGCE, Dip SpLD

Age Range. Co-educational 4–13.

Number of Children. 211. Boarding: 62 boys, 24 girls. Day: 70 boys, 31 girls. Pre-Prep 24.

Fees per term (2016–2017). Boarding £7,250, Day £4,100–£5,750, Pre-Prep (Acorns) £2,700. No compulsory extras. Extras available on request.

Set in the heart of the Shropshire countryside, between Shrewsbury and Oswestry, Packwood Haugh is a co-educational day (4–13) and boarding (7–13) school which provides an excellent all-round education in a happy and caring environment. Children benefit from a wide range of academic, sporting, musical, artistic and cultural activities which encourage them to develop enquiring minds and an enthusiasm for learning. The school espouses an atmosphere of cooperation and understanding between pupils, staff and parents and encourages good manners and consideration towards others at all times.

Packwood has always striven for academic excellence; class sizes are small (average 13) and children are prepared for all the major independent schools across the country winning a number of academic, music, sports, art and all-rounder scholarships and awards each year. The school has a thriving pre-prep department (Packwood Acorns), which takes children from Reception.

The school's facilities are superb; a state-of-the-art sports hall allows for indoor tennis, badminton, indoor cricket, fencing and five-a-side football. Incorporated in the building are fully equipped CDT and Art departments and a linked computer suite. A 280-seat theatre is used for assemblies, concerts and drama productions throughout the year.

As well as the classrooms in the main school buildings and a purpose-built new block, there are three science laboratories and two further computer suites. Park House, which accommodates Packwood Acorns and girls' boarding, is a short distance from the main school building.

Packwood has a very strong sporting tradition. As well as a large area of grass playing fields, there is a newly resurfaced full-size, floodlit AstroTurf pitch, an additional hard court area, 10 tennis courts, two squash courts, an indoor, heated swimming pool and a 9-hole golf course. In the winter terms the boys play rugby, football and hockey while the girls play netball, hockey and lacrosse. There is also cross-country running on a course within the grounds. In the summer the boys play cricket, the girls play rounders and cricket, and all take part in tennis, athletics and swimming.

Additional facilities include Forest School, a shooting range and an equestrian cross-country course as well as an adventure playground.

Charitable status. Packwood Haugh is a Registered Charity, number 528411. It exists to provide day and boarding education for boys and girls from the age of 4 to 13.

Papplewick

Windsor Road, Ascot, Berks SL5 7LH

Tel:	01344 621488
Fax:	01344 874639
email:	schoolsec@papplewick.org.uk
	registrar@papplewick.org.uk
website:	www.papplewick.org.uk

Chairman of Board of Governors: Brigadier {Retd} A R E Hutchinson, JP

Headmaster: **T W Bunbury**, BA University College Durham, PGCE

Age Range. 6–13.
Number of Boys. 209: 95 Boarders, 114 day boys.
Fees per term (2016–2017). Boarders £9,305; Day Boys: £5,145 (Year 2), £6,740 (Years 3–4), £7,145 (Years 5–6).

Papplewick is a boys-only, day, weekly and full boarding school with an exceptional Scholarship record to top Independent Schools. Day boys do prep at school and come into board from the Summer term of Year 6. Happy, confident boys abound, and a modern, family-friendly approach to boarding is adopted. Two very popular daily transport services runs to/from West London, one from Chiswick and one from Brook Green. A recent addition is a daily service from Maidenhead/South Bucks. Situated between M3 and M4, the school boasts easy access to London airports.

Papplewick exists to provide a high-quality education where – for all our academic, cultural and sporting success – the happiness of the boys come first.

Charitable status. The Papplewick Educational Trust is a Registered Charity, number 309087.

The Paragon
Junior School of Prior Park College

Lyncombe House, Lyncombe Vale, Bath BA2 4LT

Tel:	01225 310837
Fax:	01225 427980
email:	reception.paragon@priorparkschools.com
	rbraithwaite@priorparkschools.com
website:	www.priorparkschools.com
Twitter:	@ParagonBath
Facebook:	@TheParagonJunior

Chair of Governors: Mr Michael King

Headmaster: **Mr Andrew Harvey**, BA Hons, PGCE

Registrar: Mrs Rebecca Braithwaite

Age Range. 3–11 years.
Number of Pupils. 150 Boys, 120 Girls.
Fees per term (2016–2017). Juniors (Years 3–6) £3,245 including lunch; Infants (Years 1 & 2) £3,090 including lunch; Reception £2,915 including lunch. Nursery (full time) £2,780 including lunch, part time according to sessions. Sibling discounts available. Registration Fee (non-refundable) £100.

25 experienced and qualified teachers.

The Paragon is an independent, co-educational day school based in a beautiful Georgian house situated a mile from the centre of Bath. The school is set in eight acres of beautiful grounds with woodland, conservation areas, lawns and streams. It's the perfect 'outdoor classroom' and we use it right across the curriculum. We also enjoy regular access to the superb sport, science and drama facilities at our Senior School, Prior Park College.

Several factors help create the 'distinctive Paragon atmosphere'. One is undoubtedly the homely feel that comes from being based in a beautiful, former family home. Then there's our Christian ethos and strong pastoral care, as well as our belief that school at this age is about being stimulated and inspired, about laughter and spontaneity – in short, about having fun. We may be a private school and we certainly expect high standards of behaviour but we're anything but stuffy and grey.

We offer a broad curriculum taught in small classes by teachers with real passion. Academic life at The Paragon cultivates a love of learning and encourages independent and creative thinking. Our results are impressive. Our children consistently achieve well above the national average and many Year 6 children win senior school scholarships. Our facilities include a library, large gymnasium/dining hall, ICT suite, nursery with secure indoor and outdoor play areas, art studio, modern languages and music rooms.

Sport is particularly strong at The Paragon. Our sports teams take part, with considerable success, in a wide range of tournaments and festivals. We also offer a vast range of sports clubs that all children can join regardless of ability. Prior Park College offers us an indoor swimming pool, AstroTurf and grass pitches, tennis courts, athletics track and our brand new sports centre.

The Paragon's extracurricular programme is extensive. Staff run more than 60 lunchtime and after-school clubs that range from pottery and chess to Mandarin and cross-country running. The school also enjoys an enviable reputation for Music. All children receive weekly music lessons from a specialist teacher. In addition, visiting instrumental teachers offer tuition in a wide range of instruments. We offer an excellent choice of extracurricular music activities including the orchestra, two choirs, a wind band, brass group, flute choir, saxophone group and string ensemble.

The Paragon is proud of its consistently impressive academic results but we strive for much more than success in exams. We believe in developing the whole person – physically, spiritually, and emotionally as well as intellectually. As W B Yeats said: "Education is not filling a bucket but lighting a fire."

Charitable status. Prior Park Educational Trust is a Registered Charity, number 281242.

Parkside

The Manor, Stoke d'Abernon, Cobham, Surrey KT11 3PX

Tel:	01932 862749
Fax:	01932 860251
email:	office@parkside-school.co.uk
website:	www.parkside-school.co.uk
Twitter:	@parksideprep
Facebook:	/parksideprep

Chairman of Governors: Robin Southwell

Headmaster: **M J Beach**, BA Hons, Adv DipEd, MA Ed

Deputy Head: Mrs H Sayer, BEd Hons

Age Range. Boys 2½–13. Co-educational Nursery.
Numbers. 297: Prep 193, Pre-Prep 54, Nursery 50.
Fees per term (from January 2017). Day Boys £5,280, Pre-Prep £3,945, Nursery £443–£3,516.

Parkside was founded in 1879 and became a Charitable Trust in 1960. The School moved from East Horsley to its present site of over 40 acres in 1979, its centenary year. Since the move the Governors have implemented a continual development programme which has included a purpose-built, well-equipped Science Block, extending the main building to provide more Pre-Prep accommodation and a Music School with a large classroom and six practice rooms. An excellent Swimming Pool and Sports Hall complex with a stage for drama offers unrivalled facilities in the area. In addition, a £2m Classroom Block was built about 10 years ago to further enhance the facilities in the school. The Design Technology Department, Nursery and ICT suite are housed in a delightful Grade II Listed Barn which has been completely and skilfully refurbished to provide spacious, well-lit classrooms and workshops. A second Computer Room has been linked to the main network in recent years and the Art and Music facilities have been further expanded.

The school is large enough to be flexible and offer setting in major subjects yet small enough for each pupil to be known and treated as an individual. On average there are 15 pupils in a Set and the teacher : pupil ratio is 1:8. All teaching staff are highly qualified and there is a low staff turnover. Each boy is a member of a House and this helps to stimulate friendly competition for work points and many other inter-house contests.

The National Curriculum is followed to prepare all boys for entry to Senior Independent Schools by Common Entrance and Scholarship examinations. All boys pass to their first choice Senior Schools and our results in these examinations are impressive. Over the past few years many Academic, Art, Music and Sporting Scholarships have been won. Our curriculum is broad based and all boys are taught Art, Music, PE and Technology in addition to the usual Common Entrance subjects. There is a School Choir, a School Orchestra and several smaller musical groups, and over one third of the boys are receiving individual tuition in a wide variety of musical instruments. During the year, there are many opportunities for boys to perform in musical and dramatic productions.

The School has a fine sporting record and, over the past few years, many tournaments in different sports and at different age groups have been won. In addition, a number of boys have gone on to represent their County and Country in various sports. The main sports are football, hockey and cricket, but boys are able to take part in rugby, swimming, athletics, tennis, cross-country running, basketball and judo. An extensive Wednesday afternoon and After School Activity Programme (including supervised homework sessions) is available with over 40 different activities on offer, from gardening to kayaking, and table tennis to golf. Many boys have also represented the school at a high level in chess. The beautiful estate and the River Mole, which runs through the grounds, are also used to contribute to the all round education each pupil receives both in and out of the classroom.

Unusually for a Preparatory School, Parkside has a large and active Old Boys Association which runs many sporting and social events during the year.

Further details and a prospectus are available on application to the Headmaster's PA, Alison Scott, via email scotta@parkside-school.co.uk.

Charitable status. Parkside School is a Registered Charity, number 312041. It exists to provide education for children between the ages of 2½ and 13 years.

Pembridge Hall School
Alpha Plus Group

18 Pembridge Square, London W2 4ED

Tel:	020 7229 0121
email:	contact@pembridgehall.co.uk
website:	www.pembridgehall.co.uk

Headmaster: **Mr Henry Keighley-Elstub**, BA Hons, PGCE

Age Range. 4½–11.
Number of Girls. 427.
Fees per term (2016–2017). £6,865.

Pembridge girls take advantage of a vast array of learning experiences, both inside and out of the classroom. Pembridge Hall offers a 'three-dimensional education', believing that it is only by creating an environment in which teaching is inspiring and imaginative that girls will thrive. Sport and the Arts feature strongly on the curriculum.

Teachers, girls and parents work in a close partnership, ensuring that each girl is happy and achieving her maximum potential in every area of school life. Girls transfer at the end of Year Six to some of the finest senior day and boarding schools in the country.

Pennthorpe School

Church Street, Rudgwick, Nr Horsham, West Sussex RH12 3HJ

Tel:	01403 822391
Fax:	01403 822438
email:	enquiries@pennthorpe.com
website:	www.pennthorpe.com
Twitter:	@PennthorpeHead
Facebook:	/PennthorpeSchool

Where families grow together

Chairman of the Governors: Mr Mark Lucas

Headmaster: **Mr Neil Jones**, BSc, MSc, PGCE

Age Range. Co-educational 2–13.

Number of Pupils. 264 Day Pupils.

Fees per term (2016–2017). £590–£5,180.

Pennthorpe School in West Sussex lies close to the Surrey border, midway between Guildford and Horsham. The school is committed to high standards in all it does. Pennthorpe also recognises that putting the fun into the fundamentals of school life encourages the children to maximise their learning potential.

Pennthorpe has an outstanding record of 13+ Common Entrance successes, with regular academic, art, music and Performing Arts scholarships won to a number of senior schools in Sussex, Surrey and beyond. Many have also won all-rounder scholarships which reflects the school's commitment to developing its pupils into well-balanced youngsters and it is this outlook, along with the principle of putting the fun into the fundamentals, that drives Pennthorpe forward.

Developing all-rounders means offering choice, and from the very earliest stages when the two year-olds join the Pennthorpe Kindergarten, the emphasis is on breadth, both academic and outside the classroom.

The Pennthorpe Sports Department offers a wealth of sporting activities and competitive opportunities: soccer, netball, rugby, hockey, rounders, cricket and athletics are regular features on the termly fixtures calendar, while gymnastics, climbing, judo, tennis, basketball, archery and many others are available as part of the huge range of after-school options.

Pennthorpe is committed to the Arts. From the age of five, every pupil enjoys weekly Performing Arts lessons in our own dance and drama studio. There are also specialist-taught music lessons for all, including access to composition programs such as Garage Band in the iMac suite; these, along with four choirs, an orchestra, individual instrumental tuition, termly concerts and various productions involving every child in the school, provide many performing opportunities.

Pennthorpe also enjoys a cutting edge Art and Design Centre outstandingly equipped to fire the creative spirits of its pupils. The school's long-standing reputation for artistic excellence is now backed up by a 21-station iMac suite, photography studio and design room. With animation, web design, advanced programming and photo editing all embedded within the curriculum, all children can find their own ways to express their imaginations.

Complementing and building upon the classroom work, Pennthorpe's Flexiday programme of after-school activities aims to bring even more chances for every boy and girl to find their strengths and shine. Whether it is developing their computer skills, throwing a pot, scaling the climbing wall or tapping to the rhythm in the dance studio, there's something for everybody.

A continuous programme of major capital investment is under way. A recently completed Pre-Prep building with 6 new classrooms, a state-of-the-art kindergarten and large multi-purpose hall has transformed the academic life of our younger pupils. In addition to this, our new Art and Design Centre opened its doors in February 2012 and plans are already laid for a new Performing Arts and Music Centre. This is a school that never stands still!

If you would like to see how your child could thrive in this busy, happy and successful school, ask for a prospectus, visit our website (details above) and then book a visit: the Headmaster and all the staff and children will make you very welcome. There are generally two Open Mornings each term and the Headmaster is also happy to welcome parents for individual visits at any time.

Charitable status. Pennthorpe School is a Registered Charity, number 307043. It exists to provide an excellent education for boys and girls and to benefit the community.

Perrott Hill

North Perrott, Crewkerne, Somerset TA18 7SL

Tel: 01460 72051
email: admissions@perrotthill.com
website: www.perrotthill.com
Twitter: @perrotthill

Chairman of Governors: Lord Bradbury

Headmaster: **Mr Tim Butcher**, BA Warwick, PGCE

Age Range. 3–13.

Number of Pupils. 126 boys and 92 girls, of whom 41 are full, weekly or flexi boarders.

Fees per term (2016–2017). Boarders: £7,360 (full), £6,100 (weekly); Day pupils £2,085–£5,095.

Perrott Hill is a co-educational day and boarding school and is registered as an Educational Trust. Set in 25 acres of beautiful grounds in the heart of the countryside, near Crewkerne on the Somerset/Dorset border, it is served by excellent road and rail networks.

Perrott Hill is a thriving country preparatory school where children settle quickly and learn in confidence. Class sizes are small, with an average of 15 children to a form; the pupils being streamed from Year 5 onwards. Staff are dedicated and highly qualified. Facilities now include an all-weather sports area, a purpose-built sports hall, a theatre, a DT/art school, a computer centre, a new music school opened in September 2016, games fields, swimming pool and extensive Forest School.

The Nursery and Pre-Prep are housed within the converted stable courtyard next to the main school buildings, which gives the younger children their own safe, secure environment whilst allowing them to take advantage of the grounds and facilities of the Prep School. There is an emphasis on outdoor learning including weekly sessions in our on-site Forest School.

Music, Drama and Art are taught within the timetable alongside core curriculum subjects. The choir and orchestra perform at charity concerts, in competitions and school functions and the choir has recently toured Venice. There are drama productions every term.

Teaching is class-based until Year 5 and subject-based in the upper school, where all lessons are taught by specialist teachers. French, Music, IT and PE, however, are taught by specialists throughout the school.

Each child, boarding or day, has his or her own pastoral and academic tutor, while the welfare of the boarders is supervised by Ms White and Mr Sheldon. They are ably assisted by a dedicated and enthusiastic boarding staff (many of which live on site).

Sport is played every day, and matches take place on most Wednesdays as well as on Saturdays for the senior part of the school. Emphasis is placed upon skills and team work and games played include rugby, football, hockey, netball, cricket, tennis, rounders, swimming and cross-country running. The school takes part in national events, such as the IAPS Ski Championships, IAPS Sailing Regatta and the National Small Schools Rugby Sevens. Optional extras include fencing, carpentry, archery, karate, horse riding, ballet, speech and drama, cookery, Spanish, golf and craft.

Perrott Hill combines extremely high standards of academic and pastoral care. All children were offered a place at the school of their choice and scholarships have been awarded for academic, artistic, sporting, dramatic, musical, equine and all-round ability. In 2016, over half of all leavers won awards or scholarships to their schools of choice. These included Blundell's, Canford, King's College Taunton,

Leweston, Millfield, Queen's College Taunton, Sherborne Girls, Sherborne, Taunton School and Wellington School. Other destinations include Harrow, Winchester, Eton, Bryanston and King's Bruton. Academic, music, sport, art, drama and all-rounder Scholarships are offered annually in February to children in Years 3–6.

The combination of countryside, space, a family atmosphere and a forward-looking academic programme creates an ideal environment for children to thrive both academically and in their leisure pursuits – we warmly invite you to come and see the school in action.

Charitable status. Perrott Hill School Trust Limited is a Registered Charity, number 310278. It exists to give high quality education to boys and girls.

The Perse Pelican Nursery and Pre-Preparatory School

92 Glebe Road, Cambridge CB1 7TD

Tel:	01223 403940
Fax:	01223 403941
email:	pelican@perse.co.uk
website:	www.perse.co.uk

Chairman of Governors: Sir David J Wright, GCMG, LVO, MA

Headmistress: **Mrs S Waddington**, BSc, MA

Age Range. 3–7.

Number of Pupils. 150.

Ethos. We aim to awaken a thirst for learning, helping children to develop an understanding and enjoyment of the world around them. The children are enthusiastic and inspired by the opportunities on offer and delight in meeting challenges and taking risks whilst benefiting from a safe and secure environment. They learn through a range of play-based activities as well as more formal methods of learning and have many opportunities to develop their independence.

Our aim is to ensure that the children in our care are sociable, rounded, confident and inquisitive. We are proud of our broad, challenging, enticing curriculum and the spirit with which our pupils approach their learning.

Admissions. The main entry point for the Pelican is Nursery, which is for children who are three years old by 1 September in the year of entry. There are also a few spaces available for extra children in Reception. Selection takes place in the January of the year of intended entry for Nursery and in the September in the year prior to entry for Reception.

History. The buildings of the Nursery and Pre-Prep began life in 1911 as a boarding house for the Upper School. The School has been sympathetically extended inside and out, so that it provides exceptional space and excellent facilities, yet still feels like a home from home.

School life. Our pastoral care is second to none; every single child in the School is known to all and is valued for their individual characteristics. All achievements are celebrated.

Classroom routines are quickly established from the start of a child's time at the Pelican, and from day one they feel they belong. Every class benefits from a full-time teaching assistant who works alongside the teacher.

Dance, Games, Languages and Music are all taught by specialist teachers. An inclusive choir is open to everyone in Years 1 and 2 and a range of music ensembles are formed each year appropriate to the needs of the children in those year groups at the time. Our musicians regularly perform in regional and national festivals.

The children relish challenge and aim high, knowing that there is always someone to support them. We work in partnership with parents to nurture children's interests and provide opportunities to develop their potential. Pupils begin to acquire essential skills through play, topic work and a wide range of experiences and activities.

A rounded education. Regular school trips bring learning to life and being close to the centre of Cambridge the School is able to take advantage of trips to local museums and wildlife parks.

Out of school care. Children may be dropped at school from 8 am and may stay until 5.30 pm each day. We run an extended range of after school clubs catering to all tastes, from ballet to science, chess to football, and drama to gymnastics. In addition, children may attend our own holiday club, known as Club Pelican, which runs for 7 weeks of the year: five weeks in the summer holidays and one week in each of the Christmas and Lent holidays.

Moving on. By the end of Year 2, children are ready to move onto the Prep with confidence and enthusiasm. Their move is gradual and carefully managed.

Fees per term (2016–2017). Full-time (Reception, Years 1 and 2) £4,172, Part-time Nursery (six sessions per week) £2,813. Additional Nursery sessions: £38.40 per session. Nursery children attend a minimum of six sessions per week (two of which must be afternoons) but may attend up to 10 sessions per week.

Charitable status. The Perse School is a charitable company limited by guarantee (company number 5977683, registered charity number 1120654) registered in England and Wales whose registered office is situated at The Perse School, Hills Road, Cambridge CB2 8QF.

The Perse Preparatory School

Trumpington Road, Cambridge CB2 8EX

Tel:	01223 403920
Fax:	01223 403921
email:	prephmsec@perse.co.uk
website:	www.perse.co.uk

Chairman of Governors: Sir David J Wright, GCMG, LVO, MA

Head: **James Piper**, BA Hons, PGCE

Age Range. 7–11.

Number of Pupils. 282.

Ethos. At the Prep we are committed to helping your child develop as a confident, smiling, interesting and interested individual. Our School has a strong academic edge, attracting an outstanding group of specialist staff who spark in the children academic curiosity and a love of learning. Prep children thrive on challenges outside the classroom with great emphasis placed on developing breadth and balance through first-rate sport, clubs, music, art, drama and outdoor pursuits. Excellent pastoral care is at the heart of our work and ensures that our children feel completely at ease and secure in their surroundings.

Admissions. The main entry point to the Prep is Year 3 (7+). Admissions to Years 4, 5 and 6 is dependent on availability of places. Entrance tests assess the applicant's abilities in English, Maths and reasoning, and a reference from the child's current school is also sought. Selection for all year groups takes place in mid-January of the year of intended entry.

Facilities. The Prep is set in spacious mature parkland on Trumpington Road. Traditional and modern buildings are successfully combined on site, from the Victorian Leighton House to the 'New School' building which opened in 2008. Work has begun on a new state-of-the-art Science Department, at the heart of the School, fully-equipped for all types of individual practicals and group experiments. The Department will be ready for the start of the 2017/18 school year. The Prep has nine acres of playing fields on its doorstep, including a full-size AstroTurf.

Educational success. The Prep is an academically selective school with pupils of above average ability who relish challenge. Most pupils progress to the Upper School in Year 7. Pupils follow a broad curriculum which promotes intellectual curiosity and a love of learning, and we nurture creativity through a vibrant programme of drama, music and art.

The depth of academic ability throughout the School allows intellectual curiosity to flourish and pupils thrive on challenges both inside and outside the classroom. Enjoyment of learning, mutual respect and the celebration of achievement characterise life at the Prep and as a result children become independent, confident and responsible.

A supportive environment. Pastoral care is first class: Form Teachers, Heads of Year and the Assistant Head (Pastoral) all support pupils, who have access to a medical room, with a qualified nurse, and to our counselling service.

A rounded education. We make good use of technology, based on our philosophy that it should be effective, meaningful and engaging. Resources include a dedicated ICT suite, a music technology room and bookable laptops and iPads. All classrooms are equipped with SMART boards and PCs. Staff can access the school Wi-Fi (with age appropriate filtering) and we use SharePoint as our Virtual Learning Environment.

We encourage every pupil to make the most of our extra-curricular provision. There is a wide range of lunchtime and after school clubs – more than 60 currently. Music is strong with over 30 different ensembles (including numerous choirs and an orchestra comprising of a quarter of the School). Sport is a major part of a Prep education, and all children compete, whether in House Matches or against other schools. The games programme (football, rugby, cricket, netball, athletics, tennis and hockey) is designed to encourage all pupils to enjoy games and physical exercise. Music plays an important part in the curriculum and wider life of the School. The majority of pupils learn a musical instrument and there are choirs, orchestras and numerous instrumental groups, where there are many opportunities for the children to perform publicly.

Moving on. The School plans carefully for a smooth transition to the Upper School. Year 5 and 6 pupils spend days on the Upper site as part of their subject learning, helping to prepare them for the move up.

Fees per term (2016–2017). £4,845.

Bursaries. Means-tested bursaries are available for families of limited means, ranging from 5% to 100% of annual tuition fees.

Charitable status. The Perse School is a charitable company limited by guarantee (company number 5977683, registered charity number 1120654) registered in England and Wales whose registered office is situated at The Perse School, Hills Road, Cambridge CB2 8QF.

The Pilgrims' School

The Close, Winchester, Hampshire SO23 9LT

Tel:	01962 854189
Fax:	01962 843610
email:	admissions@pilgrims-school.co.uk
	info@pilgrims-school.co.uk
website:	www.thepilgrims-school.co.uk
Twitter:	@PilgrimsSchool

Acting Chairman of Governors: Mr John Pringle

Headmaster: **Mr Tom Burden**, MA Oxon

Age Range. Boys 4–13.

Number of Pupils. 255 Boys (87 boarders/weekly boarders, 112 day boys, 56 boys in Pre-Prep).

Fees per term (2016–2017). Boarders £7,630, Day boys £6,045, Pre-Prep £3,475.

Preparing boys for a broad portfolio of independent schools, with a significant number moving to Winchester College each year. Cathedral Choristers and Winchester College Quiristers are educated at the school and receive scholarships and bursaries up to the value of the full boarding fee together with free tuition in one musical instrument. All boys whether musical or not receive excellent academic and musical tuition, and the sporting tradition is equally strong. The school is noted for its happy family atmosphere, with a major focus on each boy finding his passion and talents, whether they be academic, sporting or artistic. Boarding is a popular option, either full or weekly. All enquiries about the school or singing auditions should be addressed to the Registrar.

Charitable status. The Pilgrims' School is a Registered Charity, number 1091579.

Pinewood

Bourton, Shrivenham, Wiltshire SN6 8HZ

Tel:	01793 782205
Fax:	01793 783476
email:	office@pinewoodschool.co.uk
website:	www.pinewoodschool.co.uk
Twitter:	@pinewoodprepsch

Headmaster: **Philip Hoyland**, BEd Exeter

Deputy Head: Colin Acheson-Gray, BEd

Age Range. 2–13.

Number of Pupils. 402 Boys and Girls (78 regular boarders, 42 weekly boarders) of which Nursery and Pre-Prep: 123.

Fees per term (2016–2017). Day £2,915–£5,610 inclusive, with no compulsory extras. Weekly Boarding supplement: £1,370.

Pinewood is set in 84 acres of rolling countryside. The School offers a quality, family-based environment where children are encouraged to think for themselves and a strong emphasis is placed on self-discipline, manners, trust and selflessness. Resources include a purpose-built Music School and Science Labs, a flourishing Pre-Prep and Nursery, Art and Design Workshops, Research and Reference Library, ICT Rooms, Astroturf and a state-of-the-art Sports Hall. Fortnightly exeats. Regular or weekly boarding from Year 5 upwards.

Excellent academic results are achieved through a mixture of traditional and forward-thinking teaching within a happy, friendly and stimulating learning atmosphere. Outside trips are frequent and visiting speakers prominent. Great success in Music, Art and Drama.

Sport is keenly coached and matches are played at all levels on our picturesque playing fields, which incorporate a nine-hole golf course. There is a wide range of activities and clubs both for day children and, in the evening, for boarders.

Pinewood is a school where staff, parents and children work together to find and realise the potential in every child.

Exit Schools: Marlborough, Winchester, Radley, Cheltenham College, St Edward's Oxford, Cheltenham Ladies, Sherborne, Sherborne Girls, Stowe, St Mary's Calne, Dean Close, Monkton Combe, Tudor Hall.

Charitable status. Pinewood is a Registered Charity, number 309642. It exists to provide high quality education for boys and girls.

Plymouth College Preparatory School

99 Craigie Drive, The Millfields, Plymouth, Devon PL1 3JL

Tel:	01752 201352
email:	prepschool@plymouthcollege.com
	jlearmouth@plymouthcollege.com
website:	www.plymouthcollege.com

Chairman of Governors: D R Woodgate, BSc, MBA

Headmaster: **C D M Gatherer**, BA Keele

Age Range. 3–11 Co-educational.
Number of Pupils. 220.
Fees per term (2016–2017). Infant Department: Kindergarten £2,430, Reception £2,540, Years 1 & 2 £2,985. Junior Department: Years 3–4 £3,200, Years 5–6 £3,345.

Plymouth College Preparatory School is a co-educational school for children from 3–11 years. The school was founded in 1877 and is within a few minutes' drive of Plymouth College senior school.

The primary academic aim of the school is to prepare children for entry to Plymouth College at the age of 11, ensuring that they are articulate and have taken full advantage of an education designed to stimulate the development of each child both intellectually and socially.

There are thirty full-time and three part-time members of staff, including specialist teachers in Mathematics, English, Science, Information Technology, Design Technology, Geography, History, Art, Music and French. There is a wide range of extracurricular activities.

There are two libraries, a computer room, a well-equipped laboratory, art room, theatre, music room and a sports centre.

Further information and application forms can be obtained from the Registrar, direct on 01752 831911, and appointments to view the school are welcomed.

Charitable status. Plymouth College is a Registered Charity, number 1105544. It exists to help children fulfil their wish to achieve a higher standard of education.

Pocklington Prep School

West Green, Pocklington, York, East Yorkshire YO42 2NH

Tel:	+44 (0)1759 321228
Fax:	+44 (0)1759 306366
email:	prep@pocklingtonschool.com
website:	www.pocklingtonschool.com
Twitter:	@PockPrep

Chairman of Governors: Mr T A Stephenson, MA, FCA

Headmaster: **Mr I D Wright**, BSc Hons, PGCE, NPQH

Age Range. 4–11 co-educational.
Number of Pupils. 224: 119 Boys, 105 Girls.
Fees per term (2016–2017). Day Pupils £2,425–£3,804; Full Boarders £7,154 (Year 3 Junior Boarder £6,271); 5-day Boarders £6,641.

Pocklington Prep School is the Prep School of the Pocklington School Foundation, a supportive and caring community that has been thriving in the heart of rural Yorkshire for 500 years. The school shares a 65-acre rural site on the edge of the market town of Pocklington with Pocklington School. This gives even the youngest pupils (as appropriate) access to specialist teaching facilities for sports (astroturf pitches), music and the arts (purpose-built theatre) and plenty of space to play. Classes at Pocklington Prep School are intentionally small, ensuring good individual support.

Good road and bus services from York and Hull are supplemented by the school's own minibus services. Full, weekly and flexible boarding options are available. Junior boarders live in modern single-sex houses. Boarders have a dedicated programme of weekend and after-school activities in addition to the normal school calendar.

Inspired for Life. We aim to give our pupils the care and encouragement they need to flourish into confident boys and girls who are inspired for lifelong learning so that when our pupils move on to their senior schools they are well prepared for the challenges ahead.

The formal curriculum reflects the new Primary School Review with the emphasis on creativity and enjoyment. Pocklington Prep School offers a secure and happy environment in which pupils are actively encouraged to express their natural talents and curiosity while developing their confidence in the core skills of reading, writing and numeracy to meet the challenges ahead.

Core subjects include English, maths and science but history, geography, art and design technology, music, ICT, religious studies and Modern Languages also play a prominent part, together with swimming, PE and Games. Initially forms are balanced in ability, with teachers taking care to ensure that individual children can progress at a pace according to need. From Year 5 onwards pupils are taught in ability groups in maths and English.

A wide range of sporting, cultural and other activities supports the curriculum. Pupils visit an outdoor education centre in the Yorkshire Dales, take part in fieldwork and leadership/team challenges and make full use of the excellent attractions in the area.

Games played include rugby, hockey, football, netball, cricket, tennis and rounders – with clubs and teams in athletics, swimming and trampoline also. PE and swimming form part of the weekly timetable for all pupils.

House competitions include music, art, drama, chess, creative writing, general knowledge and sport.

Extra activities take place at lunchtimes and after school and include art, computing, choir, drama, chess, orchestra, trampoline, language clubs, swimming and team coaching.

Pocklington Prep School has a strong musical tradition with a successful choir and orchestra. Individual music tuition takes place throughout the age range. Full use is made of the Theatre to perform in concerts, plays, sketches and musicals – some jointly with the senior school.

Entry Requirements: Entry to the Pre-Prep at 4+ is by informal interview and assessment. All pupils internal and external are assessed at 7+ to ensure that they are progressing in line with their peer group. Nearly all pupils go on to

Pocklington School at the end of Year 6 (age 11+). Progress is automatic for Prep School applicants provided there are no concerns about a child's behaviour or ability, which have previously been communicated to parents prior to the date of the entrance assessment. New entrants are required to sit the Pocklington School 11+ Entrance Examination.

Charitable status. The Pocklington School Foundation is a Registered Charity, number 529834.

Port Regis

Motcombe Park, Shaftesbury, Dorset SP7 9QA

Tel: 01747 857800
Fax: 01747 857810
email: admissions@portregis.com
website: www.portregis.com
Twitter: @PortRegisSchool
Facebook: /PortRegis

Chairman of the Governors: Mr Oliver Hawkins

Headmaster: **Mr Stephen Ilett**, MA Oxon, PGCE

Age Range. 3–13.
Number of Pupils. Boarders: 141 (Boys 94, Girls 47); Day Boarders: 164 (Boys 109, Girls 55).
Fees per term (2016–2017). Boarders £6,750–£8,100 (no compulsory extras); Day Boarders £2,890–£5,999 (meals included). Weekly Boarding is available.

Port Regis is a co-educational day and boarding school for children aged 3–13 which enjoys an enviable reputation as one of the leading Prep schools in the country. Located in the beautiful Dorset countryside, the school provides the perfect environment in which boys and girls can flourish and enjoy school. Our aim is to provide a first class, all-round education which will set a child up for life.

The school is located in 150 acres of parkland in the stunning Dorset countryside and enjoys a beautiful campus with facilities that are second to none in the Prep school world. Extensive woodland with nature trails sits alongside lawns, several ponds and a lake, so that the children can enjoy the space and freedom of the grounds. There are also 35 acres of games pitches, a nine-hole (18 tees) golf course, hockey pitch (Astroturf), hard tennis and netball courts, a 25m indoor swimming pool, a rifle range and an indoor sports complex, which includes two sports halls. An equestrian centre is conveniently situated close to the School.

A Pre-Prep and Nursery opened in September 1993 in the Motcombe Park grounds and enjoys full use of the Prep School's facilities.

The school's enviable reputation attracts the best teaching staff from all over the country. We are extremely fortunate to have an immensely accomplished team of staff dedicated to achieving this and who provide the happy, family atmosphere in which a child can realise their full potential.

Port Regis is extremely proud of its 100% Common Entrance success record and the high number of scholarships and awards won to senior schools every year. Learning Support is available for children with mild-to-moderate specific learning difficulties.

Extensive opportunities are provided for Music (about three-quarters of the School learn an instrument), Drama (there are up to six productions a year), and Art (in a wide choice of media), with Woodwork, Electronics, Riding, .22 Rifle Shooting, Karate, Gymnastics and Canoeing included in a list of over 70 hobby options. Major team games are Rugby, Hockey, Soccer, Netball, Cricket and Rounders. Inter-school, county and national standard competitions are entered. Home and abroad trips take place.

The high standard of boarding provision is an impressively strong feature of the school, which explains why so many boys and girls choose to board (awarded 'Outstanding' by Ofsted following their recent boarding inspection). The school was inspected by the Independent Schools Inspectorate (ISI) in June 2014 and was rated 'Excellent' in every single judgement.

Open Mornings take place each term and include tours of the school with pupils, a welcome address and Question and Answer session with the Headmaster and other key members of staff.

Academic, Music, Gymnastic, Sport and All-Rounder entrance scholarships may be awarded annually. The School also has a wealth of experience in dealing with HM Services Families and offers special awards to children of HM Services Families.

Charitable status. Port Regis School Limited is a Registered Charity, number 306218.

The Portsmouth Grammar Junior School

High Street, Portsmouth, Hampshire PO1 2LN

Tel: 023 9236 4219
Fax: 023 9236 4263
email: juniorschool@pgs.org.uk
website: www.pgs.org.uk
Twitter: @PGS_Junior
Facebook: /PGJS1732

Chairman of the Governors: B S Larkman, BSc, ACIB

Headmaster of the Junior School: **P S Hopkinson**, BA, PGCE

Deputy Headmaster: J Ashcroft, BSc, PGCE
Assistant Headmistress: Mrs P Giles, BA, PGCE
Head of Nursery: Mrs K Moore, BA, QTS

Age Range. 4–11. Nursery: 2½–4.
Number of Day Pupils. 215 boys, 141 girls.
Fees per term (2016–2017). Reception, Years 1 and 2: £3,170; Years 3 and 4: £3,341; Years 5 and 6: £3,515. (Fees quoted include direct debit discount.)

The Junior School is an integral part of The Portsmouth Grammar School under the general direction of the Governors and Headmaster. Children from 4–9 years are educated within bright and spacious classrooms that occupy a discreet space on the whole school site. The 9–11 year old pupils are educated in the historic original school building which stands in splendid isolation in close proximity to the whole school site.

The Junior School's organisation is distinct under its own Headmaster, with 31 full-time, 15 part-time members of staff, and 18 teaching assistants.

The main three-form entry is at 4+ with an additional class formed from Year 5. Pupils leave at 11 years, the majority moving on to The Portsmouth Grammar Senior School.

Whilst emphasis is placed on literacy and numeracy there is a broad curriculum which includes; Science, Geography, History, Religious Studies, ICT, Modern Foreign Languages, Music, Design Technology, Art, Drama, Physical Education, Games and PSHE. In addition, many pupils receive tuition in a wide range of musical instruments.

The school also provides a wide choice of co-curricular activities to all pupils. Currently over 30 different club activities are offered. The most recent innovations are a week's sailing instruction for all pupils in Year 4 and a

French Trip for all pupils in Year 6. There are specialist rooms for Art, DT, Music and Drama, plus a Science Laboratory and two Information Technology Centres. An innovative string scheme enables all Year 3 pupils to experience a free term's tuition in learning the violin or cello and a brass scheme offers a similar opportunity in Year 4.

Games include Rugby, Football, Netball, Hockey, Rounders, Cricket, Athletics, Tennis and Swimming. The Junior School has its own learner swimming pool and uses the Grammar School's excellent 16 acre playing fields at Hilsea, which include a floodlit Astroturf pitch.

It also has access to the Grammar School's Sports Hall, Music School and Theatre.

In September 2001 a Nursery School was opened offering up to 60 places in any one session. The architect designed building provides the children, aged from two years six months, with exciting opportunities to learn through play and exploration. All staff have early years specialism, the Head of Nursery being a fully qualified primary teacher with Early Years expertise. The Nursery School offers provision for 45 weeks a year.

Charitable status. The Portsmouth Grammar School is a Registered Charity, number 1063732. It exists to provide education for boys and girls.

Pownall Hall

Carrwood Road, Wilmslow, Cheshire SK9 5DW

Tel: 01625 523141
email: headmaster@pownallhallschool.co.uk
website: www.pownallhallschool.co.uk

Chair of Governors: Mrs Eileen MacAulay

Head: **Mr D Goulbourn**, BA Hons, PGCE Distinction

Age Range. 2–11 Co-educational.
Number of Boys and Girls. 220 (Day Children)
Fees per term (2016–2017). £2,725–£3,175.

Pownall Hall, a preparatory day school for children aged 2 to 11 and set in its own beautiful and extensive grounds, has been established for over 100 years. It is situated on the north-western side of Wilmslow, 12 miles from Manchester and within easy reach of motorway, rail and air travel.

The school has highly-trained teaching staff, who prepare children for the Entrance Examinations to the Independent Day schools in the area. A thorough grounding is given in all academic subjects extending well beyond the confines of the National Curriculum. An excellent mixture of traditional and modern techniques is used through the implementation of cutting-edge technology in and around every classroom. In Key Stage 2 each major subject has specialist teaching staff and subject rooms including a fully-equipped Science Laboratory, Maths, English, Information Technology and French rooms and, in addition, a computer-aided Library. French and German are taught from the age of two.

Pownall Hall School has two pre-school years with children entering the Nursery from the age of 2 and transferring to Kindergarten at the age of 3. From here the pupils then enter Reception and go through the school to Year 6 by which point the school will have guided parents as to where best for their child to continue their education at the age of 11.

At Pownall Hall there is an excellent staff to pupil ratio throughout the school, ensuring that pastoral care is of a very high level and also supporting the learning of children of all abilities, in conjunction with a specialist SEND provision. Children are taught in small class sizes, gaining from the individual attention they receive.

Great importance is attached to Sport, Music and Drama in order to develop the rounded education that allows all children to achieve, wherever their ability lies. The school has its own well-equipped theatre where all children perform on stage during the year. Music is offered as part of the curriculum and also additionally through a full range of peripatetic teaching staff, providing chances for the children to perform in and outside school. As well as subject specialist rooms with an outstanding range of specialist equipment, the implementation of mobile technology and 1–1 devices for both staff and children provides opportunity for outstanding teaching and learning across the school.

The facilities for sport are very impressive with the school having its own extensive grounds, alongside a fully-equipped Sports Hall and both outdoor and indoor facilities for Netball, Tennis and Football.

All children experience outdoor learning, with day and residential trips arranged as well as utilising our on-site woods for free-flow teaching and learning at all ages. Children in Years 4 to 6 also experience outdoor pursuits at a range of well-equipped sites which enhance their learning experiences. There is an extensive provision of co-curricular clubs, complementing our out-of-hours Breakfast Club and After School Care. Holiday Club runs on site throughout the year.

The school received an outstanding Full inspection Report in 2011 and an outstanding EYFS Inspection in 2014.

Charitable status. Pownall Hall School is a Registered Charity, number 525929. It exists to provide education for boys and girls, aged 2–11 yrs.

The Prebendal School

52–55 West Street, Chichester, West Sussex PO19 1RT

Tel: 01243 772220
Fax: 01243 780963
email: office@prebendalschool.org.uk
website: www.prebendalschool.org.uk

Chairman of Governors: The Very Reverend Stephen Waine, Dean of Chichester Cathedral

Headmaster: **Mr T R Cannell**, MA Ed Man, BEd Winchester

Deputy Head: Mr T Morgan, BMus Hons RCM, QTS
Bursar: Mr M Chapman, MA, MBA
Head of Pre-Prep: Miss I Carmody, MSc Ed Hons, BA Ed, HDE
Director of Studies: Mr T Bromfield, MA Ed, BEd Hons

Age Range. 3–13.
Number of Pupils. 170 pupils in total (including 15 full boarders and 9 weekly boarders): 121 in the Prep School (Years 3–8) and 49 in the Pre-Prep (Kindergarten to Year 2).
Fees per term (2016–2017). Full Boarders £6,700. Day Pupils: Years 5–8 £4,870; Years 3–4 £4,510. Weekly Boarding: £1,440 in addition to Day Fee. Pre-Prep £2,565–£2,975. Nursery/Kindergarten: £7.70 per hour. Compulsory extras: laundry and linen for Full Boarders.

The Prebendal is the oldest school in Sussex and has occupied its present building at the west end of the Cathedral (though with later additions) for over 500 years. The Cathedral Choristers are among the boys educated at the School and they receive Choral Scholarships in reduction of fees. Music and Academic Scholarships are open to boys and girls entering the school. Sibling Bursaries are also awarded as well as Scholarships for children entering Year 7. Forces families can also apply for fee remission awards.

Year 8 leavers achieve an impressive range of Scholarship awards to a range of prestigious senior schools every September.

There are excellent playing fields in the heart of the city; the main sports are football, hockey, netball, cricket, athletics, tennis, rugby and rounders. The school opened a state-of-the-art Science Laboratory in September 2016.

Approximately 95% of the children learn to play musical instruments and the School has more than 20 weekly ensembles, several orchestras, bands and a range of choirs. There are many optional extras and after-school clubs, for example Forestry Club and Sailing. Flexi boarding is available and is a popular choice for many pupils. There is a growing demand for the extended day programme, from Breakfast Club to supper, for busy families.

Former pupils, parents and staff are known as The Prebendal Associates and events are held regularly throughout each academic year. The School also has its own Toddler Group which takes place every Wednesday morning during term-time.

Charitable status. The Prebendal School is a Registered Charity, number 1157782. Registered Company No. 09038149.

Prestfelde
A Woodard School

London Road, Shrewsbury, Shropshire SY2 6NZ
Tel: 01743 245400
Fax: 01743 241434
email: office@prestfelde.co.uk
website: www.prestfelde.co.uk

Chairman of Governors: Mr Stuart Hay, MB ChB, FRCS, FRCS Orth

Head: **Mrs F Orchard**, GTCL Trinity College, PGCE Reading

Age Range. 3–13.
Number of Pupils. 282 (2 boarders, 188 day pupils, and 92 children in Little Prestfelde).
Fees per term (2016–2017). Weekly Boarders £6,260. Day: Year 8 £5,025; Years 6–7 £4,985; Year 5 £4,925; Year 4 £4,740; Year 3 £4,050; Year 2 £3,100; Year 1 £3,025; Reception £2,975; Nursery £1,590 (5 mornings).

Pupils at Prestfelde are well known for their cheerful and purposeful attitude. The school aims to maximise the potential of every individual by providing them with significant opportunities for excelling academically, and in musical, sporting and dramatic performances. A well-qualified, loyal, enthusiastic and dedicated staff form the backbone of the school's success. The use of subject specialist teachers for pupils from the age of eight adds greatly to the quality of the teaching and the enthusiasm of the pupils.

Prestfelde has excellent facilities. There has been an extensive building programme over recent years giving all age ranges the benefit of purpose-built class and specialist teaching rooms. This year two well-equipped modern science laboratories have been added. The school enjoys the benefits of thirty acres of delightful parkland playing fields on the edge of Shrewsbury. There are ample, well-maintained facilities for football, rugby, cricket, netball, rounders, lacrosse, tennis and swimming in a covered heated pool.

Although the school is non-selective, the academic standards of the school are excellent. Setting is used for pupils from the age of eight so that the curriculum meets the needs of all our children. Equally, pupils who require support have the benefit of an exceptionally successful learning support department. The great majority of pupils stay to thirteen, and talented pupils are encouraged to attempt scholarship exams to their chosen senior school. The school has an excellent reputation and 20 scholarships were gained this year to senior independent schools. 29 boys have gained academic scholarships to Shrewsbury School in the last five years with other academic awards to Westminster, Bloxham, Repton, Moreton Hall, Wrekin College and Concord College. A number of boys and girls have gained music, art, sport and all-rounder scholarships.

Prestfelde is a Woodard School, with its own Chaplain and a clear stance in promoting spiritual and moral values within the school.

Charitable status. Prestfelde School is a Registered Charity, number 1102931. It aims to provide education for boys and girls.

Prince's Mead School

Worthy Park House, Kings Worthy, Winchester, Hampshire SO21 1AN
Tel: 01962 888000
email: admin@princesmeadschool.org.uk
website: www.princesmeadschool.org.uk

Chairman of Governors: Mr B Welch

Headmistress: **Miss P Kirk**, BEd Exeter

Age Range. 4–11 co-educational.
Number of Children. 265 Day Boys and Girls.
Fees per term (2016–2017). £3,250–£4,995.

Established in 1949, Prince's Mead is a Day Preparatory School on the outskirts of Winchester. The school follows an innovative curriculum that prepares young people for what lies ahead in an every changing world. Children are encouraged to acquire sound working habits, an enthusiasm and hunger for knowledge and a desire to achieve their full potential. The pleasures and responsibilities of school life are an integral part of development and we encourage collaboration, independence and leadership qualities. Extensive playing fields and a strong sporting ethos encourage children to participate in competitive sport. The Performing Arts Department is also significant in developing the skills of all our children. The school is alive to the children's needs both now and in the future. Our Mission Statement, 'Preparing the Children of Today for the Challenges of Tomorrow' is at the core of all we do within the school and beyond.

Girls are prepared for 11+ Common Entrance and Scholarships to a wide variety of Independent Schools. Boys are prepared for entry to local Independent Day and Boarding schools at age 11. In 2015 children achieved a significant number of scholarships and were offered places at their first-choice senior schools. Our children also enter the excellent Secondary Schools in the Winchester area.

The curriculum is innovative with such subjects as Team Building, Debating and Philosophy sitting alongside the more traditional areas of study. An extensive range of extra-curricular activities enhance and enrich development.

Bursaries (financial assistance) are available from Year 3 upwards.

Charitable status. Prince's Mead School is a Registered Charity, number 288675. It exists to provide education for boys and girls.

Prior Park Prep School

Calcutt Street, Cricklade, Wiltshire SN6 6BB

Tel:	01793 750275
Fax:	01793 750910
email:	hmoffice@priorparkschools.com
website:	www.priorparkprep.com
Twitter:	@PriorParkPrep
Facebook:	/PriorParkPrep

Chair of Governors: Mr Michael King

Headmaster: **M Pearce**, BA Hons, QTS

Age Range. Rising 3–13.
Number of Pupils. 215 (30 Boarders, 185 Day).
Fees per term (2016–2017). Full Boarding £6,375–£7,410; Weekly Boarding £5,515–£6,550; Day Pupils £2,615–£5,005.

Prior Park Prep School is a thriving school situated in rural Wiltshire (Cricklade), on the edge of the Cotswolds. Established in 1946, it forms part of the Prior Park Educational Trust. The Trust has recently opened a new school – Prior Park School in Gibraltar. Awarded "Outstanding" in its recent ISI Inspection, Prior Park Prep provides a nurturing yet challenging school environment which ably prepares our children for life's journey. As a non-selective Catholic Christian school for children aged 3–13, we carefully nurture and encourage our children to flourish through identifying their gifts and talents. We have an extensive co-curricular programme that encompasses fencing, archery, orchestra, debating, art club, hockey, tennis, golf, judo and model making – to name a few. Our superb facilities include an ICT suite with 20 flat screen computers, art studio with pottery kiln, music studio, 25m heated swimming pool, extensive playing fields, astroturf and an extremely well-equipped sports hall which caters for all indoor games. We believe that sport is an essential building block of the school curriculum and fosters confidence, team work and a healthy competitive spirit. We play regular sporting fixtures and tournaments throughout the year in sports ranging from rugby, hockey and netball to tennis, swimming and athletics. Regular foreign sports tours take place, the most recent being to Barbados, South Africa, Jersey, Dubai and Paris.

In line with fostering a competitive spirit, we have a thriving house system. All children are given the opportunity to represent their house and to learn the importance of teamwork.

Our broad, balanced curriculum enables children to develop lively and enquiring young minds and our carefully planned cultural excursions broaden educational horizons. We pride ourselves on small class sizes with pupils taught in classes of between 10 and 20. Our broad-based Pre-Prep curriculum gives children an excellent start to learning with French taught to the youngest pupils as well as an exciting programme of Forest School. Our secure and friendly learning environment inspires individual excellence and ensures that children progress to their chosen senior school as confident, capable and independently-minded children. We also have an excellent scholarship record with over 35% of our children gaining scholarships at Common Entrance. Scholarships are awarded in the arts, music, drama, sport and all-rounder.

Our Learning Support Department offers support for pupils with mild to moderate dyslexia. We also support children who do not have English as their first language.

A strong boarding community lies at the heart of the school. This includes both full and flexi boarding. The school's philosophy towards boarding is to create a family atmosphere in which pupils feel happy and secure and where they develop a unique esprit de corps. Our most recent inspection highlighted the happy and caring atmosphere which pervades the whole school. Boarders are cared for by very experienced full-time members of staff who live within the boarding houses. A range of activities is organised for boarders with pupils having a say in how they spend their free time. The trip out on Sunday is always one of the highlights of the week. We are located only just over an hour from several major airports as well as having excellent road and rail links to major cities.

A limited number of HM Forces bursaries is available.

Charitable status. Prior Park Educational Trust is a Registered Charity, number 281242.

Priory Preparatory School and Nursery

Bolters Lane, Banstead, Surrey SM7 2AJ

Tel:	01737 366920
Fax:	01737 366921
email:	office@prioryprep.co.uk
website:	www.prioryprep.co.uk
Twitter:	@prioryprep

Chair of Governors: Mr Ashley Head

Headmaster: **Graham D Malcolm**, BEd, MA, FRSA, IAPS

Age Range. 2–11.
Number of Boys. 200 Day Boys.
Fees per term (2016–2017). Nursery £2,135–£2,825; Pre-Prep £3,225; Preparatory £4,110.

Priory Prep is a small, friendly school where every boy is valued and contributes fully to the various activities organised in the school. A strong pastoral framework supports the boys' learning and enjoyment of what is on offer. The boys are prepared for senior independent or grammar schools selected by their parents in consultation with the Headmaster. The aim is to provide a sound, well-balanced course designed to prepare boys for a smooth transfer to their next school. The curriculum reflects this aim and in so doing includes all school games and physical activities as a normal and necessary part of every boy's life, irrespective of ability. Soccer, Rugby, Cricket, Athletics, Basketball and Swimming are coached extensively. A multi-purpose Sports Hall greatly enhances the facilities, as does a large sports field. In 2012 an impressive Early Years outdoor play area was opened. There is specialist accommodation for Art, Science and ICT and a library. There is a strong emphasis on Music and Drama.

The Pre-Preparatory Department is highly successful having had excellent inspection reports. The Preparatory School has also had excellent reviews in recent inspections, being cited as 'Outstanding' in every section (ISI Inspection 2011).

Although most boys are prepared for the Common Entrance Examination, a large number of Scholarships have been won in recent years. The essential groundwork of a good education lies in the experienced Pre-Preparatory Department which the School possesses. Traditional values, skills and standards run parallel with modern teaching methods and an extensive range of educational visits is arranged throughout the year.

Charitable status. The Priory School (Banstead) Trust Limited is a Registered Charity, number 312035. It exists for the education of boys aged two to eleven years.

Prospect House School

75 Putney Hill, London SW15 3NT
Tel: 020 8780 0456
Fax: 020 8780 3010
email: info@prospecths.org.uk
website: www.prospecths.org.uk

Chairman of Governors: Mr Anthony Rentoul

Headmistress: **Mrs D Barratt**, MEd Newcastle-upon-Tyne

Age Range. 3–11 co-educational.
Number of Pupils. 300 day pupils.
Fees per term (2016–2017). Nursery (5 mornings) £2,735, Reception–Year 2 £5,470, Years 3–6 £5,700.

Prospect House School occupies two large buildings on Putney Hill situated just a short walk apart. Children aged 3 to 7 years occupy the Lower School building at 76 Putney Hill and children aged 7 to 11 years are based in the Upper School at 75 Putney Hill. They both have large grounds, including an all-weather sports pitch. There are multi-purpose halls where assemblies, music recitals, gymnastics and drama productions take place. There are dedicated rooms for music, ICT and special needs with art and DT also having provision within the school.

Most children join the school at 3 or 4 years of age, although occasionally there are places for older children. Selection for entry at 3 is by date of registration, with preference being given to brothers and sisters of children already in the school. An equal balance of boys and girls is kept throughout the school. There is also a good balance of male and female staff.

Although the school does not have selective entry at age 3 or 4, the academic track record is very strong. The curriculum includes all National Curriculum subjects, with the addition of French from the age of three. There are numerous specialist teachers and children from Nursery are taught by specialists for music, PE, French, ICT and dance. Children are prepared for a wide range of leading day and boarding schools for entry at 11 years of age, with some children taking academic, music and sports scholarships. There is a wide and varied sports programme with many fixtures against other preparatory schools and children from Year 3 upwards attend training sessions at a nearby sports ground under the guidance of qualified teachers.

The school was awarded 'Best Primary School' in the UK in 2009–10 for the teaching and use of ICT.

Clubs after school cater for many interests and visiting teachers also provide a wide range of individual music lessons. Children are taken on educational visits to London and the surrounding area every term, with residential field study trips being undertaken in the final three years.

Quainton Hall School

Hindes Road, Harrow, Middlesex HA1 1RX
Tel: 020 8861 8861
email: admin@quaintonhall.org.uk
website: www.quaintonhall.org.uk
Twitter: @QuaintonHall

Chairman of Governors: The Reverend V Baron, BSc, MA

Headmaster: **Mr Simon Ford**, BEd Hons

Age Range. Boys and Girls 2½–13.
Number of Pupils. 190.

Fees per term (2016–2017). £3,335–£3,675.

Established in central Harrow at the end of the nineteenth century, Quainton Hall is an IAPS Preparatory School for children between the ages of two and a half and thirteen. We have our own Nursery for girls and boys from two and a half to four, our Pre-Prep for girls and boys from four to seven and our Middle and Senior School for girls and boys from seven to thirteen. The children continue on to take 13+ entrance examinations and transfer at the end of Year 8 to a range of senior schools, mostly in North and North West London, though some go further afield and into boarding, where desired. To assist them in doing this, they undertake the Common Entrance (CE) curriculum, starting in Year 6. A number of pupils choose to leave at 11+, moving on to both independent and grammar schools. The majority of the girls leave at 11+ and transfer to North West London schools.

Quainton Hall provides a broad and balanced education, within a secure and caring environment and with a definite Christian ethos. Our children are valued as individuals and their learning experiences are stimulating. We recognise that children need to feel safe and secure in order to be motivated to learn. However, our curriculum is designed to do much more than prepare children for the next stage in their education; we teach skills and foster attitudes and values which will be of lasting benefit throughout their lives. We provide an extensive extra-curricular programme of activities, visits to places of interest and we invite speakers and theatre groups into school during the course of the school year.

Creativity, communication, teamwork, determination and a sense of the value and dignity of others are just some of the attributes we prize at Quainton Hall and where children grow to develop an understanding of the wider world, of those in need and have opportunities to raise funds for a range of charitable causes.

The life and work of the school is planned to enable children to shine in those areas and activities that they are good at and to reach their full potential. All members of staff have this objective as their aim. We also encourage the notion that learning is fun and that the acquisition of knowledge brings its own rewards. All that we do is conducted in an atmosphere and ethos that is personal, caring and family-orientated. We promote good order and self-discipline, consideration and tolerance towards others as well as personal motivation and group endeavour.

Charitable status. Quainton Hall School, under the Trusteeship of Walsingham College (Affiliated Schools) Limited, is a Registered Charity, number 312638. It exists to provide a sound education within a definite Christian framework.

Queen Elizabeth's Hospital (QEH) – Junior School

Berkeley Place, Clifton, Bristol BS8 1JX
Tel: 0117 930 3087
email: juniors@qehbristol.co.uk
website: www.qehbristol.co.uk

Chairman of Governors: D A Smart, BSc, FCA

Junior School Headmaster: **M J Morris**, BEd, BA

Age Range. Boys 7–11. Boys from age 3 are accepted as part of 'Redland High Infants with QEH' and will transfer seamlessly to QEH Junior School at the end of Year 2.
Number of Pupils. 100 day boys.

Fees per term (2016–2017). £2,975. Fees include pre- and after-school supervision until 5.00 pm.

The QEH Junior School was opened in September 2007 and is located in gracious Georgian town houses in Upper Berkeley Place backing onto the Senior School, which means it can share its first-class facilities including science, drama, music and sport. The cultural facilities of the city, such as the city museum and art gallery, are also on its door-step.

Pupils travel to the school from across the region and there is a hub for public transport on the nearby Clifton Tri-angle. The school also offers timed parking facilities for par-ents in the adjacent West End multi-storey car park, to pick up and drop off pupils, at no extra cost.

As part of the only boys' school in the city, QEH Juniors is unique in Bristol. Being small, it focuses on the individ-ual, fostering a love of learning whilst nurturing the interests and talents of each boy. In addition there is a wealth of extra-curricular activities available.

The school is a happy place with strong pastoral care, academic excellence, and high standards where the educa-tional experience is designed to be relevant and meaningful for every single child. Each boy leaves recognising himself as a lifelong learner.

Boys can therefore enter in Year 3 or Year 5 though places occasionally become available in other Years. Boys are expected to move into the Main School at 11. (*See QEH entry in HMC section.*)

Charitable status. Queen Elizabeth's Hospital is a Reg-istered Charity, number 1104871, and a Company Limited by Guarantee, number 5164477.

Queen's College Junior School
Taunton

Trull Road, Taunton, Somerset TA1 4QS

Tel: 01823 340830
Fax: 01823 323811
email: junioradmissions@queenscollege.org.uk
website: www.queenscollege.org.uk
Twitter: @QueensTaunton
Facebook: @queenstaunton

Chairman of Governors: Mr Mark Edwards

Headmistress: **Mrs Tracey Khodabandehloo**

Head of Pre-Prep: Mrs Janet Williams
Head of Nursery: Miss Elizabeth Hayes

Age Range. 0–11.
Number of Pupils. 207 with 17 children in the Junior boarding house.
Fees per term (2016–2017). £2,000–£4,070 (day); £4,430–£6,703 (boarders); £5,510–£7,800 (overseas board-ers).

Queen's College is a co-educational boarding and day school on the outskirts of Taunton, Somerset, with fine views across the playing fields to the surrounding hills.

The Pre-Prep School educates pupils up to the age of 7 and the Junior School educates pupils up to the end of Key Stage 2 (NC Year 6). Children aged 11+ will usually be admitted directly to the Senior School (*see Queen's College entry in HMC section*).

The Junior School is run as an independent unit but shares many of the excellent facilities of the adjacent Senior School. Known especially for its outstanding pastoral care and real focus on individual children, there is no doubt that pupils here are extremely happy. Specialist subject teachers,

high academic standards and a sense of fun are setting this school apart from its competitors and the outstanding Head-mistress whose excellent communication skills are admired universally means that parents are flocking towards this lovely, friendly school with its excellent facilities. Defi-nitely on the up.

Junior boarding here is growing and the House parents are kind, sympathetic and organise a wealth of activities for those away from home. Matrons read bedside stories and arrange fun weekend trips and with lots to do in the evenings the children are kept really busy and involved. Many chil-dren come from Armed Forces families and Queen's is well versed in settling pupils whose families have been posted abroad and keeping in contact. Emphasis is made on creat-ing a family-style, homely atmosphere in which the pupils can relax and unwind. Lovely, bright bedrooms and living areas with lots of games.

For every pupil the aim of the School is to find areas in which each child can succeed and develop self-confidence to help them really shine. Using different learning styles, reinforcing classroom learning with external trips and visits and a practical approach means that the children here are really inspired and enjoy their school and make excellent friendships.

The principal games are rugby, hockey and cricket for the boys, with hockey, netball and rounders for the girls. Tennis, swimming and athletics matches also take place. Fullest use is made of the excellent sporting facilities of the School, particularly the Sports Hall, tennis courts, heated indoor swimming pool and floodlit Astroturf. The school has achieved national success in hockey, cross country, swim-ming, athletics and riding this year and all abilities are wel-comed. A new hockey academy opened last year.

After-school activities include Board Games, Cookery, Chess, Computer Club, Drama, Gardening, Specialist Music Groups, Model Making, Photography, Puppets, and Fun Swim. Also arranged at an extra charge are Dancing, Speech and Drama, Climbing and Riding. Junior music is outstand-ing with many opportunities to play in groups and festivals and the performing arts is a real strength of the school with the Taunton Speech and Drama Festival run at Queen's.

Free before and after-school care is available every day until 5.45 pm and holiday clubs operate.

The Pre-Prep day school is in its own purpose-built build-ing and there is a Nursery School and recently-opened High-grove Nursery for children aged 0–4 years. Nursery and Reception are rated as outstanding and it is not difficult to see why. Outdoor gardens and facilities are superb with plenty of room to run and climb and many different things are happening at once in the classrooms. Innovative teach-ing methods, getting the children involved as well as teach-ing the foundations in small class sizes with specialist teachers means that the children have tremendous attention and support and really do achieve their potential.

Nearly all the children move on from one section of Queen's College to the next; there is no further qualifying examination.

Parent and toddler groups are held from Tuesday to Thursday.

Charitable status. Queen's College, Taunton is a Regis-tered Charity, number 310208.

Radnor House Sevenoaks – Prep School

Combe Bank Drive, Sundridge, Kent TN14 6AE
Tel: 01959 564320
Fax: 01959 560456
email: enquiries@radnor-sevenoaks.org
website: www.radnor-sevenoaks.org
Twitter: @radnorsevenoaks
Facebook: /radnorsevenoaks

Chairman of Board of Directors: Mr Colin Diggory, BSc
    Hons, PGCE, MA, EdD, CMath, FIMA, FRSA

Head: Mr David Paton, BComm Hons, PGCE, MA

Head of Prep School: **Miss Esther Wright**, MA Hons,
PGCE

Age Range. 3–11 Co-educational.
Number of Pupils. 101.
Fees per term (2016–2017). Preparatory School £3,250–
£4,150 (Lunch £235); Nursery £54 Full Day, £30 Half Day.

Radnor House Sevenoaks School was founded in 1924.
The Prep School is a flourishing independent school that
stands in 28 acres of gardens and grounds, on the Kent/Sur-
rey borders within easy reach of the centre Sevenoaks. (*See
also Radnor House Sevenoaks School entry in ISA section.*)

The Prep School is housed in an original stable block and
affords a unique environment in which the children feel
secure and comfortable. Specialist teaching rooms include
those dedicated to ICT, French, Music, PE, Speech and
Drama. The Hall includes a permanent stage with sound and
lighting systems. The older pupils have access to a purpose-
built Performing Arts Studio and the senior school's Science
and Technology Centre. The ICT suite, networked to all
classrooms, allows full class access at any time.

EYFS Nursery classes are housed within the courtyard
area, which has recently undergone refurbishment to provide first-class facilities for both indoor and outdoor activities, including a specially designed Secret Garden.

Beech Walk with its secure adventure play area gives the
children greater freedom at break times. There are two playing fields and five outdoor tennis and netball courts. A purpose-built Sports Hall allows for the teaching of multi-
sporting activities and inter-school fixtures. All pupils,
including the Nursery, use the indoor heated swimming pool
weekly throughout the year.

Academic standards are high. All pupils at Radnor House
Sevenoaks gain automatic entry to the senior school and
sixth form without re-assessments.

Drama and Music flourish in the school. Pupils have
many opportunities to perform throughout their time in the
Prep from large drama productions to musical ensembles.
The majority of study at least one musical instrument from
Year 3.

A highly dedicated staff team takes care of the academic,
physical, pastoral and extracurricular needs of the pupils.
We are committed to academic excellence for all our pupils.
We work together to raise the self-esteem of each child. We
pay particular attention to the development of thinking skills
and positively encourage independent learning. We actively
promote the development of a strong home-school partnership through parent consultation, information evenings and
social events. We also recognise the impact of Music Speech
and Drama, Art and sport in the life of the developing child.
The school is distinguished by the high standard of pastoral
care it offers. We nurture the individual.

Radnor House Sevenoaks is committed to safeguarding
and promoting the welfare of children. We achieved an 'outstanding' rating across all areas of the school at our recent
ISI inspection

Ravenscourt Park Preparatory School

16 Ravenscourt Avenue, London W6 0SL
Tel: 020 8846 9153
Fax: 020 8846 9413
email: secretary@rpps.co.uk
website: www.rpps.co.uk

Chairman of Governors: Mr Kevin Darlington

Headmaster: **Mr Carl Howes**, MA, PGCE

Deputy Head: Mr Simon Gould, BA Hons QTS
Deputy Head (*Teaching and Learning*): Miss Charlotte
    Ashworth, BA Hons, PGCE

The full staff list is available on the school website.

Age Range. 4–11 co-educational.
Number of Pupils. 413 boys and girls.
Fees per term (2016–2017). £5,405.

This non-selective school provides education of the highest quality for boys and girls, preparing them for transfer to
the best independent schools at 11 years of age. The Lower
School caters for pupils aged 4–7 and the Upper School for
7–11 years. All pupils are housed in one of the three main
buildings that make up the RPPS site. The addition of the
Gardener Building is home to a theatre, a state-of-the-art
science laboratory and an art studio. The secure site includes
a large play area, a newly refurbished outdoor learning area
for Early Years and the school makes use of the extensive
facilities of Ravenscourt Park which it adjoins.

The curriculum includes French, humanities, music, art
and craft, RE and PE for all pupils in addition to the usual
core subjects. In the Upper School the majority of subjects
are taught by specialists. All Upper School pupils attend a
Residential Week where studies across the curriculum are
applied to a non-urban environment.

There are many after-school clubs and sports activities, as
well as three choirs and two orchestras. Individual tuition is
offered in piano, harp, violin, brass, woodwind, cello, saxophone, clarinet, flute, percussion and singing. The drama
productions and concerts are a highlight of each school year.

A Day Care service, before and after school, is offered to
parents at an extra charge.

The school is noted for its warm, happy atmosphere
where parents play a full part in enriching the curriculum
and social life. Off-site visits and guest workshops presented
by noted visitors are a regular feature of education at RPPS.

The school is very popular in the local area and registration is strongly recommended on the child's first birthday. A
prospectus and registration form may be obtained from the
school secretary. Open Mornings take place each month
(dates are available on the school website).

The school was inspected by ISI in March 2016 and
received 'excellent' in all the categories. The full inspection
report is available on the school website.

Redcliffe School

47 Redcliffe Gardens, London SW10 9JH
Tel: 020 7352 9247
email: registrar@redcliffeschool.com
website: www.redcliffeschool.com

Chairman of the Board of Governors: Mr Roger Flynn

Headmistress: Mrs Susan Bourne, BSc, PGCE

Age Range. Boys 3–8, Girls 3–11.
Number of Pupils. 160 Day Pupils (65 boys, 95 girls)
Fees per term (2016–2017): £5,210. Nursery: £2,940 (morning class), £1,960 (afternoon class), £4,920 (full day).

Easily accessible from all parts of central and West London, Redcliffe is a small, friendly school with highly motivated, confident and happy children. Emphasis is placed on a combination of hard work, good manners and plenty of fun within a framework of traditional values of perseverance, courage and resilience. The balanced curriculum includes Maths, English, History, Geography, Science, IT, Art and Craft, Scripture, Current Affairs, Music, Physical Education and Drama. French is taught throughout the school. Individual attention encourages the pursuit of high academic standards and we are proud that our children gain places at their first choice of senior or prep school, including Colet Court, Sussex House, St Philip's, Downe House, Benenden, St Mary's Ascot, Queen's Gate, Godolphin and Latymer and Francis Holland. Every class has at least two hours of specialist-taught Physical Education each week including: tag rugby, netball, rounders, cricket, athletics and swimming with an option of participating in the ever-popular Friday Sports Club. After-school activities include cookery, gymnastics, ballet, computer skills and drama. Music is a strength of the school with visiting instrumental staff and a high standard of performance. Parents are encouraged to be involved with the school through Open Assemblies, Parents' Discussion Groups, the Parents' Committee and regular meetings with the teachers.

Redcliffe Robins is our nursery class for children rising 3 and access to all of Redcliffe's resources and facilities to help prepare the children for entry to the main school. Each day has a balanced timetable of phonics, mathematical skills, art and craft, music, drama and PE with ample opportunity for structured free play and the development of social skills.

Children are assessed at three years of age for entry to the main school at four. Entry for subsequent years by assessment. Tours of the school are held weekly during term time by appointment with the school office.

Charitable status. Redcliffe School Trust Ltd is a Registered Charity, number 312716. It exists to provide a high standard of education for children within a caring environment.

Reddiford School

38 Cecil Park, Pinner, Middlesex HA5 5HH
Tel: 020 8866 0660
Fax: 020 8866 4847
email: office@reddiford.org.uk
website: www.reddiford.co.uk

Chairman of Governors: Mr G Jukes

Head: Mrs J Batt, CertEd, NPQH

Age Range. 2 years 9 months to 11.

Number of Pupils. Prep: 88 Boys, 65 Girls; Pre-Prep: 43 Boys, 31 Girls; Early Years: 44 Boys, 38 Girls.
Fees per term (2016–2017). Nursery: £1,515 (mornings only), £2,685 (all day), Foundation £3,230, Reception £3,500, Pre-Prep £3,515, Prep £3,610.

Reddiford School has been established in Cecil Park, Pinner since 1913. Whilst the school maintains its Church of England status, children from all faiths and cultures are welcomed. Throughout the school the ethos is on respect for one another. Reddiford prides itself on being a town school based in the heart of Pinner; a few minutes' walk from local transport facilities.

Reddiford possesses a fine academic record, preparing its pupils for entrance at 11+ into major independent schools, many at scholarship level. There is a high teacher pupil ratio ensuring small classes leading to a friendly caring environment where all children are valued.

The Early Years Department is situated in its own building and caters for children from 2 years nine months to rising 5 years. It offers a stimulating and attractive environment where children are encouraged to be independent and active learners. The Early Years Department follows the Early Years Foundation Stage Curriculum. There is a choice of full or half day provision.

The Pre-Prep Department builds on the knowledge and skills acquired in the Early Years placing the emphasis on developing confidence and the ability to learn and work independently and with others. The Pre-Prep Department has its own computer suite and interactive whiteboards in classrooms. There is specialist teaching in French, Music and PE from reception upwards and all children are taught to swim.

In the Prep Department children are taught by specialist teachers in properly resourced subject rooms. There is a fully-equipped science laboratory, dedicated art and music rooms and an ICT suite. Pupils are prepared for entry to the many prestigious senior schools in the area, a process which involves consultation with parents from an early stage.

There is an extensive programme of extra-curricular activities throughout the school including: sports (football, cricket, netball, gymnastics), languages (French, Latin, Mandarin), art, science, and ballet. We also offer before and after school care, with a prep club for older children.

Entry to the Nursery is possible in any term once a child has reached 2 years and 9 months. Most children move from the Nursery to the Reception classes at 4+, but there are spaces for outside applicants in the Reception classes. An assessment day for these places is held on application for September entry. Means-tested bursaries may be available.

Charitable status. Reddiford School is a Registered Charity, number 312641. It exists to provide education for boys and girls.

Redmaids' High Junior School

Grange Court Road, Westbury-on-Trym, Bristol BS9 4DP
Tel: 0117 962 9451
Fax: 0117 989 8286
email: juniors@redmaids.bristol.sch.uk
website: www.redmaidshigh.co.uk
Twitter: @RedMaidsSchool
Facebook: /redmaidsschool

Chairman of Governors: Mrs J MacFarlane, BSc, MA

Headteacher: Mrs L Brown, BSc Hons Leicester, PGCE Oxford Brookes

Age Range. 7–11.

Number of Girls. 160 Day Girls.

Fees per term (2016–2017). £3,020 plus lunches.

Redmaids' High Junior School was established in 1986 alongside the Senior School which was founded in 1634. It occupies a spacious site, providing a mix of traditional and purpose-built buildings including a library, ICT suite, music room, art studio and lofty assembly hall – the perfect space for a wide range of whole-school activities. There is also a large garden for outdoor play complete with sports and climbing equipment.

The school is expanding following its recent merger with Redland High Junior School. The girls, aged 7–11, are organised into 10 classes with key points of entry at Year 3 and Year 5. The timetable is built on delivering seven learning sessions per day. Lessons range between 40 minutes to one hour. In Years 3 and 4, the girls are taught by their own class teachers with occasional input from specialists. In Years 5 and 6, a greater degree of subject specialism is introduced to help prepare for the transition to Senior School. There are opportunities for girls to work and make friends with children in all year groups. Since the girls know each other and every member of staff well, a strong community feeling is promoted within the school where girls can develop their confidence and self-esteem.

All the girls are encouraged to explore their individual talents and achieve their best through the school's broad and balanced curriculum. Whole school planning and assessment are integral to every subject area. The school uses Durham University's INCAS test to monitor girls' performance and progression, and to help with individual target setting.

In addition there is a strong emphasis on pastoral care. Through school meetings and class activities, the school teaches a sense of good citizenship as girls are encouraged to share responsibility for the care of their community and their environment.

Close links are fostered between the Junior and Senior schools through joint activities and visits. Pupils benefit from use of a science laboratory, extensive PE facilities including an all-weather pitch and shared dining facilities. At age 11, transition occurs to the Senior School (conditions apply) having sat the entrance examination and competed for academic scholarships alongside those joining from other schools. (*See Redmaids' High School entry in GSA section.*)

Extra-curricular activities are an essential part of every girl's school experience and there is a strong commitment to outdoor education.

The school enjoys close relationships with parents on a daily basis and generous support is offered to the school through a thriving Friends' Association.

Admission to Junior School: The main points of entry to the Junior School are in Year 3 and Year 5. Girls are assessed during a day visit when they also spend time with their peer group.

Charitable status. Redmaids' High School is a Registered Charity, number 1105017.

Reigate St Mary's Preparatory and Choir School

Chart Lane, Reigate, Surrey RH2 7RN

Tel: 01737 244880
email: office@reigatestmarys.org
website: www.reigatestmarys.org
Twitter: @rsmprepschool

Chairman of Governors: Mr Alan Walker

Headmaster: Marcus Culverwell, MA Ed

Age Range. 3–11.

Number of Pupils. 330 (180 boys 150 girls).

Fees per term (2016–2017). Kindergarten £1,725 (5 mornings), Reception to Year 2 £3,740, Years 3–6 £4,620.

Reigate St Mary's is an independent day school for boys and girls aged 3–11. It is the nursery and junior school of Reigate Grammar School. Set in 15 acres of beautiful parkland and sports fields, the older children also benefit from the facilities of Reigate Grammar School including the swimming pool and a further 32 acres of sports grounds. We are proud of our reputation as a lively, happy, family friendly school where each child is encouraged and known as an individual.

We aim to provide an education of considerable depth and breadth within a disciplined, happy and caring environment. All pupils are encouraged to be ambitious, to reach the best standards they can in their academic studies, in sport, in art, in music and in other performing arts.

We engender a love of learning, a zest for life and development of a caring and understanding attitude towards other people. The school places a high value on good relationships and developing inter-personal skills in our pupils to enable them to become responsible, adaptable, independent people in a changing world. With an emphasis on growth mind-sets, integration of IT into the curriculum, opportunities for public speaking and debate, plus the chance to really engage in socially responsible activities, our young people are truly being prepared for the real and rapidly changing world. We believe that all children should feel valued for who they are, not just for what they achieve.

Children at Reigate St Mary's who are on track for a successful secondary school career at Reigate Grammar do not have to sit the 11+ examination but move through from Reigate St Mary's to Reigate Grammar School by recommendation from the prep school.

We are rated 'Excellent' in all areas following an ISI Inspection in January 2016 which reported that "Pupils throughout the school are well educated, in accordance with its aims of achieving excellent standards in all areas of pupils' studies. They have high levels of knowledge, skill and understanding across all areas of learning" –"Pupils appreciate the strong Christian ethos that pervades the school, whilst also celebrating and learning to respect those of different faiths, in line with wider British values. Pupils' moral awareness is outstanding".

As a member of the Choir Schools' Association Reigate St Mary's maintains a traditional choir of boys and men under the direction of a Head of Choral Music. Choral scholarships are offered by the RGS Godfrey Searle Choir Trust.

RGS Springfield

Britannia Square, Worcester WR1 3DL

Tel: 01905 24999
email: springfield@rgsw.org.uk
website: www.rgsw.org.uk
Twitter: @RGSSpringfield
Facebook: /RGS-Springfield

Chairman of Governors: Mrs R F Ham

Headmistress: Mrs L Brown, BA Hons, PGCE

Age Range. 2–11 Co-educational.

Number of Pupils. 145.

Fees per term (2016–2017). £2,416–£3,822 including lunch.

Introduction from the Headmistress. "I am delighted to have this opportunity to welcome you to RGS Springfield, with its wonderful family atmosphere and nurturing co-educational environment, which together creates a uniquely friendly school.

Our aim is to ensure that children develop their full potential academically, socially and emotionally in a safe, caring environment.

All our pupils benefit from individual care, small class sizes, professional and dedicated teaching; all of which help children become confident, secure and considerate of the needs of others.

The school has scored highly in recent inspections, rated as consistently outstanding by Ofsted and ECERS and excellent in all areas by ISI inspectors (March 2015). There are a wealth of academic and extra-curricular opportunities to provide children with an enriching and stimulating environment, preparing them for the challenges of the 21st century, underpinned by traditional family values. The new digital learning programme adds a new dimension to classroom learning.

The school has wonderful grounds, which allow pupils to play outside in all weathers, learn from the natural environment and take part in all the fun that Forest School offers; wellies are very much encouraged!

The school, tucked away within the beautiful Georgian Britannia Square in the heart of Worcester, will provide a safe and happy place for your child to grow and develop. This website conveys only some of the ethos and spirit of RGS Springfield. Please visit us and see for yourself the happy, smiling faces of children having fun and learning in a stimulating environment. We are very much a happy family.

I look forward to welcoming you in person to our school."

Overview. RGS Springfield is the co-educational junior school for RGS Worcester (*see HMC entry*). The school educates children between the ages of 2 and 11 and is situated within a large, beautiful Georgian Town House and gardens in the centre of Worcester.

High academic standards are expected as the children are prepared to enter RGS Worcester at 11. There is a wide range of extra-curricular activities on offer and, while the school is noted for academic, creative and sporting excellence, it is of the greatest importance that the children are encouraged to be kind, considerate and well-mannered.

In 2009 an extensive refurbishment was undertaken to restore and develop the original historic site, Springfield, providing excellent modern facilities including art, design technology, science and ICT rooms alongside large, airy and warm well-equipped classrooms.

The school is set in six acres of maintained grounds and offers fantastic games facilities and outdoor space, including an extended Forest School, Walled Garden and Paddock Play Area.

Charitable status. The Royal Grammar School Worcester is a Registered Charity, number 1120644.

RGS The Grange

Grange Lane, Claines, Worcester WR3 7RR

Tel:	01905 451205
email:	grange@rgsw.org.uk
website:	www.rgsw.org.uk
Twitter:	@rgsthegrange
Facebook:	/RGS-The-Grange

Chairman of Governors: Mrs R F Ham

Headmaster: **G W Hughes**, BEd Hons

Age Range. 2–11 Co-educational.
Number of Pupils. 344.
Fees per term (2016–2017). £2,416–£3,822 including lunch.

Introduction from the Headmaster. "Welcome to a nurturing school with a big personality.

Giving a child the best possible foundations for a bright future is a true privilege. Our fantastic facilities give pupils tremendous scope for achieving the academic, sporting and creative excellence that we encourage. Just as important is the safe, secure and caring framework that we provide, giving children the support and self-belief they need to make their own individual strides forward.

I get huge satisfaction from seeing each one cross barriers and shine in a way that is uniquely theirs and with two children myself, I know the pride parents feel when they see their child thriving.

I look forward to helping your child thrive too."

Overview. RGS The Grange is one of two co-educational junior schools for RGS Worcester (*see HMC entry*). The school educates children between the ages of 2 and 11 and is situated in open countryside three miles north of Worcester in Claines.

High academic standards are expected as the children are prepared to enter RGS Worcester at 11. There is a wide range of extra-curricular activities on offer and, while the school is noted for academic, creative and sporting excellence, it is of the greatest importance that the children are encouraged to be kind, considerate and well-mannered.

The school has scored highly in recent inspections, being acknowledged as 'outstanding' and 'excellent' in all areas by ISI inspectors (March 2015). The Digital Learning Programme adds a new dimension to classroom learning across all three RGS schools and RGS The Grange is a leading school of excellence for computer science.

RGS The Grange provides excellent modern facilities including specialist art, design technology, science, food technology, French and Computing & IT rooms alongside large, airy, well-equipped classrooms.

The school is set in 49 acres of grounds and offers exceptional games facilities and outdoor space, including a full-sized floodlit Astroturf, cricket pavilion, Forest School, traverse wall and adventure play area.

Charitable status. The Royal Grammar School Worcester is a Registered Charity, number 1120644.

The Richard Pate School

Southern Road, Leckhampton, Cheltenham, Glos GL53 9RP

Tel:	01242 522086
email:	hm@richardpate.co.uk
website:	www.richardpate.co.uk

Chairman of Trustees: C Mourton, Esq

Headmaster: **R A MacDonald**, MEd, BA

Deputy Heads:
Mrs S Wade
P Lowe

Age Range. 3–11 Co-educational.
Number of Pupils. 300 (approximately an equal number of boys and girls).
Fees per term (2016–2017). Nursery: £1,070 (5 mornings), £1,422 (any 3 full days), £1,896 (any 4 full days),

£2,370 (5 full days). Preparatory: £2,405 (Reception), £2,580 (Year 1), £2,760 (Year 2). Junior: £2,885 (Year 3), £3,000 (Year 4), £3,200 (Year 5), £3,345 (Year 6).

Hot lunches are provided and included in the fees, except for 'mornings only' nursery.

The School, occupying an 11½ acre semi-rural site at the foot of the Cotswold escarpment, is part of the Pate's Grammar School Foundation which is a charity founded by Richard Pate, a Recorder of Gloucester, in 1574.

It is a non-denominational Christian school which in its present form began in 1946. The aim of the school is to provide a high academic standard and continuity of education up to the age of 11 years. The curriculum is broadly based with strong emphasis being attached to music, art, drama and sport, for these activities are seen as vital if a child's full potential is to be realised.

Facilities include a music centre with individual practice rooms; a fully equipped computer suite; an all-weather astroturf with floodlights and an enclosed pond for environmental studies. There is also a specialist wing with science labs, language suite and art studio. After-school care is available through until 5.30 pm.

At present the School is divided into three sections: Nursery 3–4½ years; Preparatory Department 5–7 and Junior 7–11. Entrance is dependent upon the availability of places but most pupils join the school at the commencement of the Nursery, Preparatory or Junior Departments.

No entry tests are taken by younger pupils but interviews and selective tests are used for assessing pupils aged 6 years and upwards. A small number of 7+ scholarships are awarded each year.

The teaching takes full account of national curriculum guidelines with children in the upper part of the school following the normal preparatory school curriculum leading to Common Entrance and Scholarship at 11+. Pupils leave at age 11 for local Grammar Schools and a variety of independent secondary schools, particularly those in Cheltenham.

The Headmaster is assisted by two deputies and 18 fully qualified teachers including specialists in Latin, French, History, Art/Design, Science, Music and Learning Support. The School employs music and dance teachers, who prepare children for participation in various competitions, in particular the Cheltenham Festival.

Charitable status. The Pate's Grammar School Foundation is a Registered Charity, number 311707.

Richmond House School

170 Otley Road, Leeds, West Yorkshire LS16 5LG
Tel: 0113 2752670
Fax: 0113 2304868
email: enquiries@rhschool.org
website: www.rhschool.org
Twitter: @RHSchoolLeeds
Facebook: /richmondhouseschool
LinkedIn: /richmond-house-school

Chairman of the Board of Governors: Ms C Shuttleworth

Headteacher: **Mrs Helen Stiles**

Age Range. 3–11.
Number of Day Pupils. 213 boys and girls.
Fees per term (2016–2017). Nursery: £1,848 (half days only), £2,888 (full time, including lunch), Reception to Year 6 £2,888, Lunches £197.

Richmond House School is an independent co-educational preparatory school providing an excellent standard of education for children aged 3 to 11 years within a happy, stimulating, family environment.

At Richmond House School, a team of dedicated staff is committed to giving each child the opportunity to develop into confident, hard-working and successful individuals.

All pupils are given the chance to learn and achieve across a broad range of activities and subject areas and the talents of each child are nurtured. The breadth of activities offered aims to challenge pupils, build self-confidence and lead pupils to discover new interests and skills.

The School boasts outstanding 11+ exam success with pupils having their choice of senior school and a substantial number being awarded scholarships.

In addition to strong academic credentials, Richmond House School is committed to providing all pupils with the opportunity to excel in other areas. The School is situated in 10 acres of land, providing excellent sports facilities and offering pupils a wide range of sports to choose from. The School also provides specialist teaching in Music, Art, Design Technology, Information Communication Technology, Languages and Science.

Pastoral Care is an important aspect of school life at Richmond House School. Our Deputy Head Teacher is responsible for leading Pastoral Care and works closely with staff, pupils and parents to ensure the well-being and progress of all pupils.

Excellent Pre and After School Care and an easily accessible car park and drop-off zone are available for busy families.

Charitable status. Richmond House School is a Registered Charity, number 505630. It exists to provide high quality education for boys and girls aged 3–11 years.

Riddlesworth Hall Preparatory School

Hall Lane, Nr Diss, Norfolk IP22 2TA
Tel: 01953 681246
Fax: 01953 688124
email: hmsec@riddlesworth-hall.com
website: www.riddlesworthhall.com

Principal: **Mrs Susan Hayes**

Age Range. Girls 2–13, Boys 2–13. Girls Boarding from age 7–13. Boys boarding from age 7–13.
Number of Pupils. 17 Boarders, 72 Day, 17 Nursery.
Fees per term (2016–2017). Full Boarders £6,200; Weekly Boarders £5,835; Day (inc Lunch): Years 3–8 £3,795; Years 1–2 £2,665; Nursery & Reception: £243.50 per am/pm session, lunch £170, £2,605 full-time inc lunch.

Riddlesworth Hall, situated in a magnificent country house on the Norfolk/Suffolk border, provides an excellent all-round education. The aim is to develop each child's potential to the full in all areas – academic, sport and creative arts. The boys and girls are prepared for Common Entrance and Scholarship examinations to independent senior schools.

Riddlesworth Hall has excellent art and pottery studios, science, domestic science and technology laboratories, a computer room, music and drama rooms and a refurbished gymnasium. French is taught from Reception. A range of sports is taught to all levels and good-quality teams are regularly produced.

The care of the children is in the hands of the Principal who is resident, supported by a team of matrons.

The school enjoys CreSTeD status and is specifically staffed to welcome dyslexic children. IEPs are prepared for these children, who enjoy all the benefits of full integration into main school activities.

Extras include speech and drama, ballet and riding. There is a very active music department with choirs, orchestra, various ensembles and a recorder group. Senior school music, drama and academic scholarships have been recently achieved.

There is a wide variety of clubs and activities including skiing, dance, ball skills, gym and cookery. A feature of Riddlesworth Hall is its Pets Corner which houses a variety of small animals brought from home and permanently resident at school.

Self-reliance, self-discipline, and tolerance are encouraged, and good manners are expected.

Ripley Court School

Rose Lane, Ripley, Surrey GU23 6NE

Tel: 01483 225217
Fax: 01483 223854
email: head@ripleycourt.co.uk
website: www.ripleycourt.co.uk

Chairman of Governors: J Evans, BA

Headmaster: **A J Gough**, BSc UED, MA

Deputy Head: G P Ryan, HDE Cape Town

Age Range. 3–13 Co-educational.

Number of Day Pupils. 276: Main School (age 7–13) 170; Little Court (age 4–7) 82; Nursery (age 3+) 24.

Fees per term (2016–2017). Main School £4,240–£4,420; Little Court £3,045–£3,250; Nursery £2,930 full-time (part-time pro rata).

Pupils start at any time from age 3, with main intakes at 3, 7 and 11 if there is room. They are prepared for Common Entrance and Scholarship Examinations for all the Boys' and Girls' Senior Independent Schools. There is a high academic standard and many Scholarships are won including for Sport, Music and Art, but there is a studious avoidance of cramming. In addition, PE, Music, Art and Craft and Food Technology are a part of every child's timetable. Forest School sessions are also taught on site from Nursery to Year 4. There are opportunities for all in orchestral, choral and dramatic productions – the school prides itself on ensuring every child can participate in all areas, including competitive sports fixtures.

Facilities include a library, science laboratories, a gymnasium, computer suite, art, music and food tech rooms. There are 20 acres of playing fields. Games and sports are Football (Association and Rugby), Hockey, Netball, Cricket, Tennis (2 hard, 2 grass courts), Athletics, Rounders, Volleyball, Stoolball; Swimming and Life Saving are taught in a large, covered, heated swimming pool.

Little Court is the Pre-Prep Department which also uses the main playing field, swimming pool and gymnasium and other specialist facilities.

The nursery, known as "The Ark", also uses all school facilities and nursery children receive specialist tuition in French, music, swimming and dance.

School transport serves Woking, Pyrford and West Byfleet.

Charitable status. Ripley Court School is a Registered Charitable Trust, number 312084. It aims to educate children and prepare them well for entry to their next school and for adult life. It offers scholarships as well as bursarial scholarships and bursaries on a means-tested basis. It is not-for-profit and all surplus funds are used to improve provision and facilities.

Rockport School

15 Rockport Road, Craigavad, Holywood, Co Down BT18 0DD, Northern Ireland

Tel: 028 9042 8372
Fax: 028 9042 2608
email: info@rockportschool.com
           schooloffice@rockportschool.com
website: www.rockportschool.com

Chairman of Governors: M J Burke, Esq

Headmaster: **George Vance**, BEd, LLB

Age Range. 3–18.

Number of Pupils. 108 Girls, 97 Boys.

Fees per term (2016–2017). Senior School: Day £4,285–£4,725, Boarding £5,5585–£8,190. Junior School: Day £2,040–£3,940, Boarding £4,590–£6,700 Nursery £1,135–£1,840.

Rockport School is the only independent preparatory and senior school in Northern Ireland. It is situated in and around a fine Victorian mansion in twenty-five acres of beautiful surroundings overlooking Belfast Lough and prides itself on bringing out the best in pupils of all abilities and talents.

The Pre-Prep and Nursery Schools are located in purpose-built buildings close to the main school. Children from ages 3 to 8 are placed in small mixed-ability classes of no more than 16 and are offered a broad curriculum, with French, Music and Sport taught by specialist teachers. The children enjoy use of all the school's facilities, particularly the outdoor space, woods and shore, whilst having their own dedicated play areas.

Pupils in the Preparatory School are prepared for 11+ examinations for transfer to local Grammar Schools or for Common Entrance and Scholarship examinations at 13+. There is an excellent record of pupils moving on to top independent schools throughout the UK.

The majority of pupils remain at the school until 18 and are prepared for GCE examinations. The school's relatively small size enables teaching to be highly individualised and annual results consistently outperform national averages and CAT predictions. The school's small and supportive Learning Support department assists this process.

Boarding is central to the life of the school and pupils are looked after by a caring staff dedicated to their welfare. With full, weekly and flexi boarding options, boarding pupils come from Northern Ireland, the rest of the UK and overseas, adding diversity to the Rockport community.

Games & Extracurricular activities. Sport, especially team games, is a significant part of the curriculum, as are Art, Music and Drama. The school takes full advantage of its beautiful location and has as varied a range of activities as any school of its size. Particular emphasis is placed on service to the environment and to others. There is a 100% participation in The Duke of Edinburgh's Award scheme in the senior school; the school's own coastal path and woodland, and the Mourne Mountains beyond are used extensively by the school.

Scholarships & Bursaries. Scholarships are awarded at 11+ to pupils who show academic excellence and Bursaries are available to children of HM Forces.

Charitable status. Rockport School Limited is a Registered Charity, number XN48119. It exists to provide education for boys and girls.

Rokeby School

George Road, Kingston-upon-Thames, Surrey KT2 7PB

Tel: 020 8942 2247
Fax: 020 8942 5707
email: hmsec@rokeby.org.uk
website: www.rokebyschool.co.uk
Twitter: @RokebyPrep

Maxim: *Smart, Skilful and Kind*

Chairman of the Governors: Mr Charles Carter

Headmaster: **Mr J R Peck**

Age Range. 4–13.
Number of Boys. 370.
Fees per term (2016–2017). £4,298–£5,352 (including lunch, books and all compulsory extras).

Rokeby has an outstanding record of success in Common Entrance and Scholarships to leading Independent Senior Schools. Boys are accepted at 4+ to the Pre-Prep and at 7+ to the Prep School.

In recent years a fabulous two-storey, energy-efficient new building was opened by HRH Princess Alexandra. It has six spacious classrooms, a multi-purpose Performing Arts Hall, as well as other lovely spaces built to house Reception, Year 1 and Year 2 Rokeby boys. The spacious and exciting playground area is enjoyed by all year groups and includes an outside classroom, an adventure playground with balance wall and an area for gardening club to grow seeds and encourage wildlife.

Science is taught in three well-equipped Laboratories. There is a large Computer Room and a very spacious Art and Design Technology Centre. Football, Rugby, and Cricket are played while other sports include Swimming, Athletics, Hockey and Basketball. There are two large Halls and an Astroturf. A full activities programme is available for boys from Chess Club to Golf. The Music Department provides Orchestra, Ensembles and four Choirs and there are fourteen visiting peripatetic teachers, who work within a sound-proofed music block.

There are a number of educational school trips arranged as well as trips overseas, including France, Italy, Iceland and a number of overseas sports tours, including Sri Lanka, Canada, Holland and Spain. The school operates a bus service to the Wimbledon and Putney areas.

Charitable status. Rokeby Educational Trust Limited is a Registered Charity, number 312653. It exists to provide an excellent education for boys aged 4–13.

Rose Hill School

Coniston Avenue, Tunbridge Wells, Kent TN4 9SY

Tel: 01892 525591
Fax: 01892 533312
email: admissions@rosehillschool.co.uk
website: www.rosehillschool.co.uk
Twitter: @rosehillschool

Chairman of Governing Body: Mr Charles Arthur

Headmaster: **P D Westcombe**, BA, PGCE

Deputy Head: W R Skottowe, BSc Hons, PGCE

Age Range. 3–13.
Number of Pupils. 173 Boys, 135 Girls.

Fees per term (2016–2017). £4,785 (Years 3–8); £3,575 (Reception–Year 2); £2,075–£2,350 (Kindergarten).

The school is situated in seventeen acres of beautiful grounds adjacent to the green belt, but within five minutes of the centre of the town. A superb Pre-Preparatory building was opened in 1991, followed by a new ICT centre. A Sports Hall was completed in 1998 and a new dining room and kitchen in 1999. Facilities also include an outdoor heated swimming pool and 6-hole golf course. A new block, comprising six classrooms, library and changing rooms, was completed in 2003 and linked to a superb Theatre and Creative Arts Centre in September 2008. An astroturf pitch was completed in 2010 and a £2.2m new teaching facility was opened in 2013. The building took 12 months to complete and is packed with state-of-the-art facilities, including a 95m² science laboratory, six teaching classrooms, two ICT suites, a learning skills suite and a surgery for the school nurse.

Children are prepared for Common Entrance and Scholarship entry to Independent Senior Schools and for competitive entry into local grammar schools at 11+ and 13+. Small classes, combined with an enriching curriculum, specialist teachers and exceptional pastoral care, ensure the pupils find and fulfil their potential.

Rose Hill was judged to be 'excellent' in all areas at its last inspection, with pastoral care particularly highlighted. The friendly and supportive atmosphere means children feel happy and secure.

Sport and the Creative Arts are highly valued. Hockey, Football, Rugby, Netball, Cricket, Rounders and Athletics are the main team games and they are supported by a range of individual sports. There is a junior and senior choir and many children receive instrumental tuition. Two major drama productions take place every year.

A full range of extracurricular clubs, including Cubs and Brownies, ensures breadth of experience. Within a secure environment, based on clear Christian principles, children are encouraged to meet new challenges with confidence.

Charitable status. Rose Hill School is a Registered Charity, number 270158. It aims to provide a high quality education to boys and girls aged 3–13.

Rosemead Preparatory School

70 Thurlow Park Road, Dulwich, London SE21 8HZ

Tel: 020 8670 5865
Fax: 020 8761 9159
email: admissions@rosemeadprepschool.org.uk
website: www.rosemeadprepschool.org.uk

Headteacher: **Mr A Bray**, Cert Ed

Age Range. 3–11.
Number of Pupils. Day: 170 Boys, 184 Girls.
Fees per term (2016–2017). £3,424–£3,912.

Rosemead is a well-established preparatory school with a fine record of academic achievement. Children are prepared for entrance to leading independent London day schools and local grammar schools at age 11, many gaining awards and scholarships. The school has a happy, family atmosphere with boys and girls enjoying a varied, balanced curriculum which includes maths, English, science, French, Spanish, information and communication technology, arts, physical education and humanities. Music and drama are strong subjects with tuition available in most orchestral instruments and various music groups meeting frequently. A full programme of physical education includes gymnastics, most major games, dance and (from age 6) swimming. Classes make regular visits to places of interest. Two residential field studies courses are arranged for children in the Prep department and activity courses are arranged during school holidays. Main entry to the school is at Nursery (age 3), following an informal assessment, and at National Curriculum Year 3, following a formal assessment. The school is administered by a board of governors elected annually by the parents.

All religious denominations welcome.

A small number of bursaries are available from Year 3.

Charitable status. Rosemead Preparatory School (The Thurlow Educational Trust) is a Registered Charity, number 1186165. It exists to provide a high standard of education in a happy, caring environment.

Rowan Preparatory School
United Learning

6 Fitzalan Road, Claygate, Esher, Surrey KT10 0LX

Tel:	01372 462627
Fax:	01372 470782
email:	school.office@rowanprepschool.co.uk
website:	www.rowanprepschool.co.uk
Twitter:	@Rowan_Prep

Rowan is a dynamic, happy school, which prepares girls (aged 2–11) for the challenges they will face in life, helping them to develop compassion, respect and a lifelong love of learning. We value all our girls as individuals and attach great importance to the quality of teaching and learning that is at the very heart of our philosophy on education.

Chairman of the Local Governing Body: Mrs Karen Bowles

Headteacher: **Mrs Susan Clarke**, BEd, NPQH

Age Range. 2–11 (Pre-Preparatory age 2–7, Preparatory age 7–11).

Number of Pupils. 320 Day Girls.

Fees per term (2016–2017). Nursery (5 mornings) £1,375; Kindergarten (5 mornings) £1,798; Reception–Year 6 £3,517–£4,666.

In 1936, Miss Katherine Millar was determined to breathe new life into the English educational system. She wished to create an environment which inspired a passion for learning. The doors of Rowan were opened wide to enable girls to develop a strong sense of self and establish lasting friendships. Three quarters of a century on, Katherine Millar's core values are firmly established in the school. Girls achieve personal excellence in a warm, family environment.

As our motto says 'Hic Feliciter Laboramus'. Here we work happily.

The school is located on two sites very close to each other in a leafy part of Claygate. Rowan Brae accommodates the Nursery and Pre-Prep and Rowan Hill, the Prep.

Upon entering the Brae you cannot fail to notice the warm, friendly and happy atmosphere. The stimulating learning environment, both indoors and outdoors, creates an inspiring and engaging place to learn. Outstanding lessons and excellent resources allow all pupils to thrive and reach their potential. Girls in Year 2 are fully prepared for the seamless transition and exciting challenges which lay ahead at the Hill.

Girls at the Hill develop a thirst for knowledge, an appreciation of all subject areas and a deeper understanding of how to analyse and apply information across different areas of learning and in everyday life. The varied creative and outdoor curriculum continues to stimulate and inspire in all subject areas of day-to-day learning. Dynamic and challeng-

ing lessons, adapted to suit the girls' needs ensure that they can truly achieve personal excellence. There is a superb ICT Suite, which was funded by the very supportive parents association, The Friends of Rowan, and well-equipped playgrounds and adventure walkways with a wooded area called The Spinney, which is held in great affection by the girls.

Admission in the Early Years is non-selective. Early registration is advisable if a place in the pre-prep is to be assured. Girls wishing to enter at other stages will be invited for a Taster Day where they will experience a day in the life of Rowan, involving assessments in maths and English.

Girls are prepared for entry to a wide variety of senior independent day and boarding schools. There is an excellent record of girls gaining places at their senior school of choice, including each year a number of girls being offered academic, music, sports or art scholarships.

Rowan offers a broad-based curriculum of work so that each pupil is able to develop her own talents and maximize her potential through an adventurous learning approach. The school welcomes visiting speakers and performers to enhance the curriculum. Day trips are also included in each term and the annual residential trips to Sayers Croft, The Isle of Wight, European ski resorts and France are both popular and highly educational in content. In addition, a wide variety of clubs are offered before and after school and at lunchtimes; they include drama, chess, art, science, foreign languages and a host of sports and musical activities. In addition, breakfast club and after-school prep clubs are available to support families.

Rowan has an excellent Music Department with all girls singing in a choir and playing the recorder. In addition, three-quarters of girls at the Hill play a further instrument. There are various ensembles, which the girls can also join in preparation for the orchestra. Girls at Rowan Brae are invited to play the violin or 'cello as part of the school's String Initiative during Year 1, a fantastic opportunity to learn about music and performance.

The school has excellent sporting opportunities and achievements. Girls have the chance to represent the school both locally and nationally for sports such as swimming, gymnastics, tennis and biathlon. Games are developed throughout the school with girls taking part in their first matches from Year 2.

Rowan is very proud of its art, providing stunning displays around both the Brae and the Hill expressing the girls' individuality and excellent capabilities.

With small classes on both sites and strong pastoral care it is Rowan's aim to provide the essential early grounding in a happy, stimulating and secure environment where every child's needs are catered for.

Prospective parents are asked to make an appointment to view the school during a normal working day or to attend one of the Open Mornings held each term. Girls entering the school at 7+ will be invited to take part in an assessment day which take place in November and January.

Assisted places and Scholarships are available and details may be obtained upon request from the school Registrar.

Charitable status. Rowan has a Local Governing Body that plays an active and supportive role in the school. Rowan is part of United Learning which is an educational trust controlled by a Board of Governors and chaired by Mr Richard Greenhalgh which comprises: UCST (a Company Limited by Guarantee, Registered in England, number 2780748, and a Registered Charity, number 1016538) and ULT (a Company Limited by Guarantee, Registered in England, number 4439859, and an Exempt Charity).

The Rowans School

19 Drax Avenue, Wimbledon, London SW20 0EG
Tel: 020 8946 8220
email: office@rowans.org.uk
website: www.rowans.org.uk

Chairman of Governors: Mrs P L Hughes, CBE

Head: **Mrs J Hubbard**, MA, BA Hons, PGCE, PG Dip
SEN

Age Range. 3–7 Co-educational.
Number of Pupils. 120.
Fees per term (2016–2017). Kindergarten £2,250,
Reception, Year 1 and Year 2 £4,100.

The Rowans School was inspected by the Independent
Schools Inspectorate (ISI) in October 2013 and was given a
rating of "Excellent" in every area, the highest rating possible.

The school is one of the few independent co-educational
schools in the area and is situated in a quiet road in Wimbledon, with beautiful grounds and large landscaped gardens,
including its own tennis court. We pride ourselves on providing a nurturing, welcoming and happy start to school life.
We have a long-standing reputation for academic and all-
round excellence and sport, music and the creative arts contribute strongly to the school's lively curriculum.

The focus of our curriculum is to build strong academic
foundations, encouraging a love of learning and enabling
our children to discover and develop their personal strengths
and talents. We prepare children for the 7+ examinations to
many of the London Day Schools and have a highly successful track record of sending to the top local prep schools.
Class sizes are kept to a maximum of 24 children, with at
least one teaching assistant in every class. Music and sport
are taught by specialist teachers and children are offered the
opportunity of learning violin and piano.

The school takes full advantage of its location with frequent outings for each year group to museums, theatres and
the local environment.

The school is very much a family school, with a warm,
friendly, child-centred atmosphere.

Charitable status. The Rowans School is owned by
King's College School, which is a Registered Charity, number 310024.

The Royal Masonic School for Girls
Pre-School, Pre-Prep and Prep Departments

Rickmansworth Park, Rickmansworth, Herts WD3 4HF
Tel: 01923 725337 (Cadogan House Pre-Prep and
            Prep Department)
            01923 725316 (Ruspini House Pre-School)
Fax: 01923 725532
email: prep@royalmasonic.herts.sch.uk
website: www.royalmasonic.herts.sch.uk

Chairman of Governors: Mr J Gould

Head: Mr K Carson, MPhil Cantab, PGCE

Head of Cadogan House Pre-Prep & Prep Departments:
Mr I Connors, BA Hons, NPQH

Acting Head of Ruspini House Pre-School: Mrs L Sumner

Age Range. Ruspini House: 2–4 Co-educational. Cadogan House: Girls 4–11.
Number of Pupils. Ruspini House 62; Cadogan House
235.
Fees per term (2016–2017). Cadogan House: Boarders
(Years 3–6): £6,450 (Full), £6,115 (Weekly); Day Pupils:
£3,485 (Reception, Years 1 and 2), £4,040 (Years 3–6). Ruspini House: please visit our website for range of fees.

Ruspini House is a small, friendly, caring community
within the larger RMS family, guided by the same inclusive
and nurturing ethos.

Housed in totally refurbished, modern and bespoke facilities and sharing our stunning grounds, Ruspini House welcomes boys and girls from 2 to 4 years. The youngest RMS
pupils quickly settle into the stimulating, happy and supportive environment where all children are encouraged to reach
their full potential through a healthy balance of learning and
play.

We follow the principles of the Early Years Foundation
Stage Curriculum and focus on each child's individual needs
and talents. We encourage each child to develop at their own
pace and they are well prepared for entry into their first
school.

Recognised by the ISI as outstanding (2014), Ruspini
House lays firm foundations for a love of learning. Boys and
girls develop independence, curiosity and enthusiasm, learn
good manners, courtesy and consideration for others within
a busy and supportive framework, where they are challenged and have fun at the same time.

Cadogan House is the stunning, spacious and refurbished home of the RMS Pre-Preparatory and Preparatory
Departments for girls aged 4 to 11 years. Recognised as
excellent in all areas, Cadogan House is a warm and vibrant
community alive with the buzz of happy, enthusiastic and
motivated young learners, each of whom is valued as an
individual.

The girls benefit from all of the facilities afforded by our
magnificent site, including a designated Outdoor Learning
Area. We have Forest School status, giving pupils experiences which complement traditional classroom learning,
while building self-esteem, confidence and well-being.

The learning opportunities are exceptionally broad with
outstanding teaching from both subject specialists and class
teachers. Small class sizes ensure that teachers quickly get
to know the girls and focus on nurturing their individual talents and strengths to enable them to become well-rounded
independent young people. In Pre-Prep, English and Maths
are taught each day as individual subject areas, whilst Science and Humanities are covered through cross-curricular
work. In Years 3 to 6, girls study English, Mathematics, Science, Art, DT, French, Geography, History, Computing,
Music, PE, PSHCE and Religious Studies, with several subjects taught by subject specialists.

Extra-curricular activities abound and sport and Performing Arts have a high profile; girls receive five PE lessons per
week, including Swimming, Gymnastics and Dance, and all
girls receive music and singing lessons each week, with
most playing at least one musical instrument.

Above all, Cadogan House girls learn to exemplify the
core RMS values of courtesy, compassion, and respect for
others.

Charitable status. The Royal Masonic School Limited is
a Registered Charity, number 276784.

Royal Russell Junior School

Coombe Lane, Croydon, Surrey CR9 5BX
Tel: 020 8651 5884
Fax: 020 8651 4169
email: juniorschool@royalrussell.co.uk
website: www.royalrussell.co.uk
Twitter: @Royal_Russell
           @RRS_Sport

Patron: Her Majesty The Queen

Chairman of Governors: Mr K Young

Headmaster: Mr James C Thompson, BA QTS St Mary's
Twickenham

Head of Lower Juniors: Mrs Amanda Burton Smith, BA
QTS, MA Ed
Head of Upper Juniors: Mrs Sarah Pain, BSc, PGCE, MA
Ed Mgt

Age Range. 3–11.
Number of Pupils. 168 Boys, 141 Girls.
Fees per term (2016–2017). Upper Juniors (Years 3–4)
£4,235 (Years 5–6) £4,410, Lower Juniors (Reception–Year
2) £3,460, Nursery £1,940–£3,460.

The Junior School stands on a magnificent wooded campus extending to over 100 acres, which it shares with Royal Russell Senior School (11–18 years). (*See Royal Russell School entry in HMC section.*)

The school is well served by road, tram and rail links and is one of the few co-educational schools in the Croydon area.

There is a fully-qualified teaching staff of 31. The school has a broad curriculum which seeks to blend the highest standards of academic work with a wide range of co-curricular activities. There are opportunities for all pupils to participate in football, netball, hockey, rounders, cross-country and cricket as team sports, and as individuals to be coached in athletics, swimming, tennis, gymnastics, trampolining and table tennis. There is an extensive fixture list of matches against other schools. Artistic development extends to include full dramatic and musical productions, and many pupils learn musical instruments. All forms of art, design and technology are actively encouraged. There are excellent teaching facilities which are complemented by an Assembly Hall, Science Laboratories, Music School, Art Room, Computer Suite, School Chapel and a Performing Arts Centre with a 200-seat auditorium. For sport, the impressive facilities include a large Sports Hall, Gymnasium, floodlit all-weather pitch for hockey and tennis, multi-use games area, netball courts, 4 grass pitches for athletics, football and cricket and an indoor swimming pool. All Junior School pupils receive weekly swimming lessons from qualified instructors.

The majority of the pupils join the school at 3 years into our Nursery, and transfer to the Senior School at 11+. Candidates for entry to the Lower Juniors and Early Years are interviewed informally, while all other entrants sit assessments in English, Mathematics and Cognitive Ability appropriate to their ages.

Prospective parents are very welcome to come and meet the Headmaster and to tour the school, by appointment.

Charitable status. Royal Russell School is a Registered Charity, number 271907. It exists solely to provide education to girls and boys.

Rupert House School

90 Bell Street, Henley-on-Thames, Oxon RG9 2BN
Tel: 01491 574263
Fax: 01491 573988
email: office@ruperthouse.oxon.sch.uk
website: www.ruperthouse.org
Twitter: @ruperthouse
Facebook: @RupertHouseSchool

Chair of Governors: Mrs A Collinson, MA Oxon

Head: Mrs C Lynas, MA Hons English St Andrews,
PGCE, MA Child Development London, NPQH

Age Range. Girls 3–11, Boys 3–7.
Number of Pupils. Girls 164, Boys 42.
Fees per term (2016–2017). £1,800 (mornings only for 3 year olds) to £4,375 (inclusive).

RUPERT HOUSE is a town school with beautiful spacious grounds and playing fields, situated on the edge of Henley. The school is a day pre-prep and prep school for girls aged 3–11 and boys aged 3–7. It has a 100% success rate for girls achieving a place at their preferred senior school with an average of 60% of the Year 6 girls winning scholarships to top independent schools. The strength and breadth of the curriculum is reflected in range of scholarships the girls attain, including Academic, Sport, Art, Music and Drama. The school also prepares girls to sit the 11+, gaining coveted grammar school places.

Rupert House offers a stimulating and varied curriculum, which includes Forest School, Path Hill Club and Outdoor Education, with access to acres of privately-owned woods nearby. The Upper School pupils enjoy residential trips, including the Year 4 Bushcraft trip, the Year 5 Field Studies trip and the Year 6 trip to France.

Drama at the school is ambitious and culminates in an annual Upper School production at the Kenton Theatre in Henley. Music is a strength with a wide range of instruments taught, orchestras, bands and renowned choirs. All pupils learn the recorder, the violin and the keyboard in their Music lessons. Sport has been given an increased allocation in the timetable and weekly fixtures are held with local prep schools. Swimming happens all year round and the children enjoy Athletics, Tennis, Cricket and Rounders in the summer. Other sports include Football, Netball, Gymnastics, Cross Country and Hockey.

The school day is enhanced by numerous after-school activities including Drumming, Jazz Dance, Musical Theatre, Film Animation, Computer Coding, Touch Typing, Think Tank and Sudoku.

Within a disciplined framework, where courtesy and consideration are expected, there is a friendly, family atmosphere in which the individual personality and aspirations of each child are respected. Indeed, the school puts great emphasis on every child's individual academic pathway. The pupils are encouraged to match their performance to potential and to meet all challenges with enthusiasm and determination. There are regular consultation evenings in addition to a half-term and an end-of-term report. Parents may consult the Head at any time by appointment.

Care is taken to ensure that pupils are well prepared for transfer to a school suited to their academic ability and personal qualities. In recent years, girls have gained admission to well-respected independent senior schools and boys to excellent prep schools.

Bursaries are offered to children from Reception through to Year 6 and a range of scholarships is available for places in the Upper School (Year 3 and above).

Charitable status. Rupert House School is a Registered Charity, number 309648. It exists to provide quality education for boys and girls.

Russell House

Station Road, Otford, Sevenoaks, Kent TN14 5QU
Tel: 01959 522352
email: head@russellhouse.kent.sch.uk
website: www.russellhouseschool.co.uk
Twitter: @RussellHouseSch
Facebook: /Russell-House

Head: **Mr Craig McCarthy**

Age Range. Co-educational 2–11+.
Number of Pupils. Boys 100, Girls 100.
Fees per term (2016–2017). Russell Robins (Under 3s) £710 (2 mornings plus optional afternoon sessions), Nursery Department (5 mornings) £1,890, Transition (5 mornings) £1,950, Reception £3,240, Years 1–2 £3,730, Year 3 £3,827 Year 4 £4,170, Years 5–6 £4,300 (including lunch).

Russell House is a family-friendly school for girls and boys aged from 2 to 11.

We have a reputation for achieving excellent academic results in a warm, caring and inclusive atmosphere where every child has access to myriad opportunities for extra-curricular activities.

Many of our pupils are successful in the 11+ examination, gaining entry to the local grammar schools, and others pass on to independent schools such as Sevenoaks. We have a consistently good record in gaining scholarships, both academic and music which goes hand in hand with an ethos which encourages individuality, self-expression, curiosity to learn and the ability to challenge accepted wisdom.

The school is careful to cultivate a calm, happy atmosphere and there is also a strong emphasis on building skills for the future and developing a sensitive awareness of the world beyond the school.

Ryde School with Upper Chine Junior School

Queen's Road, Ryde, Isle of Wight PO33 3BE
Tel: 01983 612901
email: junior.office@rydeschool.net
website: www.rydeschool.org.uk
Twitter: @rydeschool
Facebook: @rydeschool2013

Chairman of the Board of Governors: Dr C J Martin, BSc, DPhil, MBA, FIChemE, CEng

Head: **Mrs Linda Dennis**, BEd

Age Range. 2½ –11.
Number of Pupils. 124 Boys, 124 Girls.
Fees per term (from January 2017). Tuition: Foundation Stage: £2,150–£2,380 (full day), £1,090 (half day); Pre-Prep £2,580–£3,295; Junior School £3,990. Boarding (excluding tuition): £4,960 (full), £3,985 (weekly). Rates for payment by Direct Debit. Lunch included.

Scholarships may be awarded on merit to external or internal candidates for entry at 9+. All scholarships may be supplemented by bursaries, which are means tested.

Ryde Junior School and Fiveways aim to provide an ambitious, happy and supportive environment, one in which children thrive and develop a lifelong love of learning. They benefit from a varied and relevant programme of study supplemented by enriching extracurricular activities as we seek to prepare our pupils for an exciting future that we cannot even imagine.

Ryde Junior School caters for children aged 2½–11 years. Fiveways, in its own separate building, a stone's throw from the main Junior School, is home to the Foundation Stage and Early Years. Through creative and imaginative teaching in new purpose-built classrooms, a sound foundation of key skills is established. At the end of Key Stage 1 pupils are ready to move to the 'senior' part of the Junior School, having already benefited from some specialist teaching in the Junior School. Here they continue to receive the support of a well-qualified and dedicated staff, enjoying a full range of specialist facilities including a continually upgraded ICT facility, with Internet access across the school, a Creative Centre, Science Laboratory, Music room and Theatre.

A broad, balanced and rich curriculum is followed. Our pupils have the unique opportunity to study and develop a love of languages from an early age. As the original host school for the Isle of Wight Literary Festival Schools programme, our children benefit from the thrill of visiting authors, poets and script writers. Pupils are encouraged to develop their full range of talents. In Music they are able to compose and perform. Many pupils undertake individual instrumental lessons. There are choirs, music groups and an orchestra. As well as the weekly classroom drama lessons, we enter children into examinations run by the English Speaking Board and they take part in shows and festivals across the Island. Art and Design Technology are taught as discrete subjects and clubs, competitions and exhibitions also allow the children to develop their talents. Sports teams start at U8 level and we compete successfully against Island and mainland prep schools in netball, hockey, rugby, football, athletics (indoor and outdoor), cricket, rounders and cross country. Every child will be able to sail by the end of Year 6 and swimming and tennis also make up part of our extensive sports programme. Our new outdoor education programme and stunning new classroom provides an inspirational environment for the children to learn, grow and develop. There is a full and wide ranging programme of clubs and activities (which changes each term) during lunchtime and after school, offering something for everyone.

Our Senior School is on the same campus, enabling us to benefit from the use of a Sports Hall and pitches. Careful liaison between the staff and induction days in the summer term effect a smooth transition for our pupils to the Senior School (*see entry in HMC section*).

The Junior School takes weekly and full boarders who, together with Senior School boarders, have use of the range of facilities available at the Bembridge campus, situated in some 100 acres on a beautiful clifftop site approximately six miles from Ryde. Transport is provided to and from the school during the week.

Charitable status. Ryde School with Upper Chine is a Registered Charity, number 307409. The aims and objectives of the Charity are the education of boys and girls.

Rydes Hill Preparatory School

Rydes Hill House, Aldershot Road, Guildford, Surrey GU2 8BP
Tel: 01483 563160
email: admissions@rydeshill.com
website: www.rydeshill.com
Twitter: @rydeshillprep

Chairman of the Governors: Mr Dermot Gleeson, MA Cantab

Headmistress: **Mrs Stephanie Bell**, MA Oxon

Age Range. Girls 3–11, Boys 3–7. Nursery class for children 3–4.

Number of Day Pupils. 198.

Fees per term (2016–2017). £2,743–£4,083 including lunch.

Rydes Hill Preparatory School and Nursery has an exceptionally caring, family atmosphere. It has a thriving Nursery and is a Catholic School which welcomes children from all denominations and offers an excellent start academically and socially.

Although Rydes Hill Preparatory School and Nursery is non-selective academically, it achieves outstanding results and received the top rating in every category in the most recent ISI Inspection in June 2011. *"The pupils' achievements, attitudes and skills are excellent"*, *"The teaching is excellent"*, *"Pupils are keen to learn and they make excellent progress"*, *"The pupils' moral awareness is excellent"*.

Experienced and dedicated teachers encourage self-esteem and help pupils excel. Year after year, a high percentage of Year Six pupils are awarded scholarships to leading senior schools. Music, French, Ballet, Drama, Science, Sport including swimming, ICT and Art are taught by specialist teachers. Every pupil performs in one of the school's productions and the creative arts are major strengths of the School.

Extra-Curricular activities include: Speech and Drama, Ballet, Junior and Senior Choirs, Orchestra, Gymnastics, Instrumental Music Tuition (Pianoforte, Clarinet, Flute, Violin, Trumpet, Harp, Guitar, Cornet, and Cello), Tennis, French, Italian, as well as Mathematical Challenge, Netball and Cross Country Clubs. An extended school day is available from the 7.30 am Breakfast Club to the 5.30 pm Stay & Play Club, which includes a healthy afternoon tea. Supervised homework sessions are also offered every day.

Rydes Hill Preparatory School and Nursery is located in a beautiful Georgian house with a panelled Library, vaulted Dining Hall, Victorian Conservatory and galleried, panelled Entrance Hall. Facilities also include a large Science Laboratory, ICT Suite, Netball and Tennis Courts and a purpose-built Music and Performing Arts Studio.

Charitable status. Rydes Hill Preparatory School and Nursery is a Registered Charity, number 299411. It exists to ensure excellence in all aspects of education.

The Ryleys

Alderley Edge, Cheshire SK9 7UY

Tel:	01625 583241
Fax:	01625 581900
email:	info@theryleys.com
website:	www.theryleys.com
Twitter:	@TheRyleys
Facebook:	@The-Ryleys

Chairman of Governors: Mr B Staples

Headteacher: **Mrs Claire Hamilton**, BSc Hons, PGCE

Age Range. 2–11.

Number of Pupils. 206 Day Boys, 64 Day Girls.

Fees per term (2016–2017). Reception, Years 1 and 2 £3,247, Years 3–4 £3,363, Years 5–6 £3,653, Pre-School and Nursery: £26 (7.30 am to 12.30 pm), £46 (7.30 am to 4.30 pm), £56 (7.30 am to 6.30 pm).

Having a long history dating back to the 1870s, The Ryleys has developed a reputation as one of the best independent preparatory schools in the North West, with places at the school being much sought after. Situated in the idyllic village of Alderley Edge, the popular school lies in the heart of the leafy Cheshire countryside, just 15 miles south of the city of Manchester, within easy reach of the motorway and rail networks and close to Manchester Airport.

Starting at age 2, the extremely popular Nursery gently prepares its pupils for the start of their educational journey, and provides the girls and boys with the advantage of familiarity with the school as they come to take the next step on to formal education.

As the children move through the school, the small class sizes and subject specialist teaching ensures that each and every child receives the individual attention, motivation and encouragement necessary to fulfil their potential. Head-teacher Claire Hamilton aims to send children on to the next stage of their education as confident, enthusiastic and caring individuals who are ready to grasp every opportunity available to them.

The Ryleys provides so much more than just an academic education; it provides unrivalled opportunities to discover and nurture talents outside of the classroom, including music, sport, art and drama.

Children are thoroughly prepared for entry via examination into Independent Day Schools at 11. The school has an excellent academic record.

By the time they leave The Ryleys, pupils are equipped with the skills, character and confidence to see them achieve their future goals. All leavers go on to achieve places at highly regarded independent day and boarding schools of their choice, with many winning prestigious music, sports or academic scholarships.

Football, Rugby, Cricket, Athletics, Hockey, Rounders and Netball are the main team games and there is an extensive fixture list of matches against other schools at various ages. The school has undertaken sports tours to Italy and Spain in the last few years and there is an annual skiing trip to Europe or North America.

Music is another of the school's great strengths with well over 130 children receiving individual instrumental tuition from a highly-qualified staff of 9 visiting teachers. The school has a fine reputation for its concerts and musical productions. These performances take place on a full proscenium stage and every child is involved in one of the four productions each year. There are three choirs involving over 70 children.

Children are accepted into the school at various ages providing places are available and are informally assessed upon entry so that the correct educational provision can be made in order to ensure that each pupil achieves his/her full potential. Scholarships and Bursaries are available.

The school places great emphasis upon such personal qualities as good manners and consideration for others.

Charitable status. The Ryleys School Limited is a Registered Charity, number 525915. It exists to provide a quality education for children from 2 to 11 years of age.

St Albans High School for Girls Preparatory School

Codicote Road, Wheathampstead, Hertfordshire AL4 8DJ

Tel:	01582 839270
Fax:	01582 839271

email: Prep@stahs.org.uk
website: www.stahs.org.uk
Twitter: @STAHSPrep

Chair of School Council: Miss Dorothy Henderson, MA Cantab, MA Birkbeck

Head of the Preparatory School: Mrs Judy Rowe, BEd

Age Range. Girls 4–11.
Number of Pupils. 300.
Fees per term (2016–2017). Reception (age 4) £4,405 (inc Lunch), Years 1 and 2 (age 5–6) £4,650 (inc Lunch); Years 3–6 (age 7–11) £4,650 (exc Lunch).

The Preparatory School for St Albans High School for Girls is a very popular, academically selective school, with a welcoming family atmosphere, offering outstanding pastoral care. St Albans High School is uniquely placed in being able to offer all the advantages of a continuous education in two very different settings. From the ages of 4–11, the girls have the freedom to grow and develop in an attractive rural environment, before moving on to the more urban setting of the Senior School, close to the heart of the City of St Albans.

The Preparatory School is set in 18 acres of grounds within the village of Wheathampstead. It has large playing areas, a meadow and school woods, where girls engage in Forest school activities.

The curriculum is broad, embracing the National Curriculum and beyond. A central focus is placed on thinking skills, creativity and independent learning. Excellent facilities include an ICT suite and Science lab. New technologies are used to support learning, with SMART boards, laptops, iPads and Kindles, in addition to the computers in the ICT suite. Pupils at the Preparatory School use the school swimming pool located at the Senior School.

It is a happy and exciting school with a wide variety of activity days and educational visits throughout the school year. There is an extensive range of clubs including Art, Speech and Drama, Dancing, Sports, Orienteering, Karate, Fencing, Chess and Coding. Music is a real strength of the school and there are many music groups, choirs and an orchestra. Enrichment groups extend and support learning and there are opportunities for highly talented pupils to join with Senior School girls for events.

The School provides a supportive, challenging and creative environment, where girls work hard, are very successful academically and enjoy learning.

Open Days. Prep School in Action Morning: Friday 4 November 2016; Prep School Open Morning: Saturday 1 October 2016.

Charitable status. St Albans High School for Girls is a Registered Charity, number 311065.

St Andrew's Prep

Meads, Eastbourne, East Sussex BN20 7RP
Tel: 01323 733203
Fax: 01323 646860
email: admissions@standrewsprep.co.uk
website: www.standrewsprep.co.uk

Open Events: Thursday 4 May 2017, 6.00 to 8.00 pm; Friday 5 May 2017, 9.30am to 12 noon

Chairman of the Governing Body: General Sir Kevin O'Donoghue, KCB, CBE

Head: Mr Gareth Jones

Age Range. 9 months–13 years.

Number of Pupils. 254 (Prep School), 126 (Pre-Prep and Nursery).
Fees per term (2016–2017). Full boarding £7,735; Weekly Boarding £6,870; Flexible boarding – supplements from £20 per night; Day children: £5,450 (Years 4–8), £4,950 (Year 3), Pre-Prep £3,135. Nursery sessions: We offer the EYEE grant and sessions start from £20 for 3 to 4 year olds claiming the EYEE grant. For 2 to 3 year olds, sessions start from £31. For babies aged 9 to 24 months, sessions start from £32. Sessions run from 8 am to 1 pm and 1 pm to 6 pm, 8 am to 4 pm and 8 am to 6 pm. Please contact the Registrar for more details.

St Andrew's is positioned within 12 acres of beautifully tended grounds at the foot of the South Downs and is just a five minute walk to the beach. The school, founded in 1877, has a highly qualified teaching staff and children are taught in classes with a maximum size of 20 and an average number of approximately 16. A number of children in the Prep department are boarders and the school operates a popular scheme of flexi boarding allowing day children to stay any number of nights during the week on a flexible basis.

The Head is supported by a Deputy Head and a strong management team. All children in the school have a Form Teacher or Form Tutor who is responsible for their pastoral welfare and academic progress. Each section of the school has its own Head (Nursery and Pre-Prep, Junior, Middle and Senior), who coordinates, together with the Deputy Head and Academic Directors, the overall pastoral and academic work of the staff.

In addition to the expanse of playing fields, St Andrew's benefits from its own indoor swimming pool, newly refurbished netball and tennis courts and a new state-of-the-art sports hall and dance studio which was opened by Baroness Tanni Grey-Tompson in September 2016 to provide excellent sporting provision for its pupils.

There are three computer/iPad suites equipped with up-to-date software and hardware including a wireless network connection. There is an interactive whiteboard in every classroom. The equipment in the Pre-Prep suite is designed specifically for children from 3 to 7 years of age.

Other facilities include a modern purpose-built music block, an extensively equipped research and resource centre, a chapel, a Forest School and a creative arts centre with an art studio and design and technology facilities. The school strongly encourages music and drama and more than three quarters of the children play instruments and participate in orchestras, bands and choirs.

As well as music, drama is a timetabled subject and plays take place every term.

From the age of nine, children are taught by subject specialists. French is taught from the age of 5 and Latin is introduced from the age of 9. Children are introduced to working on computers from the age of two. The breadth of the curriculum means that, while the requirements of the National Curriculum are fulfilled, the children are able to experience a variety of other stimulating activities.

Accelerated sets exist from Year 5 to provide more challenging opportunities for those who are academically gifted. Academic, art, drama, music, and sports awards have been achieved to many major senior schools and over the past four years more than 100 scholarships have been won by St Andrew's pupils. The charity running St Andrews's Prep amalgamated with Eastbourne College in 2010 and the two schools are part of the Eastbourne College Charity. The school benefits from the use of College facilities including astroturf pitches, a contemporary performing arts centre and specialist staff. Approximately 65–70% of St Andrew's Prep leavers each year progress to Eastbourne College. However, it should be noted that although the schools are inter-dependent, they are also independent of each other and the Headmaster of St Andrew's advises on any number of other schools too, as appropriate to each individual.

There is a wide range of activities on offer. The Co-Curricular programme, which runs for children in Years 5 to 8, offers opportunities for all children to develop areas of interest and strength or to discover new ones. Each activity offered has its own educational objectives and challenges designed to improve children's skills and broaden their horizons. Optional Saturday morning activities for Years 4 to 8 pupils are also very popular. An extensive programme of after-school activities has always been a strong feature of St Andrew's. This starts at the Pre-Prep and runs through to Year 8. The school also operates various activity weeks and courses during the school holidays, which are run by our own staff, including cricket, rugby, football, swimming, tennis, netball and hockey.

The school's strong sporting reputation manifests itself in national honours regularly achieved in many different sports. Specialist coaches are employed to teach the skills required for all to enjoy participating in team games and opportunities are available to anyone wishing to represent the school.

Charitable status. Eastbourne College Incorporated is a Registered Charity, number 307071. The aim of the Charity is the promotion of Education.

St Andrew's School

Buckhold, Pangbourne, Reading, Berks RG8 8QA

Tel:	0118 974 4276
email:	admin@standrewspangbourne.co.uk
website:	www.standrewspangbourne.co.uk
Twitter:	@StAndrewsSch

The School is an Educational Trust controlled by a Board of Governors.

Chairman of Governors: Mrs Felicity M Rutland

Headmaster: **Mr Jonathan Bartlett**, BSc QTS Brunel

Age Range. 3–13. Weekly Boarding from age 7.
Number of Pupils. 300 including weekly boarders.
Fees per term (2016–2017). Flexi Boarders £6,106–£6,626; Day Pupils £3,370–£5,610. Nursery from £1,685 (5 mornings).

The School is fully co-educational and set in over 50 acres of private wooded estate and parkland.

The Curriculum includes all the traditional CE and Scholarship subjects and there is emphasis on Music, Speech and Drama and Modern Languages. Study Skills are an important part of the senior pupils' timetable and Information Technology is well resourced.

Academic and Sporting standards are high.

Charitable status. St Andrew's (Pangbourne) School Trust Limited is a Registered Charity, number 309090. It exists to provide education for boys and girls.

St Andrew's School, Woking

Church Hill House, Wilson Way, Horsell, Woking, Surrey GU21 4QW

Tel:	01483 760943
Fax:	01483 740314
email:	hmsec@st-andrews.woking.sch.uk
	admin@st-andrews.woking.sch.uk

website:	www.st-andrews.woking.sch.uk
Twitter:	@StAndrewsWoking
Facebook:	/standrewsschoolwoking

Chairman of Governors: Mrs Jenny Way

Headmaster: **Mr Adrian Perks**, MSc

Deputy Head: Mr Jonathan Spooner, MA Hons

Age Range. 3–13 co-educational.
Number of Pupils. Total: 311 Day pupils. Pre-Prep and Nursery 141.
Fees per term (2016–2017). Prep £4,110–£4,710. Pre-Prep £1,197–£3,470.

St Andrew's School was founded in 1937 and is an established, respected and thriving co-educational Prep school, set in 11 acres of grounds within a quiet residential area approximately half a mile from Woking town centre. The School seeks to create a nurturing and happy environment of trust and support in which all pupils are encouraged and enabled to develop their skills, talents, interests and potential to the full – intellectually, physically and spiritually, regardless of social circumstances, age or religion.

Within St Andrew's walls children feel secure and confident and are highly motivated to perform to the best of their ability in all aspects of school life. They are competitive without losing sight of their responsibility to share and they are justifiably proud of their school and their own personal achievements. In a world of changing values, self-confidence and a solid grounding are essential building blocks for life. St Andrew's hopes to provide all their children with this basic foundation as they prepare for the bigger challenges that follow. Children are prepared for entrance and scholarship exams to a wide range of independent senior schools and there are specialist teaching facilities for all subjects including science, ICT, music and art. The curriculum is broad and the school places great emphasis on music, sport and the arts.

St Andrew's is very proud of its excellent on-site facilities including an all-weather sports surface, sports pitches, tennis courts, cricket nets and outdoor heated swimming pool. We are very fortunate to enjoy the benefits of carefully designed school grounds that incorporate facilities to meet the needs of the children's physical and social development. Main school games are football, hockey, cricket, netball and rounders. Other activities include, cross-country running, swimming, tennis and athletics.

Children can be supervised at school from 8.00 am and, through our extensive after-school activities programme for Year 3 and above, until 6/6.30 pm most evenings during the week. There is also an after-school club from 4.00 pm to 6.00 pm (chargeable) for Pre-Prep and Year 3 children.

Children are assessed for entry into Year 2 and above. Contact the School for more information regarding scholarships and bursaries.

Charitable status. St Andrew's (Woking) School Trust is a Registered Charity, number 297580, established to promote and provide for the advancement of education of children.

S. Anselm's

Stanedge Road, Bakewell, Derbyshire DE45 1DP

Tel:	01629 812734
Fax:	01629 814742
email:	headmaster@anselms.co.uk
website:	www.sanselms.co.uk
Twitter:	@SAnselmsPrep

The School is an Educational Trust.

Chairman of Governors: R Howard

Headmaster: P Phillips, BH Hons London, MA Ed, PG Cert SpLD, NPQH

Age Range. 3–16.
Numbers. College (age 13 to 16), Prep School (age 7 to 13) 86 boys, 66 girls. Pre-Prep (age 3 to 7) 60 boys and girls.
Fees per term (2016–2017). Boarders: £7,500, Day: College £3,650; Prep £4,900–£6,050; Pre-Prep £3,200–£3,650.

Welcome to S. Anselm's School, the only independent co-educational prep school in Derbyshire. Situated in the heart of the glorious Peak District it offers outstanding academic, sporting and extra-curricular opportunities to all pupils. We actively welcome children of all abilities to the school and pride ourselves on cherishing each individual child and allowing their full potential to shine through.

S. Anselm's sits on the crest of a hill in the heart of the Peak National Park – a beacon of excellence in all it does. All parents seek an environment where their children can remain children for as long as possible. Here at S. Anselm's it is just so. Through everything we do this ethos remains steadfast. We are proud of our tradition and are not ashamed to say that the values we hold dear are the very reason this school is quite unique.

With an 18-acre campus in the Peak District the children are surrounded by beauty and opportunities to explore. We have 5 netball courts, an indoor swimming pool, a recently renovated sports hall, a theatre with a permanent stage, a dedicated music block, 3 fully equipped science laboratories, 2 art rooms, a new innovations centre and a newly developed library. The school is forward looking in its approach to IT having invested heavily in it over the last 2 years with iPads for learning, fully interactive whiteboards and Wi-Fi throughout the school.

The boarders enjoy a varied programme of activities including the debating club and fiercely fought tournaments of dodgeball. Those who learn music practise for 20 minutes every evening and cocoa and toast every night give a homely feel to bedtime.

Here our pupils are encouraged to be themselves; they are genuinely excited about learning and have a real thirst for knowledge. They thrive in the music and art rooms, and on the games field and stage. Pupils adore this school and are justly proud of all they do. They love learning and there is a true sense of fun.

Our small class sizes mean our staff can plan their teaching to ensure every pupil is treated as an individual. Each child is cared for and nurtured in every way they need. Our teaching staff simply want the very best for all our pupils and will do all they can to help them achieve their own personal best.

At the very centre of our values is creativity – whether through the individual or the community. It is creativity in thought and every aspect of life that sets a S. Anselm's pupil apart from others. We encourage our children to be creative in their thinking and their play and strongly believe in the importance of nurturing an environment where they can fully and confidently explore their individuality. This is a kind, caring and tolerant school and we are quite sure this wonderful environment will make a lasting impression on all who visit.

Charitable status. S. Anselm's is a Registered Charity, number 527179. It exists to provide an excellent all-round education for boys and girls.

St Anthony's School for Boys
Alpha Plus Group

90 Fitzjohn's Avenue, Hampstead, London NW3 6NP
Tel: 020 7435 3597 (Junior House)
       020 7435 0316 (Senior House)
       020 7431 1066 (Admissions)
Fax: 020 7435 9223
email: headmaster@stanthonysprep.co.uk
website: www.stanthonysprep.org.uk

Headmaster: P M Keyte, MA Oxon

Age Range. 4–13.
Number of Boys. 310 Day Boys.
Fees per term (2016–2017). £5,895–£6,025 including lunches.

Founded in the 19th century and set in the heart of Hampstead village, St Anthony's is an academic IAPS preparatory school for boys between the ages of 4 and 13. It is Roman Catholic, but welcomes boys of other faiths. The majority of boys transfer at 13, via scholarship or CE, to leading independent senior schools including Westminster, University College School, KCS Wimbledon, Habs, Merchant Taylors', St Paul's, Mill Hill, Highgate, Harrow, Eton, City of London, Ampleforth, Stonyhurst, Sevenoaks, Bedales, Tonbridge, Charterhouse and Oundle. It is one of the prestigious Alpha Plus Schools whose CEO is Julian Drinkall. The school is continuing its major rebuilding and refurbishment programme. Its new sister school, St Anthony's School for Girls, opened in September 2016.

The school accommodation consists of two large Victorian houses in close proximity. Both have their own grounds and separate playgrounds. There are eight forms in the Junior House, where boys range in age from four to eight, and ten forms in the Senior House, where boys range in age from eight to thirteen. The Senior House has a specialist Design and Technology room, a Music room, a Dance & Drama studio, wireless network, a Science laboratory and a swimming pool.

All boys receive Religious Education lessons twice a week. The course, which centres on Catholic beliefs and practices, but includes aspects of other faiths, is followed by all pupils. The school's spiritual dimension is regarded as highly important and it exists within a liberal and inclusive atmosphere. Most pupils attend mass about three times each term.

The school curriculum is stimulating and challenging: for example, it is possible for boys to study five foreign languages. All pupils study French and Mandarin from Year 1; Latin, Greek and Arabic are available from Year 6. The arts have an important place in the school with a majority of boys learning to play a musical instrument and all boys involved in drama. Sport is a further strength of the school with some pupils achieving success on a national stage. The school has use of a superb local sports club, at Brondesbury, with extensive facilities. It has recently introduced Computer Programming and Robotics courses have been very successful and all pupils can study Philosophy from Year 4 upwards.

St Anthony's still retains its famous commitment to fostering individuality with alumni such as David Suchet, Anthony Gormley and Bombay Bicycle Club underlining its notable commitment to the liberal arts. Recently, pupils have been awarded music scholarships to Eton, Harrow, Highgate and UCS. Academic awards were also achieved at St Paul's, Habs and City.

The school works hard to instil in its pupils a sense of social responsibility and charity fundraising is a key feature of school life. A former pupil was awarded the Gusi Peace

Prize (Asian equivalent of the Nobel) and the school continues to finance a kindergarten in southern India. Much work is also done with local charities.

St Aubyn's School

Bunces Lane, Woodford Green, Essex IG8 9DU

Tel: 020 8504 1577
Fax: 020 8504 2053
email: school@staubyns.com
website: www.staubyns.com
Twitter: @st_aubyns
Facebook: /St-Aubyns-School

The School was founded in 1884 and is governed by a Charitable Trust.

Chairman of the Governors: Mrs E Ruff, LLB

Headmaster: **Len Blom**, BEd Hons, BA, HDE Phys Ed, NPQH

Deputy Head: Marcus Shute, BEd

Age Range. 3–13+.
Number of Children. 530 Day.
Fees per term (from April 2016). £1,665 (Nursery) to £3,722 (Seniors) fully inclusive.

St Aubyn's provides an all-round preparatory education for children aged 3–13. The School is non-selective at its main point of entry for children aged 3 and 4. There are assessment tests for older children, principally at ages 7+ and 11+.

Classes are small, taught by well-qualified, dedicated staff. Nursery and Reception children are also supported by nursery nurses and teaching assistants. A full-time qualified nurse deals with all medical issues and emergencies.

The School offers a wide-ranging curriculum within a traditional framework, encompassing all National Curriculum and Common Entrance requirements. French is taught from 4+ and Latin from 10+. French, Music and PE are specialist-taught from an early age. All subjects are specialist-taught from Year 6.

Children progress to a range of independent and state schools at 11+ and 13+. Pupils gain a range of scholarships at both 11 and 13. Recent awards include several academic scholarships as well as awards in Sport, Technology, Music and Drama. In 2016 a total of 12 awards were gained by a total of 10 children.

The School is pleasantly situated on the borders of Epping Forest, yet is close both to the North Circular and the M11. There are three departments within the School: Pre Prep (3+, 4+, 5+, 6+); Middle School (7+, 8+, 9+) and Seniors (10+, 11+ and 12+) and each has its own base and resources. Facilities are extensive with 8 acres of grounds, large Sports Centre, all-weather pitches, fully-equipped Performing Arts Centre and Music School, Science Laboratory, Art and Design and Technology Base, a Library and two IT Suites. A computer network runs throughout the school. Games include football, cricket, hockey, rugby, tennis, netball, athletics and swimming, all coached to a high standard.

The Director of Music leads a thriving department, with a school orchestra and various instrumental groups and choirs. Children are regularly involved in performances both within and outside the School.

The School has benefited from the creation of a new dining facility and second performance space. The old dining hall has now become the designated Art and Design and Technology Base and the School has also introduced a new Food Technology facility. In 2016 a second artificial playing surface was completed to accommodate the additional extracurricular activities offered. In January 2017 we will open a new, purpose-built, state-of-the-art Nursery facility.

St Aubyn's School is a registered charity. All income from fees is for the direct benefit of its pupils. Two scholarships are available at 11+. The primary criterion for the award of a scholarship is academic ability, though special talent in music, technology, art, sport, etc may be taken into account. There is a bursary scheme at 7+.

Charitable status. St Aubyn's (Woodford Green) School Trust is a Registered Charity, number 270143. It exists to provide education for children.

Saint Bede's Preparatory School

Bishton Hall, Wolseley Bridge, Stafford, Staffordshire ST17 0XN

Tel: 01889 881277
Fax: 01889 882749
email: admin@saintbedes.co.uk
website: www.saintbedes.co.uk

(Under the patronage of His Grace the Archbishop of Birmingham)

Headmaster: **C W H Stafford Northcote**, BA

Age Range. 3–13.
Number of Pupils. 80 Boys and Girls.
Fees per term (2016–2017). £4,725 Boarders and Weekly Boarders, £2,350–£3,900 Day Pupils. Compulsory Extras Nil.

Saint Bede's is a Catholic Preparatory School, in which other faiths and denominations are welcomed.

Saint Bede's was founded in 1936 by the Grandparents of the current Headmaster. Since then, the Northcote family has educated young people as additions to their own family, treating each child with care and respect. This has helped to create an educational atmosphere unlike any other.

Bishton Hall is a Grade II* listed Georgian Mansion, surrounded by 25 acres of beautifully kept gardens and woodland and 7 acres of professionally levelled playing fields. The school has its own Chapel, hard tennis courts, indoor heated swimming pool, gymnasium/theatre and science laboratory. Situated on the edge of Cannock Chase, this rural setting provides children with a happy and safe environment in which to learn.

Pupils are prepared for all Independent Schools and many Scholarships have been won.

There is a teaching staff of 13 with visiting teachers for violin, brass instruments and guitar. A specialist Drama Teacher teaches Performing Arts to a highly proficient standard.

The Craft, Design and Technology Centre incorporates metal work and metal casting, carpentry, pottery, enamelling, jewellery making, computers, art and stone polishing.

Tennis, Rugby, Cricket, Rounders, Hockey, Netball and Volleyball are played in season.

The Headmaster is personally responsible for the health and welfare of the children. Individual care is taken of each child and good manners and consideration for others insisted upon. An acknowledged feature of the School is its family atmosphere.

For further particulars, please contact the School Office.

St Benedict's Junior School

5 Montpelier Avenue, Ealing, London W5 2XP

Tel: 020 8862 2253
Fax: 020 8862 2058
email: enquiries@stbenedicts.org.uk
website: www.stbenedicts.org.uk
Twitter: @stbenedicts
Facebook: /StBenedictsSchool
LinkedIn: /st-benedicts-school

Governing Body:
The Governing Board of St Benedict's School

Headmaster: **Mr R G Simmons**, BA Hons, PGCE

Deputy Head: Mrs T Scott, BEd

Age Range. 3–11 Co-educational.
Number of Pupils. 283.
Fees per term (2016–2017). Nursery: £2,690–£4,820 Pre-Prep: £4,040; Junior School: £4,490.

Our ethos is firmly based in the Benedictine Catholic tradition, and the pastoral and spiritual care of our pupils is central to all that we do. It is the School's mission to '*teach a way of living*' that goes beyond the acquisition of formal academic qualifications and ensures a holistic approach to education from the Nursery through to Sixth Form.

St Benedict's provides a stimulating academic education within a broad, balanced and progressive curriculum. Great importance is placed on achievements in Art, Design Technology, Drama, Information and Communications Technology, Music and Sport. In addition, we offer a wide range of co-curricular activities, including Choir and Orchestra, Dance, Eco Gardening, Fencing, Ju-Jitsu, and Swimming. High-quality teaching, exceptional pastoral care, small classes and a broad curriculum ensure that all pupils have the opportunity to achieve their potential. Interactive whiteboards are present in every classroom and the Library is very well-resourced.

Girls and boys are taught together throughout their time at St Benedict's (3–18), with the exception of traditional single-sex sports. Specialist teachers provide tuition in French, Information and Computing Technology, Science, Music and Art Design Technology. Excellent academic results across the School are matched by equally impressive value-added scores, reflecting the strong and effective partnership between pupils, parents and the staff. We rejoice in the successes of all of our pupils.

The natural points of entry in the Junior School and Nursery are at 3+, 4+ and 7+. Entry is possible at other ages subject to the availability of places.

Charitable status. St Benedict's School Ealing is a Registered Charity, number 1148512, and a Charitable Company Limited by Guarantee, number 8093330.

St Bernard's Preparatory School

Hawtrey Close, Slough, Berkshire SL1 1TB

Tel: 01753 521821
Fax: 01753 552364
email: registrar@stbernardsprep.org
website: www.stbernardsprep.org

Headteacher: **Mr N S Cheesman**, BEd

Assistant Heads:
Mrs A Underwood
Mrs A Verma

Age Range. 2½–11 co-educational.
Number of Pupils. 268.
Fees per term (2016–2017). £2,580–£3,120.

St Bernard's Preparatory has a unique ethos. We are a Catholic school, teaching the Catholic faith and living out the Gospel values which are shared by all faiths and are the foundation of all our relationships and the daily life of our school. We welcome and embrace children of all faiths and we recognise and celebrate our similarities and differences, developing mutual respect, understanding and tolerance.

We recognise the value and uniqueness of each individual, both child and adult. We celebrate the talents and gifts of each child and enable them to develop to their full potential spiritually, morally, academically, socially and physically. Our children are happy, courteous, confident, articulate young citizens, committed to the ideal of service to others.

We work in partnership with parents, recognising that they are the first and best educators of their child. We consider ourselves to be very privileged that parents have entrusted us with the care and education of their child. We ensure that parents are kept fully informed of their child's progress.

We are committed to offering a broad, balanced, creative and challenging curriculum, enriched by experiences and opportunities which enhance and consolidate the learning process. Small class sizes enable our team of highly qualified, caring, committed and enthusiastic teachers to be responsive to the needs of the individual child ensuring continuity and progression for all our children. We have developed a wide and varied range of after-school activities which broaden the curriculum and enrich the children's lives. Children are encouraged to develop new skills.

We are proud of our reputation as a school with a strong ethos and nurturing pastoral care coupled with academic excellence reflected in consistently outstanding results in local and national tests.

Our school motto 'Dieu Mon Abri' meaning 'God is my Shelter', is an inspiring reminder of God's love for each one of us. The three swords represent 'Love, Work and Prayer' which underpin and permeate the life of our school.

St Catherine's Preparatory School

Bramley, Guildford, Surrey GU5 0DF

Tel: 01483 899665; Senior School: 01483 893363
Fax: 01483 899669
email: prepschool.office@stcatherines.info
website: www.stcatherines.info
Twitter: @stcatsbramley

Chairman of the Governing Body: Mr Peter J Martin, BA, FRGS, FCCA

Headmistress: Mrs Alice Phillips, MA Cantab

Head of Preparatory School: **Miss Naomi Bartholomew**, MA London, BEd Cantab

Age Range. 4–11.
Number of Pupils. 264 Day Girls.
Fees per term (from January 2017). Pre-Prep 1 £2,860, Pre-Prep 2 £3,465, Pre-Prep 3 £4,090; Prep School £4,830.

Girls are accepted from the age of 4 to 11 when they take the Entrance Examinations for entry to Senior Schools.

Charitable status. St Catherine's School Bramley is a Registered Charity, number 1070858, which exists to provide education for girls in accordance with the principles of the Church of England.

St Cedd's School

178a New London Road, Chelmsford, Essex CM2 0AR

Tel: 01245 392810
Fax: 01245 392815
email: info@stcedds.org.uk
website: www.stcedds.org.uk

Chair of Governors: Mrs F Marshall

Head: **Dr P A Edmonds**, EdD, MEd, BEd Hons

Age Range. 3–11 Co-educational.
Number of Pupils. 400.
Fees per term (2016–2017). £3,030–£3,240 including lunch.

St Cedd's School, founded in 1931, is a leading co-educational day school for children aged three to 11. The grounds and purpose-built facilities create a vibrant and purposeful learning environment where children are encouraged to become independent, confident and caring individuals. A St Cedd's School education focuses on high standards of literacy and numeracy within an expansive academic broad and balanced curriculum, supplemented by a superb programme of sport and an extraordinary creative output of drama and the performing arts. PE, Music, Art and French are taught by specialist teachers from Nursery; Swimming and Recorders are introduced in Year 2 and International Studies is studied in Years 5 and 6. Following the 11+ entry and independent school examinations, a baccalaureate-style curriculum in Year 6 leads to the Hold Fast award which celebrates the breadth of children's achievements and talents. Music is a particular strength of the school with outstanding individual instrumental examination results. St Cedd's School is a member of the Chelmsford Choral Foundation and this link to Chelmsford Cathedral provides opportunity for our choirs to perform at Choral Evensong.

The grounded confidence the pupils have as a result of differentiated teaching and learning in a happy and supported environment, where children have fun and are encouraged to take risks, results in great personal achievements. Our boys and girls aspire to the highest levels of attainment and we can boast a successful track record of outstanding results at entry to grammar schools and scholarships to independent senior schools. We hold the International School Award (ISA) and have UNESCO Status.

Breakfast is available from 0730 and there is a very extensive array of after-school activities until 1700 with wrap-around care in our TLC club until 1800.

Charitable status. St Cedd's School Educational Trust Ltd is a Registered Charity, number 310865. It exists to provide education for boys and girls.

Saint Christina's RC Preparatory School

25 St Edmund's Terrace, London NW8 7PY

Tel: 020 7722 8784
Fax: 020 7586 4961
email: headteacherspa@saintchristinas.org.uk
website: www.saintchristinas.org.uk

Headteacher: **Miss Jenny Finlayson**, Adv Dip, BEd, MA

Age Range. Girls 3–11, Boys 3–7.

Number of Pupils. 155 girls, 30 boys.
Fees per term (2016–2017). £3,900 (inclusive).

Saint Christina's was founded in 1949 by the Handmaids of the Sacred Heart of Jesus. At Saint Christina's, children experience the joy of learning and the wonder of God and His Creation. Our purpose at Saint Christina's is to create an environment where children enjoy learning and where each individual experiences respect and acceptance enabling them to become the balanced person they are called to be.

As a School we take pride in the excellent examination results which we achieve. We value most of all our strong sense of community. We seek to ensure that children feel appreciated for themselves as individuals as much as their achievements. We believe that confidence can only grow in an atmosphere of trust and safety.

Boys are prepared for entrance tests for day and boarding schools.

Girls are prepared for Common Entrance Examination and entrance exams to day and boarding schools.

The School is purpose built in a pleasant location within a short walk of Primrose Hill and Regent's Park. Prospective parents are warmly invited to visit the School.

Charitable status. Saint Christina's is a Registered Charity, number 221319.

St Christopher's School
Hampstead

32 Belsize Lane, Hampstead, London NW3 5AE

Tel: 020 7435 1521
Fax: 020 7431 6694
email: admissions@stchristophers.london
website: www.stchristophers.london

Preparatory school for girls.

Chairman of Governors: Mr R Turnill, BA Hons

Headmistress: **Mrs C L B Symes**, BA Hons Bristol, PGCE, LGSM, RSA Dip SpLD

Age Range. 4–11.
Number of Girls. 238 Day Pupils.
Fees per term (2016–2017). £4,590 inclusive of lunch and all outings, except residential.

The School employs a fully-qualified teaching staff of 16 full-time, 6 part-time, and 7 peripatetic music teachers. Strong emphasis is placed on music. There are three choirs, quartets, ensembles and 2 orchestras; instrumental lessons are arranged within the school timetable. Whilst maintaining high standards in numeracy and literacy, the curriculum provides a wide range of subjects including art, science, computer studies, design and technology, Spanish, Latin, drama, chess, gymnastics and games.

Extra-curricular activities over the year include art, dance, debating, drama, football, gym, language, Mandarin, netball, science, sewing, striking/fielding games and yoga.

All applicants are assessed for entry. Means-tested bursaries are available, up to 100%. The girls are prepared for entrance examinations to the major London day schools and for 11+ Common Entrance to boarding schools.

Charitable status. St Christopher's School (Hampstead) Limited is a Registered Charity, number 312999. It exists to provide education for girls.

St Christopher's School
Hove

33 New Church Road, Hove, East Sussex BN3 4AD

Tel: 01273 735404
Fax: 01273 747956
email: hmsec@stchristophershove.org.uk
website: www.stchristophershove.org.uk

Chairman of Governors: Mr A J Symonds, FCIS

Headmaster: **Mr J A S Withers**, BEd Cantab

Age Range. 4–13 co-educational.
Number of Pupils. 311.
Fees per term (2016–2017). £2,680–£3,965.

Since its foundation in 1927, St Christopher's School has expanded to become a highly successful academic preparatory school, located in the middle of Brighton & Hove, England's youngest and most vibrant city.

St Christopher's School aims to provide a traditional academic education within a supportive family environment where individual talents are developed to produce confident, articulate and well-balanced children. Pupils regularly obtain top academic scholarships and awards for art, music, drama and sport. St Christopher's is a Member of the Brighton College Family of Schools and many of its pupils go on to Brighton College.

Entry to the School is at 4+, however, places are occasionally available in other age groups. In the Lower School, pupils are taught mainly by their form teachers. Particular emphasis is placed upon reading, writing and mathematics, but the curriculum is broad and a wide range of subjects is taught by specialist teachers, including French, Mandarin, Latin, Science, Music, Art, ICT, PE and Games.

Pupils move into the Middle School in Year 4, where the curriculum reflects the syllabuses of the Common Entrance and Brighton College Academic Scholarship Examinations. Formal homework is introduced at this stage. In the Upper School (Years 7 and 8), all subjects are taught by specialists, who make full use of the interactive ICT suite, music technology suite, science laboratory, art studio and library. A variety of educational day trips, an annual residential visit to France and sports trips ensure that children receive a broad and stimulating educational experience.

The boys achieve an enviable record of success in football, rugby and cricket and the girls match that success in hockey, netball and rounders. The musical life of St Christopher's is enriched by three choirs and the choice of a wide variety of instrumental and vocal tuition. All pupils are encouraged to perform on stage as part of a wide programme of drama and the development of confidence is a central aim of the school. A wide range of extra-curricular activities is on offer. After-school care is available until 5.30 pm each evening.

The Headmaster is always delighted to welcome prospective parents. Please contact the Registrar to arrange a visit.

Charitable status. St Christopher's School, Hove is a member of the Brighton College Family of Schools and is a Registered Charity, number 307061

St Columba's College Preparatory School

King Harry Lane, St Albans, Hertfordshire AL3 4AW

Tel: 01727 862616
Fax: 01727 892025

email: headofprep@stcolumbascollege.org
website: www.stcolumbascollege.org

Chairman of the Governors: Mrs J Harrison, BEd

Dean: Brother Daniel St Jacques SC, BA, PGF HG Dip Counselling, MBACP

Head: **Mrs R Loveman**, BSc

Age Range. 4–11.
Number of Pupils. 255 Boys.
Fees per term (2016–2017). Reception–Prep 2 £3,360, Prep 3 £3,795, Prep 4–6 £4,186. Fees include personal accident insurance. Additional charges are made for coaches and consumables.

The Prep School is an academically selective Catholic Day School which strives to create a welcoming community in which each boy is valued as an individual and endeavours to promote positive relationships based on mutual respect and understanding. There is a rigorous academic curriculum with an extensive range of extra-curricular opportunities. A full curriculum and sports programme is offered at Key Stage 1 and 2.

Admissions at age 4 and 7 years. Entry requirements of the school is by assessment; at age 7+ assessment is via maths, mental arithmetic, perceptual reasoning, creative writing and reading; at age 4 assessment takes place informally using a standardised test and in context in a classroom situation. Subjects include: English, Mathematics, Science, Drama, RE, French, History, Geography, IT, PE, Games, Music, Art and Design Technology.

Examinations: Pupils progress at 11+ to St Columba's College on the same site, or to other senior schools.

Academic facilities include: modern form rooms with specialist facilities for Science, IT, ADT, Music, PE, Games, RE and French, and a professionally staffed extensive library.

Sports facilities include: Rugby/Football pitches, Cricket nets and square. A swimming pool and athletics track are adjacent to the site.

There are means-tested bursaries at Prep level and a number of scholarships available to Prep School boys on entry to St Columba's College. These include academic and music scholarships.

(*See also St Columba's College entry in HMC section.*)

Charitable status. St Columba's College is a Registered Charity, number 1088480. It exists to provide a well-rounded Roman Catholic education for pupils from 4–18 years of age.

St Dunstan's College Junior School

Stanstead Road, London SE6 4TY

Tel: 020 8516 7225
Fax: 020 8516 7300
email: rscard@sdmail.org.uk
website: www.stdunstans.org.uk

Chairman of Governors: Alderman & Sheriff Sir Paul Judge, MA, MBA, LLD Hon

Head of Junior School: **Mr Paul Cozens**

Age Range. Co-educational 3–11.
Number of Pupils. Pre-Preparatory (3–7) 143, Preparatory (7–11) 176.
Fees per term (2016–2017). Nursery £3.137, Pre-Preparatory £3,998, Preparatory £3,998–£5,038. Fees include lunch.

The Junior School is an integral part of St Dunstan's College and prepares boys and girls for the Senior School (age 11–18) (*see entry in HMC section*). It shares with it a common site and many facilities. In particular the Music Centre, Refectory, Great Hall, Sports Hall, indoor Swimming Pool and playing fields increase the opportunities for all pupils in curricular and extra-curricular activities. For other work the Junior School pupils have their own buildings. The Pre-Preparatory Department is located in a Victorian house which has been beautifully converted for the specific needs of the 3–7 year olds. The Preparatory Department has its own teaching area with a library, ICT Suite, art room and activity room.

We provide an excellent all-round education with special emphasis upon the development of a high level of literacy and numeracy. The curriculum is also designed to promote learning and appreciation of Science, Humanities, Music, Art, Design and Technology, Information Technology, Drama, Languages and Study Skills. Games and Physical Education play an important part in the growth and development of each pupil and the children follow an extensive programme of activities. The children's learning is enhanced by a variety of visits and residential school journeys.

Boys and girls are encouraged to take part in various clubs and activities after school hours and at lunch times. Opportunities range from music, art and sport groups to ICT and drama.

A caring and friendly environment is provided by small class sizes and a dedicated team of well-qualified class teachers and support staff. In addition to being taught many subjects by their class teacher, Preparatory Department pupils have the advantage of being educated by specialists in Art, Music, Languages, Physical Education and Games.

An effective strong partnership exists between the home and school and parents are encouraged to participate in their children's education and the life of the Junior School. Regular contact is maintained between school and the home to ensure that parents are aware of their child's academic and social progress.

Boys and Girls are admitted at all ages from 3+ to 10+ but principally at 3+ and 4+ (Nursery and Reception) and at 7+ (Year 3).

Charitable status. St Dunstan's Educational Foundation is a Registered Charity, number 312747. It exists to provide education for boys and girls.

St Edmund's Junior School
Canterbury

Canterbury, Kent CT2 8HU
Tel: 01227 475601 (Admissions)
           01227 475600 (General Enquiries)
Fax: 01227 471083
email: admissions@stedmunds.org.uk
website: www.stedmunds.org.uk
Twitter: @stedscanterbury
Facebook: /StEdsCanterbury

Chairman of Governors: M C W Terry, FCA

Head of the Junior School: **M J Jelley**, BA Hons UEA, PGCE

Head of the Pre-Prep School: Mrs J E P Exley, BEd Hons CCCU

(*Full staff list is available on the school's website*)

Age Range. 3–13.
Numbers of Pupils. 230. Boarders: School House 19, Choir House 26; Day Pupils: Boys 97, Girls 88.

Fees per term (2016–2017). Junior School: Boarders £7,389, Weekly Boarders £6,734, Choristers £7,083, Day pupils: Years 7 & 8 £4,996, Years 3–6 £4,909. Pre-Prep: Forms 1 & 2 £3,478, Reception £3,009, Nursery £2,450.

Pupils may enter at any age from 3 to 12. Boarding begins at the age of 11.

The Junior School and the Pre-Prep School are closely linked with the Senior School (*see entry in HMC section*) but have their own identity. The Junior School uses some Senior School specialist staff, particularly in the teaching of Science, Music, Art, Technology and shares with the Senior School such amenities as the Chapel, concert theatre, sports facilities and swimming pool. There is a full-time school Chaplain. Domestic arrangements, including health and catering, are under centralised administration.

Boarding in School House offers a family experience in a stimulating environment where the individual is valued. The Canterbury Cathedral Choristers, who are St Edmund's pupils, live in the Choir House which is under the care of a married Housemaster and is situated in the precincts of Canterbury Cathedral.

Scholarships and bursaries. Academic, music, drama, sport, and all-rounder awards are available for applicants aged 11. Cathedral choristerships are available for boys from age 7. Fee concessions are also available as detailed in the Senior School entry in HMC section.

Charitable status. St Edmund's School Canterbury is a Registered Charity, number 1056382. It exists to educate the children in its care.

St Edmund's Prep School

Old Hall Green, Ware, Herts SG11 1DS
Tel: 01920 824239
email: prep@stedmundscollege.org
website: www.stedmundscollege.org
Twitter: @stedmundsware

Chairman of Governors: Mr Patrick J Mitton, MSc

Head: **Mr S Cartwright**, BSc Hons Surrey

Deputy Head: Dr F J McLauchlan, MA PhD Cantab
Assistant Head: Mr G Duddy, BEd Wales
Head of EYFS: Mrs V Penfold, BA London Metropolitan

Age Range. 3–11 Co-educational.
Number of Pupils. 224.
Fees per term (2016–2017). Day (inc Lunch): £1,475–£4,295.

St Edmund's Prep, founded in 1874, is a co-educational, independent Catholic Nursery, Pre-Prep and Prep school, situated in beautiful surroundings of wood and parkland in Old Hall Green, easily accessible from the main thoroughfares of Hertfordshire. The school embraces family values to lay the foundation for a happy and successful life. Education is seen as a joint venture involving staff, parents and children.

When you arrive at the Prep you will experience a welcome from us all that invites you and your child to be part of a very special community.

Guided by the principles of our Catholic faith and acknowledging Christ as our leader and teacher, we strive for excellence and creativity in forward-thinking education. We commit ourselves to the preparation of our children by instilling in them a sense of responsibility and strive to ensure that they leave St Edmund's Prep with a solid foundation on which to build their future in the College and beyond.

Small class sizes allow focused attention to ensure that your child becomes a confident learner both inside and outside the classroom. Our facilities shared with the College and our committed teachers ensure our pupils have the experiences they need to develop fully in all aspects of their lives. With a heritage and ethos deeply rooted in the Catholic tradition, we welcome families from all faiths who will appreciate the all-round education that we offer.

The school has a broad, balanced curriculum and it seeks to cater for the individual child at the different stages of their development. The curriculum offered is intended to improve the learners' knowledge, introduce them to a wide range of educational experiences and develop skills needed to deal critically and creatively with the world.

The Prep is committed to healthy living and we deliver this through daily home-cooked, well-balanced meals; fresh fruit is provided at break times and sport and activity for all is a priority.

Extracurricular is the norm in the Prep with a stimulating, fun range of activities run every day from chess club to junior cadets; from cookery in dedicated facilities to sport.

A breakfast and tea-time club is offered and a school bus service runs for children over 7 in Year 3.

We are fortunate to share facilities with St Edmund's College and as a result the Prep children have an opportunity to use the floodlit astroturf, all year round use of the indoor swimming pool, a large gymnasium as well as acres of grounds which the children, with supervision, can explore.

We are committed to being leaders in education in these changing times. We invite you to join us as a member of St Edmund's Prep.

Charitable status. St Edmund's College is a Registered Charity, number 311073.

St Edmund's School

Portsmouth Road, Hindhead, Surrey GU26 6BH

Tel: 01428 609875
Fax: 01428 607898
email: registrar@saintedmunds.co.uk
website: www.saintedmunds.co.uk
Twitter: @excellentsteds

Chairman of Governors: Mrs J Alliss

Headmaster: **A J Walliker**, MA Cantab, MBA, PGCE

Age Range. Boys and Girls, Nursery to GCSE.
Number of Pupils. Senior, Prep and Lower School: 400 day pupils.
Fees per term (2016–2017). Lower School £3,195–£4,380; Prep and Senior £5,115; Flexi Boarding Fee: £40 per night; Nursery from £720 (three afternoons) to £2,723 (full week) not including EYFS funded hours.

The fees are inclusive of all ordinary extras including supervised prep, orchestra/choirs, games, swimming, lectures, optional Saturday activities etc.

Scholarships and means-tested bursaries are available.

We are a fully co-educational school with an unusual flexible boarding option, from one-off nights to regular midweek boarding. Through a rich curriculum, small teaching groups and exemplary pastoral care, St Edmund's seeks to provide an excellent all round education by encouraging its pupils to achieve their very best in all that they do. "I like St Ed's, I can be myself." These words spoken by one of our pupils, capture much of what we strive to do at St Edmund's: to instil in every child a sense of self-esteem and belonging by building on their own talents, opening their eyes to new ones and giving them focused and personal support when-

ever it is needed. Academically, it is an approach that continues to pay dividends, with our pupils going on to a wide range of senior schools at both 11+ and 13+ including St Edmund's Senior.

Yet of equal importance are the discoveries, excitements and good old-fashioned fun that St Edmund's creates inside our 40 beautiful acres with facilities including an immaculate 9-hole golf course, indoor swimming pool, cross-country running course, games fields, rifle range and a floodlit all-weather pitch. The list of co-curricular activities is endless at St Ed's, from cooking to rock-climbing, scuba-diving to den building and from ballet to rifle shooting, including our unique optional Saturday Activity programme that allows us greater depth in the number of activities on offer to our pupils.

St Edmund's Senior School offers a rare and unique educational experience for those who join us. In contrast to the many larger institutions available, our dedication to small teaching groups and our strong sense of community creates an environment where pupils' confidence can be invigorated. Through high-quality teaching and resources, our aim is to provide our pupils with an inspiring and notable experience that naturally encourages an appreciation for lifelong independent learning. Our broad curriculum across Forms 7 to 11 presents a firm foundation upon which to make future educational choices, and our distinctive tutorial system enables our pupils a platform to discuss progress and achievements as well as any pastoral issues that require guidance and consideration. St Ed's Senior pupils have their own common room, kitchen and study areas.

During our latest Independent Schools Inspection, the report noted, "The quality of St Edmund's pupils' achievements and learning is 'Excellent'. Pupils' have positive attitudes to learning and they are well motivated. They show exemplary behaviour and their care for each other is special".

Charitable status. St Edmund's School Trust Limited is a Registered Charity, number 278301. Its aim is the education of children.

St Edward's Preparatory School

London Road, Charlton Kings, Cheltenham, Glos GL52 6NR

Tel: 01242 538900
Fax: 01242 538901
email: mainoffice@stedwardsprep.co.uk
website: www.stedwards.co.uk
Twitter: @StEdwards_Prep
Facebook: /StEdwardsSchoolCheltenham

Co-educational Day School.

Chairman of Governors: Dr Sue Honeywill

Headmaster: **Mr S McKernan**, BA Hons, MEd, NPQH

Age Range. 1–11 years.
Number of Pupils. 297.
Fees per term (2016–2017). £2,365–£3,780.
St Edward's Preparatory School is an independent co-educational Catholic Foundation welcoming pupils of all denominations from 1 to 11 years. We provide a supportive family atmosphere in which pupils are encouraged to develop their individual potential – academic, social, physical, creative and spiritual – in preparation for their secondary education. The school is situated on the edge of Cheltenham in forty-five acres of beautiful parkland. Our facilities are truly exceptional and give our pupils opportu-

nities for practical experience rarely available in a preparatory school, as well as enabling us to provide an unusually wide range of after-school activities. Class sizes are small which ensures the pupils receive plenty of individual attention. With a strong focus on mathematics, science, English and ICT results are good with children going to local grammar schools, successful entrance into St Edward's Senior School, many obtaining scholarships, and other independent schools. Sport is particularly strong as is music, drama and art. A new Drama Studio has enhanced our provision in this area.

Our Kindergarten is open all year round and provides a secure and stimulating introduction to school life. A new playground built on the Reggio theme uses wood and natural materials to encourage the children to develop imagination and creativity. Kindergarten children have their own ICT area where they can use dedicated software packages and explore creativity using iPads. Children move from here into our purpose-built Pre-Prep School with small classes and a rich range of extra-curricular activities. St Edward's Preparatory School provides the best possible start for a child's educational journey. In 2013 our Early Years Foundation Stage was awarded an "Outstanding" classification in every area – an exceptional achievement.

Charitable status. St Edward's School is a Registered Charity, number 293360.

St Faith's School

Trumpington Road, Cambridge, Cambridgeshire CB2 8AG

Tel:	01223 352073
Fax:	01223 314757
email:	info@stfaiths.co.uk
website:	www.stfaiths.co.uk
Twitter:	@St_Faiths
Facebook:	@StFaithsSchool
LinkedIn:	/st-faith's-school-cambridge

Chair of Governors: Mrs J Plows, BA

Headmaster: **N L Helliwell**, MA, BEd Hons

Deputy Head: J P Davenport

Age Range. 4–13.
Number of Pupils. 540.
Fees per term (2016–2017). £3,955 (Pre-Prep), £4,845 (Years 3 and 4) £4,985 (Years 5 to 8).

St Faith's, founded in 1884, is a co-educational day school set in 9 acres of grounds on the south side of Cambridge, approximately one mile from the city centre. Our pupils also have access to a further 20 acres of sports fields just 2 minutes' walk away. The School is situated close to the A10, M11 and the Park and Ride facilities. There is a school minibus in operation from the Trumpington Road Park and Ride site to the school each morning. Boys and girls enter the school at age 4 and stay until they are 13. Interviews and assessments for places occur throughout the year and scholarships are available at 7+.

St Faith's is very highly regarded in Cambridge and beyond. The 2011 ISI Report rated as 'Outstanding' the high quality of teaching, excellent academic achievements, the huge range of extra-curricular activities, the very effective links with parents and the special care and attention given to each individual child. Pupils are encouraged to develop their talents to achieve their full potential by following a curriculum that is broadly based and rigorous in its requirement. The small class sizes help accomplish this. Teaching in the early years is principally class based, while, from Year 5,

pupils work with specialist subject teachers. St Faith's prides itself on the pastoral care of the children, which operates through a House-based tutorial system. The high-quality, modern facilities and educational resources at St Faith's are a real asset to the School. The Keynes building provides enviable facilities for the teaching of Engineering, Music, Digital Literacy and Computer Science. The School is an Associate School of The Royal Society for its excellent teaching of Science and Maths. The Ashburton building houses Science labs, well-equipped Art & Design rooms, an extensive library and a Drama studio, as well as a spacious Hall, where Music concerts, Drama productions and whole-school assemblies take place. In addition to the excellent sports facilities on site, including a state-of-the-art Sports Hall, the School has the use of the swimming pool and astro-turf nearby at The Leys School.

Learning languages is a way of life at St Faith's. The School is one of ten UK schools awarded 'Associate Status' by the Spanish Embassy in recognition of the excellent teaching provided.

St Faith's has an excellent sporting tradition with rugby, netball, hockey, cricket, tennis, rounders and athletics being the main outdoor games. Basketball, cross-country running and other games are also organised, but on a more informal basis. Our sports programme involves inter-House competitions and a strong fixture list with numerous matches against other schools. Music and drama are also important at St Faith's and the School has a flourishing music department with the emphasis placed upon enjoyment as well as good performance. Pupils are able to participate in class and whole school concerts and a large number of instrumental groups, choirs and the school orchestra performs regularly. Drama is timetabled for all forms; there are performances of plays or musicals by each Year group throughout the year and the standard of performance is high.

As an Eco-School, St Faith's has earned its coveted Green Flag award and in 2014 won the Ashden Schools Award for our Eco initiatives.

Extracurricular activities range from chess, reading, art and model making to more energetic sporting pursuits. In addition there are Play Clubs, Multi-Activity Courses and a Cookery School during the holidays and teambuilding activity holidays, language trips and a ski trip for older children. Late Stay facilities operate daily and families wishing to miss the Cambridge traffic are able to enjoy breakfast in the school's dining room from 07:20 each morning.

St Faith's is part of The Leys and St Faith's Foundation and although each year approximately half of the children move on to The Leys at the end of Year 8, others prepare for entry to a variety of schools, mainly independent, many of them with scholarships.

Charitable status. The Leys and St Faith's Schools Foundation is a Registered Charity, number 1144035. The aim of the charity is the provision of first-class education.

St Francis School

Marlborough Road, Pewsey, Wiltshire SN9 5NT

Tel:	01672 563228
email:	admissions@st-francis.wilts.sch.uk
	schooloffice@st-francis.wilts.sch.uk
website:	www.st-francis.wilts.sch.uk
Twitter:	@stfrancispewsey

Chair of Governors: P Humphries-Cuff

Headmaster: **D W T Sibson**, BA Ed Hons Durham

Age Range. 2–13.

Number of Boys and Girls. 218: 109 Boys, 109 Girls.

Fees per term (2016–2017). Reception–Year 8: £2,659–£4,072 including lunch. Nursery £228 per half day session excluding lunch.

St Francis is a co-educational day school which takes children from the age of 2 to 13. Established in 1941, the School which is a charitable trust with a board of governors, is situated alongside the Kennet and Avon Canal in the lovely Vale of Pewsey some five miles south of Marlborough. Pupils travel from a wide area of mid-Wiltshire; daily minibus services operate from Marlborough and Devizes. Wrap-around care is available for all pupils, from 7.45 am until 6 pm.

Providing every child with the opportunity to fulfil his or her full potential is a feature of the school. Staff ensure that they are very positive and encouraging in their teaching. Should a child be found to need some form of specific learning assistance then appropriate help will be given. The facilities are constantly being improved. The modern Burden Block provides a Library, Design Technology room, ICT room and specialist subject teaching rooms, as well as form rooms.

The curriculum is delightfully diverse enabling the older pupils to have, for instance, CDT, Pottery, Drama, Computing, Choir and Swimming all in their normal weekly timetable. Languages are also a key part of the curriculum: French is taught from the age of three, Latin is introduced in Year 6. The majority of the pupils take up individual musical tuition and a wide range of instruments is available. Many pupils enter local music and public and choral speaking competitions.

The pupils are offered plenty of opportunity to develop and excel in their sport. All the major sports are taught both outdoors on the playing fields and also inside the Hemery Hall which doubles as a sports hall and a drama theatre. Regular matches take place against other schools and a policy of 'sport for all' allows all pupils to be involved.

Little Saints Nursery caters for children from 2 to 4 years of age. With the Reception class, this makes up the EYFS department of the school which makes use of all the facilities including the school's garden playground and woods.

The school grounds are also home to some more unexpected residents; four years ago sheep and chickens were introduced to the site, joined more recently by pygmy goats and a flock of ducks. Frankie's Farm is very popular with pupils; they especially look forward to lambing in the spring term.

Results are excellent. The pupils are mainly entered for the local senior schools, St Mary's Calne, Godolphin, Dauntsey's, Marlborough College, Stonar and Warminster, but scholarships and common entrance are also taken for boarding schools further afield. Awards are regularly achieved to all of the aforementioned.

Please write, telephone or email for a prospectus, or ask to visit and tour round the school. The Headmaster will be happy to oblige.

Charitable status. St Francis is a Registered Charity, number 298522. It exists solely to provide education for boys and girls.

St Gabriel's
Junior School

Sandleford Priory, Newbury, Berkshire RG20 9BD

Tel: 01635 555680
Fax: 01635 555698

email: info@stgabriels.co.uk
website: www.stgabriels.co.uk
Twitter: @StGabrielsNews
Facebook: /stgabrielsnewbury

Chairman of Governors: Mr N Garland, BSc Hons

Principal: Mr R Smith, MEd, MA, PGCE

Head of Junior School: **Mr P Dove**, BA Hons, PGCE

Age Range. 6 months – 11 years Co-educational.
Number of Pupils. 195.
Fees per term (2016–2017). £3,320–£4,460.

Sandleford lies at the heart of St Gabriel's and provides high-quality nursery care and Early Years education for children aged 6 months to 4 years. Sandleford offers flexible full or part-time care with an extended day provision across 50 weeks a year. At the age of four, the majority of Sandleford children move through into the Reception class of the Junior School.

The Junior School is situated adjacent to the Senior School in 54 acres of parkland on the southern outskirts of Newbury.

Subjects taught include English, Mathematics, Science, Art, Computing, Dance, Drama, Humanities (History, Geography), Modern Foreign Languages (French, Spanish, Italian, Mandarin), Music, Outdoor Education, PE, Religious Studies, Technology (Food Technology, Design Technology) and Thinking Skills

The excellent range of facilities includes a multi-discipline sports hall, theatre, dance studio, junior science laboratory, library, orienteering courses and woodland trails. All Junior School Computing lessons take place in the recently built ICT and MFL block.

Sport plays an important and integral role in the life of the school and there is a comprehensive fixtures list from Year 3 to Year 6. Athletics, Basketball, Cross-Country, Dance, Football, Gymnastics, Hockey, Netball, Rugby, Rounders and Tennis are included in the curriculum for all pupils. Swimming takes place during the Summer Term in the outdoor heated swimming pool.

Music holds an equally high profile. As well as curriculum Music lessons, there is a wide range of co-curricular music-making for all pupils with an interest in the subject. Many pupils learn instruments in school and they are given numerous opportunities to perform at concerts ranging from informal lunchtime events to major end of term extravaganzas.

In addition, pupils are offered a wide range of co-curricular activities, including Art Club, Ballet, Chess Club, Choir, Climbing Club, Creative Writing Club, Drama, Football, Film Making Club, Gymnastics, Judo, Music Theory, Recorder, Science Club, Trampolining Club and Training Orchestra. Pupils in Years 3–6 are also elected onto a School Council and a Digital Leadership Team.

Prospective pupils entering Years 1 and 2 are assessed by the class teacher and subject staff; prospective pupils entering Years 3 to 6 are assessed by the Individual Needs Department. Pupils who apply for entry to Year 6 will also be assessed on their ability to pass the 11+ entrance examinations to the Senior School.

Boys are prepared for Common Entrance Examinations and the majority of girls progress through to the Senior School at the age of 11, at which point entry is by entrance examination and interview. (For further information about the Senior School, see St Gabriel's entry in GSA section.)

Charitable status. The St Gabriel Schools Foundation is a Registered Charity, number 1062748. It exists to provide education for girls and boys from age 6 months to 11 years.

St George's Junior School, Weybridge

Thames Street, Weybridge, Surrey KT13 8NL

Tel:	01932 839400
Fax:	01932 839401
email:	contact@stgeorgesweybridge.com
website:	www.stgeorgesweybridge.com

Chairman of Board of Governors: Mr M Davie

Headmaster: **Mr A J W Hudson**, MA Cantab, PGCE, NPQH

Age Range. 3–11.

Number of Pupils. 611.

Fees per term (2016–2017). Nursery: £1,660 (mornings only), £2,720 (full days); Reception–Year 2 £3,135; Years 3–6 £4,305. Lunches (compulsory): £235.

St George's Junior School is a fully co-ed Roman Catholic Day School and all pupils attending the Junior School normally belong to one of the mainstream Christian traditions. The School was established in 1950 by a Religious Order of Priests and Brothers known as "The Josephites" who maintain a keen interest in the future of the School. Only pupils who are 'rising three' are admitted into the Nursery.

While the majority of the pupils at the school come from around North Surrey, some 13% of the pupils are from countries as far away as Australia, New Zealand, Hong Kong, South Africa, Brazil, Canada, USA as well as from most European countries including Russia. The School operates a very extensive bus service and an option for parents using cars to drop off their children at either the Junior or Senior School.

In September 2000 the Junior School moved from its previous co-located site with St George's College one mile down the road to its present 12½ acre site on the outskirts of Weybridge close to the River Thames. Since then a £1.5 million refurbishment programme has been completed involving the upgrading of most of the classrooms, the science teaching room, the library, the music room, playground equipment, an Astroturf pitch, cricket nets and the creation of a school wide computer network including three computer resources rooms, each classroom has an interactive whiteboard. In 2006, a new Development Launch focused on providing a new state-of-the-art Nursery classroom and a totally refurbished Kitchen and Dining Area, called 'The Mulberry Hall', which opened in 2008. A new Lower Years building opened in Autumn 2015 as the first part of a Master Plan which will see a Performing Arts Centre and Sports Hall erected over the coming years.

The Junior School has a genuinely happy atmosphere in which every pupil is respected and treated as an individual. The Headmaster considers the staff, pupils and parents to be constituent parts of an extended family. The School has always placed great emphasis on the importance of maintaining excellent channels of communication between members of staff, parents and pupils.

The size of classes ensures that the School is a learning community by creating the correct balance between pupil interaction and pupil-teacher contact. The pupils in the top two years of the School are taught by subject specialists. French is offered to all pupils from Year 1. The School was described in its most recent ISI report (2011) as having pupils whose "personal qualities are excellent and the emphasis on promoting the values of the Josephite tradition results in pupils who are well mannered, polite and welcoming".

All pupils are assessed on entry and when they leave at the end of Year 6 nearly all transfer to St George's College. Well over 150 scholarships, including music scholarships, have been won by pupils in Year 6 since 1989; in 2013, 7 academic, 2 Sports and 2 Music Scholarships were awarded.

While the pursuit of academic excellence is highly valued, the Mission Statement of the School stresses the importance of pupils having high personal self-esteem as well as emphasising the importance of their religious, spiritual, social and physical development. The School requires its pupils to have high moral values especially those of its school motto "Honesty and Compassion".

The Junior School has four Houses which compete against each other across a wide range of activities inside and outside the classroom including Music, Public Speaking and Sport.

Extracurricular and other enrichment activities are, likewise, considered to play an important role in the educational development of children. The extensive range of activities includes dance (ballet, modern and tap), gymnastics and clubs based on the academic subjects taught in the School. Since September 2013, Mandarin has been offered to Year 3 pupils as an after-school club. Pupils are taken to places of educational interest regularly including theatre, music and art trips and there is an annual Book Week during which pupils meet and listen to visiting authors and story-tellers.

Considerable emphasis is placed on the Creative and Performing Arts. Pupils have dance lessons throughout the school with specialist ballet and tap dance lessons being a compulsory part of the curriculum for all pupils up to the end of Reception Year. The School stages six major drama productions a year. All children from Year 2 have two lessons of music each week. Children in Year 2 learn the violin and recorder as part of the music curriculum. There is an Orchestra, Chapel Choir and Year 3 Choir which rehearse on a weekly basis as well as Violin, Brass, Guitar and Recorder ensembles. Individual music lessons are very popular with over 50% of the children in Years 2–6 learning at least one additional instrument. Concerts happen at least once every term and music lessons are supported by the use of the latest computer-based technology. Pupils have achieved considerable success at Public Speaking Competitions and achieve a very high level of attainment in their external Spoken English, Lamda and instrumental music exams. In 2013, 56 Year 6 pupils achieved 14 Distinctions and 42 Merits in their LAMDA exams, while all 29 Year 5 pupils gained Distinctions in their ESB exams.

Apart from its own sports facilities on site comprising an artificial sports pitch, netball and tennis courts, a sprung floor gymnasium and a swimming pool, the School has the use of 20 acres of outstanding sports facilities at the College including three floodlit netball/tennis courts, a floodlit artificial surface for hockey about to be completely refurbished, a four-court indoor tennis centre, three floodlit French clay courts, a sports hall and gym, three cricket squares, a tartan athletics track and six large grass fields.

The Junior School has a track record of great sporting success. In Rugby in 2013, the boys were U11 National Finalists, U10 National Quarter Finalists and the U9s were Plate Semi Finalists at the Regional Finals. In Hockey, the boys were U11 IAPS London and South East Regional Champions. In girls' Hockey, the U11s were IAPS London and South East Regional Champions and Quarter Finalists in the IAPS National Finals as well as coming second in the Surrey Cup competition.

In the midst of all this tangible success, the Junior School prides itself on ensuring that all children from Year 3 upwards have the opportunity to represent the School at least once each term in one of the mainstream sports i.e. Rugby, Hockey and Cricket for boys and Netball, Hockey and Rounders for girls.

School lunches are compulsory from Reception Year, are prepared on site and eaten in the dining rooms which can seat 320 people. The School offers a free supervised homework facility each weekday evening during term time until 4.45 pm for those children in Reception and Years 1 and 2. Children in Years 3–6 can sign up for clubs which continue until 5.00 pm.

For the last few years the school has usually had more applications for places than it can accommodate in all year groups. When vacancies do occur, pupils are admitted if they meet the School's entry criteria and successfully complete an assessment day at the School as well as receiving a satisfactory report from the current school where this is appropriate. Priority is afforded to siblings and Roman Catholics.

Charitable status. St George's College, Weybridge is a Registered Charity, number 1017853. The aims and objectives of the charity are the Christian education of young people.

St George's School

Windsor Castle, Windsor, Berks SL4 1QF

Tel: 01753 865553
Fax: 01753 842093
email: enqs@stgwindsor.co.uk
website: www.stgwindsor.org

Patron: Her Majesty The Queen

Visitor: The Lord Chancellor

Chairman of the Governors: The Revd Canon Dr H E Finlay, MA, PhD

Head Master: Mr Christopher McDade, BA Hons, FCollT, LTCL, PGCE

Deputy Head: Mr Kevin Wills, BSc Hons, PGCE

Age Range. 3–13 Co-educational.
Number of Pupils. 358 (23 boarders).
Fees per term (2016–2017). Weekly Boarders £6,953, Day Pupils £4,676–£5,239, Choristers (Boarding) £3,368, Pre-Prep £3,155–£3,578, Nursery £1,329–£1,650.

St George's School was established as part of the foundation of the Order of the Garter in 1348 when provision was made for the education of the first choristers. In 1893 the School moved into the Georgian building of the former College of the Naval Knights of Windsor situated between the mound of the Castle and the Home Park. Expansion followed with the admission of supernumerary (non-chorister) pupils. Extensions were made to the buildings in 1988 and 1996, the latter of which allowed for the opening of a Pre-Preparatory Department and Nursery. In 1997 girls were admitted to the School for the first time, entering both the Pre-Prep and the main school, and five years later the school became fully co-educational. A new Middle School building accommodating pupils in Years 3, 4 and 5, was opened in Spring 2006 by HRH Princess Alexandra. The school is a central part of the Foundation of the College of St George, within Windsor Castle. The current structure of the school is divided into the Lower School (EYFS to Year 3) and the Upper School (Year 4 to Year 8)

St George's School enjoys a long tradition of academic and musical excellence alongside impressive art, drama and sport. Many pupils gain academic, all-rounder and music

awards to some of the country's leading independent schools; in recent years they have included Eton, Hampton, King's Canterbury, Radley, Westminster and Lancing. The curriculum is broad and varied. In addition to core teaching subjects, French is introduced to Nursery children with the addition of Latin in Year 5 and Spanish in Year 6. Specialist teaching in PE and Music is provided from the Nursery upwards and in Art, DT and Drama from Year 3.

Facilities for games are excellent with pitches and playing fields on the Home Park Private, an indoor swimming pool, a recently resurfaced tennis and netball court and a gymnasium. Several areas of the school buildings have recently undergone refurbishment, including the creation of a Design Technology workshop and brand new Science laboratories opened in 2010 by HRH The Earl of Wessex. In 2013, a new Food Technology teaching room was opened and in 2015 there was a significant updating of the ICT suite. Enhanced Music facilities now include an Apple networked Music teaching room and recording studio.

The School seeks to pursue the highest standards and aims to develop happy, confident young people who aspire to achieve their potential whilst at St George's. There is a strong family ethos within the school community where each child's talents and skills are identified and nurtured. Pastoral care is excellent and each class teacher and form tutor knows the children in their care extremely well. There are frequent parents evenings for all pupils in the school, and parents are regularly invited to come in to support their children in plays, concerts and sports fixtures and to attend school services in St George's Chapel, Windsor Castle. Indeed the ISI Integrated Inspection report in February 2016 rated many key areas of the school as being Excellent.

Communications are excellent: two railway stations, the M25, M3, M4 and M40 are all close by and Heathrow is just fifteen minutes away.

Charitable status. St George's School, Windsor Castle is a Registered Charity, number 1100392. Its purpose is the education, either as boarding or day pupils, of children of pre-preparatory and preparatory school age and of the choristers who maintain the worship in the Queen's Free Chapel of Our Lady, St George and St Edward the Confessor in Windsor Castle.

St Helen's College

Parkway, Hillingdon, Middlesex UB10 9JX

Tel: 01895 234371
Fax: 01895 206948
email: info@sthelenscollege.com
website: www.sthelenscollege.com

Principals:
Mr D A Crehan, ARCS, BA, BSc, MSc, CPhys, MEd
Mrs G R Crehan, BA, MA, PGCE

Head Teacher: Mrs S Drummond, BEd Hons, MLDP

Age Range. 3–11 co-educational.
Number of Pupils. 359 Day Pupils.
Fees per term (2016–2017). £2,030–£3,700.

The aims of St Helen's College are to develop as fully as possible each child's academic potential, to provide a wide, balanced, stimulating and challenging curriculum, and to foster true values and good character based on moral and spiritual principles. The children enjoy a purposeful and happy 'family' atmosphere and are taught by committed professional teachers.

Children are prepared for independent senior schools and local grammar schools, and records of success are very good indeed. In addition to the academic subjects, sport, music and drama play an important part in the lives of the children.

A wide range of extra-curricular activities is offered, and pupils enjoy outings, day and residential, to many places of interest. There is an after-school club and summer school, and a holiday club which runs throughout the year.

St Hilary's Preparatory School

Holloway Hill, Godalming, Surrey GU7 1RZ
Tel: 01483 416551
email: registrar@sthilarysschool.com
website: www.sthilarysschool.com
Twitter: @StHilarysSchool
Facebook: /St-Hilarys-School-Trust

Chair of Governors: Mrs V J Gillman, DMS, MCMI

Headmistress: **Mrs J Whittingham**, BEd, Cert Prof Prac SpLD

Age Range. Girls 2–11, Boys 2–7.
Number of Pupils. 250 Day Pupils.
Fees per term (from January 2017). Including lunch: Reception £3,235, Year 1 £3,545, Year 2 £4,160, Year 3 £4,285, Years 4–6 £4,760. Kindergarten: £28.50 & Nursery: £29.90 per am/pm session with lunch extra.

St Hilary's is an independent preparatory day school which provides a stimulating, safe environment in which boys up to 7+ and girls up to 11+ can develop, be happy and flourish.

Situated in the heart of Godalming, St Hilary's prides itself in providing an outstanding all-round education, equipping pupils not only with strong academic standards but also the essential qualities and skills required beyond their time at our school. Ultimately we strive to ensure that all our pupils develop a real thirst for learning.

The Independent Schools Inspectorate judged our Early Years Foundation Stage 'Outstanding' in all areas in 2013/2014 and the main school achieved an outstanding school inspection report in November 2010.

Every child enjoys the benefits of well-qualified, enthusiastic staff and a broad curriculum combined with splendid facilities. Amenities include well-equipped classrooms, music wing, spacious hall for the performing arts, science room, library, modern ICT suite, design & technology and art studios, all-weather pitch, and the Hiorns Centre for drama, ballet and cooking. Small class sizes allow children to achieve their best in a dynamic and vibrant environment.

Outside the classroom, pupils can enjoy the woodland and play opportunities with the very popular Taurus Trail and exciting adventure play area. Pupils share a love of growing things in our gardens and appreciate the safe, beautiful surroundings.

Physical Education features highly at St Hilary's. The department gives all pupils equality of opportunity to participate in a broad range of activities. All pupils experience a variety of competitive and challenging situations. Our House system encourages healthy competition with matches, a swimming gala and sports days.

Children are given the opportunity to participate in a wide, varied number of extra-curricular activities, such as, gardening, football skills, drama, science, art, pottery, textiles, debating, First Aid, French, chess, gym, cross country, judo, cricket, dance, tap, choirs, woodwind, string ensemble, percussion, orchestra, recorder groups and Suzuki violin.

Speech & Drama is a highly popular option for many with pupils preparing for LAMDA (London Academy of Music and Dramatic Art) examinations. The school takes advantage of its ideal location and access to London for visits to galleries, museums and theatres.

Parents are guided in next school options and have the opportunity to make informed choices at a time when a child's true academic potential can be accurately predicted and talents in other areas identified. We have an excellent reputation in securing first-choice schools for our pupils when they leave. Boys in Year 2 and girls in Year 6 successfully move on to prestigious schools; every year many obtain academic, art, music, sport and drama scholarships.

Please do come and visit us; we will be delighted to welcome you and discuss your child's education. We hold a number of Open Days throughout the year when you can see the school in action; please visit our website for more details.

Charitable status. St Hilary's is a Registered Charity, number 312056. It exists to provide education for children.

St Hilda's School

High Street, Bushey, Hertfordshire WD23 3DA
Tel: 020 8950 1751
email: secretary@sthildasbushey.co.uk
           registrar@sthildasbushey.co.uk
website: www.sthildasbushey.com

Chairman of Governors: Mr T Barton, LLB Hons

Headmistress: **Miss S J Styles**, BA, MA

Age Range. Girls 2–11, Boys 2–4.
Number of Pupils. 130 Day Girls. Co-ed Nursery.
Fees per term (2016–2017). Prep School: £3,684–£3,961. Nursery fees upon application according to sessions chosen.

St Hilda's is an Independent Day School for girls aged 4–11, with a full-time nursery for boys and girls aged 2–4. It was founded in 1918 and has occupied its present 5-acre site since 1928. The Victorian house at the centre of the school has been continually improved, adapted and extended to provide an excellent educational environment. This includes a nature garden area, tennis courts, an indoor heated swimming pool, a large all-purpose hall, science laboratory, technology laboratory and computer suite. We teach a wide range of subjects to a high academic standard in a secure and happy environment in which every pupil can develop their academic and personal potential. We offer a broad and challenging curriculum in which art, drama and music play an important role. There is also a wide range of extra-curricular activities, including ballet, seasonal sports activities, ICT, languages and drama. Pre-school and after-school care is offered from 07.30 until 18.30 Monday to Friday during term time.

Charitable status. St Hilda's School is a Registered Charity, number 298140. It exists to provide education for girls.

St Hugh's

Carswell Manor, Faringdon, Oxon SN7 8PT
Tel: 01367 870700
Fax: 01367 870707
email: headmaster@st-hughs.co.uk
           registrar@st-hughs.co.uk
website: www.st-hughs.co.uk

Chairman of Governors: P G Daffern

Headmaster: **A J P Nott**, BA Hons, PGCE

Age Range. 3–13.

Number of Pupils. 350: 20 Weekly Boarders, 212 Day Pupils (of whom many flexi board); Pre-Prep (including Nursery) 98. (Boy-Girl ratio approximately 3:2, both boarding and day).

Fees per term (2016–2017). Upper School: Weekly Boarders £7,450, Day £6,225; Middle School: Weekly Boarders £6,970, Day £5,745; Pre-Prep £3,665–£3,995. (All fees inclusive, with very few compulsory extras.)

The School's main building is a fine Jacobean house with extensive grounds. Boys and girls are prepared for Common Entrance and Scholarship examinations to senior independent schools. The school is organised into four departments: Nursery (3–4), Pre-Prep (4–6), Middle School (7–8) and Upper School (9–13). Careful liaison ensures a strong thread of continuity throughout the school. The main entry points are at 3, 4, 7 and 9.

The School is not an academically selective school and both welcomes and accepts children from all backgrounds and a wide range of academic abilities. We aim to foster confidence and a love of learning across this range: an impressive scholarship and CE record and the provision of integral specialist support both bear testimony to our inclusive approach. The arts and sport feature strongly and pupils are encouraged to develop their talents and interests as broadly as possible.

St Hugh's is described by the Good Schools Guide as a school which "personifies what is best in prep school education".

Charitable status. St Hugh's is a Registered Charity, number 309640. It exists to provide a centre of excellence for the education of children.

St Hugh's

Cromwell Avenue, Woodhall Spa LN10 6TQ

Tel:	01526 352169
Fax:	01526 351520
email:	office@st-hughs.lincs.sch.uk
website:	www.st-hughs.lincs.sch.uk
Twitter:	@sthughslincs
Facebook:	/sthughslincs

Chairman of Governors: J Harris

Headmaster: **C A Ward**, BEd Hons

Age Range. 2–13.

Number of Pupils. 182. Boarders: 13 boys, 6 girls. Day: 53 boys, 50 girls. Pre-Prep: 16 boys, 11 girls. Nursery: 21 children.

Fees per term (2016–2017). Boarding £6,509; Day: £4,306–£4,783; Pre-Prep: £2,845.

St Hugh's School was founded by the Forbes family in 1925, became a Charitable Trust in 1964 and has continued to prosper over the years administered by a forward-thinking Governing Body.

Today the School is fully co-educational, offering both day and boarding places. The Headmaster is assisted by 21 qualified and experienced teachers. Through its Headmaster the School is a member of IAPS (The Independent Association of Prep Schools) as well as the Boarding Schools' Association.

Boys and girls are prepared for the Common Entrance and Scholarship examinations. The School's academic record is excellent, with regular awards being gained to major Independent Schools, as well as places in Lincolnshire Grammar Schools. Children with special learning needs are treated sympathetically within the mainstream, with support from specialist staff. The aim of the School is to give every child a good all-round education and to discover and develop his or her own particular talents.

The major school games for boys are rugby, hockey and cricket, and for girls netball, hockey and rounders. Both boys and girls can also enjoy cross-country, tennis, athletics and swimming. There is an annual Sports Day. All children have PE each week with time set aside for instruction in gymnastics and swimming. Skills in games such as basketball and badminton also form the basis of these lessons.

The school lays heavy emphasis on extra-curricular activities, sport of various kinds, music, the visual arts and drama. All teachers are expected to help in some way with this. There is also a strong and continuing Christian tradition at St Hugh's, where children are encouraged to consider what they believe and develop a faith of their own within the context of regular acts of Christian Worship.

The school has excellent facilities including a modern sports hall, an assembly hall with stage and lighting, a heated indoor swimming pool, extensive playing fields including an all-weather pitch, a fine library, dedicated classrooms and a large Music, Design and ICT studios. The facilities are continually being updated and added to.

Boarders are accommodated in a well-appointed House under the close supervision of Houseparents. Dormitories and common rooms are bright and cheerful and recognition is given to the importance of children having a place where they can feel at home and relaxed at the end of the day. Contact with parents and guardians is well maintained. Every half term is punctuated by an exeat weekend and arrangements are made for boarders whose parents live abroad. Minibus transport for day pupils is provided from Boston, Louth, Skegness, Lincoln, Market Rasen and Sleaford.

The Pre-Preparatory department caters for approximately 40 children, aged from 4 to 7, and is located in its own building with separate play area and staff.

The Nursery for children between 2 and 4 is attached to the Pre-Prep and accommodates approximately 45 children. The fees are fully inclusive.

Charitable status. St Hugh's School (Woodhall Spa) Limited is a Registered Charity, number 527611. It exists to provide a high standard of education and care to pupils from the age of 2 to 13.

St John's Beaumont

Priest Hill, Old Windsor, Berkshire SL4 2JN

Tel:	01784 494053
Fax:	01784 494048
email:	admissions@sjb.email
website:	www.sjb.community
Twitter:	@SJBHeadmaster
	@SJBAway
	@SJBBoarding
	@SJBSports

Chairman of Governors: M C Brenninkmeyer

Headmaster: **G E F Delaney**, BA Hons, PGCE

Age Range. 3½–13.

Number of Boys. 310 (60 Full, Weekly, Tailored Boarders; 240 Day Boys).

Fees per term (2016–2017). Boarding £8,725; Weekly Boarding £7,462; Tailored Boarding £6,951–£7,251; Day

Boys £3,916–£5,751; Pre-Preparatory (Nursery–Year 1) £3,006.

St John's is a Roman Catholic Jesuit School. Classes are small, and boys can receive individual attention according to their needs and abilities. Although following the Common Entrance syllabus for senior independent schools, St John's also promotes the National Curriculum and boys are assessed at Key Stages 1 and 2, audited by the Local Education Authority. Boys are prepared for entry to some of the top independent schools in the country and have won many scholarships in recent years.

The first purpose-built prep school in England, this pretty Victorian building stands in 70 acres on the edge of Windsor Great Park. It has a state-of-the-art sport hall and impressive ICT facilities endorsed by Microsoft awarding the school Beacon status. There is a dedicated science and art block, music school, concert hall and 25-metre indoor swimming pool. Games are played every day and the school particularly excels at rugby, cricket, tennis and swimming. The school's pool is also used by other schools and the local community. Wireless technology is available in classrooms enabling access to individual tablets and there are interactive whiteboards in all classrooms. On top of their daily curriculum schedules, there are over 40 extra-curricular activities offered after school. These include rock climbing, chess, polo, drama, art, rowing and mandarin.

The boys have daily opportunity for religious practice, as well as formal instruction and informal guidance.

An illustrated prospectus is available from the Headmaster, who is always pleased to meet parents and to show them round the school.

Charitable status. St John's is a Registered Charity, number 230165. It exists to provide education for boys.

St John's College Infant and Junior School

Grove Road South, Southsea, Hampshire PO5 3QW

Tel:	023 9281 5118
Fax:	023 9287 3603
email:	info@stjohnscollege.co.uk
website:	www.stjohnscollege.co.uk

Chairman of Governors: Mr T Forer, BA

Headmaster: **Mr R A Shrubsall**, MA Ed

Head of Pre-Prep: Mrs C Davies, BA Hons QTS

Age Range. Co-educational 2–11 years.
Number of Pupils. 150.
Fees per term (2016–2017). Junior School: Day £2,880–£3,075; Years 5 & 6 UK Boarding £8,150.

St John's College is an independent school founded to provide an academic education in a Christian environment. The College is fully co-educational, day and boarding, with approximately 600 pupils and students ranging in age from 2 to 18. We offer a continuous range of education, starting in the Nursery and progressing through the Junior and Senior schools to the Sixth Form. We are a Christian school but welcome pupils of all faiths and also those with no religious beliefs.

The Junior School is a self-contained unit but located on the main College campus. The Junior School enjoys the use of many excellent facilities: a sports centre, theatre, computer suite, library, science laboratory and music room. The attractive site is complemented by 40 acres of well-maintained playing fields, located on the outskirts of the city.

A broadly balanced and extended curriculum is offered, encompassing all aspects of the National Curriculum at Key Stages 1 and 2. Close staff liaison ensures a smooth automatic transition for pupils into the Senior School at age 11. The Early Years Foundation Stage is covered in Nursery and Reception Year (known as Little St John's).

The Junior School has a fine academic, musical and sporting tradition and there is a wide range of extra-curricular clubs which run during lunchtimes and after school. Educational and character-building residential trips are offered at holiday times.

St John's is committed to developing the whole person, but at the very heart of all that we do is teaching and learning. Our academic record is a very good one and the commitment of our staff to each pupil is outstanding.

A prospectus and further details are available from the Admissions Registrar.

St John's College School

75 Grange Road, Cambridge, Cambs CB3 9AA

Tel:	01223 353532 Headmaster
	01223 353652 Admissions Secretary
	01223 272701 Bursar
Fax:	01223 355846
email:	shoffice@sjcs.co.uk
	bhoffice@sjcs.co.uk
website:	www.sjcs.co.uk

Chairman of Governors: The Reverend Mr Duncan Dormor

Headmaster: **Mr Neil R Chippington**, MA, MEd, FRCO

Age Range. 4–13.
Number of Children. 451 girls and boys (including 20 Chorister and 16 Non-Chorister boy and girl boarders).
Fees per term (2016–2017). Choristers £2,511; Day Boys and Girls (4–13) £3,617–£4,771 (according to age); Boarders £7,534. Bursaries available for Choristers.

Profile. St John's prides itself on the quality of the academic and pastoral care it provides for each child. Through relaxed and friendly relations with children in a well-structured environment rich with opportunity; through close monitoring of progress; through communication and cooperation with parents; through expert staffing and, above all, through a sense of community that cares for the strengths and weaknesses of each of its members, St John's has consistently achieved outstanding results exemplified by over 70 scholarships during the last three years. Whilst its Choristers maintain the tradition of choral services and tour the world, St John's status as an Expert Centre for ICT, and other innovations, ensure the school's commitment to the future. Mr Neil Chippington joined St John's as the new Headmaster in September 2016, having been Head at St Paul's Cathedral School in London.

Entry. At 4–7 by parental interview; at 7–12 by parental interview, report from previous school and, as appropriate, assessment.

Curriculum. The curriculum surrounds the core of formal skills teaching with a breadth of enrichment and extension for each child's talents. In addition to the usual subjects including specialist taught DT, ICT, Art, Music, Dance and Drama, and PE for all pupils, the following are also available: French (from 4+), Latin (from 9+), Greek (optional from 11+), Spanish (11+). Pupils prepared for CE and Scholarship examinations. Philosophy and Study Skills are now regularly taught to pupils in certain year groups and all pupils are being introduced to Mindfulness.

Leavers. Virtually all go to senior independent day or boarding schools. The School works closely with parents to assist them in finding the best school for their child.

Consultation. Tutorial system (1 teacher to 10 pupils) with daily tutorial session timetabled. Half yearly academic assessments, end of year examinations, termly Parents' Evenings and weekly staff 'surgery' times.

Sports. Athletics, Badminton, Basketball, Cricket, Cross Country, Football, Golf, Gymnastics, Hockey, Netball, Rounders, Rowing, Rugby, Short Tennis, Squash, Swimming, Table Tennis, Tennis. All games are timetabled and therefore given significant status. All major sports strong.

Activities. Numerous clubs including Art, Chess, Dance, Drama, Pottery, Sketching, Design Technology, Craft, Information Technology, Maths games and puzzles, Magic, Touch-typing, Cycling Proficiency, General Knowledge, Debating, Poetry, Sewing and Wardrobe. College Choir of international status, Chamber Groups, Orchestras, School Chapel Choir, Junior Chamber Choir, Parents' Choir, Major theatrical productions, e.g. *The Sound of Music*, *Hamlet*, and theatrical opportunities for all children. A range of visits relating to curriculum plus French, Classics, skiing and outward bound trips.

Facilities. School on two sites with facilities used by all pupils.

Byron House (4–8). Outstanding facilities including Science, DT Centre, two large suites of networked PCs, computerised Library, Drama Studio, Gym, Hall, and specialist Music wing. The Byron House site has also been redeveloped and the children can now use the newly landscaped and planted 'Forest Garden'. The site now has completely redesigned classrooms and a large learning space for child-initiated learning and digital learning. The new rooms are fitted with bespoke, streamlined storage. Investigative and collaborative skills have been fostered by the use of the new 'working walls' and 'writeable tables'.

Senior House (9–13). The Senior House site has been completely redeveloped. In addition to existing facilities such as the Chapel, Theatre, Gymnasium Science Laboratory, Art Room, ICT Room, Swimming Pool and Music School, the site now boasts 14 new classrooms, an outstanding Library, a new DT and Computer Control and Graphics facility, a second Science Laboratory, a new Drama Studio, new Music facilities, a Quiet Garden, a new Multi-Sports Court and changing block, extensive new storage and excellent staff facilities.

Boarding. From age 8. Girl and boy boarders form an integral part of life at St John's and benefit from all the School's facilities whilst living in the homely, caring atmosphere of a brand new Boarding House which was completed in Spring 2011. The Boarding House accommodates up to 40 boys and girls. These improved facilities include recreation areas, a library, TV, table tennis and use of all Senior House facilities. Day boarding and 'Waiters' facilities allow the School to be flexible to the needs of parents and children alike.

Charitable status. St John's College School is part of St John's College Cambridge, which is a Registered Charity, number 1137428.

St John's School

Potter Street Hill, Northwood, Middlesex HA6 3QY
Tel: 020 8866 0067
Fax: 020 8868 8770
email: office@st-johns.org.uk
website: www.st-johns.org.uk
Twitter: @stjsnorthwood

Chairman of Governors: Mr J Armstrong, Esq

Headmaster: Mr M S Robinson, BSc, PGCE
Loughborough

Age Range. 3–13.
Number of Boys. 350 Day Boys (Prep 221; Pre-Prep and Nursery 129).
Fees per annum (2016–2017). Nursery £9,780; Pre-Preparatory £13,200; Preparatory £14,200.

Facing South, on a 35-acre site, we have outstanding views over London. Since the Merchant Taylors' Educational Trust took the School under its wing, impressive development has taken place. St John's has gained a gymnasium and changing block, two science laboratories, a six classroom Pre-Prep Department and a Junior classroom block. Another major development provided an Assembly Hall/Theatre, an Art Studio, Design & Technology Workshop, ICT Centre and a new Music Department. At the same time, other areas of the School were refurbished creating specialist teaching areas for English, French, History, Geography and Mathematics. We also acquired an area of grassland and woodland for ecological and environmental study, to add to our extensive playing fields and formal gardens.

A major extension of our Pre-Preparatory Department provided Nursery facilities, an Information Technology Suite and Library. Extra play area, including an 'indoor quiet area' and a Forest School, have also been created for our Pre-Prep and Nursery pupils. Our playing fields have been transformed with the construction of a large, all-weather multi-purpose sports area. At the same time, our four rugby pitches and athletics track were levelled and provided with excellent drainage and irrigation. Most recently, we have created a small Golf Course.

Most of the boys enter the School at either the age of three into the Nursery or at four into the Pre-Prep and there is a separate entry into the Prep School at seven. St John's has an excellent record of success in scholarship and senior school entrance examinations. Boys are prepared for all independent schools, however, our links with Merchant Taylors' School, Northwood, are particularly strong.

Although the School was originally a Church of England foundation, boys of all religions and denominations are welcome.

Charitable status. St John's School, part of the Merchant Taylors' Educational Trust, is a Registered Charity, number 1063738. It exists for the purpose of educating boys.

St John's School

Broadway, Sidmouth, Devon EX10 8RG
Tel: 01395 513984
Fax: 01395 514539
email: contact.stjohns@iesmail.com
website: www.stjohnsdevon.co.uk
Twitter: @St_Johns_School
Facebook: @stjohnsschool

Headmaster: Mr Mike Burgess, BA Hons

Age Range. 2–18 Co-educational.
Number of Pupils. Main School 200, of whom 40–50 are Boarders. The Nursery (up to 5 years) has up to 50 children. Girl/boy ratio 50:50.
Fees per term (2016–2017). Day: £2,235–£3,635; UK Boarding: £6,230–£6,835; International Boarding: £7,200–£7,835; International Study Centre: £9,580–£9,945. Full fee details are available on our website.

About St John's. St John's School is an independent day and boarding school for girls and boys aged 2–18. The school is located on a hill overlooking the sea in Sidmouth and benefits from excellent facilities, including beautiful historic buildings, extensive grounds and playing fields, indoor sports hall, adventure playground and tennis courts. With its warm, happy atmosphere, St John's prides itself on providing a caring and safe environment for all its students. Most importantly it is large enough to provide a broad study programme yet small enough to retain a special family feel that is valued by our students, parents and staff alike.

Our School is part of the wider organisation of International Education Systems (IES) and combines traditional values with a contemporary, international approach to learning. St John's is an IB World School.

Structure of St John's. St John's offers an 'all-through' education for girls and boys aged 2–18.

Nursery (Age 2–4). St John's Nursery provides a high-quality day care facility through its Early Bird department and a more structured pre-school environment in its nursery class. Nursery is located in a separate area of School but is able to benefit from the main school facilities including the swimming pool, sports hall and dining hall. Early Years Vouchers are accepted.

Junior School (Reception to Year 6). In the Junior School, the children follow an exciting 'cross-curricular' way of learning, underpinned by traditional values. We have recently become one of only 14 schools in the UK to be authorised to teach the International Baccalaureate Primary Years Programme and we are the only school in the South West of the UK to offer it.

Senior School (Year 7 to Year 11). The Senior School offers an integrated programme based on the National Curriculum, combined with a series of individual and theme-based projects to investigate and extend all topics, culminating in IGCSEs in Year 11.

Sixth Form (Years 12 and 13). As a result of the success of our Senior School, St John's opened a Sixth Form in September 2013. Our teachers are fully trained to be able to deliver a comprehensive range of A and AS Level courses across a wide range of subjects, in a small class, tutorial-style environment. Please see website for further information. A/AS Level English Language, A/AS Level English Literature, A/AS Level Mathematics, A/AS Level Physics, A/AS Level Biology, A/AS Level Chemistry, A/AS Level Applied ICT, A/AS Level Geography, A/AS Level Business Studies, A/AS Level Psychology, A/AS Level French, A/AS Level Spanish, AS Marine Science (one year only), AS Global Perspectives (one year only), A/AS Level Art, A Level Music.

Entrance Requirements. We accept students with a broad range of abilities as our focus is on providing education that is designed to challenge the individual. All students will be asked to take a small Placement Test and we would request sight of at least one School Report. Each student will be invited for a short meeting with the Headmaster.

Transport. A number of bus routes are in place across the county.

Boarding. Weekly or full boarding is available.

St Joseph's In The Park School

St Mary's Lane, Hertingfordbury, Hertfordshire SG14 2LX

Tel: 01992 513810
email: admin@stjosephsinthepark.co.uk
            marketing@stjosephsinthepark.co.uk
website: www.stjosephsinthepark.co.uk
Twitter: @fromthepark

Chair of Governors: Mrs Pauline Maile

Head: **Mr Douglas Brown**, BA Hons

Age Range. 3–11 Co-educational.
Number of Pupils. 154.
Fees per term (2016–2017). Pre School (full-time) £2,964 (fees are pro-rata for more or fewer sessions), Infants £3,819, Lower Juniors Y3 to Y4 £3,970, Upper Juniors Y5 to Y6 £3,993, Woodlands Learning Support Centre Y3 to Y6 £5,423. All fees are inclusive of books, stationery and lunches.

St Joseph's In The Park is a single-form entry, co-educational school for children between the ages of 3 and 11 years. Founded in 1898, it is one of the oldest Independent Schools in the area.

Set within 40 acres of Hertingfordbury Park on the outskirts of Hertford, St Joseph's In The Park has not only a celebrated reputation for high academic standards, but also a particularly outstanding tradition in pastoral care and a family environment. Our latest ISI inspection judged us to be 'Excellent' in all areas. This is the highest possible accolade from the largest inspection body for independent schools. The Inspectors noted that *"the pupils' achievement is excellent. It is underpinned by high quality teaching and a vibrant curriculum"*; in addition, the *"pupils thrive in the school's atmosphere of hard work, enjoyment and effort"*.

Through each Key Stage the children experience an exciting curriculum. The core focus of Literacy, Mathematics and Science is supported by a themed approach to some of the Foundation Subjects.

Our environment permits children to develop and learn in a contemporary educational setting which includes:

• a designated Wrap Around Care room providing an extended day, starting with Breakfast Club from 7.30 am and After School Care until 6.00 pm with a light tea at 4.30 pm;

• the Woodlands Department of Learning, established in 1998, providing differentiated education for children between Years 3 and 6 who need extra learning support;

• a Wednesday afternoon programme of technology, art and sport for Juniors which changes every half term during the year and may be enriched to include film making, textiles, photography, cookery, golf, forest school, skiing and street dance delivered by specialists. After exams our Year 6 are offered an Opportunities Week, which is intended to prepare them for life beyond St Joseph's and support their individual development;

• two choirs and music lessons in dedicated music rooms that include singing, guitar, drums, clarinet, violin and piano, ensuring that music is enjoyed throughout the school;

• a dedicated ICT room, wireless network across the school, interactive whiteboards in every classroom;

• an Art & Design room to provide a bespoke area for creativity;

• a separate Science Room providing space for discovery, taught by a dedicated Science Teacher;

• healthy-eating menus on a three-week rotation providing nut-free, nutritious and varied meals all prepared in the school kitchen by experienced and long-standing catering staff;

• extensive woodland setting within beautiful parkland that provides a wonderful environment for our children to learn and develop outdoors;

• an outdoor heated swimming pool, sports field and large, multi-purpose hall for drama, dance, concerts and sports;

• on-site dedicated car park.

A prospectus which further illustrates the distinctiveness of the school is available on request.

Charitable status. St Joseph's In The Park School is a Registered Charity, number 1111064.

St Lawrence College Junior School

College Road, Ramsgate, Kent CT11 7AF
Tel: 01843 572912
Fax: 01843 572913
email: jsoffice@slcuk.com
website: www.slcuk.com

Chairman of the Council: Mr David W Taylor, MA Oxon, PGCE, FRSA

Head: **Mrs Ellen Rowe**

Age Range. 3–11.
Number of Pupils. 200 boys and girls, a few of whom are boarders.
Fees per term (2016–2017). Boarders £8,275, Day £2,420–£3,785.

St Lawrence College Junior School offers a supportive, caring environment, based on traditional Christian values, in which children are given every opportunity to fulfil their potential. Academic expectations are high, but realistic and open-minded. Personal attention is given within small classes where talents are recognised and needs are catered for. There is a strong belief that education, in its truest sense, is measured not just in a student's exam results but by its ability to open young people's minds.

Most pupils transfer to the Senior School at 11+, and scholarships are regularly earned. There is also an excellent record of success at securing places in the highly-selective local grammar schools.

The Junior School is based in an attractive Victorian building in a peaceful corner of the 45-acre St Lawrence College campus. Its own independent facilities include a Music Department and Performance Hall, Science Lab, Art Studio, adventure playgrounds, tennis courts and spacious playing fields. These have recently been enhanced by the addition of a Learning Resources Centre, where library resources are integrated with the latest technology. Membership of the wider College community gives pupils the best of both worlds, and they are able to share many of the Senior School's excellent specialist facilities, including the Sports Centre and Theatre. Boarders enjoy living in Kirby House, an ultra-modern, eco-friendly development which offers accommodation of an exceptional quality.

A wide range of extracurricular opportunities includes sports such as rugby, hockey, cricket, rounders, netball, football, athletics, cross-country running, swimming and dance. There are plenty of fixtures against other schools, but, most importantly, children learn the value of fitness, cooperative teamwork and good sportsmanship. There is a proud musical tradition, and plenty of scope for drama and the creative arts. Some Activities take place at the end of the school day, but most are concentrated into the popular, informal Saturday morning programme.

St Lawrence's Christian heritage underpins all that the Junior School stands for. An atmosphere of trust and mutual respect is based on kindness, forgiveness and consideration for others. There is a strong emphasis placed on thoughtful conduct, courtesy and good manners, and on endowing young people with a clear sense of moral responsibility.

Charitable status. The Corporation of St Lawrence College is a Registered Charity, number 307921. It exists to provide education for boys and girls.

St Leonards Junior School

St Andrews, Fife KY16 9QJ
Tel: 01334 472126
Fax: 01334 476152
email: sljs@stleonards-fife.org
website: www.stleonards-fife.org
Twitter: @StLeonards_Head
Facebook: /stleonardsschool

Chairman of the St Leonards Council: James Murray, MA, LLB, DL

Headmaster: **William Goldsmith**, BA Hons Durham, QTS Reading

Age Range. 5–12.
Number of Pupils. 151 (80 girls, 71 boys).
Fees per term (2016–2017). £3,208 (Years 1–5), £3,595 (Years 6–7).

St Leonards Junior School in St Andrews is the co-educational junior school of St Leonards. The school is administered by the St Leonards Council and educates children between the ages of 5 and 12, from Year 1 to Year 7.

Pupils are prepared for entry to St Leonards Senior School. With specialist teachers and small class sizes, children benefit from individual attention. In addition to a strong academic tradition, drama, music, art, ICT and PE are included in the timetable.

Outside the classroom, a wide variety of sports are available; netball, rugby, hockey, lacrosse, tennis and cricket being the main team activities. Tuition in golf, judo and swimming is also offered. Outdoor education activities include watersports. There are also classes in Scottish Country Dancing and ballet.

Charitable status. St Leonards School is a Registered Charity, number SC010904. It exists to provide education to children between the ages of 5 and 18.

St Margaret's Junior School
Bushey

Merry Hill Road, Bushey, Hertfordshire WD23 1DT
Tel: 020 8416 4400
Fax: 020 8416 4401
email: prepoffice@smbushey.com
website: www.stmargaretsbushey.co.uk
Twitter: @StMargsBushey
Facebook: @StMargaretsBushey
LinkedIn: /St Margaret's School, Bushey

Chair of Governors: Miss M Rudland

Headmistress: Mrs R Hardy, MA Oxon, MEd, FRSA

Head of Junior School: **Mrs C Aisthorpe**, BEd Hons, LRAM

Age Range. Girls 4–11.
Number of Pupils. 118.
Fees per term (2016–2017). Years 4–6 £4,389, Transition (Year 3) £3,996, Reception, Years 1 & 2 £3,333.

St Margaret's School in Bushey, Hertfordshire is among the oldest girls' independent schools in the UK, established in 1749. It is a day and boarding school for girls aged 4 to 18. It has an excellent record of academic success, which is attributed to the School's emphasis upon providing the very best pastoral care. The School is set within 60 acres of stunning Hertfordshire countryside which offers girls abundant space to grow and be inspired in safety.

St Margaret's Junior School is distinct from the wider School. It is a day school offering a warm and nurturing environment for girls in their primary school years. Through this environment the school prides itself upon its consistent ability to stimulate and challenge girls to reach their potential and become confident members of society. Girls achieve in a myriad of ways as the school works to ensure that each fulfils her academic potential and is inspired to have a love of learning.

The Junior School's curriculum is challenging and broad in variety. It aims to identify and develop each girl's unique skill, talent and curiosity, extending her horizons and expectations. Within the School there are numerous opportunities to thrive through house, class and school-wide activities. There is a choir, an orchestra, opportunities for speech and drama through annual productions and concerts, sport, dance, numerous leadership opportunities, workshops, field trips and many other co-curricular activities. Equipped within this happy and secure education girls move confidently and seamlessly from the Junior School to the Senior School with independent and inquiring minds, a positive attitude to learning and an appetite for new experiences and challenges.

School surveys consistently feature comments from parents saying that St Margaret's is a happy, friendly and vibrant family community filled with the cheerful chatter of lively minds and the hum of purposeful activity. An exceptional team of dedicated staff are committed to bringing out the best in every girl, focusing on each as an individual.

To find out more or to arrange to visit the school, please visit our website: www.stmargaretsbushey.co.uk.

Charitable status. St Margaret's School Bushey is a Registered Charity, number 1056228.

St Margaret's Preparatory School

Curzon Street, Calne, Wiltshire SN11 0DF

Tel:	01249 857220
Fax:	01249 857227
email:	office@stmargaretsprep.org.uk
website:	www.stmargaretsprep.org.uk
Twitter:	@StMargaretsPrep

Chairman of Governors: Mr S Knight, FRICS

Headmistress: Mrs K E Cordon, GLCM, LLCM TD, ALCM

Age Range. 3–11.
Number of Pupils. 200 Day: 110 girls, 90 boys.
Fees per term (2016–2017). £1,538–£4,200.
From the Headmistress – Mrs Karen Cordon:

How do you measure an excellent education? Some would argue it's by exam results and a smooth passage to the next school, but I firmly believe that the unquantifiable aspects are every bit as important a benchmark.

St Margaret's is so much more than just a stepping-stone to academic success at 11+. In joining our vibrant community your son or daughter will start a lifelong journey of exploration. We will provide your child with endless opportunities to unearth talents, ignite interests, take risks, and experience failure as well as success. Along the way your son might discover a passion for music, or your daughter may become a gifted sportswoman.

Like you, we aspire for your child to be more than the sum of his or her academic achievement. That's why we place just as much value on building self-confidence and self-esteem, on encouraging self-assessment and personal

organisation. These qualities are harder to measure, but they are the key to your child ultimately being the best he or she can be.

Naturally, you'll be keen to understand what makes St Margaret's special? You will undoubtedly want your children to be happy and enjoy a broad and stimulating education that's rich in opportunities. But St Margaret's is so much more.

The right environment. Your child will learn in a safe, nurturing environment and spend each day in modern, stimulating and purpose-built teaching spaces. 30 acres of campus and off-site facilities mean there's space to explore, learn, play, let off steam, relax, think and grow.

Facilities and opportunities to develop potential. Wherever your child's strengths and interests lie, we have the facilities to support them. Learning spaces are contemporary, vibrant and well-equipped; these have been purpose-built in the last 10 years. These include dedicated specialist teaching rooms; a 25m indoor swimming pool; sports pitches; all-weather Astroturf; Chapel; dining hall; theatre and an outstanding Library and Computer Suite where interactive learning takes place. Additionally, outdoor space is plentiful and children enjoy time spent in the school garden, wildlife area, courtyard classroom or one of the many play areas.

A tailored learning programme. Teaching throughout the school is tailored to meet the needs of the individual child. Children are encouraged to reflect and evaluate their own learning and with support identify their next steps. Specialist teachers offer a wide range of experiences and as a result, our teaching delivers truly personalised learning for each child. An extensive range of mobile technology enhances learning across the curriculum.

Zest and vitality. Your child will join a school with real spirit and energy, which lives each day to the full. We purposefully pack excitement and learning experiences into every moment. Our staff are passionate about teaching and lessons are fun, vibrant and engaging. The children's love of learning is infectious and we hope it'll rub off on you too!

Foundations for life. Of course you want your children to be happy, alongside giving them the best possible start in life. St Margaret's is a place where friendships and special memories are created and where a love of learning is established. Your children will understand that success requires hard work, personal responsibility, respect and consideration for others. These qualities will remain with them, equipping him or her for future challenges and providing an edge in years to come.

I would really like to have the opportunity to find out more about your family and help you decide whether St Margaret's is the right place for your child's exciting journey of adventure and exploration. We welcome visitors at any time of year – please contact us to make an appointment.

St Martin's Ampleforth

Gilling Castle, Gilling East, York YO62 4HP

Tel:	01439 766600
Fax:	01439 788538
email:	headmaster@stmartins.ampleforth.org.uk
website:	www.ampleforth.org.uk/stmartins

Chairman of the Trustees: Rt Rev Cuthbert Madden

Headmaster: Dr David Moses, MA, DPhil

Age Range. 3+ to 13+ years.
Number of Pupils. 150 (40 Boarders, 110 Flexi Boarders and Day Children).

Fees per term (2016–2017). Boarding £7,509; Day £2,693–£4,991.

St Martin's Ampleforth is a boarding and day preparatory school which takes boys and girls from the age of 3+ years and prepares them for Common Entrance and Scholarship examinations. It is expected most of the pupils will enter Ampleforth College at 13+.

St Martin's Ampleforth is based in a 14th century castle with spacious and secluded gardens, 18 miles north of York and close to the North Yorkshire Moors National Park.

All Faiths are made most welcome in this Benedictine school. The Chaplaincy team is led by a monk of Ampleforth Abbey.

The highest academic standards are aimed for, within a broad and challenging curriculum. Each pupil's ability is taken into account. Very able children are provided for and coached for scholarships to Ampleforth College and other leading independent senior schools, whilst those with learning difficulties, including dyslexia, are given qualified specialist help. Each form of approximately 15 children has a tutor responsible for overall progress and pastoral support. Setting is in place from Year 6 and beyond.

There is a striking variety of extracurricular pursuits including horse riding, fencing, golf, shooting, drama, swimming and debating. The School has an enviable reputation for games and fields highly successful teams in rugby, netball, cricket, rounders, hockey, track and field and cross-country running.

Music is strong. Typically, 80% of pupils learn musical instruments and perform regularly. The School provides the trebles for the acclaimed Ampleforth College Schola Cantorum and there is an increasingly successful girls' Schola too. A purpose-built performing arts centre enhances the current provision for choral and instrumental performance as well as fostering drama throughout the school.

Parents are considered part of the School community. They are welcome at any time, especially for matches, other organised events and, of course, for Mass on Sundays and feast days.

Facilities include a sports hall, ICT room, Music School, Language School, all-weather cricket nets, a 9-hole golf course and all-weather floodlit astroturf. The extensive grounds, including woods, lakes and gardens, combine a sense of space and freedom with unrivalled beauty.

Bursaries are available.

Daily transport is provided to and from Pickering, Malton, Kirkbymoorside, Boroughbridge, Easingwold, York and Helmsley.

Charitable status. St Martin's Ampleforth, as part of the St Laurence Trust, is a registered charity, number 1063808 and exists to provide education for boys and girls.

St Martin's School

40 Moor Park Road, Northwood, Middlesex HA6 2DJ

Tel:	01923 825740
Fax:	01923 835452
email:	office@stmartins.org.uk
website:	www.stmartins.org.uk
Twitter:	@stmartinsprep

Chairman of Governors: Roy Jakes

Headmaster: **David T Tidmarsh**, BSc Hons, PGCE

Age Range. 3–13.
Number of Boys. 400 Day Boys.
Fees per term (2016–2017). Main School £4,700; Pre-Prep £4,370; Kindergarten £1,775 (mornings). Bursaries are available, details on request.

St Martin's aims to provide boys aged 3–13 with the breadth of education and experience necessary for them to realise their full potential in a safe and friendly environment. An enthusiastic staff of 40 experienced and well-qualified teachers maintains high academic standards and provides broad sporting, musical and cultural opportunities. The atmosphere is friendly and lively with great emphasis on pastoral care.

The School, which is an Educational Trust, administered by a Board of Governors, prepares boys for entry to all the Independent Senior Schools. One hundred and two Scholarship awards have been won to senior schools during the last five years. The School, which is in a pleasant residential area, stands in 12 acres of grounds. Facilities include a Kindergarten and separate Pre-Preparatory building; two Science Laboratories; a Performing Arts Centre; a Sports Centre including an indoor swimming pool; a playground; two ICT suites; an Art Studio with facilities for Design Technology; 3 Tennis Courts.

ICT, Art, DT, and Music are included in the curriculum for all boys, and a large proportion of the boys in the School learn a musical instrument. There is a varied after-school activity programme for boys to pursue their interests.

There is a pre-school and after-school club from Kindergarten age upwards enabling parents to work a full day.

The School is divided into Patrols for competitions in work and games, and senior boys make a responsible contribution towards the running of the School. Boys are taught football, rugby, cross-country running, hockey, cricket, swimming, athletics and tennis. The school has a fine reputation in inter-school matches.

Charitable status. St Martin's (Northwood) Preparatory School Trust Limited is a Registered Charity, number 312648. It exists to provide education for boys.

St Mary's School, Hampstead

47 Fitzjohn's Avenue, London NW3 6PG

Tel:	020 7435 1868
Fax:	020 7794 7922
email:	enquiries@stmh.co.uk
website:	www.stmh.co.uk

Chairman of Governors: Mrs Susan McCarron

Headmistress: **Mrs Harriet Connor-Earl**, BA

Age Range. Girls 2¾–11, Boys 2¾–7.
Number in School. 300 pupils.
Fees per term (2016–2017). Nursery £2,435 (5 mornings a week), £39.00 each additional afternoon per week; Reception to Year 6 £4,500.

St Mary's School Hampstead provides an outstanding and inspirational Catholic education to girls from 3–11 years and boys from 3–7 years.

St Mary's School celebrates the uniqueness of every pupil and their achievements. The rigorous, challenging curriculum places a strong emphasis on high academic achievement within a culture of care and support.

The School aims to instil four key habits of learning in their pupils. The children are encouraged to be risk takers, not only in their play, but also in their learning. They are also taught to be resilient and not to fall at the first hurdle. Staff ask the children to make mistakes because in the process of challenging themselves, they make more academic progress and in turn excel not only in the classroom, but in their own self-confidence. The boys and girls at St Mary's School are respectful, not just of each other, but of themselves. Finally, pupils are encouraged to be reflective, on their faith, their behaviour and their academic work.

Computer Science and digital literacy skills are integrated superbly within the classroom. Technology is used to support and enhance all curriculum areas and learning every day from Nursery to Year 6.

Music, drama, art and sports are also an essential part of life at St Mary's School and involve everyone. Children demonstrate great enthusiasm and build valuable social skills that last a lifetime.

St Mary's School is an unexpected oasis amidst the bustle and activity of Hampstead. The outdoor space is extensive and the leafy playground makes it easy to forget you are in London. The children in Nursery have their own dedicated garden, aptly named 'The Secret Garden', where they can dig in the mud, play at the water tables, dress up and spend time in the sensory room.

Leavers achieve impressive results, gaining offers and Academic Scholarships from the best schools in the country, including St Paul's Girls' School, North London Collegiate, City of London School for Girls and St Mary's Ascot.

St Mary's Preparatory School
Melrose

Abbey Park, Melrose, Roxburghshire TD6 9LN

Tel: 01896 822517
Fax: 01896 823550
email: office@stmarysmelrose.org.uk
website: www.stmarysmelrose.org.uk

Founded 1895.

Chairman of Governors: Mr G T G Baird

Headmaster: **William J Harvey**, BEd Hons

Age Range. 2–13 co-educational.
Number of Pupils. 188.
Fees per term (2016–2017). Day: Pre-Prep £4,093, Prep £5,043. Weekly Boarding: £5,697.

Curriculum. A healthy variety of subjects including traditional core studies reflecting both the Scottish and English Curriculums (English, Maths, Science, Computer Studies, French, Geography, History, Classics, Latin, RE, Art, Music, Drama and PE). The School's intention is to provide a genuinely nourishing environment allowing for the development of the whole child.

Entry requirements. Application by letter or telephone, followed by a visit to the school, if possible, and a tour guided by senior pupils. All pupils can be offered an 'Induction day' to help with placement.

Examinations offered. Common Entrance to Scholarship for independent senior schools in Scotland and England.

Academic, sports, games and leisure facilities. Classroom computers, Science Laboratory and a big open Art Room. Theatre-Arts and Assembly Hall for concerts and drama. Spacious games pitches supporting a strong tradition in rugby, cricket, hockey, netball and rounders. There is a cross-curricular Study Support Programme for talented and gifted children as well as for children with Specific Learning Difficulties.

Religious activities. Morning Assembly with hymn-singing and readings, stressing pupil participation and contribution through drama and music.

Charitable status. St Mary's School, Melrose is a Registered Charity, number SC009352. Its aim is to provide education for primary school children.

St Michael's Preparatory School

La Rue de la Houguette, Five Oaks, St Saviour, Jersey, Channel Islands JE2 7UG

Tel: +44(0)1534 856904
Fax: +44(0)1534 856620
email: clt@stmichaels.je
            office@stmichaels.je
website: www.stmichaels.je
Twitter: @stmichaelsprep
Facebook: /St-Michaels-Preparatory-School-Jersey

Headmaster: **M B S Rees**, DipEd, MEd

Senior Deputy Head: L G McAviney, Cert Ed, BEd Hons

Academic Deputy Head: Mrs L M Walsh, BA Hons QTS

Age Range. 3–14.
Number of Pupils. 178 Boys, 135 Girls.
Fees per term (2016–2017). Pre-Prep (Reception, Years 1 and 2) £3,065–£3,445; Juniors (Years 3 and 4) £4,265; Year 5 £4,385; Year 6 £4,700; Years 7 and 8 £4,730. Lunch £285.

Boys and girls are prepared for scholarship and entrance to all Independent Senior Schools. Hockey, rugby, football, gymnastics, netball, rounders, cricket, athletics and tennis are taught on spacious playing fields with pavilion and hard tennis courts which adjoin the school. The school also has a purpose-built Sports Hall (4 badminton court size), indoor swimming pool, gymnasium and dance/drama studio. Regular tours are made to Guernsey and England for sporting fixtures.

The school has flourishing and well equipped computer, art and design technology departments, in addition to networked computers in every classroom. A large variety of clubs and hobbies function within the school and many outof-door activities, including sailing and photography, are enjoyed by the children. Music, drama and art (including pottery), are all encouraged and a wide range of musical instruments are taught. There are three school choirs, two orchestras and a number of ensemble groups. The choirs participate locally and nationally in events and competitions.

For senior children there is an annual Activities Week, which takes Years 6, 7 and 8 to different locations in France and Year 5 take part in island-based activities. Each winter a party of children from Years 3 to 8 ski in Switzerland.

Care, consideration, courtesy and good manners are important aspects of behaviour that the school holds dear.

The academic and physical development, in addition to the spiritual, moral and cultural growth, of the whole child is the main aim of the school and every child is encouraged to do "a little better" than anyone thought possible.

St Michael's Preparatory School

198 Hadleigh Road, Leigh-on-Sea, Essex SS9 2LP

Tel: 01702 478719
Fax: 01702 710183
email: office@stmichaelsschool.com
website: www.stmichaelsschool.com
Twitter: @StMichaelsLeigh
Facebook: /stmichaelsschool.co.uk

Chair of Governors: Mrs Jane Attwell

Head: **Mr S Tompkins**, BSc Hons Sunderland, PGCE Leeds, MA York, NPQH

Age Range. Co-educational 3–11 years.
Number of Pupils. 289 day pupils (131 boys, 158 girls).
Fees per term (2016–2017). £1,326–£3,033.

St Michael's is a Church of England Preparatory (IAPS) School founded in 1922 to provide pupils with a well-rounded education based on Christian principles, with children welcomed from other Christian traditions and faiths. The school has its own Chapel.

The school is situated in a popular residential area in Leigh-on-Sea within easy reach of public transport. London is accessible by rail and Fenchurch Street Station is approximately 40 minutes away.

The curriculum offered is broad, balanced and tailored towards the children's needs and it aims to contribute to the intellectual, physical, creative, social and spiritual development of each child. All the children, from Nursery through to Form 6, receive specialist teaching in Music, French and PE with additional specialist teaching in the Prep department. Pupils are prepared for the end of Key Stage standardised attainment tests, 11+ entry to local grammar schools and Entrance or Scholarship examinations for independent schools. High academic standards are achieved throughout the school and the children thrive in a happy but disciplined environment.

St Michael's has a dedicated and well-qualified staff team. Class sizes are small to enable personal attention to be given. The school is well resourced with many specialist areas. Nearby playing fields are used for Games. There is a wide range of extra-curricular activities available, with Music and Drama as particular strengths.

Visits to the school are warmly welcomed.

June 2015 ISI Inspection Report: "Excellent" across all areas of its provision, "Outstanding" EYFS provision.

Charitable status. St Michael's Preparatory School is a Registered Charity, number 280688. It exists to provide education.

echoes today in a community where children from a wide variety of backgrounds and every faith are welcome.

St Michael's provides a unique environment for learning and enjoyment. The distinguished Victorian architecture of the original estate has been thoughtfully extended and upgraded. Spacious facilities for learning now include modern science, music, drama and art rooms, a large sports hall and splendid indoor 25m swimming pool. The school's wonderful wooded grounds on the slopes of the North Downs, which include a recently-built adventure playground, provide outdoor inspiration and extensive space for exploration, sport and play. They are also a truly memorable backdrop to a well-balanced education which allows every pupil to flourish.

The school prepares pupils for senior independent schools and local grammar schools (at 11+ and 13+) and has a proven academic record with many pupils gaining prestigious awards. It also has a high reputation for music, games (rugby, cricket, soccer, netball, hockey and athletics), drama and art.

A thriving Nursery, Kindergarten and Pre-Prep Department is self-contained and housed in a new purpose-built facility which opened in February 2013. Children play in the secure environment of the old walled garden.

An extensive out of school extra-curricular activity programme is offered to all pupils on a weekly basis and all classes participate in an integral programme of visits, workshops and field trips. The annual choir tour to major European cities is one of the highlights of our year.

An active Parents and Friends Association and the International Club are strengths of the school and the Old Michaelian Society is one of the longest established in the Prep School world.

St Michael's: the joy and wonder of learning.

Charitable status. St Michael's is a Registered Charity, number 1076999. It exists to provide education for boys and girls.

St Michael's Prep School
Otford

Otford Court, Row Dow, Otford, Sevenoaks, Kent TN14 5SA

Tel:	01959 522137
Fax:	01959 526044
email:	office@stmichaels.kent.sch.uk
website:	www.stmichaels.kent.sch.uk
Twitter:	@StMichaels_Prep

Chair of Governors: Ms Paula Carter

Head: **Mrs J Aisher**, BA Oxon, PGCE London, MCIL

Head of Pre-Prep Department: Mrs Z Leech, BA Hons, PGCE

Age Range. 2–13 Co-educational.
Number of Pupils. 472.
Fees per term (2016–2017). £744–£4,529.

St Michael's Prep is a thriving, friendly school in a superb setting. We offer a fully co-educational, all-round preparatory education of the highest standard in a caring, family community. With a generous staff to pupil ratio and small classes, St Michael's achieves excellent results at every stage. Boys and girls share all activities; everyone is encouraged to try their best and to take part, perform and enjoy every aspect of school life.

The school's Christian roots support its modern ethos. St Michael's Prep was founded in 1872 by London vicar Arthur Tooth who used his own fortune to create a school. The simple, egalitarian style of the founder has strong

St Neot's Preparatory School

St Neot's Road, Eversley, Hook, Hampshire RG27 0PN

Tel:	Office: 0118 973 2118
	Admissions: 0118 973 9650
email:	office@stneotsprep.co.uk
	admissions@stneotsprep.co.uk
website:	www.stneotsprep.co.uk
Facebook:	/stneotsprep

Chairman of Governors: Mr S Scott

Head: **Mrs Deborah Henderson**, BA Hons QTS

Age Range. 3 months–13 years co-educational.
Number of Pupils. 314.
Fees per term (2016–2017). Years 5–8 £4,998, Year 3–4 £4,550, Reception–Year 2 £3,407, Nursery £39 per per morning session, £22.50 per afternoon session, Tiny Tuskers £59 per day (core hours), additional hours charged at £8.20 per hour.

St Neot's, founded in 1888, is a happy, vibrant community for boys and girls from 3 months to 13 years. The school is situated on the border of Hampshire and Berkshire and is set in 70 acres of beautiful grounds and woodland.

The school's educational philosophy is to inspire children to develop a love of learning in a supportive and happy environment, where each individual is encouraged to achieve their full academic potential and beyond. Children are motivated to discover their full range of talents and to develop the passion to pursue them. They are given the opportunity to embrace challenge, think creatively, develop self-confidence and foster empathy towards others, preparing them both intellectually and emotionally for success in the 21st Century.

We aim to provide the highest standards in teaching and learning, within a well rounded educational experience and St Neot's has a very strong record of success in achieving Scholarships and Awards to numerous Senior Schools.

St Neot's is committed to providing a world of opportunity in every aspect of school life. Stimulating learning environments ensure that engaged pupils work towards the highest academic standards, whilst also enjoying a breadth of experience in sport, music, art, drama and dance.

Emphasis is placed on developing independence, self-confidence, curiosity and collaboration. Forest School and Outdoor Education programmes encourage children of all ages to develop these attributes, which are so vital in the modern world. The St Neot's journey culminates in the Years 7 and 8 leadership programme, which draws together a mix of skills through the core elements of the Prep Schools Baccalaureate (PSB).

Sport is a strength of the school and our new sports complex, comprising sports hall, 25m indoor swimming pool, all-weather astro, cricket nets, hard tennis and netball courts, significantly supplement our extensive playing fields. There is also an on-site mountain bike track and a traversing wall. Judo, dance and tennis are taught by specialist coaches and there are many after-school clubs and activities covering a wide range of interests. Holiday Clubs run in all school breaks and offer a wealth of opportunities, both sporting and creative.

St Neot's holds a Gold Artsmark award, giving recognition to our achievements in art, music, drama and dance. A number of plays, concerts and recitals take place throughout the school year for all age groups, either in the school grounds or the Performing Arts Centre.

Open Mornings take place termly and details of these can be found on the school website: www.stneotsprep.co.uk. We would also be delighted to arrange an individual tour and a meeting with the Head. Please contact Admissions on 0118 9739650; email: admissions@stneotsprep.co.uk.

Charitable status. St Neot's (Eversley) Limited is a Registered Charity, number 307324. The aim of the Charity is to try to provide the best all-round education possible to as many pupils as possible, with bursarial help according to need.

St Olave's Prep School

106–110 Southwood Road, New Eltham, London SE9 3QS

Tel:	020 8294 8930
Fax:	020 8294 8939
email:	office@stolaves.org.uk
website:	www.stolaves.org.uk

Chairman of Trustees: Mr M D Ireland, MIoD, FRSA

Head: **Mr James Tilly**, BA Hons QTS

Age Range. 3–11.
Number of Pupils. 220 Day Boys and Girls.
Fees per term (2016–2017). Nursery £1,604–£3,208; Reception & Year 1 £3,380; Years 2–6 £3,650.

In a single sentence, the school aims to bring out the best in everyone. It seeks to achieve this aim by providing an all-round education for both boys and girls aged 3 to 11 in a warm and caring environment in which each child can thrive and be happy knowing that each is accepted for who they are.

A Christian ethos permeates the pastoral life of the school, where care for others through thoughtful and responsible behaviour is expected. Praise and encouragement are emphasised and relationships between staff and pupils are relaxed and friendly. A close partnership with parents is sought.

The children in the EYFS (Nursery and Reception) and Pre-Prep (Year 1 and Year 2) are taught in mixed-ability classes where each child's progress is carefully monitored by the Class Teacher. In the Upper School (Years 3–6) the children are set across the year group for Mathematics. Throughout the school individual differences are appropriately met, with the very able and those with mild learning difficulties receiving additional support where this is thought beneficial. The school is noted for the broad curriculum it offers and for its excellent achievements in Music and Drama. A range of sporting activities is taught as part of the curriculum and there is a wide range of after school clubs and activities. Music and PE are taught by specialist teachers from the age of three, French is introduced at four years old and Latin at ten years old. The classrooms are equipped with computers and there is a networked suite which supports all areas of the curriculum. A specialist ICT teacher teaches all year groups from Reception to Year 6. Digital panels and portable devices are used to enhance learning.

St Olave's feeds a wide range of secondary schools and parents are given help in choosing the school most appropriate to meet the needs of their child.

Charitable status. St Olave's School is a Registered Charity, number 312734. It exists to provide high quality education for boys and girls.

St Olave's School, York
The Prep School of St Peter's School, York

York YO30 6AB

Tel:	01904 527416
Fax:	01904 527303
email:	enquiries@stolavesyork.org.uk
website:	www.stolavesyork.org.uk
Twitter:	@StOlavesYork
Facebook:	/stolavesyork

Chairman of the Governors: Mr W Woolley

Master: **Mr A I Falconer**, BA Hons Lancaster, MBA Leicester

Deputy Head: Mr M C Ferguson, HDipEd Capetown College of Education

Master's Secretary: Mrs C Murgatroyd

Age Range. 8–13 co-educational.
Number of Pupils. 209 Boys, 149 Girls.
Fees per term (2016–2017). Day: £3,860–£4,670; Boarding: £7,235–£7,980. Non-EU Boarder: £7,415 (Year 6), £8,180 (Years 7 & 8).

Weekly and flexi-boarding are available. Tuition fees include the costs of stationery and textbooks. There are no compulsory extras except for examination fees. Lunches are included in day fees.

St Olave's was founded in 1876. With its own halls, music school, practical subjects workshops, sports hall and magnificently appointed specialist teaching rooms, St Olave's enjoys some of the best facilities for a prep school of its type.

The school puts praise, encouragement and pastoral care of the individual as its highest priority. There is a demanding wide curriculum from the earliest age with specialist subject areas – modern foreign languages, information technology, science and music, amongst others – being taught by specialist teachers from Year 4. Progress is monitored through a regular system of effort grades, and attainment is measured through internal and externally moderated tests.

Boarding is a flourishing aspect of the school, with a co-educational House under the constant care of resident House parents and their own family. Weekly and flexi-boarding are also available. There are also five Day Houses.

Music plays an important part in the life of the school with 22 music teachers, two orchestras, a wind band and 14 ensembles playing and practising weekly. Over 200 pupils learn individual instruments, and all are encouraged to join larger groups.

Sport has an equally high profile where football, hockey, cricket, netball, rugby, tennis and swimming are major sports. Athletics, cross-country running, squash, badminton, basketball and volleyball are also available for all. The boys have won the National Schools' Seven-a-Side Rugby tournament four times in the last eleven years and won the National Cricket JET cup. The school has 23 tennis courts, a synthetic pitch and a 25m 6-lane swimming pool.

Drama has an increasing profile, and out-of-school activities flourish through clubs such as science society, chess, photography, art and trampoline.

The vast majority of boys and girls move on to St Peter's and are not required to take the Common Entrance examination.

Entrance assessments are held in January/February each year, and assessments can also be arranged at other times. Entry is possible in most year groups, although the school is heavily oversubscribed at most stages. Means-tested fee assistance is available from age 11.

Charitable status. St Peter's School, York, is a Registered Charity, number 1141329. It exists to provide education for boys and girls.

St Paul's Cathedral School

2 New Change, London EC4M 9AD
Tel: 020 7248 5156
Fax: 020 7329 6568
email: office@spcs.london.sch.uk
website: www.spcslondon.com

Chairman of Governors: The Very Revd Dr David Ison, Dean of St Paul's Cathedral

Headmaster: **Mr Simon Larter-Evans**, BA Hons, PGCE, FRSA

Age Range. 4–13 Co-educational.
Number of Pupils. Boarding Choristers 29, Day Boys 117, Day Girls 102, Pre-Prep 63
Fees per term (2016–2017). Choristers £2,685.67; Day pupils £4,400–£4,737.

There have been choristers at St Paul's for over nine centuries. The present school is a Church of England Foundation dating back over 100 years and is governed by the Dean and Chapter of St Paul's Cathedral and 7 Lay Governors. The broadening of educational expectations and the challenge of curricular developments led the Dean and Chapter to agree to expand the school in 1989 by admitting non-chorister day-boys for the first time; a decision which continues to enrich the life of the school and Cathedral. In September 1998, the school admitted girls as well as boys into its new pre-prep department for 4–7 year olds. The school became fully co-educational in September 2002. It offers a broad curriculum leading to scholarship and Common Entrance examinations. In the first three years the work is tailored to

individual needs bearing in mind the wide variety of educational backgrounds from which pupils come. The school has an excellent record in placing pupils in the senior schools of their choice, many with music scholarships. Every opportunity is taken to make use of the school's proximity to museums, libraries, galleries, theatres and the numerous attractions which London has to offer.

The 33 chorister boarders are housed on the School site and are fully integrated with the day pupils for all their academic studies and games. The choristers' cathedral choral training offers them a unique opportunity to participate in the rich musical life of St Paul's and the City.

The school was rehoused in the 60s in purpose-built premises on the eastern end of the Cathedral site. Refurbishment projects have added a new music school, art room, IT room, three pre-prep classrooms and games rooms to the existing facilities which include a hall/gymnasium, science laboratory, common room and a TV/video room. All pupils are encouraged to play a musical instrument (most pupils play two) and there are music and theory lessons with school orchestras and chamber groups.

A wide variety of games is offered including field sports at local playing fields and weekly swimming lessons. The children have their own playground and the use of the hall for indoor games and gymnastics.

Admissions procedure. Prospective pupils of 7+ years in September are given academic tests in verbal and non-verbal reasoning, usually in January of the previous academic year.

Pre-Prep children (4+) are assessed in an informal play situation in the November prior to entry.

Voice trials and tests for chorister places are held throughout the year for boys between 6½ and 8½ years old.

St Paul's Juniors (previously known as Colet Court)

Lonsdale Road, London SW13 9JT
Tel: 020 8748 3461
Fax: 020 8746 5357
email: spjheadpa@stpaulsschool.org.uk
website: www.stpaulsschool.org.uk

Chairman of Governors: J M Robertson

Head: **Maxine Shaw**, BSc London, PGCE Hull, PG Dip Brunel

Age Range. 7–13.
Number of Boys. 450.
Fees per term (2016–2017). £6,257.

St Paul's Juniors (previously known as Colet Court founded in 1881) is the junior division for St Paul's School (*see entry in HMC section*). Nearly all pupils at St Paul's Juniors transfer to St Paul's at 13. The two schools are in separate but adjacent modern buildings on the south bank of the Thames, and share many amenities, including the dining hall, sports complex, design & technology workshops and playing fields. St Paul's Juniors has its own main teaching block, hall/theatre, library, art & design room, two computer rooms and music school. A drama studio and three science laboratories are situated in a separate building.

There is close consultation with St Paul's in matters of curriculum to ensure the benefit of continuity. Some members of staff teach in both schools. Boys are not specifically prepared for scholarships to senior schools other than St Paul's. Our aim is to give every pupil the opportunity to enjoy a broad education and a wide range of activities. Music, Art, Drama and Sport are all strong.

There are two Year 3 classes and four forms per year group from Years 4 to 8. Boys join the School at 7+ and 8+ and approximately 30 places are also available at 11+. Up to 10 of these places may be offered to pupils who sit an examination in Year 5 and defer their arrival for one year. This mode of entry is available to boys from maintained primary schools only. Entrance at all levels is by competitive examination and interview. Means-tested bursaries are available at all points of entry.

Charitable status. St Paul's School is a Registered Charity, number 1119619. The object of the charity is to promote the education of boys in Greater London.

St Peter & St Paul School

Brambling House, Hady Hill, Chesterfield, Derbyshire S41 0EF

Tel: 01246 278522
email: headmaster@spsp.org.uk
website: www.spsp.org.uk

Chairman of the Board of Trustees: Mrs Dawn Graham

Headmaster: **Mr Jonathon Clark**, BA Hons, PGCE

Age Range. 4–11 years.
Number of Pupils. 130.
Fees per term (2016–2017). Infants £2,816, Juniors £2,979.

St Peter & St Paul School is a non-selective school for boys and girls in the heart of the market town of Chesterfield in Derbyshire. Our school has been providing education for the children of Chesterfield and the surrounding areas for over 70 years and has an established reputation for providing an excellent all-round education.

Our children have many opportunities to excel, as not only do we provide small class sizes and a dedicated and enthusiastic teaching team, but we also, through our exceptional life skills programme, give children the opportunity to develop their confidence by learning skills and accepting challenges that allow them to be the best they can possibly be in the security of a warm and nurturing environment. Our children have opportunities to develop their musical, artistic and dramatic talents, their sporting prowess and their academic ability. We rejoice in children's success both within school and outside school. Our focus on the academic area of school life is unashamedly to ensure that each child fulfils their potential.

We believe that every child in our care is important. We are committed to the delivery of excellent lessons which inspire our children and allow them to develop as confident and independent learners. We aim to have our children leave us proud of their achievements and courageous in tackling the challenges that lie ahead. We want our children to leave us as confident, compassionate and creative individuals. We want them to leave us understanding the value of perseverance and with the ability to learn from mistakes and to be able to deal constructively with disappointment. We want our children to be ready to meet the challenges that the next stage of their lives will bring.

Our environment is outstanding. Our extensive grounds of park and woodland, including a Scandinavian-type Forest School and sporting facilities, provide children with an extension beyond classroom learning that can only fire up the mind and the imagination. We are proud of all that we have to offer.

We have a highly successful partnership with Children 1st nurseries which allows wrap-around care from 7.30 am to 6:00 pm from birth to 11 years of age.

Charitable status. The St Peter & St Paul Trust is a registered charity, number 516113.

St Piran's

Gringer Hill, Maidenhead, Berkshire SL6 7LZ

Tel: 01628 594302
email: registrar@stpirans.co.uk
website: www.stpirans.co.uk

Chairman of Governors: Mrs Kate Taylor

Headmaster: **J Carroll**, BA Hons, BPhilEd, PGCE, NPQH

Age Range. 3–11 Co-educational.
Number of Pupils. 400 day pupils.
Fees per term (2016–2017). £3,600–£5,050. Nursery – 5 full days: £230 per week.

St Piran's is a thriving co-educational IAPS day school set amid 10 delightful acres just to the north of Maidenhead town centre. Founded as a small school in Blackheath, London in 1805.

Class sizes are small. Boys and girls benefit from individual attention in all subjects. They are provided with a wide range of exciting opportunities both inside and outside the classroom. Numerous trips to castles and museums, theatres and shows, history re-enactments, geographical fieldwork and religious sites extend the children's understanding of the world around them. In addition to the academic subjects, pupils take part in a wide range of other activities each week.

Academically, the school supports a broad curriculum at all levels in the school. French starts with our youngest classes where confidence in the spoken language is encouraged. By Year 6 we are introducing Latin and Spanish. The children enjoy specialist teaching in art, games and PE, IT, swimming and music from an early age. We support children with their entrance exams at 11+ to Grammar Schools or other Senior independent schools. Our results over the years have been excellent, supporting our desire to encourage independent thinkers, confident individuals and strong leaders of the future.

The main sports that pupils take part in are rugby, football, netball, hockey, cricket, rounders and swimming. The school has its own indoor swimming pool and large sports hall. St Piran's also has a dance studio and pupils are encouraged to take an active part in the performing arts. We are blessed with wonderful facilities which serve to enhance the varied sports programmes that we offer the children at all levels.

The school has its own Leadership programme and regular visits off site are arranged for all the children, including residential trips.

Pupils may enter the school at any age, although the main intakes occur at Nursery and Reception. Scholarships and bursaries may be offered after assessment. Please contact the school and an appointment can be arranged to talk to the Headmaster about financial support.

The school is proud of its outstanding record of achievement and the fully rounded education that it provides within a friendly caring atmosphere. We are proud of our Christian tradition and family ethos which foster high expectations and successful, happy children.

Children and parents are warmly invited to visit St Piran's to see for themselves the excellent facilities that we offer and to meet some of the staff and pupils.

Charitable status. St Piran's School Limited is a Registered Charity, number 309094.

St Pius X Prep School

200 Garstang Road, Fulwood, Preston, Lancashire PR2 8RD

Tel: 01772 719937
Fax: 01772 787535
email: enquiries@st-piusx.lancs.sch.uk
website: www.stpiusx.co.uk

Chairman of Governors: P Clegg

Headmistress: **Miss B Banks**, MA

Age Range. 2–11.
Number of Children. 255 Day Girls and Boys.
Fees per term (2016–2017). Main School £2,600, Nursery £250 per week.

The School is administered as a non-profit-making educational trust by a Board of Governors, providing education from 2–11. The children are prepared for entrance examination to independent schools and local high schools. The school has an excellent record of scholarships to senior schools and SATS results at KS1 and KS2. The school has a large Nursery division which covers the EYFS in recently-refurbished Nursery rooms. The school is in four acres of its own grounds in a pleasant suburb of Preston. All preparatory curriculum subjects covered.

Sports taught are Association Football, Cricket, Tennis, Hockey, Netball, Rugby, Table Tennis, Rounders, Athletics and Cross Country.

Ballet, piano, clarinet, flute, violin, guitar and singing lessons are some of the optional extras offered. The school has a thriving music centre.

Charitable status. St Pius X School is a Registered Charity, number 526609. Its purpose is to equip the children with an outstanding academic and social education in a Catholic Christian environment, which will enable them to achieve their full potential – the school welcomes pupils of all faiths.

Saint Ronan's

Water Lane, Hawkhurst, Kent TN18 5DJ

Tel: 01580 752271
Fax: 01580 754882
email: info@saintronans.co.uk
website: www.saintronans.co.uk
Twitter: @SaintRonans
Facebook: @SaintRonans

Chairman of Governors: Mr Colin Willis

Headmaster: **W E H Trelawny-Vernon**, BSc Hons

Deputy Head (*Pastoral*): Ross Andrew
Deputy Head (*Academic*): Matthew Bryan

Age Range. 3–13 fully co-educational.
Number of Children. 410.
Fees per term (2016–2017). Day £3,291–£5,641. We also operate a flexi boarding system (£35 per night) which can be tailored to individual needs.

Saint Ronan's is a family school as it has been since it was started in Worthing in 1883. It occupies a fine Victorian Mansion set in 249 acres of beautiful Weald of Kent countryside. There are numerous games pitches, hard tennis courts, a golf course and a swimming pool as well as a hundred-acre wood.

With an emphasis on family and pastoral care, the school has a unique and special atmosphere in which staff and children work together to achieve their aims. Small class sizes enable children to gain confidence and interact positively with their peers and the staff.

Academically we have an excellent pass rate at CE and many pupils gain Scholarships to major senior independent schools such as Eton, Sevenoaks, Benenden, Tonbridge, Harrow, King's Canterbury and Eastbourne College; we also prepare children for entry to local Grammar Schools and boast an enviable record. We have had 70 Scholarships in the last three years and a 100% Cranbrook 13+ pass rate.

Music and art play a vital role at Saint Ronan's. We have numerous choirs and ensembles including the Chamber choir and the Chapel choir, and over three-quarters of the children learn at least one musical instrument. We have an excellent orchestra and ensembles for most instruments. Music is thriving and the department regularly achieve scholarships to very competitive schools such as King's Canterbury, Harrow and Eastbourne. The Art and DT departments are flourishing and regularly achieve scholarships.

The major sports at Saint Ronan's are rugby, football, hockey, cricket and netball but we also offer coaching in athletics, tennis, swimming, dance, rounders, judo, golf, archery, fencing, lacrosse, sailing and cross country. Sports scholarships are also regularly awarded.

The Nursery and Pre-Prep are very much part of the school, in both location and ethos, and are thriving and dynamic departments taking children from age 3 to 7.

In 2006 we opened a new Nursery, Pre-Prep, Music school and IT suite, in 2010 a new Sports Hall and in 2012 a new DT suite and School Farm. In 2014 we started playing on our new astroturf. A new Drama Studio was built in 2016 and in 2017 a new classroom suite and Library come online. We have plans to open an indoor swimming pool within the next five years.

Charitable status. Saint Ronan's School is a Registered Charity, number 1066420. It exists for the advancement of education of its children.

St Swithun's Junior School

Alresford Road, Winchester, Hampshire SO21 1HA

Tel: 01962 835750
Fax: 01962 835781
email: office.juniorschool@stswithuns.com
website: www.stswithuns.com
Twitter: @stswithunsjs
Facebook: /StSwithunsJuniorSchool

Established 1884. Girls day preparatory school with pre-preparatory boys. Church of England.

School Council:
Chairman: Professor Natalie Lee, LLB

Acting Headmistress: **Ms Jane Gandee**, MA Cantab

Age Range. Girls 3–11, Boys 3–7.
Number of Pupils. 189 Girls, 13 Boys. Average class size 18. Pupil : teacher ratio 12:1.
Fees per term (2016–2017). Nursery: £1,655 (mornings inc lunch), £3,310 (all day); Reception, Years 1 & 2 £3,310; Years 3–6 £4,265.

Profile. Welcome to St Swithun's Junior School, a school in which every child is known, cherished and at the same time encouraged to be fearless.

In September 2015 we opened the doors to our brand new junior school, which provides a simply spectacular and inspiring teaching and learning environment. It is an environment in which pupils and staff have warm, respectful relationships. The development includes specialist teaching rooms, a science laboratory, an art studio, a media/computing room and, in the final phase, opened in April 2016, a new performing arts space and gym. The children enjoy going to school and the staff relish having the opportunity to share adventures, interests and laughter.

While united in their enthusiasm and energy, the children are all individuals and we encourage them to sample a wide range of experiences so that they each develop individual passions. We look always to celebrate characteristics such as the ability to bounce back from disappointment, to show compassion for others, to rise to challenges and to keep a sense of perspective. We want your children to go home every evening with slightly grubby knees and tales of what they have done at school that day.

Entry. At 3.

Curriculum. Usual subjects taught plus Spanish (from Nursery), art, technology, drama, ICT, music and PE, with due regard for National Curriculum requirements.

Leavers. Boys leave for various preparatory schools, including The Pilgrims' and Twyford. Girls go on to a range of senior independent schools, with the majority going to St Swithun's Senior School.

Consultation. Biannual reports, regular parents' evenings and PTA.

Sports. Gymnastics, netball, pop lacrosse, rounders, tag rugby, tennis, short tennis, swimming, and athletics.

Activities. These include tennis, art, drama, gymnastics, judo, science, cookery, swimming, football and dance.

Musical concerts and productions are regularly held. Three annual residential trips in Years 4–6, and regular visits from Nursery to Year 6 take place.

Special needs. Qualified Learning Support teacher.

Charitable status. St Swithun's School Winchester is a Registered Charity, number 307335.

Salisbury Cathedral School

1 The Close, Salisbury, Wilts SP1 2EQ
Tel: 01722 555300
Fax: 01722 410910
email: admissions@salisburycathedralschool.com
website: www.salisburycathedralschool.com
Twitter: @salisburycathsc
Facebook: /Salisbury-Cathedral-School

Founded in 1091. Co-educational Day and Boarding Preparatory, Pre-Preparatory and Choir School.

Chairman of Governors: Robert Key

Head Master: Clive Marriott

Age Range. 3–13.

Number of Pupils. Day pupils: 195; Boarders: 35.

Fees per term (2016–2017). Pre-Prep: £3.81 per hour (Nursery), £2,725 (Reception, Years 1 & 2), £4,085 (Year 3). Preparatory School: £4,905 (day), £7,210 (boarding).

Warm', 'caring', 'happy' –these are the three most popular words used by parents to describe Salisbury Cathedral School. Our unique setting, adjacent to one of England's finest cathedrals, helps to cultivate a strong spiritual awareness and Christian values underpin everything that we do.

Recently merged with Leaden Hall, the school now spans two iconic and beautiful sites within the Cathedral Close. The Junior Department is based on the Leaden Hall Campus with its idyllic riverside setting, while the Prep Department sits on the Palace campus site, complete with its own lake,

extensive playing fields and lessons in the thirteenth-century Bishop's Palace.

We believe a child's self-esteem is vital to their success. At SCS, we foster an unpressured environment where pupils are encouraged and congratulated every step of the way, celebrating their achievements and promoting a strong sense of self-worth. Our focus on the individual child means that all staff play a role in discovering strengths and areas that need guidance and support.

This approach works. Our academic results are impressive and consistently out-perform competing schools but, more than this, the children who leave us are confident, self-assured, well-rounded and comfortable in their own skins.

Facilities include: over 20 acres of beautiful grounds, state-of-the-art wooden classrooms, an all-weather sports pitch, tennis courts, swimming pool, outstanding music facilities, a variety of performance spaces, specialist science laboratory, art, design technology and computer suites and extensive playground facilities.

Talented sports staff coach all the major team sports and there are regular fixtures.

There are many after-school clubs open to all children in the Preparatory School. (Quality wrap-around school care is available for children in the Pre-Prep). The boarding house staff operate an "open door" policy to parents, organise many outings and activities and have achieved an enviable reputation for running a truly happy and caring boarding house.

For more information and/or to arrange a visit to the school, please telephone Jane King on 01722 439260 or visit our website.

Charitable status. Salisbury Cathedral School is a Registered Charity, number 309485. It exists to provide high quality education for children.

Sandroyd School

Rushmore, Tollard Royal, Salisbury, Wiltshire SP5 5QD
Tel: 01725 516264
Fax: 01725 516441
email: office@sandroyd.com
website: www.sandroyd.org
Twitter: @SandroydSchool

Chairman of Governors: R G L Thomas, MRICS, FAAV

Headmaster: **A B Speers**, BSc, MEd

Age Range. 2½–13 Co-educational.

Number of Pupils. 115 boarders, 60 day, plus 25 in Pre-Prep, The Walled Garden.

Fees per term (2016–2017). Boarding £8,000, Day £6,600. Year 3: Boarding £6,330, Day £4,910. Pre-Prep £2,760, Nursery: £22 (per morning), £32 (all day including lunch).

Sandroyd is a co-educational boarding and day school set in 900 acres of beautiful parkland in the heart of the Cranborne Chase on the Wiltshire/Dorset border.

The facilities which the school has to offer are second to none. They include an indoor swimming pool, all-weather hockey/tennis surfaces, cross-country riding course, squash court, extensive games fields and access to a golf course and driving range. A new Sports Hall has just been completed, with specialist gymnastic equipment, badminton courts and 4 indoor cricket nets, providing space for dance, football, indoor hockey, netball, martial arts, shooting and squash, as well as access to the indoor swimming pool.

Pets such as ponies, ferrets, hens, ducks, rabbits and hamsters are welcome. The school owns a number of mild-mannered ponies, but there are liveries available too.

On the academic side, high standards are expected and achieved. The children are prepared for Common Entrance and Scholarships to all the leading independent senior schools and, together with a number of Academic Scholarships, awards have been won in recent years for Art, Music, Sport and all-round ability. A specialist Learning Support department is in place to assist those who need extra help with their studies. The school is well known for the excellence of its music, both choral and instrumental and a new theatre caters for the many productions which the pupils put on throughout the year across all age ranges.

Pastoral care is five star. Puppet shows in the Junior dorms are a regular occurrence. Academic staff help upstairs in the evenings and the Headmaster's wife is very popular when it comes to reading bedtime stories.

Excellent opportunity: in conjunction with Bryanston, Sandroyd offers an annual full-fee bursary for academic years 7 to 13. Other bursaries are available on request.

Visitors are always welcome to meet the Headmaster and to look round the school and its exceptional grounds.

Charitable status. Sandroyd School Trust Limited is a Registered Charity, number 309490. It exists for the purpose of providing education.

Sarum Hall School

15 Eton Avenue, London NW3 3EL
Tel: 020 7794 2261
Fax: 020 7431 7501
email: admissions@sarumhallschool.co.uk
website: www.sarumhallschool.co.uk

The School, which has a Christian (Church of England) foundation, is an educational trust with a Board of Governors.

Chairman of Governors: Mr B Gorst

Headmistress: **Mrs Christine Smith**, BA Open, CertEd, RSA SpLD

Age Range. 3–11.
Number of Pupils. 180 Day Girls.
Fees per term (2016–2017). £4,280–£4,635.

Founded in 1929, the school has, since 1995, been housed in new purpose-built premises which provide excellent, spacious facilities, including a large playground, gym, dining room and specialist art, IT, music and science rooms, in addition to a French room, changing room, multi-purpose room and three individual music teaching rooms.

Girls are prepared for senior London day schools and for 11+ Common Entrance. Girls entering at age 3 are not assessed, but those joining from Year 1 are tested in English and Maths. The school is ambitious for its girls and believes that in a caring, supportive and imaginative environment, every girl can achieve her potential. They are encouraged to develop a love and interest of learning for itself and awareness that their success in all fields is dependent on their own efforts. Consequently the school has a well-established record of scholarship and examination success. Destination schools include Channing, Cheltenham Ladies' College, City of London School for Girls, Downe House, Francis Holland, Highgate, King's Canterbury, Mill Hill Foundation, North London Collegiate, Oundle School, Queen's College, Queenswood, South Hampstead High School, St Helen's, St Paul's Girls and Wycombe Abbey.

A broad curriculum is followed and a major investment in IT ensures that each girl has access to the latest technology. French is taught from Reception and Mandarin from Year 4, and a comprehensive games programme, which

takes place on site, ensures that girls have the opportunity to experience a variety of sports. Strong emphasis is placed on music, art, design and drama. Woodwind, violin, piano, cello and singing are offered. There are also two choirs, an orchestra and ensemble groups. Other extra-curricular activities include theory of music, fencing, junior and senior football, gardening, modern art, nature, netball, tennis, ICT, yoga, philosophy, photography, drama, craft, chess, cooking, classical civilisations, board games and performance.

Charitable status. Sarum Hall School is a Registered Charity, number 312721. Its purpose is education.

Seaford College Prep School
Wilberforce House

Lavington Park, Petworth, West Sussex GU28 0NB
Tel: 01798 867893
Fax: 01798 867802
email: wilberforce@seaford.org
         jhitchcock@seaford.org
website: www.seafordprep.org

Chairman of Governors: R Venables Kyrke

Head of Prep School: **Mr Alastair Brown**, BEd

Age Range. 6–13 Co-educational.
Number of Pupils. 200.
Fees per term (2016–2017). Day: £3,220–£5,410. Weekly Boarding: £6,700 (Year 6), £7,155 (Years 7 & 8).

Seaford College Prep School (Wilberforce House) is an integral part of Seaford College, having the same board of governors, but with its own buildings, playground and corporate organisation. There is very close cooperation between the two schools and there are many shared facilities such as the games fields, the Music School, Science Department, and Art and Design Department. Wilberforce House is named after Samuel Wilberforce, the son of the anti-slavery campaigner William Wilberforce. Samuel is buried in the grounds of the School's chapel. The School is set in a magnificent 400-acre site adjacent to the South Downs National Park.

The Prep School educates boys and girls from the age of 6 and the vast majority of children continue their education at Seaford College until 16 or 18. The main entry points for the Prep School are at 7+ and 11+ although children are welcome to join the school at any age.

The school aims to nurture a love of learning through a broadly based curriculum and classroom activities are often complemented by day and residential visits. In Years 2, 3, 4 and 5, the majority of lessons are taught by form teachers with subjects such as Music, French, PE/Games and Design and Technology taught by specialist staff. Year 6 are form based for English, Maths, History and Geography with all other subjects taught by subject specialists. From Year 7 all subjects are taught by specialist staff, many of whom also teach in the Senior School. All classrooms are equipped with interactive whiteboards while a Special Educational Needs Coordinator oversees the school's learning support provision which further enhances learning and achievement. The majority of children complete most of their homework in school and the school day finishes at 5.20 pm.

Boarding provision, from Year 6 upwards, is an important aspect of life in the school with the aim being to be as flexible as possible in order to meet parents' and pupils' needs as well as providing a warm and caring home-from-home atmosphere.

Pupils are able to benefit from the impressive range of games facilities on site, including an astroturf hockey pitch, swimming pool and a 9-hole golf course, with practice greens and driving range as well as the services of a golf professional. Expert coaching is provided in the main sports of football, rugby, hockey, cricket, netball, rounders, tennis, athletics and swimming. The school also has excellent facilities for music, art and design and technology.

The standard of pastoral care is high and the school has its own Chaplain who takes a weekly assembly in the school chapel. The Prep School aims to treat each pupil as an individual and to establish the firm foundations necessary for success in the Senior School and beyond. (*See Seaford College entry in HMC section.*)

Charitable status. Seaford College is a Registered Charity, number 277439.

Seaton House School

67 Banstead Road South, Sutton, Surrey SM2 5LH

Tel: 020 8642 2332
Fax: 020 8642 2332
email: office@seatonhouse.sutton.sch.uk
website: www.seatonhouse.sutton.sch.uk

Chair of Governors: Mrs J Evans

Headmistress: **Mrs D Morrison**, RSA HDipEd

Age Range. Girls 3–11, Boys 3–4 (Nursery only).
Number of Pupils. Main School 126; Nursery 26.
Fees per term (2016–2017). £1,300–£3,135.

Seaton House School was founded in 1930 by Miss Violet Henry and there is a strong tradition of family loyalty to the school. The School aims to provide children with a thorough educational grounding to give them a good start in their school lives and to instil sound learning habits in a secure, disciplined but friendly atmosphere. The girls, from Year 4, are prepared for various entrance examinations at 11+, both in the London Borough of Sutton and those required by independent day schools with a high percentage of our girls securing grammar school places at Nonsuch High School and Wallington Girls Grammar School. Our highly qualified and committed staff create a stimulating learning environment and small classes ensure that all our girls have the necessary individual attention and encouragement to achieve the highest standards.

We follow the broad outlines of the National Curriculum with generous provision for Music, French and Physical Education. There is a School Orchestra and Choir and, each year, all pupils have the opportunity to take part in dramatic productions. School sports teams enjoy considerable success when they compete regularly against neighbouring schools and each Spring we host our own Netball Tournament. Years 5 and 6 have the opportunity to experience outdoor pursuits during their annual week's residential course, but prior to that in Years 3 and 4 the girls have a one-night/two-day and two-night/three-day residential visit, respectively. The School has excellent Library and ICT resources, while the range of extracurricular activities offered is extremely varied, complementing the established provision of after-school care. There is a daily homework club and after-school care to 6.00 pm, with early-bird arrivals being looked after from 8.00 am.

Pastoral care is of the highest calibre with form staff taking a keen interest in all their pupils. Courtesy, good manners and kindness are expected as the norm and children are encouraged to develop initiative, independence and confidence. There is a strong house system in the main school which stimulates good community awareness.

The prospectus is available upon request and the Headmistress is always happy to meet parents and arrange for them to look around the School.

Charitable status. Seaton House School is a Registered Charity, number 800673. It exists to provide education for children.

Sevenoaks Preparatory School

Godden Green, Sevenoaks, Kent TN15 0JU

Tel: 01732 762336
Fax: 01732 764279
email: admin@theprep.org.uk
website: www.theprep.org.uk
Twitter: @Sevenoaksprep
Facebook: /sevenoaksprep

Chairman of Governors: Jan Berry

Headmaster: **Luke Harrison**, BA Hons, PGCE

Head of Pre-Prep: Helen Cook

Age Range. 2½ to 13.
Number of Children. 385 pupils.
Fees per annum (2016–2017). Nursery & Kindergarten £990 for one session a week, Reception £9,480, Years 1–2 £10,920, Years 3–8 £13,335.

Founded in 1919, Sevenoaks Prep School stands on a spacious 25-acre site of playing fields and woodland bordering the 1,000-acre Knole Estate. We welcome girls and boys from 2½ to 13 years of age. Our small class sizes and family atmosphere enables us to build special relationships with the children and their parents.

The curriculum is tailored to the needs of the pupils and their future aspirations. Whilst due regard is paid to the National Curriculum, our children are taught to the highest standard achievable by the individual. To this end, our teachers enhance their Programmes of Study to ensure that every pupil is motivated, challenged and prepared for 11+ or 13+ entry tests to local grammar schools or via Common Entrance examinations and scholarships to independent schools. Our academic achievements are consistently high and our pupils compete successfully for academic, music and other scholarships.

Throughout the school all classes regularly participate in a programme of visits, workshops and field trips to support their learning. Education at Sevenoaks Prep is for life not just the classroom – it is the balance of academic study and co-curricular activities that prepare the children for their future.

The school comprises the Pre-Prep (Nursery–Year 2), and the Prep School (Years 3–8).

Nursery and Kindergarten are staffed by teachers who are specially qualified in Early Years education, with a high teacher to pupil ratio. The education provided is specifically designed to match each child's needs, so that child-initiated play and teacher-directed activities are thoughtfully planned and carefully balanced.

Full-time education starts in the Reception class and from this point, through Years 1 and 2, class teachers and their assistants provide a rich and stimulating environment where curiosity and enthusiasm to learn are fostered.

On entering the Senior School in Year 3, class teaching is continued for core subjects (with specialist teaching for drama, languages, music, ICT, PE and games). By the age of ten, our pupils are taught by specialist teachers in all subjects whilst each class continues to have a form teacher who monitors their progress. Years 7 and 8 are the secondary school years and this is reflected in the teaching and levels of responsibility offered to the children. At Sevenoaks Prep they are at the top of the school and are provided with leadership opportunities and responsibilities. Heads of our destination schools say that children from the Prep enter Year 9 as rounded individuals, confident both academically and socially.

Facilities include a large multi-purpose sports hall, a state-of-the-art drama and music suite as well as a modern restaurant and kitchen. Our location provides a useful and natural extension to our teaching facilities and provide a vast playground, where children are trusted and encouraged to explore safely.

The school provides after-school care until 6.00 pm each evening and the extra-curricular activities are extensive. The school is supported by an active Social Events Committee who regularly arrange social events for parents to meet each other and to raise money for the school.

Sherborne Preparatory School

Acreman Street, Sherborne, Dorset DT9 3NY

Tel:	01935 812097
email:	registrar@sherborneprep.org
website:	www.sherborneprep.org
Twitter:	@Sherborneprep
Facebook:	@sherborneprep

Chair of Governors: Mr N Jones

Headmaster: Mr Nick Folland, BSc Hons, PGCE, MIAPS, MISI

Age Range. 3–13.
Number of Boys and Girls. 265 (Pre-Prep 77, Prep 188).
Fees per term (2016–2017). Boarders: £7,475–£7,820. Day: Nursery £2,930; Pre-Prep £2,930; Prep: £4,470 (Year 3), £5,460 (Years 4–8). Generous discounts available for Forces families and a range of scholarships available from Year 3 upwards (scholarship assessment in February each year). Bursaries available on a means-tested basis.

Sherborne Prep School aims to foster independent learning through the teaching of a broader enquiry-based curriculum with an emphasis on study and thinking skills, designed to meet the individual learning styles of the pupils.

The school is an independent co-educational day and boarding school for children aged 3–13 years. Founded in 1885, the School is set in twelve acres of attractive grounds and gardens in the centre of Sherborne and is well served by road and rail links. Although fully independent, it enjoys a long and close association with its neighbours, Sherborne School and Sherborne Girls.

The Prep School (Years 3–8) offers a broad education, leading to Common Entrance and Scholarship examinations in the penultimate and final year groups. There is a strong emphasis on languages (the school offers French, Latin, German, Spanish, Italian and Mandarin at various levels), art and design technology, and on independent thinking. In recent years the Prep has led the way in curriculum development in Geography and History, and this has been extremely well received by senior schools.

Despite being non-selective ourselves, over the last five years an impressive 38% of leavers have won scholarships or awards to leading independent schools, including Sherborne School, Sherborne Girls, Cheltenham College, Bryanston, Sedbergh School, Radley, Taunton School, Wells Cathedral School, Abingdon School, Monmouth School, St Swithun's School, St Mary's Shaftesbury, Milton Abbey, Canford School, Blundell's, King's College Taunton and Leweston School.

The Prep also offers a distinctive Saturday morning programme of various sporting, artistic, musical and cultural activities, including introductory language classes and informative lectures, to which the parents are warmly invited.

The Pre-Prep Department is housed in a fully-equipped and purpose-built classroom building, with experienced and well-qualified staff, providing an excellent ratio of teachers to children. The children enjoy weekly swimming lessons and a varied programme of after-school activities, including fun fitness, dance, music, and circus skills, and there is a thriving weekly toddler group ("Little Preppers") for children between 0 and 3.

The School's ISI report in December 2015 was outstanding, and praised the School for its success in many areas, notably in developing independent learning and positive attitudes to work and study in both boarding and day pupils.

Charitable status. Sherborne Preparatory School is a Registered Charity, number 1071494. It exists to provide an all-round education for children.

Shrewsbury House

107 Ditton Road, Surbiton, Surrey KT6 6RL

Tel:	020 8399 3066
Fax:	020 8339 9529
email:	office@shspost.co.uk
website:	www.shrewsburyhouse.net
Twitter:	@shrewsburyhouse

Chairman of the Governors: D Johns, BA Hons

Headmaster: K A Doble, BA, PDM HR, PGCE, FRSA

Second Master: C Francis, BHum Hons, PGCE

Age Range. 7–13.
Number of Boys. 320 Day Boys.
Fees per term (2016–2017). £5,795.

Shrewsbury House was founded in 1865. In 1979 it became an Educational Trust and is administered by a Board of Governors.

Boys are admitted from 7 years of age and are prepared for entry at 13+, either by Scholarship or Common Entrance, to any of the Independent Senior Schools. There are 47 full-time staff, as well as visiting music staff.

The School aims to provide both an academic and broad education; to give a comprehensive preparation for the various examinations required by independent Senior Schools; to develop sound work attitudes and habits; to promote spiritual, moral, social and cultural development and to foster individual development, including instilling self-esteem, confidence and wholeheartedness.

The School is particularly committed to offering every boy a truly broad education. Regardless of his ability – not only on the academic side but also on the non-academic – every boy is taught/coached by someone with expertise. The aims are to foster and discover talents, to aid boys to fulfil them, and, for those not so talented in a pursuit, to give them nevertheless a chance to develop an interest in and/or enjoyment for it. To this end, for instance: every boy is in a team with its own coach; every boy who wishes to be individually tutored in Music may be (currently over 80% learn at least one musical instrument); every boy is in at least one concert each year and every boy is in a play every year (there are 6 plays a year).

The School is fortunate in its extensive land, including an on-site newly completed 4G, Premiership Standard Astro-Turf facility. The original building is an Arts and Crafts Victorian mansion; its interior has been adapted, furnished and decorated for modern educational needs. There is a modern covered heated swimming pool, further playing fields nearby which include a further, floodlit all-weather playing surface.

Facilities are constantly being updated and improved. In recent years, the following facilities were added: a new Music centre, a new Theatre, a new Dining hall, a new Library and Resources room, a new Technology room, 3 new Science Laboratories, a new Art room and 8 further new Classrooms. The School has invested considerably in computer equipment and we remain at the forefront of ICT good practice. In 2015, the School launched the 'building better' development programme. This programme will see a further £15 million spent on developing the educational environment and facilities.

The main sports are Football, Rugby, Cricket and Athletics. Hockey is a new addition to the match schedule. At the same time boys are encouraged to try a variety of the more individual sports such as Swimming, Tennis, Skiing, Golf, Shooting and Sailing. In addition, there is ample opportunity for boys to discover other abilities and talents through activities in Music, technical activities and Drama.

Shrewsbury House has pupils join from many pre-prep schools including Shrewsbury Lodge, its own pre-prep School (*see Shrewsbury Lodge entry*).

Charitable status. Shrewsbury House School Trust Limited is a Registered Charity, number 277324. It seeks to provide the best possible learning environment for boys aged between 7 and 13 who have the potential for above-average academic achievement.

Shrewsbury Lodge School

22 Milbourne Lane, Esher, Surrey KT10 9EA
Tel: 01372 462781
Fax: 01372 469914
email: admin@shrewsburylodge.com
website: www.shrewsburylodge.com

Chairman of Governors: Mr Darren Johns

Head Teacher: **Mrs S Wingrove**

Age Range. 3–7 years Co-educational.
Number of Children. 140.
Fees per term (2016–2017). £2,655–£4,235.

Shrewsbury Lodge School is an IAPS independent day school for boys and girls aged from 3 to 7 years old. It is part of the Shrewsbury House School Trust.

The school aims to nurture and develop the whole child within an exciting environment of academic excellence. It offers a creative and well-balanced curriculum, where inspiring teaching staff help the children to develop lifelong skills and foster a love of learning.

Our school is a happy and welcoming one. It has a purposeful atmosphere and the children learn positive attitudes towards work and play, while building self-esteem, resilience, respect and empathy.

Shrewsbury Lodge School has extensive facilities including modern purpose-built classrooms (all with state-of-the-art interactive whiteboards), a brand new indoor school sports hall, a busy and thriving library, a large, well-equipped playground and a heated swimming pool. Children also benefit from regular sports and Forest School lessons at the school's own sports field and pavilion. Creative arts are further developed through strong Art, Music and Drama departments.

Recent popular destination schools at the 7+ stage include Shrewsbury House School and a wide range of London day schools.

Charitable status. Shrewsbury House School Trust is a Registered Charity, number 277324.

Solefield School

Solefields Road, Sevenoaks, Kent TN13 1PH
Tel: 01732 452142
email: admissions@solefieldschool.org
            office@solefieldschool.org
website: www.solefieldschool.org

Chairman of the Governors: Mr R Clewley

Headmaster: **Mr D A Philps**, BSc

Age Range. 4–13.
Number of Boys. 176.
Fees per term (2016–2017). £3,765–£4,425 including lunch.

Solefield is a day Preparatory School for boys from 4 to 13, located in the heart of Sevenoaks. Through exceptional teaching, learning and care it prepares boys for entry to independent schools such as Sevenoaks and Tonbridge at 13, along with Grammar School entry at 11. The curriculum is comprehensive and, along with core subjects and Humanities, also includes subjects such as Latin, Thinking Skills and Politics, Philosophy and Ethics. Extra-curricular endeavours are an essential part of life at Solefield and are well catered for with extensive opportunities in Sport, Drama, Music and Art. Solefield has a strong tradition of academic excellence. In the early years emphasis is placed on teaching the three Rs in a caring yet well-structured atmosphere, whilst senior boys gain numerous awards each year to senior schools. Links between parents and the school are a particular strength.

Enquiries concerning places and admissions should be made to the Registrar, Mrs Barbara Volpato.

Charitable status. Solefield School is a Registered Charity, number 293466. It aims to provide a high quality education to boys aged 4–13.

Sompting Abbotts

Church Lane, Sompting, West Sussex BN15 0AZ
Tel: 01903 235960
Fax: 01903 210045
email: office@somptingabbotts.com
website: www.somptingabbotts.com

Principal: Mrs P M Sinclair

Headmaster: **S J Douch**, MA

Bursar: D A Sinclair

Age Range. 2–13 Co-educational.
Number of Pupils. 120.
Fees per term (2016–2017). Day £2,835–£3,640 (including lunches).

The only independent, family-run school in the area!

Set in a magnificent site on the edge of the South Downs, Sompting Abbotts overlooks the English Channel with views towards Beachy Head and the Isle of Wight. The imposing Victorian House has some 30 acres of sports fields, woodlands, gardens and activity areas.

The aim of the school is to provide a well-balanced education in a caring environment, recognizing and developing the individual needs of each child, so that maximum potential academic achievement may be gained. Within the community of the school an emphasis is laid on the cultivation of courtesy, self-discipline and respect for one another in order to engender a happy atmosphere.

The school has a vibrant Pre-Preparatory Department, which includes lively Early Years classes. In the Preparatory Department well-equipped Science Laboratory and Computer Room are enjoyed by all ages. The Art and Drama departments offer wide scope for creativity, and peripatetic teachers provide tuition for a range of musical instruments. Free wrap-around care is provided from 8 am to 6 pm.

Book your child in for a Taster Day to see what life is like at our wonderful school!

South Lee School

Nowton Road, Bury St Edmunds, Suffolk IP33 2BT

Tel: 01284 754654
Fax: 01284 706178
email: office@southlee.co.uk
website: www.southlee.co.uk

Chairman of the Governors: Mr A Holliday

Headmaster: **Mr Mervyn Watch**, BEd Hons

Age Range. 2–13.
Number of Pupils. 245 Boys and Girls.
Fees per term (2016–2017). £3,060–£3,780 including lunches.

South Lee enjoys an excellent reputation for its friendly, family atmosphere. The school provides a stimulating and caring environment where children have every opportunity to learn and develop. From an early age, pupils are taught the traditional subjects, emphasising mathematics, science and English but within a wider curriculum that incorporates the use of the latest developments in technology and educational resources.

The school is situated close to the A14, has purpose-built, modern classrooms and specialist teaching areas. Sport is an important part of the curriculum and the school has the use of excellent local facilities

South Lee offers its pupils opportunities for self-expression and individual development through study of the Arts, drama, music and a broad range of outdoor, sporting and extracurricular activities.

The **Nursery**, which caters for children from 2 to 4 years of age, makes learning a fun experience from the very start.

The **Pre-Prep** is essentially class-based, though specialist staff teach French, music, ICT and Physical education.

The **Prep School** is well staffed with experienced teachers. The full range of academic subjects is taught, encompassing the national curriculum and preparing pupils for the Common Entrance 13+ examination.

Charitable status. South Lee exists to educate children from 2–13 years of age. Control is vested in a Board of Governors, the majority of whom are current parents. The school is run as a non-profit making Limited Company and is a Registered Charity, number 310491.

Spratton Hall

Smith Street, Spratton, Northampton NN6 8HP

Tel: 01604 847292
Fax: 01604 820844
email: office@sprattonhall.com
website: www.sprattonhall.com

Chairman: Mr James Coley

Head Master: **Mr Simon Clarke**, BA

Deputy Head Master: Mr Robert Dow, BA Hons, PGCE

Age Range. 4–13 Co-educational.
Number of Pupils. 395+.
Fees per term (2016–2017). Prep £4,450–£4,725, Pre-Prep £3,200. Fees include stationery, lunch, all academic books and most extra-curricular activities.

Set in 50 acres of Northamptonshire countryside, Spratton Hall is a fully co-educational day school for 4 to 13 years old.

Through highly skilled teaching we create an exciting and stimulating environment for learning, and by developing the talents of each child we believe that every pupil can succeed. The children are encouraged to become independent thinkers and to use their own initiative with confidence.

In the happy, caring Pre-Prep Department (from 4 to 7 years old) the girls and boys play imaginatively and grow in confidence. Each child is nurtured to establish a sound social and academic foundation for their future education.

Spratton has an enviable record of success at Common Entrance. Scholarships and awards are frequently won to many of the leading Independent Senior Schools.

The children enjoy a truly all-round education, achieving high academic standards as well as being recognised nationally for their success in sports and the Arts.

There are excellent facilities for Music, Art and Drama. The Performing Arts Centre provides Spratton Hall with a stage, tiered seating and a state-of-the-art sound and lighting system enabling each and every performance to be seen at its best. A wide variety of concerts, productions and exhibitions are enjoyed by all age groups throughout the year.

The Science laboratories, catering facilities and Dining Hall have been completely refurbished. Technology is constantly kept up to date and modernised to reflect the present advances in our society. The Townsend Library and Media centre incorporates books and technology exceptionally well.

The extensive playing fields together with the Jubilee Sports Dome, two all-weather surfaces and a full-size floodlit Astroturf enable all pupils to enjoy a range of sports including rugby, hockey, cricket, netball, rounders, athletics, cross-country and tennis with the Dome allowing for indoor tennis, badminton, gymnastics, dance and ballet.

In November 2010 Spratton Hall's successes were confirmed by an '*excellent*' and '*outstanding*' school inspection report in every respect by the Independent Schools Inspectorate.

For further information or to arrange a visit to see the children at work and play, please contact The Registrar on 01604 847292 or email afj@sprattonhall.com.

Charitable status. Spratton Hall is a Registered Charity, number 309925. It exists to provide education for boys and girls.

Spring Grove School

Harville Road, Wye, Kent TN25 5EZ

Tel: 01233 812337
email: office@springgroveschool.co.uk
website: www.springgroveschool.co.uk
Twitter: @SG_School
Facebook: @Spring-Grove-School-Wye

Chair of Governors: Mrs Dawne Sweetland

Headmaster: **Mr W J B Jones**, BMus Hons, PGCE
headmaster@springgroveschool.co.uk

Bursar: Mrs Sarah Peirce

bursar@springgroveschool.co.uk

Registrar: Mrs Nikki Holy
nholy@springgroveschool.co.uk

Age Range. 2–11 Co-educational.
Number of Pupils. 199.
Fees per term (2016–2017). £2,600–£3,950.

Spring Grove is a co-educational Day Preparatory School from age 2 to 11. The school was founded in 1967 and is situated on the outskirts of the beautiful village of Wye. The main building is an inspiring late 17th Century house. The facilities include an outstanding Early Years department, Science Room, School Hall, Art Room, a brand new Music Room (2014), well-equipped Classrooms, Computer Room and Changing Rooms. The grounds contain the main school buildings and 15 acres of playing fields. Qualified and graduate staff help prepare the children for entry to Independent Senior and Grammar Schools. Spring Grove has a strong tradition of academic excellence, exceptionally lively music, drama and art departments and children who are inspired with a sense of wonder about the world. Emphasis is placed on innovative and creative teaching in a caring yet well-structured atmosphere with close contact maintained between parents and teachers. 15 senior school scholarships have been awarded in the past two years.

The curriculum includes Music, Drama, Art and Technology, PE and extracurricular activities. Athletics, Cricket, Cross-Country (National U11 IAPS Champions in 2011), Football, Hockey, Netball, Rounders and Rugby are the principal games.

Enquiries concerning places and admissions should be made to the Registrar, Tel: 01233 812337.

Charitable status. Spring Grove School 2003 is a Registered Charity, number 1099823.

Staines Preparatory School

3 Gresham Road, Staines upon Thames, Middlesex TW18 2BT

Tel: 01784 450909
email: admissions@stainesprep.co.uk
website: www.stainesprep.co.uk
Twitter: @StainesPrep
Facebook: /Stainesprep

Independent Co-educational Day School founded in 1935.

Chairman of Governors: Mr M Bannister

Headmistress: **Ms Samantha Sawyer**, BEd Hons, MEd, NPQH

School Business Manager: Mrs R McLennan
Admissions Manager: Mrs N Tait

Age Range. 2½–11 Co-educational.
Number of Pupils. 217 Boys, 179 Girls.
Fees per term (2016–2017). £3,090–£3,560.

Throughout its history, Staines Preparatory School has maintained a reputation for high standards of education and care. The School aims for all pupils to attain their potential within a secure and happy environment and strives to produce boys and girls who are confident, honest, considerate and courteous.

The School believes in traditional values but is committed to providing the very best in terms of modern facilities and educational methods.

The School's philosophy of '*Educating Today's Children for the Challenges of Tomorrow*' is highlighted by the outstanding achievements of former SPS pupils in their secondary schools, with many attaining positions of responsibility as well as enjoying academic, sporting, musical and artistic success.

As Headmistress, Ms Samantha Sawyer said recently, "It is vitally important to the School that all our pupils have the chance to flourish both educationally and personally. Staines Prep provides the foundations for each and every child to strive towards their full potential and enjoy themselves in the process."

The curriculum is based upon the National Curriculum with a sharp focus on the acquisition of literacy and numeracy skills. However, it is given additional breadth by the inclusion of French from Year 2 and Latin/Classical Studies in Years 5 and 6. Sport plays an important role at SPS and there is a regular programme of fixtures against other preparatory schools. Whilst the School believes in competitive sport and has won a number of local tournaments in soccer, netball, cricket and swimming in recent years, it also believes that as many pupils as possible should be given the opportunity to play in matches at various levels. Development of abilities in the Arts is also considered highly important with opportunities provided throughout the School both in the classroom and as extra activities. Subject specialist teaching commences in Year 4 following a series of assessments at the end of Year 3. A regular programme of trips and visits enhance the curriculum and the annual Ski Trip for Year 6 much enjoyed.

The new Multi-Sports Hall, state-of-the-art teaching and performance facilities along with the The Jubilee Wing, Library, and ICT Suite all indicate the School's commitment to providing the very best facilities as well as education. In addition to the general teaching classrooms there are special facilities for Science, Art, Design and Technology and Special Needs. Hard surfaced playground areas, an all-weather floodlit court and the adjoining playing fields and environmental area provide ample space for sport and recreation. Headmistress Ms Sawyer said: "The School is exceptionally proud of its new facilities. It has been a long-awaited dream which has now come to fruition and is enjoyed by everyone, including our local community."

The School welcomes contact with parents and has a flourishing Friends' Association whose activities strengthen the links between home and school.

After-school wrap-around care is available for pupils of all ages, as well as a door-to-door minibus service that runs throughout the academic year.

Stamford Junior School

Stamford, Lincolnshire PE9 2LR

Tel: 01780 484400
email: headjs@ses.lincs.sch.uk
website: www.ses.lincs.sch.uk
Twitter: @SJS_Head
Facebook: /stamfordendowedschools

Stamford Junior School, along with Stamford High School (girls) and Stamford School (boys), is one of three schools in the historic market town of Stamford comprising the Stamford Endowed Schools Educational Charity. The schools are under a single Governing Body and overall management and leadership of the Principal and allow continuity of education for boys and girls from 3 to 18, including boarding from age 8. Each school has its own Head and staff.

Chairman of Governors: Dr Michael Dronfield

Principal of the Stamford Endowed Schools: Mr W Phelan, MBA

Headmistress: **Mrs E Smith**, BEd Hons

Age Range. 3–11.
Number of Children. 350.
Fees per term (2016–2017). Day: Year 0 £2,922, Years 1–2 £3,105, Years 3–6 £3,757; Full Boarding £6,771; Weekly Boarding £6,138; Three-night Boarding £5,393.

The Junior School educates boys and girls up to the age of 11 (including boarders from age 8), when boys move on to Stamford School and girls to Stamford High School. Admission from the Junior School to the two senior schools is based on progress and without further entrance testing.

The Junior School occupies its own spacious grounds, bordering the River Welland, overlooking the sports fields and open countryside, the boarding houses, the sports hall, floodlit artificial hockey pitch and the swimming pool on the same site. It is on the south west outskirts of Stamford within easy reach of the A1.

Entry to the School is according to registration at 4+ and assessment.

The lively and broad curriculum offers an ILIC-based (Independent Learning and Intellectual Curiosity) foundation to all academic, creative, and sporting subjects. Lessons are stimulating, energetic, and fully engaging so that the natural curiosity of our pupils can flourish. Extensive facilities, sporting opportunities, and the wide-ranging co-curricular programme promote the rounded development that we believe is essential for our children.

There are 26 full-time staff, with specialist teachers in physical education, swimming, art and music, and visiting teachers offering a variety of sports, dance, speech and drama.

There is a purpose-built nursery in the grounds of the school – Stamford Nursery School – offering first-class care and early learning for children aged 3–4. Pupils then head to the adjacent Early Years Reception Classes.

Boarding. The co-educational Boarding House (St Michael's) is run in a homely, family style under the experienced leadership of Mr and Mrs Cattell. Boys and girls are accepted as full or weekly boarders from the age of 8. Occasional or flexi boarding is accommodated where possible and according to family need. A full programme of activities takes place at weekends so that boarders enjoy a rich and varied week.

Stockport Grammar Junior School

Buxton Road, Stockport, Cheshire SK2 7AF
Tel: 0161 419 2405
email: sgjs@stockportgrammar.co.uk
website: www.stockportgrammar.co.uk
Twitter: @stockportgs
Facebook: /stockportgrammar

Chairman of Governors: C Dunn, MA

Headmaster: **T C Wheeler**, BA, MA, FRSA

Age Range. 3–11.
Number of Pupils. 420: 225 boys, 195 girls.
Fees per term (2016–2017). £2,835, plus lunch.

Entry is mainly at 3+ and 4+ following assessment, with occasional places available at other ages. Stockport Grammar Junior School is a happy school, where children are encouraged to develop their strengths. A broad curriculum is taught and academic standards are high. There are specialist facilities and teaching in Science, ICT, PE and Games, Swimming, Music, Art and Design Technology. A large number of pupils learn to play a musical instrument and tuition is available for many orchestral instruments. French and

Spanish are taught throughout. All children have swimming lessons in the School's pool. Children can choose to join in the numerous lunchtime and after-school clubs and activities.

The Junior School and the Senior School share the same site. The vast majority of pupils move into the Senior School at 11, having passed the Entrance Examination. (*See also Stockport Grammar School entry in HMC section.*)

Hockey, netball, football, rounders, cricket and athletics are the main sports. Swimming, tennis, cross-country, rugby, archery, canoeing and fencing are also offered. There is a full range of sporting fixtures and regular music and drama productions. All Junior pupils have the opportunity to participate in residential visits, which include outdoor pursuits.

Before and after school care is available and holiday play schemes are run at Easter and in the summer.

Facilities are excellent. In addition to specialist teaching rooms, which include a computer room and a science room, the Junior School has its own large all-weather surface along with a sports hall and extensive playing fields.

Charitable status. Stockport Grammar School is a Registered Charity, number 1120199. It exists to advance education by the provision and conduct, in or near Stockport, of a school for boys and girls.

Stonar Preparatory School

Cottles Park, Atworth, Wiltshire SN12 8NT
Tel: 01225 701762
Fax: 01225 790830
email: office@stonarschool.com
website: www.stonarschool.com
Twitter: @StonarSchool
Facebook: /StonarSchool

Chairman of Board of Directors:
Mr A McEwen, NACE UK Ltd

Headmaster: **Mr M Brain**, BA Ed Hons Exeter

Age Range. 2–11 Co-educational.
Number of Pupils. 133.
Fees per term (2016–2017). Day £2,710–£3,655; Boarding £6,485.

Stonar Prep School is a vibrant and exciting place to be.

Our busy, lively curriculum, delivered by the Prep School's excellent teachers, inspires creativity and intellectual curiosity. Topic-led work brings an exciting dimension to the curriculum, immersing children in a learning experience which builds skills and knowledge across the subjects. The emphasis is firmly on active learning. Pupils enjoy lots of trips and activities which support their learning and keep them stimulated and engaged.

Some pupils show obvious academic ability from an early age; others may need more encouragement. At Stonar Prep we help each child discover their aptitudes and develop their confidence as they experience numerous opportunities within and beyond the classroom. Pupils are encouraged to aim for the best in all that they do, whether it is academic, sporting, creative or performance, and we have high expectations of them.

We encourage the boys and girls to take responsibility for their own learning, behaviour and progress. This helps them become more independent. We involve parents in their child's education at every step along the way; progress is regularly and rigorously reported and the achievements of pupils are recognised and celebrated.

Because the children learn and grow within our secure and nurturing environment, they develop a caring attitude towards each other, their school and the world around them.

This is underpinned by the Prep School CARE code which was devised by the children to summarise our school rules:

Communicate kindly
Aim high – always do your best
Respect – treat others as you would be treated yourself
Enjoy – and appreciate what you have.

As part of the NACE Schools group, Prep children have unique opportunities for language immersion, exchanges and links with pupils in Spain and France. Progress is monitored by form tutors so the more able pupils receive challenging tasks that take them beyond their comfort zone; our outstanding Learning Support department is available for girls and boys with specific individual learning needs.

When pupils progress to the Senior School, we ensure that they are ready for the next stage of their education as confident learners equipped with the skills required to thrive.

Governance. Stonar is a part of NACE Educational Services Limited, Company Registration No. 8441252, Registered Address: 17 Hanover Square, London, United Kingdom W1S 1HU.

Stonyhurst St Mary's Hall

Preparatory School for Stonyhurst College

Stonyhurst, Clitheroe, Lancashire BB7 9PU

Tel:	01254 827073
Fax:	01254 827136
email:	admissions@stonyhurst.ac.uk
website:	www.stonyhurst.ac.uk

Chairman of Governors: John Cowdall

Headmaster: **Mr Ian Murphy**, BA, PGCE

Age Range. 3–13 (Boarders from age 8).
Number of Pupils. Day 218, Boarding 40.
Fees per term (2016–2017). Day £2,790–£5,195; Weekly Boarding £6,775; Full Boarding £7,995.

Stonyhurst St Mary's Hall provides a co-educational preparatory education in the Jesuit Catholic tradition for boarders (age 8–13) and day pupils (age 3–13). Stonyhurst, founded in 1593, is one of the oldest Jesuit schools in the world, and the College and Preparatory School are set within two thousand acres of outstanding natural beauty. We have impressive facilities and buildings, however, it will always be our people – children, staff, parents and families that breathe life into Stonyhurst St Mary's Hall. The positive and optimistic vision within our school community is tangible. This is an exciting time for us and our school is thriving. This is a special place where children want to be and where relationships between all members of the community are remarkable.

The children receive a high-quality rounded education. St Mary's Hall has its own dedicated teaching facilities and resources for all preparatory subjects, including French, Spanish and Latin. A new state-of-the-art Science laboratory was recently opened, and the school also enjoys the benefit of very extensive games fields, a sports hall, a fully equipped modern theatre, as well as shared use with the College of a large indoor swimming pool, and one of the finest all-weather pitches in the North. St Mary's Hall has a national reputation for rugby, but at the same time many other boys' and girls' sports flourish, as do a wide variety of cultural pursuits including drama and music. Many educational and recreational excursions take place both at home and abroad.

All pupils receive pastoral care and academic tutoring through their Class teachers and Playroom (Head of Year) Staff, who meet regularly to monitor closely pupils' progress. Early Years and Key Stage 1 pupils are taught in their own purpose-built building. The teaching staff are also closely supported by a resident Chaplaincy team, which leads the largely lay staff in the religious life of the School. Pupils of other denominations are very welcome at St Mary's Hall.

Boarders are under the care of the resident Housemaster and his wife, supported by a fantastic resident pastoral team, which ensures one of the best staff to student ratios in the country. The boarders enjoy a stimulating and wide-ranging programme of lunchtime, evening, and weekend activities. St Mary's Hall, like Stonyhurst College, provides a seven-day week boarding environment, in which the day pupils are able to participate to a great extent if they wish.

The main sports played are Rugby, Cross Country, Netball, Rounders, Hockey, Cricket, Athletics and Tennis. The wide range of extra-curricular activities available for the children in their recreational time includes Chess, Model Making, Camping (Summer), Art, Photography, Fencing, Gymnastics, Computing, Theatre Workshop, Modern Dance, Ballet, and Skiing.

Admission to St Mary's Hall of pupils from age 3 to 10+ is by previous school report (where applicable) and interview. At 11+ there is also an entrance test. Academic Scholarships are also awarded at 11+, as is an annual music scholarship. The Academic provision at the school is overseen by College Heads of Department from the age of 11 as part of a seamless transition preparing the pupils for national examinations, and whilst the pastoral care of the pupils remains in a supportive prep school environment, all pupils are effectively admitted to the College from age 11 onwards and are taught by KS3 teaching staff.

Further details and a prospectus may be obtained from the Registrar.

Charitable status. St Mary's Hall is a Registered Charity, number 230165. It exists to promote Catholic Independent Jesuit Education within the Christian Community. It also runs its own registered, pupil-led charity, Children for Children, which raises funds for a school in Zimbabwe and other worthy causes.

Stormont

The Causeway, Potters Bar, Herts EN6 5HA

Tel:	01707 654037
email:	admin@stormontschool.org
website:	www.stormontschool.org
Twitter:	@stormontschool
Facebook:	/stormontschool

The school is administered by a Board of Governors.

Chairman of Board of Governors: Mr J H Salmon, FCA

Headmistress: **Mrs S E Martin**, BSc

Age Range. 4–11.
Number of Pupils. 170 Day Girls.
Fees per term (2016–2017). £3,890–£4,080 (including lunch). There are no compulsory extras.

The School was founded in 1944 and has occupied its attractive Victorian House since then. There is a spacious, bright, purpose-built Lower School Building, which adjoins the Assembly Hall and Dining Room. Old stables have been converted to provide well-equipped rooms for Art, Pottery, Design Technology, Science and French. A Millennium Building houses a Drama/Music Studio and an Information and Communications Technology Suite. The school has two tennis courts and a playground. It has use of a two-acre playing field and a swimming pool. A well-equipped Sports Hall was opened in the Summer Term 2009.

Well-qualified and experienced staff prepare the girls for entry to a wide range of senior schools at the age of eleven.

Charitable status. Stormont School is a Registered Charity, number 311079. It exists to establish and carry on a school where children may receive a sound education.

Stover Preparatory School

Newton Abbot, Devon TQ12 6QG

Tel:	01626 354505 or 01626 331451
Fax:	01626 361475
email:	mail@stover.co.uk
website:	www.stover.co.uk

Chairman of Governors: Mr S Killick, ND, ARB

Head: **Mr David Burt**

Age Range. 3–11 Co-educational.

Number of Pupils. 142

Fees per term (2016–2017). Preparatory School: Day: Reception–Year 2 £2,560, Year 3 £2,780, Years 4–5 £3,160, Year 6 £3,440. Weekly Boarding: Year 3 £5,430, Years 4–5 £5,820, Year 6 £6,100. Full Boarding: Year 3 £6,290, Years 4–5 £6,670, Year 6 £6,950.

Stover Preparatory School enjoys a beautiful rural setting on the edge of Dartmoor National Park and close to the South Devon coast. Set in 64 acres there is ample space for pupils of all ages to experience the great outdoors, be that through play, nature walks, sport, orienteering, bushcraft, learning in our outdoor classroom or researching the history of our fine old buildings. Stover Preparatory School shares its fine site with Stover Senior School, making transfer at aged 11 years a smooth process for our pupils.

We pride ourselves on our warm, welcoming atmosphere where each individual is nurtured and encouraged to reach their full potential. Visitors frequently comment on the positive, happy feeling they experience upon entering the school. Teachers are aware of pupils' individual needs and provide support in an approachable and friendly manner.

We offer a broad, balanced curriculum with high academic standards, complemented by a wide range of extra-curricular activities. Spanish begins in Reception and French is also introduced at Year 3. Years 5 and 6 are taught all subjects by specialist teachers, whilst in the younger age groups there is a balance between specialist teaching and class teaching, depending upon the age of the pupils. Underpinning everything we do is our firm belief in Research Based Learning, where students develop their inquiry skills, taking ownership of their learning from a young age. Sport and the Performing Arts play a vital role in each child's development. We have a full fixture list for our U9 and U11 teams as well as involvement with the local Schools' Sports Partnership. Our regular school performances and concerts are a highlight of the calendar. More than 80% of our Prep School pupils choose to participate in the Prep School Choir. In addition, we offer a Pre-Prep Choir and a Chamber Choir for talented pupils in Years 5 and 6. Residential and day trips into our beautiful local environment further complement the curriculum.

Facilities include an extensive Outdoor Classroom, Sports Fields, Tennis Courts, Art room, Music room, Multi-Purpose Hall, Library and ICT suite.

Flexi, weekly and full boarding are available from the age of 8 years. Scholarships are offered at 11+. The majority of our pupils move on to Stover Senior School.

See also Stover School senior entry in The Society of Heads section.

Charitable status. Stover School Association is a Registered Charity, number 306712.

Streatham & Clapham Prep School
GDST

Wavertree Road, London SW2 3SR

Tel:	020 8674 6912
Fax:	020 8674 0175
email:	prep@schs.gdst.net
website:	www.schs.gdst.net
Twitter:	@schs_gdst

Motto: *ad sapientiam sine metu*

Chairman of Local Governors: Mrs S Wrixon, BA, PG Dip Journalism

Head: **T Mylne, BA, PGCE**

Age Range. Girls 3–11.

Number of Pupils. 212.

Fees per term (2016–2017). Prep School £4,244, Nursery £3,235.

Streatham & Clapham Prep School is a division of Streatham & Clapham High School GDST (*see the entry in the GSA section*), situated on its own extensive campus in Streatham Hill, within a mile of the Senior School. The School has a vision of excellence which aims to provide a liberal and challenging educational experience for its pupils within a caring culture of warm relationships and diversity, all the while nurturing their personal development and resilience. Its facilities include a full-size gymnasium and specialist drama, music, IT, art and design rooms; pupils also regularly benefit from specialist Senior School facilities, for instance its all-weather sports pitch. Admission to the school is by selective assessment, with individual assessment of pupils for Nursery and Reception, and an entrance examination for Year 3 entrants. Places in other year groups are occasionally available.

Curriculum. The school's broad and varied curriculum focuses on distinctive and invigorating learning through programmes such as Singapore mathematics, the 'Talk4Writing' network and Mandarin. Emphasis is placed on developing pupils' understanding of classical and cultural history, which is taught through creative topics in music, art and drama. The extent to which pupils are taught by subject specialists increases as pupils progress through the School, providing rich and intellectually stimulating challenges that nurture their skills and prepare them for life in the Senior School, to which the great majority transfer. The array of clubs, societies and events is extensive and caters for a wide range of abilities and interests, including in the social, musical, academic, sporting and artistic areas.

Personal & Pastoral Development. Great emphasis is placed on nurturing well-balanced and considerate individuals, who are ready for the challenges of adolescent and adult life. Strong pastoral and House systems reinforce this ethos, as do lessons in philosophy, myriad opportunities to build resilience, and overseas residential trips.

Charitable status. Streatham & Clapham High School is a member of The Girls' Day School Trust, which is a Registered Charity, number 306983.

Stroud School
King Edward VI Preparatory School

Highwood House, Highwood Lane, Romsey, Hampshire SO51 9ZH

Tel: 01794 513231
Fax: 01794 514432
email: enquiries@stroud-kes.org.uk
website: www.stroud-kes.org.uk

Chairman of Governors: Mr B Richards

Headmaster: Mr Joel Worrall, BSc

Deputy Head: Miss R M Lyons

Director of Studies: Mr C Jackson

Age Range. 3–13.
Number of Pupils. 318: 186 Boys, 146 Girls.
Fees per term (2016–2017). Upper School £5,300, Middle School £4,870, Pre-Preparatory £3,270, Nursery £7.00 per hour.

Stroud is a co-educational day school for children aged 2 years 9 months to 13 years. Pupils are prepared for entrance to senior Independent or Grammar Schools.

The School stands on the outskirts of Romsey in its own grounds of 20 acres, which include playing fields, a full-sized sports hall, a heated outdoor swimming pool, tennis courts, riding arena, lawns and gardens. The main team games for boys are cricket, hockey, rugby and soccer, and for girls hockey, rounders and netball. Both boys and girls play tennis.

Music and drama play an important part in the life of the School. A wide variety of instruments is taught and children are encouraged to join the school orchestra. Each year there is a musical production and the Carol Service is held in Romsey Abbey.

The Stroud School Association, run by the parents, holds many social activities and helps to raise money for amenities, but its main function is to generate goodwill.

A new Early Years building was completed in 2007.

In 2014 a £2.5 million investment included a new kitchen, dining room, as well as an art/dt/mfl block. Included in this project was a £300K Biomass Heating System.

The Study Preparatory School

Wilberforce House, Camp Road, Wimbledon Common, London SW19 4UN

Tel: 020 8947 6969
email: admissions@thestudyprep.co.uk
website: www.thestudyprep.co.uk
Twitter: @thestudyprep

Chairman of Governors: Mr Nick Brookes

Headmistress: Mrs Susan Pepper, MA Oxon

Age Range. 4–11.
Number of Girls. 320 (approximately).
Fees per term (2016–2017). £4,175.

The Study Preparatory School provides a happy and stimulating learning environment for girls from 4 to 11 on two very attractive and well-equipped sites close to Wimbledon Common.

The girls enjoy a rich diversity of experiences, both in and out of the classroom. The school is renowned for its creative ethos, and has been awarded Artsmark Gold status by Arts Council England for the second time in 2012. Each girl is encouraged to do her best academically, and excellent teaching standards encourage academic rigour and challenge. Music and sport are exceptionally strong, while drama, public speaking and a varied clubs programme play an important part. Guest speakers, fundraising events, workshops and school trips all help the children to understand important issues beyond the school gates. Good manners and consideration for others are encouraged at all times. Girls leave at 11+, very well prepared for the next stage of their education, with a zest for learning and many happy memories. Girls receive offers from leading day and boarding senior schools, many with academic or performance scholarships, with over 92 scholarships having been offered over the last five years.

Entry is by ballot at reception and by assessment thereafter. The Study has an assisted places scheme for girls aged 7+. For details contact Joint Educational Trust (JET) on 020 3217 1100.

Charitable status. The Study (Wimbledon) Ltd is a Registered Charity, number 271012. It exists to provide education for girls from 4 to 11.

Summer Fields

Mayfield Road, Oxford OX2 7EN

Tel: 01865 459204
email: admissions@summerfields.com
website: www.summerfields.com
Twitter: @SFSOxford
Facebook: Summer Fields, Oxford

Chairman of Governors: A E Reekes, MA, FRSA

Headmaster: David Faber, MA Oxon

Age Range. 8–13.
Number of Boys. 210 boarders and 45 day.
Fees per term (2016–2017). £9,357 Boarding, £7,246 Day.

Set in 72 acres of delightful grounds which lead down to the river Cherwell and yet only a few miles from the city centre, Summer Fields is often known as Oxford's *Secret Garden*.

The School has always had a strong academic reputation. In 2016, Summerfieldians secured 20 scholarships and awards to top independent schools, including three King's Scholarships to Eton and seven Music Scholarships and Exhibitions to various schools. Each year, boys pass Common Entrance to a wide variety of schools including Eton, Harrow, Radley, Winchester.

Huge emphasis is placed on providing the highest standards of pastoral care. Each boy has a personal tutor, who is responsible for his academic progress and social welfare and will be in regular contact with the boy's parents. The boarders live in comfortable Lodges within the school grounds and are looked after by an experienced and dedicated husband and wife team of Lodgeparents. More than 90% of the staff live on site, making a significant contribution to school life both in and out of the classroom.

The Music, Art, Drama, Design Technology, ICT and Sport departments are all impressive. The Choir regularly sing Evensong in Oxford Colleges. They also regularly tour abroad, most recently visiting Rome. At least one Drama production takes place every term in the Macmillan Theatre.

Every summer an Art Exhibition of boys' work is held at the school.

The facilities are outstanding, including the new Salata Pavilion, opened in October 2015, which includes purpose-built changing rooms for the boys and a large multi-functional space on the first floor. Within the school there is also a fine library, theatre and chapel; Art, Design & Technology, Music and ICT Centres and a magnificent Sports Hall, with squash and Eton fives courts, a shooting gallery and swimming pool. The extensive outdoor facilities include an astro-turf and tennis courts and all-weather cricket nets, a nine-hole golf course, the plantation where the boys camp, together with an outside classroom. A huge range of sports, activities and hobbies is on offer to the boys.

8+ Academic and Music Scholarships are available as well as 100% scholarships and bursaries for entry into Year 6 or Year 7.

For further information or to arrange a visit, please contact Mrs Christine Berry, Tel: 01865 459204 or email: admissions@summerfields.com.

Charitable status. Summer Fields is a Registered Charity, number 309683.

Sunningdale School

Dry Arch Road, Sunningdale, Berks SL5 9PY

Tel: 01344 620159
Fax: 01344 873304
email: headmaster@sunningdaleschool.co.uk
website: www.sunningdaleschool.co.uk

Headmaster: **T A C N Dawson**, MA, PGCE

Deputy Headmaster: A J Logue, BSc, PGCE

Age Range. 7–13.
Number of Boys. 110.
Fees per term (2016–2017). Boarding £7,800 (no compulsory extras).

Sunningdale is a small, mainly boarding school of around 110 boys. The unique family atmosphere means that the boys feel happy and secure and as a result are able to achieve their full potential. Our aim is to find each boy's strengths and give him the opportunity to shine in different areas of school life.

Our academic record speaks for itself, with scholarships gained on a regular basis to senior schools. The structure of our forms means that boys move through the school at their own pace, constantly challenged or supported where necessary.

Three-quarters of the boys play at least one musical instrument; many play two or even three. The chapel choir sings on Sundays and occasionally at old boys' weddings and there is a pipe band which plays on Sports Day and at other events. As well as other drama productions we produce a musical each year in which every boy appears. The art department puts on a large exhibition every year and often wins awards at senior schools.

We have a good reputation on the sports field and one of the benefits of being a small school is that almost all the boys get to represent the school in a team. This does wonders for their confidence. There is a wide range of activities on offer from judo to juggling, clay pigeons to clay modelling.

The school has a strong boarding ethos and boys can weekly board in their first year. Weekends are packed with activities to keep the boys stimulated and entertained.

Sunninghill Prep School

South Court, South Walks, Dorchester, Dorset DT1 1EB

Tel: 01305 262306
email: lhampshire@sunninghill.dorset.sch.uk
website: www.sunninghillprep.co.uk
Facebook: /SunninghillPrepSchool

Chair of Governors: Mr Richard Miller, Chartered Surveyor

Headmaster: **Mr John Thorpe**, BSc Hons, PGCE

Age Range. 3 months–13 years.
Number of Children. Baby unit (3 months–2 years 9 months) 8 girls, 5 boys, Nursery (2 years 9 months–4 years) 8 girls, 14 boys; Reception (4–5 years) 7 girls, 5 boys; Junior Prep (5–8 years) 26 girls, 35 boys; Prep School (8–13 years) 38 girls, 46 boys.
Fees per term (2016–2017). £2,830–£4,830. There are no compulsory extras. Nursery: £923.40 (based on 5 sessions per week, inclusive of Early Years Grant).

Sunninghill is a co-educational day school. There are 17 full-time and 21 part-time fully qualified teaching staff.

Founded in 1939, Sunninghill Prep became a Charitable Trust in 1969. It moved to its present site in January 1997 and has its own swimming pool, all-weather sports pitch, tennis courts and extensive grounds. Children are prepared for the Common Entrance examination to any Independent Senior School, and those with particular ability may be entered for scholarships. Over the years the school has attained many academic successes, but the broad curriculum also includes drama, art, craft, music and physical education. Friday Enrichments allow greater cross-curricular links for years 1–8, enhancing their learning further.

Team and individual sports played with PE and Games at least three times a week from years 3–8 and these include hockey, netball, lacrosse and rounders for the girls, and hockey, rugby, association football and cricket for the boys. In the summer term both boys and girls participate in athletics, swimming and tennis.

Out-of-school activities include academic clubs preparing for scholarships, such as the core subjects, humanities and art, plus debating, chess, creative arts, ballet, dance, LAMDA and various music clubs including choir and string quartet. We offer multi sports across a wide age group, all pentathlon sports and swimming and we are a member of the National Sailing Academy, with our own race team. Sunninghill Prep prides itself on its nurturing, family ethos. The school's flourishing Parents' Association ensures that parents and staff all know each other and work together for the good of the children and the School.

The prospectus is available on request.

Charitable status. Sunninghill Preparatory School is a Registered Charity, number 1024774. It exists to provide education for boys and girls.

Sunny Hill Preparatory School
Bruton School for Girls

Sunny Hill, Bruton, Somerset BA10 0NT

Tel: 01749 814400
Fax: 01749 812537
email: admissions@brutonschool.co.uk
website: www.brutonschool.co.uk
Twitter: @BrutonSchool
Facebook: @Bruton-School-for-Girls

Chairman of Governors: Mr D H C Batten

Head of Preparatory School: **Mrs Helen Snow**, BEd

Age Range. Day places for Girls and Boys aged 3–7. Day and Boarding places for Girls aged 7–11. No Saturday school.

Numbers of Pupils. 50.

Fees per term (2016–2017). Day: £3,800–£3,900 (Pre-paratory School), £1,900–£2,530 (Pre-Preparatory School), £20 per session (Nursery). Boarding (from Year 4): £6,935–£7,035 (full), £6,285–£6,385 (weekly boarding), £6,460–£6,560 (weekly boarding inc Sundays), £7,605 (Overseas Pupils including EAL support); £58.40 per day (casual boarding).

Ethos. Sunny Hill Prep aims to create a happy, caring and vibrant atmosphere where children build strong academic foundations and develop personal confidence. Pupils are encouraged to think of others in a community based on mutual respect.

Location. Situated in 40 acres in beautiful countryside, the school is conveniently located on the Somerset, Wiltshire and Dorset borders with easy access to the A303. It shares the campus with the senior school and pupils benefit from specialist teachers and facilities.

Curriculum. A carefully structured and broad curriculum, delivered using an exciting variety of teaching and learning styles ensures good foundations are laid and high standards are achieved by all. Pupils thrive on a rich mix of activities – including themed curriculum weeks, a comprehensive outdoor education programme, imaginative topic work and educational visits – all encouraging curiosity and a love of learning. Food Technology modules in specialist rooms are an integral part of Years 5 and 6 DT work. Creative and enthusiastic teachers inspire and stretch pupils. Pupils are nurtured by an excellent system of pastoral care. Children in the Nursery and Early Years Class follow the Early Years Foundation Stage curriculum with emphasis on learning through play.

A love of creative and performing arts is encouraged as are opportunities to perform – facilities include a modern theatre and an amphitheatre. Other facilities include a library, a nature reserve and a meadow. There is a wide variety of extracurricular activities, for example Latin, rugby, gymnastics, yoga, Eco club and folk group.

Sport. Hockey, netball, rounders, gymnastics, tennis, swimming and athletics are integral to the curriculum taught by specialist PE teachers. Facilities include an astroturf pitch, dance studio and heated outdoor swimming pool. Pupils participate in inter-school competitions and in addition pupils can try activities such as riding, indoor rowing, dance and trampolining.

Boarding. A high standard of care and comfort is provided in a self-contained junior boarding house with well-equipped facilities and grounds. In the evenings and at weekends, pupils enjoy a full programme of activities.

Spiritual Life. The school has a Christian ethos and welcomes pupils from all faiths or none.

Medical Care. The school has its own medical centre with a qualified nursing Sister.

Charitable status. Bruton School for Girls is a Registered Charity, number 1085577, and a Company Limited by Guarantee.

Sussex House

68 Cadogan Square, London SW1X 0EA

Tel: 020 7584 1741
email: schoolsecretary@sussexhouseschool.co.uk
website: www.sussexhouseschool.co.uk

Chairman of the Governors: John Crewe, Esq

Headmaster: **Nicholas Kaye**, MA Magdalene College Cambridge, ACP, FRSA, FRGS

Deputy Headmaster: Martin Back, BA, PGCE Sussex

Age Range. 8–13.

Number of Boys. 185.

Fees per term (2016–2017). £6,200.

Founded in 1952, Sussex House is situated in the heart of Chelsea in a fine Norman Shaw house in Cadogan Square. Its Gymnasium and Music School are housed in a converted chapel in Cadogan Street. The school is an independent charitable trust. At Common Entrance and Scholarship level it has achieved a record of consistently strong results to academically demanding schools. The school enjoys its own entirely independent character and the style is traditional yet imaginative.

There is a full-time teaching staff of 22. Creative subjects are given strong emphasis and throughout the school boys take Music and Art. Team sports take place at a nearby site and the school's football teams have an impressive record. Cricket is the main summer sport and there are opportunities for tennis, swimming, basketball, indoor football and indoor hockey. All boys have physical education classes and Sussex House is a centre of excellence for fencing and its international records are well known.

Cultural and creative activities play a major role, including theatrical productions in a West End theatre, a major annual exhibition of creative work featuring large-scale architectural models and an annual competition of poetry written by boys. There is a strong bias towards music and an ambitious programme of choral and orchestral concerts. A large number of pupils play musical instruments and there is an impressive record of music awards to senior schools. The school provides a range of sporting and cultural trips.

The school has a Church of England affiliation. There is a school chaplain and weekly services are held in St Simon Zelotes Church, Chelsea. Boys of all religions and denominations are welcomed.

Charitable status. Sussex House is a Registered Charity, number 1035806. It exists to provide education for boys.

Sutton Valence Preparatory School

Church Road, Chart Sutton, Maidstone, Kent ME17 3RF

Tel: 01622 842117
Fax: 01622 844201
email: enquiries@svprep.svs.org.uk
website: www.svs.org.uk
Facebook: /SuttonValenceSchoolKent

Chairman of Governors: B F W Baughan, Esq

Acting Head: **Miss C L Corkran**, MEd, BEd Hons Cantab

Age Range. 3–11.

Number of Day Pupils. Prep (7–11): 94 boys, 78 girls. Pre-Prep (3–6): 80 boys, 62 girls.

Fees per term (2016–2017). £2,830–£4,345. Lunch £245.

The values of our School community and the happiness of our children are central to everything we do. These provide pupils with a strong feeling of structure and security which enables them to work effectively.

At whichever point children join us they embark on their own journeys, each one different and each one with differing emphasis on the four areas we hold dear: Academic, Co-curricular, Community and Leadership and Service.

By the time they leave us at the age of 11, it is our responsibility to have equipped the children during their formative years with the essentials of character to thrive in an increasingly competitive world. To put firmly in place the qualities which will make them clear thinking, lateral thinking, robust, hardworking, determined and yet kindly citizens, who will go on to influence many people in the coming years.

We have high expectations of ourselves and of our children, both inside and out of the classroom, and we have a long history of successful preparation of children for the next stage of their education, be that for our Senior School, the Kent grammars, or other schools.

None of this should come at the expense of childhood and what the School does so successfully is find that balance between delivering in terms of education, and yet doing so kindly and with many broad, interesting and high-quality opportunities. The School is very proud of its articulate and confident pupils who move on well-equipped to work things out for themselves, so crucial in an increasingly challenging world.

To achieve this we have dedicated Art, Science and ICT facilities and a new Library. Classes are small throughout the school. The 40 teaching staff are all well qualified and there is an extensive peripatetic staff for music. Special needs are addressed by the SENCO and 3 part-time teachers. The Kindergarten to Year 2 classes all have qualified classroom assistants.

The school is situated in 18 acres of countryside overlooking the Weald and includes a hard and grass play areas, heated outdoor swimming pool, four hard tennis courts, a Sports Hall, a 13-acre games field, a full-size Astroturf and a newly established 'forest school' area, all of which support our co-curricular programme.

A solid foundation in the core subjects of English, Mathematics, Science and ICT is supplemented by Languages, Music, Drama, Art, Design Technology and Sport which are all taught by specialist teaching staff. The co-curricular programme is wide and varied providing many opportunities for children to perform in drama productions and in concerts, occasionally in conjunction with the senior school. Children are prepared for our senior school, Sutton Valence, the local Grammar schools and other independent schools with an 11+ entry.

Cricket, football, hockey, netball, rugby and rounders are the major sports, with athletics, swimming and cross-country also being available. The proximity of the senior school, Sutton Valence, allows the children to benefit from their staffing and facilities, including the use of the Sports Hall, athletics track and the indoor swimming pool. After-school activities include chess club, art, 5-a-side football, gymnastics, drama, craft, croquet, science club, ballet and judo.

The school is a Christian foundation. Assemblies, for celebration, and the use of the local church are an important facet of our lives, with the school's Chaplain visiting regularly. The school provides a fulfilling education for all its children, a thriving network for its parents and a happy workplace for all who dedicate their lives to it.

Charitable status. United Westminster Schools Foundation is a Registered Charity, number 309267. It exists to provide education for boys and girls and provides valuable resources and support.

Swanbourne House

Swanbourne, Milton Keynes, Buckinghamshire MK17 0HZ

Tel: 01296 720264
email: office@swanbourne.org

website: www.swanbourne.org
Twitter: @swanbournehouse
Facebook: @SwanbourneHouse

The School is a Charitable Trust, administered by a Board of Governors.

Chairman of Governors: J Willmott

Headmaster: S Hitchings, MA Oxon

Age Range. 3–13.

Number of Pupils. Prep: 159 Boys, 102 Girls (30 full/weekly boarders, 52 flexi boarders). Pre-Prep: 41 Girls, 59 Boys. Nursery: 11 Girls, 10 Boys.

Fees per term (2016–2017). Full/Weekly boarding £7,425; Day: Prep £5,825; 7s £4,075; Pre-Prep £3,300; Nursery £408–£1,838.

The house, which was once the home of the Cottesloe family, is a Grade II listed building, standing in 40 acres of wooded grounds and commanding extensive views of the surrounding countryside. Swanbourne has been described by Gabbitas Guardianship as 'a school you would just dream of'.

There are 40 full-time members of teaching staff, many of whom are resident. They are assisted by several peripatetic specialist teachers. The well-being of the boarders is in the hands of a resident Housemaster and his wife: they are assisted by our daily RGN staff and an Assistant Housemaster and Assistant Housemistress.

A strong musical tradition has been established. There are three choirs, an orchestra and various ensembles. Musical concerts are held throughout the school year and all pupils are encouraged to participate in drama and the Inter-House music competition. The school has its own chapel.

Boys and girls are prepared for entry to independent senior schools, usually at 13+. In 2016 all pupils passed their Common Entrance and 10 scholarships were awarded. The majority of boys and girls go on to leading senior independent schools, where the pass rate in recent years has been 100%. From age 9, pupils are taught by specialist teachers in well-equipped subject rooms. There are 2 Modern Language Laboratories and all senior pupils have the opportunity to spend a week in France.

The more practical side of the Curriculum is fully catered for in the Fremantle Hall of Technology. Art, Design Technology, Science and Information Technology are taught in this attractive building: more than 200 computers are in use throughout the school. We have two computer rooms and internet access in every classroom.

A House system operates to encourage healthy competition in work and games. The Housemasters and Housemistresses have a special responsibility and concern for the welfare of the children in their House.

For boys, the main school games are Rugby, Hockey, Football and Cricket, and for girls Hockey, Netball and Rounders. Coaching and matches are also arranged in Athletics. Both winter and summer Tennis is played. Further opportunities include Cross-country, Archery, Dance and Squash. A very wide range of extracurricular activities is available in the evenings, at weekends and on certain afternoons. Tennis and Golf facilities are excellent.

The Bridget More Hall offers outstanding facilities for Drama, Music and PE. Other facilities include a rifle range, an indoor swimming pool, two astroturf pitches, and a squash court. There are various holiday sports clubs and time to offer camping and outward-bound activities, such as canoeing, climbing, riding, skiing and leadership training.

School Prefects are taught to foster a caring concern for the well-being of every member of our community.

Children are prepared for Senior Independent Schools through lectures and workshops on international education, drugs, first aid and senior school life. All leavers at 13+ take part in a residential week of outdoor education. Our Leadership Training is first-rate and has led to the regular winning of all-rounder scholarships and the Gordonstoun Challenge.

The Pre-Preparatory Department occupies an Elizabethan Manor House, adjoining the school grounds. Whilst retaining a separate identity, the younger children are able to use the Main School facilities throughout the year.

Charitable status. Swanbourne House School is a Registered Charity, number 310640. It seeks to provide a continuous structured education for children aged 3–13 years.

Talbot Heath Junior School

Rothesay Road, Bournemouth BH4 9NJ
Tel: 01202 763360
Fax: 01202 768155
email: jsoffice@talbotheath.org
website: www.talbotheath.org

Chairman of Governors: Mr Graham Exon

Head Teacher: **Mrs Sally Weber-Spokes**, BA, PGCE

Age Range. Girls 3–11.
Number of Pupils. 222.
Our Ethos. We are immensely proud of our pupils and the happy atmosphere, in which there is a genuine love of learning that permeates the school. Being unique in the area in catering for girls from 3–18, the school is one where each individual really matters and is nurtured and valued. The School's motto, 'Honour Before Honours', underpins our community. We care for each other and support one another. Integrity and character lie at the heart of who we are.

We have a strong family atmosphere where all have a chance to achieve at their own level across every area of the broad curriculum. Perhaps, more importantly, the girls are happy and see coming to school as something enjoyable and great fun.

Talbot Heath girls are confident but not arrogant, knowledgeable but not complacent, able to express their opinions but willing to listen to those of others, independent yet supportive, strong yet compassionate, principled but fun. They value what they have and they value others. They are original but can work as a team, are keen to play a role in the wider world but have a strong sense of community.

The academic tradition and ethos of the school depends on both the encouragement of hard work and diligence and the creation of a caring community. Pupils are from a wide range of abilities and emphasis is placed on becoming rounded individuals, experiencing the full breadth of an extensive curriculum and achieving at their own personal level. Home school links are strong and positive which helps to create the caring and supportive environment of which we are so proud. Our results, right from the first steps in EYFS, are outstanding but the school places value on so much more than just results.

Facilities. The Junior School, housed in its own buildings on our woodland campus, is split into two departments, Pre-Prep (age 3–7) and Junior (age 7–11). Apart from large, spacious classrooms, Juniors have their own hall, two dining rooms, three computer suites, two libraries, a studio, a Science room and large outdoor play facilities including woodland trails, playgrounds and an adventure playground.

In addition to this they make use of all the Senior School facilities as they progress through school including the dedi-

cated Music School, the Sports Hall, athletics track, all-weather pitches, courts and gym, Science Centre and Creative Arts block. The girls are taught by subject specialists for Music and PE from Reception onwards. Once the girls reach Year 4 they are taught by academic subject specialists for the majority of their curriculum.

Fees per term (2016–2017). £2,037–£3,626.

Charitable status. Talbot Heath School Trust Limited is a Registered Charity, number 283708.

Terra Nova School

Jodrell Bank, Holmes Chapel, Cheshire CW4 8BT
Tel: 01477 571251
Fax: 01477 571646
email: office@tnschool.co.uk
website: www.tnschool.co.uk

Chairman of Governors: M C Hallam

Headmaster: **Mark Mitchell**, BSc, PGCE

Age Range. 3–13 Co-educational.
Number of Pupils. 304.
Fees per term (2016–2017). Seniors: Day £4,560–£4,695, Flexi boarding £35 per night, Weekly boarding £100 per week. Juniors: £3,200–£3,975. Pre-Prep: Reception £3,200*, Nursery £1,860–£3,100* (*Free Early Education Entitlement for three and four year olds).

Terra Nova School is nestled in 36 acres of the Cheshire countryside and caters for children from Nursery through to Year 8. Children are encouraged to aim high and believe in themselves; happiness, confidence and excellent personal achievement are our priorities.

Results from Reception to Year 8 indicate that pupils are typically working significantly higher than national levels of achievements. We have a 100% pass rate at 11+ and 13+.

Our Early Years Foundation Stage and Junior School experience is unrivalled and we have the results to prove it! Facilities include a large outdoor learning environment with woodland, outdoor classrooms, willow theatre, adventure play area, and multi-sensory zones giving children the freedom to explore beyond the classroom in a safe environment.

In the Seniors children are given opportunities to excel academically, socially and physically through our extensive sporting activities, all of which take place in our stunning grounds. They are also introduced to boarding or 'staying the night', with our flexible boarding options from Year 3.

Our Years 7 & 8 experience gives pupils great preparation for life at senior day or boarding school, as well as an extra two years in which to develop academically at a crucial time in their emotional and social development.

Based six and a half miles from Alderley Edge our location is rural but our technology connects children to the world whilst they benefit from a peaceful environment in which to thrive.

2014 was a remarkable year for Terra Nova with our Year 8 pupils moving on to some of the UK's leading independent day and boarding schools, such as Fettes College, Malvern College, Radley College, Repton School, Rugby School, Sedbergh School, Shrewsbury School, Stowe School, and Uppingham School.

For more information call Melanie Machin on 01477 572261.

Charitable status. Terra Nova School Trust Limited is a Registered Charity, number 525919. It is dedicated to all round educational excellence for children.

Terrington Hall School

Terrington, York YO60 6PR

Tel: 01653 648227
Fax: 01653 648458
email: office@terringtonhall.com
website: www.terringtonhall.com
Twitter: @TerringtonHall

Chairman of Governors: Mr Rodger Hobson

Headmaster: Mr Stephen Mulryne, BEd Hons

Age Range. 3–13 years.
Number of Children. 149: 83 boys, 66 girls (Full and Weekly boarders 8, Day 141).
Fees per term (2016–2017). Boarding: £5,940; Day: £4,440 (Years 5–8), £4,310 (Year 4), £4,210 (Year 3), £2,770 (Year 2), £2,620 (Year 1), £2,480 (Reception & Nursery).

Terrington is a co-educational day and boarding school situated in the Howardian Hills, an Area of Outstanding Natural Beauty fifteen miles from York.

The main school building, a Georgian rectory, is home to the boarders and boarding staff who live together as an extended family with family-style dining and plenty of home comforts in the bright and airy accommodation.

The school has a strong flexi-boarding community amongst its day pupils with an exciting activity programme running in the evenings. At weekends, full use is made of the surrounding countryside and heritage with trips to York, the moors and the coast.

Terrington places special emphasis on preparing pupils for entry into the senior school that best suits each child, whether locally or further afield, day or boarding. It is particularly proud of the 21 scholarships and exhibitions won by its pupils in the last three years.

The school enjoys excellent sporting facilities, with eight acres of playing fields, tennis courts, an indoor heated swimming pool and sports hall. All major sports are played and an extensive fixture list ensures that every child has ample opportunity to represent the school. Specialist tuition is available in several extra-curricular sport activities, including judo/karate, riding, swimming and tennis. All children have the opportunity to participate in the kayaking and climbing expeditions to the Ardèche and the Alps in Years Seven and Eight.

Teaching facilities are modern and well-equipped and include both computer and science suites. Music, art and drama are an integral part of the curriculum. Tuition is available for most instruments and children are prepared for Associated Board exams. The Junior and Senior choirs perform within school and at local venues, and there is a popular orchestra, rock band and wind ensemble. Drama is particularly well supported by specialist teaching within the curriculum from Nursery to Year 8, a Drama Club and private lessons available to pupils wishing to take speech and drama exams.

The School Chaplain is the local Rector who leads the school in worship at the local church every Wednesday morning and takes weekly assemblies at the school. Senior pupils are prepared for Confirmation if they so wish.

The Headmaster, his wife and children live in the school grounds and parents are fully involved in the life of the school which has a flourishing social committee.

The school welcomes overseas pupils and will arrange for pupils to be collected from or delivered to airports at the beginning and end of term.

Bursaries are available on a means-tested basis.

Charitable status. Terrington Hall is a Registered Charity, number 532362. It exists to provide a quality education for boys and girls.

Thorngrove School

The Mount, Pantings Lane, Highclere, Newbury, Berkshire RG20 9PS

Tel: 01635 253172
Fax: 01635 254135
email: admin@thorngroveschool.co.uk
website: www.thorngroveschool.co.uk
Twitter: @thorngroveprep
Facebook: @Thorngrove-school

Headmaster: Mr Adam King, BA Hons QTS Leeds, PG Dip Ed

Age Range. 2½–13 Co-educational.
Number of Pupils. 240 Day Pupils.
Fees per term (2016–2017). Reception–Year 2 £4,260; Year 3 and 4 £4,780; Year 5–8 £5,330.

Thorngrove School was founded in 1988 by Nick and Connie Broughton, the Principals. It is a co-educational day school for children aged 2½ to 13 years. The purpose-built facilities are set in former farmland in the village of Highclere, 5 miles south of Newbury and 12 miles north of Andover.

The school started with just 14 children. Due to its success and unique atmosphere the school flourished and grew in size year on year. There are currently 240 pupils at Thorngrove. Over the years, facilities have been built and extended. In 2000 The Senior Block was built. This provided exceptional facilities including a large Music room with numerous individual practice rooms; a fully resourced Science Laboratory; a light and airy Art room as well as several teaching classrooms. In 2007 an architect-designed Sports Hall was built. This magnificent building not only has a large multi-purpose hall, but also houses an IT suite, changing rooms and several teaching classrooms and offices. In 2010 a D&T centre was opened to provide a facility for children in Year 3 and above to work with resistant materials. In addition to this, a unique eco-garden was created just behind the Senior Block with chickens, raised beds and a fruit cage (much of the produce is used by the kitchens). In 2012 a new Nursery was opened next to the Reception Form in the main building to create a wonderful Early Years setting. Forest School is taught to all children from Nursery through to Year 8 and this outdoor programme makes use of the beautiful woods, covered fire pit and Mongolian Yurt. The school has recently embarked on a Mindfulness Programme. Children in Years 7 and 8 follow the .b course and younger children follow the Jigsaw programme.

The beautiful grounds have always been a key feature of the school. These have also been extended and now stretch over 25 acres. The children are lucky enough to have access to woodland areas and a small stream runs through the campus. The extensive playing fields are the envy of many a visiting team. The latest addition, partly funded by the children's school council, is an Adventure Play Area which has been positioned beside the tennis courts and astroturf pitch.

In the summer of 2009 Mr and Mrs Broughton stepped back from running the school and appointed Adam King as Headmaster. The school continues to thrive and an impressive development programme is scheduled to start in 2017 which will include a new Performing Arts Centre and further teaching block.

Thorpe House School

Oval Way, Gerrards Cross, Bucks SL9 8QA

Tel:	01753 882474
Fax:	01753 889755
email:	office@thorpehouse.co.uk
website:	www.thorpehouse.co.uk
Twitter:	@thorpehousesch
Facebook:	@thorpehousesch

Chairman of the Governors: Mr David Stanning

Headmaster: **Mr T Ayres**, BA Hons, PGCE

Age Range. Boys 3–16.

Numbers of Pupils. 299 Day Pupils.

Fees per term (2016–2017). Y7–11 £5,190, Y3–6 £4,410, Y1–2 £3,530, Reception £3,360, Nursery £1,680–£2,690.

Thorpe House was founded as a Boys' Prep School in 1923 with the Pre-Prep Department established in 1964. The School became a Charitable Trust in 1986 and in 2006 it increased its age range to become a school catering for boys between the ages of 3 and 16.

Situated on the outskirts of Gerrards Cross, Thorpe House thrives on its 'small school' environment and understanding that each boy is unique. Some are academics, some excel in sport and others in the performing arts and it is that difference that they nurture and value.

The Nursery class takes boys in the September following their 3rd birthday and then many others join Reception the following year. At the end Year 2 boys move to the Prep Department in the main school building where they are taught by the specialist staff in music, ICT, DT, French and PE/Games and specialist teaching in all subjects starts in Year 5.

At the end of Year 6 around half the boys leave to enter local grammar schools. Those who move into the Senior Department are joined by an equal number of new entrants who then form the class groups who will progress through to GCSE, although some move on to independent senior schools at 13 via the Common Entrance or scholarship examinations. Class sizes throughout the school never exceed 16 and are often as small as 12. The school's examination record at GCSE is very strong with a 100% record to date of pupils gaining at least 6 passes at C or above and pupils often gaining a full set of A and A* passes.

Although academic progress and excellence is a fundamental aspect of school life it is far from being the only focus. The boys excel at a variety of cultural activities. Music, drama, art and design technology are popular GCSE courses and boys of all ages enjoy studying these subjects and taking part in practical activities. Well over half of all recent Associated Board Music examination passes have been at Merit or Distinction level and following the latest GCSE Art exhibition one of the pupils was given a commission. The school works closely with the nearby St Mary's Girls' School to give both sets of pupils the opportunity to work together in a number of different cultural activities.

Sport is another central aspect of school life. The school has a seven-acre playing field and an outdoor swimming pool. The main team sports are rugby, football, cricket and athletics and the school puts out teams from Under 8 to Under 16 level against a wide variety of schools from the local area and further afield. These teams are very successful but the school is very proud of its Sport for All ethos and bringing on the less sporty boys is another important aspect of school life.

When the school extended its age range an extensive programme of new building and refurbishment was undertaken and the school now has improved facilities for Science, Art, Design Technology and ICT The school is now able to offer a full and modern range of facilities and all normal school experiences can take place on site. In addition the school runs a very extensive programme of extra-curricular clubs and activities, some of which such as sailing, golf and tennis involve taking advantage of local amenities.

The school offers before and after school care and arrangements to take this up are completely flexible. A bus service is also available to pick up and take home boys from certain areas.

Charitable status. Thorpe House School Trust is a Registered Charity, number 292683. It exists to provide education to boys.

Tockington Manor

Washingpool Hill Road, Tockington, Bristol BS32 4NY

Tel:	01454 613229
Fax:	01454 613676
email:	admin@tockingtonmanorschool.com
website:	www.tockingtonmanorschool.com
Twitter:	@tockingtonmanor
Facebook:	@tockingtonmanorschool

Chairman of Governors: G Sheppard

Headmaster: **Stephen Symonds**, BA Ed Hons

Age Range. Boys and Girls aged 2–13+.

Number of Pupils. 20 Boarders, 80 Day, 65 Infants, 80 Nursery.

Fees per term (2016–2017). Boarders £6,239–£7,270 (inclusive); Day £4,124–£4,742 (including meals); Lower School £3,041; Nursery £54.30 per day.

Tockington Manor School is an independent co-educational Preparatory school set in 28 acres of lovely countryside in the picturesque village of Tockington, South Gloucestershire. Pupils are welcomed from age 2 to 14 with boarding available from age 7.

We pride ourselves in delivering a varied timetable in small classes geared to the needs of each pupil but with emphasis on the core subjects of English, Mathematics and Science. We aim to provide an environment that is positive, supportive and disciplined within a warm, caring family atmosphere. Pupils are encouraged to be confident, considerate and accomplished free thinkers. All pupils take part in all aspects of school life, academic or otherwise, making the most of every moment. The boarding house has a real family atmosphere and aims to provide a caring environment which promotes the values of honesty, sharing and trust between the children.

Tormead Junior School

Cranley Road, Guildford, Surrey GU1 2JD

Tel:	01483 796073
Fax:	01483 450592
email:	head@tormeadschool.org.uk
website:	www.tormeadschool.org.uk
Twitter:	@Tormead_JS

Chair of Governors: Mrs Rosie Harris

Head of Junior School: **Mrs Louise Salmond Smith**, BA East Anglia, MMus Hull, PGCE Gloucestershire, MBA Keele

Age Range. Girls 4–11.
Number of Girls. 205.
Fees per term (2016–2017). £2,527–£4,212.

Tormead Junior School is a happy, friendly and relaxed school but with high expectations both in and outside the classroom.

Entry is selective at age 4 and 7 by assessment. When space is available, entrance to all other year groups is considered.

Our girls enjoy a broad and balanced curriculum. The school prides itself on its high academic standards and expectation of the girls whilst ensuring teaching and learning is exciting and challenging. French is taught from Year 3, with the addition of Spanish and Latin from Year 5. All girls enjoy specialist teaching in music, games and gymnastics, and from Year 2, also in Design Technology. The ICT curriculum gradually builds up the skills of the girls, and by the end of the Junior School they are confidently using computers as a tool for learning in other subjects. iPad technology is used throughout the school, but in particular with Years 5 and 6 in preparation for Senior School life.

Girls are taught by subject specialists for some subjects from Year 1; this increases as they move towards Year 6 when they are taught by different staff, from both Junior and Senior sections of the school. This provides them with the opportunity to get to know some of their Year 7 teachers before they move 'across the road', and also exposes them to expert tuition in all subject areas.

From Year 1 onwards, girls are taught 'Thinking and Learning'. This title covers a broad range of topics encompassing Philosophy, Independence, Critical Thinking and, for older girls, Study Skills and Time Management. Healthy debate on a wide variety of subjects is encouraged, with recent topics including 'Artificial Intelligence' (Year 3) and 'How Do We Measure Success?' (Year 6).

The curriculum of the Junior School achieves a dichotomy of aims; it ensures that the teachers have high expectations of the girls and that academic standards are high, whilst teaching in a way that – quite simply put – is 'fun'. By ensuring that the teaching and learning in the Junior School is interesting and motivating, the girls are fully focused on their work and keen to learn more.

In addition to their activities in the classroom, the girls enjoy numerous opportunities to be involved in extracurricular activities. The aim of the school is to offer a comprehensive range of activities to allow each girl to find something during the week that she would like to participate in and so develop her talents in this area. Extracurricular activities (in addition to sports) include: Art, Archery, Fencing, LAMDA, Jazz Band, instrumental Ensembles, two orchestras, several choirs, Photography, Gardening, computers, cookery and board games.

All sport – except swimming, where we use the excellent facilities at Surrey Sports Park – is catered for by facilities on the Junior or Senior School sites, including the use of the sprung floor gymnasium. The girls have regular fixtures with neighbouring schools in numerous sports throughout the year.

The ethos of the school means that all girls have an opportunity to be involved in all extracurricular or sporting activities, regardless of their ability. Girls with a particular talent in their chosen activity are provided with additional practice.

Personal, Social and Health Education is not just an academic subject for girls in Tormead Junior School but also a way of life. There are high expectations of how the girls will behave. Pastoral Care of the girls was described by our last Independent Schools Inspection as 'outstanding'; this is achieved by dealing with any concerns the girls may have, whether over a friendship or an activity in school, quickly and conscientiously.

Charitable status. Tormead Limited is a Registered Charity, number 312057.

Tower House School

188 Sheen Lane, East Sheen, London SW14 8LF
Tel: 020 8876 3323
Fax: 020 8876 3321
email: admissions@thsboys.org.uk
website: www.thsboys.org.uk

Chairman of Governors: Mr Jamie Forsyth

Headmaster: **Mr G Evans**, BSc, MA, PGCE

Age Range. 4–13.
Number of Boys. 190.
Fees per term (2016–2017). Reception and Year 1 £3,953, Years 2 and 3 £4,366, Senior School £4,484 (including residential trips and all school lunches).

Tower House is a day school established in 1931. The school stands in its own grounds and is conveniently situated near a number of bus routes and the local station.

Entry is at the age of 4+. Admission of boys after the age of 4+ depends very much on the availability of places. There is an entry test at this later stage and the Deputy Head interviews all boys.

The school prepares boys for Common Entrance and Scholarships to appropriate Independent Senior Schools.

The staff is fully qualified and includes specialists in art, music and games, which together with drama play an important part in the school curriculum. In addition to the full time staff, there are visiting teachers for piano, violin, woodwind, brass and guitar.

The school is well supplied with modern teaching aids, including computers. There is a well-equipped science laboratory, an art and technology room, library, and an ICT Room.

The principal games are rugby, soccer and cricket. Other sports include athletics, cross country, squash, swimming, tennis and watersports. There are many fixtures arranged with other schools.

A prospectus is available on application to the School Secretary.

Charitable status. Tower House School is a Registered Charity, number 1068844.

Town Close School

14 Ipswich Road, Norwich, Norfolk NR2 2LR
Tel: 01603 620180
Fax: 01603 618256 (Prep)
          01603 599043 (Pre-Prep)
email: admissions@townclose.com
website: www.townclose.com
Twitter: @townclose, @townclosehead

Chairman of Governors: Mr David Bolton, BSc, Dip FBA, FRAgS, FAAV

Headmaster: **Nicholas Bevington**, BA Hons, PGCE

Age Range. 3–13 Co-educational.
Number of Pupils. Prep 275, Pre-Prep 185.
Fees per term (2016–2017). £2,699–£4,133 including lunch and all single-day educational excursions. No compulsory extras.

Town Close School was founded in 1932 and became a Charitable Trust in 1968. The School is fully co-educational and is situated on a beautiful wooded site near the centre of Norwich. This location provides pupils with space and freedom and contributes substantially to Town Close's reputation as an outstandingly happy school.

There is a team of 57 talented teachers who aim to produce well-motivated, balanced, confident children, who are caring and sociable and who know the value of hard work. The children receive excellent teaching and are prepared for all major senior schools. In recent years, pupils have achieved highly in entrance and scholarship assessments to a range of the country's leading senior schools.

A modern teaching building stands at the heart of the School, containing a large, well-equipped library, an art room, an IT centre and 16 purpose-built classrooms. There are many other outstanding facilities including an indoor heated swimming pool, a new high-specification sports hall completed in July 2009, a new performance hall completed in January 2010 and a new, full-size, floodlit Astroturf opened in May 2011. Science and DT are taught in specialist buildings and the school places a high value on innovation, engineering and scientific discovery. The Pre-Prep occupies a magnificent converted house on the campus and also contains a multi-purpose hall, kitchens and a purpose-built Nursery wing opening onto fantastic outdoor facilities.

Nursery and Reception classes follow the Foundation Stage curriculum, an important element of which is outdoor learning. Children progress through a broad and varied programme of activities with a strong emphasis on the development of personal and social skills and on establishing positive attitudes to learning and to school life. Swimming, music and dance are taught by specialist teachers, while the rest of the curriculum is delivered by class teachers, ably supported by well-qualified teaching assistants.

Throughout the children's time at Town Close particular attention is paid to the teaching of good handwriting and spelling. Traditional core skills are valued very highly in addition to promoting children's use of digital technology. IT provision is extensive allowing children to become confident and proficient users. The Pre-Prep pupils use a range of children's software to develop key skills and Prep Department children build on this foundation using more sophisticated software, either in the computer room or on laptops and tablets. All sections of the School have filtered access to the internet across the network. The School Intranet contains interactive activities, images, lesson material and links to carefully selected websites. Interactive whiteboards are used throughout the School to support the curriculum.

Town Close has an excellent academic reputation and is also known for the quality of its sport, music, art, drama and its extensive co-curricular programme. Trips and expeditions form a valuable part of what is offered, and provide the balance essential for a full and rounded education. Activities take place during the lunch hour, after school, and occasionally at weekends. In terms of music, the School has a full orchestra, a variety of choirs and a wide range of ensembles. All children are encouraged to perform with regular high-quality concerts and plays.

Physical Education plays an important part in the development of each child, be they in the Nursery or in Year 8. Emphasis is placed on fostering healthy exercise, as well as encouraging a positive, competitive attitude, individual skills and teamwork. As well as providing all the usual opportunities for the major sports (rugby, netball, hockey, cricket and athletics), coaching is offered in many other sports.

A copy of the School's prospectus is available on request, while a visit to www.townclose.com will provide a fuller picture of the School, including a sight of the most recent inspection report, in which the Town Close was given the highest rating in every area.

Charitable status. Town Close House Educational Trust Limited is a Registered Charity, number 311293. It exists to provide education for children.

Truro Preparatory School

Highertown, Truro, Cornwall TR1 3QN

Tel:	01872 272616
Fax:	01872 222377
email:	prepenquiries@truroschool.com
	prepadmissions@truroschool.com
website:	www.truroschool.com/prep

Chairman of the Governors: Mr K Conchie

Headmaster of Truro School: Mr A S Gordon-Brown, BCom Hons, MSc, CA SA

Head of Preparatory School: **Miss S L Patterson**, BEd Hons

Head of Pre-Prep: Mrs S Hudson, MA, BEd Hons

Age Range. 3–11.
Number of Pupils. 239: 143 Boys, 96 Girls.
Fees per term (2016–2017). Prep (including lunch): £3,930 (Years 3–4), £4,075 (Years 5–6). Pre-Prep (including lunch): £2,850 (Nursery and Reception). £2,965 (Years 1 and 2).

Optional extras: Individual music lessons, fencing, dance, judo.

Truro School Prep was opened as Treliske School in 1936 in the former residence and estate of Sir George Smith. The school lies in extensive and secluded grounds to the west of the cathedral city of Truro, three miles from Truro School. The grounds command fine views of the neighbouring countryside. The drive to the school off the main A390 is almost 800 metres and Truro Golf Course also surrounds the school, so producing a campus of beauty and seclusion.

The keynote of the school is a happy, caring atmosphere in which children learn the value of contributing positively to the school community through the firm and structured framework of academic study and extra-curricular interests. The approach is based firmly in Christian beliefs and the school is proud of its Methodist foundation.

Building development has kept pace with modern expectations and Truro School Prep has its own large sports hall, an indoor heated swimming pool, a design and technology workshop with a computer room adjoined and purpose-built Pre-Prep.

The games programme is designed to encourage all children, from the keenest to the least athletic, to enjoy games and physical exercise. Our excellent facilities and the diverse skill of our staff enable us to offer a rich variety of sporting and recreational pursuits. There are over 20 popular clubs and activities run each week from 4.00 pm to 5.00 pm.

There is a strong school tradition in music and drama and the arts. Children may choose to learn a musical instrument from the full orchestral range. Each year the November concert, with Truro School, allows the school to show the community the excellent talents, which flourish in both schools.

Close links are maintained with the Senior School and nearly all pupils progress through at age 11 on the Head's recommendation to Truro School which is the only Independent Headmasters' and Headmistresses' Conference School in Cornwall (*see entry in HMC section*).

The prospectus and further details can be obtained from the Head's Secretary, and the Head will be pleased to show prospective parents around the school.

Charitable status. Truro School is a Registered Charity, number 306576. It is a charitable foundation established for the purpose of education.

Twickenham Preparatory School

Beveree, 43 High Street, Hampton, Middlesex TW12 2SA

Tel:	020 8979 6216
Fax:	020 8979 1596
email:	office@twickenhamprep.co.uk
website:	www.twickenhamprep.co.uk
Twitter:	@twickenhamprep

Chairman of Governors: Mr H Bates

Headmaster: **Mr D Malam**, BA Hons Southampton, PGCE Winchester

Age Range. 4–13.
Number of Pupils. Boys 150, Girls 130.
Fees per term (2016–2017). £3,415–£3,700. Lunch £185–£200.

Founded in 1969, Twickenham Prep is an independent school for boys and girls situated in Hampton. We are a happy, vibrant, and thriving school where every child is valued as an individual and inspired to achieve their full potential, personally, socially and academically. The pupils benefit from small classes, first-class facilities, specialist subject teaching and excellent pastoral care.

Our pupils achieve great success, both academic and extracurricular, moving on to excellent independent secondary schools with regular academic, sporting, musical, art and all-rounder scholarships. We are committed to working in partnership with our parents so that our pupils leave TPS as well-rounded individuals. The girls sit entrance exams at 11+ and the boys Common Entrance at 13+

Our curriculum is based on the National Curriculum with specialist teaching of PE, Games, ICT, French, Music and Think Tank (formerly Mind Lab, an innovative thinking skills programme) from Reception ensuring a balanced educational experience. Art/Design and Technology is introduced in Year 3 and from Year 4 pupils have specialist teaching in all subjects, with Latin being introduced in Year 5. Class sizes are about 18, developing each pupil to their full academic potential and promoting high academic standards. The school is well equipped to cover the full range of subjects, with purpose-built Art/DT, Science and Music facilities and a modern sports hall used for PE and termly productions.

Strong emphasis is placed on participation by all in sporting, musical and extracurricular activities. The school plays a wide range of sports and has recently formed an affiliation with Kempton Cricket Club to provide 10 acres of dedicated sporting facilities for rugby, football, cricket and rounders. The girls also play netball and hockey, with athletics and swimming also part of the sporting curriculum. Music and drama play a large part in the school with full-scale productions and concerts annually involving all pupils. There is a school choir and individual instrumental lessons are taught by visiting specialists.

Twickenham Prep are the current U11 and U13 National Independent Chess Champions and also the current National Mind Lab Champions; we represented the UK at the 2016 Mind Lab Olympics, held in Greece.

There are also many extracurricular clubs during and after school to choose from and we also provide wraparound care from 8.00 am to 6.00 pm.

Located in Hampton we offer morning minibus services to children living in Kew, Isleworth, Richmond, Twickenham, Teddington, St Margaret's, Hampton Wick, Sunbury and East Molesey.

Entry to the school is non-selective at Reception with limited places available in other year groups subject to an assessment.

Regular Open Days are held and personal tours are available – the pupils and Headmaster would be delighted to show you around. Please contact the school office.

Charitable Status. Twickenham Preparatory School is a Registered Charity, number 1067572. It exists to provide education for boys and girls.

Twyford School

Winchester, Hampshire SO21 1NW

Tel:	01962 712269
Fax:	01962 712100
email:	registrar@twyfordschool.com
website:	www.twyfordschool.com

Chairman of Governors: Mrs F Dunger

Headmaster: **Dr S J Bailey**, BEd, PhD, FRSA

Age Range. 3–13.
Number of Children. 408. Main School: 287 (167 boys, 120 girls, of whom 136 are weekly and flexi boarders); Pre-Prep: 121 (64 boys, 57 girls).
Fees per term (2016–2017). Weekly Boarding £7,790; Day: Prep Years 4–8 £6,190, Year 3 £5,163; Pre-Prep £3,022–£3,475. Fees are inclusive of all outings/trips run during the term. Bursaries are available.

Twyford School is situated at the edge of the beautiful South Downs just two miles from the historic city of Winchester and the M3. Twyford is a family school that aims to offer an all-round top-rate education with a Christian ethos. Boarding is central to life at Twyford. Most pupils start as day pupils, but by the end of their last year over 80% are weekly boarding through the school's flexi boarding system, which makes an excellent preparation for their move to senior school. The contrast between the modern facilities (classrooms, laboratories, music school, creative arts and ICT block, swimming pool and sports centre) and the Victorian chapel and hall creates a rich and stimulating environment.

The school regularly achieves scholarships – 77 awards (academic, art, design, sport and music) in the last 5 years – to major senior schools such as Winchester, St Swithun's, Canford, Marlborough, Harrow, Cheltenham Ladies' College, Wycombe Abbey, Radley and Sherborne.

Charitable status. Twyford School is a Registered Charity, number 307425. It exists to provide education for children.

Unicorn School

238 Kew Road, Richmond, Surrey TW9 3JX

Tel:	020 8948 3926
email:	registrar@unicornschool.org.uk
website:	www.unicornschool.org.uk
Twitter:	@unicornschool

Chairs of Governors: Mr Paul Rathbone and Mr Geoff Bayliss

Headmaster: **Mr Kit Thompson**

Age Range. 3–11.

Number of Children. 171 Day Pupils: 83 boys, 88 girls.
Fees per term (2016–2017). £2,165–£3,970.

Unicorn is a parent-owned IAPS co-ed primary school founded in 1970. Situated opposite Kew Gardens, the school occupies a large Victorian house and converted coach house with a spacious, superbly-equipped playground and garden.

The school has free and unrestricted access to Kew Gardens and the sports facilities at the nearby University of Westminster grounds are used for games and Pools on the Park for swimming.

Our aim is for Unicorn to be a successful, forward-thinking school that embraces children, staff and parents in an evolving, exciting, dynamic and nurturing community, enriched with creativity and supported by excellent leadership and management. Pupils are encouraged to become independent, responsible, self-aware and confident young people, who reap the benefits of a very broad curriculum to achieve considerable success.

There are 22 children per class, where a variety of teaching methods are used and the children are regularly assessed. Importance is placed upon the development of the individual and high academic standards are achieved. The main point of entry is to nursery at 3+. Children are prepared for entry at 11+ to the leading London Day Schools, as well as a variety of boarding schools.

There is a specialist IT room and networked computers in every classroom and a bank of iPads to use; a Science and Design Technology suite with interactive whiteboard technology in all classrooms; music rooms, library and a fully-equipped Art room.

The curriculum includes Drama, French (from age 5), Art and Music – with individual music lessons offered in piano, violin, cello, drums, clarinet, saxophone, flute, guitar and trumpet, as well as singing. Recorder groups, choirs, an orchestra and a wind band also flourish.

In addition to the major games of football, rugby, hockey, netball, cricket, rounders and athletics, there are optional clubs for tennis, squash, ice skating, golf, riding, sailing and karate. Other club activities include arts and crafts, cookery, pottery, chess, riding, sailing and trampolining. There are regular visits to the theatre and museums as well as the galleries of Central London. All children, from the age of seven upwards, participate in residential field study trips to Surrey, Cornwall and Cumbria.

An elected School Council, with representatives from each age group, meets weekly with the Headmaster and a weekly newsletter for parents is also produced.

A happy, caring environment prevails and importance is placed on producing kind, responsible children who show awareness and consideration for the needs of others.

Charitable status. Unicorn School is a Registered Charity, number 312578. It exists to provide education for boys and girls.

University College School – Junior Branch

11 Holly Hill, Hampstead, London NW3 6QN
Tel: 020 7435 3068
Fax: 020 7435 7332
email: juniorbranch@ucs.org.uk
website: www.ucs.org.uk

Chairman of Council of Governors: Mr S D Lewis, OBE, MA

Headmaster: **Mr L R J Hayward**, MA

Age Range. 7–11.
Number of Boys. 253.
Fees per term (2016–2017). £5,790.

The School was founded in 1891 by the Governors of University College, London. The present building was opened in 1928, but retains details from the Georgian house first used. It stands near the highest point of Hampstead Heath and the hall and classrooms face south. Facilities include a Science Laboratory, Library, Drama Studio, Music and Computer Rooms, and a Centre for Art and Technology. Boys receive their Swimming and PE lessons in the pool and Sports Hall at the Senior School, 5 minutes' walk away. The Junior School has full use of the 27 acres of playing fields on games days.

Boys enter at 7+ each year and they are prepared for transfer to the Senior School at 11+. (*See entry in HMC section.*)

Charitable status. University College School, Hampstead is a Registered Charity, number 312748. The Junior Branch exists to provide education for boys aged 7+ to 11 years.

University College School – Pre-Prep

36 College Crescent, Hampstead, London NW3 5LF
Tel: 020 7722 4433
Fax: 020 7722 4601
email: thephoenix@ucs.org.uk
website: www.ucs.org.uk/UCS-Pre-Prep

Chairman of Council: Mr S D Lewis, OBE, MA

Headmistress: **Dr Z Dunn**, BEd, PhD, NPQH

Age Range. Currently 3–7 co-educational (From 2018, 4–7, Boys only).
Number of Pupils. 128.
Fees per term (2016–2017) £3,762–£4,894.

At UCS Pre-Prep, we firmly believe that happiness and self-esteem are the keys to success in every pupil's learning journey. The well-qualified and highly-supportive staff accompany each child on a voyage of educational and social discovery during the first years of school life.

The Pre-Prep fully supports the aims and ethos of UCS: intellectual curiosity and independence of mind are developed, self-discovery and self-expression are fostered and a cooperative and collaborative approach to learning is of great importance.

For every child in our care, we provide a continuously positive and creative learning environment that allows the individual the opportunity to develop personal qualities and talents. Children enjoy specialist teaching in Music, art and Physical Education and the full primary curriculum in well resourced classrooms. The outdoor learning programme take advantage of the school's allotment and extensive space at the fields. At the end of Year 2, the children transfer to a range of local independent schools. Whilst it is hoped that most boys will transfer to the Junior Branch of UCS this is not automatic and is subject to meeting the required standard in the entrance examination. (*See separate Junior Branch entry.*)

Charitable status. UCS Pre-Prep Limited is a Registered Charity, number 1098657.

Upton House School

115 St Leonard's Road, Windsor, Berkshire SL4 3DF

Tel: 01753 862610
Fax: 01753 621950
email: info@uptonhouse.org.uk
registrar@uptonhouse.org.uk
website: www.uptonhouse.org.uk

Chairman of the Council: Mr G O J Story

Headmistress: **Mrs Rhian Thornton**

Age Range. Girls 2–11 years, Boys 2–7 years.
Number of Pupils. 280 Day: 209 Girls, 71 Boys.
Fees per term (2016–2017). £1,209–£4,690 (inclusive).

The aim of Upton House is to foster a happy and stimulating environment in which each child can prosper academically, socially and emotionally. The school will prepare all children for their continuing education and enhance their awareness of the world in which they live.

Upton House School was founded in 1936 by benefactors and has evolved over the years to provide a well-equipped environment where children can thrive.

As parents you want the best education possible for your child and at Upton House we aim to provide it. We give each child encouragement and stimulation to develop their academic abilities and we try to find something they are good at, whether it is from our broad curriculum or from our wide range of extra-curricular activities. This combined with a kind and loving environment which develops a set of pastoral values makes Upton very special.

We opened a new arts block recently. It houses a music room, an art studio and media room. We already have a kitchen for four to eleven year olds, a drama studio, gymnasium and Nursery music room.

Specialist subjects include French from 3 years old and Mandarin from 4 years old. We have iPads, laptops, interactive whiteboards and a smart table to enhance learning. Diverse sporting activities include rowing on the Thames, judo, tap and ballet.

Boys are prepared for entry to preparatory schools in the area at 7+. Girls leaving gain places at a wide range of senior schools and regularly win scholarships.

Entry is non-selective and means-tested bursaries (up to 100%) are available for those entering the school.

We provide care from 8.00 am in Early Birds until the end of the official teaching day. Children from the age of 3 are able to enjoy a late programme until 5.45 pm. A wide variety of clubs are offered in the late programmes as well as teacher-supervised prep.

We have an active PTA which organises many fundraising events through the year and helps to forge close links between the school and parents. Come and see for yourselves.

Charitable status. Upton House School is a Registered Charity, number 309095. It exists to provide an excellent all-round educational foundation for boys and girls.

The Ursuline Preparatory School Ilford

2–8 Coventry Road, Ilford, Essex IG1 4QR

Tel: 020 8518 4050
Fax: 020 8518 2060

email: urspsi@urspsi.org.uk
website: www.urspsi.org.uk
Twitter: @URSPSI

Chair of Governors: Mr Peter Nicholson

Head: **Mrs Lisa McCoy**

Age Range. 3–11 Co-educational.
Number of Pupils. 165.
Fees per term (2016–2017). Nursery: £2,186 (full-time including lunch, pre- and after-school care, holiday care), Reception–Year 6 £3,088 (including lunch, pre- and after-school care, holiday care).

The Ursuline Preparatory School Ilford is a Roman Catholic day school in the trusteeship of the Ursuline Sisters. The Ursuline Sisters first came to England in 1862 settling at Forest Gate from where they established the school in Ilford in 1903 at 73 Cranbrook Road. The school has since flourished. Formerly part of The Ursuline Academy, The Ursuline Preparatory School Ilford is now a fully independent school in its own right, but continues to share close and valued links with the Academy.

As a Catholic school we firmly believe that Religious Education is the foundation of the entire educational process. Prayers and liturgical celebrations are an important aspect of school life, unifying the hearts and minds of all associated with the school and ensuring we are all working to achieve the best possible education for the children in our care.

We provide a safe, secure and stimulating environment for our pupils to thrive. We recognise each child's unique value and are committed to encouraging self-esteem and developing each child's potential. We encourage the children to become independent learners by building on their curiosity and desire to learn and developing their skills, concepts and understanding.

While the school continues to set its own high standards, we complement these with the integration of the best of the National Curriculum. English and mathematics form the core subjects together with Religious Education, science, history, geography, ICT, PE, drama, design technology, art, music, MFL and stimulating project work. The Performing Arts have a high profile in school and the children are regularly given the opportunity to develop their talents. Well-stocked libraries, audio-visual aids and a state-of-the-art specialist Information Communication Technology department are all available throughout the nursery and school.

We offer a wide range of extra-curricular activities including ballet, speech and drama and Irish Dancing. Other clubs and sports clubs including football, cricket, basketball, netball, gymnastics and trampolining are held weekly. Individual instrumental tuition can be arranged for piano, violin, flute, clarinet and saxophone. There is also an award-winning school choir.

All teaching staff are fully qualified, experienced and dedicated to the ideals of the school. They work in close partnership with parents to ensure that each child's special individual needs are recognised. In addition, we have the help of experienced general assistants. Our pupil : teacher ratio is excellent and we are able to engage in small group teaching.

Pre- and after-school care and a holiday club are available. A variety of structured activities is planned for the children enrolled and refreshments are provided.

Charitable status. The Ursuline Preparatory School Ilford is a Registered Charity, number 245661.

Ursuline Preparatory School
Wimbledon

18 The Downs, Wimbledon, London SW20 8HR
Tel: 020 8947 0859
Fax: 020 8947 0885
email: admissions@ursuline-prep.merton.sch.uk
website: www.ursuline-prep.merton.sch.uk

A Catholic Independent day school.

Chair of Governors: Mr Francis Bacon

Headmistress: **Mrs Anne Farnish**, MA, PGCE, NPQH

Age Range. Girls 3–11, Boys 3–4.
Number of Pupils. 265+.
Fees per term (2016–2017). £3,300 full-time, £2,020 for part-time Nursery.

The Ursuline Preparatory School provides a happy and stimulating environment for girls aged 3–11 years and boys aged 3–4 years in our nursery unit.

The children enjoy a rich diversity of experiences both inside and outside of the classroom. Guest speakers, fund-raising opportunities and school trips also provide valuable experiences. Each girl is strongly encouraged to give of her best academically and to take advantage of the opportunities provided during her time at The Ursuline Preparatory School. An extensive range of extra-curricular activities are available to suit different skills and talents. A thriving after-school care facility is also available.

Girls at 11+ leave very well prepared for the next stage of their educational career with a love of learning. In the spirit of our school motto Serviam pupils show care and concern for others and strive to achieve their personal best and look to the future with confidence keen to make a difference in the world.

We are a thriving IAPS school with a vibrant Catholic ethos welcoming pupils of all faiths who would benefit from our rigorous but nurturing learning environment.

Charitable status. Ursuline Preparatory School Wimbledon Trust is a Registered Charity, number 1079754.

Victoria College Preparatory School

Pleasant Street, St Helier, Jersey, Channel Islands JE2 4RR
Tel: 01534 723468
email: admin@vcp.sch.je
website: www.vcp.sch.je

Chairman of Governors: B Watts

Headmaster: **Dan Pateman**, BA Hons

Age Range. 7–11.
Number of Boys. 275 Day Boys.
Fees per term (2016–2017). £1,756 (inclusive).

Victoria College Preparatory School was founded in 1922 as an integral part of Victoria College and is now a separate School under its own Headmaster, who is responsible for such matters as staffing, curriculum and administration. The Preparatory School shares Governors with Victoria College whose members are drawn from the leaders of the Island of Jersey with a minority representation from the States of Jer-

sey Education Committee. Members of staff are all experienced and well-qualified teachers, including specialists in Music, Dance, Art, PE and French. Entry to the Prep School is at 7 and boys normally leave to enter Victoria College at the age of 11. The school games are cricket, football, athletics, swimming, hockey, cross-country and rugby. Sporting facilities are shared with Victoria College. Special features of the school are exceptionally high standards of sport, drama, music and French. Many visits, both sporting and educational, are arranged out of the Island.

A separate Pre-Preparatory School (5 to 7 years) is incorporated in a co-educational school situated at JC Prep and offers places for boys whose parents wish them to be educated at both Victoria College and the Preparatory School. Candidates for Pre-Prep entry should be registered at JC Prep, St Helier, Jersey.

Vinehall School

Robertsbridge, East Sussex TN32 5JL
Tel: 01580 880413
Fax: 01580 882119
email: admissions@vinehallschool.com
website: www.vinehallschool.com

Chairman of Governors: Mr W Foster-Kemp, LLB, ACA

Headmaster: **Richard Follett**, BA

Age Range. 2–13 co-educational.
Number of Children. 261: 26 boarders, 235 day children.
Fees per term (2016–2017). Prep: Years 6–8: £5,679 (day), £7,406 (full boarding), £6,811 (weekly boarding); Years 3–5: £5,509 (day), £7,229 (full boarding), £6,678 (weekly boarding); Pre-Prep: Reception, Years 1 & 2 £3,045; Nursery (without Early Years funding): £33.82 per morning session, £18.75 per afternoon session, £52.53 per full day session; Nursery (with Early Years funding): £29.72 per full day session.

Founded in 1938, Vinehall School is set within 47 acres of countryside in an area of outstanding natural beauty on the East Sussex/Kent border. A flourishing Pre-Prep for boys and girls aged 2 to 7 is situated in a modern, well-resourced and purpose-built building on the same site as the Prep School.

The School's first-class facilities include a magnificent Millennium Building, comprising classrooms, IT suite and library, a science block, music building, art, design and technology centre, a purpose-built theatre with seating for 250, a sports hall and adjoining indoor swimming pool, an Astro-Turf pitch, an adventure playground and a nine-hole golf course.

The curriculum, which is based on the National Curriculum but which extends far beyond, prepares pupils for Common Entrance, local grammar school entrance and scholarship entrance to a variety of independent senior schools. The innovative 'Learning Journey' curriculum (which begins in Year 3) stimulates enquiring young minds. The academic day finishes at 4.40 pm, with a wide range of clubs and enrichment activities until 5.20 pm when school buses depart. On Saturday mornings (apart from exeat weekends) there are optional Clubs and Enrichment activities for pupils in Years 3 to 8. A dedicated learning support team is available for those children who require additional support.

Games and the Arts are an integral part of the Vinehall timetable. Pupils participate in all major team sports and everyone has a chance to represent the School. Girls' sports include netball, hockey, rounders and tennis and for boys, football, rugby, hockey, cricket and tennis. Swimming, gymnastics and athletics are also important sports throughout the year. Creative Arts are also strong, with flourishing Art, Music and Drama departments, all of which exhibit/perform regularly both inside and outside School. Carpentry and wood-turning are also offered.

Boarding is at the very heart of the School and Vinehall has a well-established boarding community, the majority being from Sussex, Kent and London. Temporary, weekly and full boarding are all available and we also offer an accompanied train service to and from London for weekly boarders each Friday and Sunday evening. There is a Junior boarding option for Years 3–6 (four nights per week) with children moving on to full or weekly boarding in Years 7 and 8. There are regular exeat weekends and a full and varied programme of weekend activities.

Charitable status. Vinehall School is a Registered Charity, number 307014. It exists to provide a secure, quality education, in particular for those in need of residential schooling.

Walden Prep School (formerly Friends' Junior School)

Mount Pleasant Road, Saffron Walden, Essex CB11 3EB
Tel: 01799 525351
Fax: 01799 523808
email: admissions@waldenschool.co.uk
website: www.waldenschool.co.uk

Head of Walden Prep: **Sally Meyrick**, BA

Curriculum Leader, Walden Prep: Kate Richardson
Curriculum Head, Walden Pre-Prep: Lucy Nicholson

Age Range. 3–11 Co-educational.
Number of Pupils. 111.
Fees per term (2016–2017). £2,875–£3,825 inc. lunch. Nursery: £22 per am session, £16 per pm session, £38 all day inc. lunch. £45 all day with before and after school care.

Walden Prep School opened in 1992 and has grown from small beginnings to a thriving school in the heart of Saffron Walden.

Children are nurtured, supported and encouraged to reach their full potential in all aspects of school life. They are encouraged to stretch themselves to ensure they produce their very best results both in academic and pastoral pursuits. Our aim is to foster a real love of learning and thirst for knowledge that will see them through their whole school career and beyond.

The high teacher/pupil ratio delivers a broad and balanced curriculum, enhanced by the use of Senior School facilities and expertise.

Music and sport opportunities are abundant at Walden Prep and there is an extensive range of extracurricular activities, including chess, cookery, orchestra, choir, drama, journalism, football, netball, hockey, cross country and cricket.

The school has outstanding facilities, including an indoor swimming pool, a floodlit all-weather mini Astroturf pitch, hard tennis/netball courts, grass tennis courts and is set in extensive grounds, including our own Forest School which every child attends at least twice a term.

Charitable status. Walden School Limited is a Registered Charity, number 1000981.

Walhampton School

Lymington, Hampshire SO41 5ZG
Tel: 01590 613300
Fax: 01590 678498
email: office@walhampton.com
website: www.walhampton.com
Twitter: @Walhamptonprep
Facebook: /walhamptonprep

Chairman of Governors: Mr Jeremy Bennett
Headmaster: **Mr Titus Mills**, BA Hons

Age Range. 2–13.
Number of Pupils. Boarding boys 20, Boarding girls 15, Day children 204, Pre-Prep 121.
Fees per term (2016–2017). Boarding £6,146–£7,571; Day £4,125–£5,550; Pre-Preparatory £2,850; Kindergarten & Nursery £25.50 per am/pm session. The only extras are: After-School Club, Riding, Individual Music, Learning Support tuition and Expeditions.

An independent day and boarding school for boys and girls aged 2–13, Walhampton lies in ancient woodland on the southern edge of the New Forest, on the coast near Lymington in Hampshire. With big vistas and broad horizons set within one hundred acres of lawns, lakes and woodland, the school's location is truly remarkable. Few prep schools can match Walhampton's setting.

Our pupils achieve consistently impressive academic results, taking their learning to the next level as they prepare for the country's leading senior schools. With small classes and outstanding teaching we prepare our boys and girls for 13+ Common Entrance and scholarships to senior independent schools including Winchester, Eton, St Swithun's, Canford, Claysemore, Marlborough, Harrow, Radley and Bryanston. Academic standards at Walhampton are excellent and were strongly endorsed in our recent ISI report. We have enjoyed 100% success rate in Common Entrance for a number of years.

Our location and facilities enable us to offer a broad and dynamic curriculum, which stretches beyond the classroom. Lessons are taught in our kitchen garden, fields and woodland bringing Maths, English and Science to life while making sure sports, music and the arts flourish alongside academic disciplines. In how many other schools would you find the Battles of Trafalgar staged on a lake, or Hastings reenacted with children in armour on horses?

As well as rigorous academic standards, Walhampton is passionate about breadth. It offers over 60 on-site extra-curricular activities including beekeeping, model railways, fishing, dance, archery, and shooting. There is a distinct 'Swallows and Amazons' spirit that burns brightly here. Sailing lessons take place on our lakes and horse riding is also popular in our equestrian centre.

Full, weekly and flexi boarders enjoy the relaxed and homely atmosphere of Bradfield House. Flexi boarding enables children to enjoy all that the school has to offer, while supporting families with busy lives.

At Walhampton, parents and children will find a school in a stunning location, with a distinctive ethos and tremendous spirit. A warm welcome awaits you at one of our Open Mornings – from 10:00 to 12:30 on Friday 3rd February, 2017 and Friday 12th May, 2017. Please contact the School Registrar on 01590 613 303 or email: registrar@walhampton.com.

Walthamstow Hall Junior School

Bradbourne Park Road, Sevenoaks, Kent TN13 3LD

Tel: 01732 453815
Fax: 01732 456980
email: registrar@whall.school
website: www.walthamstow-hall.co.uk
Facebook: /Walthamstow-Hall

Chair of Governors: Mrs J Adams, BA Joint Hons

Head of the Junior School: **Mrs D Wood**, BSc, PGCE
  Durham

Deputy Head Teacher: Mrs A J Rotchell, BEd Hons
  Westminster College Oxford, Dip SpLD York
Director of Studies: Mrs P I Potter, BEd Southampton, Dip
  MEd Roehampton Institute
Senior Teacher: Mrs C Conway, BA Hons First Class, MA
  Johannesburg, PGCE Canterbury Christ Church
Head of Pre-Prep Department: Mrs G Watts, MA Hons St
  Andrews, EYPS, QTS

Day School for Girls.
Age Range. 3–11.
Number of Girls. 215.
Fees per term (2016–2017). Nursery £295 per session
(2–10 sessions per week); Reception–Year 2 £3,680, Years
3–6 £4,640.

Walthamstow Hall Junior School is a happy and vibrant
school with a proud tradition of providing the highest quality education for girls aged 3–11 years.

From Reception upwards pupils benefit from being in
small classes (up to 20 per class) with two parallel classes in
each year group. Optimum-sized classes throughout the
Junior School guarantee individual attention, with obvious
benefits including a seamless and highly effective preparation for Senior School entrance exams without last-minute
cramming and changes to routine.

A well-planned programme of education brings out the
potential of each child as she progresses through the Junior
School. A broad curriculum is enriched with many extra-
curricular activities and clubs. After-school care is offered
until 6 pm.

Girls are well prepared for a range of senior schools and
have won awards to prestigious independent schools,
including Walthamstow Hall Senior School (*see entry in
GSA section*). Entry to our Senior School is from 11+, 13+
and 16+ with Awards, Scholarships and Bursaries offered.
Equally, our track record in the Kent test is excellent.

Walthamstow Hall was founded in 1838 and is one of the
oldest girls' schools in the country. It has built a reputation
for all-round excellence and achievements by girls are outstanding. Over recent years, many new facilities have been
added including nursery classrooms, a library with computerised lending facility and a science laboratory. Girls have
access to facilities at the nearby Senior School including the
recently refurbished Ship Theatre and swimming pool. A
new Dining Hall and Pre-Prep facilities opened at the Junior
School in 2014. The school is situated in the centre of Sevenoaks within easy reach of road and rail networks. Minibuses operate from surrounding towns and villages.

Warminster Prep School

Vicarage Street, Warminster, Wiltshire BA12 8JG

Tel: 01985 224800
Fax: 01985 218850

email: prep@warminsterschool.org.uk
website: www.warminsterschool.org.uk
Twitter: @WarminsterPrep
Facebook: /Warminster-Prep
LinkedIn: /WarminsterSchool

Co-educational, Day & Boarding.

Chairman of Governors: The Right Hon Sir David Latham,
  QC

Headmaster: P Titley, BEd

Age Range. 3–11 co-educational.
Number of Pupils. 140.
Fees per term (2016–2017). Day: Reception £2,450;
Years 1 & 2 £2,645; Year 3 £3,125; Year 4 £3,490; Years 5
& 6 £3,920. Boarding: £6,925.

Conveniently situated on the edge of Salisbury Plain with
easy access to London and the South-West, Warminster Prep
is a thriving school with a friendly, family atmosphere.
Together with our Senior School, we make up Warminster
School, providing exciting, high-quality education for children from 3 to 18 years old.

Fully-qualified and dedicated teaching staff deliver a
vibrant and stimulating curriculum enriched with many trips
and theme days. Our teaching in the Prep School is rich and
varied in its styles to suit the diverse variety of children who
thrive in our inclusive and holistic environment. We have
Learning Support for those who may need it and an 'Able &
Talented' club to ensure that all our children are achieving
their potential in a supportive and caring atmosphere.

The curriculum is broad and balanced reflecting an ethos
that values the development of skills and achievement in all
subjects and areas of school life. Whilst the pursuit of excellence in core subjects is very important, Art, Sport, Music,
Drama and Technologies are also vital areas in building confidence and self-esteem. Scholarships are available from
Year 3 upwards as well as for Years 7 and 9 in the Senior
School.

Totally flexible boarding arrangements exist for children
from 7 years upwards. Under the auspices of our experienced, dedicated Matrons and House Parents, children enjoy
a very high standard of Pastoral care with weekend trips and
outings being a highlight of the week. A number of children
are full boarders, but weekly and hotel boarding are very
popular with, and a cost-effective service for, busy working
parents. The Boarding Schools Allowance is available for
serving members of HM Forces.

Sport is an important part of life at Warminster Prep, with
a busy programme of inter-school fixtures in Rugby, Soccer,
Hockey and Cricket for boys, and Hockey, Netball and
Rounders for girls. In the summer term, children also swim
and enjoy Tennis and Athletics.

Warminster Prep School has a strong creative tradition in
the Arts; performing art in Music, Speech and Drama, visual
art in a wide range of media including sculpture and fired
clay.

The Prep (and Pre-Prep) School is well-equipped with its
own catering and Dining Hall, modern fully-equipped Science lab, ICT suite, sports pitches, AstroTurf, Art and DT
studio, well-equipped stage, tennis courts, Music and practice rooms and Library. This is in addition to the superb
facilities we share with our adjacent Senior School such as
the newly-opened Thomas Arnold Hall, swimming pool,
Library, Chapel and Sports Hall. The Courtyard Nursery
was opened in 2007 and provides superb accommodation
for the Early Years Foundation Stage. The Nursery is over-
subscribed and parents are advised to register for places in
plenty of time.

We provide, for Day and Boarding children, a wide
choice of clubs and activities including a Forest School.

These augment our timetabled curriculum and ensure that children can develop their individual tastes and interests alongside more traditionally academic abilities. We include opportunities for foreign travel with our French Trip and Ski Trip.

Interested parents are invited to ring the Headmaster's Secretary for a prospectus and to arrange a visit and free taster-day.

For information about the Senior School, please see entry in HMC section.

Charitable status. Warminster School is Registered Charity, number 1042204, providing education for boys and girls.

Warwick Junior School

Myton Road, Warwick CV34 6PP
Tel: 01926 776418
email: enquiries@warwickschool.org
website: www.warwickschool.org

Chairman of Governors: A C Firth

Headmaster of Junior School: Mr A C Hymer, BA, MA Ed, NPQH

Deputy Headmaster: Mr T C Lewis, Cert Ed

Age Range. 7–11.
Number of Pupils. 250 boys.
Fees per term (2016–2017). Tuition: £3,282 (7+), £3,586 (8+), £3,656 (9+), £3,977 (10+).

Warwick Junior School is situated on a site on the outskirts of Warwick Town adjacent to Warwick Senior School. The buildings are contained within a four-acre site and enjoy the use of the Sports and other facilities of Warwick Senior School. A programme of refurbishment has included a new extension to the school, providing six classrooms and a library, new ICT and DT rooms and most recently the Science laboratory has been refurbished.

The aim of the school is to provide a good general education based on Christian principles. Academic standards are high and in particular participation in a range of activities is encouraged. Each pupil is encouraged to develop his own personality and to realise his own potential.

The curriculum gives a good grounding in English, Mathematics, Science, Technology, ICT, History, Geography, Religious Education, French, Art, Music, Performing Arts, Drama and PE. Many sporting activities are available on the fifty acre campus of Warwick School, which includes a sports hall and indoor swimming pool. Rugby and Football are the main winter sports, with Cricket in the summer, plus Athletics, Swimming, Tennis, Squash and Cross Country. The school has won a number of national sporting championships.

The school's creative activities, dramatic productions and musical performances provide a useful focus in the development of many talents within the school. Boys benefit from an extensive extracurricular programme of activity.

Warwick Junior School provides a schedule of Curriculum Support. This support is available both for boys who need some additional assistance in English and/or Maths and also for boys with specific learning difficulties such as dyslexia or dyspraxia.

Extended day facilities are available until 5.30 pm when pupils can either do their homework or enrol in the extensive clubs and activity programme.

Boys are prepared for the Entrance Examination to Warwick Senior School at age 11. The majority of pupils who leave Warwick Junior School gain a place in the Senior School at Warwick. (*See Warwick School entry in HMC section*)

Charitable status. Warwick Independent Schools Foundation is a Registered Charity, number 1088057. It exists to provide quality education for boys.

Warwick Preparatory School

Bridge Field, Banbury Road, Warwick CV34 6PL
Tel: 01926 491545
Fax: 01926 403456
email: info@warwickprep.com
website: www.warwickprep.com

Chairman of the Governors: Mrs G Low

Headmistress: **Mrs Hellen Dodsworth**

Age Range. Boys 3–7, Girls 3–11.
Number of Children. c.490.
Fees per term (2016–2017). Nursery: £2,412 (full time, after Nursery Education Funding). Lower School (4–6 years) £3,285; Middle School (7–9 years) £3,679. Upper School (9–11 years) £3,764. (Mid-morning fruit and lunch included.)

Instrumental music tuition optional extra.

Warwick Preparatory School is an Independent School, purpose built on a 4½ acre site on the outskirts of Warwick. It is part of the Warwick Independent Schools Foundation, which includes Warwick School and the King's High School for Girls.

The Prep School has an exceptionally large staff, with specialist tuition in Art, French, Science, Music, Drama, DT, Physical Education and Computing.

Boys and girls are admitted from the age of 3+, subject to the availability of places. At the age of 7, the majority of boys continue to Warwick School, whilst the girls normally remain with us until they are 11.

Entry to King's High School is by a competitive examination and girls at the Prep School are prepared for this. Girls are also prepared for the Common Entrance and any other appropriate examinations for their secondary education.

Early registration is advised if a place in the Pre-Preparatory Dept is to be ensured. Entry to the School at the age of 7 and later requires a satisfactory level of attainment in the basic skills and may be competitive.

Charitable status. Warwick Independent Schools Foundation is a Registered Charity, number 1088057.

Waverley School

Waverley Way, Finchampstead, Wokingham, Berkshire RG40 4YD
Tel: 0118 973 1121
Fax: 0118 973 1131
email: admissions@waverleyschool.co.uk
website: www.waverleyschool.co.uk
Twitter: @waverleyschool
Facebook: @Waverley-Preparatory-School-Nursery
LinkedIn: /waverley-preparatory-school-&-nursery

Chairman of Governors: Mr Blair Jenkins

Head Teacher: Mr Guy Shore, BA Hons QTS

Age Range. 3 months–11 years.
Number of Pupils. 240.

Fees per term (2016–2017). Reception–Year 6 Core day: £2,675–£3,325. Extended day package also available. Nursery according to the broad range of flexible sessions attended. Wrap-around care available from 7.30 am to 6.00 pm.

Ethos. Providing a family environment with academic excellence and enabling every child to succeed to the best of their ability.

Pupils just love coming to school every morning at Waverley! As soon as you walk in, there is a vibrant buzz of excited children who are happy, thriving and learning.

Our priority at Waverley is to challenge every pupil to achieve academic excellence. We recognise however that only happy children, who feel supported and confident, learn to the best of their ability. Waverley's unique cheerful, nurturing environment enables every child to succeed and reach his or her full potential.

We are very proud of our position as the no. 1 Prep School in Berkshire (The Sunday Times) and no. 14 Primary School in the UK (The Sunday Times) –based upon our strong academic track record. Our school has also been in the Times Top 100 Prep Schools for the past 7 years. Our academic success is also reflected in the exceptional exam results of our Year 6 students and the secondary schools they move on to – most of our students attain scholarships, or places at selective secondary schools.

We operate small class sizes, giving each child individual attention and enabling us to closely monitor every child's progress. Our school is modern and purpose-built, enabling daily school life to flow and function easily. Our family atmosphere means that our teachers not only know every child by name – they also know what makes your child tick. This warm ethos is also visible amongst our children who play with each other freely across the year groups in the playground.

In addition to academic success, we aim to encourage self-discipline, respect, tolerance and kindness and to provide a broad, rich curriculum going far beyond national expectations.

Curriculum. Waverley's curriculum provides children with a solid foundation, particularly in the areas of literacy and numeracy. Pre-prep and Preparatory children engage in a full curriculum of subjects including English, Mathematics, ICT, French, History, Geography, Science and Art.

Gifted and Talented. We have development programmes for gifted and talented children.

Sports. Waverley School's physical education curriculum includes football, rugby, netball, cricket, athletics, golf and rounders. Swimming also takes place throughout the year as part of our ethos that every child needs to learn this life skill. The children regularly take part in sports matches and swimming galas against other local independent schools.

The Arts. We have extremely strong Speech and Drama, and Music (both choral and instrumental) departments. As well as termly productions, the School regularly takes part in local concerts in the local community and with other schools to build children's self-confidence.

Moving On. The majority of our students attain scholarships, or places at selective secondary schools.

Wellesley House

114 Ramsgate Road, Broadstairs, Kent CT10 2DG

Tel: 01843 862991
Fax: 01843 602068
email: hmsec@wellesleyhouse.net
website: www.wellesleyhouse.org

Twitter: @wellesleyschool
Facebook: /wellesleyhouseschool

Chairman of the Governors: P J Woodhouse, Esq

Headmaster: **S T P O'Malley**, MA Hons, PGCE

Age Range. 7–13.
Number of Pupils. 74 Boys, 42 Girls.
Fees per term (2016–2017). Boarding £8,354; Day: Years 5–8 £6,319, Year 4 £4,800, Year 3 £3,880.
Location. The school, which is run by an Educational Trust, stands in its own grounds of 20 acres and was purpose-built in 1898.

Trains run hourly from Victoria Station, London with a high-speed rail link from St Pancras which takes as little as 1 hour 15 minutes or under two hours by road. At the beginning of each term, and at most exeats and half-terms, the school operates coach services between Broadstairs and London via the M2 services. The school also operates a minibus at exeats and half-terms to Brentwood, Charing, near Ashford, and Benenden.

Facilities. The school has a science and technology building, which includes modern science laboratories, an ICT laboratory and a craft room. Other facilities include a library, an indoor heated swimming pool, four hard tennis courts, two squash courts, a modelling room, art room, a music wing, a .22 shooting range, fitness trail, outdoor stage and separate recreation rooms, all of which are in the school grounds. There is a spacious sports hall. The main team games are cricket, Association and rugby football, hockey, netball and rounders. Tuition is also given in fencing, squash, shooting, golf, tennis, archery, judo, scuba and swimming. Ballet, tap, modern dancing and riding are also available.

A special feature of the school is that boys between the ages of 7 and 10 live in a junior wing, Boddington House. This is linked to the main school, but self-contained under the care of resident house parents and a matron.

The girls live in a separate house, The Orchard, within the school grounds, under the care of a housemaster and his wife. The house was recently refurbished with a new conservatory added.

Education. Boys and girls are prepared for all independent senior schools. Those who show sufficient promise are prepared for scholarships and the school has a fine record of success on this front with a third of leavers gaining scholarships in recent years. The curriculum is designed to enable all children to reach the highest standard possible by sound teaching along carefully thought out lines to suit the needs of the individual.

The Headmaster and his wife are assisted by 23 teaching staff.

Charitable status. Wellesley House and St Peter Court School Education Trust Ltd is a Registered Charity, number 307852. It exists solely to provide education to boys and girls.

Wellingborough Preparatory School

London Road, Wellingborough, Northamptonshire NN8 2BX

Tel: 01933 222698
Fax: 01933 233474
email: prep-head@wellingboroughschool.org
website: www.wellingboroughschool.org
Twitter: @WboroPrepSchool

Chairman of the Governors: Dr J K Cox, MA Cantab, MB BChir, BA Hons

Headmistress: Mrs Sue Knox, BA Hons UCNW, MBA Cranfield, GradDipEd & MEdLead Macquarie University Sydney

Deputy Head, Curriculum: Mrs Katherine Owen, BSc Exeter

Deputy Head, Pastoral: Mrs Claire Petrie, BSc Loughborough

Age Range. 8–13.
Number of Pupils. 182 Boys, 121 Girls.
Fees per term (2016–2017). £4,395 (Years 4, 5 & 6), £4,595 (Years 7 & 8). Lunch is included.

The School is the Preparatory School of Wellingborough School (a registered charity). Girls and boys are admitted from 8 years old. The Preparatory School is self-contained with its own teaching centre, library, two science laboratories, computer suite and purpose-built Art Atrium. Music, sports and design technology facilities are shared with the Senior School.

The School offers a broad, well-balanced curriculum with Foundation Scholarships available at 11+, Entrance Scholarships at 13+ and an enrichment programme.

The creative arts are highly valued, with termly drama productions and a flourishing Art Department that has exhibited nationally. The School boast two orchestras and a wide variety of groups and ensembles. All the pupils have an opportunity to learn a wind instrument in Year 5 as well as learning composition and keyboard skills in other year groups. There are around 50 to 60 after-school activities to choose from during the week, as well as an optional Weekend Activities programme, which varies from term to term; some activities which might be included are: indoor skiing, equestrian, golf, dance, film school, masterclass cricket and clay pigeon shooting.

The School enjoys a strong sporting reputation which combines a desire for excellence with an 'all-inclusive sports' ethos. Games played are rugby, football, and cricket for the boys. Hockey, netball and rounders are the games played by the girls. The children are also able to represent the school at athletics, tennis cross-country golf, triathlon and sailing. There is an equestrian team whose fixture list continues to grow and Year 8 pupils can participate in sailing during the Trinity term.

The pastoral care of pupils is of paramount importance. The School is organised into six Clubs. Each Club is headed by a member of staff who oversees the academic and social progress of the girls and boys within their club.

The children work in a stimulating environment. The School aims for the pupils to become successful learners, confident individuals and responsible citizens, with parents working together in partnership with the School in the education of their children.

Almost 100% of Year 8 pupils make the transition into the Senior School with only one or two going to alternative Independent schools.

Charitable status. Wellingborough School is a Registered Charity, number 309923. It exists to provide education for girls and boys.

Wellington Prep School

South Street, Wellington, Somerset TA21 8NT
Tel: 01823 668700
email: prep@wellington-school.org.uk
website: www.wellington-school.org.uk

Chairman of Governors: Mrs Anna Govey, MSc

Headmaster: Mr Adam Gibson, BSc Hons, PGCE, NPQH, Cert Ed Cantab

Age Range. 2–11 Co-educational.
Number of Pupils. 210.
Fees per term (2016–2017). Day: £1,990–£3,620.

Wellington Prep School opened in September 1999 in purpose-built accommodation to provide one of the most stimulating educational environments for children anywhere in the country.

Wellington Prep School provides an education of unrivalled quality which both complements and enhances the national reputation of Wellington School and enables us to deliver educational excellence from nursery level through to university entrance. Our school is a place of endeavour, teamwork, integrity and laughter; a place where each child is nurtured.

We value education in its widest sense; making the most of today in order that we can make even more of tomorrow and the days, weeks, months and years that lie ahead. This is 'Learning for Life.' Our education is unbounded, as we encourage our children to be curious, to be creative and to be compassionate. At WPS Learning is not a spectator sport.

We believe that every child deserves to be inspired every day. The qualities our children will need in life are as important as their skills. This is why we have high expectations for each child, nurture and support each child and develop each child's leadership skills. We encourage our children to think independently and to 'have a go', secure in the knowledge that they can learn from mistakes.

While the headline ratio of one fully-qualified and experienced teacher for every ten children in the Prep School is striking, it is the quality of these relationships that really matters and this cannot be gauged by a simple statistic. The range of experiences our teaching team provide for our children is superb. Every person cares deeply about the children in their care and each child's happiness and fulfilment.

Our children benefit from sharing some facilities with our Senior School, giving them access to:
• Eighteen purpose-designed, modern classrooms;
• A large, attractive, central school hall, the hub of our school;
• The most modern and up-to-date education resources;
• Purpose-built ICT suite and library;
• Spacious grounds including a large playground with wooden amphitheatre;
• Our forest school in the Blackdown Hills;
• The Princess Royal Sports Complex;
• Numerous sports pitches, hard courts and the astro;
• An indoor swimming pool.

School is open from 8.00 am and there is an extensive clubs programme followed by STAR club, which is available to all children from 5.00 to 6.00 pm during term time. For children in Reception and older, holiday clubs operate at Christmas, Easter and for six weeks during the summer holidays to accommodate busy working families. Our Nursery settings are open 50 weeks a year.

Our prospectus is available from the School Registrar and can be requested via our website.

Charitable status. Wellington School is a Registered Charity, number 310268.

Wellow House School

Wellow, Newark, Notts NG22 0EA
Tel: 01623 861054
Fax: 01623 836665

email: office@wellowhouseschool.co.uk
website: www.wellowhouse.notts.sch.uk

Chairman of the Governors: Steve Cooling

Head: **Nicola Matthews**, BA Hons MA Ed Dip M

Age Range. 3–13.
Number of Pupils. 150.
Fees per term (2016–2017). Pre-Prep pupils £2,580;
Day pupils £3,845–£4,075; Boarding £21 per night. Fees
include meals for full time pupils but are charged at £5 per
lunch for part-time Pre-Prep pupils. Fees include normal
extras.

Wellow House School was founded in 1971 by the Stewart General Charitable Trust. Since 1994 it has been managed as an educational charity by the Directors and
administered by a Board of Governors. This co-educational
school has an established reputation for high academic standards, a successful sporting record, broad cultural interests
and a happy family atmosphere. Weekly and occasional
boarding has become an increasingly popular means of
encouraging self-reliance within a supportive community
and as a preparation for senior school and university.

The teaching staff of 8 men and 12 women is well qualified and experienced. A distinctive teaching style places
great emphasis on the rapport between teacher and pupil in
small classes, without slavish reliance on worksheets and
textbooks. Each pupil maintains a file of notes, as a record
and for reference. All take pride in honest hard work, confidence through encouragement, courtesy and fair discipline,
and a strong sense of belonging. The thriving house points'
system encourages much voluntary study and is the basis of
the disciplinary process.

The Headmaster, Matron and Boarding Parents look after
the boarders. They are assisted by a team of resident and
non-resident tutors, one of whom oversees the evening
activity programme. Qualified Catering Manager and
Matron supervise the pupils' boarding, catering and medical
needs. There are visiting teachers for instrumental tuition,
table tennis, judo and drama.

The school is attractively set in 20 acres of parkland and
playing fields on the fringe of the Sherwood Forest village
of Wellow. There is easy road access to this heart of Nottinghamshire from Worksop and Sheffield to the north, Mansfield and Chesterfield to the west, Nottingham and
Grantham to the south, and Lincoln and Newark to the east.
Newark lies on north-south and east-west main line rail
routes.

A continuous programme of development has provided
purpose-built classrooms, science laboratory, networked
computer room, music rooms, library, assembly hall and
dining hall to add to the original country house. The boarding accommodation was refurbished in 1997 and 2000 with
further refinements and updates in 2006 to 2008. Recent
additions to the school include studios for art and ceramics
and a sports hall with indoor cricket nets. There is an indoor
heated swimming pool, an all-weather cricket net, and an
all-weather tennis court. The Pre-Prep classes are housed in
their own building, which was totally refurbished and
extended in September 2006 and is surrounded by play-time
facilities. There are close links with the village church.

Children enter the school after an interview visit and a
trial day at any age from 3 to 11+ –the oldest often transferring from primary schools. Six Entrance Scholarships may
be awarded annually and Bursaries can give financial assistance. Pupils are prepared for Common Entrance and Scholarships to a wide range of Senior Independent Schools, both
boarding and day, and there is a continuous programme of
assessment and reporting.

There is a broad physical education programme, with
school matches in Rugby, Netball, Soccer, Hockey, Cricket,
Rounders, Cross Country, Swimming and Tennis. The
school is renowned for its pupils' prowess in Archery and
Table Tennis. Weekend and holiday expeditions for Outdoor
Pursuits in the Peak District, Yorkshire, Scotland and
beyond are popular.

There is encouragement to participate in Natural History,
the Visual Arts, Dance, Drama and Music, and more than
half of the pupils learn a musical instrument. Most are
involved in the much enjoyed regular concerts.

The school provides activity week cover during the holiday periods on Monday, Wednesday and Friday in the Pre
Prep (to include pupils in Y3 and Y4). The Prep run activity
weeks for 7–13 year olds for 2 full weeks in the summer.

Charitable status. Wellow House School is a Registered
Charity, number 528234. It exists solely to provide a high
standard of all-round education for children aged 3 to 13
years.

Wells Cathedral Junior School

**Jocelyn House, 11 The Liberty, Wells, Somerset
BA5 2ST**

Tel: 01749 834400
Fax: 01749 834401
email: juniorschool@wells-cathedral-school.com
website: www.wells-cathedral-school.com

Chairman of Governors: Canon Andrew Featherstone, MA

Head of the Junior School: **Mrs J Barrow**, BEd

Age Range. 3–11 years.
Student numbers. 167 plus 27 in the Nursery. Girl to
boy ratio: 50%
Fees per term (2016–2017). Junior School (Years 3–6):
Boarders £7,956, Weekly Boarders £6,990, Day £4,574.
Pre-Prep: £2,509 (Years 1–2), £2,424 (Reception).

The Junior School is made up of the Pre-Prep department
(age 3–7) and the Junior School (age 7–11). Pupils accepted
into the Junior School normally make a smooth transfer to
the Senior School at 11 and academic, music and sports
scholarships are awarded.

Academic Work. The Junior School prepares children
for the academic work in the senior school and takes part in
the national tests at the end of KS2, however, the school is
not restricted by the demands of the National Curriculum.
The aim of the school is to ensure high academic standards
within a friendly and stimulating environment.

Children are assessed regularly for both academic
achievement and effort, and parents have many opportunities to meet staff and receive information on their child's
progress.

Pastoral Care. The form teacher is responsible for the
pastoral care of pupils; in addition each pupil is allocated to
a House which has an assembly once a week. Work and
sports competitions take place in houses and pupils are able
to develop a good relationship not only with their own peer
group but with pupils from across the Junior School.

Creativity. We have close ties to Wells Cathedral and all
their boy and girl choristers attend our school, which is set
in beautiful grounds just to the north of the cathedral. In
addition, a number of pupils are specialist musicians enjoying the expert tuition of the music department at the school,
which is one of the four in England designated and grant-
aided by the Government's Music and Dance Scheme.
Scholarships are available for both the choristers and the
musicians.

Drama, music and dance are considered vital activities to
bring out the best in children. A full programme of concerts,
both formal and informal, takes place during the year for all

age groups as well as big productions and small year group dramas. The school takes its production to the Edinburgh Festival in alternate years and it has established drama exchange links with schools in other European countries.

A whole school arts week each summer allows all aspects of creativity to come to the fore for every pupil. Themes have included the Caribbean, Somerset and China; pupils experience workshops in the areas of art, dance, drama and music. Regular exhibitions and performances are a feature of the school. The school has received the Artsmark Gold award from Arts Council England.

Sport. The school has many excellent facilities, such as the sports hall, dance studio, astroturf pitch and swimming pool. Pupils experience a wide range of activities on the games field. Sport is played to a high standard with rugby, cross country, netball, hockey, cricket, swimming, athletics and gymnastics being the main sports; basketball and badminton are also available. A full programme of inter-school matches and house matches is available for all pupils in Year 3 to 6. Many clubs and activities run at lunchtimes or after school.

Charitable status. Wells Cathedral School is a Registered Charity, number 310212. It has existed since AD 909 to provide education for its pupils.

West Hill Park School

St Margaret's Lane, Titchfield, Hampshire PO14 4BS

Tel: 01329 842356
Fax: 01329 842911
email: admissions@westhillpark.com
website: www.westhillpark.com

Chairman of Governors: Mrs B Worsley, BA Hons, ACA

Headmaster: **A P Ramsay**, MSc, BEd Hons

Age Range. 3–13.
Number of Pupils. Prep School (age 5–13): 41 Boarders (21 girls, 20 boys); 255 Day Pupils (105 girls, 115 boys). Early Years (age rising 3 to 5): 30 boys, 27 girls.
Fees per term (2016–2017). Prep School: Day £3,540–£5,995, Boarding supplement £1,450. Early Years: according to sessions attended.

At West Hill Park pupils are prepared for Scholarships and Common Entrance to all Independent Schools.

The main building is Georgian, originally a shooting lodge for the Earls of Southampton, and provides spacious and comfortable boarding accommodation for boys and girls under the supervision of resident Houseparents. Resident matrons, academic staff and a qualified school nurse complete the Boarding team. Also in the main building are the administrative offices, the Library, the Dining Hall and the Assembly Hall with fully equipped sound and lighting equipment and stage. Further excellent facilities include the Art and Design Technology Studios, the Music School, a 25m heated indoor Swimming Pool, a fully-equipped Sports Hall, 2 Science Laboratories, two Computing Suites, the French, History, Maths and Geography Departments with Interactive Whiteboards and the purpose-built Early Years Department with its Outdoor Play Area and Woodland Classroom. West Hill Park stands in its own grounds of nearly 40 acres on the edge of Titchfield village. There are sports fields, 5 hard, 3 grass and 5 Astro tennis courts, a floodlit Riding School, a floodlit Astroturf, a cross-country course and in summer a nine-hole golf course.

There are 28 fully-qualified members of the teaching staff. 13 members of staff are resident, either in the main building or in houses in the school grounds, giving a great sense of community to the school.

A strong pastoral care system monitors the individual child's well-being regularly. There is a wide range of activities available in order to encourage children to develop individual skills and talents: choirs, orchestra, dance, aerobics, carpentry, judo, ballet, drama, golf, life-saving, computer club, string group, squash, chess, sailing, fly fishing, riding on school ponies and public speaking, as well as the more intensive training available in the Swim Squad, Tennis Squad and other sporting clubs. The Boarders enjoy many expeditions at weekends as well as fun events at school, such as orienteering, theatre workshops, cycle marathons and games evenings.

Games played include rugby, football, cricket, hockey, tennis, athletics, netball and rounders.

The school has been recently been judged by ISI Inspectors to be 'Excellent' in all areas.

Charitable status. West Hill School Trust is a Registered Charity, number 307343. It exists to educate children.

West House School

24 St James Road, Edgbaston, Birmingham B15 2NX

Tel: 0121 440 4097
Fax: 0121 440 5839
email: secretary@westhouseprep.com
website: www.westhouseprep.com
Twitter: @westhouseschool

Chairman of Governors: S T Heathcote, FCA

Headmaster: **A M J Lyttle**, BA Hons Birmingham, PGCE Birmingham, NPQH

Age Range. Boys: 4–11 years; Co-educational Nursery: 12 months to 4 years.
Number of Pupils. A maximum 230 boys aged 4–11 (Reception to Year 6) plus 100 boys and girls aged 12 months–4 years.
Fees per term (2016–2017). 4–11 year olds: £2,717–£3,695 according to age. The fees include lunches and breaktime drinks. Under 4: fees according to number of sessions attended per week. Fee list on application.

West House was founded in 1895 and since 1959 has been an Educational Trust controlled by a Board of Governors. The school has a strong academic reputation and pupils are regularly awarded scholarships to senior schools at 11+. The well-qualified and experienced staff provides a sound education for boys of all abilities. The National Curriculum has been adapted to suit the aptitudes and interests of pupils and to ensure that it provides an outstanding preparation for entry into selective senior schools. Pupils are taught in small classes which ensures that they receive much individual attention. Specialist help is available for children with Dyslexia or who require learning support. Music teachers visit the school to give individual music tuition.

The school occupies a leafy five-acre site a mile from Birmingham city centre. As well as the main teaching blocks there are two well-equipped science laboratories and a sports hall.

The Centenary Building, opened in 1998, accommodates the art and design technology department, ICT room and senior Library. Extensive playing fields, two all-weather tennis courts and all-weather cricket nets enable pupils to participate in many games and sports. Pupils also enjoy a wide range of hobby activities, and drama and music play important roles in school life.

The school is open during term time between 7.45 am and 6 pm. On-site Holiday Clubs are run by members of staff during the holidays.

Charitable status. West House School is a Registered Charity, number 528959. It exists to provide education for boys.

Westbourne House

Shopwyke, Chichester, West Sussex PO20 2BH

Tel: 01243 782739
Fax: 01243 770759
email: office@westbournehouse.org
website: www.westbournehouse.org

Chairman of the Governors: J A Ashworth, BSc Hons

Headmaster: **Martin Barker**

Age Range. 2½–13.
Number of Pupils. 448: Boarders 100; Prep Day 201; Pre-Prep 147.
Fees per term (2016–2017). Boarders £6,980; Day £5,720; Pre-Prep £3,320.

Westbourne House School was founded in 1907 and became a Charitable Trust in 1967. It has been co-educational since 1992. There is a well-qualified teaching staff of 80, plus 18 visiting music staff and 40 support staff, who all play important roles in the care of the children.

Situated in a beautiful parkland setting of 100+ acres, Westbourne House offers a warm, happy environment, which fosters learning and development. Pupils are prepared for the Common Entrance and many Scholarships have been won at an impressive list of Senior Independent Schools in recent years (34 in 2016 – which is a record number); virtually all children go on to their first-choice school at 13+. Individual academic progress is carefully monitored using the latest database technology. The average class size (16) allows plenty of individual attention, differentiation and pastoral care. The broad curriculum includes the full quota of academic subjects, as well as Music, Art, Design Technology, Ceramics, Food Technology, Drama, Physical Education & Games and Information Technology. Individual Needs, as well as the Gifted & Talented, are nurtured by a highly-qualified SENCO.

Children are encouraged to discover their talents within the wide range of activities on offer, with the aim of developing them to the full. Westbourne enjoys a proud record of sporting achievement and the children have access to excellent facilities: extensive playing fields, a full-size astroturf pitch. The School hosts the major sports (football, rugby, hockey and cricket for boys; netball, hockey, pop lacrosse and rounders for girls) and the children also engage in athletics, swimming (25-metre indoor heated pool), squash (2 courts), tennis (16 courts), as well as golf, fencing, judo and dance (dance studio). A large, well-equipped Sports Hall caters for indoor sports and also houses a newly-installed climbing wall. Music is outstanding: the children enjoy excellent facilities and teaching, with a wide range of instruments, orchestras, bands and choirs on offer. All children are encouraged to perform from an early age. Art and Technology are housed within the original stable block of the Georgian house, providing a delightful environment for the children to develop their creative skills. Drama is encouraged through a number of productions involving all the children in each year group.

Many building programmes have been undertaken in recent years: a new Junior Teaching block for Years 3, 4 and 5 was built in 1997, a purpose-built Science Department in 1999 and a Theatre seating 300 was completed in 2001. A new Dining Room, catering facilities and three new classrooms were completed in 2004, as were improvements to the library and recreational facilities. A dance studio was opened in 2008 and a full-size astroturf all-weather surface in 2009. Development in 2011 included a new 30-acre lake on the school grounds for canoeing. September 2014 saw the development of two new boarding houses, a new Food Tech Room and a new Science Lab. Extensive refurbishment took place in 2015 of the Pre-Prep which included a new Library incorporating ICT. Looking to the future – plans are now in hand for the construction of a new Music School, which will provide extensive teaching and performing opportunities, with the provision of 16 practice rooms, ensemble rooms and a 100-seat auditorium.

Charitable status. Westbourne House is a Registered Charity, number 307034.

Westbourne School

60 Westbourne Road, Sheffield, South Yorkshire S10 2QT

Tel: 0114 266 0374
Fax: 0114 263 8176
email: admin@westbourneschool.co.uk
website: www.westbourneschool.co.uk

Chairman of the Governors: Mr S Hinchliffe

Headmaster: **Mr John Hicks**, MEd Kingston, BEd Hons Exeter

Bursar: Mr Chris Heald, BA Hons Sheffield

Age Range. 3–16.
Number of Pupils. 350 day pupils, boys and girls.
Fees per term (2016–2017). £2,925–£3,995.

The fully co-educational School, founded in 1885, is an Educational Trust with a Board of Governors, some of whom are Parents. The number of entries is limited to maintain small class sizes – with an average class size of 14 throughout the school with a staff/pupil ratio of less than 1:10.

The Pre-School and Junior School are housed in a specially designed and equipped building, staffed by qualified and experienced teachers. French, Music and Games are taught by specialists. Specialist Science and Technology are introduced from Year 4 (8+), as well as specialist teaching in Computing, Art and Design, and RE. French, Science and Computers are introduced from the age of 4.

In the Junior School, some lessons are taught by specialists in Subject Rooms. There is also a Science Laboratory and ICT, Art and Music Rooms, Fiction and Reference Libraries, and a Hall with a Stage.

The Senior School provides teaching to GCSE from Year 7 to 11 up to age 16. It has its own campus immediately adjacent to the Junior School. Years 7 and 8 have the benefit of their own designated building with access to all the facilities available in Senior School. The school has a 3-form entry in Year 7 with a scholarship class. External and internal scholarships are taken in January of Year 6. All children are placed in sets in Maths and English from Year 5.

The main aim of the school is to bring out the best in every pupil according to their ability. There is a Department catering for those with Specific Learning Difficulties. Great emphasis is laid on courtesy and a mutual respect for each other.

Art, Music and Drama are strongly encouraged throughout the school, with regular concerts, plays and art exhibitions. Tuition in several instruments is available. A new Drama Studio opened in June 2015.

The main sports are Rugby, Football, Hockey, Cricket, Athletics, Netball, Rounders and Cross-Country Running with regular matches against other schools. There are also opportunities for Short Tennis, Swimming, Basketball, Volleyball, Fencing, Skiing, Badminton, Climbing, Golf and Scuba Diving. Numerous educational visits are on offer with annual trips abroad.

A supervised breakfast club runs from 7.30 am to 8.30 am. Breakfast for pupils and parents is available from 7.45 am and, while the length of day depends on the age of the child, there are after-school facilities for all pupils until 5.15 pm. There is no school on Saturdays.

Charitable status. Westbourne School is a Registered Charity, number 529381. It exists to provide education for boys and girls.

Westbrook Hay

London Road, Hemel Hempstead, Herts HP1 2RF

Tel:	01442 256143/230099
Fax:	01442 232076
email:	admin@westbrookhay.co.uk
website:	www.westbrookhay.co.uk
Twitter:	@WestbrookHaySch
Facebook:	@Westbrook-Hay-Prep-School
LinkedIn:	/westbrook-hay-prep-school

Chairman of Governors: Andrew Newland

Headmaster: **Keith D Young**, BEd Hons Exeter

Registrar: Kate Woodmansee

Age Range. Boys 3–13, Girls 3–11.
Number of Pupils. Day: 220 Boys, 107 Girls.
Fees per term (2016–2017). £2,790–£4,695. Flexi Boarding £35.50 per night.

Westbrook Hay is an outstanding independent prep school educating boys and girls from rising 3–13 years. The school's beautiful location boasts 26 acres of parkland overlooking the Bourne valley in Hertfordshire, and is just off the A41, between Berkhamsted and Hemel Hempstead. This unique setting offers a secure environment, within which children explore and enjoy all that childhood has to offer.

Through visionary teaching in small classes and with a wonderful mixture of purpose-built facilities and historic surroundings, our children achieve excellent results, enjoy a broad curriculum, and have the all-important confidence to succeed.

The Independent Schools Inspectorate (ISI) carried out a very successful inspection and regarded our school as 'Excellent' and 'Outstanding', the highest possible recognition from the ISI for both age groups.

"Pupil's achievement is excellent and they are very well educated in accordance with the school's aim for pupils to realise their intellectual, social and physical potential."

"The quality of the provision is outstanding. Through excellent understanding of differing developmental stages and careful observations, staff plan challenging and enjoyable work for each child across all learning areas."

Classes are small and each individual is encouraged and helped to achieve their potential. Individuality, honesty, a sense of humour and self-reliance are attributes which are stimulated and valued in this most friendly school, which maintains a caring, family atmosphere.

Lower and Middle School departments prepare children from rising three to eight for entry into the Upper School. Children in Years 3 and 4 are class taught primarily by their form teacher, before a move to a subject-based curriculum in Year 5. The academic focus is based on the curriculum and goals of Common Entrance, together with Senior Schools Entrance and Scholarship examinations. All children follow the National Curriculum subject areas and in many cases extend them.

The facilities of the school have benefited from significant recent improvements including a £2 million lower school building, an art studio with pottery kiln and two new fully equipped Information Technology rooms. A £3 million Performing Arts Centre, with a 300-seat theatre and full music practice and performance facilities is the most recent addition to the outstanding facilities.

Extensive playing fields give ample room for rugby, football, cricket, golf, rounders and athletics. All-weather netball and tennis courts and a heated swimming pool are complemented by a purpose-built Sports Hall which provides for badminton, table tennis, cricket nets, five-a-side football, gymnastics and a galaxy of other indoor sports.

A breakfast club, after-school care and a school bus service are also offered to accommodate the needs of working parents.

Charitable status. Westbrook Hay School is a Registered Charity, number 292537. It exists to provide education for boys and girls.

Westminster Abbey Choir School

Dean's Yard, London SW1P 3NY

Tel:	020 7654 4918
Fax:	020 7222 1548
email:	headmaster@westminster-abbey.org
website:	www.westminster-abbey.org

Chairman of Governors: The Dean of Westminster

Headmaster: **J H Milton**, BEd

Age Range. 8–13.
Number of Boys. Up to 35 all chorister boarders.
Fees per term (2016–2017). £2,746 inclusive of tuition on two instruments. Additional bursaries may be available in cases of real financial need.

Westminster Abbey Choir School is the only school in Britain exclusively devoted to the education of boy choristers. Boys have been singing services in the Abbey since at least 1384 and the 35 boys in the school maintain this tradition.

Westminster Abbey Choir School is a special place, offering boys from eight to thirteen a unique and exciting opportunity to be a central part of one of our great national institutions. Boys sing daily in the Abbey and also take part in many special services and celebrations both in the UK and abroad.

The small size of the school, the fact that all boys are boarders and the high proportion of staff who live on the premises, allow the School to have an extended family atmosphere.

A full academic curriculum is taught by specialist staff and boys are prepared for the Common Entrance and academic scholarship examinations; most boys win valuable scholarships to secondary independent schools when they leave at 13.

Music obviously plays a central part in the school. Every boy learns the piano and at least one orchestral instrument and there are 15 visiting music teachers. Concerts, both inside and outside school, are a regular feature of the year.

Besides music and academic lessons there is a thriving programme of other activities and there are many opportunities for boys to develop interests outside music.

Sports played include football, cricket, rugby, athletics, hockey, sailing, canoeing and tennis.

Entry is by voice trial and academic tests. Further details are available from Thérèse Gordon-Duffy (Headmaster's Secretary and Admissions). The Headmaster is always pleased to hear from parents who feel that their son might have the potential to become a chorister.

Charitable status. Westminster Abbey is a Registered Charity, number X8259. It is a religious establishment incorporated by Royal Charter in 1560.

Westminster Cathedral Choir School

Ambrosden Avenue, London SW1P 1QH
Tel: 020 7798 9081
email: lauger@choirschool.com
website: www.choirschool.com

President: The Most Reverend Vincent Nichols, Archbishop of Westminster

Chairman of Governors: John Gibbs

Headmaster: **Neil McLaughlan**, BA Hons

Age Range. 7–13.
Number of Boys. 179 (29 Choristers, 150 Day Boys).
Fees per term (2016–2017). Chorister Boarders £3,094; Day Boys £5,899.

Founded in 1901, Westminster Cathedral Choir School is a Day Prep School and Boarding Choir School concerned with the development of the whole person. Choristers must be Roman Catholic, but Day Boys of all denominations are welcome.

The school forms part of the precincts of Westminster Cathedral and enjoys such facilities as a large playground and a Grade 1 listed Library. The school has recently undergone a £1.3 million refurbishment, including a brand new playground and boarding facilities.

Choristers and Day Boys alike achieve a high level of music making. The Choristers sing the daily capitular liturgy in the Cathedral and are regularly involved in broadcasts, recordings and tours abroad. There is also a Day Boy Choir, two orchestras and a substantial programme of chamber music. Boys can learn the piano and any orchestral instrument in school.

The major sports played at the Choir School include football, rugby and cricket and the boys travel to Vincent Square, Battersea Park and the Queen Mother Sports Centre for Games.

There is a wide range of extracurricular activities available including: chess, computing, debating, fencing, football, judo, drama and a Saturday rugby club.

The school is justly famed for its fantastic food!

Assessment for Choristers is by academic assessment and voice trial, generally in November and February. Day Boy assessments are held in January.

Charitable status. Westminster Cathedral Choir School is a Registered Charity, number 1063761. It exists to provide a musical education for Roman Catholic boys.

Westminster Under School

Adrian House, 27 Vincent Square, London SW1P 2NN
Tel: +44 (0)20 7821 5788
Fax: +44 (0)20 7821 0458
email: lousia.lopes@westminster.org.uk
website: www.westminster.org.uk

Chairman of Governors: The Dean of Westminster, The Very Reverend Dr John Hall

Master: **Mr M O'Donnell**, BA, MA, EdM, PGDE

Deputy Master: Mr D R Smith, MA

Age Range. 7–13.
Number of Boys. 285 (day boys only).
Fees per term (2016–2017). £5,906 (inclusive of lunches and stationery).

The Under School is closely linked to Westminster School, sharing the same Governing Body, although it has its own buildings overlooking the beautiful school playing fields in Vincent Square. The school's premises were extended in 2011 with a new dining hall and a specialist suite of Art rooms located in an adjacent building. The current site was also extensively refurbished.

Boys are prepared, though not exclusively, for Westminster through the Common Entrance examinations and "The Challenge", Westminster School's scholarship exams. Most boys proceed to Westminster, but entry into the Under School does not guarantee a place at the "Great School". Each year some boys will go on to other leading senior schools, including Eton and Winchester. There is a strong academic tradition at the school.

The musical tradition is equally strong, with a junior and senior choir, an orchestra, and string, brass and jazz groups. Art is equally strong with new facilities for all areas of creative activity. The standard of Art is also very high with new facilities for many different areas of creative activity. The Art Department also organises competitions in photography and model-making. There are other school competitions in areas such as public speaking, creative writing, chess and Scrabble. The level of dramatic productions has risen in recent years and there are plays for each year group at different times of the year.

Games are played on playing fields in Vincent Square and although football and cricket are the main sports, there are opportunities to participate in athletics, basketball, cross-country, hockey, rugby, swimming and tennis. Our new sports centre, recently opened in September 2012, provides excellent facilities for all sports and after-school clubs in such activities as fencing, judo, karate, climbing and table tennis.

Approximately 20 new boys are admitted at 7+ and at 8+, and up to 28 at 11+ in September. Means-tested bursaries are available at 11+, as are music scholarships, and many boys apply at this entry point from London primary schools.

Charitable status. St Peter's College (otherwise known as Westminster School) is a Registered Charity, number 312728. It exists to provide education for boys.

Westonbirt Prep School

Westonbirt, Tetbury, Gloucestershire GL8 8QG
Tel: 01666 881400
email: prep@westonbirt.org
website: www.westonbirt.org
Twitter: @westonbirtprep
Facebook: @Westonbirt-Prep-School
LinkedIn: /westonbirt-prep-school

Chairman of Governors: Mr D McMeekin, MBA

Headmaster: **Mr Sean Price**

Westonbirt Prep School is a Preparatory Day School and Nursery for Boys and Girls aged 3–11. It successfully combines the educational quality and individual attention of an intimate family school with the facilities, resources and opportunities of a school many times larger. Westonbirt Prep offers a broad and varied curriculum, with great emphasis placed on sports, music and drama, each delivered by specialist teachers. Committed to making outdoor education part of school life, all year groups attend regular Forest School in the Spinney, a beautiful woodland clearing within the school grounds. A strong family ethos is evident throughout the school and this combination of care and sense of community creates a happy, secure and stimulating environment for boys and girls to thrive.

Age Range. 3–11.

Number of Pupils. 130 day pupils.

Fees per term (2016–2017). £2,600–£3,750.

Location. Set in 210 acres of stunning parklands, shared with Westonbirt Senior School, pupils benefit from the resources of a much larger school while maintaining the atmosphere of a small family setting. The school's idyllic rural location allows pupils the freedom to play and explore in a safe and natural environment, developing imagination and confidence.

The school is located close to Tetbury, within half an hour of the M4 and M5 and within easy reach of Cirencester, Gloucester, Swindon, Bath and Bristol.

Philosophy. Smaller class sizes and the excellent ratio of staff to pupils allow our children to be well supported throughout their development and for their individual abilities to be valued. Boys and girls are praised for their efforts and good behaviour and are encouraged to develop a sense of independence, mutual consideration, manners and respect for others. Our commitment to children's broader personal development combined with a structured preparation for senior school, makes Westonbirt Prep stand out.

Inspirational opportunities. Academic success is strong but emphasis is also placed on co-curricular activities, particularly Music, Art and Drama. Creativity is fostered and inspirational lessons fire pupil's imaginations.

Sports facilities. With our extensive grounds and fine facilities, a broad range of Physical Education and Games are offered so that every child can benefit from the integration of sport within their daily life. Facilities include a 25m swimming pool, well-maintained pitches, netball and tennis courts, cricket, athletics, a nine hole golf course and equestrian team.

Music. Music is an essential part of school life and is taught to a very high standard. Children have at least two periods of Music per week and many learn instruments in the string, brass, percussion and wind disciplines as well as taking individual singing lessons. Boys and girls often play together in the various ensembles and regularly perform at the Cheltenham Festival of Performing Arts.

Drama. Through Drama lessons, children develop confidence and communication skills. This encompasses clarity, diction, vocal and facial expression and intonation, and an early appreciation of poetry and prose. Individual Speech and Drama lessons are available and your child can work towards the LAMDA competition, Bath and Cheltenham Festival of Performing Arts or the Poetry Vanguard examinations. Children also look forward to participating in the annual whole school drama productions.

Charitable status. Westonbirt School Limited is a Registered Charity, number 311715. It exists to provide quality education in a demanding world.

Westville House School

Carter's Lane, Middleton, Ilkley, West Yorkshire LS29 0DQ

Tel:	01943 608053
Fax:	01943 817410
email:	office@westvillehouseschool.co.uk
website:	www.westvillehouseschool.co.uk
Twitter:	@WestvilleHouseS

Chairman of Governors: Mr Neil Brown, LLB

Head Master: Mr Ian D Shuttleworth, BEd Hons

Age Range. 2–11.

Number of Pupils. 130.

Fees per term (2016–2017). £1,810–£3,135.

Perched on the top of a stunning hillside location, with views across to The Cow and Calf, lies Westville House School, Ilkley's foremost provider of independent education. The gleaming white school building stands proud in acres of grounds and exudes fun, strong values, pride in tradition and a strong belief in the Westville family.

Originally based down in the town centre, the school relocated to its current site over 20 years ago and has gone from strength to strength, developing fantastic education facilities. Inspirational classrooms are to be seen throughout the school; specialist science, art and music classrooms along with a sophisticated IT suite, a state-of-the-art sports hall with attached playing fields and most recently a forest classroom stimulate learning and encourage fun.

From the minute a child begins their journey at Westville house they are valued for who they are. The Early Years Unit, which takes children from 3 years, devotes masses of energy to building foundations that will set the children up for life. Each child has education tailored to their needs – for those who are very able there is masses to challenge, whilst for those who need a little bit of extra help there is huge encouragement and a clear development of an excitement about learning.

Children progress through the Pre-Prep department (ages 3–7) and then on through the Prep department (ages 7–11). They emerge as well-rounded, confident, and above all very happy children whose memories of their time at Westville prompt them to return year after year.

Academics are brilliant here and the school is consistently ranked in the Sunday Times Top 100 Prep Schools in the UK – a fantastic achievement for a small non-selective school. Children regularly achieve scholarships to many independent senior schools and gain entrance to the local selective grammar schools.

Academics aside, there is a whole host of extracurricular activities designed to have something to suit every child. The school is particularly strong in swimming and cross country; drama and dance produce some excellent school productions. Music, in the form of choirs and instrumental lessons, is encouraged and the school ensemble is always seen as great fun. As the children progress through the school new activities and experiences are opened up to them – canoeing, fencing, first aid, street dancing – all geared to ensure that Westville children are totally prepared for their journey on to the senior school of their choice.

The school's motto '*Quotidie Opus Novum – something new every day*' really does sum up the excitement of coming to Westville House – the beginning of a lifelong education where an appetite for learning is something to be nurtured and enjoyed.

Charitable status. Westville House School is a Registered Charity, number 1086711.

Wetherby Pre-Preparatory School
Alpha Plus Group

11 Pembridge Square, London W2 4ED
Tel: 020 7727 9581
Fax: 020 7221 8827
email: learn@wetherbyschool.co.uk
website: www.wetherbyschool.co.uk

Headmaster: **Mr Mark Snell**, BA Hons, PGCE

    Age Range. Boys 2½–8.
    Number of Pupils. 350.
    Fees per term (2016–2017). £6,865.
    Wetherby School is situated at 11 Pembridge Square and 19 Pembridge Villas. The four Reception classes and Little Wetherby (a boys-only nursery opened in September 2014) are based at 19 Pembridge Villas. Each class occupies a whole floor level and there is a playground at the back for the boys to run around in. The rest of the school in based at 11 Pembridge Square.

    Whilst proud of its academic attainments for London Day School entry at 7+ and 8+ and top Boarding Schools, the priority is in producing happy, respectful, thoughtful, sociable and motivated boys. The curriculum is well balanced, with excellent sport, music and art opportunities including specialist teaching rooms for art, ICT, library and music. There is also a wide range of extra-curricular activities available. Wetherby operates a non-selective admissions procedure; registration is at birth.

Widford Lodge

Widford Road, Chelmsford, Essex CM2 9AN
Tel: 01245 352581
email: admin@widfordlodge.co.uk
    headmaster@widfordlodge.co.uk
website: www.widfordlodge.co.uk
Twitter: @widfordlodge

Proprietor: Mrs Louise Gear

Headmaster: **S C Trowell**, BHum Hons, PGCE London

    Age Range. 2½–11 years.
    Number of Pupils. Prep 140; Pre-Prep & EYFS Kindergarten 80; Pre-School Nursery: varies according to number of sessions.
    Fees per term (from April 2016). Pre-Prep £2,325, Main School £2,975. All fees include lunch, textbooks, stationery, etc.
    Widford Lodge is a co-educational day school situated on the southern fringe of Chelmsford. Founded in 1935 the school aims to provide an all-round education within a happy, caring environment. Children are encouraged to enjoy their time at school, while also learning a sense of responsibility and a positive approach to their role in school and the wider community.

    An enthusiastic staff prepare the children for grammar school via the 11+, entrance into senior independent schools through examination or scholarship and local secondary schools. A combination of form tutors, subject specialists and small classes ensure a good academic standard. The curriculum is broadly based and aims to develop a variety of interests, academic, aesthetic and sporting. The school has a well-equipped computer suite and the children are encouraged to use their computer skills in many different ways.

    The main part of the school stands in 5 acres of wooded grounds that include an outdoor Swimming Pool, a Floodlit Tennis Court, Cricket Nets, Science Laboratory, Design Technology Centre and a Performing Arts Centre. There is plenty of space for the children to play and to use their imagination. The school also owns 9 acres of playing fields.

    The children have the opportunity to play cricket, netball, rugby, hockey, soccer, athletics, swimming, cross-country, tennis, golf and rounders. Although a small school we are proud of our sporting tradition, which is underpinned by our belief that sport is for all and is ultimately played for fun.

    Music, drama and art are all encouraged and a wide range of musical instruments are taught. There is a busy school choir and an annual concert. Speech & Drama is a well-established and once a week the whole Prep School go 'off-timetable' and the teaching and learning experience is enriched by such activities as mindfulness, gardening, philosophy and cooking.

    There are many after-school activities which the children are encouraged to get involved in. These range from sports coaching in all the major games to art & crafts. The children can stay at school until 5.30 pm to do their Prep under the supervision of a member of staff.

Willington Independent Preparatory School

Worcester Road, Wimbledon, London SW19 7QQ
Tel: 020 8944 7020
email: office@willingtonschool.co.uk
website: www.willingtonschool.co.uk

Chairman of the Council: Mrs D Griffin

Headmaster: **M Chanter**, BSc Hons, PGCE, MA

    Age Range. 4–13.
    Number of Boys. 260 (all day boys).
    Fees per term (2016–2017). £3,630–£4,425 according to age.
    Willington Independent Preparatory School is a day school for boys aged 4–13. The school is set in the heart of Wimbledon and draws on a very local catchment area. Following the opening of the Johnson Building in 1999, which houses Art and History specialist rooms, the school in 2007 embarked on a major upgrading of our Worcester Road site and the rebuilding programme has created new centres for Maths, Science and Languages, a multi-purpose ICT suite, library and studio theatre and much improved Music provision. We also have our own extensive playing fields less than 10 minutes away by coach, which all boys use.

    We aim to provide a nurturing environment, where each boy is inspired to reach his full potential, not only in terms of academic, creative and sporting attainments, but also in terms of his self-confidence and happiness as a 13 year old boy, ready to meet the demands of his future life. In 2010, Willington celebrated its 125th anniversary. Throughout its history, Willington has been a welcoming independent preparatory school for boys. We take pupils from age 4 in Reception and they normally leave us at the end of Year 8 after Common Entrance, when they are 13.

    We pride ourselves on small class sizes; they average 15 across the school, with a maximum of 18. Our main intake is at Reception where we are currently over-subscribed. For over 100 years, Willington was in Putney and we moved to our present site in 1990. The school has been a charitable trust since 1961. We have recently been re-elected as a member of IAPS. We are keen to promote the highest academic standards and the number of scholarships gained over recent years is testament to this. However, we do not see this pursuit to be exclusive of a wide approach to prep school education, which involves the boys in a host of sporting and cultural opportunities.

Willington is a forward thinking school, which has traditional prep school values at heart. There is great stress here on individuality, but within a disciplined environment. We want our boys to be socially adept, confident and, not least, pleasant to each other and to the people around them. The school is founded on Christian values and is very much a family school, where parents are encouraged to participate in the day-to-day running of school life. Boys move on to a wide variety of Senior Schools on leaving Willington, including the traditional public schools. We work very closely with parents to find the right secondary school for each individual boy. It is testament to the school's unique place in Willingtonians' hearts that so many boys come back to visit.

Charitable status. Willington School Foundation Limited is a Registered Charity, number 312733. Its aim is to devote itself to the continuation and development of the School.

Wilmslow Preparatory School

Grove Avenue, Wilmslow, Cheshire SK9 5EG
Tel: 01625 524246
Fax: 01625 536660
email: secretary@wilmslowprep.co.uk
website: www.wilmslowprep.co.uk
Twitter: @wilmslowprep
Facebook: @wilmslowprep

Co-ed Day School founded 1909.

Chairman of Board of Trustees: Mr N Rudgard, MA Oxon

Headteacher: **Mrs H Rigby**, BEd Hons, NPQH

Bursar: Miss S J H Davies, BSc Hons, IPFA Hons
Secretary: Mrs S Wragg

Age Range. 3–11.
Number of Pupils. 118 day pupils.
Fees per term (2016–2017). £927–£3,455 (lunches extra).

The School is registered as an Educational Trust. It is purpose built and is situated in the centre of Wilmslow in its own spacious grounds. The facilities include an Assembly Hall, Sports Hall, a Science Room, Computer Room with networked PCs, a specialist Art Room, two well-stocked libraries and a Classroom Block with its own outdoor area for 3–5 year olds. There is a Tennis/Netball Court, a Sports field with its own stand-alone Sports Hall, and ample play areas.

The School aims to provide wide educational opportunities for all its pupils. It has a long-established excellent academic record and caters for a wide variety of entrance examinations to Independent Senior Day and Boarding Schools.

Wilmslow Preparatory School offers a variety of activities which include Music, Art and Drama. Principal sports include gymnastics, netball, football, cricket, hockey, tennis, athletics and swimming.

There are thirteen qualified and experienced teachers on the staff, as well as a highly knowledgeable and expert team of teaching support staff and management.

Charitable status. Wilmslow Preparatory School is a Registered Charity, number 525924. It exists to provide full-time education for pupils aged between 5 and 11, and part-time or full-time education to kindergarten children from the age of 3.

Wimbledon Common Preparatory School

113 Ridgway, Wimbledon, London SW19 4TA
Tel: 020 8946 1001
email: info@wimbledoncommonprep.co.uk
website: www.wimbledoncommonprep.co.uk

Chairman of Governors: Mrs P L Hughes, CBE

Head Teacher: **Mrs Tracey Buck**, BEd Hons

Age Range. Boys 4–7.
Number of Pupils. 168.

Wimbledon Common Preparatory School is a pre-prep school for boys situated in Wimbledon village, south-west London. It was founded in 1919 as a preparatory school for King's College School and other public schools, and moved to its present site in 1957. In 2006 it was bought by King's College School and is now part of their foundation and run by their board of governors.

The school's aims are to provide challenging and exciting teaching; to develop a love of learning; to encourage good study skills; to offer a variety of extra-curricular activities; to create a culture which encourages self-confidence and values tolerance, generosity, respect for others and a strong sense of community; to help boys acquire the social skills which will enable them to make a positive contribution to society; to develop sound parent partnerships, and to provide opportunities for boys to reflect upon their relationships with one another, the wider world and their God.

The school educates boys aged from four to seven years, offering Early Years Foundation Stage (EYFS) provision in its Reception classes.

Fees per term (2016–2017). £4,100.

Charitable status. Wimbledon Common Prep School is owned by King's College School, which is a Registered Charity, number 310024.

Winchester House School

High Street, Brackley, Northants NN13 7AZ
Tel: 01280 702483
Fax: 01280 706400
email: office@winchester-house.org
website: www.winchester-house.org
Twitter: @WHSprepschool

Chairman of Governors: G E S Seligman

Head: **Mrs Emma Goldsmith**, BA

Age Range. 3–13.
Number of Children. 301. Pre-Prep: 75 (52 Boys, 23 Girls); Upper School: 226 (127 Boys, 99 Girls).
Fees per term (2016–2017). Pre-Prep: £2,765–£3,480. Upper School: Day £4,970–£6,130; Boarders £7,760 inclusive.

"The quality of pupils' achievements and learning is excellent." ISI Inspection Report March 2013.

Winchester House School offers outstanding education to boys and girls aged 3–13 with day, occasional and weekly boarding available.

The School was recently nominated for Best Prep School 2017 in Tatler Magazine.

Aim. The aim of Winchester House School is to develop lifelong learners with a spirit of resourcefulness and self-reliance within a warm and purposeful community.

The School. Winchester House School sits in its own 18 acres of sports fields and gardens in the market town of Brackley, midway between Oxford and Northampton and close to the borders of Buckinghamshire, Oxfordshire and Northamptonshire. Lying just 10 minutes from the M40 and 20 minutes from the M1, it is also serviced with good rail links to London. The school operates two minibus services for day children in the local area.

Learning. Winchester House has outstanding facilities, small class sizes and all subjects from Year 5 are taught by specialist teachers. It is non-selective. Over half of the leavers last year gained scholarships to some of the top independent senior schools in the country including an Academic Scholarship to Oundle and Sports Scholarship to Whitgift. There is also a strong Learning Development department.

Opportunity. Winchester House has magnificent facilities that include a newly refurbished ICT suite and Art & Design Studios, three separate science labs and two performance spaces. Sports facilities include a full-size AstroTurf, numerous rugby, hockey and cricket pitches, tennis courts, a heated swimming pool, squash courts and a fully-fitted sports hall with indoor cricket nets. Winchester House School offers riding lessons in the after-school curriculum and hosts an annual inter-school Hunter Trials.

There is an extensive after-school activity programme including skiing, golf, dance and engineering and it offers a broad range of instrumental music teaching, music groups and three choirs. Recent major dramatic productions have included *A Midsummer Night's Dream*.

Confidence. The school understands that building a child's self-esteem is key to happiness and their ability and desire to learn. The unique Learn to Lead programme teaches leadership and team-building and includes annual expeditions for all children from Year 4 including camping in Dorset and Snowdonia.

Ambition. Winchester House encourages children to take pride in everything they do and live by the school motto: "To be their best self".

Community. There is a strong community at Winchester House. Children are encouraged to show respect and kindness (boarding have a 'Good Egg' cup for being just that) and parents are a valued part of school life, involved in school events such as the Christmas Fair and Easter Egg Hunts.

Charitable status. Winchester House School Trust Limited is a Registered Charity, number 309912.

Windlesham House School

Washington, Pulborough, West Sussex RH20 4AY

Tel: 01903 874700
Fax: +44 (0)1903 874702
email: whsadmissions@windlesham.com
website: www.windlesham.com
Twitter: @WindleshamTweet
Facebook: /windlesham

Chairman of Governors: Adam Perry

Head: Richard Foster, BEd Hons

Age Range. 4–13.
Number of Pupils. 194 boarders, 158 day (c. 50/50 boys and girls). Children can board from Year 4.

Fees per term (2016–2017). Prep: Day £5,330–£7,330 (UK & Europe), £6,330–£8,330 (International); Boarding £6,670–£8,590 (UK & Europe), £7,670–£9,590 (International). Pre-Prep: Day £2,980–£3,460.

Windlesham nestles in 65 glorious acres of the South Downs countryside in West Sussex and gives every child the opportunity to reach their potential in whatever sphere of life that may be. Established in 1837 Windlesham was one of the first schools in the country to be established as a preparatory school and in 1967 became the first IAPS co-educational school. Windlesham is one of the few prep schools to have no uniform and our children are not confined to a playground; they make dens, climb trees and camp in the woods and are free to choose what they want to do in their break times.

Today we educate approximately 352 pupils with a broad range of ability. Windlesham traditionally receives outstanding Ofsted and ISI reports which underlines our position as one of the leading prep schools in the world today. We give every child the opportunity to reach his or her full potential in whatever sphere of learning that may be. Although academic excellence is key we also encourage success in sport, music, drama and the arts whilst nurturing a friendly, family-orientated atmosphere with wonderful pastoral care.

With us children have the time and space to be children, away from the pressures of competition and urban hothousing. Windlesham is set in exceptionally beautiful grounds with magnificent buildings and facilities where children are encouraged to try a host of sports and extra-curricular activities after the academic day and at weekends. The children learn about independence, interdependence and cooperation.

At the top end of the school our overriding aim is to ensure that each child achieves the highest grades they can in their Common Entrance or Scholarship exams to some of the best senior schools in the country, as well as ensuring they follow a balanced and enjoyable curriculum. This year saw a record number of scholarships to senior schools and a 100% success rate at Common Entrance with all candidates gaining places at their first choice of school.

When the time comes to leave Windlesham children do so as confident, curious, clever and above all, kind people who are ready to make a difference in their world. Senior Schools often comment on how well prepared Windlesham children are for the next stage. Some even admit they've got a hard act to follow.

Charitable status. Windlesham House School is a Registered Charity, number 307046. It exists to provide education for girls and boys aged 4–13.

Winterfold House
Part of the Bromsgrove School Family

Chaddesley Corbett, Worcestershire DY10 4PW

Tel: 01562 777234
email: info@winterfoldhouse.co.uk
website: www.winterfoldhouse.co.uk
Twitter: @winterfoldhs

Chairman of Governors: Mr Paul West

Interim Head: **Mrs D Toms**, BA Hons QTS, NPQH

Age Range. 0–13 Co-educational.
Number of Pupils. 350 Day Boys and Girls.
Fees per term (2016–2017). Preparatory £3,570–£4,150; Pre-Prep £2,430–£2,680; Kindergarten: £33.20 per day (inc Nursery Education Funding), £49.80 per day (excluding Nursery Education Funding).

Winterfold is centred around a spacious Georgian house set in nearly 40 acres of attractive grounds, surrounded by beautiful and unspoilt Worcestershire countryside. Despite its rural setting, Winterfold is just half an hour from the centre of Birmingham, 10 miles away from Worcester, and a mere 10 minutes from the M5 and M42.

Winterfold is a Roman Catholic co-educational day preparatory school but children of all faiths are warmly welcomed and made to feel valued members of the community. The School's nursery offers day care for babies and toddlers.

The school has an excellent academic record at all levels including National Curriculum Key Stage Tests, Common Entrance and Scholarship. Children are prepared for entrance to both local independent day schools (such as RGS Worcester, King's Worcester, Bromsgrove and the King Edward's schools in Birmingham) and to independent boarding schools of national renown (such as Shrewsbury, Bromsgrove, Cheltenham College, Malvern College, Stonyhurst and Malvern St James). We have a highly regarded Learning Support Unit which provides one to one help for children with specific learning difficulties such as dyslexia. In the last 3 years our children have gained 76 scholarships to senior schools.

Winterfold places a great emphasis upon educating the whole child and aims to produce well rounded and confident boys and girls with high moral standards and good manners. In order to develop self-belief we encourage every child to achieve success in some area and thus the school fields a great number of teams and not just in the main sports of rugby, soccer, cricket, netball, hockey and rounders; but also in the minor sports which include fishing, golf, tennis, swimming, athletics, basketball, fencing and shooting. There are also a large number of clubs and societies and regular visits to theatres and concerts and other places of educational interest which gives fullness and breadth to the educational experience.

In recent years there has been considerable investment into the school which has seen the development of a brand new classroom block which has eight new classrooms, state-of-the-art Science labs and Art and CDT rooms. The school also boasts a splendid sports hall, ICT suite, chapel and a library. The entrance hall and offices have also been updated to offer a welcoming feel to children and parents. Three adventure playgrounds cater for the demands of the full age range of pupils. Music and drama are real strengths of the school and a new Performing Arts Centre, opened in 2011, is at the heart of Music in the school.

Charitable status. Winterfold House School is part of the Bromsgrove School family which is a Registered Charity, number 1098740. It exists solely to provide education for boys and girls.

Witham Hall

Witham-on-the-Hill, Bourne, Lincolnshire PE10 0JJ

Tel:	01778 590222
Fax:	01778 590606
email:	office@withamhall.com
website:	www.withamhall.com

The school was founded in 1959 and was formed into an Educational Trust in 1978.

Chairman of Governors: Mr J W Sharman

Headmaster: Mr A C Welch, BEd

Age Range. 4–13.

Number of Pupils. 249: Prep (age 8–13): 90 Boys (55 boarders, 35 day pupils); 72 Girls (50 boarders, 22 day pupils); Pre-Prep (age 4–8): 86 pupils.

Fees per term (2016–2017). Boarders £6,700, Day pupils £4,990, Pre-Prep £2,965–£3,290.

The school is situated in a superb country house setting in the village of Witham on the Hill, close to the Lincolnshire-Rutland border. Boarding is very popular (weekly and flexi are available from Year 4) and benefits from first-class provision within the original Queen Anne house, at the heart of the school.

There is a teaching staff of 40, and additional visiting teachers for instrumental music. The maximum class size is 17 and pupils benefit from outstanding pastoral care across the school. The majority of pupils join at the Pre-Prep stage, and then continue through to Common Entrance. Pupils progress to their first-choice senior school both locally (Oundle, Oakham, Uppingham and Stamford) and further afield (Eton, Rugby, Repton, Shrewsbury and Stowe). The school has an enviable scholarship record (56 awards from an average cohort of 34 pupils in the last three years) across a range of disciplines, including academic, art, drama, music and sport.

Facilities are outstanding with modern, purpose-built Prep and Pre-Prep teaching areas. Significant developments have taken place in the last three years, including a new ICT suite, two new state-of-the-art Science laboratories, and a new Library and Resource Centre. The Stimson Hall, a superb Concert Hall and Theatre, underpins a strong commitment to both Creative and Performing Arts. Most of the children learn one instrument or more and there are three bands and four choirs. Inclusivity is strong; within sport all Prep pupils represent the school on a regular basis each term. The standard is high, with teams regularly reaching National Finals in Rugby, Hockey, Netball, Cricket and Rounders (IAPS U11 National Champions 2016). A new Sports Complex, including a Dance/Drama Studio and Fitness Suite opens in 2017, complementing an Olympic-size all-weather astroturf, and magnificently maintained grass surfaces, including county-standard cricket facilities and a 9-hole golf course. The school has seen considerable growth in numbers and in almost every year group early registration is recommended.

Charitable status. Witham Hall School Trust is a Registered Charity, number 507070. It exists for the purpose of educating children.

Woodbridge School – The Abbey

Church Street, Woodbridge, Suffolk IP12 1DS

Tel:	01394 382673
Fax:	01394 383880
email:	Abbeyoffice@woodbridgeschool.org.uk
website:	www.woodbridgeschool.org.uk

Chairman of the Governors: R Finbow, MA Oxon

Head of The Abbey Prep and Queen's House Pre-Prep:
Mr John Brett, MA

Deputy Head of The Abbey: Mrs Christina Clubb
Deputy Head of Queen's House: Mrs Sarah Lindsay-Smith

Age Range. Co-educational 4–11.
Number of Pupils. 330 Day pupils.
Fees per term (2016–2017). Pre-Prep £2,788; Prep £4,299.

The Abbey is the Preparatory School for Woodbridge School for which boys and girls are prepared for entry. A small number of pupils go elsewhere. There is a highly qualified teaching staff, with additional visiting music and other specialist teachers. The academic record has been consistently good: scholarships are won regularly both to Woodbridge and to other schools. The teaching is linked to the National Curriculum and emphasis is placed on pupils reaching their full academic potential whilst also benefiting from a broad education. The school enjoys strong links with a number of European schools and exchange visits take place, and pupils learn four European languages. Music is regarded as an important part of school life with a large number of pupils receiving individual music lessons and in Year Four all pupils receive strings tuition as well as their class music lessons. In Games lessons boys play soccer, rugby, hockey and cricket and girls play netball, hockey and rounders. Children also have the opportunity to swim, play tennis and take part in athletics, cross-country, horse riding and sailing. In lunch breaks and after school, pupils are able to participate in a whole range of extra-curricular activities and hobbies.

The School is set in its own beautiful grounds of 30 acres in the middle of the town. As well as a fine Tudor Manor house, it has a well-planned and high-quality classroom and changing room block. Another major development includes a multi-purpose hall and classroom block. Recent developments have included an upgrade of Music, ICT, Art, DT and Science facilities. The grounds are extensive and include playing fields, an all-weather surface games area and a science garden. The Pre-Prep Department is at Queen's House, situated within the Senior School's grounds, a short walk from The Abbey. Here the pupils enjoy spacious accommodation and excellent facilities.

Parents of Abbey pupils are eligible to join the Parents' Association and there is a close contact maintained between parents and school.

Religious affiliation: Church of England (other denominations welcome).

Charitable status. The Seckford Foundation is a Registered Charity, number 1110964. It exists to provide education for boys and girls.

Woodcote House

Windlesham, Surrey GU20 6PF

Tel: 01276 472115
Fax: 01276 472890
email: info@woodcotehouseschool.co.uk
website: www.woodcotehouseschool.co.uk

Headmaster: **David Paterson**

Deputy Headmaster: Andrew Monk

Age Range. 7–13.
Number of Boys. 105 (80 boarders, 25 day).

Fees per term (from April 2016). £7,500 (Boarding), £5,600 (Day). No compulsory extras. Annual Scholarship Day in March.

Location. Originally a Coaching Inn on the old London to Portsmouth Road, Woodcote enjoys a beautiful, rural setting in 30 acres of grounds. The school is easily accessible from London and runs a bus service from the top of the A3. We are only 25 miles from Fulham via the M3 (Junction 3), 25 minutes from Heathrow and 40 minutes from Gatwick.

Pastoral Care. Woodcote House has been owned and run by the Paterson family for over 75 years. With a settled and committed staff, most of whom live on site with their own families, Woodcote provides an exceptionally caring and supportive environment for both Boarders and Day Boys. Our unique, graduated approach to boarding has helped solve the modern boarding conundrum faced by parents torn

between Full and Weekly options. A strong emphasis is placed on manners, consideration and respect for others. The school has its own Chapel in the woods and parents are welcome to Sunday services, as well as to school matches on Wednesdays and Saturdays (after which legendary Match Teas are served), so there is plenty of opportunity to see their boys and talk to staff and fellow parents.

Academic. There are two forms in each year group, with an average of 10 boys in each class, enabling the staff to offer all boys an enormous degree of individual attention. With SEN and EFL teaching also available, academic standards are high and the school is proud of its 100% Common Entrance and excellent Scholarship record. Woodcote boys go on to a wide variety of independent senior schools and Mr Knight takes particular care in assisting parents to choose the right school for their son.

Music and Drama. 80% of boys learn at least one musical instrument, and the young and innovative Director of Music has ensured that it is considered 'cool' to be in the excellent choir. There is an orchestra and a jazz band and the school holds regular concerts so that the boys are comfortable with public performance, both individually and as part of a group. The school produces a Junior and a Senior Play each year, in which all boys are involved one way or another.

Sports. Rugby, football, cricket and hockey are coached to a high standard and there are teams at all levels of age and ability, with a high success rate for a small school. Individual sports include tennis (the school has five courts), swimming, athletics, golf, judo, riding, squash, rifle-shooting and polo.

Hobbies and Free Time. With 'prep' done first thing in the morning, there are numerous opportunities for the boys to pursue hobbies after lessons and games, and each member of staff offers a 'club' during Hobbies Hour on Wednesday afternoons. These activities are also available at weekends, along with the traditional activities of 'hutting' (camp building in the woods), 'cooking' (frying potatoes on camp fires), and overnight camping in the grounds. Boys are also offered the opportunity to be involved in the CCF. Boys are encouraged to read and have a quiet time after lunch each day for this as well as before lights out in the evening.

Ethos. The school motto, "Vive ut Discas et Disce ut Vivas" (Live to Learn and Learn to Live), embodies the school's aim to give all boys a love of learning and to discover and nurture their individual talents in a happy and positive atmosphere.

Woodford Green Preparatory School

Glengall Road, Woodford Green, Essex IG8 0BZ

Tel: 020 8504 5045
email: admin@wgprep.co.uk
website: www.wgprep.co.uk
Twitter: @wgprep

The School is an Educational Charity, controlled by a Board of Governors.

Chairman of Governors: Dr E Hare

Head: **Mr Jonathan Wadge**, BA Hons Dunelm, PGCE, NPQH

Age Range. 3–11.
Number of Pupils. 384 (Boys and Girls).
Fees per term (2016–2017). £3,140.

The school provides an outstanding learning environment in which children achieve their best, feeling valued and secure. The School also has an outstanding record of success in 11+ examinations to Senior Independent and Grammar Schools and demand for places far outstrips availability. Parents are advised to make a very early application to the school.

Means-tested Bursaries, of up to 100% of the full fees, are available for 7+ entry.

Charitable status. Woodford Green Preparatory School is a Registered Charity, number 310930.

Wycliffe Preparatory School

Stonehouse, Gloucestershire GL10 2LD

Tel:	01453 820470
Fax:	01453 825604
email:	prep@wycliffe.co.uk
website:	www.wycliffe.co.uk

Chairman of Trustees: Brigadier [Retd] Robin Bacon

Headmaster: **A Palmer**, MA, BEd

Age Range. 2–13.
Number of Pupils. Nursery: 52 pupils; Preparatory: 51 boarding, 262 day pupils.
Fees per term (2016–2017). Day £2,200–£4,400 (Lunch £240), Boarding £6,030–£8,500.

Wycliffe Preparatory School is a co-educational day, boarding and flexi boarding school from 2 to 13 years. The School is administered by the Governors' Advisory Body and the Trustees of Wycliffe (*see Wycliffe College entry in HMC section*), but is a separate unit with its own Headmaster and full-time staff of 30 teachers (all qualified), house staff and matrons.

A range of Scholarships, both academic and non-academic, are offered by competition annually. There are also bursaries available for children from HM Forces families. The vast majority of our pupils go on to the Senior School, however, pupils are prepared for Common Entrance examinations to all schools.

Wycliffe is committed to fostering individual learning in all areas of the curriculum and pupils benefit from small class sizes with a high teacher to pupil ratio. One of Wycliffe's aims is to cultivate each pupil's unique talents and to bring out the best in its pupils by creating a supportive learning environment which promotes individual achievements in all fields. Specialist teachers ensure outstanding teaching delivery across the curriculum and a wide variety of extracurricular activities enables the school to offer a fully-rounded education designed to develop confidence and self-esteem.

There is also a dedicated CReSTeD registered SEN Department which supports children who have weaknesses in some areas of the curriculum. The school not only promotes success in the classroom, but prides itself on enabling every child to do well, whether on the sports field, in one of the many drama or musical productions or by taking part in the annual Art exhibition, hosted at the Senior School.

Academic excellence is something all pupils are encouraged to attain. Challenge for our Gifted & Talented children is something that we, as a school, provide on a regular basis, through ensuring our more able children are sufficiently stretched in the areas where they have been identified as gifted or talented. In addition to this, we offer further enrichment through the delivery of a number of specific Gifted & Talented events that provide our children with some exciting and unique learning opportunities. We have become a member of the National Association for Gifted Children (NAGC) and have recently gained the Gold Star Award.

The Preparatory School is continuing its programme to improve facilities with a state-of-the-art Years 7 and 8 learning centre opened in September 2014. This university-style facility provides eight spacious classrooms, with high-tech facilities including touchscreen smart boards, latest computer technology, common room, staff offices and two new tennis courts. A new Reception, Years 1 and 2 teaching block which is situated on the Prep campus with its own adventure playground and the extension of the boys' and girls' boarding houses by a further 16 beds. The school also boasts an all-weather pitch, refurbished Years 3 and 4 classrooms, swimming pool, art studio and craft workshop, extensive playing fields, tennis courts, sports hall, studio theatre and music school, two science laboratories, three computer rooms, a covered playground and cafeteria-style dining room. The Preparatory School uses the Chapel, Medical Centre and state-of-the-art Sports Centre at the Senior School.

The boarding houses are in the care of House staff and there are members of staff with particular responsibility for the welfare of day pupils. Vegetarian and other dietary specialities can be catered for.

As well as the usual range of sport, drama and music, there are clubs, activities and opportunities for outdoor pursuits. A number of educational trips are also arranged, including a Year 5 residential stay at the Jorvik Viking Centre, team building activity in Wales and a trip to Paris, organised by the languages department.

Charitable status. Wycliffe College Incorporated is a Registered Charity, number 311714. It is a co-educational boarding and day school promoting a balanced education for children between the ages of 2 and 18.

Yarlet School

Yarlet, Nr Stafford ST18 9SU

Tel:	01785 286568
email:	info@yarletschool.org
website:	www.yarletschool.org

Chairman of the Governors: Dr A Primrose

Headmaster: **Mr Ian Raybould**, BEd Hons, ALCM, NPQH

Age Range. Co-educational 2–13.
Number of Pupils. 151 pupils: 74 Girls and Boys in the Preparatory School (aged 7 to 13) and 77 Girls and Boys in the Nursery and Pre-Preparatory School (aged 2 to 7).
Fees per term (2016–2017). £2,375–£3,980. Flexi boarding available (Wednesday and Thursday nights) at £25 per night.

Established in 1873, Yarlet stands in 33 acres of grounds in unspoilt open countryside 3 miles north of Stafford. The school offers small classes, enthusiastic, qualified teachers, excellent facilities and a warm, friendly environment conducive to learning. All teachers keep fully abreast of the National Curriculum guidelines to Key Stage 3 and beyond.

Pupils have access to a wide range of facilities which include a new, state-of-the-art Science Laboratory, an Information Technology Centre, a CDT Centre, a purpose-built Art Studio, an indoor Sports Hall and a Music and Drama Theatre; and extensive outdoor facilities which include a nature walk, including a large wildlife pool, a heated swimming pool, four playing fields (for football, rugby, hockey, cricket and athletics), three tennis courts, a netball court, an all-weather Astroturf pitch (for football, hockey and netball) and a cross-country running course. These facilities support an extensive sports curriculum, which features a daily games lesson. The Early Years and Key Stage 1 playground areas were redeveloped in June 2015.

Music and Drama complete the picture of a Yarlet education, with termly performances from the Yarlet Academy of Music and the Academy of Performing Arts. The arts are brought to life at Yarlet, inspiring self-belief and creative confidence in all our pupils. Whatever their talent, Yarlet pupils have the chance to shine. Club and extra-curricular activities are a further feature of Yarlet and include art (painting, sculpture and pottery), model-making, music, drama, French culture, chess, photography and fishing.

Yarlet has high expectations of all its children. Children are prepared for entry to a wide variety of senior schools and their achievements in both Key Stage tests and Common Entrance examinations are a source of great pride, as too is the fact that many children leave with a Scholarship award from their Senior School.

Charitable status. Yarlet is a Registered Charity, number 528618. It exists to provide education for boys and girls from 2 to 13.

Yarm Preparatory School

Grammar School Lane, Yarm, Stockton-on-Tees TS15 9ES

Tel:	01642 781447
Fax:	01642 787425
email:	prepschool@yarmschool.org
website:	www.yarmschool.org

Chairman of Governors: A P Thomson, LLB, FCCA, FIDM

Head: **W Sawyer**, BA Hons, PGCE

Age Range. 3–11.
Number of Pupils. 330 Boys and Girls.
Fees per term (2016–2017). Preparatory School £3,090–£3,418; Pre-Prep and Nursery £2,427–£2,469; Pre-Prep and Nursery (with Nursery Grant): £1,663. Lunches: £196.

Yarm Preparatory School is a co-educational day school which educates children from 3–11 years of age (3–7 within the Nursery and Pre-Prep).

Ethos. The Preparatory School is well known as a friendly and stimulating environment that encourages children to flourish educationally whilst also developing valuable social abilities and leadership skills. Through the broad variety of extra-curricular activities, children come to excel in sport and music as well as a wide range of other pastimes.

Organisation. Pastoral care is based on both a year group and a House system. Every pupil belongs to one of four Houses. Houses exist to promote competitions, sporting events, charity and fundraising etc. Pupils have opportunities to represent their form as Form Captains, who also serve on the School Council.

Curriculum. The Preparatory School curriculum is based upon the National Curriculum, although it offers greater breadth and depth in many subject areas. In addition to the core curriculum of English, mathematics and science (in a new laboratory), full weight is given to both history and geography, whilst subjects such as design technology, ICT, art, music, religious education, PSHE, PE and games are fully catered for. Children are also taught French from age 3. Whilst form teachers deliver much of the core curriculum, subject specialist teachers are employed to cover many areas.

Games and Activities. The Preparatory School hosts a whole range of sports. However, rugby and hockey are the school's main winter games. Football and netball are played during the Spring Term, followed by cricket, athletics and rounders in the summer. In addition, cross country is also pursued at inter-school level throughout the year. There are many school activities including music, dance, drama, orienteering, chess, swimming, badminton, gardening, modelling, crafts, pottery, ICT and quizzes which are timetabled to take place during two lessons, at lunchtimes and after school each week. These activities change at least termly.

Music. The Preparatory School boasts many musical groups, choirs, choristers and a variety of traditional and modern ensembles with well over half of the school learning an instrument.

Educational Visits. A varied programme of educational day visits is undertaken by all year groups to enrich the curriculum, using the locality as a resource. From age 7, pupils have the opportunity to participate in residential trips, including visits to Whitby, York, Robinwood, Lake District and Saint-Omer, France.

Admission. Entry to the Preparatory School is by assessment which may be carried out at any time of the year if places are available. Pupils are prepared for entry to the Senior School, sitting transfer papers in January before the September in which they transfer. The results of transfer papers are considered in conjunction with ongoing assessment information made available by teachers in the Preparatory School.

Open Days. The Nursery/Pre-Prep and Preparatory School hold Open Mornings each year, normally in September and January with an Open Week in May. Prospective parents are encouraged to attend at least one Open Morning as this gives excellent opportunity to look around the school at leisure, view the new facilities, see our development plans and chat with staff. Visits are, however, welcome at any time.

Religion. The school is an interdenominational community but follows Christian traditions and ethos.

Charitable status. Yarm School is a Registered Charity, number 1093434. It exists to provide education for boys and girls from 3–18.

Yateley Manor Preparatory School

51 Reading Road, Yateley, Hampshire GU46 7UQ

Tel:	01252 405500
Fax:	01252 405504
email:	office@yateleymanor.com
website:	www.yateleymanor.com

The School is an Educational Trust controlled by a Board of Governors.

Chairman of Governors: Stephen Gorys

Headmaster: **Robert Upton**, BSc Hons, PGCE, MA Ed, NPQH

Age Range. 3–13.
Number of Pupils. Pre-Prep and Nursery: 60 Girls, 80 Boys; Prep: 100 Girls, 160 Boys.
Fees per term (2016–2017). £2,000–£4,795. Fees are fully inclusive of all normal activities, extended supervision from 8.00 am until 6.30 pm, meals, educational visits and residential field trips for Years 5, 6, 7 and 8.

Yateley Manor has a long and successful history of educating girls and boys from the age of 3 to 13.

The development of the Prep School Baccalaureate (PSB), with its focus on rigorous academic standards, coupled with a broad and balanced curriculum, delivers an education for the twenty-first century. The PSB focuses on the vital skills of independence, collaboration and leadership through pupils' thinking & learning, communication and review & improvement and its ethos is embedded throughout the school.

The School's emphasis on educating the whole child is supported by a broad enrichment programme. Activities include chess, dance, horse riding, drama and water sports and the school is always keen to find new opportunities for children to find their talents and strengths.

Nurtured in a warm, friendly and safe environment with excellent facilities and limited class sizes, children are given new experiences to explore, building confidence and stimulating a desire to learn.

Innovative, enthusiastic and committed teachers embrace the different learning styles of children and incorporate varied approaches into lessons. The result is that children may spend a day being Vikings, visiting a Hindu Temple, creating maths games to bolster understanding of probability or fractions or cooking during science to reinforce the difference between physical and chemical changes.

There is a strong culture of continuing professional development with staff regularly attending external courses, as well as weekly after-school workshops and sharing best practice. This ensures the School's innovative and committed staff are constantly challenging their own practice.

A new building housing a state-of-the-art Music School, spacious and light rooms for Art and DT and a new Modern Foreign Languages Department opened in September 2015. The School's superb teaching facilities are complemented by excellent sports amenities including a heated indoor swimming pool, a large sports hall with indoor cricket nets and provision for football, netball and basketball, a gymnasium and several pitches.

The newly developed Woodland Learning Area is an inspirational educational environment which gives younger children the freedom to explore nature in a hands-on and child-led approach. This helps build confidence, independence and self-esteem as well as giving children new life skills.

There is an informal assessment for entry to the school and the most common entrance points are at 3 into the Nursery, at 4 into Reception, and at 7 into the main school. Children are welcome to join at all other ages, at any time during the year, and many do. Means-tested bursaries are available.

A network of school coaches serves the surrounding areas including Camberley, Church Crookham, Farnborough, Fleet, Frimley, Hartley Wintney, Hook and Odiham.

Charitable status. Yateley Manor is a Registered Charity, number 307374. It is dedicated to providing the highest quality education for children of the local community.

Fees per term (2016–2017). Pre-Prep £3,120–£3,660, Middle and Upper Schools £4,160; including lunch. Nursery: £272 per half-day session (minimum 3 sessions per week).

York House School is a well-established, innovative and forward-looking school located in a Queen Anne country house standing in 47 acres of the Hertfordshire countryside. The Headmaster is assisted by a fully-qualified and caring staff. Our extended day arrangements enable pupils to attend early-morning clubs and after-school clubs between 7.45 am and 6.00 pm.

The school's aim is to encourage children to achieve the highest academic results in a happy atmosphere while promoting self-discipline and caring for others.

The school has excellent facilities which include a multi-purpose hall, library, computer suite, a science laboratory, art room and music centre.

Sporting facilities are excellent with new all-weather multi-purpose pitches for football, hockey and netball, 15 acres of playing fields for cricket, rugby, soccer, and athletics as well as a 25-metre indoor heated swimming pool.

Our smallholding includes goats, chickens, pigs and ponies that provide the children with an invaluable opportunity to experience nature first hand. This approach to Outdoor Learning is further enhanced by our 47 acres of countryside, with outdoor classrooms, use of local Woodland Trust forest, activity equipment and orienteering trails, nature pond and fruit orchard.

Pupils are prepared for Common Entrance and Independent School Scholarship. There is a Pre-Preparatory Department for children from age 4 to 7 and a Nursery for children from rising 3.

Charitable status. York House School is a Registered Charity, number 311076. It exists to provide high-quality education to boys and girls.

York House School

Sarratt Road, Croxley Green, Rickmansworth, Herts WD3 4LW

Tel:	01923 772395
email:	yhsoffice@york-house.com
website:	www.york-house.com
Twitter:	@SchoolYorkHouse
	@YHheadmaster

Founded in 1910, York House School is a non-profit making Educational Trust with a Board of Governors.

Chairman of the Governors: Mrs L Keating

Headmaster: **Mr Jon Gray**, BA Ed Hons, PGCE

Age Range. Boys 3–13, Girls 3–11.
Number of Children. All are Day pupils: 172 Prep, 131 Pre-Prep, 26 Nursery.

Entrance Scholarships

Academic Scholarships

Barrow Hills School (p. 859)

Bede's Preparatory School (p. 862)

Broughton Manor Preparatory School (p. 880)

Clayesmore Preparatory School (p. 892)

Clifton College Preparatory School (p. 893)

Cranmore School (p. 900)

Dragon School (p. 909)

Fettes College Preparatory School (p. 923)

Kingswood House School (p. 967)

Millfield Prep School (p. 984)

Milton Keynes Preparatory School (p. 985)

Rockport School (p. 1022)

St Edmund's Junior School (p. 1036)

All-Rounder Scholarships

Barrow Hills School (p. 859)

Broughton Manor Preparatory School (p. 880)

Clayesmore Preparatory School (p. 892)

Fettes College Preparatory School (p. 923)

Millfield Prep School (p. 984)

Milton Keynes Preparatory School (p. 985)

St Edmund's Junior School (p. 1036)

Art Scholarships

Barrow Hills School (p. 859)

Bede's Preparatory School (p. 862)

Clayesmore Preparatory School (p. 892)

Millfield Prep School (p. 984)

Dance Scholarships

Bede's Preparatory School (p. 862)

Drama Scholarships

Barrow Hills School (p. 859)

Bede's Preparatory School (p. 862)

St Edmund's Junior School (p. 1036)

Music Scholarships

Barrow Hills School (p. 859)

Bede's Preparatory School (p. 862)

Clayesmore Preparatory School (p. 892)

Clifton College Preparatory School (p. 893)

Cranmore School (p. 900)

Fettes College Preparatory School (p. 923)

Millfield Prep School (p. 984)

St Edmund's Junior School (p. 1036)

Sport Scholarships

Barrow Hills School (p. 859)

Bede's Preparatory School (p. 862)

Broughton Manor Preparatory School (p. 880)

Clayesmore Preparatory School (p. 892)

Clifton College Preparatory School (p. 893)

Cranmore School (p. 900)

Millfield Prep School (p. 984)

Milton Keynes Preparatory School (p. 985)

St Edmund's Junior School (p. 1036)

Other Scholarships

Chess

Millfield Prep School (p. 984)

Bursaries

Bede's Preparatory School (p. 862)

Cameron House (p. 884)

Clifton College Preparatory School (p. 893)

Dragon School (p. 909)

The Granville School (p. 932)

Milton Keynes Preparatory School (p. 985)

Prince's Mead School (p. 1013)

Rockport School (p. 1022)

St Edmund's Junior School (p. 1036)

St Martin's Ampleforth (p. 1048)

Independent Association of Prep Schools
Overseas Members

ALPHABETICAL LIST OF SCHOOLS

GEOGRAPHICAL LIST OF SCHOOLS

Individual School Entries
Overseas Members

Aiglon College Junior School

Avenue Centrale 61, Chesières-Villars 1885, Switzerland

Tel:	00 41 24 496 6141
Fax:	00 41 24 496 6142
email:	admissions@aiglon.ch
website:	www.aiglon.ch
Facebook:	/aiglon

Chairman of Governors: Tony Jhangiani-Jashanmal

Head: **Stuart Hamilton**

Age Range. 9–13.

Number of Pupils. Boys 35, Girls 34, Boarders 53, Day Children 16.

Fees per annum (2016–2017). Day: CHF 32,850–47,100; Full Boarding: CHF 66,450–73,650.

Setting. The Aiglon College Junior School provides a warm family atmosphere in the beauty and peace of the Swiss Alps for children from all over the world – with around 25 different nationalities. The intimate and caring community spirit encourages self-discipline, thought for others and joy in learning. Aiglon College Junior School's buildings and life are kept quite separate from those of the Senior School. However, it shares part of the campus of Aiglon College, and follows the principles of the founder, John Corlette. Ultimately we aim at ensuring a smooth and well-prepared transition into the Senior School.

Pastoral Care. Having a place of their own allows us to concentrate on issues most significant to this age group, such as creating and developing good habits in a positive and encouraging environment. Our main goal is to create a caring environment and, through carefully chosen experiences, build up the whole person and develop the many talents that all our pupils possess. We also aim at making the transition from Junior to Senior School a comfortable one. Learning to live and grow up with peers, listening to each other, and acquiring a taste for discovery and independence within a supportive environment; all these skills contribute, using moral and spiritual beliefs in a constructive way, to the foundation of a healthy attitude towards the challenges of teenage life. Moral principles are developed within school "meditations" (morning assemblies) especially and spiritual life is encouraged in chapel services.

Curriculum. The school also offers an EAL programme for all non-English speakers aged 9–13. The Junior School curriculum includes English, Maths, French, Science, Geography, History, Art, Music, Physical Education, Drama, Religious Studies and Computer Studies. Strong pastoral care and individual attention allows for a curriculum which has its roots in the British National Curriculum but caters for the international diversity of our recruitment. The Learning Support department aids children with special learning needs and tests all children on a yearly basis.

Sports and expeditions. Sports and "expeditions" form an essential component of a well-rounded approach to the development of our children's personalities and characters. There is a range of sports teams to choose from and we encourage full participation. "Expeditions" take place at weekends and activities include walking, map reading and orienteering, cycling, canoeing, gorge walking and rock climbing. Children participate in camping, hiking or skiing "expeditions" under expert and qualified supervision. Apart from learning to enjoy and understand nature, being outdoors together, come rain or shine, reinforces children's team spirit and respect for each other and their environment as they learn to live a little closer to nature!

Extracurricular activities. There is a wide variety of extracurricular activities called CAS activities, which encompass sports, art and crafts, music clubs, choir and bands, as well as quieter pastimes.

Further information. Further information may be obtained from the Head of Junior School or the Director of Admissions & Advancement.

Aiglon College is a non-profit making organisation, accredited by the Council of International Schools (CIS).

The Banda School

PO Box 24722, Nairobi 00502, Kenya

Tel:	00 254 20 8891220 / 254 20 5131100
	Mobiles: 00 254 726–439909 / 709–951000
email:	office@bandaschool.com
website:	www.bandaschool.com

Chairman of Governors: Mr D G M Hutchison

Headmistress: **Mrs A Francombe**, BEd Hons

Age Range. 2–13.

Number of Children. 400 (Day).

Fees per term (2016–2017). Tuition: Kshs 550,000 (Years 3–8 including lunches). Sliding fee scale Year 2 and below.

The School was founded in 1966 by Mr and Mrs J A L Chitty. It is 9 miles from Nairobi and stands in its own grounds of 30 acres adjacent to the Nairobi Game Park. Boys and girls are admitted in equal numbers and are prepared for Independent Senior School Scholarship and Common Entrance Examinations to leading secondary schools in the UK, Kenya and South Africa. The Staff consists of 48 teachers with the vast majority being UK trained graduates. The teacher-pupil ratio is about 1:10.

Facilities include a modern Weekly Boarding House, Pegasus Early Years building, Science laboratories, ICT rooms, Art room, Music rooms, Hall with well-equipped stage, two Libraries, Lower School Art Room and a Dance Studio, specialist rooms for Mathematics, French, History and Geography, Design Technology, audio-visual room, Astroturf, two Squash courts and a six-lane 25-metre Swimming Pool with three diving boards.

Sports include Rugby, Football, Hockey, Cricket, Tennis, Swimming, Netball, Rounders, Athletics, Sailing, Squash and Cross-Country. A wide range of other activities including Instrumental lessons, Dancing and LAMDA are also available. Music, Art and Drama are an important part in the life of the school.

The British International School, Cairo
The Junior School

Km 38, Alexandria Road, Beverly Hills, Cairo, Egypt

Tel: 00 202 3827 0444
Fax: 00 202 3857 1720
email: info@bisc.edu.eg
website: www.bisc.edu.eg

Chairman of Governors: Mr Yasser Hashem

Head of Junior School: **Mr Justin Durling**

Deputy Head of Junior School: Deborah Jones

Age Range. 3–11 Co-educational.
Number of Pupils. 620.
Fees per term (2016–2017). £2,851–£3,348.

The Junior School of The British International School, Cairo (BISC) is situated alongside its Senior School within a new purpose-built 65,000 square metre campus on the western outskirts of Cairo, having relocated from the School's former city centre position in the summer of 2008. BISC, founded in 1976, is the oldest established of Cairo's British international schools and is academically selective with a strong tradition of excellent academic results. The Junior School has its own dedicated and spacious classroom buildings within the whole school campus, including a large library and multimedia learning centre, science laboratory, art and design technology centres and multi-purpose hall. All classrooms are equipped with interactive 'smart' boards and computer facilities. The Junior School also shares with the Senior School a large sports hall, a gym, a 50-metre and learner swimming pools, several playing fields, an athletics track, outdoor tennis and basketball courts, and a 670-seat theatre.

The British National Curriculum is taught throughout the School and all staff are UK qualified and experienced teachers. Arabic and French are taught by qualified native speakers. Best UK educational practice is also maintained through the School's continuing professional development programme for all staff.

The school's aims are included in its mission statement: to be a first-class school preparing pupils who will eventually progress to positions of leadership in life; to provide a stimulating British education with an appreciation and understanding of Egyptian culture and Arabic; to ensure equal opportunities for pupils to develop their full intellectual, aesthetic, emotional, physical and moral potential; and to provide a broadly based education within a supportive pastoral environment, with the best possible resources and facilities. BISC seeks to foster mutual respect and tolerance and to teach essential human values such as honesty, loyalty, compassion and charity. The positive values promoted at BISC connect to those of families, the local community and the wider world, and embrace a commitment to international cooperation and understanding.

The School has over 40 nationalities represented amongst its pupil body and as such there is no affiliation to any one particular religious system. The School places a strong emphasis on moral education, both within the Personal, Social and Citizenship curriculum programme and in terms of all aspects of the life of the School. Values that characterise and permeate BISC also include a commitment to respect for others' beliefs. Regular assemblies involve participation of all pupils. The pupils' voice and developing sense of responsibility is also expressed within regular meetings of the Pupil Council and other pupil positions such as within the School's House Captaincy system.

The School's pursuit of excellence in education is also expressed in the provision of a wide programme of sporting, cultural, and artistic pursuits for all pupils, both within and as additional to the main curriculum. Concerts, choral productions and drama performances feature in every term and the Junior School has its own dedicated specialist staff for music, drama, PE and modern foreign languages, in addition to its teams of Key Stage class teachers. Junior School pupils throughout Foundation and Key Stages One and Two also enjoy regular opportunities for off-site educational visits. As pupils progress into KS2 these include Humanities trips to Luxor and El Alamein, and overseas trips in Mathematics and Sports competitions. Inter-school sporting and cultural events also take place with other schools in Cairo and Alexandria.

Learning, teaching and pastoral care structures in the Junior School are child-centred. Great importance is attached to the close monitoring of all pupils' academic progress and pastoral well being, and their progress as successful, confident and responsible learners. Regular pupil reports, parent conferences, presentation evenings and opportunities for both formal and informal meetings are all part of the natural rhythm of BISC. There is also an active PTA through which parents encourage and run many family social events, and also help to promote the wider community links of the School. Open Days for prospective parents to view the School are also held each term.

In addition to IAPS membership, BISC is also in membership of COBIS, BSME, and AGBIS. The School's most recent Inspection was undertaken by the Independent Schools Inspectorate (ISI) in 2014, and this Report is viewable on the ISI and BISC Websites.

BISC is constituted as a not-for-profit organisation of the British International Schools Society, whose elected Board members are all current parents of the School.

The British International School of New York

20 Waterside Plaza, East 23rd Street, Manhattan, New York City 10010, USA

Tel: 00 1 212 481 2700
Fax: 00 1 646 607 5970
email: info@bis-ny.org
website: www.bis-ny.org

Board of Directors contact: Abigail Snell

Headmaster: **Jason J Morrow**, MA Oxon, MA Wake Forest, North Carolina

Age Range. 3–14 Co-educational.
Number of Pupils. 270.
Fees per annum (2016–2017). $43,900.

The British International School is proud to offer a challenging curriculum which combines the inquiry-based, child-centred philosophy of the International Baccalaureate Programme with the rigour and academic quality of the English National Curriculum. As quoted in our most recent Independent Schools Inspectorate report, "The school is highly successful in meeting its ambitious aims to provide an education for pupils to inspire and stimulate a love of learning, within an international community. Standards of achievement are excellent, and pupils have outstanding speaking, listening and literacy skills for their age."

From Nursery through to Year 9, we offer a happy and nurturing environment, where students can develop a genuine love for learning and academic success. BIS-NY cultivates individual enrichment in music, the fine arts, world languages, drama and athletics. Taught by a highly-qualified faculty, content is reinforced by superior technology and resources at a stunning waterside facility on the East River in Manhattan.

BIS-NY's curriculum has been chosen for its rigorous standards of excellence and its adaptability to school systems both here in NYC and across the globe. The education provided by The British International School of New York is designed to be highly portable, preparing children for their next stage of schooling. BIS-NY graduates have enjoyed great success at some of the leading independent schools in Manhattan, the United Kingdom and other parts of the world where they continue to foster the attitudes and traits that promote international mindedness, leadership, and an application of learning that is purposeful, significant, relevant and challenging.

Application requirements for admission can be found on our website.

The British School – Al Khubairat

PO Box 4001, Abu Dhabi, United Arab Emirates

Tel:	00 971 2 446 2280
Fax:	00 971 2 446 1915
email:	registrar@britishschool.sch.ae
website:	www.britishschool.sch.ae

A member of HMC, IAPS, COBIS, BSME and BSO Inspected.

Chair of Governors: Debby Burton Shaw

Headmaster: Mark Leppard, MBE

Head of Primary School: Elaine Rawlings
Head of Secondary School: Teresa Woulfe

Age Range. 3–18.
Number of Pupils. 927 Boys, 927 Girls (all day).
Fees per term (2016–2017). Nursery: AED13,834; Reception–Year 6: AED15,467; Years 7–13: AED20,767.

Established on land generously donated by the then Ruler of Abu Dhabi, His Highness Sheikh Zayed bin Sultan Al Nahyan and sponsored since 1980 by His Highness Sheikh Khalifa Bin Zayed Al Nahyan, the President of the UAE, The British School Al Khubairat has a long tradition of success. Moving towards its 50th anniversary in 2017, it is regarded as a leading international school both within the Middle East and internationally. The school's vision is: 'To be a leading provider of British education and to be the school of choice in Abu Dhabi'.

In order to fulfil this ambitious goal, the school provides an outstanding holistic education for every one of its students. The academic record places the school comfortably alongside the top 100 schools in the UK, while its extracurricular programme offers students the opportunity to perform at the highest level in music, drama and sport. Additional to these areas, there are over 100 clubs available to students and available in wide ranging fields.

All of these exciting elements of The British School Al Khubairat are superbly housed in its purpose-built facility completed in 2013, which includes:

• 25m swimming pool
• Learner pool
• Grass pitch
• Two synthetic-turf pitches
• Auditorium
• Gym
• Multimedia suites equipped with Apple Macs
• Outstanding and creative classrooms

As a community school, The British School Al Khubairat believes in providing an individual education for every student. Its wide range of subject choices, excellent learning support provision and its outstanding staff ensures a high quality and memorable educational experience.

The school is run on a non-for-profit basis and has very close ties with the British Embassy. The Board of Governors are made up of appointments by the British Ambassador and parent elected representatives. The school undergoes regular local and British inspections.

The British School of Brussels – Primary School

Pater Dupierreuxlaan 1, 3080 Tervuren, Belgium

Tel:	+32 2 766 04 30
Fax:	+32 2 767 80 70
email:	admissions@britishschool.be
website:	www.britishschool.be
Twitter:	@BSB_Brussels
Facebook:	@britishschoolbrussels
LinkedIn:	/the-british-school-of-brussels

Patron:
Her Excellency the British Ambassador to the King of the Belgians

Chairman of the Board: Mr Ian Backhouse

Principal: Ms Melanie Warnes

***Vice Principal & Head of Primary School*: Ms Pauline Markey**

Age Range. 1–11 Co-educational.
Number of Pupils. 529 as at June 2016.
Fees per annum (2016–2017). €25,650 (Reception) to €27,000 (Years 3–6)

Introduction. The development of the whole child is at the heart of BSB's primary education programme. Learning in the Primary School is about developing personal, emotional and social skills as well as being an intellectual and academic process. We aim to help children find their voice – their own unique, personal significance. We encourage them to think about what their contribution will be in the world – how they will try to make a difference as responsible and engaged members of the school community as well as citizens of the world.

BSB has high expectations for all its learners. We pride ourselves on knowing each child as an individual in order to help them make progress. Learning opportunities are planned so that all students are challenged appropriately. Above all, we are interested in the learning process – learning how to learn and how to apply skills and knowledge across an ever-increasing spectrum of experience. From the earliest age we ensure that children have an enjoyable experience of school and are motivated to learn and improve. This positive attitude is supported by a team of highly professional teachers who are themselves engaged in lifelong learning and model effective habits of mind.

Curriculum. The curriculum is based on that of the National Curriculum for England adapted to reflect the needs of an increasingly international and multi-cultural student body and to capitalise upon the opportunities of being in Belgium at the heart of Europe. For example, our curriculum includes integrated learning themes (ILTs) unique to BSB. We aim to build on the children's background knowledge and experience to equip them with the skills, strategies and a love of learning that will inspire them to succeed whatever the next step on their educational journey. The Primary Senior Leadership Team works to ensure coherence, consistency, continuity and progression across the whole primary age range.

Facilities. The Primary School enjoys excellent resources and provides a stimulating and varied environment. The children are spread geographically across the school campus, housed in three buildings.

We seek not only to provide an environment which promotes achievement in learning, but also one of warmth, security and care. The school was purpose-built and laid out to be both light and spacious. Our visitors frequently comment not only on the beautiful site and these excellent facilities but also on the warm and happy atmosphere which infuses the school. This complements the purposeful working environment and enables our children's learning development to flourish.

Children have access to well-resourced classrooms (including computers in every classroom and interactive boards in teaching rooms), dedicated computer suites, a fully equipped gymnasium, differentiated playgrounds, the main 240-seat school theatre for drama productions, a spacious hall, the school playing field, an art, design and technology room, well-stocked libraries and smaller classrooms for additional educational needs (AEN). Rooms are also provided for English as an additional language (EAL). Both AEN/EAL provisions are integrated under the school's Inclusion Leader. We provide a French/English bilingual programme for children aged 4–14 years in addition to our English medium teaching.

Our Early Childhood Centre for children aged 1–3 provides a caring and stimulating pre-school environment with amazing facilities both indoor and outdoor.

(*See also British School of Brussels entry in HMC section.*)

The British School of Paris – Junior School

2 rue Hans List, 78290 Croissy sur Seine, France

Tel:	00 33 1 30 15 88 30
Fax:	00 33 1 73 79 15 71
email:	junior@britishschool.fr
website:	www.britishschool.fr
Twitter:	@BritishSchParis
Facebook:	@BritishSchParis

Chairman of Governors: Mr P Kett

Headmaster: Mr N Hammond

Head of the Junior School: Ms K Tuckwell

Age Range. 3–11 Co-educational.
Number of Pupils. 400.
Fees per annum (2016–2017). €17,381–€23,569.

The Junior School caters for pupils aged 3–11 and is located very close to the Senior School along the leafy banks of the river Seine. This brand new facility opened in September 2010; there are 35 classrooms accommodating up to 480 pupils, as well as 4 bespoke classrooms and 2 activity areas that are dedicated to our foundation stage/nursery section. The school was specifically designed to meet the educational and social welfare needs of junior school pupils. It is bristling with new technology and up-to-the-minute IT facilities to assist the pupils' learning and development. The British School of Paris's philosophy of education permeates throughout the Junior School and has at its core the goal of unlocking the potential of all students, by identifying strengths and supporting areas of development, while having fun and enjoying happy and strong social relationships.

Studies are based on the British National Curriculum with emphasis on English, Maths and Science, and of course, the French language. Various sports, music, drama and many other extracurricular activities are also provided.

For further details and applications, please contact the Registrar, email: registrar@britishschool.fr.

Brookhouse Preparatory School

PO Box 24987, Langata, Nairobi 00502, Kenya

Tel:	00 254 20 2430 260–3
Fax:	00 254 20 2430 269
email:	info@brookhouse.ac.ke
website:	www.brookhouse.ac.ke

Preparatory School Headteacher: Ms Michelle Forsyth, BA, PGCE

Age Range. 6 months–13 years Co-educational.
Number of Pupils. 360 boys and girls, including 30 boarders.
Fees per term (2016–2017). Tuition: Kshs 240,000–535,000 (includes lunch, but excludes transport). Transport to and from school: Kshs 50,000. Boarding: Kshs 385,000 in addition to Tuition Fees.

Established in 1981 in a leafy suburb of Nairobi about 10 minutes from the city centre, Brookhouse Preparatory School is an independent co-educational day and boarding school accredited by the Council of International Schools. Brookhouse benefits from a purpose-built "castle-style" building design that ensures a physical environment for children that is truly inspirational. The school delivers an adapted form of the British National Curriculum, catering mainly for the professional, business and diplomatic communities of the East African region. Brookhouse balances traditional values with an innovative approach to the curriculum. Our philosophy as a Round Square global member school focuses on respect for each child as an individual and the development of leadership through service to others. The school features small classes, and a particular focus on the core areas of numeracy, literacy and computer literacy. The average class size is 18.

With more than 40 nationalities represented on the student roll, the school prides itself on fostering tolerance and understanding, and promotes a diverse programme of extracurricular activities, sports and clubs to ensure the development of the whole child. Teachers are recruited from both UK and East Africa and average nearly fifteen years of classroom experience. They are carefully selected for their ability to provide both a challenging academic environment and a caring pastoral network of support for each child.

Situated on a thirteen-acre campus adjacent to Nairobi National Park, the school has on-site co-educational boarding accommodation. Academic facilities include a 'space station' computer laboratory, purpose-built science and home science laboratories, a three-storey library, Fine Art and Music studios, and a world-class performance theatre where regular drama and musical productions are staged. All classrooms are computer networked, and students have supervised email and internet access. A Learning Support Unit caters for students with Special Educational Needs (SEN) and for students who have English as an Additional Language (EAL) backgrounds, as well as providing an Academic Extension Programme (AEP) for highly able pupils.

Sporting facilities include a gym and aerobics studio, squash courts, swimming pool, indoor sports centre for tennis and basketball and irrigated playing fields to ensure a year round quality playing surface. A varied programme of team and individual sports are available.

The English School

Kuwait

PO Box 379, 13004 Safat, Kuwait

Tel:	00 965 22271385
Fax:	00 965 22271389
email:	registrar@tes.edu.kw
website:	www.tes.edu.kw

Sponsor: Mr Emad Mohamed Al-Bahar

Chair of the Governing Committee: Brigadier Piers Hankinson

Headmaster: **Kieron Peacock**

Age Range. 2–13.
Number of Pupils. 620.
Fees per annum (2016–2017). Nursery (Pre-KG and KG) KD1,1915; Pre-Preparatory (Rec, Year 1 and Year 2) KD2,800; Preparatory (Years 3–8) KD3,340.

The English School, founded in 1953 under the auspices of the British Embassy, is the longest established school in Kuwait catering for the expatriate community. The school operates as a not-for-profit, private co-educational establishment providing the highest standards in education for children of Pre-Kindergarten to Preparatory school age. The school is registered with the United Kingdom Department for Education (DfE No 703 6052) and the Headmaster is a Member of the Independent Association of Prep Schools. TES is an Accredited Member of BSME and is also accredited as a British School Overseas with the DfE and listed as a "world class British school". Uniquely in Kuwait, the language of the playground is English. The roll is predominantly British, as are the resources and texts. With the exception of foreign language teachers, the teaching staff are also predominantly British and qualified in the United Kingdom. The number of pupils in the school continues to increase although the average class size remains around 20. The school is housed in well-resourced and spacious, fully air-conditioned premises in a pleasant residential suburb of Kuwait City.

The curriculum is British, contemporary and delivers the best of traditional standards within a broad-based structure. Class teachers are supported by specialist coordinators in Art, Design and Technology, Information Technology, Music, Library and PE and Games. Music is taught to all ages and French is introduced from Year 4. The National Curriculum for England is used as the core for the curriculum, although the most able are challenged and those in need of support benefit from individual tuition. Formal end of key stage assessment takes place in Years 2 and 6. In addition the pupils are prepared for entrance tests to other schools including, where appropriate, Common Entrance Examinations at 11+, 12+ and 13+, and scholarship examinations.

Responsibility for the school is vested in the Governing Committee whose members serve in a voluntary capacity. The school provides a learning environment within which children develop their individual capacity for achievement to its fullest potential. The school's core values of Confidence, Empathy, Integrity, Positivity and Respect are at the heart of all that it does. Strong emphasis is placed on academic study, together with a wide range of non-academic activities to provide breadth and balance. The school aims to ensure that, by achieving standards at least equivalent and often better than those of competitive private and state schools in Britain, pupils are well prepared for the subsequent stages of their academic development whether in Britain, Kuwait or elsewhere in the world.

In the first instance application for enrolment should be made online via the website – please see drop-down menu: Parents, Enrolment, Online Registration Form.

The Registrar will confirm receipt of the Online Registration Form. If there are places in the year requested, the Registrar will ask for copies of current academic reports and arrange a date for the child/children to be assessed. Pupils and parents will then be invited to attend one of the school's 'Welcome and Assessment Days' prior to the start of the academic year.

The Grange Preparatory School

Chile

Av Principe de Gales 6154, La Reina, 687067, Santiago, Chile

Tel:	00 562 598 1500
Fax:	00 562 277 0946
email:	hmprep@grange.cl
website:	www.grange.cl

Co-educational Day School.

Headmaster of The Grange School: Mr Rachid Benammar

Head of the Upper Preparatory School: **Mr Carlos Packer-Comyn**

Head of the Lower Preparatory School: Mrs Carmen Gloria Gomez

Age Range. 4–12.
Number of Pupils. 1,200.
Fees per annum (2016–2017). Approximately £6,000 payable in one annual sum or 11 monthly instalments. There is a one-off incorporation fee payable on entry.

The Grange Preparatory School is the junior section of The Grange, founded in 1928 by John Jackson and based upon the British independent school which he had attended.

The Prep School is divided into the Lower Prep, which takes children from the age of 4 to the age of 8, and the Upper Prep, taking children from 8 to 12. Almost all pupils will transfer into The Grange senior school.

The ethos of the school is strongly based on giving a broad, all-round educational experience to find strengths for each child. The school may be very large but each child is valued as an individual within the team.

Entry to the school is usually at the age of 4, though entry at ages over 4 may be possible as vacancies occur in the course of the year. All teaching is in English except in those areas where the Chilean National Curriculum requires that they be taught in Spanish. The majority of the pupils are Chilean and begin an immersion course in English upon entry.

International assessment criteria are used at various stages of each pupil's career, with NFER testing in English and mathematics. The core curriculum is based largely upon the National Curriculum of England and Wales, fully encompassing and surpassing the local National Curriculum. Teaching is mainly by class teachers, though older children will find themselves being taught by specialists in many subjects. All heads of department are specialists. Approximately 30 of the teachers are expatriates.

Over the last few years strong progress has been made in the areas of Science, ICT, Music, Drama and Art and Design Technology, with new rooms having been dedicated to these subjects. There is a comprehensive after-school extra-curricular programme in which children from the age of 7 upwards are strongly encouraged to take part.

Grange School

Harold Shodipo Crescent, GRA, Ikeja, Lagos State, Nigeria

Tel: 00 234 12950493; 00 234 12713886
email: info@grangeschool.com
website: www.grangeschool.com

Chairman of the Board of Directors: Mr Dayo Lawuyi MON

CEO/Headmaster: **Mr Graham J Stothard JP**, BEd Hons Wales, NPQH Manchester, FRSA, FInstLM, FCollT, MIOD, AISTD

   Age Range. 4–16 Co-educational day and boarding.
   Number of Pupils. 750.
   Fees per annum (2016–2017). Tuition: £5,115 KS1, £6,310 KS2, £8,132 KS3, £8,540 KS4. Boarders (age 9–16): £6,000 in addition to tuition fees.

   Founded fifty-eight years ago in 1958, Grange is one of the oldest and most prestigious British International Schools in West Africa. With the Deputy British High Commissioner as its Patron, Grange is firmly rooted in British tradition inspired by Nigerian innovation. The school is located in GRA, Ikeja on the Lagos mainland. Parents and all stakeholders have high academic and social aspirations for their children almost all of whom graduate to the best of Public schools in England, America and Canada. The school has a selective admissions policy. In 2016 over 90% of IGCSE grades were A*–C. We have a balanced, wide ranging curriculum with an element of choice in KS4.

   The majority of the school's 194 staff is Nigerian with the school currently expanding its legal quota of expatriate teacher colleagues, from the UK. Approximately 85% of children are Nigerian nationals, therefore in order to acknowledge their cultural identity and heritage, clear evidence exists of using local exemplars to supplement programmes of study. This is further witnessed by the programme of co-curricular clubs and in the many school visits the children undertake both locally and further afield annually to the UK, France, Switzerland and South Africa. The school's executive team is primarily focused on 'quality first learning' across all year groups and this is reflected in Grange's vision.

   We acknowledge parental aspirations for their children through a continual drive for reflective practices both within and outside the classroom. There is regular monitoring of the quality of learning and teaching, the school learning environment and pupil progress via homework and termly assessment including optional and 'statutory' Checkpoint examinations administered by the University of Cambridge Examinations Syndicate (UCLES). Children benefit from many co-curricular activities based in classrooms, on our sports field and multi-purpose court, our 25-metre swimming pool and tennis courts at the adjoining Country Club.

   The school has embarked on an extensive building programme which has seen new boarding accommodation commissioned recently. There is an active PTA which, in addition to raising substantial amounts of money to assist in purchasing additional resources for the school and local charities, provides a constructive link with the CEO around everything from individual parental concerns to strategic matters.

Hillcrest Preparatory School

PO Box 24282, Karen 00502, Nairobi, Kenya

Tel: 00 254 (0)20 883914/16/17
email: admin_prep@hillcrest.ac.ke
website: www.hillcrest.ac.ke
Facebook: Hillcrest International Schools

Chairman of Governors: Mr Bob Kikuyu

Headteacher: **Ms Gabrielle Maina**

Deputy Head: Mrs Christina Lacey

   Age Range. 18 months – 13 years Co-educational.
   Number of Pupils. 320.
   Fees per term (2016–2017). Tuition in Hillcrest Early Years (HEY) from Play Group to Year 2 (Key Stage 1) ranges from Ksh 66,000 to 396,000 including lunch, excluding transport. Tuition in the Preparatory school from Year 3 (Key Stage 2) to Year 8 (Key Stage 3) ranges from Ksh 500,500 to 522,500. Weekly Boarding: Ksh 275,750 (in addition to Tuition fees). Weekend Boarding: Ksh 11,850 per weekend.

   Boarding is available on application from Year 6.

   Hillcrest School was founded in 1965 by Mr Frank Thompson as Founding Headmaster. It is located on an attractive, purpose-built, 20-acre campus next to our Secondary School in Karen/Langata.

   Boys and girls are accepted from the age of 18 months in HEY and 8 years at the Preparatory. Each year group has two classes of 16–20 pupils with a teaching assistant available up to the end of Year 2 (Key Stage 1). The pupils follow a broad and extensive curriculum which prepares them for Common Entrance Examinations. Some children transfer to UK Independent Secondary Schools but the majority enter the equivalent in Kenya, Hillcrest Secondary School, which prepares pupils for IGCSE and A Levels. Entry to the Senior School is achieved after successfully writing the Common Entrance.

   The school has a multinational feel with its pupils drawn from the diplomatic community including the UN, expatriate families on contract, and Kenyan residents. The friendly spirit and strong communication network that exists between staff, pupils and parents are of particular note.

   Extensive information can be found at www.hillcrest.ac.ke.

Kenton College

PO Box 30017, 00100 Nairobi, Kenya

Tel: 00 254 20 4347000 / 4347532 / 4347371
             Cell: 00 254 722 205038 / 00 254 733 687077
email: admin@kenton.ac.ke
website: www.kentonschoolnairobi.com

Chairman of the Governors: C H Banks, Esq

Headmistress: **Mrs M Cussans**, BA, PGCE, MA

   Age Range. 6–13 Co-educational.
   Number of Pupils. 322.
   Fees per term (2016–2017). Kshs 537,000/-.

   Founded in 1924 and transferred to purpose-built accommodation in 1935, Kenton College is one of the oldest schools in the country. Situated in its own secluded grounds of 35 acres, at an altitude of nearly 6000 feet, some three miles from the centre of one of Africa's most cosmopolitan capitals, Kenton is an oasis of calm amidst the rapidly sprawling urban development of the city of Nairobi.

Kenton College is an independent co-educational preparatory school, entry to which is open to both boys and girls of any race or religious persuasion, who have had their sixth birthday before the beginning of the school year in September. Most pupils remain seven years with us and leave in the July following their thirteenth birthday for senior schools in the UK, Kenya or South Africa, having followed a syllabus in the senior part of the school leading to the ISEB Common Entrance Examination. Kenton pupils frequently obtain scholarships to UK or Kenyan senior schools.

The school is based on a strong Christian foundation which is reflected in the warm and caring environment provided for its pupils, wherein positive encouragement is given towards any aspect of school life. Considerable emphasis is placed on character building, discipline and good manners, within a relaxed and happy atmosphere.

We aim for high academic achievements by offering a full curriculum in which the best of traditional and modern approaches are employed. The British National Curriculum provides the framework for our teaching throughout the school. Use is made of specialist subject teaching rooms in the senior school, to which recent additions are a Modern Languages suite, a Design Studio and two Computer rooms. There are two Science laboratories, a well-stocked Library, a 300-seat Assembly Hall with large stage, and a purpose-built Music Studio.

The academic day is balanced by opportunities for drama and music for all, together with a wide variety of sports and extra-curricular activities. Traditional British sports are played using our first class facilities which include three tennis courts, a heated swimming pool and a synthetic surface sports pitch.

Many pupils opt for extra activities such as riding, ballet, karate, music tuition, tennis or swimming coaching, speech and drama awards. Trips to facilities found in an international city are combined with expeditions and fieldwork in the unrivalled Kenyan countryside.

Academic subjects are taught by a staff complement of local and expatriate teachers numbering 43. Full use is made of accomplished musicians for music tuition, while recognised Kenyan sportsmen assist with games coaching. The average class size is 18, with 20 the maximum.

King's College School, La Moraleja

Paseo de Alcobendas 5, La Moraleja, Madrid 28109, Spain

Tel: 00 34 916 585 540
Fax: 00 34 916 507 686
email: info.lamoraleja@kingscollege.es
website: www.kingscollegeschools.org
Twitter: @KCS_Moraleja
LinkedIn: /King's College School, La Moraleja

King's College School La Moraleja opened in September 2007. It is a co-educational day school for pupils from Nursery to Year 9 and one of three King's Group schools in Madrid, the first of which was founded in 1969. The Headteacher of La Moraleja is an overseas member of IAPS and King's College School La Moraleja is also a member of COBIS.

The school is governed by the King's Group Board of Directors and the School Council. These governing bodies are composed of distinguished members from the business and academic communities.

Headteacher: Dawn Akyurek, BA Hons, PGCE, MA, NPQH

Deputy Headteacher: June Donnan, BA Hons Ulster, MEd OU
Upper School Leader: Jacky Walters, BEd Winchester
Lower School Leader: Dhamayanthi Vinthini Sangarabalan, PGCE Edinburgh
Head of Spanish Studies: Pedro García Navarro, Ddo Magistero, Ldo CAFD, CAP Madrid
Head of Admissions: Nuria Sanz, BA, MBA SIU Madrid

Age Range. 3–14 Co-educational.
Number of Pupils. 500.
Fees per term (2016–2017). €1,738–€3,004 excluding lunch and transport.

This is a day school which caters for children of approximately 35 nationalities between the ages of 3 and 14 years (Nursery to Year 9). Pupil enrolment is approximately 500 boys and girls and there are 33 fully-qualified British staff, and five qualified Spanish language teachers.

The school vision, like its sister schools in Madrid, is to "be at the forefront of British education internationally" and to provide students with an excellent all-round education while fostering tolerance and understanding between young people of different nationalities and backgrounds. It is a happy and inspiring place to learn.

At the age of fourteen, at the end of National Curriculum Year 9, pupils transfer to the school in Soto de Viñuelas to complete their final four years of study. (*See King's College entry in HMC section.*)

Location. This modern, purpose-built school is situated in the superb location of La Moraleja, one of the most highly-regarded residential areas in Madrid. The site is well connected to the city, just off the A1 and a short walk from the La Moraleja Metro station. There is an optional bus service for pupils to the city of Madrid and its outlying residential areas and all routes are supervised by a bus monitor.

Facilities. All classrooms are bright, spacious and house a complement of high-quality resources and technology to encourage interactive learning. The on-site facilities include a library, two ICT suites, science laboratory, music rooms, multi-purpose sports surface, gymnasium and infirmary.

Curriculum. Teachers deliver a broad and balanced curriculum and encourage pupils to put effort into all that they undertake academically, culturally and physically.

Pupils follow the English National Curriculum (leading to IGCSE, GCE AS and A Level examinations once pupils transfer to Soto de Viñuelas). There are Induction English Classes for children over the age of 7 who need to improve their English. There are also Beginners Spanish Classes for international children joining the school. All pupils learn Spanish.

Activities. There are choirs and musical ensembles, which participate in events throughout the year. Pupils are encouraged to explore their capabilities in the areas of music and the arts from a very early age.

Sports play an important role at the school and pupils are encouraged to take part in tournaments and local competitive events, in addition to their normal PE classes. School football and basketball teams compete in the local Alcobendas Leagues and pupils also take part in inter-school championships in athletics and cross-country.

There is a programme of optional classes which includes chess, ballet, judo, Spanish dancing, swimming and tuition in various musical instruments, as well as performing arts, language clubs and craft workshops.

Admission. Pupils wishing to enter Year 3 and above are required to sit entrance tests in English and Mathematics and to present copies of recent school reports. Further information may be obtained from The Head of Admissions, Mrs Nuria Sanz, nuria.sanz@kingsgroup.org.

Senior School. At the age of fourteen, at the end of National Curriculum Year 9, pupils transfer to King's College in Soto de Viñuelas to complete their final four years of study. (*See King's College entry in HMC section.*)

King's Infant School, Chamartín

Prieta Ureña 9–11, Madrid 28016, Spain
Tel: 00 34 913 505 843
email: info.chamartin@kingscollege.es
website: www.kingscollegeschools.org
Twitter: @KISChamartin
LinkedIn: /King's Infant School, Chamartín

King's Infant School is a co-educational day school for pupils from Nursery to Year 2 (age 3–7) based in the Chamartín area of Madrid city centre. Chamartín was the original site of the first King's College school opened in 1969. Today King's Infant School is one of seven schools in the King's Group.

The Headteacher of Chamartín is an overseas member of IAPS and King's Infant School is also a member of COBIS.

The school is governed by the King's Group Board of Directors and the School Council. These governing bodies are composed of distinguished members from the business and academic communities.

Headteacher: **Kirsty Sharp**, MA, BA Hons, QTS, AVCM Hons

Deputy Headteacher: Rachel Davies, BA Hons, QTS, NPQSL

Head of Admissions: Beatriz Eparaza

Age Range. 3–7 Co-educational.
Number of Pupils. 202.
Fees per term (2016–2017). €1,738–€2,022 excluding lunch and transport.

The Vision of King's Infant School, like its sister schools in King's Group, is to "Be at the forefront of British Education Internationally". The Group's Mission is to provide high-quality British education that delivers a transformative learning experience to all our pupils.

Location. The school occupies a modern, well-equipped and compact campus which caters ideally for young learners. It is well connected by road and public transport and is just a short walk from the nearest Metro station. There is an optional bus service for pupils to and from school which covers the city of Madrid and its outlying residential areas. All routes are supervised by a bus monitor.

Facilities. All classrooms are bright and spacious with high-quality resources and technology to encourage interactive learning. Classrooms are also fully air-conditioned in order to keep pupils cool in the hot summer months.

On-site facilities include:

• Covered play areas for use during summer and winter
• Extended outdoor play areas for Nursery and Reception class
• Mini football and netball pitch
• Music room
• SMART boards in every classroom (Reception–Year 2); IWB for use in Nursery class

Curriculum. Teachers deliver a broad and balanced curriculum, based on the English National Curriculum, and encourage pupils to put effort into all that they undertake academically, culturally and physically. King's Infant School caters for children of a variety of nationalities. There are 10 UK qualified staff, one of whom is a Spanish language teacher, as well as 7 Teaching Assistants and an Educational Psychologist. There are Induction English Classes for children who need to improve their English. There are

also Beginners Spanish Classes for international children joining the school. All pupils learn Spanish.

Activities. The school boasts an array of extracurricular activities to complement those already catered for within the curriculum. Pupils are encouraged to explore their capabilities in the areas of music and the arts from a very early age. Sport plays an important role at the school and pupils are encouraged to take part in activity days to build cooperation and confidence in addition to their normal PE classes.

Optional classes include chess, ballet, judo, modern dance, football, skating, Chinese, swimming and tuition in various musical instruments, as well as performing arts.

Admissions. Parents and pupils are invited to meet with the Head of Admissions and the Headteacher on their visit to the school.

At the age of seven, at the end of National Curriculum Year 2, pupils transfer to one of two sister schools in Madrid: King's College, Soto de Viñuelas which caters for pupils from Pre-Nursery to Year 13 (age 2 to 18) or alternatively to King's College School, La Moraleja which caters for pupils from Nursery to Year 9 (age 3 to 15). If pupils transfer to La Moraleja, they will later join the main site in Soto de Viñuelas from Year 10 in order to continue their studies leading to IGCSE, GCE AS and A Level examinations. (*See separate entry for King's College School, La Moraleja in IAPS section and King's College's entry in HMC section.*)

Lagos Preparatory School

36–40 Glover Road, Ikoyi, Lagos, Nigeria
Tel: 00 234 1 740 8325
             00 234 1 740 8323
email: admin@lagosprepikoyi.com.ng
             headteacher@lagosprepikoyi.com.ng
website: www.lagosprepikoyi.com.ng

Headmaster: **Mr Nicholas Barrett**

Age Range. 2–14 Co-educational.
Number of Pupils. 350
Fees per annum (2016–2017). Tuition: US$9,900–12,375 (payable in Naira)

Our school is an international 13+ preparatory school delivering the British National Curriculum to some 350 pupils of 33 different nationalities. English is the medium of all tuition. The majority of the school's 130+ staff is Nigerian with the school having its full legal quota of expatriate teacher colleagues, from the UK; Kenya and India. Each of the classes has (at the very least) a graduate teacher, who also possesses the PGCE qualification, and an assistant teacher. All assistant teachers are graduates, many working towards the PGCE. Y2 classes and below also have a class assistant and a Nanny working in them. The school is located in Ikoyi that part of Lagos regarded as the prime residential area of the city. Our new purpose-built premises opened in September 2011. Parents and all stakeholders have high academic and social aspirations for their children. The school has a selective admissions policy.

Approximately 51% of children are Nigerian nationals therefore in order to acknowledge their cultural identity and heritage, clear evidence exists of using local exemplars to supplement programmes of study. This is further witnessed by the programme of pre and after school clubs and in the many school visits the children undertake. The school's senior leadership team are primarily focused on 'quality first teaching' across the whole school and this is reflected in our mission statement. We acknowledge parental aspirations for their children through a continual drive for reflective practices both within and outside the classroom. There is regular monitoring of the quality of teaching and learning, the school learning environment and pupil progress via homework and bi-weekly testing (including optional and 'statutory' SATs). Children benefit from many co-curricular activities based in classrooms, our multi-purpose hall, our 25m swimming pool and on our astro surface soccer field and tennis court.

There is an active PTA which in addition to raising substantial amounts of money to assist in purchasing additional resources for the school, provides a most useful and constructive link with the Headmaster around everything from individual parental concerns through to strategic whole school development matters. In keeping with the school's mission statement it maintains a proactive stance in relation to community links. Our school has a very active staff training programme and performance management system for all staff. One member of the SLT is responsible for this crucial area of development. Over the last few years a significant number of our graduate teachers and assistant teachers have undertaken the distance learning PGCE course with the University of Sunderland, with much success.

In 2010 the school became the world's first international school to achieve the Every Child Matters Standards Award. In the Lent term of 2011 the school underwent a successful ISI inspection and accordingly became the first British school on the African continent to achieve the DfE's standards for British schools overseas. We remain the only British school in Africa to hold this accolade. A further ISI inspection in late 2015 gave an extremely glowing report. The Headmaster is a member of Independent Association of Prep Schools (IAPS) and the school is the only British school in Africa that is an Accredited Member of COBIS.

Pembroke House

PO Box 31, Gilgil 20116, Kenya
Tel: 00 254 (0)20 231 2323
           00 254 (0)734 480 439
email: headmaster@pembrokehouse.sc.ke
website: www.pembrokehouse.sc.ke

Chairman of Council: Mr Richard Vigne

Headmaster: **Mr Jason Brown**

Age Range. 5–13.
Number of Pupils. 119 boy boarders, 106 girl boarders.
Fees per term (2016–2017). Ksh 645,000 (UK£4,610).

The school was founded in 1927 and is presently owned and administered by the Kenya Educational Trust Limited. It is situated in over 40 hectares of well-maintained grounds in the Rift Valley at 2,000 metres and is 120 kms from Nairobi. The climate is sunny throughout the year affording many opportunities for an extensive education.

Facilities include Science Lab, Sen Center, Chapel, Theatre, Swimming Pool, Music School, Library, Art and Design Technology Centre, Computer Room, two Squash Courts and Tennis Courts, access to a neighbouring Golf Course, and a multi-purpose Sports Hall, Stables, Meeting Room and Café. The school has a well-equipped Surgery on site.

The main sports are Cricket, Hockey, Rugby, Rounders and Netball with Tennis, Swimming, Athletics, Squash, Golf, Horse Riding, Sailing, Soccer, Shooting and Taekwondo on offer as well.

A full range of clubs and various extras, including individual music instruction, are also offered. Drama is strong with several productions put on each year. The school also has a vibrant and varied weekend programme to support the full boarding ethos of the school. This involves much camping and other outdoor pursuits as well as many team building and leadership activities.

Children are admitted from five years as full boarders and are prepared, through the British Curriculum, for the ISEB Common Entrance Examinations which qualifies them for entry to Independent Senior Schools in the UK and South Africa as well as Kenyan schools. The School usually gains numerous academic scholarships and awards each year in addition to music and sports awards. The Learning Support Facilities at Pembroke House have been developed over many years and now provide essential help for those who require such assistance. The school currently has children from seven different countries including the United Kingdom.

The average number of pupils in each form is 15, and there are 39 fully qualified members of teaching staff plus four qualified Nurses, a Cateress, an Estate Manager, Registrar and a Bursar. Pembroke has a reputation for producing outstanding pupils. The Headmaster and the staff work together to produce kind, well-mannered, balanced children with integrity and courage who try their best at all times. This is the best preparation a child can have.

Peponi House

PO Box 23203, Lower Kabete, Nairobi 00604, Kenya
Tel: 00 254 20 2585710–712, 734881255,
           722202947
email: secretary@peponihouseschool.co.ke
website: www.peponihouseschool.co.ke

Headmaster: **Mr R J Blake**, BSc Hons, PGCE, NPQH

Age Range. 6–13.
Number of Pupils. 395 boys and girls, all day.
Fees per annum (2016–2017). Kshs 1,720,500.

Founded in 1986, Peponi House has grown to become one of the leading preparatory schools in East Africa. The attractive and spacious site in Lower Kabete houses all that a thriving prep school requires to get the very best out of the children, both in and out of the classroom.

We are a multi-cultural community which encourages respect for self and others. Our emphasis is on excellence, through a broad, balanced education which aims to maximise the potential of each pupil as a whole person. To this end, we have outstanding facilities including a 25-metre swimming pool, three hard tennis courts, purpose-built Art and Design Technology rooms and networked PCs in all rooms. Our wireless network now covers the whole site, with excellent bandwidth. We have two fully-equipped science laboratories and a new music school. Two new classrooms dedicated to History and Geography opened recently, with a senior RS room added in 2014. The school library and Computing room occupy an area that is central to the school both geographically and philosophically. These facilities help to complement the excellent work that the children and staff carry out in the well-resourced classrooms. Our extensive use of interactive whiteboards has resulted in the school being elected as a SMART Showcase School.

Whilst always striving for academic excellence, it is central to Peponi's philosophy that education is not limited to the classroom. In addition to the numerous scholarships to senior schools that our pupils have won in the last three years, we have had notable successes in sport, music, art and drama. Peponi teams have won competitions at a national level, with many individuals going on to represent their country.

We follow the British National Curriculum but this is seen very much as a framework for extension. In addition to the core subjects of Literacy, Numeracy, Science and Computing, pupils in the Junior School (Years 2 to 4) also have lessons in Music, PE and Games, Swimming, Kiswahili, Art and DT, tennis and, from Year 3, French. Junior children are taught these subjects by specialist teachers while the class teachers deliver the core subjects and humanities. All children are taught in a way that best suits their individual needs and some children do require additional support. This is carried out by our Learning Support teachers who will help children either individually or in small groups, but mainly through integrated support in the classroom. Our special needs teachers also play a vital role in advising colleagues as to the strengths and weaknesses of particular children so that teaching can be differentiated to suit everyone.

In Year 5, children are taught Humanities and English by their form teachers, who also play a vital pastoral role in preparing the children for life in the senior school. In Year 6, all subjects are delivered by subject specialists. The sciences are taught separately and there is an option for children to study Kiswahili, Spanish or Latin.

We also have a wide and varied range of extra-curricular activities. The whole school joins in the Activity Programme on Friday afternoons, with children from all year groups taking part in activities together. On Mondays, children in Years 5 to 8 take part in HOTS: higher order thinking skills activities.

Our music department flourishes in its own purpose-built accommodation. In addition to weekly class music lessons, the children have the opportunity to play in the orchestra or in one of the ensembles, or sing in either the Junior or Senior Choir. As well as the two major school concerts during the year, all children have the opportunity to perform in front of their peers and parents at our termly "Tea-Time Concerts". The Carol Service and Peponi Schools Concert offer other chances for our choirs to perform and all the children are encouraged to take part in the plays that are staged in December, March and June.

We have children from many different cultures and ethnic backgrounds and we encourage understanding and above all respect for each other. We are a Christian School and the ethos of "Love one another" is a recurring theme in our Monday Assemblies, but we are proud of our multi-faith society where children learn to appreciate and value their differences as well as their similarities.

The school's motto "A School of Many Nations, a Family of One" encapsulates all that we hold most dear. First and foremost, we are a school and the academic side of things lies at the heart of all that we do. However, we are also a family and that makes itself very clear in the day to day life of the school. We have an open door policy with our parents and encourage them to be very active in their support of what we do, either through our energetic PTA or through close consultation with the staff.

At Peponi House, we believe that our role as educators is to give our children the best possible foundation for what lies ahead. We are, after all, a preparatory school and excellent preparation is what we set out to achieve. By the time they leave us, our pupils will be confident young adults who are ready to face the future with poise and self-belief.

Postal Address:
PO Box GP 21057, Accra, Ghana

Co-educational Day School.

Governors:
Chairman: Dr Frank B Adu Jnr, BA Hons, MBA
Chair, Academic Board: Dr Joyce Aryee, BA Hons, PG Cert Public Administration

***Principal*: Mrs Valerie Mainoo**, BSc Psych, MA Ed

Age Range. 4–18.
Numbers of Pupils. 249 Boys, 283 Girls.
Fees per term (2016–2017). Junior School (Reception–Class 6): US$1,600; Senior School (Forms 1–5) US$1,900; Sixth Form US$2,000.

Established in September 2002, The Roman Ridge School aims to provide the very best of British Education whilst being firmly rooted in Ghanaian life and culture. The school is a unique facility in Ghana as it offers small class sizes (20), individual pupil attention, a family atmosphere, firm discipline, emphasis on good manners, a sound Christian foundation, a caring environment and a full programme of Sports and extra-curricular activities.

The school is noted for its Individual Learning Programmes and its Special Needs Programmes as well as its dedication to all other pupils including the high ability learners and scholars. Pupils are carefully monitored and assessed regularly in order to achieve academic success, and, parents are encouraged to help in this process.

All teaching is initially based on the English National Curriculum for the Foundation Course and Key Stage One, after which the pupils progress to the 11+ examination, then take the full range of academic subjects at the 13+ Common Entrance & the IGCSE Courses with the Cambridge Board. The school runs a thriving AS & A Level programme and offers a comprehensive range of Courses.

There are thirty classrooms at present, three ICT suites, a Multimedia Centre with a Language lab, two up-to-date Libraries with full audio-visual facilities, E-Learning facilities, junior & senior Science Labs, a Dance Studio, two Art Rooms and sporting facilities. A clinic is on site staffed by a qualified SRN.

Pupils play Football, Basketball, Volleyball, Netball, Hockey and Rounders and also enjoy a very successful Swimming programme. Pupils also benefit from an extensive extra-curricular programme which includes Karate, Ballet, Tennis, Drama Club and a highly successful Choir programme, which includes a Parent Choir. School productions and concerts take place at the end of each term.

The school also runs an excellent internal and external Community Literacy Programme, with Senior Pupils spearheading reading programmes for all age groups.

The school is open on Saturdays for extra work and pupil support programmes, swimming, games, music lessons, art and computer clubs, and special events.

Pupils thrive in The Roman Ridge School and are reluctant to go home at the end of the day.

The Roman Ridge School

No. 8 Onyasia Crescent, Roman Ridge, Accra, Ghana

Tel:	00 233 302 780456/780457
Fax:	00 233 302 780458
email:	enquiries@theromanridgeschool.com
website:	www.theromanridgeschool.com

St Andrew's Preparatory School

Private Bag, Molo 20106, Kenya

Tel:	+254 202025708
	+254 735337736
email:	officeprep@turimail.co.ke
website:	www.standrewsturi.com

Chair of Governors: Mrs Anne Aliker

Headmaster: **Mr Fergus Llewellyn**, BA

Age Range. 3–13.
Number of Pupils. 250: 126 Boys, 124 Girls.
Fees per term (2016–2017). Boarding: Kshs 563,000–676,000. Day: Kshs 281,500–439,400.

St Andrew's Preparatory School, Turi, is an international, multicultural, Christian boarding school offering British Curriculum education of the highest standard. The School aims to provide a happy, stimulating, well-rounded educational experience for children. Pupils are encouraged to grow into well-educated, confident, self-disciplined young adults with the potential to be future leaders.

The Prep School together with its Senior School is situated 200 km north west of Nairobi on a beautiful 300-acre estate at an altitude of over 2,000 metres, where the climate is both healthy and invigorating. The School has its own private airstrip within the grounds.

Boarding pupils are accepted from the age of 5 and follow the British National Curriculum and then the Common Entrance Syllabus which prepares them for entry to St Andrew's Senior School and to other independent senior schools in Britain or elsewhere.

The original School, founded in 1931, was destroyed by fire in 1944. It was completely rebuilt and is superbly designed and equipped as a modern purpose-built preparatory school. There are subject rooms for English, Mathematics, French, History, Geography and Science laboratories. Information Technology is an integral part of the curriculum throughout the School with two ICT suites and most classrooms are equipped with interactive whiteboards and data projectors. An exceptionally large Hall is used for plays, concerts and large functions. The average size of classes is 16.

Sports form a key part of school life at St Andrew's School. The grounds and playing fields are extensive. Boys play cricket and rugby; girls play rounders and netball; all play football, hockey, tennis and take part in athletics and cross country. In the newly-opened sports centre there are excellent facilities for a wide range of indoor sports including two glass-backed squash courts and a fitness suite. There are seven school tennis courts and a heated swimming pool, as well as a riding school on site where pupils of all abilities are taught by qualified instructors.

The School has a strong musical tradition. In addition to the many and varied opportunities for music within the curriculum over 80 pupils opt for specialist instrumental tuition in a wide range of instruments. Many of these pupils work towards ABRSM examinations. There are also several specialist music groups who practice and perform together and the Junior and Senior choirs.

A large and well-equipped Art Studio as well as Design Technology and Food Technology rooms allow pupils to express themselves creatively. A wealth of arts and crafts, hobbies and outdoor pursuits are actively encouraged. The School has its own Chapel and aims to give a practical Christian education in a community with high standards and in a supportive family atmosphere.

All staff live within the estate. The teaching staff are all qualified and are committed to the Christian ethos of the School.

St Andrew's Senior School offers a three-year course to IGCSE examinations with excellent academic results, and thereafter students can opt for A Levels at the incorporated St Andrew's College. The School has the same Board of Governors, but its own Headmaster, teaching staff and Management Team.

St Christopher's School

PO Box 32052, Isa Town, Kingdom of Bahrain
Tel: +973 1760 5000
Fax: +973 1760 5020
email: office.principal@st-chris.net
website: www.st-chris.net

Principal: **Mr Ed Goodwin**, BA, MA, MBA, OBE

Head of Infant School: Mr Ian Fellows, BEd, NPQH
Head of Junior School: Mrs Wendy Bataineh, BA, PGCE, MA, NPQH
Head of Senior School: Mr Nick Wilson, BSc, PGCE, NPQH

Age Range. 3–18 Co-educational.
Number of Pupils. 2,253.

St Christopher's first opened in 1961 and has grown to become an internationally renowned school with over 2,200 students from around 70 nations; a school with a fine international reputation and widely recognised as one of the world's top British schools overseas, with exceptional facilities and resources.

With a consistent record of excellent academic success, we also offer a broad programme of extra-curricular activities and personal development opportunities. The school has been rated "Outstanding" in 3 different inspection regimes – not just overall, but for every aspect of our performance.

St Christopher's is not for profit, with all income from fees being used to run and further develop the School for the benefit of our students, making us the premier choice for those parents who need and demand the very best British-style education for their children in Bahrain.

St Christopher's is a highly successful school, firmly established in the British tradition, yet with an international outlook.

St Christopher's: Caring, Learning and Communicating to give your family the very best in British-International education!

Fees per term (2016–2017). Nursery BD997; Reception–Year 2 BD1,304; Years 3–6 BD1,436; Years 7–8 BD1,735; Years 9–11 BD2,092; Years 12–13 BD2,402.

St Paul's School

Rua Juquiá 166, Jardim Paulistano, São Paulo SP 01440–903, Brazil
Tel: 00 55 11 3087 3399
Fax: 00 55 11 3087 3398
email: head@stpauls.br
website: www.stpauls.br
Twitter: @Head_StPaulsSP
Facebook: /St-Pauls-School

Chairman of the Board of Governors: Mr Anthony Jezzi

Head: **Ms Louise Simpson**

Deputy Head: Mr James Diver
Senior Master: Dr Barry Hallinan
Head of Preparatory School: Mrs Siobhain Allum
Head of Pre-Preparatory School: Ms Amy Clifford

Age Range. 3–18.
Number of Pupils. 1,106: Pre-Preparatory 234, Preparatory 278, Senior 494.

St. Paul's School was founded in 1926 and was the first British School in São Paulo. Fully co-educational, with some 1,100 pupils, aged from 3 to 18, it is a school with history and tradition, but which embraces innovation, contemporary values and technological developments. We offer a British curriculum, including the International Primary Curriculum (IPC) and courses up to IGCSE and the International Baccalaureate Diploma. At IB the following subjects are taught in the Sixth Form (and offered as standard and higher levels): English, Portuguese, Spanish, French, mathematics, mathematical studies, physics, chemistry, biology, computer science, geography, history, economics, business management, theatre, visual arts, and music.

The school prides itself on an excellent enrichment programme ranging from MUN to Duke of Edinburgh's Award, from knitting classes to a robotics programme, from mathematical olympiads to outstanding drama and music. Field trips also form an integral part of the curriculum with every year group from the age of 8 years old going on residential visits throughout Brazil and beyond.

We prepare our pupils within a bilingual and bicultural Anglo-Brazilian community for a global future. We offer a broad and balanced but rigorous curriculum where the individual pupil is at the heart of the teaching and learning. It is our aim to discover the passion and talents of every pupil, and create the right environment to develop these. Pupils leave us confident, assured and well prepared for an exciting life, and a multitude of opportunities, often at top universities.

We are a world-class school; a member of HMC and COBIS and the first officially British government accredited British School Overseas in South America. We are proud of our local, national and international reputation and we constantly strive to improve the opportunities for our pupils and staff.

The school has undertaken an almost continuous programme of building works over the past 20 years as it has gradually grown; this includes extensive refurbishment and extension of the original school building, the creation of a sixth form centre and a multimillion dollar underground state-of-the-art sports centre. In 2016 we celebrated 90 years of excellent education by opening the Queen Elizabeth II academic centre, which houses a learning resources suite, art centre, music recording facilities, and 10 modern science laboratories.

St Saviour's School, Ikoyi
Lagos, Nigeria

54 Alexander Avenue, Ikoyi, Lagos, Nigeria

Tel: 00 234 1 8990153
Fax: 00 234 1 2700255
email: info@stsavioursschikoyi.org
website: www.stsavioursschikoyi.org

St Saviour's is an Associate Member of COBIS.

Chairman of Board of Trustees: Mr L N Mbanefo, SAN

Head Teacher: **Mr Craig Heaton**, BA Hons

> **Age Range.** 4–11 Co-educational.
> **Number of Pupils.** 320.
> **Fees per term (2016–2017).** Naira 821,500.
> A truly rounded education is a preparation for life. Grounded on our core values, St Saviour's seeks to provide an education that is challenging, relevant, exciting and delivered in a caring and thoroughly professional manner. We look, unashamedly, for academic achievement in each pupil alongside equal progress in spiritual growth, friendship, independence, confidence and some appreciation of

their place in the world and their responsibilities towards others.

Christian principles are integrated into the daily life of the school which is an Anglican foundation. Children of a number of denominations and faiths attend the school and are warmly welcomed. Parents are welcomed as part of the learning cycle; communication with them is regular and their support of the school is exceptional.

The development of the whole child is at the heart of education at St Saviour's. Learning is about developing personal, emotional and social skills as well as being an intellectual and academic process. We aim to help children find their voice – their own unique, personal significance. We encourage them to think about what their contribution will be in the world – how they will try to make a difference as responsible and engaged members of the School community as well as citizens of the world.

St Saviour's has high expectations for all its learners. We pride ourselves on knowing each child as an individual in order to help them make progress. Teachers plan to scaffold success for all learners from their point of entry. This means that learning opportunities are planned so that all students are challenged appropriately, sometimes by providing work that is a little too hard and then providing support systems to enable students to work through their difficulties to achieve success.

Above all, we are interested in the learning process – learning how to learn and how to apply skills and knowledge across an ever-increasing spectrum of experience. From the earliest age we ensure that children have an enjoyable experience of school and are motivated to learn and improve. This positive attitude is supported by a team of highly professional teachers who are themselves engaged in lifelong learning and model effective habits of mind. The curriculum is based on that of the National Curriculum for England and Wales and the International Primary Curriculum adapted to reflect the needs of an increasingly international and multicultural student body We aim to build on the children's background knowledge and experience to equip them with the skills, strategies and a love of learning that will inspire them to succeed whatever the next step on their educational journey.

The school has developed and renewed its own sports facilities over the past few years and now has its own 25m swimming pool and extensive sports field, including football pitch and running track as well as informal play areas. Routinely, about 30 extracurricular Clubs operate after school each week and they are very well supported. Events such as Assemblies, Independence Day, Foundation, KS1 and KS2 Productions, Sports Day, International Week, Flower Show, Fun Day and Harvest Festival add greatly to the school's character. Our support of local orphanages flows from monies raised at some of these events.

Pupils leave the school from Y6 to attend leading Secondary schools in Nigeria and approximately 40% move on to outstanding independent schools in the UK, where they prove to be excellent ambassadors of the holistic education they have received at St Saviour's.

Tanglin Trust Junior School

95 Portsdown Road, Singapore 139299

Tel: 00 65 6778 9000
email: junior.school@tts.edu.sg
website: www.tts.edu.sg
Twitter: @TanglinTrust
Facebook: /TanglinTrustSchool
LinkedIn: /tanglin-trust-school

Chair of Governors: Mr Dominic Nixon

Chief Executive Officer: Mr Peter J Derby-Crook

Head of Junior School: **Mrs Clair Harrington-Wilcox**

Age Range. 7–11.

Number of Pupils. Junior School 770 (2,800 across Infant, Junior, Senior Schools).

Fees per term (2016–2017). S$11,030.

Building on strong foundations. Tanglin Trust School was formed in 1925 and has 90 years' experience offering British-based learning for expatriates from a wide range of nationalities, who benefit from world-class facilities combined with the highest possible standards of teaching. The school is divided into three distinct entities: Infant (3–7), Junior (7–11) and Senior (11–18) each with their own Head of School and unique set of characteristics; yet all part of the bigger Tanglin 'family'.

Broad and Balanced Curriculum. The Junior School provides a stimulating environment that inspires and motivates students in their academic, sporting, artistic and cultural development from Years 3 to 6. A creative and integrated curriculum is underpinned by a structured approach to teaching the core subjects of English, Mathematics, Science, the Humanities, Chinese and PSHCE (Personal, Social, Health and Citizenship Education) and a commitment to high standards. Alongside academic skills and knowledge, the key drivers of self-awareness and personal development and global awareness and sense of community, lead to an overall focus on students becoming well-rounded, community spirited and responsible, international young citizens. A strong pastoral system nurtures positive relationships, promoting an ethos that values and celebrates students as individuals while fostering a strong sense of community.

Entry. Students entering the School must be fluent in English, residing in Singapore with at least one parent and be able to access the curriculum independently. Prospective students may be required to sit admissions assessments.

Smooth Transition. The transition from Key Stage 1 in Tanglin's Infant School to Key Stage 2 and the Junior School presents students with exciting new challenges. The school day becomes more formally structured and students are encouraged to take on new responsibilities as they work towards becoming independent learners. The Junior School's warm and caring environment facilitates a holistic approach to learning that provides students with a wide range of opportunities to guide their academic, personal, social and physical development.

Creative Learning. All teachers (class and specialist) work creatively to capture the interest of boys and girls and to make their learning personalised, enjoyable and meaningful. A range of contemporary teaching strategies are employed. The school looks to engage and capture the imagination and interest of students right from the start of study, through themed dress-up days or practical activities involving research and collaboration as a class and in groups. The school believes that the quality of the learning experience determines the ability of the students to embrace concepts, to analyse and make connections and to see past the subject to its relevance for them beyond the classroom.

The English National Curriculum provides the basis for the programmes of study but these are enhanced and enriched to reflect the calibre of the students and the school's international setting.

Co-Curricular Activities. Students are encouraged to participate in the extensive range of Co-Curricular Activities (CCAs): over 100 activities range from cooking, cheerleading, rock climbing, soft toy making or Bollywood dancing to more traditional sport and music options. Students can learn to play a wide variety of instruments and take part in an impressive array of choirs, ensembles and orchestras. All students play sport in lesson time and are also encouraged to choose from the many sporting opportunities that are available as CCAs. Junior students are also selected to represent Tanglin in sporting events against other British schools in South and East Asia.

Building Group Identity and House System. Tanglin Junior School understands the value young people place on group membership. It ensures students are well integrated into their classes and encouraged to be part of a wide group of friends.

Each Junior student is also warmly welcomed into a House and special House days feature innovative teambuilding activities. To promote year group identity, students experience learning in large shared spaces that feature computers and comfortable reading areas and are imaginatively transformed each term into a range of settings to enrich learning.

Personal and Social Responsibility. Opportunities abound in the Junior School to build leadership skills and an appreciation of the many cultures that co-exist in Singapore. Juniors act as buddies to Infant students and can participate in the Student Council or become a Library Monitor, Junior Listener, Maths Mentor or Computer Champion. Themed assemblies celebrate cultural festivals and reinforce the importance of self management and personal and social responsibility.

Outdoor Education. Juniors also take part in challenging residential field studies that range from an overnight trip to one of Singapore's islands in Year 4 to a six-day excursion to Sarawak in Malaysia in Year 6. By valuing each individual and the contribution he or she makes and emphasising meaningful learning, self management and responsibility, Junior students are thoroughly prepared for Senior School.

Tanglin Mission. Tanglin Trust School Singapore has a long tradition of providing British-based learning with an international perspective. At Tanglin we strive to make every individual feel valued, happy and successful. Responsibility, enthusiasm and participation are actively encouraged and integrity is prized. Working together in a safe, caring yet stimulating environment, we set high expectations whilst offering strong support, resulting in a community of lifelong learners who can contribute with confidence to our world.

Tanglin's Learner Profile is a set of ten attributes which act as a framework to identify and measure the skills and attributes necessary to achieve the school's mission, in particular, the goal of nurturing 'a community of lifelong learners who can contribute with confidence to Our World.' The ten attributes are: Balanced, Caring, Risk-takers, Knowledgeable, Resilient Inquirers, Communicators, Principled, Open-minded, Thinkers, Reflective.

Not-For-Profit status. Tanglin is a not-for-profit organisation and is registered as an educational charity.

PART V
Schools whose Heads are members of the Independent Schools Association

ALPHABETICAL LIST OF SCHOOLS

The following schools, whose Heads are members of both ISA and HMC, can be found in the HMC section:

The Grange School	Princethorpe College
Lingfield Notre Dame	Winchester College

The following schools, whose Heads are members of both ISA and GSA, can be found in the GSA section:

Adcote School	St Catherine's School, Twickenham
Alderley Edge School for Girls	St Dominic's Brewood
Dodderhill School	St James Senior Girls' School
Northwood College for Girls	St Martha's

The following schools, whose Heads are members of both ISA and The Society of Heads, can be found in The Society of Heads section:

Abbey Gate College	Portland Place School
Bedstone College	Reddam House Berkshire
Bredon School	St Edward's School
Derby Grammar School	St James Senior Boys' School
Highclare School	Stafford Grammar School
LVS Ascot	Tring Park School for the Performing Arts
Pitsford School	Trinity School

The following schools, whose Heads are members of both ISA and IAPS, can be found in the IAPS section:

Abercorn School	Littlegarth School
Alleyn Court Preparatory School	Mylnhurst Preparatory School & Nursery
Collingwood School	The Old School Henstead
Crackley Hall School	Reddiford School
Cumnor House School	Rosemead Preparatory School
Gatehouse School	St Edward's Preparatory School
Holme Grange School	Shrewsbury Lodge School
Langley Preparatory School at Taverham Hall	The Study Preparatory School
Leehurst Swan School	Wilmslow Preparatory School

GEOGRAPHICAL LIST OF ISA SCHOOLS

Individual School Entries.

Abbey College Manchester
Alpha Plus Group Limited

5–7 Cheapside, King Street, Manchester M2 4WG
Tel: 0161 817 2700
Fax: 0161 817 2705
email: admin@abbeymanchester.co.uk
website: www.abbeymanchester.co.uk
Twitter: @AbbeyManchester
Facebook: /AbbeyCollegeManchester

Principal: Ms L Elam

Age Range. 15–19.
Number of Pupils. 210.
One Year GCSE, Two Year A Level and One Year A Level Retake
An independent day school with a college environment
- Year 11, Lower Sixth and Upper Sixth entry
- Very small classes (an average 7 students in each) ensure excellent progress
- Unique one year GCSEs and A Levels for those sitting for the first time or retaking
- High levels of personal support and individual responsibility gives good preparation for university life
- Expert advice is delivered for entry onto all university courses leading to strong relationships with the top universities in Britain
- City centre location means students will benefit from the unlimited arts, business, science, sports and music resources on offer

Flexible learning programmes mean that students can join at any time during the academic year, not just September.

Fees per annum (2016–2017). Year 12 (A Level) £12,250; Year 13 (A Level) £12,250; One Year A Level (1 subject) £6,250; One Year A Level (2 subjects) £12,250; Year 11 (GCSE – up to 6 subjects) £10,900.

Fees are inclusive of exam fees.

Abbey Gate Prep School

Clare Avenue, Hoole, Chester CH2 3HR
Tel: 01244 319649
email: abbeygateschool@talk21.com
            headteacher.abbeygateschool@live.co.uk
website: www.abbeygateschool.org.uk
Twitter: @AbbeyGatePrep
Facebook: /Abbey-Gate-Prep-School

Head: Mrs S A Rhodes-Leader, BA Hons, PGCE

Age Range. 3–11.
Number in School. Day: 60 Boys and Girls.
Fees per term (2016–2017). £2,600–£2,775.
Abbey Gate Prep School, founded in 1910, is a small, exclusive Christian school, comprising around 60 children and a dedicated, well-qualified staff. Small class sizes allow each child to flourish and excel as an individual. This culminates in excellent 11+ success.

It offers a broad and well-balanced curriculum and has a proven tradition of academic success both locally and nationally, as well as a growing reputation for excellence in the performing arts. Tuition is offered in a variety of musical instruments and in speech & drama and dance. Some scholarships and bursaries are available.

Specialist help is available for children with specific learning difficulties.

Extracurricular activities include chess, judo, ballet, modern dance, football, construction, computer, rhythmic gymnastics, Glee, craft, running and science clubs.

A forward-looking school, it aims to create exciting and challenging opportunities to develop academic, creative and physical skills, to produce confident and self-disciplined young people of the future. Excellent links have been established with the local community and with other schools in the area, both independent and maintained.

School opens at 8 am and has an After-School Club until 6 pm each day.

Abingdon House School
Cavendish Education Group

Broadley Terrace, London NW1 6LG
Tel: 0845 2300426
email: ahs@abingdonhouseschool.co.uk
website: www.abingdonhouseschool.co.uk

Head: Mr Roy English, MA, PGCE, Adv Dip SEN

Deputy Head: Mr Adrian Groves
Director of Studies: Mrs Claire Bredahl

Age Range. 5–14 Co-educational.
Number of Pupils. 67.
Fees per term (2016–2017). £9,850.
Abingdon House School is located in a refurbished Victorian building in London NW1 on four levels with facilities to educate up to 90 pupils aged between 5–14 years of age (Years 1–9). The school has specific expertise in the education of children who have Specific Learning Difficulties. This includes children with Dyslexia, Dyspraxia, Dyscalculia, Speech and Language Difficulties, Sensory Integration Difficulties, high-functioning Autism and so on.

The school provides a warm, nurturing environment in which the specific individual learning needs of our pupils are addressed through a multi-disciplinary approach. We provide an integrated, whole-school approach to meeting the needs of pupils who are diagnosed with a specific learning difficulty. When diagnosed early in their education, children generally respond well to intense intervention for a period of time, after which it is anticipated they would be able to return to the mainstream.

Effective learning and teaching is based on understanding a child's individual needs, nurturing a child's academic and social development and caring for a child's well-being. The environment is therefore warm and friendly and we are committed to each child's holistic development.

We aim to prepare the children for a return to mainstream schooling through:
- The provision of a holistic and individually tailored education programme.
- A whole-school teaching regime of small classes with teaching assistants, therapists and trained staff using a

range of teaching strategies and therapeutic interventions. There is an appropriately low pupil to teacher ratio. Many pupils have integrated successfully into various London day schools.

- Developing, monitoring and implementing an IEP (Individual Education Plan) for each pupil, which details SMART (Specific, Measurable, Achievable, Realistic and Timely) targets and describes the strategies and supports required to achieve those targets.
- Monitoring pupil progress through a rigorous system of assessment and tracking.
- Implementing a consistent system of positive behaviour support.
- Facilitating pupil-centred active learning.
- Placing special emphasis on the development of literacy and numeracy, social skills, language and communication and coordination, sequencing and movement.

Effort and achievement are praised and rewarded to build self-esteem. Merits and stickers are awarded daily. Certificates and rosettes are awarded each week. Pupils are given the opportunity for their efforts and achievements to be recognised and celebrated on a regular basis culminating in an end-of-term Musical Performance and Prize Giving.

We offer a full curriculum. PE/Games take place on a weekly basis at school and in local community facilities. Reading, Literacy and Maths lessons are ability grouped to enable pupils to progress as soon as they are ready. After-school clubs are offered several times a week, for example, ICT, Music, Games and Swimming.

We value teamwork and the partnership between parents and staff. Parent/Teacher meetings are held several times a term. Special Provision staff are available in weekly drop-in sessions.

ACS Cobham International School

Heywood, Portsmouth Road, Cobham, Surrey KT11 1BL

Tel: 01932 867251
Fax: 01932 869789
email: CobhamAdmissions@acs-schools.com
website: www.acs-schools.com

Head: **Tony Eysele**

Age Range. 2–18.
Number in School. Day: 827 Boys, 654 Girls; 107 Boarders.
Tuition Fees (2016–2017) per semester (2 semesters). £3,705–£12,840.
Boarding Fees (2016–2017) per semester (2 semesters). In addition to tuition fees: 7 day £9,340 (grades 7–12); 5 day £6,815 (grades 7–12).

Founded in 1967 to serve the needs of international and local families, ACS International Schools now educates 3,500 students up to age 18, from more than 70 countries, at three London area campuses in England and one in Doha, Qatar. All our schools are non-sectarian and co-educational.

The success of the programme at ACS Cobham is based on teamwork, collaboration, and the broad participation of its international community. All students are treated as unique individuals, with equal potential to make a positive contribution to the school. The goal is to instil an enthusiasm for lifelong learning and a sense of global awareness in each student, along with the necessary skills to prepare them for the challenges and changes which lie ahead.

The academic programme offers both the International Baccalaureate (IB) Diploma and Advanced Placement (AP) courses, creating a curriculum that meets the needs of a broad international student body. ACS graduates have established a tradition of attaining excellent exam results, enabling them to continue their studies at top universities around the world, including the US and UK.

Situated on 128 acres approximately 30 minutes by train from Central London, ACS Cobham enrols over 1,400 students. Exceptional facilities include an Early Childhood village; purpose-built Lower, Middle, and High School buildings; gymnasium and cafeteria complex and a Dormitory. All Lower, Middle and High School buildings have separate classrooms, science labs, libraries, computer labs, art and music studios and access to the school's state-of-the-art Interactive Learning Centre.

ACS Cobham offers extensive and varied extracurricular clubs and community service activities both locally and internationally, which encourage students to participate in the richness of school life. Students also participate in international theatre arts programmes, maths, literature and music competitions in the UK and across Europe.

The campus sports programme runs three seasons fielding teams in football, volleyball, cross country, basketball, rugby, swimming, dance, tennis, track & field, baseball, softball and golf. Sports facilities include six tennis courts, an Olympic-sized track, playing fields for football, rugby and baseball, a six-hole golf course, and a Sports Centre with 25-metre competition indoor swimming pool, basketball/volleyball show courts, dance and fitness studios, and a café.

The Dormitory provides a home-away-from-home for up to 110 students, aged 12–18. Boarders share two-person rooms with ensuite facilities and wireless internet connections; there are student lounges, kitchens, computer and study rooms. Six full-time Dormitory houseparents and over ten resident teaching staff ensure an active yet well-considered programme of pastoral care, friendship and advisor groups, house activities and weekend trips.

The admissions team is available throughout the year to answer questions, book campus visits, and assist families through the enrolment process. Students are accepted in all grades throughout the year, on non-selective criteria.

ACS Egham International School

Woodlee, London Road (A30), Egham, Surrey TW20 0HS

Tel: 01784 430800
Fax: 01784 430626
email: EghamAdmissions@acs-schools.com
website: www.acs-schools.com
Twitter: @ACSEgham

Head of School: **Mr Jeremy Lewis**

Age Range. 3–18.
Number in School. Day only: 317 Boys, 273 Girls.
Tuition Fees (2016–2017) per semester (2 semesters). £3,540–£12,010.

Founded in 1967 to serve the needs of international and local families, ACS International Schools now educates 3,500 students up to age 18, from more than 70 countries, at three London area campuses in England and one in Doha, Qatar. All our schools are non-sectarian and co-educational.

ACS Egham offers all four International Baccalaureate (IB) programmes – the IB Primary Years Programme (3–11), the IB Middle Years Programme (11–16), the IB Diploma Programme (16–18) as well as the Career-related Programme (16–18). These programmes share a common philosophy and common characteristics: they develop the whole student, helping them to grow socially, physically, aesthetically, and culturally; and provide a broad and balanced education that includes science and the humanities, languages and mathematics, technology, physical education, and the arts.

This academic programme challenges students to fulfil their potential, and offers a broad-based selection of courses and levels to meet individual needs and interests. An important characteristic of ACS Egham is individual attention to students' needs facilitated by an exceptionally well-qualified, experienced, and sympathetic faculty; many of whom are IB examiners, moderators, and teacher trainers. The success of our programme is reflected in our IB Diploma pass rate over the last six years, which has enabled our graduates to continue their studies at top universities around the world, including the US and UK.

Situated on a 20-acre campus approximately 25 miles from central London, ACS Egham enrols more than 600 students. The school has purpose-built computer labs, libraries, spacious classrooms, playgrounds and sports fields. To further enhance the teaching programme there is a 21st century Visual Arts & Design Technology Centre and a new Science wing. A new sports centre opened in September 2012.

ACS Egham runs small class sizes which afford a greater opportunity for individual attention and support for various learning styles so that students are encouraged and challenged accordingly. Child Study Teams meet with individual student's teachers, administrators and parents, to ensure that every child is appropriately challenged and supported. A Language Coordinator assists families in organising native language lessons after-school or, if possible, during the school day.

ACS Egham offers extensive and varied extracurricular clubs and community service activities both locally and internationally, which encourage students to participate in the richness of school life. Students also participate in international theatre arts programmes, maths, literature and music competitions in the UK and across Europe. The Campus sports programme runs three seasons fielding teams in football, volleyball, cross country, basketball, rugby, swimming, dance, tennis, athletics, baseball, softball and golf.

The admissions team is available throughout the year to answer questions, book campus visits, and assist families through the enrolment process. Students are accepted in all grades throughout the year.

ACS Hillingdon International School

Hillingdon Court, 108 Vine Lane, Hillingdon, Middlesex UB10 0BE

Tel: 01895 259771
Fax: 01895 818404
email: HillingdonAdmissions@acs-schools.com
website: www.acs-schools.com

Head of School: Diane Hren

Age Range. 4–18.
Number in School. Day only: 317 Boys, 263 Girls.
Tuition Fees (2016–2017) per semester (2 semesters). £5,140–£11,555.

Founded in 1967 to serve the needs of international and local families, ACS International Schools now educates 3,500 students up to age 18, from more than 70 countries, at three London area campuses in England and one in Doha, Qatar. All our schools are non-sectarian and co-educational.

The ACS Hillingdon philosophy:

- encourages a positive attitude toward education and life-long learning
- provides meaningful educational experiences that enable students to acquire and apply knowledge, concepts, and skills
- helps each student realise his/her academic, creative, and physical potential
- provides opportunities for students to understand, appreciate, and develop sensitivity for other cultures
- encourages participation in community service, and support of local and international charities
- promotes a partnership with parents to meet the needs of students, and offer programmes that addresses issues associated with a highly mobile population
- promotes students to become lifelong learners in a global community

The academic programme offers both the International Baccalaureate (IB) Middle Years and Diploma Programmes as well as Advanced Placement (AP) courses, creating a curriculum that meets the needs of our entire international student body. IB scores regularly rank it among the highest achieving non-selective schools in the UK, enabling graduates to continue their studies at top universities around the world, including the US and UK.

ACS Hillingdon accepts over 600 students aged between 4 and 18. The campus is situated on an 11-acre estate less than 15 miles from central London. A door-to-door busing service covers much of London. The campus combines Grade II listed stately mansion with a modern wing housing classrooms, computer labs, an integrated IT network, libraries, cafeteria, gymnasium, auditorium, and the Harmony House Centre for international music which houses a digital recording studio, rehearsal rooms, practice studios and a computer lab for music technology.

The campus has on-site playing fields, tennis courts and playgrounds, and off-site playing fields for football, rugby and athletics. Local swimming and golf facilities are also used by our students. The sports programme runs three seasons fielding teams in football, volleyball, cross country, basketball, rugby, swimming, dance, tennis, track & field, baseball, softball and golf.

ACS Hillingdon also offers extensive and varied extracurricular clubs and community service activities both locally and internationally, which encourage students to participate in the richness of school life. Students also participate in international theatre arts programmes, maths, literature and music competitions in the UK and across Europe.

The admissions team is available throughout the year to answer questions, book campus visits, and assist families through the enrolment process. Students are accepted in all grades throughout the year.

Alton Convent School

Anstey Lane, Alton, Hampshire GU34 2NG

Tel: 01420 82070
Fax: 01420 541711
email: enquiries@altonconvent.org.uk
website: www.altonconvent.org.uk
Twitter: @AltonConventSch
Facebook: @alton.conventschool

Motto: *Vita dulcedo spes nostra salve*

Chairman of Governors: Mr Clive Hexton

Headmaster: **Mr Graham Maher**, BA Hons, PGCE, MA

Deputy Head (*Pastoral*): Mrs Elizabeth Hoyes, BA Hons, PGCE
Deputy Head (*Curriculum*): Mrs Sally Webb, BEd Hons

Age Range. Girls 6 months–18 years, Boys 6 months–11 years.
Number in School. Day: 398 Girls, 134 Boys.
Fees per term (2016–2017). Reception–Year 1 £3,075, Preparatory £3,725, Senior School £4,365. Garden House Nursery (daily charge): 6 mths to 2 yrs 11 months £61.70; 3 yrs and Pre-Prep £74.80. EYE grants applicable.

Alton Convent School, situated in north east Hampshire, is an independent Catholic day school welcoming pupils from all faiths. It has a stimulating, friendly community promoting mutual tolerance, courtesy, care for others, a sense of self-worth and personal discipline. Inspectors noted that pupils' personal development is excellent and a strength of the school, enhanced by excellent pastoral care integral to the school's ethos. Pupils are happy, confident, courteous and articulate. Visitors comment on the calm, happy, purposeful working environment.

Alton Convent School's pupils excel across a wide and rich curriculum, with consistently outstanding exam results. Expectations are high, with exceptional success attained in the arts, sport and academic pursuits. Most recently the school celebrated national prize winners in engineering, mathematics, history, sport and the arts, culminating in an invitation to Buckingham Palace for three young engineers.

In 2014 the school was awarded the British Council's prestigious International School Award in recognition of their work to bring the world into the classroom. As an international school, possibilities extend beyond the UK, with exchange programmes in France, Germany, Spain and Colombia. Links exist and continue to flourish with sister schools around the globe including India and Peru.

Learning takes place in and outside of the classroom. Opportunities to stimulate and enrich the learning process are sought continuously from visits to law courts, art galleries and cutting-edge commercial science laboratories in the Sixth Form and Senior school to natural history field trips and museums in the Preparatory School.

The school continues to be successful in delivering its primary aims: to pursue excellence, maximize individual potential and enrich the educational experience of pupils. An environment is created where each child can shine, whilst instilling a Christian ethos, moral code and quiet confidence to enable pupils to '*be the best that they can be*'.

The Garden House Day Nursery, a purpose-built facility, is open 51 weeks a year from 8.00 am to 6.00 pm. It takes babies from 6 months and EYE grants are applicable. The quality of provision is rated as 'outstanding'.

Entry at the beginning of the Prep School is non-selective, but entry to the Senior School is by entrance examination taken in January for September entry. The school accepts girls in other years up to and including Year 10. Entry to the Sixth Form is by GCSE results and interview. Whilst academically selective, we seek to admit pupils in sympathy with our ethos who will flourish in our community. The curriculum is broad and balanced for all ages with a wide range of science, sports, languages, and expressive arts. Academic standards are high, with pupils encouraged to think for themselves and take responsibility for their own development. Boys and girls are prepared for entry into their senior schools. Senior girls take an average ten GCSEs and continue to A Level in our Sixth Form, currently selecting four AS subjects with three or four subjects continued to A2 Level.

Inspectors affirmed that A Level performance is impressive and above the national average for girls in selective and maintained schools year on year, and results at GCSE are consistently above national averages. Girls progress to prestigious universities.

Co-curricular activities include a wide range of competitive sporting opportunities, artistic activities and study workshops. Musical and dramatic opportunities are strong in both schools, with thriving choirs, orchestras, ensembles, jazz group and drama productions. All pupils are encouraged to become involved in the major music and drama productions: additional tuition in sport, dance, LAMDA and music is offered. Art is strong and has been recognised nationally in various awards. The school has retained its Gold status for the Artsmark Award marking the high expectations and provision offered in the school.

Parents have regular opportunities for consultation with staff. Open Mornings, newsletters and the school website keep parents up to date. The school is noted as having a clear vision for the future.

A range of academic scholarships are available in Year 7 (by examination) and Year 12 (by results and interview). A governors' award is also available for the Sixth Form.

Charitable status. The Alton Convent School Charity is a Registered Charity, number 1071684.

Argyle House School

19/20 Thornhill Park, Tunstall Road, Sunderland, Tyne & Wear SR2 7LA

Tel: 0191 510 0726
Fax: 0191 567 2209
email: info@argylehouseschool.co.uk
website: www.argylehouseschool.co.uk

Head: **Mr C Johnson**

Age Range. 2½–16.
Number in School. 250 Boys and Girls.
Fees per term (2016–2017). £2,215–£2,605.

Argyle House School was established in 1884 as a small independent day school for boys and girls, situated in the centre of Sunderland. Students travel from all parts of the region, by our buses, or local forms of transport. The school has maintained its high standards of academic achievement, whilst catering for a wide variety of abilities.

At Argyle House, we believe in the individual, and work with him or her to enable the achievement of each student's potential. This is due to attention to detail by fully qualified and dedicated staff, who help to mould the individual into a well-mannered and accomplished young individual, who will be able to meet future challenges.

Small class sizes and a friendly environment facilitate learning, but not all work is academic, as the school takes an active part in many sporting leagues, both within the school, and locally with other schools. We aim to offer all the facilities of a much larger school, whilst remaining at present student levels to keep the intimacy and friendliness of a smaller school, for both parents and students.

Arts Educational Schools London

Cone Ripman House, 14 Bath Road, Chiswick, London W4 1LY

Tel: 020 8987 6600
Fax: 020 8987 6601
email: rjones@artsed.co.uk
website: www.artsed.co.uk
Twitter: @ArtsEdLondon
Facebook: /artseducational

Founded in 1919.

Headteacher: **Mr Adrian Blake**

Age Range. 11–18 Co-educational.
Number in School. Day: 176 Girls, 57 Boys.
Fees per term (2016–2017). £4,833–£5,286.
"The UK's Leading Specialist Performing Arts Institution in Academic Achievement" Sunday Times, Parent Power 2007.
100% A Level Pass Rate and outstanding GCSE results.

The Arts Educational Schools London are committed to developing the full potential of each and every pupil. High quality vocational, academic and social education, in a warm, friendly, caring environment, ensures that our pupils feel challenged and fulfilled throughout the whole of their exciting careers at the school.

The school has been educating young performing artists since 1919, and there is no comparable school in the UK. Dancers learn to act and sing, actors learn to sing and dance, musicians learn to do more than play their instruments well, and everyone has the opportunity to be grounded in the visual arts, languages, humanities, sciences, and mathematics.

From Year 7 all pupils follow a course leading to eight or nine GCSEs. All pupils have access to the outstanding performance facilities, rehearsal rooms, proscenium and studio theatres. At Year 12 pupils follow a course of four AS Levels, leading to three or four A Levels, whilst receiving outstanding training in dance, drama, music and musical theatre.

In addition, students in Year 12 can opt to take a Level 3 BTEC in Musical Theatre, Acting, Dance or Production Arts, along with two A Levels as additional courses of study, where they benefit from all the expertise and excellence of the professional performance departments along with the academic reputation and pastoral guidance of the Secondary School.

Former Students of the schools include: Julie Andrews, Samantha Barks, Sarah Brightman, Darcey Bussell, Martin Clunes, Joan Collins, Adam Cooper, Bonnie Langford, Jane Seymour, Hugo Speer, Summer Strallen and Will Young.

Admission is at 11+ and 16+ and occasionally at other ages if places become available.

Charitable status. The Arts Educational Schools is a Registered Charity, number 311087. It exists solely for educational purposes.

Ashton House School

50–52 Eversley Crescent, Isleworth, Middlesex TW7 4LW

Tel: 020 8560 3902
Fax: 020 8568 1097
email: principal@ashtonhouse.com
website: www.ashtonhouse.com

Principal: Mr S J Turner, BSc

Head Teacher: **Dr James Heslop**

Age Range. 3–11.
Number in School. 119 Day Pupils: 71 Boys, 48 Girls.
Fees per term (2016–2017). £2,662–£3,696.
Founded 1930. Proprietors: P A, G B & S J Turner. Entry by interview and assessment. Prospectus on request.

Choosing a school for your child is one of the most important decisions you will be making on their behalf and we fully understand that you want to get it right. At Ashton House we do our very best to deliver a first-class education in a calm and happy atmosphere, where children learn and develop while still enjoying their childhood. Our results at 11 indicate that we are succeeding while our pupils have grown into confident, caring young people ready for the next phase in their education. Our most recent inspection judged the personal development of our pupils to be "outstanding".

Ayscoughfee Hall School

Welland Hall, London Road, Spalding, Lincolnshire PE11 2TE

Tel: 01775 724733
email: admin@ahs.me.uk
website: www.ahs.me.uk

Head: **Mrs Clare Ogden**

Age Range. 3–11 Co-educational.
Number of Pupils. 144 Day Pupils.
Fees per term (2016–2017). £1,360–£2,010.
Founded in 1920, Ayscoughfee Hall School is centred around a beautiful Georgian family home. A purpose-built extension complements the already spacious accommodation. The School houses Kindergarten, Infant and Junior Departments and has further developed its facilities to include enlarged classrooms, a dedicated Science/Art Room, Music Department, Cookery Room, Library, a large Sports Hall and a Foreign Language Room.

The guidelines and principles of the National Curriculum are followed in all subjects but go far beyond the basic requirements in order to give each child a broader, more varied understanding. Academic standards are high and progress is well monitored throughout the school. The vast majority of pupils are successful in the Lincolnshire County Council selection examination and progress to secondary selective school education very well equipped to tackle all subjects. The curriculum is continually reviewed and class teachers are supported by specialist teachers for PE, ICT, languages and music. French is taught from Reception class.

iPads support learning in the classrooms and pupils receive weekly, dedicated ICT tuition in our up-to-date ICT suite.

The School excels with its music and drama productions over the academic year, in which all children perform in front of their parents and guests.

The school competes successfully in local and regional sports activities, including football, rugby, hockey, netball, cross-country and athletics.

There is a thriving programme of extracurricular activities, including sport, drama, cookery, poetry, textiles, choir, instrumental groups and ICT. A wide variety of educational visits is offered, with the older children having the opportunity to participate in alternate foreign and activity trips, accompanied by the staff. Furthermore, regular visits by professional groups and individuals take place in school.

As a small school with small class sizes, we aim to provide a happy and caring environment where the individual child may flourish. We are proud of our academic standards but we also strive to give a broad and balanced education. Above all, we want our boys and girls to use and develop their different abilities and to enjoy the success this brings.

Charitable status. Ayscoughfee Hall School Limited is a Registered Charity, number 527294. It exists to provide education for boys and girls.

Babington House School

Grange Drive, Chislehurst, Kent BR7 5ES

Tel: 020 8467 5537
Fax: 020 8295 1175
email: enquiries@babingtonhouse.com
website: www.babingtonhouse.com
Twitter: @babingtonbr7
LinkedIn: /Babington-House-School

Chair of Governors: Mr C Turner

Headmaster: Mr T W A Lello, MA, FRSA, NPQH, PGCE

Head of Seniors: Mrs J Brown, MA, BA Hons, PGCE

Age Range. Boys 3–11, Girls 3–18, Co-ed Sixth Form.
Number in School. Day: 106 Boys, 239 Girls.
Fees per term (2016–2017). £4,082–£5,084.

Babington House School is an independent day school from 3 to 18 years, situated in a beautiful group of buildings on Grange Drive in Chislehurst, near Bromley. The school is co-educational up to 11 years old; girls only from 11 to 16 and has a mixed Sixth Form.

Our commitment is to provide an academic and well-rounded education with small class sizes which is tailored to the needs of our pupils, believing that bright children benefit from carefully monitored and well-directed learning, where self-discipline is highly prized and where each pupil is known as an individual. This helps Babington House pupils grow into confident, accomplished, creative young people with emotional intelligence and high standards.

Babington is an academic school. Our academic, social and sporting endeavours are underpinned by core Christian values which include a respect for others and an awareness of a purpose greater than ourselves. There is a strong sense of community at Babington House.

In the last inspection Babington House was praised by the ISI for achieving outstanding academic success at all key stages and providing exemplary pastoral care. The boys and girls receive a first-class education in a nurturing and supportive environment, set in pleasant suburban surroundings. Full range of courses for examinations at all levels. Schools Curriculum Award. ISA Excellence Award. "Outstanding and Excellent" in all areas of school (ISI report November 2010).

Specialist facilities for Science, Music, Drama, Art, Sport, ICT, Languages, Maths & English.

Small classes: Maximum size 20 pupils. Careers guidance by a specialist.

Wide range of sports (Athletics, Swimming, Tennis, Netball, Gymnastics, Hockey, Football, Cross Country) and extracurricular activities (Drama, Gym Club, Horse Riding, Cookery, Rock Climbing, Taekwondo, Archaeology Club, Choir, Ballet, Tap, Elocution and Instrumental Tuition).

Charitable status. Babington House School is a Registered Charity, number 307914. It exists to provide exemplary education.

Ballard School

Fernhill Lane, New Milton, Hampshire BH25 5SU

Tel: 01425 626900
Fax: 01425 638847
email: admissions@ballardschool.co.uk
website: www.ballardschool.co.uk

The School is a non-profit making Educational Trust under a Board of Governors. It is a co-educational school through to GCSE level and provides a family friendly all-round education. The school is non-selective and boasts a strong examination success record which enables students to achieve their first choice of school for the next stage of their education.

Chairman of the Board of Governors: Mr C Ford

Headmaster: Mr Alastair J Reid, MA Cantab, PGCE, NPQH

Age Range. 2 to 16 Co-educational.
Number of Children. 500 day children.
Fees per term (2016–2017). Years 9–11 £4,765, Years 6–8 £4,530, Years 3–5 £3,915–£4,405. Reception–Year 2 £2,595. Fees include the cost of school lunches.

The School is situated 2 miles from the sea and on the borders of the New Forest in 32 acres of grounds and woodlands. A good network of school buses covers the surrounding area.

Ballard School is a through school divided into four integrated areas, each catering for the specific needs of the pupils at each age range. The whole school has received an excellent ISI inspection report.

There are over 60 qualified teaching staff plus a dedicated Learning Support Unit. Academic results are consistently excellent at all stages (7+, 11+, 13+ and GCSE) with many pupils gaining scholarships and all reaching their first choice of further education. The School offers a broad curriculum with further strengths in music, visual arts, performing arts, dance and sport. More than 60 extracurricular activities are offered.

Facilities are excellent, including brand new International Standard Astro pitch, 5 science laboratories, large art department, 4 computer suites, 3 libraries, large music block including a recording studio, technology laboratory, dance studio, home economics laboratory, large sports hall, extensive playing fields, with tennis courts, netball courts, heated outdoor swimming pool, outdoor basketball court, and Performing Arts Centre seating audiences of 200.

The School has a Christian foundation and the aim of the School is to provide an all-round education where traditional values and standards are valued combined with facilities to prepare children for the 21st century.

Charitable status. Ballard School Ltd is a Registered Charity, number 307328. It exists for the education of children.

Beech Hall School

Beech Hall Drive, Tytherington, Macclesfield, Cheshire SK10 2EG

Tel: 01625 422192
Fax: 01625 502424
email: secretary@beechhallschool.org
website: www.beechhallschool.org
Twitter: @beechhall_macc
Facebook: /beechhallschool

Headmaster: Mr J D Allen, BA Ed Hons, MA, NPQH, FCoT

Age Range. 6 months–16 years.
Number of Pupils. 180.
Fees per term (2016–2017). Infants £2,950, Junior School £3,700, Senior School £3,950. The fees are inclusive of lunches and snacks.

Nursery, Infant, Junior and Senior departments offer education between 8.30 am and 4.00 pm with further supervised sporting and leisure activities available until 5.00 pm. If required, there is supervised care up until 6.00 pm for all children.

Beech Hall is a co-educational Day school situated in spacious and attractive grounds with extensive playing fields, a heated outdoor swimming pool, new food technology lab and many other facilities.

Boys and girls are prepared for entry to a wide variety of Independent Schools and Sixth Form Colleges. Classes are kept small, making individual attention possible in every lesson.

There is a very popular Nursery, Pre-School and Reception department, consisting of children between the ages of 6 months and 5 years under the care of their own specialist teachers. These classes were started with the objective of giving boys and girls a good grounding in reading, writing and arithmetic.

Beech Hall aims to provide a sound all-round education. Rugby, football, hockey and netball are played in the winter terms and in summer, cricket, athletics, and rounders are taught. There is an extensive sporting fixture list covering all sports with children playing representative sport from Year 3 upwards. Swimming is taught throughout the year and other activities include badminton and fives.

The school is situated off the main Stockport–Macclesfield road, within easy reach of Manchester International Airport and the M6 and M62 motorways.

Further details and illustrated prospectus are obtainable from the school or via the school's website.

Beech House School

184 Manchester Road, Rochdale, Greater Manchester OL11 4JQ
Tel: 01706 646309
email: info@beechhouseschool.co.uk
website: www.beechhouseschool.co.uk

Headmaster: **Mr Kevin Sartain**, BSc Hons, PGCE, Dip Spo Psy, CBiol, FIBiol

Age Range. 2–16 Co-educational.
Number of Pupils. 212.
Fees per term (2016–2017). £916–£1,980.
Beech House School is a co-educational day school for pupils aged from two to sixteen. The aim of the school is to blend the best of traditional education with the skills and resources of the modern system to ensure that pupils' talents are exercised to the full. To this end, class sizes are kept small, with 20 or fewer pupils per form at preparatory level and 16 or fewer in each secondary class. The school upholds traditional values and behaviour, providing a secure, caring and academically challenging environment. This gives Beech House its unique character as a 'family-centred' school.

The Independent Schools Association held their annual conference in 2014 at Coombe Abbey, Warwickshire. During this conference they held their awards ceremony. Nobody was more surprised and delighted than our Headmaster, when guest host, TV Presenter Juliet Morris, announced that the winner of School of the Year was Beech House School of Rochdale. The trophy was presented by Lord Lexden (OBE), the ISA President. It is a great honour for the school.

The ninth Education Business Awards, sponsored by Rathbones, were held in 2014 at The Grange Hotel, St Paul's, London. The hotel is famous for being the place where Winston Churchill planned the D Day landings. Beech House School was shortlisted for the 'Outstanding Progress Award for Independent Schools' category. The award is presented to the Independent school that has made outstanding progress and can demonstrate an increase in the educational performance of the school. Beech House was joint runners-up and Kevin Sartain, the Headmaster of the school received their award from the Olympic swimmer and television personality, Sharron Davies MBE.

For the second year running the school's Nursery was presented with the highest level in Rochdale's Early Years quality assurance award.

Bishop Challoner School

228 Bromley Road, Shortlands, Bromley, Kent BR2 0BS
Tel: 020 8460 3546
Fax: 020 8466 8885
email: admissions@bishopchallonerschool.com
website: www.bishopchallonerschool.com
Twitter: @challoner_head

Headteacher: **Mrs Paula Anderson**, BSc Hons, MBA, PGCE

Age Range. 3–18.
Number in School. 390 Day Pupils.
Fees per term (from April 2016). Seniors £3,560, Juniors £2,848, Infants £2,568, Nursery £795–£2,536.
This is a Roman Catholic Independent Co-educational School for ages 3–11 years.

Happiness, self-fulfilment and personal success are all embraced at Bishop Challoner.

The School welcomes all Faiths.

Admissions to the School follows the successful completion of an entrance examination / assessment and an interview with the Headteacher.

Scholarships and Bursaries are available.

Charitable status. Bishop Challoner School is a Registered Charity, number 1153948. It exists to provide an excellent education for boys and girls.

Bowbrook House School

Peopleton, Nr Pershore, Worcs WR10 2EE
Tel: 01905 841242/841843
Fax: 01905 840716
email: enquiries@bowbrookhouseschool.co.uk
website: www.bowbrookhouseschool.co.uk

Headmaster: **Mr C D Allen**, BSc Hons, CertEd, DipSoc

Age Range. 3½–16.
Number in School. Day: 120 Boys, 82 Girls.
Fees per term (2016–2017). £1,925–£3,456.
Bowbrook House is set in 14 acres of picturesque Worcestershire countryside yet within easy reach of Worcester, Pershore and Evesham. The school caters for the academic child and also those of average ability, who can benefit from the small classes. All pupils are able to take full advantage of the opportunities offered and are encouraged to participate in all activities. As well as the academic subjects, the school has a flourishing art department, a computer room, hard tennis courts and an open air swimming pool in addition to extensive games fields.

The Pre-Prep department of 3½–8 year olds is a self-contained unit but enjoys the use of the main school facilities.

Whilst stressing academic achievement, the school aims to provide a structured and disciplined environment in which children of all abilities can flourish, gain confidence and achieve their true potential. The small school size enables the head and staff to know all pupils well, to be able to accurately assess their strengths and weaknesses it enables each pupil to be an important part of the school and to feel that their individual attitudes, behaviour, efforts and achievements are important.

There is an extended school day from 8.15 am to 5.30 pm, with supervised prep sessions. There is also an extensive and varied extracurricular programme run by specialist coaches from basketball, gym and dance to kickboxing and fencing.

Braeside School

130 High Road, Buckhurst Hill, Essex IG9 5SD

Tel: 020 8504 1133
Fax: 020 8505 6675
email: enquiries@braesideschool.co.uk
website: www.braesideschool.co.uk

Headmistress: **Mrs C Osborn**, BA Hons, MSc, PGCE

Age Range. 2½–16.
Number in School. 200 Day Girls.
Fees per term (2016–2017). £1,950–£4,050.

Braeside School is an independent day school for girls aged between 2½ and 16. Our examination results are routinely excellent and the well-qualified staff are determined to maintain our excellent and distinctive character.

The school sets its own high standards in work and behaviour, aiming to give each pupil a sound moral and intellectual foundation for life. The education provided takes full account of each girl's capabilities and interests, and from the earliest age girls acquire a sense of responsibility and confidence, tempered with a deep consideration of others.

The school is able to offer small class sizes in both the Juniors and Seniors, with the significant advantage of teaching in small groups for many subjects in the Seniors, especially in GCSE options subjects. The high pupil-teacher ratio and individual attention builds confidence both academically and socially, and enables our pupils to reach their full potential.

A range of subject-specific outings, enhancement activities and the opportunity of a residential trip abroad all broaden the educational experience for our students.

Braeside is a happy, united school, where the potential to be part of our close-knit family from 2½ to 16 years old creates a secure and stable atmosphere. Staff and students work collaboratively to ensure that they reach their potential.

Entry, at every age apart from 2, 3 and 4, is by test and interview.

Bridgewater School

Drywood Hall, Worsley Road, Worsley, Manchester M28 2WQ

Tel: 0161 794 1463
Fax: 0161 794 3519
email: admin@bwslive.co.uk
website: www.bridgewater-school.co.uk
Twitter: @BridgewaterScho
Facebook: /BridgewaterConnected

Chair of Governors: Mr C Haighton, BSc Hons

Headmistress: **Mrs J A T Nairn**, CertEd Distinction

Age Range. 3–18 Co-educational.
Number of Pupils. 440: 230 Boys, 210 Girls.
Fees per term (2016–2017). £2,594–£3,459. Lunch is included.

Bridgewater School is a co-educational, independent day school for pupils aged between 3 and 18 years. Established as a boys' school in 1950 and having moved to its present delightful semi-rural setting soon afterwards, the school has since grown considerably – admitting girls and developing a sixth form. We draw pupils from the immediate locality, but also from a much wider area, well served as we are by the motorway network and by other major road links.

Bridgewater is by design not a large school. This enables us to provide small classes and high levels of attention to the needs of individual pupils. We seek to maximise education attainment all through a child's development, not least in the years of external examinations at GCSE and A Level.

In addition to its academic goals Bridgewater seeks to retain the intimate atmosphere it has had since its inception. We greatly value our capacity to offer provision across the full age range, from the nursery years to university entrance, for families wanting this continuity of individual attention for their children.

At the same time, however, pupils must look outward to the wider community and to the society in which they will live as adults. We see it as an integral part of Bridgewater's role to foster high standards of behaviour and self-discipline, as well as to develop an awareness of personal and social responsibility. Vital, too, are the many activities which take place outside the classroom – sport, music, drama clubs and societies, language exchange visits and outdoor activity breaks to name but a sample of the range available.

Entrusting your child's education to a school is a very big decision. We are mindful of our responsibility to justify a parent's decision to send their child to us, and of the need for that child's education to be a partnership between school and home. We aim, by the end of this partnership, to produce rounded, articulate young people who are well prepared for the challenges of adult and business life.

The School governors, staff and pupils share a sense of excitement about Bridgewater's future. The school has developed rapidly in recent years, with splendid new buildings and facilities and a considerable increase in pupil numbers. We have a commitment to continual development and improvement. If you have not yet visited us then may we recommend that you do so soon. We would be delighted to meet you and to show you how much Bridgewater School has to offer you and your child.

Charitable status. Bridgewater School is a Registered Charity, number 1105547.

Bronte School

Mayfield, 7 Pelham Road, Gravesend, Kent DA11 0HN

Tel: 01474 533805
Fax: 01474 352003
email: enquiry@bronteschool.co.uk
website: www.bronteschool.co.uk

Headmaster: **Mr Nicholas Clements**, MA, BSc

Age Range. 3–11.
Number in School. 125 Day Pupils: 71 Boys, 54 Girls.
Fees per term (2016–2017). £2,875.

Bronte is a small, friendly, family-orientated, co-educational day school serving Gravesend and surrounding villages. The children are taught in small classes and are prepared for all types of secondary education. In 1999 the school moved to its present building which has since been expanded to accommodate specialist teaching rooms. A broadly-based curriculum and an extensive number of activity clubs provide the children with every opportunity to develop their individual interests and abilities. We achieve excellent 11+ results every year.

The school was awarded Artsmark Gold status in 2013.

Entry is preferred at Kindergarten (age 3) or Reception Class (age 4) following a parental visit to the school and an interview with the Head. Children joining at a later stage are assessed informally prior to entry.

Buxlow Preparatory School

5/6 Castleton Gardens, East Lane, Wembley, Middlesex HA9 7QJ

Tel:	020 8904 3615
email:	admin@buxlowschool.org.uk
website:	www.buxlowschool.org.uk

Head Teacher: **Mrs Christina A Leach**

Director Health and Safety: Mr Michael Aherne
Director of Studies: Mr Stuart Kennedy
Director of Pastoral Care: Ms Sharon Sethi
Director Special Needs and Abilities (*Sendco*): Miss Janine Martin
School Secretary and Head's PA: Ms Alyson Parker

Age Range. 2–11 Co-educational, Nursery to Year 6.
Number of Pupils. 79.
Fees per term (2016–2017). £2,925.

Cambridge Tutors College

Water Tower Hill, Croydon, Surrey CR0 5SX

Tel:	020 8688 5284
Fax:	020 8686 9220
email:	info@ctc.ac.uk
website:	www.ctc.ac.uk

Principal: **Dr Chris Drew**, BSc Sussex, MA Bath, EdD Bath, PGCE, Dip RSA

Age Range. 15–19.
Number of Pupils. 180.
Fees per annum (2016–2017). £20,400 excluding accommodation; up to £28,900 including homestay accommodation or up to £35,400 for boarding accommodation.

2016 A Level results: 42.9% A*/A and 80% of students entering their first choice universities, mostly Russell Group.

Since 1958 Cambridge Tutors College (CTC) has been offering a very high quality academically focused education to young people from the United Kingdom and from across the world. Fundamental to the College's ethos is small group teaching – our average class size is just over 5 students – and regular testing: students sit weekly tests in every subject, under examination conditions. This combination of small classes, regular testing and expert teaching has proved to be highly successful in giving students the motivation and confidence to succeed.

CTC offers: A Level courses (two-year and 18-month), one-year GCSE course or a one-year pre-GCSE which may lead to GCSE Mathematics or Art and provides intensive amounts of English in the pathway subject areas. Also offer accelerated 12 month A Levels and two-term pre-sessional course linked to two-year A Level program.

The College's most recent ISI Inspection report in 2011 was outstanding as was the very recent 2014 Student Welfare inspection.

The college enjoys a particularly strong reputation for helping students to gain entry to the UK's most prestigious universities.

Situated in a pleasant parkside location in South Croydon, CTC is just a few minutes' walk from the town centre, East Croydon station and bus and tram routes. It is close to Central London, just 15 minutes away by train, but surrounded by parkland and quiet residential streets.

Facilities and resources are modern and well-appointed. The College has excellent technological infrastructure with fast Wi-Fi, and there is an ambitious development programme in place.

The College's welfare provision includes a team of trained professionals and all students have a personal tutor. A varied weekly programme of sporting and other activities is offered, as well as weekend excursions.

Charitable status. Cambridge Tutors Educational Trust Limited is a Registered Charity, number 312878.

Canbury School

Kingston Hill, Kingston-upon-Thames, Surrey KT2 7LN

Tel:	020 8549 8622
Fax:	020 8974 6018
email:	reception@canburyschool.co.uk
website:	www.canburyschool.co.uk

Head: **Ms L Clancy**, BEd

Age Range. 11–16.
Number in School. 65 boys and girls.

Founded in 1982, Canbury School is a unique and happy co-educational independent day school for boys and girls from the ages of 11 to 16 on the outskirts of London beside Richmond Park. With excellent transport links to the school, students come from various nearby areas such as Barnes, Putney, Wandsworth, New Malden, Richmond, Teddington, Twickenham, Hampton, Epsom, Central London, Surrey and other areas in the South East such as Esher and Effingham. We also welcome overseas students who are supported in school by our comprehensive ESOL programme. Located on the top of Kingston Hill, it affords our students the opportunity to experience the vast resources London has to offer such as museums, parks, galleries, and theatres literally via a bus ride. With class sizes of fifteen students or less, enthusiastic teaching, excellent pastoral care and a determination to target the needs of individual students, Canbury School gets the best out of students with a wide range of abilities.

Entry requirements. Educational reports need to be submitted prior to interview with the Headmistress, An assessment day(s) may be arranged to secure entry to the school.

Curriculum. We cover a full range of GCSE subjects, most students taking a total of eight or nine.

In Years 7, 8 and 9 we emphasise English, Mathematics and Science in line with the requirements of the National Curriculum. Our extended curriculum includes Spanish, Geography, History, Information Technology, Art, Design & Technology, Photography, Performing Arts, PE and Games, Music, and Personal, Social and Health Education. Later, Physics, Chemistry and Biology are taken as doubly-certificated GCSE subjects. Individual arrangements can be made for students to prepare for GCSE in Japanese, German, Chinese and other languages. GCSE Business Studies and BTEC Travel & Tourism is offered in Years 10 and 11.

We run a wide range of extracurricular activities and clubs including drama, art, karate, sports and table-tennis.

Canbury School is different in placing emphasis on small classes. No class has more than 15 students. Our aim is to bring out the talents of each student. Students participate in the school council which makes decisions in some areas of school life. The School runs an English Language programme (ESOL) for students arriving from abroad with limited skills in spoken English.

Facilities. A small, friendly school with well-equipped classrooms. We have up-to-date computer facilities, science laboratory, classrooms and Art/DT Studio with pottery area and kiln. There is also a playground and a garden area. We access local facilities for a wide range of sporting activities including athletics, cricket, netball, softball, swimming, watersports, badminton, soccer, hockey, basketball and rock climbing.

Fees per term (2016–2017). £5,370. Bursaries are available at the discretion of the School and are subject to satisfactory completion of the School's Bursary Form.

Charitable status. Canbury School is a Registered Charity, number 803766. It exists to provide education to a broad range of children including some of various nationalities who stand to benefit from being in a small school.

Cardiff Sixth Form College

1–3 Trinity Court, 21–27 Newport Road, Cardiff CF24 0AA

Tel: 02920 493121
email: marketing@ccoex.com
website: www.ccoex.com
Twitter: @CSFCOfficial
Facebook: @CardiffSixthFormCollege

Motto: Inspire, Reach and Achieve

Principal: **Mr Gareth Collier**

Age Range. 16–19 Co-educational.
Number of Students. 310.

With a reputation for outstanding educational achievement, excellent facilities and enriching extracurricular activities, Cardiff Sixth Form College (CSFC) focuses on individual care, and inspires students to make the most of their unique talents.

CSFC has been ranked, for the fourth consecutive year, top of the A Level League tables (in The Times and The Telegraph) for 2016, achieving 93% A–A*. The college has built its reputation on enabling students to gain entry to elite universities; thus, in 2016 18 students gained entry to Cambridge, 45 to medical schools, and 40 to UCL, LSE, and Imperial College. A number of students choose to study at Hong Kong University or Chinese Hong Kong University.

The college offers three core routes of study; One Year Intensive GCSEs, A Levels, and Summer School. We also run overseas study camps in the summer. Students are able to benefit from experienced teachers, many of whom have Examining/Chief Examining experience.

The Independent Schools Inspectorate (ISI) awarded the college the highest available grade (1) for all three key criteria – Teaching & Learning, Welfare, and Governance – in the last round of inspections.

The School Environment. The College offers a strong system of pastoral support, with designated members of staff to support students. The student accommodation is a newly-built facility and accommodates 300+ students. All rooms are single rooms with an en-suite shower room and have shared kitchen facilities; there are also studio rooms available which have their own cooking facilities. The complex has wardens who are on duty seven days a week, 24 hours a day, ensuring a completely safe environment. Students also have access to state-of-the-art sports facilities.

A Unique Experience. The college hosts a range of extracurricular activities which foster teamwork and discipline, including sports, music, debate and the arts. Skills acquired here carry over in work placements at home and abroad. International trips, competitions such as the Science Olympiads and NASA Space Settlement Design Competition (ISSDC) allow students to push themselves academically while adding a global dimension to their work experience portfolios. Since 2011, students from CSFC have been invited to the ISSDC competition held at the Johnson Space Centre, Houston.

Located in the vibrant city of Cardiff, a city awarded the highest 'feel good factor' in the UK Survey of best places to live, our college prides itself on the fact that its students form strong bonds with each other whilst being encouraged to participate in a wide variety of extracurricular activities in a friendly environment. The aim is to prepare students for a well-balanced, modern life.

Fees per annum (2016–2017). Day £15,000; Boarding £36,000–£40,000.

Charitable status. Cardiff Sixth Form College is Registered Charity, number: 1123262.

Carleton House Preparatory School

145 Menlove Avenue, Liverpool L18 3EE

Tel: 0151 722 0756
email: schooloffice@carletonhouse.co.uk
website: www.carletonhouse.co.uk

Chair of Governors: Mr Peter Megan

Head Teacher: **Mrs A Daniels**, MA, BA Hons, PGCE

Age Range. 3+–11 Co-educational.
Number in School. 189.
Fees per term (2016–2017). £2,515 inclusive of lunch, day trips, Spanish lessons and personal insurance cover.

Located in the leafy suburbs of south Liverpool, Carleton House is Merseyside's leading co-ed Preparatory School (16th in the Sunday Times Parent Power 2016). It is a Catholic school that welcomes children of all denominations.

They can because they think they can truly embodies the spirit of Carleton House. Our school is a lively, vibrant community that gives its pupils a first-class education for the 21st century.

Small class sizes (we endeavour to keep to a maximum of 23) and a high ratio of teaching staff to pupils enable the well-qualified and experienced staff to provide individual attention in a friendly, caring atmosphere. We nurture the development of the whole child – academically, spiritually and in the sporting and cultural aspects of their lives. Through excellent teaching and the close relationship that exists between school and home, our pupils are challenged, encouraged and supported to achieve their very best.

The implementation of all ten National Curriculum subjects ensures a broad, well-balanced curriculum is followed, but great importance is given to Maths and English as success in these subjects is central to development in other areas. Additional specialist teaching is provided for children requiring support in the basic subjects.

French has been successfully introduced in all classes including Reception with Spanish in the upper years.

All children receive music lessons and individual piano and guitar lessons are also available.

Emphasis is placed on high academic standards with children being prepared for a variety of Entrance examinations at 11 and more than 90% of pupils gain places at selective schools of their choice.

A wide range of sports and extracurricular activities is offered to both boys and girls, including football, netball, cricket, rounders, swimming, chess, lacrosse, singing and speech choir. The children compete in local sporting events as well as choral festivals.

Theatre and educational visits are encouraged along with a residential trip to Shropshire, and Paris for older pupils, which provide field and adventure activities that help build confidence and self-esteem.

Close contact with parents is promoted through regular parent/teacher meetings and reports on pupils progress.

A thriving Parent Teacher Association provides social functions for parents while raising funds for extra equipment.

After-school provision is provided by the 'Kids Club'. This operates daily from 3.30 pm until 6.00 pm and school is open from 8 am for early drop-offs.

Parents are welcome to visit the school by appointment.

Further information available from the Head Teacher.

Charitable status. Carleton House Preparatory School is a Registered Charity, number 505310. It exists to provide education for boys and girls.

Castle House School

Chetwynd End, Newport, Shropshire TF10 7JE

Tel:	01952 567600
email:	admin@castlehouseschool.co.uk
website:	www.castlehouseschool.co.uk
Twitter:	@CastleHouseSch

Chairman of Governors: Dr Martin Deahl

Headmaster: **Mark Crewe-Read**, BSc Econ Hons Wales, PGCE

Type of School. Co-educational day preparatory school.
Age Range. 2–11.
Number of Pupils. 109: 55 girls, 54 boys.
Fees per term (2016–2017). £2,365–£2,815.

Castle House is a friendly day preparatory school with a family feel. It is small enough for everybody to know and be known by everybody else, but offers a full and busy programme.

The school aims to bring the best out of every pupil by providing opportunities to excel and developing confidence to try.

Much importance is attached to the children being kind and considerate to each other, in the belief that happy children work best. We develop positive and courteous behaviour.

Since 1980 the school has been a charitable trust, run by a board of governors with varied talents and local interests. It was founded in 1944 by Miss Zellah Pitchford. The current head is the fifth.

The school's Georgian house, set in delightful gardens, is in the conservation area of Newport in east Shropshire. It serves urban and rural areas, including west Staffordshire, Market Drayton, Eccleshall, Telford and Shifnal.

Pupils are prepared for entrance exams to independent schools and to local grammar schools of which the two in Newport are unique in Shropshire. There is an excellent record of passes and scholarships, from a mixed ability intake, with children achieving their potential and beyond.

The curriculum covers all major subjects, and Art, French, Music, Spanish, ICT, PE, Games, Swimming, Gymnastics and Drama. RE and assemblies are Christian, but non-denominational, encouraging all to join in.

Our flourishing educational nursery, CHerubS, for two to four year olds, is open all year from 8.00 am to 6.00 pm. Holiday care is available all day for children up to eleven, every holiday.

A rich range of after-school activities includes moviemaking, yoga, crafts, choirs, computers, eco, gymnastics, chess, radio, football, netball, short tennis, cricket and rounders.

Matches are played in traditional team games, crosscountry and swimming. Particular success has been achieved in schools' gymnastics, with girls' teams winning silver medals at national level in GISGA (independent schools) competitions. Boys' teams have three times won national under 9 and under 11 titles and the school team has twice won the BSGA under 11 mixed teams Floor and Vault national title.

We see education as a cooperative venture with parents. There are regular progress reports and feedback meetings. Parents are encouraged to bring their concerns to the teachers and there is also a Parents' Forum. The Parents' Association is very well supported.

Further information can be obtained on our website or by telephoning the Registrar at the school.

Charitable status. Castle House School Trust Ltd is a Registered Charity, number 510515. It exists for the provision of high quality education for boys and girls.

Chase Grammar School
(formerly Chase Academy)

Convent Close, Cannock, Staffordshire WS11 0UR

Tel:	01543 501800
Fax:	01543 501801
email:	info@chasegrammar.com
website:	www.chasegrammar.com

Principal: **Mrs Jackie Medhurst**, BA Hons, PGCE

Head of Preparatory Department: Mr Ian Sterling, BEd

Age Range. 3–18.
Number in School. 6 Boarders, 197 Day.
Fees per term (2016–2017). Day £1,732–£3,748; Boarding from £6,090. Fees include lunches and most extras.

Independent day and boarding school for boys and girls from nursery to A Level.

Formerly a convent, founded in 1879, the senior school was added in 1980.

Extensive modern school on spacious urban site. Excellent science, technology, computing and language facilities, and Music School. Extensive sports facilities, including 3 floodlit astroturf pitches.

Academic work. Small classes allow attention to the individual student. The National Curriculum is shadowed throughout. Common core up to Year 9. GCSE, AS and A2 Level in: English, Mathematics, Physics, Chemistry, Biology, Design and Technology, Business Studies, History, Geography, French, German, Physical Education, Music, Drama, Art, Dance, Accounting, Latin.

A programme of early GCSE in Maths, English, Science and DT and our Grammar stream allow us to tailor timetables to individual needs.

Boarding. Delightful modern rooms, the majority of which are single or double study-bedrooms. The associated International Study Centre makes provision for overseas students who need to learn or improve their English.

Dyslexia. Support for intelligent dyslexics from a Dyslexia Institute trained teacher and within the small classes.

Sport. Football, cricket, hockey and netball are the principal sports with school facilities for tennis, volleyball, basketball, badminton and table tennis.

Music and Drama. A strong team of professional performers and first-rate teachers producing big uptake in the performing arts as extracurricular activities.

School day. 08.50–15.50. Prep/Clubs until 16.45. Facilities for early drop-off and late pick-up.

Claires Court

1 College Avenue, Maidenhead, Berkshire SL6 6AW

Tel: Registrar: 01628 411472
Fax: 01628 411466
email: registrar@clairescourt.com
website: www.clairescourt.com

Principals:
Mr H Wilding, BA, MCIM, FRSA
Mr J Wilding, BSc, FRSA

Head of Senior Boys: Mr J Rayer, BSc, PGCE
Head of Junior Boys: Mr J Spanswick, BSc, PGCE
Headteacher – Girls, *Nursery & Sixth Form*: Mr P Bevis, CertEd
Head of Junior Girls: Miss L Barlow, BA QTS
Head of Sixth Form: Mr A Giles, BSc
Head of Nursery: Mrs S Wilding, BA, DPP

Age Range. 3–18.
Number of Pupils. 622 Boys, 309 Girls. Sixth Form: Co-educational 146.
Fees per term (2016–2017). £2,850–£5,025. Sixth Form new entrants: £5,160.
Teaching Staff: 98 full time, 32 part time, 27 visiting.

Claires Court is a school for families, run by a family, providing education for young people aged 3 to 18 years. Based on three sites across Maidenhead, we are a broad ability 'diamond model' day school where boys and girls are educated separately during their main school years, but come together for trips and visits, whilst the Nursery and Sixth Form pupils benefit from a co-educational learning environment.

It is the feeling of belonging and the school's ethos that helps young people thrive and flourish in our school community. At Claires Court, we treat everyone as an individual, evaluating each child's ability to ensure we can enable them to reach their full potential, helping them achieve great results, whether that is in the classroom, on the sports field or in the creative arena. By offering the best education, strong pastoral care and a wealth of opportunities, our pupils achieve academically, feel valued and have a strong sense of self-belief and self-worth.

Pupils have access to excellent facilities across the sites, with indoor swimming pools, drama studios, extensive playing fields and ICT suites. Senior pupils have access to top-class facilities for training and playing rugby, football, cricket and hockey through our partnership agreements with local sports clubs. Sailing and rowing are also part of our sport offering with much success in regional and national competitions.

At the core of our learning philosophy are the Claires Court Essentials. Right from Nursery we make learning fun but challenging and from that springboard we focus on developing a variety of skills and behaviours that young people need to be a successful learner and individual in our fast-paced world. As they mature pupils are expected to stretch themselves, push their own boundaries and limitations; we believe it is good to be wrong as long as we learn from that experience and bounce back. We develop boys and girls who are confident and resilient, learners who are critical thinkers and risk-takers, who can solve problems and communicate, as well as be creative and work collaboratively with others.

In the Junior years, the creative, topic-based curriculum inspires a passion for learning and children quickly develop a taste for success. There is a focus on mastering the fundamental skills as well as academic attainment. Further up the school, the breadth and balance of the curriculum allows senior pupils to develop new interests and talents before focusing on their GCSEs.

The Sixth Form offers just as much variety with more than 24 A Level subjects as well BTECs in ICT and Sport available. In recent years students have achieved an overall pass rate of 100% and our value added surpasses that of most other Sixth Forms, meaning our students achieve over and above their predicted grades. Alongside this the team also offers development and training for the personal, social and work skills that are desired by universities and employers.

A warm welcome awaits visitors; please come along to one of our regular Open Morning or call the Registrar to arrange an individual tour.

Coopersale Hall School

Flux's Lane, Epping, Essex CM16 7PE

Tel: 01992 577133
Fax: 01992 571544
email: info@coopersalehallschool.co.uk
website: www.coopersalehallschool.co.uk
Twitter: @CoopersaleHSch

Headmistress: **Miss Kaye Lovejoy**, AD BEd, CertEd, BEd Hons

Age Range. 2½–11.
Number in School. 290 Day Pupils.
Fees per term (2016–2017). £1,245–£3,380.

Coopersale Hall School is a thriving, caring local independent school with a high standard of academic achievement and a wide range of activities.

The School offers small class sizes and specialist teachers for ICT, Science, PE, Sport, Music and Drama. We provide a high standard of education and enjoy success in Entrance Examinations at 11 years to a wide choice of Secondary Schools.

We encourage our pupils to develop self-confidence and to take on roles of responsibility as they move up through the school. Creativity is nurtured within a disciplined environment and traditional values such as self-discipline are promoted to maximise our pupils' effectiveness in an ever-changing world.

Coopersale Hall is situated in a large country house that is pleasantly located on the outskirts of Epping, just off Stewards Green Road and only two minutes from Epping High Street. The School has its own private road and stands in some seven acres of landscaped gardens and playing fields.

Entry requirements: Interview and assessment.

Copthill School

Barnack Road, Uffington, Stamford, Lincolnshire PE9 3AD

Tel: 01780 757506
email: mail@copthill.com
website: www.copthill.com
Twitter: @copthill
Facebook: /Copthill

Principal: Mr J A Teesdale, BA Hons, PGCE

Head of School: Mrs Helen Schofield, BA Hons, PGCE
Upper School Leader: Mr Mark Thomas, BEng, PGCE
Lower School Leader: Mrs Anne Teesdale, BEd Hons
Head of Early Years: Mrs Judy Dimbleby, BSc Hons, PGCE

Age Range. Co-educational 2–11 years.
Number of Pupils. 300 total: Main School (age 4+ to 11) 240 and Nursery/Pre-School (age 2 to 4) 60.
Fees per term (2016–2017). £2,935–£3,250.
Educational Aims.

- A welcoming, stimulating and happy environment which is friendly, caring and well disciplined, in which every pupil is encouraged to achieve and motivated to succeed.
- An open-door policy, providing the foundations for effective communication and cooperation between Home and School.
- A broad curriculum emphasising the importance of literacy and numeracy and designed to develop lifelong knowledge, skills and attitudes that allow our children to become responsible citizens, independent explorers, creative thinkers, problem solvers, team players and reflective learners.
- An emphasis on using the outdoor environment to engage and inspire our pupils, developing their knowledge, skills and attitudes across the curriculum.
- An excellent preparation for entrance to a wide range of state and independent secondary schools.

Location. Purpose-built, modern facilities set within 350 acres of farmland, including river and woodland. 2 miles from Stamford and the A1 and 15 miles from Peterborough.

School Day. Monday to Friday from 8.35 am to 4.40 pm. Crèche hours from 7.45 am to 6.00 pm. Breakfast and Tea available.

Facilities. Creative Suite, Music Suite, Library, Languages Suite, Sports Hall and playing fields including AstroTurf and a well-established on-site Forest School. High-quality catering facilities offering delicious, nutritionally balanced meals.

Pastoral Care. In addition to their forms, pupils from Year 5 onwards are also placed in small tutor groups in which their progress is closely monitored in preparation for senior school entrance. There is a genuine 'open door policy' throughout the School. Parents' Evenings and reports given twice a year.

Curriculum. A modern curriculum based on the National Curriculum. Combines traditional and innovative teaching methods. Learning support offered throughout the school where a specific need has been assessed.

Music, Speech & Drama. Music and Drama are taught as part of the curriculum. Regular drama productions encourage all pupils to participate. Pupils can also receive expert individual tuition and perform at school concerts, assemblies and in local music and drama festivals.

Sport. Rugby, Hockey (boy and girls), Football, Netball, Cross-Country, Athletics, Cricket, Rounders, Swimming, Tennis plus many extracurricular sports including Sailing and Archery.

Future Schools. Pupils leave Copthill at 11 years old with great confidence and the ability to think for themselves. Copthill is a truly independent school, offering thorough preparation to a wide variety of independent and state senior schools, both local and national, achieving a large number of scholarships and awards.

Cransley School

Belmont Hall, Great Budworth, Nr Northwich, Cheshire CW9 6HN

Tel: 01606 891747
Fax: 01606 892122
email: admin@cransleyschool.org.uk
website: www.cransleyschool.org
Twitter: @CransleySchool
Facebook: /CransleySchool

Headmaster: Mr Richard Pollock

Deputy Head: Mrs Beverley Crumpton
Operations Manager: Mrs Clare Holt

Age Range. Co-educational 4–16.
Number in School. Day: 84 Girls, 38 Boys.
Fees per term (from January 2017). £2,515–£3,547. Lunches £280.

Set in the midst of beautiful Cheshire countryside, Cransley School really is a very special place to be educated. At Cransley we offer all our children the individual support that allows them to grow in confidence and to discover what makes them unique. Our pupils are given the attention and nurturing they need to excel academically and to reach their full potential. A Cransley education is more than just the excellent academic achievements we produce; we offer our pupils a wide range of extracurricular activities and encourage them to challenge themselves to learn outside of the classroom as well as within. Once again we were thrilled with the GCSE results this year, creating firm foundations for bright and successful futures for all of our pupils.

Life is never dull at Cransley. There is a wide variety of extracurricular activities available throughout the school – there are three choirs, Duke of Edinburgh's Award expeditions and regular drama performances. Students have a choice of clubs – gymnastics, gardening, languages, rowing, football and rugby to name but a few. There are many sporting opportunities and Cransley teams regularly compete against other schools in the area.

Cransley students enjoy many visits to enrich the curriculum. We also play hosts to visiting theatre groups. We offer residential opportunities – groups have been overnight in London for theatre and museum visits; GCSE Geography students visit Llandudno and the Lake District; activity weekends are particular favourites for both Senior and Junior Department pupils; foreign travel is also on the menu.

Cransley also has a thriving 'Friends of Cransley' –they organise regular events throughout the year which raise valuable funds to support staff and students and also offer a fantastic opportunity for parents to get to know each other.

Cundall Manor School

Cundall, North Yorkshire YO61 2RW

Tel: 01423 360200
Fax: 01423 360754
email: head@cundallmanor.org.uk
website: www.cundallmanorschool.com

Twitter: @CundallManor
Facebook: /Cundall-Manor-School

Joint Heads:
Mr John Sample, BSc Hons, PGCE
Mrs Amanda Kirby, BA Hons, PGCE, NPQH

Age Range. 2–16 Co-educational.
Number of Pupils. 370.

Cundall Manor School is a thriving independent co-educational boarding school, catering for nearly 400 boys and girls from two to sixteen years of age. Described by Ofsted as 'Outstanding', it is ranked in the top 9% of independent schools in the UK. Set in 50 acres of beautiful grounds between Harrogate, Ripon and York, it is easily accessed from the A1M and A19.

Cundall Manor School blends the best traditions of honour, integrity and courtesy with up-to-the-minute teaching facilities and approaches. The school has developed a reputation for ensuring that each and every child feels happy, safe, supported and celebrated. Within this environment, children engage fully with the educational challenges and risks that maximise learning and achievement. The rural setting allows pupils to embrace their childhoods while the innovative and unique curriculum provides opportunity for all to develop the confidence, judgement and personal skills that will benefit their futures.

Children are encouraged to participate in a number of sports and events outside of the curriculum including outward bound courses, travel, charity/community work and extracurricular sports. Whilst many children do achieve top standards and awards across academia, sports and music, competing and succeeding at area, county and national level, our aim is to ensure every child has the opportunity to participate in the full range of activities, whatever their level of ability and experience. We do this by cultivating a 'yes' mentality amongst our pupils, encouraging them to engage with the wider world and to think and act independently and without inhibition.

Fees per term (2016–2017). Nursery: 1 Full Day/term £381; Reception–Year 2: Day £3,070; Year 3 & 4: Day £4,855, Weekly Boarding £6,405; Years 5–11: Day £4,925, Weekly Boarding £6,475.

Charitable status. Cundall Manor Limited is a Registered Charity, number 529540.

Daiglen School

68 Palmerston Road, Buckhurst Hill, Essex IG9 5LG
Tel: 020 8504 7108
Fax: 020 8502 9608
email: admin@daiglenschool.co.uk
website: www.daiglenschool.co.uk

Perstare et Praestare –Persevere and Excel

Head Teacher: **Mrs P Dear**, BEd

Age Range. 3–11.
Number in School. 156.
Fees per term (2016–2017). £2,685–£2,735, sibling discount available. Extras: swimming, drama (infants).

Daiglen School is a small preparatory school which provides a happy and secure environment for all pupils. Kindness to others is valued above all, and pupils are polite and considerate with each other as well as with adults. We have a strong sense of family and community, underpinned by warm supportive relationships and mutual respect, which ensures that all pupils are valued and given the chance to shine.

Confident children relish challenge and the school promotes a culture of excellence. We celebrate individual and group successes as children learn the importance of pursuing their ambitions with determination and perseverance. They are inspired to do well both by the infectious enthusiasm of their excellent teachers and by the example of older children who become their role models. Our pupils flourish in this environment and leave as caring, confident, articulate and well-mannered young people, fully prepared for the next stage in their journey through life. We are justifiably proud of our pupils' academic achievements, as well as those on the sports field and other areas, and a good proportion leave with scholarships to selective independent and state secondary schools.

Founded in 1916, Daiglen School is rich in history and tradition. The school is built around an elegant Victorian house with much of its stained glass and cornices intact. Modern features include a purpose-built gymnasium/hall, art room, science laboratory and ICT suite. It is pleasantly situated on the borders of Epping Forest and is well served by public transport.

Inspection: Daiglen School was inspected in September 2010 and received the highest accolades from the Independent Schools Inspectorate. The team praised Daiglen in glowing terms, awarding the highest possible rating in areas that include pupils' all-round achievement, personal development and the quality of teaching, and declaring the school's Early Years Foundation Stage setting to be outstanding in every respect. The full report is available to read on our website.

Choosing a school is arguably the most difficult decision you will make for your child, and one which will have the greatest consequences in his or her life. Most of our pupils come to Daiglen on personal recommendation from parents of past or present pupils. We encourage a close and mutually supportive partnership with parents. To find out more about us, you can visit our website or make arrangements to visit the school; you will receive a warm welcome.

Charitable status. The Daiglen School Trust Limited is a Registered Charity, number 273015.

Ditcham Park School

Ditcham Park, Petersfield, Hampshire GU31 5RN
Tel: 01730 825659
Fax: 01730 825070
email: admissions@ditchampark.com
website: www.ditchampark.com
Twitter: @DitchamJuniors
             @DitchamSeniors
Facebook: /DitchamParkSchool

Head Teacher: **Mr R J Connolly**, MEd, BA Hons, PGCE, NPQH

Age Range. 4–16.
Number in School. Day: 199 Boys, 154 Girls.
Fees per term (2016–2017). £2,675–£4,485 excluding lunch.

Situated high on the South Downs, the School achieves excellent results in a happy purposeful atmosphere.

Charitable status. Ditcham Park School is a Registered Charity, number 285244R. It exists for educational purposes.

The Dixie Grammar School

Market Bosworth, Leicestershire CV13 0LE

Tel: 01455 292244
Fax: 01455 292151
email: info@dixie.org.uk
website: www.dixie.org.uk
Twitter: @DixieGrammar
Facebook: @the.dixie.grammar

Headmaster: Mr Richard J Lynn, BA Cardiff

Age Range. 3–18.
Number in School. 452.
Fees per term (2016–2017). Nursery: Daily Rate (inc lunch) £46; Reception, Years 1 and 2 £2,740, Years 3 to 5 £3,140, Year 6 to Sixth Form £3,760. Scholarships, Bursaries, Vouchers/Government Funding, Monthly Payment Scheme available.

The earliest records we have of the School's existence date from 1320, but the School gained its present name when it was re-founded in 1601 under the will of an Elizabethan merchant and Lord Mayor of London, Sir Wolstan Dixie.

The most distinguished of the School's former pupils is Thomas Hooker, founder of Hartford, Connecticut, and Father of American Democracy. The best known of its teachers is undoubtedly Dr Johnson, moralist, poet and author of the famous dictionary, who taught at the School in the mid-eighteenth century.

The main building of today's School was built in 1828 and faces the historic market square of Market Bosworth, making a distinctive landmark. However, in 1969 the School was closed, as new, much larger comprehensive schools found favour.

It was to revive the best aspects of the grammar school tradition that the Leicestershire Independent Educational Trust was formed in 1983, and four years later the School was re-opened as a selective, independent, day school for boys and girls of all backgrounds between the ages of 10 and 18. Three years later our Junior School opened, moving to its present premises, Temple Hall in Wellsborough, in 2001, where we have The Pippins Nursery.

The emphasis remains the same as it ever was: to provide an excellent academic education that will be of lasting value to our children as they face the challenges of the future.

Both schools are selective and have academic achievement as their central aim. Music, drama, sport and service are also an integral part of the education offered. Both schools have an interdenominational Christian basis. The relative smallness of the schools ensures that they combine great friendliness with excellent discipline, providing a secure and well-ordered framework in which children can confidently achieve their full potential. We are ambitious for each of them.

The Grammar School offers academic, music, art, sports and sixth form scholarships.

Charitable status. The Leicestershire Independent Educational Trust is a Registered Charity, number 514407.

DLD College London
Alpha Plus Group

199 Westminster Bridge Road, London SE1 7FX

Tel: 020 7935 8411
email: dld@dld.org
website: www.dldcollege.co.uk
Twitter: @DLDcollege
Facebook: /DLDcollege

Principal: Ms Rachel Borland

Age Range. 14+ Co-educational.
Number of Pupils. 430 Day.
Fees per annum (2016–2017). £19,990.

Our oldest College, DLD, was established in 1931. After 10 years located in Marylebone, the College has merged with its younger sister, Abbey College, and moved in 2015 to brand new, purpose-built facilities in the centre of London, looking over the River Thames to the Houses of Parliament. With bright, state-of-the-art teaching facilities and secure, on-site student accommodation, all in the centre of the amazing, historic and vibrant city of London, DLD College London is a truly unique college campus, with facilities including:

- 220 secure, ensuite student bedrooms within the College
- Restaurant facilities on site, including a Starbucks franchise
- 6 high specification laboratories
- A creative arts and media faculty featuring art rooms, photography, drama, music and media suites, including a 100+ seat theatre
- Nearly 40 tutorial rooms
- Open plan library, study and ICT facilities
- Access to shared swimming pool and gymnasium facilities

DLD College is a co-educational London day school accepting pupils from the ages of 14+. There are over 430 students in the Sixth Form studying A Levels or BTECs from a choice of 40 subjects. Most are doing A Levels in the normal way over a two-year period with another cohort joining at the start of Upper Sixth. There are no subject restrictions at A Level. GCSE courses are taught over a one-year period so pupils are able to join at the beginning of Year 11. The average class size is between 6 and 8 students. The College offers a 2-year GCSE Programme for SEN students. The college also offers two BTEC programmes in Business and Media Studies.

At DLD we offer an extensive range of extra-curricular activities, which include many traditional options such as Sport, Music, Drama and Art. Our wide enrichment programme supports our academic curriculum and forms an integral part of the wider education and college experience we offer our students. Our vision is to create all-rounded students, who excel academically and develop further their emotional, inter-personal and social skills. All students are encouraged to participate in one or more of our range of extra-curricular activities. This participation is important for students both as an opportunity for recreation and as an effective way to improve the quality of their UCAS personal statement and CV in the future.

While the atmosphere at DLD is more informal than in mainstream independent schools, rules regarding academic performance are strictly enforced with an emphasis on attendance and punctuality. There are fortnightly tests in each subject and three weekly reports. Parents receive five reports each year and there are two parents' evenings and a parents' social evening.

The teaching staff are highly qualified and chosen not just for their expertise but also for their ability to relate positively to young people. The college aims to make learning interesting, active and rigorous. While clear guidelines are very important to ensure pupils establish a good working routine, the college believes strongly that pupils respond best when there is a culture of encouragement. Effort, progress, achievement and courtesy are regularly acknowledged and formally rewarded.

Dwight School London

6 Friern Barnet Lane, London N11 3LX

Tel:	020 8920 0600
Fax:	020 8211 4605
email:	admissions@dwightlondon.org
website:	www.dwightlondon.org
Twitter:	@DwightSchoolUK
Facebook:	/Dwight-School-London
LinkedIn:	/dwight-school-london

Head of School: **Mrs Alison Cobbin**, BA, Dip Ed, MBA

Age Range. 3–18.
Number in School. 350 Boys and Girls.
Fees per term (2016–2017). £1,430–£6,875.

Dwight School London provides a secure, well-ordered and happy environment with the learning process at its core, offering an International Baccalaureate (IB) education for all students in order for them to reach their full potential. Serving a cosmopolitan and diverse North London community, great importance is attached to respect, understanding and empathy with everyone's cultures, religions and backgrounds. Emphasis is placed on development of the individual student with academic, artistic, sporting, creative, practical and social skills being encouraged and individual talents nurtured. Every child has a spark of genius, we aim to ignite it!

Students follow the International Baccalaureate curriculum, starting at age 2 with the IB Primary Years Programme, moving on to the IB Middle Years Programme at age 11 and the IB Diploma Programme at age 16. The programmes are designed to encourage the development of learning skills and to meet a child's academic, social, physical, emotional and cultural needs. Through enquiry-based learning and various disciplines, subject interrelatedness is accentuated, preparing students for the pre-university IB Diploma Programme. Within the programme students must study six subjects, a research project, leading to a 4000-word essay, The Theory of Knowledge course, and Creativity, Action, Service (CAS). The CAS programme is a fundamental part of the Diploma programme, requiring students to participate in 150 hours of activities both in and out of school.

The Quest Programme is designed for students who need learning support to develop strategies to enable them to study effectively. Through one-to-one tuition with specialist staff who teach skills such as effective reading, time management, planning of work and revision and exam techniques, students can reach their full potential, further enhanced by the school's low teacher/student ratio.

Entry requirements. Students who meet the criteria are accepted for entry at any time throughout the school year subject to space. Full details can be found on the website.

Examinations offered. The International Baccalaureate Diploma.

Facilities. The Upper School has dedicated ICT, music, art Design Technology, drama and Library facilities. The Lower School has dedicated music, art, library and a multipurpose hall for sports and drama activities. The school has its own sports fields with tennis courts nearby used by both Upper and Lower School.

Music tuition is incorporated into the curriculum with the addition of individual lessons in a wide variety of instruments such as piano, guitar, drums, saxophone and violin with composition and singing also available. The school has a number of bands and groups with varying styles from jazz to rock and regular concerts highlight the very real talent within the student body.

The students' physical development is considered as important as academic development and the school's sports fields provide excellent facilities for football, cricket, athletics, hockey, tennis and softball. The school's hall, playgrounds and local amenities are also utilised to offer further activities such as basketball, badminton, squash, swimming, table tennis, ice skating and skiing. Matches and tournaments between local schools are regular fixtures.

The school's close proximity to central London allows for numerous trips to the capital's museums, galleries and theatres. A variety of overseas trips are offered, both academic and leisure, including France, Spain, skiing and our sister school, The Dwight School, in New York while the Upper School students have an opportunity to participate in the Model United Nations conferences at The Hague.

Egerton Rothesay School

Durrants Lane, Berkhamsted, Herts HP4 3UJ

Tel:	01442 865275
Fax:	01442 864977
email:	admin.dl@eger-roth.co.uk
website:	www.eger-roth.co.uk

A School with a Difference

Headteacher: **Mr Colin Parker**, BSc Hons, Dip Ed, PGCE, CMath

Age Range. 5–19 years: Poplar 5–11 years; Senior School 11–16 years; Sixth Form 16–19 years.
Number in School. 108 boys, 48 girls.
Fees per term (2016–2017). £5,085–£7,237 (lunches included).

ERS aims to provide an exciting and relevant educational experience for pupils who need that little bit more support from their school, whilst studying a mainstream curriculum.

It focuses especially on students who have found, or would find, it difficult to make progress and succeed within another school – perhaps because of an earlier, negative, educational experience or perhaps because of a specific learning difficulty, such as dyslexia or dyspraxia, a speech and language difficulty or an autistic spectrum condition. If your child has other educational difficulties the school may also be able to help with these.

Children come with a variety of learning styles and use is made of a wide range of teaching strategies in order to match these. The school provides additional levels of support both in the classroom and on an individual basis, varying to suit the need of the child. Throughout the school children are taught in small classes to match their need for support, to the level of teaching and support staff provided. The team of therapists includes Speech and Language, Occupational Therapy, Social Communications and visiting physiotherapists. Our specialist teaching team provide individual lessons in literacy and numeracy.

The Sixth Form provides for students who continue to mature beyond the age of 16 and require an additional amount of support and time in order to enable them to transfer successfully into a further education establishment or employment. The school has developed both one and two year educational programmes within a high-quality, secure and supportive environment, in which students are able to continue to mature, develop and learn whilst studying for additional examinations including GCSE, BTEC, Foundation and CREST awards. Examination results enable pupils to enter colleges and sixth forms in both state and independent schools to continue their education before university entrance, if appropriate.

Every child at Egerton Rothesay is seen as a unique person and an individual student. The school aims to make an excellent contribution into the life of each one ensuring that they can be supported in the way that they personally need to maximise their individual learning potential.

The school wants more than just to deliver a curriculum and has a learning skills approach throughout the school – aiming to prepare students not just for school and exams but for life in today's complex society and an ever changing world of work.

A child can often be able and talented in one aspect of the curriculum, yet find it difficult to make good progress in another. Some students will need support for the duration of their time in school, whilst others may only need a short amount of support to address a specific problem or to build confidence.

All activities takes place within an environment offering exceptional pastoral care and spiritual development that is driven and informed by the school's Christian foundation and its Chaplaincy team.

Transport: Egerton Rothesay is also more than just a local school – students travel to the school from all directions, many using the comprehensive bus service that the school runs over a 35-mile radius.

If you think this may be the right type of school for your child you can obtain more information from the Registrar on 01442 877060 or visit the website at www.eger-roth.co.uk.

Fairfield School

Fairfield Way, Backwell, Bristol BS48 3PD
Tel: 01275 462743
email: secretary@fairfieldschool.org.uk
website: fairfield.school

Headteacher: **Mrs Lesley Barton**, BA Hons, PGCE

Age Range. 2–11.
Number in School. 59 Boys, 58 Girls.
Fees per term (2016–2017). Nursery (full-time), Reception, Years 1–2 £2,500; Years 3–6 £2,760.

Fairfield is an independent day school for boys and girls aged 2–11. The school was founded in 1935 and aims to provide a broad, traditional education. We encourage each child to maximise his or her potential through creating a family ethos in which children feel happy, secure and valued. A fundamental aspect of our ethos is our commitment to small classes, usually of 18–20. Fairfield offers a broad and balanced curriculum, informed by the National Curriculum. Teachers and visiting coaches provide a wide range of extra-curricular lessons including music, dance, sport, drama and creative activities. Pupils are prepared for entry into all local independent senior schools as well as for the local maintained sector schools.

For further details please apply to the School Secretary.

Charitable status. Fairfield PNEU School (Backwell) Limited is a Registered Charity, number 310215.

Fairley House School

Junior Department:
218–220 Lambeth Road, London SE1 7JY
Tel: 020 7976 5456
Fax: 020 7620 1069
email: junior@fairleyhouse.org.uk

Senior Department:
30 Causton Street, London SW1P 4AU
Tel: 020 7976 5456
Fax: 020 7976 5905
email: senior@fairleyhouse.org.uk

website: www.fairleyhouse.org.uk

Headmaster: **Michael Taylor**, BA Hons, PGCE, FRGS

Age Range. 5–16.
Number of Pupils. 193 (132 Boys, 61 Girls).
Fees per term (2016–2017). £10,100.

Fairley House School is a school for children with Specific Learning Difficulties, Dyslexia and Dyspraxia. The aim of the school is to provide intensive support to help children to overcome difficulties, coupled with a full, rich curriculum designed to bring out children's strengths and talents. Most children return to mainstream schooling after two to three years. Children's learning styles have often not been catered for in their previous school, leading to failure and loss of confidence, but Fairley House offers them a 'level playing field' where everyone has similar difficulties. Children receive a stimulating educational experience integrated with therapy and specialist teaching. Teaching is multi-sensory and children learn Science, Spelling, Geography and History through interesting, hands-on activities. There is a staff: pupil ratio of 1: 3.5. This integration is one of the many things that sets us apart as a specialist day school for children with Specific Learning Difficulties.

We emphasise the development of the whole child, helping him or her to gain confidence and self-esteem through an encouraging and nurturing ethos. The children have plenty of opportunities to develop sound academic and social skills and to become independent. At Fairley House, everyone succeeds.

Falkner House

19 Brechin Place, London SW7 4QB
Tel: 020 7373 4501
email: office@falknerhouse.co.uk
website: www.falknerhouse.co.uk

Headmistress: **Mrs Anita Griggs**, BA Hons, PGCE

Age Range. Girls 4–11, Boys 4–8, Co-educational Nurseries (ages 3–4).
Number of Girls. 200.
Fees per term (2016–2017). Main School £5,870 Nursery £2,970.

Falkner House is unashamedly academically ambitious and pupils achieve notable success at 11+ to the very top day and boarding schools. This is all within a naturally self-policing, civilised atmosphere where the development of self-confidence and happiness are seen as key goals. There is a busy yet friendly environment and as a result pupils have an engaging openness, intellectual curiosity and courtesy beyond their years. "We like them to have ability and oomph" says Mrs Griggs, "but not to be sassy or precocious."

Excellent facilities include a science laboratory, art room, library and playground. State-of-the-art IT facilities now include individual iPads integrated into the curriculum. A strong musical tradition lies alongside an excellent sporting record. Pre/post school care is offered, as well as a wide range of after-school activities.

The new boys school with similar ethos and facilities is starting on a separate site in September 2017.

Entrance at 4+ for both girls and boys is by assessment.

Falkner House Nurseries cater for boys and girls aged 3–4 years. Children thrive in a stimulating atmosphere under the care of professional and thoughtful teachers. Children are encouraged to be curious, to experiment and to learn through play. Specialist staff teach subjects such as music and PE to enrich the nursery curriculum.

Entrance at rising 3 is by date of registration.

Faraday School

Old Gate House, 7 Trinity Buoy Wharf, London E14 0FH

Tel: 020 7719 9342
          020 8965 7374 (Admissions)
email: admissions@faradayschool.co.uk
          head@faradayschool.co.uk
website: www.faradayschool.co.uk

Executive Head: **Mrs Sarah Gillam**

Age Range. 4–11 Co-educational.
Number of Pupils. 104.

Founded in 2009, Faraday is a small but growing independent school in East London located at the unique setting of Trinity Buoy Wharf.

Here at Faraday we offer a traditional approach to primary education with a strong emphasis on the core skills of literacy and numeracy. Although we believe in a traditional approach, our lessons reflect modern thinking on how children learn most effectively and our small classes and quality staff allow for a very personal approach to learning.

Opportunities outside the classroom abound. Through sporting activities, first-class music, art and drama, we encourage every child to find their own particular strength. A wide range of after-school clubs, after-school care and school bus service is attractive to many working parents.

Termly school trips extend the curriculum and develop social skills. Our location on the historic wharf, home to the Faraday lighthouse, Container City and a wealth of creative tenants offers us excellent opportunities for partnerships to extend our pupils' learning. Our partially-covered playground roof, with views over the Thames to the O2 Centre, allows for all-weather play.

Entry into Reception is non selective and based on the date the completed registration form is returned to our Registrar, with siblings given priority. Entry higher up the school is by interview and informal assessment in the classroom. We offer regular open days and welcome private tours.

Faraday was the second of the New Model School Company's schools, offering a low-fee model, based on traditional teaching methods and with a Christian ethos, although we accept children of all faiths or none.

Fees per term (2016–2017). £3,044.

The Firs School

45 Newton Lane, Chester CH2 2HJ

Tel: 01244 322443
Fax: 01244 400450
email: admin@firsschool.org
          s.hunt@firsschool.org
website: www.firsschool.net

Headmistress: **Mrs L Davies**, BA Hons, PGCE, PGDCL, NPQH

Age Range. 3–11 Co-educational.
Number in School. 191: 110 Boys, 81 Girls.
Fees per term (2016–2017). £560–£2,850.

The Firs School is an independent co-educational primary school set in attractive grounds about a mile and a half north of the city of Chester. It was founded in 1945 by Mrs F A Longman.

The aim of the Firs is to help children achieve their academic potential in the context of a caring environment based upon Christian principles. Children of all faiths are welcome and we respect and learn from their beliefs and cultures. Our strengths lie in the individual attention we are able to give, a carefully planned curriculum and an effective partnership with parents. Specialist teaching for dyslexia and other educational needs is available. We have a proven record of success in preparing children for entrance to local independent and state schools. The school is well resourced with a continuous programme of investment, including our technology and pottery rooms.

Whilst placing great emphasis on the core subjects, our curriculum is enhanced through the teaching of French, Spanish, drama, the opportunity for sport and the quality of our provision of art and music throughout the school.

Our objective is to encourage the development of the whole child so that each will leave The Firs School with an understanding of the wider world and an awareness of his or her responsibility to others.

Forest Park Preparatory School
Bellevue Education

Lauriston House, 27 Oakfield, Sale, Cheshire M33 6NB

Tel: 0161 973 4835
email: post@forestparkprep.co.uk
website: www.forestparkprep.co.uk
Twitter: @ForestParkPrep
Facebook: @ForestParkPreparatorySchool

Headteacher: **Mr Nick Tucker**, BEd Hons Prim Ed, MA Ed Leadership & Mgt

Age Range. 3–11.
Number in School. 80 Day Boys, 73 Day Girls.
Fees per term (2016–2017). £2,091–£2,272.

Forest Park occupies a pleasant site in a quiet road surprisingly close to the centre of Sale, easily accessible from motorways and surrounding areas.

The school aims to discover and develop each child's particular abilities by offering a varied curriculum in a stimulating and happy atmosphere. Forest Park has a good pupil teacher ratio and offers a wide range of subjects with priority given to the traditional disciplines of English, mathematics and science. Pupils from three years of age are taught information technology by specialist staff. Swimming is taught from the age of five and games offered are football, cricket, netball, tennis and hockey. Pupils are taught French from Pre-Prep class. Older children have the opportunity to enjoy residential and activity trips to broaden their knowledge and develop self-confidence.

The confidence and social ease one expects of a private education is a product of the school. Our aim is to develop skills and knowledge through a habit of hard work in a secure and happy environment within a disciplined framework. The school prepares pupils for all independent grammar school examinations and has an excellent record in this respect.

The school prides itself on strong links and communication with a most supportive Parents' Association.

Frewen College & Frewen Preparatory School

Brickwall, Northiam, Nr Rye, East Sussex TN31 6NL

Tel: 01797 252494
Fax: 01797 252567
email: office@frewencollege.co.uk
website: www.frewencollege.co.uk

Principal: **Mr Nick Goodman**, BA Hons, PGCE, NPQH

Prep Headmistress: Mrs Sally Welch, BA Hons QTS, Dip SpLD

Age Range. 7–19 Co-educational.
Number in School. Full Boarders: 12 boys, 9 girls; Weekly Boarders: 15 boys, 7 girls; Day: 52 boys, 20 girls.
Fees per term (2016–2017). Day £5,095–£8,115; Full and Weekly Boarding £7,633–£11,265.

Frewen College is a small friendly independent specialist school catering for children with Specific Learning Difficulties (dyslexia, dyspraxia, dyscalculia) and related speech and language and sensory integration problems. We are inspected by Ofsted and rated in 2016 'Good with outstanding features' for education.

The school adopts a holistic approach to teaching, designed to enhance pupils' confidence and self-esteem, allowing them to build on their strengths while learning to cope with their difficulties. Each pupil has a comprehensive 'Provision Map' so that teaching can be tailored to individual needs. About half the children have Educational Health Care Plans and are funded, currently by 14 different Local Authorities. Services children are also welcome and their fees are fully covered by the SEN Allowance, and we have a growing number of international students from all Continents.

The number of girls increases each year. Boarding for girls was introduced in September 2009 and has already been extended twice. Our very friendly Houseparents run boarding very much like an extended family, with bedrooms of 1–4 pupils, all with en-suite facilities. Catering is 'in house', and rated by all-comers as 'excellent'! A very wide range of recreational activities is available, and transport is available to and from London each weekend.

Our separate junior school, Frewen Preparatory School, has all the benefits of a small independent school while being able to make use of specialist facilities on the adjacent senior school site. Frewen Prep employs the 'creative curriculum' approach to teaching, which has been extremely successful in engaging children in the delights of learning. As a result of the re-launch numbers are now up, with almost all pupils privately funded.

Launched in 2014, our Sixth Form offers a very wide range of courses, both in house, and through two partner Colleges. Applications are welcome from both internal and external students.

Frewen College has excellent facilities, based around a historic house located in 60 acres of playing fields, gardens and parkland. Educational provision includes three modern IT suites, a drama workshop, food and nutrition kitchens, pottery, music and music practice rooms, two newly refitted Science labs, Design & Technology workshop and an art studio. English lessons are supplemented by intensive reading sessions.

Outdoor facilities include a large open-air swimming pool, tennis and netball court, all-weather five-a-side and hockey pitch, newly refurbished fitness suite, as well as extensive playing fields. Our cricket pitch is rated one of the best village pitches in the County. We also have access to another 100 acres of ancient parkland for cross-country runs, camping, and orienteering. All Year 9 pupils are entered for the Duke of Edinburgh's Award Scheme. A recent addition to the facilities is a mountain bike trail largely designed and built by the senior pupils.

All classroom staff have specialist dyslexia training. We are Department for Education approved, a supporting corporate member of the BDA, and rated 'Dyslexia Specialist Provision' by CReSTeD.

Charitable status. The Frewen Educational Trust Limited is a Registered Charity, number 307019.

Fyling Hall School

Robin Hood's Bay, Whitby, North Yorkshire YO22 4QD

Tel: 01947 880353
Fax: 01947 881097
email: office@fylinghall.org
website: www.fylinghall.org
Twitter: @Fyling_Hall
Facebook: @FylingHallSchool

Headmaster: Mr Steven Allen, BA Hons, QTS

Deputy Head (Academic): Dr Ian Richardson, BSc, MPhil, PhD, PGCE, FGS
Deputy Head (Pastoral): Miss Adele Gilmour, BA, PGCE

Age Range. 4–18.
Number of Pupils. Boarders: Boys 32, Girls 34; Day: Boys 56, Girls 44.
Fees per term (2016–2017). Day: £2,228–£2,970; Weekly Boarding: £3,175–£3,812; Full Boarding: £5,410–£6,471.

Fyling Hall School is one of the oldest recognised co-educational schools in the country. It occupies a spectacular coastal setting within the North York Moors National Park. Pupils may safely enjoy freedom in this beautiful and peaceful rural area.

The buildings centre on a grade two listed Georgian country house in delightfully landscaped gardens incorporating an outdoor theatre overlooking Robin Hood's Bay. Recent expansion has included two new boarding houses, science laboratories and dining room in addition to the purpose-built Junior School. We have also built a spacious multi-functional sports hall and an astroturf recently.

The school is intentionally small due to its desire to educate pupils as individuals. The advantageous pupil-teacher ratio encourages effective learning. The teaching is along traditional lines with an emphasis on 'doing one's best' within a supportive yet challenging environment. A broadly based and well resourced curriculum is followed which reflects recent national initiatives, particularly in the scientific and information technology fields. A wide range of GCSE and A Level courses are offered.

Fyling Hall is a closely knit society with an emphasis on pastoral care and a real sense of communal responsibility. The chief feature is a spirit of confidence and cooperation between staff and pupils in an atmosphere which is natural for growth.

There is no entrance examination, but an interview and a report from the current school are integral parts of the admission process.

Many of the pupils stay to join the Sixth Form, where freedom and responsibility present a balance and are a useful preparation for university life.

The school takes advantage of its natural surroundings in the provision of numerous extra-curricular activities. Fyling Hall has its own ponies and these constitute a much loved part of school life. Climbing, Karate, Duke of Edinburgh's

Award and Riding are all popular. The main games are rugby, hockey, cricket and tennis, each with a full fixture list. Music enjoys a good reputation and individual tuition is available in all the usual musical instruments.

Robin Hood's Bay is remarkably accessible despite its rural splendour. Nearby Whitby and Scarborough are both railheads. Teesside Airport and the ferry port of Hull, with their frequent continental connections, are both easily reached. An experienced Secretary is able to advise on all travel arrangements.

Academic standards are high, but other abilities are valued, and aided by the small size of classes it is hoped that all pupils can be encouraged to achieve their maximum potential.

Charitable status. Fyling Hall School Trust Ltd is a Registered Charity, number 507857. It exists for the provision of high quality education for boys and girls.

Gad's Hill School

Higham, Rochester, Kent ME3 7PA

Tel:	01474 822366
Fax:	01474 822977
email:	s.fitzgerald@gadshillschool.org
website:	www.gadshill.org
Twitter:	@GadsHillSchool
Facebook:	@GadsHillSchoolOfficial

Headmaster: **Mr D G Craggs**, BSc, MA, FCollP, FRSA

Age Range. Co-educational 3–16.

Number in School. 353.

Fees per term (2016–2017). £1,995–£3,995.

Entry requirements. Interview and assessment.

Aim. To provide a good all-round education, to build confidence, establish friendships, to reward success (however small) and to ensure our students leave as mature, self-reliant young people who depart Gad's for the career or University placement of their choice.

Kindergarten (3–6 years). From the very early years in Kindergarten the children are encouraged to learn through play, music and drama. Basic letter and number work is introduced within the nursery and reception class as the children concentrate on the Early Learning Goals. In Year 1 and Year 2 they largely follow Key Stage One of the National Curriculum although in addition; from Reception upwards, all of our children are taught French and also Information and Communications Technology.

Junior School (7–11 years). Our Junior School curriculum seeks to build upon the children's undaunted love of adventure. Literacy, Numeracy and Humanities continue to be taught by Form Tutors however, the children begin to benefit from more lessons delivered by specialist tutors particularly in French, Information Technology, Design & Technology, RE, Games and Drama.

Senior School (11–16 years). Senior School concentrates very much on the preparation for GCSE success and our classes are kept to a maximum of 20 children per class. This way the children benefit from smaller class sizes and consequently our tutors get to know each child as an individual and this enables them to provide the right level of support and assistance. This goes a long way to helping them achieve their goals for GCSEs and A Levels.

Location. Gad's Hill School is centred on the former home of Charles Dickens and is surrounded by beautiful grounds, playing fields and countryside. It is a few minutes' drive from the A2 and M2, with good access to the Medway Towns, Dartford and Gravesend.

Curriculum. At Gad's we largely follow the National Curriculum although we place a strong emphasis on "communication" with all of our children benefiting from lessons in French, Information and Communications Technology and Drama as well as English. Senior School children progress to take GCSEs in English, English Literature, Maths, French, Design & Technology, Combined Science (Double Award), Geography and GNVQ ICT (4 GCSEs).

Sports and Activities. We concentrate very much on team games (rugby, hockey, soccer, netball, cricket, athletics and rounders) to ensure that our children learn the values of team work and communication. In the Kindergarten and Junior Schools all students take part in weekly swimming lessons. Because of our small class sizes almost all of our children have the opportunity to represent the school in competitive fixtures against other schools. Gad's Hill also has a thriving Combined Cadet Force. Students join the CCF in Year 8 and take part in weekly training sessions as well as termly field days and an annual camp. The CCF allows children to experience fantastic outdoor pursuits, adventurous training and leadership courses and is essentially about doing something different and challenging. Gad's Hill pupils are also able to take part in a variety of after-school activities. These range from academic pursuits to a variety of other sports and Performing Arts.

Charitable status. Gad's Hill School is a Registered Charity, number 803153. It exists for the purpose of educating children aged 3–16.

Gidea Park College

2 Balgores Lane, Gidea Park, Romford, Essex RM2 5JR

Tel:	01708 740381
Fax:	01708 740381
email:	office@gideaparkcollege.co.uk
website:	www.gideaparkcollege.co.uk

Headmistress: **Mrs Susan Gooding**, BA Hons Dunelm

Age Range. 3–11 Co-educational.

Number in School. 175 Day Pupils.

Fees per term (2016–2017). £3,080.

An established Preparatory school founded in 1924, the current Directors are the granddaughters of the founders.

The main building, a substantial Georgian/Victorian house, accommodates the 7–11 year old children, the school library, assembly room and IT room plus the kitchens. In separate outside classrooms, bounded by lawns and playgrounds, is the small Pre-school unit and accommodation for 4–7 year old pupils.

All children are known and treated as individuals with specific talents which are valued and developed. Likewise, identified areas needing extra help and encouragement are recognised.

The broad-based curriculum is delivered by highly qualified, full-time classroom staff using traditional methods, assisted by qualified support staff.

Results in selection procedures at 11+ are of a consistently high standard with scholarships and places awarded at local Independent and Grammar Schools. Our KS1 and KS2 National Assessment Testing reveals standards above the National expectations.

All National Curriculum areas are covered using whole-class teaching methods. Latin and French are introduced in the higher year groups.

A school choir performs on formal occasions and visits local care homes to sing.

Local facilities are used for PE, swimming and games lessons. Our House system fosters team spirit and enables each individual to participate in a variety of inter-house competitions as well as inter-school events.

The school has a Christian Foundation and strong links with our local parish church. However, within our diverse community those of other faiths are welcomed and their beliefs respected and festivals celebrated. Our pupils are encouraged to think of others less fortunate than themselves and arrange a variety of fundraising events for charity.

The staff supervise an early Morning and After School Club for the convenience of working parents. Those staying relax and then complete homework assignments giving quality time for parents and children at home.

New parents are made welcome by our thriving Parents' Association and encouraged to join in the various social events arranged providing a friendship base for them whilst at the school. Their fundraising provides extra equipment and fun occasions for the children.

We encourage all prospective parents to visit the school prior to applying so they may see classes in action and have an opportunity to ask any questions. We consider the partnership between pupils, parents and school to be of paramount importance in enabling each child to reach his/her potential.

Gosfield School

Cut Hedge Park, Halstead, Essex CO9 1PF
Tel: 01787 474040
Fax: 01787 478228
email: enquiries@gosfieldschool.org.uk
website: www.gosfieldschool.org.uk
Facebook: /gosfieldschool

Chair of Governors: Mr Peter Sakal

Principal: **Dr Sarah J Welch**, MA, PhD

Head of Prep: Mrs Philippa Mathews
Deputy Head: Mr Peter Flynn-Haddon

Age Range. 2–18 Boys and Girls.
Number in School. Boarders 12, Day 240.
Fees per term (2016–2017). Day £1,985–£5,085; Boarding: £5,580–£6,295 (5 nights), £6,295–£7,345 (7 nights).

Founded in 1929, Gosfield occupies a gracious, listed country house which was built in 1870 for Lady Courtauld. The school is set in a glorious 110 acre estate which borders ancient woodland and is a haven for wildlife and rare species. There are conservation areas and nature trails within the grounds.

Opened in January 2015 our new Prep School, Meadow Court, includes the latest technology and wireless connectivity, enhancing pupil learning and enabling lessons to take place inside and outside the classroom. With an academic focus on Literacy and Numeracy, pupils also follow a creative curriculum and have access to the most up to date learning materials for school work and homework.

The school is deliberately small in numbers and provides a caring family atmosphere in which every pupil will be able to develop his or her own potential to the full. Classes are small, and standards are high. The system of personal tutors ensures that every child's needs are properly looked after both in academic work and in the sporting and cultural activities in which the school encourages all pupils to participate.

There is a wide range of activities including sports, music, drama and conservation work. The programme changes termly and provides something for everyone. There are no weekend lessons.

The school day is from 8.30 am to 3.45 pm. Monday to Thursday after-school activities run until 4.45 pm with school buses departing at 5pm to various locations across Essex and into Suffolk. All pupils are encouraged to participate in after school activities. On Friday school ends at 3.45 pm with buses departing at 4 pm.

Gosfield is situated in rural North Essex only 20 miles from Stansted Airport and thirty miles from the M25. The nearest town, Halstead, is a mile away and the nearest train station is just five miles away at Braintree.

There is a daily minibus service to and from Chelmsford, Sudbury, Braintree and Colchester.

Charitable status. Gosfield School is a Registered Charity, number 310871. It exists to provide education for boys and girls.

Grangewood Independent School

Chester Road, Forest Gate, London E7 8QT
Tel: 020 8472 3552
Fax: 020 8552 8817
email: admin@grangewoodschool.com
website: www.grangewoodschool.com
Twitter: @GrangewoodSch

Head: **Mrs Beverley Roberts**, BEd Hons, PG Cert SEN

Age Range. 2–11.
Number in School. 42 boys, 25 girls.
Fees per term (2016–2017). Pre-Reception–Year 6: £1,384–£1,719. Nursery: From £1,029.60 (without EY funding) to £2,250.40 (full-time without EY funding).

School Vision Statement: "A place where potential is unlocked and where excellence is the hallmark."

Grangewood Independent School, was founded in 1979. We are a Christian, co-educational school that provides a unique and multi-faceted educational experience for children of all faiths, from two to eleven years old. 'The Christian ethos which permeates the whole school contributes a significant additional depth and relevance to the way [pupils] approach their academic and personal lives.' [Quote from last ISI Integrated Inspection of Grangewood Independent, September 2013]

Our aim is to instil a sense of respect and discipline, develop excellence in academia; whilst inspiring, motivating, and helping our pupils to realise their full potential. The achievement of our pupils in English and mathematics, including those with SEND and EAL, is consistently higher than national norms. 'The standard of reading is consistently high throughout the school and exceptional by the time pupils leave … They develop an excellent standard of handwriting, express themselves clearly on paper and are articulate in discussion.' [ISI, Sept 2013]

To ensure our pupils receive the individual attention they deserve, teaching and learning take place within small class sizes. Our pupils are happy, confident, and accustomed to establishing lasting relationships within a positive and peaceful atmosphere. We work closely with parents to identify, and inspirationally nurture, interests and talents in our pupils.

All subjects of the National Curriculum are covered by our experienced and dedicated teaching staff; and our children make tremendous progress in their levels of achievement across the board. We offer French tuition from Pre-Reception, and Spanish from Year Five. Our pupils are enabled and encouraged to develop their talents through performances in theatre and concert halls, as well as inter-school events.

Our wide range of extracurricular activities provide extended learning opportunities for our pupils within many areas including sport, art, critical thinking, and music. 'All pupils taking external music examinations up to Grade 5 have been successful.' [ISI, Sept 2013]

We provide excellent 'wrap-around' school care with a Breakfast Club and After-school Club.

We prepare our children for entrance exams, hence, after Grangewood, our children gain bursaries and entrance to independent schools; grammar schools; as well as the more popular academies and maintained schools. Year after year, we say goodbye to confident, happy, well-educated and responsible boys and girls.

We are particularly proud of the opportunity we have to offer flexible hours and assisted places in our EYFS department.

Please visit our website to arrange a visit to our school.

Charitable status. Grangewood Educational Association is a Registered Charity, number 803492.

Grantham Preparatory International School

An IES School

Gorse Lane, Grantham, Lincolnshire NG31 7UF
Tel: 01476 593293
email: contact.grantham@iesmail.com
website: www.tgps.co.uk

Head: **Mrs Kathryn Korcz**, BSc Hons, CertEd

Age Range. 3–11 Co-educational.
Number of Pupils. 127.
Fees per term (2016–2017). £2,450–£2,990.

The Grantham Preparatory School is a non-denominational independent day school for boys and girls between the ages of three and eleven. The school was established in 1981 and moved to a modern purpose-built building in 1987. It is set in nearly four acres of grounds and playing fields and, being close to the A1, it is easily accessible.

The school is owned by International Education Systems. IES is a network of seven schools (three in South Africa, two in the UK, one in Hungary and one in the United States). IES's mission is to provide excellence in education provision within an international perspective. Here at The Grantham Preparatory School we are "committed" to excellence in all areas of the curriculum, and we aim to provide the best for all our children in a happy family environment. We are now delighted to be a member of the ISA family after being accredited in November 2011.

Our children are prepared for entrance examinations to Independent senior schools and for Grammar school selection examinations. Children benefit from many specialist teachers who bring their own enthusiasm and knowledge to a particular subject. This ensures high academic standards and our broad and balanced curriculum enables our children to experience sport, art, music and drama and have the opportunity to pursue and develop their strengths, achieving their full potential. Specialist music teachers provide individual tuition in a wide variety of instruments.

Gold Artsmark was awarded in May 2010 in recognition of the very high standards achieved in music, drama and art. The school wind band, choir and recital groups continue to delight audiences with their stunning performances. The school was awarded the PE Kitemark – Gold Award for Sport (2015–2016).

Within our foundation stage there is a strong emphasis upon learning through play. We provide a stimulating and exciting curriculum which is delivered through a combination of whole-class, adult-led and child-initiated activities. There is a successful phonics programme, which begins in the Early Years classroom and continues throughout the Infant Department.

We believe that every child is an important unique individual that should be valued and nurtured during their time with us. We expect our children to leave us at age 11 as independent, confident individuals, tolerant of others and well prepared for the next stage of their education.

Greenbank Preparatory School and Day Nursery

Heathbank Road, Cheadle Hulme, Cheadle, Cheshire SK8 6HU
Tel: 0161 485 3724
Fax: 0161 485 5519
email: office@greenbankschool.co.uk
website: www.greenbankschool.co.uk
Facebook: @Greenbank-Preparatory-School

Headmistress: **Mrs Janet Lowe**, CertEd

Age Range. 6 months–11 years.
Number in School. Day: 86 Boys, 56 Girls. Daycare: 85.
Fees per term (2016–2017). £2,605 including lunches from Reception to Year Six.

Greenbank is an independent co-educational school for pupils aged three to eleven years. A separate Nursery, open fifty weeks of the year, cares for babies and children from six months to four years old.

Greenbank School was founded in 1951 by Karl and Linda Orsborn. Since 1971 the School has been administered by an Educational Trust and is registered with the Department for Education.

Greenbank is situated within extensive grounds, comprises a mixture of traditional and modern buildings including an IT Suite and Library, separate play areas for Foundation, Infant and Junior children, playing fields with a cricket pavilion, an Astroturf area and netball court. 2009 saw the opening of state-of-the-art Science, Art and Music classrooms within a new administration building. Further developments in 2012 include a brand new Preschool offering greater flexibility to parents.

The school day begins at 8.40 am and ends at 3.30 pm, however we provide wrap-around care from 7.30 am until 6.00 pm. The school also runs activity and sports clubs in the holidays.

Through its varied curricula and extracurricular activities the School provides pupils with the opportunity of expanding their natural abilities to the full. Music, drama, sport, computing and educational visits are some of the activities which play their part in providing a well-rounded programme of education. We strive to meet the social, emotional and intellectual needs of all pupils and the success of this philosophy is proven by the consistently outstanding examination results throughout the school, particularly at age eleven.

Charitable status. Greenbank School Limited is a Registered Charity, number 525930.

Greenfields Independent Day & Boarding School

Priory Road, Forest Row, East Sussex RH18 5JD
Tel: 01342 822189
Fax: 01342 825289

email: admissions@greenfieldsschool.com
website: www.greenfieldsschool.com

Head Teacher: **Mr Jeff Smith**, BSc Eng, AMIMechEng

Age Range. 2–18.
Number in School. Day: 70 Boys, 70 Girls. Boarding: 10 Boys, 10 Girls.
Fees per term (2016–2017). Tuition £1,020–£3,850, Boarding £3,250. *In July 2012 Greenfields introduced a radical new fees scheme which makes private schooling available for as little as £59 per week (subject to review).*

Greenfields Independent Day and Boarding School is an Independent Schools Association school with a Montessori-based Nursery and a Reception class (forming the Early Years Foundation Stage), an Infant and Junior School, and a Senior School including Sixth Form and long and short-term English as a Foreign Language courses.

Students aged 2 to 18 receive an all-round education for life, using the Cambridge Curriculum from Infants upwards. Greenfields utilises a unique study method which ensures children can apply what they learn for use in life – not just to pass examinations. It has a strong moral code and zero tolerance on bullying, drugs and alcohol.

Fees start from £59 a week. Situated in beautiful grounds, with its adventure playground backing onto the Ashdown Forest itself, the school is a safe and inspirational place to learn.

The main difference between Greenfields and other schools is the unique teaching method it uses. This method isolates the barriers preventing or hindering a child from learning and then provides precise tools to deal with them. Its use allows any child of any ability to learn anything.

There is a high level of open communication between students and staff that helps to prevent failure, bullying or drugs.

Every student is individually programmed and targeted to ensure each one achieves the success they are capable of.

The classes are small and an excellent curriculum, providing core subjects and peripheral studies, is available up to GCSE and Advanced Levels.

A "qualifications" department exists for checking that students have fully understood each step of their studies, and also provides extra help for any student having any trouble in class. There is also an "ethics" department that helps to resolve any personal problems the student may have.

The pre-school has Montessori trained staff who use Montessori materials to ensure the best foundation for the rest of a student's education.

Entry is by tests for literacy and numeracy. There is a pre-entry section for those who need a short programme to catch up and be ready to join their correct class.

Trains take under an hour from London to East Grinstead, which is a ten minute car ride from the school. Gatwick Airport is a twenty minute car ride away.

Charitable status. Greenfields Educational Trust is a Registered Charity, number 287037. The object for which the trust is established is the advancement of education.

The Gregg School

Townhill Park House, Cutbush Lane, Southampton SO18 3RR
Tel: 023 8047 2133
Fax: 023 8047 1080
email: office@gregg.southampton.sch.uk
website: www.gregg.southampton.sch.uk

Twitter: @TheGreggSchool
Facebook: /thegreggschool

Chairman of Board of Trustees: Mr John W Watts, MCIPS, MILT, AIGEM
Headteacher: **Mrs S Sellers**, MSc, BSc Hons, NPQH, PGCE

Age Range. 11–16 years.
Number in School. 300.
Fees per term (2016–2017). £3,990.

The Gregg School is situated to the east of Southampton and set in 23 acres of beautifully landscaped grounds. The School has a unique family atmosphere and an excellent reputation for its outstanding pastoral care. A high value is placed on identifying and developing each child's individual talents and abilities, and small classes, taught by experienced and dedicated staff, ensure that every student has the opportunity to achieve their very best.

A broad and balanced curriculum is supplemented by a wide range of extra-curricular clubs and activities, ranging from orienteering to off-road buggy building.

The School's music and drama departments provide a host of opportunities for students to perform to a range of audiences, and the School regularly achieves success in sporting disciplines at both city and county level.

A comprehensive transport service is provided for students living within a 15 mile radius of the School.

Our Trust Partner, St Winifred's School, offers a high-quality educational experience for children aged 3–11.

The Grove Independent School

Redland Drive, Loughton, Milton Keynes, Buckinghamshire MK5 8HD
Tel: 01908 690590
email: office@groveschool.co.uk
website: www.groveschool.co.uk
Twitter: @GroveSchoolMK
Facebook: /groveschool

Principal: **Mrs Deborah Berkin**

Age Range. 3 months – 13 years Co-educational.
Number of Pupils. 275.
Fees per term (2016–2017). £4,356 (47 weeks all inclusive), £4,124 (term time). Nursery: £984 per month (full time).

Hale Preparatory School

Broomfield Lane, Hale, Cheshire WA15 9AS
Tel: 0161 928 2386
email: mail@haleprepschool.com
website: www.haleprepschool.com

Headmaster: **J Connor**, JP, BSc, FCP

Age Range. 4–11.
Number in School. Day: 109 Boys, 96 Girls.
Fees per term (2016–2017). £2,470.

Hale Preparatory School is a completely independent, co-educational school for children from the age of 4 to 11.

The school's most recent ISI inspection was in the summer of 2014. The overall summary of the report reads, "*Hale Prep is a very successful school. Throughout, the teaching is excellent and the pupils' industrious approach to their studies is reflected in their rapid progress and substantial academic achievement at all levels. Indeed, in some cases, levels of progress and achievement are exceptional. The pupils reach high standards of personal fulfilment and participate enthusiastically in a wide range of extra-curricular activities. The quality of the pupils' personal development is excellent, reflecting the school's highly effective emphasis on their welfare, safeguarding and well-being."*

In recent years, the school was considered the Prep School of the Year by the Sunday Times and was referred to in two studies presented to the Department of Education: firstly, on "Best Practice in the Independent Sector" and secondly, as one of five examples of successful private schools.

One of the aims of the school is to develop each child to his or her fullest potential. This can only be achieved in a situation that emphasises a disciplined approach to school work. Teaching is carried out in a formal, traditional manner but one which also incorporates modern teaching aids. Homework is set every night.

The curriculum of the school is designed to create well-rounded children. Thus, whilst 50% of the curriculum is devoted to the core subjects of maths, English and science, all children have weekly lessons in drama, music, dance, art and design, information technology, history, geography, French, Spanish, ethics, physical education/games and Latin in year 6. Additionally, the school offers a range of extra-curricular activities including a dance club, theatre club, fencing, chess, sewing, gardening, choir, orchestra, a range of sports, outdoor pursuit holidays and continental ski trips.

The Hammond

Hoole Bank House, Mannings Lane, Chester, Cheshire CH2 4ES

Tel: 01244 305350
Fax: 01244 305351
email: info@thehammondschool.co.uk
website: www.thehammondschool.co.uk

The Hammond is the leading provider for performing arts education in the North West. Recognised and funded as a centre of excellence by the Department for Education (DfE) under the Music and Dance Scheme (MDS) and also receiving support through the Education Funding Agency's (EFA) Dance and Drama Award (DaDA) Scheme. Accredited by the CDET (Council for Dance Education and Training), The Hammond caters for a wide range of talents and interests. The Hammond has a place amongst the leading schools specialising in the field of dance, drama and music providing pupils with an academic education and training at the highest level in all aspects of the curriculum.

Principal: **Mrs M Evans**, BA, MA, PGCE, NPQH, FRSA

Age Range. 3–19+.
Number in School. 100 Boarders, 200 Day Pupils.
Fees per term (2016–2017). £3,695 for education only. Boarding extra £2,715. Prep Department £2,685.
Prep Department takes girls and boys from age 3 to 11.
Education Department takes girls and boys from 11 years to GCSE level.
Drama Department takes girls and boys from 11 years joining the Education Department with additional Drama.
Dance Department takes girls and boys from 11 years joining the Education Department with a Vocational Dance training.
Music Department takes girls and boys from 11 years joining the Education Department with additional Music.

Sixth Form takes boys and girls into the Education Department to study for A/AS Levels, also Diploma Level 6 in Musical Theatre and Dance, BTEC Level 3 in Performing Arts (Acting).

Full boarding is available.

Outreach Programme. The School is acknowledged for its commitment to the community and its varied outreach projects include:

• Hammond Dance Associates – Specialist classes for talented children, selected by audition, 9–16 years.
• Hammond Youth Theatre – weekend drama classes for 4–16 year olds.
• The Hammond's Easter and Summer schools, working with participants drawn from the community.

The Hammond is also offering a new BA Hons course in Musical Theatre Performance. This course is validated by University of Chester and students who successfully complete the programme will be eligible for a University of Chester award. The three year course will provide specialist vocational studies for a career in the professional world of musical theatre and performance. Its purpose is to nurture and develop the practical skills required to secure and sustain employment as a musical theatre performer. All students must apply through UCAS.

For a prospectus apply to The School Secretary.

The Hampshire School, Chelsea

The Main School:
15 Manresa Road, Chelsea, London SW3 6NB
Tel: 020 7352 7077

The Early Years:
5 Wetherby Place, London SW7 4NX
Tel: 020 7370 7081

email: info@thehampshireschoolchelsea.co.uk
website: www.thehampshireschoolchelsea.co.uk

Headmaster: **Mr Donal Brennan**

Age Range. 3–13.
Number in School. Day: 150 Boys, 150 Girls.
Fees per term (2016–2017). £3,960–£5,700.
Founded in 1944 and located in the London Borough of Kensington and Chelsea, just a stone's throw from the King's Road, The Hampshire School, Chelsea provides the top-class education one would expect from a traditional British preparatory school, combined with a caring approach and family feel. An independent, interdenominational day school, we cater for boys and girls between the ages of rising 3 and 13. Through personal attention from their dedicated staff and a stimulating curriculum, The Hampshire School ensures that learning is fun and that every child feels confident and valued.

In January 2009, the Pre-Preparatory and Preparatory sections made a successful move to a spacious and beautiful new site in Chelsea's old Public Library at 15 Manresa Road, London SW3. The Early Years children are based in a recently renovated Victorian town house on Wetherby Place. The children are provided with the 'home away from home' secure and nurturing environment they need at this tender young age. The EYFS curriculum is followed, with the school putting emphasis on the children becoming happy, confident and polite learners who are engaged and enthusiastic in their education.

A broad-based and balanced curriculum is provided by experienced and passionate staff. Children are given every opportunity to develop individual talents as fully as possible; a wide range of academic subjects being supported by a high level of instruction in music, art, physical education as well as the core subjects. Children are encouraged to study the history and development of their environment and culture by means of regular visit to museums, art galleries, exhibitions and places of interest.

The main school's excellent facilities include a galleried library, gymnasium, science laboratory, art and design studio, fully equipped stage, and garden.

There are a wide range of extracurricular activities offered, from judo, gymnastics, fencing and dancing to art, languages and music, as well as many in between, such as media, radio station, ukulele and cross stitch.

The school has been successful in preparing pupils for examination and scholarship entry into leading day and boarding senior independent schools. Great emphasis is placed on developing each child's individual talents. Children excel academically at The Hampshire School, Chelsea. In recent years, pupils successfully navigate the 11+ or 13+ Common Entrance Examinations to gain entry to their first-choice schools including City of London, Dulwich College, Westminster, Stowe, Ibstock Place and Latymer, to name a few.

Harvington Prep School

20 Castlebar Road, Ealing, London W5 2DS
Tel: 020 8997 1583
Fax: 020 8810 4756
email: admin@harvingtonschool.com
website: www.harvingtonschool.com
Facebook: /Harvington-School

Headmistress: **Mrs Anna Evans**, BA Hons, PGCE

Age Range. Girls 3–11, Boys 3–4.
Number in School. 120 Girls, 20 Boys (in nursery).
Fees per term (2016–2017). Early Years £3,195; Years 1–6 £4,080.

The School was founded in 1890 and made into an Educational Trust in 1970. Harvington is known for its high standards and happy atmosphere. Classes are small so that individual attention can be given by qualified and experienced staff. An academic education is offered preparing girls for senior school entrance examinations. The school continues to improve specialist facilities and also to provide a mixed nursery class for 3–4 year olds.

It is close to Ealing Broadway station and a number of bus routes.

Prospectus available from the Secretary.

Charitable status. Harvington School Education Trust Ltd is a Registered Charity, number 312621. It aims to subscribe to traditional values in behaviour and academic standards in a happy environment; to encourage a high standard of academic achievement for girls across a broad range of abilities; to encourage girls to develop their potential to the full, both in personal and academic terms; and to create an environment in which pupils will want to learn.

Hawley Place School

Fernhill Road, Blackwater, Camberley, Surrey GU17 9HU
Tel: 01276 32028
Fax: 01276 609695

email: office@hawleyplace.com
website: www.hawleyplace.com
Twitter: @HPS_School
Facebook: /hawleyplaceschool

Headmaster: **Mr Michael Stone**, BA Hons Dunelm, MA, PGCE Cantab, NPQH

Age Range. Co-educational 2–16 years.
Number in School. 340 Day Pupils.
Fees per term (2016–2017). Prep (Reception to Year 4) £3,390; Seniors (Years 5 to 11) £4,215.

Hawley Place is an idyllic independent Nursery and School, nestled in 16 acres of beautiful woodland in Camberley, Surrey. We welcome children from the age of 2 into our nursery, where they learn through play and games. From 2016 both boys and girls will be welcome to continue into Year 7 and follow through to GCSE at 16. Hawley Place is a family school and each and every child receives the individual attention they need to realise their true potential, be that in maths, science, art, sports, or all of the above!

Throughout the school, pupils are taught in small groups with an excellent teacher/pupil ratio ensuring that individual needs are met effectively in a unique family atmosphere where children can develop, thrive and succeed. We offer a broad and stimulating curriculum, a wealth of opportunities in Sport, Art, Drama and Music, which all help to mould a well-rounded and well-balanced young person.

Our pupils achieve consistently high GCSE results in the Senior School. Indeed, consistent academic excellence is one of the cornerstones of the school's success and popularity. In 2016, 100% of students obtained 5 or more passes at grade A*–C and 71% of grades were A*–B.

In the most recent Early Years Inspection, the school received the highest ranking judgment possible of Outstanding. In the latest ISI Inspection, the school was described as "full of happy purposeful young people and committed, caring staff, who are all very proud of Hawley Place". The school was praised for its outstanding levels of pastoral care and links with parents, for its high standards of education and its high quality of spiritual, moral, social and cultural development of pupils.

Hawley Place pupils not only excel within but also beyond the classroom. The school has built a strong reputation in public speaking, swimming, cross-country running and athletics and has won numerous trophies in Regional and National Finals.

Hawley Place School is part of the Minerva Education group which owns a number of private schools in London, East and South East England. Through Minerva's "Inspiring Learning" programme, we seek to share best practice and ensure the continuing improvement in every child's education.

Heathcote School

Eves Corner, Danbury, Essex CM3 4QB
Tel: 01245 223131
email: enquiries@heathcoteschool.co.uk
website: www.heathcoteschool.co.uk

Headmistress: **Mrs Caroline Forgeron**

Age Range. 2–11+.
Number in School. 105.
Fees per term (2016–2017). £2,730.

Founded in 1935, Heathcote School has achieved a high reputation as a school where every child matters. It is a small, village school that encourages excellence in all areas.

However, there is room in this happy school for children of all abilities and parents can be sure that their child's education, at all levels, will be designed to develop their particular potential.

Children may start in our Nursery from 2 years old. We offer wrap-around care from 7.30 am to 6.00 pm and have many extra-curricular activities.

Specialist subject teachers ensure the success of the high teaching standards expected at this school. Many children are prepared for scholarships, entrance examinations and the Essex Selective Schools Examination at 11+. A very high pass rate is attained in these examinations.

The School participates in many sporting fixtures including netball, football and swimming and is particularly successful in horse jumping, cross country and triathlon.

Pupils are expected to show courtesy and consideration at all times and encouraged to develop self-discipline and pride in themselves and their environment. Parents are asked to support the school in this. Regular consultations with parents are held and the Head Teacher is always available for any discussions that parents consider necessary. We have an active and dedicated "Friends of Heathcote School" who regularly hold social events and raise funds for charity and for the school.

For more information please contact us or visit our website.

Heathfield School and Day Nursery

Wolverley, Kidderminster, Worcestershire DY10 3QE
Tel: 01562 850204
Fax: 01562 852609
email: info@heathfieldschool.co.uk
website: www.heathfieldschool.co.uk
Twitter: @heathfieldsch
Facebook: /HeathfieldSchoolandDayNursery
LinkedIn: /Heathfield School & Day Nursery

Headmaster: **Mr Lawrence Collins**, MA, PGCE

Age Range. 3–16. Baby Unit for children 3 months plus.
Number in School. 205 Day pupils.
Fees per term (2016–2017). £2,265–£3,755. Pre School: £21.95 per session, £33.50 per half day, £49.15 per full day. Nursery from £22.30 (part day) to £53.60 (full day).

Heathfield is a co-educational day school with nursery provision, governed by an Educational Trust. The School is situated in spacious grounds in a green belt area north of Kidderminster, within easy reach of Worcestershire, West Midlands and Shropshire.

The curriculum is broadly based and pupils are prepared for GCSE. We also prepare children for the Common Entrance Examination at 13+. Pupils in our Junior School move up to our own Senior School at 11+. Classes are small. Careers guidance is available to senior pupils.

The school is strong in Drama, Music, Art and Sport. A wide variety of team and individual sports is offered with some pupils achieving regional and national standards.

Prospectus available from Headmaster's Secretary.

Charitable status. Heathfield Educational Trust is a Registered Charity, number 1098940. It exists to provide excellent educational opportunities at a reasonable cost.

Hemdean House School

Hemdean Road, Caversham, Reading, Berks RG4 7SD
Tel: 0118 9472590

Fax: 0118 9464474
email: office@hemdeanhouse.co.uk
website: www.hemdeanhouse.co.uk

Interim Headteacher: **Mrs Georgina Sillitto**

Age Range. Girls 3–11, Boys 3–11.
Number in School. 43 Girls, 31 Boys.
Fees per term (2016–2017). £2,500–£3,000.

Founded in 1859, Hemdean House is a school where traditional educational concepts are highly valued. We look for personal achievement in academic and other spheres, responsible behaviour and consideration for others. We aim to develop the varied talents of each and every child within our structured and caring environment; individual attention has high priority. Small classes help us to achieve our aims. We believe that school and family should work together and have opportunities to meet.

The self-contained Nursery unit offers children aged 3–4 the opportunity to begin the learning process and to develop their skills in a secure and happy environment.

We follow the National Curriculum throughout the school; Mathematics, Science, Information Technology, the Humanities and the Expressive Arts, Modern Languages, Technology and Physical Education are taught throughout the age range. French lessons begin at age 5 and recorder lessons begin at age 7 and many children learn at least one other musical instrument. Drama, Music and Art head a wide range of extra-curricular activities. For the working parent, after-school and holiday care are available if required.

National Curriculum Key Stage Tests are excellent with pupils achieving well above the national average.

The school has always been committed to Christian ethics and values, but all faiths are welcomed and understanding and appreciation of the beliefs of others is encouraged.

The most recent inspection report made some of the following statements:

Hemdean House School provides outstanding pastoral care throughout the school, where pupils are educated well and achieve their full academic potential.

The pupils are friendly, forthcoming and assured, their manners are excellent, and their behaviour throughout the school is exemplary.

Teachers know their pupils extremely well and this creates a happy, supportive environment in which the pupils thrive.

Nursery children are curious and eager to investigate.

The school successfully builds confidence and self-esteem in pupils.

Admission. Assessment during a day or half-day spent in school according to age. Scholarships and bursaries are available throughout the school.

Charitable status. Hemdean House is a Registered Charity, number 309146. Its aims include academic achievement, the development of every pupil's potential, Christian values and care for others.

Henriette le Forestier Preparatory School (formerly Virgo Fidelis Preparatory School)

147 Central Hill, Upper Norwood, London SE19 1RS
Tel: 020 8653 2169
Fax: 020 8771 0317
email: mail@hlfprep.co.uk
website: www.henrietteleforestierprepschool.co.uk

Executive Head Teacher: Adele Stedman

Head of School: **Mrs Lindsay Pollard**, BEd, CCRS

Age Range. 2–11.
Number in School. Day: 110 boys and girls.
Fees per term (2016–2017). £2,213–£3,001.

Henriette le Forestier Preparatory School offers boys and girls, aged 2 to 11, an outstanding education with excellent pastoral care and support in our safe and welcoming campus, set within beautiful grounds, in South East London.

Driven by a dedicated team of excellent teachers and staff, we provide a broad range of challenging educational experiences involving the humanities, arts, forest school, technology and sport, as well as a strong grounding in the core academic subjects. Our core values of Wisdom, Courage and Integrity permeate every aspect of school life and ensure that our pupils' social, moral and spiritual needs are given equal importance to their academic progress and learning.

Henriette le Forestier Preparatory School is a happy, warm and friendly school with high academic standards. Small class sizes, committed staff and a dynamic approach to learning means that children feel safe and secure, are inspired by their learning and enjoy their time at school. We aim to create in the mind and heart of each child a strong desire to learn and achieve success as they reach their full potential. We are proud of the school's long and successful history whilst focused and excited about its aspirational vision for the future.

Herne Hill School

The Old Vicarage, 127 Herne Hill, London SE24 9LY
Tel: 020 7274 6336
email: enquiries@hernehillschool.co.uk
website: www.hernehillschool.co.uk

Headteacher: **Mrs Ngaire Telford**

Age Range. 2–7.
Number in School. 275 boys and girls.
Fees per term (2016–2017). £1,850–£4,585.

Herne Hill School has much to offer – caring and enthusiastic staff, happy and confident children, and excellent results at 7+ years. Children join Kindergarten in the year they become 3 years old. This is by far the greatest entry point, followed by Reception and Pre-Reception. There are usually only chance vacancies for Years 1 and 2.

The school is well known as an oasis of happy learning and as the largest feeder into the reputable Dulwich schools. Its grounds and facilities lie tucked away behind St Paul's Church on Herne Hill and combine to provide a 'homely', safe and nurturing feel while at the same time being open, green and deceptively large – the perfect environment for young children to blossom and enjoy discovering how to learn.

The buildings consist of an Old Vicarage, a recent purpose-built building and a brand new hall and Kindergarten building which provides a number of additional benefits. These include a large, state-of-the-art Kindergarten room; a modern, multi-functional hall; and healthy hot lunches freshly cooked on site daily.

By focusing on Early Years education, Herne Hill School has developed strong expertise in making the critical transition from Nursery to School seamless. Children joining the Kindergarten can avoid the disruption of a 4+ change and have continuity for up to five years in what are arguably their most important formative years. Children joining in

Reception also benefit from the smooth progression from a play-based learning approach to more structured lessons.

"*Love • Care • Excellence*" encapsulates the school philosophy that love, nurture and a caring environment foster the children's self-confidence, sense of achievement and happiness, thereby stimulating their curiosity and desire to learn. The school's atmosphere lives this philosophy. It is a caring, friendly and fun place, and at the same time there is an air of achievement, respect and discipline.

The curriculum is finely balanced to take account of each child's individual needs as well as the requirements of the 7+ entry tests – and to make learning fun! It is designed to develop the skills of independent learning and to sustain the children's innate joy of learning. Music, drama, gym, dancing and French are emphasised and taught by specialists.

The latest ISI inspection report delivered a strong endorsement of the school's ethos, staff, curriculum, *modus operandi* and infrastructure by giving the highest possible rating of 'excellent' or 'outstanding' to *every* aspect of the school. The inspectors deemed overall achievement to be excellent and that pupils are very well educated and achieve very high standards in both their learning and personal development. The full report can be found on www.isi.net.

The school holds two open mornings a year, typically in March and September. Prospective parents may also see the school 'in action' by joining one of the regular tours held during school hours. The school's website contains relevant information about life at the school, its curriculum, the destination of its leavers and some useful links.

Highfield Priory School

Fulwood Row, Fulwood, Preston, Lancashire PR2 5RW
Tel: 01772 709624
email: schooloffice@highfieldpriory.co.uk
website: www.highfieldpriory.co.uk

Headmaster: **Mr J Duke**

Age Range. 6 months–11 years.
Number in School. Day: 130 Boys, 120 Girls.
Fees per term (2016–2017). £2,385.

Highfield is set in 8 acres of landscaped gardens, woodlands and playing fields and is a co-educational preparatory school for children aged 6 months to 11+ years. It is fully equipped with its own established Nursery and prepares children for all Independent, Grammar and Senior Schools in Lancashire, for which it has an excellent academic record.

Class numbers average 20 and children are taught by fully-qualified and experienced staff. Specialist facilities and teachers ensure that children are challenged and fulfilled across the curriculum, most notably in Art and CDT with a new studio in 2005, an ICT suite (since 1994), a Science Laboratory (2006) and, most recently, a Performing Arts Studio in 2013. Children from Nursery through to Year Six are also able to enjoy the school Library, Sports Hall and the school's own nature reserve, Highfield Haven.

The school has strong musical, dramatic and sporting traditions. Every child in the Junior School is given the opportunity to take part in competitive sporting fixtures and to perform in a full-scale dramatic production each year. In addition, Highfield examines the Junior children in the disciplines of Public Speaking, Elocution and Drama twice a year thereby greatly improving the children's eloquence and confidence.

Highfield holds a Step into Quality Award for its Early Years and Foundation Stage and Potential Plus UK's Three Star Gold Membership for its work with Gifted and Talented children. Highfield encourages its pupils to "Aim High" and gives them every opportunity to achieve this.

Highfield offers an extended day from 7.15 am until 6.00 pm. Extra-curricular activities include Ballet, Gardening, Choir, Design, Dance, Judo, Public Speaking, Chess, Spanish, Homework Club and Instrument Tuition. The school is well supported by an enthusiastic Parents Association. Prospective parents, and children, are encouraged to visit the school, have a tour with the Headmaster and to experience a school day.

Charitable status. Highfield Priory School is a Registered Charity, number 532262. It exists to provide independent education to all children between the ages of 6 months and 11 years within Preston and surrounding areas for all who wish to participate and to provide access to the community at large to all sporting, musical and artistic provision within the school.

Highfields School

London Road, Newark, Nottinghamshire NG24 3AL

Tel:	01636 704103
Fax:	01636 680919
email:	office@highfieldsschool.co.uk
website:	www.highfieldsschool.co.uk
Twitter:	@HighfieldsNG24
Facebook:	@highfields.newark

Head: **Mr Richard Thomson**, BEd Hons, NPQH

Age Range. 2–11 Co-educational.
Number in School. 140.
Fees per term (2016–2017). £2,920 including lunch. Day Nursery from £15 per three-hour session to £35 per school day (8.30 am – 3.30 pm), £45 per full day (7.30 am – 6.00 pm).

Highfields School is situated in fourteen acres of mature parkland and sports fields, an enviable setting for children to enjoy their education. It provides a happy, lively, caring community which allows the children to experience a sense of pride and fulfilment that comes from working to their full potential. Personal responsibility, initiative, good manners and smart appearance are encouraged and developed, in keeping with the School's pledge to combine modern methods with traditional values.

Children enter a structured course of Nursery Education in the term in which they reach the age of three. Children enter the Reception Class before their fifth birthday and proceed through the School in year groups. Each class is taught by its own teacher in the basic subjects. The maximum class size is twenty. All members of staff are fully qualified and specialist teachers assist with Art, ICT, Music, PE and Games throughout the School.

Highfields has recently adopted the Cambridge Curriculum which is an education programme designed and administered by Cambridge University for young learners that combines a world-class curriculum, high-quality support for teachers and integrated assessment. By moving the curriculum away from the National Curriculum and the controversial SATs examinations, the school has greater flexibility when making decisions about what is important when equipping the children with the skills and knowledge required for them to succeed in a global community.

Highfields has a fully deserved reputation for the quality of its pastoral care.

All children are encouraged to be creative and exhibit a delight in learning. There is the optional opportunity for speech and drama tuition and music lessons including piano, woodwind, brass and strings ensembles, choir, advanced choir, orchestra and band. Peripatetic staff offer individual

or joint music tuition in a wide variety of instruments including trumpet, saxophone, violin, cello, flute, clarinet, harp and guitar.

The School offers a wide range of extracurricular activities and sports teams compete against other independent schools as well as local schools. Highfields has fully-qualified staff who teach tennis, hockey, cricket, football, rugby and netball. The School holds an Activemark Gold Award. All children have a swimming lesson each week.

Highfields pursues a non-selective admissions policy but has an excellent academic record sending most pupils to local selective independent schools or to Grammar Schools in Lincolnshire through 11+ entry.

The School is administered by a Board of Governors, including parent governors.

Charitable status. Newark Preparatory School Company Limited is a Registered Charity, number 528261. It exists to provide and further the education of children.

Hipperholme Grammar School

Bramley Lane, Hipperholme, Halifax, West Yorkshire HX3 8JE

Tel:	01422 202256
Fax:	01422 204592
email:	secretary@hgsf.org.uk
	info@hgsf.org.uk
website:	www.hgsf.org.uk
Twitter:	@HipperholmeGS

Chairman of Governors: Mr D J Smith, BA, ACA

Headmaster: **Mr J D Williams**, BSc, PGCE

Hipperholme Grammar School Foundation was founded in 1648 by Matthew Broadley, Paymaster General to Charles I (our Alumni are known as Brodleians).

The Foundation provides a small, caring setting in which children are educated to be the very best they can be. Alongside high academic standards, all children are provided with outstanding opportunities for leadership and personal enrichment. A love of learning is developed alongside traditional values of politeness, good manners and strong moral code. The atmosphere that pervades through the School from Nursery to Sixth Form is welcoming yet challenging: all visitors to the School are given a very warm welcome. All students are provided with a range of academic and personal development challenges.

Organisation. The Hipperholme Grammar School Foundation is a co-educational day school comprising Junior School for children aged 3–11 years and Senior School for children aged 11–18 years.

The pupil roll stands at around 300 pupils with an average of 17 in each Form group. Our school is small enough to ensure individual attention for all children, yet large enough to provide a full range of subjects to GCSE and A Level. Class sizes at GCSE and A Level vary from 3 to 18 dependent on pupil choice.

Pupil Welfare. A great strength of our School is the strong commitment to provide outstanding pastoral care. Our small teaching groups, individual attention, teachers who genuinely care and excellent relationships with parents enable all children to blossom and fulfil their potential. Where necessary, individual learning programmes are devised and learning support staff ensure children make excellent progress.

Teaching and Learning. Our teachers enjoy teaching: they are enthusiastic, dedicated and exceptionally caring. Our curriculum is broadly in line with the National Curriculum to Year 9, after which students choose from a range of subjects leading to GCSE and later to A Level.

Personal Enrichment. Our Personal Enrichment programme builds self-confident and well-balanced young people with strong leadership skills. A wide range of activities is provided, including sports, music and drama, as well as a varied outdoor education programme and The Duke of Edinburgh's Award scheme.

Admission. Admission to the Junior School is non-selective and places are offered following an interview with the Headteacher and individual classroom-based assessments, if appropriate. Entry to the Senior School at 11+ follows assessment in our Entrance Examination, primary school report and interview with the Headmaster. The Senior School also selects children for their personal qualities and desire to attend the Senior School as well as academic performance. Entry to the Senior School for other year groups depends on availability and assessment during a two-day taster visit.

Fees per term (2016–2017). Junior School: Nursery £19.55 per am/pm session plus £9.50 lunchtime session; Reception to Year 6 £2,933; Senior School (Years 7–8) £3,460; Senior School (Years 9–13) £3,665. Lunch is included within the fees.

The Foundation operates a number of schemes which enable parents to spread the cost of School fees throughout the year. Transport, SEN and Individual Music Tuition are charged separately.

Bursaries and Scholarships. A number of Scholarships are awarded for entry at both Year 7 and Year 12 (Lower Sixth) for academic, musical and sporting achievement. Our Junior School children receive a fee reduction on transfer to the Senior School. Bursaries may be available throughout the School to families in financial need.

Charitable status. Hipperholme Grammar School Foundation is a Registered Charity, number 517152. It exists to provide high-quality education for boys and girls aged 3–18 in the local area and to assist those who cannot afford full fees, to finance such education.

Hopelands Preparatory School

38/40 Regent Street, Stonehouse, Gloucestershire GL10 2AD

Tel: 01453 822164
Fax: 01453 827288
email: enquiries@hopelands.org.uk
website: www.hopelands.org.uk

Chairman of Governors: Mr R D James

Head: **Mrs Sheila Bradburn**, BA Hons, PGCE

Age Range. 3–11 Co-educational.
Number of Pupils. 75.
Fees per term (2016–2017). £2,035–£2,606.
Charitable status. Hopelands Preparatory School is a Registered Charity, number 1007707.

Howe Green House School

Great Hallingbury, Bishop's Stortford, Herts CM22 7UF

Tel: 01279 657706
Fax: 01279 501333
email: schooloffice@howegreenhouse.essex.sch.uk
website: www.howegreenhouseschool.co.uk

Headmistress: **Mrs Deborah Mills**, BA Hons, QTS

Age Range. 2–11 years.
Number in School. 158.
Fees per term (2016–2017). Kindergarten £2,550, Pre-Prep £2,946, Prep £3,652.

Howe Green House offers an education of the highest quality in the widest sense. Facilities are excellent being sited in 15 acres of countryside adjacent to Hatfield Forest. It is a single-stream school which works broadly to the National Curriculum, offering additional French, Latin, Music, Drama and Sport. There is a strong parental involvement within the school whereby parents are actively encouraged to be part of their children's education. The school is seen as a community which fosters an understanding of children's development within both school and home. Children sit external examinations to senior schools both boarding and day and have been highly successful.

Entry to the school is mainly via Acorns Nursery but children are considered for entry to the Junior School by assessment and interview.

Charitable status. The Howe Green Educational Trust Ltd is a Registered Charity, number 297106. It exists to promote and provide for the advancement of education for the public benefit and in connection therewith to conduct a day school for the education of boys and girls.

Hulme Hall Grammar School

Hulme Hall Road, Cheadle Hulme, Stockport, Cheshire SK8 6LA

Tel: 0161 485 3524/0161 485 4638
Fax: 0161 485 5966
email: secretary@hulmehallschool.org
website: www.hulmehallschool.org

Headteacher: **Miss Rachael Allen**, BA Hons, MEd, PGCE

Age Range. 2–16 Co-educational.
Number in School. 250.
Fees per term (2016–2017). £1,530–£3,019.

Junior Learning Centre. We cater for girls and boys from 2 to 11 years in our Nursery, Kindergarten, Infant and Junior classes. At every stage of the learning process, we provide a caring and stimulating environment.

Given excellent resources, small classes and teachers of high calibre, children derive considerable satisfaction from their school work and experience no difficulty in realising their academic potential.

Senior School (11–16 years). The school is well staffed and equipped to deliver a curriculum covering a wide range of academic, creative and practical subjects. An extensive choice of GCSE and other external examination options enables pupils at Key Stage 4 to target optimum qualifications reflecting their personal choice of programme. The staff are consistent in the emphasis they place upon the encouragement of pupils who respond with a highly conscientious approach to their studies, which in turn ensures steady progress and excellent results.

Communication between school and home is given high priority and the regular issue of reports enables parents to monitor closely their child's educational development. At the age of 16, almost all pupils continue with A Level studies.

The school operates a bus service in conjunction with Elite Coaches, offering an extensive network of services covering a 15 mile radius of the school.

For further information please contact the School Secretary.

Charitable status. Hulme Hall Educational Trust is a Registered Charity, number 525931. The school aims to promote personal, moral, social and academic development of all pupils.

Hurst Lodge School

Bagshot Road, Ascot, Berkshire SL5 9JU
Tel: 01344 622154
email: admissions@hurstlodgesch.co.uk
website: www.hurstlodge.co.uk

Principal: **Miss V S Smit**, BSc Hons

Age Range. Girls 3–18; Boys 3–11. Weekly Boarding from age 9.
Number in School. Day: 88 Boys, 109 Girls; 12 Weekly Boarders.
Fees per term (2016–2017). Tuition: Sixth Form £2,140–£8,400, Years 7–11 £5,010, Years 5–6 £4,010, Years 3–4 £3,910; Years 1–2 £3,180, Foundation £3,110, Kindergarten (5 mornings) £1,650. Boarding Fee: £2,935.

Hurst Lodge is a small, well-established day and boarding school which successfully combines an academic and creative education. We offer excellent pastoral care and aspire to help our students realise their potential by encouraging learning for life and celebrating all achievements equally.

Small teaching groups ensure high standards, individual attention and excellent pastoral care.

We have a strong SEN department.

Hurst Lodge offers a wide breadth of academic and vocational subjects to GCSE and A Level. We specialise in Art, Textiles, Drama, Music and Dance at all levels but also have excellent academic results.

Students have Form and Personal Tutors to ensure a high level of pastoral care and support.

The Sixth Form is small and offers a full range of A Levels.

Hurtwood House School

Holmbury St Mary, Dorking, Surrey RH5 6NU
Tel: 01483 279000
Fax: 01483 267586
email: info@hurtwood.net
website: www.hurtwoodhouse.com

Headmasters: **C M Jackson**, BEd; **K R B Jackson**, MA

Age Range. 16–18.
Number in School. 330 (170 girls, 160 boys).
Fees per term (2016–2017). Boarding £13,613, Day £9,075.

Hurtwood House is the only independent boarding school specialising exclusively in the Sixth Form. It concentrates on the 16–18 age range and offers students a caring, residential structure and a commitment to a complete education where culture, sport, friendship and a full range of extracurricular activities all play an important part. Hugely successful across the whole range of academic subjects, Hurtwood House is also widely recognised as having the best Creative and Performing Arts and Media departments in the country and is therefore especially attractive to aspiring actors, directors, film directors, dancers, singers, artists and fashion designers.

Many students now want to leave the traditional school system at 16. They are seeking an environment which is structured and safe, but which is less institutional and better equipped to provide the challenge and stimulation which they are now ready for, and which is therefore better placed to develop their potential. They also require teaching methods which will prepare them for an increasingly competitive world by developing their initiative and encouraging them to think for themselves.

Hurtwood House has 330 boys and girls. It is a small and personal school, but it is a large and powerful sixth form which benefits from having specialised A Level teachers. The examination results put Hurtwood House in the top independent school league tables, but it is equally important to the school that the students develop energy, motivation and self-confidence.

In short, Hurtwood House is a stepping-stone between school and university for students who are all in the same age group and who share the same maturity and the same ambitions.

The school is situated in its own grounds high up in the Surrey Hills and offers excellent facilities in outstandingly beautiful surroundings.

Hyde Park School

Preparatory School:
24 Elvaston Place, London SW7 5NL
Tel: 020 7225 3131
Fax: 020 7590 9745
email: registrar@hydeparkschool.co.uk

Pre-Preparatory School:
The Long Garden, St George's Fields, Albion Street, London W2 2AX
Tel: 020 7262 1190
Fax: 020 7724 6980
email: admissions@hydeparkschool.co.uk

website: www.hydeparkschool.co.uk

Headmistress: **Mrs Hilary Wyatt**

Age Range. Co-educational: Prep 5–11, Pre-Prep 2–5.
Number of Pupils. Prep 120, Pre-Prep 80.
Fees per term (2016–2017). £3,300–£5,910.

Hyde Park Prep and Pre-Prep Schools occupy two separate and very different sites: the prep is housed in an elegant Victorian building in an excellent location in the heart of South Kensington; the pre-prep is situated in a wonderful large garden in W2, just north of Hyde Park. The prep school takes children aged 5 to 11 years (Year 1 to Year 6) and the pre-prep takes children from 2 to 5 years (Nursery and Reception). The schools have traditional values and our staff expect high standards of both work and behaviour, with kindness and consideration for others being of paramount importance. At the same time, the schools are well resourced with modern equipment and the children are safe, secure and exceptionally well cared for. Both schools are small, cosy, friendly establishments where no individual becomes lost in the crowd. Delicious healthy lunches are prepared by our own cooks who cater for all dietary needs.

One of the main purposes of the prep school is to prepare children for entry into the senior school of their choice. The curriculum consists of all the customary subjects plus our own additions: French from Nursery upwards and Mandarin from Form 4. We more than compensate for our limited outside space with an extensive PE curriculum including swimming from Reception and outside sports at Hyde Park. We have football and netball teams and play competitive matches against local schools. The children participate in regular trips to the nearby museums and to places of interest further afield. There is a residential trip in Forms 4, 5 and 6. We offer a wide range of after-school activities including fencing, karate, fashion design, yoga, fitness, art, drama, mini engineers, singing, street dance and coding. The children may also take ballet classes as an optional extra and there is excellent provision at both schools for children who do not have English as their first language.

The pre-prep in W2 is a paradise for young children with its wonderful garden and vast sandpit. Whatever the weather, the children have a huge array of resources to exercise their minds and bodies, and the freedom to investigate and experiment under the watchful eyes of our well-qualified and highly-experienced staff. Children who attend the pre-prep are guaranteed places at the prep school and can opt to travel between the sites by school minibus if they wish.

Hyde Park School is part of Minerva Education group which owns a number of private schools in London, East and South East England. Through Minerva's "Inspiring Learning" programme, we seek to share best practice and ensure the continuing improvement in every child's education.

Ibstock Place School

Clarence Lane, London SW15 5PY

Tel:	General Enquiries: 020 8876 9991
	Headmistress's PA: 020 8392 5802
	Bursar's Office: 020 8392 5804
	Registrar: 020 8392 5803
email:	office@ibstockplaceschool.co.uk
website:	www.ibstockplaceschool.co.uk

Chairman of Governors: Richard Jackson, MA, FRSA

Headmistress: Mrs Anna Sylvester-Johnson, BA Hons, PGCE

Deputy Headmaster: Mr Huw Daniel, BSc Hons London, PGCE
Second Master: Mr Christopher Wolsey, MA Nottingham, MEd Buckingham
Head of Pastoral Care: Mr John-Daniel Price, BSc Exeter
Tutor for Admissions: Mr Christopher Banfield, MA Leeds, MSc Open
Heads of Houses:
Mr Ross Greenwood, BA Canterbury, MA Ed St Mary's
Mr Charles Janz, MA Oxon
Mrs Emily Richardson, BA London, MEd Hertfordshire
Mr Samuel Robinson, BA Sussex
Head of Pre-Prep and Preparatory School: Miss Marion MacDonald, BA UWE

Age Range. 4–18 Co-educational.
Number in School. 970: 498 Boys, 472 Girls.
Fees per term (2016–2017). £4,995–£6,400 (including lunches).

Ibstock Place School is located in spacious grounds of some eight acres adjacent to Richmond Park with easy access to Putney, Barnes, Richmond and Hammersmith. The school offers a balanced education combining a traditional academic curriculum with an extensive range of co-curricular opportunities.

This co-educational school has grown and prospered with significant building development in recent years. A new Sports Hall opened in 2008. New School, occupying Clarence Lane and Priory wings and comprising twenty-one classrooms, six laboratories and two computer suites, opened in 2011. Additional facilities include: a new Library

accommodated over two floors, a Music Technology studio, AstroTurf and sports pitches on the adjacent Lawrence House campus site, and a swimming pool. A new Performing Arts Centre, including flexible, state-of-the-art Theatre, fully-equipped Drama Studio and backstage facilities comprising Dressing Rooms, Green Room and Workshop opened in the autumn of 2015.

The Preparatory Department and the Senior School remain distinctive and are housed separately, so that each child benefits from a small-school ambience and the younger pupils gain from many of the facilities enjoyed by the Senior School. The Prep School, which incorporates Pre-Prep, provides a rich and stimulating environment, with a wide range of curricular activity carefully planned to realise each child's abilities and talents.

The Senior School, age 11–18, offers a full range of Arts, Humanities, Languages, Science and Technology subjects. All pupils follow a core curriculum which includes a requirement to study two languages at (I)GCSE, along with many opportunities for enrichment. Co-curricular emphasis is placed on Music, Drama and Sports, and recent tours have taken pupils to China, Iceland, India, South Africa and the USA, as well as language visits to European destinations closer to home. There is an outstanding programme of outdoor education, a wide range of after-school clubs, as well as the Duke of Edinburgh's Award Scheme. All pupils are supported by a strong and effective pastoral system which operates through four houses. House Groups are vertically organised and are aspirational as well as companionable.

Our pupils' GCSE and (I)GCSE results for 2016 were outstanding: 79.3% of all GCSE and (I)GCSE entries were graded at A* or A. Our pupils' GCE A Level and Pre-U results in 2016 produced 75% of grades at A* or A, and 83.9% of all examination entries graded at A*–B. On the strength of these results, two of our pupils take up places at Oxford and Cambridge this year to read Civil Engineering and Human, Social and Political Sciences and one will study Medicine at Imperial College London. Other world-class Higher Education destinations include the universities of Bath, Birmingham, Bristol, Durham, Edinburgh, Exeter, Leeds, Nottingham, UCL and Warwick, as well as universities in the USA, France, the Netherlands and South Africa.

Entry to the Pre-Prep is by date of Registration and for subsequent years by assessment. There is no guaranteed transfer from the Prep School to the Senior School. All candidates for Senior School entry are interviewed and take examinations in Mathematics, English and Reasoning. A satisfactory report from the entrant's current school is also required.

Further information is available from the Registrar and Open Mornings and Evenings are held regularly through the year. Occasional places may arise from time to time (e.g. at 13+).

Charitable status. Ibstock Place School is a Registered Charity, number 1145565.

The Italia Conti Academy of Theatre Arts

Italia Conti House, 23 Goswell Road, London EC1M 7AJ

Tel:	020 7608 0047/8
Fax:	020 7253 1430
email:	admin@italiaconti.co.uk
website:	www.italiaconti.com

Acting Principal: Mrs S Newton

Head: Mrs Karen Dwyer-Burchill, MA, HDipEd, MEd

Age Range. 10–16.
Number in School. Day: 76.
Fees per term (2016–2017). £4,325.

For over a hundred years the Academy has been preparing young people for successful careers in the performing arts it has been aware that the profession expects excellent standards of education and training of its new entrants. Today's Producers and Directors demand that performers entering the industry be versatile and be able to take direction within the theatre, television or film studio.

The five courses offered by the Academy seek to expose students to a wide range of disciplines and techniques in the Dance, Drama and Singing fields working in the mediums of stage, television and recording studio under the careful tuition of highly qualified professional staff.

The courses are as follows:

The Theatre Arts School. For 10 to 16 year olds providing a balanced traditional academic education leading to nine GCSEs with broadly based vocational training in dance, drama and singing. Sixth Form Studies within the Performing Arts Course allows two A Levels to be studied alongside a full professional dance, drama and singing theatre arts course.

Performing Arts Course. A three-year course for students aged 16+. Accredited by the National Council for Dance Education and Training. Leading to the award of The National Diploma in Musical Theatre or a Foundation Degree in the Performing Arts

One Year Foundation Course. From age 16. Drama & Dance Award Scholarships are available for this Course.

Entry Requirements. Entry for all the above courses is by audition and assessment.

In addition to the above the Academy offers part-time Saturday classes to children aged 3½ to 18 years in Dance, Drama and Singing. Entry is by interview. Also offered is a Summer School, one week Performing Arts or Drama courses for those aged 9 to 19.

Charitable status. The Italia Conti Academy Trust is a Registered Charity, number 290261. It exists to promote education in the Performing Arts through both teaching and the provision of scholarships.

King Alfred School

Manor Wood, 149 North End Road, London NW11 7HY

Tel: 020 8457 5200
Fax: 020 8457 5249
email: kas@kingalfred.org.uk
website: www.kingalfred.org.uk
Twitter: @kingalfredsch
Facebook: /TheKingAlfredSchool

Head: **Robert Lobatto**, MA Oxon, PGCE, NPQH London

Age Range. 4–18.
Number in School. Primary: approx 300; Secondary: approx 350.
Fees per term (2016–2017). Reception, Years 1–2: £4,954, Years 3–6: £5,708, Upper School (Years 7–13): £5,972.

King Alfred School is unique among independent schools in North London. Apart from being all-age (4–18), co-ed and secular, it takes in a wide range of ability as opposed to its academically selective neighbours in the private sector.

The school's beginnings are unusual: it was founded in 1898 by a group of Hampstead parents and its governing body comprises mainly current and ex-parents. Visitors tend to comment on the pretty site (on the edge of Hampstead Garden Suburb), the "village" layout (carefully preserved by a succession of architects), and the friendly atmosphere – this is a no-uniform establishment and all are on first-name terms. The recent purchase of property across the road has enabled the school to extend classroom facilities.

Academic results are consistently impressive and constantly improving and almost 100% of the KAS Sixth Form go on to university or Art Foundation courses or music colleges and conservatoires, the vast majority to their first choice. The school prides itself on its reputation as a relaxed, informal and vibrant community that achieves academic success within a non-pressured environment.

Bursaries for Year 7 and the Sixth Form are available.

Charitable status. King Alfred School is a Registered Charity, number 312590. It exists to provide quality education for boys and girls.

Kings Monkton School

6 West Grove, Cardiff CF24 3XL

Tel: 029 2048 2854
email: mail@kingsmonkton.org.uk
website: www.kingsmonkton.org.uk
Twitter: @kings_monkton
Facebook: /kings-monkton-school

Principal: **Mr Paul Norton**

Vice Principal and Head of Primary: Mrs Karen Norton

Age Range. 3–18.
Number in School. 255.
Fees per term (2016–2017). £2,650–£3,800.

Kings Monkton School is a co-educational day school for children from nursery age right up to university entrance. The school is owned by Heathfield Independent Schools and is renowned for its caring and inclusive ethos.

Kings Monkton is one of South Wales's oldest independent schools, having educated generations of local pupils since its foundation in 1870. The school prides itself on its consistent record of academic success, its system of pastoral care and its relations with parents. Pupils are drawn from a wide catchment area including Cardiff, the Vale of Glamorgan, the Valleys and Monmouth, as well as having a number of CAS Sponsored International Pupils on Tier 4 Visas. The school is housed in purpose-built accommodation in the centre of Cardiff, close to Queen Street station and to all amenities.

Kings Monkton's primary school has small classes in which young children can receive individual care and guidance. Pupils follow a well-balanced curriculum, designed to develop and stimulate young minds to the full. Children are taught both French and Mandarin and have extensive access to sports.

In the secondary school, pupils pursue a wide curriculum with their progress being carefully monitored and receive strong pastoral support throughout their adolescent years. All pupils are encouraged to strive for high standards in their work and to contribute to the well-being of the community to which they belong. Entry to the school is non-selective, with a strict 15 pupils per class to ensure that all achieve their highest potential.

In the school's A Level college, students are taught in small tutorial groups and in addition to their academic studies participate in a number of other activities including Young Enterprise, Welsh Baccalaureate and the Extended Project Qualification as part of the school's philosophy of giving its pupils a thorough preparation for life. The minimum entry requirements to the College are five GCSE passes at grades A–C.

In 2003 the school opened its new purpose-built sixth form centre with upgraded facilities for physics, technology and music.

The school works in partnership with Oxford Royale Academy, Dragon Career Associates and Wonderland Studios, as well as having close links with China and Spain.

Kirkstone House School

Baston, Peterborough, Lincolnshire PE6 9PA

Tel:	01778 560350
Fax:	01778 560547
email:	info@kirkstonehouseschool.co.uk
website:	www.kirkstonehouseschool.co.uk

Co-Principals: Mrs B K Wyman, Mr E G Wyman, Mr J W R Wyman

Head: **Mrs C Jones**

Age Range. 3–18.
Number in School. 121: 81 boys, 40 girls.
Fees per term (2016–2017). £3,090–£3,804.

Kirkstone House prides itself on being a family run non-selective school where children of all abilities can achieve their full potential in a caring environment. The atmosphere is characterised by its supportive nature and sense of community. Classes are small and pupils and staff know each other well.

There are high aspirations for pupils and the school aims to provide the highest quality of education throughout all years by catering for the full academic range and offering a wide curriculum. Strong emphasis is placed on choice with a wide range of GCSEs and BTEC courses being offered up to the age of 18. There is also a very well established Learning Support Department providing tailored additional assistance including helping pupils to cope with dyslexia.

A wealth of extracurricular activities are enjoyed by many pupils including The Duke of Edinburgh's Award, a thriving Youth Theatre and a range of sporting pursuits. Additionally, a 60-acre site of woodlands and lakes has specific scientific interest and is used for environmental and land-based study.

Knightsbridge School

67 Pont Street, London SW1X 0BD

Tel:	020 7590 9000
Fax:	020 7589 9055
email:	registrar@knightsbridgeschool.com
website:	www.knightsbridgeschool.com

Principal: **Mr Magoo Giles**

Head: Ms Shona Colaço

Age Range. 4–13.
Number in School. 400.
Fees per term (2016–2017). £6,067–£6,460.

Knightsbridge School is a preparatory school offering a broad, balanced and challenging curriculum to prepare both boys and girls for entry to senior day and boarding schools.

Pupils are encouraged to play hard, work hard in the Junior School and work hard, play hard in the Senior School, and make the most of every opportunity open to them to achieve their full potential. They are taught all National Curriculum subjects to a high standard, and modern languages from nursery age upwards.

The school fosters a strong sense of community, and provides a supportive and warm environment. Small classes, overseen by highly qualified, dynamic and enthusiastic staff, will ensure that boys and girls benefit not only academically but also personally. By developing their self-esteem and confidence they will grow into happy, independent all-rounders of healthy body and healthy mind.

Located in the heart of Central London, the school is housed in two magnificent mansions. The premises have undergone an extensive renovation and upgrade programme. Teaching facilities include well-equipped and modern classrooms, a new science laboratory, an information and communication technology suite, music rooms, and a performing arts studio and a new library, as well as a fully catered kitchen and dining area.

Sports facilities include a gymnasium on site and the diverse and challenging sports programme makes use of local venues such as Burton's Court, Battersea Park, St Luke's recreational grounds, the Queen Mother Sports Centre and Hyde Park.

Entry to Knightsbridge School is by informal interview of both parents and children at the appropriate level. Prospective boys and girls for Year 1 and above will be expected to spend a day of assessment at the school in their relevant year group, and a report from the Head of the applicant's current school will be required.

Charitable status. Knightsbridge School Education Foundation is a Registered Charity, number 1120970.

The Knoll School

Manor Avenue, Kidderminster, Worcestershire DY11 6EA

Tel:	01562 822622
Fax:	01562 865686
email:	info@knollschool.co.uk
	head@knollschool.co.uk
website:	www.knollschool.co.uk
Facebook:	/KnollSchool

Headmaster: **N J Humphreys**, BEd Hons

Age Range. Co-educational 3 months–11 years.
Number in School. Day: 47 Boys, 45 Girls.
Fees per term (2016–2017). £873–£2,987.

2017 will be an exciting year for us as it will be our 100th birthday. Many celebrations and events are in the planning. The Knoll School, which was founded in 1917, is a small independent school situated on the outskirts of Kidderminster.

Children start at The Knoll School in our First Steps Nursery, which caters for children from 3 months to rising 3 years, and is open for 50 weeks of the year. All our staff in the nursery are NVQ3 or higher qualified and well experienced.

Children approaching their third birthday then move into to our Early Years Department.

The environment at The Knoll is that of a large, caring family. Pastoral care is of utmost importance to us and we employ a full-time Matron.

Pre- and after-school care is available from 7.30 am to 6 pm every day. Also we operate a very active holiday club during all of the school holidays, and go out regularly on trips.

The school has a busy calendar and has achieved a Gold Sing Up Award; music plays a large part at The Knoll. The children go out of school on a variety of educational outings and we offer a wide range of sporting activities, including swimming, hockey and tennis. The children enter various sporting competitions throughout the year.

We have high expectations of our pupils in all aspects of their education and our Year 6 children's achievements have enabled them to gain places at top independent schools in our area.

We are currently ranked in the top 100 independent schools in the country, being the only one in Worcestershire.

Charitable status. The Knoll School Educational Trust Limited is a Registered Charity, number 527600.

Lady Barn House School

Schools Hill, Cheadle, Cheshire SK8 1JE

Tel: 0161 428 2912
Fax: 0161 428 5798
email: info@ladybarnhouse.stockport.sch.uk
website: www.ladybarnhouse.org
Twitter: @LadyBarnHouse

Headmaster: **Mr M Turner**

Age Range. 3–11.
Number in School. Day: 260 Boys, 223 Girls.
Fees per term (2016–2017). Nursery: £2,271 (all day), £1,509 (mornings only); KS1 & KS2: £2,594. Lunches per term £179.

W H Herford, minister and educational pioneer, founded the school in 1873. His vision was to establish a co-educational school that promoted happiness, academia, whilst embracing a Christian ethos. Today, Herford's vision still drives our thriving, family-orientated community. Boys and girls flourish, learning side by side, in an exceptional educational setting.

We combine the latest educational thinking with tried and tested traditional methods. Pupils are gradually nurtured and developed so that they can confidently face their future with knowledge, understanding and the ability to be independent. Music, sport, drama, languages, outdoor adventure and a wide range of other clubs, trips and residential visits enhance our curriculum.

Pupils are prepared and supported for their 11+ entrance exams; they then move on to the best and most appropriate senior schools.

Lady Barn House School is a truly special educational institution where each and every pupil experiences success and reaches their potential. It remains one of the North West's most prestigious independent primary schools.

The School is a Charitable Trust. Bursaries are available at Year 2 and Year 3.

Charitable status. Lady Barn House School Limited is a Registered Charity, number 1042587. It exists to provide education for boys and girls.

Lime House School

Holm Hill, Dalston, Nr Carlisle, Cumbria CA5 7BX

Tel: 01228 710225
Fax: 01228 710508
email: lhsoffice@aol.com
            headmaster@limehouseschool.co.uk
website: www.limehouseschool.co.uk

Headmaster: **N A Rice**, MA, BA, CertEd

Age Range. 3+–18+. Boarders from age 9.

Number in School. Day: 28 Boys, 22 Girls; Boarding: 50 Boys, 25 Girls.
Fees per term (2016–2017). Boarding £7,000–£8,250; Day £1,800–£3,500.
Compulsory extras: Activities, Laundry.

Lime House School is a fully independent co-educational boarding and day school for pupils aged 3½ to 18. Our aim is to ensure that each pupil achieves his or her potential both academically and socially, with each child treated individually. Our pupils are cared for in a safe rural environment and every possible attempt is made to ensure that they develop confidence and self-esteem. Boarding is available to all pupils, with the majority being full boarders.

Foreign students whose first language is not English add to the cosmopolitan atmosphere of the school. They are prepared for Cambridge English examinations (KET, PET & IELTS) and follow the same curriculum as all other students.

Games and sport form an important part of school life. All students participate and a wide range of team and individual sports is offered. Most pupils take games to GCSE level, with many continuing to A Level. In 2012 the GCSE pass rate was 100% and at A Level 83% of grades were A* to C.

We would welcome a visit to our school to see it in action. Simply contact the school and we will arrange a time convenient for you.

Loreto Preparatory School

Dunham Road, Altrincham, Cheshire WA14 4GZ

Tel: 0161 928 8310
Fax: 0161 929 5801
email: info.loretoprep@btconnect.com
website: www.loretoprep.org.uk

Headteacher: **Mrs Helen Norwood**, BA Hons, PGCE

Age Range. Girls 3–11.
Number in School. 170 Day Girls.
Fees per term (2016–2017). £2,015.

Loreto Preparatory School, founded in 1909, is a modern, purpose-built school (1971), standing in pleasant grounds and offering an all-round education by well-qualified staff. Religious education and moral training are central to our teaching, based on Gospel principles. Our recent ISI Inspection stated that the school "maintains its traditional values, yet incorporates some modern thinking in the curriculum".

Music plays an important part in the life of the school. All aspects of class music are taught by a specialist. We have a school orchestra, and private individual lessons are available in most instruments. The children's dramatic ability and interest are developed through class lessons, theatre visits and regular productions. Gymnastics, swimming, netball, badminton and athletics, taught by a PE specialist, are important elements of our physical education programme and the school participates fully in local and national competitions.

Our ICT facilities are excellent and include a computer suite and interactive whiteboards in every class. There is a well-stocked, computerised library, allowing pupils to select, issue and return their own books.

We offer a wide range of extracurricular activities including Drama, Art Club, Zumbatomic, Street Dance, Computer Club and Chess.

Of equal importance is social development and each child is encouraged to reach her full potential and to care for others.

Loreto is a Catholic independent school and is one of many Loreto schools built on the foundations laid by Mary

Ward, foundress of the Institute of the Blessed Virgin Mary, according to the vision of St Ignatius of Loyola.

Visits to the school are welcome by appointment. Admission at 3+ is usually by interview and by interview and Entrance Examination for those wishing to join at 7+.

Charitable status. Loreto Preparatory School is a Registered Charity, number 250607.

Lucton School

Lucton, Leominster, Herefordshire HR6 9PN

Tel: 01568 782000
Fax: 01568 782001
email: admissions@luctonschool.org
website: www.luctonschool.org
Twitter: @LuctonSchool
Facebook: @Lucton-School
LinkedIn: /lucton-school

Headmistress: **Mrs Gill Thorne**, MA, BA Hons, PGCE, LLAM

Deputy Head: Mr D R Styles, JP, BSc Hons, MA, FCIEA, CPhys
Head of Sixth Form: Mr J Goode, MA Cantab, PGCE
Head of Prep School: Mr David Bicker-Caarten, MBA

Age Range. 6 months–19 years.
Number in School. 350.
Fees per term (2016–2017). Day £2,215–£4,315, Weekly Boarding £6,990–£8,250, Full Boarding £9,985.

About Lucton School. Founded in 1708, Lucton provides pupils with an excellent all-round education which aims to bring out their full potential. Pupils benefit from small classes, a friendly atmosphere and an idyllic rural location. There are extensive sports facilities and a good mix of day pupils, weekly boarders and full boarders.

Studying at Lucton School. Lucton has a strong academic record and an established tradition of getting the best possible results from each pupil. Subjects taught to GCSE include English language and literature, mathematics, biology, chemistry, physics, information technology, French, Spanish, German, history, geography, business studies, religious education, design & technology, art, music, drama and PE/games.

All the above GCSE subjects and more are available at AS and A2 Levels. The Sixth Form is housed in a new sixth form centre, including a new senior library and well-equipped IT suite.

School Facilities. The school is set in 55 acres of beautiful Herefordshire countryside. Facilities on site include:
- Junior and senior libraries
- Science laboratories
- ICT rooms
- Design and technology workshop
- Tennis courts
- Indoor swimming pool
- Indoor sports hall
- Games fields
- Equestrian centre.

Boarding pupils are housed in modern buildings and senior pupils have individual rooms.

Admissions. Admission can take place at any time of the year by interview and assessment. Prospective pupils are always invited to spend a taster day in the school without obligation. Examinations for academic scholarships are held in January each year.

Affiliations. The Headmistress of Lucton School is a member of the Independent Schools Association (ISA); the

Head of Lucton Prep School is a member of The Independent Association of Prep Schools (IAPS); and Lucton School is in membership of the Boarding Schools' Association (BSA).

Charitable status. Lucton School is a Registered Charity, number 518076.

The Lyceum

6 Paul Street, City of London, London EC2A 4JH

Tel: 020 7247 1588
email: admin@lyceumschool.co.uk
website: www.lyceumschool.co.uk

Head Teacher: **Mrs Vanessa Bingham**

Deputy Head Teacher: Miss Alice Riley

Age Range. 3–11 Co-educational.
Number of Pupils. 110.
Fees per term (2016–2017). £3,315–£5,020.

The Lyceum is a non-selective independent co-educational school conveniently based near Old Street station. At The Lyceum they believe that all children have the potential to achieve and excel. The school provides children with an educational atmosphere and experiences that stimulate, motivate and encourage them to achieve beyond what may be expected.

The Lyceum is a small school with a family atmosphere where children are happy, excited and challenged daily. The children in their care are offered a broad and balanced curriculum with equal emphasis on the arts, physical education, moral and spiritual education as well as academic subjects. They believe that involvement in the arts helps to build confidence and self-esteem, and that a good all-round education leads to high standards.

The Lyceum aims:

- To ensure that each child's talents are discovered and nurtured and they achieve their potential in terms of spiritual awareness, academic achievement and aesthetic appreciation.
- To ensure children go on to a suitable secondary school that matches their academic, emotional and social needs, and where their talents can be nurtured.
- To develop in children the skills which will equip them for the next stage of their lives and to enable them to positively influence their own lives.
- That children and parents look back on their time at The Lyceum as a positive and happy one.
- To ensure all children have access to a broad and balanced curriculum and a range of extra-curricular activities.
- To develop tolerance and understanding towards each other and all members of the wider community.
- To develop curiosity, a drive to learn, confidence, independence and a strong work ethic.
- To develop a positive attitude to behaviour based on traditional manners.
- To develop a responsible and independent attitude towards work and their future roles in society.
- To encourage curiosity and a positive attitude to learning.

The curriculum has a strong emphasis on using local resources, as well as the school's link to a wide range of study centres, experiences of living history and a Year 6 residential visit to a European City, usually Paris or Amsterdam.

Children who attend the Lyceum get to take advantage of their central location including the large range of museums, galleries and concert halls nearby. Children undertake at least one educational visit per half term related to the curriculum. From Year 3 (age 7) upwards children go on residential trips including 'living history' events. In addition to this authors, artists and speakers are invited to speak at the school, to enhance the curriculum.

The Lyceum is part of the Minerva Education group which owns a number of private schools in London, East and South East England. Through Minerva's "Inspiring Learning" programme, we seek to share best practice and ensure the continuing improvement in every child's education.

Lyndhurst School

36 The Avenue, Camberley, Surrey GU15 3NE
Tel: 01276 22895
email: office@lyndhurstschool.co.uk
website: www.lyndhurstschool.co.uk

Headmaster: **Mr Andrew Rudkin**

Deputy Head: Mrs Nicola Price
School Business Manager: Mrs Lesley McCready

Age Range. 3–11 years.
Number in School. Day: 63 Boys, 64 Girls.
Fees per term (2016–2017). Main School £3,100–£4,100. Little Lyndhurst: £1,725–£3,700 (five full days 8.00 am to 6.00 pm). Fees include tuition, hot lunches, 2 after-school clubs from a selective list, wrap-around care from 8.00 am to 6.00 pm and all school trips.

We are a small friendly co-educational school with a wonderful family feel. Parents and pupils comment on the 'home from home' atmosphere.

Boys and girls are accepted from the age of 3 years into the happy and friendly Early Years Department, situated in a beautiful house within the school grounds. From here until they leave the school at the age of 11, every care is taken to realise the full potential of each child.

Small class sizes ensure that, whilst teachers really know their pupils and are able to tailor the curriculum to the individual child's needs, pupils are also able to learn from each other in a challenging yet supportive environment. Our experienced staff inspire the children and set high academic standards, we achieve excellent 11+ examination results, including academic scholarships.

We make full use of the excellent local sporting facilities and the Royal Military Academy, Sandhurst. All pupils take weekly swimming lessons and are involved in a wide range of sporting activities.

Music and Drama have a significant presence within the school. We have two choirs and an orchestra, many plays throughout the year and pupils are prepared for the examinations of the Associated Board of Music. We offer an extensive after school activities programme and wrap-around care from 8.00 am to 6.00 pm.

Entry to the school can be at any age if there is a vacancy.

Happiness is the key ingredient and every child at Lyndhurst is given the chance to shine at something, whether academic, music, sport or art.

Lyonsdown School

3 Richmond Road, New Barnet, Hertfordshire EN5 1SA
Tel: 020 8449 0225
Fax: 020 8441 4690

email: enquiries@lyonsdownschool.co.uk
website: www.lyonsdownschool.co.uk

Headmistress: **Mrs Lynn Maggs-Wellings**, BEd

Age Range. Girls 3–11, Boys 3–7.
Number of Pupils. 200.
Fees per term (2016–2017). Pre-Reception: £1,260–£2,285; Reception–Year 2 £2,910; Years 3–6 £3,200.

Lyonsdown School has built on its past inheritance since its foundation in 1906, to embrace the needs of education for children of the 21st Century. Pupils are nurtured by our well-qualified, experienced and caring staff who help them to maximise their potential. The school has a tradition of high academic standards and achievements within a broad curriculum.

The personal development of each child is a high priority. A wide variety of extracurricular activities allows pupils to extend their experiences and learn new skills.

A balanced academic, physical and cultural education, together with a high level of pastoral care, enables pupils to grow and look forward to being part of the modern world.

Entry into Pre-Reception and Reception is non-selective. Pupils are considered for entry at other ages if places become available.

We aim to allow each child to move easily into the next stage of their education by preparing them for schools which best suit their needs.

Charitable status. Lyonsdown School Trust Ltd is a Registered Charity, number 312591.

Mander Portman Woodward (MPW)
London

90–92 Queen's Gate, London SW7 5AB
Tel: 020 7835 1355
Fax: 020 7259 2705
email: london@mpw.ac.uk
website: www.mpw.ac.uk

Principal: **John Southworth**, BSc, MSc

Age Range. 14–19.
Number in School. Day: 289 Boys, 253 Girls.
Fees per term (2016–2017). £8,651–£9,374.

Mander Portman Woodward (MPW) is a co-educational London day school accepting pupils from the first year of GCSE onwards. Approximately 200 new pupils join each year at the start of the sixth form. We offer a very wide range of subjects (42 at A Level and 26 at GCSE) and there are no restrictions on subject combinations at A Level. At all levels the absolute maximum number of pupils in any one class is eight.

The school has completely refurbished its Queen's Gate premises with modern facilities tastefully blended in with the traditional architecture of the buildings. There are five well equipped laboratories for Science subjects and specialist studios for Art, Ceramics, Photography, Media Studies and Drama. The school also has extensive facilities for independent study, including two supervised reading rooms and an internet library.

There is a range of compulsory extra-curricular activities for GCSE pupils, including sport, and various voluntary extra-curricular activities are offered at A Level. In keeping with our founding principles, our primary focus at all age levels is on academic goals. Entry into the sixth form is dependent on a student's academic record and performance at interview. Almost all pupils proceed to university after leaving, with about 10 each year going to read Medicine. Over the past four years an average of 7 of our full-time pupils each year have won places at the Universities of Oxford or Cambridge.

We insist on strict punctuality in the attendance of lessons and the submission of homework and there is a formal system of monthly examinations in each subject throughout a pupil's career at the school. This system is designed to ensure that sensible, cumulative revision becomes a study habit not only at school but also later on at university. We require pupils to have a strong commitment to academic discipline but our reputation is based on having created a framework in which pupils can enjoy working hard. The environment is friendly, the teachers experienced and enthusiastic and the atmosphere positive and conducive to success.

Maple Hayes Hall School for Dyslexics

Abnalls Lane, Lichfield, Staffordshire WS13 8BL

Tel: 01543 264387
Fax: 01543 262022
email: office@dyslexia.gb.com
website: www.dyslexia.gb.com

Principal: **Dr E N Brown**, PhD, MSc, BA, MSCME, MINS, AFBPsS, CPsychol

Headmaster: Dr D J Brown, DPhil, MEd Psychology of SpLD, MA Oxon, PGCE

Age Range. 7–17.
Number in School. 120 Day Boys and Girls.
Fees per term (from April 2016). £4,825–£6,450.

Maple Hayes is a specialist independent day school approved under the 1996 Education Act as a co-educational school for children of average to very high intelligence who are not achieving their intellectual potential by normal teaching methods.

This school is under the direction of Dr E Neville Brown whose work in the field of learning strategies has achieved international recognition and includes a major breakthrough in the teaching of dyslexic children. Attention is paid to the individual child by teaching the basic literacy and numeracy skills required for the child to benefit from a full curriculum (with the exception of a foreign language). The school had an excellent Ofsted report.

The very favourable teacher-pupil ratio of 1:10 or better ensures a high standard of educational and pastoral care. The children's learning is under the supervision and guidance of a qualified educational psychologist.

Maple Walk School

62A Crownhill Road, London NW10 4EB

Tel: 020 8963 3890
              020 8965 7374 (Admissions)
email: admin@maplewalkschool.co.uk
website: www.maplewalkschool.co.uk

Head Teacher: **Mrs Sarah Gillam**

Age Range. 4–11 Co-educational.
Number of Pupils. 183.

Maple Walk is a happy, thriving and vibrant independent primary school, for girls and boys aged 4–11, in North West London.

We provide a secure and supportive environment for effective learning and personal development. High standards are pursued in all subjects including English and Maths using traditional teaching methods, alongside an innovative curriculum.

We have a friendly, well-resourced, purpose-built environment with small class sizes, in which children learn and flourish.

Opportunities outside the classroom abound. Through sporting activities, first class music, art and drama, we encourage every child to find their own particular strength.

Termly school trips and residential experiences in Years 5 and 6 extend the curriculum and develop social skills.

Year 6 leavers have been offered places at a range of independent and maintained schools, including St Paul's Girls, Godolphin and Latymer, Christ's Hospital, John Lyon, Frances Holland, Slough Grammar, Notting Hill & Ealing High School, Latymer Upper, Henrietta Barnett and Highgate, to name just a few.

Founded in 2004, Maple Walk was the first of the New Model School Company's schools, offering a low-fee model, based on traditional teaching methods and with a Christian ethos.

Entry into Reception is non selective and based on the date the completed registration form is returned to our Registrar, with siblings given priority. Entry higher up the school is by interview and informal assessment in the classroom. We offer regular open days and welcome private tours.

Fees per term (2016–2017). £2,957.

Mark College

Mark, Highbridge, Somerset TA9 4NP

Tel: 01278 641632
Fax: 01278 641426
email: markcollege@priorygroup.com
website: www.priorygroup.com

Principal: **Mr Chris Sweeney**

Head Teacher: Mr Graham Scott

Age Range. 9–19.
Number in School. Boarding: 35 Boys, 2 Girls; Day: 35 Boys, 6 Girls.
Fees per term (2016–2017). Full Boarding from £9,679; Weekly Boarding from £9,308; Day from £6,847.

Mark College is a specialist secondary school for boys and girls aged 9 to 19 with specific learning difficulties. The students at Mark College have dyslexia, dyspraxia or other language disorder such as Asperger's Syndrome. Many students have struggled in mainstream schools and benefit hugely from being in an environment with other SpLD students where the level of support and teaching methods are specifically designed to overcome the challenges that dyslexic students face.

Mark College follows the National Curriculum and most students aim towards up to seven GCSEs or other forms of accreditation. Education is provided on a 35-week basis for both residential and day students. Mark College can provide places for up to 85 students. We welcome international students from all over the world and provide extra teaching with English language if required.

The sixth form allows students to study up to A Level or level 3 BTECs whilst continuing to receive the specific support they need.

Support offered includes:

- Small classes and work structured for individual student success
- Subject specialist staff, trained to teach students with SpLD
- Emphasis on educational achievement
- Information technology (IT) including personal laptops issued to every student
- Placements for international students, with English language assistance where required
- Focus on self-achievement and becoming independent learners
- Excellent sports facilities with training to both county and national level
- A caring environment where students can develop and grow
- On site SALT, OT or Art Therapy as required

Our aim. At Mark College the aim is to create an environment where students can become independent learners so that they can go on and pursue their ambitions when they leave.

We promote self-confidence, self-reliance and self-esteem and provide students with the strategies needed to meet the challenges associated with their specific learning difficulties, to enable them to go on to higher education and lead successful, independent lives.

Mayville High School

35 St Simon's Road, Southsea, Hants PO5 2PE

Tel: 023 9273 4847
Fax: 023 9229 3649
email: enquiries@mayvillehighschool.net
website: www.mayvillehighschool.com

Mayville High School – Excellence through nurture

Headteacher: Mrs R H K Parkyn, MA Oxon, MA, PGCE, MCIL

Age Range. 2+ to 16 years.
Number in School. Day Pupils: 246 Boys, 215 Girls.
Fees per term (2016–2017). £2,360–£3,470.

Mayville High School can offer your child a place from the age of 2+ to 16 years. Our close-knit community is divided into the Early Years, Pre-Prep, Junior and Senior Schools. We have a renowned Dyslexia Unit, recognised by CReSTeD, and offer a Gifted and Talented Programme. Our pupils star in numerous ways, and the Mayville family includes pupils, teachers, parents, carers and grandparents.

Mayville, a co-educational day school in Southsea, Hampshire was founded in 1897. There is a strong emphasis on traditional skills, yet Mayville adopts innovative teaching methods to help promote your child's learning. Our size is our strength, big enough to offer pupils a wide range of opportunities, we are small enough to truly treat and know each pupil as an individual.

Mayville provides a learning environment where your child is able to achieve their goals. At Mayville we want children to feel secure and valued: this enables them to take advantage of every opportunity, whether it is academic, social, physical, creative or spiritual.

Mayville sets high standards in all areas. Small class sizes encourage academic success. Boys and girls are taught separately throughout, to best meet their individual learning styles. Over the years Mayville pupils have consistently achieved high standards in GCSE examinations. Flexible teaching, varied resources, support and extension programmes coupled with high expectations help to meet the

needs of each individual learner. Art, drama, dance, music and sport play an important part in school life, the latter now enhanced by new playing fields. There are a number of clubs and after-school activities. There is something available to interest everyone.

Early Years (2+ to 5+ years). Our Early Years at Mayville encompass the statutory curriculum of the Foundation Stage; the youngest children are the 2+ year olds (Swans) who are situated in the "Cottage". In the September following their 3rd birthday the Swans graduate to the Kestrels where they complete the second year of their Foundation Stage. Our aim is to ensure that all children feel cherished and secure in a "home-from-home" environment. Our Swan and Kestrels areas have also been awarded the much coveted Flying High for Early Years Accreditation that stamps a seal of excellence on the care we provide.

When you leave your young child for the first time you want them to be cared for as they would at home. In our cosy bright buildings with their own safety surface playgrounds, children are nurtured by qualified Early Years staff. Children sit down together at lunchtime and enjoy freshly cooked nutritious meals. Close proximity to the seafront and local amenities means children are regularly taken out for trips. Our Swan and Kestrel classes are open 50 weeks of the year, 8 am to 6 pm.

For their third and final year of the Foundation Stage the children move into the Reception Class (Lower I) this class provides an early start to literacy and numeracy, and a wide range of activities designed to help them become active independent learners.

Pre-Prep Dept (6–7 years) Key Stage One. The Pre-Prep Department includes Upper I and Lower II. In these classes the curriculum widens to include science, geography, history and ICT as separate subjects. Upper I staff work closely with Lower I in order to affect a smooth transition from the Foundation stage to Key Stage One, while Lower II work closely with the Junior school in order to prepare children for Key Stage Two. All pupils in the Foundation Stage and Pre-Prep benefit from use of the the school's halls for drama, dance and PE. French and Music are taught throughout the Foundation Stage and Pre-Prep Departments.

Junior and Senior Schools. The Junior School accepts boys and girls from the age of 7+. We offer bright airy surroundings, a caring yet disciplined environment and small class sizes. While a strong emphasis is placed on the traditional skills of reading writing and numeracy, children in the Junior School enjoy a varied curriculum. Pupils are taught to appreciate that education is as much about attitudes and values, as it is about academic and sporting success. In the senior school this ethos continues, and pupils are given a wide range of opportunities to excel in: academic, creative, sporting and social settings. Pupils at KS3 follow a full curriculum. This includes thinking skills and first aid, and also study skills seminars. It is Mayville's policy to enter all pupils for their GCSE providing they have completed the course of study and any coursework. Therefore our results, which have been well above the national average for the past ten years, are a true reflection of the efforts of pupils and staff.

At Mayville we believe that confidence is the central building block to success in future life. Our commitment to Global Rock Challenge and membership of our own St John Ambulance cadet unit, allows pupils to develop teamwork and leadership skills. At Mayville we celebrate the many successes of our pupils and encourage their competitive spirit. With three houses, there are a number of inter-house competitions which also promote this. Trips to local, national and international locations are encouraged to broaden the experiences begun in the classroom.

Transport. There are good public transport links into the city from the surrounding areas. School minibuses pick up pupils from the local ferry terminals and train stations.

If you would like a prospectus, to book a tour of the school with the Head teacher, Mr Castle, or to find out about our taster days and entrance procedures, please telephone the school or visit our website. Scholarships are available from Year 2.

Charitable status. Mayville High School is a Registered Charity, number 286347. It exists to provide a traditional education to children from a wide range of academic backgrounds within a caring environment.

Mead School

16 Frant Road, Tunbridge Wells, Kent TN2 5SN

Tel:	01892 525837
email:	office@themeadschool.co.uk
website:	www.meadschool.info
Twitter:	@TheMeadSchoolTW
Facebook:	/themeadschoolTW

Headmistress: **Mrs A Culley**

Age Range. 3–11.
Number in School. 236.
Fees per term (2016–2017). Kindergarten £1,715; Infants £3,155; Juniors £3,495.

The Mead is an independent, co-educational preparatory school situated in the centre of Tunbridge Wells. We prepare children for both Kent Selection into Grammar School and for Common Entrance to a wide range of Independent Schools at 11+.

We aim to create a happy, secure and enthusiastic atmosphere in which every individual can develop his or her all round potential and thereby become well motivated, interesting and hard working members of society.

Academic standards are high and based on National Curriculum requirements. Strong emphasis is placed on individual attention and close cooperation between school and parents is encouraged.

We offer a broad range of extra-curricular activities including sport, drama, music, dance, judo, swimming.

A copy of our Prospectus and outstanding recent ISI report are available on request.

The Moat School

Bishop's Avenue, Fulham, London SW6 6EG

Tel:	020 7610 9018
email:	office@moatschool.org.uk
website:	www.moatschool.org.uk

Chair of Governors: Simon Goldhill

Headmistress: **Clare King**, EMBA, BA Hons, PGCE, Cert SpLD

Co-educational Day School.
Age Range. 11–16.
Number of Pupils. 65 Boys, 15 Girls.
Fees per term (2016–2017). £6,995–£9,600.

Set within the historic conservation area of Fulham Palace, The Moat School is a specialist school for secondary-age SpLD pupils. Mainstream in structure and specialist in nature, The Moat caters successfully for the needs of pupils with specific learning difficulties. Alongside the curriculum, the school also offers expertise in speech and language therapy, occupational therapy and a school counsellor.

All teachers complete a post-graduate BDA approved course in teaching students with SpLD within their first 2 years of appointment. Qualified Learning Support Assistants accompany pupils throughout their lessons at Key Stage 3, where class sizes are a maximum of 10. Class sizes are even smaller at Key Stage 4.

Multi-sensory teaching is combined with advanced IT provision, each pupil being provided with a laptop computer for use in school and at home. Touch-typing is taught in Year 7 and there is a state-of-the-art wireless network which enables staff and pupils to access the school intranet with its wide range of learning resources and data, as well as the internet.

At Key Stage 3, pupils follow a mainstream curriculum (with the exception of foreign languages) before selecting their GCSE options alongside the core subjects of English, Mathematics and Single or Dual Award Science. The Moat offers excellent facilities for learning, with a suite of Design Technology workshops offering state-of-the-art facilities for Food Technology, Resistant Materials and Graphics. Art, Music, Drama, ICT and Business Studies each have dedicated studios or specialist classrooms.

The Moat has an extensive enrichment programme of extracurricular activities designed to widen experience and develop self-confidence. In Drama, all Year 9 pupils take part in an annual Shakespeare play and there are several productions and workshop performances each year. The Moat's proximity to the River Thames enables pupils to experience rowing as a sport, swimming is popular and 2012 saw the introduction of Martial Arts and boxing. The Duke of Edinburgh's Award encourages pupils to test their own limits and each summer pupils in Years 7, 8 and 9 make a residential visit to an outdoor activity centre to develop independence and leadership skills.

Charitable status. The Constable Educational Trust is a Registered Charity, number 1068445. It exists to establish and support The Moat School so that it can provide education and opportunity for SpLD learners (dyslexic & dyspraxic).

Moffats School

Kinlet Hall, Bewdley, Worcs DY12 3AY

Tel:	01299 841230
Fax:	01299 841444
email:	office@moffats.co.uk
website:	www.moffats.co.uk
Twitter:	@moffatsschool
Facebook:	/moffatsschool

Head: **Mrs Robin McCarthy**, MA Oxon

Age Range. 3–13+.
Number of Children. 67.
Fees per term (2016–2017). Boarding £6,200, Day £2,275–£3,520.

Moffats is a co-educational boarding and day school in a Grade 1 historic house set in its own hundred acres of park and farmland, a glorious environment a mile from any public road. There are equal numbers of boys and girls who share the same opportunities and responsibilities in all activities. We are proud of our record since 1934, but this is not limited to academic awards or A grades in the Common Entrance Examination. Our joy and satisfaction is in bringing out the best in every child. Their achievements in music, speech and drama are outstanding. All usual games are coached daily, including athletics and cross-country running, and, with our own stables, riding is professionally taught. Weekends and spare time are filled with a multitude of activities and the annual sailing camp takes older pupils to Cornwall. Moffats is a truly family school; the personal touch of members of the same family which founded Moffats ensures the well-being and happiness of all the children in their care.

Moon Hall School for Dyslexic Children

Pasturewood Road, Holmbury St Mary, Dorking, Surrey RH5 6LQ

Tel:	01306 731464
Fax:	01306 731504
email:	enquiries@moonhallschool.co.uk
website:	www.moonhallschool.co.uk

Chairman of Governors: Mr David Baker

Headmistress: Ms Emma Fraser, BA Hons QTS, Dip SpLD, Cert Phono-Graphix

Age Range. 7–11.
Number of Children. Approximately 50.
Fees per term (2016–2017). Day Pupils £6,265–£6,515; Boarding Fee in addition payable to Belmont

Religious denomination: Church of England.

Moon Hall School, Holmbury St Mary caters for boys and girls with SpLD. Accredited by CReSTeD (SP), it has a unique relationship with Belmont Preparatory School (*see separate entry*), sharing its site and excellent facilities. Uniform is common to both schools, and pupils are fully integrated at assembly, lunch and break. They also join together for sport/teams and in dramatic and musical productions. Moon Hall pupils may transfer to Belmont classes when ready, usually into Year 7.

MHS's specialist qualified, multi-disciplinary staff deliver a full curriculum to dyslexic children from Year 3. All are taught to touch-type and are successfully entered for OCR examinations normally taken by those aged 16+. Within the well-designed, purpose-built accommodation, classes contain a maximum of 14 children, subdivided for English and Mathematics. One-to-one tuition is available as needed. Literacy and numeracy teaching is structured and multi-sensory, incorporating material devised by acknowledged experts in the field. The Phono-Graphix Programme is employed at all levels. Study/Thinking Skills are an integral part of our teaching. Great emphasis is placed upon rebuilding self-esteem.

Entry requirements: A full report by an independent Educational Psychologist showing the child to be dyslexic and of at least average intelligence. Assessment and interview at MHS.

After Year 6 children may transfer to a number of suitable mainstream senior schools, or continue their education at Moon Hall College, our own Senior School located in Leigh, near Reigate.

Charitable status. Moon Hall School is a Registered Charity, number 803481.

Moorland School

Ribblesdale Avenue, Clitheroe, Lancashire BB7 2JA

Tel:	01200 423833
Fax:	01200 429339
email:	enquiries@moorlandschool.co.uk
website:	www.moorlandschool.co.uk
Twitter:	@MoorlandSchool1
Facebook:	@MoorlandPrivateSchool

Headteacher: **Mr Jonathan Harrison**, BA Hons, PGCE

Age Range. 3 months – 18 years.
Number of Pupils. 165 including 51 boarders.
Fees per term (2016–2017). Day (Reception–Year 13): £2,332–£3,332 (exc Lunch); Full Boarding: £6,600–£8,300; Weekly Boarding: £6,000–£7,600.

Moorland School is a thriving co-educational day and boarding school located in the historic town of Clitheroe within the picturesque Ribble Valley, in the North-West of England. The school enjoys excellent transport links to Manchester. We have an outstandingly beautiful site with more than 15 acres of grounds. Around one third of children at Moorland are boarders and we find it makes for a good social mix with our day pupils from the surrounding area. The opening of our purpose-built new building means our boarders can enjoy modern and spacious facilities, fully equipped with satellite television and Wi-Fi. Moorland can now offer the seamless transition from GCSE to A Level study, through our thriving new Sixth Form Centre, which provides our students with the opportunity to settle in one place rather than having to move from school to school. Furthermore, the School boasts an outstanding elite football, elite ballet and elite music curriculum, unique to any British boarding school. These courses are led by field professionals in their respective areas.

Admission to Moorland. Parents and children are encouraged to visit the school to meet the Principal and see the school in action. Boarding or Day children are also welcome to attend Moorland for a one or two day 'taster visit'.

Kindergarten & Nursery. As well as having its own indoor soft-play area, the nursery also has a large outdoor play area within its extensive grounds, with unbroken views over Waddington Fell. The Nursery's superb layout of colourful rooms and equipment make it an ideal and exceptional learning environment.

Junior School. The Preparatory Department takes children between the ages of 4 and 11. The children have their own play area and IT suite and benefit from using the facilities of the Senior School such as science laboratories and sports hall.

The children follow Key Stages 1 and 2 of the National Curriculum with particular emphasis on numeracy and literacy. Our small class sizes allow every child to read to the Teacher on a daily basis. French is also included in the Junior curriculum.

The Senior School follows the criteria set down in the National Curriculum. We enter our pupils for the Standard Attainment Tests and for GCSE at the end of Key stage 4.

Football at Moorland. Our FA approved coach, Charles Jackson, is one of the UK's most innovative and well-respected football coaches. He teaches to a Premier League standard. He has worked at Moorland since November 2002. He also worked at the Manchester United Advanced Coaching Centre up to July 2005 and is now the Under 14 academy technical skills Development Coach at Manchester City FC. He spends 4 days per week at Moorland School teaching children from age 4–18.

Pastoral Care. At Moorland children benefit from continuous pastoral support within a friendly family environment. By day, teaching staff provide continual support within small classes. Evening and weekend care is undertaken by the teaching staff and House Parent team.

More House School

Frensham, Farnham, Surrey GU10 3AP

Tel: 01252 792303
            Admissions: 01252 797600
Fax: 01252 797601
email: schooloffice@morehouseschool.co.uk
website: www.morehouseschool.co.uk
Twitter: @MHSFrensham
Facebook: /morehouseschoolfrensham

Headmaster: **Mr Jonathan Hetherington**, BA Hons, MSc Ed QTS

Age Range. 8 to 18.
Number in School. 447: 110 Boarders, 344 Day Boys.
Fees per term (2016–2017). Full Boarding £7,199–£9,120; Weekly Boarding £6,516–£8,420; Day £4,180–£5,860.

More House School occupies a unique position in helping boys with specific learning difficulties in that multi-sensory remediation is applied across the curriculum, through carefully targeted and maintained intervention, and extra help is available in our Learning Development Centre, so that proper support is always available and individual needs met.

It is approved by the Department for Education and has been listed by CReSTeD in their Specialist Schools category. No school can help every child, so we have a very careful selection assessment to ensure that we really can help those who finally enter the school.

Founded 75 years ago, the school is a centre of excellence and prides itself in using the best modern practice to increase confidence and make children feel valued, happy and to fulfil their potential at GCSE, AS, A Level and other public examinations.

Boarding is run by caring staff and is situated in beautiful grounds with ample opportunities for outdoor pursuits. Our activities programme, which offers 18 options each day, encourages all day boys and boarders to make good use of their leisure time. There is a strong sense of community.

There is an ongoing building programme and the facilities are very good in all departments.

The 2016 Ofsted inspection recognises the exceptional progress More House pupils make throughout the school, identifying 'consistently very effective teaching' and 'highly effective support' which enable pupils to 'achieve a gamut of excellent outcomes … not only academic but [that] also relate to pupils' increased confidence, their improved sense of well-being and their ability to form meaningful social relationships'.

We have a comprehensive information pack, hold an annual 'Discover' More House open day in February and welcome new enquiries.

Charitable status. More House School is a Registered Charity, number 311872. A Catholic foundation, open to all denominations, helping boys to succeed.

Moyles Court School

Moyles Court, Ringwood, Hampshire BH24 3NF

Tel: 01425 472856/473197
Fax: 01425 474715
email: info@moylescourt.co.uk
website: www.moylescourt.co.uk

Headmaster: **Mr Richard Milner-Smith**

Age Range. 2½–16.
Number in School. Boarders: 20 boys, 15 girls. Day: 79 boys, 69 girls.
Fees per term (2016–2017). Senior Day £3,801–£4,673; Senior Boarding £8,505; Junior Day £1,864–£3,528; Junior Boarding £6,741; Nursery: £5.50 per hour (Early Years Pathfinder Scheme Funding available*).

Moyles Court is a small and successful co-educational boarding and day school for children from 2½ to 16 years. A strong pastoral ethos with traditional family values supports a broad and balanced curriculum. Academic achievement is very good.

The school is situated two miles north east of Ringwood in beautiful grounds on the edge of the New Forest, surrounded by heath, woodlands and streams. The fourteen acres provide ideal playing areas for the children and they use these extensively in their free time.

At Moyles Court, we aim to enthuse and encourage children of all academic abilities to maximise their potential in preparation for the challenging and competitive world, which lies outside the security of home and school. Education means development of the 'whole' person and this is the aim at Moyles Court.

It is the school's policy to follow the National Curriculum, within which a comprehensive range of GCSE subjects are offered. The National Curriculum is enriched in the Junior School by the International Primary Curriculum.

Moyles Court has a thriving sporting and outdoor education programme. An extensive selection of extra-curricular activities is available throughout the year including The Duke of Edinburgh's Award scheme.

Discounts apply for Service families. Sibling discounts, Scholarships and Bursaries are available. Admission is through personal interview with the Headmaster, report from previous school and a taster day at Moyles Court, during which Literacy and Numeracy assessments are conducted.

For further details visit the website at www.moyles-court.co.uk or contact Chris Young, Admissions Secretary. A warm welcome awaits you.

Moyles Court is a member of the Broadway Education Group.

New Eccles Hall School

Quidenham, Nr Norwich, Norfolk NR16 2NZ

Tel: 01953 887217
Fax: 01953 887397
email: admin@neweccleshall.com
website: www.neweccleshall.com

Headmaster: **Mr Rob Thornton**, MA Ed

Age Range. 5–18.
Number in School. 38 Boarders, 80 Day.
Fees per term (2016–2017). Day £2,365–£4,120, Boarding £5,695–£6,995.

The school offers:
• Excellent standard of teaching in small classes.
• Curriculum that covers the national requirements and more.
• Caring for the pupil as an individual is at the centre of the school's ethos.
• Large country estate providing a perfect learning environment.
• Exceptional games facilities combined with an extensive leisure programme.
• Successful Individual Teaching Unit for Specific Learning Difficulties.

- Happy relaxed atmosphere for teaching and learning.
- Attractive and comfortable boarding accommodation.
- Learning respect for each other considered essential.
- Length of the day suits working families.
- Play therapy in our Therapies Room.

Visitors to the school are welcome when the school is in session.

Norfolk House School

4 Norfolk Road, Edgbaston, Birmingham B15 3PS

Tel: 0121 454 7021
email: info@norfolkhouseschool.co.uk
website: www.norfolkhouseschool.co.uk

Headmistress: **Mrs Sarah L Morris**, BA Hons, PGCE

Age Range. 3–11.
Number in School. 154.
Fees per term (from April 2016). £2,251–£3,125 (including Prompt Payment Discount).

Norfolk House School is a Christian Independent day school situated in the pleasant suburb of Edgbaston and is ideally located for pupils and parents all over Birmingham and the surrounding areas.

The school aims to provide individual attention to each pupil, thus enabling each child to fulfil his or her potential. Small class sizes and favourable pupil : teacher ratios culminate in the best possible academic results. Many pupils move on to the various King Edward Schools, or to other Grammar Schools or senior Independent Schools as the direct result of the high standards achieved at Norfolk House.

The syllabus is designed to give each child a general academic education over a wide range of subjects – in line with the National Curriculum; the requirements of the Eleven Plus and the various Entrance Examinations are also taken into consideration.

In addition to education, Norfolk House School aims to instil in each child good manners, consideration and respect for others, and recognition of personal responsibility. Norfolk House is a small school with an emphasis on caring and traditional values, yet forward thinking in outlook. It is a happy school with high attainment, competitive fees and a family atmosphere.

Normanhurst School

68–74 Station Road, North Chingford, London E4 7BA

Tel: 020 8529 4307
Fax: 020 8524 7737
email: info@normanhurstschool.co.uk
website: www.normanhurstschool.co.uk
Twitter: @NormanhurstSch

Headmistress: **Mrs Claire Osborn**, BA Hons, MSc, PGCE

Age Range. 2½–16.
Number in School. 275 Day Pupils.
Fees per term (2016–2017). £1,230–£4,200.

Normanhurst School is a thriving, caring, local independent school with a warm, friendly atmosphere and a wide range of activities offered. The School boasts a high standard of academic achievement with excellent SATs and GCSE results.

We encourage our pupils to develop self-confidence and to take on roles of responsibility as they move up through the school. Creativity is nurtured within a disciplined environment and traditional values such as self-discipline are promoted to maximise our pupils' effectiveness in an ever-changing world.

The School offers small class sizes and a wide range of core and optional subjects up to GCSE, including English, Science, Maths, French, Spanish, Design Technology, Art, History, Geography, ICT, Business Studies, PE, Sport, Music and Drama.

Numerous clubs are provided to strengthen the important social aspect of schooling. These include Football, Netball, Gymnastics, Chess, French, Cross-country, Dance, and ICT. Homework club and Teatime club are available to all pupils, while tuition on various musical instruments takes place either as an extra-curricular activity during the day or after school.

The School is located in the centre of a tree-lined suburban street with good parking, two minutes from a mainline British Rail station and well-connected bus station.

Entry requirements: Interview and assessment.

Northease Manor School

Rodmell, Lewes, East Sussex BN7 3EY

Tel: 01273 472915
Fax: 01273 472202
email: office@northease.co.uk
            pa2headteacher@northease.co.uk
website: www.northease.co.uk

Chairman of Governors: Julie Toben

Head: **Ms Claire Farmer**

Type of School. Co-educational day and weekly boarding school.
Age Range. 10–18.
Number of Pupils. 76: 14 Girls, 62 Boys.
Fees per term (2016–2017). Day £6,939, Boarding £9,443.

Northease Manor School is a co-educational special school for pupils, aged ten to eighteen, who have specific learning difficulties. It caters for both weekly boarders and day pupils. It is approved by the Department for Education and is accredited by CReSTeD. It is set in the South Downs with Grade II listed buildings.

It provides a holistic approach to Specific Learning Difficulties within small teaching groups and provides on-site access to Speech and Language Therapy and Occupational Therapy. Most of the staff have specialist qualifications and benefit from in-house training.

Northease caters for potentially able pupils who have not realised their true potential at previous schools due to their Specific Learning Difficulties which normally results in a deficit in literacy skills but sometimes in numeracy skills as well. They receive full access to the National Curriculum and benefit from an intensive multi-sensory input which provides for all their literacy and language needs. Detailed pastoral support is given to enable pupils to feel secure and become independent learners. Everything that happens at the school is geared to the needs of the child and to ensure that each pupil experiences success in order to raise self-esteem and self-confidence.

A CReSTeD Inspection concluded that "the school has a clear and focused objective to remain one of the best schools in its field".

The ethos of the school is based upon respect for the individual and the celebration of success and achievement. All pupils have abilities and talents and it is the school's role to enable every pupil to discover and develop these talents. Pupils are encouraged to "work hard, play hard" and to have a sense of ownership. It is "our school" and everybody contributes to its well-being and development. High standards of behaviour are expected, with the onus on partnership between pupils and adults. Mistakes are seen as part of the learning process.

Charitable status. Northease Manor School Trust Ltd is a Registered Charity, number 307005. It exists for the provision of high-quality education for pupils with Specific Learning Difficulties.

Notre Dame Preparatory School

147 Dereham Road, Norwich, Norfolk NR2 3TA

Tel:	01603 625593
email:	info@notredameprepschool.co.uk
website:	www.notredameprepschool.co.uk

Chairman of Governors: Mr Richard Bailey

Headmaster: **Mr K O'Herlihy**, BA, HDipEd

Age Range. 2–11 Co-educational.
Number of Pupils. 210 Day.
Fees per term (2016–2017). £1,900–£2,010.

Notre Dame Prep School was originally founded by the Sisters of Notre Dame de Namur in 1865. The school transferred to its present site in 1971 and is now a Company with charitable status. The school maintains the traditions and the spirit of the Sisters of Notre Dame and the former name and uniform.

As a Catholic school the school and staff endeavour to nurture a love of God through Jesus Christ in all the children. The school has an ethos of love and care and embraces children of all faiths.

Children are treated as individuals, respected, nurtured and encouraged to embrace and fulfil their potential in all areas of school life. We have excellent links with High Schools in both the maintained and independent sectors.

The school achieves well above average results in external tests and has a strong academic reputation. Children are prepared for entry to selective independent schools on request. Subjects include English, Maths, Science, Computing, Design and Technology, Art, Geography, PE, History, Music, RE, French and Personal, Social and Health Education.

The school has a very strong musical tradition and has a wide range of extra-curricular musical activities on offer including Choir, Chamber Choir, Recorder, Piano, Guitar, Flute, Violin, Saxophone and Clarinet lessons.

Sports include Football, Cricket, Rugby, Netball, Rounders, Hockey, Tennis and Swimming.

The school has a wide range of extra-curricular activities including Speech and Drama, Chess, Cookery, Photography, Electronics, Arts and Crafts, Science, Sewing, Young Explorers, Creative Writing, Badminton and other sports and activities.

We have an After School Activities Club which runs until 6 pm incorporating homework club and games activities for younger children. A cooked meal is provided. Holiday clubs run throughout most of the holidays.

Charitable status. Notre Dame Preparatory School (Norwich) Limited is a Registered Charity, number 269003.

Oakfield Preparatory School

125–128 Thurlow Park Road, West Dulwich, London SE21 8HP

Tel:	020 8670 4206
Fax:	020 8766 6744
email:	info@oakfield.dulwich.sch.uk
	admissions@oakfield.dulwich.sch.uk
website:	www.oakfield.dulwich.sch.uk

Principal: **Mrs Jane Stevens**, BA Hons, PGCE, NPQH

Age Range. 2–11.
Number in School. Day: 239 Boys, 183 Girls.
Fees per term (2016–2017). Years 1–6: £3,390 including lunch. Early Years Foundation Stage fees according to sessions and Early Years funding where applicable.

Oakfield School was founded in 1887 and is today a modern co-educational prep school which prepares children for the entrance examinations of London and countrywide independent senior schools.

The School is arranged into three groups, the Nursery (age 2–3), Foundation Years and Year 1 (age 3–6) and Years 2–6 (age 6–11). Each age group has its own self-contained building and facilities. The School site of nearly three acres allows space for play and games and older children use the nearby playing field where games sessions are played. Children aged five to eleven swim once a week under instruction.

Entry to the Nursery is by observation. Once accepted the child will progress automatically into the Foundation Years (subject to the admissions policy) and Main School. Entry at 3+ and 4+ is also by observation and children should have a good idea of colours, shapes, matching, sorting and simple counting. Entry at 7+ follows an assessment and observation in a class setting.

Prospective parents – and children – would be very welcome to visit Oakfield during a school day on an Open Morning.

Oakhyrst Grange School

Stanstead Road, Caterham, Surrey CR3 6AF

Tel:	01883 343344
email:	office@oakhyrstgrangeschool.co.uk
website:	www.oakhyrstgrangeschool.co.uk

Chairman of Board of Management: Mrs Brenda Davis

Headmaster: **Mr Alex Gear**, BEd

Age Range. 4–11.
Number in School. 158 Day Boys and Girls.
Fees per term (2016–2017). £1,215–£2,664.

Oakhyrst Grange School is an independent, co-educational preparatory day school for boys and girls between 4 and 11 years.

The School was established in 1950 and moved to its present premises in Stanstead Road in 1957. Since September 1973 the School has been administered by a non-profit making trust.

Standing in five acres of open country and woodland and surrounded by the Green Belt, the School enjoys a fine position amongst the Surrey Hills.

The school has a wide and imaginative curriculum, which includes traditional teaching combined with innovative ideas. Small class sizes, with a maximum of 20 pupils, and an excellent teacher/pupil ratio enable pupils to work at their own rate and capabilities whilst being encouraged to meet new challenges.

Our pupils secure the offer of places at prominent senior schools, including scholarships and awards across the range of academic, all-rounder, music, sports and art.

There are many sporting opportunities offered and particularly high standards have been reached in cross-country, swimming, football, judo and athletics where ISA National level has been achieved. The pupils compete in many inter house, inter school and area competitions. The school also has its own heated indoor swimming pool, all-weather tennis, netball, hockey and 5-a-side court, sports pitch, cross-country course and gymnasium.

Extra-curricular music lessons are offered and much music making also takes place as part of the normal school timetable. The school has an orchestra in addition to clarinet, flute, guitar, saxophone, violin and trumpet ensembles and a choir, all of whom perform regularly. In 2014, the school was the winner of the National ISA Award for Excellence in the Arts.

In addition to the curriculum the pupils can enjoy an extensive range of clubs and activities throughout the week.

Academic excellence is encouraged and achieved, every child is expected to attain his or her individual potential. The School helps children to develop into caring, thoughtful and confident adults.

Charitable status. Oakhyrst Grange School Educational Trust is a Registered Charity, number 325043. It exists to provide an all-round education, to give the children success and the best possible start.

Oaklands School

8 Albion Hill, Loughton, Essex IG10 4RA

Tel: 020 8508 3517
Fax: 020 8508 4454
email: info@oaklandsschool.co.uk
website: www.oaklandsschool.co.uk
Twitter: @OaklandsSch

Headmistress: **Mrs S Belej**, BA Jt Hons, Cert.Ed.

Age Range. 2½–11 Co-educational.
Number in School. 245 Day Pupils.
Fees per term (2016–2017). £1,075–£3,380.

Oaklands is a long-established preparatory school, founded in 1937, and delightfully situated in extensive grounds on the edge of Epping Forest. It provides a firm foundation for girls and boys aged 2½ to 11. Great care is taken in preparing pupils for entrance examinations to their next schools.

A broad curriculum is offered, with early emphasis on literacy and numeracy, ensuring high standards, and great importance is placed on fully developing each child's potential in a secure and caring atmosphere. We have small class sizes and specialist teachers for Science, French, Music, PE, Dancing, ICT, Sport and Drama. A wide range of extra-curricular activities is offered and breakfast club operates from 7.30 am and tea time club continues after school until 6 pm. Parents enjoy easy access to their child's teachers and the headmistress has an open-door policy. Individual music tuition is available, including piano and woodwind instrumental lessons, and singing lessons.

Oaklands is a friendly, happy school where children can enjoy learning and take pride in both their own success and the achievements of others. In addition to the attainment of high standards, pupils build personal qualities of confidence, self-reliance and respect for others, in preparation for the challenges and opportunities of the modern world.

Our Lady's Convent School

Gray Street, Loughborough, Leicestershire LE11 2DZ

Tel: 01509 263901
Fax: 01509 236193
email: office@olcs.leics.sch.uk
website: www.olcs.leics.sch.uk

Headmaster: **Dr Julian Murphy**, DPhil Oxon

Age Range. Girls 4–18, Boys 4–11.
Number of Pupils. Approximately 200+.
Fees per term (2016–2017). Infants £3,084, Juniors £3,160, Seniors £3,766.

Our Lady's Convent School is a Catholic day school that extends a warm welcome to children of all faiths and denominations. Part of the Loughborough Endowed Schools Foundation it educates girls from 4 to 18 and boys from 4 to 11. The focus is very much on the individual child and their personal progress and achievement at all levels. Our next Open Day would be an excellent time to see our Senior and Primary School Departments in action on a normal working day, view our facilities and meet our Headteacher.

At all stages of their education, our students receive individual attention in small classes. They are helped, encouraged and supported rather than pressured, stretched and not stressed. Academic achievement is high at all levels. Our public examination results in 2016 were some of the best in recent memory, with 25% A*–A and 75% A*–B at A Level, and 35% A%–A and 69% A*–B at GCSE. A wide variety of GCSE and A Levels are offered in the Senior department. Academic Support is excellent for all students in all areas.

Our membership of the Endowed Schools places us in a wonderful position, where we can combine all that is best in a small school community with the benefits of the human and physical resources of a campus of two thousand two hundred students. The possibilities are numerous, to give just four examples: our budding musicians now have access to one of the finest music schools in the country; our sixth formers can choose from twenty-eight A Level courses; our youngest pupils can enjoy outdoor learning in a Forest School; and any future applicants for Oxford, Cambridge or the leading US universities will be able to access subject specialist mentoring from a large body of teaching staff stretching across three schools.

Ninety-nine per cent of our students go on to university to study a wide range of subjects. In addition there are numerous cultural, musical and sporting activities. Music and Drama have a high profile in the school; girls have taken part in the national Shakespeare Festival. A wide variety of extracurricular activities is on offer. The school successfully participates in the Combined Cadet Force (CCF), The Duke of Edinburgh's Award and Young Enterprise schemes.

The school is a registered charity and its policy is to continually enhance the facilities available to our students and to improve our service to them and their parents. All departments are well resourced and ICT facilities are excellent and updated regularly.

The School campus is an attractive walled area; an oasis of calm, near the centre of Loughborough. Open Days are held during working school days and visitors continually note the happy classroom environment and the mutual respect between students, staff and visitors. Some of our students are with us from 4 to 18 but others are very welcome to join at other stages of their education.

The Pelican Club provides before and after school care for a small additional cost. The Nursery at Loughborough Endowed Schools is based on our Campus and offers childcare 51 weeks a year from age 6 weeks to 4 years.

For further information visit our website www.olcs. leics.sch.uk.

Charitable status. Our Lady's Convent School is part of Loughborough Endowed Schools, which is a Registered Charity, number 1081765, and a Company Limited by Guarantee, registered in England, number 4038033. Registered Office: 3 Burton Walks, Loughborough, Leics LE11 2DU.

Park School

Queens Park South Drive, Bournemouth BH8 9BJ

Tel:	01202 396640
Fax:	01202 237640
email:	office@parkschool.co.uk
website:	www.parkschool.co.uk

Headmaster: **Mr Andrew D Edwards**, BA Hons, PGCE

Age Range. 2–11.
Number in School. Day: 157 Boys, 132 Girls.
Fees per term (2016–2017). £1,965–£2,800. (Fee rates apply to payment by direct debit.)

The Park is a co-educational junior day school occupying a quiet location overlooking Queens Park Golf course in a pleasant residential area near the town centre.

Pupils are taught in small classes in a caring, happy environment. The school is geared principally towards academic achievement although we do provide special help for a limited number of children with specific learning difficulties. The emphasis is on nurturing individual and academic progress whilst fostering a positive ethos and the development of the all-round child. This covers not only work in the classroom but also all other aspects of school life: games, music, the Arts and many practical activities. Pupils are prepared for entry to Senior Independent Schools and to Bournemouth and Poole Grammar Schools through their tests at 11+ years. Many children gain scholarships to Senior Independent Schools.

Many pupils join us in the Nursery at 2 years old, but there are occasional vacancies at other ages. Offer of a place is made only after prospective pupils have been formally assessed.

Parents with pupils in our Nursery classes can take advantage of our extended working day and the longer school terms should they so wish.

Park School for Girls

20–22 Park Avenue, Ilford, Essex IG1 4RS

Tel:	Office: 020 8554 2466
	Bursar: 020 8554 6022
Fax:	020 8554 3003
email:	admin@parkschool.org.uk
website:	www.parkschool.org.uk

Head Teacher: **Mrs Androulla Nicholas**, BSc Econ Hons, PGCE

Age Range. 4–16.
Number in School. 170 Day Girls.
Fees per term (2016–2017). Reception £2,130, Pre-Prep £2,355, Prep School £2,465, Senior School £3,195.

The School is situated near Valentine's Park in Ilford. It is convenient for road, rail and Central Line tube services.

Our basic aim is to provide a full educational programme leading to recognised external examinations at the age of 16.

We create a caring, well-ordered atmosphere. Our pupils are encouraged to achieve their full academic and social potential. The well-qualified staff and the policy of small classes produce well above the national average GCSE results. We do not offer a sixth form, but the majority of our leavers from Year 11 move to another school to study subjects to A Level.

In addition, the staff and I stress the development of each child as a whole person. We expect every girl to strive for self-confidence in her ability to use her talents to the full and to respect individuality. She is encouraged to make decisions and to accept responsibility for her own actions. The poise that comes from good manners and correct speech, we consider to be highly important. Honesty, reliability, courtesy and consideration for others are prime factors in the educative system.

Interested parents are welcome to visit the school, where the Head Teacher will be pleased to answer their queries.

Charitable status. Park School for Girls is a Registered Charity, number 269936. It exists to provide a caring environment in which we develop our pupils' potential to the full.

The Park School
Yeovil

The Park, Yeovil, Somerset BA20 1DH

Tel:	01935 423514
Fax:	01935 411257
email:	admin@parkschool.com
website:	www.parkschool.com
Twitter:	@Park_School
Facebook:	/theparkschoolyeovil

Head: **Mrs J Huntington**, ARAM, GRSM, LRAM, CPSEd

Age Range. 3–18 Co-educational.
Number in School. 203: 106 Boys, 97 Girls; 29 Boarders.
Fees per term (2016–2017). Day £2,120–£3,700 (including lunch); Weekly Boarding £7,170–£7,640; Full Boarding £7,400–£8,200.

The Park School, Yeovil is an Independent day and boarding school founded in 1851. It aims to provide a sound education based on Christian principles. It is a non-denominational Evangelical Christian school and has strong connections with a number of different local churches.

The School is pleasantly situated near the centre of Yeovil with easy access to surrounding towns and villages, from which day pupils are drawn, and to the main line station, Yeovil Junction, for London Waterloo. There is also a rail connection to Bristol and Weymouth from Yeovil, Pen Mill station. Transport to London Heathrow and other airports is arranged for boarders travelling abroad.

Our 'Saplings' EYFS Unit has recently been re-modelled with outdoor learning space and two classrooms for our 3–5 year olds.

Pupils flourish in a friendly, caring environment where, in small classes, they benefit from well-qualified staff. There is a wide and varied curriculum which encourages each pupil to develop their own abilities and interests to the full. In line with the National Curriculum guidelines, senior pupils choose from a range of subjects at GCSE and A Level, including: English, RE, History, Drama, Geography, French, German, Spanish, Mathematics, Science, Art, Music, Design Technology, Food Technology, ICT, Sports Studies and English for overseas pupils. Physics, Chemistry and Biology are studied as separate Sciences. Chinese is offered subject to demand. Additional subjects studied at A Level include: Business Studies, Sports Studies, Further Mathematics, Economics, Psychology and Classical Civilisation.

Physical Education is also an essential part of the curriculum. Pupils participate in a varied programme of sporting activities including: Athletics, Badminton, Basketball, Cricket, Football, Gymnastics, Hockey, Netball, Squash, Swimming, Tennis, Table Tennis, Volleyball and Cross Country. Many Senior pupils also take part in The Duke of Edinburgh's Award scheme as well as Young Enterprise.

A wide range of musical instruments are taught by the Director of Music and visiting staff. There are School Choirs and an Orchestra as well as a jazz band, rock group and a baroque ensemble. Music and drama productions are regular features of School life.

Boarders live in a newly refurbished, purpose-built School House and Bennet House. Many students occupy single study-bedrooms. They are cared for in a homely, family atmosphere by resident houseparents and assistants. At weekends a variety of interesting activities is available. On Sundays all boarders are encouraged to attend the church of their choice.

Academic standards in the School are high with The Park being consistently well placed in the GCSE league tables. However, the School is non-selective and pupils are encouraged to develop their talents as individuals with extremely favourable pupil : teacher ratios.

The school offers scholarships which may be given for academic, music, art, sport or drama ability. These are awarded by examination and interview in January of each year for entry to Years 4, 7 and 9. Sixth Form scholarship exams are held in December. Bursaries are available for children of those parents who are engaged in full-time Christian work or are members of HM Forces. In addition means-tested bursaries are available for parents on low incomes.

Charitable status. The Park School (Yeovil) Limited is a Registered Charity, number 310214. It exists to provide Christian education and care for children aged 3–18 years.

Polwhele House School

Truro, Cornwall TR4 9AE

Tel: 01872 273011
email: office@polwhelehouse.co.uk
website: www.polwhelehouse.co.uk

Headmaster: Alex McCullough, BA Hons Dunelm, PGCE, NPQH

Age Range. 3–13+.
Number in School. 100.

Fees per term (2016–2017). Day: £532–£4,200, Lunch £180–£202; Flexi Boarding (1–4 nights per week): £500–£2,000.

Polwhele House is a beautiful and historic listed building, set in over 30 acres of garden, playing fields, park and woodland. The school enjoys a glorious and secure environment only 1¼ miles from Truro Cathedral.

Uninterrupted education is provided for boys and girls during those important early years from three to thirteen. There is flexible attendance for under-fives who are taught by qualified professionals in Nursery and Reception. The school has an established reputation for high levels of care and excellent teaching.

Although mainly a day-school, weekly boarding, day boarding, and after-school care are growing in popularity. The boarders live in the Main House in comfortable sur-

roundings which include a TV lounge, en-suite facilities, quiet areas and garden. The well-being and happiness of each child is the top priority.

This flourishing family school was founded in 1976 and has a continual programme of development, building and refurbishment. Accommodation now includes a separate Pre-Prep and Prep School, built and equipped for art and craft, design technology, sciences, languages and ICT. More recently the EYFS provision was extended with larger rooms and greater free-flow access to the outdoors.

Twenty years ago an equestrian centre was built. There are now five ponies at school and almost half the pupils enjoy riding lessons and some attend competitions.

The school combines modern teaching methods with the best of traditional values. The social development of the child is carefully nurtured to help them to become confident, considerate and polite young people. Polwhele House values each child and a very strong team of skilled and caring staff is able to devote a great deal of time to every pupil in small classes.

Drama flourishes with each child participating in at least one of eight productions a year. Music is an important part of the school life with all pupils singing, and the majority playing an instrument. There are Truro Cathedral Choristerships for boys and Polwhele House Equestrian Scholarships. All the usual team games are coached.

Polwhele House is a Christian, non-denominational school and assembly is considered to be an important part of the day. The school motto is 'Karenza Whelas Karenza', Cornish for 'Love Begets Love'. Boys and girls share the same opportunities and responsibilities in all areas of school life.

The school has a fine record of academic achievement. There is a wide variety of sporting and extracurricular activities to bring out the best in every child. Pupils are prepared for a broad range of schools, and win numerous scholarships, bursaries and exhibitions to senior independent schools.

Mr McCullough takes great pleasure in meeting prospective parents and showing them around personally. Polwhele House is not just a school, more a way of life.

Prenton Preparatory School

Mount Pleasant, Oxton, Wirral CH43 5SY

Tel: 0151 652 3182
email: enquiry@prentonprep.co.uk
website: www.prentonprep.co.uk
Twitter: @prentonprep
Facebook: /prenton.prep

Directors: Mr M J and Mrs N M Aloé

Headteacher: **Mr M T R Jones**

Senior Management: Mrs A Hughes & Miss J Orme

Age Range. 2½–11.
Number in School. Day: 52 Boys, 62 Girls.

Fees per term (from January 2017). £2,475 Infants; £2,585 Juniors; from £760 part-time in Foundation Stage (with free places available for up to 15hrs)

Founded in 1935.

Prenton Preparatory School is co-educational day school for children aged 2½–11 years, situated about a mile from Junction 3 of the M53.

The building is a large Victorian house which has been carefully converted into the uses of a school. There is a large playground and gardens. Facilities include an ICT/Science block and an Art block. The Foundation Stage outdoor play area is a recent addition to the school.

The children benefit from small classes and individual attention in a holistic approach to their education within a disciplined environment which enables them to realise their full potential.

The school offers a wide range of academic subjects with emphasis on the three main National Curriculum core subjects: English, Mathematics and Science. French is taught from an early age and swimming forms a regular part of the curriculum from Year 1 upwards.

Children are prepared for entrance examinations to county, independent and grant-maintained grammar schools, gaining well above-average pass rates.

Child care facilities are available from 8 am to 6 pm. Clubs are provided at lunchtime and after school. They include football, cricket, computers and technology, karate, swimming, dance, netball, music group, speech & drama and musical instruments.

The school has a wide range of sporting teams that compete in local and regional fixtures and competitions. These include: swimming, water polo, cross-country, football, netball, cricket, rounders and athletics. Several of these teams have been successful enough to qualify for National tournaments in recent years.

Art, drama, dance and music also play an important part in school life and parents and members of the wider school community enjoy the regular performances that are part of the annual calendar.

Priory School

Sir Harry's Road, Edgbaston, Birmingham B15 2UR

Tel: 0121 440 4103/0256
Fax: 0121 440 3639
email: enquiries@prioryschool.net
website: www.prioryschool.net
Twitter: @PrioryEdgbaston
Facebook: /prioryschooledgbaston

Chairman of Governors: Mr Christopher Beesley

Headmaster: **Mr Jonathan Cramb**, BA Hons, PGCE, MEd

Age Range. 6 months – 18 years.
Number in School. 480.
Fees per term (2016–2017). £2,980–£4,505.

The school, founded on its present site in 1936 by the Sisters of the Society of the Holy Child Jesus, stands in 17 acres of parkland in the pleasant suburb of Edgbaston, only 2 miles from the centre of Birmingham. The school has extensive playing fields, excellent astroturf tennis courts, athletics facilities and football and cricket pitches. There are coaches running to and from school and frequent bus services to all parts of the city.

The school has an excellent Nursery on site which offers care for 51 weeks per annum and accepts children from the age of 6 months. All pupils are able to remain in After Care until 6.00 pm if parents so wish.

The school has a culturally diverse pupil community, based on catholic values, but welcomes all faiths. Pupils are taught by specialist teachers from the age of 9 and in the Senior School the curriculum is broad and balanced and pupils benefit from small class sizes and individual attention enabling the to make excellent progress in their academic development.

The school, whilst remaining proudly multi-ability, is justly proud of the academic achievements of the pupils. A wide range of subjects is available for GCSE, with good

facilities, including well-equipped Science Laboratories, Language Resources rooms, Information Technology facilities, Sports Centre, Performing Arts Suite and Learning Resources Centre. The school offers support for children with special needs, particularly dyslexia, with specially qualified staff.

A wide range of extra-curricular opportunities are offered in both Prep. and Senior School. These currently include photography, debating, chess, Duke of Edinburgh's Award scheme to name just a few. Private tuition is also offered in speech, singing and a wide range of musical instruments.

Entry to the school is by interview, assessment and day visit. Scholarships are awarded at 11+. Bursaries may be awarded in cases of special need.

Parents are warmly welcomed into the school to discuss individual needs. Full details prior to the visit may be obtained from the Admissions Registrar.

Charitable status. Priory School is a Registered Charity, number 518009.

Queen Ethelburga's Collegiate Foundation

Thorpe Underwood Hall, York YO26 9SS

Tel: 01423 333330
email: info@QE.org
            pj@QE.org
website: www.QE.org

Co-educational Day and Boarding School.

Principal: **Steven Jandrell**

Age Range. 3 months–18 years.
Number of Pupils. 1,500.
Fees per term (2016–2017). Day: £2,401–£5,240; Boarding: £9,542–£11,923 (UK students), £11,671–£14,706 (International students).

Founded in 1912, Queen Ethelburga's Collegiate Foundation is a day and boarding school with 1,500 pupils aged from 5 years to 18 years from over 60 different countries. Set in 120 acres of beautiful North Yorkshire countryside, the campus has some of the most impressive study, boarding and leisure facilities in the independent school sector.

2016 saw QE celebrate its best-ever A Level results. Queen Ethelburga's College was ranked the top day and boarding school in the North of England, according to the Daily Telegraph 2016 League Table for percentage A*/A A Levels and equivalent qualifications. It scored 87% which ranked it top in the North and the second UK day and boarding school overall.

The Faculty of Queen Ethelburga's, the Foundation's other Sixth Form school, scored 84% with its percentage of A*/A A Levels and equivalent qualifications in the Daily Telegraph table, placing it second in the North and fourth in the list of UK day and boarding schools.

Younger pupils study from the age of three years in Chapter House Preparatory School, starting with the Early Years Foundation Stage and child-led and adult-led activities to foster their skills in reading, language and number work. By the time the children progress through Key Stage 1 and into Key Stage 2 they will be competent readers, with good verbal and writing skills and excellent number and data handling.

King's Magna Middle School takes pupils from age 10 years to 14 years. Here the transition is made from class-based teaching to specialist teaching, so that by Years 8 and 9, all subjects will be taught by specialist teachers. The curriculum is based on the National Curriculum, but extends beyond this with a comprehensive programme of sports and creative activities.

By Year 11 students will choose to attend the College, which offers a more traditional academic route of learning with GCSEs and A Levels, or the Faculty, which offers GCSEs and A Levels but also more vocational BTEC subjects such as performing arts, fashion or sports science.

For many students though, Queen Ethelburga's is more than a school, it is their home too, and the boarding facilities are simply exemplary. Student bedrooms and apartments are all air-conditioned and have their own en-suite facilities and for the older students, their own kitchen area. Each room has a direct dial telephone, satellite plasma television with timed gaming port and DVD player. House parents are on hand 24 hours a day to help with prep, heat up hot chocolate or to listen to career ideas.

New for September 2016 are our new floodlit 3G and grassed sports pitches. We run a Cricket Academy which is being run in partnership with The Yorkshire County Cricket Club. This runs alongside our existing sporting academies – the Rugby Academy, supported by Leeds Rugby Academy and Foundation at Leeds Carnegie and the Netball Academy run by Yorkshire Jets. There will be further development of existing programmes in football, swimming, hockey and basketball, all will have the advantage of use of the facilities in our £30m Sports Village.

When homework is done, the new QE activity centre opens its doors. Complete with a go karting and speed skating track, assault course, climbing wall, 3D cinema, dj and music area, game consoles and even a stunt bike track – there's something for everyone.

Queen Ethelburga's motto is about ambition and excellence – "to be the best that I can with the gifts that I have" – it is a school rich in talent and opportunities and well deserves such a maxim.

Radnor House Sevenoaks School

Combe Bank Drive, Sundridge, Kent TN14 6AE

Tel: Senior School 01959 563720 or 01959 569011
             Preparatory School 01959 564320
Fax: Senior School 01959 561997
             Preparatory School 01959 560456
email: enquiries@radnor-sevenoaks.org
website: www.radnor-sevenoaks.org
Twitter: @radnorsevenoaks
Facebook: /radnorsevenoaks

Chairman of Board of Directors: Mr Colin Diggory, BSc Hons, PGCE, MA, EdD, CMath, FIMA, FRSA

Head: **Mr David Paton**, BComm Hons, PGCE, MA

Radnor House Sevenoaks is an independent school with entry from the term that pupils are 2½ up to the age of 18. it was founded in 1924. (*See also Preparatory School entry in IAPS section.*) In September 2014 the school became co-educational.

Aims and Ethos. Our mission is to inspire pupils to develop their talents and gifts so that they achieve academic excellence and personal success. We provide challenges in learning and opportunities for personal endeavour for all pupils at **Radnor House Sevenoaks**, so that they develop interpersonal skills, integrity and intellectual curiosity which enable them to reach their full potential in the outside world. The purposeful ethos and commitment to very good quality pastoral care are a distinctive feature of school life. High academic standards are expected.

Location. Situated in a Palladian Mansion built for the Campbell family, Dukes of Argyll and set in superb grounds with 28 acres of parkland just outside Sevenoaks, the school has excellent facilities. The Nursery, Prep School, Senior School and Sixth Form are on the same site and there are many positive links between them, so that all pupils have guaranteed access through the school until they leave at 18.

Curriculum. A modern and broad range of subjects is taught at all age levels. English, Mathematics, Sciences and RE are compulsory at GCSE. In addition pupils choose from History, Geography, IT, PE, Business Studies, Drama, Music, Art and Design, Psychology, are additional options for AS/A2. The school boasts strong Art and Music Departments with regular exhibitions and musical performances in which wide participation is achieved. **Radnor House Sevenoaks** has a well earned reputation for competitive success in PE and also provides a very wide range of sports and activities to interest all pupils. Swimming in the 25-metre covered pool is a particularly popular activity from Nursery through to Sixth Form.

Admission. Children enter the Prep school in Nursery and Reception. For the Senior School, pupils take the School's entrance examination at 11+ and 13+ Good passes at GCSE are also expected for the AS/A2 subjects of choice in order to join the Sixth Form for external candidates.

Transport. Coach transport is organized for 4 significant routes, to be paid for on a termly basis.

Fees per term (2016–2017). Senior School £4,995–£5,705 (Lunch £290); Preparatory School £3,240–£4,150 (Lunch £235); Nursery £54 full day. £50 half day (mornings) includes lunch and morning and afternoon wrap care.

Scholarships. Academic scholarships of up to half tuition fees at time of entry are awarded at 11+, 13+ and to the Sixth Form. 11+ entrance papers are taken in November. For further details go to www.radnor-sevenoaks.org

Raphael Independent School

Park Lane, Hornchurch, Essex RM11 1XY

Tel: 01708 744735
Fax: 01708 722432
email: admin@raphaelschool.com
website: www.raphaelschool.com

Headmaster: **Mr Jack Luis**, MSc

Age Range. Co-educational 4–16.
Number of Pupils. Day: 65 boys, 50 girls.
Fees per term (2016–2017). £1,995–£2,870.
Entry requirements. Interview for Early Years and Infants. Formal assessment for Juniors. Entry Tests in English and Maths for Seniors.
Aims.

• To develop the academic, social, artistic and sporting potential of each individual within a caring and welcoming school community.

• To foster respect for each other within a multi-cultural school.

• To offer a broad range of educational visits and extracurricular activities.

Location. Raphael is a ten-minute walk from Romford Main Line Station, and a fifteen-minute drive from the A12 or A127 junctions of the M25.

School day. Infants from 8.40 am, Juniors until 3.25 pm and Seniors until 4.00 pm. Our After-School Club looks after pupils until 5.45 pm.

Curriculum strengths. Computer Science, French and Spanish, English and Drama, Maths, History, Geography, Business Studies and Gateway Double Science.

Sport. We believe in competitive sport, and we offer Soccer, Rugby, Netball, Cross-Country, Swimming, Cricket and Tennis amongst others.

A prospectus containing further information may be obtained from our Office Manager, Anita Hargrove, and all prospective parents are most welcome to visit the school.

Rastrick Independent School

Ogden Lane, Rastrick, Brighouse, West Yorkshire HD6 3HF

Tel: 01484 400344
Fax: 01484 718318
email: info@rastrick-independent.co.uk
website: www.rastrick-independent.co.uk

Headmistress: **Mrs S A Vaughey**

Age Range. 0–16 co-educational. Tutorial College 16+.
Number of Pupils. 200.
Fees per term (2016–2017). £2,420–£3,800.

The philosophy of this Independent School is to provide a first-class education for all ages combined with academic excellence. This School and College are also renowned for their superb pastoral care. Situated in a small village in the heart of Yorkshire, this educational campus is flourishing in a historic and beautiful location. A 19th Century Manor House and grounds with extensive, well stocked gardens frame a collection of exquisite buildings which accommodate children and students from birth to eighteen. The academic achievement at Rastrick has been acknowledged as 'Excellent' by ISI and Ofsted. The School has achieved 100% Pass rate at 11+ and 100% A*–C at GCSE. The SATS results are outstanding at all key stages. When it comes to examination results, Rastrick succeeds far above the national and local averages.

The highly qualified team create a vibrant, exciting environment for learning. The pupils have a reputation for manners and discipline which has produced confident, happy, well adjusted young people. Life at this Independent School is extremely successful academically and daily school life is rich and rewarding. There is something very special about the atmosphere and the team at Rastrick.

Walking into the Main School, visitors experience something quite unique. The architecture and design of Rastrick has maintained the atmosphere of the historic buildings and incorporates light, air and space to create a superb learning environment. Children and Students greet invited guests, each other, their teachers and parents with a natural warmth and charm. There is a sense of mutual respect. The structure of a day here is ordered and classes for all ages take place in rooms designed to stimulate learning as well as to showcase the work being undertaken. Every child learns to take care of themselves and their peers. The pastoral care at Rastrick is outstanding.

In partnership with families, pupils achieve their potential academically but also flourish in Sports and The Arts. The School and College are open all year round to accommodate working parents. The School has taken its place in the centre of the community, taking pride in activities which reflect the daily life of the village of Rastrick.

This educational establishment has experienced a sustained record of academic success and pastoral care. The rapid growth and development of Rastrick has seen considerable investment in buildings and first-class facilities. Rastrick now welcomes Boarders, International Students and students to the Tutorial College for full or part time education beyond age the age of 16. In addition Rastrick is an Examination Centre for Private Candidates.

This environment offers an education which expects success. There is an expectation that discipline, self-worth and good manners will lead to the development of a confident, happy child.

Red House School

36 The Green, Norton, Stockton-on-Tees, Cleveland TS20 1DX

Tel: 01642 553370
Fax: 01642 361031
email: headmaster@redhouseschool.co.uk
website: www.redhouseschool.co.uk

Chairman of Governors: Mr Vinay Bedi

Headmaster: **Mr Ken James**

Head of Nursery & Infant School: Mr Simon Haywood

Age Range. 3–16.
Number in School. Approx. 175 girls and 198 boys.
Fees per term (2016–2017). Nursery £1,620*; Reception £1,760*, Years 1–2 £2,410; Years 3–6 £3,000; Years 7–11 £3,440. Lunches £190 per term.

*Nursery and Reception (under 5 years) fees are shown net of the Early Years Funding Grant. The grant is claimed by the school on behalf of the parents and is available from the term following the child's third birthday (for a total of 6 terms) until they reach their 5th birthday.

Red House School is a 3–16 co-educational independent day school. Situated on the picturesque village green at Norton, Stockton-on-Tees, Red House School has the enviable reputation as being the region's premier co-educational independent school, offering a first-class education and helping children to reach their full potential since 1929.

Our commitment to pupils and parents is summarized below:

- To provide a happy, stimulating and well disciplined environment in which children succeed.
- To encourage each child to reach their full potential and strive for excellence in all areas of school life.
- To develop pupil's self-esteem so that they have the confidence to use their individual talents, skills and knowledge effectively.
- To develop their skills of communication, analysis and independent thinking so that children are equipped to be lifelong learners prepared for a rapidly changing society.
- To develop a positive partnership between staff, parents, pupils and the wider community.

The Nursery and Infant School (Pre-Nursery to Year 3) is housed in and around the Old Vicarage, a beautiful listed building. This site has been further developed with the construction of purpose-built nursery facilities, additional classrooms and the redevelopment of 'The Barn' to provide an assembly hall and dining room. There is an ICT suite and all classrooms have interactive whiteboards. Close links are maintained with Red House Preparatory and Senior School.

The Preparatory and Senior School (Years 4–11) are housed in a beautiful Victorian building, which has been augmented over the years with purpose-built sports and assembly halls, classrooms and laboratories. The school has its own playing fields, including tennis courts. ICT is well developed within the teaching and learning across the school.

Although a selective school, Red House caters for pupils with a wide range of abilities and backgrounds. Small class sizes mean that teaching can be tailored to the needs of the individual child allowing them to reach their full potential. GCSE results have been consistently amongst the best, if not the best, of any school within the area. The academic side of the school is balanced by an extensive programme of games and activities. Pupils have regularly achieved representational honours at county, regional and national level.

Charitable status. Red House School Limited is a Registered Charity, number 527377. It exists to provide education for children and for the advancement of education for the benefit of the community.

Redcourt – St Anselm's

7 Devonshire Place, Oxton, Birkenhead, Wirral CH43 1TX

Tel:	0151 652 5228
email:	admin@redcourt.net
website:	www.redcourtstanselms.com
Twitter:	@redcourt7
Facebook:	/RedcourtStA

Chair of Governors: Mrs L Scholes

Headmistress: **Miss R M Jones**

Age Range. 3–11 Co-educational.
Number of Pupils. 200.
Fees per term (2016–2017). £2,050.

Redcourt – St Anselm's is an inclusive school welcoming all children of all abilities. There is no formal entrance examination. Prospective pupils are invited into Redcourt for a day's visit. During the day, Staff will assess the level at which the visiting child is currently working. However, most children join at nursery level. Our aim is to provide each and every child with a sound academic education in an environment which is explicitly Christian and where discipline and care go hand in hand. We endeavour to be aware of each child as an individual and we seek to encourage the development of the whole person. The school operates in an open and friendly manner, becoming something of a second home for its pupils.

The core national curriculum subjects plus RE, History, Geography, Art and Design, PE and Games, Music, ICT and French form the basis of what is taught. Children are prepared for the eleven plus and entrance examinations to grammar and selective independent schools with most children proceeding to Grammar Schools.

Charitable status. Redcourt St Anselm's is part of the Congregation of Christian Brothers which is a Registered Charity, number 254312.

Riverston School

63–69 Eltham Road, Lee Green, London SE12 8UF

Tel:	020 8318 4327
email:	office@riverstonschool.co.uk
website:	www.riverstonschool.co.uk
Twitter:	@Riverstonschool

Principal: Professsor D M Lewis

Headmistress: **Mrs S E Salathiel**

Deputy Headmaster: Mr P D Salathiel

Age Range. 9 months – 19 years.
Number in School. Day: 140 Boys, 54 Girls.
Fees per term (2016–2017). £2,900–£4,600 for mainstream pupils.

Riverston School is a small, co-educational, independent day school in South East London for children between the ages of 9 months and 19 years. Riverston was founded in the early 1900s, and in 1927 moved to its present site in Eltham Road, Lee Green. It is centrally located on the A20, close to the A2 and South Circular Roads, served by numerous bus routes and is convenient for mainline railway stations being 20 minutes from London Bridge.

The school stands in nearly three acres of carefully maintained grounds and is built around four imposing Victorian houses. It has modern purpose-built units, incorporating specialist teaching rooms, library, science laboratories, general-purpose hall, ICT suite, music room, Food Technology suite, and most recently a Design Technology room. The school also has a fully-equipped Sports Hall and two large playground areas. The Nursery and Pre-School Departments have their own separate and fully-equipped outdoor play area.

The emphasis is on "Bespoke Learning for Life" and to this end the curriculum encompasses subjects such as textiles, food technology and social communication enabling students to prepare for independent living when school life has ended. Vocational studies are at the core of the Sixth Form curriculum with BTEC courses available in various subjects as well as A Levels being delivered to students who are academically able. We have forged an educational link with Hadlow College in Mottingham where students can study Animal Management.

The school has a well-earned reputation for its teaching of children of all abilities including those who may require learning support or have special learning difficulties. There is a dedicated Riverston Plus department providing excellent specialist provision. Whilst many pupils may require additional help with their academic work, wherever possible they attend full-time mainstream lessons except for those periods determined by their individual educational programmes when they are taught individually or in small groups.

Riverston has a lively, friendly and cheerful ethos with ideals which are as strong today as they were when first conceived. A traditional school with the mission statement "Bespoke Learning for Life", Riverston endeavours to provide each pupil with an individualised curriculum, promoting a positive self-image and ensuring that all have the chance of maximising their academic potential, whilst encouraging their sporting ability. There is a considerable emphasis on pastoral care for personal happiness and a real sense of community in an environment where staff and pupils know each other very well across the year groups.

Parents are invited to visit the school on Open Mornings and by appointment only. Details can be found on our website at www.riverstonschool.co.uk

Rochester Independent College

Star Hill, Rochester, Kent ME1 1XF

Tel:	01634 828115
Fax:	01634 405667
email:	admissions@rochester-college.org
website:	www.rochester-college.org
Twitter:	@RICollege
Facebook:	@Rochester-Independent-College

Principal: **Alistair Brownlow**, MA Hons, MPhil

Age Range. 11–19 Co-educational.
Number of Pupils. 305 (including 90 single room boarding places).

Fees per year (2016–2017). Tuition: £12,000–£17,400. Weekly Boarding £11.400; Full Boarding: £13,200.

Rochester Independent College is an alternative to conventional secondary education with a happily distinctive ethos. Accepting day students from the age of 11 and boarders from 15, the focus is on examination success in a lively, supportive and informal atmosphere. Students are encouraged to be themselves and achieve exam results that often exceed their expectations. There is no uniform, no bells ring and everybody is on first-name terms. The average class size is eight.

Students enjoy being here and are treated as young adults. We encourage them to search for their own answers, to voice their opinions, to think critically, creatively and independently. They leave not only with excellent examination results but with enthusiasm for the future and new confidence about themselves and their education.

Personal Tutors work closely with students on all courses to give advice about course combinations and help students to ensure that their courses are designed to meet the requirements of university entrance. With such small class sizes individual attention is not only available, it's practically inescapable.

The College has particular academic strengths in the Sciences, Mathematics, English Literature and the Creative and Visual Arts including Film, Photography and Media.

The College's reputation for academic excellence is founded on over 30 years' experience of rigorous teaching. Students come to us for a variety of reasons and from many different backgrounds. We are not academically selective; our only entrance qualification is an honest determination to work hard. Our results however are always ranked among the best of the academically selective and students secure places at top UK universities. Direct entry into any year group is possible and the College also offers intensive one year GCSE and A Level courses as well as retake programmes. International students benefit from specialised English Language teaching support.

The College Halls combine the informality of a university residence with the supervision and pastoral support appropriate for young adults. The College offers students the opportunity to thrive in an atmosphere of managed independence and acts as a stepping stone between school and university. All accommodation is on campus and in single rooms.

Rochester Independent College is part of the Dukes Education Group.

Rookwood School

Weyhill Road, Andover, Hampshire SP10 3AL

Tel: 01264 325900
Fax: 01264 325909
email: office@rookwood.hants.sch.uk
website: www.rookwood.hants.sch.uk

Headmaster: **Dr M Whalley**, DPhil, MA, MEd, BSc Hons, PGCE, NPQH

Age Range. Co-educational 3–16 with Boarders from age 8.
Number in School. 320: 169 girls, 151 Boys (39 in the Nursery).
Fees per term (2016–2017). Boarding: £7,375–£8,655. Day: £2,965–£4,890. Nursery: £9.50 per hour (Early Years Education Funding accepted).

Hailed by the ISI as a place "where pupils make excellent progress", Rookwood is an independent non-selective day

and boarding school for girls and boys aged 3–16 years in Andover, Hampshire.

Described as "warm, welcoming and nurturing", Rookwood is known for its family atmosphere and strong pastoral care which encourages each and every child to achieve their very best with excellent results. Almost 40% of all GCSEs taken in 2016 were awarded an A*/A and 100% of students gained five A*–C grades – testament to Rookwood's small class sizes and dedicated teaching.

Set in eight acres of private grounds Rookwood has an impressive range of amenities including a state-of-the-art sports hall, outdoor swimming pool, excellent art and science facilities and a wonderful purpose-built Pre-Prep (currently deemed 'excellent' by the ISI). Both Music and Drama thrive at Rookwood, with every child encouraged to take part, whilst the Physical Education department is equally busy with several pupils advancing to represent their favourite sports at national level in recent years.

In addition to its many tangible achievements Rookwood is committed to delivering excellent pastoral care and takes great pride in seeing its pupils develop into confident, resilient and principled young adults. The School also offers a rich and varied programme of extra-curricular activities for all ages and interests giving pupils the opportunity to develop new skills, discover new passions, grow socially and emotionally and to simply enjoy themselves.

Rookwood's boarding provision was recently rated as 'excellent' in all areas by the ISI with boarders receiving a unique 'home-from-home' experience. Family-style meal times, experienced and supportive boarding staff and busy weekends all combine to ensure that Rookwood's boarders receive the best possible care.

Prospective pupils and their parents are warmly invited to attend one of Rookwood's open days (please see website for latest information). Alternatively, if you require any further information or would like to make an individual appointment, please do not hesitate to contact the Registrar directly on 01264 325910.

Admission is by school reports and individual visits.

Charitable status. Rookwood School is a Registered Charity, number 307322. It exists to provide education for children.

Roselyon School

Par, Cornwall PL24 2HZ

Tel: 01726 812110
Fax: 01726 812110
email: secretary@roselyonschool.com
website: www.roselyonschool.com

Head: **Mrs Hilary Mann**, MBA, BEd

Age Range. 2½–11.
Number in School. Day: 39 Boys, 37 Girls.
Fees per term (2016–2017). £2,875.

Roselyon School, formerly the Victorian manor house in the village of Par, near St Austell, stands in 5 acres of beautiful woodland. A new multi-purpose gymnasium and hall recently built in the centre of the campus has added greatly to the school's facilities. Roselyon is fully co-educational, taking pupils in the full time Nursery from 2½ and joining the Main School from 5–11.

The school is proud of its academic strengths and excellent examination results to local senior independent schools. It offers a broad curriculum, a variety of sports, music and drama and has an extensive range of extra-curricular activities.

Academic and Music Scholarships and Bursaries are available for pupils in Years 3 to 6, and assessments are usually taken in the Summer Term.

Roselyon is a small, friendly school where a warm family atmosphere is maintained by the committed team of caring staff.

Charitable status. Roselyon School Limited is a Registered Charity, number 306583. It exists to provide quality education to boys and girls.

Ruckleigh School

17 Lode Lane, Solihull, West Midlands B91 2AB
Tel: 0121 705 2773
Fax: 0121 704 4883
email: admin@ruckleigh.co.uk
website: www.ruckleigh.co.uk

Headmistress: **Mrs B M Forster**

Age Range. 3–11.
Number in School. Day: 120 Boys, 105 Girls.
Fees per term (2016–2017). £970–£2,795.

Ruckleigh is an independent day school offering education to boys and girls between the ages of 4 and 11 with a Nursery Department catering for children from the age of 3.

Although a high standard of work is expected this is related to the individual child, and the school is able to provide opportunities within a wide range of academic ability. Each child has every chance to develop his or her talents to the full, often resulting in achievements beyond initial expectations.

The comparatively small classes mean that every child is well known individually throughout the school creating a friendly environment.

Pupils are guided into habits of clear thinking, self-reliance and courtesy. Sound practical judgement, sensitivity towards the needs of others, and a willingness to "have a go" are the qualities that the school seeks to promote.

Rushmoor School

58–60 Shakespeare Road, Bedford MK40 2DL
Tel: 01234 352031
email: admissions@rushmoorschool.co.uk
website: www.rushmoorschool.co.uk
Twitter: @RushmoorSchool
Facebook: /RushmoorSchool

Chair of Governors: G M Bates, OBE, JP

Principal: **I M Daniel**, BA, NPQH

Age Range. Boys 2–16 (2–18 from September 2016), Girls 2–10.
Number in School. 328 Day Pupils.
Fees per term (2016–2017). £2,091–£3,500.

Rushmoor has grown and improved by investing greatly to provide excellent facilities. In partnership with our Alliance school, St Andrew's Bedford, we appreciate the importance of selecting the right school for your son or daughter; childhood is something which can be experienced only once. With this in mind, and the belief that children learn best when they feel happy and secure, we aim to develop in our pupils a lifelong interest in learning – one which encompasses the full range of intellectual, cultural, artistic and sporting achievements of our society.

We believe in individual care and attention. Visitors to the school are impressed by the friendly, positive attitude of the pupils and their energetic sense of purpose. The staff are caring and understanding, yet know the importance of effort and personal discipline in enabling pupils to achieve the highest academic standards.

At the school we ensure that all children have opportunities to develop their intellectual, physical and creative gifts, across a broad and balanced curriculum. Children in Reception and Junior classes benefit greatly from a wide range of specialist teachers.

We emphasise the individual, recognizing that all children are different and value each child in their own right. Encouraging children to develop their strengths improves their self-esteem, enabling them to find their role in the community. We promote children's personal development, encouraging lively and enquiring minds, respect for others and a high regard for truth. The stability of continuous education, spanning the ages 2–16 years (2–18 years from September 2016), is a major factor in helping us achieve this.

At Rushmoor we pride ourselves on our ability to integrate children with Specific Learning Differences within mainstream school life, whilst still providing extended challenges for our gifted and talented pupils. We believe that every child should be allowed to embrace any aspect of the curriculum. Enabling children to receive support without undermining their confidence amongst their peers is of primary importance.

Rushmoor has a fine reputation in sport and boasts a highly successful record with many pupils gaining county and national honours. Children have also gained much success in national and local drama competitions and festivals.

In 2014 Rushmoor was a finalist in the ISA Awards for excellence and winner of the 'Financial Innovation' category.

Prospective parents and children can tour the school at any time and 'taster days' can be arranged. Come and experience our caring ethos which enables our children to develop the confidence and flexibility which allows them to face the demands of modern life. To view our excellent inspection report please visit our website.

Charitable status. Rushmoor School Limited is a Registered Charity, number 307530. It exists to provide education.

Sackville School
Cognita Schools Group

Tonbridge Road, Hildenborough, Kent TN11 9HN
Tel: 01732 838888
Fax: 01732 836404
email: office@sackvilleschool.com
website: www.sackvilleschool.co.uk

Headmaster: **Mr John Hewitt**, BA, MBA

Age Range. 11–18.
Number in School. 150.
Fees per term (2016–2017). £4,860.

Sackville School is situated in Hildenborough, midway between Tonbridge and Sevenoaks. The main school building, which dates back to 1866, is set in 28 acres of magnificent parkland. The school has a newly refurbished Science block with four specialised laboratories, two dedicated Computer rooms, an impressive Sports Hall, an Art/Photography building and a new Design Suite, a modern Food Technology area, a new Drama/Music studio offering a performance area, a beautiful oak panelled Library, plus the usual range of specialist teaching rooms.

We are a mixed-ability school and our philosophy is based upon the individual and their unique learning needs. Individualised teaching is strong and successful at Sackville and all pupils benefit from this form of teaching. By concentrating on excellence the school ensures that each child has the opportunity to fulfil their true potential, and develop their gifts and talents at all levels. Students achieve excellent GCSE results and the Sixth Form offers one of the widest ranges of A Level and BTEC courses, plus Young Enterprise, Duke of Edinburgh's Award and many other life-enriching opportunities.

Our students go on to a wide variety of destinations including Oxford and other Russell Group universities.

Sackville students are cheerful, confident children who work hard and enjoy aiming high and achieving their very best – they are expected to take a full part in the life of the school. The Headmaster and staff encourage a warm, friendly working atmosphere, whilst promoting pride in achievement. Every student is valued, and their talents recognised.

The full range of academic, cultural and sporting activities are offered and all students are encouraged to try all activities. All major team games, and minor sports, are played and Sackville students have represented their County as well as National Squads. The school has a lively Music Department and over three quarters of the students are engaged in music making. The Creative Arts are particularly well represented. Art is exceptionally strong and Drama has a huge reputation for excellence. The Activities programme is an integral part of the school day and includes Orchestra, Choir, Duke of Edinburgh's Award, Drama, Golf, Film Unit, Windsurfing, Boules, Dry Slope Skiing, Archery, Self-Defence, Community Service, Horse Riding, Computing, Photography and many other activities.

The school fosters the qualities of honour, care for others, thoughtfulness and tolerance. The Headmaster is always delighted to meet with prospective parents with their sons and daughters to discuss the educational opportunities available at Sackville.

Sacred Heart School

Mangate Street, Swaffham, Norfolk PE37 7QW
Tel: 01760 721330/724577
Fax: 01760 725557
email: info@sacredheartschool.co.uk
website: www.sacredheartschool.co.uk

Headteacher: **Sister Francis Ridler**, FDC, BEd Hons, EYPS

Age Range. 3–16 Co-educational.
Number in School. 91 Day Pupils, 4 Girl Boarders.
Fees per term (2016–2017). Boarders: Termly £7,500, Weekly £5,785–£6,200; Day: £2,725 (Juniors); £3,625–£4,045 (Seniors).
Assistance with fees: Academic, Music, Art, Sport, All Rounder (Boarder) Scholarships for Year 7 (11+). Some bursaries available.
Entry requirements: Non-selective, Assessments, School Report and Interview.
Religious Affiliation: Roman Catholic (other denominations welcome).
Staff: 9 Full Time, 13 Part Time, 10 Learning Support.

The Sacred Heart School was founded by the Daughters of Divine Charity in 1914. The Sisters and lay staff work together to provide a safe and caring environment where Christian values are upheld.

Principally a day school, the school is now co-educational. Pupils study for eight to eleven GCSEs gaining consistently high A–C grades. At 16, the pupils have gained the confidence and self-possession which makes them much sought after by all Sixth Form Centres and other Independent Schools. There is a limited number of boarding places for girls aged 8–16 as well as the opportunity for flexi boarding.

All pupils are encouraged to develop their gifts in Music, Drama, Art and Sport, and the School has a fine record of success in all these areas.

Facilities include a Sports Hall, Swimming Pool and Arts Centre with Theatre, Art and Music Rooms and a Pottery Workshop.

A very active Parents' Association, loyal past pupils and parents network, together with highly-qualified Staff provide the energy, enthusiasm and friendly atmosphere which characterises the school community.

Before and after school care is available and Nursery Vouchers are accepted for the Little Pedlars Pre-School.

Charitable status. The Daughters of Divine Charity is a Registered Charity, number 237760.

Sacred Heart School

Mayfield Lane, Durgates, Wadhurst, East Sussex TN5 6DQ
Tel: 01892 783414
email: admin@sacredheartwadhurst.org.uk
website: www.sacredheartwadhurst.org.uk

Chair of Governors: Mr Anthony Moffatt

Head Teacher: **Mrs Hilary Blake**, BA, PGCE

Age Range. 3–11 Co-educational.
Number of Pupils. 120.
Fees per term (2016–2017). £2,310.
Sacred Heart School is a small independent Catholic primary school and Nursery, nestling in the heart of the Sussex countryside.

We welcome boys and girls from 3–11 and with pupil numbers around 100 we have the opportunity to know each child individually, to recognise and encourage their strengths and support them in overcoming areas of difficulty.

Our pupils enjoy a high degree of academic success, regularly obtaining places at their first choice of school, including passes at 11+ and Scholarships.

Courtesy and care for each other are important values nurtured at Sacred Heart School where children play and work well together.

Charitable status. Sacred Heart School, as part of the Arundel and Brighton Diocesan Trust, is a Registered Charity, number 252878.

St Andrew's School
Bedford

Kimbolton Road, Bedford MK40 2PA
Tel: 01234 267272
email: standrews@standrewsschoolbedford.com
website: www.standrewsschoolbedford.com
Twitter: @Standrewsschoo2
Facebook: /St-Andrews-School-Bedford

Chairman of Governors: Mr G Bates, OBE, JP

Principal: Mr I M Daniel, BA, NPQH

Head of School: **Mrs H Ryan**, BEd Hons

Age Range. 6 weeks–16 years.
Number of Pupils. 255.
Fees per term (2016–2017). £1,750–£3,680.

Founded in 1896, as a boarding school for girls, St Andrew's School is a charitable trust run by a Board of Governors. It is now a day school and nursery for girls between 6 weeks and 16, and for boys from six weeks to 11. St Andrew's School is located in central Bedford and is based around two large Victorian houses that have seen modernisation and various additions to meet the needs of our pupils. Most recently a complete refurbishment of the Physics Laboratory has been undertaken to support the strong interest of our pupils in science. In September 2013 a close working partnership between St Andrew's School and Rushmoor School was formalised to increase educational opportunities, joint ventures and the sharing of best practice. From September 2016 we will have a joint Sixth Form.

Our vision is to continually combine the best of traditional values with being at the forefront of educational advancement. Children in Reception and Junior classes benefit from a wide range of specialist teachers. By Year 9 our pupils are fully prepared to make informed choices for GCSE study.

The school's key aim is to provide the best possible standard of education and an appropriate level of challenge and support to allow each individual pupil to develop fully both academically and personally. Our GCSE results invariably demonstrate a very high degree of "value added". The high achievement at GCSE allows girls to study at competitive entry Sixth Forms, upper schools and colleges.

The older and younger girls form strong bonds outside the classroom through vertical tutor groups in Years 7–9, a pupil led House system, School Council and a wide range of co-curricular opportunities. These include team and individual sports, music, drama, science, ICT and art clubs. We offer a full range of outdoor and residential opportunities including the Blue Peris Mountain Centre and the Duke of Edinburgh's Award scheme.

Our community is a safe and peaceful environment which is both dynamic and caring, and which promotes strong values and mutual respect. To view our excellent inspection report, please visit our website.

We offer a limited number of means-tested bursaries and scholarships for pupils who excel in a particular field.

Charitable status. St Andrew's School (Bedford) Limited is a Registered Charity, number 307531.

St Anne's Preparatory School

154 New London Road, Chelmsford, Essex CM2 0AW
Tel: 01245 353488
email: headmistress@stannesprep.essex.sch.uk
website: www.stannesprep.essex.sch.uk

Headmistress: **Mrs F Pirrie**, BSc, PGCE

Age Range. 3+–11+.
Number of Children. 160.
Fees per term (2016–2017). £2,400–£2,520.

St Anne's is a co-educational day school, with its own excellent nursery facility. Established in 1925, the school is conveniently situated in the centre of Chelmsford. The building is a large Victorian house, which has been carefully converted into the uses of a school. Extensive lawned areas, astroturf, playground and Nursery play area provide ample space for both recreation and games lessons. In addition, older pupils benefit from the use of the excellent sports facilities at the nearby Essex County Cricket Club.

The children benefit from small classes and individual attention in a disciplined but happy environment, which enables them to realise their full potential. Provision is made in the school for the gifted as well as those pupils less educationally able. Classrooms are bright and well equipped and the teachers are chosen for their qualifications, experience and understanding of the needs of their pupils.

St Anne's combines modern teaching with the best of traditional values. The school maintains a high standard of academic education giving great emphasis to a secure foundation in the basic subjects whilst offering a wide curriculum with specialist teaching in many areas.

Examination results at both KS1 and KS2 levels are excellent and many pupils gain places at the prestigious Grammar and Independent schools in the county.

The school offers a wide range of extra-curricular activities and an excellent after-care facility is available for all age groups. St Anne's is rightly recognised for its friendly and supportive ethos. Parents are particularly supportive of all aspects of school life. Visitors are always welcome.

St Christopher's School

6 Downs Road, Epsom, Surrey KT18 5HE
Tel: 01372 721807
Fax: 01372 726717
email: office@st-christophers.surrey.sch.uk
website: www.st-christophers.surrey.sch.uk
Twitter: @StChrisEpsom

Headteacher: **Mrs A C Thackray**, MA, BA, Dip Mus

Age Range. 3–7.
Number in School. 180.
Fees per term (2016–2017). £3,190 (Full time including lunch), £1,620 (5 mornings).

St Christopher's School (founded in 1938) is a co-educational nursery and pre-preparatory school for children from 3–7 years.

Set in a quiet residential area a short distance from the centre of Epsom, it has attractive secure grounds with gardens and play areas. The school was found to be "excellent" in all eight areas of its 2016 ISI Inspection.

St Christopher's main purpose is to support children and parents through the early years of education. We offer a carefully managed induction programme to school life and, subsequently, a broad and challenging education within a happy, caring and secure family environment. Above all we aim to offer your child the best possible start to their education.

The children are prepared to enter a wide range of Surrey schools and we maintain a very high pass rate in a variety of entrance tests.

Breakfast Club opens at 7.45 am and After-School Care is available until 6 pm Monday to Friday. There are also a number of after-school clubs.

St Christopher's enjoys the support of an active parents association that organises a wide variety of social and fundraising events.

For further information please contact the school. Parents are welcome to visit the school by appointment with the Headteacher.

Charitable status. St Christopher's School Trust (Epsom) Limited is a Registered Charity, number 312045. It aims to provide a Nursery and Pre-Preparatory education in Epsom and district.

St Christopher's School

71 Wembley Park Drive, Wembley Park, Middlesex HA9 8HE

Tel: 020 8902 5069
email: admin@stchristophersschool.org.uk
website: www.stchristophersschool.org.uk

Headmaster: **Mr Paul Musetti**, MA, MEd

   Age Range. 2–11.
   Number in School. 48 Boys, 47 Girls.
   Fees per term (2016–2017). £2,800–£3,075. Discount for siblings 10%.
   Entry requirements: Interview and Assessment.
   St Christopher's School, a large Victorian building on Wembley Park Drive, offers a caring family atmosphere coupled with an equal emphasis on good manners, enthusiastic endeavour and academic excellence. The School, originally a Christian foundation dating from 1928, welcomes children of all faiths and cultures.
   Caring and supportive staff provide a well-structured, disciplined and stimulating environment in which children are nurtured and encouraged to develop the necessary skills – academic, social and cultural – so that when they leave us at the age of 11 they can be certain of future success. All children at St Christopher's are equal and we emphasise the qualities of equality, justice and compassion. Children benefit from a curriculum that offers both breadth and depth, an activity programme that teaches skills and develops talents, and a pastoral programme that develops social responsibility.
   The full range of academic subjects is taught based on an enriched National Curriculum. Sports and Music are seen as central elements in school life with sports matches, regular concerts and an annual carol service. In addition there is a variety of clubs and activities both at lunchtime and after school; these include Book Club, Booster Club, Choir, Cookery, First Aid, Gardening, Judo, Needlecraft, Netball and Recorders.
   Children are prepared for the full range of examinations at 11 years. Historically leavers have gained entry to a wide range of excellent schools including Haberdasher's Boys' and Girls' Schools, Merchant Taylors', Northwood College, St Helen's, North London Collegiate, Henrietta Barnett, Queen Elizabeth's Boys' School, City of London Boys and Girls, UCS, Aldenham School, John Lyon, St Paul's Girls' School and South Hampstead High.
   St Christopher's offers both Pre-School and After-School Care, from 8:00 am until 6:00 pm.
   Please phone for an appointment to view the school. We look forward to welcoming you.

St Clare's, Oxford

139 Banbury Road, Oxford OX2 7AL

Tel: 01865 552031
Fax: 01865 513359
email: admissions@stclares.ac.uk
website: www.stclares.ac.uk/ib

Principal: **Mr Andrew Rattue**, MA Oxon, MA London, PGCE London

Vice Principal Pastoral: Susan Tawse, BSc Edinburgh, PGCE
Vice Principal Academic: Cormack Kirby, BA Leeds, PGCE, MEd Bristol

   Age Range. 15–19 Co-educational.
   Number of Students. 270.
   Fees per annum (2016–2017). Boarding £37,080, Day £17,995.
   Established over 60 years St Clare's is an international college with a mission "To advance international education and understanding". The College embraces internationalism and academic excellence as core values. It is a co-educational day and residential college which has been offering the International Baccalaureate Diploma for over 35 years, longer than any other school or college in England. Students have achieved the maximum 45 points for the past 11 consecutive years.
   Students from over 45 countries study at St Clare's with a core group of British students. The atmosphere is informal and friendly with an equal emphasis on hard work and developing personal responsibility. Each student has a Personal tutor who oversees welfare and progress.
   St Clare's has an especially wide range of subjects on offer at Higher and Standard level and, in addition, currently teaches 28 different languages. The College takes a small number of transfer students each year. For students not yet ready to begin the IB Diploma, a Pre-IB course is offered with regular entry points throughout the year. There is an extensive programme of social, cultural and sporting activities and students are encouraged to take full advantage of the opportunities that Oxford provides.
   In July the College also runs a 3-week introduction to the IB Diploma and a 2-week Mid IB Visual Arts course. St Clare's is also authorised to run IB workshops for teachers.
   St Clare's is located in an elegant residential area which is part of the North Oxford Conservation Area. It occupies 28 large Victorian and Edwardian houses to which purpose-built facilities have been added. These include a beautiful library building (over 35,000 volumes, an IT suite and a Careers and Higher Education Information Centre), six science laboratories and three mathematics classes in a stunning new building on the campus, art and music studios, dining room and the popular Sugar House café. Students live in College houses close to the central campus under the care of residential staff.
   The College welcomes applications from international and UK students. Entry is based on academic results, interview and confidential school report. There is a competitive scholarship and bursary programme awarded by examination, interview and group exercises.
   St Clare's had a highly successful ISI Intermediate Boarding and Welfare inspection in 2016 and a full ISI Integrated inspection in March 2013; the reports can be accessed via the College website. The College was awarded the highest rating for the quality of its boarding provision in its Ofsted inspection in March 2009.
   Charitable status. St Clare's, Oxford is a Registered Charity, number 294085.

St David's School

23–25 Woodcote Valley Road, Purley, Surrey CR8 3AL

Tel: 020 8660 0723
Fax: 020 8645 0426
email: office@stdavidsschool.co.uk
website: www.stdavidsschool.co.uk

Head Teacher: **Miss Cressida Mardell**

   Age Range. 3+–11.
   Number in School. 156 Day: 87 boys, 69 girls.
   Fees per term (2016–2017). £1,900–£3,240 (including lunch).

We look forward to welcoming you to our happy and creative school, where we aim to achieve the highest academic standards. At St David's we offer a rich and stimulating curriculum, delivered by a talented and caring staff, giving your child the best possible start. The School has undergone many changes and developments since its foundation in 1912 and we have recently celebrated our 100th birthday! Please visit our recently re-launched website to find out more about all the exciting things that have been going on.

The small school atmosphere is, we believe, a strength and reassuring to parents and children alike. We aim to balance nurture with independence to equip your child to succeed academically and we are extremely proud of our results. Please do contact us to experience the warm inspiring environment that is the "St David's Family". Please telephone the School Office to arrange an appointment and I look forward to showing you round our school.

St David's participates fully in the Government Nursery Vouchers Scheme.

Charitable status. St David's (Purley) Educational Trust is a Registered Charity, number 312613. It aims to provide a quality education for boys and girls from 3+ to 11 years old. Bursaries are awarded in cases of financial hardship.

St Dominic's Priory School

21 Station Road, Stone, Staffordshire ST15 8EN
Tel: 01785 814181
email: info@stdominicspriory.co.uk
website: www.stdominicspriory.co.uk
Twitter: @stdomsinstone

Chair of Governors: Mr Mark Burton

Headteacher: **Mrs Rebecca Harrison**

Deputy Headteacher: Mrs Pamela Porter

St Dominic's Priory School is an outstanding independent day school and Nursery educating boys and girls from 3 months to 16 years.

We provide a friendly place of learning and are proud of our reputation for academic achievement. Our ethos and vision value the worth of each individual. High-quality teaching and small classes create an environment in which true potential can be maximised at all times.

Location. Centrally located within North Staffordshire, the school is situated in the picturesque canal town of Stone, Staffordshire, within easy reach of Newcastle-under-Lyme, Stoke-on-Trent, Stafford, Uttoxeter, Cheadle and the surrounding villages. We provide school transport from a number of locations and Stone Railway Station is only a 5 minute walk from school.

Aims and Ethos. Life is a journey, and every journey has a beginning. We aim to give each child the best possible start, to give them the tools to navigate their chosen path and the confidence to believe in themselves. Teachers and pupils work together with energy and imagination; they motivate and inspire each other in order to achieve their very best.

Boys and girls are co-educated from the age of 3 months within the purpose-built Nursery. The beginnings of reading, writing and number work are introduced at an early age.

The curriculum within the Preparatory Department encompasses all aspects of the National Curriculum with specialist teaching in many subjects including French, Drama and Music. Great emphasis is placed on high standards of presentation and regular homework reinforces the work undertaken at School.

Here at St Dominic's we aim to develop the capacity for independent thought through a rigorous and stimulating academic education. One of St Dominic's great strengths is taking pupils with a broad ability range and achieving outstanding GCSE results. With the benefit of small classes, teaching is geared to the needs of individual girls who are supported throughout by a strong pastoral care system. The School provides regular opportunities for pupils to take on positions of leadership and to develop a sense of their own worth and a determination to realise all their talents. Students leave St Dominic's with excellent academic grades, self-confidence and friends for life.

Religion. St Dominic's Priory is a Catholic School where children of all faiths are welcomed.

The Arts. The School excels in the Creative and Performing Arts and our busy programme of sport, cultural events, visits and activities ensures that there is something for everyone at St Dominic's. Pupils regularly take part in public speaking competitions, productions, festivals, concerts, recitals and exhibitions, both within and outside the School.

Sport. The School has a strong sporting tradition. Sports include tennis, badminton, hockey, netball, volleyball, gymnastics, athletics, football, tennis, cross-country running, climbing, sailing and tri-golf.

Extra-Curricular Activities. Numerous clubs and activities are held after school and during lunchtimes for both the Prep and Senior Schools. These include the Duke of Edinburgh's Award, fencing, musical theatre, choir, and percussion ensemble.

Admission. Please contact the school directly for information on admissions or visit the website.

Scholarships and Bursaries. Academic, Performing Arts, Art, Music and Sports Scholarships are awarded on the basis of performance in Entrance Assessments and Auditions for students entering year 7 and 9 in the academic year. Bursaries are available throughout the School. Details can be obtained from the Admissions Office and the school website.

Fees per term (2016–2017). Day: Reception £2,861; Primary 1–6 £3,181; Seniors £3,489 (exc lunch), £3,616 (inc lunch). Nursery: we offer different fees for those parents requiring a full year or term only nursery and a variety of session times. Please refer to the Nursery section of the school website for further details.

Further Information. The School welcomes visits from prospective parents and pupils. For more information please telephone the School Office on 01785 814181.

Charitable status. St Dominic's Priory is a Registered Charity, number 271922, providing quality education for boys and girls aged 3 months to 16 years.

St Gerard's School
Bangor

Ffriddoedd Road, Bangor, Gwynedd LL57 2EL
Tel: 01248 351656
Fax: 01248 351204
email: sgadmin@st-gerards.org
website: www.st-gerards.org

Chairman of the Governing Body: Miss C Beighton

Headteacher: **Mr C Harrison**

Age Range. 4–18.
Number in School. Day: 80 Boys, 85 Girls.
Fees per term (2016–2017). £2,180–£3,310.
Founded in 1915 by the Congregation of the Sisters of Mercy, this co-educational school is now a lay trust. The school welcomes pupils of all denominations and traditions

and has an excellent reputation locally. It has consistently attracted a high profile in national league tables also.

Class sizes in both junior and senior schools ensure close support and individual attention in order to enable all pupils to achieve their full academic potential, within an environment which promotes their development as well-rounded individuals with a keen social conscience.

The curriculum is comprehensive – pupils in the senior section usually achieve 9/10 good GCSE grades, going on to A Level and to university.

Charitable status. St Gerard's School Trust is a Registered Charity, number 1001211.

St Hilda's School

28 Douglas Road, Harpenden, Hertfordshire AL5 2ES
Tel: 01582 712307
email: office@sthildasharpenden.co.uk
website: www.sthildasharpenden.co.uk

Head: **Mr D Sayers**, BA Hons, QTS

Age Range. 3–11.
Number in School. 180 approx.
Fees per term (2016–2017). £3,515 (Forms II to VI including lunch), £3,485 (Reception & Form I including lunch), Nursery: £2,015.

St Hilda's School, situated in a residential site of 1¼ acres, has its own swimming pool, hard tennis/netball court and adjacent playing field. It also has a fully-equipped stage, a suite of music rooms, a dedicated computer suite, a science lab, a purpose-built EYFS unit, an art room, and six new classrooms.

A broad, well-balanced curriculum covering the requirements of the National Curriculum prepares girls for the Common Entrance and other senior independent school entrance examinations. Girls also enter State secondary schools if desired. Latin and French are taught to all pupils, and German and Spanish sessions are also available.

The school is well known for its high musical standards with almost all pupils learning an instrument, many two or three. The standards in drama, art and sport are also consistently high.

A prospectus is available on application to the School Secretary.

St James Junior School

Earsby Street, London W14 8SH
Tel: 020 7348 1794
email: admissions@stjamesjunior.org
website: www.stjamesjuniors.co.uk

Chair of Governors: Mr Jeremy Sinclair

Headmistress: **Mrs Catherine Thomlinson**, BA Hons

Age Range. Boys 4–11. Boys can then transfer to St James Senior Boys' School (*see entry in The Society of Heads section*) or other senior schools.

Girls 4–11. Girls then transfer to St James Senior Girls' School (*see entry in GSA section*) or other senior schools.

Number in School. 125 Boys and 127 Girls.
Fees per term (2016–2017). Reception and Year 1 £5,580, Years 2–6 £5,120.

St James provides an inspiring education. The Junior School is situated on a large Central London site and the beautiful Victorian building provides an Assembly Hall/Theatre, Gym and large airy classrooms. The playground has a climbing wall and pretty cloister gardens.

The curriculum is imaginatively and carefully balanced and, together with the impressive level of commitment from the teaching staff, high academic standards of reading, writing and arithmetic are achieved and above all a love of knowledge. Art, Drama and Music are taught with enthusiasm and results are outstanding; children sing daily and morning assemblies bring joy and a sense of unity throughout the school.

An interest and knowledge in that which is common to all traditions is cultivated. Every class has a weekly Philosophy lesson during which they explore virtues such as consideration, friendship and truthfulness. The school's philosophy curriculum is available on the website, together with curriculum details of all subjects taught.

Team sports, gymnastics or athletics are played daily and full use is made of good facilities both within school and locally. A rota of after-school clubs offers a rich choice of activities, including Ballet, French, Fencing, Cricket, Netball, Rugby and Yoga.

Creative residential holidays are organised each year for children in the Upper Junior School (7+ years) to places such as New Barn in Dorset, Chartres in France and to Northumberland, where History, Geography and Geometry become a living experience and time is enjoyed out of London with their friends and teachers.

Boys and girls are taught separately with frequent joint activities such as plays, concerts and outings. Educating the children about the environment is part of the school's wider curriculum. The Reception classes are involved with the Forest Schools programme and from Year 3 the children visit Minstead Study Centre in Dorset, where they learn about the environment and look after livestock.

The obvious happiness of the children flows from the full education offered and a level of attention and care from teachers that has become a St James trademark.

Charitable status. The Independent Educational Association Limited is a Registered Charity, number 270156. It exists to provide education for boys and girls.

St James' School
A Woodard School

22 Bargate, Grimsby, North East Lincolnshire DN34 4SY
Tel: 01472 503260
Fax: 01472 503275
email: enquiries@saintjamesschool.co.uk
website: www.saintjamesschool.co.uk
Twitter: @StJamesSchoolGY
Facebook: @stjamesschoolgrimsby

Headmaster: **Dr John Price**, BSc Hons, PhD

Director of Senior School: Mr J D Hampson, BSc Hons, PGCE
Head of Preparatory Department: Miss T Donegan, BEd Hons Liverpool John Moores
Head of Pre-Preparatory Department: Mrs C Fillingham, Cert Ed Salzburg
Director of Boarding: Mr M Park
Bursar: Mr A Major

Age Range. 2–18.
Number in School. Boarders: Boys 15, Girls 14. Day: Boys 121, Girls 113.

Fees per term (2016–2017). Tuition: Prep School: Reception £1,675 to Year 6 £2,650. Senior School Day Pupils: £3,760. Boarding: £2,000 (weekly), £2,750 (termly).

St James' School, Grimsby provides an excellent day and boarding education for children aged 2 to 18 years. The School is co-educational and a fully incorporated Member of the Woodard Corporation.

Pupils benefit from an extremely supportive environment that creates a rich and rewarding educational experience. Our highly qualified and dedicated teaching staff have the ability and experience necessary to be able to inspire and enthuse every pupil. This teaching excellence, along with the small class sizes, equips our pupils with the knowledge, skills and understanding they require to reach their academic potential.

All pupils are given the opportunity to take part in a vast range of extracurricular activities above and beyond the traditional sporting programme: from Sailing, to Archery, Horse Riding and Golf. Every pupil has a talent and such experiences ensure that we are able to discover that talent and ultimately develop the most important things, which are confidence and self-esteem.

The School offers academic scholarships and also bursaries for Choristers and candidates within the Academy Girls' Choir (both subject to voice trials).

The School operates a morning bus service calling in at villages from the Louth and Brigg areas.

Charitable status. St James' School Grimsby Ltd is a Registered Charity, number 1099060. It exists to provide education for boys and girls.

St John's School

47–49 Stock Road, Billericay, Essex CM12 0AR
Tel: 01277 623070
Fax: 01277 654288
email: registrar@stjohnsschool.net
website: www.stjohnsschool.net
Twitter: @StJBillericay
Facebook: /StJBillericay

Headmistress: **Mrs Fiona Armour**, BEd Hons

Age Range. 3–16.
Number in School. Day: 198 Boys, 150 Girls.
Fees per term (2016–2017). £1,690–£4,205.

From the moment a child enters St John's, whatever their age, they are treated as an individual. Our passion is to ensure that when a child leaves our school they have fully achieved their potential. Set in a beautiful setting across 8 acres of land overlooking Lake Meadows Park in Billericay, St John's is ideally located for public transport links and is only a five minute walk from Billericay train station.

Pupils in the Kindergarten benefit from having specialist teachers for Music, IT, Drama and PE. In the Junior School, pupils study verbal and non-verbal reasoning and have additional specialist teachers for subjects such as French, Spanish, Games, Art and Swimming. Senior School pupils follow a broad curriculum, which leads to GCSE courses commencing in Year 10. Subjects including PE, Drama and Statistics are offered alongside the more traditional subjects. Pupils make excellent progress throughout the school and GCSE pass rates are consistently high.

Sport is not only an integral part of our curriculum but also part of our extracurricular programme. Our Sport England standard Sports Hall hosts a wide range of activities including trampolining, cricket, table tennis, badminton, and basketball to name but a few. We have a proven track record

in field events with pupils participating at the ISA National events.

A wide range of extracurricular clubs and activities are offered including, karate, cookery, street dance, homework club, cheerleading, film club and gardening club. Pupils have the opportunity to participate in instrumental lessons, perform in the school orchestra and join the choir. In addition, performing arts, both musical and drama, are a pivotal part of our school, with fantastic success rates for our LAMDA examination entrants. A number of residential trips are offered each year both in the UK and in Europe. We also off an annual skiing trip for the pupils in the Senior School.

A child's education is one of the most important factors in their well-being and success. We instil all the virtues of politeness, integrity and consideration of others into our pupils, creating a magical atmosphere where learning, creativity and success is enjoyed by everyone. Although our academic success over the years has been exceptional, we are equally proud that we have educated thousands of children who are confident, successful and who genuinely make a positive contribution to society when they leave.

Means-tested scholarships are available for Year 7 places in the Senior School. For more information and to arrange a tour of the school, please contact Mrs Cox, Registrar on 01277 623070 or by email to registrar@stjohnsschool.net.

St Joseph's Convent School

59 Cambridge Park, Wanstead, London E11 2PR
Tel: 020 8989 4700
email: enquiries@stjosephsconventschool.co.uk

Chair of Governors: Sr Catherine Quane

Headteacher: **Ms Christine Glover**

Age Range. 3–11.
Number in School. 150 Day Girls.
Fees per term (2016–2017). £2,090.
Charitable status. Institute of Our Lady of Mercy is a Registered Charity, number 290544.

St Joseph's Park Hill School

Padiham Road, Burnley, Lancashire BB12 6TG
Tel: 01282 455622
email: office@parkhillschool.co.uk
website: www.parkhillschool.co.uk

Chair of Governors: Mrs Catherine McDermott

Head Teacher: **Mrs A Robinson**, BEd Hons

Age Range. 3–11 Co-educational.
Number of Pupils. 96.
Fees per term (2016–2017). £1,965.

St Joseph's was founded by the Sisters of Mercy in 1913 and has operated from its present site since 1957.

It is a small school with a warm, friendly atmosphere where the children are known personally by all the staff. We have a broad, enriched curriculum which provides many activities and opportunities, both sporting and musical. The children enjoy their learning experience and are encouraged to do their best, achieving excellent results.

The Catholic ethos permeates all areas of the school. Pupils learn to care for each other, and respect different cultures. We welcome children from all faiths.

The school has the benefit of extensive grounds and offers a morning and after-school service as well as a 3-week summer school.

Charitable status. St Joseph's School is owned by The Institute of our Lady of Mercy which is a Registered Charity, number 290544.

St Joseph's Preparatory School

Rookery Lane, Trent Vale, Stoke-on-Trent, Staffordshire ST4 5RF

Tel:	01782 417533
email:	enquiries@stjosephsprepschool.co.uk
website:	www.stjosephsprepschool.co.uk

Chair of Governors: Mr S Hulme

Head: **Mrs S D Hutchinson**, BEd

Age Range. 3–11 Co-educational.
Number of Pupils. 160 Day Pupils.
Fees per term (2016–2017). £2,330–£2,465.
Charitable status. The Congregation of Christian Brothers is a Registered Charity, number 254312.

St Joseph's School

St Stephen's Hill, Launceston, Cornwall PL15 8HN

Tel:	01566 772580
email:	registrar@stjosephscornwall.co.uk
website:	www.stjosephscornwall.co.uk

Head Teacher: **Mr Oliver Scott**

Deputy Head: Mrs Kathryn Macaulay
Junior Head: Mr Charles Gonella
Bursar: Mr Ian Barton
Registrar: Mrs Annette Goswell

Age Range. 3–16 Co-educational.
Number in School. 230.
Fees per term (2016–2017). £1,560–£4,420.

St Joseph's School, Launceston is an award-winning Independent Day School for boys and girls from 3–16.

St Joseph's has a truly unique atmosphere. The school's small size means that it is possible both to keep sight of strong family values, giving children the confidence necessary to succeed, and to allow staff and pupils to work happily together. Due to the high teacher-pupil ratio, St Joseph's is able to encourage each pupil to reach his or her full potential through positive encouragement and commendation.

In both the Junior and the Senior school, St Joseph's provides an excellent academic education for all, regardless of ability and background. Our individualised academic curriculum runs alongside a wide variety of extra-curricular activities that challenge, stimulate and inspire all pupils to unlock their potential in a safe and supportive environment. St Joseph's offers equal prospects to every individual and it is the positive response to the school's ethos that sees pupils rising to challenges both within the classroom and as highly valued members of the wider school community.

St Joseph's GCSE pupils achieve superb results. The benchmark for the percentage of pupils achieving 5 A*–C including Maths and English is outstanding: 100% of pupils achieving this in 2013, 92% in 2014 and 96% in 2015 – the first year both boys and girls took GCSEs at the school. 2016 saw 90% of pupils attain this level. This is a remarkable achievement as St Joseph's is a non-selective school, meaning there is no entrance exam and admission is possible at any time throughout a child's education. Fees are set at levels which offer tremendous value for money, particularly in light of what is on offer to all the pupils at the school and our excellent academic results.

National Honours have been gained in many areas including athletics, swimming and music. The senior chamber choir is a "flagship" choir for the South West, having appeared on both local and national television.

Academic and Sports Scholarships are offered from age 7+ and Music Scholarships from 11+. Bursaries are available and considered on an individual basis.

An extensive daily bus service (7 bus routes) allows pupils from a wide area of Devon and Cornwall to attend St Joseph's.

St Joseph's School offers a number of open events throughout the year for prospective parents. To arrange an individual visit please contact the Registrar. Further information can be found at www.stjosephscornwall.co.uk or by contacting the Registrar on 01566 772580, registrar@stjosephscornwall.co.uk.

Charitable status. St Joseph's School is a Registered Charity, number 289048.

St Joseph's School

33 Derby Road, Nottingham NG1 5AW

Tel:	0115 941 8356
email:	office@st-josephs.nottingham.sch.uk
website:	www.st-josephs.nottingham.sch.uk
Twitter:	@StJosephsNG1
Facebook:	/St-Josephs-Independent-School-and-Nursery

Head Teacher: **Mr A E Crawshaw**

Age Range. 1–11 years.
Number in School. 84 Boys, 59 Girls.
Fees per term (2016–2017). £2,576 (Main School Reception to Year 6). Nursery fees on application.

A co-educational day school providing the very highest standards to children of all abilities. Children receive individual attention in small classes. The curriculum is planned to encourage children to develop lively, enquiring minds with emphasis on literacy and numeracy. Music and Drama have a high profile in the school.

Sports include Football, Netball, Cricket, Rounders, Tag Rugby, Swimming, and Squash.

Extra-curricular activities include Karate, Archery, Dance, Speech and Drama, Chess, Piano, Drums, Violin, and Guitar.

It provides a happy and caring environment in which children can develop their full potential both socially and academically. The school is Roman Catholic but welcomes children of all faiths.

Charitable status. St Joseph's School Nottingham is a Registered Charity, number 1003916.

St Margaret's Preparatory School
Cognita Schools Group

Gosfield Hall Park, Gosfield, Halstead, Essex CO9 1SE

Tel:	01787 472134
Fax:	01787 478207
email:	admin@stmargaretsprep.com
website:	www.stmargaretsprep.com

Twitter: @StMargsPrep
Facebook: /StMargaretsPrep

Headmaster: **Mr Callum Douglas**

Age Range. 2–11.
Number of Pupils. Day: 95 Boys, 115 Girls.
Fees per term (2016–2017). £2,985–£3,585.

St Margaret's is an ISA accredited school which special-ises in the needs of children from 2 to 11 years.

Academically, St Margaret's provides excellence beyond the national standard expected, stretching each child to the best of their individual ability, but not at the expense of a full and varied childhood. Although we annually gain academic, music, art and sports scholarships to senior schools, the emphasis is on an all-round education, encompassing the academic needs, enriching aspects such as social integration and encouraging other interests of each individual.

Typically, a child at St Margaret's will have two after-noons a week of coached sport as well as a PE lesson, extra coaching sessions before school and at lunchtime for the keen and able, and numerous after-school clubs. These clubs encompass a whole range of activities including fencing, seasonal sports, speech and drama, golf, photography, choirs and ensembles, short tennis and music composition – the list goes on. They are regarded as an important and integral part of school, broadening their horizons. With a purpose-built ICT suite, art studio, music practice rooms, science lab and seven acres of grounds in a wonderful parkland setting, the children have every opportunity to excel in their chosen sphere or to experience the fun of a new challenge.

One of the school's specialities is music tuition. We offer individual lessons with 12 peripatetic music teachers on a vast range of instruments. Every child who learns an instru-ment is encouraged to join a choir or ensemble and the orchestra. Drama plays a big part too, and children partici-pate in numerous concerts and plays throughout the year. There are trips to galleries, concerts, museums, as well as taking part in festivals, competitions and local events.

Our extensive curriculum provides the children with the social confidence and academic ability to achieve their potential and to move on to their chosen senior schools as able and well-rounded individuals.

St Martin's Preparatory School

63 Bargate, Grimsby, N E Lincolnshire DN34 5AA
Tel: 01472 878907
email: secretary@stmartinsprep.co.uk
          headmaster@stmartinsprep.co.uk
website: www.stmartinsprep.co.uk

Headmaster: **Mr S Thompson**, BEd Hons

Age Range. 2–11.
Number in School. Day: 58 Boys, 64 Girls.
Fees per term (2016–2017). £1,740–£2,140.

St Martin's was founded in 1930. It aims to foster an interest in learning from an early age. A fully qualified and dedicated staff ensure that a high standard in Primary School subjects is attained throughout the school. French is taught from the age of 3 and Spanish from the age of 7. Children are taught in small classes and great attention is given to individual development. Specialist teaching is also available for children who need specific support or extension.

The purpose-built Early Years block is a modern building full of light and colour, which enhances the already excel-lent education provided by the main school.

Girls and boys are prepared for Common Entrance and the 11+ examination. The vast majority of children transfer to the local Grammar schools.

St Martin's is consistently ranked amongst the best per-forming schools in the country.

The school offers a range of clubs, including Yoga, Art, Football, Netball, Boules, Chess, Table Tennis, Computer and Drama. The school has an orchestra and two choirs. A happy and friendly atmosphere prevails throughout the school.

St Michael's School

Bryn, Llanelli, Carmarthenshire SA14 9TU
Tel: 01554 820325
Fax: 01554 821716
email: office@stmikes.co.uk
          bursar@stmikes.co.uk
website: www.stmikes.co.uk
Twitter: @StMikes
Facebook: @St-Michaels-School

Headteacher: **Alun J Millington**, MA Oxon, PGCE

Deputy Head: Kay Francis, BSc Hons, PGCE

Head of Prep School: Adrian Thomas

Age Range. 3–18.
Number in School. 383: 207 boys, 176 girls.
Fees per term (from January 2017). Tuition: Prepara-tory School £1,654–£2,686; Senior School £3,700–£4,042. Full Boarding: Years 7–10: £8,400 (twin), £9,300 (single); Years 11–13: £9,000 (twin), £9,900 (single). Weekly Board-ing: Years 7–10: £6,776 (twin), £7,480 (single); Years 11–13: £7,568 (twin), £8,184 (single). Sibling allowances available. International Students per annum (2016–2017): Twin room: Years 7–8 £20,400, Year 9 £22,500, Years 10–11 (GCSE) £22,500. Years 7–11 single room supplement £1,000. Sixth Form (A Level) £26,000 (single en-suite room).

St Michael's is very much in the pattern of the small well-disciplined grammar schools. The school has a traditional approach to learning, which does not mean it lives in the past, but places emphasis on the importance of hard work and homework in the school curriculum. The high academic standards of the school are reflected in the National League Tables. In 2013 the school was ranked 37th in The Times Top 100 Co-Educational Schools in the UK.

No school can build up such a strong reputation without a competitive, but well-disciplined atmosphere and a highly-qualified and dedicated staff. This is where we feel St Michael's is particularly fortunate.

In 2013 the school began an exciting new phase with the commissioning of two brand new developments. In addition to Park House, which is a handsome and historic mansion set in an acre of grounds in the village of Llangennech, our new, on-site, purpose-built, state-of-the-art, 31-bedroom boarding house, 'Ty Mawr', was commissioned. Both houses offer a high standard of comfort where every pupil feels safe, happy and protected. Pupils are accommodated in well-furnished and equipped, single en-suite or shared study-bedrooms. The houses provide spacious recreation rooms and pleasant grounds in which pupils may relax, play or watch TV. The Early Learning Centre for pupils aged between 3 and 7 also opened its doors for the first time in January 2013.

We have well-equipped computer laboratories where pupils have access to a computer each from 3 years of age.

Languages taught in the school are French, Spanish, Welsh and Chinese (Mandarin).

The school has an envied reputation for its academic achievement but is also proud of the wide range of traditional games and activities it offers. Pupils from Year 10 onwards pupils can also take part in The Duke of Edinburgh's Award scheme to Gold Award standard. We have a large choir and school orchestra and pupils may take music examinations at GCSE and A Level.

One of the main reasons behind the school's success is the thorough grounding that pupils receive in the 'basics' –English, Mathematics, ICT and Science in the school's Preparatory Department.

We have enjoyed outstanding sporting success over the last few years in netball, rugby, football, tennis, cricket and athletics.

Every pupil is encouraged to develop their full potential whether in academic work or in all the extracurricular activities on offer.

St Nicholas House School

Yarmouth Road, North Walsham, Norfolk NR28 9AT
Tel: 01692 403143
email: info@stnicholashouse.com
website: www.stnicholashouse.com
Twitter: @StNicksHouse
Facebook: @St-Nicholas-House-Prep-School-Nursery

Headmaster: **Mr M Castle**, BA, PGCE

Age Range. 2–11 co-educational.
Number of Pupils. 65.
Fees per term (2016–2017). £1,695. Lunch: £200 per term.

St Nicholas House School is a small caring happy environment where children are encouraged to try their best and provided with the opportunity to thrive.

In small classes children benefit from a wide and varied curriculum giving a solid grounding and foundation in English and Maths, in addition to science, history, geography, art, craft, RE and ICT. Subject specialists teach French, Music and Forest School from Reception to Year 6. In addition Peripatetic teachers offer a wide variety of musical instruments, speech and drama, dancing and singing.

Children are encouraged to try as many activities as possible through Clubs and after-school activities such as cross country, golf, pottery, Spanish and IT coding. Sport plays an important part in the curriculum and in a child's time in the school, they will have the opportunity to try football, hockey, swimming, netball, cricket, rounders and short tennis in addition to seasonal sports.

The school enjoys an excellent success rate in entrance examinations to Senior independent schools obtaining numerous academic, sporting and drama scholarships.

Please telephone for an appointment to come and see us at work and play.

Saint Nicholas School

Hillingdon House, Hobbs Cross Road, Old Harlow, Essex CM17 0NJ
Tel: 01279 429910
Fax: 01279 450224
email: office@saintnicholasschool.net
            admissions@saintnicholasschool.net

website: www.saintnicholasschool.net
Twitter: @SaintNicksSch
Facebook: /saintnicholasschoolharlow

Headmaster: **Mr D J Bown**, BA Hons, PGCE, MA, NPQH

Age Range. 2½–16.
Number in School. 375 Day Pupils: 200 Boys, 175 Girls.
Fees per term (2016–2017). Reception £3,070 to Year 11 £3,890. Pre-school fees £24 per session.

In 2014 Saint Nicholas School celebrated 75 years of excellence. Saint Nicholas is situated in a delightful rural location and combines a fresh and enthusiastic approach to learning with a firm belief in traditional values.

The academic record of the school is excellent, reflected in high pupil success rates in all competitive examinations. The dedicated team of staff involves itself closely with all aspects of pupils' educational progress and general development. High standards of formal teaching are coupled with positive encouragement for pupils to reason for themselves and develop a high degree of responsibility.

As part of the school's commitment to providing affordable, quality care to children in the community, Little Saints Pre-School opened its doors in September 2014 to children from 2½ years old. Recent building developments include magnificent junior and infant department buildings, theatre, science and technology centre, swimming pool and sports hall, and new on-site catering facilities opened in January 2015.

Main sports include hockey, netball, tennis, football, rugby, cricket, swimming, athletics and gymnastics. Optional extras include ballet, individual instrumental lessons, karate, performing arts and Spanish classes.

Charitable status. Saint Nicholas School (Harlow) Limited is a Registered Charity, number 310876. It exists to provide and promote educational enterprise by charitable means.

St Peter's School

52 Headlands, Kettering, Northamptonshire NN15 6DJ
Tel: 01536 512066
Fax: 01536 416469
email: st-petersschool@btconnect.com
website: www.st-peters.org.uk

Headmistress: **Mrs M Chapman**, MA Ed, BA Hons, PGCE

Age Range. 3–11.
Number in School. Day: 55 Boys, 60 Girls.
Fees per term (2016–2017). £2,195–£3,350.

Established in 1946, St Peter's is a small day school set in pleasant grounds on the outskirts of Kettering. It offers a sound education for boys and girls from the term of their third birthday to age 11. Pupils are thoroughly prepared for entry into their senior schools and a high rate of success in Entrance and Scholarship Examinations is regularly achieved. In addition to fulfilling the requirements of the National Curriculum the school emphasises the importance of Music, Art, Sport and Information Technology in its programme. French is introduced at Nursery.

St Peter's School is a lively, friendly school with a strong family atmosphere where children are encouraged to develop to the full their individual strengths and talents. It aims to promote, through Christian teaching, a respect for traditional values, a sense of responsibility and a concern for the needs of others.

Charitable status. St Peter's School is a Registered Charity, number 309914. It exists to maintain and manage a school for boys and girls in the town of Kettering.

St Philomena's Catholic School

Hadleigh Road, Frinton-on-Sea, Essex CO13 9HQ
Tel: 01255 674492
Fax: 01255 674459
email: generalenquiries@stphilomenas.com
website: www.stphilomenas.com

Co-educational Day School.

Chair of Governors: Mrs Josephine Geldard

Headteacher: **Mrs Barbara McKeown**, DipEd, CTC

Age Range. 4–11.
Number of Pupils. 99: 51 girls, 48 boys.
Fees per term (2016–2017). £1,945–£2,320.

St Philomena's is situated in a pleasant coastal area close to the beach. The school is dedicated to providing sound education based on Gospel values of the Whole Child within a Christian environment. Children flourish in the tangible family atmosphere throughout the school.

Very good attitudes to learning are promoted for the mixed ability intake. Pupils strive for high academic standards and have achieved a very good record in 11+ selection examinations for both the grammar schools in the maintained sector and secondary schools in the independent sector.

Staff are fully qualified, experienced and dedicated professionals who communicate well with parents. Very high standards in pupil behaviour are maintained – pupils are caring and courteous with each other and towards adults.

There is a wide range of extra-curricular activities including sports clubs, science club, Scrabble, chess, art, cycling proficiency and ICT. Tuition is offered for a wide range of musical instruments including, piano, violin, drums, guitar, flute, clarinet, trumpet and saxophone. Music lessons with a music specialist take place throughout the school and there are recorder lessons for whole classes. There are weekly swimming lessons and French lessons available for Key Stage 2. The school choirs and drama groups have achieved outstanding success in local and national competitions in recent years.

Emphasis is given to physical education. There are representative teams for football, hockey, cricket, rounders, netball, and cross country (numbers permitting). Tennis is taught to the senior children.

All children are encouraged to speak confidently and to express themselves clearly. All children from 7+ participate in an annual oral communication assessment adjudicated externally. Parents are invited to regular concerts, plays, class presentations and class assemblies.

Charitable status. St Philomena's Catholic School is a Registered Charity, number 298635. It exists to provide Roman Catholic children and those of other denominations with the opportunity to reach the highest possible standards in every area of school life.

St Piran's School, Hayle

14 Trelissick Road, Hayle, Cornwall TR27 4HY
Tel: 01736 752612
Fax: 01736 759446
email: admin@stpirans.net
website: www.stpiranshayle.net

Headteacher: **Mrs Carol A de Labat**, BEd Hons, CertEd

Age Range. 3–16.
Number of Pupils. 54.
Fees per term (2016–2017). £900–£2,300.

Established in 1988, St Piran's School is set in attractive and well-maintained premises which, at present, accommodate around seventy children, aged from three to sixteen. It is a friendly, well-ordered community with a positive ethos where pupils make good friendships with each other and relate well to staff. Pupils are treated with respect and valued equally. They have a clear sense of right and wrong. There is a good sense of community within the school and new pupils are quickly made to feel welcome. The school places a strong emphasis on good manners and politeness.

The curriculum is broad and balanced and helps to prepare the children for the next stage in their education. A wide variety of after school and lunchtime clubs provide additional activities and experiences for pupils of all ages. Educational visits to local places of interest and annual residential visits (for Year 5 and up) further enrich the curriculum.

From Years Five and Six there is greater emphasis on subjects being taught by specialists. Class size remains low, with the maximum class size being twelve. Well-qualified, conscientious and hard-working staff teach children in a supportive learning environment. Children are given the opportunity to explain their ideas and be involved in activities. There is a very well-equipped and effectively-organised computer suite, which ensures that the children are at the cutting edge of technology.

We offer our senior pupils all of the opportunities, including the Duke of Edinburgh's Award scheme, offered by larger secondary schools.

St Teresa's School

Aylesbury Road, Princes Risborough, Buckinghamshire HP27 0JW
Tel: 01844 345005
email: office@st-teresas.bucks.sch.uk
website: www.st-teresas.bucks.sch.uk

Headmaster: **Mr Simon Detre**, BA Hons QTS

Age Range. 3–11.
Number in School. 140.
Fees per term (2016–2017). £2,935 (first child), £2,755 (siblings).

St Teresa's is a Catholic prep school from which children successfully progress to the Buckinghamshire grammar schools and local independent senior schools. The size of the school is a huge advantage: everybody knows everybody and nobody is overlooked. Indeed, it is by getting to know the children well that we can help them to develop and celebrate their different gifts and abilities. Everybody has something at which they can excel – even if they have not yet discovered what it is.

Although a Catholic school, St Teresa's is open to those of all faiths and none: we are enriched by the diversity of the communities we serve.

The school is listed as the highest co-ed prep school in Buckinghamshire in The Sunday Times top 100 independent preparatory schools.

St Winefride's Convent School
Shrewsbury

Belmont, Shrewsbury, Shropshire SY1 1TE
Tel: 01743 369883
Fax: 01743 369883
email: st.winefrides@btconnect.com
website: www.stwinefrides.com

Headmistress: **Sister M Felicity**, BA Hons

Age Range. 4+–11. Nursery: 3+–4.
Number in School. Day: 83 Boys, 84 Girls.
Fees per term (from April 2016). £1,395–£1,470.

St Winifred's School

17–19 Winn Road, Portswood, Southampton SO17 1EJ
Tel: 023 8055 7352
email: office@stwinifreds.southampton.sch.uk
website: www.stwinifreds.southampton.sch.uk

Chairman of Board of Trustees: Mr John W Watts, MCIPS, MILT, AIGEM

Head Teacher: **Mr Michael Brogan**, BEd, CertEd, Cert Sp Needs

Age Range. 3–11 Co-educational.
Number of Pupils. 100.
Fees per term (2016–2017). £2,580 (Lunch £150).

St Winifred's is a small school, on a pleasant, urban road in central Southampton, close to the university. It exists to make *the most of Individual Talent – nurturing every child.* The school caters for children aged 4–11; the pre-school takes children from age three, including those receiving Nursery Education Funding. The school provides before and after care from 8.00 am until 6.00 pm.

The School aims to provide for the whole child through a varied curriculum, with a wide programme of study and opportunities to develop all aspects of every pupil's talents. The core subjects, English, Maths and Science, as well as the development of ICT skills, are at the centre of learning throughout the school. Pupils are encouraged and helped to develop a disciplined approach to personal study skills at all ages. Group and class activities help everyone to experience cooperative work and gain useful understanding of others skills and feelings.

Details of the curriculum can be found on our website. A structured academic program is covered by all age groups. This is delivered by specialist staff that enable every pupil to achieve their potential. Continuous assessment and tests prepare the upper school pupils for their entrance exams and for further achievement at secondary school.

The School provides regular feedback about pupils' progress at Parents' Evenings and through reports. Weekly newsletters are emailed to parents informing them of events pupils are involved in as well as activities happening within the school. Parents are encouraged to be involved in their children's education where ever possible.

The School is proud of its achievements in music, drama, games, swimming and dance. As well as our own two indoor hall spaces and playground, the school takes advantage of The Gregg School's sporting facilities. Weekly games, swimming and gym/dance sessions with qualified staff are provided, as well as a variety of after-school activities.

Upper school pupils gain valuable experience whilst preparing for Communication examinations. Each year many pupils achieve distinctions and merits but, most importantly, all gain much personal satisfaction and confidence that will help them in later life.

Further opportunities are provided, through extracurricular activities, to develop pupils' individual talents and personal strengths and interests. Monthly Achievement Assemblies celebrate individual and group interests in and out of school as well as focusing on pupils Endeavour and Courtesy within school. These are an opportunity for every individual to learn their own self-worth.

For taster days and further information, please contact the school secretary or visit our website.

Charitable status. The Gregg and St Winifred's Schools Trust is a Registered Charity, number 1089055.

St Wystan's School

High Street, Repton, Derbyshire DE65 6GE
Tel: 01283 703258
Fax: 01283 703258
email: head@stwystans.org.uk
website: www.stwystans.org.uk

Headmaster: **Mr P Soutar**, BEd Hons

Age Range. 2½–11.
Number in School. Day: Boys 56, Girls 53.
Fees per term (2016–2017). £2,655. Compulsory extras: Lunch £270.

St Wystan's is an independent day school for girls and boys aged 2½ to 11 years of age situated in the historic village of Repton, Derbyshire. We are only a short distance from Burton-on-Trent and the city of Derby. Nottingham and Uttoxeter are within 25 minutes of the school.

St Wystan's prides itself on a family atmosphere in which every child can grow in confidence and develop to his or her full potential as an individual. Great emphasis is placed on courtesy and good manners and a pastoral system, centred on the four School Houses, promotes a caring environment and develops teamwork and commitment.

Academic expectations are high, though the school serves a wide ability range and is non-selective. Single year classes with a maximum class size of 18 enable the children to receive individual attention and work at a pace appropriate to their ability. As a free-standing junior school, St Wystan's prepares pupils for a large number of senior schools and pupils have won a significant number of academic, sport and music scholarships.

The pre-school department provides a Nursery, headed by a fully qualified teacher and a reception class which both accept pupils on government subsidised "Early Years" places. The main school covers Key Stages 1 and 2 but is not restricted by the National Curriculum, offering a broad range of subjects and a blend of topic based teaching and specialist teaching in Music, PE and French.

St Wystan's enjoys an excellent reputation in music, sport and drama with pupils progressing to regional and national championships in football, swimming, cross country and athletics. Many pupils have instrumental tuition and there is a thriving school choir and orchestra, together with a broad range of over 35 extracurricular activities.

St Wystan's runs a very popular pre-school and after-school care facility. Children can be delivered to school from 7.30 am and looked after at school until 6.30 pm.

Scholarships are offered for 7+ entry to Year 3 and bursaries are available.

Free taster days, corporate and sibling discounts are available.

Charitable status. St Wystan's School (Repton) Limited is a Registered Charity, number 527181. It exists to provide a quality education for boys and girls.

Salesian College

119 Reading Road, Farnborough, Hampshire GU14 6PA

Tel:	01252 893000
Fax:	01252 893032
email:	office@salesiancollege.com
website:	www.salesiancollege.com

Headmaster: **Mr Gerard T Owens**, MA Hons, PGCE

Age Range. Boys 11–16 years; Co-educational Sixth Form.

Number in School. 650.

Fees per term (2016–2017). £3,696.

As a Catholic school in the Salesian tradition, the College provides a Home that welcomes; a Church where Gospel values are shared and lived out on a daily basis; a School which educates for Life and prepares for future success and realisation of individual potential; and a Playground where personal, social, moral, sporting and cultural enrichment, beyond the academic curriculum, takes place and where lasting friendships are formed. Therefore, the formation of character and the development of social conscience are at the heart of our mission.

Salesian College forms well-educated, happy and well-rounded, confident young men and women; good Christians; honest citizens who are comfortable with themselves and those around them. Students are decent, courteous, selfless people; well equipped to take their place in and make a significant contribution to society.

Staff are caring and provide an excellent all round education. Salesian has outstanding levels of academic, cultural, spiritual and physical achievement, exemplary student behaviour and a caring ethos. We are a happy and highly successful school.

Although selective, we admit students of a wide range and believe in the pursuit of excellence for all. Salesian College recognises the individual gifts and needs of all of its students as unique creations of God. As such it caters excellently for all levels of ability, providing stretch for the most able and support for those with additional learning needs.

Excellent relationships between staff and students, and the students themselves, are a key feature of the College which seeks at all times to provide a holistic approach to the education and formation of those entrusted to our care.

The recent ISI Inspection report rated Salesian College as excellent in all areas, stating that *"The excellence of academic achievement owes much to the excellence of the curriculum and the teaching. Pupils find the collaborative approach of the teaching staff very helpful and supportive. Teachers know their pupils extremely well; they plan their lessons carefully to include a variety of approaches which succeed in engaging pupils' interest and, in almost all cases, in enabling them to maintain strong progress".*

The school has its own chapel, chaplaincy and resident chaplain.

Prospective parents are always welcome to make an appointment to visit the College while in session. Please see our website for up-to-date details.

Charitable status. Salesian College Farnborough Limited is a Registered Charity, number 1130166. It exists to provide education in North East Hampshire and neighbouring counties.

Salterford House School

Salterford Lane, Calverton, Nottinghamshire NG14 6NZ

Tel:	0115 965 2127
email:	office@salterfordhouseschool.co.uk
website:	www.salterfordhouseschool.co.uk

Principal: **Mrs Marlene Venables**

Age Range. 3–11.

Number in School. Main School 71: 35 Boys, 36 Girls. Kindergarten and Pre-Prep 21: 12 Boys, 9 Girls.

Fees per term (2016–2017). £2,440–£2,470.

Salterford House is situated in rural Nottinghamshire, in a 4.5 acre woodland setting, and aims to provide a happy, family atmosphere with small classes, in order to equip children academically and socially to cope with the demands of any type of education which might follow.

Although the school is mainly Church of England, all faiths are accepted. 75% of pupils go on to senior independent schools such as Nottingham Boys' High School, Nottingham Girls' High School, Trent College and Hollygirt.

Sports include Cricket, Tennis, Swimming, Rounders, Rugby, Lacrosse, Netball, Climbing, Football, Hockey, Golf and Skiing.

The school produces 3 concerts a year and there is a recorder Group and Choir. Individual tuition in Speech and Drama, Piano, Flute, Clarinet, Guitar, Violin and Percussion is available.

Dance lessons including Ballet and Jazz/Street Dance are available.

All classrooms are equipped with computers.

Staff are easily available for discussion. Regular contact is maintained with parents via Parents Evening and newsletters.

Sancton Wood School

1–2 St Paul's Road, Cambridge CB1 2EZ

Tel:	01223 471703
email:	office@sanctonwood.co.uk
website:	www.sanctonwood.co.uk
Twitter:	@SanctonWood
Facebook:	/SanctonWood

Headmaster: **Mr Richard Settle**, BA Hons, PGCE

Age Range. 1–16 Co-educational.

Number of Pupils. 250.

Fees per term (2016–2017). £3,175–£4,135.

Sancton Wood is a school where every child finds their niche. Our small, supportive and close-knit community is often likened to a family – a kind, tolerant, school where everyone can find their place and be valued.

Our class sizes are similarly small at just 16 pupils, creating fabulous learning environments, where our teachers have time for individual pupils, where they feel comfortable airing their ideas, where imaginations soar.

Our exam results are excellent by any measure. In recent years they have been second to none in some league tables. But the school is not just about exam results; art, music, sport and a wealth of other activities are all important aspects of life here, and play their part in making well-rounded students with their lives in balance.

Sancton Wood School is part of the Minerva Education group which owns a number of private schools in London, East and South East England. Through Minerva's "Inspiring Learning" programme, we seek to share best practice and ensure the continuing improvement in every child's education.

Scarisbrick Hall School & College

Southport Road, Ormskirk, Lancashire L40 9RQ

Tel: 01704 841151
email: enquiries@scarisbrickhallschool.co.uk
website: www.scarisbrickhallschool.co.uk

Headmaster: Mr Jeff Shaw

Associate Deans: Mr G Norbury, Mrs A O'Connor, Mrs C Seddon, Mrs C Winstanley
Head of Upper First School: Mr S Meredith
Head of Lower First School and Early Years: Mrs A Evans
Nursery Manager: Ms E Fortune-Price

Age Range. 0–18.
Number of Pupils. 600.
Fees per term (2016–2017). Reception £2,175, Years 1–2 £2,175, Years 3–4 £2,420, Years 5–6 £2,435, Years 7–8 £3,130, Years 9–11 £3,450, Years 12–13 (Sixth Form) £3,450.

The essential elements of Scarisbrick Hall School are: the daily efforts of staff to provide an ambience where spiritual and cultural gifts can develop, the quality of teaching in the classroom, and the commitment of staff to extra-curricular activities.

The school follows the guidelines of the National Curriculum, but enhances these through an impressive selection of options to present a breadth and depth for all the pupils. The aim is to provide equal opportunities for all and to cater for the needs of the individual.

Throughout the school the size of classes is restricted to approximately 21 so that each pupil may receive close attention and be treated as an individual, encouraged to develop his/her abilities to the full in a friendly, caring environment.

High standards are set and expected from the pupils, with the emphasis on self-discipline. The school rules have been compiled from principles which are necessary for good order. The utmost importance is attached to the cultivation of good manners and consideration for others.

The Headmaster and staff consider the school as a partner with parents in the education of their children.

Shapwick School

Shapwick Manor, Shapwick, Nr Bridgwater, Somerset TA7 9NJ

Tel: 01278 210384
Fax: 01278 210111
email: office@shapwickschool.com
            prep@shapwickschool.com
website: www.shapwickschool.com

Principal: Mr Adrian Wylie, BEd, PG Dip, NPQH
Headteacher: Mrs Hellen Lush

Age Range. 8–18.
Number in School. Boarders: 73 boys, 32 girls; Day: 37 boys, 13 girls.
Fees per term (2016–2017). Boarders £8,086–£9,286, Day £6,173–£6,462.

Shapwick is a specialist school for boys and girls whose education would otherwise be impaired by a specific learning difficulty (SpLD). The School provides a caring and supportive atmosphere, staffed by specialist teachers across a wide curriculum offering the structured help needed by students who have dyslexia, dyscalculia, dyspraxia and associated needs. Students take up to 8 GCSE subjects and the aim is to teach to their strengths whilst their weaknesses are being overcome and their confidence grows. Supplementary courses, such as Study Skills, Keyboard Skills, and careers advice are also undertaken. The School has a full range of specialist classrooms, including three laboratories, computing rooms, design centre, art rooms, library, sports hall, recreation room and games field. Students are involved in a wide range of extracurricular activities, the Duke of Edinburgh's Award and games fixtures, to complement the formal curriculum.

Prospective entrants need a recent Educational Psychologist's report diagnosing a specific learning difficulty together with a current school report followed up by a visit to Shapwick School.

Sherborne House School
GEMS Education

39 Lakewood Road, Chandler's Ford, Hants SO53 1EU

Tel: 023 8025 2440
email: info@sherbornehouse.co.uk
website: www.sherbornehouse.co.uk

Head: Mrs Heather Hopson-Hill, BEd Hons

Age Range. 2¾–11 Co-educational.
Number of Pupils. 254 (all day pupils).
Fees per term (2016–2017). £2,620–£3,055 including lunches. Nursery Grants (vouchers and salary sacrifice schemes) available for 3–4 year olds.

Sherborne House School, founded in 1933, takes children from Chandler's Ford, Winchester, Romsey, Southampton and the surrounding villages.

Sherborne House occupies an attractive four-acre site within the Hiltingbury area of Chandler's Ford. Boys and girls between 2¾ and 11 years of age are admitted through informal assessment. Scholarships in academic subjects, art, sport and music are available.

We have an enviable reputation for excellent Common Entrance and SATs results and regularly secure scholarships to established senior schools. Our outstanding results are achieved as a result of highly qualified staff, small classes and specialist learning support. Our broad curriculum emphasises literacy, numeracy and science but not at the expense of other subjects. Performing Arts is a particular strength of the school, with all children being encouraged to perform in both musical and dramatic activities, with additional peripatetic lessons are offered on a wide range of instruments. Art and CDT are taught in a specialist craft facility and all classrooms have interactive whiteboards to support work undertaken in the IT suite. A wide variety of sports is offered, including soccer, rugby, cricket, netball, hockey, short tennis, basketball and volleyball and the school has an extensive fixtures programme. French is offered from Pre-School and Spanish is added to the curriculum in the upper school. Sherborne House also provides a strong Learning Support network for those with special needs and individual programmes are drawn up and delivered by our SENCO in collaboration with the appropriate teaching staff. School trips and workshops and specialists curriculum days are arranged for all children as are residential visits for Key Stage 2 pupils. A wide range of after-school activities and clubs is also available.

At Sherborne House we believe that a child's self-esteem is paramount. We expect children to work and play and we take pride in our multi-sensory teaching methods, high but realistic expectations and our broad, engaging curriculum to accelerate our pupils' learning. The pastoral care at Sherborne House is outstanding and the pupils are confident, disciplined, purposeful and happy.

School hours: The school day runs from 8.30 am to 3.45 pm (Reception) and 4.00 pm (pre-prep and prep). Additional supervised care is available from 7.30 am until 6.00 pm.

We are always delighted to show prospective parents around the school and have regular Open Days.

Sherborne International

Newell Grange, Sherborne, Dorset DT9 4EZ
Tel: 01935 814743
Fax: 01935 816863
email: reception@sherborne-international.org
website: www.sherborne-international.org

Principal: **Mr Tim Waters**, MA MSc Oxon

Age Range. Co-educational 11–17 (Boarding 11–17).
Number in School. 160 boarders: 80 boys, 80 girls.
Fees per term (2016–2017). £10,350 Years 7 & 8, £13,067 Years 9, 10 and 11, £14,123 1 Year I/GCSE.

Sherborne International, formerly the International College was set up by Sherborne School in 1977. It has grown to become a separate institution and is now separately recognised by the Department for Education and the Independent Schools Association.

The School aims to be the best starting point for children from non-English speaking, non-British educational backgrounds who wish to join the British educational system. Students normally stay at the School for one academic year. During this time the School aims to equip each student to take his or her place successfully at a traditional British independent boarding school.

While the full academic curriculum is provided, all teachers of all subjects at Sherborne International are trained or qualified in teaching English as a foreign language. Each student is prepared for any appropriate public examinations, for example GCSEs and IGCSEs, or Cambridge English language examinations. Each year the group taking GCSEs records very impressive results – in 2016, nearly 82% of the entries achieved A*–C grades.

The School has no entry requirements and no entry examinations for most courses. All students are non-native speakers of English, and some are complete beginners in English. However, the popular one-year GCSE/IGCSE course requires all applicants to have at least lower-intermediate standard English (IELTS 4+) or B2.

The School is housed in a purpose-built campus close to the centre of Sherborne. Its boarding houses are nearby. Students are taught in classes of up to eight students.

The School is also a member of the Boarding Schools Association, the European Council of International Schools and the British Association of International Schools with International Students (BAISIS) and is also accredited by the British Council.

Charitable status. Sherborne International is owned by Sherborne School, which is a Registered Charity, number 1081228. It exists to provide education to school-aged children.

Sherfield School

Sherfield-on-Loddon, Hook, Hampshire RG27 0HT
Tel: 01256 884800
email: info@sherfieldschool.co.uk
website: www.sherfieldschool.co.uk
Facebook: /SherfieldSchoolHampshire

Head Master: **Mr R G Jaine**, MA, FRGS

Age Range. 3 months – 18 years Co-educational.
Number in School. 425.
Fees per term (2016–2017). Day: £3,105–£5,189; Boarding: £9,166.

Based in the heart of the leafy Hampshire countryside and situated in a 19th century manor house, the school offers a first-class education for pupils aged from 3 months to 18 years, with wrap-around care from 7.30 am to 6.00 pm for 48 weeks of the year. Provision includes a range of holiday activities so that pupils can continue to extend and develop their talents. Pupils may be full or flexi boarders from Year 5.

Teaching methods are a blend of the traditional and the very best of new ideas, including interactive inquiry-based learning, whilst classroom sizes are never more than 15 pupils, providing a focused and quality educational experience. Along with the core subjects for all pupils, there are a range of options to meet the needs of each individual student. This flexible approach allows some students to take examinations early if appropriate. Our sixth form offers a range of subject choices which are studied in Years 12 and 13.

Sherfield offers sporting programmes in Equestrianism, Flying, Golf, Gymnastics, Ice Skating, Performing Arts and Tennis. Our sports partnerships are with locally-based, nationally-recognised organisations who work with us in order to provide a good balance of academic studies combined with specialist training. Sherfield's students compete at the very highest of levels, both nationally and at county level.

As part of the school's commitment to individual achievement and success, it offers outstanding opportunities for talented individuals. Scholarships are offered in sports, music, arts and academic excellence for pupils at Year 7 and upwards.

Sherfield prides itself in all aspects of academic and sporting life, providing a well-rounded experience for all of our children, preparing them well for future endeavours and ambitions.

Sherrardswood School

Lockleys, Welwyn, Hertfordshire AL6 0BJ
Tel: 01438 714282
Fax: 01438 840616
email: office@sherrardswood.co.uk
website: www.sherrardswood.co.uk

Headmaster: **Dr Markus Bernhardt**

Head of Prep: Mrs Claire Armitage
Head of Senior: Mrs Anna Wright

Age Range. 2–18.
Number in School. Day: 172 Boys, 146 Girls.
Fees per term (2016–2017). £3,200–£4,970.

Sherrardswood, founded in 1928, is a co-educational day school for pupils aged 2–18. The School is set in 28 acres of attractive parkland two miles north of Welwyn Garden City. The Junior Department is housed in a fine 18th century building whilst the Senior Department occupies a purpose-built facility. Games fields, tennis courts and woodlands trail are available on the Lockleys site for both departments.

Entry to the school is by interview or by interview and examination according to age. A broad curriculum is offered to GCSE level and a wide range of A Level subjects is available. A range of sport and extracurricular opportunities is available, both within the school day and out of school hours.

The recent ISI inspection confirmed that Sherrardswood is achieving its aims and that the quality of education and pastoral care is outstanding.

Charitable status. Sherrardswood School is a Registered Charity, number 311070. It exists solely to provide independent education for boys and girls aged 2–18.

Shoreham College

St Julian's Lane, Shoreham-by-Sea, West Sussex BN43 6YW

Tel: 01273 592681
Fax: 01273 591673
email: info@shorehamcollege.co.uk
website: www.shorehamcollege.co.uk
Twitter: @ShorehamCollege
Facebook: @shorehamcollege

Headmaster: **Richard Taylor-West**, BA King's College London, AKC, MA Sussex, PGCE

Age Range. 3–16.
Number in School. 256 Day Boys, 136 Day Girls.
Fees per term (2016–2017). £2,950–£4,775.

Shoreham College is a school that cares – it values its children as individuals, knows them well, and ensures that they feel safe, secure and happy. Within a warm friendly environment it instils traditional values of good manners and courtesy, and teaches the children to respect themselves, their peers and their community.

Teachers encourage pupils to enjoy being children, which allows them to grow. They nurture, guide, support and inspire them to develop academically, emotionally, and spiritually and are rewarded by seeing them grow into confident young adults, ready to take on the challenges of life.

Adopting a broadly non-selective approach means that the College is committed to providing a first-class all-round education to children of varied ability, ensuring that every child can achieve their potential. Ambitious for them, we ensure that they are appropriately challenged: the gifted and talented extended and children with learning differences given what they need to thrive.

We look forward to welcoming you.

Charitable status. Shoreham College (The Kennedy Independent School Trust Limited) is a Registered Charity, number 307045. It exists to provide high-quality education for boys and girls.

Slindon College

Slindon, Arundel, West Sussex BN18 0RH

Tel: 01243 814320
Fax: 01243 814702
email: registrar@slindoncollege.co.uk
website: www.slindoncollege.co.uk

Headmaster: **Mr David Quick**

Age Range. 8–18.
Number in School. 20 Boarders, 60 Day Boys.
Fees per term (2016–2017). Boarders £10,140, Day Boys £6,980.

A small school for up to 100 boys whose classes have a maximum of 12 pupils. The National Curriculum is followed where appropriate and in Years 7–9 a broad-based, balanced curriculum is provided. GCSE courses include graphics, photography, art, textiles, and design technology – all practical based and "hands-on". BTEC Food Skills & Horticulture also offered. The excellent Learning Support Department helps boys with specific learning difficulties, including dyslexia and ADD/ADHD.

A wide range of extracurricular activities is offered, including car mechanics, farm club and drama.

The school is non-denominational but has firm links with the local Anglican church.

Some bursaries are available and discount is available for Service families and second sons.

Charitable status. Slindon College is a Registered Charity, number 1028125. It aims to provide for the academic, social and personal development of each boy in a caring and purposeful environment.

Snaresbrook Preparatory School

75 Woodford Road, South Woodford, London E18 2EA

Tel: 020 8989 2394
email: office@snaresbrookprep.org
website: www.snaresbrookprep.org
Twitter: @SnaresbrookPrep
Facebook: /SnaresbrookPrep
LinkedIn: /snaresbrook-prep-school-ltd

Head: **Mr Christopher M Curl**, MA, BEd

Age Range. 3½–11.
Number in School. 165.
Fees per term (2016–2017). £2,761–£3,693.

Snaresbrook Preparatory School is a vibrant independent day school for boys and girls aged from 3½ to 11 years. Founded in the 1930s, the school occupies a substantial Victorian building, once a large private family home – something that contributes to the strong community spirit within the school. We aim to cultivate an intimate, caring family atmosphere in which children feel secure and valued. Most children join the school at age 3½ and stay with us until they reach 11 when they leave for their senior schools.

We provide a rounded education covering every aspect of your child's early development. The curriculum is designed to prepare pupils for entrance and scholarship examinations to senior independent and grammar schools. The curriculum includes Mathematics, English, Science, Current Affairs, ICT, Art, DT, Music, Drama, French, PE/Games and PSHE. Latin and Swimming are introduced in the Juniors. Year 6 undertake the Adventure Service Challenge in preparation for The Duke of Edinburgh's Award undertaken at senior school.

At age 11, we find that Snaresbrook children are confident, cheerful and courteous, with a good sense of community and a readiness to care for each other and the world around them. They have learned how to work in the ways that suit them best, are receptive to teaching and are well prepared for the next stage of their education and development.

We see ourselves as joint trustees, with parents, of the young lives in our care, bearing equal responsibility for their happiness, well being and development.

Steephill School

off Castle Hill, Fawkham, Longfield, Kent DA3 7BG
Tel: 01474 702107
email: secretary@steephill.co.uk
website: www.steephill.co.uk
Twitter: @Steephillonline
Facebook: /Steephill-School

Head Teacher: **Mrs Caroline Birtwell**, BSc, MBA, PGCE

Age Range. 3–11 co-educational.
Number of Pupils. 120.
Fees per term (2016–2017). £2,945. Pre-School Fees are pro rata.

Steephill School is a very successful School based on its academic, sporting and musical achievements. In 2014 it had 87% entry into selective schools, won many awards at music festivals and had numerous successes at inter-school sports. In its 2013 ISI inspection report the school was given an "excellent" rating in Pastoral Care, Curriculum, Extra-Curriculum and the Spiritual, Moral, Social and Cultural Development of pupils.

The School believes in high-quality teaching within a disciplined but relaxed atmosphere. The School holds traditional values and beliefs; working with and supporting each other is an important part of the ethos. There are close links with the church opposite the School. Four services per year are held there and the Rector takes a fortnightly assembly. The setting is very rural despite being only a few minutes' drive from the M2 and 5 miles from the M20 and M25. The School enjoys beautiful views of the countryside with very little traffic nearby.

The classes are a maximum of 16 and with only 120 pupils in the School, there is a close liaison between all members of the school community: children, staff, family members and governors. Parents are welcomed into the School and work closely with the teachers. There is regular feedback to parents on children's progress. Parents are also active in Friends of Steephill School, the Parents Association, to provide social and fundraising activities.

The children join the School aged 3 in the Pre-School and they leave at age 11. The curriculum is designed to support all abilities to achieve academically and in all the broader aspects of education such as drama, the arts and sports. Information Technology has been developed well over the last few years and is being continually updated.

There is a large selection of extracurricular activities at lunchtime and after school. Our Gardening Club is one of the more popular together with the choir, instruction on musical instruments, dance and football. We are very fortunate to have large grounds with a superb sports field, despite being a small school.

There is a care facility both before and after school so we are open from 7.00 am to 5.30 pm. The School is also very proud of the lunches. All the food is sourced from local shops: butcher, baker and greengrocer. The meals are carefully balanced and freshly made.

Charitable status. Steephill School is a Registered Charity, number 803152.

Stoke College

Stoke-by-Clare, Sudbury, Suffolk CO10 8JE
Tel: 01787 278141
Fax: 01787 277904
email: office@stokecollege.co.uk
website: www.stokecollege.co.uk

Headmaster: **Mr Frank Thompson**, MA, MPhil, NPQH

Age Range. 3–16+ Co-educational.
Number in School. Total 230: 131 Boys, 99 Girls. Boarders: 5 Boys, 1 Girl.
Fees per term (2016–2017). Day: £1,945–£4,752. Weekly Boarding: £6,609–£7,688.

Stoke College provides a broad, balanced and relevant curriculum up to GCSE. Weekly boarders or day pupils enjoy a caring environment in an idyllic rural situation with small classes yielding excellent results in public examinations. The College has a strong tradition in athletics and cross country and in Music and Drama. The school benefits from a new Sports/Assembly Hall, Junior School Teaching Block, Technology Rooms, a Performing Arts Centre, a swimming pool, hard tennis courts and a Nursery Department. The College aims to develop the individual's strengths and to produce a well rounded young adult to take his or her place in society.

Charitable status. Stoke College is a Registered Charity, number 310487. It is devoted to providing a full and relevant education to its pupils.

Stratford Preparatory School

Church House, Old Town, Stratford-upon-Avon, Warwickshire CV37 6BG
Tel: 01789 297993
Fax: 01789 263993
email: secretary@stratfordprep.co.uk
website: www.stratfordprep.co.uk
Facebook: @stratfordprep

Motto: *Lux et Scientia*

Principal: **Mrs C Quinn**, MBA, BEd Hons

Headmaster: Mr Neil Musk, MA, BA Hons, PGCE

Age Range. Preparatory School 4–11 years. Montessori Nursery School 2–4 years.
Number in School. Main School: 46 Boys, 52 Girls; Nursery School: 4 Boys, 8 Girls.
Fees per term (2016–2017). Junior forms £3,550; Infant forms £3,260; Reception £3,050; Nursery School: £2,200 (full-time), £1,150 (5 mornings). Compulsory extras: Lunch £145.

Stratford Preparatory School is situated in the heart of the historic town of Stratford-upon-Avon. The Preparatory school opened in September 1989 and has developed around a large town house. An additional detached house within the school's grounds provides accommodation for the Reception and Nursery children, a gymnasium, a science room and design and technology room.

The school was judged 'Outstanding' in all areas in its 2011 ISI Inspection.

The Nursery implements the Montessori philosophy of learning which encourages a structured learning environment. French and ballet are taught from the age of 2 years.

The main school offers a broad balanced learning plan adapted to the individual needs of the children using traditional teaching methods and with specific reference to the National Curriculum. All children are entered for the 11+ and independent school entrance examinations.

The school offers a high level of pastoral care and attention to personal development.

Physical education activities include: sailing, swimming, football, cricket, tennis, netball, rounders, ballet and athletics.

There are opportunities for the children to learn a variety of musical instruments. The school has two choirs and an orchestra.

Reduction in fees is offered for families with two or more children in the School.

The Headmaster is pleased to provide further details and meet prospective parents.

Study School

57 Thetford Road, New Malden, Surrey KT3 5DP
Tel: 020 8942 0754
Fax: 020 8942 0754
email: info@thestudyschool.co.uk
website: www.thestudyschool.co.uk

Headmistress: **Mrs Donna Brackstone-Drake**, BA Hons, PGCE, NPQH, MBA

Age Range. Rising 3–11 Co-educational.
Number in School. Day: 71 Boys, 72 Girls.
Fees per term (2016–2017). Nursery (mornings only) £1,565, Reception & Year 1 £3,190, Years 2–6 £3,645. Additional Nursery afternoon sessions available each day of the week: £252 per afternoon per term. All fees include a cooked school lunch. The school belongs to the Early Years Funding Scheme for 3 and 4 year olds.

Since 1923 we have successfully given our children a firm foundation in reading, writing and number skills, whilst also teaching French, Spanish, Music, Art and Games. Science, Geography, History, Design and Technology and ICT play an important part in the curriculum, with interactive whiteboards in every classroom and a full set of iPads and laptops which augment the curriculum.

Small classes allow us to stretch the most able pupils, whilst giving all our children individual attention.

Popular After School Clubs include Football, Art, Computer Coding, Drama, Dance, Science, Chess and Cookery. Individual instrumental music tuition is also available. We have Before School Care from 7.45 am and After School Care until 6.15 pm. All classes go on a school trip once a term and Years Four, Five and Six attend residential activity and field study courses and language trips abroad.

We provide a caring and stimulating atmosphere in which our children thrive. After Year Six they leave us to enter such schools at Kingston Grammar School, Wallington Boys' School, Non-Such Girls' School, Hampton School, the High Schools at Wimbledon, Sutton, Putney and Surbiton and both Tiffin Schools.

Please visit our website: www.thestudyschool.co.uk.

The Swaminarayan School

260 Brentfield Road, Neasden, London NW10 8HE
Tel: 020 8965 8381
Fax: 020 8961 4042
email: admin@tssuk.org
website: www.swaminarayan.brent.sch.uk

Chairman of Governors: Mr Piyush Amin

Headteacher, Senior School: **Mr Nilesh Manani**, BSc Hons, FRSA, PGCE

Headteacher, Prep School: Mr Umesh Raja, BSc, PGCE, NLP Masters, NPQH

Age Range. 2½–18.
Number of Pupils. 458: 258 boys, 200 girls.
Fees per term (2016–2017). £3,219–£4,310.

The Swaminarayan School was founded in 1991 by His Holiness Shree Pramukh Swami Maharaj to provide education along the lines of independent British schools, whilst reinforcing Hindu culture and tradition. It is a non-profit making, co-educational school for children aged two and a half to eighteen years.

The school admitted its first eighty or so Prep School pupils in September 1992 and the Senior School took its first intake the following September. Now there are just under 500 pupils in the school and already students from the school have gained admission to Cambridge, Oxford, Imperial, Warwick, UCL, LSE and King's.

Since those early days excellent progress has been made in all areas. The most striking aspect that always attracts comment from visitors is the purposeful atmosphere, both in classrooms and throughout the school. Teachers are able to help pupils achieve their full potential because of the generous staffing ratio, excellent behaviour of pupils and commitment from parents.

Resources and premises have also improved beyond recognition with modern libraries and computer rooms for each school. Former students from those early days dropping in to meet their teachers are amazed by the transformation!

On the curriculum front, the school has taken up the most desirable elements of the National Curriculum while developing the best practices of independent education. The cultural subjects unique to the school give it a special dimension – students have lessons in the Indian Performing Arts up to Year 8 and all students whose mother tongue is Gujarati study it up GCSE and all study Religious Education in Hinduism up to GCSE level.

In addition to their timetabled LAMDA lessons, PE lessons and club afternoons, pupils are involved in a range of extracurricular activities such as public speaking, sports, drama, dance and much more. An extensive programme of instrumental lessons, both Indian and European, is also on offer to all pupils. The school arranges regular day trips to museums, parks and other places of educational interest. The Duke of Edinburgh's Award scheme and residential outings are also a feature of the school. Whilst continuing to deliver a value based, broad and balanced curriculum, the school excels academically. Each year its excellent GCSE and A Level results put it at the top of Brent Performance tables. In The Daily Telegraph list of top independent schools, TSS has been consistently placed amongst the top ten performing schools in the country. Twenty years of vision, investment and hard work from trustees and governors, teaching and non-teaching staff as well as commitment from parents and pupils have made this a school to be proud of. The next ten years will see the school reaching even greater heights.

Charitable status. The Akshar Educational Trust is a Registered Charity, number 1023731.

Sylvia Young Theatre School

1 Nutford Place, London W1H 5YZ
Tel: 020 7258 2330
email: info@syts.co.uk
website: www.syts.co.uk

Principal: Mrs Sylvia Young OBE

Headteacher: **Ms Frances Chave**, BSc, PGCE, NPQH

Age Range. 10–16.
Number in School. Day: 78 Boys, 181 Girls. Weekly boarding is available with host families at an additional cost.
Fees per term (2016–2017). Key Stage 2 & 3 (Years 6, 7, 8 & 9): £4,500; Key Stage 4 (Years 10 & 11): £4,600.

The School has a junior department (Year 6 only) and a secondary department (Years 7–11). We aim to provide an appropriately balanced academic and vocational experience for our students. We are proud of the caring and well disciplined environment that prevails and promotes a very positive climate of individual success.

Academic subjects are delivered by highly qualified staff to the end of Key Stage 4.

GCSE Examination subjects include English, English Literature, Mathematics, Double or Triple Science, Art, Drama, Music, Media Studies, Spanish and History.

Theatrical training is given by experienced professional teachers. Pupils are prepared for examinations in Speech and Drama – LAMDA (London Academy of Music and Dramatic Art). Entry is by audition with academic ability assessed.

A vibrant array of extra-curricular activities in academic, sporting and creative subjects, coupled with our small size, enables pupils to have a high degree of participation. We recognise that success in life requires more than grades: maturity as well as social and cultural skills are also critically important. With our multi-cultural intake and strong Christian values, Thames provides a safe and inspiring environment for teenagers to become well-rounded individuals of integrity with depth of character

Our parents value the excellent communication between home and school and our competitive all-inclusive fees. A small number of scholarship awards are available annually for pupils talented in art, music, performing arts, sport or an academic area.

Situated only 5 minutes' walk from Clapham Junction station, our pupils travel to us from a wide area. A journey time of only 30 minutes covers a significant part of north and south London and the home counties.

ISI Inspection Report, March 2015:

"Behaviour is excellent and pupils feel safe, secure, valued and well supported."

"Performance across the subject range at GCSE is markedly higher than that predicted from their prior attainment."

"Almost all pupils achieve places at their first choice of schools or colleges for post-16 education, some achieving scholarships at highly competitive independent schools."

"Pupils with dyslexia make significantly greater progress, achieving on average nearly a grade higher than the average for pupils with similar abilities."

The best way to find out if our school is suitable for your child is to see for yourself what we have to offer at one of our Open Days. Alternatively please do phone 020 72283933 to make an individual appointment to see the school, especially if it is for immediate entry.

Fees per term (2016–2017). £4,720.

Charitable status. Thames Christian College Ltd is a Registered Charity, number 1081666.

Thames Christian College

Wye Street, London SW11 2HB
Tel: 020 7228 3933
Fax: 020 7924 1112
email: info@thameschristiancollege.org.uk
website: www.thameschristiancollege.org.uk

Head: **Dr Stephen Holsgrove**, PhD

Age Range. 11–16 Co-educational.
Number of Pupils. 124.

We are a small independent secondary school in London recognised for our excellent academic achievement, celebration of each individual pupil's abilities and our strong Christian ethos. Pupils excel in a wide range of subjects from the traditionally academic to the creative arts and technology. At Thames, we believe that every child is unique and has the potential to succeed. As children discover their strengths they grow in self-confidence. Confident children become enthusiastic learners who enjoy school and are keen to succeed.

As a result pupils perform very highly in their GCSE exams. in 2016 91% of pupils achieved 5 A*–C including English and Maths and 97% 5 A*–C grades. The percentage of grades attained at 93% A*–C is the best in the school's history and significantly above the national average. Pupils achieved over one grade higher than expected with one dyslexic pupil attaining an impressive 3.8 grades higher than their prediction tests indicated. Our achievements are recognised by the Good Schools Guide.

Thorpe Hall School

Wakering Road, Thorpe Bay, Essex SS1 3RD
Tel: 01702 582340
Fax: 01702 587070
email: sec@thorpehall.southend.sch.uk
website: www.thorpehall.southend.sch.uk

Headmaster: **A Hampton**, BA Hons, LTCL, MEd, NPQH

Age Range. 2–16 years.
Number in School. Approximately 340 girls and boys.
Fees per term (2016–2017). £1,218–£3,882.

Thorpe Hall School is a co-educational independent day school, pleasantly situated on green belt land on the outskirts of Southend-on-Sea, Essex. The buildings are modern and purpose-built.

Communications to London are good via the A13 and A127 and the Liverpool/Fenchurch Street railway lines. The nearest station is approximately 10 minutes' walk.

Founded in 1925, the school has been educating children for 80 years and consistently achieves excellent academic results at Key Stage 1, 2, 3 and GCSE with special emphasis being placed on the traditional values of good manners, behaviour, dress and speech.

On Monday, Tuesday and Thursday each week the school day is extended by one hour to enable all children to access library and computer facilities as well as having the opportunities to participate in Sport, Music, Drama, Mathematics and French or simply to do their homework in a suitable and supervised environment.

Refurbishment of the Science, Modern Languages, Information Systems and Resources Centre facilities has greatly enhanced the learning opportunities for all pupils.

A new building was recently completed, which houses a Theatre, Technology rooms, an extra ICT suite and an excellent Modern Art area. These new facilities ensure that Thorpe Hall School has the most modern, up-to-date and technologically advanced facilities of any independent school in South East Essex.

Thorpe Hall School has an orderly, disciplined and caring ethos that caters for the social and academic needs of children – Pre-Nursery, Nursery, Reception, Infant, Junior and Senior – not only between the hours of 9 am to 4 pm but also offers sporting opportunities in golf, tennis, karate, netball, horse riding and football at weekends and during holiday times. Youngsters have the opportunity to join our Beavers, Cubs and Scout groups while senior pupils can become involved in the Duke of Edinburgh's Award scheme.

The Charitable Trust status enables fees, which are very competitive, to be kept to a minimum. Nursery vouchers are accepted and some bursaries are available. The School is regularly inspected by the Independent Schools Inspectorate.

Charitable status. Thorpe Hall School is a Registered Charity, number 298155. It exists to provide good quality education for boys and girls in South East Essex.

Tower College

Mill Lane, Rainhill, Merseyside L35 6NE

Tel: 0151 426 4333
email: missoxley@towercollege.com
           mrtaylor@towercollege.com
           mrsknox@towercollege.com
website: www.towercollege.com

Principal: Miss R J Oxley

Vice-Principal: Mrs P Knox
Bursar: Mr M Taylor

Age Range. 3 months – 16 years.
Number in School. Day: 181 Boys, 154 Girls.
Fees per term (from April 2016). £2,113–£2,458.

Tower College is a non-denominational Christian Day School housed in a beautiful Victorian mansion set in 11 acres.

Five coaches cover a 25-mile radius including South Liverpool, Widnes, Warrington, Runcorn, St Helens, Prescot, Rainford and Ormskirk. Breakfast and after school clubs are available.

Academic and music scholarships are available.

Charitable status. Tower College is a Registered Charity, number 526611. It aims to provide a caring environment founded on Christian values, with an emphasis each individual fulfilling his/her potential.

The Towers Convent School

Upper Beeding, Steyning, West Sussex BN44 3TF

Tel: 01903 812185
Fax: 01903 813858
email: admin@thetowersconventschool.org
website: www.thetowersconventschool.org

Twitter: @TowersConvent
Facebook: /TheTowersConvent

Headmistress: **Mrs Clare Trelfa**

Age Range. Girls 2–16, Boys 2–8.
Number in School. 320.
Fees per term (2016–2017). Tuition: £2,550–£3,600.

The Towers Convent School, a Roman Catholic school for girls aged 2–16 and boys aged 2–8 years in the beautiful setting of the South Downs, is owned by a Community of Sisters. At the heart of The Towers Community is Christian love; all people of whatever race, colour, creed or status are welcome, and have equal worth and opportunity. We aim to celebrate the dignity of each individual pupil. Our motto "Always Faithful" upholds the qualities of honesty and trust, responsibility, self-discipline and forgiveness. Pupils are encouraged to achieve their full potential in everything they do, developing a love of learning and seeking "wholeness". Mathematics and science subjects are particular strengths, and the school has three times won the Whitbread Prize for GCSE results. The GCSE pass rate is consistently high and reflects a quest for high academic standards. There is a keen interest in music and drama and a major musical is produced annually. The school's achievements in sport bear witness to a fine tradition, especially in tennis, where the school has won the Sussex Shield five times; netball and gymnastics are also very strong. The on-site covered and heated pool is a real asset and is enjoyed by all ages including the nursery children.

Find enjoyment and fulfilment at affordable fees!

Charitable status. The Towers Convent School is a Registered Charity, number 229394. It exists to provide quality education for girls and boys.

Trevor-Roberts School

55–57 Eton Avenue, London NW3 3ET

Tel: 020 7586 1444
email: trsenior@trevor-robertsschool.co.uk

Headteacher: **Mr Simon Trevor-Roberts**, BA

Age Range. 5–13 Co-educational.
Number in School. 170 Day Pupils: 100 boys, 70 girls.
Fees per term (2016–2017). £4,630–£5,200.

Trevor-Roberts School was founded in Hampstead in 1955 by the headmaster's late father and moved to its present site in 1981. The school is made up of two departments but operates as one school and occupies two adjacent much-adapted late Victorian houses in Belsize Park. In addition to on-site facilities, the school makes use of nearby playing fields and a local leisure centre swimming pool.

Central to the education provided is the school's aim for all pupils to become happy and confident individuals who fulfil their potential. Strong emphasis is placed on personal organisation and pupils are encouraged to develop a love of learning for its own sake. In a happy, non-competitive atmosphere, pupils are well cared for and teachers' responses are tailored to the individual needs of pupils. It is the School's strong belief that much can be expected of a child if he or she is given self-confidence and a sense of personal worth and does not feel judged too early in life against the attainment of others.

High success rates throughout the school are achieved through small classes, individual attention and specialist teachers. The standards achieved enable almost all pupils to gain places in their first choice of school at either 11+ or 13+ into the main London day schools and academically selective independent boarding schools. In recent years a number of pupils have been awarded academic, art and music scholarships to these schools. The school aims to make pupils prepared for this process and give them the confidence to enjoy the academic challenges they will be offered.

The school provides a broad range of curricular and extra-curricular activities, contributing to pupils' linguistic, mathematical, scientific, technological, social and physical development in a balanced way. Aesthetic and creative development is strongly encouraged through art, drama and music. In the Senior Department the syllabus is extended to include Classical History, Latin, Greek and Mandarin. The curriculum is enriched at all stages by a variety of one-day educational visits as well as by residential trips for Years 6–8 on activity weekends, geography field trips and visits to France.

A range of extra-curricular activities and sporting opportunities appropriate for boys and girls of all ages is offered two afternoons a week and after school. The school's founder believed passionately in music and drama as a means of developing pupils' confidence and self-esteem and both subjects are a strong feature of the school today. All classes prepare and perform two drama performances each year in which every pupil has a speaking part.

Pupils thrive in a caring family atmosphere where the emphasis is on individual progress and expectation, and where improvement is rewarded as highly as success. It has a broadly Christian tradition, but welcomes pupils of all faiths and of none.

Trinity School

Brizes Park, Ongar Road, Kelvedon Hatch, Brentwood, Essex CM14 5TB

Tel:	01277 374123
Fax:	01277 373596
email:	enquiries@trinityschool.ac
website:	www.trinityschool.ac

Head of Senior School: **Dr M Ellis**

Head of Primary School: **Mrs V Green**

Age Range. 3–18 co-educational.
Number of Pupils. 93.
Fees per term (2016–2017). £1,444–£2,328.

Trinity School is situated in Brizes Park, a 73-acre site of magnificent parkland on the outskirts of Brentwood. An elegant Georgian mansion houses the senior section while the primary section is in modern classrooms in a beautifully landscaped walled garden.

Trinity School has a distinctively Christian ethos, and aims for its pupils to develop as grounded and successful individuals. The academic results at GCSE and A Level are consistently strong, and sporting achievements are excellent. Most pupils go on to gain good university degrees and then proceed to top jobs and careers. Many former students regularly give back to the school in various ways as a thank you for all they received here.

The school has a warm family atmosphere with many of the parents fulfilling roles in teaching, administration and support. The school is closely linked to Trinity Church, Brentwood, and one of the secrets of its success is the principle established from its foundation that the pupils should find the same standards in the school, the church and the home. This has produced happy, secure and well-motivated children who have a strong sense of service as well as a platform for success throughout life.

Charitable status. The school is a Registered Charity, number 1112705.

Ursuline Preparatory School

Great Ropers Lane, Warley, Brentwood, Essex CM13 3HR

Tel:	01277 227152
Fax:	01277 202559
email:	headmistress@ursulineprepwarley.co.uk
website:	www.ursulineprepwarley.co.uk

Headmistress: **Mrs Pauline Wilson**, MSc

Age Range. 3–11.
Number in School. Day 180.
Fees per term (2016–2017). £1,985–£3,700.

Founded in the early 1930s, the Ursuline Preparatory School enjoys a reputation as a happy family school, where pupils strive to give of their best in all areas of school life. Consequently, much emphasis is placed on encouraging the children to develop to the full their individual talents and interests, as well as fostering in each pupil a strong sense of well-being, self-reliance and team spirit. This is achieved by the frequent use of praise, by adherence to an agreed policy of consistent and fair discipline, and by the high standards, moral code and caring attitudes deriving from the strongly Catholic ethos which underpins the life of the whole school.

The Ursuline Preparatory School has well qualified and very experienced teachers and support staff. It is committed to offering to all its pupils the distinct advantages of a broad and balanced curriculum. This includes following the National Curriculum, in addition to affording many other opportunities such as the provision of French, Spanish and Information Technology to all children from 4 years upwards, Swimming Lessons, and also Extension classes where this is deemed appropriate.

A comprehensive range of extra-curricular activities are offered to the pupils. These are often taught by specialist staff and include subjects such as Theatre Club, Art Appreciation, Computing, Photography, Forest Skills, Sewing, Chess, and Speech and Drama as well as many Instrumental Classes and Sporting Activities, with which the School has considerable success in gaining individual and team awards at competition level.

The School successfully prepares children for entry to local and national independent schools, Grammar Schools or local Secondary Schools, including the Ursuline High School.

The relatively small size of the School allows for very close contact between staff, pupils and parents and provides each child with the opportunity to fulfil his or her academic potential. The pupils are encouraged to follow their own interests and to develop a sense of self-confidence and self-worth which will hopefully remain with them throughout their lives, allowing them to reflect the school motto: *A Caring School that strives for excellence.*

Charitable status. The Ursuline Preparatory School is a Registered Charity, number 1058282, which is non-profit making and managed by an independent board of voluntary trustees. It exists to provide Roman Catholic children and those of other denominations with the opportunity to reach the highest individual standards possible in every area of School life.

Vita et Pax Preparatory School

6A Priory Close, Green Road, Southgate, London N14 4AT

Tel: 020 8449 8336
Fax: 020 8440 0483
email: info@vitaetpax.co.uk
website: www.vitaetpax.co.uk

Chair of Governors: Ms Pamela Clear-Doughty

Headteacher: **Mrs Margaret O'Connor**, BEd Hons, MSc

Co-educational Day School.
Age Range. 3–11 years.
Number of Pupils. 75 Boys, 112 Girls.
Fees per term (2016–2017). £3,090.

Vita et Pax is an 'outstanding' school (ISI 2011) where staff work in close partnership with parents and children to provide a happy environment where everyone feels valued and cared for.

The school was founded 80 years ago by the Benedictine Olivetan Sisters in a spirit of ecumenism. Over the last 30 years it has evolved under lay leadership into a modern environment where pupils are prepared to be tomorrow's citizens, facing all the challenges that brings.

The school aims to instil in its pupils a love of learning from the outset. The curriculum offered encompasses the Early Years Foundation and National Curriculum with additional challenge and pace.

The school is not academically selective but has been judged (ISI 2011) to achieve exceptional standards both in academic and extra-curricular activities.

Pupils are prepared for transfer to both Independent and maintained grammar schools at age 11 and achieve considerable success through academic selection and scholarship offers.

Our highly qualified and dedicated staff nurture the pupils to become confident and considerate members of the wider community.

Charitable status. Vita et Pax School (Cockfosters) Ltd is a Registered Charity, number 281566. It exists to promote and provide for the advancement of education of infant and junior school age children.

The Webber Independent School

Soskin Drive, Stantonbury Fields, Milton Keynes, Bucks MK14 6DP

Tel: 01908 574740
Fax: 01908 574741
email: info@wis.gemsedu.co.uk
website: www.webberindependentschool.com
Twitter: @WebberIndie
Facebook: @The-Webber-Independent-School
LinkedIn: /webber-independent-school

Headmistress: **Mrs Hilary Marsden**

Age Range. 3–18.
Number in School. 165.
Fees per term (2016–2017). Early Years (3–5 years full-time places only) £2,740–£2,820; KS1 £2,860; KS2 £2,960–£3,180; KS3–KS5 £3,820.

The Webber Independent School is an exceptional private co-educational day school for students aged 3 to 18 in Milton Keynes. The school is located in attractive private grounds on a single site. It is the only private 3–18 school in Central Milton Keynes with easy access to the station, from where the school operates a pick up and drop off service.

The School inspires and supports students in achieving the highest possible standards. The School offers an exciting, challenging and enriching curriculum within a supportive community in order to promote a love of learning, which benefits students throughout their lives. They discover and nurture individual talents and promote values of respect, responsibility, effort and empathy, which enhances independent learning, academic progress and emotional well-being. The School encourages in their young people the skills, ambition and confidence required to become successful global citizens and to meet the challenges of the modern world. The Webber Independent School focuses on the attributes that are highly prized in higher education and the workplace, such as initiative, confidence, perseverance, teamwork and leadership.

The Webber Independent School offers:

- 5 star rated by the School Guide
- Outstanding results: 100% A*–C at A Level
- Excellent ISI Inspection report
- High quality teaching in small classes, teaching a stimulating curriculum
- Excellent pastoral care – a welcoming, friendly and well-mannered environment
- Door-to-door minibus service, in addition to pick up from Central Milton Keynes Station

West Lodge School

36 Station Road, Sidcup, Kent DA15 7DU

Tel: 020 8300 2489
Fax: 020 8308 1905
email: info@westlodge.org.uk
website: www.westlodge.org.uk

Chair of Governors: Mrs Chris Head-Rapson

Head Teacher: **Mrs Susan Webb**, MA

Age Range. 3–11.
Number of Pupils. 165 Day Boys and Girls.
Fees per term (2016–2017). £1,735–£2,900.

West Lodge was founded in 1940 and is now an educational trust. The main building is an extended Victorian house, well adapted to use as a school, whilst still retaining its homely atmosphere. Facilities include a newly-built extension, incorporating a science/cookery room and art room/crèche, which can also be used together as an additional hall facility, a fully-equipped gymnasium, Astroturf surface (relaid in Summer 2015), music rooms and a computer suite. There are eight classes of up to 21 pupils, one class in each year group from Nursery through to Year 6. The staff-pupil ratio is extremely high and the children are taught in smaller groups by specialist teachers for many subjects. The school is open from 8.15 am and an after-school crèche and homework club operate until 5.30 pm.

The school has a strong academic tradition and a purposeful atmosphere permeates each class. The National Curriculum is at the core of our teaching but it is enhanced and enriched by the inclusion of a wider range of subjects. These include: English, mathematics, science, French, information technology, design technology, history, geography, religious education, music, art and craft, physical education and games, swimming and drama.

Great emphasis is placed on a thorough grounding in basic learning skills, with literacy and numeracy seen as key elements in the foundation, upon which future learning will be built. Particular care is taken to extend the most gifted children and support the less able. West Lodge has a consistent record of a high level of entry to local authority selective schools and independent schools.

Music has a particularly high profile within the school and all of the children are encouraged to develop their talents. Well-qualified peripatetic staff teach both group and individual lessons and children of all ages are encouraged to join the school orchestras and choir. Concerts and dramatic performances are staged regularly and parents are warmly invited to attend.

Sports of all sorts are taught and in 2014–15, in particular, the School was thrilled to achieve competitive success at national level in netball and at a local level in kwik cricket.

The school promotes a caring attitude between all its members and aims to help each child towards the achievement of self-control and self-discipline. The Head Teacher and the class teachers know each of the children well and the excellent pastoral care and family atmosphere are major features of the school.

Home-school links are strong and the open door policy gives parents immediate access to members of staff should worries occur. The school also has strong contacts with the local community.

Extracurricular activities are given the highest priority and clubs run each afternoon after school. Regular school outings form part of the curriculum for all children, the older pupils enjoying residential visits.

Charitable status. West Lodge School Educational Trust is a Registered Charity, number 283627. It exists for the provision of high quality education for boys and girls between 3 and 11 years.

Westbourne School

Hickman Road, Penarth, Vale of Glamorgan CF64 2AJ
Tel: 029 2070 5705
email: enquiries@westbourneschool.com
website: www.westbourneschool.com
Twitter: @WestbourneS
Facebook: @WestbourneSchool

Principal: Mr K W Underhill, MA Ed

Head of Junior School: Dr Gerard Griffiths
Deputy Head of Senior School (Pastoral): Mr Colin Laity
International Baccalaureate Coordinator: Ms Virginie Gautran
Finance Director: Mr Gary Hughes
Marketing Director: Mr Nick Leiper

Age Range. 3–18.
Number in School. 89 Boys, 73 Girls.
Fees per term (2016–2017). £2,450–£4,175 (payable in advance). Fees include textbooks, sporting activities and examination charges. Boarding and Homestay £30,420 per year, fully inclusive of tuition fees, single or shared room during term time, daily breakfast, lunch and dinner, guardianship costs and annual airport transfers.

We are an Independent Co-educational school for children from Nursery age to Sixth Form, with continuity in teaching methods throughout the School, and a stable context for study. Since September 2008 we have offered the IB Diploma Programme in a brand new Sixth Form Building. In 2016, we were the top smaller IB school in the UK for the second year in a row. A wide and flexible range of subjects is offered at GCSE, and results are consistently excellent. The staff is well-qualified and settled and pupils are known

individually to all teachers and also to the Head of School; education takes place in a happy, family-like environment.

A disciplined, caring context is maintained and ample opportunity is given for a variety of sporting activities.

Entry into Year 12 is based on GCSE Results and an interview with the Principal; entry into Year 9 is by Common Entrance at which a 50% pass is required. Otherwise entrance is by interview and two day induction.

Penarth is a small seaside town on the outskirts of Cardiff, and pupils are normally drawn from Penarth, Sully, Cardiff, Barry, Cowbridge and the Vale of Glamorgan. There is a convenient train service to Penarth and the School has minibuses running each day from The Vale of Glamorgan, Cowbridge, Barry and Cardiff.

Westward School

47 Hersham Road, Walton-on-Thames, Surrey KT12 1LE
Tel: 01932 220911
Fax: 01932 242891
email: admin@westwardschool.co.uk
website: www.westwardschool.co.uk

Principals: Mr & Mrs David Townley

Headmistress: Mrs Shelley Stevenson, BEd Hons

Age Range. 3–11 Co-educational.
Number of Pupils. 155.
Fees per term (2016–2017). £1,145–£2,465.

Whitehall School

117 High Street, Somersham, Cambs PE28 3EH
Tel: 01487 840966
email: office@whitehallschool.com
website: www.whitehallschool.com
Facebook: @Whitehall-School

Principal: Ms Rebecca Hutley, BA Hons

Age Range. 6 months to 11 years.
Number in School. 90 Day children: 43 boys, 47 girls.
Fees per term (from April 2016). £891–£2,521.
'*A Unique School in Rural Cambridgeshire: A Dynamic, Forward-Thinking environment.*'

Set in extensive grounds with excellent facilities, Whitehall School provides a small, family environment where children are supported to achieve their best academically whilst also developing personality, creativity and social consciousness.

The school consists of an Edwardian house and 18th Century coach house and is set within approximately 1.5 acres of stunning grounds. Facilities include a covered heated swimming pool, playground, sensory garden, games field, library and iPad suite.

Small class sizes to a maximum of 16 allow us to support children to access the curriculum at their own pace on a 'Vertical Pathway', catering for the specific needs of each child so that they excel. Our Individual Performance Programme allows us to work in partnership with parents to encourage children to become active, independent learners.

Windrush Valley School

The Green, London Lane, Ascott-under-Wychwood, Oxfordshire OX7 6AN

Tel: 01993 831793
email: info@windrushvalleyschool.co.uk
website: www.windrushvalleyschool.co.uk

Headmaster: **Mr G A Wood**, MEd, TCert, DipSpEd, ACP, FCollP

Age Range. 3–11 Co-educational.
Number of Pupils. 103.
Fees per term (2016–2017). £2,200.

Windrush Valley School is a lively, happy community in which boys and girls thrive. Its rural location provides access to all the amenities of a beautiful Cotswold village including the 12th century church and playing fields. The school is non-selective; admission is by interview with the Headmaster. Before- and after-school care extend the school day from 8.00 am to 6.00 pm with a wide range of after-school clubs/societies. The small number of children with special educational needs are taught under the supervision of specialist staff. The school plays competitive sports in a wide range of games. Class groups are organised on a chronological age basis and the curriculum exceeds the requirements of the National Curriculum. Excellent examination results enable pupils to achieve their first choice of school on transfer to secondary education and help maintain its listing as a 'Times' top 100 preparatory school.

Woodlands School

Great Warley

Warley Street, Great Warley, Brentwood, Essex CM13 3LA

Tel: 01277 233288
Fax: 01277 232715
email: info@woodlandsschools.co.uk
website: www.woodlandsschools.co.uk

Head Teacher: **Mrs Katherine Mansfield**

Age Range. 3 months–11 years.
Number in School. 127: 60 boys, 67 girls.
Fees per term (2016–2017). £2,755–£4,390.

Woodlands School at Great Warley is set in attractive, spacious grounds, with excellent facilities for outdoor activities. The school also uses the extensive facilities of our sister school at Hutton Manor.

It is the School's principle aim to ensure that all the children are happy and secure and are as successful as possible. They are encouraged to work hard and to show kindness and consideration to their peers. The resulting ethos of the School is one of warmth, support and mutual respect.

The School provides an exciting learning experience which enables the pupils to achieve full academic potential and to develop qualities of curiosity, independence and fortitude. Classes are small. The school aims to develop high levels of self-esteem and a good attitude to learning. The School has an excellent record in public examinations. Pupils are highly successful in gaining places at the schools of their choice. Examination results in Music and LAMDA are also excellent.

A varied programme of team and individual sports aims to offer something for everyone.

There is a strong music tradition and a variety of dramatic and musical concerts and productions are staged throughout the year for children of each age group.

Modern languages are taught to a very high standard, with French introduced at the age of 3 and Spanish in the Upper School.

Pastoral care is a major feature. An 'Open House' policy is in place for parents, which results in any concern being dealt with promptly and effectively.

It is the School's view that the education of the whole child is the most important priority and is confident that the learning experience it provides is fun, truly stimulating and memorable.

The school has recently added a nursery facility offering places for children from 3 months to 3 years who will then progress automatically into Kindergarten.

Woodlands School

Hutton Manor

428 Rayleigh Road, Hutton, Brentwood, Essex CM13 1SD

Tel: 01277 245585
Fax: 01277 221546
email: info@woodlandshutton.co.uk
website: www.woodlandsschools.co.uk

Head Teacher: **Mrs Paula Hobbs**, BEd

Age Range. 3–11 Co-educational.
Number of Pupils. 140.
Fees per term (2016–2017). £3,590–£4,895.

Woodlands School at Hutton Manor is set in attractive, spacious grounds, with excellent facilities for outdoor activities. The school also uses the extensive facilities of our sister school at Great Warley.

It is the School's principle aim to ensure that all the children are happy and secure and are as successful as possible. They are encouraged to work hard and to show kindness and consideration to their peers. The resulting ethos of the School is one of warmth, support and mutual respect.

The School provides an exciting learning experience which enables the pupils to achieve full academic potential and to develop qualities of curiosity, independence and fortitude. Classes are small. The school aims to develop high levels of self-esteem and a good attitude to learning. The School has an excellent record in public examinations. Pupils are highly successful in gaining places at the schools of their choice. Examination results in Music and LAMDA are also excellent.

A varied programme of team and individual sports aims to offer something for everyone.

There is a strong music tradition and a variety of dramatic and musical concerts and productions are staged throughout the year for children of each age group.

Modern languages are taught to a very high standard, with French introduced at the age of 3 and Spanish in the Upper School.

Pastoral care is a major feature. An 'Open House' policy is in place for parents, which results in any concern being dealt with promptly and effectively.

It is the School's view that the education of the whole child is the most important priority and is confident that the learning experience it provides is fun, truly stimulating and memorable.

The school has recently added a nursery facility offering places for children from 3 months to 3 years who will then progress automatically into Kindergarten.

Entrance Scholarships

Academic Scholarships

Cundall Manor School (p. 1131)

The Dixie Grammar School (p. 1133)

Hipperholme Grammar School (p. 1146)

Radnor House Sevenoaks School (p. 1166)

St Andrew's School (p. 1171)

St Dominic's Priory School (p. 1174)

St Joseph's School (p. 1177)

Thames Christian College (p. 1188)

All-Rounder Scholarships

Cundall Manor School (p. 1131)

Radnor House Sevenoaks School (p. 1166)

Art Scholarships

Cundall Manor School (p. 1131)

The Dixie Grammar School (p. 1133)

Radnor House Sevenoaks School (p. 1166)

St Andrew's School (p. 1171)

St Dominic's Priory School (p. 1174)

Thames Christian College (p. 1188)

Dance Scholarships

Hipperholme Grammar School (p. 1146)

Drama Scholarships

Cundall Manor School (p. 1131)

Hipperholme Grammar School (p. 1146)

St Andrew's School (p. 1171)

Music Scholarships

Cundall Manor School (p. 1131)

The Dixie Grammar School (p. 1133)

Hipperholme Grammar School (p. 1146)

Radnor House Sevenoaks School (p. 1166)

St Andrew's School (p. 1171)

St Dominic's Priory School (p. 1174)

St Joseph's School (p. 1177)

Thames Christian College (p. 1188)

Sport Scholarships

Cundall Manor School (p. 1131)

The Dixie Grammar School (p. 1133)

Hipperholme Grammar School (p. 1146)

Radnor House Sevenoaks School (p. 1166)

St Andrew's School (p. 1171)

St Dominic's Priory School (p. 1174)

St Joseph's School (p. 1177)

Thames Christian College (p. 1188)

Other Scholarships

Choral

Polwhele House School (p. 1164)

Equestrian

Polwhele House School (p. 1164)

Performing Arts

St Dominic's Priory School (p. 1174)

Thames Christian College (p. 1188)

Bursaries

Cundall Manor School (p. 1131)

The Dixie Grammar School (p. 1133)

Hipperholme Grammar School (p. 1146)

St Andrew's School (p. 1171)

St Dominic's Priory School (p. 1174)

St Joseph's School (p. 1177)

INDEX OF ALL SCHOOLS